MANSION'S SHORTER
FRENCH AND ENGLISH
DICTIONARY

EDITED BY *J. E. Mansion*

D. C. HEATH AND COMPANY
Boston

Printed in the United States of America
for
D. C. HEATH AND COMPANY
New York   *Boston*   *Dallas*   *Chicago*
Atlanta   *San Francisco*   *London*

MANSION'S SHORTER
FRENCH AND ENGLISH
DICTIONARY

Part One

PREFACE

EVER since the publication in 1934 of the first part of the Standard French and English Dictionary there has been a demand for an abridged edition of this work, which should retain only that which is essential for the needs of the general reader.

The following pages embody an attempt to meet this demand in respect of Part I. Of the 58,000 words dealt with in the Standard Dictionary 31,550 have been retained, and this would appear to form a sufficiently wide range for everyday use and for the enjoyment of current French literature. But the real difficulty, in an abridgment such as we have attempted, is to sift out and retain, under each vocable, those meanings and shades of meaning which are fundamental and essential, and to retain also, in a condensed form, enough of the phraseology that gives life to the word to ensure that of our larger work something more shall remain than a mere skeleton. We hope that this has been achieved in some measure. Among other things it will be apparent that the scientific and technical aspects of our modern civilization, which bulk largely in the parent work, still receive adequate treatment. On the other hand, as this Dictionary will no doubt be used in schools, that *maxima reverentia* has been observed which is due to the young.

The plan and general arrangement of this Shorter Dictionary remain substantially the same as in the Standard Dictionary; the subdivisions of each word are presented in the same order, so that where, in schools, for instance, the larger work is available for reference, the wider range of information contained therein will be accessible with a minimum of labour.

One innovation we have made, in order to save much space and redundancy. In hundreds of cases the adjective in French has a corresponding adverb in **-ment,** where the adjective in English has also an adverb in -ly:

> *agréable, agréablement,* agreeable, agreeably; pleasant, pleasantly;
> *actif, activement,* active, actively; *grand, grandement,* great, greatly.

In all cases where this correspondence occurs without any call for fuller treatment, the article devoted to the French adjective is followed by the entry **-ment,** or **-ement,** and it will be understood that in English there exists an adverb in -ly, formed from the adjective as shown above.

There is also a frequent correspondence between the French suffix **-té** and English -ness:

> *léger, légèreté,* light, lightness;
> *bénin, bénignité,* mild, mildness.

Again, from many French verbs are formed abstract nouns in **-age, -ment, -ation,** which may be rendered in English by gerunds or verbal nouns in -ing:

> *ajuster, ajustage,* to adjust, adjusting;
> *allaiter, allaitement,* to suckle, suckling;
> *assimiler, assimilation,* to liken, likening;

and many nouns and adjectives in **-eur, -euse,** denoting the 'doer' or agent, have English counterparts in -ing, -er:

> *se moquer, moqueur,* to scoff; *a.* scoffing, *s.* scoffer.

The adjectival ending **-ant** is nearly always rendered by -ing:

> *amuser, amusant,* to amuse, amusing;

and the suffix **-able** rendered by -able:

> *accepter, acceptable,* to accept, acceptable;

with a derived noun in **-abilité,** in English -ability or -ableness:

> *acceptabilité,* acceptability, acceptableness.

The endings shown above in heavy type have been used freely to indicate the existence of French derivatives the meaning and translation of which offers no difficulty.

v

To indicate the pronunciation the symbols used are those of the *Association Phonétique Internationale*, as in the Standard Dictionary, and the abbreviations used in the body of the book are the same.

'Etymology' has not been dealt with, but when a derivative has been formed within the French language itself, and the source is not obvious, it may be helpful to give an indication of the parent word, and this has been done in the form of a hint between square brackets. Thus: avoisiner [VOISIN], affamer [FAIM], bémol [B MOL], claveau [CLEF].

October 1940   J. E. M.

REPRESENTATION OF THE PRONUNCIATION

VOWELS

[i]	vite, cygne	[y:]	mur, ils eurent
[i:]	rire, lyre, Moïse	[ø]	feu, ceux, nœud
[e]	été, donner, j'ai	[ø:]	meule, jeûne
[ɛ]	elle, très, peine, mais. Noël	[œ]	jeune, œuf, cueillir
[ɛ:]	terre, père, paire	[œ:]	fleur, sœur, œuvre
[a]	chat, là, femme, toit	[ə]	le, ce, entremets
[a:]	rare, tard, noir	[ɛ̃]	vin, plein, main, chien, examen, faim,
[ɑ]	pas, âgé, le bois		thym
[ɑ:]	sable, âge, tâche	[ɛ̃:]	prince, ceindre, plaindre
[ɔ]	donne, Paul, album	[ɑ̃]	enfant, temps, paon
[ɔ:]	fort, Laure	[ɑ̃:]	danse, centre, ample
[o]	dos, impôt, chaud	[ɔ̃]	mon, plomb
[o:]	fosse, fausse, rôle	[ɔ̃:]	honte, nombre, comte
[u]	tout, goût, août	[œ̃]	lundi, à jeun, parfum
[u:]	cour, Douvres	[œ̃:]	humble
[y]	cru, eu, ciguë		

CONSONANTS

[p]	pain, absolu	[l]	lait, aile, table
[b]	beau, bleu, abbé	[ʃ]	chose, chercher, schisme
[m]	mou, flamme, prisme	[ʒ]	Jean, gilet, manger
[f]	feu, bref, phrase	[k]	camp, képi, quatre, écho
[v]	voir, vivre, wagon	[g]	garde, guerre, second
[t]	table, net, théâtre	[ɲ]	campagne, gniaf
[d]	donner, sud	[r]	rare, marbre, rhume
[n]	né, canne, automne	[ks]	accident, extrême
[s]	sou, rébus, cire, scène, action, six	[gz]	exister
[z]	cousin, zéro, deuxième		

SEMI-CONSONANTS

[j]	yacht, piano, ration, voyage, travailler, cahier	[w]	ouate, ouest, noir, pingouin, tramway
		[ɥ]	muet, huit, lui

DIPHTHONGS

[i:j]	fille, famille	[ɑ:j]	il bâille, ferraille
[ɛ:j]	soleil, veille, paye	[œ:j]	fauteuil, œil, je cueille
[a:j]	travail, muraille		

ABBREVIATIONS

A :	Archaism; ancient; in former use	*conj.*	Conjunction	*Gr.Civ :*	Greek Civilization
		Conj. like	Conjugated like	*Gram :*	Grammar
Abs.	Absolutely, absolute use	*Const :*	Construction	*Gym :*	Gymnastics
		Coop :	Cooperage		
Ac :	Acoustics	*Corr :*	Correspondence	*Hairdr :*	Hairdressing
acc.	Accusative	*Cost :*	Costume	*Harn :*	Harness
a., adj.	Adjective	*Cr :*	Cricket	*Hatm :*	Hatmaking
Adm :	Administration	*Crust :*	Crustacea	*Her :*	Heraldry
adv.	Adverb	*Cryst :*	Crystallography	*Hist :*	History; historical
Aer :	Aeronautics	*Cu :*	Culinary; cuisine	*Hor :*	Horology
Agr :	Agriculture	*Cust :*	Customs	*Hort :*	Horticulture
Alg :	Algebra	*Cy :*	Cycles; cycling	*Hum :*	Humorous
Amph :	Amphibia			*Husb :*	Husbandry
Anat :	Anatomy	*Danc :*	Dancing	*Hyd :*	Hydraulics; hydrostatics
Ann :	Annelida	*dat.*	Dative		
Ant :	Antiquity, -ies	*def.*	(i) Definite; (ii) defective	*Hyg :*	Hygiene
Anthr :	Anthropology				
Ap :	Apiculture	*dem.*	Demonstrative	*i.*	Intransitive
Ar :	Arithmetic	*Dent :*	Dentistry	*I.C.E :*	Internal Combustion Engines
Arach :	Arachnida	*Dial :*	Dialect		
Arb :	Arboriculture	*Dipl :*	Diplomacy	*Ich :*	Ichthyology
Arch :	Architecture	*Dist :*	Distilling	*imp.*	Imperative
Archeol :	Archeology	*Dom.Ec :*	Domestic Economy	*impers.*	Impersonal
Artil :	Artillery	*Draw :*	Drawing	*ind.*	Indicative
Astr :	Astronomy	*Dressm :*	Dressmaking	*Ind :*	Industry
Astrol :	Astrology	*Dy :*	Dyeing	*indef.*	Indefinite
attrib.	Attributive			*ind.tr.*	Indirectly transitive
Aut :	Automobilism	*E :*	Engineering	*inf.*	Infinitive
aux.	Auxiliary	*Ecc :*	Ecclesiastical	*Ins :*	Insurance
Av :	Aviation	*Echin :*	Echinodermata	*int.*	Interjection
		El :	Electricity; electrical	*interr.*	Interrogative
B :	Biblical; Bible	*El.-Ch :*	Electro-Chemistry	*inv.*	Invariable
Bac :	Bacteriology	*Eng.*	English; England	*Iron :*	Ironical(ly)
Ball :	Ballistics	*Engr :*	Engraving		
Bank :	Banking	*Ent :*	Entomology	*Join :*	Joinery
Bib :	Bibliography	*Equit :*	Equitation	*Journ :*	Journalism
Bill :	Billiards	*esp.*	Especially	*Jur :*	Jurisprudence; law
Bio-Ch :	Bio-Chemistry	*etc.*	Et cetera		
Biol :	Biology	*Eth :*	Ethics	*Lap :*	Lapidary Arts
Bookb :	Bookbinding	*Ethn :*	Ethnology	*Laund :*	Laundering
Book-k :	Book-keeping	*excl.*	Exclamation; exclamative	*Leath :*	Leatherwork
Bootm :	Bootmaking			*Ling :*	Linguistics
Bot :	Botany	*Exp :*	Explosives	*Lit :*	Literary use; literature; literary
Box :	Boxing				
Breed :	Breeding	*f.*	Feminine	*Lith :*	Lithography
Brew :	Brewing	*F :*	Familiar	*Log :*	Logic
		Farr :	Farriery	*Lt.*	Latin
card.a.	Cardinal adjective	*Fb :*	Football		
Carp :	Carpentry	*Fenc :*	Fencing	*m.*	Masculine
Cav :	Cavalry	*Fin :*	Finance	*Magn :*	Magnetism
Cer :	Ceramics	*Fish :*	Fishing	*Mapm :*	Mapmaking
Ch :	Chemistry	*For :*	Forestry	*Mch :*	Machines
Chr :	Chronology	*Fort :*	Fortification	*Meas :*	Weights and measures
Cin :	Cinematography	*Fr.*	French; France		
Civ.E :	Civil Engineering	*fu.*	Future	*Mec :*	Mechanics
Cl :	Classical	*Fung :*	Fungi	*Mec.E :*	Mechanical Engineering
Clockm :	Clock and watch making	*Furn :*	Furniture		
				Med :	Medicine
Coel :	Coelenterata	*Gasm :*	Gasmaking	*Metall :*	Metallurgy
cogn.acc.	Cognate accusative	*Geog :*	Geography	*Metalw :*	Metalworking
Coll.	Collective	*Geol :*	Geology	*Metaph :*	Metaphysics
Com :	Commerce	*Geom :*	Geometry	*Meteor :*	Meteorology
Comest :	Comestibles	*ger.*	Gerund	*Mil :*	Military
comp.	Comparative	*Glassm :*	Glassmaking	*Mill :*	Milling
Conch :	Conchology	*Gr.*	Greek	*Min :*	Mining and quarrying
condit.	Conditional	*Gr.Alph :*	Greek Alphabet		

vii

Miner:	Mineralogy	phr.	Phrase	Sp:	Sport
M.Ins:	Maritime Insurance	Physiol:	Physiology	Spong:	Sponges
Moll:	Molluscs	Pisc:	Pisciculture	St.Exch:	Stock Exchange
Moss:	Mosses	pl.	Plural	sth.	Something
Mth:	Mathematics	Plumb:	Plumbing	sub.	Subjunctive
Mus:	Music	P.N:	Public notices	Sug.-R:	Sugar-Refining
Myr:	Myriapoda	Poet:	Poetical	sup.	Superlative
Myth:	Myth and legend; mythology	Pol:	Politics	Surg:	Surgery
		Pol.Ec:	Political Economy	Surv:	Surveying
		poss.	Possessive	Swim:	Swimming
n.	Nous (= we)	Post:	Postal Service		
N.	North	p.p.	Past participle	Tail:	Tailoring
N.Arch:	Naval Architecture	pr.	(i) present; (ii) pronominal	Tan:	Tanning
Nat.Hist:	Natural History			Tchn:	Technical
Nau:	Nautical	pred.	Predicate; predicative	Televis:	Television
Needlew:	Needlework			Ten:	(i) Tennis; (ii) lawn tennis
neg.	Negative	prep.	Preposition		
neut.	Neuter	Pr.n.	Proper name	Tex:	Textiles
nom.	Nominative	pron.	Pronoun	Tg:	Telegraphy
Num:	Numismatics	Pros:	Prosody	Th:	Theatre
num.a.	Numeral adjective	Prot:	Protozoa	Theol:	Theology
		Prov:	Proverb	thg	Thing
Oc:	Oceanography	Psy:	Psychology	Tls:	Tools
occ.	Occasionally	Publ:	Publishing	Toil:	Toilet
Onomat:	Onomatopoeia	Pyr:	Pyrotechnics	Tp:	Telephony
Opt:	Optics			tr.	Transitive
Orn:	Ornithology	qch.	Quelque chose	Tram:	Tramways
Ost:	Ostreiculture	qn	Quelqu'un	Trig:	Trigonometry
				Typ:	Typography
p.	(i) Participle; (ii) past	Rac:	Racing		
		Rail:	Railways	U.S:	United States
P:	Popular; slang	R.C.Ch:	Roman Catholic Church	usu.	Usually
Paint:	Painting trade				
Pal:	Paleography	rel.	Relative	v.	Verb
Paleont:	Paleontology	Rel:	Religion(s)	v.	Vous (= you)
Paperm:	Papermaking	Rel.H:	Religious History	V:	Vulgar
Parl:	Parliament	Rept:	Reptilia	Veh:	Vehicles
p.d.	Past descriptive; imperfect tense	Rh:	Rhetoric	Ven:	Venery
		Row:	Rowing	Vet:	Veterinary science
Pej:	Pejorative			Vit:	Viticulture
perf.	Perfect	S.	South	Voc:	Vocative
pers.	Person; personal	s., sb.	Substantive		
p.h.	Past historic; past definite	S.a.	See also	W.Tel:	Wireless Telephony and Telegraphy
		Sch:	Schools and universities		
Ph:	Physics			W.Tg:	Wireless Telegraphy
Pharm:	Pharmacy	Scot:	Scottish	W.Tp:	Wireless Telephony
Phil:	Philosophy	Sculp:	Sculpture	Wr:	Wrestling
Phot:	Photography	sg.	Singular		
Phot.Engr:	Photo-Engraving; process work	Sm.a:	Small arms	Y:	Yachting
		s.o.	Someone	Z:	Zoology

The symbol = is used to indicate a correspondence between French and English institutions, where the terms thus brought together cannot be considered strictly as translations one of the other. Thus: *Procureur général* = Attorney General. *Procureur de la République* = Public Prosecutor.

SHORTER
FRENCH AND ENGLISH DICTIONARY

PART ONE
FRENCH—ENGLISH

A

A, a¹ [a], *s.m.* (The letter) A, a. *F:* **Il ne sait ni A ni B,** he doesn't know A from B. **Connaître un sujet depuis A jusqu'à Z,** to know a subject from A to Z, thoroughly, inside out.

a² [a]. See AVOIR.

à [a], *prep.* (Contracts with the article *le* into **au,** with the article *les* into **aux.**)
I. **1.** Denoting direction in space, towards an end. (*a*) *Courir à qn,* to run to s.o. *Aller à l'école, à l'église,* to go to school, to church. *Voyage à Paris,* journey to Paris. *Se rendre au Japon, aux Indes,* to travel to Japan, to India. (*b*) *Au voleur! stop thief! A l'assassin!* murder! (*c*) Denoting opposition. *On se battit homme à homme,* they fought man to man. *Games: Nous sommes point à point, F:* **nous sommes point à,** the score is even. *Ten:* **Quinze A,** fifteen all. **2.** Denoting direction in time. *Du matin au soir,* from morning to night. *Attendre à plus tard,* to wait until later. *A jeudi!* good-bye until Thursday! see you on Thursday! **3.** Denoting point in space. *A la gare,* at the station. *A l'école, à l'église, à Paris,* at school, at church, in Paris. *Être au jardin,* to be in the garden. *Avoir qch. à la main,* to have sth. in one's hand. *A deux milles d'ici,* two miles away. **4.** Denoting point in time. *A deux heures,* at two o'clock. *A certains jours,* on certain days. *A mon arrivée,* on my arrival. *Arriver à temps,* to arrive in time. *Au mois de juillet,* in the month of July. **5.** Denoting mode of action. *Louer une maison à l'année,* to let a house by the year. *Vendre des marchandises à la douzaine,* to sell goods by the dozen. *Nous l'avons fait à deux, à trois,* there were two, three, of us at it. *Recevoir qn à bras ouverts,* to receive s.o. with open arms. *A la française, à l'anglaise,* (in the) French, English, fashion. *Nager à la chien,* to swim dogwise. *Manger à sa faim, boire à sa soif,* to eat, drink, one's fill. *On le voit à votre visage,* I can tell it by your face. **6.** Introducing the indirect object of a vb. *Donner qch. à qn,* to give sth. to s.o. *Parler à qn,* to speak to s.o. *Penser à qch.,* to think of sth. **7.** Forming adj. phrases. (*a*) (Purpose) *Tasse à thé,* tea-cup. (*b*) (Means of action) *Moulin à vent,* windmill. *Machine à vapeur,* steam-engine. (*c*) (Special feature) *Homme à barbe noire,* man with a black beard. *Gens à l'aspect étranger,* people of foreign appearance. *Chambre à deux lits,* double-bedded room. (*d*) (Possession) *Un livre à moi,* a book of mine. *J'ai de l'argent à moi,* I have money of my own. *Le livre est à Jean,* the book is John's. *Son idée à elle serait de . . .,* her idea would be to. . . . **8.** (*a*) Introducing a complement to an adj. *C'est très gentil à vous,* that's very nice, kind, of you. (*b*) Introducing a

complement to *être. Ce n'est pas à moi de les avertir,* it is not my business to warn them. *C'est à vous, à Pierre, de décider,* it is for you, for Peter, to decide. *C'est à vous,* it is your turn.
II. **à** introducing vb. in the infinitive. **1.** As logical subject of sentence. *Il me reste à vous remercier,* I still have to thank you. **2.** As obj. or compl. to a vb. *Il aime à se distraire,* he is fond of pleasure. *Il apprend à lire,* he is learning to read. *J'ai à faire,* I have work to do. **3.** In adj. relation to sb. or pron. *J'ai une lettre à écrire,* I have a letter to write. *Il est homme à se défendre,* he is the kind of man who will hit back. *Un spectacle à ravir,* a delightful sight. *Machine à coudre,* sewing-machine. *Vous n'êtes pas à plaindre,* you are not to be pitied. **4.** In adv. relation to adj. (*a*) *Je suis prêt à vous écouter,* I am ready to listen to you. (*b*) With numerals. *Un Samaritain fut le troisième à passer,* a Samaritan was the third to pass by. **5.** Related to vb. (*a*) Denoting time, place, circumstance. *Il est à travailler,* he is at (his) work. *J'en suis venu à lui parler,* I have got to the point of speaking to him. (*b*) With restrictive force. *A les en croire pas une âme n'aurait survécu,* if they are to be believed not a soul has survived. *A vivre ainsi vous vous abîmez la santé,* such a life is impairing your health. *A partager les mêmes périls on apprend à se connaître,* by sharing the same dangers we learn to know each other. **6.** With intensive force. *Il gèle à pierre fendre,* it is freezing hard. *Elle est laide à faire peur,* she is frightfully ugly. *Un bruit à tout casser,* a noise fit to bring the house down.

abaissant [abɛsɑ̃], *a.* Lowering (to one's self-respect, etc.).

abaissement [abɛsmɑ̃], *s.m.* **1.** *A. du bras, d'un store, des prix,* lowering of the arm, of a blind, of prices. **2.** Falling, abatement, subsidence, sinking. *A. de la température,* fall in temperature. *A. des prix,* dropping of prices. **3.** Dip (of the ground). **4.** Abasement. *A. des grands,* humbling of the great.

abaisser [abɛse], *v.tr.* **1.** To lower; to let down (drawbridge). *A. les yeux sur la foule,* to look down on the crowd. **2.** To lower (shelf, one's voice); to reduce, lessen (prices, cost, pressure, etc.). **3.** To humble, bring low, abase. *Dieu abaisse les superbes,* God humbles the proud. **4.** *Ar:* **A. un chiffre,** to bring down a figure. **5.** *Geom:* **A. une perpendiculaire à une ligne,** to let fall a perpendicular to, on, a line.

s'abaisser. 1. To fall away, dip, slope downward, go down. *Le terrain s'est abaissé,* the ground has subsided. *Ses paupières s'abaissèrent,* her eyelids drooped. **2.** *S'a. devant Dieu,* to humble oneself before God. **3.** *S'a. à, jusqu'à, faire qch.*, to, stoop so low as to do sth.; to stoop to doing sth.

abajoue [abaʒu], *s.f.* **1.** *Z:* (Monkey's) cheek-pouch. **2.** *pl. F:* Flabby cheeks.

abandon [abɑ̃dɔ̃], *s.m.* **1.** (*a*) Surrender, renunciation (of goods, rights, etc.). **Faire l'abandon de qch. à qn**, to make over, resign, surrender, sth. to s.o. (*b*) *Sp:* Giving up, withdrawal (from race). **2.** Forsaking, desertion, abandonment, neglect (of children, duty). **3.** Forlornness, neglect. *Mourir dans un a. général, universel,* to die forsaken by all. **A l'abandon**, neglected, in utter neglect. **4.** (*a*) Lack of restraint; unreserve, unconstraint, abandon. (*b*) *A. au péché,* indulgence in sin.

abandonnement [abɑ̃dɔnmɑ̃], *s.m.* **1.** = ABANDON 1, 2, 4. **2.** Profligacy, shamelessness.

abandonner [abɑ̃dɔne], *v.tr.* **1.** To forsake, desert, abandon; to leave. *Nau: A. un homme,* to maroon a man. *Ses amis l'abandonnent,* his friends are forsaking him. *Mes forces m'abandonnent,* my strength is failing me. *Abandonné de tous,* forsaken by all. *Abandonné par les médecins,* given up by the doctors. **2.** To surrender, renounce, give up. *A. ses prétentions,* to renounce, surrender, one's claims. **3.** To let go (a rope).

s'abandonner. 1. (*a*) To neglect oneself, to be careless of oneself. (*b*) To give way to despair, to grief. **2.** To be unconstrained; *F:* to let oneself go. **3.** *S'a. à qch.,* to give oneself up to sth.; to become addicted to (vice, etc.); to give way to (emotion). **4.** *S'a. à la Providence,* to commit oneself to Providence. *S'a. au sommeil,* to surrender oneself to sleep.

abandonné, -ée, *a. & s.* **1.** Forsaken (person). **Les abandonnés,** waifs and strays. *Navire a. en mer,* derelict (ship). **2.** Profligate, shameless, abandoned (person, conduct). *adv.* **-ment.**

abaque [abak], *s.m.* (*a*) Abacus, counting frame. (*b*) Chart, graph, table, scale, diagram; nomograph, plotter.

abasourd|ir [abazurdi:r, -sur-], *v.tr.* To dumbfound, astound, bewilder. *Nous restâmes abasourdis de la nouvelle,* we were flabbergasted by the news. *a.* **-issant.** *s.m.* **-issement.**

abat. See ABATTRE.

abâtardir [abɑtardi:r], *v.tr.* To cause to degenerate.

s'abâtardir, to degenerate, to deteriorate.

abâtardissement [abɑtardismɑ̃], *s.m.* Degeneracy, degeneration.

abatis [abati], *s.m.* = ABATTIS.

abat-jour [abaʒu:r], *s.m.inv.* (*a*) Lamp-shade, candle-shade. (*b*) Eye-shade. (*c*) Sun-blind, awning. (*d*) Slanting shutter. **Mettre la main en abat-jour,** to shade one's eyes with one's hand.

abattage [abata:ʒ], *s.m.* **1.** (*a*) Knocking down, throwing down. *F:* **Recevoir un abattage,** to get hauled over the coals, to get a wigging. (*b*) Felling, cutting down, clearing (of trees, etc.). **2.** Leverage. **3.** Slaughtering, killing (of oxen). *Grand a. de gibier,* heavy slaughter, heavy bag, of game.

abattant [abatɑ̃]. **1.** *a.* (*a*) Depressing. *Chaleur abattante,* heat that leaves one l.mp. (*b*) **Siège abattant,** tilting seat (of car, etc.). **2.** *s.m.* Flap (of counter, table, envelope, etc.).

abattement [abatmɑ̃], *s.m.* (*a*) (Physical) prostration. (*b*) Despondency, dejection, depression, low spirits.

abattis [abati], *s.m.* **1.** (*a*) Felling, clearing (of trees). (*b*) Killing, slaughter (of game, etc.). **2.** *A. de maisons,* heap of fallen houses. **3.** *pl.* (*a*) *Cu:* Giblets. (*b*) *P:* Limbs; hands and feet.

Tu peux numéroter tes abattis! you had better take stock of yourself (i) before I thrash you, (ii) before you face the music. **4.** *Mil:* Abatis (of trees, branches).

abattoir [abatwa:r], *s.m.* Slaughter-house; abattoir.

abatt|re [abatr], *v.tr.* (Conj. like BATTRE) **1.** (*a*) To knock down, throw down, pull down; to overthrow. *A. une maison,* to pull down a house. *F:* **Abattre de la besogne,** to get through a lot of work. (*b*) To fell, cut down, clear (trees). (*c*) To strike off, lop off, cut off, *F:* chop off (head, limb). **2.** To slaughter, kill, destroy. *A. un bœuf,* to slaughter an ox. *A. un cheval blessé,* to destroy an injured horse. **3.** To bring down. (*a*) *A. une perdrix,* to shoot a partridge. *A. un avion,* to bring down, shoot down, an aeroplane. (*b*) *A. son sabre sur la tête de qn,* to bring down one's sword on s.o.'s head. *A. violemment le couvercle,* to bang down the lid. **4.** To lower. *A. les tentes,* to strike tents. *A. l'orgueil de qn,* to lower, humble, break, s.o.'s pride. **5.** To lay (dust, wind). *Prov:* **Petite pluie abat grand vent,** small rain lays great dust. **6.** (Of wind) To blow down, beat down. *Arbre abattu par le vent,* tree blown down by the wind. **7.** To dishearten, unman, depress. *Ne vous laissez pas abattre!* bear up! **8.** *Cards: A. ses cartes, son jeu,* to lay one's cards on the table, to lay down one's hand. *s.* **-eur, -euse.**

s'abattre. 1. To fall, to crash down. *Le mât s'abattit,* the mast came crashing down. **2.** *S'a. sur qch.,* to pounce upon sth.; to swoop down, sweep down, upon sth. *Le faucon s'abat sur sa proie,* the falcon pounces on its prey. **3.** (Of fever, heat, etc.) To abate, to subside. *Le vent s'abat,* the wind is falling. **4.** To become disheartened, depressed.

abattu, *a.* **1.** Dejected, down-hearted, low-spirited. *A. par la chaleur,* limp with the heat. *Visage a.,* drawn face. **2.** See BRIDE 1.

abbaye [abɛ(j)i], *s.f.* Abbey, monastery.

abbé [abe], *s.m.* **1.** Abbot. **2.** General designation of and mode of address for a (Roman Catholic) priest. *J'en parlerai à monsieur l'abbé,* I shall mention it to the priest. *L'abbé Constantin,* Father Constantin, Abbé Constantin. **3.** *Hist:* (As applied to one having no ecclesiastical duty) Abbé.

abbesse [abɛs], *s.f.* Abbess.

abcès [apsɛ], *s.m.* Abscess, gathering. *A. au doigt,* gathered finger. *A. à la gencive,* gumboil.

abdication [abdikasjɔ̃], *s.f.* (*a*) Abdication. (*b*) Renunciation, surrender (of authority).

abdiquer [abdike], *v.tr.* To abdicate (throne); to renounce, surrender (rights, etc.).

abdomen [abdɔmɛn], *s.m.* (*a*) Abdomen. (*b*) *F:* Paunch, corporation.

abdominal, -aux [abdɔminal, -o], *a.* Abdominal.

abeille [abɛːj], *s.f.* Bee. *A. domestique,* hive-bee, honey-bee. *A. neutre, a. ouvrière,* working bee. *A. mâle,* drone. *A. mère,* queen-bee. **Nid d'abeilles,** bees' nest, honeycomb. *Serviette nid d'abeilles,* honeycomb towel. *Aut: Radiateur nid d'abeilles,* honeycomb radiator.

aberration [abɛr(r)asjɔ̃], *s.f.* **1.** *Astr: Biol: Mth: Opt:* Aberration. *A. de sphéricité,* spherical aberration. **2.** Aberration (of mind, conduct).

abhorrer [abɔr(r)e], *v.tr.* To abhor, loathe, abominate.

abîme [abiːm], *s.m.* Abyss, chasm, unfathomable depth(s). *Les profonds abîmes de l'océan,* the unfathomed deep. *F:* **Un abîme de science,** a man of immense learning.

abîmer [abime], *v.tr.* To spoil, damage, injure. *S'a. la santé,* to injure one's health. *Livre abîmé par la pluie,* book spoilt by the rain. *F: A. qn dans la presse,* to run down, slate, s.o. in the papers.

s'abîmer. **1.** (*a*) *S'a. dans les flots,* to be engulfed, swallowed up, by the sea. (*b*) *S'a. dans la douleur, dans ses pensées,* to be sunk in grief, in thought. **2.** To get spoiled; to spoil.

abject [abʒɛkt], *a.* Abject (poverty); mean, contemptible, despicable (person, conduct). *adv.* **-ement.**

abjuration [abʒyrasjɔ̃], *s.f.* Abjuration; renunciation (on oath); recantation.

abjurer [abʒyre], *v.tr.* To abjure, forswear; to renounce (on oath); to recant, retract.

ablatif, -ive [ablatif,-iːv], *a. & s.m. Gram:* Ablative (case). *A l'ablatif,* in the ablative. *A. absolu,* ablative absolute.

ablette [ablɛt], *s.f. Ich:* (Small river) bleak.

ablution [ablysjɔ̃], *s.f.* Ablution, washing. *F: Faire ses ablutions,* to perform one's ablutions.

abnégation [abnegasjɔ̃], *s.f.* Abnegation, self-sacrifice. *Faire abnégation de soi, de ses intérêts,* to sacrifice oneself, one's interests.

aboi [abwa], *s.m.* **1.** *A:* Bark, barking (of dog); bay, baying (of hound). **2.** *Aux abois,* (i) (of stag, enemy) at bay; (ii) hard pressed, hard set, with his back against the wall. *Réduire, mettre, qn aux abois,* to reduce s.o. to the last extremity; to press s.o. hard. *Ils sont aux abois,* they are in desperate straits. [ABOYER]

aboiement, aboîment [abwamɑ̃], *s.m.* Bark, barking (of dog); bay, baying (of hound).

abolir [aboliːr], *v.tr.* To abolish, suppress.

abolition [abolisjɔ̃], *s.f.* Abolition, abolishment; suppression.

abominable [abominabl], *a.* Abominable; heinous (crime). *F: Temps a.,* wretched, beastly, weather. *adv.* **-ment.**

abomination [abominasjɔ̃], *s.f.* **1.** Abomination, abhorrence, detestation. *Avoir qch. en abomination,* to abominate, loathe, sth. **2.** *Ce café est une a.,* this coffee is wretched stuff.

abominer [abomine], *v.tr.* To abominate, abhor, loathe.

abondance [abɔ̃dɑ̃s], *s.f.* **1.** Abundance, plenty. *Une a. de fruits,* an abundance of fruit. *Année d'a.,* year of plenty. *Prov: Abondance de bien(s) ne nuit pas,* store is no sore. *S.a.* CORNE[1] 4. **2.** Wealth (of expression, details). *Parler avec abondance,* to have a great flow of words. *Parler d'abondance,* to speak off-hand, extempore. **3.** *F:* Wine diluted with water (as served in schools, farms, etc.).

abond|ant [abɔ̃dɑ̃], *a.* Abundant, copious, plentiful; rich (style). *A. en qch.,* abounding in sth. *adv.* **-amment.**

abonder [abɔ̃de], *v.i.* **1.** To abound (*en, in*); to be plentiful. *Rivière qui abonde en poisson,* river well stocked with fish. **2.** *Abonder dans le sens de qn,* to be entirely of s.o.'s opinion.

abonnement [abonmɑ̃], *s.m.* **1.** Subscription (to paper, etc.). *Prendre un abonnement au 'Figaro,'* to subscribe to the 'Figaro.' **2.** (*Carte d'*)*abonnement,* season-ticket (on railway, at theatre, etc.); contract (on railway). *Prendre un a.,* to take out a season-ticket.

abonner (s') [sabone], *v.pr.* **1.** *S'a. à un journal,* to subscribe, become a subscriber, to a paper. *Être abonné à un journal,* to take in a paper. **2.** *Rail: etc:* To take a season-ticket.

abonné, -ée, *s.* **1.** Subscriber (to paper, etc.). **2.** Season-ticket holder. **3.** *Abonnés du gaz, de l'électricité,* consumers of gas, of electricity.

abord [aboːr], *s.m.* **1.** Access, approach (to land). *Ile d'un a. difficile,* island difficult of access. **2.** *pl.* Approaches (*d'un endroit,* to a place); surroundings, purlieus, outskirts (*de,* of). **3.** (*a*) Manner in which a person approaches another. *Son a. fut respectueux,* he approached, greeted, me respectfully. (*b*) Manner in which a person receives those who approach him. *Avoir l'abord facile, difficile,* to be easy, difficult, to approach. **4.** *Adv.phr.* **D'abord, tout d'abord,** (i) *A:* straightway, at once; (ii) at first, to begin with; (iii) first, in the first place, first and foremost. *Dès l'abord,* from the (very) first, from the outset. **A l'abord, au premier abord, de prime abord,** at first sight, to begin with. [ABORDER]

abordable [abordabl], *a.* **1.** Easy to land on; easy of approach, easy of access; approachable, accessible. *F: Vos prix ne sont pas abordables,* your prices are beyond my purse. **2.** Easily approached; accessible, affable, kindly.

abordage [aborda:ʒ], *s.m. Nau:* **1.** Boarding (as an act of war); grappling. *Monter, sauter, à l'abordage* (*d'un navire*), to board a ship. **2.** Collision. *Il y a eu un a. causé par le brouillard,* two ships ran foul of each other, collided, in the fog. **3.** Boarding (another boat); coming alongside.

aborder [aborde]. **1.** *v.i.* To land; to make land. *A. à un port,* to reach a port. *A. en Afrique,* to land in Africa. *A. à quai,* to berth. **2.** *v.tr.* (*a*) To accost, approach (s.o.). *Être abordé par un inconnu,* to be accosted by a stranger. (*b*) *A. une question,* to approach, tackle, a question. *A. de nouvelles études,* to take up, enter upon, new studies. (*c*) To board, grapple (ship in a fight). (*d*) To collide with, run foul of, run down (ship). [BORD]

abordeur [abordœːr], *a. & s.m.* Colliding (ship).

aborigène [aboriʒɛn]. **1.** *a.* Aboriginal (*de,* in); native (*de,* to). **2.** *s.m.* Aboriginal. *pl.* **Aborigènes,** aborigines (of a country).

Aboukir [abukiːr]. *Pr.n.m. Geog:* Abukir. *Hist:* *La bataille d'Aboukir,* the battle of the Nile.

abouler [abule], *v.tr. P:* To bring; to hand over. *Aboule ça ici!* bring that here! hand it over!

s'abouler, *P:* to come along. *S'a. en retard,* to turn up late.

aboutir [abutiːr], *v.i.* **1.** *A. à, dans, en, qch.,* to end at, in, sth.; to lead to sth.; to converge on sth.; to result in sth. *Ce sentier aboutit au grand chemin,* this path leads into, ends at, the high road. *Une pyramide aboutit en pointe,* a pyramid ends in a point. *N'a. à rien,* to lead, come, to nothing; *F:* to end in smoke. *Pour a. aux fins que nous poursuivons,* to attain the end that we have in view. **2.** *Abs.* (*a*) (Of plan, etc.) To succeed; *F:* to come off. *Ne pas aboutir,* to fail; to fall through. *Homme qui a abouti,* man who has achieved success. *Faire aboutir qch.,* to bring sth. to a successful issue. (*b*) (Of abscess) To come to a head, to burst. [BOUT]

aboutissant [abutisɑ̃], *a.* Bordering, abutting (*à, on*).

aboutissement [abutismɑ̃], *s.m.* **1.** Issue, outcome (of endeavours, etc.). **2.** *Med:* Coming to a head; bursting (of abscess).

aboyer [abwaje], *v.i.* (*j'aboie; j'aboierai*) (Of dog) To bark; (of hound) to bay. *A. à, après, contre, qn,* to bark at s.o. *A. à la lune,* (i) to bay the moon; (ii) *F:* to make useless complaint.

aboyeur, -euse [abwajœːr, -øːz], *s.* **1.** *a.* (Dog) given to barking; barking (dog). **2.** *s. F:* (*a*) Carper, fault-finder. (*b*) Tout (in front of booth, etc.).

abracadabra [abrakadabra], *s.m.* Magic key-word; abracadabra, fee-faw-fum.

abracadabrant [abrakadabrã], *a.* F: Stupendous, amazing, F: stunning. *Récit a.*, extraordinary yarn.

abrégement [abreʒmã], *s.m.* **1.** (*a*) Abridging, epitomizing (of work). (*b*) Shortening (of syllable). **2.** Abridgment, epitome.

abréger [abreʒe], *v.tr.* (j'abrège, n. abrégeons; j'abrégerai) **1.** To shorten, to cut short (life, work, etc.). *On l'appelle Toinon pour a.*, she is called Toinon for short. *Pour abréger . . .*, to be brief . . ., to cut it short. . . . **2.** To abridge, cut down (article); to abbreviate (word).
s'abréger. 1. (Of days, etc.) To grow shorter; to shorten. **2.** (Of speaker, etc.) To cut one's story short.

abrégé, *s.m.* Abridgment, précis, summary, epitome. *Faire un a. d'une correspondance,* to make a précis of a correspondence. *A. d'histoire de France,* short history of France. *Voici les faits en abrégé,* here are the facts in a few words.

abreuv|er [abrœve], *v.tr.* **1.** To water (horses, cattle, etc.); to supply (animals) with drink. **2.** To soak, drench, flood, irrigate (meadow, etc.). *L'Égypte est abreuvée par le Nil,* Egypt is watered by the Nile. **3.** *A. qn d'injures,* to heap insults on s.o. *s.m.* **-age.** *s.m.* **-ement.**
s'abreuver, (of horse) to drink; (of pers.) to drink deep, to quench one's thirst. *S'a. de sang,* to slake, sate, one's thirst for blood.

abreuvoir [abrœvwa:r], *s.m.* (*a*) Watering-place (in river, etc.); horse-pond. *Mener les chevaux à l'a.,* to water the horses. (*b*) Drinking-trough.

abréviation [abrevjasjɔ̃], *s.f.* **1.** Shortening (of term of imprisonment, etc.). **2.** Abbreviation.

abri [abri], *s.m.* Shelter, cover. *A. public,* public shelter. **Prendre abri,** to take cover. *Famille sans abri,* homeless family. **A l'abri,** sheltered, under shelter, under cover. *Mettre qch. à l'a.,* to shelter, screen, sth. *Se mettre à l'a.,* to take shelter. **A l'abri de qch.,** sheltered, screened, from sth. *A l'a. du besoin,* secure, safe, from want. *Se mettre à l'a. de la pluie,* to take shelter from the rain. *Nau: A l'a. de la côte,* under the lee of the shore.

abricot [abriko], *s.m.* Apricot.

abricotier [abrikɔtje], *s.m.* Apricot-tree.

abriter [abrite], *v.tr.* To shelter, screen, shield, shade, protect. *A. des plantes contre le vent,* to screen plants from the wind. [ABRI]
s'abriter, to take cover or shelter (contre, from); to shelter.

abrogation [abrɔgasjɔ̃], *s.f.* Abrogation, rescission, repeal (of law, etc.).

abroger [abrɔʒe], *v.tr.* (j'abrogeai(s); n. abrogeons) To abrogate, rescind, repeal (law, etc.).

abrupt [abrypt], *a.* **1.** Abrupt, sheer, steep (rock, descent). **2.** Abrupt, blunt; short of speech. *Répondre d'un ton a.,* to give an abrupt, short, answer. *adv.* **-ement.**

abrut|ir [abryti:r], *v.tr.* To brutalize, stupefy, besot. *Abruti par la boisson,* sodden with drink. *Je suis tout abruti de ce qui vient de se passer,* I am absolutely stupefied, dazed, by what has happened. [BRUT] *a.* **-issant.** *s.m.* **-issement.**
s'abrutir, to become sottish; to besot oneself; to moulder (in idleness).
abruti, *s.m.* **1.** F: Sot. **2.** P: Idiot, fool.

abscisse [apsis], *s.f.* Mth: Abscissa. *Axe des abscisses,* x-axis.

absence [apsã:s], *s.f.* **1.** Absence. *Faire de fréquentes absences,* to be often away from home. *Remarquer l'a. de qn,* to miss s.o. *A. de*

l'école, non-attendance at school, absence from school. **2.** *A de goût, d'imagination,* lack of taste, want of imagination. *A. d'esprit,* absence of mind.

absent [apsã]. **1.** *a.* (*a*) Absent, away (de, from). (*b*) Missing, wanting, absent. *Chez cet animal les dents sont absentes,* in this animal the teeth are wanting. (*c*) *Son esprit est a.,* his thoughts are far away. **2.** *s.* (*a*) (The) absent one. *Les absents ont toujours tort,* the absent are always in the wrong. (*b*) Absentee. *Liste des absents,* absentees' list.

absenter (s') [sapsɑ̃te], *v.pr.* **1.** To absent oneself; to go from home. **2.** *S'a. de l'école,* to stay, stop, away from school.

abside [apsid], *s.f.* Ecc.Arch: Apse.

absinthe [apsɛ̃:t], *s.f.* **1.** Bot: Wormwood. **2.** Absinth(e) (drink).

absolu [apsɔly], *a.* Absolute. (*a*) Zéro absolu, absolute zero. *Poser une règle absolue,* to lay down a hard and fast rule. *Refus a.,* flat refusal. (*b*) *Pouvoir a.,* absolute power. *Caractère a.,* autocratic nature. (*c*) Absolute, positive, peremptory (tone, voice).

absolument [apsɔlymã], *adv.* (*a*) (To reign, to use a verb) absolutely. **Absolument parlant . . .,** speaking generally. . . . (*b*) Entirely (unnecessary); utterly (impossible). *J'ai a. oublié,* I clean forgot. (*c*) (To speak) peremptorily. *C'est a. défendu,* it is strictly forbidden. *Je veux a.,* I insist upon it.

absolution [apsɔlysjɔ̃], *s.f.* Theol: Absolution.

absolv-ant, -ons, etc. See ABSOUDRE.

absorbant [apsɔrbã], *a.* **1.** Absorbent (substance). **2.** Absorbing, engrossing (book, task).

absorber [apsɔrbe], *v.tr.* **1.** (Of sponge, etc.) To absorb, to soak up (water, etc.). **2.** To consume (s.o.'s means, a fortune); to drink, imbibe (beer, etc.). **3.** To absorb, engross. *Son travail l'absorbe,* his work engrosses him.
s'absorber, to become absorbed, engrossed (dans, in); to give oneself up entirely (to). *Être absorbé dans ses pensées,* to be lost in thought.

absoudre [apsudr], *v.tr.* (*pr.p.* absolvant; *p.p.* absous, *f.* absoute; *pr.ind.* j'absous, il absout, n. absolvons, ils absolvent; *pr.sub.* j'absolve; *p.h. & p.sub.* are lacking; *fu.* j'absoudrai) (*a*) *A. qn de qch.,* (i) to forgive s.o. sth.; (ii) to acquit s.o. of, exonerate s.o. from, sth. (*b*) *A. qn de ses péchés,* to grant s.o. remission of his sins; to absolve s.o. from his sins.

abstenir (s') [sapstəni:r], *v.pr.* (Conj. like TENIR) *S'a. de qch.,* to abstain, refrain, from sth.; to forgo, eschew, sth. *S'a. de faire qch.,* to abstain, refrain, forbear, from doing sth. *Prov:* **Dans le doute abstiens-toi,** when in doubt, don't.

abstention [apstãsjɔ̃], *s.f.* Abstaining, abstention (de, from).

abstiendr-ai, -as, etc. See ABSTENIR (s').

abstienne, abstien-s, -t. See ABSTENIR (s').

abstinence [apstinã:s], *s.f.* Abstinence. **1.** Abstemiousness. **2.** Abstention (de, from).

abstin-s, -t [apstɛ̃]. See ABSTENIR (s').

abstraction [apstraksjɔ̃], *s.f.* Abstraction. (*a*) *Faire abstraction de qch.,* to leave sth. out of account; to disregard sth. (*b*) *Se perdre dans des abstractions,* to lose oneself in abstractions. (*c*) *Dans un moment d'a.,* in a moment of abstraction.

abstraire [apstrɛ:r], *v.tr.* (Conj. like TRAIRE) To abstract; to separate; to consider (sth.) apart (from sth.).
s'abstraire dans, en, qch., to become engrossed in sth.

abstrait, *a.* **1.** Abstracted, absorbed. **2.** Abstract (idea); abstruse, deep (question).

abstraitement [apstrɛtmã], *adv.* **1.** In the abstract. **2.** Abstractedly; in an absent-minded manner.

abstray-ons, -ez [apstrɛjɔ̃, -e]. See ABSTRAIRE.

absurde [apsyrd]. **1.** *a.* Absurd, preposterous, nonsensical. **2.** *s.m.* L'absurde, absurdity. **Réduire une théorie à l'absurde,** to reduce a theory *ad absurdum. adv.* **-ment.**

absurdité [apsyrdite], *s.f.* **1.** Absurdity, preposterousness. **2.** *Dire des absurdités,* to talk nonsense.

abus [aby], *s.m.* **1.** (a) Abuse, misuse (de, of). **Employer un terme par abus,** to misuse a term. (b) Over-indulgence (*de,* in). **Faire abus de qch.,** to indulge too freely in sth.; to make too free a use of sth. (c) Violation (of rights). **Abus de confiance,** breach of trust. **2.** Abuse; corrupt practice; evil custom or usage. *Réformer un a.,* to redress an abuse. **3.** Error, mistake. *C'est un a. (que) de crcire que . . .,* it is a mistake to suppose that. . .

abuser [abyze]. **1.** *v.i.* **A. de qch.** (a) To misuse sth. *Vous abusez de vos forces,* you are over-exerting yourself. (b) To take (an unfair) advantage of sth. *A. de l'amabilité de qn,* to impose upon s.o.'s kindness. *J'abuse de vos moments,* I am trespassing on your time. **2.** *v.tr.* To deceive, delude. *A. qn par de fausses promesses,* to delude s.o. with false promises.

s'abuser, to delude oneself; to be mistaken.

abusif, -ive [abyzif, -i:v], *a.* **1.** Contrary to usage. *Emploi a. d'un mot,* wrong use, misuse, of a word. **2.** Excessive. *Faire un emploi a. de la force,* to make an excessive, unwarranted, display of force.

abusivement [abyzivmã], *adv.* Improperly, wrongly.

abyssal [abis(s)al], *a. Oc:* Abyssal (fauna, etc.). (The *m.pl.* is uncertain.)

Abyssinie [abis(s)ini]. *Pr.n.f. Geog:* Abyssinia.

acabit [akabi], *s.m. F:* Usu. *Pej:* Nature, stamp (of person). **Ils sont du même acabit,** they are all of a piece, of the same kidney; they are tarred with the same brush.

acacia [akasja], *s.m. Bot:* **1. A. vrai,** acacia. **2.** *A. vulgaire, faux a.,* locust-tree.

académicien [akademisjɛ̃], *s.m.* Academician; esp. member of the *Académie française.*

académie [akademi], *s.f.* Academy. **1.** (a) University college or centre. (b) Educational district (of France). **2.** Society (of letters, science, or art). **L'Académie française,** the French Academy (of letters). **3.** (a) Riding-school. (b) *A. de musique,* school of music. *A. de dessin,* school of art, art school. Hence **4.** Study from the nude.

académique [akademik], *a.* Academic(al). *Séance a.,* sitting, meeting, of an Academy. **Occuper un fauteuil académique,** to sit in the French Academy.

acajou [akaʒu], *s.m.* Mahogany.

acanthe [akã:t], *s.f.* **1.** *Bot:* Acanthus, brank-ursine. **2.** *Arch:* Acanthus.

acariâtre [akarjɑːtr], *a.* (Esp. of women) Bad-tempered, cantankerous, shrewish.

acariâtreté [akarjɑtrəte], *s.f.* Cantankerousness; shrewishness.

accablant [akɑblã], *a.* **1.** Overwhelming (misfortune, proof). **2.** Overpowering (heat, etc.).

accablement [akɑbləmã], *s.m.* Dejection, despondency. *Med:* Prostration.

accabler [akɑble], *v.tr.* **1.** To overpower, overwhelm, crush. *A. qn d'injures,* to heap abuse upon

s.o. **2.** To overwhelm (in a favourable sense). *A. qn de caresses,* to load s.o. with caresses.

accablé, *a.* **1.** Overwhelmed (with work); overcome, weighed down (with grief); tired out. *A. de fatigue,* worn out with fatigue. **2.** *A. par la chaleur,* prostrated by the heat.

accalmie [akalmi], *s.f.* Lull (in the storm, in war, etc.). [CALME]

accapar|er [akapare], *v.tr.* To corner, hoard (wheat, etc.). *F: A. la conversation,* to monopolize the conversation. *A. les meilleures places,* to secure, *F:* bag, the best seats. *s.m.* **-ement.**

accapareur, -euse [akaparœːr, -øːz], *s.* (a) Buyer-up (of food, etc.); monopolist. (b) *Pej:* Grabber, shark.

accéder [aksede], *v.i.* (j'accède, n. accédons; j'accéderai) **1.** To have access (*à,* to). *On accède à la porte par un escalier,* access to the door is by a flight of steps. **2.** *A. à une requête,* to accede to, comply with, a request. *A. à une condition,* to agree, assent, to a condition.

accélérateur, -trice [akseleratœːr, -tris]. **1.** *a.* Accelerative, accelerating. **2.** *s.m. Aut: Phot: etc:* Accelerator.

accélération [akselerasjɔ̃], *s.f.* (a) Acceleration. *Aut: Pédale d'a.,* accelerator pedal. (b) Hastening, speeding up (of work).

accélérer [akselere], *v.tr.* (j'accélère, n. accélérons; j'accélérerai) To accelerate, quicken (rate of motion); to speed up (traffic, etc.).

s'accélérer, to become faster; to accelerate.

accéléré, *a.* **1.** Accelerated (motion). **2.** Quick, fast. S.a. PAS¹ 1.

accent [aksã], *s.m.* Accent. **1.** Stress. *A. tonique,* tonic accent. *Syllabe sans accent,* unaccented, unstressed, syllable. **2.** *A. grammatical,* grammatical accent. *A. aigu,* acute accent. **3.** Pronunciation. *Parler le français avec un a. anglais,* to speak French with an English accent. **4.** Tone of voice. *Son récit a l'a. de la vérité,* his account rings true. **5.** *pl.* (a) *Les accents du désespoir,* the accents of despair. (b) *Les accents de la Marseillaise,* the strains of the Marseillaise.

accentuation [aksãtɥasjɔ̃], *s.f.* **1.** Stressing (of syllables, etc.). **2.** Accentuation; placing of the grammatical accents.

accentuer [aksãtɥe], *v.tr.* **1.** To stress (syllable, etc.). *Syllabe non accentuée,* unstressed syllable. **2.** To mark (vowel) with a grammatical accent; to accentuate. **3.** To emphasize. *Traits fortement accentués,* strongly marked features. *A. le chômage,* to increase, add to, unemployment.

s'accentuer, to become accentuated, more pronounced, more marked.

accept|able [akseptabl], *a.* **1.** Acceptable (*à,* to). *Offre a.,* reasonable offer. *Cadeau très a.,* very acceptable, welcome, gift. **2.** In fair condition; that will pass muster. *s.f.* **-abilité.** *adv.* **-ablement.**

acceptation [akseptasjɔ̃], *s.f.* Acceptance.

accepter [aksepte], *v.tr.* To accept. *A. de faire qch.,* (i) to agree to do sth.; (ii) to accept an invitation to do sth. *A. que qch. se fasse,* to agree to sth. being done. *A. qn comme, pour, arbitre,* to accept s.o. as an arbitrator.

acception [aksepsjɔ̃], *s.f.* Acceptation, meaning, sense (of word, etc.).

accès [aksɛ], *s.m.* **1.** Access, approach. *Les a. de la gare,* the station approaches. **Avoir accès à qch.,** to have access to sth. **Donner accès à qch.,** to give access, to lead, to sth. **Trouver accès auprès de qn,** to gain admission to s.o. **2.** Fit, attack, outburst. *A. de fièvre,* attack, bout, of fever. *A. de faiblesse,* fainting fit. *A. de colère, de folie,* outburst of passion; fit of madness. **Travailler par accès**, to work by fits and starts.

access|ible [aksesibl], *a.* **1.** Accessible. *Charges accessibles à tout le monde*, posts accessible, open, to all. *Endroit a., F:* get-at-able place. **2.** (Of pers.) (*a*) Approachable. (*b*) *A. à la pitié*, open to pity. *s.f.* **-ibilité.**

accession [aksesjɔ̃], *s.f.* **1.** Accession (to power, etc.). *A. au trône*, accession to the throne. **2.** Union (of Brittany with France, etc.). **3.** Adherence, adhesion (to a contract, to a party).

accessit [aksesit], *s.m.* 'Proxime accessit'; honourable mention; certificate of merit.

accessoire [akseswa:r]. **1.** *a.* Accessory. *Jouer un rôle a.*, to play a subordinate part. **2.** *s.m.* Accessory, appurtenance. *pl. Th:* Properties. *adv.* **-ment.**

accident [aksidɑ̃], *s.m.* **1.** Accident. (*a*) **Je l'ai retrouvé par accident**, I found it by accident, accidentally. (*b*) Mishap. *A. de chemin de fer*, railway accident. *A. mortel*, fatality. *Être victime d'un a.*, to meet with an accident. **Nous sommes arrivés sans accident**, we arrived safely. **2.** *Mus:* Accidental. **3.** **Accident de terrain**, fold, undulation, of the ground.

accidenté, -ée [aksidɑ̃te]. **1.** *a.* (*a*) Eventful (life). (*b*) Uneven, broken (ground). **2.** *s.* Victim of an accident. *Les accidentés*, the injured, the casualties.

accident|el, -elle [aksidɑ̃tɛl], *a.* **1.** Accidental, undesigned. **2.** *Mus:* Signes accidentels, (i) accidentals, (ii) key-signature. *adv.* **-ellement.**

accidenter [aksidɑ̃te], *v.tr.* To give variety to (the landscape, etc.); to vary (one's style, etc.).

acclamation [aklamasjɔ̃], *s.f.* Acclamation, cheering. *Discours salué d'acclamations*, speech greeted with cheers.

acclamer [aklame,-klɑ-]. **1.** *v.tr.* (*a*) To acclaim, applaud, cheer; to greet (s.o.) with cheers. (*b*) *Pred. A. qn empereur*, to acclaim s.o. emperor, to hail s.o. as emperor. **2.** *v.ind.tr. A. à une proposition*, to greet a proposal with cheers.

acclimatation [aklimatasjɔ̃], *s.f.* Acclimatization. **Le Jardin d'Acclimatation**, the Acclimatization Gardens, *F:* the Zoo (in the Bois de Boulogne, near Paris).

acclimat|er [aklimate], *v.tr.* To acclimatize (à, to). *s.m.* **-ement.**
s'acclimater, to become, get, acclimatized.

accointances [akwɛ̃tɑ̃:s], *s.f.pl. Pej:* Intimacy; dealings (*avec*, with).

accointé, -ée [akwɛ̃te], *s.* Compeer, partner (in fraud, etc.).

accolade [akɔlad], *s.f.* **1.** (*a*) Embrace. (*b*) *F:* Hug or kiss. **2.** Accolade. **Recevoir l'accolade**, to be knighted. **3.** *Mus: Typ:* Brace, bracket.

accoler [akɔle], *v.tr.* To join side by side; to couple. *Typ:* To brace, bracket. *Église accolée aux murs de la ville*, church built on to the town walls.
accolé, *a.* Coupled; bracketed.

accommodant [akɔmɔdɑ̃], *a.* Good-natured, easy-going, easy to deal with, accommodating. **Peu accommodant**, not easy to deal with.

accommodation [akɔmɔdasjɔ̃], *s.f.* **1.** Adapting. *A. d'une salle aux usages d'un bureau*, adaptation, conversion, of a room to office use. **2.** *Physiol:* Accommodation (of the eye).

accommodement [akɔmɔdmɑ̃], *s.m.* Compromise, arrangement. **En venir à un accommodement**, to come to terms (*avec*, with). *Politique d'a.*, policy of compromise; give-and-take policy.

accommod|er [akɔmɔde], *v.tr.* **1.** (*a*) To make (s.o.) comfortable (in an arm-chair, etc.). (*b*) To

suit (s.o.). *Difficile à a.*, difficult to please. **2.** To cook, do up, season, dress (food). *A. une salade*, to dress a salad. **3.** *A. qch. à qch.*, to fit, adapt, sth. to sth. *a.* **-able.**

s'accommoder. **1.** To make oneself comfortable, to settle down (in arm-chair, etc.). *Il s'accommode partout, à toutes les circonstances*, he makes himself at home everywhere; he is very adaptable. **2.** *S'a. de qch.*, to make the best of sth.; to make shift, put up, with sth. *Je m'accommode de tout*, I am pleased with anything; anything suits me. **3.** *S'a. à qch.*, to adapt, accommodate, oneself to sth. **4.** *S'a. avec qn*, (i) to come to an agreement with s.o.; (ii) to compromise with s.o.; to compound (with creditor).

accompagnateur, -trice [akɔ̃paɲatœ:r, -tris], *s. Mus:* Accompanist.

accompagnement [akɔ̃paɲmɑ̃], *s.m.* **1.** (Action of) accompanying (s.o.). **2.** *Mus:* Accompaniment.

accompagner [akɔ̃paɲe], *v.tr.* **1.** To accompany. (*a*) To go, come, with (s.o.). *M'accompagnez-vous?* are you coming with me? *Faites-vous a.*, take someone with you. *A. qn un bout de chemin*, to go a bit of the way with s.o. (*b*) To escort, attend (on) (s.o. as a retinue, etc.). *Nos meilleurs vœux vous accompagnent*, our best wishes attend you, go with you. (*c*) *A. qn au piano*, to accompany s.o. on the piano. *Elle s'accompagne elle-même*, she plays her own accompaniments. **2.** *A. des remontrances de menaces*, to join threats to remonstrances.

accomplir [akɔ̃pli:r], *v.tr.* **1.** To accomplish, achieve (purpose, etc.); to carry out, perform, fulfil (order, promise, etc.). *Que la volonté du Seigneur s'accomplisse*, the Lord's will be done. **2.** To complete, finish (apprenticeship, etc.). *Il a quarante ans accomplis*, he is turned forty. **Fait accompli**, accomplished fact.
accompli, *a.* Accomplished (musician, linguist, etc.). *Scélérat a.*, out and out rascal.

accomplissement [akɔ̃plismɑ̃], *s.m.* **1.** Accomplishment, performance, carrying out, achievement (of work, duty); fulfilment (of wish). **2.** Completion.

accord [akɔ:r], *s.m.* **1.** Agreement. (*a*) Settlement. *Un a. est intervenu*, an agreement has been reached. (*b*) Harmony. **Vivre en bon accord**, to live in concord. **D'accord**, in agreement, in accordance (*avec*, with). **Mettre d'accord deux points de vue**, to reconcile two points of view. **Se mettre d'accord, tomber d'accord, avec qn**, to come to an agreement with s.o. *Être d'a. avec qn*, to agree, be at one, with s.o. **D'accord!** agreed! granted! quite so! **D'un commun accord**, by common consent. **En accord avec . . .**, in harmony, keeping, suit, with. . . . (*c*) *Gram:* Concordance (*avec*, with). **Les règles d'accord**, the concords. **2.** *Mus:* Chord. *A. parfait*, common chord. *Lit: De doux accords*, sweet strains. **3.** (*a*) *Mus:* Pitch, tune. **Être d'accord**, to be in tune. (*b*) *W.Tel: Effectuer l'a. d'un poste récepteur*, to tune a receiving-set, to tune in. **Condensateur d'accord**, tuning condenser.

accordéon [akɔrdeɔ̃], *s.m.* Accordion. *A. hexagonal*, concertina. **En accordéon**, pleated.

accord|er [akɔrde], *v.tr.* **1.** To reconcile, bring into accord (enemies, etc.). **2.** *Mus: W.Tel:* To tune (piano, receiving-set). **3.** To grant, concede; to bestow (gift); to award (damages). *A. à qn de faire qch.*, to grant s.o. leave to do sth. *A. que qch. se fasse*, to consent to sth. being done. *a.* **-able.**

s'accorder. **1.** (*a*) To agree, come to an

agreement. *S'a. sur le prix*, to agree upon the price. *Tous s'accordent à croire que* . . ., all concur in the belief that. . . . (*b*) To get on (well, badly) (*avec qn*, with s.o.). **2.** (Of fact or thg) To accord, tally, correspond, harmonize, *F:* to square, to fit in (*avec*, with). *Cela ne s'accorde pas avec son caractère*, it is not in keeping with his character. **3.** *Gram:* To agree, to be in concord (with). *Faire a. le verbe avec le sujet*, to make the verb agree with the subject. **4.** (Of article of dress, etc.) To go with, harmonize with, match (sth.). **5.** (Of instruments) To tune (up).

accordeur [akɔrdœːr], *s.m.* Tuner (of musical instruments).

accordoir [akɔrdwaːr], *s.m.* (Piano) tuning-key, -hammer.

accore [akɔːr], *a.* (Of coast) Sheer, abrupt, perpendicular, bluff; steep to.

accort [akɔːr], *a.* Pleasing, trim (maiden, etc.).

accostage [akɔstaːʒ], *s.m. Nau:* Boarding (of ship); drawing alongside (of ship, quay).

accoster [akɔste], *v.tr.* **1.** To accost (s.o.); to go, come, up to (s.o.). **2.** *A. un bateau le long du quai*, to berth a boat alongside (the quay). **3.** *Nau:* To come on board (ship).

accoter (s') [sakote], *v.pr. S'a. à, contre, un mur*, to lean against a wall. *Accoté contre* . . ., leaning against. . . .

accouchement [akuʃmã], *s.m.* Bringing forth (of child); confinement; labour, lying-in; *accouchement*.

accoucher [akuʃe], *v.i.* (Aux. usu. *être*) (*a*) To be confined; to be delivered, brought to bed (*de*, of); to lie in. *A. d'un garçon*, to give birth to a boy. (*b*) *F: A. d'un travail*, to bring forth a piece of work.

    accouchée, *s.f.* Woman in child-bed.

accoud|er (s') [sakude], *v.pr.* To lean on one's elbow(s). [COUDE] *s.m.* **-ement.**

accouplement [akupləmã], *s.m.* **1.** (*a*) Coupling, join(ing), link(ing); yoking (of oxen). *A. à débrayage*, disengaging gear, clutch coupling. *Organ:* **Pédale d'accouplement,** coupler (pedal). (*b*) *El:* Connecting. **2.** Pairing, mating.

accoupler [akuple], *v.tr.* (*a*) To couple, to join in pairs; to yoke (oxen). (*b*) To couple (up) (parts). (*c*) *El:* To connect, group (batteries, etc.).

accourir [akuriːr], *v.i.* (Conj. like COURIR. Aux. *avoir* or *être*) To hasten (up); to flock, rush, up. *Ils ont accouru, sont accourus, à mon secours*, they ran, came running, to my help.

accoutrement [akutrəmã], *s.m.* Usu. *Pej:* Dress, garb; *F:* rig-out, get-up.

accoutrer [akutre], *v.tr.* Usu. *Pej:* To rig (s.o.) out, get (s.o.) up (*de*, in). *Accoutré d'une vieille capote*, rigged out in an old military great-coat.

    s'accoutrer, to dress, rig oneself out, get oneself up (*de*, in).

accoutumer [akutyme], *v.tr. A. qn à qch.*, to accustom s.o. to sth.; to inure s.o. (to hunger, cold, etc.). *A. qn à faire qch.*, to accustom s.o. to do, to doing, sth.

    s'accoutumer. *S'a. à qch.*, to become, get, accustomed to sth.; to become inured, to inure oneself, to sth. *Je ne pouvais pas m'a. à ce qu'on me grondât*, I could not get accustomed, get used, to being scolded.

    accoutumé, -ée. 1. *a.* (*a*) Accustomed, used (*à*, to); inured (to). *Je n'étais pas à. à ce qu'on me parlât ainsi*, I was not accustomed to being spoken to in this way. (*b*) Accustomed, customary, usual. *Lit:* **Avoir accoutumé de faire qch.,** to be wont to do sth. *Adv. phr.* **Comme à l'accoutumée,** as usual, as is customary. **2.** *s. Les visiteurs*

étaient des accoutumés, the visitors were customary callers.

accréditer [akredite], *v.tr.* **1.** (*a*) *A. un ambassadeur auprès d'une cour*, to accredit an ambassador to, at, a court. (*b*) To cause (sth.) to be credited, believed. **2.** To credit, believe (sth.).

    s'accréditer, (of news, etc.) to gain credence.

accroc [akro], *s.m.* **1.** Tear, rent (in clothes, etc.). **2.** Hitch, difficulty. [ACCROCHER]

accrochage [akrɔʃaːʒ], *s.m.* **1.** (*a*) Hooking; grazing (of vehicle, etc.). *Box:* Clinch. (*b*) Hanging up (of picture, etc.). (*c*) *W.Tel: A. d'un poste*, picking up of a station. **2.** *F:* Altercation, squabble.

accroche-cœur [akrɔʃkœːr], *s.m.* Lovelock, kiss-curl. *pl. Des accroche-cœur(s).*

accrocher [akrɔʃe]. **1.** *v.tr.* (*a*) To hook; to catch (sth. by hooking). *A. un poisson*, to hook a fish. *A. sa robe à un clou*, to catch one's dress on a nail. *A. une voiture*, to run foul of, run into, collide with, a carriage or car. *F: A. qn dans la rue*, to buttonhole s.o. in the street. (*b*) *A. une voiture au train*, to hitch, couple, a carriage on to the train. (*c*) To grapple (ship). (*d*) *A. sa robe à un clou*, to hang (up) one's dress on a nail. *P:* **Accrocher sa montre,** to pawn, *P:* to pop, one's watch. *F:* **Accrocher une affaire,** to secure, clinch, a deal. (*e*) *W.Tel: A. un poste*, to pick up, tune in, a station. **2.** *v.i. Les négociations ont accroché*, there has been a hitch in the negotiations. [CROC]

    s'accrocher. 1. *S'a. à qn, à qch.*, to fasten on to, cling to, *F:* grapple on to, s.o., sth. **2.** To get caught (*à*, on). **3.** (*a*) *Box:* To clinch. (*b*) *F:* To have an altercation, a set-to.

accroire [akrwaːr], *v.tr.* (Used only in) *Faire a. à qn que* . . ., to cause s.o. to believe, delude s.o. into believing, that. . . . *En faire a. à qn*, to impose up(on) s.o., to delude s.o. *S'en faire a.*, to think too much of oneself, *F:* to fancy oneself.

accroiss-e, etc. See ACCROÎTRE.

accroissement [akrwasmã, -wa-], *s.m.* **1.** (*a*) Growth, growing (of plant, etc.). (*b*) Increase, increasing. **2.** (Amount of) increase, growth. *Mth: A. d'une fonction*, increment of a function.

accroître [akrwaːtr, -wa-], *v.tr.* (*pr.p.* **accroissant;** *p.p.* **accru;** *pr.ind.* **j'accroîs, il accroît, n. accroissons, ils accroissent;** *p.d.* **j'accroissais;** *p.h.* **j'accrus;** *fu.* **j'accroîtrai)** To increase, enlarge, add to, augment; to enhance (reputation).

    s'accroître, to increase, grow.

accroupir (s') [sakrupiːr], *v.pr.* To sit (down) (on one's hams, on one's heels); to squat (down), to crouch (down). *Accroupi*, squatting, crouching. [CROUPE]

accru, -s, -t, etc. See ACCROÎTRE.

accu [aky], *s.m. El: F:* = ACCUMULATEUR.

accueil [akœːj], *s.m.* Reception, welcome, greeting. **Faire bon accueil à qn,** to welcome s.o. *Faire mauvais a. à qn*, to give s.o. an unfriendly reception. [ACCUEILLIR]

accueillant [akœjã], *a.* Gracious, affable.

accueillir [akœjiːr], *v.tr.* (Conj. like CUEILLIR.) To receive, greet. *Bien a. qn*, to welcome s.o. *Mal a. qn*, to give s.o. a bad reception.

acculer [akyle], *v.tr.* To drive (s.o.) back (*contre*, against); to drive (s.o.) to the wall; to bring (animal) to bay, to a stand. [CUL]

    s'acculer à, contre, qch., to set one's back against sth.; to stand at bay.

accumulateur, -trice [akymylatœːr, -tris], *s.* **1.** Accumulator, hoarder (of money, etc.). **2.** *s.m. El: etc:* Accumulator. *El:* Storage cell or battery.

accumulation [akymylasjɔ̃], *s.f.* **1.** Accumulating; storage (of energy). **2.** Accumulation, hoard.

accumuler [akymyle], *v.tr.* To accumulate, amass; to gather (together); to hoard; to heap up. **s'accumuler,** to accumulate.

accusateur, -trice [akyzatœːr, -tris]. **1.** *a.* Accusatory, incriminating. **2.** *s.* Accuser, indicter, impeacher, arraigner.

accusatif, -ive [akyzatif, -iːv], *a. & s.m. Gram:* Accusative, objective (case). **Mot à l'accusatif,** word in the accusative.

accusation [akyzasjɔ̃], *s.f.* **1.** Accusation, charge. *Lancer, porter, une a. contre qn,* to raise, bring, an accusation against s.o. **2.** *Jur:* **Mettre qn en accusation,** to arraign s.o.; to commit s.o. for trial. **3.** *Pol:* Impeachment, arraignment.

accuser [akyze], *v.tr.* **1.** *A. qn de qch.,* to accuse s.o. of sth.; to charge, tax, s.o. with sth. *A. qn de faire qch.,* to accuse s.o. of, to charge, tax, s.o. with, doing sth. **2.** *A. qch.,* to own to, profess, sth. *Elle accuse trente ans,* she owns up to being thirty. *Fenc: A. un coup,* to acknowledge a hit. **3.** To define, show up, accentuate. *Esquisse qui accuse tous les muscles,* sketch that brings out every muscle. *Paroles qui accusent une grande ignorance,* words that betoken great ignorance. *L'indicateur accuse une vitesse de . . .,* the speedometer shows a speed of. . . . **4.** *Accuser réception de qch.,* to acknowledge (receipt of) sth.

accusé, -ée. 1. *a.* Prominent, pronounced, bold (feature, etc.). *Rides très accusées,* strongly marked wrinkles. **2.** *s.* Accused (of crime); (in court) defendant, prisoner at the bar. **3.** *s.m.* **Accusé de réception d'une lettre,** acknowledgment (of receipt) of a letter.

acerbe [asɛrb], *a.* **1.** Tart, sour. **2.** Sharp, harsh. *Réprimande a.,* sharp reproof. *Discussion a.,* acrid discussion.

acerbité [asɛrbite], *s.f.* Acerbity. **1.** Tartness, bitterness, sourness. **2.** Sharpness, harshness. *Répondre avec a.,* to give a sharp answer.

acérer [asere], *v.tr.* (**j'acère; j'acérerai**) (i) To point, (ii) to give a keen edge to (sth). [ACIER]

acéré, *a.* (*a*) Sharp(-pointed). (*b*) Sharp-edged, keen (blade, etc.). *Langue acérée,* sharp, stinging, tongue.

acétate [asetat], *s.m. Ch:* Acetate. *A. de cuivre,* copper acetate; verdigris.

acétique [asetik], *a. Ch:* Acetic. **Acide acétique concentré,** glacial acetic acid.

acétylène [asetile(ː)n], *s.m.* Acetylene.

achalandage [aʃalɑ̃daːʒ], *s.m. Com:* **1.** Working up of a connection. **2.** Custom, customers, connection.

achalander [aʃalɑ̃de], *v.tr.* To provide (shop) with custom. [CHALAND]

achalandé, *a. Magasin bien a.,* shop with a large custom.

acharnement [aʃarnəmɑ̃], *s.m.* (*a*) Desperate eagerness. (*b*) Relentlessness. *A. au travail, pour le travail,* passion for work. *A. à sa vengeance,* tenaciousness, relentlessness, in revenge. *Mettre de l'a. à faire qch.,* (i) to work desperately hard at sth., (ii) to be relentless in doing sth. *Se battre avec a.,* to fight tooth and nail. *Travailler avec a.,* to work (desperately) hard.

acharner (s') [saʃarne], *v.pr.* **1.** *S'a. après, contre, sur, qn,* to be dead set against s.o.; *F:* to be always on s.o.'s tracks. *Le malheur s'acharne après lui,* misfortune dogs his footsteps. **2.** *S'a. à, sur, qch.,* to work unceasingly at sth.; to persist in sth.; to slave at sth. *Il s'acharne à vous nuire,* he is bent on harming you.

acharné, *a.* **1.** Eager in pursuit. *Meute acharnée à la poursuite,* pack in hot, eager, pursuit. *Hommes acharnés les uns contre les autres,* men fighting desperately against each other. *Il est a. à votre perte,* he is bent on ruining you. **2.** *Joueur a.,* inveterate, keen, gambler. **3.** *Lutte acharnée,* stubborn, keen, desperate, contest. *Travail a.,* strenuous work.

achat [aʃa], *s.m.* Purchase. **1.** Buying. **Faire l'achat de qch.,** to purchase sth. *Aller faire ses achats (de ménage),* to go shopping. **2.** Thing bought. *Voilà tous mes achats,* these are all my purchases. [ACHETER]

acheminer (s') [saʃmine], *v.pr. S'a. sur, vers, un endroit,* to be on one's way to, towards, a place. *S'a. vers sa maison,* to proceed, to bend one's steps, to wend one's way, homeward. [CHEMIN]

acheter [aʃte], *v.tr.* (**j'achète, n. achetons; j'achèterai**) (*a*) *A. qch.,* to buy, purchase, sth. *J'ai acheté ce livre cinq francs,* I bought this book for five francs. *A. qch. (à) bon marché,* to buy sth. cheap. *F:* **Acheter chat en poche,** to buy a pig in a poke. (*b*) *A. qch. à qn,* to buy sth. from, of, s.o. (*c*) *A. qch. à, pour, qn,* to buy sth. for s.o. *Je vais lui a. un livre,* I am going to buy him a book. *s.* **-eur, -euse.**

achèvement [aʃɛvmɑ̃], *s.m.* Completion, finishing, conclusion (of work). **Travail en achèvement,** work in process of completion.

achever [aʃve], *v.tr.* (**j'achève, n. achevons; j'achèverai**) **1.** To end, conclude, finish (off), complete (piece of work, etc.). *Avant d'a. ma lettre,* before bringing my letter to a close. *Cette perte acheva sa ruine,* this loss completed his ruin. *Avant que l'année soit achevée,* before the year is out. *A. de faire qch.,* to finish doing sth. *Achève de boire ton café,* drink up your coffee. **2.** To dispatch (animal, etc.); to put (animal) out of pain. *F: Cette grosse perte l'acheva,* this heavy loss did for him. [CHEF]

s'achever. 1. To draw to a close; to end. *Le jour s'acheva tristement,* the day closed sadly. **2.** (Of work) To reach completion.

achevé. 1. *a.* (*a*) Accomplished (horseman, etc.); perfect (piece of work). (*b*) *F: Sot achevé,* downright, absolute, fool. *Coquin a.,* thorough, out-and-out, scoundrel. **2.** *s.m.* Finish, perfection (of work of art, etc.).

Achille [aʃil]. *Pr.n.m.* Achilles. *S.a.* TENDON.

achoppement [aʃɔpmɑ̃], *s.m.* Knock, stumble. **Pierre d'achoppement,** stumbling-block.

achopper (s') [saʃɔpe], *v.pr.* To stumble (*à,* against).

achromatique [akrɔmatik], *a.* Achromatic.

acide [asid]. **1.** *a.* Acid, sharp, tart, sour. **2.** *s.m.* Acid.

acidifier (s') [sasidifje], *v.pr.* To become acid; to turn sour.

acidité [asidite], *s.f.* Acidity, sourness, tartness.

acier [asje], *s.m.* Steel. *Lame d'a., en a.,* steel blade. *A. inoxydable, immaculable,* stainless steel. *A. au chrome, au nickel,* chrome steel, nickel steel. *F:* **Cœur d'acier,** heart of steel. **Regard d'acier,** steely glance.

aciérie [asjeri], *s.f.* Steel-works.

acolyte [akɔlit], *s.m.* **1.** *Ecc:* Acolyte. **2.** *F:* (*a*) Assistant, attendant, acolyte. (*b*) Confederate, accomplice.

acompte [akɔ̃ːt], *s.m.* Instalment, partial payment, payment on account. *Payer par acomptes,* to pay by instalments. *Recevoir un a.,* to receive something on account. *Un a. de cent francs,* a hundred francs on account (*sur,* of). [COMPTE]

aconit [akɔnit], *s.m. Bot:* Aconite.

Açores (les) [lɛzasoːr]. *Pr.n. f.pl.* The Azores.

à-côté [akote], *s.m.* **1.** Aside (remark). **2.** Usu. *pl.* (a) *A-côtés d'une question*, side-issues of a question. *Les à-côtés de l'histoire*, sidelights on, by-ways of, history. (b) Purlieus (of station, barracks, etc.).

à-coup [aku], *s.m.* Jerk, jolt, jar, shock; sudden stoppage. *Il travaille par à-coups*, he works by fits and starts.

acoustique [akustik]. **1.** *a.* Acoustical; acoustic (nerve, etc.). *Cornet acoustique*, ear-trumpet. *Tuyau acoustique*, speaking-tube. **2.** *s.f.* (a) Acoustics; (science of) sound. (b) *A. d'une salle*, acoustics of a hall.

acquér|ir [akeriːr], *v.tr.* (*pr.p.* acquérant; *p.p.* acquis; *pr.ind.* j'acquiers, il acquiert, n. acquérons, ils acquièrent; *pr.sub.* j'acquière, n. acquérions; *p.d.* j'acquérais; *p.h.* j'acquis; *fu.* j'acquerrai) To acquire, obtain, get, win, gain, secure. *Il acquit une belle fortune*, he acquired a handsome fortune. *Son travail lui acquit une honnête aisance*, his work secured him a decent competency. *Ce trait lui acquit l'estime publique*, this action won him the regard of the public, brought him into public esteem. *Sa protection m'est acquise*, I can count on his protection. *Prov:* Bien mal acquis ne profite jamais, ill-gotten gains seldom prosper. *s.* **-eur, -euse.**

acquis. 1. *a.* (a) Acquired (knowledge, etc.). (b) Fait acquis, established fact. **Droits acquis**, vested interests. *Je vous suis tout a.*, I am entirely yours. **2.** *s.m.* Acquired knowledge, attainments, experience.

acquiescement [akjɛsmɑ̃], *s.m.* Acquiescence, assent, consent.

acquiescer [akjese, -kie-], *v.ind.tr.* (j'acquiesçai(s); n. acquiesçons) *A. à qch.*, to acquiesce in sth.; to agree, assent, to sth.

acqui-s, -t, etc. See ACQUÉRIR.

acquisition [akizisjɔ̃], *s.f.* Acquisition. **1.** Acquiring. Faire l'acquisition de qch., to acquire, purchase, sth. **2.** (a) Thing bought or obtained; purchase. (b) *Acquisitions de l'esprit*, intellectual attainments.

acquit [aki], *s.m.* **1.** *Com:* Receipt, acquittance. Donner acquit de qch., to give a receipt for sth. "Pour acquit,' 'received (with thanks)'; 'paid.' **2.** Discharge, release (from promise). Faire qch. par manière d'acquit, to do sth. as a matter of form, for form's sake. S.a. CONSCIENCE 2.

acquittement [akitmɑ̃], *s.m.* **1.** Discharge, payment (of debt, etc.). **2.** *Jur:* Acquittal. Verdict d'acquittement, verdict of not guilty.

acquitter [akite], *v.tr.* **1.** (a) *A. qn (d'une obligation, etc.)*, to release s.o. (from an obligation, etc.). (b) *A. un accusé*, to acquit, discharge, an accused person. **2.** (a) *A. une obligation*, to fulfil an obligation. *A. une dette*, to discharge a debt. (b) *A. une facture* to receipt a bill.
s'acquitter. 1. *S'a. d'une obligation, d'un devoir*, to fulfil, carry out, discharge, an obligation, a duty. *S'a. de son devoir*, to do one's duty. *S'a. d'une dette*, to discharge a debt. **2.** *Se bien, mal, a.*, to acquit oneself well, ill.

âcre [ɑːkr], *a.* Acrid, bitter, tart, pungent. *adv.* **-ment.**

âcreté [akrəte], *s.f.* Acidity, bitterness, pungency.

acrimonie [akrimoni], *s.f.* Acrimony, acrimoniousness; bitterness (of speech, quarrel).

acrimonieu|x, -euse [akrimɔnjø, -øːz], *a.* Acrimonious, bitter (quarrel, etc.). *adv.* **-sement.**

acrobate [akrɔbat], *s.m. & f.* Acrobat, tumbler.

acrobatie [akrɔbasi], *s.f.* **1.** (a) Acrobatics. (b) Acrobatic feat. **2.** *Av:* A. aérienne, trick flying; aerobatics. *Faire de l'acrobatie*, to perform stunts.

acrobatique [akrɔbatik], *a.* Acrobatic.

acrobatisme [akrɔbatism], *s.m.* Acrobatics.

acropole [akrɔpɔl], *s.f.* Acropolis.

acrostiche [akrɔstiʃ], *a. & s.m.* Acrostic.

acte [akt], *s.m.* **1.** (a) Action, act, deed. *A. de courage*, brave deed. **Faire acte de bonne volonté**, to give proof of good will. *Faire a. de souverain*, to exercise the royal prerogative. S.a. PRÉSENCE. (b) *A. de foi, de contrition*, act of faith, of contrition. **2.** *Jur:* (a) Deed, title; any instrument embodying a transaction in real estate. *A. de vente*, bill of sale. *A. notarié, a. su. papier timbré*, deed executed and authenticated by a notary. (b) **Acte judiciaire**, writ. **Acte d'accusation**, bill of indictment. (c) Record. **Acte de naissance**, de décès, birth-, death-certificate. **Acte de dernière volonté**, last will and testament. **Prendre acte de qch.**, to record, note, take a note of, set down, sth. (d) *pl.* Records (of proceedings, etc.); transactions (of scientific body, etc.). *B:* **Les Actes des Apôtres**, the Acts of the Apostles. **3.** *Th:* Act.

acteur, -trice [aktœːr, -tris], *s.* **1.** Actor, actress; player. *Se faire a.*, to go on the stage. **2.** *Le principal a. de cet événement*, the chief actor in this event.

act|if, -ive [aktif, -iːv]. **1.** *a.* (a) Active (supporter, drug, *Gram:* verb, voice). *A. à défendre ses amis*, active in the defence of one's friends. *Armée active*, regular army. **Service actif**, active service. (b) Active, brisk, sprightly, agile, alert (person, etc.). *Faire un commerce a.*, to do a brisk trade. **2.** *s.m.* (a) *Com:* Assets; credit (account). *F:* **Mettre qch. à l'actif de qn**, to credit s.o. with sth. (b) *Gram:* **Verbe à l'actif**, verb in the active voice. *adv.* **-ivement.**

actinie [aktini], *s.f. Coel:* Actinia, sea-anemone.

actinique [aktinik], *a. Ph:* Actinic.

actinomètre [aktinɔmɛtr], *s.m. Ph: Phot:* Actinometer, exposure-meter.

action [aksjɔ̃], *s.f.* **1.** (a) Action, act. *L'a. de marcher*, the action, act, of walking. **Homme d'a.**, man of action. (b) Action, deed, exploit. **Action d'éclat**, brilliant feat of arms. **2.** (a) (i) *A. sur qch.*, action, effect, on sth. (ii) *A. sur qn*, influence over s.o. *Événements en dehors de notre a.*, events beyond our control. **Sans action**, ineffectual, ineffective. (b) *A. de l'eau, du feu, etc.*, agency, effect, of water, fire, etc. (c) Action, motion, working, functioning (of machine, etc.). **Suspendre l'action d'une loi**, to suspend the operation of a law. **Hors d'action**, out of action, out of gear. **3.** (a) Action, gesture (of orator, etc.). (b) *Th: Lit:* Action. *Scène qui retarde l'a.*, scene that delays the action. **4.** *Fin:* Share; share-certificate. *A. ordinaire*, ordinary share. *A. privilégiée*, preference share. **Compagnie par actions**, joint-stock company. *F:* **Ses actions haussent, baissent**, his stock is going up, going down. **5.** *Jur:* Action, lawsuit, trial. **Intenter une action à qn**, to bring an action against s.o.; to sue s.o. **6.** *Mil:* Action, fight, engagement.

actionnaire [aksjɔnɛr], *s.m. & f.* Shareholder.

actionner [aksjɔne], *v.tr.* **1.** *Jur:* To sue (s.o.); to bring an action against s.o. *A. qn en dommages-intérêts*, to sue s.o. for damages. **2.** *Mec.E:* To set (sth.) in action, in motion; to operate, actuate, drive, work, run (sth.). *Machine actionnée par la vapeur*, steam-driven machine. **3.** To urge on (workmen, etc.).
s'actionner, to bestir oneself.

actionné, *a.* Busy, brisk.

activer [aktive], *v.tr.* To quicken, stir (up), push on, urge on. *A. le feu,* to stir up the fire, to make the fire burn up. *A. les gens,* to rouse, stir up, the people. *A. un travail,* to hasten, expedite, accelerate, a piece of work.
s'activer. (*a*) To keep oneself busy. (*b*) To hurry up, bestir oneself ; to bustle (about).
activité [aktivite], *s.f.* Activity. **1.** *A. chimique d'un corps,* chemical activity of a body. *Maintenir l'a. de l'industrie,* to keep industry going. **2.** Quickness, briskness, dispatch. *Montrer de l'a. à faire qch.,* to show great activity in doing sth. **3.** *En activité,* in activity, in action, in operation, in progress, at work. *L'usine est en a.,* the mill is working. *Volcan en a.,* active volcano. *Être en activité (de service),* to be on active service or on the active list.
actrice. See ACTEUR.
actuaire [aktɥɛːr, -tɥeːr], *s.m. Ins:* Actuary.
actualité [aktɥalite, -tya-], *s.f.* **1.** Actuality, reality. **2.** Question, event, of the (present) day, of the moment. *Cette question est toujours d'a.,* this question has always been with us. *Les actualités,* current events. *Cin: Vues d'a.,* actualités, news reel ; topical gazette.
actuel, -elle [aktɥɛl, -tyɛl], *a.* Of the present day ; existing, current. *Le gouvernement a.,* the present government. *L'état a. du pays,* the conditions now prevailing in the country. *A l'heure actuelle,* at the present time.
actuellement [aktɥɛlmã, -tyɛl-], *adv.* (Just) now, at present, at the present time, at the moment.
acuité [akɥite], *s.f.* Acuteness, sharpness, keenness (of point, pain, etc.). *A. d'un son,* high pitch of a sound.
adage [adaːʒ], *s.m.* Adage, common saying ; wise saw ; proverb. *Selon l'adage,* as the saying goes.
Adam [adɑ̃]. *Pr.n.m.* Adam. *F:* **Se mettre dans le costume d'Adam,** to strip to the buff. S.a. ÈVE, POMME I.
adaptation [adaptasjɔ̃], *s.f.* Adaptation, adjustment (*à,* to).
adapt|er [adapte], *v.tr. A. qch. à qch.,* (i) to fit, adjust, sth. to sth. ; (ii) to adapt sth. to sth., to make sth. suitable for sth. *A. un roman à la scène,* to adapt a novel for the stage. *a.* **-able.**
s'adapter. **1.** *S'a. à qch.,* to fit, suit, sth. **2.** *S'a. aux circonstances,* to adapt oneself to circumstances. *Il sait s'a. aux circonstances,* he is very adaptable.
addenda [adɛ̃da], *s.m.inv.* Addendum (*à,* to).
addition [ad(d)isjɔ̃], *s.f.* **1.** Addition, (i) adding (*à,* to) ; (ii) adding up, totting up. **Faire l'addition des chiffres,** to cast up, sum up, tot up, the figures. **2.** (*a*) Accession, accretion. *Faire une addition à un bâtiment,* to add to a building. (*b*) *Ar:* Addition, cast, tot. (*c*) (In restaurant, etc.) Bill, reckoning.
additionnel, -elle [ad(d)isjɔnɛl], *a.* Additional.
additionner [ad(d)isjɔne], *v.tr.* **1.** To add up, cast, tot up. **2.** *Lait additionné d'eau,* watered milk, adulterated milk. *Eau additionnée d'alcool,* water with an admixture of alcohol.
adénoïde [adenɔid], *a. Med:* **Végétations adénoïdes,** adenoids.
adénome [adenoːm], *s.m. Med:* Adenoma ; glandular tumour. **Adénomes naso-pharyngiens,** adenoids.
adepte [adɛpt], *s.m. & f.* Adept.
adhérence [aderɑ̃ːs], *s.f.* **1.** *A. à un parti,* adherence, adhesion, to a party. **2.** *A. des roues (à la route),* grip of the wheels (on the road).
adhérent, -ente [aderɑ̃, -ɑ̃ːt]. **1.** *a.* Adherent (*à,* to) ; adhesive. *Substance adhérente,* sticky

substance. **2.** *s. A. d'un parti,* adherent, supporter, of a party.
adhérer [adere], *v.i.* (j'adhère, n. adhérons; j'adhérerai) **1.** To adhere, cleave, stick, cling (*aux doigts, etc.,* to the fingers, etc.). (Of wheels) *A. à la route,* to grip the road. **2.** To adhere, hold (to opinion, etc.). **3.** *A. à un parti,* to join (a party).
adhésif, -ive [adezif, -iːv]. **1.** *a.* Adhesive, sticky. **2.** *s.m.* Adhesive.
adhésion [adezjɔ̃], *s.f.* **1.** Adhesion, sticking. **Force d'adhésion,** adhesiveness. **2.** Adhesion, adherence (*à,* to). **Donner son adhésion à un projet,** to give, signify, one's adhesion to a plan. *A. à un parti,* joining of a party.
adieu, *pl.* **-eux** [adjø]. **1.** *adv.* Good-bye, farewell. **Dire adieu à qn,** to bid s.o. farewell, godspeed. **2.** *s.m.* Farewell, parting, leave-taking. **Faire ses adieux à qn,** to take one's leave of s.o. ; to say good-bye to s.o. *Baiser d'a.,* parting kiss. **Sans adieu!** this is not good-bye! [DIEU]
adipeux, -euse [adipø, -øːz], *a.* Adipose, fatty (tissue, etc.).
adjacent [adʒasɑ̃], *a.* Adjacent, contiguous (*à,* to) ; adjoining ; bordering (*à,* on). *Geom: Angles adjacents,* adjacent angles.
adject|if, -ive [adʒɛktif, -iːv]. **1.** *a.* Adjectival (phrase, etc.). **2.** *s.m.* Adjective. *A. attribut,* predicative adjective. *A. épithète,* attributive adjective. *adv.* **-ivement,** -ally.
adjoign-e, etc. See ADJOINDRE.
adjoindre [adʒwɛ̃ːdr], *v.tr.* (Conj. like JOINDRE) **1.** *A. qch. à qch.,* to unite, associate, sth. with sth. **2.** *A. qn à qn,* to give s.o. to s.o. as an assistant. *A. qn à un comité,* to add s.o. to a committee.
s'adjoindre *à d'autres,* to join (in) with others.
adjoint, -ointe. **1.** *a.* Assistant (professor, etc.). **2.** *s.* Assistant. **Adjoint au maire,** deputy mayor. **3.** *s.m. Adjoints du verbe,* adjuncts of the verb.
adjoin-s, -t. See ADJOINDRE.
adjonction [adʒɔ̃ksjɔ̃], *s.f.* **1.** Adding, adjunction. **2.** Annex (of hospital, etc.).
adjudant [adʒydɑ̃], *s.m.* **1.** *Mil:* (*a*) Company sergeant-major. (*b*) **Adjudant-major,** adjutant (of battalion). **2.** *Navy:* (*a*) Warrant-officer. (*b*) **Adjudant de pavillon,** flag-lieutenant. **3.** *Orn:* Adjutant-bird, -crane.
adjudicataire [adʒydikatɛːr]. **1.** *a. Partie a.,* (i) contracting party ; (ii) purchasing party. **2.** *s.* (*a*) Successful tenderer for a contract. (*b*) Highest bidder ; purchaser (at auction).
adjudicateur, -trice [adʒydikatœːr, -tris], *s.* Adjudicator, awarder (of contract, etc.).
adjudication [adʒydikasjɔ̃], *s.f.* (*a*) Adjudication, allocation, award ; esp. allocation of contract. (*b*) Knocking-down (of sth. to s.o.). **Mettre qch. en adjudication,** (i) to invite tenders for sth., (ii) to put sth. up for sale by auction. **Par voie d'adjudication,** (i) by tender, (ii) by auction.
adjuger [adʒyʒe], *v.tr.* (j'adjugeai(s); n. adjugeons) *A. qch. à qn,* (i) to adjudge, award, allocate, sth. to s.o. ; (ii) (at auctions) to knock down sth. to s.o. **Une fois! deux fois! adjugé! going!** going! gone! *F: S'a. qch.,* to appropriate, take possession of, sth.
adjurer [adʒyre], *v.tr.* **1.** *A. qn de faire qch.,* to adjure, beseech, s.o. to do sth. **2.** *A. un esprit,* to exorcise a spirit.
admettre [admɛtr], *v.tr.* (Conj. like METTRE) **1.** To admit ; to let (s.o.) in, let (s.o.) enter. *A. qn chez soi,* to admit, allow, s.o. into one's house. *Être admis à un examen,* to pass, get

through, an examination. **2.** *A. qn à faire qch.*, to allow, permit, s.o. to do sth. *Être admis à passer un examen*, to be allowed to sit for an examination. **3.** *(a) A. qch.*, to admit, admit of, permit, allow, sth. **L'usage admis**, the accepted custom. *Si l'on admet la vérité de . . .*, granting the truth of. *. . . Cela n'admet aucun doute*, it admits of no doubt. *(b)* **Admettre que.** *Il admet que c'est vrai*, he allows it to be true. *J'admets que j'ai tort*, I acknowledge, admit, agree, that I am in the wrong. *Je n'admets pas que j'aie tort*, I do not admit that I am in the wrong. *Admettons que j'aie tort*, let us assume, let us grant, that I am wrong.

administrateur, -trice [administratœːr, -tris], *s.* **1.** *(a)* Administrator (of colony, charity, etc.). *(b) A. foncier*, land-agent, estate-agent. **2.** Director (of company, bank, etc.).

administrat|if, -ive [administratif, -iːv], *a.* Administrative. *adv.* **-ivement.**

administration [administrasjɔ̃], *s.f.* **1.** Administering, dispensing (of justice, sacrament, etc.). **2.** *(a)* Administration, direction, management (of business, etc.). **Conseil d'administration**, board of directors. **Mauvaise administration**, mismanagement, maladministration. *(b)* Governing (of country). **3.** *(a)* Governing body; board of directors. *(b)* Government service. *Entrer dans l'a.*, to enter the civil service. *(c)* The officials.

administrer [administre], *v.tr.* **1.** To administer, manage, conduct (business, estate); to govern (country). **2.** *A. qch. à qn*, to administer sth. to s.o. *F: A. une bonne raclée à qn*, to give s.o. a good hiding.

administré, *s.m.* Person under s.o.'s administration or jurisdiction.

admirable [admirabl], *a.* Admirable, wonderful. *Quel temps a.!* what glorious weather! *adv.* **-ment.**

admirateur, -trice [admiratœːr, -tris]. **1.** *a.* Admiring. **2.** *s.* Admirer.

admirat|if, -ive [admiratif, -iːv], *a.* Admiring (gesture, etc.). *adv.* **-ivement.**

admiration [admirasjɔ̃], *s.f.* Admiration. **Regarder qch avec admiration**, to look at sth. admiringly. **Avoir de l'admiration pour qn**, to admire, be full of admiration for, s.o. **Être, devenir, faire, l'admiration de qn**, to be admired by s.o.; to excite the admiration of s.o. **Être saisi d'admiration**, to be struck with admiration.

admirer [admire], *v.tr.* To admire. *Admiré de tous*, admired by all. ●

admis, admise, etc. See ADMETTRE.

admissibilité [admisibilite], *s.f.* Admissibility. *Sch:* **Épreuves d'admissibilité** *(à l'examen oral)*, written examination.

admissible [admisibl], *a.* *(a)* Admissible, allowable (excuse, proof, conduct). *(b) A. à un emploi*, eligible for an occupation. *Sch: Candidats admissibles*, candidates who have qualified for the oral examination.

admission [admisjɔ̃], *s.f.* Admission *(à, dans, to). A. à un club*, admission to a club. **Cotisation d'admission**, entrance fee. *Mch: I.C.E: Période d'a.*, induction stroke. **Soupape d'admission**, inlet valve.

admit. See ADMETTRE.

admonestation [admɔnestasjɔ̃], *s.f.* Admonition, admonishment, reprimand.

admonester [admɔneste], *v.tr.* To admonish, censure, reprimand.

adolescence [adɔlessɑ̃ːs], *s.f.* Adolescence, youth.

adolescent, -ente [adɔlessɑ̃, -ɑ̃ːt], *s.* Adolescent, youth, lad; *f.* girl (in her teens).

Adolphe [adɔlf]. *Pr.n.m.* Adolphus.

adonner (s') [sadɔne], *v.pr.* *(a) S'a. à qch.*, to give oneself up to sth. *S'a. à l'étude*, to devote oneself to study. *S'a. à une profession*, to take up a profession. *Ils sont adonnés à la même profession*, they follow, practise, the same profession. *S'a. aux sports*, to go in for sport. *(b) S'a. à la boisson*, to take to drink; to become addicted to drink.

adopt|er [adɔpte], *v.tr.* **1.** *A. un enfant*, to adopt a child. **2.** *(a) A. un nom*, to adopt, take, assume, a name. *(b) A. un projet de loi, une résolution*, to pass, carry, a bill, a resolution. *a.* **-able.**

adoptif, -ive [adɔptif, -iːv], *a.* Adopted, adoptive (child, parent, country).

adoption [adɔpsjɔ̃], *s.f.* Adoption (of child, proposal). *Parl:* Passage, carrying (of bill).

adorable [adɔrabl], *a.* Adorable; charming. *adv.* **-ment.**

adorateur, -trice [adɔratœːr, -tris], *s.* *(a)* Adorer, worshipper. *(b) F:* Ardent admirer.

adoration [adɔrasjɔ̃], *s.f.* Adoration. **1.** Worship (of a god). **2.** *F:* Profound admiration *(de*, for). **Aimer qn à l'adoration**, to adore s.o.

adorer [adɔre], *v.tr.* **1.** To adore, worship (a god). **2.** *F:* To adore, idolize, to dote upon, to be passionately fond of (s.o., sth.). *J'adore monter à cheval*, I adore riding. *Il adorait qu'on le regardât*, he loved to be looked at.

adoss|er [adose], *v.tr.* **1.** To place (two things) back to back. **2.** *A. qch. à, contre, qch.*, to place, lean, rest, sth. (with its back) against sth.; to back sth. against sth. [DOS] *s.m.* **-ement.**

s'adosser *à, contre, qch.*, to set, lean, one's back against sth. *S'a. au mur*, to lean (back) against the wall.

adossé, *a.* **1.** Back to back. **2.** *A. à qch.*, with one's back against sth.

adouc|ir [adusiːr], *v.tr.* **1.** To soften (voice, water); to tone down (contrast, colour); to subdue (light, one's voice); to sweeten (drink). **2.** To alleviate, relieve, ease, assuage, mitigate, calm, allay (pain, sorrow, etc.). **3.** To pacify, mollify. [DOUX] *s.m.* **-issement.**

s'adoucir. **1.** (Of voice) To grow softer; to soften. **2.** (Of weather) To grow milder. **3.** (Of pain) To grow less.

adragante [adragɑ̃ːt], *a.f.* **Gomme adragante**, gum tragacanth.

adresse [adrɛs], *s.f.* **1.** Address, direction, destination. *Écrire son a.*, to put down one's name and address. **Lettre à l'adresse de qn**, letter addressed, directed, to s.o. *F:* **Une observation à votre adresse**, a hit at you. **2.** *(a)* Skill, dexterity, adroitness. **Tour d'adresse**, trick (of sleight-of-hand); feat (of skill). *(b)* Shrewdness, adroitness, tact. **Dénué d'adresse**, tactless, bungling (person). *(c)* Craftiness, cunning.

adresser [adrese], *v.tr.* **1.** To address, direct (packet, letter, etc.). **Lettre mal adressée**, misdirected letter. **2.** *On m'a adressé à vous*, I have been recommended to come to you. **3.** To aim, address (remarks, reproaches, etc.). **Adresser la parole à qn**, to speak to, to address, s.o.

s'adresser. **1.** To apply *(à*, to). "S'adresser ici," 'apply, enquire, here.' *Adressez-vous au sergent de ville*, ask the constable. **2.** *S'a. à qn*, to address s.o., to speak to s.o. **3.** *S'a. à l'imagination de qn*, to appeal to s.o.'s imagination.

Adrien [adri(j)ɛ̃]. *Pr.n.m.* **1.** Adrian. **2.** *Rom. Hist:* Hadrian.

adroit [adrwa], *a.* **1.** *(a)* Dexterous, deft, skilful, handy. *Être a. de ses mains*, to be clever with one's hands, with one's fingers. *Joueur de football a. des pieds*, footballer clever at footwork. *A. à* *faire qch.*, dexterous, skilful, handy, at doing sth. (b) *Phrase adroite*, neat way of putting it. **2.** Shrewd, adroit (answer, diplomat). *adv.* -ement.

adulateur, -trice [adylatœːr, -tris]. **I.** *a.* Adulatory, flattering, fawning, sycophantic. **2.** *s.* Sycophant; base flatterer.

adulation [adylasjɔ̃], *s.f.* Adulation, base flattery (*de*, of); sycophancy.

aduler [adyle], *v.tr.* To adulate; to fawn upon (s.o.).

adulte [adylt], *a. & s.* Adult, grown-up, full-grown. *Être arrivé à l'âge a.*, to be of adult age.

adultère¹ [adylteːr]. **I.** *a.* Adulterous. **2.** *s.* Adulterer, *f.* adulteress.

adultère², *s.m.* Adultery.

adultère|er [adyltere], *v.tr.* (j'adultère, n. adultérons; j'adultérerai) To adulterate (food, etc.); to falsify (document). *s.f.* -ation.

advenir [advəniːr], *v.* (Conj. like VENIR. Used only in the third pers.) To occur, happen; to come to pass; to befall, chance; to come (about). **I.** *v.i. Je ne sais ce qui en adviendra*, I don't know what will come of it. *Quand le cas adviendra*, when the case arises. *Le cas advenant que* + *sub.*, in the event of (something happening). **2.** *v.impers. Qu'est-il advenu de lui?* what has become of him? *Il m'advient quelquefois d'oublier*, I sometimes happen to forget. *Or, il advint que . . .*, now it came to pass that. . . . *Mais il est advenu que . .*, but it turned out, it so fell out, that. . . . *Il n'en advint que de la peine*, nothing but trouble came of it. **Advienne que pourra**, come what may.

adventice [advɑ̃tis], *a.* Adventitious; casual.

adverbe [adverb], *s.m.* Adverb.

adverbial, -aux [adverbjal, -o], *a.* Adverbial. *Locution adverbiale*, adverbial phrase. *adv.* -ement.

adversaire [adverseːr], *s.m.* Adversary, opponent.

adverse [advers], *a.* (a) *Jur: La partie a.*, the opposing party, the other side. (b) Adverse, unfortunate, unfavourable. *Fortune a.*, adverse fortune; adversity; bad luck.

adversité [adversite], *s.f.* **I.** Adversity; adverse circumstances. *Être dans l'adversité*, to be in straitened circumstances. **2.** Misfortune, trial, ill.

adviendra, advienne, advient, advint. See ADVENIR.

aède [aɛd], *s.m.* (Greek) bard.

aér|er [aere], *v.tr.* (j'aère, n. aérons; j'aérerai) **I.** (a) To ventilate (mine); to air, to renew the air of (room). (b) To air (linen); to expose (water) to the air. **2.** To aerate (water, bread). *s.m.* -age. *s.f.* -ation.

aérien, -ienne [aerjɛ̃, -jɛn], *a.* **I.** Aerial (phenomenon, plant, etc.). *Nos forces aériennes*, our air-force. *Raid aérien*, air-raid. *Ligne aérienne*, air-line. **2.** (Light and) airy (footstep, texture). **3.** *Anat:* Voies aériennes, air-, wind-passages.

aéro-club [aeroklyb, -klœb], *s.m.* Flying-club.

aérodrome [aerodroːm], *s.m.* Aerodrome, flying-ground.

aérogare [aerogaːr], *s.f.* Air-port.

aérolithe [aerolit], *s.m.* Aerolite, aerolith, meteorite.

aéronaute [aeronoːt], *s.m.* Aeronaut, balloonist.

aéronautique [aeronotik]. **I.** *a.* Aeronautical; air (service, etc.). **2.** *s.f.* Aeronautics; aerial navigation.

aéronef [aeronɛf], *s.m. or f.* Aircraft.

aéroplane [aeroplan], *s.m.* (Now usu. AVION) Aeroplane.

aéroport [aeropɔːr], *s.m.* Air-port, air-station.

aérostat [aerosta], *s.m.* Lighter-than-air craft; balloon; airship.

aérostation [aerostasjɔ̃], *s.f.* Ballooning, aeronautics.

aérostatique [aerostatik]. **I.** *a.* Aerostatic(al). *Parc aérostatique*, balloon park. **2.** *s.f.* Aerostatics.

aérostier [aerostje], *s.m. Mil:* Aeronaut, balloonist.

affabilité [afabilite], *s.f.* Graciousness, affability (*avec, envers, to*, towards).

affable [afɑbl], *a.* Gracious, affable, kindly (*à, envers, avec, to*, towards, with). *adv.* -ment.

affadir [afadiːr], *v.tr.* **I.** To render (food, etc.) insipid, tasteless. **2.** To render (sth.) dull, uninteresting. *A. une anecdote*, to take the point out of an anecdote. [FADE]

s'**affadir**, to become insipid; to lose flavour.

affaiblir [afɛbliːr], *v.tr.* To weaken. (a) To enfeeble, debilitate. (b) To lessen, reduce. *A. le courage de qn*, to damp s.o.'s courage. *Phot: A. un cliché*, to reduce (the contrasts of) a negative. [FAIBLE]

s'**affaiblir**, to grow, become, weak(er), feeble(r); to lose one's strength. *Ses forces s'affaiblissaient*, his strength was flagging. *La tempête s'affaiblit*, the storm is abating.

affaiblissement [afɛblismɑ̃], *s.m.* **I.** (a) Weakening. (b) Lessening, reducing. *Phot: A. d'un cliché*, reducing of a negative. **2.** Enfeeblement, weakness.

affaire [afɛːr], *s.f.* **I.** (a) Business, affair, concern. *Ce n'est pas votre a.*, it's no business of yours. *Ce métier n'est pas l'a. de tout le monde*, this trade is not everybody's job. *Faire son affaire de qch.*, (i) to specialize in a matter, (ii) to take charge of a matter. *J'en fais mon a.*, leave it to me; I will deal with it. *Savoir, connaître, son affaire*, to know what one is about, to know one's business. (b) Question, matter, affair. *A. d'intérêt*, money matter. *Affaire de cœur*, love-affair. *A. de goût*, matter of taste. *C'est une affaire de rien*, it is a trifling matter. *Son usine est une grande a.*, his works is a very big concern. *Ça c'est une autre affaire*, that's another question altogether; that alters the case. *Ce n'est que l'affaire d'un instant*, it won't take a minute. (c) Thing (required). *J'ai votre a.*, I have the very thing you want. *Faire l'affaire de qn*, to answer the purpose of s.o. *Cela ne fait pas l'a.*, it won't do. *F:* Il a fait son affaire, he has made his pile, his fortune. *Faire son affaire à qn*, to do for s.o.; to kill s.o. *Son affaire est faite*, he is done for, it's all up with him, *P:* his number's up. (d) (i) (Serious, difficult) business, thing, matter. *Vilaine a.*, ugly business. *Ce n'est pas une affaire*, it's no great matter. *C'est toute une a.*, it's quite an undertaking, quite a (big) business. *Ce sera l'a. de cent francs*, it will be a matter of a hundred francs. *Iron: La belle affaire!* pooh, is that all! En voici une affaire! here's a pretty kettle of fish! (ii) *Tirer qn d'affaire*, to get s.o. out of a difficulty, out of a scrape, out of trouble; to set s.o. on his legs again. *Se tirer d'a. tant bien que mal*, to muddle through. *S. a.* HORS 2. *S'attirer une* (mauvaise) *affaire*, to get into trouble, into a scrape, into hot water. *S'attirer des affaires*, to get into trouble. *Vous me faites des affaires pour douze malheureux francs!* you are making all this fuss for a beggarly twelve francs! **2.** (a) Affair, business, transaction, deal; (financial) venture. *Bonne a.*, good speculation. *Faire une bonne a.*, to do a good stroke of business. *C'est une affaire d'or*, it will be a gold mine. *Ils font des affaires* *d'or*, they are simply coining money. **Faire une mauvaise affaire**, to make a losing bargain. **Venir pour affaire(s)**, to come on business. **C'est une affaire faite!** done! that's settled! (*b*) **Avoir affaire à, avec, qn**, to deal, have to deal, have to do, with s.o. *Avoir a. à forte partie*, to be up against a strong man. **C'est affaire à vous, à lui, de . . .**, it is for you, for him, to . . . ; *F:* it is up to you, to him, to. . . . *C'est a. à un médecin*, it is a case for a doctor. **3.** *pl.* (*a*) Things, belongings. *Serrer ses affaires*, to put away one's things. (*b*) Business, trade. *Prov:* **Les affaires sont les affaires**, business is business. **Être dans les affaires**, to be in business. *Faire de bonnes affaires*, to be successful in business. *Comment vont les affaires?* how is business? **Mettre qn dans les affaires**, to set s.o. up in business. **Parler affaires**, to talk business ; *F:* to talk shop. **Homme d'affaires**, (i) business man, (ii) agent, (iii) steward, (iv) lawyer. *Être à la tête des affaires*, to be at the head of affairs. (*c*) *Les affaires de l'État*, State affairs. *F:* Ce n'est pas une affaire d'État, it is no great matter. **Le Ministère des Affaires étrangères**, the Foreign Office. **4.** *Jur:* Case, lawsuit. **5.** (*a*) **Affaire d'honneur**, duel ; affair of honour. (*b*) *Mil:* Engagement, fight. [FAIRE]

affairement [afɛrmɑ̃], *s.m.* **1.** Hurry, bustle. **2.** Ado, fuss.

affairer (s') [safere], *v.pr.* *F:* To lead a busy life, to bustle about. *S'a. à tout remettre en place*, to busy oneself tidying things away.

    affairé, *a.* Busy. **Faire l'affairé**, to pretend to be busy, to fuss around. *Porteurs affairés*, bustling porters. *Ils entrent et sortent d'un air a.*, they bustle in and out.

affaissement [afɛsmɑ̃], *s.m.* **1.** Subsidence, giving way ; collapse (of floor, roof, tyre) ; sinking (in), settling (of foundation) ; sagging (of floor, beam). **2.** Depression, dejection, despondency.

affaisser (s') [safɛse], *v.pr.* (*a*) (Of thg) To subside, give way, cave in, collapse, sink in ; (of material) to give, yield ; (of beam, etc.) to sag ; (of earth) to settle. (*b*) (Of pers.) To sink down, sink back (in chair) ; to collapse. (*c*) *Il s'affaisse de jour en jour*, he is gradually sinking. [FAIX]

affalement [afalmɑ̃], *s.m.* *F:* **1.** Discouragement, depression ; exhaustion. **2.** L'affalement final, the final crash, ruin.

affaler [afale], *v.tr. Nau:* **1.** (*a*) To haul down (rope). (*b*) To pay down (rope). **2.** To lower (object). **Affale!** lower away !

    s'affaler. 1. *Nau:* (*a*) *S'a. par un cordage*, to slide down a rope. (*b*) (Of ship) **S'affaler à la côte**, to get embayed on a lee-shore. **2.** *F:* (*a*) To fall. *S'a. par terre tout de son long*, to fall at full length on the ground. (*b*) *S'a. dans un fauteuil*, to drop, sink, *F:* flop, into an arm-chair.

affamer [afame], *v.tr.* To starve (s.o.). [FAIM]

    affamé, *a.* Hungry, starving, ravenous, famished. *Regarder qch. d'un œil a.*, to look hungrily at sth. *Être a. de qch.*, to hunger, hanker, after sth. ; to crave, yearn, long, for (pleasure, praise).

affectant [afɛktɑ̃], *a.* Affecting, touching.

affectation [afɛktasjɔ̃], *s.f.* **1.** Affectation. (*a*) Affectedness, conceit. **Sans affectation**, unaffectedly. (*b*) Simulation, pretence. *Avec une a. de générosité*, with an affectation, a show, of generosity. **2.** (*a*) *A. de qch. à qch.*, assignment, attribution, of sth. to a purpose ; appropriation for a purpose ; allotment (of money) to a purpose. (*b*) *A. de qn à un poste*, assignment of s.o. to a duty.

affecter [afɛkte], *v.tr.* **1.** (*a*) *A. qch. à un certain usage*, to assign sth. to, to appropriate, set apart, ear-mark, allocate, sth. for, a certain use. (*b*) *Mil:*

To detail, tell off, post (soldier, detachment, for a particular service). *Navy:* *Être affecté à un navire*, to be posted to a ship. **2.** To affect, feign, simulate. *A. la mort*, to feign death. *A. de faire qch.*, to pretend to do sth. **3.** To affect ; to have a predilection for, a partiality for (sth.). *A. les grands mots*, to affect big words. **4.** To assume, take on (shape, colour, etc.). **5.** (*a*) To affect, move, touch (s.o.). *Vivement affecté de la nouvelle*, much moved by the news. (*b*) To affect, to have an effect upon (career, health). *Ce gaz affecte les poumons*, this gas affects the lungs. *Mth:* *Quantité affectée d'un exposant*, quantity bearing an index.

    affecté, *a.* Affected, conceited, prim (person, manners) ; mincing (gait).

affectif, -ive [afɛktif, -iːv], *a.* Affective, emotional (use of a word, etc.).

affection [afɛksjɔ̃], *s.f.* Affection. **1.** Fondness, attachment, liking (*pour*, for). **Porter de l'affection à qn**, avoir qn en affection, to be fond of s.o. **Prendre qn en affection**, to become attached to s.o. ; to conceive a liking for s.o. **Avec affection**, affectionately. **2.** Mental state. *Les affections de l'âme*, the affections of the mind. **3.** *Med:* Disease, complaint, ailment.

affectionner [afɛksjɔne], *v.tr.* **1.** *A. qn*, to have an affection, a liking, a fondness, for s.o. ; to love, like, be fond of, s.o. *Affectionné de tous*, loved by all. **2.** *S'a. qn*, to gain s.o.'s affection.

    affectionné, *a.* Affectionate, loving. (At end of letter) **Votre affectionné(e) . . .**, your affectionate. . . . *adv.* **-ment.**

affectueu|x, -euse [afɛktuø, -øːz], *a.* Affectionate, loving, fond. *adv.* **-sement.**

afférent[1] [aferɑ̃], *a.* **1.** Assignable (*à*, to). *Traitement a. à un emploi*, salary attaching to a post. *Jur:* *Portion afférente à qn*, share falling (by right) to s.o. ; portion accruing to s.o. **2.** *Renseignements afférents à une affaire*, information relating to a matter.

afférent[2], *a. Anat:* Afferent (vessel).

afferm|er [afɛrme], *v.tr.* **1.** (*a*) To lease (farm, etc.). (*b*) *A:* To farm out (taxes). **2.** To rent ; to take (land, etc.) on lease. [FERME[2]] *s.m.* **-age.**

afferm|ir [afɛrmiːr], *v.tr.* **1.** To strengthen, steady, make firm (pillar, foundations, etc.). **2.** To strengthen, consolidate (power, belief, health, etc.). [FERME[1]] *s.m.* **-issement.**

    s'affermir, to become stronger, firmer ; to harden.

affété [afete], *a.* Affected, simpering, namby-pamby (air, tone) ; mincing (step) ; pretty-pretty (style).

afféterie [afetri], *s.f.* **1.** Affectation, primness ; affected manner. **2.** *pl.* (*a*) Vain adornments ; gewgaws. (*b*) Simpering, mincing.

affichage [afiʃaːʒ], *s.m.* (*a*) Bill-sticking, -posting ; placarding, posting-up (of bills). *Sp:* **Tableau d'affichage**, telegraph board. (*b*) *F:* Show, display, flaunting (of opinions, etc.).

affiche [afiʃ], *s.f.* (*a*) *A. murale*, placard, poster, bill. **Affiche à la main**, handbill. *A. illustrée*, picture poster. **Poser une affiche**, to stick a bill. **Panneau à affiches**, hoarding. *Annoncer une vente par voie d'affiches*, to bill, placard, a sale. *A. de théâtre*, play-bill. *Th:* **Mettre une pièce à l'affiche**, to bill a play. (*b*) Stamp, mark, sign (of fault, quality).

afficher [afiʃe], *v.tr.* **1.** To stick (up), placard, display (bill, notice, etc.). *A. une vente*, to advertise, post up, a sale. *Th:* *A. une pièce*, to bill a play. "**Défense d'afficher**," 'stick no bills.' **2.** To parade, to show (off) (sth.); to make a display, a show, of (sth.). *A. ses opinions*, to air, flaunt, one's opinions. *A. l'insouciance*, to show ostentatious carelessness. [FICHE]

s'afficher, to show off; to attract notice, to seek notoriety. *S'a. pour savant*, to set up for being learned.

afficheur [afiʃœ:r], *s.m.* Bill-sticker, bill-poster.

affidé, -ée [afide], *s.* (a) Confederate, confidant, follower. (b) Secret agent; spy. **Affidé de la police**, police spy.

affilée [afile], *s.f.* F: (Used only in the adv. phr.) **D'affilée,** occ. **à l'affilée.** *Cinq heures d'a.*, five hours at a stretch, at a time, on end. *Pendant des heures d'a.*, for hours together.

affil|er [afile], *v.tr.* 1. To sharpen, set, whet, to give an edge to, to put an edge on (blade, etc.). 2. To (wire-)draw (gold, silver). *s.m.* **-age.** **affilé,** *a.* Sharp (knife, tongue).

affiliation [afiljasjɔ̃], *s.f.* 1. *A. d'une banque à une autre*, affiliation of one bank with another. 2. Branch (of a firm, etc.).

affilier [afilje], *v.tr.* To affiliate (à, to, with).
s'affilier *à un parti*, to affiliate oneself with, to, a party. *S'a. à un complot*, to join in a conspiracy.

affin|er [afine], *v.tr.* 1. (a) To improve, refine, make better. *A. son goût en lisant*, to improve one's taste by reading. (b) To (re)fine (iron, gold). (c) To ripen, mature (cheese, etc.). 2. (a) To sharpen (the intelligence). (b) To point (nails). 3. To thin, fine down (board, etc.). [FIN] *s.m.* **-age.** *s.m.* **-ement.**
s'affiner. 1. To gain in refinement. 2. (Of cheese, etc.) To ripen, mature.

affinité [afinite], *s.f.* Affinity (*entre*, between). (a) Relationship by marriage. (b) Resemblance; similarity of character. *S'il trouve une âme qui ait des affinités avec la sienne*, if he finds a soul akin to his own, a kindred spirit. (c) *Ch: A. pour un corps*, affinity for a body.

affirmat|if, -ive [afirmatif, -i:v]. 1. *a.* (a) Affirmative, positive. *Réponse affirmative*, answer in the affirmative. **Signe affirmatif**, nod. (b) Assertive, positive (person). 2. *s.f.* **L'affirmative**, the affirmative. *adv.* **-ivement.**

affirmation [afirmasjɔ̃], *s.f.* Affirmation, asseveration, averment, assurance; assertion, statement. *Jur:* **Affirmation sous serment,** affidavit.

affirmer [afirme], *v.tr.* 1. (a) To affirm, assert, aver. *Je n'affirmerais pas que . . .*, I would not pledge my word that. . . . *Il affirme que vous avez tort*, he will have it that you are wrong. **Affirmer qch. sous, sur, par, serment,** to state sth. on oath, on affidavit. (b) *Théorie affirmée par l'expérience*, theory supported by experience. 2. *A.* son autorité, to make one's authority felt; to assert oneself.
s'affirmer. (a) To assert oneself; to assert one's authority. (b) *Sa maîtrise s'affirme dans . . .*, his mastery asserts itself in. . . . *Beaucoup de ses observations se sont affirmées justes*, many of his observations have proved correct.

affistoler [afistɔle], *v.tr.* = AFFUBLER.

affixe [afiks], *Ling:* 1. *a.* Affixed. 2. *s.m.* Affix.

afflachi [aflaʃi], *a.* F: Slack, flabby. *Personne afflachie par l'oisiveté*, person grown slack through idleness. *Câble a.*, slack cable.

affleurement [aflœrmɑ̃], *s.m.* 1. *Arch: Carp: etc:* Levelling, making flush. 2. *Geol:* Outcrop, basset.

affleurer [aflœre]. 1. *v.tr.* (a) To bring (timbers, etc.) to the same level; to make flush. (b) *A. qch.*, to be level, even, flush, with sth. 2. *v.i.* (a) To

be even, level, flush. (b) *Geol:* (Of lode) To crop out, to basset. [FLEUR]

affliction [afliksjɔ̃], *s.f.* Affliction, tribulation, sorrow.

affligeant [afliʒɑ̃], *a.* Distressing, painful, sad (news, etc.).

affliger [afliʒe], *v.tr.* (j'affligeai(s); n. affligeons) 1. To afflict (*de*, with). 2. To pain, distress, grieve.
s'affliger, to grieve, to be grieved, to sorrow (*de*, at, about, over). *Ne vous affligez pas ainsi*, F: don't be so cut up about it. *Je m'afflige de les voir dans la misère*, I grieve, I am pained, to see them in want.

affligé, *a.* 1. Afflicted. *Être a. d'une infirmité*, to be afflicted with, to suffer from, an infirmity. *s.* **Les affligés**, the afflicted. 2. *Être a. d'une nouvelle*, to be grieved at a piece of news.

afflou|er [aflue], *v.tr.* *Nau:* To refloat, float off (stranded vessel). *s.m.* **-age.**

affluence [aflyɑ̃:s], *s.f.* 1. Flow, flowing, flood (of water, etc.). F: *Quelle a. de paroles!* what a flow of words! 2. Affluence, abundance, plenty. *Vivre dans l'affluence*, to live in affluence. 3. Crowd, concourse (of people). **Heures d'affluence,** busy hours (in shops, etc.); F: rush hours.

affluent [aflyɑ̃], *s.m.* Tributary, affluent (of river).

affluer [aflye], *v.i.* 1. (Of water, etc.) To flow (*vers*, towards; *dans*, into). 2. To abound; to be plentiful. 3. *A. à, dans, un endroit*, to crowd, flock, throng, to a place.

affolement [afɔlmɑ̃], *s.m.* 1. Distraction, panic. *Causer un a.*, to create a panic. 2. *Meteor: Nau:* Perturbation, unsteadiness (of magnetic needle). 3. (a) Racing (of engine, propeller, etc.). (b) Disconnecting of pulley, etc.).

affol|er [afɔle], *v.tr.* 1. To madden, distract; to drive (s.o.) crazy; to throw (crowd) into a panic. 2. To disturb, perturb (needle of compass). 3. *Mch:* (a) To let (machine) race. (b) To disconnect (part of machine). [FOL] *a.* **-ant.**
s'affoler. 1. To fall into a panic; to stampede. 2. *S'a. de qn*, to fall madly in love with s.o., to become infatuated with s.o. 3. (a) (Of compass-needle) To spin. (b) (Of machine) To begin to race.

affolé, *a.* Crazy, distracted, demented, panic-stricken. *Épouvante affolée*, wild, crazed, terror.

affouill|er [afuje], *v.tr.* (Of water) To undermine, erode, wash away, lay bare (bank, foundation, etc.). [FOUILLER] *s.m.* **-ement.**

affranch|ir [afrɑ̃ʃi:r], *v.tr.* 1. To free; to set free; to emancipate, liberate (slave, etc.). *A. qn de qch.*, to free, release, deliver, s.o. from sth. 2. To pay the postage of, on (sth.); to frank, prepay; to stamp (letter). **Colis affranchi,** prepaid parcel. [FRANC] *s.m.* **-issement.**
s'affranchir, to become free, independent; to throw off the yoke. *S'a. de qch.*, to free, rid, oneself of, to break free from, to shake off, sth.

affranchi, -ie. 1. *a.* (a) Freed, emancipated (slave). (b) Free (*de*, of, from). 2. *s.* Freedman, -woman.

affranchisseur [afrɑ̃ʃisœ:r], *s.m.* Emancipator, liberator.

affre [afr], *s.f.* Usu. *pl.* Anguish, spasm. **Les affres de la mort,** (i) the pangs of death, the darkness of death; (ii) the death-throes, -struggle. *Être en butte aux affres du mal de mer*, to be suffering from the pangs, from the horrors, of sea-sickness; to be in the throes of sea-sickness.

affrét|er [afrete], *v.tr.* (j'affrète; j'affréterai) *Nau:* (a) To freight (= hire out) (ship) (b) To charter (ship). [FRÉTER] *s.m.* **-ètement.**

affréteur [afretœːr], *s.m. Nau:* (a) Freighter. (b) Charterer, shipper.

affreu|x, -euse [afrø, -øːz], *a.* **1.** Frightful, hideous, ghastly. *A. à contempler,* hideous to behold. **2.** Frightful, horrible, dreadful, shocking (news, crime). [AFFRE] *adv.* **-sement.**

affriand|er [afriɑ̃de], *v.tr.* **1.** *A. qn,* to entice, tempt, allure, s.o. (to eat, drink). **2.** To make (food) attractive, enticing. [FRIAND] *a.* **-ant.**

    s'affriander *de qch.,* to contract a liking, a taste, for sth.

affricher [afriʃe], *v.tr.* To let (land) lie fallow. [FRICHE]

    s'affricher, (of land) to run to waste.

affront [afrɔ̃], *s.m.* **1.** Affront, indignity, insult, snub, slight. *Faire un affront à qn,* to slight s.o. *Avaler, dévorer, un a.,* to swallow, pocket, an affront. **2.** *A:* Disgrace, shame. *Rester en affront,* to come to an ignominious halt. *Faire affront à qn,* to disgrace s.o.

affront|er [afrɔ̃te], *v.tr.* **1.** To face, confront, brave, tackle (s.o., sth.); to affront (danger). *A. une épreuve avec courage,* to meet an ordeal bravely. *A. les périls d'un voyage,* to dare the perils of a journey. **2.** To join face to face, edge to edge; to bring together (metal plates, etc.). *s.m.* **-ement.**

affublement [afybləmɑ̃], *s.m. Pej:* Get-up, rig-out; ridiculous dress.

affubler [afyble], *v.tr. Pej: A. qn de qch.,* to dress s.o. up in sth.; to rig s.o. out in sth.

    s'affubler, to dress, to rig oneself out (in sth.). *Affublé d'un antique uniforme,* got up, accoutred, in an ancient uniform.

affût [afy], *s.m.* **1.** Hiding-, lurking-place. *Chasser un animal à l'affût,* to stalk an animal. *Être, se mettre, à l'affût de qn,* to lie in wait, be on the watch, for s.o. *Attendre l'ennemi à l'a.,* to lie in wait for the enemy. *A l'a. de nouvelles,* on the look-out for news. **2.** (a) *Artil:* Gun-carriage. (b) Stand, frame, mounting (of telescope, etc.).

affût|er [afyte], *v.tr.* To grind, sharpen, whet (tool); to set (saw). *F: A. qn,* to sharpen s.o.'s wits. *P:* **S'affûter le sifflet,** to wet one's whistle; to take a whet. *s.m.* **-age.**

    affûté, *a.* Smart, sharp (child).

affûtiau, -aux [afytjo], *s.m. F:* Trinket, gew-gaw, knick-knack. ;

afin [afɛ̃], *adv.* **1.** *Afin de* (*faire qch.*), to, in order to, so as to (do sth.). **2.** *Afin que* + *sub.,* so that, in order that. [FIN]

africain, -aine [afrikɛ̃, -ɛn], *a. & s.* African.

Afrique [afrik]. *Pr.n.f. Geog:* Africa. *L'A. du Sud,* South Africa. S.a. BATAILLON.

agaçant [agasɑ̃], *a.* **1.** Annoying, irritating, provoking, *F:* aggravating. **2.** Provocative, fetching, saucy (glance, smile).

agac|er [agase], *v.tr.* (j'agaçai(s); n. agaçons) **1.** To set (teeth, nerves) on edge; to jar, grate, upon (nerves, ears). **2.** *A. qn,* (i) to provoke, annoy, irritate, s.o.; to get on s.o.'s nerves; (ii) to kindle, rouse, s.o.'s passions; to lead s.o. on. *s.m.* **-ement.**

    s'agacer, to become irritated; to get annoyed.

agacerie [agasri], *s.f.* Provocation, rousing. *Faire des agaceries à qn,* to flirt with s.o.; to lead s.o. on.

agape [agap], *s.f.* (a) *Ecc.Hist:* Agape, love-feast. (b) *F:* Reunion of old friends, of old comrades.

agate [agat], *s.f. Miner:* Agate. *A. mousseuse,* moss-agate, mocha-stone.

age [aːʒ], *s.m. Husb:* Beam (of plough).

âge [ɑːʒ], *s.m.* **1.** Age. (a) *Quel âge avez-vous?* how old are you? *Quel âge lui donnez-vous?* how old do you take him to be? *Dès son âge le plus tendre,* from his earliest years. *Ils sont du même âge,* they are (of) the same age, of an age. *Être d'âge à faire qch.,* to be of an age, old enough, to do sth. *Mourir avant l'âge,* to die before one's time. *Mourir à un âge avancé, à un bel âge,* to die at a good old age. *Être d'âge légal,* to be of age. (b) *Le bas âge,* infancy. *Enfant en bas âge,* infant. *Être à l'âge de raison,* to have arrived at years of discretion. *L'âge d'homme,* manhood. *Homme d'âge mûr,* man of middle age. S.a. INGRAT 3. (c) Old age. *Un homme d'âge,* an old, aged, man. *Prendre de l'âge,* to be getting on in years. **2.** Generation. *D'âge en âge,* from generation to generation. **3.** Period, epoch. *Archeol: L'âge de pierre,* the stone age. *L'âge de la pierre polie,* the neolithic age. *L'âge du bronze,* the bronze age. *L'âge du fer,* the iron age. *Hist: Le moyen âge,* the Middle Ages. *Myth: L'âge d'or,* the golden age. *L'âge d'airain,* the brazen age. *L'âge de fer,* the iron age.

âgé [ɑʒe], *a.* Old, aged. **1.** Agé de dix ans, aged ten, ten years old, ten years of age. *Je suis plus, moins, âgé que vous,* I am older, younger, than you. **2.** Advanced in years.

agence [aʒɑ̃ːs], *s.f.* (a) Agency. *A. d'affaires,* general business agency or office. *A. de renseignement(s),* information bureau. *A. de placement,* registry office; employment bureau. (b) Branch office.

agencement [aʒɑ̃smɑ̃], *s.m.* **1.** Arrangement, ordering, disposition (of a house); fitting up, fitting together (of parts of machine, etc.); lay-out (of wireless set, etc.). **2.** *pl.* Fixtures, fittings (of house, machine, etc.).

agencer [aʒɑ̃se], *v.tr.* (j'agençai(s); n. agençons) To arrange, dispose (house, etc.); to fit up, fit together, adjust (parts of machine, etc.). *Local bien agencé,* well-designed, well-equipped, premises. *Phrases mal agencées,* ill-balanced, badly constructed, sentences.

agenda [aʒɛ̃da], *s.m.* Memorandum-book; engagement-book; diary. *pl. Des agendas.*

agenouill|er (s') [saʒnuje], *v.pr.* To kneel (down); to fall on one's knees. *s.m.* **-ement.**

    agenouillé, *a.* Kneeling.

agent [aʒɑ̃], *s.m.* **1.** Agent, agency, medium, acting power. *Agent chimique,* chemical agent. *A. de circulation, a. monétaire,* circulating medium. **2.** (Pers.) (a) Agent. *Agent d'affaires,* general agent, man of business. *Seuls agents d'une maison,* sole agents, sole representatives, of a firm. *A. diplomatique,* diplomatic agent. (b) *Agent (de police),* policeman, police-constable. *A. vigie,* policeman on point duty. *A. pivot,* traffic police-man. (c) *Agent de change,* (i) stock-broker; (ii) mercantile broker. (d) *Mil: Agent de liaison,* liaison officer.

agglomération [aglɔmerasjɔ̃], *s.f.* Agglomeration. **1.** Massing together; packing (of snow, etc.). **2.** Mass, cluster, aggregation. **3.** Built-up area. *Les grandes agglomérations urbaines,* the great urban centres.

agglomérer [aglɔmere], *v.tr.* (j'agglomère; j'agglomérerai) To agglomerate; to mass (people, etc.) together.

    s'agglomérer, to agglomerate; to cohere, to bind; (of fuel, etc.) to cake.

    aggloméré, *s.m.* (a) Conglomerate. (b) Compressed fuel, (coal-dust) briquette.

agglutiner [aglytine], *v.tr.* To agglutinate; to bind.

s'agglutiner, to agglutinate; to bind; (of fuel, etc.) to cake.

aggrav|er [agrave], *v.tr.* **1.** To aggravate (disease, crime); to render (offence) more heinous; to worsen. *Maladie aggravée par l'anxiété,* illness heightened by anxiety. **2.** To increase, augment (penalty, difficulties). *a.* **-ant.** *s.f.* **-ation.**

s'aggraver, to worsen; to grow worse.

agile [aʒil], *a.* Agile, nimble; active, lithe; light-footed. *Avoir la langue a.,* to have a glib, ready, tongue. *Elle est a. de ses doigts,* she is nimble-fingered. *A. à faire qch.,* nimble at, in, doing sth. *adv.* **-ment.**

agilité [aʒilite], *s.f.* Agility, nimbleness, litheness.

agiotage [aʒjɔtaːʒ], *s.m. Pej:* Agiotage; gambling (on Stock Exchange).

agioteur [aʒjɔtœːr], *s.m.* Speculator, gambler (on Stock Exchange).

agir [aʒiːr], *v.i.* To act. **1.** *A. d'office,* to act officially. *A. par principe,* to act on principle. *A. en honnête homme,* to act the part of an honest man. *A. de soi-même,* to act on one's own initiative. **Faire agir qch.,** to set sth. going, working. *Bien, mal, a. envers qn,* to act, behave, well, ill, towards s.o. *Je n'aime pas sa façon d'a.,* I don't like his behaviour. **Est-ce ainsi que vous en agissez avec moi?** is that how you treat me? **2.** To act, operate, take effect. *Médecine qui agit vite,* medicine that acts quickly. *A. sur un levier,* to bear on a lever. *A. sur qn,* to bring an influence to bear upon s.o. **3.** *Jur:* Agir contre qn, to take action, proceedings, against s.o. **Faire agir la loi contre qn,** to set the law in motion against s.o.

s'agir (de), *v.impers.* (a) To concern; to be in question; to be the matter. **De quoi s'agit-il?** what is the question, the business, in hand? what is it all about? *Voici de quoi il s'agit, ce dont il s'agit,* the thing is this. *Il ne s'agit pas d'argent,* it is not a question of money. *Il s'agit de lui,* it is he who is concerned. *Il s'agit de votre vie, de votre avenir,* your life, your future, is at stake. *Il ne s'agit pas de cela,* that is not the question. (b) **S'agir de faire qch.,** to be a matter of doing sth. *Il ne s'agit que de les rendre heureux,* it is only a question of making them happy.

agissant [aʒisã], *a.* Active, busy, bustling.

agissements [aʒismã], *s.m.pl.* Usu. *Pej:* Doings, dealings, movements (of criminals ,etc.).

agitateur, -trice [aʒitatœːr, -tris]. **I.** *s.* (Political) agitator. **2.** *s.m.* Stirrer, stirring-rod.

agitation [aʒitasjɔ̃], *s.f.* Agitation. **1.** (a) Shaking, stirring; waving (of flag); wagging (of tail). (b) Discussing, discussion (of question). (c) Agitating. *L'a. ouvrière,* labour unrest. **2.** (a) (State of) perturbation; excitement. (b) Restlessness. (c) Roughness (of sea).

agit|er [aʒite], *v.tr.* **1.** (a) To agitate; to wave (handkerchief, flag). *Le chien agite sa queue,* the dog wags its tail. (b) To shake (tree, bottle, etc.). (c) To stir (mixture). **2.** (a) To agitate, excite, perturb. (b) *A. le peuple, les masses,* to stir up the masses. **3.** To discuss, debate (question). *a.* **-ant.**

s'agiter. (a) To be agitated, in movement. *S'a. dans l'eau,* to splash about, tumble (about), in the water. *S'a. dans son sommeil,* to toss in one's sleep. *Les émotions qui s'agitent dans son sein,* the emotions that struggle in his bosom. (b) To become agitated, excited.

agité, *a.* **1.** Choppy, rough (sea). **2.** Agitated, restless (patient, night); troubled (soul, sleep). **3.** Excited.

agneau [aɲo], *s.m.* Lamb, lambkin. **Peau**

---

d'agneau, lambskin. **Doux comme un agneau,** as gentle as a lamb.

Agnès [aɲɛs]. **1.** *Pr.n.f.* Agnes. **2.** *s.f.* Artless young girl.

agonie [agɔni], *s.f.* Death agony, death-struggle; pangs of death. **Être à l'agonie,** to be at one's last gasp.

agonisant, -ante [agɔnizã, -ãːt]. **I.** *a.* Dying; in the throes of death. **2.** *s.* Dying person.

agoniser [agɔnize], *v.i.* To be dying, at the point of death.

agouti [aguti], *s.m. Z:* Agouti, agouty.

agrafe [agraf], *s.f.* **1.** Hook, fastener; clasp (of medal, of album); buckle (of strap); clip (for papers). *A. de diamants,* diamond clasp. **Agrafes et portes** (*de couturière*), hooks and eyes. **2.** *Const:* etc.: Clamp; cleat; hasp or catch (of window, etc.).

agraf|er [agrafe], *v.tr.* To fasten by means of a hook, clasp, or clip. *A. une robe, un rideau, des papiers,* to do up a frock, hook up a curtain, clip papers together. **Agrafer qn,** to do up s.o.'s dress. *F: A. un voleur,* to nab a thief. *s.m.* **-age.**

s'agrafer *à qn, à qch.,* to cling to, hang on to, s.o., sth.

agraire [agrɛːr], *a.* Agrarian.

agrandir [agrãdiːr], *v.tr.* (a) To make (sth.) larger; to enlarge. (b) To make (sth.) appear larger, taller; to magnify.

s'agrandir. **1.** To grow larger; to become greater; to increase; to expand. **2.** To become richer, more powerful.

agrandissement [agrãdismã], *s.m.* **1.** (a) Enlarging, extending. (b) Enlargement, extension (of factory, etc.). *Phot:* Enlargement. **Cône d'agrandissement,** daylight or fixed-focus enlarger. **Lanterne d'agrandissement,** condenser enlarger. **2.** Increase in power; aggrandizement.

agréable [agreabl], *a.* Agreeable, pleasant, pleasing, nice. *A. au goût,* pleasant to the taste. *Choses agréables à entendre,* things pleasant to hear. *Tâche peu agréable,* disagreeable, invidious, task. *Si cela peut vous être a.,* if you care to; if you like. **Faire l'agréable,** to make oneself pleasant (*auprès de,* to). *Pour vous être a.,* to oblige you. *s.m.* **Joindre l'a. à l'utile,** to combine the pleasant with the useful. *adv.* **-ment.**

agréer [agree]. **I.** *v.tr.* To accept, recognize, approve (of), agree to (sth.). *A. un contrat,* to approve an agreement. *A. les excuses de qn,* to accept s.o.'s apologies. *A. un présent,* to be graciously pleased to accept a present. **Agréez mes salutations empressées,** believe me yours sincerely. **2.** *v.ind.tr.* To suit, please. *Si cela lui agrée,* if that suits him, suits his convenience. [GRÉ]

s'agréer *à qch.,* to take pleasure in sth.

agrégation [agregasjɔ̃], *s.f.* **1.** (a) Aggregation, binding. **Matière d'agrégation,** binding material (of road, etc.). (b) Aggregate, agglomeration. **2.** (Concours d')agrégation, competitive examination conducted by the State for admission to posts on the teaching staff of the Lycées.

agréger (s') [sagreʒe], *v.pr.* (Of matter) To unite, join together; to aggregate.

agrégé, -ée. **I.** *a.* Aggregate (matter). **2.** *a. & s. Sch:* (Professeur) agrégé, teacher who has passed the *agrégation* examination.

agrément [agremã], *s.m.* **1.** (a) Pleasure, amusement. **Voyage d'agrément,** pleasure-trip. **Ouvrages de pur a.,** works intended merely to please. **Ouvrages d'agrément,** fancy work **S.a.** ART **1.** (b) Agreeableness, attractiveness, pleasantness, charm. **2.** Usu. *pl.* (a) Amenities (of place); charms (of person). (b) Ornament(ation), embellishment. *Mus:* **Notes d'agrément,** grace-notes. **3.** *A. donné à* qch., assent, consent, to sth.; approval, approbation, acceptance, of (proposal).

agrémenter [agremãte], *v.tr.* To embellish, ornament, adorn (*de,* with). *Robe agrémentée de dentelles,* dress trimmed with lace.

agrès [agrɛ], *s.m.pl.* (*a*) Tackle, gear (of ship, balloon, etc.). (*b*) Rigging (of ship); apparatus (of gymnasium).

agresseur [agresœːr], *s.m.* Aggressor.

agress|if, -ive [agresif, -iːv] *a.* Aggressive, provocative (person, manner). *adv.* **-ivement.**

agression [agresjɔ̃], *s.f.* Aggression; unprovoked assault.

agreste [agrɛst], *a.* **I.** Rustic, uncultivated; rural (site). **2.** Uncouth, clownish, countrified (person, manners). *adv.* **-ment.**

agricole [agrikɔl], *a.* Agricultural (country, produce). **Comice agricole,** agricultural show.

agriculteur [agrikyltœːr], *s.m.* Agriculturist, husbandman, farmer.

agriculture [agrikylty:r], *s.f.* Agriculture, husbandry, farming.

agriffer [agrife], *v.tr.* F: To seize hold of (sth.) with the claws; to clutch, grip. [GRIFFE]
     s'agriffer, to clutch (*à,* at); to cling (*à,* to).

agripper [agripe], *v.tr.* F: (*a*) To clutch, clutch at, grip (sth.). (*b*) To seize, snatch, grab.
     s'agripper. I. *S'a. à* qch., to cling to, clutch at, sth. **2.** *Ils s'agrippèrent,* they came to grips.

agronome [agrɔnɔm], *s.m.* Agronomist, scientific agriculturist.

agronomie [agrɔnɔmi], *s.f.* Agronomy, husbandry.

agronomique [agrɔnɔmik], *a.* Agronomic(al).

aguerr|ir [ageriːr], *v.tr.* To harden (s.o.) to war; to accustom, inure, to (the hardships of) war; to train (troops). [GUERRE] *s.m.* **-issement.**
     s'aguerrir, to grow hardened, seasoned.
     aguerri, *a.* Seasoned, trained (army, etc.). **Peu, mal, aguerri,** raw (soldier, etc.).

aguets [agɛ], *s.m.pl.* (Used only in the adv. phr.) **Aux aguets,** watchful (*de,* for). *Être, se tenir, aux a.,* to be on the watch, on the look-out. *Avoir l'oreille aux a.,* to keep one's ears open. [GUET]

aguichant [agiʃɑ̃], *a.* P: Seductive, fetching, tantalizing, saucy (glance, smile).

aguicher [agiʃe], *v.tr.* **I.** To inflame (s.o.); to lead (s.o.) on; to carry on with (s.o.). **2.** To excite the curiosity of (s.o.).

ah [ɑ], *int.* Ah! *Ah, que c'est beau!* isn't it fine! *Ah çà, dépêchez-vous donc!* now then, do make haste!

ahur|ir [ayriːr], *v.tr.* F: To bewilder. **I.** To dumbfound, flabbergast. **2.** To confuse, stupefy, daze. [HURE] *a.* **-issant.** *s.m.* **-issement.**
     ahuri, -ie, *a.* F: Bewildered. (*a*) Dumbfounded, flabbergasted. (*b*) Confused, dazed, stupefied.

ai. See AVOIR.

aide¹ [ɛ(ː)d], *s.f.* (*a*) Help, assistance, aid. **Venir en aide à** qn, **venir à l'aide de** qn, to help s.o.; to come to the assistance of s.o. **Dieu vous soit en aide!** God help you! *Recourir à l'a. d'un médecin,* to call in a doctor. *Appeler à l'a.,* to call for help. **A l'aide!** help! *Prep.phr.* **A l'aide de** qch., with the help, assistance, of sth. (*b*) Relief, succour. *A. aux pauvres,* poor relief.

aide², *s.m. & f.* Assistant, helper. *Le bourreau et ses aides,* the executioner and his assistants. **Aide de camp,** aide-de-camp.

aide-chirurgien, *s.m.* Assistant-surgeon. *pl. Des aides-chirurgiens.*

aide-mémoire, *s.m.inv.* (*a*) Pocket-book (of formulae, etc.); manual. (*b*) Memorandum. (*c*) *Dipl:* **Aide-mémoire.**

aider [ɛde]. **I.** *v.tr.* *Aider* qn, to help, assist, aid, s.o. *A. les pauvres,* to succour, relieve, the poor. *Je me suis fait a'der,* I got some help. *S'a. de* qch., to make use of, avail oneself of, sth. *Prov:* **Aide-toi et le ciel t'aidera,** God helps those who help themselves. *A.* (*à*) qn *à faire* qch., to help s.o. to do sth. *A.* qn *à monter, à descendre, à entrer, à sortir,* to help s.o. up, down, in, out. **Dieu aidant . . .,** with God's help. **. . . Le temps aidant . . .,** with, by, the help of time. **. . . 2.** *v.ind.tr.* *A. à* qch., to help towards sth.; to contribute to(wards) sth. *A. au succès,* to further contribute to the success.

aie, -s, -nt [ɛ]. See AVOIR.

aïe [aj], *int.* (Indicating twinge of pain) Oh!

aïeul [ajœl], *s.m.* **I.** (*pl.* **Aïeuls.**) Grandfather, grandsire. **2.** (*pl.* **Aïeux** [ajø].) Ancestor, forefather; *pl.* forbears.

aïeule [ajœl], *s.f.* **I.** Grandmother. **2.** Ancestress.

aïeux. See AÏEUL 2.

aigle [ɛgl]. **I.** (*a*) *s.m. & f.* *Orn:* Eagle. *Grand a. des mers,* erne, sea-eagle. *Un regard, des yeux, d'a.,* keen, penetrating, glance. *Aux yeux d'a.,* eagle-eyed. (*b*) *s.m.* *Lit:* Genius, master mind. *F:* **Ce n'est pas un aigle,** he is no genius, is not brilliant. **2.** *s.m.* Lectern, reading-desk. **3.** *s.m.* *Ich:* **Aigle de mer,** eagle-ray. **4.** *s.m. or f.* *Mil:* Eagle, standard. *Les aigles romaines,* the Roman eagles. *L'a. noir de Prusse,* the black eagle of Prussia.

aiglefin [ɛglǝfɛ̃], *s.m.* *Ich:* Haddock.

aiglon, -onne [ɛglɔ̃, -ɔn], *s.* Eaglet; young eagle.

aigre [ɛːgr], *a.* (*a*) Sour, sharp, acid, tart. *s.m.* **Tourner à l'aigre,** to turn sour. **Sentir l'aigre,** to smell sour. (*b*) Sour(-tempered), crabbed, tart (person). (*c*)Shrill, harsh, sharp (sound). (*d*) *Vents aigres,* bitter, raw, winds.

aigre-doux, -douce, *a.* Bitter-sweet (fruit, drink, sauce). *F: Ton a.-d.,* subacid tone.

aigrefin¹ [ɛgrǝfɛ̃], *s.m.* *Ich:* = AIGLEFIN.

aigrefin², -ine [ɛgrǝfɛ̃, -in], *s.* Sharper, swindler; adventurer, adventuress.

aigrelet, -ette [ɛgrǝlɛ, -ɛt], *a.* Sourish, tart.

aigrement [ɛgrǝmɑ̃], *adv.* Acrimoniously, querulously, bitterly, tartly.

aigremoine [ɛgrǝmwan], *s.f.* *Bot:* Agrimony.

aigrette [ɛgrɛt], *s.f.* **I.** (*a*) Aigrette (of heron, of egret); crest (of peacock etc.); tuft. (*b*) *Cost:* Aigrette, plume; tuft (of feathers, gems, etc.); osprey, spray (as head ornament). (*c*) *Bot:* Egret, pappus. (*d*) *El:* Aigrette, brush (discharge). **2.** *Orn:* Egret; tufted heron.

aigreur [ɛgrœːr], *s.f.* (*a*) Sourness, tartness, acidity. (*b*) Sourness (of temper or manner); acerbity, acrimony, bitterness, crabbedness. *F:* **Échanger des aigreurs,** to exchange sour remarks, harsh words. (*c*) *pl.* **Aigreurs,** acidity of the stomach; heartburn.

aigr|ir [ɛgriːr]. **I.** *v.tr.* (*a*) To make or turn (sth.) sour; to sour (food, milk, etc.). (*b*) To sour, embitter (person). **2.** *v.i.* To turn or grow sour; to sour; (of milk) to turn. *s.m.* **-issement.**
     s'aigrir. I. To turn sour; to sour. **2.** (Of pers.) To become soured, embittered.

aigu, -uë [egy], *a.* **I.** Sharp, pointed, sharp-pointed (instrument, etc.). *Geom:* **Angle aigu,** acute angle. **2.** Acute, sharp (pain); intense (curiosity); keen, bitter (conflict, jealousy). **Ouïe aiguë,** acute hearing. **3.** Shrill, sharp, piercing, high-pitched (sound). **Voix aiguë,** shrill voice. **4.** *Gram:* **Accent aigu,** acute accent.

aiguière [egjɛːr], *s.f.* Aiguière; (silver or crystal) ewer.

aiguille [egɥiːj], *s.f.* **1.** Needle. *A. à coudre*, sewing needle. *A. à repriser*, darning-needle. *A. à passer, à lacet*, bodkin. *A. à tricoter*, knitting-needle. **Travailler à l'aiguille**, to do needlework. *Les travaux à l'a.*, needlework, needle-craft. *F:* **Discuter sur des pointes d'aiguille**, to split hairs; to cavil. **Avoir des aiguilles dans les jambes**, to have pins and needles in one's legs. S.a. FIL I. **2.** (Thing shaped like a needle) (*a*) **Aiguille de glace**, icicle. **Aiguille de pin**, pine-needle. (*b*) *A. de graveur*, etching-needle. *A. de phonographe*, gramophone needle. *A. de fusil*, firing-pin. (*c*) *Rail:* Tongue-rail, point-rail, blade. *A. de raccordement*, points, *U.S:* switches. **Changer l'aiguille**, to throw over the points. **3.** Needle, point (of obelisk, peak). *A. d'un clocher d'église*, church spire. **4.** (*a*) (Swinging) needle (of compass, galvanometer). *A. aimantée*, magnetic needle. (*b*) Index, pointer (of balance, etc.); needle, pointer (of speedometer). (*c*) Hand (of watch, clock). **Petite aiguille**, hour-hand. **Grande aiguille**, minute-hand. *A. trotteuse*, second-hand.

aiguillée [egɥije], *s.f.* Needleful (of thread, etc.).

aiguill|er [egɥije], *v.tr. Rail:* To shunt, switch off, turn off (train). *F: A. la conversation sur une autre voie*, to switch on to another subject; to divert the conversation. *s.m.* **-age.**

aiguillette [egɥijɛt], *s.f.* **1.** Aiguillette, aglet, (tagged) lace. *Mil: Navy: etc* Shoulder-knot. *Nau:* Lanyard. **2.** *Cu: A. de chair*, slice of flesh off the breast (of duck, etc.).

aiguilleur [egɥijœːr], *s.m. Rail:* Pointsman.

aiguillon [egɥijɔ̃], *s.m.* **1.** (*a*) Goad. *Piquer un bœuf de, avec, l'a.*, to prick an ox with the goad; to goad (on) an ox. *F:* **L'aiguillon du remords**, the pricks of remorse. (*b*) Spur, incentive, stimulus (of necessity, etc.). **2.** (*a*) *Bot:* Prickle, thorn. (*b*) *Ent:* Sting (of wasp, etc.).

aiguillonn|er [egɥijɔne], *v.tr.* **1.** To goad, prod (oxen). **2.** To urge on, incite (to work, etc.); to goad on (by insults, etc.); to rouse (s.o.); to whet (appetite). *s.m.* **-ement.**

aiguis|er [eg(ɥ)ize], *v.tr.* **1.** (*a*) To whet (scythe); to sharpen, set an edge on, grind (knife, etc.); to set (saw, razor). S.a. PIERRE[1]. (*b*) To point; to sharpen (tool) to a point. *A. un crayon*, to sharpen a pencil. *A. une épigramme*, to point an epigram. **2.** To make keen; to excite, stimulate (wits, appetite); to whet (appetite). *s.m.* **-age.**

s'aiguiser, (of wits, etc.) to become sharpened, keen.

aiguisé, *a.* Sharp (knife, appetite, teeth).

ail [aːj], *s.m.* Garlic. **Gousse d'ail**, clove of garlic.

aile [ɛl], *s.f.* **1.** Wing, pinion. **Coup d'aile**, stroke, flap, of the wings; waft of the wings. **Couper, rogner, les ailes à un oiseau**, *F:* à qn, to pinion a bird; *F:* to clip s.o.'s wings. **Battre de l'aile**, (i) (of bird) to beat its wings; to flutter; (ii) *F:* (of pers.) to be flustered, embarrassed; to be tired, exhausted. *Entreprise qui bat de l'a.*, concern in a bad way. **Ne (plus) battre que d'une aile**, (i) (of bird) to be wounded in one wing, (ii) *F:* (of pers.) to be on his last legs. **En avoir dans l'aile**, (i) (of bird) to be winged, (ii) *F:* (of pers.) to be hard hit. **Voler de ses propres ailes**, to depend on oneself; to stand on one's own legs. **Vouloir voler avant d'avoir ses ailes**, to want to fly before one is fledged. S.a. PLUME I, TIRE-D'AILE (à). **2.** Wing (of aeroplane, of building, of thumb-screw); wing, flank (of army); sail, whip (of windmill); arm (of semaphore); blade (of propeller, of ploughshare); aisle (of church); helix (of ear); wing, ala (of nose); wing, mudguard (of motor car). *Civ.E:* **Mur en aile**, wing-wall. S.a. DÉRIVE[1] I, ROUE.

ailé [ɛle], *a.* Winged, feathered.

aileron [ɛlrɔ̃], *s.m.* **1.** (*a*) Pinion (of bird). (*b*) Fin, flipper (of shark). (*c*) *pl. Ent:* Balancers, poisers (of diptera). **2.** *Av:* Aileron, wing-tip.

ailette [ɛlɛt], *s.f.* **1.** Small wing (of building, etc.). **2.** (*a*) Radiating plate, (cooling-)flange, rib, fin, gill (of radiator). (*b*) Lug, tenon (of machine part). **Vis à ailettes**, wing-screw, thumb-screw. (*c*) Vane (of torpedo, of fan, ventilator); blade (of turbine).

ailier [ɛlje], *s.m. Fb:* Wing (player); winger.

aill-e, -es, etc. [aːj]. See ALLER.

ailleurs [ajœːr], *adv.* **1.** Elsewhere, somewhere else. **Partout ailleurs**, everywhere else, anywhere else. **Nulle part ailleurs**, nowhere else. *J'avais l'esprit a.*, my thoughts were elsewhere. **2.** *Adv. phrs.* (*a*) **D'ailleurs**, (i) besides, furthermore, moreover; (ii) from another place, from another source. (*b*) **Par ailleurs**, (i) by another way or route, (ii) in other respects, in another connection. (iii) *Savoir une nouvelle par a.*, to have received news from another source.

aimable [emabl], *a.* **1.** Amiable, agreeable, pleasant; kind; nice. **Faire l'aimable avec qn**, to make oneself pleasant to s.o. *Être a. envers, pour, avec, qn*, to be nice to, with, s.o. **Vous êtes bien aimable, c'est très aimable à vous**, that is very kind of you, very good of you. **Le sexe aimable**, the fair sex. **Peu aimable**, ungracious. **2.** Lovable, attractive. *A. innocence*, refreshing innocence. *adv.* **-ment.**

aimant[1] [emɑ̃], *a.* Loving, affectionate.

aimant[2], *s.m.* Magnet. *A. naturel*, **pierre d'aimant**, magnetic iron ore; lodestone. *A. en fer à cheval*, horseshoe magnet.

aimantation [emɑ̃tasjɔ̃], *s.f.* Magnetization, magnetizing.

aimanter [emɑ̃te], *v.tr.* To magnetize. **Aiguille aimantée**, magnetic needle.

Aimée [eme]. *Pr.n.f.* Amy.

aimer [eme], *v.tr.* **1.** (*a*) To like, care for, to be fond of (s.o., sth.). *A. qn d'amitié*, to be good friends with s.o. *Une personne comme vous les aimez*, a person after your own heart. *Aimé des dieux*, beloved by the gods. *Aimé de tous, par tout le monde*, loved by all; beloved of all. *On l'aime beaucoup*, he is held in great affection. **Se faire aimer de qn**, to win s.o.'s affection. *A. faire qch., à faire qch.*, to like to do sth.; to like doing sth. *Il n'aime pas (à) sortir seul*, he doesn't like to go out alone, going out alone. *Il aime qu'on lui dise tout*, he likes to be told everything. **Qui m'aime me suive!** let those who love me follow me! S.a. CHÂTIER. (*b*) **Aimer autant**. *J'aime autant le cidre (que le vin)*, I like cider just as well (as wine). *J'aime(rais) autant rester ici (que de . . .)*, I would just as soon stay here (as . . .). *J'aime autant qu'il ne m'attende pas*, I would just as soon he didn't wait for me. (*c*) **Aimer mieux**. *J'aime mieux le cidre (que le vin)*, I prefer cider (to wine). *J'aime, j'aimerais, mieux rester ici*, I would rather. *J'aime mieux qu'il vienne*, I would sooner, stay here. *J'aime mieux qu'il vienne*, I prefer that he should come; I would rather he came. **2.** **Aimer qn (d'amour)**, to love s.o.; to be in love with s.o. *Ils s'aiment*, they are in love (with each other).

aine [ɛn], *s.f. Anat:* Groin.

aîné [ene], *a.* (*a*) Elder (of two); eldest (of more than two). *s.* **Nos aînés**, our elders. **Il est mon aîné**, he is older than I. (*b*) Senior. *M. Dumont a.*, Mr Dumont senior.

aînesse [ɛnɛs], *s.f.* **1.** Primogeniture. **Droit**

d'aînesse, (i) Law of Primogeniture, (ii) birthright. **2.** Seniority. [AÎNÉ]

ainsi [ɛ̃si]. **I.** adv. Thus; so; in this, in that, manner; in a like manner. **S'il en est ainsi,** if such is the case, if that is the case, if (it is) so. *Il n'en est pas a. de vous,* the case is different with you. **Et ainsi de suite,** and so on, and so forth. **Pour ainsi dire,** so to speak, as it were. **Ainsi soit-il,** (i) so- be it, (ii) *Ecc:* amen. **2.** conj. So, thus. *A. vous ne venez pas?* so you are not coming? **De même que . . ., ainsi . . .,** (just) as . . ., so. . . . **3.** *Conj.phr.* **Ainsi que,** (just) as. *Faites a. qu'il vous plaira,* do just as you please. *Cette règle a. que la suivante me paraît, me paraissent, inutile(s),* this rule, as also the next one, seems to me to be unnecessary. (The concord is usu. in the *pl.*)

air [ɛːr], *s.m.* **I. I.** (a) Air, atmosphere. *Voyage par la voie des airs,* journey by air. *Cela manque d'air ici,* it is a bit close, rather stuffy, here. **Prendre l'air,** to enjoy the fresh air. *Sortir prendre l'air,* to go for a breath of fresh air, for a breather. *F:* **Vivre de l'air du temps,** to live upon (next to) nothing, on air. **Prendre un air de feu,** to warm oneself at the fire. **S.a.** BUREAU **2. Au grand air, en plein air,** under the open sky; in the fresh air; in the open air. *Vie au grand air,* open-air life. *Jeux en plein air,* outdoor games. **Concert en plein air,** alfresco concert. **Amortisseur à air comprimé,** pneumatic shock-absorber. *Aut:* **Poste d'air,** tyre-inflating station. **S.a.** POCHE[1] **2,** TROU **2.** (b) **En l'air,** in the air. *Nous écoutions la fourchette en l'air,* we listened with poised forks. **Être en l'air,** (i) to be in a state of confusion, of disturbance; (ii) (of town) to be all agog with excitement; (iii) *Mil:* (of troops) to be unsupported, exposed, in the air. **Mettre tout en l'air,** to throw everything into confusion. **Regarder en l'air,** to look up (into the sky); to look upwards. **Contes en l'air,** idle tales, cock-and-bull stories. **Paroles en l'air,** idle talk. **Menaces en l'air,** empty threats. *F:* **Il y a quelque chose dans l'air,** there is something in the wind, something brewing. **2.** Wind, draught. **Il fait de l'air,** it is windy, breezy. **Se tenir entre deux airs,** to stand in a draught.

II. air. I. (a) Appearance, look. **Avoir bon air, grand air,** (i) (of pers.) to look distinguished; (ii) (of dress, etc.) to look well. to be becoming. **Individu de mauvais air,** ill-looking customer. **Air de famille,** family likeness. **Avoir un faux air de qn,** to bear a slight, remote, resemblance to, to have a look of, s.o. *La ville prend un air de fête,* the town assumes a holiday appearance. (b) **Avoir l'air** (= SEMBLER, PARAÎTRE), to look, seem. (The predicative adj. may agree either with *air* or with the subject.) *Elle a l'air fatigué(e),* she looks tired. *Il a un peu l'air étranger,* he has a slightly foreign appearance. *Ils ont l'air d'avoir peur,* it looks as if they were afraid. *Vous avez l'air de vous amuser,* you seem to be enjoying yourself. *Cela en a tout l'air* it looks like it. *Impers:* **Il a l'air de vouloir pleuvoir,** it looks like rain. **S.a.** TOUCHER[1] **2. 2** Manner, way. **Prendre l'air du monde,** to acquire the manners of society. **Afficher de grands airs, se donner des airs,** to give oneself airs; *F:* to put on side. *A:* **Gens du bel air,** fashionable people.

III. air. Tune, air, melody. *Vieille chanson sur un air nouveau,* old song to a new tune *F:* **Je connais des paroles sur cet air-là,** I've heard that tale before.

airain [ɛrɛ̃], *s.m.* Bronze, brass. *F:* **Bâtir sur l'airain,** to build upon a rock. **Avoir un cœur**

d'airain, to have a heart of stone. *Voix d'a.,* brazen voice. *Avoir un front d'a.,* to be brazen-faced, shameless. *Lit:* **L'airain tonne,** the cannon thunders. *L'a. retentit,* the trumpet sounds. *L'a. sonne,* the bells ring. **S.a.** ÂGE **3.**

aire [ɛːr], *s.f.* **I.** Surface; flat space; floor. *A. d'une grange,* threshing-floor. *Av:* **A. d'embarquement,** enplaning ground; the 'tarmac'. *A. d'une enclume,* flat, crown, of an anvil. **2.** Area (of field, triangle, building, etc.). **3.** Eyrie (of eagle). **4.** *Nau:* Rhumb. **Les aires de vent,** the points of the compass. *F:* **Prendre l'aire du vent,** to see which way the wind is blowing.

airelle [ɛrɛl], *s.f. Bot:* **A. myrtille,** whortleberry, bilberry. *A. coussinette,* cranberry.

ais [ɛ], *s.m.* Board, plank (of partition, etc.). *Ais de marche (d'un escalier),* tread(-board). *Ais d'un tonneau,* stave of a barrel.

aisance [ɛzɑ̃ːs], *s.f.* **I.** Ease. (a) Freedom (of movement, etc.). **Faire qch. avec aisance,** to do sth. with ease. *Donner de l'a. à qch.,* to ease sth. *A. des coudes,* elbow-room. (b) **Jouir de l'aisance,** être dans l'aisance, to be in affluence, in easy circumstances. *Un homme dans l'a.,* a well-to-do man. *Acquérir une honnête a.,* to acquire a decent competency. **2.** Easing. **Lieu, cabinet, d'aisances,** public convenience, water-closet.

aise [ɛːz]. **I.** *s.f.* (a) Ease, comfort. **Etre à l'aise, à son aise,** (i) to be comfortable, to have (elbow) room; (ii) to be well-off, in easy circumstances. **On tient à l'aise à six dans cette voiture,** this car holds six comfortably. *Ne pas être à son a.,* se sentir mal à l'aise, (i) to feel awkward, to feel uncomfortable; (ii) to feel ill. **Mettre qn à son aise,** to put, set, s.o. at his ease. **Il en prend à son aise,** (i) he takes it easy; (ii) he is a cool customer! **A votre aise!** just as you like! **Aimer ses aises,** to be fond of comfort; to like one's comforts. **Vivre à l'aise, à son aise,** to live comfortably. (b) *A:* Pleasure, joy. **Tressaillir d'a.,** to thrill with pleasure. **Ne pas se sentir d'aise,** to be overjoyed. **2.** a. **Bien aise, fort aise** [fɔrtɛːz], very glad, well pleased. *Je suis bien a. de vous voir,* I am very pleased, so pleased, so glad, to see you. *Je suis fort a. que vous soyez venu,* I am very glad you came.

aisé [ɛze], *a.* **I.** (a) Easy, free (position, manner); comfortable (clothes). (b) In easy circumstances, well-to-do (person). **2.** Easy, easily accomplished (task). **C'est plus aisé à dire qu'à faire,** it is more easily said than done. *adv.* **-ment.**

aisselle [ɛsɛl], *s.f.* Armpit.

ait [ɛ]. See AVOIR.

aîtres [ɛːtr], *s.m.pl.* Arrangement, ins and outs, of a house. **Connaître les aîtres,** to know one's way about a house.

ajonc [aʒɔ̃], *s.m. Bot:* Furze, gorse, whin.

ajour [aʒuːr], *s.m.* **I.** Opening, hole, orifice (which lets the light through). *Ménager un a. dans une cloison,* to allow an opening (for light) in a partition. **2.** (Ornamental) perforation, openwork (in wood-carving, metal-work, etc.). [JOUR]

ajouré [aʒure], *a.* (Of ornamental work) Perforated, pierced. *Woodw:* **Travail ajouré** fretwork.

ajourn|er [aʒurne], *v.tr.* (a) To postpone, put off, adjourn, defer (meeting, decision, journey). (b) *Sch:* To refer (candidate). *Mil:* To put back (conscript). *s.m.* **-ement.**

s'ajourner, to adjourn. *La Chambre s'est ajournée à huitaine,* the House adjourned for a week.

ajouter [aʒute], *v.tr.* To add. **I.** *A. des chiffres,* to add up figures. *A. qch. à qch.,* to add sth. to sth. **Ajouter l'action aux paroles,** to suit the action to the word. **2.** "*Venez aussi*," *ajouta-t-il*, "you come too," he added. *Nous devons a. que . . .*, it should also be stated that. . . .

ajustement [aʒystəmã], *s.m.* **1.** (*a*) Adjusting, adjustment (of apparatus, etc.). (*b*) Arrangement, settlement (of quarrel, etc.). **2.** *A:* Garb, attire.

ajust|er [aʒyste], *v.tr.* **1.** (*a*) To adjust, set (apparatus, tool, etc.). (*b*) To true (sth.) up. *A. une pièce à la lime*, to finish a piece with the file, to file a piece true. (*c*) To fit together, to set up (machine). (*d*) *A. son fusil*, to take aim with one's gun. *A. un coup*, to aim a shot. *A. qn (avec un fusil)*, to aim (a gun) at s.o. (*e*) *A. qch. à qch.*, to fit, adjust, adapt, suit, sth. to sth. *Cette clef s'ajuste à chacune des serrures*, this key fits each of the locks. *Corsage ajusté*, close-fitting bodice. **2.** To put (sth.) right, straight; to settle (sth.). *A. ses affaires*, to put one's affairs in order. *A. une querelle*, to settle a quarrel. *A. son chapeau*, to set one's hat straight. *a.* **-able.** *s.m.* **-age.**

ajutage [aʒyta:ʒ], *s.m.*, **ajutoir** [aʒytwa:r], *s.m.* (*a*) *Ch:* *Hyd.E:* Adjutage, ajutage. (*b*) *Mch: I.C.E: etc:* Nozzle; jet.

akène [aken], *s.m. Bot:* Achene, akene.

alacrité [alakrite], *s.f.* Alacrity, eagerness. *A. à faire qch.*, readiness to do sth.

alambic [alãbik], *s.m. Ch: Ind:* Still, *A:* alembic.

alambiquage [alãbika:ʒ], *s.m.* Excessive subtlety, over-refinement (of style, thought, etc.).

alambiquer [alãbike], *v.tr.* To refine (too much), to subtilize (style, thought, speech, etc.). S'**alambiquer le cerveau**, to puzzle, rack, one's brains. **alambiqué**, *a. F:* Fine-spun, super-subtle.

alanguir [alãgi:r], *v.tr.* To make languid; to enfeeble.
   s'**alanguir**, to grow languid; to languish, flag, droop.

alanguissement [alãgismã], *s.m.* Languor, weakness; drooping, decline.

alarmant [alarmã], *a.* Alarming; startling.

alarme [alarm], *s.f.* Alarm. **Donner, sonner, l'alarme**, to give, sound, the alarm. **Cloche d'alarme**, tocsin. *Rail:* **Tirer la sonnette d'alarme**, to pull the communication-cord. **Porter l'alarme dans un camp**, to carry the alarm into a camp.

alarmer [alarme], *v.tr.* **1.** To give the alarm to (s.o.). **2.** To frighten, startle, alarm (s.o.). *Alarmé de qch.*, alarmed at sth.
   s'**alarmer**, to take alarm, to take fright (*de*, at).

alarmiste [alarmist], *a. & s.* Alarmist; scaremonger.

albanais, -aise [albanɛ, -ɛ:z], *a. & s. Ethn:* Albanian.

Albanie [albani]. *Pr.n.f. Geog:* Albania.

albâtre [albɑ:tr], *s.m.* Alabaster.

albatros [albatrɔs, -o:s], *s.m. Orn:* Albatross.

albigeois, -oise [albiʒwa, -wa:z], *a. & s.* (Native) of Albi. *Hist:* **Les Albigeois**, the Albigenses.

albinos [albinɔs, -ɔs], *s. & a. inv.* Albino. *Une (femme) albinos*, an albino woman.

Albion [albjɔ̃]. *Pr.n.f. A.Geog:* Albion, Britain.

album [albɔm], *s.m.* **1.** Album, sketch-book. *A. à feuilles mobiles*, loose-leaf album. **2.** Trade catalogue. *pl. Des albums.*

albumine [albymin], *s.f. Ch: Biol:* Albumin.

albuminer [albymine], *v.tr. Phot:* To albumenize (paper).

albumineux, -euse [albyminø, -ø:z], *a. Biol: Bot:* Albuminous, albuminose.

alcade [alkad], *s.m.* Alcalde, sheriff (in Spain).

alcali [alkali], *s.m. Ch:* Alkali.

alcalin [alkalɛ̃], *a.* Alkaline.

alcalinité [alkalinite], *s.f.* Alkalinity.

alcarazas [alkarazɑ:s], *s.m.* Alcarraza; (porous) water-cooler.

Alceste [alsɛst]. **1.** *Pr.n.f. Gr.Lit:* Alcestis. **2.** *Pr.n.m. Fr.Lit:* (Type of) social bear or blunt-spoken critic. (From the character in Molière's *Le Misanthrope.*)

alchimie [alʃimi], *s.f.* Alchemy.

alchimiste [alʃimist], *s.m.* Alchemist.

alcool [alkɔl], *s.m.* Alcohol, *F:* spirit(s). *A. absolu*, pure alcohol. *A. dénaturé, a. à brûler*, methylated spirit; industrial alcohol.

alcoolique [alkɔlik]. **1.** *a.* (*a*) Alcoholic, spirituous. (*b*) *Med:* Alcoholic (patient). **2.** *s.* Habitual drinker; drunkard.

alcooliser [alkɔlize], *v.tr.* To alcoholize.
   s'**alcooliser**, to drink heavily; *F:* to soak.

alcoolisme [alkɔlism], *s.m. Med:* Alcoholism.

Alcoran (l') [lalkɔrɑ̃], *s.m.* = KORAN (LE).

alcôve [alko:v], *s.f.* Alcove, (bed-)recess.

alcyon [alsjɔ̃], *s.m.* **1.** *Myth:* Halcyon. **2.** *Orn:* Kingfisher.

aléa [alea], *s.m.* Risk, hazard, chance. *L'affaire présente trop d'a.*, the business is too hazardous.

aléatoire [aleatwa:r], *a.* Aleatory (contract, etc.); problematical, hazardous, risky.

Alemans [almã], *s.m.pl. Hist:* Alemanni.

alène [alɛn], *s.f. Tls:* Awl. *A. plate*, bradawl.

alentour [alɑ̃tu:r]. **1.** *adv.* Around, round about. *Le pays d'a.*, the surrounding, neighbouring, country. *Prep.phr.* **Alentour de la maison**, round about the house. **2.** *s.m.pl.* Alentours (*d'une ville, etc.*), environs, neighbourhood, vicinity, surroundings (of a town, etc.). [À L'ENTOUR]

alerte [alɛrt]. **1.** *int.* Up! to arms! **2.** *s.f.* Alarm, warning. **Donner l'alerte au camp**, to rouse the camp. *Tenir l'ennemi en a.*, to harass the enemy. **Fausse alerte**, false alarm. **3.** *a.* (*a*) Alert, brisk, quick, agile. *A. à faire qch.*, quick to do sth. (*b*) Vigilant, watchful.

alerter [alɛrte], *v.tr.* To give the alarm to (troops); to warn, send a warning to (police).

alésage [aleza:ʒ], *s.m.* **1.** *Metalw:* (*a*) Boring (out). (*b*) Broaching, reaming. **2.** Bore (of rifle barrel); internal diameter (of cylinder, bearing).

aléser [aleze], *v.tr.* (j'alèse) j'aléserai) *Metalw:* (*a*) To bore (out). (*b*) To ream out, broach.

Alexandre [alɛksɑ̃:dr]. *Pr.n.m.* Alexander.

alexandrin, -ine [alɛksɑ̃drɛ̃, -in], *a. & s.* Alexandrine; Alexandrian (school). *Pros:* (**Vers**) alexandrin, alexandrine (line).

alezan, -ane [alzɑ̃, -an], *a. & s.* Chestnut (horse).

alfa [alfa], *s.m. Bot:* Alfa(-grass), esparto.

algarade [algarad], *s.f.* **1.** Storm of abuse. *Faire une algarade à qn*, to give s.o. a good blowing-up, a good dressing-down; to bite, snap, s.o.'s head off. **2.** Escapade; prank.

algèbre [alʒɛbr], *s.f.* Algebra.

algébrique [alʒebrik], *a.* Algebraic.

Alger [alʒe]. *Pr.n. Geog:* **1.** Algiers. **2.** *m.* (The Department of) Alger.

Algérie [alʒeri]. *Pr.n.f. Geog:* Algeria.

algérien, -ienne [alʒerjɛ̃, -jɛn], *a. & s.* Algerian, Algerine; of Algeria.

algue [alg], *s.f. Bot:* Alga, seaweed.

alibi [alibi], *s.m. Jur:* Alibi. *Plaider un a.*, to set up, plead, an alibi.

aliboron [alibɔrɔ̃], *s.m.* **Un maître aliboron**, a conceited ass, an ignoramus. (From La Fontaine's fable *Les Voleurs et l'âne.*)

aliénation [aljenasjɔ̃], *s.f.* Alienation. **1.** *Jur:* Transfer (of property, etc.). **2.** Estrangement. **3.** **Aliénation mentale**, derangement of mind; insanity.

aliéner [aljene], *v.tr.* (j'aliène, n. aliénons; j'aliénerai) **1.** *Jur:* To alienate, part with (property, etc.). **2.** To alienate, estrange (a friend, etc.). *Cet acte lui aliéna tous les cœurs,* this action alienated all hearts from him. **3.** To derange, unhinge (the mind).

aliéné, -ée, *a. & s.* Lunatic, mad(man); mentally deranged, insane (person). *Maison, asile, d'aliénés,* lunatic asylum.

aliéniste [aljenist], *s.m. & f.* Alienist; mental specialist.

alignement [aliɲmã], *s.m.* **1.** (*a*) Alignment; laying out (of trees, etc.) in line. *Mil:* **A droite alignement!** right dress! (*b*) *Adm:* Making up, balancing (of accounts, etc.). **2.** Alignment, line (of wall, etc.); row (of trees, etc.). *Déborder, dépasser, l'a.,* to project beyond the building line. *Mil:* **Rentrer dans l'alignement,** to fall into line.

aligner [aliɲe], *v.tr.* To align, draw up, line up; to put (thgs) in a line, in a row. *A. un terrain,* to line out, mark out, a plot of ground. *Mil:* **A. des soldats,** to dress a line of soldiers. *F:* **Aligner des chiffres,** to go into figures; to figure out the expense.

s'aligner, to fall into line. *Mil:* To dress. **S'aligner sur le terrain,** to fight a duel.

alignée, *s.f.* Line, row (of houses, trees).

aliment [alimã], *s.m.* **1.** Aliment, food. **2.** *L'a. des pauvres,* the maintenance of the poor.

alimentaire [alimãteːr], *a.* **1.** *Régime a.,* diet(ary). *Jur:* **Pension alimentaire,** alimony; allowances for necessaries. **2.** Alimentary, nourishing (plant, product). **Conserves alimentaires,** tinned foods. **3.** *Physiol:* **Le canal, le tube, alimentaire,** the alimentary canal. *Mch:* **Pompe alimentaire,** feed-pump; donkey-pump.

alimentation [alimãtasjɔ̃], *s.f.* **1.** (*a*) Alimentation, feeding; provisioning, supply (of town, market, etc.). **Article d'alimentation,** food-stuff. (*b*) Nourishment. *A. insuffisante, défectueuse,* insufficient nourishment; malnutrition. **2.** *Mch: etc:* Feed(ing) (of boiler, etc.).

alimenter [alimãte], *v.tr.* To feed, nourish (s.o.); to supply (market) with food. *Ruisseaux qui alimentent une rivière,* streams that feed a river. *A. la haine, la sédition,* to keep hatred, sedition, alive. *El.E:* **A. une usine de courant,** to furnish, supply, a factory with current. *Fb:* **Alimenter les avants,** to feed the forward line.

alinéa [alinea], *s.m.* *Typ:* **1.** First line of paragraph; indented line. **En alinéa,** indented. **2.** Paragraph.

alise [aliːz], *s.f.* *Bot:* Sorb-apple.

alisier [alizje], *s.m.* *Bot:* Service-tree.

alitement [alitmã], *s.m.* (*a*) Confinement to bed. (*b*) State of being bed-ridden.

aliter [alite], *v.tr.* To keep (s.o.) in bed. [LIT]
s'aliter, to take to one's bed.
alité, *a.* Confined to (one's) bed; *F:* laid up.

alizé [alize], *a. & s.m.* **Les (vents) alizés,** the trade-winds.

allaiter [alɛte], *v.tr.* To suckle (child or young); to feed (child) at the breast. *s.m.* **-ement.**

allant [alã]. **1.** *a.* (*a*) Active, busy, bustling; spirited (music). *s.m.* **Avoir de l'allant,** to have plenty of go, of buoyancy, of dash. (*b*) *Ustensile a. au feu,* fire-proof utensil. **2.** *s.m.pl.* **Allants et venants,** comers and goers; passers-by. [ALLER]

allécher [al(l)eʃe], *v.tr.* (j'allèche, n. alléchons; j'allécherai) To allure, attract, entice, tempt. *a.* **-échant.** *s.m.* **-èchement.**

allée [ale], *s.f.* **1.** (Action of) going. **Allées et venues,** coming and going; running about. **2.** (*a*) Walk (esp. lined with trees); lane, avenue (through wood, etc.). (*b*) Path (in garden). (*c*) Passage, entrance, alley; carriage-drive.

allège [al(l)ɛːʒ], *s.f.* **1.** *Nau:* Lighter, hopper, barge. **2.** *Arch: Const:* (*a*) Breast-wall (of window). (*b*) Balustrade, rail (of window, etc.). [ALLÉGER]

alléger [al(l)eʒe], *v.tr.* (j'allège, n. allégeons; j'allégea(s); j'allégerai) **1.** (*a*) To lighten (ships, taxes). (*b*) To unburden; to ease the strain on (timbers, etc.). (*c*) To alleviate, relieve, mitigate (pain). **2.** *A. qn de qch.,* to relieve s.o. of (the weight of) sth. *s.m.* **-ement.**

s'alléger, to become, grow, lighter or easier.

allégorie [al(l)egɔri], *s.f.* Allegory. **Par allégorie,** allegorically.

allégorique [al(l)egɔrik], *a.* Allegorical. *adv.* **-ment.**

allègre [al(l)ɛgr], *a.* Lively, gay, jolly, merry, cheerful. *Marcher d'un pas a.,* to walk briskly.

allégresse [al(l)egrɛs], *s.f.* Gladness, joy, cheerfulness, liveliness. [ALLÈGRE]

alléguer [al(l)ege], *v.tr.* (j'allègue, n. alléguons; j'alléguerai) **1.** To allege, urge, plead. *A. l'ignorance,* to plead ignorance. *A. un prétexte,* to advance a pretext. **2.** To cite, quote (author).

alléluia [al(l)elyja, -lɥija], *s.m. & int.* *Ecc:* Hallelujah, alleluia(h).

Allemagne [alman]. *Pr.n.f. Geog:* Germany.

allemand, -ande [almã, -ãːd]. **1.** *a. & s.* German. *F:* **Querelle d'Allemand,** quarrel about nothing. **2.** *s.m.* **L'allemand,** the German language.

aller [ale]. I. *v.i.* (*pr.p.* allant; *p.p.* allé; *pr.ind.* je vais, tu vas, il va, n. allons, v. allez, ils vont; *pr.sub.* j'aille, n. allions, ils aillent; *imp.* va (vas-y), allons; *p.d.* j'allais; *p.h.* j'allai; *fu.* j'irai. Aux. *être*) **1.** To go. (*a*) *A. à Paris,* to go to Paris. *A. et venir,* to come and go. **Je ne ferai qu'aller et revenir,** I shall come straight back. **Où allons-nous?** (i) where are we going? (ii) *F:* what are things coming to? *A. par bandes,* to go about in gangs. **Aller contre la Providence,** to fly in the face of Providence. **Il va sur ses dix ans,** he is nearly ten (years old). *A. jusqu'à injurier qn,* to go so far as to call s.o. names. *F:* **Faire aller qn,** to order s.o. about. (*b*) *A. en course, à la chasse, à la pêche, à pied, à cheval, en voiture, au galop, au trot.* See these words. (*c*) (With adv. acc.) **Aller bon train,** to go at a good round pace. (With cogn. acc.) **Aller son petit bonhomme de chemin,** to jog along. (*d*) *Allez, je vous écoute,* go on, proceed, I am listening. (*e*) *Sentier qui va à la gare,* path leading to the station. **2.** (*a*) To go, be going (well, ill). *Les affaires vont, ne vont pas,* business is brisk, slack. *Ça ira!* we'll manage it! *Je vous en offre cinq francs.—Va pour cinq francs!* I'll give you five francs for it.—Five francs be it! **Cela va sans dire, cela va de soi,** that's understood, that is a matter of course. (*b*) (Of machine, clock, etc.) To go, act, work, run. *La pendule va bien, mal,* the clock is right, wrong. **Faire aller un commerce,** to run a business. **Tout va comme sur des roulettes,** everything is going like clockwork. (*c*) **Comment allez-vous?** *F:* comment cela va-t-il? how are you? how do you do? **Je vais bien,** *F:* ça va, I am well, I am all right. **3.** **Aller à qn.** (*a*) (Of colours, clothes) To suit, become, s.o. (*b*) (Of climate, food) To agree with s.o. (*c*) (Of clothes, etc.) To fit s.o. **Cela vous va comme un gant,** (i) it fits you like a glove; (ii) *F:* it suits you to a T. (*d*) (Of proposal, etc.) To be to s.o.'s liking; to suit s.o. *Vos manières ne me vont pas,* I don't like your ways. *Ça me va,*

agreed! done! *F:* Ça va! all right! O.K.!
4. (Of colours, etc.) **Aller avec qch.,** to go well
with sth.; to match sth. **5.** (*a*) **Aller** + *inf. A.
voir qn,* to go and see s.o.; to call on s.o. *A. trouver qn,* to go to s.o. **Aller se promener,** to go
for a walk. *N'allez pas vous imaginer que . . .,*
don't go and imagine that. . . . (*b*) Aux. use of
aller (*pr. & p.d.* only) To be going, to be about
(to do sth.). *Il va s'en occuper,* he is going to see
about it. *Elle allait tout avouer,* she was about to
confess everything. (*c*) **Aller** + *pr.p.* or *ger.* (i) To
be continually doing sth. *Il va épiant, écoutant,*
he is always spying, listening. (ii) *Sa santé va* (*en*)
empirant, his health is steadily growing worse.
A. en augmentant, to increase. **6.** Y **aller.** (*a*) **J'y
vais! on y va!** coming! (*b*) *Est-ce comme ça
que vous y allez?* is that how you set about it?
Y aller de tout son cœur, to put one's back
into it. **Y aller carrément,** to make no bones
about it. **Il n'y va pas par quatre chemins,** he
doesn't mince matters. **Allons-y!** well, here goes!
Vas-y! allez-y! go it! go ahead! (*c*) *F:* **Y aller de
qch.,** to lay, stake, sth. **Y aller de son reste,** to
stake one's all. **Y aller de sa personne,** to take a
hand in it oneself. **Il y est allé d'une bouteille,** he
stood (treat to the extent of) a bottle. **7.** *v.impers.*
Il va de soi que . . ., it stands to reason, it goes
without saying, that. . . . **Il en va de même pour
lui, pour moi,** it's the same with him, with me.
Il y allait de sa vie, it was a matter of life and
death. *Il y va de ma vie,* my life is at stake.
8. *int.* **Allons,** *dépêchez-vous!* come, make haste!
Allons donc! (i) come along! get a move on!
(ii) nonsense! **Allons bon!** there now! hang it!
Mais va donc! get on with it! *J'ai bien souffert,*
va! allez! I have suffered much, believe me!
　　s'en aller. (*pr.ind.* **je m'en vais;** *imp.* **va-
t'en, allons-nous-en, allez-vous-en, ne t'en va pas;**
perf. **je m'en suis allé(e), nous nous en sommes
allé(e)s,** *F:* **je me suis en allé(e))** **1.** To go away,
to depart. **Faire en aller tout le monde,** to send
everyone away. **Faire en a. des taches,** to remove
stains. *Allez-vous-en!* go away! *Il faut que je
m'en aille,* I must be going. *Ses forces s'en allaient,*
his strength was going. **Le malade s'en va,** the
patient is sinking. **2.** *F:* (= ALLER 5 (*b*)) *Je
m'en vais vous raconter ça,* I'll tell you all about it.
　　II. aller, *s.m.* **1.** Going; outward journey.
Cargaison d'aller, outward cargo. **Voyage d'aller
et retour,** journey there and back. **Billet d'aller
et retour,** return ticket. *Sp:* **Match aller,** away
match. **2. Pis aller,** last resort; makeshift; poor
substitute. **Au pis aller,** at the worst, if the worst
comes to the worst. **3. Au long aller . . .,** in the
long run. . . .
alleu, -eux [alø], *s.m. Hist:* (Franc) **alleu,**
allodium; freehold (land).
alliage [alja:ʒ], *s.m.* **1.** Alloying, blending.
2. Alloy.
alliance [aljɑ̃:s], *s.f.* **1.** Alliance. (*a*) Match,
marriage, union. *Entrer par a. dans une famille,*
to marry into a family. (*b*) Union, blending.
(*c*) **Conclure une alliance avec un pays,** to conclude an alliance with a country. *Hist:* **La Triple
Alliance,** the Triple Alliance. S.a. ARCHE[1].
2. Wedding-ring.
alli|er [alje], *v.tr.* **1.** To ally, unite. *A. une
famille à, avec, une autre,* to unite one family to
another by marriage. **2.** To alloy, mix (metals);
to harmonize, blend, match (colours); to combine, unite (qualities, words, etc.) (*à,* with).
a. **-able.**
　　s'allier. 1. (*a*) To form an alliance, to become allies, to ally. (*b*) To form a connection by

marriage. *S'a. à une famille,* to marry into a
family. **2.** (Of fluids) To mix; (of metals) to
alloy; (of colours) to harmonize, blend.
allié, -ée. 1. *a.* Allied (nation, etc.). **2.** *s.*
(*a*) Ally. (*b*) Relation by marriage.
alligator [al(l)igatɔ:r], *s.m. Rept:* Alligator.
allitératif, -ive [alliteratif, -i:v], *a.* Alliterative.
allitération [alliterasjɔ̃], *s.f.* Alliteration.
allô, allo [alo], *int. Tp:* Hullo! hallo!
allocation [allɔkasjɔ̃], *s.f.* **1.** Allocation, apportionment, assignment, granting (of sum of money,
of land, supplies, etc.). **2.** Allowance, grant.
A. de chômage, unemployment benefit.
allocution [allɔkysjɔ̃], *s.f.* Short speech; allocution. **Prononcer une allocution,** to deliver an
address (*à,* to).
allonge [alɔ̃:ʒ], *s.f.* **1.** Lengthening-piece, eking-
piece; extension(-piece); extra leaf (of table).
2. *A. d'un document,* rider to a document. **3.** *Box:*
Reach. *Être avantagé en a.,* to have the longer
reach. **4.** *Equit:* Lunging rein. [ALLONGER]
allongement [alɔ̃ʒmɑ̃], *s.m.* **1.** (*a*) Lengthening
(of dress, etc.) (*b*) Elongation (of metals, etc.).
2. Protraction, extension (of time). **3.** *F:*
= LONGUEUR.
allong|er [alɔ̃ʒe], *v.tr.* (j'allongeai(s); *n.* allon-
geons) **1.** (*a*) To lengthen; to let down (garment).
Cette robe vous allonge, this dress makes you look
taller. (*b*) To add a piece to (sth.). (*c*) To eke out
(sauce, etc.). **2.** (*a*) To stretch out (one's arm,
etc.). *Les piliers allongent de grandes ombres,* the
pillars cast long shadows. S.a. PAS[1] **1.** (*b*) *F:* **Allonger un coup à qn,** to deal s.o. a blow; to
strike out at s.o. *A. une gifle, une taloche, à qn,* to
slap s.o. in the face; to give s.o. a clout. **Allonger
l'argent,** to hand over the money. **3.** To protract,
prolong (conversation, etc.). [LONG] *a.* **-eable.**
　　s'allonger. 1. (Of days, hours, etc.) To
stretch out; to grow longer. *F: Son visage
s'allongea,* he pulled a long face. **2.** To stretch
oneself out at full length. *F:* **S'allonger par terre,**
to come a cropper.
allongé, *a.* **1.** Long. *F: Avoir une figure
allongée,* to pull a long face. **2.** Oblong; prolate
(ellipsoid).
allumage [alyma:ʒ], *s.m.* Lighting (of lamp, fire);
switching on (of electric light). *I.C.E:* Ignition.
A. par batterie, par dynamo, coil ignition. **Raté
d'allumage,** misfire. *A. prématuré,* pre-ignition.
allumer [alyme], *v.tr.* **1.** To light (lamp, fire,
pipe); to kindle, ignite, set fire to (sth.). *Abs.* To
light the lamps; to switch on the light; to light
up. **2.** To inflame, excite (passion, person).
A. l'imagination, to fire the imagination.
　　s'allumer. 1. To kindle, to take fire, to
catch alight. **2.** (Of pers.) To warm up to one's
subject.
allumé, *a.* Alight. *Haut-fourneau a.,* furnace
in blast. *F:* **Visage allumé,** face flushed with
wine, with desire.
allumette [alymɛt], *s.f.* (Lucifer) match. *A. suédoise,* safety match.
allumette-bougie, *s.f.* Wax-vesta. *pl. Des
allumettes-bougies.*
allumeur, -euse [alymœːr, -øːz], *s.* **1.** Lighter;
igniter. *A. de réverbères,* lamplighter. **2.** *s.m.*
(*a*) Lighter; igniting device. *A. électrique,* electric
igniter. *A. à gaz,* gas-lighter. (*b*) *I.C.E:* Contact-maker.
allumoir [alymwa:r], *s.m.* Lighter (for cigarettes).
allure [aly:r], *s.f.* **1.** (*a*) Walk, gait, tread, carriage, bearing. *A. dégagée,* free, easy, carriage.
Avoir de l'allure, (i) (of horse) to be a good
stepper, (ii) *F:* (of pers.) to have style. (*b*) Pace.

Marcher à une vive a., to walk at a brisk pace. (c) Speed. **A toute allure**, at full speed. *L'auto filait à toute a.*, **à grande allure**, the car was going at top speed, *F :* all out. (d) *Mch : etc :* Working (of engine, etc.). *A. régulière*, smooth motion or running. **2.** *Nau :* (a) Sailing trim. **A l'allure du plus près**, close-hauled. (b) Rate (of sailing). *A l'a. de vingt nœuds*, at the rate of twenty knots. **3.** (a) Demeanour, behaviour. *A. posée*, sedate manner. (b) Aspect, look (of things, events). *L'affaire prend une mauvaise allure*, the business is taking an ugly turn, looks bad. [ALLER]

allusion [allyzjɔ̃], *s.f.* Allusion (*à*, to); hint, innuendo. **Faire allusion à qn**, to refer to s.o.

alluvial, -iaux [allyvjal, -jo], *a.* Alluvial.

alluvion [allyvjɔ̃], *s.f. Geol :* Alluvium.

almanach [almana], *s.m.* Almanac; calendar.

almée [alme], *s.f.* Alma(h), almeh; (Egyptian) dancing-woman.

aloès [alɔɛs], *s.m. Bot :* Aloe. **Amer d'aloès**, bitter aloes.

aloi [alwa], *s.m.* **1.** (a) *A :* (= TITRE) Degree of fineness (of coin). **Monnaiᵉ d'aloi**, sterling money. (b) *F :* **Pièce de mauvais aloi**, base coin; light coin. **2.** Standard, quality. **De bon aloi**, genuine. *Marchandises de bon a.*, goods of sterling quality.

alors [alɔːr], *adv.* **1.** Then; at that time; at the time. *Que faisiez-vous a.?* what were you doing then? *La vie d'a.*, life in those days. **2.** (a) Then; well then; in that case. *A. vous viendrez?* well then, you are coming? (b) Therefore, so. *Il n'était pas là, a. je suis revenu*, he wasn't there, so I came back again. **3.** *Conj.phr.* **Alors que**, when. **Alors même que**, (i) at the very time when; (ii) even when; (iii) even though. *A. même que je le pourrais*, even though I could. **4.** (= ENSUITE) Then, next.

alose [alɔːz], *s.f. Ich :* Alose, shad.

alouette [alwɛt], *s.f. Orn :* Lark. *A. des champs*, skylark.

alourd|ir [alurdiːr], *v.tr.* **1.** To make (sth.) heavy. **2.** To make (s.o.) dull, stupid. **3.** To weigh down (s.o.). [LOURD] *s.m.* **-issement.**
s'alourdir, to grow (i) heavy, (ii) dull, stupid.

alourdissant [alurdisɑ̃], *a.* Oppressive (heat, weather, etc.).

aloyau, -aux [alwajo], *s.m.* Sirloin (of beef).

alpaga [alpaga], *s.m.* Alpaca.

alpe [alp], *s.f.* **1.** Alp, mountain. **2.** *Geog :* **Les Alpes**, the Alps.

alpestre [alpɛstr], *a.* Alpine (scenery, climate).

alphabet [alfabe], *s.m.* **1.** Alphabet. **2.** *Sch :* Spelling-book, primer.

alphabétique [alfabetik], *a.* Alphabetical. *Par ordre a.*, in alphabetical order. *adv.* **-ment.**

alpin [alpɛ̃], *a.* Alpine (club, troops).

alpinisme [alpinism], *s.m.* Mountaineering. *Faire de l'a.*, to go in for mountaineering.

alpiniste [alpinist], *s. m. & f.* Alpinist, mountaineer.

alsacien, -ienne [alzasjɛ̃, -jɛn], *a. & s.* Alsatian.

altérable [alterabl], *a.* Liable to deterioration.

altérant [alterɑ̃], *a.* Thirst-producing.

altération [alterasjɔ̃], *s.f.* **1.** Change (for the worse); impairing (of health, etc.); deterioration (of food, etc.). *A. de la voix*, faltering of the voice. *A. des roches*, weathering of rocks. **2.** Debasing, debasement (of coinage); adulteration (of food); falsification (of document). **3.** Great thirst.

altercation [alterkasjɔ̃], *s.f.* Altercation, dispute; *F :* squabble.

altérer [altere], *v.tr.* (j'altère; j'altérerai) **1.** To change (for the worse); to spoil, taint, corrupt; to impair (health). *Voix altérée par l'émotion*, husky, shaky, voice. **2.** To tamper with (sth.); to adulterate (food); to debase (coinage); to falsify (document). *A. les faits*, to give a garbled version of the facts. **3.** To make (s.o.) thirsty.
s'altérer. 1. To change (for the worse); to deteriorate, spoil; (of rocks) to weather. *Sa voix s'altéra*, his voice faltered, broke. **2.** To grow thirsty.

altéré, a. 1. Faded (colour, etc.); broken (voice); drawn, haggard (face). **2.** Thirsty. *A. de sang*, athirst for blood.

alternance [alternɑ̃ːs], *s.f.* **1.** Alternation (of seasons, etc.). **2.** *Ling :* **Alternance de voyelles**, vowel gradation; ablaut.

alternateur [alternatœːr], *s.m. El.E :* Alternating-current generator; alternator.

alternatif, -ive [alternatif, -iːv], *a.* **1.** (a) Alternate (colours, etc.). (b) *El.E :* Alternating, (current). (c) *Mec.E :* Reciprocating (engine, motion). **2.** Alternative (proposal, meaning). **3.** *s.f.* **Alternative**, alternative, option.

alternativement [alternativmɑ̃], *adv.* Alternately, in turn, turn and turn about.

alterne [altern], *a.* Alternate (leaves, angles, etc.).

alterner [alterne], *v.i.* (a) To alternate. *Faire a. les larmes et les rires*, to make s.o. cry and laugh by turns. (b) To take turns (*pour*, in + *ger.*); to take turn and turn about (*pour*, to + *inf.*, in + *ger.*); to take it in turns (*pour*, to + *inf.*). *Il alterne avec les autres pour veiller*, he takes turns with the others in sitting up. *Ils alternent pour veiller*, they take it in turns to sit up.

altesse [altɛs], *s.f.* Highness. *Son A. impériale*, his, her, Imperial Highness.

alt|ier, -ière [altje, -jɛːr], *a.* Haughty, proud. *adv.* **-ièrement.**

altimètre [altimɛtr], *s.m. Surv : Av :* Altimeter; *Av :* height gauge.

altitude [altityd], *s.f.* Altitude, height. *Av :* **Prendre de l'altitude**, to climb.

alto [alto], *s.m. Mus :* **1.** Alto (voice). **2.** Viola. **3.** Tenor saxhorn or saxophone (in E flat).

altruisme [altryism], *s.m.* Altruism.

altruiste [altryist], **1.** *a.* Altruistic. **2.** *s.* Altruist.

alumine [alymin], *s.f. Miner :* Alumina.

aluminium [alyminjɔm], *s.m.* Aluminium.

aluminothermie [alyminɔtɛrmi], *s.f. Metall :* Thermit welding.

alun [alœ̃], *s.m.* Alum. *Toil :* **Pierre d'alun**, shaving-block.

alun|er [alyne], *v.tr.* **1.** To alum. *Phot :* **Bain aluné**, hardening bath. **2.** *Phot :* To harden (negative, etc.). *s.m.* **-age.**

alvéole [alveɔl], *s.m.* **1.** (a) Alveole; cell (of honeycomb, etc.). (b) Pigeon-hole (of desk). **2.** Socket (of tooth). **3.** Cavity, pit (in stone, etc.).

alvéolé [alveɔle], *a.* **1.** Honeycombed. **2.** Pitted.

alysson [alisɔ̃], *s.m. Bot :* Alyssum, madwort.

amabilité [amabilite], *s.f.* **1.** Amiableness, amiability; kindness. **2.** *pl.* Civilities; polite attentions.

amadou [amadu], *s.m.* Amadou; (German) tinder; touchwood, *U.S :* punk.

amadou|er [amadwe], *v.tr.* **1.** To coax, wheedle, persuade. **2.** To allure, draw (customers). [AMADOU] *s.* **-eur, -euse.**

amaigr|ir [amegriːr], *v.tr.* **1.** To make thin; to emaciate. **2.** *Agr :* To impoverish (soil). [MAIGRE] *a.* **-issant.** *s.m.* **-issement.**
s'amaigrir, to grow thin, to lose flesh.

amalgamation [amalgamasjɔ̃], s.f. **1.** Amalgamation. **2.** Fin: Merger.

amalgame [amalgam], s.m. **1.** Amalgam. **2.** F: Medley, mixture.

amalgamer [amalgame], v.tr. To amalgamate.
s'**amalgamer,** to amalgamate; to blend.

amande [amɑ̃:d], s.f. Almond. Yeux en amande, almond eyes.

amandier [amɑ̃dje], s.m. Almond-tree.

amant, -ante [amɑ̃, -ɑ̃:t], s. Lover.

amarante [amarɑ̃:t]. **1.** s.f. Bot: Amarant(h). **2.** a.inv. Amaranth; purplish.

amarin|er [amarine], v.tr. Nau: **1.** To inure to the sea. **2.** To man (prize). [MARIN] s.m. **-age.**
s'**amariner,** to get used to the sea; to overcome sea-sickness; to find one's sea-legs.

amarrage [amara:ʒ], s.m. Nau: **1.** (a) Mooring. Droits d'amarrage, berthage. Aer: Mât d'amarrage, mooring mast. (b) Berth, moorings. **2.** Lashing, seizing. Faire un a. sur une corde, to lash, seize, a rope.

amarre [ama:r], s.f. (a) (Mooring) rope or line; painter, warp; pl. moorings. Navire sur ses amarres, ship at her moorings. Lâcher les amarres, to cast off (the moorings). (b) Cable, hawser.

amarrer [amare], v.tr. (a) To make fast, to moor (boat, ship, dirigible). Navire amarré au quai, boat berthed, lying, at the quay. (b) To belay (rope). (c) Const: To brace (wall, etc.).
s'**amarrer,** to make fast; to moor.

amas [amɑ], s.m. Heap, pile, accumulation. A. de neige, snow-drift. [AMASSER]

amass|er [amɑse], v.tr. **1.** To heap up, pile up. **2.** To hoard up, store up; to amass (a fortune). Il a amassé du bien, he has made his pile. **3.** To gather (troops) together. s.m. **-age.**
s'**amasser,** to pile up, accumulate.

amateur, -trice [amatœ:r, -tris], s. **1.** Lover (of sth.). A. des beaux-arts, lover, patron, of art. A. de chiens, dog-fancier. **2.** Amateur. Championnat des amateurs, amateur championship. Travailler en a., to work in dilettante fashion.

amateurisme [amatœrism], s.m. Art: Sp: Amateurism.

amazone [amazo:n], s.f. **1.** (a) Myth: Amazon. Geog: Le fleuve des Amazones, the (River) Amazon. (b) Horsewoman. (c) Lady dressed in a riding-habit. **2.** Cost: (Lady's) riding-habit.

ambages [ɑ̃ba:ʒ], s.f.pl. Circumlocution. Parler sans ambages, to speak to the point, straight out.

ambassade [ɑ̃basad], s.f. **1.** Embassy. **2.** (a) Ambassador's staff. (b) (Quarters of the ambassador's staff) Embassy.

ambassadeur [ɑ̃basadœ:r], s.m. Ambassador. L'a. d'Angleterre, the British Ambassador.

ambassadrice [ɑ̃basadris], s.f. Ambassadress.

ambiance [ɑ̃bjɑ̃:s], s.f. Surroundings, environment.

ambiant [ɑ̃bjɑ̃], a. Surrounding, encompassing, ambient (atmosphere, etc.).

ambigu, -uë [ɑ̃bigy]. **1.** a. Ambiguous. **2.** s.m. Mixture, medley. adv. **-ment.**

ambiguïté [ɑ̃bigɥite], s.f. Ambiguity, ambiguousness.

ambitieu|x, -euse [ɑ̃bisjø, -ø:z]. **1.** a. Ambitious. Être a. de faire qch., to be ambitious to do sth. **2.** s. Ambitious person. adv. **-sement.**

ambition [ɑ̃bisjɔ̃], s.f. Ambition (de, of, for). Mettre son ambition à faire qch., to make it one's ambition to do sth. L'a. de briller, the ambition to shine. Sans ambition, unambitious(ly).

ambitionner [ɑ̃bisjone], v.tr. To be ambitious

of (sth.); to covet (sth.). A. de faire qch., to aspire to do sth.

amble [ɑ̃:bl], s.m. Equit: Amble; (ambling) pace. Aller l'amble, to amble. Chevaucher a l'amble, to amble along.

ambler [ɑ̃ble], v.i. **1.** (Of horse) To pace, to amble. **2.** F: To canter along.

ambre [ɑ̃:br], s.m. **1.** Ambre gris, ambergris. **2.** Ambre jaune, yellow amber.

ambré [ɑ̃bre], a. **1.** Perfumed with amber(gris). **2.** Amber-coloured; warm (complexion, tint). **3.** Amber-tipped (cigarette).

ambroisie [ɑ̃brwazi], s.f. Gr.Myth: Ambrosia. Parfum d'ambroisie, ambrosial fragrance.

ambrosiaque [ɑ̃brɔzjak], a. Ambrosial.

ambulance [ɑ̃bylɑ̃:s], s.f. Ambulance.

ambulancier, -ière [ɑ̃bylɑ̃sje, -jɛ:r], s. Mil: Hospital orderly; f. nurse.

ambulant [ɑ̃bylɑ̃], a. Itinerant, perambulating, peripatetic. Comédiens ambulants, strolling players. Marchand ambulant, pedlar. Cirque a., travelling circus.

ambulatoire [ɑ̃bylatwa:r], s.m. Arch: Ambulatory; arcade, cloister(s).

âme [ɑ:m], s.f. **1.** Soul. (a) Avoir charge d'âmes, to have the cure of souls. Rendre l'âme, to give up the ghost. (b) (Departed) soul, spirit. Les âmes en peine, the souls in purgatory. S.a. DAMNÉ. (c) Heart, feeling, soul, spirit. Vous n'avez donc pas d'âme! have you no feelings? Mettre de l'âme à faire qch., to do sth. with feeling. Être l'âme d'une entreprise, to be the moving spirit, the life and soul, of an undertaking. (d) Population de dix mille âmes, population of ten thousand souls. Ne pas rencontrer âme qui vive, not to meet a living soul. **2.** (a) Bore (of gun, pump). (b) Core (of statue, cable). (c) Web (of girder, beam). (d) Sound-post (of violin).

Amédée [amede]. Pr.n.m. Amadeus.

Amélie [ameli]. Pr.n.f. Amelia.

amélioration [ameljɔrasjɔ̃], s.f. Amelioration, improvement, betterment; change for the better. A. de santé, improvement in health. Apporter des améliorations à qch., to effect improvements in sth.

améliorer [ameljore], v.tr. To ameliorate; to better, to improve. a. **-able.** a. **-ant.**
s'**améliorer,** to get better; to improve.

amen [amɛn, a-], int. & s.m.inv. Amen.

aménagement [amenaʒmɑ̃], s.m. **1.** See AMÉNAGER. **2.** Appointments (of house); fittings (of office, etc.).

aménager [amenaʒe], v.tr. (j'aménageai(s); n. aménageons) To fit up, to arrange (house, shop, etc.); to fit out (new ship). [MÉNAGE]

amendage [amɑ̃da:ʒ], s.m. Agr: Improving, enriching (of soil).

amende [amɑ̃:d], s.f. **1.** Fine. Frapper qn d'une amende, infliger une amende à qn, to impose a fine on s.o.; to fine s.o. Être condamné à une amende, to be fined. Games: Être mis à l'amende, to have to pay a forfeit. **2.** Faire amende honorable, (i) to make amends; (ii) to make due apology.

amend|er [amɑ̃de], v.tr. (a) To make better, to improve (health, soil, etc.). (b) Parl: To amend (bill). a. **-able.** s.m. **-ement.**
s'**amender,** to improve. (a) To mend one's ways; F: to turn over a new leaf. (b) (Of soil) To become more fertile.

amener [amne], v.tr. (j'amène; j'amènerai) **1.** To bring; to lead (hither). Amenez votre ami avec vous, bring your friend (along) with you. A. qn a son opinion, to bring s.o. round to one's opinion. A. un sujet, to lead up to a subject. Amener qn

faire qch., to bring s.o. along to do sth. *Amenez-le dîner avec nous*, bring him round to dine with us. **Amener qn à faire qch.**, to get, lead, bring, induce, s.o. to do sth. **2.** *A. une rupture*, to bring about, lead to, a rupture. *A. une mode*, to bring in a fashion. **3.** *Nau :* To strike (colours) ; to lower (sail). *Abs.* **Le vaisseau amena**, the ship struck her colours.

s'amener, *F :* to turn up ; to blow in. *Allons, amène-toi !* now then, come along !

aménité [amenite], *s.f.* **1.** Amenity, charm (of manners) ; grace (of style). **2.** *pl.* Compliments.

am₁er¹, -ère [amɛːr]. **1.** *a.* (*a*) Bitter (taste). *Poet :* **L'onde amère**, the briny deep. (*b*) *Douleur amère*, bitter grief. *Ironie amère*, biting irony. **2.** *s.m.* Bitter(s). *Prendre un a.*, to have a bitter(s). *adv.* **-èrement.**

amer², *s.m. Nau :* Sea-mark, landmark. [MER]

américain, -aine [amerikɛ̃, -ɛn], *a. & s.* American, *F :* Yankee. *F :* **Il a l'œil américain**, he keeps his eyes skinned.

Amérique [amerik]. *Pr.n.f. Geog :* America. *L'A. du Nord*, North America.

amér|ir, amerr|ir [ameriːr], *v.i. Av :* To alight (on the sea). *s.m.* **-issage.**

amertume [amɛrtym], *s.f.* Bitterness (of quinine, of sorrow). *Ressentir beaucoup d'a. de qch.*, to feel, resent, sth. bitterly.

améthyste [ametist], *s.f.* Amethyst.

ameublement [amœbləmɑ̃], *s.m.* **1.** Furnishing (of house, etc.). **2.** (*a*) Set or suite of furniture. (*b*) Furniture.

ameubl|ir [amœbliːr], *v.tr.* To loosen, break up (soil). [MEUBLE] *s.m.* **-issement.**

ameutement [amøtmɑ̃], *s.m.* **1.** Gathering into a mob. **2.** Mob.

ameuter [amøte], *v.tr.* To assemble, collect (riotous crowd). [MEUTE]

s'ameuter, to gather into a mob.

ami, -e [ami]. **1.** *s.* (*a*) Friend. *Ami de cœur*, bosom friend. *Ami d'enfance*, old playmate. **Nos amis et parents**, our kith and kin. **Sans amis**, friendless. *F :* **Être ami avec qn**, to be friendly with s.o. **Être ami de qch.**, to like, have a taste for, sth. **Mon ami**, (i) (between friends) my dear fellow, (ii) (from superior to inferior) my good man, (iii) (from wife to husband) my dear. **Mon amie**, my dear, my love. *Adv.phr.* **En ami(e)**, in a friendly manner ; as a friend. (*b*) *F :* Man- or boy-friend, *f.* woman- or girl-friend. *F :* **Bon ami, bonne amie**, lover, sweetheart. (*c*) *Les amis de la nature*, nature-lovers. **2.** *a.* (*a*) Friendly (*de*, to). (*b*) Kind, kindly.

amiable [amjabl], *a. Jur :* Friendly, conciliatory, amicable. *Arrangement à l'a.*, amicable arrangement. *Vente à l'a.*, private sale. *adv.* **-ment.**

amiante [amjɑ̃t], *s.m. Miner :* Asbestos. **Carton d'amiante**, asbestos-board.

amibe [amib], *s.f.* Amoeba.

amical, -aux [amikal, -o], *a.* Friendly. *adv.* **-ement.**

amict [ami], *s.m. Ecc.Cost :* Amice.

amidon [amidɔ̃], *s.m.* Starch. **Colle d'amidon**, starch paste.

amidonn|er [amidɔne], *v.tr.* To starch. *s.m.* **-age.**

aminc|ir [amɛ̃siːr], *v.tr.* To make thinner ; to thin down (wood). *Taille amincie*, slender, slim, figure. *Costume qui amincit*, *F :* slim-making costume. [MINCE] *s.m.* **-issement.**

s'amincir, to grow thinner, more slender.

amiral, -aux [amiral, -o], *s.m.* **1.** Admiral. *F :* **C'est un amiral suisse**, he's in the horse-

marines ; he has never seen the sea. **2.** Flagship. **3.** *Conch :* Admiral shell.

amiralissime [amiralisim], *s.m.* Commander-in-chief (of the fleet).

amirauté [amirote], *s.f.* **1.** Admiralship. **2.** **L'Amirauté**, the Admiralty.

amitié [amitje], *s.f.* **1.** Friendship, friendliness, affection. *Une étroite a.*, a close friendship. **Être sur un pied d'amitié avec qn**, to be on friendly terms, on a friendly footing, with s.o. **Prendre qn en amitié**, to take a liking for s.o. ; to take to s.o. **Se lier d'amitié avec qn, nouer amitié avec qn**, to form, to strike up, a friendship with s.o. ; to make friends with s.o. **Par amitié**, out of friendliness. **2.** (*a*) Kindness, favour. *Faites-moi l'a. de le lui dire*, will you do me the favour to tell him so. (*b*) *pl.* **Faites mes amitiés à votre frère**, remember me kindly to your brother. **Avec les sincères amitiés de . . .**, with kind regards from. . . .

ammoniac [amɔnjak], *a.m. Ch :* Gaz ammoniac, ammonia. **Sel ammoniac**, sal ammoniac.

ammoniaque [amɔnjak], *s.f. Ch :* Ammonia.

ammoniaqué [amɔnjake], *a.* Ammoniated (quinine, etc.).

amnésie [amnezi], *s.f. Med :* Amnesia.

amnistie [amnisti], *s.f.* Amnesty ; general pardon.

amnistier [amnistje], *v.tr.* To amnesty, pardon.

amoindr|ir [amwɛ̃driːr]. **1.** *v.tr.* To reduce, decrease, lessen, diminish, belittle. *A. un mal*, to mitigate an evil. *Il ne faut pas vous a.*, you must not belittle yourself. **2.** *v.i. & pr.* To diminish, to grow less. [MOINDRE] *s.m.* **-issement.**

amoll|ir [amɔliːr], *v.tr.* **1.** To soften (substance, s.o.'s heart). **2.** To weaken, enervate. [MOU] *s.m.* **-issement.**

s'amollir. **1.** To soften, to become soft. **2.** To grow weak, effeminate ; (of courage) to flag.

amonceler [amɔ̃sle], *v.tr.* (*j'amoncelle* ; *j'amoncellerai*) To pile up, heap up, bank up.

s'amonceler, to pile up ; to gather (in a heap) ; (of clouds) to bank up.

amoncellement [amɔ̃sɛlmɑ̃], *s.m.* **1.** Heaping (up), piling (up), banking up. **2.** Heap, pile. *A. de neige*, snow-drift.

amont [amɔ̃], *s.m.* Upper waters, head waters (of river, etc.). **Vent d'amont**, (i) wind from upstream, (ii) land-breeze. **En amont**, up-stream, up-river. **En amont de l'écluse, du pont**, above lock, above (the) bridge. [MONT]

amorce [amɔrs], *s.f.* **1.** Beginning. *Amorces d'indiscipline*, incipient insubordination. *Civ.E :* *A. d'un tunnel*, beginning (of the cutting) of a tunnel. **2.** (*a*) *Exp :* Primer, fuse, detonator. (*b*) *Sm.a :* Percussion cap. (*c*) *Hyd.E :* Priming (of pump). **3.** Bait. **Se laisser prendre à l'amorce**, to swallow the bait.

amor|cer [amɔrse], *v.tr.* (*j'amorçai(s)* ; *n. amorçons*) **1.** (*a*) To begin, start, initiate (building, road, subject, etc.). *A. des négociations*, to initiate negotiations. (*b*) To prime, fetch (pump). *El.E :* To start, excite (dynamo). **2.** (*a*) To bait (line, trap, etc.). (*b*) To allure, entice, decoy (animal, person). [AMORCE] *s.m.* **-çage**, *s.m.* **-cement.**

s'amorcer, (of pump, etc.) to start.

amorphe [amɔrf], *a.* Amorphous.

amortir [amɔrtiːr], *v.tr.* **1.** (*a*) To deaden, muffle (sound) ; to allay (pain) ; to subdue (light) ; to dull (pain) ; to damp (ardour) ; to cool (passion) ; to tone down, flatten (colour) ; to break (fall) ; to absorb, deaden (shock) ; to break the force of (blow). (*b*) *Ph :* To damp down, damp out (oscillations). **2.** To slack, slake (lime).

3. To redeem, pay off (debt); to allow for depreciation of affection (furniture, etc.).
s'amortir, to become deadened; (of passion) to cool. *Ph:* (Of oscillations) To die away, to damp down.
amorti, *a.* **1.** *Ph: W.Tel:* Damped (wave). *Ondes non amorties,* undamped, continuous, waves. **2. Navire amorti,** neaped ship; ship aground.
amortissable [amɔrtisabl], *a.* Redeemable.
amortissement [amɔrtismɑ̃], *s.m.* **1.** See AMORTIR I. **2.** Redemption (of debt). **Fonds, caisse, d'amortissement,** sinking-fund.
amortisseur [amɔrtisœːr], *s.m.* **1.** Damping device; dead-beat device. **2.** *Av: Aut:* Shock-absorber.
amour [amuːr], *s.m.* (Usu. *f.* in *pl.* in 1, 2.) **1.** Love, affection, passion. *A. d'une mère,* a mother's love. *Les premières amours,* first love, *F:* calf love. **S'éprendre d'amour pour qn,** to fall in love with s.o. **L'amour que vous me portez,** the love you bear me. **Mal d'amour,** lovesickness. **Mariage d'amour,** love match. *A. de, pour, qch.,* love of, for, sth. **Avoir l'amour de qch.,** to love, have a fondness for, sth. **Pour l'amour de qn,** for the sake of, for love of, s.o. **2.** (Object of one's love) *Mon a.,* my love, my sweetheart. *Une de mes anciennes amours,* an old flame of mine. **3.** Cupid, Eros, the god of Love. **Quel amour d'enfant!** what a love of a child! *Quel a. de bijou!* what a lovely jewel!
amouracher (s') [samuraʃe], *v.pr.* To fall head over ears in love (*de,* with); to become enamoured (*de,* of).
amourette [amurɛt], *s.f.* Love affair; passing fancy.
amoureu|x, -euse [amurø, -øːz]. **1.** *a.* (*a*) Loving (care, look). *Être a. de qn,* to be in love with, enamoured of, s.o. (*b*) Amorous (look, gesture); amatory (letter). **2.** *s.* Lover, sweetheart. *adv.* **-sement.**
amour-propre, *s.m.* (*a*) Self-respect; (legitimate) pride. *Blesser l'a.-p. de qn,* to hurt, wound, s.o.'s pride. *Stimuler l'a.-p. de qn,* to put s.o. on his mettle. (*b*) Self-esteem, vanity, conceit.
amov|ible [amɔvibl], *a.* **1.** (*a*) (Of office) Revocable at pleasure. (*b*) Removable (official). **2.** (Of parts of machine) Removable, detachable, interchangeable. *s.f.* **-ibilité.**
ampère [ɑ̃pɛːr], *s.m.* *El.Meas:* Ampere. *Intensité en ampères,* amperage.
ampèremètre [ɑ̃pɛrmɛtr], *s.m.* *El:* Ammeter.
amphibie [ɑ̃fibi]. **1.** *a.* Amphibious (plant, animal). **2.** *s.m.* Amphibian.
amphibiens [ɑ̃fibjɛ̃], *s.m.pl.* *Z:* Amphibia.
amphibologie [ɑ̃fibɔlɔʒi], *s.f.* Amphibology.
amphigouri [ɑ̃figuri], *s.m.* *Lit:* Amphigouri; tissue of nonsense.
amphigourique [ɑ̃figurik], *a.* *Lit:* Amphigoric; nonsensical. *Discours a.,* rambling discourse.
amphithéâtre [ɑ̃fiteɑtr], *s.m.* Amphitheatre; *Sch:* lecture-room. **En amphithéâtre,** in tiers.
amphitryon [ɑ̃fitrijɔ̃], *s.m.* Amphitryon; host; entertainer. (From Molière's play *Amphitryon.*)
amphore [ɑ̃fɔːr], *s.f.* **1.** *Archeol:* Amphora. **2.** Jar.
ample [ɑ̃pl], *a.* **1.** Ample; full (dress, skirt, etc.). **2.** Roomy, spacious (theatre, etc.). **3.** Full (account); ample (supply). *adv.* **-ment.**
ampleur [ɑ̃plœːr], *s.f.* **1.** Fullness (of garment); copiousness (of meal); volume (of voice). *A. de formes,* buxomness. **2.** Fullness (of account); breadth (of style).
ampli [ɑ̃pli], *s.m.* *F:* = AMPLIFICATEUR 3 (*c*).

amplificateur, -trice [ɑ̃plifikatœːr, -tris]. **1.** (*a*) *a.* Magnifying. (*b*) *s.* Magnifier (of trifles, etc.). **2.** *a.* Amplifying. *Phot:* (Lentille) amplificatrice, amplifier. **3.** *s.m.* (*a*) *Phot:* Enlarger. (*b*) (Sound) intensifier. (*c*) *W.Tel:* Amplifier.
amplification [ɑ̃plifikasjɔ̃], *s.f.* **1.** Amplification (of a thought, etc.). **2.** (*a*) *Opt:* Magnification. (*b*) *Phot:* Enlarging. (*c*) *W.Tel:* A. (en haute fréquence), (high-frequency) amplification.
amplifier [ɑ̃plifje], *v.tr.* **1.** To amplify; to expand (thought, etc.); to exaggerate (danger). **2.** *Opt:* To magnify.
amplitude [ɑ̃plityd], *s.f.* Amplitude (of star, oscillation).
ampoule [ɑ̃pul], *s.f.* **1.** Ampulla, phial. *Hist:* **La sainte Ampoule,** the (Holy) Ampulla. **2.** (*a*) Bulb (of thermometer, electric light). (*b*) Container (of vacuum-flask). **3.** Blister (on foot, photographic plate).
ampoulé [ɑ̃pule], *a.* **1.** Blistered. **2.** Inflated, turgid (style).
amputation [ɑ̃pytasjɔ̃], *s.f.* **1.** Amputation (of limb, etc.). **2.** Cut (in literary matter).
amputer [ɑ̃pyte], *v.tr.* **1.** *Surg:* To amputate, cut off (limb). **2.** *F:* To cut (newspaper article).
amulette [amylɛt], *s.f.* Amulet, charm.
amunitionn|er [amynisjɔne], *v.tr.* *Mil:* To provision; to supply (army, etc.) with stores. *s.m.* **-ement.**
amure [amyːr], *s.f.* *Nau:* Tack (of sail). **Être bâbord amures,** to be on the port tack. **Changer d'amures,** to go about; to change tack.
amusement [amyzmɑ̃], *s.m.* (*a*) (Action of) entertaining. (*b*) Amusement, recreation, pastime, diversion.
amus|er [amyze], *v.tr.* To amuse, entertain, divert. *a.* **-ant.**
s'amuser, to amuse, enjoy, oneself. *Bien s'a.,* to have a good time. *S'a. aux dépens de qn,* to make fun of s.o. *Dire qch. pour s'a.,* to say sth. by way of a joke, for fun. *S'a. en chemin,* to loiter on the way.
amusette [amyzɛt], *s.f.* Toy, plaything; child's play.
amygdale [amidal], *s.f.* Tonsil.
amygdalite [ami(g)dalit], *s.f.* *Med:* Tonsillitis.
an [ɑ̃], *s.m.* **1.** Year. *Tous les ans,* every year. **Avoir dix ans,** to be ten years old. *Un poulain de deux ans,* a two-year old (colt). *Ami de vingt ans,* friend of twenty years' standing. **Bon an, mal an,** taking one year with another. **En l'an 1200,** in the year 1200. **Le jour de l'an,** New Year's day. **2.** *pl.* *Lit:* *Les ans ont ralenti sa marche,* age has slackened his pace. *L'outrage des ans,* the ravages of time. *Chargé d'ans,* stricken in years.
anachorète [anakɔrɛt], *s.m.* Anchorite, recluse.
anachronisme [anakrɔnism], *s.m.* Anachronism.
anacoluthe [anakɔlyt], *s.f.* *Gram:* Anacoluthon.
anagramme [anagram], *s.f.* Anagram.
analgésique [analʒezik], *a. & s.m.* Analgesic, analgetic.
analogie [analɔʒi], *s.f.* Analogy. **Raisonner par analogie,** to argue from analogy.
analogue [analɔg]. **1.** *a.* Analogous (*à,* to, with); similar (*à,* to). **2.** *s.m.* Analogue, parallel.
analyse [analiːz], *s.f.* Analysis. **1.** (*a*) *A. grammaticale,* parsing. *A. logique,* analysis. **Faire l'analyse d'une phrase,** (i) to parse, (ii) to analyse, a sentence. (*b*) *Ch:* *A. quantitative,* quantitative analysis. (*c*) *Mth:* *A. transcendante,* the calculus. **2.** Abstract, résumé, précis.
analys|er [analize], *v.tr.* To analyse (facts, substance, etc.). *A. une phrase,* (i) to parse, (ii) to analyse a sentence. *a.* **-able.**

analytique [analitik]. **1.** *a.* Analytical. **2.** *s.f.* Analytics. *adv.* **-ment.**

ananas [anana(:s)], *s.m.* Ananas, pine-apple. **Serre à ananas,** pinery.

anapeste [anapɛst], *s.m. Pros:* Anapaest.

anarchie [anarʃi], *s.f.* Anarchy.

anarchique [anarʃik], *a.* Anarchic(al).

anarchisme [anarʃism], *s.m. Pol:* Anarchism.

anarchiste [anarʃist], *a. & s. Pol:* Anarchist.

Anastasie [anastazi]. *Pr.n.f.* **1.** Anastasia. **2.** *P:* The censorship; 'Dora'.

anastigmate [anastigmat], **anastigmatique** [anastigmatik], *a. Opt: Phot:* Anastigmatic (lens).

anathématiser [anatɛmatize], *v.tr.* To anathematize, curse (s.o., sth.).

anathème [anatɛm], *s.m.* Anathema; ban, curse. **Frapper qn d'anathème,** to anathematize s.o.

anatife [anatif], *s.m. Crust:* Barnacle.

anatomie [anatɔmi], *s.f.* Anatomy.

anatomique [anatɔmik], *a.* Anatomical.

anatomiste [anatɔmist], *s.m.* Anatomist.

ancestral, -aux [ɑ̃sɛstral, -o], *a.* Ancestral.

ancêtre [ɑ̃sɛːtr], *s.m. & f.* Ancestor, ancestress; forefather, forbear. **La maison de ses ancêtres,** his ancestral home.

anche [ɑ̃ːʃ], *s.f. Mus:* Reed, tongue (of oboe, clarinet, etc.). **Jeu d'anches,** reed-stop (of organ).

anchois [ɑ̃ʃwa], *s.m.* Anchovy. **Beurre d'anchois,** anchovy paste.

ancien, -ienne [ɑ̃sjɛ̃, -jɛn], *a.* **1.** Ancient, old. *Monument a.,* ancient monument. *Amitié ancienne,* friendship of long standing. **2.** Ancient, old(en), early, bygone, past, of yore. *Les auteurs anciens,* ancient authors. **L'Ancien Testament,** the Old Testament. *s.m.pl.* **Les anciens,** the ancients. **3.** Former, late, old; ex-; quondam (teacher, pupil, etc.). *A. élève,* old pupil, old boy (of a school). *Anciens combattants,* ex-service men. **4.** Senior (captain, officer, etc.). *Les élèves anciens, les anciens,* the senior boys. **Il est votre ancien,** he is senior to you. **5.** *s.m.* (*a*) *Ecc:* Elder. (*b*) *Scouting:* Patrol leader.

anciennement [ɑ̃sjɛnmɑ̃], *adv.* Anciently, formerly, in the old(en) days.

ancienneté [ɑ̃sjɛnte], *s.f.* **1.** Antiquity (of monument, etc.). **De toute ancienneté,** from time immemorial. **2.** Seniority; length of service. *A. de grade,* seniority in rank.

ancillaire [ɑ̃sillɛːr], *a.* Ancillary.

ancrage [ɑ̃kra:ʒ], *s.m.* **1.** Anchoring. **2.** Anchorage.

ancre [ɑ̃ːkr], *s.f.* **1.** *Nau:* Anchor. *Grosse a. de bossoir,* bower (anchor). **Ancre de veille,** *A:* **ancre de miséricorde,** sheet-anchor. *A. flottante, a. de cape,* drag, drogue, deep-sea anchor. **Mettre les ancres à poste,** to stow anchors. **Être à l'ancre,** to lie, ride, at anchor. **Jeter, mouiller, l'ancre,** to cast, drop, anchor; to anchor. **Lever l'ancre,** to weigh anchor. *Aer: A. de ballon,* balloon anchor; grapnel. **2.** *Const: etc:* Anchot, tie-plate (of wall, etc.); brace, stay (of boiler).

ancrer [ɑ̃kre], *v.tr.* **1.** *Nau: Aer:* To anchor (ship, balloon). *F:* **Idée ancrée dans la tête,** idea deep-rooted in the mind. **2.** *Const: etc:* To brace, tie, stay, anchor (chimney, etc.).

andain [ɑ̃dɛ̃], *s.m. Agr:* Swath, windrow.

andalou, -ouse [ɑ̃dalu, -uːz]. **1.** *a. & s.* Andalusian. **2.** *s.m.* Andalusian horse.

Andalousie [ɑ̃daluzi]. *Pr.n.f. Geog:* Andalusia.

Andes [ɑ̃:d]. *Pr.n.pl.* **Les Andes,** the Andes. **La Cordillère des Andes,** the Andean Belt.

Andorre [ɑ̃dɔ:r]. *Pr.n.* (Republic of) Andorra.

andouille [ɑ̃du:j], *s.f.* **1.** *Cu:* Chitterlings (made into sausages). **2.** *P:* Muff, duffer, chuckle-head, mug, mutt.

andouiller [ɑ̃duje], *s.m. Ven:* Tine (of antler). **Maître andouiller,** brow antler (of stag).

andouillette [ɑ̃dujɛt], *s.f. Cu:* Small chitterling sausage.

André [ɑ̃dre]. *Pr.n.m.* Andrew.

Andrinople [ɑ̃drinɔpl]. **1.** *Pr.n.f. Geog:* Adrianople. **2.** *s.f. Tex:* Turkey-red cotton.

Andromaque [ɑ̃drɔmak]. *Pr.n.f.* Andromache.

âne [ɑn], *s.m.* **1.** Ass; *F:* donkey. (*a*) **Faire une promenade à âne,** to go for a donkey ride. *F:* **Têtu comme un âne,** as stubborn as an ass. **Le coup de pied de l'âne,** the most unkindest cut of all. **Ressembler à l'âne de Buridan,** not to be able to make up one's mind. **Contes de Peau d'âne,** fairy tales. *Prov:* **Il y a plus d'un âne à la foire qui s'appelle Martin,** there are more Jacks than one at the fair. **Personne ne sait mieux que l'âne où le bât le blesse,** everyone knows best where his own shoe pinches. (*b*) **En dos d'âne,** ridged; razor-backed. *Colline en dos d'âne,* hog's-back (ridge). *Pont en dos d'âne,* hog-backed bridge. **2.** *F:* Fool, ass, dunce. **Mettre un bonnet d'âne à un enfant,** to put a dunce's cap on a child. **Faire l'âne pour avoir du son,** to pretend ignorance in order to achieve one's end.

anéant|ir [aneãti:r], *v.tr.* (*a*) To reduce to nothing; to annihilate, destroy. *A. les espérances de qn,* to blast, dash, s.o.'s hopes. *F: Je suis anéanti,* I am exhausted, dead-beat. (*b*) *F:* To dumbfound. (*c*) *Anéanti par la douleur,* prostrate with grief. [NÉANT] *s.m.* **-issement.**

s'anéantir, to come to nothing, to 'melt into thin air.'

anecdote [anɛgdɔt, -kd-], *s.f.* Anecdote.

anecdotier [anɛgdɔtje, -kd-], *s.m.* Anecdotist; teller of anecdotes.

anémie [anemi], *s.f. Med:* Anaemia.

anémier [anemje], *v.tr.* To render (s.o.) anaemic. **s'anémier,** to become anaemic.

anémié, *a.* Anaemic; etiolated.

anémique [anemik], *a.* Anaemic, bloodless.

anémomètre [anemɔmɛtr], *s.m. Meteor:* Anemometer; wind-gauge.

anémone [anemɔn], *s.f.* **1.** *Bot:* Anemone, wind-flower. *A. pulsatille,* pasque-flower. **2.** *Coel:* **Anémone de mer,** sea-anemone.

ânerie [ɑnri], *s.f.* *F:* **1.** Stupidity, ignorance. **2.** Foolish act or remark. **Faire des âneries,** to make an ass of oneself. [ÂNE]

anéroïde [aneroid], *a.* Aneroid (barometer).

ânesse [ɑnɛs], *s.f.* She-ass.

anesthésie [anɛstezi], *s.f. Med:* Anaesthesia.

anesthésier [anɛstezje], *v.tr.* To anaesthetize. **Se faire a.** (*chez le dentiste*), *F:* to have gas.

anesthésique [anɛstezik], *a. & s.m. Med:* Anaesthetic.

anesthésiste [anɛstezist], *s.m.* Anaesthetist.

anévrisme, anévrysme [anevrism], *s.m. Med:* Aneurism, aneurysm.

anfractueux, -euse [ɑ̃fraktɥø, -øːz], *a.* (*a*) Circuitous, sinuous, winding. (*b*) Irregular (outline); craggy (mountain).

anfractuosité [ɑ̃fraktɥozite], *s.f.* **1.** Anfractuosity, sinuosity. *pl.* Windings (of road, stream). **2.** Cragginess, unevenness.

ange [ɑ̃:ʒ], *s.m.* **1.** Angel. *A. gardien,* guardian angel. *F:* **Être aux anges,** to walk on air. **Rire aux anges,** (i) to wear a beatific smile; (ii) to smile in one's sleep. **2.** *Ich:* **Ange** (**de mer**), angel-fish.

angèle [ɑ̃ʒɛl]. *Pr.n.f.* Angela.

angélique [ɑ̃ʒelik]. **1.** *a.* Angelic(al). **La saluta-**

tion angélique, the Hail Mary. **2.** s.f. Bot: Cu: Angelica.

angélus [ãʒely:s], s.m. Angelus(-bell); ave-bell.

angevin, -ine [ãʒvɛ̃, -in], a. & s. Angevin(e).

angine [ãʒin], s.f. Med: **1.** Quinsy; tonsillitis. A. striduleuse, croup. **2.** A. de poitrine, angina pectoris; F: heart-stroke, breast-pang.

anglais, -aise [ãglɛ, -ɛ:z]. **1.** a. English (language, etc.); British (army). F: S'en aller, filer, à l'anglaise, to take French leave; to slip away. S.a. SEMAINE. **2.** s. Englishman, English-woman; Briton. **3.** s.m. English (language).

angle [ã:gl], s.m. **1.** (a) Angle. A. droit, right angle. A angles droits, rectangular. (Of house) Faire angle avec la rue, to stand at an angle to the street. Av: Angle critique, stalling angle. Mec.E: Roue d'angle, bevel-wheel, mitre-wheel. (b) Tls: Angle oblique, bevel-rule; mitre square. **2.** Corner, angle (of wall, room, etc.). Boutique d'angle, corner-shop.

Angleterre [ãglətɛ:r]. Pr.n.f. England.

anglican, -ane [ãglikã, -an], a. & s. Rel: Anglican. L'Église anglicane, the Church of England. Un anglican, a churchman.

anglicisant [ãglisizã], s.m. Student of English.

angliciser [ãglisize], v.tr. To anglicize. s'angliciser, to become English.

anglicisme [ãglisism], s.m. Anglicism; English idiom.

anglomane [ãgloman], s. m. & f. Anglomaniac.

anglo-normand, -ande, a. & s. Anglo-Norman. Les îles Anglo-normandes, the Channel Islands.

anglophile [ãglɔfil], a. & s. Anglophil(e), pro-English.

anglo-saxon, -onne, a. & s. Anglo-Saxon.

angoissant [ãgwasã], a. Alarming, distressing (news); tense (moment).

angoisse [ãgwas], s.f. Anguish; distress; agony. Les angoisses de la mort, the pangs of death. Angoisses de conscience, qualms of conscience. Poire d'angoisse, (i) Bot: choke-pear; (ii) A: iron gag; choke-pear.

angoisser [ãgwase], v.tr. To anguish; to distress. s'angoisser, to become filled with anguish.

angoisseux, -euse [ãgwasø, -ø:z], a. Fraught with anguish; full of anguish; anxious.

anguille [ãgi:j], s.f. Ich: (a) Eel. F: Il y a anguille sous roche, there's something in the wind. Soupçonner a. sous roche, F: to smell a rat. (b) Anguille de mer, conger-eel.

angulaire [ãgylɛ:r]. **1.** a. Angular. Pierre angulaire, corner-stone. **2.** s.m. Phot: Grand angulaire, wide-angle lens.

angularité [ãgylarite], s.f. Angularity.

anguleux, -euse [ãgylø, -ø:z], a. Angular, bony (face, elbows); rugged (outline).

anhydre [anidr], a. Ch: Anhydrous. Chaux anhydre, unsla(c)ked lime.

anhydride [anidrid], s.m. Ch: Anhydride. A. carbonique, carbon dioxide.

anicroche [anikrɔʃ], s.f. Difficulty, hitch, snag.

ânier, -ière [ɑnje, -jɛ:r], s. Donkey-driver; donkey-boy.

aniline [anilin], s.f. Ch: Dy: Aniline.

animal¹, -aux [animal, -o], s.m. Animal. F: Quel animal! what a brute! what a beast!

animal², -aux, a. **1.** Animal (kingdom, matter, etc.). **2.** Sensual, brutal (instinct, etc.).

animation [animasjɔ̃], s.f. **1.** Quickening; (i) coming to life, (ii) bringing to life. **2.** Animation, liveliness, briskness. L'a. des rues, the bustle the streets. Ville pleine d'a., town full of life.

…er [anime], v.tr. **1.** To animate, quicken;

to endow with life. **2.** To actuate. (a) To move, propel. (b) Animé d'un sentiment de jalousie, prompted, actuated, by feelings of jealousy. **3.** To quicken, enliven (conversation). A. un cheval, to urge on a horse. A. qn à faire qch., to incite, encourage, s.o. to do sth. A. qn contre qn, to stir up s.o.'s anger against s.o. a. -ant. a. & s. -ateur, -atrice.

s'animer. 1. To come to life. **2.** To become animated, lively. Sa figure s'anima, his face brightened up. S'a. contre qn, to become angry with s.o.

animé, a. Animated, spirited, lively. Teint a., heightened colour. Tableau a., picture full of life. Marché a., brisk market.

animosité [animɔzite], s.f. Animosity, animus, spite (contre, against). Agir par animosité, to act out of spite.

anis [ani], s.m. (a) Bot: Anise. (b) (Graine d') anis, aniseed.

anisette [anizɛt], s.f. Anisette (cordial).

ankylose [ãkilo:z], s.f. Med: Anchylosis.

ankyloser [ãkiloze], v.tr. Med: To anchylose; to stiffen.

s'ankyloser, to anchylose; to become ossified; to stiffen; F: (of pers.) to get stiff.

annales [annal], s.f.pl. Annals; (public) records.

annaliste [annalist], s.m. Annalist.

anneau, -eaux [ano], s.m. **1.** Ring. A. de rideau, curtain-ring. Anneau de mariage, wedding ring. **2.** (a) Link (of chain). F: L'anneau manquant, the missing link. (b) Ringlet, curl (of hair). (c) Coil (of serpent). Enroulé en anneaux, coiled up. (d) Nau: A. de corde, grummet.

année [ane], s.f. Year, twelvemonth. Souhaiter la bonne année à qn, to wish s.o. a happy New Year. Pendant toute une a., for a whole twelvemonth. D'un bout de l'année à l'autre, from year's end to year's end. Chargé ·d'années, stricken in years.

annelé [anle], a. Ringed (column, worm).

annélide [anelid], s.m. Z: Annelid. Les annélides, the annelida.

annexe [an(n)ɛks], s.f. **1.** (a) Annex(e), outbuilding. (b) Ecc: Chapel of ease. **2.** Dependency (of a State). **3.** (a) Rider (to bill); schedule (to act); supplement (to book). (b) Enclosure (with letter). **4.** a. Établissement annexe, annex. Lettre annexe, covering letter.

annexer [an(n)ɛkse], v.tr. **1.** To annex (territory). **2.** To append, attach (document, etc.). Pièces annexées (à une lettre), enclosures.

annexion [an(n)ɛksjɔ̃], s.f. Annexation.

Annibal [an(n)ibal]. Pr.n.m. A.Hist: Hannibal.

annihilation [an(n)iilasjɔ̃], s.f. Annihilation.

annihiler [an(n)iile], v.tr. To annihilate, destroy.

anniversaire [anivɛrsɛ:r]. **1.** a. Anniversary (festival, ceremony). **2.** s.m. (a) Anniversary (of birth, etc.). (b) F: L'a. de qn, s.o.'s birthday.

annonce [anɔ̃:s], s.f. **1.** (a) Announcement, notification, notice. Faire l'annonce de qch., to give out a notice. (b) Cards: Declaration; call. (c) Sign, indication. La baisse subite du baromètre est une a. de tempête, a sudden fall of the barometer is a sign of storm. **2.** Advertisement. Demander qch. par voie d'annonces, to advertise for sth. Annonces lumineuses, illuminated signs. A. de spectacle, play-bill.

annonc|er [anɔ̃se], v.tr. (j'annonçai(s); n. annonçons) **1.** To announce, give notice of, give out (sth.). A. une mauvaise nouvelle à qn, to break, impart, bad news to s.o. A. l'Évangile, to preach the Gospel. Cards: A. son jeu, to declare. **2.** To advertise (sale, etc.). **3.** (a) To promise, foretell,

augur, herald. *Tout semble a. le succès*, everything points to success. *Cela n'annonce rien de bon*, it bodes no good. (*b*) To give proof of (sth.) ; to show, evince, bespeak, betoken (sth.). *Visage qui annonce l'énergie*, face that indicates energy. **4.** To announce (s.o.). **Se faire annoncer (chez qn)**, to send in one's name to s.o. ; to give in one's name (at reception, etc.). *s.m.* **-eur.**
s'annoncer. 1. To announce oneself. **2.** To augur (well, ill). *Le temps s'annonce beau*, the weather promises to be fine.
annonciateur, -trice [anɔ̃sjatœːr, -tris], *s.* **1.** Announcer ; harbinger, messenger (of tidings). **2.** *s.m. Tp : etc :* Indicator-board ; annunciator.
annonciation [anɔ̃sjasjɔ̃], *s.f. Ecc :* **Fête de l'Annonciation**, Feast of the Annunciation ; Lady day.
annotation [an(n)ɔtasjɔ̃], *s.f.* **1.** Annotating. **2.** Annotation, note.
annot|er [an(n)ɔte], *v.tr.* To annotate (text, etc.). *s.* **-ateur, -atrice.**
annuaire [an(n)ɥɛːr], *s.m.* **1.** Annual, year-book. **2.** Almanac, calendar. **3.** (Yearly) list ; (telephone) directory.
annu|el, -elle [an(n)ɥel], *a.* Annual, yearly. **Plante annuelle**, annual. *adv.* **-ellement.**
annuité [an(n)ɥite], *s.f.* **1.** Annual instalment (in repayment of debt). **2.** (Terminable) annuity.
annulaire [an(n)ylɛːr]. **1.** *a.* Annular, ring-shaped. **2.** *s.m.* The ring-finger ; the third finger.
annul|er [an(n)yle], *v.tr.* To annul. (*a*) To render void ; to repeal, quash, set aside, rescind (law, will, judgment). (*b*) To cancel (contract, etc.). *a.* **-able.** *s.f.* **-ation.** *s.m.* **-ement.**
anobl|ir [anɔbliːr], *v.tr.* To ennoble (s.o.), *i.e.* to raise (s.o.) to noble rank, (in Engl.) to the peerage. *s.m.* **-issement.**
anode [anɔd], *s.f. El :* Anode ; positive pole.
anodin [anɔdɛ̃]. **1.** *a.* (*a*) Anodyne, soothing. (*b*) Mild (criticism) ; tame (poetry) ; harmless (talk). **2.** *s.m.* Palliative ; anodyne ; pain-killer.
anomalie [anɔmali], *s.f.* Anomaly.
ânon [anɔ̃], *s.m.* **1.** Ass's foal, ass's colt. **2.** *F :* Dunce, ass. [ÂNE]
ânonn|er [anɔne], *v.tr.* To stumble through (speech, recitation) ; to hum and haw ; to mumble. *s.m.* **-ement.** *s.* **-eur, -euse.**
anonymat [anɔnima], *s.m.* Anonymity. **Garder l'anonymat**, to preserve one's anonymity.
anonyme [anɔnim]. **1.** *a.* (*a*) Anonymous (writer, letter). (*b*) *Com :* **Société anonyme (par actions)**, joint-stock company, limited(-liability) company. **2.** *s.m.* Anonymous writer. **3.** *s.m.* Anonymity. **Écrire sous l'anonyme**, to write anonymously. **Garder l'anonyme**, to retain one's anonymity. *adv.* **-ment.**
anophèle [anɔfɛl], *s.m. Ent :* Anopheles.
anormal, -aux [anɔrmal, -o], *a.* Abnormal ; irregular. *Quelque chose d'a.*, something out of the ordinary. *adv.* **-ement.**
anse [ɑ̃ːs], *s.f.* **1.** Handle (of jug, cup, basket) ; ear (of bell, pitcher) ; bow (of watch, padlock). *F :* **Faire le pot à deux anses**, to stand with one's arms akimbo. (Of servant) **Faire danser l'anse du panier**, to make dishonest profits (in marketing, etc.). *Arch :* **Voûte en anse de panier**, basket-handle arch. **2.** Loop, bight (of rope, etc.). **3.** *Ph.Geog :* Bight, bay.
anspect [ɑ̃spɛk], *s.m. Nau :* Handspike.
antagonique [ɑ̃tagɔnik], *a.* Antagonistic.
antagonisme [ɑ̃tagɔnism], *s.m.* Antagonism.
antagoniste [ɑ̃tagɔnist]. **1.** *a.* Antagonistic, opposed. **2.** *s.* Antagonist, opponent.
antan (d') [dɑ̃tɑ̃]. *A. & Lit :* Of yester year.

Où sont les neiges d'antan? where are the snows of yester year?
antarctique [ɑ̃tar(k)tik], *a.* Antarctic.
antécéd|ent [ɑ̃tesedɑ̃]. **1.** *a.* Antecedent, previous, anterior (*à*, to). **2.** *s.m.* (*a*) *Gram : etc :* Antecedent. (*b*) *pl.* Previous history ; past record ; antecedents. *adv.* **-emment.**
Antéchrist [ɑ̃tekrist], *s.m.* Antichrist.
antédiluvien, -ienne [ɑ̃tedilyvjɛ̃, -jɛn], *a.* Antediluvian.
Antée [ɑ̃te]. *Pr.n.m. Gr.Myth :* Antaeus.
antenne [ɑ̃tɛn], *s.f.* **1.** *Nau :* Lateen yard. **2.** *W.Tel :* Aerial (wire). *A. de réception*, receiving aerial. **3.** Antenna, feeler, horn (of insect, etc.).
antépénultième [ɑ̃tepenyltjɛm], *a.* Ante-penultimate ; last but two.
antérieur, -eure [ɑ̃terjœːr], *a.* **1.** (*a*) Anterior (*à*, to) ; former (period) ; earlier (date) ; previous (year) (*à*, to) ; prior (engagement) (*à*, to) ; antecedent (*à*, to). (*b*) *Gram :* Futur antérieur, future perfect. Passé antérieur, past perfect historic. **2.** Fore-(limb) ; front-(wall). *adv.* **-ement.**
antériorité [ɑ̃terjɔrite], *s.f.* Anteriority ; priority.
anthère [ɑ̃tɛːr], *s.f. Bot :* Anther.
anthologie [ɑ̃tɔlɔʒi], *s.f. Lit :* Anthology.
anthracite [ɑ̃trasit], *s.m.* Anthracite.
anthrax [ɑ̃traks], *s.m. Med :* (*a*) Carbuncle. (*b*) *A. malin*, anthrax.
anthropoïde [ɑ̃trɔpɔid]. **1.** *a.* Anthropoid. **2.** *s.m. Z :* Anthropoid ape.
anthropologie [ɑ̃trɔpɔlɔʒi], *s.f.* Anthropology.
anthropologue [ɑ̃trɔpɔlɔg], *s.m.* Anthropologist.
anthropométrie [ɑ̃trɔpɔmetri], *s.f.* Anthropometry.
anthropomorphisme [ɑ̃trɔpɔmɔrfism], *s.m. Rel.H :* Anthropomorphism.
anthropophage [ɑ̃trɔpɔfaːʒ]. **1.** *a.* Cannibalistic ; man-eating. **2.** *s.* Cannibal.
anthropophagie [ɑ̃trɔpɔfaʒi], *s.f.* Cannibalism.
anti-aerien, -ienne [ɑ̃tiaerjɛ̃, -jɛn], *a.* Anti-aircraft (gun, etc.). **Défense passive anti-aérienne**, air-raid precautions ; A.R.P.
anticathode [ɑ̃tikatɔd], *s.f. X-Rays :* Anti-cathode ; target.
antichambre [ɑ̃tiʃɑ̃ːbr], *s.f.* Ante-room ; waiting-room ; antechamber. **Faire antichambre**, to cool one's heels in the waiting-room.
anticipatif, -ive [ɑ̃tisipatif, -iːv], *a.* Anticipatory ; anticipative. *Payement a.*, prepayment.
anticipation [ɑ̃tisipasjɔ̃], *s.f.* Anticipation. **Payer par anticipation**, to pay in advance.
anticiper [ɑ̃tisipe]. **1.** *v. tr.* To anticipate (sth.) ; to forestall (s.o.'s action). *A. un paiement de dix jours*, to anticipate a payment by ten days. **2.** *v.i. A. sur les événements*, to anticipate events. *A. sur ses revenus*, to spend one's income in advance.
anticlérical, -aux [ɑ̃tiklerikal, -o], *a.* Anticlerical.
anticongélateur [ɑ̃tikɔ̃ʒelatœːr], *s.m.* Anti-freezing mixture.
anticorps [ɑ̃tikɔr], *s.m. Physiol :* Anti-body.
anticyclone [ɑ̃tisiklɔːn], *s.m.* Anticyclone.
antidater [ɑ̃tidate], *v.tr.* To antedate.
antidéperditeur, -trice [ɑ̃tideperditœːr, -tris], *a. Physiol :* Anti-waste (food, etc.).
antidérapant [ɑ̃tiderapɑ̃], *a. Aut : etc :* Non-skid(ding), non-slipping (tyre, etc.).
antidote [ɑ̃tidɔt], *s.m. A. d'un poison, contre un poison*, antidote for, to, against, a poison.
antienne [ɑ̃tjen], *s.f. Ecc.Mus :* Antiphon. *F :* **Chanter toujours la même antienne**, to be always harping on the same string.

antifriction [ɑ̃tifriksjɔ̃], *s.f.* *Mec.E:* Antifriction metal; white metal.

antihalo [ɑ̃tialo]. *Phot:* **1.** *a.inv.* Plaques antihalo, non-halation plates. **2.** *s.m.* Backing.

Antilles [ɑ̃ti:j]. *Pr.n.f.pl.* *Geog:* Les Antilles, the West Indies, the Antilles. La Mer des Antilles, the Caribbean Sea.

antilope [ɑ̃tilɔp], *s.f.* *Z:* Antelope.

antimoine [ɑ̃timwan], *s.m.* *Ch:* Antimony.

antinœud [ɑ̃tinø], *s.m.* *Ph:* Antinode; loop.

antinomie [ɑ̃tinɔmi], *s.f.* Antinomy; paradox.

antinomique [ɑ̃tinɔmik], *a.* Antinomic; paradoxical.

antiobésique [ɑ̃tiɔbezik], *a. & s.m.* *Med:* Anti-fat. Régime *a.*, banting diet.

Antioche [ɑ̃tjɔʃ]. *Pr.n.f.* *A.Geog:* Antioch.

antipape [ɑ̃tipap], *s.m.* *Rel.H:* Antipope.

antipathie [ɑ̃tipati], *s.f.* *A.* pour, contre, qn, antipathy to, against, for, s.o.; aversion for, from, to, s.o.

antipathique [ɑ̃tipatik], *a.* Antipathetic. Elle lui est *a.*, he has an aversion to her.

antipatriotique [ɑ̃tipatriɔtik], *a.* Unpatriotic.

antipode [ɑ̃tipɔd]. **1.** *a.* Antipodal. **2.** *s.m.pl.* Les antipodes, the Antipodes.

antipolitique [ɑ̃tipɔlitik], *a.* Ill-advised (measure, etc.).

antiprotection(n)iste [ɑ̃tiprɔteksjɔnist]. **1.** *a.* Free-trade (policy, etc.). **2.** *s.* Free-trader.

antipyrine [ɑ̃tipirin], *s.f.* *Pharm:* Antipyrin(e).

antiquaille [ɑ̃tikɑːj], *s.f.* Worthless old stuff; lumber; old-fashioned furniture.

antiquaire [ɑ̃tikɛːr], *s.m.* (a) Antiquary, antiquarian. (b) Antiquarian bookseller.

antique [ɑ̃tik]. **1.** *a.* (a) Ancient; pertaining to the ancients. Les villes antiques, the ancient cities (of Greece and Italy). (b) Of olden time. (c) Antique (furniture, etc.). **2.** *s.m.* Dessiner d'après l'antique, to draw from the antique.

antiquité [ɑ̃tikite], *s.f.* **1.** Antiquity, ancientness (of race, etc.). **2.** Ancient times; antiquity. **3.** *pl.* Antiquities; old curiosities. Magasin d'antiquités, antique shop.

antisalle [ɑ̃tisal], *s.f.* Ante-room.

antisciens [ɑ̃tisjɛ̃], *s.m.pl.* *Geog:* Antiscians.

antisémite [ɑ̃tisemit], *s.m. & f.* Anti-Semite.

antisémitisme [ɑ̃tisemitism], *s.m.* Anti-Semitism.

antiseptique [ɑ̃tisɛptik], *a. & s.m.* *Med:* Antiseptic.

antiseptiser [ɑ̃tisɛptize], *v.tr.* *Med:* To antisepticize.

antisportif, -ive [ɑ̃tispɔrtif, -iːv], *a.* Unsportsmanlike.

antithèse [ɑ̃titɛːz], *s.f.* **1.** *Rh:* Antithesis. **2.** Direct contrary (de, to, of).

antithétique [ɑ̃titetik], *a.* Antithetic(al); in strong contrast.

antitoxine [ɑ̃titɔksin], *s.f.* *Med:* Antitoxin.

Antoine [ɑ̃twan]. *Pr.n.m.* Ant(h)ony.

Antonin [ɑ̃tonɛ̃]. *Pr.n.m.* *Hist:* Antoninus. Les Antonins, the Antonines.

antonyme [ɑ̃tonim]. *Rh:* **1.** *a.* Antonymous. **2.** *s.m.* Antonym; counter-term.

antre [ɑ̃ːtr], *s.m.* (a) Cave, cavern. (b) Den, lair, retreat (of animal, brigand).

Anvers [ɑ̃vɛːr, ɑ̃vɛrs]. *Pr.n.m.* *Geog:* Antwerp.

anxiété [ɑ̃ksjete], *s.f.* Anxiety, concern. Avec anxiété, anxiously.

anxieux, -euse [ɑ̃ksjø, -øːz], *a.* Anxious, uneasy. *A.* de l'avenir, anxious about the future. *adv.* **-sement.**

aoriste [aɔrist], *s.m.* *Gr.Gram:* Aorist.

aorte [aɔrt], *s.f.* *Anat:* Aorta.

août [u], *s.m.* **1.** August. Au mois d'août, in the month of August. Le premier, le sept, *a.*, (on) the first, the seventh, of August. **2.** *A:* Faire l'août, to harvest; to get in the corn.

Apache [apaʃ], *s.m.* **1.** *Ethn:* Apache. **2.** *F:* Un apache, a hooligan, a rough (of Paris); *U.S:* a tough.

apais|er [apɛze], *v.tr.* **1.** *A.* qn, to appease, pacify, calm, soothe, s.o. *A.* l'exaltation de qn, to allay s.o.'s excitement. Non apaisé, unappeased. **2.** To allay, alleviate (pain); to allay (hunger); to quench, slake (thirst); to quell (storm, revolt). [PAIX] *a.* **-ant.** *s.m.* **-ement.**

s'apaiser, to become appeased; to calm down; to grow quiet; (of wind) to die down; (of storm) to abate, to subside.

apanage [apanaːʒ], *s.m.* **1.** *Hist:* Ap(p)anage. **2.** Attribute, prerogative (de, of).

aparté [aparte], *s.m.* **1.** *Th:* Aside; stage-whisper. En aparté, aside; in a stage-whisper. **2.** Private conversation.

apathie [apati], *s.f.* Apathy; listlessness. Sortir de son apathie, to rouse oneself.

apathique [apatik], *a.* Apathetic; listless. *adv.* **-ment.**

apercev|oir [apɛrsəvwaːr], *v.tr.* (*pr.p.* apercevant; *p.p.* aperçu; *pr.ind.* j'aperçois, n. apercevons, ils aperçoivent; *pr. sub.* j'aperçoive, n. apercevions; *p.d.* j'apercevais; *p.h.* j'aperçus; *fu.* j'apercevrai) To perceive, see; to set eyes upon, to catch sight of (s.o., sth.). Je n'ai fait que l'a., I only caught a glimpse of him. Cela ne s'aperçoit pas, it is not noticeable. *a.* **-able.**

s'apercevoir de qch., to perceive, realize, notice, sth.; to become aware, conscious, of sth. Ne pas s'a. de qch., to be, remain, unconscious of sth. Sans s'en a., without being aware of it, without noticing it.

aperçu, *s.m.* **1.** Glimpse. *A.* sur la campagne, glimpse of the country (through an opening). **2.** Outline, sketch, survey, summary. Par aperçu, on a rough estimate; at a rough guess.

apériodique [aperjɔdik], *a.* *Mec:* *El:* Aperiodic, dead-beat (galvanometer, etc.).

apéritif [aperitif], *s.m.* Appetizer, *F:* whet. Prendre l'apéritif, to have a bitters.

aphasie [afazi], *s.f.* *Med:* Aphasia.

aphélie [afeli], *Astr:* **1.** *s.m.* Aphelion. **2.** *a.* In aphelion.

aphis [afis], *s.m.* *Ent:* Aphis; plant-louse; green-fly.

aphorisme [afɔrism], *s.m.* Aphorism.

aphte [aft], *s.m.* *Med:* Aphtha.

aphteux, -euse [aftø, -øːz], *a.* *Med:* Aphthous. *Vet:* Fièvre aphteuse, foot-and-mouth disease.

api [api], *s.m.* *Hort:* (Pomme d')api, lady-apple.

apiculteur [apikyltœːr], *s.m.* *Husb:* Bee-keeper; apiculturist. apiarist.

apiculture [apikyltyːr], *s.f.* Bee-keeping.

apitoyer [apitwaje], *v.tr.* (j'apitoie, n. apitoyons; j'apitoierai) To move (to pity); to incite to pity.

s'apitoyer sur le sort de qn, to commiserate with s.o.

aplanat [aplana], *s.m.* *Phot:* Aplanatic lens.

aplan|ir [aplaniːr], *v.tr.* **1.** To flatten, smooth (surface); to plane (wood); to planish (metal); to smooth away (difficulties). **2.** To level (road, etc.). [PLAN¹] *s.m.* **-issement.** *s.m.* **-isseur.**

s'aplanir. 1. (Of road) To grow smoother; (of difficulties) to disappear. **2.** To become level.

aplat|ir [aplatiːr], *v.tr.* **1.** To flatten; to hammer down (rivet head). *A.* qch. à coups de marteau, to beat sth. flat. **2.** *F:* *A.* qn, (i) to lay s.o. out flat; to send s.o. sprawling; (ii) to squash s.o. (by

piece of news, by rebuff). [PLAT] *s.m.* -issage.
s.m. -issement.
s'aplatir. **1.** To become flat; (of balloon)
to collapse; (of tyre) to go flat. **2.** *S'a. par terre,*
(i) to lie down flat on the ground; (ii) *F:* to fall
at full length; to come a cropper. *S'a. devant qn,*
to grovel before s.o.
   aplati, *a.* **1.** (*a*) Flattened, flat. (*b*) Deflated.
2. Oblate (spheroid, etc.).
aplomb [apl5], *s.m.* **1.** Perpendicularity; uprightness; just poise; balance (of pers., thg).
S'assurer un solide a., to take a firm stand on one's
feet. **D'aplomb,** upright; vertical(ly); plumb.
Bien d'a. sur ses pieds, steady on one's feet. *F: Je
ne suis pas d'a. aujourd'hui,* I am out of sorts, I feel
shaky, to-day. *Voilà qui vous remettra d'a.,* that
will set you up. **Hors d'aplomb,** (i) out of plumb,
(ii) *F:* wobbly. **2.** (Self-)assurance. **Il a de
l'aplomb,** he's a cool hand. **Perdre son aplomb,**
to lose one's self-possession. *Avoir l'a. de dire,
de faire, qch.,* to have the cheek, the impudence, to
say, do, sth.; to have the nerve to do sth. [PLOMB]
apocalypse [apɔkalips], *s.f. B:* **L'Apocalypse,**
the Book of Revelation; the Apocalypse.
apocalyptique [apɔkaliptik], *a.* Apocalyptic(al).
apocope [apɔkɔp], *s.f. Ling:* Apocope; elision.
apocryphe [apɔkrif], *a.* (*a*) Apocryphal. (*b*) *F:*
Of doubtful authenticity.
apodose [apɔdo:z], *s.f. Gram:* Apodosis;
'then'-clause.
apogée [apɔʒe], *s.m.* (*a*) *Astr:* Apogee. *F:* Être
à l'apogée de sa gloire, to be at the height, zenith,
acme, of one's glory. (*b*) *Mth:* Peak (of curve).
Apollon [apɔllɔ̃]. *Pr.n.m. Myth:* Apollo.
apologie [apɔlɔʒi], *s.f.* Defence, vindication,
(written) justification (*de,* of). *Faire l'a. de qn,*
to vindicate, justify, defend, s.o. NOTE. Never
= EXCUSE, *q.v.*
apologiste [apɔlɔʒist], *s.m.* Apologist.
apologue [apɔlɔg], *s.m. Lit:* Apologue, fable.
apophonie [apɔfɔni], *s.f. Ling:* Vowel gradation;
apophony; ablaut.
apophtegme [apɔftegm], *s.m.* Apophthegm.
apophyge [apɔfi:ʒ], *s.f. Arch:* Apophyge; spring
(of column).
apophyse [apɔfi:z], *s.f.* Apophysis. *Anat:* Process. *L'a. coracoïde,* the coracoid process.
apoplectique [apɔplɛktik], *a. & s. Med:*
Apoplectic.
apoplexie [apɔplɛksi], *s.f. Med:* Apoplexy.
Attaque d'apoplexie, apoplectic seizure; *F:*
stroke. **Tomber en apoplexie,** to have a stroke
(of apoplexy).
apostat, -ate [apɔsta, -at], *a. & s.* Apostate;
F: turncoat.
aposter [apɔste], *v.tr.* To station, post, set (spy,
agent, etc.). [POSTE²]
apostille [apɔsti:j], *s.f.* (Marginal) recommendation (on petition, etc.).
apostiller [apɔstije], *v.tr.* To add a (marginal)
recommendation to (petition, etc.).
apostolat [apɔstɔla], *s.m.* Apostolate, apostleship.
apostolique [apɔstɔlik], *a.* Apostolic.
apostrophe¹ [apɔstrɔf], *s.f. Rh:* Apostrophe.
Adresser une apostrophe à qn, to apostrophize s.o.
apostrophe², *s.f. Gram:* Apostrophe.
apothéose [apɔteo:z], *s.f.* **1.** Apotheosis; deification. **2.** *Th:* Grand finale; transformation
scene (of fairy play, etc.).
apothicaire [apɔtikɛ:r], *s.m.* Apothecary. *F:*
Mémoire, compte, d'apothicaire, exorbitant bill.
apôtre [apo:tr], *s.m.* Apostle. *F:* **Un bon apôtre,**
a sanctimonious knave. **Faire le bon apôtre,** to
sham the honest man.

apparaiss-ant, -e, etc. See APPARAÎTRE.
apparaître [aparɛ:tr], *v.i.* (Conj. like PARAÎTRE.
Aux. usu. *être,* occ. *avoir*) **1.** To appear; to
become visible; to come into sight. *A. à travers
le brouillard,* to loom out of the fog. *Un spectre
lui était apparu,* a ghost had appeared to him.
2. To become evident. *La vérité lui apparut,* the
truth became apparent to him, broke in upon
him.
apparat [apara], *s.m.* State, pomp, show, display.
Discours d'apparat, set speech.
apparaux [aparo], *s.m.pl. Nau:* Tackle, gear.
appareil [aparɛ:j], *s.m.* **1.** Display, magnificence,
pomp, array. *Mettre en jeu l'a. de la justice,* to
put the (machinery of the) law in motion. **2.** (*a*)
Apparatus, outfit. *Ind:* (Whether *sg.* or *pl.*)
Plant (*e.g.* for generating power). *A. de pêche,*
fishing-tackle. *L'a. digestif,* the digestive system.
A. critique d'un texte, critical apparatus of a text.
(*b*) Device, appliance, apparatus; gear; mechanism. *Appareils à gaz,* gas-fittings. *A. de levage,*
lifting appliance. (*c*) Machine, instrument.
W.Tel: A. à lampes, valve set. *Av: A. de
combat,* fighting machine or plane. *Phot:* **Appareil
(photographique),** camera. *A. instantané,* snapshot camera. *A. à pied,* field-camera, stand
camera. **3.** *Surg:* Dressing (on wound).
appareillage¹ [apareja:ʒ], *s.m.* **1.** (*a*) Installation,
fitting up (of wireless station, etc.). (*b*) *Nau:*
Getting under way; weighing. (*c*) Fitting (of
s.o.) with artificial limbs. *Adm:* Centre d'appareillage, artificial limb supply centre. **2.** (*a*) Outfit;
fittings; equipment. *A. électrique d'une auto,*
electrical equipment of a car. (*b*) *Ind:* Plant.
appareiller¹ [apareje], *v.tr.* **1.** To install, fit up
(workshop, etc.). **2.** *Nau:* (*a*) *A. une voile,* to
trim a sail. (*b*) *Abs.* To get under way; to weigh.
A. à la vapeur, à la voile, to get under steam,
under sail. [APPAREIL]
appareiller², *v.tr.* = APPARIER. [PAREIL] *s.m.*
-age². *s.m.* -ement.
apparence [aparɑ̃:s], *s.f.* **1.** (*a*) Appearance;
look. *Quelque a. de la vérité,* some semblance of
truth. *Il y a toute a. qu'il dit vrai,* there is every
indication of his speaking the truth. **Selon toute
apparence,** to all appearances. *Il se manifesta
sous l'apparence de . . .,* he appeared in the
guise, in the shape, of. . . . (*b*) (Fausse) apparence, false, fallacious, appearance. *S'introduire
chez qn sous de fausses apparences,* to force one's
way in under false pretences. **En apparence,** in
semblance, on the surface. **Plus difficile en a.**
qu'en réalité, more difficult in semblance than in
reality. *Il venait en a. pour vendre sa marchandise,*
he came ostensibly to sell his wares. **2.** Avoir de
l'apparence, (i) (of pers.) to have a good presence;
(ii) (of thg) to look well. **De belle apparence,** of
good appearance. **Sauver les apparences,** to keep
up appearances.
appar|ent [aparɑ̃], *a.* **1.** (*a*) Visible, conspicuous,
apparent. *Peu a.,* inconspicuous. (*b*) Obvious,
evident. **2.** Apparent, not real. *Mouvement a. du
soleil,* apparent motion of the sun. *adv.*
-emment.
apparenté [aparɑ̃te], *a.* Related, akin (*à, avec,*
to). **Bien apparenté,** well connected. [PARENT]
apparier [aparje], *v.tr.* To match, pair (socks,
horses, etc.); to pair off (opponents).
s'apparier, (of birds, etc.) to pair, mate.
appariteur [aparitœ:r], *s.m.* **1.** Apparitor,
beadle, mace-bearer (of University court, of
corporation). **2.** (Laboratory) attendant.
apparition [aparisjɔ̃], *s.f.* **1.** Appearance, advent; coming out; publication (of book). **Faire

son apparition, to make one's appearance; *F:* to appear on the scene. **2.** Apparition, ghost.
appartement [apartəmɑ̃], *s.m.* (*a*) Flat; suite or set of rooms. *J'ai un a. en ville*, I have a flat in town. (*b*) *Appartements de réception*, public rooms (in house).
appartenir [apartəniːr], *v.i.* (Conj. like TENIR) **1.** To belong (*à*, to). *Cette maison lui appartient en propre*, this house is his own, is his personal property. **2.** *v. impers. Il lui appartient de . . .*, it is part of his functions to . . .; it behoves him to . . .; it rests with him to . . .; it falls to him to. . . . *Il ne m'appartient pas de le critiquer*, it does not appertain to me, it is not incumbent (up)on me, to criticize him.
s'appartenir, to be one's own master.
appas [apɑ], *s.m.pl.* **1.** (Physical) charms (of woman). **2.** Lure, attraction (of wealth, etc.).
appât [apɑ], *s.m.* (*a*) Bait. *Mettre l'a. à la ligne*, to bait the line. *Mordre à l'appât*, to take the bait. (*b*) Lure (of success); attraction (of pleasure).
appâter [apɑte], *v.tr.* **1.** To lure (fish, etc.) with a bait. **2.** To feed (poultry) forcibly; to cram (geese).
appauvr|ir [apovriːr], *v.tr.* To impoverish. [PAUVRE] *s.m.* **-issement**.
s'appauvrir, to grow poor(er). *Pays appauvri d'hommes*, country impoverished in men.
appeau [apo], *s.m.* (*a*) Decoy-bird; stool-pigeon; lure. (*b*) Bird-call. *F:* **Se faire prendre à l'appeau**, to be lured into the trap.
appel [apɛl], *s.m.* **1.** Appeal. (*a*) **Faire appel à qn**, to appeal to s.o.; to call upon s.o.'s help, services. *Faire a. à tout son courage*, to summon up all one's courage. *Le moteur part au premier a.*, the engine starts at the first touch of the switch. (*b*) *Jur:* Appeal at law. **Cour d'appel**, Court of Appeal. **Interjeter appel**, to lodge an appeal. **Juger en appel** (*d'une décision*), to hear an appeal (from a decision). **Jugement sans appel**, final judgment. **2.** Call; (vocal) summons. *On a sonné l'a.* au dîner, the dinner-bell has gone. **Cri d'a.**, call for help. **Appel d'incendie**, fire-alarm. *Fin:* **Faire un appel de fonds**, to call up capital. *Mil:* **L'appel aux armes**, the call to arms. *L'a. du téléphone retentit*, the telephone bell rings. **3.** Roll-call, call-over. **Feuille d'appel**, roll, *Nau:* muster-roll. **Faire l'appel**, to call (over) the roll. *Mil:* **L'appel du soir**, tattoo. **Battre, sonner, l'appel**, to beat, sound, the (fall-in) call. *Répondre à l'a.*, to answer the roll-call; to answer (to) one's name.
appelant, -ante [aplɑ̃, -ɑ̃ːt]. (*a*) *a.* Appealing (party, etc.). (*b*) *s. A. d'un jugement*, appellant against a judgment.
appeler [aple], *v.tr.* (j'appelle, n. appelons; j'appellerai) **1.** (*a*) To call, call to (s.o.). *Il a appelé*, he called (out). *A. au secours*, to call for help. (*b*) *A. qn de la main, du geste*, to beckon (to) s.o. **2.** (*a*) To call in, send for, summon (s.o.). **Faire appeler un médecin**, to call in a doctor. *Mil:* **A. une classe**, to call up a class. *s.* **Les appelés**, the men called up. *A. qn en duel*, to call s.o. out. *Jur:* **A. qn en justice**, to summons s.o.; to sue s.o. (*b*) **Être appelé à qch.**, to be destined for sth. *Industrie appelée à un brillant avenir*, industry marked out for a brilliant future. **3.** To call (by name); to term, name. *Nous l'avons appelé Jean*, we have called him John. **4.** (*a*) To appeal to, call on, invoke (s.o., sth.). *A. la colère du ciel sur qn*, to call down the wrath of heaven upon s.o. *A. qn à faire qch.*, to call on, invite, s.o. to do sth. (*b*) To call for (sth.). *Ce problème appelle une solution immédiate*, the problem calls for an immediate solution. **5.** (*a*) To provoke, arouse. *Prov:* **Un malheur en appelle un autre**, misfortunes never come singly. (*b*) *Corps appelé par une force*, body pulled, attracted, by a force. **6.** *v.i.* (*a*) *Jur: A. d'un jugement*, to appeal against a sentence. (*b*) **En appeler à qn**, to appeal to s.o. *J'en appelle à votre témoignage*, I call you to witness.
s'appeler, to be called, named, termed. *Comment vous appelez-vous?* what is your name? *Je m'appelle . . .*, my name is. . . .
appendice [ap(p)ɛ̃dis], *s.m.* **1.** Appendix (of book). **2.** Annex(e), appendage (of building). **3.** *Anat: Bot:* (i) Appendix, (ii) appendage. *A. caudal*, caudal appendage. **L'appendice vermiforme**, the vermiform appendix.
appendicite [ap(p)ɛ̃disit], *s.f.* Appendicitis.
appentis [apɑ̃ti], *s.m. Const:* (*a*) Penthouse. Toit en appentis, lean-to roof. (*b*) Outhouse.
appesant|ir [apəzɑ̃tiːr], *v.tr.* **1.** To make (sth.) heavy; to weigh (sth.) down. *Yeux appesantis par le sommeil*, eyes heavy with sleep. **2.** To dull (the mind, etc.). [PESANT] *s.m.* **-issement**.
s'appesantir. **1.** (Of burden, etc.) To become heavy. **2.** *S'a.* (*trop*) *sur un sujet*, to dwell (too long) on a subject.
appétissant [apetisɑ̃], *a.* Tempting, appetizing.
appétit [apeti], *s.m.* **1.** Appetite. **Couper l'appétit à qn**, to spoil, take away, s.o.'s appetite. **Manger de bon appétit, avec appétit**, to eat heartily, with relish, with zest. **Bon appétit!** I hope you will enjoy your dinner. **Avoir bon appétit**, to have a hearty appetite. *Prov:* **L'appétit vient en mangeant**, when once you start eating you soon get hungry. **2.** Desire, lust (*de*, for). *A. du gain*, greed of gold. **Mettre qn en appétit**, (i) to whet s.o.'s appetite, (ii) to set s.o. agog.
applaud|ir [aplodiːr]. **1.** *v.tr.* (*a*) To applaud, clap (s.o., sth.). **Se faire applaudir à tout casser**, to bring the house down. (*b*) To applaud, approve, commend (s.o., sth.). *A. qn d'avoir fait qch.*, to commend s.o. for doing sth. **2.** *v.ind.tr. A. à qch.*, to approve sth. *s.m.* **-isseur.**
s'applaudir *de qch., d'avoir fait qch.*, to congratulate oneself on sth., on having done sth.
applaudissement [aplodismɑ̃], *s.m.* Usu. *pl.* **1.** Applause; clapping. **Salve d'applaudissements**, round of applause. **Soulever les applaudissements**, to be greeted with applause. **2.** Approval, commendation, approbation.
applic|able [aplikabl], *a.* **1.** That can be applied. *L'or est a. sur certains métaux*, gold can be applied to certain metals. **2.** Applicable. *Loi a. à un cas*, law applicable to a case. *Mot a.*, appropriate, suitable, word. *s.f.* **-abilité.**
application [aplikasjɔ̃], *s.f.* Application. **1.** (*a*) *A. de qch. à, sur, qch.*, application, superposition, laying, of sth. (up)on sth. *A. d'un bandage à une blessure*, applying of a bandage to a wound. (*b*) *A. de peinture*, coat of paint. (*c*) *Needlew:* Broderie application, appliqué work. **2.** *A. d'une loi à un cas*, application of a law to a case. *Mil: Navy:* **École d'application**, school of instruction. **3.** Diligence, steadiness (in work).
applique [aplik], *s.f.* **1.** Application (against wall, etc.). **Lampe d'applique**, bracket-lamp. **2.** Applied ornament. *Needlew:* Appliqué ornament. **3.** (*a*) (Wall-)bracket (for lamps, etc.). (*b*) Sconce, bracket-lamp. [APPLIQUER]
appliquer [aplike], *v.tr.* To apply. **1.** *A. qch. sur, à, qch.*, to apply sth. on, to, sth.; to lay sth. on sth. *A. un clairon à ses lèvres*, to set a bugle to one's lips. *N'appliquez pas trop le crayon sur le papier*, do not press too hard on the pencil

F: Appliquer une gifle à qn, to slap, smack, s.o.'s face. **2.** *A. l'algèbre à la géométrie,* to apply algebra to geometry. *S'a. un éloge,* to take praise to oneself. *Abs. A. la loi,* to bring, put, the law into operation ; to carry out, enforce, administer, the law. **3.** *A. son esprit à ses études,* to bend, turn, one's mind to one's studies.
   s'appliquer. 1. *S'a. à qch.,* to apply oneself to sth.; to work hard at sth. **2.** (Of law, etc.) To apply (à, to). *A qui s'applique cette remarque?* to whom does this remark apply?
   appliqué, *a.* **1.** Studious, diligent (person). **2.** Sciences appliquées, applied sciences.
appog(g)iature [apɔ:ʒjaty:r], *s.f. Mus:* Appoggiatura.
appoint [apwɛ̃], *s.m.* **1.** *(a) Com:* Balance ; odd money. Je vous dois dix-huit francs par appoint, the balance of what I owe you is eighteen francs. *(b)* Eau d'appoint, make-up water (for accumulator, etc.). **2.** Contribution. Apporter son appoint à qch., to contribute to sth. [POINT]
appointements [apwɛ̃tmɑ̃], *s.m.pl.* Salary, emoluments. *Ecc:* Stipend. **Toucher ses appointements,** to draw one's salary.
appontement [apɔ̃tmɑ̃], *s.m.* **1.** Gang-plank. **2.** (Wooden) wharf ; landing-stage. [PONT]
apport [apɔ:r], *s.m.* **1.** (Action of bringing) *Fin: A. de capitaux,* contribution of capital. *Civ.E: Fort:* **Terres d'apport,** earthworks. **2.** (Thing brought) *Com:* Initial share (in undertaking). *Geol: Apports d'un cours d'eau,* alluvial deposits ; silt. [APPORTER]
apport|er [apɔrte], *v.tr.* To bring. **1.** *A. du charbon, des nouvelles,* to bring coal, news (à, to). *F: Apporte-toi ici!* come here ! **2.** *A. du soin, de la précaution, du zèle, à faire qch.,* to exercise care, to use precaution, to show zeal, in doing sth. *s.* **-eur, -euse.**
apposer [apoze], *v.tr.* To affix, place, put. *A. une affiche sur un mur,* to stick a bill on a wall. *A. sa signature, son sceau, à un acte,* to set one's hand, one's seal, to a deed. S.a. SCELLÉ 2. [POSER]
appositif, -ive [apozitif, -i:v], *a. & s.m. Gram:* Appositive ; (word) in apposition.
apposition [apozisjɔ̃], *s.f.* **1.** *Adm:* Affixing (of seal, etc.). **2.** *Gram:* Apposition.
appréciable [apresjabl], *a.* Appreciable.
appréciateur, -trice [apresjatœ:r, -tris]. **1.** *a.* Appreciative. **2.** *s.* Appreciator (de, of).
appréciation [apresjasjɔ̃], *s.f.* **1.** Valuation, estimating, estimation, estimate, appraising, appraisement. **Faire l'appréciation des marchandises,** to value, appraise, goods. **2.** Appreciation (of work of art, etc.). *Une affaire d'a.,* a matter of opinion, of taste. **3.** Rise in value.
apprécier [apresje], *v.tr.* **1.** *(a)* To appraise, to estimate the value of (sth.); to value (sth.). *(b)* To determine, estimate (temperature, distance, sound). **2.** To appreciate (virtue, good thing). *Être apprécié,* to be appreciated, held in repute.
appréhender [apreɑ̃de], *v.tr.* **1.** Appréhender qn (au corps), to seize, arrest, s.o. **2.** To dread, apprehend, fear (sth.). *J'appréhende de le revoir,* I dread (the idea of) seeing him again.
appréhensif, -ive [apreɑ̃sif, -i:v], *a.* Apprehensive (de, of) ; fearful, timid.
appréhension [apreɑ̃sjɔ̃], *s.f.* **1.** Apprehension au corps, seizure, arrest. **2.** Understanding. **3.** Dread (de, of).
apprendre [aprɑ̃:dr], *v.tr.* (Conj. like PRENDRE) **1.** *(a)* To learn (lesson, trade). *A. à faire qch.,* to learn (how) to do sth. *(b)* To learn, hear of, come to know of, *F:* get to know of (news, etc.).

J'ai appris que . . ., I have heard that . . . ; it has come to my knowledge that. . . . **2.** *A. qch. à qn. (a)* To teach s.o. sth. *A. à qn à faire qch.,* to teach, show, s.o. how to do sth. *F:* Ça vous apprendra ! serve you right ! *(b)* To inform, apprise, s.o. of sth. ; to tell s.o. sth.
   appris, -e. 1. *a.* Bien appris, mal appris, well-, ill-bred. **2.** *s.* Un mal appris, a boor.
apprenti, -ie [aprɑ̃ti], *s. (a)* Apprentice. *(b)* (In legal and other professions) Articled clerk. *(c) F:* Novice, tyro.
apprentissage [aprɑ̃tisa:ʒ], *s.m. (a)* Apprenticeship. *(b)* (In liberal professions) Articles. **Mettre qn en apprentissage chez qn,** to apprentice or article s.o. to s.o. **Faire son apprentissage chez qn,** to serve one's apprenticeship with s.o. *F:* **Faire l'apprentissage de la vie,** to learn by experience.
apprêt [aprɛ], *s.m.* **1.** *pl.* Preparations (for journey, etc.). **2.** Affectation, affectedness (of speech, etc.). **3.** *Cu:* Dressing, seasoning (of food). **4.** *(a)* (Process of) dressing, finishing (fabrics, etc.). *(b)* Finish, stiffening (of fabrics, etc.). [APPRÊTER]
apprêt|er [aprɛte], *v.tr.* **1.** To prepare ; to make ready (luggage, meal, etc.). *Vous vous apprêtez bien des ennuis,* you are laying up trouble for yourself. **2.** To dress, finish, stiffen (fabrics, etc.). *s.* **-eur, -euse.**
   s'apprêter. 1. To prepare oneself, get ready. *S'a. à la lutte,* to prepare for the struggle. *S'a. à faire qch.,* to prepare to do sth. **2.** (Of storm, trouble) To be brewing.
   apprêté, *a.* Affected, stiff (style, manner).
apprîmes, apprirent, appris, apprit. See APPRENDRE.
apprivois|er [aprivwaze], *v.tr.* To tame (animal) ; to win over (s.o.). *a.* **-able.** *s.m.* **-ement.**
   s'apprivoiser, to grow, become, tame ; *F:* (of pers.) to become more sociable.
   apprivoisé, *a.* Tame.
approbateur, -trice [aprɔbatœ:r, -tris]. **1.** *a.* Approving (gesture, etc.). **2.** *s.* Approver.
approbat|if, -ive [aprɔbatif, -i:v], *a.* Approving (gesture). *adv.* **-ivement.**
approbation [aprɔbasjɔ̃], *s.f.* Approval, approbation ; (i) consent, (ii) commendation.
approchable [aprɔʃabl], *a.* Approachable, accessible (place, person).
approchant [aprɔʃɑ̃]. **1.** *a. (a)* Approximating, akin, similar (de, to). *Couleur approchante du bleu,* colour approximating to blue. *(b) Calculs très approchants,* closely approximative calculations. **2.** *prep. A:* Il y a approchant un an, (it is) well on to a year ago.
approche [aprɔʃ], *s.f.* **1.** Approach, drawing near. *L'a. de l'hiver,* the oncoming of winter. **A leur approche** *le groupe se dispersa,* when they drew near the group dispersed. **D'une approche difficile,** difficult of access. **Travaux d'approche,** approach works. S.a. LUNETTE 1. **2.** *pl. (a)* **Approches d'un camp, d'une ville,** approaches of a camp, of a town. *(b) Mth:* **Approches successives,** successive approximations ; continual approach.
approcher [aprɔʃe]. **1.** *v.tr. (a) A. qch. de qch.,* to bring, draw, sth. near (to) sth. *Approchez votre chaise,* draw up, draw in, bring up, your chair. *(b)* To approach, come near (s.o., sth.) ; to come close to (s.o., sth.). *Ne m'approchez pas,* don't come near me. **2.** *v.i. (a)* To approach, draw near. *L'heure approche,* the hour draws near. *(b) A. de qn,* to approach s.o. ; to come, draw,

near to s.o. *Nous approchons de Paris,* we are getting near Paris. (*c*) *A. de qch.,* to resemble sth.; to approximate, be akin, to sth.

s'approcher, to come near; to approach. *S'a. de qch.,* to draw, come, near (to) sth.

approché, *a.* Approximate (figure, etc.).

approfond|ir [aprɔfɔdiːr], *v.tr.* **1.** To deepen, excavate (river-bed, etc.). **2.** To go deeply, thoroughly, into (sth.); to study (sth.) thoroughly. [PROFOND] *s.m.* **-issement.**

s'approfondir, to grow deeper; to deepen.

approfondi, *a.* Elaborate, careful (study). *Enquête approfondie,* thorough, searching, enquiry. *Connaissance approfondie· du français,* thorough command of French.

appropriation [aprɔpriasjɔ̃], *s.f.* **1.** Appropriation (of property, etc.). *A. de fonds,* embezzlement. **2.** *A. de qch. à qch.,* adaptation, suiting, of sth. to sth.

approprier [aprɔprie], *v.tr.* **1.** *S'a. qch.,* to appropriate sth. (to oneself). **2.** To make appropriate; to arrange (sth.) to fit (sth.). *A. son langage aux circonstances,* to adapt one's language to the circumstances.

s'approprier *à qch.,* to adapt oneself to sth.

approprié, *a.* Appropriate, adapted (*à,* to); proper, suitable (answer, etc.).

approuver [apruve], *v.tr.* **1.** (*a*) *A. qch.,* to approve of, be pleased with, sth. *A. de la tête,* to nod approval. *A. que qn fasse qch.,* to approve of s.o.'s doing sth. (*b*) *A. qn d'avoir fait qch.,* to approve s.o. for doing sth. **2.** To consent to, agree to, sanction (expenditure, etc.). *A. un contrat,* to ratify a contract. "*Lu et approuvé,*" 'read and approved.'

approvisionnement [aprɔvizjɔnmɑ̃], *s.m.* **1.** Provisioning, supplying, victualling (of town, army); stocking (of shop). *Nau:* *A. de charbon,* coaling. **2.** Supply, stock, store.

approvisionn|er [aprɔvizjɔne], *v.tr.* To supply (*de,* with); to furnish with supplies; to provide with stores; to provision. *s.* **-eur, -euse.**

s'approvisionner, to take in, lay in, a supply (*en, de,* of); to lay in stores. *S'a. chez qn,* to get one's supplies from (a dealer).

approvisionné, *a.* Stocked, supplied (*de, en,* with). *Bien a.,* well stocked.

approximat|if, -ive [aprɔksimatif, -iːv], *a.* Approximate; rough (estimate). *adv.* **-ivement.**

approximation [aprɔksimasjɔ̃], *s.f.* Approximation. *Mth:* **Approximations successives,** continual approach. **Par approximation,** approximately; at a rough guess.

appui [apɥi], *s.m.* **1.** (*a*) Prop, stay. *Mettre un a. à un mur,* to shore up a wall. (*b*) Rest. *Arch:* Balustrade. *A. de fenêtre,* (i) window-ledge; (ii) window-rail. *A. d'escalier,* banisters. **2.** Support. (*a*) **Mur d'appui,** supporting wall. **Barre d'appui,** hand-rail. *Nau:* **Lisse d'appui,** breast-rail. **A hauteur d'appui,** breast-high; elbow-high. (*b*) *A. moral,* moral support. **Être sans appui,** to be friendless, unprotected. **Accusation avec preuves à l'appui,** accusation supported by proofs. *Il est venu à l'a. de mon dire,* he supported my statement. S.a. POINT¹ 3. **3.** *A. de la voix sur une syllabe,* stress on a syllable. [APPUYER]

appuyer [apɥije], *v.tr.* (j'appuie, n. appuyons; j'appuierai) **1.** To support. (*a*) To prop (up), shore (up) (joist, wall, etc.). (*b*) *A. une pétition,* to support a petition. **2.** (*a*) *A. qch. contre qch.,* to lean sth., rest sth., against sth. *A. la main sur la table,* to rest one's hand on the table. *A. son opinion sur qch.,* to base, rest, ground, one's opinion on sth. *Théorie appuyée sur des faits,*

theory supported by facts. (*b*) *A. son doigt sur une plaie,* to press one's finger on a wound. *Mus:* *A.* (*sur*) *une note,* to dwell on, sustain, a note. (*c*) *P:* **S'appuyer un bon dîner,** to stand oneself a good dinner. **3.** *Abs. A. sur sa plume,* to press on one's pen. *A. sur le bouton,* (i) to press the button; (ii) to touch the bell. *A. sur une syllabe,* to lay stress on a syllable. *A. à droite,* to bear to the right. *Mil:* **Appuyez à droite, à gauche!** on the right, left, close!

s'appuyer. 1. *S'a. sur, contre, à, qch.,* to lean, rest, on, against, sth. *S'a. sur qn,* (i) to lean on s.o., (ii) to rely, depend, on s.o. **2.** *S'a. d'une autorité,* to found upon, to take one's stand on, an authority.

âpre [aːpr], *a.* **1.** Rough, harsh. *Voix â.,* rasping voice. *Goût â.,* tart taste. **2.** Bitter, biting, sharp (frost, rebuke); scathing (irony). *Temps â.,* raw weather. **3.** Keen (competition, etc.). *Homme â. au gain,* grasping man. *adv.* **-ment.**

après [aprɛ]. **I.** *prep.* **1.** (Order in time, space) (*a*) After. *Il est arrivé a. moi,* he arrived after me. **Après tout . . .,** after all. . . . S.a. COUP 4. (*b*) *Je viens a. lui,* I come next to him. **2.** (Proximity, = à, CONTRE) *Épingler une carte après le mur,* to pin a card to, against, on, the wall. **3.** **Courir après qn,** to run after s.o. **Il est toujours après moi,** he is always nagging at me; *F:* he is always at me. **4.** *Prep.phr.* **D'après,** according to; after; from. *D'a. ce qu'il a dit,* according to what he said. *Peint d'a. nature,* painted from nature. *Paysage d'a. Turner,* landscape after Turner. *D'a. ce que j'ai entendu dire . . .,* from what I heard. . . . **5.** *Après + inf. perf.* **Après avoir dîné,** *il sortit,* after dining he went out.

II. après, *adv.* **1.** (*a*) Afterwards, later. *Parlez d'abord, je parlerai a.,* you speak first, I shall speak afterwards. *Six semaines a. il mourut,* six weeks later he died. **Le jour (d')après,** the next day; the day after. *F:* **Eh bien, et puis après?** well, what about it? **Et après?** what then? (*b*) *Conj.phr.* **Après que,** after, when. *A. que je fus parti,* after I had gone. *Il parlera a. que j'aurai fini,* he will speak when I have done. *Il parla a. que j'eus fini, il a parlé a. que j'ai eu fini,* he spoke when I had done. **2.** *F:* **Tout le monde leur court après,** everybody runs after them.

après-demain, *adv.* The day after to-morrow.

après-dîner, *s.m.* Evening (after dinner). **Discours d'après-dîner,** after-dinner speech.

après-guerre, *s.m.inv.* After-war period; aftermath of war.

après-midi, *s.m.* or *f. inv.* Afternoon. **Cet(te) après-midi,** this afternoon. **Trois heures de l'après-midi,** three p.m.

âpreté [ɑprəte], *s.f.* **1.** Roughness, harshness (of wine, voice, etc.). **2.** Asperity (of tone); sharpness, bitterness (of weather, reproach). **3.** *A. à faire qch.,* ruthlessness, keenness, in doing sth.

à-propos [apropo], *s.m.* **1.** Aptness, suitability (of an expression, etc.). *Le don de l'à-p.,* the knack of saying, doing, the right thing. *Votre observation manque d'à-p.,* your remark is not to the point. **2.** Opportuneness.

apside [apsid], *s.f.* = ABSIDE.

apte [apt], *a.* **1.** *Apte à faire qch., à qch.,* fit, fitted, suited, qualified, to do sth., for sth. **Élève apte,** apt, gifted, pupil. **Peu apte,** poorly gifted. **2.** Apt, suitable (example, etc.). **Peu apte,** unsuitable, irrelevant.

aptère [aptɛːr]. *Ent:* **1.** *a.* Apterous, wingless. **2.** *s.m.pl.* Aptères, aptera.

aptitude [aptityd], *s.f.* Aptitude, natural disposition, fitness (*à*, *pour*, for). *Il a des aptitudes*, he is naturally gifted. *A. à faire qch.*, capacity for doing sth.

aquafortiste [akwafɔrtist], *s.m. & f.* Etcher.

aquaplane [akwaplan], *s.m. Sp:* Surf-board.

aquarelle [akwarɛl], *s.f.* Aquarelle; water-colour. **Peindre à l'aquarelle**, to paint in water-colours.

aquarelliste [akwarelist], *s.m. & f.* Painter in water-colours.

aquarium [akwarjɔm], *s.m.* Aquarium.

aquatique [akwatik], *a.* Aquatic (bird, sport).

aqueduc [ak(ə)dyk], *s.m.* (*a*) Aqueduct. (*b*) Culvert, conduit.

aqueux, -euse [akø, -øːz], *a.* Aqueous, watery.

aquilin [akilɛ̃], *a.* Aquiline (profile, etc.). *Nez a.*, Roman nose.

aquilon [akilɔ̃], *s.m. Lit:* North wind; cutting blast.

arabe [arab]. **I.** *a. & s.* (*a*) Arab (person, horse). (*b*) *a.* Arabian (customs, etc.). **2.** (*a*) *a.* Arabic (language, numerals). (*b*) *s.m.* Arabic.

arabique [arabik], *a.* **Le golfe Arabique**, the Arabian gulf. **Gomme arabique**, gum-arabic.

arable [arabl], *a.* Arable, tillable (land).

arachide [araʃid], *s.f. Bot:* Pea-nut, earth-nut, ground-nut.

arachnides [araknid], *s.m.pl. Z:* Arachnida.

araignée [arɛɲe], *s.f.* **I.** (*a*) Spider. **Toile d'araignée**, cobweb; spider's web. *F:* **Avoir une araignée au plafond**, to have a bee in one's bonnet; to have a screw loose. S.a. FIL, PATTE **I.** (*b*) **Araignée de mer**, spider-crab. **2.** (Spider-like object, instrument) (*a*) Grapnel, drag. (*b*) *Mec.E:* Oil-tracks (of bearing). (*c*) *Veh:* Buggy, spider.

aratoire [aratwaːr], *a.* Agricultural.

arbalète [arbalɛt], *s.f.* Cross-bow.

arbalétrier [arbaletrie], *s.m.* **I.** *A:* Cross-bow-man. **2.** *Const:* Principal rafter (of roof, etc.).

arbitrage [arbitraːʒ], *s.m.* Arbitration. **L'arbitrage de la guerre**, the arbitrament of war.

arbitraire [arbitrɛːr], *a.* **I.** Arbitrary (choice, etc.); discretionary (punishment). *s.m. Laisser qch. à l'a. de qn*, to leave sth. to s.o.'s discretion. **2.** Arbitrary, despotic, overbearing (government, action). *adv.* **-ment.**

arbitral, -aux [arbitral, -o], *a.* **Tribunal arbitral**, court of arbitration.

arbitre¹ [arbiːtr], *s.m.* (*a*) *Jur:* Arbitrator, referee. (*b*) *Games:* Referee, umpire. **Arbitre de lignes**, *Fb:* **arbitre de touche**, linesman; (in Rugby) touch-judge. (*c*) Arbiter (of s.o.'s lot, of fashion).

arbitre², *s.m. Phil:* **Libre arbitre**, free will.

arbitrer [arbitre], *v.tr.* **I.** *Jur:* To arbitrate. **2.** *Games:* To referee (at), umpire (at) (match).

arborer [arbɔre], *v.tr.* To raise, set up; to hoist (flag); to step (mast). *A. l'étendard de la révolte*, to raise the standard of revolt.

arboriculteur [arbɔrikyltœːr], *s.m.* Arboriculturist; nurseryman.

arbouse [arbuːz], *s.f. Bot:* Arbutus berry.

arbousier [arbuzje], *s.m. Bot:* Arbutus, cane-apple.

arbre [arbr], *s.m.* **I.** (*a*) Tree. *A. fruitier*, fruit-tree. *A. vert*, evergreen (tree). *Prov:* **L'arbre ne tombe pas du premier coup**, Rome was not built in a day. **Au fruit on connaît l'arbre**, the tree is known by its fruit. (*b*) **Arbre généalogique**, genealogical tree. (*c*) **Arbre de Noël**, Christmas-tree. **2.** *Mec.E:* Shaft, spindle, axle. *Clockm: etc:* Arbor. *A. fou*, loose shaft. *A. coudé*, *a. manivelle*, crank-shaft. *A. moteur*, driving shaft. *A. de renvoi*, counter-shaft, lay-shaft.

arbreux, -euse [arbrø, -øːz], *a.* Woody, wooded (region).

arbrisseau [arbriso], *s.m.* Shrubby tree.

arbuste [arbyst], *s.m.* Bush; arborescent shrub.

arc [ark], *s.m.* **I.** Bow. **Tirer de l'arc**, to shoot with a bow. **Tir à l'arc**, archery. *F:* **Avoir plus d'une corde à son arc**, to have more than one string to one's bow. **Bander, tendre, l'arc**, to bend, string, the bow. **2.** Arch. (*a*) *Arch:* **Arc plein cintre**, *arc roman*, semicircular arch. **Arc en ogive**, ogival arch. **Poutre en arc**, arched girder. (*b*) **Arc de triomphe**, triumphal arch. **3.** (*a*) *Geom:* Arc (of a circle). (*b*) *El:* **Arc voltaïque**, electric arc. **Lampe à arc**, arc-lamp.

arcade [arkad], *s.f.* **I.** (*a*) Archway. (*b*) *pl.* **Arcades**, arcade. **2.** Arch (of saddle, etc.).

arc-boutant [ar(k)butã], *s.m.* **I.** Flying-buttress. *Civ.E:* Abutment pier. **2.** Strut, stay, spur. *Arcs-boutants d'un parapluie*, stretchers of an umbrella. *pl. Des arcs-boutants.*

arc-bout|er [ar(k)bute], *v.tr.* To buttress, shore up (wall, etc.). *s.m.* **-ement.**
   s'arc-bouter *contre un mur*, to set one's back against a wall (in order to resist a shock, etc.).

arceau [arso], *s.m.* **I.** Arch (of vault). **2.** Ring bow (of padlock); (croquet) hoop.

arc-en-ciel [arkãsjɛl], *s.m.* Rainbow. *pl. Des arcs-en-ciel* [arkãsjɛl].

archaïque [arkaik], *a.* Archaic.

archaïsme [arkaism], *s.m.* Archaism.

archal [arʃal], *s.m.* **Fil d'archal**, brass wire.

archange [arkãːʒ], *s.m.* Archangel.

arche¹ [arʃ], *s.f.* **L'arche de Noé**, Noah's Ark. **L'arche d'alliance**, the Ark of the Covenant.

arche², *s.f.* Arch (of bridge, etc.); (croquet) hoop.

archéo|logie [arkeɔlɔʒi], *s.f.* Archaeology. *a.* **-logique**, -logical. *s.m.* **-logue**, -logist.

archer [arʃe], *s.m.* Archer, bowman.

archet [arʃe], *s.m.* Bow. *A. de violon*, violin bow, *F:* fiddlestick. *Tls:* *A. de foret*, drill-bow. **Scie à archet**, bow-saw.

archevêché [arʃəvɛʃe], *s.m.* **I.** Archbishopric, archdiocese; archsee. **2.** Archbishop's palace.

archevêque [arʃəvɛːk], *s.m.* Archbishop.

archi- [arʃi], *pref.* (Intensive) *Archifou*, stark mad. *Architraître*, arch-traitor. *La salle était pleine et archipleine*, the house was packed and more than packed.

archidiacre [arʃidjakr], *s.m. Ecc:* Archdeacon.

archiduc [arʃidyk], *s.m.* Archduke.

Archimède [arʃimɛd], *Pr.n.m. Gr.Hist:* Archimedes. **Vis d'Archimède**, Archimedean screw.

archipel [arʃipɛl], *s.m. Geog:* Archipelago.

archiprêtre [arʃiprɛːtr], *s.m. Ecc:* Archpriest.

architecte [arʃitɛkt], *s.m.* Architect.

architecture [arʃitɛktyːr], *s.f.* Architecture.

architrave [arʃitraːv], *s.f. Arch:* Architrave.

archives [arʃiːv], *s.f.pl.* Archives. **I.** Records. **2. Les Archives** = the Record Office.

archiviste [arʃivist], *s.m. & f.* **I.** (*a*) Archivist; keeper of public records. (*b*) Palaeographer. **2.** *Com: etc:* Filing clerk.

arçon [arsɔ̃], *s.m.* **I.** *Harn:* Saddle-bow. *A. de devant*, pommel. *A. de derrière*, cantle. **Vider les arçons**, to be unhorsed, thrown; to take a toss. **2.** *Tls:* Foret à arçon, fiddle-drill, bow-drill.

arctique [arktik], *a. Geog:* Arctic.

ard|ent [ardã], *a.* **I.** Burning, hot, scorching, blazing (fire, etc.). *Charbons ardents*, live coals. *Fournaise ardente*, fiery furnace. *Rouge a.*, fiery red. **2.** Ardent, passionate, eager. *Cheval a.*, fiery, high-mettled, horse. *A. radical*, red-hot Radical. *A. sportif*, keen sportsman. *A. à la poursuite*, eager in pursuit. *adv.* **-emment.**

ardeur [ardœːr], *s.f.* **I.** Heat (of sun, fire). **2.** Eagerness, ardour. **Faire qch. avec ardeur,** to do sth. fervently, earnestly, with zeal. *A. à faire qch.,* eagerness to do sth. ; keenness on doing sth.

ardoise [ardwaːz], *s.f.* Slate. **(Couleur) gris ardoise,** slate-grey (colour). *Couvrir un toit en a.,* to slate a roof. **Ardoise à écrire,** writing slate. **Crayon d'ardoise,** slate-pencil. *F:* **Inscrire les consommations à l'ardoise,** to chalk up the drinks.

ardoiser [ardwaze], *v.tr.* To slate (roof).

ardoisière [ardwazjɛːr], *s.f.* Slate-quarry.

ardu [ardy], *a.* **I.** Steep, abrupt, difficult (path, etc.). **2.** Arduous, difficult, hard (task, etc.).

arduité [ardyite], *s.f.* Arduousness, difficulty.

are [aːr], *s.m. Meas:* (Land-measurement unit of) 100 square metres (= about 4 poles).

arec [arɛk], *s.m.* Areca palm-tree. **Noix d'arec,** areca-nut, betel-nut.

arène [arɛn], *s.f.* **I.** *Lit:* Sand. **2.** Arena. *F:* **Descendre dans l'arène,** to enter the lists, the fray. **Les arènes d'Arles,** the amphitheatre of Arles.

aréole [areɔl], *s.f.* **I.** *Anat: etc:* Areola. **2.** Halo, nimbus, ring (round the moon).

aréomètre [areɔmɛtr], *s.m. Ph: etc:* Hydrometer, areometer.

aréquier [arekje], *s.m. Bot:* Areca palm-tree.

Arès [arɛːs]. *Pr.n.m. Gr.Myth:* Ares, Mars.

arête [arɛt], *s.f.* **I.** *(a)* (Fish-)bone. **Grande arête,** backbone (of fish). **Dessin en arête de hareng,** herring-bone pattern. *(b)* Rib (of sword-blade). **2.** Line ; solid angle of intersection (of two surfaces) ; edge, arris (of beam, etc.) ; bead, chamfer, or nosing (of moulding). *A. vive,* sharp edge. *A. d'une chaîne de montagnes,* ridge, watershed, of a mountain range. *A. du nez,* bridge of the nose. *A. d'un comble,* hip of a roof. *Arch: A. de voûte,* groin, (groin-)rib, of an arch. **3.** Beard, awn (of ear of wheat).

argent [arʒɑ̃], *s.m.* **I.** Silver. **Argent orfévré,** vaisselle d'argent, (silver-)plate. **2.** Money, cash. *A. liquide,* ready money, cash (in hand). *Gagner de l'a.,* to make money. **Faire argent de tout,** to turn everything into cash. *F:* **Avoir un argent fou,** to have tons of money. **Être tout cousu d'argent,** to be rolling in wealth. **Jeter son argent par la fenêtre,** to squander one's money. **L'argent lui fond entre les mains,** he spends money like water. **En avoir pour son argent,** to have one's money's worth. **Avoir toujours de l'argent à la main,** to be always paying out. *Prov:* **Point d'argent point de Suisse,** nothing for nothing. S.a. COMPTANT I. **3.** *Her:* Argent.

argenter [arʒɑ̃te], *v.tr.* To silver. *F: La lune argentait les flots,* the moon cast a silver shimmer on the waves.

argenté, *a.* **I.** Silver(ed), silvery. **2.** Silver-plated. **3.** *F: Se trouver bien a.,* to be very flush (of money).

argenterie [arʒɑ̃tri], *s.f.* (Silver-)plate.

argentin[1], -ine [arʒɑ̃tɛ̃, -in], *a.* Silvery (waves) ; silver-toned (voice) ; tinkling (bell).

argentin[2], -ine [arʒɑ̃tɛ̃, -in], *a. & s. Geog:* Argentine, of Argentina. **La République Argentine,** the Argentine Republic.

argile [arʒil], *s.f.* *(a)* Clay. *(b)* **Argile cuite,** terra-cotta, earthenware.

argileux, -euse [arʒilø, -øːz], *a.* Clayey (soil).

argon [arʒɔ̃], *s.m. Ch:* Argon.

argonaute [argonoːt], *s.m.* **I.** *Myth:* Argonaut. **2.** *Moll:* Argonaut ; paper nautilus.

argot [argo], *s.m.* Slang. *A. de voleurs,* thieves' cant.

argotique [argɔtik], *a.* Slangy (language).

argousier [arguzje], *s.m. Bot:* Sallow thorn.

argousin [arguzɛ̃], *s.m. A:* **I.** Warder (in convict prison). **2.** *P:* Policeman. **3.** *P:* Lout, lubber.

arguer [argɥe], *v.* (j'arguë [ʒargy] ; n. arguïons [nuzargyjɔ̃]) **I.** *v.tr.* To infer, assert, deduce. *A. qch. d'un fait,* to infer, deduce, sth. from a fact. **2.** *v.i.* To argue. *A. sur tout,* to argue about everything. *Il argua de ma jeunesse pour m'exclure,* he made my youthfulness a reason for excluding me. *s.m.* **-eur.**

argument [argymɑ̃], *s.m.* **I.** Argument. **Par manière d'argument,** for argument's sake. **2.** Outline, summary (of book, etc.) ; synopsis (of contents). **3.** *Mth: etc:* *(a)* Argument ; variable. *(b)* Heading (of tables).

argument|er [argymɑ̃te]. **I.** *v.i.* *(a)* To argue (*contre,* against). *(b)* *F:* To argufy. **2.** *v.tr. A. qn,* to remonstrate with s.o. *s.* **-ateur, -atrice.** *s.f.* **-ation.**

Argus [argyːs]. *Pr.n.m. Myth:* Argus. **Aux yeux d'Argus,** Argus-eyed. *F: A. de la police,* police spy.

argutie [argysi], *s.f.* Quibble ; cavil(ling).

aria [arja], *s.m. F:* Fuss, bother. **Ne faites pas tant d'arias,** don't make so many bones about it.

Ariane [arjan]. *Pr.n.f. Gr.Myth:* Ariadne.

arianisme [arjanism], *s.m. Ecc.Hist:* Arianism.

arid|e [arid], *a.* Arid, dry, barren (country, subject, etc.). *s.f.* **-ité.**

arien, -ienne [arjɛ̃, -jɛn], *a. & s. Ecc.Hist:* Arian.

Arioste (l') [larjɔst]. *Pr.n.m.* Ariosto.

aristo [aristo], *s.m. P:* Toff, swell.

aristocrate [aristɔkrat], *s.m. & f.* Aristocrat.

aristocratie [aristɔkrasi], *s.f.* Aristocracy.

aristocratique [aristɔkratik], *a.* Aristocratic. *adv.* **-ment,** -ally.

aristoloche [aristɔlɔʃ], *s.f. Bot:* Aristolochia, birthwort.

Aristophane [aristɔfan]. *Pr.n.m. Gr.Lit:* Aristophanes.

Aristote [aristɔt]. *Pr.n.m. Gr.Phil:* Aristotle.

aristotélicien, -ienne [aristɔtelisjɛ̃, -jɛn], *a. & s.* Aristotelian.

arithméticien, -ienne [aritmetisjɛ̃, -jɛn], *s.* Arithmetician.

arithmétique [aritmetik]. **I.** *a.* Arithmetical. **2.** *s.f.* Arithmetic. **Faire de l'arithmétique,** to do sums.

arlequin [arləkɛ̃], *s.m.* **I.** *(a)* *Th:* Harlequin. **Manteau d'arlequin,** proscenium arch. *(b)* *F:* Inconsequent person, weathercock. **2.** (Plate of) broken meat ; scraps (sold off by the larger restaurants to small eating-houses).

arlequinade [arləkinad], *s.f.* *(a)* *Th:* Harlequinade. *(b)* *F:* (Piece of) buffoonery.

arlésien, -ienne [arlezjɛ̃, -jɛn], *a. & s. Geog:* Arlesian ; of Arles.

armadille [armadiːj], *s.m. or f. Crust:* Armadillo wood-louse.

armateur [armatœːr], *s.m. Nau:* *(a)* Fitter-out (of ship, expedition). *(b)* (Ship-)owner.

armature [armatyːr], *s.f.* **I.** Framework, brace, armature (of window, etc.) ; reinforcement (of concrete work) ; truss (of girder, etc.). *A. d'une raquette,* frame of a (tennis) racquet. **2.** Armouring (of electric cable). **3.** *El:* *(a)* Armature (of magnet, magneto). *(b)* Plate (of condenser). **4.** *Mus:* Key-signature.

arme [arm], *s.f.* **I.** Arm, weapon. **Armes à feu,** fire-arms. **Armes portatives,** small arms. **Armes blanches,** side arms. **Faire des armes,** to fence, go in for fencing. **Salle d'armes,** (i) armoury, (ii) fencing-school. **Maître d'armes,** fencing-master. **Hommes sous les armes,** men under arms. *Appeler la réserve sous les armes,* to call up the reserve. **Prendre les armes,** to take up arms. *F:* **Mettre bas les armes,** to cease from strife. **Aux armes!** to arms! **Faire ses premières armes sous qn,** to go through one's first campaign under s.o. **Suspension d'armes,** cessation of hostilities. *Le métier des armes,* soldiering. *Mil:* **Place d'armes,** parade-ground. **Passer par les armes,** to be (court-martialled and) shot. *Mil:* **Portez armes!** shoulder arms! S.a. PORT² 1, RENDRE 4. **2.** Arm (as a branch of the army). *Douze mille hommes de toutes armes,* twelve-thousand men of all arms. **3.** *pl. Her:* Arms. *Peint aux armes de la ville,* emblazoned with the arms of the town.

armée [arme], *s.f.* (a) Army. *A.* **permanente,** standing, regular, army. *A.* **navale,** naval forces. S.a. MÉTIER 1. (b) **L'Éternel des armées,** the Lord of Hosts. **L'Armée du Salut,** the Salvation Army.

armement [arməmã], *s.m.* **1.** (a) Arming; war preparations. **Ministère de l'Armement,** Ministry of Munitions. (b) *pl.* Armaments. **2.** Fortifying, strengthening; bracing (of girder); sheathing (of cable). **3.** *Nau:* (a) (i) Commissioning, fitting out; (ii) equipment, gear, stores. **Mettre un navire en armement,** to put a ship in commission. **Port d'armement,** port of registry. (b) (i) Manning, (ii) crew (of boat, gun). **4.** (a) Loading (of gun); arming (of fuse). (b) Setting (of camera-shutter, etc.); cocking (of loaded fire-arm). **5.** Fittings, mounting, gear.

Arménie [armeni]. *Pr.n.f. Geog:* Armenia.

arménien, -ienne [armenjẽ, -jɛn], *a. & s.* Armenian.

armer [arme]. I. *v.tr.* **1.** To arm (de, with). *Armé de pleins pouvoirs,* armed with full powers. **2.** (a) *A:* **Armer qn chevalier,** to dub s.o. a knight. (b) To fortify, strengthen, brace. **Poutre armée,** trussed beam. **Béton armé,** reinforced concrete. *A. un câble,* to sheathe, armour, a cable. **3.** *Nau:* (a) To equip, fit out, commission (ship). (b) To man (boat, prize, winch). (c) *A. les avirons,* to ship the oars. **4.** (a) *A. un canon,* to load a gun. (b) To set (an apparatus, *e.g.* camera-shutter); to cock (fire-arm). **5.** *Mus:* *A. la clef,* to put the key-signature (to a piece of music).
II. **armer,** *v.i.* **1.** *Mil:* To arm, prepare for war. **2.** *Nau:* *Le navire arme à Brest,* the ship is being commissioned at Brest.
s'armer. **1.** *S'a. d'un revolver, etc.,* to arm oneself with a revolver, etc. **2.** *S'a. de patience,* to take patience. *S'a. de tout son courage,* to summon up all one's courage.

armistice [armistis], *s.m.* Armistice. **Anniversaire de l'Armistice,** Armistice Day.

armoire [armwar], *s.f.* **1.** (a) Clothes-press. (b) Wardrobe. **Armoire à glace,** mirror-wardrobe. **2.** (a) Cupboard. *A. de cuisine,* kitchen-press. (b) *A. frigorifique,* ice-chest.

armoiries [armwari], *s.f.pl. Her:* (Coat of) arms; armorial bearings.

armoise [armwa:z], *s.f. Bot:* Artemisia.

armoricain, -aine [armɔrikẽ, -ɛn], *a. & s.* Armorican. *Lit:* **Le Cycle armoricain,** the Breton cycle.

armorier [armɔrje], *v.tr.* To (em)blazon; to adorn (sth.) with heraldic bearings.

Armorique [armɔrik]. *Pr.n.f. A.Geog:* Armorica.

armure [army:r], *s.f.* (a) Armour. *A.* **complète,** suit of armour. (b) *A. d'un cuirassé,* armour (-plating) of an iron-clad.

armurerie [armyr(ə)ri], *s.f.* **1.** Manufacture of arms. **2.** Arms factory. **3.** (a) Gunsmith's shop. (b) (In barracks) Armoury.

armurier [armyrje], *s.m.* **1.** Gunsmith. **2.** *Mil: Navy:* Armourer.

arnica [arnika], *s.f. Bot: Pharm:* Arnica.

aromate [arɔmat], *s.m.* Aromatic; spice.

aromatique [arɔmatik], *a.* Aromatic.

aromatiser [arɔmatize], *v.tr.* To aromatize.

arome [aro:m], *s.m.* **1.** Aroma. **2.** *Cu:* Flavouring.

aronde [arɔ̃:d], *s.f.* **1.** *Orn: A:* Swallow. **2.** *Carp:* **Queue d'aronde,** dovetail.

arpège [arpɛ:ʒ], *s.m.* Arpeggio; spread chord.

arpent [arpɑ̃], *s.m.* (Old French measure, roughly =) Acre. *F: Il est fier de ses arpents,* he is proud of his broad acres.

arpent|er [arpɑ̃te], *v.tr.* **1.** To survey, measure (land). **2.** *F:* **Arpenter le terrain,** to walk, stride along. *s.m.* **-age.**

arpenteur [arpɑ̃tœ:r], *s.m.* (Land-)surveyor. S.a. CHAÎNE 1. *F:* **Un grand arpenteur de terrain,** a great walker.

arpète, arpette [arpɛt], *s.f. P:* Milliner's apprentice; errand-girl.

arquebuse [arkəby:z], *s.f. A:* (H)arquebus.

arquer [arke]. **1.** *v.tr.* To bend, arch, curve (wood, iron, etc.); to camber (surface). *A. le dos,* to bend, hump, the back. **2.** *v.i.* To bend; to sag; to buckle.
s'arquer, (of the legs, back, etc.) to bend; to become bent.

arqué, *a.* Arched, curved; cambered (beam, etc.); high-bridged (nose).

arrache-clou(s), *s.m.inv. Tls:* Nail-drawer.

arrache-pied (d') [daraʃpje], *adv.phr.* Without interruption. *Travailler d'a.-p.,* to work steadily.

arrach|er [araʃe], *v.tr.* To tear (out, up, away); to pull (up, out, away); to draw (nail). *A. un arbre,* to root up, uproot, a tree. *A. qch. de qch.,* to pull sth. off, from, out of sth. *A. qch. à qn,* des mains de qn, to snatch sth. from s.o., out of s.o.'s hands. *A. le papier d'un mur,* to strip a wall. *A. une dent à qn,* to pull (out), extract, draw, s.o.'s tooth. *Se faire a. une dent,* to have a tooth out. *S'a. les cheveux,* to tear one's hair. *A. qn à la mort,* to snatch, rescue, s.o. from the jaws of death. *S'a. de ses livres,* to tear oneself away from one's books. *F: Cela lui arrache le cœur de . . . ,* it breaks his heart to. . . . *F:* **On se l'arrache,** he, she, is in great request. *s.m.* **-age.** *s.m.* **-ement.**

arracheur, -euse [araʃœ:r, -ø:z], *s.* Puller. *F:* **Arracheur de dents,** tooth-drawer. **Il ment, il est menteur, comme un arracheur de dents,** he is an arrant liar.

arraisonn|er [arɛzɔne], *v.tr. Nau:* *A. un navire,* (i) to hail, speak, a vessel (as to her destination, etc.); (ii) to stop and examine a ship. [RAISONNER] *s.m.* **-ement.**

arrangeant [arɑ̃ʒɑ̃], *a.* Accommodating, obliging.

arrangement [arɑ̃ʒmɑ̃], *s.m.* Arrangement. (a) *A. des mots dans une phrase,* (i) ordering, (ii) order, of the words in a sentence. **Mal prendre ses arrangements,** to make bad arrangements. (b) Agreement. *Prendre un a. avec qn,* to come to an arrangement, to terms, with s.o. *A. avec ses créanciers,* composition with one's creditors.

arranger [arɑ̃ʒe], *v.tr.* (j'arrangeais; n. arrangeons) To arrange. **1.** To set in order. *A. une bibliothèque,* to arrange a library. *A. sa cravate,* to put one's tie straight. *S'a. les cheveux,* to tidy one's hair. *A. une chambre,* to tidy up a room.

Bien arrangé, tidy. *F :* Je l'ai arrangé de la belle manière, I gave him a good dressing-down. 2. To contrive. *A. une fête,* to get up an entertainment. *Tout a. d'avance,* to plan everything ahead. 3. To settle (quarrel). 4. *Faire qch. pour a. qn,* to do sth. to accommodate s.o.

s'arranger. 1. To manage, contrive. *Arrangez-vous comme vous pourrez,* manage as best you can. *S'a. de ce qu'on a,* to make shift with what one has. *Il s'arrange de tout,* he is easily pleased, very adaptable. *Qu'il s'arrange!* that's his look-out! 2. *S'a. avec qn,* to come to an agreement, to terms, with s.o. *S'a. avec ses créanciers,* to compound with one's creditors.

arrérages [arera:ʒ], *s.m.pl.* Arrears.

arrestation [arɛstasjɔ̃], *s.f.* Arrest. Opérer une arrestation, to effect an arrest. Mettre qn en arrestation, to take s.o. into custody. En état d'arrestation, under arrest.

arrêt [arɛ], *s.m.* 1. Stop, stoppage; stopping, arrest (of motion). *A. d'un train,* stopping of a train. Point d'arrêt, (i) stopping place, stop-point, (ii) *Mus:* pause (over a rest). Sa langue marchait sans arrêt, her tongue ran on without a stop. *Trajet sans a.,* non-stop journey. Moment d'arrêt, short stop; pause. *Dix minutes d'a.,* ten minutes' stop. *Phot:* Bain d'arrêt, stop-bath. *Mch:* Arrêt inopiné, break-down. *Rail:* Signal à l'arrêt, signal at danger. "Arrêt fixe," 'all cars stop here.' 2. (*a*) Decree; general order. *Les arrêts de la Providence,* the decrees of Providence. (*b*) *Jur:* Judgment (delivered by a higher court). Prononcer, rendre, un arrêt, to pronounce judgment. *A. par défaut,* judgment by default. Arrêt de mort, sentence of death. 3. Seizure, impounding, attachment. Faire arrêt sur les marchandises, to attach, seize, goods. Mettre arrêt sur un navire, to put an embargo on a ship. 4. Arrest. (*a*) Mandat d'arrêt, warrant (for arrest). Lancer un mandat d'arrêt contre qn, to issue a warrant for the arrest of s.o. Maison d'arrêt, gaol. (*b*) *pl.* Mettre un officier, un élève, aux arrêts, to put an officer under arrest; to keep a pupil in rest. Garder les arrêts, to be under arrest. 5. *A:* Lance en arrêt, lance in rest. 6. (*a*) *Rugby Fb:* (i) Tackle. (ii) Arrêt de volée, fair catch. (*b*) Coup d'arrêt, *Box:* counter; *Fenc:* stop-thrust. 7. *Ven:* Set. Chien d'arrêt, setter, pointer.

arrêter [arɛte]. I. *v.tr.* 1. To stop (s.o., sth.); to check (attack); to hinder, impede; to detain, delay. *A. un cheval,* to stop, pull up, a horse. *A. qn tout court,* to stop s.o. short. *Quel obstacle vous arrête?* what is stopping you? *Cela a tout arrêté,* that put a stop to everything. *A. qn de faire qch.,* to hinder, prevent, s.o. from doing sth. *A. un mouvement,* to arrest a motion. *A. la croissance,* to arrest growth. *La flotte était arrêtée par le mauvais temps,* the fleet was weather-bound. 2. To fix, fasten (shutter, etc.). *A. ses yeux, ses soupçons, sur qn,* to fix one's eyes, one's suspicions, on s.o. *A. l'attention,* to arrest attention. 3. To arrest, seize (malefactor, s.o.'s goods); to apprehend (malefactor). Faire arrêter qn, to give s.o. into custody. 4. (*a*) To engage, hire (room, seat, servant). (*b*) To decide (sth.). *A. un jour,* to fix, appoint, a day. *A. un programme,* to draw up, settle, a programme.

II. **arrêter,** *v.i.* To stop, halt. *Arrêtez un moment,* stop a moment. *Elle n'arrête jamais de parler,* she never stops talking.

s'arrêter. 1. To stop; to come to a stop, to a standstill. *Être forcé de s'a.,* to be brought to a stand. *S'a. court,* to stop short. *S'a. en route,* to break one's journey. *S'a. de faire qch.,* to stop,

leave off, doing sth. *S'a. à contempler qch.,* to stop in contemplation before sth. 2. (*a*) *S'a. à, sur, un sujet,* to lay stress on, dwell on, a subject. (*b*) *Son regard s'arrêta sur moi,* he eyed me intently.

arrêté. 1. *a.* (*a*) (Of ideas, etc.) Fixed, decided. *Homme aux opinions arrêtées,* dogmatic person. *Dessein a.,* settled design. (*b*) *Sp:* Départ arrêté, standing start. 2. *s.m.* Decision, order, decree. Prendre un arrêté, to pass a decree.

arrhes [a:r], *s.f.pl.* (*a*) Earnest (money). (*b*) Deposit.

arrière [arjɛ:r]. 1. *adv.* (En) arrière. (*a*) Behind. Rester en a., to remain, lag, behind. *Nau:* Droit a., right abaft. *Avoir le vent en a.,* to have the wind astern. *Prep.phr.* En arrière de qch., behind sth. *En a. de son siècle,* behind the times. (*b*) In arrears. *Locataire en a. pour ses loyers,* tenant behindhand with his rent. (*c*) Backwards; backward (motion). Arrière! back! *Faire un pas en a.,* to step back a pace. Aller en arrière, to back. *Nau:* En arrière à toute vitesse! full speed astern! Marche (en) arrière, (i) backing (of engine); (ii) *Nau:* motion astern. Entrer dans le garage en marche a., to back into the garage. Faire marche arrière, to back; *Nau:* to go astern; *Aut:* to reverse. 2. *a.inv.* Back. Essieu arrière, rear axle. *Aut:* Lanterne arrière, rear light. 3. *s.m.* (*a*) Back, back part (of house, carriage, etc.). (*b*) *Nau:* Stern (of ship). Vers l'arrière, aft, abaft. (*c*) Arrears. Avoir de l'arrière, to be behindhand. 4. *Fb:* Back.

arriéré [arjere], *a.* 1. In arrears; behindhand; (payment) overdue. 2. Backward (child); (person) behind the times; old-fashioned (notion).

NOTE. In all the following compounds ARRIÈRE is inv., the noun takes the plural.

arrière-automne, *s.m.* Late autumn; back-end (of the year).

arrière-ban, *s.m. Hist:* Whole body of vassals (including the second levy); arrière-ban. *F:* Une équipe d'arrière-ban, a scratch team. *S.a.* BAN 3.

arrière-bec, *s.m.* Back starling; down-stream cutwater (of bridge pier).

arrière-boutique, *s.f.* Back-shop.

arrière-bras, *s.m.* Upper arm.

arrière-cour, *s.f.* Back-yard.

arrière-cousin, -ine, *s.* Distant cousin.

arrière-défense, *s.f. Fb:* (The) back-line defence; the backs.

arrière-garde, *s.f.* 1. *Mil:* Rear-guard. 2. *Navy:* Rear-division (of squadron).

arrière-gorge, *s.f.* Back of the throat.

arrière-goût, *s.m.* After-taste, faint taste.

arrière-grand-père, -grand'mère, *s.* Great-grandfather, -grandmother.

arrière-main, *s.m.* or *f.* 1. (*a*) Back of the hand. (*b*) *Ten:* Coup d'arrière-main, back-hand stroke. 2. (Hind)quarters (of horse).

arrière-neveu, -nièce, *s.* Grand-nephew, -niece.

arrière-pensée, *s.f.* 1. (*a*) Mental reservation. (*b*) Ulterior motive. 2. *J'ai cette a.-p. que . . . ,* I have a notion at the back of my mind that. . . .

arrière-petit-fils, -petite-fille, *s.* Great-grandson, -granddaughter.

arrière-pièce, *s.f.* Back apartment.

arrière-plan, *s.m.* Background. A l'arrière-plan, in the background; *Th:* up-stage, at the back. Artiste d'arrière-plan, artist not in the front rank.

arrière-port, *s.m.* Inner harbour.

arrière-rang, *s.m.* Rear rank.

arrière-saison, *s.f.* Late season, end of autumn, back-end (of the year).

arrière-scène, *s.f.* Th: **1.** Back of the stage. **2.** Back curtain.

arrière-train, *s.m.* **1.** (Hind)quarters (of animal). **2.** Veh: Waggon-body; hind-carriage.

arrim|er [arime], *v.tr.* (a) To stow (cargo). (b) To trim (ship). *s.m.* **-age.**

arrimeur [arimœːr], *s.m.* Nau: (a) Stower, trimmer. (b) Stevedore.

arrivage [arivaːʒ], *s.m.* Arrival (of fish, goods, etc.); new consignment (of goods).

arrivant [arivã], *s.m.* Person arriving; arrival. *Le dernier a.,* the last comer.

arrivée [arive], *s.f.* **1.** Arrival, coming, advent. *On attend son a. pour la semaine prochaine,* he is expected to arrive next week. *A mon a.,* on my arrival. **2.** Mch: Intake, admission. **3.** Sp: (Winning-)post. *Ligne d'arrivée,* finishing line.

arriver [arive], *v.i.* (Aux. *être*) **1.** (a) To arrive, come. *Il arriva en courant,* he came running up. *Il arrive de voyage,* he is just back from a journey. *Les voilà qui arrivent,* here they come. F: *Arrivez!* come on! *Il arrive donner sa leçon,* he has come to give his lesson. *La nuit arriva,* night came on. S.a. MARÉE 2, MARS 2. Impers. *Il arriva un soldat qui . . .,* there came a soldier who. . . . (b) *A. à un endroit,* to reach a place. **Arriver à bon port,** to arrive safely, duly. *A. à la vérité,* to arrive at, get at, the truth. *A. d l'âge de discrétion,* to come to, arrive at, years of discretion. *A. à un grand âge,* to attain, reach, a great age. *A. jusqu'au ministre,* to manage to see, to obtain an interview with, the minister. (c) **En arriver.** *J'en étais arrivé là lorsque . . .,* I had got thus far when. . . . *Il en était arrivé à demander l'aumône,* he was reduced to begging. *Il faudra bien en a. là,* it must come to that. **2.** To succeed. (a) *Avec du courage on arrive à tout,* with courage one can achieve anything. *C'est un (homme) arrivé,* he's a made man. *Il n'arrivera jamais à rien,* he will never come to, achieve, anything. (b) **Arriver à faire qch.,** to manage to do sth.; to succeed in doing sth. **3.** To happen. *Cela arrive tous les jours,* it happens every day. Prov: **Un malheur n'arrive jamais seul,** misfortunes never come singly. F: *Il croit que c'est arrivé,* he takes it all for gospel truth. Impers. *Il lui est arrivé un accident, un malheur,* he has met with an accident; a disaster has befallen him. *Il m'arrive souvent d'oublier,* I often forget; I am apt to forget. **Faire arriver qch.,** to bring sth. to pass. *Faire a. un accident,* to cause an accident.

arriviste [arivist], *s.m. & f.* Man, woman, of unscrupulous ambition; thruster.

arroche [arɔʃ], *s.f.* Bot: Orach.

arrogance [arɔɡãːs], *s.f.* Arrogance; overbearing manner.

arrog|ant [arɔɡã], *a.* Arrogant, overbearing. *adv.* **-amment.**

arroger (s') [sarɔʒe], *v.tr.pr.* (je m'arrogeai(s); n.n. arrogeons) *S'a. un droit, un privilège,* to arrogate a right, a privilege, to oneself; to assume a right. F: *S'a. la meilleure chambre,* to take the best room as a matter of course.

arrondir [arɔ̃diːr], *v.tr.* **1.** (a) To round (sth.) (off); to make (sth.) round. *A. sa fortune,* to round off one's fortune. *Yeux arrondis, bouche arrondie, par l'étonnement,* eyes round, mouth agape, with astonishment. (b) *A. ses manières,* to cultivate an easy manner. *Phrase bien arrondie,*

well-rounded sentence. **2.** Nau: *A. un cap,* to round, double, a cape. [ROND]

s'arrondir, to become round; to fill out.

arrondi, *a.* Rounded, round (chin, tool, etc.). *Nombres arrondis,* round numbers.

arrondissement [arɔ̃dismã], *s.m.* **1.** Rounding (off) (of sentence, territory, etc.). **2.** Fr.Adm: Each of the main subdivisions of a department; ward (in Paris).

arros|er [aroze], *v.tr.* (a) To water (streets, plants); to sprinkle, spray (lawn). *A. un rôti,* to baste a joint. F: *Yeux arrosés de larmes,* eyes bathed in tears. **Arroser ses galons,** to wet one's stripes; to pay one's footing. (b) *A. une prairie,* to irrigate a meadow. (c) F: To water, dilute (wine, milk). *s.m.* **-age.** *s.m.* **-ement.**

arroseur [arozœːr], *s.m.* Street-orderly, water-cart man.

arrosoir [arozwaːr], *s.m.* (a) Watering-pot, -can. (b) Sprinkler, spreader (of shower-bath, etc.).

arsenal, -aux [arsənal, -o], *s.m.* (a) Arsenal. (b) *A. maritime,* naval dockyard.

arsenic [arsənik], *s.m.* Arsenic.

arsouille [arsuːj]. P: **1.** *a.* Blackguardly, crapulous. **2.** *s.* Blackguard.

art [aːr], *s.m.* **1.** Art. (a) *L'art militaire, l'art de guerre,* the art of war, warcraft. **Arts d'agrément,** accomplishments. *L'art de faire qch.,* the art of doing sth. (b) **Beaux-arts,** fine arts. **Œuvre d'art,** work of art. **2.** Skill, dexterity; artistry. *Art à faire qch.,* art, skill, in doing sth. Civ.E: *Travaux, ouvrages, d'art,* (generic term for) bridges, viaducts, tunnels, etc.; constructive works. **Terme d'art,** technical term. S.a. MÉTIER 1.

artère [artɛːr], *s.f.* **1.** Anat: Artery. **2.** Channel of communication (in country); thoroughfare (in town).

artériel, -elle [arterjɛl], *a.* Arterial.

artésien, -ienne [artezjɛ̃, -jɛn], *a. & s.* Artesian; of Artois. **Puits artésien,** Artesian well.

arthrite [artrit], *s.f.* Med: Arthritis.

arthritique [artritik], *a. & s.* Med: Arthritic (patient).

arthropode [artrɔpɔd], *s.m.* Arthropod, *pl.* arthropoda.

artichaut [artiʃo], *s.m.* Globe artichoke; leaf artichoke. Cu: *Fonds d'artichauts,* artichoke bottoms.

article [artikl], *s.m.* **1.** (a) Bot: Ent: Joint, article. (b) (Critical point, moment) **Être à l'article de la mort,** to be in the article of death, at the point of death. **2.** (a) Article, clause (of treaty, etc.). *A. de foi,* article of faith. (b) **Articles de dépense,** items of expenditure. (c) Article (in newspaper, etc.). S.a. FOND 2. **3.** Com: Article, commodity; *pl.* goods, wares. **Article(s) de Paris,** fancy goods. **Faire l'article,** to puff one's goods. **4.** Gram: **Article défini, indéfini,** definite, indefinite, article.

articulaire [artikylɛːr], *a.* Articular; of the joints. *Rhumatisme a.,* rheumatism in the joints.

articulation [artikylasjɔ̃], *s.f.* **1.** (a) Anat: Articulation, joint. Bot: Node. (b) Connection, joint, link, hinge. *Accouplement à a.,* jointed coupling. *A. à rotule,* ball-and-socket joint. **2.** Articulation, utterance; (manner of) speech.

articuler [artikyle], *v.tr.* **1.** To articulate, hinge, link, joint; to connect by joints. **2.** To articulate; to utter or pronounce distinctly.

s'articuler. (Of bone) *S'a. avec un autre os,* to be jointed, to hinge, with another bone.

articulé. **1.** *a.* (a) Articulate(d); jointed (limb, coupling, etc.); hinged. (b) Articulate

artifice [artifis], _s.m._ **1.** Artifice; artificial means; guile; (guileful) expedient, contrivance. _A. de guerre_, artifice of war; stratagem. **2.** Feu d'artifice, fireworks. _Tirer un feu d'a._, to let off fireworks.

artifici|el, -elle [artifisjɛl], _a._ Artificial. **1.** _(a)_ _Lumière artificielle_, artificial light. _(b)_ _Rire a._, forced laugh. _Style a._, artificial, unnatural, style. **2.** Imitation (pearl, etc.); false (teeth, etc.). _adv._ **-ellement.**

artificieu|x, -euse [artifisjø, -ø:z], _a._ Crafty, artful, cunning, guileful. _adv._ **-sement.**

artillerie [artijri], _s.f._ **1.** Artillery, ordnance. _A. de campagne_, field-artillery. _A. lourde_, heavy artillery. **Pièce d'artillerie**, piece of ordnance. **2.** Gunnery.

artilleur [artijœːr], _s.m._ Artilleryman; gunner.

artimon [artimɔ̃], _s.m._ _Nau:_ (Mât d')artimon, mizzen-mast. _Voile d'a._, mizzen(-sail).

artisan [artizɑ̃], _s.m._ **1.** Artisan, craftsman; working man. **2.** Maker, contriver. Il a été l'artisan de ses propres malheurs, he owes his misfortunes to himself. _Il a été l'a. de sa fortune_, he is a self-made man.

artisanat [artizana], _s.m._ The working classes.

artiste [artist]. **1.** _s.m. & f._ _(a)_ Artist (including musician, etc.). _(b)_ _Th: Mus:_ Performer. _(c)_ _Th:_ Artiste (of variety stage). **2.** _a._ Artistic (temperament, style). _adv._ **-ment.**

artistique [artistik], _a._ Artistic (furniture, arrangement, etc.). _adv._ **-ment.**

aruspice [aryspis], _s.m._ _Rom.Ant:_ Haruspex.

aryanisme [arjanism], _s.m._ _Ethn:_ Aryanism.

aryen, -yenne [arjɛ̃, -jɛn], _a. & s._ _Ethn: Ling:_ Aryan; Indo-European.

as¹ [ɑːs], _s.m._ **1.** _(a)_ _Dice: Cards:_ Ace. **As de pique**, ace of spades. _P:_ Veiller à l'as, to be on the look-out. _P:_ Être aux as, to have plenty of money. _(b)_ _F:_ L'as, (table) No. 1 (in restaurants, etc.). **2.** _(a)_ _Av:_ (Military aviator who has brought down ten or more enemy machines) Ace. _(b)_ _F:_ First-rater. _Games:_ Crack player. _Aut:_ As du volant, crack racing driver.

as² [a]. See AVOIR.

asbeste [azbɛst, as-], _s.m._ _Miner:_ Asbestos.

ascaride [askarid], _s.m._ _Med:_ Ascaris; _F:_ threadworm.

ascendance [as(s)ɑ̃dɑ̃ːs], _s.f._ **1.** _Astr:_ Ascent. **2.** Ancestry.

ascendant [as(s)ɑ̃dɑ̃]. **1.** _a._ Ascending, upward (motion, etc.). _Av:_ Vol ascendant, climbing flight. _Mch:_ Course ascendante, up-stroke (of piston). _Mth:_ Progression ascendante, increasing series. **2.** _s.m._ _(a)_ Astre qui est à l'ascendant, star in the ascendant. _(b)_ Ascendancy, influence. **Prendre l'ascendant sur qn**, to gain the ascendancy over s.o. _Exercer un grand a. sur qn_, to have great influence upon s.o. _(c)_ _pl._ Ascendants, ancestry (of family).

ascenseur [asɑ̃sœːr], _s.m._ Lift; _U.S:_ elevator.

ascension [asɑ̃sjɔ̃], _s.f._ Ascent, ascension; rising (of sap, etc.). Faire l'ascension d'une montagne, to climb a mountain. Mettre un ballon en ascension, to send up a balloon. _A. en ballon_, balloon ascent. _Ecc:_ Fête de l'Ascension, Ascension Day; Holy Thursday.

ascensionnel, -elle [asɑ̃sjɔnɛl], _a._ Ascensional; upward (motion). _Aer:_ Force ascensionnelle, lifting power; lift.

ascension(n)iste [asɑ̃sjɔnist], _s.m. & f._ **1.** (Mountain) climber; mountaineer. **2.** _Aer:_ Balloonist.

ascète [asɛt], _s.m. & f._ Ascetic.

ascétique [assetik], _a. & s._ Ascetic(al).

ascétisme [assetism], _s.m._ Asceticism.

ascidie [assidi], _s.f._ _Bot:_ Ascidium, vasculum, _F:_ pitcher.

asepsie [asɛpsi], _s.f._ _Med:_ Asepsis.

aseptique [asɛptik], _a._ _Med:_ Aseptic.

aseptiser [asɛptize], _v.tr._ _Med:_ To asepticize.

asiatique [azjatik], _a. & s._ Asiatic. _F:_ Luxe asiatique, oriental splendour.

Asie [azi]. _Pr.n.f._ _Geog:_ Asia.

asile [azil], _s.m._ Shelter, home, refuge, retreat. _Lieu d'a._, (place of) refuge. Sans asile, homeless. _A. des pauvres_ = workhouse. _A. d'aliénés_, mental hospital, _F:_ lunatic asylum. _A. des marins_, sailors' home. _A:_ Salle d'asile, infant school. Donner asile à qn, to harbour, shelter, s.o.

aspect [aspɛ], _s.m._ **1.** Sight, aspect. _Trembler à l'a. de qn_, to tremble at the sight of s.o. Au premier aspect, at first sight, at a first glance. **2.** Aspect, appearance, look. _Être d'un a. repoussant_, to be repulsive-looking. Considérer une affaire sous tous ses aspects, to look at a thing in all its bearings, from all points of view.

asperge [aspɛrʒ], _s.f._ _(a)_ Asparagus. _Botte d'asperges_, bundle of asparagus. _(b)_ _F:_ Tall, gawky, young person.

asperger [aspɛrʒe], _v.tr._ (j'aspergeai(s); n. aspergeons) To sprinkle (linen, etc.) with water. _A. qn d'eau bénite_, to sprinkle s.o. with holy water.

aspérité [asperite], _s.f._ Asperity. **1.** Ruggedness, roughness (of surface, etc.). **2.** Harshness, sharpness (of character, voice).

asphalte [asfalt], _s.m._ Asphalt(um). _A. minéral_, pitch, bitumen.

asphalt|er [asfalte], _v.tr._ To cover (road, etc.) with asphalt. _s.m._ **-age.**

asphodèle [asfodɛl], _s.m._ _Bot:_ Asphodel.

asphyxiant [asfiksjɑ̃], _a._ Asphyxiating, suffocating. Obus asphyxiant, gas-shell.

asphyxie [asfiksi], _s.f._ Asphyxia, asphyxiation, suffocation. _Min: etc:_ Gassing.

asphyxier [asfiksje], _v.tr._ To asphyxiate, suffocate. _Min: etc:_ To gas.

aspic¹ [aspik], _s.m._ _Rept:_ Asp. _F:_ Langue d'aspic, venomous tongue.

aspic², _s.m._ _Cu:_ Aspic(-jelly).

aspic³, _s.m._ _Bot:_ Aspic, French lavender.

aspirant, -ante [aspirɑ̃, -ɑ̃ːt]. **1.** _a._ Sucking. Pompe aspirante, suction pump. _I.C.E:_ Course aspirante, induction stroke; admission stroke. **2.** _s._ _(a)_ Aspirant (à, to); candidate (for degree, etc.). _Les aspirants à sa main_, the aspirants to, for, after, her hand. _(b)_ _Navy:_ Midshipman.

aspirateur, -trice [aspiratœːr, -tris]. **1.** _a._ Aspiratory; suction-(device). **2.** _s.m._ (Gas-, air-) exhauster; aspirator. _A. de poussières_, vacuum-cleaner.

aspiration [aspirasjɔ̃], _s.f._ **1.** Aspiration, yearning (à, for, after). _Aspirations à la scène_, hankering after the stage. **2.** _Ling:_ Aspiration; rough breathing. **3.** _(a)_ Inspiration, inhaling (of air into the lungs). _(b)_ Suction, sucking-up (of water into pump, etc.). _(c)_ _I.C.E:_ Admission, induction. Clapet d'aspiration, intake valve.

aspirer [aspire]. **1.** _v.ind.tr._ To aspire (à, to, after). _A. à faire qch._, to aspire to do sth. **2.** _v.tr._ _(a)_ To inspire, inhale, breathe (in) (air, scent, etc.). _(b)_ To suck up, suck in, draw (up) (water, etc.). _(c)_ _Ling:_ To aspirate, breathe (a sound). Ne pas aspirer les h (en anglais), to drop one's h's.

aspiré, _a._ _Ling:_ Aspirate(d).

aspirée, _s.f._ _Ling:_ Aspirate.

aspirine [aspirin], _s.f._ _Pharm:_ Aspirin.

assag|ir [asaȝiːr], *v.tr.* To make (s.o.) wiser ; to sober (s.o.). [SAGE] *s.m.* **-issement.**
　s'assagir, to become wiser ; to sober down ; to settle down.
assaillant [as(s)ajɑ̃], *s.m.* Assailant.
assaillir [as(s)ajiːr], *v.tr.* (*pr.p.* **assaillant**; *p.p.* **assailli**; *pr. ind.* **j'assaille, n. assaillons**; *p.d.* **j'assaillais**; *p.h.* **j'assaillis**; *fu.* **j'assaillirai,** occ. **j'assaillerai**) To assail, assault, attack. *Être assailli de doutes,* to be beset, assailed, by doubts.
assain|ir [asɛniːr], *v.tr.* To make (sth.) healthier ; to cleanse, purify (atmosphere, etc.) ; to improve the sanitation of (town). *A. les finances,* to reorganize the finances. [SAIN] *s.m.* **-issement.**
assaisonnement [asɛzɔnmɑ̃], *s.m.* **1.** (Action of) seasoning, flavouring (dish) ; dressing (of salad). **2.** Condiment, seasoning, relish.
assaisonner [asɛzɔne], *v.tr.* To season (*de,* with) ; to dress (salad). *Prov:* La faim assaisonne tout, hunger is the best sauce. [SAISON]
assassin, -ine [asasɛ̃, -in]. **1.** *s.* Assassin ; murderer, *f.* murderess. **Crier à l'assassin,** to cry murder. **2.** *a.* (*a*) Murderous (horde, etc.). (*b*) Provocative, killing, bewitching (smile, glance).
assassinat [asasina], *s.m.* Assassination, murder.
assassiner [asasine], *v.tr.* **1.** To assassinate, murder. **2.** *F:* (*a*) To murder (song, etc.) ; to smash up (car, etc.). (*b*) To worry, pester, bore, (s.o.) to death (*de,* with).
assaut [aso], *s.m.* **1.** Assault, attack, onslaught. **Livrer (un) assaut, donner l'assaut, à une position,** to storm a position. **Emporter d'assaut une position,** to storm, carry, a position. **Troupes d'assaut,** storm-troops, shock troops. S.a. CHAR 2. **2.** Match, bout. *A. de lutte,* wrestling bout. *A. de boxe,* sparring match. *A. d'armes,* fencing bout, assault at arms. **Faire assaut d'esprit avec qn,** to vie in wit with s.o.
ass|écher [aseʃe], *v.* (**j'assèche, n. asséchons; j'assécherai**) **1.** *v.tr.* To dry, drain (marsh, etc.) ; to pump (mine, etc.) dry. **2.** *v.i.* & *pr.* (Of land, stream) To dry up. [SEC] *s.m.* **-èchement.**
assemblage [asɑ̃blaːȝ], *s.m.* **1.** Assemblage, gathering, collection. *A. de personnes,* gathering of people. **2.** Assembling, assembly (of parts of machine, etc.). **3.** (*a*) *Carp: etc:* Joint, jointing, joining, coupling, connection. *A. à tenon et mortaise,* mortise-and-tenon joint. (*b*) *El.E:* Connection, joining up. *A. en quantité,* parallel connection. *A. en série,* joining up in series.
assemblée [asɑ̃ble], *s.f.* Assembly. **1.** (*a*) Meeting. **Se réunir en a. publique,** to hold a public meeting. *A. de famille,* family gathering. *A. choisie,* select company. *L'a. des fidèles,* the congregation. (*b*) *Hist:* L'Assemblée législative, the Legislative Assembly. **2.** *Mil:* Battre, sonner, l'a., to beat, sound, the assembly.
assembl|er [asɑ̃ble], *v.tr.* **1.** To assemble ; to call (people) together ; to convene (committee, etc.) ; to collect, gather. *Nau:* A. l'équipage, to muster the crew. **2.** To assemble, fit together (machine, dress, etc.). *El.E:* To connect, join up (cells). *s.* **-eur, -euse.**
　s'assembler, to assemble, meet, gather. *Prov:* Qui se ressemble s'assemble, birds of a feather flock together.
assener [asəne], **asséner** [asene], *v.tr.* (**j'assène, n. assenons, n. assénons ; j'assénerai, j'asséneraî**) To deal, strike (blow). *Coup bien asséné,* telling blow.
assentiment [asɑ̃timɑ̃], *s.m.* Assent, consent, approbation. **Signe d'assentiment,** nod. *Il fit un signe d'a.,* he nodded assent.
asseoir [aswaːr], *v.tr.* (*pr.p.* **asseyant, assoyant**;

p.p. **assis**; *pr.ind.* **j'assieds** [asje], **il assied, n. asseyons, ils asseyent,** or **j'assois, il assoit, n. asseyons, ils assoient**: *pr.sub.* **j'asseye, n. asseyions,** or **j'assoie, n. assoyions**: *p.d.* **j'asseyais** or **j'assoyais**; *p.h.* **j'assis**; *fu.* **j'assiérai, j'asseyerai, j'assoirai**) **1.** (*a*) To set, seat. *Asseyez-le sur le gazon, F:* sit him down on the grass. *A. un prince sur le trône,* to set a prince on the throne. (*b*) *F:* To sit on (s.o.) ; to snub (s.o.). **2.** To lay, establish (foundations, etc.). *A. une pierre,* to bed a stone. *A. un camp,* to pitch a camp. *Av: A. l'appareil,* to pancake (the ground). *A. son opinion sur le fait que . . .,* to base, ground, found, one's opinion on the fact that. . . .
　s'asseoir, to sit down. **Faire asseoir qn,** to ask, beg, s.o. to be seated. *Asseyez-vous, messieurs,* take your seats, pray be seated, gentlemen. *P:* Va t'asseoir! go to Jericho !
　assis, *a.* Seated. *Nous étions a. auprès du feu,* we were sitting, seated, round the fire. **Demeurer assis,** to remain seated ; to keep one's seat. *Rail: Th: etc:* **Places assises,** seats. *Il n'y a plus de places assises,* 'standing room only.' **Fortune bien assise,** well-established fortune. *Sa gloire est assise sur ses romans,* his fame rests on his novels. S.a. MAGISTRATURE 2.
assermentation [asɛrmɑ̃tasjɔ̃], *s.f.* Swearing in ; attestation.
assermenter [asɛrmɑ̃te], *v.tr.* To swear (s.o.) in ; to administer the oath to (s.o.). [SERMENT]
　assermenté, *a.* Sworn (in). *Fonctionnaire a.,* sworn official.
asserv|ir [asɛrviːr], *v.tr.* (*a*) To enslave (nation, etc.) ; to reduce (nation) to slavery. (*b*) *A. qn à une tâche,* to tie s.o. down to a task. [SERF] *s.m.* **-issement.** *s.* **-isseur, -isseuse.**
　asservi, *a.* **1.** *Être a. à l'étiquette,* to be a slave to etiquette. **2.** Servo-(appliance). **Moteur asservi,** servo-motor.
assesseur [asesœːr], *s.m. Jur:* Assessor.
assey-ant, -e, -ons, etc. See ASSEOIR.
assez [ase], *adv.* **1.** Enough, sufficient, sufficiently. (*a*) *Vous travaillez bien a.,* you work quite enough. *J'aurai a. de cent francs,* I shall have enough with a hundred francs. *Tu n'es pas a. grand, tu ne marches pas a. vite,* you are not big enough, you don't walk fast enough. (*b*) *Assez de + sb. Avez-vous a. d'argent?* have you enough money ? *Oui, j'en ai a.,* yes, I have sufficient. *F:* J'en ai assez! I have had enough of it, I am sick of it ! (*c*) C'est assez + *inf. C'est a. parler,* I, you, have said enough. *C'est a. de lui faire savoir que vous êtes ici,* it is sufficient to let him know that you are here. (*d*) Assez pour + *inf.,* pour que + *sub. Soyez a. bon pour me diriger,* be kind enough to direct me. *Être a. près pour voir,* to be near enough to see. *Il n'était pas a. grand pour qu'on le laissât seul,* he was not big enough to be left alone. **2.** Rather, fairly, tolerably, passably. *Elle est a. jolie,* she is rather pretty, passably good-looking. *Je suis a. de votre avis,* I am rather inclined to agree with you. *Les deux villes sont a. semblables,* the two towns are pretty much alike. **3.** (Intensive) Est-il assez enfant! isn't he a baby ! how childish of him ! *Est-il a. grossier!* isn't he rude !
assid|u [asidy], *a.* Assiduous. (*a*) Sedulous, industrious, hard-working, steady. *Efforts assidus,* untiring efforts. *Être a. à qch., à faire qch.,* to be diligent at sth., in doing sth. ; to be persevering, assiduous, in (doing) sth. (*b*) Unremitting, unceasing (care, attention). (*c*) Regular, constant (visitor, etc.). *Être a. auprès de qn.,* to be assiduous in one's attentions to s.o. *adv.* **-ûment.**

assiduité [asidɥite], s.f. Assiduousness, assiduity. **I.** (a) Sedulousness, steadiness. A. à l'étude, close application to study. A force d'assiduité, by dint of perseverance. (b) Sch: Regular attendance. Prix d'assiduité, attendance prize. **2.** Constant attention(s). constant care.

assied, -s. See ASSEOIR.

assiégeant [asjeʒɑ̃]. **I.** a. Besieging (army, etc.). **2.** s.m. Besieger.

assiéger [asjeʒe], v.tr. (assiégeant; j'assiège, n. assiégeons; j'assiégerai) **I.** (a) To besiege, beleaguer; to lay siege to (town). (b) F: A. qn de demandes d'emploi, to besiege s.o. with requests for employment. **2.** To beset, crowd round (s.o., sth.). Ils assiègent la porte, they throng round the door. Être assiégé par des souvenirs, to be haunted by memories. [SIÈGE]

assiér-ai, -as, etc. See ASSEOIR.

assiette [asjɛt], s.f. **I.** Action of giving a stable position to sth., of laying down sth. ; laying down (of foundations) ; bedding (of stone) ; pitching (of camp). **2.** Stable position. (a) Sitting position, seat ; trim (of ship or airship). Avoir une bonne assiette, (i) to have a good seat (on horseback), (ii) (of ship or airship) to be in good trim. F: N'être pas dans son assiette, to be out of sorts ; to feel seedy ; not to be up to the mark. (b) Established position. Avoir une certaine a. dans le monde, to have, enjoy, a certain position in the world. Assiette de pied, foothold. (c) Position ; situation, site (of building, etc.) ; disposition (of camp) ; lie (of land). Golf: A. d'une balle, lie of a ball. (d) Set (of stone, beam, etc.). (Of foundation, gun) Prendre son assiette, to set, to settle ; to bed down. **3.** Support, basis. A. d'une chaussée, foundation, bottom, bed, of a road. **4.** Plate. Assiette plate, dinner plate. Assiette creuse, soup plate.

assiettée [asjɛte], s.f. Plate(ful).

assignat [asiɲa], s.m. Hist: Assignat, promissory note (as issued by the Fr. Revolutionary Government, 1790-96).

assignation [asiɲasjɔ̃], s.f. **I.** Fin: Assignment, transfer (of shares, of funds) (à, to). **2.** Jur: (a) Serving of a writ. (b) Writ of summons ; subpoena. Signifier une a. à qn, to serve a writ on s.o. **3.** A: Appointment, rendezvous. A. amoureuse, lovers' tryst.

assign|er [asiɲe], v.tr. **I.** To assign. (a) To fix, appoint (hour, etc.). A. une tâche à qn, to assign, allot, a task to s.o. A. une cause à un événement, to assign a cause to an event. A. des limites à . . ., to set limits to. . . . (b) A. une somme à un paiement, to assign, F: earmark, a sum for a payment. **2.** Jur: (a) To summon, subpoena, cite (witness, etc). (b) (i) To issue a writ against (s.o.), (ii) to serve a writ on (s.o.). a. -able.

assîmes. See ASSEOIR.

assimil|er [as(s)imile], v.tr. **I.** To assimilate (food, knowledge). **2.** To liken, compare (à, to, with). a. -able (à, to). s.f. -ation.

assis. See ASSEOIR.

assise [asiːz], s.f. **I.** Seating, laying (of foundation). **2.** (a) Seating, foundation ; bed(-plate) (of engine, etc.). Les assises de la société, the foundations of society. (b) Seat (on horseback). **3.** (a) Const: Course (of masonry) ; course, row (of bricks). (b) La montagne s'élève en assises, the mountain rises in tiers. **4.** pl. (a) Jur: Les assises, the assizes. Cour d'assises, Assize Court. (b) Assises d'un congrès, sittings of a congress. [ASSEOIR]

assistance [asistɑ̃s], s.f. **I.** Presence, attendance (esp. of magistrate or priest). **2.** (a) Audience, company. Ecc: Congregation. (b) Spectators, onlookers. **3.** Assistance, help, aid. Prêter assistance à qn, to assist s.o. A. aux vieillards, relief of old people. L'Assistance publique the Poor Law Administration.

assistant, -ante [asistɑ̃, -ɑ̃ːt], s. **I.** Usu. pl. (a) Bystander, onlooker, spectator. (b) Member of the audience. **2.** (a) Assistant (professor, priest). (b) Foreign assistant (in school).

assister [asiste]. **I.** v.i. A. à qch., to attend sth. ; to be present at sth. A. à une partie de football, to attend a football match. A. à une rixe, to witness a fight. **2.** v.tr. To help, assist, succour (s.o.). A. qn de ses conseils, to help s.o. with advice. Enfants assistés, foundlings.

association [asɔsjasjɔ̃], s.f. **I.** (a) Association (of words, ideas). (b) El: Connecting, grouping, coupling (of cells). **2.** (a) Society, company ; association, fellowship. Association ouvrière, trade-union. (b) Com: Partnership.

associ|er [asɔsje], v.tr. (a) To associate, unite, join. A. qn à qch., to make s.o. a party to sth. ; to associate s.o. with sth. A. des idées, to connect, associate, ideas. El: To connect, join up (cells, etc.). a. -able.

s'associer. **I.** S'a. à qch. (a) To share in, participate in, join in, sth. S'a. à un crime, to be a party to or a participator in a crime. (b) To join (a corporate body). **2.** S'a. à, avec, qn. (a) To enter into a combination with s.o. (b) To enter into partnership with s.o. (c) To associate with s.o.

associé, -ée, s. (a) Com: Partner. A. principal, senior partner. Prendre qn comme a., to take s.o. into partnership. (b) Associate member (of learned body).

assoiffé [aswafe], a. Etre a. de qch., to be thirsty, thirsting, athirst, eager, for sth. A. de sang, bloodthirsty. [SOIF]

assoir-ai, -as ; **assois-s, -t.** See ASSEOIR.

assol|er [asɔle], v.tr. To rotate the crops on (a piece of land). [SOLE] s.m. -ement.

assombr|ir [asɔ̃briːr], v.tr. (a) To darken, obscure. (b) To spread, cast, a gloom over (company, etc.). [SOMBRE] s.m. -issement.

s'assombrir. (a) To darken ; to become dark ; to cloud over. Tout s'assombrit, everything became dark. (b) To become gloomy, sad.

assommant [asɔmɑ̃], a. **I.** Overwhelming. Coup assommant, knock-down blow. **2.** F: Boring, tedious, wearisome, tiresome. Bavard a., deadly bore.

assommer [asɔme], v.tr. **I.** (a) A. un bœuf, to fell an ox. A. qn, to brain s.o. (b) To knock (s.o.) senseless. **2.** F: To bore ; to tire (s.o.) to death. A. qn de questions, to pester s.o. with questions.

assommeur, -euse [asɔmœːr, -øːz]. **I.** s.m. (a) Slaughterer, slaughterman. (b) Ruffian (armed with club) ; U.S: tough. **2.** s.m. & f. F: Quel assommeur que votre ami! your friend is a terrible bore !

assommoir [asɔmwaːr], s.m. **I.** (a) Pole-axe. (b) Club, bludgeon. Porter un coup d'a. à qn, to deal s.o. a staggering blow. **2.** (a) Break-back trap. (b) Ven: Deadfall ; fall-trap. **3.** Low tavern.

assomption [asɔ̃psjɔ̃], s.f. **I.** Log: Assumption. **2.** Ecc: (Fête de) l'Assomption, (feast of) the Assumption (of the Blessed Virgin).

assonance [asɔnɑ̃ːs], s.f. Ling: Pros: Assonance.

assortiment [asɔrtimɑ̃], s.m. **I.** Matching. A. parfait de couleurs, perfect match(ing) of colours. **2.** (a) Assortment. Ample a. d'échantillons, wide range of patterns. Un assortiment (de charcuterie), slices of ham, galantine, saucisson, etc., sold together. (b) Set (of tools, etc.).

assortir [asɔrtiːr], *v.tr.* (j'assortis, n. assortissons) (*a*) To assort, sort, match (colours, etc.). *A. son style à la matière*, to suit one's style to the matter. (*b*) To stock, furnish (shop, etc., with varied goods). [SORTE] **s'assortir. 1.** To match, to harmonize. **2.** *Com:* To lay in a varied stock.

assorti, *a.* **1.** Matched, paired. **Bien, mal, assorti,** well-, ill-matched. **2.** Assorted, mixed (sweets, etc.). **3. Bien assorti,** well-stocked (shop).

assoupir [asupiːr], *v.tr.* (*a*) To make (s.o.) drowsy ; to send (s.o.) to sleep. (*b*) To allay, lull, quiet (pain). **s'assoupir. 1.** To drop off to sleep ; to doze off. **2.** (Of pain, etc.) To wear away. *Le bruit s'assoupit,* the sound died away.

assoupi, *a.* **1.** Dozing. **2.** Dormant (grief, volcano).

assoupissant [asupisɑ̃], *a.* Soporific.

assoupissement [asupismɑ̃], *s.m.* **1.** Allaying, lulling (of pain). **2.** Drowsiness ; dozing, slumber.

assoupl|ir [asupliːr], *v.tr.* To make supple ; to supple. *A. du cuir,* to supple, soften, leather. [SOUPLE] *s.m.* **-issement.** **s'assouplir,** to become supple.

assourd|ir [asurdiːr], *v.tr.* **1.** To make (s.o.) deaf ; to deafen. **2.** (*a*) To deaden, damp, muffle (sound) ; to muffle (drum, bell). *Ling:* To unvoice (consonant). (*b*) To soften, subdue, tone down (light, colour). [SOURD] *s.m.* **-issement.** **s'assourdir,** (of sound) to grow fainter, to die away ; (of consonant) to become unvoiced.

assourdissant [asurdisɑ̃], *a.* Deafening.

assouv|ir [asuviːr], *v.tr.* To sate, appease, satisfy (hunger, passion). *A. sa soif,* to slake, quench, one's thirst. *s.m.* **-issement.** **s'assouvir,** to satiate, gorge, glut, oneself ; to become sated (*de,* with).

assoy-ant, -ons, etc. See ASSEOIR.

assujett|ir [asyʒetiːr], *v.tr.* **1.** (*a*) To subdue, subjugate (province, etc.) ; to bring (province, etc.) into subjection. *A. ses passions,* to govern, curb, one's passions. (*b*) *A. qn à faire qch.,* to compel, oblige, s.o. to do sth. **2.** To fix, fasten (à, to) ; to make (sth.) fast, secure. [SUJET] *s.m.* **-issement.** **assujetti,** *a.* Subject (à, to). **Etre fort assujetti,** to be tied down to, by, one's duties.

assujettissant [asyʒetisɑ̃], *a.* Tying (work).

assumer [asyme], *v.tr.* To assume ; to take upon oneself (right, responsibility, etc.).

assurance [asyrɑ̃ːs], *s.f.* **1.** Assurance. (*a*) (Self-) confidence. **Parler avec assurance,** to speak with confidence. (*b*) *Avez-vous la pleine a. de le revoir?* are you perfectly sure you will see him again? **2.** (*a*) Making sure or safe. **En lieu d'assurance,** in a place of safety. (*b*) *Com:* Insurance, assurance. **Police d'assurance,** insurance policy. **Prime d'assurance,** insurance premium. *A. sur la vie,* life-assurance. *A. contre l'incendie,* fire-insurance.

assurément [asyremɔ̃], *adv.* **1.** *Marcher a.,* to tread firmly. **2.** Assuredly, surely, undoubtedly, certainly. **Assurément non! certainly not!**

assur|er [asyre], *v.tr.* **1.** (*a*) To make (sth.) firm, steady ; to fix, secure, fasten. (*b*) *A. un résultat,* to ensure a result ; to make a result sure. *A. un pays,* to make a country secure. *A. qch. à qn,* to assure, ensure, sth. to s.o. *S'a. qch.,* to secure sth. (*c*) *A. son visage,* to put on a firm countenance. *A. qch. à qn ; a. qn de qch.,* to assure s.o. of sth. ; to vouch for sth. to s.o. *A. qn de son affection,* to assure s.o. of one's affection. *Je leur assurai que la chose était vraie,* I assured them that

it was true. *Je lui assurai l'avoir vu,* I assured him that I had seen it. **3.** *Com:* To insure. **Se faire assurer sur la vie,** to have one's life insured. *a.* **-able.** **s'assurer. 1.** *S'a. sur ses pieds, sur ses jambes,* to take a firm stand. **2.** *S'a. de qch.,* to make sure, certain, of sth. **Je vais m'en assurer,** I will go and see. *S'a. que + ind.,* to make sure, ascertain, that. . . . **3.** *S'a. de qch.,* to lay hold of, to make sure of, to secure, sth. **4.** *Com:* To get insured, to take out an insurance (*contre,* against).

assuré, *a.* Firm, sure (step, voice, etc.); assured, confident (air, person) ; certain (cure) ; secure, safe (retreat). *Voix mal assurée,* unsteady voice. *A. de l'avenir,* assured of the future. *A. du succès,* confident of success.

assureur [asyrœːr], *s.m. Com:* Insurer.

Assyrie [as(s)iri]. *Pr.n.f. A.Geog:* Assyria.

astatique [astatik], *a.* Astatic (needle). *Système a.,* astatic pair.

astérisque [asterisk], *s.m. Typ:* Asterisk.

astéroïde [asterɔid], *s.m. Astr:* **1.** Asteroid. **2.** Planetoid, minor planet.

asthénie [asteni], *s.f. Med:* Asthenia ; debility.

asthénique [astenik], *a. Med:* Asthenic.

asthmatique [asmatik], *a.* Asthmatic(al).

asthme [asm], *s.m.* Asthma.

asticot [astiko], *s.m.* Maggot. *P:* **C'est un drôle d'asticot!** he's a queer chap!

asticoter [astikɔte], *v.tr. P:* To tease, worry ; *F:* to rag, plague.

astigmatisme [astigmatism], *s.m.* Astigmatism.

astiqu|er [astike], *v.tr.* To polish, furbish (belt, brass, etc.). *s.m.* **-age.**

astragale [astragal], *s.m.* **1.** Ankle-bone. **2.** *Arch:* Astragal (of column). **3.** *Bot:* Astragalus ; milk-vetch.

astrak(h)an [astrakɑ̃], *s.m.* Astrak(h)an (fur).

astral, -aux [astral, -o], *a.* Astral (body, etc.).

astre [astr], *s.m.* Heavenly body ; star. *Poet:* **L'astre du jour,** the sun. *F:* **Louer qn jusqu'aux astres,** to praise s.o. to the skies.

astreign-ant, -ez, etc. See ASTREINDRE.

astreindre [astrɛ̃ːdr], *v.tr. (pr.p.* **astreignant ;** *p.p.* **astreint ;** *pr.ind.* **j'astreins, il astreint, n. astreignons ;** *p.d.* **j'astreignais ;** *p.h.* **j'astreignis ;** *fu.* **j'astreindrai)** To compel, oblige ; to tie down (*à un devoir,* to a duty). *Être astreint à faire qch.,* to be compelled, under compulsion, to do sth. **s'astreindre** *à un régime sévère,* to keep to a strict diet.

astringent [astrɛ̃ʒɑ̃], *a. & s.m.* Astringent.

astro|logie [astrɔlɔʒi], *s.f.* Astrology. *a.* **-logique,** -logical. *s.m.* **-logue,** -loger.

astro|nome [astronɔm], *s.m.* Astronomer. *s.f.* **-nomie,** -nomy. *a.* **-nomique,** -nomical.

astuce [astys], *s.f.* **1.** Astuteness, artfulness, wiliness, craftiness, guile. **2.** Wile.

astucieu|x, -euse [astysjø, -øːz], *a.* Astute, artful, wily, guileful, deep, crafty. *adv.* **-sement.**

asymétrie [asimetri], *s.f.* Asymmetry.

asymétrique [asimetrik], *a.* Asymmetrical, unsymmetrical.

asymptote [asɛ̃ptɔt]. *Mth:* **1.** *a.* Asymptotic(al) (line, etc.). **2.** *s.f.* Asymptote.

asynchrone [asɛ̃krɔn], *a. Ph:* Asynchronous.

asyndète [asɛ̃dɛt], *s.m. Rh:* Asyndeton.

atavique [atavik], *a. Atavistic. Biol:* **Retour atavique,** throw-back.

atavisme [atavism], *s.m.* Atavism.

ataxie [ataksi], *s.f. Med:* Ataxy, ataxia ; tabes.

atelier [atəlje], *s.m.* **1.** (*a*) (Work)shop, work-room. *A. de réparations,* repair-shop. **Chef d'atelier,** shop-foreman ; overseer. (*b*) Studio (of

artist). *Phot:* **Appareil d'atelier,** studio camera.
2. Shop-staff, work-room staff.
athée [ate]. **1.** *a.* Atheistic(al). **2.** *s.* Atheist.
athéisme [ateism], *s.m.* Atheism.
athénée [atene], *s.m.* **1.** Athenaeum. **2.** (In Belgium) Public secondary school.
Athènes [atɛn]. *Pr.n.f. Geog:* Athens.
athénien, -ienne [atenjɛ̃, -jɛn], *a. & s.* Athenian.
athlète [atlɛt], *s.m.* Athlete.
athlétique [atletik]. *a.* Athletic.
athlétisme [atletism], *s.m.* Athleticism; athletics.
atlante [atlɑ̃:t], *s.m. Arch:* Telamon. *pl.* Atlantes, telamones (supporting entablature).
atlantique [atlɑ̃tik], *a. L'océan A.,* *s.m.* **l'Atlantique,** the Atlantic (Ocean). *Le littoral a.,* the Atlantic coast-line.
Atlas [atlɑ:s]. **1.** *Pr.n.m. Myth: Geog:* Atlas. **2.** *s.m.* (*a*) *Anat:* The atlas, the first cervical vertebra. (*b*) Atlas, book of maps.
atmosphère [atmosfɛ:r], *s.f.* **1.** Atmosphere. **2.** *Ph:* (= Pressure of 30 inches of mercury) Atmosphere.
atmosphérique [atmosferik], *a.* Atmospheric. *Pression a.,* air-pressure. *W.Tel:* **Perturbations atmosphériques,** atmospherics; statics.
atoll [atɔl], *s.m. Geol:* Atoll; coral island; lagoon-reef.
atome [ato:m], *s.m. Ph:* Atom. *F: Atomes de poussière,* specks of dust. **Pas un atome de vérité,** not a jot, not an atom, of truth.
atomique [atomik], *a.* Atomic.
atomiser [atomize], *v.tr.* To atomize, to spray (liquid).
atomiseur [atomizœ:r], *s.m.* Atomizer, spray.
atone [atɔn], *a.* **1.** Dull, vacant (look life). **2.** Unstressed, atonic (syllable).
atour [atu:r], *s.m.* Usu. *pl. A. & Hum:* Finery; attire. *Parée de tous ses atours,* in fine array; decked out in all her finery.
atout [atu], *s.m.* **1.** *Cards:* Trump. **Jouer atout,** to play a trump; to play trumps. *F:* **Avoir tous les atouts dans son jeu,** to hold all the winning cards. **Avoir de l'atout,** to have pluck, courage. **2.** *F:* **Recevoir un atout,** to receive a blow; to get badly hit. [TOUT]
atrabilaire [atrabilɛ:r], *a.* Atrabilious.
âtre [ɑ:tr], *s.m.* Fireplace, hearth(-stone).
Atrée [atre]. *Pr.n.m. Gr.Lit:* Atreus.
atroce [atrɔs], *a.* (*a*) Atrocious, heinous. (*b*) *Douleur a. à voir,* grief terrible to witness. *Douleur a.,* agonizing pain. *adv.* **-ment.**
atrocité [atrosite], *s.f.* **1.** Atrociousness. **2.** Atrocious act; atrocity.
atrophie [atrofi], *s.f. Med:* Atrophy.
atrophier [atrofje], *v.tr.* To atrophy (limb, intelligence).
s'atrophier, to atrophy; to waste (away).
attabler (s') [satable], *v.pr.* To sit down to table. *Rester attablé à savourer le porto,* to sit over the port.
attachant [ataʃɑ̃], *a.* **1.** That holds the attention; interesting (book); arresting (spectacle). **2.** Engaging, winning (personality).
attache [ataʃ], *s.f.* **1.** Fastening; tying up. **Chien d'attache,** house-dog. *Nau:* **Port d'attache,** home port. **2.** Tie, fastener, fastening, attachment. (*a*) Head-rope (of horse); leash, chain (of dog). *F:* **Être toujours à l'attache,** to be tied to one's duties. *Rompre une a.,* to break a tie, a connection (with a friend, etc.). (*b*) Paper fastener, clip. *Attaches à fermoirs,* snap fasteners (of gloves). (*c*) *Anat:* Attachment (of muscle). *A.*

du pied, ankle-joint. *Membres aux fines attaches,* delicately jointed limbs. [ATTACHER]
attachement [ataʃmɑ̃], *s.m. A. pour qn,* attachment, affection, for s.o. *A. à l'étude,* fondness for study. *A. à ses devoirs,* assiduity in one's duties.
attacher [ataʃe]. **1.** *v.tr.* To attach. (*a*) To fasten, bind; to tie (up). *A. un cheval,* to tie up a horse. *A. un chien à une chaîne,* to chain up, tie up, a dog. *A. deux feuilles ensemble avec de la colle,* to gum, stick, two sheets of paper together. (*b*) *A. de l'importance à qch.,* to attach importance to sth. *Spectacle qui attache l'attention,* spectacle that rivets the attention. (*c*) To make (s.o.) attached (to s.o., sth.). *Tout ce qui nous attache à la vie,* all that makes us cling to life. **2.** *v.i. Cu:* *Les pommes de terre ont attaché,* the potatoes have caught.
s'attacher. 1. (*a*) To attach oneself, to cling, stick (à, to); to fasten (à, on). *La poix s'attache aux doigts,* pitch sticks to the fingers. *F: S'a. aux pas de qn,* to dog s.o.'s footsteps. (*b*) *S'a. à qn,* to become fond of, attached to, s.o. **2.** *S'a. à une tâche,* to apply oneself to a task. *S'a. à remplir son devoir,* to stick to one's duty.
attaché. 1. *a.* (*a*) Fastened, tied-up; chained (dog). (*b*) *Être a. à qn,* to be attached, devoted, to s.o. (*c*) *Il est a. à mes pas,* he dogs my footsteps. *Mon bonheur est a. au vôtre,* my happiness is bound up with yours. **2.** *s.m. Dipl: etc:* Attaché. *A. militaire,* military attaché.
attaquant [atakɑ̃], *s.m.* Assailant, attacker.
attaque [atak], *s.f.* **1.** (*a*) Attack, onslaught, onset, onrush. *A. de front,* direct, frontal, attack. **Lancer, déclencher, une attaque,** to launch, start, an attack. *Diriger de violentes attaques contre qn,* to attack s.o. violently. *F:* **D'attaque,** vigorously. *Il y va d'a.,* he goes at it tooth and nail. **Être d'attaque,** (i) to have plenty of pluck, to be game, (ii) *Mil:* (of troops) to be fit. (*b*) *Med: A. de goutte,* attack of gout. *A. de fièvre, de grippe,* bout of fever, of influenza. *A. d'épilepsie,* epileptic fit. **Attaque d'apoplexie,** (apoplectic) stroke. **Attaque de nerfs,** fit of hysterics. **2.** *Mec.E: A. directe,* direct drive (of motor). *Av:* **Bord d'attaque,** leading edge (of wing, propeller).
attaquer [atake], *v.tr.* **1.** To attack, assail (enemy, stronghold, etc.); to set upon (s.o.); (of acid) to attack (metal). *A. l'honneur de qn, a. qn dans son honneur,* to impeach s.o.'s honour. *Le poumon droit est attaqué,* the right lung is affected. **2.** To begin, *F:* to tackle, to wire into (meal, piece of work, etc.). *Cards:* **Attaquer trèfle,** to lead clubs. **3.** (Of piece of mechanism) To drive, operate (another piece). *a.* **-able.**
s'attaquer *à qn, à qch.,* to attack, tackle, s.o., sth. *S'a. à plus fort que soi,* to meet more than one's match. *S'a. à une difficulté,* to grapple with a difficulty.
attarder [atarde], *v.tr.* To keep (s.o.) late, beyond his time. [TARD]
s'attarder, to linger, dally, loiter; to stay late; to stay up late; to lag behind. *S'a. en route,* to tarry on the way. *S'a. à faire qch.,* to stay beyond one's time, to stay too late, doing sth.
attardé, *a.* **1.** Belated (traveller, etc.); late; behindhand. **2.** Behind the times. **3.** *Sch:* Backward (child).
atteign-ant, -ez, etc. See ATTEINDRE.
atteindre [atɛ̃:dr], *v.* (*pr.p.* atteignant; *p.p.* atteint; *pr.ind.* j'atteins, il atteint, *n.* atteignons; *p.d.* j'atteignais; *p.h.* j'atteignis; *fu.* j'atteindrai) **1.** *v.tr.* To reach; to overtake; to attain. (*a*) *A. la ville,* to reach, get to, the town. *A. qn,* to catch

s.o. up; to overtake s.o. *A. son but*, to attain, achieve, one's end. (*b*) *A. une boîte sur un rayon*, to reach for, get at, a box on a shelf. *Sa taille atteint six pieds*, he is six foot tall. (*c*) *A. le but*, to hit the target. *Ne pas a. le but*, to fall short of the mark. *A. qn d'une pierre*, to hit s.o. with a stone. *Être atteint (d'un coup de feu) au bras*, to be wounded, shot, in the arm. *Être atteint d'une maladie*, to be attacked by a disease; to catch or to have caught a disease. *Le poumon est atteint*, the lung is affected. *Gravement atteint par une faillite*, heavily hit by a bankruptcy. *Atteint dans son honneur*, wounded in his honour. **2.** *v.ind.tr. A. à qch.*, to reach, attain (to), sth.

atteinte atɛ̃t], *s.f.* **1.** Reach. **Hors d'atteinte**, beyond reach, out of reach. *Sa réputation est hors d'a.*, his reputation is unassailable. **2.** Blow, hit, stroke, attack. *Légère a. au bras*, slight blow or wound on the arm. *A. au crédit de qn*, blow to s.o.'s credit. *Sa santé n'a jamais eu d'a.*, his health has never been impaired. **Porter atteinte à l'honneur de qn**, to cast a slur on s.o.'s honour. *Porter a. aux intérêts de qn*, to interfere with, to injure, s.o.'s interests.

attelage [atla:ʒ], *s.m.* **1.** (*a*) Harnessing. (*b*) Way of harnessing. **Attelage à quatre**, four-in-hand. **2.** Team; pair (of horses, of oxen); yoke (of oxen). **3.** *Civ.E*: *etc*: Attachment. *Rail*: Coupling. **Chaîne d'attelage**, draw-chain, coupling-chain.

attel|er [atle], *v.tr.* (j'attelle, n. attelons; j'attellerai) **1.** To harness, put to (horses, etc.); to yoke (oxen). *A. un cheval à une charrette*, to harness a horse to a cart. *F*: *Toujours attelé à son travail*, always hard at it. **2.** *A. une voiture*, to put horses to a carriage. **3.** *Rail*: *A. des wagons*, to couple (up) waggons. *s.m.* **-lement**. **s'atteler** *à une tâche*, to settle down to a task.

attelle [atel], *s.f.* *Surg*: Splint.

attenance [atnɑ̃:s], *s.f.* Dependency (of house).

attenant [atnɑ̃], *a.* Contiguous (*à*, to); abutting (*à*, on); adjoining.

attendre [atɑ̃:dr], *v.tr.* **1.** To wait for (s.o., sth.), to await (s.o., sth.). *Qu'attendez-vous?* what are you waiting for? *A. la mort*, to await death. *J'attendrai mon heure*, I shall (a)bide my time. *Le sort qui l'attend*, the fate that is in store for him. **Aller attendre qn à la gare**, to go to meet s.o. at the station. **Faire attendre qn**, to keep s.o. waiting. *Se faire a.*, to be late. **Attendez donc!** wait a bit! **Ne rien perdre pour attendre**, to lose nothing by waiting. *Attendez à, de, voir le résultat*, wait until you see the result. *F*: **Attendez voir**, wait and see. *A. d'avoir soixante ans*, to wait till one is sixty. *A. que qn fasse qch.*, to wait for s.o. to do sth. *J'attendrai (jusqu'à ce) qu'il soit prêt*, I shall wait till he is ready. **En attendant**, meanwhile, in the meantime. **En attendant l'arrivée du courrier**, pending arrival of the mail. *Conj.phr.* **En attendant que** + *sub.*, till, until; pending the time when. . . . **2.** To expect. *On l'attend la semaine prochaine*, he is expected to arrive next week. *J'attends de vous aide et protection*, I look to you for assistance and protection. **s'attendre. 1.** *S'a. à qch.*, to expect sth. *Je m'y attendais*, I thought as much. *Je ne m'attends pas à ce qu'il me réponde*, I do not expect him to answer me. **2.** *Ne t'attends qu'à toi seul*, rely only on yourself.

attendrir [atɑ̃dri:r], *v.tr.* **1.** To make (meat) tender; to soften (vegetables). **2.** To soften (s.o.'s heart); to move (s.o.) to pity; to touch. *Il ne se laissa pas a.*, he would not relent. **s'attendrir. 1.** (Of meat, etc.) To become

tender. **2.** To be moved (to pity). *S'a. au spectacle de qch.*, to be softened. touched, moved to tears, at the sight of sth.

attendri, *a.* Fond, compassionate (look); full of pity.

attendrissant [atɑ̃drisɑ̃], *a.* Moving, touching, affecting.

attendrissement [atɑ̃drismɑ̃], *s.m.* (Feeling of) pity; emotion.

attendu [atɑ̃dy]. **1.** (*a*) *prep.* Considering (the circumstances); owing to (the events); in consideration of (his services). (*b*) *Conj. phr.* **Attendu que** + *ind.*, considering that . . ., seeing that . . ., *Jur*: whereas. . . . **2.** *s.m.* **Les attendus** (*d'un jugement*), the reasons adduced. [ATTENDRE]

attentat [atɑ̃ta], *s.m.* (Criminal) attempt; outrage. *Commettre un a. contre la vie de qn*, to make an attempt on s.o.'s life. [ATTENTER]

attente [atɑ̃:t], *s.f.* **1.** (*a*) Wait(ing). **Être dans l'attente de qch.**, to be waiting for sth. **Salle d'attente**, waiting-room. (*b*) *Surg*: **Ligature d'attente**, temporary ligature. **2.** Expectation(s), anticipation. **Contre toute attente**, contrary to all expectations. **Répondre à l'attente de qn**, to come up to s.o.'s expectations. **Être dans l'attente de qch.**, to be awaiting sth. "Dans l'attente de votre réponse," 'awaiting your reply.' [ATTENDRE]

attenter [atɑ̃te], *v.ind.tr.* To make an attempt (*à*, on, against). *A. à ses jours*, to lay violent hands on oneself; to attempt suicide.

attent|if, -ive [atɑ̃tif, -i:v], *a.* **1.** Attentive (*à*, to); heedful (*à*, of); careful. *A ces mots il devint a.*, at these words he pricked up his ears. *Il est a. à m'épargner toute peine*, he is careful to spare me all trouble. **2.** *Examen a.*, careful examination. *adv.* **-ivement**.

attention [atɑ̃sjɔ̃], *s.f.* Attention, care. (*a*) **Attention suivie**, close attention. **Écouter avec attention**, to listen attentively. *Son a. à ne nous laisser manquer de rien*, his care that we should want for nothing. *Appeler, porter, attirer, l'a. de qn sur un fait, signaler un fait à l'a. de qn*, to call, draw, s.o.'s attention to a fact; to point out a fact to s.o. (Of object or fact) **Arrêter, retenir, l'attention**, to arrest, hold, engage, the attention. **Attirer l'attention**, to catch the eye; to be conspicuous. **Faire attention à qch.**, to pay attention to sth. *Ne faites pas a. à eux*, never mind them. **Faites attention!** take care! **Be careful! Attention!** look out! *Faites a. (à ce) que personne ne sorte*, take care that no one leaves the house. (*b*) *Être plein d'attentions pour qn*, to show s.o. much attention.

attentionné [atɑ̃sjone], *a.* Attentive. *Être a. pour qn*, to be considerate, full of attentions, towards s.o.

atténuant [atenɥɑ̃], *a.* *Jur*: Extenuating, palliating (circumstance).

atténu|er [atenɥe], *v.tr.* **1.** (*a*) To attenuate, lessen, diminish, reduce; to tone down (colour); to dim, subdue (light); to mitigate (punishment, sentence). *A. une chute*, to break a fall. (*b*) *Phot*: To reduce (negative, etc.). **2.** To extenuate, palliate (offence). *s.f.* **-ation**. **s'atténuer**, to lessen; (of light) to grow dimmer, softer; (of sound) to diminish, to grow softer.

atterrage [atera:ʒ], *s.m.* *Nau*: **1.** (*a*) Approach (to land); shoaling. (*b*) Landing-place. **2.** Landfall.

atterrant [aterɑ̃], *a.* Overwhelming, crushing, staggering (piece of news, etc.).

atterrement [atermɑ̃], *s.m.* Stupefaction, consternation.

atterrer [atɛre], *v.tr.* To overwhelm, astound, stupefy; to strike with consternation. [TERRE]
atterré, *a.* Utterly crushed (by news). *Ils se contemplèrent atterrés,* they looked at each other in consternation.
atterrir [ateriːr]. **1.** *v.i.* (*a*) *Nau:* To sight land; to make a landfall. (*b*) (Of boat) To ground, to run ashore. (*c*) *Av:* To alight, to land. *A. brutalement,* to crash. **2.** *v.tr.* To run (boat) ashore.
atterrissage [aterisaːʒ], *s.m.* **1.** *Nau:* (*a*) Making (the) land; landfall. (*b*) Grounding (of boat); running ashore. **2.** *Av:* Landing, alighting. *A. brutal,* crash. **Terrain d'atterrissage,** landing-ground.
attestation [atɛstasjɔ̃], *s.f.* Attestation; (doctor's) certificate. *A. sous serment,* affidavit.
attester [atɛste], *v.tr.* **1.** *A. qch.,* to attest, certify, sth.; to bear testimony, bear witness, testify, to sth. *A. que qch. est vrai,* to certify that sth. is true. **2.** *A. qn (de qch.),* to call s.o. to witness (to sth.). **J'en atteste les cieux,** I call heaven to witness.
atticisme [atisism], *s.m.* ⋯ Atticism.
attiéd|ir [atjediːr], *v.tr.* To make tepid, lukewarm. [TIÈDE] *s.m.* **-issement.**
s'attiédir, to grow lukewarm. *F: Son intérêt s'est attiédi,* his interest has cooled off.
attifage [atifaːʒ], *s.m.,* **attifement** [atifmɑ̃], *s.m.* Usu. *Pej:* **1.** Dressing up. **2.** Get-up, rig-out.
attifer [atife], *v.tr.* Usu. *Pej:* To dress (s.o.) up (*de,* in). *Qui t'a attifée ainsi?* who ever got you up like that?
s'attifer, to dress oneself up; to bedeck oneself. *Comme la voilà attifée!* what a guy!
attique [atik]. **1.** *a.* Attic, Athenian. **2.** *s.m. Arch:* Attic (storey). **3.** *Pr.n.f.* L'Attique, Attica.
attirail [atiraːj], *s.m.* **1.** Apparatus, gear; outfit; set (of tools, etc.). *A. de pêche,* fishing-tackle. **2.** *F:* Pomp, show.
attirance [atirɑ̃s], *s.f.* Attraction (*vers,* to); lure (of pleasure, etc.). *L'a. du gouffre,* the lure, fascination, spell, of the abyss; the temptation to jump from a height.
attirant [atirɑ̃], *a.* Attractive, drawing (force, etc.); alluring, engaging (manners).
attirer [atire], *v.tr.* **1.** (*a*) (Of magnet, etc.) To attract, draw. (*b*) *A. qn, sur, qn,* to bring sth. on s.o. *Les malheurs que cela m'a attirés,* the misfortunes that it brought upon my head. *A. la colère de qn sur qn,* to bring down s.o.'s wrath on s.o. *S'a. un blâme,* to incur a reprimand. **2.** *A. qn dans un piège,* to lure s.o. into a trap. *A. qn par des promesses,* to entice s.o. with promises. [TIRER]
attiser [atize], *v.tr.* To stir (up), poke (up) (fire). *F:* Attiser les haines, to stir up hatred. *A. le feu d'une passion,* to fan the ardour of a passion.
attitré [atitre], *a.* Regular, appointed, recognized; ordinary (agent). [TITRE]
attitude [atityd], *s.f.* Attitude, posture. **Être toujours en attitude,** to be always posing. *A. hostile,* hostile attitude (*envers,* towards).
attouchement [atuʃmɑ̃], *s.m.* Touching, contact. *Guérir les écrouelles par a.,* to touch for king's evil.
attraction [atraksjɔ̃], *s.f.* (*a*) Attraction (of magnet, etc.). *Ph:* **Attraction universelle,** gravitation. (*b*) Attraction, attractiveness (of resort, person, etc.).
attrait [atrɛ], *s.m.* (*a*) Attraction, lure; attractiveness, allurement. *L'a. de la mer,* the appeal of the sea. *Les attraits d'une carrière dans le commerce,* the inducements of a business career. **Dépourvu d'attrait,** unattractive. (*b*) Inclination.

Se sentir de l'a. pour qn, to feel a liking, a sympathy, for s.o.
attrapade [atrapad], *s.f. F:* Quarrel; set-to.
attrapage [atrapaːʒ], *s.m. F:* **1.** Wigging, reprimand **2.** = ATTRAPADE.
attrape [atrap], *s.f.* (*a*) Trap, snare (for birds, etc.). (*b*) *F:* Trick, hoax, catch, *F:* do. **Faire une attrape à qn,** to play a trick on s.o.; to take s.o. in. [ATTRAPER]
attrape-mouches, *s.m.inv.* **1.** Fly-trap, fly-paper. **2.** *Orn:* Fly-catcher.
attrape-niais, *s.m.inv.,* **attrape-nigaud,** *s.m. F:* Booby-trap. *pl. Des attrape-nigauds.*
attraper [atrape], *v.tr.* To catch. **1.** (*a*) To (en)trap, (en)snare (animal). (*b*) *A. qn,* to trick, cheat, s.o.; to take s.o. in. **Attrapé!** sold again! **2.** (*a*) To seize (ball, thief, idea). Attrapé! take that! (*b*) *Une pierre l'a attrapé au front,* a stone hit him on the forehead. (*c*) **Attraper froid,** to catch a chill. *A. un rhume,* to catch cold. (*d*) *A. qn à faire qch.,* to catch s.o. doing sth. (*e*) *F: A. qn,* to scold s.o.; to give s.o. a good talking-to.
s'attraper. **1.** *S'a. à qch.,* to hit against, to be caught by, on, sth. *S'a. à la jambe,* (i) to knock, hit, one's leg, (ii) to get one's leg caught. **2.** *S'a. à qn,* to tackle, attack, s.o.
attrayant [atrɛjɑ̃], *a.* Attractive, engaging, alluring. **Peu attrayant,** unattractive.
attribu|er [atribɥe], *v.tr.* **1.** To assign, allot (*à,* to). *Th: A. un rôle à qn,* to cast s.o. for a part. **2.** To attribute, ascribe (fact, book) (*à,* to); impute (crime, mistake) (*à,* to); to put down, set down, ascribe (sth. to a cause). **3.** *S'a. qch.,* to assume, claim, lay claim to, sth.; to arrogate sth. to oneself. *a.* **-able.**
attribut [atriby], *s.m.* **1.** Attribute. **2.** *Log: Gram:* Predicate. **Adjectif attribut,** predicative adjective.
attributif, -ive [atribytif, -iːv], *a.* Predicative.
attribution [atribysjɔ̃], *s.f.* **1.** Assigning, attribution, attributing, ascription (*à,* to); allocation, allocating (of duties, parts). **2.** Usu. *pl.* (*a*) Prerogative; powers. **Cela rentre dans ses attributions,** this lies within his competence, his province. (*b*) Sphere of duties; functions.
attrist|er [atriste], *v.tr.* (*a*) To sadden, grieve. (*b*) To give a gloomy appearance to (sth.). [TRISTE] *a.* **-ant.**
s'attrister, to grow sad.
attristé, *a.* Sad (face); sorrowful (look).
attrition [atrisjɔ̃], *s.f.* Attrition; abrasion; wearing away.
attroupement [atrupmɑ̃], *s.m.* Unlawful assembly; *F:* mob. **Chef d'attroupement,** ringleader.
attrouper [atrupe], *v.tr.* To gather (mob, etc.) together. [TROUPE]
s'attrouper, to gather into a mob.
au [o] = *à le.* See À and LE.
aubade [obad], *s.f.* **1.** *Mus:* Aubade; morning military-band concert. **2.** *F:* Catcalling; rag (at dawn).
aubaine [obɛn], *s.f.* Windfall, godsend.
aube[1] [oːb], *s.f.* **1.** Dawn. *A l'a. du jour,* at dawn; at break of day, at daybreak. **2.** *Ecc:* Alb.
aube[2], *s.f.* (*a*) Paddle, blade, float(-board) (of wheel). **Roue à aubes,** paddle-wheel. (*b*) Blade (of turbine); vane (of fan).
aubépine [obepin], *s.f. Bot:* Hawthorn, white-thorn, may-bush. **Fleurs d'aubépine,** may.
auberge [obɛrʒ], *s.f.* (*a*) Inn. (*b*) *Auberges de la jeunesse,* youth hostels.
aubergine [obɛrʒin], *s.f. Bot:* Aubergine, egg-plant.

aubergiste [oberʒist], *s.m. & f.* Innkeeper.

aubier [obje], *s.m. Bot:* Sap-wood.

aubour [obuːr], *s.m. Bot:* (*a*) Laburnum. (*b*) Wild guelder rose.

aucun, -une [okœ̃, -yn]. **1.** *pron.* (*a*) Anyone, any. *Il travaille plus qu'a.*, he works more than anyone. (*b*) (With implied negation) *De vos soi-disant amis, a. interviendra-t-il?* of your so-called friends, will any intervene? (*c*) (With negation expressed or understood) (i) No one, nobody. *Prov:* **Aucun n'est prophète chez soi,** no man is a prophet in his own country. (ii) None, not any. *Je ne me fie à a. d'entre eux,* I don't trust any of them. (*d*) *pl. Lit:* Some people, some folk. *Aucuns, d'aucuns, prétendent qu'il est encore en vie,* some (people) maintain, some there are who maintain, that he is still alive. **2.** *a.* (*a*) Any. *Un des plus beaux livres qui aient été écrits sur a. sujet,* one of the finest books that have been written on any subject. (*b*) (With negation expressed or understood) *Vendre qch. sans a. bénéfice,* to sell sth. without any profit. *Le fait n'a aucune importance,* the fact is of no importance. **3.** *a. pl. Lit:* **D'aucunes fois . . .,** sometimes. . . .

aucunement [okynmã], *adv.* **1.** (With implied negation) In any way, at all. *Le connaissez-vous a.?* do you know him at all? **2.** (With negation expressed or understood) In no way, in no wise; not at all; by no means; not in the slightest; not in the least. *Je ne le connais a.,* I don't know him at all. *Sans a. vouloir critiquer . . .,* without in any way wishing to criticize. . . .

audace [odas], *s.f.* Audacity audaciousness. **1.** Boldness, daring. *Son a. à attaquer,* his boldness in attacking, in attack. *N'ayez pas l'a. de le toucher!* don't you dare touch him! **2.** Impudence. *Vous avez l'a. de me dire cela!* you have the face to tell me that! *Son a. à mentir, dans le mensonge,* his brazen lying.

audacieu|x, -euse [odasjø, -øːz], *a.* Audacious. **1.** Bold, daring. *Homme a. à faire qch.*, man bold to do sth. **2.** Impudent; brazen (lie, etc.). *Vêtement a.*, daring costume. *adv.* **-sement.**

au-dessous [odsu], *adv.* **1.** (*a*) Below (it); underneath. *Sur la table et a.-d.*, on the table and below it. *Les locataires a.-d.*, the occupiers below. (*b*) *Les enfants âgés de sept ans et a.-d.*, children of seven years old and under. **2.** *Prep. phr.* **Au-dessous de.** (*a*) Below, under. *A.-d. du genou*, below the knee. *Les locataires a.-d. de nous*, the occupiers below us. *Quinze degrés a.-d: de zéro*, fifteen degrees below zero. *Il est a.-d. de lui de se plaindre*, it is beneath him to complain. (*b*) *Épouser qn a.-d. de soi*, to marry beneath one. (*c*) *A.-d. de cinq ans*, under five (years of age). *Quantités a.-d. de* 30 *kilos*, quantities of less than 60 lbs. (*d*) *Son travail était a.-d. de mon attente*, his work fell short of my expectation.

au-dessus [odsy], *adv.* **1.** (*a*) Above (it). *Une cour avec un vitrage a.-d.*, a court with a glazed roof over it. (*b*) *Mille francs et a.-d.*, a thousand francs and upwards. **2.** *Prep.phr.* **Au-dessus de.** (*a*) Above. *Il a son nom a.-d. de la porte*, his name is above the door, over the door. *Nous demeurons l'un a.-d. de l'autre*, we live one above the other. *Les avions volaient a.-d. de nos têtes*, the planes were flying overhead. *Il n'est guère a.-d. d'un paysan*, he is little better than a peasant. *Il est a.-d. de cela*, he is above doing such a thing. (*b*) *A.-d. de cinq ans*, over five (years of age). (*c*) **Au-dessus de tout éloge,** beyond all praise. *La tâche est a.-d. de leurs forces, F:* the task is too much for them.

au-devant [odvã], *adv.* (Used only in such phrases as) **Aller, courir, se jeter, au-devant 1.** *Quand il y a du danger, je vais a.-d.*, when there is danger ahead, I go to meet it. **2.** *Prep.phr.* **Au-devant de.** (*a*) *Aller, courir, a.-d. de qn*, to go, run, to meet s.o. *Aller a.-d. des désirs de qn*, to anticipate s.o.'s wishes. (*b*) *Aller a.-d. d'un danger*, to provide against a danger. (*c*) *Aller a.-d. d'une défaite*, to court failure.

aud|ible [odibl], *a.* Audible. *s.f.* **-ibilité.**

audience [odjãːs], *s.f.* (*a*) Hearing. **Vous avez audience,** I am ready to hear you. (*b*) (Of king) **Tenir une audience,** to hold an audience. (*c*) *Jur:* Hearing (by the court); sitting, session, court. **Plaider en audience publique,** to plead in open court. **Lever l'audience,** to close the session, the sitting.

audit [odi]. See LEDIT.

auditeur, -trice [oditœːr, -tris], *s.* Hearer, listener. *Les auditeurs,* the audience.

audition [odisjɔ̃], *s.f.* **1.** Hearing (of sounds); audition. **2.** (*a*) *A. musicale,* (private) musical recital. *W.Tel:* **Auditions musicales,** wireless concerts. **Auditions du jour,** to-day's broadcasting. (*b*) Trial hearing (of singer, etc.). (*c*) *Jur:* **Audition des témoins,** hearing of the witnesses.

auditoire [oditwaːr], *s.m.* **1.** Auditorium, auditory. **2.** Audience (assembly of listeners). *Ecc:* Congregation.

auge [oːʒ], *s.f.* (*a*) Feeding-trough. *A. d'écurie,* manger. (*b*) *A. à mortier,* mortar-trough.

auget [oʒɛ], *s.m.* **1.** (Small) trough. *A. d'une cage,* seed-trough of a bird-cage. **2.** Bucket (of water-wheel). **Roue à augets,** bucket-wheel, overshot wheel. [AUGE]

Augias [oʒjɑːs]. *Pr.n.m. Gr.Myth:* Auge(i)as. **Les écuries d'Augias,** the Augean stables.

augmentation [ɔgmɑ̃tasjɔ̃], *s.f.* Increase, augmentation, enlargement. *Mth:* Increase (of function, etc.). *A. de gages,* rise in wages. *A. de prix,* advance in prices. **Être en augmentation,** to be on the increase.

augmenter [ɔgmɑ̃te]. **1.** *v.tr.* To increase, augment. *A. sa maison,* to enlarge one's establishment. *A. ses terres,* to extend, add to, one's estate. *Édition augmentée,* enlarged edition. *A. le prix de qch.,* to raise, advance, put up, the price of sth. *F:* **Augmenter qn,** to raise, increase, s.o.'s salary, wages, or rent. **2.** *v.i.* To increase. *Le crime augmente beaucoup,* crime is on the increase. *La rivière a augmenté,* the river has risen. *Tout a, est, augmenté de prix,* everything has risen in price.

augure[1] [ɔgyːr, o-], *s.m. Rom.Ant:* Augur.

augure[2], *s.m.* Augury, omen. *Prendre les augures,* to take the auguries. **De bon augure,** auspicious. **De mauvais augure,** ominous. **Oiseau de mauvais augure,** bird of ill omen.

augurer [ɔgyre, o-], *v.tr.* To augur, forecast. *A. bien de qch.,* to augur well of sth. *Qu'en augurez-vous?* what do you think will come of it?

Auguste[1] [ɔgyst, o-]. *Pr.n.m.* Augustus. *Lit:* **Le Siècle d'Auguste,** the Augustan Age.

auguste[2], *a.* August, majestic. *adv.* **-ment.**

aujourd'hui [oʒurdɥi], *adv.* To-day. *Cela ne se pratique plus a.,* this is not done nowadays. **D'aujourd'hui en huit, en quinze,** this day week, fortnight. **Il y a aujourd'hui huit jours,** a week ago to-day.

aumône [omoːn, -ɔn], *s.f.* Alms. **Faire l'aumône à qn,** to give alms to s.o. **Donner qch. en aumône à qn,** to give s.o. sth. out of charity. *Réduit à l'a.,* reduced to beggary. *Vivre d'a.,* to live on charity.

aumônier [omonje, -mɔ-], *s.m.* **1.** Almoner. **2.** Chaplain. *A. militaire,* army chaplain; padre.

aumônière [omonjɛːr], *s.f.* **1.** Chain purse; mesh-bag. **2.** Dorothy bag.

aunaie [onɛ], *s.f.* Plantation of alders.

aune[1] [oːn], *s.m. Bot:* Alder.

aune[2], *s.f. A:* Ell. *F:* Figure longue d'une aune, face as long as a fiddle. **Mesurer les autres à son aune,** to judge others by oneself. *Prov:* Au bout de l'aune faut le drap, all things have an end. *Cf.* FAILLIR 1.

auparavant [oparavã], *adv.* Before(hand), previously. *A. il faut s'assurer de . . .,* first we must make sure of. . . . L'année d'auparavant, the year before. *Un moment a.,* a moment before.

auprès [oprɛ], *adv.* **1.** (*a*) Close to. *Voilà l'église, la maison est tout a.,* there is the church, the house is close to it, hard by. (*b*) *Il n'y a rien à mettre a.,* there is nothing to be compared with it. **2.** Auprès de. (*a*) Close to, (hard) by, close by, beside, near. **Tout auprès de qch.,** close beside sth. **Ambassadeur auprès du roi de Suède,** Ambassador to the King of Sweden, at the Court of Sweden. *Il vit a. de ses parents,* he lives with his parents. (*b*) *Agir a. de qn,* to use one's influence with s.o. *Être bien a. de qn,* to be in favour with s.o. *Il cherche à me nuire a. de vous,* he is trying to set you against me. (*c*) (With motion) *Admettre qn a. de qn,* to admit s.o. into s.o.'s presence. (*d*) Compared with, in comparison with. *Nous ne sommes rien a. de lui,* we are (as) nothing beside him. [PRÈS]

auquel [okɛl]. See LEQUEL.

aur-a, -ai, -ons. See AVOIR.

auréole [oreol], *s.f.* **1.** (*a*) Aureola, aureole, glory, halo (of saint). (*b*) Halo (of moon). **2.** *Phot:* Halated patch.

auréolé [oreole], *a.* Haloed (martyr, etc.).

auriculaire [orikylɛːr]. **1.** *a.* Auricular (confession, etc.). **Témoin a.,** ear-witness. **2.** *s.m.* The little finger.

Aurigny [oriɲi]. *Pr.n.m. Geog:* Alderney.

aurique [orik], *a. Nau:* Fore-and-aft (sail).

auriste [orist], *s.m. Med:* Ear specialist.

aurochs [oroks], *s.m.* Aurochs; wild ox.

aurore [oroːr]. **1.** *s.f.* (*a*) Dawn, day-break; break of day. *Poet:* L'aurore aux doigts de rose, the rosy-fingered morn. **Beauté à son aurore,** budding beauty. (*b*) **Aurore boréale,** aurora borealis; northern lights. **2.** *Pr.n.f. Myth:* Aurora.

auscult|er [oskylte], *v.tr. Med:* To examine (s.o.) by auscultation; to sound (patient). *s.f.* **-ation.**

auspice [ospis], *s.m.* Usu. *pl.* (*a*) *Rom. Ant:* Auspice. **Prendre les auspices,** to take the auspices. (*b*) Omen, presage. *Mauvais a.,* ill omen. *L'année commence sous de riants auspices,* the year begins auspiciously. **Faire qch. sous les auspices de qn,** to do sth. under s.o.'s patronage, under the auspices of s.o.

aussi [osi]. **1.** *adv.* (*a*) As (in comparative sentences). **Pas aussi,** not so, not as. *Il est a. grand que son frère,* he is as tall as his brother. *Il n'est pas a. grand que vous,* he is not as tall as you. *Vous ne le connaissez pas a. bien que moi,* you don't know him so well as I do. (*b*) So. *Après avoir attendu a. longtemps,* after waiting so long, for such a long time. (*c*) (i) Also, too. *Vous venez a.,* you are coming too. (ii) So. **Moi aussi,** so can I, so do I, so shall I, so did I, etc. *J'ai froid.—Moi a.,* I am cold.—So am I. (*d*) *Conj.phr.* **Aussi bien que,** as well as; (both) . . . and. . . . *Aristote, a. bien que Platon, affirme(nt) que . . .,* Aristotle, as well as Plato, asserts that. . . . *Le paysan, a. bien que sa femme, se frotta(ien)t les*

mains, (both) the peasant and his wife rubbed their hands. (The *pl.* concord is the more usual.) **2.** *conj.* (*a*) Therefore, consequently, so. *La vie est chère ici,* aussi nous devons, aussi devons-nous, économiser, living is dear here, so (that), consequently, we have to economize. (*b*) **Aussi bien,** moreover, for that matter, in any case, besides. *Venez comme vous êtes; a. bien personne ne fait de toilette,* come as you are; for that matter, indeed, no one is dressing.

aussière [osjɛːr], *s.f. Nau:* Hawser.

aussitôt [osito]. **1.** *adv.* (*a*) Immediately, directly, at once, forthwith. **Aussitôt dit, aussitôt fait,** no sooner said than done. **Aussitôt après,** immediately after. (*b*) *Conj.phr.* **Aussitôt que** + ind., as soon as. *Il se repentit de ses paroles a. qu'il les eut prononcées,* he repented (of) his words as soon as he had uttered them. **2.** *prep.* **Aussitôt son départ, je reviens,** as soon as he is gone I shall come back.

austère [ostɛːr], *a.* Austere (life); severe (style); stern (countenance). *adv.* **-ment.**

austérité [osterite], *s.f.* Austerity. **1.** Austereness, strictness, sternness. **2.** *Pratiquer des austérités,* to practise austerities.

austral, -als, -aux [ostral, -o], *a.* Austral, southern (hemisphere, etc.).

Australasie [ostralazi]. *Pr.n.f.* Australasia.

Australie [ostrali]. *Pr.n.f.* Australia. *L'A. septentrionale,* the Northern Territory.

australien, -ienne [ostraljɛ̃, -jɛn], *a. & s.* Australian.

autan [otã], *s.m. Poet:* South wind. *Braver les autans,* to brave the elements.

autant [otã], *adv.* **1.** (*a*) As much, so much; as many, so many. *Je ne le savais pas a. respecté,* I did not know he was so much respected. **C'est autant de gagné,** it is so much to the good. **Autant en emporte le vent,** it is all idle talk. *Il a cinq voitures,* **tout le monde n'en a pas autant,** he keeps five cars, not everybody has so many. *Je consens mais* **à charge d'autant,** I consent but on condition that I may do as much for you. **Autant vous l'aimez, autant il vous hait,** he hates you as much as you love him. **Tout autant,** quite as much ; quite as many. **Encore autant, une fois autant,** twice as much; as much again; as many again. *Il se leva,* **j'en fis autant,** he got up and I did the same. (*b*) (i) **Autant vaut.** *Le travail est fini ou a. vaut,* the work is as good as finished. *A. vaut rester ici,* we may as well stay here. **Autant vaudrait dire que . . .,** one might as well say that. . . . (ii) (With ellipsis of *valoir*) **Ils ont autant dire accepté,** they have practically accepted. *A. dire mille francs,* we might as well say a thousand francs. **Autant ne rien faire du tout,** we might as well do nothing at all. S.a. AIMER 1. **2. Autant que.** (*a*) As much as, as many as. *Faites a. que vous pourrez,* do as much as you can. *Il est a. à craindre qu'elle,* he is as much to be feared as she is. *L'homme n'est responsable qu'a. qu'il est libre,* man is responsible only insomuch as he is free. *Venez tous,* **autant que vous soyez,** come all of you, however many you may be. (*b*) As far as, as near as. *A. que j'en puis juger,* as far as I can judge. **(Pour) autant que, autant que, je puisse m'en souvenir, autant qu'il m'en souvienne,** as far as, as near as, I can remember ; to the best of my recollection. S.a. SAVOIR 2. **Pour autant que nous désirions vous aider . . .,** much as we desire to help you. . . . **3. Autant de,** as much, as many, so much, so many. (*a*) *Ils ont a. de terrain, a. d'amis, que vous,* they have as much ground, as many friends, as you. *Se battre* *avec a. d'audace que d'habileté,* to fight with no less daring than skill. (*b*) **Ce sera autant de moins à payer,** it will be so much the less to pay. **C'est autant de fait,** it is so much done. **4. D'autant.** (*a*) *Nous mangeâmes comme quatre et bûmes d'a.,* we ate ravenously and were not behind with the drink. *Conj.phr.* **D'autant que . . ., d'autant plus que . . .,** more especially as. . . . *Vous devriez faire un grand voyage, d'a.* (*plus*) *que vous êtes riche,* you ought to go for a long voyage, (more) especially as you are well-to-do. (*b*) **D'autant plus, moins,** (all, so much) the more, the less. *Je l'en aime d'autant plus,* I like him (all) the better for it. *Ses défauts me le rendent d'a. plus cher,* I love him all the better for his faults. (*c*) **D'autant plus, moins,** . . . que . . ., (all) the more, the less, . . . as. . . . *J'en suis d'a. plus surpris que* . . ., I am all the more surprised as. . . . **Les aiguilles sont d'autant meilleures que leur pointe est plus fine,** the sharper the point the better the needle. *On attache d'a. plus de prix aux joies de la vie qu'elles sont moins nombreuses,* the fewer the joys of life the more we value them.

autarcie [otarsi], *s.f.* National self-sufficiency; autarky.

autel [otel], *s.m.* Altar. **Maître autel,** high altar.

auteur [otœːr], *s.m.* **1.** Author, perpetrator (of crime); promoter (of scheme). *A. d'un procédé,* originator of a process. *A. d'un accident,* party at fault in an accident. *Être l'a. de la ruine de qn,* to be the cause of s.o.'s downfall. **Les auteurs de nos jours,** our progenitors. **2.** Author, writer (of book); composer (of song); painter (of picture). **Femme auteur,** authoress. **Droit d'auteur,** copyright. **Droits d'auteur,** royalties.

authenticité [otãtisite], *s.f.* Authenticity, genuineness.

authentique [otãtik], *a.* Authentic, genuine. *C'est un fait a.,* it's a positive fact.

auto- [oto], *pref.* **1.** Auto-. *Autocéphale,* autocephalous (bishop, etc.). **2.** Self-. *Auto-équilibrant,* self-balancing. **3.** Motor. *Auto-arroseuse,* motor watering-cart.

auto [oto, o-], *s.f.* F: (= AUTOMOBILE) Motor car. *A. de tourisme,* touring-car. *Je suis venu avec l'a.,* **en auto,** I came in the car, by car. **Faire de l'auto,** to go in for motoring. **Aller en auto jusqu'à Paris,** to motor to Paris.

auto-allumage, *s.m. I.C.E:* **1.** Self-ignition. **2.** Pre-ignition, *F:* pinking.

auto-ambulance, *s.f.* Motor-ambulance. *pl.* **Des autos-ambulances.**

autobiographie [otobjografi], *s.f.* Autobiography.

autobiographique [otobjografik], *a.* Autobiographic(al).

autobus [otobyːs], *s.m. Aut:* Motor (omni)bus. *A. à trolley,* electric trolley-bus.

auto-camion [otokamjõ], *s.m.* Motor lorry. *pl.* **Des autos-camions.**

autocar [otokaːr], *s.m.* Motor coach.

autochtone [otoktoːn, -tɔn]. **1.** *a.* Autochthonal, autochthonous (race, etc.). **2.** *s.* Autochthon.

autoclave [otoklaːv], *s.m.* **1.** (*a*) *Ch: Ind:* Autoclave; digester. (*b*) Sterilizer. (*c*) *Cu:* Pressure cooker. **2.** Manhole lid.

autocopier [otokɔpje], *v.tr.* To duplicate; to hectograph or cyclostyle (circulars, etc.).

autocrate [otokrat]. **1.** *s.m.* Autocrat. **2.** *a.* Autocratic.

autocratie [otokrasi], *s.f.* Autocracy.

autocratique [otokratik], *a.* Autocratic. *adv.* **-ment,** -ally.

autodafé [otodafe], *s.m. Hist:* Auto-da-fé. *F: Faire un a. de ses manuscrits,* to commit one's manuscripts to the flames.

autodémarreur [otodemarœːr], *s.m. Aut: etc:* Self-starter.

autodidacte [otodidakt]. **1.** *a.* Self-taught. **2.** *s.* Autodidact.

autodrome [otodrom, -droːm], *s.m.* Motor-racing track.

autogène [otoʒen], *a.* Autogenous. See also SOUDURE 1.

autographe [otograf]. **1.** *a.* Autograph(ic) (letter, etc.). **2.** *s.m.* Autograph.

autographier [otografje], *v.tr.* To autograph.

autogyre [otoʒiːr], *s.m. Av:* Autogyro.

auto-inductance, *s.f. El:* Self-inductance.

auto-induction, *s.f. El:* Self-induction.

automate [otomat], *s.m.* Automaton.

automatique [otomatik], *a.* Automatic (action); self-acting (apparatus). S.a. DISTRIBUTEUR 2.

Automédon [otomedõ]. **1.** *Pr.n.m. Gr.Myth:* Automedon. **2.** *s.m. F: Hum:* Cabby.

automnal, -aux [otomnal, ot-, -o], *a.* Autumnal.

automne [oton], *s.m. or f.* Autumn, *U.S:* fall. **En automne,** in autumn.

automobile [otomobil, ot-]. **1.** *a.* (*a*) Self-propelling. **Voiture automobile,** motor vehicle. *Canot a.,* motor boat. (*b*) **Club automobile,** automobile club. **Salon automobile,** motor show. **2.** *s.f.,* occ. *m.* (Motor) car, *U.S:* automobile. **Aller en automobile,** to motor. S.a. AUTO.

automobilisme [otomobilism], *s.m.* Motoring.

automobiliste [otomobilist], *s.m. & f.* Motorist.

automoteur, -trice [otomotœːr, -tris]. **1.** *a.* Self-propelling (vehicle). **2.** *s.f.* **Automotrice,** self-propelling railway coach; rail-car.

autonome [otonom], *a.* Autonomous, self-governing.

autonomie [otonomi], *s.f.* Autonomy, self-government.

autoplastie [otoplasti], *s.f.* Plastic surgery.

autopsie [otopsi], *s.f.* Autopsy; post-mortem examination.

autorail [otoraːj], *s.m.* Rail-car.

autorisation [otorizasjõ, ot-], *s.f.* **1.** Authorization, authority; permit. *Donner à qn une a. pour faire qch.,* to authorize s.o. to do sth. *A. spéciale,* special permit. **2.** Licence. *A. de colportage,* pedlar's licence. *Avoir l'a. de vendre qch.,* to be licensed to sell sth.

autoriser [otorize, ot-], *v.tr.* **1.** To invest (s.o.) with authority. *A. qn à faire qch.,* to authorize, empower, s.o. to do sth.; to give s.o. authority to do sth. **2.** To justify, sanction (an action). **s'autoriser** *de qn,* to act on the authority of s.o.

autorisé, *a.* Authorized, authoritative; of approved authority.

autoritaire [otoritɛːr, ot-]. **1.** *a.* Authoritative, dictatorial, overbearing, self-assertive, *F:* bossy. **2.** *s.m.* Authoritarian. *adv.* **-ment.**

autorité [otorite, ot-], *s.f.* **1.** (*a*) Authority. **Il veut tout emporter d'autorité,** he wants his own way in everything. **Agir de pleine autorité,** to act with full powers. *Territoire soumis à l'a. de* . . ., area within the jurisdiction of. . . . (*b*) *L'a. de l'âge, de l'expérience,* the authority of age, of experience. **Faire autorité** *en matière de faïence,* to be an authority on china. *Sa parole a de l'a.,* his word carries weight. **2.** (*a*) **Les autorités** (*d'une ville*), the authorities (of a town). (*b*) *Alléguer des autorités,* to cite authorities.

auto-stop [otostop], *s.m. F:* Hitch-hiking. *Aller en a.-s.,* to hitch-hike.

autostrade [otɔstrad], *s.f.* Autostrada; road specially affected to motor cars.

autosuggestion [otɔsygʒɛstjɔ̃], *s.f.* Autosuggestion.

auto-taxi, *s.m.* Taxi(-cab). *pl. Des autos-taxis.*

auto-tracteur [otɔtraktœ:r], *s.m.* Motor tractor. *pl. Des autos-tracteurs.*

autour[1] [otu:r], *adv.* **I.** Round (it, them); about (it, them). *Une vieille ville avec des murs tout a.,* an old town with walls all round (it). **Il demeure ici autour,** he lives hereabouts. *Prov:* **Il ne faut pas confondre autour avec alentour,** we must not mistake one thing for another. **2.** *Prep.phr.* **Autour de,** round, about. *Assis a. de la table,* seated round the table. *F:* **Il a autour de cinquante ans,** he is (somewhere) about fifty. **Tourner autour de la question, autour du pot,** to beat about the bush. [TOUR]

autour[2], *s.m. Orn:* Goshawk.

autre [o:tr], *a. & pron.* **I.** (a) Other, further. *Les deux cents autres francs,* the other two hundred francs. *Tous les autres verbes que ceux en -er,* all verbs other than those in -er. *Un a. jour,* another day. *Les défauts des autres,* the failings of others. **D'autres vous diront que . . .,** others will tell you that. . . . *Tous les autres sont là,* all the others are there. *On vous préfère à tous autres,* they prefer you to all others. *Il y en a d'autres que lui,* there are others besides him. *Encore bien d'autres,* many more besides. **Les choux et autres légumes,** cabbages and (all) other vegetables. **Les choux et d'autres légumes,** cabbages and some other vegetables. *Sans a. perte de temps,* without further loss of time. **Parler de choses et d'autres,** to talk about one thing and another. *Je l'ai vu l'autre jour,* I saw him the other day. **C'est une raison comme une autre,** it's a good enough reason. *F:* **Comme dit l'autre,** as the saying goes; as people say. (b) (Stressing the pers. pron.) *Ils n'en savent rien eux autres,* they know nothing about it. **Vous autres hommes** (*vous*) *êtes seuls coupables,* it is you men who are alone to blame. **Nous autres Anglais,** we English. (c) *Cela peut arriver d'un jour à l'autre,* it may happen any day. *Je l'attends d'un moment à l'autre,* I expect him any moment. *Je le vois de temps à autre,* I see him now and again, now and then. *Sa réputation grandit d'une année à l'autre,* his fame is increasing from year to year. (d) **L'un et l'autre,** both. **Les uns et les autres,** (i) one and another, (ii) both parties. **L'un et l'autre a été puni, ont été punis,** both were punished. (e) **L'un ou l'autre,** either. **Ni l'un ni l'autre,** neither. *Comme l'une ou l'a. me rendrait heureux!* how happy could I be with either! *Ni l'un ni l'a. ne sont venus,* neither of them came. (f) **L'un . . ., l'autre . . .,** one . . ., the other. . . . **L'un dit ceci, l'a. dit cela,** one says this and the other says that. **Les uns . . ., les autres . . .,** some . . ., others . . .; some . . ., some. . . . *Ils s'en allèrent les uns par ci, les autres par là,* they went off some one way some another. **Sans prendre parti pour les uns ni pour les autres,** without taking either side. (g) **L'un l'autre,** each other, one another. *Lui et sa femme s'admirent l'un l'a.,* he and his wife admire one another. **Elles se moquent les unes des autres,** they make game of each other. (h) **L'un dans l'autre, on se fait trente francs,** one thing with another, on an average, we earn thirty francs. **2.** (a) Other, different. *Prov:* **Autres temps autres mœurs,** other days other ways; manners change with the times. *Quand je le revis je le trouvai (tout) a.,* when I saw him again I found him (quite) different, altered. **Une tout(e) autre**

femme, quite a different woman. *J'ai des idées autres,* my ideas are different. *F:* **En voilà bien d'une autre!** here's another business, another kettle of fish! **J'en ai vu bien d'autres,** that's nothing; I've been through worse than that. **Il n'en fait jamais d'autres!** that's just like him! (b) (Someone, something) else. *Adressez-vous à quelqu'un d'autre,* ask someone else, somebody else. **Il n'est pas plus bête qu'un autre,** he's no more stupid than anyone else. **Nul autre, personne (d')autre,** *ne l'a vu,* no one else, nobody else, saw him. (*Dites cela*) **à d'autres!** nonsense! tell that to the marines! (c) *indef.pron.m.* **Autre chose,** something else. *J'ai a. chose d'important à vous dire,* I have something else of importance to tell you. **C'est tout autre chose!** that's quite a different matter! S.a. PART[1] 3.

autrefois [otrəfwa], *adv.* Formerly; in the past. **Il y avait autrefois un roi,** once upon a time there was a king. *C'était l'usage a.,* it was the custom formerly, in times past, in olden days. *Livre a. si populaire,* book once, at one time, so popular. *Les hommes d'a.,* the men of old, of olden times, of long ago, of yore.

autrement [otrəmã], *adv.* Otherwise. **I.** (a) Differently. **Il agit autrement qu'il ne parle,** he acts differently from the way he talks. *Il ne put faire a. que d'obéir,* he could not (choose) but obey, do otherwise than obey. (b) **C'est bien autrement sérieux,** that is far more serious. *F:* **Il n'est pas autrement riche,** he is not particularly rich. **2.** *Venez demain, autrement il sera trop tard,* come to-morrow, otherwise, or else, it will be too late.

Autriche [otriʃ]. *Pr.n.f. Geog:* Austria.

autrichien, -ienne [otriʃjɛ̃, -jɛn], *a. & s.* Austrian.

autruche [otryʃ], *s.f. Orn:* Ostrich. **Plumes d'autruche,** ostrich-feathers; ostrich-plume.

autrui [otrɥi], *pron.indef.* Others; other people. *Convoiter le bien d'a.,* to covet another's property.

auvent [ovã], *s.m.* **I.** (a) Penthouse, open shed. (b) Porch roof. **2.** Hood (over hearth or part of laboratory). **3.** *Aut:* (a) Dash; scuttle. (b) *Auvents de capot,* bonnet louvres.

auvergnat, -ate [ovɛrɲa, -at], *a. & s.* (Native) of Auvergne; Auvergnat.

aux [o]. = *à les.* See À and LE.

auxiliaire [ɔksiljɛ:r, o-]. **I.** *a.* Auxiliary (verb, troops). **Bureau auxiliaire,** sub-office. **2.** *s.* Auxiliary. (a) Aid, assistant. (b) *s.m.pl.* Subsidiary troops; auxiliaries.

auxquels, -elles. See LEQUEL.

avachir [avaʃi:r], *v.tr.* To soften (leather, etc.). [VACHE]

s'avach|ir. I. To lose shape; (of leather, etc.) to perish. *F:* **Elle s'est avachie,** she has got to look very slack, very sloppy. **2.** *S'a. à ne rien faire,* to sink into sloth. *s.m.* **-issement.**

avachi, *a.* **I.** (a) (Of boots, etc.) Out of shape (through much use). (b) Slack, sloppy (figure). **2. C'est un homme avachi,** he will never do any more good.

aval[1], **-als** [aval], *s.m. Fin:* Endorsement (on bill).

aval[2], *s.m.* **I.** Lower part (of stream). *Les villages d'a.,* the villages down the stream. **En aval,** down-stream. *En a. du pont,* below the bridge. **2. Vent d'aval,** westerly wind; sea-breeze. [VAL]

avalanche [avalã:ʃ], *s.f.* Avalanche. *F:* **Avalanche d'injures,** shower of insults.

aval|er [avale], *v.tr.* **I.** To swallow (down); to drink up; to devour. *A. son repas,* to bolt one's

meal. *A. son vin à grandes gorgées*, to gulp down
one's wine. *C'est dur à avaler*, that's a bitter pill;
I can hardly stomach that. **Avaler une couleuvre,
une insulte**, to pocket an affront. *P:* **Avaler sa
langue**, (i) to keep silent, (ii) to be bored. **2.** To
lower, let down. S.a. BOTTE² 2. [VAL] *s.m.*
-ement.

avance [avɑ̃:s], *s.f.* **1.** Advance, lead. *Mouvement
d'a. et de recul*, backward and forward movement.
Avoir de l'avance sur qn, to be ahead, in advance,
of s.o.; to have the start of s.o. *Garder son a.
sur qn*, to maintain one's lead over s.o. **Prendre de
l'avance sur un concurrent**, to draw away from
a competitor. *Arriver avec cinq minutes d'a.*, to
arrive five minutes before time. *F:* **La belle
avance!** much good that will do you! *El.E: A.
d'une magnéto*, magneto-lead. *I.C.E:* **Avance à
l'allumage**, ignition advance, advance of the spark.
Mettre de l'a. à l'allumage, to advance the spark.
Levier d'avance, ignition lever. **2.** *Mec.E:* Feed
movement, travel (of tool). **3.** Projection. **Balcon
qui forme avance**, balcony that juts out. **4.** (*a*)
Avance de fonds, advance, loan. **Faire une
avance de mille francs à qn**, to advance s.o. a
thousand francs. (*b*) *pl.* **Faire des avances à qn**,
to make approaches, advances, to s.o.; to make
up to s.o. **Faire la moitié des avances**, to meet
s.o. half-way. **Faire les premières avances** (*pour
une réconciliation*), to hold out the olive-branch.
5. *Adv.phr.* (*a*) *Préparé* **d'avance**, prepared beforehand. **Payer qn d'avance**, to pay s.o. in advance.
(*b*) **Se réjouir par avance**, to rejoice beforehand.
(*c*) **Payable à l'avance**, payable in advance.
(*d*) **L'horloge est en avance**, the clock is fast.
Nous sommes en a., we are before our time. *Il est
en a. sur sa classe*, he is ahead of his class.
avancement [avɑ̃smɑ̃], *s.m.* **1.** (*a*) Advancing,
putting forward. *A. de l'outil à la pièce*, feeding
of the tool to the work. (*b*) Putting forward (of
dinner-hour, etc.); hastening (of event, etc.).
(*c*) Furtherance (of plan). (*d*) Promotion, preferment. **Avancement à l'ancienneté**, promotion
by seniority. **2.** Advance(ment), progress. *Je
suis satisfait de son a.*, I am satisfied with his
progress. **3.** Projection, jutting out (of wall
beyond alignment, etc.). **4.** Pitch (of screw).
avancer [avɑ̃se], *v.* (j'avançai(s); n. avançons)
I. *v.tr.* **1.** (*a*) To advance, put forward (one's
hand, etc.). *A. des chaises*, to set chairs (for the
company). *Chess: A. un pion*, to advance a pawn.
(*b*) *A. une proposition*, to put forward a proposal.
2. To make (sth.) earlier; to hasten (sth.) on.
A. l'heure du dîner, to put dinner forward.
3. *A. de l'argent à qn*, to advance money to s.o.
4. To promote (science, s.o.'s interests, etc.).
A quoi cela vous avancera-t-il? what good will
that do you?
II. avancer, *v.i.* **1.** To advance. (*a*) To move
forward; (of ship) to make headway. **Avancer
à grands pas**, to take, make, rapid strides. *A. d'un
pas*, to take one step forward. **Faire avancer les
troupes**, to move the troops forward. *A. en âge*,
to be getting on in years. *Montre qui avance d'une
minute par jour*, watch that gains a minute a day.
(*b*) To progress; to get on; to make headway.
Le travail avance, the work is going forward.
Prov: **Plus on se hâte moins on avance**, more
haste less speed. *A. en grade*, to advance in rank.
2. (*a*) To be ahead of time. *L'horloge avance*, the
clock is fast. *Vous avancez de dix minutes*, your
watch is ten minutes fast. *A. sur son époque*, to be
ahead of one's age. (*b*) (Of roof, etc.) To jut out,
to project.
s'avancer. 1. To move forward, to advance.

S'a. vers qch., to make one's way, to head, towards
sth. *Le bâtiment s'avançait*, the ship drew on.
2. To progress. *La nuit s'avance*, the night is
getting on. *Il s'est trop avancé pour reculer*, he
has gone too far to withdraw. **3.** (Of promontory,
etc.) To jut out.
avancé, *a.* (*a*) *Position avancée*, advanced
position. *Le plus avancé*, foremost. *Rail:* **Signal
avancé**, distant signal. (*b*) *Opinions avancées*, advanced ideas. (*c*) *Élève a.*, forward pupil. **Peu
avancé**, backward. (*d*) *A une heure avancée de la
nuit*, at a late hour of the night. (*e*) **Avancé en âge**,
well on in years. *A un âge a.*, late in life. (*f*) *F:*
Vous voilà bien avancé! a lot of good that has
done you!
avanie [avani], *s.f. F:* Insult, affront. **Faire une
avanie à qn**, to put an affront on s.o.; to snub s.o.
avant [avɑ̃]. **I. 1.** *prep.* Before. *Venez a. midi*,
come before twelve o'clock. *Pas·a. lundi*, not
before, not until, Monday. *La maison est a.
l'église*, the house comes before the church. *Les
dames a. les messieurs*, ladies before gentlemen;
ladies first. (Surtout et) *avant tout*, first of all;
above all. **2.** (*a*) *Prep.phr.* **Avant de** + *inf. Je vous
reverrai a. de partir*, I shall see you before I leave,
before leaving. (*b*) *Conj.phr.* **Avant que** + *sub.
Je vous reverrai a. que vous (ne) partiez*, I shall see
you again before you leave. (*c*) **Pas avant de, que**,
not before, not until. *Ne partez pas a. d'en recevoir
l'ordre, a. qu'on vous le dise*, don't go until you are
told. **3.** *adv.* **Il était arrivé quelques mois avant**,
he had arrived some months before. *N'allez pas
jusqu'à l'église, sa maison est avant*, do not go as
far as the church, his house comes before. **4.** *adv.*
(*a*) Far, deep. **Pénétrer très avant dans les terres**,
to penetrate far inland. *Entrer plus a. dans une
question*, to go further, more deeply, into a question. (*b*) Far, late. **Bien avant, très avant, dans
la nuit**, far into the night, very late at night.
5. *Adv.phr.* **En avant**, in front; before; forward.
Envoyer qn en a., to send s.o. on in front. *Mouvement en a.*, motion forward; forward movement.
Le plus en avant, the foremost. **Mettre en avant
une raison**, to advance a reason. *Mettre en a. un
candidat*, to put a candidate forward. *Nau:* **En
avant à toute vitesse**, full steam ahead. *Prep.phr,*
En avant de, in front of, ahead of (his class, times,
etc.). **6.** (In adj. relation to sb.) (*a*) Fore, forward,
front. **Essieu avant**, fore-axle. *Aut:* **A roue avant
motrice**, with front-wheel drive. (*b*) **La nuit
d'avant**, the night before; the previous night.
II. avant, *s.m.* **1.** (*a*) *Nau:* Bow, head (of a
ship). **Présenter l'a. à la lame**, to be head to sea.
Le logement de l'équipage est à l'avant, the crew's
quarters are forward. *Par tribord avant*, on the
starboard bow. **Aborder un navire par l'avant**, to
collide with a ship head-on. **Aller de l'avant**,
pousser de l'avant, to go, forge, ahead. (*b*) Front
(of camera, carriage, etc.). **2.** *Fb:* Forward.
Avants très vites, very speedy forwards.
avantage [avɑ̃taːʒ], *s.m.* **1.** Advantage. *Faire à
qn tous les avantages possibles*, to give s.o. every
advantage. *Plan qui offre les plus grands avantages*,
most suitable plan. **Tirer avantage de qch.**, to
turn sth. to account. **S'habiller à son avantage**,
to dress to the best advantage. *Elle est à son a. le
matin*, she looks her best in the morning. **Garder
l'avantage**, to retain the advantage. *Trouver de
l'a. à faire qch.*, to find it an advantage to do sth.
Il y a avantage à + *inf.*, it is best to + *inf.* **Avoir
l'avantage**, to have the best of it. **Avoir l'avantage
du nombre**, to have the advantage in number.
2. *Ten:* (Ad)vantage.
avantager [avɑ̃taʒe], *v.tr.* (j'avantageai(s); n.

avantageons) (*a*) To favour (s.o.); to give (s.o.) an advantage. (*b*) *L'uniforme l'avantage*, he looks well in uniform.

avantagé, *a. Être fort a. par rapport aux autres*, to enjoy many advantages over others.

avantageu|x, -euse [avɑ̃taʒø, -øːz], *a.* **1.** (*a*) Advantageous, favourable. (*b*) *Robe avantageuse*, becoming dress. **2.** Prendre un air avantageux, to preen oneself. *s.m.* Un avantageux, a coxcomb. *adv.* **-sement.**

NOTE. In all the following compounds AVANT is inv., the noun or adj. takes the plural.

avant-bassin, *s.m.* Nau: Outer basin or dock.

avant-bras, *s.m.* Forearm.

avant-centre, *s.m. Fb:* Centre-forward.

avant-corps, *s.m.* Fore-part, projecting part (of building).

avant-cour, *s.f.* Fore-court.

avant-coureur, **1.** *s.m.* Forerunner, harbinger, precursor. *Mil:* Scout. **2.** *a.m.* Precursory, premonitory (symptom).

avant-courrier, -ière, *s.* Forerunner, harbinger, herald. *Poet:* L'avant-courrière du jour, the harbinger of day.

avant-dernier, -ière, *a. & s.* Last but one; penultimate.

avant-garde, *s.f.* **1.** *Mil:* Advanced guard. *F:* Hommes d'avant-garde, men in the van (of reform, etc.); pioneers. **2.** *Navy:* Van (of fleet).

avant-goût, *s.m.* Foretaste.

avant-guerre, *s.m.* Pre-war period. *Prix d'a.-g.,* pre-war prices.

avant-hier [avɑ̃tjɛːr], *adv.* The day before yesterday.

avant-main, *s.m.* **1.** Flat of the hand. **2.** Forequarters, forehand (of horse). **3.** *Ten:* Coup d'avant-main, forehand stroke.

avant-plan, *s.m.* Foreground.

avant-pont, *s.m. Nau:* Fore-deck.

avant-port, *s.m.* Outer harbour.

avant-poste, *s.m. Mil:* Outpost.

avant-projet, *s.m.* Preliminary plan (of works, etc.); draft (of treaty).

avant-propos, *s.m.* **1.** Preface, foreword (to book). **2.** *Après quelques a.-p.,* after some preliminary remarks.

avant-scène, *s.f. Th:* Apron, fore-stage. Loge d'avant-scène, stage-box.

avant-titre, *s.m.* Half-title (of book).

avant-train, *s.m.* **1.** (*a*) Front of carriage. (*b*) Wheels (of plough). (*c*) *Artil:* Limber. *Mettre, décrocher, l'a.-t.,* to limber up, to unlimber. **2.** = AVANT-MAIN 2.

avant-veille, *s.f.* Two days before.

avare [avaːr]. **1.** *a.* (*a*) Miserly. (*b*) *Être a. de paroles*, to be sparing of one's words. **2.** *s.* Miser.

avarice [avaris], *s.f.* Avarice.

avaricieu|x, -ieuse [avarisjø, -jøːz], *a.* Avaricious, stingy. *s.* Un vieil avaricieux, an old screw. *adv.* **-sement.**

avarie [avari], *s.f.* **1.** Damage, injury (to ship, engine, etc.). *Subir une avarie*, to be damaged, to break down. **2.** *M.Ins:* Avaries-frais, average.

avari|er [avarje], *v.tr.* To damage, injure, spoil (goods, etc.). *a.* **-able.**

s'avarier, to deteriorate, go bad.

avatar [avataːr], *s.m.* (*a*) *Hindoo Rel:* Avatar. (*b*) *F:* Transformation. Esp. in *pl.* Avatars, (varied) experiences; ups and downs (of life). (*c*) *F:* Mishap, misadventure.

avec [avɛk]. **1.** *prep.* (*a*) With. *Je vous ai vu avec lui*, I saw you with him, in his company. *Avec du*

courage vous réussirez, with courage you will succeed. *Et avec cela, madame?* anything else, madam? (*b*) *Cabane construite avec quelques planches*, hut built out of a few boards. (*c*) *Cela viendra avec le temps*, that will come in time. (*d*) *Combattre avec courage*, to fight with courage. *Servir son maître avec dévouement, avec un sincère dévouement*, to serve one's master devotedly, with sincere devotion. (*e*) *Avec tous ses défauts je l'aime cependant*, with, in spite of, all his faults I love him still. (*f*) *F:* Avec cela, avec ça. *Je suis grande et avec ça mince*, I am tall, and slender to boot. *Avec ça qu'elle ne savait rien faire* . . ., as moreover, besides which, she was quite untrained. . . . *P:* Avec ca! nonsense! *Avec ça qu'on vous le permettrait!* as if they would let you! do you suppose they would let you? *Avec ça qu'il n'a pas triché!* don't say he didn't cheat! (*g*) D'avec, from. *Séparer le bon d'avec le mauvais*, to separate the good from the bad. **2.** *adv.* With it, with them. *Je saisis une pierre et lui fendis la tête avec*, I seized a stone and cracked his head with it.

avenant [avnɑ̃], *a.* **1.** Comely, pleasing, prepossessing. Mal avenant, unseemly, uncouth. **2.** A l'avenant, in keeping, in conformity, correspondingly. *Et un chapeau à l'a.,* and a hat to match. *Mœurs à l'avenant de leurs croyances,* morals of a piece with their beliefs.

avènement [avɛnmɑ̃], *s.m.* (*a*) Advent (of Christ). (*b*) *A. au trône*, accession to the throne.

avenir [avniːr], *s.m.* Future. *Prédire l'a.,* to predict the future. *Avoir un bel a. devant soi*, to have a fine future, fine prospects, before one. *Jeune homme d'un grand a.,* youth of great promise. *Dans l'avenir*, at some future date. A l'avenir, in (the) future, hereafter, henceforth.

Avent [avɑ̃], *s.m. Ecc:* Advent.

aventure [avɑ̃tyːr], *s.f.* **1.** Adventure. *A. effrayante*, terrifying experience. **2.** Chance, luck, venture. Tenter l'aventure, to try one's luck. A l'aventure, at random; at a venture. *Errer à l'a.,* to wander about aimlessly. Par aventure, d'aventure, by chance, perchance, *A:* peradventure. **3.** Dire, tirer, la bonne aventure (à qn), to tell fortunes; to tell (s.o.'s) fortune.

aventurer [avɑ̃tyre], *v.tr.* To venture, hazard, risk (one's fortune, life, etc.).

s'aventurer, to venture; to take risks.

aventureu|x, -euse [avɑ̃tyrø, -øːz], *a.* Adventurous, venturesome; rash; reckless; overbold (hypothesis, etc.). *Projet a.,* hazardous, risky, plan. *adv.* **-sement.**

aventurier, -ière [avɑ̃tyrje, -jɛːr], *s.* Adventurer; (i) soldier of fortune; (ii) sharper. *C'est un a.,* he lives by his wits. C'est une aventurière, she is an adventuress.

avenu [avny], *a.* Used in the phr. Non avenu, not having occurred; cancelled. S.a. NUL 2.

avenue [avny], *s.f.* Avenue; carriage drive.

avéré [avere], *a.* Authenticated, established (fact, etc.). Crime avéré, patent and established crime. *Ennemi a.,* avowed enemy.

Averne [avɛrn]. *Pr.n.m.* (*a*) *A.Geog:* Le lac Averne, Lake Avernus. (*b*) *Poet:* L'Averne, the infernal regions.

averse [avɛrs], *s.f.* Sudden shower; downpour. *Essuyer une a.,* to be caught in a shower.

aversion [avɛrsjɔ̃], *s.f.* Aversion (envers, pour, to, for, from); dislike (pour, to, for, of). Prendre en aversion, to take a dislike to s.o. Ma bête d'aversion, my pet aversion.

avertir [avɛrtiːr], *v.tr.* A. qn de qch., to warn, notify, advise, s.o. of sth.; to give s.o. notice of sth. *Se tenir pour averti.* to be on one's guard.

Prov: Un homme averti en vaut deux, forewarned is forearmed.

averti, a. Experienced, wide awake (observer, etc.); well-informed.

avertissement [avɛrtismɑ̃], s.m. Warning; notice. Renvoyer qn sans a. préalable, to discharge s.o. at a moment's notice. Avertissement au lecteur, prefatory note, foreword (to book).

avertisseur [avɛrtisœːr], s.m. 1. Warner. Th: Call-boy. 2. Warning signal; call-bell; alarm. Tp: Annunciator. Aut: (Motor-)horn; hooter. Avertisseur d'incendie, fire-alarm.

aveu, -eux [avø], s.m. 1. Hist: Recognition between a vassal and his overlord. F: Homme sans aveu, vagabond, vagrant. 2. Consent, authorization. Obtenir l'a. de qn pour faire qch., to obtain s.o.'s consent to do sth. 3. Avowal, confession. Faire des aveux complets, to make a full confession. De l'aveu de tout le monde . . ., by common consent. . . . De leur propre a. . . ., on their own confession. . . . [AVOUER]

aveuglant [avœglɑ̃], a. Blinding; dazzling.

aveugle [avœgl], a. Blind, sightless. 1. (a) Devenir a., to go blind. (b) s. Un aveugle, a blind man. Les aveugles, the blind. F: C'est un aveugle qui en conduit un autre, it's a case of the blind leading the blind. 2. Arch: Fenêtre aveugle, arcade aveugle, blind window, arch. 3. Blind, unreasoning (hatred); implicit (confidence, etc.). Obéissance a., blind obedience. Être a. sur les défauts de qn, to be blind to s.o.'s faults. Aller à l'aveugle, to grope one's way.

aveuglement [avœgləmɑ̃], s.m. 1. (a) Blinding. (b) Nau: Fothering (of leak). 2. (Moral, mental) blindness; infatuation. Cf. CÉCITÉ.

aveuglément [avœglemɑ̃], adv. Blindly.

aveugler [avœgle], v.tr. 1. (a) To blind (s.o.); to put (s.o.'s) eyes out. (b) To dazzle, blind. 2. Nau: A. une voie d'eau, to stop, fother, a leak.

aveuglette (à l') [alavœglɛt], adv.phr B indly. Aller à l'a., to go blindly on. Avancer à l'a. vers qch., to feel, grope, one's way to sth. Av: Voler à l'a., to fly 'blind.'

aveul|ir [avœliːr], v.tr. To enervate; to render (s.o.) indifferent, blasé; to deaden (feelings, etc.). [VEULE] a. -issant. s.m. -issement.

s'aveulir, to sink into sloth (of mind); to become indifferent to everything.

aviateur, -trice [avjatœːr, -tris], s. Aviator; flier, flyer; airman, -woman.

aviation [avjasjɔ̃], s.f. Aviation. Centre d'a., air-station.

avide [avid], a. Greedy. A. de qch., (i) greedy of sth.; avid of, for, sth.; (ii) eager for sth. Espérances avides, eager hopes. A. de sang, thirsting for blood. adv. -ment.

avidité [avidite], s.f. Avidity, greed(iness). Avec avidité, greedily; eagerly.

avil|ir [aviliːr], v.tr. 1. To render vile; to degrade, debase. 2. Com: To depreciate (currency, prices). [VIL] a. -issant. s.m. -issement.

s'avilir. 1. To debase, lower, demean, oneself. S'a. à faire qch., to demean oneself to the point of doing sth.; to stoop to do(ing) sth. 2. To lose value; to depreciate.

aviné [avine], a. Intoxicated (with wine).

avion [avjɔ̃], s.m. Aeroplane; F: plane. A. monoplace, biplace, single-seater, two-seater (machine). A. marin, seaplane. A. de combat, fighter. A. de bombardement, bombing-plane, bomber. A. de chasse, chaser. A. de reconnaissance, scouting plane. A. de transport, commercial plat e. "Par avion," 'by air-mail.' J'ai fait une partie du

trajet en a., I flew part of the way. **Descendre** d'avion, to deplane. **Pièce contre avions,** anti-aircraft gun.

aviron [avirɔ̃], s.m. 1. Oar. A. de couple, scull. A. de galère, sweep. Armer, border, les avirons, to ship the oars. Engager son aviron, to catch a crab. Coup d'a., stroke. 2. L'aviron, rowing. Cercle d'a., rowing-club Faire de l'aviron, to go in for rowing.

avis [avi], s.m. 1. (a) Opinion, judgment, decision. Exprimer, émettre, un a., to express a view, an opinion. Il exprima l'a. que l'on marchât sur Rome, he proposed that they should march on Rome. Aller aux avis, to put the question to the vote. Prov: Deux avis valent mieux qu'un, two heads are better than one. A, selon, mon avis . . ., in my opinion . . ., to my mind. . . . De l'avis de tous, in the opinion of all. Être du même a. que qn, to be of the same mind, of the same opinion, as s.o. J'ai changé d'avis, I have changed my mind. Je suis d'avis, F: m'est avis, qu'il viendra, my impression is that he will come. Je suis d'avis qu'il vienne, in my opinion he ought to come. Êtes-vous d'a. de rester ici? are you for staying here? (b) Advice, counsel. Un a. paternel, a piece of fatherly advice. Demander l'a. de qn, to ask s.o.'s advice. 2. Notice, intimation, warning, announcement. Avis au public, notice to the public. Donner avis de qch., to give notice of sth. Donner a. que . . ., to give notice that. . . . A. par écrit, notice in writing. Avis au lecteur, foreword, prefatory note (to book). Jusqu'à nouvel avis, until further notice. A moins d'avis contraire, sauf avis contraire, unless I (you) hear to the contrary.

avisément [avizemɑ̃], adv. Advisedly.

aviser [avize]. 1. v.tr. To perceive, to espy, to catch a glimpse of (sth., s.o.); F: to spot (s.o.). (b) A. qn de qch., to inform, warn, s.o. of sth. 2. v.i. A. à qch., to deal with (situation, etc.); to see about sth. A. à un cas, to take such steps as are required in a case. Vous ferez bien d'y a., you had better look to it. A. à faire qch., to see about doing sth. A. à ce que qch. se fasse, to see to it that sth. is done. [AVIS]

s'aviser de qch., to bethink oneself of sth. S'a. de faire qch., to take it into one's head to do sth. Ne vous en avisez pas! you'd better not!

avisé, a. Prudent, circumspect; far-seeing. Il est trop a. pour . . ., he knows better than to. . . . Bien avisé, well-advised. Mesures mal avisées, ill-advised measures.

aviso [avizo], s.m. Navy: Despatch-vessel, advice-boat; sloop; aviso.

aviv|er [avive], v.tr. 1. To quicken; to revive, brighten (fire, colours, etc.); to touch up (colour, picture); to irritate (wound, sore). 2. To put a keen edge on (tool, etc.). s.m. -age.

s'aviver, (of anxiety, etc.) to become more acute.

avocat, -ate [avɔka, -at], s. 1. Jur: Barrister(-at-law); counsel; Fr. & Scot: advocate. Plaider par avocat, to be represented by counsel. Être reçu avocat, to be called to the bar. Entendre les avocats des deux parties, to hear counsel on both sides. 2. Advocate, intercessor. Avocat du diable, devil's advocate.

avoine [avwan], s.f. Oat(s). Farine d'avoine, oatmeal.

avoir [avwaːr]. I. v.tr. (pr.p. ayant; p.p. eu; pr.ind. j'ai, tu as, il a, n. avons, v. avez, ils ont; pr.sub. j'aie, tu aies, il ait, n. ayons, v. ayez, ils aient; imp. aie, ayons, ayez; p.d. j'avais; p.h. j'eus, il eut, n. eûmes, v. eûtes, ils eurent; p.sub.

j'eusse; fu. j'aurai. Avoir is the auxiliary of all transitive and of many intransitive verbs.) **I.** (a) To have, possess. **A.** beaucoup d'amis, to have many friends. **A.** une grande fortune, to be the possessor of a large fortune. (b) Elle avait une robe bleue, she had on, was wearing, a blue dress. Qu'est-ce que vous avez là? what have you got there? Enfants qui ont de leur mère, children who take after their mother. (c) Pred. A. les yeux bleus, to have blue eyes. (d) Avoir dix ans, to be ten years old. Mur qui a dix pieds de haut, wall ten feet high. (e) For the phrases Avoir affaire, faim, froid, pitié, raison, etc., see under these words. **2.** To get, obtain, to come into possession of (sth.). Il a eu le prix, he got the prize. J'ai eu sa réponse ce matin, I got his answer this morning. W.Tel: Avoir Paris, to tune in, pick up, Paris. **3.** F: To get the better of (s.o.). On vous a eu! you've been had! **4.** Avoir = FAIRE, etc. (chiefly in p.h.). Elle eut une exclamation, she uttered an exclamation. Il eut un mouvement brusque, he made a sudden gesture. **5.** To ail. Qu'avez-vous? qu'est-ce que vous avez? what is the matter with you? what ails you? Il a quelque chose, there is something wrong with him. **6.** En avoir. (a) Nous en avons pour deux heures, it will take us two hours. J'en ai assez, I've had enough of it; I am tired, sick, of it. (b) En avoir à, contre, qn, to have a grudge against s.o. A qui en avez-vous? who are you getting at? Quoi qu'il en ait, whatever he may say. **7.** Avoir qch. à faire, to have sth. to do. J'ai à travailler, j'ai un devoir à finir, I have work to do, an exercise to finish. Vous n'avez pas à vous inquiéter, you have no need to feel anxious. **8.** impers. Y avoir. (a) Combien y a-t-il de blessés? how many wounded are there? Il n'y en a qu'un, there is only one. Il y en a qui disent que . . ., there are some, those, who say that. . . . Il n'y a pas de quoi, pray don't mention it. (b) Il y a quelque chose, there is something the matter. Qu'est-ce qu'il y a? what is the matter? F: what's up? (c) Il y a deux ans, two years ago. Il y avait six mois que j'attendais, I had been waiting for the last six months. Il y a de cela trente ans, that was thirty years ago. (d) Combien y a-t-il d'ici à Londres? how far is it (from here) to London? **9.** (Aux. use) J'ai fini, I have done. Attendez que nous ayons fini, wait till we have done. Je l'ai déjà vu, I have seen him before. Je l'ai vu hier, I saw him yesterday. Je l'avais vu la veille, I had seen him the day before. J'eus, j'ai eu, bientôt fini de m'habiller, I was not long dressing. Quand il eut fini de parler, il vint à moi, quand il a eu fini de parler, il est venu à moi, when he had finished speaking he came to me. J'aurai bientôt fini, I shall soon have done.

II. avoir, s.m. Property. Tout mon a., all I possess; my all. Com: Doit et avoir, debit and credit.

avoisinant avwazinã], a. Neighbouring; near by.

avoisiner [avwazine], v.tr. **A.** qch., to be near sth., close, adjacent, to sth. F: Des idées qui avoisinent la folie, ideas bordering on madness. [VOISIN]
  s'avoisiner. **I.** To be adjacent. **2.** (Of season, event) To approach, draw near.
  avoisiné, a. Être bien avoisiné, (i) to have good neighbours, (ii) to be in a good neighbourhood.

avort|er [avɔrte], v.i. To miscarry. Bot: To develop imperfectly; to fail to ripen. Faire a. un dessein, to frustrate a plan, to bring a plan to nought. s.m. **-ement.**

avorton [avɔrtɔ̃], s.m. Puny, undersized, stunted, man or child.

avoué [avwe], s.m. Jur: = Solicitor, attorney-at-law.

avou|er [avwe], v.tr. **I.** To acknowledge (s.o., debt). Pred. **A.** qn pour frère, to acknowledge, own, s.o. as one's brother. S'a. coupable, to admit one's guilt. S'a. vaincu, to acknowledge oneself beaten. **2.** To confess, to own (a misdeed, etc.). Avouez tout! make a clean breast of it! A. avoir fait qch., to own (up) to having done sth. a. **-able.**

avril [avril], s.m. April. En avril, in April. Au mois d'avril, in the month of April. Le sept a., (on) the seventh of April, (on) April (the) seventh. Le premier avril, (i) the first of April; (ii) April-fool-day; All Fools' day. Donner un poisson d'avril à qn, to make an April-fool of s.o.

axe [aks], s.m. **I.** Axis (of plant, the earth, ellipse, etc.). Grand axe, petit axe, major, minor, axis. **2.** Axle, spindle, pin. Axe d'une meule, spindle, axle, arbor, of a grindstone.

axiomatique [aksjɔmatik], a. Axiomatic(al).

axiome [aksjoːm], s.m. Axiom.

axonge [aksɔ̃ːʒ], s.f. Lard; hog's fat.

ayant [εjã]. **I.** See AVOIR. **2.** s.m. Jur: Ayant droit, rightful claimant or owner; interested party; beneficiary. pl. Des ayants droit.

ay-ez, -ons. See AVOIR.

azalée [azale], s.f. Bot: Azalea.

azimut [azimyt], s.m. Azimuth. Nau: Surv: Prendre un a., to take a bearing.

Azincourt [azɛ̃kuːr]. Pr.n.m. Agincourt.

Azor [azɔːr]. Pr.n.m. Name given to dogs. Corresponds to the English Fido.

azotate [azɔtat], s.m. Ch: Nitrate.

azote [azɔt], s.m. Ch: Nitrogen.

azoté [azɔte], a. Nitrogenous. Engrais azotés, nitrate fertilizers, F: nitrates.

azoteux, -euse [azɔtø, -øːz], a. Ch: Nitrous.

azotique [azɔtik], a. Ch: Nitric.

aztèque [aztɛk]. **I.** a. & s. Ethn: Aztec. **2.** s.m. P: Little shrimp of a man.

azur [azyːr], s.m. Azure, blue. Ciel d'a., azure sky. Geog: La Côte d'Azur, the Riviera.

azyme [azim]. **I.** a. Azymous, unleavened (bread). **2.** s.m. Azyme. Jew.Rel: Fête des azymes, feast of unleavened bread.

B, b [be], *s.m.* (The letter) B, b.
baba[1] [baba], *s.m.* *Cu:* Sponge-cake (usu. with currants) steeped in rum syrup ; baba.
baba[2], *a.inv.* *P:* Dumbfounded, flabbergasted. **En rester baba,** to be struck all of a heap
babeurre[1] [babœːr], *s.m.* Buttermilk.
babeurre[2], *s.m.* Dasher (of churn). [BAT BEURRE]
babil [babi(l)], *s.m.* **1.** Prattling ; twittering (of birds); babbling (of a brook). **2.** Prattle (of children).
babillard, -arde [babijaːr, -ard]. **1.** *a.* (Given to) prating ; talkative. *Cours d'eau b.,* babbling brook. **2.** *s.* Tattler, chatterbox.
babill|er [babije], *v.i.* To prattle ; to chatter ; (of brook) to babble. *s.m.* **-age.** *s.m.* **-ement.**
babines [babin], *s.f.pl.* *Z:* Pendulous lips (of monkey, dog, cat) ; chops (of ruminants).
babiole [babjɔl], *s.f.* Curio, knick-knack, bauble.
bâbord [baboːr], *s.m.* *Nau:* Port (side). **La barre toute à bâbord!** hard a-port! **La terre par bâbord!** land on the port side!
bâbordais [babɔrdɛ], *s.m.* *Nau:* Man of the port watch.
babou [babu], *s.m.* Baboo. *pl. Des babous.*
babouche [babuʃ], *s.f.* Turkish slipper ; babouche.
babouin [babwɛ̃], *s.m.* Baboon.
babouines [babwin], *s.f.pl.* *F:* (= BABINES) Mouth, lips. *Vous vous en lécherez les b.,* you'll lick your chops, smack your lips, over it.
babylonien, -ienne [babilɔnjɛ̃, -jɛn], *a. & s.* Babylonian. *F: Hôtel b.,* huge hotel.
bac [bak], *s.m.* **1.** (*a*) Bac (à traille), trail-bridge. (*b*) Ferry-boat (in general). *Passer qn dans un bac,* to ferry s.o. across. (*c*) Ferry. *Passer le bac,* to cross the ferry. **2.** Tank, vat ; container (of accumulator) ; pot (of electric cell) ; (miner's) truck or tub. *Bac à ordures,* dustbin.
baccalauréat [bakalɔrea], *s.m.* *B. ès lettres, ès sciences,* school leaving-certificate (giving access to the University, and essential for all liberal and civil service careers).
bacchanal [bakanal], *s.m.* No *pl.* *F:* Uproar, racket, row, rag.
bacchanale [bakanal], *s.f.* **1.** *Rom.Ant:* Les Bacchanales, the Bacchanalia. **2.** (*a*) Drinking song. (*b*) Orgy, drunken revel.
bacchante [bakɑ̃ːt], *s.f.* *Ant:* Bacchante.
bâche [bɑːʃ], *s.f.* **1.** Tank, cistern. **2.** (Coarse canvas) cover (for carts, hayricks). *B. goudronnée,* tarpaulin.
bachelier [baʃəlje], *s.m.* **1.** *A:* Bachelor ; novice in arms. **2.** *Sch:* (*f.* bachelière [baʃəljɛːr]) (*a*) **Bachelier en droit,** bachelor of law. (*b*) **Bachelier ès lettres, ès sciences,** bachelor of letters, of science (*i.e.* one who has taken his or her school-leaving certificate in the humanities or in science).
bâcher [bɑʃe], *v.tr.* To sheet (sth.) over ; to cover (sth.) with a tarpaulin. [BÂCHE]
bachique [baʃik], *a.* Bacchic. *Scène b.,* bacchanalian scene.
bachot[1] [baʃo], *s.m.* Wherry, punt.
bachot[2], *s.m.* *P:* = BACCALAURÉAT. **Four à bachot,** cramming-shop.
bachot|er [baʃɔte]. *Sch:* *P:* **1.** *v.tr.* To cram (pupil) for the *baccalauréat.* **2.** *v.i.* To cram, grind. *s.m.* **-age.**
bacille [basil], *s.m.* *Biol:* Bacillus.
bâcle [bɑːkl], *s.f.* Bar (of door).

bâcl|er [bɑkle], *v.tr.* **1.** To bar, bolt (door, etc.). **2.** *Nau:* To block up, close (port, harbour). **3.** *F:* To scamp (work) ; to hurry over (one's toilet, etc.). *s.m.* **-age.**
bâclé, *a.* **1.** Ice-bound (harbour, etc.). **2.** Slap-dash (work).
bâcleur, -euse [bɑklœːr, -øːz], *s.* *F:* **1.** *B. de besogne,* man who scamps his work. **2.** *B. d'affaires, de besogne,* hustler.
bactérie [bakteri], *s.f.* Bacterium. *pl.* Bacteria.
bactérien, -ienne [bakterjɛ̃, -jɛn], *a.* Bacterial.
bactériologie [bakterjɔlɔʒi], *s.f.* Bacteriology.
badaud, -aude [bado, -oːd], *s.* Saunterer, stroller ; gaper (in the streets) ; *U.S:* *F:* rubber-neck.
badaud|er [badode], *v.i.* To go gaping about ; to stroll about. *s.m.* **-age.**
badauderie [badodri], *s.f.* Sauntering, lounging.
Bade [bad]. *Pr.n.f.* *Geog:* Baden.
baderne [badɛrn], *s.f.* **1.** *Nau:* (*a*) Thrummed mat. (*b*) Boat-fender. **2.** *F:* Vieille baderne, old fog(e)y ; old fossil.
badigeon [badiʒɔ̃], *s.m.* **1.** (Colour-)wash, distemper (for walls, etc.). *B. blanc,* whitewash. **2.** Whitewash brush.
badigeonn|er [badiʒɔne], *v.tr.* (*a*) *B. une surface,* to brush over a surface (*de,* with). *B. un mur en blanc, en couleur,* to whitewash, to colour-wash, distemper, a wall. (*b*) *Med:* To paint (à l'iode, with iodine). *s.m.* **-age.** *s.m.* **-eur.**
badin, -ine[1] [badɛ̃, -in]. **1.** *a.* Playful, sportive, waggish. *Style b.,* light, playful, style. **2.** *s.* Wag, joker, banterer. *Petite badine,* little minx.
badine[2] [badin], *s.f.* Cane, switch.
badin|er [badine]. **1.** *v.i.* (*a*) To jest, trifle. *B. de tout,* to make sport of everything. *On ne badine pas avec l'amour,* do not trifle with love. (*b*) *B. avec sa canne,* to play, toy, with one's stick. **2.** *v.tr.* To tease, banter (s.o.). *s.m.* **-age.**
badinerie [badinri], *s.f.* Banter.
badois, -oise [badwa, -waːz], *a. & s.* *Geog:* (Native) of Baden.
baffe [baf], *s.f.* *P:* Slap, blow, cuff.
bafouer [bafwe], *v.tr.* To scoff, jeer, at (s.o.). *Amoureux bafoué,* flouted lover.
bafouill|er [bafuje], *v.tr. & i.* *F:* (*a*) To eat one's words ; to splutter, stammer. *B. quelque chose,* to stammer out something. (*b*) (Of engine) To run badly ; to miss, splutter. (*c*) *P:* To talk nonsense. *s.m.* **-age.** *s.* **-eur, -euse.**
bâfrée [bɑfre], *s.f.* *F:* Feed, tuck-in, blow-out.
bâfr|er [bɑfre]. *F:* **1.** *v.i.* To gormandize, guzzle. **2.** *v.tr.* To stuff, guzzle (food). *s.* **-eur, -euse.**
bagage [bagaːʒ], *s.m.* **1.** Baggage, impedimenta. **Plier bagage,** (i) to pack up one's traps, *Mil:* to decamp, make off. **Avec armes et bagage,** with all one's belongings. **2.** *pl.* Luggage. *Bagages non accompagnés,* luggage in advance. *Bagages à main,* hand-luggage.
bagarre [bagaːr], *s.f.* Scuffle (between crowd and police) ; affray, brawl ; free fight.
bagatelle [bagatɛl], *s.f.* Trifle. *Acheter qch. pour une b.,* to buy sth. for a mere song. *Traiter une affaire de b.,* to make light of a matter.
bagne [baɲ], *s.m.* *A:* Convict prison. *B. flottant,* hulks.
bagnole [baɲɔl], *s.f.* **1.** *Rail:* *F:* Horse-box ; cattle-truck. **2.** *P:* Motor car ; carriage.

bagou(t) [bagu], *s.m. F:* Glibness of tongue. Avoir du bagout, to have the gift of the gab.

bague [bag], *s.f.* **1.** (*a*) (Jewelled) ring. (*b*) *B. d'un cigare*, band round a cigar. (*c*) *Nau:* Grummet. (*d*) **Jeu de bagues**, tilting at the ring. **2.** *Mec.E:* B. *d'assemblage*, collar, sleeve; thimble-coupling or joint. *B. de roulement*, ball-race. *B. d'un excentrique*, strap of an eccentric. **3.** *Mch:* B. (*de garniture*) *de piston*, piston-ring, packing-ring.

bague-agrafe, *s.f.* (Fountain-pen) clip.

baguenaude [bagno:d], *s.f.* **1.** *Bot:* Bladder-senna pod. **2.** *A:* Trifle; puerile nonsense.

baguenaud|er [bagnode], *v.i. & pr. F:* To fool around; to loaf; to waste time on trifles. *s.m.* **-age.**

baguenaudier [bagnodje], *s.m.* **1.** *F:* Trifler, loafer. **2.** Ring-puzzle, tiring-irons. **3.** *Bot:* Bladder-senna.

baguette [baget], *s.f.* **1.** Rod, wand, stick. *B. de fée*, fairy's wand. *Baguettes de tambour*, drumsticks. *Mil:* B. *de fusil*, cleaning-rod, *A:* ramrod. *F:* Faire marcher qn à la baguette, to rule s.o. with a rod of iron. **Passer par les baguettes**, to run the gauntlet. **2.** *Bot:* Baguette d'or, wallflower. **3.** (*a*) *Join:* Moulding, bead, fillet. (*b*) Piping (on trousers). (*c*) Stitching (on gloves). (*d*) *Baguettes à jour*, open-work clocks (on socks).

bah [ba], *int.* **1.** Nonsense! fiddlesticks! pooh! rubbish! **2.** You don't say so!

Bahama [baama]. *Pr.n.f. Geog:* L'archipel de Bahama, the Bahamas.

bahut [bay], *s.m.* (*a*) *A:* Round-topped chest or travelling box. (*b*) Cupboard, cabinet. (*c*) *P:* School.

bai [bɛ], *a.* Bay (horse). *Bai châtain*, chestnut.

baie¹ [bɛ], *s.f. Geog:* Bay, bight.

baie², *s.f. Arch:* Bay, opening. **Fenêtre en baie**, bay-window.

baie³, *s.f. Bot:* Berry.

baignade [bɛɲad], *s.f. F:* **1.** (*a*) Bathe. (*b*) Watering (of horses). **2.** Bathing-place.

baign|er [bɛɲe]. **1.** *v.tr.* (*a*) To bathe, steep; to dip. *B. ses pieds dans le ruisseau*, to dip one's feet in the stream. *Yeux baignés de larmes*, eyes suffused with tears. (*b*) (Of sea) To wash (coast); (of river) to water (a district). (*c*) To bath, give a bath to (dog, baby). **2.** *v.i.* To soak, steep (in sth.). **Il baignait dans son sang**, he was weltering in his blood. *s.m.* **-age.**

se baigner. 1. To take a bath. **2.** (*a*) To bathe; to have a bathe. (*b*) **Faire baigner des chevaux**, to take horses to water.

baigneur, -euse [bɛɲœ:r, -ø:z], *s.* **1.** Bather. **2.** (*a*) Bath attendant. (*b*) Bathing attendant. **3.** *s.f.* Baigneuse, bathing-costume.

baignoire [bɛɲwa:r], *s.f.* **1.** Bath; (bath-)tub. **2.** *Th:* Ground-floor box (behind the pit).

bail, *pl.* **baux** [ba:j, bo], *s.m.* Lease (to tenant). **Prendre une maison à bail**, to take a lease of a house; to lease a house. *F:* Renouveler son bail de vie, to take a new lease of life. [BAILLER]

bâillant [bɑjɑ̃], *a.* Gaping (bodice); yawning (chasm); (door) ajar.

baille [ba:j], *s.f. Nau:* Tub, bucket, pail.

bâillement [bɑjmɑ̃], *s.m.* **1.** Yawn; yawning. *Étouffer un b.*, to stifle a yawn. **2.** Gaping (of seam, etc.).

bailler [bɑje], *v.tr. A:* (= DONNER) B. *un coup à qn*, to deal s.o. a blow. *F:* **Vous me la baillez belle!** tell that to the marines!

bâill|er [bɑje], *v.i.* **1.** To yawn. *F:* Bâiller à se décrocher la mâchoire, to yawn one's head off.

2. (Of seam, etc.) To gape; (of door) to stand ajar. *s.* **-eur, -euse.**

bailli [baji], *s.m. A:* Bailiff, magistrate, judge.

bâillon [bɑjɔ̃], *s.m.* Gag. **Mettre un bâillon à qn**, to gag s.o. [BÂILLER]

bâillonn|er [bɑjɔne], *v.tr.* To gag. *F:* B. *la presse*, to muzzle the press. *s.m.* **-ement.**

bain [bɛ̃], *s.m.* **1.** Bath. (*a*) *Prendre un b.*, to take, have, a bath. **Bain de pieds**, foot-bath. *B. de soleil*, sun-bath. **Salle de bains**, bath-room. (*b*) Bains publics, public baths. (*c*) *pl.* Watering-place; spa. (*d*) Bathing. **Bains de mer**, (i) sea-bathing; (ii) seaside resort. **Costume de bain(s)**, bathing-costume. **2.** *Husb:* (Sheep-)dip. *Phot:* B. *révélateur*, developing bath. B. *fixateur*, fixing-bath.

bain-marie [bɛ̃mari], *s.m.* **1.** *Ch:* Water-bath. **2.** (*a*) *Cu:* Jacketed saucepan. (*b*) Kitchen-range boiler. *pl.* Des bains-marie.

baïonnette [bajɔnɛt], *s.f.* Bayonet. **Mettre, remettre, la b.**, to fix, unfix, bayonets. *B. au canon!* fix bayonets! **Charge à la baïonnette**, bayonet charge. **Joint en baïonnette**, bayonet-joint.

baisemain [bɛzmɛ̃], *s.m.* Kissing of hands.

baiser [beze]. I. *v.tr.* (*a*) *Lit:* = EMBRASSER. *B. qn sur, à, la joue*, to kiss s.o. on the cheek. (*b*) B. *la mule du Pape*, to kiss the Pope's toe. *B. la croix*, to kiss the cross.
II. **baiser**, *s.m.* Kiss. *B. d'adieu*, parting kiss.

baissant [bɛsɑ̃], *a.* Declining, diminishing; setting (sun); failing (sight).

baisse [bɛs], *s.f.* **1.** Subsidence, going down (of water, etc.); ebb (of tide). **Température en baisse**, falling temperature. **Mouvement de monte et baisse**, up and down movement. **2.** Fall, drop, decline (in prices). **Spéculations à la baisse**, bear speculations. [BAISSER]

baisser [bese]. I. *v.* **1.** *v.tr.* To lower (curtain, price); to shut down (window, etc.); to let down, to open (carriage window). *B. une lampe*, to turn down a lamp. *Th: etc:* B. *les lumières*, to lower the lights. **Baisser la tête**, (i) to bend one's head, (ii) to hang one's head. *B. brusquement la tête*, to duck; to bob down. *Donner tête baissée dans un piège*, to fall headlong into a trap. **Baisser les yeux**, to cast down one's eyes; to look down. *B. la voix*, to lower one's voice. S.a. PAVILLON 3. **2.** *v.i.* (*a*) To be on the decline; (of tide) to ebb; (of flood) to abate; (of lamp, fire) to burn low. *La rivière baisse*, the river is going down. *Le baromètre baisse*, the glass is falling. *Le soleil baisse*, the sun is sinking. *Sa vue, sa mémoire, baisse*, his sight, memory, is failing, going. *Le malade baisse*, the patient is sinking. *B. dans l'estime de qn*, to sink in s.o.'s estimation. (*b*) (Of prices) To fall, to come down.
se baisser, to stoop; to bend down.
II. **baisser**, *s.m.* **Baisser du soleil**, sunset. *Th:* Baisser du rideau, fall of the curtain.

bajoues [baʒu], *s.f.pl.* Cheeks, chaps, chops (of pig, etc.).

bakélite [bakelit], *s.f.* Bakelite.

bal [bal], *s.m.* **1.** Ball. *Bal travesti, costumé*, fancy-dress ball. *Bal paré*, evening-dress ball. **Robe de bal**, dance-frock or ball-dress. *La reine du bal*, the belle of the ball. **2.** Bal public, dance hall. *pl.* Des bals.

balade [balad], *s.f. F:* Stroll, saunter; excursion. **Être en balade**, to be out walking, out for the day. *Faire une b.*, (i) to go for a ramble; (ii) to go on an excursion; to go for a run in the car, etc.

balader [balade]. *F:* **1.** *v.i. & pr.* To stroll, saunter. *Se b. en auto*, to go out for a spin.

P: to have a joy-ride. **P:** Envoyer balader qn, to send s.o. packing. **2.** *v.tr.* (*a*) To walk (s.o.) out, to take (dog) for a walk. (*b*) To trot (s.o.) round.

baladeur, -euse [baladœːr, -øːz], *s.* **1.** *F:* Wanderer, saunterer. **2.** *s.m. Mec.E:* Sliding collar. *Aut:* Selector rod. **Train baladeur,** sliding gear. **3.** *s.f.* **Baladeuse.** (*a*) Trailer (of tramway, motor car, etc.). (*b*) Costermonger's barrow. (*c*) *Aut:* Inspection lamp.

baladin, -ine [baladɛ̃, -in], *s.* Mountebank; buffoon.

balafre [balafr], *s.f.* **1.** Slash, gash (esp. in face); sabre-cut. **2.** Scar.

balafrer [balafre], *v.tr.* **1.** To gash, slash (esp. the face). **2.** *Visage balafré,* scarred face.

balai [balε], *s.m.* **1.** Broom. *B. de crin,* hair broom. *B. en caoutchouc,* squeegee. *B. mécanique,* carpet-sweeper. **Manche à balai,** (i) broomstick, (ii) *Av: P:* joy-stick. **Donner un coup de balai à une pièce,** to sweep out a room ; to give a room a sweep. **2.** *El.E:* Brush (of commutator). *Aut:* Blade (of windscreen-wiper). **3.** *Bot:* **Balai de sorcière,** witch-broom ; crow's-nest.

balance [balɑ̃ːs], *s.f.* **1.** (*a*) Balance ; (pair of) scales. *B. à bascule,* weigh-bridge. *B. romaine,* steelyard. **Mettre deux choses en balance,** to weigh two things one against the other. **Emporter, faire pencher, la balance,** to turn the scale. (*b*) Scale(-pan). **2.** *A:* Suspense, indecision. **Tenir qn en balance,** to keep s.o. in suspense. **3.** *B. d'un compte,* balancing of an account. **Faire la balance,** to strike the balance.

balanc|er [balɑ̃se], *v.* (je balançai(s); n. balançons) I. *v.tr.* **1.** To balance. (*a*) *B. le mal par le bien,* to (counter)balance evil with good. *B. un compte,* to balance an account. (*b*) To poise (javelin, etc.). **2.** To swing, rock (s.o. in a hammock, etc.). *B. un enfant sur ses genoux,* to rock a child on one's knees. *s.m.* **-ement.**
II. **balancer,** *v.i.* **1.** To swing ; *F:* to dangle. **2.** *A:* To waver, hesitate.
se balancer. (*a*) To swing ; to sway, rock ; *F:* to dangle. (Of ship) **Se balancer sur ses ancres,** to ride at anchor. (*b*) To see-saw.
balancé, *a.* **1.** Well-balanced ; well-poised. **2.** Swinging (blow). *s.m. Box:* **Balancé du droit,** swing in with the right.

balancier [balɑ̃sje], *s.m.* **1.** Balancing-pole (of tight-rope walker). **2.** (*a*) (i) Pendulum(-bob), (ii) balance-wheel (of watch). (*b*) Handle (of pump). (*c*) *Mch:* Beam (of beam-engine). (*d*) Fly-press, screw-press.

balançoire [balɑ̃swaːr], *s.f.* (*a*) See-saw. (*b*) (Child's) swing.

balane [balan], *s.m.* Crust: Acorn-shell.

balay|er [balεje], *v.tr.* (je balaie, je balaye; je balaierai, je balayerai) **1.** To sweep ; to sweep out (room); to sweep up (dirt). *Le vent a balayé les nuages,* the wind has swept away the clouds. **Balayer la mer,** to scour the sea. **2.** *Televis:* To scan (image). [BALAI] *s.m.* **-age.**

balayette [balεjεt], *s.f.* Small broom ; brush ; whisk.

balayeur, -euse [balεjœːr, -øːz], *s.* **1.** Sweeper. *B. de rues,* (i) crossing sweeper ; (ii) scavenger. **2.** *s.f.* **Balayeuse.** (*a*) Carpet sweeper. (*b*) Road or street sweeper.

balayures [balεjyːr], *s.f.pl.* Sweepings.

balbuti|er [balbysje], **1.** *v.i.* To stammer, mumble. **2.** *v.tr.* To stammer out (sth.). *s.m.* **-ement.**

balcon [balkɔ̃], *s.m.* **1.** Balcony. **2.** *Th:* Dress-circle.

baldaquin [baldakɛ̃], *s.m.* Baldachin, canopy (of throne, etc.) ; tester (of bed).

bale [bal], *s.f. Bot: etc:* = BALLE[2].

Bâle [baːl]. *Pr.n.f. Geog:* Basel, Basle.

baléare [baleaːr]. *Geog:* **1.** *a.* **Les îles Baléares,** the Balearic Isles. **2.** *a. & s.* Balearian.

baleine [balεn], *s.f.* **1.** Whale. **Blanc de baleine,** spermaceti. *Nau: F:* **Embarquer une baleine,** to ship a green sea. **2.** Whalebone. *Baleines d'un parapluie,* ribs of an umbrella.

baleineau [balεno], *s.m.* Whale-calf.

baleiner [balεne], *v.tr.* To (whale)bone ; to stiffen (garment).

baleinier, -ière [balεnje, -jεːr]. **1.** *a.* Whaling (industry). **2.** *s.m.* Whaler (whale-fisher or ship). **3.** *s.f.* **Baleinière,** whale-boat. *B. de sauvetage,* life-boat.

balèvre [balεːvr], *s.f.* (*a*) *A:* Under-lip. (*b*) *Pej:* **Les balèvres,** the lips. [LÈVRE]

balise [baliːz], *s.f.* (*a*) *Nau:* Beacon ; sea-mark. *B. flottante,* buoy. (*b*) *Av:* Ground-light.

balis|er [balize], *v.tr.* (*a*) *Nau:* To beacon, buoy, mark out (channel). (*b*) To provide (airport or air-routes) with ground-lights. *s.m* **-age.**

baliste [balist], *s.f. Rom.Ant:* Bal(l)ista.

balistique [balistik]. **1.** *a.* Ballistic. **2.** *s.f.* Ballistics ; gunnery.

baliveau [balivo], *s.m.* **1.** *For:* Staddle. *Hort:* Sapling. **2.** Scaffold-pole.

baliverne [balivern], *s.f. F:* (*a*) Idle story. (*b*) *pl.* Twaddle, nonsense.

balkanique [balkanik], *a.* Balkan (state, etc.).

ballade[1] [balad], *s.f. Lit:* **1.** Ballade. **2.** Ballad (poem : not song).

ballade[2], *s.f.* = BALADE.

ballader [balade], *v.* = BALADER.

ballant [balɑ̃]. **1.** *a.* Swinging, dangling (arms, etc.) ; slack (rope). **2.** *s.m. Golf:* B. ascendant, b. descendant, upward, downward, swing.

ballast [balast], *s.m.* **1.** *Civ.E:* Ballast, bottom (of road, railway track). **2.** Ballast-tank (of submarine).

balle[1] [bal], *s.f.* **1.** Ball. *B. de golf, de tennis,* golf-ball, tennis-ball. **Avoir la balle belle,** (i) to be in a good position (for playing a ball), (ii) *F:* to have a good opportunity. **Renvoyer la balle à qn,** (i) to return the ball to s.o. ; (ii) *F:* to give s.o. tit for tat. S.a. BOND. **2.** *Games:* **Balle au camp,** rounders. **Balle au mur,** fives. **2.** Bullet ; shot. *B. de fusil,* rifle bullet. *B. morte,* spent bullet. *B. perdue,* stray bullet. **Tirer à balle,** to fire ball-cartridge. **3.** *Com:* (*a*) Bale (of cotton, etc.). (*b*) (Pedlar's) pack. **Porter la balle,** to peddle.

balle[2], *s.f.* Husk, chaff (of corn). *Bot:* Glume.

ballerine [balrin], *s.f. Th:* Ballerina ; ballet-dancer.

ballet [balε], *s.m. Th:* Ballet. **Le corps de ballet,** the corps de ballet.

ballon [balɔ̃], *s.m.* **1.** Balloon. *B. d'observation,* war-balloon. **Envoyer un ballon d'essai,** (i) to send up a pilot balloon ; (ii) *F:* to put out a feeler. *Aut:* **Pneu ballon,** balloon-tyre. **2.** (*a*) (Child's large) india-rubber ball. (*b*) Football. **3.** *Ch:* Balloon-flask. *Ind:* Carboy. **4.** *Nau:* (*a*) Ball-signal. (*b*) *B. de défense,* fender. **5.** *Geog:* Rounded mountain top ; *ballon.*

ballonnant [balɔnɑ̃], *a.* Distended (stomach, etc.) ; bulgy (sleeve).

ballonn|er [balɔne], *v.i. & pr.* To swell (out), to become distended ; (of skirt, etc.) to balloon out. *s.m.* **-ement.**

ballonnet [balɔnε], *s.m.* **1.** *Aer:* (*a*) Small

balloon. (b) pl. Gas-bags (of dirigible). (c) B. compensateur, ballonet. **2.** Av: Wing-float (of hydroplane).

ballot [balɔ], s.m. **1.** Bundle, package, bale; (pedlar's) pack. **2.** P: Duffer, fat-head. [BALLE¹]

ballottage [balɔtaːʒ], s.m. **1.** Shaking, jolting. **2.** (a) Voting (by white or black balls). (b) (At parliamentary election) Second ballot.

ballott|er [balɔte]. **1.** v.tr. To toss (about), shake (about). **2.** v.i. (a) (Of door, etc.) To rattle, shake; to swing to and fro. (b) To toss (on the water). s.m. **-ement.**

balnéaire [balneːr], a. Of, pertaining to, baths. **Station balnéaire,** watering-place; (i) seaside resort; (ii) spa.

balourd, -ourde [baluːr, -urd]. **1.** a. Awkward, lumpish. **2.** s. Awkward person; lumpish creature; yokel. **3.** s.m. Mec: Want of balance.

balourdise [balurdiːz], s.f. **1.** Awkwardness, lumpishness. **2.** Stupid blunder; bloomer.

balsamique [balzamik], a. Balsamic (syrup, etc.); balmy (air); aromatic (perfume).

balte [balt], a. Geog: Baltic (port, etc.).

Balthazar [baltazaːr]. **1.** Pr.n.m. Belshazzar. **Le Festin de Balthazar,** Belshazzar's Feast. **2.** s.m. P: Square meal; blow-out; feast.

Baltique [baltik]. Geog: **1.** a. Baltic. **2.** Pr.n.f. **La Baltique,** the Baltic (Sea).

baluchon [balyʃɔ̃], s.m. P: Bundle (esp. of clothes). **Faire son baluchon,** to pack up.

balustrade [balystrad], s.f. **1.** Balustrade. **2.** (Hand-)rail; railing.

balustre [balystr], s.m. **1.** (a) Baluster. (b) pl. Banisters (of stairs). **2.** = BALUSTRADE.

balzan [balzɑ̃], a. **Cheval balzan,** horse with white stockings.

balzane [balzan], s.f. White stocking (of horse).

bambin, -ine [bɑ̃bɛ̃, -in], s. F: Little child; urchin; tiny tot.

bamboche [bɑ̃bɔʃ], s.f. **1.** (a) Puppet. (b) F: Stunted, ill-formed, person. **2.** F: Spree, lark. **Faire (une) bamboche,** to go on the spree.

bambocher [bɑ̃bɔʃe], v.i. F: To go on the spree.

bambocheur, -euse [bɑ̃bɔʃœːr, -øːz], s. F: Reveller, carouser.

bambou [bɑ̃bu], s.m. Bot: Bamboo(-cane).

bamboula [bɑ̃bula]. **1.** s.m. (a) Bamboo drum. (b) P: Negro, blackamoor. **2.** s.f. (a) Bamboula, negro dance. (b) F: = BAMBOCHE 2.

ban [bɑ̃], s.m. **1.** (a) (Public) proclamation. (b) Roll of drum. (c) F: Round of (rhythmical) applause. **Accorder un ban à qn** = to give three cheers for s.o. (d) pl. Banns (of marriage). **Publier les bans,** to publish the banns. **2.** Hist: (Proclamation of) banishment; sentence of outlawry; ban. **Mettre qn au ban,** (i) to banish s.o.; (ii) F: to send s.o. to Coventry. **Rompre son ban,** to break one's ticket-of-leave. F: **Être en rupture de ban,** to be on the loose, on the spree. **3. Le ban et l'arrière-ban,** (i) Hist: the ban and the arrière-ban, (ii) F: all one's supporters.

banal, -aux [banal, -o], a. **1.** A: Communal (mill, bakehouse). **2.** Commonplace, trite. **Événement peu banal,** unusual event. P: **Ça c'est pas banal!** that beats everything! that takes the cake! adv. **-ement.**

banaliser [banalize], v.tr. To render (sth.) commonplace.

banalité [banalite], s.f. **1.** Banality, triteness. **2.** Commonplace remark.

banane [banan], s.f. Banana.

bananier [bananje], s.m. Banana-tree.

banban [bɑ̃bɑ̃], s.m. P: **1.** Small, ill-formed, person or child. **2.** Person affected with a limp.

banc [bɑ̃], s.m. **1.** Bench, seat, settle, form. B. d'église, pew. B. de nage, thwart (of boat). Jur: B. des magistrats, magistrates' bench. B. des prévenus, dock. B. du jury, jury-box. Parl: Le B. des ministres, the Treasury bench. **2.** Bed (of lathe); table (of drilling-machine). B. d'essai, testing stand; bench (for engines). **3.** B. de sable, de vase, sand-bank or -shoal; mud-bank. B. de glace, ice-floe, -field. B. de roches, reef. B. de corail, coral-shoal. B. d'huîtres, oyster-bed. **Le Banc de Terre-Neuve,** the Banks (of Newfoundland).

bancal, pl. -als [bɑ̃kal], a. (a) Bandy-legged. **Jambes bancales,** bandy legs. (b) Wobbly, rickety (furniture, etc.).

bancroche [bɑ̃krɔʃ], a. F: = BANCAL.

bandage [bɑ̃daːʒ], s.m. **1.** (a) Bandaging, binding up (of wound). (b) Bandage. **2.** (Steel, rubber) tire, tyre. **3.** Tightening, winding (up) (of spring, etc.); stringing or bending (of bow).

bande¹ [bɑ̃ːd], s.f. **1.** (a) Band, strip (of cloth, etc.); belt (of land); (trouser) stripe. **Mettre un journal sous bande,** to put a newspaper in a wrapper. **Envoyer qch. sous bande,** to send sth. by book-post. Opt: Bandes du spectre, bands of the spectrum. W.Tel: B. de fréquence, frequency band. S.a. MOLLETIÈRE. (b) (Surgical) bandage. (c) Aut: B. de frein, brake strap. (d) Cin: Reel (of film); film. Tg: B. du récepteur, tape. (e) (Steel) tire, tyre (of wheel). (f) Bill: Cushion. **2.** Nau: (a) Side (of ship). (b) Heel, list(ing).

bande², s.f. 1. Band, party, troop. B. de voleurs, set, gang, of thieves. **Faire bande à part,** to keep to one's own clique. **Bande noire,** gang of swindlers or of terrorists. **2.** Flight, flock (of birds); pack (of wolves); herd (of buffaloes); school, shoal (of porpoises).

bandeau [bɑ̃do], s.m. **1.** (a) Bandeau, head-band. (b) Elle porte les cheveux en bandeaux, she wears her hair in bandeaux, parted down the middle. (c) Diadem. **2.** Bandage (over the eyes). **Mettre un bandeau à qn,** to blindfold s.o.

bandelette [bɑ̃dlɛt], s.f. **1.** (a) Narrow band; strip; bandage. (b) pl. Wrappings (of mummy). **2.** Archeol: Fillet (round the head).

bander¹ [bɑ̃de], v.tr. **1.** To bandage, bind (up) (wound); to put a bandage on (s.o.). B. les yeux à qn, to blindfold s.o. **2.** B. une roue, to put a tyre on a wheel. **3.** To tighten, wind up. B. un arc, (i) to bend, (ii) to string, a bow.

bander² (se), v.pr. To combine, to band together, form a league (contre, against).

banderole [bɑ̃drɔl], s.f. **1.** Banderole, streamer. **2.** Shoulder-belt. B. de fusil, rifle-sling.

bandit [bɑ̃di], s.m. (a) Bandit, brigand, highwayman. (b) F: Ruffian, villain.

bandoulière [bɑ̃duljɛːr], s.f. **1.** Shoulder-strap; (carbine) shoulder-belt. **Porter, mettre, qch. en bandoulière,** to carry, sling, sth. across one's back. **2.** Bandoleer.

banlieue [bɑ̃ljø], s.f. Suburbs; outskirts (of a town). Rail: **Ligne, gare, de banlieue,** suburban line, station.

banne [ban], s.f. **1.** Coal cart. **2.** Hamper, large basket. **3.** (a) Tarpaulin. (b) Awning (of shop). **4.** = BENNE.

banneau [bano], s.m. Fruit basket; hamper.

banneton [bantɔ̃], s.m. Basket.

bannette [banɛt], s.f. Small hamper, basket.

bannière [banjɛːr], s.f. Banner. F: **Être en bannière,** to be in one's shirt-tails.

bann|ir [bani:r], *v.tr.* To banish; to exile; to outlaw. *s.m.* **-issement.**

banni, -e. **1.** *a.* Banishḍd, outlawed. **2.** *s.* Exile, outlaw.

banque [bã:k], *s.f.* **1.** (*a*) Bank. (*b*) Banking. **La haute banque,** high finance. **Billet de banque, bank-note. Carnet, livret, de banque, bank-book; pass-book. Somme en banque,** sum at the bank. **2.** *Cards:* Bank. **Faire sauter la banque,** to break the bank. **3.** *F:* (Mountebank's) patter.

banqueroute [bãkrut], *s.f.* *Jur:* **B.** *simple,* bankruptcy. **B.** *frauduleuse,* fraudulent bankruptcy. **Faire banqueroute,** to go bankrupt.

banqueroutier [bãkrutje], *a. & s.* Fraudulent bankrupt.

banquet [bãkɛ], *s.m.* Banquet, feast. **Salle de banquet,** banqueting-hall.

banquet|er [bãk(ə)te], *v.i.* (**je banquette; je banquetterai**) To banquet, feast. *s.* **-eur, -euse.**

banquette [bãkɛt], *s.f.* **1.** Bench, seat, form; wall-sofa (in restaurant, etc.). *Th:* **Jouer devant les banquettes,** to play to empty benches. **2.** *Civ.E:* *etc:* Banquette, bank (of earth, etc.); berm. *Golf:* Bunker. [BANC]

banquier[1], **-ière** [bãkje, -jɛ:r]. **1.** *a.* Banking (house, etc.). **2.** *s.* Banker.

banquier[2], *s.m.* Newfoundland fishing boat; banker.

banquise [bãki:z], *s.f.* Ice-floe, ice-pack, ice-bank. **La Banquise,** the Great Ice Barrier.

bantou, -e [bãtu], *a. & s.* *Ethn:* Bantu.

baptême [batɛ:m], *s.m.* **1.** Baptism, christening. **Administrer le b. à qn,** to baptize s.o. **Nom de baptême,** Christian name; baptismal name. **2.** *F:* **Baptême du sang,** baptism of blood. **B.** *de l'air,* first flight.

baptiser [batize], *v.tr.* To baptize (s.o.); to christen (s.o., ship, etc.); to bless (bell, etc.). **B.** *un enfant sous le nom de Georges,* to christen a child George. *F:* **Baptiser son vin,** to water down one's wine.

baptismal, -aux [batismal, -o], *a.* Baptismal. S.a. FONTS.

Baptiste [batist]. **1.** *Pr.n.m.* Baptist. **2.** *s.m.* Clown, simpleton. **3.** *s.m.* *Ecc:* Baptist.

baptistère [batistɛ:r], *s.m.* *Ecc:* Baptist(e)ry.

baquet [bakɛ], *s.m.* **1.** Tub, bucket. **2.** *Aut:* Bucket-seat. [BAC]

bar[1] [ba:r], *s.m.* *Ich:* Sea-perch, sea-dace. **Bar** *rayé,* striped bass.

bar[2], *s.m.* (Public) bar.

bar[3], *s.m.* *Meteor. Meas:* Bar.

baragouin [baragwɛ̃], *s.m.* *F:* Gibberish, jabber.

baragouin|er [baragwine], *v.tr. & i.* *F:* To talk gibberish, to jabber. **B.** *l'anglais,* to talk broken English. *s.m.* **-age.** *s.* **-eur, -euse.**

baraque [barak], *s.f.* (*a*) Hut, shanty. *pl.* *Mil :* Huts, hutments. *P:* **Toute la baraque,** the whole lot. (*b*) Booth (at fair, etc.).

baraquement [barakmã], *s.m.* **1.** Lodging (of troops) in huts; hutting. **2.** *pl.* Camp of huts; hutments.

baraquer [barake], *v.tr.* To lodge (troops, etc.) in huts; to hut.

baratte [barat], *s.f.* Churn.

baratt|er [barate], *v.tr.* To churn (milk). *s.m.* **-age.**

barbacane [barbakan], *s.f.* **1.** *A.Fort:* (*a*) Barbican, outwork. (*b*) Loop(-hole). **2.** Draining channel (of bridge); cross-drain (of road).

Barbade (la) [labarbad]. *Pr.n.* Barbados.

barbare [barba:r]. **1.** *a.* (*a*) Barbaric; uncouth. (*b*) Barbarous, cruel, inhuman. **2.** *s.m.* Barbarian. *adv.* **-ment.**

barbaresque [barbarɛsk], *a.* *Ethn:* Barbaresque, Berber.

barbarie[1] [barbari], *s.f.* **1.** Barbarism. **2.** Barbarousness, barbarity, cruelty.

Barbarie[2]. *Pr.n.f.* *A.Geog:* Barbary.

barbariser [barbarize]. **1.** *v.tr.* To barbarize (people, one's style). **2.** *v.i.* To use barbarisms (in writing, speaking).

barbarisme [barbarism], *s.m.* *Gram:* Barbarism.

barbe[1] [barb], *s.f.* **1.** Beard. (*a*) *Homme portant b.,* bearded man. *Homme portant toute sa b.,* full-bearded man. *F:* **Rire dans sa barbe,** to laugh in one's sleeve. **Faire qch. à la barbe de qn,** de tous, to do sth. to s.o.'s face, in the face of all. **Faire la barbe à qn,** to shave s.o. **Se faire la barbe,** to shave. *"Pour la b. ou les cheveux?"* 'shave or hair-cut?' *P:* **Quelle barbe!** what a nuisance! *Ce qu'il est b.!* he's an awful bore! **La barbe!** shut up! (*b*) **Vieille barbe, barbe** - **grise,** greybeard. (*c*) Whiskers (of cat); barbel, wattle (of fish); beard, wattle (of bird); web, vane, feather (of quill); beard (of wheat). **2.** *Tchn:* (*a*) Burr (on casting, engraved plate). (*b*) *pl.* Deckle edge (of paper).

barbe[2], *s.m.* Barb; Barbary horse.

barbeau[1] [barbo], *s.m.* *Ich:* Barbel.

barbeau[2]. **1.** *s.m.* Bluebottle, cornflower. **2.** *a.inv.* (Bleu) barbeau, cornflower blue.

Barbe-bleue [barbəblø]. *Pr.n.m.* Bluebeard.

barbe-de-capucin [barbdəkapysɛ̃], *s.f.* *Bot:* *Cu:* Wild chicory. *pl.* Des barbes-de-capucin.

barbelé [barbəle], *a.* Barbed (arrow, hook). **Fil** *de fer b.,* barbed wire.

barbelure [barbəly:r], *s.f.* **1.** *Bot:* Beard, awn (of wheat). **2.** Barb (of arrow).

barber [barbe], *v.tr.* *P:* To bore, weary.

Barberousse [barbərus]. *Pr.n.m.* *Hist:* Barbarossa.

barbet [barbɛ], *s.m.* Barbet (spaniel).

barbette [barbɛt], *s.f.* **1.** *Ecc.Cost:* Barb (of nun's head-dress). **2.** *Fort:* Barbette. **Batterie (à) barbette,** barbette battery.

barbiche [barbiʃ], *s.f.* (*a*) Short beard. (*b*) Goatee.

barbier [barbje], *s.m.* Barber.

barbillon [barbijɔ̃], *s.m.* **1.** (*a*) Wattle (of cock, fish); barb, barbel (of fish); *pl.* barbels (of horse, cattle). (*b*) Barb (of fish-hook, arrow). **2.** *Ich:* = BARBEAU[1].

barbon [barbɔ̃], *s.m.* Greybeard, old fog(e)y.

barbot [barbo], *s.m.,* **barbot(t)e** [barbɔt], *s.f.* *Ich:* Eel-pout, burbot. **Petit barbot,** loach.

barbot|er [barbɔte]. **1.** *v.i.* (*a*) To paddle, splash (about). (*b*) (Of gases) To bubble. (*c*) *F:* To become confused, muddled; to flounder. **2.** *v.tr:* *B.le linge dans la lessive,* to work the linen about in the suds. *s.m.* **-age.** *s.m.* **-ement.**

barboteur, -euse [barbɔtœ:r, -ø:z], *s.* **1.** (*a*) Paddler, *F:* mudlark. (*b*) *F:* Muddler, flounderer. **2.** *s.m.* (*a*) *Ind:* Bubbler, blower. *Ch:* **B.** *pour lavage,* wash-bottle. (*b*) *Ind:* Mixer, stirrer. **3.** *s.f.* **Barboteuse,** (child's) paddling drawers.

barbouillage [barbuja:ʒ], *s.m.* **1.** (*a*) Daubing, smearing; blurring (of print). (*b*) Scrawling, scribbling. **2.** (*a*) Bad picture; daub. (*b*) Blur (in print, etc.). (*c*) Scrawl, scribble.

barbouill|er [barbuje], *v.tr.* **1.** (*a*) To daub; to smear (*de,* with). (*b*) To smear, dirty (one's face, etc.); to blot, soil (paper); to blur (printing, etc.). **2.** *F:* *B. une affaire,* to muddle, bungle, a piece of business. *Mets qui (vous) barbouille le cœur,* dish that turns one's stomach. *s.* **-eur, -euse.**

se **barbouiller**. **1.** To dirty one's face. **2.** *Le temps se barbouille,* we are going to have dirty weather.

barbouillé, *a.* (*a*) *Être b.,* to have a dirty face. (*b*) **Avoir le cœur barbouillé,** to feel sick, squeamish.

barbu, -ue [barby]. **1.** *a.* Bearded. **2.** *s.f.* **Barbue.** *Ich :* Brill.

barcarolle [barkarɔl], *s.f. Mus :* Barcarol(l)e.

bard [ba:r], *s.m.* **1.** (Wheelless) hand-barrow, stone-barrow. **2.** (Wheeled) hand-trolley.

barda [barda], *s.m. Mil : P :* Pack, kit.

bardane [bardan], *s.f. Bot :* Burdock.

barde¹ [bard], *s.f.* **1.** Pack-saddle. **2.** *Archeol :* (*a*) Bard (protecting war-horse). (*b*) *pl.* Bards (of 16th cent. armour). **3.** Slice of bacon (used to cover fowl, etc.).

barde², *s.m.* Bard, poet.

bardeau [bardo], *s.m.* **1.** *Const :* Shingle(-board). **2.** = BARDOT.

bard|**er¹** [barde], *v.tr.* **1.** To remove, carry, (stones, etc.) on a hand-barrow. **2.** *Abs. F :* To toil ; (of storm or fight) to rage. *Aujourd'hui ça barde,* to-day we're hard at it. *P :* Ça va **barder !** look out for squalls ! [BARD] *s.m.* **-age.**

barder², *v.tr.* **1.** *A :* To bard ; to arm (man or horse) with bards.· *Chevalier bardé de fer,* knight cased in steel. **2.** To bard (fowl, with bacon).

bardot [bardo], *s.m.* (*a*) Hinny. (*b*) Pack-mule.

barème [barɛːm], *s.m.* **1.** Ready-reckoner. **2.** Scale (of marks, of salaries). *B. graphique,* graph. **3.** Printed table (of charges, fares).

barguign|**er** [barɡiɲe], *v.i. F :* To hum and haw ; to shilly-shally ; to beat about the bush. *s.m.* **-age.** *s.* **-eur, -euse.**

baricaut [bariko], *s.m.* Keg.

baril [bari], *s.m.* Barrel, cask, keg. *Nau : B. de galère,* breaker, water-cask (of boat). **Mettre qch. en baril,** to barrel sth.

barillet [barijɛ], *s.m.* **1.** Small barrel, keg. **2.** Middle ear. **3.** Drum (of pressure indicator) ; barrel (of pump) ; cylinder (of revolver).

bariolage [barjɔlaːʒ], *s.m.* **1.** Variegation. **2.** Medley (of colours) ; gaudy colour scheme ; splashes of colour ; motley (of ideas).

barioler [barjɔle], *v.tr.* To variegate ; to paint (sth.) in many colours, in gaudy colours.

bariolé, *a.* Gaudy, motley ; of many colours ; splashed with colour.

bariolure [barjɔlyːr], *s.f.* = BARIOLAGE.

barnache [barnaʃ], *s.f.,* **barnacle** [barnakl], *s.f. Orn :* Barnacle-goose. *B. à collier,* brent-goose.

barnum [barnɔm], *s.m. F :* Showman.

baromètre [barɔmɛtr], *s.m.* Barometer ; *F :* weather-glass. *B. enregistreur,* recording barometer ; barograph. *Le b. est à la pluie, au beau,* the barometer points to rain, to set fair.

barométriqueʹ[barɔmetrik]ʾ, *a.* Barometric(al).

baro(métro)graphe [barɔ(metrɔ)graf], *s.m.* Barograph ; recording barometer.

baron [barɔ̃], *s.m.* Baron. *F : Les (hauts) barons de la finance, de l'industrie,* the bigwigs of finance ; the captains of industry.

baronnage [barɔnaːʒ, ba-], *s.m.* Baronage.

baronne [barɔn, ba-], *s.f.* Baroness.

baronnet [barɔnɛ, ba-], *s.m.* Baronet.

baroque [barɔk]. **1.** *a.* Quaint, odd, baroque. **2.** *s.m.* Le baroque, the baroque (style).

baroscope [barɔskɔp], *s.m. Ph :* Baroscope.

barque [bark], *s.f. Nau :* **1.** Boat. *B. de pêcheur,* fishing-boat, fishing-smack. *Patron de b.,* skipper. *F :* **Bien mener, bien conduire, sa barque,** to manage one's affairs well. *Conduire seul sa b.,* to

paddle one's own canoe. **2.** **Trois-mâts barque,** barque, bark.

barquette [barkɛt], *s.f.* **1.** Small craft ; skiff. **2.** (S. of Fr.) Light puff-biscuit.

barrage [baraːʒ, ba-], *s.m.* **1.** (*a*) Barring, stopping (of road, etc.) ; blocking (of harbour) ; damming (of valley) ; closing (of street). (*b*) Crossing (of cheque). (*c*) *Sp :* Playing off (of tie). **Troisième après barrage,** third after tying. **2.** (*a*) Barrier, obstruction ; (harbour) boom. *Hyd.E :* Barrage, dam, weir. (*b*) *Mil :* Barrage. **Tir de barrage,** barrage fire, curtain fire.

barragiste [baraʒist, ba-], *s.m. & f.* Weir-keeper.

barre [baːr, baːr], *s.f.* **1.** (*a*) Bar, rod (of metal, wood, etc.) ; (wooden) batten. *B. de chocolat,* bar, stick, of chocolate. *Gym : B. fixe,* horizontal bar. *Barres parallèles,* parallel bars. *Fb : B. du but,* cross-bar of the goal. **Fer en barres,** bar iron. *B. à T,* T iron. *Rail : B. d'attelage,* draw-bar. *Aut : B. de connexion,* cross-bar, tie-rod (of steering gear). (*b*) Bar, barrier. *B. d'appui,* hand-rail. *B. d'un tribunal,* bar of a court of justice. **Paraître à la barre,** to appear before the Court, at the bar. (*c*) (Harbour) boom. (*d*) Bar (of river or harbour). *B. d'eau,* (tidal) bore. *B. de plage,* surf. (*e*) *Mus :* Capo tasto (of guitar, etc.). **2.** *Nau :* (*a*) Bar, tiller (of boat) ; helm (of ship). *B. franche,* tiller. *B. à bras,* hand-wheel. (Of ship) **Sentir la barre,** to answer to the helm. **Homme de barre,** man at the wheel ; helmsman. **Donner un brusque coup de barre,** to put the helm hard over. (*b*) *B. des pieds (d'un canot),* stretcher. *B. à tire-veilles,* yoke (of rudder). (*c*) *Barres de hune,* cross-trees. **3.** (*a*) Line, dash, stroke, bar. *B. d'un t,* cross(-bar, -stroke) of a t. (*b*) *Mus :* Bar(-line). **4.** Stripe. *Étoffe à barres,* striped cloth. **5.** *Games :* Jeu de barres, prisoners' base.

barreau [baro], *s.m.* **1.** (*a*) Small bar ; rail. **Être sous les barreaux,** to be behind prison bars. *Barreaux d'une échelle,* rungs of a ladder. *B. de chaise,* (cross-)bar, stretcher, of a chair. (*b*) Grate-bar, fire-bar. **2.** *Jur :* Bar. **Être reçu, admis, au barreau,** to be called to the bar. *Entrée au b.,* call to the bar. *Rayer qn du b.,* to disbar s.o.

barrer [bare], *v.tr.* **1.** To strengthen (sth.) by means of a bar or bars. **2.** (*a*) To fasten (sth.) with a bar ; to bar (door, etc.). **Barrer la porte à, contre, qn,** to bar the door against s.o. ; to bar s.o. out. (*b*) To bar, obstruct (the way) ; to dam (stream) ; to block (up), close (road). "**Rue barrée,**" "no thoroughfare." *Golf :* **Trou barré,** stymie. **3.** To cross (a t, an A). *Mus :* **C barré,** barred C. *B. un chèque,* to cross a cheque. **4.** To cross out, strike out (word, etc.). **5.** *Nau :* To steer.

barrette¹ [barɛt], *s.f.* Biretta ; (cardinal's) cap.

barrette² [barɛt], *s.f.* (Small) bar. *El.E :* Connecting strip. *Cost :* Soft-collar pin. *B. de chaîne de montre,* watch-chain toggle. *B. pour les cheveux,* hair-slide. *B. de médaille,* bar of medal.

barreur [barœːr], *s.m.* **1.** *Nau :* Man at the wheel. **2.** *Row :* Coxswain, *F :* cox. [BARRE]

barricade [barikad], *s.f.* Barricade.

barricader [barikade], *v.tr.* To barricade.

barrière [barjɛːr, ba-], *s.f.* **1.** Barrier. *Rail : Barrières d'un passage à niveau,* level-crossing gates. *Geog :* **La Grande Barrière,** the Great Barrier Reef. **2.** Gate (of town, castle) ; toll-gate, turnpike. *Turf : Sp :* Starting-post.

barriquaut [bariko], *s.m.* = BARICAUT.

barrique [barik], *s.f.* Large barrel ; cask, butt, hogshead ; esp. wine-barrel of 225 litres.

Barthélemy [bartelmi]. *Pr.n.m.* Bartholomew.

baryte [barit], *s.f.* Baryta ; barium oxide.

baryté [barite], *a.* Papier baryté, baryta paper.

baryton [baritɔ̃], *a. & s.m. Mus:* Baritone, barytone (voice, saxhorn).

baryton(n)er [baritɔne], *v.i.* 1. To sing, talk, in a baritone voice. 2. To hum (tune).

baryum [barjɔm], *s.m. Ch:* Miner: Barium.

bas, basse [bɑ, bɑːs]. I. *a.* 1. Low. *Maison basse de toit, à toit b.*, low-roofed house. *Voix basse*, low, deep, voice. *Parler à voix basse*, to speak under one's breath. *Conversation à voix basse*, whispered conversation. *Maintenir les prix b.*, to keep prices down. *Box:* Coup bas, blow below the belt; foul. Enfant en bas âge, child of tender years. Avoir la vue basse, to be short-sighted, near-sighted. Mer basse, low water. S.a. BOUT[1] 1, MAIN 1, OREILLE 1. 2. Mean, base, low. *Homme de basse extraction*, man of lowly extraction. *Motif b.*, base, mean, contemptible, motive. 3. Low(er). *Les basses classes*, (i) the lower classes (of society), (ii) *Sch:* the lower forms. Terres basses, lowlands. En ce bas monde, here below. Au bas mot, at the lowest estimate.
II. **bas**, *adv.* 1. Low (down). *Quelques marches plus b.*, a few steps lower down. *Nau:* Haler bas une voile, to haul down a sail. *La malade est bien b.*, the patient is very low. S.a. ICI 1. 2. Mettre bas. (*a*) To take off (one's hat, etc.). "Chapeaux bas!" 'hats off!' *Nau:* Mettre pavillon bas, to strike the colours. (*b*) To pull down (house, etc.). (*c*) To overthrow (s.o.), to bring (s.o.) low. (*d*) (Of animals) To bring forth, drop (young). (*e*) Mettre bas les armes, to lay down one's arms. (*f*) *Nau:* Mettre b. les feux, to draw the fires. 3. Parler tout bas, to speak in a whisper, to whisper. *Rire tout b.*, to laugh to oneself.
III. **bas**, *s.m.* 1. Lower part (of sth.). *B. d'une échelle, d'une page*, foot, bottom, of a ladder, of a page. *F:* Les hauts et les bas de la vie, life's ups and downs. *Fish:* Bas de ligne, cast. *Typ:* Bas de casse, (i) lower case, (ii) small letters. *Adv.phr.* En bas, (down) below. *Aller en b.*, to go downstairs. La tête en bas, head down, upside down. *Tomber la tête en bas*, to fall head foremost. S.a. HAUT III. 3. *Prep.phr.* En bas de, at the foot of. *En bas de l'escalier*, downstairs. *Adv.phr.* A bas, down. *Mettre à b. un empire*, to lay low, overthrow, an empire. A bas les mains! hands down! hands off! *A b. les aristos!* down with the aristocrats! S.a. PATTE 1. Tomber à bas de son cheval, to fall off one's horse. 2. Bas de l'eau, low water. 3. Stocking. *F:* Un bas de laine bien garni (*d'écus*), a well-lined stocking.
IV. **basse**, *s.f.* 1. *Mus:* (*a*) Bass part. *B. fondamentale*, root, generator (of chord). *B. chiffrée*, figured bass. (*b*) Bass (voice, singer). Basse-contre, deep bass. (*c*) Bass (instrument); (i) 'cello; (ii) euphonium. 2. *Nau:* Shoal, sand-bank, (sunken) reef.

basalte [bazalt, ba-], *s.m.* Basalt.

basaltique [bazaltik, ba-], *a.* Basaltic.

basane [bazan, ba-], *s.f.* 1. Basan, sheep-skin. 2. *pl.* False boots (of cavalryman's overalls).

basaner [bazane, ba-], *v.tr. F:* To tan; to make sunburnt.
se **basaner**, to tan, become sunburnt.
basané, *a.* Sunburnt, tanned, swarthy.

bas-bleu, *s.m.* Blue-stocking. *pl. Des bas-bleus.*

bas-breton, -onne, *a. & s.* (Native) of Lower Brittany.

bas-côté, *s.m.* (Side-)aisle (of church).

basculant [baskylɑ̃], *a.* Rocking, tilting. Wagon basculant, tip-waggon. Pont basculant, draw-bridge. Siège basculant, tip-up seat.

bascule [baskyl], *s.f.* (*a*) Rocker; see-saw; bascule. *Mouvement de b.*, rocking motion. Faire la bascule, (i) to see-saw; to rock; (ii) *F:* to over-balance, tip over, topple over. Chaise, cheval, à bascule, rocking-chair, -horse. Miroir à bascule, swing-glass. (Balance à) bascule, weigh-bridge, weighing-machine. Bascule romaine, platform scales. Wagon à bascule, tip-waggon. S.a. PONT[1] 1. (*b*) *Phot:* B. arrière, swing-back (of camera).

bascul|er [baskyle], *v.tr. & i.* 1. (*a*) To rock, swing; to see-saw. *Levier basculé par une came*, lever rocked by a cam. (*b*) To tip (up). (Faire) *b. une charrette*, to tip a cart. (*c*) *Aut:* (Of head-lights) To dip. Faire b. les phares, to dip the head-lights. 2. To topple over. *s.m.* -age.

basculeur [baskylœːr], *s.m.* Swing part; rocker. *Mec.E:* Rocking-lever. *Aut:* B. de phares, head-light dipper.

base [bɑːz], *s.f.* 1. (*a*) Base (of triangle, etc.). *Surv:* Base(-line), ground-line. *Mil:* Base of operations. B. d'aviation, aviation base. (*b*) Base-plate (of machine). 2. Lower part, foot, base (of mountain, etc.). B. d'un édifice, foundations of a building. Jeter les bases, to lay the foundations. 3. Basis, foundation. *Ling:* Vocabulaire de base, basic vocabulary. Argument qui pêche par la base, fundamentally unsound argument. Sans base, ungrounded (suspicions, etc.). 4. Radix, root, basis (of logarithm). 5. *Ch:* Base (of salt).

Bas-empire (le) [ləbɑzɑ̃piːr], *s. Hist:* The Lower, Byzantine, Empire.

baser [bɑze], *v.tr.* To base, ground, found (opinion, etc.) (*sur*, on).
se **baser** *sur qch.*, to found upon (a principle).

bas-fond, *s.m.* 1. Low ground, hollow; swamp. *F:* Les bas-fonds de la société, the lowest strata of society. 2. (*a*) (= HAUT-FOND) Shallow, shoal (in sea or river). (*b*) Deep hole, pool (in river).

basilic[1] [bazilik, ba-], *s.m. Bot:* Basil.

basilic[2], *s.m. Myth: Z:* Basilisk. Regarder qn d'un œil de basilic, to cast a withering glance at s.o.

basilique [bazilik], *s.f. Arch:* Basilica.

basin [bazɛ̃], *s.m. Tex:* Dimity.

basique [bazik, ba-], *a.* Basic (salt, etc.). Scorie basique, basic slag.

bas-mât, *s.m. Nau:* Lower mast.

basoche [bazɔʃ], *s.f.* (*a*) *Hist:* Body of clerks attached to the courts of justice. (*b*) *F:* Usu. *Pej:* The legal fraternity; attorneydom.

basque[1] [bask], *a. & s. Ethn:* Basque. *F:* Courir comme un Basque, to run like a hare. S.a. TAMBOUR 1.

basque[2], *s.f.* Skirt, tail (of coat).

bas-relief [barəljɛf], *s.m.* Bas-relief, low-relief.

bass [bɑs], *s.m. Ich:* Bass.

basse. See BAS.

basse-cour, *s.f.* Farm-yard, poultry-yard. *pl. Des basses-cours.*

basse-fosse, *s.f.* Dungeon. Cul de basse-fosse, deepest dungeon. *pl. Des basses-fosses.*

bassement [bɑsmɑ̃], *adv.* Basely, meanly, contemptibly.

bassesse [bɑsɛs], *s.f.* 1. Baseness, lowness (of birth, expression, action). 2. Low, mean, contemptible, action.

basset, -ette [bɑsɛ, -ɛt], *a.* Short, low. Chien b., *s.m.* basset, basset hound. [BAS]

basse-taille, *s.f. Mus:* Basso-profondo.

basse-vergue, *s.f. Nau:* Lower yard. *pl. Des basses-vergues.*

basse-voile, *s.f. Nau:* Lower sail. *pl. Des basses-voiles.*

bassin [basɛ̃], *s.m.* **1.** Basin, bowl, pan. *Bassins de balance*, scale-pans. *B. à cracher*, spittoon. *P:* (Of pers.) Quel bassin! ce qu'il est bassin! what a bore! **2.** (*a*) Ornamental lake. (*b*) *Hyd.E:* Reservoir, tank. **3.** Dock, basin. *B. à flot*, wet dock, flooding dock. *B. de radoub*, dry dock, graving dock. **Faire passer un navire au bassin,** to dock a ship. *Entrer au b.*, to dock. **4.** (*a*) *B. d'un fleuve*, drainage basin of a river. (*b*) *B. houiller*, coal-basin, coal-measure. **5.** *Anat:* Pelvis.

bassinant [basinɑ̃], *a. P:* Boring, importunate.

bassine [basin], *s.f.* Pan. *B. à confitures*, preserving pan.

bassin|er [basine], *v.tr.* **1.** To bathe (wound, etc.). **2.** *B. un lit*, to warm a bed (with a warmingpan). **3.** *P:* To bore, plague (s.o.). *s.m.* **-age.** *s.m.* **-ement.**

bassinet [basinɛ], *s.m.* **1.** (*a*) Small (metal) basin. (*b*) *A:* Pan (of flintlock gun). **2.** *Archeol:* Basinet, basnet. **3.** *Bot:* Buttercup. [BASSIN]

bassinoire [basinwa:r], *s.f.* Warming-pan. *P:* C'est une vraie bassinoire, he's an awful bore.

basson [basɔ̃], *s.m. Mus:* Bassoon.

baste [bast], *int.* **1.** (*a*) Enough of that! (*b*) *Nau:* Hold hard! avast! **2.** Pooh! nonsense!

bastide [bastid], *s.f.* **1.** *A:* Blockhouse. **2.** *Dial:* Country-house, shooting-box (in S. of Fr.).

bastille [basti:j], *s.f.* Small fortress. *Hist:* **La Bastille,** the Bastille (State prison in Paris; destroyed 1789).

bastingage [bastɛ̃ga:ʒ], *s.m. Nau:* **1.** *A:* Hammock netting. **2.** *pl.* Bulwarks, topsides.

bastion [bastjɔ̃], *s.m. Fort:* Bastion.

bastionné [bastjɔne], *a.* Bastioned (front, etc.).

bastonnade [bastɔnad], *s.f.* Bastinado.

bastringue [bastrɛ̃:g], *s.m. P:* **1.** Low dancinghall. **2.** Noise, din, shindy. **3.** = BATACLAN.

bas-ventre, *s.m.* Lower part of the abdomen.

bat, -s [ba]. See BATTRE.

bât [bɑ], *s.m.* **1.** Pack-saddle. **Cheval de bât,** (i) pack-horse, *Mil:* bat-horse; (ii) *F:* drudge. *F:* C'est là que le bât le blesse, that's where the shoe pinches. S.a. ÂNE 1. **2.** Pack.

bataclan [bataklɑ̃], *s.m.* Belongings, traps, paraphernalia. *Vendez tout le b.!* sell the whole bang lot, the whole boiling, the whole caboodle! **bataille** [batɑ:j, -a:j], *s.f.* Battle. *Le fort de la b.,* the thick of the fight. **Champ de bataille,** battlefield. **Donner, livrer, bataille à qn,** to give battle to, join battle with, s.o. *B. rangée*, pitched battle. *A:* **Armée rangée en bataille,** army drawn up in battle array. *A:* **Chapeau en bataille,** cocked hat worn broadside on.

batailler [batɑje, -aje], *v.i.* To fight, battle (*contre*, with, against).

batailleur, -euse [batɑjœ:r, -ø:z], *a.* Fighting, quarrelsome, pugnacious.

bataillon [batɑjɔ̃], *s.m. Mil:* Battalion. **Chef de bataillon,** major. **Bataillon d'Afrique,** French punishment battalion (stationed in Africa).

bâtard, -arde [bɑta:r, -ard], *a. & s.* **1.** Bastard. (*a*) Illegitimate. *Fr.Hist:* **Le Bâtard d'Orléans,** the Bastard of Orleans. (*b*) (Not pure, mixed) *Chien b.*, mongrel, crossbred. (*c*) *Race bâtarde,* degenerate race. **2.** *Nau:* **Deux canots bâtards,** two boats alike.

bâtardeau [bɑtardo], *s.m.* **1.** *Fort:* Batardeau. **2.** *Hyd.E:* Coffer-dam, caisson.

bâtardise [bɑtardi:z], *s.f.* Bastardy.

Batave [bata:v]. *Hist:* **1.** *a.* Batavian. **2.** *s.m.pl.* **Les Bataves,** the Batavi.

bat-cul [baky], *s.m. Harn:* Swingle-tree. *pl. Des bat-culs.*

bateau [bato], *s.m.* Boat; merchant vessel.

Grands, petits, bateaux, large, small, craft. *B. à voiles*, sailing-boat. *B. à vapeur*, steamboat, steamer. *B. automobile*, motor boat, motor launch. *B. plat*, flat-bottomed boat, (i) barge, (ii) punt. *B. non ponté*, open boat. *B. à rames,* rowing-boat. *B. de pêche*, fishing-boat, -smack. *B. de sauvetage*, life-boat. **Pont de bateaux,** pontoon bridge. **Faire une partie de bateau,** to go boating. **Rail: Le train du bateau,** the boat-train. **Aller en bateau,** to go boating; to boat. *P:* Être du dernier bateau, to be in the height of fashion; to be up to date. **Monter un bateau à qn,** to hoax s.o.; to pull s.o.'s leg.

NOTE. In all the following compounds both nouns take the plural.

bateau-citerne, *s.m.* Tank boat; tanker.

bateau-école, *s.m.* School-ship, training-ship.

bateau-feu, *s.m.* Lightship.

bateau-glisseur, *s.m.* Hydroplane boat, speedboat.

bateau-hôpital, *s.m.* Hospital-ship.

bateau-maison, *s.m.* House-boat.

bateau-mouche, *s.m.* Passenger steamer (in Paris).

batelage¹ [batla:ʒ], *s.m.* Lighterage. [BATEAU]

batelage², *s.m.* Mountebank's tricks; juggling.

batelée [batle], *s.f.* Boatload; barge-load.

bateler [batle], *v.tr.* (je batelle ; je batellerai) To carry, convey, (sth.) in boats. [BATEAU]

bateleur, -euse [batlœ:r, -ø:z], *s.* Mountebank, juggler, tumbler.

batelier, -ière [batəlje, -jɛ:r], *s.* Boatman, boatwoman ; waterman ; ferryman, -woman.

batellerie [batɛlri], *s.f.* **1.** Inland water transport ; lighterage. **2.** *Coll.* Small craft.

bâter [bɑte], *v.tr. B. un mulet*, to put a packsaddle, a load, on a mule. *F:* C'est un âne bâté, he's a perfect ass. [BÂT]

bath [bat], *a.inv. P:* First-class, topping.

bâti [bɑti], *s.m.* Frame(-work), structure, support, stand. *B. de fenêtre*, window-frame. *B. d'un moteur*, frame, body, of a motor. [BÂTIR]

batifol|er [batifɔle], *v.i. F:* To frolic, skylark; to play the giddy goat. *s.m.* **-age.** *s.* **-eur, -euse.**

bâtiment [bɑtimɑ̃], *s.m.* **1.** Building trade. **Entrepreneur de bâtiment,** builder. S.a. PEINTRE. **2.** Building, edifice, structure. *Bâtiments de ferme,* farm buildings. **Usine en trois corps de bâtiment,** factory (contained) in three main buildings. **3.** Ship, vessel. **Bâtiment de guerre,** warship. *B. marchand*, merchant ship ; merchantman. *Petits bâtiments*, small craft. [BÂTIR]

bâtir¹ [bɑti:r], *v.tr.* To build, erect, construct. *B. une maison*, to build a house. *La maison se bâtit*, the house is building. *B. une fortune*, to build up a fortune. *Homme bien bâti*, well-set-up man. *Gaillard bien bâti*, strapping fellow. **Terrain à bâtir,** building-site.

bât|ir², *v.tr.* To baste, tack, (garment) together. **Coton à bâtir,** tacking thread. *s.m.* **-issage.**

bâtisse [bɑtis], *s.f.* **1.** Masonry ; bricks and mortar. **2.** (*a*) *F:* Gimcrack building, ramshackle house or shed. (*b*) *B. de bois*, frame building. [BÂTIR]

batiste [batist], *s.f. Tex:* Batiste, cambric.

bâton [batɔ̃], *s.m.* **1.** Stick, staff, rod. (*a*) *B. ferré*, iron-shod pole ; alpenstock. **Jouer du bâton,** to fence with quarterstaffs. **Martin bâton,** (i) donkey driver (armed with thick stick), (ii) thick stick, cudgel. *B. d'une chaise*, stretcher, rung, of a chair. *F:* **Vie de bâton de chaise,** life of pleasure ; fast life. **Bâton de vieillesse,** support, prop, of old age. ; **Coup de bâton,** blow, hit, with a stick. *Donner des coups de b. à qn,* to beat s.o. *F:* **Mettre des bâtons dans les roues,** to put a spoke in (s.o.'s) wheel; to interfere. (*b*) *Arch:* *Bâtons rompus,* zigzag moulding. *F:* **Travailler à bâtons rompus,** to work without method, by fits and starts. *Conversation à bâtons rompus,* desultory, rambling, conversation. (*c*) Staff, pole. *B. de pavillon,* flagstaff, flagpole. (*d*) (Wand of office) *B. pastoral,* pastoral staff, crozier. *B. de maréchal,* field-marshal's baton. *B. de magicien,* conjurer's wand. *B. de chef d'orchestre,* conductor's baton. (*e*) *Toil:* B. *d'oranger,* orangestick. **2.** Stick, roll. *B. de cire à cacheter,* stick of sealing-wax. **3.** Stroke (of the pen, etc.). *Mus:* B. *de reprise,* repeat bar. **4.** *Bot:* **Bâton de Jacob,** yellow asphodel. **Bâton d'or,** wall-flower.

bâtonner [bɑtɔne], *v.tr.* To beat, cudgel, cane.

bâtonnet [bɑtɔnɛ], *s.m.* (*a*) Square ruler. (*b*) *Games:* Tip-cat. (*c*) *Biol:* Rod-bacterium. (*d*) *Anat:* (i) Rod-like cell. (ii) *pl.* Rods (of retina). (*e*) *Toil:* Orange-stick.

bâtonnier [bɑtɔnje], *s.m.* Leader, president, of the French Bar.

bâtonniste [bɑtɔnist], *s.m.* Quarterstaff fencer.

batraciens [batrasjɛ̃], *s.m.pl.* Z: Batrachia(ns).

battage [bataːʒ], *s.m.* **1.** (*a*) Beating (of carpet, etc.); churning (of butter); threshing (of corn); ramming (of earth). (*b*) *Artil:* Field of fire (of gun). **2.** *F:* Log-rolling, self-advertisement, boosting, booming.

battant [batɑ̃]. I. *a.* **1.** (*a*) Beating. **Pluie battante,** driving, pelting, rain; downpour. **Porte battante,** (i) banging door, (ii) swing-door, (iii) folding door. **Tambour battant,** with drums beating, with beat of drum. *Mener les choses tambour b.,* to hustle things on. **Mener battant l'ennemi,** to keep the enemy on the run. *F:* **Tout battant neuf,** brand-new. (*b*) Striking. **A onze heures battant,** on the stroke of eleven. **2.** (Of signal, flag) **Être battant,** to be flying. II. **battant,** *s.m.* **1.** (*a*) Clapper, tongue (of bell). (*b*) Lift (of latch). (*c*) Fly (of flag); slab (of sail). **2.** (*a*) Leaf, flap (of table, counter); leaf (of door, shutter). **Porte à deux battants,** double door; folding doors. **Ouvrir les portes à deux battants,** to fling the gates wide open. (*b*) Door (of cupboard, etc.).

batte [bat], *s.f.* (*a*) Beater, mallet. *B. de blanchisseuse,* washerwoman's beetle. *B. à beurre,* dasher, plunger (of churn). (*b*) *La b. d'Arlequin,* Harlequin's bat or lath; slap-stick. [BATTRE]

battement [batmɑ̃], *s.m.* **1.** (*a*) Beat(ing) (of drum); stamp(ing), tap(ping) (of feet); clapping (of hands); flutter(ing) (of wings, of eyelids); flapping (of sails); banging (of door). *B. de paupières,* blink(ing). (*b*) *Ph:* (i) Beating, pulsation (of oscillations). (ii) (Interference) beat. (*c*) *Mus: Pros:* Beat. (*d*) Beat(ing), throb(bing), pulsation. *Chaque b. de cœur,* every heart-beat. **Avoir des battements de cœur,** to suffer from palpitation. (*e*) Jarring (of machinery); backlash. (*f*) Swing(ing) (of pendulum). **2.** Interval (between two events, two duties, etc.). *Rail:* B. *de vingt minutes,* wait of twenty minutes between trains.

batte-queue [batkø], *s.f.* *Orn:* Wagtail. *pl. Des batte-queue(s).*

batterie [batri], *s.f.* **1.** Fight, scuffle, rough-and-tumble. **2.** (*a*) Beat (of drum); roll (on sidedrum). (*b*) **La batterie,** (i) (in orchestra) the percussion instruments; (ii) *Mil:* the (drum and bugle) band. **3.** *Artil:* Battery. *B. de campagne,* field-battery. *Pièces en b.,* guns in action. *F:* **Dresser ses batteries,** to lay one's plans. **Montrer,**

démasquer, **ses batteries,** to show one's hand. **Démonter les batteries de qn,** to demolish s.o.'s arguments, to silence s.o.'s guns. **4.** (*a*) Set, collection. *B. de fours à coke,* battery, range, bank, of coke ovens. *B. de cuisine,* (set of) kitchen utensils. (*b*) **Batterie électrique,** electric battery. *B. de rechange,* refill (for torch, etc.).

batteur, -euse [batœːr, -øːz], *s.* **1.** (*a*) *B. d'or,* gold-beater. *B. de pieux,* pile-driver. *B. en grange,* thresher. (*b*) *Ven:* Beater. (*c*) *F:* **Batteurs de pavé,** loafers, idlers. **Batteur de grève,** beachcomber. **2.** *s.f.* **Batteuse,** threshing-machine; thresher.

battoir [batwaːr], *s.m.* **1.** Washerwoman's beetle. **2.** *Husb:* Swingle (of flail). **3.** (Wooden) bat (for ping-pong, etc.). [BATTRE]

battre [batr], *v.* (*pr.p.* battant; *p.p.* battu; *pr.ind.* je bats [ba], il bat, n. battons, ils battent; *p.h.* je battis; *fu.* je battrai) To beat. **1.** *v.tr.* (*a*) To beat, thrash, flog (s.o.). **Battre qn comme plâtre,** to beat s.o. to a jelly. *B. un tapis, un tambour,* to beat a carpet, a drum. *B. un pieu,* to drive a pile. *B. du blé,* to thresh corn. *B. le fer (avec un marteau),* to hammer iron. *Prov:* **Il faut battre le fer pendant qu'il est chaud,** we must strike while the iron is hot. S.a. FROID I.1. *B. de la monnaie,* to coin, mint, money. *F:* **Battre monnaie,** to raise the wind. *B. des œufs (en neige),* to beat (up) eggs. *B. le beurre,* to churn butter. *Artil: B. une position,* to batter a position. S.a. BRÈCHE 1. (*b*) To beat, defeat, *F:* lick (s.o.). **Battre qn à plate(s) couture(s),** to beat s.o. hollow. S.a. COUTURE 2. (*c*) **Battre la campagne,** (i) *Mil:* to scour the country; (ii) *F:* to be delirious, to wander (in one's mind). **Battre son quart,** (of policeman, etc.) to be on one's beat. S.a. PAVÉ 2, PAYS. *Ven: B. un bois,* to beat a wood. (*d*) *Nau:* **Battre un pavillon,** to fly a flag. (*e*) **Battre les cartes,** to shuffle the cards. **2.** *v.tr. & i.* (*a*) *B. la mesure,* to beat time. *La montre bat,* the watch ticks. (*b*) *B. l'alarme,* to beat the alarm. *Le tambour bat,* the drum is beating. S.a. RETRAITE 1. *Le cœur lui battait,* his heart was going pit-a-pat. *Sentir b. une machine,* to feel a machine throbbing. (*c*) *La pluie bat contre les carreaux,* the rain beats, lashes, against the panes. *Sa robe de chambre lui battait sur les talons,* his dressing-gown flapped round his heels. *Porte qui bat,* banging door. *Voile qui bat,* sail that flaps in the wind. (*d*) *B. des mains,* to clap one's hands, to applaud. *B. du pied,* to stamp one's foot. *B. des paupières,* to blink. S.a. AILE 1, ENTRECHAT, ŒIL 1, PLEIN 2, SEMELLE 1.

se battre, to fight. *Se b. avec qn,* to fight (with) s.o. *Se b. contre qn,* to fight against s.o. **Se battre en duel,** to fight a duel.

battu, *a.* **1.** *Avoir les yeux battus,* to have rings, circles, round one's eyes. **2.** *Metalw:* **Fer battu,** wrought iron. *Plancher en terre battue,* floor of beaten earth. **3.** **Chemin battu,** trodden path. *F:* **Suivre le chemin b.,** to follow the beaten track.

battue, *s.f.* (*a*) *Ven:* Battue, beat. *Nau:* **Battue en mer,** scouting cruise. (*b*) Round-up (by police).

bau, *pl.* **-aux** [bo], *s.m.* *N.Arch:* Beam. **Maître bau,** midship beam. *Navire à larges baux,* beamy ship.

baudet [bodɛ], *s.m.* **1.** (i) (He-)ass; donkey; (ii) stallion ass. **2.** *F:* (Jack)ass, dolt.

Baudouin [bodwɛ̃]. *Pr.n.* Baldwin.

baudrier [bodri(j)e], *s.m.* Cross-belt; shoulder-belt (for drum, etc.). *Astr:* **Le Baudrier d'Orion,** Orion's belt.

baudruche [bodryʃ], *s.f.* Gold-beater's skin.
bauge [bo:ʒ], *s.f.* **1.** (*a*) Lair (of wild boar).
(*b*) *F:* Pigsty. (*c*) Squirrel's nest. **2.** Clay and
straw mortar.
baume [bo:m], *s.m.* **1.** Balm, balsam. *B. de
Canada*, Canada balsam. *Pharm: B. de benjoin*,
friar's balsam. S.a. TOLU. *Iron:* **Sa réputation
fleure comme baume**, he is in very good odour.
F: Verser du b. dans le cœur de qn, to pour balm
into a wounded heart. *F:* **Baume d'acier**, the
dentist's forceps. **2.** *Bot:* **Baume des jardins**,
costmary. **Baume des champs**, wild mint.
baumier [bomje], *s.m.* Balsam(-tree).
baux¹ ². See BAIL, BAU.
bauxite [boksit], *s.f. Miner:* Bauxite.
bavard, -arde [bava:r, -ard]. **1.** *a.* (*a*) Talkative, loquacious, garrulous. *F:* **Il est bavard
comme une pie**, he would talk the hind leg off a
donkey. (*b*) Tale-bearing, gossiping. **2.** *s.* (*a*)
Chatterer, chatterbox. (*b*) Gossip-monger. [BAVER]
bavardage [bavarda:ʒ], *s.m.* Chatter(ing), chit-
chat. *Bavardages de commères*, gossip, tittle-tattle.
bavarder [bavarde], *v.i.* **1.** To chatter. **2.** To
gossip. **3.** To blab, to tell tales.
bavarois, -oise [bavarwa, -wa:z], *a. & s.* Bavarian.
bave [ba:v], *s.f.* Slaver, dribble; slobber (of dog);
slime (of snail); froth, foam (of horse, of mad
dog); spittle (of toad).
baver [bave], *v.i.* (*a*) To slaver; to drivel, dribble
(at the mouth), to slobber; (of blood) to ooze.
P: **Il en bavait**, he was furious. **Tu baves**, you
are talking drivel. (*b*) (Of pen) To run.
bavette [bavɛt], *s.f.* **1.** Bib. *F:* **Tailler une
bavette** *avec une vieille connaissance*, to have a
crack, a confab, with an old crony. **2.** *Cy: B.
garde-boue*, mud-flap. [BAVE]
baveur, -euse¹ [bavœ:r, -ø:z]. **1.** *a.* Drivelling,
slobbering. **2.** *s.* Dribbler, slobberer. **3.** *s.f.*
Ich: Baveuse, blenny.
baveux, -euse² [bavø, -ø:z], *a.* (*a*) Slobbery
(mouth). (*b*) *Omelette baveuse*, moist, juicy, omelet. *Plaie baveuse*, weeping wound. (*c*) *Lettres
baveuses*, blurred letters.
Bavière [bavjɛ:r], *Pr.n.f. Geog:* Bavaria.
bavolet [bavɔlɛ], *s.m.* **1.** *Cost:* (Peasant woman's)
bonnet. **2.** *Aut:* Valance; side-apron.
bavure [bavy:r], *s.f.* **1.** (*a*) Fin, beard (of casting).
(*b*) Wire-edge, burr. **2.** *Bavures de plume*, pen
smudges. [BAVE]
bayadère [bajadɛ:r], *s.f.* (Indian) dancing-girl,
nautch-girl.
bayer [baje, bɛ-], *v.i.* (**je baye, baie, n. bayons;
je bayerai, baierai**) *A:* To stand gaping. Still
used in **Bayer aux corneilles**, to gape at the
moon.
bazar [baza:r], *s.m.* **1.** (Oriental) bazaar. **2.** Bazaar, emporium; cheap stores. *Sch: P:* **Le
bazar**, the school, the *lycée. P: On avait invité
le maire, le curé, et* **tout le bazar**, they had invited
the mayor, the priest, and the whole boiling.
bazarder [bazarde], *v.tr. P:* To sell off (one's
effects); to turn (sth.) into money.
bê [bɛ], *onomat.* Baa.
béant [beɑ̃], *a.* Open, gaping (wound); yawning
(chasm).
béarnais, -aise [bearnɛ, -ɛ:z], *a. & s.* (Native) of
Béarn. *Hist:* **Le Béarnais**, Henry IV (of France).
béat, -ate [bea, -at], *a.* **1.** *Optimisme b.*, complacent, smug, optimism. **2.** Sanctimonious,
smug (person). *adv.* **-ement.**
béatification [beatifikasjɔ̃], *s.f.* Beatification.
béatifier [beatifje], *v.tr. Ecc:* To beatify.
béatifique [beatifik], *a.* Beatific (vision).

béatitude [beatityd], *s.f.* **1.** (*a*) Beatitude.
(*b*) Bliss. **2.** Smugness, complacency.
Béatrice [beatris]. *Pr.n.f.* Beatrix, Beatrice.
beau [bo], **bel**, *f.* **belle** [bɛl], *pl.* **beaux, belles.**
(The form *bel* is used before *m.sg.* sbs beginning
with a vowel or a 'mute' *h*, in a few phrases such
as *bel et bon*, and in archaic names.) I. *a.* **1.** Beautiful, handsome, fair. *Un bel homme*, a handsome,
good-looking, man. *Une belle femme*, (i) a beautiful woman, (ii) a fine-looking woman. **Le beau
sexe**, the fair sex. *Hist:* **Philippe le Bel**, Philip
the Fair. *De beaux arbres*, handsome, fine, trees.
2. Fine. (*a*) *De beaux sentiments*, fine, noble, lofty,
feelings. **Cela n'est pas beau à vous**, that was unworthy of you. (*b*) *Beau danseur*, fine dancer. *Bel
esprit*, pretty wit. **Un bel esprit**, a wit. *Un des
beaux esprits de l'époque*, one of the wits of the day.
Prov: **Les beaux esprits se rencontrent**, great
minds think alike. **Le bel âge**, (the days of) youth.
Un bel âge, a ripe old age. *Belle occasion*, fine
opportunity. **Avoir beau jeu**, (i) to have good
cards; (ii) to have fair play. **Avoir beau jeu à
faire qch.**, to have every opportunity to do sth.
Un beau joueur, a good loser; *F:* a sport.
S.a. MORT² I. **Voir les choses en beau**, to see
things through rose-coloured spectacles. **Voir
tout du beau côté**, to see the bright side of everything. (*c*) Smart, spruce. **Le beau monde**,
society; the fashionable set. **Se faire beau, to
smarten oneself up. Comme vous voilà beau!**
you do look smart! (*d*) *Beau temps*, fine weather,
fair weather, good weather. (*e*) **Tout cela est bel
et bon, mais . . .**, that is all well and good,
but. . . . **Il en a fait de belles**, pretty things he's
been up to! **En conter de belles sur qn**, to spread
nice reports about s.o. **Vous en avez fait une
belle!** *P:* you've been and gone and done it!
En voici d'une belle! here's a how'd-ye-do!
S.a. DRAP 2. (*f*) (Intensifying) **J'ai eu une belle
peur!** I got an awful fright! **Au beau milieu
de la rue**, in the very middle, right in the middle,
of the street. **Il y a beau jour qu'il est parti**, it's
many a long day since he went away. S.a. DENT I,
TEMPS I. **3.** *Adv. phrs.* **Bel et bien**, entirely, fairly,
quite. *Il a été bel et bien attrapé*, he was fairly
caught. **Tout beau!** steady! gently! **De plus
belle**, more than ever, worse than ever. *Il
recommença de plus belle*, he began again with
renewed vigour. **4.** *V.phrs.* (*a*) **L'échapper belle**,
to have a narrow escape, a close shave. **La manquer belle**, to miss a brilliant opportunity. (*b*) **Il
ferait beau voir cela**, that would be a fine thing
to behold. (*c*) (Of weather) **Il fait beau (temps)**,
it is fine, fair (weather); the weather is fine.
(*d*) **Avoir beau faire qch.**, (i) to be able to do sth.
with impunity, (ii) to do sth. in vain (usu. followed
by counterbalancing sentence). *Prov:* **A beau
mentir qui vient de loin**, travellers from afar can
lie with impunity. *J'avais beau chercher, je ne
trouvais rien*, search as I might, I found nothing.
Il eut beau dire . . ., in spite of his assertions
. . . . *Vous avez beau parler*, *F:* you may talk
till all's blue.
II. **beau, belle**, *s.* **1.** (*a*) Fair one, beauty.
La Belle et la Bête, Beauty and the Beast. **La
Belle au bois dormant**, the Sleeping Beauty.
(*b*) **Un vieux beau**, an old beau. **Faire e beau**,
(i) to strut, swagger; (ii) (of dog) to sit up and
beg. **2.** *s.m.* (*a*) **Le beau**, the beautiful. (*b*) **Le
plus beau de l'affaire c'est que . . .**, the best of
the thing is that. . . . (*c*) Fine (weather). **Le
temps est au beau (fixe)**, the weather is set fair.
3. *s.f.* **Belle.** (*a*) *Jouer la belle*, to play (i) the
deciding game or set (at tennis, etc.), (ii) the

rubber game (at cards). (b) *Nau:* Waist (of ship). **En belle,** abeam.

beauceron, -onne [bosrɔ̃, -ɔn], *a. & s. Geog:* (Native) of the Beauce region.

beaucoup [boku]. I. *s.m.inv.* (a) Much, a great deal, *F:* a lot. *Il reste encore b. à faire,* much still remains to be done. (b) (A great) many, *F:* a lot. **Beaucoup pensent que** . . ., many are of the opinion that. . . . **Beaucoup de,** much; (a great) many; a great deal of, *F:* lots of. *Avoir b. d'argent,* to have a great deal of money, *F:* lots of money, heaps of money. **B. de gens,** many people. *Avec b. de soin,* with much care. **Beaucoup d'entre nous, d'entre vous,** many of us, of you. *B. d'entre eux se firent tuer,* many of them fought to the death. (c) *Adv.phr.* **De beaucoup,** much, by far, by a great deal. *C'est de b. le meilleur,* it is far and away the best. S.a. PRÈS 2. 2. *adv.* Much. *Il vous aime b.,* he is very fond of you. *Elle parle b.,* she talks a great deal. *Elle parle b. trop,* she talks a great deal too much, far too much. *Il est b. plus âgé que sa femme,* he is much older than his wife. [BEAU COUP]

beau-fils [bofis], *s.m.* Stepson. *pl. Des beaux-fils.*

beau-frère, *s.m.* Brother-in-law. *pl. Des beaux-frères.*

beaune [boːn], *s.m.* Beaune (wine) (from Beaune in Burgundy).

beau-père, *s.m.* I. Father-in-law. 2. Stepfather. *pl. Des beaux-pères.*

beaupré [bopre], *s.m. Nau:* Bowsprit.

beauté [bote], *s.f.* I. Beauty, handsomeness, loveliness. *Conserver, perdre, sa b.,* to preserve, lose, one's beauty, one's good looks. **Être dans toute sa beauté,** to be in the flower of one's beauty. **Vous êtes en beauté ce soir,** you *are* looking well this evening! **Grain, tache, de beauté,** beauty spot. *F:* **La beauté du diable,** the bloom, freshness, of youth (in a woman not otherwise beautiful). **De toute beauté,** extremely beautiful. **Institut de beauté,** beauty parlour. 2. Beauty; beautiful woman. **La beauté du bal,** the belle of the ball.

beaux-arts [bozaːr], *s.m.pl.* Fine arts. **École des beaux-arts,** art school.

beaux-parents, *s.m.pl.* Parents-in-law.

bébé [bebe], *s.m.* I. Baby. **Faire le bébé,** to behave like a baby. 2. *Com:* Baby-doll.

bébête [bebɛːt], *a. F:* Childish, silly. *Rire b.,* giggle. [BÊTE]

bec [bɛk], *s.m.* I. Beak. (a) Bill (of bird). **Coup de bec,** peck. *Donner un coup de bec à qn,* (i) to peck s.o.; (ii) *F:* to have a dig, a slap, at s.o. *Il a bec et ongles,* he can look after himself. *Attaquer qn du bec et des ongles,* to go for s.o. tooth and nail. (b) Snout, beak (of certain fishes). 2. *F:* Mouth or nose. *Ils se rencontrèrent bec à bec,* they met face to face. **Fin bec,** gourmet. *F:* **Tenir qn le bec dans l'eau,** to keep s.o. in suspense. *Laisser qn le bec dans l'eau,* to leave s.o. in the lurch. *F:* **Ferme ton bec!** shut up! **River, clouer, le bec à qn,** to silence s.o.; *F:* to shut s.o. up. **Avoir bon bec,** to have the gift of the gab, a glib tongue. **Avoir le bec bien affilé,** to have a sharp tongue. **Se prendre de bec avec qn,** to have a set-to, a passage at arms, with s.o. **Prise de bec,** altercation, squabble. 3. (a) Nose (of tool); spout (of coffee-pot); peak (of bicycle saddle); mouth-piece (of clarinet); beak, horn, beak-iron (of anvil); catch, nose (of latch); cut-water (of bridge pier). (b) **Bec de plume,** pen-nib. (c) **Bec de gaz,** (i) gas burner, (ii) *F:* lamp-post. *Bec Bunsen,* Bunsen burner. *Bec Auer,* incandescent burner.

bécane [bɛkan], *s.f. P:* Bicycle, *F:* bike. **Aller à bécane,** to bike.

bécarre [bɛkaːr], *s.m. Mus:* Natural (sign).

bécasse [bɛkas], *s.f. Orn:* Woodcock. **B. de mer,** oyster-catcher. *F:* **C'est une petite bécasse,** she's a little goose.

bécasseau [bɛkaso], *s.m. Orn:* Sandpiper.

bécassine [bɛkasin], *s.f. Orn:* Snipe. *F:* **Bécassine de ruisseau,** gutter-snipe.

bec-croisé, *s.m. Orn:* Crossbill. *pl. Des becs-croisés.*

bec-de-cane, *s.m.* I. Lever handle (of shop door). 2. *Tls:* Flat-nosed pliers. *pl. Des becs-de-cane.*

bec-de-cire, *s.m. Orn:* Wax-bill. *pl. Des becs-de-cire.*

bec-de-corbin, *s.m.* (Name of various bill-headed instruments, *e.g.*) claw (for drawing nails), (caulker's) rave-hook. *F:* **Canne à bec-de-corbin,** crutch-handled walking-stick. **Nez en bec-de-corbin,** hooked nose. *pl. Des becs-de-corbin.*

bec-de-grue, *s.m. Bot: F:* Geranium; crane's-bill.

bec-de-lièvre, *s.m.* Hare-lip.

bec-en-ciseaux, *s.m. Orn:* Scissor-bill. *pl. Des becs-en-ciseaux.*

bec-en-croix, *s.m. Orn:* Common crossbill. *pl. Des becs-en-croix.*

becfigue [bɛkfig], *s.m. Orn:* (Familiar name for) the garden-warbler, the blackcap, the waxwing, and the pipit.

bec-fin, *s.m. Orn:* Warbler. *pl. Des becs-fins.*

bêche [bɛʃ], *s.f.* (a) Spade. *Labour à la b.,* digging. (b) *Artil:* Bêche de crosse, trail spade.

bêche-de-mer, *s.f. Z:* Sea-slug, trepang, sea-cucumber, bêche-de-mer. *pl. Des bêches-de-mer.*

bêch|er [beʃe], *v.tr.* I. To dig. 2. *F:* To run (s.o.) down; to pull (s.o.) to pieces. *s.m.* **-age.**

bêcheur, -euse [beʃœːr, -øːz], *s.* I. Digger (of the soil). 2. *F:* (a) Hard worker, plodder. (b) Detractor; carping critic.

bécot [beko], *s.m. F:* Little kiss; peck. [BEC]

bécoter [bekɔte], *v.tr. F:* To give (s.o.) a little kiss, a peck.

becquée [beke], *s.f.* I. Beakful, billful. 2. *L'oiseau donne la b. à ses petits,* the bird feeds its young.

becquet|er [bɛkte], *v.tr.* (je becquète, n. becquetons; je becquèterai) I. (Of birds) (a) To pick up (crumbs, etc.). (b) To peck at (sth.). 2. (a) (Of bird) To caress (another) with the beak; to bill. (b) *F:* (Of pers) To kiss. *s.m.* **-age.**

bec-rond, *s.m. Orn: F:* Bullfinch. *pl. Des becs-ronds.*

bedaine [bədɛn], *s.f. F:* Paunch, corporation.

bédane [bedan], *s.m. Mortise chisel. Metalw:* Cold chisel, cross-cut chisel. [BEC D'ÂNE]

bedeau [bədo], *s.m.* I. *A:* Beadle. 2. *Ecc:* Verger.

bédégar [bedegaːr], *s.m. Hort:* Rose-gall.

bedon [bədɔ̃], *s.m. F:* Belly, corporation. **Un gros bedon,** a big fat man.

bedonner [bədɔne], *v.i. F:* To get stout; to acquire a corporation.

bédouin, -ine [bedwɛ̃, -in], *a. & s.* Bedouin.

bée[1] [be], *s.f.* I. *Const:* Opening (for door, window); doorway. 2. (a) Mouth of mill-leet. (b) Penstock (of mill). [BAYER]

bée[2], *a.f.* Gaping. (Used in) **Bouche bée,** agape. *Regarder qch. bouche bée,* to gape at sth. [BAYER]

béer [bee], *v.i.* = BAYER.

beffroi [befrwa], *s.m.* I. Belfry. 2. Alarm-bell (hung in belfry).

bégaiement [begɛmã], *s.m.* = BÉGAYEMENT.

bégay|er [begɛje], *v.* (je bégaye, bégaie, n. béga-

5

yons; je bégayerai, bégaierai) I. v.i. To stutter, stammer. *Homme qui bégaie*, man with a stammer. 2. v.tr. B. sa leçon, to stammer out, falter through, one's lesson. [BÈGUE] s.m. -ement. s. -eur, -euse.

bègue [bɛg]. I. a. Stammering. *Il est b.*, he stammers. 2. s. Stammerer.

bégueule [begœl]. I. s.f. Prude. 2. a. Prudish, prim; strait-laced.

bégueulerie [begœlri], s.f. Prudishness, prudery.

béguin [begɛ̃], s.m. Hood (of Beguine nun); (baby's) bonnet. F: Avoir un béguin pour qn, to have an infatuation, a fancy, for s.o. C'est mon béguin, he, she, is my fancy.

béguinage [begina:ʒ], s.m. I. (Beguine) convent. 2. F: Excessive piety.

béguine [begin], s.f. I. Ecc: Beguin(e) (nun). 2. F: Very devout woman.

beige [bɛ:ʒ]. I. a. Beige; natural, raw (wool). 2. s.f. Étoffe en beige, cloth in natural colour.

beigne [bɛɲ], s.f. P: I. Bruise, bump. 2. Blow, clout, P: biff. *Donner, flanquer, une b. à qn*, to catch s.o. a clout.

beignet [bɛɲɛ], s.m. Cu: Fritter.

béjaune [beʒo:n], s.m. I. (a) Yellow beak (of young bird). (b) Young bird, nestling. 2. (a) Ninny, greenhorn. (b) Novice; freshman (at university, etc.). [BEC JAUNE]

bel [bɛl]. See BEAU.

bélemnite [belemnit], s.f. Paleont: Belemnite.

bêl|er [bɛle], v.i. To bleat. s.m. -ement.

belette [bəlɛt], s.f. Weasel.

belge [bɛlʒ], a. & s. Belgian.

belgique [bɛlʒik]. I. a. Hist: Belgic (Gaul, etc.). 2. Pr.n.f. La Belgique, Belgium.

bélier [belje], s.m. I. Z: Ram. 2. (a) Mil: A: Battering ram. (b) Civ.E: B. à pilotage, pile-driver. (c) Bélier hydraulique, hydraulic ram. 3. Astr: Le Bélier, the Ram; Aries.

bélière[1] [beljɛːr], s.f. Sheep-bell.

bélière[2], s.f. Ring (of watch); clapper-ring (of bell); shackle (of knife).

bélître [belitr], s.m. A: Cad, bounder.

belladone [bɛl(l)adɔn], s.f. Bot: Belladonna.

bellâtre [belɑːtr]. I. a. Foppish, dandified. 2. s.m. Fop.

belle [bɛl]. See BEAU.

belle-dame, s.f. Bot: (a) Garden orach. (b) Deadly nightshade.

belle-de-jour, s.f. Bot: Convolvulus minor.

belle-de-nuit, s.f. Bot: Marvel of Peru.

belle-d'onze-heures, s.f. Bot: Star of Bethlehem.

belle-fille, s.f. I. Step-daughter. 2. Daughter-in-law. pl. Des belles-filles.

bellement [bɛlmɑ̃], adv. Gently, softly.

belle-mère, s.f. I. Step-mother. 2. Mother-in-law. pl. Des belles-mères.

belles-lettres, s.f.pl. Humanities, belles-lettres.

belle-sœur, s.f. Sister-in-law. pl. Des belles-sœurs.

belligérance [bɛl(l)iʒerɑ̃:s], s.f. Belligerency.

belligérant [bɛl(l)iʒerɑ̃], a. & s.m. Belligerent.

belliqueux, -euse [bɛl(l)ikø, -øːz], a. Warlike, bellicose.

bellot, -otte [bɛlo, -ɔt], a. F: I. Pretty-pretty. 2. Dandified.

bélouga [beluga], s.m. Z: Beluga; white whale.

belvédère [bɛlvedeːr], s.m. I. Belvedere; view-point; observation tower. 2. Summer-house.

Belzébuth [bɛlzebyt]. Pr.n.m. Beelzebub.

bémol [bemɔl], s.m. Mus: Flat. Clarinette en si bémol, B-flat clarinet. [B MOL]

ben [bɛ̃], adv. P: = BIEN. *Ben oui!* why, yes!

bénarde [benard], a.f. & s.f. (Serrure) bénarde, pin-key lock, double-sided lock.

bénédicité [benedisite], s.m. Grace (before meat). Dire le bénédicité, to say grace; to ask a blessing.

bénédictin, -ine [benediktɛ̃, -in], a. & s. I. Benedictine (monk, nun). 2. s.f. Bénédictine, benedictine (liqueur).

bénédiction [benediksjɔ̃], s.f. Blessing, benediction; consecration (of colours). Donner la bénédiction, to give, pronounce, the blessing. Quelle bénédiction! what a blessing! what a godsend!

bénéfice [benefis], s.m. I. Profit, gain. Réaliser de gros bénéfices, to make big profits. Je suis en bénéfice, I am in pocket. 2. Benefit. Faire qch. au bénéfice de qn, to do sth. for s.o.'s benefit. Sous le bénéfice de cette observation . . ., (i) having made this point . . .; (ii) with this reservation. . . . Jur: Bénéfice du doute, benefit of the doubt. 3. Ecc: Living, benefice.

bénéficier [benefisje], v.i. (a) To profit (de, by). Faire bénéficier qn d'une remise, to allow s.o. a discount. (b) To make a profit (sur, on).

benêt [bənɛ]. I. a. Stupid, simple-minded. 2. s.m. Booby, simpleton, ninny.

Bénévent [benevɑ̃]. Pr.n.m. Geog: Benevento.

bénévole [benevɔl], a. I. Benevolent; kindly (reader, etc.); indulgent. 2. Gratuitous, unpaid (service). Infirmière bénévole, voluntary nurse. adv. -ment.

Bengale [bɛgal]. Pr.n.m. Bengal. Feu de Bengale, (i) Bengal light; (ii) light signal; flare.

bén|in, -igne [benɛ̃, -iɲ], a. (a) Benign, kindly. Astre bénin, benignant star. (b) Mild, gentle (remedy). Hiver b., mild winter. Forme bénigne de la rougeole, mild form of measles. adv. -ignement. s.f. -ignité.

bénir [beniːr], v.tr. (p.p. béni, bénit. The latter used chiefly as an adj. but occ. with verbal force in 2.) I. (a) To bless; to grant blessings to (s.o.). (Que) Dieu vous bénisse! God bless you! (b) To bless, ask God's blessing on (s.o.); to pronounce a blessing on (s.o.). B. un mariage, to solemnize a marriage. (c) To render thanks to (God). Le ciel en soit béni! heaven be thanked for it! 2. To consecrate (bread, water). Quand le prêtre a bénit le pain . . ., when the priest has blessed the bread. . . .

bénit, a. Consecrated, blessed. Pain bénit, consecrated bread. Eau bénite, holy water. F: Eau bénite de cour, fair promises; empty words.

bénitier [benitje], s.m. Holy-water basin; stoop, stoup.

benjoin [bɛ̃ʒwɛ̃], s.m. Gum benzoin. S.a. BAUME I.

benne [bɛn], s.f. I. Flat hamper, basket. 2. Min: etc: Skip, tub, hutch, bucket. Camion à benne basculante, tip-lorry; tipping waggon.

Benoist, Benoît [bənwa]. Pr.n.m. Benedict.

benoîte [bənwat], s.f. Bot: Herb-bennet.

benzène [bɛ̃zɛn], s.m. Ch: Benzene.

benzine [bɛ̃zin], s.f. Benzine.

benzoin [bɛ̃zwɛ̃], s.m. Bot: (Styrax) benzoin, benzoin laurel, F: benjamin-tree.

benzol [bɛ̃zɔl], s.m. Ch: Benzol.

béotien, -ienne [beɔsjɛ̃, -jɛn], a. & s. I. A.Geog: Bœotian. 2. F: Ignorant, dull-witted.

béquille [bekiːj], s.f. I. Crutch. 2. Sprag; crutch, stand (of motor cycle). Av: Tail-skid.

ber(s) [bɛːr], s.m. N.Arch: I. (Launching) cradle. 2. Boiler seatings.

berbère [bɛrbɛːr], a. & s. Ethn: Berber, Kabyle.

bercail [bɛrkaːj], s.m. Not used in the pl. (a) Husb: (Sheep)fold. (b) The fold (of the Church). Rentrer au bercail, to return to the fold.

berce [bɛrs], *s.f. Bot:* Cow-parsnip, hogweed.
berceau [bɛrso], *s.m.* **1.** Cradle; (swing-)cot. **Étouffer le mal au berceau,** to strangle evil at its birth. **2.** (*a*) *Aut: etc:* Cradle, bed, support. *B.* (*du*) *moteur,* bearer plates of the engine. (*b*) (**Voûte en**) **berceau,** cradle-vault, wagon-vault. (*c*) *Hort:* Arbour, bower.
bercelonnette [bɛrsəlɔnɛt],*s.f.* Bassinet,(swing-)cot.
berc|er [bɛrse], *v.tr.* (**je berçai(s); n. berçons**) **1.** To rock. *B. un bébé,* (i) to rock a baby (in a cradle), (ii) to dandle a baby (in one's arms). **2.** To lull; to send (s.o.) to sleep; to soften, soothe (grief). **Bercer qn de promesses,** to beguile s.o. with promises. *s.m.* **-ement.**
se bercer. 1. To rock, swing, sway. **2.** *Se b. d'une illusion,* to cherish, indulge in, an illusion.
berceuse [bɛrsøːz], *s.f.* **1.** (*a*) Swing-cot. (*b*) Rocking-chair. **2.** Lullaby, cradle-song.
béret [bɛrɛ], *s.m.* Beret. *B. écossais,* tam-o'-shanter.
bergamot(t)e [bɛrgamɔt],*s.f.* Bergamot (orange, lemon, pear).
berge [bɛrʒ], *s.f.* (Steep) bank (of river); banked edge (of railway track, of road). *Mil:* Rampart, parapet.
berger, -ère [bɛrʒe, -ɛːr], *s.* **1.** Shepherd, shepherdess. **L'Étoile du Berger,** the Evening Star. *F:* **L'heure du berger,** the auspicious hour (for lovers); the gloaming. **2.** *s.f.* **Bergère.** (*a*) Easychair. (*b*) *Orn:* Wagtail.
bergerette [bɛrʒərɛt], *s.f.* **1.** *Poet:* Young shepherdess, shepherd-maid. **2.** *Orn:* Wagtail.
bergerie [bɛrʒəri], *s.f.* **1.** Sheep-fold; pen. *F:* **Enfermer le loup dans la bergerie,** to set the fox to mind the geese. **2.** Pastoral (poem, painting).
bergeronnette [bɛrʒərɔnɛt],*s.f. Orn:* Wagtail.
berline [bɛrlin], *s.f.* (*a*) *A:* Berlin(e) (coach). (*b*) *Aut:* Limousine. (*c*) *Min:* Truck, tram. (*d*) (*Avion-*)berline, saloon air-liner.
berlingot [bɛrlɛ̃go], *s.m.* Burnt-sugar sweet; caramel.
berlinois, -oise [bɛrlinwa, -waːz]. **1.** *a.* Of Berlin. **2.** *s.* Berliner.
berloque [bɛrlɔk], *s.f. P:* = BRELOQUE 2.
berlue [bɛrly],*s.f. Med:* False vision. *F:* **Avoir la berlue,** to be blind to the facts; to see things wrong.
berme [bɛrm], *s.f.* **1.** *Fort:* Berm. **2.** *Civ.E:* Set-off, bench (with foot-path).
Bermudes [bɛrmyd]. *Pr.n.f.pl.* **Les (îles) Bermudes,** the Bermudas; the Bermuda Islands.
bernache [bɛrnaʃ], *s.f.*, **bernacle** [bɛrnakl], *s.f.* **1.** *Crust:* Barnacle. **2.** *Orn:* Barnacle; bernacle goose. *B. cravant,* brent-goose.
bernardin, -ine [bɛrnardɛ̃, -in], *s.* Reformed Cistercian monk or nun.
bernard-l'ermite [bɛrnarlɛrmit], *s.m.* Hermitcrab, soldier-crab.
berne[1] [bɛrn], *s.f.* **1.** Tossing blanket. **2.** (*a*) Tossing in a blanket. (*b*) *F:* Chaff, banter.
berne[2],*s.f.* (Used only in) **1.** *Nau:* Pavillon en berne, flag at half-mast. **Mettre en berne,** to half-mast the flag. **2.** *Mil:* Drapeau en berne, flag furled and craped.
Berne[3]. *Pr.n. Geog:* Bern(e).
bern|er [bɛrne], *v.tr.* **1.** To toss (s.o.) in a blanket. **2.** (*a*) To chaff, banter. (*b*) To hoax. *a.* **-able.** *s.m.* **-ement.** *s.* **-eur, -euse.**
bernique [bɛrnik], *int. F:* Not a bit of use! no go! nothing doing!
berrichon, -onne [bɛriʃɔ̃, -ɔn], *a. & s.* (Native) of Berry.
Berthe [bɛrt]. **1.** *Pr.n.f.* Bertha. *F:* **Du temps**

où **Berthe** filait (with reference to Berthe de Bourgogne, Xth cent.), in the days of good Queen Bess, in the days of yore. **2.** *s.f. Cost:* Bertha (collar).
berthon [bɛrtɔ̃], *s.m. Nau:* Berthon boat; collapsible dinghy.
Bertrand [bɛrtrɑ̃]. *Pr.n.m.* Bertram, Bertrand. *F:* **Bertrand et Raton,** the schemer and the cat's-paw. (From La Fontaine's fable *Le Singe et le Chat.*)
béryl [beril], *s.m. Miner:* Beryl.
besace [bazas], *s.f. A:* Double sack, double bag (with opening in the centre, carried over the shoulder by beggars); scrip. *F:* **Porter la besace,** to beg; to be very poor.
besaiguë [bazegy],*s.f.* Mortising axe; twibill.
besant [bazɑ̃], *s.m. Num: Her:* Besant, bezant.
besicles [bazikl], *s.f.pl.* **1.** *A:* Spectacles. **2.** Goggles.
bésigue [bezig], *s.m. Cards:* Bezique.
besogne [b(ə)zɔɲ], *s.f.* Work; task, job; piece of work. **Se mettre à la besogne,** to set to work. **Mourir à la besogne,** to die in harness. *Une rude b.,* a hard task or job; a stiff piece of work. **Aller vite en besogne,** to despatch work quickly; to act quickly. **Abattre de la besogne,** to get through a lot of work. **Vous n'avez pas besogne faite,** you are not at the end of your difficulties.
besogneux, -euse [bazɔɲø, -øːz], *a. & s.* Needy, impecunious; *F:* hard up (person).
besoin [bazwɛ̃], *s.m.* Want, need. **1.** Necessity, requirement. (*a*) *Pourvoir aux besoins de qn,* to provide for s.o.'s wants. *Je le ferais si le b. s'en faisait sentir,* I should do it if the necessity arose. *Pour le b. de la cause,* for the sake of the cause. *F: Faire ses (petits) besoins,* to relieve nature. **Au besoin, en cas de besoin,** in case of need, of emergency; if necessary; when required; *F:* at a pinch. (*b*) **Avoir besoin de qch.,** to need, require, want, sth. *J'ai grand b. de son aide,* I badly want his assistance. *Il n'a pas b. de venir lundi,* he need not come, there is no need for him to come, on Monday. *Je n'avais pas b. qu'on me le rappelât,* I did not need to be reminded of it. (*c*) *impers.* **Il n'est pas besoin,** there is no need. **Est-il besoin?** is there any necessity? *Il n'est pas b. de vous dire, que je vous dise, combien je vous suis reconnaissant,* I need hardly tell you how grateful I am. **Point n'est besoin d'insister,** no need to insist. **Si besoin est,** if need be. **2.** Poverty, indigence. **Être dans le besoin,** to be in want, in straitened circumstances.
besson, -onne [bɛsɔ̃, -ɔn], *a. & s. Dial:* Twin.
bestiaire [bɛstjɛːr], *s.m.* **1.** *Rom.Ant:* Bestiary, beast-fighter. **2.** *Lit:* Bestiary, book of beasts.
bestial, -aux[1] [bɛstjal, -o], *a.* Bestial, beastly, brutish. *adv.* **-ement.**
bestialité [bɛstjalite], *s.f.* Bestiality.
bestiaux[2] [bɛstjo], *s.m.pl.* Cattle, beasts, livestock. [BÊTE]
bestiole [bɛstjɔl],*s.f.* Small, tiny, beast.
bêta, f. -asse [bɛta, -as], *s. F:* Stupid, blockhead, numskull, noodle. *a. Elle est jolie mais bêtasse,* she is pretty but rather simple. [BÊTE]
bétail [betaːj], *s.m. Coll.* (No *pl.*) Cattle; livestock, grazing stock. **Gros bétail,** cattle. **Menu bétail,** smaller live-stock. [BÊTE]
bête [bɛt], *s.f.* **1.** Beast, animal; dumb creature. (*a*) *B. à cornes,* horned beast. *B. à laine,* sheep. *B. brute,* brute beast. *B. de somme,* beast of burden. *B. de trait,* draught-animal. *F:* **C'est une fine bête,** he is a shrewd fellow. *F:* **Reprendre du poil de la bête,** to take a hair of the dog that bit one. S.a. NOIR 1. (*b*) (Insect or vermin)

Fruits mangés de (petites) bêtes, fruit eaten out by 'insects. *F:* **Chercher la petite bête,** to be over-critical. **Bête à bon Dieu,** lady-bird. **2.** *F:* (a) Fool, blockhead, simpleton. **Faire la bête,** (i) to affect stupidity, (ii) to act like a fool. *(b) a.* Stupid, foolish, unintelligent. *Que je suis b.!* how silly, stupid, of me! **Pas si bête!** I am not such a fool! not if I know it! **C'est bête comme chou,** (i) it's simplicity itself, (ii) it's idiotic. *Sourire b.,* idiotic smile. *Pourquoi as-tu fait ce* **bête de voyage?** why did you go on that stupid, senseless, journey? *Ses bêtes d'idées,* his silly ideas. *adv.* **-ment.**

bétel [betɛl], *s.m.* Betel. **Noix de bétel, betel-nut.**

bêtise [beti:z], *s.f.* **1.** Stupidity, silliness. *Être d'une b. extrême,* to be exceedingly stupid. **2.** Nonsense, absurdity. *Dire des bêtises,* to talk nonsense. *Quelle b.!* what nonsense! *P:* what bosh! **Faire des bêtises,** to play the fool. **3.** Blunder; piece of stupidity. *Faire une grande b.,* to commit a great folly. **4.** Trifle. *Dépenser tout son argent en bêtises,* to fritter away one's money. **Cinq mille francs, une bêtise!** five thousand francs, a mere trifle! [BÊTE]

bétoine [betwan], *s.f. Bot:* Betony.

béton [betɔ̃], *s.m.* **Béton de ciment,** concrete, beton. **Béton armé,** ferro-concrete; reinforced concrete.

bétonn|er [betɔne], *v.tr.* To concrete; to construct (building, etc.) with concrete. *s.m.* **-age.**

bette [bɛt], *s.f. Bot:* Beet.

betterave [bɛtraːv], *s.f.* Beet(root). *B. à sucre,* sugar-beet. [BETTE RAVE]

betteraverie [bɛtravri], *s.f.* Sugar-beet factory.

beuglant [bøglɑ̃, bœ-], *s.m. P:* Low-class concert-hall.

beuglement [bøgləmɑ̃, bœ-], *s.m.* **1.** Lowing (of cattle); bellowing (of bull). *F:* (Of pers.) Bawling. **2.** Bellow.

beugler [bøgle, bœ-], *v.i.* (Of cattle) To low; (of a bull) to bellow. *F: B. une chanson,* to bawl out a song.

beurre [bœːr], *s.m.* Butter. *Cu:* **Au beurre,** cooked in butter. **Au beurre noir,** with browned butter sauce. *P:* **Avoir un œil au beurre noir,** to have a black eye. *Rond de b.,* pat of butter. *F:* **Nous sommes entrés dedans comme dans du beurre,** it, they, offered no resistance. *P:* **C'est un (vrai) beurre,** (i) it is very easy to do; (ii) it's tip-top. *F:* **Il a fait son beurre,** he has feathered his nest. **Ça fait mon beurre,** that just suits my book. **Ça mettra du beurre dans les épinards,** that will make our life more comfortable.

beurrée [bœre], *s.f.* Slice of bread and butter.

beurrer [bœre], *v.tr.* To butter. *B. des tartines,* to cut slices of bread and butter.

beurrier, -ière [bœrje, -jɛːr], **1.** *a.* **Région** *beurrière,* butter-producing district. **2.** *s.* Butter-dealer. **3.** *s.m.* Butter-dish.

bévue [bevy], *s.f.* Blunder, mistake, slip; *F:* bloomer. *Sch:* Howler. *Commettre une b.,* to make a blunder; to blunder.

biais, -aise [bjɛ, -ɛːz]. **1.** *a.* Skew, oblique, sloping, slanting, bevelled. *Voûte biaise,* skew(ed) arch. **2.** *s.m.* (a) Skew (of tool, of arch); slant (of wall); bias (of bowl). **En biais,** on the slant, slantwise; on the skew; aslant, askew. *Tailler une étoffe en b.,* to cut material on the cross. *Regarder qn de biais,* to look sideways at s.o.; to give s.o. a side-glance. *(b)* Indirect means; expedient. *Aborder de b. une question,* to approach a question indirectly. **Prendre une affaire du bon biais, du mauvais biais,** to go the right, the wrong, way to work. **Chercher un biais pour faire qch.,**

to seek some shift or expedient to do sth. *(c) Dressm:* False tuck; band cut on the cross.

biais|er [bjɛze], *v.i.* **1.** To slant; to lean over. **2.** To use evasions; to shuffle. *s.m.* **-ement.**

biatomique [biatɔmik], *a. Ch: Ph:* Diatomic.

bibasique [bibɔzik, -ba-], *a. Ch:* Bibasic, dibasic.

bibelot [biblo], *s.m.* **1.** Curio, knick-knack, trinket. **2.** *pl.* Odds and ends.

bibelot|er [biblɔte], *v.i. F:* (a) To collect curios. (b) To do odd jobs. *s.m.* **-age.** *s.* **-eur, -euse.**

biberon¹, -onne [bibrɔ̃, -ɔn]. **1.** *a.* Tippling, wine-bibbing. **2.** *s.* Tippler, wine-bibber.

biberon², *s.m.* Feeding-bottle. **Élever un enfant au biberon,** to bring up a child by hand, on the bottle.

bibi [bibi], *s.m.* **1.** *F: Mon b.,* darling; my pet. **2.** *P:* **Ça c'est pour bibi,** that's for myself.

bibiche [bibiʃ], *s.f.* Ducky. [BICHE]

Bible [bibl], *s.f.* **La Bible,** the Bible.

biblio|graphe [bibliɔgraf], *s.m.* Bibliographer. *s.f.* **-graphie,** -graphy. *a.* **-graphique,** -graphical.

bibliomane [bibliɔman], *s.m.* Bibliomaniac, book collector.

bibliomanie [bibliɔmani], *s.f.* Bibliomania, book collecting.

bibliophile [bibliɔfil], *s.m.* Bibliophile, book-lover.

bibliothécaire [bibliɔtekɛːr], *s.m.* Librarian.

bibliothèque [bibliɔtɛk], *s.f.* **1.** (a) Library (building). (b) Library (room); reading-room. **2.** Bookcase, book-stand. *B. tournante,* revolving bookcase. **3.** Library; collection of books.

biblique [biblik], *a.* Biblical.

bicarbonate [bikarbɔnat], *s.m. Ch:* Bicarbonate.

bicarré [bikare], *a. Mth:* Biquadratic.

biceps [bisɛps], *a. & s.m. Anat:* Biceps (muscle). *F:* **Avoir du biceps,** to be strong in the arm.

Bicêtre [bisɛːtr]. *Pr.n.m.* · Village near Paris, known for its mental hospital. *F:* **C'est un échappé de Bicêtre,** he's mad; he's an absolute lunatic. *Cf.* CHARENTON.

biche [biʃ], *s.f.* **1.** *Z:* Hind, doe. *a.inv.* **Ventre de biche,** reddish-white. **2.** *F:* **Ma biche,** darling, dear.

bichette [biʃɛt], *s.f.* **1.** *Z:* Young hind; small hind. **2.** *F:* = BICHE 2.

bichon, -onne [biʃɔ̃, -ɔn], *s.* **1.** Maltese dog, lap-dog. **2.** *F:* Darling, ducky.

bichonner [biʃɔne], *v.tr.* **1.** To curl, frizz (hair). **2.** To make (s.o.) spruce, smart.
se bichonner, to spruce oneself up; to titivate.

bichromate [bikrɔmat], *s.m. Ch:* Bichromate.

bichromaté [bikrɔmate], *a. Phot:* **Gomme bichromatée,** gum bichromate.

biconcave [bikɔ̃kaːv], *a.* Biconcave, double-concave.

biconvexe [bikɔ̃vɛks], *a.* Biconvex, double-convex.

bicoque [bikɔk], *s.f. F:* Poky little house; shanty.

bicorne [bikɔrn], *s.m.* (Two-pointed) cocked hat.

bicycle [bisikl], *s.m.* **1.** *A:* Velocipede, (spider) bicycle; *F:* penny-farthing. **2.** *pl. Adm:* Bicycles (in general).

bicyclette [bisiklɛt], *s.f.* Bicycle, cycle. *B. de route,* roadster. *B. de course,* racer. **Aller à bicyclette,** to ride a bicycle, to (bi)cycle. *Est-ce que vous faites de la b.?* are you a cyclist?

bicycliste [bisiklist], *s.m. & f.* (Bi)cyclist.

bidet [bidɛ], *s.m.* **1.** Nag; pony; small horse. **2.** *Hyg:* Bidet de toilette, bidet. **3.** Sawing-horse; trestle.

bidoche [bidɔʃ], *s.f. P:* Meat (esp. of inferior quality).

bidon [bidɔ̃], *s.m.* (a) Can, drum (for oil, etc.). *B. à essence,* petrol-tin, -can. *B. de secours,* spare tin. *P:* **Se remplir le bidon,** to fill one's belly. (b) *Mil:* Water-bottle.

bief [bjɛf], *s.m.* **1.** (Canal) reach, level. *B. d'amont,* head-bay. *B. d'aval,* tail-bay. **2.** Mill-course, (mill-)race, (mill-)lade.

bielle [bjɛl], *s.f.* (a) (Tie-)rod; (in compression) push-rod; crank-arm. *B. de soupape,* valve pushrod. *Aut: B. d'accouplement (des roues avant),* track-link. *B. de commande de direction,* drag-link. (b) *Mch: B. motrice,* connecting-rod, driving-rod. **Tête de bielle,** *Mch:* crank-head, *I.C.E:* big end. **Pied de bielle,** *Mch:* crosshead, *I.C.E:* small end.

bien [bjɛ̃]. **I.** *adv.* **1.** Well. *Livre b. écrit,* wellwritten book. *Il danse b.,* he dances well, is a good dancer. *Il faut b. les soigner,* we must look after them well. *Vous avez b. fait,* you did right, acted rightly. *Ma montre va b.,* (i) my watch keeps good time; (ii) my watch is right. *Tout va b.,* all's well. *Aller, se porter, b.,* to be well, in good health. **Bien!** (i) good! (ii) that's enough! that will do! (iii) all right! **Très bien!** very good! well done! (in speech) hear, hear! *F:* **Vous arrivez joliment bien,** it's deuced lucky you've come. **2.** (With adj. function) (a) Right, proper. *Comme c'est b. à vous d'être venu!* how nice of you to come! *Ce n'est pas b. de vous moquer de lui,* it's a shame to make fun of him. (b) Comfortable. **Êtes-vous bien** *dans ce fauteuil?* are you comfortable in that armchair? *Il est b. partout où il se trouve,* he is happy, feels at home, wherever he may be. *Vous ne savez pas quand vous êtes b.,* you don't know when you are well off. *F:* **Vous voilà bien!** now you're in a fine fix, in a fine pickle! (c) (Of health) **Je ne me sens pas bien,** I don't feel well. **Se trouver bien de qch.,** to derive benefit from sth. (d) **Être bien avec qn,** to be on good terms with s.o. **Être bien en cour,** to have friends at court. **Ils sont du dernier bien,** they are on very intimate terms, on a most friendly footing. (e) Of good appearance, position, quality, etc. **Elle est bien de (sa) figure,** she is good-looking. **Il est très bien,** he is very gentlemanly. **Elle est b. de sa personne,** (i) she looks a lady; (ii) she is attractive. **Ce sont des gens bien,** they are people of good position, gentlefolk. **Donnez-moi quelque chose de bien,** give me something good, of good quality. **3.** (Emphatic) (a) Indeed, really, quite. *Il y a b. deux ans que je ne l'ai vue,* it is at least two years since I saw her. *Je l'ai regardé b. en face,* I looked him full in the face. *Est-ce b. vous?* is it really you? *Qu'est-ce que ça peut b. être?* what ever can it be? *Voilà b. les femmes!* that's just like a woman! *Est-ce b. le train pour Paris?* is this the right train for Paris? **Je l'avais bien dit!** didn't I say so! *J'espère b. qu'il viendra,* I do hope he will come. **Voulez-vous bien vous taire!** (i) for shame (to speak like that)! (ii) *will* you hold your tongue! **Bien entendu,** of course. **Je m'en doutais bien,** I thought as much. *Il est b. venu, mais j'étais occupé,* he did come, but I was busy. *Je ne veux pas que tu fasses cela.*—**Mais vous le faites bien, vous!** I don't want you to do that.— Why, you do it, don't you? (b) (= TRÈS) Very. *B. malheureux,* very unhappy. *Vous venez b. tard,* you are very late in coming. **Des résultats bien autres,** very different results. (*Cf. bien d'autres* under (c).) (c) (= BEAUCOUP) Much, many, a great deal, a great many. (i) *J'ai b. souffert,* I suffered a great deal. *J'ai b. envie de lui écrire,* I have a good mind to write to him. *Ce qui est b. pis,* which is much worse, far worse, a good deal worse. (ii) (With the partitive article) **J'ai eu bien du mal, bien de la peine,** *à la convaincre,* I had much difficulty in convincing her. **Je l'ai vu bien des fois,** I have seen him many times, many a time. **Bien d'autres,** many others, *F:* lots of others. (*Cf. bien autres* under (b).) **4.** *Adv.phr.* (a) **Aussi bien,** in any case, after all, when all is said and done. *Aussi b. votre frère aurait-il pu vous avertir,* indeed your brother might have warned you. (b) **Bel et bien,** see BEAU I. 3. (c) **Tant bien que mal,** somehow (or other); after a fashion. *Je m'en suis acquitté tant b. que mal,* I muddled through. (d) **Bien plus,** nay more. (e) *Iron:* **Un peu bien,** somewhat. *Elle est un peu b. mûre,* she's on the ripe side. **5.** *Conj.phr.* (a) **Aussi bien que** (= AINSI QUE), as well as, besides. (b) **Bien que** + *sub.,* though, although. *Je le respecte, b. qu'il ne me soit pas sympathique,* I respect him though I don't like him. (c) **Si bien que** + *ind.,* so that, and so. *Il ne reparut plus, si b. qu'on le crut mort,* he failed to reappear, so that, and so, he was thought dead. (d) **Ou bien,** or else; otherwise. **6.** *int.* **Eh bien!** well!

II. bien, *s.m.* **1.** **Le bien public,** the public weal, the commonweal. **La science du bien et du mal,** the knowledge of good and evil. **Faire le bien,** to engage in good works. **Homme de bien,** good, upright, man. *C'est pour votre b.,* it is for your good. *Cela me fit beaucoup de b.,* it did me a lot of good. **Grand bien vous fasse!** much good may it do you! **Vouloir du bien à qn, vouloir le bien de qn,** to wish s.o. well. *Tout le monde dit du b. de lui,* everyone speaks well of him. *C'est peut-être un b. pour un mal,* it is perhaps a blessing in disguise. **2.** (a) Possession, property, asset, wealth, goods (and chattels). *Il a du b., de grands biens,* he is wealthy, well-to-do. *F:* **Avoir du bien au soleil,** to be a man of property. (b) *Jur:* **Biens meubles, biens mobiliers,** personal estate; personalty, chattels, movables. **Biens immeubles, biens immobiliers,** real estate. **3.** *Adv.phr.* (a) **En bien.** *Prendre la chose en b.,* to take the matter in good part. *Changement en b.,* change for the better. *Vous lui ressemblez, mais en b.,* you are like him but better looking. (b) **A bien.** *Mener une affaire à b.,* to bring a matter to a successful issue, to a satisfactory conclusion. (c) **Il a agi en tout bien, tout honneur,** he acted with the best and most honourable intentions.

bien-aimé, -ée [bjɛ̃nɛme, bjɛn-], *a. & s.* Beloved; well-beloved.

bien-être [bjɛ̃nɛːtr, bjɛn-], *s.m.* No *pl.* (a) Wellbeing; comfort. *Sentiment de b.-ê.,* feeling of well-being. (b) Welfare.

bienfaisance [bjɛ̃fəzɑ̃ːs], *s.f.* Beneficence, charity. **Bureau de bienfaisance,** relief committee.

bienfaisant [bjɛ̃fəzɑ̃], *a.* **1.** Beneficent, charitable. **2.** Beneficial, salutary (remedy, etc.).

bienfait [bjɛ̃fɛ], *s.m.* **1.** Benefit, kindness, service, good turn. **2.** Gift, blessing, boon. **Un bienfait du ciel,** a godsend.

bienfaiteur, -trice [bjɛ̃fɛtœːr, -tris], *s.* Benefactor, benefactress.

bien-fondé [bjɛ̃fɔ̃de], *s.m.* No *pl. Jur:* Cogency, justice, merits (of case, claim).

bien-fonds [bjɛ̃fɔ̃], *s.m.* Real estate; landed property. *pl.* **Des biens-fonds.**

bienheureux, -euse [bjɛ̃nœrø, bjɛn-, -øːz], *a.* **1.** Blissful, happy. **2.** *Ecc:* Blessed. *Le b. Thomas More,* the Blessed Thomas More.

biennal, -aux [bien(n)al, -o], *a.* Biennial, two-yearly.

bienséance [bjɛ̃seɑ̃:s], s.f. Propriety, decency, seemliness. *Observer les bienséances*, to observe the proprieties. *Manquer aux bienséances*, to fail in good breeding.

bienséant [bjɛ̃seɑ̃], a. Seemly, decorous, proper. *Il est b. aux jeunes gens de respecter la vieillesse*, it is seemly for young people to respect old age.

bientôt [bjɛ̃to], adv. (Very) soon; before long. *F:* **A bientôt!** good-bye, see you again soon! *P:* so long! **Il eut bientôt fait de** *dresser une échelle*, he was not long in putting up a ladder. **C'est bientôt dit!** it is easier said than done!

bienveillance [bjɛ̃vejɑ̃:s], s.f. Benevolence; kindness (*envers*, *pour*, to); good-will. **Faire qch. par bienveillance**, to do sth. out of kindness.

bienveillant [bjɛ̃vejɑ̃], a. Kind, kindly, benevolent (*envers*, *pour*, to).

bienvenir [bjɛ̃vni:r], v.i. (Used only in) **Se faire bienvenir de qn**, to ingratiate oneself with s.o.

bienvenu, -e[1], a. & s. Welcome. **Soyez le bienvenu, la bienvenue!** welcome! S.a. VENIR I.

bienvenue², s.f. Welcome. **Souhaiter la bienvenue à qn**, to welcome s.o.; to bid s.o. welcome.

bière¹ [bjɛ:r], s.f. Beer. B. *blanche, blonde*, light ale, pale ale. **Petite bière**, small beer. *F:* **Ce n'est pas de la petite bière**, (i) he's a big pot, (ii) it's not to be sneezed at.

bière², s.f. Coffin. **Mettre un corps en bière**, to coffin a body.

biez [bjɛ], s.m. = BIEF.

biffer [bife], v.tr. To cross out, strike out, put a stroke through, cancel (word, etc.). s.m. **-age**.

biffin [bifɛ̃], s.m. I. Ragman. 2. *P:* Infantryman.

biffure [bify:r], s.f. Erasure; cancelling stroke.

bifocal, -aux [bifɔkal, -o], a. Bifocal (lens, etc.).

bifteck [biftɛk], s.m. I. Beefsteak. 2. B. *de veau, d'ours*, veal steak, bear steak.

bifurcation [bifyrkasjɔ̃], s.f. Bifurcation, fork; branching (of road, tree-trunk, etc.); road fork. *Rail:* (Gare de) bifurcation, junction.

bifurquer [bifyrke] v.tr. & i. To fork, bifurcate, divide; to branch off. *La route bifurque à Noyon*, the road forks at Noyon.
se bifurquer, to fork, divide.

bigame [bigam]. I. a. Bigamous. 2. s. Bigamist.

bigamie [bigami], s.f. Bigamy.

bigarreau [bigaro], s.m. White-heart cherry; bigaroon.

bigarrer [bigare], v.tr. To variegate, mottle. *Étoffe bigarrée de rouge*, material slashed with red. *Foule bigarrée*, motley crowd.

bigarrure [bigary:r], s.f. (a) Medley; mixture (of colours). (b) Slash (of colour).

bigle¹ [bigl], a. Squint-eyed; *F:* cock-eyed.

bigle², s.m. *Ven:* Beagle.

bigorne [bigɔrn], s.f. I. (a) Two-beaked anvil. (b) Beak-iron; stake. 2. Beak, horn (of anvil).

bigorneau [bigɔrno], s.m. *Moll:* Winkle.

bigot, -ote [bigo, -ɔt]. I. a. (Over-)devout, *F:* churchy. 2. s. Zealous church-goer; religious bigot.

bigoterie [bigɔtri], s.f. Religious bigotry, *F:* churchiness.

bigoudi [bigudi], s.m. (Leather) hair-curler.

bigre [bigr], int. *P:* **Bigre!** *qu'il fait froid!* by Jove, it is cold!

bigrement [bigrəmɑ̃], adv. *Vous avez b. raison!* you are jolly well right! *Il fait b. froid*, it is awfully cold.

bigrille [bigri:j], a. *W.Tel:* **Lampe bigrille**, double-grid valve; four-electrode valve.

bigue [big], s.f. Hoisting-gin; sheers. *Nau:* Mast-crane; derrick.

bijou, -oux [biʒu], s.m. Piece of jewellery; jewel, gem. *F:* **Mon bijou!** my jewel! my pet!

bijouterie [biʒutri], s.f. I. Jeweller's trade or shop. 2. Jewellery; jewels.

bijoutier, -ière [biʒutje, -jɛ:r], s. Jeweller.

bilan [bilɑ̃], s.m. *Com:* I. Balance-sheet. **Dresser le bilan**, to strike the balance. 2. Schedule (of assets and liabilities). **Déposer son bilan**, to file one's petition (in bankruptcy).

bilatéral, -aux [bilateral, -o], a. Bilateral, two-sided (paralysis, contract, etc.).

bilboquet [bilbɔkɛ], s.m. *Toys:* (a) Cup-and-ball. (b) Tumbler (weighted figure).

bile [bil], s.f. (a) Bile, gall. (b) Bile; bad temper. **S'échauffer la bile**, to worry, fret, get angry. **Ne te fais pas de bile!** don't worry! **Épancher sa bile contre qn**, to rail at s.o. **Épanchement de bile**, (i) bilious attack; (ii) fit of bad temper.

biliaire [biljɛ:r], a. Biliary (duct, etc.).

bilieux, -euse [biljø, -ø:z], a. I. Bilious. 2. (a) Choleric, irascible, testy. (b) Morose.

bilinéaire [bilinee:r], a. *Mth:* Bilinear.

bilingue [bilɛ̃:g], a. Bilingual.

billard [bija:r], s.m. I. (Game of) billiards. 2. Billiard-table. 3. (a) Billiard-room. (b) Billiard-saloon.

bille¹ [bi:j], s.f. (Small) ball. I. (a) Billiard-ball. (b) *P:* (i) Head, *P:* noddle, nut. (ii) Face, *P:* phiz. 2. Marble, taw, alley. 3. *Mec.E:* Roulement à, sur, billes ; coussinet(s) à billes, ball-bearing(s).

bille², s.f. I. Billet (of timber). 2. Rolling pin.

billet [bijɛ], s.m. I. Note, short letter. **Billet doux**, love-letter. 2. Notice, invitation-card, circular. **Billet de faire part**, notice announcing a family event (birth, marriage, death). 3. Ticket. *Rail:* etc: B. *simple, b. d'aller*, single ticket. B. *d'aller et retour*, return ticket. B. *de correspondance*, transfer ticket. B. *de quai*, platform ticket. B. *circulaire*, tourist ticket. *Prendre un b. direct pour Paris*, to book through to Paris. (In lottery) **Tirer un billet blanc**, to draw a blank. **Billet d'entrée**, admission ticket or card. *Th:* etc: B. *de faveur*, complimentary ticket, free ticket. 4. *Com:* (a) Promissory note, bill. B. *à vue*, bill payable at sight. B. *à présentation*, bill payable on demand. B. *du Trésor*, Treasury-bill. S.a. ORDRE 5. (b) **Billet de banque**, bank-note. 5. Billet de santé, certificate, bill, of health. 6. Permit, permission. *Sch:* B. *de sortie*, exeat. 7. Billet de vote, voting paper. 8. *Mil:* Billet de logement, billeting order.

billette [bijɛt], s.f. Billet (of firewood, of metal).

billevesée [bilvəze, bij-], s.f. Crack-brained notion; nonsense.

billion [biljɔ̃], s.m. One thousand million (10^9). *U.S:* billion.

billon [bijɔ̃], s.m. I. (a) Balk (of squared timber). (b) *Agr:* Ridge of earth (formed by two plough furrows). 2. (Monnaie de) billon, copper or nickel coinage. [BILLE²]

billot [bijo], s.m. (a) Block (of wood); chopping-log. B. *de boucher*, butcher's block. (b) Executioner's block. [BILLE²]

bimane [biman], a. Bimanous.

bimbelot [bɛ̃blo], s.m. I. Toy. 2. Trumpery article; bauble.

bimbeloterie [bɛ̃blɔtri], s.f. I. Toy business or trade; cheap 'bazaar' trade. 2. Toys, knick-knacks, odds and ends.

bimensuel, -elle [bimɑ̃sɥɛl], a. Fortnightly. adv. **-ellement**.

bimétallisme [bimetalism], s.m. Bimetallism.

bimoteur [bimotœ:r], a.m. *Av:* **Appareil bimoteur**, twin-engine machine.

binaire [binɛːr], *a.* Binary.

bine [bin], *s.f. Agr: Hort:* Hoe.

bin|er [bine], *v.tr.* (*a*) *Agr:* To dig, harrow, dress, (ground) for a second time. (*b*) To hoe. *s.m.* **-age.**

binette[1] [binɛt], *s.f.* Hoe.

binette[2], *s.f.* **1.** *A:* Full-bottomed wig. **2.** *P:* Face; *P:* phiz, mug.

biniou [binju], *s.m.* Breton (ᴅag-)pipes.

binocle [binɔkl], *s.m.* Eye-glasses, pince-nez.

binôme [binoːm], *a. & s.m.* Binomial. **Le binôme de Newton,** the binomial theorem.

biochimie [biɔʃimi], *s.f.* Biochemistry.

bio|graphe [biɔgraf], *s.m.* Biographer. *s.f.* **-graphie,** -graphy. *a.* **-graphique,** -graphical.

bio|logie [biɔlɔʒi], *s.f.* Biology. *a.* **-logique,** -logical. *s.m.* **-logiste, -logue,** -logist.

bioxyde [biɔksid], *s.m. Ch:* Dioxide.

bipare [bipaːr], *a. Z:* Biparous.

biparti, *f.* **-ite** [biparti, -it], *a.* Bipartite.

bipède [biped]. **1.** *a.* Two-footed, two-legged. **2.** *s.m.* Biped.

biphasé [bifɑze], *a. El:* Two-phase (current).

biplace [biplas], *a. & s.m. Aut: Av:* Two-seater.

biplan [biplɑ̃], *s.m. Av:* Biplane.

bipolaire [bipɔlɛːr], *a. El: Ph:* Bipolar; two-pole. *Interrupteur b.,* double-throw switch.

bique [bik], *s.f.* **1.** *F:* She-goat, nanny-goat. **2.** *P:* Old horse, nag.

biquet, -ette [bikɛ, -ɛt], *s. F:* Kid.

biquotidien, -ienne [bikɔtidjɛ̃, -jɛn], *a.* Occurring or published twice a day.

birbe [birb], *s.m. P: Vieux b.,* old dotard.

biréfringent [birefrɛʒɑ̃], *a. Opt:* Doubly-refractive, birefringent, birefractive.

birman, -ane [birmɑ̃, -an], *a. & s.* Burmese. **Birmanie** [birmani]. *Pr.n.f.* Burma.

bis[1], *f.* **bise**[1] [bi, biːz], *a.* Greyish-brown; brownish-grey. **Toile bise,** unbleached linen. **Pain bis,** whole-meal bread.

bis[2][biːs]. *Lt. adv.* Twice. **1.** *No.* 10 *bis* = No. 10A (of street). **2.** (After a line of a song, etc.) Repeat. **3.** *Th:* Encore!

bisaïeul, -eule [bizajœl], *s.* Great-grandfather, great-grandmother. *pl. Des bisaïeul(e)s.*

bisannuel, -elle [bizanɥɛl], *a.* Biennial.

bisbille [bisbiːj], *s.f. F:* Petty quarrels; bickering. **Être en bisbille avec qn,** to be at loggerheads with s.o.

biscaïen, -ïenne [biskajɛ̃, -jɛn], *a. & s.* **1.** *Geog:* Biscayan. **2.** *s.m. A:* Bullet (of case-shot).

biscornu [biskɔrny], *a. F:* **1.** Mis-shapen; irregular, ill-proportioned (building, etc.). **2.** Distorted (idea); crotchety (mind); inconsequent (argument).

biscotin [biskɔtɛ̃],*s.m.* **1.** Crisp biscuit. **2.** Ship's biscuit.

biscotte [biskɔt], *s.f.* Rusk.

biscuit [biskɥi], *s.m.* **1.** Biscuit or plain cake. *B. à la cuiller,* finger biscuit, sponge-finger. **Biscuit de Savoie,** sponge-cake. **Biscuit de mer,** ship's biscuit. **2.** *Cer:* Unglazed porcelain; biscuit-ware.

bise[2][biːz], *s.f.* (*a*) North wind. (*b*) *Lit:* (The) icy blast of winter.

biseau [bizo], *s.m.* Chamfered edge; chamfer, bevel. **Taillé en biseau,** bevel-edged; bevelled, chamfered.

biseaut|er [bizote], *v.tr.* **1.** To bevel, chamfer. **2.** To mark, nick, fake (cards). *s.m.* **-age.**

bisel [bizɛl], *s.m. Ch:* Dibasic salt.

biset [bizɛ], *s.m. Orn: F:* Rock-pigeon; carrier-pigeon. [BIS[1]]

bismuth [bismyt], *s.m. Ch: Miner:* Bismuth.

bison [bizɔ̃], *s.m. Z:* Bison.

bisquain [biskɛ̃], *s.m.* Sheepskin pad of a horse's collar.

bisquant [biskɑ̃], *a. P:* Annoying.

bisque[1] [bisk], *s.f.* **1.** *Sp:* Bisque, odds. **Donner une bisque à qn,** to give s.o. odds. **2.** *P:* Vexation, ill-humour. **Prendre la bisque,** to take the pet.

bisque[2], *s.f. Cu:* Shell-fish soup; bisque.

bisquer [biske], *v.i. P:* To be vexed, in a pet; to sulk. **Faire bisquer qn,** to rile s.o.

bissac [bisak], *s.m.* Double wallet, sack, or bag.

bissecter [bisɛkte], *v.tr. Geom:* To bisect.

bissecteur, -trice [bisɛktœːr, -tris]. *Geom:* **1.** *a.* Bisecting (line, etc.). **2.** *s.f.* **Bissectrice,** bisectrix.

bisséqué [biseke], *a.* Bisected.

bisser [bise], *v.tr.* To encore (song, etc.). [BIS[2]]

bissextile [bisɛkstil], *a.f.* **Année bissextile,** leap-year.

bistouri [bisturi], *s.m. Surg:* Bistoury, lancet.

bistouriser [bisturize], *v.tr. Surg:* To lance, to cut open (abscess, etc.).

bistre [bistr]. **1.** *s.m.* Bistre. S.a. CERCLÉ 1. **2.** *a.* Blackish-brown; sepia; swarthy.

bistré [bistre], *a.* Browned, swarthy.

bistro(t) [bistro], *s.m. P:* **1.** Keeper of a public-house. **2.** Public-house, *P:* pub.

bisulfite [bisylfit], *s.m. Ch:* Bisulphite; acid sulphite.

bisulfure [bisylfyːr], *s.m. Ch:* Disulphide, bisulphide.

bitemps [bitɑ̃], *a.inv. & s.m. I.C.E:* (Moteur) **bitemps,** two-stroke motor.

bitord [bitɔːr], *s.m. Nau:* Spun-yarn.

bitte [bit], *s.f. Nau:* Bitt; bollard (on ship).

bitter[1] [bite], *v.tr. Nau:* To bitt (cable).

bitter[2] [bitɛːr], *s.m.* Appetizer, bitters.

bitture [bityːr], *s.f. P:* (*a*) *Nau:* Stiff glass of grog. (*b*) *Une bitture de qch.,* a rare tuck-in of sth. (*c*) *Prendre une bitture,* to get drunk. [BITTE]

bitume [bitym], *s.m. Miner:* **1.** Bitumen, asphalt. **2.** (Mineral) pitch, tar.

bitum|er [bityme], *v.tr.* **1.** To cover (road, etc.) with bitumen; to asphalt. **2.** To tar. **Carton bitumé,** tarred felt. *s.m.* **-age.**

bitumineux, -euse [bityminø, -øːz], *a.* **1.** Bituminous, asphaltic. **2.** Tarry.

biture [bityːr], *s.f.* = BITTURE.

bivac [bivak], *s.m.* = BIVOUAC.

bivalent [bivalɑ̃], *a. Ch:* Bivalent, divalent.

bivalve [bivalv], *s.m. Moll:* Bivalve.

bivaquer [bivake], *v.i.* = BIVOUAQUER.

bivouac [bivwak], *s.m. Mil:* Bivouac. **Feu de bivouac,** watch-fire.

bivouaquer [bivwake], *v.i.* To bivouac.

bizarre [bizaːr], *a.* Peculiar, odd, strange, queer, outlandish, bizarre, whimsical. *Le b. de l'affaire, c'est que . . .,* the strange part of the business is that. . . . *adv.* **-ment.**

bizarrerie [bizarri], *s.f.* **1.** Peculiarity, oddness. **2.** Whimsicalness; extravagance; oddity.

blackboul|er [blakbule], *v.tr.* To blackball, *F:* turn down (candidate). *s.m.* **-age.**

blafard [blafaːr], *a.* Pallid, wan, pale (moon, light, etc.); lambent (light, flame).

blague [blag], *s.f.* **1.** **Blague à tabac,** tobacco-pouch. **2.** *F:* (*a*) Tall story, humbug, bunkum. *Tout ça c'est de la b.,* that's all bosh. *Ne contez pas de blagues!* don't taradiddle! **Sans blague?** really? (*b*) Joke. *Quelle b.!* what a joke! *Il m'a joué une sale b.,* he played me a dirty trick. (*c*) Scoffing, banter. **Il traite tout à la blague,** he is never serious about anything.

blaguer [blage]. *F:* **1.** *v.i.* (*a*) To draw the long bow. (*b*) To joke. **2.** *v.tr.* To chaff, banter (s.o.); to make fun of (s.o., sth.).

blagueur, -euse [blagœːr, -øːz]. *F:* **1.** *s.* (*a*) Humbug; teller of tall stories. (*b*) Wag, joker. (*c*) Scoffer, cynic. **2.** *a.* Bantering, ironical, scoffing, mocking, cynical.

blaireau [blɛro], *s.m.* **1.** *Z:* Badger. **2.** (Badger-hair) shaving-brush. *Art:* (Badger-hair) brush; softener, blender.

blâmable [blɑmabl], *a.* Blameworthy.

blâme [blɑːm], *s.m.* **1.** Blame, disapprobation. *Rejeter, faire tomber, le b. de qch. sur qn,* to lay, cast, throw, all the blame for sth. on s.o. *Digne de b.,* blameworthy. *Vote de blâme,* vote of censure. **2.** *Adm:* *S'attirer un b.,* to incur a reprimand.

blâmer [blɑme], *v.tr.* **1.** To blame (pers. or action); to find fault with (s.o.); to pass censure on (s.o.). *B. qn d'avoir fait qch.,* to blame s.o. for doing sth. **2.** *Adm:* To reprimand.

blanc, blanche [blɑ̃, blɑ̃ːʃ]. **I.** *a.* **1.** White. *Blanc comme (la) neige,* white as snow, snow-white. *Vieillard à cheveux blancs,* white-haired, *Lit:* hoary-headed, old man. *F:* *Dire tantôt blanc tantôt noir,* to say first one thing and then another. *Drapeau blanc,* flag of truce. **2.** Light-coloured; pale. *La race blanche,* the white race. *s. Un blanc,* a white man. *Vin blanc,* white wine. *Bière blanche,* pale ale. *B. de peur,* white with fear. *Blanc comme un linge,* as white as a sheet. *Se mettre dans une colère blanche,* to become livid with anger. *Verre blanc,* colourless glass. *Monnaie blanche,* (small) silver change. *Cu:* *Sauce blanche,* white sauce, melted butter. **3.** Clean, white, pure, stainless. *Linge b.,* clean, unsoiled, linen. *F:* *C'est bonnet blanc et blanc bonnet,* it is six of one and half a dozen of the other. *Montrer patte blanche,* to show one's credentials; to give the countersign. *Se faire blanc de son épée,* to found right on might. **4.** Blank (paper, etc.). *Nuit blanche,* sleepless night. *Voix blanche,* toneless voice. *Vers blancs,* blank verse. **5.** (*a*) *Fer blanc,* tin-plate, *F:* tin. *Boîte en fer b.,* *F:* tin box, tin can; tin. (*b*) *Mil:* *Armes blanches,* side-arms.

II. blanc, *s.m.* White. **1.** *B. mat,* dead white. *Robe d'un b. sale,* dingy white dress. *Passer du blanc au noir,* to go from one extreme to the other. *Être habillé de b., être en b.,* to be dressed in white, to be in white. **2.** (White part) (*a*) *Le blanc des yeux,* the white of the eyes. *F:* *Se manger le blanc des yeux,* to have a terrific row. (*b*) *B. d'une cible,* bull's-eye of a target. *Donner dans le blanc,* to hit the bull's-eye. S.a. BUT[1] 4. (*c*) Blank. *Signer un document en blanc,* to sign an uncompleted document. *Chèque en blanc,* blank cheque. **3.** (*a*) *Saigner qn à blanc, jusqu'au blanc,* to bleed s.o. white. *Il gèle (à) blanc,* there is a white frost. *Metalw:* *Chauffer un métal à blanc,* to bring a metal to a white heat. (*b*) *Cartouche à blanc,* blank cartridge. S.a. TIRER I. 6. (Of machine) *Marche à blanc,* running light, on no load. **4.** (White substance) (*a*) *B. de volaille,* breast of chicken. *B. d'œuf,* white of egg. *Un blanc d'œuf,* the white of an egg. S.a. BALEINE I. (*b*) *Blanc d'Espagne, de Meudon,* whiting. *B. de billard,* billiard chalk. *Blanc de chaux,* whitewash. *Blanc de zinc,* zinc white. *Blanc de céruse,* white lead. (*c*) (Articles de) blanc, linen drapery. *Magasin de blanc,* linen warehouse. *Vente de blanc,* white sale.

III. blanche, *s.f.* **1.** *Bill:* White ball. **2.** *Mus:* Minim.

IV. Blanche. *Pr.n.f.* Blanche.

blanc-bec [blɑ̃bɛk], *s.m.* *F:* Callow youth; greenhorn, Johnny Raw. *pl. Des blancs-becs.*

blanc-cul [blɑ̃ky], *s.m.* *Orn:* Bullfinch. *pl. Des blancs-culs.*

blanchaille [blɑ̃ʃɑːj], *s.f.* **1.** *Fish:* Small fry. **2.** *Cu:* Whitebait. [BLANC]

blanchâtre [blɑ̃ʃɑːtr], *a.* Whitish, whity.

blancheur [blɑ̃ʃœːr], *s.f.* **1.** Whiteness, paleness. *D'une b. de perle,* pearl-white. *Les premières blancheurs de l'aube,* the first light of dawn. **2.** Purity, spotlessness (of soul).

blanchiment [blɑ̃ʃimɑ̃], *s.m. Tex:* Bleaching.

blanchir [blɑ̃ʃiːr]. **1.** *v.tr.* (*a*) To whiten; to make (sth.) white. *La colère blanchissait ses lèvres,* rage blanched his lips. (*b*) *Tex:* To bleach. *B. au pré,* to grass. (*c*) To wash, launder. *Donner du linge à b.,* to send clothes to the wash. *Qui est-ce qui vous blanchit? Chez qui vous blanchissez-vous?* who does your washing? *F:* *Il est arrivé à se b.,* he managed to clear his character. (*d*) To whitewash, limewash (ceiling, wall). *B. & F:* *Sépulcre blanchi,* whited sepulchre. (*e*) *Cu:* To scald (cabbage, meat); to blanch (almonds). S.a. NÈGRE I. **2.** *v.i.* (*a*) To whiten; to turn white. *Il commence à b.,* he is turning grey, going white. (*b*) (Of colours) To fade.

blanchissage [blɑ̃ʃisaːʒ], *s.m.* **1.** Washing, laundering. *B. de fin,* fine laundering. *Liste du b.,* laundry list. *Elle fait le b.,* she takes in washing. **2.** Whitewashing.

blanchisserie [blɑ̃ʃisri], *s.f.* **1.** (*a*) Laundering. (*b*) Laundry; laundry-works. **2.** *Tex:* Bleachery; bleaching-house, -ground.

blanchisseur, -euse [blɑ̃ʃisœːr, -øːz], *s.* **1.** (*a*) Laundryman, *f.* laundress. *Blanchisseuse de fin,* fine laundress. (*b*) *s.f.* Washerwoman. **2.** *Tex:* Bleacher.

blanc-manger [blɑ̃mɑ̃ʒe], *s.m.* Blancmange.

blanc-seing [blɑ̃sɛ̃], *s.m.* (*a*) Signature to a blank document. (*b*) Paper signed in blank. *F:* *Donner blanc-seing à qn,* to give s.o. a free hand, full power.

blandices [blɑ̃dis], *s.f.pl.* Blandishments; allurements.

blanquette [blɑ̃kɛt], *s.f.* Blanquette (stew of veal, with white sauce). [BLANC]

blaser [blaze], *v.tr.* To blunt, cloy (the palate, etc.); to surfeit (s.o.).
  se blaser, to become *blasé,* indifferent. *On se blase de ces plaisirs,* these pleasures pall.
  blasé, *a.* 'Blasé,' indifferent; surfeited (with pleasures).

blason [blazɔ̃], *s.m. Her:* (*a*) Coat of arms, armorial bearings, blazon. *F:* *Ternir, salir, son blason,* to sully, besmirch, one's escutcheon. (*b*) Blazon(ry), heraldry.

blasphémateur, -trice [blasfematœːr, -tris]. **1.** *s.* Blasphemer. **2.** *a.* Blaspheming, blasphemous, profane.

blasphématoire [blasfematwaːr], *a.* Blasphemous.

blasphème [blasfɛːm], *s.m.* Blasphemy. *Proférer des blasphèmes,* to blaspheme.

blasphémer [blasfeme], *v.tr. & i.* (je blasphème; je blasphémerai) To blaspheme.

blatte [blat], *s.f. Ent:* Cockroach, black-beetle.

blé [ble], *s.m.* **1.** (*a*) Corn. *Grenier à blé,* granary. *Halle aux blés,* corn-exchange. *F:* *Manger son blé en herbe,* to live on one's capital; to spend one's money before one gets it. (*b*) Corn-field. *F:* *Être pris comme dans un blé,* to be caught like a rat in a trap. *Faire les blés,* to cut the corn. **2.** *Blé froment,* wheat. *Blé noir,* buck-wheat. *Blé de Turquie, d'Inde,* maize; Indian corn.

blêche [blεʃ], *a. P:* **1.** Weak (in character); unreliable. **2.** Ugly.

bled [blεd], *s.m.* (In N. Africa) Rolling country. *Dans le b.*, up country.

blême [blε:m], *a.* **1.** *(a)* Livid, ghastly. *(b)* Cadaverous (face). **2.** Pale, colourless; wan (light).

blêm|ir [blemi:r], *v.i.* **1.** To turn pale, livid; to blanch; to turn ghastly pale. **2.** (Of light, etc.) To grow dim, faint, wan. *s.m.* -**issement.**

blèse [blε:z], *a.* Lisping. **Être blèse,** to lisp.

blèsement [blεzmɑ̃], *s.m.* Lisping, lisp.

blessant [blεsɑ̃], *a.* Offensive, cutting (remark).

blesser [blεse, -es-], *v.tr.* **1.** *(a)* To wound, injure, hurt. *B. qn d'un coup d'épée,* to wound s.o. with a sword(-thrust). **Blessé à mort,** mortally wounded; fatally injured. (Of saddle) To gall (horse). **2.** To offend (s.o.); to wound the feelings of (s.o.). *B. les yeux, l'oreille,* to offend the eye; to grate upon the ear. *Être blessé de qch.,* to be offended at sth. **3.** To hurt (s.o.'s interests). *B. l'honneur de qn,* to wound s.o.'s honour. *B. les convenances,* to offend, sin against, propriety.

se blesser. 1. To injure, wound, oneself *(avec,* with). **2.** To take offence *(de,* at). *Se b. d'un rien,* to take offence at trifles.

blessé, -ée, *s.* Wounded, injured, person. *Mil:* Casualty.

blessure [blεsy:r, -es-], *s.f.* Wound, hurt, injury. **Faire une blessure à qn,** to inflict a wound on s.o.; to wound s.o. **Sans blessure,** unwounded, unhurt, scatheless. *Jur:* **Coups et blessures,** assault and battery.

blet, *f.* **blette** [blε, blεt], *a.* Over-ripe, sleepy, soft (fruit).

blettir [blεti:r], *v.i.* (Of fruit) To become over-ripe, sleepy; to blet.

bleu, *pl.* **bleus** [blø]. **1.** *a.* Blue. *Enfant aux yeux bleus,* blue-eyed child. **Conte bleu,** fairy tale. **Battre qn tout bleu,** to beat s.o. black and blue. *F:* **Colère bleue,** towering rage. *Cela m'a donné une peur bleue,* it put me in a blue funk. *J'en suis resté bleu,* I was flabbergasted. **Il en a vu de bleues,** he has had a rough time of it, has had some queer experiences. *S.a.* CORDON 1. **2.** *s.m.* *(a)* Blue (colour). *B. clair,* light blue. *B. foncé,* **bleu marine,** dark blue, navy blue. *Mil:* **Bleu horizon,** horizon-blue; (French) field-service colour. **Bleu de Prusse,** Prussian blue. **Bleu d'outremer,** ultramarine (blue). *Passer du linge au bleu,* to blue linen. *F: Mon bras est couvert de bleus,* my arm is all black and blue. *(b)* **Le bleu du ciel,** the blue; the air. **Le pays du bleu,** the land of dreams. *F:* **Tout cet argent a passé au bleu,** all this money has vanished. **N'y voir que du bleu,** (i) to be puzzled, all at sea; (ii) to allow oneself to be hoodwinked; to remain blissfully unconscious of sth. **3.** *s. F:* Tyro, greenhorn. *Mil:* Recruit, conscript. **4.** *s.m.* *(a) Tchn:* Blue print. *(b) F:* **Petit bleu,** express letter (transmitted by pneumatic tube, in Paris); *(c) pl.* **Bleus,** dungarees, boiler-suit.

bleuâtre [bløɑ:tr], *a.* Bluish.

bleuet [bløε, blyε], *s.m. Bot:* = BLUET.

bleu|ir [bløi:r]. **1.** *v.tr.* To blue; to make (sth.) blue. **2.** *v.i.* To become, turn, blue. *s.m.* -**issage.** *s.m.* -**issement.**

bleuter [bløte], *v.tr.* To blue (linen) slightly; to give a blue tinge to (glass, steel).

blind|er [blε̃de], *v.tr.* **1.** To sheet, case, timber, line (trench, mine-shaft). **2.** *Mil: Navy:* To protect (building); to armour-plate (ship). **3.** *El.E:* To screen, shroud (parts). *s.m.* -**age.**

blindé, *a.* **1.** Timbered (shaft, trench).

2. Abri blindé, bomb-proof shelter; dug-out. **Train blindé,** armoured train. *Navy:* **Vaisseaux blindés,** armoured ships. *F:* **Être blindé contre le danger,** to be proof against danger. **3.** *W.Tel:* **Lampe blindée,** screened valve.

bloc [blɔk], *s.m.* **1.** Block, lump (of wood, metal, etc.). *B. de béton,* concrete block. **Acheter qch. en bloc,** to buy sth. in the lump; to buy the whole stock of sth. **Coulé en bloc,** cast in one piece. *Visser, serrer, qch. à b.,* to screw sth. tight, home. *Serrer les freins à b.,* to jam on the brakes hard. *Hisser un pavillon à b.,* to hoist a flag right up. **2.** *Pol:* Coalition (of parties). *B. du centre,* central party. **Faire bloc,** to unite *(contre,* against). **3.** *P:* Prison, lock-up, quod. *Mil:* Guard-room, cells, clink. **Mettre qn au bloc,** to put s.o. in quod. **4.** Pad (of writing-paper). *B. à dessin,* drawing-block.

blocage [blɔka:ʒ], *s.m.* **1.** Clamping, blocking-up; locking (of part). **Vis de blocage,** locking screw. **2.** Rubble(-work). **3.** *(a) El:* Blocking (of current). *(b) Mch:* Sticking, seizing, jamming (of valve, piston).

blocaille [blɔkɑ:j], *s.f.* Rubble(-stone). [BLOC]

bloc-film, *s.m. Phot:* Film-pack.

blockhaus [blɔko:s], *s.m.* **1.** *Fort:* Blockhouse, sconce. **2.** *Navy:* Conning-tower.

bloc-notes, *s.m.* Memorandum-block, writing-pad. *pl. Des blocs-notes.*

blocus [blɔky:s], *s.m.* Blockade, investment. **Faire le blocus d'un port,** to blockade a port. **Lever le blocus,** to raise the blockade. **Forcer le blocus,** to run the blockade.

blond, -onde [blɔ̃, -ɔ̃:d]. **1.** *a. (a)* Fair, flaxen (hair); blond (person). **Bière blonde,** pale ale. *(b) Tex:* Beige. **2.** *s.* Fair(-haired) man, woman; blond(e). **3.** *s.m.* Blond, flaxen (colour). *Cheveux d'un b. doré,* golden hair. **Blond ardent,** auburn. **Blond cendré,** light, silvery (hair); ash-blond(e).

blondasse [blɔ̃das], *a.* Flaxen-haired; insipidly fair.

blondin, -ine [blɔ̃dε̃, -in]. **1.** *a. & s.* Fair-haired (person). **2.** *s.m. A:* Beau, fop.

blondir [blɔ̃di:r]. **1.** *v.i.* (Esp. of corn) To turn yellow. **2.** *v.tr.* To dye or bleach (hair) blond.

blondoyer [blɔ̃dwaje], *v.i.* (il blondoie; il blondoiera) To have a yellow reflection, to gleam yellow.

bloqu|er [blɔke], *v.tr.* **1.** *(a)* To block up, fill up, (wall) with rubble. *(b)* To point (wall). **2.** To lock, clamp (piece of machinery, etc.); to jam on (brake). *B. les roues,* to lock the wheels. **3.** *Typ: B. une lettre,* to turn a letter. **4.** *(a)* To block, obstruct (road, measure, etc.); to stop (cheque). *B. le chemin à qn,* to block s.o.'s way. *(b)* To blockade (a port). *a. & s.m.* -**eur.**

se bloquer, to jam; to get jammed.

blottir (se) [sǝblɔti:r], *v.pr.* To cower, crouch, squat, hide. *Se b. dans son lit,* to curl up, snuggle down, in bed. *Blotti dans un coin,* huddled, huddling, in a corner.

blouse [blu:z], *s.f.* **1.** Loose, protecting, over-garment; overall, smock(-frock), blouse. **2.** (Woman's) sports jumper.

bluet [blyε], *s.m. Bot:* Cornflower, bluebottle.

bluette [blyεt], *s.f. (a)* (Short-lived) spark. *(b)* Flash, sparkle (of precious stones, etc.). *F: Bluettes d'esprit,* flashes, sparks, of wit.

bluffer [blœfe, bly-]. **1.** *v.tr. F:* To bluff (s.o.). **2.** *v.i. F:* To try it on.

bluter [blyte], *v.tr. Mill: etc:* To bolt, sift.

bluterie [blytri], *s.f. Mill: etc:* **1.** Bolting-mill, bolter. **2.** Bolting-reel.

blutoir [blytwa:r], *s.m.* **1.** Bolting-machine. **2.** Bolting-cloth.

boa [bɔa], *s.m.* **1.** *Rept:* Boa. **2.** (Feather-)boa.

bobard [bɔba:r], *s.m.* *P:* Tall story.

bobèche [bɔbɛʃ], *s.f.* **1.** (*a*) Socket, sconce (of candlestick). (*b*) Candle-ring ; drip-glass. **2.** *P:* Head, nut. **Se monter la bobèche,** to get excited.

bobine [bɔbin], *s.f.* **1.** (*a*) *Tex: etc:* Bobbin, spool, reel. *B. de papier,* reel, roll, of paper. *B. de coton,* reel of cotton. *Typewr: Bobines du ruban,* ribbon spools. (*b*) Reel, drum (for rope, wire, etc.). *Phot: Cin:* Spool, roll of film. (*c*) *El:* (Induction or resistance) coil. *B. d'induction,* spark-coil. *B. à rupteur,* make-and-break coil. *B. de réaction, de réactance,* choking-coil, reaction coil. **2.** *P:* Face, phiz.

bobin|er [bɔbine], *v.tr.* To wind, spool, reel (silk, etc., on bobbin). *s.m.* **-age.**

bobinette [bɔbinɛt], *s.f.* *A:* Wooden (door-) latch, bobbin(-latch).

bobinoir [bɔbinwa:r], *s.m.* (*a*) *Tex:* Winding-machine, roving-frame, bobbin-frame. (*b*) *El.E:* *Cin: etc:* Winding-bench.

bobo [bɔbo], *s.m.* *F:* (*a*) (In nursery speech) Hurt, sore. **Avoir du bobo,** to have a bump, a bruise, etc. **Est-ce que ça fait bobo?** does it hurt? (*b*) *Avoir un b. au doigt,* to have a sore on one's finger, a gathered finger.

bocage [bɔka:ʒ], *s.m.* Grove, coppice, copse.

bocal, -aux [bɔkal, -o], *s.m.* (*a*) (Wide-mouthed, short-necked) bottle or jar (for drugs, sweets, etc.). (*b*) (Glass) globe (for goldfish, etc.).

bocard [bɔka:r], *s.m.* Ore-crusher ; stamping-mill.

bocarder [bɔkarde], *v.tr.* To crush, stamp (ore).

Boccace [bɔkas]. *Pr.n.m.* Boccaccio.

bock [bɔk], *s.m.* (*a*) Beer-glass. (*b*) Glass of beer.

bœuf, *pl.* **bœufs** [bœf, bø], *s.m.* **1.** Ox, bullock. *Jeune b.,* steer. *Troupeau de bœufs,* drove of oxen. *Bœuf gras* [bøgra], fatted ox ; prize ox. *F:* **C'est un bœuf pour le travail,** he's a glutton for work. *S.a.* CHARRUE 1, ŒUF 1. *Z:* *Bœuf musqué,* musk-ox. **2.** Beef. *B. à la mode,* stewed beef. **3.** *a. P:* Colossal, tremendous, great. **C'est bœuf,** it's astounding, fine, tip-top.

bogue [bɔg], *s.f.* *Bot:* Chestnut-bur, -husk.

Bohème, Bohème[1] [bɔɛ:m]. *Pr.n.f.* Bohemia.

bohème[1]. **1.** *a. & s.* Bohemian. **Mener une vie de bohème,** to lead a Bohemian, an unconventional, a free and easy, life. **2.** *s.f.* **Bohème,** Bohemia (of the artistic world).

bohémien, -ienne [bɔemjɛ̃, -jɛn], *a. & s.* **1.** *Geog:* Bohemian. **2.** Gipsy.

boire [bwa:r]. I. *v.tr.* (*pr.p.* buvant; *p.p.* bu, bue; *pr.ind.* je bois [bwa], il boit, n. buvons, ils boivent; *pr.sub.* je boive, n. buvions; *p.d.* je buvais; *p.h.* je bus, n. bûmes; *fu.* je boirai) **1.** To drink. *B. qch. à petites gorgées, à petits coups,* to sip sth. *B. qch. d'un (seul) trait, d'un seul coup,* to drink sth. at one gulp, at a draught ; to swig off (a glass). *B. un verre jusqu'à la dernière goutte,* to drain a glass. **Boire un coup,** to have a drink. *B. un bon coup,* to have a long drink. **Boire un affront,** to swallow, pocket, an insult. **Faire boire qn,** to give s.o. a drink. *F:* **Ce n'est pas la mer à boire,** it is not so very difficult. **Croyez ça et buvez de l'eau!** don't you believe it! *S.a.* BOUILLON[2], GOUTTE 3, SANTÉ, SOIF. **2.** (Of plants, etc.) To absorb, drink up, soak up, suck in (moisture) ; (of boots) to take in water. **3.** To drink (alcoholic beverages). *Il a trop bu,* he is the worse for drink. *B. sa fortune,* to drink away one's fortune. *Abs. Il boit,* he drinks, is a drunkard. **Payer à boire à qn,** to stand s.o. a drink ; to treat s.o. **4.** To

drink in (with one's eyes, ears). **Boire qn des yeux,** to devour s.o. with one's eyes ; to look at s.o. with rapture ; to gloat over the sight of (victim, etc.). II. **boire,** *s.m.* Drink, drinking. **Le boire et le manger,** food and drink.

bois[1] [bwa], *s.m.* **1.** Wood, forest. *Petit b.,* spinney, grove, thicket. *F:* **Le Bois,** the Bois de Boulogne (outskirts of Paris). **2.** Timber(-tree). *B. en état,* standing timber. *F:* **Abattre du bois,** to work hard. **3.** Wood, timber, lumber. **Faire du bois,** to cut timber. *B. de chauffage,* firewood. *Chantier de bois,* timber-yard. *Jambe de b., en b.,* wooden leg. *Travail du bois,* wood-working. *Bois blanc,* deal. *Gravure sur bois,* (i) engraving on wood, (ii) woodcut. *S.a.* FLÈCHE 1, GUEULE 1. **Je leur ferai voir de quel bois je me chauffe,** I'll show them what stuff I'm made of. *Être du b. dont on fait les héros,* to be the stuff of which heroes are made. **Il est du bois dont on fait les flûtes,** he is a man of pliable temper ; you can twist him round your little finger. *Av:* **Casser du bois,** to crash (in landing). **Touchez du bois!** touch wood ! *S.a.* VISAGE. **4.** *Engr:* Woodcut. **5.** *pl.* **Bois de cerf,** horns, antlers, of a stag. **6. Bois de lit,** bedstead. **Les bois de justice,** the scaffold (guillotine or gallows). **Bois de fusil,** stock of a rifle. *Mus:* **Les bois,** the wood-wind instruments, *F:* the wood-wind.

bois[2] [bwa]. See BOIRE. *s*

boisage [bwaza:ʒ], *s.m.* **1.** (*a*) Timbering ; casing (of shaft, gallery, etc.) with timber. (*b*) (i) Scaffold(ing), framing. (ii) Frame, framework. (*c*) = BOISERIE 2. **2.** (*a*) Afforestation. (*b*) Young trees ; saplings.

boiser [bwaze], *v.tr.* **1.** (*a*) To panel, wainscot (room). (*b*) To timber, prop (mine). **2.** To afforest ; to put (region) under timber.

boisé, *a.* **1.** Wooded, well-timbered (country). **2.** Wainscoted, panelled.

boiserie [bwazri], *s.f.* **1.** Joiner's work. **2.** *Const:* Woodwork, wainscot(ing), panelling.

boisseau [bwaso], *s.m.* **1.** *A:* Bushel. To-day *F:* 13 litres (approx. a peck). **2.** (*a*) Drain-tile or chimney-flue tile. (*b*) Faucet-pipe. *B. de robinet,* cock-casing. (*c*) *Mch:* *I.C.E:* Throttle-chamber.

boisselier [bwasəlje], *s.m.* (Dry) cooper.

boissellerie [bwasɛlri], *s.f.* Cooper's wares ; hollow ware.

boisson [bwasɔ̃], *s.f.* Beverage, drink. **Boissons fermentées,** fermented liquors (malt liquors, wine, cider). *Adonné à la b.,* addicted to drink, to drunkenness. **Pris de boisson,** the worse for drink ; in liquor.

boîte [bwa(:)t], *s.f.* **1.** Box. *B. de, en, fer blanc,* tin box or can ; canister, *F:* tin. **Conserves en boîte,** tinned foods. *Boîte à lait,* milk-can. *B. à gants,* glove-box. **En boîte,** boxed. *B. aux lettres,* letter-box. *B. postale* 260, Post Office box 260. *B. d'allumettes,* box of matches. *B. d'outils,* tool-chest, -box. *B. à musique,* musical box. *P:* **Ferme ta boîte!** shut up ! *F:* *Elle a l'air de sortir d'une b.,* she looks as if she had just stepped out of a bandbox. *S.a.* THÉ 1. *Anat:* **Boîte du crâne,** brain-pan. **2.** *Tchn:* *B. à billes,* ball-bearing case. *Mch:* *B. à fumée,* smoke-box. *B. à vapeur,* steam-chest. *Aut:* *B. de vitesses,* gear-box. *El.E:* *B. à fusible,* fuse-box. *Organ:* *B. d'expression,* swell-box. **3.** *P:* (*a*) Uncomfortable, poky, little hole. (*b*) One's office, shop, school, etc. **Sale boîte,** rotten hole. (*c*) **Boîte de nuit,** all-night resort ; night-club. (*d*) *Mil:* Guard-room, cells, clink.

boit|er [bwate], *v.i.* To limp ; to walk or walk lame ; to hobble. *B. d'un pied,* to be lame in one foot. *B. bas*, to limp badly. *Passer en boitant*, to hobble by. *Lit: Vers qui boitent*, halting verse. *s.m.* **-ement.**

boiterie [bwatri], *s.f.* Lameness (of animals).

boiteux, -euse [bwatø, -øːz], *a.* (*a*) Lame, limping. *Jambe boiteuse*, lame, F: game, leg. *Vers b.*, halting verse. *s.* Un *b.*, *une boiteuse*, a lame man, woman. (*b*) Rickety, gimcrack (furniture, etc.). *Paix boiteuse*, patched-up peace.

boîtier [bwatje], *s.m.* Case. *B. de montre*, watch-case.

boitiller [bwatije], *v.i.* To hobble.

boiv-e, -es [bwaːv]. See BOIRE.

bol¹ [bɔl], *s.m.* (*a*) *Physiol: Bol alimentaire*, alimentary bolus. (*b*) *Pharm: Vet: Bolus*, pellet.

bol², *s.m.* (*a*) Bowl, basin. (*b*) Finger-bowl.

bolchevisme [bɔlʃəvism], *s.m.* Bolshevism.

bolcheviste [bɔlʃəvist], *a. & s.* Bolshevist.

bolduc [bɔldyk], *s.m.* (*a*) (Thin) coloured ribbon (for tying up boxes). (*b*) Red tape.

bolide [bɔlid], *s.m.* Fire-ball, meteor. *Lancé comme un b. sur la route*, hurtling along the road.

bolivien, -ienne [bɔlivjɛ̃, -jɛn], *a. & s. Geog:* Bolivian.

bombance [bɔ̃bɑ̃ːs], *s.f.* F: Feast(ing); carousing. **Faire bombance**, to feast, to junket; F: to have a good blow-out.

bombardement [bɔ̃bardəmɑ̃], *s.m.* Bombardment, shelling. *Avion de b.*, bomber.

bombarder [bɔ̃barde], *v.tr.* To bombard, shell. *Maison bombardée*, shell-struck house. *F: B. qn de pierres*, to pelt s.o. with stones. *B. qn de demandes d'argent*, to pester s.o. (with requests) for money.

bombardier [bɔ̃bardje], *s.m. Mil:* 1. *A:* Bombardier. 2. Bomber, trench-mortarman. 3. *Av:* (*a*) (Pers.) Bomber. (*b*) Bombing plane; bomber.

bombe [bɔ̃ːb], *s.f.* 1. *Mil:* Bomb. *B. aérienne*, *d'avion*, aerial bomb. *B. incendiaire*, incendiary bomb. *A l'épreuve des bombes*, bomb-proof (shelter, etc.). *F: Entrer en bombe*, to come bursting in. S.a. GARE¹. 2. (*a*) **Bombe glacée**, ice-pudding. (*b*) *Nau: Bombe de signaux*, signal-, tide-ball. 3. Huntsman's cap. 4. *P:* Feast, spree. **Être en bombe, faire la bombe**, to be on the spree, on the binge.

bomb|er [bɔ̃be]. 1. *v.tr.* (*a*) To cause (sth.) to bulge, belly. *B. la poitrine*, to throw out one's chest. (*b*) To bend, arch, *F:* hump (one's back). (*c*) To camber (road). 2. *v.i.* To bulge (out). *s.m.* **-ement.**
    se bomber, to bulge.
    bombé, *a.* Convex, bulging. *Avoir le dos'b.*, to be round-shouldered.

bombonne [bɔ̃bɔn], *s.f.* (*a*) *Ind:* Carboy. (*b*) Demijohn.

bon, bonne [bɔ̃, bɔn]. I. *a.* 1. Good, virtuous, upright, honest. *s. Les bons*, the righteous, the good. 2. Good, nice, pleasing. *J'ai trouvé le rôti bon*, I enjoyed the roast. *La bonne société*, well-bred people. **Avoir bon air**, (i) to look well; (ii) to look distinguished. *F:* **Cela est bon à dire**, it's easier said than done. *s.* **Le bon de l'histoire**, the best part, the cream, of the story. 3. (Of pers.) Clever, capable, good (at one's work, etc.). **Bon matelot**, able seaman. 4. Right, correct, proper, sound. *Si j'ai bonne mémoire . . .*, if my memory is correct. . . . *La bonne voie*, the right path. *Suis-je dans le bon train pour . . .?* am I in the right train for . . .? **En bon anglais**, in good plain English. *Ten:* **La balle tombe bonne**, the ball falls in the court, is right, is good. *Typ:* **Bon, stet.** 5. Good, kind(-hearted) (*pour, envers*, to).

Il se montre bon pour sa mère, he is kind to his mother. *C'est un bon garçon*, he's a good sort, a decent fellow. *Vous êtes bien bon de m'inviter*, it is very kind of you to invite me. **Faire bon visage à qn**, to be gracious to s.o. *Une bonne âme*, a simple, artless, soul. **Il a du bon**, there is some good in him. 6. Good, profitable, advantageous (investment, etc.). **C'est bon à savoir, à se rappeler**, it is worth knowing, worth remembering. **Acheter qch. à bon marché**, to buy sth. cheap. **A quoi bon?** what's the good of it? *A quoi bon se plaindre?* what is the use, the good, of complaining? **Puis-je vous être bon à quelque chose?** can I do anything for you, be of any service to you? 7. Good, fit, suitable. *Bon à manger*, fit to eat. *Être bon à qch.*, to be good for sth. *A quoi êtes-vous bon?* what can you turn your hand to? *F:* **Un bon à rien** [bɔnarjɛ], a good-for-nothing, *P:* a rotter. *Mil:* **Bon pour le service**, fit for duty. **Si bon vous semble**, if you think proper, if you deem it advisable. **Je ferai comme bon me semblera**, I shall do as I think fit, as I please. *Il est bon que vous sachiez . . .*, it is well that you should know. . . . S.a. TIRER 5. *Il n'est pas toujours bon de . . .*, it is not always good, advisable, to. . . . **Trouver bon de faire qch.**, to think fit, find it advisable, to do sth. 8. Good, happy, favourable (omen). **Souhaiter la bonne année à qn**, to wish s.o. a happy New Year. *Nau: Bon vent*, fair wind. 9. Good, sound, safe (security, etc.). *Il est bon pour 25,000 frs*, he is good for 25,000 frs. *En bon état*, sound; in working order. *Billet bon pour trois mois*, ticket available for three months. *F:* **Son affaire est bonne!** he's in for it! 10. *F: Prendre une bonne moitié de qch.*, to take a good half of sth. *J'ai attendu deux bonnes heures*, I waited a full two hours, for two solid hours. *Donner bonne mesure*, to give full measure. **Une bonne fois pour toutes**, once (and) for all. 11. *adv.* **Tenir bon**, to stand fast, to hold one's own. **Sentir bon**, (of flower) to smell nice; (of food) to smell good. **Il fait bon ici**, it is pleasant, comfortable, snug, cosy, here. 12. *Miscell.phrs.* **Pour de bon, tout de bon**, *F:* **pour tout de bon**, (i) for good (and all); (ii) seriously speaking, in earnest, really. *Il pleut pour de bon*, it is raining in real earnest. **Est-ce pour de bon?** are you in earnest? *F:* **La garder bonne à qn**, to owe s.o. a grudge; to have a rod in pickle for s.o. **La faire courte et bonne**, to have a short life and a merry one. **En voilà une bonne!** that's a good one! that's a good joke! **C'est bon!** that will do! *F:* enough said! 13. *int.* **Bon!** good! agreed! *Bon, je viendrai*, all right, I'll come! 14. *s. F:* **Mon bon**, my dear fellow, my dear chap. **Ma bonne**, my dear.

II. **bon,** *s.m.* 1. Order, voucher, ticket. **Bon de poste**, postal order. *Bon de caisse*, cash voucher. 2. *Fin:* (*a*) Bond, bill, draft. *Bon au porteur*, bearer bond. *Bon nominatif*, registered bond. **Bon du Trésor**, Treasury bond, Exchequer-bill. (*b*) I O U; note of hand.

III. **bonne,** *s.f.* (*a*) Maid(servant), servant. **Bonne à tout faire**, maid-of-all-work. (*b*) **Bonne d'enfants**, nursery-maid, nurse. (*c*) Waitress.

bonasse [bonas], *a. F:* Simple-minded, innocent, bland. *adv.* **-ment.**

bonbon [bɔ̃bɔ̃], *s.m.* Sweetmeat, *F:* sweet.

bonbonne [bɔ̃bɔn], *s.f.* = BOMBONNE.

bonbonnière [bɔ̃bɔnjɛːr], *s.f.* 1. Sweetmeat box. 2. Daintily furnished, neat, little house or flat.

bond [bɔ̃], *s.m.* 1. Bound, leap, jump, spring. **Faire un bond**, to leap, spring. *Franchir qch. d'un*

bond, to clear sth. at one bound. *F: Les loyers ont fait un b.*, rents have soared. **2.** (Of ball, etc.) Bounce. *Second b.*, rebound. **Prendre, saisir, la balle au bond,** (i) to catch the ball on the bounce; (ii) *F:* to seize the opportunity. **Faire faux bond,** (of ball) to break. *F:* **Faire faux bond à qn,** to fail to turn up; to leave s.o. in the lurch, to let s.o. down.

bonde [bɔ̃:d], *s.f.* **I.** (a) Bung (of cask). (b) Plug (of sink, bath). *F:* **Lâcher la bonde à sa colère,** to let loose one's anger, to pour out the vials of one's wrath. **2.** Bung-hole, plug-hole.

bonder [bɔ̃de], *v.tr.* To fill (sth.) chock-full.
   bondé, *a.* Chock-full, crammed, packed (omnibus, etc.). *Rues bondées de monde,* streets thronged with people. *Salle bondée,* packed house.

bond|ir [bɔ̃di:r], *v.i.* **I.** (a) To leap, bound; to spring up. *B. sur qch.,* to spring at, pounce on, sth. *B. à l'assaut,* to spring to the attack. **Il y a de quoi faire bondir!** it makes one wild to hear it! (b) To gambol, skip, caper. **2.** (Of ball) To bounce. *a.* **-issant.** *s.m.* **-issement.**

bondon [bɔ̃dɔ̃], *s.m.* **I.** Bung, plug. **2.** (Bung-shaped) cream-cheese.

bonheur [bɔnœːr], *s.m.* **I.** Good fortune, good luck, success. *Avoir du b.,* to be lucky. **Être en bonheur,** to be in luck. *Dieu leur accorda le b. d'avoir des enfants,* God blessed them with children. **Porter bonheur,** to bring (good) luck (à, to). **Coup de bonheur,** stroke of luck. **Quel bonheur!** what a blessing! **Par bonheur,** luckily, fortunately, by good fortune, as luck would have it. **Jouer de bonheur,** to be lucky, in luck. **Au petit bonheur,** in a haphazard manner. **Écrire avec bonheur,** to have a felicitous style of writing. **2.** Happiness, bliss. **Faire le bonheur de qn,** to be the source of s.o.'s happiness. *Si vous voulez faire mon b. . . .,* if you want to make me supremely happy. . . . **Mettre son bonheur à faire le bien,** to delight in doing good.

bonhomie [bɔnɔmi], *s.f.* Simple good-heartedness; good nature. **Avec bonhomie,** good-naturedly.

bonhomme [bɔnɔm], *s.m.*, **bonne femme,** *s.f.* (a) Simple, good-natured, man, woman. **Faux bonhomme,** sly, shifty, customer. **Il fait le bonhomme,** his simplicity is all put on. *F:* **Une petite bonne femme,** a little old woman. **Contes, remèdes, de bonne femme,** old wives' tales, remedies. *Pourquoi pleures-tu, mon b.?* why are you crying, my little man? **Il fait, va, son petit bonhomme de chemin,** he is jogging quietly along, is successful in a small way. **S.a.** NOËL 1. *a.* **Prendre un air bonhomme,** to put on an air of simplicity, of good nature. (b) **Dessiner des bonshommes,** to draw funny figures. **Bonhomme en pain d'épice,** gingerbread man. **S.a.** NEIGE. *pl. Des bonshommes* [bɔ̃zɔm].

boni [bɔni], *s.m.* **I.** *Com:* Surplus, balance in hand. **2.** Bonus, profit.

boniche [bɔniʃ], *s.f.* *P:* Young maidservant.

bonification [bɔnifikasjɔ̃], *s.f.* **I.** Improvement (of land, etc.). **2.** *Com:* Allowance, rebate, bonus.

bonifier [bɔnifje], *v.tr.* **I.** To improve, ameliorate (field, etc.). **2.** *Com:* (a) To make up, make good (shortage). (b) *B. qn d'une remise,* to allow s.o. a discount. [BON]
   se bonifier, to improve; to become better.

boniment [bɔnimɑ̃], *s.m.* (Quack's, showman's) patter, puff. **Faire du boniment à qn,** to try to coax s.o. *F: Tout ça, c'est du b.,* that's all hanky-panky, claptrap. **S.a.** GRAISSE.

bonjour [bɔ̃ʒuːr], *s.m.* Good day, good morning, good afternoon. **Souhaiter le bonjour, dire bon-**jour, à qn, to greet s.o., to pass the time of day with s.o. *Envoyer le b. à qn,* to send s.o. greetings, one's kind regards.

Bonne-Espérance [bɔnɛspɛrã:s]. *Pr.n.* **Le Cap de Bonne-Espérance,** the Cape of Good Hope.

bonne femme, *s.f.* See BONHOMME.

bonne-maman [bɔnmamã, -mãmã], *s.f.* *F:* Grand(mam)ma. *pl. Des bonnes-mamans.*

bonnement [bɔnmã], *adv.* *A:* (Still used in) **Tout bonnement,** simply, plainly. *Je lui ai dit tout b. que . . .,* I just told him that. . . .

bonnet [bɔnɛ], *s.m.* **I.** (Close-fitting and brimless) cap. **Donner un coup de bonnet à qn,** to touch one's cap to s.o. *F:* **Avoir la tête près du bonnet,** to be hot-tempered, hot-headed, of a fiery disposition. **Avoir mis son bonnet de travers,** to be in an ill humour. **Bonnet de coton,** night-cap. **Bonnet grec,** smoking-cap, fez. **S.a.** ÂNE 2, BLANC I. 3. *Mil:* **B. de police,** fatigue-cap, forage-cap. **B. à poil,** busby, bearskin. **B. de canonnier,** ear-protector. **S.a.** HUSSARD I. *F:* **Gros bonnet,** bigwig, big pot. *F:* **Opiner du bonnet,** to say ditto to s.o. **Bonnet d'évêque,** (i) bishop's mitre, (ii) *Cu:* *F:* parson's nose (of fowl). **2.** (Woman's head-dress) B. de nourrice, nurse's cap. *F:* **Elle a jeté son bonnet par-dessus les moulins,** she has thrown propriety to the winds, flung her cap over the windmills. **B. de bain,** bathing-cap. **B. de nuit,** slumber cap; *A:* night-cap. *F:* **Histoire triste comme un bonnet de nuit,** tale as dull as ditch-water.

bonneterie [bɔntri], *s.f.* Hosiery; knitted goods.

bonnetier, -ière [bɔntje, -jɛːr], *s.* Hosier.

bonnette [bɔnɛt], *s.f.* **I.** (Baby's) cap, bonnet. **2.** *Fort:* Bonnette. **3.** *Nau:* Studding-sail. **4.** *Opt:* Eye-glass shade (of telescope, etc.). **5.** *Phot:* B. d'approche, de mise au point, supplementary lens. **B. à portrait,** portrait attachment.

bon-papa [bɔ̃papa], *s.m.* *F:* Grand(pa)pa, grandad. *pl. Des bons-papas.*

bonsoir [bɔ̃swaːr], *s.m.* Good evening, good night. **Dire bonsoir, souhaiter le bonsoir, à qn,** to wish, bid, s.o. good night.

bonté [bɔ̃te], *s.f.* **I.** (a) Goodness, kindness; kindly feeling. *Avoir de la b. pour qn,* to be kind to s.o. *Sourire plein de b.,* kindly, benevolent, smile. **Ayez la bonté de me faire savoir . . .,** (will you) be so kind as, be good enough, to let me know. . . . **Bonté du ciel!** good heavens! (b) *pl.* Kindnesses, kind actions. **2.** Goodness, excellence (of things).

bonze [bɔ̃ːz], *s.m.* **I.** Bonze, Buddhist priest. **2.** *P:* **Vieux bonze,** old dodderer.

boqueteau [bɔkto], *s.m.* Small wood; copse, spinney.

borax [bɔraks], *s.m.* *Ch: Metall:* Borax.

borborygmes [bɔrbɔrigm], *s.m. pl. Med:* Rumblings (in the bowels).

bord [bɔːr], *s.m.* **I.** *Nau:* (a) Board, side (of ship). *Jeter qch. par-dessus* (le) bord, to throw sth. overboard. **Moteur hors bord,** outboard motor. *Le b. du vent,* the weather-side. *Le b sous le vent,* the lee-side. **Faux bord,** list. **Le long du bord,** alongside. **Être bord à quai,** to be alongside the quay. **Franc bord,** free-board. **S.a.** FRANC-BORD. (b) Tack, leg. **Courir un bord,** to make a tack, a board. (c) **Les hommes du bord,** the ship's company. *F:* **Être du bord de qn,** to be in the same boat, the same party, as s.o. **Journal de bord,** ship's log. **À bord d'un vaisseau,** on board, aboard, a ship. *La vie à b.,* life afloat. **À mon bord,** on board my ship. **2.** Edge (of table, etc.); border, hem (of garment); brink, verge (of precipice, of the grave); rim, brim (of hat, vase, etc.).

lip (of cup). **Être au bord du tombeau,** to be at death's door. **J'avais le mot au bord des lèvres,** I had the word on the tip of my tongue. *Auberge sur le b. de la route,* wayside inn. *Chapeau à larges bords,* broad-brimmed hat. **Remplir les verres à pleins bords,** to fill the glasses brim-full. **3.** Shore, strand (of sea); bank (of river). **Aller au bord de la mer,** to go to the seaside. *Maison au b. de la mer,* house at the seaside.

bordage [bɔrdaːʒ], *s.m.* **1.** *Nau:* Planking, sheathing (of vessel). *B. à clin,* clinker-work. *B. franc,* carvel-work. **2.** (*a*) Border(ing). *B. de pierres,* stone kerb. (*b*) Edging, taping (of dress).

bordeaux [bɔrdo], *s.m.* Bordeaux (wine). *B. rouge,* claret.

bordelais, -aise [bɔrdəlɛ, -ɛːz], *a. & s.* (Native) of Bordeaux.

border [bɔrde], *v.tr.* **1.** (*a*) To border. *Un fossé borde le jardin,* a ditch runs along the garden. (*b*) *B. qch. de qch., avec qch.,* to edge, fringe, sth. with sth. (*c*) *B. un lit,* to tuck in the bed-clothes. *B. qn dans son lit,* to tuck s.o. in. **2.** *Nau:* To plank (ship). *B. un navire en fer,* to plate a ship. **3.** To ship (oars). [BORD]

bordée, *s.f. Nau:* **1.** Broadside (guns, fire). *Lâcher une b.,* to let fly a broadside. *F:* **Lâcher une bordée de jurons,** to let fly a volley of oaths. **2.** Board, tack. **Tirer des bordées,** to tack; to beat up to windward. *F: Tirer, courir, une bordée,* to overstay one's leave; to go on the spree. **Être en bordée,** to be on the spree. **3.** Watch. *B. de tribord, de bâbord,* starboard watch, port watch.

bordereau [bɔrdəro], *s.m.* Memorandum; (detailed) statement; docket (of goods, cash, etc.); consignment note; abstract, schedule; bordereau. *B. de(s) prix,* price-list. *B. de paye,* wages docket. *Bank: B. de crédit, de débit,* credit note, debit note.

bordure [bɔrdyːr], *s.f.* **1.** (*a*) Border, rim; fringe, edging, edge (of shawl, etc.); curb or kerb (of pavement, etc.); skirt (of a wood). *Papier à b. noire,* black-edged note-paper. *Grille en b. de la rue,* railing running along the side of the street. (*b*) Binding (of hat, etc.); welt (of glove). **2.** Frame (of mirror, etc.). [BORD]

bore [bɔːr], *s.m. Ch:* Boron.

boréal, -aux [bɔreal, -o], *a.* Boreal, north(ern).

borgne [bɔrɲ], *a.* **1.** (*a*) One-eyed; blind in one eye. *F:* **Changer un cheval borgne contre un aveugle,** to make a bad bargain. (*b*) **Rue borgne,** blind alley. **2.** Suspicious, evil-looking (house, etc.); disreputable, shady (public house, etc.).

borique [bɔrik], *a.* Boric, *F:* boracic (acid).

boriqué [bɔrike], *a. Pharm:* Containing bor(ac)ic acid. *Pommade boriquée,* bor(ac)ic ointment. *Compresse en coton b.,* bor(ac)ic-lint compress.

bornage [bɔrnaːʒ], *s.m.* **1.** *Surv:* Demarcation, marking out (of land). *Pierre de b.,* boundary stone. **2.** *Nau:* Home-trade navigation.

borne [bɔrn], *s.f.* **1.** (*a*) Boundary-mark, -stone, -post. **Borne routière, kilométrique** = milestone. (*b*) *pl.* Boundaries, limits, bounds (of kingdom, etc.). *F:* **(Dé)passer toutes les bornes, n'avoir pas de bornes,** to go beyond all bounds; to know no bounds. *Cela passe les bornes,* that is going too far, beyond a joke. **Sans bornes,** boundless, unbounded. **2.** (Stone) corner-post. *Nau: B. d'amarrage,* bollard (on wharf). *F:* **Orateur de borne,** stump orator. **3.** *El:* Terminal, binding-post, binding-screw; clamp.

borne-fontaine [bɔrnəfɔ̃tɛn], *s.f.* **1.** Street fountain, drinking-fountain. **2.** *Aut:* Petrol pump. *pl. Des bornes-fontaines.*

borner [bɔrne], *v.tr.* **1.** (*a*) To mark out the boundary of (field, etc.); to peg out, stake (claim). *B. une route,* to set up milestones along a road. (*b*) To form the boundary of (country, etc.). **2.** To limit, restrict (s.o.'s view, power, the meaning of a word, etc.); to set limits, bounds, to (ambition, desires). [BORNE]

se borner, to restrict oneself, to exercise self-restraint. *Je me borne au strict nécessaire,* I confine myself to strict necessaries. *Je me suis borné à (vous) faire remarquer que . . .,* I merely, simply, observed that. . . .

borné, *a.* Limited, restricted. *Homme (d'un esprit) b.,* narrow-minded man. *Gens bornés dans leurs vues,* people of limited views.

Boschimans [bɔʃimã], *s.m.pl.* (South African) Bushmen.

Bosphore (le) [ləbɔsfɔːr]. *Pr.n.m.* The Bosporus.

bosquet [bɔskɛ], *s.m.* Grove, thicket.

bosse [bɔs], *s.f.* **1.** Hump (of camel, etc.). *F:* **Rouler sa bosse,** to knock about the world. *P:* **Se donner une bosse,** (i) to have a jolly good tuck-in, (ii) to have a spree, to go on the spree. **2.** (*a*) Bump, bruise, swelling, lump. *S.a.* PLAIE. (*b*) Unevenness, bump. *F:* **Avoir la bosse de la musique,** to have a bump for music. **3.** Dent, bruise (in tea-pot, etc.). **4.** Boss. **En bosse,** in relief, in the round. *Art:* **Dessiner d'après la bosse,** to draw from the round.

bosselage [bɔslaːʒ], *s.m.* Embossing.

bosseler [bɔsle], *v.tr.* (je **bosselle,** n. **bosselons;** je **bossellerai**) **1.** To emboss (plate, etc.). **2.** To dent. *Théière toute bosselée,* battered tea-pot.

bossellement [bɔsɛlmã], *s.m.* **1.** Denting, bruising. **2.** = BOSSELURE.

bosselure [bɔslyːr], *s.f.* Dent, bruise.

bossoir [bɔswaːr], *s.m. Nau:* **1.** (*a*) Cathead. (*b*) Bow (of ship). **Par le bossoir du bâbord,** on the port bow. *Homme de b.,* look-out man. **2.** Davit. *Les bras de b.,* the davit guys.

bossu, -ue [bɔsy]. **1.** *a.* Hunch-backed (person); humped (animal). **2.** *s.* Hunchback. *S.a.* RIRE I. 1.

bossuer [bɔsɥe], *v.tr.* = BOSSELER 2.

bot [bo], *a.* **Pied bot,** (i) club-foot, (ii) club-footed person. **Main bote,** club-hand.

botanique [bɔtanik]. **1.** *a.* Botanical. **2.** *s.f.* Botany.

botaniser [bɔtanize], *v.i.* To botanize.

botaniste [bɔtanist], *s. m. & f.* Botanist.

botte¹ [bɔt], *s.f.* Bunch, bundle (of carrots, etc.); truss, bundle (of hay). *F:* **Il y en a des bottes,** there are heaps of them.

botte², *s.f.* **1.** High boot, Wellington (boot). *Bottes à l'écuyère,* riding-boots. *Bottes de mer,* sea-boots, jack-boots. *Bottes à revers, retroussées,* top-boots. *F:* **Elle nous a dit cela à propos de bottes,** she said this suddenly, without rhyme or reason. **Il était haut comme ma botte,** he was quite a little mite. *P:* **Ça fait ma botte,** that suits me to a T. *S.a.* FOIN¹. **2.** Slip (for dog). **Avaler la botte aux limiers,** to slip the hounds. **3.** *Mil:* Bucket (for carbine, colour).

botte³, *s.f. Fenc:* Thrust, lunge, hit. **Porter, pousser, allonger, une botte à qn,** (i) to lunge, make a thrust, at s.o.; (ii) to thrust at s.o.; (ii) *F:* to play a nasty trick on s.o.; to deal s.o. a nasty blow (in debate, etc.); to have a tilt at s.o.

botteler [bɔtle], *v.tr.* (je **botelle,** n. **bottelons;** je **bottellerai**) To bundle, tie up, truss (hay, etc.); to bunch (radishes, etc.). *s.m.* -age.

botter¹ [bɔte], *v.tr.* **1.** (*a*) To put boots, shoes, on (s.o.). **Le Chat botté,** Puss in Boots. (*b*) To supply (s.o.) with boots. *Être bien botté,* to be well shod. **2.** To kick. *Fb: B. le ballon,* to kick,

F : boot, the ball. *F : B. qn,* to kick s.o.'s bottom, to boot s.o.

botter² (**se**), *v.pr.* To ball, cake, get clogged (with mud, etc.). *Nos souliers se bottent dans la boue,* our boots get caked with mud.

bottier [bɔtje], *s.m.* Bootmaker, shoemaker.

bottin [bɔtɛ̃], *s.m.* (Postal) directory (first published by Bottin).

bottine [bɔtin], *s.f.* (Half-)boot; ankle-boot. *Bottines à boutons, à lacets, à élastiques,* button boots, lace boots, elastic-sided boots.

bouc [buk], *s.m.* He-goat; *F :* billy-goat. (**Barbe de**) **bouc, goatee** (beard). **Bouc émissaire,** scapegoat.

boucan [bukɑ̃], *s.m. P :* Row, din, uproar, shindy. **Faire du boucan, faire un boucan de tous les diables,** to make the devil of a row, to raise Cain.

boucaner [bukane], *v.tr.* To smoke-dry, cure (meat, fish, etc.). *F : Populations que boucane le soleil,* sun-burnt peoples.

   boucané, *a.* Swarthy (complexion).

boucanier [bukanje], *s.m.* Buccaneer, pirate.

boucaut [buko], *s.m.* Cask (for dry goods).

bouche [buʃ], *s.f.* Mouth. **1. Faire la bouche en cœur,** to screw up one's mouth, to simper. *Avoir la b. pleine,* to have one's mouth full. **Avoir bonne, mauvaise, bouche,** to have a pleasant, a disagreeable, taste in one's mouth. **Garder qch. pour la bonne bouche,** to keep something as a tit-bit. **Être porté sur la bouche,** to make a god of one's belly. **Cela fait venir l'eau à la bouche,** it makes one's mouth water. **Faire la petite bouche,** (i) to pick at one's food, (ii) to be dainty, fastidious, namby-pamby. **Manger à pleine bouche,** to eat greedily; to gobble one's food. **Provisions de bouche,** victuals; food. **Dépense de bouche,** cost of living; housekeeping expenses. *C'est une fine bouche,* he is a gourmet. *Elle n'osait pas ouvrir la b.,* she dared not open her mouth (to speak). *Je l'ai appris de sa propre b.,* I had it from his own lips. **Son nom est dans toutes les bouches,** his name is on every tongue. **Demeurer bouche close,** to remain silent; to hold one's tongue. **2.** Mouth (of horse, ass, cattle, elephant, fish. NOTE. Of a dog and carnivorous animals *gueule* is used.) **Cheval qui a la bouche faite,** horse that has all its teeth. **Cheval qui n'a pas de bouche,** hard-mouthed horse. **3.** Mouth, opening, aperture (of crater, well, etc.); muzzle (of gun); slot (of money-box, etc.); nozzle. **Bouche à feu,** gun, piece of artillery. **Bouche d'eau,** (i) hydrant, (ii) *Rail :* water-crane. **B. d'incendie,** hydrant, fire-plug. *Geog :* **Les Bouches du Gange,** the mouths of the Ganges.

bouchée [buʃe], *s.f.* **1.** Mouthful. **Mettre les bouchées doubles,** (i) to eat quickly, to gobble up one's food; (ii) to do a job in double-quick time. **2.** *Cu : B. aux huîtres,* oyster patty. **Bouchée à la reine,** small vol-au-vent of chicken.

boucher¹ [buʃe], *v.tr. B. un trou,* to stop (up), to plug, block up, a hole. *Cela servira à b. un trou,* it will serve as a stop-gap. *B. un tonneau,* to bung a barrel. *B. une bouteille,* to cork a bottle. *B. une fenêtre,* to wall up, build in, a window. *Pluie qui bouche la vue,* rain that curtails vision, limits the view. *Se b. le nez,* to hold one's nose. *Se b. les oreilles,* to stop one's ears, to refuse to hear.

   bouché, *a.* **1.** Plugged up. *F :* **Avoir l'esprit bouché, être bouché,** to be dull-witted, dense; to be a blockhead, a duffer. **Temps bouché,** thick weather. **2.** *Flacon b. à l'émeri,* stoppered flask. **3. Cidre bouché,** bottled cider.

boucher², *s.m.* Butcher.

bouchère [buʃɛːr], *s.f.* Butcher's wife.

boucherie [buʃri], *s.f.* **1.** (*a*) Butcher's shop. (*b*) Butcher's trade. **2.** Butchery, slaughter. *Ce ne fut pas un combat, ce fut une b.,* it was not a fight, it was sheer butchery.

bouche-trou [buʃtru], *s.m.* Stop-gap, substitute; makeshift. *pl. Des bouche-trous.*

bouchon [buʃɔ̃], *s.m.* **1.** (*a*) Bush, sign (of tavern). *Prov :* **A bon vin il ne faut point de bouchon,** good wine needs no bush. (*b*) Tavern, public house. **2.** Wisp, handful (of straw). **3.** Stopper, plug, bung (of cask). *B. de liège,* cork. *Vin qui sent le b.,* corked wine. **Se noircir le visage au bouchon,** to cork one's face. *B. de verre,* glass stopper. *B. à l'émeri,* ground stopper. *I.C.E : B. de radiateur,* radiator-cap. *B. de vidange,* drain-plug. *El : B. de contact, de prise,* wall-plug. *P :* **Ramasser un bouchon,** to meet with failure; to come a cropper. **4.** *Fish :* Float, bob (of line). **5.** *El :* Wave-trap.

bouchonn|er [buʃɔne], *v.tr.* To rub down, wisp down (horse). *s.m.* **-age.** *s.m.* **-ement.**

boucle [bukl], *s.f.* **1.** Buckle, shackle. *B. de ceinture,* belt-buckle. **2.** (*a*) Loop, bow (of ribbon, string). *B. à nœud coulant,* running loop. (*b*) *Nau :* Bight, eye (of rope). (*c*) Loop, sweep (of river). (Of river) *Décrire de nombreuses boucles,* to twist and turn. **3.** Ring. *B. de rideau,* curtain ring. **Boucles d'oreilles,** ear-rings. **4.** Curl, ringlet, lock (of hair). **5.** *Sp :* Lap.

boucl|er [bukle]. **1.** *v.tr.* (*a*) To buckle (belt, etc.); to fasten (strap). *F : Se b. la ceinture,* to tighten one's belt; to go on short commons. *F :* **Boucler une affaire,** to settle, clinch, a matter. *Book-k : B. les comptes,* to close the books. S.a. BUDGET. (*b*) To loop, tie up, knot (ribbon, cord, etc.). **Boucler la boucle,** to loop the loop. (*c*) To lock up, imprison (s.o.); to put (s.o.) in irons. (*d*) *B. (les cheveux de) qn,* to curl s.o.'s hair. (*e*) *Sp :* To lap (competitor). (*f*) To ring (bull). **2.** *v.i.* (*a*) (Of metal) To buckle. (*b*) (Of hair) To curl, to be curly. *s.m.* **-ement.**

   bouclé, *a. Cheveux bouclés,* curly hair. *Tex :* **Velours bouclé,** uncut velvet; terry.

bouclier [bukli(j)e], *s.m.* **1.** Buckler, shield. *Faire un b. de son corps à qn,* to shield s.o. with one's own body. **2.** (*a*) *Civ.E :* Shield. (*b*) *Aut :* Scuttle.

Bouddha [buda]. *Pr.n.m.* Buddha.

bouddhiste [budist], *a. & s.* Buddhist.

bouder [bude]. **1.** *v.i.* To sulk. *B. contre qn,* to be sulky, in the sulks, with s.o. **Bouder à la besogne,** to be afraid of work, to be work-shy. *Dominoes :* "**Je boude**," 'pass !' 'go !' **Cheval qui boude sur son avoine,** horse off its feed. **2.** *v.tr. B. qn,* to be sulky, in the sulks, with s.o.; *F :* to be 'out of friends' with s.o.

bouderie [budri], *s.f.* Sulkiness; sulks.

boudeur, -euse [budœːr, -øːz]. **1.** *a.* Sulky. *s. Le Gouvernement fait des avances aux boudeurs,* the Government is holding out the olive-branch to those who hold aloof. **2.** *s.f.* **Boudeuse,** double back-to-back settee.

boudin [budɛ̃], *s.m.* **1.** (*a*) *Cu :* Black-pudding. *F :* (Of undertaking) **S'en aller en eau de boudin,** to fail, to fizzle out. (*b*) *F :* **Boudins,** fat, podgy, fingers. **2.** (*a*) Corkscrew curl; roll, twist (of tobacco). **Boudin d'air,** inner tube (of pneumatic tyre). S.a. RESSORT¹ I. (*b*) *Arch :* Torus, ovolo. *Mec.E : etc :* Fillet, beading; flange (on wheel).

boudoir [budwaːr], *s.m.* Boudoir; (lady's) sanctum.

boue [bu], *s.f.* **1.** Mud, mire, ooze, slush; filth,

dirt. *Tas de b.*, mud-heap. *F:* Il me méprise comme la boue de ses souliers, he treats me like dirt. Tirer qn de la boue, to raise s.o. from the gutter. S.a. TRAÎNER I. **2.** (Building) mud, clay. **3.** Sediment, mud, deposit. *Oc:* Ooze. *Mch:* Sludge. *Boues minérales*, mineral muds, mud-baths. **Bain de boues**, mud-bath.

bouée [bwe, bue], *s.f. Nau:* Buoy. **I.** B. *sonore, à sifflet*, whistling-buoy. *B. à cloche*, bell-buoy. *B. d'amarrage, de corps-mort*, mooring-buoy. *S'amarrer à, sur, une b.*, to make fast to a buoy. *F:* Je suis au vent de ma bouée, I have weathered my difficulties. **2. Bouée de sauvetage**, life-buoy.

boueur [buœːr], *s.m.* Scavenger, dustman, street orderly. [BOUE]

boueux, -euse [buø, -øːz]. **I.** *a.* (a) Muddy, miry. S.a. SOURCE. (b) Smudgy, thick (writing, print). **2.** *s.m.* = BOUEUR.

bouffant [bufɑ̃], *a.* Puffed (sleeve, etc.); baggy (trousers). *Cheveux bouffants*, (i) (man's) wavy hair, (ii) (woman's) loosely combed or padded hair.

bouffarde [bufard], *s.f. P:* (Tobacco-)pipe.

bouffe [buf], *a.* **Opéra bouffe**, opera bouffe, comic opera, musical comedy.

bouffée [bufe], *s.f.* (a) Puff (of smoke); whiff (of scent). *Lancer des bouffées de fumée*, to puff out smoke. *Tirer une b. de sa pipe*, to take a puff at one's pipe. *B. d'air*, gust; blast, puff, of air. (b) *Med:* **Bouffée de chaleur**, sudden flush.

bouffer [bufe]. **I.** *v.i.* (Of dress, etc.) To puff (out), swell out; (with puff of wind) to balloon out; (of bread) to rise. **2.** *v.tr.* (a) *B. les joues*, to puff out one's cheeks. (b) *P:* To eat (sth.) greedily. *B. son dîner*, to bolt one's dinner. (c) *P:* To blue (money).

bouffette [bufet], *s.f.* (Ribbon) rosette.

bouffir [bufiːr]. **I.** *v.tr.* To swell, blow out, bloat. **2.** *v.i.* To become swollen, puffed up, bloated.

bouffi, *a.* Puffy, puffed, swollen (eyes, cheeks); bloated (face); turgid (style). *Être bouffi d'orgueil*, to be puffed up with pride. *Com:* Hareng bouffi, bloater.

bouffissure [bufisyːr], *s.f.* Swelling; puffiness.

bouffon [bufɔ̃]. **I.** *s.m.* Buffoon, clown, fool, jester. **2.** *a.* (f. **bouffonne** [bufɔn]) Farcical, (broadly) comical.

bouffonnerie [bufɔnri], *s.f.* Buffoonery; clownery; antics.

bouge [buːʒ], *s.m.* **I.** Bilge (of cask); bulge (of wall). **2.** Den, slum, hovel. *Ils habitent dans des bouges mortels*, they dwell in foul slums. *Sa cuisine est un b.*, her kitchen is a regular pigsty.

bougeoir [buʒwaːr], *s.m.* Bed-room candlestick; flat candlestick. [BOUGIE]

bougeotte [buʒɔt], *s.f. F:* **Avoir la bougeotte**, to be fidgety; to have the fidgets.

bouger [buʒe], *v.* (je bougeai(s); n. bougeons) **I.** *v.i.* To budge, stir, move. *Rester sans b.*, to stand, remain, quite still. **2.** *v.tr. F:* Il ne faut rien b., you must not move anything.

bougie [buʒi], *s.f.* **I.** (a) Candle. *B. de cire*, wax-candle. *B. stéarique*, composite candle. *A la bougie, aux bougies*, by candlelight. (b) *B. électrique*, electric candle. **2.** *Ph.Meas:* Candle-power. **3.** *I.C.E:* **Bougie d'allumage**, sparking-plug. **4.** *Surg:* Bougie.

bougon, -onne [bugɔ̃, -ɔn]. *F:* **I.** *s.* Grumbler, grouser. **2.** *a.* Grumpy.

bougonner [bugɔne], *v.i. F:* To grumble, grouse; to scold.

bougran [bugrɑ̃], *s.m. Tex:* Buckram.

boui-boui [bwibwi], *s.m. P:* Low theatre or music-hall; low haunt. *pl. Des bouis-bouis.*

bouillabaisse [bujabɛs], *s.f. Cu:* Provençal fish-soup or -chowder; *bouillabaisse.*

bouillant [bujɑ̃], *a.* **I.** Boiling. *Boire du thé b.*, to drink scalding hot tea. *F:* **Bouillant de colère**, boiling · with anger. **2.** Fiery, hot-headed, impetuous.

bouilleur [bujœːr], *s.m.* **I.** (Brandy) distiller. **Bouilleur de cru**, farmer who distils for his own consumption; home distiller. **2.** *Mch:* Water-space, water-room (of a ship's boiler).

bouillir [bujiːr], *v.i.* (*pr.p.* **bouillant**; *p.p.* **bouilli**; *pr.ind.* je bous [bu], il bout, ils bouillent; *pr.sub.* je bouille; *p.d.* je bouillais; *p.h.* je bouillis; *fu.* je bouillirai) To boil. *L'eau bout*, the water is on the boil, is boiling. *Commencer à b.*, to come to the boil. *Cesser de b.*, to go off the boil. **Faire bouillir qch.**, to boil sth. *B. de colère*, to boil with anger. *Le sang lui bouillait*, his blood was up.

bouilli, *s.m. Cu:* Boiled beef (from which *bouillon* has been made).

bouillie, *s.f.* Pap (for infants); gruel, porridge. *F:* **Être comme de la bouillie**, to have no backbone. *Les voyageurs ont été réduits en b.*, the passengers were cut to pieces.

bouilloire [bujwaːr], *s.f.* Kettle.

bouillon [bujɔ̃], *s.m.* **I.** (a) Bubble (given off by boiling liquid). *Bouillir à gros bouillons*, to boil fast. *Cuire à petits bouillons*, to simmer. **Faire jeter un bouillon à qch.**, to bring sth. to the boil. *Le sang sortait à gros bouillons*, the blood was gushing out. (b) Bleb, air-bubble (in glass); blow-hole (in metal). (c) *Cost:* Puff, gauging. *Manches à bouillons*, puffed sleeves. **2.** (a) *Cu:* Bouillon gras, clear (meat-)soup; beef-tea; meat-stock. *B. en tablette*, soup tablet. *F:* Avaler, boire, un bouillon, to come to grief; to suffer a heavy loss. (b) *Biol:* **Bouillon de culture**, gelatine meat-broth. **3.** Restaurant. **4.** *Com:* Returns, remainders, unsold copies (of book or daily papers).

bouillonnement [bujɔnmɑ̃], *s.m.* Bubbling; boiling; seething. *F: B. de la jeunesse*, impetuousness of youth.

bouillonner [bujɔne]. **I.** *v.i.* To bubble, boil up, seethe, froth up. *F: B. de colère*, to boil, seethe, with anger. **2.** *v.tr. Dressm:* To gauge; to gather (material) into puffs.

bouillotte [bujɔt], *s.f.* **I.** (a) *Rail: etc:* Foot-warmer. (b) Hot-water bottle. **2.** = BOUILLOIRE.

bouillotter [bujɔte], *v.i.* To simmer.

boulanger¹, -ère [bulɑ̃ʒe, -ɛːr]. **I.** *s.* Baker; *f.* baker's wife. **2.** *s.f. Aut:* **Boulangère**, farmer's market van.

boulanger², *v.tr.* (je boulangeais; n. boulangeons) (a) To work (the flour, in bread-making); to make (bread). (b) *Abs:* To bake.

boulangerie [bulɑ̃ʒri], *s.f.* **I.** Bread-making, baking. **2.** Bakery, bakehouse; baker's shop.

boulant [bulɑ̃], *a.* **I.** Pigeon boulant, pouter. **2.** Sables boulants, quicksand.

boule [bul], *s.f.* **I.** (a) Ball, sphere, globe. *B. de croquet, de hockey*, croquet ball, hockey ball. **Foudre en boule**, ball-lightning. **Être rond comme une boule**, to be short and fat, podgy. (Of hedgehog, etc.) **Se rouler, se mettre, en boule**, to curl (itself) up. *F:* **Boule dans la gorge**, lump in one's throat. S.a. GOMME I, NEIGE I. (b) *P:* Face, phiz; head. **Perdre la boule**, to go off one's head; to go dotty. (c) *Mch:* Boules du régulateur, governor fly-balls. (d) Boule de scrutin, ballot-ball, voting-ball. *F:* **La boule noire lui tombe toujours**, ill-luck follows him. **2.** (a) Hot-water bottle. (b) Bulb (of thermometer). (c) *Mil:* Ration loaf. **3.** (a) *Games:* Jouer *aux boules*, to play bowls. **Jeu de boules**, bowling alley. *Partie de boules*, game of bowls ; bowling match. (*b*) *Gaming :* **La boule**, (i) the ball (thrown into the cup), (ii) (the game of) *boule.* S.a. LOTO.

bouleau [bulo], *s.m.* Birch(-tree).

boule-de-neige, *s.f.* **1.** *Bot :* Guelder-rose, snowball-tree. **2.** *F :* *Hum :* Negro, *F :* nigger, sambo. *pl. Des boules-de-neige.*

bouledogue [buldɔg], *s.m.* Bulldog.

bouler [bule]. **1.** (*a*) *v.i. F :* Envoyer bouler qn, (i) to send s.o. rolling ; (ii) to send s.o. to the right-about, to blazes. (*b*) *v.tr. F :* To make a failure of (sth.). *Th :* *B. son entrée*, to fluff one's entrance. **2.** *v.i.* (Of dough, etc.) To swell ; (of pigeon) to pout.

boulet [bulɛ], *s.m.* **1.** (*a*) *A :* Boulet de canon, cannon-ball. (*b*) *Jur :* *A :* Chain-and-ball punishment. *F :* **Traîner le boulet**, to be tied down to an uncongenial occupation. **2.** *B. de soupape*, ball of a valve. **Joint à boulet**, ball-and-socket joint. **3.** Fetlock-joint (of horse). [BOULE]

boulette [bulɛt], *s.f.* **1.** Pellet (of paper, etc.). **2.** *Cu :* Force-meat ball ; rissole. **3.** *F :* Faire **une boulette**, to make a blunder ; to drop a brick.

bouleux, -euse [bulø, -øːz], *a. & s.* **1.** Stocky (horse). *s.m.* Cob. **2.** *F :* Hard-working, plodding.

boulevard [bulvaːr], *s.m.* **1.** *A :* Bulwark, rampart. **2.** Boulevard. *F :* **Les événements du boulevard**, life in town.

boulevardier [bulvardje], *s.m.* Frequenter of the boulevards ; man about town.

bouleversant [bulvɛrsɑ̃], *a.* Upsetting, staggering, bewildering.

bouleversement [bulvɛrsəmɑ̃], *s.m.* (*a*) Overthrow, overturning, upsetting. (*b*) Disorder, confusion, upheaval.

bouleverser [bulvɛrse], *v.tr.* (*a*) To upset, overturn, overthrow ; to turn (sth.) topsy-turvy ; to throw (sth.) into confusion. (*b*) To upset, discompose (s.o.). *La nouvelle l'a complètement bouleversé, F :* the news bowled him over.

bouline [bulin], *s.f.* *Nau :* Bowline. **Naviguer à la bouline**, to sail close-hauled. **Nœud de bouline**, bowline-knot.

boulingrin [bulɛ̃grɛ̃], *s.m.* **1.** *A :* Bowling-green. **2.** Lawn, grass-plot.

boulle [bul], *s.m.* *Furn :* Buhl. *Cabinet de b.,* buhl cabinet.

boulon [bulɔ̃], *s.m.* Bolt, pin. *B. à écrou*, screwbolt. *B. à œil*, eye-bolt. *B. à oreilles*, wing-bolt.

boulonner [bulɔne], *v.tr.* To bolt (down).

boulot, -otte [bulo, -ɔt]. **1.** *a. & s. F :* Fat, dumpy, plump, chubby (person). **2.** *s.m. P :* (*a*) Work, toil. *Quel est son b.?* what is his job? (*b*) Food, grub.

boulotter [bulɔte]. *P :* **1.** *v.i.* To jog along, scrape along. *Comment ça va-t-il?*—*Ça boulotte*, how are you?—I'm getting along nicely ; I'm going strong. **2.** *v.tr.* To eat.

boum [bum], *int.* Bang ! boom !

bouquet [bukɛ], *s.m.* **1.** (*a*) Bunch of flowers, nosegay, posy, bouquet. (*b*) Cluster, clump (of trees, of electric lamps) ; plume, tuft (of feathers). **2.** Aroma (of wine, cigar) ; bouquet, nose (of wine). **3.** *Pyr :* Crowning-, finishing-piece (of display of fireworks). *F :* **Réserver qch. pour le bouquet**, to keep sth. for the last, for the grand finale. **Pour le bouquet . .**, last, but not least. . . **Ça, c'est le bouquet!** that caps all !

bouquetier, -ière [buktje, -jɛːr]. **1.** *s.* Flowerseller, esp. *f.* flower-girl **2.** *s.m.* Flower vase.

bouquetin [buktɛ̃], *s.m.* *Z :* Ibex, bouquetin.

bouquin[1] [bukɛ̃], *s.m.* (*a*) Old book ; book of no value. (*b*) *F :* Book.

bouquin[2], *s.m.* (*a*) Old he-goat or old hare. (*b*) Buck-hare, -rabbit.

bouquin|er [bukine], *v.i.* **1.** To hunt after, to collect, old books. **2.** (*a*) To read, consult, pore over, old books. (*b*) *F :* To read. *s.m.* **-age**.

bouquinerie [bukinri], *s.f.* **1.** Second-hand book-shop. **2.** Book-hunting.

bouquineur [bukinœːr], *s.m.* Lover of old books ; book-hunter.

bouquiniste [bukinist], *s.m.* Second-hand bookseller.

bourbe [burb], *s.f.* Mud (of pond, etc.) ; mire.

bourbeux, -euse [burbø, -øːz], *a.* Muddy, miry.

bourbier [burbje], *s.m.* Slough, mire, mud-pit. *F :* **Se tirer d'un bourbier**, to get out of a scrape, out of a mess. S.a. VICE I.

bourdaine [burdɛn], *s.f.* *Bot :* Alder buckthorn, black alder.

bourdalou [burdalu], *s.m.* Hat-band.

bourde [burd], *s.f.* *F :* **1.** Fib, falsehood. *Débiter des bourdes*, to tell fibs. **2.** Blunder, bloomer. **Faire une bourde**, to put one's foot in it, to drop a brick.

bourdon[1] [burdɔ̃], *s.m.* Bourdon ; pilgrim's staff.

bourdon[2], *s.m.* **1.** *Mus :* (*a*) Drone (of bagpipes, etc.). (*b*) Drone bass. **2.** Great bell. **3.** *Ent :* Humble-bee, *F :* bumble-bee.

bourdon[3], *s.m.* *Typ :* Omission ; 'out.'

bourdonn|er [burdɔne]. **1.** *v.i.* (Of insects) To buzz, hum. **2.** *v.tr.* To hum (tune). *s.m.* **-ement**.

bourdonnet [burdɔnɛ], *s.m.* *Surg :* Pledget ; (antiseptic) plug.

bourg [buːr], *s.m.* **1.** Small market-town. **2.** *Eng.Hist. :* Borough. *B. pourri*, rotten borough.

bourgade [burgad], *s.f.* Important village.

bourgeois, -oise [burʒwa, -waːz]. **I. s. 1.** (*a*) *A :* Burgess, burgher, citizen. (*b*) Commoner. **Le Bourgeois Gentilhomme**, the Cit turned Gentleman. (*c*) Civilian, townsman. **En bourgeois**, in plain clothes, *F :* in mufti, in civies. *Agent de police en b.*, plain-clothes detective. **2.** Middle-class man, woman. **Les petits bourgeois**, the lower middle class ; tradespeople, small shopkeepers. **3.** *F :* (In art circles) Philistine. **4.** *P :* (As used by workmen, etc.) Governor, boss, master, mistress.

II. bourgeois, -oise, *a.* **1.** Middle-class (family, etc.). **2.** Homely, simple, plain (cooking, tastes, etc.). **Pension bourgeoise**, private boarding-house. **3.** Common, unrefined, vulgar. *s.m.* **C'est du dernier bourgeois!** it's horribly middle-class ! *adv.* **-ement**.

bourgeoisie [burʒwazi], *s.f.* The middle class ; the bourgeoisie. **La haute bourgeoisie**, the upper middle class. **La petite bourgeoisie**, the lower middle class.

bourgeon [burʒɔ̃], *s.m.* **1.** Bud. **2.** *F :* Pimple (on the nose, etc.) ; grog-blossom.

bourgeonn|er [burʒɔne], *v.i.* **1.** *Bot :* To bud, shoot. **2.** *F :* (Of the nose, etc.) To become pimply, to break out into pimples. *s.m.* **-ement**.

bourgeonné, *a.* *F :* **Nez bourgeonné**, pimply nose.

bourgeron [burʒərɔ̃], *s.m.* (Workman's) blouse, overall. *Mil :* Fatigue-coat. *Nau :* Jumper.

bourgmestre [burgmɛstr], *s.m.* Burgomaster.

Bourgogne [burgɔɲ]. **1.** *Pr.n.f.* *Geog :* (Ancient province of) Burgundy. **2.** *s.m.* (Aussi **vin de Bourgogne**), Burgundy (wine).

bourguignon, -onne [burgiɲɔ̃, -ɔn], *a. & s.* Burgundian.

bourlinguer [burlɛ̃ge], *v.i.* (*a*) *Nau :* (Of ship) To labour, toil, strain (in a seaway) ; to make heavy weather. (b) *F:* **B.** *de par le monde,* to knock about the world.

bourrache [buraʃ], *s.f. Bot:* Borage.

bourrade [burad], *s.f.* Blow; thrust; rough word; thump (in the back); dig (in the ribs).

bourrage [buraːʒ], *s.m.* Stuffing, padding (of chair, etc.); tamping (of mines, etc.). *Sch:* Cramming. *F:* **Bourrage de crâne,** optimistic news fed to the public; eye-wash, bluff.

bourrasque [burask], *s.f.* Squall; gust of wind.

bourre [buːr], *s.f.* **1.** Flock (for stuffing or padding); waste (of cotton); linters. **B.** *de soie,* floss-silk. **2.** Plug, wad (of fire-arm).

bourreau [buro], *s.m.* Executioner; hangman. *F: que vous êtes!* inhuman wretch that you are! Être le bourreau de qn, to torment, torture, s.o.

bourrée [bure], *s.f.* Faggot; bundle of fire-wood.

bourreler [burle], *v.tr.* (je **bourrèle,** n. **bourrelons;** je **bourrèlerai**) To torment, rack (s.o. mentally). *Bourrelé de remords,* tortured by remorse; conscience-stricken.

bourrelet [burlɛ], *s.m.* **1.** (a) Pad, wad, cushion. **B.** *de porte,* draught-excluder. (b) (Horse-)collar. **2.** *Bot:* Excrescence (round tree-trunk). *F: Bourrelets de graisse,* rolls, folds, of fat (round the neck, etc.). **3.** (a) Rim, flange (of pipe, wheel); fillet. (b) Bead (of tyre).

bourrelier [burəlje], *s.m.* Harness-maker; saddler.

bourrer [bure], *v.tr.* **1.** To stuff, pad (cushion with hair, etc.); to cram, pack tight (cupboard with linen, etc.); to fill (pipe with tobacco). *F:* **B.** *un élève de latin,* to cram, stuff, a pupil with Latin. *F:* **Bourrer le crâne à qn,** to stuff s.o. with false stories; *F:* to stuff s.o. up. **2.** (a) *Mil: Min:* To ram (charge) home; to tamp (blast-hole). (b) *Mch:* To pack (piston, stuffing-box). **3.** *F:* **Bourrer qn (de coups),** to pummel, trounce, s.o.; to give s.o. a pummelling, a drubbing, a trouncing. [BOURRE]

bourriche [buriʃ], *s.f.* Basket, hamper, bass (for conveying oysters, game, etc.).

bourricot [buriko], *s.m. P:* Donkey, cuddy.

bourrique [burik], *s.f.* (a) She-ass; donkey. (b) *F:* Dunce, duffer, ignoramus.

bourriquet [burikɛ], *s.m.* Ass's colt.

bourriquier [burikje], *s.m. F:* Donkey-driver.

bourru [bury], *a.* Rough, rude, surly, churlish.

bourse [burs], *s.f.* **1.** (a) Purse, bag, pouch. **B.** *ronde, bien garnie,* well-lined purse, long purse. La bourse ou la vie! your money or your life! Tenir les cordons de la bourse, to hold the purse-strings; to look after the cash. Sans bourse délier, without spending a penny. Faire bourse commune, to share expenses, to pool resources. (b) *Z:* Pouch (of marsupial). **2.** *Sch:* **B.** *d'études,* exhibition, scholarship. **B.** *d'entretien,* maintenance grant. **3.** Stock exchange, money-market. A la Bourse, on 'Change. *Jouer à la B.,* to speculate. Bourse du Travail, Labour Exchange.

boursette [bursɛt], *s.f. Bot:* Corn salad; lamb's lettuce.

boursier, -ière [bursje, -jɛːr], *s.* **1.** Holder of a bursary; exhibitioner. **2.** Purse-holder, paymaster.

boursouflage [bursuflaːʒ], *s.m.* Bombast.

boursouflement [bursufləmɑ̃], *s.m.* Swelling, puffing up (of flesh, etc.); blistering (of paint).

boursoufler [bursufle], *v.tr.* To puff up, swell (flesh); to bloat (the face); to blister (paint).

　　se boursoufler, to rise, swell; to increase in volume; (of paint) to blister.

　　boursouflé, *a.* Swollen; bloated. *Style b.,* inflated, turgid, flatulent, style.

boursouflure [bursuflyːr], *s.f.* **1.** Swelling, puffiness (of the face, etc.); turgidity, inflation, flatulence (of style). **2.** Blister (on paint).

bous. See BOUILLIR.

bousculade [buskylad], *s.f.* Scrimmage; scuffle, hustle. Une b. vers la porte, a rush for, a general scurry towards, the door. L'heure de la bousculade, the rush hour.

bousculer [buskyle], *v.tr.* **1.** **B.** *des objets,* to knock things over, upset things, turn everything upside down. **2.** **B.** *qn,* to jostle, hustle, s.o. *s.m.* **-ement.**

bouse [buːz], *s.f.* Bouse de vache, cow-dung.

bousillage [buzijaːʒ], *s.m. F:* Bungled, scamped, botched, piece of work; bungle.

bousiller [buzije], *v.tr. F:* **B.** *un ouvrage,* to bungle, botch, scamp, a piece of work. *Av: P:* Bousiller son appareil, to crash one's plane. *s.m.* **-eur.**

boussole [busɔl], *s.f.* Compass. **B.** *de poche,* marching compass. **B.** *d'inclinaison,* dipping needle. *P:* Perdre la boussole, (i) to be all at sea, (ii) to go dotty; to lose one's head.

boustifaille [bustifaːj], *s.f. P:* **1.** Blow-out, tuck-in. **2.** Food, grub.

boustifailler [bustifɑje], *v.i. P:* To eat and swill.

bout¹ [bu], *s.m.* **1.** Extremity, end. *Au b. de la rue,* at the bottom of the street. Le haut bout de la table, the head of the table. Le bas bout de la table, the foot, bottom, of the table. Joindre les deux bouts (de l'année), to make both ends meet. D'un bout à l'autre, from end to end, from beginning to end. D'un b. à l'autre du pays, from one end of the country to the other. D'un b. de l'année à l'autre, year in year out. Au bout d'une heure, at the end of, after, an hour; when an hour had passed. Être au bout de ses écus, au bout de son rouleau, to be at the end of one's resources, at the end of one's tether. Jusqu'au bout, to the very end. Écouter, entendre, qn jusqu'au b., to hear s.o. through, to hear s.o. out. Aller jusqu'au b., (i) to go the whole way, (ii) to go on to the bitter end, to fight (it out) to a finish. Lire la lettre jusqu'au b., to read the letter through. Au bout du compte, after all. *Adv.phr.* De bout en bout, from beginning to end, from end to end; *Nau:* from stem to stern. Je connais Paris de b. en b., I know Paris through and through. Être à bout, to be exhausted, tired out. Pousser qn à bout, to aggravate s.o. to a degree, to drive s.o. to extremities. Pousser à b. la patience de qn, to exhaust s.o.'s patience, to try s.o.'s patience to breaking-point. Assembler deux planches bout à bout, to join two planks end to end, end on. *Prep.phr.* A bout de patience, at the end of one's patience. Vieillard à b. de forces, old man at the end of his tether. Nous sommes à b. d'essence, we have run out of petrol. Venir à bout de la résistance de qn, to break down s.o.'s resistance. Venir à b. d'une épidémie, to stamp out an epidemic. Venir à b. de faire qch., to succeed in doing sth.; to contrive, manage, to do sth. S.a. CHAMP¹ 1, 2. **2.** End, tip, end-piece. **B.** *du doigt, du nez, de la langue,* tip of one's finger, nose, tongue. *S.a.* DOIGT 1, LANGUE 1, LÈVRE 1. **B.** *de pipe,* mouthpiece of a pipe. **B.** *de l'archet (de violon),* point of the bow. **B.** *d'un fusil,* muzzle of a gun. A bout portant, point-blank. *Fb:* Obtenir un but à b. portant, to score from the goal-mouth. *F:* Prendre qch. par le bon bout, to tackle sth. the right way. *F:* Tenir le bon b., (i) to have the best of it; (ii) to be on the right tack, to have the right end of the stick. **3.** Bit, fragment, (fag-)end. *Nous avons un b. de jardin*, we have a bit of garden. *B. de papier*, scrap of paper. *B. de chandelle*, candle-end. S.a. ÉCONOMIE 3. *B. de cigare*, stub of a cigar. *F: Un petit bout d'homme*, a short little man. *C'est un bon bout de chemin*, it is a good step to go.

bout². See BOUILLIR.

boutade [butad], *s.f.* **1.** Whim, caprice. *Travailler par boutades*, to work by fits and starts. **2.** Sudden outburst (of ill-temper). **3.** Sally; flash of wit.

bout-dehors [budɔɔːr], *s.m. Nau:* Boom. *B.-d. de foc*, jib-boom. *pl. Des bouts-dehors.*

boute-en-train, *s.m. inv. F:* Exhilarating companion. *Le b.-en-t. d'une société*, the life and soul of a party. *C'est un b.-en-t.*, he is full of fun.

bouteille [butɛːj], *s.f.* Bottle. *Nous allons boire une b.*, we'll have a bottle (of wine) together. *B. d'eau*, bottle(ful) of water. *B. isolante*, *B. thermos* [tɛrmɔs], thermos flask. **Mettre du vin en bouteilles**, to bottle wine. S.a. ENCRE. *El: Bouteille de Leyde*, Leyden jar; electric jar. *Ind: Bouteille à gaz*, gas cylinder. *Gym:* **Bouteilles en bois**, Indian clubs.

bouteroue [butru], *s.f.* Guard-stone, -post; fender (fixed at corners of buildings, etc.).

boutique [butik], *s.f. (a)* Shop. *Tenir boutique, avoir boutique*, to keep, run, a shop. *Fermer boutique*, (i) to shut up shop; (ii) to give up one's shop. *F: Parler boutique*, to talk shop. *F: J'en ai assez de cette sale b.!* I am sick of the whole beastly place, of the whole show! *(b) B. en plein vent*, market stall.

boutiquier, -ière [butikje, -jɛːr], *s.* Shopkeeper; tradesman, tradeswoman.

boutoir [butwaːr], *s.m.* Snout (of a boar). *F: Coup de boutoir*, (i) rough or aggressive remark; thrust (at s.o.); (ii) staggering blow.

bouton [butɔ̃], *s.m.* **1.** Bud. *B. de rose*, rose-bud. *En bouton*, budding, in bud. **2.** Button. *B. à queue*, shank button. *B. de plastron de chemise*, stud. *B. de col*, collar-stud. *Boutons de manchettes jumelés*, sleeve-links. *B. à pression*, press-button, press-stud, snap-fastener. *F: Ne tenir qu'à un bouton*, to hang by a thread. **3.** *(a)* Knob, handle (of door, lock, etc.); button (of foil); button, tail-pin (of violin, etc.). *W.Tel:* Knob (of dial). *B. moleté*, milled head. **Tourner le bouton**, to switch (the wireless, etc.) on or off. *F: Faire un bouton*, to have a fencing bout. *(b) B. de sonnerie, de sonnette, d'appel*, push-button, bell-push, call button. "*Appuyez sur le bouton*," 'press the button.' **4.** Pimple, pustule (on face, etc.); pock (of smallpox); bleb. *Couvert de boutons*, pimpled, pimply. **5.** *Bot: Bouton d'argent*, (i) sneezewort, (ii) button mushroom. *Bouton d'or*, buttercup.

boutonner [butɔne]. **1.** *v.i. (a) Bot:* To bud. *(b)* (Of nose, etc.) To come out in pimples. **2.** *v.tr. (a)* To button (up) (coat, dress). *Robe qui se boutonne par derrière*, dress that buttons up at the back. *(b) Fenc:* To touch (opponent).

boutonnière [butɔnjɛːr], *s.f.* **1.** *(a)* Button-hole. *Porter une fleur à la b.*, to wear a button-hole. *(b)* Stud-hole. **2.** *Surg:* Incision, button-hole. *F: Faire une boutonnière à qn*, to pink s.o. (with a rapier). **3.** Rosette (of Legion of Honour, etc.).

bouton-pressoir, *s.m.* Push-button, bell-push. *pl. Des boutons-pressoirs.*

bouture [butyːr], *s.f. Hort:* **1.** Slip, cutting. **2.** Stem sucker.

bouturer [butyre]. **1.** *v.i.* (Of plants) To shoot suckers. **2.** *v.tr.* To propagate (plants) by cuttings. *s.m.* **-age**.

bouveret [buvrɛ], *s.m. Orn: F:* Bullfinch.

bouvet [buvɛ], *s.m. Tls:* Grooving-plane.

bouvier [buvje], *s.m. (a)* Cowherd; cowman, herdsman. *(b)* Drover, cattleman.

bouvillon [buvijɔ̃], *s.m.* Young bullock.

bouvreuil [buvrœːj], *s.m. Orn:* Bullfinch.

bovin, -ine [bɔvɛ̃, -in], *a.* Bovine.

box [bɔks], *s.m.* **1.** Horse-box, loose box (in stable). **2.** *(a)* Cubicle (in dormitory). *(b)* Pay-desk, -box. **3.** *Aut:* Lock-up garage. *pl. Des box, des boxes.*

boxe [bɔks], *s.f.* Boxing.

boxer [bɔkse], *v.i. & tr.* To box, spar. *B. qn*, to box, spar, with s.o.

boxeur [bɔksœːr], *s.m.* Boxer; prize-fighter.

boyau, -aux [bwajo], *s.m.* **1.** *F:* Bowel, gut. *Corde à, de, boyau*, (cat)gut. **2.** *(a)* Hose-pipe. *(b) Cy:* Tubular tyre. **3.** Narrow thoroughfare. *Mil:* Communication trench.

boycotter [bɔjkɔte], *v.tr.* To boycott.

brabançon, -onne [brabɑ̃sɔ̃, -ɔn], *a. & s.* Brabantine, Belgian. **La Brabançonne**, the Belgian national anthem.

bracelet [braslɛ], *s.m.* **1.** *(a)* Bracelet, bangle. *B. esclave*, slave-bangle. *B. en cuir pour montre*, wrist-watch strap. *(b)* Arm-garter. **2.** Metal band, ring.

bracelet-montre, *s.m.* Wrist-watch. *pl. Des bracelets-montres.*

brachycéphale [brakisefal], *a.* Brachycephalic; short-headed.

braconner [brakɔne], *v.tr. & i.* To poach. *F: Braconner dans la chasse de qn*, to poach on s.o.'s preserves. *s.m.* **-age**.

braconnier [brakɔnje], *s.m.* Poacher.

bractée [brakte], *s.f. Bot:* Bract.

braderie [bradri], *s.f.* Annual sale of old stock, cast-off clothing, etc., on the pavement; (yearly) jumble-sale.

brahmane [braman], *s.m.* Brahmin, Brahman.

brai [brɛ], *s.m.* Pitch, tar.

braies [brɛ], *s.f.pl. A:* Breeches. *F: Se tirer d'une affaire les braies nettes*, to get off scot-free.

braillard, -arde [brajaːr, -ard]. **1.** *a. F:* Vociferous, bawling, noisy; squalling (child). **2.** *s.* Bawler, shouter; brawler. *Petit b.*, noisy brat.

brailler [braje], *v.i. F:* To bawl, shout; (of child) to squall; to brawl. *v.tr. B. une chanson*, to bawl (out) a song. *s.m.* **-ement**.

braillerie [brajri], *s.f. F:* Shouting, vociferation, bawling; squalling.

brailleur, -euse [brajœːr, -øːz], *a. & s. F:* = BRAILLARD.

braire [brɛːr], *v.i.def. (pr.ind. il brait, ils braient; fu. il braira)* **1.** To bray. **2.** *F:* To cry, *F:* to boohoo. *s.m.* **-ment**.

braise [brɛːz], *s.f.* **1.** (Glowing) embers; live charcoal; cinders of wood. *F: Des yeux de braise*, glowing eyes. **Être sur la braise**, avoir les pieds sur la braise, to be on tenter-hooks. **2.** Small cinders; breeze.

braiser [brɛze], *v.tr. Cu:* To braise.

braisière [brɛzjɛːr], *s.f. Cu:* Braising-pan.

bramer [brame], *v.i.* (Of stag) To troat, bell. *s.m.* **-ement**.

brancard [brɑ̃kaːr], *s.m.* **1.** *Veh:* Shaft (of carriage). S.a. CHEVAL 1. **2.** Stretcher. *B. roulant*, wheeled stretcher. *B. à bretelles*, sling stretcher.

brancardier [brɑ̃kardje], *s.m.* Stretcher-bearer.

branchage [brɑ̃ʃaːʒ], *s.m. (a) Coll.* Branches, boughs (of trees). *(b) Cabane de branchages*, hut made of branches.

branche [brɑ̃ʃ], *s.f.* **1.** *(a)* Branch, limb, bough (of tree). *P: Vieille branche*, old friend; old

pal. Avoir de la branche, to look distinguished, aristocratic ; to have an air about one. (*b*) *Notre b. de la famille,* our branch of the family. (*c*) *B. d'un fleuve,* branch of a river. (*d*) *Branches du bois d'un cerf,* tines of a stag's antlers. (*e*) *Les différentes branches des sciences,* the various branches of learning. **2.** Leg (of compasses, dividers) ; side (of spectacle frame) ; prong (of pitch-fork) ; blade (of propeller) ; shank (of key). *B. à coulisse,* telescopic leg (of tripod). *B. inférieure d'un siphon,* lower limb of a siphon.

branchée [brɑ̃ʃe], *s.f.* Branchful, boughful (of fruit, etc.).

branchement [brɑ̃ʃmɑ̃], *s.m.* **1.** Branching. **Tube de branchement,** branch-pipe. *Rail : B. de voie,* junction, points. **2.** *El.E:* Lead, branch-circuit.

brancher [brɑ̃ʃe]. **1.** *v.i. & pr.* (Of bird) To perch (on a branch) ; to roost. **2.** *v.tr.* To branch. *El :* To plug in (connection). *Tp :* On *vous a mal branché,* you have been given the wrong connection. *B. une sonnerie sur le circuit de lumière,* to run a bell off the light circuit. *Se b. sur le secteur urbain,* to connect up with the town supply.

branchies [brɑ̃ʃi], *s.f.pl.* Branchiae, gills (of fish).

brande [brɑ̃:d], *s.f.* **1.** Heather. **2.** Heath.

Brandebourg [brɑ̃dbuːr]. **1.** *Pr.n.m.* Brandenburg. **2.** *s.m.pl. Cost :* Brandenburgs ; frogs and loops.

brand|ir [brɑ̃diːr], *v.tr.* To brandish, flourish (weapon, etc.). *B. un journal,* to hold up, wave about, a newspaper. *s.m.* **-issement.**

brandon [brɑ̃dɔ̃], *s.m.* (Fire-)brand ; torch (of twisted straw). **Dimanche des Brandons,** first Sunday in Lent. *F:* **Jeter des brandons de discorde,** to sow seeds of discord. **C'est un brandon de discorde,** he is a fire-brand.

branlant [brɑ̃lɑ̃], *a.* Shaky ; loose (tooth, etc.) ; tottery ; rickety, crazy (chair). *S.a.* ROCHER I.

branle [brɑ̃:l], *s.m.* **1.** (*a*) Oscillation, swing (motion). (*b*) Impulse, impetus. **Donner le branle à qch.,** to give an impetus to sth. **Mettre qch. en branle,** to set sth. going, in action, in motion. *Mettre une cloche en b.,* to set a bell swinging or ringing. **2.** *Danc : Mus : A :* Branle, brawl. **Mener le branle,** (i) to lead the dance ; to take the lead ; (ii) *F:* to set the ball a-rolling.

branle-bas, *s.m. inv.* **1.** *Navy :* (Beat, pipe, to) quarters, **Faire le branle-bas de combat,** to clear (the decks) for action. **2.** *F:* Bustle, commotion. **Toute la ville était en branle-bas,** the whole town was agog.

branle-queue, *s.m. Orn: F:* Wagtail. *pl. Des branle-queues.*

branl|er [brɑ̃le]. **1.** *v.tr.* To swing, shake (one's legs, etc.) ; to wag (one's head). **2.** *v.i.* To shake, move, rock ; to be loose. *Dent qui branle,* loose tooth. *S.a.* NEZ I. *s.m.* **-ement.**

braquage [brakaːʒ], *s.m.* **1.** Aiming, levelling, pointing (of gun, telescope, etc.). **2.** Changing the direction, deflexion (of carriage wheels, etc.). *Aut :* **Angle de braquage,** (steering) lock (of car). **Rayon de braquage,** turning circle.

braque [brak], *s.m.* (*a*) Hound. (*b*) *P:* Harebrained fellow, madcap. *a. Air b.,* daft appearance.

braquement [brakmɑ̃], *s.m.* = BRAQUAGE I.

braquer [brake], *v.tr.* (*a*) *B. un fusil sur qn, qch.,* to aim, level, point, a gun at s.o., sth. *B. une lunette sur qch.,* to fix, direct, train, a telescope on sth. ; to bring a telescope to bear on sth. (*b*) *B. les yeux sur qn,* to fix one's eye(s) on s.o. ; to stare steadily at s.o. (*c*) *Auto qui braque à 30°,* car with a lock of 30°.

bras [bra, brɑ], *s.m.* Arm. **1.** (*a*) *Il a le(s) bras long(s).* he is long in the arm. *F:* **Avoir le bras long,** to have a wide influence. *Allonger le b. vers qch.,* to make a long arm for sth. *Offrir le b. à qn,* to offer s.o. one's arm. *Avoir qn à son b.,* to have s.o. on one's arm. **Les bras m'en tombent,** I am dumbfounded. **Cette nouvelle m'a cassé bras et jambes,** this piece of news bowled me over, stunned me. *P:* **Les bras cassés,** loafers ; weary Willies. **Ouvrir, tendre, les bras à qn,** to receive s.o. with open arms. *S.a.* OUVERT. **Tendre les bras vers, à, qn,** to ask s.o.'s help. **Avoir qn sur les bras,** to have s.o. on one's hands. *F:* **Être le bras droit de qn,** to be s.o.'s right hand. **Voiture à bras,** hand-cart. **Tenir qch. à bras tendu(s),** to hold sth. at arm's length. *Prendre qn à pleins b.,* to hug s.o. **Saisir qn à bras-le-corps,** to seize s.o. round the waist ; to grapple with s.o. **Bras dessus bras dessous,** arm in arm. **En bras de chemise,** in one's shirt-sleeves. *Ş.a.* RACCOURCI I, SÉCULIER. (*b*) *pl.* Hands, workmen. **Manquer de bras,** to be short-handed. **2.** Leg (of sheers) ; arm (of lever, of anchor) ; jib (of crane) ; limb (of cross). *B. de pompe,* pump-handle. *B. d'une chaise,* arm of a chair. *B. de mer,* arm of the sea ; sound. *S.a.* BOSSOIR 2.

bras|er [braze], *v.tr.* To braze, to hard-solder. *s.m.* **-age.**

brasero [brazero], *s.m.* Brazier, charcoal-pan.

brasier [brazje], *s.m.* **1.** = BRASERO. **2.** (*a*) Fire of live coals. (*b*) Source of intense heat. **L'auto n'était plus qu'un brasier,** the car was reduced to a blazing mass. **Son cœur était un brasier,** his heart was afire.

brasiller [brazije]. **1.** (*a*) *v.tr.* To grill, broil (meat). (*b*) *v.i.* (Of meat) To sputter, sizzle (in the pan). **2.** *v.i.* (Of sea) To glitter, gleam.

brassard [brasaːr], *s.m.* Armlet, arm-badge. *B. de deuil,* mourning-band ; arm-band.

brasse [bra:s], *s.f.* **1.** Span (of the arms). *Nau :* Fathom. **Être sur les brasses,** to touch bottom. **2.** *Swim :* Stroke. **Nager à la brasse,** to swim hand over hand. *B. sur le dos,* back-stroke.

brassée [brase, brɑ-], *s.f.* Armful.

brassement [brasmɑ̃, brɑ-], *s.m.* **1.** Brewing. **2.** *F:* Mixing, mingling (of nations, etc.).

brass|er[1] [brase, brɑ-], *v.tr.* **1.** To brew, mash (beer, etc.). *F: B. une intrigue,* to brew, hatch, a plot. **2.** To mix, stir (up). *F:* **Brasser des affaires,** to handle a lot of business. *B. des écus,* to turn over a lot of money. *s.m.* **-age.**

brasser[2], *v.tr.* **1.** *Nau :* To brace (yard). *B. au vent,* to brace in, haul in. **2.** *Av :* **Brasser l'hélice,** to swing the propeller.

brasserie [brasri], *s.f.* **1.** Brewery. **2.** Brewing. **3.** Beer-saloon (often also a restaurant).

brasseur, -euse [brasœːr, -øːz], *s.* **1.** Brewer. **2.** Mixer. *F:* **Brasseur d'affaires,** (i) man who handles a lot of business, big-business man ; (ii) shady financier.

brassière [brasjɛːr], *s.f.* **1.** (*a*) Bust bodice. (*b*) Child's sleeved vest. (*c*) *B. de sauvetage,* life-jacket. **2.** *pl.* (*a*) Leading-strings (for infants). *F:* **Être en brassières,** to be in leading-strings. (*b*) Shoulder-straps, slings (of knapsack). [BRAS]

brasure [brazyːr], *s.f.* **1.** (Brazed) seam, joint. **2.** (*a*) Hard-soldering, brazing. (*b*) Hard solder.

bravache [bravaʃ]. **1.** *s.m.* Braggadocio, blusterer, bully. **2.** *a.* Swaggering, blustering, raffish, bullying. *D'un air b.,* blusteringly, raffishly.

bravade [bravad], *s.f.* Bravado, bluster. **Faire qch. par bravade,** to do sth. out of bravado.

brave [braːv], *a.* **1.** Brave, bold, gallant. **Un (homme) brave,** a brave, courageous, man.

Brave à trois poils, hard, stout, fighter. **Se conduire en brave**, to acquit oneself bravely, gallantly. **2.** Good, honest, worthy. **C'est un brave homme**, *F:* un brave type, he's a decent sort, a worthy man. **Ma brave femme de nourrice**, my good old nurse. *s.m. Je vous félicite*, **mon brave**, I congratulate you, my good man. **3.** *F:* **Comme vous voilà brave!** you do look smart! *adv.* **-ment.**
braver [brave], *v.tr.* To brave. **1.** To face (sth.) bravely. *Toujours prêt à b.* **le danger**, always ready to face danger. **2.** To defy, dare (s.o.); to set (s.o.) at defiance.
bravo¹ [bravo]. **1.** *int.* Bravo! well done! hear, hear! **2.** *s.m.* Cheer. *pl. Des bravos.*
bravo², *s.m.* Bravo, hired assassin, cut-throat. *pl. Des bravi.*
bravoure [bravu:r], *s.f.* Bravery, gallantry.
brebis [brəbi], *s.f.* **1.** Ewe. **2.** Sheep. *B. égarée*, lost sheep. *B. noire*, black sheep. *S.a.* GALEUX. *Prov:* **A brebis tondue Dieu mesure le vent**, God tempers the wind to the shorn lamb. **Qui se fait brebis le loup le mange**, mugs are always fleeced.
brèche [brɛʃ], *s.f.* Breach, opening, gap, break (in wall, hedge, etc.); hole (in ship's side); notch (in blade). **Battre en brèche une forteresse**, to batter a fortress. *F:* **Battre qn en brèche**, to disparage s.o.; to run s.o. down. *F:* **Faire une brèche à la fortune de qn**, to make a hole, a dent, in s.o.'s fortune. *Faire une b. à un pâté*, to cut into a pie.
brèche-dent, *a. & s.* Gap-toothed (person). *Elle est b.-d.*, she has a gap in her teeth.
brechet, bréchet [brəʃe, bre-], *s.m.* Breast-bone
bredouille [brədu:j], *a.inv. F:* **Être bredouille**, to have failed completely (in sth.). **Rentrer, revenir, bredouille**, to come home (from a day's shooting) with an empty bag.
bredouill|er [brəduje], *v.i.* To jabber, mumble. *v.tr. B. une excuse*, to stammer out, mumble, an excuse. *s.m.* **-age.** *s.m.* **-ement.** *s.* **-eur, -euse.**
bref, *f.* **brève** [brɛf, brɛːv]. **1.** *a.* Brief, short. *Soyez b.!* be brief! *F:* cut it short! **Raconter qch. en bref**, to relate sth. in a few words, briefly. **2.** *adv.* Briefly, in a word, in short. **Bref, il accepte**, to make a long story short, he accepts. **Parler bref**, to speak curtly. **3.** *s.m.* (Papal) brief. **4.** *s.f.* **Brève.** (a) Short syllable. (b) *Tg:* **Brèves et longues**, dots and dashes.
brelan [brəlɑ̃], *s.m.* Gaming house; gambling den.
breloque [brələk], *s.f.* **1.** Charm, trinket; esp. watch-charm. **2.** *Mil:* Dismiss. **Battre la breloque**, (i) to sound the dismiss; (ii) to sound the 'all clear' (after air-raid, etc.); (iii) *F:* to wander, ramble (in one's mind).
brème [brɛm], *s.f. Ich:* Bream.
Brème [brɛm]. *Pr.n.m. Geog:* Bremen.
Brésil [brezil]. *Pr.n.m. Geog:* Brazil.
brésilien, -ienne [breziljɛ̃, -jɛn], *a. & s.* Brazilian.
Bretagne [brətaɲ]. *Pr.n.f. Geog:* **1.** Brittany. **Basse-Bretagne**, Lower, Western, Brittany. **2.** Britain (in GRANDE-BRETAGNE).
brétailleur [bretajœ:r], *s.m. F:* Swashbuckler, fire-eater.
bretelle [brətɛl], *s.f.* **1.** Strap, brace, sling, suspender. *B. de fusil*, rifle-sling. **2.** (a) Shoulder-strap (of lady's garment). (b) (Paire de) **bretelles**, (pair of) braces. **3.** *Rail:* Cross-over.
breton, -onne [brətɔ̃, -ɔn], *a. & s.* Breton. **Breton bretonnant**, Breton-speaking Breton.
bretteur [brɛtœ:r], *s.m.* Swashbuckler, duelling bravo. *Vie de b.*, swashbuckling life.

breuvage [brœva:ʒ], *s.m.* **1.** Beverage, drink. **2.** *Med:* Draught, potion.
brève. See BREF.
brevet [brave], *s.m.* **1.** (a) A: (Letters) patent; (royal) warrant. *Mil: A:* Commission. (b) **Brevet d'inventeur, brevet d'invention**, (letters) patent. **Prendre un brevet**, to take out a patent. **2.** Diploma, certificate. *Sch:* **Brevet élémentaire**, lower certificate. *Mil:* **Brevet d'État-major** = Staff College certificate. *Nau: B. de capitaine*, master's certificate. **Passer son brevet de capitaine**, *F:* to get one's 'ticket.'
breveter [bravte], *v.tr.* (je brevète, je brevette) **1.** To grant a patent to (s.o.). **2.** To patent (invention). **Faire breveter une invention**, to take out a patent for an invention.
breveté, -ée. 1. (a) *s.* Patentee. (b) *a.* (i) **Fournisseur breveté de sa Majesté**, (tradesman) by special appointment to His Majesty. (ii) Patent. **2.** *a.* Certificated. **Officier breveté** (*d'État-major*) = officer who has 'passed Staff College.' *Instituteur b.*, certificated teacher.
bréviaire [brevjɛ:r], *s.m. Ecc:* Breviary.
brévité [brevite], *s.f.* Shortness (of vowel, etc.).
bribes [brib], *s.f.pl.* Scraps, fragments; odds and ends. *Ramasser des bribes de connaissances*, to pick up scraps of knowledge. *Bribes de conversation*, snatches of conversation. **Apprendre qch. par bribes**, to learn sth. piecemeal.
bric-à-brac [brikabrak], *s.m.* No *pl.* Odds and ends; curios, bric-à-brac. *Marchand de b.-à-b.*, dealer in old furniture, in curios.
brick [brik], *s.m. Nau:* Brig.
bricole [brikɔl], *s.f.* **1.** Strap. (a) Breast-strap, breast-harness. (b) Axle drag-rope (of gun). **2.** Rebound, ricochet. **Toucher le but par bricole**, to make an indirect hit. *Bill:* **Jouer la bricole**, to play off the cushion. **3.** Usu. *pl. F:* Odd jobs; trifles. *S'occuper à des bricoles*, to potter about the house.
bricoler [brikɔle]. **1.** *F:* (a) *v.tr. B. une affaire*, to arrange a piece of (often shady) business. *C'est une affaire bricolée*, it's a put-up job. (b) *v.i.* To do odd jobs. *B. à la maison*, to potter, tinker, about the house. **2.** *v.i. Bill:* To play off the cushion.
bricoleur [brikɔlœ:r], *s.m. F:* (a) Jack of all trades, handy-man. (b) Potterer.
bride [brid], *s.f.* **1.** (a) Bridle. **Mettre la bride à un cheval**, to bridle, put the bridle on, a horse. (b) Rein(s). *Mener un cheval par la b.*, to lead a horse. **Aller à bride abattue, à toute bride**, to ride at full speed; to ride full tilt, *F:* to ride hell for leather. *Accourir à b. abattue*, to gallop up. *S.a.* TOURNER I. **Lâcher la bride à un cheval**, *F:* **à qn**, to give rein to a horse, *F:* to s.o.; to give a horse his head; to give s.o. more liberty. *Lâcher la b. à sa colère*, to give free rein, full vent, to one's anger. *F:* **Tenir qn en bride**, to keep a tight hand over s.o. **Tenir la bride haute à qn**, to be high-handed with s.o. **Fureur sans bride**, unbridled fury. **2.** (a) String (of bonnet, etc.). (b) Bar (of button-hole, in embroidery, etc.). **3.** *Mec.E: etc:* (a) Strap, tie. *B. de bielle*, connecting-rod strap. *B. de serrage*, clamp, cramp. (b) Flange. *Tuyau à brides*, flanged pipe.
brid|er [bride], *v.tr.* **1.** (a) To bridle (horse). (b) *B. ses passions*, to check, restrain, curb, one's passions. **2.** (a) To tie up, fasten (up). *Cu:* To truss (fowl). *Mon habit me bride trop*, my coat is too tight for me. *Needlew: B. une boutonnière*, to finish off a button-hole with a bar. (b) To lash, seize, frap (cable). (c) To flange (pipe). *s.m.* **-age.**
bridé, *a.* Tied up, constricted. **Avoir les

yeux bridés, to have slits of eyes. **Sourire bridé,** constrained smile.

bridge [bridʒ], *s.m. Cards:* Bridge. *B. aux* **enchères,** auction bridge. *B.* **contrat,** contract bridge.

bridger [bridʒe], *v.i.* (je bridgeai(s); n. bridgeons) To play bridge.

bridgeur, -euse [bridʒœːr, -øːz], *s.* Bridge-player.

bridon [bridɔ̃], *s.m.* Snaffle(-bridle), bridoon.

brièvement [brièvmɑ̃], *adv.* Briefly, succinctly.

brièveté [brièvte], *s.f.* **1.** Shortness, brevity (of time). **2.** Brevity, briefness, conciseness.

brigade [brigad], *s.f.* **1.** *Mil:* Brigade. **Être de brigade avec qn,** to be brigaded with s.o. **2.** *(a)* Squad, body, detachment (of gendarmes, etc.). *(b)* Gang, party (of workmen). **Chef de brigade,** foreman. *(c)* Shift. *Travail à brigades relevées,* work(ing) in shifts.

brigadier [brigadje], *s.m.* **1.** *(a) Mil:* Corporal (of mounted arms). *(b) B. de police,* police sergeant. *(c)* Foreman (of working party). **2.** *Row:* Bow(-oar) (of boat-crew).

brigand [brigɑ̃], *s.m.* Brigand, robber; highwayman; ruffian.

brigandage [brigɑ̃daːʒ], *s.m.* Brigandage, highway robbery.

brigue [brig], *s.f.* Intrigue; underhand work.

briguer [brige], *v.tr.* To solicit, to canvass for (sth.); to court (s.o.'s favour). *B. des voix,* to canvass (for votes).

brigueur, -euse [brigœːr, -øːz], *s.* Intriguer, schemer.

brill|ant [brijɑ̃]. **1.** *a.* Brilliant. *(a)* Sparkling, glittering, bright (light, gem, etc.); glossy; sparkling (conversation). *F:* **Brillant comme un sou neuf,** as bright as a button. *(b) B. orateur,* brilliant speaker. *Spectacle b.,* splendid sight. *Le plus b. de la classe,* the brightest boy in the class. *(c) B. de santé,* radiant, beaming, with health. **2.** *s.m. (a)* Brilliancy, brilliance, brightness; glossiness. *(b)* Polish, shine (on boots, etc.). **3.** *s.m.* Brilliant (diamond). *adv.* **-amment.**

briller [brije], *v.i.* To shine, sparkle, glitter, glisten. *B. dans la conversation,* to shine in conversation. *F:* **Briller par son absence,** to be conspicuous by one's absence. *Prov:* **Tout ce qui brille n'est pas or,** all that glitters is not gold.

brimade [brimad], *s.f.* Rough joke (played on freshmen, new boys); *pl.* (bally)ragging.

brimbale [brɛ̃bal], *s.f.* **1.** Rocker-arm; rocking-lever. **2.** Handle (of pump).

brimbaler [brɛ̃bale]. **1.** *v.i. (a)* To swing (to and fro), to dangle. *(b)* (Of wheel) To wobble. **2.** *v.tr. F:* To cart (sth.) about.

brimborion [brɛ̃borjɔ̃], *s.m.* Trifle, bauble.

brimer [brime], *v.tr.* To (bally)rag (new boy).

brin [brɛ̃], *s.m.* **1.** *(a)* Shoot (of tree). *F:* **Un beau brin de fille,** a fine strapping lass; a fine slip of a girl. *(b)* Blade (of grass, corn); sprig, twig (of myrtle, etc.). **2.** *(c)* Bit, fragment. **Aller prendre un brin d'air,** to go for a breather. *B. de consolation,* grain, crumb, of comfort. *B. de malice,* touch of malice. **3.** Strand (of rope). **Laine en trois brins,** three-ply wool.

brindille [brɛ̃diːj], *s.f.* Sprig, twig, branchlet.

bringue [brɛ̃g], *s.f. F:* **1.** Piece, bit. **En bringues,** in bits; in rags and tatters. **2.** Raw-boned horse. **Grande bringue de femme,** big gawk of a woman.

brio [bri(j)o], *s.m. Mus:* Vigour, go, dash; brio. *F:* **Parler avec b.,** to talk brilliantly.

brioche [briɔʃ], *s.f. Cu:* Brioche. *P:* **Faire une brioche,** to 'drop a brick.'

brique [brik], *s.f.* **1.** *(a)* Brick. *B. vernissée,* glazed brick. **Terre à brique,** brick-clay. *(b) B. à paver,* flag, tile. **2.** *(a)* **Brique anglaise,** Bath brick. *(b) Nau:* **Brique à pont,** holy-stone.

briquet [brikɛ], *s.m. (a)* Flint and steel; tinder-box. **Battre le briquet,** to strike a light. *(b)* Gas-lighter; pipe-lighter, cigarette-lighter.

briqueter [brikte], *v.tr.* (je briquette; je briquetterai) To face with bricks; to pave or face with bricks.

briqueterie [briktri], *s.f.* Brick-field.

bris [bri], *s.m. Jur: (a)* Breaking (of seals, etc.). *(b)* **Bris de prison,** prison breaking. **Bris de clôture,** breach of close.

brisable [brizabl], *a.* Breakable.

brisant [brizɑ̃]. **1.** *a.* Shattering, disruptive. **Obus brisant,** high-explosive shell. **2.** *s.m. (a)* Reef, shoal. *(b)* Breaker. *Des brisants devant!* breakers ahead!

briscard [briskaːr], *s.m.* = BRISQUARD.

brise [briːz], *s.f.* Breeze. *Nau: Forte b.,* moderate gale; stiff breeze.

brise-bise, *s.m.inv.* **1.** Draught-tube (for doors, etc.). **2.** Short window curtain; brise-bise.

brise-circuit, *s.m.inv. El.E:* **1.** Circuit-breaker, make-and-break key. **2.** Cut-out.

brise-lames, *s.m.inv.* **1.** Breakwater. **2.** Groyne (across beach).

bris|er [brize], *v.tr.* To break, smash, shatter. *(a) B. une porte,* to break open a door. *B. une glace en mille morceaux,* to shiver, shatter, a mirror. *(b)* To break up (clods of earth, etc.); to crush (ore, etc.). **Brisé par la douleur,** crushed by grief. *(c)* To break (treaty, s.o.'s will, etc.). *B. toute résistance,* to break down all resistance. *J'ai le cœur brisé,* my heart is broken. *(d)* To break off (conversation, etc.). **Abs. Brisons là,** enough said; let us say no more about it. *(e) Abs.* **Briser avec qn,** to break with s.o. *(f) Ph:* To refract (ray). *s.m.* **-ement.** *s.* **-eur, -euse.**

se briser, to break. *Cela se brise comme du verre,* it is as brittle as glass.

brisé, *a.* **1.** Broken. *F:* **Être tout brisé,** to be sore, aching, all over. **Brisé de fatigue,** tired out. **2.** Folding (door, shutter, bedstead, etc.). *S.a.* COMBLE[1] 2.

brisées [brize], *s.f.pl. Ven: (a)* Broken boughs (to mark track of deer in wood). *(b)* Track (of deer). *F:* **Suivre les brisées de qn,** to follow in s.o.'s footsteps. **Aller, courir, sur les brisées de qn,** to rival s.o.; to compete with s.o. **Revenir sur ses brisées,** to retrace one's steps.

brise-tout, *s.m. or f. inv.* Person, child, who breaks everything.

brise-vent, *s.m.inv.* Wind-screen.

brisquard [briskaːr], *s.m. F:* Old soldier.

brisque [brisk], *s.f.* Long-service badge; war-service chevron.

bristol [bristɔl], *s.m. (a)* Bristol-board. *(b) F:* Visiting-card.

brisure [brizyːr], *s.f.* **1.** Break, crack. **2.** Break (of hinge). **Porte à brisures,** folding door. **3.** Fragment (of shell, etc.). [BRISER]

britannique [britanik], *a.* British. **Les Îles Britanniques,** the British Isles.

broc [bro], *s.m.* Pitcher; (large) jug.

brocante [brɔkɑ̃ːt], *s.f.* General dealing in second-hand goods.

brocant|er [brɔkɑ̃te]. **1.** *v.i.* To deal in second-hand goods, in curios; to buy and sell. **2.** *v.tr. F: (a) B. ses bijoux, ses effets,* to sell one's jewels, one's effects (to a second-hand dealer). *(b)* To barter. *s.m.* **-age.**

brocanteur, -euse [brɔkɑ̃tœːr, -øːz], *s.* Second-hand dealer.

brocard [brɔkaːr], *s.m.* Gibe ; lampoon. *Lancer des brocards contre qn,* to lampoon s.o. *Lancer des brocards à qn,* to gibe at s.o.

brocart [brɔkaːr], *s.m. Tex:* Brocade.

brochant [brɔʃɑ̃], *a. Her:* Brochant. *F: Et brochant sur le tout,* and to crown all, to cap it all.

broche [brɔʃ], *s.f.* **1.** *Cu:* (*a*) Spit. (*b*) Meat skewer. **2.** Peg, pin. *B. de tente,* tent-peg. *B. de charnière,* hinge-pin. *B. d'un tonneau,* spile, spigot, of a cask. *El:* Fiche à deux broches, two-pin plug. **3.** *Tex:* Spindle. **4.** *Cost:* Brooch.

broch|er [brɔʃe], *v.tr.* **1.** *Tex:* To brocade, figure (stuffs). **2.** *Bookb:* To stitch, sew (book). *Livre broché,* paper-bound book. *F: Brocher un travail,* to scamp a piece of work. **3.** *v.i. Her: Pièce qui broche sur une autre,* charge overlying another. *F: Pour brocher sur le tout . . .,* to cap it all. . . . *s.m.* **-age.** *s.* **-eur, -euse.**

brochet [brɔʃɛ], *s.m. Ich:* Pike.

brochette [brɔʃɛt], *s.f.* **1.** *Cu:* Skewer. *Rognons à la brochette,* broiled kidneys. **2.** Brochette (of decorations). **3.** *Élever des oiseaux à la b.,* to feed birds by hand. *F: Enfant élevé à la brochette,* daintily reared child.

brochure [brɔʃyːr], *s.f.* Booklet, pamphlet, brochure.

brodequin [brɔdkɛ̃], *s.m.* **1.** Laced boot ; ankleoot. **2.** The sock (in the drama of the ancients).

brod|er [brɔde], *v.tr.* To embroider. *F: Broder une histoire,* to embroider, embellish, a story. *s.* **-eur, -euse.**

broderie [brɔdri], *s.f.* **1.** (*a*) Piece of embroidery. (*b*) Embroidery work. **2.** *F:* Embellishment, embroidery (in narrative).

broiement [brwamɑ̃], *s.m.* Grinding, crushing, pounding, pulverizing. [BROYER]

brome [broːm], *s.m. Ch:* Bromine.

bromure [brɔmyːr], *s.m. Ch:* Bromide. *Phot:* **Papier au bromure,** bromide paper or gas-light paper.

bronch|er [brɔ̃ʃe], *v.i.* **1.** (Of horse) (*a*) To stumble, to flounder. (*b*) To shy. **2.** *F:* (*a*) To falter, waver. **Sans broncher,** without flinching. (*b*) To budge, move, stir. *s.m.* **-ement.**

bronches [brɔ̃ʃ], *s.f.pl. Anat:* Bronchia.

bronchial, -aux [brɔ̃ʃjal, -o], *a.* Bronchial.

bronchite [brɔ̃ʃit], *s.f. Med:* Bronchitis.

bronze [brɔ̃z], *s.m.* **1.** Bronze. *F: Cœur de bronze,* heart of steel. **2.** *Bronze à canon,* gun-metal.

bronz|er [brɔ̃ze], *v.tr.* (*a*) To bronze (statue, etc.). (*b*) To brown, blue (gun-barrels, etc.). (*c*) To tan, sunburn. *s.m.* **-age.** *s.m.* **-eur.** **se bronzer,** to tan ; to bronze.

broquette [brɔkɛt], *s.f.* Tack, tin-tack.

brosse [brɔs], *s.f.* **1.** Brush. (*a*) *B. à cheveux,* hairbrush. *B. à dents,* (i) tooth-brush ; (ii) *Mil: P:* moustache. **Donner un coup de brosse à qch., à qn,** to give sth. a brush ; to give s.o. a brush-up, a brush-down. **Cheveux taillés en brosse,** hair cut short, in a stubble. (*b*) Paintbrush. **Passer la brosse sur qch.,** to paint sth. out. **2.** *pl.* Brushwood (skirting forest, etc.).

brossée [brɔse], *s.f.* (*a*) Brushing. (*b*) *F:* Drubbing, thrashing.

bross|er [brɔse], *v.tr.* **1.** To brush ; to scrub (floor). **Brosser qn,** (i) to brush s.o.'s clothes ; (ii) *F:* to give s.o. a good thrashing. **2.** *B. les décors d'une pièce,* to paint the scenery for a play. *s.m.* **-age.**

brosseur [brɔsœːr], *s.m.* **1.** (*a*) Brusher. (*b*) *Mil:* Servant, batman. **2.** Scene-painter.

brou [bru], *s.m.* **1.** Husk (of walnut). **2.** Brou de noix, walnut stain.

brouet [bruɛ], *s.m.* (Thin) gruel ; skilly.

brouette [bruɛt], *s.f.* Wheelbarrow.

brouettée [bruɛte], *s.f.* Barrowful.

brouett|er [bruɛte], *v.tr.* To carry, convey, (sth.) in a wheelbarrow. *s.m.* **-age.**

brouhaha [bruaa], *s.m. F:* Hubbub ; hullabaloo ; hum (of conversation).

brouillage [brujaːʒ], *s.m. W.Tel:* Jamming ; interference ; *P:* mush.

brouillamini [brujamini], *s.m. F:* Confusion, disorder.

brouillard [brujaːr], *s.m.* **1.** Fog, mist, haze. **Il fait du brouillard,** it is foggy. **2.** *Com:* Day-book ; waste-book. **3.** **(Papier) brouillard,** (i) blotting-paper ; (ii) filter-paper.

brouille [bruːj], *s.f.* Estrangement. **Être en brouille avec qn,** to be at loggerheads with s.o.

brouill|er [bruje], *v.tr.* **1.** To mix up, jumble ; to throw (sth.) into confusion. *B. qn,* to confuse, embarrass, s.o. *B. des œufs,* to scramble eggs. **Brouiller les cartes,** (i) to shuffle the cards ; (ii) *F:* to spread confusion, sow discord. *B. ses papiers,* to mix up one's papers. *La pluie brouille les fenêtres,* the rain blurs the windows. *W.Tel:* Brouiller un message, to jam a message. **2.** To set (people) at variance, at loggerheads. *s.m.* **-ement.**
se brouiller. **1.** (*a*) To become mixed, confused. **Le temps se brouille,** the weather is breaking up. *F:* **Les cartes se brouillent,** things are going wrong. (*b*) *Yeux brouillés de larmes,* eyes bedimmed with tears. **2.** To quarrel, to fall out (*avec,* with).

brouillé, *a.* **1.** Jumbled, mixed, confused ; blurred (photograph) ; murky (sky). **Œufs brouillés,** scrambled eggs. **2.** *Être b. avec qn,* to be on bad terms with s.o. ; to have fallen out with s.o.

brouillerie [brujri], *s.f.* Misunderstanding, disagreement.

brouillon, -onne [brujɔ̃, -ɔn]. **1.** *a.* Unmethodical ; muddle-headed. **2.** *s.m.* (*a*) (Rough) draft ; rough copy. (*b*) = BROUILLARD 2.

broussaille [brusaːj], *s.f.* Usu. *pl.* Brushwood, underwood, scrub. **Cheveux en broussaille,** bushy, shaggy, unkempt, hair.

brousse [brus], *s.f.* (In Australia) (The) bush.

brout|er [brute]. **1.** *v.tr. B. l'herbe,* to browse on the grass ; to graze. *s.m.* **-ement.** **2.** *v.i.* (Of brake, tool) To chatter, jump. *s.m.* **-age.**

broutilles [brutiːj], *s.f.pl.* Sprigs, twigs. *F:* Trifles ; things of no importance.

broy|er [brwaje], *v.tr.* (je broie ; je broierai) To pound, pulverize. *Tex:* To brake, hackle (hemp). *B. des couleurs,* to grind colours. *F: Broyer du noir,* to be in the dumps, to have the blues. *s.m.* **-age.** *s.* **-eur, -euse.**

bru [bry], *s.f.* Daughter-in-law.

bruant [bryɑ̃], *s.m. Orn:* Yellow-hammer ; yellow-bunting. *B. des neiges,* snow-bunting.

brucelles [brysɛl], *s.f.pl.* Tweezers.

bruche [bryʃ], *s.m. Ent:* Weevil ; pea-beetle.

brugnon [brynɔ̃], *s.m. Hort:* Nectarine.

bruine [brɥin], *s.f.* Fine rain ; drizzle. **Peinture à la bruine,** spatter-work.

bruiner [brɥine], *v.impers.* To drizzle.

bru|ire [brɥiːr], *v.i.def.* (*pr.p.* bruissant ; *pr.ind.* il bruit, ils bruissent ; *p.d.* il bruyait, il bruissait ; *fu.* il bruira. The *pr.p.* **bruyant** is now used only as an adj.) To rustle ; to rumble ; to hum ; (of brook) to murmur ; (of sea) to sound. *s.m.* **-issement.**

bruit [brɥi], *s.m.* **1.** (*a*) Noise ; din ; clatter (of dishes) ; report (of a gun) ; clang (of garden

gate). *Tomber avec un bruit sourd*, to fall with a thud. **Faire du bruit**, to make a noise. S.a. MAL² I. *F:* **Un bruit de tous les diables**, the devil of a row; an awful shindy. (b) Noise, fuss. **Beaucoup de bruit pour rien**, much ado about nothing. **Sans bruit**, noiselessly, quietly. **2.** Rumour, report. **Le bruit court que . ., it is** rumoured that. . **Faire courir un bruit**, to set a rumour afloat. **Il n'est bruit que de cela**, it is the talk of the town.

brûlant [brylɑ̃], *a.* Burning; on fire. *Larmes brûlantes*, scalding tears. *Soleil b.*, scorching, blazing, fiery, sun.

brûle-gueule, *s.m. inv.* Short clay pipe; cutty.

brûle-pourpoint (à), *adv.phr.* Point-blank.

brûl|er [bryle]. **I.** *v.tr.* To burn. **1.** To burn (down) (house); to burn (up) (rubbish); to burn away (metal); to burn out (s.o.'s eyes, electric resistance). *Elle fut brûlée vive*, (i) she was burnt alive; (ii) she was burnt at the stake. **Brûler la cervelle à qn**, to blow s.o.'s brains out. **Sans brûler une amorce**, without firing a shot. **2.** To scorch. (a) *Le lait est brûlé*, the milk has caught. *B. du café*, to roast coffee. *B. les cheveux*, to singe the hair. *L'argent lui brûle la poche*, money burns a hole in his pocket. *F:* **Brûler la route, le pavé**, to scorch, tear, along the road. (b) *Train qui brûle toutes les petites stations*, train that does not stop at any of the small stations. *Aut:* **B. un village**, to pass through a village without stopping. *Rac:* **B. un concurrent**, *F:* to leave a competitor standing. S.a. ÉTAPE, POLITESSE. (c) (Of frost) To bite, nip (buds). *La fumée me brûlait les yeux*, the smoke made my eyes smart. *s.m.* **-age.**
II. brûl|er, *v.i* **1.** To burn; to be on fire, alight. *B sans flamme*, to smoulder. *Games:* **Tu brûles**, you are getting hot. **2.** *B. d'indignation*, to burn with indignation. *B. de curiosité*, to be aflame with curiosity. *B. d'amour pour qn*, to be consumed with passion for s.o. *Il brûle de prendre la parole*, he is burning to speak. **Les mains lui brûlent**, (i) his hands are hot; (ii) *F:* he is all impatience to be up and doing. **3.** (Of meat) to burn; (of milk) to catch. *s.m.* **-ement.**

brûlé. I. *a.* Burnt. *Cu:* **Crème brûlée**, caramel custard. **Vin brûlé**, mulled wine. *F:* **Cerveau brûlé**, fanatic; dare-devil. **Homme brûlé**, man who has lost his reputation. **2.** *s.m.* *Odeur de b.*, smell of burning. *F:* **Sentir le brûlé**, (of opinions) to smack of heresy.

brûleur, -euse [brylœːr, -øːz], *s.* **1.** Burner. *F:* *B. de maisons*, incendiary, fire-raiser. *B. de café*, coffee roaster. (b) Brandy distiller. **2.** *s.m.* Bunsen burner; gas-jet. *B. à couronne*, gas-ring.

brûlot [brylo], *s.m. Hist:* Fire-ship. *F:* **Brûlot d'un parti**, fire-brand of a party.

brûlure [brylyːr], *s.f.* **1.** Burn, scald. **2.** (a) Frost-nip. (b) Blight; smut (on corn).

brumailleux, -euse [brymajø, -øːz], *a.* Misty.

brumaire [brymɛːr], *s.m. Fr.Hist:* Second month of the Fr. Republican calendar (October-November).

brume [brym], *s.f.* **1.** Thick fog, haze, or mist (esp. at sea) **2. Brume artificielle**, smoke-screen.

brumeux, -euse [brymø, -øːz], *a.* Foggy.

brun, brune [brœ̃, bryn]. **1.** *a.* Brown (cloth, hair, etc.); dark, dusky (complexion). *Un (homme) b.*, *une (femme) brune*, a dark(-haired, -skinned) man, woman. **2.** *s.m.* Brown (colour). *B. foncé*, dark brown. **3.** *s.f.* A la brune, at dusk; in the gloaming.

brunâtre [brynɑːtr], *a.* Brownish.

brunet, -ette [brynɛ, -ɛt]. **1.** *a.* Brownish. **2.** *s.f.* *Jolie brunette*, pretty brunette.

brun|ir [bryniːr]. **1.** *v.i. & pr.* To become dark, tanned. **2.** *v.tr.* (a) To brown, darken, tan. (b) To burnish (gold, etc.). (c) To polish, planish (metal). *s.m.* **-issage.** *s.m.* **-issement.**

brunisseur, -euse [brynisœːr, -øːz], *s.* Burnisher.

brusque [brysk], *a.* **1.** Abrupt, blunt, offhand(ed), brusque (person, manner). **2.** Sudden. *Aut:* **Tournant brusque**, 'sharp turn,' 'sharp bend.' *adv.* **-ment.**

brusquer [bryske], *v.tr.* **1.** B. qn, to be abrupt with s.o. **2.** *B. les choses*, to precipitate, rush, matters. *Il voulut b. la fortune*, *F:* he tried to get rich quick. *Mil:* **Attaque brusquée**, rush attack; surprise attack.

brusquerie [brysk(ə)ri], *s.f.* Abruptness, bluntness, brusqueness.

brut [bryt], *a.* **1.** *Force brute*, brute force. **Bête brute**, brute beast. **2.** Raw, unmanufactured (material); unpolished (marble); undressed (timber); (statue, literary work) in the rough; unrefined (sugar); crude (acid, oil, etc.); rough, uncut (diamond). *Fonte brute*, pig-iron. **3.** *Com:* Gross (profit, value, weight). *Ph: etc:* *Résultat b.*, result uncorrected for temperature, pressure, etc. **4.** *s.f.* **Brute.** (a) Brute beast. (b) Ruffian.

brutal, -aux [brytal, -o], *a.* (a) Brutal, brutish, savage. (b) Coarse, rough. *Force brutale*, brute force. *Coup b.*, savage blow. *Le fait b.*, the blunt fact. *Vérité brutale*, plain, unvarnished, truth. *Veh: etc:* **Frein b.**, embrayage b., fierce brake, fierce clutch. *adv.* **-ement.**

brutaliser [brytalize], *v.tr.* To ill-treat, maltreat; to bully.

brutalité [brytalite], *s.f.* **1.** (a) Brutality, brutishness. (b) Brutality, savagery, savage cruelty. **2.** Brutal act; piece of brutality.

Bruxelles [brysɛl]. *Pr.n.f.* Brussels. *F:* **Filer à Bruxelles**, (of financier) to bolt.

bruy|ant [bryjɑ̃, bryijɑ̃], *a.* **1.** Noisy (street, company); resounding (success). **2.** Loud, clamorous (applause); boisterous, rollicking (laughter). [BRUIRE] *adv.* **-amment.**

bruyère [bryjɛːr, bryijɛːr], *s.f.* **1.** (a) Heather, heath. (b) Heath(-land). *Terre de b.*, heath-mould. S.a. COQ I. **2.** Briar. **Racine de bruyère**, briar root. **Pipe en bruyère**, briar pipe.

bryone [briɔn], *s.f. Bot:* Bryony.

bu. See BOIRE.

buanderie [bɥɑ̃dri], *s.f.* Wash-house. [BUÉE]

buandier, -ière [bɥɑ̃dje, -jɛːr], *s.* Laundryman, -woman; washerwoman.

bubonique [bybɔnik], *a. Med:* Bubonic (tumour, plague).

bucarde [bykard], *s.f. Moll:* Cockle.

bûche [byʃ], *s.f.* (a) (Fire-)log; billet (of fire-wood). *B. de Noël*, yule-log. *F:* **Ramasser une bûche**, to fall; to come a cropper. (b) *F:* Dolt, blockhead.

bûcher¹ [byʃe], *s.m.* **1.** Wood-shed. **2.** (a) Pile of faggots. **Monter, mourir, sur le bûcher**, to be burnt at the stake. (b) Funeral-pyre.

bûcher², *v.tr. & i. P:* To work hard; to swot. *B. son latin*, to swot up one's Latin. *B. un examen*, to grind for an examination.

bûcheron [byʃrɔ̃], *s.m.* (a) Woodcutter, woodman. (b) Lumberman, lumberer.

bûcheur, -euse [byʃœːr, -øːz], *s. F:* Plodder, hard worker, swotter.

bucolique [bykɔlik]. **1.** *a.* Bucolic, pastoral. **2.** *s.f.pl.* **Les Bucoliques**, the Bucolics (of Virgil).

budget [bydʒɛ], *s.m.* Budget. *B. de la marine, de la guerre*, navy, army, estimates. *F:* **Arriver à boucler le budget**, to make both ends meet.

budgétaire [bydʒetɛːr], *a.* Budgetary; fiscal (year); financial (period).

buée [bɥe], *s.f.* Steam, vapour (on window-panes, etc.); blur (of breath on mirror).

buffet [byfɛ], *s.m.* **1.** (*a*) Sideboard. *B. de cuisine,* dresser. (*b*) Buffet d'argenterie, set of cutlery. (*c*) Buffet d'orgue, organ-chest, -case. **2.** Buffet (at ball, etc.). *Rail:* Refreshment room.

buffle [byfl], *s.m.* **1.** *Z:* Buffalo. **Cuir de buffle,** buffalo hide; buff(-leather). **2.** Buff-stick; strop.

buffleterie [byflətri, -lɛ-], *s.f. Mil:* Leather equipment.

bugle¹ [bygl], *s.m. Mus:* Flugel horn.

bugle², *s.f. Bot:* Bugle.

buglosse [byglɔs], *s.f. Bot:* Bugloss, alkanet.

bugrane [bygran], *s.f. Bot:* Rest-harrow.

buis [bɥi], *s.m.* **1.** *Bot:* (*a*) Box(-tree). (*b*) Faux buis, butcher's-broom. **2.** (*a*) Box(-wood). (*b*) Sleeking tool.

buisson [bɥisɔ̃], *s.m.* **1.** Bush. **2.** Thicket, brake, spinney. *F:* Trouver buisson creux, to draw a blank; to find the bird flown.

buissonneux, -euse [bɥisɔnø, -øːz], *a.* Bushy.

buissonnier, -ière [bɥisɔnje, -jɛːr], *a.* That lives, lurks, in the bush. **Faire l'école buisson-nière,** to play truant.

bulbe [bylb], **1.** *s. m. or f. Bot:* Bulb, corm. **2.** *s.m. Anat:* Bulb. *B. pileux,* root of a hair.

bulbeux, -euse [bylbø, -øːz], *a.* Bulbous; bulbed (plant).

bulgare [bylgaːr], *a. & s.* Bulgarian.

Bulgarie [bylgari]. *Pr.n.f.* Bulgaria.

bulle [byl], *s.f.* **1.** (Papal) bull. **2.** (*a*) Bubble. *Faire des bulles de savon,* to blow soap bubbles. (*b*) Blister, bleb. **3. Papier bulle,** *s.m.* du bulle, Manila (paper); cap-paper.

bulletin [byltɛ̃], *s.m.* **1.** Bulletin; report. *B. météorologique,* weather report. *B. d'actualité,* news bulletin. *Sch: B. hebdomadaire,* weekly report. **2.** Ticket, receipt, certificate; (telegraph) form. *B. de vote,* voting paper. *B. de commande,* order form. *B. de consigne,* cloak-room ticket.

bulleux, -euse [byl(l)ø, -øːz], *a.* **1.** Bubbly. **2.** Vesicular (rock, fever).

bûmes. See BOIRE.

buraliste [byralist], *s. m. & f.* (*a*) Clerk (in post office, etc.). (*b*) Collector of taxes. (*c*) Tobacconist. [BUREAU]

bure [byːr], *s.f. Tex:* Frieze; rough homespun.

bureau [byro], *s.m.* **1.** Writing-table, -desk; bureau. *B. américain, à rideau,* roll-top desk. *Parl:* Déposer un projet de loi sur le bureau, to lay a bill on the table. **2.** (*a*) Office. *B. personnel,* private office. **Bureau de(s) poste(s),** post office. "Bureau restant," 'to be called for.' *Tp: B. central,* exchange. **Bureau de police,** police station. **Bureau de banque,** bank. *Th:* **Bureau de location,** box-office. **Bureau de tabac,** tobacconist's shop. *F:* **Prendre l'air du bureau,** to look in at the office. (*b*) Board, committee. *Constituer le b. (d'une société),* to elect, appoint, a committee, a board. *Mil:* **Le deuxième Bureau,** the Intelligence Department.

bureaucrate [byrokrat, -rɔ-], *s.m.* Bureaucrat.

bureaucratie [byrokrasi, -rɔ-], *s.f.* Bureaucracy; officialdom; *F:* red tape.

burette [byrɛt], *s.f.* **1.** Cruet. **2.** Oil-can; oiler.

burin [byrɛ̃], *s.m.* (*a*) Graver; etcher's needle. (*b*) *F:* Engraving, print.

buriner [byrine], *v.tr.* To engrave (copper-plate). *s.m.* **-age.** *s.m.* **-eur.**

burlesque [byrlɛsk], *a.* **1.** Burlesque. **2.** Comical, ludicrous. *adv.* **-ment.**

bus. See BOIRE.

busard [byzaːr], *s.m. Orn:* Buzzard, harrier.

busc [bysk], *s.m.* (Corset-)busk, steel.

buse¹ [byːz], *s.f.* **1.** *Orn:* Buzzard. **2.** *F:* Blockhead, dolt, fool.

buse², *s.f.* Channel, tube. **1.** Nose-piece, nozzle (of bellows, tuyere). **2.** *I.C.E:* Carburettor choke-tube.

busqué [byske], *a.* Aquiline, hooked (nose).

buss-e, -ent, -ions. See BOIRE.

buste [byst], *s.m.* **1.** Bust. **Se faire peindre en buste,** to have a half-length portrait painted of oneself.

but¹ [by(t)], *s.m.* **1.** Mark (to aim at); target, objective. **2.** (*a*) *Rac:* Goal, winning-post. *F:* **Aller droit au but,** to go straight to the point. (*b*) *Fb:* Goal; goal-posts. *Marquer, réussir, un but,* to kick, score, a goal. **3.** Object, end, aim, purpose, design. *Dans, avec, le but de faire qch.,* with the object, intention, of doing sth. *Dans le but de frauder,* with intent to defraud. *Dans ce but . . .,* with this object . . ., to this end. . . . **Errer sans but,** to wander about aimlessly. **4.** *Adv.phr.* (*a*) **But à but,** even; without any advantage to either party. (*b*) *Artil:* **Tirer de but en blanc,** to fire direct, point-blank. *F:* **Faire une offre de but en blanc,** to make an offer point-blank, on the spur of the moment.

but². See BOIRE.

butane [bytan], *s.m. Ch:* Butane.

butée [byte], *s.f.* **1.** Thrust (of ground, etc.). *Mch:* **Palier de butée,** thrust-block, -bearing. **2.** Abutment, buttress. **3.** *Mec.E:* Stop, check. **Vis de butée,** stop-screw.

buter [byte], *v.i.* (*a*) (Of thg) To butt, strike (*contre,* against). (*b*) (Of pers.) To knock (*contre,* against); to stumble (*contre,* over). (*c*) (Of beams, etc.) To abut, rest (*contre,* against). **se buter.** (*a*) *Se b. contre qch.,* to prop oneself firmly against sth. (*b*) *Se b. à un obstacle,* to come up against an obstacle. (*c*) *Se b. à faire qch.,* to be obstinately set on doing sth.

buté, *a.* Fixed, set. *Caractère b.,* obstinate nature.

butin [bytɛ̃], *s.m.* Booty, spoils, plunder.

butiner [bytine], *v.tr. & i.* **1.** *A:* To loot, plunder. **2.** (Of bees) *B. les fleurs,* to gather honey from the flowers. *s.m.* **-ement.**

butineur, -euse [bytinœːr, -øːz], *a.* Honey-gathering (insect).

butoir [bytwaːr], *s.m.* Stop, check; buffer. *Rail:* Buffer-stop. [BUTER]

butor [bytɔːr], *s.m.* **1.** *Orn:* Bittern. **2.** *F:* Churl, lout.

butte [byt], *s.f.* **1.** Knoll, hillock, mound. **2.** *Mil:* Butts (of range). *F:* **Être en butte à qch.,** to be exposed to (ridicule, etc.).

buttée [byte], *s.f.* = BUTÉE.

butter [byte], *v.tr.* To earth up (plants).

buvable [byvabl], *a.* Drinkable; fit to drink.

buv-ant, -ons, etc. See BOIRE.

buvard [byvaːr]. **1.** *a.* **Papier buvard,** blotting-paper. **2.** *s.m.* Blotter; blotting-pad.

buvetier [byvtje], *s.m.* Bar-keeper.

buvette [byvɛt], *s.f.* **1.** Refreshment bar (at station, etc.). **2.** Pump-room (at watering-place).

buveur, -euse [byvœːr, -øːz], *s.* **1.** Drinker. **2.** Toper, drunkard, wine-bibber.

Byzance [bizɑ̃ːs]. *Pr.n. A.Geog:* Byzantium.

byzantin, -ine [bizɑ̃tɛ̃, -in], *a. & s.* Byzantine.

C, c [se], *s.m.* (The letter) C, c.

c'. See CE[1].

ça [sa]. **1.** *adv.* Hither. **Çà et là,** hither and thither; here and there. **Jambe de çà, jambe de là,** astride, astraddle. **2.** *int. Ah çà!* now then! là, astride, astraddle.

cabale [kabal], *s.f.* Cabal. (*a*) Intrigue, plot. (*b*) Junto, clique, caucus.

cabal|er [kabale], *v.i.* To cabal, intrigue (*contre*, against). *s.* **-eur, -euse.**

cabalistique [kabalistik], *a.* Cab(b)alistic.

caban [kabã], *s.m.* (*a*) (Sailor's) pea-jacket. (*b*) Pilot-coat. (*c*) (Officer's) hooded overcoat. (*d*) Oilskins.

cabane [kaban], *s.f.* **1.** (*a*) Hut, shanty. (*b*) Awning (on river boat). (*c*) Cabin (of barge). **2.** *Av:* Cabane, central unit (of aeroplane).

cabanon [kabanɔ̃], *s.m.* **1.** Small hut. **2.** (*a*) Dark cell (of prison). (*b*) (Lunatic's) padded cell.

cabaret [kabarɛ], *s.m.* **1.** (*a*) Public-house, tavern. (*b*) Inn, eating-house. (*c*) (Small fashionable) restaurant. **2.** Liqueur-stand.

cabaretier, -ière [kabartje, -jɛːr], *s.* (*a*) Publican, tavern-keeper. (*b*) Inn-keeper.

cabas [kaba], *s.m.* **1.** (*a*) Frail, basket. (*b*) (Plaited two-handled) (i) shopping basket, (ii) tool-basket. **2.** *Cost:* Poke-bonnet.

cabestan [kabɛstã], *s.m.* Capstan, windlass, winch. **Grand c.,** main capstan. *Virez au c.!* heave!

cabillau(d) [kabijo], *s.m.* Codfish; fresh cod.

cabillot [kabijo], *s.m. Nau:* Toggle(-pin) or belaying-pin.

cabine [kabin], *s.f.* Cabin. (*a*) *Nau:* **La c.,** the saloon. **C. de luxe,** state-room. (*b*) Box (of bathing establishment); (telephone) call-box; cab (of locomotive). **C. de bains,** bathing-hut. *Rail:* **C. de signaux, d'aiguillage,** signal-box.

cabinet [kabine], *s.m.* **1.** Closet; small room. **C. de toilette,** dressing-room. **C. d'aisances,** *F:* **les cabinets,** water-closet. **C. de travail,** study. *Phot:* **C. noir,** dark-room. **2.** Office, room; (doctor's) consulting room. **3.** Collection (of works of art, etc.). **C. d'estampes,** print-room (in museum). **4.** (*a*) *Foreign Pol:* Government. **Le C. de l'Élysée,** the French Government. (*b*) *Home Pol:* Cabinet. (*c*) **C. d'un ministre,** minister's departmental staff. **Chef de cabinet** = principal private secretary.

câble [kɑːbl], *s.m.* (*a*) Cable, rope. **Filer le câble,** to pay out the cable. (*b*) (*De*) *Bowden,* Bowden wire. (*c*) *El.E:* (i) Cable; (ii) (in apparatus) wiring, lead. **C. souterrain, sous-marin,** underground, submarine, cable. **Poser un câble,** to lay a cable. **Aviser qn par le câble,** to cable to s.o.

câble-chaîne, *s.m.* Chain cable. *pl.* **Des câbles-chaînes.**

câbl|er [kɑble], *v.tr.* **1.** (*a*) To twist, lay (strands into cable). (*b*) *El:* To wire (up), connect up (apparatus). *s.m.* **-age.** **2.** To cable (message).

câbliau [kɑblio], *s.m.* = CABILLAUD.

câblier [kɑblie], *s.m.* Cable-ship.

câblogramme [kɑblɔgram], *s.m.* Cablegram; *F:* cable (message).

caboche [kabɔʃ], *s.f.* **1.** *P:* Head, pate. **2.** (Clou) **caboche,** heavy-headed nail; *Bootm:* hobnail.

cabochon [kabɔʃɔ̃], *s.m.* **1.** (*a*) *Lap:* Cabochon. (*b*) *Cy:* C. **rouge,** red reflector. **2.** *Furn:* (Fancy) brass-nail.

cabosse [kabɔs], *s.f.* *F:* Bruise, bump.

cabosser [kabɔse], *v.tr.* *F:* **1.** To bump, bruise. **2.** To dent (silverware); to bash in (hat).

cabotage [kabɔtaːʒ], *s.m.* Coastwise trade. **Grand c., petit c.,** off-shore, in-shore, coastal traffic.

cabotin, -ine [kabɔtɛ̃, -in], *s.* *F:* (Third-rate) play-actor, -actress; *F:* barn-stormer.

cabotinage [kabɔtinaːʒ], *s.m.* **1.** (Third-rate) acting. **2.** Life of a strolling player; *F:* barnstorming. **3.** Looseness of conduct; low bohemianism.

cabotiner [kabɔtine], *v.i.* **1.** To lead the life of a strolling player; *F:* to busk. **2.** To lead a bohemian life.

caboulot [kabulo], *s.m.* *F:* Low 'pub.'

cabrade [kabrad], *s.f.* (Of horse) **Faire une cabrade,** to rear.

cabrage [kabraːʒ], *s.m.* *Av:* Nose-lift; elevating (of plane).

cabr|er [kabre]. **1.** *v.tr.* *Av:* To elevate (plane). **2.** *v.pr.* (*a*) (Of horse) To rear. *F:* (Of pers.) **Se cabrer contre qch.,** to jib at sth. (*b*) *Av:* (Of plane) To rear, buck. *s.m.* **-ement.**

cabri [kabri], *s.m.* Kid.

cabriole [kabriɔl], *s.f.* (*a*) Leap, caper. **Faire des cabrioles,** to cut capers, to caper about. (*b*) Tumble, somersault.

cabriolet [kabriɔlɛ], *s.m.* *Veh:* (*a*) Gig. (*b*) *Aut:* Cabriolet.

cacahouette [kakawɛt], *s.f.,* **cacahuète** [kakaɥɛt], *s.f.* Peanut.

cacao [kakao], *s.m.* *Bot:* Cacao. *Com:* Cocoa.

cacatoès [kakatɔɛs], *s.m.* *Orn:* Cockatoo.

cacatois [kakatwa], *s.m.* *Nau:* Royal (sail).

cachalot [kaʃalo], *s.m.* Cachalot; sperm whale.

cache [kaʃ]. **1.** *s.f.* Hiding-place; (i) cache (of explorer); (ii) *F:* hidie-hole. **2.** *s.m.* *Phot:* Mask (for printing). [CACHER]

cache-cache, *s.m.* Hide-and-seek.

cache-col, *s.m.,* **cache-cou,** *s.m.* (Man's) scarf. *pl.* **Des cache-col(s), -cou(s).**

cache-corset, *s.m.inv.* *Cost:* Camisole.

Cachemire [kaʃmiːr]. **1.** *Pr.n.m. Geog:* Cashmere, Kashmir. **2.** *s.m.* *Tex:* Cashmere.

cache-misère, *s.m.inv.* *F:* Coat or wrap (hiding the shabbiness underneath).

cache-nez, *s.m.inv.* Muffler, comforter.

cache-pot, *s.m.inv.* Flower-pot case, cover.

cache-poussière, *s.m.inv.* *Cost:* Dust-coat.

cacher [kaʃe], *v.tr.* (*a*) To hide, secrete (sth.). (*b*) To conceal; to hide (one's face, etc.) from view; to mask, dissemble (one's feelings, etc.). *Douleur cachée,* secret grief. **C. qch. à qn,** to hide, conceal, keep back, sth. from s.o. *N'avoir rien de caché pour qn,* to have no secrets from s.o. *Il ne cache pas que . . .,* he makes no secret of the fact that. . . .

se cacher. 1. To hide, lie in hiding. **2.** (*a*) *Se c. à qn, au monde,* (i) to hide from, (ii) to shun, avoid, s.o., the world. (b) *Je ne m'en cache pas*, I make no secret of it.

cacherie [kaʃri], *s.f.* Concealing. *Pas de cacheries!* no underhand work!

cachet [kaʃɛ], *s.m.* **1.** (a) Seal, stamp (on document). *Hist:* **Lettre de cachet**, order under the King's private seal. (b) Mark, stamp, impress. *C. de la poste*, postmark. *C. d'un fabricant*, maker's trade-mark. *F:* **Le cachet du génie**, the stamp, hall-mark, of genius. *Œuvre qui manque de c.*, work that lacks character. **2.** (a) Stamp, seal (implement). (b) Signet(-ring). **3.** (a) Ticket (issued in sets, *e.g.* at restaurants); voucher (for lessons). *F:* **Courir le cachet**, to give priv te lessons (in the pupils' homes). (b) *F:* Fee (of artiste, counsel, consultant). **4.** *Pharm:* Cachet.

cachet|er [kaʃte], *v.tr.* (je cachette; je cachetterai) To seal (up) (letter, bottle, etc.). **Cire à cacheter**, sealing-wax. *s.m.* **-age.**

cachette [kaʃɛt], *s.f.* Hiding-place. **En cachette**, secretly; on the sly; on the quiet.

cachot [kaʃo], *s.m.* **1.** Dungeon; dark cell. **2.** *F:* Prison, gaol. [CACHER]

cachotterie [kaʃɔtri], *s.f.* Affectation of mystery. *Faire des cachotteries à qn*, to keep things back from s.o.

cachottier, -ière [kaʃɔtje, -jɛːr], *a. F:* Secretive, reticent, close.

cachou [kaʃu], *s.m.* (a) *Bot:* Catechu. (b) Cachou.

cacolet [kakɔlɛ], *s.m. Mil:* Mule-litter, packsaddle (for wounded men).

cacophonie [kakɔfɔni], *s.f.* Cacophony.

cactus [kaktyːs], *s.m. Bot:* Cactus.

cacuminal, -aux [kakyminal, -o], *a. Ling: L'r c.*, point r; dental r.

cadastre [kadastr], *s.m. Adm:* Cadastral survey; cadastre; plan (of commune).

cadavéreux, -euse [kadaverø, -øːz], *a.* Cadaverous.

cadavérique [kadaverik], *a.* Cadaveric. **Rigidité cadavérique**, *rigor mortis.*

cadavre [kadɑːvr], *s.m.* (a) Corpse; dead body. *F:* **Avoir son petit cadavre**, to have a skeleton in the cupboard. (b) Carcase (of animal).

cadeau [kado], *s.m.* Present; gift. **Envoyer qch. à qn en cadeau**, to send s.o. sth. as a present. **Faire cadeau de qch. à qn**, to make s.o. a present of sth.; to present s.o. with sth.

cadenas [kadnɑ], *s.m.* **1.** Padlock. **2.** Clasp, snap (of bracelet, etc.).

cadenasser [kadnɑse], *v.tr.* To padlock (door, etc.); to fasten, clasp (bracelet).

cadence [kadɑːs], *s.f.* **1.** Cadence, rhythm (of verse, motion). **En cadence**, rhythmically. *Row:* **Donner la cadence**, to set the stroke. *A une c. de . . .*, at the rate of. . . . **2.** (a) *Mus:* Cadence. (b) Intonation (of voice).

cadencer [kadɑse], *v.tr.* (je cadençai(s); n. cadençons) To give rhythm to (sth.).

 cadencé, *a.* Rhythmical; measured (step, stroke). **Prendre le pas cadencé**, (i) to fall into step; (ii) to break into quick time.

cadet, -ette [kadɛ, -ɛt], *s.* **1.** (a) (The) younger, junior. *Elle est ma cadette de deux ans*, she is my junior by two years. *Sp:* **Épreuve des cadets**, junior event. (b) Junior (in position, rank). (c) *F:* The youngest (of a family). *F:* **Le cadet de mes soucis**, the last thing I am troubling about. **2.** *s.m. Golf:* Caddie.

Cadix [kadiks], *Pr.n.* Cadiz.

cadmium [kadmjɔm], *s.m. Ch:* Cadmium.

cadran [kadrɑ̃], *s.m.* **1.** Dial. **Cadran solaire**, sun-dial. **2.** (a) Face, dial(-plate) (of clock, barometer). *F:* **Faire le tour du cadran**, to sleep

the clock round. (b) *Nau:* Engine-room telegraph.

cadrat [kadra], *s.m. Typ:* Quadrat, *F:* quad.

cadratin [kadratɛ̃], *s.m. Typ:* Em quadrat, em quad. **Demi-cadratin**, en quad.

cadre [kɑːdr], *s.m.* **1.** (a) Frame (of picture, door etc.). *W.Tel:* *C. de réception*, frame aerial. (b) Border (of map, etc.); setting (of scene) (c) Compass, limits, bounds. *Sortir du c. de ses fonctions*, to go beyond one's duties. **2.** (a) Frame(work) (of bicycle, etc.). (b) *Lit:* Outline, plan, skeleton (of book, etc.). **3.** *Mil: Navy:* (a) Cadre of (i) officers and N.C.O.'s, (ii) all ranks (in skeleton unit). **Avoir passé par les cadres**, to have risen from the ranks. (b) *C. de réserve*, reserve list. **Rayer qn des cadres**, to strike s.o. off the strength. **Hors cadre**, (i) not on the strength; (ii) specially employed.

cadrer [kadre], *v.i.* To tally, agree, square, fit in (*avec*, with).

caduc, -uque [kadyk], *a.* **1.** (a) Decaying, crumbling (house, etc.). **L'âge caduc**, declining age. (b) (Of pers.) Decrepit, broken down, frail. **2.** *Bot:* Deciduous. **3.** Null and void (legacy); lapsed (agreement); statute-barred (debt). **4.** *F:* **Mal caduc**, falling sickness; epilepsy.

cafard, -arde [kafaːr, -ard]. **1.** (a) *a. Air c.*, sanctimonious air. (b) *s. Sch:* Sneak; talebearer. **2.** *s.m.* (a) Cockroach. (b) *F:* **Avoir le cafard**, to have the hump, the blues; the pip; to be fed up.

cafard|er [kafarde], *v.i.* To sneak, peach; to carry tales. *s.m.* **-age.**

café [kafe], *s.m.* **1.** Coffee. (a) **Grain de café**, coffee-bean. *C. torréfié*, roasted coffee. (b) **Café noir, café nature**, black coffee. **Café au lait, café crème**, coffee with milk, with cream. **Café complet**, coffee, hot milk, rolls and butter. (c) *a.inv.* Coffee-coloured. **2.** Café (always licensed to sell alcoholic drinks). **Garçon de café**, waiter.

cafetier, -ière [kaftje, -jɛːr]. **1.** *s.* Owner of a café. **2.** *s.f.* Cafetière, coffee-pot.

cafouill|er [kafuje], *v.i. F:* To get into a mess; to flounder; (of rowing crew) to be (all) at sixes and sevens; (of car engine) to miss. *s.m.* **-age.**

cafre [kɑːfr], *a. & s. Ethn:* Kaf(f)ir.

cage [kaːʒ], *s.f.* **1.** (a) (Bird-)cage; (hen-)coop; cage (of lions, monkeys). (b) Cage (of mine-shaft). **2.** Cover, case (for protection); (engine) casing. **3.** Well(-hole) (of stairs); stairway; shaft (of lift). **4.** *Mec.E: C. à billes*, ball-race.

cagneux, -euse [kaɲø, -øːz], *a. & s.* (a) Knock-kneed (person). (b) (Of the legs) Crooked.

cagnotte [kaɲɔt], *s.f. Games:* Pool, kitty, pot.

cagot, -ote [kago, -ɔt]. **1.** *s.* (Canting) hypocrite. **2.** *a.* Sanctimonious.

cagoule [kagul], *s.f.* **1.** (a) Cowl. (b) Penitent's hood. **2.** *F:* Gas mask.

cahier [kaje], *s.m.* (a) (Stitched) 'paper book'; (scholar's) exercise book. *C. d'écriture*, copybook. (b) *C. de papier à lettres*, six sheets, quarter of a quire, of note paper.

cahin-caha [kaɛ̃kaa], *adv. F:* **Se porter c.-c.**, to be so-so, middling. **Marcher c.-c.**, to limp along.

cahot [kao], *s.m.* Jolt; bump (of vehicle).

cahotant [kaɔtɑ̃], *a.* **1.** Jolting (carriage). **2.** Jolty, bumpy (road).

cahot|er [kaɔte], *v.tr. & i.* To jolt, shake, bump along (in cart, etc.). **Vie cahotée**, life full of ups and downs. *s.m.* **-ement.**

cahoteux, -euse [kaɔtø, -øːz], *a.* Rough, jolty, bumpy (road).

cahute [kayt], *s.f.* **1.** Hut, shanty. **2.** Cabin (on river barge).

caïeu, -eux [kajø], *s.m.* Off-set bulb (of tulip).

caille [kɑːj], *s.f., Orn:* Quail.

caillebotis [kɑjbɔti], *s.m.* **1.** *Nau:* Grating (over hatches). **2.** *Mil:* Duckboard(s).

caillebotte [kɑjbɔt], *s.f.* Curds.

caillebotter [kɑjbɔte], *v.tr.* To curdle, clot, coagulate.
se caillebotter, to curdle.

caill|er [kɑje], *v.tr., i., & pr.* To clot, curdle; (of blood) to congeal. *s.m.* **-ement.**
caillé, *s.m.* Curdled milk; curds.

caillot [kɑjo], *s.m.* Clot (of blood, etc.).

caillou, *pl.* **-oux** [kaju], *s.m.* **1.** (*a*) Pebble. (*b*) Boulder. *Cailloux roulés,* drift boulders. (*c*) *pl.* Cobble-stones. **2.** *P:* Head, pate.

caillout|er [kajute], *v.tr.* (*a*) To ballast, metal (road, track). (*b*) To pave (road) with pebbles. *s.m.* **-age.**

caillouteux, -euse [kajutø, -øːz], *a.* Flinty, stony (road); pebbly, shingly (beach).

cailloutis [kajuti], *s.m.* **1.** Broken stones; road metal. **2.** Pebble-work surface.

caïman [kaimɑ̃], *s.m. Rept:* Cayman, caiman.

Caire (le) [lɔkɛːr]. *Pr.n.* Cairo.

caisse [kɛs], *s.f.* **1.** (*a*) (Packing-)case. *C. à claire-voie,* crate. *Mettre des marchandises en caisse,* to case goods. (*b*) Box, chest (of tea, tools); tub (for shrub); tank, cistern. *Aut: C. de l'embrayage,* casing of the clutch. **2.** Body (of vehicle). **3.** *Com:* (*a*) Cash-box; till. *C. enregistreuse,* cash-register. **Les caisses de l'État,** the coffers of the State. (*b*) (i) Pay-desk. **Payez à la caisse,** please pay at the desk. (ii) Counting-house. **Tenir la caisse,** to be in charge of the cash. (*c*) (i) Cash (in hand); (ii) takings. **Petite caisse,** petty cash. **Livre de caisse,** cash-book. **Faire la caisse,** to balance (up) one's cash. (*d*) Fund. *C. contre le chômage,* unemployment fund. *C. d'amortissement,* sinking-fund. (*e*) Bank. **Caisse d'épargne (postale),** (post-office) savings-bank. **4.** (*a*) *Mus:* Drum. **Caisse roulante,** side-drum. **Grosse caisse,** (i) bass drum, *F:* big drum; (ii) bass drummer. *F:* **Battre la grosse caisse,** to advertise. (*b*) *C. du tympan,* drum of the ear.

caissier, -ière [kɛsje, -jɛːr], *s.* Cashier.

caisson [kɛsɔ̃], *s.m.* Box. **1.** *Mil: C. à munitions,* ammunition waggon. **2.** Boot, seat-box (of carriage). **3.** *Nau:* Locker, bin. **4.** *C. hydraulique,* caisson; coffer-dam.

cajol|er [kaʒɔle], *v.tr.* To cajole, coax, wheedle. *s.* **-eur, -euse.**

cajolerie [kaʒɔlri], *s.f.* Cajolery, coaxing, wheedling; *F:* blarney.

cal [kal], *s.m.* Callosity. *pl. Des cals.*

Calabre (la) [la kalɑːbr]. *Pr.n.* Calabria.

calamine [kalamin], *s.f.* **1.** *Miner:* Calamine. **2.** *I.C.E:* Carbon (deposit). *Gratter la c.,* to decarbonize the engine.

calamité [kalamite], *s.f.* Calamity, disaster.

calamiteux, -euse [kalamitø, -øːz], *a.* **1.** Calamitous. **2.** *F:* Dilapidated, broken down.

calandre [kalɑ̃ːdr], *s.f.* **1.** (*a*) *Tex: Paperm:* Calender, roller. (*b*) *Laund:* Mangle. **2.** *Aut: C. de radiateur,* radiator shell.

calandr|er [kalɑ̃dre], *v.tr* (*a*) *Tex: Paperm: etc:* To calender, roll, press; to surface. (*b*) *Laund:* To mangle. *s.m.* **-age.** *s.* **-eur, -euse.**

calcaire [kalkɛːr]. **1.** *a.* Calcareous. *Sol c.,* chalky soil. **2.** *s.m.* Limestone.

calcédoine [kalsedwan], *s.f. Miner:* Chalcedɔny.

calcéolaire [kalseɔlɛːr], *s.f. Bot:* Calceolaria.

calcin|er [kalsine], *v.tr.* **1.** (*a*) To calcine. *F: Rôti calciné,* joint burnt to a cinder.

(*b*) *Être calciné,* to be burnt to death. **2.** *Metall:* (i) To oxidize, (ii) to roast (ores). *s.f.* **-ation.**

calcique [kalsik], *a. Ch:* Calcic. *Med: Dépôts calciques,* chalky deposits.

calcium [kalsjɔm], *s.m. Ch:* Calcium.

calcul¹ [kalkyl], *s.m.* (*a*) Calculation, reckoning. **Faux calcul,** miscalculation. **Règle à calcul(s),** slide-rule. *F:* **Faire son calcul,** to lay one's plans. **Tout calcul fait,** taking everything into account. (*b*) Arithmetic, ciphering. S.a. TÊTE 2. (*c*) Calcul infinitésimal, (differential and integral) calculus.

calcul², *s.m. Med:* Calculus, stone.

calculateur, -trice [kalkylatœːr, -tris]. **1.** *s.* Reckoner, computer, calculator. **2.** *a.* Long-headed (person, policy).

calculer [kalkyle], *v.tr.* To calculate, compute, reckon. *C. de tête,* to reckon in one's head. **Tout bien calculé,** taking everything into account. **calculé,** *a.* Premeditated (malice); deliberate (insolence).

cale¹ [kal], *s.f. Nau:* **1.** (*a*) Hold (of ship). **Fond de cale,** bilge. **A fond de cale,** down in the hold. *F:* **Être à fond de cale,** to be down and out. (*b*) *C. d'eau,* water-tank. **2.** *C. de construction, de lancement,* slip(way); (ship-building) stocks. **Mettre un navire sur cale,** to lay down a ship. **Cale sèche,** dry dock. **Cale de radoub,** graving dock. **Entrer en c. sèche,** to dry-dock.

cale², *s.f.* **1.** Wedge, chock, block. *Av: etc:* **Enlever les cales,** to withdraw the chocks. **2.** Prop, strut. **3.** Packing-piece.

calebasse [kalbɑːs], *s.f.* Calabash, gourd, water-bottle.

calèche [kalɛʃ], *s.f.* Light four-wheeled carriage (with folding hood); barouche.

caleçon [kalsɔ̃], *s.m.* (Pair of men's) drawers; pants. *C. de bain,* bathing-drawers.

calembour [kalɑ̃buːr], *s.m.* Pun; play on words.

calembredaine [kalɑ̃brədɛn], *s.f. F:* Foolish utterance or action. *Dire des calembredaines,* to jest. *Faire des calembredaines,* to play the fool.

calendes [kalɑ̃ːd], *s.f.pl. Rom.Ant:* Kalends. *F:* **Renvoyer qch. aux calendes grecques,** to put sth. off indefinitely.

calendrier [kalɑ̃dri(j)e], *s.m.* Calendar, almanac. *C. à effeuiller,* tear-off calendar.

cale-pied(s), *s.m. inv. Cy:* Toe-clip.

calepin [kalpɛ̃], *s.m.* Note-book, memorandum-book.

cal|er¹ [kale], *v.tr.* **1.** (*a*) To chock (up), wedge (up) (piece of furniture); to scotch (wheel); to clamp (telescope, etc.). (*b*) *C. un malade sur des coussins,* to prop up a patient on cushions. **2.** (*a*) To wedge, key (crank to shaft, etc.); to jam (valve). (*b*) *Aut:* To stall (the engine). *v.i.* (Of engine) To stall. **3.** To adjust; to time, tune (valve, engine). **4.** *Games:* To shoot, knuckle (a marble). *s.m.* **-age.**
calé, *a.* **1.** *Mch:* **Piston calé,** (i) jammed piston; (ii) piston at one of the dead points. **2.** *F:* (*a*) Homme calé, man of substance, of property. (*b*) *Être calé sur, en, qch.,* to be well up in a subject.

caler² [kale], *v.i. Nau: Navire qui cale vingt pieds,* ship that draws twenty feet of water.

caler³, *v.i. P:* To funk; to show the white feather. **Caler doux,** to sing small.

calfat [kalfa], *s.m.* Caulker.

calfat|er [kalfate], *v.tr.* To caulk. *s.m.* **-age.**

calfeutr|er [kalføtre], *v.tr.* To block up, stop (up) (chinks); to list (door); to make (a room) draught-proof. *F: Se c. dans sa chambre,* to make oneself snug in one's room. *s.m.* **-age.**

calibre [kalibr], *s.m.* **1.** (*a*) Calibre, bore (of

fire-arm, etc.). (b) Size, diameter (of bullet, etc.).
2. (a) *Tls:* Gauge; measuring tool. *C. de précision*, calliper gauge. *C. d'épaisseur* (*à lames*), set of feelers. (b) Template, pattern, profile. (c) *Mch.Tls:* Jig, former.
calibr|er [kalibre], *v.tr.* **I.** (a) To gauge. (b) To calibrate (thermometer, etc.). **2.** *Phot:* To trim (print). **3.** *Typ:* To cast off (copy). *s.m.* **-age.**
calice[1] [kalis], *s.m.* Chalice. *F:* Boire, avaler, le calice (d'amertume), to drain the cup (of bitterness, of woe).
calice[2], *s.m. Bot:* Calyx, flower-cup.
calicot [kaliko], *s.m.* **I.** Calico. **2.** *P:* Draper's assistant; counter-jumper.
calife [kalif], *s.m.* Caliph.
Californie [kaliforni]. *Pr.n.f.* California.
californien, -ienne [kalifornjɛ̃, -jɛn], *a. & s.* Californian.
califourchon (à) [akalifurʃɔ̃], *adv.phr.* Astride, astraddle. *Se mettre à c. sur qch.*, to bestride sth.
câlin [kɑlɛ̃], *a.* Caressing, winning (child, ways, etc.). *s. Une petite câline*, a little wheedler.
câlin|er [kaline], *v.tr.* To caress; to make much of (s.o.); to wheedle. *s.m.* **-age.**
câlinerie [kalinri], *s.f.* **I.** Caressing; wheedling. **2.** Caress.
calleux, -euse [kalø, -øːz], *a.* Horny, callous.
calligraphie [kalligrafi], *s.f.* Calligraphy, penmanship.
callosité [kallozite], *s.f.* Callosity, callus.
calmant [kalmɑ̃]. **I.** *a.* Calming; soothing. **2.** *s.m. Med:* Sedative.
calmar [kalmaːr], *s.m. Moll:* Calamary; squid.
calme[1] [kalm], *s.m.* Calm, calmness; stillness (of air, etc.). *Retrouver son c.*, to recover one's equanimity. *Nau:* Pris par le calme, becalmed. *Zones des calmes*, the doldrums.
calme[2], *a.* Calm; still, quiet (air, night); cool, composed (person, manner). *Com: Marché c.*, flat, quiet, dull, market. *adv.* **-ment.**
calmer [kalme], *v.tr.* To calm, quiet, still, allay (tempest, fears); to soothe (pain, conscience).
se calmer, to become calm; to calm down; (of storm) to abate.
calomniateur, -trice [kalɔmnjatœːr, -tris]. **I.** *s.* Calumniator, slanderer. **2.** *a.* Slanderous, libellous.
calomnie [kalɔmni], *s.f.* Calumny, slander, libel.
calomnier [kalɔmnje], *v.tr.* To slander, libel.
calomnieu|x, -euse [kalɔmnjø, -øːz], *a.* Slanderous, libellous. *adv.* **-sement.**
calorie [kalɔri], *s.f. Ph.Meas:* Calorie, calory. **Grande calorie,** (major) calory. **Petite calorie,** lesser calory, gramme-calory.
calorifère [kalɔrifɛːr]. **I.** *a.* Heat-conveying. **2.** *s.m.* (a) (Central) heating installation. (b) Slow-combustion stove.
calorifuge [kalɔrifyːʒ], *a.'* (a) Non-conducting; (heat-)insulating. (b) Heat-proof (varnish).
calorifuger [kalɔrifyʒe], *v.tr.* To insulate, lag (steam-pipe, etc.).
calorimètre [kalɔrimɛtr], *s.m. Ph:* Calorimeter.
calorimétrie [kalɔrimetri], *s.f. Ph:* Calorimetry.
calorique [kalɔrik], *s.m. Ph:* Heat; caloric.
calot [kalo], *s.m. Mil:* Forage-cap.
calotin [kalɔtɛ̃], *s.m. P:* **I.** Priest. **2.** Church-goer.
calotte [kalɔt], *s.f.* **I.** (a) Skull-cap. *Mil:* Undress cap. (b) *Ecc:* Calotte, zuc(c)hetto. *P:* La calotte, the priests, the clergy, the cloth. **2.** Calotte sphérique, portion of a sphere. Joint à calotte sphérique, ball-and-socket joint. *F:* La calotte des cieux, the vault, canopy, of heaven. **3.** *F:* Cuff; box on the ears.

calotter [kalɔte], *v.tr.* **I.** *F:* To cuff (s.o.). **2.** *Golf:* To top (the ball).
calque [kalk], *s.m.* (a) Tracing; traced design. Toile à calque, tracing-cloth. (b) *F:* Servile copy.
calqu|er [kalke], *v.tr.* **I.** To trace (sur, from); to make a tracing of (drawing). *Needlew:* To transfer (design). Dessin calqué, tracing. Toile à calquer, tracing-cloth. **2.** To copy closely. *s.m.* **-age.**
calvados [kalvadɔs], *s.m.* Cider-brandy.
calvaire [kalvɛːr], *s.m.* **I.** Le Calvaire, (Mount) Calvary. **2.** *R.C.Ch:* (a) Calvary. (b) Stations of the Cross.
calviniste [kalvinist]. **I.** *a.* Calvinistic(al). **2.** *s.* Calvinist.
calvitie [kalvisi], *s.f.* Baldness.
camaïeu, *pl.* **-eux** [kamajø], *s.m.* **I.** Cameo. **2.** Monochrome painting. *Engr:* Tint-drawing.
camail [kamaːj], *s.m.* **I.** *R.C.Ch:* Cape (worn over the surplice). **2.** Cape, cloak.
camarade [kamarad], *s.m. & f.* Comrade; fellow, mate, *F:* chum. *C. de pension*, school-fellow; school-friend (of girl). *C. de jeu*, play-mate, playfellow.
camaraderie [kamaradri], *s.f.* **I.** (a) Comradeship; good fellowship. (b) Cliquishness. **2.** Set, clique.
camard, -arde [kamaːr, -ard], *a. F:* = CAMUS. La camarde, (grim) Death.
cambiste [kãbist]. **I.** *s.m.* Exchange-broker. **2.** *a.* Place cambiste, exchange centre.
Cambodge [kãbɔdʒ]. *Pr.n.m. Geog:* Cambodia.
cambouis [kãbwi], *s.m. Mec.E:* Dirty oil or grease.
cambr|er [kãbre], *v.tr.* To bend. (a) To arch (one's foot, etc.). *C. la taille*, to throw out one's chest. (b) To camber, curve (wood, etc.). *s.m.* **-age.** *s.m.* **-ement.**
se cambrer, to brace oneself back; to throw out one's chest; to draw oneself up (to one's full height).
cambré, *a.* **I.** Cambered, arched. *Pied très c.*, highly arched foot; foot with a high instep. **2.** Bent, warped, crooked. *Jambes cambrées,* bow-legs.
cambriolage [kãbriɔlaːʒ], *s.m.* Housebreaking; *F:* burgling.
cambrioler [kãbriɔle], *v.tr.* To break into, ransack (house); *F:* to burgle.
cambrioleur, -euse [kãbriɔlœːr, -øːz], *s.* Housebreaker, *F:* burglar.
cambrure [kãbryːr], *s.f.* Camber, curve (of wood, etc.); arch (of foot), instep.
cambuse [kãbyːz], *s.f.* **I.** *Nau:* Steward's room, store-room. **2.** Canteen (in shipyard).
came [kam], *s.f. Mec.E:* Cam, lifter, wiper. Arbre à cames, cam-shaft.
camée [kame], *s.m.* Cameo.
caméléon [kameleɔ̃], *s.m.* Chameleon.
camélia [kamelja], *s.m. Bot:* Camellia.
camelot [kamlo], *s.m. F:* (a) Cheap Jack, street hawker. (b) Newsvendor.
camelote [kamlɔt], *s.f. F:* Cheap goods; shoddy goods, trash, rubbish, junk. *Meubles de c.*, gimcrack furniture. *Maison de c.*, jerry-built house.
camembert [kamãbɛːr], *s.m.* Camembert (cheese).
camera [kamera], *s.f. Cin:* Cine-camera.
camérier [kamerje], *s.m.* Chamberlain (to Pope, to cardinal).
camérière [kamerjɛːr], *s.f.* (a) Lady's maid. (b) Chambermaid.
camion [kamjɔ̃], *s.m.* Dray, waggon, lorry. *C. automobile*, motor lorry.

camionnage [kamjɔnaːʒ], *s.m.* Cartage, haulage.
camionner [kamjɔne], *v.tr.* To cart, carry, convey (goods).
camionnette [kamjɔnɛt], *s.f.* Delivery-van. *C. de police*, police loud-speaker van.
camionneur [kamjɔnœːr], *s.m.* Carrier, carman.
camisole [kamizɔl], *s.f.* **I.** (Woman's) dressing-jacket. **2.** *C. de force*, strait-waistcoat, -jacket.
camomille [kamɔmiːj], *s.f.* Camomile. **Tisane de camomille**, camomile tea.
camoufl|er [kamufle], *v.tr.* To disguise; to fake. *Mil:* *Navy:* To camouflage. *s.m.* **-age.**
camouflet [kamuflɛ], *s.m.* Affront, insult, snub.
camp [kɑ̃], *s.m.* Camp. **I.** *Mil:* **Asseoir le camp,** to pitch camp. **Lever le camp,** to strike camp. *F:* **Être en camp volant,** to be somewhere only temporarily. **Lit de camp,** camp-bed. *F:* **Fiche(r) le camp,** to decamp, to clear out. **2.** (*a*) Party, faction. *Changer de c.,* to change sides. (*b*) *Games:* Side. **Tirer les camps,** to pick sides.
campagnard, -arde [kɑ̃paɲaːr, -ard]. **I.** *a.* Country (gentleman, accent); rustic (simplicity). **2.** *s.* Countryman, -woman; rustic.
campagne [kɑ̃paɲ], *s.f.* **I.** (*a*) Plain; open country. **En rase campagne, en pleine campagne,** in the open (country). S.a. BATTRE I. (*b*) Country (-side). **A la campagne,** in the country. *Vie de c.,* country life. **Partie de campagne,** picnic. **2.** *Mil:* (The) field. **Artillerie de campagne,** field-artillery. **Tenir la campagne,** to keep the field. **Entrer, se mettre, en campagne,** (i) to take the field; (ii) *F:* to set to work. **3.** (*a*) Campaign. **Faire une campagne,** to go through a campaign. *F:* **Mener une campagne contre qn,** to lead, conduct, a campaign against s.o. *Com:* **Faire une bonne campagne,** to have a good season. (*b*) *Navy:* Cruise.
campagnol [kɑ̃paɲɔl], *s.m.* Z: (Field-)vole.
campanile [kɑ̃panil], *s.m.* Arch: Campanile; bell-tower.
campanule [kɑ̃panyl], *s.f.* Bot: Campanula.
Campêche [kɑ̃pɛʃ]. Pr.n. Geog: Campeachy. **Bois de Campêche,** logwood.
camp|er [kɑ̃pe]. **I.** *v.i.* To (en)camp; to pitch camp. **2.** *v.tr.* (*a*) To encamp (troops); to put (troops) under canvas. (*b*) *F:* To place, fix, put. *Il campa son chapeau sur sa tête,* he stuck, clapped, his hat on his head. **Camper là qn,** to leave s.o. in the lurch. *s.m.* **-ement.**
se camper. I. To encamp; to pitch one's camp. **2.** *Se c.* **solidement sur ses jambes,** to take a firm stand. *F:* **Se c. devant qn,** to plant oneself in front of s.o.
campé, *a.* *F:* **Bien c.,** well set-up (fellow).
camphre [kɑ̃fr], *s.m.* Camphor. **Essence de camphre,** camphor oil.
camphré [kɑ̃fre], *a.* Camphorated (oil, etc.).
camus [kamy], *a.* **I.** Flat-, snub-nosed (person); pug-nosed (dog). **2.** Flat, snub (nose).
can [kɑ̃], *s.m.* Edge (of board, etc.). **Sur can, de can,** on edge, edgewise.
Canada [kanada]. Pr.n.m. Canada. *Au C.,* in Canada.
canadien, -ienne [kanadjɛ̃, -jɛn], *a. & s.* Canadian.
canaille [kanɑːj, -aːj]. **I.** *s.f.* (*a*) *Coll.* Rabble, riff-raff. (*b*) Scoundrel, blackguard. **2.** *a.* Low, rascally; vulgar, coarse.
canaillerie [kanɑjri], *s.f.* *F:* **I.** Low(-down) trick; piece of blackguardism. **2.** Blackguardism.
canal, -aux [kanal, -o], *s.m.* **I.** (*a*) Channel (of river). (*b*) **Le Canal de la Manche,** the English Channel. (*c*) (i) Culvert. (ii) (Mill-)race. **2.** Canal. *C. maritime, de navigation,* ship-canal. **3.** (*a*) Pipe, conduit. *C. d'aérage,* air passage;

flue. *C. de fuite,* waste-pipe. (*b*) *Anat:* *Bot:* Duct, meatus. (*c*) *C. de graissage,* oil-groove.
canalisation [kanalizasjɔ̃], *s.f.* **I.** *Civ.E:* (*a*) Canalization (of river, etc.). (*b*) Draining (of plain). (*c*) Piping. **2.** (*a*) Pipes, pipe-work, mains. *C. électrique,* electrical mains; wiring. *C. de ville,* town mains. (*b*) Pipe-line (for mineral oils, etc.).
canaliser [kanalize], *v.tr.* **I.** To canalize (region, river). **2.** To lay down pipes, mains; to pipe (oil, etc.). *C. une maison pour l'électricité,* to wire a house for electric lighting.
canapé [kanape], *s.m.* **I.** Sofa, couch, settee. **2.** *Cu:* Slice of bread fried in butter. *C. d'anchois,* anchovy on toast.
canard [kanaːr], *s.m.* **I.** Duck; (of the male bird) drake. *C. sauvage,* wild duck. **Canard siffleur,** widgeon. *Chasse aux canards,* duck-shooting. *F:* **Mon petit canard,** ducky. **2.** (*a*) *F:* ·False report, hoax, canard. (*b*) Newspaper (of low repute); *F:* rag. **3.** *F:* Lump of sugar dipped in coffee, in brandy. **4.** *Mus:* False note (on reed instrument, etc.).
canardeau [kanardo], *s.m.* Duckling.
canarder [kanarde]. **I.** *v.i.* (Of ship) To pitch. **2.** *v.tr.* *C. qn,* to fire at s.o. from behind cover; to snipe s.o.
canardière [kanardjɛːr], *s.f.* **I.** Duck-pond. **2.** (*a*) Screen (for duck-shooting). (*b*) *Mil:* Loop-hole. **3.** Duck-gun; punt-gun.
canari [kanari], *s.m.* *Orn:* Canary.
Canaries [kanari]. Pr.n.f.pl. Les (îles) Canaries, the Canary Islands.
cancale [kɑ̃kal], *s.f.* Cancale oyster.
cancan [kɑ̃kɑ̃], *s.m.* *F:* **I.** (*a*) (Piece of) ill-natured gossip. (*b*) *pl.* Tittle-tattle, gossip. **2.** Cancan (dance).
cancaner [kɑ̃kane], *v.i.* *F:* To tittle-tattle; to talk scandal.
cancanier, -ière [kɑ̃kanje, -jɛːr]. *F:* **I.**·*a.* Fond of tittle-tattle. **2.** *s.* Gossip, scandal-monger.
cancer [kɑ̃sɛːr], *s.m.* **I.** *Astr:* Le Cancer, the Crab; Cancer. **2.** *Med:* Cancer.
cancéreux, -euse [kɑ̃serø, -øːz]. **I.** *a.* Cancerous. **2.** *s.* Cancer patient.
cancre [kɑ̃ːkr], *s.m.* **I.** Crab. **2.** *F:* Dunce, duffer.
candélabre [kɑ̃delɑːbr], *s.m.* (*a*) Candelabrum; branched candlestick. (*b*) Street lamp-post (with branched lamps).
candeur [kɑ̃dœːr], *s.f.* Ingenuousness, guileless-ness, artlessness.
candi [kɑ̃di], *a.m.* Candied. *Fruits candis,* cry-stallized fruit. **Sucre candi,** sugar-candy.
candidat [kɑ̃dida], *s.m.* Candidate, applicant (à une place, for a place); examinee. **Se porter candidat à la députation,** to stand for Parliament.
candidature [kɑ̃didatyːr], *s.f.* Candidature. **Poser sa candidature à un poste,** to offer oneself as a candidate for a post.
candide [kɑ̃did], *a.* Ingenuous, guileless, artless. *adv.* **-ment.**
Candie [kɑ̃di]. Pr.n.f. (L'île de) Candie, Crete, Candia.
cane [kan], *s.f.* Duck (as opposed to drake).
caner [kane]. **I.** *v.i.* *P:* To funk; to show the white feather. **2.** *v.tr.* *P:* *C. l'école,* to play truant from school.
caneton [kantɔ̃], *s.m.* Young (male) duck; duckling.
canette [kanɛt], *s.f.* **I.** Young (female) duck; duckling. **2.** Teal.
canevas [kanva], *s.m.* **I.** *Tex:* Canvas. *F:* **Broder le canevas,** to embroider the story. **2.** Groundwork, outline (of drawing, novel, etc.).

caniche [kaniʃ], *s. m. & f.* Poodle (dog, bitch).
caniculaire [kanikylɛːr], *a.* **1.** **Les jours caniculaires**, the dog-days. **2.** Sultry (heat, day).
canicule [kanikyl], *s.f.* The dog-days.
canif [kanif], *s.m.* Penknife.
canin [kanɛ̃], **1.** *a.* Canine. **Exposition canine**, dog-show. **2.** *s.f.* **Canine**, canine (tooth).
caniveau [kanivo], *s.m.* **1.** (*a*) Gutter-stone. (*b*) Gutter. **2.** Trough, conduit (for cables).
cannage [kanaːʒ], *s.m.* **1.** Cane-bottoming (of chairs). **2.** Cane bottom.
canne [kan], *s.f.* **1.** Cane, reed. **Canne à sucre**, sugar-cane. **Sucre de canne**, cane-sugar. **2.** Walking-stick; cane. *C. plombée*, loaded stick. (Escrime à) la canne, singlestick (play). **3.** Canne à pêche, fishing-rod.
canneberge [kanbɛrʒ], *s.f.* *Bot:* Cranberry.
canneler [kanle], *v.tr.* (je cannelle; je cannellerai) (*a*) To flute, channel. (*b*) To corrugate.
cannelier [kanəlje], *s.m.* *Bot:* Cinnamon-tree.
cannelle[1] [kanɛl], *s.f.* Cinnamon (bark).
cannelle[2], *s.f.* Spigot, faucet, tap.
cannelure [kanlyːr], *s.f.* (*a*) Groove, channel, slot. *Arch:* Fluting (of column). (*b*) Corrugation.
canner [kane], *v.tr.* To cane(-bottom) (chair).
cannetille [kantiːj], *s.f.* **1.** (Gold, silver) purl. **2.** Flat twisted braid (of gold or silver); bullion.
cannette [kanɛt], *s.f.* **1.** = CANNELLE[2]. **2.** *C. à bière*, beer-bottle (with patent stopper). **3.** (*a*) *Tex:* Cop, spool. (*b*) Spool (of sewing-machine).
cannibale [kanibal], *s.m.* Cannibal.
cannibalisme [kanibalism], *s.m.* Cannibalism.
canon[1] [kanɔ̃], *s.m.* **1.** *Mil:* *Navy:* (*a*) Gun, cannon. *C. rayé*, rifled gun. *C. de campagne*, field-gun. *C. de tranchée*, trench-mortar. **Poudre à canon**, gunpowder. *Navy:* *C. de bord*, naval gun. (*b*) *Coll.* Le gros *c.*, the heavy guns. **2.** (*a*) Barrel ((i) of rifle, (ii) of watch). **Fusil à deux canons**, double-barrelled gun. (*b*) Barrel, pipe (of key, of lock).
canon[2], *s.m.* **1.** *Ecc:* Canon, rule (of an order, of the Mass, etc.). *a.* **Droit canon**, canon law. **2.** *Mus:* Canon, round, catch.
canonique [kanɔnik], *a.* Canonical (book, etc.). **Age canonique**, (i) canonical age (for priest's housekeeper); (ii) *F:* respectable age.
canonis|er [kanɔnize], *v.tr.* *Ecc:* To canonize. *s.f.* **-ation**, -ation.
canonnade [kanɔnad], *s.f.* Cannonade; gun-fire.
canonner [kanɔne], *v.tr.* To cannonade (enemy); to batter (fort).
canonnier [kanɔnje], *s.m.* Gunner.
canonnière [kanɔnjɛːr], *s.f.* **1.** *Navy:* Gunboat. **2.** Loop-hole (for gun). **3.** *Toys:* Pop-gun.
canot [kano], *s.m.* (Open) boat; dinghy. **Faire une partie de canot**, to go boating. *Sp:* Canot glisseur, speed-boat.
canotage [kanɔtaːʒ], *s.m.* *Sp:* Boating, rowing. **Faire du canotage**, to go in for rowing.
canoter [kanɔte], *v.i.* To go in for boating, rowing.
canotier [kanɔtje], *s.m.* **1.** Rower; oarsman. **2.** Straw-hat; boater.
cantate [kɑ̃tat], *s.f.* *Mus:* Cantata.
cantatrice [kɑ̃tatris], *s.f.* (Professional) singer.
cantine [kɑ̃tin], *s.f.* **1.** (*a*) *Mil:* Canteen. (*b*) Soup-kitchen. **2.** *Mil:* (Officer's) uniform-case. **3.** *C. médicale*, field medical chest.
cantinier, -ière [kɑ̃tinje, -jɛːr], *s.* Canteen-keeper.
cantique [kɑ̃tik], *s.m.* *Ecc:* (*a*) Canticle. **Le Cantique des cantiques**, the Song of Songs. (*b*) Hymn.

canton [kɑ̃tɔ̃], *s.m.* **1.** Canton, district. **2.** *Civ.E:* Section (of road, railway).
cantonade [kɑ̃tɔnad], *s.f.* *Th:* (The) wings. **Parler à la cantonade**, to speak 'off.'
cantonal, -aux [kɑ̃tɔnal, -o], *a.* Cantonal; district (committee, etc.). *Route cantonale*, by-road.
cantonn|er [kɑ̃tɔne], *v.tr.* (*a*) To divide (district, etc.) into sections. (*b*) To confine (within circumscribed area); to isolate (sick animals, etc.). *Mil:* To quarter, billet (troops). *s.m.* **-ement**.
cantonnier [kɑ̃tɔnje], *s.m.* (*a*) Roadman, road-mender. (*b*) District road-surveyor. (*c*) *Rail:* Permanent-way man.
Cantorbéry [kɑ̃tɔrberi]. *Pr.n.m.* Canterbury.
canule [kanyl], *s.f.* *Med:* Nozzle (of syringe). *P:* **Quelle canule!** what a bore!
canuler [kanyle], *v.tr.* *P:* To bore (s.o.).
caoutchouc [kautʃu], *s.m.* **1.** (India-)rubber. **Solution de caoutchouc**, rubber solution. *Anneau en c.*, elastic band. **2.** (*a*) Waterproof(-coat); mackintosh. (*b*) *pl.* Galoshes. **3.** Solid tyre.
caoutchout|er [kautʃute], *v.tr.* **1.** To treat (sth.) with rubber; to rubberize (silk, etc.). **2.** *Roue caoutchoutée*, rubber-tyred wheel. *s.m.* **-age**.
cap [kap], *s.m.* **1.** *A:* Head. (Still used in) **De pied en cap**. See PIED 1. **2.** Cape, headland, foreland. **La colonie du Cap**, Cape Colony. **Franchir un cap**, (i) to weather, (ii) to round, a cape. **3.** *Nau:* etc: Head (of ship, airship). **Maintenir son cap**, to keep one's course. **Changement de cap**, change of course. **Mettre le cap au large**, to stand out to sea. S.a. VIRER I.
capable [kapabl], *a.* Capable. *Être c. de faire qch.*, to be capable of doing sth.; to be fit, able, to do sth.; to be equal to doing sth. **Homme très c.**, very able man. *adv.* **-ment**.
capacité [kapasite], *s.f.* **1.** Capacity (of vase, accumulator, etc.). **2.** (*a*) Capacity, ability, capability. **Homme de haute c.**, very able man. *F:* **Faire appel aux capacités**, to call for men of ability. (*b*) *Jur:* **Avoir capacité pour faire qch.**, to be (legally) entitled, qualified, to do sth.
caparacon [kaparasɔ̃], *s.m.* *Harn:* Caparison, trappings.
caparaçonner [kaparasɔne], *v.tr.* To caparison.
cape [kap], *s.f.* **1.** (Hooded) cape, cloak. **Roman de cape et d'épée**, historical romance of the cape and rapier period. *F:* **Rire sous cape**, to laugh up one's sleeve. **2.** *Nau:* **A la cape**, hove to. **Mettre à la cape**, prendre la cape, to heave to.
capel|er [kaple], *v.tr.* (je capelle; je capellerai) *Nau:* **1.** To rig (mast, spar, etc.). **2.** **Capeler une lame**, to take a green sea. *Le canot fut capelé par une lame*, the boat was swamped by a sea. *s.m.* **-age**.
capeline [kaplin], *s.f.* (*a*) *A:* Riding-hood. (*b*) Hooded cape; sun-bonnet.
Capharnaüm [kafarnaɔm]. **1.** *Pr.n.m.* Capernaum. **2.** *s.m.* *F:* Lumber-room; glory-hole.
capillaire [kapillɛːr]. **1.** *a.* Capillary (tube, attraction). *s.m.* **Les capillaires**, the capillary blood-vessels. **2.** *s.m.* Maidenhair fern.
capillarité [kapillarite], *s.f.* *Ph:* Capillarity.
capilotade [kapilɔtad], *s.f.* *Cu:* Hash. *F:* **Mis en c.**, knocked to smithereens. **Mettre qn en c.**, to beat s.o. to a jelly, black and blue.
capitaine [kapitɛn], *s.m.* (*a*) Captain. *Nau:* *C. de port*, harbour-master. *C. marchand*, ship-master. **Certificat de c.**, master's certificate. **Passer capitaine**, (i) *Mil:* to obtain one's captaincy; (ii) *Nau:* to obtain one's master's certificate. (*b*) Chief, head, leader. **Les grands capitaines de l'industrie**, the captains of industry.

capital, -aux [kapital, -o]. **I.** *a.* (*a*) Capital (crime, punishment). **La peine capitale,** the death penalty. (*b*) Essential, chief, principal. **Les sept péchés capitaux,** the seven deadly sins. *La ville capitale, s.f.* **la capitale,** the chief town ; the **capital.** *Affaire d'importance capitale,* affair of cardinal importance. (*c*) *Typ:* *Lettre capitale, s.f.* **une capitale,** capital (letter). **2.** *s.m. Fin:* Capital, assets. *C. et intérêt,* principal and interest. *C. social,* registered capital. *Les capitaux abondent,* money is plentiful.

capitalis|er [kapitalize], *v.tr.* To capitalize (interest, etc.). *Abs.* To save ; to put money by. *s.f.* **-ation.**

capitalisme [kapitalism], *s.m.* Capitalism.

capitaliste [kapitalist], *s. m. & f.* Capitalist.

capiteux, -euse [kapitø, -ø:z], *a.* (*a*) (Of wine) Heady. (*b*) Sensuous (charm, etc.).

capitonn|er [kapitɔne], *v.tr.* **I.** To upholster, pad (furniture). **2.** To quilt (petticoat, etc.). *s.m.* **-age.**

capitulation [kapitylasjɔ̃], *s.f.* Capitulation, surrender.

capituler [kapityle], *v.i. Mil:* To capitulate ; to surrender (on stipulated terms). *F: C. avec sa conscience,* to compromise with one's conscience.

capoc [kapɔk], *s.m. Com:* Kapok.

capon, -onne [kapɔ̃, -ɔn]. **I.** *a. F:* Afraid, cowardly. **2.** *s. F:* Coward, funk.

caponner [kapɔne], *v.i.* (*a*) To funk ; to show the white feather. (*b*) *Sch:* To sneak, peach ; to tell tales.

caporal, -aux [kapɔral, -o], *s.m.* **I.** Corporal. *F:* **Le petit Caporal,** Napoleon. **2.** SCAFERLATI.

caporaliser [kapɔralize], *v.tr. F:* To militarize, Prussianize.

capot¹ [kapo], *s.m.* **I.** *Mil:* Hooded great-coat. **2.** (*a*) Cover, hood, casing (of arc-lamp, etc.). *Aut:* Bonnet (of car). *Av:* Cowl(ing) (of engine). (*b*) *Nau:* Tarpaulin. **3.** *Nau:* Companion (hatch).

capot², *s.m.* **Faire capot** = CAPOTER.

capote [kapɔt], *s.f.* **I.** *Mil:* Great-coat, overcoat. **2.** (Lady's, baby's) bonnet. **3.** *Veh:* Hood. **4.** Cowl, hood (of chimney).

capot|er [kapɔte], *v.i.* **I.** *Nau:* To capsize ; to turn turtle. **2.** *Aut: Av:* To overturn. *s.m.* **-age.**

câpre [kɑ:pr], *s.f. Bot:* Caper. S.a. CAPUCINE 2.

caprice [kapris], *s.m.* Caprice, whim. **Faire qch. par caprice,** to do sth. on a sudden impulse.

capricieu|x, -euse [kaprisjø, -ø:z], *a.* Capricious, whimsical ; wayward ; temperamental (woman). *adv.* **-sement.**

capsule [kapsyl], *s.f.* **I.** *Bot: Pharm:* Capsule. **2.** *Ch: C. d'évaporation,* evaporating dish. **3.** *Sm.a: Min:* (Firing) cap ; primer. **4.** (*a*) Crown-cork (of bottle). (*b*) Seal (of bottle).

capsuler [kapsyle], *v.tr.* To seal, cap (bottle).

captage [kapta:ʒ], *s.m.* **I.** (*a*) *Hyd.E:* Collecting (of waters). *ÉLE:* Picking up (of current). (*b*) *Ind:* Recovery (of by-products). **2.** Watercatchment.

captation [kaptasjɔ̃], *s.f.* **I.** = CAPTAGE I. **2.** *Tg: Tp:* Tapping, 'milking' (of messages).

capter [kapte], *v.tr.* **I.** To obtain (sth.) by insidious means. *Tg: Tp:* To tap, 'milk' (messages). **2.** (*a*) To collect, pick up (electric current) ; to catch, impound (waters). (*b*) *Ind:* To recover (by-product).

captieu|x, -euse [kapsjø, -ø:z], *a.* Fallacious, specious, captious (argument). *adv.* **-sement.**

captif, -ive [kaptif, -i:v], *a. & s.* Captive ; prisoner.

captivant [kaptivɑ̃], *a.* Captivating ; winsome.

captiver [kaptive], *v.tr.* To captivate, enthral, charm (s.o.).

captivité [kaptivite], *s.f.* Captivity.

capture [kapty:r], *s.f.* **I.** Capture, seizure (of ship) ; apprehension (of deserter, etc.). **2.** Capture, prize.

capturer [kaptyre], *v.tr.* **I.** To capture (ship, etc.) ; to catch (whale, etc.). **2.** To collect (steam).

capuchon [kapyʃɔ̃], *s.m.* **I.** (*a*) Hood. (*b*) *Ecc:* Cowl. (*c*) Cap (of a bird). **2.** Cap, cover (of lamp) ; cap (of fountain-pen) ; chimney-cowl. *C. de valve,* valve-cap (of tyre valve).

capucin [kapysɛ̃], *s.m.* Capuchin friar.

capucine [kapysin], *s.f.* **I.** Capuchin nun. **2.** *Bot:* Nasturtium. **Câpres capucines,** nasturtium seeds. **3.** Band (of rifle).

caque [kak], *s.f.* Keg ; herring-barrel. *Prov:* **La caque sent toujours le hareng,** what's bred in the bone will come out in the flesh.

caquet [kake], *s.m.* **I.** Cackle, cackling (of hens, etc.). **2.** *A:* (Noisy) chatter ; idle gossip. **Elle lui a rabattu, rabaissé, le caquet,** she shut him up, made him sing small.

caquet|er [kakte], *v.i.* (**je caquète, je caquette** ; **je caquèterai, je caquetterai**) **I.** (Of hen, etc.) To cackle. **2.** *F:* To chatter. *s.m.* **-age.**

car¹ [ka:r], *conj.* For, because.

car², *s.m.* **I.** (Railway-, tramway-) car. **2.** (*a*) = AUTOCAR. (*b*) **Car de police,** police-van.

carabe [karab], *s.m. Ent:* Ground-beetle.

carabin [karabɛ̃], *s.m. P:* (i) Medico ; sawbones. (ii) Medical student.

carabine [karabin], *s.f.* (Cavalry) carbine ; rifle. *C. de salon,* gallery rifle.

carabiné [karabine], *a. Nau: Vent c.,* stiff gale. *F:* **Fièvre carabinée,** violent fever.

Carabosse [karabɔs]. *Pr.n.* **La fée Carabosse,** the wicked (hunch-backed) fairy.

caraco [karako], *s.m.* (Woman's) loose (working) jacket.

caracole [karakɔl], *s.f. Equit:* Caracol(e) ; halfturn. *F:* **Faire des caracoles,** to cut capers.

caractère [karaktɛ:r], *s.m.* **I.** Character ; graphic symbol. *Typ:* (Metal) type. **Écrire en petits caractères,** to write in a small hand. *Imprimer en gros caractères,* to print in large type. **2.** (*a*) Characteristic, feature. *L'affaire a pris un c. grave,* the affair has taken a serious complexion. (*b*) Official capacity (of ambassador, etc.). **Avoir caractère pour faire qch.,** to be entitled to do sth. **3.** (*a*) Nature, disposition. *Homme au c. emporté,* hot-tempered man. **Sortir de son caractère,** to lose one's temper. **Avoir mauvais caractère,** to be bad-tempered. **Avoir bon caractère,** to be good-natured. (*b*) Personality, character. *Avoir du c.,* to have character, grit. *Montrer du c.,* to show spirit. *Manquer de c.,* to lack strength of character, of will.

caractériser [karakterize], *v.tr.* To characterize. **se caractériser. I.** To assume, take on, character ; (of symptom, etc.) to become clearly marked. **2.** To be distinguished (*par,* by).

caractéristique [karakteristik]. **I.** *a.* Characteristic, distinctive ; typical (*de,* of). **2.** *s.f* Characteristic (of logarithm, etc.) ; salient feature.

carafe [karaf], *s.f.* (Glass) decanter ; waterbottle, carafe.

carafon [karafɔ̃], *s.m.* Small carafe.

caraïbe [karaib]. **I.** *a.* Caribbean. **2.** *s.m.* Carib.

carambolage [karãbɔla:ʒ], *s.m. Bill:* Cannon.

caramboler [karãbɔle]. **I.** *v.i. Bill:* To cannon.

2. *v.tr.* *F:* *Être carambolé par la foule,* to be buffeted by the crowd.

caramel [karamɛl], *s.m.* Caramel; burnt sugar.

carapace [karapas], *s.f.* Carapace, shell (of lobster, etc.). S.a. TORTUE 1.

carat [kara], *s.m.* Carat. (*a*) *Or à dix-huit carats* (*de fin*), eighteen-carat gold. (*b*) Carat (weight).

caravane [karavan], *s.f.* **1.** (*a*) Caravan; desert convoy. (*b*) *F:* Conducted party (of tourists, etc.). **2.** Caravan (vehicle).

caravanier [karavanje], *s.m.* Caravaneer.

caravansérail [karavɑ̃sɛra:j], *s.m.* Caravanserai.

caravelle [karavɛl], *s.f.* *Nau:* *A:* Caravel.

carbonate [karbɔnat], *s.m.* *Ch:* Carbonate. *C. de soude,* carbonate of soda; washing soda.

carbone [karbɔn], *s.m.* Carbon. **Papier carbone,** carbon paper.

carbonique [karbɔnik], *a.* *Ch:* Carbonic.

carbonis|er [karbɔnize], *v.tr.* (*a*) To carbonize (bones, etc.); to char (wood). (*b*) *Être carbonisé,* to be burnt to death (in house fire, accident). *s.f.* **-ation.**

carburant [karbyrɑ̃], *s.m.* Motor-fuel.

carburateur [karbyratœ:r], *s.m.* *I.C.E:* Carburettor.

carburation [karbyrasjɔ̃], *s.f.* *Ch:* Carburetting. *I.C.E:* Vaporization (of fuel).

carbure [karby:r], *s.m.* *Ch:* Carbide.

carburer [karbyre], *v.tr.* *Ch:* To carburet. *I.C.E:* To vaporize (fuel).

carcan [karkɑ̃], *s.m.* **1.** (*a*) *A:* Carcan, iron collar. (*b*) *Cost:* *Jewelry:* Choker. **2.** *P:* (Of horse) Jade, screw.

carcasse [karkas], *s.f.* **1.** Carcass, carcase. **2.** Framework; frame (of umbrella); shell, skeleton (of house, ship, etc.).

carcin [karsɛ̃], *s.m.* Green crab, shore-crab.

Cardan [kardɑ̃]. *Pr.n.m.* *Mec.E:* Joint de Cardan, à la Cardan, *s.m.* **cardan,** Cardan shaft; universal joint.

carde [kard], *s.f.* **1.** *Bot:* (*a*) Chard. (*b*) Teasel, bur. **2.** *Tex:* Carding-brush.

card|er [karde], *v.tr.* **1.** To card (wool). **2.** To teasel, raise (cloth). *s.m.* **-age.** *s.* **-eur, -euse.**

cardère [kardɛ:r], *s.f.* *Bot:* Teasel.

cardiaque [kardjak], *a.* Cardiac (murmur, etc.). *Crise cardiaque,* heart attack.

cardinal, -aux [kardinal, -o]. **1.** *a.* Cardinal (point, number, virtue). **2.** *s.m.* *Ecc:* Cardinal.

cardon [kardɔ̃], *s.m.* *Bot:* Cardoon.

carême [karɛm], *s.m.* Lent. **Faire son carême,** to keep Lent; to fast. *F:* **Figure de carême,** dismal face. S.a. MARÉE 2, MARS 2.

carénage [karena:ʒ], *s.m.* **1.** Careening (of ship). **2.** *Av:* *Aut:* Stream-lining.

carence [karɑ̃:s], *s.f.* **1.** *Jur:* Insolvency. **2.** Default(ing). **3.** *Med:* Deficiency (*de,* in, of). **Maladies de carence,** deficiency diseases.

carène [karɛn], *s.f.* Hull (of ship).

caréner [karene], *v.tr.* (je carène; je carénerai) **1.** To careen (ship). **2.** *Av:* *Aut:* To stream-line.

caresse [karɛs], *s.f.* Caress. **Faire des caresses à un chien,** to pat a dog.

caresser [karɛse], *v.tr.* **1.** To caress, fondle, stroke; to pat, make much of (animal). **Caresser qn du regard,** to look fondly at s.o. **2.** To cherish (hope, etc.).

caresseur, -euse [karɛsœ:r, -ø:z], *s.* Coaxer, wheedler.

cargaison [kargɛzɔ̃], *s.f.* Cargo, freight.

cargo [kargo], *s.m.* Cargo-boat; tramp (steamer).

cargue [karg], *s.f.* *Nau:* Brail (of sail).

carguer [karge], *v.tr.* *Nau:* To take in, clew (up) (sail).

cargueur [kargœ:r], *s.m.* *Nau:* Reefer.

caricature [karikaty:r], *s.f.* Caricature.

caricaturer [karikatyre], *v.tr.* To caricature (s.o.); to take (s.o.) off.

caricaturiste [karikatyrist], *s.m.* Caricaturist.

carie [kari], *s.f.* (*a*) Caries, decay (of bone). (*b*) Blight (of trees, etc.).

carier [karje], *v.tr.* To rot, decay. **se carier,** to rot, decay.

carillon [karijɔ̃], *s.m.* (*a*) Chime(s), carillon. **Horloge à carillon,** chiming clock. (*b*) Full peal of bells. (*c*) (In orchestra) Tubular bells.

carillonn|er [karijone], *v.i.* **1.** (*a*) To chime the bells; to ring a peal. (*b*) (Of bells) To chime. **2.** To jingle. *s.m.* **-ement.**

carillonneur [karijonœ:r], *s.m.* (*a*) Carillonneur; carillon player. (*b*) *pl.* Bell-ringers.

carlingage [karlɛga:ʒ], *s.m.* *N.Arch:* *Av:* Engine-bed, engine-bearers.

carlingue [karlɛ:g], *s.f.* **1.** *Nau:* Ke(e)lson. **2.** *Av:* (*a*) Fuselage. (*b*) *F:* Cockpit; cabin.

carlovingien [karlɔvɛ̃ʒjɛ̃], *a.* & *s.* *A:* = CAROLINGIEN.

carmagnole [karmaɲɔl], *s.f.* *Hist:* Carmagnole. (*a*) Jacket (worn by Revolutionaries in 1793). (*b*) Revolutionary dance and song.

carme [karm], *a.* & *s.m.* (**Frère**) **carme,** Carmelite Friar.

carmélite [karmelit], *s.f.* Carmelite (nun).

carmin [karmɛ̃], *s.m.* **1.** Carmine (colour). **2.** *Toil:* Rouge.

carminer [karmine], *v.tr.* To colour, dye, (sth.) carmine. *Se c. les lèvres,* to rouge one's lips.

carnage [karna:ʒ], *s.m.* Carnage, slaughter.

carnassier, -ière [karnasje, -jɛ:r]. **1.** *a.* Carnivorous, flesh-eating (animal). **2.** *s.m.* Carnivore. **3.** *s.f.* **Carnassière,** game-bag.

carnation [karnasjɔ̃], *s.f.* *Art:* (*a*) Flesh-tint, carnation. (*b*) Rendering of flesh-tints.

carnaval, pl. -als [karnaval], *s.m.* Carnival.

carné [karne], *a.* **1.** Flesh-coloured. **2.** *Med:* *Diète carnée,* meat diet.

carneau [karno], *s.m.* (Boiler) flue.

carnet [karnɛ], *s.m.* Note-book. *C. de commandes,* order-book. *C. de banque,* pass-book. *C. de chèques,* cheque-book. *C. de bal,* dance card.

carnet-répertoire, *s.m.* Address-book. *pl. Des carnets-répertoires.*

carnier [karnje], *s.m.* Game-bag.

carnivore [karnivɔ:r], *a.* Carnivorous.

carolingien, -ienne [karɔlɛ̃ʒjɛ̃, -jɛn], *a.* & *s.* *Fr.Hist:* Carolingian, Carlovingian.

Caron [karɔ̃]. *Pr.n.m.* *Myth:* Charon.

caroncules [karɔ̃kyl], *s.f. pl.* Wattles (of turkey).

carotte [karɔt, ka-], *s.f.* **1.** Carrot. *a.inv. F:* **Cheveux (rouge) carotte,** carroty, ginger, hair. **2.** Plug (of tobacco). **3.** *P:* Trick, sell. **Tirer une carotte à qn,** (i) to play a trick on s.o.; (ii) to diddle s.o. out of his money.

carott|er [karɔte, ka-], *v.tr.* *P:* (*a*) *C. qch. à qn,* to do s.o. out of sth. (*b*) *Mil:* *C. le service,* to shirk duty. *C. une permission,* to wangle a leave. *s.m.* **-age.** *s.m.* **-eur.**

Carpathes [karpat]. *Pr.n.m.pl.* **Les (monts) Carpathes,** the Carpathian Mountains.

carpe [karp], *s.f.* *Ich:* Carp. *F:* **Faire des sauts de carpe,** to flop about, to somersault. **Faire des yeux de carpe pâmée,** to show the whites of one's eyes.

carpette [karpɛt], *s.f.* Rug.

carpillon [karpijɔ̃], *s.m.* (Very) small carp.

carquois [karkwa], *s.m.* Quiver. *F:* **Il a vidé son carquois,** he has shot all his bolts.

Carrare [kara:r]. **I.** *Pr.n. Geog:* Carrara.
2. *s.m.* Carrara marble.

carré, -ée [kare]. **I.** *a.* (*a*) Square (figure,
garden, etc.).. *Mth:* Nombre carré, square number. *Dix mètres carrés* (i) ten square metres ;
(ii) ten metres square. *Nau:* Trois-mâts carré,
square-rigged three-masted vessel. *F:* Partie
carrée, pleasure party of two men and two women.
Tête carrée, (i) level-headed man ; (ii) stubborn
man. S.a. RACINE I. (*b*) *F:* Plain, straightforward, blunt (answer, person, etc.). **2.** *s.m.* (*a*)
Mth: Square. *C. d'un nombre,* square of a number. (*b*) *C. de papier,* slip of paper. *C. d'un escalier,*
landing of a staircase. *C. de choux,* cabbage-patch.
Mil: C. creux, vide, hollow square. Carré des
officiers, *Nau:* mess-room, *Navy:* ward-room.

carreau [karo], *s.m.* **I.** Small square. *Étoffe à
carreaux,* check material. **2.** (*a*) (Flooring) tile ;
flag. (*b*) Carreau de vitre, window-pane. **3.** (*a*)
Floor (of room). *F:* Rester sur le carreau, to be
left dead on the field. (*b*) (In Paris) Le carreau
des Halles, the (floor of the) market. **4.** *Cards:*
Diamonds. *F:* Se garder à carreau, to take every
precaution. **5.** *A:* Bolt, quarrel (of cross-bow).

carrefour [karfu:r], *s.m.* Cross-roads ; (in town)
square, circus. *F:* Musicien de c., street musician.

carrelage [karla:ʒ], *s.m.* **I.** Tiling. **2.** Tile-,
flagstone-pavement or floor(ing).

carreler [karle], *v.tr.* (je carrelle ; je carrellerai)
I. To lay (floor) with tiles ; to pave (yard).
2. To draw squares on (sheet of paper). Étoffe
carrelée, check material.

carrelet [karle], *s.m. Ich:* Plaice ; dab.

carrément [karemã], *adv.* Square(ly). *Se tenir
c. sur ses jambes,* to stand firmly, squarely, on
one's legs. *Agir c.,* to act (i) on the square,
(ii) without beating about the bush. *Dire c. qch.
à qn,* to tell s.o. sth. (i) straightforwardly, (ii)
bluntly, flat, straight out.

carrer [kare], *v.tr.* To square (plank, number).
se carrer. *Se c. en marchant,* to strut,
swagger, along. *Le maire se carrait dans son
fauteuil,* the mayor was sitting in his chair looking
very important.

carrier [karje], *s.m.* **I.** Quarryman. **2.** Quarry-
owner.

carrière¹ [karjɛ:r], *s.f.* **I.** *A:* Race-course,
arena. *F:* Être au bout de sa carrière, to be at
the end of one's life. *La c. du succès,* the road to
success. Ouvrir une belle carrière à qn, to open
a fine field of action for s.o. **2.** *Equit:* Donner
carrière à un cheval, to give free rein to a horse.
F: Donner libre carrière à son imagination, to
give free play to one's fancy. **3.** Career. Soldat
de carrière, regular (soldier). Embrasser une
carrière, to take up a career.

carrière², *s.f.* Stone-pit, quarry.

carriole [karjol], *s.f. Veh:* Light cart.

carrossable [karosabl], *a.* Carriageable.

carrosse [karos], *s.m. A:* Coach. *C. d'apparat,*
state-coach. *F:* Rouler carrosse, to ride in a
carriage ; to have a carriage.

carrosser [karose], *v.tr.* **I.** To convey (s.o.) in
a coach, a carriage. **2.** *Aut:* To fit the body to
(chassis).

carrosserie [karosri], *s.f.* **I.** Coach-building,
body-building. **2.** Body (of car, etc.).

carrossier [karosje], *s.m.* (*a*) Coach-, carriage-
builder. (*b*) *Aut:* Body-builder.

carrousel [karuzel], *s.m.* **I.** *A:* (*a*) Tournament.
(*b*) Tilt-yard. **2.** Merry-go-round ; roundabout.

carrure [kary:r], *s.f.* Breadth (of pers., of coat)
across the shoulders. *Homme d'une belle c.,* well-

built man. *Gaillard de forte c.,* burly fellow.
[CARRER]

cartable [kartabl], *s.m.* **I.** Writing-pad. **2.** (Cardboard) portfolio. **3.** School satchel.

carte [kart], *s.f.* **I.** *A:* Sheet of paper. Carte
blanche, (i) blank paper (bearing signature) ;
(ii) full warrant to act for the best. *F:* Donner,
laisser, carte blanche à qn, to give s.o. a free
hand. **2.** Map. *C. d'état-major,* ordnance survey
map. *C. routière,* road-map. *C. marine,* (sea-)
chart. Dresser la carte d'une région, to map a
region. Porter sur la carte, to chart (an island,
etc.). Perdre la carte, (i) to lose one's bearings ;
(ii) *F:* to get flustered. **3.** (Piece of) pasteboard
or cardboard. Carte à jouer, playing card.
Jouer aux cartes, to play cards. Faire les cartes,
to deal. Jouer cartes sur table, (i) to show one's
hand ; (ii) to act fairly and above-board. *F:*
Connaître, voir, le dessous des cartes, to be in
the know. Brouiller les cartes, to embroil matters.
On ne sait jamais avec lui de quelle carte il
retourne, you never know where you are with
him. S.a. TIRER 4. Carte de visite, visiting-card.
Faire passer sa c. à qn, to send in one's card.
Mettre des cartes chez qn, to leave cards on s.o.
C. d'entrée, admission card. Carte postale, postcard. *C. postale illustrée,* picture postcard. Carte
d'abonnement, season-ticket. *Aut:* Carte grise,
= car licence. Carte rose = driving licence.
Carte de restaurant, bill of fare ; menu. *C. du
jour,* menu for the day. C. des vins, wine-list.
Manger, dîner, à la carte, to eat, dine, à la
carte.

cartel¹ [kartel], *s.m.* **I.** *Mil: Navy:* Agreement
for exchange of prisoners. **2.** (*a*) Dial-case (of
clock). (*b*) Hanging wall-clock. **3.** *Her:* C.
d'armoiries, shield, escutcheon.

cartel², *s.m. Com:* Cartel, trust, combine, ring.
Pol: Le Cartel des Gauches, the Radical
coalition.

carte-lettre [kartəlɛtr], *s.f.* Letter-card. *pl. Des
cartes-lettres.*

carter [karte:r], *s.m.* **I.** *Cy:* Gear-case. **2.** Casing, housing (of crank, etc.). *Cin:* Spool-box.

carthaginois, -oise [kartaʒinwa, -wa:z], *a. & s.*
A. Geog: Carthaginian.

cartilage [kartila:ʒ], *s.m.* Cartilage ; *F:* gristle.

cartilagineux, -euse [kartilaʒinø, -ø:z], *a.*
Cartilaginous ; *F:* gristly.

cartographe [kartograf], *s.m.* Map-maker.

cartographie [kartografi], *s.f.* **I.** Map-making,
mapping. **2.** Collection of maps.

cartomancie [kartomãsi], *s.f.* Cartomancy ;
fortune-telling (by cards).

carton [kartɔ̃], *s.m.* **I.** Cardboard ; pasteboard.
C. épais, millboard. *C. paille,* strawboard. *
F:* Homme de carton, man of straw. Maison de
carton, jerry-built house. *F:* Déposer son carton
chez qn, to leave one's card on s.o. Poupée de c.,
papier mâché doll. *Nez en c.,* pasteboard nose,
2. Cardboard box. *C. à chapeau,* bandbox.
C. à chapeaux, hat-box. *C. à dessins,* portfolio.
C. d'écolier, satchel. *C. de bureau,* filing-case.
F: Ma demande est restée dans les cartons, my
request has been pigeon-holed, shelved. **3.** *Art:*
Cartoon ; small sketch. **4.** (*a*) *Phot: etc:* Mount.
(*b*) Miniature target (at shooting-range). *Faire un
bon c.,* to make a good score.

cartonnage [kartona:ʒ], *s.m.* **I.** *Coll.* (Cardboard)
boxes, cases. **2.** *Bookb:* (Binding in) paper
boards ; boarding, casing. *C. pleine toile,* (binding in) cloth boards. *C. souple,* limp boards.

cartonner [kartone], *v.tr.* To bind (book) in
boards ; to case (book).

cartonnier, -ière [kartɔnje, -jɛːr], s. **1.** Cardboard-maker, -seller. **2.** s.m. (Cardboard) file; file-case.

carton-pâte, s.m. inv. Papier mâché.

cartouche [kartuʃ]. **1.** s.m. Scroll (round title, etc.); cartouche. **2.** s.f. Cartridge. Cent cartouches, a hundred rounds (of ammunition). C. à balle, ball cartridge. C. de chasse, sporting cartridge.

cartouchière [kartuʃjɛːr], s.f. Cartridge-pouch.

carvi [karvi], s.m. Bot: Caraway. Graines de carvi, caraway seeds.

cas [kɑ], s.m. **1.** (a) Case, instance. Cas limite, border-line case. Cas imprévu, (i) emergency; (ii) act of God. F: C'est bien le cas de le dire, . . . and no mistake. C'est le cas ou jamais de . . ., now, if ever, is the time to. . . . Être dans le cas de faire qch., to be in a position to do sth. (b) Cas juridique, legal case, cause. (c) Cas médical, medical case. **2.** Case, matter, affair. Cela change le cas, that alters the case, the matter. **3.** Faire cas de qn, de qch., to value s.o., sth. Faire peu de cas de qch., to set little value on sth. Faire grand cas de qn, to have a high opinion of s.o. **4.** Gram: Case. Au cas nominatif, in the nominative case. **5.** En ce cas, in that case. Dans, en, aucun cas, in no case, under no circumstances, on no account. En tout cas, dans tous les cas, in any case, at all events. Le cas échéant, should the occasion arise. Selon le cas, as the case may be. En cas de nécessité, in case of need. Au cas où, dans le cas où, il viendrait, in the event of his coming. Pour le cas où vous désireriez quelque chose, in case you should want anything. Au, en, cas qu'il n'y soit pas, in case he should not be there.

casanier, -ière [kazanje, -jɛːr], a. Home-loving; stay-at-home.

casaque [kazak], s.f. **1.** Mil: A: (Musketeer's) surtout. F: Tourner casaque, to turn one's coat; F: to rat. **2.** (a) Coat, jacket (of jockey, liveried servant). (b) (Woman's) jumper.

casaquin [kazakɛ̃], s.m. (a) Dressing-jacket. (b) Jumper(-blouse).

cascade [kaskad], s.f. **1.** Cascade, waterfall. El: Batterie en cascade, battery in series. **2.** F: (a) Piece of reckless foolishness. (b) Gay time; spree. (c) Th: Gag.

cascader [kaskade], v.i. F: (a) To live a wild life; to go the pace. (b) Th: To gag.

cascadeur, -euse [kaskadœːr, -øːz], s. F: Reveller.

case [kɑːz], s.f. **1.** Small dwelling; hut, cabin. **2.** (a) Compartment, division (of drawer, etc.); pigeon-hole. Case postale, Post Office box. (b) Division, space to be filled (on printed form). (c) Square (of chess-board).

caséeux, -euse [kazeø, -øːz], a. Caseous, cheesy.

caser [kɑze], v.tr. To put, stow, (sth.) away. C. des papiers, to file, pigeon-hole, papers. F: C. qn, to find a place, employment, for s.o. C. sa fille, to find a husband for one's daughter. [CASE]
  se caser, to settle down.

caserne [kazɛrn], s.f. (a) Barracks. F: Plaisanteries de caserne, barrack-room jokes. (b) C. de pompiers, fire(-brigade) station.

casern|er [kazɛrne], v.tr. To quarter (troops) in barracks. s.m. **-ement.**

casier [kɑzje], s.m. **1.** (a) Set of pigeon-holes. (b) Casier judiciaire, record of punishments (of convict, etc.). **2.** (a) Bin, rack. C. à bouteilles, bottle-rack. (b) C. à musique, music-cabinet.

casino [kazino], s.m. Casino.

casoar [kazɔaːr], s.m. Orn: Cassowary.

caspien, -ienne [kaspjɛ̃, -jɛn], a. La mer Caspienne, the Caspian (Sea).

casque [kask], s.m. (a) Helmet. C. respiratoire, smoke-helmet. C. blindé, crash-helmet. P: Avoir le casque, to have a head (after drinking). (b) W.Tel: Casque téléphonique, (i) head bands of the receiver; (ii) head-phones, head set.

casquer [kaske], v.i. P: To pay up, fork out.

Casquets (les) [lɛkaskɛ], s.m.pl. Geog: The Caskets.

casquette [kaskɛt], s.f. Peaked cap.

cassant, a. **1.** (a) Brittle (china, etc.). (b) Crisp (biscuit, etc.). **2.** Curt, abrupt (tone of voice). Être c. avec qn, to be short with s.o.

cassation [kɑsasjɔ̃], s.f. **1.** Jur: Cassation, quashing, setting aside (of sentence, will). Cour de cassation, Supreme Court of Appeal. **2.** Reduction (of N.C.O.) to the ranks.

casse[1] [kɑːs], s.f. Typ: Case. Bas, haut, de casse, lower case, upper case.

casse[2] [kɑsɑ], s.f. **1.** Bot: Cassia. **2.** Pharm: Senna.

casse[3], s.f. (a) Breakage, damage. F: Il y aura de la casse, there will be trouble. (b) Coll. Breakages.

casse-cou, s.m.inv. **1.** Break-neck place; death-trap; Aut: dangerous corner. **2.** Dare-devil; reckless fellow.

casse-croûte, s.m.inv. **1.** Snack. **2.** Quick-lunch bar.

casse-gueule, s.m.inv. P: **1.** Raw spirit. **2.** Low dancing-hall.

casse-noisette(s), s.m.inv. **1.** (Pair of) nut-crackers. F: Menton en casse-noisette, nut-cracker chin. **2.** Orn: Nuthatch.

casse-noix, s.m.inv. (Pair of) nut-crackers.

casse-pierre(s), s.m.inv. Bot: (a) Saxifrage. (b) Samphire. (c) Pellitory.

cass|er [kɑse], v.tr. **1.** To break, snap; to crack (nuts, etc.). Casser la tête à qn, (i) to crack s.o.'s skull; (ii) F: to importune s.o. Se casser la tête, (i) to break one's head; (ii) F: to rack, cudgel, one's brains. Se casser le cou, (i) to break one's neck; (ii) F: to come a cropper. P: Ça ne casse rien, it's not up to much. Applaudir à tout casser, to bring down the house (with applause). S.a. BRAS 1, CROÛTE 1, SUCRE. **2.** To cashier, break, degrade (s.o.). C. un sous-officier (de son grade), to reduce an N.C.O. (to the ranks). **3.** Jur: To annul, quash, set aside (verdict, will). s.m. **-age.**
  se casser. **1.** To break, snap, give way, part. **2.** (Of pers.) To break up.
    cassé, a. Broken, worn out (voice, person).

casserole [kasrɔl], s.f. (Sauce)pan, stewpan. Veau en casserole, braised veal.

casse-tête, s.m.inv. **1.** (a) (War-)club, tomahawk. (b) Loaded stick, life-preserver. (c) Truncheon. **2.** Puzzling task. Casse-tête chinois, Chinese puzzle. **3.** Din, racket.

cassette [kasɛt], s.f. (a) Casket; case. (b) Money-box. A: Biens de la Cassette, Crown estates.

casseur, -euse [kasœːr, -øːz]. s. **1.** Breaker. C. de pierres, stone-breaker. F: Casseur d'assiettes, blusterer. **2.** a. (a) Domestique casseuse, maid who smashes everything. (b) Aggressive (look, manner).

cassine [kasin], s.f. **1.** Country-box, cottage. **2.** Mil: Blockhouse.

cassis[1] [kɑsi(s)], s.m. **1.** Black-currant. **2.** Black-currant liqueur.

cassis[2] [kɑsi], s.m. Cross-drain, open gutter (across road). [CASSER]

cassonade [kasɔnad], s.f. Brown sugar, moist sugar.

cassure [kɑsyːr], s.f. **1.** (a) Break, fracture. (b) Fractured edge. **2.** Broken fragment.

castagnettes [kastaɲɛt], s.f.pl. Castanets.

caste [kast], s.f. Caste. **Esprit de caste**, class consciousness. **Hors caste**, outcaste.

castel [kastɛl], s.m. (a) A: (In S. of Fr.) Castle. (b) Iron: Baronial hall.

castillan, -ane [kastijɑ̃, -an], a. & s. Castilian.

Castille [kastiːj]. Pr.n.f. Geog: Castile.

castor [kastɔːr], s.m. **1.** Beaver. **2.** Com: (a) Beaver fur. (b) A: Beaver(-hat).

castrat [kastra], s.m. Eunuch.

casuel, -elle [kazɥɛl]. **1.** a. (a) Fortuitous, accidental. (b) Gram: Flexions casuelles, case-endings. (c) Inherent in the case. **2.** s.m. Perquisites, fees (in addition to fixed salary). adv. **-ellement.**

casuiste [kazɥist], s.m. (a) Casuist. (b) F: Sophist.

casuistique [kazɥistik], s.f. Casuistry.

cataclysme [kataklism], s.m. Cataclysm, disaster.

catacombes [katakɔ̃ːb], s.f.pl. Catacombs.

catafalque [katafalk], s.m. Catafalque.

cataire [katɛːr], s.f. Bot: Catmint.

catalan, -ane [katalɑ̃, -an], a. & s. Catalan, Catalonian.

catalepsie [katalɛpsi], s.f. Catalepsy.

cataleptique [katalɛptik], a. & s. Med: Cataleptic (patient, etc.).

Catalogne [katalɔɲ]. Pr.n.f. Catalonia.

catalogue [katalɔg], s.m. Catalogue, list. C. raisonné, descriptive catalogue.

cataloguer [katalɔge], v.tr. To catalogue; to list. s.m. **-ement.** s.m. **-eur.**

catalyse [kataliːz], s.f. Ch: Catalysis.

catalytique [katalitik], a. Ch: Catalytic.

cataplasme [kataplasm], s.m. Med: Poultice. C. sinapisé, mustard-plaster. C. à mie de pain, bread-poultice.

cataracte [katarakt], s.f. **1.** Cataract, falls. F: Lâcher les cataractes, to pour out the vials of one's wrath. **2.** Med: Cataract.

catarrhe [kataːr], s.m. Med: Catarrh.

catastrophe [katastrɔf], s.f. Catastrophe. **1.** Dénouement (of tragedy, etc.). **2.** Disaster. C. financière, crash.

catéchiser [kateʃize], v.tr. **1.** (a) Ecc: To catechize. (b) F: To coach (s.o.) up (in what to say). **2.** (a) To reason with (s.o.). (b) To lecture (s.o.).

catéchisme [kateʃism], s.m. Catechism. Aller au catéchisme, to go to a catechism class.

catéchiste kateʃist], s.m. & f. Catechist, catechizer.

catégorie [kategɔri], s.f. Category.

catégorique [kategɔrik], a. (a) Categorical (proposition). (b) Categorical; explicit, clear (answer). Refus c., flat refusal. adv. **-ment.**

caténaire [katenɛːr], a. **1.** Catenary (suspension of bridge, etc.). **2.** Ch: Réactions caténaires, chain of reactions.

cathédrale [katedral], s.f. Cathedral.

Catherine [katrin]. Pr.n.f. Catherine, Katherine. F: Coiffer sainte Catherine, (of woman) to have reached one's twenty-fifth birthday without marrying.

cathode [katɔd], s.f. El: Cathode.

cathodique [katɔdik], a. El: Cathodic. Tube à rayons cathodiques, cathode ray tube.

catholicisme [katɔlisism], s.m. (Roman) Catholicism.

catholicité [katɔlisite], s.f. **1.** Catholicity, orthodoxy. **2.** The (Roman) Catholic Church.

catholique [katɔlik]. **1.** a. Orthodox. F: Ce n'est pas c., it looks, sounds, fishy. **2.** a. & s. (Roman) Catholic.

cati [kati], s.m. Tex: Gloss, lustre.

catilinaire [katilinɛːr], s.f. (a) Catiline oration (of Cicero). (b) F: Diatribe, outburst.

catimini (en) [ɑ̃katimini], adv.phr. Stealthily; on the sly. Entrer, sortir, en c., to steal in, out.

cation [katjɔ̃], s.m. El: Cation.

catir [katiːr], v.tr. Tex: To press, gloss (material). s.m. **-issage.** s. **-isseur, -euse.**

Caton [katɔ̃]. Pr.n.m. Rom.Hist: Cato.

Caucase (le) [ləkokaːz]. Pr.n. The Caucasus.

cauchemar [koʃmaːr, ko-], s.m. Nightmare. Avoir le cauchemar, to have (a) nightmare. F: Il me donne le cauchemar, he is my bugbear, my pe aversion.

cauchemarder [koʃmarde, ko-], v.tr. P: **1.** To bore (s.o.) stiff; to get on (s.o.'s) nerves. **2.** Ça me cauchemardait, it was a nightmare to me.

caudal, -aux [kodal, -o], a. Z: Caudal.

cauri [kori], s.m. Cowrie.

causailler [kozaje], v.i. F: To chatter; to indulge in small talk.

causal [kozal], a. No m.pl. Gram: Causal, causative (proposition, etc.).

causant [kozɑ̃], a. F: **1.** Chatty, talkative (person). **2.** Dîner très c., chatty dinner.

cause [koːz], s.f. **1.** Cause. C. de défiance, cause, grounds, for distrust. C. première, prime cause. C. seconde, secondary cause. Être cause de qch., to be the cause of sth. Pour quelle c.? for what reason? on what grounds? Il ne viendra pas et pour cause, he will not come and for a very good reason. Maison à céder pour cause de faillite, house for sale in consequence of bankruptcy. Absent pour c. de santé, absent for reasons of health. Prep.phr. A cause de, on account of; owing to. C'est à c. de moi qu'il a manqué le train, it was through me that he lost his train. **2.** (a) Jur: Cause, suit, action. Causes célèbres, famous trials. Avocat sans cause, briefless barrister. Être chargé d'une c., to hold a brief. Être en cause, (i) to be a party to a suit; (ii) F: to be concerned in sth. Mettre qn en cause, to implicate s.o. Mettre en c. la probité de qn, to question s.o.'s honesty. Questions hors de cause, irrelevant questions. Mettre qn hors de cause, to exonerate s.o. Agir en connaissance de cause, to act with full knowledge of the case. (b) C'est pour une bonne c., it is for a good cause. Souffrir pour une c., to suffer in a cause. Faire cause commune avec qn, to make common cause with s.o.; to side with s.o. S.a. FAIT² 2.

causer¹ [koze], v.tr. To cause. C. un changement, to bring about a change.

causer², v.i. To converse, chat. C. avec, F: à, qn, to have a chat, a talk, with s.o. Causer de la pluie et du beau temps, to talk about the weather, of one thing and the other; to indulge in small talk. C. musique, to talk music.

causerie [kozri], s.f. (a) Talk, chat. (b) Chatty lecture.

causette [kozɛt], s.f. F: Little chat. Faire la causette avec qn, to have a bit of a chat with s.o.

causeur, -euse [kozœːr, -øːz]. **1.** a. Talkative, chatty. **2.** s. Talker, conversationalist. **3.** s.f. Causeuse, small sofa or settee.

causoter [kozɔte], v.i. F: To chat familiarly; to indulge in small talk.

caustique [kostik]. **1.** a. (a) Ch: Caustic, burning. (b) Biting, caustic, cutting (remark, etc.). **2.** s.m. Pharm: Caustic. adv. **-ment.**

cauteleu|x, -euse [kotlø, -øːz], *a.* **1.** Cunning, wily, sly. **2.** Wary, cautious. *adv.* **-sement.**

cautère [koteːr], *s.m.* **1.** *Med:* Cautery. **2.** Rowel (of spur).

cautéris|er [koterize], *v.tr.* To cauterize (wound, etc.). *C. une dent,* to kill the nerve of a tooth. *s.f.* **-ation,** -ation.

caution [kosjɔ̃], *s.f.* **1.** Security, guarantee, bail-bond. Donner caution pour qn, to go bail for s.o. ; to be surety for s.o. Mettre qn en liberté sous caution, to admit s.o. to bail ; to let s.o. out on bail. *Com:* Verser une c., to pay a deposit. *F:* Sujet à caution, unreliable, unconfirmed (news, etc.). **2.** Surety, guaranty, bail(-bonds-man). Se rendre caution de qn, se porter caution pour qn, (i) to go bail for s.o. ; (ii) *Com:* to stand surety for s.o.

cautionnement [kosjɔnmɑ̃], *s.m.* *Com:* (a) Surety-bond, guarantee. (b) Caution-money.

cautionner [kosjɔne], *v.tr.* To stand surety for (s.o.). *Jur:* To go bail for (s.o.).

cavalcade [kavalkad], *s.f.* **1.** Cavalcade. **2.** Pageant(-procession).

cavale [kaval], *s.f.* *Lit:* Mare.

cavaler (se) [səkavale], *v.pr.* *P:* To run away ; to scoot.

cavalerie [kavalri], *s.f.* Cavalry.

caval|ier, -ière [kavalje, -jɛːr]. **1.** *s.* Rider ; horseman, horsewoman. *a.* Piste cavalière, (i) riding track ; (ii) bridle-path. **2.** *s.m.* (a) *Mil:* Trooper. (b) *Chess:* Knight. (c) Gentleman, gallant. *Hist:* Cavaliers et Têtes rondes, Cavaliers and Roundheads. (d) (Gentleman acting as) escort (to a lady). (e) Partner (to lady at ball) ; gentleman (in square dance). **3.** *s.m.* (a) Staple. (b) Rider (of balance). **4.** *a.* Cavalierish, off-hand ; rakish, jaunty (air). A la cavalière, in a cavalierish, off-hand, manner. *adv.* **-ièrement.**

cave¹ [kaːv], *a.* Hollow, sunken (cheeks).

cave², s.f. **1.** Cellar, vault. Avoir une bonne cave, to keep a good cellar (of wine). **2.** Cave à liqueurs, liqueur cabinet. **3.** *Aut:* Foot-well.

cave³, s.f. *Cards:* Money put up by each player (at beginning of game) ; stake.

caveau [kavo], *s.m.* **1.** Small (wine-)cellar ; vault. **2.** Burial vault.

caver¹ [kave], *v.tr.* To hollow (out), dig (out), excavate, undermine.

se caver, to become hollow.

caver². *Cards:* **1.** *v.tr.* To put up (so many counters or so much money). **2.** *v.i.* To put up a stake. *F:* C. sur la bêtise humaine, to count upon, *F:* bank on, human foolishness.

caverne [kavɛrn], *s.f.* (a) Cave, cavern. (b) Den (of thieves). (c) *Med:* Cavity (in lungs, etc.).

caverneux, -euse [kavɛrnø, -øːz], *a.* **1.** Cavernous, caverned (mountain, rock). **2.** Hollow, sepulchral (voice).

caviar [kavjaːr], *s.m.* **1.** Caviar(e). **2.** *F:* Blocked-out passage (in newspaper).

caviarder [kavjarde], *v.tr.* *F:* To suppress, block out (passage in paper, etc.).

cavité [kavite], *s.f.* Cavity, hollow ; pit (in metal).

ce¹ [s(ə)], *dem.pron.neut.* (C' before parts of *être* beginning with a vowel. Also *ç'a été, ç'aura été.*) It, that. **1.** (Used as neut. subject to *être, devoir être, pouvoir être*) (a) (With adj. or adv. complement) *C'est faux!* it is untrue ! *Ce doit être faux,* it is probably untrue. *Le voilà, ce n'est pas trop tôt!* there he is and none too soon ! *Est-ce* [ɛs] *assez?* is that enough ? (b) (With sb. or pron. as complement) (With a 3rd pers. pl. complement the verb should be in the plural, but

familiar usage allows the singular.) *C'est moi, c'est nous, ce sont eux, F: c'est eux,* it is I, we, they. Si ce n'est, except, unless. (This phr. is invariable.) *Personne si ce n'est vos parents,* no one unless it be your parents. *C'est un soldat de l'Empire,* that is a soldier of the Empire period. Note. Cp. *Il est soldat, il est vicomte* (where the sb. is adjectival). (c) Ce . . . ici = CECI. *Ce n'est pas ici une auberge!* this is not an inn ! (d) Ce . . . là = CELA. *Ce n'est pas là mon parapluie,* that is not my umbrella. (e) (Representing a subject which has been isolated in order that it may be stressed) *Paris, c'est bien loin! c'est bien loin, Paris!* it's a far cry to Paris ! *Le temps c'est de l'argent,* time is money. (f) (Anticipating the subject) *C'est demain dimanche,* to-morrow is Sunday. (g) (i) *F:* (As temporary subject when an adj. is followed by a sb. clause or an inf. subject. Careful speech requires il.) *C'était inutile de sonner,* you need not have rung. (ii) (Normally in *c'est* + *adv.* or *adv.phr.*) *C'est assez qu'il veuille bien pardonner,* that he is willing to forgive is enough. *C'est à vous de vous en occuper,* it is for you to see to it. (h) **C'est . . . qui, c'est . . . que** (used to bring a word into prominence). *C'est un bon petit garçon que Jean,* a fine little chap is John ! *C'est moi qui lui ai écrit,* it was I who wrote to him. (i) (i) **C'est que,** introducing a statement. *C'est qu'il fait froid!* it is cold and no mistake ! (ii) **Est-ce que** [ɛskə], introducing a question. *Est-ce que je peux entrer?* may I come in ? S.a. EST-CE QUI, QU'EST-CE QUI, etc. **2.** (Literary use, always [sə]) (a) (Used as subject to *devenir, laisser, sembler, venir*) *Vous devriez rougir, ce me semble,* it seems to me that you ought to blush. (b) (Used as object to *faire, dire,* etc.) **Pour ce faire . . .,** in order to do this . . . . **Ce faisant . . .,** doing which. . . . **Ce disant . . .,** saying which . . . ; so saying. . . . **3.** (Used as neut. antecedent to a rel. pron.) (a) **Ce qui, ce que,** etc. = what. *Je sais ce qui est arrivé,* I know what has happened. *Ce que de nous!* what poor mortals we are ! *Voici ce à quoi* [sakwa] *j'avais pensé,* here is what I had thought of. (b) **Ce qui, ce que,** etc. = which. *Il est parti, ce que je ne savais pas,* he has gone, which I did not know. (c) **Tout ce qui, que,** everything, all (that). *Tout ce que j'ai d'argent,* all the money I have. *Faites tout ce que vous voudrez,* do whatever you like. (d) *F:* **Ce que . . .!** how . . . ! *Ce qu'elle a changé!* how she has changed ! *Ce que tu as grandi!* well, you have grown ! **4.** (= CELA) *Registre à ce destiné,* book kept for the purpose. **Sur ce . . .,** thereupon . . . . **Depuis ce . . .,** since then. . . . S.a. NONOBSTANT. **5.** *Conj.phr.* Tenez-vous beaucoup à ce qu'il vienne? are you very anxious for him to come ? *Il profita de ce que j'avais le dos tourné* he took advantage of my having turned my back to him. **6.** *Prep.phr.* **Pour ce qui est de la qualité et du prix,** as regards quality and price. **Pour ce qui est de cela,** for the matter of that, for that matter.

ce² (cet), cette, ces [sə (sɛt), sɛt, se or sɛ], unstressed *dem. a.* (The form **cet** is used before a sb. or adj. beginning with a vowel or *h* 'mute') This, that, *pl.* these, those. **1.** *Un de ces jours,* one of these days. *Ce héros au sourire si doux,* that hero with the gentle smile. *Il y a de ces gens qui . . .,* there are those (people) who. . . . **Ce dernier,** the latter. **2.** *pl.* (Deferential use) *Que prendront ces messieurs?* what will you take, gentlemen? *Ces dames sont au salon,* the ladies are in the drawing-room. **3.** Ce . . . -ci, this.

Ce . . . -là, that. *Prenez cette tasse-ci*, take this cup.

ceci [səsi], *dem. pron. neut.* This (thing, fact, etc.). *Écoutez bien ceci*, now listen to this. NOTE. An adjective qualifying *ceci* is partitive. *Le cas offre ceci de particulier, que . . .*, the case is peculiar in this, that. . . .

cécité [sesite], *s.f.* Blindness.

cédant, -ante [sedã, -ã:t]. **1.** *a.* Granting, assigning (party). **2.** *s.* Grantor, assignor.

céder [sede], *v.* (je cède; je céderai) **1.** *v.tr.* (*a*) (i) To give up, part with, yield (*à*, to); to surrender (right). Céder le pas à qn, to give way to s.o. (ii) To transfer, make over, assign (*à*, to). Maison à céder, business for sale. *Je vous le céderai pour cent francs*, I will let you have it for a hundred francs. (*b*) Le céder à qn en qch., to yield to s.o. in sth.; to be inferior to s.o. in sth. *Pour l'intelligence elle ne (le) cède à personne*, in intelligence she is second to none. **2.** *v.i.* To yield, give way (under pressure). *Le câble céda sous l'effort*, the rope parted under the strain. *C. au sommeil*, to succumb to sleep. *C. aux circonstances*, to yield to circumstances. *Il a cédé à nos désirs*, he gave in to us.

cédille [sedi:j], *s.f. Gram:* Cedilla.

cédrat [sedra], *s.m. Bot:* (*a*) = CÉDRATIER. (*b*) Citron.

cédratier [sedratje], *s.m. Bot:* Citron-tree.

cèdre [sɛ:dr], *s.m.* Cedar(-tree, -wood).

cédulaire [sedylɛ:r], *a.* Pertaining to income-tax schedules. *Impôts cédulaires*, scheduled taxes.

cédule [sedyl], *s.f.* Schedule (of taxes).

ceign-ais, -ant, -e, -is, etc. See CEINDRE.

ceindre [sɛ̃:dr], *v.tr.* (*pr.p.* ceignant; *p.p.* ceint; *pr.ind.* je ceins, il ceint, n. ceignons; *p.d.* je ceignais; *p.h.* je ceignis; *fu.* je ceindrai) **1.** To gird. (*a*) *C. une épée*, to gird on, buckle on, a sword. (*b*) *C. qch. à qn*, to gird sth. on s.o. (*c*) *C. qn de qch.*, to gird, encircle, s.o. with sth. **2.** (Of a wreath) To encircle (s.o.'s head, etc.). **3.** To encompass, encircle (a town with walls).

ceinture [sɛ̃ty:r], *s.f.* **1.** (*a*) Girdle; (leather) belt; (silk) sash; waistband. *C. de sauvetage*, life-belt. Se serrer, se boucler, la ceinture, to tighten one's belt. (*b*) Waist, middle (of the body). *Nu jusqu'à la c.*, naked to the waist. (*c*) *Wr:* Hold round the waist. **2.** Girdle, circle (of walls); belt (of hills). **3.** *Rail:* Chemin de fer de petite, grande, ceinture, inner-, outer-circle railway.

ceinturer [sɛ̃tyre], *v.tr.* **1.** To girdle. **2.** *Rugby Fb:* *C. un joueur*, to collar, tackle, a player low.

ceinturon [sɛ̃tyrɔ̃], *s.m.* Waist-belt, sword-belt.

cela [səla, sla], *F:* ça [sa], *dem. pron. neut.* (*a*) That (thing, fact). Qu'est-ce que c'est que cela, *F:* que ça? what is that? NOTE. An adj. qualifying *cela* is always partitive. *S'il n'y a que cela de nouveau*, if that is all that is new. (*b*) That, it. (*Cela* is the pron. used as neut. subject to all verbs other than *être*, and may be used with *être* as more emphatic than *ce*) *Cela ne vous regarde pas*, that, it, is no business of yours. NOTE. As subject to *être*, *cela* resolves itself into its elements when the pred. is completed by a noun or noun-clause. *C'est là ce que je voulais dire*, that is what I meant. (*c*) *F:* (Disparagingly of people and things) *C'est ça les hommes!* that's what men are! (*d*) *F:* Ceci . . . cela. *Il m'a dit ceci et ça*, he told me this, that and the other. *Comment allez-vous?—Comme (ci comme) ça*, how are you?—So so. (*e*) Idiomatic uses. *C'est ça*, that's it, that's right. *C'est cela même!* the very thing! Il n'y a que ça, there's nothing like it. Par cela même . . ., pour cela même . . ., for that very

reason. . . . Et avec cela, madame? and what else, madam? Comme ça vous déménagez? so you are moving, are you? *F:* Allons, pas de ça! come, none of that! Il a de ça, he has wit (grit, money, etc.). Où ça? where? Comment ça? how? Ça oui! yes indeed!

céladon [seladɔ̃]. **1.** *s.m. A:* Sentimental lover. **2.** *a.inv.* Willow-green.

célèbre [selɛbr], *a.* Celebrated, famous (*par*, for).

célébr|er [selebre], *v.tr.* (je célèbre; je célébrerai) **1.** To celebrate; (i) to solemnize (rite); (ii) to observe, keep (feast). *C. des funérailles*, to hold a funeral. **2.** To extol (s.o.). *C. les louanges de qn*, to sing s.o.'s praises. *s.f.* **-ation.**

célébrité [selebrite], *s.f.* Celebrity.

celer [səle], *v.tr.* (je cèle; je celerai) *A:* To conceal, keep secret (*à*, from).

céleri [selri], *s.m.* Celery. Pied de c., head of celery. Morceau de c., stick of celery.

célérité [selerite], *s.f.* Celerity, dispatch.

céleste [selɛst], *a.* Celestial, heavenly. La voûte céleste, the vault of heaven.

célibat [seliba], *s.m.* Celibacy.

célibataire [selibatɛ:r], *a. & s.* Unmarried, single (man, woman). *s.m.* Bachelor. *s.f.* Spinster.

celle, celle-ci, celle-là. See CELUI.

cellier [selje], *s.m.* Store-room (for wine, etc.); store-cupboard (on ground floor).

cellulaire [selylɛ:r], *a.* **1.** Cellular (tissue, girder, etc.). **2.** Voiture cellulaire, police-van; *F:* Black Maria.

cellule [selyl], *s.f.* **1.** Cell (of prison, honeycomb, etc.). **2.** *Biol:* Cell.

celluloïd(e) [selyloid], *s.m. Ind:* Celluloid.

cellulose [selylo:z], *s.f. Ch: Com:* Cellulose.

celte [sɛlt]. **1.** *a. & s.m. Ling:* = CELTIQUE. **2.** *s.m. & f.* Celt, Kelt.

celtique [sɛltik]. **1.** *a.* Celtic, Keltic. **2.** *s.m.* Celtic (language).

celui, celle, *pl.* **ceux, celles** [səlɥi, sɛl, sø, sɛl], *dem. pron.* **1.** (Completed by an adj. clause) (*a*) The one; those. *Celui qui était parti le dernier arriva le premier*, the one who started last arrived first. (*b*) He, she, those. *C. qui mange peu dort bien*, he who eats little sleeps well. **2.** (Followed by *de*) *Mes livres et ceux de Jean*, my books and John's. **3.** (Completed by an adj. equivalent) *Les rails en acier et ceux en fer*, steel rails and iron ones. **4.** Celui-ci, ceux-ci, this (one), these; the latter. Celui-là, ceux-là, that (one), those; the former. **5.** *Celui-là* is used for *celui* I, when the rel. pron. does not follow at once. *Celui-là est heureux qui . . .*, he is happy who. . . .

cément [semã], *s.m.* **1.** Cement (of tooth). **2.** *Metall:* Cement; cementation powder.

cément|er [semãte], *v.tr.* To case-harden, face-harden (steel); to cement (armour-plate). *s.f.* **-ation.**

cénacle [senakl], *s.m.* **1.** *Ant:* Cenacle; esp. *B:* 'upper chamber' (of the Lord's Supper). **2.** *C littéraire*, literary group; coterie.

cendre [sã:dr], *s.f.* Ash(es), cinders. *Fosse aux cendres*, ash-pit. Mettre, réduire, une ville en cendres, to reduce a town to ashes. Mercredi des Cendres, Ash-Wednesday. *Visage couleur de c.*, ashen face.

cendrée [sãdre], *s.f. Sp:* Cinders (for track). Piste en cendrée, (i) cinder-track; (ii) dirt-track. Moto sur c., dirt-track racing.

cendrer [sãdre], *v.tr.* **1.** To colour (wall, etc.) ash-grey. **2.** To cinder (path, track).

cendré, *a.* (Ash-)grey; ashy. S.a. BLOND, LUMIÈRE I.

cendreux, -euse [sãdrø, -ø:z], *a.* **1.** Ashy; ash-grey. **2.** Full of ashes; gritty
cendrier [sãdrie], *s.m.* (*a*) Ash-bin; ash-pan (of stove); ash-pit, -hole (of furnace); ash-box (of locomotive). (*b*) Ash-tray.
Cendrillon [sãdrijõ]. **1.** *Pr.n.f.* Cinderella. **2.** *s.f. F:* (Household) drudge.
cène [sɛn], *s.f.* (*a*) La (Sainte) Cène, the Last Supper. (*b*) (In Protestant Church) Holy Communion.
cénotaphe [senɔtaf], *s.m.* Cenotaph.
cens [sã:s], *s.m.* Quota (of taxes payable); rating. *C. électoral*, property qualification.
censé [sãse], *a.* Supposed. *Je ne suis pas c. le savoir*, I am not supposed to know.
censément [sãsemã], *adv. F:* (i) Supposedly; (ii) practically. *Il est c. le maître*, (i) he is supposed to be the master; (ii) to all intents and purposes he is the master.
censeur [sãsœ:r], *s.m.* **1.** *Rom.Ant:* Censor. **2.** Censurer, critic, *F:* fault-finder. *a. Esprit c.*, carping spirit. **3.** (*a*) Censor (of plays, of the press). (*b*) *Fin:* Auditor. **4.** *Sch:* Vice-principal (of *lycée*).
censurable [sãsyrabl], *a.* Censurable; open to censure.
censure [sãsy:r], *s.f.* **1.** (*a*) *Rom.Ant:* Censorship. (*b*) Censorship (of the press, etc.). (*c*) Audit (of accounts). **2.** Censure, blame.
censurer [sãsyre], *v.tr.* **1.** To censure, find fault with (s.o., sth.). **2.** To censor (film).
cent [sã]. **1.** (*a*) *num. a.* (Takes a plural s when multiplied by a preceding numeral but not followed by another numeral. Does not vary when used as an ordinal) (A, one) hundred. *Deux cents hommes*, two hundred men. *Deux cent cinquante hommes*, two hundred and fifty men. *La page deux cent*, page two hundred. *Cent un* [sãœ̃], one hundred and one. *Faire les cent pas devant la porte de qn*, to do sentry-go in front of s.o.'s door. *Faire les cent (dix-neuf) coups*, to kick up no end of a shindy. *Être aux cent coups*, to be in desperation. *Je vous le donne en cent*, I give you a hundred guesses. (*In.* hotels) *Le numéro cent*, the w.c. (*b*) *s.m.inv.* A hundred. *Sept pour cent*, seven per cent. **2.** *s.m.var.* *Un cent d'œufs*, a hundred eggs. *F:* *Il a des mille et des cents*, he has tons of money.
centaine [sãtɛn], *s.f.* *Une c. de francs*, about a hundred francs; a hundred francs or so. *Quelques centaines de francs*, a few hundred francs. *Atteindre la centaine*, to live to be a hundred.
centaure [sãtɔ:r], *s.m. Myth:* Centaur.
centaurée [sãtɔre], *s.f. Bot:* Centaury.
centenaire [sãtnɛ:r]. **1.** *a.* Of a hundred years' standing. **2.** *s.m. & f.* Centenarian. **3.** *s.m.* Centenary (anniversary).
centennal, -aux [sãtennal, -o], *a.* Centennial.
centésimal, -aux [sãtezimal, -o], *a.* Centesimal (fraction, scale, etc.).
centiare [sãtja:r], *s.m.* Centiare (one sq. metre).
centième [sãtjɛm]. **1.** *num. a. & s.* Hundredth. **2.** *s.m.* Hundredth (part).
centigrade [sãtigrad], *a.* Centigrade.
centigramme [sãtigram], *s.m.* Centigramme (= 0.154 grain).
centilitre [sãtilitr], *s.m.* Centilitre (= nearly 3 drachms).
centime [sãtim], *s.m.* Centime (= one 100th part of franc).
centimètre [sãtimɛtr], *s.m.* **1.** Centimetre (= 0.394 in.). **2.** *F:* Tape-measure.
centinode [sãtinɔd], *s.f.* Knot-grass, hogweed.
centipède [sãtipɛd], *s.m.* Centipede.

central, -aux [sãtral, -o]. **1.** *a.* Central. (*a*) Middle (point, etc.). (*b*) Principal, head (office, etc.). La (maison) centrale = county gaol. **2.** (*a*) *s.m.* Central téléphonique, telephone exchange. (*b*) *s.f.* Centrale (électrique), power-house; electricity works. *adv.* **-ement**.
centralis|er [sãtralize], *v.tr.* To centralize. *s.f.* **-ation**, -ation.
centre [sã:tr], *s.m.* Centre; central point (of circle, etc.); middle, midst (of the country, etc.). *C. de villégiature*, holiday resort. *C. d'un levier*, fulcrum of a lever. Centre de gravité, centre of gravity.
centr|er [sãtre], *v.tr.* To centre, adjust (wheel, tool, lens, etc.). *Fb:* Centrer le ballon, to centre the ball. *s.m.* **-age**.
centrifuge [sãtrify:ʒ], *a.* Centrifugal (force).
centripète [sãtripɛt], *a.* Centripetal (force).
centuple [sãtypl], *a. & s.m.* Centuple; hundred-fold.
cep [sɛ(p)], *s.m.* Cep de vigne [sɛdviɲ, sɛpdəviɲ], vine-stock, -plant.
cépage [sepa:ʒ], *s.m.* Vine-plant.
cèpe [sɛp], *s.m. Bot:* Flap mushroom.
cependant [s(ə)pãdã]. **1.** *adv.* Meanwhile; in the meantime. **2.** *conj.* Yet, still, nevertheless, for all that. [PENDANT].
céphalique [sefalik], *a.* Cephalic.
ceps [sɛp], *s.m.* = CÈPE.
céramique [seramik]. **1.** *a.* Ceramic (arts, etc.). **2.** *s.f.* Ceramics; (art of) pottery.
cérat [sera], *s.m. Pharm:* Cerate, ointment.
Cerbère [sɛrbɛːr]. *Pr.n.m. Myth:* Cerberus.
cerceau [sɛrso], *s.m.* Hoop. *C. de baril*, barrel hoop. *Faire courir un cerceau*, to bowl, trundle, a hoop.
cercle [sɛrkl], *s.m.* **1.** Circle. (*a*) Faire cercle, to lie, stand, in a circle. *C. d'activités*, circle, sphere, of activities. Tourner dans un cercle (vicieux), to reason, argue; in a vicious circle. (*b*) Circle, set (of friends, etc.). *C. littéraire*, literary circle. (*c*) Club. *C. militaire, des officiers*, officers' club. **2.** (Binding-)hoop, ring. Vin en cercles, wine in the wood. *C. d'une roue*, tyre of a wheel. **3.** (*a*) Dial, circle. *Artil: C. de pointage*, dial (of dial-sight). (*b*) Quart de cercle, quadrant.
cercl|er [sɛrkle], *v.tr.* **1.** To encircle, to ring. *Yeux cerclés de bistre*, eyes with dark rings round them. **2.** To hoop (barrel); to tyre (wheel). *Cerclé de fer*, iron-bound. *s.m.* **-age**.
cercueil [sɛrkœːj], *s.m.* Coffin; casket. *C. de plomb*, leaden shell.
céréale [sereal], *a.f.* *Plantes céréales*, *s.f.pl.* céréales, cereal plants; cereals.
cérébral, -aux [serebral, -o], *a.* Cerebral (artery; *Ling:* consonant, etc.). *Fatigue cérébrale*, brain-fag.
cérémonial, -aux [seremɔnjal, -o]. **1.** *a.* Ceremonial. **2.** *s.m.* No *pl.* Ceremonial.
cérémonie [seremɔni], *s.f.* Ceremony. Escorter un prince en cérémonie, to escort a prince in state. Faire une visite de cérémonie, to pay a formal call (d, on). Tenue de cérémonie, full dress. *F:* Faire des cérémonies, to stand on ceremony. Maître des cérémonies, master of ceremonies.
cérémonieu|x, -euse [seremɔnjø, -øːz], *a.* Ceremonious, formal. *adv.* **-sement**.
cerf [sɛːr, occ. sɛrf], *pl.* always sɛːr], *s.m.* (*a*) Stag, hart. (*b*) *Cu:* Venison.
cerfeuil [sɛrfœːj], *s.m. Bot:* Chervil.
cerf-volant [sɛrvɔlã], *s.m.* **1.** *Ent:* Stag-beetle. **2.** (Paper) kite. *C.-v. cellulaire*, box-kite. *pl. Des cerfs-volants*.

cerisaie [s(ə)rizɛ], *s.f.* Cherry-orchard.

cerise [s(ə)riːz], **1.** *s.f.* Cherry. *F:* **Faire deux morceaux d'une cerise,** to take two bites at a cherry. **Bouche en cerise,** rose-bud mouth. **2.** *s.m. & a.inv.* Cherry-red. *Tex:* Cerise.

cerisier [s(ə)rizje], *s.m.* Cherry-tree, -wood.

cérium [serjɔm], *s.m। Ch:* Cerium.

cerne [sɛrn], *s.m.* **1.** Ring, circle (round moon, eyes, bruise). **2.** Age-ring (of tree).

cerneau [sɛrno], *s.m.* Green walnut.

cern|er [sɛrne], *v.tr.* **1.** To encircle, surround (army, etc.); to invest (town). **Avoir les yeux cernés,** to have rings under the eyes. **2.** To shell, husk (walnuts). **3.** To girdle, ring (tree). *s.m.* **-ement.**

cernure [sɛrnyːr], *s.f.* Dark ring (under the eyes).

céroplastique [serɔplastik], *s.f.* Wax-modelling.

certain, -aine [sɛrtɛ̃, -ɛn]. **I.** *a.* (*a*) Certain, sure, unquestionable. **Tenir qch. pour certain,** to look on sth. as a certainty. (*b*) *Il est c. de réussir,* he is sure he will succeed. *J'en suis c.,* I am sure, certain, of it. (*c*) Fixed, stated (date, price). **2.** *indef. a. & pron.* (*a*) Some, certain. *Certains, (de) certaines gens, affirment que . . .,* some (people) maintain that. *. . . Après un c. temps,* after a certain time. (*b*) (With shade of contempt) **Un certain M. Dupont,** one Mr Dupont. *adv.* **-ement.**

certes [sɛrt], *adv.* (Oui) **certes!** yes indeed! to be sure! \

certificat [sɛrtifika], *s.m.* Certificate. **Montrer ses certificats,** to show one's testimonials. *Cust:* **Certificat d'entrepôt,** warrant. *Breed:* **Certificat d'origine,** pedigree (of dog, etc.).

certification [sɛrtifikasjɔ̃], *s.f.* Certification, authentication. *C. d'une signature,* witnessing of a signature.

certifier [sɛrtifje], *v.tr.* To certify, attest. *C. qch. à qn,* to assure s.o. of sth. *C. une signature,* to witness, authenticate, a signature.

certitude [sɛrtityd], *s.f.* Certainty. **J'en ai la certitude,** I am sure of it.

céruse [seryːz], *s.f.* (*a*) White lead. (*b*) *Th:* Ceruse (for making up).

cerveau [sɛrvo], *s.m.* (*a*) Brain. **Rhume de cerveau,** cold in the head. *F:* **Vous me rompez le cerveau,** you give me a headache. **Vin qui monte au cerveau,** heady wine. (*b*) *F:* Mind, intellect, brains. **Cerveau creux,** dreamer, visionary. **Cerveau brûlé,** hot-head; harum-scarum.

cervelas [sɛrvəla], *s.m. Cu:* Saveloy.

cervelet [sɛrvəlɛ], *s.m. Anat:* Cerebellum.

cervelle [sɛrvɛl], *s.f.* **1.** *Anat:* Brain(s) (as matter). **Brûler, faire sauter, la cervelle à qn,** to blow s.o.'s brains out. *Cu: C. de veau,* calves' brains. **2.** *F:* Mind, brains. **Se creuser la cervelle pour . . .,** to rack, beat, one's brains to . . . . **Homme sans cervelle,** brainless individual. **Avoir une cervelle de lièvre,** to have a memory like a sieve.

cervin [sɛrvɛ̃]. **I.** *a. Z:* Cervine. **2.** *Pr.n.m.* **Le Mont Cervin,** the Matterhorn.

ces. See CE².

César [sezaːr]. *Pr.n.m.* **Jules César,** Julius Caesar.

césium [sezjɔm], *s.m. Ch:* Caesium.

cessant [sɛsɑ̃], *a.* Ceasing. **Toute affaire cessante,** to the suspension of all other business.

cessation [sɛsasjɔ̃], *s.f.* Cessation, ceasing.

cesse [sɛs], *s.f.* Cease, ceasing. **Sans cesse,** without cease; unceasingly. **Il n'aura (pas) de cesse qu'il n'ait réussi,** he will not rest till he has succeeded.

cesser [sɛse], *v.* To cease, leave off, stop. **1.** *v.i. Les collines cessent à . . .,* the hills fall away

at. . . . **Faire cesser qch.,** to put a stop to sth. *C. de faire qch.,* to cease (from) doing sth. **2.** *v.tr. C. le travail,* to cease, leave off, work. *C. les affaires,* to give up business.

cessible [sɛsibl], *a. Jur:* Transferable, assignable.

cession [sɛsjɔ̃], *s.f.* **1.** *Jur:* Transfer, assignment. **Faire cession de qch. à qn,** to transfer, surrender, sth. to s.o. **2.** Delivery (of heat); supply (of power).

cessionnaire [sɛsjɔnɛːr], *s.m. Jur:* Transferee, assignee.

c'est-à-dire [sɛtadiːr], *conj.phr.* **1.** That is (to say); *i.e.;* in other words. **2.** *F:* **C'est-à-dire que** + *ind.,* the fact is that . . .; indeed. . . .

césure [sezyːr], *s.f. Pros:* Caesura.

cet. See CE².

cétacé [setase], *a. & s.m.* Cetacean.

cette. See CE².

ceux. See CELUI.

cévenol, -ole [sevnɔl], *a. & s.* (Native) of the Cevennes region.

Ceylan [selɑ̃]. *Pr.n.m.* Ceylon.

chablis¹ [ʃabli], *s.m.* Windfallen wood.

chablis², *s.m.* Chablis (wine, from Chablis in Burgundy).

chabot [ʃabo], *s.m. Ich:* **1.** Miller's thumb. **2.** Chub.

chacal, *pl.* **-als** [ʃakal], *s.m.* Jackal.

chacun, -une [ʃakœ̃, -yn], *pron.* **1.** Each; every one; each one. *Chacune d'elles a refusé,* each (one), every one, of them has refused. *Trois francs c.,* three francs each. **2.** Everybody, everyone. **Chacun pour soi,** everyone for himself. **Chacun son goût,** every man to his taste. **Chacun son tour,** turn and turn about.

chafouin, -ine [ʃafwɛ̃, -in], *a. & s. F:* Weasel-faced, sly-looking (person).

chagrin¹ [ʃagrɛ̃], *s.m.* (*a*) Grief, sorrow, affliction, trouble. **Avoir du chagrin,** to be in sorrow. *J'ai du c. de vous voir si changé,* I am grieved to see you so altered. *Faire du c. à qn,* to grieve s.o.; to distress s.o. (*b*) Vexation, annoyance. *Chagrins domestiques,* domestic worries.

chagrin², *s.m.* Shagreen; grain-leather.

chagrin³, -ine [ʃagrɛ̃, -in], *a.* **1.** Sad; troubled (*de,* at); distressed (*de,* at). **2.** Peevish, fretful. *adv.* **-ement.**

chagrinant [ʃagrinɑ̃], *a.* (*a*) Distressing, melancholy, sad. (*b*) Provoking, vexing.

chagriner¹ [ʃagrine], *v.tr.* **1.** To grieve, distress. **2.** To vex, annoy. **se chagriner,** to grieve; to fret.

chagriner², *v.tr.* To shagreen, grain (leather). *Papier chagriné,* pebbled paper.

chah [ʃa], *s.m.* Shah.

chahut [ʃay], *s.m. F:* Rag; rowdyism. **Faire du chahut,** to kick up a shindy; to make an uproar.

chahutage [ʃayta:ʒ], *s.m. F:* (*a*) Rowdyism. (*b*) Booing (at a play, etc.). *Sp:* Barracking.

chahuter [ʃayte], *v.i.* (*a*) *F:* (*a*) To kick up a shindy. (*b*) To boo. *Sp:* To barrack.

chahuteur, -euse [ʃaytœːr, -øːz], *s. F:* Disorderly person; rowdy.

chaîne [ʃen], *s.f.* **1.** (*a*) Chain (of iron, gold, etc.). *Nau:* Cable. *C. de cou,* necklace. *C. de gilet,* watch-chain. *Nau:* **Tour de chaîne,** foul cable. *Casser sa c.,* to part one's cable. **Les chaînes,** the hawse. *C. d'arpenteur,* surveying chain. *Ind:* **Travail à la chaîne,** moving-band production. (*b*) Shackles, fetters, bonds. **Rompre sa chaîne, ses chaînes,** to burst asunder one's fetters. **Mettre un chien à la chaîne,** to chain up a dog. *F:* **Être rivé à la chaîne,** to be in hopeless bondage.

2. Chaîne de montagnes, mountain range. *C. de chalands*, string of barges. *C. d'idées*, train of thought. **3.** *Tex:* Warp.

chaînette [ʃɛnɛt], *s.f.* **1.** Small chain. **2.** *Geom:* (Arc en) chaînette, catenary (curve). **3.** *Needlew:* Point de chaînette, chain-stitch.

chaînon [ʃɛnɔ̃], *s.m.* Link (of chain).

chair [ʃɛːr], *s.f.* Flesh. **1.** *Blessure dans les chairs*, flesh-wound. *F:* Voir qn en chair et en os, to see s.o. in the flesh. Être (bien) en chair, to be nice and plump. *Avoir la c. fraîche*, to have a rosy complexion. *F:* Chair de poule, goose-flesh. Cela vous donne la chair de poule, it makes one's flesh creep. **2.** *(a)* Meat. *C. à saucisse*, sausage-meat. *F:* Battre qn en chair à pâté, (i) to make mincemeat of s.o. ; (ii) to thrash s.o. within an inch of his life. Chair à canon, cannon-fodder. N'être ni chair ni poisson, to be neither flesh, fowl, nor good red herring. *(b)* Pulp (of peach, melon, etc.).

chaire [ʃɛːr], *s.f.* **1.** Chair, throne. *C. d'un évêque*, bishop's throne. **2.** Pulpit. *Exprimer une opinion en pleine chaire*, to express an opinion from the pulpit. Monter en chaire, to ascend the pulpit. **3.** *(a)* Chair, desk, rostrum (of lecturer). *(b)* Professorship, mastership, chair.

chaise [ʃɛːz], *s.f.* **1.** *(a)* Chair, seat. *C. cannée*, cane-bottomed chair. *F:* Se trouver entre deux chaises, to find oneself between two stools. *Ecc:* Chaise de chœur, stall. *(b)* C. roulante, Bath-chair. *C. percée*, night-commode. **2.** *A:* Chaise à porteurs, sedan-chair. Chaise de poste, post-chaise. **3.** Support, bracket. *C. de coussinet*, plummer-block. *Rail:* C. de rail, rail-chair.

chaise-longue, *s.f.* Lounge-chair ; couch. *pl.* Des chaises-longues.

chaisier, -ière [ʃɛzje, -jɛːr], *s.* Chair-attendant (in parks, in church).

chaland¹ [ʃalɑ̃], *s.m.* Lighter, barge. *Transport par chalands*, lighterage

chaland², -ande, *s.* Customer, purchaser.

chaldaïque [kaldaik], *a. & s.* = CHALDÉEN.

Chaldée [kalde]. *Pr.n.f.* *A.Geog:* Chaldea.

chaldéen, -enne [kaldeɛ̃, -ɛn], *a. & s.* Chaldean.

châle [ʃɑːl], *s.m.* Shawl.

chalet [ʃalɛ, ʃa-], *s.m.* **1.** *(a)* (Swiss) chalet. *(b)* Country cottage. **2.** Chalet de nécessité, public convenience.

chaleur [ʃalœːr], *s.f.* *(a)* Heat, warmth. Il fait une grande chaleur, it is very hot. Vague de chaleur, heat-wave. "Craint la chaleur," 'to be kept in a cool place.' *Sensation de c.*, (i) glow (after cold bath) ; (ii) burning sensation. *pl.* Les chaleurs, the hot weather. *(b)* Ardour, zeal. Parler avec chaleur, to speak warmly, zealously.

chaleureu|x, -euse [ʃalœrø, -øːz], *a.* Warm (friend, thanks) ; cordial (welcome) ; gushing (compliments). *adv.* -sement.

châlit [ʃali], *s.m.* Bedstead.

chaloupe [ʃalup], *s.f.* Launch ; long-boat. *C. à vapeur*, steam-launch.

chalumeau [ʃalymo], *s.m.* **1.** Straw (for drinking). *C. de roseau*, reed. **2.** *Mus:* Pipe. **3.** Blow-pipe.

chalut [ʃaly], *s.m.* Drag-net ; trawl.

chalut|er [ʃalyte], *v.i.* To trawl. *s.m.* -age.

chalutier [ʃalytje], *s.m.* Trawler or drifter (boat or fisherman).

chalybé [kalibe], *a.* *Pharm:* Chalybeate.

Cham [kam]. *Pr.n.m.* *B.Hist:* Ham.

chamailler [ʃamaje], *v.tr.* *F:* To nag at, squabble with (s.o.).

se chamailler, to bicker, quarrel, squabble.

chamaillerie [ʃamajri], *s.f.* **1.** Bickering, quarrelling. **2.** Squabble, wrangle.

chamaillis [ʃamaji], *s.m.* Fray, scuffle.

chamarrer [ʃamare], *v.tr.* To bedizen, bedeck (uniform with braid, etc.). *F:* C. un récit, to embroider a tale.

chamarrure [ʃamaryːr], *s.f.* Bedizenment.

chambard [ʃɑ̃baːr], *s.m.* *P:* Upset, upheaval ; row.

chambard|er [ʃɑ̃barde]. *P:* **1.** *v.tr.* *(a)* To sack, rifle (room, etc.). *(b)* To upset, smash up (furniture, etc.). **2.** *v.i.* To racket. *s.m.* -ement.

chambardeur [ʃɑ̃bardœːr], *s.m.* Rowdy ; subverter, disrupter (of social order, etc.).

chambellan [ʃɑ̃belɑ̃], *s.m.* Chamberlain.

chambouler [ʃɑ̃bule], *v.tr.* *P:* Tout c., to turn everything topsy-turvy. *Ça m'a chamboulé*, it gave me quite a turn.

chambranle [ʃɑ̃brɑ̃ːl], *s.m.* **1.** Frame, casing (of door) ; (standing) window-frame. **2.** Mantelpiece.

chambre [ʃɑ̃ːbr], *s.f.* **1.** Room, chamber. *(a)* C. à coucher, (i) bedroom ; (ii) bedroom suite. *C. à un lit*, single room. *C. à deux lits*, double(-bedded) room. *C. d'ami*, spare (bed)room. *C. d'enfants*, nursery. Faire une chambre, to clean out, tidy, a room. S.a. FEMME 3, GENTILHOMME, ROBE 1. Musique de chambre, chamber-music. *(b)* C. des machines, engine-room. *C. de chauffe*, boiler-house. **2.** *Adm: Jur:* Chamber, house. *C. des députés*, Chamber of Deputies. Chambres du Parlement, Houses of Parliament. **3.** *Tchn:* Chamber, cavity, space. Chambre à air, inner tube (of tyre). *I.C.E:* C. d'explosion, combustion chamber. *Phot:* Chambre noire, (i) camera obscura ; (ii) camera (body) ; (iii) dark-room.

chambrée [ʃɑ̃bre], *s.f.* **1.** Roomful (of people sharing a room). **2.** Barrack-room.

chambrer [ʃɑ̃bre]. **1.** *v.i.* To share a room, to chum (avec, with). **2.** *v.tr.* *(a)* To confine, lock up, (s.o.) in a room. *(b)* To take the chill off (claret).

se chambrer, (of gun) to become pitted, to wear.

chambrette [ʃɑ̃brɛt], *s.f.* *F:* Little room ; attic.

chambrière [ʃɑ̃bri(j)ɛːr], *s.f.* **1.** *A:* Chamber-maid. **2.** Long whip, lunging whip. **3.** (Cart-) prop.

chameau [ʃamo], *s.m.* **1.** *(a)* Camel. *Corps de chameaux*, camelry. *(b)* P: (Of man) Scoundrel ; dirty dog. **2.** *Rail:* Shunting engine.

chamelier [ʃaməlje], *s.m.* Camel-driver ; cameleer.

chamelle [ʃamɛl], *s.f.* She-camel.

chamois [ʃamwa], *s.m.* Chamois. Peau de chamois, wash-leather, chamois leather, shammy (leather).

champ¹ [ʃɑ̃], *s.m.* Field. **1.** *(a)* C. de blé, field of corn. Prendre, couper, à travers champs, to go, cut, across country. *F:* Prendre la clef des champs, to decamp, abscond. En plein champ, in the open (fields). A tout bout de champ, repeatedly ; at every turn. *(b)* C. de foire, fair-ground. *C. d'aviation*, flying ground. *C. de courses*, race-course. Parier contre le c., to lay against the field. *C. de tir*, rifle-range. *C. de glace*, ice-field. *C. de bataille*, battle-field. Mort au champ d'honneur, died on the field of honour. S.a. MARS 1. *Mil:* Battre aux champs, to beat the general salute. *(c)* A: Champ clos, lists (for judicial combat). S.a. ÉLYSÉE. **2.** *(a)* Field of action ; range, scope. Laisser le champ libre à qn, to leave s.o. a clear field. *F:* Le champ est libre, the coast is clear. Ouvrir le champ aux conjectures, to open a wide field for conjecture,

Être à bout de champ, to be at the end of one's tether. (b) C. d'une lunette, field of a telescope. (c) Champ magnétique, magnetic field.

champ², s.m. Edge, side. Pierres (posées) de champ, sur champ, stones set on edge, edgewise.

Champagne [Šāpaɲ]. **1.** Pr.n.f. (Ancient province of) Champagne. **2.** s.m. (Also vin de Champagne) Champagne. **3.** s.f. Fine champagne, liqueur brandy.

champenois, -oise [Šāpǝnwa, -waːz], a. & s. (Native) of Champagne.

champêtre [Šāpɛːtr], a. Rustic, rural. Garde champêtre, rural policeman.

champignon [Šāpiɲ5], s.m. **1.** (a) C. comestible, mushroom. C. de couche, cultivated mushroom. Sauce aux champignons, mushroom ketchup. (Of dumdum bullet) Faire champignon, to set up, to mushroom. (b) C. vénéneux, fungus, toadstool. **2.** (a) C. de modiste, milliner's hat-stand. (b) Rail à double c., double-headed rail. (c) F: Thief, stranger (in candle).

champion, -ionne [Šāpj5, -jɔn], s. Champion.

championnat [Šāpjɔna], s.m. Championship.

chançard, -arde [Šāsaːr, -ard], a. & s. P: Lucky (chap, woman).

chance [Šāːs], s.f. **1.** Chance. Il a peu de chances de réussir, il y a peu de chances qu'il réussisse, he has little chance of succeeding. **2.** Luck, fortune. Souhaiter bonne chance à qn, to wish s.o. good luck. Avoir de la chance, to be in luck's way. Porter chance à qn, to bring s.o. luck. Rompre la chance, to break a run of (good or bad) luck.

chancelant [Šāslā], a. Pas chancelants, staggering, tottering, unsteady, footsteps. Santé chancelante, (i) delicate health; (ii) delicate constitution.

chanceler [Šāsle], v.i. (je chancelle; je chancellerai) To stagger, totter. Avancer, reculer, entrer, sortir, en chancelant, to stagger forward, back, in, out. Trône qui chancelle, tottering throne.

chancelier [Šāsəlje], s.m. Chancellor. (In Britain) Grand Chancelier, Lord Chancellor.

chancelière [Šāsəljɛːr], s.f. Foot-muff.

chancellerie [Šāselri], s.f. **1.** Chancellery. **2.** Secretaryship (of a legation).

chanceux, -euse [Šāsø, -øːz], a. F: **1.** Hazardous. C'est une affaire chanceuse, that is a risky business. **2.** Lucky, fortunate.

chancir [Šāsiːr], v.i. & pr. To go mouldy.

chancre [Šāːkr], s.m. **1.** Canker. **2.** Ulcer.

chancreux, -euse [Šākrø, -øːz], a. **1.** (Of growth) (a) Cankerous. (b) Ulcerous. **2.** (Of organ) (a) Cankered. (b) Ulcerated.

chandail [Šāda:j], s.m. Cost: Sweater.

Chandeleur (la) [laŠādlœːr], s. Candlemas.

chandelier, -ière [Šādəlje, -jɛːr], s. **1.** Candle-maker. **2.** s.m. (a) Candlestick. (b) F: Ostensible cicisbeo (screening the real paramour).

chandelle [Šādɛl], s.f. **1.** (a) (Tallow) candle. F: Économies de bouts de chandelle, cheese-paring economy. Travailler à la chandelle, to work by candlelight. F: Brûler la chandelle par les deux bouts, to burn the candle at both ends. Tenir la chandelle, to hold a candle to the devil. Voir trente-six chandelles, to see stars. (b) (Church) candle, taper. F: Je vous dois une fière chandelle, I owe you more than I can repay. **2.** (a) Chandelle de glace, icicle. (b) F: Drop (at the end of the nose). **3.** Pyr: Chandelle romaine, Roman candle. (Of aeroplane) Monter en chandelle, to rocket; to zoom. Lancer une balle en chandelle, to sky, lob, a ball. **4.** Const: etc: Stay, prop, shore, pillar, upright.

chanfrein¹ [Šāfrɛ̃], s.m. (a) Forehead (of horse, sheep). (b) Blaze (on forehead of horse).

chanfrein², s.m. Chamfered edge, chamfer, bevelled edge.

chanfreiner [Šāfrɛne], v.tr. To chamfer, bevel.

change [Šāːʒ], s.m. **1.** Fin: Exchange. Lettre de change, bill of exchange. Première de change, first of exchange. Bureau de change, foreign exchange office. Cours du change, rate of exchange. **2.** Ven: Donner le change aux chiens, to put the dogs on the wrong scent.

changeable [Šāʒabl], a. **1.** Changeable, alterable. **2.** Exchangeable.

changeant [Šāʒā], a. Changing. Caractère changeant, changeable, fickle, disposition. D'humeur changeante, fitful. Taffetas changeant, shot silk.

changement [Šāʒmā], s.m. Change; alteration. Il vous faudrait un c. d'air, d'occupation, you need a change. C. de marée, turn of the tide. C. de vent, shift of wind. C. en mal, change for the worse. Apporter un c. à une clause, to make an alteration, a change, in a clause. Mch: Aut: Changement de marche, reversing; reversing gear. Changement de vitesse, change up or down; change-speed gear. Rail: Changement de voie, points. Th: Changement à vue, transformation scene.

changer [Šāʒe], v. (je changeai(s); n. changeons) **1.** v.tr. To change or exchange. C. un billet de banque, to change a bank-note. C. des meubles contre des tableaux, to exchange furniture for pictures. **2.** v.tr. To change, alter. C. sa manière de vivre, to change one's way of living. C. une défaite en déroute, to convert, turn, a defeat into a rout. F: La campagne me changera, the country will be a change for me. **3.** v.i. (a) To undergo a change. Le temps va c., the weather is going to change. (b) C. de main, to change hands; to use the other hand. C. de mains, to change hands; to pass into s.o. else's possession. C. d'habits, abs. changer, to change one's clothes. C. d'avis, to change one's mind. C. de place, to change one's seat. F: Changer de ton, to change one's tune. **se changer. 1.** To change (en, into); to alter. **2.** To change one's clothes; F: to change.

changeur [Šāʒœːr], s.m. **1.** Money-changer. **2.** W.Tel: C. de fréquence, frequency changer.

chanoine [Šanwan], s.m. Ecc: Canon.

chanson [Šās5], s.f. **1.** Song. C. à boire, drinking-song. C. de bord, sea-shanty. F: C'est toujours la même chanson! it's the same old story! **2.** Song, lay. La Chanson de Roland, the Song of Roland.

chansonn|er [Šāsɔne], v.tr. & i. To write satirical songs (about s.o.). s.m. **-eur**.

chansonnette [Šāsɔnɛt], s.f. Comic song with patter.

chansonnier, -ière [Šāsɔnje, -jɛːr], s. **1.** Song-writer. **2.** s.m. Song-book.

chant [Šā], s.m. **1.** Singing; song. Leçon de c., singing lesson. C'était le chant du cygne, it was his swan song. C. de victoire, song of victory. C. du grillon, chirping of the cricket. Chant du coq, crowing of the cock. Au (premier) chant du coq, at cock-crow. **2.** (a) Melody, air. (b) Ecc: C. grégorien, Gregorian chant. S.a. PLAIN-CHANT. **3.** Canto (of long poem).

chantage [Šātaːʒ], s.m. Blackmail, extortion.

chantant [Šātā], a. (a) Accent c., sing-song accent. (b) Soirée chantante, musical evening. (c) Melodious, tuneful.

chanteau [Šāto], s.m. Hunch (of bread).

chanteclair [Šātklɛːr], s.m. Lit: Chanticleer.

chantepleure [Šātplœːr], s.f. **1.** (a) Wine funnel; colander. (b) Tap (of cask). **2.** (a) Weep-hole (in wall). (b) Spout (of gutter).

chanter [Šāte], v.tr. To sing. **1.** C. qch. sur l'air

de . . ., to sing sth. to the tune of. . . . **Chanter victoire sur qn,** to crow over s.o. *Ecc:* **C. la messe,** to sing mass. **Pain à chanter,** (unconsecrated) wafer. *F:* **Chanter toujours la même antienne,** to be always harping on the same string. **Faire chanter qn,** to blackmail s.o. **Faire chanter qn sur un autre ton,** to make s.o. sing another tune. **Qu'est-ce que vous me chantez?** what fairy-tale is this you are telling me? **Si ça me chante,** if it suits me. **2.** (Of birds) To sing; (of cock) to crow; (of cricket) to chirp.

chanterelle [Sɑ̃trɛl], *s.f.* **1.** (*a*) Decoy-bird. (*b*) Bird-call. **2.** *Mus:* First string (of violin).

chanteur, -euse [Sɑ̃tœːr, -øːz], *s.* Singer, vocalist. **Maître chanteur,** (i) *Mus.Hist:* master-singer; (ii) *F:* blackmailer.

chantier [Sɑ̃tje], *s.m.* **1.** Gantry, stand (for barrels). **2.** *C. de bois,* timber-yard. *C. de construction,* (i) ship(-building) yard; (ii) slip-way. *C. de l'État,* naval dockyard. *Mettre un navire en c.,* to lay down a ship. *F:* **Avoir une œuvre sur le chantier,** to have a piece of work in hand, *F:* on the stocks.

chantonn|er [Sɑ̃tɔne], *v.tr. & i.* To hum; to sing softly. *s.m.* **-ement.**

chantourn|er [Sɑ̃turne], *v.tr.* To cut, saw, (sth.) round a curved outline. **Scie à chantourner,** bow-saw; jig-saw. *s.m.* **-age.**

chantre [Sɑ̃ːtr], *s.m.* (*a*) *Ecc:* Cantor. **Grand chantre,** precentor. (*b*) *Lit:* Singer (of the past, etc.).

chanvre [Sɑ̃ːvr], *s.m.* Hemp. **Cordage en chanvre,** hempen rope. **Cheveux couleur de chanvre,** flaxen hair.

chaos [kao], *s.m.* Chaos, confusion.

chaotique [kaɔtik], *a.* Chaotic, confused.

chapard|er [Saparde], *v.tr. P:* To steal, scrounge. *s.m.* **-age.** *s.m.* **-eur.**

chape [Sap], *s.f.* **1.** *Ecc:* Cope. **2.** Covering. (*a*) *C. d'une enveloppe,* tread of a tyre. (*b*) Coping (of bridge). (*c*) *Mec.E:* etc: Cover, cap. **3.** *Mec.E:* Fork-joint, D-joint, yoke. **Chape de cardan,** cardan fork.

chapeau [Sapo], *s.m.* **1.** Hat. *C. mou,* soft felt hat. *C. gibus, c. mécanique,* opera-hat. *F:* **Recevoir le chapeau,** to be made (a) cardinal. **Saluer qn d'un coup de chapeau, donner un coup de chapeau à qn,** to raise one's hat to s.o. **Chapeau bas,** hat in hand. **2.** Cover. (*a*) *Cu:* Piecrust. (*b*) Cap (of fountain-pen, etc.). *Aut: C. de roue,* hub cap. (*c*) Hood, cowl (of chimney). **3.** *Typ:* Heading.

chapelet [Saplɛ], *s.m.* **1.** (Lesser) rosary (of fifty-five beads); (string of) beads. **Égrener, dire, son chapelet,** to tell one's beads. *C. d'oignons,* string, rope, of onions. **Réservoirs en chapelet,** reservoirs arranged in series. **2.** *Arch:* Astragal. **3.** (Pompe à) chapelet, chain-pump.

chapelier [Sapəlje], *s.m.* Hatter.

chapelle [Sapɛl], *s.f.* **1.** (*a*) Chapel (in private house, etc.); side-chapel (of church); chapel of ease (of parish). *C. de la Vierge,* Lady chapel. *Lit: Art: F:* **Petite chapelle,** clique, coterie. (*b*) *Esp. Ecc:* Choir and/or orchestra. **Maître de chapelle,** choir-master. **2.** (*a*) *C. de pompe,* pump-case. (*b*) *I.C.E:* **Soupapes en chapelle,** side-valves.

chapellerie [Sapɛlri], *s.f.* Hat-trade, -shop.

chapelure [Saplyːr], *s.f.* Bread-crumbs (for frying).

chaperon [Saprɔ̃], *s.m.* **1.** Hood. **Le Petit Chaperon rouge,** Little Red Riding Hood. **2.** Chaperon (for young woman in society). **3.** (*a*) Coping (of wall). (*b*) Protecting lid or cover. [CHAPE]

chaperonner [Saprɔne], *v.tr.* **1.** To hood (falcon). **2.** To chaperon (young woman). **3.** *Const:* To cope (wall).

chapiteau [Sapito], *s.m.* (*a*) Capital (of column). (*b*) Cornice (of wardrobe, etc.).

chapitre [Sapitr], *s.m.* **1.** *Ecc:* Chapter (of canons). *F:* **Tenir chapitre,** to hold a meeting; to deliberate (*sur,* on). S.a. VOIX 2. **2.** (*a*) Chapter (of book). (*b*) Head(ing); item (of expenditure, etc.).

chapitrer [Sapitre], *v.tr. F:* To read (s.o.) a lecture.

chapon [Sapɔ̃], *s.m. Cu:* etc: Capon.

chaque [Sak], *a.* Each, every. *C. chose a sa place,* each thing has its place.

char [Saːr], *s.m.* **1.** *A:* Chariot. **2.** Waggon (for heavy loads). *C. funèbre,* hearse. *Mil:* **Char d'assaut,** tank.

charabia [Sarabja], *s.m. F:* Jargon, gibberish.

charade [Sarad], *s.f.* Charade.

charançon [Sarɑ̃sɔ̃], *s.m. Ent:* Weevil.

charançonné [Sarɑ̃sɔne], *a.* Weevil(l)ed, weevil(l)y.

charbon [Sarbɔ̃], *s.m.* **1.** (*a*) Charbon de bois, charcoal. *F:* **Être sur des charbons ardents,** to be on tenter-hooks. (*b*) *Ch:* Carbon. *C. de cornue,* gas-carbon. **Papier au charbon,** carbon tissue. (*c*) **Charbon de terre,** (mineral) coal. *C. sans fumée,* smokeless coal. *Nau:* **Faire le charbon,** to coal. **2.** (*a*) *Agr:* Smut (of cereal); blight. (*b*) *Med: Vet:* Anthrax. *Med:* Carbuncle.

charbonnage [Sarbɔnaːʒ], *s.m.* **1.** Coal-mining. **2.** *Usu. pl.* Collieries, coal-field. **3.** Coal-depot.

charbonner [Sarbɔne], *v.tr.* **1.** To reduce to carbon; to carbonize, char. *v.i. La lampe charbonne,* the lamp is smoking. **2.** To blacken (sth.) with charcoal. *Se c. le visage,* to black one's face. **3.** *Abs.* To coal ship; to bunker.

charbonnier, -ière [Sarbɔnje, -jɛːr], **1.** *a.* (Navire) charbonnier, collier. **2.** *s.* (*a*) Charcoal-burner. *Prov:* **Charbonnier est maître chez soi,** a man's house is his castle. (*b*) Coal-merchant.

charcuter [Sarkyte], *v.tr. F:* To mangle (meat) in carving. *C. un malade,* to operate clumsily upon, to butcher, a patient.

charcuterie [Sarkytri], *s.f.* **1.** Pork-butcher's shop. **2.** Pork-butcher's meat; pig-meat.

charcutier, -ière [Sarkytje, -jɛːr], *s.* Pork-butcher.

chardon [Sardɔ̃], *s.m.* Thistle.

chardonneret [Sardɔnrɛ], *s.m.* Goldfinch.

Charenton [Sarɑ̃tɔ̃], *Pr.n.m.* Small town near Paris with a lunatic asylum. *On se croirait à C.,* you would think this was Bedlam.

charge [Sarʒ], *s.f.* **1.** Load, burden. **Bête de charge,** beast of burden. **Cheval, mulet, de charge,** sumpter-horse, -mule. **Être à charge à qn,** to be a burden to, a drag on, s.o. *Nau:* **Ligne de charge,** load-line. **Rompre charge,** to break bulk. **2.** *Tchn:* (*a*) *Mec.E:* **C. admissible, de sécurité,** safe load. (*b*) *Hyd.E:* **C. d'eau,** head of water. (*c*) *El.E:* Charge. **Conducteur en charge,** live conductor. **3.** Charge (of furnace, projectile). **4.** (*a*) Charge, responsibility, trust. **Prendre en charge les recettes et dépenses,** to take over the receipts and expenditure. **Avoir charge d'âmes,** to have the cure of souls. **Avoir la charge de faire qch.,** to have the onus of doing sth. **Cela est à votre charge,** that is part of your duty. **Femme de charge,** housekeeper. (*b*) Office. **Charges publiques,** public offices. **5.** Charge, expense. *Les frais de transport sont à notre c.,* the cost of transport is chargeable to us. **Charges de famille,** dependents. **Tomber à la charge de la**

paroisse, *F :* to come on the parish. *Prep.phr.*
A (la) charge de, on condition of. A charge de
revanche, on condition that I may do as much
for you. **6.** Loading, charging. Vaisseau en
charge, ship loading. **7.** Exaggeration (of story).
Lit : Paint : Caricature (of character, portrait).
8. *Mil :* Charge. *C. à la baïonnette*, bayonet
charge. Revenir à la charge, to return to the
charge. **9.** *Jur :* Charge, indictment. Témoin à
charge, witness for the prosecution.

chargement [ʃarʒəmɑ̃], *s.m.* **1.** (*a*) Lading (of
ship); loading-up (of waggon); loading (of gun);
charging (of accumulator). (*b*) Registration (of
letter). **2.** (*a*) Cargo, freight, load. (*b*) Registered
letter or packet.

charger [ʃarʒe], *v.tr.* (je chargeai(s); n. char-
geons) **1.** To load (*de*, with). (*a*) *C. qn de reproches*,
to heap reproaches on s.o. *L'air est chargé du
parfum des fleurs*, the air is heavy with the scent
of flowers. (*b*) *C. qch. sur son dos*, to take sth. on
one's back. *Vaisseau qui charge pour Londres*,
ship taking in freight for London. (*c*) To fill
(pipe); to load (gun); to charge (accumulator).
2. *Charger qn de qch., de faire qch.*, to charge s.o.
with sth., with doing sth.; to instruct s.o. to do
sth. *Être chargé de la correspondance*, to be in
charge of the correspondence. **3.** To turn (portrait) into a caricature. *Th :* To overact, guy
(a part). **4.** *Mil :* To charge (the enemy). **5.** *Jur :*
To indict (s.o.). *C. qn d'un crime*, to charge s.o.
with a crime. **6.** To register (letter, parcel).
   se charger. 1. *Le temps se charge*, the
weather is becoming overcast. **2.** (*a*) *Se c. d'un
fardeau*, to shoulder a burden. (*b*) *Se c. de qch.*,
to undertake sth.
   chargé, *a.* **1.** Loaded, laden. **Langue
chargée,** coated, furred, tongue. *Jour c.*, full,
busy, day. *Regard c. de reconnaissance*, look full
of gratitude. **Temps chargé,** heavy, overcast,
weather. **2.** Lettre chargée, registered letter.
3. *s.* Chargé d'affaires, ambassador's deputy;
chargé d'affaires. *Sch :* Chargé(e) de cours,
deputy lecturer; (university) reader.

chariot [ʃarjo], *s.m.* **1.** (*a*) (Four-wheeled) waggon. *Astr :* Le grand Chariot, the Great Bear;
Charles's Wain. (*b*) (Child's) go-cart. (*c*) Truck,
trolley. **2.** (*a*) Carriage (of typewriter). (*b*) *Av :*
C. d'atterrissage, under-carriage; landing gear.

charitable [ʃaritabl], *a.* Charitable (*envers*, to,
towards). *adv.* -ment.

charité [ʃarite], *s.f.* **1.** Charity, love. Faire qch.
par charité, to do sth. out of, for, charity. Dame
de charité, district-visitor. **2.** Act of charity;
alms(-giving). Maison de charité, alms-house.
Faire la charité à qn, to give alms to s.o.

charivari [ʃarivari], *s.m.* Tin-kettle music;
rough music; din. *Faire un c. de tous les diables*,
to kick up no end of a din, of a racket.

charlatan, -ane [ʃarlatɑ̃, -an], *s.* Charlatan,
quack. Remède de charlatan, quack remedy.

charlatanisme [ʃarlatanism], *s.m.* Charla-
tanism, quackery.

Charlotte [ʃarlɔt]. **1.** *Pr.n.f.* Charlotte. **2.** *s.f.*
Cu : (*a*) Apple-charlotte. (*b*) Trifle.

charmant [ʃarmɑ̃], *a.* Charming, delightful.

charme[1] [ʃarm], *s.m.* **1.** Charm, spell. Demeurer,
être, sous le charme, to be under the spell.
Rompre le charme, to break the spell. **2.** Charm,
attraction, seductiveness.

charme[2], *s.m. Bot :* Hornbeam, yoke-elm.

charmer [ʃarme], *v.tr.* **1.** To charm, bewitch,
fascinate. **2.** To charm, please, delight. *Être
charmé de faire qch.*, to be delighted to do sth.
s. -eur, -euse.

charmille [ʃarmiːj], *s.f.* (*a*) Hedge(-row).
(*b*) Bower, arbour. [CHARME[2]]

charn|el, -elle [ʃarnɛl], *a.* Carnal, fleshly
(desires); sensual (person). *adv.* -ellement.

charnier [ʃarnje], *s.m.* **1.** *Nau :* Drinking-tank.
2. Charnel-house.

charnière [ʃarnjɛːr], *s.f.* Hinge; butt-hinge.

charnu [ʃarny], *a.* Fleshy. *Bras c.*, plump arm.
Fruits charnus, fleshy, pulpy, fruit.

charogne [ʃarɔɲ], *s.f.* **1.** Carrion; decaying
carcass. **2.** *P :* (*a*) Wench. (*b*) Scoundrel.

charpente [ʃarpɑ̃ːt], *s.f.* Frame(work), framing.
Bois de charpente, timber. *F : C. d'un roman*,
framework of a novel. (Of pers.) Avoir la
charpente solide, to be solidly built.

charpent|er [ʃarpɑ̃te], *v.tr.* **1.** To cut (timber)
into shape. **2.** To frame (up) (roof, etc.). *F :*
Charpenter un roman, to frame, construct, a
novel. *s.m.* -age.
   charpenté, *a.* Built, framed. *F : Homme
solidement c.*, well-knit, well-built, man.

charpenterie [ʃarpɑ̃tri], *s.f.* **1.** Carpentry.
2. Carpenter's shop.

charpentier [ʃarpɑ̃tje], *s.m.* Carpenter.

charpie [ʃarpi], *s.f.* Lint. (*a*) Mettre de la
en charpie, to shred linen. *F :* Mettre qn en
charpie, to make mincemeat of s.o. (*b*) Tissu
charpie, charpie anglaise, (modern) lint.

charretée [ʃarte], *s.f.* Cart-load, cartful.

charretier, -ière [ʃartje, -jɛːr]. **1.** *s.m.* Carter,
carrier, carman. S.a. JURER 4. **2.** *a.* Porte charretière, carriage gate(way).

charrette [ʃarɛt], *s.f.* Cart. *C. à bras*, hand-cart;
barrow.

charriage [ʃarjaːʒ], *s.m.* **1.** Cartage, haulage.
2. Drifting (of ice, of alluvial deposit).

charrier [ʃarje], *v.tr.* **1.** To cart, carry, transport.
2. *Rivière qui charrie du sable*, river that carries,
brings down, bears down, sand. *Abs. Le fleuve
charrie*, the river is full of drift-ice.

charroi [ʃarwa], *s.m.* (*a*) Cartage, carriage;
waggon traffic. (*b*) *pl. Mil :* Transport.

charron [ʃarɔ̃], *s.m.* Cartwright (and plough-
wright); wheelwright.

charronnage [ʃarɔnaːʒ], *s.m.* Cartwright's work.

charronnerie [ʃarɔnri], *s.f.* Cartwright's trade.

charroyer [ʃarwaje], *v.tr.* (je charroie; je char-
roierai) To transport (sth.) in a cart; to cart (sth.).

charrue [ʃary], *s.f.* **1.** Plough. *Mener, pousser,
la c.*, to drive the plough. Cheval de charrue,
plough-horse. *F :* Mettre la charrue devant les
bœufs, to put the cart before the horse. **2.** Snow-
plough.

charte [ʃart], *s.f.* **1.** Charter. **2.** (Ancient) deed;
title. L'École des chartes, the School of Palaeography and Librarianship (in Paris).

charte-partie, *s.f. Nau :* Charter-party. *pl. Des
chartes-parties.*

chartreux, -euse [ʃartrø, -øːz]. **1.** *s.* Carthusian
(monk, nun). **2.** *s.f.* Chartreuse. (*a*) Carthusian
monastery. (*b*) Chartreuse (liqueur).

Charybde [karibd]. *Pr.n.m. Gr.Myth :* Charyb-
dis. *F :* Tomber de Charybde en Scylla, to fall
out of the frying-pan into the fire.

chas [ʃɑ], *s.m.* Eye (of needle).

chasse [ʃas], *s.f.* **1.** (*a*) Hunting; game shooting.
Chasse à courre, stag-hunting. *C. au lévrier*,
coursing. *C. au tir*, shooting. Aller à la chasse,
to go hunting or shooting. Fusil de chasse,
(i) sporting gun; (ii) fowling-piece. (*b*) Chasse
gardée, (game) preserve. Louer une c., to rent
a shoot. S.a. PERMIS 2. (*c*) *Nau :* Donner chasse
à un navire, to give chase to a ship. **2.** Chasse

d'eau, flush, scour. **Chasse d'air,** rush of air ; blast. **3.** *Mec.E:* Play (of wheels).
châsse [ʃɑːs], *s.f.* **1.** Reliquary, shrine. **2.** Mounting ; frame (of spectacles).
chasse-clou(s), *s.m.inv. Tls:* (Nail-)set ; punch.
chassé-croisé, *s.m.* (a) *Danc:* 'Set to partners,' *chassé-croisé.* (b) *F:* General post. *pl. Des chassés-croisés.*
chasse-marée, *s.m.inv.* **1.** Fish-cart. **2.** Coasting lugger.
chasse-mouches, *s.m.inv.* Fly-killer ; *F:* fly-swatter.
chassepot [ʃaspo], *s.m. A:* Chassepot rifle (from name of designer).
chasser [ʃase]. **1.** *v.tr.* (a) To chase, hunt. *C. le renard, la perdrix,* to go fox-hunting, partridge shooting. *C. à courre,* to ride to hounds ; to hunt. *C. au fusil,* to shoot. (b) To drive (s.o.) out, away ; to turn (s.o.) out (of doors) ; to expel (s.o. from school, etc.) ; to dismiss (servant). *Le vent chasse la pluie contre les vitres,* the wind drives the rain against the panes. *Nuages chassés par le vent,* wind-driven clouds. *C. un clou,* to drive a nail in or out. **2.** *v.i.* (a) To hunt ; to shoot. *C. au lion,* to hunt lions. (b) To drive. *Nuages qui chassent du nord,* clouds that are driving from the north. *Navire qui chasse sur ses ancres,* ship that drags her anchors. (c) *Aut:* To skid. *Nau:* (Of anchor) To drag.
chasseresse [ʃasres], *s.f. Lit:* Huntress.
chasseur, -euse [ʃasœːr, -øːz], *s.* **1.** (a) Huntsman ; hunter, huntress. (b) Sportsman with a gun. *a. Chien c.,* hound or sporting dog. **2.** *s.m.* (a) Footman, lackey. (b) *C. d'hôtel,* commissionaire ; porter ; page-boy ; *F:* buttons. **3.** *s.m. Mil:* Rifleman. **Chasseurs à pied,** light infantry. **Chasseurs à cheval,** light cavalry. **4.** *s.m. Navy: Av:* Chaser.
chassie [ʃasi], *s.f.* Rheum, matter (in the eyes).
chassieux, -euse [ʃasjø, -øːz], *a.* Rheumy (eyes) ; rheumy-eyed (person).
châssis [ʃɑsi], *s.m.* (a) Frame. *C. de porte,* door-frame. *C. de fenêtre,* window-sash, -frame. **Châssis à guillotine,** sash-window. **Châssis vitré,** skylight(-roof). *Phot: C. négatif,* dark-slide. *C. positif,* printing-frame. (b) *Hort:* Forcing-frame. **Culture sous châssis,** forcing. (c) *Aut:* Chassis. *Av:* Under-carriage. *C. d'atterrissage,* landing-gear. (d) Base-board (of wireless set).
chaste [ʃast], *a.* Chaste, pure. *adv.* **-ment.**
chasteté [ʃastəte], *s.f.* Chastity, purity.
chasuble [ʃazybl], *s.f. Ecc.Cost:* Chasuble.
chat, *f.* **chatte** [ʃa, ʃat], *s.* **1.** Cat ; *m.* tom-cat ; *f.* tabby(-cat). **Le Chat botté,** Puss in Boots. *F: Mon petit c., ma petite chatte,* ducky, darling. **Musique de chat,** caterwauling. **Il n'y avait pas un chat dans la rue,** there wasn't a soul in the street. **Appeler un chat un chat,** to call a spade a spade. **Acheter chat en poche,** to buy a pig in a poke. *Prov:* Ne réveillez pas le chat qui dort, let sleeping dogs lie. **A bon chat bon rat,** tit for tat. **Chat échaudé craint l'eau froide,** once bitten twice shy. S.a. FOUETTER I. **2. Chat à neuf queues,** cat(-o'-nine-tails). **3.** *Games:* **Jeu du chat, tag ; tig.**
châtaigne [ʃatɛɲ], *s.f.* **1.** *Bot:* (a) (Sweet) chestnut. (b) **Châtaigne d'eau,** water-caltrops. **2.** Castor, chestnut (of horse).
châtaigneraie [ʃatɛɲrɛ], *s.f.* Chestnut plantation.
châtaignier [ʃatɛɲje], *s.m.* Chestnut-tree, -wood.
châtain [ʃatɛ̃], *a.* (Usu. *inv. in fem.,* occ. **-aine**) (Chestnut-)brown (hair, horse). *Une femme châtain(e),* a brown-haired woman. **Cheveux châtain clair,** light brown hair.

château [ʃato], *s.m.* **1.** Castle. **Château fort,** fortified castle. *F:* **Bâtir des châteaux en Espagne,** to build castles in the air. **2.** (a) Country seat ; manor, hall. **Vie de château,** country-house life. (b) (Royal) palace. **Le château de Versailles,** the palace of Versailles. **3.** Château d'eau, water-tower ; *Rail:* tank.
chateaubriant [ʃatobriã], *s.m.* Grilled steak.
châtelain [ʃatlɛ̃], *s.m.* (a) Castellan ; governor (of castle). (b) Lord (of manor).
châtelaine [ʃatlɛn], *s.f.* **1.** (a) Castellan's wife. (b) Lady (of manor). **2.** Chatelaine (for keys, etc.).
châtelet [ʃatlɛ], *s.m.* Small castle.
chat-huant [ʃaɥã], *s.m.* Tawny owl ; brown owl. *pl. Des chats-huants.*
châti|er [ʃatje], *v.tr.* To punish, chastise ; to chasten (style). *C. son corps,* to mortify the body. *Prov:* **Qui aime bien châtie bien,** spare the rod and spoil the child. *s.m.* **-eur.**
  châtié, *a.* Polished (style, verse).
chatière [ʃatjɛːr], *s.f.* (a) Hole (for cat in door). (b) *F:* Secret entrance.
châtiment [ʃatimã], *s.m.* Punishment, chastisement.
chatoiement, chatoîment [ʃatwamã], *s.m.* (a) Shimmer ; sheen. (b) Glistening.
chaton¹, -onne [ʃatɔ̃, -ɔn], *s.* **1.** Kitten. **2.** *s.m. Bot:* Catkin.
chaton², *s.m. Lap:* **1.** Bezel, setting (of stone). **2.** Stone (in its setting).
chatouill|er [ʃatuje], *v.tr.* To tickle. **Chatouiller les côtes à qn,** (i) to poke s.o. in the ribs ; (ii) *F:* to give s.o. a thrashing. *s.m.* **-ement.**
chatouilleux, -euse [ʃatujø, -øːz], *a.* **1.** (Of pers.) (a) Ticklish. (b) Sensitive, touchy. **Chatouilleux sur le point d'honneur,** touchy on a point of honour. **2.** Delicate, sore (point).
chatoyant [ʃatwajã], *a.* Iridescent, chatoyant.
chatoyer [ʃatwaje], *v.i.* (il chatoie ; il chatoiera) (a) To shimmer. (b) To glisten, sparkle.
châtrer [ʃatre], *v.tr.* To castrate.
chatte. See CHAT.
chattemite [ʃatmit], *s.f. F:* Mealy-mouthed flatterer ; *F:* toady.
chatterie [ʃatri], *s.f.* **1.** Usu. *pl.* Wheedling ways ; coaxing. **2.** *pl.* Delicacies, dainties.
chatterton [ʃatɛrtɔ̃], *s.m. El.E:* Adhesive (insulating) tape.
chat-tigre, *s.m.* Tiger-cat. *pl. Des chats-tigres.*
chaud [ʃo]. **1.** *a.* (a) Warm or hot. **Avoir les pieds chauds,** to have warm feet. *F:* **Avoir la tête chaude,** to be hot-headed. *Affaire chaude,* sharp tussle ; brisk engagement. *Chaude dispute,* warm, animated, discussion. **Pleurer à chaudes larmes,** to weep bitterly. *Nouvelle toute chaude,* piping-hot news. *Tons chauds,* warm tints. *Prov:* **Il faut battre le fer pendant qu'il est chaud,** strike while the iron is hot. *F:* **Coûter chaud,** to cost a pretty penny. *V.phr.* **Il fait chaud,** it is warm (weather, or in this room). (b) Warm, warming. *Couverture chaude,* warm blanket. **Fièvre chaude,** brain-fever. **2.** *s.m.* (Warm state) **Il est au chaud dans sa maison,** he is snug and warm, nice and warm, at home. (On label) **Tenir au chaud,** to be kept in a warm place. **Cela ne fera ni chaud ni froid,** it will make no difference. **Cela ne me fait ni chaud ni froid,** it is all the same, all one, to me. **Souffler le chaud et le froid,** to blow hot and cold. **Attraper un chaud et froid,** to catch a chill. **Marqué à chaud,** branded. **Avoir chaud,** (of pers.) to be, feel, warm. **Prendre chaud,** to get over-heated. *adv.* **-ement.**

chaud-froid, *s.m. C.-f. de poulet,* cold jellied chicken. *pl. Des chauds-froids.*

chaudière [ʃodjɛːr], *s.f.* **1.** Copper (for washing, etc.). **2.** Boiler. *C. de cuisine,* range boiler. *Mch : C. à vapeur,* steam-boiler ; steam generator.

chaudron [ʃodrɔ̃], *s.m.* Ca(u)ldron.

chaudronnerie [ʃodrɔnri], *s.f.* **1.** Tinman's, coppersmith's, work or shop. **2. Grosse chaudronnerie,** (i) boiler-making ; (ii) boiler-works.

chaudronnier, -ière [ʃodrɔnje, -jɛːr], *s.* **1.** Brazier, tinman. *C. en, de, cuivre,* copper-smith ; brass-worker. **Chaudronnier ambulant,** tinker. **2.** *(a)* Boiler-smith. *(b)* Boiler-maker.

chauffage [ʃofaːʒ], *s.m.* **1.** *(a)* Warming, heating (of room, etc.). **Chauffage central,** central heating. *(b)* Firing, stoking (of boiler). *(c) P:* Cramming (of student for examination). **2.** Overheating (of bearing, etc.).

chauffard [ʃofaːr], *s.m. P:* Scorcher ; road-hog.

chauffe [ʃoːf], *s f.* **1.** Heating. **Donner une chauffe à qch.,** to warm sth. up. **2.** *Mch :* Firing, stoking. **Porte de chauffe,** fire-door ; fire-hole. **Activer la chauffe,** to fire up. *Nau :* **Chef de chauffe,** leading stoker. **Chambre de chauffe,** stokehold. **3.** Overheating (of bearings, etc.).

chauffe-assiette, *s.m.* Plate-warmer ; hotplate. *pl. Des chauffe-assiettes.*

chauffe-bain, *s.m.* Bath-heater ; geyser. *pl. Des chauffe-bains.*

chauffe-pieds, *s.m. inv.* Foot-warmer.

chauffe-plat, *s.m.* Chafing-dish. *pl. Des chauffe-plats.*

chauffer [ʃofe]. **1.** *v.tr.* *(a)* To warm, heat. *C. du linge,* to air linen. *Hort : C. une plante,* to force a plant. *(b) C. le fer à blanc, au rouge,* to bring iron to a white heat, to a red heat. *Chauffé à blanc, au rouge,* white-hot, red-hot. *C. une chaudière, une locomotive,* to stoke up, fire up, a boiler, an engine ; to raise steam. *Abs.* (Of ship, etc.) *C. au charbon, au mazout,* to burn coal, oil. *F :* **Il faut chauffer l'affaire,** we must strike while the iron is hot. *C. qn en vue d'un examen,* to cram, stuff, s.o. for an examination. *C. un examen,* to swot for an examination. S.a. BOIS¹ 3. **2.** *v.i.* *(a)* To get, become, warm, hot. *P:* **Ça va chauffer,** things are getting warm. *(b)* (Of bearing, etc.) To run hot ; to overheat.

chaufferette [ʃofrɛt], *s.f.* Foot-warmer (usu. heated with charcoal).

chauffeur, -euse [ʃofœːr, -øːz], *s.* **1.** *(a)* Stoker, fireman (of steam-engine). *(b) Sch : P:* Crammer. **2.** *Aut :* Driver ; chauffeur, chauffeuse.

chaufournier [ʃofurnje], *s.m.* Lime-burner.

chauler [ʃole], *v.tr.* To lime ; to sprinkle (ground, etc.) with lime ; to lime-wash (fruit-trees, etc.). [CHAUX] *s.m.* **-age.**

chaulier [ʃolje], *s.m.* Lime-burner.

chaume [ʃoːm], *s.m.* *(a)* Straw (of corn) ; haulm. *(b)* Thatch. *Toit de c.,* thatched roof. *(c)* (i) Stubble ; (ii) stubble-field.

chaumer [ʃome], *v.tr. Agr :* To clear (a field) of stubble. *s.m.* **-age.**

chaumière [ʃomjɛːr], *s.f.* Thatched cottage.

chaumine [ʃomin], *s.f. Poet :* Tiny (thatched) cottage ; cot.

chausse [ʃoːs], *s.f.* **1.** *pl. A :* **Des chausses,** **une paire de chausses,** hose, breeches. **Il y laissa ses chausses,** he died there. **C'est la femme qui porte les chausses,** it's the wife who wears the breeches. **2.** Straining-bag (for wine, etc.).

chaussée [ʃose], *s.f.* **1.** *(a)* Sea-wall. *(b)* Causeway (across marsh, etc.). **La Chaussée des Géants,** the Giant's Causeway. **2.** *(a)* Roadway, carriage-way. *(b)* Road ; high road. S.a. PONT¹ 1.

chausse-pied, *s.m.* Shoe-horn.

chausser [ʃose], *v.tr.* **1.** To put on (one's stockings, one's shoes). *Chaussé de pantoufles,* wearing (his) slippers. *Chaussé de ses bottes et de ses éperons,* booted and spurred. *C. les étriers,* to put one's feet into the stirrups. *F : C. ses lunettes,* to put on one's spectacles. **2.** *(a)* To put shoes on (s.o.). **Se chausser,** to put on one's shoes, boots. *F :* **Être chaussé d'une opinion,** to be fixed in an opinion. *(b)* To supply, fit, (s.o.) with footwear ; to make footwear for (s.o.). *Le cordonnier qui me chausse,* the shoemaker who makes my boots. *Être bien chaussé,* to be well shod. *F :* **Cela me chausse (bien),** that suits me (down to the ground). *(c) C. du 38,* to take 38 (in shoes) (French sizes).

chausse-trape, *s.f.* **1.** Trap (for wolves, etc.). *F :* Ruse, trick, trap. **2.** *Mil : A :* Caltrop. **3.** *Bot :* Star-thistle. *pl. Des chausse-trapes.*

chaussette [ʃosɛt], *s.f.* Sock. [CHAUSSE]

chausson [ʃosɔ̃], *s.m.* **1.** *(a) C. de lisière,* list slipper. *(b) Chaussons de danse,* (ladies') dancing sandals, opera sandals. *(c)* Gymnasium shoe. **2.** = SAVATE. **3.** *Cu :* **Chausson aux pommes,** apple turn-over. [CHAUSSE]

chaussure [ʃosyːr], *s.f.* Foot-wear, foot-gear. *Fabricant de chaussures,* boot and shoe manufacturer. *Une paire de chaussures,* a pair of boots, of shoes. *F :* **Trouver chaussure à son pied,** to find one's match. a. [CHAUSSER]

chauve [ʃoːv]. **1.** *a.* Bald. **A tête chauve,** bald-headed. *(b)* Bare, denuded (mountain, etc.). **2.** *s.m.* Bald person, bald-head, *Hum :* bald-pate.

chauve-souris, *s.f. Z :* Bat. *pl. Des chauves-souris.*

chauvin, -ine [ʃovɛ̃, -in]. **1.** *s.* Chauvinist, jingo. **2.** *a.* Chauvinist(ic), jingoist(ic).

chauvinisme [ʃovinism], *s.m.* Chauvinism ; jingoism.

chaux [ʃo], *s.f.* Lime. **Chaux vive,** quicklime. *C. éteinte,* slaked, slack(ed), lime. **Pierre à chaux,** limestone. **Eau de chaux,** lime-water. **Lait, blanc, de chaux,** lime-wash, whitewash. **Blanchir un mur à la chaux,** to whitewash a wall. *F :* **Bâtir à chaux et à sable, à chaux et à ciment,** to build firmly, solidly.

chavirer [ʃavire]. **1.** *v.i.* (Of boat, etc.) To capsize, turn turtle, upset. **2.** *v.tr.* *(a)* To turn (sth.) upside down ; to upset, capsize (boat). *(b)* To tip, shoot (refuse, etc.). *s.m.* **-ement.**

chébec [ʃebɛk], *s.m. Nau :* Xebec.

chéchia [ʃeʃja], *s.f.* (Military) cap (worn by troops serving in Africa) ; tarboosh.

chef [ʃɛf], *s.m.* **1.** *(a) A :* Head. (Still used in) **Venir à chef de son dessein,** to achieve one's end. **Il pense de son chef,** he thinks for himself. *(b) Her :* Chief (of shield). **2.** Head (of family, etc.) ; chief (of tribe, clan) ; leader (of political party) ; principal, head, chief (of business house) ; foreman (of jury) ; conductor (of orchestra) ; (scout-)master. *Chefs de service(s),* heads of departments ; departmental managers. *C. de bureau,* head clerk. **Chef de cabinet** = (minister's) principal private secretary. *C. de bande,* ringleader. **Chef de cuisine,** chef. *Mil : Navy :* **Chef de l'état-major,** chief of staff. **Chef de bataillon,** major. **Chef de file,** leading man of a file ; *Navy :* leading ship. **Chef de musique,** bandmaster. S.a. PUPITRE 3. *Nau :* **Chef de quart,** watchkeeper. *Row :* **Chef de nage,** stroke(-oar). *Sp :* **Chef d'équipe,** captain. *Rail :* **Chef de gare,** station master. **Chef de train,** guard. **Commander une armée en chef,** to be commander-in-chief of an army. **Ingénieur en chef,** chief engineer. S.a. CHAUFFE 2. **3.** Authority, right. **Faire qch. de son (propre) chef,** to do sth. on one's own (authority). **Posséder qch. de son chef,** to possess sth. in one's own right. **4.** Head(ing). *Arranger les matières d'un livre sous plusieurs chefs,* to arrange the matter of a book under several heads. *Jur :* Chef d'accusation, count of indictment. *Il importe* au premier chef *que . . .,* it is essential that. . . .

chef-d'œuvre [ʃɛdœːvr], *s.m.* Masterpiece. *pl. Des chefs-d'œuvre.*

chef-lieu [ʃɛfljø], *s.m.* Chief town (of department). *pl. Des chefs-lieux.*

cheik-[ʃɛk], *s.m.* Sheik(h).

chelem [ʃlɛm], *s.m. Cards :* Slam. **Grand** *c., petit c.,* grand, little, slam. **Faire chelem,** to make a slam.

chélidoine [kelidwan],*s.f. Bot :* Great celandine.

chemin [ʃmɛ̃],*s.m.* **I.** (a) Way, road. *C. détourné, F :* **chemin des écoliers,** roundabout way, by-road. *Il y a dix minutes de c.,* it is ten minutes away. **Faire son chemin,** to make one's way. **Chemin faisant,** on the way. **Faire un bout de chemin avec qn,** to accompany s.o. a little way. **Tout le long du chemin,** all the way. **Nous sommes dans le bon chemin,** we are on the right road. **A moitié chemin,** half-way. **Se mettre en chemin,** to set out. **Être en chemin de faire qch.,** to be well on the road to achieving sth. **S'arrêter en chemin,** to stop on the way. **Demeurer en chemin,** to stop in mid-career. **Être dans, sur, le chemin de qn,** to be, stand, in s.o.'s way. **Ne pas y aller par quatre chemins, par trente-six chemins,** to go straight to the point. S.a. CROIX I. (b) *Nau :* **Faire du chemin,** to make headway. (c) Road, path, track. *C. piéton,* footpath. **Grand chemin,** highway, high road. **Chemin battu,** beaten track. *F :* **Être toujours par voies et par chemins,** to gad about. *Mec.E :* **Chemin de roulement pour billes,** ball-race. **2. Chemin de fer,** railway. *F :* **Aller,** *voyager,* en c. de fer, to go, travel, by rail, by train. **3. Chemin de table,** (table) runner.

chemineau [ʃmino], *s.m.* **I.** Tramp, vagrant. **2.** *Nau :* Tramp (steamer).

cheminée [ʃmine], *s.f.* **I.** (a) Fireplace. **Pierre de la cheminée,** hearthstone. (b) (Manteau de) **cheminée,** chimney-piece, mantelpiece. **Garniture de cheminée,** set of chimney-piece ornaments. **2.** (a) Chimney (flue or stack). *C. d'usine,* chimney-stalk ; smoke-stack. (b) Funnel (of locomotive, steamer).

chemin|er [ʃmine], *v.i.* **I.** To tramp, walk, proceed. *C. sous la pluie,* to trudge, plod, tramp, on in the rain. **2.** *Surv :* To traverse. *s.m.* **-ement.**

cheminot [ʃmino], *s.m.* Railwayman ; esp. plate-layer.

chemise [ʃmiːz], *s.f.* **I.** (a) (For men) Shirt. *C. molle, souple,* soft shirt. *C. empesée,* stiff shirt. **En bras, en manches, de chemise,** in one's shirt sleeves. *Archeol :* C. de mailles, shirt of mail. S.a. TOILE I. (b) **Chemise de nuit,** (man's) night-shirt ; (woman's) night-dress, night-gown. (c) (For women) Chemise. *C. de tricot,* under-vest. (d) *Nau :* (Sailor's) frock, jumper. **2.** (a) Jacket (for MS. matter, etc.) ; folder. (b) Dust-jacket (of book). (c) **Pommes de terre en chemise,** potatoes cooked in their jackets. (d) Jacket(ing), casing, sheathing (of boiler, cylinder, etc.). *C. de vapeur,* steam-jacket. *C. d'eau,* water-jacket. (e) *I.C.E :* Sleeve (of sleeve-valve).

chemiser [ʃmize], *v.tr.* **I.** To jacket, case (boiler, cylinder). **2.** To line (gun, cylinder).

chemiserie [ʃmizri], *s.f.* Shirt factory or shop.

chênaie [ʃɛnɛ], *s.f.* Oak-grove, -plantation.

chenal, -aux [ʃ(ə)nal, -o], *s.m.* **I.** Channel, fairway (of river, harbour). *Au milieu du c.,* in mid-channel. **2.** Mill-race.

chenapan [ʃnapɑ̃], *s.m.* Rogue, scoundrel.

chêne [ʃɛn], *s.m.* Oak. **Chêne vert,** holm-oak.

chéneau [ʃeno], *s.m.* (Eaves-)gutter.

chêne-liège, *s.m.* Cork-oak. *pl. Des chênes-lièges.*

chenet [ʃ(ə)nɛ], *s.m.* Fire-dog ; andiron.

chènevière [ʃɛnvjɛːr], *s.f.* Hemp-field.

chènevis [ʃɛnvi], *s.m.* Hempseed.

chenil [ʃ(ə)ni], *s.m.* Kennels (of hunt).

chenille [ʃ(ə)niːj],*s.f.* **I.** (a) Caterpillar. (b) Band of caterpillar tractor. **2.** *Tex :* Chenille.

chénopode [kenɔpɔd], *s.m. Bot :* Goosefoot.

chenu [ʃ(ə)ny], *a.* (a) (Of hair, pers.) Bleached (with age) ; hoary. (b) *F :* Vin chenu, (matured) wine.

cheptel [ʃətɛl, ʃeptɛl], *s.m.* (Live-)stock. **Bail à cheptel,** lease of live-stock.

chèque [ʃɛk], *s.m.* Cheque. *C. de £60,* cheque for £60. *C. barré,* crossed cheque. *C. ouvert,* open, uncrossed, cheque. *C. prescrit,* stale cheque. *Toucher un c.,* to cash a cheque.

cher, *f.* **chère¹** [ʃɛr], *a.* **I.** Dear, beloved. *Être c. à qn,* to be dear to s.o. *s.* **Mon cher,** my dear fellow. **Ma chère,** my dear. **2.** Dear, expensive, costly. *La vie chère,* high prices. *adv. Cela se vendit c.,* it fetched a high price. **Il fait cher vivre à Paris,** the cost cf living is very high in Paris. **Cela ne vaut pas cher,** it is not worth much. **Il me le payera cher,** I will make him pay dearly for it. **Je l'ai eu pour pas cher,** I got it cheap.

chercher [ʃɛrʃe], *v.tr.* **I.** To search for, look for (s.o., sth.) ; to seek. *Je l'ai cherché partout,* I have hunted for it everywhere. *C. un mot au dictionnaire,* to look out, look up, turn up, a word in the dictionary. *C. un emploi,* to look for a situation. *C. son chemin,* to try to find one's way. *C. sa ruine,* to court one's own ruin. **Chercher aventure,** to seek adventures. S.a. BÊTE I, MIDI I. **2. Aller chercher qn, qch.,** to (go and) fetch s.o., sth. *Allez c. le médecin,* go for a doctor. **Envoyer chercher qn, qch.,** to send for s.o., sth. **3. Chercher à faire qch.,** to endeavour, attempt, to do sth.

chercheur, -euse [ʃɛrʃœːr, -øːz], *s.* **I.** Seeker, searcher ; investigator. *C. de laboratoire,* chemical research worker. *a. Esprit c.,* enquiring spirit. **2.** *s.m.* Finder (of telescope).

chère² [ʃɛːr], *s.f.* Cheer, fare, living. **Faire maigre chère,** to be on short commons. **Faire bonne chère,** to fare sumptuously. *Aimer la bonne c.,* to be fond of good living, of good cheer.

chèrement [ʃɛrmɑ̃], *adv.* **I.** Dearly, lovingly. **2.** Dearly ; at a high price. **Vendre chèrement sa vie,** to sell one's life dearly ; to die hard.

chérif [ʃerif], *s.m.* (Mohammedan) shereef, sherif.

chérir [ʃeriːr], *v.tr.* To cherish ; to love (s.o.) dearly. S.a. PRUNELLE 2.

chéri, -ie. *I. a.* Cherished, dear. **2.** *s.* Dear one. **Ma chérie,** dearest.

cherté [ʃɛrte],*s.f.* Dearness, expensiveness ; high price (of provisions, etc.).

chérubin [ʃerybɛ̃], *s.m.* Cherub. *Des chérubins,* cherubs, cherubim.

chét|if, -ive [ʃetif, -iːv], *a.* **I.** Weak, puny, sickly (person). *Arbuste c.,* puny, stunted, shrub. **2.** Poor, miserable, wretched. *adv.* **-ivement.**

cheval, -aux [ʃ(ə)val, ʃfal, -o], *s.m.* **I.** Horse. (a) *C. de trait,* draught-horse. *C. de charrette, de roulage,* cart-horse, dray-horse. *C. de brancard,* off-wheeler. *C. de selle,* saddle-horse. *C. de chasse,* hunter. *C. de course,* race-horse. *C. de bât,* pack-horse. **Voiture à deux chevaux,** carriage and pair. **A cheval,** on horseback. *Aller à c.,* to ride. **Monter à cheval,** (i) to mount one's horse; (ii) to go in for riding. **Être à cheval sur qch.,** to sit astride sth.; to straddle sth. *F:* **Être à cheval sur l'étiquette,** to be a stickler for etiquette. **Être à cheval sur l'algèbre,** to be well up in algebra. **Monter sur ses grands chevaux,** to ride the high horse. **Remède de cheval,** drastic remedy. **Fièvre de cheval,** raging fever. *(b) Ich:* **Cheval marin,** sea-horse, hippocampus. **2. Cheval de bois,** wooden horse; *Gym:* vaulting horse. *C. à bascule,* rocking-horse. **Chevaux de bois,** roundabout, merry-go-round. **3.** *Mch:* **Petit cheval,** donkey-engine, auxiliary horse. **4.** *Mec:* (= CHEVAL-VAPEUR) Horse-power. **Automobile de vingt chevaux,** *F:* **une vingt chevaux,** twenty horse-power motor car.

chevalement [ʃ(ə)valmɑ̃, ʃfal-], *s.m.* **1.** Shoring, props (of wall, etc.). **2.** Pit-head frame; gallows frame (of mine-shaft); winding-plant; derrick.

chevaleresque [ʃ(ə)valrɛsk, ʃfal-], *a.* Chivalrous, knightly. *adv.* **-ment.**

chevalerie [ʃ(ə)valri, ʃfal-], *s.f.* **1.** Knighthood. *Conférer la c. à qn,* to confer a knighthood on s.o. **2.** Chivalry. **Chevalerie errante,** knight-errantry.

chevalet [ʃ(ə)valɛ, ʃfalɛ], *s.m.* Support, stand. *(a)* Trestle, frame, stand. *C. de scieur,* saw-bench, -horse. *(b) C. de peintre,* easel. *(c) Mec:E:* Pedestal (of bearing). *(d)* (i) Clothes-horse; (ii) towel-horse. *(e)* Bridge (of violin, etc.). [CHEVAL]

chevalier [ʃ(ə)valje, ʃfal-], *s.m.* **1.** *(a)* Knight. *C. errant,* knight-errant. **Créer qn chevalier,** to knight s.o. **Armer qn chevalier,** to dub s.o. knight. *F:* **Chevalier de fortune,** soldier of fortune. **Chevalier d'industrie,** adventurer, sharper. *(b)* Chevalier (of the Legion of Honour). *(c)* Rider. **Les Quatre chevaliers de l'Apocalypse,** the Four Horsemen of the Apocalypse. **2.** *Orn:* Sandpiper.

chevalière [ʃəvaljɛːr, ʃfal-], *s.f.* **(Bague à la) chevalière,** signet-ring; seal-ring.

chevalin, -ine [ʃəvalɛ̃, ʃfalɛ̃, -in], *a.* Equine. **Boucherie chevaline,** horse-butcher's shop.

cheval-vapeur, *s.m. Mec:* (French) horse-power (= 32,549 foot-pounds per minute). *pl.* **Des chevaux-vapeur.**

chevauchant [ʃ(ə)voʃɑ̃], *a.* Overlapping.

chevauchée [ʃ(ə)voʃe], *s.f.* **1.** Ride. **2.** Cavalcade.

chevauch|er [ʃ(ə)voʃe]. **1.** *v.i. (a)* To ride (on horse). *(b) C. sur un mur,* to sit astride a wall. *(c)* To overlap. *Carp:* Joint chevauché, lapped joint. *(d)* (Of wires) To cross. *(e) Surg:* (Of fractured bones) To ride. *Geol:* To overthrust. *(f) Typ:* (Of type) To fall, drop, out of place. **2.** *v.tr.* To ride (on), straddle, to be astride (donkey, etc.). *s.m.* **-age.** *s.m.* **-ement.**

se chevaucher, (of catalogues, etc.) to overlap.

chevêche [ʃəvɛːʃ], *s.f. Orn:* Sparrow-owl.

chevelu [ʃəvly], *a.* **1.** Long-haired. **2.** *(a)* Hairy. **Cuir chevelu,** scalp. *(b) Bot:* Comose.

chevelure [ʃəvly:r], *s.f.* **1.** (Head of) hair. **Chasseurs de chevelures,** scalp-hunters. **2.** *(a)* Tail (of comet). *(b)* Coma (of seed). [CHEVEU]

chevesne [ʃ(ə)vɛːn], *s.m. Ich:* Chub.

chevet [ʃ(ə)vɛ], *s.m. (a)* Bed-head. *Livre de c.,* bedside book. *(b)* Bolster.

cheveu, -eux [ʃ(ə)vø], *s.m.* **1.** (A single) hair. **Être à un cheveu de la ruine,** to be within a hair's-breadth of disaster. **Fendre, couper, un cheveu en quatre,** to split hairs. **Comme un cheveu dans la soupe,** very inappropriate. **Voilà**

le cheveu! there's the rub! **2. Les cheveux,** the hair. (Of woman) **Être en cheveux,** to be wearing no hat. **S'arracher les cheveux,** to tear one's hair. **Argument tiré par les cheveux,** far-fetched argument. S.a. SE DRESSER, OCCASION I.

cheville [ʃ(ə)viːj], *s.f.* **1.** Peg, pin. *C. en bois,* peg, dowel(-pin). *C. en fer,* bolt. **Cheville ouvrière,** (i) king-bolt, -pin (of vehicle); (ii) *F:* mainspring (of enterprise, etc.). **2.** *(a)* Peg, plug (for filling up hole). *(b) Lit:* Expletive (word); padding (in line of verse). **3.** *Anat:* Ankle. *F:* **Il ne vous vient, monte, pas à la cheville,** he can't hold a candle to you.

chevill|er [ʃəvije], *v.tr.* **1.** To pin, bolt, peg, (sth.) together. *F:* **Avoir l'âme chevillée au dans le, corps,** to be hard to kill. **2.** To peg, plug (up). *Lit: C. un vers,* to pad, tag, a line of verse. *s.m.* **-age.**

cheviote [ʃəvjɔt], *s.f. Tex:* Cheviot (cloth). *C. écossaise,* tweed.

chèvre [ʃɛːvr], *s.f.* **1.** Goat, esp. she-goat, *F:* nanny-goat. **Barbe de chèvre,** goatee. *F:* **Ménager la chèvre et le chou,** to run with the hare and hunt with the hounds. **2.** *(a) Mec.E: Const:* etc: Gin, crab, derrick. *C. à haubans,* sheer-legs. *(b) Veh:* Jack. *(c)* Saw-horse.

chevreau [ʃəvro], *s.m.* Kid. **Gants de chevreau,** kid gloves.

chèvrefeuille [ʃɛvrəfœːj], *s.m.* Honeysuckle.

chevrette [ʃəvrɛt], *s.f.* **1.** Kid; young (she-)goat. **2.** *(a)* Tripod, trivet. *(b)* Carriage-jack. *(c)* Fire-dog, andiron. **3.** *Crust: F:* Shrimp or prawn.

chevreuil [ʃəvrœːj], *s.m.* Roe-deer; *(mâle)* roe-buck. **Peau de chevreuil,** buckskin. *Quartier de c.,* haunch of venison.

chevrier, -ière [ʃəvrie, -iɛːr], *s.* Goatherd; *f.* goat-girl.

chevron [ʃəvrɔ̃], *s.m.* **1.** Rafter (of roof). **2.** *Her:* Chevron. *Tex:* **En chevron,** in herring-bone pattern. **Engrenage à chevrons,** double helical gearing. **3.** *Mil:* Long-service stripe.

chevrotain [ʃəvrɔtɛ̃], *s.m. Z:* Musk-deer.

chevrotant [ʃəvrɔtɑ̃], *a.* Quavering, tremulous (voice).

chevrot|er [ʃəvrɔte], *v.i.* To sing, speak, in a quavering voice; to quaver. *s.m.* **-ement.**

chevrotine [ʃəvrɔtin], *s.f. (a)* (Pellet of) buck-shot, *F:* buck-shot.

chez [ʃe], *prep.* **1.** *(a)* **Chez qn,** at s.o.'s house, home, abode. *Je vais c. moi,* I am going home. *C. mon grand-père,* at my grandfather's. **Acheter qch. c. l'épicier,** to buy sth. at the grocer's. *Il demeure c. nous,* he lives with us. (On letters) **Chez . . . ,** care of . . . , c/o. . . . **Faire comme chez soi,** to make oneself at home. *Porter la guerre c. l'ennemi,* to carry the war into the enemy's country. *(b)* **Son chez-soi,** one's home, one's house. **Je pars pour chez ma sœur,** I am off to my sister's (house). **2.** With, among. *C'est une habitude c. moi,* it is a habit with me. *Il en est ainsi c. les Français,* it is so among Frenchmen. *C. les animaux,* in the animal kingdom. *C. Molière on trouve . . . ,* in Molière one finds. . . .

chic [ʃik]. **I.** *s.m. (a)* Skill, knack. **Il a le chic pour (faire) cela,** he has the knack of doing that. *(b)* Smartness, stylishness. **Il a du chic,** he has style. **Porter un monocle par chic,** to wear a monocle for effect, *F:* for swank. *(c) Art:* **Peindre de chic,** to paint without a model. **2.** *a. inv. in f.,* var. *in pl. (a)* Smart, stylish. *Dîner c.,* fashionable dinner. *Les gens chics,* the smart set. *(b) P:* Fine, first-rate. *C. dîner,* first-class, slap-up, dinner. **C'est un chic type,** he's a topping chap. *Sois c.!* come, be a sport!

chicane [ʃikan], s.f. **1.** (a) Chicanery, petti-foggery. (b) Quibbling, wrangling. Chercher **chicane à qn**, to try to pick a quarrel with s.o. (c) (At bridge) Chicane. **2.** (a) Baffle(-plate); de-flector. **Joints en chicane**, staggered joints. (b) Mil: Zigzag trench.

chicaner [ʃikane]. **1.** v.i. To chicane, quibble. C. sur les frais, to haggle over the expense. **2.** v.tr. C. qn, to wrangle with s.o. (sur, about).
  se **chicaner**, to squabble (avec, with).

chicanerie [ʃikanri], s.f. Chicanery, quibbling.

chicaneur, -euse [ʃikanœːr, -øːz], **chicanier, -ière** [ʃikanje, -jɛːr]. **1.** s. (a) Person fond of lawsuits; barrator. (b) Quibbler, haggler, caviller. **2.** a. (a) Fond of lawsuits. (b) Quibbling, haggling, captious.

chiche[1] [ʃiʃ], a. (a) (Of thg) Scanty, poor. (b) (Of pers.) Stingy, niggardly. F: Être c. de louanges, to be chary, sparing, of praise. adv. **-ment**.

chiche[2], s.m. (Pois) chiche, chick-pea.

chichi [ʃiʃi], s.m. F: **1.** Piece of false hair (in short curls). **2.** pl. Affected manners. **Gens à chichis**, over-polite people. **Faire des chichis**, (i) to put on airs; (ii) to put difficulties in the way.

chicorée [ʃikɔre], s.f. **1.** C. sauvage, chicory, succory. C. frisée, endive. **2.** (Poudre de) chicorée, (ground) chicory.

chicot [ʃiko], s.m. Stump (of tree, of tooth); hunch (of bread).

chien, f. chienne [ʃjɛ̃, ʃjɛn], s. **1.** Dog; f. bitch. **Chien de berger**, sheep-dog. C. d'attache, de garde, watch-dog. **Chien courant**, hound. **Chien d'arrêt**, pointer. **Chien couchant**, setter. F: **Faire le chien couchant auprès de qn**, to cringe to, fawn on, s.o. **Se regarder en chiens de faïence**, to stare rudely, to glare, at one another. **Avoir d'autres chiens à fouetter**, to have other, fish to fry. **Garder à qn un chien de sa chienne**, to have a rod in pickle for s.o. **Entre chien et loup**, in the twilight, in the gloaming. Prov: Qui veut noyer son chien l'accuse de rage, give a dog a bad name and hang him. F: **Vie de chien**, dog's life. **Quel temps de chien! quel chien de temps!** what awful, beastly, weather! S.a. QUILLE[1], ROMPRE 1. **2.** P: (a) **Avoir du chien**, (i) to have charm; (ii) to have pluck. (b) **Porter des chiens, être coiffée à la chien**, to wear a bang, a fringe. (c) a. **Être chien**, to be mean, stingy. **3.** Tchn: (a) Hammer (of gun). F: **Se coucher en chien de fusil**, to curl up in one's bed. (b) Mec.E: **Chien d'arrêt**, pawl, catch.

chiendent [ʃjɛ̃dɑ̃], s.m **1.** Bot: Couch-grass. P: **Voilà le chiendent!** there's the rub! **2.** Brosse en c., grass brush, whisk brush.

chiffe [ʃif], s.f. Rag. F: **Mou comme une chiffe**, as limp as a rag.

chiffon [ʃifɔ̃], s.m. **1.** (a) Rag. **Papier de chiffon**, rag-paper. (b) Piece of lace, of ribbon. F: **Causer chiffons**, to talk dress. **2.** Scrap. Hist: **Le chiffon de papier**, the scrap of paper. **3.** Tex: Chiffon.

chiffonner [ʃifɔne], v.tr. (a) To rumple (dress, etc.); to crumple (piece of paper). F: **Chiffonner l'honneur de qn**, to besmirch s.o.'s honour. **Minois chiffonné**, nice, pleasing, but irregular features. (b) To annoy, vex. s.m. **-age**.

chiffonnier, -ière [ʃifɔnje, -jɛːr]. **1.** s. Rag-man; rag-and-bone man; dustbin-raker. **2.** s.m. Small chest of drawers; chiffonier.

chiffre [ʃifr], s.m. **1.** (a) Figure, number, nu-meral. Com: **Marqué en chiffres connus**, marked in plain figures. (b) Amount, total. Com: C. d'affaires, turnover. **2.** Cipher, code. **Écriture**

en chiffre, writing in cipher. **3.** (a) Monogram. (b) Typ: Colophon.

chiffrer [ʃifre]. **1.** v.i. To calculate, reckon. **2.** v.tr. (a) To number (pages of book); to page (account book). (b) To work out (amount, etc.). **Détails chiffrés**, figures (of scheme, etc.). (c) To cipher; to write (despatch, etc.) in code. **Mot chiffré**, code word. (d) To mark (linen, etc.). (e) Mus: To figure (the bass). s.m. **-age**.

chiffre-taxe, s.m. Postage-due stamp or mark.

chignon [ʃiɲɔ̃], s.m. Coil of hair; knot of hair; chignon, F: bun. **Peigne chignon**, back-comb.

chimère [ʃimɛːr], s.f. Chimera. Le pays des chimères, the land of fancy.

chimérique [ʃimerik], a. **1.** Visionary, fanciful (mind). **2.** Chimerical. adv. **-ment**.

chimie [ʃimi], s.f. Chemistry.

chimique [ʃimik], a. Chemical. **Un produit chimique**, a chemical.

chimiste [ʃimist], s.m. Chemist. (Not pharma-ceutical chemist.)

chimpanzé [ʃɛ̃pɑ̃ze], s.m. Z: Chimpanzee.

Chine [ʃin]. Pr.n.f. Geog: China. **Encre de Chine**, Indian ink. **Papier de Chine**, rice-paper.

chiner[1] [ʃine], v.tr. Tex: To cloud, shadow, mottle (fabric). s.m. **-age**[1].

chiner[2]. **1.** v.i. To work hard; to toil and moil. **2.** v.tr. (a) To run (s.o.) down. (b) To make fun of (s.o.); to chip (s.o.). s.m. **-age**[2].

chinois, -oise [ʃinwa, -waːz]. **1.** a. Chinese. **2.** s. Chinaman, Chinese woman; Chinese.

chinoiserie [ʃinwazri], s.f. **1.** Chinese curio. **2.** F: 'Monkey' trick. Chinoiseries de bureau, red tape.

chiot [ʃjo], s.m. F: Pup(py).

chiourme [ʃjurm], s.f. Gang of convicts.

chiper [ʃipe], v.tr. P: To pinch, sneak, scrounge (sth.). s.m. **-age**. s. **-eur, -euse.**

chipie [ʃipi], s.f. F: Ill-natured woman; sour-face.

chipolata [ʃipɔlata], s.f. **1.** Onion stew. **2.** Small sausage.

chipoter [ʃipɔte]. **1.** v.i. (a) To waste time. (b) To haggle, quibble (over trifles). **2.** v.tr. To peck, nibble, at (food). s.m. **-age**.

chipotier, -ière [ʃipɔtje, -jɛːr], s. (a) Fiddle-faddler. (b) Haggler, quibbler.

chique[1] [ʃik], s.f. Quid (of tobacco).

chique[2], s.f. Ent: Chigoe, jigger.

chiqué [ʃike], s.m. P: Sham, pretence. **Faire du chiqué, la faire au chiqué**, to put it on; to make-believe. [CHIC]

chiquement [ʃikmɑ̃], adv. P: **1.** Smartly, stylishly. **2.** Like a 'sport.' [CHIC]

chiquenaude [ʃiknoːd], s.f. Fillip, flick (of the finger).

chiquer [ʃike], v.tr. To chew (tobacco). s.m. **-eur.**

chiquet [ʃikɛ], s.m. F: Scrap, morsel. **Chiquet à chiquet**, a bit at a time; bit by bit.

chiqueter [ʃikte], v.tr. (je chiquette; je chique-terai) To tear (sth.) into shreds; to shred.

chirographaire [kirɔgrafɛːr], a. Jur: Depend-ing on a simple contract. **Créance chirographaire**, unsecured debt. Obligation c., simple contract.

chiromancie [kirɔmɑ̃si], s.f. Chiromancy, pal-mistry.

chiromancien, -ienne [kirɔmɑ̃sjɛ̃, -jɛn], s. Palmist.

chirurgical, -aux [ʃiryrʒikal, -o], a. Surgical. **Subir une intervention chirurgicale**, to undergo an operation.

chirurgie [ʃiryrʒi], s.f. Surgery.

chirurgien, -ienne [ʃiryrʒjɛ̃, -jɛn], s. Surgeon. **Chirurgien dentiste**, surgeon-dentist.

chirurgique [ʃiryrʒik], *a.* Surgical.

chiure [ʃjyːr], *s.f.* Fly-speck, -mark.

chloral [klɔral], *s.m. Ch:* Chloral. *Pharm:* Hydrate de chloral, chloral (hydrate).

chlorate [klɔrat], *s.m. Ch:* Chlorate.

chlore [klɔːr], *s.m. Ch:* Chlorine.

chlorer [klɔre]. *v.tr. Ind:* To chlorinate. Eau chlorée, chlorine water.

chlorhydrate [klɔridrat], *s.m. Ch:* Hydrochlorate.

chlorhydrique [klɔridrik], *a. Ch:* Hydrochloric (acid).

chloroforme [klɔrɔfɔrm], *s.m.* Chloroform.

chloroformer [klɔrɔfɔrme], *v.tr.* To chloroform.

chloroformiser [klɔrɔfɔrmize], *v.tr. Med:* To chloroform (s.o.).

chlorophylle [klɔrɔfil], *s.f.* Chlorophyl(l).

chlorose [klɔroːz], *s.f. Med:* Chlorosis.

chlorure [klɔryːr], *s.m. Ch:* Chloride. *Phot:* F: Bain de chlorure, (gold) toning bath.

chlorurer [klɔryre], *v.tr.* To chlorinize, chlorinate.

choc [ʃɔk], *s.m.* **1.** Shock, impact (of two bodies). Tampon ᴜe choc, buffer. *C. des verres*, clink of glasses. *C. des opinions*, clash, conflict, of opinions. *Mil:* Troupes de choc, shock troops. *N.Arch:* Cloison de choc, collision bulkhead. **2.** Knock(ing), hammering (of engine, etc.). **3.** Shock (to nervous system). *Med: C. opératoire*, shock following a surgical operation.

chocolat [ʃɔkɔla]. **1.** *s.m.* Chocolate. **2.** *a.inv.* Chocolate-coloured.

chocolatier, -ière [ʃɔkɔlatje, -jɛːr], *s.* Chocolate-maker, -seller.

chœur [kœːr], *s.m.* **1.** *(a) Gr.Lit:* Chorus. *(b)* Chanter en chœur, to sing in chorus. Faire chœur au refrain, to join in the chorus. **2.** *(a)* Choir (of singers). Enfant de chœur, (i) altar-boy, (ii) chorister. *(b) Arch:* Choir, chancel.

choir [ʃwaːr], *v.i.def. A: (p.p.* chu ; *pr.ind.* je chois, il choit ; *p.h.* je chus ; *fu.* je choirai, je cherrai. The aux. is *être)* To fall. *A. & Hum:* Se laisser choir *(dans un fauteuil, etc.)*, to drop, flop, sink (into an armchair, etc.).

choisir [ʃwaziːr], *v.tr.* To choose, select, pick. *C. entre, parmi, plusieurs choses*, to choose from several things. *Nom bien choisi*, appropriate name. *C. ses mots*, to pick one's words.

    choisi, *a.* **1.** Selected. *Hommes choisis*, picked men. **2.** Select, choice. *Société choisie*, select company.

choix [ʃwa], *s.m.* Choice, selection. L'embarras du choix, the difficulty of choosing. Faites votre choix, take your choice. *Je vous laisse le c.*, choose for yourself. *Nous n'avons pas d'autre c. que de . . .*, we have no option but to. . . . Article de choix, choice article. *De tout premier choix*, of the best quality ; first-class. *Morceaux de viande de c.*, prime cuts. Hommes de choix, picked men. Avancer au choix, to be promoted by selection. *Com:* "Au choix," 'all at the same price.'

choléra [kɔlera], *s.m. Med:* Cholera.

cholérine [kɔlerin], *s.f. Med:* Cholerine ; summer cholera.

chômage [ʃomaːʒ], *s.m.* **1.** Abstention from work (on feast-days, etc.). *C. du dimanche*, Sunday closing. **2.** *C. involontaire*, unemployment. Ouvriers en chômage, men out of work. Secours de chômage, unemployment benefit, F: dole. *C. d'une usine*, shutting down of a works.

chômer [ʃome], *v.i.* **1.** To take a holiday (on feast-days, etc.). Hence *v.tr.* Chômer (la fête d')un saint, to keep a saint's day. **2.** To be idle ;

not to be working. *Ouvrier qui chôme*, unemployed workman. *Les usines chôment*, the works are at a standstill. Laisser chômer son argent, to let one's money lie idle.

chômeur [ʃomœːr], *s.m.* Unemployed workman ; out-of-work. *Les chômeurs*, the unemployed.

chope [ʃɔp], *s.f.* Beer mug, tankard.

chopine [ʃɔpin], *s.f.* Half-litre mug.

choquant [ʃɔkɑ̃], *a.* Shocking, offensive. *Un abus c.*, a gross, glaring, abuse.

choquer [ʃɔke], *v.tr.* **1.** To strike, knock, bump (sth. against sth.). *Nous choquâmes nos verres*, we clinked glasses. **2.** To shock. Être choqué de qch., to be scandalized, shocked, at, by, sth. *Idée qui choque le bon sens*, idea that offends common sense. *Je fus choqué de le voir tellement changé*, I was shocked to see such a change in him.

    se choquer. 1. To come into collision *(contre*, with). **2.** To be shocked, scandalized ; to take offence *(de*, at).

choral, *pl.* -als [kɔral]. **1.** *a.* Choral. *Société chorale*, choral society. **2.** *s.m.* Choral(e).

chorée [kɔre], *s.f. Med:* Chorea ; *F:* Saint Vitus's dance.

chorégraph|ie [kɔregrafi], *s.f.* Choreography. *a.* **-ique, -ic.**

choriste [kɔrist], *s.m.* Chorus-singer (in opera).

chorus [kɔryːs], *s.m.* (Used in) Faire chorus, to chorus s.o.'s words ; to express approval, or repeat a request, in chorus.

chose [ʃoːz]. **1.** *s.f.* Thing. *Toutes choses à tous*, all things to all men. Dire le mot et la chose, to call a spade a spade. Dites des choses aimables, bien des choses, de ma part à . . ., remember me kindly to. . . . La chose en question, the case in point. Cela n'est plus la même chose, that alters the case. Je vois la chose, I see how matters stand ; I understand. Ce n'est pas chose aisée de . . ., it is no easy matter to. . . . Ne pas faire les choses à demi, not to do things by halves. *S.a.* AUTRE I, 2, GRAND'CHOSE, LEÇON 2, PEU 1, QUELQUE CHOSE, SUR[1] I. **2.** *s.m. & f. F:* Monsieur Chose, madame Chose, Mr, Mrs, What-do-you-call-him (-her). Le petit Chose, little What's-his-name. **3.** *a.inv. F:* Être tout chose, to feel queer. *Vous avez l'air tout c.*, you look as if something had gone wrong.

chou, *pl.* -oux [ʃu], *s.m.* **1.** Cabbage. *C. pommé*, garden cabbage. *C. frisé*, kale. *C. de Bruxelles*, Brussels sprouts. *C. de Milan*, Savoy cabbage. *C. marin*, sea-kale. *F:* Planter ses choux, to live retired in the country. Faire ses choux gras, to feather one's nest. Faire chou blanc, (at games) to fail to score, to make a duck. Mon petit chou, my dear, ducky. C'est chou vert et vert chou, it's as broad as it's long. *P:* Être dans les choux, to be in a fix, in a pickle. *Rac: Arriver dans les choux*, to be nowhere. Rentrer dans le chou à qn, to attack, go for, s.o. Feuille de chou, newspaper of no standing ; *F:* rag. *S.a.* CHÈVRE. **2.** *Cost:* Cabbage-bow ; rosette (of ribbon). **3.** *Cu:* Chou à la crème, cream bun.

chouan [ʃwɑ̃], *s.m. Fr.Hist:* Chouan ; insurgent Breton royalist.

chouannerie [ʃwanri], *s.f. Fr.Hist: (a)* Militant body of Breton royalists formed in 1793. *(b)* La Chouannerie, the Chouan rising.

choucas [ʃuka], *s.m. Orn:* (Jack)daw.

chouchouter [ʃuʃute], *v.tr. F: (a)* To pet, caress, fondle. *(b)* To coddle (child). [CHOU]

choucroute [ʃukrut], *s.f. Cu:* Sauerkraut.

chouette[1] [ʃwet], *s.f.* Owl. *C. des clochers*, screech owl. *C. des bois*, wood owl, brown owl.

chouette², *a. & int. P:* Fine, topping, ripping. *adv.* **-ment.**

chou-fleur, *s.m.* Cauliflower. *pl. Des choux-fleurs.*

chou-navet, *s.m. Agr:* Swedish turnip; swede. *pl. Des choux-navets.*

chou-rave, *s.m.* Kohl-rabi. *pl. Des choux-raves.*

choyer [ʃwaje], *v.tr.* (je choie; je choierai) To pet, coddle (s.o.). *C. un espoir,* to cherish a hope.

chrême [krɛːm], *s.m. Ecc:* Chrism, holy oil.

chrestomathie [krɛstɔmati], *s.f.* Chrestomathy, anthology.

chrét|ien, -ienne [kretjɛ̃, -jɛn], *a. & s.* Christian. *adv.* **-iennement.**

chrétienté [kretjɛ̃te], *s.f.* Christendom.

Christ [krist], *s.m.* **I.** Le Christ [ləkrist], Christ. Jésus-Christ [ʒezykri], Jesus Christ. **2.** *F:* Un Christ = *un* CRUCIFIX.

christianiser [kristjanize], *v.tr.* To christianize.

christianisme [kristjanism], *s.m.* Christianity.

Christophe [kristɔf]. *Pr.n.m.* Christopher.

chromage [kromaːʒ], *s.m.* Chromium plating.

chromate [krɔmat], *s.m. Ch:* Chromate.

chromatique [krɔmatik], *a. Mus: Opt:* Chromatic. *adv.* **-ment,** -ally.

chrome [kroːm], *s.m.* **I.** *Ch:* Chromium. **2.** *Com:* Chrome. **Jaune de chrome,** chrome-yellow.

chromer [krome], *v.tr. Ind:* To chrome. **chromé,** *a.* **I.** *Cuir c.,* chrome(-tanned) leather. *Veau c.,* box-calf. *Metall: Acier c.,* chrome steel. **2.** Chromium-plated.

chromique [krɔmik, kro-], *a.* Chromic (acid).

chromo [krɔmo], *s.m. F:* Chromo(lithograph); colour-print.

chromocinématographie [krɔmɔsinematɔgrafi], *s.f.* Colour-cinematography.

chromolithographie [krɔmɔlitɔgrafi], *s.f.* **I.** Chromolithography. **2.** Chromo(lithograph).

chromophotographie [krɔmɔfɔtɔgrafi], *s.f.* Colour-photography.

chronique¹ [krɔnik], *a.* Chronic (disease, etc.). *adv.* **-ment,** -ally.

chronique², *s.f.* **I.** Chronicle. **2.** *Journ:* News, reports.

chroniqueur [krɔnikœːr], *s.m.* **I.** Chronicler. **2.** Writer of news pars; reporter.

chronologie [krɔnɔlɔʒi], *s.f.* Chronology.

chronologique [krɔnɔlɔʒik], *a.* Chronological. *adv.* **-ment.**

chronologiste [krɔnɔlɔʒist], *s.m.* Chronologist, chronologer.

chronomètre [krɔnɔmɛtr], *s.m.* Chronometer.

chronométr|er [krɔnɔmetre], *v.tr.* (je chronomètre; je chronométrerai) *Sp:* To keep the time; to time (race, etc.). *s.m.* **-age.**

chronométreur [krɔnɔmetrœːr], *s.m. Sp: Ind:* Time-keeper.

chrysalide [krizalid], *s.f. Ent:* Chrysalis, pupa. *F: Sortir de sa chrysalide,* to come out of one's shell.

chrysanthème [krizɑ̃tɛ(ː)m], *s.m. Bot:* Chrysanthemum.

chrysocale [krizɔkal], *s.m.* Pinchbeck.

chu. See CHOIR.

chuchot|er [ʃyʃɔte]. **I.** *v.i.* To whisper. *Parler en chuchotant,* to speak in a whisper. **2.** *v.tr. C. quelques mots à l'oreille de qn,* to whisper a few words in s.o.'s ear. *s.m.* **-ement.** *s.* **-eur, -euse.**

chuchoterie [ʃyʃɔtri], *s.f.* Whispering; whispered conversation.

chuinter [ʃɥɛ̃te], *v.i.* **I.** (Of owl) To hoot.

2. (*a*) *Ling:* To make a 'hushing' sound (in speaking). (*b*) (Of gas-burner) To hiss, sizzle.

chut [ʃyt, ʃt], *int.* Hush! ssh!

chute [ʃyt], *s.f.* **I.** (*a*) Fall. **Faire une chute (de cheval, de bicyclette),** to have a fall, a spill; *F:* to come a cropper. **Chute du jour,** nightfall. **Chute d'eau,** waterfall. **Hauteur de chute,** (i) fall, head (of water); (ii) drop (of pile-ram). *Th: C. du rideau,* fall of the curtain. *Com: C. de prix,* fall, drop, in prices. *El: C. de potentiel,* voltage drop. *Th: C. d'une pièce,* failure of a play. (*b*) (Down)fall. *La c. de l'homme,* the Fall. **2.** *C. d'un toit,* pitch of a roof. *C. des reins,* small of the back. *C. de la voix,* cadence of the voice. **3.** *Min: Ind:* Shoot. [CHOIR]

Chypre [ʃipr]. *Pr.n.f.* **L'île de Chypre,** Cyprus.

ci¹ [si], *adv.* (*a*) *A:* Here. (*b*) **Par-ci par-là,** here and there. **De-ci de-là,** here and there; on all sides. S.a. CE² 3, CECI, CELUI 4, GÉSIR.

ci², *dem. pron. neut. inv. A:* This. (Still used in) **Faire ci et ça,** to do this, that, and the other. **Comme ci, comme ça,** so so.

ci-après [siaprɛ], *adv.* Hereafter; later, further on (in the book, etc.).

ci-bas [sibɑ], *adv. Signature apposée ci-bas,* signature affixed below.

cibiche [sibiʃ], *s.f. P:* Cigarette, *P:* fag.

cible [sibl], *s.f.* (Round) target.

ciboire [sibwaːr], *s.m. Ecc:* Pyx, ciborium.

ciboule [sibul], *s.f.* **I.** Welsh onion, scallion. **2.** Spring onion.

ciboulette [sibulɛt], *s.f. Bot: Cu:* Chive(s).

cicatrice [sikatris], *s.f.* Scar.

cicatriciel, -ielle [sikatrisjɛl], *a.* Cicatricial (tissue, etc.).

cicatris|er [sikatrize]. **I.** *v.tr.* (*a*) To heal (wound, etc.). (*b*) To scar, mark (face, etc.). **2.** *v.i. & pr.* (Of wound, etc.) To heal (up); to scar over. *s.f.* **-ation.**

Cicéron [siserɔ̃]. *Pr.n.m. Lt.Lit:* Cicero.

cicerone [siseron, tʃitʃerone], *s.m.* Guide, cicerone. *pl. Des cicerones, ciceroni.*

ci-contre [sikɔ̃ːtr], *adv.* (*a*) Opposite; in the margin. *Book-k:* **Porté ci-contre,** as per contra. (*b*) Annexed (circular, etc.). (*c*) On the other side (of the sheet).

ci-dessous [sidsu], *adv.* Hereunder; under-mentioned.

ci-dessus [sidsy], *adv.* Above(-mentioned).

ci-devant [sidvɑ̃]. **I.** *adv.* Previously, formerly. **2.** *s.m. & f. inv.* (*a*) *Fr.Hist:* Ci-devant, aristocrat. (*b*) *F:* Old fogey.

cidre [si(ː)dr], *s.m.* Cider.

cidrerie [sidrəri], *s.f.* **I.** Cider-house. **2.** Cider-making.

ciel, *pl.* **cieux** [sjɛl, sjø], *s.m.* **I.** (*a*) Sky, firmament, heaven. *Les oiseaux des cieux,* the fowls of the air. **A ciel ouvert,** in the open air; out of doors. **Couleur bleu de ciel,** sky-blue. **Être suspendu entre ciel et terre,** to hang in mid air. (*b*) (*pl.* often **ciels**) Climate, clime, sky. *Les ciels de l'Italie,* the skies of Italy. *Art: Les ciels de Turner,* Turner's skies. **2.** Heaven. *Notre Père qui êtes aux cieux,* our Father which art in Heaven. *F:* **Tomber du ciel,** to come as a godsend. **(Juste) ciel!** (good) heavens! S.a. REMUER I. **3.** (*pl.* **ciels**) (*a*) *Ecc:* Baldachin, canopy. (*b*) **Ciel de lit,** bed-tester.

cierge [sjɛrʒ], *s.m. Ecc:* Wax candle; taper. *Brûler un c. à un saint,* to burn a candle to a saint. *F:* **Devoir à qn un beau cierge,** to have reason to be grateful to s.o.

cieux. See CIEL.

cigale [sigal], *s.f.* Ent: Cicada.

cigare [sigaːr], *s.m.* Cigar.

cigarette [sigarɛt], *s.f.* Cigarette.

ci-gisent, ci-gît. See GÉSIR.

cigogne [sigɔn], *s.f.* Stork.

ciguë [sigy], *s.f.* Bot: Med: Hemlock.

ci-inclus [siɛkly], *a.* (Is inv. when it precedes the noun) La copie ci-incluse, the enclosed copy. Ci-inclus copie de votre lettre, herewith a copy of your letter.

ci-joint [siʒwɛ̃], *a.* (Is inv. when it precedes the noun) Subjoined, herewith; hereto (annexed). Les pièces ci-jointes, the subjoined documents. Vous trouverez ci-joint quittance, please find receipt attached.

cil [sil], *s.m.* 1. (Eye-)lash. 2. Nat.Hist: Cilium, hair.

ciliaire [siljeːr], *a.* Ciliary.

cilice [silis], *s.m.* Hair-shirt.

cill|er [sije], *v.tr.* To blink (the eyes, eyelids); to nic(ti)tate. *s.m.* **-ement.**

cimaise [simɛːz], *s.f.* Arch: Cyma; ogee moulding; dado. Art: Tableau pendu sur la c., picture hung on the line.

cime [sim], *s.f.* Summit (of hill, etc.); top (of tree, mast).

ciment [simã], *s.m.* Cement. C. armé, reinforced concrete. Béton de ciment, concrete. S.a. CHAUX.

ciment|er [simãte], *v.tr.* To cement. F: C. une alliance, to cement, consolidate, an alliance. *s.m.* **-age.** *s.f.* **-ation.**

cimeterre [simtɛːr], *s.m.* Scimitar.

cimetière [simtjɛːr], *s.m.* Cemetery, graveyard.

cimier[1] [simje], *s.m.* Crest (of helmet).

cimier[2], *s.m.* Haunch (of venison); rump, buttock (of beef).

cinabre [sinaːbr], *s.m.* (a) Cinnabar. (b) Art: Vermilion.

ciné [sine], *s.m.* F: = CINÉMATOGRAPHE.

ciné-actualités, *s.m.* News theatre. pl. Des cinés-actualités.

cinéaste [sineast], *s.m.,* **cinégraphiste** [sinegrafist], *s.m.* Cin: Scenario-writer.

cinelle [sinɛl], *s.f.* Bot: Oak-gall, F: oak-apple.

cinéma [sinema], *s.m.* F: Cinema. 1. F: Pictures, U.S: movies. Faire du cinéma, to act for the films; to be a cinema actor. Gens qui font du c., film people. 2. Picture palace.

cinématique [sinematik]. 1. *a.* Kinematic(al). 2. *s.f.* Kinematics. adv. **-ment,** -ally.

cinématographe [sinematɔgraf], *s.m.* Cinematograph. F: cinema, films.

cinématographie [sinematɔgrafi], *s.f.* Cinematography.

cinématographier [sinematɔgrafje], *v.tr.* To cinematograph, F: to film.

cinématographique [sinematɔgrafik], *a.* Cinematographic; F: film (production, etc.). adv. **-ment,** -ally.

cinéprojecteur [sineprɔʒektœːr], *s.m.* Cinematograph projector.

cinéraire [sinerɛːr]. 1. *a.* Cinerary (urn, etc.). 2. *s.f.* Bot: Cineraria.

cinétique [sinetik]. Mec: 1. *a.* Kinetic, motive (energy, etc.). 2. *s.f.* Kinetics.

cinglant [sɛ̃glã], *a.* Lashing (rain, etc.); cutting, biting (wind, etc.); bitter (cold); scathing.

cingler[1] [sɛ̃gle], *v.i.* Nau: To sail (before the wind); to scud along.

cingl|er[2], *v.tr.* 1. To lash, cut, (horse, etc.) with a whip. F: La grêle lui cinglait le visage, the hail stung his face. Abs. Le vent, la pluie, cingle, it is a cutting, biting, wind, a slashing rain.

Le froid cinglait, it was bitterly cold. *s.m.* **-ement.** 2. Metall: To shingle, forge (bloom). *s.m.* **-age.**

cinglon [sɛ̃glɔ̃], *s.m.* Lash, cut (of whip, etc.).

cinglure [sɛ̃glyːr], *s.f.* Sting, smart (of lash, insult).

cinnamome [sinnamɔm], *s.m.* 1. Bot: Cinnamon(-tree). 2. Cinnamon.

cinq [sɛ̃(ː)k], num. a. inv. & *s.m.* inv. (As card.adj. before a noun or adj. beginning with a consonant sound [sɛ̃]) Five. C. (petits) garçons [sɛ̃(pti)garsɔ̃], five (little) boys. C. hommes [sɛ̃kɔm], five men. J'en ai c. [sɛ̃ːk], I have five. Le c. mars [sɛ̃kmars], March the fifth. F: Faire cinq et trois font huit, to limp; F: to dot and carry one. Il était moins cinq, it was a near thing, a close call.

cinquantaine [sɛ̃kãten], *s.f.* (About) fifty, some fifty, fifty or so. Une c. de personnes, about fifty people. Avoir passé la c., to be in the fifties. Célébrer la c., to celebrate one's golden wedding or one's jubilee.

cinquante [sɛ̃kãːt], num. a. inv. Fifty. Billet de c. francs, fifty-franc note. Page c., page fifty. Au chapitre c. de . . ., in the fiftieth chapter of. . . . Demeurer au numéro c., to live at number fifty.

cinquantenaire [sɛ̃kãtnɛːr]. 1. *s.m.* Fiftieth anniversary; jubilee. 2. *s.m. & f.* Quinquagenarian.

cinquantième [sɛ̃kãtjɛm]. 1. num. a. & s. Fiftieth. 2. *s.m.* Fiftieth (part).

cinquième [sɛ̃kjɛm]. 1. num. a. & s. Fifth. 2. *s.m.* Fifth (part). 3. *s.f.* Sch: (Classe de) cinquième, (approx. =) second form of upper school). adv. **-ment.**

cintre [sɛ̃ːtr], *s.m.* Concave surface. 1. Curve, bend. 2. (a) Arch (of tunnel). (b) Soffit (of arch). Arc plein cintre, semicircular arch. 3. Cy: Bend (of handle-bar). 4. Coat-hanger. 5. Th: Les cintres, the flies (above the stage).

cintr|er [sɛ̃tre], *v.tr.* (a) To bend, curve, (bar, etc.) to the desired shape; to camber (timber). (b) To arch (window). Const: To centre (arch). *s.m.* **-age.** *s.m.* **-ement.**

cintré, *a.* (a) Arched (window, etc.). Toit c., barrel-roof. (b) Bent, curved (timber, etc.).

cipaye [sipaːj], *a. & s.m.* Sepoy.

cirage [siraːʒ], *s.m.* 1. Waxing, polishing (of floors, etc.); polishing, blacking (of boots). 2. Polishing wax (for floors, leather). C. pour chaussures, blacking. C. à la cire, boot-polish. C. crème, shoe-cream. 3. Suit of oilskins. [CIRER]

circoncire [sirkɔ̃siːr], *v.tr.* (p.p. circoncisant; p.p. circoncis; pr.ind. je circoncis, n. circoncisons; pr.sub. je circoncise; n.h. je circoncis; fu. je circoncirai) To circumcise.

circoncision [sirkɔ̃sizjɔ̃], *s.f.* Circumcision.

circonférence [sirkɔ̃ferãs], *s.f.* 1. (a) Circumference. (b) Girth (of tree). 2. Perimeter, boundaries (of town).

circonflexe [sirkɔ̃flɛks], *a.* Circumflex (accent).

circonlocution [sirkɔ̃lɔkysjɔ̃], *s.f.* Circumlocution. Parler par circonlocution, F: to beat about the bush.

circonscription [sirkɔ̃skripsjɔ̃], *s.f.* 1. Circumscription, circumscribing. 2. Division, district. C. électorale, electoral district or ward; parliamentary division; constituency.

circonscrire [sirkɔ̃skriːr], *v.tr.* (Conj. like ÉCRIRE) To circumscribe. 1. To draw a line round (sth.). 2. To surround, encircle (par, with). 3. To limit, bound. C. son sujet, to establish the bounds of one's subject.

circonscrit, *a.* 1. Geom: Circumscribed

(*d*, to, about). **2.** Limited, restricted (space, outlook).

circonspect [sirkɔ̃spε, -spεk, -spεkt] *a.* Circumspect, prudent, cautious, wary. *adv.* **-ement.**

circonspection [sirkɔ̃spεksjɔ̃], *s.f.* Circumspection, caution, wariness. *Avec c.*, cautiously.

circonstance [sirkɔ̃stɑ̃:s], *s.f.* Circumstance, incident, event. **Dans cette circonstance,** (i) in this instance, (ii) in this emergency. **En pareille circonstance,** in such a case. **A la hauteur des circonstances,** equal to the occasion. **Eu égard aux circonstances,** all things considered. **L'homme de la circonstance,** the very man we want. **De circonstance,** (play) improvised for the occasion. *Paroles de c.*, words suited to the occasion.

circonstancié [sirkɔ̃stɑ̃sje], *a.* Circumstantial, detailed (account).

circonstanciel, -ielle [sirkɔ̃stɑ̃sjεl], *a.* (*a*) Circumstantial. (*b*) *Gram:* Adverbial (complement).

circonvallation [sirkɔ̃valasjɔ̃], *s.f.* Circumvallation.

circonvenir [sirkɔ̃vniːr], *v.tr.* (Conj. like VENIR) To circumvent, thwart; to outwit (s.o.).

circonvolution [sirkɔ̃vɔlysjɔ̃], *s.f.* *Anat: Arch:* Convolution.

circuit [sirkɥi], *s.m.* Circuit. **1.** (*a*) Circumference, compass (of town, etc.). (*b*) *Sp:* Round, lap. **2.** Deviation. *Circuits d'une rivière*, windings of a river. **3.** *El:* **Mettre (une lampe, etc.) en circuit, hors circuit,** to switch (a lamp, etc.) on, off. *Mettre l'accu hors c.*, to cut out the battery. **Mettre une ligne en court circuit,** to short-circuit a line.

circulaire [sirkylεːr]. **1.** *a.* Circular. **Billet circulaire,** tourist ticket. **Scie circulaire,** circular saw. **2.** *s.f.* Circular (letter); (administrative) memorandum. *adv.* **-ment.**

circulation [sirkylasjɔ̃], *s.f.* **1.** Circulation (of air, water, blood, etc.). *Mettre un livre en c.*, to put a book into circulation. **Mettre un bruit en circulation,** to set a rumour afloat, afoot. **2.** Traffic. *Arrêt de c.*, traffic block. **"Circulation interdite,"** 'no thoroughfare.' *C. en sens unique,* one-way traffic. *Accidents de la c.*, road accidents. *S.a.* PERMIS 2.

circuler [sirkyle], *v.ı.* **1.** (Of blood, air, etc.) To circulate, flow. *F: Faire c. la bouteille*, to pass the bottle round. **2.** To circulate, move about. **"Défense de circuler sur l'herbe!"** 'please keep off the grass!' **"Circulez!"** 'keep moving!' 'pass along!' *Des bruits circulent*, rumours are afloat, are going round.

cire [siːr], *s.f.* **1.** Wax. *C. d'abeilles*, beeswax. *C. à cacheter*, sealing-wax. *F:* **Caractère de cire,** easily moulded character. **2.** *Orn:* Cere (of beak).

cirer [sire], *v.tr.* To wax (thread, etc.); to polish, to beeswax (floors, etc.). *C. des chaussures*, to polish, black, shoes.

ciré. 1. *a.* Waxed, polished. **Toile cirée,** oilcloth, American cloth. **2.** *s.m. Nau:* (Suit of) oilskins.

cireur, -euse [sirœːr, -øːz], *s.* **1.** Polisher. **2.** Shoeblack.

cireux, -euse [sirø, -øːz], *a.* Waxy, wax-like.

cirier, -ière [sirje, -jεːr]. **1.** *a.* Wax-producing; wax-(tree, bee). **2.** *s.m.* (*a*) Wax-chandler, wax-taper maker. (*b*) *Bot:* Wax-myrtle.

ciron [sirɔ̃], *s.m.* (Cheese-, itch-)mite.

cirque [sirk], *s.m.* **1.** Circus. **2.** Cirque, corrie; amphitheatre (of mountains).

cirrus [sirryːs], *s.m. Meteor:* Cirrus; *F:* mare's tail.

cisaille [sizɑːj], *s.f.* **1.** Parings, cuttings (of metal). **2.** *sg. or pl.* Shears; nippers; wire-cutter.

cisaillement [sizɑjmɑ̃], *s.m.* **1.** (*a*) Cutting, shearing (of metal). (*b*) Nipping (of tyres). **2.** *Mec:* Shearing (stress); shear.

cisailler [sizɑje], *v.tr.* (*a*) To shear (metal). (*b*) *Chambre à air cisaillée*, nipped inner tube.

cisalpin [sizalpɛ̃], *a. A.Hist: A.Geog:* On the Roman side of the Alps; Cisalpine.

ciseau [sizo], *s.m.* **1.** Chisel. *C. à froid*, cold chisel. **2.** *pl.* (*a*) Scissors. **Coup de ciseaux,** snip of the scissors. *F:* **Travailler à coups de ciseaux,** to work with scissors and paste. (*b*) Shears. (*c*) Lazy-tongs.

ciseler [sizle], *v.tr.* (je cisèle, je ciselle; je ciselerai, je cisellerai) To chase, engrave (gold, silver); to chisel, carve (wood); to tool, emboss (leather); to cut, shear (velvet). *s.m.* **-age.** *s.m.* **-eur.**

ciselure [sizlyːr], *s.f.* **1.** Chisel(l)ing. **2.** Chasing, embossing, tooling.

cistercien, -ienne [sistεrsjɛ̃, -jεn], *a. & s.* **1.** (Native) of Cîteaux. **2.** *Ecc:* Cistercian.

citadelle [sitadεl], *s.f.* Citadel, stronghold.

citadin [sitadɛ̃], *s.m.* Citizen, townsman.

citateur, -trice [sitatœːr, -tris], *s.* Quoter, citer.

citation [sitasjɔ̃], *s.f.* **1.** (*a*) Quoting, citing. (*b*) Quotation, citation. **2.** *Jur:* (Writ of) summons. *C. des témoins*, subpoena of witnesses. **Notifier une citation à qn,** (i) to serve a summons on s.o., (ii) to subpoena s.o. **3.** *Mil:* **Citation à l'ordre du jour** = mention in dispatches.

cité [site], *s.f.* City. (*a*) (Large) town. **Droit de cité,** freedom of the city. (*b*) Housing estate. **Cité ouvrière,** workmen's garden city. **La cité universitaire,** the group of students' hostels (in Paris).

Cîteaux [sito]. *Pr.n.m. Geog:* Cîteaux. *Ecc:* **L'ordre de Cîteaux,** the Cistercian Order.

cité-jardin, *s.f.* Garden-city. *pl. Des cités-jardins.*

citer [site], *v.tr.* **1.** To quote, cite. **2.** *Jur:* To summon (s.o. before the court); to subpoena (witness). **3.** *Mil:* **Citer qn (à l'ordre du jour)** = to mention s.o. in dispatches.

citerne [sitεrn], *s.f.* Cistern, tank.

cithare [sitaːr], *s.f. Mus:* Zither(n).

citoyen, -enne [sitwajɛ̃, -εn], *s.* Citizen. **Droits de citoyen,** civic rights. *F:* **C'est un drôle de citoyen!** he's a queer customer!

citrate [sitrat], *s.m. Ch:* Citrate. *Phot:* **Papier au citrate (d'argent),** P.O.P. paper.

citrique [sitrik], *a. Ch:* Citric (acid).

citron [sitrɔ̃], *s.m.* **1.** *Bot:* (Generic term including) lemon, lime, citron. **Bois de citron,** citrus-wood. **2.** *F:* (*a*) Lemon. **Écorce de citron,** lemon peel. (*b*) *a.inv.* Lemon-coloured.

citronnade [sitrɔnad], *s.f.* Lemonade.

citronnier [sitrɔnje], *s.m. Bot:* Lemon-tree or citron-tree.

citrouille [sitruːj], *s.f.* Pumpkin, gourd.

civet [sivε], *s.m. Cu:* Stew (of venison, etc.). *C. de lièvre*, jugged hare.

civette [sivεt], *s.f.* Civet-cat.

civière [sivjεːr], *s.f.* **1.** Hand-barrow. **2.** Stretcher, litter. **3.** Bier (for coffin).

civil [sivil], *a.* Civil. **1.** (*a*) Civic (rights, etc.). *S.a.* ÉTAT 2. (*b*) *Jur:* Droit civil, common law. (*c*) Lay, secular (as opposed to ecclesiastical); civilian (as opposed to military). *s.m.* **Un civil,** (i) a layman; (ii) a civilian. **En civil,** in plain clothes; *F:* in mufti. **2.** Polite, courteous (*de*, *envers*, to, towards). *adv.* **-ement.**

civilisateur, -trice [sivilizatœːr, -tris], *s.* Civilizer.

civilisation [sivilizasjɔ̃], *s.f.* Civilization.

civiliser [sivilize], *v.tr.* To civilize.
se civiliser, to become civilized.
civilité [sivilite], *s.f.* **1.** Civility, courtesy. **2. Faire des civilités à qn,** to show s.o. courteous attention. **Mes civilités à Madame votre mère,** my kind regards to your mother.
civique [sivik], *a.* Civic (duties); civil (rights).
clabaudage [klaboda:ʒ], *s.m.,* **clabaudement** [klabodmã], *s.m.* **1.** *Ven:* Babbling, yelping, baying. **2.** *F:* Ill-natured talk, spiteful gossip, backbiting.
clabauder [klabode], *v.i.* **1.** *Ven:* (Of hound) To babble; to give tongue falsely. **2.** *F: C. sur qn,* to say ill-natured things of s.o.
clabaudeur, -euse [klabodœ:r, -ø:z], *s. F:* Gossip; scandal-monger.
clabot [klabo], *s.m. Mec.E: Aut:* Direct-drive dog-clutch.
clabotage [klabota:ʒ], *s.m. Mec.E: Aut:* Engagement by or of dog-clutch.
clac [klak], *s.m. & int.* Crack.
claie [klɛ], *s.f.* **1.** *(a)* Wattle, hurdle. **Traîner qn sur la claie,** (i) *A:* to drag s.o. to execution; (ii) *F:* to drag s.o. through the mire; to vilify s.o. *(b) C. à fruits,* (wicker) fruit-tray. **2.** Screen, riddle. **3.** Fence.
clair [klɛ:r]. **1.** *a.* Clear. *(a)* Unclouded, limpid. *Teint c.,* clear complexion. *Ciel c.,* cloudless sky. **Œuf clair,** unfertile egg. *(b)* Obvious, manifest, plain (meaning). *Explication claire,* lucid explanation. **Voilà qui est clair!** that's clear (enough)! **Règle peu claire,** ambiguously worded rule. **Clair comme le jour,** as plain as a pikestaff. *Sa conduite n'est pas claire,* his conduct is suspicious, *F:* fishy. *(c)* Bright, light (room, dress, etc.). *V.phr.* **Il fait clair,** (i) it is day(light); (ii) there is plenty of light. *Il ne fait pas c. ici,* you can't see here. *(d)* Light, pale (colour). **Robe bleu clair,** pale blue dress. *(e)* Thin (material, soup). **2.** *adv. (a)* Plainly, clearly. **Voir clair dans l'esprit de qn,** to read s.o.'s mind; *F:* to see through s.o. **Y voir clair,** (i) to be clear-sighted; (ii) to be able to see. *(b) Avoine semée c.,* thinly sown oats. **3.** *s.m. (a)* Light. **Clair de lune,** moonlight. **Au clair de (la) lune,** in the moonlight. *(b)* Clearing (in wood, etc.); thin place (in stocking, etc.). *(c)* **Message en clair,** message in plain language, in clear (*i.e.* not in cipher). *(d)* **Tirer du vin au clair,** to decant wine. *F:* **Tirer une affaire au clair,** to clear a matter up. **Sabre au clair,** with drawn sword. *adv.* **-ement.**
Claire [klɛ:r]. *Pr.n.f.* Clara, Clare.
clairet, -ette [klɛrɛ, -ɛt]. **1.** *a.* Pale, light-coloured. **(Vin) clairet,** light red wine. *Voix clairette,* thin voice. **2.** *s.f.* **Clairette.** *(a)* Lamb's-lettuce. *(b)* Light sparkling wine (of Limoux).
clair-étage, *s.m. Ecc.Arch:* Clerestory. *pl. Des clairs-étages.*
claire-voie, *s.f.* **1.** Open-work, lattice(-work). **Porte à claire-voie,** gate. **Clôture à claire-voie,** fence, paling. **Cloison à claire-voie,** grating. **Caisse à claire-voie,** crate. **2.** *(a)* Skylight. *Nau:* Deck-light. *(b) Ecc.Arch:* Clerestory. *pl. Des claires-voies.*
clairière [klɛrjɛ:r], *s.f.* Clearing, glade.
clair-obscur, *s.m. Art:* Chiaroscuro. *pl. Des clairs-obscurs.*
clairon [klɛrɔ̃], *s.m. (a)* Bugle. *(b)* Bugler.
claironnant [klɛrɔnɑ̃], *a.* Loud, brassy (sound).
clairsemé [klɛrsəme], *a.* Scattered, sparse (population, vegetation, etc.); thinly sown (corn); thin (hair).
clairvoyance [klɛrvwajɑ̃:s], *s.f.* **1.** Perspicacity,

clear-sightedness, shrewdness, acumen. **2.** Second-sight, clairvoyance.
clairvoyant, -ante [klɛrvwajɑ̃, -ɑ̃:t]. **1.** *a.* Perspicacious, clear-sighted, shrewd. **2.** *a. & s.* Clairvoyant.
clameur [klamœ:r], *s.f. (a)* Clamour, outcry. **Clameur publique,** hue and cry. *(b)* Howling, shrieking (of the wind, etc.).
clampin, -ine [klãpɛ̃, -in]. *F:* **1.** *a.* Slow, halting. **2.** *s.* Laggard; slow-coach.
clampiner [klãpine], *v.i. F:* To loiter.
clan [klã], *s.m.* **1.** Clan. **Le chef de clan,** the head of the clan. **2.** *F:* Set, clique.
clandestin [klãdɛstɛ̃], *a.* Clandestine, secret; illicit (betting, etc.).
clapet [klapɛ], *s.m.* **1.** *(a)* Valve. *C. à charnière,* clack-valve. **Boîte à clapet,** (i) clack-box; (ii) valve chest. *(b) I.C.E:* Poppet valve, mushroom valve. **2.** *El.E:* Rectifier (of current).
clapier [klapje], *s.m.* **1.** Rabbit-warren. **2.** Rabbit-hutch. **(Lapin de) clapier,** tame rabbit.
clapot|er [klapɔte], *v.i.* (Of sea) To chop, plash. *Vagues qui clapotent contre le bateau,* waves that lap against the boat. *s.m.* **-age.** *s.m.* **-ement.**
clapoteux, -euse [klapɔtø, -ø:z], *a.* Choppy (sea).
clapotis [klapɔti], *s.m.* Plash(ing), lap(ping) (of waves).
clap(p)ement [klapmã], *s.m.* **1.** Smacking (of tongue). **2.** *Ling:* Click (of Kaffirs, etc.).
clap(p)er [klape], *v.i. C. de la langue,* to smack one's tongue.
claque [klak]. **I.** *s.f.* **1.** Smack, slap. **2.** *Th:* Hired clappers (in Fr. theatres).
II. **claque,** *s.m. (a)* Opera-hat; *F:* crush-hat. *(b)* Cocked hat.
claquemurer [klakmyre], *v.tr.* To immure, mew up. **Se claquemurer,** to shut oneself up (e.g. in order to study).
claqu|er [klake]. **1.** *v.i. (a)* To clap; (of door) to bang; (of clogs, etc.) to clatter; (of piston) to slap. *C. des mains,* to clap, applaud. *Il claque des dents,* his teeth are chattering. *(b)* (i) *F:* To die. (ii) *P:* (Of business, engine, etc.) To go to pieces. *(c) I.C.E:* (Of electric lamp) To burn out. **2.** *v.tr. & i.* (Faire) **claquer,** to slam, bang (the door); to smack (one's lips); to crack (a whip); to snap (one's fingers); to click (one's heels). **3.** *v.tr. (a)* To slap, smack (child, etc.); *(b) Th:* To clap (an actor). *(c)* To burst (tyre, etc.); to rupture, tear (ligament). *s.m.* **-ement.**
claqué, *a. (a)* (Of horse) Having a trained tendon. *Tendon c.,* snapped tendon. *(b)* Fagged out, dog-tired.
claquet [klakɛ], *s.m.* Clapper (of mill-hopper).
claquette [klakɛt], *s.f. (a) Ecc:* (Wooden) clapper. *(b) F:* Chatterbox; newsmonger.
claqueur, -euse [klakœ:r, -ø:z], *s.* Hired clapper (in Fr. theatres).
clarifier [klarifje], *v.tr.* To clarify (wine, etc.).
se clarifier, (of liquid) to become clear; to clear.
clarine [klarin], *s.f.* Cattle-bell.
clarinette [klarinɛt], *s.f. (a)* Clarinet. *(b)* Clarinettist.
Clarisse [klaris]. **1.** *Pr.n.f.* Clarissa. **2.** *s.f.* **(Sœur) clarisse,** nun of the order of St Clare.
clarté [klarte], *s.f.* **1.** Clearness, clarity. *(a)* Limpidity (of water); transparency (of glass). *(b)* Lucidity, perspicuity (of style). *(c)* **Avoir des clartés sur un sujet,** to have some knowledge of a subject. **2.** Light, brightness. **A la clarté de la lune,** by the light of the moon; by moonlight.

Les premières clartés du soleil, the first gleams of the sun.
classe [klɑːs], *s.f.* **1.** Class, division (of vegetable kingdom, etc.). *Les hautes classes*, the upper classes (of society). Oranges de première classe, first-class oranges. Billet de première classe, first-class ticket. **2.** *Sch:* (*a*) Class, form; (in elementary schools) standard. *Les hautes classes*, the top forms; the upper school. *C. de français*, French class. (*b*) Aller en classe, to go to school. Être en classe, to be in school. Faire ses classes, to be at school. Faire la classe, to teach. Livre de classe, school-book. (Salle de) classe, class-room, schoolroom. S.a. RENTRÉE 1. **3.** *Mil:* Annua¹ contingent (of recruits).
classement [klɑsmɑ̃], *s.m.* **1.** Classification, classing (of plants, etc.); rating (of seaman, engine, etc.). *Sch: etc: C. de sortie*, passing-out list. **2.** (*a*) Sorting out. *Min:* Grading (of ore). (*b*) Filing (of documents).
classer [klɑse], *v.tr.* **1.** To class(ify); to rate (seaman, engine, etc.). *Ces faits se classent dans une autre catégorie*, these facts fall into another category. *Romans classés*, standard novels. **2.** (*a*) To sort out (articles). *Min:* To grade (ore). *Rail:* To marshal (trucks). (*b*) To file (documents). *F:* Classer une affaire, to shelve, pigeon-hole, an affair.
classeur [klɑsœːr], *s.m.* **1.** (*a*) Rack (for letters, etc.). (*b*) *Com:* (Index-)file; filing-cabinet. **2.** (Pers.) Sorter (of letters, coal, etc.).
classification [klasifikasjɔ̃], *s.f.* **1.** Classification, classifying (of plant, etc.); rating (of engine, etc.). **2.** Sorting out.
classifier [klasifje], *v.tr.* **1.** To classify (plant); to rate (engine, etc.). **2.** To sort (out) (articles).
classique [klasik], *a.* **1.** *Sch:* Academical; for school use. Livres classiques, school-books. **2.** (*a*) Classic(al). *Études classiques*, classical studies or education. (*b*) Standard (work); stereotyped, recognized (manner, etc.); standing (custom, joke). *F:* C'est un coup classique, that's an old dodge. **3.** *s.m.* (*a*) Les classiques grecs, français, the Greek, French, classics. (*b*) Les classiques et les romantiques, the classicists and the romanticists. *adv.* **-ment.**
claudication [klodikasjɔ̃], *s.f.* Halt(ing), limp.
clause [kloːz], *s.f. Jur:* Clause. *C. additionnelle*, rider.
claustral, -aux [klostral, -o], *a.* Claustral, monastic.
claustration [klostrasjɔ̃], *s.f.* **1.** Cloistering. **2.** Close confinement.
claustrer [klostre], *v.tr.* = CLOÎTRER.
claveau [klavo], *s.m. Const: Arch:* Arch-stone; voussoir. *C. droit*, keystone. [CLEF]
clavecin [klavsɛ̃], *s.m. A:* Harpsichord.
clavelée [klavle], *s.f. Vet:* Sheep-pox.
clavetage [klavtaːʒ], *s.m. Mec.E:* **1.** Keying, wedging, cottering (of machine parts, etc.). **2.** Key(s), wedge(s), cotter(s).
claveter [klavte], *v.tr.* (je clavette; je clavetterai) *Mec.E:* To key, wedge, cotter.
clavette [klavɛt], *s.f.* Key(-bolt), cotter(-pin).
clavicule [klavikyl], *s.f.* Clavicle; *F:* collar-bone.
clavier [klavje], *s.m.* **1.** Keyboard, finger-board (of piano, typewriter); manua! (of organ). **2.** Range, compass (of clarinet, etc.). [CLEF]
claviste [klavist], *s.m. Typ:* Machine-compositor.
clayère [klɛjɛːr], *s.f.* Oyster-park. CLAIE]
clayon [klɛjɔ̃], *s.m.* **1.** Wicker tray (for draining cheeses, etc.). **2.** Wattle enclosure. [CLAIE]

clé [kle], *s.f.*, **clef** [kle], *s.f.* **1.** Key. (*a*) *C. de maison*, latch-key. Fausse clef, skeleton key. Fermer une porte à clef, to lock a door. Donner un tour de clef à la porte, to lock the door. Tenir qch. sous clef, to keep sth. under lock and key. S.a. CHAMP¹ 1. (*b* C. d'une position, key to a position. (*c*) Key (to a cipher to a mystery); clue (to a puzzle). Roman à clef, novel introducing real characters under fictitious names. **2.** *Mus:* (*a*) Clef. *C. de sol*, treble clef. (*b*) Key-signature. **3.** Clef de voûte, keystone, crown (of arch). **4.** *Nau:* Hitch. Nœud à demi-clef, clove hitch. **5.** *Tls:* Key, wrench, spanner. Clef anglaise, screw-spanner, monkey-wrench. *C. à douilles, en tube*, box-spanner. *Aut: C. pour roues*, wheel-brace. **6.** *El:* Switch-key. *Tg: C. Morse*, Morse key, Morse sender. **7.** *Wr:* Lock.
clématite [klematit], *s.f. Bot:* Clematis.
clémence [klemɑːs], *s.f.* **1.** Clemency, mercy, leniency (*pour, envers*, to, towards) **2.** C emency, mildness (of the weather).
clément [klemɑ̃], *a.* **1.** Clement, merciful, lenient (*pour, envers*, to, towards). **2.** Mild (disease, etc.).
clenche [klɑ̃ːʃ], *s.f.*, **clenchette** [klɑ̃ʃɛt], *s.f.* Latch (of door-lock). Porte fermée à la clenche, door on the latch.
clephte [klɛft], *s.m.* Klepht; (Greek) brigand.
cleptomane [kleptoman], *s.m. & f.* Kleptomaniac.
cleptomanie [kleptomani], *s.f.* Kleptomania.
clerc [kleːr], *s.m.* **1.** *A:* (*a*) *Ecc:* Clerk, cleric, clergyman. (*b*) Learned man; scholar **2.** Clerk (in lawyer's office). Petit clerc, junior clerk. *F:* Faire un pas de clerc, to make a blunder.
clergé [klerʒe], *s.m.* (The clergy, priesthood.
clérical, -aux [klerikal, -o], *a. Ecc:* Clerical.
clic [klik], *s.m. & int* Click.
clic-clac [klikklak], *s.m.* Cracking (of whip, etc.); clatter (of sabots, etc.).
cliché [kliʃe], *s.m.* **1.** (*a*) *Typ:* Plate (of type); block of illustration. (*b*) *Typewr:* Cliché au stencil, wax stencil. **2.** *Phot:* Negative. Prendre un cliché, to make an exposure. **3.** *Lit: F:* Stock phrase; hackneyed expression; tag.
clicher [kliʃe], *v.tr. Typ:* (i) To stereotype, (ii) to take electros of (book, etc.). *s.m.* **-age.**
client, -ente [kliɑ̃, -ɑ̃ːt], *s.* (Lawyer's) client; (tradesman's) customer; (doctor's) patient; (cabman's) fare; (hotel) visitor. *F:* C'est un drôle de client, he's a queer customer.
clientèle [kliɑ̃tɛl], *s.f.* (*a*) Practice (of barrister or doctor). (*b*) *Com:* (i) Custom, (ii) customers, (iii) connection, (iv) goodwill.
clignement [kliɲmɑ̃], *s.m.* Blink(ing), wink(ing); flicker of the eyelids. *Regarder qn avec un c. d'yeux, de paupières*, to blink at s.o. Lancer un c. d'œil à qn, to wink at s.o.
cligner [kliɲe], *v.tr. & i.* **1.** (*a*) Cligner les yeux (*pour mieux voir*), to screw up one's eyes. (*b*) C. les yeux, les paupières, to blink. Il n'a pas cligné, he didn't wince. **2.** (*a*) Cligner de l'œil à qn, to wink at s.o. (*b*) Cligner des yeux, to assent with a flicker of the eyelids.
clignotant [kliɲotɑ̃], *a.* Blinking (eyes); twinkling (star) *Nau: etc:* Signal clignotant, intermittent signal.
clignoter [kliɲote], *v.i.* (*a*) Clignoter des yeux, to blink. (*b*) (Of star) To twinkle. (*c*) (Of eyelid) To twitch. (*d*) (Of arc-lamp) To flicker. *s.m.* **-ement.**
climat [klima, -mɑ], *s.m.* **1.** Climate. **2.** Region, climate. Sous d'autres climats, in other climes.

climatérique¹ [klimaterik], *a. Med :* Climacteric.

climatérique², climatique [klimatik], *a.* Climatic (conditions, etc.). **Station climat(ér)ique,** health resort.

clin¹ [klɛ̃], *s.m. Mec.E :* Joint à **clin,** lap-joint. S.a. COUTURE.

clin² d'œil [klɛ̃dœːj], *s.m.* Wink. Esp. **En un clin d'œil,** in the twinkling of an eye.

clinfoc [klɛ̃fɔk], *s.m. Nau :* Flying jib.

clinique [klinik]. **1.** *a.* Clinical (lecture, etc.). *Assister aux leçons cliniques,* to walk the hospitals. **2.** *s.f.* (*a*) Clinical lecture. (*b*) Nursing-home (esp. for surgical cases). (*c*) (Doctor's) 'surgery.'

clinomètre [klinɔmɛtr], *s.m. Av : Surv :* Clinometer ; gradient indicator.

clinquant [klɛ̃kɑ̃], *s.m.* **1.** Tinsel. *C. du style,* showiness of style. **2.** *Tchn :* Foil. *El.E :* Balai **de clinquant,** foil brush.

clique [klik], *s.f.* **1.** (Disreputable) gang, set. **2.** *Mil : F :* (Drum and bugle) band.

cliquet [klike], *s.m.* **1.** *Mec.E :* Catch, pawl. **2.** *Tls :* Ratchet (drill-)brace.

cliqueter [klikte], *v.i.* (il **cliquette** ; il **cliquettera**) (Of chains, etc.) To rattle, clank ; (of swords, etc.) to click ; (of glasses) to clink, chink ; (of keys) to jingle. *Aut :* (Of engine) To pink.

cliquetis [klikti], *s.m.* Rattling, rattle (of chain) ; clank(ing) (of fetters) ; click(ing), clash (of swords) ; clink(ing), chinking (of glasses) ; jingling, jingle (of keys). *Aut :* Pinking (of engine).

cliquette [kliket], *s.f.* (Pair of) castanets.

clisse [klis], *s.f.* (*a*) Wicker covering (of bottle). (*b*) Cheese-drainer.

clisser [klise], *v.tr.* To wicker (bottles). **Bouteille clissée,** demijohn. **Tourie clissée,** carboy.

clivage [klivaːʒ], *s.m.* **1.** Cleaving (of diamonds). **2.** Cleavage (of rocks).

cliver [klive], *v.tr.* To cleave, split (rocks, etc.).

cloaque [klɔak]. **1.** *s.f. Rom.Ant :* La grande **Cloaque,** the *Cloaca Maxima.* **2.** *s.m.* Cesspool. *F :* **Cloaque de vices,** sink of iniquity.

cloche [klɔʃ], *s.f.* **1.** Bell. *La c. du dîner,* the dinner-bell. *Ind :* **Heures hors cloche,** overtime. **Fleurs en cloche,** bell-shaped flowers. *F :* **Déménager à la cloche de bois,** to do a moonlight flit. **2.** Bell (of gasometer). *Ch :* Bell-jar. *Hort :* Bell-glass, cloche. *Dom.Ec :* Dish-cover. **Cloche à plongeur,** diving-bell. **3.** Blister, bleb. **Avoir des cloches aux mains,** to have blistered hands.

cloche-pied (à) [aklɔʃpje], *adv.phr.* **Sauter à cloche-pied,** to hop (on one foot).

clocher¹ [klɔʃe], *s.m.* Belfry, bell-tower ; steeple. **Esprit de clocher,** parochial spirit ; parochialism. **Course au clocher,** point-to-point race. [CLOCHE]

clocher² [klɔʃe], *v.i.* To limp, hobble. *F : Vers qui cloche,* halting line of verse. *Il y a quelque chose qui cloche,* there is something amiss. *s.m.* **-ement.**

clocheton [klɔʃtɔ̃], *s.m.* Pinnacle ; bell-turret.

clochette [klɔʃet], *s.f.* **1.** Small bell ; hand-bell. **2.** *Bot :* (Any) small bell-flower.

cloison [klwazɔ̃], *s.f.* **1.** Partition, division. **Mur de cloison,** dividing wall. **2.** *Nat.Hist :* Septum. **3.** (*a*) *Aut :* Baffle-plate (of silencer). (*b*) *Nau :* Bulkhead. *C. étanche,* water-tight bulkhead.

cloisonn|er [klwazɔne], *v.tr.* To partition (off) (room, etc.). *s.m.* **-age.** *s.m.* **-ement.**
    cloisonné, *a.* **1.** *Nat.Hist :* Septate(d). **2.** Cloisonné (enamel).

cloître [klwaːtr, -wɑ:-], *s.m.* **1.** Cloister(s) (of monastery, etc.). **2.** Cloister, monastery, convent. **Vie de cloître,** cloistered life.

cloîtrer [klwatre, -wɑ-], *v.tr.* To cloister (s.o.). **Nonne cloîtrée,** enclosed nun.
    se cloîtrer, to enter a convent or a monastery.

clopin-clopant [klɔpɛ̃klɔpɑ̃], *adv. F :* **Aller clopin-clopant,** to limp along, hobble about.

clopiner [klɔpine], *v.i.* To hobble, limp.

cloporte [klɔpɔrt], *s.m. Crust :* Wood-louse.

cloque [klɔk], *s.f. F :* **1.** (*a*) Lump, swelling (from insect bite, etc.). (*b*) Blister (on hand, paint). **2.** *Agr :* Rust (of corn). *Arb :* Blight.

cloqu|er [klɔke], *v.i. & pr. F :* (Of paint, skin, etc.) To blister. *s.m.* **-age.**
    cloqué, *a.* Rusty (wheat) ; blighted (leaf).

clore [klɔːr], *v.tr.def.* (= FERMER, which has taken its place in most uses) (*p.p.* **clos** ; *pr.ind.* **je clos, je clos, il clôt, ils closent** ; *fu.* **je clorai**) (*a*) To close (up), shut (up). (*b*) To enclose (park, etc.). (*c*) To end, finish (discussion) ; to conclude (bargain).

clos. **1.** *a.* (*a*) Closed ; shut up. **A la nuit close,** after dark. **Clos et coi,** snug and cosy at home. S.a. HUIS **2,** MAISON **1.** (*b*) Concluded. **2.** *s.m.* Enclosure ; close. **Clos de vigne,** vineyard.

closerie [klozri], *s.f.* (*a*) Small (enclosed) estate. (*b*) Small-holding, croft. [CLORE]

clôture [kloty:r], *s.f.* **1.** Enclosure, fence, fencing. **Mur de clôture,** (party) fence wall, enclosing wall. *Jur :* **Bris de clôture,** breach of close. **2.** (*a*) Closing, closure (of offices, theatre, etc.). *Ven : C. de la chasse,* close of season. (*b*) Conclusion, end (of sitting, etc.). **Demander la clôture** (*d'une discussion*), to move the closure (of a debate). **3.** *Com :* Closing, winding up (of account).

clôturer [klotyre], *v.tr.* **1.** To enclose, shut in (field, etc.). **2.** (*a*) To close down (factory, etc.). (*b*) To end, terminate, conclude (session). *Parl :* **Clôturer les débats,** to closure the debate. **3.** To wind up, close (accounts, etc.).

clou [klu], *s.m.* **1.** (*a*) Nail. **Souliers à gros clous,** hob-nailed boots. **Attacher qch. avec un c.,** to nail sth. up (or down). *F :* **Ne pas ficher un clou,** not to do a stroke (of work). **Mettre qch. au clou,** to pawn sth. S.a. CHASSER **1,** RIVER. (*b*) *Furn :* **Clou doré,** stud. (*c*) **Clou cavalier,** staple. **Clou à crochet,** hook. (*d*) (i) Stud (of pedestrian crossing) ; (ii) *Toil :* flapjack. (*e*) *F :* Star turn, chief attraction (of entertainment). (*f*) *Mil : P :* Cells. **Au clou,** in clink. **2.** (*a*) Boil, carbuncle. (*b*) Stab of pain ; stitch. **3.** **Clou de girofle,** clove. **4.** Old worn out motor car, etc.

clou|er [klue], *v.tr.* **1.** To nail (sth.) (up, down). **Clouer son pavillon,** to nail one's colours to the mast. *F :* **Clouer le bec à qn,** to silence s.o. ; to shut s.o. up. **2.** To pin (sth.) down ; to hold (sth.) fast. **Rester cloué sur place,** to stand stock-still, rooted to the spot. *Être cloué à son lit,* to be tied to one's bed (by illness) ; to be bed-ridden. *Chess : C. une pièce,* to pin a piece. *s.m.* **-age.**

clout|er [klute], *v.tr.* **1.** To stud. **Passage clouté,** pedestrian crossing. **2.** To fix (horse-shoe). *s.m.* **-age.**

clovisse [klɔvis], *s.f. Moll :* Cockle.

club [klyb, klɔb, klœb], *s.m.* **1.** (Political, sporting) club. **2.** (Golf-)club (implement).

coaccusé, -ée [koakyze], *s. Jur :* Co-defendant.

coacquéreur [koakerœ:r], *s.m.* Joint purchaser.

coadjuteur [koadʒytœ:r], *s.m. Ecc :* Coadjutor (to bishop).

coadministrateur [koadministratœ:r], *s.m.* (*a*) Co-director. (*b*) Co-trustee.

coagulation [koagylasjɔ̃], *s.f.* Coagulation, coagulating.

coagul|er [koagyle], *v.tr.* To coagulate, congeal (albumen, etc.) ; to curdle (milk). *a.* **-able.**
    se coaguler, (of blood, etc.) to coagulate, congeal, clot ; (of milk) to curdle.

coaliser (se) [sekoalize], *v.pr.* To form a coalition ; to unite.

coalition [kɔalisjɔ̃], *s.f.* **1.** Coalition, union. **2.** (Hostile) combination; conspiracy.

coaltar [kɔltaːr], *s.m.* (Coal-, gas-)tar.

coassler [kɔase], *v.i.* (Of frog) To croak. *s.m.* **-ement.**

coassocié, -ée [kɔasɔsje], *s.* Copartner; joint partner.

cobalt [kɔbalt], *s.m.* Cobalt. *C. d'outremer*, cobalt blue.

cobaye [kɔbaːj], *s.m. Z:* Guinea-pig; cavy.

Coblence [kɔblɑ̃ːs]. *Pr.n.m.* Coblentz.

cobra [kɔbra], *s.m. Rept:* Cobra.

cocagne [kɔkaɲ], *s.f.* Mât de cocagne, greasy pole. Pays de cocagne, land of milk and honey; land of plenty.

cocaïne [kɔkain], *s.f. Pharm:* Cocaïne.

cocaïnomane [kɔkainɔman], *s.m. & f.* Cocaine addict.

cocarde [kɔkard], *s.f.* Cockade, rosette.

cocasse [kɔkas], *a. P:* Droll, laughable.

cocasserie [kɔkasri], *s.f. P:* **1.** Comicality, oddity. **2.** *pl.* Antics (of clown, etc.).

coccinelle [kɔksinɛl], *s.f. Ent:* Coccinella; esp. lady-bird.

coche[1] [kɔʃ], *s.m. A:* Stage-coach. *F:* **Faire la mouche du coche**, to play the busybody.

coche[2], *s.f.* Notch, nick; score (on tally-stick); nock (of arrow).

cochenille [kɔʃniːj], *s.f.* Cochineal.

cochenillier [kɔʃnije], *s.m.* Cochineal-fig; nopal.

cocher[1] [kɔʃe], *s.m.* Coachman, driver. *C. de fiacre*, cabman, *F:* cabby. **Le siège du cocher**, the box. [COCHE[1]]

cocher[2], *v.tr.* To nick, notch; to score (tally).

cochère [kɔʃɛːr], *a.f.* Porte cochère, carriage gateway, main entrance. [COCHE[1]]

Cochinchine [kɔʃɛ̃ʃin]. *Pr.n.f.* Cochin-China.

cochon [kɔʃɔ̃]. **I.** *s.m.* **1.** (*a*) Pig, hog, porker. **Cochon de lait**, sucking-pig. *Troupeau de cochons*, herd of swine. **Gardeur de cochons**, swine-herd. **Étable à cochons**, pigsty, piggery. (*b*) Occ. *Cu:* Pork. **Fromage de cochon**, brawn. **2.** Cochon d'Inde, guinea-pig. **II. cochon, -onne.** *P: V:* **I.** *a.* Swinish, beastly. **2.** *s.m.* Dirty pig; swine (of a man).

cochonnerie [kɔʃɔnri], *s.f. F:* **1.** Filthiness, beastliness. **2.** Trashy stuff; rubbish. **3.** Foul trick; *P:* lousy trick.

cochonnet [kɔʃɔnɛ], *s.m.* **1.** Young pig. **2.** *Games:* (*a*) *Bowls:* Jack. (*b*) Die with twelve faces; teetotum.

coco[1] [kɔko], *s.m.* **1.** Noix de coco, coco(a)-nut. Fibre de coco, coir(-fibre). **2.** *F:* Liquorice water.

coco[2], *s.m.* **1.** (Child's word) (*a*) Cock-a-doodle. (*b*) Egg. **2.** (*a*) *P:* Fellow, individual (in bad sense). S.a. VILAIN. (*b*) *F:* **Mon coco**, my pet, my darling.

coco[3], *s.f. F:* Cocaine.

cocon [kɔkɔ̃], *s.m.* Cocoon.

cocorico [kɔkɔriko], *onomat. & s.m.* Cock-a-doodle-doo!

cocotier [kɔkɔtje], *s.m.* Coco-nut palm.

cocotte [kɔkɔt], *s.f.* **1.** (Child's word) (*a*) Hen, chicken. (*b*) Bird made out of folded paper. **2.** *F:* **Ma cocotte**, ducky; my little duck. **3.** *Cu:* Stew-pan.

code [kɔd], *s.m.* Code. **1.** Statute-book. *C. de commerce*, commercial law. *F:* **Se tenir dans les marges du code**, to keep just within the law. *Aut:* C. de la route, highway code. **Se mettre en code**, to dip and switch. **2.** *C. télégraphique*, telegraphic code.

codétenu, -ue [kɔdetny], *s.* Fellow-prisoner.

codicille [kɔdisil], *s.m.* Codicil.

codification [kɔdifikasjɔ̃], *s.f.* (*a*) Codification, classification (of laws). (*b*) Coding (of message).

codifier [kɔdifje], *v.tr.* **1.** To codify (laws). **2.** To code (message).

codirecteur, -trice [kɔdirɛktœːr, -tris], *s.* Co-director, -directress; joint-manager, -manageress.

coefficient [kɔefisjɑ̃], *s.m.* Coefficient. *Mec: C. d'écrasement, d'élasticité*, modulus of compression, of elasticity. *C. de sûreté, de sécurité*, safety factor.

cœlentérés [selɑ̃tere], *s.m.pl. Z:* Coelenterata.

coéquation [kɔekwasjɔ̃], *s.f. Adm:* Proportional assessment.

coéquipier [kɔekipje], *s.m. Sp:* Fellow-member (of team or crew).

coercible [kɔɛrsibl], *a. Ph:* Coercible (gas, etc.).

coercitif, -ive [kɔɛrsitif, -iːv], *a.* Coercive.

cœsium [sezjɔm], *s.m. Ch:* Caesium.

cœur [kœːr], *s.m.* Heart. **1.** (*a*) *Maladie de c.*, heart disease. **Serrer qn sur, contre, son c.**, to strain s.o. to one's breast, to one's bosom. **En cœur**, heart-shaped. *F:* **Faire la bouche en cœur**, to make a pretty mouth; to smirk. (*b*) **Avoir mal au cœur**, to feel sick. Cela soulève le cœur, it is nauseating; it makes one's gorge rise. **2.** Soul, feelings, mind. (*a*) **Avoir qch. sur le cœur**, to have sth. on one's mind. **En avoir le cœur net**, to get to the bottom of it; to clear the matter up. **Au fond du cœur**, in one's heart of hearts. **Parler à cœur ouvert**, to speak freely, with open heart. **Remercier qn de tout cœur**, to thank s.o. whole-heartedly. **Spectacle qui vous fend le cœur**, heart-rending sight. **Il mourut le cœur brisé**, he died of a broken heart. **Partir le cœur léger**, to set off with a light heart. **Ruiner autrui de gaîté de cœur**, to ruin others wantonly, with a light heart. S.a. GAIETÉ. **Avoir le cœur gros**, to be sad at heart. **Avoir la mort dans le cœur**, to be sick at heart. **La chose qui lui tient au cœur**, (i) the thing he has set his heart on; (ii) the thing that hurts him most. **Avoir le cœur sur les lèvres, sur la main**, to wear one's heart on one's sleeve. **Avoir trop de cœur**, to be too tender-hearted. **N'avoir point de cœur**, to have no feelings. **Manque de cœur**, heartlessness. **Si le cœur vous en dit**, if you feel like it. **Je n'ai pas le cœur à faire cela**, I am not in the mood to do that. *Je n'ai pas le c. à rire*, I am in no heart for laughing. **Vous n'aurez pas le cœur de faire cela**, you will not be so heartless as to do that. **Avoir qch. à cœur**, to have sth. at heart. **Avoir à cœur de faire qch.**, to be bent, set, on doing sth. **Prendre qch. à cœur**, to lay, take, sth. to heart. **Prendre à cœur de faire qch.**, to set one's heart on doing sth. (*b*) **Apprendre, savoir, qch. par cœur**, to learn, know, sth. by heart. **3.** Courage, spirit, pluck. **Donner du cœur à qn**, to put s.o. in good heart; to hearten s.o. *F:* **Avoir du cœur au ventre**, to have plenty of spunk. **Faire contre mauvaise fortune bon cœur**, to make the best of a bad job; to put a brave face on things. **4.** (*a*) **Avoir le cœur à l'ouvrage**, to have one's heart in one's work. **Faire qch. de bon cœur, de grand cœur**, to do sth. willingly, gladly. **Faire qch. de mauvais cœur**, to do sth. reluctantly, unwillingly. **Rire de bon cœur**, to laugh heartily. **Travailler, aller, de bon cœur**, to work heartily, with a will. S.a. JOIE. (*b*) **Donner son cœur à qn**, to lose one's heart to s.o. **Aimer qn de tout son cœur**, to love s.o. with all one's heart. **À vous de tout cœur**, yours affectionately. *Prov:* **Loin des yeux loin du cœur**, out of sight, out of mind. S.a. AFFAIRE I,

AMI 1. (c) **Avoir un grand cœur,** to be great-hearted. **C'est un bon cœur,** he is a kind-hearted sort. **Il a le cœur bien placé,** his heart is in the right place. **5.** Middle, midst. **Au cœur de la ville,** in the heart of the town. *C. d'un chou, d'un artichaut,* heart of a cabbage, of an artichoke. **Au cœur de l'hiver, de l'été,** in the depth of winter, in the height of summer. **6.** *Cards:* Hearts. *Avez-vous du c.?* have you any hearts?

coffrage [kɔfraːʒ], *s.m.* **1.** *Min: etc:* Coffering, lining (of shaft, etc.). **2.** *Const:* Framework, framing, shuttering (for concrete work).

coffre [kɔfr], *s.m.* **1.** (*a*) Chest, bin. *C. à outils,* tool-chest, -box. *C. de voyage,* trunk. *C. à linge,* linen chest. *C. à avoine,* corn bin. F: **Avoir le coffre solide,** to be sound in wind and limb. (*b*) *C. de sûreté,* safe. F: *Les coffres de l'État,* the coffers of the State; the Treasury. (*c*) Boot (of carriage). **2.** *Mch:* **Coffre à vapeur,** steam-chest, -chamber. **3.** *Nau:* Mooring-buoy; moorings. *Prendre son c.,* to pick up one's moor-ings. **4.** *Nau:* Well-deck.

coffre-fort, *s.m.* Safe. *pl. Des coffres-forts.*

coffrer [kɔfre], *v.tr.* **1.** F: To put (s.o.) into prison. **2.** *Min:* To coffer, line (shaft).

coffret [kɔfrɛ], *s.m.* Small box; tool-box or -chest. *C. à bijoux,* jewel-case; casket. *C. à documents,* deed-box.

cognac [kɔɲak], *s.m.* Cognac; brandy.

cognassier [kɔɲasje], *s.m.* Quince(-tree).

cognée [kɔɲe], *s.f.* Axe or hatchet. **Mettre la cognée à l'arbre,** to set the axe (i) to the tree, (ii) F: to the root of an evil. S.a. MANCHE[2] 1.

cogner [kɔɲe]. **1.** *v.tr.* (*a*) To drive in, hammer in (sth.). (*b*) To knock, beat, thump. *C. qn en passant,* to bump up against s.o. *Box: Il cogne dur,* he is a hard hitter. F: *Ils se sont cognés,* they had a stand-up fight. **2.** *v.i.* (*a*) To knock, thump (*sur,* on); to bump (*contre,* against). (*b*) (Of engine, etc.) To knock. *s.m.* **-ement.**

cogneur [kɔɲœːr], *s.m. Box:* Hardhitter; bruiser.

cohérence [kɔeràːs], *s.f.* Coherence.

cohérent [kɔeràː], *a.* Coherent.

cohéritier, -ière [kɔeritje, -jɛːr], *s.* Co-heir, -heiress; joint heir(ess).

cohésion [kɔezjɔ̃], *s.f.* Cohesion, cohesiveness.

cohorte [kɔɔrt], *s.f. Rom.Ant:* Cohort. F: *C. joyeuse de noceurs,* merry crew, band, of revellers.

cohue [kɔy], *s.f.* Crowd, mob, throng. *C. de voitures,* solid mass of traffic.

coi, *f.* **coite** [kwa, kwat], *a. A:* Quiet, peaceful. (Still used in) **Se tenir coi,** to keep quiet; to lie low. S.a. CLOS 1.

coiffe [kwaf], *s.f.* **1.** Head-dress, cap (esp. of peasant woman). *A.Cost:* Coif. **2.** Lining (of hat). **3.** *Nau: etc: C. blanche,* white cap-cover. **4.** Caul (of new-born child).

coiffer [kwafe], *v.tr.* **1.** (*a*) To cover (the head); to cap (bottle, etc.). *Ce chapeau vous coiffe bien,* this hat suits you. *Montagne coiffée de neige,* snow-capped mountain. S.a. CATHERINE. (*b*) *C. un chapeau,* to put on, don, a hat. *Du combien coiffez-vous?* what is your size (in hats)? **2.** *C. qn,* to dress, do, s.o.'s hair.

se coiffer. 1. To put one's hat on. *Se c. d'une casquette,* to put on or wear a cap. *Se c. en cheveux,* to go without a hat. **2.** To do, dress, one's hair. **3.** F: **Se coiffer de qn,** to become infatuated with s.o.

coiffé, *a.* **1.** *Être c. d'un chapeau,* to be wearing a hat. **Il est né coiffé,** (i) he was born with a caul; (ii) F: he was born with a silver spoon in his mouth. **2.** *Être bien c.,* to have one's hair well dressed.

coiffeur, -euse [kwafœːr, -øːz], *s.* Hairdresser.

coiffure [kwafyːr], *s.f.* **1.** Head-dress, head-gear. **2.** Style of hairdressing. *C. à la Ninon, à la Jeanne d'Arc,* bobbed hair. *C. en garçon, à la garçonne,* Eton crop. **3.** Hairdressing. S.a. SALON.

coin [kwɛ̃], *s.m.* **1.** (*a*) Corner (of street, room, etc.). **Maison du coin, qui fait le coin,** corner house. *Place de c.,* corner seat. *Mettre un enfant au c.,* to put a child in the corner (in disgrace). *Games:* **Jouer aux quatre coins,** to play puss in the corner. **Reliure avec coins,** binding with leather corners. (*b*) (Retired) spot, nook. *Petit c. rustique,* rustic spot; small country place. **Coins et recoins,** nooks and corners. (*c*) *Furn:* Corner cupboard. (*d*) **Coin de feu,** (i) smoking-jacket; (ii) corner chair. **Coin du feu,** ingle-nook. **Au coin du feu,** by the fireside. (*e*) Small piece; patch (of land, etc.). *C. de ciel bleu,* patch of blue sky. **2.** (*a*) Wedge, key, quoin, chock. *C. à fendre,* wood-splitting wedge. **Tranchant du coin,** thin edge of the wedge. *Typ: C. de serrage,* quoin. (*b*) Clock (on stocking). **3.** (*a*) Stamp, die (for striking medals, coins). (*b*) *A:* Hall-mark. **Ouvrage marqué au coin du génie,** work bearing the stamp, the hall-mark, of genius.

coin|cer [kwɛ̃se]. *v.* (je coinçai; n. coinçons) **1.** *v.tr.* To wedge (up), chock (up) (rails, etc.). *s.m.* **-cage. 2.** *v.i. & pr.* (Of machine parts, etc.) To jam, stick; to bind. *s.m.* **-cement.**

coïncidence [kɔɛ̃sidàːs], *s.f.* Coincidence.

coïncident [kɔɛ̃sidɑ̃], *a.* Coincident, coinciding.

coïncider [kɔɛ̃side], *v.i.* To coincide (*avec,* with).

coing [kwɛ̃], *s.m. Bot:* Quince.

coir [kwaːr], *s.m.* Coir; coco(a)-nut fibre.

coke [kɔk], *s.m.* Coke. **Petit coke,** breeze.

col [kɔl], *s.m.* **1.** (*a*) *A:* Neck. *Homme au col court,* short-necked man. F: **Se pousser du col,** to carry one's head high; F: to swank. *Dressm:* **Tour de col,** collar (of dress). (*b*) Neck (of bottle, etc.). **2.** *Cost:* Collar. (*a*) **Faux col,** (i) detach-able collar; (ii) F: head (of froth on glass of beer). **Col raide, mou,** stiff, soft, collar. (*b*) *Col de dentelle,* lace collar. **3.** *Geog:* Pass, col, saddle (of mountain).

colback [kɔlbak], *s.m. Mil:* Busby.

col-bleu [kɔlblø], *s.m. Navy: F:* (Pers.) Blue jacket. *pl. Des cols-bleus.*

colcotar [kɔlkɔtaːr], *s.m.* Colcothar; (jewellers') rouge.

colégataire [kɔlegatɛːr], *s.m. & f. Jur:* Co-legatee; joint legatee.

coléoptère [kɔleɔptɛːr], *s.m.* Coleopter, beetle.

colère [kɔlɛːr]. **1.** *s.f.* (*a*) Anger; *Lit:* wrath. *F:* **Colère bleue,** towering passion. **Être en colère,** to be angry, in a temper. **Mettre qn en colère,** to make s.o. angry; to anger s.o. **Se mettre, entrer, en colère,** to fly into a passion; to lose one's temper. **Décharger sa colère sur qn,** to vent one's anger on s.o. *B:* **Enfants de colère,** children of wrath. (*b*) *Il avait des colères terribles,* he was subject to terrible fits of anger. **2.** *a.* Angry (voice); irascible (person).

coléreux, -euse [kɔlerø, -øːz], *a.* Quick-tempered, irascible, choleric (person).

colérique [kɔlerik], *a.* Choleric, fiery (disposi-tion).

colériquement [kɔlerikmɑ̃], *adv.* Irritably, angrily.

colibri [kɔlibri], *s.m.* Colibri; humming-bird.

colifichet [kɔlifiʃɛ], *s.m.* Trinket, bauble. *Com: Rayon des colifichets,* fancy-goods department.

colimaçon [kɔlimasɔ̃], *s.m.* Snail. **(Escalier en) colimaçon,** spiral staircase; winding stairs.

colin-maillard [kɔlɛ̃majaːr], *s.m.* **1.** Blind-man's-buff. **2.** Blind man (in blind-man's-buff).
colique [kɔlik]. **1.** *a. Anat:* Colic (artery, etc.). **2.** *s.f.* Colic ; *F:* stomach-ache, gripes. *Avoir la colique,* to have an attack of colic.
colis [kɔli], *s.m.* **1.** Parcel, packet, package. *Colis postal,* postal packet. *Par c. postal,* by parcel post. **2.** (Article of) luggage. *Les gros c.,* heavy luggage. *C. à la main,* hand luggage.
Colisée (le) [ləkɔlize], *s. Rom.Ant:* The Colosseum, the Coliseum.
côlite [kɔlit], *s.f. Med:* Colitis.
collaborateur, -trice [kɔlabɔratœːr, -tris], *s.* Collaborator ; fellow-worker ; associate. *Collaborateurs d'une revue,* contributors to a review.
collaboration [kɔlabɔrasjɔ̃], *s.f.* Collaboration (*avec,* with) ; joint authorship.
collaborer [kɔlabɔre], *v.i.* To collaborate (*avec,* with). *C. à un journal,* to contribute to a newspaper.
collage [kɔlaːʒ], *s.m.* Gluing, sticking (of wood, etc.) ; pasting (of paper, etc.). *Phot: C. à sec,* dry mounting.
collant [kɔlɑ̃], *a.* (*a*) Sticky ; tacky. *Houille collante,* caking coal. *F: Personne collante, bur(r)*; sticker. (*b*) Tight-, close-fitting ; skin-tight (garment).
collatéral, -aux [kɔlateral, -o], *a.* Collateral. *Nef collatérale,* *s.m.* collatéral, (side) aisle. *Jur:* (Parents) collatéraux, collaterals, relatives. *adv.* **-ement.**
collation [kɔl(l)asjɔ̃], *s.f.* **1.** Granting, conferment (of degree, etc.). **2.** Collation (of documents). **3.** Light meal ; snack.
collationn|er [kɔl(l)asjɔne]. **1.** *v.tr.* To collate, compare (two written documents). *Faire collationner un télégramme,* to have a telegram repeated. **2.** *v.i.* To have a snack. *s.m.* **-ement.**
colle [kɔl], *s.f.* **1.** (i) Paste ; (ii) glue ; (iii) size. *C. de, en, pâte,* (flour) paste. *C. forte,* glue. *C. de poisson,* fish-glue ; isinglass. *Papier sans colle,* unsized paper. **2.** *F:* (*a*) Falsehood, fib. (*b*) *Sch:* (i) Poser ; (ii) oral test ; (iii) detention. *Poser une colle à un candidat,* to put a poser to a candidate.
:ollecte [kɔllɛkt], *s.f.* **1.** (*a*) *Ecc:* Collection (for the poor, etc.). (*b*) Collecting, gathering. **2.** *Ecc:* Collect.
collecteur, -trice [kɔlɛktœːr, -tris]. **1.** *s.* Collector. **2.** *a. & s.m.* (*a*) *El.E:* Collecteur, bague collectrice, collector(-ring), commutator (of dynamo, etc.). (*b*) *Civ.E:* Egout collecteur, grand collecteur, main sewer. (*c*) *I.C.E: C. d'échappement,* exhaust manifold.
collect|if, -ive [kɔlɛktif, -iːv], *a.* Collective, joint (action, report). *adv.* **-ivement.**
collection [kɔlɛksjɔ̃], *s.f.* **1.** Collecting ; gathering. **2.** Collection ; cabinet (of butterflies) ; file (of newspapers).
collectionn|er [kɔlɛksjɔne], *v.tr.* To collect (stamps, curios, etc.). *s.m.* **-ement.**
collectionneur, -euse [kɔlɛksjɔnœːr, -øːz], *s.* Collector (of curios, etc.).
collectivité [kɔlɛktivite], *s.f.* Collectivity. **1.** Community. **2.** Common ownership.
collège [kɔlɛːʒ], *s.m.* **1.** College. *Le Sacré Collège,* the College of Cardinals. *Collège électoral,* electoral body ; constituency. **2.** School. *C. communal, municipal,* secondary school (maintained by the municipality). *C. libre,* proprietary (secondary) school.
collégien, -ienne [kɔleʒjɛ̃, -jɛn], *s.* Schoolboy, -girl.

collègue [kɔllɛg], *s.m. & f.* Colleague ; fellow-worker, -officer.
collement [kɔlmɑ̃], *s.m.* Adhesion ; sticking together.
coller [kɔle]. **1.** *v.tr.* (*a*) To paste, stick, glue (*à,* to, on). *F: C. son visage à la vitre,* to press, glue, one's face to the window-pane. (*b*) (i) *F:* To put, give. *Collez ça dans un coin,* stick that in a corner. (ii) *F:* To stump, floor (s.o.). *C. un candidat,* to pluck, plough, a candidate. (*c*) To size (paper). **2.** *v.i.* To stick, adhere, cling (*à,* to). *Vêtement qui colle,* clinging, tight-fitting, garment. **se coller,** to stick, adhere closely. *Se c. contre un mur,* to stand close to a wall. *Elle se colla contre lui,* she clung close to him.
collerette [kɔlrɛt], *s.f.* **1.** Collarette, collar (of fine muslin). **2.** Flange (of pipe, joint, etc.).
collet [kɔlɛ], *s.m.* **1.** (*a*) Collar (of coat, dress). *Saisir qn par le collet, au collet,* to collar s.o. ; to seize s.o. by the scruff of the neck. *F: Un collet monté,* a stiff-necked, strait-laced, starched, person. *a.inv.* Elle est très collet monté, she is very prim (and proper), very formal. (*b*) Cape. **2.** Neck (of tooth, chisel, violin, etc.) ; shoulder (of racquet, etc.). **3.** Flange, collar (of pipe, etc.) ; journal (of shaft). **4.** Snare, springe, noose (for trapping small animals). *Prendre des lapins au collet,* to snare rabbits. [COU]
collet|er [kɔlte], *v.tr.* (je collette ; je colletterai) (*a*) To collar (s.o.). (*b*) To grapple, wrestle, scuffle, with (s.o.). *Se c.,* to come to grips. *s.m.* **-age.**
colleur [kɔlœːr], *s.m.* Gluer, paster. *C. d'affiches,* bill-sticker.
collier [kɔlje], *s.m.* **1.** Necklace, necklet. **2.** (*a*) Collar (of order, etc.). (*b*) *C. de chien, de cheval,* dog-collar, horse-collar. *Cheval de collier,* draught-horse. *Être franc du collier,* (i) (of horse) to be a good puller ; (ii) *F:* (of pers.) to be a hard worker. *Coup de collier,* sudden effort, tug (by horse). *F: Donner un coup de collier,* to put one's back into it. *S.a.* MISÈRE 1. **3.** *Mec.E:* Collar, ring. *C. de palier,* bearing collar. *C. de frein,* brake-band. **4.** Collar, ring (on birds, etc.). *Pigeon à collier,* ringed pigeon.
collimateur [kɔllimatœːr], *s.m. Astr: Surv:* Collimator ; collimating prism or lens.
colline [kɔlin], *s.f.* Hill.
collision [kɔl(l)izjɔ̃], *s.f.* Collision ; clash (of interests). *Entrer en collision avec qch.,* to collide with sth. ; to run into (ship, car, etc.).
collodion [kɔl(l)ɔdjɔ̃], *s.m. Ch: etc:* Collodion.
colloïde [kɔllɔid], *s.m. Ch: etc:* Colloid, gel.
colloque [kɔllɔk], *s.m.* Colloquy, conversation.
colloquer [kɔllɔke], *v.tr. F: C. qn au bout de la table,* to relegate s.o. to the end of the table. *C. qch. à qn,* to foist, to palm off, sth. on s.o.
collotypie [kɔllɔtipi], *s.f.* = PHOTOTYPIE.
collusion [kɔllyzjɔ̃], *s.f. Jur:* Collusion.
collusoire [kɔllyzwaːr], *a. Jur:* Collusive. *adv.* **-ment.**
collyre [kɔlliːr], *s.m. Pharm:* Eye-wash.
colmat|er [kɔlmate], *v.tr.* **1.** *Agr:* To warp (land). **2.** To fill in (pot-holes in road, etc.). **3.** To clog (up) (filter) ; to choke (up) (pipe, etc.). *s.m.* **-age. se colmater,** to clog up ; to become choked.
colocataire [kɔlɔkatɛːr], *s.m. & f.* Joint tenant ; co-tenant.
Colomb [kɔlɔ̃]. *Pr.n.m.* Christophe Colomb, Christopher Columbus.
colombe [kɔlɔ̃:b], *s.f. Orn:* Pigeon, dove.
colombier [kɔlɔ̃bje], *s.m.* Dovecot(e) ; pigeon-house.

colombin, -ine [kɔlɔ̃bɛ̃, -in]. **I.** a. (a) Dove-like. (b) Dove-coloured. **2.** s.f. **Colombine.** (a) Agr: Pigeon-dung (manure). (b) Bot: Columbine, aquilegia. (c) Pr.n. Th: Columbine.

colombophile [kɔlɔ̃bɔfil], s.m. & f. Pigeon-fancier.

colon [kɔlɔ̃], s.m. **I.** Husbandman; farmer. **2.** (a) Colonist, settler. (b) F: Colonial.

côlon [kolɔ̃], s.m. Anat: Colon.

colonel [kɔlɔnɛl], s.m. Colonel.

colonial, -aux [kɔlɔnjal, -o]. **I.** a. Colonial. **2.** s.m.pl. F: Coloniaux, colonials.

colonie [kɔlɔni], s.f. Colony, settlement. *Aux colonies,* in the colonies. **Colonie pénitentiaire,** reformatory settlement or school (for youths). **Colonie de vacances,** holiday camp (for poor children). F: La c. anglaise à Paris, the English colony in Paris.

colonisateur, -trice [kɔlɔnizatœːr, -tris]. **I.** a. Colonizing (nation, etc.). **2.** s. Colonizer.

colonisation [kɔlɔnizasjɔ̃], s.f. Colonization, settling.

coloniser [kɔlɔnize], v.tr. To colonize, settle (region).

colonnade [kɔlɔnad], s.f. Arch: Colonnade.

colonne [kɔlɔn], s.f. **I.** Column, pillar. F: **Colonne de l'Église,** pillar, mainstay, of the Church. Lit à colonnes, four-poster bed. C. d'un journal, column of a newspaper. Anat: **Colonne vertébrale,** spinal column; spine, backbone. Hyd.E: C. d'eau, head, fall, of water. **2.** (a) Mil: etc: Column. **En colonne de route,** in route column; in column of route. (b) Navy: **En colonne,** line ahead.

colophane [kɔlɔfan], s.f. Rosin, colophony.

colorage [kɔlɔraːʒ], s.m. Coloration.

coloration [kɔlɔrasjɔ̃], s.f. **I.** Colouring. **2.** Colour. C. du teint, ruddiness. **Avoir de la coloration,** to have a high colour.

colorer [kɔlɔre], v.tr. To colour, stain, tint. C. qch. en vert, to colour sth. green. F: **Colorer un récit,** to lend colour to a tale.

se colorer, (of fruit, etc.) to colour; to assume a colour, a tinge; (of complexion) to grow ruddy.

coloré, a. Coloured. Teint c., ruddy, florid, complexion. Récit c., highly coloured narrative.

colorier [kɔlɔrje], v.tr. To colour, lay colour on (map, drawing). Colorié à la main, hand-coloured. s.m. **-age.**

coloris [kɔlɔri], s.m. Colour(ing) (of painting, fruit, etc.).

coloriste [kɔlɔristj, s.m. & f. **I.** Art: Colourist. **2.** Ind: Colourer (of post-cards, toys).

colossal, -aux [kɔlɔsal, -o], a. Colossal, gigantic, huge.

colosse [kɔlɔs], s.m. Colossus; F: giant. Le **Colosse de Rhodes,** the Colossus of Rhodes.

colportler [kɔlpɔrte], v.tr. (a) To hawk, peddle (goods). (b) F: To retail, spread abroad (news). s.m. **-age.**

colporteur, -euse [kɔlpɔrtœːr, -øːz], s. (a) Pack-man, pedlar. (b) F: C. de nouvelles, newsmonger.

coltinage [kɔltinaːʒ], s.m. Porterage, carrying (of heavy articles at docks, etc.).

coltiner [kɔltine], v.tr. To carry (loads) on one's back.

coltineur [kɔltinœːr], s.m. Heavy porter. C. de charbon, coal-heaver.

colza [kɔlza], s.m. Bot: (Summer) rape; colza. **Huile de colza,** colza oil.

coma [kɔma], s.m. Coma (in all senses).

comateux, -euse [kɔmatø, -øːz], a. Comatose.

combat [kɔ̃ba], s.m. **I.** (a) Combat, fight, contest.

Livrer combat à l'ennemi, to give battle to the enemy. **Engager le combat,** to go into action. **Hors de combat,** (i) (of man) disabled; (ii) (of gun, ship) out of action. C. naval, naval engagement. (b) **Combat singulier,** single combat. (c) **Combat de taureaux, de coqs,** bull-fight, cock-fight. **2.** F: Conflict, struggle; contest (of wits, etc.).

combattable [kɔ̃batabl], a. Combatable, disputable (argument).

combattant [kɔ̃batɑ̃], s.m. Fighting man; combatant. Anciens combattants, ex-service men.

combatif, -ive [kɔ̃batif, -iːv], a. Combative, pugnacious.

combattivité [kɔ̃bativite], s.f. Combativeness, pugnacity.

combattre [kɔ̃batr], v. (Conj. like BATTRE) **I.** v.tr. To combat, to fight (against), to contend with, battle with (enemy, temptation, etc.). **2.** v.i. To fight, strive, struggle. Je n'ai pas combattu, I did not do any fighting.

combe [kɔ̃ːb], s.f. Dale, dell, coomb, combe.

combien [kɔ̃bjɛ̃], adv. **I.** (Exclamative) (a) How (much)! Vous savez c. je vous estime, you know how much I esteem you. C. peu vous me comprenez! how little you understand me! **Combien de peine cela m'a coûté!** what trouble it has cost me! (b) How many! **Combien de gens!** what a lot of people! **2.** (Interrogative) (a) How much? C. vous dois-je? how much do I owe you? **C'est combien?** how much is it? A c. sommes-nous de Paris? how far are we from Paris? **Il y a je ne sais combien de temps,** ever so long ago. (b) How many? **Combien de fois?** how many times? how often? F: **Le combien sommes-nous?** what day of the month is it? **Il y a un tram tous les combien?** how often does the tramcar run? **3. Combien d'argent qu'il se fasse,** il n'en aura jamais assez, however much money he makes, he will never have enough.

combinaison [kɔ̃binɛzɔ̃], s.f. **I.** (a) Combination, arrangement, grouping (of letters, ideas, etc.). C. financière, combine. (b) F: Plan, scheme. **Déranger les combinaisons de qn,** to upset s.o.'s plans. (c) Ch: Combination. **2.** (a) (Engineer's) overalls, dungarees. Av: Flying suit. (b) (Pair of) combinations.

combinateur, -trice [kɔ̃binatœːr, -tris], s. Combiner, contriver.

combiner [kɔ̃bine], v.tr. **I.** (a) To combine, unite (forces, etc.); to arrange, group (ideas, etc.). (b) Ch: To combine. **2.** To contrive, devise, concoct (plan).

se combiner, to combine, unite (à, avec, with).

comble¹ [kɔ̃ːbl], s.m. **I.** Heaped measure. F: **Pour comble de malheur . . .,** as a crowning misfortune. . . . **Pour y mettre le comble,** to crown all. **Ça, c'est le comble!** that beats all! **2.** (a) Roof (timbers); roofing. C. à deux pentes, span-roof. C. brisé, curb-roof.' F: **Loger sous les combles,** to live in the attics, in the garret. **De fond en comble,** from top to bottom. F: **Ruiné de fond en comble,** utterly ruined. (b) F: Highest point; heigh (of happiness); acme, summit (of fame). **Porter qch. à son comble,** to raise sth. to the highest pitch.

comble², a. (a) (Of measure, etc.) Heaped up; full o overflowing. (b) (Of hall, etc.) Packed. La pièce fait salle c., the play is drawing full houses.

combler [kɔ̃ble], v.tr. **I.** To fill (up), fill in (ditch, etc.); to make up, make good (a loss); to fill (a vacancy). **2.** To fill (measure, etc.) to

overflowing. *Train comblé de matelots*, train crowded with sailors. *C. qn de bienfaits*, to heap kindness on s.o. *C. les vœux de qn*, to gratify s.o.'s wishes to the full. *s.m.* **-ement.**
se combler, (of valley) to fill up ; (of lake, etc.) to silt up.

comburant [kɔ̃byrã]. **I.** *a.* Combustive. **2.** *s.m.* Supporter of combustion.

combustible [kɔ̃bystibl]. **I.** *a.* Combustible, inflammable. **2.** *s.m.* Fuel.

combustion [kɔ̃bystjɔ̃], *s.f.* Combustion, burning. **Poêle à combustion lente**, slow-combustion stove. **Moteur à combustion interne**, internal combustion engine.

Côme [ko:m]. *Pr.n. Geog:* Como.

comédie [kɔmedi], *s.f.* **I.** (*a*) Comedy. *C. de mœurs*, comedy of manners. *C. de salon*, private theatricals. *F:* **C'était une vraie comédie!** it was as good as a play. (*b*) **Faire, jouer, la comédie (à qn)**, to act a part (before s.o.) ; to pretend. **2.** *A:* (*a*) Play. (*b*) The drama.

Comédie-Française (la), *s.* One of the four State-aided theatres in Paris and the home of the French classical drama.

comédien, -ienne [kɔmedjɛ̃, -jɛn], *s.* Comedian ; (play-)actor, (play-)actress ; player. **Comédiens ambulants**, strolling players.

comestible [kɔmɛstibl]. **I.** *a.* Edible, eatable. *Denrées comestibles*, provisions. **2.** *s.m.* (*a*) Article of food. (*b*) *pl.* Provisions, victuals ; edibles.

comète [kɔmɛt], *s.f.* Comet.

comice [kɔmis], *s.m.* **I.** *pl. Fr.Hist:* **Comices**, electoral meeting. **2. Comice agricole**, agricultural show.

comique [kɔmik]. **I.** *Th: Lit:* (*a*) *a.* Comic (actor, author, part, etc.). **Le genre comique**, comedy. S.a. OPÉRA I. (*b*) *s.m.* (i) Comedy. **Le bas comique**, low comedy. (ii) Comic actor or comedy-writer. (iii) Comedian, humorist. **2.** (*a*) *a.* Comical, funny. (*b*) *s.m. Le c. de l'histoire c'est que* . . ., the funny part, the joke, is that . . . . *adv.* **-ment.**

comité [kɔmite], *s.m.* Committee, board. *C. consultatif*, advisory board or commission. *Th: C. de lecture*, selection committee. *Parl:* (Of the House) **Se constituer en comité**, to go into committee. *F:* **Être en petit comité**, to be a select party, an informal gathering.

commandant [kɔmɑ̃dɑ̃]. **I.** *a.* Commanding (officer, etc.). **2.** *s.m. Mil: Navy:* Commander ; commanding officer. *Av:* Squadron-leader. **Commandant en chef**, commander-in-chief. **Commandant de bataillon, d'escadron**, major. **Passer commandant**, to obtain one's majority.

commande [kɔmɑ̃:d], *s.f.* **I.** *Com:* Order. **Faire, passer, une commande à qn**, to place an order with s.o. **Fait sur commande**, made to order. **Payable à la commande**, cash with order. *Représentation de c.*, command performance. *F:* **La prudence est de commande**, prudence is essential. **Sourire de commande**, forced smile. **2.** *Mec.E:* (*a*) Control, operation. **Organes de commande**, controls. **Levier de commande**, operating lever ; *Av:* control column, *F:* joystick. (*b*) Lever. *Aut: C. du changement de vitesse*, change-speed lever. (*c*) Drive ; driving(-gear). **Machine à commande électrique**, electrically driven machine.

commandement [kɔmɑ̃dmɑ̃], *s.m.* **I.** Command, order. **Les dix Commandements**, the ten Commandments. *F:* **Obéir au commandement**, to obey with military promptness. **2.** (Position of) command, authority. **Avoir, prendre, le** commandement de qch., to be in, to assume, take, command of sth.

commander [kɔmɑ̃de]. **I.** *v.tr.* (*a*) To command, order (sth.). *C. à qn de faire qch.*, to command, order, s.o. to do sth. *Abs. Monsieur a-t-il commandé?* have you given your order, sir? *Ces choses-là ne se commandent pas*, these things are beyond our control. *Apprendre à se commander*, to learn to control oneself. (*b*) To govern (province, etc.) ; to be in command of (army, fleet). (*c*) *C. le respect*, to command, compel, respect. (*d*) (Of fort, etc.) To command, dominate (town, valley). (*e*) *Mec.E:* (i) To control, operate (motion, valve, etc.). (ii) To drive (machine, shaft, etc.). *Commandé par moteur*, motor-driven. **2.** *v.ind.tr. C. à son impatience, à ses passions*, to control, curb, one's impatience, one's passions.

commandeur [kɔmɑ̃dœ:r], *s.m. Hist:* Commander (of order of knighthood).

commanditaire [kɔmɑ̃ditɛ:r], *a. & s.m. Com:* (**Associé**) **commanditaire**, sleeping partner.

commandite [kɔmɑ̃dit], *s.f.* (*a*) (**Société en**) **commandite**, limited partnership. (*b*) Capital invested by sleeping partner.

commanditer [kɔmɑ̃dite], *v.tr.* To finance (enterprise, etc.).

comme¹ [kɔm], *adv.* **I.** (*a*) As, like. *Je l'ai eu c. maître*, I had him for, as, a master. *Faites c. moi*, do like me ; do as I do. **Tout comme un autre**, (just) like anyone else. *F:* **J'ai comme une idée que** . . ., I have a sort of idea that. . . . **Comme ça vous venez de Paris?** and so you come from Paris? S.a. CI², QUOI¹ 4. (*b*) *Doux c. un agneau*, (as) gentle as a lamb. *Blanc c. neige*, snow-white. (*c*) **Comme (si)**, as if, as though. *Il travaille c. s'il avait vingt ans*, he works as if he were twenty. *Il resta c. pétrifié*, he stood as if, as though, petrified. *F:* **C'est tout comme**, it amounts to the same thing. (*d*) *Les bois durs c. le chêne et le noyer*, hard woods such as oak and walnut. **2.** (Before verbs) As. **Faites comme il vous plaira**, do as you please. **3.** As ; in the way of. **Qu'est-ce que vous avez comme légumes?** what have you got in the way of vegetables? **4.** *Excl.* How. **Voyez comme elles courent!** see how they run ! *C. il est maigre!* how thin he is ! *C. vous avez grandi!* how you have grown ! **5.** *F:* (= COMMENT) How. **Dieu sait comme**, the Lord knows how. **Voilà comme il est**, that's how he is ; that's just like him.

comme², *conj.* **I.** As ; seeing that. *C. vous êtes là* . . ., since you are here. . . . **2.** (Just) as. *C. il allait frapper on 'arrêta*, (just) as he was about to strike he was apprehended.

commémoratif, -ive [kɔmmemɔratif, -i:v], *a.* Commemorative (*de*, of) ; memorial (service).

commémoration [kɔmmemɔrasjɔ̃], *s.f.* **En commémoration de** . . ., in commemoration of. . . .

commémorer [kɔmmemɔre], *v.tr.* To commemorate.

commençant, -ante [kɔmɑ̃sɑ̃, -ã:t], *s.* Beginner.

commencement [kɔmɑ̃smɑ̃], *s.m.* Beginning, commencement. **Au commencement**, at the outset.

commencer [kɔmɑ̃se], *v.tr. & i.* (je commençai(s); *n.* commençons) To begin, commence, start. *C. la leçon*, to begin the lesson. *Abs.* **Pour commencer**, to begin with ; first of all. *C. à, de, faire qch.*, to begin to do sth. ; to begin doing sth. *C. par faire qch.*, to begin by doing sth.

commensurable [kɔmmɑ̃syrabl], *a. Mth:* Commensurable (*avec*, with, to).

comment [kɔmɑ̃], *adv.* **I.** *Interr.* How. *C. allez-*

vous? how are you? **Comment cela?** how so? **Comment (dites-vous)?** what (did you say)? I beg your pardon? **Comment faire?** what is to be done? *C. s'appelle-t-il?* what is his name? S.a. IMPORTER² 2. **2.** *Excl.* What! why! **Comment!** vous n'êtes pas encore parti! what, haven't you gone yet! **Mais comment donc!** why, of course! by all means!

commentaire [kɔmɑ̃tɛːr], *s.m.* **1.** Commentary (*sur*, on). **Faire le commentaire d'un texte,** to comment upon a text. **Texte avec commentaire,** annotated text. **2.** Comment. **Voilà qui se passe de commentaire,** comment is needless.

commentateur, -trice [kɔmɑ̃tatœːr, -tris], *s.* Commentator, annotator.

commenter [kɔmɑ̃te], *v.tr. & i.* **1.** To comment (up)on, annotate (text, etc.). **2.** *F:* C. (*sur*) *qn, qch.,* to pass remarks upon s.o., sth.

commérage [kɔmera:ʒ], *s.m.* (Ill-natured) gossip.

commerçant, -ante [kɔmɛrsɑ̃, -ɑ̃:t]. **I.** *a.* Commercial, mercantile, business (nation, quarter, etc.). **Peu commerçant,** (i) untradesmanlike; (ii) (town, etc.) that does little trade. **2.** *s.* Merchant, tradesman. **Être commerçant,** to be in business.

commerce [kɔmɛrs], *s.m.* **1.** Commerce; trade, business (*de,* in). *C. en gros, en détail,* wholesale trade, retail trade. **Exercer un commerce,** to carry on a business, a trade. **Faire le commerce du thé,** to deal in tea; to be in the tea trade. **Le commerce,** the commercial world. **Le petit commerce,** small tradespeople. **Maison de commerce,** business house; firm. S.a. VOYAGEUR 2. **Marine de commerce,** mercantile marine. **2.** Intercourse, dealings. *C. du monde,* human intercourse. **Être en commerce avec qn,** to be in touch, in relationship, with s.o. **Être d'un commerce agréable,** to be easy to get on with, pleasant to deal with. **Rompre tout commerce avec qn,** to break off all dealings with s.o.

commercer [kɔmɛrse], *v.i.* (je commerçai(s); n. commerçons) To trade, deal (*avec,* with); to have dealings (with s.o.).

commercial, -aux [kɔmɛrsjal, -o], *a.* Commercial; trading, business (relations). *adv.* **-ement.**

commercialiser [kɔmɛrsjalize], *v.tr.* To commercialize (art, etc.).

commère [kɔmɛːr], *s.f.* **1.** Fellow-sponsor (at baptism); *A:* gossip. **2.** (*a*) Gossip, busybody. (*b*) Crony. **Les Joyeuses Commères de Windsor,** the Merry Wives of Windsor.

commérer [kɔmere], *v.i.* (je commère; je commérerai) To gossip.

commettre [kɔmɛtr], *v.tr.* (Conj. like METTRE) **1.** To lay, twist (rope). *Commis en grelin,* cable-laid. **2.** (*a*) *Il eut soin de ne pas se c.,* he was careful not to commit himself. (*b*) *C. qch. à qn,* to commit, entrust, sth. to s.o. **3.** To commit, perpetrate (crime). *C. une erreur,* to make a mistake, a slip.

comminatoire [kɔminatwaːr], *a.* (*a*) *Jur:* Comminatory (decree). (*b*) *F:* Threatening (letter).

commis¹, -isse, etc. See COMMETTRE.

commis² [kɔmi], *s.m.* **1.** Clerk; book-keeper. **2.** (*a*) (Shop-)assistant. (*b*) **Commis voyageur,** commercial traveller. **Il a un bagout de commis voyageur,** he is as glib as a bagman. [COMMETTRE]

commisération [kɔmmizerasjɔ̃],*s.f.* Commiseration, pity.

commissaire [kɔmisɛːr], *s.m.* **1.** Member of a commission; commissary, commissioner. **Commissaire de police** = police superintendent. *Commissaires d'un bal, d'une réunion,* stewards of a ball, of a meeting. *C. d'un navire,* purser. **2.** *U.S.S.R. Adm:* Commissar.

commissaire-priseur, *s.m.* **I.** Appraiser, valuer. **2.** Auctioneer. *pl. Des commissaires-priseurs.*

commissariat [kɔmisarja], *s.m.* **1.** (*a*) Commissionership, commissaryship. (*b*) *Nau:* Pursership. **2.** **Commissariat de police,** central police station.

commission [kɔmisjɔ̃], *s.f.* Commission. **1.** Péchés d'omission et de commission, sins of omission and commission. **2.** *Jur: etc:* **Avoir la commission de faire qch.,** to be commissioned, empowered, to do sth. **Vente à commission,** sale on commission. **3.** (*a*) *C. de deux pour cent,* commission of two per cent. (*b*) Brokerage, factorage. **4.** Message, errand. **Faire des commissions,** to run errands. **5.** Committee, board. *C. d'enquête,* board of inquiry; court of inquiry. **Commission du budget,** Budget Committee. *Sch:* **Commission d'examen,** board of examiners.

commissionnaire [kɔmisjɔnɛːr], *s.m.* **1.** (*a*) *Com:* Commission-agent. *C. en gros,* factor. (*b*) *C. de transport, c. expéditeur,* forwarding agent. **2.** Messenger, commissionaire. *Petit c.,* errand-boy.

commissure [kɔmisyːr], *s.f. Anat: Bot: Arch:* Commissure; line of junction.

commod|e [kɔmɔd]. **I.** *a.* (*a*) Convenient, suitable (moment, etc.); handy (tool, etc.). (*b*) Convenient, commodious, comfortable (house, etc.). *C. à faire,* easy to do; easily done. (*c*) Accommodating (disposition, etc.); easy-going, good-natured (person). *C. à vivre,* easy to live with. **Être peu commode,** to be difficult to deal with. **2.** *s.f. Furn:* Chest of drawers. *adv.* **-ément.**

commodité [kɔmɔdite], *s.f.* **1.** Convenience; comfort. **Faire qch. à sa commodité,** to do sth. at one's convenience. **2.** Commodiousness (of carriage, etc.).

commotion [kɔm(m)osjɔ̃], *s.f.* **1.** Commotion, disturbance, upheaval. *C. électrique,* electric shock. **2.** *Med:* (*a*) Shell-shock. (*b*) Concussion.

commotionné [kɔm(m)osjɔne], *a.* Suffering (i) from shell-shock, (ii) from concussion.

commuer [kɔmmɥe], *v.tr. Jur:* To commute (penalty, etc.) (*en,* to).

commun [kɔmœ̃]. **I.** *a.* (*a*) Common (*à,* to). *Choses communes,* common property. **Maison commune,** town-hall; municipal buildings. *Avoir des intérêts communs,* to have interests in common. **N'avoir rien de commun avec qn,** to have nothing in common with s.o. **Faire bourse commune,** to share expenses; to pool resources. **Faire cause commune,** to make common cause (*avec,* with). **D'un commun accord,** with one accord. *Mth:* **Facteur commun,** common factor. *Adv.phr.* **En commun,** in common. *Étude en c.,* joint study. *Agir en c.,* to co-operate. (*b*) Universal, general (custom, etc.). **Le sens commun,** common sense. **Le bien commun,** the public weal. (*c*) Usual, everyday (occurrence). **Expression peu commune,** out-of-the-way, unusual, expression. **Situation hors de l'ordre commun,** situation out of the common. (*d*) Common(-place); mediocre. (*e*) Vulgar. **2.** *s.m.* (*a*) Common run, generality (of persons, etc.). **Homme du commun,** man of common extraction. **Le commun des mortels,** the common herd. *Œuvre au-dessus, hors, du commun,* work above the average. (*b*) Common fund(s). **Vivre sur le commun,** to live at the common expense. (*c*) *pl.* **Les communs,** (i) offices and outhouses; (ii) water-closets. *adv.* **-ément.**

communal, -aux [kɔmynal, -o], *a.* **1.** Common (land, property). **2.** Communal (council, etc.). École communale = elementary school.
communauté [kɔmynote], *s.f.* **1.** Community (of interests, ideas, etc.). Vivre en communauté de biens, to have everything in common. **2.** (a) Corporation, society. (b) (Religious) community, order.
commune [kɔmyn], *s.f.* **1.** (a) Fr.Hist: Free town. Les communes, (i) the commoners, the commons; (ii) the militia. (b) (In Eng.) La Chambre des Communes, the House of Commons. **2.** Fr.Adm: (Smallest territorial division) Commune; approx. = parish.
communiant, -ante [kɔmynjã, -ã:t], *s. Ecc:* Communicant. Premier communiant, young person partaking of the sacrament for the first time.
communicable [kɔmynikabl], *a.* **1.** Communicable (disease, etc.); transferable (right). **2.** Communicating (rooms).
communicant [kɔmynikã], *a.* Communicating (vessels, rooms).
communicateur, -trice [kɔmynikatœ:r, -tris]. **1.** *a.* Connecting (wire, etc.). **2.** *s.m.* Organ of transmission.
communicatif, -ive [kɔmynikatif, -i:v], *a.* **1.** Communicative, talkative. **2.** Catching, infectious (gaiety).
communication [kɔmynikasjɔ̃], *s.f.* Communication. **1.** (a) Donner, faire, communication de qch. à qn, to communicate sth. to s.o.; to inform s.o. of sth. (b) En communication réciproque, interconnected, interrelated. Entrer, se mettre, en communication avec qn, to get into communication, into touch, with s.o. Portes de communication, communicating doors. Mettre en communication, to connect up (boilers, etc.). *Tp:* Communication locale, à longue distance, local call, trunk-call. Fausse communication, wrong number. Mettre deux abonnés en communication, to connect two subscribers. Vous avez la communication, you are through. **2.** Message.
communier [kɔmynje], *v.i.* (a) *Ecc:* To communicate; to partake of the sacrament. (b) To be, live, in communion.
communion [kɔmynjɔ̃], *s.f.* **1.** Communion. **2.** *Ecc:* (Holy) Communion; the Lord's Supper.
communiquer [kɔmynike], *v.* To communicate. **1.** *v.tr.* To impart, convey (information, heat, etc.); to transmit (a motion). **2.** *v.i.* Porte qui communique au, avec le, jardin, door that communicates with, leads into, the garden. Canal qui fait c. deux rivières, canal that connects two rivers.
se communiquer. **1.** To be communicative. **2.** (Of fire, etc.) To spread (à, to).
communiqué, *s.m.* Official statement (to the press). *W.Tel:* News.
communisme [kɔmynism], *s.m.* Communism.
communiste [kɔmynist], *s.m. & f.* Communist.
commutateur [kɔmytatœ:r], *s.m. El:* **1.** Commutator. Commutateur-collecteur, collector (of dynamo). **2.** (a) Commutateur-permutateur, change-over switch. C. à bascule, tumbler-switch. C. à couteau, knife-switch. C. à plots, step-switch. (b) *F:* Electric-light switch.
commutation [kɔmytasjɔ̃], *s.f.* **1.** Commutation (of penalty, etc.). **2.** *El.E:* Change of connection; commutation.
commutatrice [kɔmytatris], *s.f. El.E:* Rotary converter; rotary transformer.
compact [kɔpakt], *a.* Compact, close, dense (formation, etc.).

compagne [kɔpaɲ], *s.f.* **1.** (Female) companion. C. de pension, school-mate. **2.** Partner (in life); wife; (of animals) mate.
compagnie [kɔpaɲi], *s.f.* **1.** Company. Tenir compagnie à qn, to keep, bear, s.o. company. Fausser compagnie à qn, to give s.o. the slip. Dame de compagnie, (i) companion; (ii) chaperon. **2.** Company; party. Il y avait nombreuse c., there was a large party. Fréquenter la bonne, la mauvaise, c., to keep good, bad, company. Être de bonne, de mauvaise, compagnie, to be well-, ill-bred. **3.** (a) Company (of national importance). Compagnie des Chemins de fer, Railway Company. La C. du gaz, the Gas Company. (b) *Com:* La maison Durand et Compagnie (usu. et Cie), the firm of Durand and Company (usu. and Co.). **4.** *Mil:* Company.
compagnon [kɔpaɲɔ̃], *s.m.* **1.** (a) Companion, comrade, fellow. C. d'école, schoolfellow, -mate. C. de voyage, fellow-traveller. C. de bord, shipmate. C. de jeu, playfellow. Vivre en compagnons, to live together as equals. (b) *Ind:* (Workman's) mate. **2.** Journeyman, workman.
comparable [kɔparabl], *a.* Comparable (à, with).
comparablement [kɔparabləmã], *adv.* Comparably; in comparison (à, with).
comparaison [kɔparɛzɔ̃], *s.f.* **1.** Comparison. Hors de toute comparaison, beyond compare. *Prep.phr.* En comparaison de qch., par comparaison à qch., in, by, comparison with sth.; as compared with sth. **2.** *Rh:* Simile.
comparaître [kɔparɛ:tr], *v.i.* (Conj. like PARAÎTRE) *Jur:* Comparaître (en justice), to appear before a court of justice. Comparaître par avoué, to be represented by counsel. Être appelé à c., to be summoned to appear.
comparatif, -ive [kɔparatif, -i:v]. **1.** *a.* Comparative. **2.** *s.m.* Adjectif au comparatif, adjective in the comparative (degree). *adv.* -ivement.
comparer [kɔpare], *v.tr.* To compare (à, avec, to, with).
comparé, *a.* Comparative (anatomy, history).
comparse [kɔpars], *s.m.* **1.** *Th:* Supernumerary. Rôle de c., walking-on part. **2.** (a) (Conjuror's) confederate. (b) Ally, confederate (in trickery).
compartiment [kɔpartimã], *s.m.* Compartment (of railway-carriage, etc.); partition (of box, etc.); division; square (of chess-board, etc.).
comparution [kɔparysjɔ̃], *s.f. Jur:* Appearance (before the court). Non-comparution, non-appearance; default.
compas [kɔpa], *s.m.* **1.** (a) (Pair of) compasses. C. à pointe sèche, dividers. C. à réduction, proportional compasses. *F:* Tout faire au compas, to do everything by rule. (b) *Mec.E:* etc: C. à calibrer, cal(l)ipers. **2.** Compas de mer, mariner's compass. C. de route, steering-compass. Répéter le compas, to box the compass. *Surv:* C. de relèvement, azimuth compass. **3.** Standard, scale (of measurement). *F:* Avoir le compas dans l'œil, to have an accurate eye.
compassement [kɔpasmã], *s.m.* **1.** Measuring (with compasses). *Nau:* Pricking (of chart). **2.** Formality, stiffness (of manner).
compasser [kɔpase], *v.tr.* **1.** To measure (distances on map, etc.) with compasses. *Nau:* To prick (chart). **2.** To regulate, consider (one's actions, etc.); to weigh (one's words).
compassé, *a.* **1.** Stiff, formal (manner, etc.). **2.** Regular, set (life).
compassion [kɔpasjɔ̃], *s.f.* Compassion, pity. Avoir compassion de qn, to have, take, compassion on s.o. Faire compassion, to arouse compassion. Par compassion, out of compassion.

compat|ible [kɔ̃patibl], *a.* Compatible (*avec*, with). *s.f.* **-ibilité.**

compatir [kɔ̃poti:r], *v.i.* C. au chagrin de qn, to sympathize with, feel for, s.o. in his grief.

compatissant [kɔ̃patisɑ̃], *a.* Compassionate (*pour*, to, towards) ; tender-hearted.

compatriote [kɔ̃patriɔt], *s.m. & f.* Compatriot.

compendieu|x, -euse [kɔ̃pɑ̃djø, -ø:z], *a.* Compendious, concise. *adv.* **-sement.**

compensateur, -trice [kɔ̃pɑ̃satœ:r, -tris]. **1.** *a.* Compensating (spring, etc.). *El:* Equalizing (current) ; balancing (dynamo). **2.** *s.m.* Compensator (of arc-lamp, etc.) ; (pressure) equalizer.

compensation [kɔ̃pɑ̃sasjɔ̃], *s.f.* (*a*) Compensation (of loss, etc.) ; set-off. En compensation de mes pertes, as an offset to my losses. Cela fait compensation, that makes up for it. *Bank:* Chambre de compensation, clearing-house. (*b*) Equalization, balancing (of forces, etc.). (*c*) *Nau:* Adjustment (of compass). (*d*) *Mec.E:* C. de l'usure, taking up of the wear. (*e*) *Sp:* Handicapping.

compenser [kɔ̃pɑ̃se], *v.tr.* (*a*) To compensate ; to make up for (sth.). C. une perte, to make good a loss. (*b*) To compensate, balance, set off (debts). (*c*) *Mec.E:* To balance (engine). (*d*) *Nau:* To adjust (compass). (*e*) *Mec.E: etc:* C. l'usure, to take up the wear. (*f*) *Sp:* To handicap (race).

compère [kɔ̃pɛ:r], *s.m.* **1.** Godfather. **2.** Accomplice, confederate. *Th:* Announcer (in a revue). **3.** *F:* Comrade, crony. Un bon compère, a jolly good fellow.

compère-loriot, *s.m.* **1.** *Orn:* Golden oriole. **2.** *F:* Sty (on the eyelid). *pl. Des compères-loriots.*

compétence [kɔ̃petɑ̃:s], *s.f.* **1.** *Jur:* Competence, competency, jurisdiction, powers (of court of justice, etc.). Rentrer dans la c. du tribunal, to fall within the competence of the court. Sortir de sa compétence, to exceed one's powers. **2.** Competence, ability ; proficiency, skill.

compét|ent [kɔ̃petɑ̃], *a.* *Jur: etc:* Competent (authority). *F:* En lieu compétent on dit que . . ., in well-informed quarters it is said that. . . . *adv.* **-emment.**

compilateur, -trice [kɔ̃pilatœ:r, -tris], *s.* Compiler.

compilation [kɔ̃pilasjɔ̃], *s.f.* Usu. *Pej:* **1.** Compiling. **2.** Compilation.

compiler [kɔ̃pile], *v.tr.* Usu. *Pej:* To compile.

complainte [kɔ̃plɛ̃t], *s.f.* A: Plaint, lament.

complaire [kɔ̃plɛ:r], *v.ind.tr.* (Conj. like PLAIRE) C. à qn, to please, humour, s.o.
se **complaire** en, dans, qch., à faire qch., to take pleasure in sth., in doing sth.

compl-ais, -aît, -aisons. See COMPLAIRE.

complaisance [kɔ̃plɛzɑ̃:s], *s.f.* **1.** Complaisance, obligingness. Faire qch. par complaisance, to do sth. out of kindness. Faire qch. par c. pour qn, to do sth. to oblige s.o. Auriez-vous la complaisance de . . ., would you be so good, so kind, as to. . . . *Com:* Billet de complaisance, accommodation bill ; *F:* kite. **2.** Complacency ; (self-)satisfaction.

complais|ant, -ante [kɔ̃plɛzɑ̃, -ɑ̃:t]. **1.** *a.* (*a*) Obliging, complaisant (person, character). Prêter une oreille complaisante aux prières de qn, to lend a ready ear to s.o.'s requests. (*b*) Complacent, self-satisfied (smile, etc.). **2.** *s.* Flatterer ; time-server. *adv.* **-amment.**

complément [kɔ̃plemɑ̃], *s.m.* **1.** *Gram:* Complement or object (of verb). **2.** *Mil:* Full complement (of regiment, etc.).

complémentaire [kɔ̃plemɑ̃tɛ:r], *a.* Complementary (angle, colour) ; fuller (information).

compl|et, -ète [kɔ̃plɛ, -ɛt]. **1.** *a.* (*a*) Complete, entire (outfit, works, etc.). Rapport très c., very full report. *F:* Ça serait complet! that would be the last straw! (*b*) Full (bus, *Th:* house, etc.). **2.** *s.m.* (*a*) Suit (of clothes). C. veston, lounge suit. (*b*) *Adj.phr.* Au complet, complete, full. Bataillon au grand complet, battalion at full strength. *F:* Nous étions présents au grand c., we turned out in full force. *adv.* **-ètement.**

complétement [kɔ̃pletmɑ̃], *s.m.* Completion.

compléter [kɔ̃plete], *v.tr.* (je complète ; je compléterai) To complete ; to make (sth.) complete ; to finish off (a work) ; to make up (a sum). C. un bataillon, to bring a battalion up to strength.

complétif, -ive [kɔ̃pletif, -i:v], *a.* *Gram:* (*a*) Oblique (case). (*b*) Object (clause).

complexe [kɔ̃plɛks]. **1.** *a.* Complex (character, etc.) ; complicated (question) ; intricate (problem). *Gram:* Sujet complexe, compound subject. *Mth:* Nombre complexe, compound number. **2.** *s.m.* *Psy:* Complex.

complexion [kɔ̃plɛksjɔ̃], *s.f.* Constitution, temperament. Enfant de c. délicate, child of (a) delicate constitution.

complexité [kɔ̃plɛksite], *s.f.* Complexity.

complication [kɔ̃plikasjɔ̃], *s.f.* **1.** Complication ; thickening (of plot). **2.** Complexity, intricacy.

complice [kɔ̃plis], *a. & s.* Accessory (*de*, to) ; accomplice, abettor (*de*, of). Être complice d'un crime, to be party to a crime.

complicité [kɔ̃plisite], *s.f.* Complicity. *Jur:* Aiding and abetting. Agir de complicité avec qn, to act in collusion with s.o.

complies [kɔ̃pli], *s.f.pl.* *Ecc:* Compline.

compliment [kɔ̃plimɑ̃], *s.m.* **1.** Compliment. Faire des compliments à qn, to pay s.o. compliments. **2.** *pl.* Compliments, greetings. "Mes compliments à . . .," 'remember me to . . . ;' 'my kind regards to. . . .' **3.** Congratulation. Adresser des compliments à qn sur qch., to offer s.o. one's congratulations on sth.

complimenter [kɔ̃plimɑ̃te], *v.tr.* (*a*) To compliment (*de*, *sur*, on). (*b*) To congratulate (on).

compliquer [kɔ̃plike], *v.tr.* To complicate.
se **compliquer,** to become complicated (*de*, with) ; (of plot) to thicken.

compliqué, *a.* Complicated, elaborate, intricate (mechanism, etc.) ; involved (style).

complot [kɔ̃plo], *s.m.* Plot, conspiracy. Tramer un complot, to weave a plot. Chef de complot, ringleader. Mettre qn dans le complot, to let s.o. into the secret.

comploter [kɔ̃plɔte], *v.tr.* To plot, to scheme. C. de faire qch., to plot to do sth.

comploteur [kɔ̃plɔtœ:r], *s.m.* Plotter, schemer.

complu, -s, -t, etc. See COMPLAIRE.

componction [kɔ̃pɔ̃ksjɔ̃], *s.f.* **1.** Compunction. **2.** *F:* Avec componction, solemnly.

comporter [kɔ̃pɔrte], *v.tr.* **1.** To allow (of), to admit of (sth.). **2.** To call for, require (sth.). Les précautions que comporte la situation, the care which the situation demands. **3.** To comprise (sth.). Objectif qui comporte quatre éléments, lens that comprises four elements. Méthode qui comporte de grandes difficultés, method attended with great difficulties. Les inconvénients que cela comporterait, the difficulties which this would involve, entail. Les fatigues que comporte un voyage, the fatigue incidental to a journey. Les avantages que comporte la position, the advantages attaching to the position.
se **comporter,** to behave. Se comporter mal, to misbehave. Façon de se comporter, behaviour.

composant, -ante [kɔ̃pozɑ̃, -ɑ̃:t]. **1.** *a. & s.m.* Component, constituent (part). **2.** *s.f.* Composante, component (of voltage, force, velocity).
composer [kɔ̃poze]. **1.** *v.tr.* (*a*) To compose (symphony, etc.); to indite (letter, etc.); to form (ministry, etc.); to make up, compound (remedy, etc.). *Abs. Sch:* C. *en thème anglais*, to do a paper in English composition. (*b*) *Typ:* To set (type, matter). *Tp:* Composer le numéro, to dial the number. (*c*) *Les personnes qui composent notre famille*, the persons of whom our family is made up. (*d*) To arrange, settle (one's life, etc.). C. *son visage*, to compose one's countenance. **2.** *v.i.* To compound, come to terms (*avec*, with). **se composer** (*de*), to be composed (of), to consist (of).
composé. 1. *a.* (*a*) Compound (pendulum, word, interest). *Ch:* Corps composé, compound. *Gram:* Temps composé, compound tense. (*b*) *Bot:* Composite (flower). (*c*) Composed, demure (demeanour, etc.); set, impassive (countenance). **2.** *s.m.* Compound.
compositeur, -trice [kɔ̃pozitœːr, -tris], *s.* **1.** *Mus:* Composer. **2.** *Typ:* Compositor.
composition [kɔ̃pozisjɔ̃], *s.f.* **1.** (*a*) Composing, composition (of sonata, etc.); compounding, making up (of remedy, etc.). (*b*) *Typ:* Setting, composing (of type); type-setting. **2.** (*a*) Composition, compound, mixture. (*b*) *Lit: Mus:* Composition. *Sch:* Essay; (weekly or termly) test; paper. **3.** Arrangement, compromise. Entrer en composition avec qn, to come to terms with s.o.; to compound with s.o.
compost|er [kɔ̃poste], *v.tr.* To date, obliterate (ticket, etc.). *s.m.* **-age.**
compote [kɔ̃pɔt], *s.f.* Compote (of fruit); stewed fruit. En compote, stewed. *F:* Mettre qn en compote, to reduce s.o. to a jelly.
compotier [kɔ̃pɔtje], *s.m.* Fruit-dish, -stand.
compréhensible [kɔ̃preɑ̃sibl], *a.* Comprehensible, understandable.
compréhensif, -ive [kɔ̃preɑ̃sif, -iːv], *a.* **1.** Comprehensive, inclusive (statement, etc.). **2.** Intelligent, understanding (mind).
compréhension [kɔ̃preɑ̃sjɔ̃], *s.f.* Understanding; apprehension.
comprendre [kɔ̃prɑ̃:dr], *v.tr.* (Conj. like PRENDRE) **1.** To comprise, include. *Six cents francs par mois tout compris*, six hundred francs a month inclusive. Emballage non compris, exclusive of packing. Y compris . . ., including. . . . **2.** To understand, comprehend. *Ai-je bien compris que . . .?* am I to understand that . . .? *Vous la comprenez mal*, you misunderstand her. *Je comprends que vous soyez fâché*, I can understand your being angry. *Je ne comprends rien à l'algèbre*, I don't know a thing about algebra. Je n'y comprends rien, I can't make it out. Je lui ai fait comprendre que + *ind.*, I gave him to understand that. . . . Se faire comprendre, to make oneself understood. Cela se comprend, of course; naturally.
compresse [kɔ̃prɛs], *s.f. Med:* Compress.
compresseur [kɔ̃prɛsœːr], *s.m.* **1.** Compressor (of gas, air, etc.). *I.C.E:* Supercharger. *Civ.E:* (Rouleau) compresseur, road-roller. **2.** *Surg:* Constrictor.
compressible [kɔ̃prɛsibl], *a.* Compressible.
compressif, -ive [kɔ̃presif, -iːv], *a.* **1.** Compressive (stress, etc.). **2.** Repressive (measures).
compression [kɔ̃presjɔ̃], *s.f.* **1.** (*a*) Compression; squeezing. *I.C.E:* Temps de (la) compression, compression stroke. (*b*) Crushing. **2.** Repression, constraint.

comprimable [kɔ̃primabl], *a.* Compressible.
comprimer [kɔ̃prime], *v.tr.* **1.** To compress (gas, artery, etc.); to squeeze in (the waist). *Outil à air comprimé*, pneumatic tool. **2.** *F:* To repress, restrain (tears, one's feelings).
comprimé, *s.m. Pharm:* Tablet.
compr-îmes, -is, -it, etc. See COMPRENDRE.
compromettre [kɔ̃prɔmɛtr], *v.* (Conj. like METTRE) **1.** *v.tr.* (*a*) To compromise (s.o.). *Être compromis dans un crime*, to be implicated in a crime. (*b*) To endanger, jeopardize (life, etc.). **2.** *v.i.* To accept arbitration; to compromise. **se compromettre**, to compromise oneself.
compromis¹, *s.m. Jur:* Compromise. *Com:* Obtenir un compromis, to compound (with creditors).
comprom-is², -it, etc. See COMPROMETTRE.
compromission [kɔ̃prɔmisjɔ̃], *s.f.* **1.** Compromising (with one's conscience); surrender (of principle). **2.** Usu. *Pej:* Compromise.
comptabilité [kɔ̃tabilite], *s.f.* **1.** Book-keeping, accountancy. C. *en partie simple, double*, single-, double-entry book-keeping. Tenir la comptabilité d'une maison, to keep the books of a firm. Chef de comptabilité, chief accountant. **2.** Accountancy department. *Com:* Counting-house.
comptable [kɔ̃tabl]. **1.** (*a*) *a.* Book-keeping (work, etc.). Pièces comptables, original documents; vouchers. (*b*) *s.m.* Accountant, book-keeper. Expert comptable = chartered accountant. **2.** *a.* Accountable, responsible (*de*, for).
comptant [kɔ̃tɑ̃]. **1.** *a.* Argent comptant, ready money. *F:* Prendre tout pour argent comptant, to take everything for gospel truth. **2.** *adv.* Payer comptant, to pay (in) cash. **3.** *s.m.* Acheter, vendre, au comptant, to buy, sell, for cash.
compte [kɔ̃t], *s.m.* Account. (*a*) Reckoning, calculation. Faire le compte des dépenses, to add up expenses. Faire son compte de qch., to reckon, count, on sth. Cela fait mon compte, that is the very thing I want. Y trouver son compte, to get sth. out of it. Être loin de compte, to be out in one's calculations; to be wide of the mark. Le compte y est, n'y est pas, the account is correct, incorrect. *F:* Il a son compte, he is done for; that has put paid to his account. Son compte est bon, I'll settle his hash for him. Compte rond, round sum. Acheter qch. à bon compte, to buy sth. cheap. En fin de compte . . ., tout compte fait . . ., all things considered . . . A ce compte . . ., in that case . . ., things being so . . ., at that rate. . . . Tenir compte de qch., to take sth. into account, into consideration. Ne tenir aucun compte de qch., to ignore sth. Tenir le plus grand c. d'un fait, to attach the greatest importance to a fact. (*b*) Count. *Box:* Rester sur le plancher pour le compte, to be counted out. (*c*) Tenir les comptes d'une maison, to keep the accounts of a house: *F:* Régler son compte à qn, to settle s.o.'s hash. *Avoir un (petit) c. à régler avec qn*, to have a bone to pick with s.o. Régler de vieux comptes, to pay off old scores. Avoir un compte chez qn, to have an account with s.o. Compte en banque, banking account. Livre de comptes, account book. Donner son compte à qn, to pay s.o. off (on dismissal). Faire ses comptes, to make up one's accounts. Versement à compte, payment on account. *Mettre un malheur sur le c. de qn*, to ascribe, attribute, a misfortune to s.o. Dire, apprendre, qch. sur le compte de qn, to say, learn, sth. about s.o. Prendre qch. à son compte, (i) to buy sth. on one's own account; (ii) to accept responsibility for sth. Se mettre, s'établir, à son compte, to set

up in business on one's own account. **Pour mon compte . . .,** for my part. . . . **Compte à demi,** joint account. (*d*) **Demander des comptes à qn,** to call s.o. to account. **Demander compte à qn de qch.,** to bring s.o. to book for sth. *Il ne doit de comptes à personne,* he is answerable to nobody. **Rendre compte de qch.,** to render an account of sth. **Compte rendu,** report. **Faire le compte rendu d'un ouvrage,** to review a book. **Se rendre compte de qch.,** to realize, understand, sth.

compte-gouttes, *s.m.inv.* (*a*) *Pharm:* etc: Dropping-tube. (*b*) Drip-feed lubricator.

compte-pas, *s.m.inv.* Pedometer.

compt|er [kɔ̃te]. **1.** *v.tr.* (*a*) To count (up), reckon (up), compute (numbers, etc.); to number. **Dix-neuf tous comptés,** nineteen all told. **Être compté au nombre des membres,** to be counted as a member. **Marcher à pas comptés,** to walk with measured tread. **Ses jours sont comptés,** his days are numbered. **Vingt ans bien comptés,** a good twenty years. **Donner sans compter,** to give without stint(ing). **Sans compter . . .,** not counting . . .; not to mention. . . **Sans compter que . . .,** not to mention that . . .; besides the fact that. . . . **Mal compter,** to miscount. *Prep.phr.* **A compter de . . .,** (reckoning) from. . . . (*b*) *C. cent francs à qn,* to pay s.o. a hundred francs. (*c*) *Com:* To charge. *Nous ne comptons pas l'emballage,* we don't charge for packing. (*d*) To value. **Compter sa vie pour rien,** to hold one's life of no account. (*e*) **Compter faire qch.,** to expect to do sth.; to reckon on doing sth. *Je compte le voir demain,* I expect to see him to-morrow. *Je comptais qu'il serait à m'attendre,* I expected him to be waiting for me. **2.** *v.i.* (*a*) **Compter sur qn,** to reckon, count, rely, (up)on s.o. **Vous pouvez y compter,** you may depend upon it. (*b*) *C. avec qn, qch.,* to reckon with s.o., sth. (*c*) *Il compte parmi mes meilleurs amis,* he counts among my best friends. (*d*) To count; to be of consequence. **Ne compter pour rien,** to stand for nothing. *s.m.* **-age.**

compte-secondes, *s.m.inv.* Stop-watch.

compte-tours, *s.m.inv.* Revolution counter.

compteur [kɔ̃tœ:r], *s.m.* (*a*) Meter. *C. à paiement préalable,* slot-meter. (*b*) *C. de tours,* revolution counter. *C. kilométrique,* mileage recorder; cyclometer. *Aut:* *C. de trajet,* trip-recorder. (*c*) Turnstile. (*d*) Calculating machine.

compteur-indicateur, *s.m.* *Aut:* Speedometer. *pl. Des compteurs-indicateurs.*

comptoir [kɔ̃twa:r], *s.m.* **1.** *Com:* Counter. *C. de cabaret,* bar. **Garçon de comptoir,** bartender. **Demoiselle de comptoir,** (i) saleswoman; (ii) barmaid. **2.** (In the East) Godown, warehouse. **3.** **Comptoir d'escompte,** discount bank.

compulser [kɔ̃pylse], *v.tr.* To examine, check, go through (documents).

computation [kɔ̃pytasjɔ̃], *s.f.* Computation.

computer [kɔ̃pyte], *v.tr.* To compute.

comte [kɔ̃:t], *s.m.* Count. *Monsieur le c.,* my lord.

comté [kɔ̃te], *s.m.* County.

comtesse [kɔ̃tɛs], *s.f.* Countess. *Madame la c.,* my lady.

concass|er [kɔ̃kɑse], *v.tr.* To crush, break (ore). *s.m.* **-age.**

concasseur [kɔ̃kɑsœ:r], *s.m.* Crusher; crushing-mill; crushing-roller.

concave [kɔ̃ka:v], *a.* Concave.

concavité [kɔ̃kavite], *s.f.* (*a*) Concavity; concave side (of lens). (*b*) *F:* Hollow, cavity.

concéd|er [kɔ̃sede], *v.tr.* (je concède; je concéderai) **1.** To concede, grant, allow (privilege, etc.);

to grant (land). **2.** *C. qu'on a tort,* to allow, admit, that one is wrong.

concentr|er [kɔ̃sɑ̃tre], *v.tr.* **1.** To concentrate (syrup, troops, etc.); to focus (sun's rays, etc.). **2.** To hold back, contain, repress (one's feelings, etc.). *s.f.* **-ation.**

se concentrer. **1.** To concentrate, to centre (*sur, dans,* in, (up)on, round). **2.** *Se c. en soi-même,* to retire within oneself.

concentré, *a.* **1.** Concentrated. *Ch:* At high concentration. **2.** *F:* **Homme concentré,** reserved, close, man. *Air c.,* abstracted look.

concentrique [kɔ̃sɑ̃trik], *a.* *Geom:* etc: Concentric. *adv.* **-ment,** -ally.

conceptible [kɔ̃sɛptibl], *a.* Conceivable.

conception [kɔ̃sɛpsjɔ̃], *s.f.* **1.** Conception, conceiving. **Avoir la conception lente,** to be slow of apprehension. **2.** Conception, idea.

concernant [kɔ̃sɛrnɑ̃], *prep.* Concerning, about, respecting, with regard to, regarding.

concerner [kɔ̃sɛrne], *v.tr.* (Used in third pers. only) To concern, affect. **Pour ce qui concerne . . .,** concerning . . .; with regard to. . . . *Cela concerne vos intérêts,* it affects your interests. *Est-ce que cela vous concerne?* is it any concern of yours?

concert [kɔ̃sɛ:r], *s.m.* Concert. **1.** Harmony, agreement. **Agir de concert avec qn,** (i) to act in concert with s.o.; to go hand in hand with s.o.; (ii) to conspire with s.o. **2.** Musical entertainment. **Salle de concert,** concert-hall. *F:* **Ce fut un concert d'éloges,** there was a chorus of praise.

concerter [kɔ̃sɛrte], *v.tr.* (*a*) To concert, arrange (plan); to plan (scheme). *Projet concerté d'avance,* preconcerted plan. (*b*) To compose, settle (one's countenance).

se concerter (*avec qn*), (i) to act in concert (with s.o.); (ii) *Pej:* to connive (with s.o.). *Ils se concertèrent sur le moyen d'agir,* they took counsel, consulted, together as to how to act.

concerté, *a.* **1.** Concerted, united (action). **2.** Studied, stiff, composed (manner, etc.).

concertiste [kɔ̃sɛrtist], *s. m. & f.* Concert performer.

concessif, -ive [kɔ̃sɛsif, -i:v], *a.* Concessive.

concession [kɔ̃sɛsjɔ̃], *s.f.* Concession. **1.** Yielding. **Faire des concessions,** to make concessions. **2.** Grant. *C. minière,* mining concession.

concessionnaire [kɔ̃sɛsjɔnɛ:r]. **1.** *a.* Concessionary (company). **2.** *s.* Grantee (of land); licence-holder.

concevable [kɔ̃s(ə)vabl], *a.* Conceivable, imaginable.

concevoir [kɔ̃səvwa:r], *v.tr.* (*pr.p.* **concevant;** *p.p.* **conçu;** *pr.ind.* **je conçois, n. concevons, ils conçoivent;** *p.d.* **je concevais;** *p.h.* **je conçus;** *fu.* **je concevrai**) **1.** To conceive (child). **2.** (*a*) To conceive, imagine (idea, etc.). (*b*) To conceive, understand. *Je ne conçois rien à cela,* I don't understand it at all. **Conçoit-on!** fancy! (*c*) *Ainsi conçu,* (letter, etc.) worded as follows.

conchoïdal, -aux [kɔ̃kɔidal, -o], *a.* Conchoid(al).

conchoïde [kɔ̃kɔid], *s.f.* Conchoid (curve).

concierge [kɔ̃sjɛrʒ], *s. m. & f.* (House-)porter, portress; door-keeper; caretaker (of flats); lodge-keeper (of castle, etc.); keeper (of prison).

concile [kɔ̃sil], *s.m.* *Ecc:* Council, synod.

conciliabule [kɔ̃siljabyl], *s.m.* Secret meeting; *F:* confabulation.

conciliant [kɔ̃siljɑ̃], *a.* Conciliating, conciliatory.

conciliateur, -trice [kɔ̃siljatœ:r, -tris]. **1.** *a.* = CONCILIANT. **2.** *s.* Peacemaker.

conciliation [kɔ̃siljasjɔ̃], *s.f.* Conciliation.

concilier [kɔ̃silje], *v.tr.* **1.** To conciliate, reconcile (two parties, etc.). *C. un différend*, to adjust a difference. *C. des textes*, to reconcile texts. **2.** To win over, gain (hearts, esteem, etc.). **se concilier,** to agree (*avec*, with).

concis [kɔ̃si], *a.* Concise, terse.

concision [kɔ̃sizjɔ̃], *s.f.* Concision, conciseness, brevity, terseness.

concitoyen, -enne [kɔ̃sitwajɛ̃, -ɛn], *s.* **1.** Fellow-citizen. **2.** Fellow-countryman, -countrywoman.

concluant [kɔ̃klyɑ̃], *a.* Conclusive, decisive (experiment, etc.). *Peu concluant*, inconclusive.

conclure [kɔ̃kly:r], *v.tr.* (*pr.p.* **concluant;** *p.p.* **conclu;** *pr.ind.* **je conclus,** n. **concluons, ils concluent;** *p.d.* **je concluais;** *p.h.* **je conclus;** *fu.* **je conclurai**) To conclude. **1.** (*a*) To end, finish; to bring (speech, etc.) to a conclusion. (*b*) *C. la paix*, to conclude peace. *C. un marché*, to drive, strike, clinch, a bargain. **2.** (*a*) To decide, infer. *Nous avons conclu que . . .*, we have come to the conclusion that. . . . (*b*) *C. à qch.*, to conclude in favour of sth. *C. à une opération immédiate*, to decide that an immediate operation is necessary. *Le jury a conclu au suicide*, the jury returned a verdict of suicide.

conclusif, -ive [kɔ̃klyzif, -i:v], *a.* Conclusive.

conclusion [kɔ̃klyzjɔ̃], *s.f.* Conclusion. **1.** Close, end (of speech, etc.). **2.** Concluding, settlement (of treaty, agreement). **3.** (*a*) Inference. *Formuler une conclusion*, to make an inference. (*b*) *Jur:* Finding, decision. *Les conclusions du jury*, the finding(s) of the jury.

conçoi-s, -t, -ve, etc. See CONCEVOIR.

concombre [kɔ̃kɔ̃:br], *s.m.* Cucumber.

concomitant [kɔ̃kɔmitɑ̃], *a.* Concomitant, attendant (circumstance).

concordance [kɔ̃kɔrdɑ̃:s], *s.f.* **1.** Concordance, agreement (of evidence, etc.). **2.** *Gram:* Concord, agreement (of adjectives, etc.); sequence (of tenses).

concordant [kɔ̃kɔrdɑ̃], *a.* Concordant.

concordat [kɔ̃kɔrda], *s.m.* **1.** *Ecc.Hist:* Concordat, agreement. **2.** (Bankrupt's) certificate.

concorde [kɔ̃kɔrd], *s.f.* Concord, harmony.

concorder [kɔ̃kɔrde], *v.i.* (Of dates, evidence) To agree, to tally (*avec*, with).

concourant [kɔ̃kurɑ̃], *a.* Concurrent, converging.

concourir [kɔ̃kuri:r], *v.i.* (Conj. like COURIR) **1.** (Of lines, etc.) To converge; (of events, etc.) to coincide. **2.** To combine, unite. *C. avec qn*, to co-operate with s.o. **3.** *C. pour un prix*, to compete for a prize.

concours [kɔ̃ku:r], *s.m.* **1.** (*a*) Concourse, gathering (of people). *Grand c. de curieux*, great concourse of sightseers. (*b*) Concourse (of atoms, circumstances); concurrence, conjunction (of circumstances); coincidence (of events). **2.** Co-operation, assistance, help. *Prêter (son) concours à qn*, to give assistance to s.o. **3.** (*a*) Competition; competitive examination. *Mettre un prix au concours*, to offer a prize for competition. *C. de musique*, band contest. *Hors concours*, (i) not for competition; (ii) not competing (on account of acknowledged excellence). *C. d'admission*, entrance examination. (*b*) *C. agricole*, agricultural show; cattle-show. *C. hippique*, horse-show.

concret, -ète [kɔ̃krɛ, -ɛt], *a.* **1.** Concrete, solid (oil, etc.). **2.** *Gram: Log:* Concrete (term, etc.).

concréter [kɔ̃krete], *v.tr.* (je **concrète;** je **concréterai**) To solidify; to congeal (oil, blood). *Houille concrétée*, cake coal.

concrétion [kɔ̃kresjɔ̃], *s.f.* **1.** (*a*) Coagulation. (*b*) Caking. **2.** Concrete mass, concretion. *Med: Concrétions calcaires*, chalk-stones.

conçu, -s, -t, etc. See CONCEVOIR.

concurremment [kɔ̃kyramɑ̃], *adv.* **1.** Concurrently, jointly. *Agir c. avec qn*, to act jointly, in conjunction, with s.o. **2.** Competitively.

concurrence [kɔ̃kyrɑ̃:s], *s.f.* **1.** (*a*) Concurrence, coincidence (of events). (*b*) *Jusqu'à concurrence de . . .*, to the amount of. . . . **2.** Competition, rivalry. *Com: Faire concurrence à qn*, to compete with s.o.

concurrent, -ente [kɔ̃kyrɑ̃, -ɑ̃:t]. **1.** *a.* (*a*) (Of forces, actions, etc.) Co-operative. (*b*) Competitive, rival (industries, etc.). **2.** *s.* Competitor (for prize, etc.); candidate (for post, etc.).

concussion [kɔ̃kysjɔ̃], *s.f.* **1.** Misappropriation of public funds. **2.** Extortion (by public official); peculation.

condamnable [kɔ̃dɑnabl], *a.* Blamable, blameworthy.

condamnation [kɔ̃dɑnasjɔ̃], *s.f.* Condemnation. **1.** (*a*) *Jur:* Conviction, judgment, sentence. *C. à vie*, life sentence. *C. à mort*, sentence of death. *Prononcer condamnation*, to pronounce, pass, sentence or judgment. *Passer condamnation*, to admit that one is in the wrong. *Purger une condamnation*, to serve one's sentence. (*b*) Putting (of door) out of use. **2.** Reproof, censure.

condamner [kɔ̃dɑne], *v.tr.* To condemn. **1.** (*a*) *Jur:* To convict, sentence, pass judgment on (criminal, etc.). *C. qn à mort*, to condemn, sentence, s.o. to death. *Tentative condamnée à l'insuccès*, attempt doomed to failure. *Le médecin l'a condamné*, the doctor has given him up. (*b*) **Condamner une porte,** (i) to block up, fill in, a door; (ii) to forbid the use of a door; to nail or screw up a door. (*c*) **Condamner sa porte,** to be 'not at home' to visitors; *F:* (at university) to sport one's oak. **2.** To censure, reprove (s.o.'s conduct, etc.).

condamné, -ée, *s.* Convict; condemned man, woman.

condensateur [kɔ̃dɑ̃satœ:r], *s.m. El: Opt:* Condenser. *C. réglable, variable*, variable condenser.

condensation [kɔ̃dɑ̃sasjɔ̃], *s.f.* Condensation, condensing. **Machine (à vapeur) à condensation,** condensing engine.

condens|er [kɔ̃dɑ̃se], *v.tr.* To condense (gas, lecture, etc.) (*en*, into). *a.* **-able.**

se condenser, to condense.

condenseur [kɔ̃dɑ̃sœ:r], *s.m. Mch: Gasm:* Condenser.

condescendance [kɔ̃dɛsɑ̃dɑ̃:s], *s.f.* Condescension.

condescendre [kɔ̃dɛsɑ̃:dr], *v.i.* To condescend (*à faire qch.*, to do sth.).

condiment [kɔ̃dimɑ̃], *s.m.* Condiment, seasoning.

condisciple [kɔ̃disipl], *s.m.* Fellow-student, schoolfellow.

condition [kɔ̃disjɔ̃], *s.f.* Condition. **1.** (*a*) State. *En condition*, in (good) condition. *Être en c. de faire qch.*, to be in a position, in a fit state, to do sth. (*b*) *pl.* Conditions, circumstances. *Être dans les conditions requises pour agir*, to be entitled to act. *Dans ces conditions . . .*, under these conditions . . .; this being so. . . . (*c*) Rank, station. *Gens de condition*, people of fashion, of quality. *Gens de simple condition*, persons in humble circumstances. **2.** Condition, stipulation; *pl.* terms. *Faites vos conditions vous-même*, name your own terms. *Conditions de faveur*, preferential terms. *Poser des conditions à qn*, to impose conditions on s.o. *Offre sans condition*, unconditional offer. *Marchandises à condition*, goods (i) on sale or return, (ii) on approval. *A cette condition, à ces conditions,*

j'accepte, on this understanding, on these terms, I accept. **A condition de** + *inf.*, providing, provided, that. . . . **A condition que** . . ., on condition that. . . . **3. Être en condition** (*chez qn*), to be in service (with s.o.).

conditionn|el, -elle [kɔ̃disjɔnɛl]. **I.** *a.* Conditional (promise, etc., *Gram:* mood). **2.** *s.m. Gram:* Conditional mood. *adv.* **-ellement.**

conditionn|er [kɔ̃disjɔne], *v.tr.* To condition (wool, silk, etc.) ; to season (wood). *s.m.* **-ement. conditionné,** *a.* **I.** (Of work, goods) In (good, bad) condition. **Mal conditionné,** ill-conditioned. **2.** *Log:* Conditioned (proposition).

condoléance [kɔ̃dɔleɑ̃:s], *s.f.* Condolence. *Veuillez agréer mes sincères condoléances*, accept my heartfelt sympathy.

condor [kɔ̃dɔ:r], *s.m. Orn:* Condor.

conductance [kɔ̃dyktɑ̃:s], *s.f. El:* Conductance.

conducteur, -trice [kɔ̃dyktœ:r, -tris]. **I.** *s.* (*a*) Leader, guide. *C. de bestiaux,* drover. (*b*) Driver (of cart, lorry, tramcar). (*c*) *C. d'une machine,* machine-minder. (*d*) *C. des travaux,* clerk' of the works, works foreman. **2.** *a.* (*a*) *Ph: El:* Conducting, transmitting. (*b*) *Mec.E:* Driving. **3.** *s.m.* (*a*) *El: Ph:* Conductor (of heat, electricity, etc.). **Mauvais conducteur,** non-conductor. (*b*) *El.E:* Lead (wire). *C. souple,* flex.

conductibilité [kɔ̃dyktibilite], *s.f. Ph:* Conductibility. *El: C.spécifique,* conductance.

conductible [kɔ̃dyktibl], *a. Ph:* Conductive.

conduction [kɔ̃dyksjɔ̃], *s.f. Ph:* Conduction.

conductivité [kɔ̃dyktivite], *s.f. Ph:* Conductivity. *C. spécifique,* conductance.

conduire [kɔ̃dɥi:r], *v.tr.* (*pr.p.* conduisant; *p.p.* conduit; *pr.ind.* je conduis, n. conduisons, ils conduisent; *p.d.* je conduisais; *p.h.* je conduisis; *fu.* je conduirai) **I.** (*a*) To conduct, escort; to lead; to guide. *C. qn en prison,* to take s.o. to prison. *C. à bien une affaire,* to bring off an affair. *Quel est le chemin qui conduit à la gare?* which is the way to the station? *C. à un résultat,* to conduce to a result. (*b*) *C. qn à faire qch.,* to lead, induce, s.o. to do sth. **2.** (*a*) To drive (horse, car, etc.). *S.a.* PERMIS. (*b*) To steer, manage (boat). *S.a.* BARQUE I. **3.** To convey, conduct (water to mill, etc.). *Corps qui conduit bien l'électricité,* good conductor of electricity. **4.** To conduct, manage, supervise. *C. une maison,* to run a house. *C. un orchestre,* to conduct an orchestra.

se conduire, to conduct oneself, to behave. **Se mal conduire,** to misconduct oneself, to misbehave. *Se c. en honnête homme,* to act the part of an honest man.

conduit [kɔ̃dɥi], *s.m.* Passage, conduit, pipe, duct. *C. principal,* main. *C. d'admission,* steam inlet (of cylinder). *C. à gaz,* gas pipe.

conduite [kɔ̃dɥit], *s.f.* **I.** (*a*) Conducting, leading, escorting (of s.o.). **Faire un bout de conduite à qn,** to set s.o. on his way. (*b*) Driving (of cart, motor car, etc.) ; navigation (of boat, balloon). **2.** Direction, management, control (of affairs, etc.) ; command (of fleet, etc.). **Être sous la conduite de qn,** to be (i) under s.o.'s leadership, (ii) in s.o.'s care. **3.** Conduct, behaviour. **Avoir de la conduite,** to be steady, well-behaved. **Avoir une mauvaise conduite,** to lead a loose life. *Changer de c.,* to mend one's ways ; to turn over a new leaf. **4.** Piping, tubing. *C. d'eau,* (i) water-main ; (ii) channel. *C. souple,* hose. *C. de fumée,* flue.

cône [ko:n], *s.m.* **I.** Cone. *C. de pin,* pine cone. *Astr:* Cône d'ombre, umbra (of planet, etc.). **2.** Taper; tapering end. **Tailler qch. en cône,** to taper sth. **Arbre en cône,** tapering spindle.

confection [kɔ̃fɛksjɔ̃], *s.f.* **I.** Making (of machine, road, etc.) ; putting together (of parts of garment, etc.) ; manufacture (of goods) ; compounding (of drug) ; drawing up (of document). **2.** Ready-made suit or gown ; *F:* reach-me-down. **Maison de confections,** ready-made shop.

confectionn|er [kɔ̃fɛksjɔne], *v.tr.* To make (up) (dress) ; to construct (machine, etc.) ; to manufacture (clothing). **Article confectionné,** ready-to-wear article. *s.m.* **-ement.**

confectionneur, -euse [kɔ̃fɛksjɔnœ:r, -ø:z], *s.* Ready-made clothier or outfitter.

confédération [kɔ̃federasjɔ̃], *s.f.* (Con)federation, confederacy.

confédérer [kɔ̃federe], *v.tr.* (**je confédère; je confédérerai**) To confederate, unite (*avec*, with). **se confédérer,** to confederate, unite. **confédéré. I.** *a.* Confederate (nations). **2.** *s.* **Les Confédérés,** the Confederates (of the American Civil War).

conférence [kɔ̃ferɑ̃:s], *s.f.* **I.** Conference, discussion. *C. contradictoire,* (public) debate. **Tenir conférence,** to hold a conference. **2.** Lecture. **Maître de conférences,** lecturer. **Salle de conférences,** lecture-room.

conférencier [kɔ̃ferɑ̃sje], *s.m.* Lecturer.

conférer [kɔ̃fere], *v.* (**je confère; je conférerai**) **I.** *v.tr.* (*a*) To compare, collate (texts). (*b*) To confer, award (privileges, etc.). *C. le grade de docteur à qn,* to confer a doctor's degree on s.o. **2.** *v.i.* To confer (*avec*, with). *Nous avons conféré de votre affaire,* we talked your business over.

confesse [kɔ̃fɛs], *s.f.* Confession (to a priest). (Usu. in) Aller à confesse, to go to confession.

confesser [kɔ̃fese], *v.tr.* **I.** To confess, own ; to plead guilty to (sth.) ; to own (up) to (sth.). **2.** *Ecc:* (*a*) To confess (one's sins). (*b*) To confess (one's faith). **3.** (Of priest) To confess (penitent). *F:* **C'est le diable à confesser,** it is the dickens of a job. **se confesser,** to confess one's sins.

confesseur [kɔ̃fesœ:r], *s.m. Ecc:* **I.** (Father-) confessor. **2.** *Hist:* Confessor (of the faith).

confession [kɔ̃fesjɔ̃], *s.f.* **I.** Confession. **Faire la confession de qch.,** to confess, own up to, sth. **2.** *Ecc:* (*a*) Confession auriculaire, privée, auricular confession (of sins). (*b*) *C. de foi,* confession of faith. (*c*) *Adm: Mil:* Religious persuasion. **3.** *Ecc:* **Faire la confession de qn,** to hear s.o.'s confession.

confessionnal, -aux [kɔ̃fesjɔnal, -o], *s.m.* Confessional(-box).

confessionnel, -elle [kɔ̃fesjɔnɛl], *a.* Confessional ; denominational (matters, disputes).

confetti [kɔ̃fetti], *s.m.pl.* Confetti.

confiance [kɔ̃fjɑ̃:s], *s.f.* **I.** Confidence, trust, reliance. **Avoir confiance en qn,** to put trust in s.o. ; to trust s.o. *Il n'a pas c. dans les médecins,* he doesn't believe in doctors. **Acheter qch. de confiance,** to buy sth. on trust. **Il ne faut un homme de confiance,** I want a man whom I can rely on. **Abus de confiance,** breach of trust. **Digne de confiance,** trustworthy, reliable. **Maison de confiance,** reliable firm. **Commis de confiance,** confidential clerk. **Avec confiance,** (i) confidently ; (ii) trustingly. *Affirmer qch. avec c.,* to assert sth. boldly. *Parl:* **Poser la question de confiance,** to ask for a vote of confidence. **2.** Confidence, sense of security. **Confiance en soi,** self-confidence, self-assurance.

confiant [kɔ̃fjɑ̃], *a.* **I.** Confiding, trustful (*dans,* in). **2.** Confident, sanguine (disposition, etc.). **3.** Self-confident, assured (manner, etc.).

confidence [kɔ̃fidɑ̃:s], *s.f.* Confidence (imparted as a secret). **Faire une confidence à qn,** *to tell a secret to s.o.* **Faire confidence de qch. à qn,** *to confide sth. to s.o.* **Mettre qn dans la confidence,** to let s.o. into the secret. **Dire qch. en confidence,** to say sth. in confidence, as a secret.

confident, -ente [kɔ̃fidɑ̃, -ɑ̃:t], *s.* Confidant, *f.* confidante.

confidenti|el, -elle [kɔ̃fidɑ̃sjel], *a.* Confidential. **A titre confidentiel,** confidentially, in confidence. *adv.* **-ellement.**

confier [kɔ̃fje], *v.tr.* **1.** To trust, entrust, commit. *C. qch. à qn, à la garde de qn,* to entrust s.o. with sth.; to commit, consign, sth. to s.o.'s care. **2.** To confide, impart, disclose. *C. qch. à qn,* to tell s.o. sth. in confidence. **se confier** *à qn,* (i) to put one's trust in s.o.; (ii) to take s.o. into one's confidence.

configuration [kɔ̃figyrasjɔ̃], *s.f.* Configuration, outline; lie (of the land).

confiner [kɔ̃fine]. **1.** *v.i.* (Of country, etc.) *C. à un pays,* to border upon, be contiguous to, a country. *F: Courage qui confine à la hardiesse,* courage verging on foolhardiness. **2.** *v.tr.* To confine, imprison; to shut (s.o.) up. **confiné,** *a.* (a) Confined (atmosphere, etc.). (b) *Être c. au logis,* to be confined to the house.

confins [kɔ̃fɛ̃], *s.m.pl.* Confines, borders (of country).

confire [kɔ̃fi:r], *v.tr.* (*pr.p.* confisant; *p.p.* confit; *pr.ind.* je confis, n. confisons, ils confisent; *p.d.* je confisais; *p.h.* je confis; *fu.* je confirai) To preserve (fruit, etc.); to candy (peel, etc.). **Confire au sel, au vinaigre,** to pickle.

confit, *a.* Fruits confits, preserved fruit(s). *F:* Être confit en dévotion, to be steeped in piety. **Un air confit,** a sanctified air.

confirmatif, -ive [kɔ̃firmatif, -i:v], *a.* Confirmative, corroborative.

confirmation [kɔ̃firmasjɔ̃], *s.f.* **1.** Confirmation, corroboration (of news, etc.). **En confirmation de ma lettre,** confirming my letter. **2.** (Sacrament of) confirmation. **Donner la confirmation à qn,** to confirm s.o. **Recevoir la c.,** to be confirmed.

confirmer [kɔ̃firme], *v.tr.* **1.** To confirm (news, etc.); to corroborate, bear out (s.o.'s evidence). **2.** *Ecc:* To confirm (s.o.).

confis-ant, -ons, etc. See CONFIRE.

confiscation [kɔ̃fiskasjɔ̃], *s.f.* Confiscation; seizure (of property). **Perdre qch. par confiscation,** to forfeit sth.

confiserie [kɔ̃fizri], *s.f.* **1.** (a) Preserving (in sugar). (b) Confectioner's shop. (c) Confectionery, preserves. **2.** Sardine factory.

confiseur, -euse [kɔ̃fizœ:r, -ø:z], *s.* Maker, seller, of preserves and sweetmeats; confectioner.

confisquer [kɔ̃fiske], *v.tr.* To confiscate, seize.

confit. See CONFIRE.

confiture [kɔ̃fity:r], *s.f.* Usu. *pl.* Preserve(s), jam. *Tartine de confitures,* slice of bread and jam. *F:* **Avoir le bras en confiture,** to have one's arm crushed to a pulp.

confiturier [kɔ̃fityrje], *s.m.* **1.** Jam-maker, -seller. **2.** Jam-pot, -jar, -dish.

conflagration [kɔ̃flagrasjɔ̃], *s.f.* Conflagration, blaze.

conflit [kɔ̃fli], *s.m.* Conflict, struggle; clash (of arms, interests). **Être en conflit,** (i) to be at strife; (ii) (of interests, etc.) to clash (*avec,* with).

confluent [kɔ̃flyɑ̃], *s.m.* Confluence, junction (of rivers).

confluer [kɔ̃flye], *v.i.* (Of rivers) To meet, join.

confondre [kɔ̃fɔ̃:dr], *v.tr.* To confound. **1.** (a)

To merge, mingle. (b) To mistake, confuse. *C. le coupable avec l'innocent,* to mistake the innocent for the guilty. **2.** To discomfit, disconcert (one's enemies, etc.); to abash, nonplus; to put (s.o.) to confusion. *C. la calomnie,* to silence calumny. *C. les projets de qn,* to confound, baffle, s.o.'s plans. **se confondre. 1.** (a) (Of colours, etc.) To blend (*en,* into). (b) (Of streams, etc.) To intermingle, interflow. (c) (Of interests, etc.) To be identical. **2. Se confondre en excuses,** to apologize profusely. **confondu,** *a.* **1.** Disconcerted, abashed, overwhelmed. **2.** Dumbfounded (*de,* at).

conformation [kɔ̃fɔrmasjɔ̃], *s.f.* Conformation. **Mauvaise conformation,** malconformation.

conforme [kɔ̃fɔrm], *a.* Conformable, according (*à,* to); consistent, consonant (*à,* with). **Copie c. à l'original,** copy corresponding to the original. *Ses goûts sont conformes aux miens,* our tastes are identical. *Geom:* **Figures conformes,** congruent figures. *Jur:* "Pour copie conforme," 'certified true copy.'

conformément [kɔ̃fɔrmemɑ̃], *adv.* Conformably, according (*à,* to); in conformity, in accordance, in compliance (*à,* with). *C. à la loi,* according to (the) law. *Mil:* **C. au plan,** according to plan.

conformer [kɔ̃fɔrme], *v.tr.* (a) To form, shape. (b) *C. qch. à qch.,* to conform sth. to sth. **se conformer** *à qch.,* to conform to sth.; to comply with (an order). *Se c. au modèle,* to keep to the pattern. **conformé,** *a.* **Bien conformé,** well-formed (child). **Mal conformé,** mis-shapen (limb, etc.).

conformité [kɔ̃fɔrmite], *s.f.* Conformity, agreement. *Ecc:* Conformity. **Être en conformité de goûts avec qn,** to have a similarity of tastes with s.o. **Agir en c. des ordres reçus,** to act conformably to orders received.

confort [kɔ̃fɔ:r], *s.m.* Comfort(s).

confortable [kɔ̃fɔrtabl], *a.* Comfortable, snug, cosy. *adv.* **-ment.**

confraternité [kɔ̃fraternite], *s.f.* **1.** Confraternity, brotherhood. **2.** Brotherliness.

confrère [kɔ̃frɛ:r], *s.m.* (a) Colleague, fellow-member (of profession, society); brother(-writer -teacher, etc.). (b) (Newspaper) Contemporary.

confrérie [kɔ̃freri], *s.f.* (Religious) brotherhood or sisterhood; confraternity.

confrontation [kɔ̃frɔ̃tasjɔ̃], *s.f.* **1.** Confrontation (of accused person with witness). **2.** Comparison, collation (of MSS., etc.).

confronter [kɔ̃frɔ̃te], *v.tr.* **1.** To confront (prisoner) (*avec,* with). **2.** To collate (MSS.).

confus [kɔ̃fy], *a.* **1.** Confused, mixed, jumbled (heap, etc.); indistinct (noise); dim, blurred (vision); obscure, ambiguous (style, etc.). **Mélange confus,** jumble (*de,* of). **2.** Confused, abashed. *Je suis c. de vos bontés,* your kindness makes me ashamed. *adv.* **-ément.**

confusion [kɔ̃fyzjɔ̃], *s.f.* Confusion. **1.** (a) Disorder, jumble. **Tous ses papiers sont en, dans la confusion,** all his papers are in confusion, in a muddle. **Mettre la confusion parmi les troupes,** to cause confusion among the troops. *Mettre tout en c.,* to upset everything. *Med:* **Confusion mentale,** derangement of mind. (b) Mistake, error. *C. de dates,* confusion of dates. **2.** Confusion, embarrassment, abashment. *Être rouge de c.,* to blush for shame.

congé [kɔ̃ʒe], *s.m.* **1.** (a) Leave, permission (to depart). **Prendre congé de qn,** to take leave o.

s.o. (b) Leave (of absence). **En congé**, on leave ; on furlough. (c) **Être en congé**, to be on holiday. **Un après-midi de congé**, an afternoon off. **2.** (a) (Notice of) discharge, dismissal. **Donner congé à qn**, to discharge s.o. ; to give s.o. notice. **Demander son congé**, to ask to be relieved of one's duties ; to give notice. (b) **Donner c. à un locataire**, to give a tenant notice to quit. **3.** Mil : (a) Period, term, of service. (b) Discharge (from service). **Prendre son congé**, (i) Mil : to take one's discharge ; (ii) Nau : to be paid off. **4.** Authorization, permit.

congédiable [kɔ̃ʒedjabl], a. (a) Liable to be discharged. (b) Due for discharge.

congédi|er [kɔ̃ʒedje], v.tr. **I.** To dismiss (servant, etc.). **2.** (a) To take leave of, dismiss (caller). (b) To discharge (men) ; to pay off (crew) ; to disband (troops). s.m. **-ement**.

congelable [kɔ̃ʒlabl], a. Congealable, freezable.

congélateur [kɔ̃ʒelatœːr], s.m. Refrigerator.

congélation [kɔ̃ʒelasjɔ̃], s.f. (a) Congelation, congealment ; freezing (of water, etc.) ; solidification (of oil). **Viande dans la congélation**, meat in cold storage. (b) Frost-bite. (c) Coagulation.

congeler [kɔ̃ʒle], v.tr. (il **congèle**; il **congèlera**) **I.** To congeal ; to freeze (water, etc.). Esp. **Viande congelée**, frozen meat. **2.** F : To coagulate. **se congeler**, to congeal ; to freeze (up).

congénère [kɔ̃ʒeneːr]. **I.** a. Congeneric. Ling : **Mots congénères**, cognate words. **2.** s.m. Congener. F : **Lui et ses congénères**, he and his like(s).

congénital, -aux [kɔ̃ʒenital, -o], a. Congenital.

congestion [kɔ̃ʒɛstjɔ̃], s.f. Med : Congestion. **Congestion cérébrale**, F : stroke. **Congestion pulmonaire**, pneumonia.

congestionner [kɔ̃ʒɛstjɔne], v.tr. Med : To congest. **se congestionner**, to become congested.

congestionné, a. Flushed, red (face).

conglomérat [kɔ̃glɔmera], s.m. Conglomerate.

conglomérer [kɔ̃glɔmere], v.tr. (je **conglomère**; je **conglomérerai**) To conglomerate (particles of matter, etc.). **se conglomérer**, to conglomerate.

congre [kɔ̃ːgr], s.m. Conger-eel.

congrégation [kɔ̃gregasjɔ̃], s.f. Ecc : Congregation. **I.** (Monastic) community. **2.** Body of worshippers.

congrès [kɔ̃grɛ], s.m. Congress.

congru [kɔ̃gry], a. Sufficient, adequate. **Portion congrue**, (i) Ecc : adequate emolument (of priest) ; (ii) F : (income providing a) bare living.

congruent [kɔ̃gryɑ̃], a. Mth : Congruent (à, with).

conicité [kɔnisite], s.f. Conicity ; taper (of bullet).

conifère [kɔnifeːr]. Bot : **I.** a. Coniferous, cone-bearing. **2.** s.m.pl. **Conifères**, conifers.

conique [kɔnik], a. **I.** Cone-shaped, conical. **2.** Geom : **Sections coniques**, conic sections. **3.** Coned, taper(ing) (shank, pin, etc.). **Engrenage c.**, bevel gearing.

conjectural, -aux [kɔ̃ʒɛktyral, -o], a. Conjectural. adv. **-ement**.

conjecture [kɔ̃ʒɛktyːr], s.f. Conjecture, surmise, guess.

conjecturer [kɔ̃ʒɛktyre], v.tr. To conjecture, surmise, guess.

conjoindre [kɔ̃ʒwɛ̃ːdr], v.tr. (Conj. like JOINDRE) To join in marriage.

conjoint, a. **I.** Conjoined, united, joint. **Compte courant c.**, joint current account. **Légataires conjoints**, co-legatees. **2.** Jur : Married. s.m. **Les (deux) conjoints**, husband and wife.

conjointement [kɔ̃ʒwɛ̃tmɑ̃], adv. (Con)jointly. S.a. SOLIDAIREMENT.

conjoncteur [kɔ̃ʒɔ̃ktœːr], s.m. El : Circuit-closer ; switch. **Conjoncteur-disjoncteur**, make-and-break (key, etc.) ; cut-out.

conjonctif, -ive[1] [kɔ̃ʒɔ̃ktif, -iːv], a. **I.** Connective (tissue). **2.** Conjunctive (phrase, etc.). **Pronom conjonctif**, relative pronoun.

conjonction [kɔ̃ʒɔ̃ksjɔ̃], s.f. **I.** Union, connection. Astr : **En conjonction**, in conjunction ; conjoined. **2.** Gram : Conjunction.

conjonctive[2] [kɔ̃ʒɔ̃ktiːv], s.f. Anat : Conjunctiva (of the eye).

conjoncture [kɔ̃ʒɔ̃ktyːr], s.f. Conjuncture, contingency. **Se trouver dans une malheureuse c.**, to find oneself in a predicament.

conjugaison [kɔ̃ʒygɛzɔ̃], s.f. **I.** Gram : Biol : Conjugation. **2.** Pairing (of guns, etc.).

conjugal, -aux [kɔ̃ʒygal, -o], a. Conjugal. **Le domicile conjugal**, the home. **Vie conjugale**, married life. F : **Semonce conjugale**, curtain lecture. adv. **-ement**.

conjuguer [kɔ̃ʒyge], v.tr. **I.** Gram : To conjugate. **2.** To pair (engines, guns).

conjugué, a. Conjugate (leaves, foci) ; interconnected (controls, etc.). **Canons conjugués**, guns paired on turret. **Freinage conjugué**, coupled, interacting, brakes.

conjuration [kɔ̃ʒyrasjɔ̃], s.f. **I.** Conspiracy, plot. **2.** Incantation, exorcism. **3.** pl. F : Entreaties.

conjurer [kɔ̃ʒyre], v.tr. & i. **I.** To plot. (a) C. la ruine de qn, to plot s.o.'s ruin. (b) C. contre qn, to conspire against s.o. **2.** (a) To conjure up, raise (spirits) ; to exorcise (demon). (b) To avert, ward off (danger). **3.** C. qn de faire qch., to entreat, beseech, s.o. to do sth. **se conjurer**, to conspire together. **conjuré**, s.m. Conspirator.

connais. See CONNAÎTRE.

connaissable [kɔnɛsabl], a. **I.** Phil : Cognizable, knowable. **2.** Recognizable (à, by).

connaissance [kɔnɛsɑ̃ːs], s.f. **I.** (a) Acquaintance, knowledge. **Faire connaissance avec qch.**, to become acquainted with sth. **Prendre connaissance de qch.**, to make oneself acquainted with, to enquire into, sth. **Avoir c. de qch.**, to be aware of sth. **Donner connaissance de qch. à qn**, to inform, apprise, s.o. of sth. **En connaissance de cause**; **en pleine connaissance des faits**, with full knowledge of the facts. **Être en âge de connaissance**, to have arrived at years of discretion. **Une personne de ma connaissance**, someone I know, an acquaintance. **Faire connaissance avec qn, faire la connaissance de qn**, to make s.o.'s acquaintance. **Lier connaissance avec qn**, to strike up an acquaintance with s.o. **Une figure de connaissance**, a familiar face. **En pays de connaissance**, among familiar faces ; on familiar ground. (b) **C'est une de mes connaissances**, he is an acquaintance of mine. **2.** (a) Knowledge, understanding. **Avoir la connaissance de plusieurs langues**, to know several languages. (b) Jur : Cognizance. (c) Phil : Cognition. (d) pl. Learning, acquirements. **Les connaissances de droit que chacun doit posséder**, the knowledge of the law that everyone ought to possess. **3.** Consciousness. **Perdre connaissance**, to lose consciousness, to swoon. **Reprendre connaissance**, to regain consciousness ; F : to come to. **Sans connaissance**, unconscious ; in a dead faint.

connaiss-e, -es, etc. See CONNAÎTRE.

connaissement [kɔnɛsmɔ̃], s.m. Bill of lading.

connaisseur, -euse [kɔnɛsœːr, -øːz]. **I.** s. Expert, connoisseur. **Être bon connaisseur en**

qch., to be a good judge of, an authority on, sth. **2.** *a.* **Regarder qch. d'un œil connaisseur**, to look at sth. with a critical eye.

connaître [kɔnɛːtr], *v.tr.* (*pr.p.* connaissant; *p.p.* connu; *pr.ind.* je connais, il connaît, n. connaissons; *p.d.* je connaissais; *p.h.* je connus; *fu.* je connaîtrai) To know. **1.** To be acquainted with (sth.). *Un endroit de moi seul connu*, a place known to me alone. *Il ne connaît pas le monde*, he is ignorant of the world. *Je lui connaissais du talent*, I knew he had talent. *On ne lui connaît pas de domicile*, he is not known to have any place of abode. **Faire connaître qch.**, to make sth. known. *Si tu te tais, ni vu ni connu*, if you hold your tongue, no one will be any the wiser. **Il en connaît bien d'autres**, he has plenty more tricks up his sleeve. **2.** To be acquainted with (s.o.). *C. qn de nom, de vue*, to know s.o. by name, by sight. **Gagner à être connu**, to improve on acquaintance. *Pred.* **Être connu pour menteur**, to be known as a liar. *F:* **Connaître qn comme le fond de sa poche**, to know s.o. through and through. **Ça me connaît**, you can't teach me anything about that. **Connu !** that's an old story ! **Se faire connaître**, (i) to introduce oneself by name ; (ii) to come to the front. **Faire connaître qn**, (i) to reveal s.o's identity ; (ii) to bring s.o. into notice ; (iii) to show s.o. up. **3.** *Jur:* **C. de qch.**, to take cognizance of sth. **4.** (*a*) To be versed in, to have a thorough knowledge of (sth.) ; to have a thorough command of (a language). *C. aussi bien l'anglais que le français*, to be equally at home in English and French. (*b*) To distinguish. **Connaître le bien d'avec le mal**, to know good from evil.

se connaître. 1. *Se c. à, en, qch.*, to know all about, be a good judge of, sth. *F:* **Il s'y connaît**, he is an expert. *Je ne m'y connais plus*, I am all adrift, all at sea. **2. Il ne se connaît plus**, he has lost control of himself. **Il ne se connaît plus de joie**, he is beside himself with joy.

connecter [kɔnɛkte], *v.tr. El:* To connect.
connétable [kɔnetabl], *s.m. A:* High Constable.
connexe [kɔn(n)ɛks], *a. Jur: Bot:* Connected.
connexion [kɔn(n)ɛksjɔ̃], *s.f.* **1.** Connection (of parts, ideas). *Mec.E:* **Connexion directe**, positive drive. **2.** Connecting organ or part. *El.E:* Lead ; (cell-to-cell) connector.
connexité [kɔn(n)ɛksite], *s.f.* Connexity, relatedness (of ideas, etc.).
connivence [kɔnivãːs], *s.f.* Connivance, complicity. **Agir de connivence avec qn**, to act in collusion with s.o.
connu, -s, -t, etc. See CONNAÎTRE.
conque [kɔ̃ːk], *s.f.* **1.** Conch ; marine shell. **2.** *Anat:* External ear.
conquérant [kɔ̃kerã], *a.* **1.** Conquering (nation, etc.). *s.* **Guillaume le Conquérant**, William the Conqueror. **2.** *Air c.*, swagger.
conquérir [kɔ̃keriːr], *v.tr.* (*pr.p.* conquérant; *p.p.* conquis; *pr.ind.* je conquiers, n. conquérons, ils conquièrent; *p.d.* je conquérais; *p.h.* je conquis; *fu.* je conquerrai) (*a*) To conquer, subdue (country, people). (*b*) To gain over, win (over), make a conquest of (s.o.).
conquête [kɔ̃kɛːt], *s.f.* **1.** (Act of) conquest. (*a*) **Faire la conquête d'un pays**, to conquer a country. (*b*) *Faire la c. de qn*, to make a conquest of s.o. ; to win s.o.'s heart. **2.** Conquered territory ; acquisition, possession.
conquiers, conquis, etc. See CONQUÉRIR.
consacrer [kɔ̃sakre], *v.tr.* **1.** (*a*) To consecrate (altar, bread and wine, etc.). *C. un évêque, un prêtre*, to consecrate a bishop, ordain a priest.

(*b*) To dedicate (one's life to God, etc.) ; to devote (one's holidays to study, etc.) ; to assign (sum of money to a purpose, etc.). *C. toute son énergie à une tâche*, to bend, devote, (all) one's energies to a task. **2.** To sanctify, hallow (memory, place).
consacré, *a.* **1.** Consecrated, sacred (vessel, etc.) ; hallowed (ground). **2.** Sanctioned, established, time-honoured (custom, etc.). **Expression consacrée**, stock phrase.
consanguin [kɔ̃sãgɛ̃], *a.* **1.** *Jur:* **Frère c., sœur consanguine**, half-brother, half-sister, on the father's side. **2.** Inbred (horse, etc.).
conscience [kɔ̃sjɑ̃ːs], *s.f.* **1.** Consciousness. **Avoir conscience de qch.**, to be conscious, aware, of sth. *Agir avec la pleine c. des conséquences*, to act in full consciousness of the consequences. **2.** (*a*) Conscience. *C. nette*, clear, good, conscience. *C. chargée*, guilty conscience. *C. large*, accommodating conscience. **Sans conscience**, unscrupulous ; unconscionable (rogue). **(Se) faire (un cas de) conscience de faire qch.**, to scruple to do sth. **Dans le for de ma conscience**, in my heart of hearts. **Faire qch. en toute sûreté de conscience**, to do sth. with a clear conscience. **Faire qch. par acquit de conscience, pour l'acquit de sa conscience**, to do sth. for conscience' sake. *Je peux vous assurer, la main sur la conscience, que . . .*, I can assure you in all conscience that . . . , S.a. EXAMEN. (*b*) Conscientiousness. **Avoir de la conscience**, to be conscientious. **Faire qch. en conscience**, to do sth. conscientiously. (*c*) **Liberté de conscience**, liberty of conscience. **3.** *Tls:* Breast-plate (of drill, etc.).
consciencieu|x, -euse [kɔ̃sjɑ̃sjø, -øːz], *a.* Conscientious. *adv.* **-sement.**
consci|ent [kɔ̃sjɑ̃], *a.* **1.** Conscious (de, of) ; fully aware (of). **2. Être conscient**, sentient being. *adv.* **-emment.**
conscription [kɔ̃skripsjɔ̃], *s:f.* Conscription.
conscrit [kɔ̃skri]. **1.** *a. Rom.Ant:* Les pères conscrits, the conscript fathers. **2.** *s.m.* (*a*) *Mil:* Conscript. (*b*) *F:* Novice, greenhorn.
consécration [kɔ̃sekrasjɔ̃], *s.f.* **1.** Consecration (of church, bishop, etc.). **2.** Dedication (of one's life, etc.) (*à, to*). **3.** Ratification.
consécut|if, -ive [kɔ̃sekytif, -iːv], *a.* **1.** Consecutive. *Pendant trois mois consécutifs*, for three months in succession. **2.** Infirmité consécutive à une blessure, infirmity due to, following upon, a wound. *adv.* **-ivement.**
conseil [kɔ̃sɛj], *s.m.* **1.** (*a*) *A. & Lit:* Counsel, purpose, plan. **Ne savoir quel conseil prendre**, not to know what decision to make. (*b*) Counsel ; (piece of) advice. **Homme de bon conseil**, man worth consulting. **Donner conseil à qn**, to advise s.o. **Demander conseil à qn, prendre conseil de qn**, to consult s.o., seek s.o.'s advice. **Suivre le c. de qn**, to take s.o.'s advice. *Prov:* **La nuit porte conseil**, seek advice of your pillow. **2.** (*a*) *Jur:* Counsellor, counsel. **Consulter un c.**, to take counsel's opinion. **Conseil judiciaire**, guardian. (*b*) **Chimiste conseil**, consulting chemist. **Ingénieur c.**, consulting engineer. **3.** Council, committee, board. **Tenir conseil**, to hold a council. **Le conseil des ministres**, the Cabinet. **Conseil municipal** = (i) town council ; (ii) parish council, local board. *Com:* **C. d'administration**, board of directors. *Mil: Navy:* **Conseil de guerre**, (i) war-council, (ii) court-martial. **Passer en conseil de guerre**, to be court-martialled. **C. d'enquête**, court of enquiry. *Jur:* **Conseil de famille**, family council ; board of guardians. S.a. FABRIQUE 3.

conseillable [kɔsɛjabl], *a.* Advisable, recommendable.

conseill|er[1] [kɔsɛje], *v.tr.* To advise, counsel. *C. qch. à qn*, to recommend sth. to s.o. *C. à qn de faire qch.*, to advise s.o. to do sth. *s.* **-eur, -euse.**

conseiller[2], **-ère** [kɔsɛje, -ɛːr], *s.* **1.** Counsellor, adviser. **2.** *C. municipal*, town-councillor. **3.** *C. à la cour (d'appel, de cassation)*, judge of appeal.

consentement [kɔsɑ̃tmɑ̃], *s.m.* Consent, assent. *D'un commun consentement*, by common assent. *Donner son consentement à qch.*, to assent, consent, to sth.

consentir [kɔsɑ̃tiːr], *v.* (Conj. like SENTIR) **1.** *v.i.* To consent, agree. *C. à qch.*, to consent to sth. *C. à faire qch.*, to consent to do sth. *Je consens (à ce) qu'il vienne*, I consent, agree, to his coming. *Prov:* Qui ne dit mot consent, silence gives consent. **2.** *v.tr. C. un prêt*, to grant a loan. *C. une remise à qn*, to allow s.o. a discount.

conséquence [kɔsekɑ̃ːs], *s.f.* (*a*) Consequence, outcome, sequel, result. *Il faut en subir les conséquences*, we, you, must take the consequences. **En conséquence**, in consequence, consequently, accordingly. **En conséquence de . . .**, (i) in consequence of . . ., (ii) in pursuance of. . . . (*b*) Inference. **Tirer une conséquence de qch.**, to draw an inference from sth. (*c*) Importance, consequence. **Affaires de la dernière conséquence**, matters of the highest moment. *F:* **Tirer à conséquence**, to be of importance.

conséqu|ent [kɔsekɑ̃]. **1.** *a.* (*a*) Consistent, rational (mind, speech). (*b*) Following. *Septicémie conséquente d'une coupure*, septicaemia following (on) a cut. (*c*) *P:* Important (man, affair). **2.** *s.m. Gram: Log: Mth:* Consequent. *Adv.phr.* **Par conséquent**, consequently, accordingly. *adv.* **-emment.**

conservable [kɔsɛrvabl], *a.* That will keep.

conservateur, -trice [kɔsɛrvatœːr, -tris]. **1.** *s.* (*a*) Conservator, guardian, keeper. *C. de bibliothèque*, librarian. *C. d'un musée*, curator, keeper, of a museum. (*b*) *Pol:* Conservative. *a. Le parti c.*, the Conservative party. **2.** *a.* Preserving, preservative (process, etc.).

conservation [kɔsɛrvasjɔ̃], *s.f.* **1.** (*a*) Conserving, conservation ; preserving, preservation (of fruit, meat). (*b*) Preservation, care (of buildings, health, etc.) ; keeping (of archives). **Instinct de la conservation**, instinct of self-preservation. (*c*) Retaining, keeping (of rights, situation, etc.). **2.** (State of) preservation. **Meubles d'une belle conservation**, well-preserved, well-kept, furniture.

conservatoire [kɔsɛrvatwaːr]. **1.** *a. Jur:* *Mesures conservatoires*, measures of conservation. **2.** *s.m.* (*a*) Repository, museum. *C. des Arts et Métiers*, (Museum and) School of Arts and Crafts. (*b*) School, academy (of music, of dramatic art).

conserve [kɔsɛrv], *s.f.* **1.** Preserve ; preserved food. *Conserves au vinaigre*, pickles. **Bœuf de conserve**, tinned beef, corned beef ; *F:* bully beef. *Se nourrir de conserves*, to live on tinned foods. **2.** *pl.* Dark or tinted spectacles. **3.** *Nau:* Convoy, consort. **Naviguer de conserve**, to sail in company, together (*avec*, with). *F:* *Nous y sommes allés de c.*, the whole crowd of us went.

conserver [kɔsɛrve], *v.tr.* **1.** (*a*) To preserve (fruit, meat, etc.). **Aliments conservés**, tinned or bottled foods. (*b*) To preserve, take care of (building, etc.). *C. le gibier*, to preserve game. **2.** To keep, retain, maintain (rights, etc.) ; to keep up (a custom). *C. son sang-froid*, to keep

one's head. *Tp:* **Conserver la ligne**, to hold the line.

se conserver, (of goods) to keep. *Articles qui ne se conservent pas*, perishable articles.

conservé, *a.* *Tableaux bien conservés*, pictures in a good state of preservation.

considérable [kɔsiderabl], *a.* Considerable. **1.** Notable, eminent ; well-to-do (person). **2.** Large, extensive (property, population). **Peu considérable**, inconsiderable. *adv.* **-ment.**

considérant [kɔsiderɑ̃], *s.m.* Usu. *pl. Jur:* Preamble (of a law) ; grounds (of a judgment).

considération [kɔsiderasjɔ̃], *s.f.* Consideration. **1.** Attention, thought. **Agir avec, sans, considération**, to act considerately, inconsiderately. **Prendre qch. en considération**, to take sth. into consideration, into account ; to consider (offer). **En considération de**, in consideration of, on account of ; for the sake of. **2.** Reason, motive. **3.** Regard, esteem, respect. **Avoir une grande considération pour qn**, to have a great regard for s.o. *Jouir d'une grande c.*, to be highly respected. (Letter formula) **Agréez l'assurance de ma haute considération**, I am yours very truly. **Par considération pour qn**, out of consideration, out of regard, for s.o.

considérer [kɔsidere], *v.tr.* (je **considère** ; je **considérerai**) To consider. **1.** **Ce n'est pas à considérer**, it is not to be thought of. *Il faut c. que . . .*, it must be borne in mind that. . . . **A tout considérer . . ., tout bien considéré . . .**, taking all things into consideration . . . ; all things considered. . . . *Jur:* **Considérant que . . .**, whereas. . . . **2.** To contemplate, gaze on. **3.** To regard, deem. *Vous êtes considéré comme responsable*, you are held to be liable.

considéré, *a.* **1.** Circumspect (behaviour). **2.** Esteemed, respected (person). *adv.* **-ment.**

consignataire [kɔsiɲatɛːr], *s.m. & f.* **1.** *Jur:* Depositary ; trustee. **2.** *Com:* Consignee.

consignateur [kɔsiɲatœːr], *s.m.* Consignor ; shipper.

consignation [kɔsiɲasjɔ̃], *s.f.* **1.** Consignation, deposit (of money). **2.** *Com:* Consignment (of goods). **Envoyer qch. à qn en consignation**, to consign sth. to s.o.

consigne [kɔsiɲ], *s.f.* **1.** *Mil: Navy:* (*a*) Order(s), instructions (to sentry, etc.). **Manquer à la consigne**, to disobey orders. **Être de consigne**, to be on duty. **Forcer la consigne**, (i) to force a sentry ; (ii) *F:* to force one's way in. (*b*) Password, countersign. **2.** (*a*) *Mil:* Confinement (to barracks). (*b*) **Marchandises en consigne à la douane**, goods stopped, held up, at the custom-house. (*c*) *Sch:* Detention, keeping in. **3.** *Rail:* Cloak-room ; left-luggage office.

consigner [kɔsiɲe], *v.tr.* **1.** (*a*) To deposit (money, etc.). (*b*) *Com:* To consign (goods) (*à*, to). **2.** *C. qch. (par écrit)*, to write down, enter, record (fact, answer). **3.** (*a*) To confine (soldier) to barracks ; to keep in (pupil). (*b*) *Marchandises consignées par la douane*, goods stopped by the custom-house. (*c*) To refuse admittance to (s.o.). *La gare est consignée aux civils*, the station is closed to civilians. *C. un cabaret*, to put a public-house out of bounds. **4.** *Rail: C. ses bagages*, to put one's luggage in the cloak-room.

consistance [kɔsistɑ̃ːs], *s.f.* **1.** (*a*) Consistence, consistency (of syrup, etc.). *Étoffe sans c.*, flimsy material. (*b*) Stability, firmness (of mind). **Atteindre l'âge de consistance**, to attain full growth. **2.** Credit. *Homme sans c.*, man of no standing. *Bruit sans c.*, unfounded rumour.

consistant [kɔsistɑ̃], *a.* Firm, solid (substance).

Graisse consistante, (i) set grease; (ii) stiff lubricant. *Homme c.*, man who knows his own mind.
consister [kɔ̃siste], *v.i.* *C. en, dans, qch.*, to consist, to be composed, of sth.
consistoire [kɔ̃sistwa:r], *s.m.* *Ecc:* Consistory.
consolable [kɔ̃sɔlabl], *a.* Consolable.
consolateur, -trice [kɔ̃sɔlatœ:r, -tris]. **I.** *s.* Consoler, comforter. **2.** *a.* Consoling, comforting.
consolation [kɔ̃sɔlasjɔ̃], *s.f.* Consolation, solace, comfort. *Apporter de la c. à qn*, to bring comfort to s.o.; to comfort s.o.
console [kɔ̃sɔl], *s.f.* **I.** Console, corbel, bracket. **Grue à console**, wall-crane. **2.** *Furn:* Console (-table), pier-table.
consoler [kɔ̃sɔle], *v.tr.* To console, solace, comfort. *C. qn de qch.*, to console s.o. for sth.
consolidation [kɔ̃sɔlidasjɔ̃], *s.f.* **I.** Consolidation, strengthening. **Nervure de consolidation**, stiffening rib. **2.** Healing, uniting (of wound, fracture). **3.** Funding (of floating debt).
consolider [kɔ̃sɔlide], *v.tr.* **I.** To consolidate, strengthen; to brace (wall). **2.** To fund (debt). **se consolider. I.** To grow firm. **2.** *Med:* To heal, unite.
consolidé, *a.* *Dette consolidée*, funded debt. *Les fonds consolidés*, *s.* **les consolidés**, the funded debt; *F:* consols.
consommable [kɔ̃sɔmabl], *a.* Consumable (as food).
consommateur, -trice [kɔ̃sɔmatœ:r, -tris], *s.* (*a*) Consumer (of products). (*b*) Customer (in restaurant, café).
consommation [kɔ̃sɔmasjɔ̃], *s.f.* **I.** Consummation, accomplishment (of work, crime). **2.** Consumption (of wheat, petrol, etc.). **Société de consommation**, co-operative supply stores. **3.** Drink (in café).
consommer [kɔ̃sɔme], *v.tr.* **I.** To consummate, accomplish. **2.** To consume (food).
consommé. I. *a.* Consummate (skill, etc.). **2.** *s.m.* *Cu:* Stock, beef-tea; clear soup.
consomption [kɔ̃sɔ̃psjɔ̃], *s.f.* **I.** (*a*) Consumption, consuming (of food). (*b*) Consuming, destruction (by fire). **2.** *Med:* Wasting, decline. **Atteint de consomption**, in a decline, esp. in consumption.
consonant [kɔ̃sɔnɑ̃], *a.* *Mus: Ling:* Consonant.
consonne [kɔ̃sɔn], *s.f.* *Ling:* Consonant.
consort, -orte [kɔ̃sɔ:r, -ɔrt], *a.* **I.** *Eng.Hist:* Consort. **2.** *pl.* Associates (in intrigue).
consoude [kɔ̃sud], *s.f.* *Bot:* Comfrey.
conspirateur, -trice [kɔ̃spiratœ:r, -tris], *s.* Conspirator, conspirer.
conspiration [kɔ̃spirasjɔ̃], *s.f.* Conspiracy, plot.
conspirer [kɔ̃spire], *v.i.* **I.** To conspire, plot (*contre*, against). *v.tr.* *C. la mort de qn*, to plot s.o.'s death. **2.** To conspire, tend (*à*, to).
conspuer [kɔ̃spɥe], *v.tr.* **I.** To decry, run down (s.o., sth.). **2.** To boo, hoot (play, speaker).
constance [kɔ̃stɑ̃:s], *s.f.* **I.** Constancy, steadfastness. **Avec constance**, steadfastly. **2.** Persistence, perseverance. **3.** Constancy, invariability (of temperature, etc.).
const|ant, -ante [kɔ̃stɑ̃, -ɑ̃:t], *a.* **I.** (*a*) Constant, steadfast. (*b*) Firm, unshaken (perseverance, etc.). **2.** Established, patent (fact, etc.). **3.** (*a*) Constant, uniform (temperature, etc.). (*b*) *s.f.* **Constante.** *Mth: Ph:* Constant; coefficient. *adv.* **-amment.**
constatation [kɔ̃statasjɔ̃], *s.f.* Verification, establishment (of fact). *C. d'identité*, proof of identity. **Faire la constatation de qch.**, (i) to note, (ii) to acknowledge, sth. as a fact.
constater [kɔ̃state], *v.tr.* **I.** To establish, ascer-

tain (fact). *C. une erreur*, to find out a mistake. **Vous pouvez constater!** you can see for yourself! **2.** To state, record (sth.); to certify (a death).
constellation [kɔ̃stɛllasjɔ̃], *s.f.* Constellation.
consteller [kɔ̃stɛlle], *v.tr.* To constellate. *Constellé d'étoiles*, star-spangled. *Constellé de pierreries*, studded with jewels.
consternation [kɔ̃stɛrnasjɔ̃], *s.f.* Consternation, dismay.
consterner [kɔ̃stɛrne], *v.tr.* To dismay; to strike (s.o.) with consternation.
constipant [kɔ̃stipɑ̃], *a.* Constipating, binding.
constipation [kɔ̃stipasjɔ̃], *s.f.* Constipation.
constiper [kɔ̃stipe], *v.tr.* To constipate.
constipé, *a.* Constipated, costive.
constituant, -ante [kɔ̃stitɥɑ̃, -ɑ̃:t], *a.* Constituent. **I.** Component (part of a whole). *s.m.* Constituent part. **2.** *Hist:* **L'assemblée constituante**, the Constituent Assembly (of 1789). **3.** *s.* *Pol:* Elector.
constituer [kɔ̃stitɥe], *v.tr.* To constitute. **I.** (*a*) To form, make (up). (*b*) To set up, institute (committee, etc.). *Ils se constituèrent en commission*, they resolved themselves into a committee. (*c*) To incorporate (an order, a society); to empanel (jury). **2.** (*a*) *C. qn son héritier*, to make s.o. one's heir. *C. qn prisonnier*, to take s.o. into custody. *Se c. prisonnier*, to give oneself up (to justice). (*b*) *C. une dot, une rente, à qn*, to settle a dowry, an annuity, on s.o.
constitué, *a.* **I.** Constituted, organized (authority, etc.). **2.** **Enfant bien constitué**, fine healthy child.
constitution [kɔ̃stitysjɔ̃], *s.f.* **I.** Constituting, establishing. **Frais de constitution**, preliminary expenses (in company promoting). *C. de dot, de pension*, settling, settlement, of a dowry, of an annuity. **2.** Constitution. (*a*) *Avoir une bonne c.*, to have a sound constitution. (*b*) *Pol:* *C. républicaine, monarchique*, republican, monarchic, constitution. **3.** Composition (of air, water, etc.).
constitutionnel, -elle [kɔ̃stitysjɔnɛl], *a.* Constitutional (disease, government, party).
constricteur [kɔ̃striktœ:r], *s.m. & a.* **I.** *Physiol:* (Muscles) **constricteurs**, constrictors. **2.** (Boa) **constricteur**, boa-constrictor.
constructeur [kɔ̃stryktœ:r], *s.m.* Constructor; erecting engineer. **Constructeur mécanicien**, mechanical engineer. *C. de maisons*, master-builder.
constructif, -ive [kɔ̃stryktif, -i:v], *a.* Constructive.
construction [kɔ̃stryksjɔ̃], *s.f.* Construction. **I.** Constructing, erection, building. *C. en fer*, ironwork. *C. de navires*, shipbuilding. *C. de routes*, road-making. **Construction mécanique**, mechanical engineering. **2.** Edifice, structure, building.
construire [kɔ̃strɥi:r], *v.tr.* (*pr.p.* **construisant**; *p.p.* **construit**; *pr.ind.* **je construis**, **il construit**, **n. construisons**; *p.d.* **je construisais**; *p.h.* **je construisis**; *fu.* **je construirai**) To construct. **I.** To build, erect; to make, lay out (road, etc.). **2.** To assemble, put together (machine, etc.).
consul [kɔ̃syl], *s.m.* Consul. *Le c. de France*, the French consul.
consulaire [kɔ̃syle:r], *a.* Consular.
consulat [kɔ̃syla], *s.m.* Consulate; (i) consulship, (ii) consular office. *Le C. de France*, the French Consulate.
consultant, -ante [kɔ̃syltɑ̃, -ɑ̃:t]. **I.** *a.* Consulting. *Médecin c.*, consulting physician; consultant. **2.** *s.* (*a*) Person consulted. *Med:* Consultant. (*b*) Consulter.

consultatif, -ive [kɔ̃syltatif, -iːv], *a.* Consultative, advisory (committee, etc.); advisory (opinion). **Avoir une voix consultative,** to be present in an advisory capacity.

consultation [kɔ̃syltasjɔ̃], *s.f.* (*a*) Consultation, conference. (*b*) (Medical) advice; (legal) opinion. *Med:* **Cabinet de consultation,** consulting-room; surgery. **Heures de consultation,** consulting-hours.

consulter [kɔ̃sylte]. **1.** *v.tr.* To consult, to take the advice of s.o., the opinion of (s.o.). *C. un médecin,* to take medical advice. *C. un avocat,* to take legal opinion, counsel's opinion. *C. un dictionnaire,* to consult a dictionary. *Ouvrage à c.,* work of reference. **2.** *v.i. Med: etc: C. avec un confrère,* to call in a colleague.

consulteur [kɔ̃syltœːr], *a.* Consulting (doctor).

consumer [kɔ̃syme], *v.tr.* To consume. **1.** To wear away; to destroy. *Consumé par le feu,* burnt up. *Consumé de rouille,* eaten away by rust. *Consumé par l'ambition,* eaten up with ambition. **2.** To use up (fortune, energy, etc.).

se consumer, to waste away, pine away, burn away.

contact [kɔ̃takt], *s.m.* **1.** Contact, touch. **Être, entrer, en contact avec qn, qch.,** to be in contact, come into contact, with s.o., sth. **Mettre deux personnes en contact,** to bring two people into contact. **Garder, perdre, le contact,** to keep, to lose, touch. **2.** *El:* (*a*) Connection, contact. *C. de terre,* earth (connection). **Établir le contact,** to make contact; to switch on. **Rompre, couper, le contact,** to switch off. *Aut: etc: C. à la masse,* earth to frame (of car, etc.). (*b*) Switch. *C. à cheville, à fiche,* plug(-contact).

contacteur [kɔ̃taktœːr], *s.m. El.E:* Contactor; contact-maker.

contagier [kɔ̃taʒje], *v.tr. Med:* To infect (s.o.).

contagieux, -ieuse [kɔ̃taʒjø, -jøːz], *a.* **1.** Contagious, infectious, *F:* catching (disease, etc.). **2.** Noxious, pestiferous (air, etc.).

contagion [kɔ̃taʒjɔ̃], *s.f.* **1.** Contagion. **2.** *F:* Contagiousness (of laughter, etc.).

contagionner [kɔ̃taʒjɔne], *v.tr. Med:* To infect.

se contagionner, to become infected.

contamination [kɔ̃taminasjɔ̃], *s.f.* (*a*) Contamination. (*b*) *Med:* Infection.

contaminer [kɔ̃tamine], *v.tr.* (*a*) To contaminate. (*b*) *Med:* To infect.

conte [kɔ̃ːt], *s.m.* **1.** Story, tale. **Conte de fées,** conte de ma mère l'Oie, fairy-tale, nursery tale. **Contes de bonne femme,** old wives' tales. **Contes rimés,** nursery rhymes. S.a. BLEU I. **2.** *F:* Story, fib, yarn. **Conte à dormir debout,** cock-and-bull story.

contemplateur, -trice [kɔ̃tɑ̃platœːr, -tris], *s.* Contemplator.

contemplation [kɔ̃tɑ̃plasjɔ̃], *s.f.* Contemplation. **1.** *C. de qch.,* gazing upon sth. **2.** *Plongé dans la c.,* lost in contemplation, in meditation.

contempler [kɔ̃tɑ̃ple], *v.tr.* To contemplate. **1.** To behold, view (sth.); to gaze at, upon (sth.). **2.** To meditate, reflect, upon (sth.).

contemporain, -aine [kɔ̃tɑ̃pɔrɛ̃, -ɛn]. **1.** *a.* (*a*) Contemporary. (*b*) Contemporaneous (*de,* with); of the same date (as). **2.** *s.* Contemporary.

contempteur, -trice [kɔ̃tɑ̃ptœːr, -tris]. **1.** *s.* Despiser, scorner, contemner. **2.** *a.* Contemptuous, scornful (*de,* of).

contenance [kɔ̃tnɑ̃ːs], *s.f.* **1.** Capacity, content (of bottle, etc.). *C. d'un navire,* burden of a vessel. **2.** Countenance, bearing. **Se donner, se faire, une contenance,** to keep oneself in countenance. **Faire bonne contenance,** (i) to show a bold front,

put a good face on it; (ii) to keep smiling. **Perdre contenance,** to be put out of countenance. **Faire qch. par contenance,** to do sth. to keep oneself in countenance.

contenir [kɔ̃tniːr], *v.tr.* (Conj. like TENIR) **1.** To contain. *Lettre contenant chèque,* letter enclosing cheque. **2.** To restrain; to keep (crowd, feelings) in check; to control (passion). *C. ses sentiments,* to repress one's feelings.

se contenir, to contain oneself; to hold oneself in; to keep one's temper.

contenu. 1. *a.* Restrained (passion, style, etc.); pent-up (anger); reserved (character). **2.** *s.m.* Contents (of parcel, etc.).

content [kɔ̃tɑ̃]. **1.** *a.* (*a*) Content. *Être c. de son sort,* to be content, satisfied, with one's lot. (*b*) Satisfied, pleased (*de,* with). **Il a l'air content de lui,** he looks very pleased with himself. (*c*) Pleased. *Je suis très c. de vous voir,* I am very pleased to see you. (*d*) Glad. *Comme elle était contente!* how glad she was! *Je suis fort c. que vous soyez venu,* I am so glad (that) you came. **2.** *s.m. F:* **Manger tout son content,** to eat one's fill. **S'amuser tout son content,** to enjoy oneself to one's heart's content.

contentement [kɔ̃tɑ̃tmɑ̃], *s.m.* (*a*) Contentment. (*b*) Satisfaction (*de,* at, with).

contenter [kɔ̃tɑ̃te], *v.tr.* To content, satisfy (s.o.); to gratify (curiosity, whim, etc.).

se contenter *de qch., de faire qch.,* to be content, satisfied, with sth., with doing sth.

contentieux, -euse [kɔ̃tɑ̃sjø, -øːz]. **1.** *a.* Contentious (matter). **2.** *s.m. Adm:* Contentious business; matters in dispute. **Service du contentieux,** disputed claims department; legal department (of bank, etc.).

contentif, -ive [kɔ̃tɑ̃tif, -iːv], *a. Med:* Retentive (appliance, bandage).

conter [kɔ̃te], *v.tr.* To tell, relate (story, etc.). *F:* **Allez conter ça ailleurs!** go and tell that to the marines! **En conter (de belles, de fortes) à qn,** to take s.o. in, pull s.o.'s leg.

contestable [kɔ̃tɛstabl], *a.* Contestable, debatable, questionable.

contestation [kɔ̃tɛstasjɔ̃], *s.f.* Contestation, dispute. **Matières en contestation,** matters at issue. **Sans contestation possible,** beyond all question.

conteste [kɔ̃tɛst], *s.f.* **Sans conteste,** indisputably, unquestionably.

contester [kɔ̃tɛste]. **1.** *v.tr.* To contest, dispute (point, right). *C. à qn le droit de faire qch.,* to challenge s.o.'s right to do sth. **2.** *v.i.* To dispute, wrangle (*avec,* with).

conteur, -euse [kɔ̃tœːr, -øːz], *s.* **1.** Narrator, teller. **2.** Story-teller, romancer, fibber. [CONTER]

contexte [kɔ̃tɛkst], *s.m.* Context.

contien-s, -t, -ne. See CONTENIR.

contigu, -uë [kɔ̃tigy], *a.* Contiguous, adjoining. *C. à, avec, qch.,* contiguous to, next to, sth. *Geom:* **Angles contigus,** adjacent angles.

contiguïté [kɔ̃tigɥite], *s.f.* Contiguity, adjacency.

continence [kɔ̃tinɑ̃ːs], *s.f.* Continence, continency.

continent¹ [kɔ̃tinɑ̃], *a.* Continent, chaste.

continent², -s.m. **1.** Continent. **2.** Mainland.

continental, -aux [kɔ̃tinɑ̃tal, -o], *a.* **1.** Continental. **2.** Belonging to the mainland.

contingent [kɔ̃tɛ̃ʒɑ̃]. **1.** *a. Phil:* Contingent. **2.** *s.m.* (*a*) *Mil:* Contingent. (*b*) Quota (*e.g.* immigration quota).

contingenter [kɔ̃tɛ̃ʒɑ̃te], *v.tr.* **1.** To apportion, fix, quotas for (imports, etc.). **2.** To distribute, allocate, (films, etc.) according to a quota. *s.m.* **-ement.**

contin-s, -t. See CONTENIR.
contin|u [kɔ̃tiny], *a.* Continuous, unceasing; sustained (eloquence, etc.). *El: Courant c.,* continuous, direct, current. *adv.* **-ûment.**
continuateur, -trice [kɔ̃tinɥatœːr, -tris], *s.* (*a*) Continuer. (*b*) Continuator (of s.o. else's literary work).
continuation [kɔ̃tinɥasjɔ̃], *s.f.* Continuation; carrying on (of work); long spell, run (of bad weather, etc.).
continu|el, -elle [kɔ̃tinɥɛl], *a.* Continual, unceasing. *adv.* **-ellement.**
continuer [kɔ̃tinɥe], *v.tr. & i.* To continue. (*a*) To carry on (studies, tradition). *C. sa route,* to proceed on one's way. *C. à, de, faire qch.,* to continue to do sth.; to go on, keep on, doing sth. *Il continua à marcher,* he walked on. **Continuez!** go on! *Mil:* carry on! (*b*) To extend (a line).
continuité [kɔ̃tinɥite], *s.f.* Continuity; ceaselessness. S.a. SOLUTION 1.
contondant [kɔ̃tɔ̃dɑ̃], *a.* Contusive, blunt (instrument, weapon).
contorsion [kɔ̃tɔrsjɔ̃], *s.f.* Contortion. **Faire des contorsions,** to writhe.
contour [kɔ̃tuːr], *s.m.* **1.** Outline. **2.** *Surv:* Contour(-line). **3.** Circuit, circumference (of town, etc.). **4.** = CONTOURNEMENT 2.
contournement [kɔ̃turnəmɑ̃], *s.m.* **1.** Shaping, outlining (of figure, etc.). **2.** Passing round, skirting (of mountain, etc.). *Rail:* **Ligne de contournement,** loop-line. *Aut:* **Route de c.,** by-pass (road).
contourner [kɔ̃turne], *v.tr.* **1.** To shape, to trace the outline of (design). **2.** To pass round, skirt (hill, wood, etc.). *F:* **Contourner la loi,** to get round the law. **3.** To twist, warp, distort.
  contourné, *a.* **1.** Shaped. **Mal contourné,** mis-shapen. **2.** Twisted, distorted, crookęd.
contractant [kɔ̃traktɑ̃], *a.* Contracting (pafty).
contracter¹ [kɔ̃trakte], *v.tr.* **1.** (*a*) To contract (alliance, marriage). (*b*) To incur (debt). (*c*) *C. une assurance,* to take out an insurance policy. **2.** To contract, develop, acquire (habit); to catch (disease).
contracter², *v.tr.* To contract, draw together. *Traits contractés par la douleur,* features drawn with pain.
  se contracter, to contract; (of road, etc.) to narrow; (of stuff) to shrink.
contraction [kɔ̃traksjɔ̃], *s.f.* Contraction; shrinking, shrinkage; narrowing (of road, etc.).
contractuel, -elle [kɔ̃traktɥel], *a. Jur:* Contractual (obligation, etc.). *Vitesse contractuelle,* designed speed (of ship, etc.).
contradicteur [kɔ̃tradiktœːr], *s.m.* Contradictor.
contradiction [kɔ̃tradiksjɔ̃], *s.f.* **1.** Contradiction. *Il n'y a pas de c. possible,* there is no gainsaying it. **Être en contradiction avec les faits,** to be at variance with the facts. **Esprit de contradiction,** contrariness. **2.** Inconsistency; discrepancy. **En contradiction avec qch.,** inconsistent with sth.
contradictoire [kɔ̃tradiktwaːr], *a.* (*a*) Contradictory (*à,* to); inconsistent (*à,* with); conflicting (accounts, etc.). (*b*) **Examen contradictoire,** cross-examination. **Conférence contradictoire,** debate.
contraign-ant, -e, etc. See CONTRAINDRE.
contraindre [kɔ̃trɛ̃:dr], *v.tr.* (*pr.p.* contraignant; *p.p.* contraint; *pr.ind.* je contrains, n. contraignons; *p.h.* je contraignis; *fu.* je contraindrai) To constrain. **1.** To restrain, put restraint on (s.o., one's feelings). **2.** To compel. *C. qn à*

faire qch., to constrain, force, s.o. to do sth. *Je fus contraint d'obéir,* I was obliged to obey.
  se contraindre, to restrain oneself, to control oneself.
  contraint, *a.* Constrained, cramped (posture, style); forced (smile); stiff, starched (manner).
contrainte [kɔ̃trɛ̃:t], *s.f.* Constraint. **1.** Restraint. **Sans contrainte,** freely. **2.** Compulsion, coercion. **Faire qch. par contrainte,** to do sth. under constraint, under compulsion.
contraire [kɔ̃treːr], *a.* **1.** (*a*) Contrary (*à,* to); opposite (direction, etc.); opposed (interest, etc.). **A moins d'avis contraire,** unless I hear to the contrary. **Jusqu'à avis contraire,** until further notice. (*b*) *s.m. Avoir preuve du c.,* to have proof to the contrary. **Au contraire,** on the contrary. **Au contraire de . . .,** contrary to. . . . **2.** (*a*) Adverse, opposed. *Le sort lui est c.,* fate is against him. *Vent c.,* adverse, contrary, wind. *s.m.* **Aller au contraire de qn,** to run counter to s.o. (*b*) Injurious, bad. *Le vin lui est c.,* wine disagrees with him. *adv.* **-ment.**
contrariant [kɔ̃trarjɑ̃], *a.* (*a*) Provoking, contradictious (person, spirit). (*b*) Vexatious (measure); trying (circumstance, etc.); annoying.
contrarier [kɔ̃trarje], *v.tr.* **1.** To thwart, oppose, cross; to run counter to (s.o.). **2.** To vex, annoy; *F:* to put (s.o.) out. **3.** To put (colours, etc.) in contrast.
  contrarié, *a.* **1.** Thwarted. *C. dans son amour,* crossed in love. **2.** Annoyed, vexed.
contrariété [kɔ̃trarjete], *s.f.* **1.** (*a*) Contrariety; clash(ing) (of interests, etc.). (*b*) **Esprit de contrariété,** contrariness. **2.** Vexation, annoyance. **Éprouver une vive contrariété,** to be very much annoyed. *Quelle c.!* how annoying!
contraste [kɔ̃trast], *s.m.* Contrast; set-off. **Mettre une chose en contraste avec une autre,** to bring one thing into contrast with another. **Être en contraste, faire contraste, avec . . .,** to contrast with . . ., to stand out against. . . . **Comme contraste à . . .,** as a set-off to. . . .
contraster [kɔ̃traste], *v.* To contrast. **1.** *v.i. C. avec qch.,* to stand in contrast with sth.; to form a contrast to sth. **2.** *v.tr.* To put, set, (colours, etc.) in contrast.
contrat [kɔ̃tra], *s.m.* Contract, agreement, deed. **Rupture de contrat,** breach of contract. **Passer un contrat avec qn,** to enter into, conclude, an agreement with s.o. *C. de mariage,* marriage settlement. *C. d'assurance,* insurance policy. *C. de vente,* bill of sale. *Cards: Réaliser son c.,* to make one's contract.
contravention [kɔ̃travɑ̃sjɔ̃], *s.f.* Contravention, infringement, breach (*au règlement,* of regulations); minor offence. *F:* **Dresser une contravention à qn,** to take s.o.'s name and address (with a view to prosecution).
contre [kɔ̃:tr]. **1.** *prep.* Against. (*a*) *Se battre c. qn,* to fight against, with, s.o. *C. toute attente,* contrary to all expectation. (*b*) *S'abriter c. la pluie,* to shelter from the rain. *S'assurer c. l'incendie,* to insure against fire. (*c*) (In exchange) for. *Échanger une chose c. une autre,* to exchange one thing for another. *Livraison c. remboursement,* cash on delivery. (*d*) To. *Parier à cinq c. un,* to bet five to one. (*e*) (Close) to, by. *Sa maison est tout contre la mienne,* his house adjoins mine. **2.** *adv.* Against. **Parler pour et contre,** to speak for and against. **La maison est tout contre,** the house is close by, hard by. **3.** *s.m.* (*a*) Disputer le pour et le contre, to discuss the pros and cons. **Par contre,** on the other hand. **Règlement par**

contre, settlement per contra. (*b*) *Box: Fenc:* Counter. (*c*) *Bill:* Kiss. (*d*) *Cards:* Double.

NOTE. In all the following compounds CONTRE is inv.; the noun takes the plural.

contre-accusation, *s.f.* Counter-charge.
contre-allée, *s.f.* Side-walk, -lane.
contre-allumage, *s.m. I.C.E:* Back-fire.
contre-amiral, -aux, *s.m.* Rear-admiral.
contre-arbre, *s.m. Mec.E:* Countershaft.
contre-assemblée, *s.f.* Opposition meeting.
contre-assurance, *s.f.* Reinsurance.
contre-attaque, *s.f.* Counter-attack.
contre-attaquer, *v.tr.* To counter-attack.
contre-avion(s), *a.* Canon contre-avion(s), anti-aircraft gun.
contre-avis, *s.m.* **I.** Counter-advice, contrary opinion. **2.** Notification to the contrary. Sauf contre-avis, unless I hear to the contrary.
contre-balancer, *v.tr.* (je contre-balançai(s); n. contre-balançons) To counterbalance, counterpoise, offset.
contrebande [kɔ̃trəbɑ̃:d], *s.f.* **I.** Contraband, smuggling. *Articles de c.,* contraband goods. Faire la contrebande, to engage in smuggling. Faire entrer des marchandises en contrebande, to smuggle in goods. **2.** Contraband goods.
contrebandier [kɔ̃trəbɑ̃dje], *s.m.* Smuggler.
contre-bas (en), *adv.phr.* **I.** (Lower) down; below. *Être en c.-b. de qch.,* to be below the level of sth. **2.** Downwards, down.
contrebasse [kɔ̃trəbɑːs], *s.f. Mus:* (*a*) (Stringed) double-bass. (*b*) (Brass bands) Tuba, bombardon.
contrebasson [kɔ̃trəbasɔ̃], *s.m. Mus:* Double-bassoon; contra-bassoon.
contre-batterie, *s.f. Mil:* Counter-battery.
contre-bon-sens, *s.m. inv.* Absurdity.
contre-bord (à), *adv.phr. Nau:* Courir à contre-bord, to sail on opposite tacks.
contre-boutant, *s.m.* **I.** Buttress. **2.** Shore.
contre-bouter, *v.tr.* To buttress; to shore up.
contrecarrer [kɔ̃trəkare], *v.tr.* To cross, thwart, oppose (s.o., plans).
contre-chant, *s.m. Mus:* Counter-melody.
contre-charme, *s.m.* Counter-charm.
contre-cœur (à), *adv.phr.* Unwillingly, reluctantly, grudgingly.
contre-coup, *s.m.* (*a*) Rebound (of bullet, etc.); recoil. (*b*) Jar (of blow, etc.). (*c*) Repercussion, backlash (of explosion). *Mec:* Backlash. *El:* Return shock. (*d*) *F:* After-effects, consequence (of action, disaster, etc.).
contre-courant, *s.m.* Counter-current, back-current. *El:* Counter-flow. A contre-courant, against the stream.
contredanse [kɔ̃trədɑ̃:s], *s.f.* **I.** Quadrille (dance, air). **2.** (In Eng.) Country dance.
contre-déclaration, *s.f.* Counter-declaration.
contredire [kɔ̃trədiːr], *v.tr.* (*pr.ind.* je contredis, v. contredisez; other tenses like DIRE) To contradict. (*a*) To gainsay. (*b*) To be inconsistent with (sth.). *Propositions qui se contredisent,* propositions that are inconsistent.
se contredire, to contradict oneself.
contredit [kɔ̃trədi], *Adv.phr.* Sans contredit, assuredly, unquestionably.
contrée [kɔ̃tre], *s.f.* (Geographical) region; country (in an indeterminate sense).
contre-échelle, *s.f.* Diagonal scale.
contre-écriture, *s.f. Book-k:* Contra-entry.
contre-écrou, *s.m.* Lock-nut.
contre-effort, *s.m.* Counter-effort.
contre-électromoteur, -trice, *a. El:* Im-

peding (effect, etc.). *Force contre-électromotrice,* back-electromotive force; impedance.
contre-enquête, *s.f. Jur:* Counter-enquiry.
contre-épreuve, *s.f.* **I.** *Engr:* (*a*) Counter-proof. (*b*) Second proof. **2.** Repetition test.
contre-escarpe, *s.f. Fort:* Counterscarp.
contre-espion, *s.m.* Counter-spy.
contre-essai, *s.m.* Control experiment; check test.
contrefaçon [kɔ̃trəfasɔ̃], *s.f.* **I.** Counterfeiting; fraudulently copying or imitating (trade-mark, etc.); infringement (of patent, of copyright). **2.** Counterfeit, forgery, fraudulent imitation; pirated edition.
contrefaire [kɔ̃trəfɛːr], *v.tr.* (*Conj.* like FAIRE) **I.** (*a*) To imitate, mimic (s.o.'s voice, etc.). (*b*) To feign. *C. le mort, F:* to sham dead. (*c*) To disguise (one's voice, etc.). **2.** To counterfeit (coin, etc.); to forge (signature, bank-note, etc.); to pirate (book).
contrefait, *a.* **I.** Feigned (zeal, etc.); disguised (writing, etc.). **2.** Counterfeit, forged, spurious (coin, etc.). *Édition contrefaite,* pirated edition. **3.** Deformed (person).
contre-fiche, *s.f.* Brace, strut.
contre-ficher, *v.tr.* To strut, truss.
contre-fil, *s.m.* Opposite direction, wrong way (of watercourse, stuff, etc.). A contre-fil de l'eau, up-stream. Travailler du bois à contre-fil, to work wood against the grain.
contrefort [kɔ̃trəfɔːr], *s.m.* **I.** (Close) buttress; abutment. **2.** *Geog:* Counterfort, spur (of mountain); *pl.* foot-hills.
contre-griffer, *v.tr. F:* To countersign.
contre-hacher [kɔ̃trəaʃe], *v.tr. Art: Engr:* To cross-hatch.
contre-hachure [kɔ̃trəaʃyːr], *s.f. Art: Engr:* Cross-hatch(ing).
contre-haut (en) [ɑ̃kɔ̃tro]. **I.** *Adj. & adv.phr.* Higher up, on a higher level. **2.** *Prep.phr.* En contre-haut de . . ., on a higher level than. . . .
contre-indication, *s.f. Med:* Contra-indication, counter-indication.
contre-indiqué, *a. Med:* Contra-indicated (diet, etc.).
contre-jour, *s.m.* **I.** (Unfavourable) light from behind. **Tableau pendu à contre-jour,** picture hung against the light. *Assis à c.-j.,* sitting with one's back to the light, in one's own light. **2.** *Art:* Back-lighting; Rembrandt effect.
contremaître, -tresse [kɔ̃trəmɛːtr, -trɛs]. **I.** *s.* Foreman, forewoman; overseer. **2.** *s.m.* Boatswain's mate. *Navy:* Petty officer.
contremand|er [kɔ̃trəmɑ̃de], *v.tr.* To countermand, cancel, revoke (order, invitation); to call off (strike); to put off (one's guests). *s.m.* **-ement.**
contremarche [kɔ̃trəmarʃ], *s.f.* **I.** *Mil:* Countermarch. **2.** *Const:* Rise (of stair).
contre-marée, *s.f.* **I.** Undertow (of tide); counter-tide. **2.** A contre-marée, against the tide.
contremarque [kɔ̃trəmark], *s.f.* **I.** Counter-mark (on gold plate, etc.). **2.** *Th:* C. de sortie, pass-out ticket or check.
contre-ordre, *s.m.* Counter-order, counter-mand. *Sauf c.-o., à moins de c.-o.,* unless I hear to the contrary.
contre-partie, *s.f.* **I.** (*a*) Opposite view (in debate). *Soutenir la c.-p.,* to speak against the motion. (*b*) Other party (in transaction). **2.** (*a*) *Book-k:* Contra. **En contre-partie,** per contra. (*b*) Counterpart, duplicate of document, etc.). **3.** *Sp:* Revenge, return match.

contre-pas, *s.m. Mil :* **1.** Half-pace. **2.** Marcher à contre-pas, to be out of step (*de*, with).
contre-passer, *v.tr.* **1.** *Com :* To return, to endorse back (bill to drawer). **2.** *Book-k :* To reverse, contra, transfer (item, entry).
contre-pédal|er, *v.i. Cy :* To back-pedal. *s.m.* **-age.**
contre-pente, *s.f.* Reverse slope.
contre-petterie, *s.f.* Spoonerism.
contre-pied, *s.m.* No *pl. Ven :* Back-scent. *F :* Prendre le contre-pied, to take the opposite course or view (*de*, to). Prendre une observation à contre-pied, to misconstrue a remark. A contre-pied de, contrary to.
contre-plaqué, *a.* Laminated; built up in layers. *C.-p. à deux épaisseurs*, two-ply (wood).
contrepoids [kɔ̃trəpwɑ], *s.m.* (*a*) Counterweight, counterbalance; balance-weight (of clock); counterpoise. Faire contrepoids à qch., to (counter)balance sth. (*b*) Balancing-pole (of rope-dancer). (*c*) *W.Tel :* Capacity earth.
contre-poil (à), *adv.phr.* The wrong way (of the hair). *F :* Prendre qn à contre-poil, to rub s.o. the wrong way.
contrepoint [kɔ̃trəpwɛ̃], *s.m. Mus :* Counterpoint.
contre-pointe, *s.f.* **1.** (*a*) False edge (of sword). (*b*) Edge play (of fencers). **2.** Tail-stock (of lathe).
contre-pointer, *v.tr.* To quilt.
contre-poison, *s.m.* Antidote, counter-poison.
contre-porte, *s.f.* Screen-door, inner door.
contre-pression, *s.f.* Counterpressure; negative pressure. *Mch :* Back-pressure.
contre-proposition, *s.f.* Counter-proposition, counter-proposal.
contrer [kɔ̃tre]. **1.** *v.tr. Box :* To counter (blow). **2.** *v.i. Cards :* To double.
contre-révolution, *s.f.* Counter-revolution.
contre-saison (à), *adv.phr.* Out of season.
contrescarpe [kɔ̃treskarp], *s.f.* Counterscarp.
contre-sceau, *s.m.* Counter-seal.
contreseing [kɔ̃trəsɛ̃], *s.m.* Counter-signature. Avoir le contreseing de qn, to sign for s.o.
contre-sens [kɔ̃trəsɑ̃:s], *s.m.* **1.** Misinterpretation; mistranslation (of passage, etc.). Faire un contre-sens, to misunderstand a passage. Prendre le contre-sens des paroles de qn, to misconstrue, put a wrong construction on, s.o.'s words. **2.** Wrong way (of stuff). Prendre le contre-sens de la marée, to go against the tide. A contre-sens, in the wrong sense, way, direction. **3.** *Autos qui défilent à c.-s.*, cars passing in opposite directions. A contre-sens de, in the contrary direction to.
contresigner [kɔ̃trəsiɲe], *v.tr.* To countersign.
contretemps [kɔ̃trətɑ̃], *s.m.* **1.** (*a*) Mishap, hitch, untoward event. (*b*) Delay, inconvenience. **2.** Note played, step danced (i) against the beat, (ii) out of time. **3.** *Adv.phr.* A contretemps, unseasonably, inopportunely.
contre-tension, *s.f. El :* Back-pressure.
contre-torpilleur, *s.m.* (Torpedo-boat) destroyer.
contre-trame, *s.f.* Counterplot.
contre-ut [kɔ̃tryt], *s.m. Mus :* C in alt.
contrevenant, -ante [kɔ̃trəvnɑ̃, -ɑ̃:t]. **1.** *a.* Contravening. **2.** *s.* Contravener, infringer (of regulations); offender, delinquent.
contrevenir [kɔ̃trəvni:r], *v.ind.tr.* (Conj. like VENIR. Aux. *avoir*) To contravene, infringe (*à un arrêté*, an order).
contrevent [kɔ̃trəvɑ̃], *s.m.* **1.** Outside shutter (of window). **2.** *Civ.E :* Wind-brace. [VENT]
contrevent|er [kɔ̃trəvɑ̃te], *v.tr.* To brace,

stiffen, (bridge, etc.) against wind-pressure; to wind-brace. *s.m.* **-ement.**
contre-vérité, *s.f.* **1.** Untruth. **2.** Ironical statement (intended to convey the contrary).
contre-voie (à), *adv.phr. Rail :* **1.** Circuler à *c.-v.*, to travel in the reverse of the usual direction. **2.** Descendre à *c.-v.*, to get out on the wrong side of the train.
contribuable [kɔ̃tribɥabl]. **1.** *a.* Taxpaying or ratepaying. **2.** *s.* Taxpayer or ratepayer.
contribuer [kɔ̃tribɥe], *v.i.* **1.** To contribute funds (*à qch.*, to sth.). **2.** To contribute, conduce (*d*, to).
contributif, -ive [kɔ̃tribytif, -i:v], *a.* Contributive, contributory.
contribution [kɔ̃tribysjɔ̃], *s.f.* **1.** Tax or rate. Contributions directes, direct taxation. Contributions foncières, rates. Lever, percevoir, une contribution, to collect a tax. **2.** Contribution, share. Donner qch. pour sa c., to give sth. as one's contribution. Mettre qch., qn, à contribution, to lay sth., s.o., under contribution.
contristant [kɔ̃tristɑ̃], *a.* Dismal, doleful, saddening (tidings, etc.).
contrister [kɔ̃triste], *v.tr.* To sadden, grieve.
contrit [kɔ̃tri], *a.* Contrite, penitent.
contrition [kɔ̃trisjɔ̃], *s.f.* Contrition, penitence.
contrôlable [kɔ̃trolabl], *a.* That may be checked, verified.
contrôle [kɔ̃tro:l], *s.m.* **1.** *Mil : etc :* (Muster-)roll; list. *C. nominatif*, nominal roll; list of names. *C. de service*, duty roster. Porter qch. sur les contrôles, to take sth. on charge. Porter qn sur les contrôles, to take s.o. on the strength. **2.** (*a*) Testing, assaying (of gold, silver). (*b*) Hall-marking. Cachet de contrôle, hall-mark. (*c*) Assay office. **3.** (*a*) Checking, verification (of information, etc.). (*b*) *Adm :* Inspection, supervision. *Com :* Auditing, checking (of accounts). *Ind :* Contrôle de présence, time-keeping. (Bureau de) contrôle, ticket-office; *Th :* box-office. (*c*) *Sp :* (i) Check, (ii) control (point) (in reliability run).
contrôler [kɔ̃trole], *v.tr.* **1.** To hall-mark, stamp (gold, silver). **2.** To inspect, supervise (work, etc.); to check, audit (accounts); to check (tickets); to examine (passports); to verify (a fact). **3.** To hold (s.o.) in check.
contrôleur, -euse [kɔ̃trolœ:r, -ø:z], *s.* **1.** (*a*) Comptroller (of Mint). (*b*) Controller (of government department); assessor, inspector (of taxes); auditor (of accounts). (*c*) Inspector, examiner, supervisor. *Rail :* Ticket-collector; inspector. *Ind :* Time-keeper. (*d*) Driver, motor-man (of electric tram or train). **2.** *s.m.* Checking apparatus; tell-tale. *C. d'atelier*, time-recorder. *Aut : C. de marche*, throttle-control.
controuvé [kɔ̃truve], *a.* False; of pure imagination.
controversable [kɔ̃trɔversabl], *a.* Controversial, controvertible (opinion, etc.).
controverse [kɔ̃trɔvɛrs], *s.f.* Controversy. Hors de controverse, beyond dispute; indisputable.
controverser [kɔ̃trɔverse], *v.tr.* **1.** To discuss, debate (question, etc.). *Question fort controversée*, much debated question. **2.** To controvert (opinion, etc.).
contumace[1] [kɔ̃tymas], *s.f. Jur :* (*a*) Contumacy; non-appearance (in court). Condamné par contumace, sentenced in his, her, absence. (*b*) Contempt of court.
contumace[2], *s. m. & f.* Contumacious person; defaulter; absconder.
contus [kɔ̃ty], *a.* Contused, bruised.
contusion [kɔ̃tyzjɔ̃], *s.f.* Contusion, bruise.

contusionner [kɔ̃tyzjɔne], *v.tr.* To contuse, bruise.
convaincant [kɔ̃vɛ̃kã], *a.* Convincing.
convaincre [kɔ̃vɛ̃:kr], *v.tr.* (Conj. like VAINCRE) **1.** To convince (*de*, of). *Se c. d'un fait*, to convince oneself of a fact. **2.** To convict (*de*, of); to prove (s.o.) guilty (*de*, of).
convalescence [kɔ̃valɛssã:s], *s.f.* Convalescence. **Entrer en convalescence**, to become convalescent. **Maison de convalescence**, (i) convalescent home; (ii) nursing home (for rest cure).
convalescent, -ente [kɔ̃valɛssã, -ã:t], *a. & s.* Convalescent.
convenable [kɔ̃vnabl], *a.* **1.** Suitable (*d*, for, to); fit(ting), befitting, becoming, appropriate, proper. **Juger convenable de faire qch.**, to think it proper, advisable, to think fit, to do sth. **2.** Decent; well-behaved (person); seemly, decorous (behaviour). *adv.* **-ment.**
convenance [kɔ̃vnã:s], *s.f.* **1.** Conformity, agreement (of tastes, etc.). **2.** Suitability, fitness. **Pour des raisons de convenance**, on grounds of expediency. **Mariage de convenance**, marriage of convenience. **Être à la convenance de qn**, to meet s.o.'s fancy. **Faire qch. à sa convenance**, to do sth. (i) as it suits, pleases, one, (ii) at one's convenience. **3.** Propriety, decency, decorum. **Manque de convenance**, breach of (good) manners. *Observer les convenances*, to observe the proprieties. **Braver les convenances**, to defy convention, Mrs Grundy.
convenir [kɔ̃vni:r], *v.i.* (Conj. like VENIR) **1.** (Conj. with *avoir*) (*a*) To suit, fit. *C. à qn, qch.*, to suit, to be suitable to, s.o., sth. *Sa figure me convient*, I like his face. **Si cela vous convient**, if that is agreeable to you. (*b*) *Impers.* **Il convient de . . .**, it is fitting, advisable, to. . . . *Ce qu'il convient de faire*, the proper measures to take. **2.** (Conj. with *avoir*, and with *être* to denote a state of agreement) (*a*) To agree; to come to an agreement. *C. de qch.*, to agree on, about, sth. *Ils sont convenus de le faire venir*, they are agreed to send for him. *Impers. Il fut convenu que . . .*, it was agreed, arranged, that. . . . (*b*) *C. de qch.*, to acknowledge, admit, sth. *Il convient qu'il a eu tort*, he admits, owns, that he was wrong. *J'ai eu tort, j'en conviens*, I confess I was wrong.
convenu, *a.* Agreed; stipulated (price, etc.); appointed (time). **C'est convenu!** that's settled!
convention [kɔ̃vãsjɔ̃], *s.f.* Convention. **1.** (*a*) Covenant, agreement. **Convention internationale, postale**, international, postal, convention. (*b*) *pl. Jur:* Articles, clauses (of deed, etc.). **Sauf convention contraire**, unless there be any (unknown) clause to the contrary. **2.** *Les conventions sociales*, the social conventions. *Adj.phr.* **De convention**, conventional. **3.** *Parl:* (Extraordinary) assembly.
conventionn|el, -elle [kɔ̃vãsjɔnɛl], *a.* (*a*) Conventional (symbol, etc.). (*b*) *Obligations conventionnelles*, treaty obligations. *adv.* **-ellement.**
convergence [kɔ̃vɛrʒã:s], *s.f.* Convergence.
convergent [kɔ̃vɛrʒã], *a.* Convergent, converging.
converger [kɔ̃vɛrʒe], *v.i.* (convergeant; ils convergeaient) To converge.
convers, -erse [kɔ̃vɛ:r, -ɛrs], *a.* **1.** *Ecc:* Lay (brother, sister). **2.** *Log: Proposition converse, s.f.* converse, converse (proposition).
conversation [kɔ̃vɛrsasjɔ̃], *s.f.* Conversation, talk. **Lier conversation, entrer en conversation, engager la conversation, avec qn**, to enter, get, into conversation with s.o.; to engage s.o. in conversation. **Faire tous les frais de la conversation**, to do all the talking. *Parler sur le ton de la c.*,

to speak in a conversational tone. *Conversations téléphoniques*, telephone calls. **Avoir de la conversation**, to be a good conversationalist.
converser [kɔ̃vɛrse], *v.i.* To converse, talk (*avec*, with); to discourse.
conversion [kɔ̃vɛrsjɔ̃], *s.f.* **1.** Conversion (to a faith). **2.** Conversion, change (*en*, into). *C. de l'eau en vapeur*, conversion of water into steam. **3.** *Mil:* Wheel(ing); change of front, of direction.
convertible [kɔ̃vɛrtibl], *a.* Convertible (*en*, into).
convertir [kɔ̃vɛrti:r], *v.tr.* To convert. **1.** *C. qn au christianisme*, to convert s.o. to Christianity. *C. qn à ses opinions*, to bring over, win over, s.o. to one's opinions. **2.** *C. qch. en qch.*, to convert, turn, sth. into sth. **se convertir.** (*a*) To become converted (to a faith, etc.). (*b*) *La neige s'était convertie en boue*, the snow had turned (in)to slush.
converti, -e, *s.* Convert.
convertissable [kɔ̃vɛrtisabl], *a.* **1.** Convertible. **2.** Transformable (*en*, into).
convertisseur [kɔ̃vɛrtisœ:r], *s.m.* **1.** *Metall:* Converter. **2.** *El.E: C. rotatif*, rotary converter; transformer. *C. à vapeur de mercure*, mercury-vapour rectifier.
convexe [kɔ̃vɛks], *a.* Convex.
conviction [kɔ̃viksjɔ̃], *s.f.* **1.** Conviction; firm belief. **Avoir la conviction que . . .**, to be convinced that. . . . **2.** *Jur:* **Pièce à, de, conviction**, exhibit (in criminal case).
convien-s, -t, etc. See CONVENIR.
convier [kɔ̃vje], *v.tr.* **1.** To invite, bid (s.o. to a marriage, etc.). **2.** *C. qn à faire qch.*, to invite, urge, s.o. to do sth.
convié, -ée, *s.* Guest.
convin-s, -t, etc. See CONVENIR.
convive [kɔ̃vi:v], *s. m. & f.* (*a*) Guest (at table). (*b*) Table-companion.
convocation [kɔ̃vɔkasjɔ̃], *s.f.* Convocation, summons; convening (of assembly, etc.). **Recevoir une convocation**, (i) to receive notice of a meeting; (ii) *Adm:* to receive a letter fixing an appointment. (Of reservist) *Recevoir sa c.*, to be called up.
convoi [kɔ̃vwa], *s.m.* **1.** Convoy. (*a*) *C. administratif*, supply column. (*b*) *Nau:* (i) Escorting vessels. (ii) Ships under escort. **Naviguer en convoi**, to sail under convoy. **2. Convoi funèbre**, funeral procession, funeral *cortège*. **3.** Train, convoy. (*a*) *C. de prisonniers*, (i) gang of convicts; (ii) *Mil:* convoy of prisoners. (*b*) *Rail: C. de voyageurs*, passenger train. S.a. SECOURS.
convoitable [kɔ̃vwatabl], *a.* Covetable, desirable.
convoit|er [kɔ̃vwate], *v.tr.* To covet, desire; to lust after (sth.). *s.* **-eur, -euse.**
convoiteux, -euse [kɔ̃vwato, -ø:z], *a.* Covetous. **Regarder qch. d'un œil de convoitise**, to cast covetous eyes on sth. (*b*) Covetous desire. *Allumer des convoitises*, to arouse cupidity.
convoitise [kɔ̃vwati:z], *s.f.* (*a*) Covetousness.
convoler [kɔ̃vɔle], *v.i.* (Of widow) To marry again.
convolution [kɔ̃vɔlysjɔ̃], *s.f.* Convolution.
convoquer [kɔ̃vɔke], *v.tr.* **1.** (*a*) To summon, call together, convoke (assembly); to convene (meeting). (*b*) *Mil:* To call up (reservists). **2.** *Adm:* To invite (s.o.) to an interview.
convoyer [kɔ̃vwaje], *v.tr.* (je convoie; je convoierai) To convoy (train, merchant fleet, etc.).
convulser [kɔ̃vylse], *v.tr.* **1.** To convulse. **2.** *F:* To frighten (s.o.) into fits.
convuls|if, -ive [kɔ̃vylsif, -i:v], *a.* Convulsive. *adv.* **-ivement.**

convulsion [kɔ̃vylsjɔ̃], *s.f.* Convulsion. **Donner des convulsions à qn,** to throw s.o. into convulsions. **Convulsion politique,** political upheaval.
convulsionner [kɔ̃vylsjɔne], *v.tr.* To convulse.
coopérateur, -trice [kɔɔpɛratœːr, -tris], *s.* Co-operator; fellow-worker.
coopératif, -ive [kɔɔpɛratif, -iːv]. **1.** *a.* Co-operative (society, etc.). **2.** *s.f.* Coopérative, co-operative stores.
coopération [kɔɔpɛrasjɔ̃], *s.f.* Co-operation.
coopérer [kɔɔpere], *v.i.* (je coopère ; je coopérerai) To co-operate; to work together. *C. avec qn à un travail,* to co-operate with s.o. in a work.
cooptation [kɔɔptasjɔ̃], *s.f.* Co-op(ta)tion.
coopter [kɔɔpte], *v.tr.* To co-opt.
coordination [kɔɔrdinasjɔ̃], *s.f.* Co-ordination.
coordonnant [kɔɔrdɔnɑ̃], *a. Gram:* Co-ordinating (conjunction, etc.).
coordonner [kɔɔrdɔne], *v.tr.* To co-ordinate, arrange.
  coordonné, -ée. 1. *a.* (*a*) Co-ordinated. (*b*) *Gram:* Co-ordinate (clause, etc.). **2.** *s.f.pl. Mth:* Coordonnées, co-ordinates.
copahu [kɔpay], *s.m. Pharm:* Copaiba.
copain [kɔpɛ̃], *s.m. P:* Chum, pal.
copal [kɔpal], *s.m.* Copal (-resin).
copeau [kɔpo], *s.m.* Shaving (of wood) ; chip, cutting (of wood, metal). *Copeaux de tour,* turnings.
Copenhague [kɔpɛnag]. *Pr.n.f.* Copenhagen.
cophte [kɔpt, kɔft]. **1.** *s.m.* (*a*) *Ecc.Hist:* Copt. (*b*) *Ling:* Coptic. **2.** *a.* Coptic.
copie [kɔpi], *s.f.* **1.** (*a*) Copy, transcript. *Adm:* "Pour copie conforme,' 'certified true copy.' (*b*) *Journ: Typ:* Copy. *Manquer de c.,* to wait copy. (*c*) *Sch:* (i) Fair copy (of exercise). (ii) (Candidate's) paper. **2.** Copy, reproduction (of picture, etc.) ; imitation (of novel, etc.).
copier [kɔpje], *v.tr.* **1.** To copy, transcribe (manuscript, etc.). *C. qch. au propre,* to make a fair, a clean, copy of sth. **2.** To copy, reproduce (statue, picture). *C. qch. sur qch.,* to copy sth. from sth. **3.** To copy, imitate (s.o.).
copieu|x, -euse [kɔpjø, -øːz], *a.* Copious. *Repas c.,* copious, hearty, meal. *adv.* **-sement.**
copiste [kɔpist], *s. m. & f.* Copier. **1.** Copyist, transcriber. **Faute de copiste,** clerical error. **2.** Imitator.
copra(h) [kɔpra], *s.m. Com:* Copra. **Huile de coprah,** coco-nut oil.
copropriétaire [kɔprɔprietɛːr], *s. m. & f.* Co-proprietor ; joint owner.
copropriété [kɔprɔpriete], *s.f.* Co-property ; joint ownership.
copte [kɔpt], *a. & s.m.* = COPHTE.
coq¹ [kɔk], *s.m.* **1.** (*a*) Cock, *U.S:* rooster. *Jeune coq,* cockerel. **Au (premier) chant du coq,** at cock-crow. **Combat de coqs,** cock-fight. *F:* **Rouge comme un coq,** red as a turkey-cock. **Vivre comme un coq en pâte,** to live like a fighting-cock. **Coq du village, de la paroisse,** cock of the walk. *Box:* **Poids coq,** bantam-weight. (*b*) Cock, male, of various birds. *Coq-faisan,* cock-pheasant. **Coq d'Inde** [kodɛ̃ːd], turkey-cock. **Coq de bruyère,** (great) grouse, wood grouse, capercailzie. **Coq d'été,** hoopoe. **2.** Weathercock ; vane.
coq², *s.m. Nau:* (**Maître-)coq,** (ship's) cook.
coq-à-l'âne [kɔkalɑːn], *s.m.inv.* **1.** Cock-and-bull story. **2.** *Lit:* A: Skit, parody.
coque [kɔk], *s.f.* **1.** (*a*) Shell (of egg). **Un œuf à la coque,** a (soft-)boiled egg. (*b*) Shell, husk (of nut, fruit). (*c*) *Ent:* (= COCON) Cocoon. **Se renfermer dans sa coque,** to retire into one's shell. **2.** (*a*) Hull, bottom (of ship). **A double**

coque, double-bottomed. (*b*) Hull (of flying-boat). (*c*) *Mch:* Body, shell (of boiler). **3.** (*a*) Loop, bow (of ribbon, etc.). (*b*) Kink (in rope).
coquelicot [kɔkliko], *s.m. Bot:* Red poppy.
coquelourde [kɔklurd], *s.f. Bot:* **1.** Pasque-flower. **2.** Rose campion.
coqueluche [kɔklyʃ], *s.f.* **1.** *A:* Hood, cowl. *F:* **Être la coqueluche de la ville,** to be the darling of the town. **2.** (W)hooping-cough.
coquerico [kɔkriko], *s.m.* Cock-a-doodle-doo.
coque|et, -ette [kɔkɛ, -ɛt]. **1.** *a.* (*a*) Coquettish (woman, smile). (*b*) Smart, stylish, dainty (garment, etc.) ; trim (garden). **2.** *s.f.* Coquette. (*a*) Flirt, coquette. (*b*) (Botanist's) vasculum. [coq] *adv.* **-ettement.**
coqueter [kɔkte], *v.i.* (je coquette ; je coquetterai) To coquet(te), play the coquette ; to flirt. *C. avec une idée,* to toy with an idea.
coquetier, -ière [kɔktje, -jɛːr]. **1.** *s.* Wholesale egg-merchant ; egg-man, -woman. **2.** *s.m.* (*a*) Egg-cup. (*b*) *Sp:* Hum: Cup ; *F:* mug, pot.
coquetterie [kɔketri], *s.f.* **1.** (*a*) Coquetry. **Faire des coquetteries à qn,** to flirt with s.o. ; to lead s.o. on ; *F:* to carry on with s.o. (*b*) Coyness, affectation. (*c*) Love of finery. (*d*) Fastidiousness (in dress). **2.** Smartness, stylishness, daintiness (of dress).
coquillage [kɔkijaːʒ], *s.m.* **1.** Shell-fish. **2.** (Empty) shell (of shell-fish).
coquille [kɔkiːj], *s.f.* **1.** Shell (of snail, oyster, etc.). **Escalier en coquille,** spiral staircase. *F:* **Rentrer dans sa coquille,** to retire into one's shell. **2. Coquille de Saint-Jacques,** (i) scallop ; (ii) scallop-shell. *Cu:* **Huîtres en coquille,** scalloped oysters. **3.** (i) Shell (of egg, nut, etc.). *F:* **Être à peine sorti de sa coquille,** to be only just hatched. (Of boat) **C'est une vraie coquille de noix,** it's a mere cockle-shell. (*b*) *C. de beurre,* flake, shell, of butter. **4.** *Cu:* (Shell-shaped) portable grate (of Dutch oven). **5.** (*a*) Casing, housing (of motor, etc.). *Hyd.E:* Case (of spiral pump). (*b*) *Typ:* (Copper) shell (of electrotype). **6.** *Typ:* Misprint, 'literal.'
coquilleux, -euse [kɔkijø, -øːz], *a.* Shelly.
coquin, -ine [kɔkɛ̃, -in]. **1.** *s.* Rogue, rascal, knave, scamp ; *f.* hussy, jade. *Ce c. de Pierre,* that rascal of a Peter. *L'heureux c.!* the lucky dog! *Petite coquine!* you little mischief, you ! you little hussy ! **2.** *a. F:* Roguish.
coquinerie [kɔkinri], *s.f.* **1.** Knavery, roguery. **2.** Knavish or rascally trick.
cor [kɔːr], *s.m.* **1.** *Ven:* Tine (of antler). **2.** (*a*) **Cor de chasse,** hunting-horn. **Donner, sonner, du cor,** to sound, wind, the horn. *F:* **Réclamer qch. à cor et à cri,** to clamour for sth. (*b*) *Mus:* **Cor d'harmonie,** French horn. **Cor anglais,** tenor oboe ; cor anglais. **3.** Corn (on the toe).
corail, -aux [kɔra:j, -o], *s.m.* Coral. **Récif de corail,** coral-reef.
corailleur [kɔrajœːr], *s.m.* Coral fisher.
corallien, -ienne [kɔraljɛ̃, -jɛn], *a.* Coralline (limestone, etc.). **Récif c.,** coral reef.
corallin [kɔralɛ̃], *a.* Red as coral ; coral-red.
Coran (le) [lɔkɔrɑ̃], *s.* The Koran.
coraux. See CORAIL.
corbeau [kɔrbo], *s.m.* **1.** *Orn:* Crow. *Grand c.,* raven. **Noir comme un corbeau,** raven-black. **2.** (*a*) *Arch:* Corbel, bracket. (*b*) *Nau:* Nid de corbeau, crow's-nest. **3.** *F:* Bird of ill-omen.
corbeille [kɔrbɛːj], *s.f.* **1.** (Open) basket (without a bow-handle). *C. à pain,* bread-basket. *C. à papier,* waste-paper basket. **La corbeille de noces,** the wedding presents (given to bride by bridegroom). *Typewr:* **Corbeille à caractères,** type-

basket. **2.** (a) Bell, vase (of Corinthian capital). (b) (Round) flower-bed.

corbillard ⌈kɔrbijaːr], *s.m.* Hearse.

cordage [kɔrdaːʒ], *s.m.* **1.** Roping (of bales, etc.); stringing (of racquet). **2.** (a) Rope. *C. en chanvre,* hempen rope. *C. commis en câble,* cable-laid rope. **Vieux cordage,** junk. (b) *pl.* Cordage, ropes; *Nau:* gear.

corde [kɔrd], *s.f.* **1.** (a) Rope, cord, line. **Tabac en corde,** twist tobacco. *C. à linge,* clothes-line. **Danseur de corde,** tight-rope dancer. *C. à sauter,* skipping-rope. **Sauter à la corde,** to skip. *C. de traction,* tug-of-war rope. *Nau: C. de remorque,* tow-rope. (b) String. **Corde à boyau,** catgut. **Corde à fouet,** whipcord. *Mus: C. de violon,* violin string. **Instrument à cordes,** stringed instrument. **Corde à piano,** piano wire. **C'est une corde qu'il ne faut pas toucher,** it is a sore subject. S.a. ARC 1, SENSIBLE 1. (c) Halter, hangman's rope; gallows. *F:* **Se mettre la corde au cou,** to put a halter round one's own neck. **Supplice de la corde,** death by hanging. **Friser la corde,** to miss the gallows by a hair's-breadth. **Il ne vaut pas la corde pour le pendre,** he is not worth powder and shot. S.a. SAC[1] 1. (d) *Rac:* **La corde,** the cords, the rails. **Tenir la corde,** (i) to be on the inside; (ii) *F:* to have the advantage of s.o. (e) *Tex:* Thread. **Drap usé jusqu'à la corde,** cloth worn to the core, threadbare cloth. **2.** *Geom:* Chord. *Civ.E:* Span (of arch). **3.** *Anat:* (a) *Cordes vocales,* vocal cords. (b) Ligament. *C. du jarret,* hamstring.

cordé [kɔrde], *a.* Cordate; heart-shaped.

cordeau [kɔrdo], *s.m.* **1.** Tracing-line, chalk-line, string. *F:* **Tiré au cordeau,** perfectly straight. **2.** *Min:* Match, fuse. **3.** Rope, cord. *Artil: C. tire-feu,* firing lanyard. **4.** *Tex:* Selvedge.

cordelette [kɔrdəlɛt], *s.f.* (a) Small cord; string. (b) Small plait (of hair).

cordelier, -ière [kɔrdəlje, -jɛːr]. **1.** *s.* Franciscan friar or nun; grey friar or sister. *F:* **Sur la mule d'un cordelier,** on Shanks's mare. **2.** *s.f.* **Cordelière.** (a) Girdle as worn by Franciscan friar; cord of dressing-gown, pyjamas, etc. (b) *Arch:* Cable moulding.

cordelle [kɔrdɛl], *s.f.* Tow-line, warp.

corder [kɔrde], *v.tr.* **1.** To twist (hemp, etc.) into rope. **2.** (a) To cord (bale, etc.). (b) To string (racquet).

    cordée, *s.f.* **1.** *Com: C. de bois,* cord of wood. **2.** Line of roped mountain climbers; 'rope' of mountaineers.

corderie [kɔrdri], *s.f.* **1.** Ropery; rope-walk. **2.** Rope manufacture or trade.

cordial, -aux [kɔrdjal, -o], *a.* **1.** Stimulating (medicine). *s.m.* Cordial; stimulant; restorative. **2.** Cordial, hearty (welcome, etc.). *adv.* **-ement.**

cordialité [kɔrdjalite], *s.f.* Cordiality, heartiness.

cordier [kɔrdje], *s.m.* **1.** Rope-maker or -merchant. **2.** Tail-piece (of violin).

cordiforme [kɔrdifɔrm], *a.* Cordiform; heart-shaped.

cordon [kɔrdɔ̃], *s.m.* **1.** (a) Strand, twist (of cable). *Corde à trois cordons,* three-stranded rope. (b) Cord, string. *C. de coton,* cotton tape. *C. de sonnette,* bell-rope, -pull. *C. de la porte,* door-pull (controlled by the *concierge,* in French flatted (houses). "**Cordon, s'il vous plaît!**" 'door, please!' *C. de soulier,* shoe-lace. S.a. BOURSE 1. (c) Ribbon, decoration (of an order, etc.). **Cordon bleu,** (i) blue ribbon; (ii) knight of the order of the Holy Ghost; (iii) *F:* first-rate cook. (d) *El: C. souple,* flex wire. **2.** (a) Row, line (of trees,

etc.); cordon (of police). (b) *Hort:* Turf border. (c) Rim, edge-ring (of coin).

cordonner [kɔrdɔne], *v.tr.* **1.** To twist, twine, cord (silk, etc.). **2.** To edge-roll (coins).

cordonnerie [kɔrdɔnri], *s.f.* **1.** Shoemaking. **2.** Shoemaker's or cobbler's shop.

cordonnet [kɔrdɔnɛ], *s.m.* Braid, cord, twist.

cordonnier [kɔrdɔnje], *s.m.* Shoemaker, bootmaker.

Cordoue [kɔrdu]. *Pr.n.f. Geog:* Cordova.

Corée (la) [kɔre]. *Pr.n. Geog:* Korea.

coreligionnaire [kɔrəliʒjɔnɛːr], *s. m. & f.* Co-religionist.

coriace [kɔrjas], *a.* Tough, leathery (meat, etc.).

corindon [kɔrɛ̃dɔ̃], *s.m. Miner:* Corundum.

Corinthe [kɔrɛ̃t]. *Pr.n.f. Geog:* Corinth. **Raisins de Corinthe,** currants.

corinthien, -ienne [kɔrɛ̃tjɛ̃, -jɛn], *a. & s.* Corinthian.

corme [kɔrm], *s.f. Hort:* Service-berry, -apple.

cormier [kɔrmje], *s.m.* Service-tree, -wood.

cormoran [kɔrmɔrɑ̃], *s.m. Orn:* Cormorant.

cornac [kɔrnak], *s.m.* Elephant-keeper; mahout.

cornage [kɔrnaːʒ], *s.m. Vet:* Wheezing, roaring, wind-sucking (of horse).

cornaline [kɔrnalin], *s.f. Lap:* Cornelian.

cornard [kɔrnaːr], *a. & s.m. Vet:* (Cheval) cornard, roarer, wheezer.

corne [kɔrn], *s.f.* **1.** (a) Horn. **Bêtes à longues cornes, à cornes courtes,** long-, short-horned beasts. **Montrer les cornes,** (i) (of ram) to show its horns; (ii) *F:* to show fight. **Mettre des cornes à un enfant,** to put a dunce's cap on a child. **Peigne de corne,** horn comb. **Corne à souliers,** shoe-horn. S.a. TAUREAU 1. (b) Horn, feeler (of snail); horn, antenna (of stag-beetle). *F:* **Rentrer les cornes,** to draw in one's horns. **2.** (a) *Aut:* **Corne d'appel,** horn. *Nau:* **Corne de brume,** fog-horn. (b) *Nau:* Peak (of gaff). *Le pavillon à la c.,* with the flag at the peak. (c) **Chapeau à cornes,** cocked hat. *C. d'un livre,* turned down corner, dog's-ear, of a book. **Faire une corne à une carte de visite,** to turn down the corner of a visiting card. **3.** Horny matter. *Cornes cutanées,* callosities. **4. Corne d'abondance,** cornucopia; horn of plenty.

corné [kɔrne], *a.* Corneous, horny.

cornée [kɔrne], *s.f. Anat:* Cornea. *C. opaque,* sclerotic, sclera.

corneille [kɔrnɛːj], *s.f. Orn:* Crow, rook. *C. noire,* carrion crow. *C. chauve,* rook. *C. d'église,* jackdaw. S.a. BAYER.

cornemuse [kɔrnəmyːz], *s.f. Mus:* Bagpipes. **Joueur de cornemuse,** piper.

corn|er [kɔrne], *v.tr.* **1.** (a) To trumpet, proclaim (sth.). *C. une nouvelle,* to trumpet news abroad. *F:* **Corner qch. aux oreilles de qn,** (i) to shout, (ii) to din, sth. into s.o.'s ears. (b) *Abs. Aut:* To sound the horn; to hoot. *Mus:* (Of organ note) To cipher. *Vet:* (Of horse) To roar, wheeze. (c) *Les oreilles me cornent,* my ears are ringing. **2.** To turn down the corner of (visiting-card, etc.). *Page cornée,* dog's-eared page. *s.m.* **-ement.**

cornet [kɔrnɛ], *s.m.* **1.** Small horn, trumpet. *Aut:* **Cornet avertisseur,** motor horn; hooter. *Mus:* **Cornet à pistons,** cornet. **2.** (a) *C. acoustique,* ear-trumpet. **Mettre sa main en cornet,** to cup one's hand behind one's ear. (b) Mouthpiece (of microphone). (c) *C. à dés,* dice-box. *C. de papier,* screw of paper.

cornette [kɔrnɛt], *s.f.* **1.** (a) (Woman's) mob-cap. (b) (Nun's winged) coif, cornet. **2.** *Nau:* Burgee. **3.** *s.m. A:* Cornet, ensign (of cavalry).

corniche [kɔrniʃ], s.f. **1.** Arch. Cornice. **2.** Ledge (of rock). (Route en) corniche, coast road.

cornichon [kɔrniʃɔ̃], s.m. **1.** Hort: Gherkin. **2.** P: Greenhorn, noodle.

cornier, -ière [kɔrnje, -jɛːr]. **1.** a. (At the) corner. Tuile cornière, corner-tile; valley tile. **2.** s.f. **Cornière.** (a) Const: Valley (joining roofs). (b) Angle-iron, -bar; corner-iron.

cornouaillais [kɔrnwajɛ], a. Cornish.

Cornouaille(s) [kɔrnwaːj]. Pr.n.f. Cornwall. La Pointe de Cornouaille, Cape Cornwall.

cornouille [kɔrnuːj], s.f. Bot: Cornel-berry.

cornouiller [kɔrnuje], s.m. **1.** Cornel(-tree). **2.** Com: Dogwood.

cornu [kɔrny], a. Horned.

cornue [kɔrny], s.f. **1.** (a) Ch: Gasm: Retort. Charbon de cornue, gas-carbon. (b) Metall: Steel converter. **2.** Bot: Water-caltrop.

Corogne (la) [lakɔrɔɲ]. Pr.n. Geog: Corunna.

corollaire [kɔrɔlɛːr], s.m. Log: Mth: Corollary.

corolle [kɔrɔl], s.f. Bot: Corolla.

coron [kɔrɔ̃], s.m. Dial: Mining village.

corossol [kɔrɔsɔl], s.m. Bot: Custard-apple.

corporat|if, -ive [kɔrpɔratif, -iːv], a. Corporate. adv. **-ivement.**

corporation [kɔrpɔrasjɔ̃], s.f. Corporation; public body. Com.Hist: (Trade-)guild.

corporel, -elle [kɔrpɔrɛl], a. Corporeal (substance, being); corporal (punishment); bodily (infirmity, etc.); tangible (property).

corps [kɔːr], s.m. **1.** Body. F: Avoir un corps de fer, to have an iron constitution. Mortifier son corps, to mortify the flesh. Jur: Saisir qn au corps, to arrest s.o. Passer sur le corps de, à, qn, (i) to run over s.o.; (ii) to ride s.o. down. Faire bon marché de son corps, not to value one's life, one's skin. F: Avoir le diable au corps, to be full of devilment. Prendre du corps, to put on flesh. Prendre corps, to take, assume, shape. Sans corps, bodiless, disembodied. Mil: Les gardes du corps, the body-guards, the life-guards. F: C'est un drôle de corps, he's a queer chap. Jur: Séparation de corps et de biens, separation from bed and board. Saisir qn à bras le corps, to seize s.o. round the waist; to grapple with s.o. Lutter corps à corps, to struggle hand to hand. Un corps-à-corps, a tussle; hand-to-hand fight(ing); Box: a clinch. S.a. DÉFENDRE 1, PERDU 3, SAIN. **2.** Corpse, body. La levée du corps aura lieu à onze heures, the funeral will start from the house at eleven o'clock. **3.** (a) Corps simple, simple body; element. Corps composé, compound. Astr: C. célestes, heavenly bodies. (b) Étoffe qui a du corps, strong material. Vin qui a du c., full-bodied wine. C. de la voix, range, volume, and quality of the voice. Voix qui manque de corps, thin voice. **4.** Main part (of sth.); trunk (of tree); frame (of bicycle); barrel (of pump). Dressm: Body, bodice (of dress). Faire corps avec qch., to be an integral part of sth. Nau: Perdu corps et biens, lost with all hands. Caserne en trois corps de bâtiment, barracks consisting of three main buildings. **5.** (a) (Organized body of men) Le c. diplomatique, the diplomatic corps. Venir en corps, to come in a body. Mil: Corps d'armée, army corps. S.a. BALLET, ESPRIT 5, MÉTIER 1. (b) Corpus; collection of writings. C. du droit civil, corpus of civil law.

corps-de-garde, s.m.inv. Mil: Guard-house, guard-room.

corps-mort, s.m. Nau: Dolphin, moorings. Prendre le c.-m., to make fast; to moor. pl. Des corps-morts.

corpulence [kɔrpylɑːs], s.f. Stoutness, corpulence.

corpulent [kɔrpylɑ̃], a. Stout, fat, corpulent.

corpuscule [kɔrpyskyl], s.m. Corpuscle.

correct [kɔr(r)ɛkt], a. Correct, proper (language, etc.); accurate (copy, etc.). adv. **-ement.**

correcteur, -trice [kɔr(r)ɛktœːr, -tris], s. Corrector. Typ: (Proof-)reader, press-corrector.

correction [kɔr(r)ɛksjɔ̃], s.f. **1.** Correction, correcting (of exercise); reading (of proofs). Sauf correction . . ., subject to correction . . .; under correction. . . . Nau: C. des compas, adjustment of the compasses. **2.** Reproof; punishment. Administrer, infliger, une correction à qn, (i) to rebuke, reprove, s.o.; (ii) to chastise s.o. Maison de correction, reformatory, penitentiary. **3.** Correctness (of dress, speech, etc.); propriety (of speech, conduct).

correctionnel, -elle [kɔr(r)ɛksjɔnɛl], a. Jur: Délit correctionnel, minor offence. Tribunal de police correctionnelle, court of summary jurisdiction.

corrélat|if, -ive [kɔr(r)elatif, -iːv], a. & s.m. Correlative. adv. **-ivement.**

corrélation [kɔr(r)elasjɔ̃], s.f. Correlation.

correspondance [kɔrɛspɔ̃dɑ̃ːs], s.f. **1.** Correspondence, agreement (between things, etc.). **2.** (a) Communication (between places). (b) Rail: Connection (between trains); interchange service. (Of train or boat) Faire correspondance avec . . ., to connect with. . . . Billet de correspondance, transfer ticket. **3.** (a) Intercourse, dealings (avec, with). (b) Correspondence (by letter). Être en correspondance avec qn, to correspond with s.o. Ouvrir la c., to open the mail, the post.

correspondant, -ante [kɔrɛspɔ̃dɑ̃, -ɑ̃ːt]. **1.** a. (a) Corresponding (à, to, with). (b) Rail: Train c., connection. (c) Corresponding (member of learned society). **2.** s. (a) Correspondent. (b) Sch: Friend acting in loco parentis.

correspondre [kɔrɛspɔ̃ːdr], v.i. **1.** To tally, agree (à, with); to correspond (à, to, with). La théorie ne correspond pas aux faits, the theory does not square with the facts. **2.** Deux pièces qui (se) correspondent, two rooms which communicate with one another. **3.** C. avec qn, to correspond (by letter) with s.o.

corridor [kɔridɔːr], s.m. Corridor, passage. Geog: Le Corridor Polonais, the Polish Corridor.

corriger [kɔriʒe], v.tr. (je corrigeai(s); n. corrigeons) **1.** To correct (exercise, etc.); to read (proofs); to sub-edit (article); to rectify (mistake, etc.). C. qn d'une mauvaise habitude, to cure, break, s.o. of a bad habit. **2.** (a) To chastise (dog, child). (b) To set (s.o.) right.

se corriger d'une habitude, to break oneself of a habit.

corrigé, s.m. Sch: **1.** Fair copy (of exercise, after correction). **2.** Key; F: crib.

corroboration [kɔr(r)ɔbɔrasjɔ̃], s.f. Corroboration, confirmation (of statement, etc.).

corroborer [kɔr(r)ɔbɔre], v.tr. To corroborate, confirm (statement, etc.).

corrodant [kɔr(r)ɔdɑ̃], a. & s.m. Corrodent, corrosive.

corroder [kɔr(r)ɔde], v.tr. To corrode, eat away.

se corroder, to corrode, become corroded.

corrompre [kɔr(r)ɔ̃ːpr], v.tr. (a) To corrupt (morals, etc.); to deprave, spoil (taste, etc.). C. les juges, to corrupt, bribe, the judges. Essayer *de c. un témoin*, to tamper with a witness. (b) *C. la viande*, to taint meat.

se corrompre. (a) To become corrupt(ed). (b) (Of meat, etc.) To taint; to become tainted.

corrompu, a. (a) Corrupt, depraved (person, morals); vitiated (taste). (b) Tainted, putrid (meat, etc.). (c) Corrupt (text).

corrosif, -ive [kɔrrozif, -iːv], a. & s.m. Corrosive.

corrosion [kɔrrozjɔ̃], s.f. Corrosion.

corroyer [kɔrwaje], v.tr. (je corroie; je corroierai) To curry (leather); to trim, rough-plane (wood); to puddle (clay); to weld (iron, steel) in the rolling-mill. *Acier corroyé*, welded steel, wrought steel. s.m. **-age.**

corroyeur [kɔrwajœːr], s.m. Currier.

corrupteur, -trice [kɔr(r)yptœːr, -tris]. I. s. Corrupter; suborner, briber (of witness, etc.). 2. a. Corrupt(ing) (influence, etc.).

corruptible [kɔr(r)yptibl], a. Corruptible; (of pers.) bribable.

corruption [kɔr(r)ypsjɔ̃], s.f. I. Corruption; suborning, bribing (of witnesses). 2. Tainting (of food, etc.); fouling (of air, etc.). 3. Corruption, corruptness, depravity (of morals, tastes).

corsage [kɔrsaːʒ], s.m. I. Bust (of woman). 2. Bodice, body (of dress).

corsaire [kɔrseːr], a. & s.m. I. Corsair (ship); privateer. 2. (a) Corsair, privateer(sman). (b) *Croquet:* (Balle) corsaire, rover.

corse¹ [kɔrs], a. & s. Corsican.

Corse² (la). Pr.n. Corsica.

corser [kɔrse], v.tr. To give body to (wine) (by adding spirits). *C. l'action d'un drame*, to intensify the action of a drama.

se corser, (of weather, business) to take a turn for the worse. *F: L'affaire se corse*, (i) the plot thickens; (ii) things are getting serious.

corsé, a. Full-bodied (wine, etc.); stout (cloth, etc.); strong, vigorous (attack). *Histoire corsée*, broad story.

corset [kɔrse], s.m. I. Corset, pair of corsets, (pair of) stays. 2. Corset de sauvetage, life-jacket.

corsetier, -ière [kɔrsətje, -jeːr], s. Corset-maker.

cortège [kɔrteːʒ], s.m. I. Train, retinue, suite (of sovereign, etc.). 2. Procession. Aller en cortège, to walk in procession. Cortège funèbre, funeral.

corvée [kɔrve], s.f. I. A: Forced labour, statute labour. 2. Mil: etc: (a) Fatigue (task, duty). Être de corvée, to be on fatigue (duty). Tenue de corvée, fatigue dress. (b) Fatigue party. 3. F: Irksome task; piece of drudgery.

coryphée [kɔrife], s.m. I. Gr.Drama: Coryphaeus. 2. (a) Th: Leader of the ballet. (b) F: Leader (of a party).

cosaque [kozak], s.m. Cossack.

cosinus [kosinyːs], s.m. Mth: Cosine.

cosmétique [kɔsmetik], a. & s.m. Cosmetic.

cosmique [kɔsmik], a. Cosmic(al).

cosmogonie [kɔsmɔgɔni], s.f. Cosmogony.

cosmographie [kɔsmɔgrafi], s.f. Cosmography.

cosmopolite [kɔsmɔpɔlit]. I. a. Cosmopolitan (life, etc.). 2. s. Cosmopolitan, cosmopolite.

cosse [kɔs], s.f. I. Pod, husk, hull (of leguminous plants). 2. (a) Nau: Thimble, eyelet (of rope). (b) El: Eye or spade terminal; (cable) lug. 3. P: Avoir la cosse, to feel lazy.

cossu [kɔsy], a. F: Wealthy, well-to-do; monied (person). adv. **-ûment.**

costaud, costeau [kɔsto], a. & s.m. P: Strapping, hefty (individual).

costume [kɔstym], s.m. Costume, dress. En grand costume, in full dress. Th: Répéter en

costume, to have a dress rehearsal. **Costume tailleur,** (lady's) tailor-made costume.

costumer [kɔstyme], v.tr. To dress (s.o.) (up). *Se c. en Turc*, to dress up as a Turk.

costumé, a. Bal costumé, fancy-dress ball.

costumier, -ière [kɔstymje, -jeːr], s. I. Costumier; dealer in (fancy) costumes. 2. Th: Wardrobe-keeper.

cote [kɔt], s.f. I. (a) Quota, share, proportion (of expense, taxes, etc.). Cote mal taillée, rough and ready compromise. (b) Adm: Assessment. 2. (a) Cotes d'une machine, dimension figures of a machine. (b) Surv: C. de niveau, bench-mark. (c) Surv: Height from datum line. 3. (a) Com: Jur: (Classification) mark, letter, number (of document, etc.). (b) Nau: Character, classification (of ship). De première cote (au Lloyd), A1 (at Lloyds). 4. (a) St.Exch: Com: Quotation. C. des prix, (i) share-list; (ii) Com: list of prices, price-current. F: (Of pers.) Être à la cote, to be in the public eye. (b) Turf: C. d'un cheval, odds on or against a horse. Forte c., faible c., long, short, odds or price. (c) Sch: Marks awarded (for exercise, etc.).

côte [koːt], s.f. I. Rib. F: Se tenir les côtes de rire, to hold one's sides with laughter. Eng.Hist: Côtes de fer, Ironsides. Cu: C. de bœuf, rib of beef. Côte à côte, side by side. Étoffe à côtes, ribbed, corded, material. 2. (a) Slope (of hill). Vitesse en côte, speed uphill. Sp: Course de côte, hill climb. (b) Hill. A mi-côte, half-way up the hill. 3. Coast, shore. Faire côte, to run ashore, aground. Jeter un navire à la côte, to run a ship ashore; to strand a ship. F: Être à la côte, to be on the rocks, on one's beam-ends.

côté [kote], s.m. I. Side. Assis à mes côtés, sitting by my side. Passer de l'autre côté de la rue, to cross the street. Demeurer de l'autre c. de la rue, to live across the street. Appartement côté midi, flat with southern aspect. Ten: Le choix du service ou du c., the choice of service or end. La tour penche d'un côté, the tower inclines on one side, leans sideways. Nau: Présenter le c. à qch., to be broadside on to sth. Navire sur le côté, ship on her beam-ends. S.a. VENT I. Le bon côté, le mauvais côté, d'une affaire, the good side, bad side or aspect, of a matter. Le vent vient du bon côté, the wind is in the right quarter. C'est son côté faible, that is his weak spot. D'un côté à l'autre, from side to side. D'un côté . . ., de l'autre côté . . ., on the one hand . . ., on the other hand. . . De mon côté . . ., for my part. . . De tous (les) côtés, on all sides; far and wide. Vous n'êtes jamais venu de nos côtés? you have never come our way? Courir de côté et d'autre, to run about in all directions. De quel côté est l'hôtel? whereabouts is the hotel? Se diriger du côté de Paris, to go in the direction of Paris. Se ranger d'un côté, to take sides. Venez de ce côté, come (i) this way, (ii) on this side. 2. Adv.phr. (a) De côté, on one side; sideways. Pas de côté, side-step. Regard de c., sidelong glance. Mettre qch. de côté, to put sth. aside, on one side. Mettre de l'argent de côté, to put, set, money by. Laisser de côté ses vêtements d'hiver, to discard, cast (off), one's winter clothing. Laisser qn de côté, to neglect s.o. (b) A côté, to one side; near. La maison est tout à c., the house is quite near, hard by. Tirer à côté, to miss the mark. Répondre à côté, to miss the point (in one's answer). Com: Articles à côté, side-lines. A côté de, by the side of; next to; beside. Il se tenait à c. de moi, he stood at my side; he stood beside me. A c. l'un de l'autre, side by side.

Il habite. à c. de nous, he lives next door to us. *Il n'est rien à c. de vous,* he can't compare with you; *F:* he can't hold a candle to you. **coteau** [kɔto], *s.m.* **1.** Slope, hillside. *C. boisé,* hanger. **2.** (Small) hill.

côtelé [kotle], *a. Tex:* Ribbed, corduroy (velvet); corded (material).

côtelette [kotlɛt], *s.f.* (Mutton) cutlet; (mutton or pork) chop. *C. de veau,* veal cutlet.

coter [kɔte], *v.tr.* **1.** To assess. **2.** *Mec.E: Surv: etc:* To dimension (drawing, etc.); to put down references on (maps, etc.). *Croquis coté,* dimensioned sketch. **Point coté,** reference point, landmark (on map, etc.). **3.** (*a*) To classify, number (documents,etc.). (*b*) To class (ship). **4.** (*a*) *Com: St.Exch:* To quote (shares, etc.). (*b*) **Cheval très coté,** well-backed horse. **5.** *Sch:* To award marks for (exercise, etc.).

coterie [kɔtri], *s.f.* (Political, literary) set, coterie.

côtier, -ière [kotje, -jɛːr]. **1.** *a.* (*a*) Coast(ing) (pilot, etc.); coastal (defence, etc.); coastwise (trade, etc.); inshore (fishery). *Navigation côtière,* coasting. (*b*) *Chemin côtier,* hill road. **2.** *s.m.* Coaster; coasting vessel.

cotignac [kɔtiɲak], *s.m.* Quince marmalade.

cotillon [kɔtijɔ̃], *s.m.* **1.** *A:* Petticoat. **2.** *Danc:* (*a*) Cotill(i)on. *Coiffure de c.,* paper cap. (*b*) Souvenir (given away at public dance).

cotisation [kɔtizazjɔ̃], *s.f.* **1.** Clubbing together (to raise a sum). **2.** Assessment (of taxpayer). **3.** Quota, share; contribution (to common fund); subscription (to club, etc.). *C. d'admission,* entrance fee.

cotiser [kɔtize], *v.tr. Adm: C. qn à tant,* to assess s.o. at so much.

se cotiser, to subscribe, to club together (to raise sum); to get up a subscription.

cotissure [kɔtisyːr], *s.f.* Bruise (on fruit).

coton [kɔtɔ̃], *s.m.* **1.** Cotton. **Fil de coton,** sewing cotton. *C. retors,* cotton thread. **Coton azotique,** fulminant, gun-cotton. *F:* Filer un mauvais coton, to be in a bad way (in health or business). **2.** (*a*) Cotton-wool. *Med:* Coton hydrophile, absorbent cotton-wool. (*b*) Down (on plants). (*c*) Fluff (on cloth, etc.).

cotonnade [kɔtɔnad], *s.f.* (*a*) Cotton fabric. (*b*) *pl.* Cotton goods.

cotonner [kɔtɔne]. **1.** *v.tr.* To wad; to pad (with cotton-wool). **2.** *v.i. & pr.* (*a*) *Fruit qui se cotonne,* fruit that (i) becomes covered with down, (ii) becomes woolly, sleepy. *Poire cotonnée,* sleepy pear. (*b*) (Of material) To become fluffy.

cotonnerie [kɔtɔnri], *s.f.* Cotton-plantation.

cotonneux, -euse [kɔtɔnø, -øːz], *a.* Cottony; downy (leaf, etc.); fleecy (cloud); sleepy (pear).

cotonnier, -ière [kɔtɔnje, -jɛːr]. **1.** *s.* Cotton worker. **2.** *s.m.* Cotton plant.

coton-poudre, *s.m.* Gun-cotton.

côtoyer [kotwaje], *v.tr.* (je côtoie; je côtoierai) **1.** To coast along, keep close to, hug (shore, etc.); to skirt (forest). **2.** To border on (river). [CÔTE]

cotre [kɔtr], *s.m. Nau:* Cutter.

cotret [kɔtrɛ], *s.m.* (*a*) Faggot, bundle (of wood). (*b*) Stick (of faggot). **Sec comme un cotret,** as thin as a lath.

cotte [kɔt], *s.f.* (*a*) *Archeol:* Cotte d'armes, (i) tunic (worn over armour); (ii) coat of banded mail. **Cotte de mailles,** coat of mail. (*b*) Short skirt; petticoat.

Cottiennes [kɔtjɛn], *a.f.pl.* Cottian (Alps).

cotutelle [kɔtytɛl], *s.f. Jur:* Joint guardianship.

cotuteur, -trice [kɔtytœːr, -tris], *s. Jur:* Joint guardian.

cou [ku], *s.m.* Neck (of animal, bottle, etc.). **La peau du cou,** the scruff of the neck. **Couper le cou à qn,** to behead s.o. **Tendre le cou,** (i) to lay one's head on the block; (ii) to crane one's neck (in order to see). **Serrer le cou à qn,** (i) to strangle s.o.; (ii) *F:* to wring s.o.'s neck. *F:* **Être dans les dettes jusqu'au cou,** to be up to the eyes in debt. **Prendre ses jambes à son cou,** to take to one's heels.

couac [kwak], *s.m. Mus:* Squawk, goose-note.

couard [kwaːr]. **1.** *a.* Cowardly, craven. **2.** *s.m.* Coward, poltroon.

couardise [kwardiːz], *s.f.* Cowardice, cowardliness, cravenness.

cou-blanc, *s.m. Orn: F:* Wheatear. *pl. Des cous-blancs.*

couchage [kuʃaːʒ], *s.m.* **1.** (Matériel de) **couchage,** bedding; bed-clothes. **Sac de couchage,** sleeping-bag. **2.** Layering (of plants). **3.** Coating (of paper).

couchant [kuʃɑ̃]. **1.** *a.* (*a*) **Soleil couchant,** setting sun. (*b*) *A:* **Chien couchant,** setter. *F:* **Faire le chien couchant auprès de qn,** to fawn on s.o. **2.** *s.m.* (*a*) Sunset. *F:* **Être à son couchant,** (i) (of fame, etc.) to be on the decline, on the wane; (ii) (of pers.) to be nearing the end of one's life. (*b*) **Le couchant,** the west.

couche [kuʃ], *s.f.* **1.** (*a*) *Lit:* Bed, couch. (*b*) Child-bed, confinement. **Faire ses couches,** to be confined; to lie in. **Fausse couche,** miscarriage. (*c*) **Couche de bébé,** baby's (hip-) napkin. **2.** (*a*) Bed, layer, stratum (of ore, sand, etc.). *C. de houille,* coal-bed, -seam. *Hort: C. de fumier,* hotbed. *S.a.* CHAMPIGNON 1. *F: Couches sociales,* social strata; classes of society. (*b*) Coat, coating (of paint, etc.). *Première c., c. d'impression,* priming; ground coat. *C. de glace,* sheet of ice. *P:* **Il en a une couche!** did you ever see such a fool! **3.** *Mec.E:* **Arbre de couche,** main shaft.

coucher [kuʃe]. **I.** *v.* **1.** *v.tr.* (*a*) To put (child, etc.) to bed. (*b*) **Être couché et nourri chez qn,** to get board and lodging with s.o. (*c*) To lay (s.o., sth., down horizontally). *La pluie a couché les blés,* the rain has laid the corn. **Coucher un fusil en joue,** to aim a gun. *C. qn en joue,* to take aim at s.o. *C. un blessé par terre,* to lay down a wounded man. *F:* **Coucher son homme par terre,** to lay one's man out. (*d*) To lay, spread (colour on surface); to coat (paper). (*e*) **Coucher qch. par écrit,** to set, put, sth. down in writing. **Coucher qn sur son testament,** to mention s.o. in one's will. **2.** *v.i. C. à l'hôtel, chez un voisin,* to sleep, have a bedroom, at the hotel, at a neighbour's. (To dog) **Coucher!** lie down!

se coucher. (*a*) To go to bed; to retire. *Il est l'heure d'aller se c.,* it is bedtime. **Envoyer coucher les enfants,** *F:* to pack the children off to bed. *Prov:* **Comme on fait son lit on se couche,** as we make our bed so must we lie. (*b*) To lie down. *Se c. de tout son long,* to lie down at full length. (*c*) *Nau:* (Of ship) *Se c. sur le flanc,* to heel over. (*d*) (Of sun, stars) To set, go down. *Nous avons vu c. le soleil,* we saw the sun set. *Le soleil est couché,* the sun is down.

couché, *a.* Lying, recumbent (position). **Être couché,** to be in bed; to have gone to bed.

II. coucher, *s.m.* **1.** (*a*) L'heure du coucher, bedtime. (*b*) Night's lodging. **Le coucher et la nourriture,** board and lodging. (*c*) Bed(ding). **2.** Setting (of sun, star). **Au coucher du soleil,** at sunset, at sundown.

couchette [kuʃɛt], *s.f.* **1.** (Child's) cot, crib. **2.** Berth (on ship, train). *Rail:* **Wagon à couchettes,** sleeper.

coucheur, -euse [kuʃœːr, -øːz], s. Bedfellow. *Esp. F:* Mauvais coucheur, quarrelsome fellow.

couci-couça [kusikusa], adv. *F:* So so.

coucou [kuku], s.m. **1.** (a) *Orn:* Cuckoo. (b) int. Coucou! (i) cuckoo! (ii) peep-bo! (c) Cuckoo-clock. **2.** *Bot:* (a) Cowslip. (b) Daffodil. (c) Ragged robin. (d) White clover, Dutch clover.

coude [kud], s.m. **1.** Elbow. Coude à coude, side by side. Coup de coude, (i) poke with the elbow; (ii) nudge. Donner un coup de coude à qn, to nudge, jog, s.o. Jouer des coudes à travers la foule, to elbow one's way through the crowd. Se sentir les coudes, (i) *Mil:* to touch elbows; (ii) *F:* to support one another. **2.** Bend, elbow (of road, river, etc.); knee (of pipe); crank (of shaft). Arbre à deux coudes, two-throw crank-shaft.

coudée [kude], s.f. **1.** *A:* Cubit. **2.** pl. Avoir ses coudées franches, (i) to have elbow-room; (ii) to have a free hand.

cou-de-pied, s.m. Instep. pl. Des cous-de-pied.

couder [kude], v.tr. To bend (pipe, etc.); to crank (shaft, etc.).

coud|oyer [kudwaje], v.tr. (je coudoie; je coudoierai) (a) To elbow (s.o.). (b) To rub shoulders, rub elbows, with (s.o.). s.m. **-oiement.**

coudre [kudr], v.tr. (pr.p. cousant; p.p. cousu; pr.ind. je couds, il coud, n. cousons, ils cousent; p.d. je cousais; p.h. je cousis; fu. je coudrai) To sew, stitch. Machine à coudre, sewing-machine. C. une plaie, to sew up a wound.

cousu, a. Sewn. Cousu à la main, hand-sewn, -stitched. *F:* Avoir la bouche cousue, to keep one's mouth shut tight. Visage cousu de petite vérole, face pitted with smallpox. *F:* Être cousu d'or, to be rolling in wealth.

coudrier [kudrie], s.m. Hazel(-tree).

couenne [kwan], s.f. **1.** (a) (Thick) skin (of pig, porpoise). (b) Rind (of bacon); crackling (of roast pork). **2.** (Diphtheric) membrane.

couette [kwɛt], s.f. (Hare's, rabbit's) scut.

couguar [kuga:r, -gwa-], s.m. *Z:* Cougar, puma.

couic [kwik], s.m. Chirp, cheep (of young bird); squeak (of mouse). *P:* Faire couic, to die.

coulage [kula:ʒ], s.m. **1.** Pouring (of molten metal, glass, soap, etc.); casting. **2.** Leaking, leakage (of liquid). *F:* Maison où il y a beaucoup de c., house where there is much waste. **3.** Sinking, scuttling (of ship).

coulant [kulɑ̃]. **1.** a. Running, flowing (liquid). Nœud c., slip-knot; noose. Style c., easy, flowing, style. Homme coulant en affaires, accommodating man. **2.** s.m. (a) Sliding ring; scarf-ring. (b) Draw-tube, sliding tube (of microscope, etc.). (c) *Hort:* Runner (of plant).

couler [kule]. **1.** v.tr. (a) To run, pour (liquid). C. du plomb dans un joint, to run lead into a joint. C. du lait (à travers un linge), to strain milk (through a cloth). C. une statue, to cast a statue. (b) Couler (à fond) un navire, to sink a ship; (i) to send a ship to the bottom; (ii) to scuttle a ship. (c) C. une pièce dans la main de, à, qn, to slip a coin into s.o.'s hand. *Mus:* C. un passage, to slur a passage. (d) C. une vie heureuse, to lead, spend, a happy life. *P:* Se la couler douce, to take life easily. **2.** v.i. (a) (Of liquids) To flow, run. Faire couler l'eau, to turn the water on. La sueur coule sur son front, sweat trickles, runs, down his forehead. Sentiment qui coule de source, feeling that comes from the bottom of one's heart. (b) (Of barrel, etc.) To leak; (of candle) to gutter; (of nose) to run. (c) (Of ship) Couler au fond, couler bas, to sink; to founder.

(d) (Of knot) To slip. Couler sur un fait, to pass over, touch lightly on, a fact.

se couler. 1. To glide, slip. Se c. dans un trou, to creep into a hole. Se c. entre les draps, to slip into bed. Se laisser couler le long d'une corde, to slide down a rope. **2.** To ruin, *F:* do for, oneself (esp. through some scandal).

coulé. 1. a. (a) Cast (metal). Pièce coulée, casting. (b) *F:* C'est un homme coulé, he's done for (socially). **2.** s.m. *Mus:* (i) Slide, coulé. (ii) Legato. (iii) Slur.

coulée, s.f. **1.** Running, flow(ing) (of liquid); outflow (of lava). *F:* Coulée de soleil, streak of sunshine. **2.** Casting or tapping (of molten metal). Trou de coulée, tap(ping)-hole, draw-hole. Venu de coulée avec . . ., cast in one piece with. . . . **3.** (Écriture) coulée, running hand.

couleur [kulœːr], s.f. Colour. **1.** (a) Tint, hue. Personne de couleur, coloured person. Photographie en couleurs, colour photography. Couleur locale, local colour. Sous couleur d'amitié, under colour of friendship. *F:* En avoir vu de toutes les couleurs, to have had all sorts of experiences. Prendre couleur, to take, assume, colour. a.inv. Couleur de paille (etc.), straw (etc.)-coloured. *F:* Tout voir couleur de rose, to see everything through rose-coloured spectacles. (b) Complexion. Perdre ses couleurs, to become pale; to lose one's colour. Être haut en couleur, to have a high colour, a ruddy complexion. (c) pl. *Nau:* Colours, flag. Envoyer, hisser, les couleurs, to hoist one's colours. Amener, rentrer, les couleurs, to haul down, strike, the colours. **2.** Colour, paint. C. à l'huile, oil-colour, oil-paint. "Attention à la couleur!" 'wet paint.' Boîte de couleurs, box of paints; paint-box. Mettre qch. en couleur, to colour, stain, sth. Marchand de couleurs, chandler; drysalter. **3.** *Cards:* Suit. Donner de la couleur, to follow suit.

couleuvre [kulœːvr], s.f. Snake. *F:* Avaler une couleuvre, to pocket an affront or a reproof.

coulis[1] [kuli], a.m. Vent coulis, draught (through crevice, etc.). [COULER]

coulis[2], s.m. **1.** *Const:* Grout(ing); filling. **2.** *Cu:* (a) (Meat) jelly. (b) (Tomato, etc.) sauce.

coulissant [kulisɑ̃], a. Sliding (spindle, bench, electrical contact, etc.).

coulisse [kulis], s.f. **1.** (a) Groove, slot. Fenêtre, porte, à coulisse, sliding window, door. *Tls:* Pied à coulisse, slide calipers. *F:* Regard en coulisse, sidelong glance. (b) Slide. Trombone à coulisse, slide-trombone. **2.** *Needlew:* Hem (through which to pass tape). **3.** (a) *Th:* (Scenery) flat. Les coulisses, the wings, the slips. Argot de la coulisse, stage slang. *F:* Être dans la coulisse, to be pulling the strings. (b) *St.Exch:* La Coulisse, the outside market.

coulisseau [kuliso], s.m. (a) Slide (of piece of machinery). (b) Block (sliding in guides). (c) Runner (of drawer, etc.).

coulissier [kulisje], s.m. *St.Exch:* Outside broker.

couloir [kulwa:r], s.m. **1.** Strainer. **2.** Corridor, passage(-way). *Rail:* Wagon à couloir, corridor carriage. *Parl:* Couloirs de la Chambre = lobby of the House. Le Couloir de Dantzig, the Polish Corridor. **3.** Channel, gully (for water); mountain gorge. [COULER]

coup [ku], s.m. **1.** (a) Knock, blow; rap (on the door). Un petit c. discret à la porte, a tap at the door. Coup de coude, (i) poke with the elbow; (ii) nudge. Coup de tête, butt. (S.a. 4 (a).) C. de bec, peck. Coup de bâton, blow, whack (with a stick). C. sur les doigts, rap over the knuckles. Coup de couteau, de poignard, stab. Coup de sabre, (i) slash, cut (with a sword); (ii) sword wound. Coup d'épée, thrust, lunge. Coup de baïonnette, bayonet-thrust. Porter un coup à qn, to aim, strike, a blow at s.o. Porter coup, to hit home. Cela m'en a donné un coup! it gave me such a shock! Tenir le coup, (i) to withstand the blow, the shock; (ii) to hold out, F: to stick it. En venir aux coups, to come to blows. Faire d'une pierre deux coups, to kill two birds with one stone. Jur: Coups et blessures, assault and battery. Prep.phr. A coups de, with blows from (sth.). Abattre un arbre à coups de cognée, to fell a tree with an axe. Faire une traduction à coups de dictionnaire, to look up every word in the dictionary in translating a passage. S.a. CISEAU 2, ÉPÉE 1, FOUET 1, GRÂCE 3, JARNAC, MAIN 1, MARTEAU 1, ONGLE, PATTE 1, PIED 1, POING, TAMPON 5. (b) Coup de feu, shot. S.a. FEU¹ II. Coup de fusil, (i) (gun-, rifle-)shot; (ii) report (of a gun). Fusil à un coup, à deux coups, single-, double-barrelled gun. Il fut tué d'un c. de fusil, he was shot (dead). Coup de grisou, fire-damp explosion. S.a. DIANE¹, DOUBLE 1, FOUDRE¹ 1, FUSIL 3, MINE¹ 1, RETRAITE 2. (c) Coup de vent, (i) puff, gust, of wind; (ii) squall. F: Entrer dans la chambre en coup de vent, to burst into the room. Embarquer un coup de mer, to ship a green sea. Coup de roulis, roll. Coup de froid, (i) cold snap; (ii) Med: chill, cold. Coup de sang, apoplectic fit; F: stroke. S.a. LANGUE 1, SOLEIL 2. 2. Stroke (normal action of sth.). (a) Coup d'aile, stroke, flap, of the wing. Coup de dents, bite. Coup de queue, flick of the tail. Boire qch. à petits coups, to sip sth. Coup de baguette, wave, touch, of the wand. Coup de crayon, de plume, pencil-stroke; stroke of the pen. Saluer qn d'un coup de chapeau, to raise one's hat to s.o. Coup de cloche, stroke of the bell. Sur le c. de midi, on the stroke of twelve. Coup de filet, (i) cast, (ii) haul (of a net); draught (of fishes). S.a. BROSSE 1, MANQUER II. 1, ŒIL 2. (b) Games: (i) Stroke, hit, drive. Ten: C. droit, forearm stroke. (ii) Golf: Shot, stroke. C. roulé, putt. Concours par coups, stroke-play, medal-play. (iii) Fb: Kick. C. d'envoi, kick-off. (iv) Bill: Stroke, shot. Faux coup de queue, miscue. (v) Cards: Finir le coup, to finish the hand. (vi) Chess: etc: Move. S.a. DÉ¹ 1. (c) C. de bonheur, stroke of luck; piece of good fortune. C. d'audace, bold stroke. C. d'éclat, distinguished action. S.a. HASARD 1, THÉÂTRE 3, VEINE 2. (d) Clap, peal (of thunder); blast (of a whistle). C. de sonnette, ring, peal, of the bell. C. de téléphone, telephone call. 3. Influence, power; instancy, threat. Agir sous le c. de la peur, to act out of fear. Répondre sous le c. de la colère, to answer in a fit of temper. Tomber sous le c. de la loi, (i) to come within the provisions of, (ii) to fall foul of, the law. Être sous le c. d'une terrible accusation, to lie under a terrible accusation. 4. (a) Attempt; deed (often evil deed). Essayer un c., to have a try, F: a go (at it). Coup de tête, impulsive act. Faire qch. par coup de tête, to act impulsively. Il médite un mauvais c., he's up to mischief. F: Un sale coup, a dirty trick. S.a. MONTÉ 3, MONTER II.4, VALOIR. (b) F: Avoir le coup pour faire qch., to have the knack of doing sth. (c) Tout d'un coup, d'un seul coup, at one go. Faire qch. du premier coup, to do sth. at the first attempt or shot. Du coup, (i) now at last; (ii) this time, in this emergency. Du c. je

comprends, now at last I understand. Il fut tué sur le coup, he was killed outright, on the spot. Pour le coup, (i) for the moment; (ii) this time. Après coup, after the event. Réflexion après c., afterthought. Tout à coup, suddenly; all of a sudden. Coup sur coup, in rapid succession. Encore un coup . . ., once again. . . . 5. Fish: (Baited) pitch. Pêche au coup, ground-bait fishing.

coupable [kupabl]. 1. a. (a) Guilty (person). C. de vol, guilty of theft. C. envers Dieu, guilty of an offence against God. Jur: S'avouer coupable, to plead guilty. (b) Culpable (act); sinful (pleasures); unpardonable (weakness). 2. s. Culprit. Jur: Delinquent. adv. -ment.

coupant [kupã]. 1. a. Cutting, sharp. Outils coupants, edge-tools. 2. s.m. (Cutting) edge.

coup-de-poing, s.m. 1. (a) Pocket revolver. (b) C.-de-p. américain, knuckle-duster. 2. Hand oiler. pl. Des coups-de-poing.

coupe¹ [kup], s.f. Cup. (a) C. à champagne, champagne glass. F: Ma c. déborde, my cup runs over. Boire la coupe jusqu'à la lie, to drink the cup to the dregs. (b) Sp: (Gold or silver) cup.

coupe², s.f. 1. (a) Cutting (of hay, etc.); cutting out (of garment). C. de cheveux, hair-cut. Mettre un bois en coupe réglée, to make periodical cuttings in a wood. F: Mettre qn en c. réglée, to batten on, exploit, s.o. Coupe sombre, (i) slight thinning (of forest area); (ii) F: drastic cut (in personnel, estimates). (b) Cut (of a coat). C. d'un vers, division in a line of verse. (c) Section. C. transversale, cross-section. Figurer une machine en coupe, to show a machine in section. 2. Cards: Cut, cutting. (a) Être sous la coupe de qn, (i) to lead after one's opponent has cut; (ii) F: to be under s.o.'s thumb. (b) (Card tricks) Faire sauter la coupe, to make the pass. 3. Swim: Coupe indienne, overhand stroke; overarm stroke. [COUPER]

coupe-cigares, s.m.inv. Cigar-cutter.

coupe-circuit, s.m.inv. El.E: Cut-out, circuit-breaker. C.-c. à fusible, fuse.

coupée [kupe], s.f. Nau: Gangway (opening or port); gang-port. Échelle de coupée, accommodation ladder.

coupe-fil [kupfil], s.m.inv. Tls: Wire-cutters.

coupe-file, s.m.inv. (Police) pass.

coupe-gorge, s.m.inv. Cut-throat place; thieves' alley; death-trap.

coupe-jarret, s.m. (Hamstringer, hence) Cut-throat, ruffian. pl. Des coupe-jarrets.

coupe-légumes, s.m. Tls: Vegetable cutter.

coupé-lit, s.m. Rail: Sleeping compartment. pl. Des coupés-lits.

coupelle [kupel], s.f. Cupel, test. Passer de l'or à la coupelle, to assay, test, gold.

coupeller [kupelle], v.tr. To cupel, assay (gold).

coupement [kupmã], s.m. 1. Saw-cut. 2. Rail: Diamond crossing.

coupe-ongles, s.m.inv. Nail-clippers.

coupe-paille, s.m.inv. Chaff-cutter.

coupe-pain, s.m.inv. Bread-slicer.

coupe-papier, s.m.inv. Paper-knife.

coup|er [kupe], v.tr. To cut. 1. C. en morceaux, to cut up (meat). Se c. le doigt, au doigt, to cut one's finger. C. un arbre, to cut down a tree. C. la tête à qn, to cut off s.o.'s head. F: Couper bras et jambes à qn, to leave s.o. helpless. Couper dans le vif, (i) to cut to the quick; (ii) F: to take extreme measures. S.a. RACINE 1. C. les cheveux à qn, to cut, clip, s.o.'s hair. C. un vêtement, to cut out a garment. Cards: Couper

les cartes, to cut. *P: Je n'y coupe pas!* I'm not to be had! **2.** *(a)* To cut, cross, intersect. *v.i. C. à travers champs,* to cut across country. **Couper au plus court,** to take a short cut. *(b) Aut:* **Couper la route à qn,** to cut in. **3.** To cut off, interrupt, stop. *(a)* **Couper le chemin à qn,** to cut s.o. off. **Couper les vivres à l'ennemi,** to cut off the enemy's supplies. **Couper la faim, l'appétit, à qn,** to take s.o.'s appetite away. **Couper la parole à qn,** *F:* **couper qn,** to interrupt s.o.; to cut s.o. short. **Couper la communication,** to ring off. *Ne (me) coupez pas!* don't cut me off! hold the line! **Couper la respiration à qn,** to take s.o.'s breath away. *(b)* To turn off, cut off (the water); to shut off (the steam). *El: C. le courant,* to switch off the current. *(c) Cards:* To trump (opponent's card). **4.** *C. du vin,* (i) to blend wine; (ii) to water down wine. *s.m.* **-age.**
se couper. 1. (Of skin, etc.) To crack. **2.** (Of lines, roads, etc.) To intersect. **3.** To contradict oneself; to give oneself away.
coupé. 1. *a.* *(a)* Cut up, broken up; broken (sleep); jerky (style). *(b) Vin c. d'eau,* wine and water. *(c) Ten:* **Coup coupé,** drive with a cut. **2.** *s.m. Veh:* Brougham. *Aut:* Coupé.
couperet [kupre], *s.m.* **1.** (Meat) chopper; cleaver. **2.** Blade, knife (of the guillotine).
couperose [kupro:z], *s.f.* **1.** *C. verte,* green vitriol. *C. bleue,* blue vitriol. **2.** *Med:* Acne.
couperosé [kuproze], *a.* Blotchy (complexion).
coupeur, -euse [kupœ:r, -ø:z], *s.* *(a) Tail:* Cutter. *(b) C. de bourses,* pickpocket.
coupe-verre, *s.m.inv. Tls:* Glass-cutter.
couple [kupl]. **1.** *s.m.* *(a)* Pair, couple. *C. d'époux,* married couple. *C. de pigeons,* pair of pigeons (cock and hen). *(b) Mec:* **Couple (moteur),** couple (of forces); torque. *C. de démarrage,* starting torque. *(c) N.Arch:* Frame, timber. **2.** *s.f.* *(a)* Two, couple. *C. de pigeons,* brace of pigeons. *C. de bœufs,* yoke of oxen. **Avirons à couple,** double-sculls. **Nager à, en, couple,** to double-scull. *(b)* Leash (for dogs).
coupler [kuple], *v.tr.* To couple. *El:* To join up, connect (cells). *s.m.* **-age.**
couplet [kuplɛ], *s.m.* *(a)* Verse (of song). *(b) Th: F:* Tirade.
coupoir [kupwa:r], *s.m. Tls:* Cutter.
coupole [kupol], *s.f.* Cupola.
coupon [kupɔ̃], *s.m.* **1.** Portion cut off; cutting. *Coupons d'étoffe,* remnants; oddments. **2.** *(a) Fin:* Coupon. *C. de dividende,* dividend-warrant. *(b) Rail: Th:* (Part of) ticket. *C. de retour,* return half (of ticket). *Post:* **Coupon-réponse international,** international reply coupon.
coupure [kupy:r], *s.f.* **1.** *(a)* Cut, gash (on finger, etc.). *(b)* Cut(ting), drain (through marsh, etc.). **2.** *(a)* Piece cut out. *C. de journal,* newspaper cutting. *(b)* Cut, excision (in play, document). **3.** *(a)* Paper money (of small denominations). *(b) Fin:* Fractional share.
cour [ku:r], *s.f.* **1.** Court (of prince). *(a)* **A la cour,** at court. **Gens de cour,** courtiers. *F:* **Être bien, mal, en cour,** to be in favour, out of favour. *(b)* **Faire sa cour au roi,** to pay one's court to the king. **Faire la cour à une jeune fille,** to court, woo, a young lady. **2.** *C. de justice,* court of justice. **Mettre qn hors de cour,** to dismiss s.o.'s case; **to nonsuit s.o. 3.** Court, yard, courtyard. *C. d'école,* school playground. *Mil:* *C. de quartier,* barrack square.
courage [kura:3], *s.m.* Courage, valour; *F:* pluck. **Perdre courage,** to lose courage, heart. **Prendre courage,** to take courage, to take heart. **Relever le courage de qn,** to put new heart into

s.o. **Avoir bon courage,** to be of good heart. *Du courage!* courage! cheer up! bear up! **Rendre courage à qn,** to cheer s.o. up. **Une nation sans courage,** a spiritless nation. *Déployer tout son c.,* to put forth all one's courage.
courageu|x, -euse [kura3ø, -ø:z], *a.* **1.** Courageous, brave, *F:* plucky. **2.** Zealous, spirited. *Être c. au travail,* to stand up to one's work; to be a plodder. *adv.* **-sement.**
couramment [kuramɑ̃], *adv.* **1.** Easily, readily; (to read, speak) fluently. **2.** Generally, usually, currently. *C. employé,* in current use.
courant, -ante [kurɑ̃, -ɑ̃:t]. **1.** *a.* *(a)* Running. **Chien courant,** hound. (Écriture) **courante,** running, cursive, (hand)writing. *Mill:* (Meule) **courante,** running millstone; runner. *(b)* (Of measurements) Linear, running. *Prix par pied c.,* price per foot run. *(c)* Flowing. **Chambre avec eau courante,** bedroom with running water. *(d)* Current (account, etc.). **Le mois courant,** the present, current, month. **Le cinq courant,** the fifth inst. **Fin courant,** at the end of this month. *Mot d'usage c.,* word in current, general, use. **Prix courant,** price-list. *De taille courante,* of standard size. **2.** *s.m.* *(a)* Current, stream. *Suivre le c.,* to drift along. *C. de fond,* under-current (in lake, etc.). *C. sous-marin,* under-current (in sea); undertow. **Courant d'air,** draught. *F:* *Secret c.* de mécontentement, undercurrent of discontent. **Courant électrique,** electric current. **Fil hors courant,** dead wire. *(b)* Course. **Dans le courant de l'année,** in the course of the year. *C. des affaires,* course of events. **Être au courant de l'affaire,** to know all about the matter. *Quand vous serez au c.,* when you have got into the swing, into the way (of things). **Mettre qn au courant des faits,** to acquaint s.o. with the facts. *Mettre le grand-livre au c.,* to write up, post up, the ledger.
courbature [kurbaty:r], *s.f.* **1.** Stiffness, tiredness. *Avoir une c.,* to be aching all over, stiff all over. **2.** *Vet:* Founder.
courbaturer [kurbatyre], *v.tr.* **1.** To tire (s.o.) out; to knock (s.o.) up. *Courbaturé,* aching all over. **2.** To founder (horse).
courbe [kurb]. **1.** *a.* Curved. **2.** *s.f.* *(a)* Curve; sweep (of road, etc.). *(b)* Curve, graph. *C. de niveau,* contour-line.
courb|er [kurbe]. **1.** *v.tr.* To bend, curve. *Courber en deux,* to bend double. *Courbé par l'âge,* bowed with age. *C. le front, la tête,* to bow one's head. S.a. ÉCHINE 1, JOUG 1. **2.** *v.i.* To bend; to sag. *s.m.* **-ement.**
se courber, to bend, stoop. *Se c. devant qn,* to bow, *F:* ko(w)tow, to s.o.
courbette [kurbɛt], *s.f. Equit:* Curvet. *F:* **Faire des courbettes à qn,** to bow and scrape, to ko(w)tow, to s.o.
courbure [kurby:r], *s.f.* Curvature (of the earth); bend, curve (of piece of wood, etc.); camber (of road); sagging (of beam). *C. double,* S curve.
courette [kurɛt], *s.f.* Small (court)yard, small court.
coureur, -euse [kurœ:r, -ø:z], *s.* **1.** Runner; racer (on bicycle, etc.). *Sp: C. de fond,* long-distance runner stayer. *C. de vitesse,* sprinter. **2.** *(a)* Wanderer, rover. *C. de routes,* tramp, vagabond. *(b)* Gadabout. *C. de spectacles,* play-goer. *C. de cabarets, P:* pub-crawler. *(c) C. d'aventures,* seeker of adventures; adventurer. *C. de dots,* fortune-hunter.
courge [kur3], *s.f. Bot:* Gourd. *C. à la moelle, c. aubergine,* vegetable marrow.
courir [kuri:r], *v.* (*pr.p.* **courant;** *p.p.* **couru;**

pr.ind. je **cours**, n. **courons**; *p.h.* je **courus**;
fu. je **courrai**. The aux. is *avoir*) **I.** *v.i.*
To run. (*a*) *C. après qn*, to run after s.o. *J'ai
couru le prévenir*, I ran to warn him. *J'y cours*,
I'm going directly. **Monter, descendre, la colline
en courant**, to run up, down, the hill. *Arriver en
courant*, to come running up. *F:* **Elle est
toujours à courir**, she is always gadding about.
S.a. BASQUE[1], PRESSÉ 2. (*b*) *Sp:* **Turf:** To race;
to run (in a race). **Faire courir**, to keep a racing
stable. (*c*) (Of ship) To sail. *C. au large*, to stand
out to sea. *C. devant le vent*, to run, scud, before
the wind. (*d*) To be current. *Le bruit court
que . . .*, there is a report abroad that. . . .
Faire c. un bruit, to spread (abroad) a report.
Impers. *Il court des bruits*, rumours are afloat.
La mode qui court, the present, prevailing, fashion.
Par le temps qui court, nowadays; as things are
at present. *Le bail n'a plus qu'un an à c.*, the
lease has only one year to run. (*e*) *Le sang court
dans les artères*, the blood flows through the ar-
teries. **2.** *v.tr.* (*a*) To run after (sth.); to hunt,
pursue, chase (animal). (*b*) *C. un risque*, to run
a risk. *C. la chance de qch., de faire qch.*, to take
one's chance(s) of sth., of doing sth. **3.** (With
cogn. acc.) (*a*) *C. une course*, to run a race. *La
coupe se courra demain*, the cup will be competed
for to-morrow. *F:* **C'est couru**, it's a cert.
(*b*) **Courir le monde**, (i) to roam the world over;
(ii) to gad about. *C. les cafés*, to haunt the cafés.
(*c*) *C. le grand galop*, to go at full speed. *S.a.*
POSTE[1] 1. (*d*) *Nau:* *C. un bord*, to make a tack.
   couru, *a.* **1.** Sought after; popular (preacher,
etc.). *Réunion sportive très courue*, well-attended,
well-patronized, sporting event. **2. Intérêt couru**,
accrued interest.
   courlieu [kurljø], *s.m.*, **courlis** [kurli], *s.m.*
Orn: Curlew. *Petit c.*, whimbrel.
   couronne [kurɔn], *s.f.* **1.** Wreath, crown (of
flowers, laurel). *C. mortuaire*, (funeral) wreath.
2. (King's) crown; (ducal) coronet. **La triple
couronne**, the (pope's) tiara. **3.** *Num:* Crown.
Une demi-couronne, half-a-crown. **4.** Ring.
Geom: Annulus. *Bot:* Corona. *Astr:* *C. solaire*,
solar corona. **5.** (*a*) Rim (of pulley, wheel).
(*b*) Crown-wheel (of differential, etc.); sprocket-
wheel (of capstan). *C. de galets*, roller-ring.
   couronnement [kurɔnmɑ̃], *s.m.* **1.** (*a*) Crowning, coronation (of king). (*b*) Capping (of pier);
crowning, coping (of wall). **2.** Scar (on horse's
knee); broken knees.
   couronner [kurɔne], *v.tr.* **1.** (*a*) To crown (with
a wreath). *C. un élève*, to award a pupil (wreath
together with) a prize. *F:* **Pour couronner
tout . . .**, to cap, crown, it all. . . . (*b*) **Couronner qn roi**, to crown s.o. king. **2.** To cap (pier);
to cope, crown (wall). **3.** *C. un cheval*, to let a
horse down on its knees.
   couronné, *a.* **1.** (*a*) Wreathed (with flowers,
etc.). *Élève trois fois c.*, scholar who has won
three prizes. *Roman c.*, prize novel. (*b*) Crowned
(sovereign). **2.** *Cheval c.*, broken-kneed horse.
   courr-ai, -ons, etc. See COURIR.
   courre [kuːr], *v.tr. & i.* *A:* (= COURIR 2 (*a*))
(Still used in) *Chasse à courre*, hunt(ing).
S.a. CHASSER 1. **Laisser courre les chiens**, (i) to
lay on the pack; (ii) to slip the hounds.
   courrier [kurje], *s.m.* **1.** Courier; messenger.
Salle des courriers, guests' servants' hall (at hotel).
2. (*a*) Mail, post. **Par retour du courrier**, by
return of post. *Dépouiller son c.*, to open one's
mail. **Faire son courrier**, to do one's correspondence, one's mail. (*b*) Mail-boat. **3.** *Journ:*
C. des théâtres, theatrical column.

courriériste [kurjerist], *s.m.* *Journ:* Par writer.
courroie [kurwa], *s.f.* **1.** Strap. *F:* **Allonger la
courroie**, to make things go a long way. **Serrer la
courroie à qn**, to keep s.o. on a short allowance.
2. *Mec.E:* Belt(ing). *C. de transmission, de
commande*, driving-belt.
courroucer [kuruse], *v.tr.* (je courrouçai(s); n.
courrouçons) *Lit:* To anger, incense (s.o.).
   courroucé, *a.* Angry (person, voice).
courroux [kuru], *s.m.* *Lit:* Anger, wrath, ire.
Être en courroux, to be angry, wroth.
cours [kuːr], *s.m.* **I.** (*a*) Course; flow (of river);
path (of heavenly bodies). **Cours d'eau**, river,
watercourse, stream. **Poursuivre le cours de ses
idées**, to pursue the train of one's thoughts.
Donner libre cours à son imagination, to give free
rein, free play, to one's imagination. *La maladie
suit son c.*, the illness is running its course.
Affaires en cours, outstanding business. **Travail
en cours**, work in progress, on hand. **Année en
cours**, current, present, year. **En cours de route**,
on the way. **Au cours de l'hiver**, during the
winter. (*b*) *Nau:* **Long cours**, foreign trade.
Capitaine au long c., master mariner. *Voyage de
long c.*, ocean voyage. **2.** Circulation, currency
(of money). **Avoir cours**, to be legal tender.
Donner cours à un bruit, to set a rumour afloat.
3. Quotation, price. *Quel est le c. du sucre?* what
is sugar quoted at? **Cours du marché**, market
prices. *C. du change*, rate of exchange. **4.** Course
(of lectures, etc.). *Assister aux c. du soir, aux c.
d'adultes*, to attend evening classes. *Faire un c.
d'histoire*, to lecture on history. **Faire son cours
de droit**, to read law. **Finir ses cours**, to finish
one's studies.
cour-s, -t. See COURIR.
course [kurs], *s.f.* **1.** Run, running. **Au pas
de course**, at a run; *Mil:* at the double.
Prendre sa course, to set off (running). **Arrêté
en pleine course**, checked in full career. **2.** Race,
racing. *C. de chevaux*, horse-race. **Les courses**,
(i) horse-racing; (ii) the races. *C. plate*, flat race.
C. au clocher, point-to-point race. *C. d'obstacles*,
hurdle-race; obstacle-race. *C. de fond*, long-
distance race. *C. de vitesse*, sprint. *S.a.* HAIE 1,
SAC[1] 1. **Champ, terrain, de courses**, race-course.
Auto de course, racing car. *C. d'avions*, air race.
3. (*a*) Excursion, outing, trip. (*b*) Journey, run
(esp. in hired conveyance). *Payer (le prix de) sa c.*,
to pay one's fare. *Il y a une longue c. d'ici là*, it is
a long way from here. (*c*) (Business) errand.
Faire une course, aller en course, to go out on
business. **Être en course**, to be out (on business).
Faire des courses, (i) to go out shopping; (ii) to
run errands, messages. **4.** *Nau:* Privateering.
Faire la course, to privateer. **5.** (*a*) Path, way,
course (of person, planet, etc.); course, flight
(of projectile). (*b*) *Mec.E:* Travel (of tool, etc.);
stroke (of piston).
coursier [kursje], *s.m.* **1.** *Lit:* (War-)horse;
charger. **2.** Mill-race. **3.** Bow-chaser (gun).
coursive [kursiːv], *s.f.* **1.** *N.Arch:* Alley-way.
2. *Aer:* Runway, cat-walk (of dirigible).
court[1] [kuːr]. **I.** *a.* Short. (*a*) Avoir la vue courte,
to be short-sighted. **Avoir l'esprit court**, to be of
limited understanding. *Mer courte*, choppy sea.
s.m. **Prendre le plus court**, couper au court,
to take the nearest road; to take a short cut.
Tenir un chien, un cheval, de court, to hold a dog
on a short leash, a horse on a short rein. **Se
trouver à court**, to find oneself short (of money,
etc.). **A court de main-d'œuvre**, short of
hands; short-handed. (*b*) (In time) *C. intervalle*,
short, brief, interval. *F:* **La faire courte et**

bonne, to have a short life and a merry one. *De courte durée,* short-lived. **Pour (vous le) faire court . . .,** to cut a long story short. . . . (*c*) *Cu : Sauce courte,* thick sauce. **2.** *adv.* Short. **Rester court** *dans un discours,* to stop short in a speech. *Tourner c. à droite,* to turn sharp to the right. **Couper court à qch.,** to cut sth. short. **Tout court,** simply, merely.

court² [kɔrt, kuːr], *s.m. Ten :* Court. *C. sur gazon,* grass court. *C. dur,* hard court.

courtage [kurtaːʒ], *s.m. Com :* Brokerage ; (i) broking ; (ii) commission.

courtaud, -aude [kurto, -oːd], *a. & s.* **1.** *A :* Dock-tailed, crop-eared (animal). **2.** Dumpy, squat (person). [COURT¹]

court-bouclée, *a.f.* Bobbed. *pl. Court-bouclées.*

court-circuit, *s.m. El :* Short-circuit. **Mettre en court-circuit,** to short-circuit (a resistance, etc.). *pl. Des courts-circuits.*

court-circuiter, *v.tr. El :* To short-circuit.

courtepointe [kurtəpwɛ̃ːt], *s.f.* Counterpane.

courtier [kurtje], *s.m. Com :* Broker. **Courtier de commerce, courtier de, en, marchandises,** general broker, commercial broker. **Courtier en immeubles,** land-agent. **Courtier de change,** bill-broker ; jobber, dealer. **Courtier maritime, ship-broker.**

courtine [kurtin], *s.f. Mil :* Curtain (between two bastions).

courtisan [kurtizɑ̃], *s.m.* Courtier.

courtisane [kurtizan], *s.f.* Courtesan.

courtiser [kurtize], *v.tr.* (*a*) To court ; to pay court to (s.o.) ; to fawn on, toady to (the mighty). (*b*) To court, woo ; to make love to (s.o.).

courtois [kurtwa], *a.* Courteous (*envers,* to, towards) ; courtly ; polite, urbane. **Armes courtoises,** blunted weapons ; arms of courtesy. *adv.* **-ement.**

courtoisie [kurtwazi], *s.f.* **1.** Courtesy, courteousness (*envers,* to, towards) ; politeness, urbanity. **2.** (Act of) courtesy.

court-vêtue, *a.f.* Short-skirted. *pl. Court-vêtues.*

couseuse [kuzøːz], *s.f.* **1.** Sewer, seamstress. *Bookb :* Stitcher. **2.** Stitching machine.

cous-ez, -ons, etc. See COUDRE.

cousin¹, -ine [kuzɛ̃, -in], *s.* Cousin. **Cousin germain,** first cousin ; cousin german. *F :* **Cousin à la mode de Bretagne,** 'sort of relation.'

cousin², *s.m. Ent : F :* Gnat, midge.

cousinage [kuzinaːʒ], *s.m. F :* **1.** Cousinship, cousinhood. **2.** *Tout le c.,* all the cousins ; esp. all the poor relations.

cousinière [kuzinjɛːr], *s.f.* Mosquito-net.

cousoir [kuzwaːr], *s.m. Bookb :* Sewing-press.

coussin [kusɛ̃], *s.m.* Cushion.

coussiner [kusine], *v.tr.* To cushion.

coussinet [kusinɛ], *s.m.* **1.** Small cushion ; pad. **2.** *Mec.E :* (*a*) Bearing. **Coussinets à billes,** ball-bearings. (*b*) *C.* anti-friction, bearing-brasses ; bush(ing). (*c*) Die. (*d*) *Rail :* (Rail-)chair. **3.** *Bot : F :* Bilberry, whortleberry.

coût [ku], *s.m.* Cost. *Menus coûts,* petty expenses.

coûtant [kutɑ̃], *a.m.* **Au, à, prix coûtant,** at cost price.

couteau [kuto], *s.m.* Knife. (*a*) *C. fermant, pliant, de poche,* clasp-knife, jack-knife. *C. de table,* table-knife. *C. à découper,* carving-knife, carver. *C. à papier,* paper-knife. **Coup de couteau,** stab. *F :* **Figure en lame de couteau,** hatchet face. **Ils sont à couteaux tirés,** they are at daggers drawn. **Avoir le couteau sur la gorge,** to have the knife at one's throat. (*b*) *El.E :* Blade

(of switch). **Interrupteur à couteau,** knife-switch. (*c*) Knife-edge, fulcrum (of balance-beam).

coutelas [kutla], *s.m. Nau :* Cutlass.

coutelier [kutəlje], *s.m.* Cutler.

coutellerie [kutelri], *s.f.* **1.** Cutlery (trade or wares). **2.** Cutler's shop.

coûter [kute], *v.i.* **1.** To cost. **Coûter cher, peu,** to be expensive, inexpensive. *Cela vous coûtera cher,* you shall pay dearly for this. **Coûte que coûte,** at all costs ; whatever the cost. **Cela coûte les yeux de la tête,** it costs a mint of money. *Impers. Il lui en a coûté un bras, la vie,* it cost him an arm, his life. *Je voulus l'aider,* j'en m'en coûta, I tried to help him, to my cost. **2.** *Rien ne lui coûte,* (i) nothing is an effort to him ; (ii) he spares no effort. *Cela me coûte à dire, il m'en coûte de le dire,* it pains me to have to say this.

coûteu|x, -euse [kutø, -øːz], *a.* Costly, expensive. **Peu coûteux,** inexpensive. *adv.* **-sement.**

coutil [kuti], *s.m. Tex :* Drill, twill ; duck. *C. pour matelas,* ticking. **Pantalon de coutil,** ducks.

coutre [kutr], *s.m.* Coulter (of plough).

coutume [kutym], *s.f.* **1.** Custom, habit. *Selon ma c.,* as is my habit, my wont. **Avoir coutume de faire qch.,** to be in the habit of doing sth. **Comme de coutume,** as usual. *Plus tard que de c.,* later than usual.

coutumier, -ière [kutymje, -jɛːr], *a.* (*a*) *Pej :* In the habit of (doing sth.). *Il est c. du fait,* he is in the habit of doing it. (*b*) Customary. **Droit coutumier,** (i) customary law ; (ii) unwritten law, common law.

couture [kutyːr], *s.f.* **1.** Sewing, needlework. **2.** (*a*) Seam (in dress, pipe, etc.). **Sans couture,** (i) seamless ; (ii) *Metalw:* weldless. *F :* **Battre qn à plate(s) couture(s),** to beat s.o. hollow. *F :* **Savoir la vie sous toutes ses coutures,** to know the seamy side of life. (*b*) *N.Arch : C. à clin,* lapped seam.

couturer [kutyre], *v.tr.* To scar, seam, score. *Visage couturé,* scarred face.

couturier, -ière [kutyrje, -jɛːr], *s.* (*a*) *s.m. & f.* Dressmaker. (*b*) *s.f.* Seamstress ; needlewoman.

couvage [kuvaːʒ], *s.m.* Incubation, hatching.

couvain [kuvɛ̃], *s.m.* **1.** Nest of insect eggs. **2.** Brood-comb (of bees).

couvaison [kuvezɔ̃], *s.f.* Brooding time (of bird).

couvée [kuve], *s.f.* **1.** Sitting, clutch (of eggs). **2.** Brood, hatch(ing) (of chicks).

couvent [kuvɑ̃], *s.m.* (*a*) Convent, nunnery. *Entrer au c.,* to go into a convent. (*b*) Monastery.

couver [kuve]. **1.** *v.tr.* (*a*) (Of hen, etc.) To sit on (eggs) ; *abs.* to brood, sit. *Poule qui veut c.,* broody hen. (*b*) To incubate, to hatch (out) (eggs). (*c*) *F :* **Couver le feu,** to brood over the fire. *C. un complot,* to hatch a plot. *C. une maladie,* to be sickening for an illness. **Couver qn des yeux,** (i) to gaze intently at s.o. ; (ii) to look fondly at s.o. **2.** *v.i.* (Of fire, passion) To smoulder. *Un orage couvait,* a storm was brewing. *Conspiration qui couvait depuis longtemps,* conspiracy that had been hatching for a long time.

couvercle [kuverkl], *s.m.* Lid, cover ; cap (of bottle, etc.). *C. vissé,* screw-cap.

couvert. See COUVRIR.

couverture [kuvertyːr], *s.f.* **1.** Covering, cover. *C. de voyage,* travelling rug. *C. de lit,* bedspread. *C. en laine,* blanket. **Faire la couverture,** to turn down the bed. **Tirer la couverture à soi,** (i) to take all the bed-clothes ; (ii) *F :* to take the lion's share. *C. en papier,* paper wrapper (of book) ; jacket. *Mil : Troupes de c.,* covering troops. **Lettre de couverture,** covering letter.

Sous **couverture d'amitié**, under the cover, the cloak, of friendship. **2.** Roofing. **3.** *Agr:* Topping; top-dressing. **4.** *Com: Commande sans c.,* order without security, without cover.

couveuse [kuvøːz], *s.f. Husb:* **1.** Sitting hen; hatcher; brooder. **2.** *C. artificielle,* incubator (for eggs, for infants).

couvi [kuvi], *a.m.* Addle(d) (egg).

NOTE. Except where otherwise indicated, in the following compounds COUVRE is inv., the noun takes the plural.

couvre-bouche, *s.m.* Muzzle-cover (of gun).

couvre-chaîne, *s.m. Cy:* Chain-case.

couvre-chaussure, *s.m.* **1.** Galosh, overshoe. **2.** Snow-boot.

couvre-chef, *s.m. F. & Hum:* Head-dress, head-gear.

couvre-engrenages, *s.m.* Gear-box, -case.

couvre-feu, *s.m.inv.* **1.** Damper-lid (for charcoal fire). **2.** Curfew.

couvre-lit, *s.m.* Coverlet, bedspread, counterpane.

couvre-livre, *s.m. Bookb:* (Dust-)jacket; wrapper.

couvre-manche, *s.m. Ten:* Grip (for racquet).

couvre-moyeu, *s.m. Veh:* Hub-cap.

couvre-nuque, *s.m.* **1.** Sun-curtain (of cap). **2.** Rear-peak (of helmet).

couvre-objet, *s.m.* Cover-glass, cover-slip (of microscope slide).

couvre-œil, *s.m.* (Eye-)patch. *pl. Des couvre-œils.*

couvre-pied(s), *s.m.* (a) Coverlet. *C. piqué,* (eider-down) quilt. (b) Bedspread.

couvre-plat, *s.m.* Dish-cover.

couvre-radiateur, *s.m. Aut:* Radiator muff.

couvre-théière, *s.m.* Tea-cosy.

couvreur [kuvrœːr], *s.m.* Roofer. *C. en tuiles,* tiler. *C. en ardoise,* slater. *C. en chaume,* thatcher.

couvrir [kuvriːr], *v.tr.* (*pr.p.* couvrant; *p.p.* couvert; *pr.ind.* je couvre, n. couvrons; *p.d.* je couvrais; *p.h.* je couvris; *fu.* je couvrirai) To cover, to overlay, to screen (*de,* with). **1.** *Être couvert de poussière,* to be covered with dust. *C. les pauvres,* to clothe the poor. *Mur couvert de lierre,* wall overgrown with ivy. *C. ses desseins,* to conceal, keep secret, one's intentions. *C. le feu,* to cover up the fire. *Ind:* C. *les feux,* to bank (up) the fires. *Cards:* C. *une carte,* to cover a card. *C. la table,* to lay the table. *Le prix de vente couvre à peine les frais,* the selling price barely covers the cost. "*Prière de nous c. par chèque,*" 'kindly remit by cheque.' *C. une enchère,* to make a higher bid. **2.** *C. une maison,* to roof a house. *Maison couverte en ardoise, en chaume,* slated, thatched, house.

se couvrir. **1.** (a) To clothe oneself. (b) To put on one's hat. **2.** *Fenc:* To guard one's body. **3.** (Of weather) To become overcast.

couvert[1], *a.* **1.** *Allée couverte,* shady walk. *Pays c.,* wooded country. *Parler à mots couverts,* to speak (i) cryptically, (ii) not too bluntly. *Ciel c., temps c.,* overcast sky, weather. **2.** Wearing one's hat. *Rester c.,* to remain covered; to keep one's hat on. **3.** Clad.

couvert[2], *s.m.* **1.** Cover(ing), shelter. *Le vivre et le couvert,* board and lodging. **Être à couvert,** (i) to be under cover; (ii) *Com:* to be covered (for a credit). *Se mettre à couvert,* to take cover. *Mettre ses intérêts à c.,* to safeguard one's interests. *Sous le couvert de la nuit,* under cover of night. **2.** (a) Fork and spoon. (b) Cover, place (at table). *Mettre, dresser, le couvert,* to

lay, set, the table; to lay the cloth. *Oter le c.,* to clear the table. *La table est de vingt couverts,* covers are laid, the table is laid, for twenty. (c) (In restaurant) Table-money.

coxal, -aux [kɔksal, -o], *a. Anat:* Coxal. *Os coxal,* hip-bone.

coxalgie [kɔksalʒi], *s.f.* Coxalgia; hip-trouble.

coyote [kɔjɔt], *s.m. Z:* Coyote; prairie wolf.

coypou [kɔipu], *s.m. Z:* Coyp(o)u. Fourrure de **coypou,** nutria.

crabe [krɑːb], *s.m.* Crab. *F:* **Marcher en crabe,** to walk sideways, crabwise; *Av:* to drift.

crac [krak], *int. & s.m.* **1.** Crack, snap. *Crac! le voilà parti,* he was off before you could say Jack Robinson. **2.** Smash, crash (of bank, etc.).

crach [krak], *s.m.* = CRAC 2.

crachat [kraʃa], *s.m.* **1.** (a) Spittle, spit; *Med:* sputum. (b) *F:* Gob. *F:* **Se noyer dans un crachat,** to make a mountain out of a molehill. **2.** Star, Grand Cross (of an order).

crach|er [kraʃe]. **1.** *v.i.* (a) To spit; to expectorate. *F:* *Il ne faut pas cracher dessus,* it is not to be sneezed at. S.a. BASSIN 1. (b) (Of pen) To splutter. (c) *El.E:* (Of collector, etc.) To spark, spit, flash. **2.** *v.tr.* (i) To spit (out); (ii) to expectorate. *C. du sang,* cracher rouge, to spit blood. *C. des injures,* to hurl abuse. *F:* **J'ai dû cracher cinq francs,** I had to cough up five francs. (Of ship) *C. ses étoupes,* to spew, chew, oakum; to start at the seams. *s.m.* **-ement.** *s.m.* **-eur.** **craché,** *a. F:* **C'est son père tout craché,** he's the dead spit of his father.

crachin [kraʃɛ̃], *s.m.* Mizzle, fine drizzle.

crachiner [kraʃine], *v.i.* (Of weather) To mizzle, drizzle, spit.

crachoir [kraʃwaːr], *s.m.* Spittoon. *F:* **Tenir le crachoir,** to monopolize the conversation.

Cracovie [krakɔvi]. *Pr.n.f. Geog:* Cracow.

craie [kre], *s.f.* Chalk. *Écrit à la craie,* written in chalk.

craign-ant, -e, -ons, etc. See CRAINDRE.

craindre [krɛ̃ːdr], *v.tr.* (*pr.p.* craignant; *p.p.* craint; *pr.ind.* je crains, n. craignons; *p.d.* je craignais; *p.h.* je craignis; *fu.* je craindrai) (a) To fear, dread; to stand in awe of, be afraid of (s.o., sth.). *C. Dieu,* to fear God. *Je crains de le laisser entrer,* I am afraid to let him in. *Je crains qu'il (ne) soit mort,* I fear he is dead. *Il est à c., il y a lieu de c., que* . . . (*ne*) . . ., it is to be feared that. . . . *Il n'y a pas à c. qu'il revienne,* there is no fear of his coming back. *Abs. C. pour qn,* to be anxious for s.o.'s safety. *C. pour sa vie,* to go about in terror of one's life. **Faire craindre qch. à qn,** to put s.o. in fear of sth. (b) *Plante qui craint la gelée,* plant that cannot stand the frost. *Com:* "*Craint l'humidité, la chaleur,*" 'to be kept dry, cool.'

crainte [krɛ̃ːt], *s.f.* Fear, dread. **Crainte mystérieuse,** awe. *Dans la crainte de, (de) crainte de, tomber,* for fear of falling. *De crainte que* . . . (ne) + *sub.,* lest. . . . *Sans crainte,* (i) fearless, (ii) fearlessly. *Avoir des craintes au sujet de qch.,* to entertain fears regarding sth.

craint|if, -ive [krɛtif, -iːv], *a.* Timid, timorous. *adv.* **-ivement.**

crambe [krɑ̃ːb], *s.m.,* **crambé** [krɑ̃be], *s.m. Bot:* Sea-kale.

cramoisi [kramwazi], *a. & s.m.* Crimson.

crampe[1] [krɑ̃ːp], *s.f. Med:* Cramp. *C. du tennis,* tennis elbow. *Crampe de poitrine,* angina pectoris. *F:* **Avoir des crampes d'estomac,** to feel gnawing pains, an aching void.

crampe[2], *s.f.* = CRAMPON 1 (a).

crampon [krɑ̃pɔ̃], *s.m.* **1.** (a) Cramp(-iron);

clamp, holdfast. (b) Hook-nail. **2.** (a) Climbing-iron. (b) Stud (for sole of boot); calk, cog (of horseshoe). **3.** (Of pers.) Bore; P: bur, sticker.
ramponnant [krɑ̆pɔnɑ̆], a. P: Importunate, pestering (person).
cramponner [krɑ̆pɔne], v.tr. **1.** To clamp, cramp, (stones, etc.) together. **2.** P: To button-hole, pester; to stick like glue to (s.o.).
se cramponner à qch., à qn, to hold on to, hang on to, clutch, sth., s.o.
cran [krɑ̆], s.m. **1.** Notch. (a) Catch, tooth (of ratchet, etc.); cog (of wheel). Sm.a: C. de sûreté, safety-catch. Au c. de sûreté, at half-cock. F: Être à cran, to be ready to go off the deep end. (b) Distance between holes (in strap, etc.). Lâcher une courroie d'un cran, to let a strap out a hole. F: Il ne me lâche pas d'un cran, he won't leave me for a moment. Descendre d'un cran, to come down a peg, a notch. (c) Nick. Sm.a: C. de mire, (notch of the) back-sight. **2.** F: Avoir du cran, to have plenty of pluck; to be game (for anything). **3.** Mil: P: Quatre jours de c., four days' C.B.
crâne [krɑ:n]. **1.** s.m. Skull; brain-pan. Défoncer le c. à qn, to brain s.o. Fb: Réussir un c., to get in a header. **2.** a. F: (a) Plucky (conduct, etc.). (b) Jaunty (air). adv. **-ment.**
crâner [krɑne], v.i. F: To swagger, swank; to put on a jaunty air. [CRÂNE]
crânerie [krɑnri], s.f. (a) Pluck. (b) Jauntiness, swagger, swank.
crâneur, -euse [krɑnœ:r, -ø:z], s. F: Braggart, swaggerer.
crangon [krɑ̆gɔ̃], s.m. Shrimp.
cranien, -ienne [krɑnjɛ̃, -jɛn], a. Anat: Cranial. La boîte cranienne, the brain-pan.
crapaud [krapo], s.m. **1.** Toad. F: Avaler un crapaud, (i) to bring oneself to do a particularly unpleasant task; (ii) to pocket an insult. P: C'est un vilain c., he's a toad of a man. **2.** Pyr: Jumping cracker. **3.** Vet: Grease; greasy heel. **4.** (a) Tub easy-chair. (b) Baby grand (piano).
crapaudine [krapodin], s.f. **1.** Toadstone. **2.** Cu: Poulet à la crapaudine, spatchcocked chicken. **3.** Hyd.E: (a) Grating, strainer (of inlet pipe). (b) Waste hole (of bath). **4.** Mec.E: etc: (Foot)step-bearing; thrust-bearing; socket (of rudder, door, hinge).
crapouillot [krapujo], s.m. Mil: P: (a) Trench-mortar. (b) Trench-mortar shell.
crapule [krapyl], s.f. F: **1.** Debauchery, dissolute-ness, lewdness. **2.** Coll: Dissolute mob or people. **3.** Debauchee; low scoundrel.
crapuleu|x, -euse [krapylø, -ø:z], a. Debauched, dissolute; filthy (novel, etc.), foul (language). adv. **-sement.**
craque [krak], s.f. F: Cram, fib; tall story.
craqueler [krakle], v.tr. (je craquelle; je craquellerai) Cer: To crackle.
craquelé. 1. a. Crackled. **2.** s.m. Cer: Crackle-ware, -glass, -china.
craquelin [kraklɛ̃], s.m. **1.** Cracknel (biscuit). **2.** Little shrimp of a man.
craquelure [krakly:r], s.f. (i) Crack, (ii) small cracks (in paint, etc.).
craqu|er [krake], v.i. **1.** To crack; to make a cracking sound; (of dried leaves, etc.) to crackle; (of hard snow) to crunch (under the feet); (of shoes) to creak, to squeak. Faire craquer ses doigts, to crack one's finger-joints. Habit qui a craqué dans le dos, coat that has split, slit, down the back. **2.** P: To fib; to draw the long bow. s.m. **-ement.**
craqueur, -euse [krakœ:r, -ø:z], s. F: Fibber.

crassane [krasan], s.f. Bergamot (pear).
crasse [kras]. **1.** a.f. Gross, crass. Esp. **Ignorance crasse,** crass ignorance. **2.** s.f. (a) (Body) dirt. F: Né dans la crasse, born in squalor. (b) Mch: Fur, scale (in boiler). Metall: Dross, scum. Fire-arms: Fouling. (c) Avarice, stinginess. (d) F: Faire une crasse à qn, to play s.o. a scurvy trick.
crasser [krase], v.tr. To foul, clog (gun-barrel). **se crasser,** (of fire-arm) to become foul.
crasseux, -euse [krasø, -ø:z], a. (a) Dirty, filthy (hands, linen, etc.); squalid (dwelling, etc.). (b) F: Mean, stingy.
crassier [krasje], s.m. Slag-heap.
cratère [krate:r], s.m. (a) Crater (of volcano, of arc-lamp carbon). (b) Shell-hole.
cravache [kravaʃ], s.f. Riding-whip; hunting-crop.
cravacher [kravaʃe], v.tr. To flog (horse); to horsewhip (person).
cravan(t) [kravɑ̆], s.m. **1.** Moll: Barnacle. **2.** Orn: Brent(-goose).
cravate [kravat], s.f. (a) (i) (Neck-)tie; scarf; (ii) (woman's) fur tie. P: Cravate de chanvre, hempen collar; halter. (b) Wr: Hold round the neck; hold in chancery. (c) Nau: Sling. (d) Orn: Ruff, ruffle. Pigeon à cravate, ruff.
crayère [krɛjɛ:r], s.f. Chalk-pit.
crayeux, -euse [krɛjø, -ø:z], a. Chalky.
crayon [krɛjɔ̃], s.m. **1.** Pencil. C. à mine de plomb, lead pencil. Écrit au c., written in pencil. C. pastel, crayon. Dessin au crayon, pencil drawing. S.a. GRAS 3. (b) Pencil-drawing, -sketch. **2.** Stick. Med: Pencil (of caustic, etc.). El: C. de zinc, zinc rod. C. d'une lampe à arc, carbon of an arc-lamp. **3.** Chalk soil; marl.
crayonnage [krɛjɔna:ʒ], s.m. **1.** Pencilling. **2.** Pencil-sketch.
crayonner [krɛjɔne], v.tr. **1.** To make a pencil-sketch of (sth.). **2.** To pencil; to write, jot, (sth.) down (on paper); to make pencil marks on (sth.).
créance [kreɑ̆:s], s.f. **1.** Belief, credence, credit. Trouver créance, to be believed. Donner, accorder, créance à qn, à qch., to believe, give credence to, s.o., sth. **2.** Trust. Lettre(s) de créance, (i) credentials (of diplomatic agent); (ii) letter of credit (to bank). **3.** Debt. Jur: Claim. Mauvaises créances, créances véreuses, bad debts. Créances gelées, frozen credits.
créancier, -ière [kreɑ̆sje, -jɛ:r], s. Creditor.
créateur, -trice [kreatœ:r, -tris]. **1.** a. Creative (power, genius). **2.** s. Creator. (a) Le Créateur, the Creator; God. (b) Maker; establisher (of bank, etc.); inventor (of an article).
création [kreasjɔ̃], s.f. **1.** (a) Creation, creating. La c. du monde, the creation of the world. (b) Founding, establishment (of institution, etc.); creation (of peer); setting up (of a court, etc.). **2.** Les merveilles de la c., the wonders of creation, of the universe.
créature [kreaty:r], s.f. Creature. F: C'est une bonne créature, he's a good sort. Pej: (Of woman) L'insolente c.! the impudent creature!
crécelle [krɛsɛl], s.f. **1.** (Hand-)rattle. Voix de crécelle, rasping voice. **2.** F: Regular chatterbox.
crécerelle [krɛsrɛl], s.f. Orn: Kestrel.
crèche [krɛʃ], s.f. **1.** (a) Manger, crib. (b) (Christ child's crib (as shown at Christmas time). **2.** (a) (Child's) crib. (b) (Public) day-nursery; crèche. **3.** Plate-rack.
crédence [kredɑ̆:s], s.f. **1.** Sideboard, buffet. **2.** Ecc: Credence(-table).
crédibilité [kredibilite], s.f. Credibility.

crédit[1] [kredi], *s.m.* Credit, repute, influence; prestige (of country, etc.). **Mettre une opinion en crédit**, to get an opinion credited. **Nouvelle qui prend crédit**, news that is gaining credence.

crédit[2], *s.m.* Com: **1.** Credit. **Avoir du crédit en banque**, to have credit at the bank. **Crédit en blanc, à découvert**, blank, open, credit. **Vendre, acheter, qch. à crédit**, to sell, buy, sth. on credit. **Faire crédit à qn**, to give s.o. credit. **Établissement, société, de crédit**, loan-society. **Le Crédit industriel**, the Industries Bank. *Adm:* **Crédit municipal**, (municipal) pawn-office. S.a. FONCIER 1, LETTRE 3. **2.** Credit(or) side (of balance sheet). **3.** Sum voted by Parliament for supply. **Voter des crédits**, to vote supplies.

créditer [kredite], *v.tr.* **C. qn du montant d'une somme**, to credit s.o. with a sum.

créditeur, -trice [kreditœ:r, -tris]. **I.** *s.* Creditor. **2.** *a.* **Compte créditeur**, credit account. **Solde c.**, credit balance.

credo [kredo], *s.m.inv.* Creed.

crédule [kredyl], *a.* Credulous. *adv.* **-ment.**

crédulité [kredylite], *s.f.* Credulity, credulousness. **Avec c.**, credulously.

créer [kree], *v.tr.* To create. **Créer qch. de toutes pièces**, to create sth. out of nothing. **Se c. une clientèle**, to build up a connection. *Th:* **C. un rôle**, to create a part. *Pred:* **C. qn chevalier, comte**, to create s.o. a knight, a count.

crémaillère [kremajɛ:r], *s.f.* **1.** Pot-hanger, -hook. *F:* **Pendre la crémaillère**, to have a house-warming. **2.** *Mec.E:* etc: Toothed rack. **C. et pignon**, rack and pinion. **Chemin de fer à crémaillère**, rack-railway.

crémant [kremɑ̃], *a. & s.m.* Creaming (wine).

crémation [kremasjɔ̃], *s.f.* Cremation.

crématorium [krematɔrjɔm], *s.m.* Crematorium.

crème [krɛm], *s.f.* Cream. **1.** (a) **C. fouettée**, whipped cream. **Fromage à la crème**, cream-cheese. *a.inv.* **Rubans crème**, cream(-coloured) ribbons. (b) *Cu:* Custard, cream. **C. au caramel**, caramel custard. **C. glacée, glace de c.**, ice-cream. **2.** **C. pour bottines**, shoe-cream. *Ch:* **Crème de tartre**, cream of tartar.

crémer[1] [kreme], *v.tr.* (je crème; je crémerai) To cremate.

crémer[2], *v.i.* (Of milk, etc.) To cream.

crémerie [kremri], *s.f.* **1.** Creamery, dairy; milk-shop. **2.** Small restaurant.

crémeux, -euse [kremø, -ø:z], *a.* Creamy.

crémier, -ière [kremje, -jɛ:r], *s.* **1.** (a) Dairyman, dairy-woman. (b) Keeper of a small eating-house. **2.** *s.f.* **Crémière**, cream-jug.

Crémone [kremɔn]. **1.** *Pr.n.f. Geog:* Cremona. **2.** *s.f.* Casement bolt.

créneau [kreno], *s.m. Fort:* (a) Crenel(le); *pl.* battlements. **Écrou à créneaux**, castle-nut. (b) Loop-hole; look-out slit.

crénel|er [krɛnle], *v.tr.* (je crénelle; je crénellerai) **I.** *Fort:* (a) To crenel(l)ate, embattle (wall). (b) To cut loop-holes in (wall). **2.** To notch, tooth (wheel, etc.). *Num:* To mill (coin). *s.m.* **-age.**

crénelé, *a.* **1.** *Fort:* (a) Crenel(l)ated, battlemented (wall, etc.). **Écrou crénelé**, castle-nut. (b) Loop-holed. **2.** *Bot:* Crenate(d), crenelled (leaf). **3.** Toothed, notched.

crénelure [krɛnly:r], *s.f.* Crenellation.

créole [kreɔl], *a. & s. Ethn:* Creole.

créosote [kreɔzɔt], *s.f.* Creosote.

créosoter [kreɔzɔte], *v.tr.* To creosote.

crêpe [krɛp]. **I.** *s.f.* Pancake. **Virer une crêpe**, to toss a pancake. **2.** *s.m.* (a) Crape. **Crêpe de**

Chine, **crêpe de Chine**. **C. anglais**, black mourning crape. **Porter un crêpe**, to wear a mourning band. (b) **Crêpe de caoutchouc**, crêpe-rubber.

crêpelé [krɛple], *a.* (Of hair) Crimped, wavy.

crêpelu [krɛply], *a.* (Of hair) Frizzy, fuzzy.

crêpelure [krɛply:r], *s.f.* Frizziness, fuzziness.

crêp|er [krɛpe], *v.tr.* To frizz, crimp (the hair) to crisp, crimp (tissue). *P:* (Of women) S̱o crêper le chignon, to tear each other's hair; ṯo have a set-to. *s.m.* **-age.**

crêpé, *s.m.* (a) Hair-pad. (b) Switch of hair.

crépine [krepin], *s.f.* **1.** Fringe (on upholstered furniture). **2.** *Cu:* Caul. **3.** Strainer, rose (o̱f pump, etc.).

crép|ir [krepi:r], *v.tr.* **1.** Ṯo grain, pebble (leather). **2.** To rough-cast (wall). *s.m.* **-issage.**

crépit|er [krepite], *v.i.* (Of fire) To crackle; (of rain) to patter; (of candle, etc.) to sputter. *s.f.* **-ation.** *s.m.* **-ement.**

crépu [krepy], *a.* **1.** Crisp, frizzy, fuzzy (hair). **2.** Crinkled (leaf, etc.).

crépusculaire [krepyskylɛ:r], *a.* (Pertaining to) the twilight; crepuscular. **Lumière c.**, twilight, half-light.

crépuscule [krepyskyl], *s.m.* Twilight; dusk; gloaming.

cresson [krəsɔ̃], *s.m. Bot:* Cress. **C. de fontaine**, water-cress.

cressonnière [krəsɔnjɛ:r], *s.f.* Water-cress bed or pond.

crétacé [kretase], *a. Geol:* Cretaceous, chalky.

crête [krɛ:t], *s.f.* **1.** Comb, crest (of bird). **C. de coq**, cockscomb. *F:* **Lever la crête**, (i) to hold one's head high; (ii) to bristle up. **Baisser la crête**, to look crestfallen. **2.** (a) Crest (of wave, helmet). (b) Crest, ridge, comb (of roof, mountain); crest (of parapet).

crête-de-coq, *s.f. Bot:* Cockscomb.

crételle [kretel], *s.f. Bot:* Dog's-tail (grass).

crétin [kretɛ̃], *s.m.* **1.** (a) Cretin, (deformed) idiot (esp. of Alpine valleys). (b) *F:* Hopeless ass. *Sch:* Dunce.

crétinisme [kretinism], *s.m.* Cretinism.

crétois, -oise [kretwa, -wa:z], *a. & s.* Cretan.

cretonne [krətɔn], *s.f. Tex:* Cretonne.

cretons [krətɔ̃], *s.m.pl. Cu:* Greaves, cracklings.

creus|er [krøze], *v.tr.* **1.** To hollow (out); to groove; to plough (a furrow). **Front creusé de rides**, brow furrowed with wrinkles. **C. une question**, to go thoroughly, deeply, into a question. **Se c. le cerveau, l'esprit, la tête**, to rack one's brains. **2.** To excavate. (a) To dig (out) (trench, etc.); to cut (canal); to sink, bore (a well). (b) To deepen. *s.m.* **-age.** *s.m.* **-ement.**

se creuser, to grow hollow. **La mer se creuse**, the sea is rising.

creuset [krøze], *s.m.* **1.** Crucible, melting-pot. *F:* **Passer par le creuset de l'adversité**, to go through the test of adversity; to be proved by adversity. **2.** *Metall:* Crucible, well, hearth (of blast furnace).

creux, -euse [krø, -ø:z]. **I.** *a.* Hollow. **Chemin c.**, hollow, sunk(en), road. **Yeux c.**, sunken, deep-set, eyes. **Joues creuses**, gaunt, hollow, cheeks. **Voix creuse**, deep voice. **Avoir l'estomac creux**, to be sharp-set. **Avoir la tête creuse**, to be empty-headed. *adv.* **Sonner creux**, to sound hollow. **Songer creux**, to dream futile, empty, dreams. *Aut:* **Roue à base creuse**, wheel with well-base. *Rail:* etc: **Heures creuses**, slack hours. **2.** *s.m.* Hollow (of the hand); hole (in the ground); pit (of the stomach); trough (of wave). **C. de l'aisselle**, armpit. S.a. REIN 2.

crevaison [krəvɛzɔ̃], *s.f.* **1.** (a) Puncture (in

tyre). (b) Bursting (of boiler, of tyre, etc.). **2.** P: Death.

crevant [krəvɑ̃], a. P: **1.** Funny, killing (story). **2.** Killing, exhausting (work).

crevasse [krəvas], s.f. Crack (in skin, etc.); split, rift (in clouds); chink, crevice (in wall); flaw (in metal); crevasse (in glacier). Avoir des crevasses aux mains, to have chapped hands.

crevasser [krəvase], v.tr. To crack; to chap (the hands).
se crevasser, to crack; (of the hands) to get chapped.

crève-cœur, s.m.inv. Heart-breaking affair; keen disappointment.

crève-la-faim, s.m.inv. P: Starveling.

crever [krəve], v. (je crève; je crèverai) **1.** v.i. (a) To burst, split. F: C. de jalousie, to be bursting with jealousy. Crever de rire, to split (one's sides) with laughter. (b) (Of animals, P: of people) To die. F: Crever de faim, to be famished, starving. C. d'ennui, to be bored to death. **2.** v.tr. (a) To burst (balloon, bag, dam, etc.); to puncture (tyre). Crever un œil à qn, to put out s.o.'s eye. F: Ça vous crève les yeux, it's staring you in the face. (b) C. un cheval, to ride or work a horse to death.

crevé, s.m. (a) A.Cost: Slash. Manches à crevés, slashed sleeves. (b) F: A: Petit crevé, fop, dandy.

crevette [krəvɛt], s.f. C. grise, shrimp. C. rouge, prawn. Pêche à la c., shrimping.

cri [kri], s.m. (a) Cry (of persons and animals); chirp (of cricket, bird); squeak (of rat). Cri perçant, shriek (of person); squeal (of animal). (b) Shout, call. Cri de guerre, war-cry; slogan. Pousser des cris, to shout out. Pousser les hauts cris, to make shrill protest. Appeler qn à grands cris, to call loudly for s.o. S.a. RÉCLAMER 2. F: Le dernier cri, the latest fashion, style; all the go. Des chaussettes dernier cri, the latest thing, the last word, in socks.

criaill|er [kriɑje], v.i. **1.** To cry out, bawl, shout. **2.** To whine, complain, F: grouse. C. contre qn, to scold s.o.; to nag at s.o. [CRIER] s.m. **-ement.** s. **-eur, -euse.**

criaillerie [kriɑjri], s.f. Usu. pl. **1.** Crying, shouting. **2.** Whining, complaining, railing. **3.** Nagging, scolding.

criant [kriɑ̃], a. **Injustice criante,** crying, flagrant, gross, injustice.

criard, -arde [kriaːr, -ard]. **I.** a. (a) Crying, squalling, peevish. (b) Voix criarde, shrill, high-pitched, voice. Dettes criardes, pressing debts. Couleur criarde, loud, gaudy, colour. **2.** s. Bawler, squaller. Une criarde, a scold, a shrew.

crible [kribl], s.m. Sieve, riddle. Min: Civ.E: Screen. C. à gravier, gravel screen. Passer qch. au crible, to sift, screen, sth.

cribl|er [krible], v.tr. **1.** To sift, riddle; to screen (gravel, coal). **2.** C. qn, qch., de balles, to riddle s.o., sth., with bullets, with shot. C. qn de ridicule, to cover s.o. with ridicule. s.m. **-age.** s.m. **-eur.**
criblé, a. Visage c. de petite vérole, face pitted with smallpox. Criblé de dettes, head over ears in debt.

criblure [kriblyːr], s.f. Siftings; screenings.

cric¹ [krik], s.m. (Lifting) jack.

cric², int. Crack! snap!

cricri, cri-cri [krikri], s.m. **1.** Chirping (of cricket). **2.** Ent: F: Cricket.

criée [krie], s.f. Auction. Vente à la criée, sale by auction.

crier [krie]. **1.** v.i. (a) To cry; to call out, to shout; (of pig, etc.) to squeal. C. de douleur, to cry out, scream, shriek, with pain. Enfant qui crie, squalling child. C. après qn, to carp at s.o. C. contre qn, to cry out, to rail, against s.o. C. au secours, to shout for help. S.a. FAMINE, MISÈRE 2. (b) (Of mouse) To squeak; (of cricket) to chirp. (c) (Of door, axle, etc.) To creak. **2.** v.tr. (a) To cry, hawk (vegetables). F: C. qch. sur les toits, to cry sth. from the house-tops. (b) C. un ordre, to shout an order. C. à qn de faire qch., to shout to s.o. to do sth. Il cria que l'on apportât une corde, he shouted an order for a rope to be brought.

crieur, -euse [kriœːr, -øːz], s. **1.** Crier, bawler, shouter. **2.** C. public, town-crier.

crime [krim], s.m. Crime; Jur: felony. Crime capital, capital offence. Crime d'État, treason. C. d'incendie, arson.

criminaliste [kriminalist], s.m. **1.** Criminal jurist. **2.** Criminologist.

criminatoire [kriminatwaːr], a. Criminative, criminatory.

criminel, -elle [kriminɛl], a. **1.** (a) Guilty. (b) s. Criminal, felon. **2.** Criminal (law, attempt). s. Poursuivre qn au c., to take criminal proceedings against s.o.

criminellement [kriminɛlmɑ̃], adv. **1.** Criminally. **2.** Poursuivre qn c., to take criminal proceedings against s.o.

crin [krɛ̃], s.m. (a) Horsehair. Les crins, the mane and tail. Cheval à tous crins, horse with flowing mane and tail. F: Révolutionnaire à tous crins, à tout crin, out and out revolutionary. F: Être (comme un) crin, to be as cross as two sticks. (b) Crin végétal, vegetable horsehair.

crincrin [krɛ̃krɛ̃], s.m. F: Fiddle (of sorts).

crinière [krinjɛːr], s.f. Mane (of horse, lion).

crique [krik], s.f. Creek, cove.

criquet¹ [krikɛ], s.m. Ent: **1.** Locust. **2.** F: Cricket.

criquet², s.m. F: **1.** Small pony. **2.** Little shrimp (of a man or child).

crise [kriːz], s.f. **1.** Crisis. C. générale des affaires, general slump (in business). La c. du papier, the paper shortage. La c. domestique, the domestic-servant question. **2.** Attack (of gout, etc.). C. nerveuse, crise de nerfs, attack of nerves; fit of hysterics. Avoir une crise de larmes, to have a fit of crying.

crispant [krispɑ̃], a. F: Irritating, aggravating.

crispation [krispasjɔ̃], s.f. (a) Crispation, shrivelling up (of leather, etc.); puckering (of the face, etc.). (b) Nervous twitching, clenching (of the hands); wince (of pain). F: Donner des crispations à qn, to get on s.o.'s nerves.

crisper [krispe], v.tr. To contract, clench. Visage crispé par la souffrance, face contorted, F: screwed up, with pain. Cela me crispe, it gets on my nerves; it makes me wince.
se crisper, to contract; to become wrinkled; to cockle; to pucker up.

criss [kris], s.m. Creese, kris, Malay dagger.

crissement [krismɑ̃], s.m. (a) Grating, grinding (of teeth, of chalk on blackboard, etc.); squeak (of brakes, etc.). (b) pl. W.Tel: Grinders.

crisser [krise], v.tr. & i. To grate; to give a grinding, rasping, sound; (of brakes) to squeak. Crisser des dents, to grind one's teeth.

cristal, -aux [kristal, -o], s.m. **1.** Crystal. Cristal de roche, rock-crystal. **2.** Crystal(-glass). C. taillé, cut glass. C. armé, wire-glass.

cristallin [kristalɛ̃]. **1.** a. (a) Crystalline (rock). (b) Clear as crystal. **2.** s.m. Crystalline lens (of eye).

cristallisable [kristalizabl], *a.* Crystallizable.
cristallisation [kristalizasjɔ̃], *s.f.* Crystalliza-tion, crystallizing.
cristalliser [kristalize], *v.tr. & i.* To crystallize.
critérium [kriterjɔm], *s.m.*, **critère** [kriteːr], *s.m.* **1.** Criterion ; test. **2.** Selection-match,-race.
critiquable [kritikabl], *a.* Open to criticism.
critique[1] [kritik]. **1.** *a.* Critical. (*a*) Decisive, crucial. *Dans cette situation c. . . .,* in this emergency. . . . (*b*) *Examen c. d'un ouvrage,* critical examination of a work. **2.** *s.m.* Critic. *F:* Critique en chambre, armchair critic.
critique[2], *s.f.* Criticism. **1.** *C. des textes,* textual criticism. **2.** Faire la critique d'une pièce, to write a criticism of a play. **3.** Censure. *Les critiques du public,* the censure of the public.
critiqu|er [kritike], *v.tr.* (*a*) To criticize ; to write a criticism of (sth.). (*b*) To censure ; to find fault with (s.o., sth.). *s.m.* **-eur.**
croass|er [krɔase], *v.i.* (Of crow, rook) To caw ; (of raven, *F:* of person) to croak. *s.m.* **-ement.**
croate [krɔat]. **1.** *a.* Croatian. **2.** *s.* Croat.
croc [kro], *s.m.* **1.** (*a*) Hook. *C. à émerillon,* swivel hook. *C. de marinier,* boat-hook. *F:* Pendre, mettre, son épée au croc, to hang up one's sword. (*b*) Pawl, catch. **2.** Canine tooth ; fang (of wolf) ; tusk (of walrus, etc.). *F:* Mous-tache en croc, curled-up moustache.
croc-en-jambe [krɔkɑ̃ʒɑ̃ːb], *s.m.* Trip (to bring down opponent). *Faire, donner, un c.-en-j. à qn,* to trip s.o. up.
croche [krɔʃ], *s.f. Mus:* Quaver. **Double croche,** semiquaver.
crocher [krɔʃe], *v.tr.* (*a*) To hook ; to seize (sth.) with a hook. *L'ancre croche,* the anchor grips, bites. (*b*) *Nau:* To sling (hammock).
crochet [krɔʃe], *s.m.* Hook. **1.** (*a*) Clou à c., hook-nail. *C. à vis,* screw-hook. (*b*) Crochet-hook. Dentelle au crochet, crochet-work. **2.** *C. de serrurier,* picklock, skeleton key. *C. d'arrêt,* pawl, catch. *F:* Vivre aux crochets de qn, to live on, sponge on, s.o. *C. à boutons,* button-hook. **3.** (*a*) Poison fang (of serpent). (*b*) *pl.* Talons (of eagle). **4.** *pl. Typ:* Square brackets. **5.** Faire un crochet, (i) (of pers.) to swerve ; (ii) (of road) to take a sudden turn. **6.** *Box: C. du gauche,* left hook. **7.** *Mus:* Hook (of quaver).
crochetable [krɔʃtabl], *a.* (Lock) that can be picked.
crochet|er [krɔʃte], *v.tr.* (je crochète ; je cro-chéterai) **1.** To pick (lock). **2.** To crochet. **3.** *Typ:* To hook in (word). *s.m.* **-age.**
crocheteur[1] [krɔʃtœːr], *s.m.* Picklock, thief.
crocheteur[2], *s.m.* Porter, carrier.
crochu [krɔʃy], *a.* **1.** Hooked (wire, nose, etc.). *F:* Avoir les doigts crochus, les mains crochues, (i) to be light-fingered ; (ii) to be rapacious. **2.** Crooked (stick, idea).
crocodile [krɔkɔdil], *s.m.* Crocodile. *F:* Larmes de crocodile, crocodile tears.
croire [krwaːr], *v.* (*pr.p.* croyant ; *p.p.* cru ; *pr.ind.* je crois, n. croyons ; *p.d.* je croyais ; *p.h.* je crus ; *fu.* je croirai) **1.** *v.tr.* (*a*) *C. qch.,* to believe sth. Ne pas croire qch., to disbelieve sth. J'aime à croire que + *ind.,* I hope, trust, that . . . . Il est à croire que + *ind.,* it is probable that. . . . *Tout porte à c. que . . .,* there are many indications that. . . . *Je ne crois pas que cela suffise,* I don't think that will be enough. *F:* Je crois bien que . . .,* I do believe that. . . . *Je crois bien qu'il est sorti,* I fancy he is out. Je (le) crois bien! I should think so ! *Je crois que oui, que non,* I believe so ; I believe not ; I don't think so. N'en croyez rien! do not believe it !

A ce que je crois . . ., to the best of my belief . . . . *Se c. perdu,* to give oneself up for lost. *Je vous croyais Anglais,* I thought you were English. C'était à croire tous les éléments déchaînés, you would have thought that all the elements were let loose. J'ai cru bien faire, I thought I was doing right. *Il se croit de l'esprit,* he thinks him-self a wit. *Il se croit tout permis,* he thinks he may do anything. *Je lui croyais du talent,* I thought he had talent. *F:* Quel temps, crois-tu ! what beastly weather ! (*b*) *C. qn,* to believe s.o., take s.o.'s word. Me croira qui voudra, mais . . ., believe me or not, but. . . . *F:* Je te crois ! you bet ! rather ! En croire qn, (i) to take s.o.'s word for it ; (ii) to take s.o.'s advice. *Croyez-m'en,* be advised by me. *Je ne pouvais en c. mes yeux,* I couldn't believe my eyes. Il s'en croit un peu, he fancies himself a bit. **2.** *v.i.* (*a*) *C. à qch.,* to believe in (the existence or the truth of) sth. *C. aux fées,* to believe in fairies. *Le médecin crut à une fièvre scarlatine,* the doctor thought it was scarlet fever. C'est à ne pas y croire, it is beyond all belief. *C. au témoignage des sens,* to believe, trust, the evidence of one's senses. (*b*) *C. en qn,* to believe in, have faith in, s.o. *C. en Dieu,* to believe in God.
crois. See CROIRE. **croîs.** See CROÎTRE.
croisade [krwazad], *s.f. Hist:* Crusade. *Partir en c.,* to go on a crusade.
croisement [krwazmɑ̃], *s.m.* **1.** Crossing, meet-ing (of traffic). **2.** Crossing, intersection (of lines, roads, etc.). *C. dangereux,* dangerous cross-roads. **3.** (*a*) Crossing, interbreeding (of animals). (*b*) Cross-breed ; cross (entre . . . et . . ., be-tween . . . and . . .).
croiser [krwaze]. **1.** *v.tr.* (*a*) To cross. *C. le fer avec qn,* to cross swords with s.o. *C. les jambes,* to cross one's legs. **Rester les bras croisés,** (i) to stand with arms folded ; (ii) to remain idle. *C. qn sur l'escalier,* to meet, pass, s.o. on the stairs. *Leurs regards se croisèrent,* their eyes met. *Il me croise dans tout ce que je fais,* he crosses me, thwarts me, in everything I do. (*b*) To cross (sth.) out. (*c*) To cross, interbreed (animals, plants). **2.** *v.i.* (Of garment) To lap, fold over. **3.** *v.i. Nau:* To cruise.
se croiser. 1. (*a*) To (inter)cross ; to inter-sect. (*b*) *Se c. avec qn,* to meet and pass s.o. **2.** *Hist:* To take the cross.
croisé. 1. *a.* (*a*) Crossed. Mots croisés, cross-words. *Pros:* Rimes croisées, alternate rhymes. *Husb:* Race croisée, cross-breed. (*b*) Double-breasted (coat, etc.). (*c*) *Tex:* Twilled (material). **2.** *s.m.* (*a*) Crusader. (*b*) *Tex:* Twill.
croisée, *s.f.* **1.** Crossing. **Croisée des chemins,** cross-roads. **2.** Casement-window. **3.** Transept (of church). **4.** Cross-hairs (of telescope).
croiseur [krwazœːr], *s.m. Navy:* Cruiser.
croisière [krwazjɛːr], *s.f.* Cruise. Navire en croisière, ship cruising, on the, a, cruise. Faire des croisières, to cruise about. Vitesse de croisière, cruising speed ; *Av:* flying-speed under load.
croisillon [krwazijɔ̃], *s.m.* Cross-piece ; brace ; window bar.
croissance [krwasɑ̃ːs], *s.f.* Growth. **Prendre toute sa croissance,** to attain one's full growth. Arrêté dans sa croissance, stunted.
croissant[1] [krwasɑ̃], *a.* Growing (plant, etc.) ; increasing (anxiety, etc.) ; rising (prices).
croissant[2], *s.m.* **1.** (*a*) La lune est à son crois-sant, the moon is waxing. (*b*) Crescent (of moon). (*c*) *Geom:* Lune. **2.** *Cu:* Horseshoe milk-roll ; crescent(-roll). **3.** *Tls:* Bill-hook.

croiss-e, -es, etc. See CROÎTRE.

croit. See CROIRE. **croît.** See CROÎTRE.

croître [krwa:tr, -wa-], *v.i.* (*pr.p.* croissant; *p.p.* crû ; *pr.ind.* je crois, il croît, n. croissons, ils croissent; *p.h.* je crûs; *fu.* je croîtrai; *p.sub.* je crûsse) To grow, increase (in size). *C. de, en, volume,* to increase in volume. *La rivière a crû,* the river has risen. *Les jours croissent,* the days are lengthening. *C. en sagesse,* to grow in wisdom. *Aller croissant,* to go on increasing. *Prov:* **Mauvaise herbe croît toujours,** ill weeds grow apace.

croix [krwa], *s.f.* Cross. **1. La mise en croix,** the crucifixion. **Le chemin de la Croix,** the stations of the Cross. *Faire le signe de la c.,* to cross oneself. *F:* **Recevoir qn avec la croix et la bannière,** to receive s.o. with pomp and circumstance, with full honours. **La Croix rouge** (*de Genève*), the Red Cross. *Hist:* **Prendre la croix,** to take the cross (for a crusade). *Mil:* **La Croix de guerre,** the Military Cross. **En forme de croix,** cross-shaped ; crosswise. *Opt: Fils en c.,* cross-threads, -wires. *F:* **Il faut faire une croix à la cheminée,** we must mark that in red letters. **Croix de Saint-André,** St Andrew's cross. **Croix de Malte,** Maltese cross. **Croix ou pile,** heads or tails. **2.** *Typ:* Dagger, obelisk.

cromlech [krɔmlɛk], *s.m. Archeol:* Circle of standing stones.

croquant[1] [krɔkã]. **1.** *a.* Crisp (biscuit, etc.). **2.** *s.m. Cu:* Gristle, crackling.

croquant[2], *s.m. F: A:* Clod-hopper, chaw-bacon.

croque-mitaine, *s.m. F:* Bogy(-man), bugaboo. *pl. Des croque-mitaines.*

croque-mort, *s.m.* (Undertaker's) mute. *pl. Des croque-morts.*

croqu|er [krɔke]. **1.** *v.i.* To scrunch (between the teeth). **2.** *v.tr.* (*a*) To crunch, munch. **Chocolat à croquer,** eating chocolate. (*b*) To sketch. *F:* **Elle est gentille à croquer,** she is perfectly sweet. (*c*) (At croquet) To tight-croquet (the balls). S.a. MARMOT 2. *s.m.* **-ement.**

croquet[1] [krɔkɛ], *s.m. Cu:* Hard biscuit covered with almonds ; parkin ; snap

croquet[2], *s.m. Games:* Croquet.

croquignole [krɔkiɲɔl], *s.f.* **1.** Flick, fillip. **2.** Fancy biscuit.

croquis [krɔki], *s.m.* Sketch. *C. à la plume,* rough pen-drawing.

crosne [kro:n], *s.m. Hort:* Chinese artichoke.

crosse [krɔs], *s.f.* **1.** (Bishop's) crook ; crosier, crozier. **2.** *Sp:* (Hockey-)stick ; (golf-)club ; (lacrosse) stones. **3.** (*a*) Crook. **Courbé en crosse,** crooked. (*b*) *Mch:* C. **du piston,** cross-head of the piston. (*c*) Butt (of rifle) ; grip (of pistol). (*d*) *Artil:* C. **d'affût,** trail (of gun). (*e*) Scroll (of violin, etc.).

crossman, *pl.* **-men** [krɔsman, -mɛn], *s.m. Sp:* Cross-country runner.

crotale [krɔtal], *s.m.* Rattlesnake.

crotte [krɔt], *s.f.* **1.** (*a*) Dung, dropping (of horse, sheep, etc.). (*b*) **Une crotte de chocolat,** a chocolate. **2.** Mud, slush, dirt.

crotter [krɔte], *v.tr.* To dirty, soil.
se crotter, to get dirty, get covered with mud.
crotté, *a.* Dirty ; mud-bespattered.

crottin [krɔtɛ̃], *s.m.* (Horse-)dung ; (sheep-) droppings.

croulant [krulɑ̃], *a.* (Of house, etc.) Tottering, tumble-down. *Empire c.,* ramshackle empire.

croulement [krulmɑ̃], *s.m.* Collapse, falling in ; tumbling down (of building, etc.).

crouler [krule], *v.i.* (Of building, etc.) (*a*) To be on the point of collapse ; to totter. (*b*) To

collapse, crumble, tumble down, fall in. *Th: F:* **Faire crouler la salle,** to bring down the house.

croup [krup], *s.m. Med:* Croup.

croupe [krup], *s.f.* **1.** Croup, crupper, rump (of horse). **Monter en croupe,** to ride pillion. *Prendre qn en c.,* to take s.o. up behind, on the crupper. **2.** (*a*) Ridge, brow (of hill). (*b*) *Arch:* Hip. **Toit en croupe,** hipped roof.

croupetons (à) [akruptɔ̃], *adv.phr. A:* Squatting, crouching ; *F:* on one's hunkers. *Se tenir à c.,* to squat (on one's hunkers).

croupier [krupje], *s.m.* Croupier (of gaming-house).

croupière [krupjɛ:r], *s.f. Harn:* Crupper. **Tailler des croupières à l'ennemi,** to follow hot upon the enemy.

croupion [krupjɔ̃], *s.m.* (*a*) Rump (of bird). (*b*) *F:* Parson's nose (of cooked fowl).

croupir [krupi:r], *v.i.* **1.** (Of pers.) To lie, wallow (in filth, etc.). *C. dans l'oisiveté,* to lie sunk in sloth. **2.** (Of water) To stagnate, grow foul.
croupi, *a.* Stagnant, foul.

croupissant [krupisɑ̃], *a.* Stagnating.

croustillant [krustijɑ̃], *a.* **1.** Crisp, crusty (biscuit, pie). **2.** *F:* Spicy (story).

croustiller [krustije], *v.i.* (Of food) To crunch (under the teeth).

croûte [krut], *s.f.* **1.** Crust (of bread, of pie) ; rind (of cheese). **Faire croûte,** to crust, to cake. **Croûte aux champignons,** mushrooms on toast. *F:* **Casser une croûte, la croûte,** to have a snack. **2.** Scab, crust (on wound, etc.). **3.** *F:* (*a*) Daub ; badly painted picture. (*b*) *C'est une c.,* he's an old fossil, a duffer.

croûton [krutɔ̃], *s.m.* **1.** (*a*) Piece of crust. (*b*) Crusty end (of loaf). **2.** *Cu:* Sippet.

croyable [krwajabl], *a.* **1.** (Of pers.) Trustworthy. **2.** (Of thg) Believable, credible.

croyance [krwajɑ̃:s], *s.f.* Belief (*à,* in). *C. aux esprits, en Dieu,* belief in spirits, in God.

croy-ant[1], **-ons, -ez,** etc. See CROIRE.

croyant[2], **-ante** [krwajɑ̃, -ɑ̃:t]. **1.** *a.* Believing. **2.** *s.* Believer. *Les croyants,* the faithful.

cru[1] [kry], *a.* **1.** (*a*) Raw (meat, silk, material, etc.) ; crude (ore, art, drama, colour, etc.). *Cer: Pièce crue,* unfired piece. *Lumière crue,* garish light. **Dans le jour cru,** in broad daylight. **Parler en termes crus,** to speak (i) in rough, coarse, language, (ii) in plain terms. (*b*) **Mets cru à l'estomac,** indigestible dish. *Eau crue,* hard water. **2.** *Adv.phr.* **A cru,** next to the skin. *Monter (un cheval) à cru,* to ride a horse bareback(ed).

cru[2], **crû**[1] [kry], *s.m.* Locality in which vines are grown. *Les meilleurs crus,* the best vineyards. **Vin du cru,** local wine. **Sentir le cru,** to smack of the soil. S.a. BOUILLEUR 1. *F: Une histoire de son cru,* a story of his own invention.

cru[3], **crus-s, -t,** etc. See CROIRE.

crû[2], **crû-s, -t,** etc. See CROÎTRE.

cruauté [kryote], *s.f.* **1.** Cruelty (*envers,* to). **2.** Act of cruelty.

cruche [kryʃ], *s.f.* **1.** Pitcher, jug. **2.** *P:* Ass, fool, blockhead.

cruchon [kryʃɔ̃], *s.m.* **1.** Small jug ; pot (of beer). **2.** (Stoneware) hot-water bottle.

crucifères [krysifɛ:r], *s.f.pl. Bot:* Crucifers, cruciferae.

crucifi|er [krysifje], *v.tr.* To crucify. *s.m.* **-ement.**

crucifix [krysifi], *s.m.* Crucifix.

crucifixion [krysifiksjɔ̃], *s.f.* Crucifixion.

cruciforme [krysifɔrm], *a.* Cruciform ; cross-shaped.

crudité [krydite], *s.f.* **1.** Crudity (of foods); hardness (of water). **2.** Crudity, crudeness (of colouring, etc.). **3.** Coarseness (of expression).
crue [kry], *s.f.* Rising, swelling (of river); flood. Rivière en crue, river in spate. [CROÎTRE]
cru|el, -elle [kryɛl], *a.* Cruel (*envers*, to). *adv.* **-ellement.**
crûment [krymã], *adv.* Crudely, roughly.
cruss-e, -es, etc. See CROIRE.
crûss-e, -es, etc. See CROÎTRE.
crustacés [krystase], *s.m.pl.* Crustacea; shell-fish.
crypte [kript], *s.f. Arch: Anat: Bot:* Crypt.
cryptogame [kriptɔgam], *Bot:* **1.** *a.* Crypto-gamous, cryptogamic. **2.** *s.f.* Cryptogam.
cryptogramme [kriptɔgram], *s.m.* Cryptogram; cipher(-message).
cubage [kyba:ʒ], *s.m.* Cubic content; volume (of reservoir, etc.); air-space (of room).
cubain, -aine [kybɛ̃, -ɛn], *a. & s. Geog:* Cuban.
cube [kyb]. **1.** *s.m.* (*a*) *Geom: Mth:* Cube. (*b*) *pl. Toys:* Building blocks. **2.** *a.* **Mètre cube,** cubic metre.
cuber [kybe]. **1.** *v.tr.* (*a*) *Mth:* To cube (number, etc.). (*b*) To find the cubical content of (sth.). **2.** *v.i. Réservoir qui cube vingt litres,* reservoir that has a cubical content of twenty litres.
cubique [kybik], *a.* (*a*) Cubic(al). (*b*) *Mth:* **Racine cubique,** cube root.
cubisme [kybism], *s.m. Art:* Cubism.
cubitus [kybity:s], *s.m. Anat:* Cubitus, ulna.
cueillage [kœja:ʒ], *s.m.,* **cueillaison** [kœjɛzɔ̃], *s.f.* (*a*) Picking, gathering (of fruit, etc.) (*b*) Gathering time.
cueiller-ai, -as, etc. See CUEILLIR.
cueillette [kœjɛt], *s.f.* **1.** Gathering, picking (of fruit, flowers). **2.** *Nau:* **Navigation à la cueillette,** tramping.
cueilleur, -euse [kœjœ:r, -ø:z], *s.* Picker, gatherer (of fruit, etc.).
cueillir [kœji:r], *v.tr.* (*pr.p.* **cueillant;** *p.p.* **cueilli;** *pr.ind.* **je cueille, n. cueillons;** *p.d.* **je cueillais;** *p.h.* **je cueillis;** *fu.* **je cueillerai**) To gather, pick, pluck (flowers, fruit). *C. des lauriers,* to win laurels. *P: C. qn au passage,* (i) to nab s.o. as he goes by; (ii) to buttonhole s.o. **Se faire cueillir,** to get nabbed, caught.
cuiller, cuillère [kyjɛ:r, kɥijɛ:r], *s.f.* **1.** Spoon. (*a*) *C. à bouche,* table-spoon. *C. à café,* coffee-spoon. *C. à pot,* ladle. *F:* **Y aller avec le dos de la cuiller,** to act cautiously, gingerly. (*b*) *Tls:* **Mèche à cuiller,** spoon-bit. **2.** *Civ.E:* Scoop, bucket (of dredger).
cuillerée [kyjre, kɥijre], *s.f.* Spoonful.
cuilleron [kyjrɔ̃], *s.m.* **1.** Bowl (of spoon). **2.** *Ent:* Alula, winglet (of dipter).
cuir [kɥi:r], *s.m.* **1.** (*a*) *A:* Skin. (Still in) **Blessure entre cuir et chair,** wound to the quick, oblique flesh wound. *Anat:* **Cuir chevelu,** scalp. (*b*) Hide (of elephant, etc.). **2.** (*a*) Leather. *C. vert,* raw hide. *C. de molleterie,* shoe-leather. *C. jaune,* tan leather. *C. verni,* patent leather. *C. de Russie,* Russia leather. **Chaussures en cuir,** leather shoes. (*b*) **Cuir à rasoir,** razor-strop. **3.** *F:* Incorrect 'liaison,' as : *J'étais avec lui* [ʒetavɛk lɥi], *il a fait une erreur* [il a fez yn ɛrœ:r], *s'en va en guerre* [sãvãgɛ:r]. **Faire un cuir,** to make an incorrect 'liaison,' *F:* to 'drop a brick' (in speaking).
cuirasse [kɥiras], *s.f.* **1.** Cuirass, breast-plate. **Le défaut de la cuirasse,** the joints of the harness. *F: Trouver le défaut dans la c. de qn,* to find s.o.'s weak, vulnerable, spot. **2.** Armour (of (warship). **Plaque de cuirasse,** armour-plate.

cuirassement [kɥirasmã], *s.m.* **1.** Armouring (of ship). **2.** Armour(-plating).
cuirasser [kɥirase], *v.tr.* (*a*) To armour(-plate) (ship, etc.). (*b*) To enclose, protect (machine). **se cuirasser,** to put on one's cuirass. **Se cuirasser contre qch.,** to steel oneself, one's heart, against sth.
cuirassé. 1. *a.* (*a*) Armour-plated; armoured. (*b*) Enclosed, covered (dynamo, etc.). (*c*) *F: Être c. contre les supplications,* to be proof, to be steeled, hardened, against entreaties. **2.** *s.m.* Armoured ship; esp. battleship.
cuirassier [kɥirasje], *s.m. Mil:* Cuirassier.
cuire [kɥi:r], *v.* (*pr.p.* **cuisant;** *p.p.* **cuit;** *pr.ind.* **je cuis, il cuit, n. cuisons;** *p.d.* **je cuisais;** *p.h.* **je cuisis;** *fu.* **je cuirai**) **1.** *v.tr.* (*a*) To cook. *C. à l'eau,* to boil. *C. au four,* to bake or roast. *Cuit à point,* done to a turn. *Trop cuit,* overdone. *Pas assez cuit,* underdone. *F:* **Un dur à cuire,** a hardened old sinner. (*b*) To burn, fire, bake, kiln (bricks, pottery, etc.). **2.** *v.i.* (*a*) (Of food) To cook. *C. à petit feu,* to cook slowly; (in pan) to simmer. **Faire cuire un bifteck,** to cook a steak. *F:* **Cuire dans son jus,** to stew in one's own juice. (*b*) To burn, smart. *Les yeux me cuisent,* my eyes are smarting. **Il vous en cuira,** you shall smart for it; you'll be sorry.
cuite, *s.f.* **1.** Baking, firing, burning (of bricks, etc.). **2.** Batch (of things baked at one time). **3.** *P:* **Prendre une cuite,** to get drunk.
cuisant [kɥizã], *a.* Smarting, burning (pain, etc.); biting, stinging (cold). *Déception cuisante,* bitter disappointment.
cuiseur [kɥizœ:r], *s.m.* **1.** (Brick-, lime-)burner; fireman. **2.** *C. électrique,* electric cooker (utensil).
cuisine [kɥizin], *s.f.* **1.** Kitchen. *Nau:* (Cook's) galley. **Fille de cuisine,** kitchen-maid. **Articles de cuisine,** cooking utensils. **2.** (*a*) (Art of) cooking; cookery. **Livre de cuisine,** cookery book. **Faire la cuisine,** to do the cooking. (*b*) *Journ: F:* Sub-editing. **3.** (Cooked) food.
cuisiner [kɥizine], *v.tr.* To cook (meat, etc.). *F: C. des comptes,* to cook accounts. *C. un prévenu,* to interrogate, *F:* pump, *U.S:* grill, a man in custody.
cuisinier, -ière [kɥizinje, -jɛːr], *s.* **1.** Cook. **2.** *s.m.* Cookery book. **3.** *s.f.* Cuisinière, cooking-stove. *Cuisinière anglaise,* kitchen range. *Cuisinière à gaz,* gas-cooker.
cuissard [kɥisa:r], *s.m.* **1.** *Archeol:* Cuisse, thigh-piece (of armour). **2.** *pl.* (Cyclist's) overall leggings. **3.** *a.* **Bottes cuissardes,** (i) thigh-boots, jack-boots; (ii) waders.
cuisse [kɥis], *s.f.* Thigh. *Cu: C. de poulet,* chicken leg, *F:* drumstick.
cuisson [kɥisɔ̃], *s.f.* **1.** (*a*) Cooking, baking. **Le bifteck est en cuisson,** the steak is on (the grill). (*b*) Burning, firing (of bricks, etc.). **2.** Burning (sensation); smarting (pain).
cuistre [kɥistr], *s.m.* **1.** *A:* Ill-bred pedant. **2.** *F:* Cad; ill-mannered cur.
cuit, cuite. See CUIRE.
cuivre [kɥi:vr], *s.m.* **1.** **Cuivre rouge,** copper. **Doublé en c.,** copper-bottomed. **Cuivre jaune,** brass. **Faire les cuivres,** to do the brass(es). *Mus:* **Les cuivres,** the brass (wind-instruments). **2.** (*a*) *Engr:* Copper-plate. (*b*) Electrotyped plate, block.
cuivr|er [kɥivre], *v.tr.* **1.** To copper; to coat, sheath, (sth.) with copper. **2.** *C. le teint,* to bronze the complexion. **3.** *v.i.* (Of trumpet, etc.) To blare. *s.m.* **-age.**
cuivré, *a.* **1.** Copper-coloured. *Teint c.,* bronzed complexion. *Ciel c.,* lurid sky. **2.** *Voix*

cuivrée, metallic, resounding, voice. *Mus: Sons cuivrés*, brassy tones ; blare.

cul [ky], *s.m.* **I.** (*a*) *V:* Backside, bottom, behind (of person). *P:* **Cul goudronné**, sailor, tar. **Enlever le cul à qn**, to give s.o. a toe up. (*b*) Haunches, rump (of animal). **Tirer un oiseau au cul levé**, to shoot a bird on the rise. **2.** (*a*) Bottom (of bag, bottle, etc.) ; base, punt (of bottle) ; tail (of pulley-block, cart). **Mettre un tonneau à cul**, to tip up, up-end, a barrel. (*b*) Stern (of ship). **Trop sur cul**, too much by the stern.

culasse [kylas], *s.f.* **I.** Breech (of gun, rifle). *C. mobile*, bolt (of rifle). *Fusil se chargeant par la c.*, breech-loading gun. *Artil:* **Bloc de culasse**, breech-block. **2.** *I.C.E:* (Detachable) cylinder-head ; combustion head. [CUL]

cul-blanc [kyblɑ̃], *s.m. Orn:* Wheatear, stone-chat. *pl. Des culs-blancs*.

culbutant [kylbytɑ̃], *s.m.* Tumbler(-pigeon).

culbute [kylbyt], *s.f.* (*a*) Somersault. **Faire la culbute**, to turn a somersault. (*b*) Tumble ; heavy fall. *Faire une violente c.*, to come a heavy cropper. (*c*) *F:* *Faire la c.*, (of ministry) to fall ; (in business) to fail.

culbut|er [kylbyte]. **I.** *v.i.* (*a*) To turn a somersault. (*b*) *C. du haut de l'escalier*, to tumble downstairs (head over heels). **2.** *v.tr.* (*a*) To overthrow, knock over, upset (s.o., sth.). (*b*) To tip, tilt (cart, etc.) ; to dump, shoot (ore, etc.). (*c*) To trip (lever, etc.). *s.m.* **-age.**

culbuteur [kylbytœ:r], *s.m.* **I.** *Toys:* Tumbler. **2.** *El:* Interrupteur à culbuteur, tumbler-switch. **3.** *I.C.E:* (Valve) rocker. *Moteur à c.*, overhead-valve engine. **4.** (*a*) Tripper device. (*b*) Tipping apparatus (for trucks, etc.).

cul-de-jatte [kydʒat], *s.m.* Legless cripple. *pl. Des culs-de-jatte*.

cul-de-lampe [kydlɑ̃:p], *s.m.* **I.** *Arch:* (*a*) Pendant, cul-de-lampe. (*b*) Bracket, corbel. **2.** *Typ:* Tail-piece, cul-de-lampe. *pl. Des culs-de-lampe*.

cul-de-sac [kydsak], *s.m.* Blind alley, cul-de-sac. *Rail:* Blind siding. *pl. Des culs-de-sac*.

culée [kyle], *s.f.* **I.** *Civ.E:* Abutment(-pier) of bridge. **2.** *Nau:* Stern-way. [CUL]

culer [kyle], *v.i.* **I.** (*a*) To go backwards. *Faire c. une charrette*, to back a cart. (*b*) *Nau:* To make stern-way ; to drop astern. **Nagez à culer!** back water ! **2.** (Of wind) To veer astern. [CUL]

culinaire [kylinɛ:r], *a.* Culinary.

culminant [kylminɑ̃], *a.* (*a*) *Astr:* Culminant. (*b*) **Point culminant,** highest point ; zenith (of power, etc.) ; height, climax (of glory).

culot [kylo], *s.m.* **I.** Bottom (of church lamp) ; (metal) base (of sporting cartridge). *C. d'une bouteille*, punt, kick, of a bottle. *El: C. d'une lampe*, base, cap, of a lamp. *I.C.E: C. de bougie*, body of sparking-plug. *P:* **Avoir du culot,** to have plenty of cheek, of self-assurance. **2.** Dottle (in tobacco-pipe). **3.** (*a*) Last chick hatched. (*b*) *F:* Baby of the family. [CUL]

culotte [kylɔt], *s.f.* **I.** *Cu:* Rump, buttock (of beef). **2.** **Une culotte, des culottes, une paire de culottes,** a pair of breeches. *C. courte,* (i) knee-breeches ; (ii) knickerbockers ; (iii) shorts. **Culotte de peau,** (i) buckskin riding-breeches ; (ii) *F:* old officer risen from the ranks. *F:* **C'est la femme qui porte la culotte,** it is the wife who wears the breeches. **3.** *P:* **Prendre une culotte,** (i) to lose heavily (at cards) ; (ii) to get drunk.

culotter [kylɔte], *v.tr.* **I.** To breech (a child). **2.** To colour, season (pipe).

  se culotter. I. *F:* (Of painting) To mellow ; (of pipe) to colour, season. **2.** *P:* To get drunk, tight. **3.** To put on one's breeches.

culpabilité [kylpabilite], *s.f.* Culpability, guiltiness, guilt. *Jur:* **Nier sa culpabilité,** to plead not guilty.

culte [kylt], *s.m.* **I.** Worship. *Bâtiment du c.*, place of worship. *Le c. des héros*, hero-worship. **Avoir un culte pour qn,** to worship s.o. **2.** Form of worship ; cult, creed.

cultivable [kyltivabl], *a.* Arable (land).

cultivateur [kyltivatœ:r], *s.m.* **I.** Farmer. *C. de roses,* rose-grower. **2.** Cultivator ; light plough.

cultiver [kyltive], *v.tr.* **I.** To cultivate, farm, till (the soil). **2.** To cultivate (plants, one's mind). *C. des céréales,* to raise, grow, cereals.

cultivé, *a.* **I.** Cultivated (land). **2.** Cultured (mind).

cultuel, -elle [kyltɥel]. **I.** *a.* Of, pertaining to, worship. **2.** *s.f.* **Cultuelle,** church society.

culture [kylty:r], *s.f.* **I.** (*a*) Cultivation, tillage, tilling (of the soil). (*b*) *pl.* Fields, land, under cultivation. **2.** Cultivation, culture (of plants, of the mind) ; breeding (of bees, etc.). **3.** *Bac:* Culture. S.a. BOUILLON 2. **4.** *Homme de forte c.,* highly cultured man.

cumul [kymyl], *s.m.* **Cumul de fonctions,** plurality of offices ; pluralism.

cumuler [kymyle], *v.tr.* *C. des fonctions,* to hold a plurality of offices.

cumulus [kymylyːs],*s.m.inv.* *Meteor:* Cumulus ; cloud-rack.

cunéiforme [kyneifɔrm], *a.* Wedge-shaped, arrow-headed ; cuneiform (writing).

cupide [kypid], *a.* Covetous, greedy, grasping.

cupidité [kypidite], *s.f.* Cupidity, covetousness, greed.

Cupidon [kypidɔ̃]. *Pr.n.m.* Cupid.

cuprifère [kyprifɛ:r], *a.* Copper-bearing.

cuprique [kyprik], *a.* Cupric (acid).

cuproxyde [kyprɔksid], *s.m. Ch:* Cupric oxide. *El:* **Valve cuproxyde,** metal-oxide rectifying valve.

cupule [kypyl], *s.f.* Cupule ; cup (of acorn).

curable [kyrabl], *a.* Curable (disease, etc.).

curatelle [kyratɛl], *s.f. Jur:* Trusteeship, guardianship.

curateur, -trice [kyratœːr, -tris], *s. Jur:* Trustee, administrator (of vacant succession, etc.) ; guardian (of emancipated minor).

curatif, -ive [kyratif, -i:v], *a. & s.m.* Curative.

cure [ky:r], *s:f.* **I.** Care. **Prendre, avoir, cure de** qch., to take heed, notice, of sth. *Personne n'en a c.,* nobody cares. **2.** *Ecc:* (*a*) **Bénéfice avec cure,** benefice with cure (of souls). (*b*) Residence of the *curé* (= vicarage or rectory). **3.** *Med:* (Course of) treatment ; cure. **Faire une cure de** lait, to take a milk cure.

curé [kyre], *s.m.* Parish priest.

cure-dents, *s.m.inv.* Tooth-pick.

curée [kyre], *s.f.* (i) *Ven:* Quarry ; (ii) *F:* the rush for the spoils. **Être âpre à la curée,** to be eager for gain, for honours.

cure-pipe, *s.m.* Pipe-cleaner. *pl. Des cure-pipes*.

curer [kyre], *v.tr.* (*a*) To pick (one's teeth, etc.) ; to clean (one's nails). (*b*) To clear, clean out (drain, etc.) ; to dredge (river, etc.).

curieusement [kyrjøzmɑ̃], *adv.* **I.** (*a*) Interestedly, inquiringly. (*b*) Curiously, inquisitively. **2.** Curiously ; (i) delicately (worked, etc.) ; (ii) quaintly, oddly.

curieux, -euse [kyrjø, -ø:z], *a.* **I.** *A. & Lit:* (*a*) Careful (*de*, of) ; meticulous. (*b*) Inquiring (mind) ; interested (*de*, in). *C. de littérature,* interested in literature. **2.** Curious. (*a*) Interested. *Je serai c. de voir cela,* I shall be interested to see it. *s.* **Un curieux,** (i) an interested person ;

(ii) a sight-seer. (b) Inquisitive (de, about). *Caractère c.*, prying disposition. (c) Odd, peculiar. *Chose curieuse à voir*, quaint, curious, sight.

curiosité [kyrjɔzite], s.f. Curiosity. **1.** (a) Interestedness. (b) Inquisitiveness. *Par curiosité*, out of curiosity. (c) Oddness, peculiarity. **2.** (a) Curio. *Magasin de curiosités*, curiosity shop. (b) *Les curiosités de Paris*, the sights of Paris.

curseur [kyrsœːr], s.m. Cursor, slide(r), runner, traveller (of mathematical instrument). *El:* Slide contact; jockey (of rheostat).

cursif, -ive [kyrsif, -iːv]. **1.** a. (a) Cursive, running (handwriting). (b) Cursory. **2.** s.f. Cursive, running hand.

curviligne [kyrvilin], a. Curvilinear, rounded.

curvimètre [kyrvimɛtr], s.m. Curvometer; map-measurer.

cuscute [kyskyt], s.f. *Bot:* Dodder.

cuspide [kyspid], s.f. *Bot:* Cusp.

cuspidé [kyspide], a. *Bot:* Cuspidate.

custode[1] [kystɔd], s.f. (a) Altar curtain. (b) Pyx-cloth.

custode[2], s.m. or f. *Veh:* Padded side (of carriage, car); arm-rest.

cutané [kytane], a. Cutaneous. *Maladies cutanées*, skin diseases.

cuticule [kytikyl], s.f. Cuticle, epidermis.

cuti-réaction, s.f. *Med:* Skin-test (for tuberculosis, etc.).

cuve [kyːv], s.f. (a) Vat, tun. (b) Tank (*e.g.* for electro-plating); cistern. *I.C.E:* Float-chamber (of carburettor). *C. à lessive*, copper. *Phot: C. à développement*, developing-tank.

cuvée [kyve], s.f. Vatful, tunful.

cuvel|er [kyvle], v.tr. (je cuvelle; je cuvellerai) To line, timber, tub (mine-shaft, etc.). s.m. **-age.**

cuver [kyve]. **1.** v.i. (Of wine) To ferment, work. **2.** v.tr. To work, ferment (wine). *F: Cuver son vin*, to sleep off one's drink.

cuvette [kyvɛt], s.f. **1.** Wash-basin. **2.** Dish; pan (of w.c.); cistern (of barometer); bulb (of thermometer). *Nau:* Bowl (of compass). *Phot:* (Developing) dish. **3.** *Geol:* Basin.

cuvier [kyvje], s.m. Wash-tub.

cyanhydrique [sjanidrik], a. *Ch:* Hydrocyanic; *F:* prussic (acid).

cyanogène [sjanɔʒɛn], s.m. *Ch:* Cyanogen.

cyanose [sjanoːz], s.f. *Med:* Cyanosis.

cyanure [sjanyːr], s.m. *Ch:* Cyanide.

cyclable [siklabl], a. *Piste cyclable*, cycle-path.

cycle [sikl], s.m. **1.** Cycle (of events, poems, etc.). **2.** (Bi-, tri)cycle. *Fabricant de cycles*, cycle-maker.

cyclique [siklik], a. Cyclic(al).

cyclisme [siklism], s.m. *Sp:* Cycling.

cycliste [siklist], s.m. & f. Cyclist.

cycloïdal, -aux [siklɔidal, -o], a. *Mth:* Cycloidal (curve, etc.).

cycloïde [siklɔid], s.f. *Mth:* Cycloid.

cyclone [siklon], s.m. *Meteor:* Cyclone.

cyclope [siklɔp], s.m. Cyclops.

cyclopéen, -enne [siklɔpeɛ̃, -ɛn], a. Cyclopean, gigantic.

cygne [sin], s.m. Swan. *Jeune c.*, cygnet. *C. mâle*, cob. S.a. CHANT 1.

cylindre [silɛ̃ːdr], s.m. *Geom: etc:* Cylinder *I.C.E: Moteur à quatre cylindres*, four-cylinder engine. *Typ: C. d'impression*, printing drum. *C. compresseur*, (i) garden-roller, (ii) steam-roller. *F: Porter un c.*, to wear a top-hat.

cylindr|er [silɛ̃dre], v.tr. **1.** To roll (road, lawn, etc.). **2.** To calender, mangle (cloth). s.m. **-age.**

cylindrique [silɛ̃drik], a. Cylindrical.

cymbale [sɛ̃bal], s.f. *Mus:* Cymbal.

cymbalier [sɛ̃balje], s.m. Cymbal-player.

cyme [sim], s.f. *Bot:* Cyme.

cynégétique [sineʒetik]. **1.** a. Cynegetic. **2.** s.f. Cynegetics, hunting.

cynique [sinik]. **1.** a. (a) *A.Phil:* Cynic(al). (b) Shameless (morals); brazen (insolence); unblushing (indecency); bare-faced (lie). **2.** s.m. (a) *A.Phil:* Cynic. (b) Shameless, brazen, person. adv. **-ment.**

cynisme [sinism], s.m. **1.** *A.Phil:* Cynicism. **2.** Shamelessness, effrontery.

cynocéphale [sinɔsefal]. **1.** a. Cynocephalous, dog-headed. **2.** s.m. *Z:* Cynocephalus; dog-faced baboon.

cynodrome [sinɔdroːm], s.m. Greyhound racing-track.

cyprès [siprɛ], s.m. *Bot:* Cypress(-tree).

cypriote [sipriɔt], a. & s. *Geog:* Cyprian, Cypriot; of Cyprus.

cystique [sistik], a. Cystic (duct, calculus, etc.).

cytise [sitiːz], s.m. *Bot:* **1.** Cytisus. **2.** Laburnum.

cytoblaste [sitɔblast], s.m. *Biol:* Cytoblast.

czar [tsaːr, gzaːr], s.m., **czarine** [tsarin, gzarin], s.f. = TSAR, TSARINE.

D

D, d [de], s.m. (The letter) D, d. *P: Le système* D (= *débrouille-toi*), resourcefulness, wangling.

dà [da], adv. *F: Oui-dà!* yes indeed!

d'abord [dabɔːr], adv.phr. See ABORD 4.

dactyle [daktil], s.m. *Pros:* Dactyl.

dactylo [daktilo], s.m. & f. *F:* Typist.

dactylographe [daktilɔgraf], s.m. & f. Typist.

dactylographie [daktilɔgrafi], s.f. Typewriting, typing.

dactylographier [daktilɔgrafje], v.tr. To type (-write).

dactylographique [daktilɔgrafik], a. Typewriting (material, etc.).

dactyloscopie [daktilɔskɔpi], s.f. Finger-print identification.

dactyloscopique [daktilɔskɔpik], a. *Examen d.*, examination of fingerprints.

dada [dada], s.m. *F:* **1.** (In nursery language) Gee-gee. *Aller à dada*, to ride a-cock-horse. **2.** *A:* Hobby(-horse). *F: Enfourcher son dada*, to ride one's pet hobby.

dadais [dadɛ], s.m. *F:* Booby; Tony Lumpkin.

dague [dag], s.f. **1.** Dagger; *Navy:* dirk. **2.** Spike (of two-year-old deer).

daguet [dagɛ], s.m. *Ven:* Brocket, pricket.

dahlia [dalja], s.m. *Bot:* Dahlia.

daigner [dɛɲe], v.tr. To deign, condescend. *Daignez accepter ces quelques fleurs*, be pleased to accept these few flowers.

daim [dɛ̃], s.m. (Fallow-)deer; buck. **(Peau de) daim**, (i) buckskin, doeskin; (ii) suède.

daine [dɛn, *Ven*: din], *s.f.* Doe (of fallow-deer).
dais [dɛ], *s.m.* **1.** Canopy. *Recouvert d'un d.,* canopied. **2.** *A*: Dais, platform.
Dalila [dalila]. *Pr.n.f. B.Hist*: Delilah.
dallage [dalaːʒ], *s.m.* **1.** Paving (with flags, etc.). **2.** Pavement, flagging; tiled floor.
dalle [dal], *s.f.* **1.** (*a*) *Const*: Flag(stone); flooring-tile. (*b*) Slab (of marble, etc.). **2.** Slice, slab (of fish).
daller [dale], *v.tr.* To pave (with flagstones, etc.); to flag (pavement, etc.); to tile (floor).
dalmatique [dalmatik], *s.f. Ecc.Cost*: Dalmatic.
dalot [dalo], *s.m. Nau*: Scupper(-hole).
daltonien, -ienne [daltɔnjɛ̃, -jɛn], *a. & s.* Colour-blind (person).
daltonisme [daltɔnism], *s.m.* Colour-blindness.
Damas [damɑ(ːs)]. **1.** *Pr.n.m. Geog*: Damascus. **2.** *s.m.* [damɑ] (*a*) *Tex*: Damask (linen, silk, etc.). (*b*) Damson (plum).
damasquin|er [damaskine], *v.tr.* To inlay, damascene, damaskeen (blade, etc.). *s.m.* **-age.**
damasser [damɑse], *v.tr.* To damask.
  damassé. **1.** *a.* (*a*) *Linge d.,* linen damask. (*b*) *Acier d.,* Damascus steel. **2.** *s.m. Tex*: Damask linen; diaper.
dame¹ [dam], *s.f.* **1.** (*a*) (Noble) lady. *Les dames de France,* the royal princesses of France. *F*: **Elle fait la (grande) dame,** she puts on airs; she sets up for a lady. (*b*) Lady. *Que prendront ces dames.* (i) what will the ladies take? (ii) what will you take, ladies? (*c*) *A*: Dame. **Dame Nature,** Dame Nature. (*d*) (Married) lady. *F*: **Votre dame,** your good lady, *P*: your missis. *Jur*: **La dame Simon,** Mrs Simon. (*e*) **Dame d'honneur,** lady-in-waiting; maid of honour. **Dame de compagnie,** (paid) companion. **Dames de charité,** district-visitors. (*f*) (Gentleman's) partner (at dance). S.a. NOTRE-DAME. **2.** *Games*: (*a*) Jeu de dames, (game of) draughts, *U.S*: checkers. (*b*) King (at draughts); queen (at cards and chess). **Aller à dame,** (i) *Draughts*: to make a king; (ii) *Chess*: to queen. **3. Dames de nage,** rowlocks. **4.** (Paving) beetle; (earth) rammer. **5.** *Bot*: **Dame d'onze heures,** star of Bethlehem.
dame², *int.* Dame oui! well, yes! why, yes! rather! *Ça vous étonne?—D. oui!* does it astonish you?—It does indeed! *Vous y allez?—Dame!* you are going?—What else can I do?
dame-jeanne, *s.f.* Demijohn. *pl. Des dames-jeannes.*
dam|er [dame], *v.tr.* **1.** (At draughts) To crown (a piece). *F*: **Damer le pion à qn,** to go one better than s.o.; to outwit or outdo s.o. **2.** To ram, tamp (earth). *s.m.* **-age.**
damier [damje], *s.m.* Draught-board (in Fr. with 100 squares); *U.S*: checker-board. **Étoffe en damier,** check, chequered, material. **Mots en damier,** cross-word puzzle. [DAME¹]
damnable [dɑnabl], *a.* **1.** *Theol*: Deserving of damnation. **2.** *F*: Detestable, heinous.
damnation [dɑnasjɔ̃], *s.f.* Damnation.
damner [dɑne], *v.tr.* To damn.
  se damner, to incur damnation. *F*: **Faire damner qn,** to torment s.o.; to drive s.o. crazy.
  damné, -ée, *a. & s.* Damned. *F*: **Souffrir comme un damné,** to go through hell. **Être l'âme damnée de qn,** to be a mere tool in the hands of s.o.
Damoclès [damɔklɛːs]. *Pr.n.m.* **L'épée de Damoclès,** the sword of Damocles.
damoiseau [damwazo], *s.m. A*: **1.** Squire, page. **2.** *F*: Fop.
damoiselle [damwazɛl], *s.f. A*: Damozel.

dandin [dɑ̃dɛ̃], *s.m. A*: Simpleton.
dandin|er [dɑ̃dine], *v.tr.* To dandle (baby).
  se dandiner, to have a rolling gait; to waddle. *s.m.* **-ement.**
Danemark [danmark]. *Pr.n.m.* Denmark.
danger [dɑ̃ʒe], *s.m.* Danger, peril, jeopardy. *D. pour la sécurité nationale,* danger to national security. *A l'abri du d.,* out of harm's way. **Courir un danger,** to be in danger. **Courir danger de . . .,** to run the risk of. . . . *Quel d. y a-t-il à l'avertir?* what danger, what harm, is there in warning him? **Sans danger,** safe(ly); securely. **Mettre en danger la vie de qn,** to endanger, jeopardize, s.o.'s life. **En danger de mort,** in danger, peril, of death. *Être en d. de tomber,* to be in danger of falling. *F*: **Pas de danger!** never fear! *Il n'y a pas de d. qu'il vienne,* there is no fear of his coming.
dangereu|x, -euse [dɑ̃ʒrø, -øːz], *a.* Dangerous (*pour,* to). *Mil*: **Zone dangereuse,** danger zone. *adv.* **-sement.**
danois, -oise [danwa, -waːz]. **1.** *a.* Danish. **Chien danois,** Great Dane. **2.** *s.* Dane. **3.** *s.m. Ling*: Danish.
dans [dɑ̃], *prep.* **1.** (Of place) (*a*) In. *Qu'est-ce que vous avez d. la main?* what have you (hidden) in your hand? (Cp. *Un bâton à la main,* stick in hand.) *D. la France moderne,* in modern France. (Cp. *En France,* in France.) *Habiter d. Paris même,* to live in(side) Paris. (Cp. *Il est à Paris,* he is in Paris.) (*b*) Within. *D. un rayon de dix kilomètres,* within a radius of ten kilometres. (*c*) Into. *Mettre qch. d. une boîte,* to put sth. into a box. *Tomber d. l'oubli,* to sink into oblivion. (*d*) (With motion from a point within sth.) Out of. *Prendre qch. d. qch.,* to take sth. out of sth. *Boire d. un verre,* to drink out of a glass. *Copier qch. d. un livre,* to copy sth. out of, from, a book. *Découper un article d. le journal,* to cut an article out of the paper. (*e*) *Il passerait d. le feu pour elle,* he would go through fire for her sake. *Il a voyagé d. le monde,* he has travelled about the world. **2.** (Of time) (*a*) In, within, during. **Dans le temps,** long ago, formerly. *Payer d. les dix jours,* to pay within ten days. *Je serai prêt à partir d. cinq minutes,* I shall be ready to start in five minutes. (Cp. *On peut aller à Londres en cinq heures,* it takes five hours to get to London.) *F*: **Il a dans les quarante ans,** he is about forty. *Ça va faire d. les trois mois que . . .,* it is about three months since. . . . *Une somme dans les dix livres, F*: somewhere about ten pounds. (*b*) *Essayer de voir d. l'avenir,* to try to see into the future. **3.** (*a*) *Être d. le commerce,* to be in trade. (*b*) *Être d. la nécessité de . . .,* to be under the necessity of. . . . *D. ce but,* with this object. *D. cette occasion,* on that occasion.
dansant [dɑ̃sɑ̃], *a.* **1.** Dancing. **2.** *Thé dansant,* dance tea. *Donner une soirée dansante,* to give a dance.
danse [dɑ̃ːs], *s.f.* Dance, dancing. *Aimer la d.,* to be fond of dancing. *Med*: **Danse de Saint-Guy,** St Vitus's dance. *F*: **Entrer en danse,** (i) to join the dance; (ii) *F*: to join in. *F*: **Ouvrir la danse,** to start the battle. S.a. MACABRE, MAÎTRE I.
danser [dɑ̃se], *v.i.* **1.** To dance. *D. une valse,* to dance a waltz. **Faire danser qn,** (i) to dance with s.o.; (ii) *F*: to lead s.o. a dance. *Faire d. un bébé sur son genou,* to dance, dandle, a baby on one's knee. **Faire danser les écus,** to make the money fly. S.a. ANSE I. **Ne savoir sur quel pied danser,** to be all at sea. **2.** (Of horse) To prance.
danseur, -euse [dɑ̃sœːr, -øːz], *s.* **1.** (*a*) Dancer

esp. ballet-dancer. (*b*) **Dánseur de corde,** tight-rope dancer. **2.** Partner (at dance).

Dantzig [dõtsik, -dz-]. *Pr.n. Geog :* Danzig.

dard [da:r], *s.m.* **1.** (*a*) *A :* Dart, javelin. (*b*) *Fish :* (Eel-)spear. **2.** (*a*) Sting (of insect); forked tongue (of serpent). (*b*) Tongue (of flame). (*c*) Piercing ray (of sun). (*d*) Stabbing pain.

darder [darde], *v.tr.* **1.** To hurl, shoot forth, dart (pointed object). *F : Il darda sur moi un regard chargé de haine,* he shot, flashed, a glance of hatred at me. *v.i. Il a une dent qui lui darde,* he has a stabbing tooth. **2.** (*a*) To spear (eel). (*b*) *D. qn de sarcasmes,* to hurl sarcasm at s.o.

dardillon [dardijõ], *s.m.* **1.** Small dart. **2.** Barb (of fish-hook). .

dare-dare [darda:r], *adv.* In hot haste, helter-skelter, post-haste.

darne [darn], *s.f. Cu :* Slice, slab, steak (of salmon, cod).

darse [dars], *s.f.* Harbour, wet dock (at Toulon and Marseilles).

dartre [dartr], *s.f. Med :* Scurfy affection; scurf, dartre. *F : Maison plaquée de dartres,* house showing patches of decay.

dartreux, -euse [dartrø, -ø:z], *a.* Scabby, dartrous.

date [dat], *s.f.* Date. **Sans date,** undated (letter, etc.). *Erreur de d.,* mistake in the date. *Faire une erreur de d.,* to misdate an event, a document. **Prendre date pour qch.,** to fix a date for sth. (Of event) **Faire date,** to mark an epoch. **Être le premier en date,** to come first. **De fraîche date,** of recent date. **De vieille, de longue, date,** of long standing. **Je le connais de longue date,** I have known him for a long time. *Com :* **En date du 15 courant,** under date of the 15th inst. **A trente jours de date,** thirty days after date. *Fin :* **Emprunt à longue, à courte, date,** long-dated, short-dated, loan.

dater [date]. **1.** *v.tr.* To date (letter, etc.). *Non daté,* undated. **2.** *v.i.* To date (*de,* from). **A dater de ce jour,** from to-day. *A d. du 15,* on and after the 15th. *Abs. Événement qui date (dans l'histoire, etc.),* epoch-making event. *Costume qui date,* out-of-date costume.

dateur [datœ:r], *s.m.* Date-marker (for stamps).

datif [datif], *a. & s.m. Gram :* Dative (case). **Au datif,** in the dative.

datte [dat], *s.f. Bot :* Date.

dattier [datje], *s.m. Bot :* Date-palm, -tree.

daube [do:b], *s.f. Cu :* Stew. **Bœuf en daube,** stewed, braised, beef.

dauber [dobe], *v.tr. Cu :* To stew, braise (beef).

dauphin [dofɛ̃], *s.m.* **1.** Dolphin or grampus. **2.** *Hist :* Dauphin (eldest son of French king).

dauphine [dofin], *s.f. Fr.Hist :* Dauphiness, wife of the Dauphin.

davantage [davãta:ʒ], *adv.* More. *Il m'en faut d.,* I need still more. *Je n'en dis pas d.,* I shall say no more. *Je ne l'interrogeai pas d.,* I did not question him any further. *Vous êtes riche, mais il l'est d.,* you are rich but he is more so. *Nous ne resterons pas d.,* we will not stay any longer. *Se reculer d.,* to draw further back. *Se baisser d.,* to stoop lower.

davier [davje], *s.m.* **1.** *Dent :* Forceps. **2.** *Nau :* Davit.

de [də]. (Before vowels and h 'mute' d'. *De + def. art.* **le, les,** are contracted into **du, des.**) **I.** *prep.* **1.** (*a*) From. *Il vient de Paris,* he comes from Paris. *L'idée est de vous,* the idea is yours, comes from you. *Je l'ai oublié ?* C'est bien de moi, did I forget it? It's just like me. *Du matin au soir,* from morning till night. *De vous à moi . . . ,*

between ourselves. . . . *De vingt à trente personnes,* between twenty and thirty people. *De jour en jour,* from day to day. (*b*) (Time vaguely indicated) *Il partit de nuit,* he left by night. *Du temps de nos pères,* in the days of our fathers. (*c*) (Agent, means, instrument) *Accompagné de ses amis,* accompanied by his friends. *La statue est de Rodin,* the statue is by Rodin. *J'ai fait cela de ma propre main,* I did it with my own hand. *Vivre de fruits,* to live on fruit. *Vivre de sa plume,* to live by one's pen. (*d*) (Manner) *Il me regarda d'un air amusé,* he looked at me with an amused air. *Répondre d'une voix douce,* to answer in a gentle voice. (*e*) (Cause, origin) *Sauter de joie,* to leap for joy. *Je tombe de fatigue,* I am ready to drop with fatigue. *Faire qch. de soi-même,* to do sth. of one's own accord. (*f*) (Measure) *Je suis âgé de seize ans,* I am sixteen years old. *Ma montre retarde de dix minutes,* my watch is ten minutes slow. *Il est plus grand que moi de la tête,* he is taller than I by a head. *La terrasse a vingt mètres de long, est longue de vingt mètres,* the terrace is twenty metres long. (*g*) (Introducing complement of adj.) *Digne d'éloges,* worthy of praise. *Altéré de sang,* thirsting for blood. **2.** (*a*) *Le livre de Pierre,* Peter's book. *Le toit de la maison,* the roof of the house. *Le meilleur élève de la classe,* the best pupil in the class. *Les rues de Paris,* the Paris streets. (*b*) (Material) *Un pont de fer,* an iron bridge. *Robe de soie,* silk dress. (*c*) (Distinguishing mark) *Le chien de berger,* the sheep-dog. (Cp. *Le chien du berger,* the shepherd's dog.) *Le journal d'hier,* yesterday's paper. *La route de Paris,* the Paris road. *Cette réponse est d'un rustre,* such an answer is the mark of the boor. (*d*) (Partitive) *Un verre de vin,* a glass of wine. *Une livre de café,* a pound of coffee. *Quelque chose de bon,* something good. *Je n'ai pas de sœurs,* I have no, not any, sisters. **3.** (Forming compound prepositions) *Près de la maison,* near the house. *Autour du jardin,* round the garden. *A partir de ce jour-là,* from that day onward. **4.** (Connecting verb and object) *Nous approchons de Paris,* we are getting near Paris. *Manquer de courage,* to lack courage. *Convenir d'une erreur,* to admit an error.

II. de, serving as a link word. **1.** Introducing an inf. (*a*) *Il est honteux de mentir,* it is shameful to lie. *Le mieux était de rire,* it was best to laugh. *Je crains d'être en retard,* I am afraid of being late. *J'aime mieux attendre que de me faire mouiller,* I would rather wait than get wet. *Ils sont indignes de vivre,* they are unfit to live. (*b*) (The so-called 'historical infinitive') *Ainsi dit le renard, et flatteurs d'applaudir,* thus spoke the fox, and his flatterers applauded. **2.** (Introducing an apposition or a predicative complement) *La ville de Paris,* the town of Paris. *Il fut traité de lâche,* he was called a coward. *Un drôle de garçon,* a funny chap. *Il y eut trois hommes de tués,* three men were killed. *C'est un grand pas de fait,* that is a great step forward. *F : Si j'étais de vous,* if I were you.

III. de, partitive particle, not prepositional. (Used also as *pl.* of **un, une**) *N'avez-vous pas des amis ?* have you not got friends? *Sans faire de fautes,* without making any mistakes. *Il ne peut parler sans faire des fautes,* he cannot speak without making mistakes. *Je ne veux pas qu'on lui mette de collier,* I won't have a collar put on him. *De braves gens se trouvaient là,* some worthy people were there. *Je bois de l'eau,* I drink water. *Donnez-nous de vos nouvelles,* let us hear from you. *Avez-vous du pain ?* have you any bread? *Donnez-moi de ce vin,* give me some of that wine. *Vous êtes des lâches,* you are cowards. *Je m'adresserai à des amis,* I shall apply to some friends. *Donnez-moi de bon vin, F: du bon vin,* give me (some) good wine. *Manger de tous les plats,* to partake of every dish. (Intensive) **Mettre** *des heures à faire qch.,* to spend hours over sth.

dé¹ [de], *s.m.* **I.** (*a*) *Gaming:* Die. *Jeter les dés,* to throw, cast, the dice. *Dés pipés, chargés,* loaded dice. **Coup de dé,** cast of the die. *F:* **Le dé en est jeté,** the die is cast. (*b*) Domino. (*c*) *Golf:* Tee. **2.** *Arch:* Dado, die (of pedestal, baluster). **3.** *Mec.E:* Bearing(-bush), brass.

dé², *s.m.* Dé (*à coudre*), thimble.

déambuler [deãbyle], *v.i. F:* To stroll about, to walk up and down; to saunter.

débâcle [deba:kl], *s.f.* **I.** Break(ing) up (of drift-ice). **2.** (*a*) Downfall, collapse (of commercial house, of a government). *D. de la santé,* break-down in health. (*b*) *Mil: etc:* Débâcle, rout.

débâcler [debakle]. **I.** *v.i.* (Of ice) To break up. **2.** *v.tr.* To clear (harbour) (of ice).

débagouler [debagule], *v.tr. P:* To vomit. *F: D. un torrent d'injures,* to pour forth a torrent of abuse.

déballage [debala:ʒ], *s.m.* **I.** Unpacking. **2.** (Vente au) **déballage,** (i) spread of hawker's wares; (ii) clearance sale (in temporary premises).

déballer [debale], *v.tr.* To unpack (goods, cases).

déballeur [debalœ:r], *s.m.* Hawker.

débandade [debãdad], *s.f.* Rout (of army, etc.); stampede (of horses, etc.). **A la débandade,** in confusion; helter-skelter. *Marcher à la d.,* to straggle along.

débander¹ [debãde], *v.tr.* **I.** To relax (sth. under tension); to unbend (bow); to unbrace (drum); to let down (spring). *F: Se d. l'esprit,* to relax one's mind. **2.** To remove a bandage from; to unbandage, to unbind (wound).

débander², *v.tr.* To disband (troops, crew).

    se débander, (*a*) To disband; (of crowd, etc.) to disperse. (*b*) To break into a rout.

débarbouiller [debarbuje], *v.tr.* To wash (s.o.'s) face.

    se débarbouiller. I. To wash one's face. **2.** *F: Qu'il se débarbouille,* let him shift for himself. **3.** (Of weather) To clear up.

débarcadère [debarkade:r], *s.m. Nau:* Landing-stage, wharf. *Rail:* (Arrival) platform.

débarder [debarde], *v.tr.* **I.** *Nau:* To unload, discharge (timber, etc.). **2.** To convey (lumber, quarried stone) to the rail-head. *s.m.* **-age.**

débardeur [debardœ:r], *s.m.* Lumper, docker, stevedore.

débarquement [debarkəmã], *s.m.* **I.** Unloading, discharge (of cargo); landing, disembarking, disembarkment (of persons). **Carton de débarquement,** (passenger's) landing ticket. *Navy:* **Troupes de débarquement,** landing party. **2.** *Rail:* Arrival (of passengers); *Mil:* detraining. **Quai de débarquement,** arrival platform. **3.** *Nau:* Paying off, discharge (of crew).

débarquer [debarke]. **I.** *v.tr.* (*a*) To unship, unload, discharge (cargo); to disembark, land (passengers); to drop (pilot). (Of bus) To set down (passengers). (*b*) To pay off, discharge (crew). *F: D.* qn, to dismiss s.o.; to give s.o. the sack. **2.** *v.i.* To land, disembark (from boat); to alight (from train); *Mil:* to detrain. *F: C'est une nouvelle débarquée à Paris,* she is fresh from the country. *s.m.* **Au débarqué,** on arrival, on landing.

débarras [debara], *s.m.* Riddance. **Bon débarras !** good riddance ! **Chambre de débarras,** lumber-room.

débarrasser [debarase], *v.tr.* To disencumber; to clear (table, etc.). *D.* qn *de* qch., to relieve s.o. of sth. *D.* qn *de* qn, to rid s.o. of s.o. **Débarrasser le plancher,** (i) to clear the floor; (ii) *F:* to clear out. *s.m.* **-ement.**

    se débarrasser *de* qch., to get rid of sth.; to extricate, disentangle, oneself from sth.

débarrer [debare], *v.tr.* To unbar (door, etc.).

débat [deba], *s.m.* **I.** (Oral) discussion; debate. *Parl:* **Les débats,** the proceedings. **2.** Dispute. *Trancher un d.,* to settle a dispute. **Être en débat** *sur une question,* to be at issue on a question.

débâter [debate], *v.tr.* To take the pack-saddle off (horse, mule). [BÂT]

débattable [debatabl], *a.* Debatable.

débattre [debatr], *v.tr.* (Conj. like BATTRE) To debate, discuss. **Prix à débattre,** price by arrangement. *Je n'ai pas débattu le prix,* I did not haggle about the price.

    se débattre, to struggle. *Se d. dans l'eau,* to flounder, splash (about) in the water.

débauche [debo:ʃ], *s.f.* Debauch(ery), dissolute living. *Faire une petite d.,* to have a little spree.

débaucher [deboʃe], *v.tr.* **I.** To entice (s.o.) away, to lead (s.o.) astray. *D. un ouvrier,* to entice a workman away (from his work), to induce him to strike. *D. la jeunesse,* to corrupt the young. **2.** *Ind:* To discharge, turn off (hands). To reduce one's staff. *s.m.* **-age.**

    se débaucher, to go astray, to go to the dogs.

    débauché, -ée. I. *a.* Debauched, profligate. **2.** *s.* Debauchee; *s.m.* libertine, rake; *s.f.* wanton. **3.** *s.f. Ind:* **Débauchée,** knock-off time.

débile [debil], *a.* Weakly (child); weak (stomach); sickly (plant). *Avoir une volonté d.,* to be infirm of purpose.

débilitant [debilitã], *a.* Debilitating, weakening. *Remède d., s.m.* **débilitant,** debilitant.

débilité [debilite], *s.f.* Debility, weakness. *D. mentale,* mental deficiency.

débiliter [debilite], *v.tr.* To debilitate, weaken.

débine [debin], *s.f. F:* Poverty; straitened circumstances. **Être dans la débine,** to be down on one's luck.

débiner [debine], *v.tr. F:* To disparage; to speak slightingly of (s.o.); to run (s.o.) down.

débit¹ [debi], *s.m.* **I.** (*a*) (Retail) sale. *Marchandises de bon d.,* marketable, saleable, goods. (*b*) (Retail) shop. Esp. **Débit de tabac,** tobacconist's (shop). **Débit de boissons,** public house. **2.** Cutting up (of logs, meat, etc.). **3.** *Ind:* Output; discharge, delivery (of pump, etc.); flow (of river, etc.); strength, intensity (of electric current). **4.** Delivery, utterance (of orator). **Avoir le débit facile,** *F:* to have the gift of the gab, a glib tongue.

débit², *s.m. Com:* Debit. **Porter une somme au débit de** qn, to debit s.o. with a sum.

débitant, -ante [debitã, -ã:t], *s.* Retail dealer; retailer. *D. de tabac,* tobacconist.

débiter¹ [debite], *v.tr.* **I.** To retail; to sell (goods) retail. **2.** To cut up, convert (timber); to cut up (meat). **3.** To discharge, yield (so many litres an hour, etc.). *Courant débité par une dynamo,* current delivered by a dynamo. **4.** (*a*) *Th:* To pronounce, recite (one's part). (*b*) *F: Usu. Pej: D. une longue harangue,* to deliver, to spout, a long speech. *D. des mensonges,* to utter lies. *D. des histoires,* to spin yarns.

débiter², *v.tr. Com:* To debit. *D. une somme à* qn; *d.* qn *d'une somme,* to debit s.o. with an amount.

débiteur¹, -euse [debitœːr, -øːz], s. **1.** Usu. *Pej:* Utterer (of lies, etc.). *D. de calomnies,* scandal-monger. **2.** *s.m. Ind:* Feeding device.

débiteur², -trice [debitœːr, -tris]. **1.** s. Debtor. **2.** *a.* Compte débiteur, debit account.

déblai [deb{l}e], *s.m. Civ.E: Rail: etc:* **1.** Excavation, cut(ting). Route en déblai, sunk road. **2.** Spoil earth.

déblatérer [deblatere], v. (je déblatère; je déblatérerai) **1.** *v.tr. D.* des sottises, (i) to talk nonsense; (ii) to fling abuse (*contre*, at). **2.** *v.i. D. contre qn,* to rail against s.o.; to run s.o. down.

débl{a}yer [debl{e}je], *v.tr.* (je déblaye, je déblaie) **1.** To clear away, remove (spoil earth, etc.). *D. la neige,* to shovel away the snow. **2.** *D. un terrain,* to clear a piece of ground. *F:* Déblayer le terrain, to clear the ground, the way (for negotiations, etc.). *s.m.* -aiement.

débloquer [debl{ɔ}ke], *v.tr.* **1.** To raise the blockade of (town, port). **2.** To unclamp (instrument).

débobiner [debɔbine], *v.tr. El:* To unwind (coil).
se **débobiner**, *P:* to cut and run; to scoot.

déboire [debwaːr], *s.m.* **1.** (Disagreeable) aftertaste (of wine, etc.). **2.** *F:* Disappointment. *Essuyer bien des déboires,* to suffer many rebuffs.

déboisement [debwazmã], *s.m.* Deforestation.

déboiser [debwaze], *v.tr.* To deforest, untimber, clear (land). [BOIS]

déboîtement [debwatmã], *s.m.* Dislocation (of limb, etc.).

déboîter [debwate], *v.tr.* **1.** To disconnect, uncouple (pipe, etc.). **2.** To dislocate (joint). *Se d. l'épaule,* to put one's shoulder out. **3.** *Bookb:* To uncase (book). [BOÎTE]
se **déboîter**, (of shoulder, etc.) to come out of joint.

débonder [debɔ̃de], *v.tr.* To unbung (cask); to open the sluice gates of (reservoir). *F: D. son cœur,* se débonder, to pour out one's heart.

débonnaire [debɔnɛːr], *a.* Good natured, easygoing. *adv.* -ment.

débonnaireté [debɔnɛrte], *s.f.* Good-nature; easy temper.

débordant [debɔrdã], *a.* **1.** Overflowing, brimming over (*de*, with). *D. de santé,* bursting with health. **2.** Projecting, protruding; overlapping.

débordement [debɔrdəmã], *s.m.* **1.** (*a*) Overflowing (of river, etc.). *F: D. d'injures,* outburst of abuse. (*b*) Usu. *pl.* Excesses, dissipation; dissolute living. **2.** Outflanking (of enemy).

déborder [debɔrde]. **1.** *v.tr. & i.* To overflow, brim over, run over. *Verre plein à déborder,* glass full to overflowing, brim-full. *Mon cœur déborde,* my heart is overflowing. *Elle déborde de vie,* she is bubbling over with vitality. **2.** *v.tr.* (*a*) To project, jut out, stick out, protrude, extend, beyond (sth.); to overlap (sth.). *Dents qui débordent les lèvres,* protruding teeth. (*b*) *Mil:* To outflank (the enemy). (*c*) *D. les avirons,* to unship the oars. *Nau: D. les couvertures d'un lit,* to untuck a bed. *Nau: D. une embarcation d'un vaisseau, Abs.* déborder, to shove off, sheer off. (*d*) To remove the edging from (sth.). *D. une tôle,* to trim the edges of an iron plate. [BORD]

débordé, *a.* **1.** Overflowing (river, etc.). **2.** Être débordé de travail, de requêtes, to be overwhelmed, *F:* snowed under, with work, with requests. *Com:* Nous sommes débordés, we are very much rushed. **3.** Licentious, dissipated.

débotter [debɔte]. **1.** *v.tr.* To unboot (s.o.). **2.** *v.i. & pr.* To pull off one's boots; to unboot.

s.m. F: Au débotté, au débotter, immediately upon arrival.

débouché [debuʃe], *s.m.* **1.** (*a*) Outlet, opening, issue (of passage, etc.); exit (from building, etc.). (*b*) Inlet (into pond). **2.** Opening; chance of success. *Créer de nouveaux débouchés,* to open up new channels, new avenues, for trade.

débouch{er}¹ [debuʃe], *v.tr.* **1.** To clear (choked pipe, etc.). **2.** To uncork, unstopper, open (bottle). *F: D. l'intelligence d'un enfant,* to awaken, arouse, a child's intelligence. *s.m.* -age. *s.m.* -ement.

déboucher², *v.i.* To emerge, debouch, issue (forth). *Escalier débouchant sur le trottoir,* stairway opening on the pavement.

déboucler [debukle], *v.tr.* **1.** To unbuckle (belt, etc.). **2.** To take the curl out of, to uncurl (hair). se **déboucler,** (of hair) to uncurl.

débouler [debule], *v.i.* **1.** To fall head over heels. *D. l'escalier,* to roll downstairs. **2.** (Of game) To start, bolt (from cover). *s.m.* Tirer un lapin au déboulé, au débouler, to shoot a rabbit as it bolts from cover.

déboulonn{er} [debulɔne], *v.tr.* **1.** To unrivet. **2.** To unbolt. *s.m.* -age. *s.m.* -ement.

débourb{er} [deburbe], *v.tr.* **1.** To cleanse, to clear (of mud); to clean out (a cistern). *Winem: D. le vin,* to let the wine settle. **2.** To haul (carriage, etc.) out of the mire. *F: A: D. qn,* to get s.o. out of a mess. *s.m.* -age.

débourr{er} [debure], *v.tr.* **1.** To unhair (skins); to strip, clean (carding machine). **2.** To remove the wad from (fire-arm), the stuffing from (armchair, etc.), the tobacco from (pipe); to untamp (blast-hole). [BOURRE] *s.m:* -age.

débours [debuːr], *s.m.* Usu. *pl.* Disbursement; out-of-pocket expenses. *Faire des débours,* to lay out money.

débours{er} [deburse], *v.tr.* To disburse, spend, lay out (money). *Sans rien d.,* without spending a penny. *Je suis toujours à d.,* I am always dipping my hand into my pocket. *s.m.* -ement.

déboursé, *s.m.* = DÉBOURS.

debout [dəbu], *adv.* **1.** (*a*) (Of thg) Upright, on end; (of pers.) standing. *Mettre, dresser, qch. d.,* to stand on end. "Tenir debout," 'to be kept upright'; 'this end up.' Se tenir debout, to stand; (of dog) to stand on its hind legs. *Argument qui ne tient pas d.,* argument that won't hold water. Se (re)mettre debout, to stand up. Rester debout, to remain standing. Debout les gardes! up guards! "Places debout seulement," 'standing room only.' *F:* Pièce, conte, à dormir debout, play that bores one stiff; silly story. *Sp:* Record encore debout, unbeaten record. S.a. MAGISTRATURE 2. (*b*) (Of pers.) Être debout, to be up. Allons, debout! come, get up! (*c*) *Cust:* Passer debout, to have a permit for transire. **2.** *Nau: D. à la mer, à la lame, au vent,* head on to the sea, to the wind. Vent debout, head wind. [BOUT]

déboutement [debutmã], *s.m. Jur:* Nonsuit.

débouter [debute], *v.tr. Jur:* **1.** To dismiss (suit). **2.** *D. qn* (de sa demande), to nonsuit s.o.

débouté, *s.m. Jur:* Nonsuit.

déboutonner [debutɔne], *v.tr.* To unbutton. *Rire à ventre déboutonné,* to laugh immoderately.

débraillé [debraje], *a.* Untidy, all unbuttoned (person). *Tenue débraillée,* untidy, hardly decent, appearance. *Mœurs débraillées,* loose morals; bohemian habits.

débrayage [debreja:3], *s.m.* **1.** Disconnecting, declutching, throwing out of gear. **2.** *Aut:* Clutch pedal.

débrayer [debreje], *v.tr.* (je débraye, je débraie)

1. *Mec.E:* To disconnect, disengage (part); to throw (part) out of gear. **2.** *Aut:* To declutch.

débrid|er [debride], *v.tr.* **1.** To unbridle (horse, etc.), (hence) to halt. *F:* **Travailler dix heures sans débrider,** to work ten hours at a stretch. **2.** *Surg:* To incise, slit up (adhesions, etc.). *F:* **Débrider les yeux à qn,** to open s.o.'s eyes. **3.** To unsling (load). *s.m.* **-ement.**

débridé, *a.* Unbridled (appetite, tongue).

débris [debri], *s.m.pl.* Remains, debris, fragments. *Ind:* **D. de métal,** scrap.

débrouillard, -arde [debruja:r, -ard]. **1.** *a.* *F:* (*a*) Resourceful; cute. (*b*) Clear-headed. **2.** *s.* *F:* Resourceful young chap or young woman.

débrouill|er [debruje], *v.tr.* To unravel, disentangle (thread, etc.); to sort out (papers, etc.). *D. une affaire,* to clear up, straighten out, an affair. *D. une signature,* to make out, to decipher, a signature. *s.m.* **-ement.**

se débrouiller. 1. (Of the sky, complexion, etc.) To clear (up). **2.** To extricate oneself (from difficulties); to 'manage.' *Qu'il se débrouille!* let him shift for himself!

débucher [debyʃe], *v.i. Ven:* (Of big game) To break cover. **Faire débucher,** *v.tr.* **débucher, un cerf,** to unharbour, start, a stag.

débucher, *s.m.*, **débuché,** *s.m.* (i) Breaking cover; (ii) (on the horn) 'gone away.' *F:* **Au débuché . . .,** at the start. . . .

débusqu|er [debyske]. **1.** *v.tr.* (*a*) *Mil:* To drive (enemy) out of ambush. (*b*) *F:* To oust (s.o.) (from a situation). (*c*) *Ven:* = DÉBUCHER. **2.** *v.i. Mil: etc:* To come out (of ambush); to come out of hiding. *s.m.* **-ement.**

début [deby], *s.m.* **1.** *Games:* First turn, first play. *Dice:* First throw, first cast. **2.** First appearance (of actor, etc.). **Faire son début,** to make one's first appearance. (Of girl) *Faire son d. (dans le monde),* to come out. **Société à ses débuts,** association in its infancy. **3.** Beginning, start, outset. **Dès le début,** from the outset (*de, of*). **Au début des hostilités,** at the outbreak of hostilities. **Appointements de début,** commencing salary. **Discours de début,** maiden speech.

débutant, -ante [debytɑ̃, -ã:t], *s.* **1.** Beginner, tyro; actor, etc., making his first appearance. **2.** *s.f.* Débutante, girl who has just come out; débutante.

débuter [debyte], *v.i.* **1.** *Games:* To play first. *Dice:* To throw first. **2.** To make one's first appearance (on the stage, etc.). *D. dans le monde,* to start one's career. **Faire débuter une jeune fille dans le monde,** to bring out a girl. **3.** To begin, start, commence. *Vous travaillerez ici pour d,.* you will work here for a start.

deçà [dəsa], *adv.* On this side. **Deçà et delà,** here and there, on this side and that, on all sides. **Jambe deçà, jambe delà,** astraddle. **En deçà de qch.,** (on) this side of sth. [ÇÀ]

décachet|er [dekaʃte], *v.tr.* (Conj. like CACHETER) To unseal, break open (letter, etc.). *s.m.* **-age.**

décade [dekad], *s.f.* Decade. **1.** Period of ten days. **2.** Series of ten.

décadence [dekadã:s], *s.f.* Decadence, decline, decay. **Être en décadence,** to be decadent, on the down-grade.

décadent [dekadɑ̃]. **1.** *a.* Decadent; in decay. **2.** *s.m. Lit: Art:* Decadent.

décaèdre [dekaɛːdr], *Geom:* **1.** *a.* Decahedral. **2.** *s.m.* Decahedron.

décagone [dekagɔn], *s.m. Geom:* Decagon.

décagramme [dekagram], *s.m. Meas:* Decagram(me) (= ⅓ oz.).

décalamin|er [dekalamine], *v.tr. I.C.E:* To decarbonize (engine). *s.m.* **-age.**

décalcomanie [dekalkɔmani], *s.f. Cer: etc:* Transfer (process or picture).

décal|er [dekale], *v.tr.* **1.** (*a*) To unwedge, unkey. (*b*) To unscotch (wheel). **2.** To set off (part of machine, etc.); to stagger (rivets). **3.** To shift the zero of (instrument). *El.E:* To displace, shift (the brushes, etc.). *D. l'heure,* to alter the time (to summer-time). *D. tous les trains d'une heure,* to shift all the trains one hour forward or back. *Ph:* **Ondes décalées,** waves out of phase. *s.m.* **-age.**

décalitre [dekalitr], *s.m. Meas:* Decalitre.

décalque [dekalk], *s.m.* **1.** (*a*) Transferring. (*b*) Tracing off. **Papier à décalque,** (i) transfer-paper, (ii) carbon paper or tracing-paper. **2.** (*a*) Transfer. (*b*) Tracing.

décalqu|er [dekalke], *v.tr.* **1.** To transfer (design, coloured picture). **2.** To trace off (drawing). *s.m.* **-age.**

décamètre [dekamɛtr], *s.m. Meas:* Decametre.

décamper [dekɑ̃pe], *v.i.* To decamp, make off.

décantation [dekɑ̃tasjɔ̃], *s.f.* Decantation, decanting.

décanter [dekɑ̃te], *v.tr.* To decant, pour off.

décapant [dekapɑ̃], *s.m.* Scouring solution. *D. pour vernis,* varnish remover.

décap|er [dekape], *v.tr.* To scour, clean (metal, etc.); to pickle, dip (metal objects). [CAPE] *s.m.* **-age.** *s.m.* **-ement.** *s.m.* **-eur.**

décapitation [dekapitasjɔ̃], *s.f.* Decapitation, beheading.

décapiter [dekapite], *v.tr.* To decapitate, behead; to cut off the head of (s.o., sth.).

décapode [dekapɔd], *s.m. Crust:* Decapod. **Les décapodes,** the decapoda.

décapsul(at)eur [dekapsyl(at)œ:r], *s.m.* Crown-cork opener.

décarboniser [dekarbɔnize], **décarburer** [dekarbyre], *v.tr.* **1.** *Metall:* To decarbonize, decarburize (steel, iron). **2.** *I.C.E:* To decarbonize (engine).

décasyllabe [dekasillab], **décasyllabique** [dekasillabik], *a.* Decasyllabic.

décatir [dekati:r], *v.tr. Tex:* To take the gloss, the finish, off (cloth).

se décatir, *F:* to lose one's freshness, one's beauty; to show the effects of age.

décati, *a. F:* Enfeebled; broken down; the worse for wear; worn (face).

decauville [dəkovil], *s.m.* Also **Chemin de fer Decauville,** (named after the inventor) narrow-gauge railway.

décaver [dekave], *v.tr. F:* To ruin, beggar, (s.o.) at play; *F:* to clean (s.o.) out.

décavé, -ée, *a. & s. F:* Ruined, *F:* stony-broke (person).

décéder [desede], *v.i.* (Conj. like CÉDER. Aux. être) (Used only in official language) To die, to decease. *Il est décédé le premier mars,* he departed this life on the first of March.

décédé, -ée, *a. & s.* Deceased, defunct, departed.

déceler [desle], *v.tr.* (je **décèle**; je **décèlerai**) **1.** To disclose (fraud); to divulge, betray (secret). **2.** *El.E: etc:* *D. les fuites,* to test for faults.

déceleur, -euse [deslœ:r, -ø:z], *s.* **1.** Divulger. **2.** *s.m. El.E: D. de fuites,* leakage detector.

décembre [desɑ̃:br], *s.m.* December. **Au mois de décembre,** in (the month of) December.

décemment [desamɑ̃], *adv.* Decently, with decency.

décence [desɑ̃:s], *s.f.* (*a*) Decency. **Avec**

dépence, decently, modestly. (b) Propriety, decency, decorum. *Choquer la d.*, to shock the proprieties.

décennal, -aux [desɛnnal, -o], a. Decennial.

décent [desɑ̃], a. (a) Decent; modest (attire, etc.). (b) Proper, seemly (behaviour, etc.). Peu **décent,** indecent, unseemly.

décentralisation [desɑ̃tralizasjɔ̃], s.f. Decentralization.

décentraliser [desɑ̃tralize], v.tr. To decentralize (administration).

décentration [desɑ̃trasjɔ̃], s.f., **décentrement** [desɑ̃trəmɑ̃], s.m. **1.** Opt: Mec.E: etc: Decentring. Phot: Appareil à décentrement, camera with sliding front. **2.** Mec.E: etc: Eccentricity. Bowls: Bias (of bowl).

décentrer [desɑ̃tre], v.tr. Opt: Mec.E: etc: To put (lenses, axes, etc.) out of centre; to decentre. Bowls: To bias (a bowl).

décentré, a. Out of centre, out of true, eccentric.

déception [desɛpsjɔ̃], s.f. **1.** A: Deception, deceit. **2.** Disappointment.

décern|er [desɛrne], v.tr. **1.** Jur: Décerner un mandat d'arrêt contre qn, to issue a writ for the arrest of s.o. **2.** To award, bestow (a prize, etc.). *D. un honneur à qn,* to confer an honour on s.o. S.a. PALME 2. s.m. **-ement.**

décès [desɛ], s.m. (Used only in official language) Decease; (natural) death. *Notifier un d.,* to notify a death. **Acte de décès,** death certificate.

décevable [des(ə)vabl], a. Easily deceived.

décevant [des(ə)vɑ̃], a. **1.** Deceptive; delusive (appearance, etc.). **2.** Disappointing (result, etc.).

décevoir [desəvwaːr], v.tr. (Conj. like RECEVOIR) **1.** To deceive, delude. **2.** To disappoint.

déchaînement [deʃɛnmɑ̃], s.m. **1.** Letting loose, unchaining (of dog, etc.); unfettering (of prisoner). **2.** (a) Breaking loose. *Un d. de l'opinion,* a great wave of public opinion. (b) Outburst (of passion).

déchaîner [deʃɛne], v.tr. (a) To unchain, to let loose (dog, etc.); to loose the chains of, to unfetter (prisoner). *F: Les diables sont déchaînés,* hell has broken loose. (b) *D. toutes les passions,* to loose every passion.

se déchaîner, to break out. *La tempête se déchaîna,* the storm broke.

déchanter [deʃɑ̃te], v.i. *F:* To lower one's tone; to sing small. **En déchanter,** to come down a peg or two.

déchard, -arde [deʃaːr, -ard], s. *P:* Hard-up individual. [DÈCHE]

décharge [deʃarʒ], s.f. **1.** (a) Unloading (of cart, etc.); unlading, discharging (of boat, cargo). (b) Discharge, volley (of musketry, etc.). (c) *El:* Discharge. *D. disruptive,* spark discharge. *D. en retour,* back-kick. (d) Output (of accumulator). **2.** (a) Relief, relieving, easing. **Voûte de décharge,** relieving vault (of bridge). (b) *Obtenir une d. sur un impôt,* to obtain a rebate on a tax. *Com:* Décharge de 50 pour cent, composition of 10 shillings in the £. (c) *Jur:* **Témoin à décharge,** witness for the defence. (d) *Jur:* Release, acquittal (of accused person). (e) *Bank:* Letter of indemnity. **3.** (a) Discharge, outlet. **Tuyau de décharge,** exhaust-pipe; waste-pipe. *D: Dy:* Fading, rubbing off (of colour). **4.** (Lieu de) **décharge, décharge publique,** dumping ground, dump. **(Chambre de) décharge,** lumber-room, *F:* glory-hole.

déchargement [deʃarʒəmɑ̃], s.m. Unloading (of cart, fire-arm); unlading (of ship); discharging, unshipment (of cargo).

déchargeoir [deʃarʒwaːr], s.m. **1.** (a) Outfall (of culvert, etc.). (b) Sluice (of mill-race). **2.** *Mch:* Waste-pipe, exhaust-pipe. **3.** *Tex:* Cloth-beam (of loom).

décharger [deʃarʒe], v.tr. (je déchargeai(s); n. déchargeons) **1.** (a) To unload (cart, etc.); to unlade, discharge (boat); to unship, discharge (cargo); to tip, to dump down (gravel). (b) To unload (fire-arm). (c) *D. sa conscience,* to ease one's mind (de, of). *D. son cœur,* to unburden one's heart. (d) Décharger son fusil sur, contre qn, to discharge, let off, fire (off), one's gun at s.o. *D. sa colère sur qn,* to vent one's anger on s.o. (e) To discharge (accumulator). **2.** (a) To relieve, lighten, ease, (horse, ship, etc.) of part of its load; to take the strain off (beam). (b) *D. qn d'une accusation,* to acquit s.o. of a charge. *D. qn d'une dette,* to remit a debt. *Failli déchargé,* non déchargé, discharged, undischarged, bankrupt. **3.** (a) To discharge, empty (reservoir). (b) *Dy: Étoffe qui décharge (sa couleur),* stuff the colour of which rubs off or fades. *Typ: Encre qui décharge,* ink that sets off.

se décharger. 1. (a) (Of gun To go off. (b) (Of storage battery) To run down; to discharge. (c) (Of anger) To vent itself (sur, on). **2.** Se décharger de qn, de qch., to get rid of s.o., of sth. *Se d. d'un fardeau,* to put down, lay down, a burden. *Se d. sur qn du soin de qch.,* to shift the responsibility of sth. on to s.o. **3.** *Le fleuve se décharge dans la mer,* the river flows, empties itself, into the sea.

déchargeur [deʃarʒœːr], s.m. **1.** Dock labourer, docker. *D. de charbon,* coal-heaver. **2.** (Spark, lightning) arrester.

décharné [deʃarne], a. **1.** Fleshless (bones, etc.). **2.** Emaciated, scraggy (limbs, etc.); lank (body); gaunt (face); skinny, bony (fingers).

déchauss|er [deʃose], v.tr. **1.** To take off (s.o.'s) shoes. *F:* Il n'est pas digne de vous déchausser, he is not fit to tie your shoe-laces. **2.** To lay bare the roots of (tree); to bare, expose (tooth, foundations). s.m. **-ement.**

se déchausser. 1. To take off one's shoes, etc. **2.** *Ses dents se déchaussent,* his gums are shrinking.

déchaussé, a. Bare-foot(ed).

dèche [dɛʃ], s.f. *P:* Poverty, distress. **Être dans la dèche,** to be hard up, on the rocks.

déchéance [deʃeɑ̃ːs], s.f. **1.** Fall (from grace); downfall. **Nation en déchéance,** nation on the down-grade. **2.** *Jur: D. de titres,* forfeiture of shares. **Action en déchéance de brevet,** action for forfeiture of patent. *D. de propriété littéraire,* lapse of rights in literary matter. *Ins: D. d'une police,* expiration of a policy.

déchet [deʃɛ], s.m. **1.** Loss, decrease, diminution (of weight, value); loss, falling off (of reputation, authority). **2.** Usu. pl. Waste, refuse. *Déchets de coton,* cotton waste. *D. de métal,* scrap (metal). *Déchets de viande,* scraps. [DÉCHOIR]

déchiffrable [deʃifrabl], a. Decipherable (inscription); legible (writing).

déchiffr|er [deʃifre], v.tr. To decipher, make out (inscription, etc.); to decode (message); to decipher (cryptogram); to read or play (music) at sight. s.m. **-ement.** s. **-eur, -euse.**

déchiqueter [deʃikte], v.tr. (je déchiquette; je déchiquetterai) **1.** To cut, slash, tear, (stuff, flesh, etc.) into strips, into shreds. **2.** To pink out (leather).

déchiqueté, a. Jagged (edge); indented (coastline). *Papier à bords déchiquetés,* deckle-edge paper.

déchirant [deʃirɑ̃], *a.* Heart-rending, harrowing.
déchirement [deʃirmɑ̃], *s.m.* Tearing, rending (of stuff, etc.). *D. d'un muscle,* tearing of a muscle. *D. de cœur,* heart-break.
déchirer [deʃire], *v.tr.* To tear, *Lit:* to rend (garment, etc.); to tear up (paper, etc.); to tear open (envelope). *D. qch. en morceaux,* to tear sth. to pieces, to bits. *F: Le train déchira l'air de son sifflet,* the train rent the air with its shrill whistle. *Sons qui déchirent l'oreille,* ear-splitting sounds. *Cris qui déchiraient le cœur,* heart-rending cries.
  se déchirer, (of stuff, etc.) to tear.
déchirure [deʃiry:r], *s.f.* (a) Tear, rent, slit, rip. (b) Lacerated wound; laceration.
déchloruré [deklɔryre], *a. Med:* Salt-free (diet).
déchoir [deʃwa:r], *v.i.* (*pr.p.* déchéant (rare); *p.p.* déchu; *pr.ind.* je déchois, n. déchoyons, ils déchoient; *p.h.* je déchus; *fu.* je décherrai. Aux. usu. *être,* occ. *avoir*) To fall (from high estate, from honour, etc.). *Ce quartier a déchu,* the neighbourhood has gone down. *Sa popularité déchoit,* his popularity is falling off, is on the wane. *La maison déchoit de son prestige,* the firm is going down in public estimation. *D. en entrant dans une profession,* to lose caste by entering a profession.
  déchu, *a.* Fallen. **Ange déchu,** fallen angel. *Jur: Être d. de ses droits,* to have forfeited one's rights. *Ins: Police déchue,* expired policy.
de-ci, de-là [dəsidəla], *adv.phr.* See CI[1].
décidément [desidemɑ̃], *adv.* 1. Resolutely, firmly. 2. Decidedly, positively, definitely. *F: D. je n'ai pas de chance,* I am unlucky and no mistake.
décider [deside], *v.tr.* 1. (a) To decide, settle (question, dispute). *Voilà qui décide tout!* that settles it! (b) *L'Assemblée décida la guerre, la paix,* the Assembly decided on war, on peace. 2. **Décider qn à faire qch.,** to persuade, induce, s.o. to do sth. 3. *Abs.* (a) *Il faut que je décide,* I must decide, make up my mind. *D. en faveur de qn,* to decide, *Jur:* to give a ruling, in favour of s.o.; to find for (the plaintiff). (b) **Décider de qch.,** to decide, determine, sth. 4. **Décider de** + *inf.,* to decide (after deliberation) to (do sth.). **Décider que** + *ind.,* to decide, settle, that. . . . *Impers. Il fut décidé qu'on attendrait sa réponse,* it was decided to await his reply.
  se décider. 1. To make up one's mind; to come to a decision. 2. *Se d. à qch., à faire qch.,* to make up one's mind (somewhat reluctantly) to do sth. *Je ne puis pas me d. à le faire,* I cannot bring myself, I cannot find it in my heart, to do it. *Allons décidez-vous,* come, make up your mind. 3. *Se d. pour qn, pour qch.,* to decide in favour of s.o., of sth.
  décidé, *a.* 1. *Chose décidée,* settled matter. 2. Resolute, confident (person, manner); determined (character). 3. **Être décidé à faire qch.,** to be determined, resolved, to do sth.; to be bent on doing sth. 4. *Avoir une supériorité décidée sur qn,* to have a decided superiority over s.o.
décigramme [desigram], *s.m.* Decigram(me).
décilitre [desilitr], *s.m.* Decilitre.
décimal, -aux [desimal, -o], *a.* Decimal.
décimale [desimal], *s.f.* Decimal (fraction).
décimation [desimasjɔ̃], *s.f.* Decimation.
décime [desim], *s.m.* (a) One tenth of a franc. (b) Ten-centime piece.
décimer [desime], *v.tr.* To decimate. *F: La peste décima le peuple,* the plague decimated the people, took its tithe of the people.
décimètre [desimetr], *s.m. Meas:* Decimetre.
décintrer [desɛ̃tre], *v.tr.* To strike the centering of (arch). *s.m.* -age. *s.m.* -ement.

décis|if, -ive [desizif, -i:v], *a.* 1. Decisive (battle, etc.); conclusive (evidence). *Au moment décisif,* at the critical, crucial, moment. 2. Positive, peremptory (tone). *adv.* -ivement.
décision [desizjɔ̃], *s.f.* Decision. 1. (a) **Prendre, arriver à, une décision,** to arrive at, come to, reach, a decision; to make up one's mind (*quant à, au sujet de,* about, as to). **Forcer une décision,** to bring matters to a head. (b) *Jur:* Ruling, award. (c) *pl. Mil:* Regimental orders. 2. Resolution, determination.
déclamateur [deklamatœ:r], *s.m.* (a) Stump orator; *P:* tub-thumper. (b) Phrase-monger.
déclamation [deklamasjɔ̃], *s.f.* 1. (Art of) declamation; oratory. *Il a une mauvaise d.,* his delivery is bad. 2. (a) Declamation, harangue. (b) Ranting.
déclamatoire [deklamatwa:r], *a.* Declamatory, high-flown (style); ranting (speech).
déclamer [deklame], *v.tr.* 1. To declaim (speech). 2. To rant, spout. *D. contre qn,* to inveigh against s.o.
déclanchement [deklɑ̃ʃmɑ̃], *s.m.* 1. *Mec.E:* (a) Releasing, disengaging (of part). (b) Trigger action. *Phot:* (Shutter-) release. 2. Starting; setting (of sth.) in motion.
déclancher [deklɑ̃ʃe], *v.tr.* 1. To unlatch (door). 2. *Mec.E:* To release, disconnect, disengage (part). 3. *F:* To start (apparatus); to set (apparatus) in motion. *Mil: D. une attaque,* to launch an attack. [CLENCHE]
déclancheur [deklɑ̃ʃœ:r], *s.m. Phot:* Shutter-release. *D. à poire,* bulb-release.
déclarable [deklarabl], *a. Cust:* Liable to duty.
déclaration [deklarasjɔ̃], *s.f.* Declaration. (a) Proclamation, announcement. *D. de guerre,* declaration of war. (b) Notification (of birth, death, etc.). (c) **Émettre une déclaration,** to make a statement. **Déclaration sous serment,** affidavit. (d) *D. d'amour,* declaration of love. **Faire sa déclaration,** to declare oneself. (e) *Cust:* **Déclaration en douane,** customs declaration.
déclarer [deklare], *v.tr.* 1. (a) To declare, make known (one's intentions, wishes, one's love, etc.). *Il déclara qu'il n'avait rien vu,* he declared, asserted, that he had seen nothing. (b) *Cards: D. trèfle,* to declare, call, clubs. 2. To declare, proclaim, announce, make public. (a) *Pred. D. qn roi,* to declare s.o. king. *Déclaré coupable,* found guilty. *Déclaré coupable de vol,* convicted of theft. (b) To notify (birth, death). (c) *D. la guerre à qn,* to declare war on s.o. (d) *Cust: Avez-vous quelque chose à d.?* have you anything to declare?
  se déclarer. 1. (a) *Se d. pour, contre, qch.,* to declare for, against, sth. (b) To declare, avow, one's love. 2. *Se d. l'auteur du méfait,* to own up to the deed. 3. (Of fire, disease) To break out.
  déclaré, *a.* Declared, avowed, professed (enemy, intention, etc.).
déclass|er [deklɑse], *v.tr.* 1. To transfer (passengers) from one class to another. 2. To bring (s.o.) down in the world. 3. *Mil: Navy:* To abandon, dismantle (fortress); to declare (weapon) obsolete; to cast (horse). 4. *Navy:* To disrate (seaman). *s.m.* -ement.
  déclassé, -ée, *a. & s.* 1. (One) who has come down in the world, lost his social position. 2. Obsolete (ship, etc.).
déclench|er, -ement, -eur = DÉCLANCHER, etc.
déclic [deklik], *s.m.* Pawl, catch; trigger. **Chronomètre à déclic,** stop-watch.
déclin [deklɛ̃], *s.m.* Decline, close (of day); wane, waning (of moon); fall (of the year); falling-off

(of talent). **Le soleil est à, sur, son déclin,** the sun is sinking, setting. *Beauté, empire, sur son d.,* beauty, empire, on the wane. **Au déclin de sa vie,** in his declining years.

déclinable [deklinabl], *a. Gram:* Declinable.

déclinaison [deklinɛzɔ̃], *s.f.* **1.** (*a*) *Astr:* Declination (of star). (*b*) **Déclinaison magnétique,** magnetic variation. **2.** *Gram:* Declension.

décliner [dekline]. I. *v.i.* **1.** (Of compass) To deviate (from the true line). **2.** To wane; (of star) to decline. *Fièvre qui va en déclinant,* fever that is diminishing, abating. II. **décliner,** *v.tr.* **1.** To decline, refuse (offer, etc.); to decline (responsibility). **2.** (*a*) *Gram:* To decline (noun, etc.). (*b*) **Décliner son nom,** to state, give, one's name.

décliquer [deklike], *v.tr.* To release (pawl). *Civ.E:* **D. le mouton,** to release, trip, the monkey (of pile-driver).

déclive [dekliːv], *a.* Declivitous, sloping, inclined. **2.** *s.f.* Slope.

déclivité [deklivite], *s.f.* Declivity, slope, incline, gradient. **Angle de déclivité,** slope, angle, of gradient.

déclouer [deklue], *v.tr.* (*a*) To unnail, undo (packing-case, etc.). (*b*) **D. un tableau,** to take down a picture (from its nail).

décocher [dekɔʃe], *v.tr.* To shoot, let fly (bolt from cross-bow). **Décocher un coup à qn,** to hit out at s.o. **D. un juron,** to rap out an oath. **D. une épigramme,** to fire off an epigram. **D. une œillade à qn,** to flash a glance at s.o. [COCHE²]

décoiff|er [dekwafe], *v.tr.* **1.** To remove (s.o.'s) hat; to uncap (fuse). **2.** (*a*) To take (s.o.'s) hair down. (*b*) To disarrange, tousle, (s.o.'s) hair. *s.m.* **-ement.**

se décoiffer. 1. To remove one's head-dress. **2.** To take one's hair down.

décoinc|er [dekwɛ̃se], *v.tr.* (n. **décoinçons;** je **décoinçai(s)**) To loosen (jammed part); to unwedge (mast, etc.). *s.m.* **-ement.**

déçoi-s, -t, -ve. See DÉCEVOIR.

décolérer [dekɔlere], *v.i.* (je **décolère;** je **décolérerai**) *F:* To calm down. (Used esp. in the neg.) *Il ne décolérait pas,* he was in a constant state of anger; he was still fuming; *F:* he was in a fine way about it.

décollage [dekɔlaːʒ], *s.m.* **1.** Unsticking, ungluing. **2.** *Av:* Taking off; take-off.

décoller¹ [dekɔle], *v.tr.* *A:* To decapitate, behead.

décoll|er². 1. *v.tr.* (*a*) To unstick, unglue. (*b*) To loosen, disengage, release (part). **2.** *v.i.* (*a*) (Of aeroplane) To rise from the ground; to take off. (*b*) *F:* **Deux heures sans décoller,** two hours at a stretch. *s.m.* **-ement.**

se décoller, to come unstuck, undone; to work loose.

décollé, *a.* (Of ears) Projecting, standing out.

décollet|er [dekɔlte], *v.tr.* (je **décollète,** je **décollète** are theoretical forms; the pronunciation is always [dekɔlt]) **1.** To cut out the neck of (dress). **2.** *Tchn:* To cut (screw). **Tour à décolleter,** screw-cutting lathe. *s.m.* **-age.**

se décolleter, to wear a low-necked dress.

décolleté, *a.* *Femme décolletée,* woman in low-necked dress, in evening dress. *Robe décolletée,* low-necked dress. *Robe décolletée dans le dos,* dress cut low in the back.

décolorant [dekɔlɔrɑ̃], *s.m.* Bleaching agent.

décoloration [dekɔlɔrasjɔ̃], *s.f.* (*a*) Discolouration, fading. (*b*) Bleaching. (*c*) Colourlessness (of complexion).

décolorer [dekɔlɔre], *v.tr.* To discolour; to fade; to take the colour out of (sth.); to bleach (hair).

se décolorer, to lose colour, to fade, to bleach; (of pers.) to lose one's colour, to grow pale.

décombres [dekɔ̃br], *s.m.pl.* Rubbish, debris (of building).

décommand|er [dekɔmɑ̃de], *v.tr.* To countermand (order); to cancel (meeting, dinner). **D. une grève,** to call off a strike. *s.m.* **-ement.**

décomposer [dekɔ̃poze], *v.tr.* **1.** *Ph: Ch: etc:* To decompose. **D. une fraction,** to split up a fraction. **2.** To decompose, rot, decay (organic matter). **3.** To convulse, distort (features).

se décomposer. 1. To decompose, to rot, decay. **2.** (Of face, features) To become convulsed (with terror, etc.).

décomposé, *a.* (*a*) *Mch:* *Huile décomposée,* spent oil. (*b*) *Visage d.,* drawn face; face distorted by grief or terror.

décomposition [dekɔ̃pozisjɔ̃], *s.f.* **1.** *Ph: Ch: etc:* Decomposition. **2.** Decomposition, decay, rotting. **3.** Distortion, awful change (of features).

décompresseur [dekɔ̃prɛsœːr], *s.m.* *I.C.E:* (*a*) Compression tap. (*b*) Exhaust(-valve) lifter.

décompression [dekɔ̃presjɔ̃], *s.f.* *Mch: etc:* Decompression. **Robinet de décompression,** (i) *I.C.E:* compression tap; (ii) *Mch:* pet-cock.

décompte [dekɔ̃t], *s.m.* (*a*) Deduction (from sum to be paid). *F:* **Trouver du décompte,** to be disappointed (*à,* in). (*b*) Balance due.

décompter [dekɔ̃te], *v.tr.* To deduct (sum from account). *F:* **Ils ont trouvé à décompter,** they found things far short of what they expected; they were disappointed.

déconcertant [dekɔ̃sɛrtɑ̃], *a.* Disconcerting.

déconcerter [dekɔ̃sɛrte], *v.tr.* **1.** To upset, confound, frustrate (s.o.'s plans). **2.** To disconcert (s.o.); to put (s.o.) out (of countenance).

se déconcerter, to lose one's assurance; to lose countenance. **Sans se déconcerter,** unabashed.

déconcerté, *a.* Abashed, out of countenance; taken aback.

déconfit [dekɔ̃fi], *a.* Crest-fallen, discomfited.

déconfiture [dekɔ̃fityːr], *s.f.* **1.** *A:* Defeat, rout (of army). **2.** Collapse, failure, downfall, ruin; bankruptcy (of non-trader). **Tomber en déconfiture,** to fail to meet one's liabilities.

décongélation [dekɔ̃ʒelasjɔ̃], *s.f.* Thawing (of meat, etc.).

décongeler [dekɔ̃ʒle], *v.tr.* (je **décongèle;** je **décongèlerai**) To thaw (chilled meat).

décongestionner [dekɔ̃ʒɛstjɔne], *v.tr.* To relieve congestion in (the lungs, etc.); to clear.

déconnecter [dekɔnɛkte], *v.tr.* *El.E:* To disconnect (lead, etc.).

déconseiller [dekɔ̃seje], *v.tr.* **D. qch. à qn,** to advise s.o. against sth. **D. qn de faire qch.,** to advise s.o. against doing sth.

déconsidération [dekɔ̃siderasjɔ̃], *s.f.* Disrepute, discredit. **Tomber en déconsidération,** to fall into disrepute.

déconsidérer [dekɔ̃sidere], *v.tr.* (je **déconsidère;** je **déconsidérerai**) To bring (s.o., sth.) into disrepute.

décontenancement [dekɔ̃tnɑ̃smɑ̃], *s.m.* Putting (of s.o.) out of countenance; mortification, abashment.

décontenancer [dekɔ̃tnɑ̃se], *v.tr.* (je **décontenançai(s);** n. **décontenançons**) To put (s.o.) out of countenance.

se décontenancer, to lose countenance.

décontenancé, *a.* Abashed; put out.

déconvenir [dekɔ̃vniːr], *v.i.* (Conj. like VENIR. Aux. *avoir*) *D. de qch.*, to join issue with s.o. about sth. Je n'en **déconviens** pas, I do not deny it.

déconvenue, *s.f.* Disappointment, mortification; mortifying set-back.

décor [dekɔːr], *s.m.* **1.** Decoration (of house, etc.). Peintre en décor, house-painter. **2.** *Th:* Setting, arrangement (of stage); set; *pl.* scenery. Peintre de décors, scene-painter. Pièce à décors, spectacular play.

décorateur [dekɔratœːr], *s.m.* (*a*) (House-) decorator. (*b*) Stage-designer or scene-painter.

décorat|if, -ive [dekɔratif, -iːv], *a.* Decorative, ornamental. *adv.* **-ivement.**

décoration [dekɔrasjɔ̃], *s.f.* Decoration. **1.** Ornamentation, embellishment (of house, etc.). **2.** Medal; ribbon, star (of an order). Remise de décorations, investiture.

décorer [dekɔre], *v.tr.* **1.** To decorate, ornament; *F:* to do up (house, etc.). **2.** To decorate (s.o.).

décorner [dekɔrne], *v.tr.* To dehorn (cattle, etc.). *F:* Il fait un vent à décorner les bœufs, it is blowing great guns.

décortiquer [dekɔrtike], *v.tr.* To decorticate; to bark (timber); to husk (rice); to hull (barley); to shell (almonds, nuts).

décorum [dekɔrɔm], *s.m.* Decorum, seemliness, propriety; the proprieties.

découcher [dekuʃe], *v.i.* To sleep away from home, out of barracks; to sleep out.

découdre [dekudr], *v.tr.* (Conj. like COUDRE) (*a*) To unpick, unstitch (garment); to rip up (seam). (*b*) (Of horned animal) To rip open, to gore (dog, etc.). *F: A:* En découdre, to cross swords; to fight.

se découdre, to come unsewn, unstitched.

décousu, *a.* (*a*) (Of seam, etc.) Unsewn, unstitched. (*b*) Disconnected, disjointed, incoherent (words, ideas, etc.); rambling, desultory (remarks); unmethodical (work); scrappy (conversation).

découler [dekule], *v.i.* **1.** To trickle, drip, flow; to run (down). **2.** To issue, spring, be derived, proceed, follow (from). La règle découle d'elle-même, the rule follows at once.

découp|er [dekupe], *v.tr.* **1.** To cut up (paper, cake, etc.); to carve (fowl, etc.). Couteau à découper, carving-knife. **2.** To cut out (design); to stamp (out), to punch, cut (metals); to punch, pink (leather). *D. un article dans un journal,* to cut an article out of a newspaper. Scie à découper, fret-saw; jig-saw. *s.m.* **-age.**

se découper, to stand out, show up, project (*sur*, against).

découpé, *a.* (*a*) Cut out. Bois découpé, fretwork. (*b*) Jagged (edge, etc.).

découpler [dekuple], *v.tr.* **1.** To slip, uncouple (hounds). **2.** To uncouple (horses, trucks).

découplé, *a.* Usu. Bien découplé, well set up; strapping (young man).

découpure [dekupyːr], *s.f.* **1.** (*a*) Cutting out. (*b*) Punching, stamping (out). (*c*) Pinking. (*d*) Fretwork. **2.** (*a*) Piece cut out (by punch, etc.); stamping. (*b*) (Newspaper) cutting. **3.** Indentation (in coastline, etc.).

découragement [dekuraʒmɑ̃], *s.m.* Discouragement. Tomber dans le découragement, to become disheartened, despondent.

décourag|er [dekuraʒe], *v.tr.* (je décourageai(s); n. décourageons) **1.** To discourage, dishearten. *D. qn de qch., de faire qch.*, to discourage, deter, s.o. from sth., from doing sth. **2.** *D. un projet,* to discourage, discountenance, a scheme.

se décourager, to become discouraged, disheartened; to lose heart.

découragé, *a.* Discouraged, despondent, cast down.

découronner [dekurɔne], *v.tr.* **1.** To uncrown, depose (king, etc.). **2.** To pollard (tree).

décours [dekuːr], *s.m.* **1.** Waning (of the moon). Lune à son d., moon on the wane. **2.** Abatement (of fever).

décous-ant, -is, -ons, -u, etc. See DÉCOUDRE.

décousure [dekuzyːr], *s.f.* **1.** Seam-rent. **2.** Gash, rip (caused by horns or tusks).

découverte [dekuvɛrt], *s.f.* **1.** Discovery (of land, etc.). Aller à la découverte, to explore, prospect; *Mil:* to scout, reconnoitre. **2.** Discovery, exposure, detection (of plot, etc.).

découvreur [dekuvrœːr], *s.m.* Discoverer.

découvrir [dekuvriːr], *v.tr.* (Conj. like COUVRIR) **1.** (*a*) To uncover. *D. un pot,* to take the lid off a pot. *D. une maison,* to take the roof off a house. (*b*) To expose, lay bare; to unveil (statue); to disclose (secret). *Se d. la tête,* to bare one's head. *D. ses dents,* to show one's teeth. *D. son cœur,* to lay bare one's heart. *Chess: D. une pièce,* to uncover a piece. **2.** To perceive, discern. *Nau:* To sight (land). **3.** (*a*) To discover, find out (plot, etc.); to detect (error, criminal); to bring (crime, etc.) to light. *Le projecteur découvrit l'avion,* the searchlight picked out the plane. *Craindre d'être découvert,* to fear detection. (*b*) To discover (oxygen, etc.). **4.** *v.i.* (Of reef) To uncover (at low tide).

se découvrir. 1. (*a*) To bare one's head; to take off one's hat. (*b*) To take off some of one's clothing. **2.** *Fenc:* To expose oneself. **3.** (Of sky) To clear up. **4.** To become perceptible; to come into sight. **5.** To come to light. La vérité se découvre toujours, truth will out.

découvert. 1. *a.* (*a*) Uncovered. La tête découverte, bare-headed. A visage découvert, openly, frankly. (*b*) Open (country, car, etc.). *Aut:* Virage découvert, open corner. (*c*) Exposed, unprotected (town, etc.). (*d*) Compte découvert, overdrawn account. **2.** *s.m. Bank: etc:* Uncovered balance; overdraft. **3.** A découvert, uncovered, unprotected, open. Agir, parler, à découvert, to act, speak, openly. Mettre qch. à découvert, to expose sth. to view. *Crédit à d.,* unsecured credit. *St.Exch:* Vendre à découvert, *F:* to bear the market.

décrass|er [dekrase], *v.tr.* To clean, cleanse, scour; to remove the fouling from (gun-barrel); to decarbonize (engine). *D. une chaudière,* to scale, fur, a boiler. *s.m.* **-age.** *s.m.* **-ement.**

se décrasser. (*a*) To clean oneself. (*b*) *F:* To rise in the world.

décrassoir [dekraswaːr], *s.m.* Tooth-comb.

décréditer [dekredite], *v.tr.* To bring into discredit, into disrepute.

se décréditer, to fall into disrepute, into discredit (*auprès de qn,* with s.o.).

décrépi [dekrepi], *a.* Unplastered; peeling; dilapidated.

décrépit [dekrepi], *a.* Decrepit, senile; broken-down (horse); tumble-down, dilapidated (house).

décrépitude [dekrepityd], *s.f.* Decrepitude.

décret [dekrɛ], *s.m.* Decree; fiat, order. *Adm:* Décret présidentiel = Order in Council.

décréter [dekrete], *v.tr.* (je décrète; je décréterai) To decree; to enact (law). *Il avait été décrété que . . .*, it had been enacted that. . . .

décret-loi *s.m.* = Order in Council. *pl.* Des décrets-lois.

décri [dekri], *s.m.* Disparagement. *Tomber dans le d.*, to fall into disrepute, into discredit.

décrier [dekrie], *v.tr.* To disparage, decry, discredit (s.o., sth.); to run (s.o., sth.) down.

décrire [dekriːr], *v.tr.* (Conj. like ÉCRIRE) **1.** To describe (a sight, etc.). **2.** *Geom: etc:* To describe (curve, circle).

décrocher [dekrɔʃe], *v.tr.* To unhook, take down (coat from peg, etc.); to unsling (hammock); to take off, lift (telephone receiver); to uncouple, disconnect (railway carriages, etc.). *D. une agrafe*, to undo a clasp. *Se d. la mâchoire*, to dislocate one's jaw. S.a. BÂILLER 1. *F:* Décrocher les palmes, la croix, to receive a decoration. *Décrocher le grand succès*, to make a big hit. S.a. TIMBALE 2. *s.m.* **-age.** *s.m.* **-ement.**
se décrocher. *Ph:* To fall out of step, out of tune (with oscillatory system).

décrochez-moi-ça, *s.m. P:* **1.** Reach-me-down (suit). **2.** Cheap ready-made tailor's shop.

décroiser [dekrwaze], *v.tr.* To uncross (one's legs, etc.). *s.m.* **-ement.**

décroissance [dekrwasɑ̃ːs], *s.f.* Decrease; diminution (of population); decline (of strength); wane (of the moon); abatement (of fever). *Nos importations sont en décroissance*, our imports are decreasing.

décroiss-ons, -ez, etc. See DÉCROÎTRE.

décroît [dekrwa], *s.m.* Last quarter (of the moon). *Sur son d.*, in its last quarter.

décroître [dekrwaːtr,-wa-], *v.i.* (*pr.p.* décroissant; *p.p.* décru; *pr.ind.* il décroît, ils décroissent; *p.h.* il décrut; *fu.* il décroîtra) To decrease, decline, diminish. *Les jours commencent à d.*, the days are beginning to shorten, to draw in. *La lune décroît*, the moon is on the wane. *Aller (en) décroissant*, to decrease; to grow gradually less.

décrotter [dekrɔte], *v.tr.* To clean (boots, etc.); to scrape (one's boots). *s.m.* **-age.**

décrotteur [dekrɔtœːr], *s.m.* (*a*) Shoeblack, boot-black. (*b*) (In hotel) Boots.

décrottoir [dekrɔtwaːr], *s.m.* Shoe-scraper; door-scraper. *Tapis d.*, wire mat.

décru, -s, -t, etc. See DÉCROÎTRE.

décrue [dekry], *s.f.* Fall, subsidence (of river, etc.); retreat (of glacier).

décrypter [dekripte], *v.tr.* To decipher (cryptogram). *s.m.* **-ement.**

déçu, -s, -t, etc. See DÉCEVOIR.

déculotter [dekylɔte], *v.tr.* To take the breeches off (s.o.).
se déculotter, (i) to take off, (ii) to let down, one's trousers.

décuple [dekypl], *a. & s.m.* Decuple; *a.* tenfold.

décupler [dekyple], *v.tr. & i.* To decuple; to increase, multiply, tenfold. *s.m.* **-ement.**

dédaigner [dedɛɲe], *v.tr.* To scorn, disdain; *F:* to turn up one's nose at (an offer). *Cette offre n'est pas à dédaigner*, this offer is not to be disdained, *F:* is not to be sneezed at. *Il dédaigna de répondre*, he did not deign to answer.

dédaigneux, -euse [dedɛɲø, -øːz], *a.* Disdainful (de, of); contemptuous; scornful. *adv.* **-sement.**

dédain [dedɛ̃], *s.m.* Disdain, scorn (de, of); disregard (de qch., of sth., pour qn, for s.o.). *Avec dédain*, disdainfully, scornfully. *Témoigner du d. à qn*, to show contempt for s.o.; to ignore s.o. *Avoir le dédain de qch.*, to have a contempt for sth. *Prendre qn en dédain*, to begin to look down on s.o.

Dédale [dedal]. **1.** *Pr.n.m. Gr.Myth:* Daedalus. **2.** *s.m.* Labyrinth, maze (of streets, etc.).

dedans [dədɑ̃]. **1.** *adv.* Inside; within; in (it,

them, etc.). *F:* **Mettre qn dedans,** to humbug s.o.; to take s.o. in. **Donner dedans,** to fall into the trap. **De dedans,** from within. **En dedans,** (on the) inside; within. *Il n'était pas si calme en d.*, he was not so calm inwardly. **En dedans de,** within. *Par dedans la maison*, inside the house. **2.** *s.m.* Inside, interior (of house, box, etc.). **Agir du dedans,** to act from within (a party, etc.). **Au dedans,** (on the) inside; within. *Au d. et au dehors*, (i) inside and out; (ii) at home and abroad. **Au dedans de,** inside, within.

dédicace [dedikas], *s.f.* **1.** *Ecc:* Dedication, consecration. **2.** Dedication (of book, etc.).

dédicatoire [dedikatwaːr], *a.* Dedicatory.

dédier [dedje], *v.tr.* **1.** *Ecc:* To dedicate, consecrate (building). **2.** To dedicate, inscribe (book).

dédire (se) [sədediːr], *v.pr.* (Conj. like DIRE, except *pr.ind. v.v.* dédisez) **1.** *Se d. d'une affirmation*, to take back what one has said; to retract a statement. **2.** *Se d. d'une promesse*, to go back on one's word.

dédit [dedi], *s.m.* **1.** Retraction, withdrawal. **2.** Breaking (of promise). **3.** Forfeit, penalty (for breaking contract, etc.).

dédommagement [dedɔmaʒmɑ̃], *s.m.* **1.** Indemnification, indemnifying (de qn, of s.o.). **2.** Indemnity, compensation, damages. *Recevoir une somme en dédommagement de qch.*, to receive a sum as, in, compensation for sth.

dédommager [dedɔmaʒe], *v.tr.* (je dédommageai(s); n. dédommageons) To indemnify, compensate (s.o.); to make amends to (s.o.). *D. qn de qch.*, to indemnify, recoup, compensate, s.o. for sth. *D. qn d'une perte*, to make good a loss. **Se faire dédommager par qn,** to recover from s.o.
se dédommager, to recoup oneself (de, for).

dédoré [dedɔre], *a.* Tarnished; with the gilt rubbed off.

dédouanage [dedwana:ʒ], *s.m.*, **dédouanement** [dedwanmɑ̃], *s.m. Cust:* Clearance (of goods).

dédouaner [dedwane], *v.tr. Cust:* To clear (goods); to take (goods) out of bond.

dédoublable [dedublabl], *a.* Divisible into two; (train) that may run in two portions. *Phot:* Objectif d., doublet lens, convertible lens.

dédoublement [dedubləmɑ̃], *s.m.* **1.** Undoubling (of folded cloth, etc.). **2.** (*a*) Dividing, splitting, into two. *D. de la personnalité*, dual personality. (*b*) *Ch:* Double decomposition. (*c*) Running (of train) in two portions.

dédoubler [deduble], *v.tr.* **1.** To undouble (folded cloth, etc.). *D. les rangs*, to form single file. **2.** (*a*) To divide, cut, split, (sth.) into two. (*b*) To run (train) in two portions. **3.** To remove the lining of, to unline (garment).
se dédoubler. 1. To unfold. **2.** To divide, split (into two parts).

déductif, -ive [dedyktif, -iːv], *a. Phil:* Deductive (reasoning).

déduction [dedyksjɔ̃], *s.f.* **1.** Deduction, inference. **2.** *Com: etc:* Deduction, allowance, abatement. **Faire déduction des sommes payées d'avance,** to deduct, to allow for, sums paid in advance. **Sous déduction de 10%,** less 10%. **"Sans déduction,"** 'terms net cash.'

déduire [dedɥiːr], *v.tr.* (Conj. like CONDUIRE) **1.** To deduce, infer (result). **2.** To deduct. *D. 5%*, to take off, allow, 5%.

déesse [dees], *s.f.* Goddess.

défâcher [defɑʃe]. **1.** *v.tr. F:* To pacify (s.o.); *F:* to smoothe (s.o.) down. **2.** *v.i. & pr.* To calm down, cool down.

défaillance [defajɑ̃ːs], *s.f.* **1.** *A:* Extinction,

decay (of family, race). **2.** (a) (Moral, physical) lapse. *La d. de ses forces*, the failing of his strength. **Politique sans défaillance,** unflinching policy. *Moment de d.,* weak moment. *D. de mémoire,* lapse of memory. *Med:* D. *cardiaque,* heart-failure. **Coupable de défaillance,** guilty of failure to perform a duty. (b) Fainting fit; swoon. **Tomber en défaillance, avoir une défaillance,** to faint away.

défaillant, -ante [defajã, -ã:t], a. **I.** (a) A: (Of race, family) Dying out. (b) Failing (strength, etc.); waning (light); sinking (heart). (c) (Of pers.) *D. de fatigue,* dropping with fatigue. (d) (Of pers.) Faint; about to swoon. **2.** (a) a. Defaulting. (b) s. Defaulter, absconder.

défaillir [defajiːr], v.i. (pr.p. **défaillant;** p.p. **défailli;** pr.ind. il **défaille,** n. **défaillons,** ils **défaillent;** p.d. je **défaillais;** p.h. je **défaillis;** fu. occ. je **défaillerai**) (a) To become feeble, to lose strength. *Sa mémoire commence à d.,* his memory is beginning to fail. (b) *D. à son devoir,* to fail in one's duty. **Sans défaillir,** without flinching. (c) To faint, swoon. (d) *A cette nouvelle son cœur défaillit,* his heart sank at the news.

défaire [defeːr], v.tr. (Conj. like FAIRE) **I.** To demolish, destroy; to pull (sth.) to pieces; to cancel, annul (treaty); to break off (alliance, marriage). *D. des chiffons,* to pick rags. *La terreur avait défait son visage,* fear had distorted his features. **2.** (a) To undo; to untie (parcel, knot); to unwrap (parcel); to unpack (trunk); to unpick (seam); to unfasten, loose (one's dress, etc.). *D. ses cheveux,* to let one's hair down. (b) *D. qn de qn, de qch.,* to rid s.o. of s.o., of sth. **3.** To defeat, overthrow (army, etc.); to get the better of (s.o.). **4.** *Faire et d. les rois,* to make and unmake kings.

  se défaire. I. (Of clothes, knot) To come undone; (of hair) to come down; (of things joined together) to come apart. **2.** (a) *Se d. de qn,* to make away with s.o.; to kill, despatch, s.o. (b) *Se d. de qn, de qch.,* to get rid of s.o., of sth.; to rid oneself of s.o., of sth. *Je ne veux pas m'en d.,* I don't want to part with it. *Se d. d'une mauvaise habitude,* to get out of, break off, a bad habit.

défait, a. (a) Drawn, discomposed (features, face). (b) Dishevelled; disarranged (attire, hair).

défaisable [defəzabl], a. That can be undone.

défais-ant, -ons. See DÉFAIRE.

défaite [defet], s.f. **I.** Disposal. **Marchandises de prompte défaite,** goods that command a ready sale. **2.** Lame excuse; mere pretext. **3.** Defeat. **Essuyer une défaite,** to suffer (a) defeat.

défaitisme [defetism], s.m. Defeatism

défaitiste [defetist], a. & s. Defeatist.

défalcation [defalkasjɔ̃], s.f. (a) Deduction, deducting; writing-off (of bad debt). (b) Sum, weight, deducted.

défalquer [defalke], v.tr. To deduct (sum from total). *D. une mauvaise créance,* to write off a bad debt.

défass-e, -es, etc. See DÉFAIRE.

défausser[1] **(se)** [sodefose], v.pr. *Cards:* To throw out one's useless cards. *Se d. à trèfle,* to discard one's clubs. [FAUX[1]]

défausser[2], v.tr. To true, straighten (rod, blade, etc.).

défaut [defo], s.m. **I.** (a) Default, absence, (total) lack, want (of sth.). *D. de courage,* lack of courage. *D. de paiement,* failure to pay; non-payment. **Faire défaut,** (i) to be absent, wanting; (ii) to fail, give out. *Le temps me fait d.,* I cannot spare the time. *Les provisions font d.,* there is a scarcity of provisions. *La mémoire lui fait d.,*

(his) memory fails him. *Bank:* **"Défaut de provision,"** 'no funds.' **A, au, défaut de qch.,** in default of, for lack of, failing, sth. (b) Break in continuity. *Les défauts de l'armure,* the joints in the harness; *F:* the vulnerable points. S.a. CUIRASSE 1. *Glisser au d. du trottoir,* to slip off the kerb. (c) *Jur:* Default. **Faire défaut,** to fail to appear. **Jugement par défaut,** judgment by default. **2.** (a) Fault, shortcoming. *D. de caractère,* failing. **C'est là son moindre défaut,** that is the last thing one can reproach him with. (b) Defect, flaw. *Il y a un d. de fonctionnement,* there is something wrong with the works. **Sans défaut,** faultless, flawless, without blemish. (c) *Ven:* **Mettre les chiens en défaut,** to throw the hounds off the scent. *F:* **Mettre qn en défaut,** to put s.o. on the wrong track; to baffle s.o. **Prendre qn en défaut,** to catch s.o. napping, tripping, to catch s.o. out.

défaveur [defavœːr], s.f. Disfavour, discredit. **Tomber en défaveur,** to fall into disfavour, out of favour (*auprès de,* with).

défavorable [defavɔrabl], a. Unfavourable (*à,* to). *Se montrer d. à un projet,* to disfavour, discountenance, a plan. *Les conditions (nous) sont défavorables,* conditions are against us.

défectif [defektif], a. Defective (verb).

défection [defɛksjɔ̃], s.f. Defection from, desertion of, a cause. **Faire défection,** to fall away, to desert; *F:* to rat.

défectueu|x, -euse [defɛktɥø. -øːz], a. Defective, faulty, unsound. adv. **-sement.**

défectuosité [defɛktɥozite], s.f. **I.** Defectiveness. **2.** Defect, flaw.

défendable [defãdabl], a. Defensible.

défendeur, -eresse [defãdœːr, -ɔrɛs], s. *Jur:* Defendant.

défendre [defãːdr], v.tr. **I.** (a) To defend (cause, prisoner, etc.); to maintain, uphold (opinion, right); to stand up for (one's friends) (*contre,* against). *Il sait d. son opinion,* he can hold his own. *Tuer qn à son corps défendant,* to kill s.o. in self-defence. **Faire qch. à son corps défendant,** to do sth. reluctantly, under protest, under coercion. (b) To protect, shield, guard (*contre,* against, from). **2.** To forbid, prohibit. *Fruit défendu,* forbidden fruit. *D. qch. à qn,* to forbid s.o. sth. *D. à qn de faire qch.,* to forbid s.o. to do sth. *"Il est défendu de fumer,"* 'smoking prohibited.' *Il m'est défendu de fumer,* I am forbidden to smoke. *Il défendit qu'on passât par là,* he forbade anyone to pass that way. S.a. PORTE 2.

  se défendre. I. (a) To defend oneself. (b) *Se d. d'avoir fait qch.,* to deny having done sth. *Je ne m'en défends pas,* I don't deny it. **2.** *Se d. de, contre, qch.,* to protect, shield, oneself from, against, sth. **3.** *Se d. de faire qch.,* to refrain from doing sth. (Esp. in neg.) *On ne peut se d. de l'aimer,* one can't help liking him. *Il ne put se d. de sourire,* he could not refrain from smiling. **4.** (The pron. is the indirect object) *Se d. tout plaisir,* to deny oneself all pleasure.

défense [defãːs], s.f. **I.** Defence. *Combattre pour la d. de son pays,* to fight in defence of one's country. *Prendre la d. de qn,* to undertake s.o.'s defence; to champion s.o.'s cause. *D. contre avions, anti-aérienne,* anti-aircraft defence. *D. passive,* air-raid precautions. **Sans défense,** unprotected, defenceless. *Jur:* **Cas de légitime défense,** case of self-defence. **2.** pl. (a) Defences, defensive works. (b) Tusks (of elephant). **3.** Prohibition, interdiction. **"Défense d'entrer, de fumer,"** 'no admittance,' 'no smoking.' **Faire défense à qn de faire qch.,** to forbid s.o. to do sth.

défenseur [defãsœːr], *s.m.* **1.** (*a*) Protector, defender (of child, town, etc.). (*b*) Supporter, upholder (of a cause). **2.** *Jur:* Counsel for the defence.

défensif, -ive [defãsif, -iːv]. **1.** *a.* Defensive. **2.** *s.f.* **Se tenir sur la défensive,** to stand on the defensive.

défer-ai, -as, etc. See DÉFAIRE.

déférence [deferãːs], *s.f.* Deference, respect, regard (*pour,* for). **Par déférence pour . . .,** in, out of, deference to. . . .

déférer [defere], *v.* (je défère ; je déférerai) I. *v.tr.* **1.** *Jur:* (*a*) To submit, refer (case to*a court). (*b*) *D. qn à la justice,* to hand over, give up, s.o. to justice. (*c*) **Déférer le serment à qn,** to administer, tender, the oath to s.o. ; to swear (witness) ; to swear in (jury). **2.** To confer, bestow (honour) (*à,* on).
  II. **déférer,** *v.i. D. à qn,* to defer to s.o. *D. aux ordres de qn,* to comply with s.o.'s orders. *D. à une demande,* to accede to a request.

déferlant [defɛrlã], *a.* **Vague déferlante,** beachcomber ; breaker.

déferler [defɛrle]. **1.** *v.tr. Nau:* To unfurl, shake out (sail, flag) ; to break (flag, signal) ; to set (sail). **2.** *v.i.* (Of waves) To break (into foam) ; to comb.

déferrer [defɛre], *v.tr.* **1.** To remove the iron from (sth.). *D. un forçat,* to knock off a convict's irons ; to unfetter a convict. **2.** To unshoe (horse). *s.m.* **-age.**
  se déferrer, (of horse) to cast a shoe.

défeuiller [defœje], *v.tr.* To strip the leaves off (tree) ; to defoliate (shrub).
  se défeuiller, (of tree) to shed its leaves.

défi [defi], *s.m.* (*a*) Challenge. **Lancer, adresser, jeter, un défi à qn,** to challenge s.o. ; to send s.o. a challenge. **Relever un défi,** to take up a challenge. (*b*) Defiance. **Mettre qn au défi de faire qch.,** to defy, dare, s.o. to do sth. **D'un air de défi,** defiantly. **En défi de,** in defiance of.

défiance [defjãːs], *s.f.* **1.** Mistrust, distrust, suspicion. **Faire qch. sans défiance,** to do sth. unsuspectingly. **2.** *D. de soi-même,* diffidence ; lack of self-confidence.

défiant [defjã], *a.* Mistrustful, distrustful, cautious, wary.

déficeler [defisle], *v.tr.* (Conj. like FICELER). To untie, undo (parcel, etc.).
  se déficeler, to come untied, undone.

déficit [defisit], *s.m.* Deficit ; shortage. **Être en déficit,** to show a deficit. **Combler le déficit,** to make up the deficit.

déficitaire [defisitɛːr], *a.* (Account) showing a debit balance ; (budget, etc.) showing a deficit.

défier [defje], *v.tr.* (*a*) To challenge. *D. qn au combat, aux échecs,* to challenge s.o. to fight, to a game of chess. (*b*) To defy, set at defiance. *Le spectacle défie toute description,* the sight baffles all description. *D. qn de faire qch.,* to defy s.o. to do sth. (*c*) To brave, to face (danger, death).
  se défier *de qn, de qch.,* to mistrust, distrust, s.o., sth. *Se d. de soi-même,* to be diffident.

défiger [defiʒe], *v.tr.* (je défigeai(s) ; n. défigeons) To liquefy (solidified oil, etc.).
  se défiger. (*a*) (Of oil, etc.) To liquefy. (*b*) *F:* (Of pers.) (i) To thaw, (ii) to rouse oneself.

défiguration [defigyrasjɔ̃], *s.f.,* **défigurement** [defigyrmã], *s.m.* Disfigurement, disfiguration. *D. d'une statue,* defacement of a statue.

défigurer [defigyre], *v.tr.* To disfigure (s.o., sth.) ; to deface (statue) ; to distort (the truth).

défilade [defilad], *s.f.* **1.** Passing (of the fleet) in line ahead. **2.** *F:* **Aller à la défilade,** to trail along ; to trail past.

défiler[1] [defile], *v.tr.* **1.** To unstring, unthread (beads, necklace). **2.** *Mil:* To defilade (fortress) ; to put (company, etc.) under cover.
  se défiler. 1. (Of beads, etc.) To come unstrung. **2.** (*a*) *Mil: Se d. du feu de l'adversaire,* to take cover from the enemy's fire. (*b*) *P:* To make off, to clear out.

défiler[2], *v.i. Mil: etc:* (*a*) To defile ; to file off. *D. deux à deux,* to file off in twos. (*b*) To march past. (*c*) To walk in procession. *s.m.* **-ement.**

défilé, *s.m.* **1.** Defile, gorge ; (mountain) pass. **2.** *Mil: etc:* Defiling, march(ing) past. *D. de mannequins,* mannequin parade. *D. ininterrompu d'autos,* endless procession of cars.

définir [definiːr], *v.tr.* To define.
  se définir, to become clear, distinct.

défini, *a.* (*a*) Definite ; clearly defined. (*b*) *Gram:* Definite (article, etc.). **Passé défini,** past definite ; preterite ; past historic.

définissable [definisabl], *a.* Definable.

définitif, -ive [definitif, -iːv], *a.* Definitive ; final (resolution, judgment) ; permanent (installation). **Nommé à titre définitif,** permanently appointed. *Adv.phr.* **En définitive,** finally.

définition [definisjɔ̃], *s.f.* **1.** Definition. **2.** Clue (of cross-word puzzle).

définitivement [definitivmã], *adv.* Definitely ; finally ; (gone) for good.

défi-s, -t, etc. See DÉFAIRE.

déflagrateur [deflagratœːr], *s.m.* Deflagrator. *El:* Spark-gap.

déflagration [deflagrasjɔ̃], *s.f.* Deflagration, combustion.

déflagrer [deflagre], *v.i.* To deflagrate.

déflation [deflasjɔ̃], *s.f.* Deflation (of balloon, of the currency).

défleurir [deflœriːr], *v.i. & pr.* (Of tree, etc.) To lose its blooms or blossom.

déflorer [deflɔre], *v.tr.* **1.** To strip (plant) of its blooms. **2.** To take the freshness off, to spoil (piece of news, etc.). **3.** To deflower.

défoncer [defɔ̃se], *v.tr.* (je défonçai(s) ; n. défonçons) **1.** To stave in (cask, boat) ; to smash in (box, etc.) ; *F:* to knock the bottom out of (argument). **2.** To break up, cut up (road). *s.m.* **-çage.** *s.m.* **-cement.**

défoncé, *a.* **1.** Stove in ; battered, bashed-in (hat). **2.** *Chemin d.,* broken, bumpy, road.

déforestation [defɔrɛstasjɔ̃], *s.f.* Deforestation.

déformation [defɔrmasjɔ̃], *s.f.* **1.** (*a*) Deformation. (*b*) *Phot:* Distortion (of image). **2.** Buckling, warping. *D. permanente,* permanent set.

déformer [defɔrme], *v.tr.* **1.** To deform ; to put (hat) out of shape. *Phot: Image déformée,* distorted image. **2.** To warp, buckle ; to give a set to (plate, etc.).
  se déformer. 1. To get out of shape. **2.** To warp, buckle ; to take a set.

défourner [defurne], *v.tr.* To draw (pottery) from the kiln, (bread) from the oven. *s.m.* **-age.** *s.m.* **-ement.**

défraîchir [defrɛʃiːr], *v.tr.* To take away the newness, freshness, of (sth.).
  se défraîchir, to lose one's, its, freshness.

défraîchi, *a. Articles défraîchis,* (shop-)soiled goods. *Fleurs défraîchies,* faded flowers.

défrayer [defrɛje], *v.tr.* (je défraie, je défraye ; je défraierai, je défrayerai) **1.** *D. qn,* to defray, pay, s.o.'s expenses. *Être défrayé de tout,* to have all expenses paid. **2.** *F: D. la conversation,*

(i) to be the life of the conversation; (ii) to provide a topic of conversation.

défrich|er [defriʃe], *v.tr.* To clear, grub, reclaim (land for cultivation); to bring (land) into cultivation; to break (new ground). *F: D. un sujet*, to do pioneer work in a subject. *s.m.* **-ement.**

défriser [defrize], *v.tr.* To uncurl; to put (hair) out of curl. *Je suis toute défrisée*, my hair is quite out of curl.

  se défriser, (of hair) to come out of curl.

défroncer [defrɔ̃se], *v.tr.* (Conj. like FRONCER) To undo the gathers in (skirt). *Il défronça les sourcils*, he ceased to frown, his brow cleared.

défroque [defrɔk], *s.f.* **1.** Effects (of dead monk). **2.** Usu. *pl.* Cast-off clothing.

défroquer [defrɔke], *v.tr.* To unfrock, ungown (priest, monk).

défunt, -unte [defœ̃, -œ̃:t], *a. & s.* Defunct, deceased. *Le roi défunt,* the late King.

dégagement [degaʒmɑ̃], *s.m.* **1.** Redemption (of pledge, mortgage); taking out of pawn. **Dégagement de sa parole,** (i) carrying out of one's promise; (ii) retraction of one's word. **2.** *(a)* Disengagement, release (of brake, etc.). *Mil:* Extrication (of troops); relieving, relief (of town). *(b)* Loosening, slackening (of bolt, etc.). *(c)* Relieving of congestion; clearing (of road, of the lungs, etc.). **Escalier de dégagement,** (i) private staircase; (ii) emergency stairs. *(d) Dégagements d'un théâtre,* exits of a theatre. *(e) Fb:* Clearing kick. **3.** *(a)* Escape, release (of steam, gas, etc.). **Tuyau de dégagement,** waste-pipe. *(b)* Emission, liberation (of heat). **4.** Clearance (of car above ground).

dégager [degaʒe], *v.tr.* (je **dégageai(s);** n. **dégageons) 1.** To redeem (pledge, mortgage); to take (sth.) out of pawn. **Dégager sa parole,** (i) to make good one's promise; (ii) to take back one's word. **2.** *(a)* To disengage. *D. le frein,* to release the brake. *D. une troupe,* to extricate a body of troops (from critical position). *D. une ville,* to relieve a town. *D. qn d'une promesse,* to release, absolve, s.o. from a pledge. *D. des titres,* to release (pledged) securities. *D. son esprit de préjugés,* to clear one's mind of prejudices. *D. la vérité de l'erreur,* to separate, sift out, truth from error. *(b)* To relieve the congestion in, to clear (road, deck). *(c) D. des conclusions d'un récit,* to draw conclusions from an account. *D. le sens intime d'un passage,* to bring out the inner meaning of a passage. *D. son style,* to give ease, freedom, to one's style. *(d)* To free (a part); to loosen, slacken (bolt). *Fenc:* To disengage (the blade). *Box:* To break away. *Fb:* To kick over the touch-line; to clear. **3.** To emit, give off (vapour, smell); to exhale (odour, etc.); to emit, give out (heat).

  se dégager. 1. To free oneself, to get free *(de,* from); to get clear *(de,* of); to break loose, break away *(de,* from); to disengage oneself *(de,* from); to extricate oneself *(de,* from). *Se d. d'une promesse,* to back out of a promise. *Le ciel se dégage,* the sky is clearing. *Sa toux se dégage,* his cough is easier. **2.** (Of gas, odour, etc.) To be given off *(de,* by); to escape, emanate *(de,* from); to arise, to come off. **3.** To emerge, come out. *La silhouette du navire se dégagea du brouillard,* the ship loomed up out of the fog. *Enfin la vérité se dégage,* at last the truth is coming out. *Cette nécessité se dégage de l'étude des faits,* this need becomes apparent after a study of the facts.

  dégagé, *a.* *(a)* Free, untrammelled (movements, etc.). *Allure dégagée,* swinging stride. *(b)* Pert, perky, free and easy (tone, manner).

Propos dégagés, somewhat free conversation. *(c) Vue dégagée,* open view.

dégaine [degɛn], *s.f.* Gait; usu. awkward gait.

dégainer [degene], *v.tr.* To unsheathe, draw (sword). *Abs.* To draw.

déganter (se) [sədegɑ̃te], *v.pr.* To take off one's gloves.

dégarn|ir [degarniːr], *v.tr.* To dismantle (room, etc.); to untrim (dress); to strip (bed, etc.); to withdraw the garrison from (fort); to unrig (ship, capstan). *s.m.* **-issement.**

  se dégarnir. 1. (Of tree) To lose its leaves; (of head) to get bald. **2.** (Of hall, etc.) To empty. **3.** To run oneself short of ready money.

dégarni, *a.* Empty; depleted; stripped *(de, of).* *Armoire dégarnie,* bare cupboard. *Arbre d.,* tree bare of leaves. *D. d'argent,* short of money.

dégâts [degɑ], *s.m.pl.* Damage. *Les gelées ont fait des dégâts dans les vignobles,* the frosts have wrought havoc in, made havoc of, the vineyards.

dégauch|ir [degoʃiːr], *v.tr.* To rough-plane, to try up, shoot (board, etc.); to straighten, to true up (piece of machinery, etc.). *s.m.* **-issage.** *s.m.* **-issement.**

dégauchisseuse [degoʃisøːz], *s.f.* Planing machine (for surfacing).

dégel [deʒɛl], *s.m.* Thaw. **Le temps est, se met, au dégel,** the thaw is setting in; the frost has broken.

dégelée [deʒle], *s.f.* *F:* Shower of blows.

dégeler [deʒle], *v.tr. & i., v.impers.* **(il dégèle; il dégèlera)** To thaw.

dégénération [deʒenerasjɔ̃], *s.f.* Degeneration, degeneracy.

dégénérer [deʒenere], *v.i.* **(je dégénère; je dégénérerai)** To degenerate *(de,* from; *en,* into). *Il croirait d. en acceptant,* he would think he was lowering himself if he accepted.

  dégénéré, -ée, *a. & s.* Degenerate.

dégénérescence [deʒenerɛssɑ̃:s], *s.f.* *Med:* Degeneration.

dégingandé, -ée [deʒɛ̃gɑ̃de], *a. & s.* *F:* Awkward, ungainly, loosely built (person).

déglacer [deglase], *v.tr.* (Conj. like GLACER) To thaw, to melt the ice on (pond, etc.); to defrost (refrigerator).

dégoiser [degwaze], *v.tr.* *F:* To spout (abuse, a speech). *D. ses prières,* to rattle off one's prayers.

dégomm|er [degɔme], *v.tr.* **1.** To ungum, unstick (sth.). **2.** *F: (a)* To dismiss (s.o. from office). *(b)* To push out, oust (s.o.). *(c)* To beat, *F:* to lick (s.o.) (at a game).

dégonfl|er [degɔ̃fle], *v.tr.* **1.** To deflate, let the air out of (balloon, etc.). *Elle dégonfla son cœur,* (i) she had her say out; (ii) she had her cry out. **2.** To reduce, bring down (swelling). **3.** *P:* To debunk (hero). *s.m.* **-ement.**

  se dégonfler. *(a)* (Of tyre, balloon, etc.) To collapse, to go flat. *(b)* (Of swelling) To subside.

dégonflé, *a.* Flat or soft (tyre).

dégorg|er [degɔrʒe], *v.* **(je dégorgeai(s);** n. **dégorgeons) 1.** *v.tr.* *(a)* To disgorge. *F:* **Faire d. qn,** to make s.o. disgorge (ill-gotten gains). *(b)* To free, clear, unstop (passage, pipe). *(c)* To purify, scour (wool, leather). **2.** *v.i. & pr.* (Of sewer, pond) To flow out, to discharge *(dans,* into). **3.** *v.i.* (Of gutter, stream) To overflow. *s.m.* **-ement.**

dégot|er [degɔte], *v.tr.* **1.** *F:* *(a)* To oust, supplant (s.o.). *(b)* To surpass, beat, lick (s.o.). **2.** *P:* To get, find, unearth (curio, etc.).

dégouliner [deguline], *v.i.* *F:* **1.** *D. l'escalier,* to tumble downstairs. **2.** (Of water) To trickle, drip, run.

dégourd|ir [degurdi:r], *v.tr.* (*a*) To remove stiffness, numbness, from (the limbs); to revive (by warmth, movement). *D. les mains à qn*, to chafe s.o.'s hands. *F: D. une recrue*, to lick a recruit into shape. *Paris l'a dégourdi*, Paris has smartened, brightened, him up. (*b*) (Faire) **dégourdir de l'eau**, to take the chill off water. *s.m.* **-issement.**

se dégourdir. 1. To restore the circulation; to lose one's numb, stiff, feeling; to stretch one's limbs. **2.** (Of water) To grow warm. **3.** To grow smarter, more alert.

dégourdi, *a.* (Of pers.) Alive, wide-awake, sharp, cute.

dégoût [degu], *s.m.* Disgust, distaste, loathing, dislike. **Prendre qch. en dégoût**, to take a dislike to sth. *Avoir du d. pour qch.*, to feel a dislike for sth., an aversion from sth.

dégoûtant [degutã], *a.* Disgusting, loathsome, nauseating, nasty (sight, smell, etc.).

dégoûter [degute], *v.tr.* To disgust. *D. qn de qch.*, to disgust s.o. with sth.; to give s.o. a distaste for sth.

se dégoûter *de qn, de qch.*, to take a dislike to s.o., sth. *Je suis dégoûté de la vie*, I am sick, tired, weary, of life.

dégoûté, *a.* **1.** Disgusted (*de*, with); sick (of); *F:* fed up. *D. de la viande*, off meat. **2.** Overnice, fastidious, squeamish. *F:* **Vous n'êtes pas dégoûté!** you don't want much!

dégouttant [degutã], *a.* Dripping (*de*, with).

dégoutter [degute], *v.i.* **1.** To drip, trickle, to fall drop by drop (*de*, from). **2.** To be dripping (*de*, with).

dégouttures [deguty:r], *s.f.pl.* Drippings.

dégradant [degradã], *a.* Degrading, lowering.

dégradateur [degradatœ:r], *s.m. Phot:* Vignetting mask; vignetter.

dégradation¹ [degradasjõ], *s.f.* **1.** Degradation (from rank, etc.). *D. civique*, loss of civil rights. **2.** (Moral) degradation. **Tomber dans la dégradation**, to sink into the mire. **3.** (*a*) Defacement; weathering (of rock). (*b*) Usu. *pl.* Damage; dilapidation; wear and tear (of house, etc.).

dégradation², *s.f.* Shading off, graduation (of colours, light). *Phot:* Vignetting.

dégrader¹ [degrade], *v.tr.* **1.** To degrade (s.o.) (from rank, etc.). **2.** To degrade, besot. **3.** To deface, damage, dilapidate.

se dégrader. 1. To lower oneself; to lose caste. **2.** To sink into vice. **3.** To fall into disrepair.

dégrader², *v.tr.* To shade off, to graduate (colours, light). *Phot:* To vignette.

dégrafer [degrafe], *v.tr.* To unhook, unfasten, undo (dress, etc.); to unclasp (bracelet).

se dégrafer. (Of garment) To come undone. **2.** (Of pers.) To undo one's dress.

dégraiss|er [degrɛse], *v.tr.* **1.** (*a*) To take, skim, the fat off (soup). (*b*) *Se d. les cheveux*, to shampoo one's hair. **2.** To clean (clothes, file); to scour (wool). *s.m.* **-age.**

degré [dagre], *s.m.* **1.** (*a*) Step (of stair, ladder); degree (of musical scale). (*b*) Degree (of circle, heat). **2.** Degree (of relationship, comparison). *Cousins au troisième d.*, cousins thrice removed. **Tuberculeux au dernier degré**, in the last stage of tuberculosis. **Passer par tous les degrés**, to pass through all the stages. *Un tel d. d'insolence*, such a pitch of insolence. *Par degrés*, by degrees, gradually. *Équation du second, du troisième, d.*, quadratic, cubic, equation.

dégré|er [degree], *v.tr. Nau:* To unrig (mast, etc.); to dismantle, take down (crane); to unsling (hammock). *s.m.* **-age.** *s.m.* **-ement.**

dégr|ever [degrəve], *v.tr.* (**je dégrève; je dégrèverai**) **1.** To reduce, diminish (tax). **2.** To relieve (s.o.) of a tax; to derate (industry); to reduce the rates on (building). **3.** To disencumber (estate); to clear off the mortgage on (an estate). *s.m.* **-èvement.**

dégringolade [degrɛ̃gɔlad], *s.f. F:* **1.** Tumble (downstairs, down hill). **2.** Downfall (of financier); collapse (of prices, etc.).

dégringoler [degrɛ̃gɔle], *v.tr. & i. F:* **1.** To tumble down, to come clattering down. **2.** To shoot down (bird, etc.); to bring (the Government) toppling down.

dégris|er [degrize], *v.tr.* (*a*) To sober (s.o.). (*b*) *F:* To disillusionize (s.o.); to bring (s.o.) to his senses. [GRIS 2] *s.m.* **-ement.**

se dégriser. (*a*) To sober down. (*b*) *F:* To come to one's senses.

dégross|ir [degrosi:r], *v.tr.* To give a preliminary dressing to (sth.); to rough down (timber); to rough-hew (stone); to rough out (plan). *F: D. qn*, to polish s.o. up; to lick s.o. into shape. *s.m.* **-issage.** *s.m.* **-issement.**

déguenillé [degnije], *a.* Ragged, tattered, in rags, in tatters. *s. Un petit d.*, a little ragamuffin.

déguerp|ir [degerpi:r], *v.i.* (*a*) (Of tenant) To move out. **Faire déguerpir un locataire**, to evict a tenant. (*b*) To clear out, decamp. *D. au plus vite*, *F:* to skedaddle. *s.m.* **-issement.**

déguisement [degizmã], *s.m.* **1.** (*a*) Disguise, get-up, make-up. (*b*) Fancy dress. **2.** Dissimulation. **Sans déguisement**, plainly, openly.

déguiser [degize], *v.tr.* **1.** To disguise. *D. un enfant en clown*, to get a child up as a clown. **2.** To disguise, conceal (truth, etc.). *Parler sans rien d.*, to speak plainly, openly.

se déguiser. (*a*) To disguise oneself; to make up. (*b*) To put on fancy dress.

dégustation [degystasjõ], *s.f. Com:* Tasting (of wines, tea, etc.).

déguster [degyste], *v.tr.* To taste, sample (tea, wines). *F: D. sa liqueur*, to sip one's liqueur.

déhanch|er (**se**) [sədeãʃe], *v.pr.* (*a*) (Of horse) To dislocate its hip. (*b*) *F:* To sway one's hips (in walking). *s.m.* **-ement.**

déharnach|er [dearnaʃe], *v.tr.* To unharness (horse). *s.m.* **-ement.**

dehors [dəɔ:r]. **1.** *adv.* (*a*) Out, outside. *Coucher, dîner, d.*, to sleep, dine, (i) out of doors, in the open, (ii) away from home. **Mettre qn dehors**, (i) to put, turn, s.o. out (of doors); (ii) *F:* to give s.o. the sack. **"Ne pas se pencher dehors!"** 'do not lean out of the window!' *Nau:* **Toutes voiles dehors**, with every sail set. (*b*) *Box:* **Compter qn dehors**, to count s.o. out. (*c*) **De dehors**, from outside, from without. **En dehors**, (on the) outside; outwards. **En dehors de la maison**, outside the house. *En d. de mes pouvoirs*, not within my competence. *En d. du sujet*, beside the question. *Cela s'est fait en d. de moi*, it was done (i) without my knowledge, (ii) without my participation. **2.** *s.m.* (*a*) Outside, exterior (of house, etc.). **Affaires du dehors**, foreign affairs. **Agir du dehors**, to act from without (a party, etc.). *Mettre une embarcation au d.*, to get out a boat. **Au dehors de ce pays**, outside, beyond, this country. (*b*) Usu. in *pl.* (Outward) appearance. *Maison aux d. imposants*, house with an imposing exterior. **Sous les dehors de la religion**, under the cloak of religion. **3.** *prep.* **Dedans et dehors le royaume**, within and without the realm.

déifier [deifje], *v.tr.* To deify; to make a god of (s.o., sth.).

déité [deite], *s.f.* Deity.

déjà [deʒa], *adv.* **1.** Already. **2.** Before, previously. *Je vous ai d. vu,* I have seen you before. **3.** *F: Vous avez d. trop d'amis,* you have too many friends as it is. *Ça n'est déjà pas si mal,* indeed it is not at all bad (for a start).

déjeter [deʒte, deʃte], *v.tr.* (il déjette; il déjetera) To make lopsided; to warp (wood); to buckle (metal). *Elle a la taille déjetée,* she has one shoulder higher than the other.

se déjeter, to grow lopsided; (of wood) to warp; (of metal) to buckle.

déjettement [deʒetmã], *s.m.* Lopsidedness; warping; buckling; curvature (of the spine).

déjeuner [deʒœne]. **I.** *v.i.* (*a*) To breakfast (*de,* off). (*b*) To lunch; to have, take, lunch. **II. déjeuner,** *s.m.* (*a*) (Premier) déjeuner, breakfast. **Petit déjeuner,** coffee with rolls, etc. (*b*) (Second) déjeuner, lunch, luncheon.

déjouer [deʒwe], *v.tr.* To thwart, (plan); to baffle, foil (the police); to frustrate (plot).

déjucher [deʒyʃe], *v.i.* (Of fowls) To come off the roost. *F:* **Faire déjucher qn,** to make s.o. come down from his perch.

delà [d(ə)la]. Beyond. **1.** *prep.* **Delà les monts,** beyond the mountains. **Par delà les mers,** beyond the seas. **De delà les mers,** from beyond the seas. **2.** *adv.* **Deçà et delà,** see DEÇÀ. **Au delà,** beyond. **En delà,** further away. *s.m.* **L'au-delà,** the beyond. **Au delà de,** beyond. *N'allez pas au d. de dix francs,* don't go above ten francs. *Il est allé au d. de ses promesses,* he was better than his word. [LÀ]

délabrement [delabrəmã], *s.m.* Ruinous condition; disrepair, decay.

délabrer [delabre], *v.tr.* To dilapidate; to wreck, ruin (house, fortune, health, digestion).

se délabrer, (of house, etc.) to fall into decay; (of health) to become impaired.

délabré, *a.* Out of repair; broken-down (furniture); tumble-down (house); impaired (health). *Chapeau d.,* battered hat.

délacer [delase], *v.tr.* (je délaçai(s); n. délaçons) To unlace; to undo (shoes, etc.).

se délacer, to come unlaced, undone.

délai [delɛ], *s.m.* **1.** Delay. **Sans délai,** without delay; forthwith. **2.** Respite, time allowed (for completion of a work, etc.). **A court délai,** at short notice. **Dans le délai prescrit, dans les délais voulus,** within the required time. **Dans le plus bref délai,** as soon as possible. *Com: D. de payement, de congé,* term of payment, of notice. *Livrable dans un d. de trois jours,* can be delivered at three days' notice.

délaissement [delɛsmã], *s.m.* **1.** (*a*) Desertion, abandonment, neglect (of wife, children, etc.). (*b*) Loneliness. *Être dans un grand d.,* to be completely friendless. **2.** Relinquishment, renunciation (of right); abandonment (of ship to insurer).

délaisser [delɛse], *v.tr.* **1.** To forsake, desert, abandon (s.o.). **2.** *Jur:* To relinquish, forgo (right, succession); to abandon (ship to insurer).

délassement [delɑsmã], *s.m.* Rest, relaxation.

délasser [delɑse], *v.tr.* To rest, refresh (s.o.).

se délasser, to take some rest, some relaxation.

délateur [delatœːr], *s.m.* Informer, spy.

délation [delasjɔ̃], *s.f.* Delation.

délavé [delave], *a.* Washed out (colour, complexion); wishy-washy (food).

délayer [deleje], *v.tr.* (je délaie, délaye; je

délaierai, délayerai) (*a*) To add water to (powdered material, etc.); to thin (paint, etc.) (*dans,* with); to water (liquid). *D. de la farine dans du lait,* to mix flour with milk. (*b*) *F:* **Délayer un discours,** to spin out, pad, a speech. *s.m.* **-age.**

délayé, *a.* (*a*) Thin, watery. **Sol délayé,** sodden ground. (*b*) Wordy (style).

déléatur [deleatyːr], *s.m.inv. Typ:* Delete (mark); dele.

délectable [delɛktabl], *a. A:* Delectable; delicious, delightful, pleasant. *adv.* **-ment.**

délectation [delɛktasjɔ̃], *s.f. A:* Delectation, enjoyment, relish.

délecter [delɛkte], *v.tr. A:* To delight.

se délecter *à qch., à faire qch.,* to take delight in sth., in doing sth.

délégation [delegasjɔ̃], *s.f.* **1.** (*a*) Delegation (of authority). **Agir par délégation,** to act on the authority of s.o. (*b*) Delegation, deputing (of representatives). (*c*) Assignment (of debt, pay, etc.). **2.** *Coll.* Delegation; body of delegates.

déléguer [delege], *v.tr.* (je délègue; je déléguerai) **1.** *D. qn pour faire qch.,* to delegate, depute, s.o. to do sth. **2.** To delegate, hand over (powers). *D. une créance,* to assign a debt.

délégué, -ée, *a. & s.* (*a*) Delegate (at meeting, etc.). (*b*) Deputy (professor, etc.).

délester [delɛste], *v.tr.* (*a*) To unballast (ship). (*b*) *F: D. qn d'un fardeau,* to relieve s.o. of a burden. *Se d. le cœur,* to unload one's heart; to unbosom oneself. *s.m.* **-age.**

délétère [deletɛːr], *a.* Deleterious; noxious (gas); offensive (smell); pernicious (doctrine).

délibérant [deliberã], *a.* Deliberative (assembly).

délibératif, -ive [deliberatif, -iːv], *a.* Deliberative (function). **Avoir voix délibérative,** to be entitled to speak and vote.

délibération [deliberasjɔ̃], *s.f.* **1.** Deliberation, debate, discussion. **Question en délibération,** question under consideration. **2.** Reflection, cogitation. *Après mûre d.,* after due deliberation. **3.** Resolution, decision, vote (of an assembly).

délibérer [delibere], *v.* (je délibère; je délibérerai) **1.** *v.i.* (*a*) To deliberate; to take counsel. *D. (avec qn) de, sur, qch.,* to deliberate (with s.o.) on sth. (*b*) To reflect, ponder. *D. (avec soi-même) de, sur, qch.,* to turn sth. over in one's mind. **2.** *v.tr.* (*a*) To deliberate over (a question); to turn (a question) over in one's mind. (*b*) To debate, discuss (a matter). *C'est une affaire délibérée,* the matter is settled, decided.

délibéré. 1. *a.* Deliberate. (*a*) Determined, resolute (tone). (*b*) Intentional. **Agir de propos délibéré,** to act deliberately, of malice prepense. **2.** *s.m. Jur:* Consultation, private sitting (of judges). *adv.* **-ment.**

délicat [delika], *a.* Delicate. **1.** Dainty (dish, etc.). **2.** Fine, refined, discerning (taste, person); tactful (behaviour). **3.** Sensitive, tender (skin, flower, etc.); delicate, frail, weak (health). **4.** Difficult, critical, *F:* ticklish (situation, problem); tricky (job). **5.** Scrupulous, nice, particular, tender (conscience). *D. sur le point d'honneur,* touchy on points of honour. *D. sur la nourriture,* dainty, fastidious, about one's food. *Peu d. en affaires,* not over-scrupulous in one's dealings. *adv.* **-ement.**

délicatesse [delikates], *s.f.* Delicacy. **1.** Fineness, softness (of texture, colouring, etc.). *Délicatesses de table,* table delicacies. **2.** Refinement, nicety (of taste); delicacy (of ear); scrupulousness (of conduct); fastidiousness (of taste); tactfulness (of behaviour). **Avec délicatesse,** tactfully. **Fausse**

délicatesse, false modesty. **3.** Fragility, frailness, weakness; delicate state (of health). **4.** Difficulty, awkwardness (of situation, etc.). **Nous sommes en délicatesse**, our relations are slightly strained.

délice [delis], *s.m.* Delight; extreme pleasure.

délices, *s.f.pl.* Delight(s), pleasure(s). **Faire les délices de qn**, to be the delight of s.o. **Faire ses délices de qch.**, to delight in sth.

délicieu|x, -euse [delisjø, -ø:z], *a.* Delicious (food); delightful, charming (scenery, etc.). *adv.* **-sement.**

délictueux, -euse [deliktɥø, -ø:z], *a.* *Jur:* **1.** Punishable. **Acte délictueux**, misdemeanour, offence. **2.** Felonious (design); malicious (intent).

délié [delje]. **1.** *a.* Slender, fine. *Taille déliée*, slim, supple, figure. *Un esprit d.*, (i) a sharp, subtle, mind; (ii) a nimble wit. *Avoir la langue déliée*, to have a glib tongue. **2.** *s.m. Typ:* etc: Thin stroke.

délier [delje], *v.tr.* **1.** To untie, undo, unbind; to loose (fetters, prisoner). *D. les mains à qn*, to untie, unbind, s.o.'s hands. *Le vin délie la langue*, wine loosens the tongue. S.a. BOURSE I. **2.** *D. qn d'un serment*, to release s.o. from an oath.

se délier, to come undone, unbound; to come loose. *Sa langue se déliait*, (i) his tongue was beginning to wag; (ii) he was beginning to find his tongue.

délimitation [delimitasjɔ̃], *s.f.* Delimitation. *Poteau de délimitation*, boundary post.

délimiter [delimite], *v.tr.* To delimit, demarcate (territory); to define (powers).

délinéation [delineasjɔ̃], *s.f.* Delineation, outlining.

délinéer [delinee], *v.tr.* To delineate, outline.

délinquant, -ante [delɛ̃kɑ̃, -ɑ̃:t], *s. Jur:* Offender, delinquent.

délirant [delirɑ̃], *a.* Delirious, raving, lightheaded. *Joie délirante*, frenzied joy.

délire [deli:r], *s.m.* Delirium. **Avoir le délire**, **être en délire**, to be delirious; to wander (in one's mind).

délirer [delire], *v.i.* To be delirious, lightheaded; to wander (in one's mind); to rave.

délit [deli], *s.m. Jur:* Misdemeanour, offence. S.a. FLAGRANT.

délivrance [delivrɑ̃:s], *s.f.* **1.** Deliverance, rescue, release. **2.** Delivery, handing over (of property, certificate); issue (of tickets).

délivrer [delivre], *v.tr.* **1.** To deliver; to rescue (captive, etc.); to release (prisoner). *D. qn de ses liens*, to loose s.o. from his bonds. **2.** To deliver, hand over (goods, etc.); to deliver, issue (certificate, ticket).

se délivrer *de qn, de qch.*, to rid oneself, to get rid, of s.o., of sth.

déloger [delɔʒe], *v.* (Conj. like LOGER) **I.** *v.i.* (*a*) To remove (to another abode). (*b*) To go off, get away. *F:* **Déloger sans tambour ni trompette**, to steal away. **2.** *v.tr.* To oust; to drive (s.o.) out; to eject (tenant); to dislodge (the enemy).

déloyal, -aux [delwajal, -o], *a.* Disloyal, unfaithful, false (friend, etc.); dishonest, unfair (practice). *Sp:* *Jeu d.*, foul play. *Coup d.*, foul. *adv.* **-ement.**

déloyauté [delwajote], *s.f.* **1.** Disloyalty, perfidy, treachery. **2.** *Commettre une d.*, (i) to play s.o. false; (ii) to act unfairly.

Delphes [delf]. *Pr.n.f.pl. A.Geog:* Delphi.

delphien [delfjɛ̃], *a.* Delphic (oracle).

delta [delta], *s.m. Gr.Alph: Geog:* Delta.

deltoïde [deltɔid], *a. & s.m.* Deltoid (muscle).

déluge [delyːʒ], *s.m.* (*a*) Deluge, flood; torrent (of abuse). **Après nous le déluge!** when we are gone let happen what may! (*b*) *F:* Downpour (of rain).

délurer [delyre], *v.tr.* To sharpen (s.o.'s) wits. **se délurer**, to lose one's shyness.

déluré, *a.* Sharp, knowing, smart, cute.

démagnétiser [demanetize], *v.tr.* **I.** *Ph:* To demagnetize. **2.** To demesmerize (s.o.).

démagogie [demagɔʒi], *s.f.* Demagogy.

démagogue [demagɔg], *s.m.* Demagogue.

demain [dəmɛ̃], *adv. & s.m.* To-morrow. *D.* (*au*) *soir*, to-morrow evening. **De demain en huit**, to-morrow week. **A demain!** good-bye till to-morrow. *Le journal de d.*, to-morrow's paper. *La mode de d.*, coming fashions.

démanch|er [demɑ̃ʃe]. **I.** *v.tr.* (*a*) To remove the handle of s., to unhaft (tool, etc.). (*b*) *Se d. le bras, la mâchoire*, to put one's arm, one's jaw, out (of joint). **2.** *v.i. Mus:* To shift (in playing the violin). *s.m.* **-ement.**

demande [d(ə)mɑ̃:d], *s.f.* **I.** (*a*) Request, petition, application (*de*, for). **Faire la demande de qch.**, to ask for sth. *D. en mariage*, offer, proposal, of marriage. **Faire qch. sur la demande de qn**, to act at s.o.'s request. (*b*) *Com:* Demand. *L'offre et la d.*, supply and demand. (*c*) *D. en divorce*, action for divorce. **2.** Question, enquiry. *Demandes et réponses*, questions and answers.

demander [d(ə)mɑ̃de], *v.tr.* **I.** To ask (for). *D. qch. à grands cris*, to call out for sth. **Demander permission**, to ask permission. **Demander pardon**, to beg pardon. *D. la paix*, to beg, sue, for peace. *D. des dommages-intérêts*, to claim damages. **On vous demande**, somebody wants to see you. **Combien demandez-vous pour . . .?** how much do you charge for . . .? **Demander qch. à qn**, to ask s.o. for sth. *On nous demanda nos passeports*, we were asked for our passports. *Il demande qu'on lui rende justice*, he asks that justice may be done him. **Demander à faire qch.**, to ask (permission) to do sth. *Je demande à être entendu*, I ask to be heard. *D. à manger*, to ask for something to eat. **Demander à qn de faire qch.**, to ask s.o. to do sth. *Puis-je vous d. de me passer le journal*, I will thank you for the paper. **2.** To desire, want, need, require. *On demande maçon*, bricklayer wanted. *Article très demandé*, in great demand. *La situation demande à être maniée avec tact*, the situation needs, wants, calls for, tactful handling. S.a. MIEUX I. **3.** To demand. *D. un discours à qn*, to call on s.o. for a speech. *Faire ce que demande sa position*, to do what one's position requires of one. **En demander trop à qn**, to be too exacting with s.o. **4.** To ask, enquire. *D. quelle heure il est*, to ask the time. *D. son chemin à un agent*, to enquire one's way of a policeman. *D. à qn son avis*, to ask s.o.'s opinion. *Cela ne se demande pas*, it's obvious. *Je me demande pourquoi*, I wonder why.

demandeur, -eresse [d(ə)mɑ̃dœ:r, -ɜres], *s. Jur:* Plaintiff.

démangeaison [demɑ̃ʒɛzɔ̃], *s.f.* Itching. *F: Une d. de faire qch.*, a longing, an itching, to do sth.

démanger [demɑ̃ʒe], *v.i.* (il démangea(it). Always with dative of person) To itch. *L'épaule me démange*, my shoulder is itching.

démanteler [demɑ̃tle], *v.tr.* (je démantèle; je démantèlerai) To dismantle (fortress, ship); to disable (ship) (by gunfire).

démantibuler [demɑ̃tibyle], *v.tr.* To dislocate (the jaw); to put (the jaw) out of joint. *F: D. une machine*, to take or smash a machine to pieces.

démarcation [demarkasjɔ̃], *s.f.* Demarcation. Ligne de démarcation, dividing line.

démarche [demarʃ], *s.f.* 1. Gait, step, walk. *D. majestueuse,* majestic bearing. *Il avait une d. digne,* he moved with dignity. 2. Step. **Faire une démarche auprès de qn,** to approach s.o. **Faire les premières démarches,** to make the advances. **Faire les démarches nécessaires,** to take the necessary steps.

démarquage [demarka:ʒ], *s.m.* 1. Removal of the mark (from linen, etc.). 2. Plagiarism.

démarqu|er [demarke], *v.tr.* 1. To remove the identification marks from (linen, plate, etc.). 2. To plagiarize (a book), to dish up its contents in another form. *s.m.* **-eur.**

démarrage [demara:ʒ], *s.m.* 1. Unmooring (of boat). 2. (*a*) Start, starting (of train, car, etc.). *D. doux,* smooth get-away. **Bouton de démarrage,** self-starter switch. (*b*) *Sp :* (Sudden) spurt.

démarrer [demare]. 1. *v.tr.* (*a*) To unmoor, cast off (ship). (*b*) To start (car, etc.). 2. *v.i.* (*a*) (Of boat) To cast off. (*b*) (Of train, motor car, etc.) To start, move off, get away; (of driver) to drive away, to drive off. **Faire démarrer,** to start (car, etc.). (*c*) *Sp :* To put on a spurt.

démarreur [demarœ:r], *s.m. Aut :* Self-starter.

démasquer [demaske], *v.tr.* To unmask; to expose, to show up (impostor). *F :* **Démasquer ses batteries,** to show one's hand.

se démasquer, (i) to take off one's mask; (ii) *F :* to drop the mask.

démâter [demɑte], *v.tr.* To dismast (ship). *F :* **Démâter qn,** to disconcert s.o.; to take s.o. aback.

démêl|er [demele], *v.tr.* (*a*) To disentangle, unravel (string, silk, etc.); to comb out (hair); to tease (out) (wool). *F : D. un malentendu,* to clear up a misunderstanding. *F :* **Avoir quelque chose à démêler avec qn,** to have a crow to pluck with s.o. (*b*) *F : D. qn dans l'ombre,* to discern, make out, s.o. in the gloom. *Je ne peux pas d. ses raisons,* I can't make out, fathom, his reasons. *D. qch. de, d'avec, qch.,* to distinguish sth. from sth. *s.m.* **-age.**

se démêler. (*a*) To extricate oneself (from difficulty). (*b*) *F : La vérité se démêle,* the truth is coming out.

démêlé, *s.m.* Usu. *pl.* Contention; (unpleasant) dealings.

démêloir [demelwa:r], *s.m. Toil :* Rake-comb.

démélures [demely:r], *s.f.pl.* Combings.

démembrement [demɑ̃brəmɑ̃], *s.m.* Dismembering (of body); dismemberment, disruption (of empire, etc.); breaking up (of ship).

démembrer [demɑ̃bre], *v.tr.* To dismember; to cut up (chicken); to divide up (kingdom).

se démembrer, (of ship, empire) to break up.

déménagement [demenaʒmɑ̃], *s.m.* Removal; moving house. **Voiture de déménagement,** furniture van; pantechnicon.

déménager [demenaʒe], *v.tr.* (je déménageai(s); n. déménageons) *D.* (*ses meubles*), to move house, to remove. *P :* **Déménager à la cloche (de bois),** to shoot the moon. *F :* **Il, sa tête, déménage,** he has taken leave of his senses. [MÉNAGE]

déménageur [demenaʒœ:r], *s.m.* Furniture remover.

démence [demɑ̃:s], *s.f.* Insanity, madness. *Jur :* Lunacy. *Med :* Dementia. **Être en démence,** to be insane, demented, of unsound mind.

démener (se) [sədemne], *v.pr.* (Conj. like MENER) 1. To fling about, throw oneself about; to struggle. 2. *F :* To bestir oneself.

dément, -ente [demɑ̃, -ɑ̃:t], *a. & s.* Crazy, mad (person). *Jur :* Lunatic.

démentir [demɑ̃ti:r], *v.tr.* (Conj. like MENTIR) 1. To give the lie to, to contradict (s.o., sth.); to deny (fact). 2. To belie. *Il a démenti nos espérances,* he has not come up to our expectations; he has disappointed us.

se démentir, to contradict oneself; to go back on one's word. *Politesse qui ne se dément jamais,* unfailing courtesy.

démenti, *s.m.* 1. (Flat) denial, contradiction. *Donner un d. formel à qn,* to give the lie direct to s.o. 2. Failure (of efforts); disappointment (of pectations).

démesuré [demzyre], *a.* Beyond measure, huge, unmeasured; inordinate (pride); immoderate (thirst); unbounded (ambition). *adv.* **-ment.**

démettre[1] [demetr], *v.tr.* (Conj. like METTRE) To dislocate (joint). **Se démettre l'épaule,** to put one's shoulder out (of joint).

démettre[2] **(se),** *v.pr. Se d. de ses fonctions,* to resign (office); to resign one's post; to demit office; to retire.

démeubl|er [demœble], *v.tr.* To remove the furniture from (house, etc.); to strip (house, etc.) of its appurtenances. *s.m.* **-ement.**

demeurant [dəmœrɑ̃], *s.m.* (*a*) *A :* Remainder. (*b*) *Adv.phr.* Au demeurant, after all, all the same, howbeit.

demeure [dəmœ:r], *s.f.* 1. (*a*) *A :* Tarrying, delay. (Still so used in) **Sans plus longue demeure,** without further delay. **'Il y a péril en la demeure,** there is danger in delay. (*b*) **Mettre qn en demeure de faire qch.,** to call upon s.o. to do sth. **Mise en demeure** (*de faire qch.*), formal notice, summons (to do sth.). (*c*) Stay, sojourn. **A demeure,** fixed; permanent(ly). *Meuble à d.,* fixture. *Institutrice à d.,* resident governess. *Canalisation électrique à d.,* permanent wiring. 2. (Place of) residence, dwelling place; abode. **Livraison à demeure,** goods delivered at any address. **Dernière demeure,** last resting-place.

demeurer [dəmœre], *v.i.* 1. (Aux. *être*) To remain; to stay, stop (in a place). *Je demeure convaincu que . . .,* I remain convinced that. . . . *L'affaire n'en demeurera pas là,* the matter will not rest there. *Demeurons-en là,* let us leave it at that. *Ne pouvoir d. en place,* to be unable to keep still. **Demeurer sur place, y demeurer,** to be killed on the spot. **Demeurer court dans son discours,** to stop short, break down, in one's speech. **Demeurer en reste avec qn,** to remain under an obligation to s.o. *La victoire nous demeure,* the victory rests with us. 2. (Aux. *avoir*) To live, reside, *Lit :* to have one's abode, to dwell. *D. à la campagne,* to live in the country.

demi [dəmi]. 1. *a.* (*a*) Half. **Deux heures et demie,** (i) two and a half hours, two hours and a half; (ii) half-past two. *Un demi-congé,* a half-holiday. *Une demi-heure,* half an hour. (*b*) Semi-. *Demi-cercle,* semicircle. (*c*) Demi-. **Demi-dieu,** demigod. (*d*) Demi-cuit, half-cooked. 2. *s.m.* (*a*) **Deux plus un demi,** two plus one half. (*b*) *Fb :* Les demis, the half-backs. *Rugby : D. à la mêlée,* scrum half. *Les demis aile,* the wing halves. (*c*) **A demi.** (i) Half. *A d. mort,* half-dead. **Faire les choses à demi,** to do things by halves. S.a. COMPTE (*c*). (ii) Semi-. *A d. transparent,* semi-transparent. 3. *s.f.* **Demie,** half-hour. **Il est la demie,** it is half-past.

NOTE. In all the following compounds DEMI is inv.; the second component takes the plural.

demi-arrière, *s.m. Fb :* Half-back.

demi-bosse, *s.f.* Half-relief, mezzo-rilievo.
demi-botte, *s.f.* Half-boot; Wellington boot.
demi-bouteille, *s.f.* Half-bottle.
demi-cercle, *s.m.* Semicircle, half-circle. *En d.-c.,* semicircular.
demi-circulaire, *a.* Semicircular.
demi-clef, *s.f. Nau:* Half-hitch.
demi-congé, *s.m.* Half-holiday.
demi-coupe, *s.f. Draw:* Half-section.
demi-deuil, *s.m.* Half-mourning.
demi-dieu, *s.m.* Demigod.
demi-fin, *a. & s.m.* Twelve-carat (gold). Bracelet **(en) demi-fin,** twelve-carat bracelet.
demi-fond, *s.m.inv. Sp:* (Course de) demi-fond, middle-distance race.
demi-frère, *s.m.* Half-brother; step-brother.
demi-gros, *s.m. Commerce de d.-g.,* wholesale dealing in small quantities.
demi-heure, *s.f. Une d.-h.,* half an hour. *Deux demi-heures,* two half-hours. **De demi-heure en demi-heure, toutes les demi-heures,** every half-hour.
demi-jour, *s.m.* **1.** *Art:* Half-light. **2.** (a) Half-light (of dawn); morning twilight. (b) Occ. Gloaming, dusk.
démilitaris|er [demilitarize], *v.tr.* To demilitarize. *s.f.* **-ation.**
demi-litre, *s.m.* Half-litre.
demi-lune, *s.f.* **1.** Half-moon. **2.** *Fort:* Demi-lune.
demi-mal, *s.m. F:* Small harm. **Il n'y a que demi-mal,** it might have been worse.
demi-monde, *s.m.* Demi-monde; outskirts of society.
demi-mort, *a.* Half-dead.
demi-mot (à), *adv.phr. Entendre (qn) à d.-m.,* to (know how to) take a hint.
demi-opaque, *a.* Semi-opaque.
demi-pension, *s.f.* Partial board.
demi-pensionnaire, *s.m. & f.* Person taking partial board. *Sch:* Day-boarder.
demi-place, *s.f.* Half-fare (when travelling); half-price (at theatre, etc.).
demi-pose, *s.f. Phot:* Bulb exposure.
demi-queue, *s.m.inv.* Grand or half-grand piano.
demi-reliure, *s.f. Bookb:* Quarter-binding. *D.-r. à petits coins,* half-binding.
démis [demi]. See DÉMETTRE.
demi-saison, *s.f.* Between-season. *Étoffes de d.-s.,* spring suitings.
demi-sœur, *s.f.* Half-sister; step-sister.
demi-solde. 1. *s.f. Mil:* Half-pay. **En demi-solde,** on half-pay. **2.** *s.m. inv.* Half-pay officer.
demi-soupir, *s.m. Mus:* Quaver rest.
démission [demisjɔ̃], *s.f.* Resignation. **Donner sa démission,** to tender, send in, one's resignation; to resign.
démissionnaire [demisjɔnɛːr], *a. & s.* Resigner; resigning (officer, etc.); out-going (ministry).
démissionner [demisjɔne], *v.i. = Donner sa démission, q.v.* under DÉMISSION.
demi-teinte, *s.f.* Half-tone; half-tint.
demi-ton, *s.m. Mus:* Semitone.
demi-tour, *s.m.* Half-turn; *Mil:* about turn. **Faire demi-tour,** (i) to turn back; (ii) to turn (right-)about. *Mil:* **Demi-tour à droite!** (right-)about turn! *Faire faire d.-t. à son cheval,* to turn one's horse.
demi-varlope, *s.f. Tls:* Jack-plane.
demi-voix (à), *adv.phr.* **1.** In an undertone; under one's breath. **2.** *Mus:* Mezza voce.
demi-volée, *s.f. Ten:* Half-volley.

démobilisation [demɔbilizasjɔ̃], *s.f.* Demobilization, demobilizing (of troops); discharge (of men after active service).
démobiliser [demɔbilize], *v.tr.* To demobilize (troops); to discharge (men after active service).
démocrate [demɔkrat], *s.m. & f.* Democrat.
démocratie [demɔkrasi], *s.f.* Democracy.
démocratique [demɔkratik], *a.* Democratic. *adv.* **-ment,** -ally.
démoder (se) [sədemɔde], *v.pr.* (Of clothes, etc.) To go out of fashion.
démodé, *a.* Old-fashioned; out of fashion; obsolete, out of date.
demoiselle [dəmwazɛl], *s.f.* **1.** (a) Spinster; single woman, unmarried woman. **Son nom de demoiselle,** her maiden name. (b) **Demoiselle d'honneur,** (i) maid of honour; (ii) bridesmaid. **Demoiselle de compagnie,** lady-companion. *D. de magasin,* shop-assistant, shop-girl. **2.** Young lady. **3.** *F:* (a) *Orn:* Long-tailed tit. (b) *Ent:* Dragon-fly. **4.** Paving beetle.
démolir [demɔliːr], *v.tr.* To demolish, pull down (house, etc.); to break up (ship); *F:* to overthrow (government); *F:* to ruin (health).
se démolir, to break up; to go to pieces.
démolisseur, -euse [demɔlisœːr, -øːz], *s.* **1.** Demolisher, overthrower (of argument, government). **2.** *Tchn:* (a) Housebreaker. (b) Ship-breaker.
démolition [demɔlisjɔ̃], *s.f.* Demolition; pulling down (of structure). **Chantier de démolition,** (i) housebreaker's yard; (ii) ship-breaker's yard.
démon [demɔ̃], *s.m.* **1.** *Myth:* Daemon; (good, evil) genius. **2.** Demon, devil, fiend. *Cet enfant est un petit d.,* that child is a little imp. *Le d. de la jalousie,* the demon of jealousy.
démonétiser [demɔnetize], *v.tr.* To call in, withdraw, (coinage, etc.) from circulation.
démoniaque [demɔnjak]. **1.** *a.* Demoniac(al); possessed of the devil. **2.** *s.* Demoniac.
démonstrateur [demɔ̃stratœːr], *s.m. Sch:* Demonstrator; professor's assistant.
démonstratif, -ive [demɔ̃stratif, -iːv], *a.* **1.** (Logically) conclusive. **2.** *Gram:* Demonstrative. **3.** Demonstrative, expansive (person). *Peu démonstratif,* undemonstrative, staid.
démonstration [demɔ̃strasjɔ̃], *s.f.* Demonstration. **1.** (a) Proof (of theorem, etc.). (b) *Box:* **Assaut de démonstration,** sparring match. **2.** (a) *Mil:* Show of force. (b) *Esp. pl.* **Faire de grandes démonstrations d'amitié à qn,** to make great demonstrations of friendship to s.o.
démontable [demɔ̃tabl], *a.* (Of machine, etc.) That takes to pieces; portable (building); collapsible (boat).
démonte-pneus, *s.m.inv.* Tyre-lever.
démont|er [demɔ̃te], *v.tr.* **1.** To unhorse, unseat (rider). *F: La nouvelle m'a démonté,* I was greatly upset by the news. **Se laisser démonter,** to get upset. *Il ne se laisse pas d.,* he isn't easily flummoxed, abashed. **2.** To take down, take to pieces, dismantle; to dismount (gun); to unhinge, unhang (door); to remove (pneumatic tyre); to unset, unmount (diamond); to release spring of (clock). *s.m.* **-age.**
se démonter. (a) (Of mechanism) To run down. (b) *F: Il ne se démonte pas pour si peu,* he is not so easily put out.
démonté, *a.* **1.** Dismounted (cavalry). **2.** Stormy, raging (sea). **3.** *F:* (of pers.) Abashed, flustered. **4.** (Of clock, etc.) Run down.
démonte-soupapes, *s.m.inv. Aut:* Valve-spring lifter.
démontrable [demɔ̃trabl], *a.* Demonstrable.
démontrer [demɔ̃tre], *v.tr.* **1.** To demonstrate.

2. *Action qui démontre la bonté,* act that betokens, evinces, kindliness.

démoralisation [demɔralizasjɔ̃], *s.f.* Demoralization.

démoraliser [demɔralize], *v.tr.* To demoralize. **I.** To corrupt, deprave. **2.** To dishearten.

se démoraliser, to become demoralized.

démordre [demɔrdr], *v.i.* (*a*) To let go one's hold (with the teeth). (*b*) *F:* (Usu. with negative) **Ne pas démordre de ses opinions,** to stand by, to stick to, one's opinions. **Il ne veut pas en démordre,** he won't give up his point; he sticks to it.

démoul|er [demule], *v.tr.* (*a*) To withdraw (pattern) from the mould. (*b*) *Cu:* To turn out (a jelly, a cake). *s.m.* **-age.**

démultiplicateur [demyltiplikatœːr], *a. & s.m.* (**Engrenage**) démultiplicateur, reducing-gear. *W.Tel:* Vernier. *Bouton d.,* slow-motion knob.

démultiplication [demyltiplikasjɔ̃], *s.f. Mec.E:* **I.** Gearing down. **2.** Reduction ratio (of gears).

démultiplier [demyltiplie], *v.tr. Mec.E:* To reduce the gear ratio; to gear down.

démunir (se) [sɔdemyniːr], *v.pr. Se d. de qch.,* (i) to allow oneself to run short of sth.; (ii) to part with sth.

démuni, *a.* **I.** Unprovided (*de,* with). **2.** *Com: Être d. de qch.,* to be out of sth., sold out of sth.

démuseler [demyzle], *v.tr.* (**je démuselle; je démusel!erai**) To unmuzzle (dog).

dénantir (se) [sɔdenãtiːr], *v.pr.* To part with one's securities. *F: Se d. de tout ce qu'on possède,* to give up all that one possesses.

dénatalité [denatalite], *s.f.* Fall in the birth-rate.

dénationaliser [denasjɔnalize], *v.tr.* To denationalize.

dénatter [denate], *v.tr.* To unbraid (one's hair).

dénaturaliser [denatyralize], *v.tr.* To denaturalize, denationalize (person).

dénaturation [denatyrasjɔ̃], *s.f.* Denaturation, changing the nature (of sth.). *D. de l'alcool,* denaturing of alcohol.

dénaturer [denatyre], *v.tr.* **I.** (*a*) To denature (alcohol, etc.). (*b*) To misrepresent, pervert, distort (words, actions). *D. les faits,* to garble the facts. **2.** To render unnatural; to pervert (the soul).

dénaturé, *a.* **I.** Denatured. **2.** Unnatural; hard-hearted (father); perverted (taste).

dénégation [denegasjɔ̃], *s.f.* Denial.

dengue [dãːg], *s.f. Med:* Dengue(-fever).

déni [deni], *s.m. Jur:* Denial, refusal (of sth. which is due).

déniais|er [denjeze], *v.tr.* To educate (s.o.) in the ways of the world. [NIAIS] *s.m.* **-ement.**

déniaisé, *a.* Smartened up; who has been taught a thing or two; *F:* up to snuff.

dénich|er [deniʃe], *v.tr.* **I.** *v.tr.* (*a*) To take (bird, eggs) out of the nest. (*b*) To find, discover, (bird or eggs) in a nest. *F: Nous avons déniché un bon chauffeur,* we have discovered, unearthed, a good chauffeur. (*c*) To dislodge (bird); to rout out (animal). **2.** *v.i.* (Of birds) To forsake the nest. *F: Dénicher sans tambour ni trompette,* to move off quietly, on the quiet. *s.m.* **-ement.**

dénicheur [deniʃœːr], *s.m.* **I.** Bird('s)-nester. **2.** *F:* Searcher, ferreter out. *D. de curiosités,* curio-hunter.

denier [dɔnje], *s.m.* **I.** (*a*) *Rom.Ant:* Denarius. (*b*) *A:* (Fr.) Denier, (Eng.) penny. *F: Le d. de la veuve,* the widow's mite. **Denier à Dieu,** gratuity (to newly engaged servant, etc.); (when

taking a house) key-money. **Le denier de saint Pierre,** Peter's pence. **Payer jusqu'au dernier denier,** to pay to the uttermost farthing. **2.** *A:* (Rate of) interest. (Still used in) **Prêter à un denier honnête,** to lend at fair interest. **3.** Money, funds. *Deniers personnels,* one's own money. **Acheter qch. à (beaux) deniers comptants,** to buy sth. for hard cash.

dénier [denje], *v.tr.* **I.** To deny (crime, etc.); to disclaim (responsibility). **2.** *D. la justice à qn,* to refuse, deny, s.o. justice.

dénigr|er [denigre], *v.tr.* To disparage; to run down (s.o., sth.). *s.m.* **-ement.**

dénigreur, -euse [denigrœːr, -øːz], *s.* Disparager; detractor; denigrator.

déniveler [denivle], *v.tr.* (Conj. like NIVELER) **I.** To make (surface, etc.) uneven; to put out of level. **2.** *Surv:* To determine differences in level; to contour (survey).

se déniveler, (of supports, piers, etc.) to subside, to sink, to settle.

dénivelé, *a.* Uneven, unlevel (roadway).

dénivellation [denivɛlasjɔ̃], *s.f.,* **dénivellement** [denivɛlmã], *s.m.* **I.** Difference in level (of supports of girder, etc.). *D. d'une route,* (i) unevenness, (ii) gradients, ups and downs, of a roadway. **2.** Subsidence, sinking; settling (of piers, etc.). **3.** *Surv:* Contouring.

dénombrement [denɔ̃brɔmã], *s.m.* Enumeration, counting; census (of population).

dénombrer [denɔ̃bre], *v.tr.* To count, enumerate; to take a census of (population).

dénominateur [denɔminatœːr], *s.m.* Denominator.

dénomination [denɔminasjɔ̃], *s.f.* Denomination, name, appellation.

dénommer [denɔme], *v.tr.* To denominate, name.

dénoncer [denɔ̃se], *v.tr.* (**je dénonçai(s)**; n. **dénonçons**) **I.** (*a*) To declare, proclaim (war). (*b*) *D. un traité,* to denounce a treaty. (*c*) *Son visage dénonce la grossièreté de sa vie,* his face betrays, proclaims, the coarseness of his life. **2.** (*a*) To denounce (s.o.); to inform against (s.o.). *Se d.,* to give oneself up. (*b*) To expose (vice); to make known (misdeeds).

dénonciateur, -trice [denɔ̃sjatœːr, -tris]. **I.** *s.* Informer, denouncer. **2.** *a.* Tell-tale (look, etc.).

dénonciation [denɔ̃sjasjɔ̃], *s.f.* **I.** Notice of termination (of treaty, etc.). **2.** Denunciation; information (*de qn,* against s.o.).

dénoter [denɔte], *v.tr.* To denote, betoken, show (energy, contempt, etc.).

dénouement, dénoûment [denumã], *s.m.* **I.** Untying, undoing (of knot, etc.). **2.** Issue, upshot, result, outcome (of event); solution (of difficulty); ending (of plot, story).

dénouer [denwe], *v.tr.* **I.** To unknot; to untie, undo, loose (knot, etc.). *D. ses cheveux,* to undo, let down, one's hair. *D. une intrigue,* to clear up, unravel, untangle, a plot. **2.** To make (limbs, etc.) more supple; to loosen (the tongue).

se dénouer. I. To come undone. **2.** (Of story) To end, to wind up. **3.** *Sa langue se dénouait,* he was finding his tongue.

denrée [dãre], *s.f.* Commodity; food-stuff. Usu. *pl.* Produce. *Denrées alimentaires,* food products; foodstuffs.

dense [dãːs], *a.* **I.** *Ph:* Dense. **2.** Dense, crowded; close (formation of troops); thick (atmosphere).

densité [dãsite], *s.f.* **I.** *Ph:* Density. **Flacon à densité,** specific-gravity flask. **2.** Denseness, density (of population, etc.).

dent [dɑ̃], s.f. **1.** (a) Tooth. *Grosses dents, dents du fônd*, back teeth; molars. *D. de sagesse*, wisdom tooth. *Dents de lait*, milk-teeth, first teeth. **Sans dents**, toothless. **Faire, percer, ses dents**, to cut one's teeth; to be teething. **Mal de dents**, toothache. **Avoir mal aux dents**, to have toothache. *Se faire arracher une d.*, to have a tooth out. **Coup de dent(s)**, bite. (Of dog) **Donner un coup de dent à qn**, to snap at s.o. **N'avoir rien à se mettre sous la dent**, to have nothing to eat. **Manger à belles dents**, to eat away steadily, hungrily. **Jouer des dents**, to ply one's teeth. **Rire à belles dents**, to laugh heartily. **Manger du bout des dents**, to pick at one's food. **Rire du bout des dents**, to force a laugh. **Avoir les dents longues**, (i) to be very hungry; (ii) to be grasping. **Montrer les dents**, to show one's teeth, to show fight. **Avoir une dent contre qn**, to have a grudge against s.o. **Son qui agace les dents**, sound that sets one's teeth on edge. **Il n'a pas desserré les dents**, he didn't open his mouth. **Parler entre ses dents**, to mumble. **Être sur les dents**, to be done up, worn out. *Mettre son personnel sur les dents*, to work one's staff to death. S.a. MORS 2, SERRER 3. (b) *D. d'éléphant*, elephant's tusk. **2.** Tooth (of comb, saw); cog (of wheel); prong (of fork). **En dents de scie**, serrated. **Roue à dents**, cogged wheel.

dentaire [dɑ̃tɛːr], a. (a) Dental, dentary (pulp, etc.). (b) *L'art d.*, dentistry. *Pièce d.*, denture, *F:* plate.

dental, -aux [dɑ̃tal, -o]. **1.** a. Dental. **2.** s.f. **Dentale**, dental consonant.

dent-de-loup [dɑ̃dlu], s.f. **1.** Pin, bolt (of carriage). **2.** Gullet-tooth (of saw). **3.** *Aut:* Ratchet-tooth, skew dog, catch (engaging the starting handle).

denté [dɑ̃te], a. Cogged, toothed (wheel); dentate (leaf). **Roue dentée**, cog-wheel.

denteler [dɑ̃tle], v.tr. (je dentelle; je dentellerai) (a) To notch, jag. (b) To pink (out) (leather).

dentelé, a. Jagged, notched, indented; serrated (leaf); scalloped (design).

dentelle [dɑ̃tɛl], s.f. (a) Lace. *D. à l'aiguille*, point-lace. *D. aux fuseaux*, pillow-lace. (b) Wrought ironwork (of balustrade, etc.).

dentellerie [dɑ̃tɛlri], s.f. Lace manufacture.

dentellière [dɑ̃tɛljɛːr], s.f. Lace-maker.

dentelure [dɑ̃tlyːr], s.f. Denticulation, indentation; serration (of leaf); perforation (at edge of postage-stamp); ins and outs (of coast-line).

dentier [dɑ̃tje], s.m. Set of false teeth; denture, *F:* plate.

dentifrice [dɑ̃tifris]. **1.** s.m. Tooth-paste, -powder; mouth-wash. **2.** a. **Pâte dentrifrice**, tooth-paste.

dentiste [dɑ̃tist], s.m. Dentist. **Chirurgien dentiste**, dental surgeon.

dentition [dɑ̃tisjɔ̃], s.f. Dentition. (a) Cutting of the teeth; teething. (b) Permanent teeth. (c) Arrangement of the teeth.

denture [dɑ̃tyːr], s.f. **1.** Set of (natural) teeth. **2.** Serrated edge. **3.** *Mec.E:* Teeth, cogs, gearing.

dénudation [denydasjɔ̃], s.f. Denudation; laying bare; stripping.

dénuder [denyde], v.tr. To denude, to lay bare. *D. un arbre (de son écorce)*, to strip a tree of its bark. *Dénudé de tous ses biens*, stripped of all his worldly goods.

dénudé, a. Bare, denuded (country); stripped (tree); bald (pate); *El:* bare (wire).

dénuement [denymɑ̃], s.m. Destitution, penury,

need. *Être dans le d.*, to be destitute, to be in want. *D. d'idées*, dearth of ideas.

dénuer [denye], v.tr. To divest, strip (*de*, of). [NU] **se dénuer** *de ses biens*, to part with all one's possessions; to leave oneself penniless.

dénué, a. (a) *D. d'argent*, without money; out of cash. (b) *Projet d. de sens*, plan devoid of sense. *D. de raison*, senseless. *D. d'intelligence*, unintelligent.

dénûment [denymɑ̃], s.m. = DÉNUEMENT.

déodoris|er [deɔdɔrize], v.tr. To deodorize; to sweeten (the air, etc.). s.f. **-ation**.

dépannage [depanaːʒ], s.m. Emergency repairs (to engine, etc.); road repairs (to motor car). **Équipe de dépannage**, break-down gang.

dépanner [depane], v.tr. To repair and set going (broken-down engine, car, etc.). [PANNE]

dépanneur [depanœːr], s.m. *Aut:* Break-down mechanic.

dépanneuse [depanøːz], s.f. Break-down lorry.

dépaquet|er [depakte], v.tr. (like PAQUETER) To unpack (goods, etc.). s.m. **-age**.

dépareiller [depareje], v.tr. To spoil, break (set, collection).

dépareillé, a. Odd, unmatched. *Com:* *Articles dépareillés*, oddments.

déparer [depare], v.tr. **1.** To strip (sth.) of ornaments. **2.** To mar; to spoil the beauty of (s.o., sth.).

déparier [deparje], v.tr. To remove one of a pair of, to spoil a pair of (objects). *Gant déparié*, odd glove.

départ [depaːr], s.m. **1.** Division, separation, sorting (out). **Faire le départ entre qch. et qch.**, to sort out sth. from sth.; to discriminate between sth. and sth. **2.** Departure, starting; sailing (of ship); start (of race, etc.). **Être sur son départ**, to be on the point of starting, of leaving. **Point de départ**, starting point. *Com:* **Prix de départ**, upset price (at auction). **Au départ**, at the outset. *Golf:* **Tertre de d.**, teeing ground. *Sp:* **D. lancé**, flying start. **D. arrêté**, standing start. *Rac:* **Faux départ**, false start. **3.** (a) *Rail:* Departure platform. (b) *Sp:* Starting-post. (c) Foot (of flight of stairs).

départager [departaʒe], v.tr. (Conj. like PARTAGER) To decide between (opinions, etc.). *D. les voix*, to give the casting vote.

département [departəmɑ̃], s.m. *Adm:* Department. (a) Ministry, *U.S:* Department. *F:* **Cela n'est pas de mon département**, this is not within my province. (b) *Adm:* Subdivision (of France) administered by a prefect; department.

départemental, -aux [departəmɑ̃tal, -o], a. Departmental. S.a. ROUTE 1.

départir [departiːr], v.tr. (Conj. like PARTIR) (a) To divide (property amongst heirs, etc.). (b) To dispense, deal out (favours, etc.). **se départir**. (Conj. like FINIR) **1.** *Se d. de qch.*, to part with, give up, sth. **2.** *Se d. de ses instructions*, to depart from one's instructions. *Se d. de son devoir*, to swerve, deviate, from one's duty.

dépasser [depɑse], v.tr. **1.** (a) To pass beyond, go beyond (s.o., sth.); to run past (signal, etc.). **Dépasser le but**, to overshoot the mark. **Dépasser les bornes**, to overstep the bounds. *Il a dépassé la trentaine*, he has turned thirty. (b) *D. qn (à la course)*, to overtake, outrun, outstrip, s.o.; to draw ahead of s.o. **2.** *D. qch. en hauteur*, to (over-)top sth. *D. qn de la tête*, to stand a head taller than s.o. *Maison qui dépasse l'alignement*, house that projects beyond the others. *Votre jupon dépasse*, your petticoat is showing (below your skirt). *Il les dépasse tous en mérite*, he transcends them all in merit. *Cela dépasse mon entendement, F :* cela me dépasse, it is above my comprehension. **3.** To exceed. *D. son congé*, to overstay one's leave. *D. ses instructions*, to go beyond one's instructions. *D. la limite de vitesse*, to exceed the speed-limit.

dépav|er [depave], *v.tr.* To unpave. *s.m.* **-age.**

dépays|er [depe(j)ize], *v.tr.* **1.** To remove (s.o.) from his usual surroundings, from his element. **2.** To embarrass, bewilder (s.o.). *s.m.* **-ement.** **dépaysé**, *a.* Out of one's element. *Il a l'air d.*, he seems lost, at a loss.

dép|ecer [depəse], *v.tr.* (je dépèce ; je dépècerai) To cut up (carcass, etc.) ; to dismember, to carve (fowl). [PIÈCE] *s.m.* **-ècement.**

dépêche [depɛ(:)ʃ], *s.f.* (*a*) (Official) despatch. (*b*) *D. télégraphique*, telegram, *F :* wire.

dépêcher [depeʃe], *v.tr.* **1.** To dispatch ; to do (sth.) speedily. **2.** To dispatch, put to death. **3.** *D. un courrier*, to dispatch a messenger.

se dépêcher, to hasten, to make haste ; to be quick. *Dépêchez-vous !* look sharp ! hurry up ! *Se d. de faire qch.*, to hasten to do sth.

dépeigner [depɛɲe], *v.tr.* To ruffle, rumple (s.o.). *Personne dépeignée*, person with tousled hair ; unkempt person.

dépeindre [depɛ̃:dr], *v.tr.* (Conj. like PEINDRE) To depict, picture, describe (s.o., sth.).

dépenaillé [depnaje], *a.* Ragged, tattered, torn ; in rags, in tatters.

dépendance [depãdã:s], *s.f.* **1.** Dependence, depending. **2.** (*a*) Dependency (of a country). (*b*) *pl.* Outbuildings, offices. **3.** Dependence, subjection, subordination. *Être sous la dépendance de qn*, to be under s.o.'s domination.

dépendant [depãdã], *a.* Dependent (*de*, on).

dépendre[1] [depã:dr], *v.tr.* To take down (hanging object).

dépendre[2], *v.i.* To depend (*de*, on). **1.** *Il dépend de vous de + inf.*, it lies, rests, with you to . . . . Cela dépend, that depends ; we shall see. **2.** (*a*) (Of land, etc.) To be a dependency (*de*, of) ; to appertain to, belong to (the Crown). (*b*) (Of ship) To hail (from a port). **3.** To be subordinate, subject (*de*, to). *Ne d. que de soi*, to be one's own master ; to stand on one's own legs.

dépens [depã], *s.m.pl.* *Jur :* Costs. *Com :* Cost, expenses. *Être condamné aux dépens*, to be ordered to pay costs. *Aux dépens de*, at the expense of (s.o., sth.). *S'amuser aux d. de ses études*, to amuse oneself to the detriment of one's studies. *Il apprit à ses d. que . . .*, he learnt to his cost that. . . .

dépense [depã:s], *s.f.* **1.** Expenditure, expense, outlay (of money). *Faire des dépenses*, to incur expenses. *Faire la d. d'une voiture*, to go to the expense of hiring a car. *Faire trop de d.*, to spend too much money. *Se mettre en dépense*, (i) to incur expense ; (ii) *F :* to put oneself to a great deal of trouble. *On ne regardait pas à la dépense*, there was no stinting ; they spared no expense. *Faire de folles dépenses*, to spend money extravagantly. *Recettes et dépenses*, receipts and expenditure(s). **2.** *D. de vapeur, d'essence*, steam, petrol, consumption. *D. à vide*, wasted energy. **3.** Store-room, buttery, pantry.

dépenser [depãse], *v.tr.* **1.** To spend (money). *D. sans compter*, to spend lavishly. **2.** To spend, consume (time, energy, etc.).

se dépenser. *Se d. en vains efforts*, to spend oneself, waste one's energy, in useless efforts. *Se d. pour qn*, to spare no trouble on s.o.'s behalf.

dépensier, -ière [depãsje, -jɛːr]. **1.** *s.* Dispenser

(of hospital) ; storekeeper. **2.** (*a*) *a.* Extravagant, thriftless. (*b*) *s.* Spendthrift.

déperdition [deperdisjɔ̃], *s.f.* Waste, wastage, destruction (of tissue, etc.) ; loss, leakage (of heat, energy) ; dwindling (of capital).

dépér|ir [deperiːr], *v.i.* To waste away, pine, dwindle ; (of health) to decline ; (of trees, flowers) to wither, decay ; (of race) to die out. *s.m.* **-issement.**

dépêtrer [depetre], *v.tr.* To extricate, free (s.o.) (from entanglement).

se dépêtrer, to extricate oneself.

dépeupl|er [depœple], *v.tr.* To depopulate (country, etc.) ; to unstock (pond) ; to thin, clear (forest). *s.m.* **-ement.**

se dépeupler, to become depopulated.

déphasage [defazaːʒ], *s.m.* *El.E :* Phase displacement ; difference in phase. *D. en avant*, (phase) lead. *D. en arrière*, lag.

déphasé [defaze], *a.* *El.E :* (Of current) Out of phase. *D. en arrière*, lagging (current). *D. en avant*, leading (current).

dép|iécer [depjese], *v.tr.* (je dépièce, n. dépiéçons ; je dépiéçai(s) ; je dépiécerai) To pull, cut, (chicken, etc.) to pieces ; to dismember. *s.m.* **-iècement.**

dépiquer [depike], *v.tr.* (*a*) To unquilt. (*b*) To unstitch.

dépister[1] [depiste], *v.tr.* To track down (game) ; to run (game, *F :* s.o.) to earth.

dépister[2], *v.tr.* To put (hounds, *F :* s.o.) off the scent ; to baffle, outwit (police).

dépit [depi], *s.m.* Spite, spleen, resentment, chagrin. *Par dépit*, out of spite. *Pleurer de dépit*, to cry with vexation. *En dépit de . . .*, in spite of, in defiance of. . . . *En dépit de ce que + ind.*, in spite of the fact that. . . .

dépiter [depite], *v.tr.* To vex. *Je l'ai dit pour la d.*, I said it to spite her.

se dépiter, to take offence, to be annoyed. *Il se dépitait de ne rien découvrir*, he was vexed that he could not find out anything.

déplacement [deplasmã], *s.m.* **1.** (*a*) Displacement, shifting ; removing (of wreck, etc.) ; transfer (of official). *Parl :* *D. de quatre voix*, turn-over of four votes. (*b*) Altering of the time (of a train, etc.). **2.** Travelling ; moving ; journey. *Frais de déplacement*, travelling or removal expenses. *Nau :* *Déplacements*, movements of ships. **3.** *N.Arch :* *D. à vide, d. lège*, light displacement. *D. en charge*, displacement fully loaded ; load displacement.

déplacer [deplase], *v.tr.* (je déplaçai(s) ; n. déplaçons) **1.** (*a*) To displace, shift (an object) ; to change the place of (s.o., sth.). *D. un fonctionnaire*, to transfer, move, a civil servant. (*b*) To alter the time of (train, etc.). **2.** To oust, take the place of (s.o.). **3.** *Nau :* *Ce navire déplace dix mille tonneaux*, this ship has a displacement of ten thousand tons.

se déplacer. (*a*) To change one's place, one's residence. (*b*) To move about, to travel.

déplacé, *a.* **1.** Out of its place ; displaced (heart, etc.). **2.** Out of place, misplaced, ill-timed ; uncalled-for (remark).

déplaire [deplɛːr], *v.ind.tr.* (Conj. like PLAIRE) (*a*) To displease. *D. à qn*, (i) to displease, offend, s.o. ; (ii) to fail to please s.o. ; to be displeasing to s.o. *Odeur qui déplaît*, disagreeable smell. *Ils se déplaisent*, they dislike each other. (*b*) *Impers.* *Il me déplairait de vous contredire*, I should not like to contradict you. *N'en déplaise à la compagnie*, with all due deference to those present. *N'en déplaise à votre Altesse !* may it please your

Highness! **Ne vous en déplaise,** if you have no objection ; with your permission.
se déplaire, to be displeased, dissatisfied. *Se d. à Paris,* to dislike (living in) Paris.
déplaisant [deplɛzã], *a.* Unpleasing, unpleasant, disagreeable.
déplaisir [deplɛziːr], *s.m.* Displeasure, annoyance, vexation, chagrin.
déplant|er [deplɑ̃te], *v.tr.* **1.** To take up (plant). **2.** To transplant. *s.m.* **-age.**
déplantoir [deplɑ̃twaːr], *s.m.* Garden trowel.
déplier [deplie], *v.tr.* To unfold, open out, spread out (newspaper, etc.).
se déplier, to unfold ; to open out.
déploiement, déploîment [deplwamã], *s.m.* **1.** (*a*) Spreading out, unfolding (of wings, etc.); unfurling (of flag). (*b*) Deployment (of troops or ships). **2.** Display, show (of goods, courage).
déplomb|er [deplɔ̃be], *v.tr.* **1.** To remove the custom-house seals from (package). **2.** To unstop (tooth). *s.m.* **-age.**
déplorable [deplɔrabl], *a.* (*a*) Deplorable, lamentable. (*b*) Pitiable (sight). *adv.* **-ment.**
déplorer [deplɔre], *v.tr.* To deplore, lament (sth.). *D. la mort de qn,* to grieve over, to mourn, s.o.'s death. *D. son destin,* to bewail one's lot.
déployer [deplwaje], *v.tr.* (je déploie ; je déploierai) **1.** To unfold, open out, spread out (wings, etc.); to unfurl (flag) ; to spread (sails). *Mil:* To deploy (troops). **2.** To display, show (goods).
se déployer. 1. (*a*) (Of sail, flag) To unfurl. (*b*) (Of breaker) To spread. **2.** *Mil: Navy:* To deploy.
déplu, -s, -t, etc. See DÉPLAIRE.
déplumer [deplyme], *v.tr.* To pluck (chicken).
se déplumer. 1. (Of bird) **To** moult. **2.** *F:* (Of pers.) To become bald.
déplumé, *a.* Featherless ; bald ; shabby.
dépolariser [depɔlarize], *v.tr.* To depolarize.
dépol|ir [depɔliːr], *v.tr.* **1.** To dull (surface). **2.** To grind, frost (glass). *s.m.* **-issage.**
se dépolir, to become dull.
dépoli. 1. *a.* Ground, frosted (glass). **2.** *s.m. Phot:* Focusing screen.
déponent [depɔnã], *a. Gram:* Deponent (verb).
dépopulation [depɔpylasjɔ̃], *s.f.* Depopulation.
déportation [depɔrtasjɔ̃], *s.f.* **1.** Deportation (of alien, etc.). **2.** Transportation (of convict).
déportements [depɔrtəmã], *s.m.pl.* Misbehaviour, misconduct, excesses.
déporter[1] [depɔrte], *v.tr.* **1.** To deport (alien). **2.** To transport (convict).
déporté, -ée, *a. & s.* **1.** Deported (person). **2.** Transported (convict).
déporter[2]. **1.** *v.tr.* (*a*) To carry (sth.) out of its course. (*b*) *Mec.E: etc:* To offset (part). **2.** *v.i. Av:* To drift.
déposant, -ante [depozã, -ãːt], *s.* **1.** Depositor (of money). **2.** *Jur:* Deponent, witness.
déposer [depoze], *v.tr.* **1.** (*a*) To deposit ; to lay, set, (sth.) down. *Mon auto vous déposera à l'hôtel,* my car will set you down, *F:* will drop you, at the hotel. *D. sa carte chez qn,* to leave one's card on s.o. *D. les armes,* to lay down one's arms ; to surrender. *D. le masque,* to lay aside, put off, the mask. (*b*) (Of liquid) To deposit (sediment) ; to settle. **2.** (*a*) *D. son argent, des documents, à la banque,* to lodge, deposit, one's money, documents, at the bank. (*b*) *Com:* To register (trademark). (*c*) *Jur: D. une plainte contre qn,* to prefer a charge, lodge a complaint, against s.o. *Com: D. son bilan,* to file one's petition (in bankruptcy). (*d*) *D. un projet de loi (sur le bureau*

de la Chambre), to table, bring in, a bill. (*e*) *Abs. Jur:* **Déposer (en justice),** to give evidence (*contre,* against) ; to depose. **3.** To depose (monarch, etc.).
se déposer, (of matter) to settle ; to form a deposit.
dépositaire [depoziteːr], *s.m. & f.* **1.** Depositary, trustee. *D. de valeurs,* holder of securities on trust. **2.** (*a*) Sole agent (for s.o.'s products). (*b*) Newsagent.
déposition [depozisjɔ̃], *s.f.* **1.** *Jur:* Deposition ; statement (made by witness). **2.** Deposing, deposition (of king, etc.).
déposséder [deposede], *v.tr.* (je **dépossède** ; je **déposséderai**) To dispossess (*de,* of) ; to oust (*de,* from) ; to deprive (*de,* of).
dépôt [depo], *s.m.* **1.** (*a*) Depositing ; handing in (of telegram). **Récépissé de dépôt,** safe-custody receipt. **Société de dépôt,** joint-stock bank. *D. légal d'un livre,* copyrighting of a book (by depositing duty copies). (*b*) Deposit. *D. sacré,* sacred trust. *D. en banque,* bank deposit. **Compte de dépôts,** deposit account. (*c*) **Avoir qch. en dépôt,** to hold sth. in trust, on trust. **Marchandises en dépôt,** (i) *Cust:* goods in bond ; (ii) *Com:* goods on sale or return. **2.** Depository, repository, store, depot ; police station. **Écroué au dépôt,** committed to the cells. *D. de mendicité,* workhouse. *D. de marchandises,* warehouse. *D. de bois,* timber yard. *D. de charbon,* coal yard ; *Nau:* coaling-station. *Rail: D. des machines,* engine shed. *Aut: D. d'essence,* petrol station. **3.** (*a*) Deposition, settling (of mud, etc.). (*b*) Deposit, sediment ; silt (of harbour, etc.).
dépot|er [depote], *v.tr.* **1.** To decant (liquid). **2.** To unpot (plants) ; to plant out, bed out (seedlings). **3.** To dump (night-soil). *s.m.* **-age.**
dépotoir [depotwaːr], *s.m.* Night-soil dump.
dépouille [depuːj], *s.f.* **1.** Skin, hide (taken from animal). *Le serpent jette sa dépouille,* the serpent casts its slough. **Dépouille mortelle,** mortal remains. **2.** (*a*) Usu. *pl.* Spoils, booty (of war). (*b*) Effects (of deceased person). **3.** Relief, clearance (of machine-tool).
dépouill|er [depuje], *v.tr.* **1.** (*a*) To skin (eel, etc.). *L'hiver dépouille les champs,* winter strips the fields. (*b*) To cast off, lay aside. *D. ses vêtements,* to throw off one's clothes ; to strip. **2.** To deprive, strip, despoil. *D. qn de ses droits,* to deprive, rob, s.o. of his rights. *D. un pays,* to despoil a country. *El.E: D. un câble,* to strip a cable. **3.** To analyse (inventory). *D. un compte,* to make an abstract of an account. *D. le scrutin,* to count the votes. *D. son courrier,* to open, go through, one's mail. *D.* To back off, give clearance to (drill, etc.). *s.m.* **-ement.**
se dépouiller. 1. (Of insect, reptile) To cast (off) its skin, its slough ; (of tree) to shed its leaves. **2.** *Se d. de qch.,* to divest, rid, oneself of sth. ; to cast sth. aside. *Se d. de ses vêtements,* to strip off one's clothes.
dépourvoir [depurvwaːr], *v.tr.* (Used only in the *inf., p.p.* **dépourvu,** and compound tenses) To deprive (s.o.) (*de,* of).
dépourvu, *a.* Destitute, bereft, short, devoid (*de,* of) ; -less. *Pays d. d'arbres, de pluie,* treeless, rainless, country. *Être d. d'argent,* to be without money. **Être pris au dépourvu,** to be caught off one's guard ; to be caught napping, unawares.
dépoussiéreur [depusjerœːr], *s.m.* Vacuum-cleaner.
dépravant [depravã], *a.* Depraving.
dépravation [depravasjɔ̃], *s.f.* **1.** Depravation (of taste, etc.). **2.** (Moral) depravity.

dépraver [deprave], *v.tr.* To deprave.
 se dépraver, to become depraved.
dépréciateur, -trice [depresjatœ:r, -tris]. I. *s.*
 (*a*) Depreciator (of currency, etc.). (*b*) Disparager.
2. *a.* (*a*) Depreciatory. (*b*) Disparaging.
dépréciation [depresjasjɔ̃], *s.f.* I. Depreciation.
 (*a*) Fall in value. (*b*) Wear and tear. **2.** (*a*) Underrating, undervaluing. (*b*) Disparagement.
déprécier [depresje], *v.tr.* I. To depreciate
 (coinage, etc.). **2.** (*a*) To underrate, undervalue.
 (*b*) To disparage, belittle (s.o.).
  se déprécier. I. To depreciate. **2.** To make
  oneself cheap.
déprédateur, -trice [depredatœ:r, -tris]. I. *s.*
 (*a*) Depredator. (*b*) Peculator. **2.** *a.* Depredatory.
déprédation [depredasjɔ̃], *s.f.* I. Depredation.
 2. Peculation ; misappropriation.
dépression [depresjɔ̃], *s.f.* I. Hollow, dip (in
 floor, ground). **2.** (*a*) Fall (in value) ; lowering
 of (barometric) pressure. (*b*) *Meteor :* Depression, storm. **3.** (Moral) depression ; dejection.
déprimer [deprime], *v.tr.* To depress.
  se déprimer, to get depressed, miserable.
  déprimé, *a.* Depressed. (*a*) Low, flat. *Front
  d.,* low forehead. (*b*) *Pouls d.,* feeble pulse.
  Marché d., depressed market. *Malade d.,* patient
  in a low state. (*c*) Down-hearted ; low-spirited ;
  F : down in the mouth.
depuis [dəpɥi], *prep.* I. (*a*) (Of time) Since, for.
 D. quand êtes-vous ici? how long have you been
 here ? *Je suis ici d. trois jours,* I have been here
 for three days. *D. combien?* how long since ?
 since when ? *D. ce temps-là,* since then, since that
 time. *D. son enfance,* from a child. (*b*) *adv.* Since
 (then) ; afterwards, later. (*c*) Depuis que + *ind.,*
 since. . . . **2.** (Of time, place) From. *D. le
 matin jusqu'au soir,* from morning till night.
 3. *W.Tel :* Broadcast from. . . .
dépuratif, -ive [depyratif, -i:v], *a.* & *s.m.*
 Med : Depurative ; blood-cleansing.
dépurer [depyre], *v.tr.* To depurate, cleanse,
 clear (the blood) ; to purify (metal, etc.).
députation [depytasjɔ̃], *s.f.* I. (*a*) Deputing,
 delegating (of s.o.). (*b*) Deputation, delegation.
 2. Membership (of Parliament). **Se présenter à
 la députation,** to stand for Parliament. **Candidat
 à la députation,** parliamentary candidate.
députer [depyte], *v.tr.* To depute (s.o.) ; to
 appoint (s.o.) as deputy (*à, vers,* to).
 député, *s.m.* Deputy, delegate. **La chambre
 des Députés,** the Chamber of Deputies.
déracin|er [derasine], *v.tr.* I. To uproot, grub
 up ; to tear (tree, etc.) up by the roots. *Se sentir
 déraciné,* to feel oneself in a strange land, to feel
 like a fish out of water. **2.** To eradicate (fault,
 abuse). *s.m.* **-ement.**
déraidir [deredi:r], *v.tr.* I. To unstiffen. **2.** *F :*
 To unstarch (one's manners, smile, etc.).
  se déraidir. I. (Of limb, etc.) To lose its
  stiffness. **2.** *F :* (Of pers.) To unbend, to thaw.
déraill|er [deraje], *v.i.* (*a*) (Of train, tram) To
 jump the metals ; to become derailed. **Faire
 dérailler un train,** to derail a train. (*b*) (Of
 gramophone needle) To jump the sound groove.
 s.m. **-ement.**
déraison [derezɔ̃], *s.f.* Unreasonableness ; foolishness ; unreason.
déraisonnable [derezɔnabl], *a.* Unreasonable,
 irrational ; preposterous ; unwise, senseless,
 foolish. *adv.* **-ment.**
déraisonn|er [derezɔne], *v.i.* To talk nonsense ;
 (in illness) to rave. *s.m.* **-ement.**
dérangement [derɑ̃ʒmɑ̃], *s.m.* Derangement.

(*a*) Disarrangement (of furniture, etc.). (*b*) Disturbance, trouble. (*c*) Disturbed or unsettled
state ; upset. *D. de cerveau,* mental derangement.
D. atmosphérique, atmospheric disturbance. *D. de
corps,* diarrhoea. (*d*) *El.E : etc :* Fault.
déranger [derɑ̃ʒe], *v.tr.* (**je dérangeai(s) ; n.
 dérangeons**) To derange. (*a*) To disarrange
 (papers). (*b*) To disturb, trouble. *Pardon si je
 vous dérange,* excuse my disturbing you. (*c*) To
 put (sth.) out of order ; to upset (plans). *D. la
 raison de qn,* to unsettle s.o.'s reason ; to derange
 s.o.'s mind.
  se déranger. I. To move, stir. *Ne vous
  dérangez pas,* please don't move, don't trouble.
  Se d. pour obliger qn, to go out of one's way to
  oblige s.o. **2.** To deviate from the path of virtue ;
  F : to run wild. **3.** (Of machine) To get out of
  order ; (of mind) to become deranged.
dérap|er [derape], *v.tr.* & *i.* I. *Nau :* (*a*) To trip,
 weigh, the anchor. (*b*) (Of anchor) To drag ; (of
 ship) to drag its anchor. **2.** *Aut : etc :* To skid,
 to side-slip. *s.m.* **-age.**
dérater [derate], *v.tr.* To spleen (dog, etc.). *F :
 Courir comme un dératé,* to run like a hare.
dératisation [deratizasjɔ̃], *s.f.* Extermination of
 rats. **Semaine de dératisation,** rat week.
dératiser [deratize], *v.tr.* To clear (place) of rats.
derechef [dərəʃef], *adv.* A second time ; yet
 again ; once more.
dérèglement [deregləmɑ̃], *s.m.* I. Disordered
 state (of house, imagination, etc.) ; irregularity
 (of pulse) ; (mental) derangement. **2.** Dissolute-
 ness, profligacy.
dérégler [deregle], *v.tr.* (**je dérègle ; je déréglerai**)
 I. To put (clock, etc.) out of order. **2.** To upset,
 disarrange, disorder (habits, etc.) ; to unsettle
 (trade, the stomach).
  se dérégler. I. (Of clock, etc.) To get out
  of order. **2.** (Of pers.) To get into evil ways.
  déréglé, *a.* I. (Of clock, etc.) Out of order.
  2. Disordered (mind) ; irregular (pulse). **3.** Lawless, wild (life) ; immoderate (desires).
dérider [deride], *v.tr.* To smoothe, to unwrinkle ;
 F : to cheer (s.o.) up.
  se dérider, to brighten up, to cease to frown.
dérision [derizjɔ̃], *s.f.* Derision, mockery.
 Tourner qn en dérision, to hold s.o. up to ridicule.
 Dire qch. par dérision, to say sth. derisively,
 in mockery. **Rires de dérision,** derisive laughter.
dérisoire [derizwa:r], *a.* Ridiculous, laughable
 (offer, etc.) ; absurdly low (price). *adv.* **-ment.**
dérivation[1] [derivasjɔ̃], *s.f.* I. (*a*) Diversion,
 tapping (of watercourse). **Fossé de dérivation,**
 drain. **Canal de dérivation,** head-race, penstock.
 (*b*) *El.E :* Shunt(ing), branching, tapping (of
 current). **Excité en dérivation,** shunt-wound
 (motor, etc.). **Monter un condensateur en
 dérivation,** to shunt a condenser. **Piles en d.,** cells
 in parallel. (*c*) *Rail :* Loop(-line). **2.** *Ling :*
 Derivation (of word).
dérivation[2], *s.f.* *Nau : etc :* Drift.
dérive [deri:v], *s.f.* *Nau :* Leeway, drift. *Av :*
 Drift. **Aller en dérive,** to drift. **A la dérive,**
 adrift. **(Quille de) dérive,** drop-keel ; centreboard. **(Aile de) dérive,** lee-board.
dériver[1] [derive], *v.* I. *v.tr.* (*a*) To divert, tap
 (stream). *El.E :* To shunt, branch (current).
 (*b*) *Ling : Mth :* To derive (de, from). **2.** *v.i.*
 (*a*) (Of stream) To be diverted (*de,* from).
 (*b*) To spring, arise, be derived (from a source).
  dérivé, -ée, *a.* & *s.* I. *Ling : etc :* Derived,
  secondary (meaning, etc.). **Un dérivé,** a derivative. *Produit d.,* by-product. **2.** *Mth :* Derived
  (function). *s.f.* **Dérivées continues,** derivatives.

3. *El:* Shunt(ed) (current, etc.). **4.** *Mus:* Accord dérivé, inversion of a chord.

dériver, *v.tr.* To unrivet.

dériver, *v.i. Nau:* To drift. *D. à vau-l'eau,* to drift down stream.

dériveter [derivte], *v.tr.* (je dérivette ; je dérivetterai) To unrivet.

dérivomètre [derivɔmɛtr], *s.m. Av:* Drift indicator.

dermatologie [dɛrmatɔlɔʒi], *s.f.* Dermatology.

derme [dɛrm], *s.m. Anat:* Derm ; cutis.

dernier, -ière [dɛrnje, -jɛːr], *a. & s.* **I.** Last, latest. *(a) Au d. moment,* at the last moment. *Faire un d. effort,* to make a final effort. *Mettre la dernière main à qch.,* to give the finishing, the final, touches to sth. *J'ai payé jusqu'au d. sou,* I paid to the last farthing. *Jusqu'à mon d. jour, jusqu'à ma dernière heure,* to my dying day. *Il veut toujours avoir le dernier mot, F:* avoir le dernier, he must always have the last word. *Il arriva le d.,* he arrived last, was the last to arrive. *Dans ces derniers temps,* l atterly ; of late years. *Informations de la dernière heure,* latest news. *La dernière mode,* the latest fashion, the latest thing. S.a. BATEAU, CRI. *St.Exch:* **Dernier cours,** closing price. *(b)* (Last of series) *Le mois d.,* last month. *Les six derniers,* the last six. **Le d. rang,** the rear rank. *La dernière moitié de juin,* the latter half of June. **En dernier ressort,** in the last resort. *Com: Le d. enchérisseur,* the highest bidder. *Le d. élève de la classe,* the last, bottom, boy in the form. *(c)* **Ce dernier répondit . . .,** the latter answered. . . . **2.** *(a)* Utmost, highest. *De la dernière importance,* of the utmost, greatest, importance. *Au d. degré,* to the utmost, highest, degree. *Entrer dans les derniers détails,* to enter into the minutest details. *Le d. supplice,* the extreme penalty. *Dans la dernière misère,* in dire want. *Je suis du d. bien avec lui,* I am on the very best terms with him. *(b)* Lowest, worst. *Le d. prix,* the lowest price. **Le dernier de mes soucis,** the least of my worries. *Le d. des hommes,* the vilest, meanest, of men. **Le dernier des derniers,** the lowest of the low.

dernièrement [dɛrnjɛrmɑ̃], *adv.* Lately, latterly, of late, not long ago.

dernier-né, *s.m.* Last-born child. *pl. Les derniers-nés.*

dérober [derɔbe], *v.tr.* **I.** *(a)* To steal, to make away with (sth.). *On m'a dérobé mon argent,* I have been robbed of my money. *D. un baiser,* to steal a kiss. *(b) D. qn au danger,* to rescue, save, s.o. from danger. **2.** To hide, conceal. *D. une batterie aux coups,* to cover, screen, a battery from fire. *Mur qui dérobe la vue,* wall that hides, intercepts, the view.

se dérober. I. *(a)* To escape, steal away, slip away *(à,* from). *Se d. à l'étreinte de qn,* to get out of s.o.'s clutches. *Se d. aux regards,* to escape observation. *Se d. aux coups,* to dodge the blows. *Se d. à un devoir,* to evade, shirk, a duty. *(b)* (Of horse) To swerve, shy (at a jump) ; to jib ; to refuse. **2.** To give way. *Le sol se déroba sous nos pas,* the ground gave way under our feet.

dérobé, *a.* **I.** Culture, récolte, dérobée, catch-crop, snatch-crop. **2.** Hidden, concealed, secret (staircase, door, etc.). **A la dérobée,** stealthily, secretly, on the sly. *Regarder qn à la d.,* to steal a glance at s.o. *Sortir à la d.,* to steal out.

dérocher [derɔʃe], *v.tr. Metalw:* To scour, pickle. *s.m.* **-age.**

dérogation [derɔgasjɔ̃], *s.f.* Derogation, impairment *(à une loi,* of a law). **Faire dérogation à l'usage,** to make a departure from custom.

Par, en, **dérogation à cette règle,** this rule notwithstanding.

déroger [derɔʒe], *v.i.* (je dérogeai(s) ; n. dérogeons) *(a) D. à l'usage, à la loi,* to depart from custom, from the law. *D. à une condition,* not to conform to a condition. *(b)* To derogate *(à,* from). *D. à son rang,* to lose caste. *D. jusqu'à faire une chose pareille,* to stoop to such a thing. **Sans déroger,** without derogation *(à,* from).

dérouiller [deruje], *v.tr.* To take, rub, the rust off (sth.). *F: Se d. les jambes,* to stretch one's legs. *Se d. la mémoire,* to polish up, refresh, one's memory. *D. son français,* to brush up one's French. *s.m.* **-ement.**

dérouler [derule], *v.tr.* To unroll (map, etc.) ; to unwind, unreel, uncoil (cable) ; to uncoil, let down (one's hair). *F: D. ses plans à qn,* to unfold one's plans to s.o. *s.m.* **-ement.**

se dérouler. I. (Of map, etc.) To come unrolled ; (of cable, etc.) to come unwound. **2.** To unfold, to develop. *Le paysage se déroule devant nous,* the landscape unfolds (itself), stretches out, before us. *Les événements qui se déroulent à Paris,* the events that are taking place in Paris. *La manifestation s'est déroulée sans désordre,* the demonstration passed off without disorder.

déroute [derut], *s.f. (a)* Rout. **Être en (pleine) déroute,** to be in (full) flight. **L'armée fut mise en déroute,** the army was put to flight, was routed. *(b) F:* Ruin, downfall (of a family, etc.).

dérouter [derute], *v.tr.* **I.** To throw, lead, (s.o., sth.) out of the right way. **Dérouter les soupçons,** to throw people off the scent. *Ces interruptions me déroutent,* these interruptions put me off. **2.** To confuse, baffle, nonplus.

derrière [dɛrjɛːr]. **I.** *prep. (a)* Behind, at the back of (s.o., sth.). *Caché d. le rideau,* hidden behind the curtain. *Laisser qn d. soi,* to leave s.o. behind. *(b) Nau:* (i) Abaft ; (ii) astern of (the ship). **2.** *adv. (a)* Behind, at the back, in the rear. **Attaquer qn par derrière,** to attack s.o. from behind, from the rear. **Wagons de derrière,** rear waggons. **Porte de derrière,** back-door. **Pattes de derrière,** hind legs. S.a. DEVANT[1] 2. *(b) Nau:* (i) Aft ; (ii) astern. **3.** *s.m. (a)* Back, rear (of building, etc.). *Mil:* **Les derrières d'une armée,** the rear of an army. *(b) F:* Behind, backside, bottom. *Chien assis sur son d.,* dog sitting on its haunches.

derviche [dɛrviʃ], *s.m.,* **dervis** [dɛrvi], *s.m.* Dervish.

des [de, dɛ] = *de les.* See DE, LE[1], and UN.

dès [dɛ], *prep.* Since, from ; as early as. *Dès ce moment elle l'aima,* she loved him from that moment. *Dès sa jeunesse . . .,* from childhood . . . *Dès l'abord,* from the outset ; from the (very) first. *Dès maintenant, dès à présent,* already ; henceforth. *Dès 1840,* as far back as 1840. *Dès le matin,* first thing in the morning. *Dès mon retour,* immediately on my return. *Je commencerai dès aujourd'hui,* I will begin this very day. *Conj.phr.* **Dès que** *+ ind.* **Dès qu'il sera arrivé,** as soon as he arrives. *Adv.phr.* **Dès lors,** (i) from that time onwards ; ever since (then) ; (ii) consequently. *Conj.phr.* **Dès lors que** *+ ind.,* since, seeing that. . . .

désabusement [dezabyzmɑ̃], *s.m.* **I.** Disabusing, undeceiving. **2.** Disillusionment.

désabuser [dezabyze], *v.tr.* To disabuse, disillusion, undeceive *(de,* with regard to).

se désabuser *(de qch.),* to lose one's illusions (about sth.) ; to have one's eyes opened.

désaccord [dezakɔːr]. *s.m.* **I.** *(a)* Disagreement,

dissension. **Se trouver en désaccord avec qn sur qch.**, to be at variance, at issue, with s.o. about sth. **Sujet de désaccord**, bone of contention. (b) Clash (of interests, etc.). *Le d. entre la théorie et les faits*, the discordance between the theory and the facts. **2.** (a) *Mus:* Discord. **En désaccord**, out of tune. (b) *W.Tel:* Detuning.

désaccorder [dezakɔrde], *v.tr.* **1.** To set (persons) at variance. **2.** *Mus:* To put (instrument) out of tune.

désaccoutumance [dezakutymɑ̃:s], *s.f. D. de qch.*, loss of the habit of, of familiarity with, sth.

désaccoutumer [dezakutyme], *v.tr.* To disaccustom. *D. qn de faire qch.*, to break s.o. of, to get s.o. out of, the habit of doing sth.

se désaccoutumer *de qch., de faire qch.* **1.** To become unused to sth., to doing sth. **2.** To get out of the habit of doing sth.

désaffectation [dezafɛktasjɔ̃], *s.f.* Putting (of public building, etc.) to another purpose; deconsecration, secularization (of church).

désaffecter [dezafɛkte], *v.tr.* To put (public building, etc.) to another purpose. *Église désaffectée*, deconsecrated, secularized, church.

désaffection [dezafɛksjɔ̃], *s.f.* Disaffection (*envers*, to).

désaffectionner [dezafɛksjɔne], *v.tr.* **1.** To alienate (s.o.'s) affections. **2.** To disaffect (followers, etc.).

désagréable [dezagreabl], *a.* Disagreeable, unpleasant (*à*, to); surly, grumpy (nature); offensive, nasty (smell). *D. au goût*, distasteful, unpalatable. *adv.* **-ment.**

désagrégation [dezagregasjɔ̃], *s.f.* Disaggregation, disintegration; breaking up (of family).

désagréger [dezagreʒe], *v.tr.* (*je désagrège*, n. **désagrégeons;** je **désagrégeai(s);** je **désagrégerai**) To disaggregate, disintegrate.

se désagréger, to break up.

désagrément [dezagremɑ̃], *s.m.* Source of annoyance; unpleasant occurrence. *Attirer à qn des désagréments*, to get s.o. into trouble.

désaimantation [dezemɑ̃tasjɔ̃], *s.f.* Demagnetization, demagnetizing.

désaimanter [dezemɑ̃te], *v.tr.* To demagnetize.

désajust|er [dezaʒyste], *v.tr.* (a) To disarrange. (b) To throw (mechanism) out of adjustment. *s.m.* **-ement.**

se désajuster, to become disarranged; to work loose; to fall out of adjustment.

désaligné [dezaliɲe], *a.* Out of alignment; out of line.

désaltérant [dezalterɑ̃]. **1.** *a.* Thirst-quenching. **2.** *s.m.* Thirst-quencher.

désaltérer [dezaltere], *v.tr.* (je **désaltère;** je **désaltérerai**) To slake, quench, (s.o.'s) thirst.

se désaltérer, to slake, quench, one's thirst; to have some refreshment.

désamor|cer [dezamɔrse],*v.tr.* (je **désamorçai(s);** n. **désamorçons**) To unprime (shell, siphon, etc.). *s.m.* **-çage.**

se désamorcer. 1. (Of pump, etc.) To fail. **2.** (Of dynamo) To run down.

désappointement [dezapwɛ̃tmɑ̃], *s.m.* Disappointment.

désappointer [dezapwɛ̃te], *v.tr.* To disappoint.

désapprendre [dezaprɑ̃:dr], *v.tr.* (Conj. like APPRENDRE) To forget (what one has learnt); to unlearn. *Faire d. qch. à qn*, to unteach s.o. sth.

désapprobateur, -trice [dezaprɔbatœːr, -tris]. **1.** *s.* Disapprover, censurer (*de*, of). **2.** *a.* Disapproving, censorious.

désapprobation [dezaprɔbasjɔ̃], *s.f.* Disapproval, disapprobation (*de*, of).

désapprouver [dezapruve], *v.tr.* To disapprove of, object to (s.o., sth.). *Il désapprouve que je vienne*, he objects to my coming.

désarçonnant [dezarsɔnɑ̃], *a. F:* Dumbfounding, staggering (news, etc.).

désarçonn|er [dezarsɔne], *v.tr.* **1.** (Of horse) To unseat (rider). **2.** *F:* To dumbfound, stagger (s.o.). *s.m.* **-ement.**

désargenter [dezarʒɑ̃te], *v.tr.* **1.** To desilver (plated object). **2.** *F:* To drain (s.o.) of his cash.

désargenté, *a.* **1.** That has lost its silver. **2.** *F:* Short of cash, out of cash.

désarmement [dezarməmɑ̃], *s.m.* **1.** Disarming (of s.o.). **2.** Disarmament. **3.** *Nau:* Laying up, paying off (of ship).

désarmer [dezarme]. **1.** *v.tr.* (a) To disarm (soldier, criticism, etc.). (b) *Mil:* (i) To unload (gun); (ii) to uncock (rifle); (iii) to remove guns from (fort). (c) *Nau:* To lay up, pay off (ship); to put (ship) out of commission. (d) To unship (oars). **2.** *v.i.* (a) To disarm; to disband one's naval or military forces. (b) (Of ship) To be laid up, put out of commission.

désarmé, *a.* **1.** (a) Disarmed. (b) (Ship) out of commission. **2.** (a) Unarmed, defenceless. (b) Unloaded (gun).

désarrim|er [dezarime], *v.tr. Nau:* **1.** To unstow (cargo). **2.** To put (ship) out of trim. *s.m.* **-age.**

se désarrimer, (of cargo) to shift.

désarroi [dezarwa], *s.m.* Disarray, disorder, confusion.

désarticuler [dezartikyle], *v.tr.* (a) *Surg:* To disarticulate, disjoint. (b) To dislocate.

désassembl|er [dezasɑ̃ble], *v.tr.* To take (sth.) to pieces, apart; to disengage, disconnect (joints, etc.). *s.m.* **-age.**

désassocier [dezasɔsje], *v.tr.* To disassociate, dissociate (*de*, from).

se désassocier *de qn*, to sever one's connection with s.o.

désassortir [dezasɔrtiːr], *v.tr.* (Conj. like ASSORTIR) (a) To spoil, break up (collection). *Service de table désassorti*, dinner service made up of odd pieces. (b) *Com: Je suis désassorti de cet article*, I am out of this article.

désastre [dezastr], *s.m.* Disaster, calamity.

désastreu|x, -euse [dezastrø, -øːz], *a.* Disastrous, calamitous. *adv.* **-sement.**

désattrister [dezatriste], *v.tr.* To cheer, comfort.

se désattrister, to cheer up.

désavantage [dezavɑ̃ta:ʒ], *s.m.* Disadvantage, drawback. *Avoir le désavantage*, (i) to be handicapped; (ii) to get the worst of it.

désavantager [dezavɑ̃taʒe], *v.tr.* (je **désavantageai(s);** n. **désavantageons**) To affect (s.o.) unfavourably. *Être désavantagé par suite de qch.*, to be handicapped by sth.

désavantageu|x, -euse [dezavɑ̃ta:ʒø, -øːz], *a.* Disadvantageous, unfavourable. *adv.* **-sement.**

désaveu [dezavø], *s.m.* Disavowal, denial; disowning (of s.o.); disclaimer.

désaveugler [dezavœgle], *v.tr.* To disabuse.

désavouer [dezavwe], *v.tr.* To disavow, repudiate, deny (promise); to disclaim (authorship); to disown (offspring); to retract (opinion).

désaxé [dezakse], *a.* **1.** (a) Eccentric (cam, etc.). (b) *Roue désaxée*, (i) splayed, dished, wheel; (ii) wheel out of true. (c) *I.C.E:* Offset (cylinders). **2.** *F:* Unbalanced (mind).

descell|er [desele], *v.tr.* **1.** To unseal, to break the seal of (document, etc.); to force (**safe**).

2. To loosen (iron post from stonework, etc.). *s.m.* **-ement.**

descendance [dɛsɑ̃dɑ̃ːs, de-], *s.f.* **1.** Descent, lineage. **2.** *Coll.* Descendants.

descendant, -ante [dɛsɑ̃dɑ̃, de-, -ɑ̃ːt]. **1.** *a.* Descending (scale, curve, etc.); downward (motion); down-(stroke of piston). *Mil:* **Garde descendante,** old guard (about to be relieved). *Rail:* **Train, quai, descendant,** up-train, -platform. **2.** *s.* Descendant. *D. d'une famille noble,* scion of a noble family.

descendre [dɛsɑ̃ːdr, de-]. **I.** *v.i.* (Aux. *être,* occ. *avoir*) **1.** (*a*) To descend; to come down, go down. *D. d'un arbre,* to come down from a tree. *D. en glissant,* to slide down, to slither down. *La marée descend,* the tide is falling, going down. *Le baromètre descend,* the glass is falling. *Jur:* **Descendre sur les lieux,** to visit the scene (of a crime, etc.). *La police est descendue, a descendu, dans le dancing,* the police raided the night-club. *Av: D. en vol plané,* to volplane to the ground. *D. à plat,* to pancake to the ground. S.a. GARDE² 4. (*b*) To come, go, downstairs. *Je descends dîner,* I am going down to dinner. *Il n'est pas encore descendu,* he is not down yet. **Faites-le descendre,** (i) send him down, (ii) call him down. (*c*) To lower oneself, condescend. *D. jusqu'au mensonge,* to stoop to lying. **2.** (*a*) To alight (from carriage). *D. de cheval,* to dismount. *C'est ici que je descends,* this is where I get off (from bus, etc.). *"Tout le monde descend!"* 'all change!' *D. à terre,* to go ashore. (*b*) *D. à un hôtel,* to put up at a hotel. **3.** To extend downwards. *Le chemin descend jusqu'à la vallée,* the road stretches down to the valley. **4.** To be descended (from). *Sa famille descend des croisés,* his family goes back to the crusaders.

II. descendre, *v.tr.* (Aux. *avoir*) **1.** *D. les marches, la colline, la rue,* to go down the steps, the hill, the street. **2.** (*a*) To take, bring, (sth.) down. *D. les bagages,* to carry down, bring down, the luggage. (*b*) To lower, let down (man by rope, etc.). (*c*) To shoot down, bring down (partridge, man). (*d*) To set down (passenger).

descente [dɛsɑ̃ːt, de-], *s.f.* Descent. **1.** (*a*) Coming down, going down (from a height). *D. de cheval,* dismounting. **Mouvement de descente,** descending motion; down-stroke (of piston, etc.). S.a. GARDE² 4. (*b*) *D. à un hôtel,* putting up at a hotel. (*c*) Raid. *Faire une descente dans un pays,* to make an incursion into a country. *Jur:* **Descente sur les lieux,** visit to the scene (of a crime, etc.). *D. de police,* police raid. *Fb: Une d. des avants,* a dash by the forwards. **2.** Letting down, lowering. *Art:* **La Descente de croix,** the Descent from the Cross. **3.** (*a*) Place where sth. descends. *D. dangereuse,* dangerous hill. *Sentier en forte d.,* steep path. (*b*) **Descente de bain,** bath-mat. **Descente de lit,** (bed-side) rug. (*c*) *W.Tel:* **Descente d'antenne,** down-lead.

descriptible [deskriptibl], *a.* Describable.

descriptif, -ive [deskriptif, -iːv], *a.* Descriptive.

description [deskripsjɔ̃], *s.f.* Description. Conforme à la description, as represented.

desdits, *see* LEDIT.

déséchou|er [dezeʃwe], *v.tr. Nau:* To refloat (ship). *s.m.* **-age.** *s.m.* **-ement.**

désembarqu|er [dezɑ̃barke], *v.tr.* To put ashore, to disembark (person); to unship (goods). *s.m.* **-ement.**

désemparer [dezɑ̃pare]. **I.** *v.tr.* (*a*) *Nau:* To disable (ship). (*b*) To undo (coupling, etc.). **2.** *v.i.* **Sans désemparer,** without intermission.

désemparé, *a.* (Ship) in distress, crippled. *F: Être tout d.,* to be all at sea.

désemplir [dezɑ̃pliːr]. **1.** *v.tr.* To half-empty. **2.** *v.i. & pr. Son magasin ne (se) désemplit pas,* his shop is always full (of customers).

désenchaîner [dezɑ̃ʃene], *v.tr.* To unfetter.

désenchantement [dezɑ̃ʃɑ̃tmɑ̃], *s.m.* (*a*) Disenchantment. (*b*) Disillusion.

désenchanter [dezɑ̃ʃɑ̃te], *v.tr.* (*a*) To disenchant. (*b*) To disillusion.

désenchanteur, -eresse [dezɑ̃ʃɑ̃tœːr, -ərɛs], *a.* Disillusioning.

désencombr|er [dezɑ̃kɔ̃bre], *v.tr.* To disencumber; to clear, free (passage). *s.m.* **-ement.**

désencrasser [dezɑ̃krase], *v.tr.* To clean. *I.C.E:* To decarbonize (engine).

désenfiler [dezɑ̃file], *v.tr.* To unthread (needle); to unstring (beads, etc.). **se désenfiler,** to come unthreaded; (of beads) to come unstrung.

désenfler [dezɑ̃fle]. **1.** *v.tr.* (*a*) To reduce the swelling of (ankle, etc.). (*b*) To deflate (balloon, etc.). **2.** *v.i. & pr.* To become less swollen; (of swollen part, of tyre) to go down.

désenfumer [dezɑ̃fyme], *v.tr.* To clear (room) of smoke; to renovate (picture).

désengager [dezɑ̃gaʒe], *v.tr.* (je désengageai(s); n. désengageons) **1.** (*a*) To free (s.o.) from an obligation. (*b*) *D. sa parole,* to obtain release from a promise. **2.** To take (sth.) out of pawn. **3.** To disengage (pulley).

désengorg|er [dezɑ̃gɔrʒe], *v.tr.* (je désengorgeai(s); n. désengorgeons) To unchoke, clear (pipe, etc.). *s.m.* **-ement.**

désengouer (se) [sədezɑ̃gwe], *v.pr. F:* To get over one's infatuation (de, for).

désengren|er [dezɑ̃grəne], *v.tr.* (Conj. like ENGRENER) To disengage (toothed wheels); to throw (machine) out of gear. *s.m.* **-age.**

désenivrer [dezɑ̃nivre], *v.tr.* To sober (s.o.). **se désenivrer,** to sober off.

désennuyer [dezɑ̃nɥije], *v.tr.* (je désennuie; je désennuierai) To amuse (s.o. who is bored). **se désennuyer,** to find entertainment, diversion (à faire qch., in doing sth.).

désenrayer [dezɑ̃rɛje], *v.tr.* **1.** To release (brake, mechanism). **2.** To unscotch (wheel).

désensibilisateur, -trice [desɑ̃sibilizatœːr, -tris]. *Phot:* **1.** *a.* Desensitizing. **2.** *s.m.* Desensitizer.

désensibiliser [desɑ̃sibilize], *v.tr. Phot:* To desensitize.

désensorceler [dezɑ̃sɔrsəle], *v.tr.* (je désensorcelle; je désensorcellerai) **1.** To disenchant (sth.); to free (sth.) from a magic spell. **2.** *F:* To turn (s.o.'s) luck (at cards, etc.).

désenterrer [dezɑ̃tere], *v.tr.* To disinter (body); *F:* to dig up (old grievances, etc.).

désenthousiasmer [dezɑ̃tuzjasme], *v.tr.* To damp the enthusiasm of (s.o.). **se désenthousiasmer,** to lose one's enthusiasm.

désentortiller [dezɑ̃tɔrtije], *v.tr.* To untwist (thread, etc.); to disentangle, unravel (wool, intricate business).

désenvenimer [dezɑ̃vnime], *v.tr.* To cleanse (wound, etc.).

déséquilibrer [dezekilibre], *v.tr.* To unbalance; to throw (sth.) out of balance.

déséquilibré, *a.* **1.** Out of balance. **2.** Unbalanced (person, mind).

désert¹ [dezɛːr], *a.* **1.** Deserted, forsaken (place). **2.** Desert, uninhabited (island, etc.); lonely (spot); unfrequented (resort).

désert², *s.m.* Desert, wilderness. **Prêcher dans le désert,** to preach in the wilderness.
désert|er [dezɛrte], *v.tr.* To desert. *D. son poste,* to abandon, quit, one's post. *Abs. Soldat qui déserte,* deserter. *D. à l'ennemi,* to go over to the enemy. *s.m.* **-eur.**
désertion [dezɛrsjɔ̃], *s.f.* Desertion.
désespérance [dezɛsperɑ̃:s], *s.f. Lit:* Loss of hope; despond.
désespérant [dezɛsperɑ̃], *a.* Heart-breaking; that drives one to despair.
désespérément [dezɛsperemɑ̃], *adv.* **1.** Despairingly, hopelessly. **2.** Desperately (in love, etc.).
désespérer [dezɛspere], *v.* (**je désespère; je désespérerai**) **1.** *v.i.* To despair; to lose hope. *D. de qn,* to despair of s.o. *D. de faire qch.,* to despair of doing sth. **2.** *v.tr.* To drive (s.o.) to despair.
se désespérer, to be in despair.
désespéré, -ée. 1. *a.* Desperate. (*a*) Hopeless; to be despaired of. (*b*) *Lutte désespérée,* desperate struggle, life-and-death struggle. (*c*) Driven to despair. *F: Être d. de qch., d'apprendre qch.,* to be dreadfully sorry about sth. **2.** *s.* Desperate person. *F:* **Travailler en désespéré,** to work like mad.
désespoir [dezɛspwa:r], *s.m.* **1.** Despair. **Être au désespoir, dans le désespoir,** to be in despair. **Coup de désespoir,** act of despair. **2.** Desperation. *Réduire qn au d.,* to drive s.o. to desperation, to despair. **En désespoir de cause,** in desperation; as a last resource.
désétabl|ir [dezetabli:r], *v.tr.* To disestablish. *s.m.* **-issement.**
déshabiller [dezabije], *v.tr.* To undress (s.o.).
se déshabiller. 1. To undress; to take off one's clothes; *F:* to strip. **2.** To change into everyday garments.
déshabillé, *s.m.* **1.** Boudoir wrap, tea-gown. **2. Être en déshabillé,** to be (i) in dishabille, (ii) in undress.
déshabituer [dezabitye], *v.tr. D. qn de qch.,* to disaccustom s.o. to sth.; to break s.o. of (the habit of) doing sth.
se déshabituer. 1. To grow unused (*de,* to). **2.** To break oneself of the habit (*de,* of).
déshérence [dezerɑ̃:s], *s.f. Jur:* Default of heirs. **Tomber en déshérence,** to escheat.
déshériter [dezerite], *v.tr.* To disinherit (s.o.); to will one's property away from (s.o.). *F: Les déshérités,* the outcasts of fortune.
déshonnête [dezɔnɛt], *a.* Improper, unseemly.
déshonneur [dezɔnœ:r], *s.m.* Dishonour, disgrace. **Faire déshonneur à qn,** to disgrace s.o. **Tenir à déshonneur de . . .,** to consider it dishonourable to. . . .
déshonorant [dezɔnɔrɑ̃], *a.* Dishonouring, discreditable.
déshonorer [dezɔnɔre], *v.tr.* (*a*) To dishonour, disgrace. (*b*) To disfigure, spoil (picture, tree).
se déshonorer, to disgrace oneself.
déshydrater [dezidrate], *v.tr.* To dehydrate.
désignation [deziɲasjɔ̃], *s.f.* Designation. **1.** (*a*) Indication, pointing out (of s.o., sth.). (*b*) Description (of goods, etc.). **2.** *D. de qn pour un poste,* appointment, nomination, of s.o. to a post.
désigner [deziɲe], *v.tr.* **1.** To designate, show, indicate. *D. qch. à l'attention de qn,* to call s.o.'s attention to sth. *D. qch. du doigt,* to point sth. out. **2.** (*a*) To appoint, set, fix (day, meeting-place). *D. un fondé de pouvoir,* to nominate an agent. (*b*) *D. qn à, pour, un poste,* to appoint, nominate, s.o. to a post. *Mil: D. qn pour un service,* to detail, tell off, s.o. for a duty.

désillusion [dezillyzjɔ̃], *s.f.* Disillusion.
désillusionn|er [dezillyzjɔne], *v.tr.* To disillusion. *a.* **-ant.** *s.m.* **-ement.**
désinence [dezinɑ̃:s], *s.f. Gram:* Termination (of word); flexional ending.
désinfectant [dezɛ̃fɛktɑ̃], *a. & s.m.* Disinfectant.
désinfecter [dezɛ̃fɛkte], *v.tr.* To disinfect.
désinfection [dezɛ̃fɛksjɔ̃], *s.f.* Disinfection.
désintégration [dezɛ̃tegrasjɔ̃], *s.f.* Disintegration, breaking up; weathering (of rocks).
désintégrer [dezɛ̃tegre], *v.tr.* (**je désintègre; je désintégrerai**) To disintegrate; to split (atom).
désintéressement [dezɛ̃teresmɑ̃], *s.m.* **1.** Disinterestedness; (i) impartiality; (ii) unselfishness. **2.** Buying out (of partner); paying off (of creditor).
désintéresser [dezɛ̃terɛse], *v.tr.* To buy out (partner); to pay off (creditor).
se désintéresser *de qch.,* to take (i) no further interest, (ii) no part, in sth.
désintéressé, *a.* **1.** Not involved, not implicated. **2.** (*a*) Disinterested, unprejudiced, unbiased (advice, etc.). (*b*) Unselfish (motive).
désinviter [dezɛ̃vite], *v.tr.* To cancel an invitation to (s.o.).
désinvolte [dezɛ̃vɔlt], *a.* (*a*) Easy, free (gait). (*b*) Airy, detached, unembarrassed, unselfconscious (manner). (*c*) *F:* Cheeky (answer).
désinvolture [dezɛ̃vɔlty:r], *s.f.* (*a*) Unconstraint, unselfconsciousness; ease (of movement). (*b*) Free and easy manner; off-hand, airy, manner. (*c*) Lack of deference (towards one's elders, etc.). **Avec désinvolture,** in an off-hand manner; airily; cheekily.
désir [dezi:r], *s.m.* Desire (*de,* for); wish. *D. de plaire,* wish to please. *Ardent d. de réussir,* eagerness to succeed. **Sur, selon, le désir de son père,** at, by, his father's wish.
désirable [dezirabl], *a.* Desirable. **Peu désirable,** undesirable.
désirer [dezire], *v.tr.* To desire, want; to wish for (sth.); to be desirous of (sth.). *D. ardemment qch.,* to yearn, long, for sth. *Je désire le voir,* I want, wish, to see him. *Je désire qu'il vienne,* I want him to come. *Il est à désirer que . . .,* it is to be desired that. . . . *Cela laisse à désirer,* it is not quite satisfactory, not quite up to the mark. *Cela ne laisse rien à désirer,* it is all that one could wish for; it is quite satisfactory. *Com: Madame désire?* what can I show you, madam?
désireux, -euse [dezirø, -ø:z], *a.* Desirous (*de,* of). *D. de plaire,* anxious to please.
désistement [dezistəmɑ̃], *s.m.* Desistance (*de,* from). (*a*) Waiver (of claim); withdrawal (of suit). (*b*) Withdrawal of one's candidature.
désister (se) [sədeziste], *v.pr.* (*a*) *Se d. d'une poursuite,* to desist from, to withdraw, an action. *Se d. d'une demande,* to waive a claim. (*b*) *Abs.* to désister, to withdraw (one's candidature); to stand down.
désobéir [dezɔbei:r], *v.ind.tr. D. à qn,* to disobey s.o. *D. à une règle,* to break a rule. (May be used in the passive) *Je ne veux pas être désobéi,* I won't be disobeyed.
désobéissance [dezɔbeisɑ̃:s], *s.f.* Disobedience (*à un ordre,* of an order, *à qn,* to s.o.).
désobéissant [dezɔbeisɑ̃], *a.* Disobedient (*à,* to).
désobligeance [dezɔbliʒɑ̃:s], *s.f.* (*a*) Disobligingness. (*b*) Disagreeableness, unkindness (*envers qn,* to s.o.).
désobligeant, -ante [dezɔbliʒɑ̃, -ɑ̃:t], *a.* (*a*) Disobliging. (*b*) Disagreeable, unkind, ungracious (person, manner).
désobliger [dezɔbliʒe], *v.tr.* (**je désobligeai(s);**

n. **désobligeons**) **1.** To disoblige (s.o.); to be disobliging to (s.o.). **2.** To offend.

désobstruer [dezɔpstrye], v.tr. To clear, free, (sth.) of obstructions; to clear (pipe, etc.).

désodoriser [dezodɔrize], v.tr. = DÉODORISER.

désœuvré [dezœvre], a. (Of pers.) Unoccupied, idle; F: at a loose end. [ŒUVRE]

désœuvrement [dezœvrəmã], s.m. Idleness, leisure. Par désœuvrement, for want of something to do.

désolant [dezɔlã], a. Distressing, sad, disheartening (news, etc.).

désolation [dezɔlasjɔ̃], s.f. Desolation. **1.** (a) Devastation, laying waste. (b) Desolateness (of region, etc.). **2.** Grief, sorrow.

désoler [dezɔle], v.tr. To desolate. **1.** To devastate, ravage (country). **2.** To distress, grieve. se **désoler**, to grieve.

désolé, a. **1.** (a) Desolate, dreary (region). (b) Devastated (country). **2.** Very sorry; grieved. Nous sommes désolés d'apprendre . . ., we regret very much to hear. . . . Air d., woe-begone look.

désopilant [dezɔpilã], a. F: Screamingly funny.

désopiler (se) [sədezɔpile], v.pr. F: To shake, roar, with laughter.

désordonner [dezɔrdɔne], v.tr. To throw (sth.) into disorder, into confusion.

désordonné, a. **1.** Disordered (ranks, etc.); ill-regulated (life). Maison désordonnée, (i) untidy house; (ii) ill-managed house. **2.** Disorderly, dissolute (person, life).

désordre [dezɔrdr], s.m. **1.** (a) Disorder, confusion. Tout est en désordre, everything is in disorder. Cheveux en d., tangled, untidy, hair. Mettre le d. dans les rangs, to throw the ranks into disorder, into confusion. (b) Med: D. nerveux, nervous disorder. **2.** Disorderliness, licentiousness. **3.** pl. Disturbances, riots.

désorganisation [dezɔrganizasjɔ̃], s.f. Disorganization.

désorganiser [dezɔrganize], v.tr. To disorganize; to upset (plans).

désorientation [dezɔrjãtasjɔ̃], s.f. **1.** Confusion as to one's bearings. **2.** F: Confusion, bewilderment.

désorienter [dezɔrjãte], v.tr. **1.** To make (s.o.) lose his bearings. **2.** F: To disconcert, bewilder. **désorienté**, a. F: Puzzled, bewildered; at a loss. Je suis tout d., I am all at sea.

désormais [dezɔrmɛ], adv. Henceforth; from now on(wards); in future.

désoss|er [dezose], v.tr. To bone (meat, fish). s.m. -ement.

désoxyder [dezɔkside], v.tr. Ch: To deoxidize, deoxygenate.

despote [dɛspɔt], s.m. Despot.

despotique [dɛspɔtik], a. Despotic (power). adv. -ment, -ally.

despotisme [dɛspɔtism], s.m. Despotism.

desquamer (se) [sədɛskwame], v.pr. Med: To desquamate; to scale off, to peel.

dessaisir [desezi:r], v.tr. Jur: D. qn de qch., to disseize, dispossess, s.o. of sth. se **dessaisir** de qch., to relinquish sth.; to part with, give up, sth.

dessaler [desale], v.tr. To remove the salt from (meat, fish); to put (meat, fish) in soak. **dessalé**, a. **1.** Freed of salt. **2.** F: Wideawake, knowing (person); up to snuff.

dessangler [desãgle], v.tr. To ungirth (horse).

dess|écher [deseʃe], v.tr. (je dessèche; je dessécherai) **1.** To dry up (ground). **2.** To season (wood); to desiccate (food-stuffs). **3.** (a) (Of wind, heat) To wither (plant); to dry (the skin);

to parch (the mouth). (b) (Of illness, etc.) To waste, emaciate (the body); to wither (limb). s.m -**èchement**. se **dessécher**. **1.** To dry up. **2.** To wither; to waste away. **desséché**, a. **1.** Dry (pond, bed of torrent). **2.** Withered.

dessein [desɛ̃], s.m. **1.** Design, plan, scheme, project. Marcher sans dessein, to walk about aimlessly. **2.** Intention, purpose. Avoir le d. de faire qch., to have the intention of, to purpose, doing sth. Dans ce dessein . . ., with this intention, . . . Sans dessein, unintentionally. Avec dessein, designedly. A dessein, on purpose, intentionally, advisedly.

desseller [desɛle], v.tr. To unsaddle.

desserr|er [desɛre], v.tr. To loosen (screw); to ease, slacken (belt); to unclamp; to unscrew (nut); to unclench (fist, teeth); to release (brake). D. son étreinte, to relax one's hold. F: Je n'ai pas desserré les dents, les lèvres, I did not open my lips. s.m. -**age**. se **desserrer**. **1.** To work loose. **2.** (Of grip, etc.) To relax.

dessert[1] [desɛːr], s.m. Dessert.

dessert[2]. See DESSERVIR.

desservant[1] [desɛrvã], s.m. Ecc: Priest in charge.

desservir[1] [desɛrviːr], v.tr. (Conj. like SERVIR) **1.** Ecc: To minister to (chapel of ease, etc.). **2.** (Of railway, etc.) To serve (district).

desservir[2], v.tr. (Conj. like SERVIR) **1.** To clear (the table). Abs. To clear away. **2.** To be a bad friend to (s.o.); to do (s.o.) a disservice, an ill turn. Cela desservirait mes intérêts, it would be detrimental to my interests.

dessiccation [desikasjɔ̃], s.f. Ind: Desiccation; drying; seasoning (of wood).

dessin [desɛ̃], s.m. **1.** (a) (Art of) drawing, sketching. D. à main levée, free-hand drawing. (b) Drawing, sketch. D. à la plume, pen-and-ink sketch. Cin: D. animé, animated cartoon. **2.** Design, pattern. **3.** Tchn: (L'art du) dessin, draughtsmanship.

dessinateur, -trice [desinatœːr, -tris], s. **1.** (a) Sketcher, drawer. (b) Black-and-white artist. **2.** Designer (of wall-papers, etc.); dressdesigner. **3.** Draughtsman, -woman.

dessiner [desine], v.tr. **1.** To draw, sketch. D. qch. d'après nature, to draw sth. from nature. D. à l'encre, à la craie, to draw in ink, in chalk. **2.** To design (wall-paper, etc.); to lay out (garden). **3.** To show, delineate, outline (sth.). Vêtement qui dessine bien la taille, garment that shows off the figure. Visage bien dessiné, finely chiselled face. se **dessiner**, to stand out, take form; to be outlined. Une forme se dessina dans l'obscurité, a form loomed up in the darkness. Nos projets se dessinent, our plans are taking shape.

dessouder [desude], v.tr. **1.** To unsolder (sth.). **2.** To reopen (brazed or welded seam).

dessouler [desule]. **1.** v.tr. To sober (s.o.). **2.** v.i. & pr. To become sober; to sober off.

dessous [dəsu]. **1.** adv. Under(neath), below, beneath. Marcher bras dessus bras dessous, to walk arm-in-arm. Vêtements de dessous, under-clothing. Dents de dessous, lower teeth. En dessous, underneath; down(wards). Regarder qn en d., to look at s.o. furtively, stealthily. Agir en dessous, to act in an underhand way. S.a. SENS 4. **2.** s.m. (a) Lower part, underpart, bottom. Dessous de plat, table-mat. Dessous de bouteille, (i) bottle-mat; (ii) coaster. F: Avoir le dessous, to get the worst of it; to be defeated. Cost:

Dessous de robe, (under-)slip. (b) *Les d. de la politique,* the shady side of politics. S.a. CARTE 2. **3.** *prep. Blessure d. le sein,* wound under the breast. *Ses boucles ressortaient de dessous son chapeau,* her curls peeped out from under her hat. S.a. AU-DESSOUS, CI-DESSOUS, LÀ-DESSOUS, PAR-DESSOUS.

dessus [dəsy]. **I.** *adv.* Above, over; (up)on (it, them). *On a répandu de l'encre d.,* someone has spilt ink over it. *La terre et tout ce qu'il y a d.,* the earth and all that is thereon. *Mettre la main d.,* to lay hands on it, on them. **Dents de dessus,** upper teeth. **Vêtement de dessus,** outer garment; top garment. **Nau:** *Avoir le vent dessus,* to be aback. **En dessus,** on top; above. *I.C.E:* Soupapes en dessus, overhead valves. S.a. SENS 4. **2.** *s.m.* (a) Top, upper part (of table, etc.). **Dessus de plateau,** tray-cloth. **Dessus d'assiette,** doily. **Dessus de lit,** coverlet, bedspread. **Dessus de cheminée,** mantelpiece. **Th:** Les dessus, the flies. *F:* **Le dessus du panier,** the pick of the basket. (b) **Avoir le dessus,** to have the upper hand. **Prendre le dessus,** to rally (from illness). **Nau:** **Avoir le dessus du vent,** to have the weather-gauge. **3. De dessus,** from, off. *Tomber de d. sa chaise,* to fall off one's chair. S.a. AU-DESSUS, CI-DESSUS, LÀ-DESSUS, PAR-DESSUS.

destin [dɛstɛ̃], *s.m.* Fate, destiny.

destinataire [dɛstinatɛːr], *s.m. & f.* Addressee (of letter); consignee (of goods); payee (of money order).

destination [dɛstinasjɔ̃], *s.f.* **1.** Destination. *Ce paquet est à votre destination,* this parcel is addressed to you. **Trains à destination de Paris,** trains for, (running) to, Paris. *Navire à d. de Bordeaux,* ship bound for Bordeaux. **2.** Intended purpose (of building, sum of money, etc.).

destinée [dɛstine], *s.f.* **1.** (a) Destiny. **Unir sa destinée à celle de qn,** (i) to throw in one's lot with s.o.; (ii) to marry s.o. (b) *pl.* Destinies, fortunes. **2.** = DESTIN.

destiner [dɛstine], *v.tr.* **1.** To destine. *Destiné à mourir sur l'échafaud,* destined, fated, doomed, to die on the scaffold. **2.** (a) *D. qch. à qn,* to intend, mean, sth. for s.o. *La balle vous était destinée,* the bullet was aimed at you. (b) *Il avait destiné son fils au barreau,* he had intended his son for the bar. (c) *D. une somme d'argent à un achat,* to assign a sum of money to a purchase. **se destiner** *à qch.,* to intend to take up sth. (as a profession).

destituer [dɛstitɥe], *v.tr.* To dismiss, discharge (s.o.); to remove (official) from office.

destitué, *a.* Deprived (*de,* of); lacking (*de,* in); without.

destitution [dɛstitysjɔ̃], *s.f.* Dismissal (of official, etc.).

destrier [dɛstri(j)e], *s.m.* A: (Battle-)steed.

destructeur, -trice [dɛstryktœːr, -tris]. **I.** *a.* Destroying (agent); destructive (child, war). **2.** *s.* Destroyer, destructor.

destructible [dɛstryktibl], *a.* Destructible.

destructif, -ive [dɛstryktif, -iːv], *a.* Destructive.

destruction [dɛstryksjɔ̃], *s.f.* Destruction, destroying.

désuet, -ète [desɥɛ, -ɛt], *a.* Obsolete (word); antiquated, out-of-date (theory).

désuétude [desɥetyd], *s.f.* Disuse, desuetude. **Tomber en d.,** to fall into disuse; (of right, etc.) to lapse; (of law) to fall into abeyance. *Mot tombé en d.,* obsolete word.

désunion [dezynjɔ̃], *s.f.* Disunion (of people, etc.); disconnection (of parts, etc.).

désunir [dezyniːr], *v.tr.* To disunite, divide (people); to disjoin, disconnect (parts, etc.). **se désunir. 1.** To become disunited, estranged. **2.** (Of parts) To come asunder; to work loose.

désuni, *a.* (Of people) Disunited, at variance; (of parts, etc.) disjoined, disconnected.

détachant [detaʃɑ̃]. **I.** *a.* Stain-removing. **2.** *s.m.* Stain-remover.

détachement [detaʃmɑ̃], *s.m.* **1.** Detaching, cutting off (of sth.). **2.** Indifference (*de,* to); lack of interest (*de,* in); detachment (*de,* from). **Détachement de ce monde,** otherworldliness, unworldliness. **3.** *Mil:* Detachment, draft (of troops). *D. de corvée,* fatigue party.

détacher[1] [detaʃe], *v.tr.* To detach. (a) To (un)loose, to unfasten, untie, unbind, unlash; to uncouple (truck); to untether (horse); to unhook (curtain). *F: Je ne peux pas en d. mes yeux,* I cannot take my eyes off it. (b) To separate, disjoin (*de,* from); to cut off, pull off, break off, bite off, saw off, chisel off. *D. un chèque du carnet,* to tear out a cheque from the book. *D. qn de ses amis,* to detach, alienate, s.o. from his friends. (c) *D. une compagnie d'un bataillon,* to detach a company from a battalion. *D. un officier auprès de qn,* to detach an officer to serve with s.o. *Être détaché à un autre service,* to be seconded to another branch. (d) *F:* **Détacher un coup à qn,** to hit out at s.o. (Of horse) *D. une ruade,* to fling out. **se détacher. 1.** (a) (Of knot, etc.) To come undone, unfastened, loose. (b) (Of animal) To break loose. **2.** To break off, break loose, become detached; (of parts) to come apart. *Un bouton s'est détaché,* a button has come off. *Se d. de sa famille,* to separate, break away, from one's family. *Se d. des rangs,* to step forward from the ranks. **3.** *Se d. sur le fond,* to stand out against the background.

détaché, *a.* **1.** (a) Loose, detached (part); untethered (horse, etc.). (b) Isolated (farm, etc.). **2.** Detached, unconcerned (manner, etc.).

détacher[2], *v.tr.* To remove stains, spots, from (clothing, etc.). *s.m.* **-age.**

détail [detaːj], *s.m.* **1.** (a) Dividing up, cutting up (of cloth, meat). (b) *Com:* Retail. **Vendre au détail,** to sell (goods) retail. **Marchand au détail,** retailer. **2.** Detail. *Donner tous les détails,* to go into all the details. *Le d. d'un compte,* the items of an account. **3.** *Adm: Mil:* (a) Internal economy. **Service de détail,** executive duties. (b) Special duty.

détaillant, -ante [detajɑ̃, -ɑ̃ːt], *s.* Retailer.

détailler [detaje], *v.tr.* **1.** (a) To divide up, cut up (piece of stuff, side of beef, etc.). (b) To retail (goods). **2.** To detail, enumerate; to relate in detail; to itemize (account).

détaler [detale], *v.i.* To decamp, to take oneself off, to scamper away.

détartrer [detartre], *v.tr.* **1.** To scale, fur (boiler). **2.** *I.C.E:* To decarbonize (engine). *s.m.* **-age.**

détecteur [detɛktœːr]. **I.** *s.m. El:* W.Tel: etc: Detector. El.E: *D. de fuites,* fault-finder. **2.** *a.* (With *f.* **détectrice**) *W.Tel:* Lampe détectrice, detecting valve.

détection [detɛksjɔ̃], *s.f.* W.Tel: Detection.

détective [detɛktiːv], *s.m.* **1.** (English) detective. **2.** *Phot:* Box-camera.

déteign-ais, -ant, -is, etc. See DÉTEINDRE.

déteindre [detɛ̃ːdr], *v.* (Conj. like TEINDRE) **1.** *v.tr.* To take the colour out of (sth.). **2.** *v.i. & pr.* (a) To fade, to lose colour. (b) (Of colour) *Se d. au lavage,* to run in the wash.

dételer [detle], *v.tr.* (je **dételle**; je **détellerai**)
1. (*a*) To unharness. (*b*) To unhitch, take out
(horse(s)); to unyoke (oxen). **2.** *Rail:* To
uncouple (trucks, etc.). *s.m.* **-age.**
détendre [detã:dr], *v.tr.* **1.** To slacken, relax,
loosen (sth. that is taut); to unbend (bow).
D. l'esprit, (i) to relax, give relaxation to, the
mind; (ii) to calm the mind. **2.** To unhang,
take down (curtains). **3.** *Mch:* **Détendre la
vapeur,** to expand, cut off, the steam.
   se détendre. 1. To become slack; to
slacken, relax. *Son visage se détendit dans un
sourire,* his face relaxed into a smile. *Le temps se
détend,* the weather is becoming milder. *La
situation se détend,* the situation is easing. **2.** (Of
steam) To expand.
   détendu, *a.* Slack.
détenir [detni:r], *v.tr.* (Conj. like TENIR) **1.** To
hold, to be in possession of (sth.). *D. le record,*
to hold the record. **2.** (*a*) To detain (s.o.); to
keep (s.o.) prisoner. (*b*) To withhold, keep back
(property, etc.).
   détenu, -e, *s.* Prisoner. *Prison des jeunes
détenus,* reformatory.
détente [detã:t], *s.f.* **1.** (*a*) Relaxation, loosening,
slackening (of sth. that is taut); relaxing (of
muscles). (*b*) Easing (of political situation). *D. du
temps,* mild spell of weather. (*c*) *Sm.a:* Pull-off
(of trigger). **Arme dure à la détente,** fire-arm
hard on the trigger. *F:* **Personne dure à la
détente,** close-fisted, stingy, person. **2.** (*a*) Expansion (of steam, of gases). **Machine à détente,**
expansion steam-engine. *D. triple,* triple expansion. (*b*) *I.C.E:* Explosion stroke, power stroke.
3. Trigger (of gun).
détenteur, -trice [detãtœ:r, -tris], *s.* **1.** (*a*)
Holder (of securities, challenge cup, record).
D. de titres, stockholder. (*b*) Owner (of copyright,
etc.). **2.** Withholder (of property, etc.).
détention [detãsjɔ̃], *s.f.* **1.** Holding (of securities). **2.** Detention, imprisonment, confinement
(of s.o.). **Maison de détention,** house of detention. **3.** Withholding (of property, etc.).
détérioration [deterjɔrasjɔ̃], *s.f.* **1.** Deterioration. **2.** *pl. Jur:* (i) Dilapidations; damage (to
property); (ii) wear and tear.
détériorer [deterjɔre], *v.tr.* To make (sth.)
worse; to spoil, damage.
   se détériorer, to deteriorate; to spoil.
déterminant [determinã]. **1.** *a.* Determinant,
determinative. **2.** *s.m. Mth:* Determinant.
déterminatif, -ive [determinatif, -i:v], *a. & s.m.*
Determinative (word, etc.).
détermination [determinasjɔ̃], *s.f.* **1.** Determination (of species, date, area, etc.). **2.** Determination, fixity of purpose. **3.** Resolve. *Prendre
une d.,* to make up one's mind.
déterminer [determine], *v.tr.* **1.** To determine
(species, noun, etc.); to fix, settle (meeting-
place). **2.** To cause; to give rise to (sth.); to
bring (sth.) about. **3.** (*a*) *D. de faire qch.,* to
resolve, decide, to do sth. (*b*) *D. qn à faire qch.,*
to induce, move, s.o. to do sth.
   se déterminer, to determine, to make up
one's mind (*à faire qch.,* to do sth.).
   déterminé, *a.* **1.** Determined, definite, well-
defined; specific, particular (aim). *Dans un sens
d.,* in a given direction. **2.** (*a*) Determined,
resolute. (*b*) *Être d. à faire qch.,* to be resolved,
determined, to do sth.
déterrer [detɛre], *v.tr.* To dig up, unearth
(buried treasure, etc.); to bring (sth.) to light;
to exhume, disinter (corpse).

détestable [detɛstabl], *a.* Detestable, hateful;
execrable (work, weather). *adv.* **-ment.**
détestation [detɛstasjɔ̃], *s.f.* Detestation.
détester [detɛste], *v.tr.* To detest, hate. *Je
déteste être dérangé,* I hate to be disturbed. **Se
faire détester de tous, par tout le monde,** to get
oneself disliked by everyone.
détirer [detire], *v.tr.* To stretch (linen, etc.).
détonant [detɔnã]. **1.** *a.* Detonating, explosive.
2. *s.m.* Explosive.
détonateur [detɔnatœ:r], *s.m.* Detonator. *Rail:*
Fog-signal.
détonation [detɔnasjɔ̃], *s.f.* (*a*) Detonation.
(*b*) Report (of fire-arm).
détoner [detɔne], *v.i.* To detonate, explode.
Faire détoner, to detonate (dynamite, etc.).
détonner [detɔne], *v.i.* (*a*) To be, play, sing, out
of tune. (*b*) (Of colours) To jar, clash.
détordre [detɔrdr], *v.tr.* To untwist (yarn, etc.);
to unlay (rope).
   se détordre, to come untwisted.
détortiller [detɔrtije], *v.tr.* **1.** To untwist.
(*b*) To disentangle. (*c*) To unwrap (mummy).
détour [detu:r], *s.m.* **1.** Turning, deviation (from
direct way); roundabout way, circuitous way.
Faire un détour, to go a roundabout way. *Faire
un long d.,* to go a long way round. **Sans détour(s),**
plainly, frankly. *Répondre sans détours,* to give a
plain, straightforward, answer. **2.** Turn, curve,
bend (in road, river). *Suivre tous les détours du
fleuve,* to follow all the windings of the river.
détournement [deturnəmã], *s.m.* **1.** Diversion
(of watercourse, etc.). **2.** (*a*) Misappropriation
(of funds); embezzlement. (*b*) Abduction.
détourner [deturne], *v.tr.* **1.** (*a*) To divert
(watercourse, etc.); to turn (weapon) aside.
D. l'attention de qn, to divert s.o.'s attention.
D. de son devoir, to seduce, entice, s.o. from
his duty. *D. qn de la bonne voie,* to lead s.o. astray.
D. la conversation, to turn, change, the conversation. *D. les soupçons,* to avert suspicion. (*b*) To
turn away, avert (one's eyes, etc.). *S.a.* REGARD I.
2. To misappropriate, embezzle (funds).
   se détourner, to turn away, turn aside (*de,*
from).
   détourné, *a.* **1.** Indirect, circuitous, roundabout (road). *Chemin d.,* by-road. **2.** Unfrequented, secluded (locality, etc.).
détracteur, -trice [detraktœ:r, -tris], *s.* Detractor, disparager.
détraquement [detrakmã], *s.m.* (*a*) Putting (of
mechanism, etc.) out of order. (*b*) Breakdown (of
mechanism, health, etc.).
détraquer [detrake], *v.tr.* To put (apparatus)
out of order; to throw (mechanism) out of gear.
Son intervention a tout détraqué, his intervention
has upset everything. *Se d. l'estomac, les nerfs,*
to wreck one's digestion, one's nerves.
   se détraquer, (of mechanism, digestion)
to get out of order; (of health) to break down.
détrempe [detrã:p], *s.f.* (*a*) *Art:* Distemper
(-painting). (*b*) *Paint:* Distemper, size-colouring.
détremper[1] [detrã:pe], *v.tr.* To moisten, soak
(sth.). *D. la chaux,* to slake lime. *Champ détrempé,*
sodden, soppy, field.
détremper[2], *v.tr.* To anneal, soften (steel).
   se détremper, (of steel) to lose its temper.
détresse [detrɛs], *s.f.* Distress. **1.** Grief, anguish.
2. (*a*) (Financial) straits, difficulties. (*b*) Esp.
Nau: Danger. **Navire en détresse,** ship in
distress, in difficulties. **Signal de détresse,** distress
signal; *F:* S O S.
détresser [detrɛse], *v.tr.* To unbraid, unplait.
détriment [detrimã], *s.m.* Detriment, loss. **Au**

détriment de qn, to the detriment, prejudice, of s.o. *Je l'ai appris à mon d.,* I found it out to my cost.

détritus [detrity:s], *s.m.* (*a*) Detritus (of rock, etc.). (*b*) Rubbish. (*c*) Refuse.

détroit [detrwa],*s.m. Ph. Geog:* **1.** Strait, straits, sound. **2.** (Mountain) pass.

détromper [detrɔ̃pe], *v.tr.* To undeceive.

détrôn|er [detrone], *v.tr.* **1.** To dethrone. **2.** *F:* To supersede (method, etc.). *s.m.* **-ement.**

détrousser [detruse], *v.tr.* **1.** To untuck, let down (one's sleeves, etc.). **2.** To rob (s.o.) on the highway ; to rifle (s.o.'s) pockets.

détrousseur, -euse [detrusœ:r, -ø:z], *s.* Highwayman, footpad.

détruire [detrɥi:r], *v.tr.* (*pr.p.* **détruisant** ; *p.p.* **détruit** ; *pr.ind.* **je détruis, n. détruisons** ; *p.d.* **je détruisais** ; *p.h.* **je détruisis** ; *fu.* **je détruirai**) **1.** (*a*) To demolish, pull down (building, etc.) ; to overthrow (empire, etc.). (*b*) To break up (old ship, etc.). **2.** To destroy, ruin.

dette [dɛt], *s.f.* Debt. **Faire des dettes,** to run into debt. **Avoir des dettes,** to be in debt. **Être perdu, criblé, accablé, de dettes ; avoir des dettes par-dessus la tête,** to be head over ears in debt. **Dettes actives,** book-debts ranking as assets. **Dettes passives,** liabilities. **La Dette publique,** the National Debt. *D. sacrée envers la patrie,* sacred duty towards one's country. *F:* **Payer sa dette à la nature,** to pay one's debt to nature. S.a. HONNEUR 1, JEU 4.

deuil [dœ:j], *s.m.* **1.** (*a*) Mourning, sorrow (for the loss of s.o.). *F:* **Faire son deuil de qch.,** to give sth. up as lost. (*b*) Bereavement. **2.** (*a*) Mourning (clothes, etc.). **Grand deuil,** deep mourning. **Demi-deuil,** half-mourning. **Se mettre en deuil,** to go into mourning. **Être en deuil de qn,** to be in mourning for s.o. **Quitter le deuil,** to go out of mourning. (*b*) Funeral procession. **Conduire le deuil,** to be chief mourner.

deux [dø ; before a vowel sound in the same word group, døz], *num.a.inv. & s.m.* Two. *Deux enfants* [døzɑ̃fɑ̃], two children. *Charles Deux,* Charles the Second. *Il est arrivé d. ou troisième,* he arrived second or third. *Chapitre d.,* chapter two. *F:* **C'est clair comme deux et deux font quatre,** it's as plain as a pikestaff. **Deux fois,** twice. **Tous (les) deux,** both. *Des d. côtés du fleuve,* on either side of the river. **Tous les deux jours, de deux jours l'un,** every other day ; on alternate days. *F:* **C'est entre les deux,** it is betwixt and between. **Casser qch. en deux,** to break sth. in two. *Diviser, couper, une ligne en d.,* to bisect a line. **Marcher deux par deux,** to walk two and two, in pairs. **Entrer deux par deux,** to come in two by two. **Entre deux âges,** of uncertain age. *Voiture à d. chevaux,* two-horse carriage. **A nous deux maintenant !** now we two will have it out ! *Ten:* A deux, deuce. A deux de jeu, five (games) all. **Il fera ça en moins de deux,** he will do it in two ticks. **C'est à deux pas d'ici,** it is close at hand. S.a. EAU 2, MOT, SOU.

deuxième [døzjɛm], *num. a. & s.* Second. *Appartement au d.* (*étage*), flat on the second floor. *Équation du deuxième degré,* quadratic equation. *adv.* **-ment.**

deux-mâts, *s.m.* Two-masted vessel.

deux-pièces, *s.m.* (Lady's) two-piece suit.

deux-points, *s.m.* Colon.

dévaler [devale]. **1.** *v.i.* To descend, go down ; (of stream) to rush down. **2.** *v.tr. D. la colline, l'escalier,* to hurry down the hill, the stairs. *D. la rue à toute vitesse,* to race down the street. [VAL]

dévaliser [devalize], *v.tr.* To rob (s.o. of his money, etc.). *D. une maison,* to rifle, *F:* burgle, a house. [VALISE]

dévaliseur, -euse [devalizœ:r, -ø:z], *s.* Robber. *D. de maisons, F:* burglar.

dévalorisation [devalɔrizasjɔ̃], *s.f.* **1.** Devaluation (of currency). **2.** *Com:* Fall in value.

dévaloriser [devalɔrize], *v.tr.* To devaluate (currency).

devanc|er [d(ə)vɑ̃se], *v.tr.* (je **devançai**(s); n. **devançons**) **1.** To precede ; to go or come before (s.o., sth.). **2.** To leave (the others) behind ; to outdistance, overtake, outstrip. *Je vous ai devancé,* (i) I got here before you ; (ii) I anticipated, forestalled, you. *D. son époque,* to be ahead of one's times. **3.** To forestall. *D. les désirs de qn,* to anticipate s.o.'s desires. *s.m.* **-ement.**

devancier, -ière [d(ə)vɑ̃sje, -jɛ:r], *s.* (*a*) Precursor. (*b*) Predecessor.

devant[1] [d(ə)vɑ̃]. **1.** *prep.* Before, in front of (s.o., sth.). *Marchez tout droit d. vous,* go straight ahead. *Être courageux d. le danger,* to be courageous in the face of danger. *Égaux d. la loi,* equal in the eyes of the law. *Vaisseau d. Calais,* ship off Calais. *D. cet état de choses . . .,* in view of this state of affairs. *. . .* **2.** *adv.* Before, in front. **Aller devant,** to go in front ; to lead the way. **Porter qch. sens devant derrière,** to wear sth. back side foremost, back to front. **Un navire devant !** ship ahead ! *Nau:* **Être pris devant,** to be taken aback. **Saisir qch. par devant,** to seize sth. in front. *F: Il revint plus effaré que d.,* he came back more scared than before. S.a. GROSJEAN. **3.** *s.m.* Front (part), fore-part ; breast (of coat). **Devant de chemise,** shirt front. **Devant de cheminée,** fire-screen. **Chambre sur le devant,** front-room. **Dents de devant,** front teeth. **Prendre les devants,** to go on ahead. **Gagner les devants,** to take the lead. S.a. AU-DEVANT, CI-DEVANT.

devant[2]. See DEVOIR.

devanture [d(ə)vɑ̃ty:r], *s.f.* (*a*) Front(age) (of building). (*b*) *D. de magasin,* shop-front, shop-window.

dévastateur, -trice [devastatœ:r, -tris]. **1.** *s.* Devastator, ravager. **2.** *a.* Devastating.

dévastation [devastasjɔ̃], *s.f.* Devastation.

dévaster [devaste], *v.tr.* To lay waste, to ravage ;

déveine [devɛn], *s.f. F:* (Run of) ill-luck. **Avoir la déveine, être en déveine, dans la déveine,** to be out of luck, down on one's luck. [VEINE]

développement [devlɔpmã], *s.m.* **1.**(*a*) Spreading out (of wings, of folded paper). (*b*) *Alg:* Expansion (of contracted expression). *Geom:* Evolution (of curve). **2.**(*a*) Spread (of branches) ; length (of road, etc.). (*b*) Bicyclette avec un d. de 5 m. 25, bicycle geared to 66 inches. **3.** Development, growth (of the body) ; development (of flower, faculties, *Phot:* of image).

développer [devlɔpe],*v.tr.* **1.**(*a*) To spread out, open out (wings, etc.) ; to stretch out (arm) ; to unroll (map) ; to unwrap, undo (parcel). (*b*) *Alg:* To expand (contracted expression). *Geom: D. un cube,* to develop a cube. (*c*) *Bicyclette qui développe . . .,* bicycle that is geared to . . . **2.** To develop (muscles, faculties, *Phot:* a negative). *D. un projet,* to work out a plan.

se développer. 1. To spread out, open out. **2.** (Of organs, the intelligence, etc.) To develop.

développée, *s.f. Geom:* Evolute (curve).

devenir [dəvni:r], *v.pred.* (Conj. like VENIR. Aux. être) (*a*) To become. *Il devint général,* he became a general. *Qu'est-il devenu ?* what has become of him ? (*b*) To grow into. *C'était devenu un beau gars,* he had grown into a fine young fellow. (c) D. grand, (i) to grow tall ; (ii) to grow up. D. vieux, to grow, get, old. D. blanc de rage, to go, turn, white with rage. Il devint agriculteur, he turned farmer. C'est à devenir fou! it is enough to drive one mad !

dévergondage [devɛrgɔ̃da:ʒ], s.m. Licentiousness, profligacy.

dévergonder (se) [sədevɛrgɔ̃de], v.pr. To fall into dissolute ways.

dévergondé, -ée. 1. a. Licentious, profligate, shameless. **2.** s. Profligate.

dévernir [devɛrni:r], v.tr. To take the varnish, the polish, off (sth.).

déverrouiller [deveruje], v.tr. To unbolt.

devers [dəvɛ:r], prep. (a) A : Towards. (b) Prep. phr. Par devers. (i) Retenir ses papiers par d. soi, to keep papers in one's possession. (ii) A. Par d. les juges, in the presence of the judges.

dévers [devɛ:r]. **1.** a. Warped (timber, etc.); out of true. **2.** s.m. (a) Inclination, slope ; banking (of road at a bend). (b) Warp, twist (in timber).

déversement¹ [devɛrs(ə)mã], s.m. = DÉVERS 2.

déversement², s.m. Discharge, overflow (of liquid) ; tipping (of cart). Lieu de déversement, dump.

déverser¹ [devɛrse]. **1.** v.tr. (a) To slope, slant (wall) ; to bank (road). (b) To warp (timber). **2.** v.i. & pr. (a) To lean ; to get out of plumb. (b) To warp.

déversé, a. **1.** Sloping. **2.** Lopsided.

déverser², v.tr. **1.** To divert (channel). **2.** To pour, discharge (water) ; to tip, dump (material). **se déverser,** to flow, pour (dans, into).

déversoir [devɛrswa:r], s.m. Overflow ; wasteweir ; outfall.

dévêtir [devɛti:r], v.tr. (Conj. like VÊTIR) (a) To undress, strip (s.o.) ; to unrobe (s.o.). (b) To take off (garment).
se dévêtir. 1. (a) To undress, strip ; to unrobe. (b) To leave off some of one's clothing. **2.** Se d. de son bien, to divest oneself of one's property.

déviation [devjasjɔ̃], s.f. Deviation (de, from) ; variation (of compass) ; curvature (of the spine).

dévid|er [devide], v.tr. (a) To unwind. (b) To reel off (thread, etc.). F: Il me dévida toute l'histoire, he reeled off the whole story to me. s.m. -age. s. -eur, -euse.

dévidoir [devidwa:r], s.m. (a) Reeling machine. (b) Hose-reel ; El.E: drum (for cable).

dévier [devje]. **1.** v.i. To deviate, swerve, diverge (de, from). Faire dévier une balle, to deflect a bullet. **2.** v.tr. To turn (blow, etc.) aside ; to deflect (ray, etc.) ; Surg: to abduct (organ).
se dévier, (of the spine, etc.) to become, grow, crooked ; (of timber) to warp.

dévié, a. Route déviée, loop-way. Rayon d., refracted ray.

devin [dəvɛ̃], s.m. A: Soothsayer. F: Je ne suis pas devin, I'm not a wizard.

deviner [d(ə)vine], v.tr. To guess (riddle, etc.) ; to predict (the future). Je lui devine de l'intelligence, I should say he has intelligence. F: Cela se devine, that's obvious.

devinette [d(ə)vinɛt], s.f. Riddle, conundrum.

devis [dəvi], s.m. Estimate (of work to be done) ; specification ; bill of quantities.

dévisager [devizaʒe], v.tr. (je dévisageai(s) ; n. dévisageons) To stare at (s.o.).

devise [dəvi:z], s.f. **1.** (a) Her: Device. (b) Motto. (c) F: Slogan. (d) Nau: Name (of ship). **2.** Fin: Currency. Esp. Devises étrangères, foreign bills.

deviser [dəvize], v.i. To chat, gossip.

déviss|er [devise], v.tr. To unscrew (bolt, nut) ; to screw out (breech-block). s.m. -age.
se dévisser, to come unscrewed.

dévoiement [devwamã], s.m. **1.** Canting, tilting. **2.** Diverting (of flue). **3.** Diarrhoea.

dévoiler [devwale], v.tr. **1.** To unveil. **2.** To reveal, disclose (secret) ; to unmask (conspiracy).

devoir [dəvwa:r]. I. v.tr. (pr.p. devant ; p.p. dû, f. due ; pr.ind. je dois, n. devons, ils doivent; p.d. je devais ; p.h. je dus ; fu. je devrai) **1.** (Duty) Should, ought. (a) (General precept) Tu dois honorer tes parents, you should honour your parents. Il refusa comme faire se devait, he very properly refused. Fais ce que dois, advienne que pourra, do your duty come what may. (b) (Command) Vous devez, devrez, vous trouver à votre poste à trois heures, you must be at your post at three o'clock. (c) Je ne savais pas ce que je devais faire, I did not know what (I ought) to do. Vous devriez lire Dickens, you ought to read Dickens. Il aurait dû m'avertir, he should have warned me. Il crut devoir se retirer, (i) he thought it his duty to retire, (ii) he deemed it advisable to retire. **2.** (Compulsion) Must, have to. Tous les hommes doivent mourir, all men must die. Enfin j'ai dû, je dus, céder, at last I had to yield. **3.** (Futurity) Am to. (a) Je dois partir demain, I am to start to-morrow. Je devais venir, mais . . ., I was to have come, but. . . . Dût-il m'en coûter la vie, were I to die for it. Dussé-je, quand je devrais, tout perdre, even though I were to lose everything. (b) Il ne devait plus les revoir, he was (destined) never to see them again. Cela devait être, it was meant to be. **4.** (Opinion expressed) Must. Vous devez avoir faim, you must be hungry. Il dut, a dû, avait dû, me prendre pour un autre, he must have taken me for someone else. Il doit y avoir beaucoup de gens qui . . ., there must be many people who. . . . **5.** Devoir qch. à qn, to owe s.o. sth. Tout l'argent qui m'est dû, all the money owing to me. Il doit de tous les côtés, he owes money all round. Est-ce à vous que je dois cela? am I indebted to you for that? Je dois à mes amis de leur éviter ce chagrin, I owe it to my friends to spare them this sorrow. La peine due à ces forfaits, the penalties which these crimes deserve.
II. devoir, s.m. **1.** (a) Duty. Manquer à son devoir, to fail in one's duty. S.a. INFRACTION, MANQUEMENT. Rentrer dans le devoir, (of mutineers, etc.) to return to duty. Faire, remplir, son devoir envers qn, to do one's duty by s.o. Se faire un devoir de faire qch., to make a point of doing sth. Se mettre en devoir de faire qch., to prepare to do sth. Il est de mon devoir de . . ., it is my duty to. . . . (b) Sch: Exercise, task. Un devoir de latin, a Latin exercise. Je n'ai pas encore fait mes devoirs, I haven't done my home-work yet. **2.** pl. Rendre ses devoirs à qn, to pay one's respects to s.o. Mes devoirs à madame votre mère, my duty to your mother. Rendre à qn les derniers devoirs, to pay the last honours to s.o.

dû, due. I. a. Due. (a) Owing. En port dû, carriage forward. (b) Proper. En temps dû, in due course. Contrat rédigé en bonne et due forme, contract drawn up in due form. **2.** s.m. Due. F: A chacun son dû, give the devil his due.

dévolt|er [devɔlte], v.tr. El.E: To step down (current). s.m. -age. [VOLT]

dévolteur [devɔltœ:r], s.m. El.E: Step-down transformer.

dévolu [devɔly]. **1.** a. Jur: Devolved ; devolving (d, to, upon). **2.** s.m. F: Jeter son dévolu sur qch.,

(i) to have designs on sth.; (ii) to lay claim to sth.; (iii) to choose sth.

dévolution [devɔlysjɔ̃], s.f. Jur: (a) Devolution, transmission (of property). (b) Ecc: Lapsing (of benefice).

dévorant [devɔrɑ̃], a. Ravenous (wolf, etc.); consuming (fire, thirst); devouring (passion).

dévorateur, -trice [devɔratœːr, -tris]. **1.** s. Devourer. **2.** a. Devouring, consuming.

dévorer [devɔre], v.tr. To devour. D. qn des yeux, to devour s.o. with one's eyes; to gaze intently on s.o. Les flammes ont dévoré le bâtiment, the flames consumed the building. La soif me dévore, I am consumed with thirst. D. la route, to tear along; to eat up the miles.

dévot, -ote [devo, -ɔt]. **1.** a. Devout, religious. Être dévot à un saint, to be a votary of a saint. F: Être d. à la bouteille, to be addicted to the bottle. **2.** s. Devout person. **Faux dévot,** hypocrite. adv. **-ement.**

dévotion [devosjɔ̃, -vɔ-], s.f. Devotion; esp. devoutness, piety. **Tomber, se jeter, dans la dévotion,** to take to religion. Tableau de d., religious picture. **Faire ses dévotions,** to make one's devotions.

dévouement [devumɑ̃], s.m. **1.** Self-sacrifice; devotion to duty. **2.** Devotion, devotedness. Servir qn avec d., to serve s.o. devotedly. Croyez, monsieur, à mon entier d., I am yours obediently.

dévouer [devwe], v.tr. **1.** To dedicate, consecrate (s.o., sth.) (d, to). **2.** To devote, sacrifice (one's energy to a cause, etc.).
 se dévouer. **1.** To devote oneself, dedicate oneself. Se d. au secours des pauvres, to devote oneself to the poor. **2.** Se d. pour qn, to sacrifice oneself for s.o.
 dévoué, a. Devoted, staunch, loyal (friend, etc.). **Votre tout dévoué,** yours faithfully; (more intimately) yours sincerely.

dévoyer [devwaje], v.tr. (je dévoie; je dévoierai) **1.** To mislead; to lead (s.o.) astray. **2.** To give (s.o.) diarrhoea. [VOIE]
 se dévoyer, to go astray; to stray (from the path of duty).

devr-a, -ai, -as, etc. See DEVOIR.

déwatté [dewate], a. El: Wattless (current).

dextérité [deksterite], s.f. Dexterity, skill (d, in).

diabète [djabɛt], s.m. Med: Diabetes.

diabétique [djabetik], a. & s. Diabetic (subject).

diable [djɑːbl], s.m. **1.** Devil. F: **Faire le diable,** to be noisy, to romp. **Faire le diable à quatre,** to kick up a shindy. **Tirer le diable par la queue,** to be hard up. **Du diable si je le sais!** hanged, blowed, if I know! **Allez au diable!** go to blazes! **Que le diable l'emporte!** the devil take him! confound him! **Il demeure au diable,** he lives miles away. **Aller au diable vauvert, au diable auvert, au diable au vert,** to go a long way; to disappear. C'est au d. auvert, it's miles from anywhere. **C'est le diable pour lui faire entendre raison,** it is the very deuce to make him see reason. **Ce n'est pas le diable,** (i) it is not so very difficult; (ii) it is nothing to worry about. Où d. est-il allé? where the devil has he gone? **Bruit de tous les diables,** devil of a din. **A la diable,** anyhow; in a harum-scarum sort of way. **Pauvre diable!** poor beggar! Un grand d., a big, strapping, fellow. C'est un bon d., he is not a bad fellow. **Ce diable de parapluie,** that wretched umbrella. **Quelle diable de langue que l'anglais!** English is a devilish language! a. **Il est très diable,** he is full of fun, of mischief. **Il n'est pas aussi diable qu'il est noir,** he is not so black as he is painted. S.a. AVOCAT 2, BEAUTÉ 1, CORPS 1.

2. (a) (Two-wheeled) trolley; (railway porter's) barrow, truck. (b) Toys: **Diable (à ressort).** Jack-in-the-box. (c) Ich: Angler-fish.

diablement [djɑbləmɑ̃], adv. F: Devilish, awfully (funny, difficult, etc.).

diablerie [djɑblərï], s.f. **1.** A: Devilry, sorcery. **2.** F: Mischievousness, fun.

diablesse [djɑbles], s.f. F: **1.** She-devil. **2. Une grande diablesse de paysanne,** a great strapping peasant-woman.

diablotin [djɑblɔtɛ̃], s.m. **1.** Little devil; imp. **2.** (Christmas) cracker.

diabolique [djabɔlik], a. Diabolical, fiendish. adv. **-ment.**

diacre [djakr], s.m. Ecc: Deacon.

diacritique [diakritik, dja-], a. **1.** Ling: Diacritic(al) (sign). Signe d., diacritic. **2.** Med: Characteristic (symptom).

diadème [djadɛm], s.m. Diadem.

diagnostic [djagnɔstik], s.m. Med: Diagnosis.

diagnostique [djagnɔstik], a. Med: Diagnostic.

diagnostiquer [djagnɔstike], v.tr. Med: To diagnose.

diagonal, -aux [djagɔnal, -o]. **1.** a. Diagonal. **2.** s.f. Diagonale, diagonal (line). **En diagonale,** diagonally. adv. **-ement.**

diagramme [djagram], s.m. Diagram.

dialectal, -aux [djalɛktal, -o], a. Dialectal.

dialecte [djalɛkt], s.m. Dialect.

dialogue [djalɔg], s.m. Dialogue.

dialoguer [djalɔge], v.i. To hold a dialogue; to converse.

diamant [djamɑ̃], s.m. Diamond. D. de première eau, diamond of the first water. D. brut, rough diamond. Tls: D. de vitrier, glazier's diamond.

diamanté [djamɑ̃te], a. Set with diamonds.

diamétral, -aux [djametral, -o], a. Diametrical. adv. **-ement.**

diamètre [djametr], s.m. Diameter. La roue a 60 cm. de d., the wheel is 60 cm. in diameter.

diane¹ [djan], s.f. Mil: Reveille. **Battre, sonner, la diane,** to sound the reveille. Navy: **Coup de canon de diane,** morning-gun.

Diane². Pr.n.f. Diana.

diantre [djɑ̃ːtr], int. A. & Lit: (Softened form of DIABLE) Que diantre désirez-vous? what the deuce do you want?

diantrement [djɑ̃trəmɑ̃], adv. A. & Lit: = DIABLEMENT.

diapason [djapazɔ̃], s.m. Mus: **1.** Diapason, pitch. **2.** Tuning-fork. D. de bouche, pitch-pipe. **3.** Compass, range (of the voice).

diaphane [djafan], a. (a) Diaphanous; translucent. (b) F: Transparent.

diaphanéité [djafaneite], s.f. Diaphaneity; translucence.

diaphragme [djafragm], s.m. **1.** Physiol: Diaphragm, midriff. **2.** Tchn: (a) Diaphragm, dividing plate. Phot: Diaphragm stop (of lens). D. iris, iris-diaphragm. (b) Sound-box (of gramophone). Membrane du d., diaphragm of the sound-box.

diapositif [diapozitif], s.m., **diapositive** [diapoziti:v], s.f. Phot: Transparent positive; transparency; lantern-slide.

diaprer [djapre], v.tr. To variegate, mottle, speckle.
 diapré, a. Variegated, diapered. **Toile diaprée,** diaper.

diaprure [djapryːr], s.f. Variegated appearance or pattern.

diarrhée [djare], s.f. Med: Diarrhoea.

diathermie [diatermi], s.f. Med: Diathermy.

diathèse [diatɛ:z], *s.f. Med:* Diathesis, disposition, tendency, predisposition (to disease).

diatomée [diatɔme], *s.f. Algae:* Diatom.

diatomique [diatɔmik], *a. Ch:* Diatomic.

diatonique [djatɔnik], *a. Mus:* Diatonic (scale).

diatribe [djatrib], *s.f.* Diatribe.

dibasique [dibazik], *a. Ch:* Dibasic, bibasic.

dichotomie [dikɔtɔmi], *s.f.* Dichotomy.

dicotylédone [dikɔtiledɔn]. *Bot:* **1.** *a.* Dicotyledonous. **2.** *s.f.* Dicotyledon.

dictagraphe [diktagraf], *s.m.* Dictagraph.

dictame [diktam], *s.m.* **1.** *Bot:* Dittany. **2.** *A:* Solace, comfort, balm.

dictateur [diktatœ:r], *s.m.* Dictator.

dictatorial, -aux [diktatɔrjal, -o], *a.* Dictatorial. *adv.* **-ement.**

dictature [diktaty:r], *s.f.* Dictatorship.

dicter [dikte], *v.tr.* To dictate.

dictée, *s.f.* Dictation. Écrire qch. sous la dictée de qn, to write sth. at, from, s.o.'s dictation.

diction [diksjɔ̃], *s.f.* Diction; delivery. Professeur de diction, teacher of elocution.

dictionnaire [diksjɔnɛ:r], *s.m.* Dictionary, lexicon. *D. de géographie,* gazetteer.

dicton [diktɔ̃], *s.m.* Common saying; by-word; (wise) saw; maxim.

didactique [didaktik]. **1.** *a.* Didactic. **2.** *s.f.* Didactics. *adv.* **-ment,** -ally.

dièdre [djɛ:dr]. *Geom:* **1.** *a.* Dihedral (angle). **2.** *s.m.* Dihedron.

diélectrique [dielɛktrik], *a. & s.m. El:* Dielectric.

dieppois, -oise [djɛpwa, -wa:z], *a. & s. Geog:* (Native) of Dieppe.

diérèse [dierɛ:z], *s.f.* (a) Diaeresis; division of one syllable into two. (b) *A:* = TRÉMA.

dièse [djɛ:z], *s.m. Mus:* Sharp. *Fa d.,* F sharp.

diéser [djeze], *v.tr.* (je dièse; je diéserai) *Mus:* To sharp, sharpen (note).

diète¹ [djɛt], *s.f.* Diet, regimen. *D. absolue,* starvation diet. Être à la diète, to be (i) on a low, short, diet, (ii) on starvation diet.

diète², *s.f. Hist: Pol:* Diet.

diététique [djetetik]. *Med:* **1.** *a.* Dietetic. **2.** *s.f.* Dietetics.

dieu, -ieux [djø], *s.m.* God. **1.** Grands dieux! heavens! Se faire un dieu de qn, to make a (little) god of s.o. **2.** (a) *La voix de Dieu,* the voice of God. Un homme tout en Dieu, a very devout man. S'il plaît à Dieu, God willing; D.V. Dieu merci! thank God! (b) *F:* Le bon Dieu, God. S.a. BÊTE 1. (c) *F:* Dieu merci! thank heaven! Pour l'amour de Dieu, for goodness' sake. Dieu sait si j'ai travaillé, heaven knows I have worked hard enough! C'est la maison du bon D., it is a very hospitable house. **3.** *int. F:* Mon Dieu! grand Dieu! dear me! bless me! Mon D., mon D.! dear, dear! Mon D. oui! why, yes! Mon D. non! well, no! Mon D. je n'en sais rien! indeed I don't know!

diffamant [diffamɑ̃], *a.* Slanderous, libellous.

diffamateur, -trice [diffamatœ:r, -tris], *s.* Slanderer, libeller.

diffamation [diffamasjɔ̃], *s.f.* Defamation, slander, libel.

diffamatoire [diffamatwa:r], *a.* Defamatory, slanderous, libellous.

diffamer [diffame], *v.tr.* To slander, libel.

différence [diferɑ̃:s], *s.f.* Difference. *D. de goûts,* differences of taste. *La d. de A à B, entre A et B, de A et de B,* the difference between A and B. *Quelle d. avec . . . !* what a difference from . . .! Faire la différence d'une chose avec une autre, entre une chose et une autre, to distinguish, discriminate, between two things. *D. d'âge,* disparity in years. *A la différence de . . .,* unlike *. . ., contrary to. . . . A la différence que . . .,* with this difference that *. . .,* except that. *. . .*

différenciation [diferɑ̃sjasjɔ̃], *s.f.* Differentiation.

différencier [diferɑ̃sje], *v.tr.* To differentiate (de, from). *Mth: Expression non différenciée,* undifferentiated expression.

différend [diferɑ̃], *s.m.* Difference, dispute, disagreement (entre, between). Partager le différend, to split the difference. Vider un différend, to settle a difference.

différ|ent [diferɑ̃], *a.* Different. *Différentes personnes l'ont vu,* divers persons saw him. A différentes reprises, at various times; off and on. *adv.* **-emment.**

différentiel, -elle [diferɑ̃sjɛl]. **1.** *a.* Differential (calculus, gear, etc.); discriminating (duty, tariff). **2.** *s.m. Aut: etc:* Differential. **3.** *s.f.* Différentielle. *Mth:* Differential.

différer [difere], *v.* (je diffère; je différerai) **1.** *v.tr.* To defer, postpone (judgment); to put off, hold over (payment). *D. à,* occ. *de, faire qch.,* to defer, put off, doing sth. **2.** *v.i.* To differ. *Ils diffèrent entre eux par la taille,* they differ from one another in height. *Ils diffèrent de race et d'idiome,* they are different in race and speech. *D. d'opinion,* to differ in opinion.

difficile [difisil], *a.* **1.** Difficult. *Raisonnement d. à suivre,* argument that is difficult, hard, to follow. *Circonstances difficiles,* trying circumstances. *Les temps sont difficiles,* times are hard. *Il m'est d. d'accepter,* it is difficult for me to accept. **2.** *F:* Difficult to get on with; hard to please. *Il est d. à vivre,* he is difficult to get on with. *Il est d. sur la nourriture,* he is particular, faddy, about his food. *s.* Faire le difficile, to be hard to please. *Ne faites pas le d.,* don't be squeamish about it.

difficilement [difisilmɑ̃], *adv.* With difficulty.

difficulté [difikylte], *s.f.* Difficulty. *Cela ne présente aucune d.,* there is no difficulty about it. Faire, élever, des difficultés, to create obstacles, raise objections, make difficulties. *Faire des difficultés pour accepter,* to make difficulties about accepting. *Avoir de la d. à faire qch.,* to have difficulty in doing sth. Susciter des difficultés à qn, to put difficulties in s.o.'s way. Avoir une légère difficulté avec qn, to have a slight tiff with s.o.

difforme [difɔrm], *a.* Deformed, misshapen.

difformité [difɔrmite], *s.f.* Deformity.

diffracter [difrakte], *v.tr. Opt:* To diffract.

diffraction [difraksjɔ̃], *s.f. Opt:* Diffraction.

diffringent [difrɛ̃ʒɑ̃], *a. Opt:* Diffracting, diffractive.

diffus [dify], *a.* Diffused (light). *Éclairs diffus,* sheet-lightning. *F: Style d.,* diffuse, prolix, style.

diffusément [difyzemɑ̃], *adv.* Diffusely, wordily, verbosely; in a long-winded fashion.

diffuser [difyze], *v.tr.* **1.** To diffuse (light, heat, etc.). Lumière diffusée, flood-lighting. **2.** *W.Tel:* To broadcast (news, a speech, etc.).

diffuseur [difyzœ:r], *s.m.* **1.** *I.C.E:* Mixing cone, spray-cone. **2.** *W.Tel:* (a) (Of pers.) Broadcaster. (b) Cone loud-speaker.

diffusion [difyzjɔ̃], *s.f.* **1.** Diffusion (of light, heat, etc.); spread (of disease, etc.). **2.** Broadcasting (of news, etc.). **3.** Verbosity, wordiness, diffuseness.

digérer [diʒere], *v.tr.* (je digère; je digérerai) **1.** (a) To digest (laws, etc.). (b) To digest, assimilate (what one reads or learns). **2.** (a) To digest (food). *Je ne digère pas le porc,* pork does not agree with me. (b) F: To brook, stomach, put up with (insult, etc.).

digestible [diʒɛstibl], a. Digestible.

digestif, -ive [diʒɛstif, -iːv], a. Digestive. Le tube d., the alimentary canal.

digestion [diʒɛstjɔ̃], s.f. Digestion. F: Un affront de dure d., an insult difficult to swallow, to stomach. S.a. VISITE 1.

digital, -aux [diʒital, -o]. 1. a. Digital (nerve, etc.). Empreinte digitale, finger-print. 2. s.f. Digitale. Bot: Digitalis. D. pourprée, foxglove.

digitaline [diʒitalin], s.f. Ch: Pharm: Digitalis, digitalin.

digne [diɲ], a. 1. (a) Deserving, worthy (de, of). D. d'éloges, praiseworthy. D. de remarque, noteworthy. D. de pitié, pitiable. Livre d. d'être lu, book worth reading. F: C'est bien digne de lui, that's just like him. (b) F: Un digne homme, a worthy man. 2. Dignified. adv. -ment.

dignitaire [diɲitɛːr], s.m. Dignitary.

dignité [diɲite], s.f. 1. Dignity. Air, ton, de d., dignified air, tone. La d. d'un sujet, the seriousness, importance, of a subject. 2. High position; dignity. D. de chancelier, dignity of chancellor. S'élever aux dignités, to rise to high rank.

digression [digresjɔ̃], s.f. Digression. Faire une digression; se perdre, se lancer, dans une digression, to digress; to wander from the point.

digue [dig], s.f. (a) Dike, dam; embankment (of waterway, etc.). (b) Breakwater or pier (of stone); sea-wall; jetty. Opposer une digue aux eaux, à la colère, to stem the waters, anger.

dilapidation [dilapidasjɔ̃], s.f. 1. Wasting, squandering (of fortune, etc.). 2. Peculation.

dilapider [dilapide], v.tr. 1. To waste, squander (fortune). 2. To misappropriate (funds).

dilatable [dilatabl], a. Dilatable.

dilatation [dilatasjɔ̃], s.f. (a) Dila(ta)tion, expansion. D. des gaz, expansion of gases. Const: Joint à dilatation libre, expansion joint. (b) Distension (of stomach).

dilater [dilate], v.tr. (a) To dilate, expand. (b) To distend (the stomach).
  se dilater. (a) To dilate, swell, expand. (b) To become distended.

dilemme [dilɛm], s.m. Log: Dilemma. Les termes d'un dilemme, the horns of a dilemma.

dilettante [dilɛttãːt], s.m. Dilettante, amateur.

dilettantisme [dilɛttãtism], s.m. Dilettantism.

diligence [diliʒãːs], s.f. 1. (a) Diligence, industry, application. (b) Haste, dispatch. En toute diligence, with all possible dispatch. Faire diligence, to hurry, to make haste. 2. (Stage-)coach.

diligent [diliʒã], a. Diligent, industrious; busy (bee); assiduous (care). adv. -emment.

diluer [dilɥe], v.tr. To dilute (de, with); to water down (drink, etc.). Fin: D. le capital, to water the stock.

dilution [dilysjɔ̃], s.f. Dilution; watering down.

diluvial, -aux [dilyvjal, -o], **diluvien, -ienne** [dilyvjɛ̃, -jɛn], a. 1. Diluvian (fossils). 2. F: Torrential (rain).

dimanche [dimãːʃ], s.m. Sunday. D. des Rameaux, Palm Sunday. Observer le d., to keep the sabbath. Venez me voir d., come and see me on Sunday. Il vient le dimanche, he comes on Sundays. Habits du dimanche, one's Sunday best.

dîme [diːm], s.f. A: Tithe.

dimension [dimãsjɔ̃], s.f. Dimension, size. Géométrie à deux, à trois, dimensions, two-, three-dimensional geometry. Prendre les dimensions de qch., to take the measurement of sth. Mettre à dimension(s), to size (a hole, etc.).

diminuer [diminɥe]. 1. v.tr. To lessen; to diminish, reduce; to shorten. Cela vous diminuerait aux yeux du public, it would lower you in the eyes of the public. D. le son, to reduce the volume of sound. 2. v.i. To diminish, lessen, grow less; (of fever) to abate; (of attendance, profits) to fall off; (of prices) to fall; (of cold) to relax. D. de vitesse, to slow down. Les jours diminuent, the days are drawing in. Nau: D. de toile, to shorten sail. (Of water) D. de profondeur, de fond, to shoal.

diminutif, -ive [diminytif, -iːv], a. & s.m. Diminutive.

diminution [diminysjɔ̃], s.f. Diminution, lessening; reduction, decrease, lowering (of price, etc.); abatement (of fever, etc.); curtailing, cutting down (of expenses); slackening (of speed). Faire une d. à une robe, (i) to shorten, (ii) to take in, a dress.

dinanderie [dinãdri], s.f. Coppersmith's work.

dinandier [dinãdje], s.m. Coppersmith.

dinde [dɛ̃ːd], s.f. 1. Turkey-hen. Cu: Turkey. 2. F: Dull or stupid woman.

dindon [dɛ̃dɔ̃], s.m. 1. Turkey-cock. 2. F: Être le dindon de la farce, to be fooled, duped; to have to pay the piper.

dindonneau [dɛ̃dono], s.m. Young turkey.

dîner [dine]. 1. v.i. To dine; to have dinner. D. en ville, to dine out. Prov: Qui dort dîne, (i) he who sleeps forgets his hunger; (ii) no work no dinner. Dîner sur l'herbe, to picnic.
  II. **dîner,** s.m. Dinner; dinner-party. Faire son dîner de, F: avec, qch., to dine off, (up)on, sth. Dîner sur l'herbe, picnic.

dînette [dinɛt], s.f. 1. Dolls' dinner-party. 2. Dînette sur l'herbe, picnic.

dîneur, -euse [dinœːr, -øːz], s. Diner.

dingue [dɛ̃ːg], a. P: Cracked, daft, off his nut.

diocésain [djɔsezɛ̃], a. & s.m. Ecc: Diocesan.

diocèse [djɔsɛːz], s.m. Ecc: Diocese.

Diogène [djɔʒɛn]. Pr.n.m. Gr.Hist: Diogenes.

dionée [djɔne], s.f. Bot: Venus's fly-trap.

dioptrie [djɔptri], s.f. Opt: (Unit of refractive power) Diopter.

diphasé [difaze], a. El.E: Two-phase (system).

diphtérie [difteri], s.f. Med: Diphtheria.

diphtongue [diftɔ̃ːg], s.f. Ling: Diphthong.

diplomate [diplɔmat], s.m. Diplomatist.

diplomatie [diplɔmasi], s.f. 1. Diplomacy. F: User de d., to use tact, discretion. 2. Entrer dans la d., to enter the diplomatic service.

diplomatique [diplɔmatik], a. Diplomatic (service, F: answer). adv. -ment, -ally.

diplôme [diploːm], s.m. Diploma.

diplômer [diplome], v.tr. To grant a diploma to (s.o.). Institutrice diplômée, certificated teacher.

dipsomane [dipsɔman], a. & s. Dipsomaniac.

dipsomanie [dipsɔmani], s.f. Dipsomania.

diptère [diptɛːr]. Ent: 1. a. Dipterous. 2. s.m. pl. Les diptères, the diptera.

diptyque [diptik], s.m. Diptych.

dire [diːr]. I. v.tr. (pr.p. disant; p.p. dit; pr.ind. je dis, n. disons, vous dites, ils disent; p.h. je dis; fu. je dirai) 1. To say, tell. D. qch. à qn, to tell s.o. sth.; to say sth. to s.o. Vous ne m'en avez jamais rien dit, you never mentioned it. Envoyer d. à qn que . . ., to send word to s.o. that. . . . Ce disant . . ., with these words . . . . D. du mal de qn, to speak ill of s.o. Qu'en dira-t-on? what will people say? F: what will Mrs Grundy say? S.a. QU'EN-DIRA-T-ON. Il n'y a rien à d. à sa conduite, no fault can be found with his behaviour. D. un secret, to tell a secret. D. ce

qu'on pense, to speak one's mind. *Quand je vous le disais! je vous l'avais bien dit!* didn't I tell you so? **Dire bonjour, adieu, à qn,** to bid s.o. good day, farewell. **Comme dit l'autre; comme on dit,** as the saying goes. *Comment est-ce que cela se dit en français?* what is the French for that? *Cela ne se dit pas,* that is not said. *Qu'est-ce qui me dit que vous payerez?* how do I know whether you will pay? *F:* **A qui le dites-vous?** don't I know it? **Dites toujours!** go on! say it! *D. que oui,* to say yes. *Je vous dis que non,* I tell you, no. **Je ne sais comment dire,** I don't know how to put it. *Je me disais que tout était fini,* I thought all was over. *Que dites-vous de ce tableau?* what do you think of this picture? **A vrai dire . . .,** to tell the truth. . . . **Pour ne pas dire . . .,** not to say. . . . **Pour tout dire . . .,** in a word . . . . **C'est tout dire,** I need say no more. **Tout est dit,** that is an end to the matter. **Tout n'est pas dit,** we haven't heard the last of it. **Pour ainsi dire,** so to speak. **Comme qui dirait . . .,** as you might say. . . . *A ce qu'il dit,* according to him. **Vous l'avez dit,** quite so; exactly. **Ainsi dit, ainsi fait,** no sooner said than done. **Cela va sans dire,** that goes without saying. **Tenez-vous cela pour dit,** don't let me have to tell you that again. **Alors c'est dit,** well then, that's settled, decided. **On dit que . . .,** the story goes that. . . . **On dirait que . . .,** one would think that. . . . *On dirait qu'il va pleuvoir,* it looks like rain. **On aurait dit que . . .,** it seemed as though. . . . **Il n'y a pas à dire,** there is no denying it. **Dites donc,** *en voilà assez!* look here, I say, that's enough! **Et dire qu'il n'a que vingt ans!** and to think that he is only twenty! *S.a.* ENVOYER, PARLER I. (*b*) *Pred.* **On le dit mort,** he is reported (to be) dead. (*c*) **Faire dire qch. à qn,** to send word of sth. to s.o. **Il ne se le fit pas dire deux fois,** he didn't wait to be told twice. (*d*) **Faire dire qch. à qn,** to make s.o. say or tell sth. (*e*) **Faire dire qch. par qn,** to send word of sth. through s.o. **2.** (*a*) **Dire à qn de faire qch.,** to tell, order, s.o. to do sth; to bid s.o. do sth. *Faites ce qu'on vous dit,* do as you are bidden, as you are told. (*b*) **Dire que** + *sub. Dites qu'on le fasse entrer,* bid them show him in. *Il avait dit qu'on le réveillât à six heures,* he had given orders to be awakened at six o'clock. **3. Dire des vers,** to recite poetry. *D. son chapelet,* to tell one's beads. **4.** (*a*) To express, betoken. *Horloge qui dit l'heure,* clock that tells the time. *Cela en dit beaucoup sur son courage,* it speaks volumes for his courage. *Ce nom ne me dit rien,* the name conveys, means, nothing to me. *Cela ne me disait rien de bon,* I didn't like the look of it. (*b*) *Cette musique ne me dit rien,* I don't care for this music. *Son offre ne me dit rien,* I don't fancy his offer. **5.** (*a*) **Vouloir dire,** to mean. *Que voulez-vous d. par là?* what do you mean by that? (*b*) **Qu'est-ce à dire?** what does this mean? **Est-ce à dire que . . .?** do you mean to imply that . . .? **Ce n'est pas à dire que** + *sub.,* it does not follow that. . . .
II. **dire,** *s.m.* Statement, assertion. *Je reviens à mon d.,* I reaffirm what I said before. **Selon dire d'expert,** according to expert opinion. **Selon son dire . . .,** according to him . . .; by his own account. . . .

dit. I. *a.* (*a*) Settled, fixed. **Prendre qch. pour dit,** to take sth. for granted. *A l'heure dite,* at the appointed time. (*b*) (So-)called. *La zone dite tempérée,* the so-called temperate zone. **2.** *s.m.* Maxim, saying.

direct [dirɛkt], *a.* Direct, straight. *Démenti d.,*

flat denial. *Gram:* **Complément direct,** direct object. *Rail:* **Train direct,** through train.
directement [dirɛktəmã], *adv.* Directly, straight. *Se diriger d. au nord,* to go due north.
directeur, -trice [dirɛktœːr, -tris]. **I.** *s.* Director, directress; manager, manageress; head (of industrial concern, etc.); head-master, head-mistress (of school); principal (of school); governor (of reformatory); governor, warden (of prison); editor (of paper); leader (of under-taking). *D. gérant,* managing director. **Directeur général des postes, télégraphes, et téléphones,** Postmaster General. **2.** *a.* Directing, managing, controlling (force, etc.); guiding (principle). **Roue directrice,** (i) *Aut:* steering-wheel; (ii) *Cy:* front wheel.
directif, -ive [dirɛktif, -iːv]. **I.** *a.* Directing, guiding (rule, etc.). **2.** *s.f.pl.* **Directives,** rules of conduct; broad lines (laid down); main lines, general lines (of a policy).
direction [dirɛksjɔ̃], *s.f.* **I.** (*a*) Guidance, direction; conduct (of undertaking); management, control (of business house, etc.); directorate (of railways, etc.); editorship (of newspaper); head-mastership (of school); leadership (of a party). (*b*) Board of directors. **2.** Direction, driving, guiding (of engine, etc.). *Aut: Nau:* Steering. **3.** Direction, course. *Nau:* Bearing. *Quelle d. ont-ils prise?* which way did they go? *Train d. de Bordeaux,* train for Bordeaux. *Imprimer une d. à l'opinion,* to shape the course of opinion. **4.** *pl.* Directions, instructions.
Directoire (le) [lədirɛktwaːr], *s.m. Fr.Hist:* The Directory (1795-9).
directorat [dirɛktɔra], *s.m.* (*a*) Directorate; directorship. (*b*) Managership.
dirigeable [diriʒabl]. **I.** *a.* Dirigible. *W.Tel:* **Antenne d.,** directional aerial. **2.** *s.m. Aer:* Dirigible (balloon); airship.
dirigeant [diriʒã], *a.* Directing, guiding (power, principle, etc.). *Classes dirigeantes,* ruling classes.
diriger [diriʒe], *v.tr.* (**je dirigeai(s); n. dirigeons**) **I.** To direct, control, manage; *F:* to run (business, etc.); to conduct (orchestra); to edit (newspaper); to superintend, conduct (proceedings). **Mal diriger une entreprise,** to misdirect, mismanage, an undertaking. **2.** (*a*) To direct, guide, lead; to drive (horse, car); to steer, navigate (ship). *Efforts mal dirigés,* misguided, misdirected, efforts. (*b*) **Diriger ses pas vers . . .,** to bend, direct, one's steps towards. . . . *D. des accusations contre qn,* to level, aim, accusations at s.o. (*c*) To aim (rifle) (*sur,* at); to train (gun) (*sur,* on); to level, point (telescope) (*sur,* at); to bring (telescope) to bear (*sur,* on). *W.Tel:* **Onde dirigée,** directional wave. **Émission aux ondes dirigées,** beam transmission.
se diriger. I. (*a*) *Se d. vers un endroit,* to make, wend, one's way towards a place. *Le vaisseau se dirigea vers le port,* the vessel steered, headed, for the harbour. (*b*) *Se d. vers qn,* to go up to s.o. **2.** (Of river, etc.) *Se d. du nord au sud,* to run north and south.
dis-, -ais, -ant, -e, -ons, etc. See DIRE.
discernable [disɛrnabl], *a.* Discernible, visible.
discernement [disɛrnəmã], *s.m.* **I.** Perception, distinguishing; discrimination. **2.** Discernment, judgment; (age of) understanding.
discerner [disɛrne], *v.tr.* To discern, distinguish (sth.). *D. qch. de qch.,* to discriminate between sth. and sth. *D. le bien du mal,* to tell right from wrong.
disciple [disipl], *s.m.* Disciple, follower.
disciplinaire [disiplinɛːr]. **I.** *a.* Disciplinary (punishment, etc.). **2.** *s.m.* Disciplinarian.

discipline [disiplin], *s.f.* **1.** Scourge (for self-flagellation). **2.** Discipline. *Garder la d.*, to maintain discipline, order. *Il ne sait pas maintenir la d.*, he cannot keep discipline; he is no disciplinarian. (Fr. army) **Compagnies de discipline**, disciplinary companies.

discipliner [disipline], *v.tr.* To discipline (school); to bring (troops, etc.) under control, under discipline.

discontinu [diskɔ̃tiny], *a.* Discontinuous.

discontinuation [diskɔ̃tinɥasjɔ̃], *s.f.* Discontinuance.

discontinuer [diskɔ̃tinɥe], *v.tr. & i.* To discontinue.

discontinuité [diskɔ̃tinɥite], *s.f.* Discontinuity.

disconvenance [diskɔ̃vnɑ̃:s], *s.f.* **1.** Unsuitableness. **2.** Disparity, dissimilarity; incongruity.

disconvenir [diskɔ̃vni:r], *v.i.* (Conj. like VENIR. Aux. *avoir*) **1.** *D. à qn, à qch.*, to be unsuited to, unsuitable for, s.o., sth. **2.** *D. de qch.*, not to agree with (a statement). **On ne peut pas en disconvenir**, there is no gainsaying it. *Je n'en disconviens pas*, I don't deny it.

discordance [diskɔrdɑ̃:s], *s.f.* Discordance, dissonance (of sounds); clashing (of colours); difference (of opinions); disagreement (of evidence, etc.).

discordant [diskɔrdɑ̃], *a.* Discordant, inharmonious (sound); grating, jarring (noise); clashing (colours); conflicting (opinions, etc.).

discorde [diskɔrd], *s.f.* Discord, dissension, strife. **Semer la discorde**, to make trouble.

discoureur, -euse [diskurœ:r, -ø:z], *s.* (Great) talker; speechifier.

discourir [diskuri:r], *v.i.* (Conj. like COURIR) To discourse; to air one's opinions (*sur*, on); *F:* to speechify.

discours [disku:r], *s.m.* **1.** Talk. *pl.* **Discours en l'air**, idle talk. **2.** Discourse, dissertation. **3.** Speech, oration, address. **Prononcer, faire, un discours**, to make, deliver, a speech. **4.** Diction, language. *Gram:* **Parties du discours**, parts of speech. *D. indirect*, reported speech.

discourtois [diskurtwa], *a.* Discourteous.

discrédit [diskredi], *s.m.* Discredit; disrepute.

discréditer [diskredite], *v.tr.* To disparage, run down (s.o., s.o.'s work); to throw discredit on (statement); to bring discredit on (s.o.'s authority, on a firm, etc.).

discr|et, -ète [diskrɛ, -ɛt], *a.* **1.** (*a*) Discreet, cautious. **Discret comme la tombe**, silent as the tomb. (*b*) Quiet, unobtrusive; sober, quiet (dress); modest (request, etc.). **2.** *Mth:* Discrete, discontinuous (quantity). *adv.* **-ètement.**

discrétion [diskresjɔ̃], *s.f.* Discretion. **1.** Prudence, circumspection. **Age de discrétion**, age, years, of discretion. **2. Être à la discrétion de qn**, to be (i) at s.o.'s disposal, (ii) at s.o.'s mercy. **A discrétion**, at discretion. *Se rendre à d.*, to surrender unconditionally.

disculpation [diskylpasjɔ̃], *s.f.* Exculpation, exoneration.

disculper [diskylpe], *v.tr.* To exculpate, exonerate (*de*, from).

se disculper, to exculpate oneself (*de*, from); to clear oneself (*de*, of)

discursif, -ive [diskyrsif, -i:v], *a.* Discursive.

discussion [diskysjɔ̃], *s.f.* Discussion, debate. *La question en discussion*, the question under discussion, at issue. *Sans d. possible*, indisputably. **Entrer en discussion avec qn**, to enter into an argument with s.o.

discutable [diskytabl], *a.* Debatable, arguable.

discuter [diskyte], *v.tr.* (*a*) To discuss, debate.

Discutons la chose, let us talk the matter over; let us talk it over. *Abs. D. avec qn sur qch.*, to argue with s.o. about sth. *S.a.* AIGUILLE I. (*b*) To question, dispute. *D. un droit*, to call a right into question.

disert [dizɛ:r], *a.* Eloquent, fluent (orator).

disette [dizɛt], *s.f.* Scarcity, dearth. *D. d'eau*, drought. *La guerre amène la d.*, war brings famine in its train.

diseur, -euse [dizœ:r, -ø:z], *s.* (*a*) Monologuist; reciter. *D. de chansonnettes*, entertainer; humorist. (*b*) **Diseuse de bonne aventure**, fortune-teller. (*c*) **Beau diseur**, fine talker. [DIRE]

disgrâce [dizgrɑ:s], *s.f.* Disfavour, disgrace.

disgracier [dizgrasje], *v.tr.* To dismiss (s.o.) from favour.

disgracié, *a.* Out of favour. *s. Les disgraciés de la fortune*, the unlucky, the unfortunate.

disgracieu|x, -euse [dizgrasjø, -ø:z], *a.* **1.** Uncouth, awkward, ungraceful. **2.** Ungracious (answer). *adv.* **-sement.**

disjoindre [dizʒwɛ̃:dr, dis-], *v.tr.* (Conj. like JOINDRE) To disjoin, sever, disjoint.

se disjoindre, to come apart.

disjoncteur [dizʒɔ̃ktœ:r], *s.m. El.E:* (*a*) Circuit-breaker, cut-out, switch. *Bouton d.*, disconnecting key. (*b*) Underload release.

disjonctif, -ive [dizʒɔ̃ktif, -i:v], *a.* Disjunctive.

dislocation [dislɔkasjɔ̃], *s.f.* **1.** Dislocation; taking down (of machine, etc.); dismemberment (of empire). **2.** *Geol:* Fault.

disloquer [dislɔke], *v.tr.* To dislocate; to put (limb) out of joint; to put (machine) out of order; to dismember (state).

se disloquer, to break up.

disparaître [disparɛ:tr], *v.i.* (Conj. like PARAÎTRE. Aux. *avoir* or *être*) To disappear. **1.** To vanish. *D. aux yeux de qn*, to vanish before s.o's eyes. *La côte disparut de l'horizon*, the coast faded from the horizon. *Ces vieux amis ont, sont, disparu(s)*, these old friends have passed away. **Faire disparaître qn, qch.**, (i) to make away with s.o., sth.; to remove (stain, etc.); to smooth out (crease); (ii) to put s.o., sth., out of sight. *Cette mode disparaît*, this fashion is going out. **2.** *La muraille disparaît sous le lierre*, the wall is hidden under the ivy.

disparu, *a.* **1.** *Mil:* Missing. **2.** Extinct (race, etc.).

disparate [disparat]. **1.** *a.* (*a*) Dissimilar. (*b*) Ill-matched, ill-assorted; jarring. *Couleurs disparates*, clashing colours. **2.** *s.f.* (*a*) Disparity. (*b*) Incongruity.

disparition [disparisjɔ̃], *s.f.* **1.** Disappearing, vanishing. **2.** Disappearance.

dispendieux, -euse [dispɑ̃djø, -ø:z], *a.* Expensive, costly.

dispensaire [dispɑ̃sɛ:r], *s.m.* (Public) dispensary; out-patients' department; welfare centre.

dispensation [dispɑ̃sasjɔ̃], *s.f.* **1.** Dispensation; distribution (of favours, etc.). **2.** *Pharm:* Dispensing.

dispense [dispɑ̃:s], *s.f.* **1.** (*a*) Exemption (from military service); waiving (of age limit). (*b*) *Ecc:* Dispensation. **2.** Certificate of exemption. *D. de bans*, marriage licence.

dispenser [dispɑ̃se], *v.tr.* **1.** *D. qn de qch., de faire qch.*, to dispense, exempt, excuse, s.o. from sth., from doing sth. *D. qn d'une tâche*, to excuse s.o. from, to let s.o. off, a task. *D. qn du service militaire*, to exempt s.o. from military service. **2.** (*a*) To dispense, mete out, distribute (charity, etc.); to administer (the sacraments). (*b*) *Pharm:* To dispense, make up (medicine).

se **dispenser** de qch., de faire qch., to excuse oneself from sth.; to get out of doing sth.

dispers|er [disperse], v.tr. **1.** To disperse, scatter; to spread (far and wide). D. une armée, to rout an army. **2.** Opt: (i) To disperse, split up (light); (ii) to scatter (light). s.m. **-ement.** se **disperser,** to disperse, scatter.

dispersion [dispersjɔ̃], s.f. **1.** Dispersion, dispersal; rout (of army); spread, scattering (of shot). **2.** Scattering (of light). El: Leakage.

disponibilité [disponibilite], s.f. **1.** Availability (of seats, capital, etc.). Avoir la d. de qch., to have the disposal of sth. Mil: Être en disponibilité, to be unattached, on half-pay. **2.** pl. (a) Available time or means. (b) Available funds; liquid assets.

disponible [disponibl], a. Available; at (s.o.'s) disposal. Actif d., s.m. le **disponible,** available assets; liquid assets. Officier d., unattached officer; half-pay officer.

dispos [dispo], a.m. (a) Fit, well, in good form. S.a. FRAIS[1] **1.** (b) Esprit d., fresh, alert, mind.

disposer [dispoze]. **1.** v.tr. (a) To dispose, set out, arrange; to lay out (garden). L'homme propose et Dieu dispose, man proposes but God disposes. (b) D. qn à qch., à faire qch., to dispose, incline, s.o. to sth., to do sth. **2.** v.ind.tr. (a) D. de qch., to dispose of sth.; to have sth. at one's disposal. Droit des peuples de d. d'eux-mêmes, right of peoples to self-determination. Disposez de moi, I am at your service. Les moyens dont je dispose, the means at my disposal. (b) D. de ses biens en faveur de qn, to make over one's property to s.o. **3.** (Of law, act) To provide, enjoin (que, that). se **disposer** à faire qch., to make ready to do sth. Se d. au sommeil, à dormir, to compose oneself to sleep.

disposé, a. **1.** Disposed. Être bien, mal, d., to be in a good, bad, humour. Être bien d. pour, envers, qn, to be well disposed towards s.o. Être, se sentir, d. à faire qch., to feel disposed, in the mood, to do sth. Je suis tout d. à pardonner, I am fully prepared to forgive. **2.** Être d. au rhumatisme, to have a predisposition to rheumatism.

dispositif [dispozitif], s.m. Apparatus, device, contrivance, appliance. D. de commande, driving-gear, controlling-gear. D. de sûreté, safety device; locking device.

disposition [dispozisjɔ̃], s.f. Disposition. **1.** Arrangement, ordering (of house, etc.); laying out, lay-out (of garden, etc.). D. du terrain, lie of the land. **2.** (a) State (of mind, body); frame of mind. Être en bonne disposition pour faire qch., to be disposed, inclined, in the humour, to do sth. (b) Predisposition; tendency (to malady, etc.). Avoir une d. à s'enrhumer, to be liable to catch cold. (c) pl. Natural aptitude; aptness (for sth.). Dispositions naturelles pour la musique, natural bent for music. Avoir des dispositions pour la peinture, to have a turn for painting; F: to be cut out for an artist. Enfant qui a des dispositions, naturally gifted child. **3.** pl. (a) Arrangements. Prendre des dispositions pour faire qch., to prepare, arrange, for doing sth. Prendre toutes dispositions utiles, to take all useful steps. (b) Provisions, dispositions (of will, law, treaty); clauses (of law). **4.** Disposal. Avoir la libre d. de son bien, to be free to dispose of one's property. Libre disposition de soi-même, self-determination. Fonds à ma disposition, funds at my disposal. Mettre qch. à la disposition de qn, to place sth. at s.o.'s disposal.

disproportion [disproporsjɔ̃], s.f. Disproportion, want of proportion.

disproportionné [disproporsjɔne], a. Dispro-

portionate (à, to); out of proportion (à, with) adv. **-ment.**

disputable [dispytabl], a. Disputable, debatable.

disputailler [dispytaje], v.i. F: To wrangle, bicker (sur, about).

disputailleur, -euse [dispytajœ:r, -ø:z], a. Fond of wrangling; contentious.

dispute [dispyt], s.f. **1.** A: Debate, dispute. Sujet en dispute, subject under discussion. **2.** Altercation, quarrel. Chercher dispute à qn, to pick a quarrel with s.o.

disputer [dispyte], v.tr. & i. **1.** A: Disputer qch., de qch., sur qch., to dispute, argue, about sth.; to discuss sth. **2.** Disputer qch., de qch., to dispute, contest, sth. D. le terrain, to dispute every inch of ground. D. qch. à qn, to contend with s.o. for sth. Deux chiens qui se disputent un os, two dogs fighting over a bone. D. un match, to play a match. D. une course sur 1600 mètres, to run a race over a mile. **3.** v.i. To quarrel, wrangle. se **disputer,** to quarrel, wrangle, argue (pour, over, about).

disputeur, -euse [dispytœ:r, -ø:z]. **1.** a. Contentious, quarrelsome. **2.** s. Wrangler, arguer.

disqualification [diskalifikasjɔ̃], s.f. Sp: Disqualification (of horse, boxer, etc.).

disqualifier [diskalifje], v.tr. Sp: To disqualify.

disque [disk], s.m. **1.** Gr.Ant: Discus. **2.** (a) Disk, disc (of moon, etc.). (b) D. d'embrayage, clutch-plate. D. d'excentrique, eccentric-sheave. D. de phonographe, gramophone record. (c) Rail: (Disk-)signal. D. à distance, distance signal. Siffler au disque, (i) to whistle for the road, (ii) F: to endeavour to obtain a favour from s.o.

disquisition [diskizisjɔ̃], s.f. Disquisition.

disrupteur [disryptœ:r], s.m. El.E: (Spark-) interrupter; break.

dissection [diseksjɔ̃], s.f. Dissection.

dissemblable [dis(s)ãblabl], a. Dissimilar (à, de, to); different (from); unlike.

dissemblance [dis(s)ãblã:s], s.f. Dissimilarity (entre, between); unlikeness.

dissémination [dis(s)eminasjɔ̃], s.f. Scattering (of seeds); spreading (of germs, ideas, etc.); dissemination.

disséminer [dis(s)emine], v.tr. To scatter (seeds, etc.); to spread, disseminate (germs, ideas, etc.).

dissension [dis(s)ãsjɔ̃], s.f. Dissension, discord.

dissentiment [dis(s)ãtimã], s.m. Disagreement, dissent.

disséquer [dis(s)eke], v.tr. (je dissèque; je disséquerai) To dissect.

dissertateur [disertatœ:r], s.m. Dissertator. F: Grand d., great talker, great speechifier.

dissertation [disertasjɔ̃], s.f. (a) Dissertation (sur, (up)on). (b) Sch: D. française, French essay; exercise in composition.

disserter [diserte], v.i. D. sur un sujet, to dissert, F: to hold forth, (up)on a subject.

dissidence [dis(s)idã:s], s.f. Dissidence, schism; dissent.

dissident [dis(s)idã]. **1.** a. Dissident, dissentient; disaffected (tribe, etc.). **2.** s. (a) Dissentient. (b) Ecc: Dissenter, nonconformist.

dissimilaire [dis(s)imilɛ:r], a. Dissimilar, unlike.

dissimulateur, -trice [dis(s)imylatœ:r, -tris], s. Dissimulator, dissembler.

dissimulation [dis(s)imylasjɔ̃], s.f. **1.** Dissimulation; deceit. User de dissimulation, to dissemble. **2.** Concealment (of the truth).

dissimuler [dis(s)imyle], v.tr. To dissemble, dissimulate, conceal (feelings); to conceal (trench); to cover up (fault). Abs. To dis-

semble. *D. qch. à qn*, to hide sth., keep sth. back, from s.o. *Il n'y a pas à se d. que . . .*, there is no blinking the fact that. . . .
  se dissimuler *derrière les rideaux*, to hide, skulk, behind the curtains.
  dissimulé, *a.* **I.** Dissimulating, secretive. **2.** Latent (electricity).
dissipateur, -trice [disipatœːr, -tris]. **I.** *s.* Spendthrift, squanderer. **2.** *a.* Wasteful (administration).
dissipation [disipasjɔ̃], *s.f.* **I.** *(a)* Dissipation, dispersion (of clouds, etc.). *(b)* Dissipation, wasting (of time, etc.); squandering (of fortune). **2.** *(a)* Dissipation, dissolute living. *(b)* Frivolous conduct (in school, etc.); fooling; inattention.
dissiper [disipe], *v.tr.* **I.** *(a)* To dissipate, disperse, scatter, dispel (clouds, etc.); to clear up (misunderstanding); to dispel (fears). *(b)* To dissipate, waste (fortune, time); to squander (money). **2.** To divert; to occupy the spare time of (s.o.). *Ces petits travaux me dissipent,* these little jobs come as a relaxation.
  se dissiper. **I.** (Of suspicions, etc.) To vanish, disappear; (of fog) to lift, clear; (of storm) to blow over. **2.** *(a)* To amuse oneself, seek relaxation. *(b)* To fall into dissipated ways. *(c)* To be frivolous, inattentive (in school, etc.).
dissipé, *a.* *(a)* Dissipated; gay (life). *(b) Sch:* Inattentive.
dissociation [dis(s)ɔsjasjɔ̃], *s.f. Ch:* Dissociation.
dissocier [dis(s)ɔsje], *v.tr. Ch:* To dissociate.
dissolu [dis(s)ɔly], *a.* Dissolute, loose, profligate.
dissolution [dis(s)ɔlysjɔ̃], *s.f.* **I.** Disintegration, dissolution (of body, etc.). **2.** *(a)* Dissolving (of substance in liquid). *(b)* Solution. *D. de caoutchouc,* rubber solution (for tyres). **3.** Dissolution (of parliament, marriage); breaking up (of meeting). **4.** Dissoluteness, profligacy.
dissolv-ant¹, -ez, -ons, etc. See DISSOUDRE.
dissolvant² [dis(s)ɔlvã], *a. & s.m.* (Dis)solvent.
dissonance [disɔnãːs], *s.f.* **I.** Dissonance. **2.** *Mus:* Discord.
dissonant [disɔnã], *a* Dissonant, discordant.
dissoudre [dis(s)udr], *v.tr.* (*pr.p.* dissolvant; *p.p.* dissous, *f.* dissoute; *pr.ind.* je dissous, il dissout, n. dissolvons; *p.d.* je dissolvais; *p.h. & p.sub.* are lacking; *fu.* je dissoudrai) To dissolve. **I.** To melt (substance) in a liquid. **2.** *(a)* To disintegrate, decompose; to disperse (tumour). *(b)* To dissolve (parliament, partnership, etc.).
  se dissoudre. **I.** *Se d. dans l'eau,* to dissolve, melt, in water. *Faire dissoudre une substance,* to dissolve, melt, a substance. **2.** (Of assembly) To break up.
dissuader [dis(s)ɥade], *v.tr. D. qn de qch. de faire qch.,* to dissuade s.o. from sth., from doing sth. *D. qn de partir,* to persuade s.o. not to go.
dissyllabe [disil(l)ab]. **I.** *a.* Di(s)syllabic (word). **2.** *s.m.* Di(s)syllable.
dissyllabique [disil(l)abik], *a.* Di(s)syllabic.
distance [distãːs], *s.f.* Distance. *On ne voyait rien à cette d.,* one could see nothing from that distance. *Suivre qn à distance,* to follow s.o. at a distance. *La ville est à deux lieues de distance,* the town is five miles distant, five miles away. *A quelle d. sommes-nous de la ville?* how far are we from the town? *A courte d.,* within easy reach (*de,* of). *De distance en distance,* at intervals. *Tenir qn à distance,* to keep s.o. at a distance. *Mec.E: Commande à d.,* remote control. S.a. OBSERVER. *Opt: D. focale,* focal length. *Artil: A petite d., à faible d.,* at short range. *Nau: D. parcourue,* day's run.

distanc|er [distãse], *v.tr.* (**je distançai(s)**; **n.** distançons) *Rac: etc:* **I.** To outdistance, outrun, outstrip. *Nau:* To outsail. *Se laisser distancer,* to drop away; to fall behind. **2.** To disqualify (winner). *s.m.* **-ement.**
distant [distã], *a.* **I.** Distant. **2.** *F:* Standoffish, aloof.
distendre [distãːdr], *v.tr.* **I.** To distend (stomach, etc.); to over-inflate (balloon). **2.** To overstretch, strain (muscle).
distension [distãsjɔ̃], *s.f.* **I.** Distension (of stomach). **2.** Overstretching, straining (of muscle).
distillateur [distilatœːr], *s.m.* Distiller.
distillation [distilasjɔ̃], *s.f.* Distillation, distilling. *D. fractionnée,* fractional distillation.
distiller [distile], *v.tr.* *(a)* To distil, exude, secrete (drops of moisture, etc.). *(b) Ind:* To distil (spirits); to condense (water).
distillerie [distilri], *s.f.* **I.** Distillery. **2.** Distilling (trade).
distinct, -incte [distɛ̃(ːkt], -ɛ̃ːkt], *a.* **I.** Distinct, separate (*de,* from). **2.** Distinct, clear (outline, voice). *adv.* **-ement.**
distinctif, -ive [distɛ̃ktif, -iːv], *a.* Distinctive, characteristic, distinguishing (sign, feature, etc.). *Trait distinctif,* characteristic, peculiarity.
distinction [distɛ̃ksjɔ̃], *s.f.* Distinction. **I.** *Faire une d. entre deux choses,* to make a distinction, to discriminate, distinguish, between two things. *Sans distinction,* indiscriminately. **2.** *(a)* Distinction, honour. *(b)* Decoration (*e.g.* medal, star). **3.** Distinction, eminence. *Avoir de la d. dans les manières,* to have a distinguished bearing, a polished manner.
distinguable [distɛ̃gabl], *a.* Distinguishable.
distinguer [distɛ̃ge], *v.tr.* To distinguish. **I.** To mark, characterize. **2.** To honour; to single (s.o.) out for distinction. **3.** *D. entre deux choses,* to distinguish between two things. *D. qch. de qch., d'avec qch.,* to distinguish, tell, sth. from sth. **4.** To discern, perceive, make out. *Il faisait trop noir pour bien d.,* it was too dark to see clearly.
  se distinguer. **I.** To distinguish oneself. **2.** *Se d. des autres,* to be distinguishable, marked off, from others (*par,* by). **3.** To be noticeable, conspicuous; to stand out.
  distingué, *a.* Distinguished. **I.** Eminent, noted (writer, etc.). **2.** *(a)* Refined, polished (taste, bearing, etc.). *Avoir un air d.,* to look distinguished. *(b)* Smart (costume, etc.).
distique [distik], *s.m. Pros:* **I.** Distich (in Gr. or Lt. verse). **2.** Couplet (in Fr. verse).
distorsion [distɔrsjɔ̃], *s.f.* Distortion (of limb, of optical image, of wireless reproduction).
distraction [distraksjɔ̃], *s.f.* **I.** *(a)* Division, severance (of part from a whole, etc.). *(b)* Appropriation. *(c)* Misappropriation (of funds, supplies). **2.** Absence of mind, inadvertence, abstraction. *Par distraction,* inadvertently, absent-mindedly. **3.** Diversion, amusement.
distraire [distrɛːr], *v.tr.* (Conj. like TRAIRE) **I.** *(a)* To divert, separate (part from whole). *(b)* To abstract, misappropriate (funds, etc.). **2.** To distract, divert (s.o.'s attention, etc.). *D. qn de son chagrin,* to take s.o.'s mind off his sorrow. *D. qn de ses travaux,* to take s.o. off his work. **3.** To divert, entertain, amuse.
  se distraire, to seek, take, relaxation; to amuse oneself. *Le besoin de se d.,* the need for relaxation.
  distrait, *a.* *(a)* Absent-minded. *(b)* Inattentive, listless. *adv.* **-ement.**
distray-ais, -ez, -ons, etc. See DISTRAIRE.

distrayant [distrɛjɑ̃], *a.* Diverting, entertaining.
distribuer [distribɥe], *v.tr.* To distribute, give out (alms, etc.); to issue, serve out, portion out (provisions, etc.); (of postman) to ˙ deliver (letters). *D. les cartes,* to deal out the cards. *Th:* D. *les rôles,* to cast the parts (in a play).
distributeur, -trice [distribytœ:r, -tris]. **1.** *s.* Distributor, dispenser (of alms, etc.). **2.** *s.m.* **Distributeur automatique,** automatic machine; (i) penny-in-the-slot machine, (ii) petrol pump. *I.C.E:* D. *de courant,* distributor. *Mch:* D. *de vapeur,* steam-valve.
distribution [distribysjɔ̃], *s.f.* Distribution; allotment (of duties, cabins, etc.); issue (of rations); delivery (of letters). *Sch:* D. *de prix,* prize-giving; speech-day. *Th:* D. *des rôles d'une pièce,* (i) casting, (ii) cast, of a play. D. *d'eau (de la ville),* water supply. *El.E:* **Tableau de distribution,** switchboard.
district [distrik(t)], *s.m.* District, region.
dit, dites, dîtes. See DIRE.
diurne [djyrn], *a.* Diurnal (motion, etc.).
diva [diva], *s.f.* Diva, prima donna.
divagation [divagasjɔ̃], *s.f.* Divagation, wandering; digression (in a speech, etc.).
divaguer [divage], *v.i.* **1.** To divagate, wander. **2.** *F:* (a) To digress; to wander away from the point. (b) To ramble (in delirium, etc.).
divalent [divalɑ̃], *a. Ch:* Divalent, bivalent.
divan [divɑ̃], *s.m.* Divan; couch.
divergence [diverʒɑ̃:s], *s.f.* Divergence; spread (of bullets, etc.); differences (of opinion).
divergent [diverʒɑ̃], *a.* Divergent.
diverger [diverʒe], *v.i.* **(il divergea(it); n. divergeons)** To diverge (de, from).
divers [dive:r], *a.* **1.** *A:* Changing, varying (nature, etc.). **2.** *pl.* (a) Diverse, different, varied. **(Frais) divers,** sundry expenses. *Remarques diverses,* miscellaneous remarks. *Journ:* **Faits divers,** news items. (b) *Indef. adj.* (Always preceding the sb.) Various, sundry. **En diverses occasions,** on various, divers, occasions. *adv.* **-ement.**
diversifier [diversifje], *v.tr.* To diversify, vary (conversation, pursuits, etc.); to variegate (colours).
diversion [diversjɔ̃], *s.f.* **1.** *Mil:* Diversion. **2.** Diversion, change. **Faire diversion,** to create a diversion.
diversité [diversite], *s.f.* Diversity.
divertir [diverti:r], *v.tr.* To divert, entertain, amuse.
se divertir, to amuse oneself.
divertissant [divertisɑ̃], *a.* Diverting, amusing, entertaining.
divertissement [divertismɑ̃], *s.m.* **1.** Misappropriation (of funds). **2.** Diversion; entertainment, amusement, recreation, relaxation.
divette [divɛt], *s.f.* (Music-hall or light opera) star.
dividende [dividɑ̃:d], *s.m. Mth: Fin:* Dividend. **Dividende provisoire,** interim dividend.
divin [divɛ̃], *a.* Divine; holy (word, etc.); sacred (blood, etc.). *F: Poésie divine,* exquisite, sublime, divine, poetry.
divinateur, -trice [divinatœ:r, -tris]. **1.** *s.* Diviner, soothsayer. **2.** *a.* Foreseeing.
divination [divinasjɔ̃], *s.f.* Divination, soothsaying.
divinatoire [divinatwa:r], *a.* Divinatory. **Baguette divinatoire,** divining-rod, dowsing-rod.
divinité [divinite], *s.f.* Divinity. **1.** Godhead (of Christ). **2.** Deity; god, goddess.
diviser [divize], *v.tr.* To divide. *Mth:* D. *un*

nombre par un autre, to divide one number by another. *Montagnes qui divisent la France d'avec l'Espagne,* mountains that divide, separate, France from Spain. *Maison divisée contre elle-même,* house divided against itself.
se diviser, to divide, to break up (*en,* into).
diviseur [divizœ:r], *s.m.* **1.** *Mth:* Divisor. *Plus grand commun d.,* highest common factor, greatest common measure. D. *premier,* prime factor. **2.** Divider. *El:* D. *de courant,* current-divider.
divisible [divizibl], *a.* Divisible.
division [divizjɔ̃], *s.f.* Division. **1.** Partition (*en,* into); dividing. *Mth:* Division. D. *du travail,* division of labour. D. *par arrondissements,* division into wards. **2.** Part, portion, section (of whole); (administrative) department, branch. *Mil:* Division. **3.** Discord, dissension, disagreement. **4.** (a) *Typ:* Hyphen. (b) *Mus:* Double bar.
divorce [divɔrs], *s.m.* Divorce. **Intenter une action en divorce** *contre qn,* to take divorce proceedings against s.o. *Demander le d.,* to sue for a divorce.
divorcer [divɔrse], *v.i.* **(je divorçai(s); n. divorçons)** D. *(d')avec qn, se d. de qn,* to divorce s.o.
divulgation [divylgasjɔ̃], *s.f.* Divulgation, divulgement, disclosure (*de,* of).
divulguer [divylge], *v.tr.* To divulge, reveal, disclose.
dix, *num.a.inv. & s.m.* Ten. **1.** *card a.* (At the end of the word-group [dis]; before sb. or adj. beginning with a vowel sound [diz]; before sb. or adj. beginning with a consonant [di]) *Il est dix heures* [dizœ:r], it is ten o'clock. *J'en ai dix* [dis], I have ten. **2.** (Always [dis]) (a) *Dix et demi,* ten and a half. (b) *Le dix mai* [lədismɛ], the tenth of May. *Charles Dix,* Charles the Tenth.
dix-huit [dizɥi(t)]. **1.** Eighteen. **2.** *Le dix-huit mai,* the eighteenth of May.
dix-huitième [dizɥitjɛm]. Eighteenth.
dixième [dizjɛm]. **1.** *num. a. & s.* Tenth. **2.** *s.m.* Tenth (part).
dix-neuf [diznœ(f)]. **1.** Nineteen. **2.** *Le dix-neuf mai,* the nineteenth of May.
dix-neuvième [diznœvjɛm]. Nineteenth.
dix-sept [dissɛt]. **1.** Seventeen. **2.** *Le dix-sept mai,* the seventeenth of May.
dix-septième [dissɛtjɛm]. Seventeenth.
dizain [dizɛ̃], *s.m. Pros:* Ten-line stanza.
dizaine [dizɛn], *s.f.* (About) ten; half a score. *Une d. de personnes,* ten or a dozen people. *Compter par dizaines,* to count in tens.
djinn [dʒin], *s.m.* Jinn(ee). *Les djinns,* the jinn, *F:* the jinns.
do [do], *s.m. Mus:* (The note) C.
docile [dɔsil], *a.* (a) Docile, teachable (pupil, etc.). (b) Submissive, manageable, amenable (child); tractable (animal, etc.); flexible (engine). *adv.* **-ment.**
docilité [dɔsilite], *s.f.* Docility.
dock [dɔk], *s.m.* **1.** *Nau:* (a) Dock. **Mettre un navire au dock,** to dock a ship. (b) Dock(s), dockyard. *Droits de d.,* dock-dues. **2.** *Com:* (Dock-)warehouse.
docte [dɔkt], *a. Iron:* Learned. *adv.* **-ment.**
docteur [dɔktœ:r], *s.m.* Doctor. **1.** *D. en droit,* Doctor of Laws. D. *ès lettres,* Doctor of Literature. **2. Docteur (en médecine),** doctor (of medicine); physician. *Entrez, d.,* come in, Doctor. *Le d. Petit,* Dr Petit.
doctoral, -aux [dɔktɔral, -o], *a.* Doctoral; pompous, heavy (manner); grandiloquent (tone). *adv.* **-ement.**

doctorat [dɔktɔra], *s.m. Sch:* Degree of Doctor; doctorate.

doctrinaire [dɔktrinɛːr], *s.m.* Doctrinarian.

doctrine [dɔktrin], *s.f.* Doctrine, tenet.

document [dɔkymɑ̃], *s.m.* Document.

documentaire [dɔkymɑ̃tɛːr], *a.* Documentary (proof, etc.). *Film d.,* instructional film.

documentation [dɔkymɑ̃tasjɔ̃], *s.f.* **1.** Documentation. **2.** *Coll.* Documents.

documenter [dɔkymɑ̃te], *v.tr.* To document (question). *D. qn sur une question,* to post s.o. up on a question.

dodécaèdre [dɔdekaɛdr], *s.m.* Dodecahedron.

dodécagone [dɔdekagoːn, -gɔn], *s.m.* Dodecagon.

dodelin|er [dɔdline]. **1.** *v.i.* (Of old pers.) *D. de la tête,* to wag one's head; to nod. **2.** *v.tr.* To dandle (child). *s.m.* **-ement.**

dodo [dɔdo], *s.m.* (In nursery language) (*a*) Sleep, bye-bye. *Faire dodo,* to go to sleep; to sleep. (*b*) *Aller au dodo,* to go to bed, to bye-bye.

dodu [dɔdy], *a.* Plump.

doge [dɔːʒ], *s.m. Hist:* Doge.

dogmatique [dɔgmatik], *a.* Dogmatic. *adv.* **-ment,** -ally.

dogmatiser [dɔgmatize], *v.i.* To dogmatize.

dogme [dɔgm], *s.m.* Dogma, tenet.

dogue [dɔg], *s.m.* Large watch-dog. *D. anglais,* mastiff.

doigt [dwa], *s.m.* **1.** Finger; *Anat:* Z: digit. (*a*) *Le doigt indicateur,* the forefinger, the index finger. *Troisième d., grand d.,* second finger, middle finger. *F: Mon petit doigt me l'a dit,* a little bird told me so. *Porter une bague au doigt,* to wear a ring on one's finger. *Promener ses doigts sur qch.,* to finger, feel, sth. *Donner sur les doigts à qn,* to rap s.o. over the knuckles. *Savoir qch. sur le bout du doigt,* to have sth. at one's finger tips. *Anglais jusqu'au bout des doigts,* every inch an Englishman. *Il lui fit signe du doigt,* he beckoned to him. *Montrer qch. du doigt,* to point at sth. *Fourrer le doigt partout,* to interfere with everything. *P: Se fourrer le doigt dans l'œil,* to be entirely mistaken. *Se mordre les doigts,* to bite one's nails with impatience. *S'en mordre les doigts,* to repent (of) it, to rue it. (*b*) Finger's breadth. *Être à deux doigts de la mort,* to be within an ace of death. (*c*) *Doigt de pied,* toe. **2.** Iron finger; pawl. *D. d'entraînement,* catch-pin (of lathe).

doigter [dwate], *v.tr.* To mark (music) with the proper fingering.

doigté, doigter, *s.m.* **1.** *Mus:* Fingering (of piece of music). **2.** *F:* Adroitness; tact; judgment. *Manquer de d.,* to be tactless.

doigtier [dwatje], *s.m.* Finger-stall.

dois-, -t, -ve. See DEVOIR.

doit [dwa], *s.m. Com:* Debit, liability. *Doit et avoir,* debit and credit.

doléances [dɔleɑ̃ːs], *s.f.pl.* Complaints; whining. *Conter ses d.,* to tell one's tale of woe; to air one's grievances.

doll|ent [dɔlɑ̃], *a.* **1.** Whining, doleful, plaintive, complaining (voice, person, etc.). **2.** Painful, swollen (arm, etc.). *adv.* **-emment.**

dolman [dɔlmɑ̃], *s.m.* **1.** (Short-skirted) jacket (of hussars, etc.). **2.** (Lady's) pelisse.

doloire [dɔlwaːr], *s.f.* (Carpenter's) broad axe, chip-axe; (cooper's) adze.

domaine [dɔmɛn], *s.m.* **1.** Domain; (real) estate, property. *Jur:* Demesne. *Domaine public, de l'État,* public property. *Le d. forestier,* the national forests. *Ouvrage tombé dans le d. public,* work out of copyright. **2.** *F:* Field, scope (of a

science). *Ce n'est pas de mon d.,* that is not within my province, not within my sphere.

dôme [doːm], *s.m.* **1.** (*a*) *Arch:* Dome, cupola. (*b*) *F:* Vault, canopy (of heaven, etc.). **2.** (*a*) *Mch:* D. de prise de vapeur, steam-dome. (*b*) *D. du palais,* roof of the mouth.

domesticité [dɔmestisite], *s.f.* **1.** (*a*) Menial condition; (state of) dependence. (*b*) Domesticated state; domesticity (of animal). **2.** *Coll.* Staff of servants.

domestique [dɔmestik]. **1.** *a.* (*a*) Domestic (animal, life). *Économie domestique,* domestic economy; housekeeping. (*b*) Domestic, menial (service). **2.** *s.m. & f.* (Domestic) servant; man-servant, woman-servant.

domestiquer [dɔmestike], *v.tr.* To domesticate (animal).
   se domestiquer, to become domesticated.

domicile [dɔmisil], *s.m.* Residence; (place of) abode; dwelling(-place). *Jur:* Domicile. *Sans d. fixe,* with no fixed abode. *Jur:* Élire domicile dans un endroit, to elect domicile at a place. S.a. RÉINTÉGRER 2. *A domicile,* at one's private house. *Franco à domicile,* carriage paid. *Institutrice à domicile,* visiting governess.

domicilier [dɔmisilje], *v.tr. Com:* To domicile (bill at banker's, etc.).
   se domicilier, to take up one's residence, one's abode (à, at).
   domicilié, *a.* Resident, domiciled (à, at).

dominance [dɔminɑ̃ːs], *s.f.* **1.** Dominance, dominion, sway. **2.** Predominance, preponderance (of colour, opinion, etc.).

dominant, -ante [dɔminɑ̃, -ɑ̃ːt], *a.* **1.** Dominating, dominant, ruling (power, etc.). **2.** Predominating, prevailing (colour, opinion); outstanding (feature). **3.** *s.f.* **Dominante.** *Mus:* Dominant.

dominateur, -trice [dɔminatœːr, -tris], *a.* Domineering, overbearing (person, tone).

domination [dɔminasjɔ̃], *s.f.* Domination, rule, sway.

dominer [dɔmine]. **1.** *v.i.* To rule, hold sway. *D. sur qn,* (i) to have dominion over s.o.; (ii) to domineer over s.o. *Couleur qui domine,* predominating colour. **2.** *v.tr.* To dominate. (*a*) To rule, sway; to master, control, overcome (one's scruples). *Sa voix dominait toutes les autres,* his voice rose above, was heard above, all others. *Sp: D. la partie,* to have the best of the game. (*b*) To tower above (sth.); to overlook. *Le château domine la vallée,* the castle looks down upon the valley.

dominicain, -aine [dɔminikɛ̃, -ɛn], *a. & s.* **1.** *Ecc:* Dominican. **2.** *Geog:* **La République Dominicaine,** the Dominican Republic; Santo Domingo.

dominical, -aux [dɔminikal, -o], *a.* Dominical (letter, etc.). *L'oraison dominicale,* the Lord's prayer.

domino [dɔmino], *s.m. Cost: Games:* Domino. *Jouer aux dominos,* to play (at) dominoes.

dommage [dɔmaːʒ], *s.m.* **1.** (*a*) Damage, injury. *Causer du d. à qn,* to do s.o. harm. (*b*) *F: Quel dommage!* what a pity! *C'est dommage qu'elle ne soit pas venue,* it is a pity that she did not come. **2.** *pl.* (*a*) Damage (to property, etc.). *Réparer les dommages,* to repair, make good, the damage. (*b*) *Jur:* **Dommages-intérêts,** damages.

domptable [dɔ̃tabl], *a.* Tamable.

dompt|er [dɔ̃te], *v.tr.* To tame (animal); to break in (horse); to subdue, master (one's passions). *s.m.* **-age.**

dompteur, -euse [dɔ̃tœ:r, -øːz], s. Tamer (of wild beasts); horse-breaker.
don [dɔ̃], s.m. **1.** Giving (à, to); bestowal (à, on). **2.** (a) Gift, present. **Faire don à qn de qch.**, to make a present of sth. to s.o. (b) Gift; natural quality; talent. *D. de séduction*, gift of fascination. *Avoir le don de faire qch.*, to have a talent, a genius, for doing sth.
donation [dɔnasjɔ̃], s.f. Donation, gift.
donc [dɔ̃:k]. **1.** *conj.* Therefore, hence, consequently, so. *Je pense, donc je suis*, I think, therefore I am. **2.** *adv.* [dɔ̃, but in oratory often dɔ̃:k] (a) (Emphatic) *Que voulez-vous d.?* what ever do you want? *Mais taisez-vous d.!* do hold your tongue! *Allons d.!* (i) nonsense! not a bit of it! (ii) come on! look sharp! *Pensez d.!* just think! (b) (After digression) Donc [dɔ̃:k], *pour en revenir à notre sujet*, well, to come back to our subject.
dondon [dɔ̃dɔ̃], s.f. F: **Grosse dondon**, big lump of a lass, of a woman.
donjon [dɔ̃ʒɔ̃], s.m. Keep (of castle).
donne [dɔn], s.f. Cards: Deal. **Faire la donne**, to deal.
donner [dɔne], v.tr. To give. **1.** *D. un bal*, to give a ball. *D. aux pauvres*, to give to the poor. *Prov:* **Qui donne tôt donne deux fois**, he gives twice who gives quickly. *D. un coup de brosse à son chapeau*, to give one's hat a brush. *D. le bonjour à qn*, to bid, wish, s.o. good day. *D. des conseils*, to give advice. *D. à boire à qn*, to give s.o. something to drink. *Je lui ai donné à entendre que . . .*, I gave him to understand that. . . . *Je vous en donne dix francs*, I will give you ten francs for it. *Je vous le donne en vingt*, I give you twenty guesses. *F:* **C'est donné**, it's dirt cheap; it's a gift. *Cela se donne*, it can be had for the asking. *D. un cheval pour, contre, un âne*, to give a horse in exchange for a donkey. **S'en donner (à cœur joie)**, to enjoy oneself (to the full); to have a good time. *D. au plaisir*, to give oneself up to pleasure. *D. à qn sa fille en mariage*, to give one's daughter to s.o. in marriage. *D. la main à qn*, to shake hands with s.o. *Elle lui donna sa main*, she gave him her hand (in marriage). *D. les cartes*, to deal (the cards). **Mal donner**, to misdeal. **2.** (a) To provide, furnish; (of crops) to yield. *Arbre qui donne des fruits*, tree that bears fruit. *D. des preuves à qn*, to furnish s.o. with proofs. *Cela donne à penser*, this gives, provides, food for reflection. *Cela donne l'idée que . . .*, it conveys the idea that. . . . *D. un bon exemple*, to set a good example. *D. la leçon pour demain*, to set the lesson for to-morrow. *D. une pièce de théâtre*, to produce, perform, a play. **A un point donné**, at a given, certain, point. *Étant donné qu'il est mineur*, inasmuch as he is not of age. *Abs. Si les blés donnent cette année*, if there is a good crop of wheat this year. (b) **Donner faim, soif, sommeil, chaud, à qn**, to make s.o. hungry, thirsty, sleepy, hot. *D. la fièvre à qn*, to throw s.o. into a fever. **3.** To ascribe, attribute (sth. to s.o.). *Elle se donne trente ans*, she professes to be thirty. *Je lui donne vingt ans*, I put him down as twenty. *Se d. pour un honnête homme*, to claim to be, to put oneself forward as, an honest man. **Donner tort, donner raison, à qn**, to disagree, agree, with s.o. **4.** (a) **Fenêtre qui donne sur la cour**, window that looks out on the yard. **Cette porte donne (accès) sur le jardin**, this door leads out into the garden. *Le soleil donne sur la porte*, the sun shines on, beats down upon, the door. (b) *D. de la tête contre qch.*, to knock, strike, bump, run, one's head against sth. *D. dans le piège*, to fall into the trap. *F:* **Donner dedans**, to walk right into the

trap. *D. dans le luxe*, to have a taste for expensive things. **Il me donne sur les nerfs**, he gets on my nerves. *F:* **Donner dans l'œil de, à, qn**, to strike s.o.'s fancy. *La cavalerie n'a pas donné*, the cavalry did not engage. *I.C.E:* **Moteur qui donne mal**, engine running or firing badly. (c) *Le toit donne*, the roof is giving way.
donnée, s.f. **1.** Datum (of problem, etc.); fundamental idea (of novel, etc.). **2.** *pl.* Data.
donneur, -euse [dɔnœ:r, -øːz], s. (a) Giver. *Med:* **D. de sang**, blood donor. (b) *Cards:* Dealer.
dont [dɔ̃], *rel.pron.* (= de qui, duquel, desquels, etc.) (a) From, by, with, whom or which. *Les aïeux d. je suis descendu*, the ancestors from whom I am descended. *La chaîne d. il était attaché*, the chain by which he was fastened. *La femme d. il est amoureux*, the woman he is in love with. (b) (Of, about, concerning) whom, which. *Le livre d. j'ai besoin*, the book (that) I want. *Voici ce d. il s'agit*, this is what it is all about. (c) Whose, of whom, of which. *La dame d. je connais le fils, vous connaît*, the lady whose son I know. *La dame d. le fils vous connaît*, the lady whose son knows you.
donzelle [dɔ̃zɛl], s.f. F: Wench, hussy.
dorade [dɔrad], s.f. Ich: Dorado, dolphin.
dorénavant [dɔrenavɑ̃], adv. Henceforth.
dor|er [dɔre], v.tr. **1.** To gild. *F:* **Dorer la pilule**, to gild the pill. **2.** *Bookb:* Dorer à froid, to stamp (cover) in blind. **3.** *Cu:* (a) To glaze (cake). (b) To brown (meat, etc.). s.m. **-age.**
doré, a. Gilded, gilt. *Bookb: D. sur tranches*, gilt-edged.
doreur, -euse [dɔrœ:r, -øːz], s. Gilder.
dorique [dɔrik], a. Arch: Doric (order).
dorloter [dɔrlɔte], v.tr. To fondle, coddle; to pamper.
se dorloter, to coddle oneself.
dormant [dɔrmɑ̃]. **1.** a. (a) Sleeping. (b) Dormant (account); (capital) lying idle; stagnant (water). (c) Fixed, immovable (post, fan-light). *Nau:* **Manœuvres dormantes**, standing rigging. **2.** s.m. Frame, casing (of door, window).
dormeur, -euse [dɔrmœ:r, -øːz], s. (a) Sleeper. (b) *F:* Sleepy-head, sluggard.
dormir [dɔrmi:r], v.i. (*pr.p.* dormant; *p.p.* dormi; *pr.ind.* je dors, n. dormons; *p.d.* je dormais; *p.h.* je dormis) **1.** To sleep; to be asleep. *D. profondément*, to be fast asleep. *D. du sommeil du juste*, to sleep the sleep of the just. *Il n'en dort pas*, he can't sleep for thinking of it. *D. trop longtemps*, to oversleep oneself. **Dormir la grasse matinée**, to lie late abed. S.a. DÎNER I. *F:* **Dormir à poings fermés, comme un sabot**, to sleep soundly, like a top, like a log. **Ne dormir que d'un œil**, to sleep with one eye open. **Vous pouvez dormir sur les deux oreilles**, you need have no cause for uneasiness. **Il dormait debout**, he couldn't keep his eyes open. **Une histoire à dormir debout**, (i) a boring, tedious, tale; (ii) a tall yarn. **2.** To be dormant. *Laisser d. une affaire*, to let an affair lie dormant. *Eau qui dort*, stagnant water. *Prov:* **Il n'y a pire eau que l'eau qui dort**, still waters run deep.
dormitif [dɔrmitif], s.m. Sleeping-draught.
dortoir [dɔrtwa:r], s.m. Dormitory. *Nau:* Sleeping cabin. *Ind:* Men's sleeping-quarters.
dorure [dɔry:r], s.f. **1.** (a) Gilding. (b) *Bookb: D. à froid*, blind tooling. (c) *Cu:* (i) Glazing (with yolk of egg). (ii) Browning. **2.** Gilt.
dos [do], s.m. Back. **1.** *Avoir le dos rond*, to be round-shouldered. **Voir qn de dos**, to have a back view of s.o. **Tourner le dos à qn**, to turn

one's back on s.o.; to stand, sit, with one's back to s.o. *Il va nous tomber sur le dos*, he will be bursting in upon us. **Faire le gros dos**, (of cat) to arch up, set up, its back; (of pers.) to put on important airs. **Monter à dos, to ride bareback**. **Se mettre tout le monde à dos**, to set everybody against oneself. *F:* **Avoir qn sur le dos**, to be saddled with s.o. **Il a bon dos**, the blame is always put on him. *P:* **J'en ai plein le dos**, I am fed up with it. S.a. ÂNE 1. **2.** Back (of chair, blade, page, etc.); bridge (of nose). *Scie à dos*, backed saw. *"Voir au dos,"* 'turn over.'

dose [do:z], *s.f.* **1.** *Ch: etc:* Proportion, amount (of constituent). **2.** Dose (of medicine).

dos|er [doze], *v.tr. Ch: etc:* To proportion, titrate (constituent). *s.m.* **-age.**

dossard [dosa:r], *s.m. Sp:* Number (fastened on the back of competitor).

dossier [dosje], *s.m.* **1.** Back (of seat). *D. de malade*, bed-rest. **2.** (a) Documents, file (relating to an affair). (b) Record (of official, prisoner, etc.). *Avoir un d. lourdement chargé*, to have a very bad record.

dossière [dosjɛ:r], *s.f.* **1.** *Harn:* Back-strap (supporting the shafts). **2.** Back-plate (of cuirass).

dot [dɔt], *s.f.* Dowry, dower; marriage portion. *F:* Coureur de dots, fortune-hunter.

dotal, -aux [dɔtal, -o], *a.* Dotal (property, etc.). **Apport dotal**, dowry.

dotation [dɔtasjɔ̃], *s.f.* Endowment (of hospital, etc.); foundation.

doter [dɔte], *v.tr.* (a) To dower (bride). (b) To endow (hospital, etc.).

douaire [dwɛ:r], *s.m.* **1.** (Widow's) dower. **2.** Jointure; marriage settlement in favour of wife.

douairière [dwɛrjɛ:r], *a. & s.f.* Dowager.

douane [dwan], *s.f. Adm:* Customs. *Visite de la d.*, customs examination. *Aut:* **Carnet de passage en douane**, International Customs Pass. **Passer des marchandises en douane**, to clear goods. **Marchandises en douane**, bonded goods. **(Bureau de) douane**, custom-house. **Franc de douane**, duty paid.

douanier, -ière [dwanje, -jɛːr]. **1.** *a. Tarif d.*, customs tariff. *Union douanière*, customs union. *Barrières douanières*, tariff-walls. **2.** *s.m.* Custom-house officer. *Nau:* Tide-waiter.

double [dubl]. **1.** *a.* Double, twofold. **Mot, expression, à double entente**, word, phrase, with a double meaning. **Mot à double sens**, ambiguous word. **Faire coup double**, to kill two birds at one shot. **Fermer une porte à double tour**, to double-lock a door. *Pompe à d. effet*, double-acting pump. **Comptabilité en partie double**, double entry book-keeping. *Quittance d.*, receipt in duplicate. *I.C.E:* D. allumage, dual ignition. *F:* **Un d. coquin**, an arrant rascal. **2.** *adv.* **Voir double**, to see double. **3.** *s.m.* (a) Double. *J'ai le d. de votre âge*, I am twice your age. *Plus lent du d.*, twice as slow. **Plier qch. en double**, to fold sth. in half. **Bontés rendues au double**, kindnesses returned twofold. *Ten:* **Double messieurs, double dames**, men's, ladies', double. (b) Duplicate, counterpart. **Facture en double**, invoice in duplicate. *adv.* **-ment[1].**

double-corde, *s.f. Mus:* Double-stopping (on violin, etc.).

doubl|er [duble]. **1.** *v.tr.* (a) To double (the size, etc.). (b) To fold (sheet of paper) in half, in two; to double (sheet of paper). *Nau:* D. un cap, to double, 'make,' weather, a cape. *Sch:* D. une classe, to repeat a class. *Th:* D. un rôle, to understudy a part. D. le pas, to quicken one's pace. *Aut:* **Défense de doubler**, overtaking and

passing forbidden. (c) To line (coat, etc.). *Caisse doublée de zinc*, zinc-lined case. *Fourchettes doublées d'argent*, silver-plated forks. *Haine qui se double de mépris*, hatred to which contempt is added. (d) *Cin:* To dub (a film). **2.** *v.i.* (Of population, etc.) To double, to increase twofold. *s.m.* **-age.** *s.m.* **-ement[2].**

doublé, *s.m.* Gold-, silver-cased jewellery; rolled gold. *D. d'argent*, silver-plated wares.

doublet [dublɛ], *s.m. Ling: Phot:* Doublet.

doublure [dubly:r], *s.f.* **1.** Lining (of garment, etc.); sheathing (of hull, etc.). **2.** *Th:* Understudy.

douce. See DOUX.

douce-amère, *s.f. Bot:* Woody nightshade, bitter-sweet.

douceâtre, douçâtre [dusɑ:tr], *a.* Sweetish.

doucement [dusmɑ̃], *adv.* Gently, softly; (to run, work) smoothly. **Allez-y doucement!** gently does it! easy does it! *Prov:* **Qui va doucement va loin**, slow and steady wins the race.

doucereu|x, -euse [dusrø, -ø:z], *a.* **1.** Sweetish, sickly; mawkish (taste, etc.). **2.** Mealy-mouthed, smooth-tongued (person). *adv.* **-sement.**

doucet, -ette [dusɛ, -ɛt]. **1.** *a. & s.* Meek, mild, demure (person). **2.** *s.f.* **Doucette**, corn salad; lamb's-lettuce.

douceur [dusœ:r], *s.f.* **1.** (a) Sweetness (of honey, perfume, etc.). (b) *pl.* Sweets; sweet things. **2.** Softness (of sound, material, etc.); smoothness (of trot, etc.); meekness (of disposition). **3.** (a) Pleasantness. (b) Pleasant thing. *Les douceurs de la vie*, the comforts, sweets, of life. **4.** Gentleness (of character, etc.); sweetness (of smile); mellowness (of colour, wine); mildness (of climate). **En douceur**, cautiously, carefully. *Allez-y en d.!* gently does it!

douche [duʃ], *s.f.* **1.** Shower-bath. **Jeter une douche froide sur l'enthousiasme de qn**, to throw cold water on s.o.'s enthusiasm. **2.** *Med:* Douche.

doucher [duʃe], *v.tr.* **1.** To give (s.o.) a shower-bath. **2.** *Med:* To douche.

doucine [dusin], *s.f. Arch:* Cyma, ogee.

douer [dwe], *v.tr.* To endow (s.o.) (de, with).

doué, *a.* Gifted. *Il est d. pour les mathématiques*, he has a natural gift for mathematics.

douille [du:j], *s.f.* Tubular casing. (a) Socket (of tool, bayonet). *El.E:* Contact-socket, holder (of electric-light bulb). (b) Case (of cartridge). (c) *Mec.E:* Sleeve, boss (of wheel, etc.). **Accouplement à douille**, sleeve-coupling.

douillet, -ette [dujɛ, -ɛt]. **1.** *a.* (a) Soft, downy (cushion, etc.). (b) (Of pers.) Soft; timorous of pain. *Un d.*, a molly-coddle. **2.** *s.f.* **Douillette.** *Cost:* Quilted overcoat (of priest).

douillettement [dujɛtmɑ̃], *adv.* Softly, delicately; cosily. *Élever un enfant d.*, to coddle a child.

douleur [dulœ:r], *s.f.* Suffering. **1.** Pain, ache. *Se sentir des douleurs par tout le corps*, to ache all over. *Sans douleur*, painless (operation, etc.). **2.** Sorrow, grief, woe.

douloureu|x, -euse [dulurø, -ø:z], *a.* Painful. **1.** Aching; sore, tender. S.a. TIC. **2.** Sad, distressing, grievous (loss, etc.); pained, sorrowful (look). *adv.* **-sement.**

doute [dut], *s.m.* Doubt, uncertainty, misgiving. **Être en doute, dans le doute**, to be in doubt. **Avoir des doutes sur qch.,**, to have misgivings, suspicions, about sth. **Mettre, révoquer, qch. en doute**, to call sth. in question; to question sth. *Mettre en d. la parole de qn*, to challenge s.o.'s word. **C'est hors de doute, il n'y a pas de doute,** it is beyond doubt, beyond (all) question. **Il est hors de doute que** + *ind.*, it is beyond doubt that .... **Nul doute qu'il (ne) soit mort,** there is no doubt that he is dead. **Sans doute,** (i) doubtless(ly), without doubt; (ii) no doubt, I dare say, to be sure. *F*: **Sans doute qu'il oubliera,** I dare say he will forget. S.a. ABSTENIR (s').

douter [dute], *v.i.* To doubt. *D. du zèle de qn,* to doubt, to question, to have doubts about, s.o.'s zeal. *D. de qn,* to mistrust s.o. **Il était à n'en point douter courageux,** his courage was beyond all question. *Je ne doute pas de le voir bientôt,* I have no doubt I shall see him before long. *Je doute qu'il soit assez fort,* I doubt whether he is strong enough. *Je ne doute pas qu'il (ne) vous vienne en aide,* I do not doubt but that he will help you. *F*: *Il ne doute de rien,* he is full of self-confidence.

se douter de qch., to suspect, surmise, conjecture, sth. *Il se doute de quelque chose,* he suspects something. *Il ne se doute de rien,* he suspects nothing. *Je ne me doutais pas qu'il fût là,* I had no suspicion, no idea, that he was there.

douteu|x, -euse [dutø, -øːz], *a.* **1.** Doubtful, uncertain, questionable. *Créance douteuse,* doubtful debt. *Clarté douteuse,* dubious, uncertain, light. **Il est douteux que** + *sub.*, it is doubtful whether .... **Il n'est pas douteux que ...** (ne) + *sub.*, more usu. **que** + *ind.*, there is no doubt (but) that. .... **2.** *Je suis d. sur ce que je dois faire,* I am in doubt what to do. *adv.* **-sement.**

douve [duːv], *s.f.* **1.** Trench, ditch; moat (of castle). **2.** *Coop:* Stave. **3.** *Bot:* **Grande douve,** spearwort. **4.** *Vet:* Fluke(-worm).

Douvres [duːvr]. *Pr.n.f. Geog:* Dover.

doux, *f.* **douce** [du, dus], *a.* (*a*) Sweet; smooth, soft (to the touch). **Eau douce,** (i) fresh water, (ii) soft water. S.a. MARIN 2. (*b*) Pleasant, agreeable. *J'ai eu la vie douce,* my life has been a pleasant one. **Tenir de doux propos,** to say sweet nothings. S.a. ŒIL 2. (*c*) Gentle (movement); soft, subdued (light, colour); mellow (light); mild (climate); quiet (horse). **Voiture douce,** smooth-running car. *Temps d.,* mild, open, weather. *Lime douce,* smooth file. *Tabac d.,* mild tobacco. (*d*) Gentle (remonstrance); meek (nature); mild (rule). *Prix d.,* moderate price. *F*: **Doux comme un agneau,** meek as a lamb. (*e*) *adv. F*: **Filer doux,** to obey; to sing small. **Tout doux!** gently!

douzaine [duzɛn], *s.f.* Dozen. *Trois douzaines d'œufs,* three dozen eggs. *Une d. de personnes,* about a dozen people. *Une demi-douzaine,* half a dozen. **A la douzaine,** by the dozen. **Il ne s'en trouve pas à la douzaine,** they are not to be picked up every day.

douze [duːz], *num.a.inv. & s.m.inv.* Twelve. *Le d. mai,* the twelfth of May. *Louis D.,* Louis the Twelfth. *Rail: etc:* **Douze heures,** twelve o'clock (at noon).

douzième [duzjɛm], **1.** *num. a. & s.* Twelfth. **2.** *s.m.* Twelfth (part).

doyen, -enne [dwajɛ̃, -ɛn], *s.* **1.** (*a*) *Ecc: Sch:* Dean. (*b*) Doyen (of diplomatic corps). **2.** *Être le d., la doyenne, de qn,* to be s.o.'s senior.

draconien, -ienne [drakɔnjɛ̃, -jɛn], *a.* Draconian; harsh, unduly severe (regulations).

dragage [dragaːʒ], *s.m.* **1.** Dredging. **2.** Minesweeping; dragging (of river for body, etc.).

dragée [draʒe], *s.f.* (*a*) Sugar(ed) almond. *F*: **Tenir la dragée haute à qn,** to make s.o. dance to one's tune. (*b*) *Pharm:* Sugar-coated pill. *F*: **Avaler la dragée,** to swallow the pill.

drageon [draʒɔ̃], *s.m. Arb: Hort:* Sucker.

dragon [dragɔ̃], *s.m.* **1.** Dragon. **2.** *Mil:* Dragoon.

dragonne [dragɔn], *s.f.* (*a*) Sword-knot. (*b*) Tassel (of umbrella).

drague [drag], *s.f.* (*a*) Dredger. *D. à godets,* bucket dredger. (*b*) Drag, grappling-hook. (*c*) *Fish:* Dredge, drag-net.

draguer [drage], *v.tr.* **1.** To dredge (river, harbour). **2.** (*a*) To drag (pond, etc.); to sweep (channel). (*b*) To dredge for (oysters, etc.).

dragueur [dragœːr]. **1.** *s.m.* Dredger-man. **2.** *a. & s.m.* (*a*) (Bateau) **dragueur,** dredger. (*b*) *D. de mines,* mine-sweeper.

drain [drɛ̃], *s.m.* **1.** Drain(-pipe). **2.** *Surg:* Drainage-tube.

drain|er [drɛne], *v.tr.* To drain (soil, abscess). *s.m.* **-age.**

dramatique [dramatik], *a.* Dramatic. *L'art d.,* the drama. *Chanteur d.,* operatic singer. *Auteur d.,* playwright. *adv.* **-ment, -ally.**

dramatiser [dramatize], *v.tr.* To dramatize.

dramatiste [dramatist], *s.m. & f.,* **dramaturge** [dramatyrʒ], *s.m.* Dramatist, playwright.

drame [dram], *s.m.* **1.** Flag; (regimental) *a.* (*a*) Drama (as a literary genre). (*b*) Play. *D. lyrique,* opera. **2.** *F*: Sensational affair; drama.

drap [dra], *s.m.* **1.** Cloth. *D. fin,* broadcloth. *D. mortuaire,* pall. *D. d'or,* gold brocade. *Hist:* **Le Camp du drap d'or,** the Field of the Cloth of Gold. **2.** Drap de lit, bed-sheet. *F*: **Être dans de beaux, mauvais, draps,** (i) to be in a fine mess, in a sorry plight; (ii) to be in a bad way.

drapeau [drapo], *s.m.* Flag; (regimental) colour. *D. parlementaire,* flag of truce. **Arborer un d.,** to hoist a flag. **Être sous les drapeaux,** to serve with the colours.

draper [drape], *v.tr.* **1.** To drape, cover, hang, (doorway, etc.) with black (as a sign of mourning). **2.** To drape (article of furniture, etc.).

draperie [drapri], *s.f.* Drapery.

drapier, -ière [drapje, -jɛːr], *s.* **1.** (*a*) Draper, clothier. (*b*) Cloth manufacturer. **2.** *s.f.* **Drapière,** blanket pin.

drêche [drɛʃ], *s.f. Brew: Dist:* Draff.

drelin [drəlɛ̃], *onomat. & s.m.* Ting-a-ling; tinkle.

Dresde [drɛzd]. *Pr.n.f. Geog:* Dresden.

dress|er [drese], *v.tr.* **1.** To erect, set up, raise (mast, monument, etc.); to set (trap); to set, lay (table); to pitch (tent). *D. la tête,* (i) to hold up one's head; (ii) to look up. *D. les oreilles,* to prick up one's ears. **2.** To prepare, draw up (plan, contract); to make out (cheque, invoice); to draw up (list). **3.** To adjust, arrange (sth.); to trim, true up (piece of wood); to square (block of stone). **4.** To train (animal, person); to break in (horse); to drill (recruit). *s.m.* **-age.**

se dresser. (*a*) To stand up, rise. *Se d. contre qch.,* to rise up (in protest) against sth. *Se d. sur la pointe des pieds,* to rise on tiptoe. *C'était à faire dresser les cheveux (sur la tête),* it was enough to make one's hair stand on end. *Au centre se dresse une statue,* in the centre stands a statue. (*b*) To sit up, straighten up (in one's chair); to become all attention. (*c*) (Of horse) To rear.

dresseur, -euse [drescœːr, -øːz], *s.* **1.** Erector; adjuster. **2.** Trainer (of animals). *D. de chevaux,* horse-breaker.

dressoir [dreswaːr], *s.m.* Sideboard, dresser.

drille¹ [driːj], *s.m. F*: *Un joyeux d.,* a merry fellow; a gay dog. *Pauvre d.!* poor devil!

drille², *s.f. Tls:* Hand-drill.

drisse [dris], *s.f. Nau:* Halyard.

drogue [drɔg], *s.f.* **1.** (*a*) Drug, nostrum. (*b*) Chemical (as a commercial article). **2.** *F:* Worthless stuff; trash.

droguer [drɔge]. **1.** *v.tr.* To physic (person); to dope, nobble (race-horse, etc.). *Se d.,* to take drugs. **2.** *v.i. F:* To be kept waiting. **Faire droguer qn,** to keep s.o. waiting.

droguerie [drɔgri], *s.f.* Drysaltery.

droguiste [drɔgist], *s.m.* Drysalter.

droit[1] [drwa], *a.* **1.** Straight, upright; plumb (wall, etc.). *Se tenir d.,* to stand upright. *Col d.,* stand-up collar. *Angle d.,* right angle. *Geom. Draw:* Section droite, cross-section. **2.** (*a*) Direct, straight (road, etc.). *Nau:* **D. la barre!** helm amidships! (*b*) *Ligne droite, s.f.* droite, straight line. **En ligne droite,** in a straight line. (*c*) *adv. Marcher d.,* to walk straight. *Allez tout d.,* keep straight on. *Nau:* **Droit devant, droit debout,** right ahead. **3.** Straightforward, upright (person, conduct). **4.** (*a*) Right (hand, side, etc.). **Être le bras droit de qn,** to be s.o.'s right-hand man. (*b*) *s.f.* **Droite,** right hand; right(-hand) side. *Tenir la droite,* to keep to the right. *Nau:* **A droite (la barre)!** starboard!

droit[2], *s.m.* **1.** Right. *Droits civils,* civil rights. *D. de passage,* right of way. *D. de cité,* freedom of a city. *Droit d'aînesse,* birthright. *Droit d'auteur,* copyright. **"Tous droits réservés,"** 'all rights reserved.' *Faire valoir son droit,* to vindicate one's rights. **Droits acquis,** vested interests. **Avoir droit à qch.,** to have a right to sth. **Donner droit à qn,** to give a decision in favour of s.o. **Avoir le droit, être en droit, de faire qch.,** to be entitled to do sth. **S'adresser à qui de droit,** to apply to the proper quarter. **Être dans son droit,** to be within one's rights. **A bon droit,** with good reason. **Faire droit à une demande,** to accede to a request; to allow a claim. **2.** Charge, fee, due. *Droits d'auteur,* royalties. *Droits de port,* harbour dues. *Cust:* **D. de douane,** duty. *Marchandises assujetties aux droits, exemptes de droits,* dutiable goods, duty-free goods. *D. d'inscription,* registration fee. **3.** *Law. D. écrit,* statute law. *D. coutumier,* common law. **Par voies de droit,** by legal process. **Responsable en droit,** legally responsible. **Faire son droit,** to study, read, law. *Étudiant en d.,* law student.

droitier, -ière [drwatje, -jɛːr], *a. & s.* **1.** Right-handed (person). **2.** *Pol:* Member of the Right.

droiture [drwatyːr], *s.f.* Uprightness, straightforwardness, rectitude.

drolatique [drɔlatik], *a.* (*a*) Comic, humorous. (*b*) Spicy, ribald (tale, song).

drôle[1] [droːl], *s.m.* Rascal, knave, scamp.

drôle[2], *a.* Funny, droll, odd. **Un drôle de garçon,** a funny, rum, chap; *F:* a queer fish. *Une d. de fille,* a funny girl. *Quelle d. d'idée!* what a funny idea! *adv.* **-ment.**

drôlerie [droːlri], *s.f.* **1.** Drollery, (i) oddness; (ii) jesting. **2.** Quip, jest.

drôlesse [droːles], *s.f.* Jade, strumpet, hussy.

dromadaire [drɔmadɛːr], *s.m. Z:* Dromedary.

drosère [drɔzɛːr], *s.f. Bot:* Sundew. *D. à feuilles rondes,* moor-grass.

dru [dry]. **1.** *a.* Thick, strong, close-set (corn, etc.); dense, thick-set (undergrowth). *Pluie fine et drue,* fine, close rain. **2.** *adv. Tomber dru,* to fall thick and fast. *Pousser dru,* to grow thickly. *Frapper dru,* to shower blows (on s.o.).

druide, *f.* **druidesse** [drɥid, drɥidɛs], *s.* Druid, druidess.

druidique [drɥidik], *a.* Druidic(al).

drupe [dryp], *s.m. or f. Bot:* Drupe; stone-fruit.

du [dy] = *de le.* See DE and LE[1]. **dû.** See DEVOIR.

dubitatif, -ive [dybitatif, -iːv], *a.* Dubitative.

duc [dyk], *s.m.* **1.** Duke. **2.** Horned owl.

ducal, -aux [dykal, -o], *a.* Ducal.

duché [dyʃe], *s.m.* Duchy, dukedom.

duchesse [dyʃes], *s.f.* Duchess.

ductile [dyktil], *a.* Ductile; *F:* tractable, pliable (nature).

ductilité [dyktilite], *s.f.* Ductility; *F:* pliableness, docility.

due. See DEVOIR.

duègne [dɥɛɲ], *s.f.* (*a*) Duenna. (*b*) *F:* Chaperon.

duel[1] [dɥɛl], *s.m.* Duel, encounter. **Provoquer, appeler, qn en duel,** to call s.o. out.

duel[2], *s.m. Gram:* Dual (number).

duelliste [dɥelist], *s.m.* Duellist.

dulcifier [dylsifje], *v.tr.* To sweeten, dulcify.

dulcinée [dylsine], *s.f. F:* Dulcinea, inamorata, lady-love.

dûment [dymɑ̃], *adv.* Duly; in due form.

dûmes. See DEVOIR.

dune [dyn], *s.f.* Dune, sand-hill; down.

dunette [dynet], *s.f. Nau:* Poop(-deck).

Dunkerque [dœ̃kerk]. *Pr.n.f. Geog:* Dunkirk.

duo [dyo], *s.m. Mus:* Duet.

duodécimal, -aux [dyɔdesimal, -o], *a.* Duodecimal.

duodénal, -aux [dyɔdenal, -o], *a.* Duodenal.

duodénum [dyɔdenɔm], *s.m.* Duodenum. *Ulcère au d.,* duodenal ulcer.

dupe [dyp], *s.f.* Dupe, *F:* gull.

duper [dype], *v.tr.* To dupe, to gull, to fool (s.o.).

duperie [dypri], *s.f.* **1.** Dupery, deception. **2.** Take-in.

duplicité [dyplisite], *s.f.* Duplicity, double-dealing, deceit.

duquel. See LEQUEL.

dur [dyːr], *a.* **1.** Hard; tough (meat, wood). *Œufs durs,* hard-boiled eggs. **Être dur à cuire,** (i) (of food) to take a lot of cooking; (ii) *F:* (of pers.) to be a tough nut. *Eau dure,* hard water. *s.f.* **Coucher sur la dure,** to sleep on bare boards or on the bare ground. **2.** Hard, difficult. *C'est dur à croire,* it is difficult to believe. **Avoir la vie dure,** (i) to be hard to kill; (ii) to have a hard time of it. *adv.* **Travailler dur,** to work hard. **3.** (*a*) *Dur à la fatigue,* hardened, inured, to fatigue. (*b*) **Avoir l'oreille dure, être dur d'oreille,** to be hard of hearing. **Avoir la tête dure,** to be dull-witted. *Avoir le sommeil dur,* to be a heavy sleeper. **4.** Hard, harsh (treatment, voice). *Traits durs,* hard features. *Avoir le cœur dur,* to be hardhearted. *Hiver dur,* hard, severe, winter.

durabilité [dyrabilite], *s.f.* Durability.

durable [dyrabl], *a.* Durable, lasting.

durant [dyrɑ̃], *prep.* (May follow a sb. sounded as one syllable) During. *Il travailla d. toute sa vie, sa vie d.,* he worked during his whole life, he worked his whole life long. *Parler des heures d.,* to talk for hours on end.

durcir [dyrsiːr]. **1.** *v.tr.* To harden; to make (sth.) hard. **2.** *v.i. & pr.* To harden; to grow hard or tough. *s.m.* **-issement.**

durée [dyre], *s.f.* **1.** Lasting quality; wear; life (of electric bulb). *Essai de durée,* endurance test. **2.** Duration; continuance (of reign, war, etc.). *Bonheur de courte durée,* short-lived happiness. *Quelle est la d. de votre congé?* how long is your leave?

durement [dyrmɑ̃], *adv.* **1.** Hard; hardly (earned). *Vivre d.,* to live a hard life. **2.** Harshly, severely, unkindly.

durent[1,2]. See DEVOIR, DURER.

durer [dyre], *v.i.* **1.** To last, endure. *Étoffe qui durera*, stuff which will wear well. *Voilà trois ans que cela dure*, it has been going on for three years. **2.** (Of pers.) To hold out. *Il ne peut pas d. en place*, he simply can't keep still.

dureté [dyrte], *s.f.* **1.** Hardness; toughness (of meat). **2.** (a) Difficulty (of task, etc.). (b) *D. d'oreille*, hardness of hearing. **3.** Harshness, callousness. *D. de cœur*, hardness of heart. *D. du froid*, severity of the cold. *Parler avec dureté*, to speak harshly.

durillon [dyrijɔ̃], *s.m.* Callosity (on hand, etc.); corn (on sole of foot).

durite [dyrit], *s.f. Aut: Av: etc:* Flexible connection piping.

du-s, -t, etc.; **dusse, -s,** etc. See DEVOIR.

duvet [dyvɛ], *s.m.* Down (on chin, young bird, peach, etc.). *D. de l'eider, du cygne,* eider-down, swan's down.

duveteux, -euse [dyvtø, -øːz], *a.* Downy, fluffy.

dynamique [dinamik]. **1.** *a.* Dynamic(al). **2.** *s.f.* Dynamics.

dynamite [dinamit], *s.f.* Dynamite.

dynamit|er [dinamite], *v.tr.* To dynamite; to blow up (building, etc.). *s.m.* **-age.**

dynamo [dinamo], *s.f. El.E:* Dynamo.

dynamo-démarreur, *s.f. Aut:* Dynamotor. *pl. Des dynamos-démarreurs.*

dynastie [dinasti], *s.f.* Dynasty.

dynastique [dinastik], *a.* Dynastic.

dyne [din], *s.f. Ph.Meas:* Dyne.

dysenterie [disɑ̃tri], *s.f. Med:* Dysentery.

dysentérique [disɑ̃terik], *a. Med:* Dysenteric.

dyspepsie [dispɛpsi], *s.f.* Dyspepsia.

dyspepsique [dispɛpsik], **dyspeptique** [dispɛptik], *a. & s. Med:* Dyspeptic.

dyssymétrie [dis(s)imetri], *s.f.* Asymmetry.

E

E, e [e], *s.m.* (The letter) E, e.

eau [o], *s.f.* Water. **1.** *Eau douce,* (i) fresh water; (ii) soft water. *Laver le plancher à grande eau,* to swill the floor. *Eau de vaisselle,* dish-water. S.a. BÉNIT, MARIN 2, SAVON 1. *Eau rougie,* wine and water. *F:* Mettre de l'eau dans son vin, to draw in one's horns. *Sans eau,* undiluted; neat, raw (spirits). S.a. BOIRE I. 1, SELTZ. *Ville d'eau,* watering-place; spa. *Prendre les eaux,* to take, drink, the waters. *Aller aux eaux,* to go to a watering-place. S.a. THERMAL. (Of locomotive, ship) *Faire de l'eau,* to water; to take in water. *Caisse à eau,* tank. S.a. NIVEAU 2. **2.** (a) *Cours d'eau,* waterway, stream. *Jet d'eau,* fountain. *Pièce d'eau,* (ornamental) lake or pond. *Au bord de l'eau,* at the waterside. S.a. NAGER 2. *Tomber à l'eau,* dans l'eau, (i) to fall into the water; (ii) (of plan, etc.) to fall through. (b) *Eau de pluie,* rain-water. Il tombe de l'eau, it is raining. *Le temps est à l'eau,* it is rainy, wet, weather. (c) *Mortes eaux,* neap tides. *Vives eaux,* spring-tides. *Hautes, basses, eaux,* high, low, water. (Of ship) *Faire eau,* to leak; to spring a leak. *Souliers qui prennent l'eau,* leaky shoes. *Être dans les eaux d'un bâtiment,* to be in the wake of a ship. *Mettre un navire à l'eau,* to launch a ship. S.a. FLEUR 2. (d) *Service des eaux,* water supply. *Château d'eau,* water-tower. *Conduite d'eau,* water-main. *Faire mettre l'eau courante,* to have the water laid on. *Eau courante dans les chambres,* hot and cold water in the rooms. **3.** (a) *Eau d'un fruit,* juice of a fruit. *Diamant de la première eau,* diamond of the first water. *F:* Cela lui fait venir l'eau à la bouche, it makes his mouth water. *Être tout en eau,* to be dripping with perspiration. (b) *Eau oxygénée,* hydrogen peroxide. *Eau régale,* aqua regia.

eau-de-vie, *s.f.* Spirits; brandy.

eau-forte, *s.f.* **1.** *Ch:* Aqua fortis; nitric acid. **2.** *Engr:* Etching. S.a. GRAVURE 1. *pl. Des eaux-fortes.*

ébahir [ebaiːr], *v.tr.* To astound, flabbergast.

s'ébahir, to gape, to stare; to stand amazed, dumbfounded (*de,* at).

ébahissement [ebaismɑ̃], *s.m.* Amazement, astonishment, wonder.

ébarb|er [ebarbe], *v.tr.* To trim; to remove the rough edges from (sth.); to fettle (casting); to clip (hedge, etc.). [BARBE¹] *s.m.* **-age.**

ébarbure [ebarbyːr], *s.f.* Burr, paring (of metal, etc.); *pl.* trimmings.

ébats [eba], *s.m.pl.* Gambols, revels, frolic. *Prendre ses ébats* = S'ÉBATTRE.

ébattre (s') [sebatr], *v.pr.* (Conj. like BATTRE) To gambol, frolic, play, sport; to frisk about.

ébaub|ir (s') [sebobiːr], *v.pr. F:* = S'ÉBAHIR. *s.m.* **-issement.**

ébauche [eboːʃ], *s.f.* Rough sketch (of picture); skeleton, outline (of novel, etc.). *É. d'un sourire,* suspicion, ghost, of a smile.

ébauch|er [eboʃe], *v.tr.* To rough (sth.) out; to sketch out, outline (picture, plan); to rough-hew (statue, etc.); to rough-forge. *É. un sourire,* to give a faint smile. *s.m.* **-age.** *s.m.* **-eur.**

ébauchoir [eboʃwaːr], *s.m. Tls:* (Sculptor's) boaster; roughing-chisel; paring-chisel.

ébène [eben], *s.f.* Ebony.

ébéniste [ebenist], *s.m.* Cabinet-maker.

ébénisterie [ebenistri], *s.f.* **1.** Cabinet work. **2.** Cabinet (for wireless set, etc.).

éberluer [eberlɥe], *v.tr. F:* = ÉBAHIR.

éblouir [ebluiːr], *v.tr.* To dazzle.

éblouissement [ebluismɑ̃], *s.m.* **1.** Dazzling, dazzle(ment). **2.** Dizziness, vertigo.

ébonite [ebonit], *s.f.* Ebonite, vulcanite.

éborgn|er [eborɲe], *v.tr. É. qn,* to blind s.o. in one eye; to put s.o.'s eye out. *s.m.* **-ement.**

ébou|er [ebue], *v.tr.* To scavenge (streets); to clean out (boiler). *s.m.* **-age.** *s.m.* **-eur.**

ébouillanter [ebujɑ̃te], *v.tr.* To scald.

éboulement [ebulmɑ̃], *s.m.* **1.** Falling in (of mine, etc.); caving in (of wall). **2.** Fall of stone. *É. de terre,* land-slide, landslip.

ébouler (s') [sebule], *v.pr.* To fall in, crumble, cave in; (of cliff) to slip.

éboulis [ebuli], *s.m.* **1.** Mass of fallen earth, of debris. **2.** (Mountain) scree.

ébouriffant [eburifɑ̃], *a. F:* Amazing, astounding (success, etc.).

ébouriffer [eburife], *v.tr.* **1.** To dishevel, ruffle, tousle (s.o.'s hair). *Pierre l'Ébouriffé,* Shock-headed Peter. **2.** To amaze (s.o.); to take (s.o.'s) breath away; to take (s.o.) aback.

ébranch|er [ebrɑ̃ʃe], *v.tr.* To lop off the branches from (tree); to strip (tree) of its branches. *s.m.* **-age.** *s.m.* **-ement.**

ébranlable [ebrɑ̃labl], *a.* **1.** Easily shaken or moved. **2.** (*a*) Easily daunted. (*b*) Accessible to pity.

ébranlement [ebrɑ̃lmɑ̃], *s.m.* **1.** Shaking; shock. **2.** Perturbation, agitation, commotion. *É. de la raison,* unhinging of the mind.

ébranler [ebrɑ̃le], *v.tr.* **1.** (*a*) To shake; to loosen (tooth, etc.); to shake, to unsettle (s.o.'s faith). (*b*) **Se laisser ébranler,** to allow oneself to be moved (to pity). **2.** To set in motion. *É. une cloche,* to set a bell a-ringing. [BRANLER]

　s'ébranler. **1.** To shake, totter. **2.** (Of troops, etc.) To get under way, to move off; (of train) to start.

Èbre (l') [lɛbr]. *Pr.n.m.* The (river) Ebro.

ébréch|er [ebreʃe], *v.tr.* (**j'ébrèche;** **j'ébrécherai**) (*a*) To notch; to make a notch in (sth.); to chip (a plate); to break (a tooth). *Couteau ébréché,* jagged knife. (*b*) *F:* To damage, impair (reputation); to make a hole in (fortune). [BRÈCHE]

ébriété [ebriete], *s.f.* Ebriety; drunken state.

ébrouer (s') [sebrue], *v.pr.* **1.** (Of horse) To snort. **2.** (Of bird) *S'é. dans la poussière,* to take a dust bath.

ébruit|er [ebrɥite], *v.tr.* To make known; to noise abroad. [BRUIT] *s.m.* **-ement.**

　s'ébruiter, (of news, etc.) to become known, to spread.

ébullition [ebylisjɔ̃], *s.f.* (*a*) Ebullition, boiling. **Entrer en ébullition,** to begin to boil. (*b*) *F:* Ferment; turmoil.

écaille [ekɑːj], *s.f.* **1.** (*a*) Scale (of fish, etc.). (*b*) Flake; chip (of marble); splinter (of wood). *F:* **Les écailles lui tombèrent des yeux,** the scales fell from his eyes. **2.** Shell (of oyster, etc.). **Écaille de tortue,** tortoise-shell.

écaill|er [ekɑje], *v.tr.* (*a*) To scale (fish); to open (oyster). (*b*) To scale (boiler). *s.m.* **-age.**

　s'écaill|er, to scale off, peel off; to flake (off). *s.m.* **-ement.**

écailler², *s.m.* Oyster-seller or -sheller.

écailleux, -euse [ekɑjø, -øːz], *a.* Scaly; splintery (wood); flaky (paint).

écale [ekal], *s.f.* Shell, pod (of peas); hull, husk (of walnut); shuck (of chestnut).

écaler [ekale], *v.tr.* To shell (peas); to hull, husk (walnuts); to shuck (chestnuts).

écarlate [ekarlat], *s.f. & a.* Scarlet.

écarquill|er [ekarkije], *v.tr.* To open (the eyes) wide; to straddle, spread out (the legs). *É. les yeux,* to stare. *s.m.* **-ement.**

écart¹ [ekaːr], *s.m.* **1.** Motion or distance apart; divergence. (*a*) *É. de cent francs entre deux comptes,* difference of a hundred francs between two accounts. *É. entre deux lectures (d'un appareil scientifique),* variation between two readings. *É. du plomb,* spreading, scattering, of small shot. (*b*) Separation, spreading out; straddling (of the legs). **Faire le grand écart,** to do the splits. (Of horse, etc.) *Se donner un é.,* to strain its shoulder. **2.** Deviation. (*a*) Deflection (of compass needle). (*b*) *Artil: etc:* Error (in range). (*c*) Swerve; step(ping) aside. **Faire un écart,** to step aside; (of horse) to shy. *Écarts de conduite,* delinquencies; slips of behaviour. *Écarts de jeunesse,* errors of youth. (*d*) Digression (in speech, etc.). **3.** À l'écart, aside; on one side. **Se tenir à l'écart,** to keep out of the way; to stand aside. **Tenir qn à l'écart,** to keep s.o. in the background. **Mettre**

de l'argent à l'écart, to put money by. **Prendre qn à l'écart,** to take s.o. aside.

écart², *s.m. Cards:* **1.** Discarding. **2.** Discard.

écarteler [ekartəle], *v.tr.* (**j'écartèle**) To quarter ((i) criminal, (ii) shield).

écartement [ekartəmɑ̃], *s.m.* **1.** (*a*) Separation; spacing. **Pièce d'écartement,** distance piece. (*b*) Setting aside (of objects). **2.** Space, gap, clearance (between bars, etc.); gauge (of railway track). *Veh: É. des essieux,* wheel-base. *É. des roues,* track (of wheels).

écarter¹ [ekarte], *v.tr.* **1.** To separate, part (the fingers, branches, etc.); to draw aside (curtains); to open (one's arms); to spread (one's legs); to square (one's elbows). **2.** To move, thrust, brush, (s.o., sth.) aside. *É. qch. d'une poussée,* to push, shove, sth. aside. *É. un coup,* to ward off, avert, turn aside, a blow. *É. une objection,* to brush aside, rule out, dismiss, an objection. *É. une réclamation,* to turn down a claim. **3.** To divert (suspicion, etc.). *É. qn de la bonne voie,* to lead s.o. astray.

　s'écarter. **1.** To move aside. *S'é. pour laisser passer qn,* to step aside, stand aside, to allow s.o. to pass; to make way for s.o. **2.** To move apart, diverge; (of shot) to spread. **3.** To deviate, stray (*de,* from). *Maison écartée du chemin,* house standing back from the road. *S'é. du sujet,* to deviate, wander, from the subject.

écarté¹, *a.* **1.** Isolated, lonely, secluded, remote (house, spot). *Chemin, sentier, é.,* by-lane, by-path. **2.** (Far) apart.

écarter², *v.tr. Cards:* To discard.

écarté², *s.m. Cards:* (Game of) écarté.

ecclésiastique [ɛklezjastik]. **1.** *a.* Ecclesiastical; clerical (hat, garb). **2.** *s.m.* (*a*) Ecclesiastic clergyman. (*b*) *B.Lit:* **L'Ecclésiastique,** Ecclesiasticus.

écervelé, -ée [esɛrvəle]. **1.** *a.* Thoughtless, hare-brained, scatter-brained (person). **2.** *s.* Harum-scarum. [CERVELLE]

échafaud [eʃafo], *s.m.* **1.** Scaffolding, staging; stand. **2.** Scaffold. *Monter sur l'é., à l'é.,* to go to the scaffold.

échafaudage [eʃafodaːʒ], *s.m.* **1.** Erection of a scaffolding. **2.** Scaffolding.

échafauder [eʃafode]. **1.** *v.i.* To erect a scaffolding. **2.** *v.tr.* To pile up (objects); to build up, construct (system).

échalas [eʃala], *s.m.* **1.** (*a*) Vine-prop. (*b*) Hop-pole. **2.** *F:* Long, thin, person.

échalote [eʃalɔt], *s.f. Bot:* Shallot, scallion.

échancrer [eʃɑ̃kre], *v.tr.* To make a circular or V-shaped cut in (neck of dress, etc.); to notch, gap (plank, etc.). *Mouchoir échancré,* scalloped handkerchief. *Littoral échancré,* indented coast-line. *Robe trop échancrée,* dress cut too low.

échancrure [eʃɑ̃kryːr], *s.f.* Cut-out part, opening (in garment); notch, nick (in wood, etc.); indentation (in coast-line, etc.).

échange [eʃɑ̃ːʒ], *s.m.* Exchange. *Com:* Exchange, barter. **Libre échange,** free trade. **Faire un échange de qch. pour, contre, qch.,** to exchange, barter, sth. for sth. **Recevoir qch. en échange de qch.,** to receive sth. in exchange, in return, for sth.

échangeable [eʃɑ̃ʒabl], *a.* Exchangeable.

échanger [eʃɑ̃ʒe], *v.tr.* (**j'échangeai(s);** n. **échangeons**) To exchange. **Échanger qch. pour, contre, qch.,** to exchange, barter, sth. for sth. *Nous échangeons des timbres,* we swap postage stamps.

échanson [eʃɑ̃sɔ̃], *s.m. Hist:* Cup-bearer.

échantillon [eʃɑ̃tijɔ̃], *s.m.* Sample (of wine, etc.); sample, pattern (of cloth, etc.); specimen (of one's work, etc.). *Prendre des échantillons de . . .*, to sample. . . . **Conforme, pareil, à l'échantillon,** up to sample.

échantillonn|er [eʃɑ̃tijɔne], *v.tr.* **1.** *Com:* To prepare patterns, samples, of (sth.). **2.** *(a)* To verify, check, (articles) by the samples. *(b)* To sample (wine, etc.). *s.m.* **-age.**

échappatoire [eʃapatwaːr], *s.f.* Subterfuge, way out; loop-hole (of escape from obligation, etc.).

échappement [eʃapmɑ̃], *s.m.* **1.** Escape, leakage (of gas, water). **2.** *Mch:* (i) Exhaust, release (of steam); (ii) exhaust stroke. **Tuyau d'échappement,** (i) waste-steam pipe; (ii) *I.C.E:* exhaust (-pipe). **3.** *Clockm:* Escapement.

échapper [eʃape], *v.i.* (Aux. *être* or *avoir*) To escape. **1.** *(a) É. à qn, à qch.*, to escape s.o., sth. *É. à la potence, F:* to cheat the gallows. *Il n'y a pas moyen d'y é.*, there is no escaping it, no escape from it. *Ce fait a, est, échappé à mon attention*, this fact had escaped my attention; I had overlooked this fact. *Il n'a échappé à personne que . . .*, it will not have escaped the notice of anyone that. . . . *Ce propos m'a échappé*, I failed to hear this remark. *Il est vrai que ce propos m'est échappé*, it is true that I let slip this remark. *Son nom m'échappe*, his name has slipped my memory. *É. à toute définition*, to baffle definition. *(b)* (Aux. *avoir*) *É. à un coup*, to dodge a blow. *F:* **Vous l'avez échappé belle,** you have had a narrow escape. *(c)* **Laisser échapper qn,** to let s.o. escape; to set s.o. free. *Laisser é. l'air d'un ballon*, to let out the air from a balloon. *Laisser é. une larme*, to let fall a tear. *Laisser é. une faute*, to overlook a mistake. *(d) Impers. Il lui échappa de la tutoyer*, he forgot himself and called her '*tu.*' **2.** *É. de qch.*, to escape from, out of, sth. *La plume m'est échappée des mains*, the pen slipped from my fingers. *É. d'une maladie, d'un naufrage*, to survive an illness, a wreck.

s'échapper, to escape; to break free, loose. **1.** *S'é. de prison*, to escape from prison; to break prison. *Échappez-vous!* run away! *Cheval échappé*, runaway horse. **2.** *Le gaz s'échappe*, the gas leaks out. *Sa douleur s'échappe en reproches*, his grief finds vent in reproaches.

échappée, *s.f.* **1.** *(a)* Escape (of cattle into field, etc.). **A l'échappée,** stealthily. *(b) Sp:* Sudden spurt. *(c)* Escapade. **2.** Space, interval. *É. de vue*, vista (*sur*, over); glimpse (of). *É. de soleil*, sunburst. *É. de beau temps*, spell of fine weather. *F:* **Faire qch. par échappées,** to do sth. by fits and starts. **3.** Turning space.

écharde [eʃard], *s.f.* Prickle, splinter, that has lodged under the skin or nail.

écharpe [eʃarp], *s.f. (a)* Shoulder sash or (municipal) sash worn round the waist. *(b)* (Lady's) scarf. *É. de fourrure*, fur stole. *(c) Surg:* Arm-sling. *(d)* **En écharpe,** slantwise, aslant; oblique(ly). *Porter le bras en é.*, to carry one's arm in a sling.

écharper [eʃarpe], *v.tr. (a)* To slash, gash, hack. *(b)* To hack (up) (fowl); to cut up (troops, etc.). *F:* **Vous allez vous faire é.!** they will tear you to pieces!

échasse [eʃaːs], *s.f.* Stilt. **Etre monté sur des échasses,** (i) to be on stilts; (ii) *F:* to be pompous; to ride the high horse.

échassier [eʃasje], *s.m. Orn:* Wader.

échaud|er [eʃode], *v.tr.* To scald. *F:* **Se faire échauder dans une affaire,** to burn one's fingers over sth. *s.m.* **-age.**

échaudé, *s.m.* Canary-bread.

échaudure [eʃodyːr], *s.f.* Scald.

échauffant [eʃofɑ̃], *a.* **1.** Heating; binding (food). **2.** *F:* Exciting (discussion, etc.).

échauffement [eʃofmɑ̃], *s.m.* **1.** Heating (of bearings); overheating (of engine). **2.** *Med:* (i) Overheating (of the body); (ii) constipation. **3.** Over-excitement. **4.** Heating (of corn, hay).

échauffer [eʃofe], *v.tr.* **1.** *(a)* To overheat (room, blood, etc.). *Abs. Aliments qui échauffent*, binding food. *F:* **Échauffer la bile de qn,** to anger, provoke, s.o. S.a. BILE 2. *(b)* To warm. **2.** To cause fermentation in, to heat (corn, hay).

s'échauffer. **1.** *(a)* To become, get, overheated. **Ne vous échauffez pas,** (i) don't overheat yourself; (ii) *F:* don't get excited. *La dispute s'échauffait*, feeling began to run high. *(b)* To warm (up). **2.** (Of engine) To run hot.

échauffourée [eʃofure], *s.f.* Scuffle; clash (between mobs). *Mil:* Affray.

échauffure [eʃofyːr], *s.f. Med:* Heat-rash.

échauguette [eʃoget], *s.f. A:* Watch-tower.

échéance [eʃeɑ̃s], *s.f.* **1.** Date (of payment); maturity (of bill). **Venir à l'échéance,** to fall due. **Payable à l'échéance,** payable at maturity. **Billet à longue échéance, à courte échéance,** long-dated, short-dated, bill. **A trois mois d'échéance,** at three months' date. **2.** Expiration (of tenancy).

échéant [eʃeɑ̃]. **1.** *a.* Falling due. **2.** See ÉCHOIR.

échec [eʃɛk], *s.m.* **1.** *(a)* Check (at chess). **Échec et mat,** checkmate. **En échec,** (i) in check; (ii) *F:* (of army, etc.) stopped, unable to advance. *Tenir l'ennemi en é.*, to hold the enemy in check. *(b) F:* Check, failure, defeat. *Essuyer, subir, un é.*, to meet with a check, with a repulse. **Faire échec à (qch.),** to put a check on, to check (activities, etc.). **2.** *pl. (a)* Chess. **Partie d'échecs** [eʃɛk, eʃe], game of chess. *(b)* Chessmen.

échelle [eʃɛl], *s.f.* **1.** *(a)* Ladder. *É. à incendie, é. de sauvetage*, fire-escape. *É. brisée*, folding steps. *É. de corde*, rope-ladder. S.a. HAUT III. **2.** **Faire la courte échelle à qn,** to give s.o. (i) a leg up, (ii) a helping hand. *F:* **Après lui il faut tirer l'échelle,** (i) we can never better that; (ii) *Pej:* *P:* he's the limit. *(b) Nau:* **Faire échelle,** to put into port; to call (*à*, at). *(c)* Scale (of colours, prices). *É. de marée*, tide-gauge. **L'échelle sociale,** the social scale, the social ladder. **Etre au bout de l'échelle,** to be at the top of the ladder. *(d)* Ladder (in stocking). **2.** Scale (of plan, map, etc.). **Carte à grande échelle,** large-scale map. *F:* **Faire les choses sur une grande échelle,** to do things on a large scale.

échelon [eʃlɔ̃], *s.m.* **1.** Rung, round (of ladder). *F:* **Monter par échelons,** to rise by degrees. **2.** *Mil:* Echelon (formation). **En échelon,** in echelon; stepped (gearing, etc.).

échelonn|er [eʃlɔne], *v.tr.* **1.** To dispose (troops) in echelon. **2.** *(a)* To space out (objects). *(b)* To spread out (payments); to stagger (holidays, etc.). *(c)* To step (gears). *(d) El.E:* To stagger (brushes). *s.m.* **-ement.**

échenill|er [eʃnije], *v.tr.* To clear (fruit-trees, etc.) of caterpillars. *s.m.* **-age.**

écherra [eʃera], **échet** [eʃe]. See ÉCHOIR.

écheveau [eʃvo], *s.m.* Hank, skein (of yarn, etc.).

échevelé [eʃəvle], *a. (a)* Dishevelled (hair, person). *(b)* Wild, disorderly (dance, etc.).

échevin [eʃvɛ̃], *s.m.* **1.** *A:* Municipal magistrate. **2.** (In Belgium) Deputy-mayor.

échine [eʃin], *s.f.* Spine, backbone; (of animals) chine. *F:* **Crotté jusqu'à l'échine,** all over mud. **Courber l'échine devant qn,** to fawn on, toady to, s.o. **Avoir l'échine souple,** to be obsequious.

échiner [eʃine], *v.tr. (a)* To break (s.o.'s) back. *(b) F:* To tire out.

s'échiner, *F:* to knock oneself up. *S'é. à un travail,* to slave, fag, at a piece of work.

échinoderme [ekinɔdɛrm], *s.m.* Echinoderm.

échiquier [eʃikje], *s.m.* **1.** Chess-board. **En échiquier,** chequerwise; chequered. **2.** (In Engl.) **Chancelier de l'Échiquier,** Chancellor of the Exchequer.

écho [eko], *s.m.* **1.** Echo. **Faire écho,** to echo(-back). **2.** *Journ:* **Échos,** news items.

échoir [eʃwaːr], *v.i.* (*pr.p.* échéant; *p.p.* échu; *pr.ind.* il échoit, il échet, ils échoient, ils échéent; *p.d.* il échoyait, il échéait; *p.h.* il échut; *fu.* il écherra. Aux. usu. *être*) **1.** Échoir en partage à qn, to fall to s.o.'s share. **Le cas échéant,** should the occasion arise; in case of need. **2.** (*a*) (Of bill) To fall due, to mature. **Billets échus,** bills (over)due. **Intérêts échus,** outstanding interest. (*b*) (Of tenancy) To expire.

échoppe[1] [eʃɔp], *s.f.* (*a*) Booth; street stall. (*b*) (Cobbler's) small workshop.

échoppe[2], *s.f. Tls:* Graver.

échopp|er [eʃɔpe], *v.tr. Engr: etc:* To grave, gouge, scoop; to rout (out). *Wood Engr:* To cut away. **-age.**

échouage [eʃwaːʒ], *s.m. Nau:* **1.** (*a*) Stranding, running aground. (*b*) Beaching (of vessel). **2.** Beaching strand; graving-beach.

échouement [eʃumã], *s.m.* **1.** *Nau:* = ÉCHOU-AGE 1 (*a*). **2.** Failure; miscarriage (of plan).

échouer [eʃwe]. **1.** *v.i.* (*a*) *Nau:* To run aground, to be stranded, to ground. **Échoué à sec,** high and dry. (*b*) To fail, miscarry, prove abortive. *Son plan a échoué,* his plan broke down. *L'affaire échoua,* the business fell through. *É. dans, à, un examen,* to fail, to be ploughed, at an examination. **Faire échouer un projet,** to bring about the failure of a plan; to wreck a plan. **2.** *v.tr.* To beach; to run (ship) aground.

échu. See ÉCHOIR.

écim|er [esime], *v.tr.* To top, pollard (tree). [CIME] *s.m.* **-age.**

éclaboussement [eklabusmã], *s.m.* Splashing, (be)spattering. *Mec.E:* **Graissage par éclaboussement,** splash-lubrication.

éclabousser [eklabuse], *v.tr.* To splash, (be)-spatter (with mud, etc.).

éclaboussure [eklabusyːr], *s.f.* Splash, spatter (of mud, ink, etc.).

éclair [eklɛːr], *s.m.* **1.** Flash of lightning; *pl.* lightning. **Il fait des éclairs,** it is lightening. **Rapide comme un éclair,** quick as lightning. **2.** Flash (of a gun). *Bijoux qui lancent des éclairs,* flashing, glittering, jewels. *É. de génie,* flash of genius. **3.** *Cu:* Éclair.

éclairage [eklɛraːʒ], *s.m.* **1.** (*a*) Lighting; illumination. *É. des rues,* street-lighting. *É. par projecteurs,* flood-lighting. **Heure d'éclairage,** lighting-up time (for vehicles). (*b*) Light. *Mauvais é.,* bad light. **2.** *Mil: Navy:* Scouting.

éclairant [eklɛrã]. **1.** *a.* Lighting; illuminating (power). **2.** *s.m.* Illuminant.

éclaircie [eklɛrsi], *s.f.* **1.** Break, opening, rift (in clouds, etc.). **2.** Clearing (in forest).

éclaircir [eklɛrsiːr], *v.tr.* **1.** To clear (up). *S'é. la voix,* to clear one's throat. **2.** (*a*) To lighten; to make (sth.) clear. *É. le teint,* to clear the complexion. (*b*) To solve, explain, clear up (mystery). (*c*) *É. qn sur qch.,* to enlighten s.o. on sth. **3.** To thin (forest, sauce); to thin out (seedlings, etc.). **4.** To clarify (liquid). **s'éclaircir. 1.** (*a*) (Of the weather) To clear (up). (*b*) *Je veux m'é. sur ce point,* I wish to enlighten myself on this point. **2.** (Of hair, plants, etc.) To get thin; to thin.

éclaircissement [eklɛrsismã], *s.m.* (*a*) Enlightenment; elucidation. (*b*) Clearing up (of mystery).

éclaire [eklɛːr], *s.f. Bot:* Celandine.

éclair|er [eklɛre]. **1.** *v.tr.* (*a*) To light, illuminate. *Venez nous é.,* come and light the way. *Salle éclairée par six fenêtres,* hall lighted by six windows. *Maison éclairée à l'électricité,* house lighted by electricity. (*b*) *Abs.* (Of lamp, etc.) To give a good light. *Cette lampe n'éclaire pas,* this lamp gives a poor light. (*c*) *Mil:* **É. le terrain, la marche,** to reconnoitre (the ground); to scout. (*d*) To enlighten. **2.** *v.impers.* **Il éclaire,** it is lightening. *s.m.* **-ement.**

s'éclairer. 1. To light up, brighten up. **2.** To clear up, become clear.

éclairé, *a.* Enlightened; well-informed.

éclaireur [eklɛrœːr], *s.m.* **1.** (*a*) *Mil: Navy:* Scout. (*b*) Boy scout. **Chef éclaireur,** scoutmaster. **2.** *Aut:* É. de tablier, dash-board light.

éclat [ekla], *s.m.* **1.** Splinter, chip (of wood, stone, etc.). **Voler en éclats,** to fly into pieces; to be shattered, shivered. **2.** Burst (of thunder, laughter, etc.). **Partir d'un grand éclat de rire,** to burst out laughing. **Rire aux éclats,** to laugh heartily. **Faire (de l')éclat,** to create a stir, a scandal. **Sans éclat,** quietly; without any scandal. **3.** (*a*) Flash (of light, of gun). *Nau:* **Feu à éclats,** flashing light. (*b*) Glare (of the sun, etc.); glitter, lustre (of diamond, etc.); brilliancy, vividness (of colours); brilliancy, dash (of musical execution). **Action d'éclat,** brilliant feat of arms. **Être dans tout l'éclat de sa beauté,** to be in the full bloom of one's beauty. **Aimer l'é.,** to be fond of show, of display. **Faux éclat,** false glamour; tawdriness. **Prêter de l'éclat à . . .,** to lend a glamour to. . . . [ÉCLATER]

éclatant [eklatã], *a.* **1.** Bursting. *F:* **Être éclatant de santé,** to be bursting with health. **2.** Loud, ringing (sound, etc.). **3.** Glaring; dazzling, brilliant (light); bright, vivid (colour); sparkling, glittering, flashing (jewels, etc.); brilliant, illustrious (deed).

éclatement [eklatmã], *s.m.* Bursting; shivering, flying (of glass). *El.E:* **Pont d'éclatement,** spark-gap.

éclater [eklate]. **1.** *v.tr.* To split, splinter (mast); to burst (tyre). **2.** *v.i.* (Of boiler, shell) To burst, explode; (of mine) to blow up; (of tyre) to burst; (of glass) to fly (into pieces); (of mast) to split, splinter. **Faire éclater qch.,** to burst, explode, shatter, split, sth. *La guerre, l'incendie, éclata,* war, fire, broke out. **La salle éclata en applaudissements,** the house burst into applause. **Laisser éclater sa colère,** to give vent to one's anger. **Éclater de rire,** to burst out laughing. **3.** *v.i.* (Of jewels, etc.) To sparkle, glitter, flash.

éclateur [eklatœːr], *s.m. El: W.Tel:* Spark-gap; discharger. *É. tournant,* rotary discharger.

éclipse [eklips], *s.f.* Eclipse. **Cible à éclipse,** disappearing target. *Nau:* **Feu à éclipses,** occulting light.

éclipser [eklipse], *v.tr.* (*a*) To eclipse; *F:* to surpass, outshine. (*b*) To obscure (light).

s'éclipser, to become eclipsed; to disappear, vanish.

éclisse [eklis], *s.f.* **1.** Split-wood. **2.** Cheese-tray. **3.** *Surg:* Splint. **4.** *Rail:* Fish-plate.

éclisser [eklise], *v.tr. Surg:* To put (limb) in splints.

écloper [eklɔpe], *v.tr.* (*a*) To lame (s.o., horse). (*b*) *F:* To hurt (s.o.) badly; to cripple (s.o.).

éclopé, *a.* Footsore, lame, crippled.

éclore [eklɔːr], *v.i. def.* (*p.p.* éclos; *pr.ind.* il éclôt, ils éclosent; *p.d.* il éclosait; no *p.h.; fu.*

il éclora. Aux. usu. *être*, occ. *avoir*) **1.** (Of eggs, chicks) To hatch (out); to be hatched. **2.** (Of flowers) To open, to blossom (out); (of buds) to burst. *Le jour est près d'é.*, dawn is at hand. Faire éclore un projet, to realize a plan.

éclosion [eklozjɔ̃], *s.f.* **1.** Hatching. **2.** Opening, blossoming; birth (of passion, etc.).

écluse [eklyːz], *s.f.* **1.** (*a*) (Canal) lock. **Porte d'écluse**, flood-gate, lock-gate, sluice(-gate). **Lâcher une écluse**, to open a sluice-gate. (*b*) Sluice(-gate), flood-gate, lock-gate; tide-gate (of dock). **2.** *Geog:* L'Écluse, Sluys.

éclusier, -ière [eklyzje, -jɛːr], *s.* Lock-keeper.

écœurant [ekœrɑ̃], *a.* Disgusting, loathsome; sickening, nauseous.

écœurement [ekœrmɑ̃], *s.m.* Disgust.

écœurer [ekœre], *v.tr.* **1.** To disgust, sicken, nauseate. **2.** To dishearten. [CŒUR]

école [ekɔl], *s.f.* **1.** (*a*) School. *É. primaire*, elementary school. *É. maternelle*, infant school. **Maison d'école**, school-house. **Maître d'école**, schoolmaster. **Tenir école**, to keep a school. **Aller à l'école**, to go to school. *F:* **Prendre le chemin de l'école**, to go a roundabout way. (*b*) **L'École polytechnique** = the Military Academy (of Artillery and Engineering). **École supérieure de Guerre** = Staff College. (In Paris) **Le quartier des Écoles**, the Latin quarter. S.a. NORMAL I. (*c*) *Mil:* *Navy:* School, drill, training. *É. du soldat*, recruit drill. *É. de tir*, musketry instruction. (*d*) *É. d'équitation*, riding-school. **Haute école**, higher horsemanship. **2.** School (of thought). **Faire école**, (i) to found, be leader of, a school; (ii) *F:* to set a fashion.

écolier, -ière [ekɔlje, -jɛːr], *s.* (*a*) Schoolboy, -girl; scholar. *Bévue d'é.*, (i) schoolboy howler, (ii) foolish mistake. *F:* **Le chemin des écoliers**, the longest way round. (*b*) Novice, beginner, tyro. (*c*) **Papier écolier**, foolscap.

éconduire [ekɔ̃dɥiːr], *v.tr.* (Conj. like CONDUIRE) To get rid of (s.o.) (politely); to show (an importunate person) to the door.

économat [ekɔnɔma], *s.m.* (*a*) Stewardship; treasurership; bursarship. (*b*) Steward's, treasurer's, bursar's, office.

économe [ekɔnɔm]. **1.** *s. m. & f.* Treasurer, bursar (of college, etc.); steward, housekeeper (of castle, etc.); agent (of estate). **2.** *a.* Economical, thrifty (person). **Économe de paroles**, sparing of words.

économie [ekɔnɔmi], *s.f.* **1.** (*a*) Economy, management. **Économie politique**, political economy. S.a. DOMESTIQUE I. (*b*) Harmonious arrangement (of body, system). **2.** Economy, saving, thrift. **Faire une économie de temps**, to save time. **3.** *pl.* Savings. **Faire des économies**, to save money; to save (up). *F:* **Faire des économies de bouts de chandelles**, to pursue a cheese-paring policy.

économique [ekɔnɔmik], *a.* **1.** Economic (problem, doctrine). **2.** Economical, inexpensive. *adv.* **-ment**, -ally.

économiser [ekɔnɔmize], *v.tr.* To economize, save (money, time); to husband (resources, strength). *É. ses paroles*, to be sparing of one's words.

économiste [ekɔnɔmist], *s.m.* Economist.

écope [ekɔp], *s.f.* Ladle. *Nau:* Bailer.

écoper [ekɔpe]. **1.** *v.tr.* To bail out. **2.** *v.i.* *P:* To be hit, wounded; *P:* to cop it.

écorce [ekɔrs], *s.f.* Bark (of tree); rind, peel (of orange, etc.); husk (of rice). *L'é. du globe*, the earth's crust.

écor|cer [ekɔrse], *v.tr.* (j'écorçai(s); n. écorçons)

To bark (tree); to peel (orange, etc.); to husk (rice). *s.m.* **-çage**. *s.m.* **-cement**.

écorch|er [ekɔrʃe], *v.tr.* **1.** To flay (large animal); to skin (eel). *F:* *É. une langue*, to murder a language. *Marchand qui écorche ses clients*, shopkeeper who fleeces his customers. **Écorcher l'anguille par la queue**, to set to work the wrong way; to begin at the wrong end. **2.** (*a*) To graze, rub off (the skin); to graze, bark (one's elbow, one's shin). (*b*) To scrape, scratch (furniture); to rasp (throat). **Son qui écorche l'oreille**, sound that grates on the ear. *s.m.* **-ement**. *s.m.* **-eur**.

écorchure [ekɔrʃyːr], *s.f.* (*a*) *Med:* Abrasion. (*b*) *F:* Scratch, graze.

écorner [ekɔrne], *v.tr.* **1.** To remove the horns of (animal). *F:* **Vent à écorner les bœufs**, tearing wind. **2.** To break, chip, the corner(s) off (sth.). *É. un livre*, (i) to dog('s)-ear a book; (ii) to break the corner of a (bound) book. *F:* *É. son capital*, to make a hole in one's capital.

écornifl|er [ekɔrnifle], *v.tr.* *F:* To cadge, scrounge (meal, etc.); to sponge. *s.* **-eur, -euse**.

écossais, -aise [ekɔsɛ, -ɛːz]. **1.** *a.* Scotch, Scottish. **2.** *s.* Scot; Scotchman, -woman; Scotsman, -woman. **3.** *s.m.* Scotch; Scots (dialect).

Écosse [ekɔs]. *Pr.n.f.* *Geog:* Scotland. **La Nouvelle-Écosse**, Nova Scotia. **Fil d'Écosse**, Lisle thread.

écosser [ekɔse], *v.tr.* To shell (peas, etc.). [COSSE]

écot [eko], *s.m.* **1.** Share, quota. **Payer chacun son écot**, to pay share and share alike. **2.** Score, reckoning, (of meal).

écoulement [ekulmɑ̃], *s.m.* **1.** (*a*) (Out)flow, discharge (of liquid); *Fossé d'é.*, drain. *Trou d'é.*, plug-hole (of sink). *É. catarrhal*, catarrhal discharge. (*b*) Waste-pipe (of bath, etc.) **2.** *Com:* Sale, disposal (of goods). **Marchandises d'écoulement facile**, goods that have a ready sale.

écouler [ekule]. **1.** *v.pr.* (*a*) (Of liquid, etc.) To flow out, run out. *Son argent s'écoule*, his money is melting away. **Faire écouler l'eau**, to run off, drain off, the water. **Faire écouler la foule**, to get the crowd (i) to empty the building, (ii) to move on. (*b*) (Of time) To pass, elapse, slip away. **2.** *v.tr.* To sell (off), dispose of, get rid of (goods, etc.).

écoulé, *a.* *Com:* Of last month; ultimo, *F:* ult. **Payable fin écoulé**, due at the end of last month.

écourter [ekurte], *v.tr.* (*a*) To shorten (dress, etc.); *F:* to curtail, to cut short (speech, etc.). (*b*) To dock (dog's tail, dog); to crop (dog's ears, dog). S.a. QUEUE I.

écoute[1] [ekut], *s.f.* **1.** Listening-place. *Mil:* Listening-post. *F:* **Se tenir aux écoutes**, (i) to eavesdrop; (ii) to keep one's ears open. **2.** *W.Tel:* Receiving, reception, listening in. **Faire l'écoute**, se **mettre à l'écoute**, prendre l'écoute, veiller à l'écoute, to listen in. "Ne quittez pas l'écoute!" 'hold on a minute!'

écoute[2], *s.f.* *Nau:* Sheet (of sail). **Nœud d'écoute**, sheet bend.

écouter [ekute], *v.tr.* **1.** (*a*) To listen to (s.o., sth.). **N'écouter que d'une oreille**, to be only half listening. **Écouter de toutes ses oreilles**, to be all ears. *É. à la porte*, aux portes, to eavesdrop. **Écoutez!** look here! I say! (*b*) *W.Tel:* To listen in. **2.** To pay attention to (s.o.). *Si on m'écoutait . . .*, if I were listened to. . . . *F:* **S'écouter trop**, to coddle oneself.

écouteur, -euse [ekutœːr, -øːz], *s.* **1.** (*a*) Listener. *É. aux portes*, eavesdropper. (*b*) *W.Tel:*

écoutille] Listener-in. **2.** *s.m.* (Telephone) receiver. *W.Tel:* Ear-phone.

écoutille [ekuti:j], *s.f. Nau:* Hatchway.

écouvillon [ekuvijɔ̃], *s.m.* (a) (Gun-)sponge; (rifle) cleaning-brush. (b) *Med:* Swab.

écouvillonn|er [ekuvijɔne], *v.tr.* To brush out (rifle, tube, etc.); to sponge out, swab, scavenge (gun). *Med:* To swab. *s.m.* **-age.**

écrabouiller [ekrabuje], *v.tr. P:* To crush; to squash; to reduce (sth.) to pulp.

écran [ekrɑ̃], *s.m.* **1.** Screen. **Présenter, mettre, un roman à l'écran,** to put a novel on the screen. *Phot:* É. *coloré, é. filtre,* (light) filter. **2.** (Candle-)shade.

écrasant [ekrazɑ̃], *a.* Crushing (weight, defeat).

écrasement [ekrazmɑ̃], *s.m.* Crushing, squashing (of fruit, etc.); defeat (of army); collapse (of building, etc.); crashing (of aeroplane).

écraser [ekraze], *v.tr.* To crush, bruise; to flatten out (tin can, etc.); to squash (fruit, blackbeetle). **Se faire écraser,** to get run over. **Écraser un peuple d'impôts,** to overburden a people with taxes. *Écrasé de travail,* overwhelmed with work. *Ten:* É. *la balle,* to kill, smash, the ball.

s'écraser. 1. To collapse, crumple up. (Of pers.. or aeroplane) *S'é. sur le sol,* to crash (to earth). **2.** *On s'écrasait aux portes,* there was a dreadful crush at the doors.

écraseur [ekrazœːr], *s.m.* **1.** (a) Crusher. (b) *Aut: F:* Road-hog. **2.** Steam-roller.

écrém|er [ekreme], *v.tr.* (j'écrème; j'écrémerai) To cream; (i) to separate, (ii) to skim (milk). *Lait crémé,* skim milk. *s.m.* **-age.**

écrémeuse [ekremøːz], *s.f.* (Cream) separator.

écrevisse [ekrəvis], *s.f.* **1.** (Fresh-water) crayfish. *F:* **Rouge comme une écrevisse,** as red as a boiled lobster. **2.** *Astr:* Cancer; the Crab.

écrier (s') [sekrie], *v.pr.* (a) To cry (out), to shout (out). (b) To exclaim.

écrin [ekrɛ̃], *s.m.* (Jewel-)case.

écrire [ekriːr], *v.tr.* (pr.p. **écrivant**; p.p. **écrit**; pr.ind. **j'écris, n. écrivons, ils écrivent**; p.h. **j'écrivis**; fu. **j'écrirai**) To write. (a) *Il écrit bien,* (i) he is a good writer (of fiction, etc.); (ii) he writes a good hand. **Machine à écrire,** typewriter. **Écrire une lettre à la machine,** to type a letter. *É. une lettre à qn,* to write s.o. a letter. *É. un mot à la hâte,* to scribble a note. *Je lui ai écrit de venir,* I have written to him to come. (b) To write (sth.) down. *É. l'adresse de qn,* to jot down s.o.'s address. *F:* **Il est écrit que je serai en retard,** it is fated that I shall be late. (c) To write, compose (book, song, etc.).

écrit. 1. *a.* Written (word, law, etc.). **2.** *s.m.* (a) Writing. **Coucher qch. par écrit,** to set down sth. in writing. *Convention en, par, é.,* written agreement. (b) Written document; written work. *Il tira un é. de sa poche,* he took from his pocket a paper with something written on it. (c) *Sch:* Written examination.

écri-s, -t. See ÉCRIRE.

écriteau [ekrito], *s.m.* Placard, bill, notice.

écritoire [ekritwaːr], *s.f.* **1.** *A:* Writing-desk. **2.** Inkstand.

écriture [ekrityːr], *s.f.* **1.** (Hand-)writing. *Avoir une belle é.,* to write a good hand. *É. à la machine,* typewriting, typing. **2.** (a) *pl.* (Legal, commercial) papers, documents, records. **Tenir les écritures,** to keep the accounts. *Commis aux écritures,* book-keeper. (b) *Book-k:* Entry, item. *Écritures en partie double,* double entry. (c) **L'Écriture sainte, les saintes Écritures,** Holy Scripture.

écrivaill|er [ekrivaje], *v.i. F:* To penny-a-line; to scribble. *s.* **-eur, -euse.**

écrivain [ekrivɛ̃], *s.m.* **1.** *A:* Scrivener, scribe; (public) letter-writer. **2.** Author, writer. **Femme é.,** woman writer; authoress.

écrou[1] [ekru], *s.m.* Committal to gaol. **Levée d'écrou,** release; discharge from prison.

écrou[2], *s.m. Mch: etc:* (Screw-)nut. É. *ailé, à oreilles,* thumb-nut, wing-nut. É. *à créneaux, à entailles,* castellated nut, castle-nut.

écrouelles [ekruɛl], *s.f.pl. F:* Scrofula.

écrouer [ekrue], *v.tr.* To commit, consign, (s.o.) to prison. *Écroué au dépôt, F:* run in.

écrou|ir [ekruiːr], *v.tr. Metalw:* (a) To hammer-harden, to cold-hammer. (b) To cold-draw. *s.m.* **-issage.** *s.m.* **-issement.**

écroulement [ekrulmɑ̃], *s.m.* Collapse, tumbling down, falling in; fall (of earth); ruin, downfall (of hopes). *É. de la santé,* break-down in health.

écrouler (s') [sekrule], *v.pr.* (Of roof, etc.) To collapse, fall in, give way, tumble down. *Nos plans s'écroulèrent,* our plans fell about our ears. *F: S'é. sur une chaise,* to drop, flop, on to a chair.

écru [ekry], *a.* (Of material) Unbleached, écru, natural-coloured. *Soie écrue,* raw silk. *Toile écrue,* holland.

ectropion [ɛktrɔpjɔ̃], *s.m. Med:* Ectropion; eversion of the eyelid.

écu [eky], *s.m.* **1.** (a) *Archeol:* Shield. (b) *Her:* Escutcheon; coat of arms. **2.** *Num: A:* (a) Crown (= three francs). (b) Five-franc piece. *F:* **Avoir des écus,** to have plenty of money, a pot of money. **C'est le père aux écus,** he is rolling in wealth. **3.** *Ent:* Scutum.

écuanteur [ekɥɑ̃tœːr], *s.f. Veh:* Dish(ing) of wheels).

écubier [ekybje], *s.m.. Nau:* Hawse-hole.

écueil [ekœːj], *s.m.* Reef, shelf. (Of ship) **Donner sur les écueils,** to strike the rocks. *F: La vie est pleine d'écueils,* life is full of dangers.

écuelle [ekɥɛl], *s.f.* Bowl, basin.

écuellée [ekɥɛle], *s.f.* Bowlful.

éculer [ekyle], *v.tr.* É. *ses souliers,* to wear one's shoes down at heel.

écumant [ekymɑ̃], *a.* Foaming, frothing (sea, beer, etc.).

écume [ekym], *s.f.* **1.** (a) Froth (on liquid); foam (on waves, etc.); lather (of soapy water). (b) Scum (on soup, jam, etc.). *F:* **Écume de la société,** scum, dregs, of society. **2. Écume de mer,** meerschaum.

écum|er [ekyme], *v.tr.* To scum, skim (soup, molten metal, etc.). *F:* **Écumer la mer, les mers,** to scour (= rove, the seas. *S.a.* MARMITE. **2.** *v.i.* (Of wine, beer, the sea) To foam, froth. *F: É. de rage,* to foam (at the mouth) with rage. *s.m.* **-age.**

écumeur [ekymœːr], *s.m.* **Écumeur de mer,** sea-rover; pirate. *F:* **Écumeur de marmites,** parasite; hanger-on.

écumeux, -euse [ekymø, -øːz], *a.* Foamy, frothy; scummy (liquid).

écumoire [ekymwaːr], *s.f.* Skimmer.

écur|er [ekyre], *v.tr.* To clean, scour (pots, pans); to clean out (a well). *s.m.* **-age.** *s.m.* **-eur.**

écureuil [ekyrœːj], *s.m.* Squirrel.

écurie [ekyri], *s.f.* (a) Stable. *Mettre les chevaux à, dans, l'é.,* to stable the horses. É. *de courses,* racing stable; racing stud. (b) Boxing school.

écusson [ekysɔ̃], *s.m.* **1.** *Her:* Escutcheon, shield, coat of arms. **2.** Keyhole scutcheon. **3.** *Hort:* Shield-bud (for grafting). *S.a.* GREFFE 2. **4.** *Ent:* Scutellum.

écussonner [ekysɔne], *v.tr.* To graft a shield-bud on (fruit-tree).

écuyer, -ère [ekɥije, -ɛːr], *s.* **1.** *s.m. A:* (a) Squire. (b) Equerry. **2.** *s.m. & f.* Rider; horseman, horsewoman. *Être bon é., bonne écuyère*, to be a good rider. *É. de cirque*, circus rider. **Bottes à l'écuyère**, riding-boots. (Of lady) **Monter à l'écuyère**, to ride astride.

eczéma [ɛgzɛma], *s.m. Med :* Eczema.

eczémateux, -euse [ɛgzɛmatø, -øːz], *a. Med :* Eczematous.

Éden (l') [lɛdɛn], *s.m. B :* (The Garden of) Eden.

édenter [edɑ̃te], *v.tr.* To break the teeth of (comb, saw) ; to take out (s.o.'s) teeth. **édenté**, *a.* **1.** Toothless (person, etc.). **2.** *Z :* Edentate (mammal).

édicter [edikte], *v.tr.* To enact, decree (penalties).

édicule [edikyl], *s.m.* (*a*) Kiosk, shelter. (*b*) *F :* Public convenience.

édifiant [edifjɑ̃], *a.* Edifying (example, etc.).

édification [edifikasjɔ̃], *s.f.* **1.** Erection, building ; setting (up) (of monument, etc.). **2.** (*a*) (Moral) edification. (*b*) Enlightenment. *Pour votre é., sachez que . . .*, to be fully informed, you should know that . . .,

édifice [edifis], *s.m.* Building, edifice. *Tout l'é. social*, the whole fabric, structure, of society.

édifier [edifje], *v.tr.* **1.** To erect, set up (temple). **2.** (*a*) To edify. (*b*) To enlighten, instruct (s.o.).

édile [edil], *s.m.* (*a*) *Rom.Ant :* Aedile. (*b*) *F :* Often *Hum :* Municipal official ; town-councillor.

Édimbourg [edɛ̃buːr]. *Pr.n. Geog :* Edinburgh.

édit [edi], *s.m.* Edict.

éditer [edite], *v.tr.* **1.** To edit (text, etc.). **2.** To publish (book, etc.) ; to run (magazine).

éditeur, -trice [editœːr, -tris], *s.* **1.** Editor, editress (of text). **2.** Publisher.

édition [edisjɔ̃], *s.f.* **1.** Edition, issue, impression (of work). **Édition originale, édition princeps,** first edition. **2.** Publishing. **Maison d'édition,** publishing house.

éditorial, -aux [editɔrjal, -o]. *Journ :* **1.** *a.* Editorial. **2.** *s.m.* Leading article ; leader.

Édouard [edwaːr]. *Pr.n.m.* Edward.

édredon [edrədɔ̃], *s.m.* **1.** Eider-down. **2.** (*a*) *É. piqué, é. américain*, eider-down quilt. (*b*) Large eider-down pillow (covering most of bed).

éducateur, -trice [edykatœːr, -tris], *s.* **1.** Educator, instructor. **2.** *É. de vers à soie*, silkworm-breeder. *É. d'abeilles*, bee-keeper.

éducatif, -ive [edykatif, -iːv], *a.* Educative.

éducation [edykasjɔ̃], *s.f.* **1.** (*a*) Education, bringing up. **Faire l'éducation de qn**, to educate s.o. *É. professionnelle*, vocational training. *É. physique*, physical training. (*b*) Training (of animals). (*c*) Upbringing, breeding. **Personne sans éducation**, ill-bred person. **2.** Rearing, breeding (of silkworms, etc.) ; keeping (of bees).

édulcorant [edylkɔrɑ̃], **1.** *a.* Sweetening. **2.** *s.m.* Sweetener.

édulcorer [edylkɔre], *v.tr.* To sweeten (medicine, etc.).

éduquer [edyke], *v.tr.* **1.** To bring up, educate (child). **Mal éduqué**, ill-bred. **2.** To train (animal).

effacement [ɛfasmɑ̃], *s.m.* **1.** Obliteration ; wearing away (of carvings, etc.). **2.** *E. du corps*, sideways position of body (in fencing). **3.** Retirement, unobtrusiveness ; self-effacement.

effacer [ɛfase], *v.tr.* (j'effaçai(s) ; n. effaçons). **1.** To efface, obliterate, delete. *E. un mot avec une gomme*, to rub out a word. *E. une tache*, to wash out a stain. *E. qch. de sa mémoire*, to blot sth. out of one's memory. **2.** To throw (s.o. else) in the shade. **3.** *Fenc :* *E. le corps*, to stand sideways. **4.** *Av :* To retract (under-carriage).

s'effacer. 1. To become obliterated ; to wear away. *Cela s'effacera à l'eau*, it will wash

off. *Impression, souvenir, qui s'efface vite*, impression, memory, that soon fades, that soon dies out, grows dim. **2.** To stand aside. **3.** *Fenc :* To stand sideways, to show less front.

effacé, *a.* Unobtrusive ; retired (life).

effarement [ɛfarmɑ̃], *s.m.* Fright, alarm.

effarer [ɛfare], *v.tr.* To frighten, scare, startle. **s'effarer**, to be frightened, scared, startled (*de*, at, by) ; to take fright (*de*, at).

effarouch|er [ɛfaruʃe], *v.tr.* To startle, scare away, frighten away (animal). *s.m.* **-ement.** **s'effaroucher**, to be startled (*de*, at, by) ; to take fright (*de*, at) ; to be shocked (*de*, at).

effectif, -ive [efɛktif, -iːv]. **1.** *a.* (*a*) Effective, efficacious (treatment). **Rendre un traité e.**, to implement a treaty. (*b*) Effective, actual. **Valeur effective**, real value. **2.** *s.m.* (*a*) *Mil :* Effective (force) ; total strength (of army, etc.). *Nau :* Complement. *Effectifs en temps de paix*, peace establishment. **Crise d'effectifs**, shortage of man-power. (*b*) *Ind :* Stock (of material, etc.).

effectivement [efɛktivmɑ̃], *adv.* **1.** Effectively. **2.** Actually, in reality ; in actual fact. **3.** (As an answer) That is so.

effectuer [efɛktɥe], *v.tr.* To effect, carry out, accomplish, execute (scheme, operation). *E. un vol*, to carry out a flight. *Mth :* *E. une addition*, to perform an addition.

efféminant [efeminɑ̃], *a.* Weakening, enervating.

efféminer [efemine], *v.tr.* To render effeminate. **s'efféminer**, to become effeminate.

efféminé, *a.* Effeminate, unmanly.

effervescence [efɛrvɛsɑ̃ːs], *s.f.* **1.** Effervescence. **2.** *F :* Excitement ; restlessness, restiveness (of the people).

effervescent [efɛrvɛsɑ̃], *a.* Effervescent.

effet [efɛ], *s.m.* **1.** Effect, result. **Avoir de l'effet sur le résultat**, to affect the result. **Avoir, faire, son effet**, to take effect. **A cet effet, for this purpose ; to this end. A l'effet de, for the purpose of. Sans effet**, ineffective, ineffectual ; without avail. **2.** Action, performance, operation, working. (*a*) **Mettre un projet à l'effet, en effet**, to put a plan into action ; to carry out a plan. (Of law) **Prendre effet**, to become operative. *S.a.* NUL 2. (*b*) *Cr :* *Ten :* Screw, break, twist. **Donner de l'effet à la balle**, to put a spin on the ball. *Bill :* *E. de côté*, side(-screw). (*c*) *Mch :* A simple effet, à double effet, single-acting, double-acting. (*d*) **En effet**, as a matter of fact ; indeed. *Vous oubliez vos paquets!—En e.!* you are forgetting your parcels!—So I am! **3.** (*a*) Impression. *Voilà l'e. que cela m'a produit*, that is how it impressed me. *F :* *Ça m'a fait un e. de la voir si pâle*, it gave me quite a turn to see her so pale. **Faire de l'effet**, to make a show, attract attention. *Cela fait bon e.*, it looks well. **Manquer son effet**, to fail to attract attention ; (of joke, etc.) to miss fire ; to fall flat. **Phrases à effet**, words meant for effect ; claptrap. (*b*) *Art :* *E. de lune*, moon-light effect or study. **4.** **Effet de commerce**, negotiable instrument ; *F :* bill. **Effets à payer**, bills payable. **Effet à vue**, sight draft. **Effets publics**, public bonds. **5.** *pl.* Possessions, belongings, effects ; clothes. **Effets mobiliers**, personal effects ; goods and chattels.

effeuillaison [efœjɛzɔ̃], *s.f.* Fall of the leaves.

effeuillement [efœjəmɑ̃], *s.m.* **1.** = EFFEUIL-LAISON. **2.** Bareness (of woods, etc.).

effeuill|er [efœje], *v.tr.* To thin out the leaves of (fruit-tree) ; to pluck off the petals of (flower). *s.m.* **-age.**

s'effeuiller, (of tree) to shed its leaves ; (of flower) to shed its petals.

efficace [efikas]. **I.** *a.* Efficacious, effectual, effective. *Prêter à qn un appui e.*, to give s.o. effectual support. *El : Watt e.*, true watt. **2.** *s.f. Theol :* Efficacity (of grace, etc.). *adv.* -**ment.**

efficacité [efikasite], *s.f.* Efficacy, effectiveness (of remedy) ; efficiency (of work).

effigie [efiʒi], *s.f.* Effigy. **Brûler qn en effigie,** to burn s.o. in effigy.

effilage [efila:ʒ], *s.m.* Fraying, ravelling out (of material).

effilement [efilmɑ̃], *s.m.* Tapering.

effiler [efile], *v.tr.* **I.** *Tex :* To fray, unravel, ravel out. **2.** To taper. **3.** To string (beans). **s'effiler. I.** To fray out. **2.** To taper.

effilé, *a.* **I.** *Tex :* Frayed, fringed (material). **2.** Slender, slim, slight (figure) ; taper, tapering (fingers). *Aut :* Stream-lined.

effiloch|er [efiloʃe], *v.tr.* (*a*) To ravel out, tease out. (*b*) To fray (material). *s.m.* -**age.**

effilochure [efiloʃy:r], *s.f.* Ravelled or frayed material.

effilure [efily:r], *s.f.* **I.** = EFFILOCHURE. **2.** Ladder (in stocking).

efflanqué [eflɑ̃ke], *a.* Lean(-flanked), *F :* skinny.

effleurement [eflœrmɑ̃], *s.m.* **I.** (*a*) (Light, gentle) touch. (*b*) Skimming (of the water). **2.** Graze.

effleurer [eflœre], *v.tr.* To touch or stroke lightly ; to skim (the surface of the water) ; to graze, brush (solid surface). *F : E. un sujet,* to touch (lightly) on a topic. [FLEUR]

effloraison [eflɔrɛzɔ̃], *s.f. Bot :* Flowering.

efflorescence [efflɔrɛssɑ̃:s], *s.f.* Efflorescence.

effluve [efly:v], *s.m.* **I.** Effluvium, emanation. **2.** *El :* Brush discharge.

effondrement [efɔ̃drəmɑ̃], *s.m.* **I.** Breaking down, caving in ; subsidence ; collapse (of bridge) ; falling in (of roof) ; slump (in prices). **2.** *Geol : etc :* Sink-hole.

effondrer [efɔ̃dre], *v.tr.* To break (sth.) in, down ; to stave in (barrel). **s'effondrer,** to fall in, cave in, break down ; (of credit, prices) to slump ; (of government) to collapse. *F : S'e. dans un fauteuil,* to sink, subside, *F :* flop, into an armchair.

efforcer (s') [sefɔrse], *v.pr.* (**je m'efforçai(s)** ; **n.n. efforçons)** *S'e. de faire qch.*, to strive, do one's utmost, to do sth.

effort [efɔ:r], *s.m.* **I.** Effort, exertion. *Faire un e. sur soi-même,* to try to control oneself. **Faire tous ses efforts pour . . .,** to do one's utmost to. . . . *Consacrer tous ses efforts à une tâche,* to bend, devote, all one's energies to a task. **Sans effort,** easily. **Après bien des efforts,** after much exertion, much hard work. **2.** (*a*) *Mec.E : etc :* Strain, stress. *E. de tension,* tensile stress ; pull. *E. de traction,* pull. (*b*) *Med : Vet :* Strain, (w)rick. **Se donner, attraper, un effort,** to (w)rick one's back.

effraction [efraksjɔ̃], *s.f.* Housebreaking. **Vol de nuit avec effraction,** burglary.

effraie [efrɛ], *s.f.* Barn owl, screech owl.

effray|ant [efrejɑ̃], *a.* **I.** Frightful, terrifying, dreadful, appalling. **2.** *F :* Tremendous, awful. *adv.* -**amment.**

effrayer [efreje], *v.tr.* (**j'effraie, j'effraye** ; **j'effraierai, j'effrayerai**) To frighten, scare, startle (s.o.). **s'effrayer,** to get frightened ; to take fright. *S'e. de qch.*, to be frightened of, at, sth.

effréné [efrene], *a.* Unbridled, unrestrained (passion, etc.) ; frantic (efforts). *adv.* -**ment.**

effrit|er [efrite], *v.tr.* To cause (sth.) to crumble ; to disintegrate. **s'effriter,** to crumble (to dust) ; (of rock) to weather. *s.m.* -**ement.**

effroi [efrwa], *s.m.* Fright, terror, fear. *E. religieux,* awe.

effronté [efrɔ̃te], *a.* Shameless, bold ; impudent (child) ; barefaced, brazen-faced (lie, liar) ; rakish (swagger). [FRONT] *adv.* -**ment.**

effronterie [efrɔ̃tri], *s.f.* Effrontery, insolence, impudence, *F :* cheek(iness). **Payer d'effronterie,** to brazen it out.

effroyable [efrwajabl], *a.* Frightful, fearful, dreadful ; hideous (face) ; *F :* awful, tremendous (expense, etc.). *adv.* -**ment.**

effusion [effyzjɔ̃, efy-], *s.f.* **I.** Effusion, outpouring, overflowing. **Effusion de sang,** (i) haemorrhage, (ii) bloodshed. **2.** Effusiveness. **Avec effusion,** effusively, gushingly.

égailler [egaje], *v.tr.* To flush, scatter (birds). **s'égailler,** (of birds, etc.) to disperse, scatter.

égal, -aux [egal, -o], *a.* **I.** (*a*) Equal (*à,* to). **Toutes choses égales (d'ailleurs),** other things being equal. **Combattre à armes égales,** to fight on equal terms. *s.* **Traiter qn d'égal à égal,** to treat s.o. as an equal. *Prep.phr.* **A l'égal de,** as much as ; equally with. (*b*) Level, even, regular (road, etc.) ; steady (pace). **2.** (All the) same. **Cela m'est (bien) égal,** it is all the same, all one, to me. *Si cela vous est é.,* if you don't mind. *Cela vous est-il é. de venir?* do you mind coming ? *F :* **C'est égal,** *il nous doit des excuses,* all the same, he ought to apologize.

égalable [egalabl], *a.* That can be equalled (*à,* to, with).

également [egalmɑ̃], *adv.* **I.** Equally, alike. **2.** Also, likewise. *J'en veux é.,* I also want some ; I want some as well.

égaler [egale], *v.tr.* **I.** To consider as equal (*à,* to). **2.** To equal, be equal to (s.o., sth.) *Deux et deux égalent quatre,* two and two make four. *Rien ne peut é. cette élégance,* nothing can compare with, come up to, this elegance.

égalis|er [egalize], *v.tr.* **I.** To equalize, adjust (pressure, etc.) ; to screen (coal) ; to size (small shot, etc.). **Égaliser une expression à zéro,** to equate an expression to zero. **2.** To level ; to make (ground) even. *s.f.* -**ation.**

égalitaire [egalitɛ:r], *Pol :* **I.** *a.* Levelling (spirit, policy). **2.** *s.m.* Equalitarian ; leveller.

égalité [egalite], *s.f.* **I.** Equality. **Être sur un pied d'égalité avec qn,** to be on an equal footing, on equal terms, with s.o. *Games :* **A égalité,** equal in points ; *Golf :* all square ; *Ten :* deuce. *Ten :* **Égalité à rien,** love all. **Course à égalité,** dead heat ; tie. *Turf :* **Parier à égalité sur un cheval,** to lay evens on a horse. **A égalité de . . .,** where there is equality of. . . . **2.** Evenness, regularity (of surface, of breathing, etc.).

égard [ega:r], *s.m.* Consideration, respect. (*a*) **Avoir égard à qch.,** to allow for sth. ; to pay regard to sth. **Eu égard à . . .,** in consideration of . . . ; having regard to. . . . **A tous (les) égards,** in all respects. **N'ayez aucune crainte à cet égard,** have no fear in this connection, on that score, about that. **A l'égard de,** with regard to ; with respect to. *Être injuste à l'é. de qn,* to be unjust to(wards) s.o. *A l'é. de votre demande . . .,* in reference to your request. . . . (*b*) *Témoigner des égards pour qn,* to show regard for s.o. *Devoir des égards à qn,* to owe s.o. respect. **Faire qch. par égard pour qn,** to do sth. (i) out of respect for s.o., (ii) for s.o.'s sake. **Être plein d'égards pour qn,** to be full of attentions to s.o. **Manquer d'égards envers qn,** to slight s.o.

égarement [egarmɑ̃], *s.m.* **I.** (*a*) Miscarriage (of letter, etc.). (*b*) Mislaying (of object). (*c*) Bewilderment. **Égarement d'esprit,** mental aberration. **2.** Deviation (from virtue, etc.); wildness (of conduct). **3.** Frenzy (of grief, etc.).

égarer [egare], *v.tr.* **1.** (a) To lead (s.o.) astray; to mislead, misguide (s.o.). (b) To mislay (sth.). **2.** To bewilder, derange (s.o.).
s'égarer. 1. To lose one's way. *Colis qui s'est égaré*, parcel that has miscarried, gone astray. **2.** *Son esprit s'égare*, his mind is becoming unhinged.

égaré, *a.* **1.** Stray, lost (sheep, etc.). *Balles égarées*, stray bullets. *Village é.*, out-of-the-way village. **2.** Distraught, distracted (face, etc.).

égayant [egɛjɑ̃], *a.* Cheerful, cheery, lively (conversation, etc.).

égayement [egɛjmɑ̃], *s.m.* Enlivenment. *Au grand é. de la compagnie*, to the great amusement of the company.

égayer [egɛje], *v.tr.* (j'égaie, j'égaye; j'égaierai, j'égayerai) To cheer up (patient); to amuse (the company); to enliven (the conversation); to brighten (up) (room). [GAI]
s'égayer. (a) To make merry (together) (de, about). (b) To amuse oneself.

égide [eʒid], *s.f.* (a) *Gr.Myth:* Aegis, shield. (b) *F:* Protection, defence. *Sous l'égide de . . .*, under the care of . . ., under the aegis of. . . .

églantier [eglɑ̃tje], *s.m. Bot:* Wild rose, dog-rose (bush). *É. odorant*, sweet briar.

églantine [eglɑ̃tin], *s.f. Bot:* Wild rose, dog-rose (flower). *É. odorante*, sweet briar; eglantine.

église [egliːz], *s.f.* Church. *L'É. anglicane*, the Church of England. *L'É. et l'État*, Church and State. *F:* **Petite église,** small coterie. *Aller à l'é.*, to go to church.

églogue [eglɔg], *s.f. Lit:* Eclogue.

égoïsme [egɔism], *s.m.* Selfishness.

égoïste [egɔist]. **1.** *s. m. & f.* Selfish person. **2.** *a.* Selfish. *adv.* **-ment.**

égorgement [egɔrʒmɑ̃], *s.m.* **1.** Sticking, cutting the throat (of pig, etc.). **2.** Massacre, slaughter.

égorger [egɔrʒe], *v.tr.* (j'égorgeai(s); n. égorgeons) **1.** To cut the throat of, *F:* to stick (pig, sheep); to slit (s.o.'s) throat. **2.** To butcher, massacre, slaughter (persons). *s.m.* **-eur.**

égosiller (s') [segozije], *v.pr.* To bawl; to shout (oneself hoarse).

égout [egu], *s.m.* **1.** (a) Draining, drainage (of liquid). (b) Slope (of roof). **2.** (a) (i) Sewer, (ii) drain. *Eaux d'égout*, sewage, *F:* sewerage. *É. collecteur*, main sewer. (b) Eaves (of roof).

égoutier [egutje], *s.m.* Sewerman.

égouttement [egutmɑ̃], *s.m.* Drip(ping) (of water, etc.); *F:* drip-drip (of water).

égoutter [egute], *v.tr. & i.* To drain (cheese, etc.). *Mettre la vaisselle à é.*, to put the dishes to drain (in rack). *Faire égoutter l'eau*, to drain off the water. *s.m.* **-age.**
s'égoutter, to drain, drip.

égouttoir [egutwaːr], *s.m.* Drainer (for bottles); plate-rack.

égoutture [egutyːr], *s.f.* Drops, drippings.

égratigner [egratiɲe], *v.tr.* To scratch.

égratignure [egratiɲyːr], *s.f.* **1.** Scratch. **2.** *F:* Gibe; dig (at s.o.).

égrènement [egrɛnmɑ̃], *s.m.* **1.** *É. d'un chapelet*, telling of beads. **2.** *É. de lumières*, dotted line of lights.

égrener [egrəne], *v.tr.* (j'égrène; j'égrènerai) (a) To shell (peas); to pick off (grapes from the bunch). *Les marronniers égrènent leurs feuilles*, the chestnut-trees shed their leaves one by one. *s.m.* **-age.**

s'égrener, (of corn, grapes, etc.) to fall, drop, from the ear, from the bunch; to seed. *Des lumières s'égrènent le long du quai*, a dotted line of lights runs along the quay.

égrillard [egrijaːr], *a.* (a) Lewd, ribald. (b) Naughty, spicy (story, etc.).

Égypte [eʒipt]. *Pr.n.f. Geog:* Egypt.

égyptien, -ienne [eʒipsjɛ̃, -jɛn], *a. & s.* Egyptian.

égyptologie [eʒiptɔlɔʒi], *s.f.* Egyptology.

eh [e], *int.* Hey! **Eh bien!** well! now then! *Eh! là-bas*, hullo there!

éhonté [eɔ̃te], *a.* Shameless, unblushing.

eider [edɛːr], *s.m. Orn:* Eider(-duck).

éjecteur [eʒɛktœːr], *s.m. Mch: Sm.a:* Ejector.

éjection [eʒɛksjɔ̃], *s.f.* Ejection.

élaboration [elabɔrasjɔ̃], *s.f.* Elaboration.

élaborer [elabɔre], *v.tr.* To elaborate.

élaguer [elage], *v.tr. Arb:* To prune (tree); to lop (off, away) (branches). *F:* To curtail, cut down (play, book). *É. des détails*, to cut out details. *s.m.* **-age.**

élan¹ [elɑ̃], *s.m.* **1.** (a) Spring, bound, dash. *Avancer par élans*, to advance by rushes. *D'un seul é.*, at one bound. **Prendre son élan,** to take off (for a spring). **Saut sans élan,** avec élan, standing jump, running jump. (b) *L'é. merveilleux de nos troupes*, the wonderful *élan*, dash, of our troops. (c) Impetus. **L'élan vital,** the vital impulse. **2.** Burst, outburst (of feeling, etc.). **Mouvement de premier élan,** first impulse.

élan², *s.m. Z:* Elk, moose.

élancement [elɑ̃smɑ̃], *s.m.* **1.** Transport (of feeling). **2.** Shooting pain; twinge.

élancer [elɑ̃se], *v.i.* (j'élançai(s); n. élançons) (Of part of the body) To throb, shoot (with pain).
s'élancer. 1. *S'é. en avant*, to spring, bound, dash, shoot, forward. *S'é. sur son cheval*, to spring, leap, on to one's horse. *S'é. sur qn*, to rush at s.o.; to make a spring at s.o. **2.** (Of child, plant) To shoot up.

élancé, *a.* Tall and slim; slender.

élargir [elarʒiːr], *v.tr.* **1.** (a) To widen (road); to let out (dress); to stretch (shoes). *Acteur qui a élargi son jeu*, actor who has broadened his style. (b) To enlarge, extend (one's estate, ideas); to expand (tube); to enlarge (hole). **2.** To set (prisoner) free, at large; to release (prisoner). *s.m.* **-issement.**
s'élargir. (a) To widen out, broaden out. (b) (Of shoes, etc.) To stretch. (c) (Of estate, circle of friends) To grow, extend.

élasticité [elastisite], *s.f.* Elasticity.

élastique [elastik]. **1.** *a.* (a) Elastic. (b) *F:* Springy. **Gomme élastique,** india-rubber. *D'un pas é.*, with a springy, buoyant, step. **2.** *s.m.* (a) (India-)rubber. (b) *Dressm: etc:* Elastic. (c) Elastic band; rubber band.

élatère [elatɛːr], *s.m. Ent:* Elater, *F:* skipjack.

électeur, -trice [elɛktœːr, -tris], *s.* **1.** *German Hist:* Elector, *f.* electress. **2.** Elector; voter.

électif, -ive [elɛktif, -iːv], *a.* Elective.

élection [elɛksjɔ̃], *s.f.* **1.** *Pol:* Election; polling. *Élections législatives*, parliamentary election. **2.** Election, choice, preference. *Jur:* **Faire élection de domicile,** to elect domicile.

électoral, -aux [elɛktɔral, -o], *a.* Electoral. *Comité é.*, election committee. *Consulter le corps é.*, to go to the country.

électorat [elɛktɔra], *s.m.* **1.** Electorate. **2.** Franchise.

électrice. See ÉLECTEUR.

électricien [elɛktrisjɛ̃], *s.m.* Electrician. **Ingénieur électricien,** electrical engineer.

électricité [elɛktrisite], *s.f.* Electricity. **Usine d'électricité**, power station. *Éclairé à l'é.*, lighted by electricity. *F:* **Allumer, donner, l'électricité,** to switch on the light. **Éteindre, couper, l'électricité,** to switch off the light.

électrification [elɛktrifikasjɔ̃], *s.f.* Electrification (of railway, etc.).

électrifier [elɛktrifje], *v.tr.* To electrify.

électrique [elɛktrik], *a.* **1.** Electric (current, lighting, etc.). **2.** Electrical (unit).

électrisable [elɛktrizabl], *a.* Electrifiable.

électrisation [elɛktrizasjɔ̃], *s.f.* Electrification.

électriser [elɛktrize], *v.tr.* To electrify (substance, audience, etc.).

électro-aimant [elɛktrɔɛmɑ̃], *s.m.* (Electro-) magnet.

électrocuter [elɛktrɔkyte], *v.tr.* To electrocute.

électrocution [elɛktrɔkysjɔ̃], *s.f.* Electrocution.

électrode [elɛktrɔd], *s.f.* Electrode.

électrogène [elɛktrɔʒɛn], *a. El.E:* Generating (plant, etc.). *Groupe é.*, generating set.

électrolyse [elɛktrɔliːz], *s.f.* Electrolysis.

électrolyte [elɛktrɔlit], *s.m.* Electrolyte; battery solution.

électromobile [elɛktrɔmɔbil], *a.* Electrically driven (vehicle).

électromoteur, -trice [elɛktrɔmɔtœːr, -tris]. **1.** *a.* Electromotive. **2.** *s.m.* Electromotor.

électron [elɛktrɔ̃], *s.m. Ph:* Electron.

électronique [elɛktrɔnik], *a.* Electronic. **Lampe,** valve, électronique, thermionic valve.

électroscope [elɛktrɔskɔp], *s.m.* Electroscope.

électrothérapie [elɛktrɔterapi], *s.f. Med:* Electro-therapy; electro-therapeutics.

électrothermique [elɛktrɔtɛrmik], *a.* Thermo-electric(al).

électrotype [elɛktrɔtip], *s.m. Typ:* Electrotype.

électrotyper [elɛktrɔtipe], *v.tr.* To electrotype.

élégance [elegɑ̃ːs], *s.f.* Elegance; stylishness.

élég|ant [elegɑ̃]. **1.** *a.* Elegant, well-dressed; stylish; tasteful (drawing-room, etc.). **2.** *s.* Man of fashion. *Une élégante*, a woman of fashion. *Elle veut faire l'élégante, F:* she puts it on. *adv.* **-amment.**

élégiaque [eleʒjak], *a.* Elegiac. **Poète élégiaque,** elegist.

élégie [eleʒi], *s.f.* Elegy.

élément [elemɑ̃], *s.m.* **1.** Element. *F:* **Être dans son élément,** to be in one's element. **2.** (*a*) Component unit or member (of sectional structure, etc.); ingredient (of medicine, etc.). (*b*) *El:* Cell (of battery). **3.** *pl.* (*a*) Rudiments, first principles (of science, etc.). (*b*) Data.

élémentaire [elemɑ̃tɛːr], *a.* **1.** Elementary (knowledge, algebra, etc.). *Sch:* **Classes élémentaires,** lower forms or standards. **2.** Rudimentary.

éléphant [elefɑ̃], *s.m.* Elephant. *É. mâle, femelle,* bull, cow, elephant.

éléphantesque [elefɑ̃tɛsk], *a. F:* Elephantine, gigantic, enormous.

élevage [elvaːʒ], *s.m.* **1.** Breeding, raising, rearing (of stock); stock-farming. **Élevage des moutons,** sheep-farming. **2.** (Stock-)farm; ranch; (in Australia) sheep-station.

élévateur, -trice [elevatœːr, -tris]. **1.** *a. & s.m.* Elevator (muscle). **2.** *s.m.* Elevator, lift, hoist.

élévation [elevasjɔ̃], *s.f.* **1.** (*a*) Elevation, lifting, raising. *É. de l'eau*, pumping (up) of water. *É. des prix*, putting up of prices. (*b*) Erection, setting up (of statue, etc.). **2.** Rise (in temperature, etc.). **3.** (*a*) Loftiness, height, altitude. *É. de style*, grandeur, nobility, of style. *É. d'esprit, d'âme*, high-mindedness. (*b*) Altitude (of star,

etc.). **4.** *Arch: Geom:* Elevation; vertical section. **5.** High ground, height, eminence.

élévatoire [elevatwaːr], *a.* Elevatory, lifting, hoisting (apparatus, etc.). **Usine élévatoire,** waterworks.

élève [elɛːv]. **1.** *s.m. & f.* Pupil (in school); student (at college); apprentice (to architect, etc.). **2.** *s.f.* (*a*) Young rearing animal. (*b*) Seedling.

élever [elve], *v.tr.* (j'élève; j'élèverai) **1.** To elevate, raise. *É. un mur de deux mètres*, to raise a wall by two metres. *É. la voix*, to raise, lift up, one's voice. *É. les prix*, to put up prices. **Élever** qn aux nues, to laud s.o. to the skies. **2.** (*a*) To erect, set up (temple, statue). (*b*) *É. une objection, de nouvelles difficultés*, to raise an objection, fresh difficulties. **3.** To bring up, rear (child); to raise (stock); to breed (horses, rabbits); to keep (bees). **s'élever. 1.** To rise (up). *Le brouillard s'élève*, the fog is lifting. *Le vent s'élève*, the wind is rising. *Le compte s'élève à mille francs*, the bill comes to a thousand francs. *S'il s'élève des difficultés . . .*, if difficulties arise. . . . *Des cris s'élevèrent*, cries were uttered. **2.** (*a*) To raise oneself. *S'é. à force de travail*, to work one's way up. (*b*) *S'é. contre une accusation*, to protest against an accusation.

élevé, *a.* **1.** High (mountain, price); noble, lofty (style, mind). *L'officier le plus é. en grade*, the senior officer. *Plafond peu élevé*, low ceiling. **2. Bien élevé,** well brought up; well-bred. **Mal élevé,** ill-mannered; ill-bred.

éleveur, -euse [elvœːr, -øːz]. **1.** *s.* Stock-breeder. *É. de chiens*, dog-fancier. **2.** *s.f.* **Éleveuse,** incubator (for chickens).

elfe [ɛlf], *s.m.* Elf, brownie.

élider [elide], *v.tr.* To elide (vowel).

éligibilité [eliʒibilite], *s.f.* Eligibility.

éligible [eliʒibl], *a.* Eligible.

élimer [elime], *v.tr.* To wear the nap off (clothes). **s'élimer,** (of clothes) to wear threadbare.

éliminateur, -trice [eliminatœːr, -tris]. **1.** *a.* Eliminating, eliminative. **2.** *s.m.* Eliminator.

élimination [eliminasjɔ̃], *s.f.* Elimination.

éliminatoire [eliminatwaːr], *a.* Eliminatory (examination, etc.). *Sp:* **Épreuves éliminatoires,** preliminary heats.

éliminer [elimine], *v.tr.* To eliminate, get rid of (s.o., sth.). *É. les incapables*, to weed out the inefficient. *Mth: etc:* (Of quantities) **S'éliminer,** to cancel out. *Phot: É. l'hyposulfite*, to eliminate, *F:* kill, the hypo.

élingue [elɛ̃ːg], *s.f.* Sling(s).

élire [eliːr], *v.tr.* (Conj. like LIRE) **1.** To elect, choose (s.o.). *É. qn président*, (i) to elect s.o. president; (ii) to vote s.o. into the chair. **2. Élire domicile** (*dans un endroit*), to take up one's residence, *Jur:* to elect domicile (in a place).

élu, -e. 1. *a.* Chosen; successful (candidate). **2.** *s.* (*a*) *Les élus*, the elect. (*b*) *Nouvel élu*, newly elected member.

élision [elizjɔ̃], *s.f. Ling:* Elision.

élite [elit], *s.f.* Élite; flower, pick (of the army, etc.). *Personnel d'é.*, picked personnel. *Régiment d'é.*, crack regiment.

elle, elles [ɛl], *pers.pron.f.* **1.** (Unstressed, clinging to the verb or its adjuncts) (Of pers.) She, they; (of thg) it, they. *Elle m'a vu*, she saw me. **2.** (Stressed) (*a*) (Subject) She, it, they. *C'est elle, ce sont elles*, it is she, it is they. *Je fais comme elle*, I do as she does. *Elle-même l'a vu*, she saw it herself. (*b*) (Object) Her, it, them. *Chez elle*, with her, at her house. *Elle ne pense qu'à elle*, she thinks only of herself. *Chacune* *d'elles travaille pour elle-même,* each of them works for herself. *Il aimait sa patrie et mourut pour elle,* he loved his country and died for it.

ellébore [ɛl(l)ebɔːr], *s.m. Bot:* Hellebore.

ellipse [ɛllips], *s.f.* **1.** *Gram:* Ellipsis. **2.** *Geom:* Ellipse.

elliptique [ɛlliptik], *a. Gram: Geom:* Elliptic(al). *adv.* **-ment,** -ally.

élocution [elɔkysjɔ̃], *s.f.* Elocution.

éloge [elɔːʒ], *s.m.* **1.** Eulogy, panegyric. **2.** (Deserved) praise. (*Cf.* LOUANGE.) Faire l'éloge de qn, to praise s.o.; to speak highly of s.o. *Digne d'éloges,* praiseworthy, commendable.

élogieux, -euse [elɔʒjø, -øːz], *a.* Eulogistic, laudatory. *Parler en termes é. de qn,* to speak in high terms of s.o.

éloignement [elwaɲmã], *s.m.* **1.** Removal, removing, putting away (of s.o., sth.); postponement (of departure, etc.); deferment (of payment). **2.** (*a*) Absence. (*b*) Distance, remoteness (in place, time). **Voir qch. dans l'éloignement,** to see sth. in the distance. **Vivre dans l'éloignement du monde,** to live apart, aloof, from the world. (*c*) Aversion. *Avoir de l'é. pour qn, pour qch.,* to have an antipathy to s.o., an aversion to sth. (*d*) Distance (of manner).

éloigner [elwaɲe], *v.tr.* (*a*) To remove (s.o., sth.) to a distance, further off; to get (s.o., sth.) out of the way. *É. qch. de qch.,* to move sth. away from sth. *Éloignés d'un mille,* a mile apart. *F: É. toute crainte,* to banish all fears. *É. une pensée,* to dismiss, put away, a thought. *É. les soupçons,* to avert suspicion. *É. qn de faire qch.,* to put s.o. off doing sth. (*b*) To postpone, put off (departure); to defer (payment). (*c*) *É. qn de qn,* to alienate, estrange, s.o. from s.o. [LOIN]

s'éloigner. 1. To move off, retire, withdraw. *Nau:* To stand away, bear off (*de,* from). *S'é. en toute hâte,* to hurry away. *S'é. de son devoir,* to deviate from one's duty. **2.** To assume a distant position. (*a*) *Voudriez-vous vous é. un peu?* would you please stand further away, further back? (*b*) *Votre opinion ne s'éloigne pas beaucoup de la mienne,* your opinion does not differ much from mine.

éloigné, a. Far (away); distant; remote (place, time). *La ville est éloignée de deux lieues,* the town is five miles distant. *Le plus é.,* farthest, furthermost. *Parent é.,* distant relation. *Avenir peu éloigné,* near future. *Se tenir é. de qch.,* to hold (oneself) aloof from sth.

élongation [elɔ̃gasjɔ̃], *s.f.* Elongation.

éloquence [elɔkɑːs], *s.f.* (*a*) Eloquence. (*b*) *É. de la chaire,* pulpit oratory.

éloquent [elɔkã], *a.* Eloquent. *adv.* **-emment.**

élu, -s, -t, etc. See ÉLIRE.

élucidation [elysidasjɔ̃], *s.f.* Elucidation.

élucider [elyside], *v.tr.* To elucidate, clear up (mystery, etc.).

éludable [elydabl], *a.* Eludible, evadable.

éluder [elyde], *v.tr.* To elude, evade, dodge (law, difficulty).

Élysée [elize]. **1.** *Pr.n.m.* (*a*) *Myth:* L'Élysée, Elysium. (*b*) (**Le palais de**) l'Élysée, the official residence of the President of the French Republic. **2.** *a.* **Les Champs Élysées,** (i) *Myth:* the Elysian Fields; (ii) the Champs Élysées (avenue in Paris).

élytre [elitr], *s.m. Ent:* Elytron, wing-sheath.

émaciation [emasjasjɔ̃], *s.f.* Emaciation.

émacié [emasje], *a.* Emaciated; wasted (figure).

émail, *pl.* **émaux** [emaːj, emo], *s.m.* **1.** (*a*) Enamel. *Émaux de niellure,* niello enamels. (*b*) *Her:* Tincture. (*c*) Enamel (of the teeth). **2.** (*a*) Enamelling material; enamel. (*b*) *Cer:* Glaze.

émaill|er [emaje], *v.tr.* **1.** *Art: etc:* To enamel. *Émaillé au four,* stove-enamelled. **2.** *Cer:* To glaze (porcelain). **3.** (Of flowers, etc.) To dot, fleck (the fields). *F: Style émaillé de métaphores,* style studded with metaphors. *s.m.* **-age.**

émailleur [emajœːr], *s.m.* Enameller.

émaillure [emajyːr], *s.f.* **1.** Enamel work. **2.** Spot, speckle (of colour in nature, etc.).

émanation [emanasjɔ̃], *s.f.* Emanation.

émancipateur, -trice [emɑ̃sipatœːr, -tris]. **1.** *a.* Emancipatory. **2.** *s.* Emancipator.

émancipation [emɑ̃sipasjɔ̃], *s.f.* Emancipation.

émanciper [emɑ̃sipe], *v.tr.* To emancipate.

s'émanciper. 1. To free oneself from control. *Esprit émancipé de toute influence,* mind freed from all influence. **2.** *F:* (Of young pers.) To get out of hand.

émancipé, a. *F:* (*a*) Holding advanced opinions. (*b*) (Of young pers.) Free in his (her) manners; forward.

émaner [emane], *v.i.* To emanate, to issue, proceed (*de,* from). *Ordres émanant de qn,* orders emanating from, sent out by, s.o. *Pétition émanant de . . .,* petition from. . . .

émargement [emarʒəmã], *s.m.* **1.** *Bookb:* Trimming. **2.** Initialling (of account, etc.) in the margin. **Feuille d'émargement,** pay-sheet.

émarger [emarʒe], *v.tr.* (j'émargeai(s); n. émargeons) **1.** *Bookb:* To trim the margins of (sheets). **2.** To receipt, initial (an account) (in the margin). Hence *Abs.* To draw one's salary.

émaux. See ÉMAIL.

embâcle [ɑ̃baːkl], *s.m.* Obstruction, blockage; esp. ice-jam (in waterway).

emballage [ɑ̃balaːʒ], *s.m.* **1.** (*a*) Packing, wrapping (of parcels, etc.). **Papier d'emballage,** packing paper. (*b*) Packing-cases; wrappings. **Emballages vides,** (returned) empties. **2.** *Rac:* Burst of speed; spurt.

emballement [ɑ̃balmã], *s.m.* **1.** (Of machine, engine) Racing. **2.** *F:* Burst of enthusiasm, of energy, etc.; *Com:* boom.

emballer [ɑ̃bale], *v.tr.* **1.** To pack (goods, etc.); to wrap up, do up (article in paper, etc.). **2.** (*a*) *Abs. Rac:* To spurt. (*b*) *I.C.E:* E. le moteur (à vide), to race the engine (without a load). **3.** To fire (s.o.) with enthusiasm; to excite (s.o.).

s'emballer. (*a*) (Of horse) To bolt, run away. *Cheval emballé,* runaway horse. (*b*) (Of engine) To race. (*c*) *F:* To be carried away (by excitement, anger, enthusiasm). *Ne vous emballez pas!* keep cool! **Être emballé pour, sur, qn,** to be gone on s.o.; to be keen on s.o.

emballeur [ɑ̃balœːr], *s.m.* Packer.

embarcadère [ɑ̃barkadɛːr], *s.m.* **1.** *Nau:* Landing-stage; wharf, quay; loading dock. **2.** *Rail:* (Departure) platform.

embarcation [ɑ̃barkasjɔ̃], *s.f.* Boat; esp. ship's boat. *E. à vapeur,* steam-launch.

embardée [ɑ̃barde], *s.f.* (*a*) *Nau:* Yaw, lurch. *F: E. hors du sujet,* digression from the subject. (*b*) *Aut:* Skid, swerve. **Faire une embardée,** (i) (of boat) to yaw; (ii) (of car) to swerve or skid; (iii) *F:* (of pers.) to lurch across the road.

embard|er [ɑ̃barde], *v.i.* (*a*) (Of ship) To yaw, lurch. (*b*) (Of motor car) To skid, swerve; to steer wildly. *s.m.* **-age.**

embargo [ɑ̃bargo], *s.m. Nau: etc:* Embargo. **Mettre l'embargo sur un navire,** to lay an embargo on a ship. *F: Mettre l'e. sur un journal,* to suspend a newspaper.

embarquement [ɑ̃barkəmã], *s.m.* **1.** Embarkation, embarking (of passengers); shipment, shipping (of goods); hoisting in (of boats). **2.** Entrainment (of troops). **3.** *Av:* Enplaning. **embarquer** [ɑ̃barke]. **I.** *v.tr.* (*a*) To embark (passengers); to ship (goods); to take (goods) aboard; to hoist in (boat). *F:* **Embarquer de** l'eau, to ship a sea. (*b*) To entrain (troops). (*c*) *Av:* To enplane (passengers). **2.** *v.i. & pr.* To embark. *Embarquez!* all aboard! *S'e. dans un train*, to entrain; to get into a train. *S'e. en avion*, to enplane. *F: S'e. dans une dissertation*, to embark upon, launch out into, a dissertation.

embarras [ɑ̃barɑ], *s.m.* **I.** Obstruction, obstacle, encumbrance; hold-up (in traffic); impediment (of speech). **Embarras de richesses**, superfluity of good things. *Med:* **Embarras gastrique**, bilious attack. **2.** (*a*) Difficulty, trouble. **Se trouver dans l'embarras**, (i) to be in difficulties; (ii) to be in embarrassed circumstances. **Tirer qn d'embarras**, to help s.o. out of a difficulty. *Je vous donne beaucoup d'e.*, I am putting you to a lot of trouble. (*b*) *F:* **Faire des embarras**, to be fussy; to make a fuss. **Sans plus d'embarras**, without any more ado. **3.** Embarrassment. (*a*) Perplexity, hesitation. **N'avoir que l'embarras du choix**, to have only too much to choose from. (*b*) Confusion, abashment.

embarrassant [ɑ̃barɑsɑ̃], *a.* **I.** Cumbrous, cumbersome (parcel, etc.). **2.** (*a*) Perplexing, puzzling (question). (*b*) Embarrassing, awkward.

embarrasser [ɑ̃barase], *v.tr.* To embarrass. **I.** To (en)cumber, hamper; to block, obstruct (passage). *E. la circulation*, to hold up the traffic. *E. qn de qch.*, to (en)cumber s.o. with sth. **2.** (*a*) To trouble, inconvenience. (*b*) To perplex, nonplus, puzzle (s.o.). (*c*) To confuse (s.o.); to put (s.o.) out (of countenance).

s'embarrasser. I. *S'e. de qch.*, to burden, hamper, oneself with sth. **2.** To trouble oneself (about sth.).

embarrassé, *a.* **I.** Encumbered, obstructed (path, etc.); involved (style); congested (traffic). **2.** Embarrassed. (*a*) Perplexed, nonplussed, puzzled. *Être e. pour trouver un mot*, to be at a loss for a word. (*b*) Bashful, sheepish, diffident.

embarriquer [ɑ̃barike], *v.tr.* To barrel.

embase [ɑ̃baːz], *s.f.* Base; shoulder (of chisel, knife, etc.); flange, collar (of shaft, etc.); bed-plate, base-plate (of machine). **Écrou à embase**, collar nut.

embauch|er [ɑ̃boʃe], *v.tr.* **I.** To engage, take on, sign on (workmen); to hire (farm-hands). **2.** (*a*) To crimp (soldiers, sailors). (*b*) To entice (soldiers) over to the enemy. *s.m.* **-age.**

embaucheur, -euse [ɑ̃boʃœːr, -øːz], *s.* **I.** Labour contractor. **2.** Crimp.

embauchoir [ɑ̃boʃwaːr], *s.m.* Boot-tree.

embaum|er [ɑ̃bome], *v.tr.* **I.** To embalm (corpse). **2.** To embalm, perfume, scent. *Air embaumé*, balmy air. *Abs. Ces fleurs embaument*, these flowers have a delightful scent. (With cogn. acc.) *Sa chambre embaumait la violette*, her room was fragrant of violets. *s.m.* **-ement.** *s.m.* **-eur.**

embéguiner [ɑ̃begine], *v.tr. F: E. qn d'une idée*, to infatuate s.o. with an idea. **S'embéguiner de qn**, to become infatuated with s.o.

embellir [ɑ̃beliːr]. **I.** *v.tr.* To embellish; to beautify. **2.** *v.i.* To improve in looks.

embellie, *s.f. Nau:* Clearing (in the weather); lull (in wind, etc.); smooth (in sea).

embellissement [ɑ̃belismɑ̃], *s.m.* **I.** Embellishing, beautifying. **2.** Improvement (in looks). **3.** Embellishing touch; ornament.

emberlificot|er [ɑ̃berlifikɔte], *v.tr. F:* **I.** To

entangle (s.o.). **2.** To cajole, wheedle; to get round (s.o.). *s.* **-eur, -euse.**

embêtant [ɑ̃bɛtɑ̃], *a. F:* = ENNUYANT, ENNUYEUX.

embêtement [ɑ̃bɛtmɑ̃], *s.m. F:* = ENNUI.

embêter [ɑ̃bɛte], *v.tr. F:* = ENNUYER. [BÊTE]

emblée (d') [dɑ̃ble], *adv.phr.* Directly; right away; straight off.

emblématique [ɑ̃blɛmatik], *a.* Emblematic(al).

emblème [ɑ̃blɛːm], *s.m.* **I.** (*a*) Emblem, device. (*b*) Badge, crest. **2.** Symbol, sign.

embobeliner [ɑ̃bɔbline], *v.tr. F:* To coax, wheedle; get round (s.o.).

emboire (s') [sɑ̃bwaːr], *v.pr.* (Of paint) To soak in; to become flat, dull.

emboîtage [ɑ̃bwataːʒ], *s.m.* **I.** (*a*) Packing in boxes. (*b*) Box, casing. **2.** *Bookb:* (*a*) French binding. (*b*) Cover, case (of book).

emboîtement [ɑ̃bwatmɑ̃], *s.m.* **I.** (*a*) Encasing; nesting (of boxes). (*b*) Fitting, jointing (of pipes, etc.). **2.** Fitment; joint; housing; socket.

emboîter [ɑ̃bwate], *v.tr.* **I.** (*a*) To encase; to nest (boxes). (*b*) *Bookb:* To case (book). **2.** (*a*) To pack (sardines, etc.) in tins, boxes. *P: E. qn*, to run s.o. in. (*b*) To fit (things) together; to joint, interlock, dovetail. (*c*) **Emboîter le pas**, to fall into step (*d, sur*, with); to lock (in marching).

emboîture [ɑ̃bwatyːr], *s.f.* **I.** Fit, interlock (of two things). **2.** Socket.

embolie [ɑ̃bɔli], *s.f. Med:* (*a*) Embolism. (*b*) Clot of blood (in artery, etc.).

embonpoint [ɑ̃bɔ̃pwɛ̃], *s.m.* Stoutness, plumpness. **Prendre de l'embonpoint**, to put on flesh; to get fat.

emboucher [ɑ̃buʃe], *v.tr.* To put (wind instrument) to one's mouth; to blow (trumpet, etc.).

embouché, *a. F:* **Mal embouché**, foul-mouthed; coarse (of speech).

embouchure [ɑ̃buʃyːr], *s.f.* **I.** Mouthpiece (of telephone, wind instrument, etc.). **2.** (*a*) Opening, mouth (of sack, etc.). (*b*) Mouth (of river).

embouquer [ɑ̃buke], *v.tr. & i. Nau: E. la passe, dans la passe*, to enter the channel.

embourb|er [ɑ̃burbe], *v.tr.* To mire, bog (vehicle). *s.m.* **-ement.**

s'embourber, to stick in the mud, in the mire; to get bogged.

embourser [ɑ̃burse], *v.tr.* = EMPOCHER.

embout [ɑ̃bu], *s.m.* Ferrule, tip (of umbrella, stick); chape (of scabbard).

embouteillage [ɑ̃butejaːʒ], *s.m.* **I.** Bottling. **2.** Bottling up (of harbour). **3.** *F:* Congestion (of traffic); bottle-neck.

embouteiller [ɑ̃buteje], *v.tr.* **I.** To bottle. **2.** To bottle up, block up (harbour mouth, fleet). *Circulation embouteillée*, congested traffic.

embout|ir [ɑ̃butiːr], *v.tr.* (*a*) To stamp, press (metal). (*b*) To emboss. *s.m.* **-issage.**

s'emboutir. (Of car, etc.) *S'e. contre un mur*, to crash, cannon, into a wall.

embranchement [ɑ̃brɑ̃ʃmɑ̃], *s.m.* **I.** Branching (off). **2.** Branch. (*a*) Road junction; fork (of road). (*b*) Branch-road. *Rail:* Branch-line or siding. (*c*) Pipe junction. (*d*) Spur (of mountain-range). **3.** *Nat.Hist:* Sub-kingdom.

embrancher [ɑ̃brɑ̃ʃe], *v.tr.* To join up (roads, pipes).

s'embrancher, (of road) (i) to form a junction, (ii) to branch off (*sur*, from).

embraquer [ɑ̃brake], *v.tr.* To haul (rope) taut.

embrasement [ɑ̃brazmɑ̃], *s.m.* **I.** Burning, conflagration (of town, ship, etc.). **2.** Illumination (of public building, etc.).

embraser [ɑ̃braze], *v.tr.* **I.** To set fire to (sth.);

to set (sth.) ablaze. *E. l'imagination*, to fire the imagination. **2.** To illuminate (public building).
s'embraser, to catch fire, to blaze up.
embrasé, *a.* Blazing (ship, etc.); glowing (coal, etc.); fiery (sky); sweltering (day).
embrassade [ăbrasad], *s.f. F:* Embrace.
embrasse [ăbras], *s.f.* **1.** Curtain-loop. **2.** Arm-rest (of carriage, etc.).
embrassement [ăbrasmă], *s.m.* Embrace.
embrasser [ăbrase], *v.tr.* To embrace. **1.** (*a*) To put one's arms round (s.o., sth.); to hug (s.o.). *F: Le lien qui embrasse un fagot*, the cord that binds a faggot. S.a. ÉTREINDRE. (*b*) To kiss. (Letter formula) "**Je vous embrasse de tout mon cœur,**" 'with much love.' (*c*) To adopt, take up (career, etc.); to espouse (cause); to embrace (doctrine). **2.** To contain, include, take in. *L'explication n'embrasse pas tous les faits*, the explanation does not cover all the facts.
embrasure [ăbrazy:r], *s.f.* (*a*) Embrasure; window-recess. (*b*) *Nau:* Gun-port.
embrayage [ăbrɛja:ʒ], *s.m.* **1.** Connecting, coupling; engaging (of the clutch); throwing into gear (of engine parts). **2.** Connecting gear; coupling, clutch. *E. à disques*, multi-disc clutch.
embrayer [ăbrɛje], *v.tr.* (j'embraie, j'embraye; j'embraierai, j'embrayerai) *Mec.E:* To connect, couple, engage; to throw (parts) into gear. *Abs. Aut:* To let in the clutch.
embrigader [ăbrigade], *v.tr.* **1.** To brigade (troops). **2.** To enrol (body of men).
embroch|er [ăbrɔʃe], *v.tr.* **1.** (*a*) *Cu:* To spit (piece of meat). (*b*) *F:* To run (s.o.) through (with a bayonet). **2.** *El.E:* To wire (station) on to a circuit. [BROCHE] *s.m.* **-ement.**
embrouillamini [ăbrujamini], *s.m. P:* = BROU-ILLAMINI.
embrouillarder (s') [săbrujarde], *v.pr.* (Of weather) To become misty, foggy.
embrouillement [ăbrujmă], *s.m.* **1.** Entanglement (of thread, etc.). **2.** Confusion (of ideas, etc.); jumbled state; intricacy (of question).
embrouiller [ăbruje], *v.tr.* **1.** To ravel, tangle (thread, etc.). **2.** To confuse, tangle up, muddle (business); to mix up (papers); to confuse (s.o.).
s'embrouiller. 1. To get tangled, into a tangle. **2.** (*a*) (Of pers.) To get muddled, confused. (*b*) *L'affaire s'embrouille*, the affair is getting intricate. **3.** (Of sky) To cloud over.
embrouillé, *a.* **1.** Tangled (skein, etc.); complicated, involved (style, business). **2.** Dull (weather).
embroussaillé [ăbrusaje], *a.* Covered with bushes. *F: Cheveux embroussaillés*, tousled hair.
embrumer [ăbryme], *v.tr.* To cover (landscape, etc.) with mist, haze. [BRUME]
s'embrumer, to become misty, hazy. *Son visage s'embruma*, his face clouded (over).
embrumé, *a.* Misty (weather); hazy (horizon); clouded (countenance).
embrun [ăbrœ̃], *s.m.* **1.** Spray, spindrift. **2.** Fog.
embrunir [ăbryni:r], *v.tr.* To embrown, darken.
embryologie [ăbriɔlɔʒi], *s.f.* Embryology.
embryon [ăbriõ], *s.m. Biol:* Embryo. Œuvre encore en embryon, work still in embryo.
embryonnaire [ăbriɔnɛ:r], *a. Biol:* (*a*) Embryonic (period, etc.); (plan) still in embryo. (*b*) Embryonary (state).
embûche [ăby(:)ʃ], *s.f.* **1.** *A:* Ambush. **2.** *F:* Dresser, tendre, une embûche à qn, to lay a trap for s.o.; to waylay s.o.
embuer [ăbɥe], *v.tr.* (Of steam, damp) To dim, cloud (glass, etc.).
embuscade [ăbyskad], *s.f.* Ambush, ambuscade.

Dresser, tendre, une embuscade à qn, to lay an ambush for s.o. **Attirer qn dans une embuscade,** to ambush, waylay, s.o. **Se tenir en embuscade,** to lie in ambush.
embusquer [ăbyske], *v.tr.* To place (troops, etc.) in ambush, under cover.
s'embusquer. (*a*) To lie in ambush. (*b*) To take cover. (*c*) *F:* (In war) To shirk active service.
embusqué, *s.m.* **1.** Man (i) in ambush, (ii) under cover. **2.** *F:* Shirker (from active service).
éméché [emeʃe], *a. F:* Slightly the worse for drink; a bit screwed.
émeraude [ɛmro:d]. **1.** *s.f.* Emerald. **2.** *a.inv.* Emerald green.
émergence [emɛrʒɑ̃:s], *s.f.* Emergence; emersion.
émerger [emɛrʒe], *v.i.* (j'émergeai(s); n. émergeons) **1.** To emerge. **2.** To come into view.
émeri [ɛmri], *s.m.* Emery; emery-powder. **Toile (d')émeri,** emery-cloth. **Meule d'émeri,** emery wheel. **Flacon bouché à l'émeri,** stoppered bottle. **Bouchon à l'émeri,** ground stopper.
émerillon [emrijõ], *s.m.* **1.** *Orn:* Merlin. **2.** Swivel(-hook).
émerillonné [ɛmrijɔne], *a.* (*a*) Bright (eye). (*b*) Roguish, mischievous (eye).
émérite [emerit], *a.* **1.** *A:* Retired, superannuated (official, etc.). *Professeur é.*, emeritus professor. **2.** Practised, experienced (player,etc.).
émerveillement [emɛrvɛjmă], *s.m.* Amazement, wonder.
émerveiller [emɛrvɛje], *v.tr.* To amaze; to fill (s.o.) with wonder, with admiration.
s'émerveiller, to marvel, be amazed (*de*, at).
émerveillé, *a.* Amazed, wonder-struck.
émétique [emetik], *s.m.* Emetic.
émetteur, -trice [emetœ:r, -tris]. **1.** *s.m.* (*a*) Issuer (of bank-notes, etc.). (*b*) *W.Tel:* Transmitter. **2.** *a.* Issuing (bank, etc.). *W.Tel:* Poste émetteur, **station émettrice,** (i) transmitting station; (ii) broadcasting station.
émettre [emɛtr], *v.tr.* (Conj. like METTRE) **1.** (*a*) To emit, send out (sound, heat, etc.); to utter (sound); to give off (fumes, etc.). (*b*) *É. une opinion*, to express an opinion. (*c*) *W.Tel:* (i) To send out, transmit; (ii) to broadcast. **2.** To issue (bank-notes, loan, tickets).
émeu [emø], *s.m. Orn:* Emu. *pl. Des émeus.*
émeu-s, -t, etc. See ÉMOUVOIR.
émeute [emø:t], *s.f.* Riot. **Chef d'émeute,** ringleader.
émeutier [emøtje], *s.m.* Rioter.
émiettement [emjɛtmă], *s.m.* Crumbling.
émietter [emjɛte], *v.tr.* To crumble. *É. sa fortune*, to fritter away one's fortune. [MIETTE]
s'émietter, to crumble (away).
émigrant, -ante [emigră, -ă:t]. **1.** *a.* Emigrating (population); migratory (bird). **2.** *s.* Emigrant.
émigration [emigrasjõ], *s.f.* **1.** Migration (of birds). **2.** Emigration.
émigrer [emigre], *v.i.* **1.** (Of birds) To migrate. **2.** (Of pers.) To emigrate.
émigré, -ée, *s.* (Political) exile, refugee.
éminemment [eminamã], *adv.* Eminently; to, in, a high degree.
éminence [emin ̄:s], *s.f.* Eminence. **1.** (*a*) Rising ground; rise. (*b*) *É. osseuse*, bony protuberance. (*c*) (Moral, intellectual) superiority, prominence. **2.** *Ecc:* **Son Éminence le Cardinal,** his Eminence the Cardinal.
éminent [eminã], *a.* Eminent; high; distinguished.

émir [emiːr], *s.m.* Emir, Ameer.
émi-s, -t, etc. See ÉMETTRE.
émissaire [emiseːr], *s.m.* Emissary. *a.* Bouc émissaire, scapegoat.
émission [emisjɔ̃], *s.f.* 1. (*a*) Emission (of sound, light, etc.); utterance (of sound). (*b*) *W.Tel:* (i) Sending out, transmission; (ii) broadcasting. Antenne d'émission, transmitting aerial. Station, poste, d'émission, transmitting station; broadcasting station. 2. Issue, issuing (of bank-notes, tickets); issue (of loan).
emmagasinage [ãmagazinaːʒ], *s.m.*, **emmagasinement** [ãmagazinmã], *s.m.* 1. Storage, warehousing (of goods). 2. Storing up, accumulation (of electrical energy).
emmagasiner [ãmagazine], *v.tr.* 1. To store, warehouse (goods). 2. To store up, to accumulate (energy, etc.).
emmaillot|er [ãmajɔte], *v.tr.* To swaddle (infant); to swathe, to bind (up) (limb, etc.). [MAILLOT] *s.m.* -ement.
emmanch|er [ãmãʃe], *v.tr.* 1. To fix a handle to, to haft, to helve (tool, etc.). 2. To joint (pipes, etc.); to fit (pipes, etc.) together. *F: E. une affaire,* to start, set about, an affair. Affaire mal emmanchée, business muddled at the start. *s.m.* -ement.
emmanchure [ãmãʃyːr], *s.f.* Arm-hole.
emmêlement [ãmɛlmã], *s.m.* 1. (*a*) Tangling. (*b*) Mixing up, muddling (of facts). 2. (*a*) Tangle. (*b*) Mix-up; muddle.
emmêler [ãmɛle], *v.tr.* (*a*) To tangle. (*b*) To mix up (facts); to muddle (story).
   s'emmêler, to get into a tangle, a muddle.
emménag|er [ãmenaʒe], *v.* (j'emménageai(s); *n.* emménageons) 1. *v.tr.* (*a*) To move (s.o.) into a new house; to install (s.o., the furniture, etc.). (*b*) *Nau:* To fit up the accommodation in (a ship). 2. *v.i.* To move in. *s.m.* -ement.
emmener [ãmne], *v.tr.* (j'emmène; j'emmènerai) To lead, take, (s.o.) away, out. *Emmené en prison,* taken off to gaol. *E. les chevaux,* to lead away the horses. *Je vous emmène avec moi,* I am taking you with me. [MENER]
emmitoufler [ãmitufle], *v.tr.* To muffle (s.o.) up (dans, de, in).
émoi [emwa], *s.m.* Emotion, agitation. Être (tout) en émoi, to be all of a flutter. *Toute la ville était en é.,* the whole town was agog with excitement, was in a commotion. Mettre en émoi, to excite; to flutter.
émollient [emɔljã], *a. & s.m.* Emollient.
émoluments [emɔlymã], *s.m.pl:* Emoluments, remuneration, salary.
émond|er [emɔ̃de], *v.tr.* 1. To prune, trim. 2. To clean (grain, etc.). *s.m.* -age. *s.m.* -eur.
émotion [emosjɔ̃], *s.f.* Emotion; thrill; excitement. *Parler avec é.,* to speak feelingly.
émotionnable [emosjɔnabl], *a.* (Of pers.) Emotional; excitable.
émotionnant [emosjɔnã], *a.* Exciting, thrilling.
émotionner [emosjɔne], *v.tr.* *F:* To thrill, move, touch (s.o.).
   s'émotionner, to get excited.
émouchet [emuʃɛ], *s.m.* *Orn:* Kestrel.
émoudre [emudr], *v.tr.* (Conj. like MOUDRE) To grind, sharpen, whet (tool, etc.).
émoulu, *a.* Sharpened, newly ground (tool). *F: Frais é. du collège,* fresh from school.
émouleur [emulœːr], *s.m.* (Tool-)grinder.
émoulu. See ÉMOUDRE.
émouss|er [emuse], *v.tr.* (*a*) To blunt; to take the edge off (tool). (*b*) To dull, deaden, blunt

(the senses, etc.); to take the edge off (appetite). [MOUSSE³] *s.m.* -ement.
   s'émousser. (*a*) (Of tool, etc.) To lose its edge. (*b*) (Of senses, passions) To become blunted, dull, less keen.
émoussé, *a.* Blunt.
émoustillant [emustijã], *a.* *F:* Exhilarating; rousing.
émoustiller [emustije], *v.tr.* *F:* (*a*) To exhilarate, rouse. (*b*) To kindle the senses of (s.o.).
émouvant [emuvã], *a.* Moving. (*a*) Touching. (*b*) Stirring, thrilling.
émouvoir [emuvwaːr], *v.tr.* (*p.p.* ému; otherwise conj. like MOUVOIR) To move. 1. *F:* Émouvoir la bile à qn, to move s.o. to anger. 2. (*a*) To stir up, rouse (mob, passion, etc.). (*b*) To affect, touch. Émouvoir qn jusqu'aux larmes, to move s.o. to tears. Facile à émouvoir, emotional; easily moved.
   s'émouvoir. 1. To get excited, roused. 2. To be touched, affected, moved. *Sans s'é.,* calmly.
ému, *a.* Affected (by emotion): moved. *Voix émue,* voice touched with emotion. *Parler d'une voix émue,* to speak in tones of emotion. *Se sentir un peu ému,* to feel a bit nervous.
empaill|er [ãpaje], *v.tr.* 1. To pack (goods, etc.) in straw; to cover up (plants) with a straw litter. 2. To bottom (chair seat) with straw. 3. To stuff (animal). [PAILLE] *s.m.* -age.
empailleur, -euse [ãpajœːr, -øːz], *s.* 1. Chair-bottomer. 2. Taxidermist.
empaler [ãpale], *v.tr.* To impale.
empanacher [ãpanaʃe], *v.tr.* To plume; to adorn with plumes. *F: Style empanaché,* pompous, flowery, style. [PANACHE]
   s'empanacher, *F:* to don all one's finery.
empapilloter [ãpapijɔte], *v.tr.* To put (hair) in curl-papers.
empaquet|er [ãpakte], *v.tr.* (j'empaquette; j'empaquetterai) To pack (sth.) up; to make (sth.) into a parcel. *E. qch. dans du papier,* to wrap up, do up, in paper. *s.m.* -age.
emparer (s') [sãpare], *v.pr. S'e. de qch.,* to lay hold of, take hold of, lay hands on, seize (upon), secure, take possession of, sth. *F:* S'emparer de la conversation, to engross, monopolize, the conversation.
empâtement [ãpatmã], *s.m.* 1. Pasting (of accumulator plate, etc.). 2. *E. de la voix,* thickness, huskiness, of the voice. *E. des chairs,* (i) putting on of flesh; (ii) fleshiness. 3. Fattening, cramming (of fowls).
empâter [ãpate], *v.tr.* 1. To paste (accumulator plate, etc.). 2. *E. une lime,* to clog a file. *S'e. les mains,* to make one's hands sticky. 3. To fatten up, cram (fowls).
   s'empâter, *F:* to put on flesh.
   empâté, *a.* Clogged, choked. *Langue empâtée,* 'woolly' tongue. *Voix empâtée,* thick voice. *Visage e.,* fleshy, bloated, face.
empattement¹ [ãpatmã], *s.m.* 1. Foundation; footing (of wall). 2. Wheel-base (of car). 3. *Typ:* Serif (of letter).
empatter¹ [ãpate], *v.tr.* To give footing to (a wall, a crane).
empatt|er², *v.tr.* (*a*) To foot, tenon, joint (timbers). (*b*) To join, lay in (strands for splice). *s.m.* -ement².
empaumer [ãpome], *v.tr.* (*a*) To catch (ball) in the palm of the hand; to strike (ball) with the palm of the hand. *F: Empaumer la balle,* to seize the opportunity. (*b*) *F: E. une affaire,* to get a thorough grip of an affair.

empêchement [ăpɛʃmã], *s.m.* (*a*) Obstacle, hindrance, impediment. **Mettre empêchement à qch.**, to put an obstacle in the way of sth. *Sans e.*, without let or hindrance. (*b*) **Empêchement de la langue**, impediment of speech.
empêcher [ăpeʃe, -pɛ-], *v.tr.* **I.** To prevent, hinder, impede. *E. un mariage*, to prevent, put a stop to, a marriage. *Je ne peux pas l'e.*, I cannot prevent it. *E. qn de faire qch.*, ·to prevent, keep, s.o. from doing sth. *Je ne peux pas l'en e.*, I cannot prevent him. *Cela n'empêche pas qu'elle soit honnête*, that doesn't prevent her from being virtuous. *Impers.* (Il) **n'empêche que cela nous a coûté cher**, all the same, nevertheless, it has cost us dear. **2.** (Of garment, etc.) *E. qn*, to hamper s.o.'s movements ; to be in s.o.'s way. **s'empêcher. I.** (Always in the negative) To refrain (*de*, from). *Je ne pus (pas) m'e. de rire*, I couldn't help laughing. **2.** To get entangled (in seaweed, etc.).
empêché, *a.* **I.** Puzzled ; at a loss. **2.** *Être e. de sa personne*, to be awkward. **3.** Unavoidably absent. **4.** (Of rope) Fouled.
empêcheur, -euse [ăpeʃœːr, -øːz], *s.* F: Hinderer. *E. de danser en rond*, spoil-sport.
empeigne [ăpɛɲ], *s.f.* Vamp, upper (of shoe).
empennage [ăpɛnaːʒ], *s.m.* (*a*) Feathering, feathers (of arrow) ; vanes (of bomb) ; fin (of dirigible). (*b*) Empennage (of aeroplane).
empenné [ăpɛne], *a.* Feathered (arrow) ; finned, vaned (bomb).
empereur [ăprœːr], *s.m.* Emperor.
empeser [ăpəze], *v.tr.* (j'empèse; j'empèserai) To starch (linen, etc.). F: *E. son style*, to impart stiffness to one's style.
empesé, *a.* F: Stiff, starchy, formal.
empester [ăpɛste], *v.tr.* **I.** (*a*) To make (place) stink. *Air empesté par le tabac*, air reeking of tobacco. (*b*) *Il nous empestait de son haleine*, his breath was dreadful. **2.** *Abs.* To stink. *E. l'alcool*, to reek of alcohol. [PESTE]
empesté, *a.* Foul.
empêtrement [ăpetrəmã], *s.m.* Entanglement.
empêtrer [ăpetre], *v.tr.* **I.** To hobble (animal). **2.** To entangle ; to trammel. *S'e. les pieds dans les broussailles*, to catch one's feet in the undergrowth. F: *E. qn dans une querelle*, to involve s.o. in a quarrel.
s'empêtrer, to become entangled, embarrassed. *S'e. de colis*, to hamper oneself with luggage. *Empêtré dans le varech*, floundering among the seaweed.
emphase [ăfaːz], *s.f.* Bombast, turgidity, grandiloquence ; rotundity (of style). *Écrire avec e.*, to write in a high-flown style.
emphatique [ăfatik], *a.* Bombastic, grandiloquent, turgid. *adv.* **-ment.**
empiècement [ăpjɛsmã], *s.m.* Yoke (of dress).
empierrement [ăpjɛrmã], *s.m.* **I.** (*a*) Metalling (of road). *Rail:* Ballasting. (*b*) Paving. **2.** Macadam ; (road) metal. *Rail:* Ballast.
empierrer [ăpjɛre], *v.tr.* (*a*) To metal, macadamize (road). *Rail:* To ballast (track). (*b*) To pave. [PIERRE]
empiétement [ăpjetmã], *s.m.* Encroachment, trespass (*sur*, on) ; infringement (*sur*, of).
empiéter [ăpjete], *v.* (j'empiète; j'empiéterai) **I.** *v.i. E. sur le terrain, l'autorité; les loisirs, de qn*, to encroach (up)on s.o.'s land, authority, leisure. *E. sur les droits de qn*, to infringe s.o.'s rights. **2.** *v.tr. E. un arpent sur le champ d'un voisin*, to filch an acre from a neighbour's field. [PIED]
empiffrer [ăpifre], *v.tr.* F: To cram, stuff (s.o. with food).

s'empiffrer, to gorge (*de*, on).
empil|er [ăpile], *v.tr.* **I.** To stack, to pile (up) (wood, coal, etc.). **2.** *P:* To cheat, rob (s.o.). *s.m.* **-age.** *s.m.* **-ement.** *s.* **-eur, -euse.**
empire [ăpiːr], *s.m.* **I.** (*a*) Sovereign authority; dominion ; sway. **Sous l'empire d'un tyran**, under the rule of a tyrant. (*b*) Influence, control ; sway. *Il a perdu son e. sur l'opinion*, he has lost his hold on, his sway over, opinion. **Empire sur soi-même**, self-command, self-control. **2.** Empire. **Le Saint Empire Romain**, the Holy Roman Empire.
empirer [ăpire], *v.* To worsen. **I.** *v.tr.* To make (sth.) worse ; to aggravate (an ill). **2.** *v.i.* To become, grow, worse. [PIRE]
empirique [ăpirik], *a.* Empiric(al) ; rule-of-thumb (method). *adv.* **-ment, -ally.**
empirisme [ăpirism], *s.m.* Empiricism.
emplacement [ăplasmã], *s.m.* **I.** (*a*) Site (of, for, building, etc.). (*b*) Location (of works, etc.). (*c*) Place, spot. **2.** *Mil:* Emplacement (of gun); gun-pit. *Nau: E. de chargement*, loading berth.
emplanture [ăplătyːr], *s.f.* (*a*) Step (of mast). (*b*) Socket (of aeroplane wing).
emplâtre [ăplɑːtr], *s.m.* **I.** *Pharm:* Plaster. F: *C'est mettre un emplâtre sur une jambe de bois*, it's no earthly use. **2.** Gaiter (for repair of tyre).
emplette [ăplɛt], *s.f.* Purchase. **Aller faire ses emplettes**, to go shopping. **Faire emplette d'un chapeau**, to purchase a hat.
emplir [ăpliːr], *v.tr.* To fill (up).
s'emplir, to fill up.
emploi [ăplwa], *s.m.* **I.** Use, employment (of sth.). **Emploi du temps**, time-table (of work). **Faire emploi de la force**, to resort to force. **Mot qui fait double emploi**, word that is a useless repetition. **2.** Employment, occupation, post. **Être sans emploi**, to be out of work, out of employment, *F:* out of a job. *E. public*, public office. *Journ:* "**Demandes d'emploi**," 'situations wanted.' "**Offres d'emploi**," 'situations vacant.' *Th: E. d'un acteur*, special line of an actor. **Tenir l'emploi de père noble**, to play heavy fathers.
employ|er [ăplwaje], *v.tr.* (j'emploie ; j'emploierai) **I.** To employ, use (sth.). *E. son argent à l'achat de livres*, to use, lay out, one's money in buying books. *Bien e. son temps*, to make good use of one's time. *Mal e. son temps*, to mis-spend, misemploy, one's time. **2.** To employ (workmen, etc.). *E. qn comme secrétaire*, to employ s.o. as secretary. *a.* **-able.**
s'employer, to occupy oneself. *Il s'emploie à jardiner*, he spends his time gardening. *S'e. pour qn*, to exert oneself in, on s.o.'s behalf.
employé, -ée, *s.* Employee. *E. de magasin*, (male) shop-assistant. *Employée de magasin*, (female) shop-assistant ; shop-girl, -woman. *E. à la vente*, salesman. *E. de banque*, bank clerk. *E. des chemins de fer*, railway-servant.
employeur, -euse [ăplwajœːr, -øːz], *s.* Employer (of labour).
emplumer [ăplyme], *v.tr.* To feather (sth.).
empocher [ăpoʃe], *v.tr.* To pocket (money, *F:* an insult). *F: E. un coup*, to be hit ; to receive a blow.
empoignant [ăpɔɲã, -pwa-], *a.* Thrilling, stirring.
empoigner [ăpɔɲe, -pwa-], *v.tr.* **I.** (*a*) To grasp, seize, grab ; to lay hold of (s.o., sth.). F: **Empoigner l'occasion**, to seize the opportunity. (*b*) F: *Ils se sont empoignés*, they had a set-to.

2. To catch, arrest (criminal, etc.). **3.** To thrill, grip (reader, spectator). [POING]

empois [ăpwɑ], *s.m.* (a) Starch(-paste). (b) *Tex:* Dressing.

empoisonnant [ăpwazɔnã], *a.* F: Poisonous; putrid (smell); rotten (play).

empoisonn|er [ăpwazɔne], *v.tr.* **1.** To poison (s.o.). **2.** (a) To poison (food, etc.); to infect (the air). (b) *Abs. F:* To stink. (With cogn. acc.) *Ça empoisonne le tabac ici,* this room is reeking of tobacco. *s.m.* **-ement.**
s'empoisonner, to take poison.

empoisonneur, -euse [ăpwazɔnœːr, -øːz], *s.* Poisoner.

empoissonner [ăpwasɔne], *v.tr.* To stock (pond, etc.) with fish.

emportement [ăpɔrtəmã], *s.m.* Transport (of anger). *Dans l'e. de la discussion,* in the heat of debate. *Répondre avec e.,* to make a heated reply.

emporte-pièce, s.m.inv. *Tls:* Punch. *Découper qch. à l'e.-p. (dans la tôle),* to stamp sth. out (of sheet-iron). *Mots à l'emporte-pièce,* biting, cutting, words; words that tell.

emporter [ăpɔrte], *v.tr.* **1.** To carry away, take away, bear away. *Vin à emporter,* wine for off-consumption. F: **(Que) le diable l'emporte!** the devil take him! **2.** (a) To carry, tear, sweep, away. *Le vent emporta son chapeau,* the wind blew off his hat. S.a. AUTANT 1. *F: Cette moutarde vous emporte la bouche,* this mustard is very hot. (b) À un fort, to carry, take, a fort (by assault). (c) *Outil qui emporte les pièces,* tool that stamps out, punches out, the parts. *F:* **Emporter la pièce, le morceau,** to be very trenchant. (d) **Emporter la balance,** to turn the scale. **3.** To carry (s.o., sth.) along. **Se laisser emporter à la colère,** to give way to anger. *Ce point essentiel emporte tout le reste,* everything hangs on this essential point. **4. L'emporter sur qn,** to prevail over, get the better of, s.o. *L'e. dans une discussion,* to have the best of an argument. *L'e. en nombre sur . . .,* to outnumber. . . .
s'emporter. 1. To lose one's temper; to fly into a passion. *S'e. contre qn,* to flare up at s.o. **2.** (Of horse) To bolt.

emporté, a. 1. Quick-tempered; hot-headed; fiery. *Caractère e.,* passionate nature. **2.** Runaway (horse).

empot|er [ăpɔte], *v.tr.* To pot (plants, jam). *s.m.* **-age.**

empoté, -ée, a. & s. F: Awkward, clumsy.

empourprer [ăpurpre], *v.tr.* To tinge (sth.) with crimson; to give a purple tinge to (sth.).
s'empourprer. 1. (Of pers.) To flush (up). **2.** (Of sky, etc.) To turn crimson.

empourpré, *a.* Crimson.

empreindre [ăprɛ̃ːdr], *v.tr.* (*pr.p.* empreignant; *p.p.* empreint; *pr.ind.* j'empreins, n. empreignons, ils empreignent; *p.h.* j'empreignis; *fu.* j'empreindrai) To impress, imprint, stamp. *Visage empreint de mélancolie,* face stamped with sadness. *Visage empreint de terreur,* face full of terror.

empreinte, s.f. (a) Impress(ion), (im)print, stamp. *E. en plâtre,* plaster cast. *E. des roues,* trace, track, of the wheels. *E. du pied, de pas,* footprint. *E. digitale,* finger-print. **Prendre l'empreinte de qch.,** to take an impression of sth. (b) *Typ:* Mould (from standing type).

empressement [ăprɛsmã], *s.m.* (a) Eagerness, readiness, alacrity (*à faire qch.,* to do sth.). **Faire qch. avec empressement,** to do sth. readily, with alacrity. **Peu d'empressement à faire qch.,** reluctance to do sth. (b) Bustling zeal.

empresser (s') [săprɛse], *v.pr.* **1.** To hurry, hasten (*de faire qch.,* to do sth.). **2.** *S'e. à faire qch.,* to show eagerness, zeal, in doing sth. *S'e. auprès de qn,* (i) to dance attendance on s.o.; (ii) to pay marked attention(s) to s.o.

empressé, -ée. 1. *a.* Eager, zealous, fervent. *Corr:* **"Agréez mes salutations empressées,"** 'I am yours faithfully.' **2.** *s.* Busybody. **Faire l'empressé auprès de qn,** to fuss, buzz, around s.o.; to show marked attention(s) to s.o.

emprise [ăpriːz], *s.f.* **1.** Expropriation or acquisition (of land for public purposes). **2.** Ascendancy (over person or mind); hold (*sur,* on).

emprisonnement [ăprizɔnmã], *s.m.* Imprisonment. *E. cellulaire,* solitary confinement.

emprisonner [ăprizɔne], *v.tr.* To imprison; to put (s.o.) in prison.

emprunt [ăprœ̃], *s.m.* Borrowing or loan. **Faire un emprunt à qn,** to borrow (money) of, from, s.o. **Offrir qch. à qn à titre d'emprunt,** to offer sth. to s.o. as a loan, on loan. **Nom d'emprunt,** feigned, assumed, name. *E. d'État,* government loan. *Contracter un e.,* to raise a loan.

emprunter [ăprœ̃te], *v.tr.* To borrow (*à,* from). *Mot emprunté du latin,* word taken from Latin. *E. un nom,* to assume a name. *Le cortège emprunta la rue de Rivoli,* the procession took the Rue de Rivoli.

emprunté, a. 1. (a) Assumed, false (name, etc.); sham (learning). (b) Derived (meaning); borrowed (idea, etc.). **2.** Self-conscious, stiff, awkward (manner).

emprunteur, -euse [ăprœ̃tœːr, -øːz], *s.* Borrower.

empyrée [ăpire], *a. & s.m.* Empyrean.

ému. See ÉMOUVOIR.

émulateur, -trice [emylatœːr, -tris], *s.* Rival, competitor.

émulation [emylasjɔ̃], *s.f.* Emulation, rivalry, competition.

émule [emyl], *s. m. & f.* Emulator, rival, competitor.

émulsion [emylsjɔ̃], *s.f.* Emulsion.

émulsionner [emylsjone], *v.tr.* To emulsify.

en¹ [ã], *prep.* **1.** (Place) (a) In, (in)to. *Être, aller, en ville,* to be in town, to go (in)to town. *En province,* in the country. *Venir en tramway,* to come by tram. *En tête, en queue,* at the head, in the rear. (With *f.* names of countries) *Être, aller, en France, en Amérique,* to be in, to go to, France, America. S.a. under ARRIÈRE 1, AVANT I. 5, BAS III. 1, etc. (b) (With pron.) *Il y a quelque chose en lui que j'admire,* there is something I admire about him. *Un homme en qui, en lequel, j'ai confiance,* a man whom I trust. (c) (With def. art., poss. adj., etc.) *En l'honneur de qn,* in honour of s.o. *En votre honneur,* in your honour. *Regarder en l'air,* to look up at the sky. **2.** (Time) In. *En été, en hiver, en automne,* in summer, autumn, winter. *Né en 1905,* born in 1905. *D'aujourd'hui en huit,* to-day week. *On peut aller à Londres en cinq jours,* one can go to London in five days. *En l'an 1800,* in the year 1800. *En ce temps-là,* in those days. **3.** (a) (State) *Être en deuil,* to be in mourning. *Être en guerre,* to be at war. *En réparation,* under repair. *En congé,* on leave. *En faction,* on guard. *Une femme en cheveux,* a woman without a hat. (b) (Material) *Montre en or,* gold watch. (c) (Manner) *Escalier en spirale,* spiral staircase. *Faire cent à l'heure en palier,* to do 100 kilom. an hour on the level. *Docteur en médecine,* doctor of medicine. (d) (Change, division) Into. *Il fut changé en serpent,* he was changed into a serpent. *Traduire une lettre en français,* to translate a letter into French.

Briser qch. en morceaux, to break sth. into bits. *Casser qch. en deux*, to break sth. in two. (*e*) **De mal en pis**, from bad to worse. *De fleur en fleur*, from flower to flower. **4.** (Introducing a pred. complement) *Envoyer qch. en cadeau*, to send sth. as a present. *Il m'a traité en gentilhomme*, he treated me (i) like the gentleman he is, (ii) as was due to a gentleman. *Prendre la chose en philosophe*, to take the thing philosophically. **5.** (With gerund) *Il répondit en riant*, he answered laughingly, with a laugh. *Travailler en chantant*, to sing at one's work. *On apprend en vieillissant*, we learn as we grow older. *En arrivant à Paris* . . ., on arriving in Paris. . . . *En attendant*, while waiting; in the meantime. *Tout en filant elle nous racontait des histoires*, while she span she told us stories. *Elle sortit en dansant*, she danced out, out of the room. *Elle s'endormit en pleurant*, she cried herself to sleep.

en², *unstressed adv. and pron.* **I.** *adv.* **I.** From there; thence. *Vous avez été à Londres?—Oui, j'en arrive*, you have been to London?—Yes, I've just come from there. **2.** On that account. *Si vous étiez riche, en seriez-vous plus heureux?* if you were rich, would you be happier on that account, any the happier? **II. en**, *pron.inv.* **I.** (*a*) (Standing for a sb. governed by *de*) *Vous avez appris la nouvelle? —Oui, nous en parlions*, you have heard the news?—Yes, we were speaking of it, about it. *J'aime mieux n'en pas parler, ne pas en parler*, I would rather not speak about it. *Les rues en sont pleines*, the streets are full of it, of them. *Il l'aime et il en est aimé*, he loves her and is loved by her. (*b*) (With expressions of quantity) *Combien avez-vous de chevaux?—J'en ai un, trois, plusieurs*, how many horses have you got?—I have one, three, several. (*c*) (Replacing the possessive, when the possessor is inanimate) *Nous avons visité l'église et en avons admiré les vitraux*, we visited the church and admired its stained glass. (*d*) (Standing for a clause) *Vous remplacer, il n'en est pas capable*, he is not fit to take your place. **2.** (Standing for a partitive sb.) Some, any. *J'en ai*, I have some. *Je n'en ai pas*, I have none. *En avez-vous?* have you any? **3.** (Indeterminate uses) *Je n'en ai pas encore fini avec lui*, I have not done with him yet. *Si le cœur vous en dit*, if you feel so inclined. *On s'en est donné*, we had a great time. **4.** (After imperative) *Prenez-en*, take some. *Prenez-en dix*, take ten.

enamourer (s') [sãnamure], *v.pr.* To fall in love (de, with).

  enamouré, *a.* Enamoured (*de*, of); in love (*de*, with).

en-avant [ãnavã], *s.m.inv. Fb:* Forward pass.

encablure [ãkɑblyːr], *s.f. Nau:* Cable('s-length) (= one tenth of a nautical mile).

encadrement [ãkɑdrəmã], *s.m.* **I.** (*a*) Framing. (*b*) *Mil:* Officering (of unit). **2.** Framework; frame (of picture); setting (of story). *E. de porte*, door-, window-frame.

encadrer [ãkɑdre], *v.tr.* **I.** To frame (picture, etc.). *E. un journal de noir*, to put a black border round a paper. *Jardin encadré de haies*, garden enclosed by hedges. **2.** *Mil:* (*a*) To officer (battalion). (*b*) To straddle (target).

encadreur [ãkɑdrœːr], *s.m.* Picture-framer.

encaissage [ãkɛsaːʒ], *s.m. Hort:* Planting in tubs; tubbing. **2.** Boxing (of goods).

encaisse [ãkɛs], *s.f.* Cash (in hand). *E. de 1000 francs*, cash balance of 1000 francs. *E. or et argent d'un pays*, gold and silver holding of a country.

encaissement [ãkɛsmã], *s.m.* **I.** (*a*) Incasing, encasing; packing into cases; boxing (of goods); planting in tubs; tubbing. (*b*) *Com:* Encashment, collection (of bills). **2.** (*a*) Embanking (of river). (*b*) Embankment.

encaisser [ãkɛse], *v.tr.* **I.** (*a*) To pack (goods) into cases; to box, case (goods); to plant (trees) in tubs; to tub. (*b*) To encash, collect (bill). *F:* (Of boxer) *Apprendre à e. les coups*, to learn to take a blow; to learn to stand punishment. *Il a encaissé*, he was severely punished. *E. une observation*, to take a remark in good part. **2.** To embank (river).

  encaissé, *a.* Boxed in; deeply embanked (river); sunk (road). *Tournant e.*, blind corner.

encaisseur [ãkɛsœːr], *s.m. Com:* (*a*) Collector (of bill, etc.); payee; (bank) cashier. (*b*) Bank messenger. (*c*) Collector (of gas company).

encan [ãkã], *s.m.* (Public) auction. **Mettre qch. à l'encan**, to put sth. up for auction.

encanailler (s') [sãkɑnɑje], *v.pr.* To frequent low company; to get into low habits. [CANAILLE]

encapuchonner [ãkapyʃɔne], *v.tr.* To put a hood, a cowl, on (s.o.); to hood, cover (machine).

  s'encapuchonner, to put on a hood; to wrap up one's head.

encaqu|er [ãkake], *v.tr.* To barrel (herrings, etc.). [CAQUE] *s.m.* **-ement**.

encart [ãkaːr], *s.m. Bookb:* Inset (of 4 or 8 pages).

encartage [ãkartaːʒ], *s.m. Bookb:* **I.** Insetting. **2.** Inset; inlay.

encarter [ãkarte], *v.tr. Bookb:* To inset.

en-cas [ãkã], *s.m.inv.* **I.** Article kept for emergencies; emergency supply. *Avoir une somme en réserve comme en-cas*, to have a sum put by to fall back upon. **2.** = EN-TOUT-CAS.

encastrement [ãkastrəmã], *s.m.* **I.** Embedding, fixing, housing (of sth.) (in recess). **2.** (*a*) Recess; housing. (*b*) Frame, casing.

encastrer [ãkastre], *v.tr.* To embed, to set in, to house (beam, etc.); to recess (rivet-head, etc.).

  encastré, *a.* Imbedded; built-in; countersunk (rivet).

encaustique [ãkostik, -kɔ-]. **I.** *a. & s.f. Art:* Encaustic (painting). **2.** *s.f.* (Bees-)wax polish.

encaustiqu|er [ãkostike, -kɔ-], *v.tr.* To beeswax (floor, etc.); to polish (table). *s.m.* **-age**.

enceindre [ãsɛ̃ːdr], *v.tr.* (Conj. like CEINDRE) To gird, surround, encompass.

  enceinte¹, *s.f.* **I.** (*a*) Surrounding wall; fence. (*b*) *Parc qui a deux lieues d'e.*, park five miles in circumference. **2.** Enclosure. *Box:* *Turf:* Ring.

  enceinte² [ãsɛ̃ːt], *a.f.* With child; pregnant.

encens [ãsã], *s.m.* **I.** Incense. *E. mâle*, frankincense. **2.** *Bot:* Rosemary.

encens|er [ãsãse], *v.tr.* (*a*) *Ecc:* To cense (altar etc.). (*b*) To burn incense to, before (idols). (*c*) To flatter. *s.m.* **-ement**.

encenseur [ãsãsœːr], *s.m.* (*a*) *Ecc:* Thurifer, censer-bearer. (*b*) *F:* Flatterer, sycophant.

encensoir [ãsãswaːr], *s.m.* Censer. *F: Coup d'encensoir*, (piece of) fulsome flattery.

encéphalite [ãsefalit], *s.f. Med:* Encephalitis.

encercl|er [ãsɛrkle], *v.tr.* To encircle; to shut in. *s.m.* **-ement**.

enchaînement [ãʃɛnmã], *s.m.* **I.** Chaining (up) (of dog, etc.). **2.** Chain, series, concatenation (of events, etc.); (logical) sequence.

enchaîner [ãʃene], *v.tr.* **I.** To chain up (dog etc.). *E. un prisonnier*, to put a prisoner in chains in irons. *F: E. les passions*, to curb the passions. **2.** To link (up), connect (machinery, ideas, etc.).

On voit comme les choses s'enchaînent, one sees how things hang together.

enchantement [ãʃãtmã], *s.m.* **I.** Enchantment, magic; (magic) spell. **2.** Charm; glamour. **3.** Delight.

enchanter [ãʃãte], *v.tr.* **I.** To enchant, bewitch (s.o., sth.); to lay (s.o.) under a spell. **2.** To charm, delight, enrapture (s.o.).

enchanté, *a.* **I.** (a) Enchanted, under a spell, bewitched. *"La Flûte enchantée,"* 'the Magic Flute.' (b) *F:* Charming, delightful (spot). **2. Être enchanté de qch.,** to be delighted, charmed, at, with, sth.

enchanteur, -eresse [ãʃãtœ:r, -rɛ:s]. **I.** *s.* Enchanter, enchantress; *F:* charmer. **2.** *a.* Bewitching; entrancing (beauty); charming.

enchâss|er [ãʃase], *v.tr.* **I.** To enshrine (relic, etc.). **2.** To set, mount (jewel). *s.m.* **-ement.**

enchère [ãʃɛ:r], *s.f.* Bid(ding). **Vente à l'enchère,** aux enchères, sale by auction. **Mettre enchère,** to make a bid (*sur,* for). **Mettre qch. aux enchères,** to put sth. up to, for, auction. **Folle enchère,** irresponsible bid that cannot be made good. *F:* **Payer la folle enchère,** to pay for one's folly, for one's rashness. S.a. BRIDGE. [ENCHÉRIR]

enchérir [ãʃeri:r]. **I.** *v.tr.* To put up the price of (goods, etc.). *F:* **Sans rien enchérir,** without exaggeration. **2.** *v.i.* (a) To go up in price; to grow dearer. (b) To make a higher bid. **Enchérir sur qn,** (i) to outbid s.o.; (ii) *F:* to go one better than s.o. [CHER]

enchérissement [ãʃerismã], *s.m.* Rise, increase (in price, in the cost of living).

enchérisseur, -euse [ãʃerisœ:r, -ø:z], *s.* **I.** Bidder. **Dernier enchérisseur,** highest bidder. **2.** *F: E. sur . . .,* improver upon (offer, etc.).

enchevêtrement [ãʃvetrəmã], *s.m.* **I.** Tangling up. **2.** Tangle (of string, traffic, etc.).

enchevêtrer [ãʃvetre], *v.tr.* **I.** To halter (horse). **2.** To mix up, confuse, tangle up.
s'enchevêtrer, to get mixed up, confused, entangled; (of horse) to get tangled up.

enchevêtré, *a.* Tangled (skein, etc.); confused, involved (style).

enchifrènement [ãʃifrɛnmã], *s.m.* Cold in the head; *F:* snuffles.

enchifrener [ãʃifrəne], *v.tr.* (**j'enchifrène; j'enchifrènerai**) To give (s.o.) a cold in the head. *Être enchifrené,* to have a cold in the head; to snuffle.

enclancher [ãklãʃe], *v.tr.* = ENCLENCHER.

enclave [ãkla:v], *s.f.* Enclave; gore (of land).

enclav|er [ãklave], *v.tr.* **I.** To wedge in, dovetail (timbers). **2.** To enclave (land). *s.m.* **-ement.**

enclenchement [ãklãʃmã], *s.m. Mec.E:* Throwing into gear; interlocking (of parts). **Appareil d'enclenchement,** interlocking gear, engaging gear.

enclencher [ãklãʃe], *v.tr. Mec.E:* To lock, engage; to throw (parts) into gear. [CLENCHE]
s'enclencher, to engage; to come into gear (*avec,* with).

enclin [ãklɛ̃], *a.* Inclined, disposed (*à qch., à faire qch.,* to sth., to do sth.). *Nature encline au mal,* nature prone to evil.

encliquetage [ãklikta:ʒ], *s.m.* (Pawl-and-) ratchet mechanism. **Doigt d'encliquetage,** pawl.

enclitique [ãklitik], *a. & s.f. Gram:* Enclitic.

enclore [ãklɔ:r], *v.tr.* (Conj. like CLORE) To enclose; to fence in, wall in.

enclos [ãklo], *s.m.* **I.** Enclosure; paddock. **2.** Ring-fence; (enclosing) wall.

enclouer [ãklue], *v.tr.* **I.** To prick (horse) (in shoeing). **2.** To spike (gun). [CLOU]

s'enclouer. I. (Of horse) To prick itself. **2.** *F:* To get into a fix.

enclume [ãklym], *s.f.* Anvil. *F:* **Être entre l'enclume et le marteau,** to be between the devil and the deep sea.

encoche [ãkɔʃ], *s.f.* (a) Notch, nick (in tallystick, etc.). (b) Slot. (c) *Bookb:* *Avec encoches,* with thumb-index.

encocher [ãkɔʃe], *v.tr.* (a) To notch, nick (stick, etc.). (b) To slot.

encoignure [ãkɔɲy:r], *s.f.* **I.** Corner, angle (of room, street). **2.** Corner-cupboard.

encoll|er [ãkɔle], *v.tr.* (a) To glue (wood, etc.). (b) To gum, paste (paper, etc.). *E. une carte,* to mount a map. (c) To size. *s.m.* **-age.**

encolure [ãkɔly:r], *s.f.* **I.** (a) Neck and withers (of horse). *Turf:* *Gagner par une e.,* to win by a neck. (b) *F:* *Homme de forte e.,* thick-set, stocky, man. **2.** (a) Neck-opening (of dress). (b) Size in collars. **3.** Crown (of anchor).

encombrant [ãkɔ̃brã], *a.* Cumbrous, cumbersome; clumsy (furniture, etc.); bulky (luggage); (man) always in the way.

encombre [ãkɔ̃:br], *s.m.* (Used in the phr.) *Sans encombre,* without let or hindrance.

encombrement [ãkɔ̃brəmã], *s.m.* **I.** (a) Litter (of articles); congestion (of traffic, etc.); glut (of goods); block (of vehicles). (b) Overcrowding. **2.** (a) Cumbersomeness, bulkiness (of article). (b) Floor or ground space (required); room occupied (by engine, etc.). *E. hors tout,* over-all dimensions.

encombrer [ãkɔ̃bre], *v.tr.* To encumber; to congest (the streets). *Table encombrée de papiers,* table encumbered, littered, with papers. *E. le marché,* to glut, to overstock, the market. *"N'encombrez pas le passavant,"* 'stand clear of the gangway.'

encontre (à l') [alãkɔ̃:tr], *adv.phr.* In opposition; to the contrary. *Je n'ai rien à dire à l'e.,* I have nothing to say against it. **A l'encontre de,** against; in opposition to. *Aller à l'e. du danger,* to go out to meet danger. *Aller à l'e. de la loi,* to run counter to the law. *A l'e. des idées reçues,* contrary to received ideas.

encorbellement [ãkɔrbelmã], *s.m. Arch:* Corbelling (out) (of wall); overhang (of upper storey). *Poutre en e.,* overhung girder, cantilever girder. *Fenêtre en e.,* oriel window.

encore [ãkɔ:r], *adv.* **I.** (a) Still. *Il est à. ici,* he is still here. *Hier encore je lisais un de ses livres,* only yesterday, as recently as yesterday, I was reading a book of his. (b) Yet. *Je ne suis e. qu'étudiant,* I am only a student yet, so far. **Pas encore,** not yet. *Un homme que je n'avais e. jamais vu,* a man I had never seen before. (c) More, again. *E. un mot,* (just) one word more. *En voulez-vous e.?* will you have some more? *E. une tasse de café,* another, one more, cup of coffee. **Quoi encore?** what else? *Pendant trois mois e.,* for three months longer. *Réduire e. le prix,* to reduce the price still further. **Encore une fois,** once more. **Encore autant,** as much again. **2.** Moreover, furthermore. **Non seulement . . ., mais encore . . .,** not only . . ., but also . . . **3.** (Restrictive) (a) *Encore si on pouvait lui parler,* if even one could speak to him. (b) (With inversion) *Je n'ai qu'un ciseau, e. est-il émoussé,* I have only one chisel and even that is a blunt one. *E. vous aurait-il fallu me prévenir,* for all that you should have let me know. (c) *Il vous en donnera dix francs et encore!* he will give you ten francs for it, if that! (d) *Conj.phr.* **Encore (bien) que** + *sub.,* (al)though; even though. *E. qu'il ne me* *soit rien*, although he is nothing to me. *Temps agréable e. qu'un peu froid*, pleasant weather if rather cold. **4.** *Il s'est montré très discret.—*Mais **encore!** he was very reticent.—But what *did* he say?

encourageant [ăkuraʒă], *a.* Encouraging, cheering; cheerful (news).

encouragement [ăkuraʒmă], *s.m.* Encouragement. *E. à la vertu*, incentive to virtue. *Recevoir peu d'e. à faire qch.*, to receive little encouragement, little inducement, to do sth. *Sch:* **Prix d'encouragement,** prize for meritorious work.

encourager [ăkuraʒe], *v.tr.* (j'encourageai(s); n. encourageons) **1.** To encourage, hearten (s.o.). *E. qn à faire qch.*, to encourage s.o. to do sth. **2.** To encourage, foster (the arts). *E. une croyance*, to foster a belief. *Industrie encouragée*, State-aided industry.

encourir [ăkuriːr], *v.tr.* (Conj. like COURIR) To incur (reproaches, expense, etc.). *E. un risque*, to take a chance.

encrasser [ăkrase], *v.tr.* To dirty, soil, grease (one's clothes, etc.); to foul (gun); to oil up; to soot up (sparking-plug); to clog, choke (machine, etc.). [CRASSE] *s.m.* **-ement.**

s'encrasser, to get dirty, greasy; to get foul; to foul; to soot up, oil up.

encre [ăːkr], *s.f.* Ink. *E. de Chine*, Indian ink. *E. d'impression*, printing ink. *E. sympathique*, invisible ink. **Écrit à l'encre,** written in ink. *F:* **C'est la bouteille à l'encre,** there's no making head or tail of it.

encrer [ăkre], *v.tr. Typ:* To ink. *s.m.* **-age.**

encrier [ăkrie], *s.m.* Inkpot; inkstand; ink-well.

encroûtant [ăkrută], *a.* (a) Encrusting. (b) *F:* Soul-killing (occupation, etc.).

encroûtement [ăkrutmă], *s.m.* **1.**(a) Encrusting, crusting over. (b) *F:* Sinking into the rut. **2.** Crust. *E. calcique*, chalky deposit.

encroûter [ăkrute], *v.tr.* To encrust; to cake (with mud, etc.). *E. un mur*, to rough-cast a wall.

s'encroûter. 1. To become encrusted, caked (*de*, with). **2.** *F:* To sink into a rut; to become fossilized.

encroûté, *a.* Crusted. *F: Vieux bonhomme e.*, old fossil, old stick-in-the-mud.

encyclique [ăsiklik], *s.f. Ecc:* Encyclical (letter).

encyclopédie [ăsiklɔpedi], *s.f.* Encyclop(a)edia.

encyclopédique [ăsiklɔpedik], *a.* Encyclop(a)edic.

encyclopédiste [ăsiklɔpedist], *s.m.* Encyclop(a)edist.

endaubage [ădoba:ʒ], *s.m.* **1.** (a) Stewing (of meat). (b) Stew. **2.** Tinned beef.

endauber [ădobe], *v.tr.* **1.** To stew (meat). **2.** To tin, preserve (meat). [DAUBE]

endémie [ădemi], *s.f.* Endemic disease; endemic.

endémique [ădemik], *a.* Endemic.

endenter [ădăte], *v.tr.* **1.** (a) To tooth, cog (wheel, etc.). (b) To mesh (wheels). **2.** To join (timbers) by a scarf-joint. *s.m.* **-ement.**

endetter [ădete], *v.tr.* To get (s.o.) into debt.

s'endetter, to get, run, into debt. *Endetté*, in debt.

endeuiller [ădœːje], *v.tr.* To plunge into mourning. *Maison endeuillée*, house of mourning.

endêver [ădeve], *v.i. P:* To be furious, angry.

endiabler [ădjable], *v.i.* **Faire endiabler qn,** to torment, rag, s.o.

endiablé, *a.* (a) Reckless, devil-may-care (courage, etc.). (b) Wild, frenzied (music, etc.).

endiamanté [ădjamăte], *a.* Studded, covered, with diamonds.

endiguement [ădigmă], *s.m.* **1.** (a) Damming

(up). (b) Embanking (of river, etc.). **2.** (a) Dam. (b) Sea-wall. (c) Embankment, dyke, dike.

endiguer [ădige], *v.tr.* **1.** To dam up (river, etc.). **2.** To (em)bank (river, etc.); to dike (land). **3.** To impound (water).

endimancher [ădimăʃe], *v.tr.* To dress (s.o.) in (his, her) Sunday best. *s.m.* **-ement.**

endive [ădiːv], *s.f. Bot:* **1.** Endive. **2.** Broad-leaved chicory.

endocardite [ădɔkardit], *s.f. Med:* Endocarditis.

endocrine [ădɔkrin], *a.f. Anat:* Endocrine, ductless (gland).

endogamie [ădɔgami], *s.f. Anthr:* Endogamy; in-breeding.

endolorir [ădɔlɔriːr], *v.tr.* To make (limb) ache.

s'endolorir, to become painful.

endolori, *a.* Painful, sore; tender.

endolorissement [ădɔlɔrismă], *s.m.* Ache, pain (in limb, etc.); tenderness.

endommager [ădɔmaʒe], *v.tr.* (j'endommageai(s); n. endommageons) To damage, injure; to do damage to (sth.).

endormant [ădɔrmă], *a.* **1.** Soporific. **2.** *F:* Boring, wearisome.

endormeur, -euse [ădɔrmœːr, -øːz], *s. F:* (a) Cajoler, humbug. (b) Bore.

endormir [ădɔrmiːr], *v.tr.* (Conj. like DORMIR) **1.** (a) To put, send, lull, (s.o.) to sleep. (b) *F:* To bore (s.o.). (c) *Med:* To anaesthetize; to chloroform. **2.** To benumb (limb, etc.); to lull, deaden (pain). **3.** *F:* To cajole, humbug, hoodwink (s.o.). *E. les soupçons*, to allay suspicion.

s'endormir, to fall asleep; to go to sleep; to drop off to sleep.

endormi, -ie, *a.* **1.** (a) Asleep, sleeping. *s.* Sleeper. **Faire l'endormi,** to pretend to be asleep. (b) Sleepy, drowsy. *s. F:* Sleepy-head. (c) Dormant (passion). **2.** (Of limb etc.) Numb; 'gone to sleep.'

endos [ădo], *s.m.* Endorsement (on cheque).

endosmose [ădɔsmoːz], *s.f. Ph:* Endosmosis.

endossataire [ădɔsateːr], *s.m. Com:* Endorsee.

endosser [ădose], *v.tr.* **1.** To don, put on (clothes). *F: E. une responsabilité*, to assume, shoulder, a responsibility. **2.** *Com:* To endorse (cheque, etc.); to back (bill). **3.** *Bookb:* To back (book). *s.m.* **-ement.**

endosseur [ădosœːr], *s.m. Com:* Endorser.

endossure [ădosyːr], *s.f. Bookb:* Backing, rounding.

endroit [ădrwa], *s.m.* **1.** Place, spot; passage (in book). **Par endroits,** here and there; in places. *Rire au bon e.*, to laugh in the right place. S.a. SENSIBLE 1. **2.** Side, aspect. **Prendre qn par son endroit faible,** *F:* to get on the soft side of s.o. **A l'endroit de qn, de qch.,** regarding, with regard to, s.o., sth. **3.** Right side (of material). **A l'endroit,** right side out. **Étoffe à deux endroits,** reversible material.

enduire [ădɥiːr], *v.tr.* (pr.p. enduisant; p.p. enduit; pr.ind. j'enduis, ils enduisent; p.h. j'enduisis; fu. j'enduirai) To smear, coat, plaster. *E. des pierres de goudron*, to coat stones with tar.

enduit, *s.m.* **1.** (a) Coat, coating (of tar, paint, etc.). (b) Plastering; coat of plaster. **2.** (Water)proofing (of cloth, etc.). **3.** *Cer:* Glaze. **4.** *Phot:* Enduit antihalo, backing.

endurable [ădyrabl], *a.* Endurable.

endurance [ădyrăːs], *s.f.* Endurance. **1.** Long suffering. **2.** Resistance to wear and tear. *Aut: etc:* **Épreuve d'endurance,** reliability trial.

endurant [ãdyrã], *a.* Patient; long-suffering. **Peu endurant,** quick-tempered.

endurcir [ãdyrsiːr], *v.tr.* **I.** To harden, indurate. **2.** To inure (à, to). *Enduroi à la fatigue,* inured, hardened, to fatigue. [DUR] **s'endurcir.** **I.** To harden, indurate; to become hard; *F:* to become callous. **2.** To become hardened, fit, tough. **endurci,** *a.* **I.** Hardened; *Tchn:* indurated. **2.** Hard, callous (heart); hardened (sinner); inveterate (hatred).

endurcissement [ãdyrsismã], *s.m.* **I.** (a) Hardening, induration. (b) Inuring (to fatigue). **2.** (a) Hardness (of heart). (b) Obduracy.

endurer [ãdyre], *v.tr.* To endure, bear (hardship, etc.). *E. des railleries,* to put up with chaff.

énergétique [enɛrʒetik], *a.* **I.** Energizing (medicine, food). **2.** *Dépense é.,* expenditure of energy.

énergie [enɛrʒi], *s.f.* Energy. **I.** (a) Force, vigour. *Apporter, appliquer, toute son é. à une tâche,* to devote, bend, direct, all one's energies to a task. *Avec énergie,* energetically. *Sans énergie,* listless(ly). (b) Efficacy (of remedy). **2.** (a) *É. cinétique,* kinetic energy. *É. potentielle,* potential energy. (b) *Ind: É. consommée,* power consumption.

énergique [enɛrʒik], *a.* (a) (Of pers.) Energetic. (b) Strong, drastic (measures); forcible (language); emphatic (gesture). *Remède é.,* (i) powerful medicine; (ii) *F:* drastic remedy; kill-or-cure remedy. *adv.* **-ment,** -ally.

énergumène [enɛrgymɛn], *s.m. & f.* **I.** Energumen. *F:* **Crier comme un énergumène,** to scream like one possessed. **2.** *F:* Ranter, tub-thumper.

énervant [enɛrvã], *a.* **I.** Enervating (climate, etc.). **2.** *F:* Aggravating, nerve-racking.

énervement [enɛrvəmã], *s.m.* State of jangled nerves; nervous irritation; state of nerves.

énerver [enɛrve], *v.tr.* **I.** (a) To enervate, weaken (body, will). (b) To hamstring. **2.** *É. qn,* to get on s.o.'s nerves; to set s.o.'s nerves on edge. **s'énerver.** **I.** To become flabby; to lose one's stamina. **2.** To become irritable, fidgety, 'nervy'; to get excited.

enfance [ãfãːs], *s.f.* **I.** (a) Childhood. **Première enfance,** infancy. *Industrie encore dans son e.,* industry still in its infancy. (b) Boyhood; girlhood. **2.** *Tomber en enfance,* to sink into one's second childhood, into one's dotage. **3.** *Coll.* Children.

enfant [ãfã], *s.m. & f.* Child; boy or girl; *F:* youngster. *E. en bas âge, e. du premier âge,* infant. **Enfant trouvé,** foundling. *E. de chœur,* choir-boy. *F:* **Ce n'est qu'un jeu d'enfant,** it is mere child's play. **Se conduire en enfant, faire l'enfant,** to behave childishly. *a.* **Ne soyez pas si enfant,** don't be so childish. S.a. CHAMBRE I, TERRIBLE, VOITURE 2. *F: Allons-y, mes enfants!* come on, lads! *a.* **Bon enfant,** good-natured. *Sourire e.,* childlike smile. **Mourir sans enfants,** to die childless, *Jur:* without issue. *F: Un e. de Paris,* a native of Paris.

enfantement [ãfãtmã], *s.m.* **I.** Childbirth. **2.** Giving birth (to literary work, etc.).

enfanter [ãfãte], *v.tr.* To bear, to give birth to (child). *F: La discorde enfante le crime,* discord begets crime.

enfantillage [ãfãtijaːʒ], *s.m.* Childishness; childish act or saying.

enfantin [ãfãtɛ̃], *a.* **I.** Infantile. *Classe enfantine,* infant class. **2.** Childish (voice, etc.). *Littérature enfantine,* juvenile literature.

15

---

enfariner [ãfarine], *v.tr.* To flour (sth.); to cover (sth.) with flour. *F:* **Aborder qn la langue enfarinée,** to address s.o. (i) in a bumptious manner, (ii) in a mealy-mouthed manner.

enfer [ãfɛːr], *s.m.* Hell. **Les enfers,** the underworld; Hades. *Lit:* **L'Enfer de Dante,** Dante's Inferno. *Hist: L'e. de Verdun,* the inferno of Verdun. **Aller un train d'enfer,** (i) to ride hell for leather; (ii) (of car, etc.) to scorch along. S.a. JEU 4.

enfermer [ãfɛrme], *v.tr.* **I.** To shut (s.o., sth.) up. *E. ses papiers,* to lock up one's papers. *Tenir qn enfermé,* to keep s.o. in confinement. *F:* **Il est bon à enfermer,** he ought to be shut up. (Of room) **Sentir l'enfermé,** to smell stuffy. **2.** To shut (sth.) in; to enclose, surround. **s'enfermer,** to lock oneself in; to shut oneself up. *Enfermé dans ses pensées,* wrapped in his thoughts. *Vivre trop enfermé,* to live too much indoors.

enferrer [ãfɛre], *v.tr.* To run (s.o.) through. **s'enferrer.** **I.** (a) To spit oneself (on opponent's sword). (b) (Of fish) To swallow the hook. **2.** *F:* To give oneself away; to be hoist with one's own petard.

enfieller [ãfjele], *v.tr.* *F:* To embitter, sour (s.o.'s life, etc.). [FIEL]

enfiévrer [ãfjevre], *v.tr.* (j'enfièvre; j'enfiévrerai) **I.** To give (s.o.) fever; to make (s.o.) feverish. **2.** *F:* To fire, animate (s.o.). **s'enfiévrer.** **I.** To grow feverish. **2.** To get excited.

enfilade [ãfilad], *s.f.* **I.** Succession, series (of doors, etc.); suite (of rooms); row (of houses); string (of insults). **2.** *Mil:* Enfilade. **Tir d'enfilade,** raking, enfilading, fire.

enfiler [ãfile], *v.tr.* **I.** To thread (needle); to file (papers on spike file); to string (beads). **Enfiler qn,** to run s.o. through. **2.** To take, go along (a street). *F:* **Enfiler la venelle,** to cut and run. **3.** *E. ses vêtements,* to slip on one's clothes. *E. son pantalon, ses bas,* to pull on, draw on, one's trousers, one's stockings. **Blouse à enfiler,** slip-on blouse. **4.** *Mil:* To enfilade, rake (trench, etc.). *s.m.* **-ement.**

enfilure [ãfilyːr], *s.f.* **I.** String (of beads, etc.). **2.** *F:* Series (of events, etc.).

enfin [ãfɛ̃]. **I.** *adv.* (a) Finally, lastly. (b) In fact, in a word, in short. (c) At last, at length. *E. vous voilà! vous voilà e.!* here you are at last! **2.** *int.* (a) At last! (b) *Mais e., s'il acceptait!* but still, if he did accept! (c) *E.! ce qui est fait est fait,* well, well! what is done is done.

enflammer [ãflame], *v.tr.* **I.** To inflame. To ignite; to set (sth.) on fire, ablaze. **2.** To inflame (wound). **3.** To excite, fire, stir up (s.o.); to enflame (mob). *s.m.* **-ement.** **s'enflammer.** **I.** To catch fire; to ignite. **2.** (Of wound, etc.) To become inflamed. **3.** *F:* (Of pers.) To fire up, flare up. **enflammé,** *a.* **I.** Burning, blazing; fiery (sun, sunset). **2.** Blazing, glowing (cheeks).

enflèchure [ãfleʃyːr], *s.f. Nau:* Ratline.

enfler [ãfle], *v.tr.* (a) To swell; to cause (sth.) to swell. *E. les joues,* to puff out, blow out, one's cheeks. *E. le nombre, la dépense,* to swell the number, the expenditure. (b) *E. son style,* to inflate one's style. **2.** *v.i. & pr.* To swell. *Son bras (s')enfle,* his arm is swelling. *La rivière (s')enfle,* the river is rising. *s.m.* **-ement.** **enflé,** *a.* Swollen. *Style e.,* turgid, high-flown, style. *F:* **Enflé d'orgueil,** puffed up with pride.

enflure [ãflyːr], *s.f.* Swelling (of cheek, limb, etc.); inflation, turgidity (of style).

enfoncement [ãfɔ̃smã], *s.m.* **1.** Driving (in) (of nail, etc.); breaking open (of door). **2.** Hollow, depression (in the ground). *Arch:* Alcove, recess. *Nau:* Bay, bight.

enfoncer [ãfɔ̃se], *v.* (j'enfonçai(s); n. enfonçons) **1.** *v.tr.* (*a*) To drive (in) (pile, nail). *E. la main dans sa poche,* to thrust one's hand into one's pocket. *E. son chapeau sur sa tête,* to cram one's hat on one's head. *S'e. une épine dans le pied,* to run a thorn into one's foot. (*b*) To break open, beat in, burst in (door, etc.); to stave in (cask). *E. un carreau,* to break a window-pane. *E. tous les obstacles,* to break through all obstacles. (*c*) *F:* To get the better of (s.o.); to best (s.o.). **2.** *v.i.* To sink (into mud, sea). *Le navire enfonçait,* the ship was settling.

s'enfoncer, to penetrate, plunge, go deep (into sth.). *Le navire s'enfonça sous les eaux,* the ship sank to the bottom. *Le plancher s'enfonçait,* the floor was subsiding, was giving way. *La balle s'enfonça dans le mur,* the bullet bedded itself in the wall. *S'e. dans une rue, F:* to dive into a street.

enfoncé, *a.* **1.** Smashed (in), broken (in); stove in (cask). **2.** (*a*) Sunken, deep (cavity). *Yeux enfoncés,* deep-set, sunken, eyes. *E. dans l'étude,* deep in study. (*b*) Low-lying (ground).

enfonçure [ãfɔ̃sy:r], *s.f.* Cavity; depression, hollow (in ground); recess (in cavern, etc.).

enfou|ir [ãfwi:r], *v.tr.* To hide (sth.) in the ground; to bury (dead animal, money). *s.m.* **-issement.**

enfouisseur [ãfwisœ:r], *s.m.* **1.** Burier. **2.** *Ent:* Sexton-beetle.

enfourcher [ãfurʃe], *v.tr.* **1.** To thrust a (pitch-) fork into (sth.). **2.** (*a*) To bestride, get astride, mount (horse, bicycle). (*b*) *F:* To ride (hobby) to death.

enfourchure [ãfurʃy:r], *s.f.* Fork, crotch (of tree); fork (of legs).

enfourn|er [ãfurne], *v.tr.* To put (bread) in the oven, (pottery) in the kiln. *s.m.* **-ement.**

enfreindre [ãfrɛ̃:dr], *v.tr.* (*pr.p.* enfreignant; *p.p.* enfreint; *pr.ind.* j'enfreins, n. enfreignons, ils enfreignent; *p.h.* j'enfreignis; *fu.* j'enfreindrai) To infringe, transgress, break (the law).

enfuir (s') [ãfɥi:r], *v.pr.* (Conj. like FUIR) **1.** (*a*) To flee, fly (*de,* from); to run away. *Les côtes s'enfuient,* the coast recedes. (*b*) (Of embezzler, etc.) To abscond. (*c*) (With lover) To elope. **2.** (Of liquid) To leak out, run out.

enfum|er [ãfyme], *v.tr.* **1.** To fill with smoke. **2.** To blacken (sth.) with smoke. **3.** To smoke out (bees, etc.). *s.m.* **-age.**

enfumé, *a.* **1.** Smoky (room, etc.). **2.** Smoke-blackened (walls, etc.). *Verres enfumés,* smoked glasses.

engageant [ãgaʒã], *a.* Engaging, prepossessing, winning (manners, etc.); inviting (meal, etc.).

engagement [ãgaʒmã], *s.m.* **1.** (*a*) Pawning, pledging. (*b*) Receipt (for object pledged). **2.** (*a*) Engagement, promise. *Tenir ses engagements; faire honneur, faire face, à ses engagements,* to keep, observe, carry out, one's engagements; to meet one's obligations. *Contracter, prendre, un engagement,* to enter into a contract, into an engagement. (*b*) Engagement, appointment (of employee). *Mil:* Voluntary enlistment. *Se trouver sans e.,* to be out of a job. (*c*) *Sp:* (i) Entering, (ii) entry (for event); (iii) fixture. **3.** *Mil:* Navy: Engagement, action.

engager [ãgaʒe], *v.tr.* (j'engageai(s); n. engageons) **1.** To pledge, pawn (jewellery, etc.). *E. sa parole,* to pledge one's word. *Cette lettre ne vous* engage pas, this letter does not bind you, does not commit you. *S.a.* HONNEUR I, RESPONSABILITÉ. **2.** To engage (servant, etc.); to take on (hands); to sign on (ship's company). **3.** (*a*) To catch, foul, entangle (rope, etc.); to jam (part of machine, etc.). *E. une ancre,* to foul an anchor. *E. un aviron,* to catch a crab. *F: E. qn dans une querelle,* to involve s.o. in a quarrel. (*b*) To engage (machinery); to put (machinery) into gear. *E. la clef dans la serrure,* to fit, insert, the key in the lock. **4.** To begin, start; to set (sth.) going; to open (conversation, fight, etc.). *E. le combat,* to join battle. *E. des négociations,* to enter into, start upon, negotiations. *Mil: E. des troupes,* to bring troops into action; to engage troops. **5.** *E. qn à faire qch.,* to invite, urge, advise, s.o. to do sth. **6.** *v.i.* (*a*) (Of machinery) To come into gear. (*b*) (Of ship) To roll gunwale under.

s'engager. 1. *S'e. à faire qch.,* to undertake, bind oneself, pledge one's word, to do sth. *S'e. par traité à faire qch.,* to contract to do sth. *Sans s'e. à rien,* without pinning himself down to anything. *Je suis trop engagé pour reculer,* I have gone too far to draw back. **2.** (*a*) To take service (*chez qn,* with s.o.). (*b*) To enlist; to volunteer. **3.** (*a*) (Of rope, propeller) To foul; to become fouled; (of machine) to jam; (of aeroplane) to get out of control. (*b*) *Un tube s'engage dans l'ouverture,* a pipe fits into the opening. *L'armée s'engagea dans le défilé,* the army entered the pass. (*c*) (Of battle) To begin.

engagé. 1. *a.* (Of ship) Gunwale under; on her beam-ends. **2.** *s.m. Mil:* Engagé (volontaire), volunteer.

engainer [ãgɛne], *v.tr.* To sheathe (dagger, etc.).

engazonn|er [ãgazɔne], *v.tr.* **1.** To turf (over). **2.** To sow with grass-seed. *s.m.* **-ement.**

engeance [ãʒã:s], *s.f.* **1.** *A:* Breed (of poultry, etc.). **2.** *F: E. de scélérats,* brood of scoundrels. *Sale e.!* dirty crew!

engelure [ãʒly:r], *s.f.* Chilblain.

engendrement [ãʒãdrəmã], *s.m.* **1.** Begetting (of children). **2.** *F:* Production; generation (of heat); breeding (of disease).

engendrer [ãʒãdre], *v.tr.* **1.** To beget (child). **2.** To engender (strife, etc.); to generate, develop (heat, etc.); to breed (disease). *Prov: La familiarité engendre le mépris,* familiarity breeds contempt.

engin [ãʒɛ̃], *s.m.* **1.** Engine, machine; device, contrivance. *Engins de pêche,* fishing tackle. **2.** *A:* Snare, gin.

englober [ãglɔbe], *v.tr.* To include, embody.

englout|ir [ãgluti:r], *v.tr.* **1.** To swallow; to gulp (sth.) down. **2.** To engulf; to swallow up (ship, fortune). *s.m.* **-issement.**

s'engloutir, (of ship) to be engulfed; to sink.

engluer [ãglye], *v.tr.* (*a*) To lime (twigs or bird). *F: Se laisser e.,* to allow oneself to be caught in the toils. (*b*) *Coque engluée de boue,* hull slimed all over with mud. [GLU]

engoncé [ãgɔ̃se], *a.* **1.** Bundled up in one's clothes. *Avoir l'air e.,* to look awkward and stiff. **2.** *Taille engoncée,* hunched-up shoulders.

engorgement [ãgɔrʒəmã], *s.m.* **1.** Choking, stopping (up), blocking, clogging. **2.** Obstruction, stoppage. *Med:* Engorgement, congestion.

engorger [ãgɔrʒe], *v.tr.* (j'engorgeai(s); n. engorgeons) To choke (up), stop (up); to block, clog.

s'engorger, to become choked (up), blocked (up), clogged; (of pump) to foul. *Med:* To become engorged, congested.

engouement [ãgumã], *s.m.* Infatuation.
engouer (s') [sãgwe], *v.pr. S'e. de qn,* to become infatua:ed with, to go crazy over, s.o.
engouffr|er [ãgufre], *v.tr.* To engulf. *F:* To swallow up (fortune). *s.m.* **-ement.**
s'engouffrer, to be engulfed, swallowed up, lost to sight. *Le vent s'engouffre par la porte,* the wind sweeps in, rushes in.
engoulevent [ãgulvã], *s.m. Orn:* Nightjar.
engourdir [ãgurdi:r], *v.tr.* To (be)numb. **s'engourdir. 1.** (Of limb, etc.) To grow numb ; *F:* (of foot) to go to sleep. **2.** (Of the mind) To become dull, sluggish.
engourdi, *a.* **1.** Numb(ed). *J'ai le pied e.,* my foot has gone to sleep. **2.** Dull, sluggish (mind). **3.** *Nau:* Stiff (rope).
engourdissement [ãgurdismã], *s.m.* **1.** Numbness. **2.** Dullness, sluggishness (of mind).
engrais [ãgrɛ], *s.m.* **1.** *Husb:* Fattening food. **2.** *Agr:* Manure. *E. chimique,* fertilizer.
engraiss|er [ãgrɛse]. **1.** *v.tr.* (*a*) To fatten (animals) ; to cram (fowls) ; to make (s.o.) fat. (*b*) To manure, fertilize (land). **2.** *v.i.* To grow stout ; to put on flesh. *s.m.* **-age.** *s.m.* **-ement.**
engrang|er [ãgrãʒe], *v.tr.* (j'engrangeai(s); n. engrangeons) To garner, get in (the corn). [GRANGE] *s.m.* **-ement.**
engrav|er [ãgrave]. **1.** *v.tr. Nau:* To strand (ship). **2.** *v.i. & pr.* (*a*) (Of boat) To ground ; to settle into the sand. (*b*) (Of harbour) To silt up. *s.m.* **-ement.**
engrenage [ãgrəna:ʒ], *s.m.* **1.** Gearing, engaging, throwing into gear ; meshing. **2.** (Toothed) gearing ; gear ; gear-wheels. *Système, jeu, d'engrenages,* train, set, of gear-wheels. **Turbine à engrenage(s),** geared turbine. *F: E. de circonstances,* mesh of circumstances.
engrener [ãgrəne], *v.* (j'engrène ; j'engrènerai) **1.** *v.tr.* To connect, engage, mesh (toothed wheels). *F: E. une affaire,* to set a thing going. **2.** *v.i. & pr. Roues qui* (s')*engrènent,* wheels that mesh with one another.
engrenure [ãgrəny:r], *s.f.* **1.** *Mec.E:* (*a*) Engaging, meshing (of toothed wheels). (*b*) Gear ratio. **2.** *Anat:* Serrated suture.
engueuler [ãgœle], *v.tr. P:* To abuse, slang, jaw (s.o.) ; to give (s.o.) a blowing up.
enguignonné [ãgiɲɔne], *a. F:* Out of luck.
enhardir [ãardi:r], *v.tr.* To embolden. *E. qn à faire qch.,* to encourage s.o. to do sth.
s'enhardir, to pluck up courage. *S'e. à faire qch.,* to venture, make bold, to do sth.
énigmatique [enigmatik], *a.* Enigmatic(al).
énigme [enigm], *s.f.* Enigma, riddle. *Proposer une énigme* (à qn), to ask (s.o.) a riddle ; to put, propound, a riddle (to s.o.). **Trouver le mot de l'énigme,** to find the answer, the clue, to the riddle ; to solve the riddle.
enivrant [ãnivrã], *a.* Intoxicating, heady.
enivrement [ãnivrəmã], *s.m.* **1.** Intoxication, inebriation. **2.** *F:* Ecstasy (of joy).
enivrer [ãnivre], *v.tr.* To intoxicate. **1.** To inebriate ; to make (s.o.) drunk. **2.** *F:* To elate.
s'enivrer, to become intoxicated, inebriated (de, with) ; to get drunk.
enjambement [ãʒãbmã], *s.m. Pros:* Enjambment ; run-on line.
enjamber [ãʒãbe]. **1.** *v.tr.* (*a*) To bestride (horse). (*b*) To step over, stride over (obstacle). *Trois ponts enjambent le fleuve,* three bridges span the river. **2.** *v.i.* (*a*) To step out ; to walk with long strides. (*b*) *E. sur qch.,* (i) to project over sth. ; (ii) to encroach on sth. [JAMBE]
enjambée, *s.f.* Stride.

enjeu, -eux [ãʒø], *s.m. Gaming:* Stake. **Retirer son enjeu,** (i) to withdraw one's stake ; (ii) *F:* to back out (of an undertaking).
enjoindre [ãʒwɛ̃:dr], *v.tr.* (Conj. like JOINDRE) To enjoin (silence, etc.). *E.* (*strictement*) *à qn. de faire qch.,* to enjoin, to call upon, to charge, s.o. to do sth.
enjôlement [ãʒolmã], *s.m.* **1.** Cajoling, wheedling. **2.** Cajolery, blandishment.
enjôler [ãʒole], *v.tr.* To coax, wheedle ; to humbug, blarney (s.o.) ; to talk (s.o.) over.
enjôleur, -euse [ãʒolœ:r, -ø:z]. **1.** *s.* Coaxer, cajoler, wheedler. **2.** *a.* Coaxing, cajoling, wheedling.
enjolivement [ãʒolivmã], *s.m.* **1.** Beautifying, embellishing. **2.** Embellishment ; ornamental piece ; scroll.
enjoliver [ãʒolive], *v.tr.* To beautify, embellish. *F: E. un récit,* to embroider a tale. [JOLI]
enjoliveur, -euse [ãʒolivœ:r, -ø:z], *s.* **1.** Beautifier, embellisher. **2.** *s.m. Aut:* Hub-cap.
enjolivure [ãʒolivy:r], *s.f.* Small embellishment.
enjoué [ãʒwe], *a.* Playful, sprightly.
enjouement [ãʒumã], *s.m.* Sprightliness ; playfulness.
enkyster (s') [sãkiste], *v.pr.* (Of tumour) To become encysted.
enlac|er [ãlase], *v.tr.* (j'enlaçai(s); n. enlaçons) **1.** To intertwine, interlace. **2.** (*a*) To entwine, enlace. (*b*) To clasp (s.o.) in one's arms ; to hug (s.o.) ; to hem in (enemy). *s.m.* **-ement.**
s'enlacer. (Of plants, etc.) (*a*) To intertwine. (*b*) *S'e. autour de qch.,* to twine round sth.
enlaid|ir [ãledi:r]. **1.** *v.tr.* To make (s.o.) ugly ; to disfigure (s.o.). **2.** *v.i.* To grow ugly, plain. [LAID] *s.m.* **-issement.**
enlevable [ãlvabl], *a.* Removable ; detachable.
enlevage [ãlva:ʒ], *s.m. Row:* Spurt.
enlevant [ãlvã], *a.* Rousing (speech, tune).
enlèvement [ãlevmã], *s.m.* **1.** Removal, removing ; carrying away. **2.** Kidnapping, carrying off. *L'e. des Sabines,* the rape of the Sabines. **Mariage par enlèvement,** runaway match. **3.** *Mil:* Storming, carrying (of position). **4.** Sending up (of balloon).
enlever [ãlve], *v.tr.* (j'enlève ; j'enlèverai) **1.** (*a*) To remove ; to carry away, take away ; to carry off ; to take up (carpet) ; to take down (curtains). *E. l'écorce, la peau,* to peel off, strip off, the bark ; to peel off, tear off, the skin. *E. le couvert,* to clear away ; to clear the table. *E. une tache,* to remove, take out, a stain. *Enlevé par la mer,* carried away, washed away, by the sea. (*b*) *E. qch. à qn,* to deprive s.o. of sth. ; to take sth. from s.o. *Un obus lui enleva une jambe,* a shell took off one of his legs. **2.** To carry off, steal (s.o.s.) ; to kidnap (s.o.) ; to abduct (girl). **Se faire enlever par qn,** to elope with s.o. **3.** *Mil:* To carry, storm (position). **4.** To raise ; to bear upwards. *E. le couvercle,* to lift the lid. *E. un ballon,* to send up a balloon. *E. son cheval,* (i) to lift one's horse (to a hurdle, etc.) ; (ii) to set one's horse at full speed. *F: La foule fut enlevée par ces paroles,* the crowd was carried away by these words. *E. un morceau (de musique),* to play a piece of music brilliantly, with brio.
s'enlever. 1. To come off. *La peau s'enlève,* the skin is peeling (off). *Cela s'enlèvera par l'usure,* it will wear off. **2.** (*a*) (Of balloon) To rise. (*b*) (Of milk) To boil over, up. *F:* (Of pers.) **S'enlever (comme une soupe au lait),** to flare up.
enliasser [ãljase], *v.tr.* To tie (papers, etc.) into bundles ; to file (papers). [LIASSE]

enlis|er, enliz|er [ălize], *v.tr.* (Of quicksand, bog) To suck in, engulf. *s.m.* **-ement.**
s'enliser, to sink, be sucked down (into quicksand) ; (of car, etc.) to get bogged.
enluminer [ălymine], *v.tr.* **1.** (*a*) To illuminate (MS.). (*b*) To colour (print, map). **2.** *F: Visage enluminé par la boisson,* face flushed with drink.
enluminure [ălyminy:r], *s.f.* **1.** (*a*) Illuminating (of MS.) ; colouring (of prints). (*b*) *F:* High colour. **2.** Illuminated design ; illumination.
enneigé [ănɛʒe], *a.* Snow-clad, -covered.
ennemi, -ie [ănmi]. **1.** *s.* Enemy ; *Lit:* foe. **Passer à l'ennemi,** to go over to the enemy. **2.** *a.* Hostile (*de,* to).
ennobl|ir [ănɔbli:r], *v.tr.* To ennoble (action) ; to elevate (mind). *s.m.* **-issement.**
ennui [ănɥi], *s.m.* **1.** Worry, anxiety ; *F:* bother. **Avoir des ennuis,** to be worried. *Petits ennuis,* petty annoyances. **Attirer, créer, susciter, des ennuis à qn,** to make trouble for s.o. **Aller au-devant des ennuis,** to ask for trouble ; to meet trouble half-way. **Quel ennui!** what a nuisance! **2.** Boredom, wearisomeness, tedium, tediousness, ennui. **Ils me font mourir d'ennui,** they bore me to death.
ennuyant [ănɥijă], *a.* Annoying, vexing.
ennuyer [ănɥije], *v.tr.* (j'**ennuie** ; j'**ennuierai**) **1.** (*a*) To annoy, worry, vex. *Cela vous ennuierait-il d'attendre?* would you mind waiting? (*b*) To importune ; *F:* to bother (s.o.). **2.** To bore, weary (s.o.). *F: Il m'ennuie à mourir,* I get dreadfully tired of him ; *P:* he bores me stiff.
s'ennuyer, to be bored ; to feel dull ; to weary ; to suffer from ennui. *Je m'ennuie à ne rien faire,* I weary for want of something to do.
ennuyeu|x, -euse [ănɥijø, -øːz], *a.* **1.** (*a*) Boring, tedious, tiresome, dull. *Mortellement e.,* deadly dull. (*b*) Importunate. **2.** = ENNUYANT. *adv.* **-sement.**
énoncer [enɔ̃se], *v.tr.* (j'**énonçai(s)** ; n. **énon-çons**) **1.** To state, to set forth (opinion, fact, etc.). *É. une vérité,* to state a truth. **2.** To articulate (word, syllable).
s'énoncer, to express oneself (clearly, etc.).
énoncé, *s.m.* Statement (of facts, etc.). *É.d'un problème,* terms of a problem. *É. d'un acte,* text, wording, of an act.
énonciation [enɔ̃sjasjɔ̃], *s.f.* **1.** Stating, expressing (of fact). **2.** Enunciation ; articulation.
enorgueillir [ănɔrgœji:r], *v.tr.* To make proud.
s'enorgueillir, to become proud, elated. *S'e. de qch., d'avoir fait qch.,* to pride oneself on sth., on having done sth.
énorme [enɔrm], *a.* Enormous, huge. *Crime é.,* shocking, outrageous, crime. *Perte é.,* grievous loss. *Mensonge é.,* whopping lie. *Ça m'a fait un bien é.,* it did me no end of good.
énormément [enɔrmemă], *adv.* **1.** Enormously, hugely ; *F:* tremendously. *Je le regrette é.,* I'm awfully sorry. **2.** A great deal (of) ; a great many. *Il y a é. de gens qui . . .,* there are any amount of people who. . . .
énormité [enɔrmite], *s.f.* **1.** (*a*) Enormity ; outrageousness (of demand, etc.) ; heinous-ness (of crime). (*b*) Enormousness, vastness, hugeness. **2.** *F:* **Commettre une énormité,** to make a gross blunder. **Dire des énormités,** to say the most awful things.
enquérir (s') [săkeri:r], *v.pr.* (Conj. like ACQUÉRIR) To inquire, make inquiries (*de,* after). *S'e. du prix,* to ask the price.
enquête [ăkɛ:t], *s.f.* Inquiry, investigation. **Faire, procéder à, une enquête sur qch.,** to hold an inquiry, to inquire, into sth.

enquêter [ăkɛte], *v.i.* To hold an inquiry ; to make investigations. *E. sur une affaire,* to inquire into an affair.
enqui-s, -t, etc. See ENQUÉRIR (s').
enracin|er [ărasine], *v.tr.* (*a*) To dig in (tree, foundations). (*b*) *F:* To establish, implant (principles, etc.). *s.m.* **-ement.**
s'enraciner. (*a*) To take root. (*b*) *F:* (Of habit) To become established, deeply rooted.
enraciné, *a.* Deep-rooted ; deep-seated.
enrageant [ăraʒă], *a.* Maddening ; *F:* aggra-vating.
enrager [ăraʒe], *v.* (j'**enrageai(s)** ; n. **enrageons**) **1.** *v.tr.* (*a*) To enrage, madden (s.o.). (*b*) To excite (s.o.) ; to drive (s.o.) wild (with desire, etc.). **2.** *v.i.* To (fret and) fume. *E. des dents,* to be mad with toothache. *J'enrage rien que d'y penser,* it makes me wild only to think of it. **Faire enrager qn,** to tease s.o.
enragé, -ée. 1. *a.* (*a*) Mad (dog). (Of dog) *Devenir e.,* to go mad. S.a. VACHE **1.** (*b*) *F:* Rabid, out-and-out (radical, etc.) ; enthusiastic, keen (angler) ; inveterate (gambler). **2.** *s.* *Un e. de golf,* a golf enthusiast, a keen golfer.
enray|er [ărɛje], *v.tr.* **1.** (*a*) To lock, skid (wheel) ; to put (i) the brake, (ii) the drag, on (wheel). *Mil:* To check, slow up (attack). *E. une maladie,* to arrest, check, a disease. *F:* **Il est temps d'enrayer,** it is time to call a halt. (*b*) To jam, stop (machinery). **2.** To furnish (wheel) with spokes. *s.m.* **-age.** *s.m.* **-ement.**
enrégimenter [ăreʒimăte], *v.tr.* **1.** To form (troops) into regiments. **2.** *F:* To enrol (body of helpers, etc.).
enregistrement [ărəʒistrəmă], *s.m.* **1.** (*a*) Regis-tration, registry, recording ; booking, entering (up) (of an order). **Bureau d'enregistrement,** registry office. *E. d'une compagnie,* incorporation of a company. (*b*) *Gramoph: Cin:* Recording (of music, etc.). **2.** *Adm:* Registry (office) ; register office.
enregistrer [ărəʒistre], *v.tr.* **1.** To register, record. *E. une naissance,* to register a birth. **Société enregistrée,** incorporated company. *Rail: E. des bagages pour Paris,* to book, register, luggage for Paris. **2.** To record (for gramophone reproduction). *Musique enregistrée,* music on (gramophone) records. *Cin:* (Of actor) *E. la joie, le dédain,* to register joy, disdain. **3.** *Fb:* To score (a goal).
enregistreur, -euse [ărəʒistrœːr, -øːz]. **1.** *a.* (Self-)recording, registering (apparatus, device). S.a. CAISSE **3. 2.** *s.m.* (*a*) Registrar. (*b*) (Auto-matic) recording instrument.
enrhumer [ăryme], *v.tr.* To give (s.o.) a cold.
s'enrhumer, to catch (a) cold ; to take cold. *Être enrhumé du cerveau,* to have a cold in the head.
enrichir [ăriʃi:r], *v.tr.* To enrich ; to make (s.o.) wealthy.
s'enrichir. 1. To grow rich ; to make money. **2.** To grow richer (*en, de,* in).
enrichi, -ie, *a. & s.* New-rich, parvenu.
enrichissement [ăriʃismă], *s.m.* Enrichment.
enrob|er [ărɔbe], *v.tr.* To coat, cover, (sth.) with, wrap (sth.), in a protecting envelope. *E. des pierres de goudron,* to coat stones with tar. *s.m.* **-age.**
enrôlement [ărolmă], *s.m.* (*a*) Enrolment. (*b*) *Mil:* Enlistment.
enrôler [ărole], *v.tr.* (*a*) To enrol, recruit (labour). (*b*) *Mil:* To enlist.
s'enrôler. (*a*) To enrol oneself. (*b*) To enlist.
enrôlé, *s.m.* Person on the rolls.

enrouement [ārumã], *s.m.* Hoarseness, huskiness.

enrouer [ārwe], *v.tr.* To make hoarse, husky. **s'enrouer,** to get hoarse. **enroué,** *a.* Hoarse, husky (person, voice).

enroul|er [ārule], *v.tr.* (*a*) To roll up (map, etc.); to wind (cable, etc.). (*b*) To wrap up (*dans*, in). *s.m.* **-ement.** **s'enrouler,** to wind, coil (*autour de*, round).

enroutiné [ārutine], *a.* Bound by routine, by red-tape.

enrubanner [ārybane], *v.tr.* To decorate, trim, with ribbon(s); to beribbon.

ensabler [āsoble], *v.tr.* **1.** To strand; to run (ship) aground. **2.** (Of flood, etc.) To cover (land) with sand. *E. un port,* to silt up a harbour. **s'ensabler. 1.** (Of ship) To settle in the sand. **2.** To silt up; (of pipes) to get choked up.

ensanglanter [āsãglãte], *v.tr.* To cover, stain, with blood. *Mains ensanglantées,* blood-stained, bloody, hands.

enseignable [āsɛnabl], *a.* Teachable.

enseignant [āsɛnã], *a.* Teaching. *Le corps e.,* the teaching profession.

enseigne [āsɛn]. **1.** *s.f.* (*a*) Sign, index, token, mark (of quality, etc.). *A bonnes enseignes,* (i) deservedly; (ii) on good authority. *A telles enseignes que . . .,* the proof being that . . .; so much so that. . . . (*b*) Sign(-board); shop sign. *E. lumineuse,* electric sign. *F: Nous sommes tous logés à la même enseigne,* we are all in the same boat. *Prov: A bon vin point d'enseigne,* good wine needs no bush. (*c*) *Mil:* Ensign, colour(s). **2.** *s.m.* (*a*) *Mil: A:* Standard-bearer. (*b*) *Navy:* Sub-lieutenant.

enseignement [āsɛnmã], *s.m.* **1.** (*a*) Teaching. *Entrer dans l'e.,* to go in for teaching. *Il est dans l'e.,* he is a teacher. (*b*) *Tirer un e. de qch.,* to draw a lesson from sth. **2.** Education, instruction. *E. privé,* private tuition.

enseigner [āsɛne], *v.tr.* **1.** To show; to point out. **2.** (*a*) *E. les enfants,* to teach, give lessons to, children. (*b*) *E. la grammaire à qn,* to teach s.o. grammar. *E. à qn à faire qch.,* to teach s.o. to do sth. *E. l'anglais,* to teach English.

ensemble [āsãbl]. **1.** *adv.* Together. *Ils se marièrent e.,* they married each other. *Être bien ensemble,* to be good friends. *Être mal ensemble,* to have fallen out. *Choses qui vont ensemble,* things that belong, go, together. *Le tout ensemble,* (i) the general effect; (ii) the whole lot. *Agir d'ensemble,* to act in concert, as a body. **2.** *s.m.* (*a*) Whole, entirety. *Vue d'ensemble,* comprehensive view; general view. *Enquête d'ensemble,* general enquiry. *Étude d'ensemble,* comprehensive study; conspectus. *Dans l'ensemble . . .,* on the whole . . .; in the aggregate. (*b*) Cohesion, unity. *Mouvement d'ensemble,* combined movement. *E. d'un morceau de musique,* (i) general unity, (ii) general effect, of a piece of music. *Avec ensemble,* all together; harmoniously; as one. *E. de couleurs,* harmonious group of colours. (*c*) Set (of tools, etc.).

ensemenc|er [āsmãse], *v.tr.* (j'ensemençai(s); n. ensemençons) To sow (field). *s.m.* **-ement.**

enserr|er [āsɛre], *v.tr.* (*a*) To enclose, encompass (sth.); to hem in (army, etc.). (*b*) (Of brake-band, etc.) To grip round (drum). (*c*) To squeeze, crush. *s.m.* **-ement.**

ensevelir [āsəvliːr], *v.tr.* **1.** To bury, entomb (corpse). **2.** To shroud (corpse).

ensevelissement [āsəvlismã], *s.m.* **1.** Burial, entombment. **2.** Shrouding (of corpse).

ensoleillé [āsɔlɛje], *a.* Sunny (countryside, smile).

ensommeillé [āsɔmɛje], *a.* Sleepy, drowsy.

ensorcelant [āsɔrsəlã], *a.* (Be)witching.

ensorceler [āsɔrsəle], *v.tr.* (j'ensorcelle; j'ensorcellerai) (*a*) To bewitch; to cast, put, a spell (up)on (s.o., sth.). (*b*) *F:* To captivate (s.o.); to turn (s.o.'s) head. **ensorcelé,** *a.* Bewitched; under a spell.

ensorceleur, -euse [āsɔrsəlœːr, -øːz]. **1.** *s.* (*a*) Sorcerer, sorceress. (*b*) *F:* Charmer. **2.** *a.* = ENSORCELANT.

ensorcellement [āsɔrsɛlmã], *s.m.* **1.** Sorcery, witchcraft. **2.** Charm, spell.

ensouple [āsupl], *s.f.* Beam, roller (of loom).

ensuite [āsɥit], *adv.* After(wards), then. *Et e. il m'a dit . . .,* and then he said to me. . . . *Et ensuite?* what then? *F: Ensuite de quoi . . .,* after which. . . . *Ensuite de cela . . .,* after that. . . . *Les sapeurs marchaient en tête, ensuite venait la musique,* the sappers led the van, next came the band.

ensuivre (s') [sãsɥiːvr], *v.pr.* (Conj. like SUIVRE. Used only in the third pers.) To follow, ensue, result. *Impers. Il s'ensuit que nous sommes ruinés,* it follows that we are ruined. *F: Et tout ce qui s'ensuit,* and what not.

entablement [ātabləmã], *s.m.* **1.** Entablature (of building). **2.** *Const:* Coping (of wall, etc.).

entacher [ātaʃe], *v.tr.* **1.** To sully, besmirch; to cast a slur on (s.o.'s honour, etc.). *Religion entachée de superstition,* religion tainted with superstition. **2.** *Jur:* To vitiate (contract, etc.).

entaille [ātaːj], *s.f.* (*a*) Notch, jag, nick, cut (in wood, etc.); groove, slot; tommy-hole (in circular nut). *A entailles,* slotted. *Assemblage à entailles,* notched joint. (*b*) Gash, cut, slash.

entailler [ātaje], *v.tr.* (*a*) To notch, nick (piece of wood, etc.); to groove, slot. (*b*) To gash, cut, slash.

entame [ātam], *s.f.* **1.** First cut, outside slice (of loaf, etc.). **2.** *Cards:* Opening (of a suit).

entam|er [ātame], *v.tr.* **1.** To cut into (loaf, etc.); to broach (cask); to open (bottle); to penetrate (defence, armour-plate). *E. la peau,* to break the skin. *E. son capital,* to break into one's capital. **2.** To begin, commence, start (conversation, etc.). *E. des relations avec qn,* to enter into relations with s.o. *E. un sujet,* to broach a subject. *Cards: E. trèfle,* to open clubs. *s.m.* **-ement.**

entamure [ātamyːr], *s.f.* = ENTAME 1.

entartr|er [ātartre], *v.tr.* (Of water) To incrust, fur, scale (boiler, etc.). [TARTRE] *s.m.* **-age.** **s'entartrrer,** to fur; to become furred.

entassement [ātasmã], *s.m.* Accumulation. **1.** (*a*) Piling (up), heaping (up); stacking (of cases, etc.). (*b*) Crowding (up), overcrowding; congestion. **2.** Pile (of goods, etc.).

entasser [ātase], *v.tr.* (*a*) To accumulate; to pile (up), heap (up) (stones, etc.); to stack (up) (cases); to amass (money). (*b*) To pack, crowd, cram, (passengers, cattle, etc.) together. [TAS] **s'entasser. 1.** (Of thgs) To accumulate; to pile up. **2.** To crowd, huddle, together.

ente [āːt], *s.f.* **1.** *Hort:* (*a*) Scion; grafted shoot. (*b*) Stock. **2.** Handle (of brush).

entendement [ātãdmã], *s.m.* Understanding. *Homme d'e.,* man of sense, of good judgment.

entendeur [ātãdœːr], *s.m.* (Used in the phr.) *A bon entendeur salut!* (i) a word to the wise (is enough); (ii) if the cap fits, wear it.

entendre [ātãːdr], *v.tr.* **1.** To intend, mean. *E. faire qch.,* to intend, mean, to do sth. *Il n'y entend pas malice,* (i) he means no harm; (ii) he takes what you say at its face value. *Faites comme vous l'entendrez,* do as you think best. *J'entends que vous veniez,* I expect you to come ; you must come. *Je n'entends pas qu'on le vende,* I won't have it sold. **2.** (*a*) To hear. *J'entendis un cri,* I heard a cry. *On l'entend à peine,* it is scarcely audible. **Faire entendre des cris,** to utter cries. *Je l'entendis rire,* I heard him laugh. *On l'entendit rire,* he was heard to laugh. **Entendre parler de qn, de qch.,** to hear of (s.o.), of sth. *C'est la première fois que j'en entends parler,* this is the first I have heard of it. *Il ne veut pas en e. parler,* he won't hear of it. **Entendre dire que** + *ind.,* to hear it said that. . . . **Entendre dire qch. à qn,** (i) to hear sth. said or told to s.o. ; (ii) to hear s.o. say sth. *Abs.* **Il entend mal, dur,** he doesn't hear well ; he is hard of hearing. **On ne s'entend pas ici,** one can't hear oneself speak here. (*b*) To listen to, hearken to (s.o., sth.). *Veuillez m'e.,* give me a hearing. *L'affaire sera entendue demain,* the case comes up for hearing to-morrow. **A vous entendre** . . ., judging from what you say . . . ; according to you. . . . **Entendre raison,** to listen to reason. **Faire entendre raison à qn,** to bring s.o. to reason. **3.** (*a*) *E. une langue,* to understand a language. **Donner à entendre à qn que** . . ., **faire entendre à qn que** . . ., (i) to lead s.o. to believe, (ii) to give s.o. to understand, that. . . . **Laisser entendre qch.,** to throw out hints about sth. ; to insinuate, imply, sth. *Il n'entend pas la plaisanterie,* he can't take a joke. **Cela s'entend,** that is understood. **C'est entendu,** agreed ; all right. **Bien entendu!** of course! certainly! (*b*) To know all about (sth.) ; to be skilled in (sth.). **Je n'y entends rien,** I am quite a duffer at it. **s'entendre. 1.** To understand one another ; to agree. *Nous ne sommes pas faits pour nous e.,* we are not suited to each other. *S'e. directement avec qn,* to come to a direct understanding with s.o. *S'e. pour commettre un crime,* to conspire to commit a crime. **Ils s'entendent comme larrons en foire,** they are as thick as thieves. **2.** To be skilled (*à,* in). *S'e. en musique,* to understand, know about, music. *S'e. à faire qch.,* to know, understand, how to do sth. **entendu,** *a.* **1.** (*a*) Business-like, sensible (person). *Être e. aux affaires,* to be well versed in business matters. *Petite fille très entendue,* very capable little girl. (*b*) Knowing, shrewd (smile, look, etc.). **Faire l'entendu,** to pretend to know all about it ; to pose as an expert. **2. Maison bien entendue,** well-arranged house. **Zèle mal entendu,** mistaken zeal.

enténébrer [ãtenebre], *v.tr.* (il **enténèbre** ; il **enténébrera**) To envelop, plunge, (scene, etc.) in darkness, in gloom. [TÉNÈBRES]
　s'enténébrer, to grow dark, gloomy.
enténébré, *a.* Dark, gloomy.
entente [ãtã:t], *s.f.* **1.** (*a*) Understanding (*de,* of) ; skill (*de,* in). **Avoir l'entente des affaires,** to have a good head for business. (*b*) **Mot à double entente,** word with a double meaning. **2.** Agreement, understanding (*entre,* between). *Bonne e.,* good feeling. **Entente cordiale,** friendly understanding.
enter [ãte], *v.tr.* **1.** To graft (tree, etc.). **2.** *Carp:* To scarf (timbers) ; to assemble (timbers) by mortises. *Canne entée,* jointed cane.
entériner [ãterine], *v.tr. Jur:* To ratify, confirm.
entérique [ãterik], *a. Med:* Enteric.
entérite [ãterit], *s.f. Med:* Enteritis.
enterrement [ãtɛrmã], *s.m.* (*a*) Burial, interment. (*b*) Funeral.

enterrer [ãtɛre], *v.tr.* **1.** To put (sth.) in the earth ; to plant (bulbs). **2.** To bury, inter (corpse).
enterré, *a.* Sunken, deep (trench, road).
en-tête [ãtɛ:t], *s.m.* **1.** Heading (of letter, document). **2.** Headline (of page). *pl. Des en-têtes.*
entêtement [ãtɛtmã], *s.m.* Obstinacy, stubbornness. *E. à faire qch.,* persistency in doing sth.
entêter [ãtɛte], *v.tr.* (Of odour, etc.) To give (s.o.) a headache ; to make (s.o.) giddy ; to intoxicate. *F: Ces louanges l'entêtaient,* this praise went to his head. [TÊTE]
　s'entêter, to be obstinate, stubborn. *S'e. dans une opinion, à faire qch.,* to persist in an opinion, in doing sth.
entêté, *a.* Obstinate, headstrong.
enthousiasme [ãtuzjasm], *s.m.* Enthusiasm, rapture.
enthousiasmer [ãtuzjasme], *v.tr.* To fire (s.o.) with enthusiasm.
　s'enthousiasmer, to become enthusiastic. *S'e. pour qn, de qch.,* to be enthusiastic, go into raptures, over s.o., sth.
enthousiaste [ãtuzjast]. **1.** *s.m. & f.* Enthusiast. **2.** *a.* Enthusiastic.
entichement [ãtiʃmã], *s.m.* Infatuation.
enticher (s') [sãtiʃe], *v.pr. S'e. de qn,* to become infatuated with, to take a fancy to, s.o.
entiché, *a.* Infatuated (*de qn,* with s.o.) ; keen (on sport). *E. d'une opinion,* wedded to an opinion.
entier, -ière [ãtje, -jɛ:r], *a.* **1.** Entire, whole. *La France entière,* the whole of France. *Pendant des heures entières,* for hours on end. *Conserver sa réputation entière,* to keep one's reputation intact. *Mth:* **Nombre entier,** integer ; whole number. *Payer place entière,* to pay full fare. **2.** Complete, full (authority, etc.). *L'entière direction de qch.,* the entire, sole, management of sth. **3.** *F:* **Homme entier,** (i) bluff, plain-spoken, man ; (ii) headstrong man. **4.** *s.m.* Entirety. *Raconter une histoire dans son e.,* to relate a story in its entirety. *Adv.phr.* **En entier,** entirely, in full. *Nom en e.,* name in full.
entièrement [ãtjɛrmã], *adv.* Entirely, wholly, quite, fully, completely.
entité [ãtite], *s.f. Phil:* Entity.
entoiller [ãtwale], *v.tr.* **1.** To mount (map, etc.) on linen or canvas. *Carte entoilée,* map mounted on cloth. **2.** *Av: etc:* To cover (fuselage) with canvas, with fabric. *s.m.* **-age.**
entomologie [ãtɔmɔlɔʒi], *s.f.* Entomology.
entomologique [ãtɔmɔlɔʒik], *a.* Entomological.
entonner¹ [ãtɔne], *v.tr.* To barrel (wine, etc.). *F: S'e. du vin dans le gosier,* to swig wine.
　s'entonner, (of the wind) to rush in, up, down (as into a funnel) ; to blow (*dans,* into).
entonner², *v.tr. Mus:* **1.** To intone (psalm, etc.). **Entonner les louanges de qn,** to sing s.o.'s praises. **2.** To begin to sing (a song) ; to strike up (a song).
entonnoir [ãtɔnwa:r], *s.m.* **1.** Funnel. **2.** (*a*) Shell-hole, crater. (*b*) Hollow (among hills).
entorse [ãtɔrs], *s.f.* Sprain, wrench, twist (esp. of the ankle). **Se donner une entorse,** to sprain, twist, wrench, one's ankle. *F: Donner une e. à la vérité,* to twist the truth.
entortiller [ãtɔrtije], *v.tr.* (*a*) *E. qch. dans qch., autour de qch.,* to wind, twist, twine, sth. in sth., round sth. (*b*) *F:* To wheedle ; to get round (s.o.). *s.m.* **-ement.**
　s'entortiller, to twist, twine, coil (*autour de,* round). *S'e. dans qch.,* to get entangled in sth.
entortillé, *a.* Involved (style).

entour [ătu:r], *s.m.* (Used in) A l'entour, around, round about. *Les villages à l'e.*, the surrounding villages. A l'entour de, round (the town, etc.). *Cf.* ALENTOUR 1.

entourage [ătura:ʒ], *s.m.* **1.** Surroundings (of place); setting, framework (of sth.). **2.** Set, circle (of friends, etc.); environment, entourage.

entourer [ăture], *v.tr.* To surround, encompass (de, with); to fence in (field, etc.); to encircle (army). *Une affaire entourée de mystère,* an affair wrapped in mystery. *Entouré de dangers,* beset with dangers. [TOUR²]

entournure [ăturny:r], *s.f.* Arm-hole.

en-tout-cas [ătukɑ], *s.m.* Umbrella-sunshade.

entr'acte [ătrakt], *s.m.* Th: **1.** Interval. **2.** Entr'acte, interlude. *pl. Des entr'actes.*

entr'aide [ătre(:)d], *s.f.* No *pl.* Mutual aid.

entr'aider (s') [sătrɛde], *v.pr.* To help one another.

entrailles [ătrɑ:j], *s.f.pl.* **1.** Entrails, bowels. *Les e. de la terre,* the bowels of the earth. **2.** F: Bowels of mercy; heart, compassion. *Secoué jusqu'au fond de ses e.,* stirred to the depths of his soul. Être sans entrailles, to be ruthless, unfeeling; to have no bowels of mercy.

entr'aimer (s') [sătrɛme], *v.pr.* To love one another.

entrain [ătrɛ̃], *s.m.* Liveliness, briskness; spirit; F: go. Être plein d'e., to be full of life, of go. *Musique pleine d'e.,* lively music. *Y mettre de l'e.,* to go briskly at it. **Manger avec entrain,** to eat with gusto. *Travailler avec e.,* to work with spirit. *Jouer avec e.,* to play with zest. *Attaque menée avec e.,* attack carried out with dash, smartly carried out. **Faire qch. sans entrain,** to do sth. in a half-hearted manner.

entraînant [ătrɛnɑ̃], *a.* Inspiriting, stirring.

entraînement [ătrɛnmɑ̃], *s.m.* **1.** (a) Dragging (or being dragged) along; carrying away. (b) (i) Feed (of machine-tool). (ii) Drive (of machine). *E. par courroie,* belt transmission. (c) Enthusiasm. **2.** Leading (or being led) astray; allurement. *Préserver qn des mauvais entraînements,* to keep s.o. from being led astray. *E. d'une mélodie,* lure, witchery, of a tune. **3.** *Sp:* Training; coaching (of team). **Partie d'entraînement,** practice match.

entraîner [ătrɛne], *v.tr.* **1.** (a) To drag, draw, carry, along; to carry away; to wash away or down; to sweep along or away (gravel, etc.). *E. qn en prison,* to drag s.o. off to prison. *Entraîné par le courant,* borne along, swept along, by the current. *Il a été entraîné dans le désastre,* he was involved in the disaster. (b) To drive (part of machine, etc.). **2.** To seduce, inveigle (s.o.). *E. qn à faire qch.,* to lead s.o. to do sth. *Être entraîné dans un piège,* to be lured into a trap. *Se laisser entraîner,* to allow oneself to be led into temptation, led astray, carried away. **3.** To produce (sth.) as a consequence; to entail, involve. *Cela entraînera un retard,* it will involve, lead to, delay. **4.** *Sp:* To train (race-horse, athlete); to coach (team). *Entraîné à fond,* in thorough training.

entraîneur [ătrɛnœ:r], *s.m.* Trainer (of horses, etc.); coach (of team).

entrant, -ante [ătrɑ̃, -ɑ̃:t], **1.** *a.* Incoming, ingoing; newly-appointed (official). **2.** *s.* Incomer, ingoer; (at cards) player cutting in. *Entrants et sortants,* comers and goers.

entr'apercevoir [ătrapɛrsɘvwa:r], *v.tr.* (Conj. like APERCEVOIR) To catch a fleeting, a momentary, glimpse of (sth.).

entravant [ătravɑ̃], *a.* Hampering, impeding.

entrave [ătra:v], *s.f.* **1.** (a) Shackle, fetter. (b) Hobble. **2.** É. à qch., hindrance, impediment, to sth. Agir sans entraves, to act without hindrance.

entraver [ătrave], *v.tr.* **1.** To shackle, fetter; to hobble (a horse). **2.** To hinder, hamper, clog impede. *E. la circulation,* to hold up the traffic.

entravé, *a.* Jupe entravée, hobble-skirt. *Ling:* Voyelle entravée, checked vowel.

entre [ɑ̃:tr]. I. *prep.* **1.** Between. *Femme e. deux âges,* middle-aged woman. **Entre les deux,** betwixt and between; neither one thing nor the other. *Être e. la vie et la mort,* to be betwixt life and death. **2.** (a) Among(st). *Nous sommes e. amis,* we are among friends. *Elle était belle e. toutes,* she was beautiful beyond all others. *Ce problème est délicat e. tous,* there is no more delicate question. *Ce jour e. tous,* this day of all days. *E. autres choses il a dit que . . .,* among other things he said that. . . . *Moi entre autres . . .,* I, for one. . . . (b) *Tomber e. les mains de l'ennemi,* to fall into the enemy's hands. (c) **D'entre,** (from) among. (Used instead of de with pers. pron.) *L'un d'e. eux,* one of their number. *Beaucoup, peu, plusieurs, d'e. nous,* many, few, several, of us. **3.** In relation to (one another). *Ils s'accordent e. eux,* they agree among themselves. *Ils se marient e. eux,* they intermarry. **Soit dit entre nous,** (be it said) between ourselves. II. **entre-** used as *pref.* **1.** (Reciprocity) *S'entre-tuer,* to kill one another. **2.** (a) (Crossing) *Entrecouper,* to intersect. (b) (Connecting) *S'entre-communiquer,* to inter-communicate. (c) ('Between') *S'entremettre,* to interpose. **3.** ('Half', 'partially') *Entrebâiller,* to half-open.

entrebâillement [ătrɘbajmɑ̃], *s.m.* **1.** Narrow opening; chink (of door, etc.); slit, gap (between curtains). **2.** Casement-stay.

entrebâiller [ătrɘbaje], *v.tr.* To set (door) ajar; to half-open.

entrechats [ătrɘʃa], *s.m.pl.* Danc: F: Cross-capers. Battre des entrechats, to cut capers.

entre-choquement, *s.m.* Shock, clash.

entre-choquer (s'), *v.pr.* **1.** To collide, clash. (b) (Of bottles, etc.) To knock against one another; (of glasses) to chink.

entre-clos, *a.* Half-closed; half-drawn (curtains); (door) ajar.

entrecôte [ătrɘko:t], *s.f.* Steak cut from the ribs (of beef); F: rib of beef.

entrecouper [ătrɘkupe], *v.tr.* **1.** To intersect. **2.** To interrupt.

s'entrecouper, to intersect.

entrecoupé, *a.* Interrupted, broken (sleep, etc.). *Voix entrecoupée (de sanglots),* broken voice.

entre(-)croisement [ătrɘkrwazmɑ̃]. *s.m.* Intersection; interlacing.

entre(-)croiser [ătrɘkrwaze], *v.tr.* To intersect, cross (lines); to interlace (threads).

s'entre(-)croiser, to intersect, interlace; to criss-cross.

entre-deux, *s.m. inv.* **1.** Space between; interspace, interval. *Prendre un e.-d.,* to take a middle course. **2.** (a) Partition. (b) *Dressm:* Insertion.

entrée [ătre], *s.f.* **1.** (a) Entry, entering. *E. en scène d'un acteur,* actor's entrance (on the stage). *Faire son e.,* to make one's entrance. *Sch:* Entrée en vacances, breaking-up. *Av:* Nau: Arête d'entrée, leading edge (of propeller). *W.Tel:* (Fil d')entrée de poste, lead-in. (b) *pl.* Arrivals (of ships). **2.** Admission, admittance to club, etc.). **Avoir son entrée, ses entrées, dans un lieu,** to have one's entrée to a place. **Avoir ses entrées libres dans une maison,** to be free of a house.

"Entrée interdite," 'no admittance.' *Cust :* Droit d'entrée, import duty. **3.** (*a*) Way in ; entrance. (*b*) **A l'entrée de l'hiver,** at the beginning of winter. (*c*) *Mch :* Admission, inlet (of cylinder, etc.). *I.C.E : E. d'air,* air intake. **4.** *Cu :* Entrée.

entrefaite [ãtrəfɛt], *s.f.* **Sur l'entrefaite, sur ces entrefaites,** (i) meanwhile ; wħile this was going on ; (ii) at this moment.

entrefer [ãtrəfɛːr], *s.m.* Air-gap (of dynamo, etc.).

entrefilet [ãtrəfilɛ], *s.m.* Paragraph (in newspaper) ; *F :* par.

entregent [ãtrəʒã], *s.m.* Tact (in handling people) ; worldly wisdom ; *F :* gumption.

entrelacement [ãtrəlasmã], *s.m.* Interlacing ; interweaving (of threads, etc.) ; intertwining ; network (of branches).

entrelacer [ãtrəlase], *v.tr.* (Conj. like LACER) To interlace (ribbons, twigs) ; to interweave (threads, etc.) ; to intertwine (branches). *Typ :* To ligature (letters).

s'entrelacer, to intertwine.

entrelacs [ãtrəla], *s.m.* Interlacing, intertwining ; knotwork, strapwork (in embroidery).

entrelarder [ãtrəlarde], *v.tr.* (*a*) To lard (meat). (*b*) To interlard (speech with quotations).

entrelardé, *a.* (Of pork, etc.) Streaky.

entre-ligne, *s.m.* Space between lines (of print, etc.). *pl. Des entre-lignes.*

entre-ligner, *v.tr.* To interline.

entremêlement [ãtrəmɛlmã], *s.m.* **1.** (Inter)-mingling. **2.** (Inter)mixture, jumble, medley.

entremêler [ãtrəmɛle], *v.tr.* *E. qch. de, parmi, qch.,* to (inter)mix, (inter)mingle, sth. with sth. *E. des couleurs,* to blend colours. *Ordres entre-mêlés de jurons,* orders interspersed with oaths.

s'entremêler. 1. To (inter)mix, (inter)-mingle. **2.** *S'e. dans une affaire,* to interfere.

entremets [ãtrəme], *s.m. Cu :* (*a*) Side-dish. (*b*) E. sucré, sweet (as dinner course).

entremetteur, -euse [ãtrəmɛtœːr, -øːz], *s.* Intermediary ; go-between. *Com :* Middleman.

entremettre (s') [sãtrəmɛtr], *v.pr.* (Conj. like METTRE) To interpose, intervene ; to act as a go-between.

entremise [ãtrəmiːz], *s.f.* (*a*) Intervention. (*b*) Mediation. **Agir par l'entremise de qn,** to act through s.o.

entre-nuire (s') [ãtrəmyiːr], *v.pr.* (Conj. like NUIRE) To injure, be harmful to, one another.

entrepénétrer (s') [sãtrəpenetre], *v.pr.* To interpenetrate.

entrepont [ãtrəpɔ̃], *s.m. Nau :* Between-decks. **Passager d'entrepont,** steerage passenger.

entreposer [ãtrəpoze], *v.tr.* To warehouse, store. *Cust :* To bond (goods). *s.m.* **-age.**

entreposeur [ãtrəpozœːr], *s.m.* Warehouseman.

entrepositaire [ãtrəpozitɛːr], *s.m.* Bonder.

entrepôt [ãtrəpo], *s.m.* **1.** Warehouse, store. *E. maritime,* wharf. *E. de la douane,* bonded warehouse. **Marchandises en entrepôt,** bonded goods. **2.** (Ammunition) depot.

entreprenant [ãtrəprənã], *a.* Enterprising.

entreprendre [ãtrəprãːdr], *v.tr.* (Conj. like PRENDRE) **1.** To undertake ; to take (sth.) in hand. *E. une étude,* to enter upon a study. *E. de faire qch.,* to undertake to do sth. **2.** To contract for (piece of work).

entrepreneur, -euse [ãtrəprənœːr, -øːz], *s.* Contractor. **Entrepreneur en bâtiments,** building contractor. *E. de déménagements,* furniture remover. **Entrepreneur de pompes funèbres,** undertaker.

entreprise [ãtrəpriːz], *s.f.* **1.** Undertaking ; venture. *E. commerciale,* business concern. *E. de*

transports, de roulage, carrying company. **2. Travail à l'entreprise,** work by, on, contract. **Mettre qch. à l'entreprise,** to put sth. out to contract.

entre-quereller (s'), *v.pr.* To quarrel (with one another) ; to bicker.

entrer [ãtre], *v.i.* (Aux. *être*) **1.** (*a*) To enter ; to go in, to come in ; to step in. *Entrez !* come in ! **"Défense d'entrer," "on n'entre pas,"** 'no admittance.' **Faire entrer qn,** (i) to show s.o. in ; (ii) to call s.o. in. **Laisser entrer qn,** to let s.o. in ; to admit s.o. *E. en passant, F :* to drop in, look in (on s.o.). *Empêcher qn d'e.,* to keep s.o. out. *Pièce qui entre dans une autre,* piece that fits into another. *Faire e. qch. dans qch.,* to insert sth. in sth. *Th :* Hamlet entre, enter Hamlet. *E. en courant,* to run in. *E. précipitamment,* to dash in. *E. furtivement,* to steal in. *Parvenir à e.,* to (manage to) get in. (*b*) *E. dans l'armée, dans une carrière,* to join the army, to take up a career. *E. en fonction,* to enter upon one's duties. *Mil : E. en campagne,* to take the field. *E. en ménage,* to set up house(keeping). *E. au collège,* to go to school (for the first time). *E. en vacances,* to break up (for holidays). (*c*) *E. en colère,* to get angry. *E. en ébullition,* to begin to boil ; to come to the boil. **2.** To enter into, take part in (sth.). *Vous n'entrez pour rien dans l'affaire,* you are in no way concerned with the business. *E. dans une catégorie,* to fall under a category. *Dans tout ceci l'imagination entre pour beaucoup,* in all this imagination plays a large part. *Pilules où il entre de l'arsenic,* pills that contain arsenic. **3.** *v.tr.* (Aux. *avoir*) To bring, let, put, (sth.) in. **Entrer des marchandises en fraude,** to smuggle in goods.

entre-rail, *s.m.* Rail : Gauge (of track).

entre-regarder (s'), *v.pr.* To look at one another.

entresol [ãtrəsɔl], *s.m.* Entresol ; mezzanine (floor).

entre-temps, entretemps [ãtrətã]. **1.** *s.m. inv.* Interval. **Dans l'entre-temps,** meanwhile ; in the meantime. **2.** *adv.* Meanwhile ; in the meantime ; between-whiles.

entretenir [ãtrətniːr], *v.tr.* (Conj. like TENIR) **1.** To maintain ; to keep (sth.) up. *E. une correspondance avec qn,* to keep up a correspondence with s.o. *E. une agitation,* to foster an agitation. *S'e. la main,* to keep one's hand in. *E. le feu,* to keep the fire burning. **2.** (*a*) To maintain, support, keep (family). *E. qn de vêtements,* to keep s.o. in clothes. *Il ne gagne pas de quoi s'e.,* he does not earn enough to keep himself. (*b*) *E. des soupçons,* to entertain, harbour, suspicions. **3.** *E. qn (de qch.),* to converse with, talk to, s.o. (about sth.).

s'entretenir. 1. To talk, converse (*avec,* with ; *de,* about). **2.** *Sp :* To keep fit.

entretenu, *a. Ph : Ondes entretenues,* undamped, continuous, waves.

entretien [ãtrətjɛ̃], *s.m.* **1.** Upkeep, maintenance (of roads, etc.) ; maintenance (of accumulator) ; keeping in repair, in good order. **2.** Support, maintenance (of family). *Ce qu'il gagne ne suffit pas à son e.,* he does not earn his keep. **3.** (*a*) Conversation ; interview. (*b*) Subject, topic (of conversation). **Faire l'entretien du public,** to be the talk of the town.

entretoise [ãtrətwaːz], *s.f. Const : etc :* Brace, cross-bar, cross-piece, distance-piece.

entretoiser [ãtrətwaze], *v.tr.* To (cross-)brace ; to stay, strut, tie. *s.m.* **-ement.**

entreverr-ai, -as, etc. See ENTREVOIR.

entrevi-s, -t, etc. See ENTREVOIR.

entre-voie, s.f. Rail: Space between tracks.

entrevoir [ãtrəvwa:r], v.tr. (Conj. like VOIR) To catch sight, catch a glimpse, of (s.o., sth.). F: Il entrevoyait la vérité, he had an inkling of the truth. Laisser e. qch. à qn, to drop a hint, give an indication, of sth. to s.o.

entrevue [ãtrəvy], s.f. Interview.

entr'ouïr [ãtrui:r], v.tr. (Conj. like OUÏR) To half-hear.

entr'ouvrir [ãtruvri:r], v.tr. (Conj. like OUVRIR) To half-open; to set (door) ajar.
   s'entr'ouvrir. 1. To half-open. 2. (Of chasm, etc.) To gape, yawn.
   entr'ouvert, a. 1. Half-open (window, flower); (door) ajar. 2. Gaping, yawning (chasm).

enture [ãty:r], s.f. 1. Incision, cut (for grafting). 2. (a) Peg, pin (of a peg ladder). (b) Scarf-joint. E. à goujon, pin-joint. [ENTER]

énucléation [enykleasjɔ̃], s.f. 1. Surg: Enucleation. 2. Stoning (of fruit).

énucléer [enyklee], v.tr. 1. Surg: To enucleate (tumour, tonsils). 2. To stone (fruit).

énumérateur, -trice [enymeratœːr, -tris], s. Enumerator.

énumération [enymerasjɔ̃], s.f. Enumeration; telling (of votes).

énumérer [enymere], v.tr. (j'énumère; j'énumérerai) To enumerate; to count up.

envah|ir [ãvai:r], v.tr. 1. To invade, to overrun (country, etc.). Envahi par l'eau, flooded. Quand la crainte nous envahit, when fear assails us, comes over us. 2. To encroach upon (neighbour's land). s.m. **-issement.**

envahisseur [ãvaisœːr], s.m. Invader.

envas|er [ãvaze], v.tr. To silt; to choke (up) (canal, etc.) with mud. [VASE²] s.m. **-ement.**
   s'envaser. 1. (Of harbour, etc.) To silt up. 2. (Of ship) To settle down in the mud.

enveloppe [ãvlɔp], s.f. 1. (a) Envelope, cover-(ing) (of letter); wrapper, wrapping (of parcel). E. à fenêtre, window envelope. (b) E. de voyage, hold-all. 2. Exterior; external appearance. 3. Sheathing, casing; lagging (of boiler); outer cover (of tyre). El: E. d'induit, armature casing.

envelopp|er [ãvlɔpe], v.tr. 1. To envelop. (a) To wrap (s.o., sth.) up. Enveloppé de bandages, swathed in bandages. Crime enveloppé de mystère, crime shrouded, hidden, in mystery. Enveloppé de brume, shrouded in mist. (b) To cover, case (tube, etc.); to jacket, lag (boiler). (c) To surround, encircle, hem in (enemy, etc.). La nuit nous enveloppa, darkness closed in upon us. 2. E. qn dans un désastre, to involve s.o. in a disaster. s.m. **-ement.**

envenimement [ãvnimmã], s.m. 1. Envenoming; poisoning (of wound). 2. Irritation; aggravation (of quarrel).

envenimer [ãvnime], v.tr. 1. To envenom, poison (wound, etc.). 2. To irritate, aggravate (wound, quarrel).
   s'envenimer, (of wound) to fester, suppurate; to go septic. F: La discussion s'envenime, the discussion grows acrimonious.

envergure [ãvergy:r], s.f. Spread, breadth, span (of bird's wings, of aeroplane). F: De grande envergure, far-reaching, wide-spreading. [VERGUE]

enverr-ai, -as, etc. See ENVOYER.

envers¹ [ãvɛːr], s.m. Wrong side, reverse, back (of material, etc.). Étoffe sans envers, étoffe à deux envers, reversible material. F: L'e. de la vie, the seamy side of life. L'e. de la médaille, the reverse of the medal. A l'envers, (i) inside out; (ii) wrong way up. Le monde à l'e., topsy-turvy-dom. J'ai la tête à l'e., my brain is in a whirl.

envers², prep. Towards. Bien intentionné e. nous, well-intentioned towards us. Agir loyalement e. qn, to deal honestly, fairly, with s.o. Soutenir une opinion envers et contre tous, to maintain an opinion against all comers.

envi [ãvi], s.m. (Used in the adv.phr.) A l'envi, emulously. A l'envi de, in emulation of.

enviable [ãvjabl], a. Enviable.

envie [ãvi], s.f. 1. Desire, longing. Avoir envie de qch., to want, to have a fancy for, sth. Avoir e. de faire qch., to wish, have a mind, to do sth. J'avais e. de pleurer, I felt like crying. Jeter sur qch. des regards d'envie, to cast longing looks on sth.; to look enviously at sth. Avec envie, longingly. 2. Envy. Dévoré d'e., eaten up with envy. Faire envie à qn, to make s.o. envious. Porter envie à qn, to envy s.o. 3. (a) Agnail; F: hangnail. (b) Birthmark.

envier [ãvje], v.tr. To envy. 1. To covet; F: to hanker after (sth.). 2. To be envious of (s.o.). E. qch. à qn, (i) to envy s.o. sth.; (ii) to begrudge s.o. sth.

envieu|x, -euse [ãvjø, -øːz], a. Envious (de, of). adv. **-sement.**

environ [ãvirɔ̃]. 1. adv. About. Il a e. quarante ans, he is about forty. 2. s.m.pl. Environs, surroundings, outskirts, neighbourhood, environs (of a place). Habiter aux, dans les, environs de Paris, to live in the vicinity of Paris. Aux environs de Noël, round about Christmas.

environnement [ãvirɔnmã], s.m. Surroundings; environment.

environner [ãvirɔne], v.tr. To surround.

envisager [ãvizaʒe], v.tr. (j'envisageai(s); n. envisageons) To face, envisage. (a) To look (s.o.) in the face. (b) To consider, contemplate (possibility, etc.). E. l'avenir, to look to the future. On n'avait pas envisagé ce fait, this event had not been anticipated. Cas non envisagé, unforeseen case. Je n'envisage pas la chose ainsi, I do not view the matter in that light.

envoi [ãvwa], s.m. 1. Sending, dispatch, forwarding, consignment. E. par mer, shipment. Com: Lettre d'envoi, letter of advice. Envoi de fonds, remittance of funds. Fb: Coup d'envoi, (i) kick-off; (ii) place-kick. 2. Consignment, parcel. 3. Poetry: Envoy.

envol [ãvɔl], s.m. 1. (a) (Of birds) Taking flight, taking wing. (b) (Of aeroplane) Taking off. Piste d'envol, tarmac. 2. (a) Flight. (b) Take-off.

envolée [ãvɔle], s.f. (a) Flight. Av: Take-off. (b) F: E. d'éloquence, flight of oratory.

envol|er (s') [sãvɔle], v.pr. (a) (Of bird) To fly away, to fly off; to take flight; to take wing. (b) (Of aeroplane) To take off. (c) (Of hat, etc.) To blow off. F: Le temps s'envole, time is flying. s.m. **-ement.**

envoûtement [ãvutmã], s.m. Sympathetic magic; hoodoo.

envoûter [ãvute], v.tr. To practise sympathetic magic on (s.o.) (by means of a wax effigy); to hoodoo; F: to cast a spell on (s.o.).

envoûteur [ãvutœːr], s.m. Worker of spells.

envoy|er [ãvwaje], v.tr. (j'envoie; fu. j'enverrai) To send. E. une dépêche, to dispatch a telegram. E. sa démission, to send in one's resignation. E. un baiser à qn, to blow s.o. a kiss. E. un soufflet à qn, to fetch s.o. a box on the ears. Envoyer chercher qn, to send for s.o. Envoyer dire que . . ., to send word that. . . . F: Je ne le lui ai pas envoyé dire, I told him straight. F: Envoyer promener qn, to send s.o. to the right-about. S.a. PAÎTRE. P: Ça c'est envoyé! that's got him! a. **-able.**

envoyé, *s.m.* Messenger, representative; esp. (Government) envoy.

envoyeur, -euse [ãvwajœːr, -øːz], *s.* Sender; remitter (of money).

enzyme [ãzim], *s.f. Ch:* Enzyme.

éolien, -ienne [eɔljɛ̃, -jen], *a. & s.* **I.** *Gr.Hist:* Aeolian. **Harpe éolienne,** Aeolian harp. **2.** *s.f.* Éolienne, wind-mill (for pumping); air-motor.

éon [eɔ̃], *s.m.* Aeon, eon.

épagneul, -eule [epaɲœl], *s.* Spaniel.

épais, -aisse [epɛ, -ɛːs], *a.* Thick. *Mur e. de deux pieds,* wall two foot thick. *Feuillage é.,* dense foliage. *Avoir la taille épaisse,* to be thick-set. *F:* **Avoir l'esprit épais,** to be dense, dull-witted. *Avoir la langue épaisse,* to be thick of speech. *adv.* **Semer épais,** to sow thick.

épaisseur [epesœːr], *s.f.* **I.** Thickness (of wall, etc.); depth (of layer). *Le mur a deux pieds d'é.,* the wall is two foot thick. *Courroie en trois épaisseurs,* three-ply belt. *Mec.E:* **Feuilles d'épaisseur,** feelers. **2.** Density, thickness (of foliage, fog, etc.). *F: É. d'intelligence,* dullness of mind.

épaiss|ir [epesiːr], **I.** *v.tr.* To thicken; (of smoke, etc.) to make (the air) dense. **2.** *v.i. & pr.* To thicken, become thick; (of pers.) to grow stout; (of mind) to grow dense, dull; (of darkness) to deepen. *s.m.* **-issement.**

épanchement [epɑ̃ʃmɑ̃], *s.m.* **I.** (a) Pouring out, discharge, overflow (of liquid); effusion (of blood). S.a. BILE 2. (b) Outpouring, effusion (of feeling). **2.** *pl. F:* Effusiveness.

épancher [epɑ̃ʃe], *v.tr.* To pour out (liquid); to shed (blood). *F:* **Épancher sa bile,** to vent one's spleen. S.a. BILE 2. *É. son cœur,* to pour out one's heart; to unbosom oneself.

s'épancher, (a) (Of liquid) To pour out, overflow. (b) To unbosom oneself.

épandage [epɑ̃daːʒ], *s.m.* Spreading, scattering (of manure, sewage). **Champs d'épandage,** sewage farm.

épandre [epɑ̃ːdr], *v.tr.* To spread, scatter (manure, etc.); to shed (light).

s'épandre, (of water, fire) to spread.

épanou|ir [epanwiːr], *v.tr.* To cause (flower, etc.) to open out. *F: Un large sourire lui épanouit le visage,* his face broadened into a grin.

s'épanouir. I. (Of flower) To open out, bloom, blow. **2.** (Of face) To beam; to light up. *s.m.* **-issement.**

épanoui, *a.* In full bloom; full-blown. *Visage épanoui,* beaming face.

épargne [eparɲ], *s.f.* **I.** Saving, economy, thrift. **Caisse d'épargne,** savings-bank. **2. Vivre de ses épargnes,** to live on one's savings.

épargner [eparɲe], *v.tr.* **I.** To save (up), economize, put by (money, etc.). *E. le beurre,* to be sparing with the butter. *É. ses forces,* to husband one's strength. **2.** To save, spare (energy, time). *É. à qn la peine de faire qch.,* to save s.o. the trouble of doing sth. **3.** To spare, have mercy on (prisoner, etc.).

éparpill|er [eparpije], *v.tr.* To disperse, scatter; to spread (sth.) about. *s.m.* **-ement.**

s'éparpiller, to scatter, to disperse.

épars [epaːr], *a.* Scattered. *Cheveux é.,* (i) dishevelled hair; (ii) thin hair.

éparvin [eparvɛ̃], *s.m. Vet:* Spavin.

épat|ant [epatã], *a. F:* Wonderful; stunning; fine, **capital,** splendid. *C'est un type é.,* he's a topping chap. *Un dîner é.,* a top-hole dinner. *adv.* **-amment.**

épate [epat], *s.f. F:* Swank, swagger. **Faire de l'épate,** to show off, swank, cut a dash.

épatement [epatmɑ̃], *s.m. F:* Stupefaction, astonishment.

épater [epate], *v.tr. F:* To astound, flabbergast, amaze; to bowl (s.o.) over. **Pour épater le bourgeois,** to startle the old fogeys.

s'épater, to get rattled. *Il ne s'épate de rien,* nothing surprises him.

épateur [epatœːr], *s.m. F:* Swanker, bouncer.

épaulard [epolaːr], *s.m. Z:* Grampus, orc.

épaule [epoːl], *s.f.* Shoulder. **Large d'épaules,** broad-shouldered. **Hausser les épaules,** to shrug one's shoulders. **Épaule de mouton,** (i) *Cu:* shoulder of mutton; (ii) *Nau:* leg-of-mutton sail. **Coup d'épaule,** (i) shove; (ii) effort; (iii) leg-up. *Charger un fardeau sur son é.,* to shoulder a burden. *L'arme sur l'é.,* with rifle at the slope.

épaulement [epolmɑ̃], *s.m.* **I.** *Const:* Revetment wall. *Fort:* Breastwork. **2.** Shoulder(ing) (of tenon); bolster (of penknife).

épauler [epole], *v.tr.* (a) To bring (gun) to the shoulder. *Abs.* To level one's gun, to take aim. (b) *Carp:* To shoulder (beam).

épaulette [epolet], *s.f. Cost:* (a) Shoulder-strap. (b) *Mil:* Epaulet(te). **Obtenir l'épaulette,** to obtain a commission.

épaulière [epoljɛːr], *s.f. Cost:* Shoulder-strap.

épave [epaːv], *s.f.* (a) Unclaimed object. (b) Waif, stray. (c) *Nau:* Wreck; derelict. *Épaves d'un naufrage,* wreckage. *Épaves flottantes,* flotsam. *Épaves rejetées,* jetsam.

épée [epe], *s.f.* Straight sword; rapier. **Faire de l'épée,** to go in for fencing. **Se battre à l'épée,** to fight with swords. **Mettre l'épée à la main,** to draw one's sword. **Passer une garnison au fil de l'épée,** to put a garrison to the sword. **Poursuivre qn l'épée dans les reins,** to be in hot pursuit of s.o.; to press hard upon s.o. **Coup d'épée,** sword-thrust. *F:* **Coup d'épée dans l'eau,** wasted effort; beating the air.

épeler [eple], *v.tr.* (j'épelle; j'épellerai) **I.** To spell (word). **2.** To spell out (message, etc.).

épellation [epelasjɔ̃], *s.f.* Spelling.

épépin|er [epepine], *v.tr.* To take out the seeds or pips (of melon); to stone (raisins). *s.m.* **-age.**

éperdu, *a.* Distracted, bewildered. *Résistance éperdue,* desperate resistance. *E. de joie,* wild with delight. [PERDRE]

éperdument [eperdymɑ̃], *adv.* Distractedly, madly. *Aimer qn é.,* to love s.o. to distraction.

éperlan [eperlã], *s.m. Ich:* Smelt.

éperon [eprɔ̃], *s.m.* **I.** *Equit:* Spur. **Donner l'éperon à son cheval, piquer de l'éperon,** to spur, clap spurs to, one's horse. **2.** Spur (of mountain range, cock's leg); ram (of warship); cutwater; fender (of bridge).

éperonner [eprɔne], *v.tr.* (a) To spur, put spurs to (horse); to spur, urge, (s.o.) on. (b) To ram (enemy ship).

épervier [epervje], *s.m.* **I.** *Orn:* Sparrow-hawk. **2.** *Fish:* Sweep-net.

épeuré [epœre], *a.* Frightened, scared.

éphèdre [efeːdr], *s.f. Bot:* Shrubby horsetail.

éphémère [efemeːr], **I.** *a.* Ephemeral; *F:* short-lived, transitory, fleeting (happiness, etc.). **2.** *s.m. Ent:* Day-fly; may-fly.

éphéméride [efemerid], *s.f.* **I.** *Astr:* Ephemeris. **2.** *Calendrier é.,* tear-off calendar, block-calendar. **2.** *pl.* Ephemerides; astronomical tables; nautical almanac.

éphialte [efjalt], *s.m.* Incubus, nightmare.

éphod [efɔd], *s.m. Jew.Ant:* Ephod.

épi [epi], *s.m.* **I.** Ear (of grain); spike (of flower). **Blés en épi,** corn in the ear. (Of corn) **Monter en épi,** to ear. *F: Épi de cheveux,* tuft of hair;

cow-lick. **2.** Cluster (of diamonds). **3.** *(a) Const:* Appareil en épi, herring-bone work. *(b) Surg:* Spica (bandage). *(c)* Parting (of horse's mane). **4.** *Hyd.E:* Wharf, jetty. **5.** *Bot:* Épi d'eau, pondweed.

épice [epis], *s.f.* Spice. **Pain d'épice,** ginger-bread.

épicéa [episea], *s.m. Bot:* Picea; spruce(-fir).

épicentre [episɑ̃:tr], *s.m.* Epicentre (of earth-quake); epicentrum.

épicer [epise], *v.tr.* **(j'épiçai(s); n. épiçons)** To spice (cake, etc.).
épicé, *a.* Highly spiced; hot (seasoning). *F: Conte é.*, spicy tale.

épicerie [episri], *s.f.* **I.** Spices. **2.** *(a)* Groceries. Être dans l'é., to be in the grocery business. *(b)* Grocer's shop.

épicier, -ière [episje, -jɛːr], *s. (a)* Grocer. *(b) F:* Philistine.

épicrâne [epikrɑːn], *s.m.* Epicranium, scalp.

épicurien, -ienne [epikyrjɛ̃, -jɛn]. **I.** *a. & s. Gr.Phil:* Epicurean. **2.** *s. F:* Epicure, sybarite.

épicurisme [epikyrism], *s.m.* **I.** *Gr.Phil:* Epicureanism. **2.** Epicurism.

épicycloïde [episiklɔid], *s.f. Geom:* Epicycloid.

épidémie [epidemi], *s.f.* Epidemic; outbreak (of disease).

épidémique [epidemik], *a.* Epidemic(al).

épiderme [epiderm], *s.m.* Epiderm(is). *F:* Avoir l'épiderme sensible, délicat, to be thin-skinned.

épidermique [epidermik], *a.* Epidermal, epi-dermic (tissue). S.a. GREFFE[1] 2.

épier[1] [epje], *v.tr.* **I.** To watch (s.o.); to spy upon (s.o.). *É. un secret,* to be on the watch for a secret. **2.** To be on the look-out for (opportunity, etc.).

épier[2], *v.i.* (Of grain) To ear, to head.
épié, *a.* Spicate (flower, etc.).

épieu [epjø], *s.m.* Boar-spear.

épigastre [epigastr], *s.m. Anat:* Epigastrium.

épigrammatique [epigramatik], *a.* Epigram-matic. *adv.* **-ment,** -ally.

épigramme [epigram], *s.f.* Epigram.

épilage [epila:ʒ], *s.m.,* **épilation** [epilasjɔ̃], *s.f.* Depilation; removal of superfluous hairs; plucking (of eyebrows).

épilatoire [epilatwa:r], *a. & s.m.* Depilatory.

épilepsie [epilɛpsi], *s.f.* Epilepsy.

épileptique [epilɛptik], *a. & s.* Epileptic.

épiler [epile], *v.tr.* To depilate; to remove (s.o.'s) superfluous hairs; to pluck (eyebrows).

épileur, -euse [epilœ:r, -øːz], *s.* Depilator.

épilogue [epilɔg], *s.m.* Epilogue.

épiloguer [epilɔge]. **I.** *v.tr.* To find fault with (s.o.'s actions, etc.). **2.** *v.i. É. sur qch.*, to carp at, cavil at, about, sth.

épilogueur, -euse [epilɔgœːr, -øːz], *s.* Caviller, fault-finder.

épinaie [epinɛ], *s.f.* Brake, thicket.

épinard [epina:r], *s.m. (a) Bot:* Spinach. *(b) pl. Cu:* Épinards au naturel, en branches, boiled spinach. *Mil:* Épaulettes à graines d'épinards, bullion-fringe epaulets. S.a. BEURRE.

épin|cer [epɛ̃se], *v.tr.* **(j'épinçai(s); n. épinçons) I.** *Tex:* To burl (cloth). **2.** *Arb:* To disbud (tree). *s.m.* **-çage.**

épine [epin], *s.f.* **I.** Thorn-bush. *É. blanche,* hawthorn. *É. noire,* blackthorn, sloe(-bush). *F:* Fagot d'épines, crusty, cross-grained, fellow. **2.** Thorn, prickle. *F:* Être sur des épines, to be on thorns. **Une épine au pied,** a thorn in one's side. **Tirer à qn une épine du pied,** (i) to get s.o. out of a mess; (ii) to relieve s.o.'s mind. **3.** Épine dorsale, spine, backbone.

épinette [epinɛt], *s.f.* **I.** *Bot:* Spruce. **2.** *Mus: A:* Spinet, virginal.

épineux, -euse [epinø, -øːz], *a.* Thorny, prickly, spiky. *F:* Affaire épineuse, thorny, ticklish, matter.

épine-vinette [epinvinɛt], *s.f. Bot:* Barberry.

épingle [epɛ̃:gl], *s.f.* **I.** Pin. *É. de cravate,* tie-pin. *É. de sûreté, de nourrice,* safety-pin. *É. à cheveux,* hair-pin. *É. à linge,* clothes-peg. **Tête d'épingle,** pin-head. *F:* **Tiré à quatre épingles,** dapper; spick and span. **Tirer son épingle du jeu,** to get out of a venture without loss. **Coups d'épingle,** pin-pricks, petty annoyances. **Chercher une épingle dans une botte de foin,** to look for a needle in a bottle of hay. **2.** *pl. A: (a)* Pin-money. *(b)* Present, douceur.

épingl|er [epɛ̃gle], *v.tr.* To pin; to fasten (sth.) with a pin. *É. une carte au mur,* contre, *après,* le mur, to pin a map to, on, against, the wall. *É. ses cheveux,* to pin up one's hair. *s.m.* **-age.**

épinglier [epɛ̃gli(j)e], *s.m.* Pin-tray.

épinière [epinjɛːr], *a.f.* **Moelle épinière,** spinal cord.

épinoche [epinɔʃ], *s.f. Ich:* Stickleback.

Épiphanie [epifani], *s.f.* Epiphany; Twelfth Night.

épique [epik], *a.* Epic. **Poème épique,** epic.

épiscopal, -aux [episkɔpal, -o], *a.* Episcopal.

épiscopat [episkɔpa], *s.m. Ecc:* Episcopate.

épisode [epizɔd], *s.m.* Episode. **Film à épisodes,** serial film.

épisodique [epizɔdik], *a.* Episodic(al).

épisser [epise], *v.tr.* To splice (rope, wire cable).

épissoir [episwa:r], *s.m.,* **épissoire** [episwa:r], *s.f. Nau:* Marline-spike.

épissure [episy:r], *s.f.* Splice (in rope).

épistolaire [epistɔlɛːr], *a.* Epistolary.

épistolier, -ière [epistɔlje, -jɛːr], *s. F:* Letter-writer.

épistyle [epistil], *s.m. Arch:* Epistyle, architrave.

épitaphe [epitaf], *s.f.* Epitaph.

épithélial, -aux [epiteljal, -o], *a.* Epithelial.

épithète [epitɛt], *s.f.* Epithet. *Gram:* Attribu-tive adjective.

épithétique [epitetik], *a.* Epithetic(al).

épitoge [epitɔ:ʒ], *s.f. Rom.Ant:* Cloak (worn over the toga).

épitomé [epitɔme], *s.m.* Epitome, abridgment.

épître [epi:tr], *s.f.* Epistle. *Ecc:* **Côté de l'épître,** south side, epistle-side (of altar).

épizootie [epizɔɔti, -si], *s.f.* Epizootic disease.

éploré [eplɔre], *a.* Tearful, weeping.

épluch|er [eplyʃe], *v.tr.* **I.** *(a)* To clean, pick (salad, wool, etc.). *(b)* To peel, pare (potatoes, etc.). **2.** *F: (a)* To examine, criticize, (work) closely, in detail. *É. une question,* to sift a ques-tion. *(b)* To review (work) hypercritically. *É. une réputation,* to canvass a reputation. *s.m.* **-age.** *s.m.* **-ement.**

éplucheur, -euse [eplyʃœːr, -øːz], *s.* **I.** *(a)* Clea-ner. *É. de laine,* wool-picker. S.a. POUBELLE. *(b) É. de pommes de terre,* potato peeler (person). **2.** *F:* Hypercritical person.

épluchoir [eplyʃwa:r], *s.m.* Paring-knife; potato-knife.

épluchures [eplyʃy:r], *s.f.pl.* Peelings, parings (of potatoes, etc.); refuse.

époint|er [epwɛ̃te], *v.tr.* To break or blunt the point of (needle, etc.); to trim (hair). *s.m.* **-age.**
s'épointer, (of pencil, etc.) to lose its point.
épointé, *a.* **I.** Blunt(-pointed) (pencil, etc.). **2.** (Of horse) Hip-shot.

éponge [epɔ̃:ʒ], *s.f.* **I.** Sponge. **Effacer une tache**

à l'éponge, d'un coup d'éponge, to sponge out a stain. *F:* Passons l'éponge là-dessus, let us say no more about it. *Box:* Jeter l'éponge, to throw up the sponge. *Tex:* Tissu éponge, sponge-cloth. **2.** *É. métallique,* metallic sponge. *É. de fer,* spongy iron. S.a. PLATINE².

épong|er [epɔ̃ʒe], *v.tr.* (j'épongeai(s); n. épon-geons) **1.** To sponge up, mop up (liquid). **2.** To sponge, mop (surface); to sponge down (horse). *S'é. le front avec un mouchoir,* to mop one's brow with a handkerchief. *s.m.* **-eage.**

épontille [epɔ̃ti:j], *s.f. Nau:* **1.** Pillar, stanchion. **2.** Shore, prop.

épontill|er [epɔ̃tije], *v.tr. Nau:* To prop, shore (up). *s.m.* **-age.**

épopée [epɔpe], *s.f.* Epic (poem).

époque [epɔk], *s.f.* **1.** Epoch, era, age. *L'é. glaciaire,* the ice age. *Faire époque,* to mark an epoch. **2.** Time, period, date. **A l'époque de sa naissance,** at the time of his birth. **Il y a un an à pareille époque,** this time last year.

épouffer (s') [sepufe], *v.pr. F:* To lose one's breath; to get puffed. *S'é. de rire,* to burst with laughter; to guffaw.

époufflé, *a. F:* Breathless, out of breath, puffed.

épouill|er [epuje], *v.tr.* To cleanse (s.o., sth.) of vermin; to delouse. [POU] *s.m.* **-age.**

époumoner [epumɔne], *v.tr.* To try the lungs of, to puff (s.o.).

    s'époumoner, to shout oneself out of breath. *S'é. à crier,* to shout oneself hoarse.

épousailles [epuzɑ:j], *s.f.pl. A. & Dial:* Es-pousals, nuptials, wedding.

épouse. See ÉPOUX.

épouser [epuze], *v.tr.* **1.** To marry, wed; to take (woman) to wife. **2.** To espouse, take up, adopt (cause, doctrine, etc.). **3.** *É. la forme de qch.,* to follow the exact shape of sth.; to fit sth. exactly.

épousé, -ée, *s.* Bridegroom, *f.* bride.

épouseur [epuzœr], *s.m.* Suitor, wooer. *Ici, peu d'épouseurs,* here there are few (i) marrying men, (ii) eligible men.

épousset|er [epuste], *v.tr.* (j'époussette; j'épous-setterai; or *F:* j'époussete [epust]; j épous-seterai) To dust (furniture, etc.); to beat (the dust from) (clothes, etc.); to rub down (horse). *F: É. qn,* to dust s.o.'s jacket for him. *s.m.* **-age.**

époussette [epusɛt], *s.f.* Feather-duster; whisk.

épouvantable [epuvɑ̃tabl], *a.* Dreadful, fright-ful; appalling. *adv.* **-ment.**

épouvantail [epuvɑ̃ta:j], *s.m.* **1.** Scarecrow. **2.** *F:* Bugbear, bogy.

épouvante [epuvɑ̃:t], *s.f.* Terror, fright. *Saisi d'é.,* terror-stricken.

épouvant|er [epuvɑ̃te], *v.tr.* To terrify; to frighten (s.o.) out of his wits. *s.m.* **-ement.**

    s'épouvanter, to take fright; to become terror-stricken, panic-stricken.

époux, -ouse [epu, -u:z], *s.* Husband, *f.* wife; *Jur:* spouse. *Les deux époux,* the married couple.

épreindre [eprɛ̃:dr], *v.tr.* (*pr.p.* épreignant; *p.p.* épreint; *pr.ind.* j'éproins, n. épreignons; *p.h.* j'épreignis; *fu.* j'épreindrai) **1.** To squeeze (lemon, etc.). **2.** To squeeze out (juice).

éprendre (s') [seprɑ̃:dr], *v.pr.* (Conj. like PRENDRE) To become enamoured (*de,* of). *S'é. de qn,* to fall in love with s.o.; to lose one's heart to s.o. *S'é. de qch.,* to take a fancy to sth.

    épris, *a. É. de qn, de qch.,* in love with s.o., with sth.; enamoured of s.o., of sth.

épreuve [eprœ:v], *s.f.* **1.** (a) Proof, test, trial. *Subir une é.,* to undergo a test. **Soutenir, sup-**

porter, l'épreuve, to pass, stand, the test. **Faire l'épreuve de qch., mettre qch. à l'épreuve,** to try, test, sth.; to put sth. to the test. **Amitié à l'épreuve,** sure, staunch, friendship. **Acheter qch. à l'épreuve,** to buy sth. on trial, on approval. **A l'épreuve de qch.,** proof against sth. *A l'é. du feu,* fire-proof. S.a. BOMBE I. **Mécanisme à toute épreuve,** fool-proof mechanism. (b) *Sch:* (Examination) test, paper. (c) *Sp:* Event (at athletic meeting). *É. éliminatoire,* preliminary heat. *É. nulle,* dead heat. (d) *A: L'é. du feu,* ordeal by fire. **2.** Trial, affliction, ordeal. **3.** (a) *Typ: Engr:* Proof. *É. en première,* (i) foul proof; (ii) galley-proof. *É. de révision, deuxième é.,* revise. *É. en bon à tirer,* press-proof, press-revise. *Engr: É. avant la lettre,* proof before letters; proof engraving. (b) *Phot:* Print.

épris. See ÉPRENDRE (s').

éprouver [epruve], *v.tr.* **1.** To test, try (s.o., sth.); to put (s.o., sth.) to the test. **2.** To feel, experience (sensation, pain, etc.). *É. une perte,* to sustain, suffer, a loss. *É. des difficultés,* to meet with difficulties. **L'émotion que cette nouvelle nous fit éprouver,** the emotion which this news aroused within us.

    éprouvé, *a.* **1.** *Remède é.,* well-tried remedy. **2.** *Troupes très éprouvées,* troops that have suffered severely. *Région éprouvée,* stricken district.

éprouvette [epruvɛt], *s.f.* **1.** (a) Test-tube. (b) *Metall:* Test-piece, -bar. **2.** Assay spoon.

épuisable [epɥizabl], *a.* Exhaustible.

épuisant [epɥizɑ̃], *a.* Exhausting.

épuisement [epɥizmɑ̃], *s.m.* **1.** Exhausting, using up (of provisions, etc.); emptying, drain-ing (of cistern); pumping out (of a mine). **2.** Exhaustion. *É. nerveux,* nervous breakdown. *É. cérébral,* brain-fag.

épuiser [epɥize], *v.tr.* To exhaust. **1.** To use up, consume (provisions, etc.); to drain, empty (well, etc.). *É. une mine,* (i) to work out, exhaust, (ii) to drain, pump out, a mine. *F: É. un sujet,* to exhaust a subject. **2.** To wear, tire, (s.o.) out.

    s'épuiser, to become exhausted. **1.** (Of spring, etc.) To dry up, to run dry; (of stock, etc.) (i) to run out, give out, (ii) to run low. **2.** To wear oneself out (with work). *F: Mais je m'épuise à vous le dire,* I've told you so till I'm blue in the face.

    épuisé, *a.* Exhausted. **1.** Worked-out (mine); (edition) out of print; spent (acid, energy). **2.** Tired out, worn out.

épuisette [epɥizɛt], *s.f.* **1.** *Nau:* Scoop, bailer. **2.** *Fish:* Landing-net.

épurateur [epyratœ:r], *s.m.* Purifying appara-tus; purifier (of liquids, etc.). *É. d'eau,* water-softening plant. *Ind: I.C.E: É. d'air,* air-filter, air scrubber.

épuratif, -ive [epyratif, -i:v], *a.* Purifying.

épuration [epyrasjɔ̃], *s.f.* Purification, puri-fying; purging (of morals); filtering, scrubbing (of gas); expurgation (of a text).

épure [epy:r], *s.f.* **1.** Working drawing. **2.** Fin-ished design (of engine, etc.).

épurer [epyre], *v.tr.* To purify, filter (gas, water, etc.); to scrub, clean (gas). *Nau: É. l'eau,* to sweeten the water.

épurge [epyrʒ], *s.f. Bot:* Spurge.

équanimité [ekwanimite], *s.f.* Equanimity.

équarrir [ekari:r], *v.tr.* **1.** To square (timber, etc.). **2.** To broach, ream (hole). **3.** To quarter the carcass of (horse, mule, etc.).

équarrissage [ekarisa:ʒ], *s.m.,* **équarrisse-ment** [ekarismɑ̃], *s.m.* **1.** Squaring (of timber, stone). Bois d'équarrissage, scantling(s). **2.** Quartering, cutting up (of animal carcasses). **Chantier d'équarrissage,** knacker's yard.

équarrisseur [ekarisœ:r], *s.m.* **1.** Squarer (of wood, etc.). **2.** Knacker.

équarrissoir [ekariswa:r], *s.m.* **1.** *Tls:* Broach, reamer. **2.** (*a*) Knacker's knife. (*b*) Knacker's yard.

équateur [ekwatœ:r]. **I.** *s.m.* Equator. *Sous l'é.,* at the equator. **2.** *Pr.n.m. Geog:* Ecuador.

équation [ekwasjɔ̃], *s.f. Mth: Ch: Astr: Psy:* Equation. *Mth: É. du premier, du deuxième degré,* simple equation, quadratic equation. **Mettre un problème en équation,** to find the equation of a problem.

équatorial, -aux [ekwatɔrjal, o], *a.* Equatorial.

équerrage [ekera:ʒ], *s.m. Carp:* **1.** (*a*) Squaring. (*b*) Bevelling (of timber). **2.** Square or bevel angle.

équerre [ekɛ:r], *s.f.* **1.** *Tls:* Square. *É. à dessin,* set square. **Fausse équerre,** bevel-square. *É. à onglet,* mitre square. *Surv: É. d'arpenteur,* optical square. **2.** *Const:* (Angle d')équerre, right angle. **En équerre, d'équerre,** at right angles. **Hors d'équerre,** out of square, out of perpendicular. **Couper qch. à fausse équerre,** to cut sth. askew, on the bevel. **3.** Angle-iron; corner-plate; iron knee.

équerrer [ekere], *v.tr. Carp:* (*a*) To square. (*b*) To bevel (timber, etc.).

équestre [ekɛstr, -kɥ-], *a.* Equestrian (statue, order, etc.).

équidistant [ekɥidistɑ̃], *a. Geom:* Equidistant.

équilatéral, -aux [ekɥilateral, -o], *a.* Equilateral.

équilibration [ekilibrasjɔ̃], *s.f.* **1.** Equilibration, counterbalancing, counterpoising. **2.** Balancing (of budget).

équilibre [ekilibr], *s.m.* Equilibrium, balance, (equi)poise; stability (of aeroplane). **Mettre qch. en équilibre,** to balance sth. **Se tenir en équilibre,** to keep one's balance. **Perdre l'équilibre,** to lose one's balance. **Rétablir l'équilibre budgétaire,** to balance the budget. *Pol: É. européen,* balance of power in Europe.

équilibr|er [ekilibre], *v.tr.* To balance, (counter)poise, equilibrate. *É. le budget,* to balance the budget. *s.m.* **-age.**

s'équilibrer, (of weights, etc.) to balance.

équilibré, *a.* In equilibrium; balanced. *Mal é.,* ill-balanced; unbalanced (mind); cranky (boat).

équilibreur, -euse [ekilibrœ:r, -ø:z]. **I.** *a.* Balancing (action, etc.). **2.** *s.m. Av:* Stabilizer.

équilibriste [ekilibrist], *s. m. & f.* Equilibrist; rope-walker.

équin [ekɛ̃], *a.* Equine. **Pied équin,** club-foot.

équinoxe [ekinɔks], *s.m.* Equinox. *Vent d'é.,* equinoctial gale.

équinoxial, -aux [ekinɔksjal, -o], *a.* Equinoctial.

équipage [ekipa:ʒ], *s.m.* **1.** *Nau:* Crew; ship's company. **Maître d'équipage,** boatswain. **2.** *Mil:* Train, equipment. **Train des équipages,** baggage train, waggon-train; = Army Service Corps. **3.** Equipage. (*a*) Retinue, suite, train. *F:* **Arriver en grand équipage,** to arrive in state. (*b*) Carriage and horses; turn-out. **Avoir équipage,** to keep a carriage. **4.** *Ven:* Pack of hounds; hunt. **Maître d'équipage,** master of the hounds. **5.** Apparel, attire; *F:* **get-up, rig-out. 6.** (General sense of 'requisites') *É. d'engrenage(s),* gear-train (of lathe, etc.). *É. d'outils,* outfit, set, of tools.

équipe [ekip], *s.f.* **1.** Train of barges. **2.** Gang

(of workmen). *Mil:* Working party. **Travailler par équipes,** to work in shifts. **Travail d'équipe,** team-work. **Chef d'équipe,** foreman; ganger. *É. volante,* (police) flying squad. **3.** *Sp:* (*a*) Team; side. (*b*) Crew (of rowing-boat).

équipement [ekipmɑ̃], *s.m. Nau: Mil:* Equipment. **1.** (*a*) Fitting out. (*b*) Rigging up, fitting up (of sheers, etc.). **2.** Outfit (of ship, soldier). *Petit é.,* kit.

équiper [ekipe], *v.tr.* To equip (s.o., sth.); to fit (s.o.) out. *É. un navire,* (i) to equip, fit out, (ii) to man, a vessel. *Comme vous voilà équipé!* what a guy you look!

équipée, *s.f. F:* Escapade, lark.

équipier [ekipje], *s.m.* **1.** One of a gang (of workmen). **2.** *Sp:* Member of a team.

équitable [ekitabl], *a.* (*a*) Equitable, fair, just. (*b*) Fair-minded. *adv.* **-ment.**

équitation [ekitasjɔ̃], *s.f.* Equitation, horsemanship. *École d'é.,* riding-school.

équité [ekite], *s.f.* Equity, equitableness, fairness.

équivalence [ekivalɑ̃:s], *s.f.* Equivalence (*d*, to).

équivalent [ekivalɑ̃], *a. & s.m.* Equivalent (*d*, to).

équivaloir [ekivalwa:r], *v.i.* (Conj. like VALOIR) To be equivalent, equal in value (*d*, to). *F: Cela équivaut à l'appeler lâche,* that is tantamount to calling him a coward.

équivaut. See ÉQUIVALOIR.

équivoque [ekivɔk]. **I.** *a.* (*a*) Equivocal, ambiguous. (*b*) Questionable, doubtful, dubious (conduct, etc.). **2.** *s.f.* (*a*) Ambiguity (of expression). **Sans équivoque,** unequivocal(ly). User d'équivoque, to quibble. (*b*) Ambiguous expression. (*c*) Misunderstanding.

équivoquer [ekivɔke], *v.i.* To equivocate; to quibble.

érable [erabl], *s.m. Bot:* Maple(-tree, -wood). **Sucre d'érable,** maple sugar.

éradication [eradikasjɔ̃], *s.f.* Eradication.

érafl|er [erafle], *v.tr.* (*a*) To scratch, graze. *S'é. les tibias,* to bark one's shins. (*b*) To score (inside of gun, etc.). *s.m.* **-ement.**

éraflure [erafly:r], *s.f.* Slight scratch; graze; abrasion.

éraillement [erajmɑ̃], *s.m.* **1.** (*a*) Unravelling, fraying (of material). (*b*) Grazing, chafing. **2.** *Med: É. de la paupière,* ectropion. **3.** Raucousness, hoarseness (of the voice).

érailler [eraje], *v.tr.* **1.** To unravel, fray out (material). **2.** To graze, chafe (the skin, etc.). **3.** To roughen (the voice).

s'érailler. 1. To come unravelled; to fray. **2.** (Of skin, voice) To grow rough.

éraillé, *a.* **1.** Frayed (collar, etc.); scratched (surface). **2.** Bloodshot or red-rimmed (eyes). **3.** Raucous, harsh (voice).

éraillure [erajy:r], *s.f.* **1.** Frayed part (of garment, etc.). **2.** = ÉRAFLURE.

ère [ɛ:r], *s.f.* Era; epoch. **En l'an 1550 de notre ère,** in 1550 A.D.

érectile [erɛktil], *a.* Erectile.

érection [erɛksjɔ̃], *s.f.* Erection; setting up (of statue, etc.).

éreintage [erɛ̃ta:ʒ], *s.m. F:* = ÉREINTEMENT 2.

éreintant [erɛ̃tɑ̃], *a. F:* Back-breaking, killing, fagging (work, etc.).

éreintement [erɛ̃tmɑ̃], *s.m. F:* **1.** Exhaustion. **2.** (Of literary criticism) Slating, cutting up; savage attack.

éreinter [erɛ̃te], *v.tr.* **1.** To break the back of (horse, etc.). **2.** *F:* To exhaust; to tire (s.o.) out. **3.** *F:* (*a*) To smash up, ruin (car, etc.). (*b*) To criticize (author, etc.) unmercifully; to slate, slash (literary work, etc.); to pull (performance) to pieces. [REIN]

s'éreinter. (a) To exhaust oneself; to tire oneself out. (b) To drudge, toil (d, at).

éreinteur [erɛ̃tœːr], s.m. F: Slashing critic.

érésipèle [erezipɛl], s.m. F: = ÉRYSIPÈLE.

erg [ɛrg], s.m. Ph.Meas: Erg.

ergot [ɛrgo], s.m. **1.** (a) Spur (of cock, etc.). F: Monter, se dresser, sur ses ergots, to get on one's high horse; to bristle up. (b) Dew-claw (of dog, etc.). **2.** (a) Stub (on fruit-tree, etc.). (b) Agr: Pharm: Ergot. **3.** Mec.E: etc: Catch, pin, stop. E. d'arrêt, stop-pin.

ergot|er [ɛrgɔte], v.i. F: To quibble, cavil (sur, about); to split hairs. s.m. Ergotage.

ergoterie [ɛrgɔtri], s.f. F: = ERGOTAGE.

ergoteur, -euse [ɛrgɔtœːr, -øːz]. **1.** a. Cavilling, quibbling. **2.** s. Caviller, quibbler.

ériger [eriʒe], v.tr. (j'érigeai(s); n. érigeons) **1.** To erect, set up, raise (statue, etc.). **2.** To establish, set up (office, tribunal). **3.** F: To elevate, exalt. É. la corruption en système, to exalt bribery to a system.

s'ériger en critique, to set up for (being) a critic; to pose as a critic.

érigéron [eriʒerɔ̃], s.m. Bot: Erigeron, flea-bane.

erminette [ɛrminɛt], s.f. Tls: Adze.

ermitage [ɛrmitaːʒ], s.m. Hermitage.

ermite [ɛrmit], s.m. Hermit, eremite.

éroder [erɔde], v.tr. To erode, abrade; to eat away (metal, coast, etc.).

érosif, -ive [erɔzif, -iːv], a. Erosive.

érosion [erɔzjɔ̃], s.f. Erosion; wearing away.

érotique [erɔtik], a. Erotic; amatory (poem).

érotisme [erɔtism], s.m. Erotism.

érotomane [erɔtɔman], s. m. & f. Erotomaniac.

erpétologie [ɛrpetɔlɔʒi], s.f. Herpetology.

errant [ɛrɑ̃], a. **1.** Rambling, roaming, roving, wandering. Le Juif errant, the Wandering Jew. Chien .., stray dog. S.a. CHEVALIER 1, CHEVA-LERIE 2. **2.** Erring, misguided (person).

erratique [ɛr(r)atik], a. Erratic (block, pulse).

erratum [ɛr(r)atɔm], s.m. Typ: Erratum; misprint. pl. Des errata.

erre [ɛːr], s.f. **1.** Nau: (Head)way (of ship). Prendre de l'erre, to gather, fetch, headway. Avoir de l'erre, to have headway, to have way on. Casser l'erre, to check the way. **2.** Ven: Track, spoor (of stag, etc.).

errements [ɛrmɑ̃], s.m.pl. Erring ways; mistaken ideas.

errer [ɛre], v.i. **1.** To roam, wander (about). E. par les rues, to wander about the streets. Barques errant sur les flots, boats drifting on the waves. F: Laisser errer ses pensées, to let one's thoughts run on. **2.** To err; to be mistaken.

erreur [ɛrœːr], s.f. Error. **1.** Mistake, blunder, slip. E. de date, mistake in the date. E. de jugement, error of, in, judgment. E. typographique, misprint. Commettre une erreur, to make a mistake, a slip. Par erreur, by mistake. Sauf erreur, if I am not mistaken. Com: Sauf erreur ou omission, errors and omissions excepted. **2.** False belief, mistaken opinion; delusion; fallacy. Être dans l'erreur, to labour under a misapprehension; to be mistaken. Induire qn en erreur, to mislead s.o. Tirer qn d'erreur, to undeceive s.o. **3.** Les erreurs de la jeunesse, the errors of youth.

erroné [ɛrɔne], a. Erroneous, wrong, mistaken. adv. -ment.

éructation [eryktasjɔ̃], s.f. Eructation; belch.

éructer [erykte], v.i. To eruct, to belch.

érudit [erydi]. **I.** a. Erudite, scholarly, learned. **2.** s.m. Scholar.

érudition [erydisjɔ̃], s.f. Erudition, learning, scholarship.

éruption [erypsjɔ̃], s.f. **1.** Eruption. Faire éruption, to erupt. **2.** Med: Eruption, rash.

érysipèle [erizipɛl], s.m. Med: Erysipelas.

es [ɛ]. See ÊTRE.

ès [ɛs], contracted article = en les. Docteur ès lettres, doctor of literature. Geog: Saint-Pierre-ès-liens [eljɛ̃], literally 'St Peter in bonds.'

esbrouf(f)ant [ɛzbrufɑ̃], a. P: Amazing; unheard of; loud (dress).

esbrouf(f)e [ɛzbruf], s.f. P: Showing off; bounce. Faire de l'esbrouf(f)e, (i) to show off, to bounce, to put on side; (ii) to hector. Vol à l'esbrouf(f)e, pocket-picking by hustling one's victim; hustling.

esbrouf(f)er [ɛzbrufe], v.tr. P: To impress (s.o.) by one's bounce; to shock, P: knock (s.o.).

esbrouf(f)eur, -euse [ɛzbrufœːr, -øːz]. P: **I.** a. (a) Sidy. (b) Hectoring. **2.** s. (a) Bouncer, hustler. (b) Snatch-and-grab thief.

escabeau [ɛskabo], s.m. **1.** (Wooden) stool. **2.** Step-ladder.

escadre [ɛskɑːdr], s.f. Navy: Squadron. Chef d'escadre, commodore; squadron commander.

escadrille [ɛskadriːj], s.f. **1.** Navy: Flotilla. **2.** Av: Squadron.

escadron [ɛskadrɔ̃], s.m. Mil: Squadron (of cavalry). Chef d'escadron, major.

escalade [ɛskalad], s.f. **I.** (a) Scaling, climbing (of wall, cliff). (b) Climb. Mil: Escalade. **2.** Jur: Housebreaking.

escalader [ɛskalade], v.tr. To scale, climb (wall, etc.). Mil: To escalade (fortress, etc.).

escale [ɛskal], s.f. Nau: Av: **1.** Port or place of call. **2.** Call. Faire escale à Bordeaux, to put in, call, at Bordeaux. Av: Vol sans escale, non-stop flight.

escalier [ɛskalje], s.m. Staircase; (flight of) stairs. Rencontrer qn dans l'e., to meet s.o. on the stair(s). E. de service, de dégagement, backstairs. E. tournant, en vis, spiral stair(s). S.a. ESCARGOT. E. roulant, moving staircase; escalator. F: Esprit de l'escalier, after-wit. Nau: E. de commande, accommodation ladder. E. central, main companion.

escalope [ɛskalɔp], s.f. Collop, cutlet (of veal).

escamotable [ɛskamotabl], a. Concealable; disappearing. Av: Retractable (under-carriage).

escamotage [ɛskamota:ʒ], s.m. **1.** Legerdemain, conjuring, sleight of hand. E. d'une carte, conjuring away of a card. F: E. d'un devoir, scamping of a duty. Phot: E. d'une plaque, changing of a plate (in a changing-box). **2.** F: Sneaking, filching.

escamoter [ɛskamote], v.tr. **1.** (Of conjuror, etc.) To conjure (sth.) away; to make (sth.) vanish; to whisk (sth.) away; to cause (card, etc.) to disappear. Av: To retract (under-carriage). E. la vraie question, to burke the question. Phot: E. une plaque, to change a plate (in the changing-box). **2.** F: To sneak, filch. On m'a escamoté ma montre, F: my watch has been pinched.

escamoteur [ɛskamotœːr], s.m. Conjuror.

escampette [ɛskɑ̃pɛt], s.f. F: (Used in) Prendre la poudre d'escampette, to bolt, skedaddle.

escapade [ɛskapad], s.f. Escapade; prank.

escarbille [ɛskarbiːj], s.f. (a) (Half-burnt) cinder. (b) pl. Clinkers, ashes.

escarbot [ɛskarbo], s.m. Ent: **1.** Hister. E. doré,

rose-chafer. **2.** *F:* (*a*) Cockchafer. (*b*) Dung-beetle.

escarboucle [ɛskarbukl], *s.f. Lap:* Carbuncle.

escarcelle [ɛskarsɛl], *s.f. A:* Wallet.

escargot [ɛskargo], *s.m.* Snail. *E. comestible*, edible snail. *F:* (**Escalier en**) **escargot**, winding stair(s).

escargotière [ɛskargɔtjɛːr], *s.f.* Snailery.

escarmouche [ɛskarmuʃ], *s.f.* Skirmish.

escarmoucher [ɛskarmuʃe], *v.i.* To skirmish.

escarmoucheur [ɛskarmuʃœːr], *s.m.* Skirmisher.

escarole [ɛskarɔl], *s.f. Hort:* Endive.

escarpe[1] [ɛskarp], *s.f. Fort:* Escarp, scarp.

escarpe[2], *s.m. F:* Cut-throat.

escarpé [ɛskarpe], *a.* Steep, precipitous, abrupt (slope); bluff, sheer (cliff).

escarpement [ɛskarpəmɑ̃], *s.m.* **1.** Steepness. **2.** (*a*) *Fort: etc:* Escarpment. (*b*) Abrupt descent.

escarpin [ɛskarpɛ̃], *s.m.* (Dancing-)shoe; pump.

escarpolette [ɛskarpɔlɛt], *s.f.* (Child's) swing.

Escaut (**l'**) [lɛsko]. *Pr.n.m.* The (river) Scheldt.

eschare [ɛskaːr], *s.f. Med:* **1.** Scab, slough. **2.** Bed-sore.

escient [ɛsjɑ̃], *s.m.* Knowledge, cognizance. (Used in) **A bon escient**, deliberately, wittingly; *Jur:* scienter. **A mon, ton, son, escient**, to my, your, his, (certain) knowledge.

esclaffement [ɛsklafmɑ̃], *s.m. F:* Burst, roar, of laughter.

esclaffer (**s'**) [sɛsklafe], *v.pr. F:* To burst out laughing; to roar, shake, with laughter.

esclandre [ɛsklɑ̃ːdr], *s.m.* Scandal. **Faire de l'esclandre**, to make a scene.

esclavage [ɛsklavaːʒ], *s.m.* Slavery; *Lit:* bondage. **Réduire qn en esclavage**, to enslave s.o.; to reduce s.o. to slavery.

esclavagiste [ɛsklavaʒist], *s.m. U.S.Hist:* Partisan of negro slavery.

esclave [ɛsklaːv], *s. m. & f.* Slave; *A:* bondman, bondwoman. **Marchand d'esclaves**, slave-trader. *Être* (*l'*)*e. de la mode, du devoir*, to be a slave to, the slave of, fashion, duty. *Il est e. de sa parole*, his word is his bond.

escogriffe [ɛskɔgrif], *s.m.* **Un grand escogriffe**, a great lout of a fellow.

escompte [ɛskɔ̃ːt], *s.m.* **1.** *Com:* Discount, rebate. **Escompte au comptant**, discount for cash. **A escompte**, at a discount. **2.** *Fin: E. officiel*, le taux d'escompte, Bank rate of discount; the Bank rate. **Faire l'escompte**, to discount bills.

escompt|er [ɛskɔ̃te], *v.tr.* **1.** *Com:* To discount (bill). **2.** *F: E. les variations du marché*, to anticipate, allow for, the variations in prices. *E. un succès*, to reckon upon, anticipate, a success; *F:* to bank on a success. *s.a.* **-able**. *s.m.* **-eur.**

escopette [ɛskɔpɛt], *s.f. A:* Blunderbuss.

escorte [ɛskɔrt], *s.f. Mil: etc:* Escort. *Navy:* Convoy. **Sous l'escorte de . . .**, under the escort of . . .; *Navy:* convoyed by. . . . **Vaisseau d'escorte**, convoy.

escorter [ɛskɔrte], *v.tr.* To escort. *Navy:* To convoy, escort.

escorteur [ɛskɔrtœːr], *s.m. Navy:* Escort vessel.

escouade [ɛskwad], *s.f.* **1.** Squad, gang (of workmen). **2.** *Mil:* Section (of infantry).

escrime [ɛskrim], *s.f.* Fencing, swordsmanship. **Faire de l'escrime**, (i) to fence; (ii) to go in for fencing. *E. à la baïonnette*, bayonet exercise. **Maître d'escrime**, fencing-master.

escrimer (**s'**) [sɛskrime], *v.pr. F:* To spar, fight; to struggle. *S'e. de sa canne*, to make play with one's stick. *S'e. des pieds et des mains*, to fight tooth and nail. *S'e. contre qn*, to have a tussle with s.o. *S'e. à faire qch.*, to try hard to do sth.

escrimeur [ɛskrimœːr], *s.m.* Fencer, swordsman.

escroc [ɛskro], *s.m.* Swindler, sharper; crook.

escroquer [ɛskrɔke], *v.tr.* **1.** *E. qch. à qn*, to cheat, rob, s.o. of sth.; to trick s.o. out of sth. **2.** *E. qn*, to swindle, defraud, s.o.

escroquerie [ɛskrɔkri], *s.f.* **1.** (Obtaining of sth. by) false pretences; swindling. **2.** Swindle, fraud.

esculent [ɛskylɑ̃], *a.* Esculent, eatable.

Ésope [ezɔp]. *Pr.n.m. Gr.Lit:* Aesop.

espace [ɛspas]. **I.** *s.m.* Space. **1.** (*a*) Distance, interval (between two objects). (*b*) Interval (of time). *Dans l'e. d'un an*, within the space, course, of a year. **2.** Void, infinity. *Regarder dans l'e.*, to stare into space, into vacancy. *S.a.* GÉOMÉTRIE. **II.** **espace**, *s.f. Typ:* Space. *E. fine*, hair-space. *E. forte*, thick space.

espac|er [ɛspase], *v.tr.* (**j'espaçai(s); n. espaçons**) **1.** To space. *Typ: E. les lignes*, to lead, space, white out, the lines. **2.** (Of time) *Il faut e. nos rencontres*, we must meet at longer intervals, make our meetings less frequent. *s.m.* **-ement.** **s'espacer. 1.** *Les maisons s'espaçaient*, the houses became fewer and farther between. **2.** *Ses visites s'espacent*, his visits are becoming less frequent.

espacé, *a.* Far between, far apart; at wide intervals.

espadon [ɛspadɔ̃], *s.m.* Sword-fish.

espadrille [ɛspadriːj], *s.f.* (*a*) Canvas shoe (with jute or esparto sole). (*b*) Bathing sandal.

Espagne [ɛspaɲ]. *Pr.n.f.* Spain.

espagnol, -ole [ɛspaɲɔl]. **1.** *a.* Spanish. **2.** *s.* Spaniard. **3.** *s.m. Ling:* Spanish.

espagnolette [ɛspaɲɔlɛt], *s.f.* Espagnolette, fastener (of French window).

espalier [ɛspalje], *s.m.* Espalier ((i) tree, (ii) wall).

espèce [ɛspɛs], *s.f.* **1.** (*a*) Kind, sort. **Gens de toute espèce**, people of all kinds. *F:* **Espèce de . . .**, takes the gender and number of the following noun. *Cet e. d'idiot, cette e. d'idiote*, that silly fool. *Ces espèces d'idiots*, these silly fools. *Ces espèces de gens*, these sort of people. *P:* **Espèce d'idiot!** you (bally) idiot! (*b*) *Jur: etc:* Case in question. **Dans chaque cas d'espèce**, in each specific case. (*c*) *pl. Fin:* **Espèces (monnayées)**, specie, cash, coin. **Payer en espèces**, to pay in specie, in cash. **2.** *Nat.Hist:* Species (of plants, animals). **L'espèce humaine**, mankind. **3.** *Theol:* (Eucharistic) species. *Communion sous les deux espèces*, communion in both kinds.

espérable [ɛsperabl], *a.* That may be hoped for.

espérance [ɛsperɑ̃ːs], *s.f.* Hope. **Fonder son espérance sur qn**, to found one's hopes on s.o. **Être dans l'espérance de qch.**, to be in hopes of sth. **Garçon de grande espérance**, hopeful, promising, lad. **Avoir des espérances**, to have expectations (of a fortune).

espérantiste [ɛsperɑ̃tist]. *Ling:* **1.** *s.m. & f.* Esperantist. **2.** *a.* Esperanto (society, etc.).

espéranto [ɛsperɑ̃to], *s.m. Ling:* Esperanto.

espérer [ɛspere], *v.tr.* (**j'espère; j'espérerai**) **1.** To hope. *E. qch.*, to hope for sth. *J'espère vous revoir*, I hope to see you again. *J'espère que tout ira bien*, I hope, trust, (that) all will go well. *Espérez-vous que je le fasse, que je le ferai?* do you hope I may, shall, do it? *Un jour viendra, je l'espère, où . . .*, a day will come, I hope, when. . . . *E. en qn, en qch.*, to hope, trust, in s.o., in sth. **2.** *Dial: A: E. qn*, to expect s.o.

espiègle [ɛspjɛgl], *a. & s.* Mischievous, roguish (child, etc.). *Regard e.*, arch look. **Petit(e) espiègle**, little mischief.

espièglerie [ɛspjɛglɔri], *s.f.* **I.** Mischievousness, roguishness. **2.** Prank; roguish trick.
espion, -onne [ɛspjɔ̃, -ɔn], *s.* **I.** Spy. **2.** *s.m.* (*a*) Concealed microphone (in room, etc.); detectaphone. (*b*) Window-mirror, busybody.
espionnage [ɛspjɔnaːʒ], *s.m.* Espionage, spying.
espionner [ɛspjɔne], *v.tr.* To spy (up)on (s.o.). *Abs.* To spy.
esplanade [ɛsplanad], *s.f.* Esplanade; promenade, parade.
espoir [ɛspwaːr], *s.m.* Hope. *Avoir l'e. de faire qch.*, to have hopes of doing sth. **Avoir bon espoir,** to be full of hope. **Mettre (tout) son espoir en qch., en qn,** to set one's hopes on sth., on s.o. *Mettre son e. en Dieu*, to trust in God. **Nourrir l'espoir de faire qch.,** to live in hopes of doing sth. [ESPÉRER]
esprit [ɛspri], *s.m.* **I.** *Phil: Theol:* Spirit. (*a*) **Le Saint-Esprit,** the Holy Ghost, the Holy Spirit. **Rendre l'esprit,** to give up the ghost. **L'Esprit malin,** the Evil One. (*b*) Ghost, phantom. *Il revient des esprits dans cette maison*, this house is haunted. (*c*) (Of Puck, Ariel, etc.) Sprite. **2.** (*a*) Vital spirit. **Recueillir ses esprits,** to pull oneself together. **Reprendre ses esprits,** to regain consciousness; to come to. (*b*) *Ch: etc:* (Volatile) spirit. **Esprit de vin,** spirit(s) of wine. *Com:* **E. de sel,** spirit(s) of salt; hydrochloric acid. **3.** *Gr.Gram:* **Esprit rude,** rough breathing. **Esprit doux,** smooth breathing. **4.** (*a*) Mind. *Avoir l'e. tranquille*, to be easy in one's mind. **Avoir l'esprit de travers,** to have an awkward temper. *Elle avait l'e. ailleurs*, her thoughts were elsewhere. *Prov:* **Les grands esprits se rencontrent,** great minds think alike. **Perdre l'esprit,** to go out of one's mind. *Il a perdu l'e.*, his mind is unhinged, deranged. **Présence d'esprit,** presence of mind. **Conserver toute sa présence d'esprit,** to keep all one's wits about one. **Il m'est venu à l'esprit que . . .,** it occurred to me, struck me, that. . . . **Avoir l'esprit des affaires,** to have a genius, a turn, for business. **Un esprit fort,** a free-thinker. (*b*) Wit. **Il fait de l'esprit,** he is trying to be funny. *Trait d'esprit*, flash of wit. **Mots d'esprit, traits d'esprit,** witticisms. S.a. BEAU I. 2, ESCALIER. **5.** Spirit, feeling. *Esprit de corps*, corporate feeling. *Personnes de bon e.*, well-disposed people. **Entrer dans l'esprit de qch.,** to enter into the spirit of sth.
esquif [ɛskif], *s.m.* Small boat, skiff; wherry.
esquille [ɛskiːj], *s.f.* *Surg:* Splinter (of bone).
esquilleux, -euse [ɛskijø, -øːz], *a. Surg:* Comminuted (fracture); splintered (bone).
Esquimau, -aux [ɛskimo], *s. & a.* Eskimo; *U.S:* Husky.
esquinancie [ɛskinãsi], *s.f. Med:* Quinsy.
esquintant [ɛskɛ̃tã], *a. P:* Exhausting, killing (work, etc.).
esquinter [ɛskɛ̃te], *v.tr.* **I.** To exhaust; to tire (s.o.) out. **2.** To smash (sth.); to do (s.o.) in. *E. sa santé*, to ruin one's health.
esquisse [ɛskis], *s.f.* Sketch; draft; outline (of portrait, landscape, novel, etc.). *E. d'un bâtiment*, rough plan of a building. *E. au crayon, à la plume*, pencil-sketch, pen-and-ink sketch.
esquisser [ɛskise], *v.tr.* To sketch, outline (portrait, plan, etc.). *E. un sourire*, to give, put on, the ghost of a smile.
esquive [ɛskiːv], *s.f. Box: Fb: etc:* Dodging. *E. de la tête*, duck(ing).
esquiver [ɛskive], *v.tr.* To avoid, dodge, evade (blow, s.o., etc.). *Abs. Box: E. de la tête*, to duck.
s'esquiver, to slip away, off; to steal off; to make oneself scarce.

essai [ɛsɛ], *s.m.* **I.** (*a*) Trial, test(ing). **Essai d'usine,** shop-trial; bench-test. *E. de vitesse*, speed-trial. **En essai,** undergoing trials. **Mettre qn, qch., à l'essai,** to put s.o., sth., to the test. **Prendre qch. à l'essai,** to take sth. on trial, on approval. S.a. BALLON I. (*b*) *Metall:* Assay(ing) (of ore). **2.** (*a*) Attempt(ing), try. **Coup d'essai,** first attempt; *F:* trial shot. (*b*) *Lit:* Essay. (*c*) *Rugby Fb:* Try. **Transformer un essai (en but),** to convert a try. **3.** *Com:* Sample.
essaim [ɛsɛ̃], *s.m.* Swarm (of bees, etc.). (Of hive) **Jeter un essaim,** to throw off a swarm.
essaim|er [ɛsɛme], *v.i.* (Of bees) To swarm. *s.m.* **-age.**
essarter [ɛsarte], *v.tr. Husb:* To grub up (trees, roots); to clear (ground).
essay|er [ɛseje], *v.tr.* (j'essaie, j'essaye; j'essaierai, j'essayerai) **I.** (*a*) To test, try (machine, etc.); to taste (wines). (*b*) To try on (garment, etc.). (*c*) *Metall:* To assay (ore). (*d*) *E. de qch.*, to try, make trial of (wine, dish, etc.). **2.** *E. de faire qch.*, to try, attempt, endeavour, to do sth. *Essayez de l'attraper*, try and catch him. *s.m.* **-age.**
s'essayer *à, dans, qch., à faire qch.*, to try one's hand at sth., at doing sth.
essayeur, -euse [ɛsɛjœːr, -øːz], *s.* **I.** *Ind:* Assayer (of metals). **2.** *Tail:* Fitter; trier-on.
esse [ɛs], *s.f.* **I.** (The letter) **s. 2.** *Tchn:* (*a*) S-shaped hook. (*b*) *Veh:* Linchpin. **3.** Sound-hole, *f*-hole (of violin).
essence [ɛsãːs], *s.f.* **I.** *Phil: Theol:* Essential being; essence. **2.** (*a*) (Essential) oil; attar (of roses). *E. de térébenthine*, oil of turpentine. S.a. VERNIS I. (*b*) Motor spirit, petrol, *U.S:* gasoline. **Poste d'essence,** filling-station. (*c*) (Concentrated) essence, extract. **3.** (*a*) Nature, spirit, natural quality. *L'e. de l'affaire*, the essence, gist, of the matter. (*b*) *For:* Species, variety (of tree).
essentiel, -elle [ɛsãsjɛl], **I.** *a.* Essential (truth, character, oil, etc.). **2.** *s.m.* L'essentiel, the great thing, the main point. *adv.* **-ellement.**
esserter [ɛserte], *v.tr.* To lop, prune (tree).
esseulé [ɛsœle], *a.* Solitary, lonely (person).
esseulement [ɛsœlmã], *s.m.* Isolation, solitude.
essieu, -eux [ɛsjø, ɛ-], *s.m.* Axle(-tree) (of wheel); pin (of pulley-block). *E. fixe*, dead axle. *E. tournant*, live axle. S.a. ÉCARTEMENT 2.
essor [ɛsɔːr], *s.m.* Flight, soaring. **Donner l'essor à un oiseau,** to release a bird. **Donner libre essor à son génie,** to give full scope to one's genius. **Prendre son essor,** (i) (of bird) to take wing, to soar; (ii) *F:* to spring into vigorous action. *F: E. d'une industrie*, rise of an industry.
essor|er [ɛsɔre], *v.tr.* To dry (clothes, etc.); to wring (linen) dry. *Phot:* To wipe, blot off (negative). *s.m.* **-age.**
essoreuse [ɛsɔrøːz], *s.f.* **I.** Drying-machine, centrifugal dryer. **2.** *E. à rouleaux*, wringing-machine, wringer; mangle.
essoriller [ɛsɔrije], *v.tr.* To crop the ears of (dog, horse).
essouch|er [ɛsuʃe], *v.tr.* To stub up, grub up, the stumps of trees from (land). [SOUCHE] *s.m.* **-ement.**
essoufflement [ɛsufləmã], *s.m.* Breathlessness, panting; *F:* puffing.
essouffler [ɛsufle], *v.tr.* To blow, wind (horse, man); *F:* to puff s.o. [SOUFFLER]
s'essouffler, to get out of breath; to get winded, blown, puffed.
essoufflé, a. Out of breath, short of breath; *F:* puffed. *Voix essoufflée*, breathless voice. *Essoufflé d'avoir couru*, breathless with running.

essuie-glace, *s.m. Aut:* Windscreen wiper. *pl. Des essuie-glaces.*

essuie-main(s), *s.m.inv.* Towel.

essuie-pieds, *s.m.inv.* Door-mat.

essuie-plumes, *s.m.inv.* Pen-wiper.

essuy|er [esɥije], *v.tr.* (**j'essuie**; **j'essuierai**) **1.** To wipe (dish, etc.); to wipe (sth.) clean; to wipe up, mop up (water, etc.). *s.m.* **-age. 2.** To suffer, endure, be subjected to (defeat, insults, etc.). *E. un refus,* to meet with a refusal. *E. une perte,* to suffer a loss.

est[1] [ɛst]. **1.** *s.m.* No *pl.* East. *Un vent (d')est,* an easterly wind. *Le vent d'est,* the east wind. *Vers l'est,* eastward. *Borné à l'est par . . .,* bounded on the east by. . . . **2.** *a.inv. Les régions est de la France,* the easterly parts of France.

est[2] [ɛ]. See ÊTRE.

estacade [ɛstakad], *s.f.* **1.** Line of stakes or piles. (*a*) *Fort:* Stockade. (*b*) *Nau:* (i) Breakwater. (ii) Pier (on piles); pier at sea-side resort. **2.** *E. flottante,* (harbour) boom.

estafette [ɛstafɛt], *s.f.* Estafette, courier. *Mil:* Mounted orderly; dispatch-rider.

estafier [ɛstafje], *s.m. A:* **1.** (Armed) attendant. **2.** (*a*) Bully; hired ruffian. (*b*) Pimp.

estafilade [ɛstafilad], *s.f.* (*a*) Gash in the face (from razor, sword). (*b*) Slash (in clothing).

estagnon [ɛstaɲɔ̃], *s.m.* Drum (for oil, etc.).

estame [ɛstam], *s.f. Tex:* Worsted.

estaminet [ɛstaminɛ], *s.m.* **1.** Public house. **2.** Bar (in hotel); tap-room.

estampe [ɛstɑ̃:p], *s.f.* **1.** = ÉTAMPE. **2.** Print, engraving. *E. en bois,* woodcut.

estamp|er [ɛstɑ̃pe], *v.tr.* **1.** To stamp, emboss; to impress (pattern on clay, etc.). **2.** = ÉTAMPER. *Metalw: Pièce estampée,* punched piece. **3.** *P:* To swindle (s.o.). *s.m.* **-age.**

estampeur, -euse [ɛstɑ̃pœ:r, -ø:z], *s.* **1.** Stamper, embosser. **2.** *P:* Swindler.

estampille [ɛstɑ̃pi:j], *s.f.* (Official) stamp. *Com:* Trade-mark.

estampill|er [ɛstɑ̃pije], *v.tr.* To stamp (weights, document, etc.); to mark (goods). *s.m.* **-age.**

estarie [ɛstari], *s.f. Nau:* (*Jours d'*)estarie, lay-days.

esthète [ɛstɛt], *s. m. & f.* Aesthete.

esthétique [ɛstetik]. **1.** *a.* Aesthetic. **2.** *s.f.* Aesthetics. *adv.* **-ment,** -ally.

estimable [ɛstimabl], *a.* **1.** Estimable. **2.** Fairly good (work, etc.).

estimateur, -trice [ɛstimatœ:r, -tris], *s.* **1.** Estimator. *Com:* Appraiser, valuer. **2.** Appreciator, esteemer (of merit, etc.).

estimatif, -ive [ɛstimatif, -i:v], *a.* Estimated (cost, etc.). *Devis estimatif,* estimate.

estimation [ɛstimasjɔ̃], *s.f.* (*a*) Estimation (of the value of sth.); valuing, appraising (of goods, etc.). (*b*) Estimate, valuation.

estimatoire [ɛstimatwa:r], *a.* Estimatory.

estime [ɛstim], *s.f.* **1.** Guesswork. *Nau:* Reckoning. *Adv.phr.* **A l'estime,** by guesswork; *Nau:* by dead reckoning. **2.** (*a*) Estimation, opinion. (*b*) Esteem, regard. *Témoigner de l'e. pour qn,* to show regard for s.o. **Tenir qn en grande, en médiocre, estime,** to think highly, little, of s.o.

estimer [ɛstime], *v.tr.* **1.** (*a*) To estimate; to value, appraise (goods); to assess (damage). (*b*) To calculate (distance, etc.). *Nau:* To reckon. *Latitude estimée,* latitude by dead reckoning. **2.** (*a*) To consider, deem; to be of (the) opinion (that). *S'e. heureux,* to think, deem, oneself lucky; to account oneself lucky. (*b*) To esteem (s.o.); to have a high opinion of (s.o., sth.); to value (sth.).

estival, -aux [ɛstival, -o], *a.* (A)estival, summer (plant, illness, etc.).

estivant, -ante [ɛstivɑ̃, -ɑ̃:t], *s.* Summer visitor (at holiday resort).

estiv|er [ɛstive]. **1.** *v.tr.* To summer (cattle, etc.) (in mountain pastures). **2.** *v.i.* To spend the summer (at a resort); to summer. *s.m.* **-age.**

estoc [ɛstɔk], *s.m.* **1.** Stock, trunk (of tree). *F:* **Être de bon estoc,** to be of good stock, of good lineage. **2.** *Fenc:* Coup d'estoc, thrust. **Frapper d'estoc et de taille,** (i) to cut and thrust; (ii) *F:* to lay about one with might and main.

estocade [ɛstɔkad], *s.f.* (*a*) Stab-wound. (*b*) *Fenc:* Thrust.

estomac [ɛstɔma], *s.m.* Stomach. *Creux de l'e.,* pit of the stomach. **Le mal d'estomac,** the stomach-ache. *F:* **Avoir l'estomac dans les talons,** (i) to be faint with hunger; (ii) to have one's heart in one's boots. **Avoir de l'estomac,** (i) to have plenty of pluck; (ii) to have plenty of cheek; (iii) to be financially strong.

estomaquer [ɛstɔmake], *v.tr. F:* To take (s.o.'s) breath away; to stagger, astound (s.o.).

estompe [ɛstɔ̃:p], *s.f. Art:* (*a*) Stump. (*b*) Stump drawing.

estomper [ɛstɔ̃pe], *v.tr. Art:* To stump; to soften off, shade off, (drawing) with a stump. **estompé,** *a.* Soft, blurred (outline).

Estonie [ɛstɔni]. *Pr.n.f. Geog:* Esthonia.

estonien, -ienne [ɛstɔnjɛ̃, -jɛn], *a. & s. Geog:* Esthonian.

estourbir [ɛsturbi:r], *v.tr. P:* To kill (s.o.); to do (s.o.) in.

estrade[1] [ɛstrad], *s.f. A:* Road. (Still used in) **Battre l'estrade,** (i) *Mil:* (of cavalry) to scout; (ii) *F:* to roam about; (iii) to be on the tramp; (iv) (of highwayman) to be on the look-out for travellers. **Batteur d'estrade,** (i) *Mil:* scout; (ii) *F:* tramp, vagabond; (iii) footpad.

estrade[2], *s.f.* Dais; platform, stage.

estragon [ɛstragɔ̃], *s.m. Bot: Cu:* Tarragon.

estrapade [ɛstrapad], *s.f.* **1.** *A:* (*a*) Strappado (punishment). (*b*) *Nau:* Dipping from the yard-arm. **2.** *Equit:* Buck-jump. **3.** *Gym:* Skinning the cat. **Faire l'estrapade,** to skin the cat.

estrope [ɛstrɔp], *s.f. Nau:* Strop, grommet (of pulley-block, toggle-pin).

estropi|er [ɛstrɔpje], *v.tr.* (*a*) To cripple, lame, maim. (*b*) *F: E. le français,* to murder French. *s.m.* **-ement.** **estropié, -ée. 1.** *a.* Crippled, disabled, maimed. *Être e. du bras,* to have a game arm. **2.** *s. Les estropiés,* the maimed.

estuaire [ɛstɥɛ:r], *s.m.* Estuary.

esturgeon [ɛstyrʒɔ̃], *s.m. Ich:* Sturgeon.

et [e], *conj.* And. *Et son frère et sa sœur,* both his brother and his sister. *J'aime le café; et vous?* I like coffee; do you? *F: Et les dix francs que je vous ai prêtés?* and (what about) the ten francs I lent you? NOTE. There is no 'liaison' with *et. J'ai écrit et écrit* [ʒeekrieekri].

étable [etabl], *s.f.* Cow-shed, -house; cattle-shed; *Scot:* byre. *E. à pourceaux,* pigsty.

établ|er [etable], *v.tr.* To stall (cattle); to stable (horses). *s.m.* **-age.**

établi [etabli], *s.m.* (Work-)bench.

établir [etabli:r], *v.tr.* **1.** (*a*) To establish (business house, etc.); to set up (statue, agency); to put up (building, etc.); to construct (dam, railway); to settle, fix (one's place of abode); to install, fix up (machinery, etc.); to set (a sail). *E. un camp,* to pitch a camp. *E. un record,* to set up a record. *Route solidement établie,* well-laid road. (*b*) To establish, prove (fact). **2.** To work

16

out (plan, proposition, etc.); to draw up (plan). **Considérer qch. comme chose établie,** to take sth. for granted. *Com: É. un compte, un bilan, un budget,* to draw up, make up, an account, a balance-sheet; to draw up a budget. *É. une balance,* to strike a balance. **3.** To institute, create (tax, tribunal, etc.); to prescribe, lay down (rule); to found (colony, factory). **4.** To set (s.o.) up in business.

s'établir. 1. To establish oneself, to take up one's abode (in a place). **2.** *S'é. épicier,* to set up as a grocer. **3.** (Of custom, etc.) To become established.

établissement [etablismã], *s.m.* Establishment. **1.** (*a*) Setting up, putting up, installing (of machinery, etc.); establishing, building up (of reputation, etc.). **Frais de premier établissement,** initial expenses. (*b*) Establishment, proving (of innocence, guilt). **2.** Working out (of design, etc.); proving, establishing (of facts, etc.); drawing up, making up (of accounts, etc.). **3.** Instituting, creating, forming (of government, etc.); laying down (of rules); founding (of colony, industry). **4.** (*a*) Institution. *É. de charité,* charitable institution. *É. colonial,* colonial settlement. (*b*) Trading centre (in colony, etc.); factory. (*c*) Premises.

étage [eta:ʒ], *s.m.* **1.** Stor(e)y, floor (of building); level (of mine). *A deux étages,* two-storied; *U.S:* three-storied. **2.** (*a*) Tier, range, step. *F:* **Menton à deux étages,** double chin. (*b*) *F:* Degree, rank. *Cabaret de bas é.,* low, third-rate, public house. (*c*) *Geol:* Stage, layer, formation. (*d*) *Mch: etc:* Stage. *Compression par étages,* compression by stages. *W.Tel:* *É. amplificateur,* amplifying stage.

étag|er [etaʒe], *v.tr.* (j'étageai(s); n. étageons) **1.** (*a*) To range (seats, etc.) in tiers. *Jardin étagé,* terraced garden. *Poulie étagée,* cone-pulley. (*b*) To stagger (rivets, holidays, etc.). **2.** To perform (operation) by stages. *s.m.* **-ement.**

s'étager, to rise in tiers.

étagère [etaʒɛ:r], *s.f.* (*a*) What-not. (*b*) Rack; (set of) shelves. (*c*) *F:* Shelf.

étai¹ [ete], *s.m.* *Nau:* Stay. **Voile d'étai,** staysail.

étai², *s.m.* *Const:* Stay, prop, shore, strut. *É. de mine,* pit-prop. *F:* *É. de la société,* mainstay of society.

étain [etɛ̃], *s.m.* **1.** Tin. **Étain battu, étain en feuilles,** tinfoil. **2.** Pewter. **Vaisselle d'étain,** pewter (plate).

étal, -aux, occ. **-als** [etal, -o], *s.m.* Butcher's stall; meat stall.

étalage [etala:ʒ], *s.m.* *Com:* (*a*) Display, show (of goods, etc.). *É. de bouquiniste,* second-hand bookstall. (*b*) Window-dressing. **Faire l'étalage,** (i) to set out one's wares; (ii) to dress the window(s). **Mettre qch. à l'étalage,** to put sth. in the window. (*c*) *F:* Show-off. **Faire étalage de ses bijoux, de son savoir,** to show off, to display, parade, one's jewels, one's knowledge. *Faire é. de ses opinions,* to air one's opinions.

étalager [etala:ʒe], *v.tr.* (j'étalageai(s); n. étalageons) To expose, display, (goods) for sale.

étalagiste [etala:ʒist], *s. m. & f.* *Com:* (*a*) Stall-keeper, -holder. (*b*) Window-dresser.

étale [etal]. *Nau:* **1.** *a.* Slack (tide); steady (breeze). **2.** *s.m.* (*a*) Slack (of rope). (*b*) **Étale du flot,** slack water.

étal|er [etale], *v.tr.* **1.** *Nau:* (*a*) To stem (the current); to weather out, ride out (gale). (*b*) *É. l'erre,* to check the way. **2.** (*a*) *Com:* To display (goods); to set out (one's wares); to expose (goods) for sale. (*b*) To spread out, lay out (linen

to dry, etc.). (*c*) *Cards:* To lay down (one's cards). (*d*) *F:* To flaunt, show off (one's wealth, etc.). *s.m.* **-ement.**

s'étaler, to stretch oneself out; to sprawl (in an arm-chair, etc.). *S'é. sur un sujet,* to hold forth on a topic. *S'é. par terre,* (i) to lie down at full length; (ii) *F:* to come a cropper.

étalinguer [etalɛ̃ge], *v.tr.* *Nau:* To bend (cable) to the anchor; to clinch, shackle (cable).

étalingure [etalɛ̃gy:r], *s.f.* *Nau:* Clinch (of cable to anchor).

étalon¹ [etalɔ̃], *s.m.* Stallion; stud-horse.

étalon², *s.m.* Standard (of weights, measures, etc.). *Fin:* **L'étalon or,** the gold standard. *Nau:* **Compas étalon,** standard compass.

étalonn|er [etalɔne], *v.tr.* **1.** To standardize (weights, etc.); to calibrate (tube, etc.); to test, gauge, adjust (instrument). *W.Tel:* *É. les stations,* to log the stations. **2.** To stamp, mark (standardized weights, etc.). *s.m.* **-age.**

étambot [etãbo], *s.m.* *Nau:* Stern-post.

étam|er [etame], *v.tr.* **1.** To tin (copper, etc.); to tin(-plate) (iron). **2.** (*a*) To galvanize, zinc (metals). (*b*) To (quick)silver (mirror). *s.m.* **-age.**

étameur [etamœ:r], *s.m.* **1.** (*a*) Tinner, tinsmith. (*b*) *É. ambulant,* tinker. **2.** Silverer (of mirrors).

étamine¹ [etamin], *s.f.* **1.** (*a*) Coarse muslin; bolting-cloth. (*b*) *É. à pavillon,* bunting. **2.** Sieve, strainer. **Passer qch. par l'étamine,** (i) to sift, bolt, sth.; (ii) *F:* to sift (evidence, etc.).

étamine², *s.f.* *Bot:* Stamen.

étampe [etã:p], *s.f.* **1.** Stamp, die. **2.** *Tls:* (*a*) Punch. (*b*) Swage.

étamp|er [etãpe], *v.tr.* **1.** To stamp (sheet metal, etc.); to punch (horseshoe, etc.). **2.** (*a*) To swage. (*b*) To drop-forge. **Pièce étampée,** drop-forging. *s.m.* **-age.** *s.m.* **-eur.**

étamure [etamy:r], *s.f.* **1.** Coating of tin. **2.** Tinning-metal.

étanche [etã:ʃ], *a.* **1.** Tight, impervious. *É. à l'eau, à l'air,* water-, air-tight. **Cloisons étanches,** watertight bulkheads. **2.** *El.E:* Insulated.

étanchéité [etãʃeite], *s.f.* *É. à l'eau, à l'air,* water-, air-tightness.

étanch|er [etãʃe], *v.tr.* **1.** (*a*) To check the flow of (liquid); to sta(u)nch (blood). *É. une voie d'eau,* to stop a leak. (*b*) To quench, slake (one's thirst). (*c*) To clear (ship, land) of water; to dry up (land). **2.** To make (vessel) watertight, air-tight. *s.m.* **-ement.**

étançon [etãsɔ̃], *s.m.* (*a*) *N.Arch:* Pillar, stanchion. (*b*) Prop, stay, shore.

étançonn|er [etãsɔne], *v.tr.* To stay, to prop (up), to shore (up) (wall, deck, etc.); to underpin (building). *s.m.* **-ement.**

étang [etã], *s.m.* Pond, pool, mere.

étape [etap], *s.f.* *Mil: etc:* (*a*) Stage (of journey). (i) Halting-place. **Brûler une étape,** to pass a halting-place without stopping. (ii) Distance between two halting-places. (*b*) **Faire, fournir, une étape,** to do a day's march.

état [eta], *s.m.* **1.** State, condition. **État de choses,** state of things; circumstances. **En l'état . . .,** this being the case. . . . **Vêtements à l'état de guenilles,** clothes reduced to rags. **En (bon) état,** in good condition, in good order; (house) in good repair. **En mauvais état, hors d'état,** out of repair, out of order, in bad condition; (house) in bad repair. **Hors d'état de rendre aucun service,** totally unfit for use. **Mettre ses affaires en état,** to put one's affairs in order. **Remettre qch. en état,** to put sth. to rights; to overhaul (engine, etc.). **En état d'ivresse,** in a state of intoxication. *É. d'esprit,* state, frame, of mind. *É. de guerre,*

(i) state of war; (ii) war footing. **Être en état de faire qch.**, to be (i) fit, in a fit state, (ii) able, ready, to do sth. **Mettre qn en état de faire qch.**, to enable s.o. to do sth. **Hors d'état de faire qch.**, unable, not in a position, to do sth. F: **Être dans tous ses états**, to be in a great state. **2.** (a) Statement, report, list, return. **État des dépenses, état de compte**, statement of expenses, statement of account. *Jur:* **É. de frais**, bill of costs. **É. mensuel**, monthly return. **État des lieux**, inventory of fixtures (as between landlord and tenant). **É. nominatif**, list of names; (nominal) roll. **Rayer qn des états**, to strike s.o. off the rolls. (b) **Faire état de qch.**, (i) to take sth. into account; to note (a fact); (ii) to depend, count, on sth. **En tout état de cause . . .**, whatever the circumstances . . .; in any case. . . . **Faire grand état de qn**, to think highly of s.o. (c) *Adm:* **État civil**, (i) civil status; (ii) registry office. *Actes de l'é. civil*, certificates of births, marriages, deaths. *Officier de l'é. civil*, mayor, etc., acting as registrar. **3.** Profession, trade. *Il est militaire, épicier, de son é.*, he is a soldier by profession, a grocer by trade. **4.** *Pol:* (a) Estate (of the realm). **Le tiers état**, the third estate, the commonalty. *Hist:* Les **États généraux**, the States General. (b) State; (form of) government. **É. monarchique**, monarchic form of government. **Coup d'État**, coup d'état. **Homme d'État**, statesman. *Prisonnier d'É.*, prisoner of State. (c) Nation, state. *Servir l'É.*, to serve the nation, the State.

étatisme [etatism], *s.m.* State management or control; State socialism.

état-major [etamaʒɔːr], *s.m. Mil: Navy:* (a) (General) staff. **Officier d'état-major**, staff officer. **Carte d'état-major**, ordnance (survey) map. S.a. BREVET 2, CHEF 2. (b) Headquarters. *pl. Des états-majors.*

États-Unis (les) [lezetazyni]. *Pr.n.m.pl.* The United States (of America).

étau, -aux [eto], *s.m. Tls:* Vice. **É. à main**, hand-vice. **É. d'établi**, bench-vice. *Tel: etc:* **É. tendeur**, draw-vice.

étayer [eteje], *v.tr.* (j'étaie, j'étaye; j'étaierai, j'étayerai) (a) To stay, prop (up), shore (up), support. (b) F: To support, back up (statement, etc.). *s.m.* **-iement, -yement.** *s.m.* **-yage.**

s'étayer *contre un choc*, to steady oneself against a shock. F: **S'é. sur qn**, to lean upon s.o.

été¹ [ete], *s.m.* Summer. **En été**, in summer. **Se mettre en été**, to put on summer clothing. **Heure d'été**, summer-time. F: **Été de la Saint-Martin**, St Martin's summer, Indian summer.

été². See ÊTRE.

éteign-ant, -is, -ons, etc. See ÉTEINDRE.

éteignoir [etɛɲwaːr], *s.m.* (Candle) extinguisher.

éteindre [etɛ̃ːdr], *v.tr.* (Conj. like TEINDRE) **1.** To extinguish, put out (fire, light); to turn off (the gas); to switch off (electric light). *É. les feux d'un fourneau*, to draw the fires of a furnace. *Abs. Éteignez*, turn out, switch off, the light. **2.** To extinguish (race, family); to pay off (a debt); to abolish (a right). **É. la soif**, to slake, quench, thirst. **3.** (a) To slake, slack, kill (lime). (b) *Metalw:* To quench (red-hot iron, etc.). **4.** To fade, soften (colour); to smother, deaden (sound); to appease, allay (passion); to dim (light, flashing eyes, etc.).

s'éteindre. 1. (a) (Of fire, light) To go out, to die out. (b) (Of colour, etc.) To fade, grow dim; (of sound) to die down, to die away; to subside; (of passion) to die down. *Le jour s'éteint*, daylight is failing. **2.** (a) (Of race, family) To become extinct, to die out. (b) *Vieillard*

qui s'éteint, old man who is nearing his end. *Il s'éteignit entre mes bras*, he passed away in my arms.

éteint, *a.* (a) Extinguished. *Le feu est é.*, the fire is out. (b) Extinct (race, volcano). (c) Dull; dim, faint (colour, sound). *Yeux éteints*, dull, *Lit:* lack-lustre, eyes. *Voix éteinte*, faint, toneless, far-away, voice.

étendage [etɑ̃daːʒ], *s.m.* **1.** (a) Hanging out (of washing); spreading (of butter). (b) Stretching. **2.** (a) Clothes-lines. (b) Drying yard.

étendard [etɑ̃daːr], *s.m.* (a) *Mil:* Standard (of mounted arms); colour(s). (b) F: (War-)flag, standard. **Lever l'étendard de la révolte**, to raise the flag of rebellion.

étendoir [etɑ̃dwaːr], *s.m.* (a) Clothes-line. (b) Drying-yard, -room.

étendre [etɑ̃ːdr], *v.tr.* **1.** To spread, stretch. *É. de la paille dans la rue*, to spread straw over the street. *É. du beurre sur du pain*, to spread butter on bread. *É. la lessive*, to hang out the washing. *É. le bras*, to stretch out one's arm. (Of bird) *É. ses ailes*, to spread its wings. *É. qn par terre d'un coup de poing*, to knock s.o. down; *F:* to lay s.o. out. **2.** (a) To stretch (sth.) out (to more than original size). *É. l'or*, (i) to beat out gold; (ii) to wire-draw gold. *Cu:* **É. la pâte**, to roll out the dough. *É. ses connaissances*, to extend, enlarge, improve, one's knowledge. *É. sa propriété*, to enlarge one's estates. (b) To dilute (wine, milk, etc.) (de, with).

s'étendre. 1. (a) To stretch oneself out; to lie down at full length. (b) *S'é. sur un sujet*, to dwell, enlarge, expatiate, (up)on a subject. **2.** (a) To extend, stretch. *La ligne s'étend depuis . . . jusqu'à . . .*, the line stretches, runs, from . . . to . . . (b) To spread. *Empêcher l'incendie de s'é.*, to prevent the fire from spreading. (Of dye) *S'é. au lavage*, to run in the wash.

étendu, -ue. 1. *a.* (a) Extensive (knowledge); far-reaching (influence); wide (plain). (b) Outspread (wings); outstretched (hands). **2.** *s.f.* **Étendue**, extent, size, area; scale (of calamity, etc.); stretch (of water, etc.); reach (of the mind). *Vaste é. de mer*, vast stretch, expanse, of sea. *É. d'une voix*, compass, range, of a voice.

étern|el, -elle [etɛrnɛl], *a.* (a) Eternal. *s.m.* **L'Éternel**, God, the Lord. S.a. ARMÉE. (b) Everlasting, endless. *F: Soucis éternels*, never-ending worries. S.a. NEIGE. *adv.* **-ellement.**

éterniser [etɛrnize], *v.tr.* (a) To eternize, perpetuate. *É. la mémoire de qn*, to immortalize s.o.'s memory. *Si nous pouvions é. cette heure*, if only we could make this hour last for ever. (b) *F:* To drag on (discussion) (interminably).

s'éterniser, to last for ever; to drag on; to go on and on.

éternité [etɛrnite], *s.f.* Eternity. *F:* **De toute éternité**, from time immemorial. *Il y a une é. que je ne vous ai vu*, it is ages since I saw you.

éternuement [etɛrnymɑ̃], *s.m.* = ÉTERNÛMENT.

éternuer [etɛrnɥe], *v.i.* To sneeze.

éternûment [etɛrnymɑ̃], *s.m.* **1.** Sneezing. **2.** Sneeze.

étésiens [etezjɛ̃], *a.m.pl.* Etesian (winds).

étêt|er [etete], *v.tr.* (a) To remove the head from (fish, nail, etc.). (b) To pollard (tree). [TÊTE] *s.m.* **-age.** *s.m.* **-ement.**

éther [etɛːr], *s.m. Ph: Ch: Med:* Ether.

éthéré [etere], *a.* **1.** Ethereal, airy (regions). **2.** *Ch:* Ethereal (salt).

Éthiopie [etjɔpi]. *Pr.n.f.* Ethiopia; Abyssinia.

éthiopien, -ienne [etjɔpjɛ̃, -jɛn], *a. & s.* Ethiopian; Abyssinian.

éthique [etik]. **1.** *a.* (*a*) Ethical (problem, etc.). (*b*) Datif éthique, ethic dative. **2.** *s.f.* Ethics.

ethnique [ɛtnik], *a.* **1.** *Rel.H:* Ethnic(al), gentile. **2.** Ethnological, ethnical (influences).

ethnographe [ɛtnɔgraf], *s.m. & f.* Ethnographer.

ethnographie [ɛtnɔgrafi], *s.f.* Ethnography.

ethnologie [ɛtnɔlɔʒi], *s.f.* Ethnology.

ethnologue [ɛtnɔlɔg], *s. m. & f.* Ethnologist.

éthylamine [etilamin], *s.f. Ch:* Ethylamine.

éthyle [etil], *s.m. Ch:* Ethyl.

éthylène [etilɛn], *s.m. Ch:* Ethylene.

étiage [etjaːʒ], *s.m.* Lowest water-level, low water (of river). Échelle d'étiage, floodometer. *F: Un é. social plus élevé,* a higher social plane.

Étienne [etjɛn]. *Pr.n.m.* Stephen.

étinceler [etɛ̃sle], *v.i.* (il étincelle; il étincellera) **1.** To throw out sparks. **2.** (Of diamond, etc.) To sparkle, glitter, gleam, flash.

étincelle [etɛ̃sɛl], *s.f.* Spark. *Lancer des étincelles,* to throw out sparks; to sparkle, flash. *El.E: É. disruptive,* spark discharge. *I.C.E:* Allumage par étincelle, spark ignition.

étincellement [etɛ̃sɛlmɑ̃], *s.m.* Sparkling, glittering, scintillation (of gem); twinkling (of stars).

étiolement [etjɔlmɑ̃], *s.m.* (*a*) *Bot: Med:* Chlorosis, etiolation. (*b*) Drooping, wilting (of flowers); atrophy (of the mind).

étioler [etjɔle], *v.tr.* **1.** To etiolate, blanch (celery, etc.). **2.** To make (s.o.) weakly, pale.
  s'étioler. (*a*) To etiolate, blanch. (*b*) (Of flowers, etc.) To droop, wilt.

étique [etik], *a.* **1.** *A:* Consumptive. **2.** Emaciated; all skin and bone.

étiquet|er [etikte], *v.tr.* (j'étiquète; j'étiqueterai) To label (luggage); to ticket (goods). *s.m.* **-age.** *s.* **-eur, -euse.**

étiquette [etikɛt], *s.f.* **1.** Label, docket, ticket. *É. à œillets,* tie-on label; tag. *É. gommée,* stick-on label. *É. de vitrine,* show-card. **2.** Etiquette, formality, ceremony. *Il n'est pas d'é. de . . . ,* it is not etiquette to. . . .

étirable [etirabl], *a.* (Of metal) Ductile, drawable; (of tissue) elastic.

étir|er [etire], *v.tr.* To stretch; to draw out (sth.). *É. le fil,* to draw wire. Banc à étirer, draw-bench. *s.m.* **-age.** *s.* **-eur, -euse.**
  s'étirer, to stretch oneself, one's limbs.

étoc [etɔk], *s.m. Arb:* = ESTOC 1.

étoffe [etɔf], *s.f.* **1.** Material (used in fabrication of sth.). *F:* Avoir de l'étoffe, to have plenty of grit. *Il a de l'é.,* there is something in him, there is good stuff in him. *Il y a en lui l'é. d'un écrivain,* he has the makings of a writer. **2.** *Tex:* Stuff, material, fabric. *Riches étoffes de soie,* rich silken fabrics.

étoffer [etɔfe], *v.tr.* **1.** (*a*) To use ample material in making (sth.). (*b*) To stuff (cushion, etc.); to upholster (armchair, etc.). **2.** To stiffen (gum, etc.); to beat up (cream, etc.).
  s'étoffer, (of horse, *F:* of pers.) to fill out.

étoffé, *a.* Ample, full (garment); stuffed (cushion); upholstered (armchair); rich, full (voice). *Homme bien é.,* (i) stout, thick-set, man; (ii) well-to-do man. *Cheval é.,* stout, stocky, horse.

étoile [etwal], *s.f.* Star. **1.** *É. filante,* shooting star. *L'é. polaire,* the pole star. *A la clarté des étoiles,* in the starlight. *F:* Coucher, dormir, à la belle étoile, to sleep in the open. *Né sous une bonne, une mauvaise, étoile,* born under a lucky, an unlucky, star. S.a. PÂLIR 1. **2.** (*a*) Decoration. *É. de la Légion d'honneur,* cross of the Legion of Honour. (*b*) *Typ:* Asterisk, star. (*c*) = ROND-

POINT. (*d*) Étoile de mer, star-fish. **3.** *É. de cinéma,* film-star.

étoiler [etwale], *v.tr.* **1.** To stud, bespangle, (sth.) with stars. **2.** To make a star-shaped crack in, to star (glass, etc.).
  s'étoiler. 1. (Of the sky) To light up (with stars). **2.** (Of window-pane, etc.) To star.
  étoilé, *a.* **1.** Starry, starlit (sky). La Bannière étoilée, the Star-spangled Banner (of the U.S.A.). **2.** Star-shaped.

étole [etɔl], *s.f. Ecc:* Stole.

étonn|ant [etɔnɑ̃], *a.* Astonishing, surprising. *Rien d'é. à cela,* that is no wonder. *Ce n'est pas é. qu'il soit malade,* no wonder, little wonder, it is not to be wondered at, that he is ill. *adv.* **-amment.**

étonnement [etɔnmɑ̃], *s.m.* Astonishment, surprise, wonder, amazement. Jeter qn dans l'étonnement, to astonish, dumbfound, s.o. Faire l'étonnement de tout le monde, to be the talk of the town.

étonner [etɔne], *v.tr.* **1.** (*a*) *A:* To stun. (*b*) To shake, loosen (structure); to crack, fissure (arch, etc.). **2.** To astonish, amaze, surprise. *Cela m'étonne que + sub.,* I am astonished that. . . . *Cela ne m'étonnerait pas,* I shouldn't wonder (at it). *Ce qui m'étonne, c'est que . . . ,* the wonder to me is that. . . .
  s'étonner. 1. To become loose; to crack, fissure. **2.** To be astonished, surprised, to wonder (de, at). *Je m'étonne de vous voir,* I am surprised to see you. *Je m'étonne que + sub.,* I wonder that. . . .

étouffant [etufɑ̃], *a.* Stifling, suffocating, stuffy (atmosphere); sultry (weather); sweltering (heat).

étouffée [etufe], *s.f. Cu:* Cuire qch. à l'étouffée, to braise (meat).

étouffement [etufmɑ̃], *s.m.* **1.** Suffocation, stifling (of s.o.); smothering (of fire). **2.** Choking sensation; fit of breathlessness.

étouffer [etufe]. **1.** *v.tr.* (*a*) To suffocate, choke, smother (s.o.). On s'étouffait pour entrer, people crushed in. (*b*) To stifle (cry, passion, industry); to smother (fire); to stamp out (epidemic); to quell, suppress (revolt); to damp (sound). *El:* To quench (spark). *É. une affaire,* to hush up a matter. *É. un sanglot,* to choke down a sob. **2.** *v.i.* & *pr.* (*a*) To suffocate, choke. *É. de rage,* to choke with rage. (*b*) On étouffe ici, it is stifling here.

étoupe [etup], *s.f.* **1.** (*a*) *É. blanche,* tow. (*b*) *É. noire,* oakum. (*c*) *É. de coton,* cotton waste. *F:* Mettre le feu aux étoupes, to set a match to the train. **2.** Packing, stuffing (of piston-rod).

étouper [etupe], *v.tr.* **1.** To stop up (crevice, etc.) with tow or oakum; to caulk (boat). **2.** *Mec.E:* To stuff (gland, etc.).

étoupille [etupiːj], *s.f.* **1.** *Artil:* (*a*) *A:* Quick-match. (*b*) Firing-tube. **2.** *Min:* Fuse.

étourderie [eturdəri], *s.f.* **1.** Thoughtlessness, inadvertence. *Par é.,* inadvertently. **2.** Thoughtless action; oversight, blunder; careless mistake.

étourdir [eturdiːr], *v.tr.* **1.** To stun, daze; to make (s.o.) dizzy. *F: Cet enfant nous étourdit,* that child is making an awful din. **2.** (*a*) To (be)numb, deaden (pain); to allay, assuage (grief). (*b*) *É. l'eau,* to take the chill off water.

étourdi, -ie. **1.** *a.* Thoughtless, scatter-brained; foolish (answer). **2.** *s.* Scatter-brain, harum-scarum. **3.** *Adv.phr.* A l'étourdie, thoughtlessly, heedlessly. *adv.* **-ment.**

étourdissant [eturdisɑ̃], *a.* **1.** Deafening, ear-splitting. **2.** *F:* Staggering, astounding (news).

étourdissement [eturdismɑ̃], *s.m.* **1.** Giddiness, dizziness. *Avoir un é.*, to feel giddy. *Cela me donne des étourdissements*, it makes my head swim. **2.** Numbing, deadening (of pain); dazing (of the mind).

étourneau [eturno], *s.m.* (*a*) *Orn:* Starling. (*b*) *F:* = ÉTOURDI 2.

étrange [etrɑ̃:ʒ], *a.* Strange, peculiar, odd, queer. *adv.* -**ment.**

étranger, -ère [etrɑ̃ʒe, -ɛ:r]. **1.** (*a*) *a.* Foreign. Ministre des affaires étrangères, Minister of Foreign Affairs. (*b*) *s.* Foreigner, alien. (*c*) *s.m.* Foreign parts. *Vivre à l'étranger*, to live abroad. **2.** (*a*) *a.* Strange, unknown. *Sa voix m'est étrangère*, his voice is unknown to me. (*b*) *s.* Stranger. **3.** *a.* Extraneous, foreign; not belonging (to sth.); irrelevant (*à*, to). *Cela est é. à la question*, that is beside the point. *Être é. au complot*, to have no part in the plot.

étrangeté [etrɑ̃ʒte], *s.f.* Strangeness, quaintness, oddness (of conduct, style, etc.).

étranglement [etrɑ̃gləmɑ̃], *s.m.* **1.** (*a*) Strangling, strangulation. (*b*) Constriction, narrowing; jamming (of cable). *Mch:* Throttling. **2.** Narrows (of river); bottle-neck (of thoroughfare).

étrangler [etrɑ̃gle], *v.tr.* **1.** (*a*) To strangle, throttle (s.o.). (*b*) *v.i.* *É. de colère*, to choke with rage. **2.** To constrict, compress. *Mch:* To throttle (steam). **3.** *F:* *É. un complot au berceau*, to nip a plot in the bud.

étranglé, *a.* Constricted, narrow (passage); choked, choking (voice); strangulated (hernia).

étrangleur, -euse [etrɑ̃glœ:r, -ø:z], *s.* **1.** Strangler, garrotter; thug. **2.** *I.C.E:* Strangler, choke.

étrave [etra:v], *s.f.* *Nau:* Stem, stern-post (of ship). *Lame d'é.*, bow-wave.

être [ɛ:tr]. I. *v.i. & pred.* (*pr.p.* étant; *p.p.* été; *pr.ind.* je suis, tu es, il est, n. sommes, v. êtes, ils sont; *pr. sub.* je sois, il soit, n. soyons, ils soient; *imp.* sois, soyons, soyez; *p.d.* j'étais; *p.h.* je fus, n. fûmes, ils furent; *p. sub.* je fusse; *fu.* je serai) **1.** To be, to exist. *Cesser d'être*, to cease to be. *Elle n'est plus*, she is no more. *Cela étant*, that being the case. *Cela n'est pas!* that is not so! *Eh bien, soit!* well, so be it! *Ainsi soit-il*, so be it; *Ecc:* amen. **2.** (As copula) (*a*) *Il est le chef de gare*, he is the stationmaster. *Il est chef de gare*, he is a stationmaster. *Soit a la base d'un triangle*, let *a* be the base of a triangle. *Nous étions deux, trois*, there were two, three, of us. *Comment êtes-vous avec vos chefs?* how do you stand with your chiefs? *Nous sommes le dix*, to-day is the tenth. *Quand il fut pour sortir*, just as he was about to leave. *Être à l'agonie*, to be dying. *Vous n'êtes pas à ce que je dis*, you are not paying attention to what I say. *Il est tout à son travail*, he is entirely engrossed in his work. *Il est d'un bon caractère*, he is good-tempered. *Il est de Londres*, he is from London. *Voulez-vous être des nôtres?* will you join our party, make one of us? *Il est de mes amis*, he is a friend of mine. (*b*) *Il est à travailler*, he is at work. *Il fut trois ans à l'écrire*, he took three years to write it. (*c*) (i) (With *ce* as neuter subject) See CE¹ 3: (ii) (With ellipsis of *ce*) *Je le ferais (si ce) n'était que* . . ., I should do it were it not that . . ., only that . . ., but that. . . . *N'était mon rhumatisme* . . ., were it not for my rheumatism, but for my rheumatism . . . . (*d*) (Impers. uses) (i) *Il est midi*, it is twelve o'clock. *Il est vrai que* . ., it is true that. . . . *Il est de mon devoir de + inf.*, it is my duty to + *inf.* *Comme si de rien n'était*, as if nothing had happened. *Abs. Trois chemises à quinze francs,*

soit 45 fr., three shirts at fifteen francs, that is 45 fr. *S.a.* SOIT, TANT 1. **Soit dit sans offense, be** it said without offence. (ii) *Il est un Dieu*, there is a God. *Il était une fois une fée*, there was once upon·a time a fairy. *Un héros*, *s'il en fut jamais*, a hero, if ever there was one. (*e*) (With indeterminate *en*) (i) *Où en sommes-nous?* how far have we got? *Nous en sommes à la page 10*, we have got to, have reached, page 10. *Il en est à mendier son pain*, he has come down to begging. (ii) *J'en suis pour mon argent*, I've spent my money to no purpose. *J'en suis pour mille francs*, I am the poorer by a thousand francs. (iii) *J'en suis pour ce que j'ai dit*, I stick to what I said. (iv) *J'en suis!* I'm game! I'm on! (v) *C'en est trop!* this is past bearing, beyond words! *C'en est assez!* enough! (vi) (Impers.) *Il en est de l'homme comme de la Nature*, it is' with man as with Nature. *Il n'en est rien!* nothing of the kind! (vii) *Il en est qui disent que* . . ., there are some, those, who say that. . . . **3.** (*a*) *Être à qn*, to belong to s.o. *A qui sont ces livres?* whose books are these? *Je suis à vous dans un moment*, I shall be at your service in a moment. (*b*) *C'est à vous de jouer*, it is your turn to play. *C'est à nous de mener l'affaire à bien*, it rests with us to see the business through. **4.** (Aux. use) (*a*) (With intr. vbs. denoting change of place or state, etc.) *Il est arrivé*, he has arrived. *Il est arrivé hier*, he arrived yesterday. (*b*) (With pronominal verbs) *Nous nous sommes trompés*, we (have) made a mistake. *Elle s'est fait mal*, she (has) hurt herself. **5.** (As aux. of the passive voice) *Il fut puni par son père*, he was punished by his father. *Il est aimé de tout le monde*, he is beloved by everyone. *J'entends être obéi*, I mean to be obeyed. **6.** *F:* (*a*) = ALLER (in compound tenses and in *p.h.*) *J'avais été à Paris*, I had been to Paris. *J'ai été voir Jones*, I've been, I went, to see Jones. *On a été jusqu'à prétendre que* . . ., people have gone so far as to claim that. . . (*b*) = S'EN ALLER (in *p.h.* only) *Il s'en fut ouvrir la porte*, he went off to open the door.

II. **être,** *s.m.* **1.** Being, existence. **Lettres encore en être**, letters still in existence. **2.** Being, nature. *L'être véritable des choses*, the true nature of things. **3.** Being, individual. **L'Etre suprême,** the Supreme Being. *Un être humain*, a human being. *Pauvres petits êtres!* poor little creatures! poor little things!

étréc/ir [etresi:r], *v.tr.* To narrow (street, etc.). *É. une robe*, (i) to take in, (ii) to shrink, a dress. *s.m.* -**issement.**

s'étrécir. 1. To become narrower; to narrow; to contract. **2.** (Of material) To shrink.

étreign-ant, -is, -ons, etc. See ÉTREINDRE.

étreindre [etrɛ̃:dr], *v.tr.* (*pr.p.* étreignant; *p.p.* étreint; *pr.ind.* j'étreins, il étreint, n. étreignons; *p.h.* j'étreignis; *fu.* j'étreindrai) **1.** To embrace, hug; to clasp. *É. qch. dans la main*, to grasp, grip, sth. *É. la main de qn*, to wring s.o.'s hand. *L'émotion qui m'étreint*, the emotion that wrings my heart. *Prov:* **Qui trop embrasse mal étreint,** grasp all, lose all. **2.** To fetter, impede (thought).

étreinte [etrɛ̃:t], *s.f.* **1.** (*a*) Embrace, hug. (*b*) Grasp, grip. (*c*) *Wr:* Lock. **2.** *Sous l'é. de la misère*, under the pressure of want.

étrenne [etrɛn], *s.f.* **1.** Usu. *pl.* New-Year's gift. **2.** Handsel. **Avoir l'étrenne de qch.,** to have the first use of sth.

étrenner [etrɛne], *v.tr.* **1.** To be the first to buy from (shopkeeper). **2.** To handsel, *F:* to christen (object); to wear (dress) for the first time.

êtres [ɛ:tr], *s.m.pl.* = AÎTRES.

étrésillon [etrezijɔ̃], *s.m.* Prop, strut, brace.
étrésillonn|er [etrezijɔne], *v.tr.* To prop; to shore (across); to strut, brace (wall, trench). *s.m.* **-ement.**
étrier [etrie], *s.m.* **1.** (*a*) Stirrup. **Vider les étriers,** (i) to lose one's stirrups; (ii) to be unhorsed. **A franc étrier,** at full gallop. **Le coup de l'étrier,** the stirrup-cup. (*b*) *pl.* Climbing-irons. **2.** *Anat:* Stirrup-bone (of ear). **3.** *Tchn:* Stirrup-piece; clip, yoke. *Tp:* É. *du récepteur,* receiver rest.
étrille [etriːj], *s.f.* Curry-comb.
étrill|er [etrije], *v.tr.* **1.** To curry(-comb) (horse). **2.** *P:* To thrash, trounce, drub (s.o.); *F:* to tan (s.o.'s) hide. *s.m.* **-age.**
étrip|er [etripe], *v.tr.* To gut (fish); to draw (chicken); to disembowel (horse). *s.m.* **-age.**
étriqué [etrike], *a.* Skimpy, tight (coat, etc.). *Position étriquée,* cramped position.
étrivière [etrivjeːr], *s.f.* Stirrup-leather. *A:* **Donner les étrivières à qn.** to thrash, strap, s.o.; to give s.o. a belting.
étroit [etrwa], *a.* **1.** Narrow (space, ribbon, etc.); confined (space). *La voie étroite,* the strait way, the narrow way. *Esprit é.,* narrow mind. **2.** Tight, close (knot, bond, etc.); tight(-fitting) (coat, etc.). *Dans le sens le plus é. du mot,* in the strictest sense of the word. **3.** *Adv.phr.* **Être à l'étroit,** (i) to be cramped for room; (ii) to be in straitened circumstances. *adv.* **-ement.**
étroitesse [etrwates], *s.f.* **1.** Narrowness. *É. d'esprit,* narrow-mindedness. **2.** Tightness, closeness (of bond, etc.).
étrusque [etrysk], *a. & s.* Etruscan.
étude [etyd], *s.f.* **1.** (*a*) Study. *L'é. des langues,* the study of languages. **Faire ses études à . . .,** to be educated at. . . . **Programme d'études,** curriculum. *Sch:* **L'étude du soir,** evening preparation; *F:* evening prep. S.a. MAÎTRE 1. **Pièce à l'étude,** play in, under, rehearsal. **Mettre une pièce à l'étude,** to put a play in rehearsal. **Faire son étude de qch., mettre son étude à qch.,** to make sth. one's study. **Cela sent l'étude,** it smells of midnight oil. (*b*) Research, investigation. *Civ.E:* Survey. **Bureau d'études,** research department. **Faire les études d'un chemin de fer,** to survey a railway. **Mettre une question à l'étude,** to go into, to examine, a question. **2.** *Mus:* É. *pour le violon,* violin study. *Art:* É. *de tête,* study of a head. **3.** (*a*) Office (of notary, solicitor); chambers (of advocate). (*b*) (Lawyer's) practice.
étudiant, -ante [etydjã, -ãːt], *s.* Student; undergraduate. É. *en médecine,* medical student. É. *de première année,* freshman.
étudier [etydje], *v.tr.* (*a*) To study. *Sch:* To prepare, con over (lessons); to read (law, medicine). (*b*) To investigate, go into, *F:* look into (question); to make a study of (a case).
     s'étudier *à faire qch.,* to endeavour to do sth.; to make a point of doing sth. *Il s'étudiait à m'éviter,* he studiously avoided me.
étudié, *a.* Studied (calm); elaborate, deliberate (effect); set (speech). *Manières étudiées,* artificial, affected, manners.
étui [etɥi], *s.m.* Case, box, cover. É. *de cartouche,* cartridge-case. É. *à lunettes,* spectacle-case. É. *à cigares,* cigar-case.
étuve [etyːv], *s.f.* **1.** Sweating-room (of baths). É. *humide,* vapour-bath. **2.** *Ch: Ind:* (*a*) Drying-room. (*b*) Drying cupboard. É. *à linge,* hot (linen) press.
étuv|er [etyve], *v.tr.* **1.** *Ind: etc:* To dry; to

heat; to stove, bake (contaminated clothing). **2.** To stew; to steam (potatoes). *s.m.* **-age.**
étymologie [etimɔlɔʒi], *s.f.* Etymology.
étymologique [etimɔlɔʒik], *a.* Etymological.
étymologiste [etimɔlɔʒist], *s. m. & f.* Etymologist.
eu, -e [y]. See AVOIR.
eucalyptus [økaliptyːs], *s.m.* Eucalyptus; gum-tree. *Essence d'e.,* eucalyptus oil.
eucharistie (**l'**) [løkaristi], *s.f. Ecc:* The eucharist; the Lord's Supper.
eucharistique [økaristik], *a.* Eucharistic(al).
euh [ø], *int.* (Expressing surprise, incredulity). Hm !
eûmes [ym]. See AVOIR.
eunuque [ønyk], *s.m.* Eunuch.
euphémique [øfemik], *a.* Euphemistic.
euphémisme [øfemism], *s.m.* Euphemism.
euphonie [øfɔni], *s.f.* Euphony.
euphonique [øfɔnik], *a.* Euphonic, euphonious.
euphorbe [øfɔrb], *s.f. Bot:* Euphorbia, spurge.
euphorie [øfɔri], *s.f.* Well-being.
eurent [yːr]. See AVOIR.
Europe [ørɔp]. *Pr.n.f.* Europe.
européen, -enne [ørɔpeẽ, -ɛn], *a. & s.* European.
eurythmie [øritmi], *s.f.* Eurhythmy. *E. d'un passage,* happy rhythm, swing, of a passage.
eurythmique [øritmik], *a.* Eurhythmic.
euss-e, -es, etc. [ys]. See AVOIR.
Eustache [østaʃ]. **1.** *Pr.n.m.* Eustace. S.a. TROMPE 3. **2.** *s.m. F:* Clasp-knife.
eut [y], **eûtes** [yt]. See AVOIR.
euthanasie [øtanazi], *s.f.* Euthanasia.
eux [ø]. See LUI².
évacuable [evakɥabl], *a. Mil:* (Of wounded man) Fit to be moved.
évacuation [evakɥasjɔ̃], *s.f.* **1.** Evacuation, voiding (of matter from the body, etc.); draining off (of water); eduction (of steam). *I.C.E:* Exhaust-stroke. **2.** (*a*) Removal, clearing out. *Mil:* Evacuation, withdrawal (of troops, wounded men). *Hôpital d'é.,* clearing hospital. *Centre d'é.,* casualty clearing station. (*b*) Vacating (of apartment, etc.); evacuation (of fortress). **3.** *Med:* Evacuated matter; evacuation.
évacuer [evakɥe], *v.tr.* **1.** To evacuate, void (matter from the body, etc.); to drain (off) (water). É. *l'eau d'une chaudière,* to empty, blow out, a boiler. **2.** To evacuate, withdraw (troops, wounded, etc.). **3.** To vacate (apartment, etc.); to evacuate (fortress). *Nau:* É. *le bâtiment,* to abandon ship.
évader (s') [sevade], *v.pr.* To escape (by stealth); to run away. *S'é. de prison,* to escape from prison; to break gaol.
évadé, -ée, *a. & s.* Escaped (prisoner).
évaluateur [evalɥatœːr], *s.m.* Valuer, appraiser.
évaluation [evalɥasjɔ̃], *s.f.* Valuation, appraisement (of property, etc.); assessment (of damages); estimate (of weight, etc.). *Typ:* Cast(ing) off (of MS.).
évalu|er [evalɥe], *v.tr.* To value, appraise (property, etc.); to assess (damages); to estimate, reckon (weight, number). *a.* **-able.**
évangélique [evãʒelik], *a.* **1.** *Ecc:* Evangelic; according to the Gospel. **2.** Evangelical, protestant (Church, etc.).
évangélisateur [evãʒelizatœːr], *s.m.* Evangelizer.
évangéliser [evãʒelize], *v.tr.* To evangelize.
évangéliste [evãʒelist], *s.m.* Evangelist.
évangile [evãʒil], *s.m.* Gospel. *F:* **Prendre qch. pour parole d'Évangile,** to take sth. for gospel (truth). *Côté de l'é.,* north side, gospel-side (of altar).

évanouir (s') [sevanwi:r], *v.pr.* **1.** To vanish, disappear; to die away. **2.** To faint, swoon. **Tomber évanoui,** to fall down in a faint, in a swoon.

évanouissement [evanwismã], *s.m.* **1.** Vanishing, disappearance (of ghost, hopes, etc.); dying away (of sound). *W.Tel:* Fading. **2.** Faint(ing fit); swoon.

évaporateur [evapɔratœ:r], *s.m. Ch.: Ind:* Evaporator.

évaporation [evapɔrasjɔ̃], *s.f.* **1.** Evaporation. **2.** *F:* Frivolousness, flightiness.

évaporer [evapɔre], *v.tr. A:* To evaporate (liquids). **Évaporer sa bile,** to vent one's spleen.
  s'évaporer. 1. To evaporate. **Faire évaporer un liquide,** to evaporate, dry off, a liquid. **2.** *F:* To grow frivolous.
  évaporé, -ée, *a. F:* Feather-brained, flighty, irresponsible. *s. C'est une évaporée,* she is a harum-scarum.

évasement [evɑzmã], *s.m.* **1.** Widening out, splaying. **2.** Bell-mouth (of vessel, pipe); flare (of skirt); splay.

évaser [evɑze], *v.tr.* To widen (out) the opening of (vessel); to open out (pipe); to flare (skirt).
  s'évaser, to widen out at the mouth. *Dressm:* To flare (out).
  évasé, *a.* Bell-mouthed, wide-mouthed (pipe, etc.); flared (skirt, etc.); splayed (opening).

évas|if, -ive [evazif, -i:v], *a.* Evasive. *adv.* **-ivement.**

évasion [evazjɔ̃], *s.f.* **1.** Escape (from prison, etc.). *É. de capitaux,* exodus of capital. **2.** Quibble, evasion.

évasure [evazy:r], *s.f.* Bell-mouthed or funnel-shaped opening; splay.

Ève [ɛːv]. *Pr.n.f.* Eva. *B.Lit:* Eve. *F:* **Je ne le connais ni d'Ève ni d'Adam,** I don't know him from Adam.

évêché [eveʃe], *s.m.* **1.** Bishopric, diocese, see. **2.** Bishop's palace.

éveil [evɛːj], *s.m.* **1.** (*a*) Awakening. (*b*) Wide-awake state; state of alertness. **Être en éveil,** to be wide-awake; to be on the alert. *Tenir qn en é.,* to keep s.o. on the alert. **2.** Warning (*contre,* against). **Donner l'éveil,** to raise the alarm. **Donner l'éveil à qn,** to warn s.o.; to put s.o. on his guard.

éveiller [evɛje], *v.tr.* To awake(n); to wake (s.o.) up. *É. l'envie,* to arouse envy.
  s'éveiller, to awake(n), to wake (up). *Il s'éveilla en sursaut,* he woke with a start.
  éveillé, *a.* **1.** Awake. *Tenir qn é.,* to keep s.o. awake. *É. ou endormi,* waking or sleeping. **2.** Wide-awake, alert. *Cerveau é.,* active brain.
  éveillée, *s.f. F: Quelle é.!* what an awakening!

événement [evɛnmã], *s.m.* Event. **1.** (*a*) *A:* Issue, outcome. (Still so used in) **Dans l'événement,** en l'événement, as things turned out. (*b*) *Th:* Climax. **2.** Occurrence, incident. **Faire événement,** to cause quite a stir. **En cas d'événement,** in case of emergency. **A tout événement,** in order to provide against emergencies.

évent [evã], *s.m.* **1.** Fresh air. **Mettre qch. à l'évent,** to air sth. *F:* **C'est une tête à l'évent,** she is a feather-brain. **2.** Mustiness (of food); flatness (of beverage). **Sentir l'évent,** to smell stale, musty. **3.** (*a*) *Z:* Blow-hole, spout (of whale). (*b*) *Tchn:* Vent-(hole). S.a. TUYAU I.

éventail [evãta:j], *s.m.* Fan. **En éventail,** fan-shaped, fan-wise. **Fenêtre en éventail,** fan-light.

éventaire [evãtɛːr], *s.m.* (Hawker's) flat basket or tray.

évent|er [evãte], *v.tr.* **1.** (*a*) To air; to expose (grain, etc.) to the air. (*b*) *Mil: A: É. une mine, la mèche,* to lay bare a mine, the match. *F:* **Éventer la mèche,** (i) to divulge the secret, to let the cat out of the bag; (ii) (by confusion with 3 (*b*)) to discover the secret. **2.** To fan. **3.** (*a*) (Of hounds) To scent, get the scent of (game). (*b*) *F:* To get wind of (sth.). *s.m.* **-age.**
  s'éventer, (of food, etc.) to spoil (from exposure to the air); (of beverage) to go flat, stale.
  éventé, *a.* (*a*) Stale, musty (food, etc.); flat (beer, etc.). (*b*) *F:* Hare-brained, harum-scarum.

éventrer [evãtre], *v.tr.* To disembowel, eviscerate (animal); to gut (fish); to rip open, tear open (parcel, envelope); to break open, smash open (cask, box, etc.).

éventualité [evãtɥalite], *s.f.* Possibility, contingency, eventuality.

éventuel, -elle [evãtɥɛl]. **1.** *a.* (*a*) Possible, contingent. **A titre éventuel,** as a possible event. **Sortie éventuelle,** emergency-exit. (*b*) Eventual (profits, etc.). **2.** *s.m.* Eventuality, contingency.

éventuellement [evãtɥɛlmã], *adv.* Possibly, contingently; should the occasion arise; on occasion.

évêque [evɛːk], *s.m.* Bishop.

évertuer (s') [severtɥe], *v.pr.* To do one's utmost; to exert oneself. *S'é. à, pour, faire qch.,* to do one's utmost to achieve sth.

éviction [eviksjɔ̃], *s.f.* Eviction.

évidement [evidmã], *s.m.* **1.** = ÉVIDAGE. **2.** Hollow, groove, slot, cavity.

évidemment [evidamã], *adv.* **1.** Evidently, obviously. **2.** Certainly; of course.

évidence [evidã:s], *s.f.* (*a*) Obviousness, manifestness, clearness (of fact). **Se rendre à l'évidence,** to bow to the facts. **Comment nier l'évidence même?** how can we deny obvious, patent, facts? **Il est de toute évidence que . . .,** it is obvious that. . . . (*b*) Conspicuousness. **Être en évidence,** to be in a conspicuous, prominent, position. **Mettre des marchandises en évidence,** display, show off, goods.

évident [evidã], *a.* Evident, obvious, plain. **C'est évident,** that stands to reason. **Il est évident que . . .,** it stands to reason that . . .

évid|er [evide], *v.tr.* **1.** To hollow out, scoop out. **2.** To groove, channel (needle, etc.). **3.** To cut away, slope out (neck of dress). **4.** To pink (leather). [VIDE] *s.m.* **-age.**
  s'évider, to form a cavity.
  évidé, *a.* **1.** Hollow; hollow-ground (razor); gaunt (face). **2.** Grooved. **3.** Cut away.

évier [evje], *s.m.* (Scullery) sink.

évinc|er [evɛ̃se], *v.tr.* (j'évinçai(s); n. évinçons) **1.** *Jur:* To evict, eject, *F:* turn out (tenant). **2.** To oust, supplant (s.o.). *s.m.* **-ement.**

éviscérer [evisere], *v.tr.* (j'éviscère: j'éviscérerai) To eviscerate, disembowel.

évitable [evitabl], *a.* Avoidable.

évitage [evita:ʒ], *s.m.,* **évitée** [evite], *s.f. Nau:* **1.** Swinging (of ship); **2** Room to swing; searoom; width of channel.

évitement [evitmã], *s.m.* **1.** Shunning (of s.o., sth.). **2.** (*a*) *Rail:* Shunting (of train). **Gare d'évitement,** siding. (*b*) **Route d'évitement,** by-pass road. **3.** Passing-place; loop.

éviter [evite]. **1.** *v.tr.* (*a*) To avoid, shun; to give (s.o.) a wide berth; to keep out of (s.o.'s) way; to keep clear of (s.o.). *É. un danger,* to evade a danger. *É. un coup,* to dodge a blow. *É. de la tête,* to duck. *É. de faire qch.,* to avoid doing sth. *Évitez qu'on ne vous voie,* avoid being seen. (*b*) *F:* (= ÉPARGNER) *É. une peine à qn,* to spare s.o. trouble. **2.** *v.i. Nau :* (Of ship) *É. sur l'ancre,* to swing at anchor.

évocable [evɔkabl], *a.* Evocable (spirit, memory, etc.). *Jur :* **Cause évocable,** case that may be summoned, evoked, to a higher court.

évocateur, -trice [evɔkatœːr, -tris], *a.* Evocative *(de,* of).

évocation [evɔkasjɔ̃], *s.f.* (*a*) Evocation ; calling forth, conjuring up, raising (of spirits, etc.). (*b*) Conjuring up, calling up (of the past).

évocatoire [evɔkatwaːr], *a.* Evocatory.

évoluer [evɔlɥe], *v.i.* **I.** (Of ship, troops, etc.) To perform evolutions ; to manœuvre. **2.** (Of wheel, etc.) To revolve, go round. **3.** To evolve, develop. *Biol : etc :* To advance.

évolution [evɔlysjɔ̃], *s.f.* **I.** *Mil : Nau :* Evolution, manœuvre. *Évolutions tactiques,* tactical exercises. **2.** *Biol :* Evolution ; development.

évolutionniste [evɔlysjɔnist]. *Biol : etc :* **I.** *a.* Evolutionistic. **2.** *s. m. & f.* Evolutionist.

évoquer [evɔke], *v.tr.* (*a*) To evoke, call forth, conjure up, raise (spirit). (*b*) To call to mind, conjure up (memory).

exact [ɛgzakt], *a.* Exact. (*a*) Accurate, correct (calculation, etc.). *Les sciences exactes,* the exact sciences. *L'heure exacte,* the right, correct, time. *E. à un millimètre près,* correct to a millimetre. *C'est exact,* it is quite true. (*b*) Strict, rigorous (diet, etc.) ; close (copy). (*c*) Punctual. *Être e. au bureau,* to be punctual at the office. *E. à payer son loyer,* punctual in paying his rent. *adv.* **-ement.**

exacteur [ɛgzaktœːr], *s.m.* **I.** Exactor (of what is due). **2.** (*a*) Extorter (*de,* of). (*b*) Extortioner.

exaction [ɛgzaksjɔ̃], *s.f.* **I.** Exaction (of tax, etc.). **2.** Extortion.

exactitude [ɛgzaktityd], *s.f.* (*a*) Exactness, exactitude, correctness, accuracy. (*b*) Punctuality. *Avec e.,* (i) accurately, (ii) punctually.

ex æquo [ɛgzeko], *Lt.adj.phr.* Of equal merit. *Premier prix ex æquo,* first prize divided. *Être troisième ex æquo,* to tie for third place.

exagérateur, -trice [ɛgzaʒeratœːr, -tris]. *s.* Exaggerator.

exagération [ɛgzaʒerasjɔ̃], *s.f.* Exaggeration ; overstatement.

exagérer [ɛgzaʒere], *v.tr.* (**j'exagère ; j'exagérerai**) To exaggerate, magnify (danger) ; to overstate (truth) ; to over-estimate, overrate (qualities).

exaltant [ɛgzaltɑ̃], *a.* Exciting, stirring.

exaltation [ɛgzaltasjɔ̃], *s.f.* **I.** (*a*) Exaltation (of the Cross). (*b*) Exalting, glorifying, extolling (of virtue, etc.). **2.** (*a*) Exaltation ; rapturous emotion ; excitement. (*b*) *Med :* Overexcitement.

exalter [ɛgzalte], *v.tr.* **I.** To exalt, magnify, extol. **2.** To excite, inflame (courage, imagination). **3.** To exalt, dignify, ennoble.
　　s'exalter, to grow enthusiastic ; to enthuse.
exalté, -ée. I. *a.* (*a*) Impassioned (speech, etc.). (*b*) Hot-headed ; quixotic (person). (*c*) Uplifted (state of mind). **2.** *s.* Excitable person ; hot-head, fanatic.

examen [ɛgzamɛ̃], *s.m.* Examination. (*a*) Investigation ; overhauling (of machine). *Après un e. attentif de l'horizon,* after a careful scrutiny of the horizon. *E. de la vue,* sight-testing. **Question à l'examen,** matter under examination, under consideration. **Examen de conscience,** self-examination. (*b*) *Sch :* **Être reçu, refusé, à un e.,** to pass, fail in, an examination. *E. de passage,* end-of-year examination. *E. pour permis de conduire,* driving-test. **Jury d'examen,** examining body ; **the examiners.**

examinateur, -trice [ɛgzaminatœːr, -tris], *s.* (*a*) *Ind :* Inspector. (*b*) *Sch :* Examiner.

examiner [ɛgzamine], *v.tr.* To examine. (*a*) To investigate, inspect, scrutinize. *E. une machine, un malade,* to overhaul a machine, a patient. *E. attentivement l'horizon,* to scan, survey, the horizon. *E. les comptes,* to go through the accounts. (*b*) *Sch :* *E. qn en algèbre,* to examine s.o. in algebra.
　　s'examiner, to examine one's conscience.

exanthème [ɛgzɑ̃tɛm], *s.m. Med :* Exanthema, rash.

exaspération [ɛgzasperasjɔ̃], *s.f.* **I.** Aggravation (of pain, etc.). **2.** Exasperation, irritation.

exaspérer [ɛgzaspere], *v.t.* (**j'exaspère ; j'exaspérerai**) **I.** To aggravate, exacerbate (pain). **2.** To exasperate, irritate ; to provoke (s.o.) beyond measure.
　　s'exaspérer, (of pers.) to lose all patience.

exau|cer [ɛgzose], *v.tr.* (**j'exauçai(s) ; n. exauçons**) (Of the Deity) **I.** *E. qn,* to grant, give ear to, answer, the prayer of s.o. **2.** To fulfil (wish, desire). *s.m.* **-ement.**

excavateur [ɛkskavatœːr], *s.m. Civ.E :* Digging machine ; (steam-)navvy, excavator.

excavation [ɛkskavasjɔ̃], *s.f.* **I.** Excavation, digging (out) (of channel, etc.). **2.** Excavation, hollow, pit.

excaver [ɛkskave], *v.tr.* To excavate, to dig out.

excédant [ɛksedɑ̃], *a.* **I.** Surplus (sum, etc.) ; excess(ive) (luggage, etc.). **2.** Tiresome (visitor) ; overpowering (smell).

excédent [ɛksedɑ̃], *s.m.* Excess, surplus. **Somme en excédent,** sum in excess. *E. de poids,* overweight. *E. de bagages,* excess luggage.

excéder [ɛksede], *v.tr.* (**j'excède ; j'excéderai**) **I.** To exceed, go beyond (a certain limit). *E. ses pouvoirs,* to exceed one's powers. **2.** (*a*) To tire (s.o.) out ; to wear (s.o.) out ; to overwork (horse). *Excédé de fatigue,* worn out ; fagged out. (*b*) To overtax (s.o.'s) patience. *J'étais excédé,* I was out of all patience.

excellence [ɛkselɑ̃ːs], *s.f.* **I.** Excellence, pre-eminence. **Par excellence,** (i) pre-eminently ; (ii) supremely, above all. **2. Votre Excellence,** your Excellency.

excell|ent [ɛkselɑ̃], *a.* Excellent ; *F :* first-rate, A1. *adv.* **-emment.**

exceller [ɛksele], *v.i.* To excel (*à faire qch.,* in doing sth.).

excentr|er [ɛksɑ̃tre], *v.tr. Mec.E :* To throw off centre ; to offset. *s.m.* **-ement.**
　　excentré, *a.* Eccentric (shaft, etc.).

excentricité [ɛksɑ̃trisite], *s.f.* **I.** *a.* (*a*) Eccentricity (of orbit, etc.). *Mec.E :* Throw (of eccentric). (*b*) Remoteness (of suburb, etc.). **2.** Eccentricity, oddity (of manner).

excentrique [ɛksɑ̃trik]. **I.** *a.* (*a*) Eccentric (orbit, etc.). (*b*) Remote, outlying (suburb, etc.). (*c*) Eccentric, odd, whimsical (person). **2.** *s.* Odd, queer eccentric, fellow, etc. **3.** *s.m. Mec.E :* (*a*) Eccentric (gear). (*b*) Cam. *adv.* **-ment.**

excepter [ɛksepte], *v.tr.* To except, exclude (s.o., sth.) (*de,* from). *Personne, elle exceptée, n'a rien entendu,* no one but she, save her, heard anything.
　　excepté, *prep.* Except(ing), but, save. *Personne e. lui,* none but he, save him. *Conj.phr.* **Excepté que + ind.,** except that . . ., but that. . . .

exception [ɛksɛpsjɔ̃], *s.f.* **I.** Exception. **Faire une exception à une règle,** to make an exception to a rule. **Faire exception à une règle,** to be an exception to a rule. *Tous sans e. refusèrent,* they one and all declined. **Sauf exception,** with certain exceptions. **A quelques exceptions près,** with a few exceptions. **A titre d'exception,** by way of an exception. **A l'exception de . . .,** exception faite de . . ., except . . ., save . . ., with the exception of. . . . **2.** (a) *Jur:* Exception; incidental plea (of defence). (b) *Question résolue sans soulever la moindre e.,* question solved without anyone taking exception to the decision, without any protest being raised.

exceptionn|el, -elle [eksɛpsjɔnɛl], a. Exceptional; out of the ordinary. adv. **-ellement.**

excès [eksɛ], s.m. (a) Excess. *E. des dépenses sur les recettes,* excess of expenditure over revenue. *E. d'huile,* too much oil. **Pécher par excès de zèle,** to be over-zealous. *Phot:* E. de pose, over-exposure. **(Jusqu')à l'excès,** to excess. *Scrupuleux à l'e.,* scrupulous to a fault; over-scrupulous. *Consciencieux à l'e.,* hyper-conscientious. (b) pl. Commettre des excès, to commit excesses; to be intemperate. (c) *Jur:* E. de pouvoir, action *ultra vires.* *Révoqué pour e.* de pouvoir, recalled for exceeding his powers.

excess|if, -ive [eksɛsif, -i:v], a. Excessive, extreme; undue (optimism, etc.); exorbitant (price); immoderate (eating); inordinate (pride); exaggerated. adv. **-ivement.**

exciser [eksize], v.tr. *Surg:* To excise, cut out.

excision [eksizjɔ̃], s.f. Excision, cutting out.

excitabilité [eksitabilite], s.f. Excitability.

excitable [eksitabl], a. Excitable.

excitant [eksitɑ̃]. **1.** a. Exciting, stimulating. **2.** s.m. *Med:* Excitant, stimulant.

excitateur, -trice [eksitatœ:r, -tris]. **1,** a. Exciting (cause, etc.); provocative (de, of). **2.** s. Exciter, instigator (de, of).

excitation [eksitasjɔ̃], s.f. **1.** Excitation (of the senses, etc.). *E. à la révolte,* instigation, incitement, to rebellion. **2.** (State of) excitement (of a nerve, etc.). **3.** *El:* Excitation.

exciter [eksite], v.tr. To excite. (a) To arouse, stir up (envy, etc.). *E. la pitié de qn,* to move s.o. to pity. (b) To animate, inflame. *E. qn à la révolte, à se révolter,* to incite s.o. to revolt. *E. qn contre qn,* to set s.o. against s.o. (c) To stimulate (thirst, etc.).

s'exciter, to get excited, worked up.

exclamatif, -ive [eksklamatif, -i:v], a. Exclamative, exclamatory.

exclamation [eksklamasjɔ̃], s.f. Exclamation. *Gram:* **Point d'exclamation,** exclamation mark.

exclamer (s') [eksklame], v.pr. (a) To exclaim. (b) To protest loudly.

exclure [ekskly:r], v.tr. (pr.p. excluant; p.p. exclu; pr.ind. j'exclus, n. excluons; p.d. j'excluais; p.h. j'exclus; fu. j'exclurai) (a) To exclude, shut out, leave out. (b) *Deux qualités qui s'excluent,* two qualities that are incompatible, that are mutually exclusive.

exclus|if, -ive [eksklyzif, -i:v], a. Exclusive, sole (right, etc.). *Com: Article e.,* exclusive article; speciality. adv. **-ivement.**

exclusion [eksklyzjɔ̃], s.f. Exclusion, excluding, debarring (de, from). *A l'exclusion de . . .,* excluding . . ., exclusive of . . ., to the exclusion of. . . .

exclusivité [eksklyzivite], s.f. **1.** Exclusiveness. **2.** Sole rights. Film en exclusivité, exclusive film.

excommunication [ekskɔmynikasjɔ̃], s.f. Excommunication.

excommunier [ekskɔmynje], v.tr. To excommunicate.

excoriation [ekskɔrjasjɔ̃], s.f. Excoriation.

excorier [ekskɔrje], v.tr. To excoriate; to peel off (the skin). **s'excorier,** (of the skin) to peel (off).

excrément [ekskremɑ̃], s.m. *Physiol:* Excrement.

excréter [ekskrete], v.tr. (j'excrète; j'excréterai) *Physiol:* To excrete.

excréteur, -trice [ekskretœ:r, -tris], a. *Physiol:* Excretive; excretory (duct, etc.).

excrétion [ekskresjɔ̃], s.f. *Physiol:* Excretion.

excroissance [ekskrwasɑ̃:s], s.f. Excrescence.

excursion [ekskyrsjɔ̃], s.f. **1.** Excursion; (i) tour, trip; (ii) jaunt, outing. *E. à pied,* walking tour; *F:* hike. *Faire une e. en Belgique,* to go on a trip to Belgium; to go on a tour through Belgium. *Rail:* **Billet d'excursion,** excursion ticket. **2.** *Mil:* Raid; inroad (dans, on). **3.** *F:* Digression, excursion (in speech, etc.).

excursionniste [ekskyrsjɔnist], s.m. & f. Excursionist, tourist, tripper.

excusabilité [ekskyzabilite], s.f. Excusableness, excusability.

excusable [ekskyzabl], a. Excusable, pardonable. adv. **-ment.**

excuse [ekskyːz], s.f. **1.** Excuse. **Il n'y a rien à dire à son excuse,** there is nothing to be said in excuse for him. *F:* **Faites excuse!** pardon me! **2.** pl. Apology. **Faire, présenter, ses excuses à qn,** to make one's apologies, to apologize, to s.o.

excuser [ekskyze], v.tr. **1.** To make excuses, to apologize, for (s.o.). **2.** To excuse, pardon (s.o.). *E. qn de faire qch.,* to excuse s.o. (i) for doing sth., (ii) from doing sth.

s'excuser, to excuse oneself; to apologize. *S'e. auprès de qn,* (i) to make one's apologies to s.o.; (ii) to send excuses for not coming. *S'e. de faire qch.,* (i) to apologize for doing sth.; (ii) to excuse oneself from doing sth. *S'e. sur sa jeunesse,* to plead the inexperience of youth. *S'e. sur sa tenue,* to apologize for one's attire. **Se faire excuser,** to decline; *F:* to cry off. *Prov:* **Qui s'excuse s'accuse,** excuses always proceed from a guilty conscience.

exeat [egzeat], s.m. *Ecc: Sch:* Exeat.

exécrable [egzɛkrabl], a. Execrable; abominable; extremely bad (taste, verse, etc.); loathsome (crime). adv. **-ment.**

exécration [egzɛkrasjɔ̃], s.f. Execration, detestation. **Avoir qn en exécration,** to hold s.o. in execration; to loathe s.o.

exécrer [egzekre], v.tr. (j'exècre; j'exécrerai) To execrate, loathe, detest.

exécutable [egzekytabl], a. Practicable, feasible.

exécutant, -ante [egzekytɑ̃, -ɑ̃:t], s. *Mus:* Performer (in band, etc.); executant.

exécuter [egzekyte], v.tr. **1.** To execute; to follow out, carry out (plan); to perform, fulfil (promise); to perform, play (piece of music). **2.** (a) To execute, put to (criminal, etc.) to death. (b) *Jur:* To distrain upon (debtor). (c) *St.Exch:* To hammer (defaulter).

s'exécuter. 1. To submit, comply. **2.** To oblige (at the piano, etc.). **3.** To pay up.

exécuteur, -trice [egzekytœ:r, -tris], s. **1.** (a) Executor, performer (of undertaking). (b) *Jur:* Exécuteur, -trice, testamentaire, executor, -trix. **2.** *A:* **Exécuteur des hautes œuvres,** executioner; hangman.

exécutif, -ive [egzekytif, -i:v], a. Executive. *Le pouvoir e.,* s. l'exécutif, the Executive.

exécution [egzekysjɔ̃], s.f. **1.** Execution, performance, carrying out (of plan, orders); fulfilment (of promise); enforcement (of the law). *E. d'un opéra,* production, performance, of an opera. **Mettre une idée à exécution,** to carry an idea into effect, into execution. **Travaux en voie d'exécution,** work in progress. **2.** *(a) E. capitale,* carrying out of the death sentence ; execution. **Ordre d'exécution,** death-warrant. *(b) Jur :* Distraint, distress. *(c) St.Exch :* Hammering (of defaulter). *(d) Sp :* Suspension (of player).

exécutoire [egzekytwaːr]. *Jur :* **1.** *a. (a)* (Of decree, contract, etc.) Enforceable ; to be put in force. *(b)* Executory (formula, etc.). **2.** *s.m.* Writ of execution. *E. de dépens,* order to pay costs.

exemplaire[1] [egzɑ̃plɛːr], *a.* Exemplary. *adv.* **-ment.**

exemplaire[2], *s.m.* **1.** Exemplar, pattern. **2.** *(a)* Sample, specimen (of work). *(b)* Copy (of book, engraving, etc.).

exemple [egzɑ̃ːpl], *s.m.* Example. **1.** Donner l'exemple, to set an, the, example. Suivre l'exemple de qn, prendre exemple sur qn, to follow s.o.'s example. Prêcher d'exemple, to practise what one preaches. Joindre l'exemple au précepte, to suit the action to the word. Être un exemple de vertu, to be a model of virtue. *Prep.phr.* A l'exemple de (qn), following the example of (s.o.); after the example of (s.o.). **2.** Lesson, warning, caution. Faire un exemple de qn, to make an example of s.o. Servir d'exemple à qn, to be a lesson, a warning, to s.o. **3.** Instance, precedent. Sans exemple, unexampled ; without parallel. Par exemple . . ., for instance . . ., for example. . . . *int.* Par exemple! (i) the idea! upon my word! (ii) (Intensive) *Cela vous serait utile, mais c'est cher, par e.!* it would be useful to you but it's very expensive. *Ah non, par e.!* no indeed!

exempt, -empte [egzɑ̃, -ɑ̃ːt]. **1.** *a.* Exempt, free (*de*, from). *E. de soucis,* care-free. *Com : E. de droits,* duty-free. **2.** *s. Sp :* Player who has a bye.

exempter [egzɑ̃te], *v.tr. E. qn (de qch.)*, to exempt, free, excuse, s.o. (from sth.). *E. qn de faire qch.,* to exempt s.o. from doing sth. **s'exempter** *de faire qch.,* to abstain from, get out of, doing sth.

exemption [egzɑ̃psjɔ̃], *s.f.* Exemption (*de*, from); immunity (from service, tax, etc.); freedom (from anxiety, etc.).

exerçant [egzɛrsɑ̃], *a.* Practising (doctor, etc.).

exercer [egzɛrse], *v.tr.* (j'exerçai(s); n. exerçons) To exercise. **1.** *(a) E. son oreille,* to train one's ear. *E. qn à faire qch.,* to train s.o. to do sth. *(b) Mil :* To drill, train (soldiers). **2.** *(a)* To exert, make use of (force, etc.). *E. son influence sur qn,* to exert, exercise, one's influence on s.o. *E. une pression sur qch.,* to exert a pressure on sth. *E. ses droits,* to exercise one's rights. *(b)* (Of medicine, etc.) *E. une action sur . . .,* to have an action upon . . ., to act upon. . . . **3.** To practise, follow, pursue, carry on (profession, business); to ply (a trade). *Abs. Médecin qui n'exerce plus,* doctor no longer in practice. **s'exercer. 1.** *S'e. à qch., à faire qch.,* to practise sth., doing sth. **2.** *La pression qui s'exerce sur . . .,* the pressure exerted on. . . .

exercé, *a.* Experienced, practised (*à,* in). *Oreille exercée à saisir tous les sons,* ear attuned to every sound.

exercice [egzɛrsis], *s.m.* Exercise. **1.** *(a)* Prendre de l'exercice, to take exercise. *(b) Mil : etc :* Drill(ing), training. Être à l'exercice, to be on parade. Faire l'exercice, to drill. *(c) Exercices scolaires,* school exercises. **2.** *(a)* (Putting into) practice ; use (of power, etc.); carrying out (of mandate). Entrer en exercice, to enter upon one's duties. Dans l'exercice de ses fonctions, in the

---

exercise, discharge, of one's duties. Avocat en exercice, practising barrister. *(b) L'e. du culte,* public worship. **3.** *(a)* Financial year ; year's trading. *(b)* Balance-sheet.

exergue [egzɛrg], *s.m. Num :* Exergue. *F :* Portant en exergue . . ., bearing inscribed below. . . .

exfoliation [ɛksfɔljasjɔ̃], *s.f.* Exfoliation.

exfolier [ɛksfɔlje], *v.tr.* To exfoliate, scale (bone). **s'exfolier,** to exfoliate, scale off.

exhalaison [ɛgzalɛzɔ̃], *s.f.* Exhalation, effluvium.

exhalation [ɛgzalasjɔ̃], *s.f.* Exhalation, exhaling.

exhaler [ɛgzale], *v.tr.* To exhale, emit, give out (smell, vapour, etc.); to breathe (a sigh); to vent (one's wrath). **s'exhaler,** (of gas, smell, vapour, etc.) to exhale, to pass off into the air.

exhaussement [ɛgzosmɑ̃], *s.m.* **1.** Raising, increasing the height (of house, etc.). **2.** *E. du terrain,* rise in the ground ; mound.

exhausser [ɛgzose], *v.tr.* To raise, to increase the height of (house, etc.). **s'exhausser,** (of ground, etc.) to rise.

exhaustion [ɛgzostjɔ̃], *s.f.* Exhaust(ion) (of liquid, gas).

exhéréder [ɛgzerede], *v.tr.* (j'exhérède ; j'exhérédérai) To exheredate, disinherit.

exhiber [egzibe], *v.tr.* **1.** To present, show, produce (ticket, passport). **2.** *(a)* To exhibit, show (animals, etc.). *(b) Pej :* To show off, display (knowledge, diamonds). **s'exhiber.** *Pej :* To make an exhibition of oneself.

exhibition [egzibisjɔ̃], *s.f.* **1.** Producing, showing (of passport, etc.). **2.** Show (of cattle, etc.); exhibition (of pictures).

exhortation [ɛgzɔrtasjɔ̃], *s.f.* Exhortation (*à,* to); admonishment.

exhorter [ɛgzɔrte], *v.tr.* To exhort, urge (*à faire qch.,* to do sth.).

exhumation [ɛgzymasjɔ̃], *s.f. (a)* Exhumation, disinterment. *(b) F :* Unearthing.

exhumer [ɛgzyme], *v.tr. (a)* To exhume, disinter (body). *(b) F :* To unearth, bring to light, dig out (old documents, etc.).

exigeant [ɛgziʒɑ̃], *a.* Exacting ; hard to please.

exigence [ɛgziʒɑ̃ːs], *s.f.* **1.** Exactingness. **2.** *(a)* Unreasonable or arbitrary demand. *(b)* Exigence, exigency, demand(s), requirement(s). Selon l'exigence du cas, as may be required. *Satisfaire les exigences,* to meet requirements.

exiger [ɛgziʒe], *v.tr.* (j'exigeai(s); n. exigeons) **1.** To exact, demand, require (*de,* from); to insist upon (sth.). *Trop e. des forces de qn,* to overtax s.o.'s strength. **2.** To require, necessitate, call for (care, etc.).

exigible [ɛgziʒibl], *a.* Exigible (*de,* from); claimable ; (payment) due.

exigu, -uë [ɛgzigy], *a.* Exiguous, tiny (abode); scanty (resources); slender (income).

exiguïté [ɛgziguite], *s.f.* Exiguity (of abode, etc.); scantiness (of resources); slenderness (of income); diminutiveness (of stature).

exil [egzil], *s.m.* Exile, banishment. Envoyer qn en exil, to send s.o. into exile.

exiler [egzile], *v.tr.* To exile, banish.

exilé, -ée, *s.* Exile.

existant [egzistɑ̃], *a. (a)* Existing, living, existent. *(b)* Extant (species). *(c)* (Supplies, etc.) on hand.

existence [egzistɑ̃ːs], *s.f.* **1.** *(a)* Existence ; (state of) being. *(b)* Life. Prix de l'existence, cost of living. Moyens d'existence, means of subsistence. **2.** *pl. Com :* Stock (on hand).

exister [ɛgziste], *v.i.* (*a*) To exist, be; to have one's being; to live. (*b*) To be extant.

ex-libris [ɛkslibriːs], *s.m.* Book-plate, ex-libris.

exode [ɛgzɔd], *s.m. B.Hist: etc:* Exodus.

exonération [ɛgzɔnerasjɔ̃], *s.f.* Exoneration; exemption (from military service).

exonérer [ɛgzɔnere], *v.tr.* (j'exonère; j'exonérerai) (*a*) To exonerate (*de*, from); to free (from duty, etc.); to exempt (from military service). (*b*) To take the duty off (goods).

exorbitant [ɛgzɔrbitɑ̃], *a.* Exorbitant.

exorcisation [ɛgzɔrsizasjɔ̃], *s.f.* Exorcizing.

exorcis|er [ɛgzɔrsize], *v.tr.* To exorcize (demon, or one possessed); to cast out (devil); to lay (ghost). *s.m.* **-eur.**

exorcisme [ɛgzɔrsism], *s.m.* **1.** Exorcizing. **2.** Exorcism.

exorciste [ɛgzɔrsist], *s. m. & f.* Exorcist, exorcizer.

exorde [ɛgzɔrd], *s.m. Rh:* Exordium.

exosmose [ɛgzɔsmoːz], *s.f. Ph:* Exosmosis.

exostose [ɛgzɔstoːz], *s.f. Med: Bot:* Exostosis.

exotique [ɛgzɔtik], *a.* Exotic.

expansibilité [ɛkspɑ̃sibilite], *s.f.* **1.** *Ph:* Expansibility (of gas, etc.). **2.** *F:* Expansiveness (of disposition).

expansible [ɛkspɑ̃sibl], *a. Ph:* Expansible.

expansif, -ive [ɛkspɑ̃sif, -iːv], *a.* **1.** Expansive (force, etc.). **2.** (Of pers.) Expansive, exuberant.

expansion [ɛkspɑ̃sjɔ̃], *s.f.* **1.** Expansion. **Machine à triple expansion,** triple-expansion engine. **L'univers en expansion,** the expanding universe. **2.** *F:* Expansiveness, unreserve.

expatriation [ɛkspatriasjɔ̃], *s.f.* Expatriation.

expatrier [ɛkspatrie], *v.tr.* To expatriate.
    s'expatrier, to leave one's own country.
    expatrié, -ée, *s.* Exile.

expectant [ɛkspɛktɑ̃], *a.* Expectant (attitude, medicine, etc.); 'wait-and-see' (policy).

expectatif, -ive¹ [ɛkspɛktatif, -iːv], *a.* Expectative.

expectative², *s.f.* Expectation, expectancy (of inheritance, etc.). **Avoir qch. en expectative,** to expect sth.; to have hopes of sth. *Triste e.,* sad prospect.

expectorant [ɛkspɛktɔrɑ̃], *a. & s.m. Med:* Expectorant.

expectoration [ɛkspɛktɔrasjɔ̃], *s.f.* **1.** Expectoration. **2.** Sputum.

expectorer [ɛkspɛktɔre], *v.tr.* To expectorate.

expédient [ɛkspedjɑ̃]. **1.** *a.* Expedient. *Il est e. de . . .,* it is expedient to. . . . **2.** *s.m.* Expedient, device, shift. *Vivre d'expédients,* to live by one's wits. **Homme d'expédients,** man of resource.

expédier [ɛkspedje], *v.tr.* To dispatch. **1.** To get rid of, dispose of (s.o.); to get (s.o.) out of the way. **2.** (*a*) To expedite, hasten on (task, business). *E. son déjeuner,* to hurry through one's lunch. (*b*) *Cust:* E. des marchandises en douane, to clear goods. **3.** *Jur:* To draw up (contract, deed). **4.** To forward, send off (letter).

expéditeur, -trice [ɛkspediːtœːr, -tris], *s.* **1.** Sender (of letter, etc.). **2.** (*a*) Shipper, consigner. (*b*) Forwarding agent.

expéditif, -ive [ɛkspeditif, -iːv], *a.* Expeditious.

expédition [ɛkspedisjɔ̃], *s.f.* **1.** (*a*) Expedition, dispatch (of business, etc.). (*b*) *Cust:* Expédition en douane, clearance. **2.** (i) Copying, (ii) copy (of deed, etc.). **En double expédition,** in duplicate. **3.** (*a*) Dispatch(ing), forwarding (of parcels, etc.). **E. par mer,** shipping, shipment. **Bulletin d'expédition,** way-bill. (*b*) Consignment. **4.** Ex-

pedition (= march or voyage). *E. au pôle sud,* expedition to the South Pole.

expéditionnaire [ɛkspedisjɔnɛːr]. **1.** *s.m.* (*a*) Sender. (*b*) Forwarding agent. **2.** *a. & s.m.* (Commis) expéditionnaire, copying clerk. **3.** *a. Mil:* Expeditionary (force).

expérience [ɛksperjɑ̃ːs], *s.f.* **1.** Experience. **Avoir l'expérience de qch.,** to have experience of, in, sth. *Il a l'e. du monde,* he is a man of the world. **Faire l'expérience de qch.,** to experience sth. **Connaître qch. par expérience,** to know sth. from experience. **Sans expérience,** inexperienced (*de*, in). **2.** Experiment, test. **Faire, procéder à, une expérience,** to carry out an experiment.

expérimental, -aux [ɛksperimɑ̃tal, -o], *a.* Experimental. *Les sciences expérimentales,* the applied sciences. *adv.* **-ement.**

expérimentateur, -trice [ɛksperimɑ̃tatœːr, -tris], *s.* Experimenter.

expérimentation [ɛksperimɑ̃tasjɔ̃], *s.f.* Experimentation, experimenting.

expérimenter [ɛksperimɑ̃te], *v.tr.* To test, try (remedy, model). *Abs.* To make an experiment.
    expérimenté, *a.* Experienced; skilled.

expert [ɛkspɛːr]. **1.** *a.* Expert, skilled (*en, dans,* in); able. **2.** *s.m.* Expert; connoisseur. *Com:* Valuer, appraiser. **A dire d'experts,** according to expert advice. *adv.* **-ement.**

expert-comptable [ɛkspɛrkɔ̃tabl], *s.m.* = Chartered accountant. *pl. Des experts-comptables.*

expertise [ɛkspɛrtiːz], *s.f.* **1.** *Com:* Expert appraisement; valuation. *Nau:* E. d'avarie, damage survey. **Faire l'expertise des dégâts,** to appraise the damage. **2.** Expert's report.

expertiser [ɛkspɛrtize], *v.tr. Com:* To appraise, value. *Nau:* To survey (ship for damage).

expiable [ɛkspjabl], *a.* Expiable.

expiation [ɛkspjasjɔ̃], *s.f.* Expiation. *Theol:* Atonement.

expiatoire [ɛkspjatwaːr], *a.* Expiatory.

expier [ɛkspje], *v.tr.* To expiate, atone for, pay the penalty of (sin, etc.).

expiration [ɛkspirasjɔ̃], *s.f.* Expiration. **1.** Breathing out (of air). **2.** Expiry, termination, end (of lease, etc.).

expirer [ɛkspire], *v.* To expire. **1.** *v.tr.* To breathe out (air). **2.***v.i.* (*a*) To die. (*b*) To come to an end; (of lease) to run out. *Ce passeport expire le . . .,* the validity of this passport expires on. . . .
    expiré, *a.* At an end. *Mon congé est e.,* my leave is up.

explétif, -ive [ɛkspletif, -iːv], *a. & s.m.* Expletive.

explicable [ɛksplikabl], *a.* Explicable, explainable.

explicatif, -ive [ɛksplikatif, -iːv], *a.* Explanatory.

explication [ɛksplikasjɔ̃], *s.f.* Explanation. **Demander une explication à qn,** to call s.o. to account. **Avoir une explication avec qn,** to have it out with s.o.

explicite [ɛksplisit], *a.* Explicit, clear, plain. *adv.* **-ment.**

expliquer [ɛksplike], *v.tr.* (*a*) To explain, expound, elucidate. (*b*) To explain, account for (action, etc.). *Je ne m'explique pas pourquoi . . .,* I can't understand why. . . .
    s'expliquer, to explain oneself, one's conduct. *S'e. avec qn,* to have it out with s.o.

exploit [ɛksplwa], *s.m.* **1.** Exploit; feat (of arms, etc.); achievement; (heroic) deed. **2.** *Jur:* Writ, process, summons. *Signifier un e. à qn,* to serve a writ on s.o.

exploitable [ɛksplwatabl], *a.* **1.** Workable (quarry); paying (ore, etc.). **2.** Exploitable. (person).

exploitant [ɛksplwatɑ̃]. **1.** *a.* (*a*) *Ind:* Operating (staff, etc.). (*b*) *Jur:* Huissier exploitant, process-server. **2.** *s.m.* (*a*) Owner or operator (of mine, etc.); cultivator (of land). (*b*) *Cin:* Exhibitor.

exploitation [ɛksplwatasjɔ̃], *s.f.* **1.** Exploitation, exploiting. (*a*) Working (of mine, etc.); getting, winning (of coal); cultivation (of land). *Frais d'e.*, working expenses. (*b*) Taking (unfair) advantage (of s.o., s.o.'s ignorance); sweating (of labour). **2.** Workings; mine.

exploit|er [ɛksplwate], *v.tr.* To exploit. **1.** To work (mine, patent, etc.); to operate (railway, etc.); to get, win (coal); to cultivate (land). **2.** To take (unfair) advantage (of s.o.); to trade upon (s.o.'s ignorance). *s.* **-eur, -euse.**

explorable [ɛksplɔrabl], *a.* Explorable.

explorateur, -trice [ɛksplɔratœːr, -tris]. **1.** *s.* Explorer. **2.** *a.* Exploring, exploratory *Cin:* *Televis:* Scanning (cell, etc.).

exploratif, -ive [ɛksplɔratif, -iːv], *a.* Explorative, exploratory.

exploration [ɛksplɔrasjɔ̃], *s.f.* Exploration. *Televis:* Scanning.

explorer [ɛksplɔre], *v.tr.* (*a*) To explore (country, etc.); to probe (wound). (*b*) *E. les poches de qn*, to go through s.o.'s pockets. (*c*) *Cin:* *Televis:* To scan (sound-track, image).

exploser [ɛksploze], *v.i.* (Of boiler) To explode, to blow up; (of shell) to explode. *I.C.E:* (Of mixture) To fire, burn.

explosible [ɛksplozibl], *a.* Explosive.

explosif, -ive [ɛksplozif, -iːv]. **1.** *a.* Explosive, detonating. *El:* *Distance explosive*, sparking distance; spark-gap. **2.** *s.m.* Explosive. *Haut e., e. puissant, grand e.*, high explosive.

explosion [ɛksplozjɔ̃], *s.f.* Explosion, bursting. *Faire explosion*, to explode, blow up; (of boiler) to burst. *Moteur à explosion*, internal combustion engine. *F: E. de fureur, de rires*, outburst of fury, burst of laughter.

exponentiel, -elle [ɛksponɑ̃sjɛl]. *Mth:* **1.** *a.* Exponential. **2.** *s.f.* Exponentielle, exponential.

exportateur, -trice [ɛkspɔrtatœːr, -tris]. **1.** *s.* Exporter. **2.** *a.* Exporting.

exportation [ɛkspɔrtasjɔ̃], *s.f.* Exportation (of goods). *Les exportations*, (i) the export trade; (ii) exports.

export|er [ɛkspɔrte], *v.tr.* To export. *a.* **-able.**

exposant, -ante [ɛkspozɑ̃, -ɑ̃ːt]. **1.** *a.* (*a*) *Jur:* Petitioning. (*b*) Exhibiting. **2.** *s.* (*a*) *Jur:* Petitioner. (*b*) Exhibitor (of work of art, etc.). **3.** *s.m.* *Mth:* Exponent; (power) index.

exposer [ɛkspoze], *v.tr.* **1.** (*a*) To exhibit, show, display (goods, works of art). (*b*) To set forth, set out (plans, etc.). *Je leur ai exposé ma situation*, I explained to them how I was placed. **2.** (*a*) To expose; to lay (s.o., sth.) open (to sth.). *Après avoir été exposé au soleil . . .*, after exposure to the sun. . . . *Phot: E. le papier à la lumière*, to expose the paper (to the light). *Maison exposée au nord*, house with a north aspect, facing north. *E. sa vie*, to imperil one's life. *S'e. à des critiques*, to lay oneself open to criticism. (*b*) *Le corps fut exposé pendant deux jours*, the body lay in state for two days. **3.** (*a*) To expose, lay bare (roots, etc.). (*b*) To expose (hypocrite).

exposé. **1.** *a.* (*a*) In an exposed position; in danger, in peril. (*b*) Liable, apt (*à*, to). (*c*) Open (*à*, to). *E. à tous les vents*, open to every wind. **2.** *s.m.* Statement, account (of facts, etc.). *Faire*

un exposé complet de la situation, to give a full account of the position of affairs.

exposition [ɛkspozisjɔ̃], *s.f.* **1.** (*a*) Exhibition, show (of goods, flowers, etc.); lying in state (of body). *E. internationale*, international exhibition. *Salle d'exposition*, show-room. (*b*) Exposure (to danger, to cold). (*c*) Exposition, statement, setting forth (of facts, reasons, etc.). **2.** Aspect, exposure (of house).

expr|ès¹, -esse [ɛksprɛ, -ɛːs]. **1.** *a.* Express, distinct, explicit (order, warning, etc.). *"Défense expresse de fumer,"* 'smoking strictly prohibited.' **2.** [ɛksprɛːs], *a.* & *s.m.* Express (messenger). *Lettre à remettre par exprès*, express letter. *adv.* **-essément.**

exprès² [ɛksprɛ], *adv.* Designedly, on purpose, intentionally. *Je ne l'ai pas fait e.*, I didn't do it on purpose. *C'est comme un fait exprès!* you would think that everything was conspiring to annoy me, to thwart me!

express [ɛksprɛːs], *a.* & *s.m.* Express (train).

express|if, -ive [ɛksprɛsif, -iːv], *a.* Expressive (face, smile). *Mus:* Clavier expressif, swell-organ. *adv.* **-ivement.**

expression [ɛksprɛsjɔ̃], *s.f.* Expression. **1.** Squeezing, pressing (of juice, etc.). **2.** Utterance, voicing (of opinion, etc.); show, manifestation (of feelings). *Au delà de toute expression*, inexpressible. *Sans expression*, expressionless. S.a. BOÎTE 2. **3.** Term, phrase. *Selon l'expression de . . .*, in the words of. . . . *Expressions vives*, strong language. S.a. FAMILIER 2.

exprimable [ɛksprimabl], *a.* Expressible.

exprimer [ɛksprime], *v.tr.* To express. **1.** *E. le jus d'un citron*, to squeeze (out), press, the juice from a lemon. **2.** (*a*) To voice, give utterance to (thoughts, etc.). *E. l'espoir que . . .*, to express the hope that. . . . (*b*) (Of looks, gestures, etc.) To show, betoken (pain, etc.). *Attitude qui exprime le dédain*, attitude expressive of disdain. **s'exprimer**, to express oneself.

expropriation [ɛksprɔpriasjɔ̃], *s.f.* *Jur:* Purchase under compulsion; expropriation.

exproprier [ɛksprɔprie], *v.tr.* To expropriate ((i) proprietor, (ii) property).

expugnable [ɛkspygnabl], *a.* Pregnable (fortress).

expulser [ɛkspylse], *v.tr.* To expel; to eject (s.o.); to turn (s.o.) out; to evict (tenant); to blow out (air).

expulsif, -ive [ɛkspylsif, -iːv], *a.* Expulsive.

expulsion [ɛkspylsjɔ̃], *s.f.* Expulsion; deportation (of alien); eviction (of tenant).

expurgation [ɛkspyrgasjɔ̃], *s.f.* Expurgation; bowdlerizing (of book).

expurger [ɛkspyrʒe], *v.tr.* (j'expurgeai(s); n. expurgeons) To expurgate; to bowdlerize.

exquis [ɛkski], *a.* Exquisite. *adv.* **-ement.**

exsangue [ɛksɑ̃ːg], *a.* (*a*) Anaemic, bloodless. (*b*) *F:* Cadaverous.

exsuder [ɛksyde], *v.tr.* & *i.* To exude.

extase [ɛkstaːz], *s.f.* Ecstasy. **1.** *Psy:* *Med:* Trance. **2.** *F:* Rapture.

extasier (s') [ɛkstazje], *v.pr.* To be in, go into, ecstasies (*devant*, before; *sur*, over).

extatique [ɛkstatik], *a.* **1.** *Psy:* *Med:* Ecstatic. **2.** *F:* Rapturous, enraptured.

extenseur [ɛkstɑ̃sœːr]. **1.** *a.* & *s.m.* *Anat:* Extensor (muscle). **2.** *s.m.* (*a*) *Gym:* Chest expander. (*b*) Trouser-stretcher.

extensibilité [ɛkstɑ̃sibilite], *s.f.* Extensibility.

extensible [ɛkstɑ̃sibl], *a.* Extensible; extending (table, etc.); expanding (bracelet, etc.).

extensif, -ive [ɛkstāsif, -iːv], *a.* **1.** Tensile (force, etc.). **2.** Extensive.

extension [ɛkstãsjɔ̃], *s.f.* **1.** Extension. (*a*) Stretching. *Mec:* **Travail à l'extension**, tensile stress. (*b*) Straining (of muscle). (*c*) Spreading, enlargement; spread (of disease). *Donner de l'e. à qch.*, to extend, enlarge, sth. *Prendre de l'e.*, to spread, grow. **2.** Extent. *Gram:* Extended meaning (of word). **Par extension,** in a wider sense.

exténuation [ɛkstenɥasjɔ̃], *s.f.* **1.** Extenuation, softening (of terms, etc.). **2.** (*a*) Emaciation (of body). (*b*) Exhaustion (of body or mind).

exténuer [ɛkstenɥe], *v.tr.* **1.** To extenuate, soften (judgment, etc.). **2.** (*a*) To emaciate, waste (the body). (*b*) To exhaust. *Être exténué (de fatigue)*, to be tired out, worn out.

s'exténuer, to work oneself to death.

extérieur [ɛksterjœːr]. **1.** *a.* (*a*) Exterior, outer, external. *Jardin e. à ma propriété*, garden that lies outside my grounds. (*b*) Foreign (trade, policy). **2.** *s.m.* (*a*) Exterior, outside (of building, etc.). **A l'extérieur,** (i) (on the) outside, out of doors; (ii) abroad. **A l'extérieur de la gare,** outside the station. (*b*) Foreign countries. (*c*) (Outward) appearance, looks.

extérieurement [ɛksterjœrmã], *adv.* **1.** Externally, on the outside, outwardly. **2.** On the surface; in appearance.

exterminateur, -trice [ɛkstɛrminatœːr, -tris]. **1.** *s.* Exterminator, destroyer. **2.** *a.* Exterminating, destroying (angel, etc.).

extermination [ɛkstɛrminasjɔ̃], *s.f.* Extermination; *F:* wiping out (of race, etc.).

exterminer [ɛkstɛrmine], *v.tr.* To exterminate, destroy; *F:* to wipe out (army, etc.).

s'exterminer, *F:* to work oneself to death (*à faire qch.*, doing sth.).

externat [ɛkstɛrna], *s.m.* **1.** Day-school. **2.** Non-resident medical studentship (at hospital); dressership. **3.** Out-patients' department.

externe [ɛkstɛrn]. **1.** *a.* (*a*) External, outside, outer. *Angle e.*, exterior angle. *Pharm:* **Pour l'usage externe,** for outward application. (*b*) *Élève e.*, day-pupil. *Malade e.*, out-patient (at hospital). **2.** *s.* (*a*) Day-pupil. (*b*) Non-resident medical student, dresser (at hospital).

exterritorialité [ɛkstɛritorjalite], *s.f. Jur:* Ex(tra)territoriality (of ambassador, etc.).

extincteur, -trice [ɛkstɛ̃ktœːr, -tris]. **1.** *a.* Extinguishing (material, etc.). **2.** *s.m.* Fire-extinguisher.

extinctif, -ive [ɛkstɛ̃ktif, -iːv], *a.* Extinctive.

extinction [ɛkstɛ̃ksjɔ̃], *s.f.* Extinction. **1.** (*a*) Extinguishing, putting out (of fire, etc.). *Tchn: E. du fer rouge*, quenching of red-hot iron. *E. de la chaux*, slaking, slacking, of lime. (*b*) Abolition, suppression; paying off, wiping out (of debt); termination (of contract). **2.** (*a*) Dying out (of race, species). (*b*) Loss (of voice, of sight).

extirpateur [ɛkstirpatœːr], *s.m.* (*a*) Extirpator, remover (of corns). (*b*) Uprooter (of tree, evil).

extirpation [ɛkstirpasjɔ̃], *s.f.* Extirpation; uprooting; eradication; removal (of corns).

extirper [ɛkstirpe], *v.tr.* To extirpate, eradicate, root out; to remove (corn).

extorquer [ɛkstɔrke], *v.tr.* To extort; to wring (money, promise) (*à qn*, from s.o.).

extorsion [ɛkstɔrsjɔ̃], *s.f.* Extortion.

extra [ɛkstra]. **1.** *s.m.* Usu. *inv.* Extra. *Du vin d'e.*, extra-special wine. *Payer les extra(s)*, to pay for the extras. *Faire un peu d'e.*, to do things a little better than usual. **2.** *a.inv.* Extra-special (wine, etc.); tip-top (entertainment). **3.** *adv.* (*a*) Extra-(fine, strong, etc.). (*b*) Extra (= additional)

(current, etc.). (*c*) Extra-(territorial). *L'extra-monde*, the beyond.

extracteur [ɛkstraktœːr], *s.m.* **1.** Drawer, extractor (of teeth, etc.). **2.** *Tls:* Extractor.

extraction [ɛkstraksjɔ̃], *s.f.* Extraction. **1.** Extracting. (*a*) Drawing (of teeth, etc.); getting, winning (of coal); quarrying (of stone). (*b*) Drawing up. *Min:* **Machine d'extraction,** winding-gear. (*c*) *Mth:* Extraction (of root). **2.** Descent, lineage, origin. *De basse e.*, of low extraction. *De haute e.*, high-born.

extrader [ɛkstrade], *v.tr. Jur:* To extradite.

extradition [ɛkstradisjɔ̃], *s.f. Jur:* Extradition.

extrados [ɛkstrado], *s.m. Arch:* Extrados.

extra-fin [ɛkstrafɛ̃], *a.* Superfine.

extra-fort [ɛkstrafoːr], *a.* Extra-strong.

extraire [ɛkstrɛːr], *v.tr.* (Conj. like TRAIRE) To extract, draw out, take out, pull out; to draw, pull (tooth); to get, win (coal, ore); to quarry (stone). *Mth: E. une racine,* to extract a root. *S'e. d'une position difficile,* to get out of an awkward position.

extrait, *s.m.* **1.** Extract. *E. de viande,* meat extract, essence. **2.** Extract, excerpt (from book); abstract (of deed, account). *E. de naissance,* birth-certificate. *E. de compte,* statement of account.

extrajudiciaire [ɛkstraʒydisjɛːr], *a. Jur:* Extrajudicial. *adv.* **-ment.**

extra-muros [ɛkstramyroːs]. **1.** *adv.* Outside the town. **2.** *a.inv.* Extramural, suburban (district).

extraordinaire [ɛkstr(a)ordinɛːr], *a.* Extraordinary. (*a*) Special (meeting, messenger, etc.). (*b*) Unusual, unwonted; out of the common; wonderful; above the ordinary. **Par extraordinaire,** (i) for a wonder; (ii) for once in a while. *adv.* **-ment.**

extravagance [ɛkstravagɑ̃ːs], *s.f.* Extravagance; absurdity, folly (of action, etc.); exorbitance (of price); immoderateness (of desires). *Il a dit un tas d'extravagances,* he talked a lot of wild nonsense.

extravag|ant [ɛkstravagɑ̃], *a.* Extravagant; absurd, foolish (action, etc.); exorbitant (demand); immoderate (desire). *adv.* **-amment.**

extravaguer [ɛkstravage], *v.i.* (*a*) To be delirious; to rave. (*b*) *F:* To talk nonsense.

extravaser (s') [sɛkstravaze], *v.pr.* (Of blood, sap, etc.) To extravasate.

extray-ant, -ons, etc. See EXTRAIRE.

extrême [ɛkstrɛːm]. **1.** *a.* Extreme. (*a*) Farthest, utmost (point, etc.). *L'e. lointain,* the extreme distance. (*b*) Intense, excessive (cold, etc.). (*c*) Drastic, severe (measure). **2.** *s.m.* Extreme limit. **Scrupuleux à l'extrême,** scrupulous in the extreme, to a degree. *Pousser les choses à l'e.,* to carry matters to extremes. *adv.* **-ment.**

extrême-onction, *s.f. Ecc:* Extreme unction.

extrême-Orient (l'), *s.m.* The Far East.

extrémiste [ɛkstremist], *s. m. & f.* Extremist.

extrémité [ɛkstremite], *s.f.* **1.** (*a*) Extremity, end (of rope, etc.); tip (of finger, etc.); point (of needle, etc.). *Les extrémités de la terre,* the uttermost ends of the earth. (*b*) Extremity, extreme, last degree (of misery, etc.). **Pousser qch. à l'extrémité,** to carry sth. to extremes. *L'e. d'un besoin,* the urgency of a need. **Dans cette extrémité . . .,** in this exigency. . . . **Être à l'extrémité à toute extrémité,** to be at death's door, in the last extremity. **2.** *pl.* **Pousser qn à des extrémités,** to drive s.o. to extremities.

extrinsèque [ɛkstrɛ̃sɛk], *a.* Extrinsic.

extroverti, -ie [ɛkstrɔverti], *s. Psy:* Extrovert.

extrusion [ɛkstryzjɔ̃], *s.f.* Extrusion.
exubérance [ɛgzyberɑ̃:s], *s.f.* Exuberance, super-abundance.
exubérant [ɛgzyberɑ̃], *a.* Exuberant, super-abundant. *E. de santé,* bursting with health.

exultation [ɛgzyltasjɔ̃], *s.f.* Exultation.
exulter [ɛgzylte], *v.i.* To exult, rejoice.
ex-voto [ɛksvɔto], *s.m.inv.* Ex-voto; votive offering.
Ézéchias [ezekjɑ:s]. *Pr.n.m. B.Hist:* Hezekiah.

F

F, f [ɛf], *s.f.* (The letter) F, f.
fa [fa], *s.m.inv. Mus:* (The note) F. *Clef de fa,* bass clef, F-clef.
fabagelle [fabaʒɛl], *s.f. Bot:* Bean-caper.
fable [fɑ:bl], *s.f.* (a) Fable.' (b) Story, tale. **Être la fable de toute la ville,** to be the laughing-stock of the town. **Célèbre dans la fable,** famous in story.
fabliau, -aux [fablio], *s.m. A:* Short tale in verse; fabliau.
fablier [fablie], *s.m.* Book of fables.
fabricant, -ante [fabrikɑ̃, -ɑ̃:t], *s.* (a) Maker, manufacturer (de, of). (b) Mill-owner.
fabricateur, -trice [fabrikatœ:r, -tris], *s. Pej:* Fabricator (of lies, etc.); coiner; forger (of a document).
fabrication [fabrikasjɔ̃], *s.f.* **1.** Manufacture, making. *N'employer que la meilleure f.,* to employ only the best workmanship. **2.** Forging (of document); coining (of counterfeit money). *C'est de la pure f.,* it's pure fabrication.
fabrique [fabrik], *s.f.* **1.** Making, manufacture. **Prix de fabrique,** manufacturer's price. **Marque de fabrique,** trade-mark. **2.** Factory, works; (cloth-, paper-, oil-)mill. **Valeur en fabrique,** cost price. **3.** *Ecc:* Fabric (of church). **Conseil de fabrique,** church council; vestry.
fabriquer [fabrike], *v.tr.* **1.** (a) *Ind:* To manufacture. (b) *F:* To make (sth.). *Qu'est-ce que vous fabriquez là?* (i) what's that you're making? (ii) what are you up to? **2.** *Pej:* To fabricate; to forge (document).
fabuleux, -euse [fabylø, -ø:z], *a.* **1.** Fabulous. **2.** *F:* Incredible; prodigious. *adv.* **-sement.**
fabuliste [fabylist], *s.m.* Fabulist.
façade [fasad], *s.f.* Façade, front(age). **Local en façade sur deux rues,** premises with frontages on two streets. *Γ:* **Patriotisme de façade,** patriotism all on the surface.
face [fas], *s.f.* Face. **1.** (a) *A. & F: Jeter la vérité à la f. de qn,* to cast the truth in s.o.'s face. *F:* **Sauver la face,** to save (one's) face. **Perdre la face,** to lose face. (b) *La f. des eaux, de la terre,* the face of the waters, of the earth. **2.** (a) Face (of sth.). *F. avant,* front. *F. arrière,* back. *F:* **Considérer qch. sous toutes ses faces,** to consider sth. from all sides. (b) Obverse (of medal); head side (of coin). S.a. PILE³. *Disque à double f.,* double-sided record. **3.** (a) **Faire face à qn,** à qch., to face s.o., sth. *Faire f. à ses échéances,* to meet one's liabilities. *Faire f. à des difficultés,* to cope with difficulties. (b) Portrait **de face,** full-face portrait. *Vue de f.,* front-view. *Se présenter de f.,* to face (the observer, etc.). **La maison (d')en face,** the house opposite. **Regarder qn (bien) en face,** to look s.o.. full, straight, in the face. **Face à face,** face to face *(avec,* with). **4.** *Prep.phr.* **Face à, en face de,** opposite; over against. *En f. l'un de l'autre, l'un en f. de l'autre,* opposite each other; facing each other.

face-à-main, *s.m.* Lorgnette. *pl. Des faces-à-main.*
facétie [fasesi], *s.f.* Joke, jest. *Dire des facéties,* to crack jokes. **Faire des facéties à qn** to play pranks on s.o.
facétieux, -euse [fasesjø, -ø:z], *a.* Facetious, waggish. *adv.* **-sement.**
facette [fasɛt], *s.f.* Facet. **(Taillé) à facettes,** (cut) in facets.
fâcher [fɑʃe], *v.tr.* **1.** To grieve. **2.** To anger; to make (s.o.) angry. **Soit dit sans vous fâcher,** if I may say so without offence.
se fâcher. **1.** To get angry; to lose one's temper. *Ne pas se f.,* to keep one's temper. *F: Se f. tout rouge,* to flare up, blaze up. **2.** *Se f. avec qn,* to fall out with s.o.
fâché, *a.* **1.** Sorry. *Être f. de qch., pour qn,* to be sorry about sth., for s.o. **2.** Angry. *Être f. contre qn,* to be annoyed, vexed, with s.o. **3.** *Être f. avec qn,* to have fallen out with s.o.
fâcherie [fɑʃri], *s.f. F:* Quarrel, tiff.
fâcheux, -euse [fɑʃø, -ø:z]. **1.** *a.* Troublesome, tiresome, trying, annoying. **Position fâcheuse,** awkward, trying, position. *Il est f. que + sub.,* it is unfortunate, a pity, that. . . . **2.** *s.m. A:* (Society) bore; intrusive fellow. *adv.* **-sement.**
facial, -aux [fasjal, -o], *a. Anat: etc:* Facial. *Névralgie faciale,* face-ache.
faciès [fasjɛs], *s.m.* **1.** *Bot: Med: Z:* Facies, aspect, appearance (of plant, features, etc.). **2.** *F:* Cast of features.
facile [fasil], *a.* **1.** Easy. (a) *F. à faire,* easy to do, easily done. *C'est f. à dire,* it is more easily said than done. (b) (i) *Homme f. à vivre,* man easy to get on with. (ii) Pliable, weak; frail (virtue, etc.). **2.** Facile, ready, quick. *Avoir le style, la parole, f.,* to have a fluent style, tongue. *Je n'ai pas la parole f.,* I am not a ready speaker. *adv.* **-ment.**
facilité [fasilite], *s.f.* **1.** (a) Easiness (of task, etc.); ease (with which a thing is done). **Avec facilité,** easily, with ease. (b) **Avoir la facilité de faire qch.,** to enjoy facilities for doing sth. *Com: Facilités de paiement,* facilities for payment; easy terms. **2.** Aptitude, talent, facility. *F. à faire qch.,* gift, aptitude, for doing sth. *F. de parole,* readiness of speech; fluency. **3.** Pliancy; complaisance.
faciliter [fasilite], *v.tr.* To facilitate; to make (sth.) easier, easy; to promote (progress).
façon [fasɔ̃], *s.f.* **1.** (a) (i) Making, fashioning; (ii) make; workmanship. *F. d'un habit,* cut of a coat. **Tailleur à façon,** jobbing tailor. **"On prend, travaille, à façon,"** 'customers' own materials made up.' **Plat de sa façon,** dish of her own making. (b) *Ciseau f. américaine,* American pattern chisel. *Cuir f. porc,* imitation pigskin. (c) *Ind: Matière et f.,* material and labour. **2.** (a) Manner, mode, way (of acting, speaking, etc.). *Vivre à la façon des sauvages,* to live after the fashion of savages, like savages. *Avoir une f.*

à soi de faire qch., to have a way of one's own of doing sth. **Je le ferai à ma façon,** I shall do it (in) my own way. **Façon de parler,** manner of speaking. **Je lui dis, façon de rire, que . . .,** I said to him, by way of a joke, that. . . . *Parler d'une f. absurde,* to talk in an absurd manner. *Ils agissent tous de la même f.,* they all act alike. *De quelque f. qu'il s'y prenne . . .,* whatever way he sets about it. . . . *Regardez de quelle f. il tient son archet,* look how he holds his bow. **De la bonne façon,** properly ; in good style. **Arranger qn de (la) belle, de bonne, façon,** to give s.o. a good dressing down. (*b*) **Homme sans façon,** rough-and-ready man. **Il entra sans façon(s),** he entered unceremoniously. **Traiter qn sans façon(s),** to treat s.o. in an off-hand manner. **Sans plus de façons,** without any more ado. **Faire des façons,** to stand on ceremony ; to make a fuss. (*c*) **De cette façon,** thus. *Ne me parlez pas de cette f.,* don't speak to me like that. **De façon ou d'autre, d'une façon ou d'une autre,** (in) one way or another, some way or other. **De toute façon j'irai,** anyhow, in any case, I shall go. **En aucune façon!** not at all! by no means! **En quelque façon,** in a way, in a sense. **3.** *Conj.phr.* (*a*) **De façon à,** so as to. *Parlez de f. à vous faire comprendre,* speak so that one may understand. (*b*) **De (telle) façon que.** (i) + *ind.* *Il pleuvait de telle f. que je fus obligé de rentrer,* it was raining so hard that I had to go home. *Il pleuvait, de f. que je fus obligé de rentrer,* it was raining, (and) so I had to go home. (ii) + *sub.* *Parlez de f. qu'on vous comprenne,* speak so as to be understood.

faconde [fakɔ̃:d], *s.f.* Fluency of speech ; ready flow of language ; *F:* the gift of the gab.

façonn|er [fasɔne], *v.tr.* To work, shape (wood, metal, etc.) ; to fashion (clay, etc.). *F. une robe,* to make (up) a dress. *F. la terre,* to dress, work, the soil. *F: F. un enfant,* to mould, form, a child's character. *Se f. à la discipline,* to accustom oneself to discipline. *s.m.* **-age.** *s.m.* **-ement.**

façonnier, -ère [fasɔnje, -ɛ:r], *a. & s.* **1.** *Ouvrier f.,* home-worker. **2.** Fussy, over-ceremonious.

fac(-)similé [faksimile], *s.m.* Facsimile ; exact copy. *pl. Des fac(-)similés.*

factage [fakta:ʒ], *s.m.* (*a*) Carriage (and delivery) ; transport (of goods). (*b*) Porterage. (*c*) Delivery (of letters). [FACTEUR]

facteur, -trice [faktœ:r, -tris], *s.* **1.** (Musical) instrument maker. *F. d'orgues,* organ-builder. **2.** (*a*) Carrier ; transport agent. (*b*) Carman (delivering parcels). (*c*) Postman. **3.** *Com:* Agent, middleman, factor. **4.** *s.m. Mth:* Factor. *F: Le facteur humain,* the personal factor. *Mec.E: F. de sûreté, de sécurité,* safety factor ; coefficient of safety.

factice [faktis], *a.* Factitious ; artificial, imitation (gems, etc.) ; dummy (box of chocolates, etc.). *s.m. Factices de caoutchouc,* rubber substitutes. *adv.* **-ment.**

factieux, -euse [faksjø, -ø:z]. **1.** *a.* Factious. **2.** *s.* Sedition-monger.

faction [faksjɔ̃], *s.f.* **1.** Sentry-duty, guard. **Faire faction, être de faction, être en faction,** to be on sentry-go. **Mettre (qn) en faction,** to post (a sentry). **Relever (qn) de faction,** to relieve (a sentry). *Mettre les grévistes en f.,* to place strikers on picket-duty. **2.** Faction ; factious party.

factionnaire [faksjɔnɛ:r], *s.m.* (*a*) Sentry, sentinel. (*b*) Man on picket-duty.

factotum [faktɔtɔm], *s.m.* Factotum ; man-of-all-work, handy man.

facture¹ [fakty:r], *s.f.* **1.** (*a*) Treatment (of work

of art). *Mus: F:* **Morceau de facture,** show piece. (*b*) *Com:* Get-up, make, workmanship. **2.** Manufacturing (of musical instruments).

facture², *s.f. Com:* Invoice ; bill (of sale). *Faire, dresser, établir, une f.,* to make out an invoice. *F. simulée,* pro forma invoice. **Selon, suivant, facture,** as per invoice.

facturer [faktyre], *v.tr.* To invoice.

facturier [faktyrje], *s.m.* **1.** Invoice clerk. **2.** Sales-book.

facultat|if, -ive [fakyltatif, -i:v], *a.* Optional, facultative. *adv.* **-ivement.**

faculté [fakylte], *s.f.* **1.** (*a*) Option, right, faculty. **Avoir (la) faculté de faire qch.,** to have (i) the option of doing sth., (ii) power to do sth. (*b*) Faculty, ability, power. **Jouir de toutes ses facultés,** to be in possession of all one's faculties. *Homme doué de grandes facultés,* man of great abilities ; man of parts. *L'aimant a la f. d'attirer le fer,* the magnet has the property of attracting iron. (*c*) *pl.* Resources, means. **2.** Faculty (of law, medicine, etc.). *F:* **La Faculté,** the (medical) Faculty, the Doctors. *Les différentes facultés (d'une université),* the different schools.

fadaise [fadɛ:z], *s.f.* (*a*) Piece of nonsense ; silly remark. (*b*) *pl.* Twaddle, nonsense. *Débiter des fadaises,* to talk twaddle.

fade [fad], *a.* Insipid, flavourless, tasteless (dish, etc.) ; pointless (joke). **Avoir le cœur fade,** to feel squeamish. *adv.* **-ment.**

fadette [fadɛt], *s.f. Dial:* Fairy.

fadeur [fadœ:r], *s.f.* (*a*) Insipidity ; sickliness (of taste, smell, etc.). (*b*) *pl.* Dire des fadeurs à qn, to pay insipid compliments to s.o. (*c*) Pointlessness, tameness (of joke). [FADE]

fafiot [fafjo], *s.m. P:* Bank-note ; *P:* flimsy.

fagot [fago], *s.m.* **1.** Faggot ; bundle of firewood. *Fort: F. de sape,* fascine. **Il y a fagots et fagots,** all men, things, are not alike. **Sentir le fagot,** to savour of heresy. **Bouteille de vin de derrière les fagots,** bottle of wine from the hidden store. **2.** *A:* Bundle (of clothes, etc.). *F: S'habiller comme un f.,* to be dowdy.

fagotage [fagota:ʒ], *s.m.* **1.** (*a*) Faggoting. (*b*) *F:* Botching (of work). **2.** (*a*) Faggot-wood. (*b*) *F:* Botched piece of work. **3.** *F:* Ridiculous get-up.

fagoter [fagote], *v.tr.* **1.** To faggot (firewood). **2.** To botch (work). **3.** *P:* To dress (s.o.) without taste. **Mal fagoté,** ridiculously dressed.

faiblard [fɛblar], *a. F:* Weak(ish) ; feeblish.

faible [fɛbl]. **1.** *a.* (*a*) Feeble, weak. *F. d'esprit,* weak-, feeble-minded. *s.* **Protéger les faibles,** to protect the weak. (*b*) *Brise f.,* light breeze. *Voix f.,* (i) weak voice ; (ii) faint voice. *F. son,* faint sound. *Café f.,* weak, thin, coffee. *F. espérance,* faint hope. *Prix f.,* (i) low price ; (ii) discount price. *Minerai à f. teneur (d'or, etc.),* low-grade ore. *Faibles ressources,* small resources, scanty means. *Nau: F. tirant,* shallow draught. *Phot: Cliché f.,* thin negative. **2.** *s.m.* Weakness, failing, foible. *Le f. de qn,* the weak side in s.o. **Avoir un faible pour qch.,** to have a weakness, a partiality, a liking, for sth. ; to be partial to sth. *adv.* **-ment.**

faiblesse [fɛblɛs], *s.f.* **1.** (*a*) Feebleness, weakness. (*b*) Fainting fit. **Tomber en faiblesse,** to fall down in a faint ; to swoon, faint. (*c*) *La f. humaine,* human weakness, frailty. (*d*) Smallness (of sum, number). **2.** *F. chez qn,* failing in s.o. *Je l'aime pour toutes ses faiblesses,* I love him in spite of all his failings.

faiblir [fɛbli:r], *v.i.* To weaken ; to grow weak(er) ; *I.C.E:* (of engine) to lose power.

Ma vue faiblit, my sight is failing. *Le vent faiblit,* the wind is abating.

faïence [fajɑ̃ːs], *s.f.* Crockery; earthenware, stone-ware. *F. fine,* china.

faïencerie [fajãsri], *s.f.* **1.** Crockery, earthenware. **2.** (*a*) Earthenware-shop. (*b*) Pottery.

faïencier [fajãsje], *s.m.* Crockery-, earthenware-maker or dealer.

faille[1] [faːj], *s.f.* Coarse-grained silk material; faille.

faille[2], *s.f.* *Geol: Min:* Fault, break (in lode).

faille[3]. See FALLOIR.

faillibilité [fajibilite], *s.f.* Fallibility.

faillible [fajibl], *a.* Fallible.

faillir [fajiːr], *v.i.* (*pr.p.* **faillant;** *p.p.* **failli;** *pr.ind.* **je faux, il faut, n. faillons;** *p.h.* **je faillis;** *fu.* **je faillirai, je faudrai**) **1.** To fail. (*a*) *Si je faux à mon devoir,* if I fail in my duty. *F. à une promesse,* to fail to keep a promise. **Sans faillir,** without fail. S.a. AUNE[2]. (*b*) *Com: A: = Faire faillite.* **2.** **Faillir** + *inf.* (only in past hist. and compound tenses) *J'ai failli manquer le train,* I all but missed the train; I nearly missed the train. *Il faillit être écrasé,* he narrowly missed being run over.

failli, *s.m.* (Adjudicated) bankrupt.

faillite [fajit], *s.f.* *Com:* Failure, bankruptcy, insolvency. **Être en état de faillite,** to be bankrupt, insolvent. **Tomber en faillite, faire faillite,** to go bankrupt; to fail. **Déclarer, mettre, qn en faillite,** to adjudicate, adjudge, s.o. bankrupt. S.a. JUGEMENT 1.

faim [fɛ̃], *s.f.* Hunger. **Avoir faim, se sentir faim,** to be, feel, hungry. *F:* **Avoir une faim de loup,** to be ravenously hungry. **Manger à sa faim,** to eat one's fill. **Mourir de faim,** (i) to die of starvation; (ii) *F:* to be starving, to be famished. *F:* **Avoir f. de gloire,** to hunger, thirst, for glory.

faîne [fɛːn], *s.f.* **1.** Beech-nut. **2.** *pl.* Beech-mast.

fainéant, -ante [fɛneɑ̃, -ãːt]. **1.** *a.* Idle, lazy, slothful. **2.** *s.* Idler, sluggard, lazy-bones. [NÉANT]

fainéanter [fɛneɑ̃te], *v.i.* To idle; to loaf.

fainéantise [fɛneɑ̃tiːz], *s.f.* Idleness, laziness, sloth.

faire [fɛːr], *v.tr.* (*pr.p.* **faisant** [fəzɑ̃]; *p.p.* **fait** [fɛ]; *pr.ind.* **je fais, il fait, n. faisons** [fəzɔ̃], v. **faites** [fɛt], **ils font;** *pr.sub.* **je fasse;** *imp.* **fais, faisons, faites;** *p.h.* **je fis;** *fu.* **je ferai**) I. To make. **1.** *Dieu a fait l'homme à son image,* God made, created, man in his own image. *Les vieilles gens sont ainsi faits,* old people are like that. *Il n'est pas fait pour être soldat,* he is not cut out for a soldier. **2.** (*a*) *Statue faite en, de, marbre,* statue cut, made, out of marble. **Vêtements tout faits,** ready-made clothes. *F:* **Comme vous voilà fait!** what a sight you are! (*b*) *F. la guerre,* to wage war. *F. un miracle,* to work a miracle. *Le mariage ne se fera pas,* the marriage will not take place. S.a. AFFAIRE 2. (*c*) *F:* *F. de l'œil à qn,* to wink at s.o. **3.** (*a*) *F. sa fortune,* to make one's fortune. *Se f. des amis,* to make friends. (*b*) *Faire des provisions,* to lay in provisions. (Of locomotive, ship) *F. de l'eau, du charbon,* to take in water, coal. (*c*) *P:* *On vous a fait,* you've been had.

II. **faire,** to do. **1.** (*a*) *Il n'a rien fait,* he did nothing. *Qu'est-ce qu'il y a à f.?* what is there to do? **Il n'y a rien à faire,** there is no help for it. **Que faire?** what is to be done? **Je ne sais que faire,** I don't know what to do. *Est-ce que je peux ouvrir la fenêtre?—Faites donc!* may I open the window?—Do! By all means! *Faites vite!* look sharp! **Avoir fort à faire,** to have a great deal to do. **Vous allez avoir de quoi faire,** you have your work cut out. **Homme à tout faire,** handy-man.

Bonne à tout faire, maid-of-all-work; general servant. *Ces choses-là ne se font pas,* those things are not done. **Grand bien vous fasse!** much good may it do you! **C'est bien fait!** it serves you right! (*b*) (To say) *"Vous partez demain!" fit-il,* "you leave to-morrow!" he said, he ejaculated. *Il fit un petit "oh" de surprise,* he gave a little "oh" of surprise. **2.** (To perform, practise) (*a*) *F. son devoir,* to do one's duty. *F. la ronde,* to go one's rounds. *Com: Quel article faites-vous?* what is your line? **Voilà qui est fait,** that's done, settled. **Toute réflexion faite . . .,** all things considered. . . . (*b*) *F. du sport, de l'auto,* to go in for sport, for motoring. *J'ai fait de l'anglais à l'école,* I did English at school. *Il fait sa médecine,* he is doing medicine, studying medicine. *Il fait son droit,* he is reading law. **3.** *F. quelques pas dans le sentier,* to go, take, a few steps along the path. *F. une promenade,* to go for a walk. *F. soixante milles à l'heure,* to go sixty miles an hour. **4.** *Combien cela fait-il?* how much does that come to? *Deux fois deux font quatre,* twice two is four. **5.** To be, constitute. *F. l'admiration de tous,* to be the admiration of all. *Cela fera mon affaire,* that will suit me. S.a. AFFAIRE 1. *Prov:* **L'habit ne fait pas le moine,** it is not the cowl that makes the friar. **6.** To matter. **Qu'est-ce que ça fait?** what does it matter? who cares? *Qu'est-ce que cela vous fait?* what is that to you? **Si cela ne vous fait rien,** if you don't mind. *Rien ne lui fait,* nothing affects him. **Cela ne fait rien,** that makes no difference; never mind. **7.** (Faire replacing a head verb in the second term of a comparison) *Charles XII voulait braver les saisons comme il faisait ses ennemis,* Charles XII wanted to defy the seasons as he did his enemies. *Pourquoi agir comme vous le faites?* why do you act as you do?

III. **faire.** **1.** To form. *Ce professeur fait de bons élèves,* this master produces, turns out, good pupils. *Démarche faite pour m'étonner,* step calculated to astonish me. **2.** To arrange. *F. la chambre,* to clean, *F:* to do, the room. *F. sa malle,* to pack one's trunk. *F. ses ongles,* to (polish and) trim one's nails. *F. les cartes,* (i) to shuffle, (ii) to deal, the cards. **A qui de faire?** whose deal is it? **3.** *Faire qn qch., faire qch. de qn,* to make s.o. sth. *Dieu a fait tous les hommes égaux,* God made all men equal. *Qu'allez-vous f. de votre fils?* what are you going to make of your son? *F. d'un théâtre un cinéma,* to turn a theatre into a cinema. **N'avoir que faire de qch.,** to have no occasion, no need, for sth. *F: Cela fait riche,* it gives an appearance of wealth. *On le faisait mort,* he was alleged, given out, to be dead. *Il se fait plus pauvre qu'il ne l'est,* he makes himself out to be poorer than he is. **4.** *Il fait Hamlet,* he acts Hamlet. *F. le malade,* to sham illness. *Il fait le mort,* he is shamming dead. *F. le gros monsieur,* to come the heavy swell. *F. l'imbécile,* to play the fool.

IV. **faire.** **1.** **En faire.** (*a*) *Il n'en fait qu'à sa tête,* he follows his own inclination. *N'en faites rien,* do no such thing. (*b*) *C'en est fait,* the worst has happened. *C'(en) est fait de lui,* it's all up with him; he is done for. **2.** **Y faire.** *Rien n'y fit,* nothing availed; it was all of no use. *Qu'y faire?* how can it be helped? *Que voulez-vous que j'y fasse?* how can I help it? **3.** *F:* **La faire.** *On ne me la fait pas!* nothing doing! I am not to be had! *La f. à la vertu,* to come the virtuous. S.a. BON 12.

V. **faire,** *impers.* **1.** **Quel temps fait-il?** what is the weather like? **Il fait beau (temps),** it is

fine (weather). *Il fait du soleil*, the sun is shining. *Par le froid qu'il fait*, in this cold weather. **2.** *Il fait mauvais voyager par ces routes*, it is hard travelling on these roads. **3.** *Il fait soif, faim, après un travail pareil*, one feels, gets, thirsty, hungry, after work like that.
VI. faire. (Syntactical constructions) **1.** *Il ne fait que lire toute la journée*, he does nothing but read all day. *Je n'ai fait que le toucher*, I only touched it. **2.** *Je ne fais que d'arriver*, I have only just arrived. **3.** *Vous n'aviez que faire de parler*, you had no business to speak. **4.** (*a*) Faire que + *ind*. *C'est ce qui fait que je suis venu si vite*, that is why I came so quickly. (*b*) Faire que + *sub*. *Fasse le ciel qu'il vienne à temps!* heaven grant that he (may) come in time! *Faites qu'il se trouve là demain*, arrange, see to it, that he is there to-morrow.
VII. faire + *inf*. = causative verb. **1.** (The noun or pron. object is the subject of the inf.) (*a*) *Le soleil fait fondre la neige*, the sun causes the snow to melt, melts the snow. *Je le fis chanter*, I made him sing. *On le fit chanter*, he was made to sing. *Il nous a fait venir*, he sent for us. *Faites-le entrer*, show him in. *Ne me faites pas attendre*, don't keep me waiting. (*b*) Faire + *v.pr*. (i) (Reflexive pron. omitted) *F. asseoir qn*, to make s.o. sit down. *F. coucher un enfant*, to put a child to bed. (ii) (Reflexive pron. retained) *C'est moi qui les ai fait se connaître*, it was I who made them acquainted with one another. *Je le fis s'arrêter*, I made him stop. **2.** (The noun or pron. is the object of the inf.) (*a*) *F. bâtir une maison*, to have, to get, a house built. **Faire faire deux exemplaires**, to have two copies made; to cause two copies to be made. *Je le fis arrêter*, I had him arrested. (*b*) **Se faire** + *inf*. *Se faire photographier*, to have, *F:* get, oneself photographed; to have one's photograph taken. *Un bruit se fit entendre*, a noise was heard. *Ne vous faites pas tant prier*, don't take so much asking. *Il ne se le fit pas dire deux fois*, he did not require twice telling. **3. Faire faire qch. à qn**, to cause, get, s.o. to do sth.; to get, have, sth. done by s.o. *Il fit lâcher prise à son adversaire*, he made his opponent let go. *Faites-lui lire cette lettre*, get him to read, make him read, this letter. *Je lui ai fait observer que . . .*, I called his attention to the fact that. *. . . Faites-lui comprendre que . . .*, give him to understand that. . . .
VIII. faire, *s.m*. **1.** Doing, making (of sth.). *Il y a loin du faire au dire*, there is a great difference between doing and saying. **2.** *Art: Lit:* Technique; handling. **Tableau d'un faire libre et élégant**, picture of free and elegant execution.
se faire. 1. (*a*) To develop, mature. *Ce fromage se fera*, this cheese will ripen. *Son style se fait*, his style is forming. (*b*) To become. *Se f. vieux*, to become, grow, get, old. *Se f. soldat*, to become a soldier. *Se f. catholique*, to turn Roman Catholic. *La nuit se fait*, night is falling. (*c*) To adapt oneself. **Se faire à qch.**, to get used, accustomed, to sth. *Se f. à la fatigue*, to become inured to fatigue. *Mec.E:* *Permettre aux engrenages de se f.*, to run in the gears. (*d*) *La mer, le vent, se fait*, the sea, the wind, is getting up. **2.** *Impers.* (*a*) *Il se fait tard*, it is growing late. (*b*) *Il se fit un long silence*, a long silence followed, ensued. *Comment se fait-il que vous soyez en retard?* how does it happen, come about, that you are late? how is it that you are late?
fait[1], *a*. Fully developed. *Homme f.*, (i) (full-) grown man; (ii) man of ripe experience. *Fromage f.*, ripe cheese. *Temps f.*, settled weather.

fait[2], *s.m*. **1.** Act, deed, feat, achievement. **Faits et dits**, sayings and doings. **Fait d'armes**, feat of arms. **Cela est du fait d'un tel**, this is so-and-so's doing. **Prendre qn sur le fait**, to catch s.o. in the act, red-handed. **Se porter à des voies de fait**, to resort to force, to violence. **Parler n'était pas son fait**, speaking was not his strong point. **Dire son fait à qn**, *F:* to talk straight to s.o. *Elle lui a dit son f.*, she told him what she thought of him. *S.a.* GESTE[2] 2. **2.** (*a*) Fact. **Fait accompli**, accomplished fact. **Fait de fait, actual possession. Prendre fait et cause pour qn**, to take up the cudgels for s.o. **Roi de nom plutôt que de fait**, king in name rather than in fact. **Il est de fait que** + *ind*., it is a fact that. . . . **Aller droit au fait**, to go straight to the point. **En venir au fait et au prendre, arriver au fait**, to come to the point. **Être au fait de la question**, to know how things stand. **Mettro qn au fait**, to give s.o. full information; to make s.o. acquainted with the facts. **Mettre, poser, qch. en fait**, to lay sth. down as a fact. *Adv.phr.* (i) **Au fait, que venez-vous faire ici?** after all, what have you come here for? (ii) **En fait, par le fait, dans le fait, de fait**, as a matter of fact, in point of fact, in actual fact. *De f. cela est un refus*, that is in effect a refusal. (iii) **De ce fait**, thereby; on that account. **Du fait que . . .**, owing to the fact that. . . . *Prep.phr.* **En fait de**, as regards. *Qu'est-ce que vous avez en f. de rôti?* what have you in the way of a joint? (*b*) Occurrence, happening. *Ces faits sont assez rares*, these occurrences are few; this seldom occurs.

faire-part [fɛrpaːr], *s.m.inv*. (= *lettre de faire part*, *q.v.* under PART[1] 2) **Faire-part de décès**, notification (to friends) of death.

fais [fɛ]. See FAIRE.

faisable [fəzabl], *a*. Practicable, feasible.

fais-ais, -ant, etc. See FAIRE.

faisan [fəzɑ̃], *s.m*. (Coq) faisan, (cock-)pheasant.

faisander [fəzɑ̃de], *v.tr*. *Cu:* To hang (meat).

se faisander, to get high.

faisandé, *a*. (*a*) High, gamy (meat). (*b*) *F:* Spicy (story).

faisanderie [fəzɑ̃dri], *s.f*. Pheasantry.

faisandier [fəzɑ̃dje], *s.m*. Pheasant breeder.

faisane [fəzan], *s.f*. Hen-pheasant.

faisceau [fɛso], *s.m*. Bundle (of sticks, etc.). *Anat:* Fasciculus, bundle (of fibres). *F. d'ampoules électriques*, cluster of electric bulbs. *Mil:* F. d'armes, pile of arms. *Former les faisceaux*, to pile arms. *Opt:* F. lumineux, de lumière, pencil of rays. F. parallèle, parallel beam.

faiseur, -euse [fəzœːr, -øːz], *s*. **1.** Maker, doer. *F. de miracles*, miracle worker. *F. de projets*, schemer. **Chapeau du bon faiseur**, hat from a good house. *F. de mariages*, match-maker. **2.** *F:* Bluffer, humbug.

fait [fɛ]. See FAIRE.

faîtage [fɛtaː3], *s.m*. *Const:* **1.** Roof-tree. **2.** Ridge tiling or sheathing. **3.** Roof timbers.

fait-divers [fɛdivɛːr], *s.m*. *Journ:* News item. *Faits-divers*, news in brief.

faîte [fɛt], *s.m*. **1.** (*a*) *Const:* Ridge (of roof). (*b*) *Geog:* Ligne de faîte, watershed, crest line. **2.** Top, summit (of house, tree). *F: Le f. de la gloire*, the pinnacle of glory.

faites. See FAIRE.

faîtière [fɛtjɛːr], *s.f*. Ridge-tile.

faix [fɛ], *s.m*. Burden, load. *F: Le f. des années*, the weight of years.

falaise [falɛːz], *s.f*. Cliff.

falbalas [falbala], *s.m.pl*. Furbelows, flounces.

fallacieu|x, -euse [falasjø, -øːz], *a.* Fallacious, deceptive, misleading. *adv.* **-sement.**

falloir [falwaːr], *v. impers. def.* (No *pr.p.; p.p.* **fallu;** *pr.ind.* il **faut;** *pr.sub.* il **faille;** *p.d.* il **fallait;** *p.h.* il **fallut;** *fu.* il **faudra**) **1.** To be wanting, lacking, necessary, requisite. *Il lui faut un nouveau pardessus,* he wants a new overcoat. *Avez-vous tout ce qu'il (vous) faut?* have you got all you require? *Faut-il de tout cela?* is all that necessary? *Il m'a fallu trois jours pour le faire,* it took me three days to do it. *Il faudrait des volumes pour raconter . . .,* it would take volumes to relate. *. . . C'est plus qu'il n'en faut,* that's more than enough. **S'en falloir,** to be lacking, wanting. *Il s'en faut de beaucoup,* it falls far short of it. *Il s'en faut de trois pieds qu'il m'ait donné la mesure,* he has given me three feet short measure. *Je ne suis pas satisfait, il s'en faut de beaucoup,* tant s'en faut, I am not satisfied, far from it, not by any means, not by a long way. *Tant s'en faut, bien s'en faut, qu'il soit artiste,* he is far from being an artist. **Peu s'en faut,** very nearly. *Peu s'en fallut qu'il ne pleurât,* he almost cried; he all but cried. **Comme il faut,** proper(ly). *Se conduire comme il faut,* to behave in a proper, gentlemanly, manner. *Un jeune homme très comme il faut,* a very gentlemanly young man. *Elle est très comme il faut,* (i) she is very ladylike; (ii) she is very prim and proper. **2.** (a) **Falloir** + *inf.,* falloir que + *sub.,* to be necessary. *Il faut partir,* I, we, you, etc., must start. *Il nous faut le voir, il faut que nous le voyions,* we must see him. *Il faut nous dépêcher,* we must hurry. *Il m'a fallu y renoncer,* I had to give it up. *Il fallait voir ça!* you ought to have seen it! **Il fallait le dire!** why didn't you say so! *Il n'aurait pas fallu attendre,* you ought not to have waited. *F: Faut-il qu'il soit bête!* well, he *is* a fool! *F: C'est ce qu'il faudra voir!* we must see about that! *Faut-il le faire ou non?* am I to do it or not? *La police a arrêté l'homme qu'il ne fallait pas,* the police have arrested the wrong man. (b) (With *le* = nounclause) *Il viendra s'il le faut,* he will come if need be, if necessary, if required.

falot[1] [falo], *s.m.* (Hand) lantern; (stable) lamp.

falot[2], **-ote** [falo, -ɔt], *a.* **1.** Quaint, droll, odd (person, idea). **2.** Wan (light); colourless (style).

falsificateur, -trice [falsifikatœːr, -tris], *s.* Falsifier; forger (of documents).

falsification [falsifikasjɔ̃], *s.f.* Falsification; forging, forgery (of documents, etc.); adulteration (of food).

falsifier [falsifje], *v.tr.* To falsify, tamper with (text, etc.); *F:* to fake (document); to adulterate (milk).

famé [fame], *a.* **Bien, mal, famé,** of good, evil, repute.

famélique [famelik], **1.** *a.* Famished-looking; half-starved. **2.** *s.* Starveling.

fameusement [famøzmɑ̃], *adv. F:* Famously, toppingly. *On s'est f. amusé,* we had rare fun.

fameu|x, -euse [famø, -øːz], *a.* **1.** Famous. *F. dans l'histoire,* renowned in history. **2.** *F:* Fameuse idée, capital idea. **Vous êtes un fameux menteur!** you are a precious liar! *Un f. dîner,* a rare, tip-top, dinner. **Ce n'est pas fameux,** it isn't up to much.

famili|al, -aux [familjal, -o], *a.* Family (life, ties, etc.). *Salle familiale,* living-room.

familiariser [familjarize], *v.tr.* To familiarize (à, avec, with).

  se familiariser. 1. To familiarize oneself, make oneself familiar (avec, with). **2.** To grow familiar; to make over-free.

familiarité [familjarite], *s.f.* Familiarity. (a) *Être admis dans la f. des grands,* to be intimate with the great; *F:* to hob-nob with the great. (b) *Prendre trop de familiarités avec qn,* to be too familiar, to take liberties, with s.o.

famili|er, -ère [familje, -ɛːr], *a.* **1.** Domestic; of the family. *Dieux familiers,* household gods. **2.** Familiar. (a) *Être f. avec qn,* to be on familiar terms, to be intimate, with s.o. *Expression familière,* colloquialism. *s. Un des familiers de la maison,* a regular frequenter of the house. (b) *Visage qui lui est f.,* face which is familiar, well-known, to him. *adv.* **-èrement.**

famille [famiːj], *s.f.* Family; household. **A-t-il de la famille?** has he any family? **Charges de famille,** dependants. **Chef de famille,** head of the family or of the household. **Soutien de famille,** bread-winner. **Fils de famille,** youth of good social position. *Rentrer dans sa f.,* to go home (after absence). **En famille,** as a family party. *Cela tient, vient, de famille,* it runs in the family. **Esprit de famille,** clannishness. *Jur: Prévenir la f.,* to inform the next of kin.

famine [famin], *s.f.* Famine, starvation. **Crier famine,** to complain of hard times. *Salaire de f.,* starvation wages.

fanal, -aux [fanal, -o], *s.m.* (a) Lantern, light. *F. de tête,* head-light (of locomotive, motor car). (b) Beacon-light. (c) *Nau:* Navigation light.

fanatique [fanatik]. **1.** *a.* Fanatic(al). **2.** *s.* Fanatic. *adv.* **-ment,** -ally.

fanatisme [fanatism], *s.m.* Fanaticism, zealotry.

fanchon [fɑ̃ʃɔ̃], *s.f.* Kerchief.

fane [fan], *s.f.* (a) Leaves for litter. (b) *Fanes de navets,* turnip-tops. [FANER]

faner [fane], *v.tr.* **1.** To ted, toss (hay). **2.** To make (flowers, etc.) fade. *F: Beauté fanée,* faded beauty. [FOIN]

  se faner, (of flowers, etc.) to droop, wither, wilt, fade; (of colours, etc.) to fade.

faneur, -euse [fanœːr, -øːz], *s.* **1.** Tedder; haymaker. **2.** *s.f.* **Faneuse,** tedding machine.

fanfare [fɑ̃faːr], *s.f.* **1.** (a) Flourish (of trumpets or bugles). (b) Fanfare (on hunting horns). **2.** (a) Brass band. (b) *Mil:* Bugle band. **Chef de fanfare,** bandmaster.

fanfaron, -onne [fɑ̃farɔ̃, -ɔn]. **1.** *a.* Boasting. **2.** *s.* Braggart, boaster, swaggerer.

fanfaronnade [fɑ̃farɔnad], *s.f.* Piece of brag, of boasting, of bounce.

fanfreluche [fɑ̃frəly§], *s.f.* **1.** *A:* Trifle, bauble. **2.** *pl.* Fallals; frills and furbelows.

fange [fɑ̃ːʒ], *s.f.* Mud, mire, filth. **Vivre dans la fange,** to live in vice, in degradation. *F: Il est sorti de la f.,* he rose from the gutter.

fangeu|x, -euse [fɑ̃ʒø, -øːz], *a.* **1.** Miry, muddy. **2.** Filthy (mind, etc.).

fanion [fanjɔ̃], *s.m. Mil:* (a) (Distinguishing) flag. (b) Lance-pennon.

fanon [fanɔ̃], *s.m.* **1.** *Ecc:* (i) Maniple, fanon. (ii) Pendant, vitta (of mitre). **2.** *Z:* (a) Dewlap (of ox). (b) Wattle (of bird). (c) Fetlock (of horse). **3.** Whalebone, baleen.

fantaisie [fɑ̃tezi], *s.f.* **1.** (a) Imagination, fancy. *De fantaisie,* imaginary. (b) *Mus:* (i) Fantasia. (ii) *F. sur "Faust,"* selection from 'Faust.' **2.** (a) Fancy, whim. *Chacun s'amusait à sa fantaisie,* everyone amused himself as he pleased. **Articles, prix, de fantaisie,** fancy goods, prices. (b) Freakish notion; freak, vagary.

fantaisiste [fɑ̃tezist], *a. & s.* Whimsical, freakish.

fantasmagorique [fɑ̃tasmagɔrik], *a.* Weird, fantastic.

fantasque [fɑ̃task], *a.* Odd, whimsical (person, idea); temperamental, humoursome (person).

fantassin [fɑ̃tasɛ̃], *s.m.* Foot-soldier, infantryman.

fantastique [fɑ̃tastik], *a.* **1.** Fantastic, fanciful; weird, eerie (light). **2.** *F:* Luxe *f.*, incredible luxury. *adv.* **-ment.**

fantoche [fɑ̃tɔʃ], *s.m.* Marionette, puppet.

fantomatique [fɑ̃tɔmatik], *a.* Spectral, ghostly.

fantôme [fɑ̃toːm], *s.m.* Phantom, ghost, spectre, apparition, spirit. Le Vaisseau Fantôme, the Flying Dutchman.

faon [fɑ̃], *s.m.* Fawn; roe calf. *F. femelle*, hind calf.

faquin [fakɛ̃], *s.m.* Low fellow; cad.

farad [farad], *s.m. Magn. Meas:* Farad.

faraud [faro]. **1.** *a. F:* Vain, affected (country bumpkin); (youth) toffed up. **2.** *s.m. F:* Bumpkin dressed up to cut a dash. **Faire le faraud,** to put on side.

farce [fars], *s.f.* **1.** *Cu:* Stuffing, force-meat. **2.** (*a*) *Th:* Farce. (*b*) *F:* Practical joke; prank. **Faire des farces à qn,** to play tricks on s.o. (*c*) **Faire des farces,** to run wild. (*d*) *F:* **Dire des farces à qn,** to joke with s.o. **3.** *a. P:* Funny, comical.

farceur, -euse [farsœːr, -øːz], *s.* **1.** Practical joker. **2.** Wag, joker, humorist; humbug. *C'est un f. qui vous aura dit cela,* somebody's been pulling your leg.

farcir [farsiːr], *v.tr. Cu:* To stuff (poultry, etc., with force-meat).

fard [faːr], *s.m.* Paint, rouge, make-up (for the face). *F: Sans fard,* without pretence, without disguise, plainly. *Parler sans f.,* to speak candidly. *P:* **Piquer un fard,** to blush.

fardeau [fardo], *s.m.* Burden, load. *F: Le f. des ans,* the weight of years.

farder[1] [farde], *v.tr.* To rouge; to make (s.o.) up. *F. la vérité,* to camouflage, disguise, the truth. **se farder,** to make up, to rouge.

farder[2], *v.i.* (*a*) To weigh heavy (*sur,* upon). (*b*) (Of wall, etc.) To settle (down); to sink.

fardier [fardje], *s.m.* Trolley, dray, truck, lorry (for carrying building-stones, etc.).

farfadet [farfadɛ], *s.m.* (Hob)goblin, brownie; sprite, elf.

farfouill|er [farfuje], *v.tr. & i.* To rummage (in, among); to grope (among). *F.* (*dans*) *un tiroir,* to rummage (about in) a drawer. [FOUILLER] *s.m.* **-ement.** *s.* **-eur, -euse.**

faribole [faribɔl], *s.f.* Idle tale; stuff and nonsense.

farinacé [farinase], *a.* Farinaceous, flour-like.

farine [farin], *s.f.* Flour or meal. *Fleur de f.,* pure wheaten flour. *Folle f.,* mill-dust. *F. de maïs,* Indian meal. *F. d'avoine,* oatmeal. *F. de riz,* ground rice. *F: Ce sont gens de (la) même farine,* they are birds of a feather.

fariné [farine], *a.* Floury; covered with flour.

farineux, -euse [farinø, -øːz], *a.* **1.** Farinaceous; floury, mealy (potato). **2.** Covered with flour.

farlouse [farluːz], *s.f. Orn:* Meadow titlark.

farniente [farnjɛ̃te], *s.m.* No *pl.* (Pleasant, luxurious) idleness.

faro [faro], *s.m.* Brussels beer.

farouch(e)[1] [faruʃ], *s.m. Agr:* Crimson clover.

farouche[2], *a.* **1.** Fierce, wild, savage. *Tyran f.,* grim, cruel, tyrant. **2.** (*a*) Shy, timid, coy. (*b*) Unsociable.

fasce [fas], *s.f.* **1.** *Arch:* Fascia (of column). **2.** *Her:* Fess(e).

fascicule [fasikyl], *s.m.* **1.** *Bot: Z:* Fascic(u)le, bunch, cluster (of hairs). **2.** Instalment, part, section (of publication).

fascinant [fas(s)inɑ̃], **fascinateur, -trice** [fas(s)inatœːr, -tris], *a.* Fascinating.

fascination [fas(s)inasjɔ̃], *s.f.* Fascination, charm, witchery.

fascine [fasin], *s.f.* Fascine, faggot (of brush-wood).

fasciner[1] [fassine], *v.tr.* (*a*) To fascinate. (*b*) *F:* To entrance, bewitch.

fasciner[2], *v.tr.* To fascine (river bank, earth-works); *U.S:* to corduroy (road).

fascisme [fas(s)ism], *s.m. Pol:* Fascism.

fasciste [fas(s)ist], *s. m. & f. Pol:* Fascist.

fass-e, -ions, etc. See FAIRE.

faste [fast], *s.m.* Ostentation, display. *Mariage sans f.,* quiet wedding.

fastes [fast], *s.m.pl.* (*a*) *Rom.Ant:* Fasti. (*b*) *F:* Annals, archives, records (of great deeds).

fastidieu|x, -euse [fastidjø, -øːz], *a.* **1.** Dull, tedious, wearisome, irksome. *Besognes fastidieuses,* drudgery. *Orateur f.,* prosy speaker. **2.** (Food) that palls; fulsome (compliments). *adv.* **-sement.**

fastueu|x, -euse [fastɥø, -øːz], *a.* Ostentatious; showy; sumptuous. *adv.* **-sement.**

fat [fat]. **1.** *a.m.* Conceited, foppish. **2.** *s.m.* Conceited ass; fop.

fatal, -als [fatal], *a.* **1.** Fatal (*d,* to). *Heure fatale,* fatal hour; hour of death. *Coup f.,* fatal, mortal, blow. **2.** Fated, inevitable. *Aboutissement f. d'une action,* inevitable result of an action. *C'est fatal,* it is bound to happen. *adv.* **-ement.**

fatalisme [fatalism], *s.m.* Fatalism.

fataliste [fatalist]. **1.** *s.* Fatalist. **2.** *a.* Fatalistic.

fatalité [fatalite], *s.f.* **1.** Fate, fatality. *C'est comme une f.!* it was bound to happen! **2.** Mischance, calamity.

fatidique [fatidik], *a.* Fatidical (number, etc.); fateful (word).

fatigant [fatigɑ̃], *a.* **1.** Tiring, fatiguing. **2.** Tiresome, tedious.

fatigue [fatig], *s.f.* **1.** (*a*) Fatigue, tiredness, weariness. **Tomber de fatigue,** to be dropping with fatigue. **Brisé de fatigue,** dog-tired; deadbeat. (*b*) **Souliers de fatigue,** strong walking shoes. **Habits de fatigue,** working clothes. **Cheval de fatigue,** cart-horse. *Mec.E:* **Pièces de fatigue,** parts subject to strains. **2.** Wear and tear (of machines, clothes, etc.).

fatiguer [fatige]. **1.** *v.tr.* (*a*) To fatigue, tire; to make (s.o.) weary *Se f. les yeux (à faire qch.),* to strain one's eyes (doing sth.). (*b*) To overwork (animal, etc.); to overdrive (machine, etc.); to strain (ship). *F. un livre,* to give a book hard usage. **2.** *v.i.* (Of ship, engine) To labour. *Poutre qui fatigue,* beam that bears a heavy strain. **se fatiguer,** to tire; to get tired. *Se f. de qch.,* to tire, get tired, of sth. *Se f. à faire qch.,* to tire oneself out doing sth.

fatras [fatrɑ], *s.m.* (*a*) Jumble, medley, hotchpotch (of ideas, papers, etc.). (*b*) Lumber, rubbish. *F. de connaissances,* farrago of useless knowledge.

fatuité [fatɥite], *s.f.* Self-conceit, self-satisfaction, self-complacency. [FAT]

fauber(t) [foberr], *s.m. Nau:* (Deck-)swab, mop.

faubourg [fobuːr], *s.m.* Suburb, outlying part (of town). *Parler avec l'accent des faubourgs,* to speak with a common accent.

faubourien, -ienne [foburjɛ̃, -jɛn]. **1.** *a.* Suburban. *Accent f.,* common accent. **2.** *s.* Suburbanite; common person.

faucard [fokaːr], *s.m.* Long-handled scythe (for clearing ponds, etc.).

fauchaison [foʃɛzɔ̃], *s.f.* Mowing-time.

fauchard [toʃaːr], *s.m. Hort:* Double-edged slasher; slash-hook.

fauch|er [foʃe], *v.tr.* **I.** To mow, cut, reap (field, corn). *Rugby Fb: F. son homme,* to bring down one's man. **2.** (*a*) To mow down (troops). (*b*) To sweep (the ground) (with machine-gun fire). *s.m.* **-age.**

 fauché, *a. P:* Stony-broke; cleaned out.

faucheur, -euse [foʃœːr, -øːz], *s.* **I.** Mower, reaper. **2.** *s.m. Arach:* Harvester, harvest-spider, *U.S:* daddy-long-legs. **3.** *s.f.* **Faucheuse,** (mechanical) reaper; mowing-machine.

faucheux [foʃø], *s.m.* = FAUCHEUR 2.

faucille [fosiːj], *s.f.* Sickle; reaping-hook.

faucon [fokɔ̃], *s.m. Orn:* Falcon, hawk. *F. mâle,* tercel, tiercel. *Falconry; hawking.*

fauconneau [fokono], *s.m.* **I.** Young falcon. **2.** *Archeol:* Falconet (gun).

fauconnerie [fokɔnri], *s.f. Ven:* **I.** Hawk house, falcon house. **2.** Falconry; hawking.

fauconnier [fokɔnje], *s.m.* Falconer.

faudr-a, -ai, -as, etc. See FAILLIR and FALLOIR.

faufil [fofil], *s.m.* Tacking thread, basting thread.

faufil|er [fofile], *v.tr.* (*a*) To tack, baste (seam, etc.); to tack on, baste on (braid, etc.). (*b*) To insert, introduce, (s.o., sth.) stealthily; to slip (s.o., sth.) in. [FIL] *s.m.* **-age.**

 se faufiler, to thread one's way. *Se f. dans la faveur de qn,* to insinuate oneself into s.o.'s favour. *Se f. dans un endroit, hors d'un endroit,* (i) to edge into, out of, a place; (ii) to sneak in, out. *Se f. le long du mur,* to creep along the wall.

faufilure [fofilyːr], *s.f.* Tacked seam.

faune[1] [foːn], *s.m. Myth:* Faun.

faune[2], *s.f.* Fauna, animal life (of region, etc.).

faussaire [foseːr], *s.m. & f.* Forger (of documents, etc.); perverter (of the truth, etc.).

fausse. See FAUX[1].

faussement [fosmɑ̃], *adv.* Falsely, erroneously, untruly.

fausser [fose], *v.tr.* (*a*) To make false; to falsify (the truth, etc.). *F. les faits,* to alter the facts. *F. les idées de qn,* to warp s.o.'s ideas. **Fausser parole à qn,** to break one's word to s.o. S.a. COMPAGNIE I. (*b*) To force (a lock); to bend, buckle, warp. *Essieu faussé,* sprung axle. (*c*) To put (instrument) out of tune.

 se fausser. (*a*) (Of appliance, etc.) To get out of order. (*b*) To bend, buckle. (*c*) (Of voice) (i) To get out of tune; (ii) to crack.

fausset[1] [fosɛ], *s.m. Mus:* Falsetto.

fausset[2], *s.m.,* **fosset** [fosɛ], *s.m.* Spigot, vent-plug. *Trou de fausset,* vent-hole.

fausseté [foste], *s.f.* **I.** Falseness, falsity. **2.** Falsehood, untruth. **3.** Duplicity.

faut. See FAILLIR and FALLOIR.

faute [foːt], *s.f.* **I.** Lack, need, want. **Faire faute,** to be lacking. **Vous lui faites faute,** he misses you. **Ne se faire faute de rien,** to deny oneself nothing. **Sans faute,** without fail. **Faute de,** for want of, for lack of. *F. d'argent,* for want of money. *Faute de quoi . . .,* failing which. . . . **Faute de mieux,** for want of something better. **Faute d'essayer,** for want of trying. **2.** (*a*) Fault, mistake. **Être en faute,** to be in fault. **Trouver, prendre, qn en faute,** to find, catch, s.o. in fault, in error. **Il n'y a pas de faute de ma part, ce n'est pas (de) ma faute,** it is not my fault. *A qui la f.?* whose fault is it? *La f. en est à moi,* the blame lies with me. *F. d'orthographe,* spelling mistake. *F. de jugement,* error of judgment. *F. d'impression,* misprint. (*b*) Transgression, delinquency, offence. *F. grave,* serious offence.

F. légère, peccadillo. (*c*) *Fb: etc:* Foul. (*d*) *Ten:* Fault. *F. de pied,* foot-fault.

fauter [fote], *v.i. F:* (*a*) To fall into sin. (*b*) *F. par un endroit,* to be defective in sth.

fauteuil [fotœːj], *s.m.* **I.** Arm-chair, easy-chair. *F. à bascule,* rocking-chair. *F. pliant,* folding-chair. *Th: F. d'orchestre,* orchestra stall. *F. de premier balcon,* dress-circle seat. **2.** Chair (at meeting). **Occuper le fauteuil,** to be in the chair. S.a. ACADÉMIQUE, PRÉSIDENTIEL.

fauteur, -trice [fotœːr, -tris], *s.* Abettor, supporter (*de,* of); instigator (of rising). *F. de troubles,* agitator.

faut|if, -ive [fotif, -iːv], *a.* **I.** Faulty, incorrect. *Calcul f.,* miscalculation. **2.** Sinning, offending, in fault. *adv.* **-ivement.**

fauve [foːv]. **I.** *a.* (*a*) Fawn-coloured, fulvous; tawny (hair, etc.); (of deer) fallow. (*b*) *Odeur f.,* musky smell. **2.** *s.m.* (*a*) Fawn (colour). (*b*) *Le f., les (bêtes) fauves,* deer. (*c*) *Les (grands) fauves,* (fulvous) wild beasts (lions, tigers, etc.).

fauvette [fovɛt], *s.f. Orn:* Warbler.

faux[1], **fausse** [fo, foːs]. I. *a.* False. **I.** Untrue. *Nouvelle fausse,* false report. *F. témoin,* false witness. *Témoignage f., f. témoignage,* perjury. **2.** Not genuine. (*a*) **Il y a un faux air de famille entre eux,** there is a sort of family likeness between them. *Fausse monnaie,* spurious, counterfeit, base, coin(age). *Fausse clef,* skeleton key. *Fausse adresse,* wrong, false, address. *Fausse cartouche,* dummy cartridge. *Bijouterie fausse,* imitation jewellery. *Fausse fenêtre,* blind window. *Acte f.,* forged deed. *F. bilan,* fraudulent balance-sheet. *Typ:* **Faux titre,** half-title, bastard title. *adv.* **Rire qui sonne faux,** laugh that has a false ring. (*b*) (Usu. after noun) Treacherous. *F:* **Faux bonhomme,** shifty, sly, customer. **3.** Wrong, mistaken. *Fausse date,* wrong date. **Être dans un faux jour,** to be in the wrong light. **Présenter la conduite de qn sous un faux jour,** to place s.o.'s conduct in a false light. *Balance fausse,* inaccurate balance. *F. poids,* unjust weight. **Faire un faux pas,** (i) to take a false step; (ii) to blunder, to make a *faux pas.* **Faire fausse route,** to take the wrong road; *F:* to be on the wrong track or tack. *Bill:* **Faire fausse queue,** to miscue. *Ling:* **Faux sens,** wrong shade of meaning (in translation). *Mus:* **Fausse note,** wrong note. *adv.* **Chanter faux,** to sing out of tune. *Adv.phr.* **A faux,** wrongly. *Interpréter qch. à f.,* to put a false interpretation on sth. **Frapper à faux,** to miss one's mark. *Argument qui porte à faux,* argument that (i) rests on erroneous premises, (ii) is irrelevant, beside the point. (Of wheel) **Tourner à faux,** to run untrue, out of true. S.a. BOND 2, PORTE-À-FAUX.

 II. **faux,** *s.m.* **I.** (*a*) *Le f.,* the false, the untrue. **Plaider le faux pour savoir le vrai,** to angle for the truth with a lie. *Jur:* **S'inscrire en faux contre qch.,** to dispute the validity of sth.; to deny sth. (*b*) **Bijouterie en faux,** imitation jewellery. **2.** *Jur:* Forgery. **Inscription de faux,** plea of forgery.

faux[2], *s.f.* **I.** Scythe. **2.** *Anat:* Falx.

faux[3]. See FAILLIR.

faux-filet [fofilɛ], *s.m. Cu:* Sirloin.

faux-fuyant [fofɥijɑ̃], *s.m.* Subterfuge, shift, quirk, evasion. *pl. Des faux-fuyants.*

faux-monnayeur [fomɔnɛjœːr], *s.m.* Coiner.

faveur [favœːr], *s.f.* Favour. **I.** (*a*) **Gagner la f. de qn,** to obtain s.o.'s favour, s.o.'s interest. **Être en f. auprès de qn,** to be in favour with s.o. **Rentrer en f.,** to be restored to favour. **Trouver faveur auprès de qn,** to find favour with s.o.

Com: Prix de faveur, preferential price. Jours de faveur, days of grace. Billet de faveur, complimentary ticket ; free ticket. A la faveur de . . ., by the help of . . . ; by means of. . . . *A la f. de la nuit*, under cover of (the) night. (*b*) Faire une faveur à qn, to do s.o. a favour, a kindness. **2.** *F. de soie*, silk favour, silk ribbon.

favorable [favɔrabl], *a.* **I.** Favourable (*à*, to). *Se rendre les dieux favorables*, to propitiate the gods. **2.** Favourable, propitious (circumstances, wind) ; auspicious (occasion). **Peu favorable**, unfavourable, unpropitious (*à*, to). *adv.* **-ment.**

favori, -ite [favɔri, -it]. **I.** *a. & s.* Favourite. **2.** *s.m.pl.* (Side-)whiskers.

favoriser [favɔrize], *v.tr.* To favour, to be partial to (s.o., sth.). *Être favorisé par, de, qn*, to be favoured by s.o. *F. la croissance*, to promote growth. *F. les arts*, to patronize, encourage, promote, the arts.

favoritisme [favɔritism], *s.m.* Favouritism.

fayot [fajo], *s.m. P:* Haricot bean, kidney-bean.

féal, -aux [feal, -o], *a. A:* Faithful, trusty. A nos féaux sujets, to our trusty lieges.

fébrifuge [febrify:ʒ], *a. & s.m. Med:* Febrifuge.

fébrile [febril], *a.* (*a*) *Med:* Febrile (pulse, etc.). (*b*) *F:* Feverish (preparations).

fécal, -aux [fekal, -o], *a. Ch: Physiol:* Faecal.

fécond [fekɔ̃], *a.* Prolific, fruitful, fertile, fecund ; productive (*en*, of). *Esprit f. en inventions*, mind fertile, rich, in inventions.

féconder [fekɔ̃de], *v.tr.* To fecundate.

fécondité [fekɔ̃dite], *s.f.* Fecundity. **I.** Fruitfulness. **2.** Fertility (of land, etc.).

fécule [fekyl], *s.f.* F(a)ecula, starch.

féculent [fekylɑ̃]. **I.** *a.* Starchy. **2.** *s.m.* Starchy food.

fédéral, -aux [federal, -o], *a. & s.m.* Federal.

fédéraliser [federalize], *v.tr.* To federalize.

fédéraliste [federalist], *a. & s.* Federalist.

fédération [federasjɔ̃], *s.f.* Federation.

fédérer [federe], *v.tr.* (**je fédère** ; **je fédérerai**) To federate, federalize.
   se fédérer, to federate.

fédéré, *a. & s.m.* Federate.

fée [fe], *s.f.* Fairy. *Conte de fées*, fairy-tale. **Pays des fées**, fairyland. *F:* Vieille fée, old hag. S.a. CARABOSSE.

féerie [feri], *s.f.* **I.** Enchantment, fairyhood. **2.** Fairyland. **3.** *Th:* Fairy play.

féerique [ferik], *a.* **I.** Fairy, magic (castle, etc.). **2.** Fairy-like, enchanting (sight, etc.).

feignant¹ [feɲɑ̃], *s.m. P:* = FAINÉANT.

feign-ant², -ais, -is, etc. See FEINDRE.

feindre [fɛ̃:dr], *v.* (*pr.p.* feignant ; *p.p.* feint ; *pr.ind.* je feins, il feint, n. feignons ; *p.h.* je feignis ; *fu.* je feindrai) **I.** *v.tr.* To feign, simulate, sham (death, illness, etc.). *Feindre de faire qch.*, to pretend to do sth. **2.** *v.i.* (Of horse) To limp slightly.
   feinte, *s.f.* **I.** (*a*) Feint, sham, pretence. (*b*) *Box: Fenc:* Feint. *Rugby Fb:* Faire une feinte de passe, to give, sell, the dummy. **2.** Slight limp.

feld-maréchal [fɛldmareʃal], *s.m.* Field-marshal. *pl.* Des feld-maréchaux.

feldspath [fɛlspat], *s.m. Miner:* Fel(d)spar.

fêler [fele], *v.tr.* To crack (glass, china, etc.).
   se fêler, (of glass, etc.) to crack.

fêlé, *a.* Cracked. *F:* Inventeur à l'esprit fêlé, crack-brained inventor. *Il a le cerveau f.*, *le timbre f.*, he is a bit cracked.

félicitations [felisitasjɔ̃], *s.f. pl.* Congratulations, felicitations. **Faire des félicitations à qn,** to congratulate s.o.

félicité [felisite], *s.f.* Felicity, bliss(fulness).

féliciter [felisite], *v.tr.* *F. qn de qch., d'avoir fait qch.,* to congratulate, compliment, s.o. on sth., on having done sth.
   se féliciter *de qch.,* to be pleased with sth. ; to express satisfaction at sth.

félin, -ine [felɛ̃, -in], *a.* Feline. (*a*) *Z:* Cat (family, etc.). *s. Les grands félins*, the great felines, the great cats. (*b*) *F:* Catlike.

félon, -onne [felɔ̃, -ɔn]. **I.** *a. A:* Disloyal, false, felon. **2.** *s.m. A:* Felon, caitiff.

felouque [fəluk], *s.f. Nau:* Felucca.

fêlure [fely:r], *s.f.* Crack (in china, etc.) ; split (in wood). *F. du crâne*, fracture of the skull. *F:* Il a une fêlure, he's a bit cracked. [FÊLER]

femelle [fəmɛl], *s.f. & a.* (*a*) Female (animal) ; she-(animal) ; cow-(elephant, etc.) ; hen-(bird). (*b*) *s.f. P:* (Not in polite use) Woman, female.

féminin [feminɛ̃]. **I.** *a.* Feminine (gender, etc.). *Le sexe f.*, the female sex. *Voix féminine*, (i) woman's voice ; (ii) womanish voice. **2.** *s.m. Gram:* Feminine gender. **Ce mot est du féminin**, this word is feminine.

femme [fam], *s.f.* **I.** Woman. **Femme auteur**, woman author ; authoress. **Femme médecin**, lady doctor. **2.** Wife. **Chercher femme,** to seek a wife. **Prendre femme,** to take a wife. **Avoir femme,** to have a wife ; to be married. **3.** **Femme de chambre**, housemaid ; *Nau:* stewardess. **Femme de charge**, housekeeper. **Femme de journée**, charwoman, daily help, *F:* 'daily.' **Femme de ménage,** (i) charwoman ; (ii) housekeeper. **4.** *F:* **Bonne femme.** See BONHOMME, CONTE I, REMÈDE.

femmelette [famlɛt], *s.f. F:* (*a*) Little woman. (*b*) (Of man) Weakling.

fémoral, -aux [femɔral, -o], *a. Anat:* Femoral.

fémur [femy:r], *s.m. Anat:* Femur, thigh-bone.

fenaison [fənɛzɔ̃], *s.f.* **I.** Haymaking ; hay-harvest. **2.** Haymaking time. [FOIN]

fendeur [fɑ̃dœ:r], *s.m.* (*a*) Splitter, slitter (of slates, etc.) ; cleaver (of diamonds). (*b*) *F:* Wood-cutter.

fendille [fɑ̃di:j], *s.f.* (Surface) crack.

fendill|er [fɑ̃dije], *v.tr.* To fissure ; to crack (wood, etc.) ; to crackle (glaze). *s.m.* **-ement.**
   se fendiller, (of wood, paint) to crack ; (of china) to crackle.

fendoir [fɑ̃dwa:r], *s.m. Tls:* Chopper, cleaver.

fend|re [fɑ̃:dr], *v.tr.* To cleave (lengthwise) ; to split (wood, etc.) ; to fissure. *F. l'air*, (of sound) to rend the air. **Fendre la foule**, to force, elbow, one's way through the crowd. **Il gèle à pierre fendre**, it is freezing hard. *C'était à fendre l'âme*, it was heart-breaking, heart-rending. *Bruit à f. la tête, à vous f. les oreilles*, ear-splitting noise. S.a. OREILLE I. *s.m.* **-age.**
   se fendre, **I.** To split, crack. **2.** *Fenc:* To lunge. **3.** *P:* Se fendre (de vingt francs), to fork out, stump up (twenty francs).

fenêtre [f(ə)nɛ:tr], *s.f.* **I.** Window. *F. à coulisse, à guillotine,* sash-window. *F. croisée, à battants,* casement-window. *F. en saillie*, bay-window *Regarder par la f.,* to look out of the window. *F:* Il faut passer par là ou par la fenêtre, it is absolutely inevitable ; there is nothing else for it. **Mettre la tête à la fenêtre,** to thrust one's head out of the window. S.a. JETER. **2.** Blank, space (in document). **3.** Window (in envelope).

fenil [fəni], *s.m. A:* Hayloft.

fenouil [fənu:j], *s.m. Bot:* Fennel.

fente [fɑ̃:t], *s.f.* **I.** (*a*) Crack, crevice, split, slit, fissure, chink. (*b*) Slot, cut (in head of screw, etc.). *Av:* Aile à fentes, slotted wing. **Fente de poche,** pocket-hole. **2.** *Fenc:* Lunge.

féodal, -aux [feɔdal, -o], *a.* Feudal.

féodaliser [feɔdalize], *v.tr.* To feudalize.

féodalité [feɔdalite], *s.f.* The feudal system.

fer [fɛːr], *s.m.* Iron. **1.** *Fer coulé, de fonte,* cast iron. *Fer en saumon, en gueuse,* pig-iron. *Fer forgé, soudé, battu,* wrought iron. *Fer en tôle, en feuilles,* sheet-iron. *Fer plat, fer feuillard,* hoop-iron. **Fil de fer,** wire. *F:* **Discipline de fer,** iron discipline. **Le peuple croit dur comme le fer à l'existence de . . .,** the people have a cast-iron belief in the existence of. . . . *S.a.* ÂGE 3, BATTRE I. **2.** (*a*) **Fer de lance,** spear-head. *Fer de flèche,* arrow-head. *Fer d'un lacet,* tag of a lace. *Fer de rabot,* plane-iron. (*b*) Shoe, band, cap (of pile). (*c*) Sword. **Croiser le fer avec qn,** to cross swords with s.o. *F:* **Battre le fer,** to fence. **Porter le feu et le fer dans un pays,** to put a country to fire and sword. **3.** *Tls: etc: Fer à souder,* soldering-iron, soldering-bit. *Fer à marquer,* branding-iron. **Marquer qn au fer rouge,** to brand s.o. *Fer à friser,* curling-tongs. *Fer à repasser,* flat-iron, laundry iron. **Coup de fer tailleur,** pressing (of suit of clothes). *Golf:* **Grand fer,** driving-iron. **4.** *pl.* Irons, chains, fetters. **Être aux fers,** to be in irons. **5. Fer à, de, cheval,** horseshoe. (Of horse) *Perdre un fer,* to cast a shoe. *F:* **Tomber les quatre fers en l'air,** to go sprawling. **Table en fer à cheval,** horseshoe table. *S.a.* LOCHER.

fer-ai, -as, etc. See FAIRE.

fer-blanc [fɛrblɑ̃], *s.m.* See BLANC I. 5.

ferblanterie [fɛrblɑ̃tri], *s.f.* **1.** (*a*) Tin-plate. (*b*) *Ind:* Tin-shop. **2.** Tin(-plate) ware.

ferblantier [fɛrblɑ̃tje], *s.m.* Tinman, tinsmith.

férié [ferje], *a.* **Jour férié,** (general) holiday.

férir [feriːr], *v.tr.* (Used only in inf. and in *p.p.* **féru**) To strike. **Sans coup férir,** without striking a blow; without firing a shot. **Être féru de qn, d'amour pour qn,** to be madly in love with s.o., to be enamoured of s.o. **Être féru d'une idée,** to be set on an idea.

se férir. (Used in inf. and compound tenses) *Se f. de qn,* to fall (madly) in love with s.o. *Elle s'était férue du théâtre,* she had become stage-struck.

ferl|er [fɛrle], *v.tr.* To furl (sail). *s.m.* **-age.**

fermage [fɛrmaːʒ], *s.m.* **1.** (Tenant) farming. **2.** Rent (of farm).

fermail [fɛrmaːj], *s.m.* (Ornamental) clasp.

fermant [fɛrmɑ̃], *a.* Closing. **Arriver à portes fermantes,** to arrive as the gates are closing. **A jour fermant, à nuit fermante,** at close of day.

ferme¹ [fɛrm]. **1.** *a.* (*a*) Firm, steady. *Poutre f.,* firm, rigid, beam. **Terre ferme,** (i) firm land; (ii) mainland. *Être f. dans ses desseins,* to be firm, steadfast, in one's intentions. *Mil:* **De pied ferme,** at the halt. *F:* **Attendre qn de pied ferme,** to wait resolutely for s.o. (*b*) **Vente ferme, offre ferme,** firm, definite, sale, offer. **2.** *adv.* Firmly. **Tenir ferme,** to stand fast. **Frapper ferme,** to hit hard. **J'y travaille ferme,** I am hard at it. **Croire fort et ferme aux esprits,** to be a firm believer in spirits. **Manger ferme,** to eat steadily through the courses. *Com:* **Vendre ferme,** to make a firm sale.

ferme², *s.f.* **1.** (*a*) Farming lease. **Prendre une terre à ferme,** to take a lease of, to rent, a piece of land. (*b*) Farm. **Valet de ferme,** farm-hand. **2.** (*a*) Truss (of roof, bridge, etc.). (*b*) Trussed girder. **3.** *Th:* Rigid flat; set piece.

ferme³, *s.f.* *P:* (Used only in) **La ferme!** shut up! hold your jaw! [FERMER]

fermement [fɛrməmɑ̃], *adv.* Firmly, steadily, steadfastly.

ferment [fɛrmɑ̃], *s.m.* Ferment.

fermentation [fɛrmɑ̃tasjɔ̃], *s.f.* **1.** Fermentation. **2. Fermentation populaire,** unrest among the people. *Esprits en f.,* minds in a ferment.

fermenter [fɛrmɑ̃te], *v.i.* **1.** (Of wine, etc.) To ferment, *F:* to work; (of dough, etc.) to rise. **2.** *Les esprits fermentaient,* men's minds were in a ferment.

fermer [fɛrme]. **1.** *v.tr.* (*a*) To close, shut. **Fermer violemment la porte,** to slam, bang, the door. **Fermer sa porte à qn,** to close one's door against s.o. *F. la porte à clef, au verrou,* to lock, to bolt, the door. *F. les rideaux,* to draw the curtains. **Fermer boutique,** to shut up shop. *On ferme!* closing time! *F. un trou,* to stop up, block up, a hole. *F. un robinet,* to turn off a tap. **Fermer le gaz,** (i) to turn out the gas; (ii) to turn off the gas (at the meter). **Fermer l'électricité, la lumière,** to switch off the light. *S.a.* ŒIL I. *El:* *F. un circuit,* to close a circuit; to switch on (current). (*b*) **Fermer la marche,** to bring up the rear. **2.** *v.i.* (Of door, etc.) To close, shut.

se fermer, to close, shut.

fermé, *a.* **1.** Closed (door, window). *Rade fermée,* landlocked roadstead. **A la nuit fermée,** when night had fallen. *F:* **Être fermé à qch.,** to have no taste for, no appreciation of, sth. **2. Visage fermé,** inscrutable countenance. **3.** *Monde très f.,* very exclusive society.

fermeté [fɛrməte], *s.f.* Firmness; steadfastness, steadiness (of purpose). **Agir avec fermeté,** to act firmly.

fermeture [fɛrmətyːr], *s.f.* **1.** Closing, shutting. **Fermeture des ateliers,** (i) knock-off (from work); (ii) closing down of the workshops; (iii) lock-out. *F. de la pêche,* close of the fishing season. *Com:* *F. d'un compte,* closing of an account. *Mch:* *F. de l'admission,* cut-off (of steam). **2.** Closing apparatus. **Fermeture éclair,** zip fastener. *F. à rouleau,* revolving shutter. *Sm.a:* **Fermeture de culasse,** rifle-bolt.

fermier, -ière [fɛrmje, -jɛːr], *s.* **1.** (*a*) Tenant (of farm). *F. d'une pêche,* lessee of a fishery. (*b*) Farmer; *f.* farmer's wife, farm-mistress. **2.** *Fr.Hist:* Tax-farmer. **Fermier général,** farmer-general.

fermoir¹ [fɛrmwaːr], *s.m.* **1.** Clasp, hasp, snap, catch, fastener (of book, lady's bag, etc.). *Bouton f. à pression,* snap fastener. **2.** *Sm.a:* Cut-off (of box-magazine). [FERMER]

fermoir², *s.m.* *Tls:* Firmer (chisel).

féroce [ferɔs], *a.* Ferocious, savage, wild, fierce. *Bêtes féroces,* wild beasts. *adv.* **-ment.**

férocité [ferɔsite], *s.f.* Ferocity, ferociousness.

Féroé [ferɔe]. *Pr.n.* *Geog:* **Les îles Féroé,** the Faroe Islands.

ferraille [fɛraːj], *s.f.* Old iron, scrap-iron. **Bruit de ferraille,** clanking noise. [FER]

ferraillement [fɛrajmɑ̃], *s.m.* **1.** Hammer-and-tongs fighting. **2.** Rattle, drumming (of car).

ferrailler [fɛraje], *v.i.* **1.** *F:* To slash about with the swords. **2.** *F:* To fence clumsily. **3.** (Of car) To drum.

ferrailleur [fɛrajœːr], *s.m.* *F:* **1.** Sword rattler, bully, swashbuckler. **2.** Poor fencer.

ferrant [fɛrɑ̃], *a.* **Maréchal ferrant,** shoeing smith; farrier.

ferrate [fɛrrat], *s.m.* *Ch:* Ferrate.

ferr|er [fɛre], *v.tr.* **1.** To fit, mount, (sth.) with iron; to put a ferrule on (stick); to tag (lace); to tyre, shoe (wheel). **Ferrer un cheval,** to shoe a horse. **2.** To metal (road). **3.** *Fish:* To strike (fish). *s.m.* **-age.**

ferré, *a.* *(a)* Fitted, mounted, with iron; iron-shod. *Souliers ferrés,* hobnailed shoes. **Voie ferrée,** (i) permanent way (of railway); (ii) railway (line). *Cheval f. à glace,* rough-shod horse. *F:* **Être ferré (à glace) sur un sujet,** to know all about a subject. **Être ferré en mathématiques,** to be well up in mathematics. *(b) Route ferrée,* metalled, macadamized, road.

ferret [fɛrɛ], *s.m.* Tag, tab, a(i)glet (of bootlace, of aiguillette). [FER]

ferreux, -euse [fɛrø, -øːz], *a. Ch: Miner:* Ferrous (metal).

ferrique [fɛrrik], *a. Ch:* Ferric (salt, etc.).

ferro-chrome [fɛrɔkroːm], *s.m. Metall:* Ferrochrome, -chromium; chrome iron.

ferrocyanure [fɛrrɔsjanyːr], *s.m. Ch:* Ferrocyanide.

ferronnerie [fɛrɔnri], *s.f.* **1.** Iron works. **2.** Ironmongery.

ferronnier [fɛrɔnje], *s.m.* **1.** Ironworker, blacksmith. **2.** Ironmonger.

ferrotypie [fɛrɔtipi], *s.f. Phot:* Ferrotype.

ferroviaire [fɛrɔvjeːr], *a.* Pertaining to a railway. *Trafic f.,* railway traffic.

ferrugineux, -euse [fɛrryʒinø, -øːz], *a.* Ferruginous. *Source ferrugineuse,* chalybeate spring.

ferrure [fɛryːr], *s.f.* **1.** Piece of ironwork. *Ferrures de porte,* door fittings. *Ferrures en cuivre,* brass fittings. **2.** Shoeing (of horse, etc.).

fertile [fɛrtil], *a.* Fertile, fruitful *(en,* in); rich (land). *Semaine f. en événements,* eventful week. *adv.* **-ment.**

fertilisant [fɛrtilizã]. **1.** *a.* Fertilizing. **2.** *s.m.* Fertilizer.

fertilisation [fɛrtilizasjɔ̃], *s.f.* Fertilization, fertilizing.

fertilis|er [fɛrtilize], *v.tr.* To fertilize; to make (sth.) fertile, fruitful. *a.* **-able.**

fertilité [fɛrtilite], *s.f.* Fertility; fruitfulness.

féru. See FÉRIR.

férule [feryl], *s.f.* **1.** *Bot:* Ferula; giant fennel. **2.** *Sch:* Cane; *A:* ferule. **Donner de la férule à qn,** to cane s.o. *F:* **Être sous la férule de qn,** to be ruled with a rod of iron by s.o.

ferv|ent, -ente [fɛrvã, -ãːt]. **1.** *a.* Fervent, ardent, earnest. **2.** *s.* Enthusiast; devotee *(de,* of). *adv.* **-emment.**

ferveur [fɛrvœːr], *s.f.* Fervour *(à faire qch.,* in doing sth.); ardour, earnestness.

fesse [fɛs], *s.f.* **1.** Buttock. **Donner sur les fesses à qn,** to give s.o. a spanking. **2.** *pl. Nau:* Buttocks, tuck (of ship).

fessée [fɛse], *s.f.* Spanking.

fesse-mathieu [fɛsmatjø], *s.m.* 'Skinflint, screw. *pl. Des fesse-mathieux.* [FESSER]

fesser [fɛse], *v.tr.* To spank (s.o.).

festin [fɛstɛ̃], *s.m.* Feast, banquet. **Salle de festin,** banqueting-hall. **Faire (un) festin,** to feast, banquet.

festiner [fɛstine]. **1.** *v.i.* To feast. **2.** *v.tr.* To feast (s.o.).

feston [fɛstɔ̃], *s.m.* **1.** Festoon. **2.** *Needlew:* Scallop. **Point de feston,** button-hole stitch.

festonner [fɛstɔne], *v.tr.* **1.** To festoon. **2.** To scallop (hem, etc.).

festoyer [fɛstwaje], *v.* (je festoie; je festoierai) **1.** *v.tr.* To regale, feast (s.o.). **2.** *v.i.* To feast, carouse. [FÊTE]

fêtard, -arde [fɛtaːr, -ard], *s. F:* Reveller; roisterer; man or woman of pleasure.

fête [fɛːt], *s.f.* **1.** Feast, festival. **Jour de fête,** feast-day, holiday. **Faire fête,** (i) to hold high festival; (ii) to keep holiday. *F.* **légale,** public holiday (= bank-holiday). **Fête de qn,** s.o.'s name-day. **Souhaiter la fête, une bonne fête, à qn,** to wish s.o. many happy returns. **Ce n'est pas tous les jours fête,** we'll make this an occasion. **2.** Fête, entertainment. **3.** Festivity. **Le village était en fête,** the village was holiday-making. **Faire la fête,** to carouse; to have one's fling. **Faire fête à qn,** to receive s.o. with open arms; to welcome s.o. **Être de la fête,** to be one of the festive party. *Il ne s'était jamais vu à pareille f.,* he had never had such a good time.

fête-Dieu [fɛtdjø], *s.f. Ecc:* Corpus Christi.

fêter [fɛte], *v.tr.* **1.** *(a)* To keep (day, etc.) as a holiday, as a festival. **Fêter la naissance de qn,** to celebrate s.o.'s birthday. *(b) F.* **un saint,** to keep a saint's day. **2. Fêter qn,** (i) to fête s.o.; (ii) to entertain s.o. *Dîner pour f. le nouveau membre,* dinner to welcome the new member.

fétiche [fetiʃ], *s.m.* Fetish. *Aut:* Mascot.

fétide [fetid], *a.* Fetid, stinking.

fétidité [fetidite], *s.f.* Fetidness.

fétu [fety], *s.m.* Straw. *F:* **Je m'en soucie comme d'un fétu,** I don't care a straw, a rap, about it.

fétuque [fetyk], *s.f. Bot:* Fescue.

feu¹, feux [fø], *s.m.* Fire. I. **1.** *(a)* **Craindre qch. comme le feu,** to stand in dread of sth. **Faire feu des quatre pieds,** (i) (of horse) to make the sparks fly; (ii) *F:* to make a great effort. *F:* **Il fait feu de tout bois,** nothing comes amiss to him. **Mettre (le) feu à qch.,** to set fire to sth. *Ustensiles qui vont au feu,* fire-proof utensils. **Cheminée en feu,** chimney on fire. **Mettre l'Europe en feu,** to set Europe ablaze. **Visage en feu,** flushed face. S.a. SACRÉ I. **Prendre feu,** (i) to catch fire; (ii) *F:* to fly into a passion. **Pompe à feu,** fire-engine. **Faire la part du feu,** (i) to clear the ground (to prevent fire spreading); (ii) *Com: F:* to cut one's losses. *F:* **Jeter feu et flamme contre qn,** to rage and fume at s.o. **Voulez-vous bien me donner du feu?** will you kindly give me a light? S.a. FOLLET. *(b)* Heat, ardour. *Dans le premier feu de sa colère,* in the heat of his resentment. **2.** *(a)* **Faire du feu,** to light a fire. **Garniture de feu,** set of fire-irons. **Feu de joie,** bonfire; beacon. **Feu d'artifice,** fireworks. *Leur amitié ne fera pas long feu,* their friendship will not last long. S.a. COIN I, PAILLE I. *(b) Mch:* **Mettre une chaudière en feu,** to fire up a boiler. **Pousser les feux,** to make all steam. **Mettre bas les feux,** to draw the fires. *(c)* **Condamner qn au feu** to condemn s.o. to (be burnt at) the stake. **J'en mettrais la main au feu,** I would swear to it. **Épreuve du feu,** ordeal by fire. **Brûler qn à petit feu,** to torture s.o. (on the grill). **Faire mourir qn à petit feu,** (i) to kill s.o. by inches; (ii) to keep s.o. on tenter-hooks. *(d) Cu:* **Cuire qch. à un feu doux, vif,** to cook sth. in a gentle, brisk, oven. **A grand feu, petit feu,** on a fierce, a slow, fire. **Fourneau à pétrole à quatre feux,** four-burner oil-stove. *(e)* **Hameau de cinquante feux,** hamlet of fifty homes. **N'avoir ni feu ni lieu,** to have neither hearth nor home. **3.** **Armes à feu,** fire-arms. **Bouche à feu,** piece of ordnance. **Faire feu,** to fire. **Faire feu sur qn,** to shoot at s.o. *(Of pistol, fuse)* **Faire long feu,** to hang fire. *F:* **Projet qui fait long feu,** plan that is hanging fire. **Tué au feu,** killed in action. *F:* **Un feu roulant de questions,** a running fire of questions. S.a. NOURRI 2. **4.** *(a)* Light (of lighthouse, etc.). **Feu tournant,** revolving light. **Feu à éclats,** flashing light. *Feu d'avant d'une locomotive,* head-light of a locomotive. *Feu d'arrière,* tail-light. *Nau:* **Feux de route,** navigation lights. *Adm:* **Feux de circulation,** traffic lights. *(b)* **N'y voir que du feu,**

(i) to be dazzled; (ii) *F:* to be completely hoodwinked. **II. coup de feu. 1.** (a) Browning (of joint). (b) Burning (of bread, joint, etc.). (c) *F:* Rush hour. *Com: etc:* Être dans son coup de feu, to be at one's busiest. **2.** (Gun-, pistol-)shot. *Recevoir un coup de feu,* to receive a gunshot wound. **3.** Fire-damp explosion.

feu², *a.* Late (= deceased). **1.** (Between article and sb., and variable) *Le feu roi, la feue reine,* the late king, the late queen. **2.** (Preceding the article or poss. adj., and inv.) *Feu la reine,* the late queen.

feuillage [fœja:ʒ], *s.m.* Foliage.

feuille [fœːj], *s.f.* **1.** Leaf (of plant). Feuille morte, dead leaf. *Av:* Descente en feuille morte, falling-leaf roll. Feuille de chou, (i) cabbage-leaf; (ii) *F:* insignificant journal; rag. **2.** *F.* de métal, sheet of metal. Fer en feuilles, sheet-iron. *F.* d'or, gold-leaf, -foil. *F.* d'un contrevent, leaf of a shutter. Feuille anglaise, sheet-rubber. **3.** *F.* de papier, sheet of paper. Feuille volante, mobile, loose sheet. Feuille de route, (i) way-bill (of carrier); (ii) *Mil:* marching orders. Feuille quotidienne, daily (news)paper. *Med:* Feuille de température, temperature chart.

feuillé [fœje], *a.* Leafy; in full leaf.

feuillée [fœje], *s.f.* **1.** (a) Foliage (in painting, etc.). (b) Arbour. **2.** *Mil:* Les feuillées, the latrines (in camp).

feuillet [fœjɛ], *s.m.* **1.** (a) Leaf (of book). (b) *Adm:* Form (for a return); return sheet. **2.** Thin sheet, plate (of wood, etc.).

feuillet|er [fœjte], *v.tr.* (je feuillette; je feuilletterai) **1.** To divide (wood, etc.) into sheets, leaves. *Cu:* To roll and fold (pastry). **2.** To turn over the pages of (book). Livre bien feuilleté, well-thumbed book. *s.m.* **-age.**

se feuilleter, (of mineral, etc.) to split up, to flake, to cleave.

feuilleté, *a.* Foliated, laminated. *Cu:* Pâte feuilletée, puff paste.

feuilleton [fœjtɔ̃], *s.m.* Feuilleton. (a) Literary or scientific article. (b) Serial story (in newspaper).

feuillette¹ [fœjɛt], *s.f.* Small leaf; leaflet.

feuillette², *s.f.* (Approx. =) Quarter-cask.

feuillu [fœjy]. **1.** *a.* Leafy. **2.** *s.m.* Foliage.

feuillure [fœjy:r], *s.f. Carp:* Groove, rabbet.

feutre [føːtr], *s.m.* **1.** Felt. **2.** Felt hat. **3.** Stuffing, padding (of saddle, etc.).

feutr|er [føtre], *v.tr.* **1.** To felt (hair, etc.). **2.** To felt; to cover (boiler, etc.) with felt. *F:* A pas feutrés, with noiseless tread; with velvet tread. *s.m.* **-age.**

fève [fɛːv], *s.f.* (a) Bean. *F:* Rendre à qn fève pour pois, to give s.o. tit for tat. (b) Fève de cacao, cocoa-nib.

février [fevrie], *s.m.* February. Au mois de février, in (the month of) February.

fez [fɛːz], *s.m.* Fez (as worn in the Near East).

fi [fi], *int.* Fie! for shame! Faire fi de qch., to despise sth.; to turn up one's nose at sth.

fiacre [fjakr], *s.m.* Hackney-carriage; cab. *Cocher de f.,* cab-driver. Fiacre automobile, taxi-cab.

fiançailles [fjɑ̃sɑːj], *s.f.pl.* Betrothal, engagement (avec, to).

fiancer (se) [səfjɑ̃se], *v.pr.* To become engaged (à, to).

fiancé, -ée, *s.* Fiancé, fiancée; *A. & Lit:* betrothed.

fiasco [fjasko], *s.m.inv.* Fiasco. Leurs projets ont fait fiasco, their plans have failed.

fibre [fibr], *s.f.* Fibre. *F.* du bois, fibre, grain, of the wood. *F:* Avoir la fibre sensible, to be susceptible, impressionable.

fibreux, -euse [fibrø, -øːz], *a.* Fibrous, stringy.

fibrille [fibril], *s.f.* Fibril(la).

fibrine [fibrin], *s.f. Ch: Physiol:* Fibrin.

fibroïde [fibroid], *a. & s.m. Med:* Fibroid.

fibrome [fibroːm], *s.m. Med:* Fibroma; fibrous tumour.

ficaire [fikɛːr], *s.f. Bot:* Lesser celandine; pilewort.

ficel|er [fisle], *v.tr.* (je ficelle; je ficellerai) To tie up, do up. *s.m.* **-age.**

ficelle [fisɛl], *s.f.* (i) String, twine; (ii) packthread. *F.* à fouet, whipcord. *F:* C'est lui qui tient les ficelles, he pulls the strings. Connaître les ficelles, to know the ropes. Montrer la ficelle, (of underhand work, etc.) to show up. *a.* Avocat ficelle, tricky, wily, knowing, lawyer.

fichant [fiʃɑ̃], *a.* **1.** *Mil:* Plunging (fire). **2.** *P:* Annoying.

fiche [fiʃ], *s.f.* **1.** Peg, pin (of iron, wood); stake. *El:* Plug, key. *Surv:* Pin, arrow. **2.** (a) Slip (of paper); memorandum slip; voucher. *Adm:* Fiche policière, (hotel) registration form. (b) Card, ticket (of membership, etc.). (c) Index card. Jeu de fiches, card-index. (d) Tie-on label. **3.** *Cards: etc:* Counter, marker; fish. *F:* Fiche de consolation, crumb, scrap, of comfort.

ficher [fiʃe], *v.tr.* **1.** To drive in (stake, nail, etc.). *F.* une épingle dans qch., to stick a pin into sth. *F:* Ficher les yeux sur qch., to fix, fasten, one's eyes on sth. **2.** *P:* (p.p. fichu; the inf. is usu. fiche) (a) (= METTRE) Fiche(r) qn à la porte, to throw s.o. out. *F.* qn dedans, to cheat s.o.; to take s.o. in. On m'a fichu dedans, I've been done! (b) (= DONNER, ENVOYER) *F.* une gifle à qn, to give, fetch, s.o. a clout, a box on the ear. Fichez-moi la paix! shut up! (c) (= FAIRE) Il n'a rien fichu de la journée, he hasn't done a stroke of work all day. (d) Fichez(-moi) le camp! out you go! hop it! Va te faire fiche! go to blazes!

se fiche(r). *P:* **1.** Se ficher par terre, to fall. **2.** (a) Se fiche(r) de qn, de qch., to make fun of s.o., of sth. *Vous vous fichez de moi,* what do you take me for? (b) Je m'en fiche (pas mal)! I don't care a rap! Ce que je m'en fiche! as if I cared!

fichu¹, *a. P:* **1.** Beastly, rotten (weather, etc.). **2.** Il est fichu, he is done for; it is all up with him. **3.** Être fichu comme quatre sous, to be dressed like a guy. **4.** N'être pas fichu de faire qch., not to be able, fit, to do sth.

fichier [fiʃje], *s.m.* Card-index; card-index cabinet. [FICHE]

fichtre [fiʃtr], *int. P:* **1.** (Admirative) My word! **2.** Hang it!

fichu² [fiʃy], *s.m.* Small shawl; fichu, neckerchief.

fict|if, -ive [fiktif, -iːv], *a.* Fictitious, imaginary. *adv.* **-ivement.**

fiction [fiksjɔ̃], *s.f.* Fiction, invention, fabrication.

fidéicommis [fideikɔmi], *s.m. Jur:* Trust.

fidéicommissaire [fideikɔmisɛːr], *s.m. Jur:* Beneficiary (of a trust).

fidèle [fidɛl], *a.* Faithful, loyal, staunch. *Être f.* à ses opinions, to hold fast to one's opinions. *s. Ecc:* Les fidèles, (i) the faithful; (ii) the congregation. *adv.* **-ment.**

fidélité [fidelite], *s.f.* Fidelity, faithfulness. Serment de fidélité, oath of allegiance.

fiduciaire [fidysjɛːr]. **1.** *a.* Fiduciary (loan, etc.). *Circulation f.,* monnaie f., fiduciary currency; paper money. **2.** *s.m.* Fiduciary, trustee.

fief [fjɛf], *s.m. Jur: A:* Fief, feoff, fee.

fieffé [fjefe], *a.* **1.** *Jur: A:* (*a*) (Of pers.) Enfeoffed. (*b*) (Of land) Given in fief. **2.** *F: Pej:* Arrant (liar); egregious (fool); rank (impostor). **fiel** [fjɛl], *s.m.* (*a*) Gall (of animal). *F. de bœuf,* ox gall. (*b*) *F:* **Épancher son fiel,** to vent one's spleen (*sur,* on). **N'avoir point de fiel,** to be without malice.

fielleux, -euse [fjɛlø, -øːz], *a.* (*a*) Gall-like, bitter. (*b*) *F:* Rancorous, bitter (remark, etc.)

fiente [fjãːt], *s.f.* Dung; droppings (of cattle, birds).

filer¹ [fjɛːr], *a.* **1.** (Legitimately) proud. *Être trop f. pour mendier,* to be too proud to beg. **Être fier de qch.,** to be proud of, to glory in, sth. **Il est fier d'avoir réussi,** he is proud of having succeeded. **2.** Proud, haughty, stuck-up. *F:* **Fier comme Artaban,** as proud as Lucifer. **3.** *F:* Rare, fine, famous. *Tu m'as fait une fière peur,* a fine, rare, fright you gave me. *adv.* **-èrement.**

fier² [fje], *v.tr. A:* = CONFIER.

se fier, to trust. **Se fier à qn,** occ. **en qn,** to rely on s.o.; to trust s.o. **Se fier à qn du soin de qch.,** to trust s.o. with a task. **Fiez-vous à moi,** leave it to me. *Je me fie à lui pour* . . ., I depend on him to. . . . **Se fier à ses yeux,** to trust, believe, one's eyes. **Ne vous y fiez pas,** (i) beware! (ii) don't reckon on it.

fierté [fjɛrte], *s.f.* **1.** Pride, self-respect. **2.** Pride, haughtiness.

fièvre [fjɛːvr], *s.f.* Fever. *F: F. de cheval,* raging fever. **Avoir la fièvre,** (i) to have fever; (ii) to be feverish. *F:* To have a temperature. **Dans la fièvre de la mêlée,** in the heat of the battle. S.a. DONNER 2.

fiévreu|x, -euse [fjevrø, -øːz]. **1.** *a.* (*a*) Causing fever. *Marécage f.,* fever swamp. (*b*) Feverish (person, pulse, haste); fevered (brow). **2.** *s.* Fever patient. *adv.* **-sement.**

fifre [fifr], *s.m.* Fife.

figement [fiʒmã], *s.m.* Coagulation, congealing (of oil, blood); clotting (of blood, cream).

figer [fiʒe], *v.tr.* (figeant; il figeait) To coagulate, congeal. *F: Cris qui vous figent le sang,* blood-curdling cries.

se figer, (of oil, blood) to coagulate, congeal; (of blood) to clot; (of the features) to set. *Sourire figé,* set smile.

fignol|er [fiɲɔle]. *F:* **1.** *v.i.* To finick, to fiddle-faddle. **2.** *v.tr.* To fiddle, finick, niggle, over (job). *s.m.* **-age.**

se fignoler, to titivate oneself.

fignoleur, -euse [fiɲɔlœːr, -øːz]. *F:* **1.** *a.* Finicking, finical. **2.** *s.* Fiddle-faddler; niggler.

figue [fig], *s.f.* **1.** Fig. *F:* Moitié figue, moitié raisin, half one thing and half another. **2.** Figue banane, plantain. Figue de Barbarie, prickly pear.

figuier [figje], *s.m.* **1.** Fig-tree. **2.** *F. de Barbarie,* prickly pear.

figurant, -ante [figyrã, -ãːt], *s. Th:* (*a*) Walker-on; supernumerary, *F:* super. (*b*) *s.f.* Figurante, ballet-dancer; figurante.

figurat|if, -ive [figyratif, -iːv], *a.* Figurative, emblematic. *adv.* **-ivement.**

figuration [figyrasjɔ̃], *s.f.* **1.** Figuration, representation. **2.** *Coll. Th:* Supers, extras.

figure [figyːr], *s.f.* **1.** Figure, form, shape. *Portrait de demi-figure,* half-length portrait. *Figures de cire,* waxworks. *Figures géométriques,* geometrical figures, diagrams. **Figure de mots,** figure of speech. **Figure de proue,** figure-head (of ship). **2.** (*a*) Face, countenance. **Jeter qch. à la figure de qn,** to throw sth. in s.o.'s face. **Faire longue figure,** to pull a long face. *Th:* **Faire sa figure,** to make up. *Cards:* **Les figures,** the court-cards. S.a. CONNAISSANCE I. (*b*) Appearance.

Faire figure avec peu de fortune, to cut a figure on small means.

figurer [figyre]. **1.** *v.tr.* To represent. **Figurer un personnage sur la scène,** to act, take the part of, a character. **2.** *v.i.* To appear, figure. *Vases qui figurent bien sur la cheminée,* vases that look well on the mantelpiece. *Th:* **Figurer sur la scène,** to walk on.

se figurer qch., to imagine sth.; to fancy sth. *Figurez-vous la situation,* picture the situation to yourself. *Je me figure bien que cela puisse arriver,* I can imagine it happening.

figuré, *a.* (*a*) Decorated with figures. (*b*) Figurative (meaning). *Adv.phr.* **Au figuré,** in the figurative sense; figuratively. (*c*) *Étoffe figurée,* figured stuff.

figurine [figyrin], *s.f.* Figurine, statuette.

fil [fil], *s.m.* **1.** (*a*) Thread. *Fil d'Écosse,* Lisle thread. *Gants de fil,* cotton gloves. *Fil de lin,* linen thread. *Fil d'emballage,* packthread. *F:* **Sa vie ne tenait qu'à un fil,** his life hung by a thread, by a hair. **Finesses cousues de fil blanc,** obvious tricks. **De fil en aiguille elle m'a raconté toute l'affaire,** little by little, bit by bit, she told me the whole business. **Brouiller les fils,** to muddle things up. **Perdre le fil de ses idées,** to lose the thread of one's ideas. **Fil d'araignée,** (i) spider's thread; (ii) *Opt:* cross-hair. **Fils de la Vierge,** gossamer. *Const:* **Fil à plomb,** plumb-bob, -line. S.a. RETORDRE 2. (*b*) *Fil métallique,* wire. **Fil de fer,** iron wire; *F:* wire. S.a. ARCHAL. *Tp:* **Être au bout du fil,** to be on the phone, to be speaking. **Télégraphie sans fil,** wireless telegraphy. *F:* **Un sans-fil,** a wireless message. S.a. TÉLÉPHONIE. *F:* **Il n'a pas inventé le fil à couper le beurre,** he will never set the Thames on fire. *F:* **C'est lui qui tient les fils,** it is he who pulls the strings. **2.** Grain (of wood, meat). **Contre le fil, à contre-fil,** against, across, the grain. **De droit fil,** with the grain. **3.** *Fil de l'eau,* current. **Au fil de l'eau,** with the stream. **4.** (Cutting) edge. *Donner le fil à un rasoir,* to put an edge on a razor. *Passer des prisonniers au fil de l'épée,* to put prisoners to the (edge of the) sword.

filament [filamã], *s.m.* Filament.

filandreux, -euse [filãdrø, -øːz], *a.* Stringy (meat, toasted cheese). *F:* **Explication filandreuse,** long-drawn, involved, explanation.

filant [filã], *a.* **1.** Ropy (liquid). **2.** Etoile filante, shooting star.

filasse [filas], *s.f.* **1.** Tow. *F:* **Cheveux de filasse,** tow-like hair. **2.** Oakum.

filateur [filatœːr], *s.m.* **1.** Spinner; owner of a spinning-mill. **2.** (Private detective's) spy; shadower; informer.

filature [filatyːr], *s.f.* **1.** Spinning. **2.** Spinning-mill, -factory. **3.** Shadowing (by detective).

file [fil], *s.f.* File (of soldiers, etc.). *F. creuse,* blank file. **Chef de file,** (i) front-rank man, file-leader; (ii) leader (of a party, etc.); (iii) (parliamentary) whip. **Aller à la file,** to go in file, one behind another. **En file indienne,** in Indian file; *Nau: etc:* in single file. **Deux heures à la file,** two hours on end. **Prendre la file,** to join one's car on to the end of the line; to line up, to queue up. *Navy:* **En ligne de file,** (single) line ahead. *Mil:* **Par f. à droite!** right wheel!

fil|er [file]. **I.** *v.tr.* **1.** To spin (flax, etc.). *F:* **Filer doux,** to sing small. S.a. BERTHE I, COTON I. **2.** (*a*) *Nau:* To pay out (cable). *Filez de la chaîne!* ease off the cable! *F. le corps mort,* to cast off from the buoy. *F:* **Filer son nœud,** to slip one's painter; (i) to make off; (ii) to die.

(b) *F. une barrique*, to lower a cask (into a cellar).
(c) To prolong, draw out (sound, story); to pour out (oil) in a trickle. **3.** (Of detective) To shadow (s.o.). **4.** *Cards:* **Filer sa carte,** (i) to palm, (ii) to palm off, a card. *s.m.* **-age.**
    II. **filer,** *v.i.* **1.** (a) To flow smoothly; (of oil) to run. (b) *La lampe file,* the lamp is smoking. **2.** To slip by. *Le temps file,* time flies. **Laisser filer un câble,** to pay out a cable. *Les autos filaient sur la route,* cars were bowling along the road. *Nau:* **Filer à grande vitesse, à vingt nœuds,** to proceed at a high speed, at twenty knots. *F:* **Filer (en vitesse),** to cut and run. **Allez, filez!** take yourself off! cut along! buzz off! **Filer à l'anglaise,** to take French leave.

filé, *s.m.* Thread. *F. de coton,* yarn. *F. d'or,* gold thread.

filet[1] [file], *s.m.* **1.** Small thread. (a) *F. de lumière,* thin streak of light. *F. d'eau,* thin trickle of water. *Ajoutez-y un f. de citron,* add a dash of lemon. (b) *F. d'une vis,* screw thread. (c) *Anat:* Frenum. *F:* **Avoir le filet,** to be tongue-tied. (d) Fillet (of column). (e) *Typ:* (Brass) rule. **2.** *Cu:* *F. de poisson,* fillet of fish. *F. de bœuf,* fillet, undercut, of beef. S.a. **FAUX-FILET. 3.** *Harn:* (a) Snaffle-bridle. (b) Snaffle(-bit).

filet[2], *s.m.* Net(ting). *F. de pêche,* fishing-net. **Faire du filet,** to net. *Être pris au f.,* to be caught in the net. *F. pour cheveux,* hair-net. *Rail:* *F. à bagages,* luggage rack. *Ten:* Jeu au filet, net play. S.a. **COUP 2.**

filet|er [filte], *v.tr.* (je filète; je filèterai) **1.** To (wire-)draw (metal). **2.** To cut a thread on (bolt, etc.); to thread (bolt, etc.). *s.m.* **-age.**

fileur, -euse [filœːr, -øːz], *s.* *Tex:* (a) Spinner. (b) (Silk-)thrower, throwster.

filial, -als, -aux [filjal, -o]. **I.** *a.* Filial. *Peu f.,* unfilial; undaughterly. **2.** *s.f.* Filiale. (a) *Com:* Sub-company, subsidiary company. (b) Provincial branch (of association). *adv.* **-ement.**

filiation [filjasjɔ̃], *s.f.* **1.** (a) Consanguinity in direct line. **En filiation directe,** in direct line. (b) Descendants. **2.** *F. des idées,* filiation of ideas.

filière [filjɛːr], *s.f.* **1.** (a) (Stock and) die. (b) *F. à étirer,* draw(ing)-plate. **Travailler un métal à la filière,** to draw a metal. *F:* **Il a passé par la filière,** he has worked his way up (to a good position), has gone through the whole mill. **La filière administrative,** the usual official channels. **2.** Ridge-rope (of tent). *Nau:* *F. d'envergure,* jack-stay. **3.** Spinneret (of spider, etc.). [FIL]

filiforme [filifɔrm], *a.* Filiform, thread-like.

filigrane [filigran], *s.m.* **1.** Filigree (work). **2.** Watermark (of bank-notes, etc.).

filin [filɛ̃], *s.m.* Rope. *Vieux f.,* junk. [FIL]

fille [fiːj], *s.f.* **1.** Daughter. **2.** (a) Girl. **Petite fille,** little girl; child. **Jeune fille,** girl, young woman. **Nom de jeune fille,** maiden name. **Grande f.,** full-grown girl. *École de filles,* girls' school. **Vieille fille,** old maid, spinster. **Rester fille,** to remain single, unmarried. *Habitudes de vieille f.,* old-maidish habits. (b) **Fille d'honneur,** (i) maid of honour (attached to queen); (ii) brides-maid. **3.** *Ecc:* *Les filles de Port-Royal,* the sisters, nuns, of Port-Royal. **4.** Fille de service, maidservant. *F. de cuisine,* kitchen-maid. *F. de salle,* waitress.

fillette [fijɛt], *s.f.* **1.** Little girl. **2.** *P:* Half-bottle (of wine).

filleul, -eule [fijœl], *s.* God-child.

film [film], *s.m.* Film. *Cin:* **Tourner un film,** (i) to record a film; (ii) to act a film part. **Film muet,** silent film; *F:* movie. **Film parlant, parlé,**

talking picture; *F:* talkie. *F. d'actualité,* news film, news reel.

filmer [filme], *v.tr.* *Cin:* To film (scene).

filoche [filɔʃ], *s.f.* *Tex:* Netting, esp. silk netting.

filon [filɔ̃], *s.m.* *Min:* Vein, seam, lode (of metal, etc.); reef (of gold). *P:* **C'est le filon,** that's a cushy job. **Il tient le filon, il a déniché le bon filon,** he has struck it rich; he has struck oil.

filoselle [filɔzɛl], *s.f.* Floss-silk.

filou [filu], *s.m.* Pickpocket, thief. *F:* Rogue, swindler.

filout|er [filute], *v.tr.* **1.** *F. qch. à qn,* to rob s.o. of sth. **2.** *F. qn,* to swindle, cheat, s.o. *s.m.* **-age.**

filouterie [filutri], *s.f.* **1.** = FILOUTAGE. **2.** Swindle, fraud.

fils [fis], *s.m.* **1.** Son. *Ses deux fils,* her two boys. *F:* **Fils à papa,** young man with an influential father. **C'est bien le fils de son père,** he's a chip of the old block. **Être le fils de ses œuvres,** to be a self-made man. **M.** Duval fils, Mr Duval junior. S.a. **PÈRE 1. 2.** *F:* Boy, lad, fellow. *C'est un bon f.,* he's a decent chap.

filtrant [filtrɑ̃], *a.* Filterable (virus).

filtration [filtrasjɔ̃], *s.f.* Filtration, percolation.

filtre [filtr], *s.m.* **1.** Filter, strainer, percolator. *Papier à f.,* filter-paper. *Cu:* *F. à café,* perco-lator. **2.** *W.Tel:* By-pass, filter.

filtr|er [filtre]. **1.** *v.tr.* (a) To filter, strain. (b) *W.Tel:* *F. un poste émetteur,* to by-pass a station. **2.** *v.i. & pr.* To filter, percolate. **Laisser filtrer une nouvelle,** to let a piece of news leak out. *s.m.* **-age.**

fin[1] [fɛ̃], *s.f.* **1.** End, close, termination. *Com:* *Fin de mois,* monthly statement. **Vis sans fin,** endless screw. **Mettre fin à qch.,** to put an end, a stop, to sth.; to bring sth. to an end. **Prendre fin,** avoir une fin, to come to an end. **Mener une affaire à bonne fin,** to bring a matter to a success-ful issue. **L'année tire, touche, à sa fin,** the year is drawing to an end, to a close. **Jusqu'à la fin des temps, des siècles,** till the end of time; until the crack of doom. **A la fin il répondit,** at last he answered. *F:* **Tu es stupide à la fin!** you really are very stupid! **A la fin du compte,** en fin de compte, in the end; to cut a long story short. *Com:* **Payable fin courant, fin prochain,** payable at the end of the current month, of next month. **2.** End, aim, purpose, object. (a) **La fin justifie les moyens,** the end justifies the means. **En venir, arriver, à ses fins,** to attain one's end. **A cette fin il faut . . . ,** to this end one must. . . . **A quelle fin?** for what purpose? to what end? **A deux fins,** serving a double purpose. **Aux fins de faire qch.,** with a view to doing sth. *Prov:* **Qui veut la fin veut les moyens,** where there's a will there's a way. (b) *Jur:* **Renvoyer qn des fins de sa plainte,** to nonsuit s.o. **Fin de non-recevoir,** demurrer, plea in bar, estoppel. *Rendre une fin de non-recevoir,* to dismiss a case.

fin[2], **fine** [fɛ̃, fin], *a.* **1.** *A:* Farthermost. *F:* **Dans le fin fond du hangar,** at the very back of the shed. S.a. **MOT 1. 2.** (a) Fine, first-class. **Vins fins,** choice wines. **Or fin,** pure, fine, gold. **Linge fin,** fine linen. *s.f.* *F:* **Une fine** = fine champagne, *q.v.* under CHAMPAGNE 3. **Fine à l'eau,** brandy and soda. S.a. **HERBE 1.** (b) Subtle, shrewd. **Fine ironie,** subtle irony. **Avoir l'oreille fine,** to be quick of hearing. **Fin comme l'ambre,** sharp as a needle. **Bien fin qui le prendra,** it would take a smart man to catch him. **Plus fin que lui n'est pas bête,** he's no fool. *s.m.* **Jouer au plus fin,** to have a battle of wits. **Savoir le fort et le fin d'une affaire,** to know the ins and outs of sth. (c) Fine, small (rain, etc.). *Traits* *fins*, delicate features. *Écriture fine*, small hand-writing. *adv.* **-ement.**

final, -als [final], *a.* Final. **1.** (*a*) Last (letter, etc.). *Sp:* Les (*épreuves*) *finales*, the finals. (*b*) Ultimate (success, etc.). **2.** (*a*) *Phil:* Cause finale, final cause. (*b*) *Gram:* Proposition finale, final clause. *adv.* **-ement.**

final(e) [final], *s.m. Mus:* Finale (of sonata, etc.).

finale, s.f. 1. End syllable (of word). **2.** *Mus:* Key-note, tonic.

finaliste [finalist], *s. m. & f. Sp:* Finalist.

finalité [finalite], *s.f.* Finality.

finance [finãːs], *s.f.* **1.** *A:* Ready money. *F:* Faire qch. moyennant finance, to do sth. for a consideration. **2.** Finance. La haute finance, (i) high finance; (ii) the financiers, the bankers. **3.** *pl.* Finances, resources. Ministre des Finances, minister of Finance, = Chancellor of the Exchequer. Le Ministère des Finances = the Exchequer, *U.S:* the Treasury.

financ|er [finãse], *v.tr.* (je finançai(s); n. finançons) To finance (undertaking). *s.m.* **-ement.**

financier, -ière [finãsje, -jɛːr]. **1.** *a.* Financial. *Le marché f.*, (i) the money-market; (ii) the stock-market. **2.** *s.m.* Financier.

finasser [finase], *v.i. F:* To finesse.

finasserie [finasri], *s.f.* **1.** Cunning, foxiness. **2.** (*a*) Piece of cunning. (*b*) *pl.* Wiles.

finassier, -ière [finasje, -jɛːr]. **1.** *a.* Artful, wily. **2.** *s.* Petty trickster; artful rogue.

finaud, -aude [fino, -oːd]. **1.** *a.* Wily, cunning. **2.** *s.* Sly fox; artful miss or old lady. *Petite finaude*, little sly-boots. [FIN²]

finesse [fines], *s.f.* Fineness. **1.** Good quality (of material, etc.); delicacy (of execution). **2.** (*a*) Subtlety, shrewdness. *F. d'ouïe*, quickness of hearing. *F. d'esprit*, shrewdness of mind. (*b*) Cunning, guile. (*c*) Piece of cunning. **3.** Fineness (of dust, etc.); slenderness (of waist); sharpness (of optical image, wireless tuning).

finir [finiːr]. **1.** *v.tr.* To finish, end. **2.** *v.i.* To end, come to an end, finish. Voir finir qch., to see sth. out, through. Il finira mal, he will come to a bad end. Tout est bien qui finit bien, all's well that ends well. En finir avec qn, qch., to be, have, done with s.o., sth. Cela n'en finit pas, there is no end to it. Pour en finir, to cut the matter short. Histoires à n'en plus finir, (i) never-ending stories; (ii) no end of stories. Finir de faire qch., to finish, leave off, doing sth. Finissez de pleurer, have done (with) crying. *F. en pointe*, to end, terminate, in a point. Finir par faire qch., to end in, by, doing sth.

fini, a. 1. Finished, ended, over. *L'orage est f.*, the storm is over. C'est fini; tout est fini, it's all over, all done with. *F:* Il est fini, c'est un homme fini, he's done for. C'est fini de rire, we've done with laughter! **2.** (*a*) Accomplished, finished. *Acteur f.*, consummate actor. (*b*) *s.m.* Finish.. *Articles d'un beau f.*, highly finished goods. **3.** Finite (space, tense, etc.).

finisseur, -euse [finisœːr, -øːz], *s. Ind:* Finisher.

finlandais, -aise [fɛ̃lɑ̃dɛ, -ɛːz]. **1.** *a.* Finnish. **2.** *s.* Finlander.

Finlande [fɛ̃lɑ̃ːd]. *Pr.n.f. Geog:* Finland.

finnois, -oise [finwa, -waːz]. **1.** *a.* Finnish. **2.** (*a*) *s.* Finn. (*b*) *s.m. Ling:* Finnish.

fiole [fjɔl], *s.f.* (*a*) Phial, flask. (*b*) *P:* Head, mug. Se payer la fiole de qn, to make a fool of s.o.

fion [fjɔ̃], *s.m. P:* **1.** Finish (of an article). Donner le coup de fion à qch., to give the finishing touch(es) to sth. **2.** Avoir le fion pour faire qch., to have the knack of sth.

Fionie [fjɔni]. *Pr.n. Geog:* Fünen, Fyen.

fioritures [fjɔrityːr], *s.f.pl.* Flourishes (to handwriting, etc.).

firmament [firmamɑ̃], *s.m.* Firmament, sky.

firme [firm], *s.f.* **1.** (Business) firm. **2.** Style of firm. *Publ:* Imprint.

fi-s, -t. See FAIRE.

fisc (le) [lefisk], *s.m.* (*a*) The Treasury, the Exchequer. (*b*) The Inland Revenue.

fiscal, -aux [fiskal, -o], *a.* Fiscal. Dans un but fiscal, for purposes of revenue. *L'administration fiscale*, the taxation authorities. *Aut:* Puissance fiscale, Treasury rating (of car).

fiss-e, -es, etc. See FAIRE.

fissure [fis(s)yːr], *s.f.* Fissure, cleft (in rock, etc.).

fissurer [fis(s)yre], *v.tr.* To fissure, split. se fissurer, to fissure, crack.

fiston [fistɔ̃], *s.m. P:* Son, youngster. [FILS]

fistule [fistyl], *s.f. Med:* Fistula.

five-o'clock [fivɔklɔk], *s.m. F:* Afternoon tea.

five-o'clocker [fivɔklɔke], *v.i. F:* To have tea.

fixage [fiksaːʒ], *s.m.* **1.** Fixing; fastening. *Phot:* Bain de f., fixing bath. **2.** Deciding.

fixatif [fiksatif], *s.m.* (*a*) Fixative (for drawings). (*b*) Fixature (for hair).

fixation [fiksasjɔ̃], *s.f.* (*a*) Fixing (of date, shelf, etc.). *Vis de f.*, fixing screw. Fixation des impôts, assessment of taxes. (*b*) Fixation (of nitrogen).

fixe [fiks], *a.* **1.** Fixed, firm. *Idée f.*, fixed idea. *Regard f.*, intent gaze. *Mil:* Fixe! eyes front! **2.** Fixed, regular, settled. A prix fixe, at fixed prices. *Traitement f.*, *s.m.* fixe, fixed salary. Beau (temps) fixe, set fair. *P.N:* Arrêt fixe, all cars stop here. *adv.* **-ment.**

fixe-chaussettes, *s.m.inv.* Sock-suspender(s).

fixer [fikse], *v.tr.* **1.** (*a*) To fix; to make (sth.) firm, rigid, fast. Les vis qui fixent la serrure, the screws that hold the lock. F. qch. dans sa mémoire, to fix sth. in one's memory. Fixer l'attention de qn, to engage, hold, arrest, s.o.'s attention. Fixer les yeux sur qch., to fix one's eyes on sth.; to gaze, stare, at sth. Fixer qn, to stare at s.o. (*b*) *Ch: Phot:* To fix. **2.** To fix, determine. Le jour reste à fixer, the day remains to be fixed, decided upon. F. l'heure et le lieu, to appoint the time and the place.

se fixer. **1.** *Se f. dans un pays*, to settle in a country. **2.** (Of spawn, etc.) Se f. sur qch., to set on sth.

fixé, a. 1. *Se réunir à des époques fixées*, to meet at fixed, stated, times. **2.** Être fixé sur qch., to entertain no further doubts about sth.

fixité [fiksite], *s.f.* Fixity.

flac [flak], *s. m. & int.* Slap; crack (of whip); plop (into water). Faire flac, to plop.

flaccidité [flaksidite], *s.f.* Flaccidity, flabbiness.

flache [flaʃ], *s.f.* **1.** Wane, flaw (of plank). **2.** (*a*) (Pot-)hole (in road). (*b*) *F. d'eau*, puddle.

flacon [flakɔ̃], *s.m.* Bottle; (stoppered) flask. *F. à odeur*, scent-bottle. *F. à liqueur*, liqueur-decanter.

fla-fla [flafla], *s.m. F:* Ostentation, show. Faire du fla-fla, to make a show, a display.

flagellation [flaʒɛllasjɔ̃], *s.f.* Flagellation, scourging; flogging.

flageller [flaʒɛlle], *v.tr.* To scourge, flog.

flageoler [flaʒɔle], *v.i.* (Of legs) To shake, tremble, give way.

flageolet¹ [flaʒɔlɛ], *s.m. Mus:* Flageolet.

flageolet², *s.m. Cu:* Flageolet; (small) kidney-bean.

flagorner [flagɔrne], *v.tr.* To flatter; to fawn upon (s.o.); to toady to (s.o.).

flagornerie [flagɔrnəri], *s.f.* Flattery, toadyism.

flagorneur, -euse [flagɔrnœːr, -øːz], *s.* Flatterer, toady, lick-spittle.

flagrant [flagrã], *a.* Flagrant, glaring (injustice). **Pris en flagrant délit**, caught in the act, red-handed.

flair [flɛːr], *s.m.* (*a*) (Of dogs) Scent, (sense of) smell; nose. (*b*) *F:* (Of pers.) Flair. **Avoir du flair**, to have a gift for nosing things out. **Avoir du flair pour qch.**, to have a flair for sth.

flairer [flɛre], *v.tr.* (*a*) (Of dog) To scent, smell (out), nose out (game). *F: F. le danger*, to smell danger. (*b*) To smell, sniff (flower).

flamand, -ande [flamã, -ãːd]. **1.** *a.* Flemish. **2.** *s.* Fleming. **3.** *s.m. Ling:* Flemish.

flamant [flamã], *s.m. Orn:* Flamingo.

flambage [flãbaːʒ], *s.m.* **1.** (*a*) Singeing. (*b*) Charring. **2.** = FLAMBEMENT **1.**

flambant [flãbã], *a.* Blazing, flaming. *adv.* **Habit (tout) flambant neuf, robe (toute) flambant neuve**, brand-new coat, frock.

flambard, -arde [flãbaːr, -ard], *a. P:* Smartly dressed (person). *s.* **Faire le flambard**, to swank.

flambeau [flãbo], *s.m.* **1.** (*a*) Torch. **A la lueur des flambeaux**, by torch-light. S.a. RETRAITE **1.** (*b*) Candle. **2.** Candlestick. *F. électrique*, electric table-standard.

flambement [flãbmã], *s.m.* **1.** Buckling, collapse (of metal plate, etc.). **2.** = FLAMBOIEMENT.

flamber [flãbe]. **1.** *v.i.* (*a*) To flame, blaze. *F:* **Faire flamber la maison**, to set the house ablaze. (*b*) (Of metal bar, etc.) To buckle, yield. **2.** *v.tr.* To singe (fowl, cloth); to char (end of stake, etc.). *Surg: F. une aiguille*, to sterilize a needle (in flame). *F:* **C'est de l'argent flambé**, it is so much money lost. **Il est flambé**, he is done for; his goose is cooked.

flambée, *s.f.* Blaze; blazing fire.

flamberge [flãbɛrʒ], *s.f. A. & F:* Sword, blade. **Mettre flamberge au vent**, to draw (one's sword).

flamboyant [flãbwajã], *a.* **1.** Flaming, blazing (fire); blazing (eyes). **2.** Flamboyant (speech); gaudy, dazzling (get-up).

flamb|oyer [flãbwaje], *v.i.* (il flamboie) (Of fire) To blaze. *F:* **Ses yeux flamboyaient de colère**, his eyes blazed, glowed, flashed, with anger. *s.m.* **-oiement.**

flamingant, -ante [flamɛ̃gã, -ãːt]. **1.** *a.* Flemish-speaking (town, person). **2.** *s.* Flemish speaker.

flamme [flɑːm], *s.f.* **1.** (*a*) Flame. **Tout en flammes**, on fire; ablaze. **Par le fer et la flamme**, with fire and sword. S.a. FEU[1] **1.** **Retour de flamme**, (i) back-flash (from gun); (ii) spitting back, popping back (in the carburettor). *Tex: etc:* **Passer le drap à la flamme**, to singe the cloth. (*b*) *Poet. & F:* Passion, love. **Avouer sa flamme**, to declare one's passion. *F: Une de mes anciennes flammes*, an old flame of mine. **2.** *Mil: Nau:* Pennant, pendant, pennon, streamer. *Navy: F. de guerre*, action pennant.

flammèche [flamɛʃ], *s.f.* Spark, flake (of fire).

flan [flã], *s.m.* **1.** *Cu:* Baked-custard tart. *P:* **Du flan!** nothing doing! **2.** *Num: etc:* Blank. *Mec.E: F. de fraise*, milling-cutter blank. **3.** *Typ:* Mould (from standing type); (news-paper) flong. **4.** *P:* A la flan, (i) happy-go-lucky; (ii) in a happy-go-lucky fashion. **Travail fait à la flan**, work done anyhow.

flanc [flã], *s.m.* Flank, side. **Route à flanc de coteau**, road following the hill-side. *Se coucher sur le f.*, (i) to lie down on one's side; (ii) (of ship) to heel over. *F:* **Être sur le flanc**, (i) to be laid up (in bed); (ii) to be quite done up. **Se**

battre les flancs, (i) (of tiger) to lash its tail; (ii) *F:* to make desperate efforts. *Mil:* **Par le flanc droit!** by the right! **Attaquer de flanc**, to attack on the flank. **Prêter le flanc à la critique**, to lay oneself open to criticism. *P:* **Tirer au flanc**, to skrimshank, to malinger, to swing the lead. **Tireur au flanc**, skrimshanker.

flancher [flãʃe], *v.i. P:* **1.** (*a*) To flinch; to give in. (*b*) To jib, to rat. **2.** (Of motor car, etc.) To break down.

flanchet [flãʃɛ], *s.m. Cu:* Flank (of beef).

Flandre [flãːdr]. *Pr.n.f. Geog:* Flanders.

flandrin [flãdrɛ̃], *s.m. F:* **Un grand flandrin**, a tall, lanky, fellow; a great lout of a lad.

flanelle [flanɛl], *s.f.* **1.** Flannel. *F. de coton*, flannelette. **2.** Flannel under-vest.

flâner [flɑne], *v.i.* To air one's heels; to lounge about; to stroll. *Perdre son temps à f.*, to idle away one's time.

flânerie [flɑnri], *s.f.* Dawdling, idling. *Flâneries le long du boulevard*, strolls along the boulevard.

flâneur, -euse [flɑnœːr, -øːz], *s.* **1.** (*a*) Idler, dawdler; stroller. (*b*) Loafer. **2.** *s.f.* Flâneuse, lounge-chair.

flânocher [flɑnɔʃe], *v.i. F:* = FLÂNER.

flanquer[1] [flãke], *v.tr.* To flank.

flanquer[2], *v.tr. F:* To throw, pitch, chuck. **Flanquer un coup de pied à qn**, to land s.o. a kick. **Flanquer qn à la porte**, to throw, *F:* boot, chuck, s.o. out. *Se f. par terre*, to fall; to come a cropper.

flapi [flapi], *a. F:* **1.** Fagged out, done up, washed out. **2.** (Of thg) The worse for wear.

flaque [flak], *s.f.* **1.** Puddle, pool, plash. **2.** **Flaque de neige**, patch of snow.

flasque[1] [flask], *a.* Flaccid (flesh); flabby (hand, style). *Se sentir f.*, to feel limp.

flasque[2], *s.f.* **1.** *A:* Powder-horn. **2.** *Com:* Flask (of mercury, etc.).

flasque[3], *s.m.* **1.** Cheek (of gun-carriage); cheek, web (of crank). **2.** *pl. Nau:* Whelps (of capstan). **3.** *Aut:* Wheel-disk.

flatter [flate], *v.tr.* **1.** To stroke, caress. **Flatter un cheval**, to make much of, to pat, a horse. **2.** To delight, please, charm. *Spectacle qui flatte les yeux*, sight that is pleasant to the eye. **Flatter les caprices de qn**, to humour s.o.'s fancies. **3.** To flatter. *Être flatté de qch.*, to feel flattered by sth. **Flatter le portrait de qn**, to draw a flattering portrait of s.o.

se flatter, to flatter oneself, delude oneself. **Elle se flattait de réussir**, she flattered herself, felt sure, that she would succeed. **Se flatter de générosité, d'avoir fait qch.**, to take credit for oneself, *F:* to pat oneself on the back, for generosity, for doing sth.

flatté, *a. Portrait f.*, flattering portrait.

flatterie [flatri], *s.f.* Flattery, blandishment.

flatteu|r, -euse [flatœːr, -øːz]. **1.** *a.* (*a*) Pleasing, pleasant (taste, etc.); fond (hope). (*b*) Flattering (remark, etc.). **2.** *s.* Flatterer; sycophant. *adv.* **-sement.**

flatueux, -euse [flatyø, -øːz], *a.* Flatulent; *F:* windy (food).

flatulence [flatylãːs], *s.f. Med:* Flatulence.

flatulent [flatylã], *a. Med:* Flatulent.

fléau, -aux [fleo], *s.m.* **1.** *Husb:* Flail. **2.** Scourge; plague, pest, bane. *Attila, le f. de Dieu*, Attila, the scourge of God. **3.** (*a*) Beam, arm (of balance). (*b*) Bar (of door).

flèche[1] [flɛʃ], *s.f.* **1.** (*a*) Arrow. **Fer de flèche**, arrow-head. **Faire flèche de tout bois**, to use every means to attain an end. (*b*) Direction-sign, arrow. (*c*) Pointer (of balance). **2.** (*a*)

Spire (of church); leading shoot (of tree). (b) Jib, boom (of crane). (c) *Nau:* (i) *F. d'un mât*, pole of a mast. **Mât de flèche**, top-mast. (ii) Topsail (of cutter). (d) Beam (of plough); pole (of carriage); trail (of gun). (e) **Cheval de flèche**, head horse. *Chevaux en f.*, horses driven tandem. **3.** (a) *Geom:* Sagitta; versed sine. *Arch: etc:* Rise (of arch); rise of camber (of road). (b) Sag, dip (of cable, etc.). **Faire flèche**, to sag, dip.

flèche², *s.f.* Flitch (of bacon).

fléchette [fleʃɛt], *s.f. Games:* Dart.

fléch|ir [fleʃiːr]. **1.** *v.tr.* (a) To bend. *F. le genou (devant qn)*, to bend, bow, the knee (to s.o.). (b) To flex (the arm). (c) To move (s.o.) to pity, to mercy. **2.** *v.i.* (a) To give way, bend; to sag. *Ses jambes fléchissaient*, his legs were giving way. (b) (Of sound, current, etc.) To grow weaker. *Son attention fléchit*, his attention flags. *s.m.* **-issement.**

flegmatique [flɛgmatik], *a.* Phlegmatic. **1.** Lymphatic (person, etc.). **2.** *F:* Calm, imperturbable, stolid. *adv.* **-ment.**

flegme [flɛgm], *s.m.* Phlegm.

flémard, flemmard, -arde [flɛmaːr, -ard]. *P:* **1.** *a.* Idle, lazy. **2.** *s.* Idler, slacker.

flémarder, flemmarder [flɛmarde], *v.i. P:* To laze.

flème, flemme [flɛm], *s.f. P:* Laziness, slackness. *Il a la flème*, he has a lazy fit. **Battre sa flème**, to be on the laze. [FLEGME]

Flessingue [flesɛ̃ːg]. *Pr.n. Geog:* Flushing.

flet [flɛ], *s.m. Ich:* Flounder.

flétan [fletɑ̃], *s.m. Ich:* Halibut.

flétrir¹ [fletriːr], *v.tr.* To fade; to wither up (flowers); to blight (hopes).

  se flétrir, to fade; (of flowers) to wither, wilt.

flétrir², *v.tr.* **1.** To brand (convict, etc.); to stigmatize (crime, etc.). **2.** To sully, stain. *F. la réputation de qn*, to cast a slur on s.o.'s character.

flétrissure¹ [fletrisyːr], *s.f.* Fading; withering.

flétrissùre², *s.f.* **1.** Brand (on a criminal). **2.** (Moral, etc.) blemish, blot, stigma.

fleur [flœːr], *s.f.* **1.** Flower. (a) Blossom, bloom. *Arbre en fleur(s)*, tree in blossom. *Tissu à fleurs*, flowered material. S.a. LIS. (b) *F:* **Être dans, à, la fleur de l'âge**, to be in the prime, heyday, of life. **Dans la première fleur de la jeunesse**, in the flower, bloom, blush, of youth. **La fine fleur de la race**, the flower of the race. (c) Bloom (on peach, grapes). (d) **Fleur d'antimoine, de soufre**, flowers of antimony, of sulphur. S.a. FARINE. **2.** (= SURFACE) A fleur de, on the surface of, on a level with. **A fleur d'eau**, at water-level. *Voler à fleur d'eau*, to skim the water. *Ten: Balle à f. de corde*, ball that just grazes, skims, the net. **Émotions à fleur de peau**, skin-deep emotions. **Yeux à fleur de tête**, prominent eyes; *F:* goggle eyes. **3.** *Tan:* Hair-side (of skin).

fleurdeliser [flœrdəlize], *v.tr.* **1.** To adorn, ornament, (sth.) with fleurs-de-lis. **2.** *A:* To brand (criminal).

fleurer [flœre], *v.i.* To smell; to be fragrant. *Fleurer la violette*, to smell of violets.

fleuret [flœrɛ], *s.m.* **1.** (a) (Fencing) foil. (b) *Min:* Borer. **2.** Floss-silk; ferret.

fleurette [flœrɛt], *s.f.* Floweret. *A:* **Conter fleurette à qn**, to say sweet nothings to s.o.; to flirt with s.o.

fleurir [flœriːr]. **1.** *v.i.* (a) (Of plants) To flower, bloom, blossom. (b) (*pr.p.* florissant; *p.d.* il florissait) To flourish, prosper. **2.** *v.tr.* To decorate (table) with flowers; to deck (s.o.) out

with flowers. **Fleurir sa boutonnière**, to put a flower in one's buttonhole.

fleuri, *a.* **1.** (a) In bloom; in flower or in blossom. (b) **Avoir la boutonnière fleurie**, (i) to have a flower in one's buttonhole; (ii) *F:* to sport a decoration. **2.** Flowery (path, etc.); flowery, florid (style). *Teint f.*, florid complexion.

fleuriste [flœrist], *s.m. & f.* **1.** Florist. **2.** Artificial flower maker.

fleuron [flœrɔ̃], *s.m.* **1.** *Bot:* Floret (of compositae, etc.). **2.** Flower-shaped ornament; rosette; fleuron. *Arch:* Finial. *F:* **C'est encore un fleuron à sa couronne**, that's another feather in his cap.

fleuve [flœːv], *s.m.* (Large) river.

flexibilité [flɛksibilite], *s.f.* Flexibility; pliability (of disposition); suppleness (of body).

flexible [flɛksibl]. **1.** *a.* Flexible, pliable; pliant (disposition). **2.** *s.m. El:* Flexible lead; *F:* flex. *Mec.E:* Bowden wire.

flexion [flɛksjɔ̃], *s.f.* **1.** (a) Flexion, bending, sagging. **Effort de flexion**, bending stress. *Gym:* **Flexion du corps**, trunk exercise. (b) *Mec:* Buckling, collapse (of rod, etc.). **2.** *Ling:* Inflexion (of word). *F. casuelle*, case-ending.

flibuste [flibyst], *s.f.* Buccaneering, freebooting.

flibuster [flibyste], *v.i.* To freeboot, buccaneer.

flibusterie [flibystri], *s.f.* = FLIBUSTE.

flibustier [flibystje], *s.m.* **1.** (a) Pirate, freebooter, buccaneer, filibuster. (b) Privateer. **2.** *F:* Cheat, rogue.

flic [flik], *s.m. P:* (a) Policeman, bobby. (b) Detective.

flic flac [flikflak], *s.m.* **1.** Crack (of whip); slap. **2.** Heel-and-toe dance; clog-dance.

flingot [flɛ̃go], *s.m. P:* Rifle.

flirt [flœrt], *s.m. F:* **1.** Flirtation, flirting. **2.** Philanderer.

flirtage [flœrtaːʒ], *s.m.* **1.** Flirting. **2.** Flirtation.

flirter [flœrte], *v.i.* To flirt.

floche [flɔʃ], *a.* Flossy. *Soie f.*, floss-silk.

flocon [flɔkɔ̃], *s.m.* (a) Flake. *F. d'écume*, foam-flake. (b) *F. de laine*, tuft, flock, of wool.

floconneux, -euse [flɔkɔnø, -øz], *a.* **1.** Fleecy, fluffy. **2.** *Ch:* Flocculent (precipitate).

floral, -aux [flɔral, -o], *a.* Floral.

flore [flɔːr], *s.f. Bot:* Flora.

florès [flɔrɛs]. (Used in) *F:* **Faire florès**, to prosper; to shine (in society); to be in vogue.

florilège [flɔrilɛːʒ], *s.m.* Florilegium, anthology.

florin [flɔrɛ̃], *s.m.* Florin.

floriss-ait, -ant, etc. See FLEURIR.

florissant [flɔrisɑ̃], *a.* Flourishing, prosperous.

flot [flo], *s.m.* **1.** (a) Wave. (b) Cascade (of ribbons). (c) (**Marée de) flot**, flood-tide. **Demi-flot**, half-tide. **Bassin à flot**, wet dock. (d) *F:* **Flots de larmes**, floods of tears. **Un flot de sang lui monta au visage**, a flush rose to his cheek. *F. pressé d'hommes*, surging mass of men. *Entrer à flots*, to stream in. *Couler à flots*, to gush forth. **2.** Floating. **A flot**, afloat. **Mettre un navire à flot**, (i) to launch a ship; (ii) to refloat, float off, a ship. *F:* **Remettre qn à flot**, to restore s.o.'s fortunes. **Choses de flot et de mer**, flotsam and jetsam. **3.** Timber-raft.

flottaison [flɔtɛzɔ̃], *s.f.* Floating. *Nau:* (**Ligne de) flottaison**, water-line, -mark. *F. en charge*, load-line. *F. lège*, light water-mark.

flottant [flɔtɑ̃], *a.* (a) Floating (island, debt, etc.). *Robe flottante*, flowing robe. (b) Irresolute, undecided (mind). **Avoir une volonté flottante**, to be infirm of purpose.

flotte¹ [flɔt], *s.f.* **1.** (a) Fleet. *F. de ligne, de combat*, battle-fleet. (b) *F:* *Son fils est dans la f.*

his son is in the navy. **2.** *P:* Water, rain. ‖ *tombe de la flotte,* it's raining.

flotte², *s.f.* Float (of net, cable) ; (mooring-)buoy.

flottement [flɔtmã], *s.m.* Undulation ; swaying (of line of troops) ; flapping (of flag) ; wobble. *F:* **Les flottements du cœur humain,** the wavering, irresolution, of the human heart.

flotter [flɔte]. **I.** *v.i.* (*a*) To float. (*b*) To wave, float, stream (in the wind). (*c*) To waver, hesitate. *F. entre l'espérance et la crainte,* to fluctuate between hope and fear. **2.** *v.tr. F. du bois,* to float timber (down a stream). *Bois flotté,* (i) drift-wood ; (ii) raft-wood.

flotteur [flɔtœːr], *s.m.* **I.** Raftsman. **2.** (*a*) Float (of fishing-line, carburetter, etc.). (*b*) Ball (of ball-tap, etc.). **Robinet à flotteur,** ball-cock.

flottille [flɔtiːj], *s.f. Navy:* Flotilla.

flou [flu]. **I.** *a.* Woolly (outline, sound) ; hazy, blurred (horizon). *Opt:* Unsharp, fuzzy (image). *Cheveux flous,* soft, fluffy, hair. **2.** *s.m.* Softness, woolliness, fuzziness (of outline).

flouer [flue], *v.tr. P:* To swindle, do, have (s.o.).

flouerie [fluri], *s.f. P:* **I.** Swindling. **2.** Swindle.

fluctuation [flyktɥasjɔ̃], *s.f.* Fluctuation.

fluctuer [flyktɥe], *v.i.* To fluctuate.

fluet, -ette [flyɛ, -ɛt], *a.* Thin, slender.

fluide [flyid], *a. & s.m.* Fluid.

fluidité [flyidite], *s.f.* Fluidity.

fluor [flyɔːr], *s.m. Ch:* Fluorine. *Miner:* **Spath fluor,** fluor-spar, fluorite.

fluorescence [flyɔres(s)ãːs], *s.f.* Fluorescence.

fluorescent [flyɔres(s)ã], *a.* Fluorescent.

fluorhydrique [flyɔridrik], *a. Ch:* Hydro-fluoric.

flûte [flyːt], *s.f.* **I.** Flute. *Grande f.,* concert flute. *Petite f.,* piccolo. *F:* **Ajustez, accordez, vos flûtes,** settle your differences. *Prov:* **Ce qui vient de la flûte s'en va par le tambour,** easy come easy go. S.a. BOIS¹ 3. **2.** (*a*) Long thin roll (of bread). (*b*) Tall champagne glass. (*c*) *F:* **Jouer des flûtes, se tirer des flûtes,** to run ; to show a clean pair of heels. **3.** *int. P:* = ZUT.

flûter [flyte]. **I.** *v.i.* (*a*) To play the flute. (*b*) *P:* To tipple. **2.** *v.tr. F. un litre,* to swig off a litre (of wine, etc.).

flûté, *a. Voix flûtée,* (i) soft, flute-like, voice ; (ii) piping voice.

flûtiste [flytist], *s.m.* Flutist, flautist.

fluvial, -aux [flyvjal, -o], *a.* Fluvial ; river (police). *Voie fluviale,* waterway.

flux [fly], *s.m.* **I.** Flow. (*a*) *Un flux de sang lui monta au visage,* a flush, blush, rose to his cheeks. (*b*) *Le f. et le reflux,* the ebb and flow. **2.** *Med:* Flux. *F. de ventre,* diarrhoea. *F. de sang,* dysentery. **3.** *Ch: El: Metall:* Flux.

fluxion [flyksjɔ̃], *s.f. Med:* Fluxion, inflammation. *F. à la joue,* gumboil. *F:* **Fluxion de poitrine,** pneumonia.

foc [fɔk], *s.m. Nau:* Jib. *Grand foc,* main jib. **Bâton de foc,** jib-boom.

focal, -aux [fɔkal, -o], *a. Geom: Opt:* Focal.

foène [fwɛn], *s.f. Fish:* Fish-gig ; pronged harpoon.

fœtal, -aux [fetal, -o], *a. Biol:* Fœtal.

fœtus [fetyːs], *s.m. Biol:* Fœtus.

foi [fwa], *s.f.* Faith. **I.** (*a*) *Acheteur de bonne foi, bona fide* purchaser. *Il est de bonne foi,* he is quite sincere. *Mauvaise foi,* (i) dishonesty, insincerity ; (ii) unfairness. *Engager sa foi,* to plight one's troth. *Manquer de foi à qn,* to break faith with s.o. *Manque de foi,* breach of faith. **Ma foi, oui!** indeed yes ! *Foi d'honnête homme,* on the word of a gentleman. *Sur la foi de sa lettre,* on the strength of his letter. (*b*) *Hist:*

Fealty. S.a. PRESTATION 2. **2.** Belief, trust, confidence. *Avoir foi en qn,* to have faith in s.o. *Ajouter foi, attacher foi, à une nouvelle,* to credit, to believe (in), a piece of news. *Témoin digne de foi,* reliable witness. *Texte qui fait foi,* authentic text. *Jur:* **En foi de quoi,** in witness whereof. **3.** (Religious) faith, belief. *Profession de foi,* (i) profession of faith ; (ii) *F:* candidate's statement of policy. *F:* **Il n'a ni foi ni loi,** he respects neither law nor religion.

foie [fwa], *s.m.* Liver. *Huile de foie de morue,* cod-liver oil. *P:* **Avoir les foies,** to be in a funk.

foin¹ [fwɛ̃], *s.m.* Hay. *Faire les foins,* to make hay. *Tas de foin,* haycock. **Fièvre,** *F:* **rhume, des foins,** hay-fever. *F:* **Mettre du foin dans ses bottes,** to feather one's nest.

foin², *int. A:* **Foin de . . .,** a fig for. . . . *Faire foin des convenances,* to snap one's fingers at etiquette or at Mrs Grundy.

foire¹ [fwaːr], *s.f.* Fair. *Le champ de foire,* the fair-ground.

foire², *s.f. P:* Diarrhoea.

fois [fwa], *s.f.* Time, occasion. *Une fois,* once. *Il y avait une fois . . .,* once upon a time there was. . . . *Deux fois,* twice. *Trois fois,* three times. *Encore une fois,* once more, once again. *Une (bonne) fois pour toutes,* once (and) for all. *Cette f.,* this time. *De fois à autre,* from time to time. *Combien de f.?* how many times ? how often ? *Faire beaucoup en une f.,* to do a great deal at once. *Toutes les fois que . . .,* as often as, every time that. . . . *A la fois,* at one and the same time. *Faire deux choses à la f.,* to do two things at a time.

foison [fwazɔ̃], *s.f.* Abundance, plenty. *A foison,* plentifully ; in abundance.

foisonnant [fwazɔnã], *a.* **I.** Abundant, plentiful. **2.** Festering (and swollen).

foisonn|er [fwazɔne], *v.i.* **I.** To abound (*de,* in, with). **2.** (*a*) (Of lime, etc.) To swell, to expand. (*b*) To rot, fester (and swell). **3.** (Of metals, etc.) To buckle. *s.m.* **-ement.**

fol [fɔl], *a.* See FOU.

folâtre [fɔlɑːtr], *a.* Playful, frisky, frolicsome. *adv.* **-ment.**

folâtrer [fɔlɑtre], *v.i.* To sport, romp, frolic, gambol ; to frisk (about).

folâtrerie [fɔlɑtrəri], *s.f.* **I.** Playfulness, friskiness. **2.** Frolic, romp.

folding [fɔldiŋ], *s.m.* Folding camera.

folichon, -onne [fɔliʃɔ̃, -ɔn], *a.* Playful, larky, frolicsome, full of fun.

folichonner [fɔliʃɔne], *v.i.* To play about; to lark; *F:* to play the giddy goat.

folichonnerie [fɔliʃɔnri], *s.f.* **I.** Playing, frisking ; larkiness. **2.** Lark, frolic.

folie [fɔli], *s.f.* **I.** Madness. *Être pris de folie,* to go mad. *Avoir un grain de folie,* to be a little touched. *Aimer qn à la folie,* to love s.o. to distraction. **2.** Folly ; piece of folly, act of folly. *Il a eu la folie de . . .,* he was so foolish as to. . . . *Dire des folies,* to talk wildly, extravagantly. *Faire des folies,* (i) to act irrationally ; (ii) to have one's fling ; (iii) to be extravagant.

folio [fɔljo], *s.m. Typ: etc:* Folio.

foliot|er [fɔljɔte], *v.tr.* (i) To folio, (ii) to paginate (book). *s.m.* **-age.**

folle. See FOU.

follement [fɔlmã], *adv.* Madly. **I.** Foolishly, unwisely. **2.** Extravagantly.

follet, -ette [fɔlɛ, -ɛt], *a.* **I.** Merry, lively. *Esprit follet,* elfish spirit ; sprite. *Feu follet,* will-o'-the-wisp. **2.** *Poil follet,* down. *Cheveux follets,* stray lock(s) of hair. [FOU]

omentation [fɔmãtasjɔ̃], *s.f.* Fomentation.

omenter [fɔmãte], *v.tr.* To foment (wound, sedition); to stir up (strife).

on|cer [fɔ̃se], *v.* (**je fonçai(s)**; *n.* **fonçons**) **I.** *v.tr.* (*a*) To bottom (cask). (*b*) To drive (in) (pile, etc.); to sink, bore (well, mine-shaft). (*c*) To deepen, darken, the colour of (sth.). **2.** *v.i.* (*a*) *F.* **sur** *qn*, to rush, charge, swoop (down), upon *s.o.*; (of bull, footballer) to charge *s.o.* (*b*) (Of whale) To sound. *s.m.* **-çage.**
se foncer, to grow darker, deeper (in colour).
foncé, *a.* Dark (colour). **Des rubans bleu foncé**, dark-blue ribbons.

foncier, -ière [fɔ̃sje, -jɛːr], *a.* **I.** Of the land. **Propriété foncière**, landed property; real estate. **Le propriétaire foncier**, the ground-landlord. **Rente foncière**, ·ground-rent. **Crédit Foncier**, land bank. **2.** Deep-seated, fundamental. *Bon sens* f., innate common sense.

foncièrement [fɔ̃sjɛrmã], *adv.* Fundamentally; at bottom.

fonction [fɔ̃ksiɔ̃], *s.f.* **I.** Function, office. (*a*) *Fonctions publiques*, public offices. **Entrer en fonctions**, to take up one's duties. **Faire fonction de . . .**, to serve, act, as. . . . *Adjectif qui fait f. d'adverbe*, adjective that functions as an adverb. (*b*) *Fonctions de l'estomac, du cœur*, functions of the stomach, of the heart. **2.** *Mth:* Function. *F. inverse*, inverse function. *Exprimer une quantité en f. d'une autre*, to express one quantity in terms of another.

fonctionnaire [fɔ̃ksjɔnɛːr], *s.m.* Official; esp. civil servant.

fonctionnement [fɔ̃ksjɔnmã], *s.m.* Functioning, working (of the organs, etc.). **Machine en bon état de fonctionnement**, machine in good running order. *Mch:* **Pression de fonctionnement**, working pressure.

fonctionner [fɔ̃ksjɔne] *v.i.* **I.** (Of committee, etc.) To function. **2.** To act, work. *Les trains ne fonctionnent plus*, the trains are no longer running. *Les freins n'ont pas fonctionné*, the brakes failed to act; the brakes refused to act. **Faire fonctionner une machine**, to run, operate, a machine.

fond [fɔ̃], *s.m.* **I.** (*a*) Bottom (of well, etc.). *Abîme sans fond*, bottomless chasm. *F. d'une culotte, d'une chaise*, seat of a pair of breeches, of a chair. *Boîte à double f.*, box with a false bottom. *Mch: F. de cylindre, de chaudière*, cylinder-head, boiler-head. **Au fond du cœur**, ·at the bottom of one's heart. **Aller au f. d'une affaire**, to get to the bottom, to go to the root, of a matter. **Au fin fond de . . .**, at the very bottom of. . . . *Bateau à f. plat*, flat-bottomed boat. *F. de cale*, bilge. (*b*) Bottom, bed (of the sea). *F. de sable*, sandy bottom. (Of anchor) **Prendre fond**, to bite, grip. *Grands fonds*, ocean deeps. *Hauts, petits, fonds*, shallows. **Courant de fond**, undertow. **Trouver le fond, prendre le fond**, to take soundings. (Of swimmer) **Perdre fond**, to get out of one's depth. *Adv.phr.* **A fond**, thoroughly. *Visser une pièce à f.*, to screw a piece home. **Connaître un sujet à fond**, to have a thorough knowledge of a subject; to be an adept in a subject. *Se lancer à f. dans une description de . . .*, to plunge headlong into a description of. . . . S.a. COULER I, TRAIN 2. **2.** Foundation. **Rebâtir une maison de fond en comble**, to rebuild a house from top to bottom. *F:* **Être ruiné de fond en comble**, to be utterly ruined. *Needlew:* **Broderie sur f. de soie**, embroidery on a silk foundation, on a silk ground. **Faire fond sur qch.**, to rely, depend, on sth.; to build upon·(promise). *Je n'aime ni la forme ni le fond de sa lettre*, I like neither the form nor the

substance of his letter. **Cheval qui a du fond**, horse with staying power. **Course de fond**, long-distance race. **Question de fond**, fundamental question. *Journ:* **Article de fond**, leading article; leader. *Mus:* **Jeu de fond**, pipe-stop (of organ); foundation-stop. **Bruit de fond**, (i) scratching (of gramophone needle); (ii) *Cin:* ground noise. **Au fond**, **dans le fond**, fundamentally; at bottom. **3.** Back, furthermost part, far end. *F:* **Fonds de boutique**, oddments; old stock. *F. d'un tableau*, background of a picture. *Ten:* **Lignes de fond**, base-lines, back-lines. **Jeu de fond**, back-line play. *Th:* **Le fond**, the back of the stage.

fondamental, -aux [fɔ̃damãtal, -o], *a.* Fundamental; basic (principle). **Pierre fondamentale**, foundation stone. **Couleurs fondamentales**, primary colours. *adv.* **-ement.**

fondant [fɔ̃dã]. **I.** *a.* Melting. **2.** *s.m.* (*a*) *Metall:* Flux. (*b*) Fondant, bon-bon.

fondateur, -trice [fɔ̃datœːr, -tris], *s.* Founder. *Fin:* Promoter (of company). **Parts de fondateur**, founder's shares.

fondation [fɔ̃dasjɔ̃], *s.f.* **I.** (*a*) Founding (of empire, etc.). (*b*) (Fund for) endowment; foundation. (*c*) (Endowed) establishment, institution. **2.** *Fondations d'une maison*, foundations of a house.

fondement [fɔ̃dmã], *s.m.* **I.** (*a*) *Const:* Substructure; foundation; base. **Jeter les fondements d'un édifice**, to lay the foundations of a building. (*b*) **Il n'y a pas de fondement à faire sur sa parole**, there is no reliance to be placed on his word. **Soupçons sans fondement**, groundless suspicions; unfounded suspicions. **2.** *Anat:* Fundament; *F:* buttocks, bottom.

fonder, *v.tr.* **I.** To found, lay the foundations of (building, business). *F. un commerce, une maison de commerce*, to start, set up, a business. *F. ses espérances sur qch.*, to ground, base, one's hopes on sth. **2.** *Fin:* To fund (debt).
se fonder sur qch., to place one's reliance on sth.; to build upon (promise, etc.). *Sur quoi se fonde-t-il pour nier que . . . ?* what are his grounds for denying that . . . ?
fondé. **I.** *a.* (*a*) Founded, grounded, reasonable, justified. *Nous ne sommes pas fondés à leur refuser ce droit*, we are not entitled to refuse them this right. (*b*) Funded (debt). **2.** *s.m.* **Fondé de pouvoir**, (i) *Jur:* agent (holding power of attorney); proxy; (ii) *Com:* manager, managing director; (iii) signing clerk. S.a. BIEN-FONDÉ.

fonderie [fɔ̃dri], *s.f.* **I.** (*a*) Smelting. (*b*) Founding, casting (of metals). **2.** (*a*) Smelting works. (*b*) Foundry.

fondeur [fɔ̃dœːr], *s.m.* (*a*) Smelter. (*b*) (Metal-)founder, caster.

fondre [fɔ̃dr]. **I.** *v.tr.* (*a*) To smelt (ore). (*b*) To melt (snow, wax, etc.); to melt down (metal, etc.). (*c*) To cast, found (bell, gun). (*d*) To dissolve, melt (salt, sugar, etc.). (*e*) To blend (colours). **2.** *v.i.* (*a*) To melt. *El:* **Le fusible fond**, the fuse blows (out). *F:* **L'argent lui fond entre les mains**, money melts in his hands. *Sp: F:* **Se faire fondre**, to train down. (*b*) (Of salt, etc.) To melt, dissolve. *F:* **Fondre en larmes**, to dissolve in(to) tears. **3.** *v.i.* To pounce, swoop down (upon the prey, etc.).
fondu, *s.m. Cin:* Fading in or out.
fondue, *s.f. Cu:* Cheese soufflé.

fondrière [fɔ̃driɛːr], *s.f.* (*a*) Hollow (in ground). (*b*) Bog, quagmire. (*c*) Muddy hole (in road).

fonds [fɔ̃], *s.m.* **I.** **Fonds de terre**, estate. **2.** (*a*) **Fonds de commerce**, business, goodwill.

(b) Stock(-in-trade). *Avoir un f. de science*, to have a stock of knowledge. **3.** (a) Funds. **Faire les fonds d'une entreprise**, to supply the capital for an undertaking. **Mise de fonds**, paid-in capital. **Rentrer dans ses fonds**, to get one's outlay, one's money, back. **Appel de fonds**, call upon shareholders. (b) Fund (for special purpose). **Fonds de roulement**, working capital, trading capital. (c) Means, resources. **Placer son argent à fonds perdu**, to purchase a life annuity. *F:* **Prêt à fonds perdu**, loan without security. **Être en fonds**, to be in funds. (d) **Fonds d'État, fonds publics**, Government stock(s).

font. See FAIRE.

fontaine [fɔ̃tɛn], *s.f.* **1.** (a) Spring; pool (of running water). (b) Spring, source, well. **2.** Fountain. *Les fontaines Wallace*, the Wallace drinking fountains (in Paris). **3.** Cistern.

fontainier [fɔ̃tɛnje], *s.m.* **1.** Fountain-maker. **2.** *Adm:* Turncock. **3.** Well-borer, -sinker.

fonte¹ [fɔ̃ːt], *s.f.* **1.** (a) Melting; thawing (of snow). (b) Smelting (of ore). (c) Casting, founding. **Pièces de fonte**, castings. **Cylindres venus de fonte ensemble**, cylinders cast in one piece. **2.** Cast iron. **Fonte d'acier**, cast steel. **3.** *Typ:* Fount. [FONDRE]

fonte², *s.f.* **1.** (Saddle) holster (for pistol). **2.** *Aut:* Leather pocket.

fonts [fɔ̃], *s.m.pl. Ecc:* Font. **Tenir un enfant sur les fonts (baptismaux)**, to stand godfather or godmother to a child.

football [futbal], *s.m.* (Association) football.

footballeur [futbalœːr], *s.m.* Footballer.

footing [futɛ̃ŋ, -tiŋ], *s.m.* Walking (training or exercise). *Course de f.*, walking race.

for [fɔːr], *s.m.* **1.** *A:* Tribunal. **2.** **Le for intérieur**, the conscience. **Dans, en, son for intérieur**, in his heart of hearts.

forage [fɔraːʒ], *s.m.* **1.** Drilling, boring; sinking (of well). **2.** Bore-hole, drill-hole.

forain, -aine [fɔrɛ̃, -ɛn]. **1.** *a.* (From) outside; foreign. See MOUILLAGE 3, RADE. **2.** *a. & s.* Itinerant. **Spectacle forain**, travelling show (at a fair). **(Marchand) forain**, (i) packman, pedlar; (ii) stall-keeper (at a fair, etc.).

forban [fɔrbɑ̃], *s.m.* Corsair, pirate, buccaneer.

forçage [fɔrsaːʒ], *s.m.* **1.** Forcing (of plant, etc.). **2.** Excess in weight (of coin).

forçat [fɔrsa], *s.m.* Convict. *F:* **Mener une vie de forçat**, to drudge and slave.

force [fɔrs], *s.f.* **1.** Strength, force, might, vigour. (a) **Mourir dans la force de l'âge**, to die in the prime of life. **Être à bout de forces**, to be exhausted. **Travailler de toutes ses forces**, to work with all one's might, with might and main. *Const:* **Jambes de force**, *s.f.pl.* forces, force-pieces, struts. *Mec:* **F. de résistance à la tension**, tensile strength. (b) **Il est d'une belle force au tennis**, he is a crack tennis-player. **Ils sont de force (égale)**, they are equally matched. **Boxeur de première force**, first-rate boxer. **Il est de force à vous renverser**, he is strong enough to overthrow you. **Tour de force**, feat (of strength or skill); *tour de force.* (c) Force, violence. **Force majeure**, circumstances outside one's control. **Faire qch. de vive force**, to do sth. by sheer, main, force. **Entrer, pénétrer, de force, par force, dans une maison**, to force one's way into a house. **Faire entrer qch. de force dans qch.**, to force sth. into sth. **Faire force sur** (*un câble, etc.*), to bring a strain on (a cable, etc.). *Nau:* **Faire force de voiles**, to crowd on (all) sail. **Force lui fut d'obéir**, he had no alternative but to obey. *Prov:* **La force prime le droit** might is right. **De gré ou de force**,

willy-nilly. **De toute force il nous faut . . .**, we absolutely must. . . . **A toute force**, in spite of all opposition; at all costs. S.a. CAMISOLE 2, MAISON 1. **2.** Force, power. (a) **F. motrice** motive power. **Force d'inertie**, vis inertiae. **Force vive**, kinetic energy. **Dans toute la force du mot**, in every sense of the word. **Par la force des choses . . .**, owing to the force of circumstances. . . . (b) **F. d'un régiment**, strength of a regiment. (c) **La force publique**, police force. **La force armée**, (i) armed force; (ii) the military. *F:* **Nous étions présents en force(s)**, we had turned out in (full) force. **3.** *a.inv.* **Force gens**, many plenty of, people. **Boire f. bière**, to drink a copious amount of beer. **4.** **A force de.** (i) By dint of, by means of. **A f. de travailler**, by dint of hard work. **A f. de volonté**, by sheer force of will (ii) **A force de bras**, by sheer strength (of arm).

forcement [fɔrsəmɑ̃], *s.m.* Forcing open, breaking open.

forcément [fɔrsemɑ̃], *adv.* Perforce. **1.** Under compulsion. **2.** Necessarily, inevitably.

forcené, -ée [fɔrsəne]. **1.** *a.* Frantic, mad, frenzied. **2.** *s.* Madman, madwoman.

forcer [fɔrse], *v.tr.* (je forçai(s); n. forçons) To force. **1.** To compel. **F. la main à qn**, to force s.o.'s hand. **F. le respect de qn**, to compel respect from s.o. **Forcer qn à faire qch.**, to force, compel, s.o. to do sth. **Être forcé de faire qch.**, to be forced to do sth. **2.** (a) **Forcer qn, qch.**, to do violence to s.o., sth. **Forcer la consigne**, to force one's way in. **F. un poste**, to take a post by storm, by force. **F. une serrure**, to force a lock. **F. la caisse**, to break into the till. **F. sa prison**, to break jail. S.a. BLOCUS. (b) **To strain** (mast); to bend, buckle (plate). **Se f. l'épaule**, to wrench one's shoulder. **Se f. le cœur**, to strain one's heart. *F:* **Forcer la note**, to overdo it. **F. un cheval**, to overwork, override, a horse. **Forcer le pas**, to force the pace. **F. des fleurs**, to force flowers. **Forcer un cerf**, to bring a stag to bay. (c) To increase (dose). **3.** *v.i.* **F. de voiles**, to crowd on sail. **F. de vitesse**, to increase speed.

se forcer. 1. To overstrain oneself. **2.** To do violence to one's feelings.

forcé, -a. Forced. **1.** Compulsory (loan). *Av:* **Atterrissage f.**, forced landing. S.a. TRAVAIL² 1. **2.** Strained. **Exemple f.**, far-fetched example. **Sourire f.**, forced, wry, smile.

forcerie [fɔrsəri], *s.f. Hort:* Forcing house.

forcir [fɔrsiːr], *v.i. F:* **1.** To get fat. **2.** (Of child) To grow (strong).

forer [fɔre], *v.tr.* To drill, bore; to sink (a well).

forestier, -ière [fɔrɛstje, -jɛːr], *a.* Pertaining to a forest. **Exploitation forestière**, lumbering. **(Garde) forestier**, forest-ranger.

foret [fɔrɛ], *s.m. Tls:* (a) Drill. **F. à hélice**, *f. hélicoïdal*, twist-drill. (b) Gimlet. **F. de charpentier**, auger. (c) (Brace-)bit.

forêt [fɔrɛ], *s.f.* Forest.

foreur [fɔrœːr], *s.m.* Borer, driller.

foreuse [fɔrøːz], *s.f.* Drill(ing-machine).

forfaire [fɔrfɛːr], *v.ind.tr.* (Conj. like FAIRE. Used only in *inf.*, compound tenses, and occ. *pr.ind.sg.*) **F. à l'honneur**, to forfeit one's honour. **F. à sa parole**, to break one's word.

forfait¹ [fɔrfɛ], *s.m.* Heinous crime.

forfait², *s.m.* Contract. **Travail à forfait**, (i) work by contract; (ii) (of workman) job work. **Acheter qch. à forfait**, to buy sth. outright.

forfait³, *s.m. Turf:* Fine, forfeit (paid for scratching a horse from a race). **Déclarer forfait pour un cheval**, to scratch a horse.

forfaitaire [fɔrfɛtɛːr], *a.* Contractual. **Marché**

forfaitaire, (transaction by) contract; outright purchase. *Payement f.*, lump sum.

forfaiture [fɔrfɛtyːr], *s.f.* 1. Abuse (of authority); maladministration. 2. **Forfaiture au devoir, à l'honneur**, breach of duty, of honour.

forfanterie [fɔrfɑ̃tri], *s.f.* Impudent boast(ing).

forficule [fɔrfikyl], *s.f.* *Ent:* Earwig.

forge [fɔrʒ], *s.f.* 1. (*a*) Forge; smith's hearth. **Pièce de forge**, forging. (*b*) **Forge maréchale**, smithy. *Mener un cheval à la f.*, to take a horse to the blacksmith's. 2. Usu. *pl.* Ironworks. **Maître de forges**, ironmaster.

forge|r [fɔrʒe], *v.tr.* (je forgeai(s); n. forgeons) To forge. 1. *Fer forgé*, wrought iron. *Prov:* **En forgeant on devient forgeron**, practice makes perfect. 2. To forge (document); to make up, invent (story, excuse). *a.* **-able.** *s.m.* **-age.**

forgeron [fɔrʒərɔ̃], *s.m.* (Black)smith.

forgeur, -euse [fɔrʒœːr, -øːz], *s.* 1. Inventor, fabricator (of news, lies). 2. *s.m.* = FORGERON.

formaldéhyde [fɔrmaldeid], *s.f.*, **formaline** [fɔrmalin], *s.f.* *Ch:* Formaldehyde, formalin(e).

formaliser [fɔrmalize], *v.tr.* To give offence to (s.o.); to offend.

se formaliser, to take offence (*de*, at).

formalisme [fɔrmalism], *s.m.* Formalism.

formaliste [fɔrmalist]. 1. *a.* Formal, stiff, precise (mind, etc.). 2. *s.* Formalist, precisian.

formalité [fɔrmalite], *s.f.* 1. Formality. **C'est une pure formalité**, it is a mere matter of form. *F:* **Sans autre formalité**, without further ado. 2. *F:* Ceremoniousness. Esp. **Sans formalité(s)**, without ceremony.

format [fɔrma], *s.m.* (*a*) Format (of book). *F. de poche*, pocket size. (*b*) *Phot:* Size (of plates).

formation [fɔrmasjɔ̃], *s.f.* Formation. 1. Forming; moulding (of character). **Une nation en voie de formation**, a nation in the making. 2. Make-up (of train, etc.).

forme [fɔrm], *s.f.* 1. Form, shape; lines (of ship). **En forme de cloche**, bell-shaped. **Sous la forme d'une nymphe**, in the form, shape, of a nymph. **Statistiques sous forme de tableau**, statistics in tabular form. **Dire qch. par forme d'avertissement**, to say sth. by way of warning. **Sans forme**, shapeless, formless. 2. Form; method of procedure. (*a*) **Quittance en bonne forme, dans les formes**, receipt in order, in proper form. **Renvoyer qn sans autre forme de procès**, to dismiss s.o. without ceremony. **Avertir qn dans les formes**, to give s.o. formal, due, warning. **Faire qch. dans les formes**, to do sth. with due decorum. **Pour la forme**, as a matter of form; for form's sake. (*b*) *pl.* Manners. *Y mettre des formes*, to be polite; to use tact. (*c*) *Sp:* **Être en forme**, to be in form. **Équipe bien en f.**, team at the top of its form. 3. *Ind:* Former. *Bootm:* Last; *pl.* boot-trees. *Hatm:* (i) Block; (ii) body; (iii) (of woman's hat) shape, hood. *Paperm:* Mould, form. **Chapeau à haute forme**, top hat. **Papier à forme**, hand-made paper. 4. *F. d'un lièvre*, hare's form. 5. *Nau:* Dock. 6. *Typ:* Form(e). *Serrer une f.*, to lock up a form. 7. (Choir) stall.

formel, -elle [fɔrmɛl], *a.* Formal, strict (rule, order); explicit (declaration); categorical.

formellement [fɔrmɛlmɑ̃], *adv.* Formally. **Il est formellement interdit de . . .**, it is absolutely, strictly, expressly, forbidden to. . . .

former [fɔrme], *v.tr.* To form. 1. To make, create; to draw up (plan); to formulate (objections). 2. To shape, fashion. (*a*) *F. son style sur celui de . . .*, to form one's style on that of . . .

(*b*) To school (child, horse); to train (servant); to mould (a child's character).

se former, to form; to take form. *Nos plans se forment*, our plans are taking shape. **Le fruit se forme**, the fruit is setting. **Se former aux affaires**, to acquire a business training.

formé, *a.* Formed, full-grown; (of fruit) set.

formidable [fɔrmidabl], *a.* (*a*) Fearsome, formidable. (*b*) *F:* Tremendous. **C'est formidable!** well, I never! *adv.* **-ment.**

formulaire [fɔrmylɛːr], *s.m.* 1. (*a*) Formulary. (*b*) Pharmacopoeia. 2. = FORMULE 2.

formule [fɔrmyl], *s.f.* 1. (*a*) *Mth:* *Ch:* etc: Formula. *Pharm:* Recipe. (*b*) (Set) form of words; (turn of) phrase; formula. 2. *Adm:* etc: (Printed) form. *Post:* Telegraph form. *F. de chèque*, cheque form; blank cheque.

formuler [fɔrmyle], *v.tr.* To formulate (doctrine); to draw up (document); to give expression to (wish); to put (proposal) into words. *F. une plainte*, to lodge, bring forward, a complaint. *F. une règle*, to lay down a rule.

fors [fɔːr], *prep.* *A:* Except, save. **Tout est perdu fors l'honneur**, all is lost save honour.

fort [fɔːr]. I. *a.* 1. (*a*) Strong. *Je suis plus f. des bras que vous*, I am stronger in the arms than you. **Trouver plus fort que soi**, to meet one's match. **C'est une tête forte, une forte tête**, he has a good head on his shoulders. **Esprit fort**, free-thinker. **Être fort en mathématiques**, to be good at mathematics. *Semelle forte*, stout sole. *Terre forte*, heavy soil. *Tabac f.*, strong tobacco. *Avoir une forte odeur*, to have a strong smell. *Liqueurs fortes*, strong drink. *Forte fièvre*, high fever. *Forte mer*, heavy sea. *D'une voix forte*, in a loud voice. **C'est plus fort que moi!** I can't help it! *Ce qu'il y a de plus f., c'est que . . .*, (i) the most outrageous, (ii) the best, part of it is that. . . . (*b*) **Ville, place, forte**, fortified town; fortress. (*c*) **Se faire fort de faire qch.**, to engage, undertake, to do sth. **Elles se font fort, fortes, de le retrouver**, they undertake to find him again. 2. Large. *Femme forte*, stout woman. *Forte barbe*, heavy beard. *Il y avait une forte rosée*, there was a heavy dew. *Forte somme*, large sum of money. *Fortes ressources*, ample means. *Forte différence*, great difference. *Forte baisse de prix*, big drop in price. *Forte pente*, steep gradient. **Armée forte de cinq mille hommes**, army five thousand strong. *Com:* **Prix fort**, full price, catalogue price. *adv.* **-ement.**

II. **fort**, *adv.* 1. Strongly. **Frapper fort**, to strike hard. *F:* **Y aller fort**, (i) to go hard at it; (ii) to exaggerate. *Crier de plus en plus f.*, to shout louder and louder. 2. Very, extremely. *Il a été f. mécontent*, he was highly displeased. **J'ai fort à faire**, I have a great deal to do.

III. **fort**, *s.m.* 1. Strong part. **Le fort et le faible d'une affaire**, the strong and weak points of an affair. *Le f. de l'hiver*, the depth of winter. **Au (plus) fort du combat**, in the thick of the fight. **Le plus fort est fait**, the most difficult part is done. **La politesse n'est pas son fort**, politeness is not his strong point. 2. (*a*) Strong man. **Les forts de la Halle**, the market porters. (*b*) *Prov:* **La raison du plus fort est toujours la meilleure**, might is right. 3. Fort, stronghold.

forte [fɔrte], *adv.* & *s.m.inv.* *Mus:* Forte.

forteresse [fɔrtərɛs], *s.f.* Fortress, stronghold.

fortifiable [fɔrtifjabl], *a.* Fortifiable.

fortifiant [fɔrtifjɑ̃]. 1. *a.* Fortifying, strengthening, invigorating. 2. *s.m.* Tonic, fortifier.

fortification [fɔrtifikasjɔ̃], *s.f.* Fortification. 1. Fortifying (of town, etc.). 2. Defence work(s).

18

Usu. *pl. Les fortifications,* the fortifications (of a town).

fortifier [fɔrtifje], *v.tr.* To strengthen; to fortify (town); to invigorate (the body).
se fortifier, to become stronger.

fortin [fɔrtɛ̃], *s.m.* Small fort.

fortuit [fɔrtɥi], *a.* Fortuitous; (by) chance. *Rencontre fortuite,* chance, casual, meeting. *Cas fortuit,* (i) accidental case, accident; (ii) *Jur:* act of God. *adv.* **-ement.**

fortuité [fɔrtɥite], *s.f.* Fortuitousness.

fortune [fɔrtyn], *s.f.* **1.** Fortune, chance, luck. *Coup de fortune,* stroke of luck. *Tenter (la) fortune,* to try one's luck. *Compagnons de fortune,* chance companions. *Officier de fortune,* officer risen from the ranks. *Venez dîner à la fortune du pot,* come and take pot-luck. *Dispositif de fortune,* makeshift. *Réparations de f.,* breakdown repairs. *Nau:* **Mât, gouvernail, de fortune,** jury-mast, jury-rudder. *M.Ins:* **Fortune de mer,** sea-risks. **2.** Piece of (good, bad) luck, fortune. *F:* **En quête de bonnes fortunes,** on the prowl. *Mauvaise fortune,* misfortune. *Avoir la bonne, mauvaise, f. de rencontrer . . .,* to have the good, bad, luck to meet. . . . **3.** Fortune, riches. **Faire fortune,** to make one's fortune. **Avoir de la fortune,** to be well off.

fortuné [fɔrtyne], *a.* **1.** Fortunate, happy, successful. **2.** Rich, well-off, well-to-do.

forure [fɔryːr], *s.f.* Bore(-hole); esp. pipe (of a key).

fosse [foːs], *s.f.* **1.** Pit, hole. *Aut:* Inspection pit. *Hyg: F. d'aisance,* cesspool. **2.** Grave. *F:* **Avoir un pied dans la fosse, être au bord de la fosse,** to have one foot in the grave. **3.** *Anat:* Fossa. *Fosses nasales,* nasal fossae.

fossé [fose], *s.m.* (a) Ditch, trench, drain. *Creuser des fossés,* to trench, to ditch. (b) *Fort:* Moat. *F:* **Sauter le fossé,** to take the plunge.

fossette [fosɛt, fɔ-], *s.f.* (a) Pit, chuck-hole (in game of marbles). **Jouer à la fossette,** to play at chucks, at pits. (b) Dimple. *Joues à fossettes,* dimpled cheeks. [FOSSE]

fossile [fɔsil], *a. & s.m.* Fossil.

fossiliser (se) [səfɔsilize], *v.pr.* To fossilize; to become fossilized. *F: Un bonhomme fossilisé,* an old fossil.

fossoyer [foswaje, fɔ-], *v.tr.* (je fossoie; je fossoierai) To trench, drain, ditch (field, etc.). [FOSSE] *s.m.* **-age.**

fossoyeur [foswajœːr], *s.m.* Grave-digger.

fou [fu], **fol, folle** [fɔl]. (The form 'fol,' used in the *m.* before a vowel within the word-group, is confined to sense I (b).) **1.** *a.* (a) Mad, insane. **Fou à lier,** raving mad; crazy. *Il était fou de douleur,* he was mad, frantic, with pain. **Fou de joie,** beside oneself with joy. **Être fou de qn,** to be madly in love with s.o. *S.a.* RIRE II, TERREUR. (b) Foolish, extravagant, silly. **Les vierges folles,** the foolish virgins. *Un fol espoir,* a foolish, mad, hope. (c) Excessive (in size, number); prodigious, enormous. **Succès fou,** tremendous success. *Mal de tête fou,* splitting headache. *Il gagne un argent fou,* he makes no end, tons, of money. *A une allure folle,* at a break-neck speed. *Il y avait un monde fou,* the place was crowded. (d) Wafted here and there; not under control. *Des mèches folles sortaient de son bonnet,* wisps of hair peeped from under her cap. *Herbes folles,* rank weeds. *Poulie folle,* loose pulley. *Nau:* **Vent fou,** unsteady wind. **Aiguille (de compas) folle,** crazy (compass-)needle. **2.** *s.* (Never *fol*) (a) Madman, madwoman; lunatic. **Fou furieux,** raving lunatic; maniac.

F: **Maison de fous,** lunatic asylum; madhouse. (b) Fool. **Fou de cour,** court fool; jester. **Plus on est de fous plus on rit,** the more the merrier. **3.** *s.m.* (a) *Chess:* Bishop. (b) *Orn:* Gannet; solan goose.

fouailler [fwaje], *v.tr.* To flog, lash (with a whip).

foucade [fukad], *s.f.* Passing whim, fancy. *Travailler par foucades,* to work by fits and starts. [FOUGUE]

foudre¹ [fudr], *s.* **1.** (a) *f.* Thunderbolt, lightning. *La foudre est tombée à . . .,* the lightning struck at. . . . *Coup de foudre,* (i) flash of lightning; (ii) thunderbolt; (iii) *F:* bolt from the blue. (b) *m. Les foudres de Jupiter,* Jupiter's thunderbolts. **2.** *m. A:* **Un foudre de guerre,** a great captain. *F. d'éloquence,* powerful orator. [FOUGUE]

foudre², *s.m.* Tun, hogshead, large cask.

foudroyant [fudrwajɑ̃], *a.* (a) Striking (down), terrifying, crushing; smashing (attack); overwhelming, crushing (news). (b) *F:* Of lightning speed. *Aut: Reprise foudroyante,* lightning pick-up; terrific acceleration.

foudr|oyer [fudrwaje], *v.tr.* (je foudroie; je foudroierai) To strike down (by lightning); to blast. *Arbre foudroyé,* blasted tree. *L'apoplexie l'a foudroyé,* he was struck down by apoplexy. *J'étais foudroyé de ses paroles,* I was thunderstruck, dumbfounded, by what he was saying. *s.m.* **-oiement.**

fouet [fwɛ, fwa], *s.m.* **1.** Birch(-rod). **Donner le fouet à un enfant,** to birch a child. **2.** (a) Whipcord. (b) Whip, lash. **Donner le fouet à qn,** to whip, flog, s.o. **Coup de fouet,** (i) cut, lash (of whip); (ii) fillip, stimulus (to the system); (iii) whipping, whip, lashing, surging (of cable); (iv) *Med:* tearing of ligament. *F:* **Donner un coup de fouet à la circulation,** to give a fillip, a stimulus, to the circulation. **Faire claquer son fouet,** (i) to crack one's whip; (ii) *F:* to blow one's own trumpet. *Artil:* **Tir de plein fouet,** direct fire.

fouettement [fwɛtmɑ̃, fwa-], *s.m.* Lashing; esp. flapping (of sail); surging (of cable); whipping (of rod, etc.).

fouett|er [fwɛte, fwa-], *v.tr.* (a) To birch, spank (child). (b) To whip, flog, lash (horse, person); to beat, whisk (eggs); to whip (cream). **Fouette, cocher!** off we go! **Il n'y a pas là de quoi fouetter un chat,** there is nothing to make such a fuss about. **Avoir d'autres chiens, d'autres chats, à fouetter,** to have other fish to fry. *Brise qui fouette le sang,* breeze that makes the blood tingle. *Être fouetté par le désir,* to be stimulated, spurred on, by desire. *La pluie fouette (contre) les vitres,* the rain lashes against the panes. (c) *Abs.* (Of moving part) To lash, whip; (of cable) to surge; (of sail) to flap. *s.m.* **-age.**
    fouettée, *s.f.* Whipping, spanking.

fougeraie [fuʒrɛ], *s.f.* Fern-patch, -brake.

fougère [fuʒɛːr], *s.f. Bot:* Fern. *F. arborescente,* bracken.

fougue [fug], *s.f.* Fire, ardour, dash, spirit. **Cheval plein de fougue,** high-mettled, mettlesome, fiery, horse.

fougueu|x, -euse [fugø, -øːz], *a.* Fiery, ardent, spirited; impetuous. *adv.* **-sement.**

fouille [fuːj], *s.f.* **1.** Excavation. **2.** *F. d'un suspect,* search(ing) of a suspected person.

fouill|er [fuje]. **I.** *v.tr.* (a) To dig, excavate. **Machine à fouiller,** excavating machine. (b) To search. **Fouiller qn,** to search s.o. *F. un tiroir,* to ransack a drawer. *F. un bois,* to scour a wood. **2.** *v.i. F. dans une armoire,* to search, rummage, in a cupboard. *F. dans sa poche pour un mouchoir,*

to grope in one's pocket for a handkerchief. *F. pour trouver qch.*, to rummage, forage, for sth. *s.m.* **-ement.**
   se fouiller, to go through one's pockets. *P :* **Tu peux te fouiller!** nothing doing!
   fouillé, *a.* Showing great detail; elaborate.
fouilleur, -euse [fujœːr, -øːz], *s.* **1.** (*a*) Excavator. (*b*) Rummager, searcher. **2.** *s.f.* **Fouilleuse.** (*a*) Subsoil plough. (*b*) Excavator.
fouillis [fuji], *s.m.* Jumble, muddle (of papers).
fouinard [fwinaːr], *a. P:* (*a*) Inquisitive, ferrety. *s.* Nosy Parker. (*b*) Sly, sneaking. [FOUINE]
fouine [fwin], *s.f. Z:* Stone-marten. *F:* **A figure de fouine,** weasel-faced.
fouiner [fwine], *v.i.* To ferret; to nose about.
foui|r [fwiːr], *v.tr.* To dig (underground). *Animaux qui fouissent le sol,* animals that burrow in the soil. *s.m.* **-issement.**
fouisseur, -euse [fwisœːr, -øːz], *a. & s.* Burrowing (animal); burrower.
foulant [fulɑ̃], *a.* Pressing, crushing. **Pompe foulante,** force-pump.
foulard [fulaːr], *s.m.* **1.** *Tex:* Foulard, silk. **2.** Silk neckerchief; scarf; silk handkerchief.
foule [ful], *s.f.* **1.** Pressing, crushing. (*a*) Fulling, milling (of cloth). (*b*) Treading (of grapes). **2.** Crowd; throng (of people). **Faire foule autour de qn,** to crowd round s.o. **Magasin qui fait foule,** shop that draws crowds.
foul|er [fule], *v.tr.* **1.** To press. (*a*) To crush, crumple, rumple (dress); to trample (down), tread down (grass); to tread, crush (grapes). *F. qch. aux pieds,* to tread, trample, sth. under foot. (*b*) *Tex:* To full (cloth). **2.** To sprain, strain, wrench. **Se fouler le poignet,** to sprain one's wrist. *F:* **Ne pas se fouler la rate,** *P:* **ne pas se la fouler,** to take it easy. *s.m.* **-age.** *s.m.* **-ement.**
   se fouler. *F:* (*a*) To put oneself out; to take pains. (*b*) To hurry. **Ne pas se fouler,** to take it easy.
   foulée, *s.f.* **1.** Tread (of stair). **2.** (*a*) Print, tread (of horse's hoof). (*b*) Usu. *pl.* Stride. *Parcourir les guérets à longues foulées,* to stride over the fields. (*c*) *pl. Ven:* Foil, spoor (of game). **3.** Compression (of bellows).
fouleur, -euse [fulœːr, -øːz], *s.* **1.** *Tex:* Fuller. **2.** Wine-presser.
foulon [fulɔ̃], *s.m. Tex:* Fuller. **Chardon à foulon,** fuller's teasel. **Terre à foulon,** fuller's earth.
foulque [fulk], *s.f. Orn:* Coot.
foulure [fulyːr], *s.f.* **1.** Sprain, wrench. *F. au genou,* sprained knee. (*b*) *Equit:* Saddle-gall (of horse). **2.** Fulling, milling (of skins).
four [fuːr], *s.m.* **1.** (*a*) (Kitchen or baker's) oven. *F. à gaz,* gas-oven, gas-cooker. *Plat allant au f.,* fireproof dish. *Sch: P:* **Four à bachot,** cramming shop. (*b*) **Petits fours,** fancy biscuits. **2.** Kiln, furnace. *F. à chaux,* lime-kiln. *F. à recuire,* annealing furnace. *F. à sécher le houblon,* oast-house. **3.** *F:* Esp. *Th:* Failure. **La pièce fit four,** the play was a failure, a fiasco, a frost; the play fell flat. S.a. NOIR 1.
fourbe [furb]. **1.** *a.* Rascally, knavish (person). **2.** *s. A:* Cheat, knave, rascal.
fourberie [furbəri], *s.f.* **1.** Imposture, deceit, cheating, double-dealing. **2.** Swindle; piece of roguery.
fourb|ir [furbiːr], *v.tr.* To furbish, rub up, polish up. *s.m.* **-issage.**
   fourbi, *s.m. P:* (Soldier's) kit or equipment. **Tout le fourbi,** every blessed thing; lock, stock, and barrel.

fourbu [furby], *a.* (Of horse) Foundered, broken-down. *F:* (Of pers.) Tired out, dead-beat.
fourche [furʃ], *s.f.* Fork. **1.** *F. à foin,* hay-fork, pitchfork. **Remuer le sol à la fourche,** to fork the ground. **2.** Arbre, chemin, qui fait la fourche, tree, road, that branches, forks. S.a. PATIBULAIRE 1.
fourchée [furʃe], *s.f.* Pitchforkful (of hay, etc.).
fourch|er [furʃe]. **1.** *v.i.* (Of roads, etc.) To fork, divide, branch. *F:* **La langue lui a fourché,** he made a slip of the tongue. **2.** *v.tr. F. le sol,* to fork, dig, the ground. *s.m.* **-ement.**
fourchet [furʃɛ], *s.m.* **1.** *Agr:* Two-pronged fork. **2.** *Vet:* Foot-rot.
fourchette [furʃɛt], *s.f.* **1.** (Table) fork, dinner fork. **Repas à la fourchette,** knife-and-fork meal. *F:* **C'est une bonne fourchette,** he is a good trencherman. **2.** (*a*) *Artil:* Bracket, fork (in ranging). (*b*) *Cards:* Tenace. **3.** (*a*) Wish-bone, merry-thought (of fowl). (*b*) Frog (of horse's hoof). **4.** *Mec.E:* Belt-guide, -shifter. *F. de débrayage,* clutch throw-out fork.
fourchu [furʃy], *a.* Forked, bifurcated. **Pied fourchu,** cloven hoof.
fourchure [furʃyːr], *s.f.* Fork (of road, etc.).
fourgon¹ [furgɔ̃], *s.m.* Poker, (fire-)rake.
fourgon² [furgɔ̃], *s.m.* Van, wag(g)on. *Mil:* General service waggon. *F. automobile,* motor van. *Rail: F. à bagages,* luggage van, guard's van. *F. à marchandises,* covered goods waggon. *F. à bestiaux,* cattle-truck.
fourgonner [furgone]. **1.** *v.i. F:* To poke, rake, the fire. *F. dans un tiroir,* to poke about in a drawer. **2.** *v.tr.* To poke, prick (the fire).
fourgonnette [furgonɛt], *s.f. Aut:* Light van.
fourmi [furmi], *s.f.* **1.** *v.i.* (*a*) Ant. (*b*) **Fourmi blanche,** termite, white ant. *F:* **Avoir des fourmis dans les jambes,** to have a tingling, pins and needles, in one's legs.
fourmilier [furmilje], *s.m. Z:* Ant-eater.
fourmilière [furmiljɛr], *s.f.* Ant-hill, ants' nest.
fourmillement [furmijmɑ̃], *s.m.* **1.** Swarming, coming and going (of ants, etc.). **2.** Pricking or tingling sensation; pins and needles.
fourmiller [furmije], *v.i.* **1.** To swarm; to teem. *L'avenue fourmillait de voitures,* the avenue was alive with vehicles. **2.** *Le pied me fourmille,* I have pins and needles in my foot. [FOURMI]
fournaise [furnɛz], *s.f. Lit:* (Fiery) furnace.
fourneau [furno], *s.m.* **1.** (*a*) Furnace (of boiler, etc.); bowl (of pipe). (*b*) **Fourneau de cuisine,** kitchener, (kitchen-)range. *F. à gaz,* gas-stove, -cooker. **Fourneau philanthropique,** soup-kitchen. (*c*) **Haut fourneau,** blast-furnace. **2.** *Min: F. de mine,* mine chamber, blast-hole.
fournée [furne], *s.f.* Batch (of loaves, etc.).
fournil [furni], *s.m.* Bakehouse.
fourniment [furnimɑ̃], *s.m.* (Soldier's) equipment.
fournir [furniːr], *v.tr.* **1.** *A:* To complete, to fill. *F:* **Fournir sa carrière, une longue carrière,** to have a long career; to live to a great age. **2.** To supply, furnish, provide. *L'effort fourni par . . .,* the effort put forth by. . . . **Fournir qch. à qn,** **fournir qn de qch.,** to supply s.o. with sth. *Magasin bien fourni,* well-stocked shop. *Cards: F. du trèfle,* to follow the club lead. **3.** *v.ind.tr. F. aux dépenses,* to defray the expenses. *F. aux besoins de qn,* to supply s.o.'s wants.
   se fournir. **1.** (Of beard, etc.) To grow thick. **2.** (*a*) *Se f. de qch.,* to provide oneself with sth. (*b*) *Il se fournit chez nous,* he is a customer of ours.

fourni, *a.* **1.** Thick (hair, etc.); bushy (beard). **2.** *Sp:* *Champ f.*, big field of starters.

fournisseur, -euse [furnisœːr, -øːz], *s.* (a) Supplier, purveyor, caterer. *F. de navires, de la marine,* ship-chandler. (b) **Les fournisseurs,** the tradesmen (with whom we deal).

fourniture [furnityːr], *s.f.* **1.** Supplying, providing. **2.** *pl.* Supplies, requisites. *Fournitures pour chapeaux,* hat trimmings. *Fournitures de navires,* ships' chandlery. *Fournitures de bureau,* office requisites; stationery.

fourrage [furaːʒ], *s.m.* **1.** *Husb: etc:* Forage, fodder. **2.** *Mil:* Foraging. *Aller au f.,* to forage.

fourrager[1] [furaʒe], *v.* (n. **fourrageons; je fourrageai(s)**) **1.** *v.i.* (a) To forage. *F:* **Fourrager dans des papiers,** to search, rummage, among papers. (b) To foray. **2.** *v.tr.*(a) To pillage, ravage (country). (b) To rumple (s.o.).

fourrager[2], **-ère** [furaʒe, -ɛːr]. **1.** *a.* (a) Pertaining to forage. *Mil:* **(Corde) fourragère,** (i) forage rope; (ii) aiglet or lanyard (worn by certain units round the left shoulder); shoulder-braid. (b) *Plante fourragère,* fodder plant. **2.** *s.f.* **Fourragère.** (a) Forage waggon. (b) *Aut:* Luggage-carrier.

fourrageur [furaʒœːr], *s.m.* Forager. **Cavaliers dispersés en fourrageurs,** cavalry in extended order; in open order.

fourreau [furo], *s.m.* (a) Sheath, cover, case; scabbard (of sword). **Tirer l'épée du fourreau,** to unsheathe, bare, one's sword. *Remettre l'épée au f.,* to sheathe one's sword. (b) *Mec.E:* Sleeve. *Joint à f.,* expansion joint.

fourrer [fure], *v.tr.* **1.** (a) To cover or line with fur. (b) *F. un coup,* to serve, keckle, a cable. **2.** To stuff, cram. *F. ses mains dans ses poches,* to stuff, bury, one's hands in one's pockets. *Je les avais fourrés dans le coin,* I had stuck them in the corner. *Où est-il allé se fourrer?* where ever has he gone and hidden himself? **Fourrer son nez partout,** to poke one's nose into everything. **Se fourrer dans la conversation,** to butt into the conversation. *P:* **S'en fourrer jusque-là,** to gorge. *F:* **Fourrer qn dedans,** (i) to let s.o. down badly; (ii) to run s.o. in. S.a. DOIGT 1.

fourré. 1. *a.* (a) Lined (gloves, etc.); thickly wooded (country). *Chocolats fourrés à la crème,* chocolate creams. (b) *Paix fourrée,* hollow peace. *Médaille fourrée,* plated medal (palmed off as solid gold). *Fenc:* **Coup fourré,** exchanged hit, double hit. *F:* **Porter un coup fourré à qn,** to deal s.o. a back-handed blow. (c) *F:* **Être toujours fourré chez qn,** to be constantly at s.o.'s house. **2.** *s.m.* (a) Thicket; brake. (b) Jungle.

fourre-tout [furtu], *s.m. inv.* **1.** Lumber-room. **2.** Hold-all (for travelling).

fourreur [furœːr], *s.m.* Furrier.

fourrier [furje], *s.m. Mil:* Sergent **fourrier** = assistant to quartermaster sergeant.

fourrière [furjɛːr], *s.f.* Pound (for animals). *Mettre un chien en f.,* to impound a dog.

fourrure [furyːr], *s.f.* **1.** (a) Fur, skin. *F. de peau de mouton,* sheepskin (coat, rug, etc.). (b) Hair, coat (of heavy-coated animal). **2.** Filling or lining material; packing (of joint). *Mec.E:* *F. d'antifriction,* antifriction lining or bushing.

fourv|oyer [furvwaje], *v.tr.* (je **fourvoie;** je **fourvoierai**) To mislead; to lead (s.o.) astray. *s.m.* **-oiement.**

se fourvoyer, to lose one's way; to go astray. **Être fourvoyé,** to be on the wrong track.

fox [fɔks], *s.m. F:* Fox-terrier.

foyer [fwaje], *s.m.* **1.** Fire(-place), hearth, grate; fire-box (of steam-engine). *F. de chaudière,*

boiler furnace. **2.** (a) *F. de chaleur,* source of heat. *F:* **Un foyer d'érudition,** a centre of learning. (b) *Med:* Focus, seat (of disorder). *F:* **Foyer d'intrigue,** hotbed of intrigue. **3.** (a) Hearth, home. **Le foyer familial,** the home. **Rentrer dans ses foyers,** to come (back) home (*e.g.* from military service). **Foyer du soldat,** soldiers' home. (b) *Th:* **Foyer du public,** foyer, crush-room. **Foyer des artistes,** green-room. **4.** Focus (of lens, curve, etc.).

frac [frak], *s.m.* Dress-coat.

fracas [fraka], *s.m.* Din; (sound of a) crash; clash (of arms). *F:* **Faire du fracas,** to kick up a dust, a row, a shindy.

fracasser [frakase], *v.tr.* To smash (sth.) to pieces; to shatter.

fraction [fraksjɔ̃], *s.f.* **1.** *A:* Breaking. **2.** Fraction; fractional part. *Mth:* **Fraction ordinaire,** vulgar fraction. **Fraction périodique,** recurring decimal. **3.** (Political) group.

fractionnaire [fraksjɔnɛːr], *a.* Fractional. **Nombre fractionnaire,** improper fraction.

fractionn|er [fraksjɔne], *v.tr.* **1.** To divide into (fractional) parts; to split (up) (shares, etc.). **2.** *Ch: Ind:* (a) To fractionate (distillation). (b) To crack (mineral oils). *s.m.* **-ement.**

se fractionner, to split up; to divide into groups.

fracture [fraktyːr], *s.f.* **1.** Breaking open, forcing (of lock, door). **2.** Fracture (of bone, etc.). *Réduire une f.,* to set a fracture.

fracturer [fraktyre], *v.tr.* **1.** To force (lock); to break open (door). **2.** To fracture (bone).

se fracturer, to fracture, break.

fragile [fraʒil], *a.* **1.** Fragile; brittle. **2.** Frail (virtue, health).

fragilement [fraʒilmã], *adv.* Fragilely, weakly.

fragilité [fraʒilite], *s.f.* **1.** Fragility; brittleness. **2.** Frailty (of virtue, health).

fragment [fragmã], *s.m.* Fragment; chip (of stone, etc.); snatch, scrap (of song).

fragmentaire [fragmãtɛːr], *a.* Fragmentary.

fragmentation [fragmãtasjɔ̃], *s.f.* Fragmentation; breaking up (of an empire, etc.).

fragmenter [fragmãte], *v.tr.* To divide (sth.) into fragments.

frai [frɛ], *s.m.* **1.** Abrasion, wear (of coins). **2.** (a) Spawning (of fishes). (b) Spawn.

fraîche. See FRAIS[1].

fraîchement [frɛʃmã], *adv.* **1.** Coolly. **2.** Freshly, recently.

fraîcheur [frɛʃœːr], *s.f.* **1.** Coolness, chilliness. **Dans la fraîcheur du soir,** in the cool of the evening. **Attraper une fraîcheur,** to catch a chill. **2.** Freshness, bloom (of flowers, complexion).

fraîchir [frɛʃiːr], *v.i. Meteor:* **1.** To grow colder. *Impers.* **Il fraîchit,** it is getting cooler. **2.** *Le vent fraîchit,* the wind is freshening.

frairie [freri], *s.f. A:* Jollification; feast.

frais[1], **fraîche** [frɛ, frɛʃ]. **1.** *a.* Fresh. (a) Cool (wind, etc.). (b) *Nau:* *Vent f.,* fresh gale. *Vent grand f.,* stormy gale. (c) New, recent. *De fraîche date,* of recent date. *Œufs frais,* new-laid eggs. *Pain f.,* new bread. *Eau fraîche,* freshly drawn water. **"Peinture fraîche,"** 'wet paint.' **Roses toutes fraîches cueillies,** freshly gathered roses. (d) *Teint, visage, f.,* fresh complexion. **Frais et dispos,** hale and hearty. *F. et dispos pour le travail,* fit and fresh for work. **2.** (a) *s.m.* **Prendre le frais,** to take the air; to enjoy the cool of the evening. **A mettre au frais,** to be kept in a cool place. **De frais,** freshly. *Peint de f.,* freshly painted. (b) *s.f.* **La fraîche,** the cool of the day.

frais², *s.m.pl.* Expenses, cost. Faux frais, incidental expenses. **Menus frais**, (i) petty expenses ; (ii) pocket-money. *F. d'un procès*, costs of a law-suit. **Être condamné aux frais**, to be ordered to pay costs. **Faire les frais de qch.**, to bear the cost of sth. **Faire, couvrir, ses frais**, to cover one's expenses ; to get back one's money. **Faire les frais de la conversation**, (i) to contribute a large share of the talk ; (ii) to be the subject of the conversation. **Faire qch. à ses frais**, to do sth. at one's own expense. **A grands frais, à peu de frais**, at great, at little, cost. **Se mettre en frais**, to go to expense. **Faire des frais**, to lay oneself out to please. **J'en suis pour mes frais**, I've had all my trouble for nothing. *Com:* **Frais généraux**, trade expenses. **Exempt de frais, sans frais**, (i) free of charge ; (ii) (on bill) no expenses. **Frais scolaires**, school fees. **S.n. DÉPLACEMENT 2.**

fraise¹ [frɛːz], *s.f.* (a) Strawberry. (b) *F:* Naevus ; strawberry mark.

fraise², *s.f.* **1.** *Cu:* Crow (of calf or lamb). **2.** (a) *A.Cost:* Ruff. (b) Wattle (of turkey). **3.** *Fort:* Fraise. **4.** *Ven:* Rose (of stag's horn). **5.** *Tls:* Milling cutter. (b) Countersink.

frais|er [frɛze], *v.tr.* **1.** To frill, to goffer. **2.** *Mec.E:* (a) To mill. (b) To countersink (hole). *s.m.* **-age.**

fraisier [frɛzje], *s.m.* Strawberry-plant.

fraisil [frɛzi], *s.m.* Coal cinders ; breeze.

fraisure [frɛzyːr], *s.f.* Countersunk hole.

framboise [frɑ̃bwaːz], *s.f.* Raspberry.

framboisé [frɑ̃bwaze], *a.* Raspberry-flavoured.

framboisier [frɑ̃bwazje], *s.m.* Raspberry-cane.

franc¹ [frɑ̃], *s.m.* Franc (= 1.3d. ; *A:* = 9.6d.).

franc², **franche** [frɑ̃, frɑ̃ːʃ], *a.* **1.** Free. **Franc arbitre** [frɑ̃karbiːtr], free will. *F. de tout droit,* duty-free. *F. de port,* post-free ; carriage paid. *Fb:* **Coup franc**, free kick. **S.a. COUDÉE 2.** **2.** (a) Frank ; open, candid. **Dire la franche vérité**, to speak the candid truth. **Avoir son franc parler**, to speak one's mind. **Y aller de franc jeu**, to be quite straightforward about it. **Jouer jeu franc, franc jeu** (*avec, contre, qn*), (i) to play a straightforward game ; (ii) to play the (square) game, to play fair (with s.o.). *adv.* **Pour parler franc . . .**, frankly speaking . . ., candidly speaking. . . . (b) Real, true, downright. *Cassure franche*, clean break. *Une franche canaille*, a downright scoundrel. (c) *Huit jours francs*, eight clear days.

franc³, **franque** [frɑ̃, frɑ̃ːk]. *Hist:* (a) *a.* Frankish. (b) *s.* Frank.

français, -aise [frɑ̃sɛ, -ɛːz], **1.** *a.* French. **2.** *s.* Frenchman, Frenchwoman. *Les Français,* the French. **3.** *s.m. Le f.,* (the) French (language).

franc-alleu [frɑ̃kalø], *s.m.* *Hist:* Freehold. *pl. Des francs-alleux.*

franc-bord, *s.m.* *Nau:* **1.** Free-board. **2.** Carvel (work).

France [frɑ̃ːs]. *Pr.n.f. Geog:* France. *La F. est bornée par . . .*, France is bounded by. . . . *En F.*, in France. *Les vins de F.*, French wines.

franche. See FRANC².

franchement [frɑ̃ʃmɑ̃], *adv.* **1.** Frankly, candidly, openly. **2.** *F:* Really, quite. *C'était f. stupide*, it was sheer stupidity. *J'en suis f. dégoûté*, I am heartily sick of it.

franch|ir [frɑ̃ʃiːr], *v.tr.* (a) To clear (obstacle) ; to jump (over) (ditch) ; to shoot (rapids) ; to run past (danger-signal) ; to get over (difficulty). (b) To pass through ; to cross. **Franchir le Rubicon**, to cross, pass, the Rubicon. *F. le seuil,* to step over, cross, the threshold. *Il a franchi la*

quarantaine, he has turned forty. *a.* **-issable.** *s.m.* **-issement.**

franchise [frɑ̃ʃiːz], *s.f.* **1.** (a) Freedom (of a city). (b) *Hist:* (i) Right of sanctuary. (ii) Sanctuary, asylum. (c) (Diplomatic) immunity. **2.** Exemption. **Importer qch. en franchise**, to import sth. free of duty, duty-free. *Bagages en f.*, free (allowance of) luggage. *Post:* En *f.* = O.H.M.S. **3.** Frankness, openness, candour. *Avouer en toute f. que . . .*, to confess quite frankly that. . . .

franciser [frɑ̃size], *v.tr.* To gallicize ; *F:* to Frenchify (foreign word, etc.).

franc-maçon *s.m.* Freemason. *pl. Des francs-maçons.*

franc-maçonnerie *s.f.* Freemasonry.

franco [frɑ̃ko], *adv.* Free, carriage-free. **Livré franco**, delivery free (of charge) ; post(age) paid. **Franco à bord**, free on board ; F.O.B. *F. quai*, free alongside ship ; F.A.S.

François [frɑ̃swa]. *Pr.n.m.* Francis, Frank.

Françoise [frɑ̃swaːz]. *Pr.n.f.* Frances.

franc-parler, *s.m.* Frankness, candour ; bluntness of speech ; plain speaking.

franc-tireur, *s.m.* (a) *Fr.Hist:* Franc-tireur. (b) *Mil:* Sniper. (c) Free-lance journalist. *pl. Des francs-tireurs.*

frange [frɑ̃ːʒ], *s.f.* Fringe.

franger [frɑ̃ʒe], *v.tr.* (je **frangeai(s)**; n. **frangeons**) To fringe.

frangible [frɑ̃ʒibl], *a.* Frangible, breakable, brittle.

frangin, -ine [frɑ̃ʒɛ̃, -in], *s. P:* Brother, sister.

franquette [frɑ̃kɛt], *s.f.* (Used in) **A la bonne franquette**, simply ; without ceremony. *Homme à la bonne f.*, easy-going sort of chap. [**FRANC²**]

frappant [frapɑ̃], *a.* Striking (likeness, etc.).

frappe [frap], *s.f.* **1.** (a) Striking, minting (of coins). (b) *Typewr:* Striking (of the keys) ; touch. **2.** Impression, stamp (on coin, etc.).

frapp|er [frape], *v.tr.* **1.** (a) To strike, hit. *F. la table du poing*, to bang one's fist upon the table. *Se f. les cuisses*, to slap one's thighs. *F. un coup*, to strike a blow. **Frapper des marchandises d'un droit**, to impose, levy, a duty on goods. *Son qui me frappa l'oreille*, sound that smote my ear, that fell upon my ear. **Être frappé d'une maladie**, to be stricken with a disease. **Être frappé de mutisme**, to be struck dumb. *F. la porte*, to slam the door. **Frapper à la porte**, to knock at the door. *On frappa à la porte*, there was a knock, a tap, at the door ; a knock, tap, came at the door. **On frappe**, there's a knock. **Entrer sans frapper**, to walk straight in. **Frapper du pied**, to stamp (one's foot). S.a. JUSTE 3. (b) To strike (medal, coin) ; to mint (coins) ; to stamp, emboss (wallpaper, etc.). (c) To punch (out), cut out (paper pattern). (d) To type (letter). **2.** *Nau:* To bend, frap. *F. une drisse*, to bend a halyard. **3.** To ice (champagne). *s.m.* **-age.**

se frapper, *F:* to become demoralized, alarmed, *F:* panicky. *Ne vous frappez pas*, don't get excited.

frappeur, -euse [frapœːr, -øːz], *s.* (a) Hitter, striker. *Metalw:* Hammerman. *Psychics: Esprit f.*, rapping spirit. (b) Stamper ; embosser. (c) Cutter-out, puncher (of patterns, etc.).

frasque [frask], *s.f.* *F:* Prank, escapade.

fratern|el, -elle [fratɛrnɛl], *a.* Fraternal, brotherly. *adv.* **-ellement.**

fraternisation [fratɛrnizasjɔ̃], *s.f.* Fraternizing.

fraterniser [fratɛrnize], *v.i.* To fraternize.

fraternité [fratɛrnite], *s.f.* Fraternity, brotherhood.

fratricide¹ [fratrisid]. **1.** *s.m. & f.* Fratricide, brother-slayer. **2.** *a.* Fratricidal.

fratricide², *s.m.* Fratricide (as a crime).

fraude [froːd], *s.f.* **1.** Fraud, deception. **Fraude aux droits de douane**, smuggling. **En fraude**, fraudulently. **Entrer, passer, qch. en fraude**, to smuggle sth. through the customs. **2.** Fraudulence, deceit. **Par fraude**, under false pretences.

frauder [frode]. **1.** *v.tr.* (*a*) To defraud, cheat, swindle (s.o.). (*b*) *Lait fraudé*, adulterated milk. **2.** *v.i.* To cheat.

fraudeur, -euse [frodœːr, -øːz], *s.* **1.** Defrauder, cheat. **2.** Smuggler.

frauduleu|x, -euse [frodylø, -øːz], *a.* Fraudulent. *adv.* **-sement.**

fraxinelle [fraksinɛl], *s.f.* *Bot :* False dittany.

frayer [frɛje], *v.* (je fraye, je fraie; je frayerai, je fraierai) **1.** *v.tr.* (*a*) To scrape, rub. **Frayer des pièces d'or**, (i) (through use) to wear away gold coins ; (ii) (fraudulently) to sweat gold coins. *Vet :* **Frayer un cheval**, to gall a horse. (*b*) *F. un chemin*, to open up, trace out, clear, a path. **Le chemin frayé**, the beaten track. **Se frayer un passage**, (i) to clear a way (for oneself) ; (ii) to force, break, one's way in. **Frayer la voie à qn**, to clear the way for s.o. **2.** *v.i.* (*a*) (Of fishes) To spawn. (*b*) *F. avec qn*, to consort with, associate with, frequent, s.o. **Je ne fraye pas avec eux**, I don't mix with them. (*c*) (Of coins) To wear thin.

frayeur [frɛjœːr], *s.f.* Fright ; fear, dread (*de*, of).

fredaine [frədɛn], *s.f.* Prank, escapade. **Faire des fredaines**, to sow one's wild oats.

fredonn|er [frədɔne], *v.tr.* To hum (tune, song). *s.m.* **-ement.**

frégate [fregat], *s.f.* **1.** Frigate. **Capitaine de frégate**, commander. **2.** *Orn :* Frigate-bird.

frein [frɛ̃], *s.m.* **1.** (*a*) Bit ; (in wider sense) bridle. **Ronger son frein**, (of horse) to champ the bit ; *F :* (of pers.) to fret, chafe, under restraint. *F :* **Mettre un frein aux désirs de qn**, to curb, bridle, s.o.'s desires. **Curiosité sans frein**, unbridled, uncurbed, curiosity. (*b*) *Anat :* Fraenum. *F. de la langue*, string(s) of the tongue. **2.** Brake. *F. sur jante*, rim-brake. *F. à ruban, à collier, à bande*, band-brake. *F. à sabots*, shoe-brake. *F. à levier, à main*, hand-brake. *F. à pédale, au pied*, foot-brake. **Serrer, mettre, le frein**, to apply the brake ; to brake. *F :* **Donner un coup de frein à qn**, to pull s.o. up short.

freinage [frɛnaːʒ], *s.m.* **1.** Braking. **2.** Brake-system ; brakes (collectively). S.a. CONJUGUÉ.

freiner [frɛne], *v.tr.* **1.** (*a*) *F. une roue*, to brake, apply the brake(s) to, a wheel. (*b*) *Abs.* To put on the brakes. **2.** *F. la production*, to check, restrain, production.

frelatage [frəlataːʒ], *s.m.*, **frelatation** [frəlatasjɔ̃], *s.f.*, **frelatement** [frəlatmɑ̃], *s.m.*, **frelaterie** [frəlatri], *s.f.* Adulteration.

frelater [frəlate], *v.tr.* To adulterate (food).

frêle [frɛːl], *a.* Frail, weak (health, person).

frelon [frəlɔ̃], *s.m.* *Ent :* Hornet.

freluche [frəlyʃ], *s.f.* Tuft (of tassel, etc.).

freluquet [frəlykɛ], *s.m.* *F :* Whipper-snapper.

frémir [fremiːr], *v.i.* **1.** To quiver ; (of leaves) to rustle ; (of wind) to sough ; (of water) to simmer. **2.** To tremble, shake, quake, shudder. *F. de crainte*, to shake, quiver, with fear.

frémissement [fremismɑ̃], *s.m.* **1.** Quivering, rustling ; simmering ; sighing, soughing. **2.** (*a*) Shuddering, quaking. (*b*) Shudder, tremor.

frênaie [frɛnɛ], *s.f.* Ash plantation.

frêne [frɛːn], *s.m.* Ash(-tree or timber).

frénésie [frenezi], *s.f.* Frenzy, madness. **Applaudir avec frénésie**, to applaud frantically.

frénétique [frenetik], *a.* Frantic, frenzied.

frénétiquement [frenetikmɑ̃], *adv.* Frantically.

fréquence [frekɑ̃ːs], *s.f.* Frequency. *Courant à haute, basse, F.*, high-, low-frequency current. *F. du pouls*, quickness of the pulse ; pulse-rate.

fréqu|ent [frekɑ̃], *a.* **1.** Frequent. **2.** *Pouls f.*, quick, rapid, pulse. *adv.* **-emment.**

fréquentation [frekɑ̃tasjɔ̃], *s.f.* Frequentation, frequenting. **1.** (*a*) *F. des sacrements*, constant attendance on the means of grace. (*b*) **Mauvaises fréquentations**, evil associates, evil company. **2.** *F. d'une route*, (amount of) traffic on a road.

fréquenter [frekɑ̃te]. **1.** *v.tr.* To frequent ; to visit (place) frequently ; to attend (school). *Endroit très fréquenté*, place of great resort. **Fréquenter les sacrements**, to frequent the sacraments. (*b*) *F. qn*, to associate with, consort with, s.o. **Quels gens fréquente-t-il?** what company does he keep? **2.** *v.i.* *F. chez qn*, to be on visiting terms with s.o.

frère [frɛːr], *s.m.* **1.** Brother. S.a. CONSANGUIN 1. **Frères d'armes**, brothers-in-arms. **Frère de lait**, foster-brother. *Ecc :* **Mes très chers frères**, dearly beloved brethren. **2.** *Ecc :* Friar. **Frère lai**, lay brother.

frérot [frero], *s.m.* *F :* Little brother.

fresque [frɛsk], *s.f.* *Art :* Fresco. *Peinture à f.*, painting in fresco.

fressure [fresyːr], *s.f.* Pluck (of calf, sheep, etc.).

fret [frɛ], *s.m.* Freight. **1.** Freightage. **2.** Chartering. **Prendre un navire à fret**, to charter a ship. **3.** Load, cargo. **Faux fret**, dead freight.

fr|éter [frete], *v.tr.* (je frète ; je fréterai) **1.** To freight (out) (ship). **2.** (= AFFRÉTER) To charter (ship). *s.m.* **-ètement.**

fréteur [fretœːr], *s.m.* Ship-owner.

frétillant [fretijɑ̃], *a.* **1.** (Of fish) Wriggling ; (of dog's tail) wagging. **2.** Full of life ; lively.

frétill|er [fretije], *v.i.* (Of fish, etc.) To wriggle. **Le chien frétille de la queue**, the dog wags its tail. *F. d'impatience*, to fidget, quiver, with impatience. *s.m.* **-ement.**

fretin [frətɛ̃], *s.m.* **1.** *Fish :* Fry. *Menu f.*, small fry. **2.** *F :* Objects of no value ; rubbish.

frette¹ [frɛt], *s.f.* (Binding) hoop, collar, ferrule ; band (of axle, etc.). **Frette de moyeu**, nave-ring.

frette², *s.f.* *Arch :* Her : Fret.

frett|er [frɛte], *v.tr.* To bind (sth.) with a ring, with a ferrule ; to band, hoop (sth.). *s.m.* **-age.**

freux [frø], *s.m.* Rook. **Colonie de freux**, rookery.

friabilité [friabilite], *s.f.* Friability, friableness.

friable [friabl], *a.* Friable, crumbly.

friand, -ande [friɑ̃, -ɑ̃ːd], *a.* (*a*) Fond of delicacies. *F. de sucreries*, fond of sweets. (*b*) *Morceau f.*, dainty morsel.

friandise [friɑ̃diːz], *s.f.* **1.** Love of good food ; epicurism. **2.** Dainty, delicacy, tit-bit.

fricandeau [frikɑ̃do], *s.m.* Stew of larded veal.

fricasser [frikase], *v.tr.* *Cu :* To fricassee. *F :* **Fricasser tout son bien**, to squander, run through, all one's property.

fricassée, *s.f.* (*a*) Fricassee. (*b*) *F :* Jumble, medley.

fricasseur, -euse [frikasœːr, -øːz], *s.* Indifferent cook. *F :* *F. d'héritages*, squanderer of legacies ; prodigal.

friche [friʃ], *s.f.* Waste land, fallow land. (Of land) **Rester, être, en friche**, to lie fallow.

frichti [friʃti], *s.m.* *P :* (*a*) Food, grub (in general). (*b*) = FRICOT.

fricot [friko], *s.m.* *F :* Made-up dish ; stew.

fricot|er [frikɔte], *v.tr. & i.* *F :* **1.** To stew ; to cook. *Elle fricote bien*, she is a good cook. **2.** (*a*) To act on the sly. **Je me demande ce**

qu'il **fricote**, I wonder what mischief he's up to. *F. des comptes*, to cook accounts. (*b*) To make a bit on the side. **3.** *Mil: P:* (*a*) To skrimshank. (*b*) To maraud. *s.m.* **-age.** *s.* **-eur, -euse.**

friction [friksjɔ̃], *s.f.* **1.** (*a*) *Med:* Rubbing, chafing (of. the limbs, etc.); *Sp:* rub-down. **Gant à friction,** flesh-glove. (*b*) Dry shampoo; scalp massage. **2.** *Mec:* Friction. *Embrayage à f.,* friction-clutch.

frictionner [friksjɔne], *v.tr.* To rub, massage (*avec,* with); to give (s.o.) a rub-down. *F. la tête de qn,* to give s.o. a dry shampoo.

frigo [frigo], *s.m.* *P:* Chilled meat; frozen meat.

frigorification [frigɔrifikasjɔ̃], *s.f.* Refrigerating, chilling (of meat).

frigorifier [frigɔrifje], *v.tr.* To refrigerate. *Viande frigorifiée,* chilled meat.

frigorifique [frigɔrifik]. **1.** *a.* Refrigerating, chilling; frigorific. **Appareil frigorifique,** refrigerator. **Wagon** *f.,* refrigerator van. **Entrepôt frigorifique,** *s.m.* **frigorifique,** cold store. **2.** *s.m.* *F:* Chilled or frozen meat.

frileusement [friløzmɑ̃], *adv.* Cosily, snugly.

frileux, -euse [frilø, -øːz]. **1.** *a.* Sensitive to the cold; chilly (person). **2.** *s.f.* **Frileuse,** head shawl.

frimaire [frimɛːr], *s.m.* *Hist:* Third month of the Fr. Republican calendar (Nov.-Dec.).

frimas [frima], *s.m.* (Hoar-)frost; rime. *Poet:* Les frimas, winter(-time).

frime [frim], *s.f.* *F:* Sham, pretence, make-believe; *P:* bunkum, eye-wash.

frimousse [frimus], *s.f.* *F:* (Nice, roguish) little face. *Gentille f.,* nice little phiz.

fringale [frɛ̃gal], *s.f.* *F:* Pang of hunger; keen appetite. **Avoir la fringale,** to be sharp-set, to have a twist.

fringal|er [frɛ̃gale], *v.i. Aut:* To skid (during braking). *s.m.* **-age.**

fringant [frɛ̃gɑ̃], *a.* Brisk, spirited, lively, frisky (horse); *F:* smart, dashing (person). **Faire le fringant,** to cut a dash.

fringuer [frɛ̃ge], *v.i.* To prance; to frisk.

fringues [frɛ̃g], *s.f.pl.* *P:* Clothes, togs.

friper [fripe], *v.tr.* To crumple, crush (dress). **se friper,** (of garment) to get crushed, shabby. **Visage fripé,** worn face; tired face.

friperie [fripri], *s.f.* **1.** (*a*) Second-hand goods (esp. clothes). (*b*) *F:* Rubbish, frippery. **2.** Old-clothes-shop.

fripier, -ière [fripje, -jɛːr], *s.* Wardrobe dealer; old-clothes-man, -woman.

fripon, -onne [fripɔ̃, -ɔn]. **1.** *s.* Rogue, rascal, knave. *Petite friponne!* you wicked little thing! you little baggage! **2.** *a.* Roguish, knavish.

friponnerie [fripɔnri], *s.f.* **1.** Roguery, knavery. **2.** Piece of roguery; knavish trick.

fripouille [fripuːj], *s.f.* *P:* Rascal, rotter, bad lot; cad.

frire [friːr], *v.tr. & i.def.* (Has only *p.p.* frit; *pr.ind.* **je fris, tu fris, il frit,** no *pl.*; *fu.* **je frirai.** For the *v.tr.* the parts wanting are supplied by *faire frire*) To fry. **Je fris, fais frire,** *des pommes de terre,* I am frying potatoes.

frit, *a.* **1.** Fried. **Pommes de terre frites,** *s.f. F:* **frites,** fried potatoes; *F:* chips. **2.** *P:* Il est frit, he's done for.

frise[1] [friːz], *s.f.* **1.** *Arch:* Frieze. **2.** *Th:* Les frises, the borders, sky pieces.

frise[2], *s.f.* *Tex:* Frieze, dreadnought (cloth).

Frise[3]. *Pr.n.f. Geog:* Friesland. *Mil:* **Chevaux de frise,** (i) *A:* chevaux de frise; (ii) (any form of) portable wire entanglement.

fris|er [frize]. **1.** (*a*) *v.tr.* To curl, wave. *F. les* cheveux de qn, *f.* qn, to curl s.o.'s hair. **Fer à friser,** curling-tongs. (*b*) *v.i.* (Of hair, etc.) To curl. **2.** *v.tr.* To touch, skim, graze. **Friser la prison,** to scrape clear of prison. *S.a.* CORDE 1. Il frisait la soixantaine, he was bordering on sixty. *s.m.* **-age.**

frisé, *a.* Curly; crisp (hair). *Laitue frisée,* curly lettuce. *Velours f.,* uncut velvet.

frisette [frizet], *s.f.* Ringlet; small curl.

frisoir [frizwaːr], *s.m.* **1.** Hair-curler, curling-pin. **2.** Curling-tongs.

frison[1] [frizɔ̃], *s.m.* Wave (of curl); curl (of hair).

frison[2], **-onne** [frizɔ̃, -ɔn], *a. & s. Geog:* Frisian.

frisotter [frizɔte]. **1.** *v.tr.* To crimp, frizz, (s.o.'s) hair. **2.** *v.i.* To curl; to be frizzy.

frisquet, -ette [friskɛ, -ɛt], *a.* *F:* Chill(y). Il fait frisquet, it is a bit chilly.

frisson [frisɔ̃], *s.m.* (*a*) Shiver (from cold). **Avoir le frisson,** to have the shivers. (*b*) Shudder, thrill. **J'en ai le frisson,** it makes me shudder, it gives me the shudders. (*c*) Thrill (of pleasure).

frissonnement [frisɔnmɑ̃], *s.m.* **1.** Shivering; shuddering. **2.** Slight shiver, shudder.

frissonner [frisɔne], *v.i.* (*a*) To shiver, shudder. (*b*) *F. de joie,* to be thrilled with delight. (*c*) To quiver (with impatience).

frisure [frizyːr], *s.f.* Curling; curliness.

frit. See FRIRE.

friture [frityːr], *s.f.* **1.** (*a*) Frying (of foods). (*b*) *Tp: W.Tel:* (**Bruits de**) **friture,** crackling (noise), sizzling (noises); sizzle. **2.** Fry; esp. fried fish. **3.** Fat, grease (for frying).

frivole [frivɔl], *a.* Frivolous, shallow. *Jeune fille f.,* flighty girl. *adv.* **-ment.**

frivolité [frivɔlite], *s.f.* **1.** (*a*) Frivolity; shallowness (of mind). (*b*) Trifle. **2.** *Needlew:* Tatting.

froc [frɔk], *s.m.* (Monk's) (i) cowl, (ii) frock, gown. **Jeter le froc aux orties,** (i) (of monk) to unfrock oneself; to throw one's frock away; (ii) *F:* to change one's profession.

froid [frwa]. **I.** *a.* **1.** Cold. **A froid,** in the cold state. *F:* **Faire de l'enthousiasme à froid,** to sham enthusiasm. **Il fait froid,** it is cold. **Avoir froid,** to be, feel, cold. **J'ai froid aux mains,** my hands are cold. *F:* **Il n'a pas froid aux yeux,** (i) he has plenty of pluck; (ii) he has plenty of cheek. **Prendre froid,** to catch a chill. **2.** Cold, irresponsive (person); chilly (manner). *Sourire f.,* frigid smile. *Style f.,* frigid style. **Se montrer froid, être froid, avec, pour, qn,** to be cold towards s.o. **Battre froid à qn,** to cold-shoulder s.o. **Ne sentir ni froid ni chaud pour qn,** to be, feel, quite indifferent about s.o. *adv.* **-ement.** **II. froid,** *s.m.* **1.** Cold. **Conservation par le froid,** cold storage. **Il fait un froid de loup,** it is bitterly cold. *F:* **Souffler le chaud et le froid,** to blow hot and cold. *S.a.* CHAUD 2. **Coup de froid,** (i) *Med:* chill; (ii) *Meteor:* cold snap. **2.** Coldness. **Il y a du froid entre eux, ils sont en froid,** there is a coolness between them.

froideur [frwadœːr], *s.f.* **1.** Coldness of (temperature). **2.** (*a*) Coldness, chilliness, frigidity (of manner). (*b*) Irresponsiveness. *Contempler le spectacle avec f.,* to look coldly on; to look on coldly. (*c*) Frigidity (of style).

froidure [frwadyːr], *s.f.* **1.** Coldness; cold weather. **2.** *Med:* Frost-bite.

froissant [frwasɑ̃], *a.* Hurtful to the feelings.

froissement [frwasmɑ̃], *s.m.* **1.** (Slight) bruising; rumpling, crumpling (of paper, etc.); rustle (of silk); jostling (in crowd). **Froissement d'intérêts,** slight conflict, clash, of interests.

2. Giving or taking offence. *Éviter tous froissements*, to avoid wounding any susceptibilities.
froisser [frwase], *v.tr.* **I.** To bruise slightly (muscle, etc.); to rumple, crumple (up) (paper, etc.). *F. qn en passant*, to brush past s.o. *Être froissé dans la foule*, to be jostled in the crowd. **2.** *F. qn*, to give offence to s.o.; to hurt, ruffle, wound, s.o.'s feelings.
se froisser, to take offence, to take umbrage (*de*, at); *F:* to take the huff.
frôl|er [frole], *v.tr.* To touch lightly (with a glancing motion); to brush, rub. *Il a frôlé la mort*, he very nearly died. *s.m.* **-ement.**
fromage [fromaːʒ], *s.m.* **I.** Cheese. **Rôtie au fromage,** toasted cheese. S.a. POIRE I. *P:* Gentil petit fromage, nice job. **2.** *F. de cochon, f. d'Italie*, pork brawn.
fromager, -ère [fromaʒe, -ɛːr]. **I.** *a.* Pertaining to cheese-making. *L'industrie fromagère*, the cheese industry. **2.** *s.* Cheesemonger.
fromagerie [fromaʒri], *s.f.* Cheesemongery.
froment [fromɑ̃], *s.m.* Wheat. *Pain de f.,* wheaten bread (of first quality).
fronce [frɔ̃ːs], *s.f.* (*a*) (Accidental) pucker; crease. (*b*) *Needlew:* Gather, fold-in.
froncement [frɔ̃smɑ̃], *s.m.* Wrinkling, puckering. *F. de(s) sourcils*, frown; scowl.
froncer [frɔ̃se], *v.tr.* (je fronçai(s); n. fronçons) (*a*) To wrinkle, pucker. *F. les sourcils*, to knit one's brows; to frown. (*b*) *Needlew:* To gather.
frondaison [frɔ̃dɛzɔ̃], *s.f.* **I.** Foliation, leafing. **2.** Foliage.
fronde[1] [frɔ̃ːd], *s.f. Bot:* Frond.
fronde[2], *s.f.* (*a*) Sling. (*b*) (Toy) catapult.
fronder [frɔ̃de]. **I.** *v.tr.* To sling (stone, etc.). **2.** *v.i.* Fronder contre qn, *v.tr.* fronder qn, to criticize s.o. irreverently; to banter s.o.
frondeur, -euse [frɔ̃dœːr, -øːz]. **I.** *s.* (*a*) Slinger. (*b*) *F:* Banterer; critic of the authorities. **2.** *a.* Bantering, irreverent.
front [frɔ̃], *s.m.* **I.** Forehead, brow. **Donner du front contre qch.,** to butt, run, into sth. **Montrer un front serein,** to show an unruffled countenance. **Et vous avez le front de me dire cela!** you have the face, the impudence, to tell me that! **2.** Face, front (of building, etc.); brow (of hill). *Mil: F. de bataille*, battle front. **Faire front à qch.,** to face sth. **3. De front.** (i) Abreast. **Mener plusieurs choses de front,** to have several things on hand at once. *Navy:* **En ligne de front,** line abreast. (ii) *Vue de f.*, front view. *Attaque de f.,* frontal attack.
frontal, -aux [frɔ̃tal, -o], *a.* Frontal, front. *Os f., s.m.* **frontal,** frontal bone.
frontalier [frɔ̃talje], *s.m.* Frontiersman, borderer.
frontière [frɔ̃tjɛːr], *s.f.* Frontier(-line); border (-line). **Ville frontière,** frontier town.
frontispice [frɔ̃tispis], *s.m.* **I.** Frontispiece. **2.** Title-page.
fronton [frɔ̃tɔ̃], *s.m. Arch:* (*a*) Fronton, pediment. (*b*) *F:* Ornamental front; façade.
frottement [frɔtmɑ̃], *s.m.* (Intransitive action of) rubbing. **I.** Chafing. *Phot: Marques de f.*, stress marks. **2.** *Mec.E:* (*a*) Friction. *F. de glissement*, sliding friction. **User qch. par le frottement,** to abrade sth. (*b*) Fit (of parts). *F. doux*, easy fit. **3.** *F. du monde*, rubbing shoulders with other people.
frott|er [frɔte]. **I.** *v.tr.* To rub. *Se f. les mains*, to rub one's hands. *F. le parquet avec un chiffon*, to rub up, polish, the floor with a rag. **Frotter une allumette,** to strike a match. *F:* **Frotter les oreilles à qn,** to warm s.o.'s ears. **2.** *v.i. La roue frotte contre le frein*, the wheel rubs, grinds,

against the brake. **3.** *v.tr. Art:* To scumble (sky, background). *F:* **Être frotté de latin,** to have a smattering of Latin. *s.m.* **-age.**
se frotter. I. *Se f. contre qch.*, to rub against sth. **2.** *Se f. à qn*, to associate with s.o. **3.** *Se f. à qn, à qch.*, to come up against s.o., sth. **Qui s'y frotte s'y pique,** gather thistles, expect prickles. **Ne vous y frottez pas!** have a care!
frottée, *s.f. P:* Hiding, thrashing, drubbing.
frotteur, -euse [frɔtœːr, -øːz], *s.* **I.** Floor polisher. **2.** *s.m. El.E:* Sliding contact.
frottis [frɔti], *s.m.* **I.** (*a*) *Art:* Scumble. (*b*) *Med: etc:* Smear (for microscopic examination). **2.** *Prendre un f. d'une inscription*, to take a rubbing of an inscription
frottoir [frɔtwaːr], *s.m.* (*a*) Rubber, polisher; scrubbing brush. (*b*) Friction-strip (of match-box).
frou-frou, froufrou [frufru], *s.m.* Rustle, rustling, swish (of silk dress, etc.). *F:* **Faire du frou-frou,** to make a great show; to show off. **Une petite frou-frou,** a fluffy little thing.
froussard, -arde [frusaːr, -ard], *a. & s. P:* Funky, cowardly (person); coward.
frousse [frus], *s.f. P:* Funk, fear. **Avoir la frousse,** to be in a funk; to have the wind up; to have the jitters.
fructiculture [fryktikylty:r], *s.f.* Orcharding.
fructidor [fryktidɔːr], *s.m Hist:* Twelfth month of the Fr. Republican calendar (Aug.-Sept.).
fructification [fryktifikasjɔ̃], *s.f.* **I.** Fructification. **2.** Fruition (of idea, etc.).
fructifier [fryktifje], *v.i.* To fructify; to bear fruit.
fructueu|x, -euse [fryktɥø, -øːz], *a.* Fruitful, advantageous, profitable.. *adv.* **-sement.**
frugal, -aux [frygal, -o], *a.* Frugal (person, meal). *adv.* **-ement.**
frugalité [frygalite], *s.f.* Frugality.
fruit[1] [frɥi], *s.m.* Fruit. **Arbre à fruit,** fruit-tree. **Porter fruit,** to bear fruit. *Sch: F:* **Un fruit sec,** a student who has failed to qualify; a failure. *Les fruits de la paix*, the fruits, advantages, of peace. **Étudier avec fruit,** to study to good purpose. **Sans fruit,** fruitlessly.
fruit[2], *s.m. Civ.E:* Batter (of wall, abutment). **Avoir du fruit,** to batter.
fruiterie [frɥitri], *s.f.* **I.** Store-room for fruit. **2.** Fruiterer's, greengrocer's shop.
fruitier, -ière [frɥitje, -jɛːr]. **I.** *a.* **Arbre fruitier,** fruit-tree. **2.** *s.* Fruiterer, greengrocer.
frusques [frysk], *s.f.pl. P:* Clothes, togs, duds.
fruste [fryst], *a.* Worn, defaced (coin, medal); rough, unpolished (style); simple-minded (population); rough (manners).
frustration [frystrasjɔ̃], *s.f.* **I.** Frustration. **2.** Cheating, defrauding (of creditors).
frustrer [frystre], *v.tr.* **I.** To frustrate, disappoint. **Frustrer qn dans son espoir, frustrer l'espoir de qn,** to frustrate, baffle, s.o.'s hopes. **2.** *F. qn de qch.*, to defraud s.o. of sth.
fucus [fykyːs], *s.m. Algae:* Fucus; *F:* sea-wrack.
fugace [fygas], *a.* Fugacious, fleeting.
fugacité [fygasite], *s.f.* Fugacity, transience.
fugit|if, -ive [fyʒitif, -iːv], *a. & s.* **I.** Fugitive; runaway. **2.** *Désir f.*, transitory, passing, desire. *Passion fugitive*, fleeting, ephemeral, passion. *Mémoire fugitive*, short memory. *adv.* **-ivement.**
fugue [fyg], *s.f.* **I.** *Mus:* Fugue. **2.** *F:* Flight, escapade. **Faire une f.,** to break out; to go on the loose.
fuir [fɥiːr], *v.* (*pr.p.* **fuyant;** *p.p.* **fui;** *pr.ind.* je **fuis,** ils **fuient;** *p.d.* je **fuyais;** *p.h.* je **fuis;** *fu.* je **fuirai**) **I.** *v.i.* (*a*) To flee, fly, run away.

Le temps fuit, time flies time is flying. *Nau :* F. *devant le vent*, to scud, run, before the wind. (*b*) (Of horizon, etc.) To recede. (*c*) (Of tap, cask, etc.) To leak. **2.** *v.tr.* To shun, avoid. *Tout le monde le fuit*, he is shunned by everybody.
fuite ǀfɥit], *s.f.* **I.** (*a*) Flight, running away, absconding. **Prendre la fuite, to take to flight ;** *F :* to take to one's heels. **Mettre l'ennemi en fuite, to put the enemy to flight.** (*b*) *Art :* Point **de fuite,** vanishing point. **2.** Leak ; escape (of steam, etc.) ; leakage (of official secrets, etc.). **3.** Shunning, avoidance.
fulgurant [fylgyrɑ̃], *a.* Fulgurating, flashing.
fulguration [fylgyrasjɔ̃], *s.f.* Fulguration.
fuligineux, -euse [fyliʒinø, -øːz] *a.* Fuliginous, smoky, sooty ; murky (sky, etc.).
fulmicoton [fylmikɔtɔ̃], *s.m. Exp :* Gun-cotton.
fulminant [fylminɑ̃], *a.* Fulminating, fulminant.
fulminate [fylminat], *s.m. Ch :* Fulminate.
fulminer [fylmine]. **I.** *v.tr.* To fulminate (Papal bull). **2.** *v.i.* F. *contre un abus*, to fulminate, inveigh, thunder forth, against an abuse. **3.** *v.i.* To fulminate, detonate.
fumant [fymɑ̃], *a.* (*a*) Smoking. *F :* **Fumant de colère,** fuming with anger. (*b*) Steaming (soup).
fume-cigare [fymsigaːr], *s.m.* Cigar-holder. *pl. Des fume-cigare(s).*
fume-cigarette [fymsigaret], *s.m.* Cigarette-holder. *pl. Des fume-cigarette(s).*
fumée [fyme], *s.f.* (*a*) Smoke. **Charbon sans fumée,** smokeless coal. **Noir de fumée,** lamp-black. *Mes rêves s'en vont en f.*, my dreams end in smoke. *Prov :* **Il n'y a pas de fumée sans feu,** there is no smoke without fire. S.a. BOÎTE 2, RIDEAU I. (*b*) Steam (of soup, etc.) ; fumes (of charcoal). *Les fumées du vin*, the fumes of wine.
fumer[1] [fyme]. **I.** *v.i.* (*a*) To smoke. (*b*) (Of soup, etc.) To steam ; (of horse) to steam, smoke. *F :* **Fumer de colère,** to fume, to rage. **2.** *v.tr.* (*a*) To smoke-cure (fish). (*b*) F. *du tabac, une pipe*, to smoke tobacco, a pipe. **Défense de fumer,** no smoking.
fumer[2], *v.tr. Agr :* To dung, manure (land, etc.).
fumerie [fymri], *s.f.* **I.** Smoking (of tobacco). **2.** F. *d'opium*, opium den.
fûmes [fym]. See ÊTRE.
fumet [fymɛ], *s.m.* **I.** (Pleasant) smell (of cooking) ; bouquet (of wine). **2.** *Ven :* Scent.
fumeterre [fymtɛːr], *s.f. Bot :* Fumitory.
fumeur, -euse[1] [fymœːr, -øːz], *s.* (*a*) Smoker (of tobacco). (*b*) F. *de poisson*, fish-smoker, fish-curer.
fumeux, -euse[2] [fymø, -øːz], *a.* **I.** Smoky, smoking. *Idées fumeuses*, hazy ideas. **2.** Heady (wine).
fumier [fymje], *s.m.* **I.** Stable-litter, manure, dung. **2.** Dunghill ; manure heap.
fumigation [fymigasjɔ̃], *s.f.* Fumigation.
fumigène [fymiʒen]. **I.** *a.* Smoke-producing ; smoke(-shell). **2.** *s.m.* Smoke-producer.
fumiger [fymiʒe], *v.tr.* (je fumigeai(s) ; n. fumigeons) To fumigate.
fumiste [fymist], *s.m.* **I.** Stove-setter. **2.** *P :* (*a*) Wag ; practical joker. (*b*) Humbug. [FUMER]
fumisterie [fymistri], *s.f.* **I.** Stove-setting. **2.** *P :* Practical joke ; hoax.
fumivore [fymivɔːr], *a.* Smoke-consuming.
fumoir [fymwaːr], *s.m.* **I.** Smoking-room (of hotel, etc.). **2.** Smoke(-curing) house.
funambule [fynɑ̃byl], *s.m. & f.* Funambulist ; tight-rope walker.
funambulesque [fynɑ̃bylɛsk], *a.* Fantastic, grotesque (story, etc.).
funèbre [fynɛbr], *a.* **I.** Funeral (ceremony, etc.).

Marche f., dead-march. **2.** Funereal, dismal, gloomy. *adv.* **-ment.**
funérailles [fyneraːj], *s.f.pl.* (Elaborate) funeral (*e.g.* of public man) ; obsequies.
funéraire [fynerɛːr]. *a.* Funeral, funerary. **Pierre funéraire,** tombstone. *Drap f.*, pall.
funeste [fynɛst], *a.* Deadly, fatal (*d*, to) ; baleful ; bad (*d*, for). *Influence f.*, baneful influence. *adv.* **-ment.**
funiculaire [fynikylɛːr]. **I.** *a.* Funicular. **2.** *s.m.* Funicular railway, cable-railway. **3.** *s.f. Mth :* Catenary curve.
fur [fyːr], *s.m. A :* Rate. *Adv.phr.* **Au fur et à mesure,** (in proportion) as ; progressively. *On inspecte les articles et on les emballe au fur et à mesure*, the articles are inspected and packed as the inspection proceeds, as soon as they are ready. *Fournir des articles au fur et à mesure des besoins*, to supply articles as they are wanted. *Envoyez-moi l'argent au fur et à mesure que vous le recevrez*, send me the money as fast as you receive it. *Au fur et à mesure de l'ouvrage*, as the work proceeds.
furent [fyːr]. See ÊTRE.
furet [fyrɛ], *s.m.* (*a*) *Z :* Ferret. **Jeu du furet,** hunt-the-slipper. (*b*) *F :* Inquisitive person ; Nosy Parker, Paul Pry.
furet|er [fyrte], *v.i.* (je **furette ; je furetterai**) (*a*) To ferret, go ferreting. (*b*) F : F. *dans les armoires*, to ferret, pry about, nose about, in the cupboards. *s.m.* **-age.**
fureteur, -euse [fyrtœːr, -øːz], *s.* **I.** Ferreter. **2.** *F :* Nosy Parker, Paul Pry.
fureur [fyrœːr], *s.f.* **I.** Fury, rage, wrath. **Etre en fureur,** to be in a rage: **2.** Fury, passion. **Aimer qn avec fureur, à la fureur, to be passionately fond of s.o. Avoir la fureur de bâtir,** to have a craze for building ; to be building mad. **Chanson qui fait fureur,** song that is all the rage.
furibond [fyribɔ̃], *a.* Furious ; full of fury.
furie [fyri], *s.f.* **I.** *Myth :* Les Furies, the Furies. *F :* **C'est une furie,** she's a termagant, a fury. **2.** (*a*) Fury, rage. **Entrer, se mettre, en f.,** to become furious. (*b*) *F :* Applaud avec furie, to applaud frantically.
furieusement [fyrjøzmɑ̃], *adv.* **I.** Furiously, passionately. **2.** *F :* Tremendously. *Il est f. bavard*, he's a tremendous talker.
furieux, -euse [fyrjø, -øːz], *a.* **I.** Furious, raging ; in a passion. **Etre furieux contre qn,** *F :* **après qn,** to be furious, in a rage, *F :* wild, with s.o. **Rendre qn furieux,** to infuriate s.o. *s.* **Un furieux, une furieuse,** a madman, mad-woman. S.a. FOU 2. **2.** *F :* **C'est un furieux mangeur,** he's a tremendous eater.
furolle [fyrɔl], *s.f.* Jack-o'-lantern,will-o'-the-wisp.
furoncle [fyrɔ̃kl], *s.m. Med :* Furuncle ; boil.
furt|if, -ive [fyrtif, -iːv], *a.* Furtive, stealthy. *adv.* **-ivement.**
fus [fy]. See ÊTRE.
fusain [fyzɛ̃], *s.m.* **I.** *Bot :* Spindle-tree. **2.** (*a*) Drawing charcoal. (*b*) Charcoal sketch.
fusant [fyzɑ̃], *a Exp :* Fusing. **Obus fusant,** time-shell.
fuseau [fyzo], *s.m.* **I.** *Tex :* Spindle. F. *de quenouille*, distaff. *F :* **Jambes de, en, fuseau,** spindle-shanks. **2.** (*a*) *Geom :* Spherical lune. (*b*) F. *horaire*, time-belt, -zone. (*c*) *Aer :* Gore (of balloon).
fusée [fyze], *s.f.* **I.** Spindle (of shaft, axle) ; barrel (of capstan). *Aut :* Stub axle. **2.** (*a*) Roc-ket. F. *éclairante*, flare. F. *de signaux*, signal rocket. F. *à pétard*, maroon. F. *porte-amarre*, rocket apparatus. *Pistolet à f.*, Verey-light pistol. (*b*) Fuse. F. *fusante, à temps*, time-fuse. F.

percutante, percussion-fuse. **3.** *De longues fusées de rires*, long ripples of laughter.
fuselage [fyzla:ʒ], *s.m. Av:* Fuselage.
fuseler [fyzle], *v.tr.* (**je fuselle; je fusellerai**) To shape like a spindle; to taper.
   fuselé, *a.* Spindle-shaped. *Aut:* Streamlined. *Doigts fuselés*, tapering, slender, fingers.
fuser [fyze], *v.i.* **1.** (Of colour) To spread, run. **2.** (*a*) To fuse, melt. (*b*) (Of lime) To slake. **3.** (Of fuse, etc.) To burn slowly.
fusibilité [fyzibilite], *s.f.* Fusibility.
fusible [fyzibl]. **1.** *a.* Fusible; easily melted. **2.** *s.m. El.E:* Fuse; fuse-wire. **Fusible de sûreté**, safety-fuse; cut-out.
fusiforme [fyzifɔrm], *a.* Spindle-shaped; slender.
fusil [fyzi], *s.m.* **1.** Steel (of tinder-box). **Pierre à fusil**, flint. **2.** (*a*) (Sharpening) steel. (*b*) Whetstone. **3.** Gun. (*a*) *F. de chasse*, sporting-gun. *F. à aiguille*, needle-gun. *F. à bascule*, hinged breech-loader. *F. à deux coups*, double-barrelled gun. *F. à vent*, air-gun. (*b*) *F. rayé*, rifled musket; rifle. *F. à répétition*, magazine-rifle. **A une portée de fusil d'ici**, within a gunshot from here. (*c*) **Coup de fusil**, (i) gunshot, musket-shot; rifle-shot; (ii) report (of a gun); (iii) *P:* fleecing (in restaurant, etc.). **Essuyer le coup de fusil**, to be stung, fleeced.
fusilier [fyzilje], *s.m.* Fusilier. *F. marin*, marine.
fusillade [fyzijad], *s.f.* Fusillade, rifle-fire.
fusiller [fyzije], *v.tr.* (*a*) To shoot (down) (men). (*b*) To execute (by shooting); to shoot (spy).
fusion [fyzjɔ̃], *s.f.* **1.** (*a*) Fusion, melting (by heat). **Point de f.**, melting-point. **Fer en f.**, molten iron. **Entrer en fusion**, to begin to melt. (*b*) Smelting. **2.** Dissolving, melting. **3.** Coalescing (of ideas, etc.). **4.** *Com:* Merger.

fusionner [fyzjɔne], *v.tr., i., & pr. Com: etc:* To amalgamate, unite, merge.
fuss-e, -ions, etc. See ÊTRE.
fustig|er [fystiʒe], *v.tr.* (**je fustigeai(s); n. fustigeons**) To thrash, beat. *s.f.* **-ation.**
fut, fût[1] [fy]. See ÊTRE.
fût[2], *s.m.* **1.** Stock (of rifle, plane, anvil); handle (of saw, etc.); brace (for bit). **2.** (*a*) Shaft (of column, chimney); stem (of candelabra); shank (of rivet). (*b*) Bole (of tree). **3.** Cask, barrel. *Tirer la bière du fût*, to draw beer from the wood. *Fût d'un tambour*, barrel, body, of a drum.
futaie [fytɛ], *s.f.* Wood, forest. **Arbre de haute futaie**, full-grown tree; timber-tree.
futaille [fytɑ:j], *s.f.* Cask, tun.
futaine [fytɛn], *s.f. Tex:* Fustian.
futé [fyte], *a.* Sharp, smart, astute. **Futé comme un renard**, cunning as a fox. *Une petite futée*, a little sly-boots.
fûtes [fyt]. See ÊTRE.
futile [fytil], *a.* Futile, trifling; idle (pretext). *adv.* **-ment.**
futilité [fytilite], *s.f.* Futility. *S'occuper à des futilités*, to busy oneself with trifles. *Dire des futilités, F:* to talk piffle.
futur [fyty:r]. **1.** *a.* (*a*) Future; (life) to come. (*b*) *s. F:* **Mon futur, ma future**, my intended (husband, wife). **2.** *s.m. Gram:* Future (tense). **Verbe au futur**, verb in the future.
fuy-ais, -ons, etc. See FUIR.
fuyant [fɥijɑ̃], *a.* **1.** Fleeing, flying (animal, etc.); fleeting (moment). **2.** Receding (forehead, line). *Aut:* **Ligne fuyante**, stream-line. **3.** *Yeux fuyants*, shifty eyes.
fuyard, -arde [fɥija:r, -ard], *s.* (Panic-stricken) fugitive; runaway.

G

G, g [ʒe], *s.m.* The letter G, g.
gabare [gaba:r], *s.f.* **1.** Sailing-barge; lighter. **2.** Drag-net.
gabarier[1] [gabarje], *s.m. Nau:* **1.** Skipper (of barge). **2.** Lighterman, bargee.
gabarier[2], *v.tr.* **1.** *N.Arch:* To shape, mould. **2.** *Metalw:* To gauge (metal plate).
gabarit [gabari], *s.m.* **1.** (*a*) Model (of ship); mould. (*b*) *Mec.E:* Templet, former. *G. de mécanicien*, engineer's jig. **Tour à gabarit**, copying lathe. (*c*) *F:* = ACABIT. **2.** Gauge. *Rail: G.* (*de pose*) *de voie*, track(-laying) gauge.
gabegie [gabʒi], *s.f. P:* **1.** Intrigue, trickery; underhand dealings. **2.** Waste, muddle.
gabelle [gabel], *s.f. A:* Salt-tax.
gabelou [gablu], *s.m. P:* Custom-house officer.
gabier [gabje], *s.m. Nau:* Topman. *G. breveté*, able(-bodied) seaman.
gâche [gɑ:ʃ], *s.f.* **1.** *Locksm:* (*a*) (Box-)staple; (latch-)catch. (*b*) Striking-box or -plate. **2.** Notch (for paw). **3.** Wall-hook; clip.
gâch|er [gɑʃe], *v.tr.* **1.** To mix (mortar); to slack (lime). **Gâcher serré**, (i) to temper (clay) hard; (ii) *P:* to go hard at it. **2.** (*a*) To spoil (sheet of paper, etc.); to bungle (job). (*b*) To waste; to squander. *G. sa vie*, to make a mess of one's life. *s.m.* **-age.**
gâchette [gɑʃet], *s.f.* **1.** (*a*) Tumbler, sear (of gun-lock). (*b*) *F:* Trigger. **2.** Spring-catch (of lock). **3.** Pawl.

gâcheur [gɑʃœ:r], *s.m.* **1.** Mason's labourer. **2.** Bungler, botcher.
gâcheux, -euse [gɑʃø, -ø:z], *a.* **1.** Muddy, miry (road). **2.** Damaged (fruit).
gâchis [gɑʃi], *s.m.* **1.** Wet mortar. **2.** (*a*) Mud or slush. (*b*) *F: Quel g.!* what a mess!
gadouard [gadua:r], *s.m.* Scavenger.
gadoue [gadu], *s.f.* (*a*) Night-soil; (town) refuse. (*b*) *F:* Dirt, slush.
gaélique [gaelik], *a.* Gaelic. *s.m.* **Le gaélique**, Gaelic.
gaffe [gaf], *s.f.* **1.** (*a*) Boat-hook. (*b*) *Fish:* Gaff. *P:* **Avaler sa gaffe**, to die. **2.** *F:* Social solecism; blunder. **Faire une gaffe**, to put one's foot in it; to make a blunder; to drop a brick.
gaffer [gafe]. **1.** *v.tr.* To hook (floating object); to gaff (salmon). **2.** *v.i. F:* = *Faire une gaffe.*
gaffeur, -euse [gafœ:r, -ø:z], *s. F:* Blunderer.
gaga [gaga]. *P:* **1.** *s.m.* Dodderer, driveller. **2.** *a.inv.* Doddering; in senile decay.
gage [ga:ʒ], *s.m.* **1.** Pledge, pawn, security. **Mettre qch. en gage**, to pawn, pledge, sth. **Prêteur sur gages**, pawnbroker. **2.** Token, sign. *G. d'amour*, love-token. **3.** Forfeit. **4.** *pl.* Wages, pay. **Homme à gages**, hired servant. **Être aux gages de qn**, to be in the pay of s.o. **Casser qn aux gages**, to discharge s.o.
gager [gaʒe], *v.tr.* (**je gageai(s); n. gageons**) **1.** To wager, bet (*avec, contre*, with, against). *Gage que si!* I'll bet it is! (To bet at races, etc.,

is PARIER.) **2.** (*a*) To pay wages to (s.o.). (*b*) To hire (servant). *Commis gagé*, salaried clerk.

gageure [gaʒyːr], *s.f.* Wager, bet.

gagiste [gaʒist], *s.m.* **I.** *Th:* Supernumerary actor; *F:* super. **2.** *Jur:* Pledger, pawner.

gagnant, -ante [gɔɲɑ̃, -ɑ̃ːt]. **I.** *a.* Winning (ticket, etc.). **2.** *s.* Winner.

gagne-pain [gɑɲpɛ̃], *s.m.inv.* **I.** (Means of) living; livelihood. **2.** Bread-winner; support (of the family).

gagne-petit [gɑɲpəti], *s.m.inv.* **I.** (Itinerant) knife-grinder. **2.** Cheap-jack.

gagn|er [gɑɲe], *v.tr.* **I.** (*a*) To earn. *G. gros*, to make big money. *G. sa vie*, to earn, make, one's living. *F: Il l'a bien gagné*, it serves him right. (*b*) To gain; to be the gainer (*à*, by). *C'est autant de gagné*, it is so much gained, so much to the good. *G. au change*, to be a gainer by the exchange. *G. à faire qch.*, to profit by doing sth. *J'y gagnerai*, I shall gain by it. **2.** (*a*) To win, gain (a victory). (*b*) *G. la partie, la course*, to win the game, the race. *Donner gagné à qn*, to give s.o. best. S.a. MAIN **I**. (*c*) *G. qn à une cause*, to win over, bring over, s.o. to a cause. *G. tous les cœurs*, to win (over) all hearts. *G. sur qn qu'il fasse qch.*, to prevail on s.o. to do sth. (*d*) To get, catch (a disease, etc.). *Maladie qui se gagne*, infectious disease. **3.** To reach, arrive at. *G. son domicile*, to reach home. *G. les montagnes*, to escape to the mountains. *G. le port*, to fetch into port. S.a. LARGE 2. **4.** To gain (up)on, overtake. *Se laisser g.*, to let oneself be caught up. *G. un navire*, to gain (up)on, overhaul, a ship. S.a. DEVANT¹ 3, VITESSE. *La nuit nous gagna*, darkness overtook us. *La mer gagne du terrain*, the sea is encroaching on the land. *Nous fûmes gagnés par cette vague d'enthousiasme*, we were caught up in this wave of enthusiasm. *Gagné par le sommeil*, overcome by sleep. *Nau: G. (dans) le vent, g. au vent*, to fetch to windward. *G. de l'avant*, to forge ahead. *s.* **-eur, -euse.**

gai [ge, gɛ], *a.* **I.** Gay. (*a*) Merry, lively (person, song). *Gai comme un pinson*, blithe as a lark. *Gai et dispos*, in high feather. *Avoir le vin gai*, to be merry in one's cups. (*b*) Bright, cheerful (colour, etc.). **2.** (Of bolt, etc.) Free; having play; loose. **3.** *Hareng gai*, shotten herring. *adv.* **-ement.**

gaïac [gajak], *s.m.* *Bot:* Guaiacum. **Bois de gaïac,** lignum vitae.

gaieté, gaîté [gete, gɛ-], *s.f.* **I.** Gaiety, mirth, cheerfulness. *Faire qch. de gaîté de cœur*, to do sth. out of, from, sheer wantonness. **2.** *pl.* (*a*) Escapades; *F:* larks. (*b*) Jollities.

gaillard, -arde [gajaːr, -ard]. **I.** *a.* (*a*) Strong, well, vigorous. *Frais et gaillard*, hale and hearty. (*b*) Merry, lively, cheery. (*c*) Free, ribald. (*d*) Fresh (wind); bracing (weather). **2.** *s.m.* (*a*) (Merry) fellow; (jolly) chap. (*b*) Sharp fellow, sly fellow. **3.** *s.m. Nau:* **Gaillard d'avant,** forecastle, fo'c'sle. **Gaillard d'arrière,** quarter-deck. **4.** *s.f.* **Gaillarde.** (*a*) (i) Bold young woman; hussy, wench. (ii) Strapping young woman. (*b*) *Danc:* Galliard. *adv.* **-ement.**

gaillardise [gajardiːz], *s.f.* **I.** Gaiety, jollity. **2.** *Conter des gaillardises*, to tell risky stories; to crack broad jokes.

gaillet [gajɛ], *s.m. Bot:* Cheese-rennet; yellow bedstraw.

gaîment [gɛmɑ̃], *adv.* = GAIEMENT.

gain [gɛ̃], *s.m.* **I.** (*a*) Gain, profit. (*b*) Earnings. **2.** (*a*) Winning (of contest, etc.). **Donner gain de cause à qn,** to decide in favour of s.o. **Avoir gain de cause,** to win one's case. (*b*) Winnings. **Être en gain,** to be in pocket.

gaine [gɛːn], *s.f.* **I.** Sheath, cover, case, casing. **Câble sous gaine,** sheathed cable. **2.** *Cost:* Sheath corset. **3.** *Arch:* Terminal.

gain|er [gɛne], *v.tr.* To sheath. *Gainé cuir*, cased, covered, in leather. *s.m.* **-age.**

gala [gala], *s.m.* Festivity, fête, gala. **Habit de gala,** full dress. **Dîner en grand gala,** to dine in state.

galamment [galamɑ̃], *adv.* **I.** Gallantly; like a gentleman. (*a*) Politely, courteously. (*b*) Bravely, honourably.

galant [galɑ̃]. **I.** *a.* (*a*) Gay, elegant. (*b*) Attentive to women; gallant [ga'lant]. (*c*) *Femme galante*, 'gay' woman. *Fête galante*, gay party or entertainment. *Intrigue galante*, love-affair. (*d*) *Galant homme*, man of honour; gentleman. **2.** *s.m.* Lover, gallant; ladies' man.

galanterie [galɑ̃tri], *s.f.* **I.** Politeness (esp. to ladies). **2.** *Usu. pl.* (*a*) Love-affair, intrigue. (*b*) Pretty speech.

galantine [galɑ̃tin], *s.f. Cu:* Galantine.

galbe [galb], *s.m.* **I.** Curve (of furniture, etc.); curves, contour (of the human figure); sweep, outline, lines (of car). **Avoir du galbe,** to be well-proportioned; to have a good figure. **2.** *P:* Smartness, style.

gale [gal], *s.f.* **I.** *Med:* (The) itch; scabies. **2.** *Vet:* Scab, mange. **3.** *Bot:* Scurf.

galée [gale], *s.f. Typ:* Composing galley.

galène [galɛn], *s.f. Miner:* Galena; lead glance.

galère [galɛːr], *s.f.* (*a*) Galley (rowed by slaves). *F:* Vogue la galère! let's chance it! **Mais que diable allait-il faire dans cette galère?** but what the deuce was he doing there? (Spoken by Géronte in Molière's *Les Fourberies de Scapin.*) (*b*) *A:* Convict-ship. *pl.* Hulks.

galerie [galri], *s.f.* **I.** (*a*) Gallery or long room. *G. de portraits*, portrait gallery. (*b*) *A:* Gallery (round tennis-court). *F:* **Faire galerie,** to be a looker-on. **Jouer pour la galerie,** to play to the gallery. (*c*) Arcade; covered walk. **2.** *Th:* Balcony, gallery. *Seconde g.*, upper circle. *Troisième g.*, gallery; *F:* the gods. **3.** *Min:* Gallery, drift. *Mil: G. d'écoute*, listening-gallery. **4.** Cornice, moulding. **5.** Luggage-rail (of cab).

galérien [galerjɛ̃], *s.m.* *A:* (*a*) Galley-slave. (*b*) Convict.

galet [galɛ], *s.m.* **I.** (*a*) Pebble. *Gros g.*, boulder. (*b*) *pl.* Shingle. **2.** *Mec.E:* (*a*) Roller. **Couronne de galets,** roller ring. (*b*) Small pulley. *G. de renvoi*, idle pulley. **3.** Float (of net).

galetas [galta], *s.m.* (*a*) Garret, attic. (*b*) Hovel.

galette [galɛt], *s.f.* **I.** (*a*) Girdle-cake. *G. des Rois*, Twelfth-cake. *G. aux pommes*, apple-tart. (*b*) *Nau:* Ship's biscuit. **2.** *P:* Money, brass.

galeux, -euse [galø, -øːz], *a.* (Child, etc.) with the itch; mangy (dog). *F:* **Brebis galeuse,** black sheep (of the family). [GALE]

Galilée¹ [galile]. *Pr.n.f. B.Geog:* Galilee.

Galilée². *Pr.n.m. Hist:* Galileo.

galimafrée [galimafre], *s.f.* **I.** Hotchpotch. **2.** *F:* Tuck-in, blow-out.

galimatias [galimatja], *s.m.* Farrago; jumble of words; grandiloquent nonsense.

galion [galjɔ̃], *s.m. Nau: A:* Galleon.

galipette [galipɛt], *s.f. F:* Somersault.

galipot [galipo], *s.m.* Galipot; white resin.

galle [gal], *s.f. Bot:* Gall(-nut).

Galles [gal]. *Pr.n.f. Geog:* **Le pays de Galles,** Wales. **Le Prince de Galles,** the Prince of Wales. **La Nouvelle-Galles du Sud,** New South Wales.

gallican,-ane [galikã,-an], a. & s. Ecc: Gallican.

gallicisme [galisism], s.m. French turn or phrase; Gallicism.

gallinacé [gal(l)inase]. Orn: 1. a. Gallinaceous. 2. s.m.pl. Gallinacés, gallinaceae.

gallique[1] [gallik], a. Hist: Gallic; of Gaul.

gallique[2], a. Ch: Gallic (acid).

gallois, -oise [galwa, -waːz]. 1. a. Welsh. 2. s. Welshman,-woman. Les Gallois, the Welsh.

gallo-romain [gallorɔmɛ̃], a. Gallo-Roman.

galoche [galɔʃ], s.f. (a) Clog (with wooden sole and leather upper. Cf. SABOT). P: Vieille galoche, old fogey. (b) Overshoe.

galon [galɔ̃], s.m. 1. Braid, galloon. 2. pl. Mil: (N.C.O.'s) stripes; (officer's) bands, gold braid. Priver qn de ses galons, to reduce s.o. to the ranks.

galonner [galɔne], v.tr. To trim, ornament, with braid or lace; to braid.

galop [galo], s.m. 1. Gallop. Prendre le galop, to break into a gallop. Aller au galop, to gallop. Au grand galop, (at) full gallop. Au petit galop, at a canter. Partir au g., to gallop away. F: Faire qch. au galop, to gallop, rattle, through sth. Faire déjeuner qn au g., to rush s.o. through lunch. 2. Danc: Galop. 3. Mouvement de galop, hunting (of locomotive). 4. P: Scolding, wigging.

galopade [galɔpad], s.f. Galloping, gallop; canter. F: Son imagination prend la galopade, his imagination runs away with him. Expédier son repas à la galopade, to bolt one's meal.

galopant [galɔpɑ̃], a. Phtisie galopante, galloping consumption.

galoper [galɔpe]. 1. v.i. To gallop. 2. v.tr. C. un cheval, to gallop a horse.

galopin, -ine [galɔpɛ̃, -in], s. (a) Errand-boy, -girl. (b) Urchin; young scamp.

galopiner [galɔpine], v.i. To run wild in the streets.

galoubet [galubɛ], s.m. Three-holed (fipple-) flute (of Provence); tabor pipe.

galuchat [galyʃa], s.m. Shark-skin, shagreen.

galurin [galyrɛ̃], s.m. P: Hat, tile.

galvanique [galvanik], a. Galvanic. Dorure galvanique, electro-gilding.

galvaniser [galvanize], v.tr. 1. To galvanize (corpse, etc.). F: To give new life to (under-taking). 2. Metall: To galvanize; (i) to (electro-)plate; (ii) to zinc.

galvano [galvano], s.m. Typ: F: Electrotype (plate); F: 'electro.'

galvanomètre [galvanɔmetr], s.m. El: Gal-vanometer.

galvanoplastie [galvanɔplasti], s.f. Galvano-plasty; electroplating.

galvauder [galvode], v.tr. 1. To botch (work). 2. To besmirch (s.o.'s name, honour). se galvauder. 1. To sully one's name, one's honour. 2. To go to the bad.

galvaudeur, -euse [galvodœːr, -øːz], **galvau-deux, -euse** [galvodø, -øːz], s. 1. Tramp; vagabond. 2. Loose liver.

gambade [gɑ̃bad], s.f. Leap, gambol. Faire des gambades, to gambol; to cut capers.

gambader [gɑ̃bade], v.i. To leap, caper; to frisk (about); to gambol.

gambette [gɑ̃bɛt], s.m. Orn: Red-shank.

gamelle [gamɛl], s.f. Pannikin, bowl, tin-can. Mil: Navy: Mess-tin, -kettle.

gamin, -ine [gamɛ̃, -in]. 1. s. (a) Street-boy, -girl; street-arab; urchin. (b) F: Boy, young-ster; f. little girl. (c) s.f. Hoyden, romp. 2. a. Mœurs gamines, manners of the street.

gaminer [gamine], v.i. 1. To play about the streets. 2. To play pranks.

gaminerie [gaminri], s.f. Child's prank, trick.

gamme [gam], s.f. 1. Mus: Scale, gamut. F: Changer de gamme, to alter one's tone, to change one's tune. 2. Range, series, scale (of colours, etc.).

gammée [game], a.f. Croix gammée, swastika.

ganache [ganaʃ], s.f. 1. (Lower) jaw, jowl (of horse, P: of person). Cheval chargé de ganache, heavy-headed horse. 2. F: (a) Blockhead; stick-in-the-mud. (b) Old dotard, old fogey.

Gand [gɑ̃], Pr.n.m. Geog: Ghent.

gandin [gɑ̃dɛ̃], s.m. F: A: Dandy, masher.

ganga [gɑ̃ga], s.m. Orn: Pin-tailed grouse.

ganglion [gɑ̃gliɔ̃], s.m. Ganglion.

gangrène [gɑ̃grɛn], s.f. 1. Med: Gangrene, mortification. G. gazeuse, gas gangrene. G. des os, necrosis. 2. Bot: Canker. F: La paresse est la g. de l'âme, idleness is the canker of the soul.

gangrener [gɑ̃grəne], v.tr. (il gangrène; il gan-grènera) 1. Med: To gangrene. 2. To canker, corrupt. se gangrener. 1. To mortify, gangrene. 2. To become cankered.

gangreneux, gangréneux, -euse [gɑ̃grənø, gɑ̃grenø, -øːz], a. 1. Gangrenous, gangrened. 2. Cankerous, cankered.

gangue [gɑ̃ːg], s.f. Gang(ue), matrix (of precious stone, etc.).

ganse [gɑ̃ːs], s.f. 1. Braid, (plaited) cord, gimp, piping. 2. Rope handle; loop.

gant [gɑ̃], s.m. 1. Glove. Archeol: Gauntlet. (a) Mettre ses gants, to draw on, pull on, one's gloves. Cela vous va comme un gant, it fits you like a glove. Jeter le gant à qn, to throw down the gauntlet to s.o. Relever le gant, to take up the gauntlet. (b) Gants bourrés, boxing-gloves. (c) Gant de crin, flesh-glove, friction glove. 2. pl. A: Glove-money. Se donner les gants d'une affaire, to take credit to oneself for sth.

gantelé [gɑ̃tle], a. Gauntleted. F: La main gantelée, the mailed fist.

ganter [gɑ̃te], v.tr. To glove. Être bien ganté, to be well gloved. G. du sept, to take sevens in gloves. F: Ça me gante, that suits me down to the ground, to a T. se ganter, to put, pull, draw, slip, on one's gloves.

ganterie [gɑ̃tri], s.f. 1. Glove-making or -trade. 2. Glove-factory, -shop, or -counter.

gantier, -ière [gɑ̃tje, -jeːr], s. Glover.

garage [garaːʒ], s.m. 1. (a) Docking (of boats). (b) Dock, basin (of canal). 2. Rail: Shunting, side-tracking. Voie de garage, siding. 3. (a) Stor-age (of bicycles, etc.). (b) Parking. 4. (a) G. pour autos, garage. G. pour canots, boat-house. G. de tramway, tram-depot. (b) Car-park. [GARER]

garagiste [garaʒist], s.m. Aut: Garage keeper.

garance [garɑ̃ːs], s.f. 1. Bot: Madder(-wort). 2. (a) Madder (dye). (b) a.inv. Madder(-red).

garant[1], **-ante** [garɑ̃, -ɑ̃ːt], s. (a) Guarantor, surety, bail. Se rendre, se porter, garant de qn, (i) to answer for s.o.; (ii) to go bail for s.o. Prendre qn à garant de qch., to call on s.o. to vouch for sth. Être garant pour ses faits, to be answer-able for one's actions. (b) Authority, guarantee.

garant[2], s.m. Nau: (Tackle-)fall.

garantie [garɑ̃ti], s.f. 1. (a) Guarantee (contre, against). Prendre des garanties contre les abus, to insure against abuses. (b) Guarantee, pledge (of execution of contract); guaranty (of pay-ment). Verser une somme en garantie, to leave a deposit. Donner une garantie pour qn, to stand security for s.o. (c) Com: Warranty, guarantee (of quality, etc.). Sans garantie, without warranty.

2. *Fin:* Underwriting. **Syndicat de garantie,** underwriters.

garantir [garɑ̃tiːr], *v.tr.* **1.** (*a*) To warrant, guarantee. *Créance garantie,* secured debt. *G. un fait,* to vouch for a fact. *F:* **Je vous garantis qu'il viendra,** he'll come, I warrant you. (*b*) *Fin:* To underwrite (issue of shares, etc.). **2.** To shelter, protect (*de,* from; *contre,* against). **3.** *G. une maison contre l'incendie,* to insure a house against fire.

garbure [garbyːr], *s.f.* Hotchpotch of cabbage, bacon, goose fat, and rye-bread.

garce [gars], *s.f. P:* Trollop.

garcette [garsɛt], *s.f. Nau:* **1.** Gasket, becket. *G. de ris,* reef-point. **2.** Rope-end, rope's end, cat-o'-nine-tails.

garçon [garsɔ̃], *s.m.* **1.** (*a*) Boy, lad. *F:* **C'est un garçon manqué,** she's a tomboy. *S.a.* COIFFURE 2. (*b*) *F:* Son. **2.** Young man. **Garçon d'honneur,** best man; groomsman. *F:* **Brave garçon, bon garçon,** decent chap. **Il est beau garçon,** he is a good-looking fellow. **3.** Bachelor. *Il est encore g.,* he is still single. **4.** Servant, employee. **Garçon de café,** waiter. *G. de bureau,* office-messenger. *G. d'ecurie,* (h)ostler. *G. de cabine,* steward.

garçonne [garsɔn], *s.f.* Bachelor girl; mannish girl. *S.a.* COIFFURE 2.

garçonnet [garsɔnɛ], *s.m.* Little boy.

garçonnier, -ière [garsɔnje, -jɛːr]. **1.** *a. Habitudes garçonnières,* (i) bachelor habits; (ii) (woman's) mannish habits or ways. **2.** *s.f.* **Garçonnière,** bachelor's establishment.

garde¹ [gard], *s.m. & f.* **1.** (*a*) Keeper. **Garde des sceaux,** Keeper of the Seals. (*b*) Watchman. **Garde champêtre,** rural policeman. *G. forestier,* ranger. (*c*) = GARDE-BARRIÈRE, GARDE-CHASSE, GARDE-PÊCHE I, etc. **La maison du garde,** the lodge (occupied by gamekeeper, forester, etc.). (*d*) *f.* = GARDE-MALADE. **2.** *Mil:* Guardsman. **Gardes du corps,** life-guards.

garde², *s.f.* **1.** (*a*) Guardianship, care, custody (of person); care (of thing). **Chien de garde,** watch-dog. **Commettre qch. à la garde de qn,** to entrust s.o. with the care of sth. **A la garde de Dieu,** in God's keeping. **Être sous bonne garde,** to be in safe custody. **Avoir qch. en garde,** to have charge of sth. **Prendre qn en sa garde,** to take charge of s.o. (*b*) Nursing. (*c*) Guarding, protection (of frontier, machinery, etc.). (*d*) Keeping. **Vin de garde,** good keeping wine. **De bonne garde,** worth keeping. **2.** (*a*) Watch(ing). **Faire la garde,** to keep watch. **Faire bonne garde,** to keep a good watch. (*b*) Care, guard. **Mettre qn en garde contre qch.,** to put s.o. on his guard against sth. *Fenc:* **Se mettre en garde,** to take one's guard. **En garde!** on guard! **Être, se tenir, sur ses gardes,** to be, stand, on one's guard. **Garde à toi!** look out! beware! *Mil:* **"Garde à vous!"** 'attention!' "shun!" *A. & Lit:* **N'avoir garde de faire qch.,** to be far from doing sth. *Je n'eus g. de le désabuser,* I took good care not to undeceive him. **3. Prendre garde.** (*a*) *Prendre g. à qn, à qch.,* to beware of s.o., of sth. **Prenez garde!** take care! (*b*) *Prendre g. à qch.,* to attend to, be careful of, to notice, sth. *Un fait auquel on n'a pas pris g.,* a fact that has been left out of consideration. **Faire qch. sans y prendre garde,** to do sth. without meaning to it, inadvertently. (*c*) *Prendre g. à, de, faire qch.,* to be careful to do sth.; to take (good) care to do sth. (*d*) *Prendre g. de faire qch.,* to be careful not to do sth. **Prenez garde de tomber,** mind you don't fall. (*e*) *Prendre g. que . . . (ne) + sub.,* to be careful lest (sth. should happen). *Prenez g.*

qu'il (ne) vous voie, take care he doesn't see you. **4.** Guard. (*a*) **Soldat de garde à la porte,** soldier on guard at the door. **Être de garde,** to be on guard, on duty. **Descendre de garde,** to come off guard, off duty. *Descente de g.,* coming off guard. **Monter la garde,** to mount guard; to go on guard. (*b*) *G.* **montante,** new guard, relieving guard. (*c*) **La garde,** the Guards. *La g. à cheval,* the Horse-guards. *La g. à pied,* the Foot-guards. **5.** *Cards:* Covering card; guard. *J'ai la g. au roi,* my king is guarded. **6.** (*a*) (Hilt-)guard (of sword or foil). *F:* **S'enferrer jusqu'à la garde,** to give oneself completely away. (*b*) Ward (of lock). **7.** (*a*) Fly-leaf (of unbound book). (*b*) End-paper (of bound book).

garde-à-vous, *s.m.* No *pl. Mil:* (Position of) attention. *Au g.-à-v.,* at attention. *S.a.* GARDE² 2.

garde-barrière, *s. m. & f.* Gate-keeper (at level-crossing). *pl. Des gardes-barrière(s).*

garde-boue, *s.m.inv.* Splash-board (of vehicle); mudguard (of bicycle, car).

garde-cendre(s),*s.m.inv.* **1.** Ashpan. **2.** Fender.

garde-chasse, *s.m.* Gamekeeper. *pl. Des gardes-chasse(s).*

garde-corps, *s.m.inv.* **1.** Parapet, balustrade. **2.** Railing, guard-rail (of bridge, etc.).

garde-côte, *s.m.* **1.** Coast-guard(sman). *pl. Des gardes-côte(s).* **2.** *Inv.* (*a*) Coast-guard vessel. (*b*) Coast-defence ship.

garde-crotte, *s.m.inv.* = GARDE-BOUE.

garde-feu, *s.m.* **1.** Fireman (in theatre, etc.). *pl. Des gardes-feu.* **2.** *Inv.* (*a*) Fender. (*b*) Fire-guard; fire-screen.

garde-fou, *s.m.* = GARDE-CORPS. *pl. Des garde-fous.*

garde-frein(s), *s.m. Rail:* Brakesman. *pl. Des gardes-frein(s).*

garde-magasin, *s.m.* Warehouseman, store-keeper. *pl. Des gardes-magasin.*

garde-malade. 1.*s.m.* Male nurse. **2.** *s.f.* (Sick-)nurse. *pl. Des gardes-malades.*

garde-manger, *s.m.inv.* **1.** Larder, pantry. **2.** Meat-safe.

garde-meuble, *s.m.* (*q*) Furniture-repository, -warehouse. (*b*) Lumber-room. *pl. Des garde-meubles.*

garde-nappe, *s.m.* **1.** Dinner-mat. **2.** Doily. **3.** (Table-)runner. *pl. Des garde-nappe(s).*

garde-pêche, *s.m.* **1.** Water-bailiff. *pl. Des gardes-pêche.* **2.** *Inv.* Fishery protection vessel.

garde-phare, *s.m.* Lighthouse-keeper. *pl. Des gardes-phare(s).*

garde-place(s), *s.m.inv. Rail:* **1.** (Office for) reservation of seats. **2.** *Ticket g.-p.,* ticket for reserved seat(s).

garder [garde], *v.tr.* To keep. **1.** To guard, protect; to keep watch over (s.o., sth.). **Que les anges te gardent!** angels guard thee! *G. la boutique,* to mind the shop. *G. un troupeau,* to tend a flock. **Garder qn à vue,** to keep a close watch on s.o. **2.** (*a*) To retain. *G. un vêtement,* (i) to keep a garment; (ii) to keep on a garment. (*b*) To preserve. *F:* **Garder une poire pour la soif,** to put by something for a rainy day. **Garder rancune à qn,** to harbour resentment against s.o. *S.a.* BON I. 12. **Viande qui ne se garde pas bien,** meat that does not keep well. **3.** To remain in (a place). *G. sa chambre,* to keep to one's room. *G. le lit,* to be laid up, confined to bed. **4.** To observe, respect. *G. un secret, sa parole,* to keep a secret, one's word.

se garder. 1. To protect oneself. **Garde-toi!** look out for yourself! *Cards: Se g. en trèfle,* to keep a guard in clubs. *S.a.* CARREAU 4.

2. (*a*) **Se garder de** qn, de qch., to beware of s.o., sth. (*b*) **Se garder de faire** qch., to take care not to do sth.

garderie [gard(ə)ri], *s.f.* Day-nursery; crèche.

garde-robe, *s.f.* **I.** (*a*) Wardrobe. (*b*) Clothes. **2.** (*a*) Water-closet. (*b*) Night-commode. (*c*) *Med:* Stool(s), motion. *pl. Des garde-robes.*

gardeur, -euse [gardœːr, -øːz], *s.* Keeper (of animals); herdsman. *G. de cochons*, swine-herd. *Gardeuse d'oies*, goose-girl.

garde-voie, *s.m.* Rail: Track-watchman. *pl. Des gardes-voie.*

garde-vue, *s.m.inv.* **I.** Eye-shade. **2.** Lamp-shade.

gardien, -ienne [gardjɛ̃, -jɛn], *s.* Guardian, keeper; care-taker (of public building, etc.); warder (of prison). *G. d'autos*, car-park attendant. **Gardien de la paix**, policeman (in Paris). *Fb:* **Gardien du but**, goal-keeper. *a.* **Ange gardien**, guardian angel.

gardon [gardɔ̃], *s.m. Ich:* Roach.

gare[1] [gaːr], *int.* Look out! mind yourself! *F:* **Gare la bombe!** look out for squalls! *G. à lui si . . .*, woe betide him if. . . . **Sans crier gare**, without warning.

gare[2], *s.f.* **I.** Siding (of canal). Rail: *G. d'évitement*, siding. S.a. TRIAGE. **2.** (Railway) station. *G. maritime*, harbour-station. *G. de bifurcation*, junction. **Chef de gare**, station-master. *Le train est en g.*, the train is in. **Colis à prendre en gare**, parcel to be fetched from the station.

garenne [garɛn], *s.f.* **I.** (Rabbit-)warren. **Lapin de garenne**, *F:* un garenne, wild rabbit. **2.** (Fishing) preserve.

garer [gare], *v.tr.* **I.** To dock (vessel). **2.** To shunt (train) on to a siding. **3.** (*a*) To put into the garage; to garage (car). (*b*) To park (car). **se garer. I.** To get out of the way (*de*, of). **Garez-vous!** (i) stand aside! (ii) take cover! **2.** (Of car, etc.) To pull to one side. **3.** (Of train) To shunt on to a siding.

gargantua [gargɑ̃tɥa], *s.m. F:* Glutton, guzzler.

gargantuesque [gargɑ̃tɥɛsk], *a.* Gargantuan.

gargariser [gargarize], *v.tr.* To gargle (throat). **se gargariser**, to gargle.

gargarisme [gargarism], *s.m.* Gargle.

gargote [gargɔt], *s.f.* Low-class eating house.

gargotier, -ière [gargɔtje, -jɛːr], *s.* **I.** Keeper of a cook-shop. **2.** *F:* Wretched cook.

gargouille [garguːj], *s.f.* (*a*) (Water-)spout (of roof-gutter). (*b*) *Arch:* Gargoyle.

gargouill|er [garguje], *v.i.* **I.** (Of water) To gurgle, bubble. **2.** (Of the bowels) To rumble. *s.m.* **-ement.**

gargousse [gargus], *s.f. Artil:* (i) Cartridge (of big gun); (ii) cartridge-bag.

garnement [garnəmɑ̃], *s.m. F:* Usu. **Mauvais garnement**, scapegrace, scamp, rogue.

garn|ir [garniːr], *v.tr.* **I.** To strengthen, protect. *G. une place de guerre*, to garrison a stronghold. **2.** To furnish, provide (*de*, with). *G. une boutique*, to stock a shop. *G. qch. à l'intérieur*, to line sth. *Coffret garni de . . .*, case fitted (out) with. . . . *Salle garnie de monde*, (i) room full of company; (ii) large audience. *G. une lampe*, to fill a lamp (with oil). **3.** To trim (dress, hat, etc.). **4.** *Tchn:* To stuff (chair); to lag (boiler); to pack (piston); to line (brake). *Phot: G. un châssis*, to load, fill, a slide. *s.m.* **-issage.** *s.* **-isseur, -euse.** **garni. I.** *a.* **I.** (*a*) **Bourse bien garnie**, well-lined purse (*b*) **Choucroute garnie**, sauerkraut with sausages. **2.** Usu. *Pej:* **Chambre garnie**, room ready furnished (in 'hôtel' of the poorer class). *Chambres garnies*, 'furnished apartments.'

II. garni, *s.m.* Usu. *Pej:* Furnished room(s). **Loger en garni**, to live in lodgings.

garnison [garnizɔ̃], *s.f.* Garrison. *Ville à g.*, garrison town. **Être en garnison dans une ville**, to be garrisoned, stationed, in a town. *Changer de g.*, to change station.

garniture [garnityːr], *s.f.* **I.** Fittings. *G. de lit*, bedding. *G. intérieure d'une voiture*, upholstery of a carriage. **2.** (*a*) Trimming, decoration (of dress, hat). (*b*) Trimming(s). **3.** (Complete) set (of buttons, furs, etc.). *G. de toilette*, toilet-set. *G. de feu, de foyer*, set of fire-irons. **4.** Garnish(ing), trimmings (of dish). **5.** (*a*) *Mch:* Packing (of stuffing-box); (packing-)ring (of piston). *Boîte à g.*, stuffing-box. (*b*) *Mch:* Lagging (of boiler). (*c*) *G. de frein*, brake-lining.

garrot[1] [garo], *s.m.* **I.** *Surg:* Tourniquet. **2.** Racking-stick. **3.** **Supplice du garrot**, gar(r)otting, gar(r)otte.

garrot[2], *s.m.* Withers (of horse).

garrotte [garɔt], *s.f.* = GARROT[1] 3.

garrott|er [garɔte], *v.tr.* **I.** To rack down (goods on a truck, etc.). **2.** To pinion (prisoner, etc.). **3.** To gar(r)otte, strangle. *s.m.* **-age.**

garrulité [garylite], *s.f.* Garrulousness, garrulity.

gars, gas [gɑ], *s.m. F:* Young fellow; lad. *Un petit g.*, a small urchin. **Allons-y, les gars!** come on, boys!

Gascogne [gaskɔɲ]. *Pr.n.f. Geog:* Gascony. **Le Golfe de Gascogne**, the Bay of Biscay.

gascon, -onne [gaskɔ̃, -ɔn]. **I.** *a. & s. Ethn:* Gascon. **Faire le Gascon**, to boast, brag; to draw the long-bow. **2.** *s.m.* The Gascon dialect.

gasconnade [gaskɔnad], *s.f.* Gasconade. **I.** Bragging. **2.** Piece of brag; tall story.

gasconner [gaskɔne], *v.i.* **I.** To speak with a Gascon accent. **2.** *F:* To boast, brag.

gaspill|er [gaspije], *v.tr.* To waste, squander (money); to waste, spoil (paper, cloth). *G. sa vie*, to make a hash of one's life. *s.m.* **-age.** *s.* **-eur, -euse.**

gastéropode [gasterɔpɔd]. *Moll:* **I.** *a.* Gasteropodous. **2.** *s.m.* Gasteropod.

gastralgie [gastralʒi], *s.f. Med:* Stomach pains.

gastrique [gastrik], *a.* Gastric.

gastrite [gastrit], *s.f. Med:* Gastritis.

gastronome [gastrɔnɔm], *s.m.* **I.** Gastronome. **2.** Writer on gastronomy.

gastronomie [gastrɔnɔmi], *s.f.* Gastronomy.

gastronomique [gastrɔnɔmik], *a.* Gastronomical.

gât [gɑ], *s.m.* Quay steps.

gâteau [gɑto], *s.m.* **I.** (*a*) Cake; (open) tart. *G. de riz*, rice shape. **Gâteau des Rois**, Twelfth-cake. *F:* **Papa gâteau**, fond parent. **Marraine gâteau**, fairy godmother. (*b*) *G. de chien*, dog-biscuit, puppy-cake. **2.** Lump, cake (of any material). **Gâteau de miel**, honeycomb.

gâte-métier, *s.m.inv.* Spoil-trade.

gâte-papier, *s.m.inv. F:* Scribbler.

gât|er [gɑte], *v.tr.* To spoil. **I.** *La grêle gâte le blé*, hail damages the corn. *Les mouches gâtent la viande*, the flies taint the meat. *Cela ne gâte rien*, that won't do any harm. **Il a tout gâté**, he has spoiled everything. *G. le plaisir de* qn, to mar s.o.'s pleasure. **2.** To pamper (child, etc.). *s.* **-eur, -euse.** **se gâter**, to spoil, deteriorate. *Le temps se gâte*, the weather is breaking up. *Les affaires se gâtent*, things are going wrong.

gâté, *a.* Spoilt. (*a*) *Viande gâtée*, tainted meat. *Dents gâtées*, decayed teeth. (*b*) **Enfant gâté**, (i) spoilt, pampered, child; (ii) pet, favourite.

gâterie [gɑtri], *s.f.* **I.** Over-indulgence (to faults of others). **2.** *pl.* Treats, goodies (for children).
gâteux, -euse [gɑtø, -øːz]. **I.** *s.* Old dotard. **2.** *a.* In senile decay.
gâtisme [gɑtism], *s.m.* Senile decay.
gauche [goːʃ], *a.* **I.** Warped, crooked; out of true; skew (surface, etc.). **2.** Awkward, clumsy. **3.** Left. (*a*) *Main g.*, left hand. (*b*) *s.f.* Assis à ma gauche, seated on my left. *Mon voisin de g.*, my left-hand neighbour. (*c*) *s.m.* (= *poing gauche*) *Box:* Feinter du gauche, to feint with the left. (*d*) *s.m.pl. Pol:* Les Gauches, the Left, the Radical party. **4.** *Adv.phr.* A gauche, on the left, to the left. *Tournez à g.*, turn to the left. La première rue à gauche, the first street on the left. *F:* Emprunter à droite et à gauche, to borrow right and left, on every hand. *Mil: P:* Passer l'arme à gauche, to go west; to peg out. Vis à pas à gauche, left-handed screw.
gauchement [goʃmã], *adv.* Awkwardly, clumsily.
gaucher, -ère [goʃe, -ɛːr], *a. & s.* **I.** Left-handed (person). **2.** *Pol:* Member of the Left.
gaucherie [goʃri], *s.f.* **I.** Left-handedness. **2.** Awkwardness, clumsiness, *gaucherie.* Commettre des gaucheries, to make awkward mistakes.
gauch|ir [goʃiːr]. **I.** *v.i. A:* To flinch; to give way; to dodge (blow). **2.** *v.i. & pr.* (Of wood, etc.) To warp; to shrink out of true; (of iron) to buckle. **3.** *v.tr. Av: G. l'aileron*, to warp the aileron; to bank. *s.m.* -issement.
  gauchi, *a.* Out of true.
gaude [goːd], *s.f.* Yellow-weed, dyer's weed.
gaud|ir (se) [sɔgodiːr], *v.pr. A. & F:* **I.** To enjoy oneself. **2.** Se gaudir de qn, to laugh at, make fun of, s.o. *s.m.* -issement.
gaudriole [godriɔl], *s.f. F:* Broad joke or joking. *Dire des gaudrioles,* to crack broad jokes.
gaufrage [gofraːʒ], *s.m.* **I.** Embossing (of leather, etc.); goffering, fluting (of linen); corrugating; crinkling. **2.** Embossed work; corrugation(s); goffers, fluting; chequered pattern.
gaufre [goːfr], *s.f.* **I.** Waffle. **2.** *Cu:* Honeycomb. Moule à gaufres, waffle-iron.
gaufr|er [gofre], *v.tr.* **I.** (*a*) To figure, emboss (leather, velvet); (*b*) To goffer, flute, crimp (linen). Fer à gaufrer, goffering-iron. (*c*) To corrugate; to crinkle (paper). **2.** *Tex:* To diaper (cloth). *s.m.* -eur, -euse.
gaufrette [gofret], *s.f. Cu:* Wafer biscuit.
gaufrure [gofryːr], *s.f.* **I.** Stamped design (on leather, etc.). **2.** Goffering (on linen).
gaule¹ [goːl], *s.f.* **I.** (Long thin) pole, stick. *G. de pavillon,* (small) flagstaff. **2.** (One-piece) fishing-rod. **3.** (Riding-)switch.
Gaule². *Pr.n.f. A.Geog:* Gaul.
gaul|er [gole], *v.tr.* To beat (fruit-tree, walnut-tree). *s.m.* -age.
gaulois, -oise [golwa, -waːz]. **I.** *a.* Gallic; of Gaul. *F:* Esprit gaulois, (broad) Gallic humour. **2.** *s.* (*a*) Les Gaulois, the Gauls. (*b*) Le gaulois, (the) Gallic (tongue).
gauloiserie [golwazri], *s.f.* Broad joke; joyous tale.
gausser (se) [sɔgose], *v.pr.* Se g. de qn, to poke fun at s.o.
gausserie [gosri], *s.f. F:* Mockery, banter, chaff.
gausseur, -euse [gosœːr, -øːz]. **I.** *s.* Mocker, banterer. **2.** *a.* Mocking, bantering.
Gautier [gotje]. *Pr.n.m.* Walter.
gave [gaːv], *s.m.* Mountain-torrent (in the Pyrenees).
gav|er [gave], *v.tr.* To cram (poultry). *Med:* To feed (s.o.) forcibly *F:* Se gaver de nourriture,

to gorge; to stuff oneself with food. *s.m.* -age.
gavroche [gavrɔʃ], *s.m.* Street-arab (of Paris) ragamuffin. (From the character in V. Hugo' *Les Misérables.*)
gaz [gɑːz], *s.m.* **I.** Gas. *Gaz d'éclairage,* illuminating gas, coal-gas. Usine à gaz, gas-works. Fourneau à gaz, gas-stove. Réchaud à gaz, gas-ring. Moteur à gaz, gas-engine. *Aut:* Ouvrir, mettre, les gaz, to open out the throttle; *U.S:* *F:* to tread on the gas. A pleins gaz, with the throttle full open; flat out. *Gaz asphyxiant,* toxique, de combat, asphyxiating gas; *F:* poison gas. **2.** *F:* Avoir des gaz, to suffer from flatulence, *F:* from wind.
gaze [gɑːz], *s.f.* Gauze. *G. métallique,* wire gauze. *F:* Raconter les choses sans gaze, to tell the story without any reticence.
gazéifier [gɑzeifje], *v.tr.* **I.** *Ch:* To gasify, volatilize. **2.** To aerate (mineral waters, wine).
gazelle [gazɛl], *s.f. Z:* Gazelle.
gazer¹ [gɑze], *v.tr.* To cover with gauze. *F:* Sans rien gazer, without glossing over anything.
gazer². **I.** *v.tr.* To gas (troops). **2.** *v.i. P:* (*a*) *Aut:* Ça gaze! we're slipping along! (*b*) Ça va gazer! we're in for trouble! look out for squalls!
gazette [gazɛt], *s.f.* Gazette; news-sheet.
gazeux, -euse [gazø, -øːz], *a.* **I.** Gaseous. *El:* Lampe à atmosphère gazeuse, gas-filled lamp. **2.** Aerated (water, etc.); fizzy (drink).
gazier [gɑzje], *s.m.* (*a*) Employee at gas-works. (*b*) Gas-fitter.
gazogène [gɑzɔʒɛn]. **I.** *a.* (*a*) Gas-producing. (*b*) Aerating. **2.** *s.m.* (*a*) Gas-generator. (*b*) Gasogene, seltzogene.
gazomètre [gɑzɔmɛtr], *s.m.* Gasometer, gasholder.
gazon [gɑzɔ̃], *s.m.* **I.** (*a*) (Fine, short) grass; turf, sward. (*b*) Lawn, green. **2.** Turf, sod. **3.** *Bot:* Gazon d'Olympe, thrift.
gazonn|er [gɑzɔne], *v.tr.* To cover with sods or turf; to turf. *Talus gazonné,* turfed slope *s.m.* -age. *s.m.* -ement.
gazonneux, -euse [gɑzɔnø, -øːz], *a.* Turfy.
gazouill|er [gazuje], *v.i.* (Of bird) To twitter, warble; (of water) to babble, purl; *F:* (of child) to prattle. *s.m.* -ement.
gazouillis [gazuji], *s.m.* = GAZOUILLEMENT.
geai [ʒe], *s.m. Orn:* Jay. *F:* Le geai paré des plumes de paon,* the jackdaw in borrowed feathers.
géant, -ante [ʒeã, -ãːt]. **I.** *s.* Giant, giantess. *Gym:* Pas de géant, giant's stride. Avancer à pas de géant, to advance with giant strides; to make astonishing progress. **2.** *a.* Gigantic.
géhenne [ʒeɛn], *s.f.* Gehenna, Hell.
geign-ais, -ant, -is, etc. See GEINDRE.
geignard, -arde [ʒeɲaːr, -ard]. **I.** *a.* Fretful; (given to) whining; peevish. **2.** *s.* Whiner.
geignement [ʒeɲmã], *s.m.* **I.** Whining, whimpering. **2.** Whine, whimper.
gei|ndre [ʒɛdr], *v.i.* (*pr.p.* geignant; *p.p.* geint; *pr.ind.* je geins, il geint, n. geignons; *p.h.* je geignis; *fu.* je geindrai) To whine, whimper; *P:* to grizzle. *s.m.* -gneur, -euse.
gel [ʒɛl], *s.m. Geol: etc:* Frost, freezing.
gélatine [ʒelatin], *s.f.* Gelatin(e).
gélatineux, -euse [ʒelatinø, -øːz], *a.* Gelatinous.
gélatino-bromure [ʒelatinɔbrɔmyːr], *s.m. Phot:* Gelatino-bromide. Papier au gélatino-bromure, bromide paper.
gélatino-chlorure [ʒelatinɔklɔryːr], *s.m. Phot:* Gelatino-chloride. Papier au gélatino-chlorure, gas-light paper.
geler [ʒ(ə)le], *v.* (je gèle; je gèlerai) **I.** *v.tr.* To

convert into ice; to freeze. **2.** *v.i.* (*a*) To become frozen; to freeze. **On gèle dans cette salle,** this room is like an ice-house. (*b*) *Impers.* **Il gèle dur, à pierre fendre,** it is freezing hard. **Il a gelé blanc,** there was a white frost.

se geler, *v.pr.* To freeze, solidify.

gelé, *a.* **I.** Frozen. **2.** (*a*) Frost-bitten (nose, toe). (*b*) Frost-nipped. **3.** *Fin:* **Dettes gelées,** frozen debts.

gelée, *s.f.* **I.** Frost. **Forte g.,** hard frost. **Temps à la gelée,** frosty weather. **2.** Jelly.

gelinotte [ʒ(ə)linɔt], *s.f.* **I.** Hazel-grouse, hazel-hen. **2.** Fattened pullet.

gelure [ʒəlyːr], *s.f. Med:* Frost-bite.

Gémeaux (les) [leʒemo], *s.m.pl. Astr:* Gemini; the Twins.

géminé [ʒemine], *a.* Geminate, twin (leaves, etc.). *Sch:* **Classes géminées,** forms taught together.

gémir [ʒemiːr], *v.i.* To groan, moan, wail. *G. sur son sort,* to bemoan one's fate.

gémissement [ʒemismã], *s.m.* Groan(ing), moan(ing); wail(ing). *Pousser un profond g.,* to give, utter, a deep groan.

gemme [ʒem]. **I.** (*a*) *s.f.* Gem; precious stone. (*b*) *a. Pierre g.,* gem stone. **Sel gemme,** rock-salt. **2.** *s.f.* Pine resin.

gemmer [ʒemme]. **I.** *v.i.* (Of tree) To bud. **2.** *v.tr.* To tap (tree for resin).

gémonies (les) [leʒemɔni], *s.f.pl. Rom.Ant:* The Gemonies.

gênant [ʒɛnɑ̃], *a.* **I.** Cumbersome; in the way. **2.** Embarrassing, awkward (situation, silence).

gencive [ʒɑ̃siːv], *s.f. Anat:* Gum. S.a. ABCÈS.

gendarme [ʒɑ̃darm], *s.m.* **I.** Gendarme; soldier of the police militia; approx. = constable. *F:* **C'est un vrai gendarme,** she's a martinet. **2.** *F:* Spark (from crackling fire). **3.** *P:* Red herring. **4.** Flaw (in jewel).

gendarmer [ʒɑ̃darme], *v.tr.* To stir up, rouse (public opinion, etc.).

se gendarmer (*contre qn, qch.*), to be up in arms (against s.o., a proposal); to flare up.

gendarmerie [ʒɑ̃darməri], *s.f.* **I.** The force of gendarmes; approx. = the constabulary. **2.** Barracks, headquarters (of the gendarmes).

gendre [ʒɑ̃ːdr], *s.m.* Son-in-law.

gêne [ʒɛ(ː)n], *s.f.* **I.** *A:* Torture. *F: Se mettre l'esprit à la g.,* to rack one's brains. **2.** Discomfort, constraint, embarrassment. **Sans gêne,** unconstrained, unconventional, free and easy. *Il est sans g.!* he's a cool customer! he makes himself at home! **3.** Want; financial embarrassment or pressure. **Être dans la gêne,** to be in straitened, reduced, embarrassed, circumstances; to be in want.

généalogie [ʒenealɔʒi], *s.f.* Genealogy; pedigree, descent; pedigree (of cattle, horses, etc.).

généalogique [ʒenealɔʒik], *a.* Genealogical. **Arbre généalogique,** family-tree; pedigree. *adv.* **-ment.**

généalogiste [ʒenealɔʒist], *s.m.* Genealogist.

gêner [ʒene], *v.tr.* **I.** To constrict, cramp. *Mes souliers me gênent,* my shoes pinch. **On est gêné ici,** we are too crowded here. **2.** To hinder, obstruct, impede; to be in (s.o.'s) way. *G. la vue,* to obstruct, block, the view. *Cette valise vous gêne-t-elle?* is this bag in your way? **3.** To inconvenience, embarrass. *La fumée (de tabac) vous gêne-t-elle?* do you mind my smoking? *Cela me gênerait de le rencontrer,* it would be embarrassing for me to meet him.

se gêner. To put oneself under some restraint. *Je ne me suis pas gêné pour le lui dire,* I did not scruple to tell him so. *Il ne se gêne pas*

---

avec nous, he does not stand on ceremony with us; he makes himself at home. **2.** To put oneself to inconvenience.

gêné, *a.* **I.** Embarrassed; ill at ease; uneasy. **Il n'est pas gêné** = *il est sans gêne, q.v.* under GÊNE 2. **Silence g.,** awkward silence. **2. Gêné d'argent,** in straitened circumstances; *F:* hard up.

général, -ale, -aux [ʒeneral, -o]. **I.** *a.* General (rule, appearance, etc.). **En règle générale,** as a general rule. **D'une façon générale,** generally speaking, broadly speaking. *Th:* **Répétition générale,** *s.f.* **générale,** dress-rehearsal. S.a. QUARTIER 3. **En général,** in general, generally; generally speaking; for the most part. **2.** *s.m. Mil:* General. *G. de division,* (lieutenant-) general. *G. de brigade,* brigadier-general. **3.** *s.f.* **Générale.** (*a*) The general's wife. (*b*) Alarm call. **Battre la générale,** to call to arms. *adv.* **-ement.**

généralisateur, -trice [ʒeneralizatœːr, -tris]. **I.** *a.* Generalizing. **2.** *s.* Generalizer.

généralisation [ʒeneralizasjɔ̃], *s.f.* **I.** Generalizing. **2.** Generalization.

généraliser [ʒeneralize], *v.tr.* To generalize.

se généraliser, to become general; (of habit, etc.) to spread.

généralissime [ʒeneralisim], *s.m.* Generalissimo, commander-in-chief.

généralité [ʒeneralite], *s.f.* Generality. **Dans la g. des cas,** in most cases. **S'en tenir à des généralités,** to confine oneself to generalities.

générateur, -trice [ʒeneratœːr, -tris]. **I.** *a.* Generating (machine, function); generative (force, organ); productive (*de,* of). *El.E:* **Station, usine, génératrice,** generating station; power-house. **2.** *s. El.E:* **Générateur, génératrice, de courant,** current-generator; dynamo.

génération [ʒenerasjɔ̃], *s.f.* **I.** (Act of) generation; generating. **2. La génération actuelle,** the present generation, the present age. **De génération en génération,** from generation to generation.

générer [ʒenere], *v.tr.* (je **génère;** je **générerai**) **I.** To generate, engender. **2.** To generate, produce (electricity, etc.).

généreu|x, -euse [ʒenerø, -øːz], *a.* **I.** Noble, generous (soul). *Cœur g.,* warm heart. *Vin g.,* generous wine. **2.** Liberal, generous, open-handed. *Il est trop g.,* he is too free with his money. *adv.* **-sement.**

générique [ʒenerik], *a.* Generic (term, etc.). *adv.* **-ment,** -ally.

générosité [ʒenerozite], *s.f.* Generosity; munificence, bounteousness.

Gênes [ʒɛn]. *Pr.n.f. Geog:* Genoa.

genèse [ʒənɛːz], *s.f.* Genesis, origin, birth. *B:* **La Genèse,** (the Book of) Genesis.

genet [ʒ(ə)nɛ], *s.m.* Jennet (horse).

genêt [ʒ(ə)nɛ], *s.m. Bot:* Genista; esp. broom.

gêneur, -euse [ʒenœːr, -øːz], *s.* Spoil-sport; intruder. [GÊNER]

Genève [ʒ(ə)nɛːv]. *Pr.n.f. Geog:* Geneva.

genévrier [ʒ(ə)nevrie], *s.m. Bot:* Juniper(-tree).

génial, -aux [ʒenial, -o], *a.* Inspired; full of genius. *Œuvre géniale,* work of genius. **Idée géniale,** brilliant idea. *adv.* **-ement.**

génie [ʒeni], *s.m.* **I.** *a.* (Guardian) spirit; (presiding) genius. *Son mauvais g.,* his evil genius. (*b*) Genie, jinnee. **Les génies des contes arabes,** the genii, the jinn, of the Arabian Nights. **2.** *Homme de g.,* man of genius. **Suivre son génie,** to follow the bent of one's genius. **3.** (Pers.) Genius. **4.** *Tchn:* (*a*) **Génie civil,** engineering. (*b*) *Mil:* **Le corps du génie, le génie,** the engineer corps; the sappers.

genièvre [ʒənjɛːvr], *s.m.* **1.** *Bot:* Juniper-berry or -tree. **2.** Gin, Hollands.

génisse [ʒenɪs], *s.f.* Heifer.

génital, -aux [ʒenital, -o], *a.* Genital.

géniteur [ʒenitœːr], *s.m.* Sire, begetter.

génitif [ʒenitif], *s.m. Gram:* Genitive (case). Au génitif, in the genitive.

génois, -oise [ʒenwa, -waːz], *a. & s.* Genoese.

genou, -oux [ʒənu], *s.m.* **1.** Knee. Enfoncé jusqu'aux genoux dans la boue, knee-deep in mud. Se mettre à genoux, fléchir le(s) genou(x), to bend the knee ; to kneel down. Un genou à, en, terre, on one knee. A genou(x) ! down on your knee(s) ! kneel down ! Tenir un enfant sur ses genoux, to hold a child on one's knees, on one's lap. Ronds de genoux, 'knees' (in one's trousers). **2.** *Mec.E:* (Joint à) genou, (i) elbow joint ; (ii) ball-and-socket joint ; (iii) toggle-joint.

genouillère [ʒ(ə)nujɛːr], *s.f.* **1.** *(a)* Knee-piece, knee-cap (of armour). *(b)* (Workman's) knee-pad, knee-guard. **2.** *Mec.E :* Articulation à genouillère, knuckle-joint, ball-and-socket joint.

genre [ʒãːr], *s.m.* **1.** Genus, family, kind. Le genre humain, the human race ; mankind. **2.** Kind, manner, sort, way. Quel g. de vie mène-t-il? what kind of a life does he lead? C'est plus dans son genre, that's more in his line. C'est un artiste dans son genre, he is an artist in his way. Vin blanc genre sauternes, white wine of the Sauterne type. Étui g. maroquin, case in imitation morocco. **3.** (Artistic, literary) style, manner. Le g. comique, comedy. Peinture de genre, genre painting. Tableau de genre, subject picture. **4.** Manners, fashion, taste. C'est bon, mauvais, genre, it is good, bad, form. Elle a du genre, there is a style about her. Se donner du genre, to put on airs ; *F:* to put it on. **5.** *Gram :* Gender.

gens [ʒã], *s.m.pl.* (Was originally feminine, being the plural of GENT, *q.v.*, and most attributive adjectives preceding gens still take the feminine form, the word-group being nevertheless felt as masculine. Ces bonnes gens sont venus me trouver. Heureux les petites gens éloignés des grandeurs ! Quels sont ces gens? Quels or quelles sont ces bonnes gens? Tout varies according as the attributive adjective has a distinctive feminine ending or not : Toutes ces bonnes gens, but tous ces pauvres gens. Jeunes gens, and the compounds of group 2 *(b)* below, never have a feminine adjective. De bons petits jeunes gens. Les malheureux gens de lettres.) **1.** People, folk(s), men and women. Beaucoup de g., bien des g., l'ont vu, many people have seen it. Qui sont ces gens-là? who are these people? Il y a des g. qui . . ., there are those who. . . . **2.** *(a)* Jeunes gens, (i) young people, young folk ; (ii) young men. *(b)* G. du monde, society people. G. de bien, honest folk. G. d'église, (i) clergy(men), priests ; (ii) church(y) people. G. de lettres, men of letters. G. de robe, lawyers. *(c)* Petites gens, people of small account, of small means. *(d)* Servants, domestics ; retinue ; attendants, retainers. Les g. du Cardinal, (i) the Cardinal's train ; (ii) the Cardinal's people. G. de maison, servants. **3.** Nations, peoples. Esp. Le droit des gens, the law of nations.

gent [ʒã], *s.f. A:* (Still used humorously after the manner of La Fontaine) Tribe, race, brood. La g. moutonnière, the woolly race, the sheep. La g. ailée, the feathered tribe.

gentiane [ʒãsjan], *s.f.* **1.** *Bot:* Gentian. **2.** Gentian-bitters.

gentil[1], -ille [ʒãti, -iːj], *a. (a)* Pretty, pleasing, nice. Un gentil enfant (no 'liaison' [ʒãtiãfã]), a

pretty child ; a nice child. C'est gentil à vous de m'écrire, it is very kind, very nice, of you to write to me. *(b)* Sois gentil(le), be a good boy. a good girl.

gentil[2], *s.m. Hist:* Gentile.

gentilhomme [ʒãtijɔm], *s.m.* Man of gentle birth ; gentleman (in this restricted sense). Gentilhomme de la Chambre du Roi, gentleman of the Privy Chamber. S.a. BOURGEOIS 1. 1. *pl.* Des gentilshommes [ʒãtizɔm].

gentillâtre [ʒãtijɑːtr], *s.m. A:* Squireen.

gentillesse [ʒãtijɛs], *s.f.* **1.** *(a)* Prettiness, graciousness, engaging manner. *(b)* Auriez-vous la gentillesse de . . ., would you be so very kind as to. . . **2.** *pl.* Dire des gentillesses à une dame, to say nice things, sweet nothings, to a lady

gentillet, -ette [ʒãtijɛ, -ɛt], *a.* Rather nice ; prettyish ; engaging (child).

gentiment [ʒãtimã], *adv.* Nicely ; prettily.

génuflexion [ʒenyflɛksjõ], *s.f. Ecc:* Genuflexion. Faire une g., to genuflect.

géoclase [ʒeɔklaːz], *s.f. Geol :* Fault.

géodésie [ʒeɔdezi], *s.f.* Geodesy, surveying.

géodésique [ʒeɔdezik], *a.* Geodetic(al), geodesic.

Geoffroi [ʒɔfrwa]. *Pr.n.m.* Godfrey, Geoffrey.

géographe [ʒeɔgraf], *s.m.* Geographer.

géographie [ʒeɔgrafi], *s.f.* Geography. G. dans l'espace, solid geometry.

géographique [ʒeɔgrafik], *a.* Geographic(al). Carte g., map. *adv.* **-ment**, -ally.

geôle [ʒoːl], *s.f. A :* Gaol, jail ; prison.

geôlier [ʒolje], *s.m.* Gaoler, jailer, turnkey.

géologie [ʒeɔlɔʒi], *s.f.* Geology.

géologique [ʒeɔlɔʒik], *a.* Geological. *adv.* **-ment**.

géologue [ʒeɔlɔg], *s.m.* Geologist.

géométral, -aux [ʒeɔmetral, -o]. **1.** *a.* Flat (projection, elevation). **2.** *s.m.* Flat projection.

géomètre [ʒeɔmetr]. **1.** *s.m.* Geometer, geometrician. **2.** *s.f. Ent :* Geometer moth.

géométrie [ʒeɔmetri], *s.f.* Geometry. G. dans l'espace, solid geometry.

géométrique [ʒeɔmetrik], *a.* Geometric(al). *adv.* **-ment**, -ally.

géophone [ʒeɔfɔn], *s.m.* Geophone, sound-detector.

Georges [ʒɔrʒ]. *Pr.n.m.* George.

gérance [ʒerãːs], *s.f.* **1.** *(a)* Management (of business, newspaper). *(b)* Managership. **2.** Board of directors. [GÉRANT]

géranium [ʒeranjɔm], *s.m.* **1.** *Bot:* Geranium, crane's-bill. **2.** *Hort:* Pelargonium, *F:* geranium.

gérant, -ante [ʒerã, -ãːt], *s.* Manager, director ; *f.* manageress, directress ; managing director (of company). Rédacteur gérant, managing editor.

gerbe [ʒɛrb], *s.f.* **1.** Sheaf (of corn). G. d'étin-celles, shower of sparks. G. d'eau, (cone-shaped) spray of water ; column of water (raised by shell, etc.). **2.** *Mil :* Cone of fire.

gerbée [ʒɛrbe], *s.f.* **1.** Fodder straw (with a little corn left in it). **2.** Corn cut in the green (for fodder). **3.** Rye-straw.

gerb|er [ʒɛrbe], *v.tr.* **1.** To bind, sheave (corn, etc.). **2.** To stack, pile (shells). *s.m.* **-age**.

gerbier [ʒɛrbje], *s.m.* **1.** Stack (of corn). **2.** Barn.

gerboise [ʒɛrbwaːz], *s.f. Z:* Jerboa.

gerce [ʒɛrs], *s.f.* **1.** *(a)* Crack, fissure (in wood). *(b)* Crack, chap (in the skin). **2.** Clothes-moth.

gerc|er [ʒɛrse], *v.tr.* (il gerçait ; il gerça) To crack (wood, etc.) ; to chap (the hands). *s.m.* **-ement**. se gercer, (of skin) to crack, chap.

gerçure [ʒɛrsyːr], *s.f.* Crack, cleft, fissure ; flaw (in wood) ; chap (in skin).

gérer [ʒere], *v.tr.* (je gère ; je gérerai) To manage,

19

run (newspaper, hotel). *Mal g. ses finances*, to mismanage one's finances.

gerfaut [ʒɛrfo], *s.m. Orn:* Gerfalcon.

germain¹, -aine [ʒɛrmɛ̃, -ɛn]. *Hist:* **1.** *a.* Germanic. **2.** *s.* German.

germain², -aine, *a. Frère g.*, own brother, full brother, brother-german. *Cousin g.*, first cousin.

germandrée [ʒɛrmãdre], *s.f. Bot:* Germander.

Germanie [ʒɛrmani]. *Pr.n.f. Hist:* Germania.

germanique [ʒɛrmanik], *a. Hist:* (*a*) Germanic. (*b*) **L'empire germanique,** the German Empire.

germaniser [ʒɛrmanize], *v.tr.* To Germanize.

germanisme [ʒɛrmanism], *s.m. Ling:* Germanism ; esp. German phrase or idiom.

germe [ʒɛrm], *s.m. Biol:* Germ. (Of potatoes) *Pousser des germes*, to sprout. **Étouffer une rébellion dans son germe,** to crush a rebellion in the bud.

germer [ʒɛrme], *v.i.* To germinate ; to shoot, spring (up) ; (of potatoes) to sprout.

germinal [ʒɛrminal], *s.m. Hist:* Seventh month of the Fr. Republican calendar (March-April).

germination [ʒɛrminasjɔ̃], *s.f.* Germination.

gérondif [ʒerɔ̃dif], *s.m. Gram:* **1.** Gerund. **2.** Gerundive. **Au gérondif,** in the gerund(ive).

gésier [ʒezje], *s.m.* Gizzard.

gésir [ʒeziːr], *v.i. def.* (*pr.p.* gisant ; *pr.ind.* il gît, n. gisons, v. gisez, ils gisent ; *p.d.* je gisais, etc.) (Of pers.) To lie (helpless or dead) ; (of thg) to lie. (On gravestone) **Ci-gît, ci-gisent . . .,** here lies, here lie. . . . **C'est là que gît le lièvre,** that's the point ; there's the rub.

gesse [ʒɛs], *s.f. Bot:* Vetch ; everlasting pea. *G. odorante*, sweet pea.

gestation [ʒɛstasjɔ̃], *s.f.* Gestation, pregnancy.

geste¹ [ʒɛst], *s.m.* **1.** Gesture, motion, movement. *D'un geste de la main*, with a wave, a motion, of the hand. **Faire un geste,** to make a gesture. **Joindre le geste à la parole,** to suit the action to the word. *Mil:* **Commandements au geste,** control signals. **2. Beau geste,** handsome gesture, gesture of sympathy (on the part of a state, etc.).

geste², *s.f.* **1.** (**Chanson de**) **geste,** mediaeval verse-chronicle (of heroic exploits). **2. Faits et gestes,** doings, exploits.

gesticuller [ʒɛstikyle], *v.i.* To gesticulate. *s.f.* **-ation.**

   gesticulé, *a.* Expressed in gestures, in dumb show.

gestion [ʒɛstjɔ̃], *s.f.* (*a*) Management (of works, etc.) ; administration ; care (of public money). *Mauvaise g.*, maladministration. (*b*) Administratorship.

gestionnaire [ʒɛstjɔnɛːr]. **1.** *a.* **Administration gestionnaire,** administration by agent or factor. **2.** *s.* Manager, administrator ; *f.* manageress, administratrix.

geyser [ʒezeːr, ʒe-], *s.m. Geol:* Geyser.

ghetto [ɡɛt(t)o], *s.m.* Ghetto.

gibbeux, -euse [ʒib(b)ø, -øːz], *a.* **1.** Gibbous. **2.** Humped, hunch-backed.

gibbon [ʒib(b)ɔ̃], *s.m. Z:* Gibbon (ape).

gibbosité [ʒib(b)ozite], *s.f.* Gibbosity ; hump.

gibecière [ʒipsjɛːr], *s.f.* **1.** Game-bag, -pouch. **2.** Wallet ; (school) satchel.

Gibelin [ʒiblɛ̃], *s.m. Hist:* Ghibelline.

gibelotte [ʒiblɔt], *s.f.* Fricassee of rabbit or hare.

giberne [ʒibɛrn], *s.f.* **1.** *A:* Cartridge-pouch. **2.** (Bandsman's) wallet. **3.** (School) satchel.

gibet [ʒibɛ], *s.m. A:* Gibbet, gallows.

gibier [ʒibje], *s.m.* Game (= wild animals). *Gros g.*, big game. *Menu g.*, small game. *G. d'eau*, wild-fowl. *F:* **Gibier de potence,** gallows-bird.

giboulée [ʒibule], *s.f.* **1.** Sudden shower (usu. with snow or hail). **2.** *P:* Drubbing.

giboyer [ʒibwaje], *v.i.* (**je giboie ; je giboierai**) To spend one's time shooting ; to pot at small game. [GIBIER]

giboyeux, -euse [ʒibwajø, -øːz], *a.* Well stocked with game.

gibus [ʒibyːs], *s.m.* Crush-hat, opera-hat.

giclage [ʒikla:ʒ], *s.m. I.C.E:* Spraying (of petrol).

giclée [ʒikle], *s.f.* Spirt, squirt (of water, blood).

giclement [ʒikləmɑ̃], *s.m.* Splashing up, squelching (of mud) ; squirting, spirting (of blood).

gicler [ʒikle], *v.i.* **1.** To squirt out ; (of blood, etc.) to spirt (out). **2.** To splash up ; to squelch.

gicleur [ʒiklœːr], *s.m. I.C.E:* (Spray) nozzle ; atomizer, jet. *G. de ralenti*, pilot jet.

gifle [ʒifl], *s.f.* Slap, smack, in the face ; box on the ear. **Appliquer,** *F:* **flanquer, une gifle à qn,** to slap s.o.'s face.

gifler [ʒifle], *v.tr.* To slap, smack, (s.o.'s) face ; to box (s.o.'s) ears.

gigantesque [ʒiɡɑ̃tɛsk], *a.* Gigantic ; huge. *adv.* **-ment,** -ally.

Gigogne [ʒiɡɔɲ], *s.f.* **La mère Gigogne =** the Old Woman who lived in a shoe. **Table gigogne,** nest of tables, *Vaisseau g.*, mother ship.

gigot [ʒiɡo], *s.m.* Leg of mutton.

gigoter [ʒiɡɔte], *v.i. F:* **1.** To kick, fling about. **2.** To jig it ; to shake a leg.

gigue¹ [ʒiɡ], *s.f. Danc:* Jig.

gigue², *s.f.* (*a*) Haunch (of venison). (*b*) *pl. F:* Legs, stumps.

gilet [ʒilɛ], *s.m.* Waistcoat, vest. *G. tricoté*, cardigan. *G. à manches*, sleeved vest. **Gilet de corps,** singlet. **Gilet de force,** strait waistcoat. **Gilet de sauvetage,** life-saving jacket. **Gilet d'armes,** fencing jacket.

giletier, -ière [ʒiltje, -jeːr], *s.* Waistcoat-maker, waistcoat-hand.

Gilles [ʒil]. **1.** *Pr.n.m.* Giles. **2.** *s.m. A:* Tom Fool ; clown, ninny.

gingembre [ʒɛ̃ʒɑ̃:br], *s.m.* Ginger.

gingin [ʒɛ̃ʒɛ̃], *s.m. P:* Common sense ; gumption.

ginguet, -ette [ʒɛ̃ɡɛ, -ɛt], *a. F:* Weak, thin (wine, style). *Femme ginguette*, pretty doll (of a woman).

girafe [ʒiraf], *s.f. Z:* Giraffe.

girandole [ʒirãdɔl], *s.f.* **1.** Girandole, chandelier. **2.** Épergne, centre-piece (for table). **3.** Cluster (of blooms) ; girandole (of jewels).

giration [ʒirasjɔ̃], *s.f.* Gyration. *Nau:* **Cercle de giration,** turning circle (of ship).

giratoire [ʒiratwaːr], *a.* Gyratory ; *F:* roundabout (traffic).

giries [ʒiri], *s.f.pl. P:* **1.** Querulous complaints ; (hypocritical) whining. **2. Faire des giries,** to make a fuss.

girofle [ʒirɔfl], *s.m. Bot:* Clove. **Un clou de girofle,** a clove. *Huile de g.*, oil of cloves.

giroflée [ʒirɔfle], *s.f. Bot:* G. des jardins, grande g., stock(-gillyflower). *G. jaune, des murailles*, wallflower.

girol(l)e [ʒirɔl], *s.f. Bot:* **1.** Skirret. **2.** Chanterelle (mushroom).

giron [ʒirɔ̃], *s.m.* **1.** Lap. *Tenir un enfant dans son g.*, to hold a child in one's lap. **Le giron de l'Église,** the bosom of the Church. **2.** *Arch:* Tread (of step).

gironde [ʒirɔ̃:d], *a.f. P:* Plump, comely.

girondin, -ine [ʒirɔ̃dɛ̃, -in], *a. & s. Hist:* Girondist.

girouette [ʒirwɛt], *s.f.* (*a*) Weathercock ; vane.

F : **Graisser la girouette (avant de souffler dessus),** to pave the way. (*b*) *F :* (Of pers.) Weathercock.

gisais, gisent, etc. See GÉSIR.

gisant [ʒizã]. **I.** *a.* (Of pers.) Lying (helpless or dead). *For :* **Bois gisant,** felled timber. *Mill :* **Meule gisante,** nether millstone. **2.** *s.m.* Recumbent figure (on tomb).

gisement [ʒizmã], *s.m.* **I.** (*a*) *Geol :* Layer, bed, stratum. **Gisement pétrolifère,** oil-field. (*b*) *Min :* Lode, vein. **Gisements houillers,** coal-measures. **2.** *Nau :* Bearing (from the ship); lie (of the coast).

gît. See GÉSIR.

gitane [ʒitan], *s. m. & f.* (Spanish) gipsy.

gîte¹ [ʒit], *s.m.* **I.** (*a*) Resting-place. *N'avoir pas de g.,* to have nowhere to lay one's head. (*b*) Lair (of deer); form (of hare). S.a. LIÈVRE. **2.** Stratum, bed, deposit (of ore). **3.** Leg of beef, gravy-beef. **Gîte à la noix,** silverside.

gîte², *s.f.* (Of ship) **Avoir, prendre, de la gîte,** to have, take, a list.

gîter [ʒite]. **I.** *v.i.* (*a*) To lodge, lie. (*b*) (Of animal) To couch; (of bird) to perch. (*c*) (Of ship) (i) To run aground; (ii) to list, heel. **2.** *v.tr.* To house, shelter (s.o.).

givre [ʒiːvr], *s.m.* Hoar-frost, rime.

givrer [ʒivre], *v.tr.* (*a*) To cover (sth.) with hoar-frost, with rime. (*b*) To frost (cake).

glabre [glɑːbr], *a. Nat.Hist :* Glabrous, smooth. *F :* **Visage glabre,** clean-shaven face.

glace [glas], *s.f.* **I.** Ice. *Glaces de fond,* ground ice, anchor ice. *G. flottante,* drift ice, ice-floe. **Montagne de glace,** iceberg. *Champ de g.,* ice-field. **Retenu, pris, par les glaces,** ice-bound. **Rompre la glace,** to break the ice. **2.** (*a*) (Plate-) glass. *Phot :* **Glace dépolie,** focussing screen. (*b*) (Looking-)glass, mirror. *G. à main,* hand-mirror. (*c*) *Rail : Veh :* Window; light. *Baisser les glaces,* to lower, open, the windows. (*d*) *Aut :* **Glace brise-vent,** wind-screen. **3.** *Cu :* (*a*) Glaze, (meat-)jelly. (*b*) (Sugar-)icing. (*c*) Ice(-cream). *G. à la vanille,* vanilla ice.

gla|cer [glase], *v.tr.* (je glaçai(s); n. glaçons) **I.** (*a*) To freeze. **Cela me glace le sang,** it makes my blood run cold. (*b*) To ice (water, champagne). (*c*) To ice, frost (cake). **2.** To glaze (thread, pastry, etc.); to surface (paper). *Phot : G. une épreuve,* to glaze, gloss, a print. **3.** *Dressm :* To tack in (lining). *s.m.* **-çage.**

se glacer, to freeze. *Sens glacés d'effroi,* senses numbed with terror.

glacé, *a.* **I.** (*a*) Frozen (river, etc.). (*b*) Chilled, icy, cold. **J'ai les pieds glacés,** my feet are as cold as ice. **Glacé jusqu'aux os,** chilled to the bone. *Politesse glacée,* frigid, icy, politeness. (*c*) Iced (coffee, etc.). **2.** Glazed, glossy. *Gants glacés,* glacé-kid gloves. *Soie glacée,* watered silk. *Phot. Épreuve glacée,* glossy print.

glaciaire [glasjɛːr], *a. Geol :* Glacial (erosion); glacier (mud). **La période glaciaire,** the ice-age.

glacial, -als [glasjal]. **I.** *a.* Icy (temperature); frosty (air). **La Zone glaciale,** the Frigid Zone. *Politesse glaciale,* icy, frigid, politeness. **2.** *s.f. Bot :* **Glaciale,** ice-plant.

glacier¹ [glasje], *s.m. Geol :* Glacier.

glacier², *s.m.* **I.** Ice-cream man. **2.** Maker of mirrors.

glacière [glasjɛːr], *s.f.* **I.** Ice-house. **2.** Ice-box, -safe, -chest.

glacis [glasi], *s.m.* **I.** Slope, bank (in garden). *Fort :* Glacis. **2.** *Art :* Scumble, glaze. **3.** *Dressm :* Tacking.

glaçon [glasõ], *s.m.* (*a*) Block of ice; floe. *bl.* Drift-ice. (*b*) Icicle.

glaçure [glasyːr], *s.f. Cer :* Glaze, glazing.

gladiateur [gladjatœːr], *s.m.* Gladiator.

glaïeul [glajœl], *s.m. Bot :* Gladiolus, sword-lily. *G. des marais,* sword-flag.

glaire [glɛːr], *s.f.* **I.** (*a*) White of egg; glair. (*b*) Mucus, phlegm. **2.** Flaw (in diamond).

glaireux, -euse [glɛrø, -øːz], *a.* (*a*) Glaireous, glairy. (*b*) (Throat) full of phlegm.

glaise [glɛːz], *s.f.* Clay, loam. **Terre glaise,** (i) clay; (ii) potter's clay.

glais|er [glɛze], *v.tr.* **I.** To clay; to dress (soil) with clay. **2.** To line (sth.) with clay; to loam. *Hyd.E :* To puddle, pug (reservoir). *s.m.* **-age.**

glaiseux, -euse [glɛzø, -øːz], *a.* Clayey, loamy.

glaisière [glɛzjɛːr], *s.f.* Clay-pit.

glaive [glɛːv], *s.m. Lit :* Sword, blade.

gland [glã], *s.m.* **I.** (*a*) Acorn. (*b*) *pl.* Mast. **2.** Tassel. *Orné de glands,* tasselled. **3.** *Mch : G. de presse-étoupe,* stuffing-gland.

glande [glãːd], *s.f.* Gland. *F :* **Avoir des glandes au cou,** to have swollen glands.

glandée [glãde], *s.f.* Acorn-crop; mast, pannage.

glandiforme [glãdiform], *a.* Glandiform. **I.** Acorn-shaped. **2.** Gland-like.

glane [glan], *s.f.* **I.** Gleaning. **2.** Rope (of onions); cluster (of pears).

glan|er [glane], *v.tr.* To glean. *s.m.* **-age.** *s.* **-eur, -euse.**

glanure [glanyːr], *s.f.* Gleaning(s).

glap|ir [glapiːr], *v.i.* To yelp, yap; (of fox) to bark. *s.m.* **-issement.**

glas [glã], *s.m.* (*a*) Knell. **Sonner le glas,** to toll the passing-bell. *Sonner le g. de . . .,* to ring the knell of. . . . (*b*) Salvo of guns (at military or State funeral).

glauque [gloːk], *a.* Glaucous; sea-green.

glèbe [glɛb], *s.f.* **I.** Clod (of earth); sod. **2.** *Lit :* Soil, land (under cultivation); glebe.

glène¹ [glɛn], *s.f. Anat :* Glene, socket.

glène², *s.f. Nau :* Coil (of rope).

glissade [glisad], *s.f.* **I.** Slip. *Av :* **Glissade sur l'aile,** side-slip. **Glissade sur la queue,** tail-dive. *Geol :* **Glissade de terre,** landslip, land-slide. **2.** (*a*) Sliding. **Faire une glissade,** to have a slide. (*b*) *Mus :* (i) Portamento; (ii) rapid scale passage. **3.** Slide (on snow or ice).

glissant [glisã], *a.* **I.** Slippery. **Il fait glissant,** it is slippery walking. **2.** Sliding. **Porte glissante,** sliding door. *El : Contact g.,* slider.

glissement [glismã], *s.m.* **I.** (*a*) Sliding, slipping; slip. (*b*) Gliding; glide. **2.** Landslip, land-slide.

glisser [glise]. I. *v.i.* **I.** (*a*) To slip. (*b*) (Of wheel) To skid. *Av :* **Glisser sur l'aile,** to side-slip. **2.** To slide (on ice, etc.). **Se laisser glisser le long d'une corde,** to slide down a rope. **3.** To glide (over the water, etc.). **4.** (*a*) *L'épée lui glissa sur les côtes,* the sword glanced off his ribs. (*b*) **Glissons là-dessus!** we will not dwell on that; let that pass. II. **glisser,** *v.tr. G. qch. dans la poche de qn,* to slip sth. into s.o.'s pocket. *G. un mot dans l'oreille à qn,* to whisper, drop, a word in s.o.'s ear.

se glisser, to glide, creep, steal (*dans,* into).

glisseur, -euse [glisœːr, -øːz], *s.* **I.** Slider. **Bateau glisseur,** hydroplane boat; *F :* speed-boat. **2.** *s.m. Av :* Glider.

glissière [glisjɛːr], *s.f.* **I.** Groove, slide. **Porte à glissières,** sliding-door. **2.** *Mch :* Slide-bar. *Artil :* Recoil-slide. **3.** Shoot (for coal etc.).

glissoir [gliswɑːr], *s.m.* **I.** *Mch :* Slide; sliding block. *For :* Timber-slide.

glissoire [gliswaːr], *s.f.* Slide (on ice or snow),

global, -aux [glɔbal, -o], *a.* Total, aggregate, inclusive (sum) ; lump (payment).

globalement [glɔbalmã], *adv.* In the aggregate.

globe [glɔb], *s.m.* **I.** (*a*) Globe, sphere. **Faire le tour du globe,** to go round the globe, round the earth. *Le g. du soleil,* the orb of the sun. (*b*) Orb (of regalia). **2.** *G. de lampe,* lamp-globe. *G. électrique,* electric-light globe **3. Globe de l'œil,** eyeball ; globe of the eye. **4.** *Meteor :* **Globe de feu,** fire-ball.

globulaire [glɔbylɛ:r], *a.* Globular.

globule [glɔbyl], *s.m.* Globule.

globuleux, -euse [glɔbylø, -ø:z], *a.* Globular ; globulous.

gloire [glwa:r], *s.f.* **I.** Glory. *G. à Dieu!* glory be to God! *F :* **Travailler pour la gloire,** to work for nothing. **Parti pour la gloire,** slightly fuddled. **2.** Boast, pride ; vainglory. **Se faire gloire de qch.,** to glory in sth. **Mettre sa gloire à, en, qch.,** to boast of, glory in, sth. **3.** Glory, halo, nimbus.

glomérule [glɔmeryl], *s.m.* Glomerule, tuft.

gloria [glɔrja], *s.m. F :* Coffee served with spirits.

gloriette [glɔrjɛt], *s.f.* Summer-house, arbour.

glorieu|x, -euse [glɔrjø, -ø:z], *a.* **I.** Glorious. **Les glorieux, the saints in glory. 2.** Vainglorious, proud. *G. de qch.,* vain of, conceited about, sth. **3.** *s.m.* Boaster, braggart. **Faire le glorieux,** to brag, to swagger. *adv.* **-sement.**

glorification [glɔrifikasjɔ̃], *s.f.* Glorification.

glorifier [glɔrifje], *v.tr.* To praise, glorify ; to crown with glory.

se glorifier, to boast. *Se g. de qch., de faire qch.,* to glory in sth., in doing sth. ; to boast of sth., of doing sth.

gloriole [glɔrjɔl], *s.f.* Notoriety, vainglory. **Pour la gloriole,** for the sake of kudos ; *F :* for swank. **Faire de la gloriole,** to talk big.

glose [glo:z], *s.f.* **I.** Gloss, commentary ; (marginal) note. **2.** Comment, criticism. *La vérité sans glose,* the truth and nothing but the truth.

gloser [gloze]. **I.** *v.tr.* To gloss, expound (text). **2.** *v.i.* **Gloser de, sur, qch.,** to find fault with sth. ; to carp at sth.

glossaire [glɔsɛ:r], *s.m.* Glossary, dictionary.

glotte [glɔt], *s.f. Anat :* Glottis. *Ling :* **Coup de glotte,** glottal stop.

glouglou [gluglu], *s.m.* **I.** Glug-glug, gurgle, bubbling. **Faire glouglou,** to gurgle, to bubble. **2.** Gobble-gobble (of turkey) ; coo (of pigeon).

glouglouter [gluglute], *v.i.* **I.** (Of liquid) To gurgle, bubble. **2.** (Of turkey) To gobble.

glouss|er [gluse], *v.i.* (Of hen) To cluck ; (of turkey) to gobble ; (of pers.) to chuckle, to gurgle ; *F :* to chortle. *s.m.* **-ement.**

glouteron [glutrɔ̃], *s.m. Bot :* **I.** Burdock, burr. **2.** Bedstraw.

glout|on, -onne [glutɔ̃, -ɔn]. **I.** *a.* Greedy, gluttonous. **2.** *s.* (*a*) Glutton, gormandizer. (*b*) *s.m. Z :* Glutton, wolverine. *adv.* **-onnement.**

gloutonnerie [glutɔnri], *s.f.* Gluttony.

gloxinie [glɔksini], *s.f. Bot :* Gloxinia.

glu [gly], *s.f.* (*a*) Bird-lime. *F :* **Être pris à la glu,** to be inveigled, caught in the trap. **Il a de la glu aux mains,** money sticks to his fingers. (*b*) **Glu marine,** marine glue.

gluant [glyã], *a.* Sticky, gummy, gluey.

gluau, -aux [glyo], *s.m.* Lime-twig, snare.

glucose [glyko:z], *s.f.; in Ch :* usu. *s.m.* Glucose, grape-sugar.

gluer [glye], *v.tr.* To lime (twigs). *F :* **Cela vous glue les mains,** it makes one's fingers sticky.

glume [glym], *s.f.* (*a*) *Bot :* Glume. (*b*) Chaff.

gluten [glytɛn], *s.m.* Gluten.

glutineux, -euse [glytinø, -ø:z], *a.* Glutinous.

glutinosité [glytinozite], *s.f.* Glutinosity.

glycérine [gliserin], *s.f.* Glycerin(e).

glycériner [gliserine], *v.tr.* To rub (sth.) over, treat (sth.), with glycerin(e).

glycine [glisin], *s.f.* **I.** *Bot :* Wistaria. **2.** *Phot :* Glycin(e).

glyphe [glif], *s.m. Arch :* Glyph, groove, channel.

gnan-gnan [ɲɑ̃ɲɑ̃]. **I.** *a.inv. F :* Languid, lackadaisical, peevish. **2.** *s.* Peevish person.

gneiss [gnɛs], *s.m. Geol :* Gneiss.

gniaf [ɲaf], *s.m. P :* **I.** Cobbler. **2.** (*a*) Bad workman ; bungler. (*b*) Dirty scoundrel.

gniole [ɲo:l], **gnole** [ɲɔl], **gnôle** [no:l], *s.f. Mil : P :* Rum, brandy.

gnome [gno:m], *s.m.* Gnome.

gnomon [gnomɔ̃], *s.m.* **I.** Gnomon. **2.** Sun-dial.

gnon [ɲɔ̃], *s.m. P :* Blow, biff, punch.

gnou [gnu], *s.m. Z :* Gnu, wildebeest.

go [go]. Used in the *adv.phr.* **Tout de go. I.** Easily ; without a hitch. *Avaler qch. tout de go,* to swallow sth. at a gulp. **2.** Without ceremony ; all of a sudden.

gob(b)e [gɔb], *s.f.* Ball, bolus. (*a*) Poison-ball (for destroying animals). (*b*) Food-ball (for fattening poultry).

gobelet [gɔblɛ], *s.m.* Goblet, cup. **Verre gobelet,** tumbler. **Joueur de gobelets,** thimble-rigger. **Tour de gobelet,** conjuring trick.

gobeleterie [gɔbletri], *s.f.* Hollow-glass trade or ware.

gobelin [gɔblɛ̃], *s.m.* Goblin, hobgoblin, imp.

Gobelins (les) [legɔblɛ̃]. *Pr.n.m.pl.* The State factory of Gobelin tapestry (in Paris).

gobe-mouches [gɔbmuʃ], *s.m.inv.* **I.** *Orn :* Fly-catcher. **2.** *Bot :* Fly-trap. **3.** *P :* Gaper, simpleton.

gober [gɔbe], *v.tr.* (*a*) To swallow, gulp down (oyster, etc.). **Gober l'appât, le morceau, la mouche,** to swallow the bait. *F :* **Gober des mouches,** to stand gaping. *Il gobe tout ce qu'on lui dit,* he takes it all in. (*b*) *F :* To have a strong liking for (s.o.) ; to think no end of (s.o.).

se gober, *F :* to be self-conceited ; *F :* to think a lot of oneself ; to fancy oneself.

goberger (se) [sɔgɔbɛrʒe], *v.pr.* (je me gobergeai(s) ; n.n. gobergeons) To feast, guzzle.

gobet|er [gɔbte], *v.tr.* (je gobette ; je gobetterai) *Const :* **I.** To rough-cast. **2.** To render (with plaster). **3.** To stop (cracks) ; to point (wall, etc.). *s.m.* **-age.**

gobetis [gɔbti], *s.m. Const :* **I.** Rough-cast. **2.** Rendering, roughing-in coat (of plaster).

gobeur, -euse [gɔbœ:r, -ø:z], *s. F :* Simpleton, gull. *a. Il est très g.,* he is easily taken in. [GOBER]

gobie [gɔbi], *s.m. Ich :* Goby.

godaille [gɔda:j], *s.f. P :* Feast, revel, guzzle.

godailler [gɔdaje], *v.i. P :* (*a*) To go pub-crawling. (*b*) To gormandize, feast.

godailleur [gɔdajœ:r], *s.m. P :* **I.** Pub-crawler. **2.** Great guzzler.

godasses [gɔdas], *s.f.pl. Mil : P :* Boots.

Godefroi [gɔdfrwa]. *Pr.n.m.* Godfrey.

godelureau [gɔdlyro], *s.m. F :* Countrified young gallant ; Tony Lumpkin.

god|er [gɔde], *v.i.* (Of cloth) To pucker, to ruck (up) ; (of paper) to cockle. (Of trousers) *G. aux genoux,* to bag at the knees. *s.m.* **-age.**

godet [gɔdɛ], *s.m.* **I.** (*a*) (Wooden) bowl, (drinking-)cup, mug. (*b*) *G. à couleur,* saucer for mixing water colours ; pan (of moist colour). *G. à huile,* waste-oil cup (of lamp, machine) ; drip receiver. (*c*) Socket (for foot of machine, etc.). *Mil :* Bucket (for butt of lance, etc.). (*d*) (Noria) scoop ; bucket (of dredger, excavator, water-wheel). **Roue à godets,** overshot wheel. (*e*) *Bot :* Cup (of acorn).

2. (a) Pucker, ruck (in cloth). (b) *Dressm:* Flare, gore. **A godets,** flared, fluted.

godiche [gɔdiʃ], **godichon, -onne** [gɔdiʃɔ̃, -ɔn]. *F:* **1.** *a.* Awkward, lumpish, simple. **2.** *s.* (a) Simpleton. (b) Lout, bumpkin.

godille [gɔdiːj], *s.f.* **1.** Stern-oar; scull. **Aller à la godille,** to (single-)scull. **2.** *pl.* Pair of sculls.

godill|er [gɔdije], *v.i.* To (single-)scull, to single. *s.m.* **-eur.**

godillot [gɔdijo], *s.m. F:* Hobnailed boot.

godiveau [gɔdivo], *s.m. Cu:* **1.** Force-meat. **2.** Force-meat ball. **3.** Pasty, pie.

godron [gɔdrɔ̃], *s.m.* **1.** *Arch:* Gadroon, godroon. **2.** (a) Pleat, goffer; *pl.* fluting (of coif, etc.). (b) Goffering-iron.

godronner [gɔdrɔne], *v.tr.* **1.** To goffer, flute (coif, etc.). **2.** To mill (head of screw, etc.).

goéland [gɔelɑ̃, gwa-], *s.m. Orn:* (Sea-)gull.

goélette [gɔelɛt, gwa-], *s.f.* Schooner. *G. franche,* fore-and-aft schooner. *G. carrée,* topsail schooner.

goémon [gɔemɔ̃, gwe-], *s.m.* Seaweed.

gogo¹ (à) [agogo], *adv.phr. F:* In abundance.

gogo², *s.m. P:* Juggins, gull.

goguenard [gɔgnaːr], *a.* Mocking, bantering. *D'un ton g.,* banteringly, jeeringly.

goguenarder [gɔgnarde], *v.i.* To banter, chaff.

gogueneau [gɔgno], **goguenot** [gɔgno], *s.m.* **1.** (Algerian troops') camp-kettle. **2.** *pl. P:* Latrines.

goguette [gɔgɛt], *s.f. A:* Jollity. *F:* **Faire goguette, être en goguette(s),** to be on the spree. **Conter des goguettes,** to tell smoking-room stories.

goinfre [gwɛ̃ːfr], *s.m. F:* Guzzler.

goinfrer [gwɛ̃fre], *v.i. F:* To guzzle, gorge.

goinfrerie [gwɛ̃frəri], *s.f.* Gluttony, guzzling.

goitre [gwaːtr], *s.m.* Goitre; *F:* wen.

goitreux, -euse [gwatrø, -øːz], *a.* Goitrous.

golf [gɔlf], *s.m.* Golf. **Terrain de golf,** *F:* un golf, golf-links. *En tenue de g.,* in plus-fours.

golfe [gɔlf], *s.m.* Gulf, bay. **Le Courant du Golfe,** the Gulf-Stream. S.a. GASCOGNE.

gomme [gɔm], *s.f.* **1.** (a) Gum. *G. arabique,* gum-acacia, gum-arabic. **Gomme laque,** shellac. (b) Boule de gomme, jujube, gum. **2.** *G. élastique, à crayon, à effacer,* (india-)rubber; eraser. **3.** *F: A:* **La (haute) gomme,** the smart set, the swells. **Faire de la gomme,** to swank.

gomme-gutte, *s.f.* Gamboge.

gommelaquer [gɔmlake], *v.tr.* To shellac.

gomm|er [gɔme], *v.tr.* **1.** To gum. S.a. TAFFETAS. **2.** To erase, rub out. **3.** *v.i.* To stick, jam. *Piston gommé,* gummed piston. *s.m.* **-age.**

gomme-résine, *s.f.* Gum resin.

gommeux, -euse [gɔmø, -øːz], **1.** *a.* Gummy, sticky. **2.** *s.m. F: A:* Swell, toff.

gommier [gɔmje], *s.m. Bot:* Gum-tree.

gonade [gɔnad], *s.f. Biol:* Gonad.

gond [gɔ̃], *s.m.* Hinge-pin (of door). **Mettre une porte sur ses gonds,** to hang a door. *F:* **Sortir (hors) de ses gonds,** to lose one's temper; *P:* to fly off the handle.

gondolant [gɔ̃dɔlɑ̃], *a. F:* Excruciatingly funny.

gondole [gɔ̃dɔl], *s.f.* Gondola.

gondol|er [gɔ̃dɔle], *v.i.* (Of wood) To warp; (of paper) to cockle; (of sheet iron) to buckle. *s.m.* **-age.** *s.m.* **-ement.** **se gondoler. 1.** = GONDOLER. **2.** *P:* To shake with laughter.

gondolier [gɔ̃dɔlje], *s.m.* Gondolier.

gonfalon [gɔ̃falɔ̃], *s.m. A:* Gonfalon, banner, streamer.

gonflage [gɔ̃flaːʒ], *s.m. Aut: etc:* Inflation. **Tableau de gonflages,** table of tyre pressures.

gonflement [gɔ̃fləmɑ̃], *s.m.* Inflating, inflation (of tyres, balloon); distension (of stomach).

gonfler [gɔ̃fle]. **1.** *v.tr.* (a) To inflate, distend; to blow up, pump up (tyre); to puff out, blow out, bulge (one's cheeks); to puff (rice). (b) To swell. *Torrent gonflé par les pluies,* torrent swollen by the rains. **2.** *v.i. & pr.* To become inflated; (of stomach) to become distended.

gonfleur [gɔ̃flœːr], *s.m. Aut:* Inflator; air-pump.

gong [gɔ̃g], *s.m.* Gong.

goniomètre [gɔnjɔmɛtr], *s.m.* Goniometer; angle gauge. *Artil:* Dial-sight.

gonne [gɔn], *s.f.* Barrel, drum (for tar, etc.).

gonze [gɔ̃ːz], *s.m. P:* Man, bloke, cove.

gonzesse [gɔ̃zɛs], *s.f. P:* Woman.

gord [gɔːr], *s.m. Fish:* Kiddle, stake-net.

gordien [gɔrdjɛ̃], *a.* Gordian (knot).

gorenflot [gɔrɑ̃flo], *s.m. Cu:* Sponge-cake soaked in rum or kirsch.

goret [gɔrɛ], *s.m.* **1.** Little pig; porker; piglet. **2.** *F:* (a) Dirty little urchin. (b) Dirty pig of a man. **3.** *Nau:* Scrub-broom; hog.

goret|er [gɔrte], *v.tr.* (je gorette; je goretterai) *Nau:* To hog down (hull). *s.m.* **-age.**

gorge [gɔrʒ], *s.f.* **1.** (a) Throat, neck. **Couper la gorge à qn,** to cut s.o.'s throat. *F:* **Je le tiens à la gorge,** I have a strangelhold on him. S.a. COUTEAU. (b) Bosom, bust (of woman). *G. d'un pigeon,* pigeon's breast. **2.** Throat, gullet. **Avoir mal à la gorge,** to have a sore throat. **Avoir la gorge serrée,** to have a lump in one's throat. **Crier à pleine gorge,** to shout at the top of one's voice. **Avaler qch. à pleine gorge,** to gulp sth. down. **Rire à gorge déployée,** to laugh heartily. **Rire sous gorge,** to chuckle. **3.** *Ven:* Gorge. **Rendre gorge,** (i) to bring up food, to vomit; (ii) *F:* to disgorge, make restitution. **Gorge chaude,** tit-bit from prey given to hawk. *F:* **Faire des gorges chaudes de qch.,** to gloat over sth. **4.** Gorge, pass, defile. **5.** Groove. *Arch:* Moulure à gorge, grooved moulding.

gorge-de-pigeon, *a.inv.* Dove-coloured shot (silk, etc.).

gorgée [gɔrʒe], *s.f.* Mouthful, draught (of wine, etc.); gulp. *Petite g.,* sip.

gorger [gɔrʒe], *v.tr.* (je gorgeai(s); n. gorgeons) To stuff, gorge. *Husb:* To cram (fowls).

gorgerette [gɔrʒərɛt], *s.f.* **1.** *A:* Front, gorget (for lady's dress). **2.** *Orn:* Blackcap.

Gorgone [gɔrgɔn], *s.f. Myth:* Gorgon.

gorille [gɔriːj], *s.m. Z:* Gorilla.

gosier [gozje], *s.m.* Throat; (i) gullet, (ii) windpipe. **Rire à plein gosier,** to laugh heartily.

gosse [gɔs], *s.m. & f. P:* Youngster, kid; *P: m.* nipper; *f.* flapper.

gothique [gɔtik]. **1.** *a.* Gothic. **2.** *s.m. Arch: Ling:* Gothic. **3.** *s.f. Typ:* Black letter.

goton [gɔtɔ̃], *s.f.* **1.** *F:* Country wench. **2.** *P:* Trollop.

gouache [gwaʃ], *s.f. Art:* Body-colour, gouache. **Peindre à la gouache,** to paint in *gouache.*

gouailler [gwaje], *v.tr.* To banter, chaff (s.o.).

gouaillerie [gwajri], *s.f.* Banter, chaff.

gouailleur, -euse [gwajœːr, -øːz]. **1.** *a.* Waggish (humour); bantering (tone). **2.** *s.* Banterer.

gouape [gwap], *s.f. P:* **1.** *Coll.* Riff-raff, blackguards. **2.** Blackguard, bad lot.

gouaper [gwape], *v.i. F:* To loaf; to live a disreputable life.

goudron [gudrɔ̃], *s.m.* Tar. *G. de gaz, de houille,* coal-tar. *G. de bois,* wood-tar. *G. à calfater,* (navy) pitch. *Med:* Eau de goudron, tar-water.

goudronn|er [gudrɔne], *v.tr.* **1.** To tar. *Nau:*

To pay. **Toile goudronnée,** tarpaulin. **Papier goudronné,** tar-lined paper. **2.** *Huile goudronnée,* gummed oil. *s.m.* **-age.**

goudronnerie [gudrɔnri], *s.f.* **1.** Tar-works. **2.** Tar-shed.

goudronneux, -euse [gudrɔnø, -ø:z], *a.* (*a*) Tarry. (*b*) Gummy (oil).

gouet [gwɛ], *s.m.* **1.** Bill-hook. **2.** *Bot:* Wild arum ; lords and ladies.

gouffre [gufr], *s.m.* (*a*) Gulf, pit, abyss. *G. béant,* yawning chasm. (*b*) Whirlpool, vortex.

gouge [gu:ʒ], *s.f. Tls:* Gouge ; hollow chisel.

gouger [guʒe], *v.tr.* (je gougeai(s) ; n. gougeons) To gouge ; to scoop out..

goujat [guʒa], *s.m.* **1.** Farm-hand. *G. de maçon,* hodman. **2.** Boor, churl, cad.

goujaterie [guʒatri], *s.f.* **1.** Caddishness. **2.** Caddish action.

goujon[1] [guʒɔ̃], *s.m. Ich:* Gudgeon. *F:* Avaler le goujon, to swallow the bait.

goujon[2], *s.m.* **1.** (*a*) Gudgeon, joggle (in stonework). (*b*) Projecting stud ; *Carp:* tenon. **2.** (*a*) *Carp:* Coak. *G. perdu,* dowel. (*b*) *G. de jonction,* assembling pin. *G. de charnière,* pin, pintle, of a hinge.

goujonner [guʒɔne], *v.tr. Carp:* (*a*) To dowel. (*b*) To joggle. (*c*) To pin, to bolt.

goule [gul], *s.f.* Ghoul.

goulée [gule], *s.f. A. & F:* Big mouthful ; gulp.

goulet [gulɛ], *s.m.* Narrow part, neck (of object) ; gully (in mountains). *Nau:* Gut, bottle-neck, narrows (of harbour). **Le Goulet de Brest,** the Brest Channel.

goulot [gulo], *s.m.* **1.** Neck (of bottle). **2.** *P:* Gullet, mouth.

goul|u, -ue [guly]. **1.** *a.* Greedy, gluttonous. **2.** *s.* Glutton. *adv.* **-ûment.**

goum [gum], *s.m.* **1.** Tribe, family (among the Arabs). **2.** *Mil:* Arab (Algerian) contingent.

goupil [gupi], *s.m. A:* (Reynard the) Fox.

goupille [gupi:j], *s.f.* (Linch)pin ; gudgeon. *G. fendue,* split pin ; cotter. *G. d'arrêt,* stop-bolt.

goupiller [gupije], *v.tr. Tchn:* To pin, key.

goupillon [gupijɔ̃], *s.m. Ecc:* Aspergillum, sprinkler (for holy water). **2.** Brush (for gum, lamp, bottle).

gourbi(l) [gurbi], *s.m.* (Arab) hut ; shack.

gourd [gu:r], *a.* Numb(ed), benumbed ; stiff, swollen (with cold).

gourde [gurd], *s.f.* **1.** (*a*) *Bot:* Gourd. (*b*) *P:* Fool, fat-head. **2.** Calabash, water-bottle ; flask (of brandy, etc.).

gourdin [gurdɛ̃], *s.m.* Club, cudgel, bludgeon.

gourer [gure], *v.tr. P:* **1.** To adulterate, doctor (drugs). **2.** To cheat, trick.

se gourer, to be mistaken.

gourgandine [gurgɑ̃din], *s.f.* **1.** *A:* Trollop, trull. **2.** Venus shell ; *Com:* cockle.

gourgane [gurgan], *s.f. F:* Horse-bean. *pl. Nau:* Dried beans.

gourganier [gurganje], *s.m. P:* Old sailor, old salt, old shellback. [GOURGANE]

gourmade [gurmad], *s.f. F:* Slap, cuff.

gourmand, -ande [gurmɑ̃, -ɑ̃:d]. **1.** *a.* (*a*) Greedy. **Herbes gourmandes,** parasitical weeds. (*b*) Fond of sweet things. **2.** *s.* (*a*) Gourmand, glutton. (*b*) Epicure. **3.** *s.m. Hort:* Sucker.

gourmander [gurmɑ̃de]. **1.** *v.i.* To guzzle. **2.** *v.tr.* (*a*) To rebuke, chide. (*b*) To treat roughly ; to saw (horse's mouth).

gourmandise [gurmɑ̃di:z], *s.f.* **1.** Greediness, gluttony. **2.** *pl.* Sweetmeats, dainties.

gourme [gurm], *s.f.* **1.** *Med:* (*a*) Impetigo. (*b*) Teething rash. **2.** *Vet:* Strangles. **Jeter sa**

gourme, (i) (of horse) to run at the nose ; (ii) *F:* (of pers.) to sow one's wild oats ; (iii) *F:* (of pers.) to blow off steam, to get over one's temper.

gourmé [gurme], *a.* Stiff, starched, stuck-up.

gourmet [gurmɛ], *s.m.* Gourmet, epicure.

gourmette [gurmɛt], *s.f.* **1.** *Harn:* Curb(-chain). *F:* **Lâcher la gourmette à qn,** to give s.o. a free hand. **2.** (*a*) Curb watch-chain. (*b*) Curb-bracelet.

gournable [gurnabl], *s.f. N.Arch:* Treenail.

goussant [gusɑ̃], **goussaut** [guso], *a. & s.m.* Thick-set, stocky (horse, *F:* person).

gousse [gus], *s.f.* Pod, shell, husk (of peas, etc.). *G. d'ail,* clove of garlic.

gousset [gusɛ], *s.m.* **1.** Arm-pit. **2.** *Cost:* (*a*) Gusset. (*b*) Fob (pocket) or waistcoat pocket. **3.** (Shoulder-)bracket, stay-plate.

goût [gu], *s.m.* **1.** (Sense of) taste. **Avoir le goût fin,** to have a fine palate. **2.** Flavour, taste ; bouquet (of wine). *G. de terroir,* native tang. **Sans goût,** tasteless(ly). **Plat de haut goût,** highly seasoned dish. *F: Contes de haut g.,* spicy stories. **3.** (Pleasure, preference) *On ajoute du sucre et du citron selon son g.,* you add sugar and lemon to taste. *Le g. du jour,* the reigning fashion. **Avoir du goût pour,** le **goût de, qch.,** to have a taste for sth. **Prendre goût à qch.,** to develop a taste for sth. **Chacun** (à) **son goût,** *Prov:* il ne faut pas disputer des **goûts,** everyone to his taste ; there is no accounting for tastes. **Faire qch. par goût,** to do sth. from inclination. **Affaire de goût,** matter of taste. **4.** (Discernment, right judgment) *Toilette d'u' g. parfait,* dress in perfect taste. **Les gens (** *)* **goût,** people of taste. **C'est de mauvais goût,** it is bad form, in bad taste. **5.** Style, manner. *Plat dans le g. de Watteau,* painted in the Watteau manner. *Quelque chose dans ce g.-là,* something of that sort, in that style.

goûter [gute]. **I.** *v.tr.* **1.** To taste (food). **2.** To enjoy, appreciate, relish. *G. la musique,* to enjoy music. **3.** **Goûter à qch.,** to taste sth. (critically) ; to take a little of sth. **4.** *Abs.* (*a*) To take a snack (between meals). (*b*) To picnic. **II. goûter, goûté,** *s.m.* (Afternoon) snack.

goutte [gut], *s.f.* **1.** Drop (of liquid). **Goutte à goutte,** drop by drop. (Of liquid) **Tomber goutte à goutte,** to drip. *F:* **C'est une goutte d'eau dans la mer,** it is a drop in the ocean. **2.** Spot, splash (of colour) ; speck ; fleck. **3.** *F:* (*a*) Small quantity ; sip, sup. *Prendre une g. de bouillon,* to take just a mouthful of soup. (*b*) Nip, drop (of brandy, etc.). **Il aime la goutte,** he likes a dram. **Boire la goutte,** to tipple, to nip. *F:* **Il a bu une goutte,** (i) he was nearly drowned ; (ii) he had a heavy loss ; (iii) (of actor) he got hissed, *F:* got the bird. **4.** *Adv.phr. F:* **Ne . . . goutte,** not at all (thus used to-day only with *comprendre, entendre, voir*). **Je n'y vois goutte,** (i) I can't see at all here ;' (ii) I can make nothing at all of it. *On n'y voyait g.,* it was pitch-dark. **5.** *Med:* Gout.

goutte-de-suif, *s.f. El.E:* Stud, contact-point (of switch-board). *pl. Des gouttes-de-suif.*

gouttelette [gutlɛt], *s.f.* Droplet, globule.

goutteux, -euse [gutø, -ø:z], *a.* Gouty.

gouttière [gutjɛ:r], *s.f.* **1.** *Const:* (*a*) (Roof-)gutter, (rain-water) guttering. (*b*) *pl.* Eaves (of roof). **2.** Spout, rain-pipe. **3.** Groove (of bone sword). **4.** *Surg:* Cradle ; (cradle-like) splint **5.** Fore-edge (of book).

gouvernail [guverna:j], *s.m.* (*a*) *Nau:* Rudder, helm. **Monter, démonter, le gouvernail,** to ship

unship, the rudder. **Roue du gouvernail**, (steering-)wheel. **Tenir le gouvernail**, to be at the wheel, at the helm ; to steer. (*b*) *Av* : *G. vertical, de direction*, vertical rudder. *G. d'altitude, de profondeur*, horizontal rudder ; elevator.

gouvernante [guvɛrnɑ̃:t], *s.f.* **1.** Housekeeper (of bachelor, priest). **2.** *A* : Governess.

gouverne [guvɛrn], *s.f.* **1.** Guidance, direction. **Pour votre gouverne**, for your guidance. **2.** *pl. Av* : Rudders and ailerons ; controls.

gouvernement [guvɛrnəmɑ̃], *s.m.* **1.** (*a*) Government, management. *G. monarchique*, monarchical government. (*b*) Governorship. (*c*) Steering, handling (of boat). **2.** (The) Government, (the) Cabinet.

gouvernemental, -aux [guvɛrnəmɑ̃tal, -o], *a.* Governmental.

gouvern|er [guvɛrne], *v.tr.* **1.** *Nau* : To steer, handle (ship). **Gouvernez droit!** steady ! **2.** To govern, rule, control, direct. *Dieu gouverne l'univers*, God is the ruler of the universe. *Mouvement gouverné par un pendule*, movement regulated, controlled, by a pendulum. **3.** (*a*) To manage, administer. (*b*) To govern (country). **4.** *Gram* : *Verbe qui gouverne l'accusatif*, verb that governs, takes, the accusative. **5.** *v.i. Nau* : *Navire qui ne gouverne plus*, ship that no longer answers to the helm. *a.* **-able**.

gouverneur [guvɛrnœ:r], *s.m.* Governor (of province, bank, etc.) ; commanding officer (of fortified position). **Gouverneur général**, governor-general.

goyave [gwaja:v], *s.f. Bot* : Guava (fruit).

grabat [graba], *s.m.* Mean bed, litter (of straw, etc.) ; pallet. *F* : *Mourir sur un grabat*, to die in abject poverty.

grabuge [graby:ʒ], *s.m. F* : Squabbling, row. *Il y aura du g.*, there'll be ructions.

grâce [grɑ:s], *s.f.* **1.** Grace, gracefulness, charm. (*a*) **Avoir bonne grâce à faire qch.**, to do sth. in a becoming manner. **Danser avec grâce**, to dance gracefully. *F* : **Faire des grâces**, to attitudinize. (*b*) **De bonne grâce**, willingly, readily. **De mauvaise grâce**, unwillingly, ungraciously. (*c*) *Myth* : **Les trois Grâces**, the three Graces. **2.** Favour. **Trouver grâce devant qn, auprès de qn**, to find favour in s.o.'s eyes. **Se mettre dans, obtenir, les bonnes grâces de qn**, to get into favour with s.o. ; to get into s.o.'s good graces. **Rentrer en grâce**, to reingratiate oneself (*auprès de*, with). **De grâce!** for pity's sake ! **for goodness' sake! 3.** (*a*) (Act of) grace. **Faire une grâce à qn**, to do s.o. a favour, a kindness. *Demander une g. à qn*, to ask a favour of s.o. **Coup de grâce**, finishing stroke ; quietus. **C'est trop de grâces que vous me faites!** you really are too kind ! *Com* : **Jours, terme, de grâce**, days of grace. (*b*) *Theol* : **En état de grâce**, in a state of grace. **L'an de grâce 1802**, the year of grace 1802. *F* : **A la grâce de Dieu**, we must trust in God. **4.** (*a*) *Jur* : Free pardon. **Lettre(s) de grâce**, reprieve. **Faire grâce à qn**, to grant s.o. a free pardon. *F* : *Je vous fais g. cette fois-ci*, I will let you off this time. *S.a.* RECOURS. (*b*) **Demander grâce, crier grâce**, to cry for mercy. **Faire grâce de qch. à qn**, to spare s.o. sth. ; *F* : to let s.o. off sth. *Je vous fais g. du reste*, you needn't do, say, any more. **5.** Thanks. (*a*) *pl.* **Action de grâces**, thanksgiving. (*b*) *Prep.phr.* **Grâce à**, thanks to, owing to. *G. à vos soins*, thanks to your care.

graci|er [grasje], *v.tr.* To pardon, reprieve. *a.* **-able**.

gracieusement [grasjøzmɑ̃], *adv.* **1.** Gracefully. **2.** Graciously, kindly. **3.** Gratuitously.

gracieuseté [grasjøzte], *s.f.* **1.** Graciousness, affability. **2.** *Faire une g. à qn*, to do s.o. a kindness, a favour.

gracieux, -euse [grasjø, -ø:z], *a.* **1.** Graceful, pleasing (figure, style). **2.** (*a*) Gracious (manner, etc.). (*b*) **A titre gracieux**, as a favour ; gratis, free of charge. **3.** *Notre g. souverain*, our gracious Sovereign.

gracile [grasil], *a.* Slender ; gracile, slim.

gracilité [grasilite], *s.f.* Slenderness, slimness.

Gracques (les) [legrak]. *Pr.n.m.pl. Rom.Hist* : The Gracchi.

gradation [gradasjɔ̃], *s.f.* Gradation ; gradual process. *Avec une g. lente*, by slow degrees. **Par gradation**, gradually.

grade [grad], *s.m.* **1.** Rank, dignity, degree, grade. *Détenir un g.*, to hold a rank. **2.** (University) degree. **Prendre ses grades**, to take one's degree. **3.** (*a*) *Mil* : Rank. *G. honoraire*, brevet rank. **Monter en grade**, to be promoted. (*b*) *Navy* : Rating.

gradé [grade], *s.m.* **1.** *Mil* : Non-commissioned officer ; N.C.O. *Tous les gradés*, all ranks (commissioned and non-commissioned). **2.** *Navy* : Rated man.

gradin [gradɛ̃], *s.m.* **1.** Step, tier ; stepped row of seats. *F* : *Quand j'étais sur les gradins*, when I was at school. **2.** Poulie à gradins, cone-pulley, step-pulley. *El.E* : **Disposer les balais en gradins**, to stagger the brushes (of a dynamo).

graduation [gradɥasjɔ̃], *s.f. Ph* : **1.** Graduating (of scale). **2.** Graduation. **3.** Scale.

graduel, -elle [gradɥɛl]. **1.** *a.* Gradual, progressive. **2.** *s.m. Ecc* : Gradual.

graduellement [gradɥɛlmɑ̃], *adv.* Gradually ; by degrees.

graduer [gradɥe], *v.tr.* **1.** To graduate (thermometer, etc.). **2.** To grade (studies, etc.).

gradué, *a.* (*a*) Graduated. *Verre g.*, measuring glass ; graduated measure. (*b*) Graded, progressive (exercises, etc.).

graillement [grajmɑ̃], *s.m.* **1.** Huskiness (owing to phlegm). **2.** Hawk (of phlegm). **3.** Hoarse sound.

grailler [graje], *v.i.* **1.** To speak huskily. **2.** To hawk up phlegm.

graillon¹ [grajɔ̃], *s.m.* **Sentir le graillon**, to smell of burnt fat ; to taste greasy.

graillon², *s.m. F* : Clot of phlegm.

graillonn|er [grajɔne], *v.i. F* : To hawk up phlegm ; to hawk. *s.m.* **-ement**.

grain¹ [grɛ̃], *s.m.* **1.** (*a*) Grain. *G. de blé*, grain of wheat. *G. d'orge*, barleycorn. (*b*) Corn. *La récolte des grains*, the (corn-)harvest. **Poulet de grain**, plump (corn-fed) pullet. **2.** Berry, bean (of coffee). *G. de poivre*, peppercorn. *G. de raisin*, grape. *F* : **Grain de beauté**, beauty spot ; mole. **3.** Particle, atom ; grain (of salt, of sand) ; speck, particle (of dust). *G. de plomb*, pellet. *Metall* : *Cassure à grains*, granular fracture. *Pas un g. de bon sens*, not a grain, not an atom, of common sense. *F* : **Il a un grain**, he is not quite right in his head. **Avoir son grain**, to be slightly tipsy, fuddled. **4.** *Meas* : *A* : Grain (= 0.053 gramme). **5.** (*a*) Bead. (*b*) Bead-sight (of fire-arms). (*c*) *El* : **Grains platinés**, platinum points. **6.** Grain, texture (of substance). **Contre le grain**, against the grain.

grain², *s.m. Nau* : Squall ; gust of wind. **Temps à grains**, squally weather. *G. noir*, black squall. *S.a.* PARER² 1, 2, VEILLER 1.

grain-d'orge, *s.m. Tls* : Diamond-point chisel. **2.** *F* : Sty(e) (in the eye). *pl. Des grains-d'orge*.

graine [grɛn], s.f. **1.** Seed (of plants). *G. de lin*, linseed. **Monter en graine**, to run to seed· *F:* (of girl) to be getting on in years. *F: C'est une mauvaise graine*, he's a bad lot. **2.** *F:* **Graines de vers à soie**, silkworm eggs; graine.

grainer [grɛne], v.tr. **1.** To granulate, corn (metal, etc.). **2.** To grain (paper, leather).

graineterie [grɛntri], s.f. Seed-trade or -shop.

grainetier, -ière [grɛntje, -jɛːr], s. Seedsman, -woman; corn-chandler.

graissage [grɛsaːʒ], s.m. Greasing, oiling, lubrication. *G. par barbotage*, splash lubrication. *G. sous pression*, *g. forcé*, forced-feed lubrication. **Huile de graissage**, lubricating oil.

graisse [grɛːs], s.f. **1.** Grease, fat. *G. de rognon*, suet. *G. de rôti*, dripping. *G. de porc*, lard. *G. de baleine*, blubber. *F:* **Prendre de la graisse**, to put on fat. **Boniments à la graisse d'oie**, blarney, bluff. *G. pour essieux*, axle-grease. **2.** (Of wine) **Tourner à la graisse**, to get ropy.

graisser [grɛse], v.tr. **1.** To grease, oil, lubricate. *F:* **Graisser ses bottes**, to prepare (i) for a long journey, (ii) for the other world. **Graisser la patte à qn**, to oil, grease, s.o.'s palm. **2.** To soil with grease; to grease (one's clothes).

graisseur [grɛsœːr], s.m. **1.** (Pers.) Greaser, oiler. **2.** Lubricator, grease-cup. *Aut: G. à graisse*, grease-gun.

graisseux, -euse [grɛsø, -øːz], a. **1.** (a) Greasy, oily, unctuous. (b) Fatty, adipose (tissue). **2.** Ropy (wine).

graminé [gramine]. *Bot:* **1.** a. Gramineaceous. **2.** s.f.pl. Graminées, graminaceae.

grammaire [grammɛːr], s.f. Grammar. **Classes de grammaire**, lower forms (of secondary school).

grammairien, -ienne [grammɛrjɛ̃, -jɛn], s. Grammarian.

grammatical, -aux [grammatikal, -o], a. Grammatical. *S.a.* ANALYSE I. adv. **-ement**.

gramme [gram], s.m. *Meas:* Gram(me).

gramophone [gramɔfɔn], s.m. Gramophone.

grand, grande [grã, grãːd], a. **1.** (a) Tall (in stature); large, big (in size). *Homme g.*, tall man. *Un g. homme blond*, a tall, fair man. *Grands bras*, long arms. *Grands pieds*, big feet. *Grande distance*, great distance. S.a. AIR I. I, MER. (b) Chief, main. *G. amiral*, chief admiral. *G. chemin*, main road, highway, high road. *La Grande rue*, the High Street, the Main Street. *Nau: Le g. mât*, the mainmast. *La grande messe*, high mass. *G. ressort*, mainspring. (c) *Quand tu seras g.*, when you are grown up, when you are old enough. *Sch:* **Les grandes classes**, the upper forms. (d) adv. **Voir, faire, grand**, to see, do, things in a big way, on a large scale. *Porte(s) grande(s) ouverte(s)*, wide-open door(s). *Adv.phr.* **En grand**, (i) on a large scale; (ii) full size. *Se faire peindre en g.*, to have one's portrait painted life-size. **2.** (Of number, quantity) Large, many. *Pas g. monde*, not many people. *Le g. public*, the general public. **En grande partie**, largely, to a great extent, in a large measure. **3.** (Of worth, rank, fame) *Les grands hommes*, great men. *De grande naissance*, of noble birth. **Le grand monde**, (high) society. *Grands vins*, high-class wines. *Alexandre le Grand*, Alexander the Great. *Se donner de grands airs*, to give oneself airs of importance. *Une grande dame*, a great lady, a grand lady. *Le G. Hôtel de Brighton*, the Brighton Grand (Hotel). *s.m.* **Donner dans le grand**, to be fond of display. **4.** *Grandes pensées*, great, noble, thoughts. *La grande manière*, the grand

manner. **5.** *Grande différence*, wide, great, difference. *Avec g. plaisir, de g. cœur*, with great pleasure, very willingly. *G. froid*, severe cold. *Il fait g. jour*, it is broad daylight. *Il est g. temps de partir*, it is high time we were off. *Grandes pluies*, heavy rains. *Les grands blessés*, the seriously wounded. *Grande jeunesse*, extreme youth. *Tex:* **Couleur grand teint**, fast dye. **6.** *s.* (a) *m.* Grandee. (b) *Grands et petits*, old and young (c) *Les grands de la terre*, the great ones of the earth.

grand'chose [grãʃoːz], indef. pron. *m.* (Nearly always coupled with *pas* or *sans*) Much. *Cela ne fait pas grand'chose*, it is of no great importance; it doesn't matter much.

grand'croix [grãkrwa]. **I.** s.f.inv. Grand Cross (of the Legion of Honour). **2.** s.m. Grand-croix, Knight Grand Cross. *pl. Des grands-croix.*

grand-duc, s.m. **1.** Grand duke. **2.** *Orn:* Eagle-owl, great horned owl. *pl. Des grands-ducs.*

grand-duché, s.m. Grand duchy. *pl. Des grands-duchés.*

Grande-Bretagne. *Pr.n.f.* Great Britain.

grande-duchesse, s.f. Grand duchess. *pl. Des grandes-duchesses.*

grandement [grãdmã], adv. **1.** Grandly, nobly. *Faire les choses g.*, to do things on a noble scale. **2.** Greatly, largely. *Avoir g. raison*, to be altogether right. *Avoir g. le temps*, to have ample time. *Il est g. temps*, it is high time.

grandeur [grãdœːr], s.f. **1.** (a) Size; height (of tree). **Étoile de troisième grandeur**, star of the third magnitude. **De grandeur naturelle**, full-size(d). (b) Extent (of voyage); scale (of undertaking). **2.** Greatness. (a) Importance; magnitude (of offence); grandeur (of conception). (b) Majesty, splendour, grandeur. *F:* **Regarder qn du haut de sa grandeur**, to look down on s.o. (c) Nobility (of character, etc.). **3.** Sa Grandeur, his Highness.

grand'garde [grãgard], s.f. *Mil:* Outpost picket. *pl. Des grand'gardes.*

grandiloquence [grãdilɔkɑ̃ːs], s.f. Grandiloquence.

grandiose [grãdjoːz], a. Grand, imposing.

grandir [grãdiːr]. **I.** v.i. (a) (i) To grow tall; (ii) to grow up. *Il est grandi*, he has grown, he is taller. **En grandissant**, as one grows up. (b) *G. en sagesse*, to grow in wisdom. **2.** v.tr. (a) To make (sth.) greater; to increase. *Souvenirs qui grandissent la France*, memories that exalt France. (b) To magnify.

grandissement [grãdismã], s.m. (a) Growth, increase. (b) *Opt:* Magnification.

grand(-)livre, s.m. Ledger. *pl. Des grands-livres.*

grand'maman [grãmamã], s.f. *F:* Grand-mamma.

grand'mère [grãmɛːr], s.f. Grandmother.

grand'messe [grãmes], s.f. *Ecc:* High mass.

grand-oncle [grãtɔ̃kl], s.m. Great-uncle. *pl. Des grands-oncles.*

grand-papa, s.m. *F:* Grandpapa.

grand'peine (à) [agrãpen], adv.phr. See PEINE 4.

grand-père, s.m. Grandfather. *pl. Des grands-pères.*

grand-prêtre, s.m. High priest. *pl. Des grands-prêtres.*

grand'route [grãrut], s.f. Highway, high road.

grand'rue [grãry], s.f. High street, main street.

grands-parents, s.m.pl. Grandparents.

grand'tante [grãtãːt], s.f. Great-aunt.

grange [grãːʒ], s.f. Barn. **Mettre le blé en grange**, to garner the corn.

granit [grani(t)], *s.m.* Granite. *F:* Cœur de granit, heart of stone.

graniteux, -euse [granitø, -øːz], **granitique** [granitik], *a.* Granitic; granite (formation).

granulaire [granylɛːr], *a.* Granular.

granulation [granylasjɔ̃], *s.f.* Granulation.

granule [granyl], *s.m.* Granule.

granuler [granyle], *v.tr.* **1.** To granulate. **2.** *Engr:* To stipple.

granuleux, -euse [granylø, -øːz], *a.* Granular, granulous.

granulosité [granylozite], *s.f.* Coarseness of grain.

graphique [grafik]. **1.** *a.* Graphic (sign, method). **2.** *s.m.* Diagram, graph. *adv.* **-ment,** -ally.

graphite [grafit], *s.m.* Graphite, black-lead, plumbago.

grappe [grap], *s.f.* **1.** Cluster, bunch (of grapes). *G. d'oignons,* string of onions. *F:* Mordre à la grappe, to jump at the offer. **2.** *Bot:* Raceme.

grappill|er [grapije], *v.tr. & i.* **1.** To glean (in vineyard). **2.** *F:* (a) To make petty profits. (b) To pilfer, cadge. *s.m.* **-age.** *s.* **-eur, -euse.**

grappillon [grapijɔ̃], *s.m.* Small bunch, cluster (of grapes, etc.).

grappin [grapɛ̃], *s.m.* **1.** (a) *Nau:* Grapnel, hook; (b) Grab-dredger; grab. *F:* Mettre le grappin sur qch., to lay hands on, get hold of sth. **2.** *pl.* Climbing-irons.

gras, grasse [grɑ, grɑːs], *a.* **1.** (a) Fat (meat); fatty (tissue). (b) Rich (food). *Régime g.,* meat diet. *Potage g.,* potage au gras, meat soup. *Ecc:* Jour gras, meat day. Faire gras, to eat meat (on a fast-day). S.a. CHOU I, MARDI. (c) *s.m.* Fat (of meat). **2.** (a) Fat, stout (person). *F:* En serez-vous plus gras? will you be any the richer for it? (b) Fatted (animal); plump (pullet). Tuer le veau gras, to kill the fatted calf. **3.** Greasy, oily (rag, hair). Crayon gras, stick of grease-paint. *Blanc g.,* white grease-paint. *s. Entretenir le mécanisme au gras,* to keep the machinery well greased. **4.** Thick. (a) *Boue grasse,* thick, slimy, mud. *Toux grasse,* loose, phlegmy, cough. *Conte g.,* broad story. *adv.* Rire gras, to give a fat laugh. *Temps g.,* thick, foggy, weather. (b) *Poutre grasse,* thick beam. *Plante grasse,* thick-leaved plant. *Typ:* Caractères gras, heavy, bold-faced, type. *s.m.* Le gras de la jambe, the calf of the leg. *F:* Il n'y en a pas gras, there is not much of it. S.a. MATINÉE I. **5.** *Contours g.,* softened, woolly, outlines. *Pierre grasse,* soft stone.

gras-double, *s.m. Cu:* Tripe.

grassement [grɑsmɑ̃], *adv.* **1.** *Vivre g.,* to live in plenty, on the fat of the land. **2.** *Récompenser qn g.,* to reward s.o. handsomely, liberally.

grasset, -ette [grɑsɛ, -ɛt]. **1.** *a. F:* Plump; chubby. **2.** *s.m.* Stifle(-joint) (of horse).

grassey|er [grɑseje], *v.i.* To speak with a strongly marked r ; to roll one's r's. *s.m.* **-ement.**

grassouillet, -ette [grɑsujɛ, -ɛt], *a. F:* Plump; chubby.

grateron [gratrɔ̃], *s.m.* Goose-grass, cleavers.

graticule [gratikyl], *s.m.* Framework of squares (for enlargement of maps, etc.).

graticuler [gratikyle], *v.tr.* To divide (drawing, etc.) into squares.

gratification [gratifikasjɔ̃], *s.f.* (a) Gratuity, tip. (b) Bonus, bounty.

gratifier [gratifje], *v.tr. G. qn de qch.,* (i) to confer, bestow, sth. upon s.o.; (ii) *F:* to attribute, ascribe, sth. to s.o.

gratin [gratɛ̃], *s.m.* (a) Burnt portion adhering to the pan. (b) Au gratin, (cooked) with bread-crumbs and grated cheese. (c) *F:* Le gratin, the

upper crust (of society) ; the pick of the basket.

gratiné [gratine], *a. Cu:* Bread-crumbed. *Sole gratinée,* sole fried with egg and bread-crumbs.

gratis [gratis], *adv.* Gratis ; free of charge. Entrée gratis, admission free

gratitude [gratityd], *s.f.* Gratitude, gratefulness.

gratte [grat], *s.f. F:* Pickings, perquisites, rake-off ; graft. Faire de la gratte, to get pickings.

gratte-ciel, *s.m.inv.* Sky-scraper.

gratte-huile, *a.inv. I.C.E:* Bague gratte-huile, scraper-ring (of piston).

gratte-papier, *s.m.inv. F:* Quill-driver ; (literary) hack.

gratte-pieds, *s.m.inv.* (Door-, shoe-)scraper.

gratt|er [grate], *v.tr.* **1.** (a) To scrape, scratch. *Il est toujours à se g.,* he is always scratching himself. *P:* Tu peux te gratter, you may whistle for it ! *Plume qui gratte,* scratchy pen. *F:* Gratter le papier, to drive a quill. *P:* En gratter pour qn, to be gone on s.o., keen on s.o. (b) *Tex:* Laine grattée, brushed wool. **2.** To erase (a word). **3.** *F: G. un concurrent,* to overtake, pass, a competitor. *s.m.* **-age.** *s.* **-eur, -euse.**

grattoir [gratwaːr], *s.m.* Scraper. *G. de bureau,* erasing knife, scraper-eraser.

gratuit [gratɥi], *a.* Gratuitous. (a) Free. *École gratuite,* free school. A titre gratuit, gratis, free of charge. (b) *Insulte gratuite,* gratuitous, wanton, unprovoked, insult. *adv.* **-ement.**

gratuité [gratɥite], *s.f.* Gratuitousness.

gravats [grava], *s.m.pl.* = GRAVOIS.

grave [graːv], *a.* **1.** *A:* Heavy. *Ph:* Corps grave, heavy body. **2.** (a) Grave (face); solemn (tone) ; sober (countenance). (b) Important, weighty (business) ; severe (wound). *Subir une g. opération,* to undergo a serious operation. **3.** *Mus:* Note g., low(-pitched), deep, note. **4.** *Gram:* Accent grave, grave accent. *adv.* **-ment.**

gravel|er [gravle], *v.tr.* (jə gravelle ; je gravel-lerai) To gravel, cover with gravel. *s.m.* **-age.**

graveleux, -euse [gravlø, -øːz], *a.* **1.** Gravelly (soil) ; gritty (pencil, pear). **2.** Smutty (story). **3.** *Med:* Suffering from gravel.

gravelle [gravɛl], *s.f. Med:* Gravel.

graver [grave], *v.tr.* To cut, engrave, carve (material or design). *G. à l'eau-forte,* to etch. *F: Cela reste gravé dans ma mémoire,* it remains graven on my memory.

graveur [gravœːr]. **1.** *s.m.* Engraver ; carver (on stone, etc.). *G. à l'eau-forte,* etcher. **2.** *a.* Bain graveur, etching-bath.

gravier [gravje], *s.m.* **1.** Gravel, grit. **2.** Usu. *pl. Med:* Gravel.

gravir [graviːr], *v.tr.* To climb ; to ascend (mountain); to mount (ladder). *G. un échelon social,* to climb a rung of the social ladder.

gravitation [gravitasjɔ̃], *s.f. Ph:* Gravitation.

gravité [gravite], *s.f.* **1.** *Ph:* Gravity. Centre de gravité, centre of gravity. **2.** (a) Gravity, seriousness. (b) Severity (of illness) ; seriousness (of operation). **3.** *Mus:* Low pitch, deepness (of note).

graviter [gravite], *v.i.* **1.** To gravitate (*vers,* towards). **2.** To revolve (*autour de,* round).

gravois [gravwa], *s.m.pl.* **1.** Screenings (of plaster). **2.** (Plaster) rubbish.

gravure [gravyːr], *s.f.* **1.** Engraving. (a) *G. en creux,* (i) intaglio-engraving; (ii) die-sinking. (b) *G. en taille-douce,* copper-plate engraving. *G. à l'eau-forte, g. en creux,* etching. *G. en simili,* half-tone work. **2.** Print, picture, engraving, etching. *G. en taille-douce, g. sur cuivre,* copper-plate. *G. sur bois,* woodcut. *G. en couleurs,* colour-print. *Livre plein de gravures*, book full of illustrations. *G. avant la lettre*, proof before letters.

gré [gre], *s.m.* **I.** Liking, taste. **A mon gré, selon mon gré**, (i) to my liking, to my taste ; (ii) in my opinion. **Au gré de mes désirs**, (i) just as I could wish ; (ii) to my heart's content. **2.** Will, pleasure. **De mon propre gré, de mon plein gré**, of my own free will, of my own accord. **Bon gré mal gré**, whether we like it or not ; willy-nilly. **Au gré des flots**, at the mercy of the waves. **De gré à gré**, by (mutual) agreement. S.a. FORCE I. **3.** **Savoir (bon) gré à qn de qch., de faire qch.**, to be grateful to s.o. for sth., for doing sth. **Savoir mauvais gré à qn de qch.**, to be annoyed with s.o. about sth. ; to take sth. ill.

grèbe [grɛb], *s.m. Orn :* Grebe.

grec, grecque [grɛk]. **I.** *a.* Greek ; *occ.* Grecian. *Les orateurs grecs*, the Greek orators. *Coiffure à la grecque*, hair done in the Grecian style. **2.** *s.* (a) Greek. (b) *P : A :* Un grec, a (card-)sharper, a Greek, a rook. **3.** *s.m.* Le grec, (the) Greek (language). **4.** *s.f. Art :* Grecque, Greek key-pattern, Greek border.

Grèce [grɛs]. *Pr.n.f. Geog :* Greece.

gréco-romain, -aine, *a.* Gr(a)eco-Roman.

grecque. See GREC.

gredin, -ine [grədɛ̃, -in], *s.* Rogue, scoundrel ; *f.* jade.

gredinerie [grədinri], *s.f.* **I.** Roguery. **2.** Rascally trick.

gréement [gremã], *s.m. Nau :* **I.** Rigging. **2.** Rig (of ship). **3.** Gear (of tree, etc.).

gré|er [gree], *v.tr. Nau :* (a) To rig (mast, vessel, etc.). *Gréé en carré*, square-rigged. (b) To sling (hammock). *s.m.* **-age.** *s.m.* **-eur.**

greffe¹ [grɛf], *s.f.* **I.** *Arb : Hort :* Graft, slip. *Surg :* Graft (of skin, tissue). **2.** Grafting. *G. par œil détaché*, budding. *G. en écusson*, shield grafting, shield budding. *Surg : G. épidermique*, skin grafting.

greffe², *s.m.* **I.** *Jur :* Office of the clerk of the court. **2.** *Fin :* Registry (of joint-stock company).

greff|er [grɛfe], *v.tr. Arb : Hort : Surg :* To graft. *s.m.* **-age.** *s.m.* **-eur.**

greffier [grɛfje], *s.m.* **I.** *Jur :* Clerk (of the court). **2.** *Adm : Fin :* Registrar.

grégaire [gregɛːr], *a.* Gregarious.

grège [grɛːʒ], *a.* Raw (silk).

grégeois [greʒwa], *a.m. A :* (= GREC) Feu grégeois, Greek fire.

Grégoire [gregwaːr]. *Pr.n.m.* Gregory.

grégorien, -ienne [gregɔrjɛ̃, -jɛn], *a.* Gregorian (chant, etc.).

grêle¹ [grɛːl], *a.* Slender, thin (leg, etc.); thin, high-pitched (voice). *Anat :* Intestin grêle, small intestine.

grêle², *s.f.* (a) Hail. *Orage accompagné de g.*, hail-storm. (b) *F : G. de coups, de balles*, shower of blows ; hail of bullets.

grêler [grɛle]. **I.** *v.impers.* Il grêle, it hails. **2.** *v.tr.* To damage (crops) by hail. **3.** *v.tr.* To pock-mark.

grêlé, *a.* Pock-marked, (pock-)pitted.

grelin [grəlɛ̃], *s.m. Nau :* Cablet, hawser, warp.

grêlon [grɛlɔ̃], *s.m.* **I.** Hail-stone. **2.** *F :* Sty(e) (on the eyelid).

grelot [grəlo], *s.m.* **I.** (Small globular) bell ; sleigh-bell. *F :* **Attacher le grelot**, to bell the cat. **Faire sonner son grelot**, to put one's word in. **2.** *Bot : F :* Grelot blanc, snowdrop.

grelott|er [grəlɔte], *v.i.* **I.** To tremble, shake, shiver (with cold, fear). *Il grelottait de froid*, he was shaking with cold. **2.** To jingle. *a.* **-ant.**

grémil [gremil], *s.m. Bot :* Gromwell.

grenade¹ [grənad], *s.f.* **I.** *Bot :* Pomegranate (fruit). **2.** (a) Grenade, bomb. *G. à main*, hand-grenade. (b) *G. extinctrice*, fire-grenade. (c) *G. sous-marine*, depth-charge.

Grenade². *Pr.n.f. Geog :* Granada (in Spain).

grenadier¹ [grənadje], *s.m.* Pomegranate(-tree).

grenadier², *s.m. Mil :* (a) *A. & Br.Army :* Grenadier. (b) Bomber.

grenadière [grənadjɛːr], *s.f.* Lower band (of rifle). **A la grenadière**, (of rifle) slung.

grenadine [grənadin], *s.f.* **I.** *Tex :* Grenadine. **2.** Grenadine (syrup).

grenaille [grənaːj], *s.f.* **I.** Refuse grain ; tailings. **2.** Granular metal. *G. de plomb*, lead shot. **En grenaille**, granulated. **3.** *Tp :* Granular filling (of capsule) ; carbon granules.

grenaill|er [grənaje], *v.tr.* To granulate ; to shot (metal). *s.m.* **-ement.**

grenat [grəna]. **I.** *s.m.* Garnet. **2.** *a.inv.* Garnet-red.

grener [grəne], *v.* (je grène ; je grènerai) **I.** *v.i.* (Of cereals) To seed ; to corn. **2.** *v.tr.* (a) To corn, granulate (gunpowder). (b) *Engr :* To stipple.

grené, *s.m.* Stipple.

grèneterie [grɛntri], *s.f.* (a) Corn-chandlery. (b) Seed-trade.

grènetier, -ière [grɛntje, -jɛːr], *s.* (a) Corn-chandler. (b) Seedsman, -woman.

grènetis [grɛnti], *s.m.* Milled edge (of coin).

grenier [grənje], *s.m.* **I.** Granary, storehouse. *Hist :* Greniers d'abondance, public granaries. *G. à foin, à grain*, hayloft, corn-loft. **2.** Attic, garret. **3.** *Nau :* Dunnage.

grenouille [grənuːj], *s.f.* **I.** Frog. **2.** *P :* Messfunds, club-money ; funds (of a society). **Manger la grenouille**, to make off with the cash.

grenouillère [grənujɛːr], *s.f.* (a) Marsh, swamp ; froggery. (b) *F :* Paddling-pool.

grenu [grəny], *a.* **I.** (Of corn) Grainy, full of grain. **2.** (a) Granular (fracture, etc.). (b) Grained (leather, etc.). **3.** *s.m.* Granularity.

grès [grɛ], *s.m.* **I.** Sandstone. *G. dur*, grit. *G. à bâtir*, freestone. **2.** Poterie de grès, grès cérame, stoneware. *Cruche de g.*, stone jug.

grésière [grezjɛːr], *s.f.* Sandstone quarry.

grésil [grezi], *s.m.* **I.** Frozen pellets of snow. **2.** Pounded glass.

grésill|er¹ [grezije], *v.impers.* (Of frozen snow) To patter. *s.m.* **-ement¹.**

grésill|er², *v.i.* (a) (Of fire) To crackle ; (of flame) to sputter ; (of frying-pan, of gas) to sizzle. (b) (Of crickets) To chirp. *s.m.* **-ement².**

grève [grɛːv], *s.f.* **I.** (a) Strand, (sea-)shore ; (sandy) beach. (b) (Sandy) bank, strand (of river). **La Grève**, the Strand (open space on banks of Seine where dissatisfied workmen assembled. Whence) **2.** Strike (of workmen). **Se mettre en grève**, to go on strike. **Faire grève**, to strike, to be on strike. **Grève perlée**, (i) ca'canny strike ; (ii) underhand sabotage. **Faire la grève de la faim**, to go on hunger-strike.

grever [grəve], *v.tr.* (je grève ; je grèverai) **I.** To burden, encumber (estate). *Grevé d'un impôt*, saddled with a tax. **2.** (a) To entail (estate). (b) To mortgage (property). **3.** *Adm :* To lay a rate on (a building).

gréviste [grevist], *s. m. & f.* Striker. *G. de la faim*, hunger-striker.

gribouillage [gribujaːʒ], *s.m.* Scrawl, scribble.

Gribouille [gribuːj]. *Pr.n.m.* Simpleton, ninny.

gribouill|er [gribuje], *v.tr. F :* = GRIFFONNER. *s.* **-eur, -euse.**

gribouillis [gribuji], *s.m.* = GRIBOUILLAGE.

grief [grief], *s.m.* Grievance; ground for complaint. **Faire grief à qn de qch.**, to harbour resentment against s.o. on account of sth.

grièvement [grievmã], *adv.* Severely, grievously, gravely (wounded); deeply (offended).

griffe [grif], *s.f.* **1.** (*a*) Claw (of tiger, etc.); talon (of hawk). **Coup de griffe**, scratch. **Tomber sous les griffes de qn**, to fall into s.o.'s clutches. (*b*) Claw, clip, clamp. *G. d'embrayage*, coupling-dog, -claw. *Griffes de prise directe*, direct-drive dogs. **Marteau à griffe**, claw-hammer. **Griffe à papiers**, paper-clip. **Griffes de monteur**, climbing-irons. (*c*) *Bot:* Tendril (of vine). **2.** (*a*) Stamped signature. (*b*) (Signature) stamp.

griffer [grife], *v.tr.* **1.** To scratch, claw. **2.** To stamp (circular, etc.) with a signature.

griffon [grifɔ̃], *s.m.* **1.** Griffin, gryphon. **2.** Griffon (terrier). **3.** *Orn:* Griffon-vulture.

griffonnage [grifɔnaːʒ], *s.m.* **1.** Scribbling. **2.** Scrawl, scribble.

griffonner [grifɔne], *v.tr.* To scrawl, scribble (off) (letter, etc.). *s.* -**eur**, -**euse**.

grignoter [griɲɔte], *v.tr.* To nibble, nibble at (sth.); to pick at, toy with (food). *s.m.* -**age**. *s.m.* -**ement**. *s.* -**eur**, -**euse**.

grigou [grigu], *s.m.* *F:* Miser; old screw; skinflint. *pl. Des grigous.*

gril [gri], *s.m.* **1.** *Cu:* Grid(iron), grill. *F:* **Être sur le gril**, to be on tenterhooks, on the rack. **2.** *Th:* Le gril, the upper flies.

grillade [grijad], *s.f.* Grill, grilled meat; esp. grilled steak. *G. de pain*, piece of toast.

grillage¹ [grijaːʒ], *s.m.* **1.** Grilling, broiling (of meat); toasting (of bread). **2.** Calcining; roasting (of ores). **3.** *El:* Burning out (of bulb).

grillage², *s.m.* (*a*) (Metal) grating; lattice-work. *G. en fil de fer*, wire-netting. (*b*) Grid, frame (of accumulator plate).

grillager [grijaʒe], *v.tr.* (je grillageai(s); n. grillageons) **1.** To lattice. **2.** To surround with wire-netting.

grille [griːj], *s.f.* **1.** (*a*) (Iron) bars; grill(e) (of convent parlour). (*b*) Iron gate, entrance gate (to grounds, etc.). (*c*) Railings. (*d*) Grating (of sink, etc.). (*e*) Fire-grate. **2.** *Aut:* Gate(-quadrant). **Secteur à grille**, visible gate. **3.** *El:* Grid ((i) of accumulator, (ii) of thermionic valve). **4.** (Cipher-)stencil.

griller¹ [grije], *v.tr.* **1.** To grill, broil (meat); to toast (bread, etc.); to roast (coffee); to calcine (ore). **2.** (*a*) To burn, scorch. *F:* *G. une cigarette*, to smoke a cigarette. *P:* **Il est grillé**, he has been found out, shown up. (*b*) (Of sun or frost) To scorch (vegetation). (*c*) *F:* *G. un concurrent*, to race past a competitor; to leave a competitor standing. **3.** *v.i.* (*a*) *Cu:* (Of meat) To grill; (of bread) to toast. (*b*) *F:* **La lampe a grillé**, the (incandescent) bulb has burnt out. (*c*) *F:* *G. d'envie de faire qch.*, to be burning, itching, to do sth.

griller², *v.tr.* (*a*) To rail in, rail off (garden, etc.). (*b*) To grate, bar (window, etc.).

grillon [grijɔ̃], *s.m.* *Ent:* Cricket.

grimace [grimas], *s.f.* (*a*) Grimace, grin, wry face. **Faire la grimace**, to make, pull, a face. (*b*) *F:* **Faire des grimaces**, to put on airs; to mince.

grimacer [grimase], *v.i.* (je grimaçai(s); n. grimaçons) **1.** To grimace; to grin; to make faces. *G. un sourire*, to force a smile; to give a wry smile. (*b*) *F:* To simper.

grimaceries [grimasri], *s.f.pl.* (*a*) Grimaces, grimacing. (*b*) Affectation.

grimacier,-ière [grimasje,-jɛːr]. **1.** *a.* (*a*) Grimacing, grinning. (*b*) Affected. **2.** *s.* Affected-person.

grimaud [grimo], *s.m.* *A:* Ignoramus, scribbler.

grime [grim], *s.m.* *Th:* Dotard, old fogey. *Jouer les grimes*, to play old men.

grimer [grime], *v.tr.* *Th:* To make up (an actor) (for an elderly part).

se grimer, to make up (one's face).

grimoire [grimwaːr], *s.m.* **1.** *A:* Wizard's book of spells; black book. **2.** Scrawl; unintelligible scribble.

grimper [grɛ̃pe], *v.i.* **1.** To climb (up), clamber (up). **Il a, est, grimpé sur la muraille**, he climbed (up) the wall. *G. à un mât*, to swarm up a pole. *G. au pouvoir*, to climb to power. *v.tr. G. une montagne*, to climb a mountain. **2.** (Of plants, liquids) To creep; (of plants) to climb.

grimpeur, -euse [grɛ̃pœːr, -øːz]. **1.** *a.* Climbing, scansorial (bird). **2.** *s.* Climber.

grincer [grɛ̃se], *v.i.* (je grinçai(s); n. grinçons) To grate; to grind; to creak. *G. des dents*, to grind, gnash, one's teeth. *Plume qui grince sur le papier*, scratchy pen. *s.m.* -**ement**.

grincheux, -euse [grɛ̃ʃø, -øːz]. **1.** *a.* Grumpy, crabbed, cross-grained. **2.** *s.* Grumbler, grouser.

gringalet [grɛ̃galɛ], *s.m.* (*a*) Shrimp (of a man, of a boy); puny little fellow. (*b*) Whipper-snapper.

griot [grio], *s.m.* *Mill:* Seconds.

griotte [griɔt], *s.f.* Morello (cherry).

griottier [griɔtje], *s.m.* Cherry-tree.

grippage [gripaːʒ], *s.m.* *Mch:* Seizing, binding, jamming (of bearing, piston, valve, etc.).

grippe [grip], *s.f.* **1.** Dislike, aversion. **Prendre qn en grippe**, to take a dislike to s.o. **2.** *Med:* Influenza, *F:* 'flu.

gripper [gripe]. **1.** *v.tr.* *F:* To seize, pounce upon, snatch. **2.** *v.i. & pr.* (Of bearings) (i) To run hot; (ii) to seize (up); to bind, jam.

grippé, *a.* **1.** Suffering from influenza. *Être g.*, to have influenza. **2.** *Med:* Pinched, drawn (face).

grippe-sou, *s.m.* *F:* Old miser; skinflint. *pl. Des grippe-sou(s).*

gris [gri], *a.* **1.** Grey. (*a*) *Une jupe gris bleu*, a blue-grey skirt. *Cheval g. pommelé*, dapple-grey horse. (*b*) Grey-haired, grey-headed. *Barbe grise*, grey, grizzly, beard. (*c*) *Vin gris*, pale-red wine (of Anjou). (*d*) *Temps g.*, cloudy, dull, grey, weather. *Faire grise mine*, to look anything but pleased. *Faire grise mine à qn*, to give s.o. a poor welcome, the cold shoulder. **En faire voir de grises à qn**, to give s.o. a rough time; to lead s.o. a dance. **2.** *F:* (Slightly) tipsy, fuddled.

grisaille [grizaːj], *s.f.* *Art:* (*a*) Grisaille. (*b*) *Engr:* Tint drawing. *F: Les grisailles du soir*, the greyness of the evening.

grisailler [grizaje], *v.i.* (Of hair) To turn, become, grey.

grisâtre [grizaːtr], *a.* Greyish.

griser [grize], *v.tr.* *F:* To make (s.o.) tipsy. *Grisé par le succès*, intoxicated by success.

se griser, to get tipsy, fuddled.

griserie [grizri], *s.f.* **1.** Tipsiness. **2.** Intoxication, exhilaration, excitement, rapture.

grisette [grizɛt], *s.f.* *A:* Young (grey-clad) milliner, etc., of easy virtue. [GRIS]

grison, -onne [grizɔ̃, -ɔn], *a. & s. Geog:* (Native) of the Canton of Grisons.

grisonner [grizɔne], *v.i.* (Of pers., of hair) To grow grey, to go grey. *a.* -**ant**. *s.m.* -**ement**.

grisou [grizu], *s.m.* *Min:* Fire-damp. **Coup de grisou**, fire-damp explosion.

grive [griːv], *s.f.* *Orn:* Thrush. *Prov:* **Faute de grives on mange des merles**, beggars can't be choosers; half a loaf is better than no bread.

grivelé [grivle], *a.* Speckled (plumage).

grivois [grivwa], *a.* Licentious, loose, broad (story, song, joke).
grivoiserie [grivwazri], *s.f.* Broad joke.
Groenland [grɔɛnlɑ̃(:d)]. *Pr.n.m. Geog:* Greenland. *Au G.,* in Greenland.
groenlandais, -aise [grɔɛnlɑ̃dɛ, -ɛːz]. **I.** *a.* Of Greenland. **2.** *s.* Greenlander.
grog [grɔg], *s.m.* Toddy.
grognard, -arde [grɔɲaːr, -ard]. *F:* **I.** *a.* Grumbling; given to grousing. **2.** *s.* (*a*) Grumbler, grouser. (*b*) *Hist:* Soldier of Napoleon's Old Guard; veteran.
grognement [grɔɲmɑ̃], *s.m.* **I.** (*a*) (i) Grunting; (ii) grunt. (*b*) (i) Growling; (ii) growl. **2.** *F:* (*a*) Grumbling, grousing. (*b*) Snarling; snarl.
grogn|er [grɔɲe], *v.i.* **I.** (*a*) To grunt. (*b*) To growl. **2.** To grumble; to grouse. *s.* **-eur, -euse.**
grognerie [grɔɲri], *s.f.* Grumbling, growling; grousing.
grognon [grɔɲɔ̃]. **I.** *a. inv. in f.* Grumbling, peevish. *Une petite fille g.,* a little cross-patch. **2.** *s. m. & f.* Grumbler; cross-patch.
grognonner [grɔɲɔne], *v.i. F:* (*a*) To grouse, to grumble. (*b*) To show peevishness.
grognonnerie [grɔɲɔnri], *s.f. F:* Grumbling, grousing; peevishness.
groin [grwɛ̃], *s.m.* Snout (of pig, etc.).
grolle[1] [grɔl], *s.f. F:* Crow, rook, or jackdaw.
grolle[2], *s.f. P:* Shoe, boot.
grommel|er [grɔmle], *v.i.* (je **grommelle**; je **grommellerai**) To grumble, mutter. *G. un juron,* to mutter an oath. *s.m.* **-lement.**
grondement [grɔ̃dmɑ̃], *s.m.* **I.** Growl(ing), snarl(ing). **2.** Rumble, rumbling (of thunder); roaring (of the storm); booming (of the waves, of guns).
gronder [grɔ̃de]. **I.** *v.i.* (*a*) To growl, snarl. (*b*) (Of thunder, etc.) To rumble, mutter; (of storm, etc.) to boom. (*c*) *G. contre qn,* to grumble at s.o.; to find fault with s.o. **2.** *v.tr.* To scold, chide, rate. *G. qn d'avoir fait qch.,* to scold s.o. for doing sth.
gronderie [grɔ̃dri], *s.f.* Scolding; rating.
grondeur, -euse [grɔ̃dœːr, -øːz]. **I.** *a.* Grumbling, scolding. **2.** *s.* Grumbler; *f.* scold, shrew.
grondin [grɔ̃dɛ̃], *s.m. Ich:* Red gurnet.
groom [grum], *s.m.* **I.** (= PALEFRENIER) Groom. **2.** Page(-boy), 'buttons.'
gros, grosse [gro, groːs]. **I.** *a.* (*a*) Big, bulky, stout. *Monsieur gros et gras,* portly gentleman. *Grosse corde,* thick, stout, rope. *G. bout,* thick end (of stick, etc.). *G. caractères,* large characters (in writing). *G. murs,* main walls (of building). *G. moteur,* high-powered, heavy, motor. *Grosse pièce de forge,* heavy forging. *Gros doigt du pied,* big toe. *Grosse toile,* coarse linen. *G. sel,* coarse salt. *Affaire de gros bon sens,* matter of plain common sense. *G. rire,* (i) loud laugh; (ii) coarse laugh. *Grosse voix,* gruff voice; big voice. *Gros mot,* coarse expression, foul word, *F:* swear word. *Grosse cavalerie,* heavy cavalry. *Grosse somme,* large sum. *Jouer gros (jeu),* to play for high stakes. *Avoir la grosse faim,* to be very hungry. *G. rhume,* heavy, violent, cold. *Grosse faute,* gross, serious, mistake. *Faire la grosse besogne,* to do the rough work. *Grosse mer,* heavy sea, high sea. *Gros temps,* heavy, foul, bad, weather. *Gros bourgeois,* solid, substantial, citizen. *G. propriétaire,* big landowner. *F:* Les gros bonnets, *P:* les gros légumes, the bigwigs, the nobs. *S.a.* CŒUR 2, ŒIL 2. (*b*) *Femme grosse,* pregnant woman. *Action grosse de conséquences,* action big with consequences. (*c*) *adv.* **Gagner gros,** to earn a great deal; *F:* to make big money.

2. *s.m.* (*a*) Bulk, chief part, biggest or thickest part. *G. de l'avant-bras,* swell of the forearm. *Le g. de la cargaison,* the bulk of the cargo. *Le plus gros est fait,* the hardest part of the job is done. *G. de l'été, de l'hiver,* height of summer, depth of winter. (*b*) *En gros.* (i) Roughly, broadly, approximately, on the whole, in the main. *Évaluation en g.,* rough estimate. (ii) *Écrire en gros,* to write in large characters. *Écrit en g.,* writ(ten) large. (iii) *Acheter en g.,* to buy in bulk. (*c*) *Com:* Wholesale (trade). **Marchand en gros,** wholesale dealer, wholesaler. **3.** *s.f.* **Grosse.** (*a*) Round-hand (writing). *Écrire en grosse,* to engross. (*b*) *Com:* Gross; twelve dozen. *Six grosses de plumes,* six gross pens.
gros-bec, *s.m. Orn:* Grosbeak, hawfinch. *pl. Des gros-becs.*
groseille [grozɛːj], *s.f.* **I.** **Groseille à grappes,** currant. **2.** **Groseille à maquereau,** gooseberry.
groseillier [grozeje], *s.m.* **I.** Currant-bush. **2.** Groseillier à maquereau, gooseberry-bush.
Gros-Jean, *s.m. F:* Man of low degree; Hodge. *Le voilà Gros-Jean comme devant! le beggar is back to his hedge again! C'est Gros-Jean qui en remontre à son curé,* it's like teaching your grandmother to suck eggs.
grosse. See GROS.
grossesse [grosɛs], *s.f.* Pregnancy.
grosseur [grosœːr], *s.f.* **I.** Size, bulk, volume; thickness (of lips, etc.). **2.** *Med:* Swelling, tumour, growth.
grossi|er, -ère [grosje, -ɛːr], *a.* (*a*) Coarse, rough (food, cloth). (*b*) *Stupidité grossière,* rank stupidity. *Ignorance grossière,* gross, crass, ignorance. *Faute grossière,* glaring blunder. (*c*) Rude, unmannerly (*envers,* to); vulgar, coarse, gross. *G. personnage,* unmannerly fellow. *Il a été on ne peut plus grossier,* he was most rude. [GROS] *adv.* **-èrement.**
grossièreté [grosjɛrte], *s.f.* **I.** (*a*) Coarseness, roughness (of object). (*b*) Rudeness, vulgarity, coarseness (of manner, etc.). (*c*) Grossness, glaring nature (of mistake). **2.** Dire des grossièretés à qn, to be rude, offensive, to s.o.
grossir [grosiːr]. **I.** *v.tr.* To enlarge, increase, magnify. *Torrent grossi par les pluies,* torrent swollen by the rain. *Objet grossi trois fois,* object magnified three times. **Grossir sa voix,** to put a threatening tone into one's voice. **2.** (*a*) *v.i.* To increase, swell; to grow bigger, larger. (*b*) *v.i. & pr.* La foule (se) grossissait, the crowd was increasing.
grossissant [grosisɑ̃], *a.* **I.** Growing, swelling. **2.** Magnifying, enlarging (lens, etc.). **Verre grossissant,** magnifying glass.
grossissement [grosismɑ̃], *s.m.* **I.** Increase in size; swelling. **2.** (*a*) Magnifying, enlargement (through lens, etc.). (*b*) Magnification, amplification, magnifying power (of lens, etc.). **Jumelles à fort grossissement,** high-power field-glasses.
grossiste [grosist], *s.m.* Wholesaler.
grotesque [grɔtɛsk], *a.* (*a*) *Art:* Grotesque. (*b*) *F:* Ludicrous, absurd. *adv.* **-ment.**
grotte [grɔt], *s.f.* Grotto.
grouill|er [gruje], *v.i.* To crawl, swarm, be alive (*de,* with). *Leurs habits grouillaient (de vermine),* their clothes were alive with vermin. *Le peuple grouille dans les rues,* the streets are swarming, teeming, with people. *a.* **-ant.** *s.m.* **-ement.**
se grouiller, *P:* To hurry up, to look alive.
groupe [grup], *s.m.* (*a*) Group (of people, things); clump (of trees, etc.); cluster (of stars, etc.); party (of people). (*b*) Set. *El.E:* G. électrogène, generator set. (*c*) Unit. *Mil:* G. de combat,

section, cell. *Av:* G. *de bombardement,* bombardment unit. *(d) Nat.Hist:* Division.

groupement [grupmɑ̃], *s.m.* **1.** *(a)* Grouping. *(b) El:* Connecting up; coupling. **2.** Group.

grouper [grupe], *v.tr.* **1.** To group; to arrange (in groups). G. *des efforts,* to concentrate efforts. **2.** *El:* To connect up, group, couple (cells, etc.). **se grouper,** to form a group; to gather; to bunch (together).

gruau [gryo], *s.m.* **1.** *(a)* (Finest) flour of wheat. **Pain de gruau,** fine wheaten bread. *(b)* Gruau d'avoine, (i) groats; (ii) oatmeal. **2.** *Cu:* Gruel.

grue [gry], *s.f.* **1.** *Orn:* Crane. *F:* **Faire le pied de grue,** to kick, cool, one's heels; to be kept waiting. *Cou de g.,* long scraggy neck. **2.** *F:* *Grande g.,* great gawk of a woman. **3.** (Hoisting) crane. G. *à vapeur,* steam-crane. G. *à pivot,* revolving crane. *Rail:* **Grue alimentaire,** water-pillar, water-crane.

gruger [gryʒe], *v.tr.* (je grugeai(s); n. grugeons) **1.** To crunch (piece of sugar, etc.); to crumble (glass). **2.** *F:* To eat (up), swallow. G. *qn sans merci,* to eat s.o. out of house and home.

grume [grym], *s.f.* **1.** Bark (left on felled tree). **Bois en grume,** rough timber. **2.** Log.

grumeau [grymo], *s.m.* (Finely divided) curd (of milk, soap, etc.).

grumeler (se) [səgrymle], *v.pr.* (il se grumelle; il se grumellera) To clot, curdle.

grumeleux, -euse [grymlø, -øːz], *a.* **1.** Curdled, clotted. **2.** Gritty (pear).

gruyère [gryjɛːr], *s.m.* Gruyere (cheese).

guano [gwano], *s.m.* Guano.

gué [ge], *s.m.* Ford. **Passer une rivière à gué,** to ford a river; to wade through a river.

guéable [geabl], *a.* Fordable. **Non guéable,** unfordable.

guède [gɛd], *s.f. Bot:* Woad, pastel.

guéer [gee], *v.tr.* **1.** To ford (stream). **2.** To water (horse).

guelfe [gɛlf], *s.m. Hist:* Guelph.

guelte [gɛlt], *s.f. Com:* Commission, percentage (on sales).

guenille [gəniːj], *s.f.* Tattered garment, old rag. **En guenilles,** in rags (and tatters).

guenilleux, -euse [gənijø, -øːz], *a.* Ragged.

guenipe [gənip], *s.f. F:* Trollop, strumpet.

guenon [gənɔ̃], *s.f.* **1.** *Z:* *(a)* Long-tailed monkey. *(b)* She-monkey (in general). **2.** *F:* Ugly woman; fright.

guépard [gepaːr], *s.m. Z:* Cheetah.

guêpe [gɛːp], *s.f. Ent:* Wasp. *F:* **Taille de guêpe,** wasp-waist.

guépéou [gepeu], *s.m. Russian Adm:* Ogpu.

guêpier [gepje], *s.m.* **1.** Wasps' nest. *F:* **Donner, tomber, dans un guêpier,** to bring a hornets' nest about one's ears. **2.** *Orn:* Bee-eater.

guère [gɛːr], *adv.* (Always with neg. expressed or understood) Not much, not many, only little, but little. *Je ne l'aime g.,* I don't care much for him. *Il ne tardera g. à venir,* he will not be long in coming. **Ne plus guère,** (i) hardly any more; (ii) not much longer. **Il n'y a guère plus de six ans,** it is barely more than six years ago. **Il ne s'en faut de guère,** there is not much wanting; it is not far short. **Sans guère avoir d'amis, il était respecté,** although he had but few friends, he was respected.

guéret [gerɛ], *s.m. Agr:* **1.** *(a)* Ploughed land. *(b)* Fallow land. *(c) pl. Lit:* Les guérets, the fields. **2.** (= SILLON) Furrow.

guéridon [geridɔ̃], *s.m.* Pedestal table.

guérilla [gerija, -illa], *s.f.* Band or troop of guerrillas. **Guerre de guérillas,** guerrilla warfare.

guérir [geriːr]. **1.** *v.tr.* *(a)* To cure, heal (s.o.); to restore (s.o.) to health. G. *qn d'une habitude,* to cure, break, s.o. of a habit. *(b)* G. *un rhume,* to cure a cold. *F: Cela ne guérit rien,* that's no cure; that doesn't help much. **2.** *v.i.* *(a)* To be cured; to recover. G. *de la fièvre,* to get over, recover from, fever. *Il n'en guérira pas,* he won't get over it. *(b)* (Of wound) To heal.

guérison [gerizɔ̃], *s.f.* **1.** Recovery. *En voie de g.,* on the way to recovery. **2.** *(a)* Cure (of disease). *(b)* Healing (of wound).

guérissable [gerisabl], *a.* *(a)* Curable. *(b)* That can be healed.

guérisseur, -euse [gerisœːr, -øːz]. **1.** *s.* *(a)* Healer. *(b)* Quack(-doctor). **2.** *a.* Healing.

guérite [gerit], *s.f.* **1.** *Mil:* Sentry-box. **2.** Cabin, shelter (for watchman, etc.); look-out turret. G. *téléphonique,* call-box. *Rail:* G. *à signaux,* signal-box. **3.** Hooded (wicker) chair.

Guernesey [gɛrnəze]. *Pr.n.m. Geog:* Guernsey.

guerre [gɛːr], *s.f.* War, warfare. **1.** Grande g., war on a large scale. *Petite g.,* (i) minor operations; (ii) sham fighting. G. *sur mer,* naval warfare. G. *de course,* commerce destroying. **Se mettre en guerre,** to go to war. **Être en guerre avec, contre, . . .,** to be at war with. . . . **En pleine guerre,** in the midst of war. **Faire la guerre à, contre, un pays,** to wage war, make war, on, against, a country. *F:* **C'est de bonne guerre,** it is quite fair. **S'en aller en guerre,** to go to the wars. **A la guerre comme à la guerre,** (i) one must take the rough with the smooth; (ii) we, you, have got to rough it. **Le Ministère de la Guerre,** the War Office. S.a. CONSEIL 3, CRI, MARINE 3, NAVIRE, PARTISAN 2, USURE². **2.** Strife, contention, quarrel, feud. **Faire la guerre à qn sur, au sujet de, qch.,** to fight s.o. over sth. *G. à outrance, à mort,* war to the knife. G. *de plume,* paper warfare. S.a. NOM 1. *Adv.phr.* **De guerre lasse j'y consentis,** for the sake of peace and quietness I gave in.

guerrier, -ière [gɛrje, -jɛːr]. **1.** *a.* Warlike, martial. *Danse guerrière,* war-dance. **2.** *s.m.* Warrior.

guerroyant [gɛrwajɑ̃], *a.* Bellicose.

guerroyer [gɛrwaje], *v.i.* (je guerroie; je guerroierai) To war, to wage war, (contre, against).

guerroyeur, -euse [gɛrwajœːr, -øːz]. **1.** *s.m.* Fighter, knight-errant. **2.** *a.* Fighting (spirit).

guet [ge], *s.m.* **1.** Watch(ing); look-out. **Être au guet,** to be on the watch. **Avoir l'œil au guet,** to keep a sharp look-out. **Faire le guet,** (i) to be on the watch; (ii) to go the rounds. **Chien de bon guet,** good watch-dog. **2.** *A:* **Le guet,** the (constables of the) watch. **Mot du guet,** password, watchword.

guet-apens [getapɑ̃], *s.m.* **1.** Ambush, ambuscade, snare, trap. **Dresser un guet-apens à qn,** to waylay s.o. **2.** *Jur:* Lying in wait. **De guet-apens,** with premeditation.

guêtre [gɛtr], *s.f.* **1.** Gaiter. *Demi-guêtres,* spats. *A: Il y laissa ses guêtres,* he died there (esp. on the field of battle). **2.** *Aut:* Sleeve, gaiter, patch (for punctured tyre).

guetter [gete], *v.tr.* *(a)* To lie in wait for, to be on the look-out for, to watch for (s.o.). *(b)* **Guetter l'occasion,** to watch one's opportunity.

guetteur [getœːr], *s.m.* **1.** *A:* Watchman, watcher. **2.** Look-out (man) (in trenches, etc.).

gueulard, -arde [gœlaːr, -ard]. **1.** *s.P:* Bawler, mouther. **2.** *s.m.* *(a)* *P:* Nau: Speaking-trumpet. *W.Tel:* Extra-loud loud-speaker. *(b)* Mouth (of sewer); mouth, throat (of blast-furnace); muzzle (of gun). [GUEULE]

gueule [gœl], *s.f.* **1.** (*a*) Mouth (of carnivorous animals, of dog). (*b*) *P:* **Tais ta gueule! ta gueule!** shut up! *Quelle vilaine g.!* what an ugly mug! **Faire sa gueule,** to sulk. **Casser la gueule à qn,** to bash s.o.'s face. **Avoir la gueule de bois,** to have hot coppers; to feel chippy. (*c*) *F:* = BOUCHE 1. *Dépenser beaucoup pour la g.,* to spend a great deal on food. **2.** Mouth (of sack, tunnel); muzzle (of gun). (Of mill) **Marcher à gueule bée,** to work with all sluice-gates open.

gueule-de-lion, *s.f. Bot:* Antirrhinum, snapdragon.

gueule-de-loup, *s.f.* **1.** = GUEULE-DE-LION. **2.** (Chimney-)cowl.

gueuler [gœle]. *P:* **1.** *v.i.* To bawl, shout. **2.** *v.tr.* To bawl out (song, etc.).

gueules [gœl], *s.m. Her:* Gules.

gueuleton [gœltɔ̃], *s.m. P:* (*a*) Big feed, blowout, tuck-in. (*b*) Banquet.

gueuletonner [gœltɔne], *v.i. P:* To feast.

gueusaille [gøzɑːj], *s.f. F:* Riff-raff, rabble.

gueuse[1] [gøːz], *s.f. Metall:* G. de fonte, pig. **Fer en gueuse,** pig-iron; *Nau:* kentledge.

gueuse[2]. See GUEUX.

gueuser [gøze], *v.i. F:* To beg.

gueuserie [gøzri], *s.f.* **1.** Begging, mendicity. **2.** Wretched affair; 'poor show.'

gueux, -euse [gø, -øːz]. **1.** *s.* (*a*) Beggar; tramp. *Hist:* **Gueux de mer,** sea-beggar. (*b*) *F: Mon g. de neveu,* my scamp of a nephew. **2.** *a.* Poor, beggarly, poverty-stricken. *F:* **Gueux comme un rat d'église,** as poor as a church mouse.

gui[1] [gi], *s.m. Bot:* Mistletoe.

gui[2], *s.m. Nau:* **1.** Boom. **2.** Guy(-rope).

Gui[3]. *Pr.n.m.* Guy.

guibolle [gibɔl], *s.f. P:* Leg. **Jouer des guibolles,** to stir one's stumps.

guibre [giːbr], *s.f. N.Arch:* Cutwater. *A:* Figure de guibre, figure-head.

guichet [giʃɛ], *s.m.* **1.** (*a*) Wicket(-gate) (of prison, etc.). (*b*) Spy-hole, grille, grating (in door). **2.** Turnstile; entrance gate. *Rail:* (Platform) barrier. **3.** (*a*) Pay-desk (of bank, etc.). (*b*) *Rail:* (Booking-office) window. *Th:* Boxoffice (window). **4.** *Cr:* Wicket.

guichetier [giʃtje], *s.m.* Turnkey (of prison).

guide[1] [gid], *s.m.* **1.** (*a*) Guide (for journey, etc.); conductor. *G. alpestre,* Alpine guide. (*b*) *Mil. Hist:* Soldier of the Guides (under the Empire). **2.** Guide(-book). **3.** *Tchn:* G. de courroie, belt-guide.

guide[2], *s.f.* Rein. **Leçons de guide,** driving lessons. **Conduire à grandes guides,** to drive (i) tandem, (ii) four-in-hand. *F:* **Mener la vie à grandes guides,** to live in lavish style.

guide-âne, *s.m.* **1.** Book of standing instructions (in office, etc.). **2.** Black lines (supplied with writing-block, etc.). *pl.* Des guide-âne(s).

guider [gide], *v.tr.* To guide, direct, lead (s.o.); to drive (car, horse); to steer (boat).

guidon [gidɔ̃], *s.m.* **1.** *Cy:* Handle-bar. **2.** *Mil:* Foresight, bead (of gun, rifle). **3.** *Nau:* (*a*) Pennant. (*b*) Burgee. **4.** *Mil:* Guidon.

guignard, -arde [giɲaːr, -ard], *s.* **1.** *F:* Unlucky person; 'Jonah.' **2.** *s.m. Orn:* Dotterel.

guigne[1] [giɲ], *s.f.* Heart-cherry.

guigne[2], *s.f. F:* Bad luck, ill-luck. **Porter la guigne à qn,** to bring s.o. bad luck.

guigner [giɲe], *v.tr. F:* **1.** To cast an (envious) eye upon (sth.). (At cards) *Il guigne votre jeu,* he is looking over your hand. **2.** To ogle (s.o.).

guignol [giɲɔl], *s.m.* **1.** (*a*) Punch. (*b*) Punch and Judy show. **2.** *Av:* (*a*) King-post (of aeroplane). (*b*) Elevator lever.

guignolet [giɲɔlɛ], *s.m.* Cherry-liqueur.

guignon [giɲɔ̃], *s.m. F:* Bad luck, ill-luck. **Je suis en guignon,** I am out of luck.

Guillaume [gijoːm]. **1.** *Pr.n.m.* William. **2.** *s.m. Tls:* Rabbet(ing)-plane.

guilledou [gijdu], *s.m.* (Used in) *F:* **Courir le guilledou,** to frequent night haunts.

guillemets [gijmɛ], *s.m.pl. Typ:* Inverted commas, quotation marks, *F:* quotes. **Ouvrir, fermer, les guillemets,** to begin, close, the inverted commas. *Mots entre guillemets,* words quoted, in inverted commas.

guillemot [gijmo], *s.m. Orn:* Guillemot.

guiller [gije], *v.i.* (Of beer) To work, ferment.

guilleret, -ette [gijrɛ, -ɛt], *a.* Lively, gay, brisk.

guillochage [gijɔʃaːʒ], *s.m.* **1.** *Metalw:* (Rose-) engine turning; chequering. **2.** = GUILLOCHIS.

guillocher [gijɔʃe], *v.tr.* To engine-turn; to chequer.

guillochis [gijɔʃi], *s.m.* Guilloche (pattern), chequered pattern (on gold, silver, etc.).

guillotine [gijɔtin], *s.f.* **1.** Guillotine. **2.** Fenêtre à guillotine, sash-window. **Obturateur à guillotine,** drop shutter (of camera).

guillotin|er [gijɔtine], *v.tr.* To guillotine. *s.m.* **-ement.**

guimauve [gimoːv], *s.f. Bot:* Marsh-mallow. *F:* **Guimauve blonde,** insipid writing.

guimbarde [gɛ̃bard], *s.f.* **1.** Jew's-harp. **2.** *P:* Ramshackle vehicle; old rattletrap. **3.** *Tls:* Router-plane.

guimpe [gɛ̃p], *s.f.* (Nun's) wimple.

guindeau [gɛ̃do], *s.m. Nau:* Windlass.

guind|er [gɛ̃de], *v.tr.* To hoist, raise (with a windlass). *F:* **Guinder ses manières,** to affect a stiff, starched, manner. *s.m.* **-age.**

se guinder, to affect a lofty manner.

guindé, *a.* Stiff, *F:* starchy (person); stilted, stiff (style).

Guinée [gine]. **1.** *Pr.n.f. Geog:* Guinea. **La Nouvelle Guinée,** New Guinea. **2.** *s.f. Num:* Guinea.

guingan [gɛ̃gɑ̃], *s.m. Tex:* Gingham.

guingois [gɛ̃gwa], *s.m.* Skew. **De guingois,** awry, askew. *Esprit de g.,* cross-grained disposition. *Entrer en g.,* to sidle in.

guinguette [gɛ̃gɛt], *s.f.* Suburban place of refreshment (with music and dancing); pleasure gardens.

guipage [gipaːʒ], *s.m.* (Action of, material for) winding, taping, wrapping, lapping, covering.

guiper [gipe], *v.tr.* To wind (about); to tape, wrap, lap. **Fil guipé coton,** cotton-lapped wire.

guipure [gipyːr], *s.f.* **1.** Point-lace, pillow-lace. **2.** *El.E:* Wrapping, lapping (of cable, etc.).

guirlande [girlɑ̃d], *s.f.* Garland, festoon, wreath. (Of rope) **Faire guirlande,** to sag.

guirlander [girlɑ̃de], *v.tr.* To garland, festoon.

guise [giːz], *s.f.* Manner, way, fashion. **Faire, agir, à sa guise,** to do as one pleases; to go one's own way. **A votre guise!** please yourself! **En guise de,** (i) by way of; (ii) instead of.

guitare [gitaːr] *s.f. Mus:* Guitar. *F:* **C'est toujours la même guitare,** it's the same old story.

gustatif, -ive [gystatif, -iːv], *a.* Gustative; gustatory (nerve, etc.).

gustation [gystasjɔ̃], *s.f.* Gustation, tasting.

gutta-percha [gytaperka], *s.f.* Gutta-percha.

guttural, -aux [gytyral, -o]. **1.** *a.* Guttural; throaty (voice). **2.** *s.f. Ling:* Guttural, guttural. *adv.* **-ement.**

Guy [gi]. *Pr.n.m.* Guy. S.a. DANSE.

Guyane (la) [laguijan]. *Pr.n.f. Geog:* Guiana.

Guyenne (la) [lag(ɥ)ijɛn]. *Pr.n.f. A.Geog:* Guienne.

gymnase [ʒimnɑːz], *s.m.* Gymnasium.
gymnaste [ʒimnast], *s.m.* Gymnast.
gymnastique [ʒimnastik], **1.** *a.* Gymnastic. S.a. PAS¹ **1.** **2.** *s.f.* (*a*) Gymnastics. (*b*) *Sch :* *F :* Gymnasium.
gymnote [ʒimnɔt], *s.m.* *Ich :* Gymnotus ; *F :* electric eel.
gynécée [ʒinese], *s.m.* Gynaeceum.
gypaète [ʒipaɛt], *s.m.* *Orn :* Gypaetus ; esp. lammergeier.

gypse [ʒips], *s.m.* **1.** *Miner :* Gypsum, plaster-stone. **2.** *Com :* Plaster of Paris.
gyration [ʒirasjɔ̃], *s.f.* = GIRATION.
gyratoire [ʒiratwaːr], *a.* = GIRATOIRE
gyrin [ʒirɛ̃], *s.m.* *Ent :* Whirligig-beetle.
gyro [ʒiro], *a.* *Adm :* **Sens gyro,** 'roundabout.' *F :* electric eel.
gyrocompas [ʒirɔkɔ̃pɑ], *s.m.* *Nau :* Gyro-compass.
gyroscope [ʒirɔskɔp], *s.m.* Gyroscope.
gyroscopique [ʒirɔskɔpik], *a.* Gyroscopic.

H

Words beginning with an 'aspirate' h are
shown by an asterisk.

H, h [aʃ], *s. m. & f.* (The letter) H, h. h muet(te), 'mute' h.
*ha [ɑ], *int.* **1.** = AH. **2.** (As laughter) *Ha, ha!* ha ha! haw haw!
habile [abil], *a.* (*a*) Clever, skilful, able, capable (workman, etc.) ; cunning, smart, artful, crafty (rogue, etc.). *Mains habiles,* skilled hands. Façonner qch. d'une main habile, to fashion sth. skilfully, with a cunning hand. *H. à faire qch.,* clever at doing sth. (*b*) *Jur :* Habile à succéder, able, competent, to inherit. *adv.* -ment.
habileté [abilte], *s.f.* (*a*) Ability, skill, skilful-ness. (*b*) Cleverness, smartness.
habilité [abilite], *s.f.* *Jur :* Ability, title. Avoir habilité à hériter, to be entitled to succeed.
habiliter [abilite], *v.tr.* *Jur :* H. qn à faire qch., to enable, entitle, s.o. to do sth.
habillant [abijɑ̃], *a.* = HABILLÉ 2.
habillement [abijmɑ̃], *s.m.* **1.** Clothing, dress-ing. Effets d'habillement, wearing apparel ; clothing. **2.** Clothes, dress ; apparel, raiment. *H. complet,* suit of clothes.
habill|er [abije], *v.tr.* **1.** To prepare. (*a*) *Cu :* To draw and truss (poultry) ; to clean (fish) ; to trim (meat). (*b*) *Arb :* To prune, trim (tree). (*c*) To put (watch, etc.) together ; to assemble (parts). **2.** (*a*) To dress. *F :* Habiller qn de (la) belle façon, to give s.o. a good dressing-down. (*b*) To clothe ; to provide (s.o.) with clothes. *s.m.* -age.
s'habiller, to dress ; to put one's things on ; (of priest, etc.) to robe.
habillé, *a.* **1.** Dressed. *H. en femme,* dressed up, got up, as a woman. *H. chaudement,* warmly clad. **2.** (Of clothes) Becoming, smart, *F :* dressy.
habilleur, -euse [abijœːr, -øːz], *s. Th :* Dresser.
habit [abi], *s.m.* **1.** Dress, costume ; *pl.* clothes. Mettre ses habits, to put on one's clothes. *H. complet,* suit of clothes. Marchand d'habits, old-clothes man. **2.** (*a*) Coat. Mettre habit bas, to take off one's coat. *H. de cheval,* riding-habit. *F :* Les habits rouges, the redcoats (English soldiers). Habit vert, member of the *Académie française.* (*b*) *H. de soirée,* (evening) dress-coat. Être en habit, to be in evening-dress. **3.** (Monk's, nun's) habit ; (monk's) frock. Prendre l'habit, to take the habit, to enter religion.
habitabilité [abitabilite], *s.f.* Habitability ; fit-ness for habitation.
habitable [abitabl], *a.* Habitable.
habitacle [abitakl], *s.m.* **1.** *B.Lit :* Habitation. **2.** *Nau :* Binnacle. **3.** *Av :* Cockpit.
habitant, -ante [abitɑ̃, -ɑ̃ːt], *s.* (*a*) Inhabitant ; resident, dweller. *Ville de 10,000 habitants,* town

of 10,000 inhabitants. (*b*) Occupier (of house). (*c*) Inmate (of house).
habitat [abita], *s.m.* Habitat (of animal, plant).
habitation [abitasjɔ̃], *s.f.* **1.** Habitation ; dwell-ing, inhabiting. *Le problème de l'h.,* the housing problem. **2.** Dwelling(-place), residence, abode. *N'avoir point d'h.,* to have no fixed abode. Avoir son habitation à . . ., to reside at. . . .
habiter [abite]. **1.** *v.tr.* (*a*) To inhabit, to dwell in, live in (a place). *Pays peu habité,* country sparsely inhabited. (*b*) To occupy (house). **2.** *v.i.* To live, reside, dwell ; to have one's home (à, at). *H. à la campagne,* to live in the country.
habitude [abityd], *s.f.* (*a*) Habit, custom, prac-tice, use. Faire qch. par pure habitude, to do sth. from mere habit. Prendre, contracter, l'habitude de faire qch., to grow, get, into the habit of doing sth. Se faire une habitude de . . ., to make it one's practice to. . . . Être dans l'habitude, avoir l'habitude, avoir pour habitude, de faire qch., to be in the habit of doing sth. Se défaire d'une habitude, to get out of a habit. Faire perdre une habitude à qn, to break s.o. of a habit. D'habitude, usually, ordinarily. Comme d'habitude, as usual. Ses vêtements d'habitude, his usual clothes. (*b*) Knack. *Je n'en ai plus l'h.,* I'm out of practice.
habitu|el, -elle [abityɛl], *a.* Usual, customary, regular ; habitual (à, to). *adv.* -ellement.
habituer [abitye], *v.tr.* To accustom, habituate, make familiar. *H. qn à faire qch.,* to get s.o. into the habit of doing sth. *H. qn à la fatigue,* to inure s.o. to fatigue.
s'habituer, to get used, to get, grow, accus-tomed, to become habituated (à, to).
habitué, -ée, *s.* Frequenter ; regular attendant ; regular customer.
*hâbler [ɑble], *v.i.* To boast, brag ; to talk big.
*hâblerie [ɑblɔri], *s.f.* **1.** Bragging, boasting. **2.** Piece of brag.
*hâbleur [ɑblœːr], *s.m.* Boaster, braggart.
*hache [aʃ], *s.f.* Ax(e). *H. à main,* hatchet. Fait, taillé, à coups de hache, rough-hewn, hacked out. *Archeol :* H. d'armes, battle-axe. *H. de guerre,* tomahawk. *F :* Enterrer la hache de guerre, to bury the hatchet.
*hach|er [aʃe], *v.tr.* **1.** (*a*) To chop (up) ; to hash (meat, etc.). Hacher menu, to mince. *F :* Hacher qn menu comme chair à pâté, to make mincemeat of s.o. (*b*) To hack (up), mangle. **2.** To (cross-) hatch, to hachure (drawing). *s.m.* -age.
haché, *a.* **1.** Staccato, jerky (style). **2.** *Mer hachée,* cross sea ; choppy sea.
*hachette [aʃet], *s.f.* Hatchet.

**hache-viande* [aʃvjɑ̃:d], *s.m.inv.* Mincer.
**hachis* [aʃi], *s.m. Cu:* Minced meat; mince. En hachis, hashed or minced.
**hachisch* [aʃiʃ], *s.m.* Has(c)hish; bhang.
**hachoir* [aʃwa:r], *s.m.* (a) Chopping-knife, chopper. (b) Chopping-board.
**hachure* [aʃy:r], *s.f. Engr: Mapm:* Hatching, hachure. Carte en hachures, hachured map.
**hachurer* [aʃyre], *v.tr.* To hatch, hachure.
**hagard* [aga:r], *a.* 1. Faucon hagard, haggard. 2. Haggard, wild(-looking) (appearance, etc.); drawn (face).
hagiographe [aʒjɔgraf], *s.m.* Hagiographer.
hagiographie [aʒjɔgrafi], *s.f.* Hagiography.
**haie* [ɛ], *s.f.* (a) Hedge(-row). *H. vive,* quickset hedge. (b) Hurdle. *Sp:* Course de haies, (short-distance) hurdle-race; *F:* the hurdles. (c) Line, row (of trees, police, troops). Faire, former, la haie, to line the streets.
**haillon* [ajɔ̃], *s.m.* Rag (of clothing). Etre en haillons, to be in rags.
**haillonneux, -euse* [ajɔnø, -ø:z], *a.* Ragged, tattered.
**haine* [ɛːn], *s.f.* Hatred (de, contre, of); detestation; *Lit:* hate. Avoir la haine de qch., avoir qch. en haine, to hate, detest, sth. Prendre qch. en haine, to conceive a strong aversion for sth. En haine de qch., out of hatred of sth.
**haineusement* [ɛnøzmɑ̃], *adv.* In a tone, with a look, of bitter hatred.
**haineux, -euse* [ɛnø, -ø:z], *a.* Full of hatred.
**haïr* [ai:r], *v.tr.* (je hais [ɛ], tu hais, il hait, n. haïssons, etc.; *imp.* hais; otherwise regular) To hate, detest. Haïr qn comme la peste, to hate s.o. like poison, like the plague. *Être haï de, par, qn,* to be hated by s.o.
**haire* [ɛːr], *s.f.* 1. Hair-shirt. 2. Hair-cloth.
**hais.* See HAÏR.
**haïssable* [aisabl], *a.* Hateful, detestable.
**halage* [ɑla:ʒ], *s.m.* (a) Warping, hauling (of ship). (b) Towing. Chemin, corde, de halage, tow(ing)-path, -line. [HALER]
**halbran* [albrɑ̃], *s.m. Orn:* Young wild duck.
halcyon [alsjɔ̃], *s.m. Orn:* Halcyon, kingfisher.
**halde* [ald], *s.f. Min:* 1. Dump(-heap). 2. Mouth (of mine).
**hâle* [ɑːl], *s.m.* 1. (a) Tanning, browning (of skin by weather); sunburn. (b) Tan; sunburnt complexion. 2. Hot, dry, wind. [HÂLER]
haleine [alɛn], *s.f.* Breath. Retenir son haleine, to hold one's breath. Tout d'une haleine, all in one breath. Avoir de l'haleine, to have plenty of wind, of staying power. Avoir l'haleine courte, to be short-winded. (Re)prendre haleine, (i) to take breath; (ii) to recover one's breath, to get one's second wind. Donner haleine a qn, à un cheval, to give s.o. time to breathe; to breathe a horse. Perdre haleine, to get out of breath. Hors d'haleine, out of breath; breathless Travail de longue haleine, long and exacting labour. En haleine, in good condition, in good form. Tenir qn en haleine, to hold s.o. breathless; to keep s.o. in suspense.
halenée [aləne, -len-], *s.f.* Strong breath (usu. unpleasant); wh ff (of drink, etc.).
**haler* [ɑle], *v.tr.* 1. (a) To warp (ship). (b) To tow (barge, etc.). (c) *H. une embarcation au sec,* to haul up a boat (on the beach). 2. *Nau:* To pull, haul in, heave (rope, etc.). *v.i. H. sur une manœuvre,* to haul, pull on, a rope; to heave at a rope. 3. *Nau:* Haler le vent, se haler dans le vent, to haul upon the wind. *s.m.* -eur.
**hâler* [ɑle], *v.tr.* (Of sun) To burn brown, tan (s.o.); to burn up (vegetation).

se hâler, to get sunburnt.
hâlé, *a.* Sunburnt, tanned weather-beaten.
**haletant* [altɑ̃], *a.* Panting, breathless, out of breath; gasping (for breath).
**haleter* [alte], *v.i.* (je halète; je halèterai) To pant; to gasp (for breath). *s.m.* -ètement.
**hall* [al, ɔl], *s.m.* 1. (Palatial) entrance hall; (hotel) lounge. 2. (a) *Ind:* Bay, shop, room. *H. de montage,* erecting shop. (b) Open garage.
hallali [alali], *s.m. Ven:* Mort. Assister à l'h., to be in at the death, at the finish.
**halle* [al], *s.f.* (Covered) market. Les Halles (centrales), the Central Market (in Paris). *F:* Langage des halles = billingsgate. S.a. BLÉ.
**hallebarde* [albard], *s.f. Archeol:* Halberd, halbert; bill. *F:* Il pleut, tombe, des hallebardes, it is raining cats and dogs.
**hallebardier* [albardje], *s.m.* Halberdier
**hallier* [alje], *s.m.* Thicket, copse, brake.
hallucination [al(l)ysinasjɔ̃], *s.f.* Hallucination, delusion.
halluciner [al(l)ysine], *v.tr.* To hallucinate.
**halo* [alo], *s.m.* 1. *Meteor:* Halo. 2. (a) *Opt:* Blurring. (b) *Phot:* Halation.
halogène [alɔʒɛn], *s.m. Ch:* Halogen.
haloïde [alɔid], *a. & s.m. Ch:* Haloid.
**halte* [alt], *s.f.* 1. Stop, halt. Faire une h., to make a halt; to halt. Faire halte, (i) *Mil:* to halt; (ii) *Rail:* (of train) to stop, to call (at station). Halte là! halt! 2. (a) Stopping-place resting-place. (b) *Rail:* Halt; wayside station.
haltère [altɛ:r], *s.m.* Dumb-bell.
**hamac* [amak], *s.m.* Hammock. *Crocher, décrocher, un h.,* to sling, unsling, a hammock.
hamadryade [amadriad], *s.f.* 1. *Gr.Myth:* Hamadryad, dryad, wood-nymph. 2. King-cobra.
**hambourgeois, -oise* [ɑ̃burʒwa, -wa:z] *Geog:* 1. *a.* Of Hamburg. 2. *s.* Hamburger.
**hameau* [amo], *s.m.* Hamlet.
hameçon [amsɔ̃], *s.m.* (Fish-)hook. Prendre l'hameçon, (of fish) to take the hook; *F:* (of pers.) to swallow the bait. Mordre à l'hameçon, to nibble at the bait.
**hammam* [amam], *s.m.* Turkish baths.
**hampe* [ɑ̃:p], *s.f.* 1. Staff, pole (of flag, etc.); stave, shaft (of spear, etc.); shank (of fish-hook). 2. *Bot:* Scape, stem.
**hamster* [amstɛ:r], *s.m. Z:* Hamster.
**han* [ɑ̃], *int.* Sound of breath accompanying violent effort. *Pousser un han à chaque coup,* to give a grunt at every stroke.
**hanap* [anap], *s.m. A:* Goblet, tankard, hanap.
**hanche* [ɑ̃:ʃ], *s.f.* 1. Hip. Les (deux) poings sur les hanches, with arms akimbo. Tour de hanches, (i) measurement round the hips; (ii) *Wr:* cross-buttock. 2. Haunch (of horse); *pl.* hind-quarters. 3. *Nau:* Quarter (of ship). Par la hanche, on the quarter
**hanché* [ɑ̃ʃe], *a.* (At drill) *Dans la position hanchée,* (standing) at ease.
**handicap* [ɑ̃dikap], *s.m. Sp:* Handicap.
**handicaper* [ɑ̃dikape], *v.tr Sp:* To handicap. *s.m.* -age. *s.m.* -eur.
**hangar* [ɑ̃ga:r], *s.m.* 1. (Open) shed; lean-to. *H. à bateaux,* boat-house. 2. *Av:* Hangar.
**hanneton* [antɔ̃], *s.m.* 1. *a) Ent:* Cockchafer, may-bug. *F:* Avoir un hanneton dans le plafond = avoir une araignée dans le plafond, q.v. under ARAIGNÉE (b) *F:* Harum-scarum.
**hanse* [ɑ̃:s], *s.f. Hist:* Hanse. La Hanse, the Hanseatic League, the Hanse towns.
**hanséatique* [ɑ̃seatik], *a. Hist:* Hanseatic.
**hanter* [ɑ̃te], *v.tr.* To frequent, haunt. *Maison hantée (par les revenants),* haunted house Être

hanté par une idée, to be obsessed, possessed, by an idea. *s.m.* **-ement.** *s.* **-eur, -euse.**

*hantise [ɑ̃tiːz], *s.f.* Haunting memory; obsession.

*happe [ap], *s.f.* **1.** (*a*) Cramp; (joiner's) dogs. (*b*) *Metall:* Crucible tongs. (*c*) Cramp-iron. **2.** Staple. *Anneau à happe*, ring and staple.

*happ|er [ape]. **1.** *v.tr.* (Of birds, etc.) To snap up, snatch, seize, catch (insects, etc.). *F: Être happé par un gendarme*, to be nabbed by a policeman. **2.** *v.i.* (Of clay, etc.) To stick, adhere, cleave (to the tongue, to the lips). *s.m.* **-ement.**

*haquenée [akne], *s.f.* (*a*) *A:* Palfrey. (*b*) Hack; ambling mare. *Aller à la haquenée*, to amble along. *F: Une grande haquenée*, a tall gawky woman.

*haquet [ake], *s.m.* (Narrow) dray (for casks).

*harangue [arɑ̃ːg], *s.f.* Harangue; speech. *F: Faire une harangue à qn*, to jaw s.o.

*haranguer [arɑ̃ge], *v.tr.* (*a*) To harangue. (*b*) *F:* To lecture (s.o.).

*harangueur [arɑ̃gœːr], *s.m.* (*a*) Orator, speaker. (*b*) *F:* Speechifier, tub-thumper.

*haras [arɑ], *s.m.* **1.** Stud-farm; horse-breeding establishment. **2.** Stud.

*harasse [aras], *s.f.* Crate (for glass, etc.).

*harass|er [arase], *v.tr.* (*a*) To tire (out), exhaust; to override (horse). (*b*) To harass, worry. *s.m.* **-ement.**

*harcelant [arsəlɑ̃], *a.* Harassing, harrying, tormenting, worrying.

*harcèlement [arsɛlmɑ̃], *s.m.* = HARCELAGE.

*harcel|er [arsəle], *v.tr.* (je harcèle; je harcèlerai) To harass, worry, torment; to harry (the enemy); to bait (an animal). *H. qn de questions*, to pester, plague, s.o. with questions. *Harcelé par ses créanciers*, dunned, harried, by one's creditors. *s.m.* **-age.** *s.* **-eur, -euse.**

*harde¹ [ard], *s.f.* (*a*) *Ven:* Herd, bevy (of deer). (*b*) Flock (of birds).

*harde², *s.f. Ven:* Leash (for hounds).

*hardes [ard], *s.f.pl.* (Worn) clothes; wearing apparel; *F:* togs. *Marchand(e) de hardes*, wardrobe dealer.

*hardi [ardi], *a.* Bold, audacious. (*a*) Daring, fearless. *Écriture hardie*, bold hand(-writing). *H. à agir*, bold to act. (*b*) Rash, venturesome (undertaking). (*c*) Impudent, forward, brazen. (*d*) *int.* Courage! go it! *adv.* **-ment.**

*hardiesse [ardjɛs], *s.f.* **1.** Boldness, hardihood. (*a*) Daring, pluck. *Prendre la hardiesse de faire qch.*, to make so bold as to do sth. (*b*) Impudence, forwardness, effrontery. *Il a eu la h. de m'écrire*, he had the audacity, *F:* the cheek, to write to me. **2.** Bold, daring, act.

*harem [arɛm], *s.m.* Harem.

*hareng [arɑ̃], *s.m.* Herring. *H. bouffi*, bloater. *H.* (*salé et*) *fumé, h. doux*, kipper. *H. saur*, red herring. *S.a.* CAQUE.

*harengaison [arɑ̃gɛzɔ̃], *s.f.* (*a*) Herring-season. (*b*) (Season's) catch of herrings.

*harengère [arɑ̃ʒɛːr], *s.f.* Fish-woman, -wife.

*harenguet [arɑ̃gɛ], *s.m. Ich:* Sprat.

*harenguier [arɑ̃gje], *s.m.* **1.** Herring-boat. **2.** Herring-fisher.

*hargneu|x, -euse [arɲø, -øːz], *a.* Snarling (dog); peevish, cross, cross-grained, cantankerous (person); nagging (woman); ill-tempered, vicious (horse).

*haricot [ariko], *s.m.* **1.** *Cu: H. de mouton*, Irish stew, haricot mutton. **2.** *H. blanc*, haricot bean, kidney bean. *Haricots verts*, French beans. *Haricots d'Espagne*, scarlet runners.

*haricot-beurre, *s.m.* Butter-bean. *pl. Des haricots-beurre.*

*haridelle [aridɛl], *s.f. F:* (*a*) Old horse; screw. (*b*) Tall gaunt woman.

*harle [arl], *s.m. Orn:* Merganser.

harmonica [armɔnika], *s.m.* **1.** Harmonica; musical glasses. **2.** *H. à bouche*, mouth-organ.

harmonie [armɔni], *s.f.* **1.** (*a*) Harmony, consonance; accord, agreement. *En harmonie avec . . .*, in keeping with . . . ; of a piece with. . . . *Vivre en harmonie*, to live harmoniously. (*b*) Harmoniousness. **2.** *Mus:* (*a*) Harmony. *Table d'harmonie*, sounding-board (of piano, etc.). (*b*) Brass and reed band.

harmonieu|x, -euse [armɔnjø, -øːz], *a.* (*a*) Harmonious, melodious, tuneful (sound). (*b*) Harmonious (family, etc.). *Peu harmonieux*, inharmonious, discordant. *adv.* **-sement.**

harmonique [armɔnik]. **1.** *a.* Harmonic. **2.** *s.m. Mus:* Harmonic. *Harmoniques supérieurs*, overtones.

harmoniser [armɔnize], *v.tr.* **1.** To harmonize, attune (ideas); to match (colours). **2.** *Mus:* To harmonize (melody, etc.). **s'harmoniser**, to be in keeping, to harmonize, agree (*avec*, with). (Of colours) *S'h. avec qch.*, to tone in with sth.

harmoniste [armɔnist], *s. m. & f. Mus:* Harmonist.

harmonium [armɔnjɔm], *s.m.* Harmonium.

*harnachement [arnaʃmɑ̃], *s.m.* **1.** Harnessing. **2.** (*a*) Harness, trappings. (*b*) Saddlery.

*harnacher [arnaʃe], *v.tr.* (*a*) To harness. (*b*) *Pej:* To accoutre.

*harnais [arnɛ], *s.m.* **1.** (*a*) Harness. *Cheval de harnais*, draught-horse. (*b*) Saddlery. **2.** *A:* Harness; armour. *F:* Blanchi sous le harnais, grown grey in the service. *Reprendre le harnais*, to go back to work again. **3.** Train (of gearwheels); gearing.

*haro [aro], *int. & s.m.* (*Clameur de*) *h.*, outcry; hue and cry. *Crier haro*, to raise a hue and cry (*sur*, against).

harpagon [arpagɔ̃], *s.m. F:* Skinflint, miser. (Character in Molière's *L'Avare*.)

*harpe [arp], *s.f. Mus:* Harp. *Jouer, pincer, de la h.*, to play the harp.

*harpie [arpi], *s.f.* **1.** (*a*) *Myth:* Harpy. (*b*) *F:* Harpy, shrew, hell-cat. **2.** Harpy-eagle.

*harpin [arpɛ̃], *s.m.* Boat-hook.

*harpiste [arpist], *s. m. & f.* (*a*) Harpist (in orchestra). (*b*) Harper.

*harpon [arpɔ̃], *s.m.* **1.** Harpoon. *H. à trois branches*, grains. **2.** (Two-handed) cross-cut saw. **3.** Wall-staple; tie.

*harponn|er [arpɔne], *v.tr.* To harpoon. *s.m.* **-age.** *s.* **-eur.**

*hart [aːr], *s.f.* **1.** (*a*) Withe (for hurdling). (*b*) Band, binder (for bundling faggots). **2.** *A:* Rope, noose (for hanging). *Sous peine de la h.*, under penalty of the gallows.

*hasard [azaːr], *s.m.* **1.** (*a*) Chance, luck, accident. *Coup de hasard*, (i) stroke of luck; (ii) fluke. *Par un coup de h.*, by a mere chance. *Jeu de hasard*, game of chance. *Ne rien laisser au h.*, to leave nothing to chance. *Le hasard fit que + ind.* or *sub.*, chance so ordained that. . . . *Au hasard*, at a guess, at haphazard, at random. *Par hasard*, by accident, by chance. *Si par h. vous le voyez*, if you (should) happen to see him. *Sauriez-vous son adresse par h.?* do you by any chance know his address? (*b*) Risk, danger, hazard. *Courir le hasard*, to run the hazard, the risk. *Au hasard d'un refus, de tout perdre*, at the risk of a refusal, of losing everything. *A tout hasard*, (i) at all hazards; (ii) on the off chance;

(iii) to make assurance double sure. **2.** (a) *Golf:* Hazard. (b) *Ten:* (Of ball) **Faire hasard,** to break.

*hasarder [azarde], *v.tr.* To risk, venture, hazard (one's life, etc.). *H. une opinion,* to venture an opinion.

se hasarder, to take risks; to run risks. *Se h. à faire qch.,* to venture to do sth.

hasardé, *a.* Hazardous, risky, rash, foolhardy (action); indiscreet (words). *Chanson hasardée,* risky song.

*hasardeux, -euse [azardø, -ø:z], *a.* **1.** Hazardous, perilous, risky. **2.** Daring, foolhardy.

*hase [ɑ:z, a:z], *s.f.* (a) Doe-hare. (b) Doe-rabbit.

hast [ast], *s.m.* *A:* Shaft. **Arme d'hast,** shafted weapon; pike, spear.

*hasté [aste], *a.* *Bot:* Hastate (leaf, etc.).

*hâte [ɑ:t], *s.f.* Haste, hurry, precipitation. **Faire hâte,** to hurry, make haste. **Avoir hâte de faire qch.,** (i) to be in a hurry, in haste, to do sth.; (ii) to be eager, to long, to do sth. **A la hâte,** in a hurry, in haste, hastily, hurriedly. *Déjeuner à la h.,* to make a hurried breakfast. **Avec hâte,** en hâte, hastily; in haste. **En toute hâte,** with all possible speed; *F:* post-haste.

*hâter [ate], *v.tr.* To hasten; to hurry (sth.) on; to accelerate (proceedings); to expedite (work). **Hâter le pas,** to quicken one's pace.

se hâter, to hasten, hurry. *Se h. de faire qch.,* to make haste to do sth.; to lose no time in doing sth. *Prov:* **Hâtez-vous lentement,** more haste less speed.

*hâtier [atje], *s.m.* *Cu:* Spit-rack.

*hâtif, -ive [atif, -i:v], *a.* (a) Forward, early (spring, fruit); premature (old age); precocious (fruit, mind). (b) Hasty, hurried, ill-considered (measure, etc.). *adv.* **-ivement.**

*hauban [obã], *s.m.* *Nau:* (a) Shroud. *H. bâtard,* swifter. (b) Guy, stay. *Haubans de cheminée,* funnel-stays.

*hauban(n)er [obane], *v.tr.* To guy, stay, anchor, brace (post, etc.). *s.m.* **-age.**

*haubert [obɛ:r], *s.m.* *Archeol:* Hauberk; shirt or coat of mail.

*hausse [o:s], *s.f.* **1.** Rise, rising. **Baromètre à la hausse,** en hausse, barometer on the rise. *H. des prix,* advance, inflation, of prices. **Marchandises en hausse,** goods on the rise. **Jouer à la hausse,** to speculate on a rise; to bull the market. **Spéculateur à la hausse,** bull. **2.** (a) Prop, block, stand. (b) *Typ:* (i) Underlay; (ii) overlay. **3.** *Mil:* (a) (Back-)sight (of rifle). (b) *Artil:* Tangent-scale; sighting-gear. (c) Elevation, range.

*haussement [osmã], *s.m.* Raising; lifting. **Haussement d'épaules,** shrug(ging) of the shoulders; *F:* shrug.

*hausser [ose]. **1.** *v.tr.* To raise, lift; to heighten (wall); to put up (prices). *H. la voix,* to raise one's voice. **Hausser les épaules,** to shrug one's shoulders; *F:* to shrug. **2.** *v.i.* (a) To rise; (of prices) to go up. (b) *Nau:* (Of ship, land, etc.) To heave in sight.

se hausser. 1. To raise oneself. *Se h. pour voir,* to crane one's neck. **2.** *Le temps se hausse,* the clouds are lifting, the weather is clearing.

*haussier [osje], *s.m.* *St.Exch:* *F:* Bull.

*haut [o]. **I.** *a.* **1.** High. (a) Tall; lofty; towering (cliff). *Homme h. de taille, de haute taille,* tall man. **Mur haut de six pieds,** wall six foot high. *Hautes terres,* highlands. *Hautes eaux,* high water. *Haute mer,* open sea, high seas. **A mer haute,** at high water, at high tide. (b) Exalted, important, great. **Le Très-Haut,** the Most High (God). *De h. rang,* of high rank. *De hauts faits,*

doughty deeds. *La haute finance,* high finance. *Haute cuisine,* high-class cooking. (c) Raised. *Marcher la tête haute,* to carry one's head high. *Voix haute,* (i) loud voice; (ii) high voice. **Lire à haute voix,** to read aloud. (d) *Haute trahison,* high treason. **Être haut en couleur,** to have a high colour, a florid complexion. *Les hauts temps,* remote antiquity. *Mch:* *Haute pression,* high, heavy, pressure. **2.** Upper, higher. *Les hauts étages,* the upper stories. *Le plus h. étage,* the top floor. *Les hautes classes,* (i) the upper classes (of society); (ii) the higher, upper, forms (of school). *Les hautes mathématiques,* higher mathematics. **Le haut Rhin,** the Upper Rhine. **La Haute Écosse,** the Highlands. *S.a.* MAIN 1.

II. haut, *adv.* **1.** High (up), above, up. **Haut les mains!** hands up! *S.a.* MAIN 1. **Parler haut,** to speak loudly. *Parlez plus h.!* speak up! **Parler, penser, tout haut,** to talk, think, aloud. *Estimer qch. h.,* to set a high value on sth. **On homme haut placé,** a highly-placed man. *Viser h.,* to aim high. **2.** Back. *Remonter plus h. (dans le temps),* to go further back. *Comme il est dit plus h.,* as aforesaid.

III. haut, *s.m.* **1.** Height. *Le mur a six pieds de haut,* the wall is six foot high. **Traiter qn de son haut,** to patronize s.o. **Tomber de son haut,** (i) to fall flat on the ground; (ii) to fall from one's high estate. **Penser tomber de son haut,** to be very much taken aback; to be dumbfounded. **2.** Top; upper part. *F:* **Être au haut de l'échelle,** to be at the top of the ladder, of the tree. *S.a.* PAVÉ 2. *H. de la table,* head of the table. **Crier du haut de sa tête,** to cry out at the top of one's voice. **Les hauts et les bas,** the ups and downs (of life, etc.). *H. de l'eau,* high water; top of the flood. *Les hauts (d'un navire),* the topsides, upper works. *Typ:* **Haut de casse,** upper case; *F:* caps. **3.** De haut en bas, (i) downwards; (ii) from top to bottom. *Regarder qn de h. en bas,* to look at s.o. contemptuously; to look down on s.o. **Du haut en bas,** from top to bottom. **En haut,** (i) above, *Nau:* aloft; (ii) upstairs. *Nau:* **En h. tout le monde!** all hands on deck! **Je l'aperçus en haut de l'échelle,** I espied him at the top of the ladder.

*hautain [otɛ̃], *a.* Haughty. *adv.* **-ement.**

*hautbois [obwa], *s.m.* *Mus:* Oboe.

*hautboïste [oboist], *s.m. & f.* Oboe-player.

*haut-de-chausse(s), *s.m.* *Cost:* *A:* Breeches, trunk-hose.

*hautement [otmã], *adv.* **1.** Highly (esteemed, etc.). **2.** (a) Loudly, openly, boldly. **3.** Loftily, nobly.

*hauteur [otœ:r], *s.f.* **1.** (a) Height, elevation; altitude (of star, triangle). *Av:* **Prendre de la hauteur,** to climb. *Le peu de hauteur du plafond,* the lowness of the ceiling. *F:* **Tomber de sa hauteur,** to be dumbfounded. **A la hauteur de qch.,** abreast of, level with, sth. *A la h. de l'œil,* at eye level. *Être à la h. d'une tâche,* to be equal to a task. **Se montrer à la hauteur de la situation,** to prove equal to the occasion. *F:* **Être à la hauteur,** to be up to snuff. *Nau:* *A la h. du cap Horn,* off Cape Horn. (b) Depth (of bridge arch). **Hauteur sous clef,** rise (of arch). **Hauteur libre, de passage,** head-room. (c) *Mus:* Pitch (of note). (d) Loftiness (of ideas, etc.). **2.** Haughtiness, arrogance. **3.** High place; eminence, rising ground; hill-top.

*haut-fond, *s.m.* Shoal, shallow (in sea or river). *pl. Des hauts-fonds.*

*haut(-)fourneau, *s.m.* See FOURNEAU 1. *pl. Des hauts(-)fourneaux.*

*haut-le-cœur, *s.m.inv.* Heave (of stomach). *Avoir des h.-le-c.*, to retch, to feel sick.

*haut-le-corps, *s.m.inv.* Sudden start, jump.

*haut-le-pied, *a.inv.* **1.** *Mil:* (Of horse, etc.) Spare; in reserve. **2.** *Rail:* (Of engine) Running light; (of train) running empty.

*haut-mal, *s.m.* No *pl.* See MAL² 2.

*haut-parleur, *s.m.* *W.Tel:* Loud-speaker. Réception en haut-parleur, reception (i) on a loud-speaker, (ii) of loud-speaker strength. *pl. Des haut-parleurs.*

*haut-relief, *s.m.* *Art:* High relief, alto-relievo. *pl. Des hauts-reliefs.*

*hauturier, -ière [otyrje, -jɛːr], *a.* Of the high seas. Navigation hauturière, ocean navigation. Pilote hauturier, deep-sea pilot, 'proper pilot.'

*Havane [avan]. **1.** *Pr.n.f.* *Geog:* La Havane, Havana. **2.** *(a) s.m.* Havana (cigar). *(b) a.inv.* Cuir havane, brown leather.

*hâve [ɑːv], *a.* Haggard, gaunt (face); sunken (cheeks).

*havir [aviːr], *v.tr.* To scorch, burn (meat).

*havre [ɑːvr]. **1.** *s.m.* Harbour, haven, port. **2.** *Pr.n.m.* Le Havre, Havre.

*havresac [avrəsak], *s.m. (a) Mil: A:* Knapsack, pack. *(b)* (Workman's) tool-bag.

hawaïen, -ienne [avajɛ̃, -wa-, -jɛn], *a. & s. Geog:* Hawaiian.

*Haye (la) [laɛ]. *Pr.n.f.* The Hague.

*hé [e], *int.* **1.** (To call attention) Hullo! hi, there! I say! **2.** (Surprise) Hey! what! **3.** *Hé! hé!* well, well! **4.** *Hé bien . . .,* well. . . .

*heaume [oːm], *s.m.* *Archeol:* Helm(et).

hebdomadaire [ɛbdɔmadɛːr]. **1.** *a.* Weekly. **2.** *s.m. F:* Weekly (paper).

hebdomadairement [ɛbdɔmadɛrmɑ̃], *adv.* Weekly; once a week.

héberg|er [ebɛrʒe], *v.tr.* (j'hébergeai(s); n. hébergeons) To harbour; to lodge, shelter (and feed). *s.m.* **-ement.** *s.* **-eur, -euse.**

hébétement [ebetmɑ̃], *s.m.* Stupefaction.

hébéter [ebete], *v.tr.* (j'hébète; j'hébéterai) To dull, stupefy (the senses, etc.); to daze. **hébété**, *a.* Dazed, vacant, bewildered (expression). *s. Il agit comme un h.,* he acts as if he were in a daze.

hébétude [ebetyd], *s.f.* **1.** *Med:* Hebetude. **2.** *F:* Dazed, stunned, condition.

hébraïque [ebraik], *a.* Hebraic, Hebrew.

hébreu, -eux [ebrø]. **1.** *a.m.* (HÉBRAÏQUE is used for the *f.*) Hebrew. **2.** *s.m. Ling:* L'hébreu, Hebrew.

hécatombe [ekatɔ̃ːb], *s.f. (a)* Hecatomb. *(b) F:* Great slaughter.

hectare [ektaːr], *s.m.* Hectare (= 2·47 acres).

hectique [ektik], *a. Med:* Hectic.

hectogramme [ektɔgram], *s.m.* Hectogramme.

hectolitre [ɛktɔlitr], *s.m.* Hectolitre (= 2·75 bushels).

hédonisme [edɔnism], *s.m. Eth:* Hedonism.

hégémonie [eʒemɔni], *s.f.* Hegemony.

hégire [eʒiːr], *s.f. Moham.Rel:* Hegira.

*hein [ɛ̃], *int. (a)* (Expressing surprise) Eh? what? *(b) = n'est-ce pas.*

hélas [elɑːs], *int.* Alas!

Hélène [elen]. *Pr.n.f.* Helen, Helena; *F:* Ellen.

*héler [ele], *v.tr.* (je hèle; je hélerai) To hail, call (s.o., a taxi); to hail (a ship).

hélianthe [eljɑ̃ːt], *s.m.* Helianthus, sunflower.

héliaque [eljak], *a. Astr:* Heliac(al).

hélice [elis], *s.f.* **1.** *Geom:* Helix; spiral line. Escalier en hélice, spiral staircase. **2.** *(a) Mec.E:* Archimedean screw; conveyance worm. *(b) Nau:*

(Screw-)propeller, screw. Vapeur à deux hélices, twin-screw steamer. *Av:* H. tractive, air-screw. H. propulsive, propeller. **3.** *Moll:* Helix.

hélicoïdal, -aux [elikɔidal, -o], *a.* Helicoid(al), helical. *Tls:* Mèche hélicoïdale, twist drill.

hélicoïde [elikɔid], *a. & s.m. Geom:* Helicoid.

hélicon [elikɔ̃], *s.m. Mus:* (Helicon) bombardon.

hélicoptère [elikɔptɛːr], *s.m. Av:* Helicopter.

héliochromie [eljɔkrɔmi], *s.f.* Heliochromy; colour photography.

héliographe [eljɔgraf], *s.m.* Heliograph.

héliograveur [eljɔgravœːr], *s.m.* Photogravure worker.

héliogravure [eljɔgravyːr], *s.f.* Photogravure.

héliostat [eljɔsta], *s.m.* **1.** *Astr: Surv:* Heliostat. **2.** *Mil:* Heliograph.

héliothérapie [eljɔterapi], *s.f. Med:* Heliotherapy; sunlight treatment.

héliotrope [eljɔtrɔp], *s.m. (a) Bot:* Heliotrope; turnsole. *(b) a.inv.* Heliotrope(-coloured).

hélium [eljɔm], *s.m. Ch:* Helium.

hélix [eliks], *s.m. Anat:* Helix (of the ear).

hellébore [ellebɔːr], *s.m. Bot:* = ELLÉBORE.

hellène [ɛllɛn]. **1.** *a.* Hellenic. **2.** *s.* Hellene.

hellénique [ɛllenik], *a. Hist:* Hellenic.

helvète [ɛlvɛt]. **1.** *a. & s. Ethn:* Helvetian. **2.** *s.m.pl. Hist:* Les Helvètes, the Helvetii.

Helvétie [ɛlvesi]. *Pr.n.f. A. & Poet:* Helvetia.

helvétique [ɛlvetik], *a.* Helvetic, Swiss.

*hem [ɛm], *int.* (A)hem! hm!

hématie [emati], *s.f.* Red blood corpuscle.

hématite [ematit], *s.f. Miner:* Haematite.

hémicranie [emikrani], *s.f. Med:* Hemicrania, migraine.

hémicycle [emisikl], *s.m. Arch:* Hemicycle.

hémione [emjon], *s.m. Z:* Hemione, dziggetai.

hémiplégie [emipleʒi], *s.f. Med:* Hemiplegia.

hémiptère [emiptɛːr]. *Ent:* **1.** *a.* Hemipterous, hemipteral. **2.** *s.m.* Hemipter.

hémisphère [emisfɛːr], *s.m.* Hemisphere.

hémisphérique [emisferik], *a.* Hemispheric(al).

hémistiche [emistiʃ], *s.m. Pros:* Hemistich.

hémoglobine [emɔglɔbin], *s.f.* Haemoglobin.

hémophilie [emɔfili], *s.f. Med:* Haemorrhagic diathesis; haemophilia.

hémophilique [emɔfilik], *s.m. & f. Med:* Haemophile; *F:* bleeder.

hémorragie [emɔraʒi], *s.f. Med:* Haemorrhage; bleeding.

hémorroïdes [emɔrɔid], *s.f.pl. Med:* Haemorrhoids, piles.

hendécagone [ɛ̃dekagon], *s.m. Med:* Hendecagon.

*henné [enne], *s.m. Bot: Toil:* Henna.

*hennir [aniːr, ɛn-], *v.i.* To whinny; to neigh.

*hennissement [anismɑ̃, ɛn-], *s.m. (a)* Whinnying, neighing. *(b)* Whinny, neigh.

Henri [ɑ̃ri]. *Pr.n.m.* Henry.

Henriette [ɑ̃rjɛt]. *Pr.n.f.* Henrietta.

hépatique [epatik]. **1.** *a.* Hepatic. **2.** *s.f. Bot:* Hepatica; *F:* liverwort.

heptagonal, -aux [ɛptagonal, -o], *a.* Heptagonal.

heptagone [ɛptagon]. *Geom:* **1.** *a.* Heptagonal. **2.** *s.m.* Heptagon.

heptamètre [ɛptamɛtr], *s.m. Pros:* Heptameter.

heptarchie [ɛptarʃi], *s.f. Hist:* Heptarchy.

héraldique [eraldik]. **1.** *a.* Heraldic; armorial. **2.** *s.f.* Heraldry.

*héraut [ero], *s.m. (a)* Herald. *(b)* Harbinger (of spring, etc.).

herbacé [ɛrbase], *a. Bot:* Herbaceous.

herbage [ɛrbaːʒ], *s.m.* **1.** Grass-land; pasture. **2.** Grass, herbage.

herbag|er¹ [ɛrbaʒe], *v.tr.* (j'herbageai(s); n.

herbageons) To put (animals) out to grass. **s.m. -ement.**

herbager², *s.m.* Grazier.

herbe [ɛrb], *s.f.* **1.** Herb, plant, weed. **Herbes potagères,** pot-herbs. **Fines herbes,** herbs for seasoning. *Omelette aux fines herbes,* savoury omelet. **Herbes marines,** seaweed. **Mauvaise herbe,** weed. S.a. CROÎTRE. *F: Sur quelle herbe avez-vous marché?* what's the matter with you? **2.** Grass. **Brin d'herbe,** blade of grass. **Faire de l'herbe,** to cut grass (for cattle). **Mettre un cheval à l'herbe,** to turn a horse out to grass. *F: Couper l'herbe sous le pied à qn,* to cut the ground from under s.o.'s feet. **Dîner sur l'herbe,** to picnic. **3.** En herbe, (i) green, unripe (corn, etc.); (ii) *F:* budding (poet). *Diplomate en h.,* diplomatist in embryo. S.a. BLÉ. **4.** *Bot:* (Familiar appellations) *H. aux chats,* catmint, *U.S:* catnip. *H. au cœur, aux poumons,* lungwort. *H. aux écus,* money-wort. *H. à éternuer,* sneezewort. *H. à loup,* wolf's-bane, monk's-hood. *H. aux puces,* flea-bane.

herbette [ɛrbɛt], *s.f.* (a) Lawn-grass. (b) *Poet:* (Green)sward.

herbeux, -euse [ɛrbø, -øːz], *a.* Grassy.

herbier [ɛrbje], *s.m.* **1.** (a) Herbal. (b) Herbarium. **2.** Loft or shed for cut grass.

herbivore [ɛrbivɔːr]. *Z:* **1.** *a.* Herbivorous, grass-eating. **2.** *s.m.* Herbivore.

herboris|er [ɛrbɔrize], *v.i.* To herborize; to botanize. *s.f.* **-ation.**

herboriste [ɛrbɔrist], *s. m. & f.* Herbalist.

herboristerie [ɛrbɔristri], *s.f.* Herbalist's shop.

herbu [ɛrby], *a.* Grassy; grass-grown.

*****herche** [ɛrʃ], *s.f. Min:* Waggon; skip, tub.

*****herch|er** [ɛrʃe], *v.i. Min:* To haul coal, ore. *s.m.* **-age.**

*****hercheur, -euse** [ɛrʃœːr, -øːz], *s. Min:* Haulage-man, -boy, -girl.

Herculanum [ɛrkylanɔm]. *Pr.n.m. A.Geog:* Herculaneum.

Hercule [ɛrkyl]. *Pr.n.m.* Hercules. *F: Travail d'Hercule,* Herculean task.

herculéen, -enne [ɛrkyleɛ̃, -ɛn], *a.* Herculean.

*****hère** [ɛːr], *s.m. F: Un pauvre h.,* a poor luckless wight (lacking in character, devoid of means). *Pauvre h.!* poor devil!

héréditaire [ereditɛːr], *a.* Hereditary; (disease) that runs in the family. *adv.* **-ment.**

hérédité [eredite], *s.f.* **1.** *Jur: Biol:* Hereditary principle; heredity. **2.** Right of inheritance; heirship.

hérésie [erezi], *s.f.* Heresy.

hérétique [eretik]. **1.** *a.* Heretical. **2.** *s.* Heretic.

*****hériss|er** [erise], *v.tr.* (a) To bristle (up). (Of bird) *H. ses plumes,* to ruffle up, put up, its feathers. (b) To make (sth.) bristle; to cover, surround, with spikes. *s.m.* **-ement.**

se hérisser, to bristle (up); (of hair) to stand on end; *F:* (of pers.) to get one's back up.

hérissé, *a.* **1.** Bristling (de, with). **2.** (a) Spiky (hair); bristly (moustache). *Bot:* Prickly (stem, fruit). (b) Shaggy, rough (hair, etc.).

*****hérisson** [erisɔ̃], *s.m.* **1.** *Z:* Hedgehog. (b) Hérisson de mer, (i) sea-urchin; (ii) porcupine-fish. (c) *F:* Cross-grained person. **2.** (a) Row of spikes (on wall, etc.). (b) Bottle-drainer. **3.** *Mec.E:* Sprocket-wheel; pin-wheel. **4.** (a) (Sweep's) flue-brush. (b) Bottle-brush.

héritage [erita:ʒ], *s.m.* Inheritance, heritage. **Part d'héritage,** portion. **Faire un héritage,** to come into money, into a legacy. *H. de honte,* legacy of shame.

hériter [erite]. **1.** *v.i. H. d'une fortune,* to

inherit, succeed to, come into, a fortune. **2.** *v.tr. H. qch. de qn,* to inherit sth. from s.o.

héritier, -ière [eritje, -jɛːr], *s.* Heir, *f.* heiress. *H. de qch., de qn,* heir to sth., to s.o. **Héritier présomptif,** (i) next-of-kin; (ii) heir apparent. **Héritier légitime,** heir-at-law, rightful heir.

hermétique [ɛrmetik], *a.* **1.** Hermetic (philosophy). **2.** Tight(-closed), hermetically sealed. *Joint h.,* (air-, water-)tight joint. *adv.* **-ment,** -ally.

hermine [ɛrmin], *s.f.* **1.** *Z:* Stoat, ermine. **2.** *Com:* Ermine (fur).

herminette [ɛrminɛt], *s.f. Tls:* Adze.

hermite [ɛrmit], *s.m.* = ERMITE.

*****herniaire** [ɛrnjɛːr]. **1.** *a.* Hernial (tumour, etc.). **Bandage herniaire,** truss. **2.** *s.f. Bot:* Rupturewort.

*****hernie** [ɛrni], *s.f.* **1.** Hernia, rupture. **2.** *Aut: Cy:* Bulge, swelling (in tyre).

*****hernieux, -euse** [ɛrnjø, -øːz], *a.* Suffering from hernia; ruptured.

héroï-comique [erɔikɔmik], *a.* Heroi-comic, mock-heroic.

héroïne¹ [erɔin], *s.f.* Heroine.

héroïne², *s.f. Ch:* Heroin.

héroïque [erɔik], *a.* Heroic(al). *adv.* **-ment,** -ally.

héroïsme [erɔism], *s.m.* Heroism.

*****héron** [erɔ̃], *s.m. Orn:* Heron.

*****héronneau** [erɔno], *s.m.* Young heron.

*****héronnière** [erɔnjɛːr], *s.f.* Heronry.

*****héros** [ero], *s.m.* Hero.

herpès [ɛrpɛs], *s.m. Med:* Herpes, tetter.

herpétique [ɛrpetik], *a. Med:* Herpetic.

*****herse** [ɛrs], *s.f.* **1.** *Agr:* Harrow. **2.** *A.Fort:* Portcullis, herse. **3.** (a) *Ecc:* (Taper-)hearse. (b) *pl. Th:* Stage lights; battens.

*****hers|er** [ɛrse], *v.tr. Agr:* To harrow. *s.m.* **-age.** *s.m.* **-eur.**

hertzien, -ienne [ɛrtsjɛ̃, -jɛn], *a. El:* Hertzian.

hésitation [ezitasjɔ̃], *s.f.* Hesitation, hesitancy, wavering. **Parler avec hésitation,** to speak hesitatingly. **Sans hésitation,** unhesitatingly.

hésit|er [ezite], *v.i.* **1.** To hesitate, waver. *H. sur ce qu'on fera,* to hesitate as to what one will do. *H. à, pour, faire qch.,* to hesitate, be reluctant, to do sth.; to hold back. *Il n'hésite devant rien,* he sticks at nothing. **2.** To falter. *a.* **-ant.**

hétéroclite [eterɔklit], *a.* **1.** *Gram:* Heteroclite, irregular (noun, etc.). **2.** Unusual, strange, odd, queer; uncouth (behaviour).

hétérodoxe [eterɔdɔks], *a.* Heterodox.

hétérodoxie [eterɔdɔksi], *s.f.* Heterodoxy.

hétérodyne [eterɔdin], *a. & s.m. W.Tel:* Heterodyne (receiver).

hétérogène [eterɔʒɛn], *a.* (a) Heterogeneous, dissimilar. (b) *F:* Incongruous (collection, etc.); mixed (society).

hétérogénéité [eterɔʒeneite], *s.f.* Heterogeneousness, heterogeneity.

*****hêtraie** [ɛtrɛ], *s.f.* Beech-grove, -plantation.

*****hêtre** [ɛːtr], *s.m.* Beech (tree or timber). *H. rouge, pourpre,* copper beech.

*****heu** [ø], *int.* (a) Ah! (b) (Doubt) H'm! (c) (Contempt) Pooh! hmph! (d) (In speech) . . . er. . . .

heur [œːr], *s.m. A. & Lit:* Luck, chance; usu. good luck. *Il n'est qu'heur et malheur,* we must take the rough with the smooth. *Iron: Je n'ai pas l'h. de la connaître,* I have not the pleasure of her acquaintance.

heure [œːr], *s.f.* Hour. **1.** (a) *A toutes heures du jour,* at all hours of the day. **D'heure en heure,** hour by hour; hourly. **Deux lieues à l'heure,** five miles an hour. *Travail à l'h.,* time-work.

Être payé à l'h., to be paid by time. **Homme à l'heure**, casual labourer. *Journ:* **La dernière heure**, (i) the latest news; (ii) stop-press news. *Ind:* **Heures hors cloche**, **supplémentaires**, overtime. (b) (Time of day) *L'h. de Greenwich*, Greenwich mean time. *H. astronomique*, sidereal time. *H. légale*, civil time. *H. d'été*, summer time. **Quelle heure est-il?** what is the time? what o'clock is it? *Cinq heures moins dix*, ten minutes to five. *Dix heures cinquante*, ten fifty. *Où serai-je demain à cette heure-ci?* where shall I be this time to-morrow? *Jouer au bridge jusqu'à pas d'heure*, to play bridge till all hours. **Mettre sa montre à l'heure**, to set one's watch (right). *Ecc:* **Livre d'heures**, prayer-book. (c) (Appointed hour) *L'h. du dîner*, dinner-time. *Aut:* **H. d'éclairage**, lighting-up time. *A l'h. dite*, at the appointed time. **Être à l'heure**, to be punctual. *Arriver à l'h.*, to arrive on time. *Il est l'h.*, (i) the hour has come ; (ii) the hour is striking ; (iii) time is up. (d) (Present time) **Pour l'heure**, for the present, for the time being. *La question de l'h.*, the question of the hour. **A l'heure qu'il est**, (i) by this time ; (ii) nowadays, just now. (e) Time. *Il y eut une h. où . . .*, there was a time when. . . . **2.** *Adv.phrs.* **De bonne heure**, (i) early, betimes, in good time ; (ii) at an early period. *Il est de trop bonne h. pour rentrer*, it is too early to go home. *De meilleure h.*, earlier. *Faire qch. sur l'heure*, to do sth. at once, right away. *Je vais le faire dès cette heure*, I will do it at once. **Tout à l'heure**, (i) just now, a few minutes ago ; (ii) presently, in a few minutes, *F:* directly. *A tout à l'heure!* so long ! see you later ! **3.** *int.* **A la bonne heure!** well done ! capital ! that's right !

heureusement [œrøzmã], *adv.* Happily. (a) Successfully. (b) Luckily, fortunately. *H. que j'étais là*, it is a good thing that I was there. (c) *Commencer h.*, to begin auspiciously. (d) *Des pensées h. exprimées*, felicitously expressed thoughts.

heureux, -euse [œrø, -ø:z], *a.* **I.** Happy. *Une heureuse ignorance*, blissful ignorance. *H. du bonheur des autres*, happy, rejoicing, in the happiness of others. *Je suis très h. de vous faire savoir que . . .*, I am very happy, pleased, to inform you that. . . . *Nous serions h. que vous acceptiez*, we should be glad if you would accept. **2.** (a) Successful. *Voyage h.*, prosperous voyage. *L'issue heureuse des négociations*, the happy issue of the negotiations. (b) Lucky, favoured. *H. au jeu, en amour*, lucky at cards, in love. *Le feu roi, d'heureuse mémoire*, the late king, of blessed memory. *B:* *H. sont les pauvres en esprit*, blessed are the poor in spirit. **3.** (a) Favourable, lucky, fortunate. *C'est h., il est fort h., que vous soyez libre*, it is a (very) good thing that you are free. *Par un h. accident . . .*, by a fortunate accident. . . . (b) *Début h.*, auspicious beginning. **4.** Felicitous, happy, apt (phrase, etc.). [HEUR]

*heurt** [œ:r], *s.m.* Shock, blow, knock, bump. **Tout s'est fait sans heurt**, everything went smoothly.

*heurtement** [œrt(ə)mã], *s.m.* Clashing, clash.

*heurter** [œrte], *v.tr. & i.* **I.** (a) To knock (against), run against, run into (s.o., sth.). *H. de la tête contre une muraille*, to run one's head against a wall. *H. du pied contre une pierre*, to stub one's toe, to stumble, against a stone. (b) *H. à la porte*, to knock at the door. **2.** To shock, offend (s.o.'s feelings, etc.). *H. toutes les idées reçues*, to go against, run counter to, all conventions.

se heurter. **I.** *Se h. à, contre, avec, qn*, to

run (slap) into s.o. *Se h. à une difficulté*, to come up against a difficulty. **2.** To collide.

heurté, *a.* **I.** *Phot:* Contrasty, hard (negative). **2.** *Lit:* Abrupt or halting (style).

*heurtoir** [œrtwa:r], *s.m.* **I.** Door-knocker. **2.** (a) Door-stop. (b) *Mec.E:* (i) Catch, stop. (ii) Driver, tappet. (c) *Rail:* Bumping post (of siding). **3.** Sill (of lock-gate).

*heuse** [ø:z], *s.f.* Plunger, bucket (of pump).

*hévé** [eve], *s.m.* Hevea ; Para rubber plant.

hexacorde [εgzakɔrd], *s.m. Mus:* Hexachord.

hexaèdre [εgzaεdr]. **I.** *a.* Hexahedral. **2.** *s.m.* Hexahedron.

hexagonal, -aux [εgzagɔnal, -o], *a.* Hexagonal.

hexagone [εgzagɔn]. **I.** *a.* Hexagonal. **2.** *s.m.* Hexagon.

hexamètre [εgzamεtr]. *Pros:* **I.** *a.* Hexametric(al). **2.** *s.m.* Hexameter.

hiatus [iaty:s], *s.m.* **I.** Gap, break (in narrative, etc.). **2.** *Pros: Anat:* Hiatus.

hibernal, -aux [ibεrnal, -o], *a.* Hibernal (germination, etc.) ; wintry (temperature).

hibernant [ibεrnã], *a.* Hibernating (animal).

hibernation [ibεrnasjɔ̃], *s.f.* Hibernation.

hiberner [ibεrne], *v.i.* To hibernate.

*hibou, -oux** [ibu], *s.m. Orn:* Owl. *Jeune h.*, owlet. *F:* **Faire le hibou**, to mope.

*hic** [ik], *s.m. F:* (Used in the phr.) **Voilà le hic!** there's the rub !

*hideur** [idœ:r], *s.f.* (a) Hideousness. (b) Hideous sight.

*hideux, -euse** [idø, -ø:z], *a.* Hideous. *H. à voir*, hideous to behold. *adv.* **-sement.**

*hie** [i], *s.f.* **I.** (Paviour's) beetle, (earth-)rammer. **2.** Pile-driver.

hièble [jεbl], *s.f. Bot:* Dwarf elder.

hiémal, -aux [iεmal, jε-, -o], *a.* Hiemal ; winter (solstice, etc.).

hier [iε:r]. **I.** *adv.* Yesterday. *H. (au) matin*, yesterday morning. *H. (au) soir*, last night. *Je ne suis arrivé que d'h.*, I only arrived yesterday. **2.** *s.m. Vous aviez tout h. pour vous décider*, you had all yesterday to make up your mind.

*hiérarchie** [jerarʃi], *s.f.* Hierarchy.

*hiérarchique** [jerarʃik], *a.* Hierarchical. **Par voie hiérarchique**, through the official channels.

*hiérarchiquement** [jerarʃikmã], *adv.* Hierarchically ; through the usual channels.

hiéroglyphe [jerɔglif], *s.m.* (a) Hieroglyph. (b) *pl.* Hieroglyphics.

hiéroglyphique [jerɔglifik], *a.* Hieroglyphic(al).

*hi-han** [iã], *onomat.* (Donkey's) Hee-haw.

hi hi [ii], *onomat.* (Sound of tittering) He, he !

hilarant [ilarã], *a.* Mirth-provoking. *Ch:* **Gaz hilarant**, laughing gas.

hilare [ila:r], *a.* Hilarious, mirthful.

hilarité [ilarite], *s.f.* Hilarity, mirth, laughter.

*hile** [il], *s.m. Anat: Bot:* Hilum.

hiloire [ilwa:r], *s.f. N.Arch:* **I.** Binding-strake (of deck). **2.** *H. de panneau*, hatch-coaming.

hindou, -oue [ɛ̃du], *a. & s. Ethn:* Hindu.

hippique [ippik], *a.* Relating to horses ; equine. **Concours hippique**, (i) horse-show ; (ii) race-meeting.

hippisme [ippism], *s.m.* Horse-racing.

hippocampe [ippokã:p], *s.m. Ich:* Hippocampus, sea-horse.

hippodrome [ip(p)ɔdrɔm, -drɔːm], *s.m.* **I.** Hippodrome, circus. **2.** Race-course.

hippomobile [ippɔmɔbil], *a.* Horse-drawn.

hippophagie [ippɔfaʒi], *s.f.* Hippophagy.

hippophagique [ippɔfaʒik], *a.* **Boucherie hippophagique**, horse-butcher's.

hippopotame [ip(p)ɔpɔtam], *s.m.* Z: Hippopotamus.

hircin [irsɛ̃], *a.* Hircine, goatish.

hirondeau [irɔ̃do], *s.m.* Young swallow.

hirondelle [irɔ̃dɛl], *s.f.* **1.** Orn: Swallow. H. domestique, common swallow. H. de fenêtre, house-martin. H. de rivage, sand-martin. Prov: Une hirondelle ne fait pas le printemps, one swallow does not make a summer. **2.** Small river steamboat (for passengers).

hirsute [irsyt], *a.* **1.** Hirsute, hairy, shaggy. **2.** F: Rough, boorish.

hispanique [ispanik], *a.* Hispanic, Spanish.

hispanisant [ispanizɑ̃], *s.m.* Student of Spanish.

hispide [ispid], *a.* Hispid ; hairy, rough.

***hiss|er** [ise], *v.tr.* To hoist (up), pull up; to trice (up) (sail) ; to hoist in (boat) ; to run up (signal). S.a. BLOC 1. *s.m.* **-age.**

  se hisser. Se h. jusqu'à la fenêtre, to pull, hoist, oneself up to the window. Se h. le long du mur, to climb up the wall. Se h. sur la pointe des pieds, to raise oneself, stand, on tiptoe.

histoire [istwaːr], *s.f.* **1.** (a) History. Tableau, peintre, d'h., historical painting, painter. Livre d'h., history-book. (b) Histoire naturelle, natural history. **2.** Story, tale, narrative. H. de marin, sailor's yarn. Livre d'histoires, story-book. F: C'est toujours la même histoire, it's the old, old story. Le plus beau de l'h., c'est que . . ., the best of the story, of the business, is that. . . . F: Il est sorti, histoire de prendre l'air un peu, he went out merely, just, to get a breath of fresh air. S.a. RIRE 2. F: En voilà une histoire! here's a pretty go, a pretty kettle of fish ! C'est toute une histoire, (i) it's a long story ; (ii) it's no end of a job. Iron: La belle histoire! what about it? **3.** F: Fib, story. Tout ça c'est des histoires, that's all bunkum ; it's all my eye (and Betty Martin). **4.** F: Faire des histoires, un tas d'histoires, to make a fuss, a to-do. Faire des histoires à qn, to put difficulties in s.o.'s way ; to make trouble. Il faut éviter d'avoir des histoires, you, we, must keep out of trouble.

histologie [istɔlɔʒi], *s.f.* Histology.

historien, -ienne [istɔrjɛ̃, -jɛn], *s.* Historian.

historier [istɔrje], *v.tr.* To illustrate, embellish, illuminate (Bible, etc.).

  historié, *a.* Historiated (initials) ; illuminated (Bible, etc.) ; storied (window).

historiette [istɔrjɛt], *s.f.* Anecdote ; short story.

historique [istɔrik]. **1.** *a.* Historic(al). F: C'est historique, it actually happened. Gram: Présent h., historic present. **2.** *s.m.* Historical account ; recital of the facts. adv. **-ment,** -ally.

histrion [istriɔ̃], *s.m.* (a) Histrion, play-actor. (b) F: (Political, etc.) mountebank.

histrionique [istriɔnik], *a.* Histrionic ; stagy.

hiver [iveːr], *s.m.* Winter. En hiver, in winter. A l'hiver, when winter is at hand. Temps d'h., wintry weather. Lit: Il compte soixante hivers, he has seen sixty winters. F: Le bonhomme Hiver, Jack Frost.

hivernage [ivernaːʒ], *s.m.* **1.** (a) Wintering (of cattle, etc.). (b) Laying up (of ships) for the winter. **2.** Winter season. **3.** Winter quarters. Nau: Winter harbour. **4.** Winter fodder.

hivernal, -aux [ivernal, -o], *a.* Winter (cold, etc.) ; wintry (weather).

hivernant [ivernɑ̃], *a.* Wintering. *s.m.pl.* Winter visitors (on the Riviera, etc.).

hivern|er [iverne], *v.i.* (a) To winter ; (of ship) to lie up (for the winter). (b) (Of animal) To hibernate. *s.* **-eur, -euse.**

***ho** [o], *int.* **1.** (Call) Hi ! **2.** (Surprise) Oh !

***hobereau** [ɔbro], *s.m.* **1.** Orn: Hobby. **2.** F: Squireen.

***hoche** [ɔʃ], *s.f.* Notch, nick (on tally, etc.).

***hochepot** [ɔʃpo], *s.m.* Cu: Hotch-potch.

***hochequeue** [ɔʃkø], *s.m.* Orn: Wagtail.

***hoch|er**[1] [ɔʃe], *v.tr. & i.* H. (de) la tête, (i) to shake one's head ; (ii) to nod ; (iii) (of pers. or horse) to toss the head. *s.m.* **-ement.**

***hocher**[2], *v.tr.* To notch, nick (tally, etc.).

***hochet** [ɔʃe], *s.m.* (a) (Child's) rattle or coral. (b) Bauble, toy.

hodomètre [ɔdɔmɛtr], *s.m.* = ODOMÈTRE.

hoir [waːr], *s.m.* Jur: Heir.

hoirie [wari], *s.f.* Jur: Inheritance, succession.

***holà** [ɔla], *int.* **1.** Hallo ! **2.** Stop ! enough ! Mettre le holà, to interfere (in a fight). Mettre le h. au désordre, to put a stop to disorder.

***hollandais, -aise** [ɔlɑ̃dɛ, -ɛːz]. **1.** *a.* Dutch. **2.** *s.* Dutchman, -woman. **3.** *s.m.* Ling: Le Hollandais, Dutch.

***Hollande** [ɔlɑ̃ːd]. **1.** Pr.n.f. Geog: Holland. **2.** *s.m.* (Also fromage de Hollande) Dutch cheese. **3.** *s.f.* Holland (cambric).

holocauste [ɔlɔkost], *s.m.* Holocaust ; (i) burnt-offering, (ii) sacrifice.

holoèdre [ɔlɔɛdr]. Cryst: **1.** *a.* Holohedral. **2.** *s.m.* Holohedron.

holographe [ɔlɔgraf], *a.* = OLOGRAPHE.

holothurie [ɔlɔtyri], *s.f.* Echin: Holothurian, sea-slug, sea-cucumber.

***homard** [ɔmaːr], *s.m.* Lobster. H. épineux, crayfish.

homélie [ɔmeli], *s.f.* Homily.

homéopathe [ɔmeɔpat]. Med: **1.** *a.* Homoeopathic. **2.** *s.m.* Homoeopath.

homéopathie [ɔmeɔpati], *s.f.* Homoeopathy.

homéopathique [ɔmeɔpatik], *a.* Homoeopathic.

Homère [ɔmɛːr]. Pr.n.m. Gr.Lit: Homer.

homérique [ɔmerik], *a.* Homeric.

homicide[1] [ɔmisid]. **1.** *s.m. & f.* Homicide. **2.** *a.* Homicidal ; Poet: murderous (weapon).

homicide[2], *s.m.* Jur: Homicide (as a crime). H. volontaire, murder. H. excusable, justifiable homicide. H. par imprudence, h. involontaire, manslaughter (through negligence).

hommage [ɔmaːʒ], *s.m.* **1.** Homage. Faire, rendre, hommage à qn, (i) to do, render, homage, to pay obeisance to s.o. ; (ii) to pay a tribute to s.o. **2.** *pl.* Respects, compliments. Présenter ses hommages à une dame, (i) to pay one's respects, (ii) to send one's compliments, to a lady. **3.** Tribute, token (of respect, esteem). H. de l'éditeur, exemplaire en h., complimentary copy, presentation copy.

hommasse [ɔmas], *a.* F: (Of woman) Masculine, mannish.

homme [ɔm], *s.m.* Man. (a) Mankind. Tous les hommes, all men, all mankind. De mémoire d'homme, within living memory. Les droits de l'h., the rights of man. (b) (Opposed to woman or boy) Soyez un h.! be a man ! Homme fait, grown man. Jeune homme, see JEUNE. Se battre homme à homme, to fight man to man. F: Mon homme, my husband. (c) (Individual, pl. hommes or gens, q.v.) Il n'est pas mon h., he is not the man for me. Trouver son homme, to meet one's match. Homme à tout, man of all work. Homme d'État, statesman. Homme de mer, seafaring man. Homme de journée, de peine, (day-)labourer. S.a. AFFAIRE 3, BIEN II. 1, BRAVE 2, MONDE 1, PAILLE 1. (d) Z: Homme des bois, orang-outang.

homocentrique [ɔmɔsɑ̃trik], *a.* Homocentric.

homogène [ɔmɔʒɛn], *a.* Homogeneous.

homogénéité [ɔmɔʒeneite], *s.f.* Homogeneousness, homogeneity.

homologation [ɔmɔlɔgasjɔ̃], *s.f. Jur :* Confirmation, *Scot :* homologation (of deed, etc.) ; probate (of will).

homologie [ɔmɔlɔʒi], *s.f.* Homology.

homologue [ɔmɔlɔg]. *Biol : Geom : etc :* **1.** *a.* Homologous. **2.** *s.m.* Homologue.

homologuer [ɔmɔlɔge], *v.tr. Jur :* **1.** To confirm, endorse (deed, etc.) ; to ratify (decision) ; to grant probate (of will). **2.** To prove (will).

homoncule [ɔmɔ̃kyl], *s.m.* = HOMUNCULE.

homonyme [ɔmɔnim]. **1.** *a.* Homonymous. **2.** *s.m.* (*a*) Homonym. (*b*) *F :* Namesake.

homothétie [ɔmɔteti], *s.f. Geom :* Similarity (in construction and position). *Centre d'h.,* centre of similarity.

homuncule [ɔmɔ̃kyl], *s.m.* **1.** *A :* Homunculus. **2.** *F :* Manikin, dwarf.

*****hongre** [ɔ̃ːgr]. **1.** *a.m.* Gelded, castrated (horse). **2.** *s.m.* Gelding.

*****hongrer** [ɔ̃gre], *v.tr. Vet :* To geld, castrate.

*****Hongrie** [ɔ̃gri]. *Pr.n.f. Geog :* Hungary.

*****hongrois, -oise** [ɔ̃grwa, -waːz], *a. & s. Geog :* Hungarian.

honnête [ɔnɛt], *a.* **1.** Honest, honourable, upright. *Homme h., h. homme,* honest man. *Fille h.,* straight, decent, girl. **Peu honnête,** dishonourable. **2.** Courteous, well-bred ; civil, polite (*envers,* to). *A :* **Honnête homme,** gentleman. **3.** Decent, seemly, becoming (behaviour, etc.). *Attitude peu h.,* unseemly, unbecoming, attitude. **4.** Reasonable, moderate, fair (price, etc.). *Moyens honnêtes,* fair means. *adv.* **-ment.**

honnêteté [ɔnɛtte], *s.f.* **1.** Honesty, uprightness, integrity. **2.** Courtesy civility, politeness. **3.** Decency, propriety, decorum. **4.** Fairness ; fair dealing.

honneur [ɔnœːr], *s.m.* Honour. **1.** *Homme d'honneur,* man of honour, honourable man. **Être engagé d'honneur à faire qch.,** to be bound in honour, in honour bound, to do sth. **Soutenir l'honneur du corps,** to show *esprit de corps.* (*Ma*) *parole d'honneur!* on my word of honour ! **Se faire honneur de qch., de faire qch.,** to be proud of sth., proud to do sth. **Piquer qn d'honneur,** to put s.o. (up)on his mettle. **Tenir à honneur de faire qch.,** (i) to consider it an honour to be allowed to do sth. ; (ii) to consider oneself in honour bound to do sth. **Faire qch. en tout honneur,** to do sth. in all good faith. **Affaire d'honneur,** affair of honour ; duel. **Faire une réparation d'honneur à qn,** to make a full apology to s.o. **Dette d'honneur,** debt of honour. S.a. CHAMP[1] I, LÉGION. *Assis à la place d'h.,* occupying the seat of honour. *Cour d'h.* (*d'un lycée*), main quadrangle. *Escalier d'h.,* grand staircase. S.a. DEMOISELLE I, GARÇON 2, VIN. **2.** (*a*) Réception en l'honneur de qn, at-home in honour of s.o. **Faire honneur à qn,** to do honour to s.o. *F :* *Faire h. au dîner,* to do justice to the dinner. *J'ai l'h. de vous faire savoir que . . .,* I beg to inform you that. . . . *F :* **En quel honneur vous voit-on ici?** what is the occasion of your being here? *Games : A vous l'h.,* your honour. **Jouer pour l'honneur,** to play for love. (*b*) **Faire honneur à son pays,** to be an honour, a credit, to one's country. **On doit dire à leur honneur que . . .,** it must be said to their credit that. . . . **Il en est sorti à son honneur,** he came out of it with credit, with flying colours. **3.** *pl.* (*a*) Regalia (at coronation, etc.). (*b*) (Marks of esteem) **Rendre les derniers honneurs, les honneurs suprêmes, à qn,** to pay the last (funeral) honours

to s.o. **Faire à qn les honneurs de la maison,** to do the honours of the house to s.o. *Mil :* **Rendre les honneurs à qn,** to present arms, pay compliments, to s.o. **4. Faire honneur à sa signature,** to honour one's signature. *Com :* **Faire honneur à une traite,** to honour, meet, a bill. **Acceptation par honneur,** acceptance (of a bill) for honour. **5.** (*a*) *Cards :* Les honneurs, honours. *Quatre d'honneurs,* four by honours. *Honneurs partagés,* honours even. (*b*) **Partie d'honneur,** deciding game or match.

*****honnir** [ɔniːr], *v.tr. A :* To disgrace, to dishonour. **Hon(n)i soit qui mal y pense,** evil be to him who evil thinks. *Honni de tous,* spurned by all.

honorabilité [ɔnɔrabilite], *s.f.* (*a*) Honourable character. (*b*) Respectability. (*c*) Standing (of a firm).

honorable [ɔnɔrabl], *a.* (*a*) Honourable. *Vieillesse h.,* respected old age. *Vit : Année h.* vintage year. S.a. AMENDE 2. (*b*) Respectable, reputable (family, profession) ; creditable (performance). *adv.* **-ment.**

honoraire [ɔnɔrɛːr]. **1.** *a.* Honorary (duty, member, etc.). **2.** *s.m.pl. Occ. sg.* Fee(s) (of professional man) ; honorarium ; (lawyer's) retainer ; (author's) royalty.

honorer [ɔnɔre], *v.tr.* **1.** (*a*) To honour (s.o.) ; to respect (s.o.'s good qualities, etc.). *Com.Corr :* **Votre honorée du . . .,** your favour of the. . . . (*b*) To do honour to (s.o.). *H. qn de sa présence, d'une invitation,* to honour, favour, s.o. with one's presence, with an invitation. (*c*) *Com :* To honour, meet (bill). **2.** To be an honour to, do credit to (s.o.) ; to reflect honour on (s.o.).

s'honorer. (*a*) To gain distinction. (*b*) To consider oneself honoured (*de,* by).

honorifique [ɔnɔrifik], *a.* **1.** Honorary (title, rank, etc.). **2.** Honorific.

*****honte** [ɔ̃ːt], *s.f.* **1.** (*a*) (Sense of) shame. **Avoir perdu toute honte, tout sentiment de honte ;** *A :* avoir toute honte bue, to be lost, dead, to all sense of shame. **Honte à vous!** shame (on you) ! **Sans honte,** shameless. **Avoir honte,** to be ashamed. *Avoir h. de faire qch. ; avoir, éprouver, de la honte à faire qch.,* to be, feel, ashamed to do sth. **Faire honte à qn,** to make s.o. ashamed ; to put s.o. to shame. (*b*) **Fausse honte, mauvaise honte,** self-consciousness, bashfulness. **2.** (Cause of) shame, disgrace, dishonour. **Couvrir qn de h.,** to cover s.o. with shame, with disgrace ; to bring shame on s.o. **Faire, être, la honte de qn,** to be a disgrace to s.o.

*****honteu|x, -euse** [ɔ̃tø, -øːz], *a.* **1.** Ashamed. *Être h. d'avoir fait qch.,* to be ashamed of having done sth. **2.** Bashful, shamefaced, sheepish. *Prov :* **Jamais honteux n'eut belle amie,** faint heart never won fair lady. **3.** Shameful, disgraceful (conduct). *adv.* **-sement.**

*****hop** [ɔp], *int. Allez hop!* out you go ! *P :* hop it !

hôpital, -aux [ɔpital, -o], *s.m.* **1.** (*a*) Hospital, infirmary. **Faire les hôpitaux,** to walk the hospitals. (*b*) *Navy :* **H. du bord,** sick-bay. **Vaisseau hôpital,** hospital ship. **2.** (= HOSPICE 2) Poorhouse ; *A :* asylum. *H. des orphelins,* orphans' home. *F :* **Prendre le chemin de l'hôpital,** to be on the road to ruin. **3.** *Hist :* **Ordre de l'Hôpital,** order of the Knights Hospitallers.

*****hoquet** [ɔkɛ], *s.m.* **1.** Hiccough, hiccup. **Avoir le hoquet,** to have the hiccups. **2.** Gasp (of surprise, terror, etc.). **Être au dernier hoquet,** to be at one's last gasp.

horaire [ɔrɛːr]. **1.** *a.* Horary. *Signal h.,* time-signal. *Astr : Cercle h.,* horary circle, hour circle

S.a. FUSEAU 2. *Ind*: *Puissance h.*, output per hour. **2.** *s.m.* Time-table.

*****horde** [ɔrd], *s.f.* Horde (of nomads, etc.).

hordéole [ɔrdeɔl], *s.m. Med*: Sty(e) (on eyelid).

*****horion** [ɔrjɔ̃], *s.m.* Blow, punch, knock.

horizon [ɔrizɔ̃], *s.m.* Horizon, sky-line. *A l'h.*, *au-dessus de l'h.*, on the horizon, on the sky-line. *Art*: **Ligne d'horizon**, vanishing line.

horizontal, -aux [ɔrizɔ̃tal, -o]. **I.** *a.* Horizontal. **2.** *s.f.* Horizontale, horizontal line. *adv.* **-ement**.

horloge [ɔrlɔːʒ], *s.f.* **I.** Clock (esp. town or church clock). *H. comtoise, de parquet*, grandfather('s) clock. *H. marine, de bord*, ship's chronometer. *Il est deux heures à l'h.*, it is two by the clock. *J'ai attendu une bonne heure d'h.*, I waited for a full hour by the clock. **2.** *Ent*: **Horloge de la mort**, death-watch (beetle).

horloger [ɔrlɔʒe], *s.m.* Clock and watch-maker.

horlogerie [ɔrlɔʒri], *s.f.* **I.** Clock and watch-making. **Mouvement d'horlogerie**, clockwork. **2.** Clock-maker's shop.

*****hormis** [ɔrmi], *prep.* (No liaison; *hormis elle* [ɔrmiɛl]) Except, but, save. *Personne h. vous*, no one but you; no one besides yourself. *Conj.phr.* **Hormis que** + *ind.*, except that, save that; apart from the fact that. **Hormis que . . . ne** + *sub.*, unless, except. [HORS]

hormones [ɔrmɔn], *s.f.pl. Physiol*: Hormones.

horoscope [ɔrɔskɔp], *s.m.* Horoscope. **Faire, dresser, tirer, l'horoscope de qn**, to cast s.o.'s horoscope, s.o.'s nativity.

horreur [ɔrœːr], *s.f.* Horror. **I.** *A ma grande h.*, to my unspeakable horror. *Frappé d'h.*, horror-stricken. **2.** Repugnance, disgust, abhorrence. **Faire horreur à qn**, to horrify s.o.; to be repulsive to s.o. **Avoir qch. en horreur, avoir horreur de qch.**, to have a horror of sth.; to hate, detest, abhor, abominate, sth. **Être en horreur à qn**, to be held in abhorrence by s.o. **3.** Awfulness. *Silence plein d'h.*, awful silence. **4.** (*a*) (Cause, object, of) horror. *Quelle h. d'enfant!* what a horrid child! *Oh, la vilaine h.!* the horrid thing! (*b*) **Commettre des horreurs**, to commit atrocities. *Dire des horreurs de qn*, to say horrid things about s.o.

horrible [ɔribl], *a.* Horrible, horrifying, awful; *F*: horrid. *H. à voir*, awful to behold; appalling. *adv.* **-ment**.

horrifier [ɔrifje], *v.tr. F*: To horrify. *Être horrifié de qch.*, to be horrified at sth.

horrifique [ɔrifik], *a. F*: Horrific, hair-raising.

horripilant [ɔripilɑ̃], *a.* **I.** Hair-raising (adventure). **2.** *F*: Exasperating, maddening.

horripilation [ɔripilasjɔ̃], *s.f.* **I.** *Med*: Horripilation, goose-flesh. **2.** *F*: Exasperation.

horripiler [ɔripile], *v.tr.* **I.** To give (s.o.) goose-flesh; *F*: to make (s.o.'s) flesh creep. **2.** *F*: To exasperate.

*****hors** [ɔːr], *prep.* (Liaison with *r*: *hors elle* [ɔrɛl]) **I.** (*a*) Out of, outside. *Longueur h. tout*, over-all length. *Fourneau h. feu*, furnace out of blast. S.a. CONCOURS 3, COURANT 2, JEU 2, LIGNE I, LOI I, SERVICE I. (*b*) Except. *Tous h. un seul*, all but one. *Conj.phr.* **Hors que** + *ind.*, except that, save that. **Hors que . . . ne** + *sub.*, unless, except. **2.** *Prep.phr.* **Hors de**, out of, outside (of). (*a*) *H. de la ville*, outside the town. *Dîner h. de chez soi*, to dine out. **Hors d'ici!** begone! **Hors d'haleine**, out of breath. **Hors de combat**, (i) (of gun, ship, etc.) out of action; (ii) (of man) disabled. *Fb*: **Hors des touches**, out of touch. **Être hors d'affaire**, to have got through one's difficulties; (of sick person) to be out of danger.

Être hors de soi, to be beside oneself (with rage, etc.). S.a. CAUSE 2, COUR 2, PORTÉE 3, PRIX I, VOIX I. (*b*) *H. de le battre*, unless they had beaten him; short of beating him. **3.** *Adj.phr.* **Hors d'œuvre**, (i) out of the alignment; projecting; (ii) (of precious stone) unmounted, unset. S.a. HORS-D'ŒUVRE.

*****hors-bord**, *s.m.inv.* Outboard motor boat.

*****hors-caste**, *s. m. & f.inv.* Outcaste, untouchable.

*****hors-d'œuvre**, *s.m.inv.* **I.** *Arch*: Annexe. outwork. **2.** *Cu*: Hors-d'œuvre, side-dish. *Les hors-d'œuvre*, the hors-d'œuvres.

*****hors-la-loi**, *s.m.inv.* Outlaw.

*****hors-texte**, *s.m.inv. Bookb*: (Inset) plate.

hortensia [ɔrtɑ̃sja], *s.m. Bot*: Hydrangea.

horticole [ɔrtikɔl], *a.* Horticultural; flower-(show, etc.).

horticulteur [ɔrtikyltœːr], *s.m.* Horticulturist.

horticulture [ɔrtikyltyːr], *s.f.* Horticulture, gardening.

hosanna [ɔzan(n)a]. **I.** *int.* Hosanna! **2.** *s.m.* (Cry of) hosanna; song of praise.

hospice [ɔspis], *s.m.* **I.** Hospice (on the Saint-Bernard, etc.). **2.** Alms-house, home, asylum, charitable institution, house of refuge (for the aged, for incurables). *F*: **Mourir à l'hospice**, to die in the poorhouse. **3.** *F*: (= HÔPITAL I) Hospital.

hospitalier[1], -ière [ɔspitalje, -jɛːr], *a.* Hospitable.

hospitalier[2], -ière, *a.* Pertaining to hospices, poorhouses or hospitals. *Religieux h.*, *s.m.* hospitalier, hospitaller.

hospitalisation [ɔspitalizasjɔ̃], *s.f.* (*a*) Ordering, admission, to a home or hospital. (*b*) Hospital care or treatment.

hospitaliser [ɔspitalize], *v.tr.* To send, admit (s.o.) (i) to a home, to a charitable institution, (ii) to a hospital.

hospitalisé, -ée, *s.* **I.** Inmate (of home, etc.); almsman, -woman. **2.** Man, soldier, woman, in hospital; in-patient.

hospitalité [ɔspitalite], *s.f.* Hospitality. **Établissement d'hospitalité de nuit**, casual ward.

hostie [ɔsti], *s.f.* **I.** *Jew.Ant*: Victim, offering (for sacrifice). **2.** (Eucharistic) host.

hostile [ɔstil], *a.* Hostile; unfriendly (action). **Être h. à, envers, qn**, to be hostile, opposed, adverse, to s.o. *adv.* **-ment**.

hostilité [ɔstilite], *s.f.* **I.** Hostility (*contre*, to); enmity, ill-will. **Acte d'hostilité**, act of war. **2.** *pl.* Hostilities.

hôte, hôtesse [oːt, otɛs], *s.* **I.** Host, *f.* hostess; entertainer (of guests); landlord, landlady (of tavern, etc.). **Compter sans son hôte**, to reckon without one's host. **Dîner à la table d'hôte**, to dine at the *table d'hôte*; to take the (set) dinner. **2.** (*a*) Guest, visitor. (*b*) Dweller; denizen. *Hôtes d'un hospice*, inmates of an alms-house.

hôtel [otɛl, ot-], *s.m.* **I.** Mansion, town-house. S.a. MAÎTRE I. **2.** Public building. **Hôtel de ville**, town-hall. **L'Hôtel des Monnaies**, the Mint. **Hôtel des Postes**, General Post Office. **L'Hôtel des Invalides**, the Military Pensioners' Hospital. *L'H. des Ventes*, the general auction rooms (in Paris). **3.** (*a*) Hotel, hostelry. (*b*) *H. meublé, garni*, residential hotel (providing lodging but not board); often *Pej*: apartments, lodgings.

hôtel-Dieu, *s.m.* Principal hospital (in many French towns). *pl.* **Des hôtels-Dieu**.

hôtelier, -ière [otəlje, -jɛːr], *s.* Innkeeper; landlord, landlady; host, hostess (of an inn).

hôtellerie [otɛlri], *s.f.* **I.** Hostelry, inn. **2.** Guest quarters (of a convent). **3.** L'hôtellerie, the hotel trade.

*hotter [ɔt], *s.f.* **1.** Basket (carried on the back); dosser, pannier; (mason's) hod. **2.** Hood (of forge, laboratory, over fire place).

*hottentot, -ote [ɔtɑ̃to, -ɔt], *a. & s.* Hottentot.

*hou [u], *int.* **1.** (Imitating the howl of the wolf) Boo! **2.** *Hou! la vilaine!* fie! you naughty girl!

*houache [waʃ], *s.f.* Wake, wash (of ship).

*houblon [ublɔ̃], *s.m.* *Bot:* *Brew:* Hop(s). Cueilleur, -euse, de houblon, hop-picker, hopper. Perche à houblon, hop-pole.

*houblonner [ublɔne], *v.tr.* To hop (beer)

*houblonnier, -ière [ublɔnje, -jɛːr]. **1.** *a.* Hop (-growing) (district, etc.). **2.** *s.m.* Hop-grower. **3.** *s.f.* Houblonnière, hop-field.

*houe [u], *s.f.* *Tls:* Hoe.

*houer [ue], *v.tr.* To hoe. *s.m.* -age.

*houille [uːj], *s.f.* **1.** (Pit-)coal. Mine de houille, coal-mine, -pit; colliery. **2.** Houille blanche, (electricity generated by) water-power; white coal.

*houiller, -ère [uje, -ɛːr]. **1.** *a.* (*a*) Carboniferous, coal-bearing. Dépôt, bassin, h., coal-bed, -basin. (*b*) Production houillère, output of coal. **2.** *s.f.* Houillère, coal-pit, -mine; colliery.

*houilleur [ujœːr], *s.m.* Collier, (coal-)miner.

*houilleux, -euse [ujø, -øːz], *a.* Carboniferous, coal-bearing.

*houle [ul], *s.f.* Swell, surge (of sea). Grosse h., heavy swell. H. de fond, ground-swell.

*houlette [ulɛt], *s.f.* **1.** (*a*) (Shepherd's) crook. (*b*) *A:* (Bishop's) crozier. **2.** Trowel.

*houleux, -euse [ulø, -øːz], *a.* Swelling, surging (sea). *F:* Réunion houleuse, stormy meeting.

*houp [up], *int.* Allons h.! now then, heave! Saute, h.! jump, (h)up!

*houppe [up], *s.f.* **1.** (*a*) Bunch, tuft (of feathers, wool); pompon. H. à poudrer, powder-puff. (*b*) Tassel, bob. **2.** (*a*) Tuft, crest (of hair); topknot. (*b*) (Bird's) tuft, crest (of feathers). (*c*) Crest (of tree). **3.** *Cryst:* *Opt:* Brush; absorption figure.

*houppé [upe], *a.* Tufted, crested.

*houppelande [uplɑ̃ːd], *s.f.* (*a*) *A:* Great-coat; (coachman's) box-coat. (*b*) Cosy outdoor overgarment (esp. as worn by priest); surcoat.

*houppette [upɛt], *s.f.* **1.** Small tuft (of wool, feathers). **2.** Powder-puff.

*hourdage [urdaːʒ], *s.m.* *Const:* **1.** (*a*) Roughcasting. (*b*) Nogging, pugging. **2.** Rough masonry or plaster-work; rubble-work.

*hourder [urde], *v.tr.* *Const:* (*a*) To rough-cast. (*b*) To nog, pug.

*hourdis [urdi], *s.m.* = HOURDAGE 2.

*houri [uri], *s.f.* *Moham.Rel:* Houri.

*hourra [ura], *int. & s.m.* Hurrah! huzza!

*hourvari [urvari], *s.m.* **1.** Huntsman's call to hounds to cast back. **2.** *F:* Uproar, tumult.

*housard [uzaːr], *s.m.* *A:* = HUSSARD.

*houseaux [uzo], *s.m.pl.* *A:* Spatterdashes; leggings; long leather gaiters.

*houspiller [uspije], *v.tr.* **1.** To hustle (s.o.); to knock (s.o.) about; to jostle; to handle (s.o.) roughly; to bully (s.o.). **2.** To abuse, rate (s.o.). *s.m.* -ement.

*houssaie [usɛ], *s.f.* Holly-plantation, -grove.

*housse [us], *s.f.* **1.** (*a*) Covering; (furniture) cover; (protecting) bag. *Aut:* Spare-tyre cover. (*b*) Dust-sheet. **2.** *Harn:* Housing, horse-cloth.

*housser [use], *v.tr.* To dust, switch (furniture).

*houssine [usin], *s.f.* (*a*) Switch (for beating furniture). (*b*) (Riding-)switch.

*houssiner [usine], *v.tr.* To switch (clothes, etc.). H. son cheval, to touch up one's horse.

*houssoir [uswaːr], *s.m.* Feather-brush; whisk.

*housson [usɔ̃], *s.m.* *Bot:* Butcher's-broom, knee-holly.

*houx [u], *s.m.* *Bot:* Holly.

*hoyau, -aux [wajo], *s.m.* **1.** Mattock, grubbing-hoe. **2.** *Min:* Pickaxe.

*huard [yaːr], *s.m.* *Orn:* **1.** Black-throated diver. **2.** Osprey.

*hublot [yblo], *s.m.* *Nau:* Scuttle, side-light, port-hole. Verre de hublot, bull's-eye.

*huche [yʃ], *s.f.* **1.** Kneading-trough. **2.** Bin. La h. au pain, the bread-bin. **3.** Hopper (of flour-mill).

*hucher (se) [səyʃe], *v.pr.* *F:* = SE JUCHER.

*hue [y], *int.* (To horse) Gee (up)!

*huer [ye]. **1.** *v.i.* (*a*) To shout, halloo, whoop. (*b*) (Of owl) To hoot. **2.** *v.tr.* To hoot, boo (actor, etc.). *Sp:* To barrack (player).

huée, *s.f.* **1.** *Ven:* Hallooing. **2.** (*a*) Boo, hoot. (*b*) *pl.* Booing, hooting; jeering, jeers. Quitter la scène au milieu des huees, to be hooted, booed, off the stage.

*huguenot, -ote [ygno, -ɔt], *a. & s.* **1.** *Hist:* Huguenot. **2.** (Marmite) huguenote, pipkin.

*Hugues [yg]. *Pr.n.m.* Hugh.

hui [ɥi], *adv.* *A:* To-day. *Jur:* Ce jour d'hui, this day. S.a. AUJOURD'HUI.

huile [ɥil], *s.f.* Oil. **1.** H. à manger, pour la salade, salad-oil. H. de lin, linseed oil. H. cuite, boiled oil. Peinture à l'huile, oil-painting. H. de baleine, train-oil, sperm oil. S.a. MORUE 1. H. de graissage, lubricating oil. H. d'éclairage, lampante, lamp oil. *F:* Ouvrage qui sent l'huile, work that smells of the lamp, of the midnight oil. Il n'y a plus d'huile dans la lampe, his life is flickering out. Tache d'h., oil stain. *F:* Mauvais exemple qui fait tache d'huile, bad example that spreads. *F:* Huile de bras, de coude, elbow-grease. *P:* Les huiles, (i) the big pots, the big bugs; (ii) the toffs. **2.** H. minérale, mineral oil. Moteur à huile lourde, heavy-oil engine. **3.** H. essentielle, essential oil. H. de pomme de terre, fusel oil, potato-spirit. S.a. VITRIOL.

huiler [ɥile], *v.tr.* To oil; to lubricate, grease. *s.m.* -age.

huilerie [ɥilri], *s.f.* **1.** Oil-works. **2.** Oil-store.

huileux, -euse [ɥilø, -øːz], *a.* Oily, greasy.

huilier [ɥilje], *s.m.* **1.** (*a*) Oil-can. (*b*) Oil and vinegar cruet. **2.** Oilman.

huis [ɥi], *s.m.* *A:* Door. (Still used in) Entretien à huis clos, conversation behind closed doors. *Jur:* Entendre une cause à huis clos, to hear a case in camera. (The h is 'aspirate' in Ordonner le h. clos, (i) to clear the court; (ii) to order a case to be heard in camera.)

huisserie [ɥisri], *s.f.* Door-frame, -casing.

huissier [ɥisje], *s.m.* **1.** (Gentleman) usher. **2.** *Jur:* (*a*) Process-server; = sheriff's officer, bailiff. (*b*) H. audiencier, court usher.

*huit [ɥit], *num.a.inv. & s.m.inv.* (As card. adj. before a noun or adj. beginning with a consonant sound [ɥi]) Eight. Huit (petits) garçons [ɥi(pti)-garsɔ̃], eight (little) boys. Huit [ɥit] hommes, eight men. Le huit mai [ɥitmɛ], the eighth of May. Huit jours, a week. D'aujourd'hui en huit, to-day week, this day week. Donner ses huit jours à qn, (of master or servant) to give s.o. a week's notice.

*huitaine [ɥiten], *s.f.* **1.** (About) eight. **2.** Week. Dans une huitaine de jours, in a week or so. Dans la huitaine, in the course of the week. *Ind:* Mettre le personnel en huitaine, to close down for a week.

*huit-de-chiffre(s) [ɥidʃifr], *s.m.* **I.** Figure-of-eight bandage. **2.** *Tls:* Figure-of-eight calipers. *pl. Des huits-de-chiffres.*

*huitième [ɥitjɛm]. **I.** *num. a. & s.* Eighth. **2.** *s.m.* Eighth (part). **3.** *s f. Sch:* (Classe de) huitième, approx. second form of lower school. *adv.* **-ment.**

huître [ɥiːtr], *s.f.* **I.** Oyster. *H. perlière, à perle,* pearl oyster. **2.** *P:* Fool, mug.

*huit-reflets [ɥirəfle], *s.m.inv. F:* Top hat.

huîtrier, -ère [ɥitrie, -ɛːr]. **I.** *a.* Of, pertaining to, oysters. **2.** *s.f.* Huîtrière, oyster-bed.

*hulan [ylɑ̃], *s.m. Mil:* Uhlan.

*hulotte [ylɔt], *s.f. Orn:* Common wood-owl.

*hululer [ylyle], *v.i.* = ULULER.

*hum [hm, ɔm], *int.* Hem! hm!

humain [ymɛ̃], *a.* **I.** Human. *Le genre h.,* mankind. *Organ:* Voix humaine, vox humana (stop). **2.** Humane. *adv.* **-ement.**

humaniser [ymanize], *v.tr.* To humanize. **I.** To make human. **2.** To make (s.o.) more humane.
s'humaniser. (a) To become more humane. (b) *F:* To become more sociable; to thaw.

humaniste [ymanist], *s.m.* Humanist; classical scholar.

humanitaire [ymanitɛːr], *a. & s.* Humanitarian. *Œuvre h.,* humane task.

humanité [ymanite], *s.f.* **I.** Humanity. (a) Human nature. (b) Mankind. (c) Kindness, humaneness. **2.** *pl.* Humanities. *Sch:* *Les classes d'humanités,* the classical side (of school).

humble [œ̃:bl], *a.* Humble, lowly. *H. de cœur,* humble-hearted. *adv.* **-ment.**

humect|er [ymɛkte], *v.tr.* To damp, moisten. *F: S'h. le gosier,* to wet one's whistle. *s.m.* **-age.** *s.f.* **-ation.**
s'humecter, to become moist, damp.

*humer [yme], *v.tr.* To suck in, up. *H. l'air frais,* to breathe in the fresh air. *H. une prise,* to take a pinch of snuff. *H. un œuf,* to take off, swallow, an egg (raw).

huméral, -aux [ymeral, -o], *a. Anat:* Humeral.

humérus [ymerys], *s.m. Anat:* Humerus.

humeur [ymœːr], *s.f.* **I.** (a) *A.Med:* Humour. (b) *pl. Med: F:* Tissue-fluids, body-fluids. *F:* Humeurs froides, scrofula. (c) *Anat:* *H. aqueuse, h. vitrée,* aqueous humour, vitreous humour (of the eye). **2.** (a) Humour, mood. *Être de bonne humeur,* to be in a good humour. *Mauvaise h.,* ill-humour. *De méchante h.,* out of temper; cross. *Être d'une h. noire,* (i) to feel depressed, to have a fit of the blues; (ii) to be out of temper. *Être d'humeur à refuser net,* to be in the mood to refuse point-blank. *Être en humeur de faire qch.,* to be in the mood, vein, to do sth. *En h. de lire,* in a reading mood. (b) Temper. *Avoir l'h. vive,* to be quick-tempered. *Homme d'h. égale,* even-tempered man. *Mouvement d'humeur,* outburst of temper. *Montrer de l'h.,* to show (ill-)temper. *Avec humeur,* testily, pettishly.

humide [ymid], *a.* Damp, moist, humid; watery, wet. *Draps humides,* damp sheets. *Temps h. et chaud,* muggy weather. *Temps h. et froid,* raw weather.

humidifier [ymidifje], *v.tr.* To damp, moisten.

humidité [ymidite], *s.f.* Humidity, damp(ness), moisture, moistness, wet(ness). "Craint l'humidité," 'to be kept dry.' *Taches d'humidité,* mildew. *Taché d'h.,* mildewed.

humiliant [ymiljɑ̃], *a.* Humiliating, mortifying.

humiliation [ymiljasjɔ̃], *s.f.* Humiliation, mortification; affront.

humilier [ymilje], *v.tr.* To humiliate, humble.
s'humilier *jusqu'à faire qch.,* to stoop to doing sth.

humilité [ymilite], *s.f.* Humility, humbleness.

humoriste [ymɔrist]. **I.** *a.* Humorous (writer, etc.). **2.** *s.* Humorist.

humoristique [ymɔristik], *a.* Humorous.

humour [ymuːr], *s.m.* Humour. *L'h. de Shakespeare et le comique de Molière,* Shakespeare's humour and Molière's laughter.

humus [ymyːs], *s.m. Hort:* Humus, leaf-mould.

*hune [yn], *s.f. Nau:* Top. *H. de vigie,* crow's-nest. **Grand'hune,** main-top. **Mât de hune,** topmast. *Ohé de la h.!* aloft there!

*hunier [ynje], *s.m. Nau:* Topsail.

*huppe¹ [yp], *s.f. Orn:* Hoopoe.

*huppe², *s.f.* Tuft, crest (of bird).

*huppé [ype], *a.* **I.** *Orn:* Tufted, crested. **2.** *F:* Smart, well-dressed; in high society.

*hure [yːr], *s.f.* **I.** (a) Head (of boar, pig); jowl (of salmon). (b) *P:* Head, mug. **2.** Potted head.

*hurlement [yrləmɑ̃], *s.m.* Howl(ing) (esp. of wolf or dog); yell(ing), roar(ing). (Of dog, etc.) *Pousser un h.,* to give a howl.

*hurler [yrle]. **I.** *v.i.* (Of dog, wolf) To howl; (of wind, storm) to roar; (of pers.) to howl, roar, yell. *F:* Hurler avec les loups, to cry with the pack. **2.** *v.tr.* To bawl out (song, etc.).

*hurleur, -euse [yrlœːr, -øːz]. **I.** *a.* Howling, yelling. **2.** *s.* Howler, yeller. **3.** *s.m.* (a) Howler (monkey). (b) *W.Tel:* *F:* Extra-loud loud-speaker.

hurluberlu [yrlyberly], *a. & s.* Harum-scarum; scatter-brain(ed).

*hussard [ysaːr], *s.m. Mil:* Hussar. **Bonnet de hussard,** busby.

*hussarde [ysard], *s.f.* **A la hussarde.** (a) Cavalierly, brusquely. (b) *Pantalon à la hussarde,* full trousers. *Culotte à la hussarde,* riding-breeches. *Bottes à la hussarde,* riding-boots.

*hussite [ysit], *s.m. Rel.H:* Hussite.

*hutte [yt], *s.f.* Hut, shed, shanty.

hyalin [ialɛ̃], *a.* Hyaline, glassy. **Quartz hyalin,** rock-crystal.

hyaloïde [ialɔid], *a. Anat: etc:* Hyaloid.

hybridation [ibridasjɔ̃], *s.f. Biol:* Hybridization; cross-breeding.

hybride [ibrid], *a. & s.m. Biol: Ling:* Hybrid.

hybrider [ibride], *v.tr.* To hybridize, to cross.

hydarthrose [idartroːz], *s.f. Med:* Hydrarthrosis. *H. du genou, F:* water on the knee.

hydratation [idratasjɔ̃], *s.f. Ch:* Hydration.

hydrate [idrat], *s.m. Ch:* Hydrate, hydroxide. *H. de potasse,* caustic potash. *H. de carbone,* carbohydrate.

hydraté [idrate], *a. Ch:* Hydrated, hydrous.

hydraulique [idrolik]. **I.** *a.* Hydraulic. *Roue h.,* water-wheel. *Usine h.,* waterworks. **2.** *s.f.* (a) Hydraulics. (b) Hydraulic engineering.

hydraviation [idravjasjɔ̃], *s.f.* Marine aviation.

hydravion [idravjɔ̃], *s.m.* Sea-plane, hydroplane.

hydre [iːdr], *s.f.* Hydra.

hydrique [idrik]. **I.** *a.* Hydrous. **2.** *a.suff. Ch:* (a) Hydro-. *Chlorhydrique,* hydrochloric (acid). (b) -hydric. *Sulfhydrique,* sulphydric (acid, etc.).

hydrocarbure [idrɔkarbyːr], *s.m.* Hydrocarbon.

hydrocéphale [idrɔsefal]. *Med:* **I.** *a. & s.* Hydrocephalic, hydrocephalous (subject). **2.** *s.f.* = HYDROCÉPHALIE.

hydrocéphalie [idrɔsefali], *s.f. Med:* Hydrocephalus; *F:* water on the brain.

hydroélectrique [idrɔelɛktrik], *a.* Hydro-electric.

hydrofuge [idrɔfy:ʒ], *a.* Waterproof, damp-proof; (of coat, etc.) rainproof. *Const:* **Couche hydrofuge**, damp-course.

hydrofuger [idrɔfyʒe], *v.tr.* (**j'hydrofugeai(s)**; **n. hydrofugeons**) To waterproof (garment, etc.).

hydrogène [idrɔʒɛn], *s.m. Ch:* Hydrogen.

hydrogéner [idrɔʒene], *v.tr.* To hydrogenate, hydrogenize.

hydroglisseur [idrɔglisœ:r], *s.m.* Hydroglider; hydroplane (motor boat); speed-boat.

hydrographe [idrɔgraf], *a. & s.m.* (Ingénieur) **hydrographe**, hydrographer. *Navire h.*, survey vessel.

hydrographie [idrɔgrafi], *s.f.* Hydrography.

hydrographique [idrɔgrafik], *a.* Hydrographic(al). *Navy: Le service h.*, the survey department.

hydromètre [idrɔmɛtr], *s.m.* **1.** (= ARÉOMÈTRE) Hydrometer. **2.** *Oc: etc:* Depth-gauge.

hydrophile [idrɔfil], *a.* Absorbent (cotton-wool).

hydrophobe [idrɔfɔb]. *Med:* **1.** *a.* Hydrophobic. **2.** *s.* Hydrophobic subject.

hydrophobie [idrɔfɔbi], *s.f. Med:* Hydrophobia, rabies.

hydropique [idrɔpik]. *Med:* **1.** *a.* Dropsical. **2.** *s.* Dropsical subject.

hydropisie [idrɔpizi], *s.f. Med:* Dropsy.

hydroplane [idrɔplan], *s.m. Av:* Hydroplane, sea-plane.

hydroplaner [idrɔplane], *v.i. Av:* To taxi along (on water).

hydroquinone [idrɔkinɔn], *s.f. Ch: Phot:* Hydroquinone, quinol.

hydroscope [idrɔskɔp], *s.m.* Water-diviner; dowser.

hydroscopie [idrɔskɔpi], *s.f.* Water-divining; dowsing.

hydrosphère [idrɔsfɛ:r], *s.f.* Hydrosphere.

hydrostatique [idrɔstatik]. **1.** *a.* Hydrostatic(al). **2.** *s.f.* Hydrostatics.

hydrothérapie [idrɔterapi], *s.f.* Hydrotherapeutics; water cure.

hydrothérapique [idrɔterapik], *a.* Hydrotherapeutic.

hydrure [idry:r], *s.m. Ch:* Hydride.

hyène [jɛn], *s.f. Z:* Hyena.

hygiène [iʒjɛn], *s.f.* Hygiene. *H. publique*, public health. **Ministère de l'Hygiène**, Ministry of Health. *Conférence d'h.*, health conference.

hygiénique [iʒjenik], *a.* Hygienic; healthy; sanitary. **Peu hygiénique**, unhealthy (work); unsanitary (building). *adv.* **-ment**, -ally.

hygiéniste [iʒjenist], *s.m.* Hygienist; public health specialist.

hygroma [igrɔma], *s.m. Med:* Hygroma. *H. du genou, F:* housemaid's knee.

hygromètre [igrɔmɛtr], *s.m. Ph:* Hygrometer.

hygrométrie [igrɔmetri], *s.f. Ph:* Hygrometry.

hygrométrique [igrɔmetrik], *a. Ph:* Hygrometric(al).

hygroscope [igrɔskɔp], *s.m. Ph:* Hygroscope.

hymen [imɛn], *s.m.*, **hyménée** [imene], *s.m. Poet:* Marriage.

hyménoptère [imenɔptɛ:r]. *Ent:* **1.** *a.* Hymenopterous. **2.** *s.m. pl.* **Hyménoptères**, hymenoptera.

hymnaire [imnɛ:r], *s.m.* Hymn-book hymnal.

hymne [im(n)]. **1.** *s.m.* Song (of praise); patriotic song. **2.** *s.f. Ecc:* Hymn. *H. nationale*, national anthem.

hyoïde [iɔid], *a. & s.m. Anat:* Hyoid (bone).

hyperbole [ipɛrbɔl], *s.f.* **1.** *Rh:* Hyperbole, exaggeration. **2.** *Geom:* Hyperbola.

hyperbolique [ipɛrbɔlik], *a.* Hyperbolic(al). *adv.* **-ment**, -ally.

hyperboloïde [ipɛrbɔlɔid], *s.m. Geom:* Hyperboloid.

hypercritique [ipɛrkritik]. **1.** *a.* Hypercritical, over-critical. **2.** *s.m.* Hypercritic, severe critic.

hyperémier (s') [sipɛremje], *v.pr. Med:* To become congested.

hyperesthésie [ipɛrɛstezi], *s.f.* Hyperaesthesia.

hyperfocal, -aux [ipɛrfɔkal, -o], *a. Phot:* Hyperfocal (distance).

hypermétropie [ipɛrmetrɔpi], *s.f. Med:* Hypermetropia, long-sightedness.

hypersensible [ipɛrsɑ̃sibl], *a.* Supersensitive (person, *Phot:* plate).

hypertension [ipɛrtɑ̃sjɔ̃], *s.f.*, **hypertonie** [ipɛrtɔni], *s.f. Med:* Hypertension. *H. artérielle*, high blood pressure.

hypnose [ipno:z], *s.f.* Hypnosis; trance.

hypnotique [ipnɔtik], *a.* Hypnotic.

hypnotiser [ipnɔtize], *v.tr.* To hypnotize.

hypnotiseur, -euse [ipnɔtizœ:r, -ø:z], *s.* Hypnotizer.

hypnotisme [ipnɔtism], *s.m.* Hypnotism.

hypnotiste [ipnɔtist], *s. m. & f.* Hypnotist.

hypocondre [ipɔkɔ̃:dr]. **1.** *s.m.* Hypochondrium. **2.** *a. & s.* = HYPOCONDRIAQUE.

hypocondriaque [ipɔkɔ̃driak]. **1.** *a.* Hypochondriac(al); *F:* melancholy, depressed. **2.** *s.* Hypochondriac.

hypocondrie [ipɔkɔ̃dri], *s.f.* Hypochondria.

hypocrisie [ipɔkrizi], *s.f.* Hypocrisy; cant.

hypocrite [ipɔkrit]. **1.** *a.* Hypocritical. **2.** *s.* Hypocrite. *adv.* **-ment**.

hypodermique [ipɔdɛrmik], *a.* Hypodermic.

hypogastre [ipɔgastr], *s.m. Anat:* Hypogastrium.

hypogastrique [ipɔgastrik], *a. Anat:* Hypogastric. *Ceinture h.*, abdominal belt.

hypogée [ipɔʒe], *s.m. Archeol:* Hypogeum.

hypophosphate [ipɔfɔsfat], *s.m. Ch:* Hypophosphate.

hypostyle [ipɔstil], *a. Arch:* Hypostyle, pillared.

hyposulfite [ipɔsylfit], *s.m. Ch:* Hyposulphite, thiosulphate. *H. de soude*, sodium thiosulphate, hyposulphite of soda; *Phot: F:* hypo.

hypoténuse [ipɔteny:z], *s.f.* Hypotenuse.

hypothécable [ipɔtekabl], *a.* Mortgageable.

hypothécaire [ipɔtekɛ:r]. **1.** *a.* Pertaining to mortgage. *Prêt h.*, loan on mortgage. *Contrat h.*, mortgage deed. *Créancier h.*, mortgagee. *Débiteur h.*, mortgagor **2.** *s.* Mortgagee.

hypothèque [ipɔtɛk], *s.f.* Mortgage. **Franc, libre, d'hypothèques**, unencumbered, unmortgaged. **Prendre, lever, une hypothèque**, to raise a mortgage. *Prêt sur h.*, mortgage loan. **Purger une hypothèque**, to pay off, redeem, a mortgage.

hypothéquer [ipɔteke], *v.tr.* (**j'hypothèque**; **j'hypothéquerai**) **1.** To mortgage (estate, etc.). **2.** To secure (debt) by mortgage.

hypothèse [ipɔtɛ:z], *s.f.* Hypothesis, assumption.

hypothétique [ipɔtetik], *a.* Hypothetical.

hypsométrie [ipsɔmetri], *s.f.* Hypsometry, altimetry.

hypsométrique [ipsɔmetrik], *a.* Hypsometric(al). *Courbe hypsométrique*, contour-line.

hysope [izɔp], *s.f. Bot:* Hyssop.

hystérèse [istere:z], *s.f.* Hysteresis; magnetic lag.

hystérie [isteri], *s.f. Med:* Hysteria.

hystérique [isterik], *a. Med:* Hysteric(al).

I, i [i], *s.m.* **1.** (The letter) I, i. **Mettre les points sur les i** (à qn), to speak plainly, unambiguously (to s.o.). **2. i grec**, (the letter) Y, y.

ïambe [jã:b], *s.m. Pros:* **1.** (*a*) Iamb, iambus. (*b*) Iambic. **2.** *pl.* Satirical poem.

ïambique [jãbik], *a. Pros:* Iambic (line, verse).

ibère [ibɛːr], *a. & s. Ethn:* Iberian.

Ibérie [iberi]. *Pr.n.f. A.Geog:* Iberia.

ibérien, -enne [iberjɛ̃, -ɛn], *a. & s.* Iberian.

ibérique [iberik], *a. Geog:* Iberian. **La péninsule Ibérique**, the Spanish, Iberian, Peninsula.

ibex [ibɛks], *s.m. Z:* Ibex.

ibis [ibis], *s.m. Orn:* Ibis.

icaque [ikak], *s.f. Bot:* **1.** (**Prune d'**)**icaque**, coco-plum. **2.** Coco-plum (tree).

icaquier [ikakje], *s.m. Bot:* Coco-plum tree.

iceberg [isberk], *s.m.* Iceberg.

ichneumon [iknømɔ̃], *s.m.* **1.** *Z:* Ichneumon, Pharaoh's rat. **2.** *Ent:* Ichneumon (fly).

ichtyocolle [iktjɔkɔl], *s.f.* Fish-glue, isinglass.

ichtyologie [iktjɔlɔʒi], *s.f.* Ichthyology.

ichtyologique [iktjɔlɔʒik], *a.* Ichthyologic(al).

ichtyophage [iktjɔfa:ʒ]. **1.** *a.* Ichthyophagous, fish-eating. **2.** *s.* Ichthyophagist.

ichtyophagie [iktjɔfaʒi], *s.f.* Ichthyophagy.

ichtyosaure [iktjɔsɔːr], *s.m.* Ichthyosaurus.

ici [isi], *adv.* **1.** Here. **Ici et là**, here and there. *Je ne suis pas d'ici*, I am a stranger (in these parts). **Ici-bas**, here below, on earth. *Hors d'ici!* begone! *Il y a vingt milles d'ici* (d) *Londres*, it is twenty miles (from here) to London. *Il demeure par ici*, *près d'ici*, he lives hereabouts. *Passez par ici*, step this way. *C'est ici*, this is the place. *L'autobus vient jusqu'ici*, the bus comes as far as this. *Tp:* **Ici Dupont**, Dupont speaking. *W.Tel:* **Ici Toulouse**, Toulouse calling. **2.** Now. **Jusqu'ici**, up to now; hitherto. **D'ici**, from to-day; henceforth. *D'ici (à) lundi*, between now and Monday; by Monday. **D'ici là**, between now and then; by that time. **D'ici peu**, before long.

icone [ikɔn, -oːn], *s.f. Ecc:* Icon, ikon.

iconoclasie [ikɔnɔklazi], *s.f.*, **iconoclasme** [ikɔnɔklasm], *s.m.* Iconoclasm.

iconoclaste [ikɔnɔklast]. **1.** *a.* Iconoclastic. **2.** *s.m.* Iconoclast.

iconoscope [ikɔnɔskɔp], *s.m.* **1.** *Phot:* View-finder. **2.** *Televis:* Electric eye.

ictère [ikteːr], *s.m. Med:* Icterus, jaundice.

ictérique [ikterik]. *Med:* **1.** *a.* (*a*) Icteric(al) (disorder). (*b*) Jaundiced (pers., eyes). **2.** *s.* Sufferer from jaundice.

idéal [ideal]. **1.** *a.* (*pl.* idéaux [ideo]) Ideal. **Le beau idéal**, the ideal of beauty. **2.** *s.m.* (*pl.* idéals, idéaux) Ideal. *adv.* **-ement.**

idéaliser [idealize], *v.tr.* To idealize.

idéalisme [idealism], *s.m.* Idealism.

idéaliste [idealist]. **1.** *a.* Idealistic. **2.** *s.* Idealist.

idéalité [idealite], *s.f.* Ideality.

idée [ide], *s.f.* **1.** Idea. (*a*) Notion. *Je n'en ai pas la moindre i.*, I haven't the least idea; *F:* I haven't the ghost of a notion. On n'a pas idée de cela, you can't imagine it. *Quelle idée!* the idea! **Une bonne idée!** a good idea! a happy thought! **J'ai (l')idée que . . .**, I have an idea, I rather fancy, that. . . . *L'i. me vint tout à coup que . . .*, it flashed through my mind that. . . . **Donner des idées** à qn, to put ideas into s.o.'s head. **Femme à idées**, woman of, with, ideas. *Essayez de vous faire une i. de notre situation*, try

to imagine our position. **Voir qch. en idée**, to see sth. in the mind's eye. **Se faire des idées**, to imagine things. **Idée fixe**, obsession. (*b*) View, opinion. **Avoir des idées arrêtées sur qch.**, to have settled ideas, very decided views, on sth. **Agir selon son idée**, **faire à son idée**, to act according to one's own ideas. *En faire à son i.*, to do just what one likes. **Changer d'idée**, to change, alter, one's mind. (*c*) Whim, fancy. **Comme l'idée m'en prend**, just as the fancy takes me. **Avoir des idées noires**, to have (a fit of) the blues. *Il faut la laisser se marier à son i.*, we must let her marry according to her fancy. **2.** Mind. **J'ai dans l'idée que . . .**, I have a notion that. . . . **Il me vient à l'idée que . . .**, it occurs to me that. . . . *Je ne peux pas lui ôter cela de l'i.*, I can't get that out of his head. **Cela m'est sorti de l'idée**, it has gone clean out of my mind. **Il me revient à l'idée que . . .**, now I remember that. . . . **3.** *F:* Une i. *de vanille*, just a suspicion of vanilla. *Ruban une i. trop bleu*, ribbon a thought too blue.

idem [idem], *adv.* Idem, id.; ditto.

identification [idãtifikasjɔ̃], *s.f.* Identification.

identifier [idãtifje], *v.tr.* To identify. **1.** To consider as identical. **2.** To establish the identity of (s.o., sth.).

s'identifier à *une cause*, to identify oneself, to become identified, with a cause.

identique [idãtik], *a.* Identical (d, with); the very same. *adv.* **-ment.**

identité [idãtite], *s.f.* Identity. *Mil:* **Plaque d'identité**, identification disk. *Adm:* **Carte d'identité**, identity card. *Établir son i.*, to prove one's identity.

idéologie [ideɔlɔʒi], *s.f.* Ideology.

idéologique [ideɔlɔʒik], *a.* Ideologic(al).

idéologue [ideɔlɔg], *s.m.* Ideologist, ideologue.

ides [id], *s.f.pl. Rom.Ant:* Ides.

idiomatique [idjɔmatik], *a.* Idiomatic(al).

idiome [idjoːm], *s.m.* (*a*) Idiom, dialect. (*b*) Language.

idiosyncrasie [idjɔsɛ̃krazi], *s.f.* Idiosyncrasy.

idiot, -ote [idjo, -ɔt]. **1.** *a.* (*a*) *Med:* Idiot (child, etc.). (*b*) *F:* Idiotic, absurd; senseless (joke, etc.). **2.** *s.* (*a*) *Med:* Idiot, imbecile; *F:* natural. (*b*) *F:* Idiot, fool; silly ass.

idiotement [idjɔtmɑ̃], *adv. F:* Idiotically.

idiotie [idjɔsi], *s.f.* **1.** *Med:* (*a*) Idiocy, imbecility. (*b*) Mental deficiency. **2.** *F:* (*a*) Rank stupidity. (*b*) Piece of rank stupidity.

idiotisme [idjɔtism], *s.m.* Idiom; idiomatic expression or phrase.

idolâtre [idolɑːtr]. **1.** *a.* Idolatrous. **2.** *s.* Idolater, *f.* idolatress.

idolâtrer [idolɑtre], *v.tr.* To be passionately fond of (s.o., sth.).

idolâtrie [idolɑtri], *s.f.* Idolatry.

idole [idɔl], *s.f.* Idol, image. **Faire une idole de qn**, to idolize s.o. **Faire son idole de l'argent**, to make a god of money.

idylle [idil], *s.f.* Idyll; romance.

idyllique [idilik], *a.* Idyllic.

if [if], *s.m.* **1.** *Bot:* Yew(-tree). **2.** (*a*) Triangular frame (for illumination lights, etc.). *Ecc:* Taperhearse. (*b*) Draining rack (for bottles).

Ignace [iɲas]. *Pr.n.m.* Ignatius.

igname [inam, iɲ-], *s.f. Yam:* Indian potato.

ignare [iɲaːr]. **1.** *a.* Ignorant. **2.** *s.* Ignoramus.

igné [igne], *a. Geol:* Igneous (rock, etc.).

ignifuge [ignify:ʒ]. **1.** a. (a) Non-inflammable, fire-resisting, fire-proof. (b) **Grenade ignifuge,** fire-extinguisher. **2.** s.m. Fire-proof or fire-proofing material.

ignifug|er [ignifyʒe], v.tr. (j'ignifugeai(s): n. ignifugeons) To fire-proof. s.f. **-ation.**

ignition [ignisjɔ̃], s.f. (State of) ignition. (Cp. ALLUMAGE = act of ignition.)

ignoble [iɲɔbl], a. (a) Ignoble ; base (person) ; vile, disgraceful, unspeakable (conduct, etc.). (b) Wretched, filthy (dwelling, etc.). adv. -ment.

ignominie [iɲɔmini], s.f. Ignominy, shame, disgrace.

ignominieu|x, -euse [iɲɔminjø, -ø:z], a. Ignominious, shameful, disgraceful. adv. **-sement.**

ignorance [iɲɔrɑ̃:s], s.f. **1.** Ignorance. Par **ignorance,** through, out of, ignorance. **Laisser qn dans l'ignorance de qch.,** to keep s.o. in ignorance of sth., F : in the dark about sth. **Les siècles d'ignorance,** the dark ages. *Peuple plongé dans l'i.,* benighted people. *Jur :* **Prétendre cause d'ignorance,** to plead ignorance. **2.** pl. Errors, mistakes, blunders.

ignor|ant, -ante [iɲɔrɑ̃, -ɑ̃:t]. **1.** a. (a) Ignorant, illiterate, uninstructed. (b) *I. de, en, qch.,* ignorant of (a fact) ; unacquainted with (Latin, etc.). **2.** s. Ignoramus, dunce. adv. **-amment.**

ignorantisme [iɲɔrɑ̃tism], s.m. Ignorantism, obscurantism.

ignorantiste [iɲɔrɑ̃tist], a. & s. Ignorantist, obscurantist.

ignorer [iɲɔre], v.tr. Not to know ; to be ignorant of (sth.) ; to be unaware of (sth.). *Il ignore tout de . . .,* he knows nothing whatever about. . . . *Ignoré de, par, ses contemporains,* (i) unknown to, (ii) ignored by, his contemporaries. **Ne pas ignorer qch.,** to be (quite, fully) aware of sth. *Je n'ignore pas que + ind.,* occ. + sub., I am not unaware that. . . . *Personne n'ignore que . . .,* there is nobody who does not know that. . . . *Un fusil qu'il ignorait être chargé,* a gun which he did not know to be loaded.

ignoré, a. Unknown (document, etc.).

iguane [igwan], s.m. Rept : Iguana.

il, ils [il]. **1.** pers. pron. nom. m. (Of pers.) He, they ; (of thg) it, they ; (of ship) she, they. **2.** inv. It, there. (a) *Il est, il doit être, six heures,* it is, it must be, six o'clock. *Il est honteux de mentir,* it is shameful to lie. *Il est vrai que j'étais là,* it is true that I was there. *Il arriva deux bataillons d'infanterie,* there arrived two battalions of infantry. *Il était une fois une fée,* there was once upon a time a fairy. (b) (With impers. vbs) *Il pleut,* it is raining. *Il faut partir,* we must start. *Il y a quelqu'un à la porte,* there is someone at the door.

île [il, i:l], s.f. **1.** Island, isle. *Habiter dans une île,* to live on an island. **Les îles Normandes,** the Channel Islands. **L'Ile de France,** Mauritius. **2.** (a) Block of houses (surrounded by streets). (b) Island site.

iléon [ileɔ̃], s.m. Anat : Ileum.

iles [il], s.m.pl. Anat : Ilia, flanks.

ilex [ilɛks], s.m. Ilex. **1.** Holly. **2.** Holm-oak.

Iliade [l'] [iljad], s.f. Gr.Lit : The Iliad.

iliaque [iljak], a. Anat : Iliac. **Os iliaque,** hip-bone.

illégal, -aux [illɛgal, -o], a. Illegal, unlawful. adv. **-ement.**

illégalité [illegalite], s.f. Illegality.

illégitime [illeʒitim], a. Illegitimate (child, etc.) ; unlawful (marriage, etc.). adv. **-ment.**

illégitimité [illeʒitimite], s.f. Illegitimacy (of child) ; unlawfulness (of marriage).

illettré [illɛtre], a. Illiterate, uneducated.

illicite [illisit], a. Illicit, unlawful. *Sp :* **Coup i.,** foul. adv. **-ment.**

illico [illiko], adv. *F :* At once ; then and there.

illimitable [illimitabl], a. Illimitable, boundless.

illimité [illimite], a. Unlimited, boundless, unbounded. *Congé i.,* indefinite leave.

illiquide [illikid], a. *Fin :* Unrealizable, unmarketable, unavailable (assets).

illisibilité [illizibilite], s.f. Illegibility.

illisible [illizibl], a. Illegible, unreadable. adv. **-ment.**

illogicité [illɔʒisite], s.f. Illogicality, illogicalness ; inconsequence ; inconsistency.

illogique [illɔʒik], a. Illogical ; inconsequent ; inconsistent. adv. **-ment.**

illogisme [illɔʒism], s.m. = ILLOGICITÉ.

illuminant [illyminɑ̃]. **1.** a. Illuminating. **2.** s.m. Illuminant.

illuminateur [illyminatœ:r], s.m. **1.** Illuminator (of building, etc.). **2.** Illuminer (of the soul or mind) ; enlightener.

illumination [illyminasjɔ̃], s.f. Illumination. **1.** (a) Lighting. *I. par projecteurs,* flood-lighting. (b) pl. Lights, illuminations. **2.** (Inward) light ; enlightenment.

illuminer [illymine], v.tr. **1.** (a) To illuminate (in token of festivity). (b) To light up. *I. une question,* to throw light upon a question. **2.** To enlighten.

illusion [illyzjɔ̃], s.f. **1.** Illusion. *I. d'optique,* optical illusion. *Se nourrir d'illusions,* to cherish illusions, to dream empty dreams. **Se faire illusion à soi-même,** to deceive oneself. **2.** Delusion. **Se faire illusion,** to labour under a delusion. *Une douce i.,* a fond delusion.

illusionner [illyzjone], v.tr. **1.** To work off an illusion on (s.o.). **2.** To delude (s.o.). **s'illusionner,** to labour under a delusion ; to delude oneself ; to deceive oneself.

illusionniste [illyzjonist], s. m. & f. Illusionist ; conjurer.

illusoire [illyzwa:r], a. Illusory, illusive.

illustrateur [illystratœ:r], s.m. **1.** Illustrator (of books, etc.). **2.** *I. d'une ville,* one who has shed lustre upon a town.

illustration [illystrasjɔ̃], s.f. **1.** (a) Shedding of lustre (upon town, etc.). (b) Celebrated person ; celebrity. **2.** *Art :* Illustration. (a) Illustrating. (b) Picture. *I. en couleur,* coloured illustration.

illustre [illystr], a. Illustrious, famous, renowned.

illustrer [illystre], v.tr. **1.** To render illustrious. **2.** To illustrate (book, etc.). *Carte postale illustrée,* picture postcard.

s'illustrer, to become famous (par, for, through) ; to win fame, renown.

illustré, s.m. Pictorial paper.

illutation [illytasjɔ̃], s.f. **1.** *Const :* Coating with mud ; luting. **2.** Mud-bath ; mud-cure.

illuter [illyte], v.tr. To bathe (patient) in mud.

îlot [ilo], s.m. **1.** Islet, small island ; holm. **2.** Small block (of houses).

ilote [ilɔt], s.m. *Gr.Hist :* Helot.

ilotisme [ilɔtism], s.m. *Gr.Hist :* Helotism.

image [ima:ʒ], s.f. Image. **1.** (a) Reflection (in water, etc.). (b) *Opt :* **I. réelle,** real image. *I. virtuelle,* virtual image. (c) *Cin :* Frame. *Televis : Émission à 25 images par seconde,* emission at 25 frames per second. **2.** (a) *L'i. vivante de son père,* the living image of his father. **A l'image de qn,** in the likeness of s.o. (b) *Pict :* Picture, figure. *Livre d'images,* picture-book. *Écriture en images,* pictorial writing. **3.** Mental picture, idea, impression. **Expression qui fait image,** vivid expression, effective phrase. **4.** Simile, metaphor.

imagé [imaʒe], *a.* Vivid, picturesque (style, etc.); full of imagery.

imagerie [imaʒri], *s.f.* **1.** Imagery. **2.** Picture-sheet or colour-print (i) trade, (ii) printing works.

imaginable [imaʒinabl], *a.* Imaginable.

imaginaire [imaʒinɛːr], *a.* Imaginary; fancied; make-believe. *Mth:* Imaginary (root). *Malade i.,* hypochondriac.

imaginatif, -ive [imaʒinatif, -iːv], *a.* Imaginative.

imagination [imaʒinasjɔ̃], *s.f.* Imagination. (*a*) **Voir qch. en imagination,** to see sth. in one's mind's eye, in imagination. (*b*) Fancy, invention. *De pure i.,* baseless, unfounded, devoid of foundation. **Se faire des imaginations,** to fancy, imagine, all sorts of things.

imaginer [imaʒine], *v.tr.* To imagine. **1.** To conceive, invent, devise. *I. une méthode,* to devise, think out, a method. *I. un dispositif,* to contrive a device. **2.** To fancy, picture. *Imaginez(-vous) un peu le plaisir que cela m'a fait,* just imagine the pleasure it gave me. **Comme on peut (se) l'imaginer . . .,** as may well be imagined. . . . **Tout ce qu'on peut imaginer de plus beau,** the finest thing imaginable. *Vous plaisantez, j'imagine,* you're joking, I suppose.

s'imaginer, to delude oneself with the thought or fancy (that . . .); to think, fancy, suppose (that . . .). *Elle s'imagine que tout le monde l'admire,* she thinks, fancies, that everyone admires her. **Il s'imagine tout savoir,** he fancies he knows everything.

imago [imago], *s.f. Ent:* Imago.

imbattable [ɛ̃batabl], *a.* Invincible; unbeatable.

imbattu [ɛ̃baty], *a.* Unbeaten (champion); unbroken (record).

imbécile [ɛ̃besil]. **1.** *a.* (*a*) Imbecile, half-witted. (*b*) *F:* Silly, idiotic. **2.** *s.* (*a*) Imbecile. (*b*) *F:* Idiot, fool; fat-head. **Mécanisme à l'épreuve des imbéciles,** fool-proof mechanism. *Faire l'i.,* to act the fool.

imbécilement [ɛ̃besilmã], *adv. F:* Idiotically.

imbécillité [ɛ̃besilite], *s.f.* **1.** (*a*) Imbecility; feebleness of mind. (*b*) *F:* Silliness, stupidity. **2.** *F:* Stupid act or speech. *Dire des imbécillités,* to talk nonsense.

imberbe [ɛ̃bɛrb], *a.* Beardless; callow (youth).

imbiber [ɛ̃bibe], *v.tr.* **1.** *I. qch. de qch.,* to soak, steep, sth. in sth.; to imbue, impregnate, sth. with sth. *Imbibé d'eau,* wet. *F: Être imbibé de préjugés,* to be steeped in, imbued with, prejudice. **2.** (Of liquid) To permeate, drench, soak (sth.). **3.** To soak up, absorb, imbibe (sth.).

s'imbiber. 1. To become saturated (*de,* with); to absorb. **2.** (Of liquids) To become absorbed; to sink in.

imbibition [ɛ̃bibisjɔ̃], *s.f.* **1.** Soaking. **2.** Absorption.

imbrication [ɛ̃brikasjɔ̃], *s.f.* Imbrication: overlap(ping) (of tiles, scales, etc.).

imbrifuge [ɛ̃brifyːʒ], *a.* Rain-proof, waterproof.

imbriqué [ɛ̃brike], *a.* Imbricate(d), overlapping.

imbrisable [ɛ̃brizabl], *a.* Unbreakable.

imbroglio [ɛ̃brɔ(l)jo], *s.m.* Imbroglio.

imbrûlable [ɛ̃brylabl], *a.* Unburnable, fire-proof.

imbu [ɛ̃by], *a.* Imbued, soaked. *Papier i. d'huile,* (i) oily paper; (ii) oiled paper. *I. de préjugés,* steeped in prejudice.

imbuvable [ɛ̃byvabl], *a.* Undrinkable.

imitateur, -trice [imitatœːr, -tris]. **1.** *s.* Imitator. **2.** *a.* Imitative, imitating, apish.

imitatif, -ive [imitatif, -iːv], *a.* Imitative.

imitation [imitasjɔ̃], *s.f.* Imitation. **1.** (*a*) Imitating, copying. **A l'imitation de qch.,** in imitation, on the model, of sth. (*b*) Mimicking, mimicry. (*c*) Forging (of signature, etc.); counterfeiting (of money). **2.** (*a*) Copy. **(Bijoux en) imitation,** imitation jewellery. (*b*) Forgery, counterfeit.

imiter [imite], *v.tr.* To imitate. (*a*) To copy; to model (*de,* upon). (*b*) To mimic; to take (s.o.) off. (*c*) To forge (signature); to counterfeit.

immaculable [immakylabl], *a.* Unstainable. **Acier immaculable,** stainless steel.

immaculé [immakyle], *a.* Immaculate; stainless; undefiled.

immanent [immanã], *a.* Immanent.

immangeable [immãʒabl, ɛ̃mãʒabl], *a.* Uneatable.

immanquable [ɛ̃mãkabl], *a.* Certain, inevitable.

immanquablement [ɛ̃mãkabləmã], *adv.* Inevitably, without fail, for certain.

immatérialité [immaterjalite], *s.f.* Immateriality.

immatéri|el, -elle [immaterjɛl], *a.* **1.** Immaterial, unsubstantial. **2.** Intangible (assets, etc.). *adv.* **-ellement.**

immatriculation [immatrikylasjɔ̃], *s.f.* **1.** Registering, registration (of deed, of rolling-stock, etc.). **2.** Enrolment, enrolling.

immatricule [immatrikyl], *s.f.* **1.** = IMMATRICULATION. **2.** Registration-number, -certificate.

immatriculer [immatrikyle], *v.tr.* To enter (s.o., sth.) on a register; to register (document, car, etc.); to enrol (s.o.).

immaturité [immatyrite], *s.f.* Immaturity.

immédiat [immedja(t)], *a.* Immediate. **1.** (*a*) Direct (cause, successor). *Ch: Analyse immédiate,* proximate analysis. (*b*) Close at hand; near. (*c*) Urgent (question, etc.). **2.** Without delay. *adv.* **-ement.**

immémorial, -aux [immemɔrjal, -o], *a.* Immemorial. **De temps immémorial,** time out of mind; from, since, time immemorial.

immen|se [immãːs], *a.* **1.** Immeasurable, boundless. **2.** Immense, vast, huge. *adv.* **-sément.**

immensité [immãsite], *s.f.* **1.** Immensity, infinity. **2.** Vastness, boundlessness.

immerger [immɛrʒe], *v.tr.* (j'immergeai(s); n. immergeons) **1.** (*a*) To immerse, plunge, dip. *Tg: I. un câble,* to lay a cable. (*b*) To drop (a body) overboard (in funeral at sea); to commit (a body) to the deep. **2.** *Astr:* To occult.

s'immerger. 1. (Of ship) To settle. **2.** *Astr:* To be occulted.

immérité [immerite], *a.* Unmerited, undeserved.

immersion [immɛrsjɔ̃], *s.f.* **1.** Immersion, dipping. *Tg:* Laying (of cable). *Astr:* Occultation. **2.** Submergence, submersion (of submarine). **3.** *Nau:* Committal to the deep.

immesurable [ɛ̃mazyrabl], *a.* Immeasurable.

immeuble [immœbl]. *Jur:* **1.** *a.* Real, fixed. **Biens immeubles,** real estate. **2.** *s.m.* (*a*) Real estate, landed property. (*b*) *F:* House, mansion (in flats). (*c*) Premises (of business).

immigrant, -ante [immigrã, -ã:t], *a. & s.* Immigrant.

immigration [immigrasjɔ̃], *s.f.* Immigration.

immigrer [immigre], *v.i.* To immigrate.

immigré, -ée, *s.* Immigrant, settler.

imminence [imminãːs], *s.f.* Imminence.

imminent [imminã], *a.* Imminent, impending.

immiscer [immise], *v.tr.* (j'immisçai(s); n. immisçons) To mix up, involve (s.o.) (*dans,* in).

s'immiscer *dans une affaire,* to interfere in, (inter-)meddle with, in, an affair.

immiséricordieux, -euse [immizerikɔrdjø, -øːz], *a.* Merciless, pitiless ; hard-hearted.

immixtion [immikstjɔ̃], *s.f. I. dans une affaire,* unwarrantable interference in, with, a business.

immobile [immɔbil], *a.* **I.** Motionless, still, unmoved. *Visage i.,* set face. **2.** Immovable ; firm, steadfast.

immobilier, -ière [immɔbilje, -jɛːr], *a. Jur :* Real. **Biens immobiliers,** real estate, landed estate, realty. **Vente immobilière,** sale of property. **Société immobilière,** building society. **Agence immobilière,** estate-agency. **Agent immobilier,** estate-agent. S.a. SAISIE.

immobilisation [immɔbilizasjɔ̃], *s.f.* **I.** Immobilization, immobilizing. **2.** *Jur :* Conversion into real estate. **3.** (a) Locking up, tying up, tie-up (of capital). (b) *pl.* **Immobilisations,** fixed assets, capital assets.

immobiliser [immɔbilize], *v.tr.* **I.** To immobilize. (a) To bring to a standstill. (b) To fix (sth.) in position. **2.** *Jur :* To convert (personaly) into realty. **3.** To lock up, tie up (capital).

immobilité [immɔbilite], *s.f.* Immobility, motionlessness ; fixity.

immodéré [immɔdere], *a.* Immoderate, excessive, inordinate. *adv.* **-ment.**

immodeste [immɔdɛst], *a.* Immodest, shameless. *adv.* **-ment.**

immodestie [immɔdɛsti], *s.f.* Immodesty.

immolation [immɔlasjɔ̃], *s.f.* Immolation.

immoler [immɔle], *v.tr.* To immolate, sacrifice.

immonde [immɔ̃ːd], *a.* **I.** *Rel.H :* Unclean. **2.** (Unspeakably) foul ; filthy ; vile.

immondices [immɔ̃dis], *s.f.pl.* Dirt, refuse, street sweepings. "**Défense de déposer des immondices,**" (i) 'shoot no rubbish' ; (ii) 'commit no nuisance.'

immoral, -aux [immɔral, -o], *a.* Immoral. *adv.* **-ement.**

immoralité [immɔralite], *s.f.* **I.** Immorality. **2.** Immoral act.

immortaliser [immɔrtalize], *v.tr.* To immortalize.

immortalité [immɔrtalite], *s.f.* Immortality.

immortel, -elle [immɔrtɛl], **I.** *a.* Immortal (life, etc.); everlasting, undying (fame, etc.). **2.** *s.m.pl.* **Les immortels,** the immortals, esp. *F :* the members of the Académie française. **3.** *s.f. Bot :* **Immortelle,** everlasting (flower); immortelle. *adv.* **-ellement.**

immuabilité [immɥabilite], *s.f.* = IMMUTABILITÉ.

immuable [immɥabl], *a.* Immutable, unalterable ; fixed, unchanging. *adv.* **-ment.**

immunisation [immynizasjɔ̃], *s.f. Med :* Immunization.

immuniser [immynize], *v.tr. Med :* To immunize ; to render (s.o.) immune (*contre,* from).

immunité [immynite], *s.f.* Immunity.

immutabilité [immytabilite], *s.f.* Immutability.

impact [ɛ̃pakt], *s:m.* Impact, shock.

impair [ɛ̃pɛːr]. **I.** *a.* (a) Odd, uneven (number). *Jouer à pair ou i.,* to play at odd or even. *Rail :* **Voie impaire,** down line. (b) *Anat :* Single, azygous (bone). **2.** *s.m. F :* Blunder, bloomer, break. *Commettre un impair,* to drop a brick ; to put one's foot in it.

impalpable [ɛ̃palpabl], *a.* Impalpable, intangible.

impaludé [ɛ̃palyde], *a.* Malarious.

impaludisme [ɛ̃palydism], *s.m. Med :* = PALUDISME.

impardonnable [ɛ̃pardɔnabl], *a.* Unpardonable.

imparfait [ɛ̃parfɛ], *a.* **I.** Unfinished, uncompleted. **2.** Imperfect, defective. **3.** *s.m.* **Verbe à l'imparfait,** verb in the imperfect.

imparfaitement [ɛ̃parfɛtmɑ̃], *adv.* Imperfectly.

imparité [ɛ̃parite], *s.f.* **I.** Inequality, disparity. **2.** *Mth :* Oddness (of number).

impartageable [ɛ̃partaʒabl], *a.* **I.** Indivisible. **2.** That cannot be shared.

impartial, -aux [ɛ̃parsjal, -o], *a.* Impartial, unbiassed, fair-minded, unprejudiced ; evenhanded (justice). *adv.* **-ement.**

impartialité [ɛ̃parsjalite], *s.f.* Impartiality.

impartir [ɛ̃partiːr], *v.tr.* (j'impartis, n. impartissons) *Jur :* To grant (right, favour) (*à,* to).

impassable [ɛ̃pɑsabl], *a.* Impassable ; unfordable (river).

impasse [ɛ̃pɑːs], *s.f.* **I.** Blind alley, dead-end, *cul-de-sac. P.N :* Impasse, no thoroughfare. **2.** Position from which there is no escape ; dead-lock. *Se trouver dans une i.,* to find oneself in a dilemma, *F :* in a fix. *Aboutir à une i.,* to come to a dead-lock. **3.** *Cards :* **Faire une impasse,** to finesse. [PASSE]

impassibilité [ɛ̃pasibilite], *s.f.* Impassibility, impassiveness.

impassible [ɛ̃pasibl], *a.* Impassive. **I.** Unmoved ; unconcerned. **2.** (a) Unimpressionable. (b) Callous. *adv.* **-ment.**

impatience [ɛ̃pasjɑ̃ːs], *s.f.* **I.** *Lit :* Intolerance (*de,* of). *I. du joug,* chafing under the yoke. **2.** (a) Impatience. *Avec impatience,* impatiently. (b) Eagerness. *Avoir une grande i. de faire qch.,* to be all impatience, most eager, to do sth. **3.** *pl.* Fits of impatience.

impatient, -ente [ɛ̃pasjã, -ãːt], *a.* (a) *Lit :* Intolerant (*de,* of). *I. du joug,* chafing under the yoke. (b) Impatient. *D'un air i.,* impatiently. (c) *Être i. de faire qch.,* to be eager, anxious, all agog, to do sth. *adv.* **-emment.**

impatienter [ɛ̃pasjãte], *v.tr.* To put (s.o.) out of all patience ; to provoke (s.o.). *a.* **-ant.** **s'impatienter,** to lose patience ; to grow impatient (*contre qn,* with s.o.).

impatroniser [ɛ̃patrɔnize], *v.tr.* **I.** To set (stranger) in authority (over one's household, etc.). **2.** To introduce and impose (practice) ; to set (fashion). **s'impatroniser,** to make one's authority or influence felt ; *F :* to get one's foot in.

impayable [ɛ̃pejabl], *a.* **I.** Inestimable, invaluable, priceless. **2.** *F :* Highly amusing, killingly funny ; priceless (joke).

impayé [ɛ̃peje], *a.* Unpaid (debt, etc.); dishonoured (bill).

impeccabilité [ɛ̃pɛkabilite], *s.f.* Impeccability. (a) Sinlessness. (b) Faultlessness (of attire, etc.).

impeccable [ɛ̃pɛkabl], *a.* Impeccable. (a) Infallible. (b) Faultless (style, taste); flawless (technique).

impécunieux, -euse [ɛ̃pekynjø, øːz], *a.* Impecunious.

impédance [ɛ̃pedɑ̃ːs], *s.f. El :* Impedance. **Bobine d'impédance,** choking coil ; *F :* choke.

impédimenta [ɛ̃pedimɛ̃ta], *s.m.pl.* Impedimenta.

impénétrabilité [ɛ̃penetrabilite], *s.f.* **I.** Impenetrability ; imperviousness. **2.** Inscrutableness, inscrutability.

impénétrable [ɛ̃penetrabl], *a.* **I.** Impenetrable (forest, etc.). *I. à l'eau,* impervious to water. **2.** Inscrutable (face); unfathomable (mystery); close (secret). *adv.* **-ment.**

impénitence [ɛ̃penitãːs], *s.f.* Impenitence, unrepentance ; obduracy.

impénitent [ɛ̃penitɑ̃], a. Impenitent, unrepentant.

impérat|if, -ive [ɛ̃peratif, -iːv]. **I.** a. Imperious, imperative, peremptory. **2.** s.m. Gram: A l'impératif, in the imperative. adv. **-ivement.**

impératrice [ɛ̃peratris], s.f. Empress.

impercept|ible [ɛ̃pɛrsɛptibl], a. Imperceptible, unperceivable, undiscernible. s.f. **-ibilité.** adv. **-iblement.**

imperdable [ɛ̃perdabl], a. That cannot be lost.

imperfection [ɛ̃perfɛksjɔ̃], s.f. Imperfection. **I.** Incompletion, incompleteness. **2.** (a) Defectiveness. (b) Defect, fault, flaw, blemish.

impérial, -aux [ɛ̃perjal, -o]. **I.** a. Imperial. **2.** s.f. **Impériale.** (a) Outside, top(-deck) (of tram, bus, etc.); (railed in) top (of taxi, etc.). (b) Imperial; tuft (on lower lip) (as worn by Napoleon III).

impérialisme [ɛ̃perjalism], s.m. Imperialism.

impérieux, -euse [ɛ̃perjø, -øːz], a. **I.** Imperious, haughty, lordly, domineering. **2.** Imperative, pressing (necessity, etc.).

impérissable [ɛ̃perisabl], a. Imperishable.

impéritie [ɛ̃perisi], s.f. Incapacity, incompetence.

imperméabiliser [ɛ̃permeabilize], v.tr. To (water)proof (cloth).

imperméabilité [ɛ̃permeabilite], s.f. Impermeability; imperviousness (à, to).

imperméable [ɛ̃permeabl]. **I.** a. Impervious (à, to); impermeable. I. à l'eau, waterproof, watertight. I. au gaz, gas-tight. I. à la poussière, dust-proof. **2.** s.m. Cost: Waterproof, mackintosh; rain-coat.

impersonnalité [ɛ̃personalite], s.f. Impersonality.

impersonnel, -elle [ɛ̃personɛl], a. Impersonal.

impertinence [ɛ̃pertinɑ̃ːs], s.f. Impertinence. **I.** Jur: Irrelevance. **2.** Pertness, rudeness. Dire des impertinences, to utter impertinences.

impertin|ent, -ente [ɛ̃pertinɑ̃, -ɑ̃ːt], a. Impertinent. **I.** Jur: Irrelevant. **2.** Pert, rude. s. Impertinent fellow, f. saucy wench. adv. **-emment.**

imperturbabilité [ɛ̃pertyrbabilite], s.f. Imperturbability.

imperturbable [ɛ̃pertyrbabl], a. Imperturbable, unruffled. adv. **-ment.**

impétigo [ɛ̃petigo], s.m. Med: Impetigo.

impétr|ant, -ante [ɛ̃petrɑ̃, -ɑ̃ːt], s. **I.** Grantee (of title, diploma, etc.). **2.** F: Candidate.

impétueu|x, -euse [ɛ̃petɥø, -øːz], a. Impetuous; hot-headed, impulsive. adv. **-sement.**

impétuosité [ɛ̃petɥozite], s.f. Impetuosity; impulsiveness.

impie [ɛ̃pi], a. Impious, ungodly; blasphemous.

impiété [ɛ̃pjete], s.f. **I.** (a) Impiety, godlessness; ungodliness. (b) Impiousness (of wish). **2.** (a) Blasphemy. (b) Impious deed.

impitoyable [ɛ̃pitwajabl], a. (a) Pitiless (à, envers, towards); ruthless, merciless, unmerciful. (b) Relentless, unrelenting. adv. **-ment.**

implacabilité [ɛ̃plakabilite], s.f. Implacability.

implacable [ɛ̃plakabl], a. Implacable, relentless, unrelenting (à, pour, à l'égard de, towards). adv. **-ment.**

implant|er [ɛ̃plɑ̃te], v.tr. (a) To plant; to implant, ingraft (idea, etc.). (b) Surg: To graft, ingraft. s.f. **-ation.**
  s'implanter, to take root. F: S'i. chez qn, to plant, foist, oneself on s.o.

implicite [ɛ̃plisit], a. Implicit. (a) Implied (intention, etc.) (b) Absolute (faith, confidence).

implicitement [ɛ̃plisitmɑ̃], adv. Implicitly. (a) By implication; impliedly. (b) Unquestioningly.

impliquer [ɛ̃plike], v.tr. **I.** To implicate, involve. Véhicule impliqué (dans un accident), vehicle involved. **2.** Log: Impliquer contradiction, to imply a contradiction.

implorateur, -trice [ɛ̃plɔratœːr, -tris], s. Implorer, beseecher.

imploration [ɛ̃plɔrasjɔ̃], s.f. Imploring, imploration, entreaty.

implorer [ɛ̃plɔre], v.tr. To implore, beseech, entreat.

imployable [ɛ̃plwajabl], a. Unbending.

impoli [ɛ̃pɔli], a. Impolite, unmannerly, uncivil, rude (envers, avec, to). adv. **-ment.**

impolitesse [ɛ̃pɔlitɛs], s.f. **I.** Impoliteness. (a) Discourtesy, incivility. (b) Rudeness, unmannerliness, ill-breeding. **2.** Act of discourtesy or rudeness; breach of (good) manners.

impolitique [ɛ̃pɔlitik], a. Impolitic, ill-advised.

impondérable [ɛ̃pɔ̃derabl], a. Imponderable.

impondéré [ɛ̃pɔ̃dere], a. **I.** Ill-considered (action). **2.** (Nature) lacking ballast.

impopulaire [ɛ̃pɔpylɛːr], a. Unpopular.

impopularité [ɛ̃pɔpylarite], s.f. Unpopularity.

importable[1] [ɛ̃pɔrtabl], a. Importable (goods).

importable[2], a. Unwearable; not fit to wear.

importance [ɛ̃pɔrtɑ̃ːs], s.f. Importance. (a) Consequence, moment. De peu d'importance, of little moment, of slight consequence. Sans importance, unimportant; trifling (matter). Événement de la première importance, de toute importance, all-important event. Avoir de l'importance, to be important, of importance. Mettre, attacher, prêter, de l'importance à qch., to attach importance to sth. Rail: I. du retard, number of minutes (train is) late. I. d'une blessure, gravity of a wound. I. du dommage, extent of the damage. Adv.phr. Tancer qn d'importance, to give s.o. a good talking-to. Rosser qn d'i., to thrash s.o. soundly. (b) Social importance, position. Faire l'homme d'importance, to set up for a man of consequence.

important, -ante [ɛ̃pɔrtɑ̃, -ɑ̃ːt]. **I.** a. (a) Important; large, considerable (sum). Personnage i., person of importance, of consequence. Il est i. qu'on le sache, it is important that it should be known. Peu important, unimportant, immaterial. (b) Consequential, self-important; F: bumptious. **2.** s. Busybody.

importateur, -trice [ɛ̃pɔrtatœːr, -tris]. **I.** s. Importer. **2.** a. Importing (firm, etc.).

importation [ɛ̃pɔrtasjɔ̃], s.f. Importation. **I.** Importing. **2.** (Thing imported) Import.

importer[1] [ɛ̃pɔrte], v.tr. To import (goods).

importer[2], v.i. (Only used in the third pers., participles, and inf.) To be of importance, of consequence; to matter, to signify. **I.** Les choses qui importent, the things that matter. Que m'importe la vie! what is life to me! **2.** Impers. Il importe que + sub., it is essential that. . . . Il importe à tout le monde de le faire, it behoves everyone to do so. Il importe peu que . . ., peu importe que . . ., it matters little whether. . . . Peu m'importe, I don't mind; it is all one to me. N'importe, no matter, never mind. Qu'importe qu'il vienne ou non? what does it signify whether he comes or not? Que m'importe? what do I care? Faire qch. n'importe comment, où, quand, to do something no matter how, where, when; to do sth. anyhow, anywhere, any time. N'importe quelle autre personne, anybody else. Venez n'importe quel jour, come any day. N'importe qui, anyone (at all); no matter who. N'importe quoi, anything; no matter what.

importun, -une [ɛ̃pɔrtœ̃, -yn]. **I.** *a.* Importunate; obtrusive tiresome (person); harassing (thought, etc.); unseasonable (request); unwelcome (visitor). *Je crains de vous être i.*, I am afraid I am disturbing you; I fear I intrude. **2.** *s.* Intruder; nuisance (of a man). *adv.* **-ément.**

importuner [ɛ̃pɔrtyne], *v.tr.* To importune. (*a*) To bother, pester (s.o.); to obtrude oneself on (s.o.). *Être importuné par ses créanciers*, to be dunned by one's creditors. (*b*) To annoy, trouble, inconvenience (s.o.).

importunité [ɛ̃pɔrtynite], *s.f.* Importunity; obtrusiveness; dunning (by creditors).

imposable [ɛ̃pozabl], *a.* (*a*) Taxable (person, income). (*b*) Ratable, assessable (property).

imposant [ɛ̃pozɑ̃], *a.* Imposing (figure, ceremony); commanding, stately, dignified.

imposer [ɛ̃poze]. **I.** *v.tr.* **I.** (*a*) *Ecc:* To lay on (hands). (*b*) *Typ:* To impose (sheet). **2.** To give, assign (name). **3.** To impose, prescribe; to set (task). *I. une règle*, to lay down, enforce, a rule. *Sujet imposé aux concurrents*, set subject. *I.* (*le*) *silence à qn*, to enjoin silence on s.o. *I. sa manière de voir*, to carry one's point. *I. du respect à qn*, to inspire s.o. with respect. *I. le respect*, to command respect. *S'i. un labeur*, to undertake a task. *S'i. de faire qch.*, to make it a duty to do sth. **4.** *Adm:* (*a*) *I. des droits sur qch.*, to impose, put, a tax on sth.; to tax sth. (*b*) *I. qn*, (i) to tax s.o.; (ii) to rate s.o. *I. qch.*, to make sth. taxable. *I. un immeuble*, to levy a rate on a building; to assess a building.
II. imposer, *v.i.* **I.** (En) imposer, to inspire respect, awe. **2.** (En) imposer à qn, to impose on s.o.; to deceive s.o., to take s.o. in.
s'imposer. I. To assert oneself; to compel recognition. *S'i. à l'attention*, to command attention. *La conviction s'imposa à mon esprit que . . .*, the conviction forced itself upon me that. . . . .2. *S'i. à qn, chez qn*, to foist, thrust, force, oneself upon s.o. **3.** To be indispensable. *La discrétion s'impose*, discretion is imperative.
imposé, -ée, *s.* (*a*) Tax-payer. (*b*) Rate-payer.

imposition [ɛ̃pozisjɔ̃], *s.f.* **I.** (*a*) *Ecc:* Imposition, laying on (of hands). (*b*) *Typ:* Imposing, imposition. **2.** Giving, assigning (of name). **3.** Imposing, laying down (of conditions); setting, prescribing (of task). **4.** (*a*) Imposition, putting on (of tax); taxation. (*b*) Assessment (of property). **5.** (*a*) Tax, duty. (*b*) Rates.

impossibilité [ɛ̃pɔsibilite], *s.f.* Impossibility. *Il y a i. à cela*, it is impossible that it should be so. *Être dans l'i. matérielle de faire qch.*, (i) to find it impossible to do sth.; (ii) to be unavoidably prevented from doing sth. **Il est de toute impossibilité** *qu'il vienne à le savoir*, it is impossible that he should come to know of it.

impossible [ɛ̃pɔsibl], *a.* Impossible. *Cela m'est i.*, I cannot. *Il m'est i. de le faire*, I cannot do it. *Il m'est i. de ne pas croire que . . .*, I cannot but believe that. . . . *C'est i. à faire*, it cannot be done. **Il a fait l'impossible** *pour nous secourir*, there is nothing he did not do to help us. *Il est i. qu'il revienne en temps voulu*, he cannot possibly be back in time. *Prov:* **A l'impossible nul n'est tenu,** no one is expected to perform impossibilities. **Si par impossible** *il est encore vivant*, if, by any remote chance, he is still alive. *F: Il a fallu nous lever à une heure i.*, we had to get up at an unearthly hour.

imposte [ɛ̃pɔst], *s.f.* (*a*) Impost (of bearing arch); springer. (*b*) Transom-window; fanlight.

imposteur [ɛ̃pɔstœːr], *s.m.* Impostor, humbug.

imposture [ɛ̃pɔstyːr], *s.f.* Imposture. **I.** Deception, trickery. **2.** Swindle, piece of trickery.

impôt [ɛ̃po], *s.m.* Tax, duty. *I. foncier*, land tax. *I. cédulaire sur le revenu*, income tax. *I. sur le luxe*, luxury tax. *I. du timbre*, stamp duty. **Mettre un impôt sur qch., frapper qch. d'un impôt,** to tax sth.; to lay, levy, a tax on sth.

impotence [ɛ̃pɔtɑ̃ːs], *s.f.* Helplessness, lameness, infirmity.

impotent, -ente [ɛ̃pɔtɑ̃, -ɑ̃ːt]. **I.** *a.* Helpless, crippled. *Être i. de la jambe gauche*, to be lame in, to have lost the use of, the left leg. **2.** *s.* Cripple; helpless invalid.

impraticable [ɛ̃pratikabl], *a.* **I.** Impracticable, unfeasible, unworkable; unpractical. **2.** Impassable. *Chemin i. aux automobiles*, road unfit for motor traffic.

impratiqué [ɛ̃pratike], *a.* Unfrequented, untrodden (path, etc.).

imprécation [ɛ̃prekasjɔ̃], *s.f.* Imprecation, curse. **Faire des imprécations contre qn,** to call down curses upon s.o.

imprécatoire [ɛ̃prekatwaːr], *a.* Imprecatory.

imprécis [ɛ̃presi], *a.* Lacking in precision. **I.** Vague, unprecise, indefinite; inexplicit. **2.** Inaccurate (fire).

imprécision [ɛ̃presizjɔ̃], *s.f.* Lack of precision. **I.** Looseness (of terminology); vagueness (of statement). **2.** Inaccuracy (of fire).

imprégnation [ɛ̃preɲasjɔ̃, -ɛgn-], *s.f.* Impregnation; permeation.

imprégner [ɛ̃preɲe], *v.tr.* (j'imprègne; j'imprégnerai) To impregnate (*de*, with); to permeate. **s'imprégner,** to become saturated (*de*, with). *S'i. d'eau*, to soak up, soak in, water.

imprémédité [ɛ̃premedite], *a.* Unpremeditated, undesigned.

imprenable [ɛ̃prǝnabl], *a.* Impregnable.

imprésario [ɛ̃prezarjo], *s.m.* **I.** Impresario. **2.** Business manager (for athlete, etc.).

imprescriptible [ɛ̃preskriptibl], *a.* *Jur:* Imprescriptible, indefeasible (right, etc.).

impression [ɛ̃presjɔ̃], *s.f.* **I.** Impressing. (*a*) *Tex: Typ:* Printing. *Livre à l'i.*, book in the press. **Faute d'impression,** misprint. (*b*) Stamping (of coins). (*c*) *Paint:* Priming. **2.** (*a*) Impression (of a seal upon wax). *I. de pas sur le sol*, imprint of footsteps, footprints, on the ground. (*b*) *Publ: Troisième i. d'un livre*, third impression, third printing, of a book. (*c*) *Engr: etc:* Print. *I. en couleurs*, colour-print. (*d*) Impress (on coin). **3.** (Mental) impression. **Faire impression,** to make an impression; to create a sensation.

impressionnable [ɛ̃presjɔnabl], *a.* **I.** Impressionable; excitable. **2.** *Ch: Phot:* Sensitive (plate, etc.). *Papier i.*, sensitized paper.

impressionnant [ɛ̃presjɔnɑ̃], *a.* Impressive; moving (sight, voice); sensational (news).

impressionner [ɛ̃presjɔne], *v.tr.* **I.** To impress, affect, move; to make an impression upon (s.o.). **2.** To act on (the retina); to produce an image on (sensitized paper, etc.).
s'impressionner, to be strongly affected (by piece of news, etc.). *Ne vous impressionnez pas*, don't get excited; *F:* don't get panicky.

impressionnisme [ɛ̃presjɔnism], *s.m.* *Art:* Impressionism.

imprévisible [ɛ̃previzibl], *a.* = IMPRÉVOYABLE.

imprévision [ɛ̃previzjɔ̃], *s.f.* Want of foresight.

imprévoyable [ɛ̃prevwajabl], *a.* Unforeseeable.

imprévoyance [ɛ̃prevwajɑ̃ːs], *s.f.* (*a*) Want of foresight. (*b*) Improvidence.

21

imprévoyant [ɛ̃prevwajɑ̃], a. (a) Wanting in foresight. (b) Improvident.

imprévu [ɛ̃prevy]. I. a. Unforeseen, unlooked for, unexpected. S.a. CAS I. 2. s.m. (a) Unexpected character (of event). (b) Unforeseen events. Sauf imprévu, à moins d'imprévu, barring accidents; unless some unforeseen obstacle occurs. En cas d'imprévu, in case of an emergency. Imprévus, unforeseen expenses or contingencies.

imprimable [ɛ̃primabl], a. Printable.

imprimer [ɛ̃prime], v.tr. I. To communicate (direction, etc.) (à, to). I. le mouvement à un corps, to impart, transmit, motion to a body. I. le respect, to inspire respect. 2. (a) To (im)print, impress, stamp (sth. on sth.). (b) To (im)print (material). Indienne imprimée, printed calico; print. 3. Typ: To print. Presse à imprimer, printing-press. 4. Paint: To prime, ground (canvas).
    imprimé, s.m. Printed paper or book. Remplir un i., to fill up a form. "Imprimés," 'printed matter.'

imprimerie [ɛ̃primri], s.f. I. (Art of) printing. 2. Printing-office, -works, -house; press.

imprimeur [ɛ̃primœ:r], s.m. I. (a) (Master-) printer. Imprimeur-libraire, printer and publisher. (b) (Working) printer. 2. I. d'indiennes, calico printer.

imprimeuse [ɛ̃primø:z], s.f. Hand-press.

improbabilité [ɛ̃prɔbabilite], s.f. Improbability, unlikelihood.

improbable [ɛ̃prɔbabl], a. Improbable, unlikely.

improbateur, -trice [ɛ̃prɔbatœ:r, -tris]. I. a. Disapproving. 2. s. Disapprover, censurer.

improbatif, -ive [ɛ̃prɔbatif, -i:v], a. Disapproving; (sign) of disapproval.

improbité [ɛ̃prɔbite], s.f. Dishonesty.

improductif, -ive [ɛ̃prɔdyktif, -i:v], a. Unproductive (land); non-productive (assets).

improductivité [ɛ̃prɔdyktivite], s.f. Unproductiveness.

impromptu [ɛ̃prɔ̃(p)ty]. I. adv. Without preparation; impromptu. 2. a.inv. Unpremeditated (departure, etc.); impromptu (meal, etc.); extempore (speech). 3. s.m. Lit: Mus: Impromptu. pl. (Des) impromptus.

imprononçable [ɛ̃prɔnɔ̃sabl], a. Unpronounceable.

impropre [ɛ̃prɔpr], a. (a) Incorrect, wrong (term). (b) I. à qch., à faire qch., unfit, unsuitable, for sth.; unfit to do sth. adv. -ment.

impropriété [ɛ̃prɔpriete], s.f. Impropriety; incorrectness (of word).

improvisateur, -trice [ɛ̃prɔvizatœ:r, -tris], s. Mus: Improviser, improvisator; extempore player.

improvisation [ɛ̃prɔvizasjɔ̃], s.f. Improvisation. I. Improvising; extempore playing. 2. Extemporization (on organ, etc.); extempore speech.

improviser [ɛ̃prɔvize], v.tr. I. To improvise. I. un discours, to make an extempore speech. 2. Abs. (a) To speak extempore. (b) Mus: I. à l'orgue, to improvise on the organ.

improviste (à l') [alɛ̃prɔvist], adv.phr. Unexpectedly; without a moment's warning. Prendre qn à l'i., to take s.o. unawares.

improvoqué [ɛ̃prɔvɔke], a. Unprovoked.

imprudence [ɛ̃prydɑ̃:s], s.f. Imprudence; rashness. Commettre des imprudences, to act rashly, imprudently.

imprud|ent [ɛ̃prydɑ̃], a. Imprudent, foolhardy, rash; unwise. adv. -emment.

impubère [ɛ̃pybɛ:r], a. Jur: Under the age of puberty.

impuberté [ɛ̃pybɛrte], s.f. Impuberty.

impubliable [ɛ̃pybliabl], a. Unpublishable.

impudence [ɛ̃pydɑ̃:s], s.f. I. Impudence. (a) Effrontery. (b) Shamelessness, immodesty. 2. Piece of impudence.

impud|ent [ɛ̃pydɑ̃], a. I. Shamelessly immodest. 2. Impudent, insolent. adv. -emment.

impudeur [ɛ̃pydœ:r], s.f. Shamelessness. I. Immodesty. 2. Effrontery.

impudicité [ɛ̃pydisite], s.f. Unchastity, impudicity, lewdness.

impudique [ɛ̃pydik], a. Unchaste, immodest, lewd. adv. -ment.

impuissance [ɛ̃pɥisɑ̃:s], s.f. I. Impotence, powerlessness, helplessness. I. à faire qch., powerlessness to do sth. Je suis dans l'impuissance de le sauver, it is beyond my power to save him. 2. Med: Impotence.

impuissant [ɛ̃pɥisɑ̃], a. (a) Impotent, powerless, helpless. I. à faire qch., powerless to do sth. (b) Unavailing, ineffective (effort, etc.).

impulsif, -ive [ɛ̃pylsif, -i:v], a. Impulsive.

impulsion [ɛ̃pylsjɔ̃], s.f. I. (a) Mec: Impulse. Force d'i., impulsive force. El.E: I. de courant, current impulse. (b) F: Impulse, impetus. Donner de l'i. au commerce, to give a stimulus, an impulse, to trade. Les affaires ont reçu une nouvelle i., business has received fresh impetus. 2. Sous l'impulsion du moment, under the impulse of the moment, on the spur of the moment.

impunément [ɛ̃pynemɑ̃], adv. With impunity.

impuni [ɛ̃pyni], a. Unpunished. (Of crime) Rester i., to go unpunished.

impunité [ɛ̃pynite], s.f. Impunity.

impur [ɛ̃py:r], a. (a) Impure; foul, tainted. (b) (Morally) impure; lewd. adv. -ement.

impureté [ɛ̃pyrte], s.f. I. (a) Impurity, foulness (of water, etc.). (b) (Moral) impurity; lewdness. 2. pl. Impurities (in water, etc.).

impurifié [ɛ̃pyrifje], a. Unpurified.

imputable [ɛ̃pytabl], a. I. Imputable, ascribable, attributable (à, to). 2. Frais imputables sur un compte, expenses chargeable to an account.

imputation [ɛ̃pytasjɔ̃], s.f. I. Imputation, charge. Imputations calomnieuses, slanderous charges. 2. Com: I. d'une somme sur une quantité, deduction of a sum from a quota.

imputer [ɛ̃pyte], v.tr. I. To impute, ascribe, attribute. I. un crime à un innocent, to impute a crime to an innocent person. Imputez-le à mon ignorance, put it down to my ignorance. I. à qn d'avoir fait qch., to charge s.o. with having done sth., with doing sth. 2. Com: I. qch. sur qch., (i) to deduct sth. from sth.; (ii) to charge sth. to sth. I. des frais à, sur, un compte, to charge expenses to an account.

imputrescible [ɛ̃pytressibl], a. Imputrescible, incorruptible; rot-proof.

inabondance [inabɔ̃dɑ̃:s], s.f. Dearth, scarcity.

inabordable [inabɔrdabl], a. (a) Unapproachable, inaccessible (coast, person, etc.). (b) Prohibitive (price).

inabrité [inabrite], a. Unsheltered, unprotected.

inabrogé [inabrɔʒe], a. Unabrogated, unrepealed.

inabstinent [inapstinɑ̃], a. Intemperate.

inaccentué [inaksɑ̃tɥe], a. I. Unaccented (vowel). 2. Unstressed (syllable, etc.).

inacceptable [inakseptabl], a. Unacceptable.

inacceptation [inakseptasjɔ̃], s.f. Non-acceptance.

inaccepté [inaksepte], a. Unaccepted, declined.

inaccessibilité [inaksesibilite], s.f. Inaccessibility, unapproachableness.

inaccessible [inaksɛsibl], *a.* **1.** Inaccessible; unapproachable; *F:* un-get-at-able. **2.** *I. à la pitié*, inaccessible to pity, incapable of pity. *I. à la flatterie*, proof against flattery.

inacclimaté [inaklimate], *a.* Unacclimatized.

inaccompagné [inakɔ̃paɲe], *a.* Unaccompanied.

inaccompli [inakɔ̃pli], *a.* Unaccomplished.

inaccomplissement [inakɔ̃plismɑ̃], *s.m.* Non-fulfilment, non-accomplishment.

inaccordable [inakɔrdabl], *a.* **1.** (*a*) Irreconcilable (facts). (*b*) Untunable (instrument). **2.** Ungrantable, inadmissible (request, etc.).

inaccoutumé [inakutyme], *a.* Unaccustomed. **1.** Unused (*à*, to). **2.** Unusual, unwonted.

inachevé [inaʃve], *a.* Unfinished, uncompleted.

inachèvement [inaʃɛvmɑ̃], *s.m.* Incompletion.

inact|if, -ive [inaktif, -i:v], *a.* Inactive; idle; *Ch:* inert (body) *Com:* Marché i., dull market. *adv.* **-ivement.**

inactinique [inaktinik], *a. Ph:* Inactinic.

inaction [inaksjɔ̃], *s.f.* Inaction, idleness.

inactivité [inaktivite], *s.f.* **1.** Inactivity. *Ch:* Inertness. *Com:* Dullness (of market). **2.** (Of civil servant, etc.) Être en inactivité, to be unemployed.

inadmissibilité [inadmisibilite], *s.f.* **1.** Inadmissibility (of proof, request). **2.** *Sch:* Failure to qualify at the written examination.

inadmissible [inadmisibl], *a.* **1.** Inadmissible (request, etc.). *C'est i.!* who ever heard of such a thing! **2.** *Candidat i.*, candidate who has not qualified at the written examination.

inadmission [inadmisjɔ̃], *s.f.* Non-admission.

inadvertance [inadvɛrtɑ̃:s], *s.f.* **1.** Inadvertence, inadvertency. Par inadvertance, inadvertently; by an oversight; through carelessness. **2.** (*a*) Oversight, mistake. (*b*) Lapse of attention.

inadvert|ant [inadvɛrtɑ̃], *a.* Inadvertent, heedless, careless. *adv.* **-amment.**

inaliénabilité [inaljenabilite], *s.f. Jur:* Inalienability; indefeasibility (of right).

inaliénable [inaljenabl], *a. Jur:* Inalienable, untransferable, unassignable (property right); indefeasible (right). *adv.* **-ment.**

inaliéné [inaljene], *a. Jur:* Unalienated.

inaltérabilité [inalterabilite], *s.f.* **1.** Resistance to deterioration; permanence. **2.** (*a*) Unalterableness (of planetary motion, etc.). (*b*) Unfailingness (of good humour, etc.).

inaltérable [inalterabl], *a.* **1.** That does not deteriorate. *I. à l'air*, unaffected by air. **2.** (*a*) Unalterable (course of the stars. etc.). (*b*) Unfailing, unvarying (good humour).

inamabilité [inamabilite], *s.f* Unamiableness.

inamical, -aux [inamikal, -o], *a.* Unfriendly.

inamovibilité [inamɔvibilite], *s.f.* Fixity of tenure; irremovability (of judge, etc.).

inamovible [inamɔvibl], *a.* Irremovable. **1.** (*a*) Holding appointment for life. (*b*) (Post) held for life. **2.** Fixed; built in.

inanimé [inanime], *a.* **1.** Inanimate, lifeless. *Marché i.*, dull market. **2.** Senseless, unconscious, in a swoon.

inanité [inanite], *s.f.* **1.** Inanity, futility. **2.** Inane remark.

inanition [inanisjɔ̃], *s.f.* Inanition, starvation. *F Tomber d'i.*, to be starving.

inapaisable [inapɛzabl], *a.* Inappeasable (hunger, etc.); unquenchable (thirst); (grief) that nothing can assuage, that nothing can soothe.

inapaisé [inapɛze], *a.* Unappeased (hunger, etc.); unslaked, unquenched (thirst); unassuaged (grief, etc.).

inapercevable [inapɛrsəvabl], *a.* (*a*) Unperceivable. (*b*) Out of sight.

inaperçu [inapɛrsy], *a.* (*a*) Unseen, unperceived, unobserved. (*b*) Unnoticed, unremarked. Passer inaperçu, to escape notice; to pass unnoticed.

inapparent [inaparɑ̃], *a.* Unapparent; inconspicuous.

inapplicable [inaplikabl], *a.* Inapplicable.

inapplication [inaplikasjɔ̃], *s.f.* Want of assiduity, of application.

inappliqué [inaplike], *a.* **1.** Wanting in application; careless. **2.** Unapplied (method, etc.); (law) in abeyance.

inappréciable [inapresjabl], *a.* **1.** Inappreciable. *I. à l'œil*, not discernible by, not perceptible to, the eye. **2.** Inestimable, invaluable, priceless. *adv.* **-ment.**

inapprécié [inapresje], *a.* Unappreciated.

inapprenable [inaprənabl], *a.* Unlearnable.

inapprêté [inaprɛte], *a.* Unprepared, uncooked (food); undressed (cloth); unrehearsed (speech).

inapprivoisable [inaprivwazabl], *a.* Untamable.

inapprivoisé [inaprivwaze], *a.* Untamed; wild (bird, etc.); shy

inapte [inapt], *a.* Inapt, unapt; unfit (*à*, for); unsuited (*à*, to). Les inaptes, the unemployable.

inaptitude [inaptityd], *s.f.* Inaptitude; unfitness (*à*, for).

inarticulable [inartikylabl], *a.* Unpronounceable.

inarticulé [inartikyle], *a.* (*a*) Inarticulate (sound, etc.). (*b*) Not jointed. *Z:* Inarticulate(d).

inassermenté [inasɛrmɑ̃te], *a.* Unsworn. *Hist:* Non-juring (priest).

inasservi [inasɛrvi], *a.* Unsubdued, unenslaved.

inassiduité [inasidɥite], *s.f.* Want of assiduity.

inassisté [inasiste], *a.* Not in receipt of (poor-)relief.

inassociable [inasɔsjabl], *a.* Incompatible, incongruous.

inassouvi [inasuvi], *a.* Unappeased, unsated (hunger, desire); unquenched (thirst).

inassouvissable [inasuvisabl], *a.* Insatiable.

inattaquable [inatakabl], *a.* Unassailable (position); unimpugnable, unquestionable (right). *I. par les acides, aux acides*, acid-proof, acid-resisting; incorrodible.

inattendu [inatɑ̃dy], *a.* Unexpected, unlooked for, unforeseen.

inattentif, -ive [inatɑ̃tif, -i:v], *a.* Inattentive (*à*, to); unobservant, careless, heedless (*à*, of).

inattention [inatɑ̃sjɔ̃], *s.f.* (*a*) Inattention (*à*, to); carelessness; negligence, unobservance (*à*, of). (*b*) *Faute d'i.* careless mistake; slip.

inattesté [inateste], *a.* Unattested.

inaud|ible [inodibl], *a.* Inaudible.

inaugural, -aux [inogyral, -o], *a.* Inaugural.

inaugurateur, -trice [inogyratœ:r, -tris], *s.* Inaugurator.

inauguration [inogyrasjɔ̃], *s.f.* Inauguration; opening (of fête, etc.); unveiling (of statue). *Discours d'i.*, inaugural address.

inaugurer [inogyre], *v.tr.* To inaugurate (building, etc.); to unveil (statue); to open (fête, etc.); to usher in (epoch).

inauthentique [inotɑ̃tik], *a.* Unauthentic.

inautorisé [inotɔrize], *a.* Unauthorized, unwarranted.

inaverti [inavɛrti], *a.* (*a*) Unwarned. (*b*) Uninformed, inexperienced.

inavouable [inavwabl], *a.* Unavowable; shameful; *F:* low-down (attempt at fraud, etc.).

inavoué [inavwe], *a.* Unacknowledged; unconfessed, unavowed.

incalculable [ɛ̃kalkylabl], *a.* Incalculable; beyond computation. *Nombre i. de . . .*, countless number of . . . *adv.* **-ment.**

incandescence [ɛ̃kɑ̃dɛssɑ̃:s], *s.f.* Incandescence; white heat. *Bec de gaz à i.*, incandescent gasburner. *El : Lampe à i.*, glow-lamp

incandescent [ɛ̃kɑ̃dɛssɑ̃], *a.* Incandescent; glowing; white hot.

incantation [ɛ̃kɑ̃tasjɔ̃], *s.f.* Incantation.

incapable [ɛ̃kapabl], *a.* **1.** Incapable, unfit; inefficient (person): **2.** *I. de faire qch.*, (i) incapable of doing sth.; (ii) unfit to do sth.; (iii) unable to do sth.

incapacité [ɛ̃kapasite], *s.f.* **1.** Incapacity, incapability, unfitness, inefficiency (of person). **2.** *I. de faire qch.*, incapability of doing sth. *Adm : I. permanente*, permanent disablement.

incarcération [ɛ̃karsɛrasjɔ̃], *s.f.* Incarceration.

incarcérer [ɛ̃karsere], *v.tr.* (*j'incarcère; j'incarcérerai*) *(a)* To incarcerate, imprison. *(b)* To impound (animal).

incarnadin [ɛ̃karnadɛ̃], *a.* Incarnadine, rosy, pink.

incarnat [ɛ̃karna]. **1.** *a.* Rosy, pink; fleshcoloured. **2.** *s.m.* Rosy tint (of dawn); rosiness (of complexion).

incarnation [ɛ̃karnasjɔ̃], *s.f.* **1.** *(a)* Incarnation (of Christ). *(b) F :* Embodiment (of vice, etc.). **2.** Ingrowing (of the nails).

incarner [ɛ̃karne], *v.tr.* To incarnate, embody. **s'incarner.** **1.** To become incarnate. **2.** (Of nail) To grow in.

incarné, -ée. **1.** *a.* Incarnate. *La vertu incarnée,* the embodiment of virtue. **2.** **Ongle incarné,** ingrowing nail.

incartade [ɛ̃kartad], *s.f.* **1.** (Verbal) attack, outburst; violent tirade (*contre,* against). **2.** Freak, prank.

incassable [ɛ̃kɑsabl], *a.* Unbreakable.

incendiaire [ɛ̃sɑ̃djɛ:r]. **1.** *a.* Incendiary (bomb); inflammatory (speech). **2.** *s.* (Of pers.) *(a)* Incendiary. *(b)* Fire-brand.

incendie [ɛ̃sɑ̃di], *s.m.* (Outbreak of) fire; conflagration; burning (of town, etc.). **Poste d'incendie,** fire-station. **Échelle à incendie,** fireescape. **Pompe à incendie,** fire-engine. *I. volontaire, par malveillance,* arson. **Provoquer un incendie,** (i) to cause, start, a fire; (ii) to commit arson.

incendier [ɛ̃sɑ̃dje], *v.tr.* To set (house, etc.) on fire; to set fire to (sth.); to set ablaze. **incendié, -ée.** **1.** *a.* (Of house) Burning; burnt down. **2.** *s.* Sufferer by a fire.

incertain [ɛ̃sɛrtɛ̃], *a.* *(a)* Uncertain, doubtful; dubious (result). *Temps i.,* unsettled, broken, weather. (Of pers.) *I. de qch.,* (i) uncertain of, as regards, sth.; (ii) undecided about sth. *(b)* Unreliable; undependable.

incertitude [ɛ̃sɛrtityd], *s.f.* *(a)* Uncertainty, incertitude, doubt; dubiousness (of result, etc.). *(b)* Indecision, perplexity (of mind).

incessamment [ɛ̃sesamɑ̃], *adv.* **1.** Unceasingly, incessantly. **2.** Immediately, without delay, at once, forthwith.

incessant [ɛ̃sesɑ̃], *a.* Unceasing, ceaseless.

incessible [ɛ̃sesibl], *a.* *(a)* Inalienable (right). *(b)* Not negotiable; untransferable.

inceste [ɛ̃sɛst], *s.m.* Incest.

incestueu|x, -euse [ɛ̃sɛstɥø, -øːz], *a.* Incestuous. *adv.* **-sement.**

inchavirable [ɛ̃ʃavirabl], *a.* Uncapsizable.

inchoatif, -ive [ɛ̃kɔatif, -iːv], *a. & s.m. Gram :* Inceptive, inchoative (verb, etc.).

incidemment [ɛ̃sidamɑ̃], *adv.* Incidentally.

incidence [ɛ̃sidɑ̃:s], *s.f.* Incidence. *Opt :* **Angle d'incidence,** angle of incidence.

incident, -ente [ɛ̃sidɑ̃, -ɑ̃:t]. **1.** *a.* *(a)* Incidental (question, etc.). *Gram :* Parenthetical (clause). *(b) Opt :* Incident (ray). **2.** *s.m.* Incident. *(a)* Occurrence, happening. *(b)* Difficulty, hitch. **3.** *s.f.* **Incidente,** parenthetical clause.

incinérateur [ɛ̃sinɛratœːr], *s.m.* Incinerator.

incinération [ɛ̃sinɛrasjɔ̃], *s.f.* *(a)* Incineration. *(b)* Cremation.

incinérer [ɛ̃sinere], *v.tr.* (*j'incinère; j'incinérerai*) *(a)* To incinerate; to burn to ashes. *(b)* To cremate.

incirconcis [ɛ̃sirkɔ̃si], *a.* Uncircumcised.

incise [ɛ̃si:z], *s.f. Gram :* Interpolated clause, incidental clause.

inciser [ɛ̃size], *v.tr.* To incise, cut; to lance (tumour). *I. un pin,* to tap a pine-tree (for resin).

incis|if, -ive [ɛ̃sizif, -iːv], *a.* **1.** Incisive, sharp, cutting (remark). **2.** *Dent incisive, s.f.* **incisive,** incisor (tooth). *adv.* **-ivement.**

incision [ɛ̃sizjɔ̃], *s.f.* Incision. **1.** Cutting; lancing (of tumour). **2.** Cut.

incitant [ɛ̃sitɑ̃], **1.** *a.* Inciting, stimulating. **2.** *s.m. Med :* Tonic.

incitateur, -trice [ɛ̃sitatœːr, -tris]. **1.** *a.* Inciting. **2.** *s.* Inciter (*à,* to); urger on.

incitation [ɛ̃sitasjɔ̃], *s.f.* Incitement (*à,* to).

inciter [ɛ̃site], *v.tr.* To incite; to urge (on). *I. qn à faire qch.,* to incite, prompt, s.o. to do sth.

incivil [ɛ̃sivil], *a.* Uncivil, rude, discourteous. *adv.* **-ement.**

incivilisable [ɛ̃sivilizabl], *a.* Uncivilizable.

incivilisé [ɛ̃sivilize], *a.* Uncivilized.

incivilité [ɛ̃sivilite], *s.f.* **1.** Incivility, rudeness, discourtesy. **2.** Piece of incivility.

inclassable [ɛ̃klɑsabl], *a.* Unclass(ifi)able, nondescript.

inclémence [ɛ̃klemɑ̃:s], *s.f.* Inclemency.

inclément [ɛ̃klemɑ̃], *a.* Inclement; severe (climate).

inclinable [ɛ̃klinabl], *a.* Tilting, inclinable.

inclinaison [ɛ̃klinɛzɔ̃], *s.f.* **1.** *(a)* Tilting, canting. *(b)* Incline, gradient, slope (of hill, etc.); inclination (of line, star); pitch, slant (of roof, etc.); tilt (of camera, hat); heel, list (of ship); rake (of mast); dip (of magnetic needle). *Comble à forte, faible, i.,* high-pitched, low-pitched, roof. **Aiguille d'inclinaison,** dipping needle. **2.** (= INCLINATION) Nod (of the head).

inclination [ɛ̃klinasjɔ̃], *s.f.* Inclination. **1.** Bending, bow(ing) (of body); nod of head. **2.** *(a)* Bent, propensity. *Avoir de l'i., se sentir d'i., à faire qch.,* to be, feel, inclined to do sth. *(b)* Attachment, love. **Mariage d'inclination,** lovematch. *Faire un mariage d'i.,* to marry for love.

incliner [ɛ̃kline]. **1.** *v.tr.* To incline. *(a)* To slant, slope, cant. *(b)* To tip up; to tilt. *(c)* To bend, bow (the head, etc.). *(d) I. qn à faire qch.,* to predispose, influence, s.o. in favour of doing sth. **2.** *v.i.* *(a)* To lean, slope; (of ship) to list. *(b) I. à la pitié,* to incline, be disposed, to pity. **Incliner à faire qch.,** to be, feel, inclined to do sth. **s'incliner.** **1.** To slant, slope; (of ship) to heel (over). *Av :* To bank. **2.** *(a) S'i. sur qn,* to bend over s.o. *(b) S'i. devant qn,* to bow before s.o. *S'i. devant les arguments de qn,* to bow, yield, to s.o.'s arguments.

incliné, -e. *a.* **1.** Inclined. *(a) La tête inclinée,* with bowed head. *(b)* Sloping, a-tilt. **2.** *I. à, vers, qch., à faire qch.,* inclined, disposed, to do sth.

inclinomètre [ɛ̃klinɔmɛtr], *s.m.* Inclinometer.

inclure [ɛ̃kly:r], *v.tr.* (Conj. like CONCLURE except

p.p. **inclus**, but little used except in *p.p.*) To enclose (document in letter, etc.).

inclus, *a.* (*a*) Enclosed (in letter, etc.). *s.f.* **L'incluse**, the enclosed (note). S.a. CI-INCLUS. (*b*) *Jusque la page 5 incluse*, up to and including page 5.

inclus|if, -ive [ɛklyzif, -iːv], *a.* Inclusive. *adv.* **-ivement**.

inclusion [ɛklyzjɔ̃], *s.f.* (*a*) Enclosing (of document in letter). (*b*) Inclusion (of consequence in theory).

incognito [ɛkɔɲito, -gn-]. **1.** *adv.* Incognito, *F:* incog. **2.** *s.m.* *Garder l'i.*, to preserve one's incognito.

incohérence [ɛkɔɛrɑ̃ːs], *s.f.* Incoherence, incoherency (of particles, thought, speech); disjointedness (of speech, etc.).

incohérent [ɛkɔɛrɑ̃], *a.* Incoherent.

incohésion [ɛkɔezjɔ̃], *s.f.* (*a*) *Ph:* Incohesion. (*b*) Lack of cohesion (in patty, etc.).

incolore [ɛkɔlɔːr], *a.* Colourless.

incomber [ɛkɔ̃be], *v.i.* (Used only in third pers.) *I. à qn*, to devolve upon, be incumbent on, behove, s.o. *Les devoirs qui lui incombent*, the duties which fall on him. *Impers. Il nous incombe à tous de . . .*, it behoves us all to. . . .

incombustible [ɛkɔ̃bystibl], *a.* Incombustible, uninflammable, fire-proof.

incomestible [ɛkɔmɛstibl], *a.* Inedible.

incommensurable [ɛkɔm(m)ɑ̃syrabl], *a.* **1.** *Mth:* Incommensurable (*avec*, with); incommensurate. *Racine i.*, irrational root. **2.** *F:* Immeasurable, huge. *adv.* **-ment.**

incommodant [ɛkɔmɔdɑ̃], *a.* Unpleasant, disagreeable, annoying.

incommod|e [ɛkɔmɔd], *a.* **1.** Inconvenient; incommodious (room); uncomfortable (chair, heat); unhandy, clumsy, awkward (tool). **2.** *A:* Disagreeable (person); unpleasant (smell). *adv.* **-ément.**

incommoder [ɛkɔmɔde], *v.tr.* **1.** To inconvenience, incommode, hinder (s.o.). *La fumée ne vous incommode pas?* you don't mind my smoking? **2.** (Of food, etc.) To make (s.o.) unwell; to disagree with (s.o.); to upset (s.o.).

incommodité [ɛkɔmɔdite], *s.f.* (*a*) Inconvenience; incommodiousness. (*b*) Discomfort; awkwardness (of situation).

incommuable [ɛkɔmmɥabl], *a.* Incommutable.

incommunicable [ɛkɔmynikabl], *a.* Incommunicable.

incommutable [ɛkɔmytabl], *a Jur:* **1.** Nontransferable. **2.** (Owner) who cannot be dispossessed.

incomparable [ɛkɔ̃parabl], *a.* Incomparable, unrivalled, matchless. *adv.* **-ment.**

incompatibilité [ɛkɔ̃patibilite], *s.f.* Incompatibility (of duties, etc.). **Incompatibilité d'humeur**, incompatibility of temper.

incompatible [ɛkɔ̃patibl], *a.* Incompatible, inconsistent, at variance (*avec*, with). *adv.* **-ment.**

incompétence [ɛkɔ̃petɑ̃ːs], *s.f.* Incompetence, incompetency (of person, tribunal). *I. à faire qch.*, lack of authority to do sth.

incompétent [ɛkɔ̃petɑ̃], *a.* Incompetent. (*a*) Inefficient. (*b*) *Jur:* Not qualified, unqualified (to try case). *I. à faire qch.*, incompetent to do sth.

incomplaisant [ɛkɔ̃plɛzɑ̃], *a.* Uncomplaisant, disobliging.

incompl|et, -ète [ɛkɔ̃plɛ, -ɛt], *a.* Incomplete. *adv.* **-ètement.**

incompréhensibilité [ɛkɔ̃preɑ̃sibilite], *s.f.* Incomprehensibility.

incompréhensible [ɛkɔ̃preɑ̃sibl], *a.* Incomprehensible. *C'est i.*, I can't make it out. *adv.* **-ment.**

incompréhension [ɛkɔ̃preɑ̃sjɔ̃], *s.f.* Lack of understanding; obtuseness.

incompressible [ɛkɔ̃prɛsibl], *a.* Incompressible.

incompris [ɛkɔ̃pri], *a.* Misunderstood; unappreciated.

inconcevable [ɛkɔ̃s(ə)vabl], *a.* Inconceivable, unthinkable, unimaginable. *adv.* **-ment.**

inconciliabilité [ɛkɔ̃siljabilite], *s.f.* Irreconcilability, incompatibility (of theories, etc.).

inconciliable [ɛkɔ̃siljabl], *a.* Irreconcilable, incompatible (*avec*, with).

inconditionn|el, -elle [ɛkɔ̃disjɔnɛl], *a.* Unconditional (consent); absolute (liability). *adv.* **-ellement.**

inconduite [ɛkɔ̃dɥit], *s.f.* Loose living; laxity of conduct. *Jur:* Misconduct.

incongelable [ɛkɔ̃ʒ(ə)labl], *a.* Uncongealable; non-freezing.

incongru [ɛkɔ̃gry], *a.* **1.** Incongruous, foolish (remark, etc.). **2.** Improper, unseemly (question).

incongruité [ɛkɔ̃gryite], *s.f.* **1.** (*a*) Incongruity, incongruousness, absurdity. (*b*) Impropriety, unseemliness. **2.** Foolish, tactless, or improper remark or action.

inconnu, -ue [ɛkɔny]. **1.** *a.* Unknown (*de, à, to*). *I. de tout le monde*, unknown to all. **2.** *s.* (*a*) Unknown person; (i) stranger, (ii) (mere) nobody. (*b*) *s.m.* **L'inconnu**, the unknown. **3.** *s.f. Mth:* **Inconnue**, unknown (quantity).

inconscience [ɛkɔ̃sjɑ̃ːs], *s.f.* Unconsciousness (*de, of*); inconscience.

inconsci|ent [ɛkɔ̃sjɑ̃], *a.* Unconscious (act); (person) (i) oblivious to everything, (ii) unconscious of the nature of his actions. *adv.* **-emment.**

inconséquence [ɛkɔ̃sekɑ̃ːs], *s.f.* (*a*) Inconsistency, inconsequence. *Un tissu d'inconséquences*, a tissue of absurdities. (*b*) Inconsequentiality.

inconséqu|ent [ɛkɔ̃sekɑ̃], *a.* (*a*) Inconsistent, inconsequent (reasoning, etc.). (*b*) Irresponsible, inconsequential (behaviour, person); rambling (speech). *adv.* **-emment.**

inconsidération [ɛkɔ̃siderasjɔ̃], *s.f.* **1.** Thoughtlessness, inconsiderateness. **2.** *Tomber dans l'i.*, to fall into disrepute.

inconsidéré [ɛkɔ̃sidere], *a.* **1.** Thoughtless, inconsiderate (person). **2.** Unconsidered, illconsidered, rash (act).

inconsistance [ɛkɔ̃sistɑ̃ːs], *s.f.* **1.** Unsubstantiality; looseness (of ground, etc.). **2.** Inconsistency.

inconsistant [ɛkɔ̃sistɑ̃], *a.* **1.** Unsubstantial; soft (mud); loose (ground). **2.** Inconsistent (conduct, person).

inconsolable [ɛkɔ̃sɔlabl], *a.* Inconsolable, unconsolable; disconsolate (person). *adv.* **-ment.**

inconstance [ɛkɔ̃stɑ̃ːs], *s.f.* **1.** Inconstancy, fickleness, flightiness. **2.** Changeableness (of weather).

inconstant [ɛkɔ̃stɑ̃], *a.* **1.** Inconstant, fickle. **2.** Changeable (weather).

inconstitutionnel, -elle [ɛkɔ̃stitysjɔnɛl], *a.* Unconstitutional.

incontestable [ɛkɔ̃tɛstabl], *a.* Incontestable, undeniable; beyond all question. *adv.* **-ment.**

incontesté [ɛkɔ̃tɛste], *a.* Uncontested, undisputed.

incontinence [ɛkɔ̃tinɑ̃ːs], *s.f.* Incontinence.

incontinent¹ [ɛkɔ̃tinɑ̃], *a.* Incontinent.

incontinent², *adv.* At once, forthwith, straightway.

incontrôlable [ɛ̃kɔ̃trolabl], *a.* Difficult to verify, to check.

incontrôlé [ɛ̃kɔ̃trole], *a.* Unchecked, unverified.

incontroversé [ɛ̃kɔ̃trɔvɛrse], *a.* Uncontradicted, uncontroverted, undisputed.

inconvaincu [ɛ̃kɔ̃vɛ̃ky], *a.* Unconvinced.

inconvenance [ɛ̃kɔ̃vnɑ̃:s], *s.f.* **1.** (*a*) Unsuitableness. *(b)* Impropriety, indecorousness (of conduct); indecency. **2.** Improper act or utterance; indecency.

inconvenant [ɛ̃kɔ̃vnɑ̃], *a.* Improper, indecorous, unseemly; indecent.

inconvénient [ɛ̃kɔ̃venjɑ̃], *s.m.* Disadvantage, drawback. *Pouvez-vous sans inconvénient me prêter . . .?* can you conveniently lend me . . .? *Je n'y vois pas d'inconvénient,* I see no objection to it.

inconvertible [ɛ̃kɔ̃vɛrtibl], *a.* Inconvertible.

inconvertissable [ɛ̃kɔ̃vɛrtisabl], *a.* Beyond hope of conversion; past praying for.

inconvié [ɛ̃kɔ̃vje], *a.* Uninvited; unbidden.

incorporation [ɛ̃kɔrpɔrasjɔ̃], *s.f.* Incorporation.

incorporel, -elle [ɛ̃kɔrpɔrɛl], *a.* Incorporeal.

incorporer [ɛ̃kɔrpɔre], *v.tr.* To incorporate. *I. un champ à un domaine,* to incorporate a field in an estate.

incorrect [ɛ̃kɔr(r)ɛkt], *a.* Incorrect. **1.** (*a*) Inaccurate, wrong. *(b)* Untrue. **2.** Contrary to etiquette, to use and wont.

incorrectement [ɛ̃kɔr(r)ɛktəmɑ̃], *adv.* Incorrectly. *Écrire un mot i.,* to mis-spell a word. *Citer un auteur i.,* to misquote an author.

incorrection [ɛ̃kɔr(r)ɛksjɔ̃], *s.f.* **1.** (*a*) Incorrectness, inaccuracy, error. *(b)* Incorrectness (of attire, etc.). **2.** Incorrect act.

incorrigible [ɛ̃kɔr(r)iʒibl], *a.* Incorrigible (child, etc.); irreclaimable, *F:* hopeless (drunkard, etc.); past praying for.

incorruptibilité [ɛ̃kɔr(r)yptibilite], *s.f.* Incorruptibility.

incorruptible [ɛ̃kɔr(r)yptibl], *a.* Incorruptible.

incrédibilité [ɛ̃kredibilite], *s.f.* Incredibility.

incrédule [ɛ̃kredyl]. **1.** *a.* (*a*) Incredulous (*à l'égard de,* of). *(b) Theol:* Unbelieving. **2.** *s.* Unbeliever, infidel.

incrédulité [ɛ̃kredylite], *s.f.* **1.** Incredulity. **2.** *Theol:* Unbelief.

incrément [ɛ̃kremɑ̃], *s.m. Mth:* Increment.

increvable [ɛ̃krəvabl], *a.* Unpuncturable (tyre).

incriminable [ɛ̃kriminabl], *a.* **1.** (Person) liable to prosecution. **2.** Indictable (offence).

incrimination [ɛ̃kriminasjɔ̃], *s.f.* **1.** Incriminating. **2.** Accusation, charge; indictment.

incriminer [ɛ̃krimine], *v.tr. Jur:* **1.** To (in)criminate, accuse, indict (s.o.). **2.** *I. la conduite de qn,* to hold up s.o.'s conduct as indictable.

incriminé, -ée, *a. & s.* Accused.

incrochetable [ɛ̃krɔʃtabl], *a.* Unpickable (lock); burglar-proof (safe).

incroyable [ɛ̃krwajabl]. **1.** *a.* Incredible, unbelievable; beyond belief. **2.** *s.* (Extravagantly dressed) beau or belle (of the French Directory period). *adv.* **-ment.**

incroyant, -ante [ɛ̃krwajɑ̃, -ɑ̃:t]. **1.** *a.* Unbelieving. **2.** *s.* Unbeliever.

incrustant [ɛ̃krystɑ̃], *a.* Petrifying (well, etc.). *Ind:* Hard (water).

incrustation [ɛ̃krystasjɔ̃], *s.f.* Incrustation. **1.** (*a*) Encrusting. *Join:* Inlaying. *(b) Mch:* Furring (up) (of boiler). **2.** (*a*) Inlaid work. *Avec incrustations de nacre,* inlaid with mother of pearl. *(b) Dressm:* Insertion. *(c) Incrustations de chaudière,* fur(ring); boiler scale.

incruster [ɛ̃kryste], *v.tr.* **1.** To encrust. *Join:*

To inlay (*de,* with). **2.** To encrust, form a crust on (sth.).

s'incruster. 1. To become encrusted; to fur (up). **2.** *F:* To dig oneself in.

incubateur [ɛ̃kybatœ:r], *s.m.* (*a*) Incubator. *(b) Pisc:* Grille.

incubation [ɛ̃kybasjɔ̃], *s.f.* (*a*) Incubation, hatching (of eggs). *(b)* Sitting (of hens). *(c) Période d'i.,* incubation period (of disease).

incube [ɛ̃kyb], *s.m.* Incubus, nightmare.

inculpabilité¹ [ɛ̃kylpabilite], *s.f.* Guiltlessness.

inculpabilité², *s.f.* Liability to be charged (with an offence).

inculpable [ɛ̃kylpabl], *a. Jur:* Chargeable, indictable.

inculpation [ɛ̃kylpasjɔ̃], *s.f.* Indictment, charge, inculpation. *I. de vol,* indictment for theft.

inculper [ɛ̃kylpe], *v.tr.* To indict, charge. *I. qn de coups et blessures,* to charge s.o. with assault and battery.

inculpé, -ée, *s. Jur: L'inculpé,* the accused (of a DÉLIT, *q.v.*); the defendant.

inculquer [ɛ̃kylke], *v.tr.* To inculcate (*d,* upon); to instil (*d,* into).

inculte [ɛ̃kylt], *a.* Uncultivated, wild (garden); waste (land); unkempt (hair).

incultivé [ɛ̃kyltive], *a.* Untilled, uncultivated (land); uncultured (mind).

incunable [ɛ̃kynabl], *s.m.* Early printed book; incunabulum, *pl.* incunabula.

incurable [ɛ̃kyrabl], *a. & s.* Incurable.

incurie [ɛ̃kyri], *s.f.* (*a*) Carelessness, negligence. *(b)* Lack of interest (*de,* in).

incurieux, -euse [ɛ̃kyrjø, -ø:z], *a.* Incurious (*de,* of).

incuriosité [ɛ̃kyrjɔzite], *s.f.* Want of curiosity; incuriosity.

incursion [ɛ̃kyrsjɔ̃], *s.f.* Inroad, foray, raid, incursion.

incurvation [ɛ̃kyrvasjɔ̃], *s.f.* Incurvation; bend.

incurver [ɛ̃kyrve], *v.tr.* To incurvate, incurve.

incurvé, *a.* (*a*) Incurv(at)ed. *(b)* Concave.

Inde [ɛ̃:d]. *Pr.n.f. Geog:* (*a*) India. *L'I. anglaise,* British India. *La Compagnie anglaise des Indes,* the East India Company. *(b)* **Les Indes,** the Indies. **Les Indes occidentales,** the West Indies.

indébrouillable [ɛ̃debrujabl], *a.* (*a*) (Skein, etc.) that cannot be disentangled. *(b) F:* Inextricable, tangled (situation).

indécence [ɛ̃desɑ̃:s], *s.f.* Indecency, immodesty. *Commettre des indécences,* to commit indecencies.

indéc|ent [ɛ̃desɑ̃], *a.* **1.** Indecent, improper; immodest. **2.** Indecorous. *adv.* **-emment.**

indéchiffrable [ɛ̃deʃifrabl], *a.* **1.** Undecipherable (inscription); illegible (writing). **2.** Unintelligible, incomprehensible.

indéchiffré [ɛ̃deʃifre], *a.* Undeciphered.

indéchirable [ɛ̃deʃirabl], *a.* Untearable.

indécis [ɛ̃desi], *a.* **1.** Unsettled, open (question, etc.); doubtful (victory, etc.); vague, blurred (outline). *Bataille indécise,* drawn battle. **2.** (Of pers.) (*a*) *Être i. quant au parti à prendre,* to be undecided, in two minds, how to act. *(b)* Irresolute, hesitating.

indécisif, -ive [ɛ̃desizif, -i:v], *a.* Indecisive.

indécision [ɛ̃desizjɔ̃], *s.f.* **1.** Indecision, irresolution. **2.** Uncertainty.

indéclinable [ɛ̃deklinabl], *a.* **1.** That cannot be refused or declined. **2.** *Gram:* Indeclinable.

indécomposable [ɛ̃dekɔ̃pozabl], *a.* **1.** Indecomposable, irresolvable (element, etc.).

indécousable [ɛ̃dekuzabl], *a.* That cannot come unsewn; non-ripping (seam).

indécouvrable [ɛ̃dekuvrabl], *a.* Undiscoverable.

indécrottable [ɛ̃dekrɔtabl], *a.* **1.** Uncleanable. **2.** *F:* Incorrigible; hopeless (dunce, etc.).
indédoublable [ɛ̃dedublabl], *a.* **1.** *Ch:* Indecomposable (body). **2.** *Phot:* Unconvertible (anastigmat).
indéfendable [ɛ̃defɑ̃dabl], *a.* Indefensible.
indéfini [ɛ̃defini], *a.* **1.** Indefinite. *Gram:* **Pronom indéfini**, indefinite pronoun. **Passé indéfini**, indefinite past (tense); perfect (tense). **2.** Undefined. *adv.* **-ment.**
indéfinissable [ɛ̃definisabl], *a.* Indefinable, undefinable (term, etc.); nondescript (colour).
indéformable [ɛ̃defɔrmabl], *a.* That will not lose its shape.
indéfrisable [ɛ̃defrizabl]. **1.** *a.* (Hair) that will not come out of curl. **2.** *s.f. Hairdr:* Permanent wave.
indélébile [ɛ̃delebil], *a.* Indelible (ink, stain).
indéliberé [ɛ̃delibere], *a.* Undeliberated, unconsidered.
indélicat [ɛ̃delika], *a.* (*a*) Indelicate; coarse (nature); tactless (action). (*b*) Dishonest, unscrupulous. *adv.* **-ement.**
indélicatesse [ɛ̃delikatɛs], *s.f.* **1.** (*a*) Indelicacy; tactlessness. (*b*) Unscrupulousness. **2.** Indelicate, tactless, or unscrupulous action.
indémaillable [ɛ̃demajabl], *a.* Ladderproof (stocking).
indemne [ɛ̃dɛmn], *a.* (*a*) Without loss; without (material or moral) damage. (*b*) Undamaged. (*c*) Uninjured, unhurt, unscathed, scatheless.
indemnisable [ɛ̃dɛmnizabl], *a.* Entitled to compensation.
indemnisation [ɛ̃dɛmnizasjɔ̃], *s.f.* Indemnification.
indemniser [ɛ̃dɛmnize], *v.tr.* To indemnify, compensate. *I. qn d'une perte*, to recoup s.o. for a loss. *I. qn en argent*, to pay s.o. compensation in cash.
indemnité [ɛ̃dɛmnite], *s.f.* **1.** (*a*) Indemnity, indemnification, compensation (for loss sustained). (*b*) Penalty (for delay, non-delivery). (*c*) Allowance, grant. *I. de chômage*, unemployment benefit; *F:* dole. *I. de charges de famille*, child bounty. *I. de route, de déplacement*, travelling expenses or allowance. *I. parlementaire*, emoluments of a member of parliament. **2.** *Parl:* **Bill d'indemnité**, act, bill, of indemnity.
indémontrable [ɛ̃demɔ̃trabl], *a.* Undemonstrable.
indémontré [ɛ̃demɔ̃tre], *a.* Undemonstrated.
indéniable [ɛ̃denjabl], *a.* Undeniable.
indénouable [ɛ̃denwabl], *a.* That cannot be untied, unravelled.
indentation [ɛ̃dɑ̃tasjɔ̃], *s.f.* Indentation.
indépendance [ɛ̃depɛ̃dɑ̃ːs], *s.f.* Independence (*de, à l'égard de*, of).
indépendant [ɛ̃depɑ̃dɑ̃], *a.* **1.** (*a*) Independent (*de*, of); free. *État i.*, free state. (*b*) Self-reliant. **2.** Self-contained (flat, etc.). *adv.* **-amment.**
indéracinable [ɛ̃derasinabl], *a.* Ineradicable.
indéréglable [ɛ̃dereglabl], *a.* Fool-proof (mechanism); that cannot get out of order.
indescriptible [ɛ̃dɛskriptibl], *a.* Indescribable; beyond description.
indésirable [ɛ̃dezirabl], *a. & s. Adm:* Undesirable.
indesserrable [ɛ̃desɛrabl], *a.* **1.** *F:* Unyielding (grip). **2.** **Écrou indesserrable**, self-locking nut.
indestructible [ɛ̃destryktibl], *a.* Indestructible.
indéterminable [ɛ̃detɛrminabl], *a.* Indeterminable, unascertainable.
indétermination [ɛ̃detɛrminasjɔ̃], *s.f.* Indetermination. **1.** Indefiniteness. **2.** Irresoluteness.

indéterminé [ɛ̃detɛrmine], *a.* **1.** Undetermined, indefinite. *Mth:* Indeterminate (problem). **2.** Irresolute, undecided.
indéveloppable [ɛ̃devlɔpabl], *a. Geom:* Skew (surface).
indevinable [ɛ̃d(ə)vinabl], *a.* Unguessable.
indévot [ɛ̃devo], *a.* Undevout, indevout.
indévotion [ɛ̃devosjɔ̃], *s.f.* Indevotion, irreligion.
index [ɛ̃dɛks], *s.m.inv.* **1.** (*a*) Forefinger, index(-finger). (*b*) Pointer (of balance, etc.); indicator. **2.** (*a*) Index (of book). **Faire l'index d'un livre**, to index a book. (*b*) *R.C.Ch:* **Mettre un livre à l'Index**, to ban, prohibit, a book.
indicateur, -trice [ɛ̃dikatœːr, -tris]. **1.** *a.* Indicatory (*de*, of). (**Doigt**) **indicateur**, forefinger, index-finger. **Poteau indicateur**, sign-post, finger-post. **Lampe indicatrice**, tell-tale lamp. **2.** *s.* Informer; (police) spy. **3.** *s.m.* (*a*) (Railway) time-table, guide; (street) directory. (*b*) Indicator, pointer (of weather-glass, etc.); gauge (of boiler, etc.); tell-tale. *I. de vitesse*, speed-indicator; *Aut:* speedometer. *I. de pente*, clinometer. *I. jauge d'essence*, petrol-gauge.
indicatif, -ive [ɛ̃dikatif, -iːv]. **1.** *a.* Indicative (*de*, of); indicatory. **2.** *a. & s.m. Gram:* (**Mode**) **indicatif**, indicative (mood). **A l'indicatif**, in the indicative. **3.** *s.m. Tg:* *W.Tel:* etc: **Indicatif d'appel**, call-sign, -number.
indication [ɛ̃dikasjɔ̃], *s.f.* Indication. **1.** Indicating, pointing out. **2.** (*a*) (Piece of) information. **Fausse indication de revenu**, false declaration of income. **A titre d'indication**, for your, my, guidance. (*b*) Sign, token (of guilt, etc.); clue. (*c*) *Indications topographiques*, survey marks or data. **3.** Esp. *pl.* Instruction(s). *Indications du mode d'emploi*, directions for use. **Sauf indication contraire . . .**, except where otherwise stated. . . .
indice [ɛ̃dis], *s.m.* **1.** Indication, sign; mark, token. **2.** Index. *Opt: I. de réfraction*, refractive index. **Nombres indices du coût de la vie**, index numbers of the cost of living.
indicible [ɛ̃disibl], *a.* (*a*) Inexpressible, unutterable; unspeakable (grief, rage). (*b*) Indescribable. *adv.* **-ment.**
indien, -ienne [ɛ̃djɛ̃, -jɛn]. **1.** *a. & s.* Indian (of India, of America). S.a. **FILE.** **2.** *s.f.* **Indienne.** (*a*) *Tex:* (i) Printed calico; print. (ii) Chintz. (*b*) *Swim:* Overarm stroke.
indiennerie [ɛ̃djɛnri], *s.f.* (*a*) Calico printing. (*b*) Printed cotton goods.
indifférence [ɛ̃diferɑ̃ːs], *s.f.* Indifference (*pour, to, towards*); unconcern; apathy.
indifférent [ɛ̃diferɑ̃], *a.* **1.** (*a*) Indifferent (*à, to*); unaffected (*à, by*); unconcerned; apathetic. **Rester à tout**, to take no interest in anything. *Je lui suis i.*, I am indifferent to him; he is, feels, indifferent about me. (*b*) Cold, insensible, emotionless (heart, etc.). **2.** Immaterial, unimportant. *adv.* **-emment.**
indigence [ɛ̃diʒɑ̃ːs], *s.f.* Poverty, indigence, want. *Tomber dans l'i.*, être réduit à l'i., to be reduced to poverty. *I. d'idées*, poverty of ideas.
indigène [ɛ̃diʒɛn]. **1.** *a.* Indigenous (*à, to*); native (population, troops). **2.** *s.* Native (esp. of foreign country, of colony).
indigent, -ente [ɛ̃diʒɑ̃, -ɑ̃ːt]. **1.** *a.* Poor, needy, poverty-stricken, indigent. **2.** *s.* Pauper.
indigeste [ɛ̃diʒɛst], *a.* **1.** Indigestible; stodgy (food). **2.** Undigested, confused, heavy (book).
indigestion [ɛ̃diʒɛstjɔ̃], *s.f.* Indigestion. *Avoir une i.*, to have an attack of indigestion.
indignation [ɛ̃diɲasjɔ̃], *s.f.* Indignation.
indigne [ɛ̃diɲ], *a.* Unworthy. **1.** (*a*) Undeserving (*de*, of). (*b*) *Jur: I. de succéder*, debarred from

succeeding, from inheriting. **2.** Shameful (action, conduct). *adv.* **-ment.**
indigner [ɛ̃dine], *v.tr.* To rouse (s.o.) to indignation ; to make (s.o.) indignant.
  s'indigner, to become or be indignant. *S'i. de qch., contre qn,* to be indignant at sth., with **s.o. S'indigner que** + *sub.,* **de ce que** + *ind.,* to be indignant that. . . .
    indigné, *a.* Indignant (*de,* at). *D'un air, d'un ton, i.,* indignantly.
indignité [ɛ̃dinite], *s.f.* **1.** (*a*) Unworthiness. (*b*) Baseness, vileness (of an action). **2.** *Souffrir des indignités,* to suffer indignities, humiliations.
indigo [ɛ̃digo], *s.m.* **1.** Indigo. *a.inv. Des rubans indigo,* indigo-blue ribbons. **2.** = INDIGOTIER.
indigotier [ɛ̃digɔtje], *s.m. Bot:* Indigo-plant.
indiquer [ɛ̃dike], *v.tr.* To indicate. (*a*) To point to ; to point out. *I. qch. du doigt,* to point to sth. ; to point sth. out. (*b*) To mark, show. *Point indiqué sur la carte,* point shown on the map. (*c*) *Indiquez-moi un bon médecin,* tell me of a good doctor. (*d*) To betoken. *Cela indique de l'intelligence,* it gives token of intelligence. (*e*) To appoint, name (a day, etc.). *A l'heure indiquée,* at the appointed hour. (*f*) *C'était indiqué,* it was the obvious thing to do. *Un sujet de plaisanterie tout indiqué,* a ready subject for jokes.
indirect [ɛ̃direkt], *a.* (*a*) Indirect (route, *Gram:* object, etc.) ; oblique (oration) ; collateral (heirs). (*b*) *Jur:* Circumstantial (evidence). (*c*) *Attaque indirecte,* covert attack. *Moyens indirects,* crooked, underhand, methods. *adv.* **-ement.**
indisciplinable [ɛ̃disiplinabl], *a.* Indisciplinable, intractable.
indiscipline [ɛ̃disiplin], *s.f.* Indiscipline.
indiscipliné [ɛ̃disipline], *a.* Undisciplined, unruly.
indiscr|et, -ète [ɛ̃diskrɛ, -ɛt]. **1.** *a.* Indiscreet. (*a*) Imprudent, unguarded. (*b*) Pushing (person) ; tactless (question). *A l'abri des regards indiscrets,* safe from prying eyes. (*c*) (Person) given to blabbing. **2.** *s.* (*a*) Tactless, pushing, person. (*b*) Tell-tale, blabber. *adv.* **-ètement.**
indiscrétion [ɛ̃diskresjɔ̃], *s.f.* Indiscretion. **1.** Indiscreetness. **2.** Indiscreet action or remark. *Il lui échappe des indiscrétions,* he blurts out (i) tactless things, (ii) secrets.
indiscutable [ɛ̃diskytabl], *a.* Indisputable, unquestionable. *adv.* **-ment.**
indispensable [ɛ̃dispɑ̃sabl], *a.* Indispensable. **1.** Obligatory. **2.** Essential (*à,* to) ; absolutely necessary. *Il nous est i.,* we can't spare him. *s.m. Ne prenez que l'i.,* don't take more than is strictly necessary. *adv.* **-ment.**
indisponibilité [ɛ̃disponibilite], *s.f.* **1.** *Jur:* Inalienability. **2.** Unavailability (of funds, of man for a duty).
indisponible [ɛ̃disponibl], *a.* **1.** *Jur:* Inalienable (property) ; entailed (estate). **2.** (*a*) Not available (for duty). (*b*) Unavailable (capital).
indisposer [ɛ̃dispoze], *v.tr.* **1.** To make (s.o.) unwell ; (of food) to upset (s.o.), to disagree with (s.o.). **2.** To antagonize (s.o.). *I. qn contre qn,* to set s.o. against s.o.
  indisposé, *a.* **1.** Indisposed, unwell ; *F:* out of sorts. **2.** *I. contre qn,* unfriendly to s.o. ; ill-disposed towards s.o.
indisposition [ɛ̃dispozisjɔ̃], *s.f.* Indisposition, illness.
indisputable [ɛ̃dispytabl], *a.* Indisputable, incontestable, unquestionable. *adv.* **-ment.**
indissolubilité [ɛ̃dissɔlybilite], *s.f.* **1.** Insolubility (of salt, etc.). **2.** Indissolubility (of marriage).

indissoluble [ɛ̃dissɔlybl], *a.* **1.** Insoluble (salt, etc.). **2.** Indissoluble (bond, friendship).
indistinct [ɛ̃distɛ̃(:kt)], *a.* Indistinct ; hazy, blurred ; faint (inscription). *adv.* **-ement.**
indistinguible [ɛ̃distɛ̃gibl], *a.* Indistinguishable (*de,* from).
individu [ɛ̃dividy], *s.m.* **1.** *Nat.Hist: etc:* Individual. *F: Soigner son i., avoir soin de son i.,* to look after oneself well. **2.** *F:* Usu. *Pej:* Individual, person, fellow. *Un i. louche,* a shady customer, a suspicious character.
individualiser [ɛ̃dividɥalize], *v.tr.* To individualize ; to specify, particularize (case).
individualité [ɛ̃dividɥalite], *s.f.* Individuality.
individu|el, -elle [ɛ̃dividɥel], *a.* Individual ; personal (liberty, etc.) ; private (fortune, etc.). *adv.* **-ellement.**
indivis [ɛ̃divi], *a.* *Jur:* **1.** Undivided, joint (estate). **2.** Joint (owners). **Par indivis,** jointly.
indivisibilité [ɛ̃divizibilite], *s.f.* Indivisibility.
indivisible [ɛ̃divizibl], *a.* Indivisible.
indivulgable [ɛ̃divylgabl], *a.* Unrevealable.
indivulgué [ɛ̃divylge], *a.* Unrevealed.
in-dix-huit [ɛ̃dizɥit], *a. & s.m.inv. Typ:* Decimo-octavo, eighteenmo.
Indo-Chine [ɛ̃dɔʃin]. *Pr.n.f.* Indo-China.
indocile [ɛ̃dɔsil], *a.* Intractable, disobedient, indocile. *adv.* **-ment.**
indocilité [ɛ̃dɔsilite], *s.f.* Intractableness, intractability, indocility.
indo-européen, -enne [ɛ̃dɔørɔpeɛ̃, -ɛn], *a. & s.* Indo-European.
indolence [ɛ̃dɔlɑ̃:s], *s.f.* **1.** Indolence, apathy, sloth. **2.** *Med:* Indolence, painlessness.
indol|ent, -ente [ɛ̃dɔlɑ̃, -ɑ̃:t], *a.* **1.** Indolent, apathetic, slothful. **2.** *Med:* Painless, indolent (tumour). *adv.* **-emment.**
indomptable [ɛ̃dɔ̃tabl], *a.* Unconquerable (nation) ; untam(e)able (animal) ; unmanageable (horse) ; indomitable (pride) ; ungovernable (passion). *adv.* **-ment.**
indompté [ɛ̃dɔ̃te], *a.* Unconquered (nation) ; untamed (animal).
indou, -oue [ɛ̃du], *a. & s. Ethn:* = HINDOU.
in-douze [ɛ̃du:z], *a. & s.m.inv. Typ:* Duodecimo, twelvemo.
indu [ɛ̃dy], *a.* **1.** (Of money) Not owed, not due. **2.** Undue (haste, etc.) ; unwarranted (remark, etc.). *Il rentre à des heures indues,* he comes home at all hours of the night.
indubitable [ɛ̃dybitabl], *a.* Beyond doubt, indubitable, unquestionable. *adv.* **-ment.**
inductance [ɛ̃dyktɑ̃:s], *s.f. El:* Inductance. (*a*) Coefficient of self-induction. (*b*) Inductance coil.
inducteur, -trice [ɛ̃dyktœ:r, -tris]. *El:* **1.** *a.* Inductive (capacity) ; inducing (current). **2.** *s.m.* Inductor ; field magnet (of dynamo).
inductif, -ive [ɛ̃dyktif, -i:v], *a.* Inductive.
induction [ɛ̃dyksjɔ̃], *s.f.* Induction. **1.** *Raisonner par i.,* to reason by induction. **2.** *El:* **Courant d'induction,** induced current. **Bobine d'induction,** induction coil.
induire [ɛ̃dɥi:r], *v.tr.* (*pr.p.* induisant ; *p.p.* induit ; *pr.ind.* j'induis, n. induisons, ils induisent ; *p.h.* j'induisis ; *fu.* j'induirai) **1.** Usu. *Pej:* To induce. *I. qn à faire qch.,* to lead, induce, tempt, s.o. to do sth. **2.** *Log:* To infer, induce (conclusion).
  induit. *El:* **1.** *a.* Induced, secondary (circuit). **2.** *s.m.* (*a*) Induced circuit. **Charge d'induit,** induced charge. (*b*) Armature (of large dynamo). *Ouverture d'i.,* armature gap. Cp. ARMATURE 3.

indulgence [ɛ̃dylʒɑ̃:s], *s.f.* **1.** Indulgence, leniency. Avec indulgence, indulgently, leniently. *Montrer, avoir, de l'i. envers qn, pour qn*, to be indulgent to s.o., to show forbearance to s.o. **2.** *Ecc: I. plénière*, plenary indulgence.

indulgent [ɛ̃dylʒã], *a.* Indulgent, lenient, long-suffering. *Être i. à, pour, envers, qn*, to be indulgent to, lenient with, s.o.

indûment [ɛ̃dymã], *adv.* Unduly; improperly.

induration [ɛ̃dyrasjɔ̃], *s.f. Med:* Induration.

indurer [ɛ̃dyre], *v.tr. Med:* To indurate, harden. **s'indurer**, to indurate, harden.

industrialiser [ɛ̃dystrialize], *v.tr.* To industrialize.

industrialisme [ɛ̃dystrialism], *s.m.* Industrialism.

industrie [ɛ̃dystri], *s.f.* **1.** (*a*) Activity; industry (of. bees, etc.). (*b*) Ingenuity, cleverness, skill. *Vivre d'industrie*, to live by one's wits. S.a. CHEVALIER 1. **2.** Industry, trade, manufacture. *L'i. mécanique*, engineering. *Les industries du bâtiment*, the building trades.

industri|el, -elle [ɛ̃dystriel]. **1.** *a.* Industrial (product, etc.). **2.** *s.m.* Manufacturer, industrialist. *adv.* **-ellement.**

industrieu|x, -euse [ɛ̃dystriø, -ø:z], *a.* Busy, activé, industrious. *adv.* **-sement.**

inébranlable [inebrãlabl], *a.* Unshak(e)able. (*a*) Immovable, solid, firm (wall, etc.). (*b*) Resolute, constant, steadfast (person); unswerving (purpose, etc.); unflinching, unwavering (courage). *adv.* **-ment.**

inéclairci [ineklɛrsi], *a.* Unelucidated.

inéclairé [ineklɛre], *a.* Unlighted, unlit (passage, etc.); unenlightened (mind, etc.).

inédit [inedi], *a.* **1.** Unpublished (book, etc.). **2.** *F:* New, original (show, plan).

ineffable [inefabl], *a.* Ineffable, unutterable.

ineffaçable [inefasabl], *a.* Ineffaceable (mark, memory); indelible (stain). *adv.* **-ment.**

inefficace [inefikas], *a.* Ineffectual (measure); inefficacious (remedy). *adv.* **-ment.**

inefficacité [inefikasite], *s.f.* Ineffectualness; inefficacy (of remedy).

inégal, -aux [inegal, -o], *a.* **1.** Unequal (parts, etc.). **2.** (*a*) Uneven, rough (ground). (*b*) Irregular (pulse); changeable (wind). *adv.* **-ement.**

inégalé [inegale], *a.* Unequalled.

inégalité [inegalite], *s.f.* **1.** Inequality, disparity (*entre*, between). **2.** (*a*) Unevenness, inequality (of ground). *Les inégalités du chemin*, the bumps in the road. (*b*) Inégalité d'humeur, capriciousness; crotchetiness (of temper).

inclastique [inelastik], *a.* Inelastic.

inélégance [inelegã:s], *s.f.* Inelegance.

inélégant [inelegã], *a.* Inelegant.

inéligible [ineliʒibl], *a.* Ineligible.

inéluctable [inelyktabl], *a.* Ineluctable; from which there is no escape. *adv.* **-ment.**

inéludable [inelydabl], *a.* That cannot be eluded; unescapable.

inemployé [inãplwaje], *a.* Unemployed, unused (time, capital).

inénarrable [inenarabl], *a.* Untellable; beyond words. .

inentamé [inãtame], *a.* Intact; uncut (loaf, etc.); unshaken (faith).

inepte [inɛpt], *a.* Inept, foolish, idiotic (remark).

ineptement [inɛptəmã], *adv.* Ineptly, foolishly, idiotically.

ineptie [inɛpsi], *s.f.* Ineptitude. **1.** Ineptness. **2.** *Dire des inepties*, to utter ineptitudes, to talk nonsense.

inépuisable [inepɥizabl], *a.* Inexhaustible; unfailing (patience, etc.). *adv.* **-ment.**

inépuisé [inepɥize], *a.* Unexhausted, unspent.

inéquitable [inekitabl], *a.* Inequitable, unfair. *adv.* **-ment.**

inerte [inɛrt], *a.* (*a*) Inert (mass, etc.); sluggish (nature); dull (intelligence). (*b*) *Résistance i.*, passive resistance.

inertie [inɛrsi], *s.f.* **1.** Inertia. **Force d'inertie**, vis inertiae. *Mec:* Moment d'inertie,· moment of inertia. **2.** Sluggishness, dullness.

inespéré [inespere], *a.* Unhoped-for, unexpected, unlooked-for.

inessayé [inesɛje], *a.* **1.** Unattempted. **2.** Untried, untested.

inestimable [inestimabl], *a.* Inestimable, invaluable, priceless.

inétudié [inetydje], *a.* Unstudied (pose, style).

inévitable [inevitabl], *a.* **1.** Unavoidable (accident, engagement). **2.** Inevitable (result). *C'est inévitable*, it is bound to happen. *adv.* **-ment.**

inexact [inɛgzakt], *a.* **1.** Inexact, inaccurate, incorrect; wrong (amount, etc.). *Esprit i.*, inaccurate mind. **2.** (*a*) Unpunctual. (*b*) **Inexact à remplir ses devoirs**, remiss, slack, lax (in one's duty). *adv.* **-ement.**

inexactitude [inɛgzaktityd], *s.f.* **1,** Inaccuracy, inexactitude. (*a*) Inaccurateness, incorrectness. (*b*) Mistake. **2.** (*a*) Unpunctuality. (*b*) Remissness, slackness.

inexcusable [inɛkskyzabl], *a.* Inexcusable; unwarrantable (action). *adv.* **-ment.**

inexécutable [inɛgzekytabl], *a.* Inexecutable, impracticable; (order) that cannot be carried out.

inexécuté [inɛgzekyte], *a.* Unperformed; unfulfilled (promise); (order) not carried out.

inexécution [inɛgzekysjɔ̃], *s.f.* Non-performance; non-fulfilment (of promise).

inexercé [inɛgzerse], *a.* **1.** Unexercised, untrained. **2.** Unpractised, unskilled (*d*, in).

inexigible [inɛgziʒibl], *a.* **1.** Inexigible (debt). **2.** Not due.

inexistant [inɛgzistã], *a.* Non-existent.

inexistence [inɛgzistã:s], *s.f.* Non-existence.

inexorable [inɛgzɔrabl], *a.* Inexorable, unrelenting. *adv.* **-ment.**

inexpérience [inɛksperjã:s], *s.f.* Inexperience.

inexpérimenté [inɛksperimãte], *a.* **1.** Inexperienced; unpractised, unskilled (hand, etc.). **2.** Untried, untested (process).

inexpiable [inɛkspjabl], *a.* Inexpiable, unatonable.

inexpié [inɛkspje], *a.* Unatoned.

inexplicable [inɛksplikabl], *a.* Inexplicable, unexplainable, unaccountable. *adv.* **-ment.**

inexpliqué [inɛksplike], *a.* Unexplained, unaccounted for.

inexploitable [inɛksplwatabl], *a.* Unworkable (mine); uncultivable (land).

inexploité [inɛksplwate], *a.* Unworked, unwrought (mine); undeveloped (land).

inexploré [inɛksplɔre], *a.* Unexplored.

inexplosible [inɛksplɔzibl], *a.* Non-explosive.

inexpressif, -ive [inɛkspresif, -i:v], *a.* Inexpressive; expressionless, soulless (countenance).

inexprimable [inɛksprimabl], *a.* Inexpressible; beyond words; unutterable. *adv.* **-ment.**

inexprimé [inɛksprime], *a.* Unexpressed.

inexpugnable [inɛkspygnabl], *a.* Impregnable, inexpugnable; storm-proof (fortress).

inextensible [inɛkstãsibl], *a.* Inextensible.

inextinguible [inɛkstɛ̃g(ɥ)ibl], a. Inextinguishable; unquenchable (fire, thirst); irrepressible, uncontrollable (laughter).
inextirpable [inɛkstirpabl], a. Ineradicable.
inextricable [inɛkstrikabl], a. Inextricable. adv. **-ment.**
infaillibilité [ɛ̃fajibilite], s.f. Infallibility.
infaillible [ɛ̃fajibl], a. Infallible. **I.** Unerring. **2.** Certain, sure, unfailing (remedy). adv. **-ment.**
infaisable [ɛ̃fəzabl], a. Unfeasible; impossible of execution.
infamant [ɛ̃famɑ̃], a. **I.** Defamatory. **2.** Ignominious, dishonourable. **Peine infamante,** penalty involving loss of civil rights.
infâme [ɛ̃fɑːm], a. Infamous; foul (deed); unspeakable (behaviour); vile, squalid (slum).
infamie [ɛ̃fami], s.f. **I.** Infamy, dishonour. *Être noté d'i. comme escroc,* to be branded as a swindler. **2.** Vile, foul, deed. *Dire des infamies sur le compte de qn,* to vilify s.o.
infant, -ante [ɛ̃fɑ̃, -ɑ̃ːt], s. *Spanish Hist:* Infante, f. infanta.
infanterie [ɛ̃fɑ̃tri], s.f. Infantry. *Soldat d'i.,* infantryman, foot-soldier. **Infanterie de marine,** Marine Light Infantry.
infanticide[1] [ɛ̃fɑ̃tisid], s. m. & f. Infanticide, child-murderer.
infanticide[2], s.m. Infanticide, child-murder.
infantile [ɛ̃fɑ̃til], a. Infantile (disease, etc.).
infatigable [ɛ̃fatigabl], a. Indefatigable, untiring, tireless. *I. à faire le bien,* never weary in well-doing. adv. **-ment.**
infatuation [ɛ̃fatɥasjɔ̃], s.f. (a) Infatuation (de, for, over). (b) Self-conceit.
infatuer [ɛ̃fatɥe], v.tr. To infatuate.
s'infatuer de, pour, qn, to become infatuated with s.o. *Infatué de soi-même,* eaten up with self-conceit.
infécond [ɛ̃fekɔ̃], a. Barren, sterile; unfruitful (suggestion).
infécondité [ɛ̃fekɔ̃dite], s.f. Barrenness, sterility.
infect [ɛ̃fɛkt], a. Stinking (food); foul (air); noisome (smell); filthy (book). *Odeur infecte,* stench. *F: Temps i.,* beastly weather.
infecter [ɛ̃fɛkte], v.tr. **I.** To infect (de, with). **2.** To pollute, taint. *Abs. Viande qui infecte,* meat that stinks. *Il infecte le tabac,* he reeks of tobacco.
infectieux, -euse [ɛ̃fɛksjø, -øːz], a. Infectious.
infection [ɛ̃fɛksjɔ̃], s.f. **I.** Infection. *I. bactérienne,* bacterial contamination. *Med: I. purulente,* pyaemia, *F:* blood-poisoning. *I. putride,* septicaemia, *F:* blood-poisoning. **2.** Stink, stench.
inféoder [ɛ̃feɔde], v.tr. *A:* To enfeoff.
s'inféoder à un parti, to give one's allegiance to a party.
inférence [ɛ̃ferɑ̃s], s.f. *Log:* Inference.
inférer [ɛ̃fere], v.tr. (**j'infère; j'inférerai**) To infer (de, from).
inférieur, -eure [ɛ̃ferjœːr], a. Inferior. **I.** (a) (In place or amount) Lower. *L'Égypte inférieure,* Lower Egypt. *La lèvre inférieure,* the lower lip, the nether lip. (b) (In quality) Poor (goods, harvest, etc.). (c) (In position) *D'un rang i.,* of an inferior rank, of a lower rank. **2.** *Inférieur à,* inferior to; below. *I. au niveau de la mer,* below sea-level. *Être i. à qn par le mérite,* to be inferior to s.o. in merit. **3.** s. *Être l'i. de qn,* to be s.o.'s inferior.
inférieurement [ɛ̃ferjœrmɑ̃], adv. **I.** In a lower position; on the under side. **2.** In an inferior manner.
infériorité [ɛ̃ferjɔrite], s.f. Inferiority. (a) *I. du*

nombre, inferiority in numbers. (b) *I. de niveau,* difference (= drop) in, of, level.
infernal, -aux [ɛ̃fernal, -o], a. Infernal. **I.** Of Hell or of Hades. **2.** *F:* Diabolical, devilish. **3. Machine infernale,** infernal machine.
infertile [ɛ̃fertil], a. Infertile, unfruitful, barren.
infertilité [ɛ̃fertilite], s.f. Infertility, unfruitfulness, barrenness.
infester [ɛ̃feste], v.tr. (Of vermin, etc.) To infest, overrun; (of ghost) to haunt. *Infesté de bandes noires,* gang-ridden.
infidèle [ɛ̃fidɛl]. **I.** a. Unfaithful. (a) False, faithless; unfaithful (à, to). (b) Dishonest; defaulting (cashier, etc.). (c) Misleading, incorrect; unfaithful (translator). **2.** s. Infidel, unbeliever. adv. **-ment.**
infidélité [ɛ̃fidelite], s.f. Infidelity (envers, to). (a) Unfaithfulness, faithlessness. (b) Dishonesty. (c) Inaccuracy (in translation, etc.). (d) (Religious) unbelief.
infiltration [ɛ̃filtrasjɔ̃], s.f. Infiltration. **I.** Percolation, seepage. **2.** Filtering through (of traffic).
infiltrer (s') [sɛ̃filtre], v.pr. **I.** (a) (Of fluid) To infiltrate, percolate, seep (dans, into; à travers, through); to soak in, filter in. (b) (Of idea, etc.) To trickle in, filter in, soak in. **2.** (Of troops) To progress, advance, by infiltration.
infime [ɛ̃fim], a. **I.** Lowly, mean (rank, etc.). **2.** *F:* Tiny, minute; infinitesimal (majority).
infini [ɛ̃fini]. **I.** a. Infinite; boundless, immeasurable (space); endless (bliss, etc.); innumerable (favours). **2.** s.m. **L'infini,** the infinite. *Phot: Régler à l'i.,* to focus for infinity. Adv.phr. **A l'infini,** to infinity, ad infinitum; boundlessly.
infiniment [ɛ̃finimɑ̃], adv. Infinitely. *I. plus intelligent,* infinitely, ever so much, more intelligent. *Se donner i. de peine,* to give oneself no end of trouble. *Je regrette i., F:* I am awfully sorry.
infinité [ɛ̃finite], s.f. (a) *Mth: etc:* Infinity. (b) Infinitude, boundlessness (of space). *F: Une i. de raisons,* no end of reasons.
infinitésimal, -aux [ɛ̃finitezimal, -o], a. *Mth: etc:* Infinitesimal. S.a. CALCUL[1].
infinitif, -ive [ɛ̃finitif, -iːv], a. & s.m. *Gram:* Infinitive (mood). *A l'infinitif,* in the infinitive.
infirme [ɛ̃firm]. **I.** a. (a) Infirm (old man, etc.). (b) Disabled, crippled. (c) Weak, feeble, frail (body, spirit). **2.** s. (a) Invalid. (b) Cripple.
infirmer [ɛ̃firme], v.tr. **I.** (a) To show up the weakness of (proof, argument, etc.). (b) To weaken (s.o.'s authority). (c) To weaken, invalidate (evidence, claim). **2.** *Jur:* To annul, quash (judgment); to set (verdict) aside. (b) To cancel (letter, etc.).
infirmerie [ɛ̃firmɔri], s.f. (a) Infirmary, hospital. (b) Sick-room.
infirmier, -ère [ɛ̃firmje, -ɛːr]. **I.** s.m. Hospital attendant; male nurse; ambulance man. *Mil:* Medical orderly. *Navy:* Sick-berth attendant. **2.** s.f. Infirmière, (hospital) nurse; sick-nurse; ambulance nurse. *Infirmière en chef,* matron.
infirmité [ɛ̃firmite], s.f. (a) Infirmity. (b) Physical disability. (c) Weakness, frailty.
inflammabilité [ɛ̃flamabilite], s.f. Inflammability, inflammableness.
inflammable [ɛ̃flamabl], a. Inflammable.
inflammation [ɛ̃flamasjɔ̃], s.f. **I.** Inflammation, ignition, firing (of explosives, etc.). **Point d'inflammation,** flash-point (of mineral oil). **2.** *Med:* Inflammation.
inflation [ɛ̃flasjɔ̃], s.f. *Pol.Ec:* Inflation.
infléchir [ɛ̃fleʃiːr], v.tr. To bend, inflect (ray).
s'infléchir. I. To bend, deviate. *Opt:* (Of

ray) To be inflected. **2.** (Of structure) To
cave in.

nfléchissable [ɛ̃fleʃisabl], *a.* (*a*) Unbendable,
rigid (*b*) = INFLEXIBLE.

nflexibilité [ɛ̃flɛksibilite], *s.f.* Inflexibility.

nflexible [ɛ̃flɛksibl], *a.* Inflexible, unbending;
unyielding (will); rigid (virtue); (heart) not to
be swayed. *I. à toutes les prières*, inexorable to all
entreaties. *adv.* **-ment.**

nflexion [ɛ̃flɛksjɔ̃], *s.f.* Inflexion, inflection.
I. *Mth: Opt:* Bend(ing); change of direction
(of curve, ray). **2.** Modulation (of voice).

nfliction [ɛ̃fliksjɔ̃], *s.f.* *Jur:* Infliction (of
penalty) (*d*, upon).

nfliger [ɛ̃fliʒe], *v.tr.* (j'infligeal(s); n. infligeons)
To inflict. *I. une peine à qn*, to impose a penalty
on s.o.

nflorescence [ɛ̃flɔrɛssɑ̃:s], *s.f.* Inflorescence.

nfluençable [ɛ̃flyɑ̃sabl], *a.* Susceptible to
influence.

nfluence [ɛ̃flyɑ̃:s], *s.f.* Influence. *Exercer une
i. sur qch., sur qn*, to have an effect upon sth.; to
exercise an influence, an ascendancy, over s.o.
Avoir peu d'i., to have little weight; to be of
very small account.

nfluencer [ɛ̃flyɑ̃se], *v.tr.* (j'influençai(s); n.
influençons) To influence; to put pressure upon
(s.o.); to sway (public opinion).

nfluent [ɛ̃flyɑ̃], *a.* Influential. **Peu influent**,
uninfluential.

nfluenza [ɛ̃flyɔ̃za], *s.f.* Influenza; *F:* flu(e).

nfluer [ɛ̃flye], *v.i.* *I. sur qn*, to influence s.o.; to
exercise, have, (an) influence on, over, s.o. *I. sur
qch.* to have an effect upon sth.

nflux [ɛ̃fly], *.m.* **I.** Influx (of ideas, etc.).
2. Influx nerveux, nerve-impulse.

in-folio [ɛ̃fɔljo]. **I.** *a.inv.* *Volume in-f.*, folio
volume. **2.** *s.m.inv.* Folio.

informateur, -trice [ɛ̃fɔrmatœːr, -tris], *s.*
Informant.

informatif, -ive [ɛ̃fɔrmatif, -iːv], *a.* Informative, informatory.

information [ɛ̃fɔrmasjɔ̃], *s.f.* (*a*) Inquiry.
Jur: Preliminary investigation (of a case).
Ouvrir une information, to begin legal proceedings. *Prendre des informations (sur qn)*, to make
inquiries (about s.o.). *Mil:* Service d'informations, intelligence service. **Agence d'informa-
tion(s)**, (i) trade-protection society; (ii) news
agency. (*b*) **Je vous envoie, pour votre information . . .**, I am sending you for your
information. . . . *pl.* *W.Tel:* **Informations**,
news(-bulletin).

informe [ɛ̃fɔrm], *a.* (*a*) Formless, shapeless (mass,
etc.); crude (plan). (*b*) Ill-formed, unshapely;
mis-shapen (monster, etc.).

informer [ɛ̃fɔrme]. **I.** *v.tr.* *I. qn de qch.*, to
inform, apprise, s.o. of sth.; to acquaint s.o.
with (a fact). **Mal informé**, misinformed.
2. *v.i.* *Jur:* (*a*) *I. sur un crime*, to investigate a
crime, to inquire into a crime. (*b*) *I. contre qn*,
to inform against s.o.; to lay information
against s.o.

s'informer, to make inquiries. *S'i. de qch.*,
to inquire about sth.

informé, *s.m.* *Jur:* **Renvoyer une cause à
plus ample informé**, to defer a case for further
inquiry.

infortune [ɛ̃fɔrtyn], *s.f.* Misfortune, calamity.
Tomber dans l'infortune, to fall on evil days.
Compagnons d'infortune companions in dis-
tress; fellow-sufferers.

infortuné [ɛ̃fɔrtyne], *a.* Unfortunate, hapless,
unlucky.

infraction [ɛ̃fraksjɔ̃], *s.f.* Infraction. **I.** Infringement (of rights). **2.** *I. à la loi*, infraction of
the law. *I. à la paix*, breach of the peace. *I. au
devoir*, breach of duty.

infranchissable [ɛ̃frɑ̃ʃisabl], *a.* Impassable;
insuperable (difficulty).

infra-rouge [ɛ̃fraruːʒ], *a.* *Opt:* Infra-red.

infrastructure [ɛ̃frastryktyːr], *s.f.* Substructure,
understructure; underframe (of bridge); bed
(of roadway).

infréquent [ɛ̃frekɑ̃], *a.* Infrequent, rare.

infréquenté [ɛ̃frekɑ̃te], *a.* Unfrequented.

infructueu|x, -euse [ɛ̃fryktɥø, -øːz], *a.* (*a*) Un-
fruitful, barren (land, etc.). (*b*) Fruitless,
unavailing (efforts). (*c*) Unprofitable (investment). *adv.* **-sement.**

infus [ɛ̃fy], *a.* Infused, inborn (knowledge,
etc.).

infuser [ɛ̃fyze], *v.tr.* To infuse. **I.** To instil (*à*,
into). **2.** To steep, macerate (herbs, etc.).

s'infuser, to infuse; (of tea) to draw. **Faire
infuser le thé**, to infuse the tea.

infusé, *s.m.* *Pharm:* Infusion.

infusible [ɛ̃fyzibl], *a.* Infusible, non-fusible,
non-melting.

infusion [ɛ̃fyzjɔ̃], *s.f.* Infusion.

infusoires [ɛ̃fyzwaːr], *s.m.pl.* Infusoria.

ingambe [ɛ̃gɑ̃ːb], *a.* Nimble, alert; still active.

ingénier (s') [ɛ̃ʒenje], *v.pr.* *S'i. à faire qch.*, to
exercise one's wits, strain one's ingenuity, in
order to do sth.

ingénieur [ɛ̃ʒenjœːr], *s.m.* Engineer. *I. conseil*,
consulting engineer. *I. des ponts et chaussées*,
Government civil engineer. *I. maritime, de la
marine*, naval architect. *I. de l'artillerie navale*,
naval ordnance officer. *Cin:* *I. du son*, monitor
man.

ingénieu|x, -euse [ɛ̃ʒenjø, -øːz], *a.* Ingenious,
clever. *I. à plaire*, expert at pleasing. *adv.*
-sement.

ingéniosité [ɛ̃ʒenjɔzite], *s.f.* Ingenuity, ingeniousness; cleverness (of person).

ingénu, -ue [ɛ̃ʒeny]. **I.** *a.* Ingenuous, artless,
simple. **Faire l'ingénu**, to affect simplicity. **2.** *s.f.*
Ingénue. (*a*) Artless girl. (*b*) *Th:* *Ingénue.*
adv. **-ment.**

ingénuité [ɛ̃ʒenɥite], *s.f.* Ingenuousness, artlessness, simplicity.

ingérence [ɛ̃ʒerɑ̃ːs], *s.f.* (Unwarrantable) interference, (inter)meddling.

ingérer [ɛ̃ʒere], *v.tr.* (j'ingère; j'ingérerai) To
ingest (food).

s'ingérer *d'une affaire, dans une affaire*, to
interfere in, (inter)meddle with, a business.
S'i. de faire qch., to take it upon oneself to do sth.

inglorieu|x, -euse [ɛ̃glɔrjø, -øːz], *a.* Inglorious.
adv. **-sement.**

ingouvernable [ɛ̃guvɛrnabl], *a.* **I.** Ungovernable, unruly. **2.** Unmanageable (ship, etc.).

ingrat [ɛ̃gra], *a.* **I.** Ungrateful (*envers, to,
towards*). **2.** Unproductive, unprofitable (soil,
etc.); intractable (material); thankless (task);
barren (subject). **3.** (*a*) Unpleasing, repellent
(work, etc.). (*b*) **L'âge ingrat**, the awkward age.

ingratitude [ɛ̃gratityd], *s.f.* **I.** Ingratitude,
ungratefulness. **2.** Thanklessness, unprofitable-
ness (of task).

ingrédient [ɛ̃gredjɑ̃], *s.m.* Ingredient, constituent.

inguéable [ɛ̃geabl], *a.* Unfordable.

inguérissable [ɛ̃gerisabl], *a.* Incurable.

inguinal, -aux [ɛ̃gɥinal, -o], *a.* *Anat:* Inguinal.

ingurgitation [ɛ̃gyrʒitasjɔ̃], *s.f.* Ingurgitation,
swallowing.

ingurgiter [ɛ̃gyrʒite], *v.tr.* To swallow, gulp down (dose, etc.).

inhabile [inabil], *a.* **I.** Inapt (*à*, at); unskilled (in); unfitted (to); clumsy, awkward. **2.** *Jur:* *I. à tester,* incompetent to make a will.

inhabilement [inabilmɑ̃], *adv.* Unskilfully; awkwardly.

inhabileté [inabilte], *s.f.* Want of skill (*à faire qch.,* in doing sth.); clumsiness.

inhabilité [inabilite], *s.f.* Legal incapacity or disability. *I. à succéder,* incompetency to succeed.

inhabitable [inabitabl], *a.* Uninhabitable.

inhabité [inabite], *a.* Uninhabited.

inhabitude [inabityd], *s.f.* Unaccustomedness (*de,* to).

inhabitué [inabitɥe], *a.* Unaccustomed (*à,* to).

inhalateur [inalatœːr], *s.m.* Inhaling apparatus.

inhalation [inalasjɔ̃], *s.f.* Inhalation.

inhaler [inale], *v.tr.* To inhale (ether, etc.).

inharmonieux, -euse [inarmɔnjø, -øːz], *a.* Inharmonious, discordant; unmusical.

inhérent [inerɑ̃], *a.* Inherent (*à,* in).

inhiber [inibe], *v.tr.* To inhibit (feeling, etc.).

inhibition [inibisjɔ̃], *s.f.* Inhibition.

inhospitalier, -ière [inɔspitalje, -jɛːr], *a.* Inhospitable.

inhumain [inymɛ̃], *a.* Inhuman; unfeeling.

inhumanité [inymanite], *s.f.* Inhumanity.

inhumation [inymasjɔ̃], *s.f.* Burial, inhumation.

inhumer [inyme], *v.tr.* To bury, inhume, inter.

inimaginable [inimaʒinabl], *a.* Unimaginable; inconceivable, unthinkable.

inimitable [inimitabl], *a.* Inimitable; matchless. *adv.* **-ment.**

inimitié [inimitje], *s.f.* Enmity, hostility, ill-feeling.

inimprimé [inɛ̃prime], *a.* Unprinted.

ininflammable [inɛ̃flamabl], *a.* Non-inflammable; fire-proof. *Cin:* Non-flam (film).

inintelligence [inɛ̃teliʒɑ̃s], *s.f.* Want of intelligence; obtuseness.

inintelligent [inɛ̃teliʒɑ̃], *a.* Unintelligent; obtuse. *adv.* **-emment.**

inintelligible [inɛ̃teliʒibl], *a.* Unintelligible.

ininterrompu [inɛ̃terɔ̃py], *a.* Uninterrupted, unintermitting; unbroken (sleep).

inique [inik], *a.* Iniquitous. *adv.* **-ment.**

iniquité [inikite], *s.f.* Iniquity.

initial, -aux [inisjal, -o]. **I.** *a.* Initial (letter, cost); starting (price). **2.** *s.f.* **Initiale,** initial (letter).

initiateur, -trice [inisjatœːr, -tris]. **I.** *s.* Initiator. **2.** *a.* Initiatory.

initiation [inisjasjɔ̃], *s.f.* Initiation (*à,* into).

initiative [inisjatiːv], *s.f.* Initiative. *I. privée,* voluntary effort. **Prendre l'initiative d'une réforme,** to initiate a reform. *Mil:* **Garder l'i.,** to keep the initiative. **Faire qch. de sa propre initiative,** to do sth. on one's own initiative. **Syndicat d'initiative,** association for the encouragement of touring.

initier [inisje], *v.tr.* To initiate (s.o.) (*à,* in); to receive (s.o.) among the initiates.
  initié, -ée, *s.* (*a*) Initiate. (*b*) *F:* Person in the know.

injecter [ɛ̃ʒekte], *v.tr.* To inject.
  s'injecter, (of eyes, etc.) to become bloodshot, injected.
  injecté, *a.* Congested, inflamed, injected. *Yeux injectés de sang, de bile,* bloodshot, jaundiced, eyes.

injecteur [ɛ̃ʒektœːr], *s.m.* *Mch:* Injector.

injection [ɛ̃ʒeksjɔ̃], *s.f.* Injection.

injonction [ɛ̃ʒɔ̃ksjɔ̃], *s.f.* Injunction, behest.

injouable [ɛ̃ʒwabl], *a.* Unplayable (music, ball); unperformable, unactable (play).

injudicieu|x, -euse [ɛ̃ʒydisjø, -øːz], *a.* Injudicious. *adv.* **-sement.**

injure [ɛ̃ʒyːr], *s.f.* **I.** Wrong, injury. *Jur:* Tort. **Faire injure à qn,** to wrong s.o. **Tenir à injure un refus,** to feel insulted by a refusal. **2.** Insulting word or remark; insult; *pl.* abuse. *Débiter des injures à qn,* to abuse, slang, s.o.

injurier [ɛ̃ʒyrje], *v.tr.* To abuse (s.o.); to call (s.o.) names.

injurieu|x, -euse [ɛ̃ʒyrjø, -øːz], *a.* Insulting, abusive, injurious (language). *adv.* **-sement.**

injuste [ɛ̃ʒyst]. **I.** *a.* (*a*) Unjust, unfair (*envers, avec, pour,* to). (*b*) Unrighteous. **2.** *s.m.* **Le juste et l'injuste,** right and wrong. *adv.* **-ment.**

injustice [ɛ̃ʒystis], *s.f.* **I.** Injustice, unfairness (*envers,* to, towards). **2.** *Faire une i. à qn,* to do s.o. an injustice; to wrong s.o.

injustifiable [ɛ̃ʒystifjabl], *a.* Unjustifiable, unwarrantable.

injustifié [ɛ̃ʒystifje], *a.* Unjustified, unwarranted.

inlassable [ɛ̃lɔsabl], *a.* Untiring, unflagging, unwearying (efforts, etc.); tireless (person). *adv.* **-ment.**

innavigable [innavigabl], *a.* **I.** Unnavigable, innavigable. **2.** Unseaworthy (ship).

inné [inne], *a.* Innate, inborn.

innocence [inɔsɑ̃s], *s.f.* Innocence. (*a*) Guiltlessness, blamelessness. (*b*) Guilelessness, artlessness, simplicity. (*c*) Harmlessness (of joke).

innoc|ent [inɔsɑ̃], *a.* **I.** Innocent; guiltless, not guilty (*de,* of). **2.** (*a*) Simple, guileless, artless. *s.* Simpleton. (*b*) Harmless, inoffensive (joke, etc.). *Jeux innocents,* parlour games. (*c*) *s.* Innocent, natural, idiot. **L'innocent du village,** the village natural. *adv.* **-emment.**

innocenter [inɔsɑ̃te], *v.tr.* **I.** *I. qn (d'une accusation),* to clear s.o. (of a charge); to declare s.o. not guilty. **2.** To excuse, justify (conduct).

innocuité [innɔkɥite], *s.f.* Innocuousness, harmlessness.

innombrable [innɔ̃brabl], *a.* Innumerable, numberless, countless.

innom(m)é [innɔme], *a.* Unnamed, nameless.

innovateur, -trice [innɔvatœːr, -tris]. **I.** *a.* Innovating, innovative. **2.** *s.* Innovator.

innovation [innɔvasjɔ̃], *s.f.* Innovation.

innover [innɔve], *v.i.* To innovate; to introduce changes, innovations.

inobservance [inɔpsɛrvɑ̃ːs], *s.f.* Non-observance, unobservance.

inobservation [inɔpsɛrvasjɔ̃], *s.f.* Non-observance, disregard (of the law); non-compliance (*de,* with).

inobservé [inɔpsɛrve], *a.* Unobserved. **I.** Unnoticed. **2.** (Of rule) Not kept, not complied with.

inoccupation [inɔkypasjɔ̃], *s.f.* Unemployment, inoccupation.

inoccupé [inɔkype], *a.* Unoccupied. **I.** Idle, unemployed. **2.** Vacant (seat, house); uninhabited (house).

in-octavo [inɔktavo], *a.* & *s.m.inv.* Octavo.

inoculable [inɔkylabl], *a.* *Med:* Inoculable.

inoculation [inɔkylasjɔ̃], *s.f.* *Med:* Inoculation.

inoculer [inɔkyle], *v.tr.* **I.** *I. une maladie à qn,* to infect s.o. with a disease. *Elle nous a inoculé sa gaieté,* she has infected us with her gaiety. **2.** *I. qn (contre une maladie),* to inoculate s.o. (against a disease).

inodore [inɔdɔːr], *a.* Inodorous, odourless; scentless (rose).

inoffens|if, -ive [inɔfãsif, -iːv], *a.* Inoffensive; harmless; innocuous (snake). *adv.* **-ivement.**

inondable [inɔ̃dabl], *a.* (Of land) (*a*) Liable to inundation. (*b*) Easily flooded.

inondation [inɔ̃dasjɔ̃], *s.f.* Inundation; flood. *F:* *I. de maux,* deluge of misfortunes.

inonder [inɔ̃de], *v.tr.* To inundate, flood (fields, etc.); to glut (the market). **inondé, -ée. I.** *a.* Flooded. *Pays i.,* country under water *Visage i. de larmes,* face suffused with tears. *I. d'invitations,* deluged, snowed under, with invitations. **2.** *s.* Flood victim.

inopérable [inɔpɛrabl], *a.* *Surg:* Inoperable (tumour, patient).

inopérant [inɔpɛrã], *a.* *Jur:* Inoperative.

inopiné [inɔpine], *a.* Sudden, unexpected, unforeseen. *adv.* **-ment.**

inopportun [inɔpɔrtœ̃], *a.* **1.** Inopportune. **2.** Unseasonable, ill-timed. *adv.* **-ément.**

inopportunité [inɔpɔrtynite], *s.f.* **1.** Inopportuneness. **2.** Unseasonableness (of remark, etc.).

inorganique [inɔrganik], *a.* Inorganic.

inoubliable [inubliabl], *a.* Unforgettable.

inoublié [inublie], *a.* Unforgotten.

inouï [inui, -w-], *a.* Unheard of. (*a*) Unparalleled, extraordinary. (*b*) *F:* Outrageous (behaviour, etc.).

inoxydable [inɔksidabl], *a.* Unoxidizable; rustproof. *Acier inoxydable,* stainless steel.

inqualifiable [ɛ̃kalifjabl], *a.* Unqualifiable; beyond words; unspeakable (behaviour).

in-quarante-huit [ɛ̃karãtɥit], *a.* & *s.m.inv. Typ:* Forty-eightmo.

in-quarto [ɛ̃kwarto], *a.* & *s.m. inv. Typ:* Quarto.

inquiet, -ète [ɛ̃kjɛ, -ɛt], *a.* (*a*) Restless, fidgety. (*b*) Anxious, apprehensive, uneasy; *F:* worried. *I. de qn, sur le compte de qn,* uneasy about s.o. *Avoir l'esprit i.,* to be uneasy in one's mind.

inquiétant [ɛ̃kjetã], *a.* Disquieting, disturbing, upsetting.

inquiéter [ɛ̃kjete], *v.tr.* (j'inquiète; j'inquiéterai) To make (s.o.) anxious or uneasy; to disquiet, trouble, disturb.
s'inquiéter, to become anxious, to trouble (oneself), to worry, to get uneasy (*de, au sujet de,* about). *Je ne m'inquiète guère de ce qu'on dit,* I care little what they say.

inquiétude [ɛ̃kjetyd], *s.f.* Disquiet. (*a*) Restlessness. *F:* **Avoir des inquiétudes dans les jambes,** to have twitchings in one's legs. (*b*) Anxiety, concern, misgivings, uneasiness. *Être dans l'i.,* to be anxious, uneasy. *Dissiper les inquiétudes de qn, tirer qn de son i.,* to set s.o.'s mind at ease. **État d'inquiétude,** state of anxiety; anxious state of mind. *Éprouver quelques inquiétudes,* to experience a few qualms.

inquisiteur [ɛ̃kizitœːr]. **I.** *s.m. Ecc.Hist:* Inquisitor. **2.** *a.m.* (*a*) Inquisitorial (tribunal). (*b*) *F:* Inquisitive, prying (glance).

inquisition [ɛ̃kizisjɔ̃], *s.f.* Inquisition.

inrouillable [ɛ̃rujabl], *a.* Rustless (steel, etc.).

insaisissable [ɛ̃sezisabl], *a.* **1.** (*a*) That cannot be grasped. (*b*) Difficult to catch; elusive. (*c*) Imperceptible (sound, difference). **2.** *Jur:* Not distrainable, not attachable.

insalissable [ɛ̃salisabl], *a.* Unsoilable, dirtproof.

insalubre [ɛ̃salybr], *a.* Insalubrious (climate); unhealthy (climate, occupation); insanitary (dwelling).

insalubrité [ɛ̃salybrite], *s.f.* Insalubrity, unhealthiness; insanitariness.

insanité [ɛ̃sanite], *s.f.* Insanity.

insatiabilité [ɛ̃sasjabilite], *s.f.* Insatiability.

insatiable [ɛ̃sasjabl], *a.* Insatiable (*de,* of); unquenchable (thirst). *adv.* **-ment.**

insciemment [ɛ̃sjamã], *adv.* Unknowingly, unconsciously, unwittingly.

inscripteur, -trice [ɛ̃skriptœːr, -tris], *a.* Recording (device). **Tambour inscripteur,** drum-recorder.

inscriptible [ɛ̃skriptibl], *a.* *Geom:* Inscribable.

inscription [ɛ̃skripsjɔ̃], *s.f.* **1.** (*a*) Writing down, inscribing. (*b*) Registration, enrolment. **Droit d'inscription,** registration fee, entrance fee. **Feuille d'inscription,** entry form. **Prendre son inscription,** to enter one's name. *Fr.Navy:* **Inscription maritime,** seaboard conscription for the navy. S.a. FAUX[1] II. 2. (*c*) *Gramophones:* *I. sur cire,* wax recording. **2.** (*a*) Inscription (on tomb, etc.). (*b*) Directions (on sign-post, etc.); notice.

inscrire [ɛ̃skriːr], *v.tr.* (*pr.p.* **inscrivant**; *p.p.* **inscrit**; *pr.ind.* **j'inscris, il inscrit, n. inscrivons**; *p.h.* **j'inscrivis**; *fu.* **j'inscrirai**) **I.** (*a*) To inscribe, write down. *I. une question à l'ordre du jour,* to place a question on the agenda. (*b*) To register (marriage, etc.); to enrol(l) (s.o.); to enter (s.o.'s) name. **Se faire inscrire à un cours,** to enter, put down, one's name, to enrol(l), for a course. **2.** To inscribe, engrave (epitaph, etc.). **3.** *Geom:* To inscribe (triangle, etc.) (*dans,* in).
s'inscrire, (*a*) To put down one's name. (*b*) To have oneself registered. S.a. FAUX[1] II. 1.

inscrit, *s.m. Fr.Navy:* **Inscrit maritime,** man enrolled for naval conscription.

inscrutable [ɛ̃skrytabl], *a.* Inscrutable, unfathomable. *adv.* **-ment.**

insécable [ɛ̃sekabl], *a.* Indivisible.

insecte [ɛ̃sɛkt], *s.m.* Insect.

insecticide [ɛ̃sɛktisid], *a.* & *s.m.* Insecticide. *Poudre i.,* insect-powder.

insectivore [ɛ̃sɛktivɔːr]. **I.** *a.* Insectivorous. **2.** *s.m.* Insect-eater, insectivore.

insécurité [ɛ̃sekyrite], *s.f.* Insecurity.

in-seize [ɛ̃sɛːz], *a.* & *s.m.inv. Typ:* Sixteenmo.

insensé, -ée [ɛ̃sãse], *a.* (*a*) Mad, insane. *s.* Madman, -woman. (*b*) Senseless, foolish (action, etc.). (*c*) Extravagant, *F:* hare-brained (scheme).

insensibilisateur [ɛ̃sãsibilizatœːr], *s.m.* Anaesthetic.

insensibilisation [ɛ̃sãsibilizasjɔ̃], *s.f.* Anaesthetization.

insensibiliser [ɛ̃sãsibilize], *v.tr.* *Med:* To insensibilize, anaesthetize.

insensibilité [ɛ̃sãsibilite], *s.f.* Insensitiveness. (*a*) Insensibility. (*b*) Indifference, callousness (*envers,* to).

insensible [ɛ̃sãsibl], *a.* Insensible. **I.** (*a*) Insensitive. (*b*) Indifferent (*à,* to); unfeeling; callous (*à,* to). *I. à la flatterie,* proof against flattery. **2.** Imperceptible; hardly perceptible (difference, etc.). *adv.* **-ment.**

inséparable [ɛ̃separabl]. **I.** *a.* Inseparable. **2.** *s.m.pl. Orn:* Love-birds. *adv.* **-ment.**

insérer [ɛ̃sere], *v.tr.* (j'insère; j'insérerai) To insert (clause in an agreement, etc.).

insertion [ɛ̃sɛrsjɔ̃], *s.f.* Insertion.

inserviable [ɛ̃sɛrvjabl], *a.* Disobliging.

insidieu|x, -euse [ɛ̃sidjø, -øːz], *a.* Insidious. *adv.* **-sement.**

insigne[1] [ɛ̃siɲ], *a.* **I.** Distinguished (*par,* for); remarkable. *Faveur i.,* signal favour. **2.** *Pej:* Notorious; arrant (liar, etc.).

insigne[2], *s.m.* Usu. *pl.* Distinguishing mark; badge. *F: sportif,* sporting badge. *Insignes de la royauté,* insignia of royalty.

insignifiance [ɛ̃siɲifjãːs], *s.f.* Insignificance, unimportance.

insignifiant [ɛ̃siɲifjɑ̃], *a.* **1.** Insignificant, unimportant ; trivial, trifling (loss, sum). **2.** Vacuous (face) ; lacking in personality.

insinuant [ɛ̃sinɥɑ̃], *a.* Insinuating, insinuative.

insinuation [ɛ̃sinɥasjɔ̃], *s.f.* Insinuation. **1.** Introduction (*e.g.* of probe into wound). **2.** Innuendo.

insinuer [ɛ̃sinɥe], *v.tr.* To insinuate. **1.** To introduce, insert (gently). **2.** To hint at (sth.). *Que voulez-vous i.?* what are you hinting at?
   s'insinuer, to penetrate ; to creep (in, into) ; to steal (in, into). *S'i. dans les bonnes grâces de qn,* to insinuate oneself into s.o.'s good graces.

insipide [ɛ̃sipid], *a.* Insipid. (*a*) Tasteless (dish). (*b*) Dull, vapid, flat, uninteresting (conversation, etc.) ; tame (story, ending).

insipidité [ɛ̃sipidite], *s.f.* Insipidity. (*a*) Tastelessness. (*b*) Dullness, vapidness, vapidity, flatness (of conversation) ; tameness (of ending).

insistance [ɛ̃sistɑ̃ːs], *s.f.* Insistence (*à faire qch.,* on doing sth.). **Avec insistance,** earnestly, insistently.

insister [ɛ̃siste], *v.i.* To insist. *I. sur un fait,* to dwell, lay stress, (up)on a fact. *I. sur ses demandes,* to stand out for, insist on, persist in, one's claims. *I. à, pour, faire qch.,* to insist on doing sth. *I. auprès de qn,* to take a matter up strongly with s.o. *N'insistez pas trop,* do not be too insistent.

insobriété [ɛ̃sɔbriete], *s.f.* Intemperance.

insociabilité [ɛ̃sɔsjabilite], *s.f.* Insociability, unsociableness.

insociable [ɛ̃sɔsjabl], *a.* Unsociable, insociable.

insolation [ɛ̃sɔlasjɔ̃], *s.f.* Insolation. **1.** (*a*) *Phot :* Daylight printing. (*b*) Sun-bathing. **2.** = *coup de soleil, q.v.* under SOLEIL **2.**

insolence [ɛ̃sɔlɑ̃ːs], *s.f.* **1.** Insolence, impertinence ; *F :* impudence. **Répondre avec insolence,** to answer insolently. **2.** Piece of impudence.

insol|ent, -ente [ɛ̃sɔlɑ̃, -ɑ̃ːt]. **1.** *a.* (*a*) Insolent, impertinent, *F :* impudent (*envers, avec,* to). (*b*) Haughty, overbearing. **2.** *s.* Insolent fellow, impudent hussy. *adv.* **-emment.**

insoler [ɛ̃sɔle], *v.tr.* To insolate ; to expose (sth.) to the sun.
   s'insoler, to take a sun-bath.

insolite [ɛ̃sɔlit], *a.* Unusual, unwonted.

insolubiliser [ɛ̃sɔlybilize], *v.tr.* To render insoluble.

insolubilité [ɛ̃sɔlybilite], *s.f.* Insolubility.

insoluble [ɛ̃sɔlybl], *a.* **1.** Insoluble (substance). **2.** Insoluble, insolvable, unsolvable (problem). *Situation i.,* dead-lock.

insolvabilité [ɛ̃sɔlvabilite], *s.f.* Insolvency.

insolvable [ɛ̃sɔlvabl], *a. Com :* Insolvent.

insomnie [ɛ̃sɔmni], *s.f.* Insomnia, sleeplessness. *Nuit d'i.,* sleepless night.

insondable [ɛ̃sɔ̃dabl], *a.* **1.** Unsoundable, fathomless (sea). **2.** Unfathomable (mystery).

insonore [ɛ̃sɔnɔːr], *a. Cin :* **1.** Sound-proof (studio, etc.). **2.** Sound-deadening (material).

insonoriser [ɛ̃sɔnɔrize], *v.tr. Cin :* To insulate, silence (the studio, etc.).

insouciance [ɛ̃susjɑ̃ːs], *s.f.* (*a*) Freedom from care ; unconcern, insouciance. (*b*) Thoughtlessness, casualness.

insouci|ant [ɛ̃susjɑ̃], *a.* (*à*) Careless, free from care, unconcerned. *I. du lendemain,* careless of the morrow. (*b*) Heedless, thoughtless, casual. *adv.* **-amment.**

insoucieux, -euse [ɛ̃susjø, -øːz], *a.* Heedless (*de,* of). *I. de l'avenir,* regardless of the future.

insoumis, -ise [ɛ̃sumi, -iːz], *a.* **1.** Unsubdued, unsubjugated. **2.** (*a*) Unsubmissive, refractory, unruly. (*b*) *a. & s.m. Mil :* Absentee (conscript or reservist).

insoumission [ɛ̃sumisjɔ̃], *s.f.* Insubordination, unsubmissiveness.

insoupçonnable [ɛ̃supsɔnabl], *a.* Beyond suspicion ; above suspicion.

insoupçonné [ɛ̃supsɔne], *a.* Unsuspected (*de,* by).

insoutenable [ɛ̃sutnabl], *a.* **1.** Untenable (opinion) ; unwarrantable, unmaintainable (assertion) ; indefensible (position). **2.** Unbearable, unendurable (agony, etc.).

inspecter [ɛ̃spɛkte], *v.tr.* To inspect (school, etc.) ; to survey (field of battle) ; to examine (accounts).

inspecteur, -trice [ɛ̃spɛktœːr, -tris], *s.* Inspector, *f.* inspectress ; overseer (of works, etc.) ; shop-walker ; surveyor (of mines, etc.) ; examiner (of commercial books, etc.). *Adm : I. de la sûreté,* detective inspector. *I. des contributions directes,* inspector of taxes. *Sch : I. d'Académie,* secondary-school inspector (one is assigned to each *département*).

inspection [ɛ̃spɛksjɔ̃], *s.f.* **1.** (*a*) Inspection, inspecting ; examination, examining ; survey. **Faire l'inspection de** = INSPECTER. **Passer l'inspection** *d'une compagnie,* to inspect a company. (*b*) Tour of inspection. **2.** Inspectorship ; surveyorship.

inspirateur, -trice [ɛ̃spiratœːr, -tris]. **1.** *a.* (*a*) Inspiratory (muscle, etc.). (*b*) Inspiring, inspiriting. **2.** *s.* Inspirer.

inspiration [ɛ̃spirasjɔ̃], *s.f.* Inspiration. **1.** Breathing in, inhaling. **2.** Suggestion, prompting. *Sous l'inspiration du moment,* on the spur of the moment.

inspirer [ɛ̃spire], *v.tr.* To inspire. **1.** (*a*) *I. qch. à qn,* to inspire s.o. with sth. *I. le respect,* to inspire respect. *I. à qn de faire qch.,* to prompt s.o. to do sth. (*b*) *I. qn,* to inspire s.o. *Inspiré par la jalousie,* prompted, actuated, by jealousy. *Régime inspiré du principe de liberté,* régime imbued with the spirit of liberty. **2.** To breathe in, inhale (air, smoke, etc.).
   s'inspirer *de qn, de qch.,* to take, draw, one's inspiration from s.o., from sth.

instabilité [ɛ̃stabilite], *s.f.* Instability. (*a*) Shakiness, unsteadiness. *Nau :* Crankiness (of ship). (*b*) Inconstancy, fickleness ; uncertainty (of fortune, etc.).

instable [ɛ̃stabl], *a.* Unstable. (*a*) Shaky, unsteady. *Nau :* Cranky (ship). **Équilibre instable,** unstable equilibrium. (*b*) Inconstant, unreliable.

installation [ɛ̃stalasjɔ̃], *s.f.* **1.** (*a*) Installation (of a judge, of a bishop). (*b*) Setting up (of machine, house) ; fitting up, equipping (of workshop) ; fixing (of curtains, etc.). **2.** (*a*) Arrangements, appointments (of a flat, etc.) ; fittings (of workshop, etc.). (*b*) *Ind :* Plant. (*c*) *I. de radio,* wireless station or set.

installer [ɛ̃stale], *v.tr.* (*a*) To install (president, bishop). *F : I. qn dans un fauteuil,* to make s.o. comfortable in an armchair. (*b*) To set up (machine, etc.) ; to fit up, equip (factory, etc.) ; to fix (curtains, etc.). *Maison bien installée,* well-appointed house. *I. sa famille à la campagne,* to settle one's family in the country.
   s'installer, to install oneself ; to settle (down). *S'i. à la campagne,* to take up one's abode in the country.

instamment [ɛ̃stamɑ̃], *adv.* Insistently, earnestly. *On demande i. un médecin,* a doctor is urgently required.

instance [ɛ̃stɑ̃ːs], *s.f.* **1.** (*a*) Instancy, solicitation. *Sur l'instance de . . .,* at the instance of. . . . **Prier avec instance,** to pray earnestly. (*b*) *pl.* Requests, entreaties. *Faire de vives instances* *auprès de qn,* to make earnest representations to s.o. (c) *Jur :* Process, suit. **Introduire une instance (en justice),** to institute an action. *Ils sont en i. de divorce,* their divorce proceedings are taking place. **Tribunal de première instance,** court of first instance (= Engl. County Court). **Acquitté en seconde instance,** acquitted on appeal. **2.** Immediacy. **Être en instance de départ pour . . .,** to be on the point of departure for. . . .

instant[1] [ēstā], *a.* Pressing, urgent, instant.

instant[2], *s.m.* Moment, instant. **A chaque instant, à tout instant,** continually; at every moment. **Par instants,** off and on. **Un instant!** wait a moment! *Adv.phr.* **A l'instant,** (i) a moment ago; (ii) immediately, at once. **Dès l'instant que** + *ind.,* (i) from the moment when . . .; (ii) since, seeing that. . . .

instantané [ēstātane]. **I.** *a.* Instantaneous (death); sudden (fright). **2.** *s.m. Phot :* Snapshot. *adv.* **-ment.**

instar de (à l') [alēsta:rdə], *prep.phr.* After the fashion, manner, of; like. *Grand cinéma à l'i. de Paris,* grand cinema as in Paris, equal to anything in Paris.

instaurateur, -trice [ēstɔratœːr, -tris], *s.* Founder, establisher.

instauration [ēstɔrasjō], *s.f.* Founding (of republic, of liberty); setting up.

instaurer [ēstɔre], *v.tr.* To found (temple, etc.); to set up (republic, etc.).

instigateur, -trice [ēstigatœːr, -tris], *s.* Instigator (*de,* of); inciter (*de,* to).

instigation [ēstigasjō], *s.f.* Instigation, incitement (*à,* to). **Agir à l'instigation de qn,** to act at, on, s.'s instigation.

instiller [ēstil(l)e], *v.tr.* To instil.

instinct [ēstē], *s.m.* Instinct. **Par instinct,** by instinct. **D'instinct,** instinctively.

instinct|if, -ive [ēstēktif, -iːv], *a.* Instinctive. *adv.* **-ivement.**

instituer [ēstitɥe], *v.tr.* To institute. (a) To establish, set up, found (institution, etc.); to lay down (a rule). *I. des poursuites contre qn,* to inst'tute, initiate, proceedings against s.o. (b) To appoint (official).

institut [ēstity], *s.m.* Institute, institution. **L'Institut (de France),** the Institute (composed of the five Academies).

instituteur, -trice [ēstitytœːr, -tris] *s.* **I.** Founder, foundress. **2.** (a) (School-)teacher; (elementary) schoolmaster, schoolmistress. (b) *s.f.* **Institutrice,** governess.

institution [ēstitysjō], *s.f.* **I.** Institution. **2.** (Educational, etc.) establishment; (young gentlemen's) academy.

instructeur [ēstryktœːr], *s.m.* **I.** Instructor, teacher; esp. drill-master. *Sergent i.,* drill-sergeant. **2.** *Jur :* **Juge instructeur,** examining magistrate.

instructif, -ive [ēstryktif, -iːv], *a.* Instructive.

instruction [ēstryksjō], *s.f.* Instruction. **I.** (a) **Travailler à l'instruction de qn,** to work under s.o.'s direction. (b) *pl.* Instructions, directions, orders. **Conformément aux instructions,** as directed, as requested. **2.** (a) Education, schooling. *Mil :* Training (of troops). *I. primaire,* elementary education. *I. professionnelle,* vocational training. **Avoir de l'instruction,** to be well educated. **Sans instruction,** uneducated. (b) Lesson. *Tirer des instructions salutaires de qch.,* to draw useful lessons from sth. **3.** *Jur :* Preliminary investigation (of case). **Juge d'instruction,** examining magistrate.

instruire [ēstrɥiːr], *v.tr.* (*pr.p.* **instruisant;** *p.p.* **instruit;** *pr.ind.* **j'instruis, il instruit,** n. **instruisons;** *p.h.* **j'instruisis**) **I.** *I. qn de qch.,* to inform s.o. of sth. **2.** (a) To teach, educate, instruct. *I. qn dans, en, qch., à faire qch.,* to instruct s.o. in sth., how to do sth. (b) To train, drill (troops). **3.** *Jur :* To examine, investigate.

s'instruire, to educate oneself; to improve one's mind.

instruit, *a.* **I.** (a) Educated, learned; well-read. (b) Trained (soldier). **2.** *I. de qch.,* acquainted with sth.; aware of sth.

instrument [ēstrymā], *s.m.* (a) Instrument, implement, tool. (b) (Musical) instrument. (c) (Legal) instrument (deed, contract, writ, etc.).

instrumental, -aux [ēstrymātal, -o], *a.* Instrumental (music).

instrumentation [ēstrymātasjō], *s.f. Mus :* Scoring, instrumentation, orchestration.

instrumenter [ēstrymāte]. **I.** *v.i. Jur : I. contre qn,* to order proceedings to be taken against s.o. **2.** *v.tr.* To score, instrument (opera, etc.).

instrumentiste [ēstrymātist], *s.m. Mus :* Instrumentalist; instrumental performer.

insu [ēsy], *s.m.* (Used in the phr.) **A l'insu de,** without the knowledge of. **A mon insu,** without my knowledge.

insubmersible [ēsybmɛrsibl], *a.* Insubmersible, unsinkable (life-boat, etc.).

insubordination [ēsybɔrdinasjō], *s.f.* Insubordination.

insubordonné [ēsybɔrdɔne], *a.* Insubordinate.

insuccès [ēsyksɛ], *s.m.* Unsuccess; failure; miscarriage (of plan).

insuffisance [ēsyfizãːs], *s.f.* **I.** Insufficiency, deficiency; shortage (of labour); inadequacy (of means). *Phot :* **Insuffisance de pose,** under-exposure. **2.** Incapacity, incompetence.

insuffis|ant [ēsyfizã], *a.* **I.** Insufficient; inadequate (means); short (weight). **2.** Incapable, incompetent. *adv.* **-amment.**

insuffler [ēsyfle], *v.tr.* **I.** (a) To insufflate; to blow, breathe (air into sth.). (b) *Med :* To spray (the throat, etc.). **2.** To inflate, blow up (bladder).

insulaire [ēsylɛːr]. **I.** *a.* Insular. **2.** *s.* Islander.

insularité [ēsylarite], *s.f.* Insularity.

insuline [ēsylin], *s.f. Med :* Insulin.

insultant [ēsyltā], *a.* Insulting, offensive.

insulte [ēsylt], *s.f.* Insult. *Faire une i. à qn,* to insult s.o.

insulter [ēsylte]. **I.** *v.tr.* To insult, affront (s.o.). **2.** *v.ind.tr. I. à qn,* to revile s.o. *I. au malheur,* to jeer at misfortune.

insulteur [ēsyltœːr], *s.m.* Reviler; insulter.

insupportable [ēsypɔrtabl], *a.* Unbearable, unendurable (pain); intolerable (conduct); insufferable (person). **Il est insupportable!** he is very trying! *adv.* **-ment.**

insurger (s') [ēsyrʒe], *v.pr.* (je m'insurgeai(s); n. n. insurgeons) To rise (in rebellion); to revolt (*contre,* against).

insurgé, -ée, *s.* Insurgent, insurrectionist, rebel.

insurmontable [ēsyrmōtabl], *a.* Insurmountable, insuperable; unconquerable (aversion).

insurpassable [ēsyrpasabl], *a.* Unsurpassable, unexcelled.

insurrection [ēsyr(r)eksjō], *s.f.* Insurrection, rising, rebellion. **En état d'insurrection,** insurgent.

intact, *a.* Intact. (a) Untouched; undamaged, unbroken, whole. (b) Unsullied, unblemished (reputation).

intaille [ēta:j], *s.f. Lap :* Intaglio (work, gem).

intangibilité [ɛ̃tãʒibilite], *s.f.* Intangibility, intangibleness.

intangible [ɛ̃tãʒibl], *a.* Intangible.

intarissable [ɛ̃tarisabl], *a.* Inexhaustible (well, etc.); unfailing; endless (chatter). *adv.* **-ment.**

intégral, -aux [ɛ̃tegral, -o], *a.* **1.** Integral, entire, whole. *Paiement i.*, payment in full. *Texte i.*, full text. *Édition intégrale*, unexpurgated edition. **2.** *Mth:* (*a*) **Calcul intégral,** integral calculus. (*b*) *s.f.* **Intégrale,** integral.

intégralement [ɛ̃tegralmã], *adv.* Wholly, entirely, fully, in full.

intégralité [ɛ̃tegralite], *s.f.* Integrality, entireness, wholeness.

intégrant [ɛ̃tegrã], *a.* Integral, integrant (part, etc.). **Faire partie intégrante de . . .,** to be part and parcel of . . .

intégration [ɛ̃tegrasjɔ̃], *s.f. Mth:* Integration.

intègre [ɛ̃tegr], *a.* Upright, honest. *adv.* **-ment.**

intégrer [ɛ̃tegre], *v.tr.* (**j'intègre; j'intégrerai**) *Mth:* To integrate.

intégrité [ɛ̃tegrite], *s.f.* Integrity. **1.** Entirety, wholeness. **2.** Uprightness, honesty.

intellect [ɛ̃tɛllɛkt], *s.m.* Intellect, understanding.

intellectu|el, -elle [ɛ̃tɛl(l)ɛktɥɛl]. **1.** *a.* Intellectual; mental (culture). *Travail i.*, *F:* brainwork. S.a. SURMENAGE. **2.** *s.* Intellectual; brain-worker; *F:* high-brow. *adv.* **-ellement.**

intelligence [ɛ̃tɛl(l)iʒã:s], *s.f.* **1.** Understanding, comprehension. *Avoir l'i. des affaires,* to have a good knowledge of business. *Pour l'i. de ce qui va suivre . . .,* in order to understand what follows. . . . **2.** Intelligence, intellect; brainpower. **Aiguiser l'intelligence de qn,** to sharpen s.o.'s wits. **3.** (*a*) **Être, vivre, en bonne, mauvaise, intelligence avec qn,** to be, live, on good, bad, terms with s.o. **Être d'intelligence avec qn,** to have an understanding, be in collusion, with s.o. (*b*) *pl. Entretenir des intelligences avec qn,* to keep up a secret correspondence with s.o. **Avoir des intelligences avec l'ennemi,** to have dealings with the enemy.

intellig|ent [ɛ̃tɛl(l)iʒã], *a.* Intelligent; sharp, clever. *Il est i., F:* he has brains; he is brainy. *adv.* **-emment.**

intelligibilité [ɛ̃tɛlliʒibilite], *s.f.* Intelligibility.

intelligible [ɛ̃tɛlliʒibl], *a.* (*a*) Intelligible, understandable. (*b*) Clear, distinct. *adv.* **-ment.**

intempérance [ɛ̃tãpɛrã:s], *s.f.* Intemperance.

intempérant [ɛ̃tãperã], *a.* Intemperate.

intempéré [ɛ̃tãpere], *a.* Unrestrained, immoderate.

intempérie [ɛ̃tãperi], *s.f.* Inclemency (of weather). **Imperméable aux intempéries,** weatherproof.

intempest|if, -ive [ɛ̃tãpɛstif, -iːv], *a.* Untimely, ill-timed; unseasonable (remark); inopportune (arrival). *adv.* **-ivement.**

intenable [ɛ̃tnabl], *a.* Untenable, unmaintainable (position, etc.).

intendance [ɛ̃tãdã:s], *s.f.* Intendance, intendancy. **1.** (*a*) Stewardship (of estate). (*b*) Managership. **2.** *Fr.Hist:* Administration (of province). **3.** *Mil:* The Commissariat.

intendant [ɛ̃tãdã], *s.m.* Intendant. **1.** (*a*) Steward, bailiff. (*b*) Manager. **2.** *Fr.Hist:* Administrator (of province). **3.** *Mil:* Senior Commissariat officer.

intense [ɛ̃tã:s], *a.* Intense; severe (cold, pain, etc.); high (fever); intensive (propaganda); deep (blue, etc.). *Temps d'un froid i.*, intensely cold weather.

intensif, -ive [ɛ̃tãsif, -iːv], *a.* Intensive. *El: Courant i.*, heavy flow (of current).

intensifier [ɛ̃tãsifje], *v.tr.* To intensify.

intensité [ɛ̃tãsite], *s.f.* **1.** Intensity, intenseness; loudness (of sound); force (of wind); depth or strength (of colour). *El: I. du courant,* current strength. **2.** *Ling:* **Accent d'intensité,** stress.

intenter [ɛ̃tãte], *v.tr. Jur: I. une action, un procès, à, contre, qn,* to bring, enter, an action against s.o.

intention [ɛ̃tãsjɔ̃], *s.f.* Intention. (*a*) Purpose, design. *Jur:* Intent. **Avec intention délictueuse,** with malicious intent. **Sans mauvaise intention,** with no ill intent. **Avoir l'intention de faire qch.,** to intend to do sth.; to mean to do sth. **Faire qch. dans la meilleure intention,** to do sth. with the best intentions. **Faire qch. avec intention,** to do sth. deliberately, on purpose.. **Sans intention,** unintentionally, undesignedly. (*b*) Will, wish. *Mon i. est que vous le fassiez,* it is my will that you should do it; I intend you to do it. **Accepter l'intention pour le fait,** to take the will for the deed. **L'enfer est pavé de bonnes intentions,** (the road to) hell is paved with good intentions. **A l'intention de,** in honour of; for the sake of. *Voici un châle que j'ai acheté à votre i.*, here is a shawl that I bought expressly for you. *Cette remarque est à votre i., F:* that's a dig at you. **Dans l'intention de faire qch.,** with a view to doing sth. (*c*) *Surg:* **Réunion par première intention,** healing, reunion, by first intention.

intentionné [ɛ̃tãsjɔne], *a.* (Used only in) (*a*) **Bien, mal, intentionné,** well-, ill-disposed (*envers,* towards). **Mieux intentionné,** better disposed. (*b*) *Personne, démarche, bien intentionnée,* well-intentioned person, step.

intentionn|el, -elle [ɛ̃tãsjɔnɛl], *a.* Intentional, wilful, deliberate. *adv.* **-ellement.**

interallié [ɛ̃tɛralje], *a.* Interallied.

intercalaire [ɛ̃tɛrkalɛːr], *a.* **1.** Intercalary (day, year, etc.). **2.** *Bookb:* **Feuille i.,** interpolated sheet. *Feuillet i.,* inset.

intercalation [ɛ̃tɛrkalasjɔ̃], *s.f.* Intercalation, insertion. *El:* Switching in (of resistance).

intercaler [ɛ̃tɛrkale], *v.tr.* To intercalate (day in year, etc.). *El:* To cut in, switch in (resistance). *Le wagon-restaurant est intercalé à Orléans,* the dining-car is coupled up at Orleans.

intercéder [ɛ̃tɛrsede], *v.i.* (Conj. like CÉDER) To intercede (*auprès de,* with).

intercepter [ɛ̃tɛrsɛpte], *v.tr.* To intercept (letter, etc.); to shut out (light); to cut off, shut off (steam).

interception [ɛ̃tɛrsɛpsjɔ̃], *s.f.* Interception.

intercesseur [ɛ̃tɛrsɛsœːr], *s.m.* Intercessor.

intercession [ɛ̃tɛrsesjɔ̃], *s.f.* Intercession.

interchangeable [ɛ̃tɛrʃãʒabl], *a.* Interchangeable.

intercommunication [ɛ̃tɛrkɔmynikasjɔ̃], *s.f.* Intercommunication, through-communication (between railway carriages, etc.). *Train à i.,* corridor train.

interdiction [ɛ̃tɛrdiksjɔ̃], *s.f.* Interdiction. **1.** Prohibition, forbidding. **2.** *Jur:* (*a*) State of minority declared by court; deprival of control over money. (*b*) Suspension of civil rights (on account of a conviction).

interdire [ɛ̃tɛrdiːr], *v.tr.* (Conj. like DIRE, except *pr.ind.* v. **interdisez** and *imp.* **interdisez**) **1.** To forbid, prohibit. (*a*) *I. qch. à qn,* to forbid s.o. sth. "**Entrée interdite (au public),**" 'no admittance.' "**Passage interdit,**" 'no thoroughfare.' *Questions interdites à nos recherches,* questions into which we are forbidden to enquire. *Pièce interdite par la censure,* play banned by the censor. *I. à qn de faire qch.,* to prohibit s.o. from doing sth.; to forbid s.o. to do sth. (b) *I. qn de ses fonctions*, to suspend s.o. from the execution of his duties. *I. un prêtre*, to lay a priest under an interdict. *Jur:* **Faire interdire qn**, to have s.o. declared incapable of managing his own affairs. **2.** To disconcert, nonplus, bewilder.

interdit, -e. I. *a.* Disconcerted, nonplussed; abashed; taken aback. **2.** *s. Jur:* (a) Prodigal, lunatic, or convict under judicial disability. (b) **Interdit de séjour**, ex-convict prohibited from entering a certain area. **3.** *s.m. Ecc:* Interdict. **Frapper qn d'interdit**, to lay s.o. under an interdict.

interéssant [ɛ̃teresɑ̃], *a.* Interesting. *Son cas est i.*, his is a worthy case. *Prix intéressants*, attractive prices.

interésser [ɛ̃terese], *v.tr.* To interest. (a) *I. qn dans un commerce*, to give s.o. a financial interest, a partnership, in a business. (b) To affect, concern. *Cela m'intéresse peu*, that hardly concerns me, hardly affects me. (c) To be interesting to (s.o.). *Sujet qui m'intéresse beaucoup*, subject which interests me greatly, in which I am greatly interested. (d) *I. qn à une cause*, to interest s.o. in a cause.

s'intéresser. (a) *S'i. dans une affaire*, to become interested, to take up a partnership, in a venture. (b) *S'i. à qn, à qch.*, to take, feel, an interest in s.o., in sth.

interéssé, *a.* **I.** Interested. *Les parties intéressées*, *s.* **les intéressés**, the interested parties, the persons concerned. *Les premiers intéressés*, those most directly affected. **2.** Selfish, self-seeking. **Amour intéressé**, cupboard love.

intérêt [ɛ̃terɛ], *s.m.* Interest. **I.** Share, stake (in business, etc.). **Avoir un intérêt au jeu**, to have a stake in the game. **Mettre qn hors d'intérêt**, to buy, pay, s.o. out. **2.** Advantage, benefit. **Il y a intérêt à . . .**, it is desirable to. . . . **Il est de mon intérêt de le faire, j'ai intérêt à le faire**, it is to my interest to do it. *Agir dans son i.*, to act in, for, one's own interest. *L'i. public*, public interest. *Agir dans l'i. commun des peuples*, to act for the common good of the people. *Rail:* **Ligne d'intérêt local**, branch-line, local line. **3.** (Feeling of) interest. **Porter intérêt à qn**, to take an interest in s.o. *Ressentir de l'i. pour qn*, to feel interested in s.o. *Livre sans intérêt*, uninteresting book. **4.** *Fin:* **I. simple, composé**, simple, compound, interest. **Placer son argent à 5% d'intérêt**, to invest one's money at 5% interest. **Prêt à intérêt**, loan bearing interest. **Intérêt(s) couru(s)**, accrued interest. **Intérêts à échoir**, accruing interest. S.a. DOMMAGE 2.

interférence [ɛ̃terferɑ̃s], *s.f. Ph:* Interference.

interfolier [ɛ̃terfɔlje], *v.tr.* To interleave; to interpage (book).

intérieur [ɛ̃terjœːr]. **I.** *a.* (a) Interior; inner (room); internal (part); inland (sea). (b) Inward (feelings). *Vie intérieure*, inner life. (c) Domestic (administration). *Commerce i.*, home trade, inland trade. **2.** *s.m.* (a) Interior, inside. *Place d'i.*, inside seat (of bus). **A l'intérieur**, inside; on the inside. *A l'intérieur de la gare*, inside the station. *Dans l'i. du pays*, inland. (b) Home, house. *Vie d'i.*, home life, domestic life. *Femme d'i.*, domesticated woman. *Robe d'i.*, indoor frock. (c) *Adm:* **Le Ministère de l'Intérieur** = the Home Office. *Le Ministre de l'I.* = the Home Secretary. **3.** *s.m. Fb:* **Intérieur gauche**, inside left (player).

intérieurement [ɛ̃terjœrmɑ̃], *adv.* Inwardly, internally, inside, within. *Rire i.*, to laugh to oneself.

intérim [ɛ̃terim], *s.m.* Interim. **Dans l'intérim,**

in the interim; (in the) meanwhile. *Fin:* **Dividende par intérim**, (ad) interim dividend. **Faire l'intérim (de qn)**, to deputize (for s.o.); to act as locum tenens. *Assurer l'i.*, to carry on (during vacancy or absence).

intérimaire [ɛ̃terimɛːr]. **I.** *a.* Temporary, provisional, ad interim (duty, etc.). **2.** *s.* Deputy; locum tenens.

interjecter [ɛ̃terʒɛkte], *v.tr.* To ejaculate, to utter (cry of surprise, etc.).

interjection [ɛ̃terʒɛksjɔ̃], *s.f.* **I.** *Gram:* Interjection. **2.** *Jur:* **Interjection d'appel**, lodging of an appeal.

interjeter [ɛ̃terʒəte], *v.tr.* (Conj. like JETER) **I.** To interject (remark); to observe, bring in, (remark) incidentally. **2.** *Jur:* **Interjeter appel** (*d'un jugement*), to give notice of appeal.

interligne [ɛ̃terliɲ]. **I.** *s.m.* Space between two lines. *Mus:* Space (on the stave). *Dans les interlignes*, between the lines. **2.** *s.f. Typ:* Lead.

interlign|er [ɛ̃terliɲe], *v.tr.* **I.** To write between the lines of (a text); to interline. **2.** *Typ:* To lead out (type). *s.m.* **-age.**

interlinéaire [ɛ̃terlineɛːr], *a.* Interlinear (translation, etc.).

interlocuteur, -trice [ɛ̃terlɔkytœːr, -tris], *s.* Interlocutor, *f.* interlocutress; speaker (engaged in conversation).

interlocutoire [ɛ̃terlɔkytwaːr]. **I.** *a.* Interlocutory (judgment); provisional (order). **2.** *s.m.* Provisional order.

interlope [ɛ̃terlɔp], *a.* (a) Unauthorized, illegal, shady (trade, trader). (b) *F:* Suspect, dubious, shady (house, society, etc.).

interloquer [ɛ̃terlɔke], *v.tr.* To disconcert, nonplus, abash (s.o.).

s'interloquer, to be overcome by shyness; to get nervous (at interview, etc.).

intermède [ɛ̃termɛd], *s.m.* **I.** Medium, intermediary. **Par l'intermède de qch.**, through the medium, agency, of sth. **2.** *Th:* Interlude.

intermédiaire [ɛ̃termedjɛːr]. **I.** *a.* Intermediate, intervening (state, time). *Distance i.*, *plan i.*, middle distance. *Commerce i.*, middleman's business. *Mec.E:* **Arbre intermédiaire**, countershaft. **2.** *s.m.* Agent, intermediary, go-between. *Com:* Middleman. **3.** *s.m.* Intermediary, agency. (a) **Par l'intermédiaire de qn**, through the instrumentality of s.o.; through s.o. (b) *I.C.E:* **I. de poussoir**, tappet. *Phot:* **I. pour plaques**, plate-carrier, adapter. (c) *Mec.E:* Step-up gear, step-down gear. **4.** *s.m.* **Sans intermédiaire**, (to pass from one idea to another) without transition.

intermezzo [ɛ̃termedzo], *s.m. Mus:* Intermezzo.

interminable [ɛ̃terminabl], *a.* Interminable; endless (task); never-ending. *adv.* **-ment.**

intermittence [ɛ̃termittɑ̃s], *s.f.* Intermittency, intermittence. **Par intermittence**, intermittently.

intermitt|ent [ɛ̃termittɑ̃], *a.* Intermittent; irregular (pulse). *El:* **Courant intermittent**, make-and-break current. *adv.* **-emment.**

internat [ɛ̃terna], *s.m.* **I.** (a) Living-in (system, period). *Sch:* Boarding-in. (b) Resident medical studentship. **2.** Boarding-school.

international, -aux [ɛ̃ternasjɔnal, -o], *a.* International. *adv.* **-ement.**

interne [ɛ̃tern]. **I.** *a.* (a) Internal; inward (purity, etc.); inner (side). *Geom:* **Angle interne**, interior angle. *Gram:* **Objet interne**, cognate accusative. S.a. COMBUSTION. (b) *Élève i.*, boarder. **2.** *s.* (a) *Sch:* Boarder. (b) Resident medical student (in hospital).

intern|er [ɛ̃terne], *v.tr.* To intern (alien, etc.); to shut up, confine (madman). *s.m.* **-ement.**

internissable [ɛ̃tɛrnisabl], *a.* Untarnishable.

interpellateur, -trice [ɛ̃tɛrpɛl(l)atœːr, -tris], *s.* Interpellator.

interpellation [ɛ̃tɛrpɛl(l)asjɔ̃], *s.f.* **1.** (Sharp) question; interpellation, interruption (at meeting, etc.). **2.** Challenge (by sentry).

interpeller [ɛ̃tɛrpɛl(l)e], *v.tr.* **1.** *I. qn de dire la vérité,* to call upon s.o. to tell the truth. *Mil:* (Of sentry) To challenge (stranger). **2.** *Jur:* To summon (s.o.) to answer. **3.** *Pol:* (In Fr. Chamber) To call upon (minister, etc.) to account for his action; to interpellate.

interplanétaire [ɛ̃tɛrplanetɛːr], *a.* Interplanetary.

interpolation [ɛ̃tɛrpɔlasjɔ̃], *s.f.* Interpolation.

interpoler [ɛ̃tɛrpɔle], *v.tr.* To interpolate.

interposer [ɛ̃tɛrpoze], *v.tr.* To interpose, place (*entre,* between).
　s'interposer, to interpose, intervene; to come between.

interposition [ɛ̃tɛrpɔzisjɔ̃], *s.f.* **1.** Interposition. **2.** Intervention.

interprétation [ɛ̃tɛrpretasjɔ̃], *s.f.* **1.** Interpreting (of speech). **2.** (*a*) Interpretation. **Fausse interprétation,** misinterpretation, misconstruction (of statement). (*b*) *Mus: Th:* Rendering, interpretation. **3.** *Th:* Cast (of a play).

interprète [ɛ̃tɛrprɛt], *s.m. & f.* Interpreter.

interpréter [ɛ̃tɛrprete], *v.tr.* (j'interprète; j'interpréterai) To interpret. (*a*) To act as interpreter. *I. un discours,* to interpret a speech. (*b*) To explain (text, etc.). *I. des signaux,* to read, make out, signals. *Mal i. un signal,* to misread a signal. (*c*) *Mus: Th:* To render (work, part).

interrègne [ɛ̃tɛrrɛɲ], *s.m.* Interregnum.

interrogateur, -trice [ɛ̃tɛrɔɡatœːr, -tris]. **1.** *a.* Interrogatory, inquiring, questioning. **2.** *s.* Questioner, interrogator; *Sch:* examiner.

interrogatif, -ive [ɛ̃tɛrɔɡatif, -iːv], *a.* *Gram:* Interrogative.

interrogation [ɛ̃tɛrɔɡasjɔ̃], *s.f.* Interrogation. **1.** Questioning. *Gram:* Point d'interrogation, note of interrogation; question-mark. **2.** Question, query. *Sch:* Oral test; *F:* oral.

interrogatoire [ɛ̃tɛrɔɡatwaːr], *s.m.* (*a*) *Jur:* Interrogatory, examination (of defendant, etc.). *I. contradictoire,* cross-examination. (*b*) *Mil:* Questioning (of prisoners).

interroger [ɛ̃tɛrɔʒe], *v.tr.* (j'interrogeai(s); n. interrogeons) (*a*) To examine, interrogate (witness, etc.); to examine (candidate). (*b*) To consult (history, etc.); to sound (one's conscience).

interrompre [ɛ̃tɛrɔ̃ːpr], *v.tr.* (Conj. like ROMPRE) (*a*) To interrupt. (*b*) To intercept, interrupt (flow of river, etc.). (*c*) To stop, suspend (traffic, etc.); to cut short (conversation); to break off (negotiations); to break (journey) (*d*, at). *El:* To break, switch off (the current).
　s'interrompre, to break off; to stop (talking).

interrupteur, -trice [ɛ̃tɛryptœːr, -tris]. **1.** *s.* Interrupter. **2.** *s.m.* *El.E:* (*a*) Switch, contact-breaker, circuit-breaker. *I. à culbuteur, à bascule,* tumbler-switch. *I. d'escalier,* two-way switch. (*b*) Cut-out.

interruption [ɛ̃tɛrypsjɔ̃], *s.f.* (*a*) Interruption. (*b*) Stoppage, break; severance (of communication, etc.); breaking off (of negotiations). *El.E:* Disconnection, switching off; breaking (of current). **Sans interruption,** unceasingly; without a break.

inter-saison [ɛ̃tɛrsɛzɔ̃], *s.f.* *Sp:* Off season.

intersecté [ɛ̃tɛrsɛkte], *a.* *Arch:* Intersecting, interlacing.

intersection [ɛ̃tɛrsɛksjɔ̃], *s.f.* (*a*) Intersection. (*b*) Crossing (of roads, tracks).

intersession [ɛ̃tɛrsɛsjɔ̃], *s.f.* (Parliamentary) recess.

interstice [ɛ̃tɛrstis], *s.m.* Interstice; chink.

interurbain [ɛ̃tɛryrbɛ̃], *a.* Interurban. *Tp:* Lignes interurbaines, trunk-lines.

intervalle [ɛ̃tɛrval], *s.m.* Interval. **1.** Distance, gap, space (*entre,* between). **2.** Period (of time). *Visites à de longs intervalles,* visits at long intervals. **Par intervalles,** at intervals; now and then. *Dans l'i. . . .,* in the meantime. . . .

intervenir [ɛ̃tɛrvəniːr], *v.i.* (Conj. like VENIR. Aux. *être*) **1.** To intervene. (*a*) To interpose; *F:* to step in. *I. dans une conversation,* to break in on a conversation; *F:* to cut in. *Faire i. la force armée,* to call out the military. (*b*) To interfere. **2.** To happen, occur, arise. *Un accord est intervenu,* an agreement has been reached, concluded, arrived at.

intervention [ɛ̃tɛrvɑ̃sjɔ̃], *s.f.* **1.** Intervening, intervention. *Offre d'i.,* offer of mediation. **2.** Interference.

interversion [ɛ̃tɛrvɛrsjɔ̃], *s.f.* Inversion, transposition (of order, of dates).

intervertir [ɛ̃tɛrvɛrtiːr], *v.tr.* To invert, transpose; to reverse (the order of . . .). *Maintenant les rôles sont intervertis, F:* now the tables are turned.

interviewer [ɛ̃tɛrvju(v)e], *v.tr.* To interview.

intestat [ɛ̃tɛsta], *a.inv.* *Mourir i.,* to die intestate. **Hériter ab intestat,** to succeed to an intestate estate.

intestin¹ [ɛ̃tɛstɛ̃], *a.* Intestine. (*a*) Internal (parasites). (*b*) Domestic, civil (war).

intestin², *s.m.* *Anat:* Intestine, bowel, gut. *Gros i.,* large intestine. *I. grêle,* small intestine. **Les intestins,** the bowels.

intestinal, -aux [ɛ̃tɛstinal, -o], *a.* Intestinal.

intimation [ɛ̃timasjɔ̃], *s.f.* **1.** Notification (*d'un ordre,* of an order). *I. de vider les lieux,* notice to quit. **2.** *Jur:* Notice of appeal.

intime [ɛ̃tim], *a.* Intimate. **1.** Interior, inward, deep-seated (conviction, grief, etc.). *Sens i. d'un passage,* inner meaning of a passage. **2.** Close. *Ami i.,* particular, intimate, close, friend. *Dîner i.,* homely, quiet, dinner. *s.* Un, une, intime, an intimate friend. *Ses intimes savent que . . .,* his intimates know that. . . . **3.** *Secrétaire i.,* private secretary. *adv.* **-ment.**

intimer [ɛ̃time], *v.tr.* *I. qch. à qn,* to intimate sth. to s.o.; to notify s.o. of sth.

intimé, -ée, *s.* Respondent, defendant (before Court of Appeal).

intimidable [ɛ̃timidabl], *a.* Easily intimidated.

intimidant [ɛ̃timidɑ̃], *a.* Intimidating, awe-inspiring.

intimidateur, -trice [ɛ̃timidatœːr, -tris]. **1.** *a.* Intimidating, intimidatory. **2.** *s.* Intimidator.

intimidation [ɛ̃timidasjɔ̃], *s.f.* Intimidation; threatening; undue influence.

intimider [ɛ̃timide], *v.tr.* (*a*) To intimidate, frighten; to cow. *Il nous intimidait,* we stood in awe of him. *Nullement intimidé,* nothing daunted. (*b*) *Jur:* To threaten; to exert undue influence on (s.o.).
　s'intimider, to become self-conscious; to get nervous.

intimité [ɛ̃timite], *s.f.* **1.** Deepest parts, depths (of one's being, etc.). *Dans l'i. de la conscience,* in his inner conscience. **2.** Intimacy. (*a*) Close connection (between actions, etc.). (*b*) Closeness (of friendship). (*c*) *L'i. du chez-soi,* the privacy of one's home. **Il avait des goûts d'intimité,** he enjoyed home life.

intituler [ɛ̃tityle], *v.tr.* To entitle, give a title to (book, person, etc.). *Article intitulé* . . ., article headed. . . .
   intitulé, *s.m.* Title (of document, of book, etc.); heading (of chapter, etc.).
intolérable [ɛ̃tɔlɛrabl], *a.* Intolerable, insufferable, unbearable, unendurable. *Vie i.*, life that is not worth living. *adv.* **-ment.**
intolérance [ɛ̃tɔlerɑ̃:s], *s.f.* Intolerance.
intolér|ant [ɛ̃tɔlerɑ̃], *a.* Intolerant (*de*, of). *adv.* **-amment.**
intonation [ɛ̃tɔnasjɔ̃], *s.f.* Intonation.
intoxicant [ɛ̃tɔksikɑ̃], *a.* Poisonous, toxic.
intoxication [ɛ̃tɔksikasjɔ̃], *s.f. Med:* Poisoning.
intoxiquer [ɛ̃tɔksike], *v.tr. Med:* To poison; esp. (of food, etc.) to cause auto-intoxication.
intrados [ɛ̃trado], *s.m. Arch:* Inner surface, soffit, intrados (of arch).
intraduisible [ɛ̃tradɥizibl], *a.* Untranslatable.
intraitable [ɛ̃trɛtabl], *a.* **1.** *Med:* Beyond treatment. **2.** (*a*) Intractable, unmanageable. (*b*) Obstinate, stiff-necked, uncompromising.
intra-muros [ɛ̃tramyro:s], *a.* **1.** *adv.* Within the (city) walls. **2.** *a.inv.* Intramural.
intransférable [ɛ̃trɑ̃sferabl], *a.* Untransferable. *Jur:* Unassignable (right, etc.).
intransigeance [ɛ̃trɑ̃ziʒɑ̃:s], *s.f.* Intransigence; uncompromisingness; strictness.
intransigeant [ɛ̃trɑ̃ziʒɑ̃], *a.* Intransigent (in politics); uncompromising, strict (moral code, etc.); peremptory (tone).
intransit|if, -ive [ɛ̃trɑ̃zitif, -i:v], *a. Gram:* Intransitive. *adv.* **-ivement.**
intransportable [ɛ̃trɑ̃spɔrtabl], *a.* (*a*) Untransportable. (*b*) (Of wounded man) Not fit to travel.
intraversable [ɛ̃traversabl], *a.* Untraversable; that cannot be crossed.
in-trente-deux [ɛ̃trɑ̃tdø], *a. & s.m.inv. Typ:* Thirtytwomo.
intrépide [ɛ̃trepid], *a.* Intrepid, dauntless, undaunted, bold, fearless. *Menteur i.*, brazen(-faced) liar. *adv.* **-ment.**
intrépidité [ɛ̃trepidite], *s.f.* Intrepidity, dauntlessness, fearlessness.
intrigant, -ante [ɛ̃trigɑ̃, -ɑ̃:t]. **1.** *a.* Intriguing, scheming, designing. **2.** *s.* Intriguer, schemer, wire-puller.
intrigue [ɛ̃trig], *s.f.* Intrigue. **1.** (*a*) Plot, scheme. *Une i. de cour*, a court intrigue. (*b*) (Love-)affair, intrigue. **2.** Plot (of play).
intriguer [ɛ̃trige]. **1.** *v.tr.* To puzzle; *F:* to intrigue (s.o.). **2.** *v.i.* To scheme, plot, intrigue.
intrinsèque [ɛ̃trɛ̃sɛk], *a.* Intrinsic; specific (value). *adv.* **-ment,** **-ally.**
introducteur, -trice [ɛ̃trɔdyktœ:r, -tris], *s.* (*a*) Introducer. (*b*) Usher (at reception).
introductif, -ive [ɛ̃trɔdyktif, -i:v], *a.* Introductory introductive.
introduction [ɛ̃trɔdyksjɔ̃], *s.f.* Introduction. **1.** (*a*) Insertion (of probe in wound, etc.). *Mch:* Admission, induction (of steam, gas, etc.). (*b*) Introducing, bringing in (of s.o. into s.o.'s presence, etc.). *Lettre d'i.*, letter of introduction (*de la part de*, from). **2.** Introductory matter or chapter. *Après quelques mots d'i.*, after a few introductory words.
introduire [ɛ̃trɔdɥi:r], *v.tr.* (*pr.p.* introduisant; *p.p.* introduit; *pr.ind.* j'introduis, il introduit, n. introduisons; *p.h.* j'introduisis; *fu.* j'introduirai) To introduce. (*a*) To insert, put (key in lock, etc.). (*b*) To bring in (goods, etc.); to admit, let in (steam). *I. une mode*, to bring in a fashion. (*c*) To usher in. *Introduisez ce monsieur*, show the gentleman in.

s'introduire, to get in, enter. *S'i. dans la société*, to worm one's way into society. *L'eau s'introduit partout*, the water is penetrating, creeping in, everywhere.
introït [ɛ̃trɔit], *s.m. Ecc:* Introit.
intronisation [ɛ̃trɔnizasjɔ̃], *s.f.* **1.** Enthroning, enthronement (esp. of bishop). **2.** Establishment (of system, etc.).
introniser [ɛ̃trɔnize], *v.tr.* **1.** To (en)throne (king, bishop). **2.** To set up, establish (new religion, etc.).
   s'introniser. (*a*) *S'i. chez qn*, to establish oneself in s.o.'s household. (*b*) (Of custom, etc.) To become established.
introspectif, -ive [ɛ̃trɔspɛktif, -i:v], *a.* Introspective.
introspection [ɛ̃trɔspɛksjɔ̃], *s.f.* Introspection.
introuvable [ɛ̃truvabl], *a.* (*a*) Undiscoverable; not to be found; untraceable. (*b*) *F:* Peerless, matchless.
introverti, -ie [ɛ̃trɔvɛrti], *a. Psy:* Introverted. *s.* Introvert.
intrus, -use [ɛ̃try, -y:z]. **1.** *a.* Intruding. **2.** *s.* Intruder; *F:* gate-crasher. *Jur:* Trespasser.
intrusion [ɛ̃tryzjɔ̃], *s.f.* (*a*) Intrusion. **Faire intrusion auprès de qn**, to intrude upon s.o. (*b*) *Jur:* Trespass.
intuit|if, -ive [ɛ̃tɥitif, -i:v], *a.* Intuitive. *adv.* **-ivement.**
intuition [ɛ̃tɥisjɔ̃], *s.f.* Intuition.
intumescence [ɛ̃tymɛssɑ̃:s], *s.f.* Swelling (up), intumescence.
intumescent [ɛ̃tymɛssɑ̃], *a.* Intumescent.
inusable [inyzabl], *a.* Hard-wearing; that wears for ever; everlasting.
inusité [inyzite], *a.* (*a*) Unusual. (*b*) Not in common use.
inutile [inytil], *a.* (*a*) Useless, unavailing, unprofitable; vain, bootless (effort). *Je suis i. ici*, I am of no use here. (*b*) Needless, unnecessary. *C'est i.!* (i) it's no good! (ii) you need not trouble. **Inutile de dire que** . . ., needless to say that. . . . *adv.* **-ment.**
inutilisable [inytilizabl], *a.* Unserviceable.
inutilisé [inytilize], *a.* Unutilised.
inutilité [inytilite], *s.f.* **1.** (*a*) Inutility, uselessness. (*b*) Needlessness, unnecessariness. **2.** *Apprendre des inutilités*, to learn useless things.
invaincu [ɛ̃vɛ̃ky], *a.* Unconquered, unvanquished.
invalidation [ɛ̃validasjɔ̃], *s.f. Jur:* Invalidation (of document, election).
invalide [ɛ̃valid]. **1.** *a.* (*a*) Invalid, infirm; disabled (soldier, etc.). (*b*) *Jur:* Invalid (will, etc.); null and void. **2.** *a.* (*a*) Invalid. (*b*) *s.m.* Disabled soldier; pensioner. **L'Hôtel des Invalides,** *s.m.pl.* **les Invalides,** the army pensioners' hospital (in Paris).
invalider [ɛ̃valide], *v.tr. Jur:* To invalidate (will, election, etc.); to quash (election).
invalidité [ɛ̃validite], *s.f.* **1.** (*a*) Infirmity. *Adm:* Disablement, disability. (*b*) Chronic ill-health; invalidism. **2.** *Jur:* Invalidity (of will, etc.).
invar [ɛ̃va:r], *s.m.* Invar (metal); invar steel.
invariabilité [ɛ̃varjabilite], *s.f.* Invariability.
invariable [ɛ̃varjabl], *a.* Invariable, unvarying. *adv.* **-ment.**
invasion [ɛ̃vazjɔ̃], *s.f.* Invasion; inroad. *Faire une i. dans un pays*, to invade a country.
invective [ɛ̃vɛkti:v], *s.f.* (*a*) Invective. (*b*) *pl.* Abuse.
invectiver [ɛ̃vɛktive]. **1.** *v.i. I. contre qn*, to inveigh against s.o. **2.** *v.tr. F:* To abuse, blackguard (s.o.); to call (s.o.) names.

invendable [ɛ̃vãdabl], *a.* Unsaleable.

invendu [ɛ̃vãdy], *a.* Unsold.

inventaire [ɛ̃vãtɛːr], *s.m.* Inventory. (*a*) Faire, dresser, un inventaire, to draw up an inventory. Sous bénéfice d'inventaire, conditionally ; with reservations. *Accepter une succession sous bénéfice d'i.*, to accept an estate, without liability to debts beyond the assets descended. (*b*) *Com*: Stocklist. Établissement, levée, d'inventaire, stocktaking. Faire, dresser, l'inventaire, to take stock.

inventer [ɛ̃vãte], *v.tr.* To invent. (*a*) To find out, discover. *F*: Il n'a pas inventé la poudre, he will never set the Thames on fire. *(b)* To devise, contrive (machine, etc.) ; to make up (story).

inventeur [ɛ̃vãtœːr], *s.m.* (*a*) Inventor, discoverer (of process, etc.). (*b*) *Jur*: Finder (of lost object, etc.).

inventif, -ive [ɛ̃vãtif, -iːv], *a.* Inventive.

invention [ɛ̃vãsjɔ̃], *s.f.* **1.** (*a*) Invention, inventing, contriving. Nécessité est mère d'invention, necessity is the mother of invention. (*b*) Imagination, inventiveness. **2.** (*a*) Invention, contrivance, device. (*b*) Fabrication, lie.

inventorier [ɛ̃vãtɔrje], *v.tr.* To inventory, make a list of (goods, etc.). *Abs.* To take stock.

invérifiable [ɛ̃verifjabl], *a.* Unverifiable.

invérifié [ɛ̃verifje], *a.* Unverified (statement).

inversable [ɛ̃vɛrsabl], *a.* That cannot overturn ; uncapsizable (boat).

inverse [ɛ̃vɛrs]. **1.** *a.* Inverse, inverted, opposite, contrary. En sens inverse (*de qch.*), in the opposite direction (to sth.). En ordre inverse, in the reverse order. *Mth*: En raison inverse de qch., in inverse ratio to sth. *Book-k*: *Écriture i.*, contra entry ; set-off. **2.** *s.m.* Opposite, reverse. A l'inverse du bon sens, (in a manner) contrary to reason. **3.** *s.f. Mth*: Inverse (function, etc.) ; reciprocal. *adv.* **-ment.**

inverser [ɛ̃vɛrse], *v.tr.* To reverse (current, image, result, etc.). *I.C.E*: Carburateur inversé, down-draught carburettor.

inverseur [ɛ̃vɛrsœːr], *s.m.* Reversing device. *El.E*: *I. du courant*, current reverser ; change-over switch.

inversion [ɛ̃vɛrsjɔ̃], *s.f.* **1.** (*a*) *Gram*: *Mus*: Inversion. (*b*) Transposition. **2.** Reversal (of current). *Mch*: Inversion de marche, reversing.

invertébré [ɛ̃vɛrtebre], *a.* Invertebrate.

invertir [ɛ̃vɛrtiːr], *v.tr.* **1.** To reverse (motion, etc.). **2.** *Opt*: To invert, reverse, erect, the image of (object).

investigateur, -trice [ɛ̃vɛstigatœːr, -tris]. **1.** *a.* Investigating, inquiring ; searching (glance). **2.** *s.* Investigator, inquirer.

investigation [ɛ̃vɛstigasjɔ̃], *s.f.* Investigation, inquiry.

investir¹ [ɛ̃vɛstiːr], *v.tr.* To invest. Investir qn d'une fonction, to endue, invest, vest, s.o. with an office.

invest|ir², *v.tr.* To beleaguer, hem in, invest (town, etc.). *s.m.* **-issement.**

investir³, *v.tr.* To invest (money).

investiture [ɛ̃vɛstityːr], *s.f.* Investiture ; induction (of bishop).

invétérer (s') [sɛ̃vetere], *v.pr.* (il s'invétère ; il s'invétérera) (Of evil, etc.) To take deep root ; to become inveterate.

invétéré, *a.* Inveterate ; deeply rooted (hatred, etc.) ; confirmed, irreclaimable (drunkard, criminal) ; intractable (disease).

invincibilité [ɛ̃vɛ̃sibilite], *s.f.* Invincibility.

invincible [ɛ̃vɛ̃sibl], *a.* Invincible, unconquerable ; insuperable (difficulty). *adv.* **-ment.**

inviolabilité [ɛ̃vjɔlabilite], *s.f.* Inviolability, inviolacy ; sacredness (of office).

inviolable [ɛ̃vjɔlabl], *a.* Inviolable ; sacred (office, etc.). *adv.* **-ment.**

invisibilité [ɛ̃vizibilite], *s.f.* Invisibility.

invisible [ɛ̃vizibl], *a.* Invisible.

invitant [ɛ̃vitã]. **1.** *a.* Attractive, inviting. **2.** *s.m. Sp*: Les invitants, the challengers.

invitation [ɛ̃vitasjɔ̃], *s.f.* Invitation. *Venir sur l'i.* de qn, to come at s.o.'s invitation, at s.o.'s request. Venir sans invitation, to come uninvited.

invite [ɛ̃vit], *s.f.* **1.** Invitation, inducement. **2.** *Cards*: Lead ; call (for a suit). *I. d'atout*, call for trumps. *Répondre à l'i. de qn*, (i) to return s.o.'s lead ; (ii) *F*: to respond to s.o.'s advances.

inviter [ɛ̃vite], *v.tr.* To invite. **1.** *I. qn à dîner*, to invite, ask, s.o. to dinner. *Être déjà invité pour ce soir*, to be already engaged, booked, for this evening. *I. qn à entrer*, to invite s.o. in. **2.** (*a*) *I. le désastre*, to court disaster. (*b*) *I. qn à faire qch*, (i) to invite, request, s.o. to do sth. ; (ii) to tempt s.o. to do sth. *Cards*: Inviter atout, to call for trumps.

invité, -ée, *s.* Guest.

invocation [ɛ̃vɔkasjɔ̃], *s.f.* Invocation.

invocatoire [ɛ̃vɔkatwaːr], *a.* Invocatory.

involontaire [ɛ̃vɔlɔ̃tɛːr], *a.* Involuntary, unintentional. *adv.* **-ment.**

involution [ɛ̃vɔlysjɔ̃], *s.f.* Involution.

invoquer [ɛ̃vɔke], *v.tr.* **1.** (*a*) To call upon, to invoke (the Deity, etc.). *I. l'aide de la justice*, to appeal to the law. (*b*) To invoke, call forth (a spirit). **2.** *I. une raison, un motif*, to set forth, put forward, a reason, a motive.

invraisemblable [ɛ̃vrɛsãblabl], *a.* Lacking in verisimilitude ; unlikely, improbable ; hard to believe. *adv.* **-ment.**

invraisemblance [ɛ̃vrɛsãblãːs], *s.f.* **1.** Unlikelihood, unlikeliness, improbability. **2.** Fact or statement hard to believe.

invulnérabilité [ɛ̃vylnɛrabilite], *s.f.* Invulnerability.

invulnérable [ɛ̃vylnɛrabl], *a.* Invulnerable. *adv.* **-ment.**

iode [jɔd, iɔd], *s.m.* Iodıne. Teinture d'iode, tincture of iodine.

ioder [jɔde, iɔ-], *v.tr. Med*: *Phot*: To iodize.

iodhydrique [jɔdidrik], *a. Ch*: Hydriodic.

iodique [jɔdik, iɔ-], *a. Ch*: Iodic.

iodoforme [jɔdɔfɔrm, iɔ-], *s.m.* Iodoform.

iodoformé [jɔdɔfɔrme], *a.* Iodoformized (gauze).

iodure [jɔdyːr, iɔ-], *s.m. Ch*: Iodide.

iodurer [jɔdyre, iɔ-], *v.tr.* To iodize.

ion [iɔ̃], *s.m. El*: *Ph*: *Ch*: Ion.

ionique¹ [iɔnik], *a. Arch*: Ionic (order, etc.).

ionique², *a. W.Tel*: Thermionic (valve).

ionisant [iɔnizã], *s.m. El*: *Ph*: *Ch*: Ionizer.

ionisation [iɔnizasjɔ̃], *s.f.* Ionization.

ioniser [iɔnize], *v.tr. Ph*: *Ch*: To ionize.

iota [jɔta], *s.m. Gr.Alph*: Iota. *F*: Pas un iota, not a jot, not an iota ; not one jot or tittle.

iouler [jule], *v.i. Mus*: To yodel.

ipécacuana [ipɛkakyana], *s.m.*, *F*: **ipéca** [ipɛka], *s.m. Pharm*: Ipecacuanha, ipecac.

ipréau [ipreo], *s.m. F*: White poplar.

ir-ai, -as, etc. See ALLER.

Irak [irak]. *Pr.n. Geog*: Irak, Iraq.

irakien, -ienne [irakjɛ̃, -jɛn], *a. & s.* Iraqui.

irascibilité [irassibilite], *s.f.* Irascibility, irascibleness ; hot temper ; testiness.

irascible [irasibl], *a.* Irascible, irritable, testy, *F*: peppery.

iridescence [iridɛssãːs], *s.f.* Iridescence.

iridescent [iridɛssã], *a.* Iridescent.

iridium [iridjɔm], *s.m. Ch:* Iridium.
Iris [iris]. **1.** *Pr.n.f. Myth:* Iris. **2.** *s.m.* (a) Iris, rainbow(-like play of colours); prismatic halo. (b) *Anat:* Iris (of eye). *Phot:* Diaphragme iris, iris diaphragm. **3.** *s. m. or f. Bot:* Iris, flag. *I. jaune, des marais,* yellow iris. **Racine d'iris,** orris-root.
irisation [irizasjɔ̃], *s.f.* Iridescence, irisation.
iriser [irize], *v.tr.* To make iridescent. **s'iriser,** to become iridescent.
irisé, *a.* Iridescent, rainbow-hued.
irlandais, -aise [irlɔ̃dɛ, -ɛːz]. **1.** *a.* Irish. **2.** *s.* Irishman; Irishwoman, Irish girl. **Les Irlandais,** the Irish. **3.** *s.m. Ling:* Irish, Erse.
Irlande [irlɑ̃ːd]. *Pr.n.f. Geog:* Ireland.
ironie [irɔni], *s.f.* Irony.
ironique [irɔnik], *a.* Ironic(al). *adv.* **-ment,** -ally.
ironiser [irɔnize], *v.i.* To speak ironically.
ironiste [irɔnist], *s.m. & f.* Ironist.
iroquois, -oise [irɔkwa, -waːz], *a. & s.* Iroquois (Indian). *A:* **Drôle d'Iroquois,** rum old card.
irraccommodable [irrakɔmɔdabl], *a.* Unmendable.
irradiation [irradjasjɔ̃], *s.f.* Irradiation. *Phot:* Halation.
irradier [irradje], *v.i.* To (ir)radiate; (of pain, cancer, etc.) to spread.
irraisonnable [irrɛzɔnabl], *a.* Irrational, unreasoning. *adv.* **-ment.**
irraisonné [irrɛzɔne], *a.* Unreasoned.
irrassasiable [irrasazjabl], *a.* Insatiable (de, of).
irrationnel, -elle [irrasjɔnɛl], *a.* Irrational (action, *Mth:* quantity).
irréalisable [irrealizabl], *a.* Unrealizable.
irrecevable [irrəsəvabl], *a.* Inadmissible (evidence); unacceptable (theory).
irréconciliable [irrekɔ̃siljabl], *a.* Irreconcilable. *adv.* **-ment.**
irrécouvrable [irrekuvrabl], *a.* Irrecoverable, unrecoverable (loss).
irrécusable [irrekyzabl], *a.* Unimpeachable, unexceptionable, irrecusable (evidence, etc.); unchallengeable (juryman, evidence).
irréductible [irredyktibl], *a.* **1.** Irreducible (equation, dislocation). *Ar: Fraction i.,* fraction in its lowest terms. **2.** Indomitable; unshakeable (attachment to s.o.); unyielding.
irréel, -elle [irreel], *a.* Unreal.
irréfléchi [irrefleʃi], *a.* **1.** Unconsidered, thoughtless (action). **2.** Hasty, rash, unthinking.
irréflexion [irreflɛksjɔ̃], *s.f.* Thoughtlessness.
irréfragable [irrefragabl], *a.* Irrefragable.
irréfutable [irrefytabl], *a.* Irrefutable, indisputable. *adv.* **-ment.**
irréfuté [irrefyte], *a.* Unrefuted.
irrégularité [irregylarite], *s.f.* **1.** Irregularity. **2.** Unpunctuality.
irrégulier, -ière [irregylje, -jɛːr]. **1.** *a.* (a) Irregular. (b) Unpunctual. **2.** *s.m.* Guerrillero; partisan. Esp. *pl.* Irregulars. *adv.* **-èrement.**
irréligieux, -euse [irrelixjø, -øːz], *a.* Irreligious.
irrémédiable [irremedjabl], *a.* Irremediable (loss); irreparable (injury). *adv.* **-ment.**
irremplaçable [irrɔ̃plasabl], *a.* Irreplaceable.
irréparable [irreparabl], *a.* Irreparable (wrong); irretrievable (loss, mistake). *adv.* **-ment.**
irespréhensible [irrepreɑ̃sibl], *a.* Blameless.
irrépressible [irrepresibl], **irréprimable** [irreprimabl], *a.* Irrepressible.
irréprochable [irreprɔʃabl], *a.* Irreproachable; faultless (attire, etc.). *adv.* **-ment.**
irrésistible [irrezistibl], *a.* Irresistible. *adv.* **-ment.**

irrésolu [irrezɔly], *a.* **1.** Irresolute, wavering (nature); faltering (steps). **2.** Unsolved (problem). *adv.* **-ment.**
irrésoluble [irrezɔlybl], *a.* **1.** Irresolvable (nebula). **2.** Unsolvable (problem).
irrésolution [irrezɔlysjɔ̃], *s.f.* Irresolution, indecision.
irrespectueu|x, -euse [irrɛspɛktɥø, -øːz], *a.* Disrespectful (pour, envers, to, towards). *adv.* **-sement.**
irrespirable [irrɛspirabl], *a.* Unbreathable, irrespirable (gas, etc.).
irresponsabilité [irrɛspɔ̃sabilite], *s.f.* Irresponsibility.
irresponsable [irrɛspɔ̃sabl], *a.* Irresponsible.
irrévérence [irreverɑ̃ːs], *s.f.* Irreverence.
irrévérencieux, -euse [irreverɑ̃sjø, -øːz], *a.* Irreverent; disrespectful, *F:* cheeky.
irréversible [irreversibl], *a. Mec.E:* Irreversible (gear, etc.); non-reversing.
irrévocable [irrevɔkabl], *a.* Irrevocable; binding (agreement). *Jur: Décret i.,* decree absolute. *adv.* **-ment.**
irrigable [irrigabl], *a.* (a) Irrigable. (b) Floodable.
irrigateur [irrigatœːr], *s.m.* (a) Garden-hose, street-hose. (b) Enema, douche.
irrigation [irrigasjɔ̃], *s.f.* **1.** *Agr:* (a) Irrigation. (b) Flooding. **2.** Spraying (of wound, etc.); douching.
irriguer [irrige], *v.tr.* **1.** *Agr:* (a) To irrigate. (b) To flood. **2.** *Med:* To irrigate, spray, douche.
irritabilité [irritabilite], *s.f.* Irritability. **1.** Sensitiveness; reaction to stimulus. **2.** Irritableness (of temper); testiness, touchiness.
irritable [irritabl], *a.* Irritable. **1.** Sensitive (skin, etc.). **2.** Testy, touchy.
irritant [irritɑ̃]. **1.** *a.* Irritating, *F:* aggravating. **2.** *a. & s.m. Med:* Irritant.
irritation [irritasjɔ̃], *s.f.* Irritation.
irriter [irrite], *v.tr.* To irritate. **s'irriter. 1.** To grow angry (contre qn, with s.o.; de qch., at sth.). **2.** (Of sore, etc.) To become irritated, inflamed.
irruption [irrypsjɔ̃], *s.f.* Irruption. (a) Invasion, raid. **Faire irruption dans une salle,** to burst, rush, into a room. (b) Overflow, flood (of river); inrush (of water).
Isabelle [izabɛl]. **1.** *Pr.n.f.* Isabel(la). **2.** *a.inv.* Biscuit-coloured, cream-coloured. *Cheval i.,* light-bay horse.
Isaïe [izai]. *Pr.n.m. B.Hist:* Isaiah.
isard [izaːr], *s.m. Z:* Izard; wild goat.
Isengrin [izɑ̃grɛ̃]. *Pr.n.m.* Isengrim. (The Wolf in the *Roman de Renart.*)
Islam [islam], *s.m. Rel:* Islam.
islamique [islamik], *a.* Islamic, Islamitic.
islamisme [islamism], *s.m.* Islamism.
islandais, -aise [islɑ̃dɛ, -ɛːz]. *Geog:* **1.** *a.* Icelandic. **2.** (a) *s.* Icelander. (b) *s.m. Ling:* **L'islandais,** Icelandic.
Islande [islɑ̃ːd]. *Pr.n.f. Geog:* Iceland.
isobare [izɔbaːr], **isobarique** [izɔbarik], **isobarométrique** [izɔbarɔmetrik], *a. Meteor:* Isobaric. *s.f. Isobare,* isobaric curve; isobar.
isocèle [izɔsɛl], *a. Geom:* Isosceles (triangle).
isochromatique [izɔkrɔmatik], *a. Opt: Phot:* Isochromatic.
isochrone [izɔkrɔn], **isochronique** [izɔkrɔnik], *a. Mec:* Isochronous, isochronal, isochronic.
isolable [izɔlabl], *a.* **1.** Isolable. **2.** Insulatable.
isolant [izɔlɑ̃]. **1.** *a.* (a) Isolating. (b) Insulating. **Bouteille isolante,** vacuum-flask, thermos flask.

Cabine isolante, sound-proof box. *El.E: Ruban i.*, insulating tape. **2.** *s.m.* Insulator.

isolateur, -trice [izɔlatœːr, -tris]. *El:* **1.** *a.* Insulating. **2.** *s.m.* Insulator. *I. d'étincelles*, spark-box.

isolement [izolmɑ̃], *s.m.* **1.** Isolation, loneliness. **2.** *El.E:* Insulation.

isolément [izɔlemɑ̃], *adv.* Separately, individually; solitarily; singly.

isoler [izole], *v.tr.* **1.** To isolate (*de, d'avec*, from). **2.** *El.E:* To insulate.

isolé, *a.* **1.** Isolated; detached (house, etc.); lonely, remote (spot, etc.). *Il se tient i. de la foule*, he stands aloof from the crowd. **2.** *El.E:* Insulated.

isoloir [izɔlwaːr], *s.m.* **1.** *El:* Insulator. **2.** Polling-booth.

isomère [izɔmɛːr]. **1.** *c. Ch:* *Bot:* Isomerous, isomeric. **2.** *s.m. Ch:* Isomer.

isomérie [izɔmeri], *s.f.,* **isomérisme** [izɔmerism], *s.m. Ch:* Isomerism.

isomorphe [izɔmɔrf]. **1.** *a. Cryst: Mth: etc:* Isomorphous, isomorphic. **2.** *s.m.* Isomorph.

isoscèle [izɔsɛl], *a.* = ISOCÈLE.

isotherme [izɔtɛrm]. *Meteor:* **1.** *a.* Isothermal (line). **2.** *s.f.* Isotherm.

isotope [izɔtɔp], *s.m. Ch:* Isotope.

isotrope [izɔtrɔp], *a. Ch: Ph:* Isotropic.

Israël [israɛl, iz-]. *Pr.n.m. B.Hist:* Israel.

Israélite [israelit, iz-]. *B.Hist:* **1.** *s.m. & f.* Israelite, Jew. **2.** *a.* Israelitish (woman, etc.); Israelitic (history).

issu [isy], *a.* Descended (*de*, from); born (*de*, of).

issue [isy], *s.f.* **1.** Issue, end, conclusion. *A l'issue de la réunion*, at the end, close, of the meeting. **2.** Exit; outlet (of tunnel, etc.). *Chemin sans issue*, blind path; dead-end. *Se ménager une issue*, to prepare a loop-hole of escape. **3.** (*a*) (Butchery) offal. (*b*) *pl. Mill: Issues de blé*, sharps, middlings. (*c*) *pl. Ind:* By-products.

Istamboul [istɑ̃bul]. *Pr.n.m. Geog:* Istanbul.

isthme [ism], *s.m. Geog: Anat:* Isthmus.

isthmien, -ienne [ismjɛ̃, -jɛn], *a.,* **isthmique** [ismik], *a.* Isthmian, isthmic (canal, games, etc.).

itague [itag], *s.f. Nau:* Tie. **Palan sur itague,** runner and tackle.

Italie [itali]. *Pr.n.f.* Italy. S.a. PAILLE 1, PÂTE 1.

italien, -ienne [italjɛ̃, -jɛn], *a. & s.* Italian.

italique [italik]. **1.** *a. Typ:* Italic (type). **2.** *a. & s.m. Typ:* Italic (type); italics. **2.** *a. Ethn:* Italic (race).

item [itɛm], *adv.* Item, likewise, also.

itérat|if, -ive [iteratif, -iːv], *a.* **1.** *Jur:* Reiterated (prohibition, etc.). **2.** *Gram:* Iterative (verb). *adv.* **-ivement.**

itération [iterasjɔ̃], *s.f.* Repetition; iteration.

Ithaque [itak]. *Pr.n.f. A.Geog:* Ithaca.

itinéraire [itinerɛːr]. **1.** *a.* Concerning roads. *Mesures itinéraires*, road measurements. *Colonne i.*, direction-post. **2.** *s.m.* Itinerary. (*a*) Route, way. (*b*) Road-book, guide-book.

itinérant [itinerɑ̃], *a.* Itinerant.

iule [jyl], *s.m.* **1.** *Bot:* Catkin, spike, amentum. **2.** *Myr:* Iulus, galley-worm.

ivoire [ivwaːr], *s.m.* Ivory. **1.** *I. vert*, raw ivory, live ivory. **Noir d'ivoire,** ivory-black. *Geog:* **La Côte d'Ivoire,** the Ivory Coast. **2.** Ivory (statuette, curio, etc.).

ivoirerie [ivwarəri], *s.f.* **1.** Ivory trade. **2.** Ivory work.

ivraie [ivrɛ], *s.f. Bot:* **1.** (*a*) Cockle, darnel. (*b*) *B.Lit:* Tares. **Séparer l'ivraie d'avec le bon grain,** to separate the wheat from the tares. **2.** Ivraie vivace, fausse ivraie, rye-grass.

ivre [iːvr], *a.* Drunk, intoxicated. *A moitié i.*, half-tipsy; *F:* half-seas-over. *I. mort*, dead drunk. *I. de joie*, mad with joy.

ivresse [ivrɛs], *s.f.* (*a*) Intoxication, inebriety. *Jur:* En état d'ivresse publique = drunk and disorderly. (*b*) *Lit:* Rapture, ecstasy.

ivrogne [ivrɔɲ]. **1.** *s.m.* Drunkard, tippler, toper. *Nez d'i.*, bibulous nose. **2.** *a.* Addicted to drink; drunken.

ivrogner [ivrɔɲe], *v.i. F:* To tipple, to soak; to go on the booze.

    s'ivrogner. **1.** = *ivrogner.* **2.** To become an habitual drunkard; to take to drink.

ivrognerie [ivrɔɲri], *s.f.* Habitual drunkenness.

ivrognesse [ivrɔɲɛs], *s.f. F:* Woman given to drink; drunkard.

izard [izaːr], *s.m. Z:* = ISARD.

J

J, j [ʒi], *s.m.* The letter J, j.

jabot [ʒabo], *s.m.* **1.** Crop (of bird). **Faire jabot;** enfler, gonfler, le jabot, (i) (of pigeon) to pout; (ii) *F:* (of pers.) to throw a chest; to strut. *F: Se remplir le jabot*, to fill one's maw. **2.** *Cost:* (*a*) Shirt-frill, ruffle, jabot. (*b*) Frill (of blouse).

jabot|er [ʒabɔte], *v.i.* **1.** *A:* (Of bird) To gobble. **2.** *F:* To jabber, chatter. *s.m.* **-age.** *s.* **-eur, -euse.**

jacasse [ʒakas], *s.f. F:* (Of woman) Chatter-box.

jacasser [ʒakase], *v.i. F:* (Of magpie or pers.) To chatter, jabber.

jacasserie [ʒakasri], *s.f. F:* Chatter; idle talk.

jacée [ʒase], *s.f. Bot:* **1.** Brown radiant knapweed. **2.** Petite jacée, wild pansy.

jachère [ʒaʃɛːr], *s.f. Agr:* Unploughed land; fallow. **Champ en jachère,** fallow field. **Mettre la terre en jachère,** to lay land fallow.

jacinthe [ʒasɛ̃ːt], *s.f.* **1.** *Bot:* Hyacinth. *J. des bois*, wild hyacinth; blue-bell. **2.** *Miner:* Jacinth.

jack [ʒak], *s.m. Tp: etc:* Jack.

Jacob [ʒakɔb]. *Pr.n.m.* Jacob. **L'échelle de Jacob,** Jacob's ladder. *F:* **Bâton de Jacob,** (i) *Astr:* Orion's belt; (ii) *Bot:* yellow asphodel.

jacobée [ʒakɔbe], *s.f. Bot:* Ragwort.

jacobin, -ine [ʒakɔbɛ̃, -in], *s.* **1.** *Ecc:* Dominican friar or nun. **2.** *Fr.Hist:* (1789): Jacobin (*i.e.* member of a political club that met in an old *couvent de jacobins*).

jacobinisme [ʒakɔbinism], *s.m.* Jacobinism.

jacobite [ʒakɔbit], *a. & s.m.* Jacobite.

jacquard, jacquart [ʒakaːr], *s. m. or f. Tex:* Jacquard loom.

jacquerie [ʒakri], *s.f. Fr.Hist:* Jacquerie (peasant rising; primarily that of 1358).

Jacques [ʒɑːk]. *Pr.n.m.* James. *F:* **Maître Jacques,** Jack-of-all-trades. (From the servant in Molière's *L'Avare*.) **Jacques Bonhomme,**

(i) *Hist:* the French peasant (at the time of the Jacquerie); (ii) *F:* friend Hodge.

jacquet [ʒakɛ], *s.m.* Backgammon.

jacquot [ʒako]. **I.** *Pr.n.m. F:* = Jim, Jimmy. **2.** *s.m.* Poll(-parrot), Polly.

jactance [ʒaktɑ̃:s], *s.f.* **I.** Boastfulness, vaingloriousness, boasting, brag. Discours plein de jactance, boastful speech. Parler avec jactance, to speak boastfully. **2.** Boast; piece of brag.

jade [ʒad], *s.m.* Jade(-stone); nephrite.

jadis [ʒadis], *adv. Lit:* Formerly, once, of old. Au temps jadis, in the olden time, in the days of yore.

jaguar [ʒagwa:r], *s.m.* Jaguar; American tiger.

jaill|ir [ʒaji:r], *v.i.* To spring (up); to shoot forth; (of water) to gush (forth), to spout up or out, to squirt (out); (of blood) to spurt; (of sparks) to fly; (of light) to flash. Faire jaillir des étincelles d'une pierre à fusil, to strike sparks from a flint. *s.m.* **-issement.**

jaillissant [ʒajisɑ̃], *a.* Gushing, spouting, spurting; flying (sparks). Puits jaillissant, (mineral oil) gusher.

jais [ʒɛ], *s.m. Miner:* Jet. Noir comme du jais, *a.inv.* noir de jais, jet-black.

jalap [ʒalap], *s.m. Bot: Pharm:* Jalap.

jalon [ʒalɔ̃], *s.m.* (a) (Surveyor's) staff; (range-)pole; stake, rod. *F:* Jeter des jalons (dans une science, etc.), to show the way; to blaze a trail. (b) *Mil:* Alignment picket. (c) *Artil:* Aiming-post

jalonn|er [ʒalɔne], *v.tr. Surv:* To lay out, stake out, mark out; to peg (out) (claim). *F: Ils ont jalonné la route à ceux qui suivront*, they have shown the way, blazed the trail for, their successors. *Événements qui jalonnent une epoque*, events that stand out as landmarks in a period. *s.m.* **-age.** *s.m.* **-ement.**

jalonneur [ʒalɔnœ:r], *s.m. Surv:* Staffman.

jalouser [ʒaluze], *v.tr.* To envy (s.o.).

jalousie [ʒaluzi], *s.f.* **I.** Jealousy. *J. de métier*, professional jealousy. **2.** (a) (Lattice-work) screen. (b) Venetian blind, sun-blind. **3.** *Bot:* Sweet-william.

jalou|x, -ouse [ʒalu, -u:z], *a.* (a) Jealous (de, of). Observer qn d'un œil jaloux, to keep a jealous, a watchful, eye on s.o. (b) Zealous, careful. *J. de faire qch.*, anxious, desirous, to do sth. *adv.* **-sement.**

Jamaïque (la) [laʒamaik]. *Pr.n.f.* Jamaica.

jamais [ʒamɛ], *adv.* **I.** Ever. *Plus cher que j.*, dearer than ever. A jamais, pour jamais, for ever. A tout jamais, for ever and ever; for evermore. **2.** (With neg. expressed or understood) Never. *J. homme ne fut plus admiré*, never was a man more admired. Sans jamais y avoir pensé, without ever having thought of it. *C'est le cas ou j.*, now or never. *On n'en avait encore jamais entendu parler*, it had never been heard of before. On ne le voit presque jamais, one hardly ever sees him. On ne le verra plus jamais, jamais plus, we shall never see him again. Jamais de la vie! never! out of the question! Jamais! well I never! *Prov:* Mieux vaut tard que jamais, better late than never. **3.** *s.m.* Au grand jamais! never, never!

jambage [ʒɑ̃ba:ʒ], *s.m.* **I.** Jamb(-post) (of door, window); jamb, side, cheek (of fireplace). **2.** Leg, standard (of crane, etc.). **3.** Downstroke (of written letter). *Sch:* Faire des jambages, to make pot-hooks.

jambe [ʒɑ̃:b], *s.f.* **I.** (a) Leg. Jambe deçà, jambe delà, astride, astraddle. *Hist:* Edouard Longues-jambes, Edward Longshanks. *Nau:* (Nœud de)

jambe de chien, sheepshank. Il s'enfuit à ⸱outes jambes, he ran off as fast as his legs could carry him, at full speed. *F:* Prendre ses jambes à son cou, to take to one's heels, to show a clean pair of heels. Jouer des jambes, to leg it. Par-dessous la jambe, without care or exertion. *Travail fait par-dessous la j.*, scamped work. Faire la belle jambe, to strut about; to show off. C'est ça qui me fera une belle jambe! a lot of good that will do me! Avoir les jambes rompues, to be worn out, done up, knocked up. N'avoir plus de jambes, to be tired out, fagged out. Jambe de bois, wooden leg, peg-leg; *F:* pin. (b) *J. d'un verre*, stem of a glass. *Jambes d'un pantalon*, legs of a pair of trousers. **2.** Jambe de force, strut, prop, brace; *Aut:* stay(-rod), torque-rod.

jambé [ʒɑ̃be], *a.* (Used in) Bien, mal, jambé, with shapely, unshapely, legs.

jambier, -ière [ʒɑ̃bje, -jɛ:r]. **I.** *a. Anat:* Tibial (muscle, etc.). **2.** *s.m.* (Butcher's) gambrel. **3.** *s.f.* Jambière. (a) *Archeol:* Greave. (b) *Surg:* Elastic stocking. (c) *pl.* (Infantry) leggings; (cyclist's) mackintosh leggings, overall leggings; *Fb:* shin-guards.

jambon [ʒɑ̃bɔ̃], *s.m.* Ham. Œufs au j., ham and eggs.

jambonneau [ʒɑ̃bɔno], *s.m.* **I.** Knuckle of ham. **2.** Foreleg ham; hand of pork.

janissaire [ʒanisɛ:r], *s.m.* Janissary.

janot [ʒano], *s.m. F:* (= JEANNOT) Simpleton, silly Billy. *J. tête-en-l'air*, jay-walker.

janoterie [ʒanɔtri], *s.f.* **I.** Silliness, simplicity. **2.** Silly or ingenuous remark.

jansénisme [ʒɑ̃senism], *s.m. Rel.H:* Jansenism.

janséniste [ʒɑ̃senist], *a. & s. Rel.H:* Jansenist.

jante [ʒɑ̃:t], *s.f.* Felloe, felly (of wheel); rim (of cycle or car wheel). *Aut: J. à base creuse*, well-base rim. *J. à rebord*, beaded rim.

janvier [ʒɑ̃vje], *s.m.* January. En janvier, ⸱n January. Au mois de janvier, in the month of January. Le premier j., (on) January (the) first; (on) the first of January.

japhétique [ʒafetik], *a.* Japhetic; Aryan.

Japon (le) [ləʒapɔ̃]. **I.** *Pr.n.m. Geog:* Japan. *Au J.*, in, to, Japan. Papier du Japon, Japanese vellum. **2.** *s.m.* Japan porcelain; fine porcelain.

japonais, -aise [ʒapɔnɛ, -ɛ:z]. **I.** *a. & s.* Japanese. **2.** *s.m. Ling:* Japanese.

japonaiserie [ʒapɔnɛzri], *s.f.*, **japonerie** [ʒapɔnri], *s.f.* **I.** Craze for Japanese curios. **2.** *pl.* Japanese curios.

japp|er [ʒape], *v.i.* (Of dog, fox) To yelp, yap. *s.m.* **-ement.**

jaquemart [ʒakma:r], *s.m.* Jack(-o'-the-clock) (striking the hours).

jaquette [ʒakɛt], *s.f.* (a) (Man's) tail-coat, morning coat. (b) (Woman's) jacket.

jardin [ʒardɛ̃], *s.m.* Garden. *J. potager*, kitchen garden. *J. d'agrément*, pleasure garden. *J. des plantes*, botanical garden. *J. alpin*, rock-garden. *S.a.* ACCLIMATATION. *Sch:* Jardin d'enfants, kindergarten.

jardinage [ʒardina:ʒ], *s.m.* **I.** (a) Gardening. (b) Garden-stuff, -produce. **2.** Flaw (in diamond).

jardiner [ʒardine], *v.i.* To garden.

jardinet [ʒardinɛ], *s.m.* Small garden.

jardinier, -ière [ʒardinje, -jɛ:r]. **I.** *a. Plantes jardinières*, garden plants. **2.** *s.* Gardener. **3.** *s.f.* Jardinière. (a) Flower-stand. (b) Bottle stand (in café). (c) Market-gardener's cart; spring-cart.

jargon [ʒargɔ̃], *s.m.* (a) Jargon. (b) Cant, slang.

jargon², *s.m. Miner:* Jargon, jargoon.

jargonner [ʒargɔne], *v.i.* To talk jargon.

Jarnac [ʒarnak]. *Pr.n.m.* (Used in) **Coup de Jarnac**, treacherous stroke; stab in the back.

jarre [ʒaːr], *s.f.* (Large glazed) earthenware jar.

jarret [ʒarɛ], *s.m.* **1.** Bend of the knee; hough, hock (of horse, etc.). *F:* **Tendre le jarret**, to make a leg. **Plier le jarret**, to bend the knee. **Avoir le jarret solide, avoir du jarret**, to be strong on one's legs. **Couper les jarrets à un cheval**, to hamstring a horse. **2.** *Cu:* Knuckle (of veal); shin (of beef).

jarreté [ʒarte], *a.* **1.** Gartered. **2.** (Of horse) Close-hocked.

jarretelle [ʒartɛl], *s.f.* (Stocking) suspender.

jarretière [ʒartjɛːr], *s.f.* **1.** Garter. **Ordre de la Jarretière**, Order of the Garter. **2.** (*a*) Picketing rope. (*b*) Tug-of-war rope. *Lutte à la j.*, tug of war. (*c*) *Nau:* Gasket.

jars[1] [ʒaːr], *s.m.* Gander.

jars[2], *s.m.* P: Slang. **Il entend les jars**, he's a knowing one, a cute 'un.

jas [ʒɑ], *s.m. Nau:* Stock (of anchor). **Sans jas**, stockless.

jaser [ʒɑze], *v.i.* (*a*) To chatter (*de*, about); to gossip. **Jaser comme une pie (borgne)**, to talk nineteen to the dozen. **Faire jaser les gens**, to set tongues wagging. (*b*) To blab; to tell tales. **Faire jaser qn**, to make s.o. talk; *F:* to pump s.o.

jaserie [ʒɑzri], *s.f.* Chatter; tittle-tattle; gossip.

jaseur, -euse [ʒɑzœːr, -øːz]. **1.** *a.* Talkative. **2.** *s.* Chatterbox; gossip. **3.** *s.m. Orn:* Waxwing.

jasmin [ʒasmɛ̃], *s.m. Bot:* Jasmine, jessamine.

jaspe [ʒasp], *s.m.* **1.** *Miner:* Jasper. **J. sanguin**, bloodstone. **2.** = JASPURE.

jasp|er [ʒaspe], *v.tr.* To marble, mottle. *Bookb*: (i) To marble, (ii) to sprinkle (edges). **Papier jaspé**, marbled paper. *s.m.* **-age.**

jaspure [ʒaspyːr], *s.f. Bookb:* (*a*) Marbling. (*b*) Sprinkling.

jatte [ʒat], *s.f.* Bowl; (milk-)pan, basin.

jauge [ʒoːʒ], *s.f.* **1.** (*a*) Gauge (of cask, etc.). (*b*) *Nau:* Tonnage, burden (of ship). **J. brute**, gross tonnage. **2.** (*a*) Gauging-rod. *Aut:* (i) Petrol-gauge, (ii) dip-stick (of crank-case). (*b*) *Mec.E: etc:* Gauge, templet. **J. micrométrique**, vernier cal(l)iper. (*c*) *Mch:* **Jauge de vapeur**, steam-gauge. **Robinet de jauge**, gauge-cock.

jaug|er [ʒoːʒe], *v.tr.* (je jaugeai(s); n. jaugeons) **1.** To gauge; to measure the capacity of (cask), the tonnage of (ship). *F:* **J. un homme**, to take a man's measure; to size up a man. **2.** *Nau:* (Of ship) (*a*) **J. 300 tonneaux**, to be of 300 tons burden. (*b*) **J. deux mètres d'eau**, to draw six feet of water. *s.m.* **-eage.**

jaugeur [ʒoːʒœːr], *s.m.* Gauger.

jaunâtre [ʒonɑːtr], *a.* Yellowish; sallow.

jaune [ʒoːn]. **1.** *a.* Yellow. *F:* **Jaune comme un coing**, comme un citron, yellow as a guinea. **Chaussures jaunes**, brown boots. **Fièvre jaune**, yellow fever, *F:* yellow jack. *Adm:* **Livre jaune** = Blue Book. **Feu, lumière, j.**, amber light. *a.inv.* **Des gants jaune paille**, straw-yellow gloves. **J. serin**, canary yellow. *adv.* **Rire jaune**, to give a sickly smile. **Voir jaune**, to see everything with a jaundiced eye. **2.** *s.m.* (*a*) Yellow (colour). **J. d'ocre**, yellow ochre. (*b*) **Jaune d'œuf**, yolk (of egg). **3.** *s.m. F:* Non-union workman; blackleg, scab.

jauneau [ʒono], *s.m. Bot:* Lesser celandine.

jaun|ir [ʒoniːr], *v.tr. & i.* To yellow. **1.** To colour (sth.) yellow. **2.** To grow, turn, yellow; to fade. *s.m.* **-issement.**

jaunisse [ʒonis], *s.f. Med:* Jaundice.

javanais, -aise [ʒavanɛ, -ɛːz]. **1.** *a. & s.* Java-

---

nese. **2.** *s.m. A:* A form of cant. **To every syllable was added *av* or *va* (*jeudi* becoming *javeudavi*). **3.** *s.f. Danc:* Javanaise, Javanaise.

Javel [ʒavɛl], *s.m.* **Eau de Javel**, *F:* **eau de javelle**, bleaching-water.

javell|er [ʒavle], *v.* (je javelle; je javellerai) **1.** *v.tr. Agr:* To lay (corn) in swaths. **2.** *v.i.* (Of corn) To turn yellow. *s.m.* **-age.**

javelé, -e, *a. Agr:* **Avoine javelée**, oats that have rotted in the swath.

javeline [ʒavlin], *s.f.* Javelin.

javelle [ʒavɛl], *s.f.* **1.** *Agr:* Swath; loose sheaf. **2.** Bundle (of hop-poles, etc.).

javellis|er [ʒavelize], *v.tr. Hyg:* To sterilize (water) with potassium chloride; to chlorinate. *s.f.* **-ation.**

javelot [ʒavlo], *s.m.* Javelin.

je, before vowel sound **j'** [ʒ(ə)], *pers.pron.nom.* **1. 1.** **Je vois**, I see. **J'ai**, I have. **J'en ai**, I have some. **Que vois-je** [vwaːʒ]? what do I see? **2.** (Stressed [ʒə]) *Jur:* **Je, soussigné . . .**, I, the undersigned. . .

Jean [ʒɑ̃]. *Pr.n.m.* John. (Saint) **Jean-Baptiste** [batist], (St) John the Baptist. **La Saint-Jean**, Midsummer Day. *Hist:* **Jean sans Terre**, John Lackland.

Jeanne [ʒɑ(ː)n]. *Pr.n.f.* Jane, Joan, *Scot:* Jean. **Jeanne d'Arc**, Joan of Arc. **Cheveux à la Jeanne d'Arc**, bobbed hair with a fringe.

Jeanneton [ʒantɔ̃]. **1.** *Pr.n.f.* Jenny. **2.** *s.f. F:* Serving wench.

Jeannette [ʒanɛt]. **1.** *Pr.n.f.* Jenny, Janet. **2.** *s.f.* (*a*) Small gold cross (worn by peasants). (*b*) Sleeve-board. (*c*) *Bot:* **Jeannette jaune**, daffodil. **Jeannette blanche**, pheasant's eye.

Jeannot [ʒano]. **1.** *Pr.n.m. F:* Johnny, Jack. **2.** *s.m.* = JANOT.

jenny [ʒeni], *s.f. Tex:* Spinning-jenny.

jérémiade [ʒeremjad], *s.f.* Jeremiad, lamentation, doleful story.

Jérémie [ʒeremi]. *Pr.n.m.* Jeremiah.

jersey [ʒɛrzɛ], *s.m.* **1.** *Cost:* Jersey. **2.** Fine machine-knitted or woven material; stockinet.

jersiais, -aise [ʒɛrzjɛ, -ɛːz], *a. & s.* (Native) of Jersey. (**Vache**) **jersiaise**, Jersey cow.

jésuite [ʒezɥit], *s.m. Ecc:* Jesuit.

jésuitique [ʒezɥitik], *a.* Usu. *Pej:* Jesuitic(al); plausible, specious.

Jésus [ʒezy]. *Pr.n.m.* Jesus. **Jésus-Christ**, Jesus Christ. **En l'an 44 avant J.-C.** in the year 44 B.C.

jet [ʒɛ], *s.m.* **1.** (*a*) Throwing, casting; throw, cast (of net, dice, etc.). **A un jet de pierre de . . .**, within a stone's throw of. . . . *Art: Lit:* **Premier jet**, first sketch, rough outline; rough draft (of novel). **Du premier jet**, at the first attempt. **Force de jet**, impetus. (*b*) *Metall:* Cast, casting. **Couler qch. d'un seul jet**, to cast sth. in one piece. *F:* **Faire qch. d'un seul jet**, to do sth. at one go. (*c*) **Jet (de marchandises) à la mer**, jettison(ing), throwing overboard (of cargo). **2.** (*a*) Jet, gush, stream (of liquid); spurt (of blood); flash, ray (of light); new swarm (of bees). **Jet de vapeur**, steam jet; blast of steam. **Jet d'eau**, fountain. **Jet de flamme**, (i) burst of flame; (ii) blowpipe flame. **A jet continu**, in one continuous stream. (*b*) Young shoot (of tree). *F:* **Elle est tout d'un jet**, she is tall and slender. **3.** *Jet* (of nozzle, etc.); spout (of pump, watering-can, etc.). **Jet à pomme**, rose (of watering-can).

jeter [ʒəte, ʃte], *v.tr.* (je jette; je jetterai) To throw, fling, cast. **J. qch. de côté**, to toss sth. aside. **J. son argent par la fenêtre**, to fling, throw, one's money out of the window; to play ducks and drakes with one's money. **J. qch. à la tête de qn**, to throw sth. at s.o.'s head. *J. qch. au nez, à la figure, de qn,* to cast sth. in s.o.'s teeth ; to cast sth. up to s.o. *J. un filet,* to cast a net. **Jeter bas qch., jeter qch. à terre,** to throw sth. down. *Mch : J. bas les feux,* to draw the fires. *J. loin qch.,* to fling sth. away. *J. ses armes,* to throw away one's weapons. **Le dé en est jeté,** the die is cast. **Jeter un cri,** to utter a cry. *J. un soupir,* to heave a sigh. *J. un regard sur qn,* to cast a glance at s.o. *J. une ombre,* to cast a shadow. *J. qn en prison,* to throw, cast, s.o. into prison. *J. des racines,* to throw out roots ; to strike (root). *J. les fondements d'un édifice,* to lay the foundations of a building. **Abeilles qui vont jeter** (*un essaim*), bees about to swarm. **Jeter** (*une statue*) **en fonte,** to cast (a statue). *Nau : J. le plomb, la sonde,* to heave the lead. *J. l'ancre,* to cast anchor.

se jeter. *Se j. par la fenêtre,* to throw oneself out of the window. *Se j. à bas de son lit,* to jump out of bed. *Se j. sur qn,* to fall upon s.o. ; to attack s.o. *Se j. au cou de qn,* to fall on s.o.'s neck. *Cours d'eau qui se jette dans la Seine,* stream that flows into the Seine.

jeté, *s.m. Knitting :* Jeté simple, jeté double, single over, double over.

jetée, *s.f.* **1.** Jetty, pier. **2.** (= BRISE-LAMES) Breakwater. **3.** Jetée d'abeilles, swarm.

jeton [ʒətɔ̃, ʃtɔ̃], *s.m.* (*a*) *Cards : etc :* Counter. (*b*) *J. de présence,* tally, token (issued as voucher for attendance at meeting). **Toucher ses jetons,** to hand in one's checks, to draw one's fees.

jettature [ʒɛttaty:r], *s.f.* Evil eye.

jeu, jeux [ʒø], *s.m.* **1.** (*a*) Play, sport. **Jeu de mots,** play on words ; pun. **Jeu d'esprit,** witticism. *Jeux de la fortune,* tricks of fortune. **Par un jeu de la Fortune . . .,** through a freak of chance. . . . *Jeu de la nature,* freak (of nature). **Se faire** (**un**) **jeu de qch., de faire qch.,** to make light of sth., of doing sth. ; to make nothing of doing sth. **Ils se faisaient un jeu de le tourmenter,** they made a sport of baiting him. (*b*) (Manner of) playing ; acting (of actor) ; execution, playing (of musician). *Jeu muet,* dumb show. *Jeux de scène,* stage business. *Jeu brillant,* brilliant execution. *S.a.* VIEUX 2. **2.** (*a*) *Jouer à un jeu,* to play (at) a game. *Jeux d'adresse,* games of skill. *Jeux olympiques,* Olympic games. *Jeux de société, petits jeux,* parlour games, forfeit games. *Jeux de hasard,* games of chance. *Terrain de jeux,* sports-ground. **Ce n'est pas de jeu, cela passe le jeu,** that's not fair. **Jouer beau jeu,** to play the game ; to play fair. *Prov :* **A beau jeu beau retour,** one good turn deserves another. *F : Vous avez beau jeu,* now's your chance. **Il a fait mon jeu,** he played into my hands. **Jouer bon jeu bon argent,** (i) to play a straight game ; (ii) to mean business. *Ten : Jeu et partie,* game and set. *Fb :* (i) **Hors jeu,** off side. (ii) *Ballon hors jeu,* ball out of play. **Mettre la balle en jeu,** to bring the ball into play ; *Hockey :* to bully off. *S.a.* FRANC² 2. (*b*) (Place) *Jeu de tennis,* (lawn-)tennis courts. *Jeu de boules,* (in Fr.) bowling-alley ; (in Eng.) bowling-green. *Jeu de quilles,* skittle-alley. **3.** Set. *Jeu d'échecs,* set of chessmen. *Jeu de cartes,* pack of cards. *Jeu d'outils,* set of tools. *Jeu de voiles,* suit of sails. *Jeu de fiches,* card-index. *Mus : Jeu d'orgue,* (organ) stop. **4.** (*a*) Gaming, gambling, play ; carding ; dicing. **Maison de jeu,** gaming-house. *Perdre au jeu,* to have gaming losses. *Perdre une fortune au jeu,* to gamble away a fortune. *Dettes de jeu,* gambling-debts. *Table de jeu,* gaming-table or card-table. **Jouer gros jeu,** to play high. *Jouer un jeu d'enfer,* to plunge recklessly. **Faites votre jeu, vos jeux !** put down

your stakes ! **Mettre tout en jeu,** (i) to stake one's all ; (ii) to leave no stone unturned. *Les intérêts en jeu,* the interests at issue, at stake. *F :* **Le jeu ne vaut pas la chandelle,** the game isn't worth the candle. *F :* **Jouer double jeu,** to play a double game. **Cacher son jeu,** to play an underhand game. (*b*) *St.Exch :* Speculating. **5.** (Activity, action) **Les forces en jeu,** the forces at work. **Mettre qch. en jeu,** to set sth. in action ; to bring, call, sth. into play. *Jeu d'un piston,* length of stroke of a piston. *Jeu de lumière,* play of light. *Th : Jeux de lumière,* lighting effects. *Mec.E :* **En jeu,** in gear. **6.** *Mec.E :* (*a*) **Jeu** (utile), clearance, play, free motion. *Donner du jeu à un organe,* to ease, slacken, a part. (*b*) **Jeu** (nuisible), looseness, play, (back-)lash. **Prendre du jeu,** to work loose.

jeudi [ʒødi], *s.m.* Thursday. **Jeudi saint,** Maundy Thursday. **Jeudi gras,** Thursday before Shrove Tuesday. *F :* **Dans la semaine des quatre jeudis,** to-morrow come never.

jeun (à) [aʒœ̃], *adj.phr.* **1.** Fasting. *Boire à j.,* to drink on an empty stomach. **2.** Sober.

jeune [ʒœn], *a.* (*a*) Young ; juvenile or youthful. **Jeune homme,** *pl.* **jeunes gens,** *occ.* **jeunes hommes,** young man, youth, lad. *J. personne,* young person ; young lady. **Jeune fille,** see FILLE 2. **Jeunes gens,** (i) young folk, young people ; (ii) young men. *J. aveugle,* blind boy or girl. (*b*) Younger. **Mon j. frère,** my younger brother. **M. Dupont jeune,** Mr Dupont junior. (*c*) *Vin j.,* new wine.

jeûne [ʒøːn], *s.m.* (*a*) Fast. *Rompre le j.,* (i) to break one's fast ; (ii) *Ecc :* to break the rule of fasting. (*b*) Fasting. **Jour de jeûne,** (i) day of fasting ; (ii) *Ecc :* fast-day.

jeune-premier, -ière, *s. Th :* Juvenile lead ; *f.* leading lady.

jeûner [ʒøne], *v.i.* To fast (*de,* from).

jeunesse [ʒœnɛs], *s.f.* **1.** (*a*) Youth ; boyhood, girlhood. **Je le connais de jeunesse,** I have known him from my youth. *La toute première j.,* earliest youth ; infancy. *Livres pour la j.,* juvenile books. **Il faut que jeunesse se passe,** youth will have its fling. (*b*) Youthfulness, juvenility (of appearance, etc.). **2.** *F :* Girl, flapper.

jeûneur, -euse [ʒønœːr, -øːz], *s.* One who fasts ; faster.

joaillerie [ʒwajri], *s.f.* **1.** Jeweller's trade or business. **2.** Jewellery, trinkets.

joaillier, -ière [ʒwaje, -jɛːr], *s.* Jeweller.

jobard [ʒɔbaːr], *s.m. F :* Person easily taken in (by beggars, etc.) ; easy prey ; *F :* easy mark ; mug, juggins.

jobarder [ʒɔbarde], *v.tr. F :* To dupe, gull (s.o.) ; to take (s.o.) in.

jobarderie [ʒɔbardri], *s.f.,* **jobardise** [ʒɔbardiːz], *s.f. F :* **1.** Gullibility. **2.** Piece of misplaced philanthropy.

jockey [ʒɔkɛ], *s.m.* (*a*) Jockey. (*b*) Outrider. (*c*) Groom, tiger.

jocko [ʒɔko], *s.m. F :* Orang-outang or chimpanzee.

jocrisse [ʒɔkris], *s.m.* **1.** Stupid servant. **2.** Fool, simpleton ; hen-pecked husband.

joie [ʒwa], *s.f.* **1.** Joy ; delight ; gladness, glee. *Plein de j.,* full of joy ; in high glee. *Sauter de j.,* to leap for joy. **A ma grande joie, on me permit . . .,** to my great joy, I was allowed. . . . **Être en joie,** to be full of joy ; to be joyful. **Faire la joie de qn,** (i) to be s.o.'s joy ; (ii) to make s.o. happy. **Se faire une joie de servir qn,** to delight, to take a delight, in serving s.o. **Feu de joie,** bonfire. **Joie de vivre,** joy of life ; exhilaration.

Adv.phr. A cœur joie, to one's heart's content.
2. (*a*) Mirth, merriment. (*b*) *Aimer la j.*, to be fond of pleasure.

joign-ant, -ons, -is, etc. See JOINDRE.

joindre [ʒwɛ̃:dr], *v.tr.* (*pr.p.* joignant; *p.p.* joint; *pr.ind.* je joins, il joint, n. joignons, ils joignent; *p.h.* je joignis; *fu.* je joindrai) **1.** To join. (*a*) To bring together. *J. les mains,* to join, fold, one's hands. *J. un tube à chaud,* to weld a tube. S.a. BOUT[1] **1.** (*b*) To add (*d*, to). *J. le geste à la parole,* to suit the action to the word. *J. l'utile à l'agréable,* to combine business with pleasure. (*c*) *J. son régiment, son navire,* to join one's regiment, one's ship. **2.** To adjoin. *Notre maison joint la sienne,* our house is next to his.

　　se joindre. 1. To join, unite. *Se j. à, avec, qn pour faire qch.,* to join with s.o. in doing sth. **2.** To adjoin; to be contiguous.

　　joint. 1. *a.* Joined, united. *Pieds joints,* feet close together. *Saut à pieds joints,* standing jump. *A mains jointes,* with clasped hands. *Corr:* **Pièces jointes,** enclosures. *Conj.phr.* **Joint** (à ce) que, besides which, added to which. S.a. CI-JOINT. **2.** *s.m.* (*a*) Joint, join. *F:* **Trouver le joint,** to hit upon the right plan; to find a way. *J. biseauté,* scarf-joint. *J. en charnière,* knuckle-joint. *J. articulé, de Cardan,* universal joint, Cardan joint. *J. à rotule,* ball(-and-socket) joint. *J. à brides,* flange joint. (*b*) *pl.* Jointing (of wall). (*c*) *Mch:* Packing (of piston or gland). *I.C.E: J. de culasse,* gasket.

jointé [ʒwɛte], *a.* Jointed.

jointement [ʒwɛtmɑ̃], *s.m.* Jointing.

jointif, -ive [ʒwɛtif, -i:v], *a. Const:* Joined; placed edge to edge.

joint|oyer [ʒwɛtwaje], *v.tr.* (je jointoie) je jointoierai) *Const:* **1.** To point, joint (wall, etc.). **2.** To grout. *s.m.* **-oiement.**

jointure [ʒwɛty:r], *s.f.* **1.** Joint, join. *J. du genou,* knee-joint. *Les jointures des doigts,* the knuckles. *Jointures de la cuirasse,* joints of the harness. **2.** Often = JOINT **2.**

joli [ʒɔli], *a.* Pretty; good-looking (girl); nice. *Jolie comme un cœur, jolie à croquer,* sweetly pretty; pretty as a picture. *J. de jolies choses,* to say nice things. *Iron: Voilà une jolie conduite!* that's a nice way to behave! *Voilà du j.!* here's a pretty state of things!

joliment [ʒɔlimɑ̃], *adv.* **1.** Prettily, nicely, finely. **2.** *F: J. amusant,* very amusing, awfully funny. *Il danse j. bien!* he's a jolly good dancer. *Je suis j. content!* I'm awfully pleased! I'm jolly glad!

Jonas [ʒɔnɑ:s]. *Pr.n.m. B.Hist:* Jonah.

jonc [ʒɔ̃], *s.m.* (*a*) *Bot:* Rush. *J. fleuri,* flowering rush. *J. odorant,* sweet calamus, sweet rush. *J. à balais,* reed. *J. marin,* whin, furze. (*b*) Jonc d'Inde, rattan. *Canne de jonc,* Malacca cane; rattan (walking-stick).

jonchaie [ʒɔ̃ʃɛ], *s.f.* **1.** Plantation of rushes. **2.** Cane-plantation, -brake.

jonchée [ʒɔ̃ʃe], *s.f.* Scattering (of branches, flowers). *Une j. de roseaux, de morts, recouvrait le sol,* the ground was strewn with rushes, with dead.

jonch|er [ʒɔ̃ʃe], *v.tr. J. la terre de fleurs,* to strew the ground with flowers. *Les débris de la statue jonchaient le pavé,* fragments of the statue lay scattered about the pavement. *Des journaux jonchaient la table,* newspapers littered the table. [JONC] *s.m.* **-ement.**

jonchets [ʒɔ̃ʃɛ], *s.m.pl.* Games: Spillikins. [JONC]

jonction [ʒɔ̃ksjɔ̃], *s.f.* Junction, joining. *Point de j.,* junction-point. *Tuyau de j.,* joint-pipe. **Gare de jonction,** junction (station). *Voie de j.,*

cross-over. (Of troops) **Opérer une jonction,** to come together; to join hands.

jongler [ʒɔ̃gle], *v.i.* To juggle.

jonglerie [ʒɔ̃gləri], *s.f.* **1.** Juggling, jugglery. **2.** Trickery, imposture; trick.

jongleur [ʒɔ̃glœ:r], *s.m.* **1.** *A:* Jongleur; (mediaeval) tumbler. **2.** Juggler, mountebank.

jonque [ʒɔ̃:k], *s.f. Nau:* (Chinese) junk.

jonquille [ʒɔ̃ki:j]. **1.** *s.f. Bot:* Jonquil. **2.** *a.inv. & s.m.* Pale yellow.

Josué [ʒɔzųe]. *Pr.n.m. B.Hist:* Joshua.

jottereaux [ʒɔtro], *s.m.pl. Nau:* Cheeks, hounds (of mast).

jouable [ʒwabl], *a.* Playable.

joubarbe [ʒubarb], *s.f. Bot:* Houseleek.

joue [ʒu], *s.f.* **1.** Cheek (of person, horse). **Mettre, coucher, qn en joue,** to aim (with a gun) at s.o. **2.** Side (of arm-chair, etc.); cheek (of bearing, mortise, etc.); flange (of wheel); web (of girder, etc.). *Aut: J. d'aile,* wing flange. **3.** *N.Arch:* **Les joues,** the bows.

jouée [ʒwe], *s.f. Arch:* Reveal (of window). [JOUE]

jouer [ʒwe], *v.* To play. **I.** *v.i.* **1.** (*a*) *J. avec qn,* to play with s.o. *J. avec sa chaîne de montre,* to toy, fiddle, with one's watch-chain. *J. sur les mots,* to play upon words. (*b*) *J. à qch.,* to play at sth. *J. à la marchande,* to play at keeping shop. *J. aux cartes,* to play cards. *C'est à qui de jouer?* whose turn is it to play? (*c*) *J. du piano, de la harpe,* to play the piano, the harp. *J. de l'éventail,* to flirt one's fan. *J. des coudes,* to elbow one's way. *J. des dents,* to ply one's teeth. **2.** (*a*) To gamble. *Prov:* **Qui a joué, jouera,** once a gambler always a gambler. (*b*) *Fin: J. à la hausse,* to gamble, speculate, on a rise; to operate for a rise. **3.** (*a*) To come into play; to work, to act. *Les eaux joueront dimanche,* the fountains will play on Sunday. **Faire jouer qch.** to bring sth. into play; to set sth. in motion. *Faire j. une mine,* to spring, touch off, a mine. *Faire j. un ressort,* to work, touch, release, a spring. (*b*) (Of regulation, etc.) To be, become, operative. (*c*) (Of wood) To warp; to shrink or swell. (*d*) (Of part) To fit loosely; to have too much play.

　　II. jouer, *v.tr.* **1.** (*a*) To stake. *J.* cinq *francs,* to stake five francs. *J. gros jeu,* to play for high stakes; to play high. *J. de malheur,* to be unlucky. (*b*) *Turf:* To back (horse). *J. un cheval gagnant et placé,* to back a horse each way. **2.** (*a*) To play (card, pawn). *J. trèfle,* (i) to play clubs; (ii) to lead clubs. *Bien j. ses cartes,* to play one's cards well. *Chess: J. une pièce,* to move a piece. (*b*) To act, play, perform (a play). *J. un rôle,* to act a part. *F: J. un rôle dans une affaire,* to play a part in an affair. *F:* **Jouer la surprise,** to affect, feign, surprise. **3.** To trick, fool, make a fool of (s.o.).

　　se jouer. 1. *Faire qch. en se jouant,* to make child's-play of sth.; to do sth. with great ease. **2.** *Se j. de qn,* to make game of s.o. **3.** *Se j. à qn,* to venture to confront s.o. *Se j. au feu,* to play with fire.

jouet [ʒwɛ], *s.m.* Toy, plaything. *F: Être le j. de la fortune, des vents,* to be the sport of fortune, of every wind.

joueur, -euse [ʒwœ:r, -ø:z], *s.* **1.** (*a*) Player (of game). *J. de golf, de boules,* golfer, bowler. *J. aux cartes,* card-player. *Être beau j.,* to be a sport, a good loser. *Être mauvais j.,* to be a bad loser. *a.* **Enfant joueur,** child fond of play. (*b*) Performer, player (on an instrument). **2.** (*a*) Gambler, gamester. *a.* Given to gambling, fond of gambling. (*b*) *St.Exch:* Speculator, operator.

Joueur à la hausse, bull. Joueur à la baisse, bear.

joufflu [ʒufly], *a.* Chubby.

joug [ʒu(g)], *s.m.* **1.** Yoke. **Mettre les bœufs au joug**, to yoke the oxen. *Courber un peuple sous le j.*, to bend a people under the yoke. **Secouer le joug**, to throw off the yoke. **2.** (*a*) Beam (of balance). (*b*) Yoke, cross-head (of engine).

jouir [ʒwiːr], *v.i.* To enjoy. (*a*) *J. de la vie, d'un bon dîner*, to enjoy life, a good dinner. (*b*) *J. de toutes ses facultés*, to be in the enjoyment of all one's faculties. *J. d'une bonne réputation*, to bear a good character. (*c*) *Abs. Gens qui ne pensent qu'à jouir*, people who think only of enjoyment.

jouissance [ʒwisãːs], *s.f.* Enjoyment. (*a*) *Le travail est une j. pour lui*, work is a pleasure to him. (*b*) Possession, tenure. **Avoir la jouissance de certains droits**, to enjoy certain rights. **Entrer en jouissance de ses biens**, to enter into possession of one's property. **Maison à vendre avec jouissance immédiate**, house for sale with vacant possession. **Jouissance de passage**, right of way.

jouisseur, -euse [ʒwisœːr, -øːz]. **1.** *s.* Sensualist. **2.** *a.* Sensual.

joujou, -oux [ʒuʒu], *s.m. F:* (*a*) Toy, plaything. (*b*) **Faire joujou** *avec un enfant*, to play with a child.

joule(-seconde) [ʒul(səgɔ̃ːd)], *s.m. El.E:* Joule (-second). *pl. Des joules(-seconde).*

jour [ʒuːr], *s.m.* Day. **1.** (Day)light. (*a*) *Voyager le j., de j.*, to travel by day. *Travailler j. et nuit*, to work day and night. **Le petit jour**, the morning twilight. *Éveiller qn au j.*, to rouse s.o. at daybreak. **Au grand jour, en plein jour**, (i) in broad, full, daylight; (ii) publicly. **Chambre qui prend jour sur la cour**, room that looks out on the yard. **Il fait jour**, it is growing light. **Il fait grand jour**, it is broad daylight. *Le j. se faisait dans mon esprit*, I was beginning to understand. (*b*) **Mettre qch. au jour**, to bring sth. to light; to publish (fact). **Mise au jour d'un mystère**, elucidation of a mystery. **Mettre au jour un enfant, donner le jour à un enfant**, to give birth to a child. *Lit:* **J'ai vu le jour à Paris**, I first saw the light, I was born, in Paris. **Attenter aux jours de qn**, to make an attempt on s.o.'s life. *Hum:* **L'auteur de mes jours**, the author of my being. (*c*) Lighting. **Voir qch. sous son vrai jour**, to see sth. in its true light. *Présenter une affaire sous un j. favorable*, to put a matter in a favourable light. S.a. FAUX¹ I. 3. *Vous êtes dans mon j.*, you are standing in my light. **2.** (*a*) Aperture, opening. *Pratiquer un j. dans un mur*, to make, cut, an opening, a hole, in a wall. **Jour de l'escalier**, well-hole (of stair). *Percer (qch.) à jour*, (i) to bore, go, right through (sth.); (ii) to see through (plan, etc.); to penetrate (a design). **Garniture, bas, à jour(s)**, open-work trimming, stockings. (*b*) **Se faire jour**, to make a way for oneself. *La vérité se fait j. dans son esprit*, the truth is dawning (up)on him. **3.** (Period of time) *Un j. je me promenais . . .*, one day I was walking. . . . *Un j. je vous le dirai*, some day I will tell you. **Prendre jour pour qch.**, to appoint a day, make an appointment, for sth. *Le journal du j.*, to-day's newspaper. **Plat du jour** (*dans un restaurant*), *F:* 'to-day's special.' *Com: Les prix du j.*, the ruling prices. **Être de jour**, to be on duty for the day. **De nos jours**, nowadays. *Il y a six ans jour pour jour*, six years ago to the very day. **L'an dernier à pareil jour**, a year to-day. **Leur beauté n'est que d'un jour**, their beauty is ephemeral, is but for a day. **Vivre au jour le jour**, to live from day to day, from hand to mouth. **Je l'ai vu** l'autre jour, I saw him the other day. **Un jour ou l'autre**, some time or other. **D'un jour à l'autre**, de jour en jour, from day to day. **Du jour au lendemain**, (i) soon; (ii) at a moment's notice. **Tous les jours**, every day. **A un de ces jours!** *F:* so long! **Mes beaux jours sont passés**, I have had my day. **Mourir plein de jours**, to die full of years. S.a. AN 1, BEAU I. 2, HUIT, QUINZE 2. **Mettre** (*une liste*) **à jour**, to bring (a list) up to date. *Tenir qn à j.*, to keep s.o. posted up on recent affairs. *Com:* **Intérêts à ce jour**, interest to date. *Jur:* **Ce jour d'hui** = AUJOURD'HUI.

journal, -aux [ʒurnal, -o], *s.m.* **1.** Journal, diary, record. *Book-k:* Day-book. **Tenir un journal**, to keep a diary. *Nau: J. de navigation*, log(-book). *J. de bord*, (i) (mate's) log(-book); (ii) log-book in harbour. **2.** Newspaper, journal. **Le journal d'aujourd'hui**, to-day's paper. *J. de modes*, fashion paper. **Les journaux**, the Press. *Marchand de journaux*, news-agent. **Style de journal**, journalese. *W.Tel:* **Journal parlé**, 'news.'

journalier, -ière [ʒurnalje, -jɛːr]. **1.** *a.* Daily (task); everyday (occurrence). **2.** *s.m.* (*a*) Day-labourer, journeyman. (*b*) *Aut:* (Totalisateur) journalier, trip-recorder (of speedometer).

journalisme [ʒurnalism], *s.m.* Journalism. *L'influence du j.*, the influence of the Press.

journaliste [ʒurnalist], *s. m. & f.* Journalist, pressman; reporter.

journalistique [ʒurnalistik], *a.* Journalistic.

journée [ʒurne], *s.f.* **1.** Day(time). *Pendant la j.*, in the daytime. **Toute la journée**, all day (long); the whole day. *Dans la j.*, in the course of the day. *J. de travail*, (i) day's work; (ii) working day. **Il ne fait rien de la journée**, he does nothing all day long. **2.** (*a*) Day's work. **Travailler à la journée**, to work by the day. **Homme de journée**, (day-)labourer. **Femme de journée**, charwoman, daily help, *F:* Aller en journée, to go out charring. (*b*) Day's wages. (*c*) Day's march. **Voyager à petites journées**, to journey by easy, short, stages. (*d*) Historic day; day of battle. *La j. d'Austerlitz*, the day, battle, of Austerlitz. **Gagner la journée**, to win the day.

journellement [ʒurnɛlmã], *adv.* Daily; every day. *Employé j.*, in daily use.

joute [ʒut], *s.f.* **1.** *A:* Joust, tilt, tilting. **2.** Contest, match. *J. de coqs*, cock-fight. *J. oratoire*, contest in eloquence.

jouter [ʒute], *v.i.* **1.** *A:* To joust, tilt. **2.** (Of cocks, etc.) To fight. **3.** *F: J. avec qn*, to break a lance with s.o.; to have a tilt at s.o.

jouteur [ʒutœːr], *s.m.* **1.** *A:* Tilter. **2.** *F: Un rude j.*, a formidable antagonist.

jouvence [ʒuvãːs], *s.f. A:* Youth. **La Fontaine de Jouvence**, the Fountain of Youth.

jouvenceau [ʒuvãso], *s.m. A:* Stripling, youth.

jovial, -aux [ʒɔvjal, -o], *a.* Jovial, jolly, merry; breezy. *adv.* **-ement.**

jovialité [ʒɔvjalite], *s.f.* Joviality, jollity; breeziness.

joyau, -aux [ʒwajo], *s.m.* Jewel. **Les joyaux de la Couronne**, the Crown jewels; the regalia. *F: C'est le plus beau j. de mon écrin*, it is the brightest jewel in my crown.

joyeuseté [ʒwajøzte], *s.f.* Piece of drollery; prank; joke. *Dire des joyeusetés*, to crack jokes.

joyeu|x, -euse [ʒwajø, -øːz], *a.* Merry, mirthful, joyous; *Lit:* blithe. *J. Noël!* a merry Christmas! *J. et gai*, blithe and gay. *adv.* **-sement.**

jubé [ʒybe], *s.m. Ecc:* Rood-screen or rood-loft.

jubilant [ʒybilɑ̃], *a. F:* Jubilant; in high glee.

jubilation [ʒybilasjɔ̃], *s.f.* Jubilation; high glee.

jubilé [ʒybile], *s.m.* Jubilee; golden wedding.

jubiler [ʒybile], *v.i.* To exult, jubilate.

jucher [ʒyʃe]. **1.** *v.i.* (Of birds) To go to roost; to perch. *F:* Où *juchez-vous?* where do you hang out? **2.** *v.tr.* On *m'avait juché au dernier étage*, they had perched me on the top floor. **se jucher. 1.** (Of fowls) To go to roost. **2.** *Se j. sur un haut tabouret*, to perch oneself on a high stool.

juchoir [ʒyʃwaːr], *s.m.* Perch (for fowls); roosting-place; hen-roost.

judaïque [ʒydaik], *a.* Judaic (law, etc.); Jewish (history).

judaïsme [ʒydaism], *s.m.* Judaism.

Judas [ʒydɑ(s)]. **1.** *Pr.n.m.* Judas (Iscariot). *F:* **Poil de Judas,** carroty hair. *Baiser de J.,* Judas kiss. **2.** *s.m.* (*a*) *F:* Traitor, betrayer. (*b*) Judas(-hole, -trap); spy-hole (in door).

judéo-allemand, -ande [ʒydeoalmɑ̃, -ɑ̃ːd], *a. & s.m. Ling:* Yiddish.

judiciaire [ʒydisjɛːr]. **1.** *a.* Judicial, judiciary, legal. *Vente judiciaire,* sale by order of the court. *A:* **Combat judiciaire,** trial by combat. *Éloquence j.,* forensic eloquence. *Nouvelles judiciaires,* law reports. **2.** *s.f.* (Sound) judgment; *F:* nous. *adv.* **-ment.**

judicieu|x, -euse [ʒydisjø, -øːz], *a.* Judicious, sensible, discerning. *Peu judicieux,* injudicious. *adv.* **-sement.**

juge [ʒyːʒ], *s.m.* (*a*) Judge. **Juge d'instruction,** examining magistrate. **Juge de paix,** (i) conciliation magistrate (in commercial cases); (ii) police-court magistrate. *Les juges,* the Bench. *F:* **Je vous en fais juge,** I appeal to you. (*b*) Umpire. *Turf:* Judge. *Fb: J. de touche,* linesman.

jugement [ʒyʒmɑ̃], *s.m.* Judgment. **1.** *Jur:* (*a*) Trial (of case). **Mettre, faire passer, qn en jugement,** to bring s.o. to trial. **Mise en jugement,** arraignment. **Passer en jugement,** to be brought up for trial, to stand one's trial. **Jugement par défaut,** judgment by default. *Le jugement dernier,* doomsday. (*b*) Decision, award; (in criminal cases) sentence. *Prononcer un j.,* to pass judgment; to adjudicate. *Rendre un j. arbitral,* to make an award. *J. provisoire,* decree nisi. *J. déclaratif de faillite,* adjudication in bankruptcy. **2.** Opinion, estimation. *Au j. de bien des gens,* in the opinion, view, of many people. **3.** Discernment, discrimination. *Montrer du j.,* to show sound judgment, good sense. *Erreur de j.,* error of judgment. **Avoir perdu le jugement,** to be out of one's senses.

jugeotte [ʒyʒɔt], *s.f. F:* Common sense; *F:* gumption, nous. [JUGER]

juger [ʒyʒe]. **I.** *v.tr.* (je jugeai(s); n. jugeons) **1.** (*a*) To judge; to try (case, prisoner); to pass sentence on (prisoner); to adjudicate, adjudge (claim); to adjudicate (*entre*, between). (*b*) *J. un livre,* to pass judgment on, to criticize, a book. *Mal j. qn* to misjudge s.o. *J. les gens sur la mine,* to judge people from, by, appearances. **2.** (*a*) To think, believe; to be of opinion. *On le jugeait fou,* people took him to be mad. *J. à propos, nécessaire, de faire qch., que qch. se fasse,* to deem it advisable, necessary, to do sth., that sth. should be done. (*b*) **Juger de qch.,** to judge of sth. *Jugez de ma surprise, jugez quelle fut ma surprise,* judge of my surprise. **A en juger par . . .,** to judge by . . .; judging by. . . . **Autant que j'en puis juger,** to the best of my judgment. **II. juger, jugé,** *s.m.* **Faire qch. au jugé,** to do sth. by guess-work. *Tirer au j.,* to fire at a venture.

jugoslave [ʒygoslaːv], *a. & s.* Jugo-Slav.

jugulaire [ʒygylɛːr]. **1.** *a. & s.f.* Jugular (vein). **2.** *s.f.* Chin-strap, -chain (of helmet).

juguler [ʒygyle], *v.tr.* (*a*) To strangle, throttle. *Med:* To jugulate (disease). (*b*) To cut the throat of (s.o.).

juif, f. juive [ʒɥif, ʒɥiːv]. **1.** *a.* Jewish; Jew (money-lender, etc.). **2.** *s.* Jew, *f.* Jewess. *F:* **Le petit juif,** the funny-bone. *S.a.* ERRANT I.

juillet [ʒɥijɛ], *s.m.* July. **En juillet,** in July. **Au mois de juillet,** in the month of July. *Le premier j.,* (on) the first of July; (on) July (the) first.

juin [ʒɥɛ̃], *s.m.* June. **En juin,** in June. **Au mois de juin,** in the month of June. *Le premier j.,* (on) the first of June; (on) June (the) first.

juiverie [ʒɥivri], *s.f.* **1.** (*a*) Jewry, ghetto. (*b*) The Jews; Jewry. **2.** *F:* Usury; sharp practice.

jujube [ʒyʒyb], *s.m. Pharm:* Jujube (lozenge).

julien, -ienne [ʒyljɛ̃, -jɛn]. **I.** *a.* Julian. *Chr:* **Année julienne,** Julian year. **II. julienne,** *s.f.* (*a*) *Bot:* Rocket. (*b*) (**Potage à la**) **julienne,** julienne soup.

jumeau, -elle [ʒymo, -ɛl]. **I.** *a. & s.* Twin. *Trois jumeaux,* triplets. *Lits jumeaux,* twin beds. *Vapeur à hélices jumelles,* twin-screw steamer. *Navire j.,* sister ship. **II. jumelles,** *s.f.pl.* **1.** Binoculars. *Jumelles de théâtre,* opera-glasses. *Jumelles de campagne,* field-glass(es). **2.** (*a*) *Mec.E:* Cheeks, side-pieces; slide-bars (of lathe-bed). (*b*) *Veh:* (Spring-)shackles. (*c*) *Her:* Gemels.

jumel|er [ʒymle], *v.tr.* (je jumelle; je jumellerai) **1.** (*a*) To pair; to arrange in pairs. (*b*) To fix (beams, etc.) longitudinally together. **2.** To strengthen by means of cheeks; to fish (mast, beam, etc.). *s.m.* **-age.**

jumelé, Arranged in pairs; coupled. *Aut:* **Pneus jumelés,** twin tyres; dual tyres.

jument [ʒymɑ̃], *s.f.* Mare.

jungle [ʒɔ̃ːgl], *s.f.* Jungle.

Junon [ʒynɔ̃]. *Pr.n.f. Myth:* Juno.

junte [ʒɔ̃ːt], *s.f.* **1.** *Hist:* Junta (in Spain, Italy). **2.** *F:* Clique, cabal.

jupe [ʒyp], *s.f.* **1.** (Woman's) skirt. *J. de dessous,* (i) petticoat; (ii) slip. *F:* **Pendu aux jupes de sa mère,** tied to his mother's apron-strings. **2.** Skirt (of frock-coat).

jupe-culotte, *s.f.* Divided skirt. *pl. Des jupes-culottes.*

Jupiter [ʒypitɛːr]. *Pr.n.m. Myth:* Jupiter, Jove.

jupon [ʒypɔ̃], *s.m.* Petticoat, underskirt.

jurement [ʒyrmɑ̃], *s.m.* (Profane) swearing; oath. *Proférer des jurements,* to curse and swear.

jurer [ʒyre], *v.tr.* To swear. **1.** *J. sa foi,* (i) to pledge one's word; (ii) to plight one's troth (*à*, to). *J. le ciel,* to call heaven to witness. *Abs. J. sur la Bible,* to swear on the Bible. **2.** (To promise) *J.* (*la*) *fidélité à qn,* to swear, vow, fidelity to s.o. **Faire jurer le secret à qn,** to swear s.o. to secrecy. *J. de faire qch.,* to swear to do sth. **3.** (To assert) *Je le jure sur mon âme,* I swear it on my soul and conscience. **J'en jurerais,** I would swear to it. *Prov:* **Il ne faut** (**jamais**) **jurer de rien,** you never can tell. **4.** *Abs.* (*a*) To swear (profanely); to curse. *F:* **Jurer comme un charretier,** to swear like a trooper. (*b*) (Of colours, etc.) To clash, jar (*avec,* with).

juré. 1. *a.* **Ennemi j. de qn,** sworn enemy of s.o. **Expert j.,** sworn expert. **2.** *s.m.* Juryman, juror. *Les jurés,* the jury.

juridiction [ʒyridiksjɔ̃], *s.f.* Jurisdiction. *F:* **Cela n'est pas dans ma juridiction,** that is not within my province.

juridique [ʒyridik], *a.* Juridical, judicial; legal (tie, claim). **Conseiller j.,** legal adviser.

jurisconsulte [ʒyriskɔ̃sylt], *s.m.* Jurisconsult; jurist; legal expert.

jurisprudence [ʒyrisprydõːs], *s.f.* **I.** Jurisprudence. **2.** Statute law.

juriste [ʒyrist], *s.m.* Jurist; legal writer.

juron [ʒyrɔ̃], *s.m.* (Profane) oath; *F:* swearword. *Lâcher un j.,* to rap out an oath.

jury [ʒyri], *s.m.* **I.** *Jur:* Jury. **Dresser la liste du jury,** to empanel the jury. **Chef du jury,** foreman of the jury. **Membre du jury,** juryman, juror. **2.** Selection committee (*e.g.* for the Salon). *J. d'examen,* board of examiners.

jus [ʒy], *s.m.* **I.** Juice. *F:* **Le jus de la treille,** the juice of the grape; wine. *F:* **C'est jus vert et verjus,** it is six of one and half a dozen of the other. *P:* **Y mettre du jus,** to put some vim into it. **2.** Gravy. **3.** *P:* (a) Water. *Il est tombé dans le jus,* he fell in. (b) Coffee. (c) Petrol; *P:* juice. (d) Electric current; *P:* juice.

jusant [ʒyzã], *s.m.* Ebb(-tide).

jusque [ʒysk(ə)], *prep.* **I.** As far as; up to. *Jusqu'ici,* thus far, so far. *Jusque-là* [ʒyskala], thus far; up to that point. *Jusqu'où?* how far? *Depuis Londres jusqu'à Paris,* all the way from London to Paris. *Jusqu'à un certain point,* up to a certain point. *Aller jusqu'à faire qch.,* to go so far as to do sth. *J. chez lui,* up to his very door. *Plaisanter j. sur l'échafaud,* to jest even on the scaffold. *Compter jusqu'à dix,* to count up to ten. *Ils furent tués jusqu'au dernier,* they were killed to a man. **2.** (a) Till, until. *Attendez jusqu'après les vacances,* wait till after the holidays. *Jusqu'ici,* till now, up to the present (time), as yet. *Jusque-là,* until then. *Jusqu'à présent,* up to now; hitherto. *Jusqu'à hier, à dix heures,* until yesterday, ten o'clock. *Jusqu'(à) aujourd'hui,* until to-day. *Jusqu'au jour que . . . , jusqu'au jour où . . . , jusqu'au moment que, où . . . ,* (i) until such time as . . . ; (ii) until the time when. . . . (b) *Si nous remontons jusqu'en 1800,* if we go as far back as the year 1800. **3.** (Intensive) (a) *Il sait jusqu'à nos pensées,* he knows our very thoughts. *Jusqu'à mon père était indigné,* even my father was indignant. *Jusqu'à dix personnes l'ont vu,* as many as ten people saw it. *Noter jusqu'aux moindres détails,* to make a note of the smallest details. *Il n'est pas jusqu'aux enfants qui ne sachent cela,* the very children know that. (b) *Il se montra sévère jusqu'à mériter le reproche d'être cruel,* he showed himself so severe as to deserve the reproach of cruelty. **4.** *Conj.phr.* **Jusqu'à ce que,** usu. + *sub.,* till, until.

jusqu'auboutiste [ʒyskobutist], *s. m. & f. F:* **I.** Whole-hogger. **2.** Die-hard, last-ditcher.

jusques [ʒyska(z)], *prep. Rh. &, Poet:* = JUSQUE. *Jusques à quand, ô Catilina . . . !* how long, Catiline . . . ! (Always in) **Jusques et y compris . . . ,** up to and including . . .

jusquiame [ʒyskjam], *s.f. Bot:* Henbane.

jussion [ʒysjɔ̃], *s.f. Hist:* **Lettres de jussion,** iussive letter.

justaucorps [ʒystokɔːr], *s.m. A.Cost:* Jerkin.

juste [ʒyst], *a.* **I.** Just, right, fair. (a) *Traitement j.,* fair play, just treatment. *J. colère,* legitimate, righteous, anger. **Rien de plus juste,** nothing could be fairer. *s.* **Le juste et l'injuste,** right and wrong. (b) *Magistrat j.,* just, upright, judge. *s. Les justes et les repentis,* the just and the repentant. **2.** Right, exact, accurate. (a) *Quelle est l'heure j.?* what is the right time? *Le mot j.,* the exact word, the right word. *Raisonnement j.,* sound reasoning. *Avoir l'oreille j.,* to have a good ear (for music). *Votre réponse n'est pas j.,* you have got the answer wrong. *Balance j.,* accurate scales. *Arriver à l'heure j.,* to arrive on the stroke of time. **C'est juste,** that is so! that's

right! **Rien de plus juste,** you are perfectly right. **Comme de juste,** of course. *Mus: Quarte j.,* perfect fourth. (b) *Ration bien j.,* very scanty, bare, allowance. *Bottines trop justes,* tight boots. *Vis j.,* tight screw. *Vêtement (bien) j.,* tight-fitting, skimpy, garment. *C'est bien j.,* there is barely enough (food, etc.) to go round. **C'est tout juste s'il ne me frappa pas,** he all but struck me. *Com:* **Au plus juste prix,** at rock-bottom price. **3.** *adv.* (a) Rightly. *Parler j.,* to speak to the point. *Frapper j.,* to strike home. *Chanter j.,* to sing in tune. *Voir j.,* to take a right view of things. *S.a.* TOMBER I. 4. (b) Exactly, precisely. *J. au milieu,* right, plumb, in the centre. *C'est j. l'homme qu'il nous faut,* he is the very man we want. *C'est j. ce qu'il faut,* that is the very thing. (c) Barely. *N'avoir que j. le temps,* to have barely time, to have no time to spare. **Échapper tout juste,** to escape by the skin of one's teeth. **4.** *Adv.phr.* **Je ne sais pas au juste si . . . ,** I do not exactly know whether. . . . **Comme de juste,** as is only fair, only just.

justement [ʒystəmã], *adv.* **I.** Justly, rightly, properly, deservedly. **2.** Precisely, exactly, just. *Voici j. la lettre que j'attendais,* here comes the very letter I was waiting for.

justesse [ʒystɛs], *s.f.* **I.** Exactness, correctness, accuracy. *J. d'une vis,* exact fit of a screw. *J. d'une opinion,* soundness of an opinion. *Raisonner avec j.,* to argue soundly, rightly. **2. Arriver de justesse,** to arrive just in time; *F:* to cut it fine.

justice [ʒystis], *s.f.* **I.** Justice. **C'est justice que** + *sub.,* it is only right, fair, that. . . . **Il est de toute justice de l'entendre,** it is only fair to give him a hearing. **En toute justice,** by rights. **Avec justice,** justly, deservedly. **Faire justice à qn,** (i) to mete out justice to s.o.; (ii) to right s.o.'s wrongs. *Se faire j. à soi-même,* to take the law into one's own hands. **Faire justice de qn,** to treat s.o. as he deserves. **Faire justice de qch.,** to make short work of sth. **Rendre justice à qn,** to do s.o. justice. **2.** Law; legal proceedings. **Palais de Justice,** Law Courts. **Gens de justice,** (i) officers of the law; (ii) lawyers. **Action en justice,** action at law. **Citer qn en justice,** to go to law with s.o. **Poursuivre qn en justice,** to institute legal proceedings against s.o.; to take action against s.o.

justiciable [ʒystisjabl], *a. & s. J. d'un tribunal,* justiciable to, in a court. *Cette question n'est pas j. des règles ordinaires,* this question is not amenable to ordinary rules.

justicier, -ière [ʒystisje, -jɛːr], *s.* (a) Lover of justice. (b) Justiciary. *F: J. de la mode,* arbiter of fashion.

justifiable [ʒystifjabl], *a.* Justifiable, warrantable. *adv. -ment.*

justificateur, -trice [ʒystifikatœːr, -tris]. **I.** *a.* Justificatory, justifying. **2.** *s.* Justifier.

justificatif, -ive [ʒystifikatif, -iːv], *a.* Justificatory, justificative. **Pièce justificative,** *s.m.* **justificatif,** *Com:* voucher; *Jur:* relevant paper.

justification [ʒystifikasjɔ̃], *s.f.* **I.** Justification, vindication. **2.** Proof (of fact, of identity). **3.** *Typ:* (a) Justification (of lines). (b) Type area.

justifier [ʒystifje], *v.tr.* **I.** To justify, vindicate (s.o.'s conduct, etc.); to warrant (action, expenditure). *J. qn d'une imputation,* to clear s.o. of, from, an imputation. **2.** To prove, give proof of, make good (assertion). **3.** *Typ:* To justify, adjust (line of type or length of column). **4.** *v.ind.tr. Jur: J. de ses mouvements,* to give a

satisfactory account of one's movements. *J. de son identité*, to prove one's identity.
se justifier, to clear oneself; to justify oneself; to vindicate one's character.
jute [ʒyt], *s.m. Tex:* Jute. *Sac en j.*, gunny bag.
iuter [ʒyte], *v.i.* To be juicy; to drip juice.
juteux, -euse [ʒytø, -øːz]. **1.** *a. (a)* Juicy. *(b) P:* Elegant, smart. **2.** *s.m. Mil: P:* = ADJUDANT I *(a)*.

juvénile [ʒyvenil], *a.* Juvenile; youthful.
juvénilité [ʒyvenilite], *s.f.* Juvenility.
juxtalinéaire [ʒykstalineːr], *a.* **Traduction juxtalinéaire,** juxtalinear translation; 'construe' with text and translation arranged in parallel vertical columns.
juxtaposer [ʒykstapoze], *v.tr.* To place side by side; to juxtapose.
juxtaposition [ʒykstapozisjɔ̃], *s.f.* Juxtaposition.

K

K, k [kɑ], *s.m.* (The letter) K, k.
kaïnite [kainit], *s.f. Miner:* Kainite.
kakatoès [kakatoɛs], *s.m.* = CACATOÈS.
kaki[1] [kaki], *s.m. & a.inv. Tex:* Khaki.
kaki[2], *s.m. Bot:* (Chinese) persimmon.
kaléidoscope [kaleidoskop], *s.m.* Kaleidoscope.
kaléidoscopique [kaleidoskopik], *a.* Kaleidoscopic.
kangourou [kãguru], *s.m. Z:* Kangaroo.
kantien, -ienne [kãtjɛ̃, -jen], *a. Phil:* Kantian.
kaolin [kaolɛ̃], *s.m. Cer:* Kaolin, porcelain clay.
kauri [kɔri], *s.m.* **1.** *Bot:* Kauri(-pine). **2.** Kauri gum.
kawcher, -ère [kɔʃɛːr], *a. Jew.Rel:* Kosher.
keepsake [kipsek], *s.m.* **1.** (Young lady's) autograph album. **2.** Souvenir.
Kénia [kenja]. *Pr.n.m. Geog:* Kenya (Colony).
képi [kepi], *s.m.* Kepi; peaked cap.
kermès [kɛrmɛs], *s.m.* **1.** *Ent: Com:* (Al)kermes. **2.** *Bot:* **Chêne kermès,** kermes-oak.
kermesse [kɛrmɛs], *s.f.* (Flemish) kermis; village fair.
khaki [kaki], *s.m. & a.inv.* = KAKI[1].
kick [kik], *s.m. Motor Cy:* Kick-starter.
kif-kif [kifkif], *a. P:* Same, likewise. *C'est k.-k.,* it's all one; it's as broad as it's long.
kilocycle [kilɔsikl], *s.m. Ph: El.E:* Kilocycle.
kilogramme [kilɔgram], *s.m. Meas:* Kilogram(me) (= 2.2 lbs).
kilomètre [kilɔmɛtr], *s.m. Meas:* Kilometre (= 0.624 mile).
kilométr|er [kilɔmetre], *v.tr.* (je kilomètre; je kilométrerai) *(a)* To measure (road, etc.) in kilometres. *(b)* To mark off (road) with kilometre stones. *s.m.* **-age.**
kilométrique [kilɔmetrik], *a.* Kilometric(al). **Borne kilométrique,** kilometre stone; = milestone.
kilovolt-ampère [kilɔvɔltɑ̃pɛːr], *s.m. El:* Kilovolt-ampère. *pl. Des kilovolts-ampères.*
kilowatt [kilɔwat], *s.m. El:* Kilowatt.
kimono [kimɔno], *s.m. Cost:* Kimono.

kinétoscope [k netɔskɔp], *s.m. Cin:* Kinetoscope.
king-charles [kinʃarl, kɛ̃k-], *s.m.inv.* King Charles spaniel.
kinkajou [kɛ̃kaʒu], *s.m.* Kinkajou, honey-bear.
kiosque [kjɔsk], *s.m.* **1.** *(a)* Kiosk. *K. de musique,* bandstand. *K. de jardin,* summer-house. *(b)* Newspaper- or flower-stall (on Paris boulevards, etc.). **2.** *Nau: (a) K. de la barre,* wheelhouse. *K. de navigation,* chart-house, -room. *(b)* Conning-tower (of submarine).
kiwi [kiwi], *s.m. Orn:* Kiwi, apteryx.
klaxon [klaksɔ̃], *s.m. Aut:* Klaxon, hooter.
klephte [klɛft], *s.m.* Klepht; (Greek) brigand.
kleptomane [kleptɔman], *a. & s.* Kleptomaniac.
kleptomanie [kleptɔmani], *s.f.* Kleptomania.
knock-out [nɔkut], *a.inv. Box:* **Mettre** (qn) **knock-out,** to knock (s.o.) out.
knockouter [nɔkute], *v.tr. Box:* To knock out.
knout [knut], *s.m.* Knout; Russian scourge.
knouter [knute], *v.tr.* To knout.
koala [kɔala], *s.m. Z:* Koala; koolah; Australian bear.
kodak [kɔdak], *s.m.* Kodak camera.
kola [kɔla], *s.m. Bot:* Cola, kola.
kopeck [kɔpek], *s.m. Num:* Copeck, kopec(k).
Koran (le) [lɔkɔrɑ̃]. *Pr.n.m.* The Koran.
korrigan, -ane [kɔrigɑ̃, -an], *s.* (In Brittany) Goblin; evil sprite.
koumis(s) [kumis], *s.m. Cu:* Koumiss, kumiss.
kourde [kurd], *a. & s. Ethn:* Kurd.
Kourdistan [kurdistɑ̃]. *Pr.n.m.* Kurdistan.
krach, krack [krak], *s.m.* '(Financial) crash; failure, smash (esp. of a bank).
kummel [kymel], *s.m.* Kümmel (liqueur).
kymrique [kimrik], *a. & s.m. Ling:* Cymric.
kyrielle [kirjɛl], *s.f.* **1.** *A:* Litany. **2.** *F:* Rigmarole; long string (of words, etc.). *Toute une k. de noms, d'enfants,* a whole string of names, of children.
kyste [kist], *s.m. Med:* Cyst. *K. synovial,* ganglion, *pl.* ganglia.
kystique [kistik], *a. Med:* Cystic (tumour).

L

L, l [ɛl], *s.f.* (The letter) L, l. *L mouillée,* liquid l, palatal(ized) l.
l'. See LE[1], [2].
la[1] [la], *def. art. & pron. f.* See LE[1], [2].
la[2], *s.m.inv. Mus:* *(a)* (The note) A. *Morceau en la,* piece in A. *(b)* The A string (of violin, etc.).
là [la], *adv.* **1.** (Of place) There. *(a) Là où vous êtes . . .*, where you are. . . . *Quand il n'est pas*

là, when he is away. *Les choses en sont là que . . .*, matters are at such a point that. . . . *A cinq pas de là se tenait . . .*, five paces away stood. . . . *F: Otez-vous de là!* get out of that! **Passez par là,** go that way. S.a. CE I. *(b)* (Emphatic use) *C'est là la question,* that is the question. *Que dites-vous là?* what is that you are saying? *Ce, cette, etc., . . . -là,* see CE[1] I, CE[2] 3. *Celui-là,*

celle-là, see CELUI 4. (c) P: *Pour la pêche je suis (un peu) là,* when it comes to fishing I'm all there. *Comme menteur il est un peu là!* he isn't half a liar! 2. (Of time) Then. **D'ici là,** between now and then; in the meantime. *A quelques jours de là,* some days after (that); a few days later on. 3. (= CELA) *Qu'entendez-vous par là?* what do you mean by that? *Il suit de là que . . . ,* it follows from that, therefrom, that. . . . *On l'avait filouté, de là sa fureur,* he had been swindled, hence his rage. *Je n'ai rien à dire là-contre,* I have nothing to say against it. 4. *int.* (a) *Là!* there now! (b) A: Moderately. *Est-il riche?—Là, là!* is he rich?—So so, fairly. (c) Oh là là! (i) oh dear me! (ii) (jeeringly) look at him!

là-bas [laba], adv. (Over) yonder. *Le voilà là-bas,* he is over there.

labeur [labœːr], *s.m.* Labour, toil, hard work.

labial, -ale, -aux [labjal, -o], a. Labial. Ling: *Consonne labiale,* s.f. **labiale,** lip consonant; labial.

labié [labje], a. Bot: Labiate, lipped.

labio-dental [labjɔdɑ̃tal], a. Ling: Labio-dental.

laboratoire [labɔratwaːr], *s.m.* Laboratory.

laborieusement [labɔrjøzmɑ̃], adv. Laboriously.

laborieux, -euse [labɔrjø, -øːz], a. 1. Toilsome, arduous, hard (work, etc.); laboured (diction, etc.). *Digestion laborieuse,* sluggish digestion. 2. (Of pers.) Laborious, hard-working. *Les classes laborieuses,* the working classes.

labour [labuːr], *s.m.* Tilling, tillage; esp. ploughing. *Donner un l. à un champ,* to plough a field. *Chevaux de labour,* plough-horses. **Terres de labour,** les labours, ploughed land.

labourable [laburabl], a. Arable.

labourage [laburaːʒ], *s.m.* Tilling, ploughing.

labourer [labure], v.tr. (a) To till, esp. to plough (land). *Commencer à labourer,* to break ground. *F: Le canon laboure le rempart,* the cannon ploughs up the rampart. *Les chagrins ont labouré son front,* sorrow has furrowed his brow. (b) Nau: *Labourer le fond,* (of ship) to graze the bottom; (of anchor) to drag.

laboureur [laburœːr], *s.m.* Agr: 1. Tillage farmer. 2. Farm-labourer; esp. ploughman.

laboureuse [laburøːz], s.f. Steam plough, tractor plough.

labyrinthe [labirɛ̃ːt], *s.m.* 1. Labyrinth, maze. 2. Anat: Labyrinth (of the ear).

lac [lak], *s.m.* Lake. *Lac de cirque,* tarn. *Les lacs de l'Écosse,* the lochs of Scotland. P: *Être dans le lac,* to be in the soup, in Queer Street, in a fix.

laccifère [laksifɛːr], a. Bot: Lac-bearing.

Lacédémone [lasedemɔn]. Pr.n.f. A.Geog: Lacedaemon, Sparta.

lacédémonien, -ienne [lasedemɔnjɛ̃, -jɛn], a. & s. Lacedaemonian.

lacer [lase], v.tr. (je laçai(s); n. laçons) (a) To lace (up) (shoe). (b) *L. un filet,* to make a net; to net. (c) Nau: To belay (rope). *s.m.* **-çage.** *s.m.* **-cement.**

se lacer, to lace up one's shoes, etc.; (of woman) to lace oneself in.

lacération [laserasjɔ̃], s.f. Laceration. 1. Tearing. 2. Tear; jagged wound.

lacérer [lasere], v.tr. (je lacère; je lacérerai) To tear, lacerate; to slash (sth.) to pieces.

laceron [lasrɔ̃], *s.m.* Bot: = LAITERON.

lacet [lase], *s.m.* 1. Lace (of shoe, etc.); boot-lace, shoe-lace, stay-lace. Nau: Lacing (of sail). *Mouvement de lacet,* (i) Rail: swaying, rocking

(of carriages); hammering (of engine); (ii) Av: yaw(ing). 2. Hairpin bend (in road). **Sentier en lacet(s),** winding path; zigzag path. 3. Noose, springe, snare (for rabbits, etc.); pl. toils. **Prendre un lapin au lacet,** to snare a rabbit. **Tendre un lacet,** to set a snare. F: **Pris dans ses propres lacets,** caught in his own toils.

lâchage [lɑʃaːʒ], *s.m.* 1. Releasing (of bomb from aeroplane). 2. F: Dropping (of acquaintance); jilting.

lâche [lɑːʃ], a. 1. Loose, slack; loosely fitting (garment); lax (discipline); slipshod (style). 2. Cowardly, faint-hearted; dastardly, unmanly. *s.m.* **Un lâche,** a coward, a dastard.

lâchement [lɑʃmɑ̃], adv. 1. Indolently, slackly. 2. In a cowardly manner.

lâcher [lɑʃe]. I. v.tr. To release. (a) To slacken, loosen (spring, etc.). *L. la détente (d'un fusil),* to release, pull, the trigger. *L. un coup de fusil à qn,* to fire a shot at s.o. *L. une bordée,* to fire, let fly, a broadside. *L. un coup de pied à qn,* to let fly at s.o. with one's foot. *L. une écluse,* to open a lock. S.a. BRIDE 1. (b) To let go; to leave go of (sth.); to drop (sth.). Av: To release (bomb). *Lâchez-moi!* let me go! F: *L. un emploi,* to throw up, fling up, a job. **Lâcher pied,** to give ground, to give way. S.a. OMBRE[1] 4, PRISE 1. F: **Lâcher qn,** (i) to drop s.o., s.o.'s acquaintance; (ii) to leave s.o. in the lurch. (c) To set free (prisoner, bird); to let (animal) loose. *L. un chien,* to unleash a dog; Ven: to slip a dog. *L. les eaux d'une écluse,* to let the water out of a lock. Mch: *L. la vapeur,* to blow off steam. F: *L. un juron,* to let out, rap out, an oath. *L. un secret,* to blurt out, let out, a secret. II. **lâcher,** *s.m.* Release (of pigeons, etc.).

lâche, a. Slovenly, slipshod (work, style).

lâcheté [lɑʃte], s.f. 1. (a) Cowardice, cowardliness. (b) Piece of, act of, cowardice. 2. (a) Dastardliness, despicableness. (b) Dastardly action.

lâcheur, -euse [lɑʃœːr, -øːz], s. F: Fickle, unreliable, person; quitter. [LÂCHER]

lacis [lasi], *s.m.* Network (of trenches, wire entanglements).

laconique [lakɔnik], a. Laconic; (man) of few words. adv. **-ment,** -ally.

'acrymal, -aux [lakrimal, -o], a. Lachrymal; tear-(gland, etc.).

lacrymogène [lakrimɔʒɛn], a. Gaz lacrymogène, lachrymatory gas, tear-gas.

lacs [lɑ], *s.m.* 1. Knotted cord. **Lacs d'amour,** love-knot. 2. Noose, snare, springe (for trapping). F: **Tendre des lacs à qn,** to set traps for s.o.

lacté [lakte], a. 1. Lacteous, milky. *Diète lactée, régime l.,* milk diet. Astr: **La Voie lactée,** the Milky Way, the Galaxy. 2. Anat: Lacteal (duct).

lactifère [laktifɛːr], a. Lactiferous, milk-bearing; lacteal (duct).

lactique [laktik], a. Ch: Lactic (acid).

lacune [lakyn], s.f. Lacuna, gap, hiatus (in text); break (in succession); blank (in memory).

lacustre [lakystr], a. Lacustrine (animal, etc.); lacustrian (dwelling, etc.). *Habitation l.,* lake-dwelling, pile-dwelling.

lad [lad], *s.m.* Stable-boy (in racing stable).

là-dedans [ladədɑ̃], adv. In there; within.

là-dehors [ladəɔːr], adv. Without, outside.

là-dessous [latsu], adv. Under that; under there.

là-dessus [latsy], adv. On that. *L.-d. il est parti,* thereupon he went away.

ladite, See LEDIT.

ladre [laːdr] 1. a. Niggardly, mean, stingy. 2. s. (f. **ladresse** [ladrɛs]) Niggard, skinflint. *Un vieux l.,* an old screw.

ladrerie [lɑdrəri], *s.f.* Meanness, stinginess.
lagon [lagɔ̃], *s.m.* **1.** Lagoon. **2.** Salt-water pool.
lagopède [lagɔpɛd], *s.m.* *Orn:* Lagopus. L. *des Alpes*, ptarmigan. L. *rouge d'Écosse*, (red) grouse.
lagune [lagyn], *s.f.* Lagoon.
là-haut [lao], *adv.* Up there.
lai¹ [lɛ], *s.m. Lit: Pros:* Lay (in eight-foot verse).
lai². **1.** *a.* Frère lai, sœur laie, lay-brother, -sister. **2.** *s.m.* Layman.
laîche [lɛʃ], *s.f. Bot:* Sedge.
laïcis|er [laisize], *v.tr.* To laicize, secularize (school, etc.). *s.f.* **-ation,** -ation.
laid [lɛ]. **1.** *a.* (*a*) Ugly; unsightly; plain (of face). *F:* **Laid comme les sept péchés capitaux, comme une chenille,** as ugly as sin. (*b*) Unseemly, unhandsome, mean, shabby, low-down (action, etc.). **2.** *s.* (*a*) Plain(-faced) person. (*b*) *F: Oh, la laide!* oh, the naughty girl!
laidement [lɛdmɑ̃], *adv.* Shabbily, meanly.
laideron [lɛdrɔ̃], *s.m. or f.* Ill-favoured woman or girl; plain Jane.
laideur [lɛdœːr], *s.f.* **1.** Ugliness, unsightliness; plainness (of features). **2.** Unseemliness, meanness, shabbiness (of conduct, etc.).
laie¹ [lɛ], *s.f.* (Wild) sow.
laie², *s.f. For:* Ride. L. *sommière,* major ride.
lainage [lɛnaːʒ], *s.m.* **1.** (*a*) Fleece (of sheep). (*b*) Woollen article. *pl.* Woollen goods, woollens. **2.** *Tex:* Teaseling, napping.
laine [lɛn], *s.f.* **1.** Wool. *Bêtes à l.,* woolly-haired animals. L. *peignée,* worsted. L. *filée,* yarn. L. *de Berlin, l. à tricoter,* Berlin wool. *Bas de l.,* woollen stockings. *F:* **Manger la laine sur le dos à qn,** to fleece s.o. **2.** (*a*) Woolly hair (of negro). (*b*) **Laine de bois,** wood fibre, wood-wool.
lainer [lɛne], *v.tr. Tex:* To teasel, nap (cloth).
lainerie [lɛnri], *s.f.* (*a*) Manufacture of woollens. (*b*) Woollen mill. (*c*) Woollen goods, woollens. (*d*) Wool-shop.
laineux, -euse [lɛnø, -øːz], *a.* Fleecy (cloth, etc.); woolly (sheep, hair, etc.).
lainier, -ière [lɛnje, -jɛːr]. **1.** *a.* Wool(len) (trade, etc.). **2.** *s.* Woollen-goods manufacturer.
laïque [laik]. **1.** *a.* Laic; lay (dress, etc.); secular (education). École laïque, undenominational school. **2.** *s.* Layman, laywoman. *Les laïques,* the laity.
lais [lɛ], *s.m.* **1.** *For:* Staddle. **2.** *Geol:* Silt, alluvium, warp. [LAISSER]
laisse¹ [lɛs], *s.f.* **1.** Leash, lead; *Ven:* slip. *F:* **Mener, tenir, qn en laisse,** to keep a tight hand over s.o. **2.** Hat-guard.
laisse², *s.f.* **1.** *Lit:* Old French epic strophe. **2.** (*a*) Beach (of shore). L. *de haute, basse, marée,* high-, low-water mark. (*b*) Wrack.
laissé-pour-compte, *s.m. Com:* Returned or rejected article; tailor's misfit. *pl. Des laissés-pour-compte.*
laisser [lɛse], *v.tr.* **1.** To let, allow. *Il le laissa partir,* he let him go, allowed him to go. *On le laissa partir,* he was suffered to go. *Je les ai laissés dire,* I let them talk away. *Elle se laissa embrasser,* she allowed herself to be kissed. **Laisser voir qch.,** to reveal sth. L. *voir son mécontentement,* to show one's displeasure. S.a. TOMBER I. **1.** **Laisser tout aller,** *F:* to let things slide. **Se laisser aller,** to get into slovenly ways. *Se l. aller dans un fauteuil,* to sink into, loll in, an arm-chair. *Ne vous laissez pas aller comme ça!* don't carry on like that! *F: Ce fruit se laisse manger,* this fruit is toothsome, palatable. *Laissez-les, -leur, boire un verre de vin,* let them have a glass of wine. *Je vous le laisse raconter,*

je vous laisse le raconter, I will let you tell it. **Laissez-le faire!** leave it to him! *Laissons faire aux dieux,* let us leave it in the hands of the gods. *Il se laissa faire* he offered no resistance. **2.** (*a*) To leave (s.o. or sth. somewhere). L. *sa valise à la consigne,* to leave one's bag in the cloak-room. L. *une veuve et trois enfants,* to leave a widow and three children. L. *qch. de côté,* to cast sth. aside. **Laisser là qn,** to leave s.o. in the lurch. L. *là qch.,* to give up doing sth.; to throw up (a job). (*b*) (i) L. *la fenêtre ouverte,* to leave, keep, the window open. L. *une page en blanc,* to leave a blank page. *Je vous laisse libre d'agir,* I leave you free to act. *Nous l'avions laissé pour mort,* we had left him for dead. (ii) To leave (s.o., sth.) alone. *Laissons cela jusqu'à demain,* we will leave that, let that stand over, till to-morrow. L. *les détails,* to pass over, leave out, the details. **Laissez donc!** please do not trouble. (iii) **Vous pouvez nous laisser,** you may leave us; you may depart. (*c*) **Laisser qch. à qn.** *Laissez-lui son secret,* let him keep his secret. L. *à qn un héritage,* to leave s.o. a legacy. *Laissez-moi vos clefs,* leave me, let me have, your keys. *Je vous le laisserai à bon compte,* I will let you have it cheap. (*d*) *Je vous laisse à penser notre bonheur,* I leave you to picture our happiness. **Cela laisse (beaucoup) à désirer,** it leaves much to be desired. (*e*) **Ne pas laisser de faire qch.,** to do sth. nevertheless; not to fail to do sth. *On ne peut l. d'admirer ce travail,* it is impossible to refrain from admiring this work. *Cela ne laisse pas (que) de m'inquiéter,* I feel anxious all the same, nevertheless.
laisser-aller [lɛseale], *s.m.inv.* **1.** Unconstraint, free-and-easiness. **2.** Carelessness, slovenliness.
laisser-faire, *s.m.* Non-interference. Politique de laisser-faire, policy of inaction, or drift.
laissez-passer, *s.m.inv.* Pass, permit. *Dipl:* Laissez-passer. *Cust:* Transire. *Rail:* Platform-ticket.
lait [lɛ], *s.m.* Milk. **1.** L. *chaud,* (i) new milk; (ii) hot milk. L. *écrémé,* skim-milk. L. *battu, de beurre,* buttermilk. L. *clair,* whey. L. *concentré,* condensed milk. **Vache à lait,** milch-cow. **Boîte à lait,** (domestic) milk-can. **Pot à lait,** milk-jug. **Dents de lait,** milk-teeth, first teeth. **Frère, sœur, de lait,** foster-brother, -sister. **Cochon de lait,** sucking-pig. **Se mettre au lait,** to go on to a milk diet. S.a. POULE 1, SOUPE 1. **2.** (*a*) L. *de coco,* coco-nut milk. (*b*) L. *de chaux,* milk of lime; whitewash. *Const:* L. *de ciment,* grout.
laitage [lɛtaːʒ], *s.m.* Dairy produce. *Vivre de l.,* to live on milk foods, on a milk diet.
laitance [lɛtãːs], *s.f.,* **laite** [lɛt], *s.f. Ich:* Milt. *Cu:* Soft roe.
laité [lɛte], *a.* Soft-roed (fish).
laiterie [lɛtri], *s.f.* **1.** Dairy. **2.** (*a*) Dairy-work. (*b*) Dairy-farming.
laiteron [lɛtrɔ̃], *s.m. Bot:* Sow-thistle.
laiteux, -euse [lɛtø, -øːz], *a.* **1.** Lacteous, milky. **2.** Milk-like, milky.
laitier¹, -ière [lɛtje, -jɛːr]. **1.** *a. L'industrie laitière,* the milk-industry; dairying. **Vache laitière,** milch-cow. **2.** *s.* (*a*) Milkman; milk-woman, milkmaid. (*b*) Dairyman; dairy-woman, dairymaid.
laitier², *s.m. Metall:* Dross, slag. L. *basique,* basic slag.
laiton [lɛtɔ̃], *s.m.* Brass.
laitue [lɛty], *s.f.* Lettuce. L. *pommée,* cabbage lettuce. L. *romaine,* cos lettuce.
laïus [lajyːs], *s.m. P:* Speech, lecture. **Piquer un laïus,** to deliver a speech.

laïusser [lajyse], *v.i.* *P:* To make a speech; *F:* to spout.

lama[1] [lama], *s.m.* (Buddhist) lama.

lama[2], *s.m.* *Z:* Llama.

lamanage [lamana:ʒ], *s.m.* In-shore pilotage.

lamaneur [lamanœ:r], *s.m.* In-shore pilot.

lamantin [lamɑ̃tɛ̃], *s.m.* *Z:* Manatee, sea-cow.

lambeau [lɑ̃bo], *s.m.* **1.** Scrap, bit, shred (of cloth, etc.). *Vêtements en lambeaux,* clothes in rags, in tatters. *(Of garment)* **S'en aller en lambeaux,** to go, fall, to pieces. **Mettre qch. en lambeaux,** to tear sth. to shreds, to rags. **2.** *Surg:* Flap (over wound).

lambin, -ine [lɑ̃bɛ̃, -in]. *F:* **1.** *a.* Dawdling, slow. **2.** *s.* Dawdler, slow-coach.

lambiner [lɑ̃bine], *v.i.* *F:* To dawdle.

lambourde [lɑ̃burd], *s.f.* **1.** *Arb:* Fruit-shoot. **2.** *Const:* (a) Wall-plate, beam-bearing. (b) Bridging-joist; sleeper (of flooring).

lambrequin [lɑ̃brəkɛ̃], *s.m.* **1.** *Her:* Mantling (of helmet). **2.** *Furn:* Valance, pelmet.

lambris [lɑ̃bri], *s.m.* **1.** Panelling, wainscoting (in wood); casing, lining (in marble, etc.). *L. d'appui,* dado. **2.** (Panelled) ceiling. *F:* **Né sous des lambris dorés,** born in the sumptuous dwellings of the rich.

lambriss|er [lɑ̃brise], *v.tr.* To wainscot, panel, line (room, etc.). *s.m.* **-age.**

lambruche [lɑ̃bryʃ], *s.f.,* **lambrusque** [lɑ̃brysk], *s.f.* Wild vine.

lame [lam], *s.f.* **1.** (a) Lamina, thin plate, strip (of metal, etc.); leaf (of spring). *Needlew:* Foil, tinsel. *L. de platine,* platinum foil. *L. de jalousie,* slat of a Venetian blind. (b) Blade (of sword, razor, etc.). *Canif à deux lames,* two-bladed penknife. *F:* **C'est une fine lame,** he's a fine swordsman. **Visage en lame de couteau,** hatchet-face. **2.** Wave; *Poet:* billow. **Lame de fond,** ground-swell. *L. de houle,* roller. *Recevoir une l.,* to be struck by a sea.

lamé [lame]. **1.** *a.* **Lamé d'argent, d'or,** spangled, worked, with silver, with gold. **2.** *s.m.* **Lamé d'or,** gold lamé, gold spangles.

lamellaire [lamelle:r], *a.* Lamellar; foliated. *El:* *Noyau l.,* laminated core (of transformer).

lamelle [lamɛl], *s.f.* (a) Lamella, lamination; lamina (of slate); thin sheet or plate (of iron); scale, flake (of mica). (b) *Sm.a:* Leaf (of sight).

lamellé [lamɛlle], **lamelleux, -euse** [lamɛllø, -øːz], *a.* Lamellate(d); foliated, fissile; flaky.

lamentable [lamɑ̃tabl], *a.* Lamentable, deplorable (accident); pitiful, pitiable (fate); woeful (voice). *adv.* **-ment.**

lamentation [lamɑ̃tasjɔ̃], *s.f.* Lamentation. **1.** (Be)wailing. **2.** Lament. *Cri de l.,* wail.

lamenter (se) [səlamɑ̃te], *v.pr.* To lament; to wail. *Se l. sur son sort,* to bewail one's lot.

lame-ressort, *s.f.* Flat spring. *pl. Des lames-ressorts.*

laminaire [lamine:r]. **1.** *a.* Laminar; *F:* flaky. **2.** *s.f. Algae:* Laminaria, sea-tangle.

lamin|er [lamine], *v.tr.* **1.** To laminate, flat(ten), roll (metal); to calender, plate-glaze (paper). **2.** *Mch:* To throttle (the steam). *s.m.* **-age.** *s.m.* **-eur.**

lamineux, -euse [laminø, -øːz], *a.* Laminous, laminose; *F:* scaly.

laminoir [laminwa:r], *s.m.* **1.** *Metalw:* (a) Flatting-mill, rolling-mill. *L. de finissage,* finishing rolls. (b) Roller (of mill). **2.** *Paperm:* Calendering machine.

lampadaire [lɑ̃pade:r], *s.m. Furn:* **1.** Standard lamp. **2.** Candelabrum.

lampant [lɑ̃pɑ̃], *a.* **Huile lampante,** lamp-oil, illuminating oil. *S.a.* PÉTROLE.

lampe [lɑ̃:p], *s.f.* Lamp. **1.** *L. à huile,* oil-lamp, paraffin lamp. *Min:* *L. de sûreté,* safety-lamp. **A la lampe,** by lamplight, in the lamplight. *P:* **S'en mettre plein la l.,** to have a good blow-out. **2.** (a) *L. à incandescence,* incandescent lamp. *L. ampoule,* electric-light bulb. *L. à arc,* arc-light. *L. à vapeur de mercure,* vapour lamp. *L. de poche,* electric torch; flash-lamp. *Cin:* *L. à lueur,* glow-lamp. *S.a.* TÉMOIN 3. (b) *L. radio-électrique, l. valve,* (wireless) valve. *L. à filament sombre,* dull-emitter valve. *L. de puissance,* power-valve. *L. amplificatrice,* amplifying valve. *S.a.* OSCILLATEUR 1, TRIODE. **3.** *L. à alcool,* spirit-lamp or -stove. *L. à souder,* brazing-lamp, blow-torch.

lampée [lɑ̃pe], *s.f.* Draught, gulp (of wine, etc.).

lamper [lɑ̃pe], *v.tr.* To swig, toss off (drink).

lampion [lɑ̃pjɔ̃], *s.m.* (a) Fairy light (for illuminations). (b) Chinese lantern.

lampiste [lɑ̃pist], *s.m. & f.* **1.** Lamp-maker. **2.** Lamplighter; lampman.

lampisterie [lɑ̃pistəri], *s.f.* **1.** Lamp-making. **2.** *Rail:* etc: Lamp-room.

lamproie [lɑ̃prwa], *s.f. Ich:* Lamprey.

lampyre [lɑ̃pi:r], *s.m.* Fire-fly, glow-worm.

lance [lɑ̃:s], *s.f.* **1.** (a) Spear. **Percer un animal d'un coup de lance,** to spear an animal. **Fer de lance,** (i) spear-head; (ii) *Rept:* fer de-lance. *Bot:* **En fer de lance,** lanceolate. (b) Lance. *F:* **Rompre une lance avec qn,** to break a lance with s.o. (c) Harpoon. **2.** (a) *L. de drapeau,* flagstaff. (b) *L. d'arrosage, l. à eau,* water-hose nozzle.

lance-bombes, *s.m.inv.* **1.** *Artil:* Trench mortar. **2.** *Av:* Bomb-releasing apparatus; bomb rack.

lance-flammes, *s.m.inv. Mil:* Flame-projector.

lancéolé [lɑ̃seɔle], *a.* Lanceolate, spear-shaped.

lance-pierres, *s.m.inv.* Catapult.

lanc|er [lɑ̃se]. **I.** *v.tr.* (je lançai(s); n. lançons) **1.** To throw, fling, cast, hurl. *L. une pierre à qn,* to throw, *F:* shy, a stone at s.o. *L. des bombes,* to throw bombs; (of aircraft) to drop bombs. *L. un avion,* to catapult a plane. *L. de la fumée,* to puff out smoke. *L. de l'eau sur qch.,* to play water on sth. *L. un coup à qn,* to deal s.o. a blow. *L. un coup d'œil à qn,* to dart a glance at s.o. *L. un mandat d'amener contre qn,* to issue a warrant against s.o. *L. un juron,* to rap out an oath. **2.** To start, set, (s.o., sth.) going. (a) *L. un cheval,* to start a horse off at full gallop. *L. un chien contre qn,* to set a dog on s.o. *Si vous le lancez sur ce sujet il ne tarira pas,* if you start him on this subject he will never stop. (b) To launch (ship, scheme, attack); to release (bomb, parachute); to send up (balloon); to float, promote (company); to bring out (actress, etc.); to initiate, set (fashion). *El.E:* To switch on (current). *Aut:* *L. le moteur,* to start (up) the engine. *Av:* *L. l'hélice,* to swing the propeller. *L. une marchandise,* to put an article on the market. *L. une souscription,* to start a fund. **Lancer qn** *(dans les affaires, etc.),* to set s.o. on his feet (in business, etc.); to give s.o. a start. *s.m.* **-ement.**

se lancer *en avant,* to rush, dash, shoot, forward. *Se l. à la poursuite de qn,* to dash off in pursuit of s.o. *Se l. dans les affaires,* to launch out into business. *Se l. (à fond) dans la description de qch.,* to plunge (headlong) into a description of sth. *F:* **Il se lance!** he's going it!

II. lancer, *s.m.* **1.** *Ven:* (a) Release (of pigeons, etc.). (b) Pêche au lancer, casting, spinning.

lancé, *a.* **1.** *Train l. à toute vapeur,* train going at full speed. *Sp:* **Départ lancé,** flying

start. Le voilà lancé, (i) now he has got a start (in life) ; (ii) F : now he's on his pet subject. Il est éloquent une fois l., he is eloquent when once he gets going. Il était un peu l., his tongue was wagging ; he'd had a drop. **2.** Actrice lancée, actress who has made her name.

lance-torpille, s.m. Navy: Torpedo-tube. pl. Des lance-torpilles.

lancette [lɑ̃sɛt], s.f. **1.** Surg: Lancet. **2.** Arch: (Arc à) lancette, lancet-arch.

lanceur, -euse [lɑ̃sœːr, -øːz], s. **1.** Thrower. **2.** Promoter, floater (of company, etc.) ; initiator (of fashion).

lancier [lɑ̃sje], s.m. **1.** Mil: Lancer. **2.** (Quadrille des) lanciers, lancers.

lancinant [lɑ̃sinɑ̃], a. Lancinating, shooting (pain).

lanciner [lɑ̃sine], v.i. (Of pain) To shoot; (of finger, etc.) to throb.

lançon [lɑ̃sɔ̃], s.m. Ich: Sand-eel, -lance.

landau, -aus [lɑ̃do], s.m. Veh: Landau.

lande [lɑ̃ːd], s.f. Sandy moor ; heath ; waste.

Landerneau [lɑ̃dɛrno]. Pr.n. (Small town near Brest, in Brittany) F : = Little Pedlington, Slocum-in-the-Hole.

landier[1] [lɑ̃dje], s.m. Andiron, fire-dog.

landier[2], s.m. F : (= AJONC) Furze, gorse.

langage [lɑ̃gaːʒ], s.m. Language ; speech (of the individual, as opposed to the common language of a whole people. Cp. LANGUE 3). Correction du l., correctness of speech, of language. Tenir un langage aimable, grossier, à qn, to speak amiably, rudely, to s.o. Vous tenez là un étrange l., that is a strange way to talk. F : Changer de langage, to sing another tune. En voilà un l.! that's no way to talk ! En l. ordinaire, in common parlance.

lange [lɑ̃ːʒ], s.m. (a) Baby's napkin. (b) pl. Swaddling-clothes.

langoureu|x, -euse [lɑ̃gurø, -øːz], a. Languid, languorous. Amant l., languishing lover. adv. **-sement.**

langouste [lɑ̃gust], s.f. Spiny lobster ; F. & Com: crayfish.

langoustine [lɑ̃gustin], s.f. Norway lobster.

langue [lɑ̃ːg], s.f. **1.** Tongue. Tirer la langue, (i) to put out one's tongue (à qn, at s.o.) ; (ii) (of dog) to hang out its tongue ; F : (of pers.) to be near the end of one's tether. Avoir la langue liée, to be tongue-tied. Avoir la langue déliée, bien pendue, to have a glib tongue, F : the gift of the gab. F : Je l'avais sur le bout de la langue, I had it on the tip of my tongue. Coup de langue, (i) click (of the tongue) ; tonguing (on wind instrument) ; (ii) lick ; (iii) cutting remark. Faire aller les langues, to set people's tongues wagging. Jeter, donner, sa langue aux chiens, au chat, (with reference to riddle, etc.) to give it up. Mauvaise langue, backbiter, mischief-maker. S.a. AVALER 1. **2.** Tongue (of flame) ; spit (of land) ; gore (of sail). **3.** Language, speech, tongue (of a people). L. maternelle, mother tongue. Langues étrangères, foreign languages. Professeur de langues vivantes, modern-language master. Don des langues, gift of tongues. F : Langue verte, slang.

langue-de-cerf, s.f. Bot: Hart's-tongue.

langue-de-chat, s.f. Cu: (Wafer-like) finger-biscuit. pl. Des langues-de-chat.

languette [lɑ̃gɛt], s.f. Small tongue (of wood, metal) ; strip (of tin-foil) ; tongue (of shoe). Ph: Pointer (of balance). Mec.E: Feather(-key), spline. Carp: Assemblage à rainure et languette,

groove-and-tongue joint. El: Contact à languette, snap contact.

langueur [lɑ̃gœːr], s.f. **1.** Languor, languidness ; listlessness. Maladie de langueur, decline. **2.** Languishment. Regard plein de l., languishing look.

languir [lɑ̃giːr], v.i. To languish, pine. L. d'amour, to be sick for love. L. d'ennui, to yawn one's life away. Languir pour qn, to long, pine, yearn, for s.o. L. après qch., to long for sth. Ne nous faites pas languir, don't keep us on tenter-hooks. Ne pas laisser l. la conversation, to keep the conversation alive. Th: L'action languit, the action drags.

languissant [lɑ̃gisɑ̃], a. **1.** Languid, listless. Marché l., dull market. **2.** Languishing (look).

lanière [lanjɛːr], s.f. Thin strip of material ; esp. thin strap ; thong ; (leather) lace ; lash (of whip). Drapeau réduit en lanières, flag reduced to ribbons.

lanigère [laniʒɛːr], a. Lanigerous, wool-bearing.

lansquenet [lɑ̃skənɛ], s.m. Lansquenet.

lanterne [lɑ̃tɛrn], s.f. **1.** (a) Lantern. L. sourde, dark lantern. L. vénitienne, Chinese lantern. L. magique, magic lantern. L. de poche, pocket lamp. L. (de) tempête, hurricane-lamp. S.a. VESSIE 1. (b) L. de voiture, de bicyclette, carriage-, cycle-lamp. Aut: L. à feu blanc, side-light. L. à feu rouge, l. arrière, tail-light. (c) A : L. de rue, street-lamp. Fr.Hist: (During the Revolution) A la lanterne! string him up ! **2.** Arch: Lantern(-turret). Mec.E: (Roue à) lanterne, lantern(-wheel), trundle(-wheel).

lanterneau [lɑ̃tɛrno], s.m. Skylight (over staircase) ; lantern(-light).

lanterner [lɑ̃tɛrne]. F : **1.** v.i. To trifle ; to dilly-dally. **2.** v.tr. (a) To shilly-shally with (s.o.) ; to put (s.o.) off. (b) To bother, importune.

lanternier, -ière [lɑ̃tɛrnje, -jɛːr], s. (a) Lantern-maker. (b) Lamplighter.

lantiponner [lɑ̃tipone], v.i. F : = LANTERNER 1.

lantur(e)lu [lɑ̃tyrly], int. (Burden of old songs) **1.** You don't catch me ! I'm not having any ! **2.** Wait and see !

La Palice, La Palisse [lapalis]. Pr.n.m. F : Vérité de (monsieur de) La Palice, self-evident truth ; truism.

lapalissade [lapalisad], s.f. = Vérité de La Palice.

lapier [lape], v.tr. (Of dog, cat) To lap (up) (milk, etc.). s.m. **-ement.**

lapereau [lapro], s.m. Young rabbit.

lapidaire [lapidɛːr]. **1.** a. Lapidary (inscription, style) ; concise (style). **2.** s.m. Lapidary.

lapidateur, -trice [lapidatœːr, -tris], s. **1.** Stoner. **2.** pl. F : Vilifiers.

lapidation [lapidasjɔ̃], s.f. Lapidation, stoning.

lapider [lapide], v.tr. To lapidate ; to stone (s.o.) to death ; F : to throw stones at (dog). L. qn dans les journaux, to vilify s.o., to hurl abuse at s.o., in the Press.

lapilleux, -euse [lapijø, -øːz], a. Gritty (pear).

lapin, -ine [lapɛ̃, -in], s. Rabbit, f. doe (of tame rabbit). Cf. HASE. L. mâle, buck rabbit. L. de garenne, wild rabbit. L. domestique, de clapier, F : l. de choux, tame rabbit. Com: Peau de lapin, cony(-skin). P : Poser un lapin à qn, to fail to turn up ; to hoax s.o. C'est un rude lapin, (i) he is a fine fellow ; (ii) he's a plucky one ! F : Être en lapin, (i) to sit beside the driver or chauffeur ; (ii) to sit bodkin in car, etc.).

lapis-lazuli [lapislazyli], s.m.inv. Lapis lazuli. a.inv. Robe l.-l., bright-blue dress.

lapon, -one [lapɔ̃, -ɔn]. **1.** a. Lappish, Lapp. **2.** s. Lapp, Laplander.

Laponie [laponi]. Pr.n.f. Lapland.

laps¹ [laps], *s.m.* **Un laps de temps,** a lapse, space, of time.

laps², *a. Ecc:* **Être laps et relaps,** *f.* **être lapse et relapse,** to have relapsed into a former heresy.

lapsus [lapsy:s]. *Lt.s.m.* Slip, mistake, lapse. *L. linguae,* slip of the tongue. *L. calami,* slip of the pen. *L. de mémoire,* lapse of memory.

laquais [lakɛ], *s.m.* Lackey, footman. *Pej: F:* Flunkey. **Petit laquais,** buttons.

laque [lak]. **I.** *s.f.* (*a*) Lac. **Gomme laque,** gum lac. *L. en écailles, en plaques,* shellac. (*b*) *Paint:* Lake. **2.** *s.m.* Lacquer. **Laque de Chine,** japan.

laquelle [lakɛl], *pron.f.* See LEQUEL.

laquer [lake], *v.tr.* (*a*) To lacquer, to japan. (*b*) *F:* **Meubles laqués de blanc,** white-enamelled furniture. *s.* **-eur, -euse.**

larbin [larbɛ̃], *s.m. F:* Flunkey.

larcin [larsɛ̃], *s.m. Jur:* Larceny; petty theft.

lard [la:r], *s.m.* (*a*) Back-fat, flare, fleed (esp. of pig). *F:* **Faire du lard,** to grow stout. **Rentrer dans le lard à qn,** to go for s.o. (*b*) Bacon. (*c*) *L. de baleine,* blubber.

larde [lard], *s.f. Cu:* Larded joint.

larder [larde], *v.tr.* To lard (piece of meat). *F:* *L. qn de coups d'épée,* to inflict numerous (stab-)wounds on s.o. *L. qn d'épigrammes,* to shower epigrams on s.o. *L. ses écrits de citations,* to (inter)lard one's writings with quotations.

lardoire [lardwa:r], *s.f. Cu:* Larding-needle.

lardon [lardɔ̃], *s.m.* (*a*) Piece of larding bacon; lardon, lardoon. (*b*) *F:* Jibe; cutting remark.

lare [la:r], *s.m. Rom.Ant:* Household god; lar. *Esp. pl.* **Dieux lares,** Lares.

largable [largabl], *a. Av:* (Of petrol-tank, etc.) That can be dropped; releasable. [LARGUER]

large [larʒ]. **I.** *a.* (*a*) Broad, wide. *L. d'épaules,* broad-shouldered. *Route l. de vingt pieds,* road twenty feet wide. *D'un geste l.,* with a broad, sweeping, gesture. *Critique à l'esprit l.,* broad-minded critic. *Au sens le plus l. du mot,* in the most liberal sense of the word. *Être l. en affaires,* to be generous, free, liberal, in business. *adv.* **Peindre large,** to paint boldly, broadly. *Calculer l.,* to allow a good margin for error. *Rac:* **Prendre le tournant l.,** to take the turning wide. *Portes larges ouvertes,* wide-open doors. (*b*) Large, big, ample. **Prendre une l. part dans la direction,** to take a large share in the management. **2.** *s.m.* (*a*) Room, space. **Vous êtes au large ici,** you have plenty of room here. (*b*) *Nau:* Open sea. **Brise du l.,** sea-breeze. **Prendre le large,** (i) to put to sea; (ii) *F:* to decamp. *Mettre le cap au l.,* to stand out to sea. **Gagner au large,** to get an offing. *Se tenir au l.,* to keep out at sea. **Au large,** (i) in the offing; (ii) (to small boat) keep away! keep off! *Au l. de Cherbourg,* off Cherbourg. *Trop au l.,* too far from the shore. (*c*) Breadth. *Route qui a vingt pieds de l.,* road twenty feet wide. **Se promener de long en large,** to walk up and down, to and fro.

largement [larʒəmɑ̃], *adv.* (*a*) Broadly, widely. *Services l. rétribués,* highly-paid services. *Opinion l. répandue,* widely held opinion; wide-spread opinion. *Art:* **Peindre l.,** to paint in a free, broad, style. (*b*) Amply. *Avoir l. de quoi vivre,* to have ample means.

largesse [larʒɛs], *s.f.* **1.** Liberality (*envers,* towards). **2.** *A. & Hum:* Bounty, largess(e). **Faire largesse,** to make handsome presents.

largeur [larʒœːr], *s.f.* Breadth, width; beam (of ship); span (of arch); gauge (of railway track). *L. de vues, d'esprit,* broadness of outlook, of mind. *Avoir trois pieds de l.,* to be three feet wide.

largue [larg], *a. Nau:* **1.** (Of rope, etc.) Loose,

slack. **2.** (Of wind) Large, free. **Naviguer vent largue,** to sail off the wind; to run free.

larguer [large], *v.tr.* **1.** *Nau:* (*a*) To let go, loose (rope). *L. l'amarre,* to cast off, slip, the mooring rope. *Largué!* all gone! *Av:* *L. un réservoir,* to release, drop, get rid of, a tank. (*b*) To let out, unfurl (sail). *S.a.* RIS². **2.** (*a*) To blow off, let off (steam). (*b*) To release (balloon). **3.** *v.i. Nau:* (Of seams) To start, to gape.

larme [larm], *s.f.* Tear. **Fondre en larmes,** to burst into tears. *Elle eut une crise de larmes,* she burst into tears. **Pleurer à chaudes larmes,** to weep copiously, bitterly. *Faire venir des larmes aux yeux de qn,* to bring tears to s.o.'s eyes. *Elle était (tout) en larmes,* she was in tears. **Avoir la larme facile, avoir toujours la larme à l'œil,** to be easily moved to tears. **Il a ri (jusqu')aux larmes,** he laughed till he cried, till the tears came. *F:* Y aller de sa (petite) larme, to shed a (perfunctory) tear. *Larmes de commande, de crocodile,* crocodile tears. *F:* **Prendre une l. de rhum dans son café,** to take just a drop of rum in one's coffee.

larmier [larmje], *s.m.* **1.** *Anat:* (*a*) Inner canthus; corner (of the eye). (*b*) Tear-bag (of deer). **2.** *Arch:* Drip(-stone); gutter-overhang; weather-moulding.

larmoyant [larmwajɑ̃], *a.* **1.** (*a*) Weeping, tearful. (*b*) *Med:* *Yeux larmoyants,* watering eyes. **2.** *Pej:* Lachrymose, doleful, maudlin (voice); soppy (sentimentality).

larm|oyer [larmwaje], *v.i.* (je **larmoie;** je **larmoierai**) **1.** (Of the eyes) To water. **2.** *Pej:* To shed tears, to snivel. *s.m.* **-oiement.**

larron [larɔ̃], *s.m.* **1.** (*a*) *A:* Robber, thief. *F:* **S'entendre comme larrons en foire,** to be as thick as thieves. *S.a.* OCCASION 1. (*b*) Thief (in candle). **2.** *Typ:* Bite (in the paper).

larvaire [larvɛ:r], *a.* (*a*) Larval. (*b*) Immature.

larve [larv], *s.f.* Larva; grub (of insect).

laryngien, -ienne [larɛ̃ʒjɛ̃, -jɛn], *a.* Laryngeal.

laryngite [larɛ̃ʒit], *s.f. Med:* Laryngitis. *L. striduleuse,* false croup, child-crowing.

laryngoscope [larɛ̃goskop], *s.m.* Laryngoscope.

laryngotomie [larɛ̃gotomi], *s.f.* Laryngotomy.

larynx [larɛ̃:ks], *s.m. Anat:* Larynx.

las¹ [lɑ(s)], *int. A:* Alack! alas!

las², lasse [lɑ, lɑs], *a.* Tired, weary. *Être las de qch.,* to be (sick and) tired of sth. *S.a.* GUERRE 2.

lascar [laska:r], *s.m.* **1.** Lascar. **2.** *P:* (Fine, clever, lazy, etc.) fellow.

lasc|if, -ive [lasif, -i:v], *a.* Lascivious, lewd. *adv.* **-ivement.**

lasciveté [lasivte], *s.f.* Lasciviousness, lewdness.

lasser [lɑse], *v.tr.* To tire, weary; to exhaust (s.o.'s patience).

se lasser, to grow tired or weary; to tire. *Se l. de qch.,* to get tired of sth. *Se l. d'attendre,* to grow weary of waiting.

lassitude [lɑsityd], *s.f.* Lassitude, tiredness, weariness.

lasso [laso], *s.m.* Lasso. *Prendre un cheval au l.,* to lasso a horse.

latanier [latanje], *s.m. Bot:* Latania. *L. de Bourbon,* Bourbon palm.

latent [latɑ̃], *a.* Latent (disease, *Phot:* image, *Ph:* heat); hidden, concealed.

latéral, -aux [lateral, -o], *a.* Lateral. *Rue latérale,* side-street or cross-street. *Entrée latérale,* side-entrance. *adv.* **-ement.**

latin, -ine [latɛ̃, -in]. **I.** (*a*) *a. & s.* Latin (people, etc.). **Le Quartier latin,** the students' quarter (of Paris). (*b*) *a. Nau:* *Voile latine,* lateen sail. **2.** *s.m. Ling:* Latin. **Bas l.,** low Latin. *F:* **Latin de cuisine,** dog-Latin. **Être au bout de son**

latin, to be at one's wits' end. **J'y perds mon latin,** I can't make head or tail of it.
latinité [latinite], *s.f.* Latinity.
latitude [latityd], *s.f.* Latitude. **1.** Scope, freedom. **2.** *Geog:* *Être sous telle ou telle l.,* to be in such and such a latitude. *Par 30° (de) l. nord,* in latitude 30° North.
Latran [latrɑ̃]. *Pr.n.m.* **Le palais de Latran,** the Lateran Palace. **Saint-Jean de Latran,** Saint John Lateran.
latrines [latrin], *s.f.pl.* Latrines.
latte [lat], *s.f.* **1.** Lath, batten, slat. *L. volige,* slate-lath, roof-batten. *Fer en lattes,* slat-iron. **2.** Straight (heavy cavalry) sword.
latt|er [late], *v.tr.* To lath; to batten. *Mch:* To lag (cylinder). *s.m.* **-age.**
lattis [lati], *s.m.* **1.** Lathing, lath-work. **2.** Lattice-work.
Latvie [latvi]. *Pr.n.f. Geog:* Latvia.
laudanisé [lodanize], *a.* Containing laudanum.
laudanum [lodanɔm], *s.m.* Laudanum.
laudatif, -ive [lodatif, -iːv], *a.* Laudatory.
lauracé [lorase]. *Bot:* **1.** *a.* Lauraceous. **2.** *s.f.pl.* **Lauracées,** lauraceae.
lauréat, -ate [lɔrea, -at], *s.* Laureate, prizeman; (prize-)winner.
Laurent [lɔrɑ̃]. *Pr.n.m.* Lawrence.
lauréole [lɔreɔl], *s.f. Bot:* Daphne.
laurier [lɔrje], *s.m. Bot:* Laurel. *L. commun,* bay-laurel, sweet bay. **Couronne de lauriers,** bay wreath; bays. *F:* **Cueillir, moissonner, des lauriers,** to reap, win, laurels, glory. **Se reposer sur ses lauriers,** to rest on one's laurels.
laurier-cerise, *s.m.* Cherry-laurel.
laurier-rose, *s.m.* Common oleander, rose-laurel.
laurier-sauce, *s.m.* = *laurier commun.*
lavable [lavabl], *a.* Washable.
lavabo [lavabo], *s.m.* **1.** *Ecc:* Lavabo (ritual or towel). **2.** Lavatory-basin, wash-hand basin. **3.** (Place for washing) (*a*) Lavatory (in schools, etc.). (*b*) Pit-head baths.
lavallière [lavaljɛːr], *s.f.* Loosely tied bow.
lavande [lavɑ̃ːd], *s.f. Bot:* Lavender. **Eau de lavande,** lavender-water.
lavandière [lavɑ̃djɛːr], *s.f.* **1.** Washerwoman; laundress. **2.** *Orn:* (Grey) wagtail.
lavaret [lavarɛ], *s.m. Ich:* Lavaret, pollan.
lavasse [lavas], *s.f.* Thin, watery, soup or wine; *F:* slops, cat-lap, dish-water; *P:* hog-wash.
lavatory [lavatɔri], *s.m.* Public lavatory (and convenience).
lave [laːv], *s.f. Geol:* Lava.
lavement [lavmɑ̃], *s.m.* (Rectal) injection; enema.
lave-pieds [lavpje], *s.m. inv.* Foot-bath.
lav|er [lave], *v.tr.* To wash. (*a*) *Se l.,* to wash (oneself); *F:* to have a wash. *Se l. les mains,* to wash one's hands. *L. le plancher à grande eau,* to swill the floor. *L. la vaisselle,* to wash up. *L. une plaie,* to bathe a wound. *Ind: L. un gaz,* to scrub a gas. *S.a.* LINGE 1. *F:* **Laver la tête à qn,** to haul s.o. over the coals; to give s.o. a good dressing-down. *P:* **Laver sa montre,** to sell one's watch. (*b*) *L. un dessin,* to wash a drawing. (*c*) (Of stream) *L. un pré,* to wash against, flow along, a meadow. *s.m.* **-age.**
lavé, *a.* *Couleur lavée,* faint, washed-out, colour. *Bleu l.,* light blue.
lavette [lavɛt], *s.f.* (*a*) (Dish-)mop; saucepan-brush. *L. métallique,* scrubber. (*b*) Dish-cloth.
laveur, -euse [lavœːr, -øːz]. **1.** *s.* (Pers.) Washer; scrubber (of gas). *Laveuse de linge,* washer-woman. *Laveuse de vaisselle,* scullery maid,

F: washer-up. **2.** *a. Ch:* Flacon lavour, scrubber, washing-bottle (for gases). **3.** *s.f.* **Laveuse mécanique,** (laundry) washing-machine.
lavis [lavi], *s.m.* **1.** Washing, tinting (of drawing). **2.** Wash-tint. **Épure au lavis,** wash-drawing, tinted drawing.
lavoir [lavwaːr], *s.m.* (*a*) Wash-house. (On the Seine) Boat wash-house. (*b*) Washing and rinsing board by riverside.
lavure [lavyːr], *s.f.* **1.** (Kitchen) swill, dish-water, hog-wash. **2.** Metal turnings and filings.
laxatif, -ive [laksatif, -iːv], *a. & s.m. Med:* Laxative, aperient.
layet(t)erie [lɛjɛtri], *s.f.* **1.** Box-making. **2.** Baby-linen making.
layetier [lɛjtje], *s.m.* Packing-case maker, box-maker.
layette [lɛjɛt], *s.f.* **1.** Packing-case; box. **2.** Set of baby garments; layette.
layon [lɛjɔ̃], *s.m.* **1.** Tail-board (of cart). **2.** *For:* Cross-ride; service-path.
lazaret [lazarɛ], *s.m.* Lazaret(to); quarantine station or camp.
lazzi [lazi, ladzi], *s.m.pl.* (*a*) Piece of buffoonery. (*b*) Jeers, hooting, catcalls.
le¹, les [lə, le, la, lɛ], *def.art.* (*Le* and *la* are elided to l' before a vowel or h 'mute.' *Le* and *les* contract with *à, de,* into *au, aux; du, des.*) The. **1.** (Particularizing) (*a*) *Ouvrez la porte,* open the door. *Il est venu la semaine dernière,* he came last week. *J'apprends le français,* I am learning French. *La province a perdu le quart de ses habitants,* the province has lost a quarter of its inhabitants. *L'un . . . l'autro,* (the) one . . . the other. *Il est arrivé le lundi 12,* he arrived on Monday 12th. (*b*) *La France,* France. *Le Mont Blanc,* Mont Blanc. (*c*) *L'empereur Guillaume,* the Emperor William. *Le roi Édouard,* King Edward. *Le colonel Chabot,* Colonel Chabot. *Le petit Robert,* little Robert. (*d*) *Le Dante,* Dante. *Le Tasse,* Tasso. *Le Havre,* Havre. *Le Caire,* Cairo. *Je me rends au Caire,* I am going to Cairo. *Le peintre Le Brun,* the painter Le Brun. *Les tableaux de Le Brun,* Le Brun's pictures. (*e*) (With most feast-days) *La Toussaint,* All Saints' Day. *F: A la Noël,* at Christmas. (*f*) (Often with parts of the body) *J'ai mal à la gorge,* I have a sore throat. *Elle a les yeux bleus,* she has blue eyes. *Hausser les épaules,* to shrug one's shoulders. *Elle ferma les yeux,* she closed her eyes. *Il s'est pincé le doigt,* he pinched his finger. *Les yeux leur cuisaient,* their eyes were smarting. **2.** (Forming superlatives) *Dès les temps les plus anciens,* from the earliest times. *Mon amie la plus intime,* my most intimate friend. *C'est elle qui est la plus heureuse,* she is (the) happiest (one). *C'est elle qui travaille le mieux,* she works best. *Elle est le plus heureuse quand elle est seule,* she is happiest when she is by herself. **3.** (Generalizing) *Je préfère le café au thé,* I prefer coffee to tea. **4.** (Distributive) *Trois fois l'an,* three times a year. *Cinq francs la livre,* five francs a pound. **5.** Partitive *du, de la, des.* See DE III.
le², la, les, *pers.pron.* **1.** (Replacing sb.) Him, her, it, them. (*a*) *Je vous le, la, présenterai,* I will introduce him, her, to you. *Je ne le lui ai pa donné,* I did not give it to him. *Êtes-vous le parents de cet enfant?—Nous les sommes,* are you the parents of this child?—We are. *Les voilà* there they are! (*b*) (Following the vb.) *Donnez le-lui,* give it to him. *Donne-le à ton frèr* [dɔnlɔatɔ̃frɛːr], give it to your brother. **2.** *Neut pron.* Le. (*a*) (Replacing an adj. or a sb. used a an adj.) *Malheureux, je l'étais certainement*

unhappy I certainly was. *Étes-vous mère?—Je le suis,* are you a mother?—I am. (b) (Replacing a clause) (i) So. *Il me l'a dit,* he told me so. *On me l'a dit,* I was told so. (ii) *Il est plus riche que vous (ne) le pensez,* he is richer than you think (he is). *Vous le devriez,* you ought to.

lé [le], *s.m.* **1.** *Tex:* Width, breadth (of cloth). **2.** Towage-way (between field and stream).

lebel [labɛl], *s.m. Sm.a:* Lebel rifle.

léchage [leʃa:ʒ], *s.m.* **Surface de léchage,** air-surface (of radiator, etc.). [LÉCHER]

lèche[1] [lɛʃ], *s.f. F:* Thin slice (of bread, meat).

lèche[2], *s.f. P:* **Faire de la lèche auprès de qn,** to suck up to s.o.; to toady to s.o. [LÉCHER]

lèchefrite [lɛʃfrit], *s.f. Cu:* Dripping-pan.

lécher [leʃe], *v.tr.* (je lèche; je lécherai) **1.** To lick. *Le chat lécha tout le lait répandu,* the cat licked up all the spilt milk. *Se l. les doigts,* to lick one's fingers. *F:* **Il s'en léchait les doigts,** he smacked his lips over it. **Lécher les bottes de qn,** to lick s.o.'s boots; to toady to s.o. *Surface léchée par les flammes,* surface exposed to the flames. **2.** To over-polish (work, style).

leçon [ləsɔ̃], *s.f.* **1.** (a) Reading (of a manuscript, etc.). *Bonne l.,* true reading. (b) *Ecc:* Lesson (at Matins, etc.). **2.** *Sch:* Lesson. *L. de choses,* object-lesson. *Leçons particulières,* private lessons. *Prendre des leçons de français,* to take lessons in French. *Leçons de chant,* singing lessons. **Donner une leçon à qn,** (i) to give s.o. a lesson; (ii) to teach s.o. a lesson. *Que cela vous serve de l.,* let that be a lesson, a warning, to you. **Faire la leçon à qn,** (i) to prime, drill, s.o. (in what he has to say or do); (ii) to sermonize s.o. *Faire réciter les leçons,* to hear the lessons.

lecteur, -trice [lɛktœ:r, -tris], *s.* **1.** (a) Reader. S.a. AVIS 2. (b) *Typ:* (Proof-)reader. (c) *Mus:* **Être bon lecteur,** to be a good reader at sight. **2.** (a) Reader aloud. (b) Lecturer (in German university); foreign assistant (in French university). **3.** *s.m.* (a) *Phot:* Retouching desk. (b) *Cin:* Lecteur des sons, lecteur phonique, sound-reproducing unit; sound pick-up.

lecture [lɛkty:r], *s.f.* Reading. (a) *Enseigner la l. à qn,* to teach s.o. to read. *Livre d'une l. agréable,* book that makes pleasant reading. *Cabinet de lecture,* (i) reading-room or news-room (of library); (ii) lending library. **Livre en lecture,** book 'out.' **Prendre lecture d'un contrat,** to read through a contract. (b) **Lecture à haute voix,** reading aloud. **Faire la lecture à qn,** to read aloud to s.o. **Donner lecture de l'ordre du jour,** to read out the agenda. (c) *Lecture sonore d'un film,* reproduction of a sound film; sound pick-up.

ledit, ladite, *pl.* **lesdits, lesdites** [lədi, ladit, ledi, ledit], *a. Jur:* The aforesaid (Dupont, etc.).

légal, -aux [legal, -o], *a.* Legal; statutory. *Fête légale,* statutory holiday. **Avoir recours aux moyens légaux,** to have recourse to the law. *Médecine légale,* forensic medicine. *adv.* **-ement.**

légalisation [legalizasjɔ̃], *s.f.* Authentication, certification (of signature, etc.).

légaliser [legalize], *v.tr.* **1.** To legalize (holiday). **2.** To attest, certify, authenticate (signature).

légalité [legalite], *s.f.* Legality, lawfulness. **Rester dans la légalité,** to keep within the law.

légat [lega], *s.m. Ecc:* *Rom.Ant:* Legate.

légataire [legatɛ:r], *s.m. & f. Jur:* Legatee, devisee, heir. *L. universel,* residuary legatee. *L. d'une propriété,* heir to an estate.

légation [legasjɔ̃], *s.f.* Legation.

lège [lɛ:ʒ], *a.* (Of ship) Light. **Tirant d'eau en lège,** light draught. S.a. DÉPLACEMENT 3, FLOTTAISON.

légendaire [leʒãdɛ:r], *a.* (a) Legendary (story, etc.). (b) *F:* Epic (combat, etc.).

légende [leʒã:d], *s.f.* **1.** Legend. *Le domaine de la l.,* the region of fable. **2.** (a) Inscription, legend (on coin, etc.). (b) Caption, legend (of drawing, etc.). *Typ:* Underline. (c) List of references; key (to diagram, etc.).

lég|er, -ère [leʒe, -ɛ:r], *a.* **1.** (a) Light (weight, artillery, food, etc.). *L. à la course,* light, fleet, of foot. **Achille au pied léger,** swift-foot(ed) Achilles. **Avoir le cœur léger,** to be light-hearted. **Avoir le sommeil léger,** to be a light sleeper. **Avoir la main légère,** to be quick, clever, with one's hands. *Être l. d'argent,* to have a light purse. **Avoir le style léger,** to write with a light touch. *Conduite légère,* flighty conduct; fickle conduct. *Propos légers,* (i) frivolous, idle, talk; (ii) free talk. (b) Slight (pain, mistake); gentle (breeze); mild (tobacco, beer); weak (tea, coffee); faint (sound). *Il y a un l. mieux,* there is a slight improvement. *Perte légère,* trivial loss. **2.** *Adv.phr.* **A la légère,** (i) lightly; (ii) without due consideration; wantonly. *Vêtu à la légère,* lightly clad. *Prendre un engagement à la légère,* to commit oneself without due reflection. *Conclure à la légère,* to jump to conclusions. *adv.* **-èrement.** *s.f.* **-èreté,** -ness.

légiférer [leʒifere], *v.i.* (je légifère; je légiférerai) To legislate (*sur,* on).

légion [leʒjɔ̃], *s.f.* Legion. **La Légion étrangère,** the Foreign Legion. **La Légion d'honneur,** the Legion of Honour. *F:* *L. de moucherons,* host, swarm, of gnats. **Ils s'appellent légion,** their name is legion.

légionnaire [leʒjɔnɛ:r], *s.m.* **1.** (a) *Rom. & Fr.Hist:* Legionary. (b) Soldier of the Foreign Legion. **2.** Member of the Legion of Honour.

législateur, -trice [leʒislatœ:r, -tris]. **1.** *s.* Legislator, lawgiver. **2.** *a.* Legislative (power).

législatif, -ive [leʒislatif, -i:v], *a.* (a) *Fr.Hist:* **L'Assemblée législative,** the Legislative Assembly. (b) *Élection législative,* parliamentary election.

législation [leʒislasjɔ̃], *s.f.* (a) Legislation. (b) (Set of) laws. *L. criminelle,* criminal law.

législature [leʒislaty:r], *s.f.* Legislature; legislative body.

légiste [leʒist], *s.m.* Legist, jurist.

légitimation [leʒitimasjɔ̃], *s.f.* **1.** Legitimation (of child). **2.** (a) Official recognition (of title, etc.). (b) Submission of credentials.

légitime [leʒitim], *a.* **1.** Legitimate, lawful (child, wife, etc.). S.a. HÉRITIER. **2.** (a) Justifiable, rightful; well-founded (fears, etc.). *Jur:* **Légitime défense,** self-defence. (b) Sound (deduction). *adv.* **-ment.**

légitimer [leʒitime], *v.tr.* **1.** To legitimate, legitimatize (child, etc.). **2.** To justify (claim, etc.). **3.** To recognize (title).

légitimisme [leʒitimism], *s.m. Fr.Hist:* Legitimism; adherence to the elder branch of the Bourbon dynasty.

légitimiste [leʒitimist], *a. & s.* Legitimist.

légitimité [leʒitimite], *s.f.* **1.** Legitimacy (of child, of title). **2.** Lawfulness (of measure, etc.).

legs [lɛ], *s.m.* Legacy, bequest. *Faire un l. à qn,* to leave a legacy to s.o. *F:* **Coureur de legs,** legacy-hunter.

léguer [lege], *v.tr.* (je lègue; je léguerai) To bequeath, leave (personalty); to devise (realty).

légume [legym], *s.m.* **1.** (a) Vegetable. *Légumes verts,* greens. (b) *Bot:* Legume(n), pod. **2.** *F:* **Gros légume,** *P:* **grosse légume,** bigwig.

légumier [legymje], *s.m.* Vegetable dish.

Léman [lemɑ̃]. *Pr.n.m.* **Le lac Léman,** the Lake of Geneva.

lémur(e) [lemyːr], *s.m.* Z: Lemur.

lendemain [lɑ̃dmɛ̃], *s.m.* Next day; morrow. *Le l. de la bataille,* the day after the battle. *Le l. matin,* the next morning, the morning after. *Du jour au lendemain il devint célèbre,* he awoke to find himself famous. **Des succès sans lendemains,** short-lived successes.

lendit [lɑ̃di], *s.m.* Inter-schools athletic sports competition.

lénifier [lenifje], *v.tr.* Med: To assuage, soothe.

lénitif, -ive [lenitif, -iːv]. **I.** *a.* Lenitive, soothing. **2.** *s.m.* Med: Lenitive.

lent, lente[1] [lɑ̃, lɑ̃ːt], *a.* Slow. *Mort lente,* lingering death. *L. à agir,* slow to act, slow in action. *L. à croire,* slow of belief. *Avoir la parole lente,* to be slow of speech. *adv.* **-ement.**

lente[2], *s.f.* Nit; egg (of louse).

lenteur [lɑ̃tœːr], *s.f.* **I.** Slowness. *Mettre de la l. à faire qch.,* to be slow in doing sth. **Avec lenteur,** slowly; with due deliberation. *L. à répondre,* (i) slowness to answer; (ii) dilatoriness, remissness, in answering. **2.** *pl.* *Les lenteurs de l'administration,* the delays, dilatoriness, of the government departments.

lenticule [lɑ̃tikyl], *s.f.* Bot: Duckweed.

lentigo [lɑ̃tigo], *s.m.* Med: Lentigo, freckles.

lentille [lɑ̃tiːj], *s.f.* **I.** Bot: (a) Cu: Lentil. *B.Lit:* **Plat de lentilles,** (Esau's) mess of pottage. (b) **Lentille d'eau,** duckweed. **2.** Bob, ball (of pendulum). **3.** Opt: (a) (Spectacle) lens; single lens. (b) Component (of photographic lens, etc.): *Objectif à quatre lentilles,* four-component lens. (c) Crystalline lens (of eye). **4.** Freckle.

lentisque [lɑ̃tisk], *s.m.* Bot: Lentiscus; F: mastic-tree.

léonin [leɔnɛ̃], *a.* Leonine, lion-like. **Part léonine,** lion's share.

léopard [leɔpaːr], *s.m.* Leopard. *L. des neiges,* snow-leopard; ounce.

lépidoptère [lepidɔptɛːr]. Ent: **I.** *a.* Lepidopterous. **2.** *s.m.* Lepidopteran. *pl.* **Lépidoptères,** lepidoptera.

léporide [lepɔrid], *s.m.* Leporide; Belgian hare.

lèpre [lepr], *s.f.* Leprosy.

lépreux, -euse [leprø, -øːz]. **I.** *a.* Leprous. **2.** *s.* Leper.

léproserie [leprozri], *s.f.* Leper-hospital.

lepte [lept], *s.m.* Arach: Leptus. *L. automnal,* harvest-bug; harvest-mite.

lequel, laquelle, lesquels, lesquelles [ləkɛl, lakɛl, lekɛl], *pron.* (Contracted with *à* and *de* to **auquel, auxquel(le)s, duquel, desquel(le)s**) **I.** *rel.pron.* Who, whom; which. (a) (Of thgs after prep.) *Les adresses auxquelles il devait m'écrire,* the addresses at which he was to write to me. *Décision par laquelle . . .,* decision whereby. . . . (b) (Of pers.) *Ont comparu trois témoins, lesquels ont déclaré . . .,* three witnesses appeared, who averred. . . . *Les deux officiers entre lesquels elle était assise,* the two officers between whom she was seated. *La dame avec laquelle elle était sortie,* the lady with whom she had gone out. *La dame chez laquelle je l'ai rencontrée,* the lady at whose house I met her. (c) (To avoid ambiguity) *Le père de cette jeune fille, lequel est très riche,* the girl's father, who is very rich. *Il épousa une sœur de Colin, laquelle le rendit très heureux,* he married one of Colin's sisters, who made him very happy. (d) (Adjectival) *Voici cent francs, laquelle somme vous était due,* here are a hundred francs, which sum was owing to you. *Il écrira peut-être, auquel cas . . .,*

perhaps he will write, in which case. . . . **2.** *interr.pron.* Which (one)? *Lequel de ces chapeaux préférez-vous?* which of these hats do you prefer? *Lequel d'entre nous?* which one of us? *Lesquels préférez-vous?* which do you prefer?

lérot [lero], *s.m.* Z: Lerot; garden dormouse.

les[1]. See LE[1], [2].

lès, les[2] [lɛ, le], *prep.* (In place names) Near(-by). *Plessy-les-Tours,* Plessy near Tours.

lesdit(e)s. See LEDIT.

lèse [lez], *a.f.* Injured. *Crime de lèse-humanité,* outrage against humanity.

lèse-majesté *s.f.* High treason, lese-majesty.

léser [leze], *v.tr.* (je lèse; je léserai) (a) To wrong (s.o.); to wound, injure (s.o., s.o.'s pride, etc.). *La partie lésée,* the injured party. (b) (Of action) To prove injurious to (s.o.'s interests). (c) *Le coup a lésé un nerf,* the blow has injured a nerve.

lésine [lezin], *s.f.* Stinginess, niggardliness.

lésiner [lezine], *v.i.* To be stingy, close-fisted; to haggle (*sur,* over).

lésinerie [lezinri], *s.f.* **I.** Stingy act; piece of stinginess. **2.** = LÉSINE.

lésineur, -euse [lezinœːr, -øːz]. **I.** *a.* Close-fisted, niggardly. **2.** *s.* (Old) hunks; niggard.

lésion [lezjɔ̃], *s.f.* Injury, hurt. Med: Lesion. *Jur:* Wrong.

lesquels, -elles. See LEQUEL.

lessive [lɛsiːv], *s.f.* **I.** Lye. **2.** (Household) washing. (a) **Faire la lessive,** to do the washing. *Envoyer qch. à la l.,* to send sth. to the wash. (b) Soiled linen (going to the wash). (c) Articles washed. *Étendre la l.,* to hang out the washing.

lessiv|er [lɛsive], *v.tr.* **I.** (a) To wash (linen, etc.) in lye; to buck, boil (linen). (b) To scrub, swill (floor, etc.). F: **Lessiver la tête à qn,** to haul s.o. over the coals. **2.** P: *L. sa montre,* to sell one's watch; to turn one's watch into money. *s.m.* **-age.**

lessiveuse [lɛsivøːz], *s.f.* Washing-machine.

lest [lest], *s.m.* No *pl.* Ballast (of ship or balloon). *Navire sur lest,* ship in ballast(-trim). *L. en gueuses,* kentledge. **Faire son lest,** to take in ballast. **Jeter du lest,** (i) to discharge ballast; (ii) F: to make sacrifices (in order to attain one's end). *Il a besoin de l.,* he lacks ballast.

leste [lest], *a.* **I.** Light; nimble, agile (person, animal); smart, brisk. F: **Avoir la main leste,** to be free with one's hands. **2.** (a) Unceremonious, unscrupulous (behaviour); sharp (practice). (b) *Être l. dans ses discours,* to be free, broad, in one's conversation. *adv.* **-ment.**

lest|er [leste], *v.tr.* **I.** To ballast (ship, balloon). F: *Se l. l'estomac,* to have a good feed. **2.** To weight (fishing-net, etc.). *s.m.* **-age.**

léthargie [letarʒi], *s.f.* (a) Med: Death-trance. (b) Lethargy, apathy.

léthargique [letarʒik], *a.* Lethargic(al).

Léthé [lete]. *Pr.n.m.* Myth: (The river) Lethe.

léthifère [letifɛːr], *a.* Lethiferous; deadly (juice); lethal (weapon); death-dealing (device).

lette [let], *s.m.,* **lettique** [let(t)ik], *s.m.* Ling: Lettic, Lettish.

letton, -one [letɔ̃, -ɔn]. **I.** *a. & s.* (a) Ethn: Lett. (b) Geog: Latvian. **2.** *s.m.* Ling: = LETTE.

Lettonie [letɔni]. *Pr.n.f.* Geog: Latvia.

lettrage [letraːʒ], *s.m.* Lettering.

lettre [letr], *s.f.* Letter. **I.** **Écrire qch. en toutes lettres,** to write sth. out in full. **2.** **Selon la lettre de la loi,** according to the letter of the law. **A la lettre, au pied de la lettre,** to the letter; literally. **Rester lettre morte,** to remain a dead letter. S.a. ÉPREUVE 3. **3.** (a) Epistle, missive. *L. recommandée,* registered letter. **Cela a passé comme**

une lettre à la poste, it went down easily, without any difficulty. *Post:* L. *de rebut,* dead letter, unclaimed letter. (*b*) **Lettre de grâce,** reprieve. *pl.* **Lettres patentes,** letters patent. *Lettres de noblesse,* letters patent of nobility. **Lettre de crédit,** letter of credit. S.a. CHANGE 1, CRÉANCE 2. (*c*) **Lettre de voiture,** way-bill, consignment note. S.a. MARQUE². **4.** *pl.* Literature, letters, humanities. **Homme de lettres,** man of letters. *Avoir des lettres,* to be well read.

lettré [letre]. **1.** *a.* Lettered, well-read, literate (person). **2.** *s.m.* Scholar.

lettrine [letrin], *s.f. Typ:* **1.** Reference letter, superior letter. **2.** (Ornamental) initial letter.

leu [lø], *s.m. A: =* LOUP. (Used in the phr.) **A la queue leu leu,** (i) in single file, in Indian file; (ii) helter-skelter.

leucocyte [løkɔsit], *s.m. Physiol:* Leucocyte; white blood-corpuscle.

leucome [løko:m], *s.m. Med:* Leucoma, albugo.

leur¹ [lœ(:)r]. **1.** *poss.a.* [lœr]. Their. *Leur oncle et leur tante,* their uncle and (their) aunt. *Leurs père et mère,* their father and mother. **2. Le leur** [lœːr], **la leur, les leurs.** (*a*) *poss.pron.* Theirs. *J'ai écrit à mes amis et aux leurs,* I wrote to my friends and to theirs. (*b*) *s.m.* (i) Their own (property, etc.). *Ils n'y mettent pas du leur,* they don't pull their weight, they don't do their share. (ii) *pl.* Their own (friends, followers, etc.). *Je m'intéresse à eux et aux leurs,* I am interested in them and in theirs. (iii) *F: Ils continuent à faire des leurs,* they go on playing their old tricks.

leur², *pers.pron.* See LUI¹.

leurre [lœːr], *s.m.* (*a*) Lure (for hawks). (*b*) Decoy (for birds); (artificial) bait, lure (for fish). (*c*) Allurement, catch, take-in.

leurrer [lœre], *v.tr.* (*a*) To lure (hawk, etc.). (*b*) To bait (fish); to decoy (bird). (*c*) *F:* To allure, entice, gull (s.o.). *Se l. d'illusions,* to delude oneself.

levage [ləva:ʒ], *s.m.* **1.** Lifting (up), hoisting, raising. *Câble de l.,* hoisting cable. *Cric de l.,* lifting jack. **2.** Levying (of taxes, etc.).

levain [ləvɛ̃], *s.m.* Leaven. *L. de bière,* barm, yeast. **Poudre levain,** baking-powder. **Pain sans levain,** unleavened bread.

levant [ləvɑ̃]. **1.** *a.m.* **Soleil levant,** rising sun. **2.** *s.m.* (*a*) **Le levant,** the east. (*b*) *Geog:* **Le Levant,** the Levant.

levantin, -ine [ləvɑ̃tɛ̃, -in], *a. & s.* Levantine.

lève-glace(s), *s.m.inv. Aut:* Window-raiser; winder.

lever [ləve]. **I.** *v.tr.* (**je lève; je lèverai**) **1.** (*a*) To raise, to lift (up) *L. les épaules,* to shrug one's shoulders. **J'en lève la main,** I swear to it. **Lever la main sur qn,** to raise one's hand against s.o. *L. la tête,* (i) to hold up one's head; (ii) to raise one's head, to look up. *L. les yeux,* to look up. *L. le store,* to pull up, draw up, the blind. **Lever l'ancre,** to weigh anchor. *Ven: L. le gibier,* to put up, flush, the birds. *L. un étendard,* to raise a standard. (*b*) To raise (siege, interdict); to strike (camp); to cancel (arrest); to close, adjourn (meeting). *L. une saisie,* to lift an embargo. (*c*) *L. un complet sur une pièce d'étoffe,* to cut off a suit-length from a web. (*d*) *L. une difficulté,* to remove a difficulty. *L. tous les doutes,* to remove all doubts. **Lever les scellés,** to break, remove, the seals. *L. une sentinelle,* to withdraw a sentry. **2.** To collect, gather (crops); to raise, levy (troops); to levy (tax). *L. les lettres,* to collect the letters. *L. une boîte,* to clear a letter-box. **3.** **Lever un plan,** to make, draw, get out, a plan; to effect a survey. **4.** *v.i.* (*a*) (Of plants) To shoot.

(*b*) (Of dough) To rise. **Faire lever la pâte,** to raise the dough.

se lever. (*a*) To stand up. *Se l. de son siège,* to rise from one's seat. *Se l. de table,* to leave the table. (*b*) To get up (from bed); to rise (early, late). *Je me lève de bonne heure,* I am an early riser. *F: Se lever du pied gauche,* to get out of bed on the wrong side. **Faire lever qn,** (i) to rouse s.o. (from his sleep, etc.); (ii) to make s.o. get up or stand up. (*c*) *Le jour se lève,* day is breaking, is dawning. *Le vent se lève,* the wind is rising. (*d*) **Faire lever une perdrix,** to put up, flush, a partridge.

II. lever, *s.m.* **1.** (*a*) Rising; getting up (from bed). (*b*) Levee (of sovereign, etc.). (*c*) **Lever du soleil,** sunrise. **2.** *Th:* **Lever du rideau,** rise of the curtain. **Un lever de rideau en un acte,** a one-act curtain-raiser. **3.** = LEVÉ 2.

levé. 1. *a.* (*a*) Raised. **Voter à main levée,** to vote by a show of hands. **Dessin à main levée,** (i) free-hand drawing; (ii) sketch. **Pierre levée,** standing stone; menhir. (*b*) *Blé l.,* wheat spearing. *Pâte bien levée,* well raised dough. (*c*) (Of pers.) Up, out of bed; (of sun, etc.) up. *Rester l. à attendre qn,* to wait up for s.o. **2.** *s.m.* (*a*) **Voter par assis et levé,** to give one's vote by rising or remaining seated. (*b*) *Surv: L. d'un terrain,* plan, survey, of a piece of land. **Faire le levé d'un terrain,** to survey a piece of ground.

levée, *s.f.* **1.** (*a*) Raising, lifting. **Puissance de levée,** lifting power (of crane). (*b*) Raising (of siege); striking (of camp); lifting (of embargo); cancellation (of arrest); closing, adjourning (of meeting). S.a. ÉCROU¹. (*c*) Breaking (of seals). (*d*) Gathering (of crops); levy(ing) (of troops, taxes). *Post:* Collection (of letters); clearing (of letter-boxes). *La l. est faite,* the box has been cleared. **2.** (*a*) Spearing (of corn). (*b*) Rising (of court, etc.). (*c*) *Nau: L. de la lame,* surge, swell. (*d*) *Mch:* (Up) stroke (of piston); lift (of cam). **3.** (*a*) Embankment, sea-wall, dike, levee. (*b*) *Mec.E:* Cam, lifter. (*c*) *Cards:* **Faire une levée,** to take a trick.

lève-roues, *s.m. inv. Veh:* Wheel-jack.

lève-soupapes, *s.m.inv. Tls:* Valve-spring lifter.

levier [ləvje], *s.m.* **1.** Lever. **Force de levier,** leverage. **Bras de levier,** (i) lever arm; (ii) leverage. **Faire levier sur qch.,** to prize against sth. *L. de commande,* control lever. *L. de pompe,* pump-handle. *Aut: L. des vitesses,* gear lever. **2.** Crow-bar. **3.** *Sm.a:* Bolt-lever (of rifle).

lévite [levit]. **1.** *s.m. B:* Levite. **2.** *s.f. Cost:* (Man's) warm indoor gown; dressing-gown.

levraut [ləvro], *s.m.* Leveret; young hare.

lèvre [lɛːvr], *s.f.* **1.** Lip. *F:* **J'ai le mot sur le bord des lèvres,** I have the word on the tip of my tongue. S.a. CŒUR 2. **Du bout des lèvres,** in a forced, artificial, manner. *Rire du bout des lèvres,* to force a laugh. **Pincer les lèvres,** to prim (up) one's mouth; to purse, screw up, one's lips. S.a. DESSERRER, MORDRE 1. **2.** (*a*) Rim (of crater). (*b*) Lip (of wound).

levrette [ləvrɛt], *s.f.* Greyhound (bitch).

lévrier [levrje], *s.m.* Greyhound. *L. d'Écosse,* deer-hound. *L. russe,* borzoi. *Courses de lévriers,* greyhound racing; *F:* gracing.

levure [ləvyːr], *s.f.* Yeast. *L. de bière,* barm.

lexicographe [leksikɔgraf], *s.m.* Lexicographer.

lexicographie [leksikɔgrafi], *s.f.* Lexicography.

lexicologie [leksikɔlɔʒi], *s.f.* Lexicology.

lexique [leksik], *s.m.* (*a*) Lexicon. (*b*) Glossary; vocabulary (at end of book, etc.).

Leyde [lɛd]. *Pr.n.f. Geog:* Leyden. *El:* **Bouteille de Leyde,** Leyden jar.

lez [le], *prep.* = LÈS.

lézard [lezaːr], *s.m.* Lizard. *L. des murailles,* wall lizard. *F: Faire le lézard,* to bask in the sun.

lézarde [lezard], *s.f.* Split, crevice, cranny, chink (in wall, plaster).

lézarder [lezarde]. **1.** *v.tr.* To crack, split (plaster, etc.). **2.** *v.i. F:* (*a*) To bask in the sun; to sun oneself. (*b*) To lounge, loaf. **se lézarder,** (of wall) to crack, split. **lézardé,** *a.* (Of wall, plaster) Cracked, full of cracks; crannied.

liais [ljɛ], *s.m.* Hard limestone.

liaison [ljezɔ̃], *s.f.* **1.** (*a*) Joining, binding. *Const:* (i) Bonding (of bricks, etc.); (ii) mortar, cement. *Mus:* (i) Slur; (ii) tie, ligature. (*b*) *Ling:* Sounding of final consonant before initial vowel sound; liaison. (*c*) *Cu:* Thickening (of sauce). (*d*) *Mil:* Liaison, intercommunication, touch (between units). S.a. AGENT 2. **2.** Intimacy; intimate relationship. *L. d'affaires,* business connection.

liaisonner [ljezɔne], *v.tr.* **1.** To bond (bricks, etc.). **2.** To grout, point (stonework).

liane [ljan], *s.f. Bot:* Liana; (tropical) creeper.

liant [ljɑ̃]. **1.** *a.* (*a*) Winning, good-natured, responsive. *Il est l. avec tout le monde, U.S:* he is a good mixer. *Peu liant,* stand-offish. (*b*) Flexible, pliant, springy (rod, etc.); tough (metal); easily worked (dough, etc.). **2.** *s.m.* (*a*) Winning manner, responsiveness, amiability. *Avoir du liant,* to have an engaging manner. (*b*) Flexibility, pliability, springiness. **3.** *s.m. Civ.E:* Binding material (of road). [LIER]

liard [ljaːr], *s.m. A:* Liard, half-farthing. *F: Il n'a pas un* (rouge) *liard,* he hasn't a red cent.

liarder [ljarde], *v.i. F:* To haggle over every halfpenny.

liardeur, -euse [ljardœːr, -øːz], *s. F:* **1.** Haggler. **2.** Skinflint.

lias [ljɑ(s)], *s.m. Geol:* Lias.

liasse [ljas], *s.f.* Bundle, packet (of letters, etc.); wad (of bank-notes); file (of papers).

libage [libaː3], *s.m.* Rubble; rough ashlar.

Liban [libɑ̃]. *Pr.n.m. Geog:* Lebanon.

libation [libasjɔ̃], *s.f.* Libation; drink-offering. *F: Faire d'amples libations,* to indulge in copious potations.

libelle [libɛl], *s.m.* Lampoon; scurrilous satire.

libeller [libɛlle], *v.tr.* To draw up, word (document, etc.); to sign and date (sketch, etc.). **libellé,** *s.m.* **1.** Drawing up, wording (of document). **2.** Wording, terms used (in document).

libelliste [libɛllist], *s.m.* Lampoonist.

libellule [libɛllyl], *s.f. Ent:* Dragon-fly.

liber [libɛr], *s.m. Bot:* Inner bark; bast.

libéral, -ale, -aux [liberal, -o]. **1.** *a.* Liberal. (*a*) Broad, wide (education, etc.). (*b*) Generous; bountiful; open-handed. **2.** *a. & s. Pol:* Liberal. *adv.* **-ement.**

libéralité [liberalite], *s.f.* Liberality. **1.** (*a*) Breadth (of outlook). (*b*) Generosity; open-handedness. **2.** Act of liberality; gift. *Faire des libéralités à qn,* to give liberally to s.o.

libérateur, -trice [liberatœːr, -tris]. **1.** *a.* Liberating. **2.** *s.* Liberator, deliverer.

libération [liberasjɔ̃], *s.f.* (*a*) Liberation, freeing, releasing; exemption (from military service); discharge (of prisoner). (*b*) Payment in full; discharge.

libératoire [liberatwaːr], *a. Monnaie libératoire,* legal tender (currency). (Of money) *Avoir force libératoire,* to be legal tender.

libérer [libere], *v.tr.* (je libère, je libérerai)

(*a*) To liberate, release; to set (s.o.) free; to discharge (prisoner, debtor). *L. un soldat,* to discharge a soldier (to the reserve). (*b*) To free from debt. **se libérer,** to free oneself. *Se l. d'une dette,* to redeem a debt.

liberté [libɛrte], *s.f.* **1.** Liberty, freedom. (*a*) *Animaux en liberté,* animals in freedom. *Mettre qn en liberté,* to set s.o. free; to liberate s.o. *L'hydrogène est mis en l. à la cathode,* hydrogen is released, comes off, at the cathode. *Jur:* (*Mise en*) *liberté provisoire sous caution,* bail. *Avoir pleine liberté d'action,* (i) to have full liberty of action; (ii) (of engine part) to have free play. *L. de conscience, de la presse,* liberty, freedom, of conscience, of the press. *Parler avec liberté, en toute liberté,* to speak freely, without restraint. *Prendre la l. de faire qch.,* to take leave to do sth. *Mon jour de l.,* my free day, my day off. (*b*) *Il fait tout avec l. et grâce,* he is free and graceful in all his actions. *Art: L. de crayon, de pinceau,* breadth, boldness, of touch. **2.** *Prendre des libertés avec qn,* to take liberties, make free, with s.o.

libertin, -ine [libɛrtɛ̃, -in]. **1.** *a.* (*a*) *A:* Free-thinking. (*b*) Licentious, dissolute. (*c*) Wayward, freakish (imagination). **2.** *s.* (*a*) *A:* Free-thinker. (*b*) Libertine, rake.

libertinage [libɛrtinaːʒ], *s.m.* Libertinage.

libidineux, -euse [libidinø, -øːz], *a.* Libidinous, lustful.

libraire [librɛːr], *s.m., occ. f.* Bookseller.

libraire-éditeur, *s.m.* Publisher. *pl. Des libraires-éditeurs.*

librairie [librɛri], *s.f.* (*a*) Book-trade, bookselling. *Inédit en librairie,* not published in book form. *Ouvrages en l.,* published books. (*b*) Bookshop. *L. de neuf et d'occasion,* new and secondhand bookseller. (*c*) Publishing house.

libre [libr], *a.* Free. **1.** (*a*) *Homme né l.,* man born free. *Traduction l.,* free translation. *Vers libres,* free verse. (To porter) *Êtes-vous l.?* are you disengaged? *Quand je suis l.,* when I am off duty. *Être libre de faire qch.,* to be free to do sth. *Je suis l. de mon temps,* my time is my own. *Libre arbitre,* free will. *Libre parole,* free speech. *Libre penseur,* free-thinker. S.a. ENTRÉE 2, PRATIQUE² 6. (*b*) *L. de préjugés,* free from prepossessions. *L. de soucis,* free from care; carefree. (*c*) *Jeune fille d'allures libres,* free-mannered young woman. *Conversation l.,* free, broad, conversation. (*d*) *Jeune fille à la taille l.,* well set up, supple, young woman. *Art: Avoir la main l.,* to draw or paint boldly, broadly. **2.** (*a*) Clear, open (space, road); vacant, unoccupied (table, seat). *Avoir du temps de l.,* to have some time free. *On m'a donné un jour l.,* I have been given a day off. *F: Le champ est libre,* the coast is clear. *Rail:* "*Voie libre,*" 'line clear.' *Tp:* "*Pas libre,*" 'line engaged.' (Taxi sign) "*Libre,*" 'for hire.' (*b*) *Mec.E:* Disengaged, running free, out of gear. *Cy:* **Roue libre,** free wheel. *adv.* **-ment.**

libre-échange, *s.m. Pol.Ec:* Free trade.

libre-échangiste, *s.m.* Free-trader. *pl. Des libre-échangistes.*

librettiste [librɛttist], *s.m. Th:* Librettist.

libretto [librɛtto], *s.m.* Libretto, *F:* book of an opera). *pl. Des libretti, des librettos.*

lice¹ [lis], *s.f. A:* Lists. *Entrer en lice contre qn,* (i) to enter the lists against s.o.; (ii) *F:* to have a tilt at s.o.

lice², *s.f. Ven:* Hound bitch.

lice³, *s.f. Tex:* **1.** Heddle. **2.** Warp. **Tapisserie**

de haute lice, de basse lice, high-warp, low-warp, tapestry.

licence [lisã:s], *s.f.* Licence. **1.** (a) Leave, permission. *L. de débitant,* liquor licence. *Détenteur d'une l.,* licensee. (b) *Sch :* Licentiate's degree. *L. ès lettres, ès sciences, en droit,* degree in arts, in science, in law. **Passer sa licence,** to take one's degree. **2.** (a) Abuse of liberty. *L. poétique,* poetic licence. **Prendre des licences avec qn,** to take liberties with s.o. (b) Licentiousness.

licenci|er [lisãsje], *v.tr.* To disband. *s.m.* **-ement.**

licencié, -ée, *s.* **1.** Licentiate. *L. ès lettres,* (approx. =) master of arts. *L. en droit* = bachelor of laws. **Être reçu licencié,** to take one's degree. **2.** Licensee, licence-holder.

licencieu|x, -euse [lisãsjø, -ø:z], *a.* Licentious, ribald. *adv.* **-sement.**

licet [liset], *s.m.* Permit, leave.

lichen [likɛn], *s.m. Bot :* Lichen. *L. d'Islande,* Iceland moss.

lich|er [liʃe], *v.tr. P :* **1.** To lick. **2.** (a) To drink up (tot of spirits, etc.). (b) *Abs.* To drink, to tipple. *s.* **-eur, -euse.**

licite [lisit], *a.* Licit, lawful, permissible. *adv.* **-ment.**

licol [likɔl], *s.m. Harn :* Halter; head-stall.

licorne [likɔrn], *s.f.* **1.** *Myth :* Unicorn. **2.** *Z :* **Licorne de mer,** sea-unicorn, narwhal. **3.** *Astr :* **La Licorne,** Monoceros; the Unicorn.

licou, *pl.* **-ous** [liku], *s.m.* = LICOL.

licteur [liktœ:r], *s.m. Rom.Ant :* Lictor.

lie[1] [li], *a.f. A :* Joyous. **Faire chère lie,** to live well.

lie[2], *s.f.* Lees, dregs. **Boire le calice jusqu'à la lie,** to drain the cup (of sorrow, etc.) to the dregs. **Lie de vin,** (i) lees of wine (in cask); (ii) *a.inv.* purplish red, lie-de-vin. *F : La lie du peuple,* the scum, dregs, of the populace.

liebig [libig], *s.m.* Beef extract.

liège [ljɛ:ʒ], *s.m.* **1.** *Bot :* Cork-oak. **2.** (a) Cork. **Cigarettes à bouts de liège,** cork-tipped cigarettes. (b) *Fish :* Cork, float.

lien [ljɛ̃], *s.m.* **1.** Tie, bond. **Rompre ses liens,** to burst one's bonds, one's fetters. *Liens du sang,* ties of blood. *L. d'amitié,* bond of friendship. **2.** Diagonal brace, tie, strap, band.

li|er [lje], *v.tr.* **1.** (a) To bind, fasten, tie, tie up. *L. les pieds et les mains à qn,* to bind s.o. hand and foot. **S.a.** FOU 1. *L. les lacets de ses souliers,* to tie, knot, one's shoe-laces. *Ce contrat vous lie,* you are bound by this agreement. *L'intérêt nous lie,* we have common interests. *L. des idées,* to connect, link, ideas. *L. deux lettres,* to join (up) two letters. *L. deux mots,* to link two words (in pronunciation); to sound the liaison. *Mus : L. deux notes,* to tie two notes. (b) *Cu : L. une sauce,* to thicken, give body to, a sauce. **2. Lier connaissance avec qn,** to strike up an acquaintance with s.o. **Lier conversation avec qn,** to enter into conversation with s.o. *s.m.* **-age.**

se lier. 1. *Se l. (d'amitié) avec qn,* to form a friendship with s.o.; to become intimate with s.o. **2.** (a) (Of sauce) To thicken. (b) (Of gravel, concrete) To bind.

lié, *a.* **1.** Bound. **Avoir la langue liée,** to be tongue-tied. **2.** *Être (très) lié avec qn,* to be intimately acquainted with s.o. **3.** *Notes liées,* (i) tied, (ii) syncopated, notes. **4. Jouer une partie liée,** to play the best (out) of three (games).

lierre [ljɛr], *s.m.* **1.** Ivy. **2. Lierre terrestre,** rampant, ground-ivy.

liesse [ljɛs], *s.f. A :* Jollity, gaiety. **La ville était en liesse,** the town was given up to rejoicing; it was a gala occasion.

lieu, -eux [ljø], *s.m.* **1.** Place. (a) Locality, spot. **Mettre qch. en lieu sûr,** to put sth. in a safe place. **En tout lieu,** everywhere. **En aucun lieu,** nowhere. *En quelque l. que ce soit,* wherever it be. **En haut lieu,** in high circles, in high places. *Je tiens ce renseignement de bon l.,* I have this information from a good source. *Le l. du sinistre,* the scene of the disaster. **J'étais sur le lieu, sur les lieux,** I was on the spot. **Un mauvais lieu,** an evil haunt. **En (tout) premier lieu,** in the first place, first of all, firstly. *En troisième l.,* in the third place, thirdly. **En dernier lieu,** last of all, lastly. **S.a.** TEMPS 1. (b) *pl.* House, premises. *Jur :* **Sur les lieux,** on the premises. **S.a.** VIDER 1. (c) *pl. F :* **Lieux d'aisances,** (i) privy, w.c.; (ii) latrines. **2.** (a) **Avoir lieu,** to take place. *La réunion aura l. à . . .,* the meeting will be held at. . . . (b) Ground(s), cause. **Il y a (tout) lieu,** *j'ai lieu, de supposer que + ind.,* there is, I have, (good) ground, (every) reason, for supposing that. . . . *Il y a l. d'attendre,* we had to be (as) well to wait. *Je vous écrirai s'il y a l.,* I shall write to you if need be, should occasion arise. **Donner lieu à des désagréments,** to give rise to trouble. *Tout donne l. de croire que . . .,* everything leads us to believe that. . . . (c) **Tenir lieu de qch.,** to take the place of, stand instead of, sth. *La caisse nous tenait l. de table,* the box stood us instead of a table. **Au lieu de,** instead of, in lieu of. *Au l. de son frère,* in his brother's stead. **Au lieu que** + *ind.,* whereas. **3.** *Geom :* Locus. **4. Lieux communs,** commonplaces, platitudes.

lieue [ljø], *s.f.* League (= 4 kilometres). *Deux lieues* = five miles. **Être à mille lieues de croire qch.,** to be far from believing sth. *Bottes de sept lieues,* seven-league boots.

lieur, -euse [ljœ:r, -ø:z]. **1.** *s.* Binder (of sheaves, etc.). **2.** *s.f.* Lieuse, (mechanical) sheaf-binder.

lieutenance [ljøtnã:s], *s.f.* Lieutenancy.

lieutenant [ljøtnã], *s.m.* (a) *Mil : Navy :* Lieutenant. *L. de vaisseau,* lieutenant-commander. (b) *Mercantile Marine :* Mate. **Premier l.,** second mate. (c) *L. de port,* harbour-master.

lieutenant-colonel, *s.m.* Lieutenant-colonel.

lièvre [ljɛ:vr], *s.m. Z :* Hare. *F :* **C'est vous qui avez levé le lièvre,** you started it. **Prendre le lièvre au gîte,** to catch s.o. napping. **Courir deux lièvres à la fois,** to try to do two things at once. **Mémoire de lièvre,** memory like a sieve. **S.a.** CERVELLE 2, GÉSIR.

lift [lift], *s.m.* Lift; *U.S :* elevator.

liftier, -ière [liftje, -jɛːr], *s.* Lift-man, -boy; lift-girl; lift-attendant.

ligament [ligamã], *s.m.* Ligament.

ligature [ligaty:r], *s.f.* **1.** Tying, binding. **Fil de ligature,** binding wire. **2.** (a) *Mus :* Tie. (b) Splice (in cable). (c) *Surg : Typ :* Ligature.

ligaturer [ligatyre], *v.tr.* To bind, whip, splice; to tie (sth.) up. *Surg :* To ligature (artery, etc.).

lignage [liɲa:ʒ], *s.m.* Lineage, descent. **Demoiselle de haut lignage,** maiden of high degree.

lignard [liɲa:r], *s.m. F :* Soldier of the line.

ligne [liɲ], *s.f.* Line. **1.** (a) Cord. **Ligne de pêche,** fishing-line. *L. droite,* straight line. *Mth : La l. des x,* des *y,* the x, y, axis (for co-ordinates). **Tracer une ligne,** to draw a line. *Fb : L. de touche,* touch-line. *Ten : L. de fond,* base-line. (c) (Out)line. *Fermeté, pureté, des lignes,* boldness, purity, of line (in picture). **Auto qui a de la ligne,** car with clean lines. **Grandes lignes d'une œuvre,** broad outline of a work. (d) *L. de flottaison,* water-line (of ship). *Ph : L. de force,* line of force. *L. de conduite,* line of conduct. *Suivre la l. du devoir, de l'honneur,* to follow the path of duty, of honour. *Descendre en l. directe de* . . ., to be lineally descended from. . . . (*e*) *L. de maisons,* row of houses. *Se mettre en ligne,* to line up ; to draw up in a line. *Question qui vient en première ligne,* question of primary importance. *Hors ligne,* out of the common ; outstanding, incomparable (artist, etc.). (*f*) *L. d'écriture,* line of writing. *Écris-moi deux lignes,* drop me a line. *Lire entre les lignes,* to read between the lines. *Aller à la ligne,* to begin a new paragraph. **2.** (*a*) *Mil: Lignes de retranchement,* the lines. **Rentrer dans ses lignes,** to retire within one's lines. (*b*) **Bataillon, vaisseaux, en ligne,** battalion, ships, in line. **Ligne de bataille,** line of battle, battle-line. **Infanterie de ligne,** line infantry ; infantry of the line. *Navy:* **Vaisseau de ligne,** ship of the line ; man-of-war. S.a. FRONT 3. **3.** (*a*) *Ligne de chemin de fer,* railway line. *L. de paquebots,* steamship line. *L. d'autobus,* bus service. (*b*) *L. télégraphique,* telegraph line. *El.E: Les fils de l.,* the mains.

lignée [liɲe], *s.f.* Issue ; (line of) descendants. *De bonne l. puritaine,* of good puritan stock. *Chien de bonne l.,* pedigree dog.

ligneux, -euse [liɲø, -øːz], *a.* Ligneous, woody.

lignite [liɲit], *s.m.* Lignite ; brown coal.

lignosité [liɲozite], *s.f.* Woodiness.

ligot|er [liɡɔte], *v.tr.* To bind (s.o.) hand and foot ; to tie (s.o.) up ; to lash (thgs) together. *s.m.* **-age.**

ligue [liɡ], *s.f.* League, confederacy.

liguer [liɡe], *v.tr.* To league, bond, (nations, etc.) together. *Être ligué avec qn,* to be in league with s.o.
se liguer, to league, to form a league.

lilas [lila], **1.** *s.m. Bot :* Lilac. **2.** *a.inv.* Lilac.

liliacées [liljase], *s.f.pl. Bot :* Liliaceae.

lilial, -aux [liljal, -o], *a.* (*m.pl.* form usu. avoided) Lily-like, lily-white.

lilliputien, -ienne [lilipysjɛ̃, -jɛn], *a. & s.* Lilliputian.

limace [limas], *s.f.* **1.** *Moll :* Slug. **2.** Archimedean screw.

limaçon [limasɔ̃], *s.m.* **1.** (*a*) Snail. *Escalier en limaçon,* spiral staircase. (*b*) **Limaçon de mer,** periwinkle. **2.** Cochlea (of the ear). **3.** = LIMACE 2.

limaille [limaːj], *s.f.* Filings. *L. de fer,* iron filings.

limande [limɑ̃ːd], *s.f.* **1.** *Ich :* Dab. **2.** *Carp :* Graving piece. **3.** Straight-edge (of carpenter, etc.). **4.** *Nau :* Parcelling (of rope).

limbe [lɛ̃ːb], *s.m.* **1.** *Bot : Mth :* Limb. *Astr :* Rim, edge (of the sun, etc.). **2.** *Theol :* Les Limbes, limbo.

lime[1] [lim], *s.f.* **1.** *Tls :* File. *L. triangulaire,* three-square file. *Grosse l.,* rasp. *L. à ongles,* nail-file. *L. de carton, d'émeri,* emery-board. *Aiguiser un outil à la lime,* to file up a tool. *Enlever une saillie à la lime,* to file off a projection. *Donner un coup de lime à qch.,* to give sth. a touch up with a file. **2.** *Moll :* Lima.

lime[2], *s.f. Bot :* Sweet lime.

lim|er [lime], *v.tr.* To file ; to file up ; to file off ; to file down. *s.m.* **-age.** *s.m.* **-eur.**

limeuse [limøːz], *s.f.* Filing-machine ; shaping-machine.

limier [limje], *s.m.* Bloodhound ; sleuth-hound. *F: Les limiers de la police,* the police sleuth-hounds ; the detective force.

liminaire [liminɛːr], *a.* **1.** *Typ : Pièces liminaires,* preliminary pages ; *F:* prelims. **2.** **Épître liminaire,** foreword.

limitatif, -ive [limitatif, -iːv], *a.* Limiting, restrictive.

limitation [limitasjɔ̃], *s.f.* **1.** Limitation, restriction. **2.** Marking off (of ground).

limite [limit], *s.f.* **1.** Boundary (of field, etc.) ; limit (of power, etc.). *Marquer les limites du terrain,* to mark out the ground. *L. d'âge,* age limit. **Donner des limites à l'autorité de qn,** to set bounds to s.o.'s authority. *F : Franchir, dépasser, les limites,* to pass all bounds. *Mettre des limites à* . . ., to set limits to. . . . *Dans les limites où les circonstances le permettent,* so far as circumstances permit. **A la dernière limite de l'exaspération,** exasperated beyond measure. **Sans limites,** unbounded, limitless. *Mec : L. critique de résistance,* breaking(-down) point. *Sp : Limites du jeu,* boundary(-lines). **2. Cas limite,** border-line case. **Vitesse limite,** maximum speed.

limiter [limite], *v.tr.* **1.** To bound, to mark the bounds of (country, etc.). **2.** To limit ; to restrict ; to set bounds, limits, to (power, etc.).

limité, *a.* Limited, restricted.

limiteur [limitœːr], *s.m.* Limiting device. *El.E :* Flickerer (of domestic electric-light installation).

limitrophe [limitrɔf], *a.* Limitrophe, adjacent (*de,* to) ; abutting (*de,* on) ; bordering (on).

limoger [limɔʒe], *v.tr. F :* To supersede (general, etc., by sending him to Limoges) ; = to 'stellenbosch.'

limon[1] [limɔ̃], *s.m.* Mud, silt. *F :* **Il se croit d'un autre limon que nous,** he thinks he is formed of a different clay.

limon[2], *s.m.* **1.** *Veh :* Shaft, thill. **2.** *Const :* Stringer (of staircase).

limon[3], *s.m. Bot :* Sour lime.

limonade [limɔnad], *s.f.* **1.** Lemonade. *L. gazeuse,* effervescing lemonade. **2.** *pl.* Mineral waters ; *F :* minerals, soft drinks.

limonadier, -ière [limɔnadje, -jɛːr], *s.* **1.** Occ. Dealer in mineral waters, in soft drinks ; *U.S:* soda-fountain keeper. **2.** Keeper of a bar, of a small 'pub.'

limoneux, -euse [limɔnø, -øːz], *a.* (Of water, etc.) Muddy ; charged with mud.

limonier[1] [limɔnje], *s.m.* Shaft horse ; wheeler.

limonier[2], *s.m. Bot :* Sour-lime (tree).

limousin, -ine [limuzɛ̃, -in]. **1.** *a. & s.* (Native) (i) of Limoges, (ii) of the ancient province of Limousin. **2.** *s.m.* Stonemason. **3.** *s.f.* **Limousine.** (*a*) (Carter's) rough woollen great-coat. (*b*) *Aut :* Limousine (car).

limpide [lɛ̃pid], *a.* Limpid, clear.

limpidité [lɛ̃pidite], *s.f.* Limpidity, clarity.

limures [limyːr], *s.f.pl.* = LIMAILLE.

lin [lɛ̃], *s.m.* **1.** Flax. **Graine de lin,** linseed. **Huile de lin,** linseed oil. **Farine de lin,** linseed meal. *a.inv.* **Bleu de lin,** flax-blue. **2. (Tissu de) lin,** linen. **Fil de lin,** linen thread or yarn.

linaire [linɛːr], *s.f. Bot :* Linaria, *F :* toad-flax.

linceul [lɛ̃sœl, -œːj], *s.m.* Winding-sheet, shroud.

linéaire [lineɛːr], *a.* Linear (equation, etc.). *Mesures linéaires,* measures of length. **Dessin linéaire,** geometrical drawing.

linéal, -aux [lineal, -o], *a.* Lineal (heir, etc.). *adv.* **-ement.**

linéament [lineamɑ̃], *s.m.* Lineament, feature.

linge [lɛ̃ːʒ], *s.m.* **1.** (Made-up) linen or calico. *L. de table,* napery ; table-linen. **(Gros) linge de maison,** house linen, household napery. *L. de corps, de dessous,* body linen ; underlinen. *F :* **Laver son linge sale en famille,** to wash one's dirty linen at home. **2.** Piece of linen or calico. *Essuyer qch. avec un l.,* to wipe sth. with a cloth. S.a. BLANC I. 2.

lingère [lɛ̃ʒɛːr], *s.f.* (*a*) Wardrobe keeper. (*b*) Sewing-maid (in boarding-school, etc.).

lingerie [lɛ̃ʒri], s.f. **1.** (a) Linen-drapery. (b) Underclothing, linen. L. pour dames, lingerie. Vente de lingerie, white sale. **2.** Linen-room.

lingot [lɛ̃go], s.m. **1.** Metall: Ingot. Or, argent, en lingots, bullion. **2.** Sm.a: Typ: Slug.

lingual, -aux [lɛ̃gwal, -o]. **1.** a. Lingual (nerve, consonant); tongue (consonant). **2.** s.f. Linguale. Ling: Lingual.

linguet [lɛ̃gɛ], s.m. Mec.E: Pawl, catch.

linguiforme [lɛ̃gчiform], a. Linguiform, tongue-shaped.

linguiste [lɛ̃gчist], s. m. & f. Linguist.

linguistique [lɛ̃gчistik]. **1.** a. Linguistic. **2.** s.f. Linguistics.

linière [linjɛːr], s.f. Flax-field.

liniment [linimɑ̃], s.m. Med: Liniment.

linoléum [linoleɔm], s.m. **1.** Linoléum incrusté, linoleum. **2.** Linoléum imprimé, (floor) oilcloth.

linon [linɔ̃], s.m. Tex: **1.** Lawn. **2.** Buckram.

linotte [linɔt], s.f. Orn: (Cock- or hen-)linnet; redpoll. F: Tête de linotte, empty-headed, feather-brained person.

linotype [linɔtip], s.f. Typ: Linotype (machine).

lint [lɛ̃t], s.m. Lint. L. boriqué, boracic lint.

linteau [lɛ̃to], s.m. **1.** Lintel. **2.** L. de baie, breastsummer.

lion, -onne [ljɔ̃, -ɔn], s. **1.** (a) Lion, f. lioness. Hardi comme un lion, as bold as a lion. Homme au cœur de lion, lion-hearted man. F: La part du lion, the lion's share. C'est l'âne couvert de la peau du lion, it's the ass in the lion's skin. (b) Lion marin, lion de mer, sea-lion. **2.** F: Celebrity of the day; (social) lion. **3.** Geog: Le golfe du Lion, the Gulf of Lions.

lionceau [ljɔ̃so], s.m. Lion's cub.

lippe [lip], s.f. Thick (lower) lip; blubber lip. Faire la lippe, to pout.

lippée [lipe], s.f. A: Mouthful. A: Franche lippée, good tuck-in at someone else's expense.

lippu [lipy], a. Thick-lipped; blubber-lipped.

liquéfaction [likefaksjɔ̃], s.f. Liquefaction.

liquéfiable [likefjabl], a. Liquefiable (gas).

liquéfier [likefje], v.tr. To liquefy; to reduce (gas, etc.) to the liquid state.
   se **liquéfier**, to liquefy.

liqueur [likœːr], s.f. **1.** (a) Liquor, drink. Liqueurs fortes, strong drink. (b) Liqueur de dessert, liqueur. **2.** Ch: Liquid, solution. L. titrée, standard solution.

liquidateur [likidatœːr], s.m. Jur: Liquidator.

liquidation [likidasjɔ̃], s.f. **1.** Liquidation. (a) L. judiciaire, winding up (of company, etc.). Entrer en liquidation, to go into liquidation. (b) Clearing of (accounts). St.Exch: Settlement. Chambre de liquidation, (bankers') clearing-house. **2.** Com: Selling off; clearance sale.

liquide [likid]. **1.** a. Liquid. Argent l., ready money. **2.** s.m. (a) Liquid. Mesures pour les liquides, fluid measures. (b) Drink. **3.** s.f. Liquid consonant.

liquider [likide], v.tr. **1.** To liquidate. (a) To wind up (a business). (b) Abs: To go into liquidation. (c) To clear, settle (account). F: Liquider son passé, to wipe out one's past. **2.** To realize (one's fortune, etc.); to sell off.

liquoreux, -euse [likɔrø, -øːz], a. Liqueur-like (wine, etc.); sweet.

liquoriste [likɔrist], s.m. Wine and spirit merchant.

lire [liːr], v.tr. (pr.p. lisant; p.p. lu; pr.ind. je lis, n. lisons; p.h. je lus; fu. je lirai) To read. **1.** L. tout haut, à haute voix, to read aloud. L. qch. dans un livre, to read sth. (i) in a book, (ii) (aloud) out of a book. L. à vue, to read

(music) at sight. Avoir beaucoup lu, to be well read. L. dans la pensée de qn, to read s.o.'s thoughts. "Dans l'attente de vous lire," 'hoping to hear from you.' **2.** L. une communication, to read out, give out, a notice.

lis [lis], s.m. Lily. Lis tigré, tiger-lily. Lis des vallées, de mai, lily of the valley. Lis d'eau, des étangs, lis jaune, yellow pond-lily, water-lily. Teint de lis, lily-white complexion. Her: Fleur de lis [flœrdəli(s)], fleur-de-lis, A: flower-de-luce.

lis-ant, -e, -ons, etc. See LIRE.

Lisbonne [lizbon]. Pr.n.f. Geog: Lisbon.

lise [liːz], s.f. Quicksand.

Lise[2]. Pr.n.f. F: Eliza, Lizzie.

liserer [lizre], li*sérer* [lizere], v.tr. (je lisère; je lisèrerai) Needlew: (a) To border, edge. (b) To pipe; to trim with piping.
   liseré, liséré, s.m. (a) Needlew: Border, edge, edging. (b) Piping, binding (of skirt). (c) Mapm: Hatching.

liseron [lizrɔ̃], s.m. Bindweed, convolvulus.

Lisette [lizɛt]. Pr.n.f. F: Lizzie, Eliza. Lit: Gay, light-hearted, work girl (of popular songs). Th: Jouer les Lisettes, to take the soubrette parts.

liseur, -euse [lizœːr, -øːz]. **1.** (a) a. Fond of reading. Le public l., the reading public. (b) s. C'est un l., he is a great reader. Liseur d'âmes, thought-reader. **2.** s.f. Liseuse. (a) Book-marker and paper-knife combined. (b) Book-rest, reading-stand. (c) Reading-lamp. (d) (Lady's) rest-gown or bed-jacket.

lisibilité [lizibilite], s.f. Legibility.

lisible [lizibl], a. Legible. adv. -ment.

lisière [lizjɛːr], s.f. **1.** (a) Selvedge, list (of cloth). Chaussons de lisière, list slippers. (b) (Child's) leading-strings. F: Mener qn en lisière, to keep s.o. in leading-strings. **2.** Edge, border (of field); skirt (of forest, etc.).

lisse[1] [lis], s.f. N.Arch: **1.** (a) Ribband (of the hull); rail, strake. Lisses de l'avant, harpings. (b) Hand-rail (of the bulwarks). L. de couronnement, taffrail. **2.** pl. Lines (of ship, as laid down on plan).

lisse[2], s.f. = LICE[3].

lisse[3], a. Smooth, glossy, polished; sleek.

liss|er [lise], v.tr. To smooth, gloss, polish; to glaze (paper, etc.); to burnish (metal). (Of bird) Se l. les plumes, to preen its feathers. L. des amandes, to sugar almonds. s.m. -age. s. -eur, -euse.

lissoir [liswaːr], s.m. Tls: Smoothing-tool; polishing-iron.

liste [list], s.f. List, roll, register. Mil: Roster. L. officielle de taux, schedule of charges. Listes électorales, register (of voters). Dresser, faire, une liste, to draw up a list. Grossir la liste, to swell the numbers. S.a. SCRUTIN I.

listeau, -eaux [listo], s.m., **listel, -eaux** [listɛl, -o], s.m., **liston** [listɔ̃], s.m. **1.** Arch: etc: Listel, fillet, moulding. **2.** Rim, edge-ring (of coin). **3.** N.Arch: (a) Sheer-rail. (b) Rubbing strake.

lit [li], s.m. **1.** Bed. Lit clos, box-bed. Lit de sangle, camp-bed, trestle-bed. Lit à colonnes, four-poster. Lit d'ami, spare bed. Lit d'enfant, à galerie, crib, cot. Mettre un enfant au lit, to put a child to bed. Se mettre au lit, to get into bed. Prendre le lit, to take to one's bed. Être au lit, garder le lit, to be in bed (usu. through illness); to be laid up. Cloué au lit, bed-ridden. Faire les lits, to make the beds. Chambre à un lit, à deux lits, single-, double-bedded room. Enfant du second lit, child of the second marriage. Aveu fait au lit de mort, death-bed confession. Prov: Comme on fait son lit on se couche, as you make

your bed so you must lie on it. S.a. PARADE¹ 2.
(b) **Bois de lit**, bedstead. *Lit de fer*, iron bedstead.
2. (a) *Lit de plume*, (i) feather-bed; (ii) *F:* cushy
job. (b) *Ven:* (Stag's) harbour; (hare's) form.
3. (a) Bed, layer (of mortar, etc.). *Hyd.E: Lit de
filtrage*, filter-bed. *Lit de pose*, seating (of engine,
etc.). (b) Bed, bottom (of river). **4.** Set (of the
tide, etc.). *Être dans le lit de la marée*, to be in
the tideway. **Dans le lit du vent**, in the wind's eye.

litanie [litani], *s.f.* (a) *pl.* Litany. (b) *sg. F:* Rigmarole, rambling story. *Réciter toujours la même
l.*, to keep harping upon one string.

lit-armoire [liarmwa:r], *s.m.* Box-bed. *pl. Des
lits-armoires.*

litée [lite], *s.f.* Litter (of young).

literie [litri], *s.f.* Bedding.

litharge [litar3], *s.f. Ch: Ind:* Litharge.

lithium [litjɔm], *s.m. Ch:* Lithium.

lithographe [litɔgraf], *s.m.* Lithographer.

lithographie [litɔgrafi], *s.f.* **1.** Lithography.
2. Lithograph. **3.** Lithographic printing works.

lithographier [litɔgrafje], *v.tr* To lithograph.

lithographique [litɔgrafik], *a.* Lithographic.

lithopone [litɔpɔn], *s.m. Ind:* Lithopone.

lithotomie [litɔtɔmi], *s.f. Surg:* Lithotomy;
operation for stone.

Lit(h)uanie [lituani]. *Pr.n.f. · Geog:* Lithuania.

lit(h)uanien, -ienne [lituanjɛ̃, -jɛn], *a. & s.
Geog:* Lithuanian.

litière [litjɛ:r], *s.f.* **1.** (Stable-)litter. **Cheval sur
la litière**, sick horse. *F:* **Faire litière de l'honneur
de qn**, to trample s.o.'s reputation under foot.
2. Litter, palanquin. *Être porté en l.*, to be
carried in a litter.

litige [liti:3], *s.m.* Litigation; dispute at law;
suit. *Cas en litige*, case at issue.

litigieux, -euse [litiʒjø, -ø:z], *a.* Litigious.

litre [litr], *s.m. Meas:* Litre (1000 cubic cm.
= about 1¾ pint).

lit-sac, *s.m.* Sleeping-bag. *pl. Des lits-sacs.*

lits-salon, *s.m. Rail:* First-class sleeping-car.
pl. Des lits-salons.

littéraire [litetɛ:r], *a.* Literary. *Agent l.*, literary
agent. S.a. PROPRIÉTÉ 1. *adv.* **-ment.**

littéral, -aux [literal, -o], *a.* **1.** Literal (translation, etc.). **2.** *Jur:* **Preuve littérale**, documentary
evidence. *adv.* **-ement.**

littérateur [literatœ:r], *s.m.* Literary man; man
of letters.

littérature [literaty:r], *s.f.* Literature.

littoral, -aux [litɔral, -o]. **1.** *a.* Littoral, coastal.
2. *s.m.* Coastline; littoral; seaboard.

liturg|ie [lityrʒi], *s.f.* Liturgy. *a.* **-ique**, -ical.

liure [ljy:r], *s.f.* **1.** Lashing (of load on cart, etc.).
2. *Nau:* Gammoning, frapping. [LIER]

livarde [livard], *s.f. Nau:* Sprit. **Voile à livarde**,
spritsail.

livide [livid], *a.* Livid; ghastly (pale).

lividité [lividite], *s.f.* Lividity, lividness;
ghastliness.

Livourne [livurn]. *Pr.n. Geog:* Leghorn.

livrable [livrabl], *a. Com:* Ready for delivery.

livraison [livrɛzɔ̃], *s.f.* **1.** Delivery (of goods,
shares, etc.). *L. franco*, free delivery, delivered
free. **Payable à la livraison**, payable on delivery.
Faire livraison de qch., to deliver sth. **Prendre
livraison de qch.**, to take delivery of sth. **Voiture
de livraison**, delivery van. **2.** Part, instalment (of
book published in parts).

livre¹ [li:vr], *s.f.* Pound. **1.** (Weight) **Vendre qch.
à la livre**, to sell sth. by the pound. **2.** (Money)
(a) *L. sterling*, pound sterling. (b) *F. & A:*
(= FRANC) *Dix mille livres de rente*, private income
of ten thousand francs a year.

livre², *s.m.* Book. (a) *L'industrie du l.*, the book-
trade. *L. de classe*, school-book. *L. de prix*, prize-
book. *L. d'images*, picture-book. *F: Parler
comme un l.*, to speak like a book. *Traduire un
passage, jouer un morceau, à livre ouvert*, to translate a passage, play a piece, at sight. (b) **Livre
de raison**, (i) record book, register (of a district);
(ii) family record book. *Nau:* **Livre de bord**,
ship's book, ship's register. (c) *L. de comptabilité*,
account-book. *Tenir les livres*, to keep the
accounts. **Tenue des livres**, book-keeping.
Teneur de livres, book-keeper. (d) *Turf:* **Livre
de paris**, betting-book. **Faire un livre**, to make
a book.

livrée [livre], *s.f.* **1.** Livery. **Grande l.**, full livery.
Valet en l., liveried servant. **Porter la livrée d ' qn**,
(i) to be in s.o.'s service; (ii) *F:* to be a follower
of s.o. **2.** *Ven:* Coat (of horse, deer, etc.);
plumage (of certain birds).

livrer [livre], *v.tr.* **1.** (a) To deliver, surrender;
to give up. *L. qn à la justice*, to deliver, hand
over, s.o. to justice. *L. un corps à la tombe*, to
commit a body to the grave. *Livré à soi-même*,
left to oneself. *L. un secret*, to betray a secret.
L. ses secrets à qn, to confide one's secrets to s.o.
(b) *L. un assaut à l'ennemi*, to deliver an attack
on the enemy. **Livrer bataille**, to join battle (à,
with); to give battle (à, to). **2.** To deliver
(goods, etc.).

se livrer. 1. *Se l. à la justice*, to surrender to
justice; *F:* to give oneself up. *Se l. à qn*, to
confide in s.o.; to put oneself in s.o.'s hands.
2. *Se l. à un vice*, to indulge in, surrender to, a
vice. *Se l. à la boisson*, (i) to take to drink; (ii) to
be a heavy drinker. *Se l. à la joie*, to give oneself
up to rejoicing. *Se l. au désespoir*, to give way to
despair. *Se l. à l'étude*, to devote onself to study.

livresque [livrɛsk], *a.* (a) Acquired from books.
Connaissances livresques, book-learning. (b) Bookish (mind).

livret [livrɛ], *s.m.* **1.** Small book, booklet; handbook. *L. de banque*, pass-book. *L. de caisse
d'épargne*, savings-bank book. **2.** *Mus:* Libretto,
book (of opera).

livreur, -euse [livrœ:r, -ø:z]. **1.** *s.* (a) Delivery-
man; delivery-boy, -girl; roundsman. (b) Car-
man. **2.** *s.f.* **Livreuse**, delivery-van.

lixivier [liksivje], *v.tr.* To lixiviate.

lloyd [lɔid], *s.m. M.Ins:* (Any) association of
marine brokers and underwriters.

lobe [lɔb], *s.m.* **1.** Lobe (of ear, etc.); flap (of
ear). **2.** *Arch:* Foil.

lobé [lɔbe], *a. Nat.Hist:* Lobed, lobate (leaf).

lobélie [lɔbeli], *s.f. Bot:* Lobelia.

lober [lɔbe], *v.tr. Ten:* To lob (ball).

lobule [lɔbyl], *s.m. Anat:* Lobule. *Bot:* Lobelet.

local, -aux [lɔkal, -o]. **1.** *a.* Local. *Bonne
mémoire locale*, *F:* bump of locality. *Loi locale*,
by-law. *Couleur locale*, local colour. **2.** *s.m.*
(a) Premises, building. (b) *Nau:* **Locaux affectés
au personnel**, crew's quarters. *adv.* **-ement.**

localiser [lɔkalize], *v.tr.* **1.** To localize (epidemic, etc.). **2.** To locate (leak, etc.).

se localiser. 1. To fix one's abode (in a
place). **2.** (Of disease, etc.) To become localized

localité [lɔkalite], *s.f.* Locality, place, spot.

locataire [lɔkatɛ:r], *s.m. & f.* **1.** Tenant, occupier (of property). *Jur:* Lessee, leaseholder.
2. Lodger.

locatif¹, -ive [lɔkatif, -i:v], *a.* **1.** Valeur locative,
rental (value). *Prix l.*, rent. *Réparations locatives*,
repairs incumbent upon the tenant. **2.** Maison
locative, tenement house.

locatif², *s.m. Gram:* Locative (case).

location [lɔkasjɔ̃], s.f. (a) (i) Hiring (ii) letting out on hire (of boat, etc.). **En location**, let out on hire. (b) (i) Renting, tenancy; (ii) letting (of house). **Agent de location**, house-agent. (c) Th: etc: **Booking** (of seats). **Bureau de location**, box-office, booking-office.

loch [lɔk], s.m. Nau: (Ship's) log. **Ligne de l.**, log-line. **Filer le loch**, tc heave, to stream, the log **Livre de loch**, log-book.

loche [lɔʃ], s.f. **1.** Ich: Loach. **2.** Moll: Grey slug.

locher [lɔʃe], v.i. F: (Of horseshoe) To be loose. F: **Il y a quelque fer qui loche**, there's something wrong somewhere.

lock-out [lɔk(a)ut], s.m. inv. Ind: Lock-out.

locomobile [lɔkɔmɔbil]. **1.** a. Locomotive; travelling (crane). **2.** s.f. Transportable steam-engine.

locomoteur, -trice [lɔkɔmɔtœːr -tris], a. Locomotor(y). Med: **Ataxie locomotrice progressive**, locomotor ataxy.

locomotif, -ive [lɔkɔmɔtif, -iːv]. **1.** a. (a) Transportable (engine, etc.). **Grue locomotive**, travelling crane. (b) Physiol: Locomotive (organs, faculty). **2.** s.f. Locomotive. (a) Rail: Locomotive, engine. (b) **Locomotive routière**, traction-engine.

locomotion [lɔkɔmɔsjɔ̃], s.f. Locomotion.

locuste [lɔkyst], s.f. Ent: Locust.

locution [lɔkysjɔ̃], s.f. Expression, phrase. L. **vicieuse**, incorrect expression.

loess [løs], s.m. Geol: Loess.

lof [lɔf], s.m. Nau: **1.** Windward side (of ship). **Venir, aller, au lof**, to sail into the wind. **Virer lof pour lof**, to wear. **2.** (a) Luff, weather-leech (of sail). (b) pl. Tacks and sheets (of a sail).

lof(f)er [lɔfe], v.i. Nau: To luff.

logarithme [lɔgaritm], s.m. Logarithm.

logarithmique [lɔgaritmik], a. Logarithmic.

loge [lɔːʒ], s.f. **1.** Hut, cabin; (gardener's, freemasons') lodge. **2.** Th: (a) Box. **L. d'avant-scène**, stage-box. (b) **Loges des artistes**, artists' dressing-rooms. **3.** El.Rail: (Driver's) cabin. **4.** Arch: Loggia, stanza.

logeable [lɔʒabl], a. (Of house) Tenantable; fit for occupation.

logement [lɔʒmɑ̃], s.m. **1.** Lodging, housing (of people); quartering, billeting (of troops); stabling (of horses, etc.). **2.** (a) Accommodation; lodgings. **Logement garni**, furnished apartment(s). **Le logement et la nourriture**, board and lodging. **Chercher un l. pour la nuit**, to look for a night's lodging. (b) Mil: Quarters; (in private house) billet. S.a. BILLET 8. **3.** (i) Seating, bedding (of machine part); housing (of shaft). (ii) **L. de clef**, cotter slot, key-way.

loger [lɔʒe] v. (je logeai(s); n. logeons) **1.** v.i. To lodge, live; (of troops) to be quartered, billeted. **L. en garni**, to be in lodgings; F: to live in digs. S.a. ENSEIGNE 1. **2** v.tr. (a) To lodge, accommodate, house (s.o.); to quarter, billet (troops); to stable (horses). (Ici) **on loge à pied et à cheval**, good accommodation for man and beast. (b) To place, put. **L une balle dans la cible**, to plant a shot on the target **L. l'arbre dans les paliers**, to set the shaft in its bearings.

se loger. 1. To build a house or to find a suitable abode. **2.** (a) **Mon ballon s'est logé sur le toit**, my ball has lodged on the roof. (b) **Le soupçon se logea dans son cœur**, suspicion fixed itself in his heart.

logeur, -euse [lɔʒœːr, -øːz], s. (a) Landlord, -lady (of furnished apartments). **Logeurs et logés**, householders and lodgers. (b) Lodging-house keeper. (c) **L. de chevaux**, stable-keeper.

logicien, -ienne [lɔʒisjɛ̃, -jɛn], s. Logician.

logique [lɔʒik]. **1.** a. Logical; reasoned (diet, etc.). S.a. ANALYSE 1 **2.** s.f. Logic. adv. -ment.

logis [lɔʒi], s.m. (a) Home, house, dwelling. **Garder le logis**, to stay in; to stay at home. **Corps de logis**, main (portion of) building. (b) (Temporary) lodgings. **Bon l. à pied et à cheval**, good accommodation for man and beast. S.a. MARÉCHAL 3. (c) Hostelry.

loi [lwa], s.f. **1.** (a) Law. **Homme de loi**, lawyer. **Consulter un homme de loi**, to take legal advice. **Tomber sous le coup de la loi**, to come under the law. **La loi de Moïse**, the law of Moses. **C'est lui qui donne la loi**; **sa parole fait loi**, his word is law. **Faire la loi à qn**, to lay down the law, to dictate, to s.o. **Se faire une loi de faire qch.**, to make a rule, a point, of doing sth. **Subir la loi de qn**, to be ruled by s.o.; to be under s.o.'s thumb. **Hors la loi**, outlawed. **Mettre qn hors la loi**, to outlaw s.o. **Mise hors la loi**, outlawry. S.a. NÉCESSITÉ. (b) Act (of Parliament); law, enactment, statute. **Projet de loi**, bill. **2.** **Les lois de la pesanteur**, the laws of gravity. **Loi de Grimm**, Grimm's law. **Les lois du jeu**, the rules of the game.

loin [lwɛ̃], adv. Far. **Plus loin**, farther (on); further. **1.** (Of place) (a) **Est-ce l. d'ici?** is it far from here? **Jeune homme qui ira l.**, young man who will go a long way. Prov: **Loin des yeux, loin du cœur**, out of sight, out of mind. **Il y a loin de la coupe aux lèvres**, there's many a slip 'twixt the cup and the lip. S.a. DOUCEMENT. **Rejeter bien l. une proposition**, to dismiss a proposal with scorn; to scorn a proposal. S.a. COMPTE. **Être l. de faire qch.**, to be far from doing sth. **Je ne suis pas mécontent**, (bien) **loin de là**, I am not ill-pleased, far from it. **Vous allez trop l.**, you are carrying things too far. Conj.phr. **Loin que les crimes aient diminué ils ont augmenté**, far from diminishing, crime has increased. (b) s.m. **Apercevoir qn au loin**, to see s.o. afar, in the distance. **Admirer qn de loin**, to admire s.o. at a distance, from afar. Conj.phr. **Du plus loin qu'il les voit**, as soon as he sees them. S.a. REVENIR 3. **2.** (Of time) **Famille qui remonte bien l.**, family that goes far back. **Ce jour est encore l.**, that day is still distant. Conj.phr. **(D')aussi loin qu'il me souvienne**, as far back as I remember. **De loin en loin**, at long intervals; now and then.

lointain [lwɛ̃tɛ̃]. **1.** a. Distant, remote, far-off (country, period). **Mes souvenirs les plus lointains**, my earliest recollections. **Des jours lointains**, far-off days. **Dans un avenir l.**, in a distant, remote, future. **2.** s.m. **Dans le lointain**, in the distance, in the background.

loir [lwaːr], s.m. Z: Dormouse.

loisible [lwazibl], a. Permissible, optional. **Il lui est l. de refuser**, it is open to him to refuse. **S'il ne vous est pas l. de venir**, if it is not convenient for you to come.

loisir [lwaziːr], s.m. Leisure. **Être de loisir**, to be free, at leisure. **Avoir du loisir, des loisirs**, to have some spare time. **Dans mes heures de l.**, pendant mes loisirs, in my leisure hours. **Examiner qch. à loisir**, to examine sth. at leisure.

lolo [lolo], s.m. F: (Child's word) Milk.

lombaire [lɔ̃bɛːr], a. Anat: Lumbar.

lombes [lɔ̃b], s.m.pl. Lumbar region; loins.

lombric [lɔ̃brik], s.m. Earthworm.

londonien, -ienne [lɔ̃dɔnjɛ̃, -jɛn]. **1.** a. Of London. **2.** s. Londoner.

Londres [lɔ̃ːdr]. Pr.n. Usu. f. Geog: London.

londrès [lɔ̃drɛs], s.m. Havana cigar.

long, longue [lɔ̃, lɔ̃:g]. **1.** *a.* Long. (*a*) (Of space) *Ruban l. de cinq mètres*, ribbon five metres long. S.a. BRAS 1, DENT 1. **Prendre (le chemin) le plus long**, to go the longest way (round). (*b*) (Of time ; PROLONGÉ is preferable after a noun) *Un long hiver* [lɔ̃kiveːr], a long, protracted, winter. *Longue histoire*, long-spun, lengthy, story. *L. soupir*, long-drawn sigh. *Être l. à faire qch.*, to take a long time to do sth. *Elle fut longue à s'en remettre*, she was a long time getting over it. *Com: Papiers à longue échéance*, long-dated bills. S.a. FEU[1] 1.3. **A la longue**, in course of time ; in the long run. (*c*) *Cu: Sauce longue*, thin sauce. **2.** *adv.* Length. (*a*) (Of space) *Table qui a six pieds de l.*, table six foot long, six feet in length. **En long**, lengthwise. **De long en large**, up and down, to and fro. **Étendu de tout son long**, tout **de son long**, stretched at full length. **S'amarrer le long d'un navire**, to moor alongside a ship. *Se faufiler le l. du mur*, to creep along the wall. **Raconter qch. (tout) au long**, to relate sth. at full length. (*b*) (Of time) *Tout le l. du jour*, all day long, the whole day long. (*c*) (Of amount) *Inutile d'en dire plus l.*, I need say no more. **Regard qui en dit long**, look which speaks volumes. **Je ne cherche pas à en savoir plus long**, I don't want to know any more. *Je n'en sais pas plus l. pour cela*, I am not any the wiser. **3.** *s.f.* Longue. (*a*) *Pros:* Long syllable. (*b*) *Cards:* **Attaquer dans sa longue**, to lead from one's long suit.

longanime [lɔ̃ganim], *a.* Long-suffering.

longanimité [lɔ̃ganimite], *s.f.* Long-suffering, forbearance, longanimity.

long-courrier, *a. & s.m. Nau:* **1.** Ocean-going (ship) ; liner. **2.** Deep-sea (sailor) ; captain of a liner. *pl. Des long-courriers.*

longe[1] [lɔ̃:ʒ], *s.f. Harn:* (*a*) Leading-rein, head-rope, halter. (*b*) Lunging-rein.

longe[2], *s.f. Cu:* Loin (of veal or venison).

longer [lɔ̃ʒe], *v.tr.* (je longeai(s) ; n. longeons) To keep to the side of (road, etc.) ; to skirt (forest). *L. la côte, le mur*, to hug the coast, the wall.

longeron [lɔ̃ʒrɔ̃], *s.m.* **1.** *Civ.E:* Stringer, longitudinal girder ; beam (of bridge, etc.). **2.** *Aut:* Side-member (of frame). **Faux longerons**, sub-frame. **3.** *Av:* Longeron, tail-boom (of fuselage) ; spar (of wing).

longévité [lɔ̃ʒevite], *s.f.* Longevity, long life.

longicaude [lɔ̃ʒikoːd], *a. Z:* Long-tailed.

longicorne [lɔ̃ʒikɔrn], *a. & s.m. Ent:* Longicorn.

longirostre [lɔ̃ʒirɔstr], *a. Orn:* Long-billed.

longitude [lɔ̃ʒityd], *s.f.* Longitude. *Par* 10° (de) *l. ouest*, in (the) longitude (of) 10° west. **Bureau des longitudes**, Central Astronomical Office.

longitudinal, -aux [lɔ̃ʒitydinal, -o], *a.* Longitudinal. *Nau:* Fore-and-aft. *adv.* **-ement**.

longrine [lɔ̃grin], *s.f.* Longitudinal beam, girder, or member. *L. de faîtage*, ridge-bar.

longtemps [lɔ̃tɑ̃], *adv.* **1.** Long ; a long time. *Cela ne pouvait durer l.*, it could not last long. *Être l. à faire qch.*, to be long (i) in doing sth., (ii) before one does sth. *Rester trop l.*, to stay too long. **2.** Il y a longtemps, long ago, a long time ago. *Il n'y a pas l.*, not long ago. *Il y a l. qu'il est mort*, he has been dead (for) a long time. *Cela existe depuis longtemps*, it has existed for a long time. **Avant qu'il soit longtemps**, before long, ere long. *Cela ne se fera pas de longtemps*, it will not happen for a long time to come. *Je n'en ai pas pour l.*, (i) it won't take me long ; (ii) I haven't much longer to live.

longuement [lɔ̃gmɑ̃], *adv.* **1.** For a long time.

2. Slowly, deliberately. **3.** *Plaider l. une cause*, to argue a case at length. *S'étendre trop l. sur les détails*, to dwell at too great length on details.

longuet, -ette [lɔ̃gɛ, -ɛt], *a. F:* (*a*) Rather long, longish ; on the long side. (*b*) Slender.

longueur [lɔ̃gœːr], *s.f.* Length. **1.** *L. totale, l. hors tout*, length over all, over-all length. **Mesures de longueur**, linear measures. *Jardin qui a cent pieds de l.*, garden a hundred feet long. **Couper qch. en longueur, dans le sens de la longueur**, to cut sth. lengthwise. **Tirer un discours en longueur**, to spin out a discourse. *Traîner, tirer, en l.*, (of lawsuit, etc.) to drag (on). **2.** (*a*) *Roman où il y a des longueurs*, novel with tedious passages. **Cette scène fait longueur**, this scene drags, slows down the action. (*b*) *Gagner par une l.*, to win by a length.

longue-vue, *s.f.* Telescope, field-glass, *F:* spyglass. *pl. Des longues-vues.*

looch [lɔk], *s.m. Pharm:* Soothing emulsion (to be sipped).

looping [lupiŋ], *s.m. Av:* **Faire un looping**, to loop the loop.

lopin [lɔpɛ̃], *s.m.* **1.** *L. de terre*, piece, patch, plot, of ground ; allotment. **2.** *Metall:* Bloom, billet.

loquace [lɔkwas], *a.* Loquacious, talkative.

loquacité [lɔkwasite], *s.f.* Loquacity, talkativeness, garrulity.

loque [lɔk], *s.f.* Rag. **Être en loques**, to be in rags, in tatters. *F:* (Of pers.) **Être comme une loque**, to be worn out, absolutely limp.

loquèle [lɔkyɛl], *s.f.* Flow of language. **Avoir de la loquèle**, to have the gift of the gab.

loquet [lɔkɛ], *s.m.* **1.** Latch (of door). **Fermer la porte au loquet**, to latch the door. **2.** **Couteau à loquet**, clasp-knife.

loqueteux, -euse [lɔktø, -øːz], *a.* **1.** In rags, in tatters, ragged. **2.** *s.* Tatterdemalion.

lorgnade [lɔrɲad], *s.f.* (*a*) Sidelong glance. (*b*) Ogle.

lorgn|er [lɔrɲe], *v.tr.* **1.** (*a*) To cast a sidelong glance, sidelong glances, at (sth.). *F: L. une dot, une place*, to have one's eye on an heiress, on a post. (*b*) To ogle, to make eyes at (s.o.). **2.** To stare at (s.o., sth.) through a lorgnette or through opera-glasses. *s.m.* **-ement**.

lorgnette [lɔrɲɛt], *s.f.* (Pair of) opera-glasses.

lorgnon [lɔrɲɔ̃], *s.m.* (*a*) Pince-nez, eye-glasses. (*b*) (Handled) lorgnette.

loriot [lɔrjo], *s.m. Orn:* Oriole. S.a. COMPÈRE-LORIOT 1.

lorrain, -aine [lɔrɛ̃, -ɛn]. **1.** *a.* Lorrainese. **2.** *s.* Lorrainer.

lors [lɔːr], *adv.* **1.** *A:* = ALORS. **2.** (Still used in) (*a*) **Depuis lors**, from that time, ever since then. *F:* **Pour lors . . ., so . . . ; then.** S.a. DÈS. (*b*) **Lors . . . que** (= LORSQUE), when. **Lors même que** *nous sommes heureux*, even when we are happy. **Lors donc qu'il arriva . . .**, thus when he arrived. . . . **Lors de sa naissance**, at the time of his birth ; when he was born.

lorsque [lɔrsk(ə)], *conj.* (At the time, moment) when. *L. j'entrai*, when I entered ; on my entering. S.a. LORS 2.

losange [lɔzɑ̃:ʒ], *s.m.* **1.** *Her:* Lozenge. **En losange**, diamond-shaped. **2.** *Geom:* Rhomb(us).

lot [lo], *s.m.* **1.** (*a*) Share (of estate) ; portion, lot. *Avoir son lot de tourments*, to have one's share of worries. (*b*) Prize (at a lottery). **Gros lot**, first prize. *Fin:* Emprunt à lots, lottery loan. **Tirage à lots**, prize-drawing. **2.** Lot, parcel (of goods) ; batch.

loterie [lɔtri], *s.f.* (*a*) Lottery. (*b*) Raffle, draw. **Mettre une montre en loterie**, to raffle a watch.

lotion [lɔsjɔ̃], *s.f.* **1.** Washing, bathing (of wound). **2.** *Pharm:* Lotion.

lotionner [lɔsjɔne], *v.tr.* To wash, bathe (wound).

lotir [lɔtiːr], *v.tr.* **1.** (a) To divide (sth.) into lots; to parcel out (estate). (b) *Com:* To sort (out) (hides, grain, etc.); to parcel out (goods). **2.** *L. qn de qch.*, to allot sth. to s.o. *F:* Être bien loti, to be well provided for; to be favoured by fortune; to be well off.

lotissement [lɔtismɑ̃], *s.m.* **1.** (a) Dividing into lots; parcelling out. (b) Making up into sets. (c) Allotment, apportionment. (d) Development (of building land). **2.** Building plot.

loto [lɔto], *s.m. Games:* **1.** Lotto. *F:* Yeux en boules de loto, goggle eyes. **2.** Lotto set.

lotte [lɔt], *s.f. Ich:* Burbot, eel-pout.

lotus [lɔtyːs], *s.m.* **1.** *Bot:* (a) Lotus. *L: sacré*, Indian lotus. (b) Lotus-tree. **2.** *Gr.Myth:* Lotus. *F:* Manger du lotus, to live in a state of dreamy content. Mangeur de lotus, lotus-eater.

louable [lwabl, lu-], *a.* Laudable, praiseworthy; commendable (*de*, for). *adv.* **-ment.**

louage [lwaːʒ, lu-], *s.m.* **1.** Letting out, hiring out. Donner qch. à louage, to let sth. out on hire. **2.** Hiring, hire (of labour, horses, etc.). Prendre qch. à louage, to hire sth.; to take sth. on hire. Voiture de louage, hackney-carriage. *Bicyclette de l.*, hired bicycle.

louange [lwɑ̃ːʒ], *s.f.* Praise; laudation; commendation; esp. adulatory praise. *Cf.* ÉLOGE. Chanter, entonner, les louanges de qn, to laud s.o. to the skies. Chanter ses propres louanges, to blow one's own trumpet. *Combler qn de louanges*, to belaud s.o. Dire qch. à la louange de qn, to say sth. in praise of s.o.

louangeur, -euse [lwɑ̃ʒœːr, -øːz], *s.* Adulator, praiser, lauder.

louche[1] [luʃ], *a.* **1.** Cross-eyed, squint-eyed (person). *Yeux louches*, eyes that squint. **2.** *F:* (a) Ambiguous (expression, etc.). (b) Shady, suspicious (house, character, etc.). *s.m. Il y a du l. dans cette affaire*, there's something shady in the business. (c) Cloudy (wine, pearl, etc.).

louche[2], *s.f.* **1.** (a) (Soup-)ladle. (b) Basting-spoon, -ladle. **2.** *Tls:* (a) Reamer, broach. (b) Countersink bit.

louch|er [luʃe], *v.i.* To squint; to be cross-eyed. *L. de l'œil gauche*, to have a cast in the left eye. *s.m.* **-ement.** *s.* **-eur, -euse.**

loucherie [luʃri], *s.f.* Strabismus, squint(ing).

louchon [luʃɔ̃], *s.m. & f. P:* Cross-eyed person; squint-eyes.

louer[1] [lwe, lue], *v.tr.* **1.** (a) To hire out, let (out) (*à*, to). Maison à louer, house to let. (b) (Of farm-hand) Se l. pour la saison to engage oneself for the season. **2.** To hire (horse, etc.); to rent (house) (*à*, from). *L. une place d'avance*, to reserve or book a seat.

lou|er[2], *v.tr.* To praise, laud, commend. *L. qn de qch.*, to praise s.o. for sth. Loué de tous, par ses maîtres, pr. ised by all, by his masters. Dieu soit loué! praise be to God! *Le ciel en soit loué! F:* thank Heaven (for that)! *s.* **-eur**[1], **-euse.**

se louer. Se l. de qch., to be pleased, well satisfied, with sth. Se l. d'avoir fait qch., to congratulate oneself upon having done sth. *Je n'ai qu'à me l. de lui, de sa conduite*, I have nothing but praise for him, for his conduct.

loueur[2], **-euse** [lwœːr, lu-, -øːz], *s.* Hirer out; letter; renter out. *L. de bateaux*, boat-keeper. *L. de chevaux, de voitures*, job-master.

louf [luf], **loufoque** [lufɔk], *a. F:* Loony, eccentric; *P:* dippy.

loufoquerie [lufɔkri], *s.f. F:* Eccentricity.

lougre [lugr], *s.m. Nau:* Lugger.

Louis [lwi, lui]. **1.** *Pr.n.m.* Lewis; (of French kings) Louis. **2.** *s.m. A:* Louis(-d'or), twenty-franc piece.

Louise [lwiːz]. *Pr.n.f.* Louisa, Louise.

loulou, -outte [lulu, -ut], *s. F:* **1.** Dear, ducky. **2.** Loulou de Poméranie, Pomeranian (dog), *F:* pom.

loup [lu], *s.m.* **1.** (a) Wolf. *F:* Crier au loup, to cry wolf. Marcher à pas de loup, to walk stealthily; to steal along. Avoir une faim de loup, to be ravenously hungry. Il fait un froid de loup, it is bitterly cold. Se jeter dans la gueule du loup, to jump, rush, into the lion's mouth. Tenir le loup par les oreilles, to have the wolf by the ears; to be in a fix. Il est connu comme le loup blanc, he is known everywhere. *Prov:* Quand on parle du loup on en voit la queue, talk of the devil and he will appear. Les loups ne se mangent pas entre eux, dog won't eat dog. *F:* (To man or woman) Mon petit loup, mon gros loup, my darling, my pet. S.a. BREBIS 2, CHIEN 1. (b) Loup de mer, (i) *Ich:* sea-perch, sea-dace; (ii) *F:* old salt, sea-dog, jack-tar. **2.** *F:* (a) Flaw (in timber, etc.); *Ind:* defect. (b) *Th:* Fluff; fluffed entrance. **3.** Black velvet mask (worn at a masked ball).

loup-cervier, *s.m. Z:* Lynx. *pl. Des loups-cerviers.*

loupe [lup], *s.f.* **1.** (a) *Med:* Wen. (b) Excrescence, gnarl (on tree). **2.** *Metall:* Bloom. **3.** Lens, magnifying-glass.

louper [lupe]. *P:* **1.** *v.i.* To be slack, lazy. **2.** *v.tr.* To botch, bungle (piece of work); to miss (one's turn or opportunity). *Av: L. son atterrissage*, to crash. *Th: L. son entrée*, to fluff one's entrance.

loup-garou, *s.m.* **1.** (a) *Myth:* Wer(e)wolf. (b) *F:* Bugaboo. **2.** *F:* Recluse, bear. *pl. Des loups-garous.*

loupiot [lupjo], *s.m. P:* Child, urchin, kid.

lourd [luːr], *a.* **1.** (a) Heavy (load, sleep, food); heavily-built, ungainly (person); ponderous (style). *Poids l.*, heavy weight. *Terrain l.*, heavy ground. *Entrer, sortir*, d'un pas lourd, to lumber in, out. A la main lourde, heavy-handed. *F:* Il n'en reste pas lourd, there isn't much left. *adv.* Peser lourd, to weigh heavy. (b) Clumsy, awkward; dull (mind, speech); dull-witted, stupid (person). *Avoir l'esprit l., l'intelligence lourde*, to be dull-witted. (c) Lourde bévue, gross blunder. (d) Incident l. de conséquences, incident big with consequences. (e) Close, sultry (weather). Il fait lourd, it is very close, very sultry. *adv.* **-ement.**

lourdaud, -aude [lurdo, -oːd]. **1.** *a.* (a) Loutish (fellow); lumpish, awkward, clumsy (fellow or girl). (b) Dull-witted, thick-headed. **2.** *s.* (a) Lout, bumpkin. (b) Dullard, blockhead.

lourdeur [lurdœːr], *s.f.* Heaviness; ponderousness (of style); clumsiness, awkwardness, ungainliness; dullness (of intellect); sultriness, closeness (of the weather).

loustic [lustik], *s.m. F:* Joker, wag.

loutre [lutr], *s.f.* **1.** *Z:* (a) Otter. Casquette de loutre, otter-skin cap. (b) *L. d'Amérique*, nutria. **2.** *Com:* (Peau de) loutre, sealskin. Fourrure genre loutre, coney-seal.

louve [luːv], *s.f. Z:* She-wolf.

louveteau [luvto], *s.m. Z: Scouting:* Wolf-cub.

louveterie [luvtri], *s.f.* Wolf-hunting. *Hist:* Lieutenant de louveterie, master of the wolf-hunt.

louv|oyer [luvwaje], *v.i.* (je louvoie; je louvoierai)

(a) *Nau:* To tack, to beat about; to beat to windward. *L. à petits bords,* to take short tacks. (b) *F:* To scheme, manœuvre (to attain one's end). *s.m.* **-oiement.**

louvre [luːvr], *s.m. A:* Royal Palace. **Le Palais du Louvre,** the Louvre (in Paris).

lov|er [lɔve], *v.tr.* To coil (down) (rope). *s.m.* **-age.**

se lover, (of snake, etc.) to coil up.

loxodromique [lɔksɔdrɔmik], *a. Nau:* Loxodromic (sailing); plane (sailing).

loyal, -aux [lwajal, -o], *a.* **1.** Honest, fair, straight(forward). *Être l. en affaires,* to be upright, straightforward, in business. *Jeu l.,* fair play. **2.** Loyal, faithful (servant); true (friend). *adv.* **-ement.**

loyauté [lwajote], *s.f.* **1.** Honesty, straightforwardness, uprightness. **Manque de loyauté,** (i) dishonesty; (ii) unfairness. **2.** Loyalty, fidelity (*envers,* to).

loyer [lwaje], *s.m.* Rent. **Prendre une maison à loyer,** to rent a house. **Donner à loyer,** to let.

lu. See LIRE.

lubie [lybi], *s.f.* Whim, fad, freak, crotchet.

lubricité [lybrisite], *s.f.* Lubricity, lewdness.

lubrifiant [lybrifjã]. **1.** *a.* Lubricating. **2.** *s.m.* Lubricant.

lubrification [lybrifikasjõ], *s.f.* Lubrication, greasing.

lubrifier [lybrifje], *v.tr.* To lubricate; to grease or oil (machinery).

lubrique [lybrik], *a.* Libidinous, lustful.

Luc [lyk]. *Pr.n.m.* Luke.

lucarne [lykarn], *s.f.* (a) Dormer-window, attic window. (b) Skylight.

Lucayes (les) [lelyka:j]. *Pr.n.f.pl. Geog:* The Bahama Islands.

lucide [lysid], *a.* Lucid, clear (mind). **Somnambule lucide,** clairvoyant(e). *adv.* **-ment.**

lucidité [lysidite], *s.f.* **1.** Lucidity, clearness. **2.** Clairvoyance.

luciole [lysjɔl], *s.f. Ent:* Fire-fly, glow-worm.

Lucques [lyk]. *Pr.n. Geog:* Lucca.

lucrat|if, -ive [lykratif, -iːv], *a.* Lucrative, profitable. *adv.* **-ivement.**

lucre [lykr], *s.m.* Lucre, profit.

ludion [lydjõ], *s.m. Ph:* Cartesian diver; *F:* bottle-imp.

luette [lɥɛt], *s.f. Anat:* Uvula.

lueur [lɥœːr], *s.f.* **1.** Gleam, glimmer. *Les premières lueurs de l'aube,* the first rays of dawn. **A la lueur des étoiles,** by starlight. **2.** *L. momentanée,* flash; blink of light. **Jeter une lueur,** to flash.

luge [lyːʒ], *s.f.* Luge; Swiss toboggan.

lug|er [lyʒe], *v.i.* (**je lugeai(s); n. lugeons**) To luge, to toboggan. *s.m.* **-eage.** *s.* **-eur, -euse.**

lugubre [lygybr], *a.* **1.** Lugubrious, dismal, gloomy. **2.** Ominous, dire (news, etc.); baleful (sight). *adv.* **-ment.**

lui¹, *pl.* **leur** [lɥi, lœ(ː)r], *pers. pron. m. & f.* (To) him, her, it, them. (a) (Unstressed) *Je le lui donne,* I give it (to) him, (to) her. *Donnez-lui-en,* give him some. *Cette maison leur appartient,* this house belongs to them. (b) (Stressed in *imp.*) *Donnez-le-lui,* give it him. *Montrez-le-leur,* show it to them.

lui², *pl.* **eux** [lɥi, ø], *stressed pers.pron. m.* (a) He, it, they. *C'est lui,* it is he, *F:* it's him, that's him. *Ce sont eux, F: c'est eux,* it is they, *F:* that's them. *Lui et sa femme,* he and his wife. *Lui, il a raison; c'est lui qui a raison,* he is right. *C'est lui-même qui me l'a dit,* he told me so himself. (b) Him, it, them. *J'accuse son frère et lui,* I accuse

him and his brother. *Lui, je le connais,* him I know. *Je n'ai vu que lui,* I have seen only him. *Ce livre est à lui, à eux,* this book is his, is theirs. (c) (Refl.) Him(self), it(self), them(selves). *Il les rassembla autour de lui,* he gathered them round him. *Ils ne pensent qu'à eux,* they think of nobody but themselves.

lui³. See LUIRE.

luire [lɥiːr], *v.i.* (*pr.p.* **luisant;** *p.p.* **lui** (no *f.*); *pr.ind.* **il luit, ils luisent;** *p.h.* **il luisit** is rare; *fu.* **il luira**) To shine. *Le soleil luit,* the sun is shining. *Son couteau luisait dans l'ombre,* his knife gleamed in the dark. *Le jour luit,* day is breaking.

luis-ait, -ent, etc. See LUIRE.

luisant [lɥizã]. **1.** *a.* Shining, bright; shiny, glossy (surface, etc.); gleaming (eyes, etc.). *S.a.* VER 2. **2.** *s.m.* Shine, gloss, sheen.

lumachelle [lymaʃɛl], *s.f. Miner:* Lumachel(le), fire-marble.

lumen [lymɛn], *s.m. Ph.Meas:* Lumen.

lumière [lymjɛːr], *s.f.* **1.** Light. *L. du gaz, du jour, du soleil,* gaslight, daylight, sunlight. *L. oxhydrique,* limelight. *L. électrique,* electric light. *Th: etc:* **Couper la lumière,** to black out. **A la lumière de la lune,** by moonlight. *Apportez de la l.,* bring in a light. *Mettre en l. les défauts de . . .,* to bring out the faults of. . . . **Porter la lumière dans un sujet,** to throw light on a subject. **Faire la lumière sur une affaire,** to clear up a business. *Les lumières de la raison,* the light of reason. *Difficultés au-dessus de mes lumières,* difficulties beyond my understanding. **La Ville Lumière,** the City of Light; Paris. *Art:* **Hautes lumières,** high lights. *Astr:* **Lumière cendrée** (*de la lune*), earth-light, **-shine. 2.** Aperture (of sighting-vane); oil-hole (of bearing); slot (in piston wall); port (of cylinder-valve). *L. d'échappement,* exhaust port.

lumignon [lyminõ], *s.m.* **1.** Snuff (of candle). **2.** Candle-end. **3.** Dim light.

luminaire [lyminɛːr], *s.m.* (a) Luminary, light; star, sun. (b) *Coll.* Lights, lighting (at church ceremony, etc.).

luminescence [lyminɛssã:s], *s.f.* Luminescence. *Éclairage par luminescence,* neon-tube lighting.

luminescent [lyminɛssã], *a.* Luminescent, self-luminous.

lumineu|x, -euse [lyminø, -øːz], *a.* Luminous (body, sea, mind). *F: Yeux l.,* bright eyes. *Ph: Onde lumineuse,* light-wave. *adv.* **-sement.**

luminosité [lyminozite], *s.f.* **1.** Luminosity, luminousness, brightness; sheen. **2.** Patch of light.

lunaire [lynɛːr]. **1.** *a.* Lunar (month, caustic). **2.** *s.f. Bot:* Lunaria; *F:* honesty, satin-flower.

lunatique [lynatik], *a. & s.* **1.** Whimsical, capricious (person). **2.** *B:* Lunatic. **3.** *Vet:* Œil lunatique, moon-eye (of horse).

lunch [lœ̃ʃ], *s.m.* (a) Lunch(eon). (b) Light meal; snack.

lundi [lœ̃di], *s.m.* Monday. **Le lundi gras,** Shrove Monday. *Le l. de Pâques,* Easter Monday. *F:* **Faire le lundi,** to take Monday off.

lune [lyn], *s.f.* **1.** Moon. *Pleine l.,* full moon. *Nouvelle l.,* new moon. **Clair de lune,** moonlight. *Au clair de la l.,* by moonlight. **Nuit sans lune,** moonless night. *Paysage éclairé par la l.,* moonlit landscape. **Lune rousse,** April moon. **Lune de miel,** honeymoon. **Demander la lune,** to ask for the moon and stars. **Faire un trou à la lune,** to shoot the moon; (of banker, etc.) to abscond. **Être dans la lune,** to be wool-gathering. *S.a.* ABOYER. **2.** Crescent-shaped object or aperture. *En forme de l.,* crescent-shaped. **3.** Vagary, caprice, whim. **Avoir des lunes,** to have moods, to be moody. *Il est dans sa mauvaise l.*, he is in one of his bad moods. **4. Pierre de lune,** moonstone.

luné [lyne], *a.* **1.** Lunate, crescent-shaped. **2.** *F:* **Être bien, mal, luné,** to be in a good, bad, mood.

lunetier [lyntje], *s.m.* Spectacle-maker; optician.

lunette [lynɛt], *s.f.* **1. Lunette d'approche,** (refracting) telescope; field-glass. *L. viseur,* sighting telescope. *Surv:* **Coup de lunette,** observation, sight. **2.** *pl.* (*a*) **(Paire de) lunettes,** (pair of) spectacles. *Porter (des) lunettes,* to wear spectacles. *Lunettes d'automobiliste, d'aviateur,* goggles. **Serpent à lunettes,** Indian cobra, spectacled snake. (*b*) *Harn:* Blinders. **3.** *Cu:* Merrythought, wish(ing)-bone (of fowl). **4.** (*a*) *Arch: Fort:* Lunette. (*b*) Lunette (of guillotine). **5.** (*a*) Seat (of water-closet). (*b*) Cab-window (of locomotive). *Aut:* **Lunette arrière,** back-light, backwindow.

lunetterie [lynɛtri], *s.f.* Making of spectacles, of optical instruments.

lunettier [lynɛtje], *s.m.* = LUNETIER.

lupercales [lypɛrkal], *s.f.pl. Rom.Ant:* Lupercalia.

lupin [lypɛ̃], *s.m. Bot:* Lupin(e).

lupinelle [lypinɛl], *s.f.* **1.** Clover. **2.** Sainfoin.

lurette [lyrɛt], *s.f.* (Used only in) *F:* **Il y a belle lurette** *qu'il est parti,* he went away a long time ago, ages ago.

luron, -onne [lyrɔ̃, -ɔn], *s. F:* (*a*) *m.* Jolly chap; strapping fellow. *C'est un gai l.,* he's a gay dog. (*b*) *f.* Strapping lass; tomboy; bold hussy.

lu-s, -t. See LIRE.

lusol [lyzɔl], *s.m.* Commercial benzine.

lustral, -aux [lystral, -o], *a. Rom.Ant:* Lustral.

lustre[1] [lystr], *s.m.* **1.** Lustre, polish, gloss, glaze (of silk, etc.). *F:* **Mettre qch. dans tout son lustre,** to show sth. to the best advantage. **2.** (Ornamented) chandelier. *L. à gaz,* gas pendant. *L. électrique,* electrolier.

lustre[2], *s.m.* Lustrum; period of five years.

lustr|er [lystre], *v.tr.* To glaze, gloss, polish (up), lustre (leather, etc.). *Le poil lustré du chat,* the cat's glossy coat. *Toile lustrée,* glazed cloth. *F: Étoffe lustrée par l'usure,* cloth shiny with wear. *s.m.* **-age.**

lustrine [lystrin], *s.f.* Cotton lustre, linenette.

lut [lyt], *s.m. Cer: Ind:* Lute, luting, cement.

Lutèce [lytɛs]. *Pr.n.f. A.Geog:* Lutetia (Roman name of Paris).

luter [lyte], *v.tr.* To lute; to seal with luting.

luth [lyt], *s.m. Mus:* Lute.

luthéranisme [lyteranism], *s.m.* Lutheranism.

lutherie [lytri], *s.f.* Stringed-instrument industry.

luthérien, -ienne [lyterjɛ̃, -jɛn], *a. & s. Rel.H:* Lutheran.

luthier [lytje], *s.m.* Stringed-instrument maker, violin-maker.

lutin, -ine [lytɛ̃, -in]. **1.** *s.m.* (*a*) Mischievous sprite; imp. (*b*) *F:* (Of child) Imp. **2.** *a.* Mischievous, impish.

lutiner [lytine]. **1.** *v.tr.* To tease, plague, torment (s.o.). **2.** *v.i.* To play the imp.

lutrin [lytrɛ̃], *s.m. Ecc:* Lectern; singing-desk.

lutte [lyt], *s.f.* **1.** Wrestling. *L. libre,* catch-ascatch-can. **2.** (*a*) Contest, struggle, tussle. *Entrer en lutte avec qn,* to join battle with s.o. *Les partis en l.,* the contending parties. *L. à mort,*

life-and-death struggle. *L. pour l'existence,* struggle for life. *Adv.phr.* **De haute lutte,** by force, by sheer fighting, by force of arms. *Trophée remporté de haute l.,* hard-won trophy. **De bonne lutte,** fair(ly), above-board. *C'est de bonne l.,* it is quite fair. *Sp:* **Lutte à la corde de traction,** tug-of-war. (*b*) Strife. *La l. des classes,* the class war.

lutt|er [lyte], *v.i.* **1.** To wrestle (*avec, contre,* with). **2.** To struggle, contend, fight, compete (*contre,* with, against). *L. contre l'incendie,* to battle with the fire. *L. contre un abus,* to make a stand against an abuse. *L. de vitesse avec qn,* to race s.o. *s.m.* **-eur.**

luxation [lyksasjɔ̃], *s.f.* Luxation, dislocation.

luxe [lyks], *s.m.* Luxury. (*a*) **Gros luxe,** vulgar display of wealth. *Se payer le l. d'un cigare,* to indulge in the luxury of a cigar. **Articles de luxe,** articles of luxury. *Édition de l.,* de luxe edition. **Train de luxe,** first-class and Pullman train. **Taxe de luxe,** luxury tax. (*b*) Abundance, profusion, superfluity (of food, etc.). *L. de précautions,* extravagant precautions.

luxer [lykse], *v.tr.* To luxate, dislocate (joint). *Se l. le genou,* to put one's knee out (of joint).

luxueu|x, -euse [lyksɥø, -ø:z], *a.* Luxurious; rich (dress); sumptuous (feast). *adv.* **-sement.**

luxure [lyksy:r], *s.f.* Lewdness.

luxurieu|x, -euse [lyksyrjø, -ø:z], *a.* Lewd, lustful. *adv.* **-sement.**

luzerne [lyzɛrn], *s.f.* Lucern(e); purple medick.

luzernière [lyzɛrnjɛ:r], *s.f.* Lucern(e)-field.

lycanthrope [likɑ̃trɔp], *s.m.* Lycanthrope.

lycanthropie [likɑ̃trɔpi], *s.f.* Lycanthropy.

lycée [lise], *s.m.* **1.** *Gr.Ant:* Le Lycée, the Lyceum. **2.** (In Fr.) State-supported secondary school; *lycée.*

lycéen, -éenne [liseɛ̃, -eɛn], *s.* Pupil at a *lycée*; schoolboy, -girl.

lychnide [liknid], *s.f.,* **lychnis** [liknis], *s.m. Bot:* Lychnis, campion. *L. diurne,* red campion. *L. des prés,* ragged robin.

lycopode [likɔpɔd], *s.m. Bot:* Lycopod(ium), club-moss.

lyddite [lidit], *s.f. Exp:* Lyddite.

lydien, -ienne [lidjɛ̃, -jɛn], *a. & s. A.Geog: Mus:* Lydian.

lymphatique [lɛ̃fatik]. **1.** *a. & s.* Lymphatic (gland, subject). **2.** *s.m.* Lymphatic (duct).

lymphe [lɛ̃:f], *s.f.* Lymph.

lynch|er [lɛ̃ʃe], *v.tr.* To lynch. *s.m.* **-age.**

lynx [lɛ̃:ks], *s.m.* Lynx. **Aux yeux de lynx,** lynx-eyed.

Lyon [ljɔ̃]. *Pr.n. Geog:* Lyons.

lyonnais, -aise [ljɔnɛ, -ɛ:z], *a. & s. Geog:* (Native) of Lyons.

lyre [li:r], *s.f.* **1.** *Mus:* Lyre. **Toute la lyre,** the whole range (of poetic emotion, etc.). **2.** *Astr:* Lyra. **3. Oiseau lyre,** lyre-bird.

lyrique [lirik], *a.* (*a*) Lyric(al). (*b*) **Théâtre lyrique,** opera-house.

lyrisme [lirism], *s.m.* **1.** Lyricism. **2.** Poetic enthusiasm.

lyrure [liry:r], *s.m. Orn:* Lyrure des bouleaux, black-cock; (*femelle*) grey-hen.

lys [lis], *s.m. A:* = LIS.

lysimachie [lizimaki], *s.f.,* **lysimaque** [lizimak], *s.f. Bot:* Loosestrife. *L. nummulaire,* money-wort, creeping jenny.

lysol [lizɔl], *s.m. Pharm:* Lysol.

M, m [ɛm], *s.f.* (The letter) M, m.

m'. 1. See ME. **2.** *A: poss.a.f.* = *ma. M'amie,* my dear.

ma [ma], *poss.a.f.* See MON.

maboul, -oule [mabul]. *P:* **1.** *a.* A bit mad; cracked, *P:* dippy. **2.** *s.* Loony.

macabre [makɑːbr], *a.* (*a*) La Danse macabre, the dance of Death. (*b*) Macabre; gruesome (discovery); ghoulish, grim (humour, etc.). *adv.* **-ment.**

macadam [makadam], *s.m.* **1.** Macadam. *M. au goudron,* tar macadam. **2.** Macadamized road.

macadamis|er [makadamize], *v.tr.* To macadamize (road). *s.m.* **-age.**

macaque [makak], *s.m. Z:* Macaque.

macareux [makarø], *s.m. Orn:* Puffin.

macaron [makarɔ̃], *s.m.* **1.** *Cu:* Macaroon. **2.** Coat-hanger. **3.** *pl. Hairdr:* Coils (over the ears); *F:* ear-phones.

macaroni [makarɔni], *s.m.* Macaroni.

macaronique [makarɔnik], *a.* Macaronic (verse).

Mac(c)habée [makabe]. **1.** *Pr.n.m.* Maccabeus. **2.** *s.m. P:* Corpse.

Macédoine [masedwan]. **1.** *Pr.n.f.* Macedonia. **2.** *s.f.* (*a*) *M. de fruits,* fruit salad. *M. de légumes,* vegetable hotchpotch. (*b*) Medley, miscellany; *Pej:* farrago.

macédonien, -ienne [masedɔnjɛ̃, -jɛn], *a. & s.* Macedonian.

macération [maserasjɔ̃], *s.f.* Maceration.

macér|er [masere], *v.tr.* (je macère; je macérerai) To macerate. **1.** To steep, soak. **2.** To mortify (the flesh).

macfarlane [makfarlan], *s.m.* Inverness cape.

mâche [mɑːʃ], *s.f.* Corn-salad, lamb's-lettuce.

mâchecoulis [mɑʃkuli], *s.m. A.Fort:* Machicolation.

mâchefer [mɑʃfɛːr], *s.m.* Clinker, slag.

mâch|er [mɑʃe], *v.tr.* (*a*) To chew, masticate; *F:* to munch (biscuit, etc.); (of animal) to champ (fodder). (Of horse) *M. le mors,* to champ the bit. *F: L'usine mâche à vide,* the factory is eating its head off. Je ne vais pas lui mâcher les mots, I shall not mince words with him. **Mâcher la besogne à qn,** to half-do s.o.'s work for him. (*b*) (Of blunt tool, etc.) *M. le bois,* to chew up the wood. *s.m.* **-ement.**

mâché, *a.* Worn, fretted, galled (rope, etc.). *Plaie mâchée,* jagged, ragged, wound.

Machiavel [makjavel]. *Pr.n.m.* Machiavelli.

machiavélique [makjavelik, maʃ-], *a.* Machiavellian.

mâchicoulis [mɑʃikuli], *s.m.* = MÂCHECOULIS.

machin [maʃɛ̃], *s. F:* **1.** Monsieur, madame, machin, Mr, Mrs, what's his (her) name, what d'ye call him (her); Thingumbob. **2.** *s.m.* Thing(amy). *Qu'est-ce que c'est que ce m.-là?* what's that gadget?

machinal, -aux [maʃinal, -o], *a.* Mechanical, unconscious (action). *adv.* **-ement.**

machinateur, -trice [maʃinatœːr, -tris], *s.* Machinator, hatcher (of plot, etc.).

machination [maʃinasjɔ̃], *s.f.* Machination, plot.

machine [maʃin], *s.f.* **1.** Machine. (*a*) *M. à coudre,* sewing-machine. *M. à écrire,* typewriter. **Écrire une lettre à la machine,** to type a letter. **Écriture à la machine,** typewriting, typing. *M. de guerre,* engine of war. *M. de hissage, d'extraction,* winding-engine, hoist(ing-engine). *M. à forger,*

forging-press. *M. à composer,* type-setting machine. *pl.* **Les machines,** the machinery. **Les grosses machines,** the heavy plant. *Th:* **Pièce à machines,** play with stage-effects. (*b*) Bicycle. *M. à cadre,* diamond-frame bicycle. *M. de course,* racing bicycle. *Monter sur sa m.,* to get on one's bicycle or motor cycle. (*c*) (Machine-tools) *M. à aléser,* boring machine, fine borer. *M. à fraiser,* milling-machine, shaper. *Travailler le métal à la m.,* to machine metal. **Fait à la machine,** machine-made. (*d*) *F:* Thing, gadget, contraption. **2.** Engine. (*a*) *M. motrice,* prime mover. *M. thermique,* heat engine. *M. à combustion interne,* internal-combustion engine. *M. à gaz,* gas engine. *M. à pétrole,* oil engine. **Machine à vapeur,** steam-engine. *M. à triple détente,* triple-expansion engine. *M. auxiliaire,* donkey-engine. (*b*) (i) *Rail:* Locomotive. *M. de manœuvre,* shunting-engine. (ii) *M. routière,* traction-engine. **3.** *El:* Dynamo. *M. alternative,* alternating-current dynamo.

machine-outil, *s.f.* Machine-tool. *pl. Des machines-outils.*

machin|er [maʃine], *v.tr.* **1.** To scheme, plot, machinate. *Affaire machinée d'avance,* put-up job. **2.** To supply (sth.), fit (sth.) up, with mechanical contrivances.

machinerie [maʃinri], *s.f.* **1.** Machine construction. **2.** (*a*) *Ind:* Machine shops. (*b*) *Nau:* Engine-room. **3.** *Ind:* Plant.

machiniste [maʃinist], *s.m.* **1.** Occ. = MÉCANICIEN. **2.** *Th:* Scene-shifter, stage-hand. **Chef machiniste,** stage-setter.

mâchoire [mɑʃwaːr], *s.f.* **1.** (*a*) Jaw (of person, animal). *La m., les mâchoires,* the jaws. *F:* **Jouer de la mâchoire, des mâchoires,** to ply one's jaws, to eat with an appetite. (*b*) Jaw-bone. **2.** *Mâchoires d'un étau,* jaws, chaps, chops, of a vice. *M. d'une poulie,* flange of a pulley. *Aut: Mâchoires du frein,* brake-shoes.

mâchonn|er [mɑʃɔne], *v.tr.* **1.** To chew (food) with difficulty; to munch; to chew (cigar); (of horse) to champ (the bit). **2.** To mutter (threats, etc.); to mumble (prayer). *s.m.* **-ement.**

mâchure [mɑʃyːr], *s.f.* Bruise (on pear, flesh).

mâchurer[1] [mɑʃyre], *v.tr. Typ:* To smudge, mackle, blur (sheet).

mâchurer[2], *v.tr.* **1.** To bruise. *Mec.E:* To dent, bruise (metal part in the vice). **2.** To reduce (handkerchief, etc.) to pulp.

macis [masi], *s.m. Bot: Cu:* Mace.

macle [makl], *s.f.* **1.** *Cryst:* Macle; twin(ned) crystal. **2.** *Fish:* Wide-meshed net.

maçon [masɔ̃, mɑ-], *s.m.* **1.** (*a*) Mason. *M. en briques,* bricklayer. (*b*) = FRANC-MAÇON. **2.** *a. Ent:* **Abeille maçonne** [masɔn], mason-bee.

mâcon [mɑkɔ̃], *s.m.* (Also **vin de Mâcon**) Mâcon (wine) (from Mâcon in Burgundy).

maçonnage [masɔnaːʒ], *s.m.* Mason's work; bricklaying.

maçonn|er [masɔne], *v.tr.* **1.** (*a*) To build (wall, etc.). (*b*) To mason (wall); to face (wall, etc.) with stone. (*c*) To wall up, brick up (door, etc.). **2.** *F:* To bungle, mess up (job).

maçonnerie [masɔnri], *s.f.* **1.** Masonry; stonework or bricklaying. **2.** = FRA..C-MAÇONNERIE.

maçonnique [masɔnik], *a.* Masonic (lodge, etc.).

macqu|er [make], *v.tr.* **1.** *Tex:* To brake (flax, hemp). **2.** *Metall:* To squeeze (bloom). *s.m.* **-age.**

macre [makr], s.f. Bot: Water caltrops.
macreuse [makrø:z], s.f. Orn: Scoter(-duck).
macrocéphale [makrɔsefal], a. Macrocephalic; large-headed.
macrocéphalie [makrɔsefali], s.f. Macrocephaly.
macrocosme [makrɔkɔsm], s.m. Macrocosm.
macropode [makrɔpɔd]. 1. a. Nat.Hist: Macropodous. 2. s.m. Ich: Paradise fish.
macroscopique [makrɔskɔpik], a. Macroscopic.
maculage [makyla:ʒ], s.m., **maculation** [makylasjɔ̃], s.f. Maculation, spot. Typ: (i) Setting off. (ii) Set-off, offset.
maculature [makylaty:r], s.f. Typ: Waste sheets; waste.
macule [makyl], s.f. (a) Stain, spot, blemish. Sans macule, immaculate, spotless, without blemish. (b) Astr: Macula, sun-spot. (c) Birth-mark.
maculer [makyle]. 1. v.tr. To stain, maculate, spot. 2. v.i. & pr. (Of paper) To mackle, blur; (of engraving) to fox.
   maculé, a. Z: etc: Spotted.
madame, pl. **mesdames** [madam, mɛdam], s.f.
1. (a) Madame, Mme, Dupont, Mrs Dupont. Mesdames, Mmes, Dupont, the Mrs Dupont, the Dupont ladies. Madame la marquise, la comtesse, de . . ., the Marchioness, the Countess, of. . . . Madame la comtesse, etc., her ladyship Je voudrais parler à madame la directrice, I want to speak to the manageress. Comment va madame votre mère? how is your mother? (b) (Used alone) (pl. ces dames) Voici le chapeau de madame, here is Mrs X's hat. Ces dames n'y sont pas, the ladies are not at home. 2. (a) (In address) Madam, F: ma'am; (to titled lady) your ladyship. Non, madame, no (,madam). Entrez, mesdames, come in, ladies. (b) (In letter writing) Madame (always written in full), Dear Madam. (Implying previous acquaintance) Chère Madame, Dear Mrs X. 3. F: (Often with pl. madames) Lady. Jouer à la madame, to play the fine lady. Il peint des belles madames, he paints fine ladies.
madapol(l)am [madapɔlam], s.m. Madapol-(l)am; fine calico.
madécasse [madekas], a. & s. Geog: Malagasy, Madagascan.
Madeleine [madlɛn]. 1. Pr.n.f. (a) B.Hist: Magdalen(e). (b) Madeline. 2. s.f. Sponge-cake.
mademoiselle, pl. **mesdemoiselles** [madmwazɛl, medmwazɛl], s.f. 1. Miss. Mademoiselle, Mlle, Smith, Miss Smith. Mesdemoiselles Smith, the Misses Smith. Voici le chapeau de mademoiselle, here is Miss Smith's, Miss Mary's, hat. Voici mademoiselle la directrice, here is the manageress. Comment va mademoiselle votre cousine? how is your cousin? 2. (a) (In address) Merci, mademoiselle, thank you, Miss Mary, Miss Smith, etc. (b) (pl. ces demoiselles) Mademoiselle est servie, dinner is served, madam. Que prendront ces demoiselles? what can I offer you, ladies? (c) (In letter writing) Mademoiselle (always written in full), Dear Madam. (Implying previous acquaintance) Chère Mademoiselle, Dear Miss X.
Madère [madɛ:r]. 1. Pr.n.f. Geog: Madeira. 2. s.m. Madeira (wine). Gâteau au madère, tipsy-cake.
madone [madɔn], s.f. Madonna.
madrague [madrag], s.f. Fish: Tunny-net.
madré [madre], a. 1. Veined, mottled. Savon m., mottled soap. Érable m., bird's-eye maple. 2. Sly, crafty, wily. s.m. Sly fox.
madrépore [madrepɔ:r], s.m. Coel: Madrepore.
madrier [madrie], s.m. (Piece of) timber; beam; joist; thick board, plank.

madrigal, **-aux** [madrigal, -o], s.m. Madrigal.
madrilène [madrilɛn], a. & s. Of Madrid; Madrilenian.
madrure [madry:r], s.f. Mottle (on wood); spot (on animal fur). pl. Speckles (of birds' feathers).
maestria [maɛstria], s.f. Art: Masterliness (of execution). Avec m., in a masterly manner; brilliantly; with dash.
maestro [maɛstro], s.m. Mus: Maestro.
mafflu [mafly], a. F: Heavy-jowled.
magasin [magazɛ̃], s.m. 1. (a) (Large) shop. Grand m., emporium, stores. Commis, demoiselle, de magasin, shop-assistant. Garçon de magasin, porter. (b) Store, warehouse. Garçon de magasin, warehouseman, storeman. Marchandises en magasin, stock in hand. Magasins généraux, bonded warehouse(s). (c) M. à poudre, powder magazine. M. d'armes, armoury. 2. Magazine (of rifle, camera).
magasinage [magazina:ʒ], s.m. 1. Warehousing, storing (of goods). 2. (Droits de) magasinage, warehouse dues; storage (charges).
magasinier [magazinje], s.m. 1. Warehouseman, storekeeper. 2. Com: Stock-book.
magazine [magazin], s.m. (Illustrated) magazine.
mage [ma:ʒ], s.m. Magus. Les trois Mages, (i) B.Hist: the Three Magi, the Three Wise Men; (ii) Astr: Orion's belt.
magenta [maʒɛta], a.inv. Magenta (colour).
magicien, **-ienne** [maʒisjɛ̃, -jɛn], s. Magician, wizard, sorcerer; f. sorceress.
magie [maʒi], s.f. Magic, wizardry. M. noire, black magic, the black art. M. blanche, white magic. F: La m. des mots, the witchery of words.
magique [maʒik], a. Magic(al). Baguette m., magic wand. Lanterne magique, magic lantern. adv. **-ment**, -ally.
magister [maʒistɛ:r], s.m. A: Schoolmaster, dominie.
magistral, **-aux** [maʒistral, -o], a. (a) Magisterial, authoritative; F: pompous; masterful (manner). (b) Masterly (work). adv. **-ement**.
magistrat [maʒistra], s.m. Magistrate; justice; judge. Il est m., he sits on the Bench.
magistrature [maʒistraty:r], s.f. Magistrature. 1. Magistrateship. 2. Magistracy. La magistrature assise, the judges, the Bench. La magistrature debout, the body of public prosecutors; the law-officers of the State. Entrer dans la magistrature, to be appointed judge or public prosecutor.
magnalium [magnaljɔm], s.m. Metall: Magnalium.
magnanerie [maɲanri], s.f. 1. Silkworm rearing-house; cocoonery. 2. Silkworm breeding; sericulture.
magnanier, **-ière** [maɲanje, -jɛ:r], s. Silkworm breeder; sericulturist.
magnanime [maɲanim], a. Magnanimous. adv. **-ment**.
magnanimité [maɲanimite], s.f. Magnanimity.
magnésie [maɲezi], s.f. 1. Ch: Pharm: Magnesia, magnesium oxide. 2. Pharm: Sulfate de magnésie, Epsom salts.
magnésite [maɲezit], s.f. Magnesite, meerschaum.
magnésium [maɲezjɔm], s.m. Ch: Magnesium. Phot: Lampe au magnésium, flash-lamp.
magnétique [maɲetik], a. Magnetic. adv. **-ment**, -ally.
magnétiser [maɲetize], v.tr. 1. (= AIMANTER) To magnetize (iron, etc.). 2. To mesmerize, hypnotize. F: Auditoire magnétisé, spell-bound audience.

magnétisme [maɲetism], *s.m.* **1.** *Ph:* Magnetism. *M. remanent,* residual magnetism. **2.** (*a*) Mesmerism. (*b*) *M. personnel,* personal magnetism.

magnétite [maɲetit], *s.f.* Magnetite, lodestone.

magnéto [maɲeto], *s.f. I.C.E:* Magneto.

magnéto-électrique [maɲetoelɛktrik], *a. Ph:* Magneto-electric.

magnificence [maɲifisɑ̃:s], *s.f.* **1.** Magnificence, splendour. **2.** Munificence.

magnifier [maɲifje], *v.tr.* To magnify, glorify.

magnifique [maɲifik], *a.* **1.** (*a*) Magnificent, grand; sumptuous; gorgeous (sight). (*b*) Grandiloquent, pompous (tone). (*c*) High-sounding (promises). *F: Vous êtes magnifique!* it's easy to talk! **2.** Liberal, open-handed. *adv.* **-ment.**

magnitude [maɲityd], *s.f.* Magnitude (of star).

magnolia [maɲɔlja, -gn-], *s.m. Bot:* Magnolia.

magnolier [maɲɔlje, -gn-], *s.m.* Magnolia(-tree).

magot[1] [mago], *s.m. F:* Hoard (of money); savings, *F:* pile.

magot[2], *s.m.* **1.** Barbary ape, pigmy ape; macaque, magot. **2.** (*a*) Chinese grotesque porcelain figure. (*b*) *F:* (With *f.* **magotte**) Ugly person; *F:* fright.

magyar [maʒja:r], *a. & s. Ethn:* Magyar.

mahari [maari], *s.m.* Racing dromedary.

Mahomet [maɔmɛ]. *Pr.n.m.* Mohammed, Mahomet.

mahométan, -ane [maɔmetɑ̃, -an], *a. & s.* Mohammedan, Mahometan, Moslem.

mahomét(an)isme [maɔmet(an)ism], *s.m.* Mohammedanism, Moslemism.

mahout [mau], *s.m.* Mahout; elephant-driver.

mai [mɛ], *s.m.* **1.** May. *En mai,* in May. *Au mois de mai,* in the month of May. *Le sept mai,* (on) the seventh of May, (on) May (the) seventh. *Le premier mai,* May-day. **2.** Maypole.

maigre[1] [mɛ:gr]. **1.** *a.* (*a*) Thin, skinny, lean. *F: Maigre comme un clou, comme un hareng saur,* as thin as a lath, as a rake. *Homme grand et m.,* tall spare man. (*b*) Lean (meat, coal); meagre (fare); scanty (vegetation); unfertile, poor (land). **Maigre repas,** scanty, frugal, meal. **Repas maigre,** meatless meal (on fast-days). **Jour maigre,** fast-day, day of abstinence. *Faire maigre,* to fast, to abstain from meat. *M. bagage de latin,* scanty store of Latin. *Faire m. chère, m. réception, à qn,* to show s.o. meagre hospitality; to give s.o. a poor reception. *adv.* Peindre, dessiner, *maigre,* to lack breadth of brush, of pencil. **2.** *s.m.* Lean (part of meat). *Voulez-vous du gras ou du m.?* will you have fat or lean? *adv.* **-ment.**

maigre[2], *s.m. Ich:* Meagre, maul.

maigrelet, -ette [mɛgrəlɛ, -ɛt], *a.* Thin, slight (person); *F:* skinny.

maigreur [mɛgrœ:r], *s.f.* **1.** (*a*) Thinness, leanness. (*b*) Emaciation. **2.** Poorness, meagreness, scantiness (of a meal, etc.); baldness (of style).

maigrichon, -onne [mɛgriʃɔ̃, -ɔn], **maigriot, -ote** [mɛgrio, -ɔt], *a. F:* Thin, skinny (urchin).

maigrir [mɛgri:r]. **1.** *v.i.* To grow thin, lean; to lose flesh. *J'ai maigri ae vingt livres,* I have lost twenty pounds. **2.** *v.tr.* (*a*) (Of illness) To make (s.o.) thinner. (*b*) (Of garment) To make (s.o.) look thin(ner). (*c*) To thin (piece of wood).

mail [ma:j], *s.m.* **1.** (*a*) *A:* Mall (game, club, or alley). (*b*) Avenue, promenade. **2.** Sledgehammer.

maille[1] [mɑ:j], *s.f.* **1.** (*a*) Stitch (in knitting, etc.). *Mailles endroit, mailles envers,* plain and purl. *Arrêter les mailles,* to cast off. (*b*) Link (of chain). (*c*) *Arm:* (Chain-)mail. *Cotte de mailles,* coat of mail. **2.** Mesh (of net). *Filet à larges mailles,* wide-mesh net. **3.** Speckle, spot (on partridge feather, etc.).

maille[2], *s.f. Num: A:* Mail. *F:* Il n'a ni sou ni maille, he hasn't a penny to bless himself with. *Avoir maille à partir avec qn,* to have a bone to pick, a crow to pluck, with s.o.

maillechort [majʃɔ:r], *s.m.* German silver, nickel silver.

mailler [maje], *v.tr.* **1.** (*a*) To net (a purse, etc.). (*b*) To make (sth.) in lattice-work. **2.** To shackle (two chains).

maillet [majɛ], *s.m.* (*a*) *Tls:* Mallet or maul; beetle. (*b*) Polo-stick, -mallet; croquet-mallet.

mailloche [majɔʃ], *s.f.* **1.** Beetle; large mallet. **2.** Bass-drumstick.

maillon [majɔ̃], *s.m.* **1.** (*a*) Link (of a chain). *M. tournant,* swivel. (*b*) *W.Tel: M.isolateur,* shell insulator; buckle insulator. **2.** *Nau:* (Length of chain of 30 metres) Shackle.

maillot[1] [majo], *s.m.* Swaddling-clothes. **Enfant encore au maillot,** baby not yet 'shortened.'

maillot[2], *s.m.* (*a*) *Th: etc:* Tights. (*b*) *M. de bain, de natation,* bathing costume; swimming costume. (*c*) *Sp:* (Football) jersey; (running, boxing) vest, singlet.

main [mɛ̃], *s.f.* **1.** Hand. (*a*) *F: Se laver les mains de qch.,* to wash one's hands of sth. **Soin des mains,** manicure, manicuring. *F: Faire la belle main,* to attitudinize. *Donner la m. à qn,* (i) to take s.o.'s hand, to lead s.o. by the hand; (ii) to shake hands with s.o. **Se donner la main,** to shake hands. **Donner sa main à qn,** (i) to shake hands with s.o.; (ii) (of woman) to give one's hand in marriage to s.o. *Je lui serrai la m.,* I shook hands with him. **Prêter la main à qn,** to lend s.o. a helping hand. *Mettre, porter, la m. à son chapeau,* to touch one's hat (to s.o.). **Porter la main sur qn,** to lay a hand on s.o. *F:* Je n'en mettrais pas la main au feu, I shouldn't like to swear to it. **Mariage de la main gauche,** (i) morganatic marriage, left-handed marriage; (ii) marriage over the broomstick. **En venir aux mains,** to come to blows. *Ils en sont aux mains,* they are at grips. **Enlèvement à main armée,** abduction by force of arms. **N'y pas aller de main morte,** to put one's back into it; to go at it hard. **Faire main basse sur une ville,** to pillage a town. *F: Faire main basse sur les vivres,* to make a clean sweep of the victuals. **Haut les mains!** hands up! **A bas les mains!** hands off! **Faire qch. sous main,** to do sth. in an underhand way. **Avoir qch. sous la main,** to have sth. (near) at hand. **Coup de main,** *Mil:* raid, surprise attack. *Tenter un coup de m. contre une position,* to attempt to carry a position by surprise. **Donner un coup de main à qn,** to lend s.o. a helping hand; to bear a hand. *F: Passer la main dans le dos, dans les cheveux, à qn,* to soft-sawder s.o. S.a. CŒUR 2, NOUVELLE[2] 1, REVERS 1. (*b*) (Hand used for gripping sth.) **Il a des mains de beurre,** he's a butter-fingers. **Prendre son courage à deux mains,** to take one's courage in both hands. **Épée à deux mains,** two-handed sword. **Il signa le contrat des deux mains,** he signed the contract eagerly. **Donner de l'argent à pleine(s) main(s),** to ladle out money by the handful. **Avoir de l'atout plein les mains,** to have a handful of trumps. **Avoir sans cesse l'argent à la main,** to be constantly paying out money. **Argent en main(s),** money in hand. **Outil bien en mains, bien à la main,** handy tool. **Tenir le succès entre ses mains,** to have success within one's grasp. **Tomber entre les mains de l'ennemi,** to fall into the enemy's hands. **Être en bonnes mains,** to be in good hands, in safe keeping. **Prendre une affaire en main**, to take a matter in hand. **Mettre la main sur qn**, *F:* to collar, nab, nail, s.o. *Mettre la m. sur qch.*, to lay hands on, take possession of, sth. **Je ne peux pas mettre la main sur sa lettre**, I cannot lay my hand on his letter. **Acheter qch. de première, seconde, main**, to buy sth. (at) first, second, hand. *Renseignements de première m.*, first-hand information. **De main en main**, from hand to hand. **Payer de la main à la main**, to hand over the money direct (without receipt or other formality). (*c*) *Faire, fabriquer, qch. à la m.*, to do, make, sth. by hand. *Travail fait à la m.*, handwork. *Scie à m.*, hand-saw. *Écrire une lettre de sa propre m.*, to write a letter in one's own hand. *Notes écrites à la m.*, hand-written notes. **Faire qch. en un tour de main**, to do sth. in a twinkling, in a jiffy. S.a. TOUR² 5. **Mettre la main à l'œuvre**, *F:* to put one's hand to the plough. S.a. PÂTE I. **Mettre la main à la plume**, to put pen to paper. **Se faire la main**, to get one's hand in; to acquire the knack of sth. *S'entretenir la m.*, to keep one's hand in. **Il a perdu la main**, he is out of practice. S.a. LEVÉ I, NET I, TRAVAIL² I. (*d*) *Equit:* **Rendre la main à son cheval**, to give one's horse its head. **Cheval à main, de main**, led horse. **Cheval à toute main**, horse for riding or driving. *F:* **Homme à toute main**, man ready to do anything. **Cheval bien en main, bien dans la main**, horse well in hand, under control. *Être sous la m. de qn*, to be under s.o.'s thumb. **Agir de haute main**, to act with a high hand, in a high-handed way. **Avoir la haute main sur . . .**, to have supreme control over. . . . **Gagner haut la main**, (i) *Turf:* to win in a canter; (ii) *F:* to win easily, hands down. (*e*) *Adv.phr.* **De longue main**, for a long time (past). *Ami de longue m.*, friend of long standing. **2.** (*a*) *Hand(writing).* *Avoir une belle m.*, to have a fine hand; to write well. (*b*) *Com:* **Main courante**, waste book, rough book. **3.** *Cards:* (*a*) Hand. *Avoir une m. longue*, to have a long suit in trumps. (*b*) **Avoir la main**, to have the deal. **Passer la main**, (i) to pass the deal; (ii) *F:* to stand aside; to give someone else a chance. (*c*) **Avoir la main**, to have the lead. **4.** (*a*) (Grocer's, etc.) scoop. (*b*) **Mains de caoutchouc**, rubber gloves. (*c*) Handle (of drawer, etc.). (*d*) *Aut:* **Main de ressort**, dumbiron, spring-carrier arm. **5.** **Main de papier** (25 *feuilles*), approx. = quire (24 sheets). **6.** Feel (of cloth, etc.). *Papier qui a de la m.*, paper with some substance, that handles easily. **7.** **Main courante**, hand-rail (of stair); hand-rope. **8.** **Main de fer**, (i) hand-hold (on wall, etc.); (ii) handled hook (of rag-pickers).

main-d'œuvre, *s.f.* **1.** Labour; man-power. *Embaucher de la m.-d'œ.*, to take on hands. **2.** Cost of labour. **3.** Workmanship.

main-forte, *s.f.* Help, assistance (to authority or of authority). **Prêter main-forte à la justice**, to give assistance to the law.

mainlevée [mɛlve], *s.f.* *Jur:* Mainlevée de saisie, replevin; restoration of goods (taken in distraint). *M. d'opposition à mariage*, withdrawal of opposition to marriage. *Ecc:* *M. d'interdit*, removal of interdict.

mainmise [mɛ̃mi:z], *s.f.* **1.** *A:* Manumission; freeing (of bondman). **2.** Seizure (*sur*, of); distraint (upon property).

mainmorte [mɛ̃mɔrt], *s.f.* *Jur:* Mortmain.

maint [mɛ̃], *a.* *A. & Lit:* Many (a . . .). *M. auteur*, many an author. **Maintes et maintes fois,**

à maintes reprises, en mainte (et mainte) occasion, many a time and oft.

maintenant [mɛtnɑ̃], *adv.* Now. *A vous m.*, your turn next. **Dès maintenant**, (i) henceforth, from now onwards; (ii) even now.

maintenir [mɛtni:r], *v.tr.* (Conj. like TENIR) To maintain. **1.** (*a*) To keep, hold, (sth.) in position. *Colonnes qui maintiennent la voûte*, columns that keep up, hold up, support, the roof. *M. qn dans ses fonctions*, to maintain s.o. in his post, to continue s.o. in office. (*b*) *M. sa famille par son travail*, to maintain, support, one's family by one's work. (*c*) To uphold, keep (the law, discipline, opinion); to abide by (a decision). *Je maintiens que c'est faux*, I maintain that it is untrue. **2.** *M. un fou furieux sur sa couchette*, to hold down a raving lunatic on his bed.

se maintenir. 1. (*a*) To last well. (*b*) (Of casting-mould, etc.) To hold together. **2.** To hold on. *Se m. dans les bonnes grâces de qn*, to keep in favour with s.o. *Se m. contre les attaques de l'ennemi*, to hold one's own, to keep one's ground, against the enemy. *Les prix se maintiennent*, prices are keeping up. **3.** To be maintained, to continue. *Cela ne peut pas se m. longtemps*, it cannot last long.

maintien [mɛtjɛ̃], *s.m.* **1.** Maintenance, upholding, keeping (of order, etc.). **2.** Bearing, carriage, deportment. *Il n'a pas de m.*, he is awkward, loutish. **Perdre son maintien**, to lose countenance.

maintien-gorge, *s.m.inv.* Bust-supporter.

maire [mɛ:r], *s.m.* Mayor.

mairesse [mɛres], *s.f.* *F:* Mayoress.

mairie [mɛri], *s.f.* Town-hall; municipal buildings.

mais [mɛ]. **1.** *adv.* (*a*) *A:* More. (Still so used in) **N'en pouvoir mais**, (i) to be exhausted, at the end of one's tether; (ii) to be too disconcerted to protest. (*b*) (Emphatic) **Mais oui!** why, certainly! **Mais non!** not at all! **Mais qu'avez-vous donc?** why, what is the matter? **Mais c'est que c'est vrai!** indeed, it's quite true! **2.** *conj.* But. *Famille pauvre m. honnête*, poor but honest family. *Non seulement . . ., m. encore . . .*, not only . . ., but also. . . .

maïs [mais], *s.m.* Maize, Indian corn. **Farine de maïs**, cornflour.

maison [mezɔ̃], *s.f.* **1.** House. (*a*) *M. d'habitation*, dwelling-house. *M. de ferme*, farm-house. S.a. RAPPORT I.1. *M. d'éducation*, educational establishment. *M. religieuse*, convent. **Maison de ville**, **maison commune**, municipal buildings; town-hall. *M. de santé*, (i) nursing home; (ii) home for the insane. *M. de fous*, lunatic asylum, madhouse. *M. de correction*, (i) *A:* bridewell; (ii) reformatory school. *M. d'arrêt*, lock-up; prison, gaol. *M. de force*, prison. *M. de jeu*, gambling-house. *Prov:* **Les maisons empêchent de voir la ville**, you can't see the wood for the trees. *F:* **Faire des demandes par-dessus les maisons**, to make extravagant, exorbitant, demands. (*b*) **Maison de commerce**, business house: firm. (*c*) Home. *M. de ville*, town-house. *M. de campagne*, country-house, country-seat. ·**Se faire une maison**, to set up house. **A la maison**, at home. **Garder la maison**, to stay at home, to stay in(doors). **Tenir maison ouverte**, to keep open house. **Tenir la maison de qn**, to keep house for s.o. **Trouver maison nette**, to find the house empty. (*d*) *Astrol:* House, mansion. **2.** Family. (*a*) *Le fils de la m.*, the son of the house. **Il est de bonne maison**, he belongs to a family of good standing. **Être de la maison**, to be one of the family. (*b*) Dynasty. **La Maison des Bourbons**, the House of Bourbon.

(c) Household, staff. *Un valet et deux servantes composent toute sa m.*, his household consists of a valet and two maids. *La m. du Roi*, the Royal Household. **Faire maison nette**, to make a clean sweep of all the servants or employees.

maisonnée [mɛzɔne], *s.f.* F: Household, family.

maisonnette [mɛzɔnɛt], *s.f.* Small house; cottage.

maistrance [mɛstrã:s], *s.f.* (a) Petty officers (of the navy). (b) Dockyard staff.

maître, -esse [mɛ:tr, mɛtrɛs], *s.* 1. (a) Master, *f.* mistress. **Parler à qn en maître**, to speak authoritatively to s.o. *Être m. de la situation*, to be master of the situation. **Être maître absolu de faire qch.**, to be entirely free to do sth. *F:* **Faire le maître**, to lord it. **Trouver son maître**, to meet one's master. **Être maître, maîtresse, de soi(-même)**, to be master, mistress, of oneself. *Le mécanicien n'était plus m. du train,* the driver had lost control of the train. *Navire qui n'est pas m. de sa manœuvre,* ship out of control. **Devenir, se rendre, maître de qch.**, (i) to become the owner of sth., to take possession of sth.; (ii) to master sth. *Il est toujours m. de son auditoire,* he always commands the attention of his audience. *Prov:* **Tel maître, tel valet**, like master, like man. (b) **Maître, maîtresse, d'école, de pension**, schoolmaster, schoolmistress. **Maître d'étude** = RÉPÉTITEUR (a). **Maître de danse**, (i) dancing-master; (ii) *Tls:* in and out calipers. *M. d'armes, d'escrime,* fencing-master. *M. de chapelle,* choir-master. (c) **Maître charpentier, maître maçon,** master carpenter, master mason. **Main de maître,** master hand. *C'est fait de main de m.,* it is a masterpiece. **Coup de maître,** master stroke. **Être passé maître en qch.,** to be a past master in sth. (d) Works owner. **Maître de forges,** ironmaster. (e) Employee in charge. **Maître d'œuvre,** foreman. *M. clerc,* (lawyer's) managing clerk. **Maître, maîtresse, de poste,** postmaster, postmistress. *Navy:* **Premier maître,** chief petty officer. **Second maître,** second-class petty officer. **Maître d'équipage,** boatswain. **Maître d'hôtel,** (i) major-domo, house-steward, butler; (ii) head waiter; (iii) *Nau:* chief steward. *Cu:* **Sauce à la maître d'hôtel,** melted butter with parsley and lemon juice. (f) (Title applied to notaries and advocates) Maître. 2. *N.Arch:* Midships. **Demi-coupe au maître,** half-midship section. 3. *Attrib.* (a) **Maîtresse femme,** capable, managing, woman. *F:* **Maître sot,** utter fool. *M. filou,* arrant knave. (b) Chief, principal. **Maîtresse poutre,** main girder, main beam. *Idée maîtresse d'un ouvrage,* governing idea of a work. *Games:* **Carte maîtresse,** master card. 4. *s.f.* **Maîtresse,** mistress, *A:* paramour.

maître-autel, *s.m.* Ecc: High altar.

maître-couple, *s.m.* N.Arch: Midship(s) frame.

maître-timonier, *s.m.* Navy: Yeoman of the signals. *pl. Des maîtres-timoniers.*

maîtrise [mɛtri:z], *s.f.* 1. (a) Mastership. Sch: *M. de conférences,* lectureship. (b) Choir-mastership (of cathedral). (c) Choir school. 2. Mastery (of passions, of an art). *M. de soi,* self-control. *M. des mers,* command of the seas.

maîtriser [mɛtrize], *v.tr.* To master (a horse); to subdue (a fire); to get (fire) under control; to curb, bridle (passion). *M. une voie d'eau,* to overcome, stop, a leak. **Ne pas savoir se maîtriser,** to have no control over oneself.

majesté [maʒɛste], *s.f.* 1. Majesty. *Sa M. le Roi, la Reine,* His Majesty the King, Her Majesty

the Queen. *Leurs Majestés,* Their Majesties. 2. (a) Stateliness; augustness. (b) Grandeur (of style, of landscape).

majestueu|x, -euse [maʒɛstɥø, -ø:z], *a.* Majestic. *adv.* **-sement,** -ally.

majeur [maʒœ:r], *a.* (a) Major, greater. *La majeure partie de qch.,* the greater part, the bulk, of sth. *La majeure partie du temps,* most of the time. **En majeure partie,** for the most part. **Le doigt majeur,** *s.* **le majeur,** the second finger. *Geog:* **Le lac Majeur,** Lake Maggiore. (b) *Affaire majeure,* business of first importance. *Raison majeure de qch.,* chief reason for sth. **Être absent pour raison majeure,** to be unavoidably absent. **Cas de force majeure,** case of absolute necessity. (c) *Jur:* Of full age. **Devenir m.,** to attain one's majority; to come of age.

majolique [maʒɔlik], *s.f.* Cer: Majolica.

major [maʒɔ:r], *s.m.* 1. *Mil:* Regimental adjutant (with administrative duties). *M. général,* chief of staff (of group of armies). *M. de la garnison,* town-major. S.a. ÉTAT-MAJOR, TAMBOUR-MAJOR. 2. *Navy:* *M. de la flotte,* port-admiral. 3. *Mil. & Navy:* (**Médecin**) major, medical officer; M.O.

majoration [maʒɔrasjɔ̃], *s.f.* 1. (a) Over-estimation, overvaluation (of assets, etc.). (b) Additional charge (on bill). 2. (a) Increase (in price). (b) Increased allowance.

majordome [maʒɔrdɔm], *s.m.* Major-domo; steward.

majorer [maʒɔre], *v.tr.* 1. To over-estimate, overvalue (assets, etc.). 2. To make an additional charge on (bill). *M. une facture de 10%,* to put 10% on an invoice. 3. To raise, put up, the price of (sth.).

majorité [maʒɔrite], *s.f.* 1. Majority. **Emporter la majorité,** to secure a majority; to carry a vote. **Décision prise à la majorité (des voix),** decision taken by a majority. 2. *Jur:* Majority; coming of age. **Atteindre sa majorité,** to come of age. 3. *Mil:* Function of adjutant or chief of staff.

Majorque [maʒɔrk]. Pr.n.f. Geog: Majorca.

majuscule [maʒyskyl], *a. & s.f.* (Large) capital (letter).

mal¹ [mal], *a.* *A:* = MAUVAIS. (Still used in) **Bon an, mal an,** year in, year out. **Bon gré, mal gré,** willy-nilly. S.a. MALEMORT, MALEPESTE.

mal², *pl.* **maux** [mal, mo], *s.m.* 1. Evil. (a) Hurt, harm. **Faire du mal,** to do harm. **Faire du mal à qn,** to do s.o. harm; to injure s.o. *Il fait plus de bruit que de mal,* his bark is worse than his bite. *S'en tirer sans aucun mal,* to escape uninjured, unhurt, unscathed. *Vouloir du mal à qn,* to wish s.o. evil. *Je ne lui veux pas de mal,* I mean him no harm. *Cela fera plus de mal que de bien,* it will do more harm than good. *Souffrir de grands maux,* to suffer great ills. **Il n'y a pas de mal à cela,** there is no harm in that. **Il n'y a pas grand mal!** there's no great harm done! **Mal lui en a pris,** he has had cause to rue it. (b) **Dire du mal de qn,** to speak ill of s.o. **Changement en mal,** change for the worse. **Prendre qch. en mal,** to take sth. amiss. **Tourner qch. en mal,** to put the worst interpretation on sth. (c) Wrong(doing). **Le bien et le mal,** right and wrong, good and evil. *Rendre le bien pour le mal,* to return good for evil. **Il ne songe pas à mal,** he doesn't mean any harm. 2. (a) Disorder; malady, disease; ailment; pain, ache. *Quel est votre mal?* what is wrong with you? *Esp:* *Vous allez prendre du mal* you will catch your death of cold. *F:* **Attraper du mal à faire qch.,** to catch an illness, a complaint, through doing sth. **Mal de tête,** headache. **Mal**

de dents, toothache. **Mal de cœur,** sickness, nausea. S.a. ESTOMAC. **Mal de mer,** seasickness. **Avoir le mal de mer,** to be seasick. **Mal de gorge,** sore throat. *A : Tomber du haut mal,* to have an epileptic fit. **Mal blanc,** gathering; esp. gathered finger. **Avoir mal à la tête, aux dents, à la gorge,** to have a headache, toothache, a sore throat. **Vous me faites (du) mal,** you are hurting me. *Mes os me font mal,* my bones ache. *Spectacle qui fait mal,* painful sight. **Avoir le mal du pays,** to be homesick. (b) **Se donner du mal pour faire qch.,** to take pains to do sth. **Avoir du mal à faire qch.,** to have difficulty in doing sth. **mal³,** *adv.* **I.** (a) Badly, ill. *Se conduire mal,* to behave badly. **Mal à l'aise,** ill at ease. *Biens mal acquis,* ill-gotten gains. *Faire qch.* tant **bien que mal,** to do sth. fairly well, after a fashion. **Aller de mal en pis,** to go from bad to worse. **S'y mal prendre,** to go the wrong way to work. *Vous êtes mal informé,* you are ill-informed. *Vous ne trouvez pas mal que je corrige vos fautes?* you do not mind my correcting your mistakes? *Vous ne feriez peut-être pas mal de . . .,* it wouldn't be a bad plan to. . . . (b) **Aller, se porter, mal,** to be ill, in bad health. *Comment allez-vous?*—**Pas mal! pas trop mal!** how are you?—Not so bad! pretty well! **Être au plus mal,** to be dangerously ill, at death's door. (c) *F:* **Pas mal** *(de qch.),* a fair amount (of sth.). *Il (n')y en a pas mal,* there are a good many, a good few. *Cela m'a pris pas mal de temps,* it took me a good time. *Pas mal de gens,* a good many people. **2.** (With adj. function) (a) Not right. *Vous savez ce qui est bien et ce qui est mal,* you know what is right and wrong. *C'est très mal à lui,* (i) that's too bad of him; (ii) that's very unkind of him. (b) Uncomfortable; badly off. *Nous ne sommes pas mal ici,* we are quite comfortable, not at all badly off, here. **Être mal dans ses affaires,** to be in a bad way of business. (c) **Ils sont mal ensemble,** they are on bad terms (with each other). (d) (Of health) *Se sentir mal,* to feel ill, sick, faint, *F:* bad. **Se trouver mal,** to faint, to swoon. (e) *F:* **Pas mal,** of good appearance, quality, etc. *Ce n'était pas mal du tout, F:* it wasn't half bad. *Elle n'est pas mal,* she is rather good-looking.

malachite [malakit], *s.f. Miner:* Malachite.

malade [malad]. **I.** *a.* Ill, sick, poorly, unwell; diseased. *Être m.,* to be ill, poorly. *Dent m.,* (i) aching tooth; (ii) decaying tooth. *Jambe m.,* bad leg. *J'ai l'estomac m.,* my stomach is out of order. **Tomber malade,** to fall ill, to be taken ill. *M. de la fièvre typhoïde,* ill, *F:* down, with typhoid fever. **Il en est malade,** he is quite upset about it. **Malade à mourir,** sick to death. *M. d'esprit et de corps,* diseased in body and mind. *Être m. du cœur, de l'estomac,* to have heart trouble, stomach trouble. *Esprit m.,* disordered mind. *Mil:* **Se faire porter malade,** to report sick. **2.** *s.* Sick person; invalid. *Med:* Patient, *F:* case. *Les malades,* the sick. *Mil: etc:* Rôle des malades, sick-list. **Faire le malade,** to malinger.

maladie [maladi], *s.f.* Illness, sickness, disease, disorder, complaint. *M. de l'enfance,* child's complaint; ailment. **Faire une longue maladie,** to have a long illness. **Par suite de maladie,** through illness. *M. cutanée,* skin disease. *M. de foie,* liver complaint. *M. mentale,* mental disease. *Maladies des plantes,* diseases of plants. *Vet:* **Maladie des chiens,** distemper.

maladif, -ive [maladif, -i:v], *a.* Sickly; morbid.

maladministration [maladministrasjɔ̃], *s.f.* Maladministration.

maladrerie [maladrəri], *s.f. A :* Leper-house.

maladresse [maladrɛs], *s.f.* **I.** (a) Clumsiness, awkwardness. (b) Maladroitness, impolicy (of speech, etc.). **2.** Blunder.

maladroit, -oite [maladrwa, -wat]. **I.** *a.* (a) Unskilful, clumsy, awkward (person); clumsy, maladroit (compliment, etc.). (b) Blundering, maladroit (speech). **2.** *s.* (a) Awkward person. (b) Blunderer. *adv.* **-ement.**

Malaga [malaga]. **I.** *Pr.n. Geog:* Malaga. **2.** *s.m.* Malaga (wine).

malais, -aise¹ [malɛ, -ɛ:z], *a. & s.* Malay(an).

malaise² [malɛ:z], *s.m.* **I.** Uneasiness, discomfort, malaise. *Sentiment de m.,* (i) uneasy feeling; (ii) sickish feeling. **2.** Indisposition; fit of faintness.

malaisé [malɛze], *a.* Difficult. *Chose malaisée à faire,* thing difficult to do.

malaisément [malɛzemɑ̃], *adv.* With difficulty.

Malaisie [malɛzi]. *Pr.n.f. Geog:* The Malay Archipelago.

malandre [malɑ̃:dr], *s.f.* **I.** Rotten knot, defect (in wood). **2.** *Vet:* Malanders.

malandreux, -euse [malɑ̃drø, -ø:z], *a.* **I.** (Of wood) Rotten at the knots. **2.** *Vet:* (Of horse) Malandered.

malandrin [malɑ̃drɛ̃], *s.m.* **I.** *Hist:* Disbanded mercenary (preying on the people). **2.** *F:* Brigand, robber, highwayman; marauder.

malappris, -ise [malapri, -i:z]. **I.** *a.* Uncouth, ill-bred. **2.** *s.* Ill-bred person; lout.

malard [mala:r], *s.m.* Wild drake; mallard.

malaria [malarja], *s.f.* Malaria, marsh-fever.

malavisé, -ée [malavize]. **I.** *a.* Ill-advised, blundering (act); unwise, injudicious (person, etc.). **2.** *s.* Dunderhead.

malax|er [malakse], *v.tr.* To malaxate (pills); to knead (dough); to work (butter); to mix (cement); to pug (clay). *s.m.* **-age.**

malaxeur [malaksœ:r], *s.m.* Mixer. **I.** Butterworker. **2.** Cement-mixer. **3.** *Brickm:* Pug-mill.

malbâti [malbɑti], *a.* Uncouth.

malchance [malʃɑ̃:s], *s.f.* **I.** Bad luck, ill luck. **Par malchance,** as ill luck would have it. **2.** Mishap.

malchanceux, -euse [malʃɑ̃sø, -ø:z], *a.* Unfortunate, unlucky.

maldonne [maldɔn], *s.f. Cards:* Misdeal. **Faire maldonne,** to misdeal.

mâle [mɑ:l], *a. & s.m.* **I.** Male; cock (bird); buck (rabbit, antelope); dog (fox, wolf); bull (elephant, etc.). *Héritier m.,* male heir. Also (of animals) He-. *Un ours m.,* a he-bear. *Un âne m.,* a he-ass. **2.** *Courage m., m. courage,* manly courage. *Style m.,* virile style.

malechance [malʃɑ̃:s], *s.f.* = MALCHANCE.

malédiction [malediksjɔ̃], *s.f.* Malediction, curse. *Être sous le coup d'une m.,* to be under a curse. *int.* **Malédiction!** *il m'a échappé,* curse it! he has escaped me.

maléfice [malefis], *s.m.* Malefice; evil spell.

maléfique [malefik], *a.* Maleficent; malefic (star, etc.); baleful, evil (influence).

malemort [malmɔ:r], *s.f. A:* Foul death. *Mourir de malemort,* to come to a tragic end; to die a violent death.

malencontre [malɑ̃kɔ̃:tr], *s.f. F:* Misfortune, mishap, unfortunate occurrence. **Par malencontre,** unfortunately.

malencontreu|x, -euse [malɑ̃kɔ̃trø, -ø:z], *a.* **I.** (a) Untoward, unfortunate (event, etc.). (b) (Person, etc.) of ill omen. **2.** Unlucky, unfortunate (person). *adv.* **-sement.**

malendurant [malɑ̃dyrɑ̃], *a.* Impatient, short tempered, testy.

mal-en-point, *adj.phr. inv.* In a bad way; in a sorry plight.

malentendu [malɑ̃tɑ̃dy], *s.m.* Misunderstanding, misapprehension.

malentente [malɑ̃tɑ̃:t], *s.f.* Dissension, disagreement.

malepeste [malpɛst]. *A:* **1.** *s.f. La m. soit de lui!* plague take him! **2.** *int.* Zounds! the devil! plague take him!

malfaçon [malfasɔ̃], *s.f.* Bad work(manship); defect.

malfaire [malfɛːr], *v.i.* (Used only in the inf.) To do evil, wrong.

malfaisance [malfəzɑ̃s], *s.f.* **1.** Maleficence, evil-mindedness. **2.** *Jur:* Malfeasance.

malfaisant [malfəzɑ̃], *a.* Maleficent; evil-minded (person); noxious, harmful (food, etc.); evil (influence). *Jur:* Malfeasant.

malfaiteur, -trice [malfɛtœːr, -tris], *s.* Malefactor, wrong-doer, evil-doer.

malfamé [malfame], *a.* In bad repute; of ill fame.

malformation [malfɔrmasjɔ̃], *s.f.* Malformation.

malgache [malgaʃ], *a. & s.* = MADÉCASSE.

malgracieu|x, -euse [malgrasjø, -øːz], *a.* Ungracious, churlish, rude. *adv.* **-sement.**

malgré [malgre], *prep.* **1.** In spite of; notwithstanding. *M. cela, m. tout,* for all that; nevertheless; yet . . .; in spite of all. . . . *Je l'ai fait m. moi,* I did it against my will. **2.** *Conj.phr.* **Malgré que** + *sub.* (i) *M. que vous en ayez,* in spite of all you may say, do. (ii) = QUOIQUE.

malhabile [malabil], *a.* Unskilful; clumsy, awkward. *adv.* **-ment.**

malhabileté [malabilte], *s.f.* Lack of skill, of experience; clumsiness, awkwardness.

malherbe [malɛrb], *s.f. Bot:* **1.** Plumbago. **2.** Daphne mezereon.

malheur [malœːr], *s.m.* Misfortune. **1.** Untoward occurrence; calamity, accident. *Ils ont eu des malheurs,* they have seen better days. *F:* Faire un malheur, to do something desperate; to commit murder or suicide. *Iron:* **Le grand malheur!** that's nothing much to complain about! *Prov:* **Un malheur ne vient jamais seul,** misfortunes never come singly. **2.** Bad luck, ill luck. **Messager de malheur,** bird of ill omen. **Porter malheur à qn,** to bring s.o. bad luck. **Malheur à vous!** woe betide you! *En ce jour de m.,* on this ill-fated day. **Par malheur,** unfortunately. **Quel malheur que je ne l'aie pas su!** what a pity I didn't know of it! **Enfant qui fait le malheur de ses parents,** child that is a sore trial to its parents. **Jouer de malheur,** être en malheur, to be unlucky; to be out of luck. *C'est jouer de m.,* it is most unfortunate. *Prov:* **A quelque chose malheur est bon,** it's an ill wind that blows nobody good. **C'est dans le malheur qu'on connaît ses vrais amis,** a friend in need is a friend indeed.

malheureusement [malœrøzmɑ̃], *adv.* Unfortunately, unhappily, unluckily.

malheureux, -euse [malœrø, -øːz], *a.* (a) Unfortunate, unhappy, wretched (person, affair); poor, badly off (person); woeful (countenance). *s. Secourir les m.,* to help the unfortunate, the poor. **Le malheureux!** (the) poor man! **Malheureux!** wretched man! wretch! (b) Unlucky. *M. au jeu,* unlucky at play. *Entreprise malheureuse,* ill-starred adventure. *C'est bien m. pour vous!* it is hard lines on you! **Avoir la main malheureuse,** (i) to be unlucky; (ii) to be clumsy, awkward, with one's hands. *Le voilà enfin, ce n'est pas m.!* here he comes at last, and a good job too! (c) *F:* Paltry, wretched. *Une malheureuse pièce de cinq francs,* a beggarly five-franc piece.

malhonnête [malɔnɛt], *a.* (a) Dishonest.

(b) Rude, impolite. (c) Indecent (gesture); improper. *adv.* **-ment.**

malhonnêteté [malɔnɛtte], *s.f.* **1.** (a) Dishonesty. (b) Dishonest action. **2.** (a) Rudeness, incivility. (b) Rude word or remark.

malice [malis], *s.f.* **1.** (a) Malice, maliciousness, spitefulness. **Ne pas voir malice à qch.,** (i) to see no harm in sth.; (ii) to mean no harm by sth. S.a. ENTENDRE 1. (b) Mischievousness, roguishness, naughtiness. **2.** (a) Smart remark; dig (at s.o.). **Dire des malices à qn,** to chaff s.o. (b) Trick, prank. **Faire une malice à qn,** to play a trick on s.o. *La belle m.!* there's nothing very clever in that!

malicieu|x, -euse [malisjø, -øːz], *a.* **1.** *A:* Malicious, spiteful. **Cheval malicieux,** unreliable horse. **2.** (a) Mischievous, naughty. (b) Waggish, bantering, sly, arch. *adv.* **-sement.**

maligne. See MALIN.

malignement [maliɲmɑ̃], *adv.* **1.** Malignantly, spitefully. **2.** Mischievously, slyly, archly.

malignité [maliɲite], *s.f.* **1.** (a) Malignity, malignancy (of pers., of disease). (b) Spite(fulness). **2.** Act of spite.

malin, -igne [malɛ̃, -iɲ], *a.* **1.** Malignant. (a) Evil(-minded), wicked. **L'Esprit malin, le Malin,** the Evil One, the Devil. (b) Malicious (pleasure, etc.). (c) *Tumeur maligne,* malignant tumour. **2.** (a) *F:* Shrewd, cunning; *F:* knowing, sharp, cute. **Il est plus malin que ça,** he knows better. *s.* **C'est un malin,** *F:* he knows a thing or two. *Un vieux m.,* an old fox. *Une petite maligne,* a little slyboots, a little imp. *Prov:* **A malin malin et demi,** diamond cut diamond. (b) *P:* Smart Alec. **Faire le malin, faire son malin,** to try to be smart. (c) *P:* **C'est pas malin!** that's not difficult! that's easy!

Malines [malin]. **1.** *Pr.n.f. Geog:* Malines, Mechlin. **2.** *s.f.* Mechlin lace.

malingre [malɛ̃ːgr], *a.* Sickly, puny.

malintentionné, -ée [malɛ̃tɑ̃sjɔne], *a. & s.* Evil-, ill-intentioned (person) (*envers,* towards).

mal-jugé, *s.m. Jur:* Miscarriage of justice.

malle [mal], *s.f.* **1.** (a) Trunk, box. *M.* (de) *paquebot, m.* (de) *cabine,* cabin-trunk. *M. en osier,* basket-trunk. **Faire sa malle,** to pack (one's trunk). *Défaire sa m.,* to unpack. (b) (Pedlar's) pack. **2.** *A:* (a) Mail-bag (hung from horse's saddle). (b) = MALLE-POSTE. (c) Mail-boat.

mallé|able [malleabl], *a.* (a) Malleable (metal, etc.). (b) *F:* Plastic, soft, pliable, malleable (nature). *s.f.* **-bilité.**

malle-armoire, *s.f.* Wardrobe-trunk. *pl. Des malles-armoires.*

malléole [malleɔl], *s.f. Anat:* Malleolus, ankle.

malle-poste, *s.f. Mail(-coach).*

malletier, -ière [maltje, -jɛːr], *s.* Bag and trunk maker.

mallette [malɛt], *s.f.* **1.** (a) Small case. *M. de camping,* tea-basket. (b) (Small) suit-case. (c) Attaché case. **2.** *Bot:* Shepherd's-purse.

malmener [malməne], *v.tr.* (Conj. like MENER) (a) To maltreat, ill-treat, ill-use (s.o.); to mishandle, misuse (sth.). (b) To abuse, *F:* slate (s.o.). *adv.* **-age.**

malodorant [malɔdɔrɑ̃], *a.* Evil-smelling, malodorous.

malotru [malɔtry]. **1.** *a.* Coarse, vulgar, ill-bred; uncouth. **2.** *s.m.* Boor; low fellow.

malouin, -ine [malwɛ̃, -in], *a. & s. Geog:* (Native) of Saint-Malo.

malpeigné, -ée [malpeɲe]. **1.** *a.* Unkempt, tousled, untidy (hair, person). **2.** *s.* Sloven; *f.* slut, slattern.

malplaisant [malplɛzɑ̃], *a.* Unpleasant, displeasing.

malpropre [malprɔpr], *a.* **1.** *A:* Ill-fitted (for sth., to do sth.). **2.** *(a)* Dirty, grubby (hands, etc.); slovenly, untidy (appearance). *(b) F:* Smutty (story, etc.); dirty, unsavoury (business, conduct). *adv.* **-ment.**

malpropreté [malprɔprəte], *s.f.* **1.** *(a)* Dirtiness. *(b)* Indecency, smuttiness (of story); unsavouriness (of business). **2.** *pl. (a)* Dirt. *(b) Dire des malpropretés*, to talk smut.

malsain [malsɛ̃], *a.* **1.** *(a)* Unhealthy (person, climate). *(b) Nau:* Dangerous (coast). **2.** Unwholesome (food); pernicious (literature).

malséance [malseɑ̃:s], *s.f.* Unseemliness.

malséant [malseɑ̃], *a.* Unseemly; unbecoming.

malsonnant [malsɔnɑ̃], *a.* Offensive (to the ear).

malt [malt], *s.m. Brew:* Malt.

maltais, -aise [maltɛ, -ɛːz], *a. & s.* Maltese.

Malte [malt]. *Pr.n.f. Geog:* Malta. *Mec.E:* Croix de Malte, Maltese cross; *Cin:* star-wheel.

malterie [malt(ə)ri], *s.f.* Malt-house.

maltraiter [maltrete], *v.tr.* To maltreat, ill-treat, ill-use; to treat (s.o.) badly (by word or deed); to handle (s.o.) roughly.

malvacées [malvase], *s.f.pl. Bot:* Malvaceae, *F:* mallows.

malveillance [malvejɑ̃:s], *s.f. (a)* Malevolence, ill-will (*pour, envers*, to, towards). *(b)* Foul play.

malveill|ant [malvejɑ̃], *a. (a)* Malevolent, ill-willed; malicious. *(b)* Spiteful (remark). *adv.* **-ament.**

malvenu [malvəny], *a.* Ill-advised; unwarranted. **Vous êtes malvenu à critiquer,** you are the last one who ought to criticize. S.a. VENIR 1.

malversation [malversasjɔ̃], *s.f.* Malversation, embezzlement, malpractice.

maman [mamɑ̃, mãmã], *s.f. F:* Mam(m)a, mum(my). **Bonne maman,** granny.

mamellaire [mamɛlɛːr], *a. Anat:* Mammary.

mamelle [mamɛl], *s.f. Anat:* Mamma; breast (of man or woman); udder (of animal). *Enfant à la m.*, child at the breast.

mamelon [mamlɔ̃], *s.m.* **1.** *Anat:* Mamilla. *(a)* Nipple, teat. *(b)* Dug (of animal). **2.** (Small excrescence) *(a) Anat:* Papilla (of the tongue). *(b) Geog:* Mamelon; rounded hillock. **3.** *Mec.E: (a)* Boss, swell. *(b)* Gudgeon (on axle). *(c)* Nipple (for lubrication).

m'amie [mami], *s.f. A:* My dear.

mamillaire [mamilɛːr], *a.* Mamillary.

mammaire [mammɛːr], *a. Anat:* Mammary.

mammifère [mammifɛːr], *a.* **1.** *a.* Mammalian. **2.** *s.m.* Mammal.

mammouth [mammut], *s.m.* Mammoth.

m'amour, mamour [mamuːr], *s.m.* **1.** My love, my dear. **2.** *pl.* Billing and cooing. **Faire des mamours à qn,** to caress, fondle, s.o.

mam'selle, mam'zelle [mamzɛl], *s.f. F:* = MA-DEMOISELLE.

manant [manɑ̃], *s.m.* **1.** *A:* Peasant, villager. **2.** *F:* Churl, boor.

mancenille [mɑ̃sniːj], *s.f.* Manchineel apple.

manche[1] [mɑ̃:ʃ], *s.f.* **1.** Sleeve. *(a) Être en manches de chemise,* to be in one's shirt-sleeves. *Fausses manches,* oversleeves. **Mettre qch. dans sa manche,** to put sth. up one's sleeve. *F: Avoir qn dans sa manche,* to have s.o.'s services at command. **Jambes en manches de veste,** bow-legs. *Se faire tirer la m. pour faire qch.*, to do sth. with great reluctance. **Ça, c'est une autre paire de manches!** that's quite another matter, another story! **Avoir la manche large,** to be easy-going, broad-minded (in matters of conscience).

(b) Tchn: **Manche à eau, manche en toile,** (canvas) hose(-pipe). *M. d'incendie,* fire-hose. *Nau:* Manche à vent, à air, (i) (canvas) windsail; (ii) (metal) air-shaft, ventilator, ventilating-cowl. *M. à charbon,* coal-shoot. **2.** *(a) Cards:* Hand (played); single game. **Nous sommes manche à manche,** (i) we are even, game all; (ii) *F:* we are neck and neck. *(b) Sp:* Heat. *(c) Ten:* Set. **3.** *Geog:* Strait, channel. **La Manche,** the (English) Channel.

manche[2], *s.m.* **1.** Handle (of hammer, whip, etc.); haft (of dagger, etc.); stock (of whip); helve (of axe, etc.); loom (of oar); stick (of umbrella); neck (of violin, etc.). **Manche à balai,** (i) broomstick; (ii) *Av: F:* direction-stick, *F:* joy-stick. *Couteau à m. d'ivoire,* ivory-handled knife. *F:* **Jeter le manche après la cognée,** to throw the helve after the hatchet. **2.** *Moll:* **Manche de couteau,** razor-shell.

Manche[3] **(la).** *Pr.n.f. A.Geog:* La Mancha (old province of Spain). S.a. MANCHE[1] 3.

mancheron[1] [mɑ̃ʃrɔ̃], *s.m. Dressm: (a)* Short sleeve. *(b)* Cuff.

mancheron[2], *s.m.* Handle, stilt (of plough).

manchette [mɑ̃ʃɛt], *s.f.* **1.** *(a)* Cuff. *M. mousquetaire,* double cuff, turn-back cuff (of shirt). *(b)* Gauntlet (of glove). *(c)* Wristband (of shirt-sleeve). **2.** *(a)* Head-line (of newspaper). *(b) Typ:* Shoulder-note; side-note.

manchon [mɑ̃ʃɔ̃], *s.m.* **1.** Muff. **2.** *Tchn: (a)* Casing. *M. de refroidissement,* cooling-jacket. *Nau:* M. d'écubier, hawse-pipe. *(b)* Sleeve. *M. d'accouplement,* coupling-sleeve. *(c)* Bush(ing) (of bearing); socket (of pivot). *(d) Aut: M. d'embrayage,* clutch. *(e)* Flange. *(f)* Neck (of balloon). *(g)* Gas-mantle.

manchot, -ote [mɑ̃ʃo, -ɔt]. **1.** *a. & s.* One-armed, one-handed (person). *F:* **Il n'est pas manchot,** he is clever with his hands; he's all there. **2.** *s.m. Orn:* Penguin, *F:* Johnny.

mandant [mɑ̃dɑ̃], *s.m.* **1.** Mandator. *Jur:* Principal (in transaction). **2.** *pl. Pol:* Le député et ses mandants, the member and his constituents.

mandarin [mɑ̃darɛ̃], *s.m. (a)* (Chinese) mandarin. *(b)* (Grotesque figure) Nodding mandarin.

mandarine [mɑ̃darin], *s.f.* Mandarin orange; tangerine.

mandarinier [mɑ̃darinje], *s.m.* Mandarin orange-tree.

mandat [mɑ̃da], *s.m.* **1.** *(a)* Mandate; commission. *Territoire sous m.,* mandated territory. *(b) M. de député,* member's (electoral) mandate. *Fonctionnaire sans m.,* unauthorized official. *(c) Jur:* Power of attorney; proxy. **2.** Warrant. *(a) Jur: M. de perquisition,* search warrant. *M. d'arrêt,* warrant for arrest. *M. de comparution,* summons (to appear). *Lancer un m.,* to issue a warrant. *(b) Fin: M. du Trésor,* Treasury warrant. **3.** Order (to pay); money order; draft. *Post: M. international,* foreign money order.

mandataire [mɑ̃datɛːr], *s.m. & f.* **1.** Mandatory (of electors, etc.). **2.** Proxy (at meeting). **3.** *Jur:* Authorized agent; attorney. **4.** Trustee.

mandat-poste, *s.m. Post:* Money order. *pl.* **Des mandats-poste.**

mandchou, -oue [mɑ̃tʃu], *a. & s. Ethn:* Man-chu, Manchurian.

Mandchourie [mɑ̃tʃuri]. *Pr.n.f.* Manchuria.

mander [mɑ̃de], *v.tr.* **1.** *(a) A: M. une nouvelle à qn,* to send news (by letter) to s.o. *(b) Journ: On mande de ...,* it is reported from. . . . **2.** *M. à qn de faire qch.,* to send word to s.o., to instruct s.o., to do sth. **3.** To summon (s.o. to attend); to send for (subordinate).

mandibule [mãdibyl], *s.f. Z:* Mandible.
mandoline [mãdɔlin], *s.f. Mus:* Mandolin(e).
mandragore [mãdragɔ:r], *s.f. Bot:* Mandragora, *F:* mandrake.
mandrill [mãdril], *s.m. Z:* Mandrill.
mandrin[1] [mãdrɛ̃], *s.m.* **1.** (*a*) Mandrel (of lathe). (*b*) Chuck, face-plate (of lathe). *M. porte-foret,* drill collet. (*c*) Pad (of a brace). **2.** *Metalw:* (*a*) Mandrel, swage. (*b*) Punch. **3.** *El:* Coilformer.
mandrin[2], *s.m. F:* Bandit, ruffian.
manécanterie [manekãtri], *s.f.* Choir school (attached to a church).
manège [manɛ:ʒ], *s.m.* **1.** (*a*) Horsemanship, riding. **Maître de manège,** riding-master. (*b*) Training, breaking (in) (of a horse). (*c*) (*Salle de*) **manège,** riding-school. (*d*) Manège de chevaux de bois, merry-go-round; roundabout. **2.** *F:* Wile, stratagem, trick. *J'observais leur m.,* I was watching their little game. **3.** Horse-driven mill (for threshing, etc.).
mânes [mɑːn], *s.m.pl. Rom.Ant:* Manes, shades, spirits (of the departed).
maneton [mantɔ̃], *s.m.* Crank-pin (of crankshaft); wrist(-pin).
manette [manɛt], *s.f.* (*a*) Handle, hand-lever. *Aut: M. de commande,* control-lever (on steeringwheel). *M. du frein,* trigger of the hand-brake. *El: M. de contact,* contact finger. (*b*) *Tg:* Key (of Morse apparatus). (*c*) *Nau:* Spoke (of the wheel).
manganate [mãganat], *s.m. Ch:* Manganate.
manganèse [mãganɛːz], *s.m.* Manganese.
mangeable [mãʒabl], *a.* Edible, eatable.
mangeaille [mãʒaːj], *s.f.* **1.** (Soft) food; feed (for fowls, etc.). **2.** *F:* Victuals, *F:* grub.
mangeoire [mãʒwaːr], *s.f.* **1.** Manger. **2.** Feeding-trough.
manger [mãʒe]. **I.** *v.tr.* (je mangeai(s); n. mangeons) **1.** To eat. *Il a tout mangé,* he has eaten up everything. *M. dans de l'argenterie,* to eat off plate. **Salle à manger,** dining-room. *Donner à m. aux poules,* to feed the fowls. *Donner à m. à qn,* to give s.o. food, something to eat. **Manger à son appétit, à sa faim,** to eat one's fill. *F:* **Manger comme quatre,** to make a huge meal. **Manger comme un ogre,** to eat like a wolf, like a horse. **Bon à manger,** good to eat. *La rouille mange l'acier,* rust eats into, eats away, steel. *Mangé des vers,* worm-eaten. **Manger ses mots,** (i) to mumble, to speak indistinctly; (ii) to clip one's words. *F: M. qn des yeux,* to devour s.o. with one's eyes. *M. qn de caresses,* to smother s.o. with caresses. *P:* **Manger de la prison,** to do time. **2.** *M. son argent,* to squander, run through, one's money. (Of horse, etc.) *M. le chemin,* to devour the way.
II. manger, *s.m.* Food. "A prendre après manger," 'to be taken after a meal.' S.a. BOIRE II.
mangerie [mãʒri], *s.f. F:* (*a*) Gorging, guzzling. (*b*) Gorge, guzzle.
mange-tout [mãʒtu], *s.m.inv.* **1.** Squanderer, spendthrift. **2.** (*a*) Sugar-pea. (*b*) String-bean.
mangeur, -euse [mãʒœːr, -øːz], *s.* Eater. *Beau m.,* gros *m.,* good trencherman, great eater. *F: M. de livres,* devourer of books. *M. d'argent,* squanderer, spendthrift. *M. de petits enfants,* boaster, braggart.
mangeure [mãʒyːr], *s.f.* Place nibbled, eaten (by insects, mice). *Étoffe criblée de mangeures,* motheaten cloth.
mangle [mãːgl], *s.f. Bot:* Mangrove-fruit.
manglier [mãglie], *s.m. Bot:* Mangrove(-tree).

mangouste[1] [mãgust], *s.f.* Mangosteen (fruit).
mangouste[2], *s.f. Z:* Mongoose.
mangue [mãːg], *s.f.* Mango. (fruit).
manguier [mãgje], *s.m. Bot:* Mango(-tree).
maniabilité [manjabilite], *s.f.* Handiness (of tool, ship); manageableness (of aeroplane, etc.).
maniable [manjabl], *a.* Manageable; easy to handle, to control; handy (tool, ship). **Peu maniable,** unhandy (tool, ship); awkward (tool). *Fer m.,* easily wrought iron. [MANIER].
maniaque [manjak], *a. & s.* **1.** Maniac; raving mad(man, -woman). **2.** Finical, faddy (person). *s.* Faddist.
maniaquerie [manjakri], *s.f. F:* **1.** Finicalness, faddiness. **2.** Fad.
manicure [manikyːr], *s. m. & f.* = MANUCURE.
manie [mani], *s.f.* **1.** Mania. (*a*) *Med:* Mental derangement. (*b*) *F:* Craze; inveterate habit. *Avoir la manie des tableaux,* to have a mania, a craze, for pictures. **2.** Idiosyncrasy. *Il a ses petites manies,* he has his little fads, his little ways.
mani|er [manje]. **I.** *v.tr.* **1.** To feel (cloth, etc.); to handle (tool, rope, etc.). *Fb:* **Ballon manié,** handled ball. **2.** To handle (affair); to wield (sword, pen); to handle, manage, control (horse, business). *M. les avirons,* to ply, pull, the oars. *s.m.* **-ement.**
II. manier, *s.m.* Feel (of cloth). *Juger au m.,* to judge by the feel.
manière [manjɛːr], *s.f.* **1.** (*a*) Manner, way (of doing sth.). **Manière d'être,** state, condition. *Laissez-moi faire à ma manière,* let me do it my own way. *S'y prendre de la bonne m.,* to set about it the right way. **De cette manière,** thus; in this way. *F:* **Tancer qn de la belle manière,** to give s.o. a good dressing-down. **De manière ou d'autre, d'une manière ou d'une autre,** somehow or other, by some means or other. **D'aucune manière,** in no wise. **Par, en, manière de consolation,** by way of consolation. **En quelque manière,** in a way. **De (telle) manière que,** so that. (i) (+ *ind.,* result) *Il a agi de m. que tout le monde a été content,* he so acted that everyone was pleased. (ii) (+ *sub.,* purpose) *Agissez de m. qu'on n'en sache rien,* act so that nobody knows anything about it. *F:* **De manière à ce que = de manière que** (ii). (*b*) *Art: Lit:* **Tableau à la manière de Degas,** painting after the manner of Degas. *Il a sa m.,* he has his mannerisms. **2.** *pl.* Manners. *Avoir de bonnes, de belles, manières,* to be well-mannered. *Avoir de mauvaises manières,* to be ill-mannered. *F:* **Faire des manières,** (i) to put on an affected air; to· mince; (ii) to affect reluctance.
maniéré [manjere], *a.* **1.** Affected, finical (person); mincing, genteel (tone of voice, etc.). **2.** *Art: Lit:* Mannered (style).
maniérisme [manjerism], *s.m.* Mannerism, affectedness.
manieur, -euse [manjœːr, -øːz], *s.* Handler. *Esp.* **Manieur d'argent,** (i) financier; (ii) financial adventurer.
manifestant, -ante [manifɛstã, -ãːt], *s.* (Political) demonstrator.
manifestation [manifɛstasjɔ̃], *s.f.* (*a*) Manifestation (of feeling, etc.). (*b*) (Political) demonstration.
manifeste[1] [manifɛst], *a.* **1.** Manifest, evident, patent, obvious (truth, etc.); palpable (error). **2.** *Jur:* Overt (act). *adv.* **-ment.**
manifeste[2], *s.m.* **1.** Manifesto, proclamation. **2.** *Nau:* (Ship's) manifest.
manifester [manifɛste], *v.tr.* **1.** To manifest, reveal; to evince (opinion); to show, exhibit

(confusion). *M. sa volonté*, to give expression to one's will. **2.** *Abs.* To make a public demonstration ; to manifest.

se manifester, to appear ; to show itself.

manigance [manigɑ̃:s], *s.f.* *F:* (*a*) Intrigue. (*b*) *pl.* Underhand practices ; wire-pulling.

manigancer [manigɑ̃se], *v.tr.* (*je manigançai* ; *n.* **manigançons**) *F:* To scheme, to plot ; to work (sth.) underhand. *Il se manigance quelque chose*, there's something in the wind. *M. une élection*, to gerrymander an election.

Manille[1] [mani:j]. **I.** *Pr.n. Geog:* Manilla. **2.** *s.m.* (*a*) Manilla cheroot. (*b*) Manilla straw hat.

manille[2], *s.f.* Cards : (*a*) Manille (in games of manille, ombre). (*b*) (French game of) manille.

manille[3], *s.f.* **I.** Manilla, (native's) anklet. **2.** Shackle (of chain).

manill|er [manije], *v.tr.* To shackle (chains). *s.m.* **-age**.

manipulateur, -trice [manipylatœːr, -tris], *s.* **I.** Manipulator ; handler (of money, goods). **2.** *s.m. Tg:* (Sending) key.

manipulation [manipylasjɔ̃], *s.f.* Manipulation ; handling.

manipuler [manipyle], *v.tr.* **I.** To manipulate ; to handle, operate (apparatus). **2.** *F:* To manœuvre, gerrymander (an affair).

manitou [manitu], *s.m.* **I.** Manitou (of American Indians). **2.** *P:* Grand Panjandrum (of an undertaking) ; bit pot (in the business world).

manivelle [manivɛl], *s.f.* **I.** (*a*) Crank. **Arbre (à) manivelle**, crank-shaft. (*b*) Pedal-crank (of bicycle). **2.** Crank-handle. *Aut: M. de mise en marche*, starting-handle.

manne[1] [man], *s.f.* **I.** *B:* Manna. **2.** *Pharm: M. du frêne*, manna.

manne[2], *s.f.* Basket, hamper ; crate ; (fishwife's) creel.

mannequin[1] [mankɛ̃], *s.m.* Small hamper.

mannequin[2], *s.m.* **I.** (Anatomical) manikin. **2.** (*a*) *Art:* Lay figure. (*b*) *Dressm:* Dummy ; dress-stand. **3.** *Occ. f.* (Lady) mannequin.

manœuvrable [manœvrabl], *a.* (Of ship) Manageable, handy.

manœuvre [manœːvr]. **I.** *s.f.* (*a*) Working, managing, driving (of machine, etc.). (*b*) *Nau:* Handling, manœuvring (of ship) ; seamanship. **Maître de manœuvre**, boatswain. *Navire qui n'est pas maître de sa m.*, ship not under command. (*c*) (i) Drill, exercise. *Champ de manœuvres*, drill-ground. (ii) Tactical exercise ; manœuvre. *Grandes manœuvres*, army manœuvres. (*d*) Shunting, marshalling (of trains). *Voie de m.*, shunting track. (*e*) *F:* Scheme, manœuvre, intrigue. (*f*) *pl.* Scheming. *Manœuvres frauduleuses*, swindling. **2.** *s.f.* (*a*) *Nau:* Rope. *Manœuvres dormantes*, standing rigging. (*b*) *Av:* Control. **3.** *s.m.* (Unskilled) labourer. **Travail de manœuvre**, (i) manual labour ; (ii) *F:* hack-work.

manœuvrer [manœvre]. **I.** *v.tr.* (*a*) To work, operate (machine, etc.) ; to ply (spade, etc.). (*b*) To manœuvre, handle (ship). (*c*) *Rail:* To shunt ; to marshal (trucks). **2.** *v.i.* (*a*) *Mil: Nau:* To manœuvre. (*b*) *F:* To scheme, manœuvre.

manoir [manwaːr], *s.m.* (*a*) (Feudal) manor. (*b*) *F:* Country-house, country-seat.

manomètre [manɔmɛtr], *s.m.* Manometer, pressure-gauge. *M. pour pneus*, tyre-gauge.

manouvrier, -ère [manuvrie, -ɛːr], *s.* Day labourer ; woman by the day.

manquant, -ante [mɑ̃kɑ̃, -ɑ̃:t]. **I.** *a.* (*a*) Missing, absent. (*b*) Wanting, lacking. **2.** *s.* (*a*) Absentee ; defaulter. (*b*) *Mil: etc:* Les manquants, the missing.

manque [mɑ̃:k], *s.m.* **I.** Lack, want ; deficiency ; shortage. *M. de cœur*, heartlessness. *M. de parole*, breach of faith. *M. de convenances*, breach of good manners. *M. de poids*, deficiency in weight ; short weight. **Dix livres de manque**, ten pounds short. (**Par**) **manque de**, for lack of, for want of. **2.** *Bill:* **Manque de touche, manque à toucher**, miss. **3.** *P:* A la manque (= RATÉ), feeble, poor. *Artiste à la m.*, dud artist.

manquement [mɑ̃kmɑ̃], *s.m.* Failure, shortcoming, omission, lapse. *M. à une règle*, violation of a rule. *M. à la discipline*, breach, infraction, of discipline. *M. au devoir*, breach of duty. *M. à l'appel*, failure to answer one's name ; absence from roll-call.

manquer [mɑ̃ke]. **I.** *v.i.* **I.** (*a*) *M. de qch.*, to lack, want, be short of, sth. *Je manque d'argent*, I am short of money. *M. de politesse*, to be lacking in politeness. *M. de courage*, to lack courage. **Ne manquer de rien**, to want for nothing. (*b*) *M. de faire qch.*, narrowly to miss doing sth. *Il a manqué (de) tomber*, he nearly fell. (*c*) *Impers.* Il s'en manque de beaucoup, far from it. *Il s'en est manqué de peu qu'il ne gagnât la partie*, he very nearly won the match. **2.** To fail. (*a*) To be missing, wanting, deficient. *Les vivres commencent à m.*, provisions are running short. *Les mots me manquent pour exprimer . . .*, I am at a loss for words to express. *. . . La place me manque*, I have no room. *Impers. Il ne manque pas de candidats*, there is no lack of candidates. *F:* Il ne manquait plus que cela! that's the last straw ! *Il manque quelques pages*, there are a few pages missing. *Il me manque dix francs*, I am ten francs short. (*b*) To give way. *Son cœur lui manqua*, his heart failed him. *Prenez garde que le pied ne vous manque*, take care you don't miss your footing. (*c*) (Of pers.) To be absent, missing. *M. à un rendez-vous*, to fail to keep an appointment. **Manquer à qn**, to be missed by s.o. (*d*) To fall short. *M. à son devoir*, to fail in one's duty. *M. à sa parole*, to break one's word. *M. à la consigne*, to disregard orders. *M. à une règle*, to violate a rule. *M. à qn*, to be disrespectful to s.o. *Se m. à soi-même*, to do sth. derogatory to one's position. *Bill:* **Manquer de touche**, to miss. *Abs. Le coup a manqué*, the attempt miscarried. (*e*) (i) *A:* **Manquer à faire qch.** to fail, omit, to do sth. (ii) **Ne pas manquer de faire qch.**, not to neglect, not to omit, to do sth. *Ne manquez pas de nous écrire*, be sure to write to us. *Cela ne pouvait manquer d'arriver*, it was bound to happen. **II. manquer**, *v.tr.* **I.** (*a*) To miss (target, train, etc.). *M. une occasion*, to lose, miss, an opportunity. **Manquer son coup**, to miss one's aim ; to miss one's blow, one's stroke, one's shot ; to make an abortive attempt. **Il l'a manqué belle**, he missed a splendid chance. (*b*) *Pourquoi avez-vous manqué l'office?* why were you absent from church ? why did you miss church ? **2.** *M. sa vie*, to make shipwreck of one's life. *M. un tableau*, to make a failure of a picture.

manqué, *a.* **I.** Missed (opportunity, etc.) ; unsuccessful, abortive (attempt, etc.). **Coup manqué**, (i) miss ; (ii) failure. *Vie manquée*, wasted life. *Vêtement m.*, misfit. **2.** *F:* C'est un médecin manqué, he ought to have been a doctor. *C'est un garçon m.*, she's a regular tomboy.

mansarde [mɑ̃sard], *s.f.* *Arch:* **I.** (*a*) **Toit, comble, en mansarde**, mansard roof. (*b*) (**Fenêtre en**) **mansarde**, garret window, dormer-window. **2.** Attic, garret.

mansardé [mɑ̃sarde], *a.* Mansard-roofed. *Chambre mansardée*, attic.

mansuétude [mɑ̃sɥetyd], *s.f.* Mansuetude.
mante[1] [mɑ̃:t], *s.f. A:* (Woman's) mantle.
mante[2], *s.f. Ent:* Mantis. *M. religieuse,* praying mantis.
manteau [mɑ̃to], *s.m.* **1.** Cloak, mantle, wrap. *M. du soir,* (lady's) evening cloak. *M. de sport,* sports-coat. *F: Sous le manteau de la religion,* under the cloak of religion. *M. de neige,* mantle of snow. *Avancer sous le m. de la nuit,* to advance under (the) cover of darkness. **2.** (*a*) **Manteau de cheminée,** mantelpiece. *F:* **Faire qch. sous le manteau (de la cheminée),** to do sth. secretly, under the rose. (*b*) *Th:* **Manteau d'Arlequin,** proscenium arch.
mantelé [mɑ̃tle], *a. Orn:* Hooded (crow).
mantelet [mɑ̃tlɛ], *s.m.* **1.** *Cost:* Tippet, mantlet. **2.** (*a*) *Harn:* (Cart-)saddle, pad. (*b*) *Veh:* (Carriage-)apron. **3.** Shutter; *Nau:* port-lid, dead-light.
mantille [mɑ̃ti:j], *s.f. Cost:* Mantilla.
mantisse [mɑ̃tis], *s.f.* Mantissa (of logarithm).
manucure [manyky:r], *s.m. & f.* Manicurist.
manu|el, -elle [manɥel]. **1.** *a.* Manual (labour). **2.** *s.m.* Manual, handbook. *adv.* **-ellement.**
manufacture [manyfakty:r], *s.f.* (Manu)factory; (textile, iron) mill; works.
manufactur|er [manyfaktyre], *v.tr.* To manufacture. *a.* **-able.**
manufacturier, -ière [manyfaktyrje, -jɛ:r]. **1.** *a.* Manufacturing (town, etc.). **2.** *s.m.* Manufacturer; mill-owner.
manumission [manymisjɔ̃], *s.f.* Manumission; freeing (of slave).
manuscrit [manyskri], *a. & s.m.* Manuscript.
manutention [manytɑ̃sjɔ̃], *s.f.* **1.** Management, administration. **2.** Handling (of stores, materials). **3.** *Mil: Navy:* (*a*) Storehouse; stores. (*b*) Bakery.
manutentionner [manytɑ̃sjɔne], *v.tr.* **1.** To handle (stores, materials). **2.** *Mil: Navy:* (*a*) To store. (*b*) To bake.
manxois, -oise [mɑ̃kswa, -wa:z]. *Geog:* **1.** *a.* Manx. **2.** *s.* Manxman, Manxwoman.
maori, -ie [maɔri], *a. & s. Ethn:* Maori.
mappemonde [mapmɔ̃:d], *s.f.* Map of the world in two hemispheres. *M. céleste,* planisphere.
maquette [makɛt], *s.f.* (*a*) *Sculp:* Clay model. (*b*) *Art:* Small figure (for arranging groups, etc.). (*c*) Model (of a stage setting); mock-up (of aeroplane). (*d*) *Publ:* Dummy (of book).
maquignon, -onne [makiɲɔ̃, -ɔn], *s.* **1.** Horse-dealer; coper. **2.** *Pej:* (Shady) go-between; jobber.
maquignonnage [makiɲɔna:ʒ], *s.m.* **1.**(*a*) Horse-dealing. (*b*) Horse-faking; bishoping. **2.** Sharp practice.
maquignonner [makiɲɔne], *v.tr.* **1.** To fake up, bishop (horse). **2.** To arrange (business, etc.) by sharp practice. *Affaire maquignonnée,* put-up job.
maquillage [makija:ʒ], *s.m. Th:* (*a*) Making up. (*b*) Make-up.
maquill|er [makije], *v.tr.* (*a*) *Th:* To make up (face for a part). (*b*) To fake up (picture); *Phot:* to work up (negative). *s.* **-eur, -euse.** **se`maquiller,** to make up (one's complexion); *F:* to paint.
maquis [maki], *s.m.* Scrub, bush (in Corsica).
marabout [marabu], *s.m.* **1.** (*a*) Marabout (priest or shrine). (*b*) *F:* Ugly or mis-shapen man. **2.** (Round-bodied) hot-water jug. **3.** (*a*) Marabou(-stork). (*b*) Marabou (feathers).
maraîchage [mareʃa:ʒ], *s.m.* Market-gardening.

maraîcher, -ère [mareʃe, -ɛ:r]. **1.** *a.* (*a*) Pertaining to marshland. (*b*) Market-gardening (industry). **2.** *s.* Market-gardener.
marais [mare], *s.m.* **1.** (*a*) Marsh(land); bog, fen. *M. tourbeux,* peat-bog. **Gaz des marais,** marsh-gas. (*b*) **Marais salant,** salt-pan. **2.** Market-garden.
marasme [marasm], *s.m.* (*a*) *Med:* Marasmus, wasting; tabes. (*b*) Stagnation (of business). (*c*) Depression (of mind).
marasquin [maraskɛ̃], *s.m.* Maraschino (liqueur).
marathon [maratɔ̃], *s.m. Sp:* Marathon (race); long-distance race.
marâtre [marɑ:tr], *s.f.* (Unnatural, cruel) step-mother or mother.
maraud, -aude[1] [maro, -o:d], *s. A:* Villain, rascal, rogue; *f.* wench, hussy.
maraude[2], *s.f.* (*a*) Marauding, plundering. **Aller à la maraude,** to go looting or marauding. (*b*) Petty thieving (from orchards, etc.). (*c*) *F: Taxi en m.,* crawling taxi.
marauder [marode], *v.i.* (*a*) To maraud, plunder. (*b*) To thieve (from market-gardens, etc.). (*c*) *F:* (Of taxicabs) To crawl (in search of fares).
maraudeur, -euse [marodœ:r, -ø:z], *s.* (*a*) Marauder, plunderer. (*b*) Filcher, petty thief.
marbre [marbr], *s.m.* **1.** (*a*) Marble. *F: Cœur de m.,* stony heart. (*b*) Marble (statue, etc.). *Collection de marbres,* collection of marbles. **2.** *Bookb:* Marbling (on book edges). **3.** *Mec.E:* Surface-plate, face-plate. **4.** *Typ:* (*a*) Imposing-stone. (*b*) Bed (of press); press-stone. **Livre sur le marbre,** book in type, at press.
marbrer [marbre], *v.tr.* To marble; (i) to mottle, (ii) to vein. *F: Le froid marbre la peau,* the cold mottles, blotches, the skin.
marbré, *a.* Marbled; (i) mottled, (ii) veined, (iii) (beaten) black and blue. *Savon m.,* mottled soap.
marbrier, -ère [marbrie, -ɛ:r]. **1.** *a.* Marble (industry). **2.** *s.m.* Monumental mason. **3.** *s.f.* **Marbrière,** marble-quarry.
marbrure [marbry:r], *s.f.* **1.** Marbling, veining. **2.** (*a*) Mottling (of the skin). (*b*) Mark of a bruise.
marc [ma:r], *s.m.* **1.** (*a*) Marc (of grapes, olives, etc.); rape(s) (of grapes). (*b*) Eau de vie de marc, white brandy (distilled from marc). **2.** (Used) tea-leaves; coffee-grounds.
marcassin [markasɛ̃], *s.m.* Young wild boar.
marchand, -ande [marʃɑ̃, -ɑ̃:d]. **1.** *s.* Dealer, shopkeeper, merchant; tradesman, tradeswoman. *M. de chevaux,* horse-dealer. *M. de fer,* ironmonger. *M. de fromage,* cheesemonger. *M. de poisson,* fishmonger. *M. de grains,* corn-chandler. *M. de tabac,* tobacconist. *M. de vin,* publican. *M. en plein vent,* stall-keeper. *M. des quatre saisons,* costermonger; hawker (of fruit and vegetables). *M. en gros,* wholesale dealer, wholesaler. *M. en détail,* retailer. S.a. AMBULANT, HABIT I, SABLE[1] I, SOUPE 2. **2.** *a.* (*a*) Saleable, marketable (article, etc.). **Fer marchand,** commercial iron. (*b*) Trading. *Ville marchande,* commercial town. *Place marchande,* shopping centre. **Navire marchand,** merchant ship, merchantman. S.a. MARINE 3. *Prix m.,* wholesale price, trade price. *Valeur marchande,* market value.
marchand|er [marʃɑ̃de], *v.tr.* **1.** (*a*) M. qch. avec qn, to haggle with s.o. over sth. *M. qn,* to haggle over the price with s.o. (*b*) *M. les éloges à qn,* to grudge one's praise. *Il ne marchande pas sa peine,* he spares no pains. **2.** To job (contract); to sub-contract (job). *s.m.* **-age.** *s.* **-eur, -euse.**

marchandise [marʃãdiːz], s.f. **1.** Merchandise, goods, wares. **Train de marchandises,** goods train. *Vanter, faire valoir, sa marchandise,* to puff one's wares. **2.** *Une m.,* a commodity.

marche¹ [marʃ], s.f. **1.** March, border. **2.** Marchland, borderland.

marche², s.f. **1.** (a) (i) Step, stair (of stairs). (ii) Tread (of step). *La m. du bas,* the bottom stair. *Les marches du trône,* the steps of the throne. (b) Treadle (of lathe, etc.). **2.** (a) Walking. *Aimer la m.,* to be fond of walking. *Avoir une m. gracieuse,* to have a graceful walk, gait. *Ralentir sa marche,* to slacken one's pace. **Continuer sa marche,** to walk on. **Se mettre en marche,** to set out, start off. *Deux heures de m.,* two hours' walk. (b) March. (i) *Colonne en m.,* column on the march. *Ordres de m.,* marching orders. *Mettre les troupes en m.,* to set the troops in motion. **Ouvrir la marche,** to lead the way. **Fermer la marche,** to bring up the rear. **Gagner une marche sur l'ennemi,** to steal a march on the enemy. (ii) *Mus:* *M. nuptiale, funèbre,* wedding-march, dead march. **3.** (a) Running (of trains, etc.); sailing (of ships). **Mettre en marche un service,** to start or run a service. (b) *M. arrière,* (i) backing (of train); (ii) reversing (of motor car). *Entrer dans le garage en m. arrière,* to back into the garage. **Navire en marche,** ship under way. *Tramway en m.,* moving tram. **4.** (a) Running, going, working (of machine, etc.). **Être en marche,** (i) (of machine) to be going, running; (ii) (of furnace) to be in blast. *Aut:* **Mettre l'interrupteur sur marche,** to switch on the engine. (b) Course (of events, etc.); march (of time); progress (of malady). *M. à suivre,* course to be followed; procedure. (c) *M. d'un poème,* course, progression of ideas, of a poem. (d) *Mus:* **Marche harmonique,** harmonic progression.

marché [marʃe], s.m. **1.** (a) Dealing, buying. *Faire son marché,* to do one's shopping. *Être en m. avec qn,* to be negotiating with s.o. (b) Deal, bargain, contract. *Faire, conclure, un m.,* to strike a bargain. *M. de fourniture,* supply contract. *C'est marché fait,* it is a bargain; *F:* done! **Mettre à qn le marché en main,** to invite s.o. to take it or leave it. **Par-dessus le marché,** into the bargain. (c) **Bon marché,** cheapness (de, of). *Acheter, vendre, qch. à bon m.,* to buy, sell, sth. cheap, at a cheap rate. *A meilleur m.,* more cheaply, cheaper. *Articles bon m.,* low-priced goods, *F:* bargains. **Faire bon marché des conseils de qn,** to hold s.o.'s advice cheap. **Vous vous en êtes tiré à bon marché,** you got off lightly. **2.** Market. (a) *Jour de marché,* market-day. *M. en plein vent,* open-air market. *Aller au m.,* to go to market. (b) (State of the) market. *M. ferme,* steady, strong, firm, market.

marchepied [marʃəpje], s.m. (a) Steps (of altar); step (of carriage). (b) *Veh:* Footboard. *Aut:* Running-board. (c) *Row:* Stretcher. (d) Pair of steps, step-ladder.

marcher [marʃe], v.i. **1.** To tread. **Marcher sur le pied à qn,** to tread on s.o.'s foot, on s.o.'s toes. **Marcher sur les traces,** sur les pas, de qn, to follow, tread, in s.o.'s footsteps. **2.** (a) To walk, go. *Le bébé ne marche pas encore,* the child isn't walking yet. *Façon de m.,* gait. *Il boite en marchant,* he is walking lame. *Deux choses qui marchent toujours ensemble,* two things that always go together. S.a. PAIR 1. *L'État marche à la ruine,* the State is heading for ruin. (b) *F:* To obey orders. *Il marchera,* he will do as he's told. **Faire marcher qn,** (i) to order s.o. about; (ii) to deceive, fool, s.o.; to pull s.o.'s leg. (c) *Mil:*

etc: To march. **En avant, marche!** quick march! *M. à l'ennemi,* to advance, move, against the enemy. **3.** (a) (Of trains, etc.) To move, travel, go; (of ships) to sail, steam; *F:* to proceed, progress. (Of ship, etc.) *M. à toute allure, à toute vitesse,* to proceed at full speed. *Le temps marche,* time goes on. *Les affaires marchent,* business is brisk. **Faire marcher la maison,** to run the house. *Faire m. le feu,* to make the fire burn. *Est-ce que ça marche?* are you getting along all right? *Ça ne marche pas si mal,* we are doing not so badly. *La répétition a bien marché,* the rehearsal went well. (b) (Of machine) To work, run, go. *Ma montre ne marche plus;* je ne peux pas la faire marcher, my watch has stopped, is out of order; I can't get it to go.

marcheur, -euse [marʃœːr, -øːz]. **1.** s. (a) Walker. *Bon m.,* good walker; (of horse) good goer. (b) *F:* **Vieux marcheur,** old rake; old reprobate. **2.** a. Walking (animal). *Navire bon m.,* fast-sailing boat, good sailer. **3.** s.f. *Th:* **Marcheuse,** walker-on; figurante (in ballet).

marconigramme [markɔnigram], s.m. *Tg:* Marconigram.

marcotte [markɔt], s.f. *Hort:* **1.** Layer. **2.** Runner, sucker.

marcott|er [markɔte], v.tr. To layer. s.m. **-age.**

mardi [mardi], s.m. Tuesday. **Mardi gras,** Shrove Tuesday.

mare [maːr], s.f. (Stagnant) pool; pond.

marécage [mareka:ʒ], s.m. (a) Fen, marshland. (b) Bog, slough, swamp.

marécageux, -euse [marekaʒø, -øːz], a. Boggy, marshy, swampy.

maréchal, -aux [mareʃal, -o], s.m. **1.** **Maréchal ferrant,** shoeing-smith; farrier. **2.** Marshal (of royal household, etc.). **3.** *Mil:* (a) **Maréchal de France,** field-marshal. (b) **Maréchal des logis,** sergeant (in mounted arms).

maréchalerie [mareʃalri], s.f. Horse-shoeing, farriery.

maréchaussée [mareʃose], s.f. *Hist:* **1.** Marshalsea. **2.** Corps of mounted constabulary.

marée [mare]. s.f. **1.** Tide. *M. haute,* high water, high tide. *M. basse,* low water, low tide. *M. montante,* flood-tide. *M. descendante,* ebb-tide. *Grande m.,* spring-tide. **Fleuve à marée,** tidal river. **Contre vent et marée,** (i) against wind and tide; (ii) *F:* in spite of all opposition. *F:* **Avoir vent et marée,** to have everything in one's favour. *Port à m., de m.,* tidal harbour. **2.** Fresh (sea-water) fish. **Train de marée,** (i) fish-train; (ii) *F:* boat-train. *F:* **Arriver comme marée en carême,** to arrive just at the right moment, in the nick of time.

marelle [marɛl], s.f. *Games:* Hopscotch.

marennes [marɛn], s.f. Marenne oyster (from Marennes, near La Rochelle).

mareyage [mareja:ʒ], s.m. The fish trade.

mareyeur, -euse [marɛjœːr, -øːz], s. **1.** Fishmonger. **2.** Fish porter.

margarine [margarin], s.f. Margarine.

marge [marʒ], s.f. **1.** (a) Border, edge (of ditch, road). *F:* **Vivre en marge de la société,** to live on the fringe of society. (b) Margin (of book). *Écrire qch. en m.,* to write sth. in the margin. **Note en marge,** marginal note. **2. Avoir de la marge,** to have time or means enough and to spare; to have plenty of margin.

margelle [marʒɛl], s.f. Curb(-stone) (of a well).

marginal, -aux [marʒinal, -o], a. Marginal (note); fringing (reef, etc.).

margotin [margɔtɛ̃], s.m. Bundle of firewood.

margrave [margra:v]. *Hist:* **I.** *s.m.* Margrave. **2.** *s.f.* Margravine.

Marguerite [margərit]. **I.** *Pr.n.f.* Margaret. **2.** *s.f.* (*a*) *A. & B:* Pearl. Jeter des marguerites aux pourceaux, to cast pearls before swine. (*b*) *Bot:* (Petite) marguerite, daisy. Grande marguerite, ox-eye daisy, marguerite.

marguillier [margije], *s.m.* Churchwarden.

mari [mari], *s.m.* Husband. S.a. PUISSANCE 2.

mariable [marjabl], *a.* Marriageable.

mariage [marja:ʒ], *s.m.* **I.** Marriage. (*a*) Wedlock, matrimony. (*b*) Wedding, nuptials. *M. d'inclination*, love-match. *M. religieux*, wedding (in church). *M. civil*, civil marriage (before mayor). Acte de mariage, marriage certificate. Demande en mariage, proposal of marriage. *Enfant né hors du m.*, child born out of wedlock. *Le m. de l'esprit et de la beauté*, the joining of wit to beauty. **2.** *Nau:* Marrying (of two ropes).

Marianne [marjan]. *Pr.n.f.* **I.** Marian(ne). **2.** *F:* The (French) Republic.

Marie [mari]. *Pr.n.f.* Mary, Maria.

marier [marje], *v.tr.* **I.** To marry. (*a*) (Of priest, etc.) To unite (man and woman) in wedlock; to join in marriage. (*b*) To give (one's daughter, etc.) in marriage; to find a husband, a wife, for (s.o.). *Fille à m.*, marriageable daughter. **2.** (*a*) To join, unite. *M. des couleurs*, to blend colours. (*b*) *M. des cordages*, to marry ropes. **se marier.** (*a*) To marry, to get married; *Lit:* to wed. *Se m. à, avec, qn*, to marry s.o. (*b*) (Of colour, etc.) One. *M. avec qch.*, to go with sth.; to harmonize with sth.

marié, -ée, *a. & s.* **I.** Married (person). Nouveau marié, nouvelle mariée, (i) newly-married man, woman; (ii) bridegroom, *f.* bride. **2.** *s.m.* Bridegroom, *s.f.* bride (about to be married). Robe de mariée, wedding-dress, bridal attire.

marie-salope, *s.f. F:* **I.** Slut. **2.** (*a*) (Dredger's) mud-barge; hopper(-barge). (*b*) Mud-dredger. *pl. Des maries-salopes.*

marieur, -euse [marjœːr, -øːz], *s.* Matchmaker.

marin, -ine [marɛ̃, -in]. **I.** *a.* Marine (plant, engine, etc.). *Carte marine*, sea-chart. Mille marin, nautical mile. *Costume m.*, sailor suit. *F:* Avoir le pied marin, to have found one's sea legs; to be a good sailor. **2.** *s.m.* (*a*) Seafaring man (officer or seaman); mariner. (*b*) Sailor, seaman. *M. d'État, F:* bluejacket. Se faire marin, to go to sea. *F:* Marin d'eau douce, land-lubber; swab.

marine, *s.f.* **I.** *Art:* Seascape, seapiece. **2.** Seamanship. *Terme de m.*, nautical term. **3.** The sea service. La marine marchande, the merchant service, the mercantile marine. La marine de guerre, the Navy. Officier de marine, naval officer. **4.** Sentir la marine, to smell, taste, of the sea.

marinade [marinad], *s.f.* Pickle; brine, souse. *M. de chevreuil*, soused venison.

marin|er [marine], *v.tr.* To pickle; to souse (mackerel, etc.). *s.m.* -age.

maringot(t)e [marɛ̃gɔt], *s.f.* **I.** Spring cart. **2.** Caravan (of strolling players, gipsies).

maringouin [marɛ̃gwɛ̃], *s.m. Ent:* Mosquito (in W. Indies).

marinier, -ière [marinje, -jɛːr]. **I.** *a.* Marine, naval. S.a. OFFICIER[2]. **2.** *s.m.* Waterman, bargeman, bargee. **3.** *s.f.* Marinière, side-stroke (in swimming).

mariol [marjɔl], *a. P:* Knowing, cute, shrewd. *s.* Faire le mariol, to show off; to talk big.

marionnette [marjɔnɛt], *s.f.* **I.** (*a*) Marionette,

puppet. Théâtre de marionnettes, puppet-show. (*b*) *F:* (Of pers.) Puppet, tool. **2.** *Nau:* Ninepin block.

mariste [marist], *s.m. Ecc:* Marist (father).

marital, -aux [marital, -o], *a.* Marital. *adv.* -ement.

maritime [maritim], *a.* Maritime (navigation, plant, province, etc.). *Ville m.*, seaboard town, seaside town. *Commerce m.*, sea-borne trade. *Assurance m.*, marine insurance. *Courtier m.*, ship-broker. *Agent m.*, shipping-agent. *Arsenal m.*, naval dockyard. *Navire affecté à la navigation m.*, sea-going vessel. *Rail:* Gare maritime, harbour station.

maritorne [maritɔrn], *s.f.* Sloven, slut; untidy wench.

marivaudage [marivoda:ʒ], *s.m.* Witty and affected conversation (in the style of Marivaux); mild flirting.

marivauder [marivode], *v.i.* To talk like the characters in the plays of Marivaux; to bandy airy trifles; to flirt.

marjolaine [marʒɔlɛn], *s.f.* (Sweet) marjoram.

mark [mark], *s.m. Num:* (German) mark.

marlou [marlu], *s.m. P:* **I.** Pimp, bully. **2.** = VOYOU.

marmaille [marma:j], *s.f. Coll. F:* Children. *Rue pleine de m.*, street swarming with noisy little brats.

Marmara [marmara]. *Pr.n. Geog:* La mer de Marmara, the Sea of Marmora.

marmelade [marməlad], *s.f.* (*a*) Compote (of fruit). *M. de pommes*, stewed apples. (*b*) *M. d'orange(s)*, orange marmalade. (*c*) *F:* Viande en marmelade, meat cooked to shreds. Mettre qn en marmelade, to pound s.o. to a jelly.

marmite [marmit], *s.f.* **I.** (*a*) (Cooking-)pot, boiling-pot; pan. *M. à conserves*, preserving-pan. *M. suédoise, norvégienne*, hay-box. Écumer la marmite, (i) to skim the pot; (ii) *F:* to cadge, sponge. *F:* Faire bouillir la marmite, to keep the pot boiling. (*b*) *Mil:* Dixy, camp-kettle. **2.** *Mil: P:* Heavy shell.

marmit|er [marmite], *v.tr. P:* To bombard (place) with heavy shells; to shell. *s.m.* -age.

marmiteux, -euse [marmitø, -øːz], *a. & s.* Poor, miserable (wretch).

marmiton [marmitɔ̃], *s.m.* Cook's boy; pastry-cook's errand-boy.

marmonner [marmɔne], *v.tr.* To mumble, mutter.

marmoréen, -enne [marmɔreɛ̃, -ɛn], *a.* Marmoreal.

marmot [marmo], *s.m.* **I.** Child, brat, urchin. **2.** *A:* Grotesque figure (esp. as door-knocker). (Hence) *F:* Croquer le marmot, to be kept waiting; to cool one's heels.

marmottage [marmɔta:ʒ], *s.m.* **I.** Mumbling, muttering. **2.** Mumble, mutter.

marmotte [marmɔt], *s.f.* **I.** *Z:* Marmot. **2.** Kerchief (tied over the forehead).

marmottement [marmɔtmɑ̃], *s.m.* = MARMOTTAGE.

marmott|er [marmɔte], *v.tr.* To mumble, mutter. *s.* -eur, -euse.

marmouset [marmuzɛ], *s.m.* (*a*) Quaint figure (in ivory, china); grotesque. (*b*) *F:* Little chap; urchin. (*c*) Fire-dog (with grotesque head).

marne [marn], *s.f. Agr:* Marl.

marn|er [marne], *v.tr.* To marl (soil). *s.m.* -age.

marnière [marnjɛːr], *s.f.* Marl-pit.

Maroc (le) [ləmarɔk]. *Pr.n.m.* Morocco.

marocain, -aine [marɔkɛ̃, -ɛn], *a. & s.* Moroccan. *Tex:* Crêpe marocain, marocain.

maronner [marɔne], *v.tr. & i. F:* To growl, grumble; to growl out (oath).

maroquin [marɔkɛ̃], *s.m.* (a) Morocco(-leather). (b) *F:* Minister's portfolio.

maroquinerie [marɔkinri], *s.f.* (a) Morocco-leather goods or trade. (b) Fancy-leather goods or trade.

marotte [marɔt], *s.f.* 1. (Court fool's) bauble; cap and bells. 2. *F:* Fad, hobby, fancy. *Chacun a sa m.*, everyone has a bee in his bonnet.

maroufle[1] [marufl], *s.m. A:* Rogue, scoundrel; low individual.

maroufle[2], *s.f.* Strong paste (for re-mounting pictures).

maroufler [marufle], *v.tr.* 1. (a) To re-mount (picture) on a new foundation. (b) *Aer: etc:* M. *une couture*, to tape a seam. *Bande à maroufler*, taping, tape. 2. To prime, size (canvas).

maroute [marut], *s.f. Bot:* Stinking camomile.

marquant [markã], *a.* 1. Prominent, outstanding (incident, personage). 2. *Carte marquante, s.f.* marquante, card that counts.

marque[1] [mark], *s.f.* 1. Mark. M. *d'identité*, identification mark. **Marque de fabrique, de commerce**, trade-mark; brand. M. *déposée*, registered trade-mark. **Bicyclette de première marque**, bicycle of the best make. **Vin de marque**, wine of a well-known brand. *F: Personnages de m.*, distinguished, prominent, people. **Marque de l'État**, government stamp. *Navy:* La m. de l'amiral, the admiral's flag. M. *au crayon, à la plume, à la craie*, pencil-mark, pen-mark, chalk-mark. *Porter la m. du génie*, to bear the stamp of genius. *Marques d'amitié, de respect*, tokens of friendship, of respect. *Rugby Fb:* **Faire une marque**, to make one's mark. 2. Marking-tool, branding-iron, marker. 3. (a) *Com:* Tally. (b) *Games:* Scoring-board; marker. (c) *Games:* Score. **Tenir la marque**, to keep the score. (d) *Games:* Counter.

marque[2], *s.f. A:* Reprisals. *Hist:* **Lettres de marque**, letters of marque (and reprisal).

marque-mal, *s.m.inv. F:* Suspicious-, shady-looking fellow.

marquer [marke]. 1. *v.tr.* To mark. (a) To put a mark on (sth.). M. *du linge*, to mark linen. *Com:* **Prix marqué**, (i) catalogue price; (ii) price marked in plain figures. *Figure marquée par, de, la petite vérole*, pock-marked face. M. *un criminel*, to brand a criminal. M. *un arbre*, to blaze a tree. *Rail: etc:* M. *sa place*, to leave one's hat, etc., on a seat (to show that it is engaged). (b) To record, note; to make a note of, jot down (sth.). *Games:* M. *les points*, to keep the score. (c) To indicate, show. *L'horloge marque l'heure*, the clock tells the time. *La pendule marque dix heures*, the clock points to ten o'clock. M. *la mesure avec son bâton*, to beat time with one's baton. **Marquer le pas**, to mark time. **Cheval qui marque**, horse with mark of mouth. *F:* **Il marque son âge**, he shows his age. M. *à qn son estime*, to give s.o. proof, a token, of one's esteem. 2. *v.i.* To stand out, make a mark. *Notre famille n'a jamais marqué*, our family has never been remarkable. **Marquer mal**, to be of unprepossessing appearance. *s.m.-age.*

marqué, *a.* 1. (a) Marked (card, etc.). **Être né marqué**, to be born with a birth-mark. (b) **Papier marqué**, stamped paper. 2. Marked, decided, unmistakable (difference, etc.); pronounced (features). 3. **Au jour marqué**, on the appointed day.

marqueter [markəte], *v.tr.* (je **marquette**; je

marquetterai) 1. To spot, speckle (fur, imitation tiger-skin, etc.). 2. To inlay (table, etc.).

marqueterie [markɔtri], *s.f.* 1. Inlaid-work, marquetry. 2. *F:* Patchwork (literary composition, etc.).

marqueur, -euse [markœːr, -øːz]. 1. *s.* Marker. (a) Stamper, brander; stenciller (of boxes, etc.). (b) Scorer (at games). (c) Tally-keeper. 2. *s.m.* (a) *Ten:* M. *à chaux*, court-marking machine. (b) M. *de plis*, (sewing-machine) tucker, tuck-creaser.

marquis [marki], *s.m.* Marquis, marquess.

marquisat [markiza], *s.m.* Marquisate.

marquise [markiːz], *s.f.* 1. Marchioness. 2. (a) Awning (on pleasure-boat, etc.). (b) Marquee (tent). (c) (Overhanging) shelter; glass porch (at hotel entrance).

marraine [marɛn], *s.f.* (a) Godmother; sponsor (at baptism). (b) Presenter (of débutante).

marrant [marã], *a. P:* 1. (Screamingly) funny. 2. Wearisome, boring.

marre [maːr], *s.f. P:* **J'en ai marre**, I'm fed up with it; it bores me stiff.

marrer (se) [səmare], *v.pr. P:* To split one's sides with laughing.

marri [mari], *a. A:* Sad, sorry, grieved.

marron[1] [marɔ̃], *s.m.* 1. (a) (Large edible) chestnut. **Tirer les marrons du feu pour qn**, to be s.o.'s cat's-paw. **Marrons glacés**, iced chestnuts, *marrons glacés*. (b) **Marron d'Inde**, horse-chestnut. 2. *Pyr:* Maroon. 3. *a. inv. in f.* Chestnut(-colour); maroon.

marron[2], **-onne** [marɔ̃, -ɔn], *a.* 1. *Nègre m., s.* marron, maroon, runaway negro slave. **Animal m.**, animal that has gone to the bush. 2. Unlicensed (trader, cabman, etc.); unqualified (doctor). *Sp:* **Amateur m.**, sham amateur.

marronner[1] [marɔne], *v.i.* 1. (Of runaway slave) To live in hiding. 2. To carry on a trade, profession, without legal qualification.

marronner[2], *v.i. P:* = MARONNER.

marronnier [marɔnje], *s.m.* Chestnut-tree. **Marronnier d'Inde**, horse-chestnut tree.

marrube [maryb], *s.m. Bot:* Hoarhound, horehound. M. *aquatique*, gipsy-wort.

Mars [mars]. 1. *Pr.n.m. Myth: Astr:* Mars. *Mil:* **Champ de Mars**, parade-ground. 2. *s.m.* March. **Au mois de mars**, in the month of March. *Le premier m.*, (on) the first of March, (on) March (the) first. *Blé de m., pl.* **les mars**, spring wheat. *Bière de m.*, March beer, March ale. *F:* **Arriver comme mars en carême**, to come round as regularly as clock-work.

marseillais, -aise [marsɛje, -ɛːz], *a. & s. Geog:* Marseillais, -aise. **La Marseillaise** (national song of the Fr. Republic), the Marseillaise.

Marseille [marsɛːj]. *Pr.n. Geog:* Marseilles.

marsouin [marswɛ̃], *s.m.* 1. (a) *Z:* Porpoise. (b) *P:* Colonial infantry soldier. 2. (a) *Nau:* Forecastle awning. (b) *N.Arch:* M. *arrière*, sternson. M. *avant*, stemson.

marsupial, -aux [marsypjal, -o], *a. & s.m. Z:* Marsupial.

marteau [marto], *s.m.* 1. (a) Hammer. M. *à panne fendue*, claw-hammer. M. *à deux mains*, sledge-hammer. **Coup de marteau**, hammer-stroke. *S.a.* ENCLUME. *P:* **Il a un coup de marteau, il est un peu marteau**, he isn't all there, he's a bit cracked. (b) (Auctioneer's) hammer. **Passer sous le marteau**, to be sold under the hammer. (c) Knocker (of door). **Coup de marteau**, knock (at the door). *F:* **Graisser le marteau**, to tip the door-keeper. 2. *Ich:* Hammer-head (shark).

marteau-pilon, *s.m. Metall:* Power-hammer.
martel [martɛl], *s.m. A:* = MARTEAU. *F:* Avoir
martel en tête, to be uneasy in one's mind; to
be anxious.
martel|er [martəle], *v.tr.* (je martèle; je marte-
lerai) (*a*) To hammer. *Metalw:* M. à froid, to
cold-hammer. *F:* Marteler le cerveau à qn, to
worry, torment, plague, s.o. (*b*) *Abs.* (Of water
in pipes, etc.) To hammer. *I.C.E:* (Of engine)
To knock. *s.m.* -age.
  martelé, *a.* 1. Hammer-wrought. 2. *Style*
m., laboured style (of writing).
marteleur [martəlœːr], *s.m.* Hammersmith,
hammerman.
martial, -aux [marsjal, -o], *a.* 1. Martial,
soldierlike; warlike (humour, etc.). 2. Loi
martiale, martial law. Code martial, articles of
war. Cour martiale, court-martial. *adv.* -ement.
Martin [martɛ̃]. *Pr.n.m.* (*a*) Martin. (*b*) Name
frequently given to a donkey; = Neddy. *Prov:*
Il y a à la foire plus d'un âne qui s'appelle Martin,
there are more Jacks than one at the fair. (*c*) Ours
Martin, Bruin; Teddy Bear.
martinet[1] [martinɛ], *s.m.* 1. *Metall:* Tilt-
hammer; drop-stamp. 2. Strap, *Scot:* tawse
(for chastising child).
martinet[2], *s.m. Orn:* Swift, martlet.
martingale [martɛ̃gal], *s.f.* 1. (*a*) *Harn:* Martingale. (*b*) *Cost:* Half-belt (of greatcoat, sports-
coat). 2. *Gaming:* Martingale.
martin-pêcheur, *s.m. Orn:* Kingfisher. *pl.* Des
martins-pêcheurs.
martre [martr], *s.f. Z:* Marten. Martre zibeline, sable. Martre du Canada, mink. Martre
des palmiers, palm-cat, civet. *F:* Prendre martre
pour renard, to be taken in by a resemblance.
martyr, -yre[1] [martiːr], *s.* Martyr. *F:* Être
du commun des martyrs, to be an insignificant
person. *a.* Un peuple m., a martyred people.
martyre[2], *s.m.* Martyrdom. Souffrir le m., to
suffer martyrdom. *F:* Mettre qn au m., to
agonize s.o.
martyriser [martirize], *v.tr.* 1. To martyr (s.o.
for his faith). 2. To martyrize; to make a
martyr of (s.o.).
marxisme [marksism], *s.m.* Marx(ian)ism.
marxiste [marksist]. 1. *a.* Marxian. 2. *s.* Marx-
ist.
maryland [marilɑ̃], *s.m.* Maryland tobacco.
mas [mɑ(s)], *s.m.* (In S. of Fr.) Small farmhouse.
mascarade [maskarad], *s.f.* Masquerade.
mascaret [maskarɛ], *s.m.* Bore, tidal wave (in
estuary).
mascaron [maskarɔ̃], *s.m.* (Grotesque) mask (on
keystone of arch, etc.); mascaron.
mascotte [maskɔt], *s.f.* Mascot, charm.
masculin [maskylɛ̃], *a.* 1. Male (sex, attire).
2. Masculine. (*a*) Mannish (woman). (*b*) *Gram:*
Le (genre) m., the masculine gender. *Pros:* Rimes
masculines, masculine rhymes.
masque[1] [mask], *s.m.* 1. Mask. (*a*) Sous le
masque de la vertu, under the mask of virtue.
Oter, arracher, le masque à qn, to unmask s.o.
Lever le masque, to throw off the mask. *Mil:*
M. à gaz, contre le gaz, gas-mask. *Toil:* M. anti-
rides, face-pack. (*b*) M. mortuaire, death-mask.
(*c*) (Expression of the) face; features (as a
whole). Il a le m. mobile, he has mobile features.
2. (*a*) *Th:* Masque. (*b*) Masquerader, masker,
mummer. 3. *Artil:* Shield or hood (of gun).
masque[2], *s.f.* Petite m., little minx, hussy.
masquer [maske], *v.tr.* To mask. 1. (*a*) To put
a mask on (s.o.). Se m., to put on a mask. Bal
masqué, masked ball. (*b*) To hide, screen (sth.).

M. qch. à qn, to conceal sth. from s.o. M. une
odeur, to disguise a smell. *Aut:* Virage masqué,
blind corner. *Mil:* Masquer une batterie, to
conceal a battery. *Nau:* Naviguer à feux masqués,
to steam without lights, with all lights obscured.
2. *Nau:* To back (sail). Être masqué, *v.i.*
masquer, to be caught aback, taken aback.
massacrante [masakrɑ̃ːt], *a.f.* (Used in the phr.)
Être d'une humeur massacrante, to be in a very
bad temper; to be as cross as two sticks.
massacre [masakr], *s.m.* (*a*) Massacre, slaughter;
F: butchery. (*b*) Jeu de massacre, (game played
at fairs similar to) Aunt Sally. *F:* Il a une tête
de massacre, he's got a face you'd like to punch.
massacr|er [masakre], *v.tr.* 1. To massacre,
butcher, slaughter. 2. *F:* To bungle, spoil,
make a hash of (work); to murder (music); to
ruin (clothes). 3. *Ten:* M. un lob, to kill, smash,
a lob. *s.m.* -eur.
massage [masaːʒ], *s.m.* (*a*) *Med:* Massage.
(*b*) Rubbing down (of horse). (*c*) Shampoo.
masse[1] [mas], *s.f.* 1. Mass. (*a*) Marchandise en
masse, goods in bulk. Se prendre en masse, to
solidify, coagulate. Tomber comme une m., to fall
like a log. (*b*) *Mil:* Mass formation. (*c*) *Mec:*
Mass (of moving body). (*d*) M. de gens, mass.
crowd, body, of people. Émouvoir les masses, to
move the masses, the mob. En masse, in a body.
Exécutions en m., mass executions. Il faut voir les
choses en m., you must look upon things as a
whole. 2. (*a*) Fund, stock. *Jur:* M. des biens
(de la faillite), (bankrupt's) total estate. M. passive, liabilities. M. active, assets. (*b*) *Mil:*
Company funds. (*c*) (Prisoner's) earnings
(handed to him on liberation). 3. *El.E:* Earth
(constituted by frame of machine). Mettre le
courant à la masse, to earth the current.
masse[2], *s.f.* 1. Sledge-hammer. M. en bois,
beetle. 2. (*a*) *A:* Masse d'armes, mace.
(*b*) (Ceremonial) mace. 3. *Bot:* Masse d'eau
= MASSETTE 2.
masselotte [maslɔt], *s.f.* 1. *Metall:* Dead-head
(of casting); sprue, runner. 2. Inertia block
(of fuse, etc.).
massepain [maspɛ̃], *s.m.* Marzipan cake or
biscuit.
masser[1] [mase], *v.tr.* To mass (soldiers, etc.).
  se masser, to mass; to form a crowd.
masser[2], *v.tr.* (*a*) To massage. (*b*) To rub down
(horse). (*c*) To shampoo.
massette [masɛt], *s.f.* 1. Two-handed hammer.
2. *Bot:* Bulrush, reed-mace, cat's-tail.
masseur, -euse [masœːr, -øːz], *s. Med:* Masseur, *f.* masseuse.
massicot[1] [masiko], *s.m.* Massicot, yellow lead.
massicot[2], *s.m. Bookb:* Guillotine, trimmer.
massier[1], -ière [masje, -jɛːr], *s.* Treasurer;
student in charge (in Fr. art studio).
massier[2], *s.m.* Mace-bearer, macer; beadle.
massif, -ive [masif, -iːv]. 1. *a.* (*a*) Massive,
bulky; gross, material (mind, etc.). (*b*) Argent
m., solid silver. (*c*) Action massive contre l'ennemi,
mass attack against the enemy. 2. *s.m.* (*a*) Solid
mass (of masonry, etc.); body (of a pier).
(*b*) Clump (of shrubs). (*c*) *Geog:* Mountain mass.
massique [masik], *a. Ph:* Pertaining to the mass.
Puissance massique, power-to-weight ratio (of
engine).
massivement [masivmɑ̃], *adv.* Massively,
ponderously; heavily.
massue [masy], *s.f.* (*a*) Club, bludgeon. Coup
de massue, (i) bludgeon stroke; (ii) *F:* staggering blow. (*b*) *pl.* Indian clubs.
mastic [mastik], *s.m.* 1. Mastic (resin). 2. (*a*)

Cement, mastic compound. *M. à vitres*, (glazier's) putty. (*b*) *Dent:* Filling, stopping. (*c*) *Aut: Cy. M pour enveloppes*, tyre-stopping.

mastication [mastikasjɔ̃], *s.f.* Mastication; chewing (of food).

masti|quer[1] [mastike], *v.tr.* To fill in (cracks, etc.) with cement; to putty (window). *Dent:* To fill stop (teeth). *s.m.* **-cage.**

mastiquer[2], *v.tr.* To masticate, chew.

mastoc [mastɔk], *s.m. F:* Lubberly, lumpish, fellow.

mastodonte [mastɔdɔ̃:t], *s.m.* Mastodon.

mastoïde [mastɔid], *a. Anat:* Mastoid (bone)

mastroquet [mastrɔkɛ], *s.m. P:* Pub-keeper.

masure [mazy:r] *s.f.* Tumbledown cottage; hovel, shanty.

mat[1] [mat], *a.* Mat, unpolished, dull (metal). *Teint mat*, mat complexion. *Son mat*, dull, dead, sound; thud.

mat[2] [mat]. **1.** *a.inv. Chess:* Checkmated. **2.** *s.m.* (Check)mate. *Faire (échec et) mat en trois coups*, to mate in three.

mât [mɑ], *s.m.* Mast, pole. (*a*) *Nau:* **Grand mât**, mainmast. *Mât de misaine*, foremast. *Bas mât*, lower mast. *Mât de hune*, topmast. *Mât de charge*, derrick. *Mât de pavillon*, flagstaff, ensign staff. **Navire à trois mâts**, three-masted ship; three-master. (*b*) *Mât de tente*, tent-pole. **Mât de cocagne**, greasy pole. (*c*) *Av:* Strut.

matamore [matamɔ:r], *s.m.* Braggart; swashbuckler. **Faire le matamore**, to bully, to hector.

match [matʃ], *s.m. Sp:* Match.

maté [mate], *s.m.* Paraguay tea; maté.

matelas [matlɑ], *s.m.* (*a*) (Overlay) mattress. *M. à eau*, water-bed. **Toile à matelas**, ticking. *La toile du matelas*, the tick. (*b*) Cushion (of chair); padding (of carriage). *Mch: M. de vapeur*, steam cushion.

matelasser [matlase], *v.tr.* To pad, cushion (chair, carriage, etc.). *Chambre matelassée*, padded room. *Porte matelassée*, baize door.

matelassier, -ière [matlasje, -jɛ:r], *s.* **1.** Mattress-maker. **2.** Mattress-cleaner.

matelot [matlo], *s.m.* **1.** Sailor, seaman. *M. (breveté) de première classe*, leading seaman. *M de deuxième classe*, able seaman. *Servir comme simple m.*, to sail before the mast. **2.** Consort (ship). **3.** (Child's) sailor suit.

matelote [matlɔt], *s.f.* **1.** Fish stew. **2.** *A la matelote*, sailor-fashion.

mat|er[1] [mate], *v.tr.* **1.** To mat, dull (metals, etc.). **2.** (*a*) To caulk, hammer (boiler seams). (*b*) To batter, bruise (working parts). *s.m.* **-age.**

mater[2], *v.tr.* (*a*) *Chess:* To (check)mate. (*b*) *F:* **Mater qn**, to bring s.o. to heel. *M. l'orgueil de qn*, to humble, bring down, s.o.'s pride.

mât|er [mate], *v.tr.* (*a*) To mast (ship). (*b*) *M. les avirons*, to toss oars. *s.m.* **-age.**

matérialisation [materjalizasjɔ̃], *s.f.* Materialization, materializing.

matérialiser [materjalize], *v.tr.* To materialize. **se matérialiser**, to materialize.

matérialisme [materjalism], *s.m.* Materialism.

matérialiste [materjalist]. **1.** *a.* Materialistic. **2.** *s.* Materialist.

matériau [materjo], *s.m. Civ.E: Const:* (Building, constructional material).

matériaux [materjo], *s.m.pl.* Materials.

matériel, -elle [materjɛl]. **1.** *a.* (*a*) Material, physical (body). (*b*) Materialistic, gross, sensual. (*c*) *Besoins matériels*, bodily needs. **2.** *s.m.* Plant; working stock (of factory); implements (of a farm, etc.). *M. d'école*, school furniture. *M. de*

guerre, war material. *Rail:* **Matériel roulant**, rolling stock.

matériellement [materjɛlmɑ̃], *adv.* (*a*) Materially. *Avoir de quoi vivre m.*, to have enough for one's material needs. *Chose m. impossible*, thing physically impossible. (*b*) Materialistically, sensually.

matern|el, -elle [matɛrnɛl], *a.* Maternal. **1.** Motherly (care, etc.). **École maternelle**, *s.f.* **maternelle** infant school. **2.** (*a*) *Aïeul m.*, maternal grandfather. (*b*) *Langue maternelle*, mother tongue. *adv.* **-ellement.**

maternité [matɛrnite], *s.f.* **1.** Maternity, motherhood. **2.** Maternity hospital, lying-in hospital.

mathématicien, -ienne [matematisjɛ̃, -jɛn], *s.* Mathematician.

mathématique [matematik]. **1.** *a.* Mathematical. **2.** *s.f.* Usu. *pl.* Mathematics. *Sch: Mathématiques spéciales*, higher mathematics. *adv.* **-ment.**

mathurin [matyrɛ̃], *s.m.* **1.** Mathurin (friar). **2.** *F:* Jack Tar.

matière [matjɛ:r], *s.f.* **1.** Material. **Matières premières**, raw materials. **2.** Matter, substance. *Être enfoncé dans la m.*, to be engrossed in material things. *M. grise*, grey matter (of the brain). **3.** Subject (of speech, etc.); topic, theme (for discussion). **Table des matières**, table of contents. **Entrer en matière**, to broach the subject; to begin (one's discourse). **Il n'y a pas matière à rire**, it is no laughing matter. **Être bon juge en matière de musique**, to be a good judge of music.

matin [matɛ̃]. **1.** *s.m.* Morning, *Poet:* morn. *Quatre heures du m.*, four o'clock in the morning; *4 a.m. Au matin*, in the morning, the next morning. *C'est le m. que je travaille le mieux*, I work best in the morning(s). *Demain m.*, to-morrow morning. **Tous les lundis matin**, every Monday morning. **De grand, bon, matin**: **le matin de bonne heure**, early in the morning, in the early morning. **Il était grand matin**, it was very early (in the day). **Un de ces (quatre) matins, un beau matin**, one of these (fine) days. **2.** *adv.* Early (in the morning). *Se lever très m.*, to get up very early.

mâtin [matɛ̃], *s.m.* **1.** (*a*) Mastiff. (*b*) Large mongrel; watch-dog. **2.** *F:* (*f.* **mâtine** [matin]). **Sacré mâtin!** you sly dog, you! *Petite mâtine!* you little minx! *int.* **Mâtin!** by Jove!

matinal, -aux [matinal, -o], *a.* **1.** Morning (breeze, etc.); *Lit:* matutinal. *A cette heure matinale* . . ., at this early hour . . . **2.** (Of pers.) *Comme tu es m. aujourd'hui!* you are down very early this morning! *s. C'est un m.*, he is an early riser.

matinalement [matinalmɑ̃], *adv.* Early (in the morning).

mâtiné [matine], *a.* Mongrel, cross-bred.

matinée [matine], *s.f.* **1.** Morning, forenoon. *Dans la m.*, in the course of the morning. *A onze heures de la m.*, at eleven in the forenoon. *Je ne l'ai pas vu de toute la m.*, I haven't seen him all morning. *F:* **Dormir, faire, la grasse matinée**, to sleep all the morning, to lie late abed. **2.** *Th: etc:* Matinée; afternoon performance. **3.** (Woman's) wrapper (worn in the morning).

matines [matin], *s.f.pl. Ecc:* Matins.

matineux, -euse [matino, -o:z]. **1.** *a.* Early rising. **2.** *s.* (Habitual) early riser.

matité [matite], *s.f.* Deadness, dullness (of sound, etc.). [MAT[1]]

matoir [matwa:r], *s.m.* **1.** Matting tool. **2.** Caulking chisel. **3.** Riveting hammer.

25

matois, -oise [matwa, -waːz]. **1.** *a.* Sly, cunning, crafty. **2.** *s.* Crafty person. Esp. **Fin matois,** long-headed old chap; sly fox.

matou [matu], *s.m.* **1.** Tom-cat. **2.** *F:* Curmudgeon.

matraque [matrak], *s.f.* Bludgeon.

matriarcal, -aux [matriarkal, -o], *a.* Matriarchal.

matricaire [matrikɛːr], *s.f. Bot:* Feverfew.

matrice [matris], *s.f.* **1.** Matrix. (*a*) *Anat:* Womb. (*b*) *Metalw:* Die; lower half of diestamp. (*c*) *Typ:* Type mould. **2.** *Adm:* Original (of register of taxes).

matri|cer [matrise], *v.tr.* To stamp (metal). *Pièce matricée,* (i) stamping; (ii) drop-forging. *s.m.* **-çage.**

matricide[1] [matrisid]. **1.** *s. m. & f.* Matricide. **2.** *a.* Matricidal.

matricide[2], *s.m.* Matricide (as a crime).

matricule [matrikyl]. **1.** *s.f.* (*a*) Roll, register, list. *Mil:* Regimental roll. (*b*) Inscription, registration; enrolment. (*c*) Registration certificate. **2.** *Numéro m., s.m.* **matricule,** (regimental or administrative) number.

matriculer [matrikyle], *v.tr.* **1.** To enter (s.o.'s) name on a register; to enrol (soldier). **2.** To stamp the number on (car engine, etc.).

matrimonial, -aux [matrimɔnjal, -o], *a.* Matrimonial (agency, etc.).

matrone [matron], *s.f.* **1.** Matron (= married woman). **2.** Midwife.

Matthieu [matjø]. *Pr.n.m.* Matthew.

maturation [matyrasjɔ̃], *s.f.* Maturation, ripening (of fruit, abscess, etc.).

mâture [matyːr], *s.f.* **1.** Masts; masts and spars. **Dans la mâture,** aloft. **2.** Mast crane, sheer-legs. **Mâture flottante,** sheer-hulk.

maturément [matyremɑ̃], *adv.* With, after, mature consideration.

maturité [matyrite], *s.f.* (*a*) Maturity, ripeness. *Arriver à m.,* to come to maturity. (*b*) *L'œuvre de sa m.,* the work of his maturity, of his middle years. **Avec maturité,** after mature consideration.

matutinal, -aux [matytinal, -o], *a.* Matutinal.

maubèche [mobɛʃ], *Orn:* Sandpiper.

maud|ire [modiːr], *v.tr.* (*pr.p.* maudissant; *p.p.* maudit; *pr.ind.* je maudis, n. maudissons, v. maudissez, ils maudissent; *pr.sub.* je maudisse; *p.h.* je maudis; *fu.* je maudirai) To curse, to call down curses upon (s.o., sth.); to anathematize. *s.m.* **-issement.**

maudit. 1. *a.* (*a*) (Ac)cursed (crime, etc.). *F: A: M. soit le coquin!* hang the fellow! confound the fellow! (*b*) *F: Quel m. temps!* what damnable weather! **2.** *s.* **Le Maudit,** the Evil One. **Les maudits,** the accursed, the damned.

maugréer [mogree], *v.i.* To curse, fume; to grumble (*après, contre,* about, at).

Maure [moːr]. *Ethn:* **1.** *s.m.* Moor. **2.** *a.m.* Moorish.

mauresque [morɛsk]. **1.** (*a*) *a.f.* Moorish (woman etc.). (*b*) *a.* Moresque (architecture, design). **2.** *s.f.* (*a*) Moorish woman; Moresque. (*b*) Moresque (pattern).

Maurice [moris]. *Pr.n.m.* Maurice. **L'île Maurice,** Mauritius.

mausolée [mozole], *s.m.* Mausoleum.

maussade [mosad], *a.* (*a*) Surly, sullen, glum; peevish; *F:* crusty, grumpy, disgruntled. *D'un ton m.,* irritably. (*b*) *Temps m.,* dull, cheerless, weather. *adv.* **-ment.**

maussaderie [mosadri], *s.f.* Sullenness, peevishness.

mauvais [movɛ], *a.* (*a*) Evil, ill (thought, omen, etc.); bad, wicked (person). **Mauvaise action,** ill deed; wrong. *De plus en plus m.,* worse and worse. *Le plus m.,* the worst. **Avoir l'air mauvais,** (i) to look evil-minded; (ii) to look fierce, vicious. *Son m. ange,* his bad angel. *Né sous une mauvaise étoile,* born under an unlucky star. **Le mauvais œil,** the evil eye. (*b*) Ill-natured (*pour,* towards). **C'est une mauvaise langue,** he has a venomous tongue. S.a. SUJET[2] 2, TÊTE 2. (*c*) Nasty, displeasing, unpleasant. **Mauvais pas,** dangerous situation. *M. temps,* bad weather. *Mer mauvaise,* rough sea. **Trouver qch. mauvais,** to dislike sth. **Trouver mauvais que qn fasse qch.,** to disapprove of, take exception to, s.o.'s doing sth. **Prendre qch. en mauvaise part,** to take exception to sth.; to take offence at sth. *Adv.* **Sentir mauvais,** to smell bad, to stink. **Il fait mauvais être pauvre,** it is wretched to be poor. **Il fait mauvais,** the weather is bad. (*d*) *M. pour la santé, pour la digestion,* bad for, injurious to, the health, the digestion. (*e*) Imperfect, poor, inadequate. **Avoir mauvais air,** (i) to look ill; (ii) to have a poor appearance. *Mauvaise santé,* poor health. *Avoir mauvaise vue,* to have bad eyesight. *Faire de mauvaises affaires,* to be doing badly. *M. frein,* defective brake. (*f*) Wrong; due to a mistake. *C'est la mauvaise clef,* it is the wrong key. *Venir dans un m. moment,* to come at an inconvenient time. *Rire au m. endroit,* to laugh in the wrong place. **Tenir qch. par le m. bout,** to hold sth. by the wrong end. S.a. HONTE 1.

mauvaisement [movɛzmɑ̃], *adv.* Evilly, wickedly; ill-naturedly.

mauve[1] [moːv]. **1.** *s.f. Bot:* Mallow. **2.** *a. & s.m.* Mauve, purple.

mauve[2], *s.f. Orn: Dial:* Sea-gull.

mauviette [movjɛt], *s.f.* (*a*) *Cu:* Lark (in season). *F: Elle mange comme une mauviette,* she doesn't eat enough to keep a sparrow alive. (*b*) *F:* Slight, frail, person.

maxillaire [maksilɛːr], *a. Anat:* Maxillary. **Os maxillaire,** jaw-bone.

maxima. See MAXIMUM.

maxime [maksim], *s.f.* Maxim. *Il tenait pour m. que . . . ,* it was a maxim of his that. . . .

maximum [maksimɔm]. Maximum. **1.** *s.m. M. de rendement,* highest efficiency, maximum efficiency. *Porter la production au m.,* to raise production to a maximum. *Thermomètre à maxima,* maximum thermometer. *pl. Des maxima, des maximums.* **2.** *a.* Usu. *inv. Pression maximum,* maximum pressure. *El.E: etc: Débit maximum,* peak load.

Mayence [majɑ̃ːs]. *Pr.n.f. Geog:* Mainz.

mayonnaise [majonɛːz], *s.f. Cu:* Mayonnaise.

mazagran [mazagrɑ̃], *s.m.* Glass of black coffee.

mazarinade [mazarinad], *s.f. Hist:* Lampoon (on Cardinal Mazarin).

mazette [mazɛt], *s.f. F:* **1.** *A:* Poor horse; screw. **2.** (*a*) Duffer (at a game, etc.); *F:* rabbit. (*b*) *Mil:* Recruit. **3.** *int.* My word! crikey!

mazout [mazu], *s.m.* Fuel oil, oil fuel.

mazurka [mazyrka], *s.f.* Mazurka.

me, before a vowel sound **m'** [m(ə)], *pers.pron.* (*a*) (*Acc.*) Me. *Il m'aime,* he loves me. *Me voici,* here I am. (*b*) (*Dat.*) (To) me. *Il me l'a dit,* he told me so. *Donnez-m'en,* give me some. (*c*) Myself. *Je me lave,* I wash myself. (*d*) *Je me dis que . . . ,* I said to myself that. . . .

mea-culpa [meakylpa], *s.m. inv.* Faire, dire, son mea-culpa, to acknowledge one's sins.

méandre [meɑ̃ːdr], *s.m.* Meander, sinuosity, winding, bend (of stream); winding path.

mécanicien, -ienne [mekanisjɛ̃, -jɛn]. **I.** *s.m.* (*a*) Mechanic. *Navy:* Engine-room artificer. (*b*) Mechanician. (*c*) *Rail:* Engine-driver. *Nau:* Engineer. **2.** Ingénieur **mécanicien**, mechanical engineer. **3.** *s.f.* **Mécanicienne**, machinist; sewing-woman (in factory).

mécanique [mekanik]. **I.** *a.* Mechanical. *Métier m.*, power-loom. *Chemin de fer m.*, (toy) clockwork railway. *Dentelle m.*, machine-made lace. **2.** *s.f.* (*a*) (Science of) mechanics. (*b*) Mechanical skill (in an art). *La m. du piano*, piano technique. (*c*) Mechanism, piece of machinery. **Fait à la mécanique**, machine-made. *M. du piano*, piano-action. *adv.* **-ment.**

mécanisation [mekanizasjɔ̃], *s.f.* Mechanization (of industry, of army).

mécaniser [mekanize], *v.tr.* To mechanize.

mécanisme [mekanism], *s.m.* **I.** Mechanism, machinery. *M. d'une montre*, works of a watch. **2.** Working, technique.

mécano [mekano], *s.m.* *P:* = MÉCANICIEN I (*a*).

Mécène [mesɛn]. *Pr.n.m. Lt.Lit:* Maecenas.

méchanceté [meʃɑ̃ste], *s.f.* **I.** (*a*) Wickedness, naughtiness, mischievousness. (*b*) Unkindness, spitefulness, ill-nature. **Faire qch. par méchanceté**, to do sth. out of malice. **2.** Spiteful act or word. *Faire une m. à qn*, to do s.o. an ill turn.

méchant [meʃɑ̃], *a.* **I.** (*a*) Miserable, wretched, poor, sorry (dwelling, etc.). *Un m. billet de cent francs*, a paltry hundred-franc note. *Méchante excuse*, lame excuse. (*b*) Unpleasant, disagreeable (business, etc.). *Être de méchante humeur*, to be out of temper, as cross as two sticks. **2.** (*a*) Wicked, evil (person, deed); naughty, mischievous (child). *Le chien est-il m.?* does the dog bite? *F:* **Pas méchant**, harmless. *s. Oh, le m.!* *la méchante!* oh, the naughty boy! the naughty girl! *Les méchants*, the wicked. (*b*) Spiteful, ill-natured; vicious (horse). *Auteur m.*, spiteful author. *s.* **Ne faites donc pas le méchant**, don't be nasty. *adv.* **-amment.**

mèche [mɛʃ], *s.f.* **I.** (*a*) Wick (of candle, lamp). (*b*) Match (for firing explosives); touch, fuse (of mine). *F:* **Découvrir la mèche**, to discover the plot. **Vendre la mèche**, to give the show away; to blab. **Il n'y a pas mèche**, it's quite impossible. **Être de mèche avec qn**, to be in collusion, in league, with s.o. *S.a.* ÉVENTER I. **2.** (*a*) Cracker (of whip). (*b*) Lock (of hair); wisp (of wool, etc.); tassel (of nightcap). *Surg:* Tent. **3.** (*a*) Core, heart (of cable, etc.). *El.E:* *Charbon à m.*, cored carbon. (*b*) *Nau:* Spindle (of capstan). **4.** *Tls:* (*a*) Bit, drill. *M. anglaise*, à *trois pointes* centre-bit. *M. hélicoïdale, torse*, twist-bit, auger-bit. (*b*) *Carp:* Auger, gimlet.

mécompte [mekɔ̃t], *s.m.* **I.** Miscalculation, miscount, error. *M. de chronologie*, error in chronology. **2.** Mistaken judgment; foiled expectation, disappointment. *Il a eu un grave m., F:* he has been badly let down.

méconnaissable [mekɔnɛsabl], *a.* Hardly recognizable, unrecognizable.

méconnaissance [mekɔnɛsɑ̃s], *s.f.* (*a*) Failure to recognize or to appreciate (s.o.'s talent, etc.); misappreciation; misreading (of the facts). (*b*) Disavowal, repudiation (of an action).

méconnaître [mekɔnɛtr], *v.tr.* (Conj. like CONNAÎTRE) To fail to recognize. (*a*) To misprize, to misappreciate, not to appreciate (s.o.'s talent, etc.); to belittle (plan etc.); to disregard (duty). *M. les faits*, to ignore blink, the facts. (*b*) To disown, disavow, repudiate.

méconnu, *a.* Unrecognized, misappreciated, unappreciated; misunderstood.

mécontent, -ente [mekɔ̃tɑ̃, -ɑ̃:t]. **I.** *a.* (*a*) Discontented, displeased, dissatisfied (*de*, with). *Être m. que + sub.*, to be annoyed, vexed, that. . . . (*b*) Disaffected. **2.** *s.* Malcontent.

mécontentement [mekɔ̃tɑ̃tmɑ̃], *s.m.* Dissatisfaction (*de*, with); displeasure (*de*, at); disaffection. *Marquer son m.*, to show or express one's displeasure.

mécontenter [mekɔ̃tɑ̃te], *v.tr.* To dissatisfy, displease, annoy (s.o.); to cause (s.o.) dissatisfaction.

Mecque (la) [lamɛk]. *Pr.n.f. Geog:* Mecca.

mécréant, -ante [mekreɑ̃, -ɑ̃:t]. **I.** *a.* (*a*) Misbelieving. (*b*) Unbelieving. **2.** *s.* (*a*) Misbeliever. (*b*) Unbeliever, infidel. (*c*) *F: A:* Miscreant, wretch.

médaille [medɑ:j], *s.f.* **I.** Medal. **Le revers de la médaille**, (i) the reverse of the medal; (ii) *F:* the other side, the dark side, of the picture. **2.** (Porter's, hawker's) badge. **3.** *Arch:* Medallion.

médaillé, -ée [medaje]. **I.** *a.* (*a*) Holding a medal; decorated. (*b*) *Commissionnaire m.*, badged porter. **2.** *s.* Holder of a medal; medallist; medal-winner, prize-winner.

médaillier [medaje], *s.m.* Collection of medals.

médaillon [medajɔ̃], *s.m.* **I.** (*a*) Medallion. (*b*) *Journ: etc:* Inset. Portrait **dans le médaillon**, inset portrait (in corner of larger illustration). **2.** Locket.

médecin [metsɛ̃, medsɛ̃], *s.m.* Medical man, doctor, physician. **Femme médecin**, lady doctor. *M. chirurgien*, general practitioner. *M. consultant*, consulting physician, consultant. *M. sanitaire*, medical officer.

médecine [metsin, medsin], *s.f.* **I.** (Art of) medicine. **Docteur en médecine**, doctor of medicine; M.D. **Étudiant en médecine**, medical student. *École de m.*, medical school. **2.** (Dose of) medicine. *M. noire*, black draught. **Prendre (une) médecine**, to take a dose of medicine, of physic. *F:* **Avaler la, sa, médecine**, to take one's gruel, one's punishment.

médial, -als, -aux [medjal, -o]. *Ling:* **I.** *a.* Medial (letter). **2.** *s.f.* **Médiale**, medial consonant, medial letter. *adv.* **-ement.**

médian [medjɑ̃], *a.* Median (nerve, line); mesial (line of the body). *Hairdr: Raie médiane*, parting in the middle.

médianique [medjanik], *a. Psychics:* Mediumistic.

médiat [medja], *a.* Mediate. *adv.* **-ement.**

médiateur, -trice [medjatœ:r, -tris]. **I.** *a.* Mediating, mediatory, mediative. **2.** *s.* Mediator; intermediary.

médiation [medjasjɔ̃], *s.f.* Mediation.

médical, -aux [medikal, -o], *a.* Medical. *Med:* **Matière médicale**, materia medica. **Certificat médical**, medical certificate.

médicament [medikamɑ̃], *s.m.* Medicament, *F:* medicine.

médicamenter [medikamɑ̃te], *v.tr. F:* To doctor, physic, dose (s.o.).

médicinal, -aux [medisinal, -o], *a.* Medicinal.

Médicis [medisis], *s.m.pl. Hist:* Medici (family). *Catherine de M.*, Catherine de' Medici.

médico-légal, -aux, *a.* Medico-legal.

médiéval, -aux [medjeval, -o], *a.* Medi(a)eval.

médiéviste [medjevist], *s.m. & f.* Medi(a)evalist.

médiocre [medjɔkr]. **I.** *a.* Medi'ocre; indifferent (work); feeble (performance); second-rate; moderate (ability); *F:* only so so. *Vin m.*, poor wine. **2.** *s.m.* Mediocrity. *adv.* **-ment.**

médiocrité [medjɔkrite], *s.f.* Mediocrity. **Vivre**

dans la médiocrité, to live (i) undistinguished, (ii) on a bare competency. *Ministère composé de médiocrités*, Ministry of second-raters.

médire [medi:r], *v.i.* (Conj. like DIRE, except *pr.ind.* and *imp.* **médisez**) *M. de qn*, to speak ill of s.o. ; to slander, vilify, s.o.

médisance [medizɑ̃:s], *s.f.* **1.** Slander, back-biting, scandal-mongering. *L'École de la médisance*, the School for Scandal. **2.** Piece of slander.

médisant, -ante [medizɑ̃, -ɑ̃:t]. **1.** *a.* Back-biting, scandal-mongering. **2.** *s.* Slanderer, back-biter, scandal-monger.

méditatif, -ive [meditatif, -i:v], *a.* Meditative.

méditation [meditasjɔ̃], *s.f.* Meditation, cogitation ; musing.

méditer [medite]. **1.** *v.i.* To meditate, to muse (*sur*, upon, over). **2.** *v.tr.* To contemplate (a journey, etc.) ; to ponder (sth.) ; to have (sth.) in mind. *M. la mort*, to contemplate suicide. *M. de faire qch.*, to be thinking of doing sth.

méditerrané [mediterane], *a.* Mediterranean, inland, landlocked. *La (mer) Méditerranée*, the Mediterranean (Sea).

méditerranéen, -enne [mediteraneɛ̃, -ɛn], *a.* Mediterranean (climate, etc.).

médium [medjɔm], *s.m. Psychics :* Medium.

médiumnique [medjɔmnik], *a. Psychics :* Mediumistic.

médius [medjy:s], *s.m.* Middle finger.

médoc [medɔk], *s.m.* (Also *vin de Médoc*) Medoc (claret).

médullaire [medylle:r], *a.* Medullary.

médulleux, -euse [medyllø, -ø:z], *a. Bot :* Medullary ; full of pith.

Méduse [medy:z]. **1.** *Pr.n.f. Gr.Myth :* Medusa. *F :* C'est la tête de Méduse, it is paralysing in its effect. **2.** *s.f. Coel :* Medusa, jelly-fish.

méduser [medyze], *v.tr. F :* To petrify ; to paralyse with fear or astonishment.

méfait [mefɛ], *s.m.* Misdeed, ill deed. *Méfaits d'un orage*, damage wrought by a storm. *Se déclarer l'auteur du m.*, to own up to the deed.

méfiance [mefjɑ̃:s], *s.f.* Distrust, mistrust. *Avoir de la m. envers, à l'égard de, qn*, to distrust s.o. *Regarder qn avec m.*, to eye s.o. distrustfully.

méfiant, *a.* Distrustful, mistrustful, suspicious (*à l'égard de, à l'endroit de,* of).

méfier (se) [səmefje], *v.pr.* (a) *Se m. de qn*, to distrust, mistrust, s.o. *Méfiez-vous des voleurs*, beware of pickpockets. (b) *Abs.* To be on one's guard.

mégalithe [megalit], *s.m.* Megalith.

mégalithique [megalitik], *a.* Megalithic.

mégalocéphale [megalɔsefal], *a. & s.* Megalocephalic, megalocephalous.

mégalocéphalie [megalɔsefali], *s.f.* Megalocephaly.

mégalomane [megalɔman], *s. m. & f.* Megalomaniac.

mégalomanie [megalɔmani], *s.f.* Megalomania.

mégaphone [megafɔn], *s.m.* Megaphone.

mégarde (par) [parmegard], *adv.phr.* Inadvertently ; through carelessness.

mégavolt [megavɔlt], *.m. El.Meas :* Megavolt.

mégère [meʒɛ:r], *s.f.* Shrew, termagant, scold. *La Mégère mise à la raison*, the Taming of the Shrew.

mégerg [megɛrg], *s.m. Mec.Meas :* Megerg, megaerg ; a million ergs.

mégir [meʒi:r], **mégisser** [meʒise], *v.tr.* To taw, dress (light skins).

mégis [meʒi], *a.m.* Cuir mégis, tawed leather, white leather.

mégisserie [meʒisri], *s.f.* · **1.** Tawing (of skins). **2.** Tawery.

mégissier [meʒisje], *s.m. Tan :* Tawer.

mégohm [mego:m], *s.m. El.Meas :* Megohm.

mégot [mego], *s.m. F :* Fag-end (of cigarette) ; stump, butt (of cigar).

méhalla [meala], *s.f.* (In N. Africa) **1.** Desert camping place. **2.** Column of troops.

méhari [meari], *s.m.* Fast dromedary ; racing camel. *pl. Des méhara.*

meilleur, -eure [mejœːr], *a.* **1.** Better, etc. (*Cf.* the several meanings of BON. *Rendre qch. m.*, to improve sth. *Devenir m.*, to grow better ; to improve. *De meilleure heure*, earlier. *Les choses prennent une meilleure tournure*, things are taking a turn for the better. *adv.* Il fait meilleur, the weather is better. *Il fait m. ici*, it is pleasanter, milder, here. **2.** *Le meilleur*, (i) the better (of two) ; (ii) the best. *Nous sommes les meilleurs amis du monde*, we are the best of friends. *s. Le m. est de s'en aller*, it is best to go away. *Nous avons bu de son meilleur*, we drank of his best. *Du meilleur de mon cœur*, with all my heart.

méjuger [meʒyʒe], *v.tr.* (Conj. like JUGER) *A :* To misjudge.

mélancolie [melɑ̃kɔli], *s.f.* **1.** Melancholy, dejection, mournfulness. **2.** *Med :* Melancholia.

mélancolique [melɑ̃kɔlik], *a.* **1.** Melancholy, dejected, gloomy, mournful. **2.** *Med :* Melancholic.

mélancoliquement[melɑ̃kɔlikmɑ̃],*adv.* Mournfully, gloomily.

Mélanésie [melanezi]. *Pr.n.f. Geog :* Melanesia.

mélange [melɑ̃:ʒ], *s.m.* **1.** Mixing ; blending (of tea, etc.) ; crossing (of breeds) ; mingling. **2.** Mixture ; blend (of tea, etc.) ; intermixture (of breeds, etc.) ; mix (of cement, etc.). *I.C.E : M. explosif, tonnant*, explosive mixture. *Lit : Mélanges en prose*, prose miscellany.

mélanger [melɑ̃ʒe], *v.tr.* (je mélangeai(s) ; n. mélangeons) To mix, to mingle ; to blend (teas). **se mélanger**, (of liquids, etc.) to mix, to mingle, to blend.

mélangeoir [melɑ̃ʒwa:r], *s.m.*, **mélangeur** [melɑ̃ʒœːr], *s.m.*, **mélangeuse** [melɑ̃ʒø:z], *s.f.* Mixer, mixing-machine. *Cin :* Mélangeur de sons, mixing panel ; mixer.

mélasse [melas], *s.f.* Molasses, *F :* treacle. *M. raffinée*, golden syrup. *P :* Être dans la mélasse, to be in the soup.

mêlée [mele], *s.f.* (a) Conflict, fray, mêlée. (b) *F :* Scuffle, tussle, free fight. (c) Scramble. (d) *Rugby :* Scrimmage, *F :* scrum.

mêler [mele], *v.tr.* To mix, mingle, blend. (a) *M. qch. avec, à, qch.*, to mix sth. with sth. Il mêle toujours son mot à la conversation ; il mêle partout son mot, he is always putting his word in every pie. Il est mêlé à tout, *F :* he has a finger in every pie. *M. son vin d'eau*, to mix water with one's wine. (b) To put out of order ; to throw into confusion ; to tangle. Mêler les cartes, to shuffle the cards. *F :* Vous avez bien mêlé les cartes! a nice tangle, a nice mess, you've made of it ! *M. une serrure*, to tangle up, spoil, a lock. (c) *M. qn à, dans, qch.*, to implicate s.o., involve s.o., in sth. *M. qn à la conversation*, to bring s.o. into the conversation. *s.m.* **-ement.** **se mêler**, to mix, mingle, blend. *Se m. à, dans, la foule*, to mingle with, lose oneself in, the crowd. *Se m. à la conversation*, to take part in the conversation ; *F :* to chip in. *Se m. de qch.*, to take a hand in sth. Ce n'est pas à moi de m'en mêler, it's not for me to interfere. *F :* Le diable s'en mêle! the devil's in it ! Se mêler de politique, to dabble in politics.

mêlé, *a.* Tangled (skein, hair) ; tous r

(hair); involved (business). *F:* **Avoir la langue mêlée,** to speak thickly (when intoxicated).
mélèze [melε:z], *s.m.* Larch(-tree or -wood).
mélilot [melilo], *s.m.* Melilot; sweet clover.
méli-mélo [melimelo], *s.m. P:* Jumble (of facts, etc.); hotchpotch; medley (of people, etc.); clutter (of furniture).
mélinite [melinit], *s.f. Exp:* Melinite.
mélique [melik], *s.f. Bot:* Melic(-grass).
mélisse [melis], *s.f. Bot:* Melissa, balm. **Eau de mélisse,** melissa cordial.
melliflu [mεllifly], *a.* Mellifluous, honeyed, sugary (eloquence, etc.).
mélo [melo], *s.m. F:* **Le mélo** = the transpontine melodrama.
mélodie [melɔdi], *s.f.* **1.** Melody, tune. **2.** Melodiousness (of verse, etc.).
mélodieu|x, -euse [melɔdjø, -ø:z], *a.* Melodious, tuneful. *adv.* **-sement.**
mélodique [melɔdik], *a. Mus:* Melodic.
mélodramatique [melɔdramatik], *a.* Melodramatic.
mélodrame [melɔdram], *s.m.* Melodrama. *Auteur de mélodrames,* melodramatist.
mélomane [melɔman], *a. & s* Melomaniac. *Être m.,* to be music-mad.
melon [mɔlɔ̃], *s.m.* **1.** *Bot:* Melon. *M. d'eau,* water-melon. **2.** *P:* Simpleton, fat-head. **3.** (Chapeau) melon, bowler (hat), billycock.
melonnière [mǝlɔnjε:r], *s.f.* Melon bed.
mélopée [melɔpe], *s.f. Mus:* **1.** Art of recitative. **2.** (*a*) Chant, recitative. (*b*) Singsong.
membrane [mãbran], *s.f.* **1.** (*a*) Membrane. (*b*) Web (of web-footed bird). (*c*) *M. poreuse,* porous membrane, diaphragm. **2.** *Tp:* **Membrane phonique,** diaphragm. *Gramophones: M. du diaphragme,* diaphragm of the sound-box.
membrané [mãbrane], *a.* (*a*) Membranous; membranated. (*b*) Webbed (fingers, toes).
membraneux, -euse [mãbranø, -ø:z], *a.* Membranous.
membre [mã:br], *s.m.* Member. **1.** (*a*) Limb. (*b*) Member or fellow (of an association). *M. du Parlement,* member of Parliament. **2.** Constituent part. (*a*) *Les membres de la phrase,* the members of the sentence. *Premier m. d'une équation,* left-hand side of an equation. (*b*) Rib or timber (of ship).
membré [mãbre], *a.* **Cheval bien membré,** well-limbed horse. *Homme fortement m.,* strong-limbed man.
membrure [mãbry:r], *s.f.* **1.** (*a*) Coll. Limbs. *Homme à forte m.,* powerfully built man. (*b*) Frame(work) (of building, etc.). (*c*) *Coll.* The ribs (of ship). **2.** Flange (of web-girder).
même [mε:m]. **I.** *a.* (*a*) Same. *Une seule et m. chose,* one and the same thing. *Ils sont du m. âge, de m. taille,* they are of an age, of a size. *Ce m. jour . . .,* the same day. . . . **En même temps,** at the same time; at once. *Il (Elle) est toujours le (la) m.,* he (she) is always the same. *Pron.neut.* *Cela revient au même,* it comes, amounts, to the same thing. (*b*) (Following the noun) Very. *Il habite ici m.,* he lives in this very place, or in this very house. **C'est cela même,** that's the very thing. *Donner les chiffres mêmes,* to give the actual figures. (*c*) Self. *Elle est la bonté même,* she is kindness itself. **Moi-même,** myself. **Toi-même,** thyself. **Lui-même,** himself, itself. **Elle-même,** herself, itself. **Soi-même,** oneself. **Nous-mêmes,** ourselves. **Vous-même,** yourself. **Vous-mêmes,** yourselves. **Eux-mêmes, elles-mêmes,** themselves. *Il l'a fait lui-même,* he did it himself. **Faire qch. de soi-même,** to do sth. of one's own

accord. *Un autre lui-même,* a second self. **2.** *adv.* Even. *Aimer m. ses ennemis,* to love even one's enemies. *Je n'ai pas m. le prix de mon voyage,* I haven't so much as my fare. *M. si je le savais,* even if I knew. *S.a.* QUAND **1. 3. De même,** in the same way; likewise. **Faire de même,** to do likewise; to do the same. *Il en est de m. des autres,* so it is with the others. *Il en est de m. pour . . .,* the same holds true, holds good, in respect of. . . . **De même que,** (just) as, like. *De même que + ind. . . . de même + ind. . . .,* (just) as . . . so (also). . . . **Tout de même,** all the same; for all that. *Je l'aime tout de m.,* I like him nevertheless. **Boire à même la bouteille,** to drink straight out of the bottle. *Des maisons bâties à m. le trottoir,* houses built flush with the pavement. *Tout cela se passait à m. la rue,* all this took place in the very street. *Escalier taillé à m. la pierre,* steps cut out of the solid rock. *Il prit un abricot et mordit à m.,* he took an apricot and bit into it. **Être à même de faire qch.,** to be able to do sth.; to have it in one's power, to be in a position, to do sth. *Il n'est pas à m. de faire le voyage,* he is not equal to, up to, taking the journey. *Mettre les chômeurs à m. de gagner leur vie,* to put the unemployed in the way of earning their living.
mémento [memε̃to], *s.m.* **1.** (*a*) Memorandum, note. *Bloc m.,* scribbling block. (*b*) Memento, reminder. **2.** (*a*) Note-book, memorandum-book. (*b*) *Sch:* *M. de chimie,* synopsis of chemistry.
mémo [memo], *s.m. F:* = MÉMORANDUM.
mémoire[1] [memwa:r], *s.f.* Memory. (*a*) *Je n'ai pas le nom, des noms,* I have no memory for names. **Si j'ai bonne mémoire,** if I remember rightly. *F:* **Mémoire de lièvre,** memory like a sieve. (*b*) Recollection, remembrance. *Perdre la m. de qch.,* to forget sth. *Garder la m. de qch.,* to keep sth. in mind. *Avoir m. de qch.,* to remember sth. *Rappeler qch. à la m. de qn,* to recall sth. to s.o.'s mind. *Je vais lui rafraîchir la m.,* I'll send him a reminder. *Jamais de m. d'homme,* never within living memory. **En mémoire de qn, à la mémoire de qn,** (monument, etc.) in memory of s.o., to the memory of s.o.
mémoire[2], *s.m.* **1.** (*a*) Memorial; (written) statement (of case); specifications (of patent). (*b*) Memoir, dissertation, thesis. **2.** (Contractor's) account; bill (of costs). *S.a.* APOTHICAIRE. **3.** *pl.* (*a*) (Historical) memoirs. (*b*) Transactions (of learned society).
mémorable [memɔrabl], *a.* Memorable, noteworthy; eventful (year). *adv.* **-ment.**
mémorandum [memɔrãdɔm], *s.m.* **1.** Memorandum, note. **2.** Note-book.
mémorial, -aux [memɔrjal, -o], *s.m.* **1.** Memorial; memoirs. **2.** *Com:* Waste-book, day-book.
mémorisation [memɔrizasjɔ̃], *s.f.* Memorizing, memorization.
menaçant [mǝnasã], *a.* Menacing, threatening; forbidding (look); lowering (sky).
menace [mǝnas], *s.f.* Threat, menace. *pl. Jur:* Intimidation. *Menaces en l'air,* empty threats, idle threats. *Menaces de part et d'autre,* threats and counter-threats.
menacer [mǝnase], *v.tr.* (je menaçai(s); n. menaçons) To threaten, menace. (*a*) **Menacer qn du doigt, du poing,** to wag one's finger at s.o.; to shake one's fist at s.o. *M. qn d'un procès,* to threaten s.o. with legal proceedings. *M. de faire qch.,* to threaten to do sth. (*b*) **Menacer ruine,** to be in danger of falling to pieces.
ménade [menad], *s.f.* Maenad, bacchante.
ménage [mena:ʒ], *s.m.* **1.** (*a*) Housekeeping,

housewifery; domestic arrangements. **Faire ménage avec qn,** to keep house with s.o. **Entrer en ménage,** to set up house(keeping). *Pain de m.,* household bread, home-made bread. (b) **Faire le ménage,** to do the housework. **Faire des ménages,** to go out charring. **Femme de ménage,** (i) charwoman; (ii) housekeeper. **2.** Household goods. *M. de poupée,* set of doll's furniture. **Je suis dans mon ménage,** I have furnished a house of my own. **3.** Household, family. (a) *Jeune ménage,* young (married) couple. *"On demande un m. recommandable,"* 'respectable couple wanted.' **Se mettre en ménage,** to set up house; to enter upon married life. (b) **Faire bon, mauvais, ménage** (*ensemble*), to live, get on, happily, unhappily, together. **4.** *A:* Thrift. **Vivre de ménage,** to live thriftily.

ménagement [menaʒmã], *s.m.* Caution, care, circumspection, consideration. **Avoir des ménagements pour qn,** to treat s.o. with consideration; to have regard for s.o., for s.o.'s feelings. **Parler sans ménagement(s),** to speak bluntly.

ménager[1] [menaʒe], *v.tr.* (**je ménageai(s)**; n. **ménageons**) **1.** (a) To save; to be sparing of (sth.); to use (sth.) economically. *M. ses ressources,* to husband one's resources. *M. sa santé,* to take care of one's health. *M. son cheval,* to spare, nurse, one's horse. *Prov:* **Qui veut aller loin ménage sa monture,** slow and steady wins the race. *M. qn,* to deal tactfully, gently, with s.o. **Ne le ménagez pas,** don't spare him. S.a. CHÈVRE 1. (b) To use (words) with circumspection, with tact. **Sans ménager ses termes,** without mincing one's words. **2.** To contrive, arrange. (a) *M. à qn l'occasion de faire qch.,* to arrange, make, provide, an opportunity for s.o. to do sth. *M. une surprise à qn,* to prepare a surprise for s.o. (b) *M. une ouverture pour les fils,* to make, adjust, an opening for the wires. *M. une sortie,* to provide an exit.

ménager[2], **-ère** [menaʒe, -ɛːr]. **1.** *a.* (a) Connected with the house. *Travaux ménagers,* housework. *Enseignement m.,* domestic science. *Eau ménagère,* water for domestic use. *Eaux ménagères,* waste water; slops. (b) Housewifely (virtues, etc.). (c) Thrifty, sparing. *s.* **Être bon ménager du temps,** to know how to make the most of one's time. *Être m. de ses éloges,* to be chary, sparing, of praise. **2.** *s.f.* **Ménagère.** (a) (i) Housekeeper, housewife. (ii) Charwoman. (b) Cruet-stand.

ménagerie [menaʒri], *s.f.* Menagerie.

menant [mənã], *a.* *Mec.E:* Driving. *Brin m.,* driving side (of belt).

mendiant, -ante [mãdjã, -ãːt]. **1.** *a.* Mendicant, begging (friar, etc.). **2.** *s.* Mendicant; beggar(-man, -woman). **Les quatre mendiants,** (i) *Ecc.Hist:* the four mendicant orders; (ii) *F:* almonds, raisins, nuts and figs.

mendicité [mãdisite], *s.f.* (a) Mendicity, mendicancy, begging. **Dépôt de mendicité,** workhouse. (b) *Réduit à la m.,* reduced to beggary.

mendier [mãdje]. **1.** *v.i.* To beg. *Faire son chemin jusqu'à Paris en mendiant,* to beg one's way to Paris. **2.** *v.tr. M. son pain,* to beg (for) one's bread. *M. sa vie,* to live by begging.

meneau [məno], *s.m.* *Arch:* *M. vertical,* mullion. *M. horizontal,* transom.

menée [məne], *s.f.* **1.** *Ven:* Track. **Chasser menée,** to follow the track. **2.** Underhand manœuvre, intrigue. *pl.* Schemings (of political party, etc.). *Déjouer les menées de qn,* to thwart s.o.; to outwit s.o.

mener [məne, mne], *v.tr.* (**je mène**; **je mènerai**)

1. To lead. (a) *M. qn à sa chambre,* to conduct, take, s.o. to his room. *M. qn voir qch.,* to take s.o. to see sth. *Danc: M. une dame,* to partner a lady. *Geom: M. une ligne entre deux points,* to draw a line between two points. (b) To be or go ahead (of). *M. la danse,* to lead the dance. *M. le deuil,* to be chief mourner. *Games: M. par huit points,* to lead by eight points. (c) *Chemin qui mène à la ville,* road that leads to the town. *Cela nous mène à croire que . . .,* that leads us to believe that. . . . (d) To control, manage. *Mari mené par sa femme,* hen-pecked husband. *M. ses gens au doigt et à l'œil,* to have one's people well trained, well schooled. **2.** To drive (horse, motor car); to ride (motor cycle); to steer (boat). *M. trois chevaux de front,* to drive three horses abreast. *F:* **Mener plusieurs choses de front,** to have several irons in the fire. S.a. TRAIN 2. *Mec.E:* **Roue menée,** driven wheel. **3.** To manage, conduct (business, etc.). **Mener qch. à bonne fin, à bien,** to bring sth. to a successful issue; to carry through, carry out (mission, etc.); to work out (plan). *M. une vie triste,* to lead a sad life. *F:* **N'en pas mener large,** to be in a tight corner.

ménestrel [menestrɛl], *s.m.* Minstrel, gleeman.

ménétrier [menetrie], *s.m.* (Strolling) fiddler.

meneur, -euse [m(ə)nœːr, -øːz], *s.* (a) Leader (of blind man, etc.); partner (of lady in a dance). (b) Ringleader (of revolt, etc.); agitator. (c) Driver (of machine, etc.). (d) *M. de bœufs,* cattle-drover. *M. d'ours,* bear-leader.

menhir [meniːr], *s.m.* Menhir; standing stone.

méninge [menɛ̃ːʒ], *s.f.* *Anat:* Meninx. **Les trois méninges,** the three meninges.

méningite [menɛ̃ʒit], *s.f.* *Med:* Meningitis.

ménisque [menisk], *s.m.* Meniscus.

menotte [mənɔt], *s.f.* **1.** (a) *F:* (Child's) little hand. (b) Handle (of winch). **2.** (a) *pl.* Handcuffs, manacles. **Mettre les menottes à qn,** to handcuff s.o. (b) Link, shackle (of shaft, spring).

menotter [mənɔte], *v.tr.* To handcuff.

men-s, -t. See MENTIR.

mensonge [mãsɔ̃ːʒ], *s.m.* (a) Lie, untruth, falsehood; *F:* story. **Faire, dire, un mensonge,** to tell a lie, a story. *M. blanc,* white lie. *Gros m.,* whopping lie; whopper. (b) Error, fallacy, delusion. *Tout n'est que m.,* all is vanity.

mensonger, -ère [mãsɔ̃ʒe, -ɛːr], *a.* Lying, untrue, mendacious (story); deceitful (look); vain, illusory (hope).

mensongèrement [mãsɔ̃ʒɛrmã], *adv.* Falsely, untruthfully, mendaciously.

mensualité [mãsɥalite], *s.f.* (a) Monthly nature (of payments, etc.). (b) Monthly payment or remittance. *Payer par mensualités,* to pay by monthly instalments.

mensuel, -elle [mãsɥel], *a.* Monthly.

mensuellement [mãsɥelmã], *adv.* Monthly; each month.

mensur|able [mãsyrabl], *a.* Mensurable, measurable. *s.f.* **-abilité.**

mensuration [mãsyrasjɔ̃], *s.f.* Measurement. **1.** Measuring; *Geom:* mensuration. **2.** *Anthr:* **Prendre les mensurations de qn,** to take s.o.'s measurements.

mentagre [mãtaːgr], *s.f.* Sycosis; barber's itch.

mental, -aux [mãtal, -o], *a.* Mental (arithmetic, etc.). S.a. ALIÉNATION 3. *adv.* **-ement.**

mentalité [mãtalite], *s.f.* Mentality.

menterie [mãtri], *s.f.* *F:* Fib, story.

menteu|r, -euse [mãtœːr, -øːz]. **1.** *a.* (a) Lying, mendacious, fibbing, story-telling (person); given

to lying. (b) False, deceptive (appearance).
2. s. Liar, fibber, story-teller. adv. **-sement.**

menthe [mã:t], s.f. Bot: Mint. M. verte, spearmint, garden mint. M. anglaise, poivrée, peppermint. Pastilles de m., peppermint lozenges; peppermints.

menthol [mɛ̃tɔl], s.m. Menthol.

mention [mɑ̃sjɔ̃], s.f. (a) Mention. Faire m. de qch., to make mention of, to refer to, to mention, sth. Sch: Reçu avec mention, passed with distinction. (b) Post: Endorsement (on envelope, etc.). M. "inconnu," endorsed 'not known.' Publ: Mention de réserve, Journ: mention d'interdiction, copyright notice. (c) Reference (at head of letter).

mentionner [mɑ̃sjɔne], v.tr. To mention. Mentionné ci-dessus, above-mentioned, aforesaid.

mentir [mɑ̃ti:r], v.i. (pr.p. mentant; p.p. menti; pr.ind. je mens, il ment, n. mentons, ils mentent; p.h. je mentis; fu. je mentirai) To lie, F: to fib; to tell lies, stories. Sans mentir! honour bright! Il en a menti par la gorge! he lies in his throat! Faire m. un proverbe, to belie a proverb. S.a. ARRACHEUR, BEAU I. 4.

menton [mɑ̃tɔ̃], s.m. Chin. M. de, en, galoche, slipper-chin, undershot jaw. M. effacé, receding chin. F: S'en mettre jusqu'au menton, to gorge; to have a good tuck-in.

mentonnet [mɑ̃tɔne], s.m. (a) Catch (of latch, etc.); stop (on moving part of machine). (b) Mec.E: Tappet, cam. (c) Rail: Flange (of wheel). (d) Lug; ear (of bomb).

mentonnière [mɑ̃tɔnjɛ:r], s.f. (a) Archeol: Chin-piece (of helmet). (b) (Bonnet-)string. Mil: Check-strap, -chain. Surg: Chin-bandage. (c) Mus: Chin-rest (of violin).

mentor [mɛ̃tɔ:r], s.m. Mentor; 'guide, philosopher and friend.'

menu [mǝny]. **I.** a. Small. (a) Fine (gravel, etc.); slender, slim, slight (figure); tiny, little (fragment). Menu plomb, small shot, bird shot. Menue monnaie, small change. S.a. BÉTAIL. (b) Trifling (incident, etc.). Menues réparations, minor repairs. Menus détails, small, minute, details. Menus frais, (i) petty expenses; (ii) pocket-money. Le menu peuple, the humbler classes. Menus propos, small talk. **2.** adv. Small, fine. Hacher menu, to chop (meat, etc.) up small; to mince (sth.). Il pleuvait dru et menu, the rain came down in a steady drizzle. **3.** s.m. (a) M. du charbon, small coal. (b) Raconter qch. par le menu, to relate sth. in detail. (c) Bill of fare, menu (of a meal).

menuet [mǝnɥɛ], s.m. Minuet.

menuiser [mǝnɥize], v.tr. **1.** To cut down, plane down (wood to size). **2.** Abs. To do joiner's work, woodwork. s.m. **-age.**

menuiserie [mǝnɥizri], s.f. **1.** Joinery, woodwork, carpentry. **2.** Joiner's shop.

menuisier, -ière [mǝnɥizje, -jɛ:r]. **1.** a. Abeille menuisière, carpenter bee. **2.** s.m. Joiner. M. en meubles, cabinet-maker. M. en bâtiments, carpenter.

ménure [meny:r], s.m. Orn: Menura, lyre-bird.

méphitique [mefitik], a. Mephitic, foul, noxious, noisome.

méplat [mepla]. **1.** a. (a) Flat. Const: (Of joist) Flat-laid. Fer méplat, flat bar-iron. Bois méplat, wood in planks. (b) Art: Lignes méplates, lines showing up the different planes (of the face, etc.). **2.** s.m. (a) Flat part; flatted end; ledge (of rock). (b) Art: Méplats du visage, planes that build up the face.

méprendre (se) [sǝmeprɑ̃:dr], v.pr. (Conj. like

PRENDRE) To be mistaken, to make a mistake (sur, quant à, about, regarding). Se m. sur un motif, to mistake, misjudge, a motive. Il n'y a pas à s'y méprendre, there can be no mistake about it. Il imitait le maître à s'y m., he could imitate the master to the life.

mépris [mepri], s.m. Contempt, scorn. M. des richesses, contempt for, scorn of, riches. Tenir qn en m., to hold s.o. in contempt. Avoir un souverain m. pour qn, to hold s.o. in sovereign contempt. Faire mépris de qch., to despise sth. Au, en, mépris de qch., in contempt of sth. Avec mépris, scornfully, contemptuously. Sourire de m., contemptuous smile. Prov: La familiarité engendre le mépris, familiarity breeds contempt.

méprisable [meprizabl], a. Contemptible, despicable.

méprisant [meprizɑ̃], a. Contemptuous, scornful.

méprise [mepri:z], s.f. Mistake, misapprehension. Par méprise, by mistake.

mépriser [meprize], v.tr. To despise, scorn; to hold (s.o.) in contempt. Méprisé de, par, qn, despised by s.o. M. de faire qch., to scorn to do sth. M. les dangers, to make light of dangers.

mer [mɛ:r], s.f. Sea. (a) La haute mer, la grande mer, the open sea, the high seas. En haute mer, en pleine mer, on the high seas, out at sea. Le bord de la mer, the seaside. Mal de mer, sea-sickness. Avoir le mal de mer, to be sea-sick. Homme, gens, de mer, seaman, seamen; sea-faring man, men. Grosse mer, heavy sea. Il y a de la mer, there is a heavy sea. Essuyer un coup de mer, to be struck by a heavy sea. Tomber à la mer, to fall overboard. Un homme à la mer! man overboard! Sur mer, afloat. Servir sur mer, to serve afloat, to serve at sea. Prendre la mer, to set sail; to put (out) to sea. Mettre une embarcation à la mer, to get out, lower, a boat. Tenir la mer, to keep the sea, to remain at sea. Vaisseau qui tient bien la mer, ship that behaves well in a sea-way. S.a. BOIRE I. 1, COUP 1. (b) (= MARÉE) Tide. Mer haute, pleine mer, high tide. Basse mer, low tide.

mercanti [mɛrkãti], s.m. **1.** (a) (Oriental) bazaar-keeper. (b) Mil: A: Camp-follower. **2.** F: Low-class profiteer; shark.

mercantile [mɛrkãtil], a. **1.** Mercantile (operation, etc.); commercial. **2.** Esprit m., grabbing, money-making, spirit.

mercantilisme [mɛrkãtilism], s.m. Pej: Mercantilism, money-grabbing, profiteering.

mercenaire [mɛrsǝnɛ:r]. **1.** a. Mercenary, venal. **2.** s.m. Mil: Mercenary.

mercerie [mɛrsǝri], s.f. **1.** Small wares, haberdashery. **2.** Small-ware shop.

merceriser [mɛrsǝrize], v.tr. Tex: To mercerize. s.m. **-age.**

merci [mɛrsi]. **1.** s.f. (a) A: Favour. F: Dieu merci, by the favour of God; thank God. (b) A: Pleasure, discretion. A merci, at pleasure. A: Se rendre à merci, to surrender unconditionally. (c) Mercy. Être à la m. de qn, to lie at s.o.'s mercy. Crier merci, to cry quarter. Sans merci, merciless(ly), pitiless(ly). **2.** adv. (a) Thank you. Merci bien, thank you very much. (b) No, thank you. Prenez-vous du thé? —Merci! Will you have some tea? —No, thank you! no, thanks! **3.** s.m. Adresser un cordial m. à qn, to thank s.o. heartily. Usu. Iron: Grand merci! no, thank you!

mercier, -ière [mɛrsje, -jɛ:r], s. Small-ware dealer; haberdasher.

mercredi [mɛrkrədi], *s.m.* Wednesday. **Le mercredi des Cendres**, Ash-Wednesday.

Mercure [mɛrky:r]. **1.** *Pr.n.m.* Mercury. **2.** *s.m. Ch:* Mercury, quicksilver. S.a. LAMPE 2.

mercuriale[1] [mɛrkyrjal], *s.f. Bot:* Mercury. *M. vivace*, dog's mercury.

mercuriale[2], *s.f.* Reprimand, dressing-down.

mercuriale[3], *s.f.* Market price-list, market prices (of corn, etc.).

mercuriel, -elle [mɛrkyrjɛl], *a. Pharm:* Mercurial (ointment, etc.).

mère[1] [mɛ:r], *s.f.* Mother. **1.** (*a*) *Elle est m. de famille*, she is the mother of a family. **Enfants sans mère**, motherless children. *M. nourrice*, foster-mother. (*b*) *Husb:* (i) *M. poule*, mother-hen. (ii) *Dam* (of a beast). (*c*) *F:* **La mère Dupont**, old Mrs Dupont. *P:* **Eh dites donc, la petite mère!** I say, Missis! S.a. CONTE 1. (*d*) *Ecc:* **Mère supérieure**, mother superior (of nunnery). **2.** (Source, origin) (*a*) *L'oisiveté est la m. de tous les vices*, idleness is the source, the root, of all evil (*b*) (i) *Mould*, matrix (for plaster casts, etc.). (ii) *Mec.E:* Die (of screw-thread). **3.** *Attrib.* (*a*) **La Reine Mère**, the Queen Mother. (*b*) **Langue mère**, mother language (of other languages). *Biol:* **Cellule m.**, mother cell. *Com:* **Maison mère**, parent establishment.

mère[2], *a.f.* Pure. **1. Vin de la mère goutte**, wine from the first pressing. **2. Mère laine**, mother wool.

mère-patrie, *s.f.* Parent state (of colonies); metropolis. *pl. Des mères-patries.*

merganser [mɛrgɑ̃sɛ:r], *s.m. Orn:* Merganser, goosander.

méricarpe [merikarp], *s.m. Bot:* Mericarp.

méridien, -ienne [meridjɛ̃, -jɛn]. **1.** *a.* (*a*) Meridian, meridional (line, etc.). (*b*) *Chaleur méridienne*, midday heat. *Ombre méridienne*, shadow at noon. *Cercle m.*, transit(-circle). **2.** *s.m.* Meridian. *Sous le m. de vingt degrés à l'ouest de Greenwich*, twenty degrees west of Greenwich. (Of star) *Passer le méridien*, to south. **3.** *s.f.* **Méridienne.** (*a*) (i) Meridian line. (ii) Meridian altitude. (*b*) *F:* Midday nap; siesta.

méridional, -aux [meridjɔnal, -o]. **1.** *a.* (*a*) Meridional (distance, etc.). (*b*) South(ern). **2.** *s.* Southerner; meridional (esp of France).

meringue [mərɛ̃g], *s.f. Cu:* Meringue.

meringuer [mərɛ̃ge], *v.tr. Cu:* **1.** To enclose (sweet, etc.) in a meringue shell. **2.** *Pommes meringuées*, apple snow.

mérinos [merinɔs], *s.m.* Merino (sheep, cloth).

merise [məri:z], *s.f.* Wild cherry; gean.

merisier [mərizje], *s.m.* Wild cherry(-tree).

méritant [meritɑ̃] *a.* Meritorious, deserving. **Peu méritant**, undeserving.

mérite [merit], *s.m.* Merit. (*a*) Desert, worth. *Chose de peu de m.*, thing of little worth. *S'attribuer le m. de qch.*, to take the credit for sth. *Il faut dire à son m. que . . . .*, it must be said to his credit, in his praise, that. . . . (*b*) Excellence, talent. *Homme de m.*, man of talent, of ability.

mériter [merite], *v.tr.* **1.** To deserve, merit. *Il n'a que ce qu'il mérite*, he has only got his deserts. *Bien m. de sa patrie*, to deserve well of one's country. *Cela mérite réflexion*, it is worth thinking over. *Cela mérite d'être vu, entendu*, it is worth seeing, hearing. **2.** *Voilà ce qui lui a mérité cette faveur*, that is what earned him, entitled him to, this favour.

méritoire [meritwa:r], *a.* Meritorious, deserving.

merlan [mɛrlɑ̃], *s.m. Ich:* Whiting. *P:* **Faire des yeux de merlan frit à qn**, (i) to gaze ecstatically at s.o.; (ii) to cock up one's eyes at s.o.

merle [mɛrl], *s.m. Orn:* **1.** Blackbird. *F:* **Jaser comme un merle**, to chatter like a magpie. *C'est un fin merle*, he's a cunning old bird. **Merle blanc**, (i) white crow; (ii) *F:* rara avis. S.a. GRIVE. **2. Merle d'eau**, water-ouzel.

merlette [mɛrlɛt], *s.f.* Hen-blackbird.

merlin[1] [mɛrlɛ̃], *s.m. Nau:* Marline; small stuff.

merlin[2], *s.m.* Axe, cleaver; felling-axe; pole-axe.

Merlin[3]. *Pr.n.m. Medieval Lit:* Merlin.

merluche [mɛrlyʃ], *s.f.* **1.** *Ich:* Hake. **2.** Dried cod, stockfish.

mérovingien, -ienne [merɔvɛ̃ʒjɛ̃, -jɛn], *a. & s. Hist:* Merovingian.

merrain [mɛrɛ̃], *s.m.* **1.** Cask wood, stave-wood; wood for cooperage. **2.** Beam (of deer's antlers).

merveille [mɛrvɛ:j], *s.f.* Marvel, wonder. **Les sept merveilles du monde**, the seven wonders of the world. **Faire merveille, faire des merveilles**, to work, perform, wonders. **Crier merveille**, to exclaim in admiration. *Les Aventures d'Alice au pays des Merveilles*, Alice's Adventures in Wonderland. **A merveille**, excellently; wonderfully well. *Cette robe vous va à m.*, this dress suits you to a T. *Se porter à m.*, to be in excellent health. *Ce chèque tombe à m.*, this cheque is most welcome. S.a. MONT.

merveilleu|x, -euse [mɛrvɛjø, -ø:z]. **1.** *a.* Marvellous, wonderful. *s. Je ne crois pas au m.*, I don't believe in the supernatural. **2.** *s. Hist:* = INCROYABLE. *adv.* **-sement.**

mes. See MON.

mésalliance [mezaljɑ̃:s], *s.f.* Improper alliance (esp. by marriage); misalliance. *Faire une m.*, to marry beneath one.

mésallier (se) [səmezalje], *v.pr.* To marry beneath one, below one's station.

mésange [mezɑ̃:ʒ], *s.f. Orn:* Tit(mouse). *M. charbonnière*, great tit, tomtit.

mésaventure [mezavɑ̃ty:r], *s.f.* Misadventure, mishap, mischance.

mesdames, -demoiselles. See MADAME, MADEMOISELLE.

mésentente [mezɑ̃tɑ̃:t], *s.f.* Misunderstanding, disagreement.

mésentère [mezɑ̃tɛ:r], *s.m. Anat:* Mesentery.

mésestimation [mezɛstimasjɔ̃], *s.f.* Underestimation, underrating, undervaluing.

mésestime [mezɛstim], *s.f.* Disesteem, low esteem. *Tenir qn en m.*, to have a poor opinion of s.o. *Encourir la m. de qn*, to fall in s.o.'s opinion.

mésestimer [mezɛstime], *v.tr.* **1.** To underestimate, undervalue, underrate. **2.** To hold (s.o.) in low esteem.

mésintelligence [mezɛ̃teliʒɑ̃:s], *s.f.* Disagreement. **Être en mésintelligence avec qn**, to be at variance, at loggerheads, with s.o.

mésinterprétation [mezɛ̃tɛrpretasjɔ̃], *s.f.* Misinterpretation.

mésinterpréter [mezɛ̃tɛrprete], *v.tr.* (Conj. like INTERPRÉTER) To misinterpret, misconstrue.

mesmérique [mɛsmerik], *a.* Mesmeric.

mesmérisme [mɛsmerism], *s.m.* Mesmerism.

mésocarpe [mezɔkarp], *s.m. Bot:* Mesocarp.

mésoderme [mezɔdɛrm], *s.m. Biol:* Mesoderm.

Mésopotamie [mezɔpotami]. *Pr.n.f.* Mesopotamia.

mesquin [mɛskɛ̃], *a.* (*a*) Mean, shabby (appearance); paltry, petty (excuse, etc.). (*b*) Mean, niggardly, stingy. *adv.* **-ement.**

mesquinerie [mɛskinri], *s.f.* **1.** Meanness. (*a*) Pettiness, paltriness. (*b*) Niggardliness. **2.** Shabby action.

message [mɛsaːʒ], *s.m.* Message.
messager, -ère [mɛsaʒe, -ɛːr], *s.* **1.** Messenger. Messager d'État, messenger of State. *Lit:* M. du *printemps*, harbinger of spring. *a.* Pigeon messager, carrier pigeon. **2.** *s.m.* Carrier.
messagerie [mɛsaʒri], *s.f.* Carrying trade. Service de messageries, parcel post, parcel delivery. Messageries maritimes, (i) sea transport of goods; (ii) shipping line. Bureau de(s) messageries, (i) A : stage-coach office; (ii) shipping office; (iii) *Rail:* parcels office.
messe [mɛs], *s.f. Ecc:* Mass. Messe haute, grande messe, high mass. Messe basse, low mass. Messe des morts, requiem (mass). Livre de messe, mass-book, = book of Common Prayer.
messéance [meseãːs], *s.f.* Unseemliness, impropriety (of conduct).
messéant [meseã], *a.* (*a*) Unbecoming (*à*, to). (*b*) Unseemly, improper.
messeigneurs. See MONSEIGNEUR.
messeoir [meswaːr], *v.ind.tr., def.* (*pr.p.* messeyant; *p.p.* is lacking; *pr.ind.* il messied, ils messeyent; *pr.sub.* il messeye; *p.d.* il messeyait; *p.h.* is lacking; *fu.* il messiéra) To be unbecoming, unseemly; to misbecome. *Il lui messied de* . . ., it ill becomes him to. . . . [SEOIR]
messer [mɛsɛːr], *s.m. A: Hum:* = MESSIRE. *M. Gaster*, the stomach, the inner man.
messey-ait, -e. See MESSEOIR.
messianique [mɛsjanik], *a.* Messianic.
messianisme [mɛsjanism], *s.m.* Messianism.
Messidor [mɛsidɔːr], *s.m.* Tenth month of the French Republican calendar (June-July).
Messie [mɛsi]. *Pr.n.m.* Messiah.
messied [mesjɛ]. See MESSEOIR.
messiéra [mesjéra]. See MESSEOIR.
messieurs. See MONSIEUR.
messire [mɛsiːr], *s.m. A:* Sir, master.
mesurable [məzyrabl], *a.* Measurable, mensurable.
mesure [məzyːr], *s.f.* Measure. **1.** (*a*) Prendre la mesure de qn, (i) to take s.o.'s measurements, to measure s.o.; (ii) *F:* to size s.o. up. Complet fait sur mesure, suit made to measure. *F:* Donner sa mesure, to show what one is capable of. Dans une certaine mesure, in some degree; to a certain extent. *Je vous aiderai dans la m. de mes forces*, I shall help you to the best of my ability. *Adv.phr.* A mesure, in proportion; successively; one by one. S.a. FUR. A mesure que, (in proportion) as. *A m. que je reculais il s'avançait*, as (fast as) I retired he advanced. (*b*) Prendre des mesures, to take action, to adopt measures. *Prendre des mesures pour faire qch.*, to take measures, steps, to do sth. *Prendre des mesures contre qch.*, to make provision against sth. *Prendre ses mesures*, to make one's arrangements (*pour que*, in order that). *Par m. d'économie*, as a measure of economy. **2.** (*a*) *Mth:* M. commune, common measure. (*b*) Gauge, standard. M. de longueur, measure of length. M. de superficie, square measure. M. de volume, cubic measure. S.a. LIQUIDE 2. *Poids et mesures*, weights and measures. (*c*) M. en ruban, tape measure. (*d*) (Quantity measured out) Verser une m. de vin, de rhum, à qn, to pour s.o. out a measure of wine, of rum. **3.** (*a*) Standard size or amount. Pièces qui ne sont pas de mesure, pieces that are not to size. *F:* Garder la mesure, to keep within bounds. Dépasser la mesure, (i) to overstep the line; (ii) to overdo it. Ne garder aucune m., oublier toute m., to fling aside all restraint, to go beyond all bounds. Ambition sans mesure, unbounded ambition. S.a. OUTRE² 1. (*b*) *Fenc:*

Measure, reach, distance. *F:* Être en mesure de faire qch., to be in a position to do sth. **4.** *Mus:* (i) Bar. (ii) Time. M. à quatre temps, common time. Battre la mesure, to beat time. En mesure, in strict time. Aller en m., to keep time.
mesure-étalon, *s.f.* Standard measure. *pl. Des mesures-étalons.*
mesur|er [məzyre], *v.tr.* **1.** (*a*) To measure (dimensions); to measure out (corn); to measure up (land); to measure off (cloth). (Of tailor) M. un client, to take the measurements of a customer. Mesurer qn des yeux, to eye s.o. up and down. *F:* Mesurer le sol, la terre, to measure one's length on the ground. (*b*) Colonne qui mesure vingt pieds, column that measures twenty feet. (*c*) Mesurer la nourriture à qn, to ration s.o. in food; to grudge s.o. his food. **2.** To calculate; to weigh (one's words, etc.). M. sa depense sur ses profits, to proportion one's expenditure to one's gains. M. la distance à la vue, to judge, estimate, gauge, distance by the eye. *Prov:* A brebis tondue Dieu mesure le vent, God tempers the wind to the shorn lamb. *s.m.* -age. *s.* -eur, -euse.
se mesurer avec, contre, qn, to measure one's strength, to measure oneself, against s.o.; to try conclusions with s.o. *Vous n'êtes pas de force, de taille, à vous m. avec lui*, you are no match for him.
mesuré, *a.* Measured (tread, etc.); temperate, moderate, restrained (language).
mésusage [mezyzaːʒ], *s.m.* Misuse.
mésuser [mezyze], *v.ind.tr.* **1.** M. de son bien, to misuse one's wealth. **2.** M. de son pouvoir, to abuse one's power.
métabisulfite [metabisylfit], *s.m. Ch:* Metabisulphite.
métabolique [metabɔlik], *a.* Metabolic.
métabolisme [metabɔlism], *s.m.* Metabolism.
métacarpe [metakarp], *s.m. Anat:* Metacarpus.
métacentre [metasãːtr], *s.m. Hyd: N.Arch: Av:* Metacentre.
métairie [meteri], *s.f.* Small farm (held on métayage agreement).
métal, -aux [metal, -o], *s.m.* **1.** Metal. Métal blanc, white metal; babbitt. M. (blanc) anglais, Britannia metal. **2.** *Fin:* M. en barres, bullion.
métallifère [metallifɛːr], *a.* Metal-bearing.
métallin [metallɛ̃], *a.* Metalline, metallic (sheen).
métallique [metallik], *a.* Metallic. Câble m., wire rope. Plume m., steel pen. Rendre un son m., to clang, to ring.
métalliser [metallize], *v.tr.* **1.** To metallize. **2.** To cover with metal; to plate.
se métalliser. *Phot:* To bronze.
métallographie [metallɔgrafi], *s.f.* Metallography.
métalloïde [metallɔid], *a. & s.m.* Metalloid.
métallurgie [metallyrʒi], *s.f.* Metallurgy.
métallurgique [metallyrʒik], *a.* Metallurgic(al). Usine métallurgique, ironworks.
métallurgiste [metallyrʒist], *s.m.* Metallurgist. (*a*) Ironmaster. (*b*) Metal-worker.
métamorphique [metamɔrfik], *a. Geol:* Metamorphic, metamorphous.
métamorphisme [metamɔrfism], *s.m. Geol:* Metamorphism.
métamorphose [metamɔrfoːz], *s.f.* Metamorphosis, transformation.
métamorphos|er [metamɔrfoze], *v.tr.* To metamorphose, transform. *a.* -able.
se métamorphoser, to change completely.
métaphore [metafɔːr], *s.f.* Metaphor; figure of speech. M. disparate, mixed metaphor.

métaphorique [mɛtafɔrik], *a.* Metaphorical; figurative. *adv.* **-ment.**

métaphysicien, -ienne [mɛtafizisjɛ̃, -jɛn], *s.* Metaphysician.

métaphysique [mɛtafizik]. **1.** *a.* Metaphysical; *F:* abstract, abstruse. **2.** *s.f.* Metaphysics.

métapsychique [mɛtapsiʃik]. **1.** *a.* Psychic (phenomenon). **2.** *s.f.* Psychics.

métapsychisme [mɛtapsiʃism], *s.m.* Psychics.

métapsychiste [mɛtapsiʃist], *s.m. & f.* Psychist.

métatarse [metatars], *s.m. Anat:* Metatarsus.

métatarsien, -ienne [mɛtatarsjɛ̃, -jɛn], *a. & s.m. Anat:* Metatarsal (bone).

métathèse [mɛtatɛːz], *s.f. Ling: Surg:* Metathesis.

métayage [mɛtɛjaːʒ], *s.m. Husb:* Métayage system (by which farmer pays rent in kind).

métayer, -ère [mɛtɛje, -ɛːr], *s.* (a) Métayer; farmer who pays rent in kind. (b) *F:* Farmer.

métazoaire [mɛtazɔɛːr]. *Biol:* **1.** *a.* Metazoan. **2.** *s.m.* Metazoon. *pl. Métazoaires,* metazoa.

méteil [mɛtɛːj], *s.m. Agr:* (Mixed crop of) wheat and rye; *Dial:* maslin.

métempsyc(h)ose [mɛtɑ̃psikoːz], *s.f.* Metempsychosis; transmigration of souls.

météore [meteɔːr], *s.m.* Atmospheric phenomenon; meteor.

météorique [meteɔrik], *a.* Meteoric.

météorisation [meteɔrizasjɔ̃], *s.f. Med:* Meteorism; flatulence. *Vet:* Hoove, blast.

météoriser [meteɔrize], *v.tr. Med:* To distend (abdomen). *Vet:* To hove (sheep, cattle).
  météorisé, *a.* (Of sheep, etc.) Hoven, blown, blasted.

météorisme [meteɔrism], *s.m.* = MÉTÉORISATION.

météorite [meteɔrit], *s. m. or f.* **1.** Meteorite. **2.** Meteorolite.

météorologie [meteɔrɔlɔʒi], *s.f.* Meteorology.

météorologique [meteɔrɔlɔʒik], *a.* Meteorological. *Bulletin m.,* weather report, weather forecast.

météorologiste [meteɔrɔlɔʒist], *s.m.,* **météorologue** [meteɔrɔlɔg], *s.m.* Meteorologist.

métèque [metɛk], *s.m. F:* (a) Foreigner, alien. (b) *F:* Dago; *U.S:* wop. (c) *P:* Bloke, beggar, blighter.

méthane [metan], *s.m. Ch:* Methane; marsh gas. *Min:* Fire-damp.

méthode [metɔd], *s.f.* **1.** Method, system. *Il a beaucoup de m.,* he is very methodical. **Faire qch. avec méthode,** to do sth. methodically, systematically. **2.** Primer, grammar, method.

méthodique [metɔdik], *a.* Methodical, systematic. *adv.* **-ment,** -ally.

méthodiste [metɔdist], *a. & s. Ecc:* Methodist.

méthyle [metil], *s.m. Ch:* Methyl.

méthylène [metilɛn], *s.m. Ch:* Methylene.

méthylique [metilik], *a. Ch:* Methyl(ic).

méticuleu|x, -euse [metikylø, -øːz], *a.* Meticulous, punctilious (person, care, civility); scrupulously careful (person). *Par trop méticuleux,* over-scrupulous, over-particular. *adv.* **-sement.**

méticulosité [metikylozite], *s.f.* Meticulosity, over-carefulness; punctiliousness.

métier [metje], *s.m.* **1.** (a) Trade, profession, craft. *M. manuel,* handicraft. **Arts et métiers,** arts and crafts. **Homme de métier,** craftsman. **Gens de métier,** experts, professionals. **Terme de métier,** technical term. **Armée de métier,** professional army. *Exercer un m.,* to carry on, follow, ply, a trade; to follow a calling. **Il est charpentier de métier,** he is a carpenter by trade. *F: Vous faites là un vilain m.!* that's a dirty game you are playing! **Tours de métier,** tricks

of the trade. **Parler métier,** to talk shop. *F:* **Quel métier!** what a life! *Hist:* **Corps de métier,** corporation, g(u)ild; trade association. **Chacun son métier,** everyone to his trade. (b) Craftsmanship. *Il manque encore de m.,* he still lacks experience. **2.** *Tex:* (a) **Métier à tisser,** loom. *M. mécanique,* power-loom. *F:* **Avoir un ouvrage sur le métier,** to have a piece of work in hand, on the stocks. (b) *M. à filer,* spinning-frame. (c) *M. à tapisserie,* tapestry frame.

métis, -isse [meti, -is]. **1.** *a.* Half-bred, crossbred; mongrel (dog). *Plante métisse,* hybrid plant. **2.** *s.* Half-breed; mongrel (dog, etc.).

métissage [metisaːʒ], *s.m.* Cross-breeding.

métisser [metise], *v.tr.* To cross (breeds).

métonymie [metɔnimi], *s.f.* Metonymy.

métonymique [metɔnimik], *a.* Metonymical.

métrage [mɛtraːʒ], *s.m.* **1.** (a) Measuring, measure(ment). (b) *Civ.E:* Quantity-surveying. **2.** (a) (Metric) length. *Cin:* Footage, length (of film). (b) Metric area. (c) Metric volume.

mètre[1] [mɛtr], *s.m. Pros:* Metre.

mètre[2], *s.m.* **1.** *Meas:* Metre (= 3·281 ft). S.a. CARRÉ 1, CUBE 2. **2.** (Metre) rule. *M. pliant,* folding rule. *M. à ruban,* tape-measure.

métrer [mɛtre], *v.tr.* (je mètre; je métrerai) **1.** To measure (by the metre). **2.** *Civ.E:* To survey (for quantities).

métreur [mɛtrœːr], *s.m.* Quantity-surveyor.

métrique[1] [metrik]. **1.** *a. Pros:* Metrical. **2.** *s.f.* Prosody, metrics.

métrique[2], *a.* Metric. **Le système métrique,** the metric system.

Métro (le) [ləmetro], *s.m. F:* The Underground (railway) (in Paris).

métronome [metrɔnɔm], *s.m.* Metronome.

métropole [metrɔpɔl], *s.f.* Metropolis. *(a)* Capital. *(b)* Parent state. *(c)* See (of archbishop). *a. Église m.,* metropolitan church.

métropolitain [metrɔpolitɛ̃], *a.* **1.** Metropolitan. **Chemin de fer métropolitain,** *s.m.* **le Métropolitain,** the Underground (railway) (in Paris). **2.** Armée métropolitaine, home army. **3.** *Ecc:* (a) Metropolitan (church); archiepiscopal. (b) *s.m.* Metropolitan; archbishop.

mets[1] [mɛ], *s.m.* (Article of prepared) food; viand; dish (of food).

mets[2]. See METTRE.

mettable [mɛtabl], *a.* (Of clothes, etc.) Wearable. *Pas m.,* not fit to be worn.

metteur, -euse [mɛtœːr, -øːz], *s.* **1.** Metteur en œuvre, mounter (of jewellery, etc.). **2.** *Rail:* **Metteur de rails,** plate-layer. **3.** Metteur en scène, (i) *Th:* producer, (ii) *Cin:* director.

mettre [mɛtr], *v.tr. (pr.p.* mettant; *p.p.* mis; *pr.ind.* je mets, il met, n. mettons, ils mettent; *p.h.* je mis; *fu.* je mettrai) **1.** (a) To put, lay, place, set. *M. la nappe sur la table,* mettre la table, mettre le couvert, to lay the cloth, the table. *M. la main sur qn,* to lay hands on s.o. *M. des cartes chez qn,* to leave cards on s.o. *M. un manche à un balai,* to fit a handle to a broom. *M. les chevaux à la voiture,* to put the horses to. *Aut: M. le bras avant de stopper,* to stick out one's arm before stopping. **Mettre qn à la porte,** to turn s.o. out (of doors). **M. les volets,** to put up the shutters. *Gaming: M. un enjeu, une somme,* to lay a stake, a sum. **Mettre le tout pour le tout,** to stake one's all on one throw. *Abs.* **Mettre dans le blanc,** to make a bull's-eye, a bull. *Il me met dans toutes ses affaires,* he tells me all his business. S.a. BAS II.2, DEDANS 1. *J'y mettrai tous mes soins,* I will give the matter every care. *Il a mis de la modération dans ses paroles,* he observed moderation in what he said. **Mettre le feu à qch.**, to set fire to sth. ; to set sth. on fire. S.a. FEU[1] I. 1. **Mettre le siège à une ville,** to lay siege to a town. *M. du temps à faire qch.*, to take time over sth. S.a. SIEN 2. (*b*) To put (clothes) on. *Qu'est-ce que je vais mettre?*—*Mettez votre smoking,* what shall I wear?—Put on your dinner-jacket. *J'ai du mal à m. mes souliers,* I find it difficult to get my shoes on. *M. ses gants,* to draw on one's gloves. (*c*) **Mettre sécher du linge,** *m. du linge à sécher,* to put linen out to dry. *Quand on le met à causer . . .,* if once you start him talking. . . . **2.** To set, put (in a condition). *M. une machine en mouvement,* to set a machine going. *M. des vers en musique,* to set verse to music. *M. du latin en français,* to turn Latin into French. *M. son argent en fonds de terre,* to invest one's money in real estate. *M. qn à la torture,* to put, subject, s.o. to torture. S.a. RAISON 2. *Nau: M. une voile au vent,* to hoist, set, a sail. *Abs.* **Mettre à la voile,** to set sail. **3.** (*a*) To admit, grant. *Mettons que vous ayez raison,* say that you are right ; suppose you are right. *Mettons cent francs,* let's say a hundred francs. (*b*) *Mettez que je n'ai rien dit,* consider that unsaid.

se mettre. 1. (*a*) To go, get. *Se m. derrière un arbre,* to get behind a tree. *Se m. au lit,* to go to bed. *Se m. à table,* to sit down to table. *Nau: Se m. à, sur, une manœuvre,* to man a rope. *Se m. au service de qn,* to enter s.o.'s service. *Se m. d'une société,* to join an association. (*b*) To begin, to set about (sth.). *Se m. à l'œuvre, au travail,* to set to work ; to set to, to fall to. **Il est temps de s'y mettre,** it is time to set about it. (*c*) **Se mettre à faire qch.,** to set about doing sth. ; to begin to do sth. *Se m. à rire,* to begin to laugh, to start laughing. *Ils se mirent à manger,* they fell to. *Il se mit à écrire,* (i) he began to write ; (ii) he took to writing (as a profession). *Impers. Il se mit à pleuvoir,* it began to rain ; it came on to rain. **2.** To dress. *Se m. à la mode, simplement,* to dress fashionably, simply. *Se m. en smoking,* to put on a dinner-jacket. **Être bien, mal, mis,** to be well, badly, dressed. S.a. TRENTE[1]. **3.** *Se m. en rage,* to get into a rage. *Se m. en route,* to start on one's way. *Se m. au pas,* (i) to fall into step ; (ii) to subside into a walk (after running). S.a. FRAIS[2], QUATRE. **4.** *Le temps se met au beau,* the weather is turning out, setting in, fine.

meublant [mœblɑ̃], *a.* (Of cloth, etc.) Fit for furnishing. *Brimborions meublants,* knick-knacks that help to furnish, that help to make a home.

meuble [mœbl]. **1.** *a.* (*a*) Movable. *Jur:* **Biens meubles,** *s.m.* movables, personal estate, chattels, personalty. (*b*) *Agr:* **Terre m.,** light, running, soil. **2.** *s.m.* (*a*) Piece of furniture. **Être dans ses meubles,** to have one's own furniture ; to have a home of one's own. (*b*) Suite of furniture. *M. de salon,* drawing-room suite.

meubler [mœble], *v.tr.* To furnish ; to stock (farm, cellar, memory) (*de,* with).

se meubler, to furnish one's home.

meublé. 1. *a.* Furnished. **Non meublé,** unfurnished. *Pièce pauvrement meublée,* barely furnished room. **Cave bien meublée,** well-stocked cellar. *F:* **Bouche bien meublée,** fine set of teeth. **2.** *s.m.* Furnished apartment(s). **Habiter en meublé,** to live in lodgings.

meugler [mœgle], *v.i.* (Of cow) To low ; *F:* to moo. *s.m.* **-ement.**

meule [mœl], *s.f.* **1.** (*a*) Millstone. (*b*) *M. à aiguiser,* grindstone. *M. en émeri,* emery-wheel. *M. à polir,* buffing-wheel. (*c*) **Meule de fromage,** round cheese. **2.** (*a*) Stack, rick (of hay, etc.) ;

(charcoal) stack or pile ; clamp (of bricks). **Mettre le foin en meule,** to stack, rick, the hay. *M. de foin,* haystack, hayrick. (*b*) *Hort:* Hotbed. (*c*) Manure heap. **3.** Burr (of deer's antler).

meuler [mœle], *v.tr.* To grind (chisel, etc.) ; to grind (down) (lens, etc.). *s.m.* **-age.**

meulette [mœlɛt], *s.f.* **1.** Small haystack. **2.** Shock, stook (of corn). *M. de foin,* haycock.

meulière [mœljɛ:r], *s.f.* **1.** Millstone grit ; millstone. **2.** Millstone quarry.

meunerie [mønri], *s.f.* **1.** (Flour-)milling. **2.** Milling-trade.

meunier, -ière [mønje, -jɛ:r]. **1.** *s.* Miller. *Garçon m.,* mill-hand. **2.** *s.f. Orn:* **Meunière,** (i) long-tailed tit ; (ii) hooded crow, saddle-back crow.

meur-e, -s, -t [mœr]. See MOURIR.

meurt-de-faim, *s.m.inv. F:* Starveling.

meurtre [mœrtr], *s.m. Jur:* (*a*) Murder. (*b*) Voluntary manslaughter. **Au meurtre!** murder ! *F: C'est un m. de retoucher ces tableaux,* it is a crime, rank vandalism, to touch up these pictures.

meurtrier, -ère [mœrtrie, -ɛ:r]. **1.** *a.* (*a*) Murderous (war) ; deadly (weapon). (*b*) (Of pers.) Guilty of murder. **2.** *s.* Murderer, *f.* murderess. **3.** *s.f. Fort:* Meurtrière, loop-hole.

meurtrir [mœrtri:r], *v.tr.* To bruise (one's arm, fruit). *M. qn de coups,* to beat s.o. black and blue.

meurtri, *a.* Bruised (arm, fruit, etc.). **Visage meurtri,** (i) battered face ; (ii) ravaged face. **Être tout meurtri,** to be black and blue all over.

meurtrissure [mœrtrisy:r], *s.f.* Bruise.

meu-s, -t [mø]. See MOUVOIR.

Meuse [mø:z]. *Pr.n.f.* (The river) Meuse, Maas.

meute [mø:t], *s.f.* (*a*) *Ven:* Pack (of staghounds, etc.). (*b*) *F:* Crowd, mob, pack (of people in pursuit). **Chef de meute,** ringleader.

meuv-e, -ent [mœ:v]. See MOUVOIR.

mévente [mevɑ̃:t], *s.f.* **1.** Sale (of goods) at a loss. **2.** Slump, stagnation (of business). [VENTE]

mexicain, -aine [mɛksikɛ̃, -ɛn], *a. & s.* Mexican.

Mexique (le) [ləmɛksik]. *Pr.n.m.* Mexico.

mezzanine [mɛdzanin], *s.f.* Mezzanine (storey or window).

mezzo-tinto [mɛdzotinto], *s.m.inv. Engr:* Mezzotint.

mi[1] [mi], *adv.* (*a*) Half, mid, semi-. *Paupières mi-closes,* half-closed eyelids. *Acier mi-doux,* semi-mild steel. *La mi-avril,* mid-April. *A mi-hauteur,* half-way up. *Faire qch. mi de gré mi de force,* to do sth. half willingly half under compulsion. (*b*) In half. *Her: Écu mi-coupé,* shield divided down the centre.

mi[2], *s.m.inv. Mus:* (*a*) (The note) E. *Morceau en mi,* piece in E. (*b*) First string, E string (of violin).

miaou [mjau], *s.m.* Miaow, mew (of cat).

mi-août [miu], *s.f.inv.* Mid-August.

miasmatique [mjasmatik], *a.* Miasmatic, miasmal, noxious (exhalation).

miasme [mjasm], *s.m.* Miasma.

miauler [mjole], *v.i.* To mew, miaow ; to caterwaul. *s.m.* **-ement.**

mi-bois (à), *adv.phr. Carp:* Assemblage à mi-bois, halved joint.

mica [mika], *s.m. Miner:* Mica.

micacé [mikase], *a.* Micaceous.

mi-carême, *s.f.* Mid-Lent. **Dimanche de la mi-carême,** Simnel-Sunday.

miche [miʃ], *s.f.* Round loaf ; cob (of bread).

Michel [miʃel]. *Pr.n.m.* Michael. **La Saint-Michel,** Michaelmas.

Michel-Ange [mikelɑ̃:ʒ]. *Pr.n.m.* Michelangelo.

mi-chemin (à), *adv.phr.* Half-way.

micmac [mikmak], *s.m.* F: Underhand intrigue, scheming.

micocoulier [mikɔkulje], *s.m. Bot:* Nettle-tree.

mi-corps (à), *adv.phr.* To the waist. *Portrait à mi-c.*, half-length portrait. *Saisi à mi-c.*, caught round the waist.

mi-côte (à), *adv.phr.* Half-way up the hill.

micro [mikro], *s.m.* F: = MICROPHONE. *W.Tel:* Le micro, F: the mike. Parler au micro, to speak on the air.

microbe [mikrɔb], *s.m.* Microbe, F: germ.

microbicide [mikrɔbisid]. **I.** *a.* Microbicidal, germ-killing. **2.** *s.m.* Germ-killer.

microbien, -ienne [mikrɔbjɛ̃, -jɛn], *a.* Microbial, microbic (disease, etc.).

microbiologie [mikrɔbjɔlɔʒi], *s.f.* Microbiology.

microcéphale [mikrɔsefal]. **I.** *a.* Microcephalous, microcephalic, small-headed. **2.** *s.* Microcephalic.

microcéphalie [mikrɔsefali], *s.f.* Microcephaly.

microcosme [mikrɔkɔsm], *s.m.* Microcosm.

microfarad [mikrɔfarad], *s.m. El:* Microfarad.

micromètre [mikrɔmɛtr], *s.m.* Micrometer.

micrométrique [mikrɔmetrik], *a.* Micrometric(al). *Vis m.*, micrometer screw.

micron [mikrɔ̃], *s.m.* Micromillimeter, micron.

micro-objectif, *s.m.* **I.** Photo-micrographic object-glass. **2.** Microscope object-lens.

micro-organisme, *s.m.* Micro-organism.

microphone [mikrɔfɔn], *s.m.* Microphone; transmitter, mouthpiece (of telephone); *W.Tel:* F: mike. *M. électrodynamique*, moving-coil microphone.

microphoniste [mikrɔfɔnist], *s. m. & f. W.Tel:* Announcer.

microphotographie [mikrɔfɔtɔgrafi], *s.f.* **I.** Photomicrography. **2.** Photomicrograph.

microscope [mikrɔskɔp], *s.m.* Microscope. *Visible au m.*, visible under the microscope.

microscopique [mikrɔskɔpik], *a.* Microscopic(al).

microthermie [mikrɔtermi], *s.f. Ph.Meas:* Microtherm.

microtome [mikrɔtɔm], *s.m.* Microtome.

microzoaire [mikrɔzɔɛːr], *s.m.* Microzoon.

miction [miksjɔ̃], *s.f.* Urination.

midi [midi], *s.m.* No *pl.* **I.** Midday, noon, twelve o'clock. *Il est m.*, it is twelve o'clock. Arriver sur le midi, F: sur les midi, to arrive about noon. Avant midi, ante meridiem; a.m. Après midi, post meridiem; p.m. *M. et demi*, half-past twelve. En plein midi, (i) in broad daylight; (ii) F: in the full light of day. F: Chercher midi à quatorze heures, to look for difficulties where there are none; to miss the obvious. F: *Être au m. de la vie*, to be in the heyday of life. **2.** (a) South. *Chambre au m.*, room facing south. (b) Southern part (of country). Esp. **Le Midi** (de la France), the South of France.

midinette [midinɛt], *s.f.* F: Work-girl; esp. young milliner or dressmaker (who goes home to lunch at midday).

mi-distance, *s.f.* Middle distance.

mi-drisse (à), *adv.phr. Nau:* Pavillon à mi-drisse, flag at the dip.

mie[1] [mi], *s.f.* **I.** Crumb (of loaf, as opposed to crust). *P:* Excuses à la mie de pain, worthless excuses. **2.** A: (a) = MIETTE. (b) *adv.* Still used as a literary mannerism in Ne . . . mie (= ne . . . point), not at all.

mie[2], *s.f.* (= AMIE) Used only with *ma, ta, sa.* Ma mie (= A: m'amie), my pet; darling.

miel [mjɛl], *s.m.* Honey. F: Elle était tout sucre

et tout miel, she was all sugar and honey. Paroles de miel, honeyed words. Faire son miel de qch., to turn sth. to advantage. S.a. LUNE I, RAYON[3] I.

miellé [mjɛle], *a.* **I.** Sweetened with honey. **2.** = MIELLEUX.

mielleusement [mjɛløzmɑ̃], *adv.* Blandly; with honeyed words.

mielleux, -euse [mjɛlø, -øːz], *a.* **I.** *Goût m.*, taste of honey. **2.** F: Honeyed, sugary (speech, etc.); bland (smile); soapy, smooth-tongued, mealy-mouthed, soft-spoken (person).

mien, mienne [mjɛ̃, mjɛn]. **I.** *Occ. poss.a.* Mine. Un mien ami, a friend of mine. **2.** Le mien, la mienne, les miens, les miennes, mine. (a) *poss. pron. Je pris ses mains dans les deux miennes*, I took her hands in both of mine. (b) *s.m.* (i) My own (property, etc.); mine. Le mien et le tien, mine and thine. *Tels sont les faits, je n'y mets rien du m.*, such are the facts, I am not adding anything of my own (invention). (ii) *s.m.pl. J'ai été renié par les miens*, I have been disowned by my own people, by my own folk. (c) *s.f.pl.* On dit que j'ai encore fait des miennes, they say I've been up to my old tricks again.

miette [mjɛt], *s.f.* (a) Crumb (of broken bread). (b) F: Morsel. *Mettre un vase en miettes*, to smash a vase to atoms, F: to smithereens.

mieux [mjø], *adv.* **I.** *Comp.* Better. (a) *Il faut m. les surveiller, les m. surveiller*, you must watch them more closely. Vous feriez mieux de m'écouter, you would do better to listen to me. *Prov:* Mieux vaut tard que jamais, better late than never. *Ça va m.*, things are improving. Pour mieux dire . . ., to be more exact. . . . Pour ne pas dire mieux, pour ne pas mieux dire, to say the least of it. De mieux en mieux, better and better. *M. encore . . .*, better still. . . . *Adv.phr. Faire qch.* à qui mieux mieux, to vie with one another in doing sth. *Tous travaillaient à qui m. m.*, all worked their hardest. Il va mieux, he is (feeling) better. S.a. TANT I, VALOIR I. (b) (With adj. function) (i) C'est on ne peut mieux, it couldn't be better. *Ce qui est m.*, qui mieux est . . .*, what is better . . .; better still. . . . (ii) *Vous serez m. dans ce fauteuil*, you will be more comfortable in this armchair. (iii) *Il est m.*, he is (feeling) better. (iv) *Il est m. que son frère*, he is better-looking than his brother. (c) *s.neut.* (i) Le mieux est l'ennemi du bien, leave well alone. Faute de mieux, for want of something better. *Elle ressemble à sa mère, mais en mieux*, she is very like her mother, but better-looking. Je ne demande pas mieux, I shall be delighted (to do so, to have it so). (ii) *Med: etc:* Un mieux, du mieux, a change for the better. **2.** *Sup.* Le mieux, (the) best. (a) *La femme le m. habillée de Paris*, the best-dressed woman in Paris. Il s'en est acquitté le mieux du monde, nobody could have done it better. (b) (With adj. function) (i) *Ce qu'il y a de m.* à faire, c'est de . . ., the best course to take is to. . . . *C'est tout ce qu'il y a de m.*, there is absolutely nothing better. (ii) Être le mieux du monde avec qn, to be on the best of terms with s.o. (iii) C'était la mieux des trois sœurs, she was the best-looking of the three sisters. (c) *s.neut.* Faire, agir pour le mieux, to act for the best. *Le m. serait de . . .*, the best plan would be to. . . . En mettant les choses au mieux . . ., at best. . . . Agir au mieux des intérêts de qn, to act in the best interests of s.o. Faire qch. de son mieux, to do sth. to the best of one's ability. Faire de son mieux, to do one's best. Être au mieux avec qn, to be on the best of terms with s.o.

mièvre [mjɛːvr], *a.* (*a*) Fragile, delicate (child, etc.). (*b*) Finical, affected (style). *adv.* -ment.

mièvrerie [mjɛvrəri], *s.f.*, **mièvreté** [mjɛvrəte], *s.f.* (*a*) Fragility, delicateness. (*b*) Finicalness, affectation (of style).

mignard [miɲaːr], *a.* Affected, mincing, simpering; pretty-pretty. *adv.* -ement.

mignarder [miɲarde]. **1.** *v.tr.* To pat, caress, fondle. *M. son style*, to be finical (in one's style). **2.** *v.i.* To mince, simper.
se mignarder, (of a man) to doll oneself up.

mignardise [miɲardiːz], *s.f.* **1.** (*a*) Affectation; mincing manners. (*b*) Finicalness; prettiness (of style, etc.). **2.** *Bot:* Garden pink.

mignon, -onne [miɲɔ̃, -ɔn]. **1.** *a.* Dainty, tiny, delicate (person, etc.). *Est-elle mignonne!* isn't she sweet! *Son péché mignon*, his besetting sin. **2.** *s.* Pet. darling, favourite.

mignonnette [miɲɔnɛt], *s.f.* **1.** (*a*) London-pride. (*b*) Wild succory. (*c*) Clover. **2.** Mignonette lace. **3.** Coarse-ground pepper.

mignoter [miɲɔte], *v.tr.* To fondle, caress; to pet (child).
se mignoter, to coddle oneself.

migraine [migren], *s.f.* Sick headache; migraine.

migrateur, -trice [migratœːr, -tris], *a.* Migrating, migratory (bird); migrant (people).

migration [migrasjɔ̃], *s.f.* Migration.

migratoire [migratwaːr], *a.* Migratory.

mijaurée [miʒɔre], *s.f.* Conceited, affected, woman.

mijoter [miʒɔte]. **1.** *v.tr.* To stew (sth.) slowly; to let (sth.) simmer. *F:* Mijoter un projet, to turn a scheme over in one's mind. *Il se mijote quelque chose*, there's something in the wind. **2.** *v.i.* To simmer, stew.

mil¹ [mil], *s.m. Gym:* Indian club.

mil², *a.* (Used only in legal documents in writing out dates A.D.) Thousand. *L'an mil neuf cent trente*, the year nineteen hundred and thirty.

mil³ [miːj], *s.m. Bot:* = MILLET I.

mi-laine [milɛn], *s.f. Tex:* Half-wool cloth; union.

milan [milɑ̃], *s.m. Orn:* Kite.

mildew, mildiou [mildju], *s.m. Vit:* Mildew; brown rot. *Atteint de m.*, mildewed.

miliaire [miljɛːr], *a.* Resembling millet-seed. *Med:* Miliary (gland, fever, etc.).

milice [milis], *s.f.* Militia.

milicien [milisjɛ̃], *s.m.* Militiaman.

milieu, -eux [miljø], *s.m.* **1.** Middle, midst. *Au milieu de*, amid(st). *Au beau milieu de la rue*, right in the middle of the street. *Au m. du navire*, amidships. *Le m. du jour*, noon. *Au m. de l'été, de l'hiver, de la nuit*, in the height of summer, in the depth of winter, at dead of night. *La table du milieu*, the middle table. *Geom: Le m. d'une droite*, the middle point of a straight line. **2.** (*a*) *Ph:* Medium. (*b*) Surroundings, environment; (social) sphere, circle. *Dans les milieux autorisés*, in responsible quarters. *Les différents milieux*, the different social classes. *Je n'appartiens pas à leur m.*, I don't belong to their set, class, circle. **3.** Middle course; mean. *Il n'y a pas de m.*, there is no middle course. *Le juste milieu*, the golden mean, the happy medium. *Tenir le milieu entre . . . et . . .*, to be something between . . . and . . .

militaire [militɛːr]. **1.** *a.* (*a*) Military (art, profession, etc.). *F: A huit heures, heure militaire*, at eight o'clock sharp. *Allure m.*, soldierlike bearing. (*b*) *La marine militaire*, the Navy. **2.** *s.m.* Military man; soldier. *Les militaires*, the military. *adv.* -ment.

militant [militɑ̃]. **1.** *a.* Militant (church, etc.). **2.** *s.m. M. d'une idée*, fighter for an idea.

militarisation [militarizasjɔ̃], *s.f.* Militarization.

militariser [militarize], *v.tr.* To militarize.

militarisme [militarism], *s.m.* Militarism.

militariste [militarist], *s.m.* Militarist.

militer [milite], *v.i.* To militate (*pour, en faveur de*, in favour of). *Cela milite en sa faveur*, that tells in his favour.

mille¹ [mil]. **1.** *num.a.inv. & s.m.inv.* Thousand. *M. hommes*, a thousand men. *Trois cent m. hommes*, three hundred thousand men. *Ils moururent par centaines de mille*, they died in hundreds of thousands. *M. un*, a thousand and one. (But) *Les Mille et une Nuits*, the Arabian Nights. *F: J'étais à mille lieues de supposer que . . .*, I should never have dreamt that. . . . *Il a des mille et des cents*, he has tons of money. *Hist:* L'an mille, the year one thousand. **2.** *s.m.* (*a*) *Un m. de briques*, a thousand bricks. (*b*) *Mettre dans le mille*, (i) to make a 'thousand' throw (at the game of *tonneau*); (ii) *F:* to be successful.

mille², *s.m.* Mile (= 1609 metres).

mille-feuille, *s.f.* **1.** *Bot:* Milfoil, yarrow. **2.** *Cu:* Genoese pastry.

millénaire [milleneːr]. **1.** *a.* Millennial, millenary. **2.** *s.m.* Thousand years; millenary, millennium.

millénium [millenjɔm], *s.m.* Millennium.

mille-pattes, *s.m.* Centipede, millepede.

mille-pertuis, *s.m.inv. Bot:* St John's wort.

millésime [mil(l)ezim], *s.m.* (*a*) Date (on coin, etc.). (*b*) *Ind:* Year of manufacture.

millet [mijɛ], *s.m.* **1.** *Bot:* Wood millet-grass. *M. long*, canary-grass. (Grains de) millet, bird-seed, canary-seed. **2.** *Med:* Miliary eruption.

milliaire [miljɛːr], *a.* Borne, pierre, milliaire, milestone.

milliampère [milliɑ̃pɛːr], *s.m.* Milliampere.

milliard [miljaːr], *s.m.* Milliard; one thousand million(s).

milliardaire [miljardɛːr], *a. & s.m.* Multi-millionaire.

millième [miljɛm], *num. a. & s.* Thousandth. **2.** *s.m.* (One-)thousandth (part).

millier [milje], *s.m.* (About a) thousand; *F:* a thousand or so. *Des milliers*, thousands

milligramme [milligram], *s.m.* Milligram(me).

millimètre [mil(l)imetr], *s.m.* Millimetre.

millimétrique [mil(l)imetrik], *a. Échelle m.*, millimetre scale.

million [miljɔ̃], *s.m.* Million. *Quatre millions d'hommes*, four million men. *F: Riche à millions*, worth millions.

millionième [miljɔnjɛm], *a. & s.* Millionth.

millionnaire [miljɔnɛːr], *a. & s.* Millionaire (in French currency).

millithermie [millitermi], *s.f. Ph:* Large calorie.

milord [milɔːr], *s.m.* **1.** (In address) My Lord. **2.** (*a*) (English) nobleman. (*b*) *F:* Immensely wealthy man. **3.** *Veh:* Victoria.

milouin [milwɛ̃], *s.m. Orn:* Pochard.

mi-lourd [miluːr], *a. & s.m. Box:* (Poids) mi-lourd, light heavy-weight; cruiser weight.

mi-mât [mimɑ], *adv.phr.* (Flag, etc.) at half-mast.

mime [mim], *s.m.* **1.** *Gr: & Lt.Ant:* Mime. **2.** Mimic.

mimer [mime], *v.tr.* **1.** To mime. *M. une scène*, to act a scene in dumb show; to mime a scene. **2.** To mimic, to ape (s.o.).

mimétisme [mimetism], *s.m. Biol:* Mimesis.

mimi [mimi], *s.m. F:* Pussy. *F: Mon petit m.*, ducky, darling. [MINET]

mimique [mimik]. **1.** *a.* (*a*) Mimic. *Langage m.*, (i) sign language; (ii) dumb show. (*b*) *Z:* Mimetic. **2.** *s.f.* (*a*) Mimic art; mimicry. (*b*) *F:* Dumb show.

mimosa [mimoza], *s.m. Bot:* Mimosa.
minable [minabl], *a.* **1.** Mineable (fort, etc.).
2. *F:* Sorry-looking, seedy-looking (person);
shabby, pitiable (appearance).
minaret [minarɛ], *s.m.* Minaret.
minauder [minode], *v.i.* To simper, smirk.
minauderie [minodri], *s.f.* Simpering, smirking.
minaudier, -ière [minodje, -jɛːr], *a. & s.* Simpering, smirking, affected (person).
mince [mɛ̃ːs]. **1.** *a.* Thin (board, cloth); slender,
slight, slim (person); *F:* small, scanty (income).
2. *int. P:* **Mince de pluie!** what a downpour!
Mince alors! well I never! *adv.* **-ment.**
mincer [mɛ̃se], *v.tr.* (je minçai(s); n. minçons)
Cu: To mince.
minceur [mɛ̃sœːr], *s.f.* Thinness; slenderness,
slimness.
mine¹ [min], *s.f.* **1.** Mine. (*a*) *M. de houille,*
coal-mine, -pit; colliery. *M. d'or,* gold-mine.
Exploitation des mines, mining. *F:* *Une m. de*
renseignements, a mine, a store-house, of information. (*b*) *Mil:* *Faire jouer une m.,* to spring,
touch off, a mine. *Coup de mine,* blast, shot.
S.a. ÉVENTER 1. *Navy:* *M. flottante,* floating
mine. *Champ de mines,* minefield. *Poser, mouiller,*
une m., to lay a mine. *Poseur, mouilleur, de*
mines, mine-layer. **2.** **Mine de plomb,** graphite,
black-lead. *Passer le poêle à la m. de plomb,* to
black-lead the stove.
mine², *s.f.* Appearance, look, mien. (*a*) *Juger*
qn sur la m., to judge s.o. by appearances. **Avoir**
belle mine, avoir de la mine, to be good-looking.
Homme de bonne mine, man of prepossessing
appearance. *Individu de mauvaise m., de méchante*
m., shady-looking individual. **Il porte la mine**
d'un fripon, he looks a rascal. **Il ne paye pas de**
mine, his appearance goes, is, against him; *F:* he
is not much to look at. (*b*) (Of health) **Avoir**
bonne mine, mauvaise mine, to look well, ill.
(*c*) **Faire une laide mine,** to scowl, to look black.
Faire bonne mine à qn, to be pleasant to s.o.
Faire bonne mine à mauvais jeu, to smile in the
face of adversity; to grin and bear it. **Faire grise**
mine, to look anything but pleased. **Faire la**
mine, to look sulky. **Faire des mines,** to simper.
Faire mine d'être fâché, to make a show of being
angry. *Il fit m. de me suivre,* he made as if to
follow me. *Il me fit m. de le suivre,* he signed to
me (by a play of features) to follow him. *Avoir m.*
de (vouloir) faire qch., to look like doing sth.
miner [mine], *v.tr.* To mine, undermine (fortress,
etc.). *La fièvre l'a miné,* fever has sapped,
undermined, his strength. *Miné par l'envie,*
eaten up, consumed, with envy.
se miner, to waste away; to pine.
minerai [minrɛ], *s.m.* Ore. *M. de fer,* iron ore.
minéral, -aux [mineral, -o]. **1.** *a.* Mineral.
(*a*) *Chimie minérale,* inorganic chemistry. (*b*) *Eau*
minérale, mineral water(s). *Source minérale,*
mineral spring; spa. **2.** *s.m.* Mineral.
minet, -ette [minɛ, -ɛt], *s.* **1.** Puss(y); *f.* tabby;
F: pet, darling. **2.** *s.f. Bot:* Minette, black
medic(k).
mineur¹, -euse [minœːr, -øːz]. **1.** *a.* Burrowing
(insect). **2.** *s.m.* (*a*) Miner. (*b*) *Mil:* Sapper.
mineur², -eure [minœːr]. **1.** *a.* (*a*) Minor,
lesser. (*b*) *Jur:* Under age. (*c*) *Mus:* Minor
(scale). **2.** *s.* Minor; *Jur:* infant.
miniature [minjatyːr], *s.f.* Miniature. *Peintre*
en m., miniature-painter. *Adv.phr.* **En miniature,**
in miniature; on a small scale.
miniaturiste [minjatyrist], *s.m. & f.* Miniaturist, miniature-painter.
minier, -ière [minje, -jɛːr]. **1.** *a.* Mining

(industry, district). **2.** *s.f.* **Minière,** surface mine.
minime [minim], *a.* Small; trivial (loss);
trifling (value). *s.m.pl.* **Classe des minimes,** tiny
tots' class.
minimum [minimɔm]. Minimum. **1.** *s.m. M. de*
vitesse, minimum speed. **Réduire les frais au**
minimum, to reduce expenses to a minimum.
Thermomètre à minima, minimum thermometer.
pl. Des minima, des minimums. **2.** *a. La largeur,*
les largeurs, minimum or *minima,* minimum
width(s).
ministère [ministɛːr], *s.m.* **1.** (*a*) Agency. *User*
du m. de qn, to make use of s.o.'s services.
(*b*) *Ecc:* **Le saint ministère,** the ministry.
2. *Adm:* Ministry. (*a*) Office. *Entrer au m.,* to
take office. (*b*) *Former un m.,* to form a ministry,
a government. (*c*) Government department. **Le**
Ministère des Affaires Étrangères, the Foreign
Office. **Ministère de l'Intérieur,** Home Office.
Ministère de la Guerre, War Office, War Department. **Ministère de l'Air,** Air Ministry. (*d*) *Jur:*
Le Ministère public, the (Department of the)
Public Prosecutor.
ministéri|el, -elle [ministerjel], *a.* Ministerial.
Journal m., Government organ. *Crise ministé-*
rielle, cabinet crisis. *Jur: Officier m.,* law official
(*avoué, huissier,* or *notaire*). *adv.* **-ellement.**
ministre [ministr], *s.m.* **1.** (*a*) *A. & Lit:* Ser-
vant, agent (of God, of prince, etc.). (*b*) *Ecc:*
(Protestant) minister; clergyman. **2.** Minister;
Secretary of State. **Premier ministre,** Prime
Minister. **Ministre des Affaires Étrangères =**
Foreign Secretary. **Ministre de l'Intérieur =**
Home Secretary. **Ministre de la Guerre,** Secretary of State for War. **Ministre de l'Air,** Air
Minister. **Papier ministre,** petition paper;
= official foolscap.
minium [minjɔm], *s.m.* Minium; red lead.
minois [minwa], *s.m. F:* Pretty face (of child,
young woman).
minorité [minɔrite], *s.f.* Minority. **1.** Nonage;
Jur: infancy. **2.** **Être en minorité,** to be in the,
in a, minority.
Minorque [minɔrk], *Pr.n. Geog:* Minorca.
minot [mino], *s.m. Nau:* Bumpkin.
minoterie [minɔtri], *s.f.* **1.** (Large) flour-mill;
flour-milling works. **2.** Flour-milling.
minotier [minɔtje], *s.m.* **1.** (Flour-)miller.
2. Flour-factor.
minuit [minɥi], *s.m.* Midnight; twelve o'clock
(at night). *M. et demi,* half-past twelve at night.
Sur le minuit, F: sur les minuit, about midnight.
minuscule [minyskyl], *a.* (*a*) Small, minute, tiny.
(*b*) **Lettre minuscule,** *s.f.* minuscule, small letter;
Typ: lower-case letter.
minus habens [minysabɛ̃ːs], *s.m.inv.* Mental
defective.
minute [minyt], *s.f.* **1.** Minute (of hour, degree).
Faire qch. à la minute, to do sth. at a minute's
notice, at a moment's notice. *Vous êtes à la m.,*
you are punctual to a minute. **Réparations à la**
minute, repairs while you wait. *P:* **Minute!**
.gently! wait a bit! **2.** (*a*) Minute, draft (of
contract, etc.). *Faire la m. d'un acte,* to draft an
act. (*b*) Record (of deed, of judgment).
minuter [minyte], *v.tr.* (*a*) To minute, draw up
(agreement, etc.). (*b*) To record, enter (deed,
judgment).
minuterie [minytri], *s.f.* **1.** (*a*) *Clockm: etc:*
Motion-work, train of wheels. (*b*) *M. d'enregistre-*
ment, counting mechanism (of meter). **2.** Automatic time-switch (on stair-landing).
minutie [minysi], *s.f.* **1.** (*a*) Minute detail; trifle.
(*b*) *pl.* Minutiae. **2.** Attention to minute detail.

minutieu|x, -euse [minysjø, -ø:z], *a.* Scrupulously careful (person) ; close, thorough, minute, detailed (inspection, etc.). *adv.* **-sement.**

miocène [mjɔsɛn], *a. & s.m. Geol:* Miocene.

mioche [mjɔʃ], *s. m. & f. F:* Small child ; mite, urchin.

mi-parti, *a.* (*a*) Equally divided (opinions, etc.) ; halved. (*b*) Parti-coloured. (*c*) *Her:* (Shield) parted per pale.

mi-pente (à), *adv.phr.* Half-way up or down the hill.

mirabelle [mirabɛl], *s.f.* Mirabelle plum.

miracle [mira:kl], *s.m.* **I.** Miracle. **Faire, opérer, un miracle,** to work, accomplish, a miracle. **Fait à miracle,** marvellously well done. **Échapper comme par miracle,** to have a miraculous escape, a hairbreadth escape. **Par miracle . . .,** for a wonder. . . . *F:* **On cria au miracle, "a miracle"** was the cry. **2.** Miracle play ; miracle.

miraculeu|x, -euse [mirakylø, -ø:z], *a.* Miraculous ; *F:* marvellous. *adv.* **-sement.**

mirage [mira:ʒ], *s.m.* Mirage.

mire [mi:r], *s.f.* **I.** Sighting, aiming (of fire-arm). **Ligne de mire,** line of sight. *Point de m.,* aim. *F:* **Point de mire de tous les yeux,** cynosure of all eyes. **2.** (*a*) Sighting-mark. (*b*) Surveyor's pole ; (levelling-)staff. (*c*) Foresight (of rifle) ; bead. S.a. CRAN I.

mirer [mire], *v.tr.* **I.** (*a*) To aim at, take aim at (sth.). *F: M.* **une dot,** to have one's eye on a dowry. (*b*) *Surv:* To take a sight on (sth.). **2.** *M.* **un œuf,** to candle an egg. **3.** *P:* = REGARDER. **se mirer,** to look at, admire, oneself (in mirror, etc.).

mirette [mirɛt], *s.f.* **I.** *Bot:* Venus's looking-glass. **2.** *pl. P:* Eyes ; *P:* optics, peepers.

mirifique [mirifik], *a. F:* Wonderful, mirific. *adv.* **-ment.**

mirliton [mirlitɔ̃], *s.m.* Toy musical instrument with vibrating parchment reinforcing the voice, usu. adorned with strips of paper and humorous verse. *U.S:* Hewgag. *F:* **Vers de mirliton,** vulgar doggerel, trashy verse.

mirobolant [mirɔbɔlɑ̃], *a. F:* Wonderful ; astounding (news, etc.).

miroir [mirwa:r], *s.m.* **I.** (*a*) Mirror, looking-glass. *Geol:* **Miroirs de faille,** slickensides. (*b*) *Bot: F:* **Miroir de Vénus,** (i) Venus's looking-glass ; (ii) corn-salad. **2.** *Cu:* **Œufs au miroir,** eggs fried in butter. **3.** Speculum (on wing of bird) ; eye, ocellus (on peacock's feather).

miroitant [mirwatɑ̃], *a.* Flashing ; glistening (armour) ; shimmering (lake) ; sparkling (jewel).

miroit|er [mirwate], *v.i.* To flash ; to gleam, glisten ; to shimmer ; (of jewel) to sparkle. *F:* **Faire miroiter l'avenir aux yeux de qn,** to hold out bright prospects to s.o. *s.m.* **-ement.**

miroité, *a.* Dappled bay (horse).

miroiterie [mirwatri], *s.f.* Mirror manufacture or trade.

miroton [mirɔtɔ̃], *s.m. Cu:* Yesterday's beef done up with onion sauce ; stew.

mis, -e [mi, mi:z]. See METTRE.

misaine [mizɛn], *s.f. Nau:* (Voile de) **misaine,** (square) foresail. S.a. MÂT.

misanthrope [mizɑ̃trɔp]. **I.** *s.m.* Misanthropist, misanthrope. **2.** *a.* Misanthropic(al) (disposition).

misanthropie [mizɑ̃trɔpi], *s.f.* Misanthropy.

miscellanées [misɛllane], *s.f.pl. Lit:* Miscellany, miscellanea.

miscible [missibl], *a.* Miscible (*avec,* with).

mise [mi:z], *s.f.* **I.** (*a*) Placing ; putting (of sth. in a place). *M.* **en place** (*de qch.*), putting (of sth.) in its place ; setting (of boiler, etc.). *M.* **en plis,** setting (of the hair). **Mise à l'eau,** launching (of ship). *M.* **à terre,** landing (of goods). (*b*) Setting (of sth. in a condition, in a state). *M.* **en jeu de forces,** bringing of forces into play. *M.* **en musique d'un poème,** setting of a poem to music. *M.* **en liberté,** releasing, release. **Mise en retraite,** pensioning (off). **Mise en marche,** starting (of engine). *Aut: etc: M.* **en marche automatique,** self-starter. (*c*) **Être de mise,** (i) (of money) to be in circulation ; (ii) (of clothes) to be in fashion, to be worn. *La familiarité n'est pas de m.,* familiarity is quite out of place. **2.** Dress, attire, get-up. *M.* **irréprochable,** faultless dress or attire. **3.** (*a*) *Gaming: Cards:* Staking or stake. (*b*) Bid (at auction-sale). (*c*) *Com:* **Mise de fonds,** putting up of money. **Mise sociale,** working capital (of company). *M. d'un associé,* partner's holding (in business concern).

mise-bas, *s.f.* **I.** (*a*) Dropping of young. (*b*) Litter (of young). **2.** Cast-off clothing. **3.** *Ind:* Downing of tools.

miser [mize], *v.tr.* (*a*) *Gaming:* To stake (*sur,* on). (*b*) To bid (at auction). [MISE]

misérable [mizerabl]. **I.** *a.* Miserable. (*a*) Unhappy, unfortunate (person) ; wretched, abject (dwelling, etc.). (*b*) Despicable, mean (behaviour). **2.** *s.* (*a*) Poor wretch. (*b*) Scoundrel, wretch, villain. *adv.* **-ment.**

misère [mize:r], *s.f.* **I.** Misery. (*a*) **Manger le pain de misère,** to eat the bread of affliction. **Reprendre le collier de misère,** to go back to drudgery. (*b*) Trouble, ill. *Misères domestiques,* domestic worries. **Lit de misère,** (i) bed of sickness ; (ii) childbed. **Faire des misères à qn,** to tease s.o. unmercifully. **2.** Extreme poverty ; destitution. **Dans la misère,** poverty-stricken. *Réduire qn à la m.,* to reduce s.o. to destitution, to want. *Dames réduites à la m.,* distressed gentlewomen. **Crier misère,** to make a poor mouth. *Vêtements qui crient misère,* shabby, threadbare, garments. **3.** *F: Trifle. Cent francs? Une misère!* a hundred francs? a mere nothing! **4.** *Cards:* Misère.

miséreux, -euse [mizerø, -ø:z], *a. & s.* **I.** Poverty-stricken, destitute. **2.** Shabby-genteel.

miséricorde [mizerikɔrd], *s.f.* **I.** Mercy, mercifulness. **Crier miséricorde,** to cry for mercy. *Être à la m. de qn,* to be in s.o.'s hands. **Faire miséricorde à qn,** to be merciful to s.o. **A tout péché miséricorde,** no sin but should find mercy. S.a. ANCRE I. **2.** *int.* Mercy upon us! goodness gracious!

miséricordieu|x, -euse [mizerikɔrdjø, -ø:z], *a. & s.* Merciful (*envers,* to). *adv.* **-sement.**

misogame [mizɔgam], *s.m. & f.* Misogamist.

misogyne [mizɔʒin]. **I.** *a.* Misogynous. **2.** *s.m.* Misogynist, woman-hater.

misogynie [mizɔʒini], *s.f.* Misogyny.

missel [misɛl], *s.m.* Missal ; (altar) mass-book.

mission [misjɔ̃], *s.f.* Mission. (*a*) *Avoir m. de faire qch.,* to be commissioned to do sth. *Ministre en m. spéciale à Paris,* minister on (a) special mission to Paris. *Mil:* **En mission,** on detached service. (*b*) *Ecc: Missions étrangères,* foreign missions.

missionnaire [misjɔnɛ:r], *s.m.* Missionary.

missive [misi:v], *s.f.* Often *Iron:* Missive, letter.

mistenflûte [mistɑ̃flyt], *s.m. F:* Thingumbob, what's-his-name.

mistigri [mistigri], *s.m. F:* Puss ; grimalkin.

mistral [mistral], *s.m.* Mistral ; cold N.E. wind (blowing from the Alps down the Rhone valley).

mitaine [mitɛn], *s.f.* Mitten. *F:* **Y aller avec**

des mitaines, to go to work with great caution.
Dire qch. sans mitaines, to tell sth. bluntly.
mite [mit], s.f. **1.** Mite. M. du fromage, cheese-mite. **2.** (a) Moth-worm. (b) Clothes-moth. Rongé des mites, moth-eaten.
mité [mite], a. Moth-eaten.
mi-temps, s.f. Fb: La mi-t., half-time; interval. La première, seconde, mi-t., the first, second, half.
miteux, -euse [mitø, -øːz], a. P: **1.** Blear-eyed. **2.** Shabby (furniture, etc.); shabbily-dressed, seedy-looking (individual).
mitigation [mitigasjɔ̃], s.f. Mitigation.
mitiger [mitiʒe], v.tr. (je mitigeai(s); n. mitigeons) **1.** To mitigate (pain, penalty). **2.** To relax (rule, law).
miton[1] [mitɔ̃], s.m. Woollen wristlet.
miton[2], s.m. F: Crumb (of the loaf).
miton[3]. (Found in the phr.) **Onguent miton mitaine,** innocuous (and worthless) salve. Explications miton mitaine, F: eye-wash.
mitonner [mitɔne]. **1.** v.tr. (a) Cu: To let (bread) simmer (in the soup); to let (the soup) simmer. F: M. un projet, to nurse a project. (b) F: To coddle, pamper (child, etc.). **2.** v.i. (Of soup) To simmer.
mitoyen, -enne [mitwajɛ̃, -ɛn], a. Intermediate. Mur m., party wall. Cloison mitoyenne, dividing wall (between two rooms). Puits m., well common to two habitations.
mitoyenneté [mitwajɛnte], s.f. Joint ownership (of party wall, hedge, etc.).
mitraille [mitraːj], s.f. A: **1.** (a) M. de fer, scrap-iron. (b) Mil: Case-shot, grape-shot. **2.** F: Copper coinage; coppers.
mitrailler [mitraje], v.tr. Mil: To pepper, rake, (enemy) with machine-gun fire.
mitrailleur [mitrajøːr], s.m. Machine-gunner. a. Fusil mitrailleur, automatic rifle.
mitrailleuse [mitrajøːz], s.f. Machine-gun.
mitral, -aux [mitral, -o], a. Mitral (valve of the heart).
mitre [mitr], s.f. **1.** Mitre (of bishop). **2.** (a) Chimney-pot. (b) Chimney-cowl.
mitré [mitre], a. Mitred (abbot).
mitron [mitrɔ̃], s.m. A: **1.** (Baker's) paper cap. **2.** Journeyman baker. [MITRE]
mi-vent, s.m.inv. Half-grown fruit-tree in an exposed position.
mi-vitesse (à), adv.phr. At half-speed.
mi-voix (à), adv.phr. In an undertone, under one's breath, in a subdued voice.
mixte [mikst], a. **1.** Mixed (race, bathing). Commission m., joint commission. s.m. Ten: **Mixte double,** mixed doubles. **2.** Serving a double purpose. Train m., composite train (goods and passengers).
mixtion [mikstjɔ̃], s.f. **1.** Compounding (of drugs, etc.). **2.** Pharm: Mixture.
mixture [mikstyːr], s.f. Mixture (esp. of drugs).
mnémonique [mnemɔnik]. **1.** a. Mnemonic. **2.** s.f. Mnemonics.
mnémoniser [mnemɔnize], v.tr. To memorize.
mnémotechnie [mnemɔtɛkni], s.f. Mnemonics.
mobile [mɔbil]. **1.** a. (a) Mobile, movable. **Fête mobile,** movable feast. (b) Unstable, changeable, fickle (nature); restless, excitable (population). (c) Detachable. Objectif m., detachable lens. Album à feuilles mobiles, loose-leaf album. S.a. TIMBRE 2. (d) Moving (target, etc.); shifting, changing (expression). Organes mobiles, sliding, working, parts. Escalier m., moving stairway. Med: Rein m., floating kidney. Mil: Colonne m., flying column. Fr.Hist: Garde mobile, militia (of 1848, of 1868-71). **2.** s.m. (a) Moving body;

body in motion. (b) Driving power. (i) (Of pers.) Premier m. dans un complot, prime mover in a plot; originator of a plot. (ii) M. d'un crime, motive of a crime.
mobilier, -ière [mɔbilje, -jɛːr]. **1.** a. Jur: Movable, personal. Biens mobiliers, personal estate, chattels, personalty. Fin: Valeurs mobilières, stocks and shares. **2.** s.m. (a) Furniture. (b) Set, suite, of furniture.
mobilisation [mɔbilizasjɔ̃], s.f. Mobilization (of troops); liquidation, liberation (of capital).
mobilis|er [mɔbilize], v.tr. To mobilize (troops); to call out, call up (reservist); to liberate (capital). Anciens mobilisés, ex-service men. a. **-able.**
mobilité [mɔbilite], s.f. **1.** Mobility, movableness. **2.** Changeableness, instability (of character).
mocassin [mɔkasɛ̃], s.m. Moccasin.
moche [mɔʃ], a. P: Rotten (conduct, etc.); poor, shoddy (work); ugly (individual).
modal, -aux [mɔdal, -o], a. Jur: Log: Mus: Modal.
modalité [mɔdalite], s.f. **1.** Phil: Modality. **2.** Mus: Form of scale. **3.** pl. Jur: (Restrictive) clauses. Modalités de paiement, methods of payment. Fin: Modalités d'une émission, terms and conditions of an issue.
mode[1] [mɔd], s.f. **1.** Fancy, fashion. (a) Vivre à sa mode, to live according to one's own fancy. (b) Mener la mode, to set the fashion. Lancer la mode de qch., mettre qch. à la mode, to bring sth. into fashion. Être de mode, à la mode, to be in fashion, in vogue. Devenir à la m., to come into fashion. Passer de mode, to go out of fashion. A l'ancienne m., in the old style. Robe à la m., fashionable, modish, stylish, dress. A la mode de . . ., after the style, manner, of . . . . S.a. BŒUF 2. **2.** pl. Com: (a) Ladies' dresses; fashions. Gravures de modes, fashion-plates. (b) (Articles de) modes, millinery. Magasin de modes, milliner's shop.
mode[2], s.m. **1.** Log: Mode, mood. **2.** Gram: Mood. **3.** Mus: (a) Mode (in plainsong). (b) (Major, minor) mode or mood. **4.** Method, mode. "Mode d'emploi," 'directions for use.'
modèle [mɔdɛl]. **1.** s.m. (a) Model, pattern. M. de broderie, sampler. M. d'écriture, hand-writing copy. Machines toutes bâties, établies, sur le même m., machines all built to one pattern, on the same lines. M. déposé, registered pattern. Prendre modèle sur qn, to take s.o. as one's model, as one's pattern. (b) Mec.E: Template. Metall: Pattern (of casting). Cost: Model frock or hat. **2.** s.m. (Artist's) model. Servir de m. à un artiste, to sit for an artist. **3.** a. Un époux m., a model, exemplary, husband.
model|er [mɔdle], v.tr. (je modèle; je modèlerai) To model; to mould (clay, etc.). F: M. la destinée de qn, to shape s.o.'s destiny. s.m. **-age.** s.m. **-eur.**
se modeler sur qn, to take s.o. as a pattern; to take pattern by s.o.
modelé, s.m. (a) Art: Relief. (b) Surv: Hill-shading.
modelliste [mɔdelist], s. m. & f. Dress-designer.
modérateur, -trice [mɔderatœːr, -tris]. **1.** a. Moderating, restraining. **2.** s. Moderator, restrainer. **3.** s.m. Regulator, governor (of engine, etc.). El: Damper (of magnetic needle). M. de son, volume-control (of wireless set).
modération [mɔderasjɔ̃], s.f. **1.** Moderation, restraint; temperateness. Aveo modération, temperately. **2.** M. de prix, reduction in price. M. de peine, mitigation of penalty.

modérer [mɔdere], *v.tr.* (je modère; je modérerai) **1.** (*a*) To moderate, restrain (passion, etc.); to slacken (speed); to regulate (machine). *M. son impatience*, to curb one's impatience. (*b*) *El:* To damp (magnetic needle). **2.** To reduce (price); to mitigate (penalty).
　se modérer. **1.** To control oneself; to keep calm; to calm down. **2.** (Of storm, etc.) To abate, to subside.
　modéré, *a.* Moderate; temperate (person); reasonable (price, etc.); subdued (cheers). *adv.* **-ment.**

moderne [mɔdɛrn], *a.* Modern. *Enseignement m.,* modern side (in schools). *Bâtir à la moderne,* to build in the modern style.

modernement [mɔdɛrnəmɑ̃], *adv.* In a modern, up-to-date manner.

modernis|er [mɔdɛrnize], *v.tr.* To modernize. *s.f.* **-ation.**

modernisme [mɔdɛrnism], *s.m.* Modernism.

modernité [mɔdɛrnite], *s.f.* **1.** Modernity, modernness. **2.** Modern times.

modeste [mɔdɛst], *a.* Modest; unassuming, unpretentious; quiet (dress). *adv.* **-ment.**

modestie [mɔdɛsti], *s.f.* Modesty (of person); unpretentiousness. **Faire de la modestie,** to belittle oneself.

modicité [mɔdisite], *s.f.* Moderateness; slenderness (of means); lowness, reasonableness (of price).

modificateur, -trice [mɔdifikatœːr, -tris]. **1.** *a.* Modifying, modificatory. **2.** *s.* Modifier. **3.** *s.m.* *Mec.E:* Engaging or disengaging gear. *M. instantané,* trip-gear.

modificatif, -ive [mɔdifikatif, -iːv], *a.* Modifying (clause, etc.); modal (verb).

modification [mɔdifikasjɔ̃], *s.f.* Modification, alteration. *Apporter, faire, une m. à qch.,* to modify sth.; to amend (a plan).

modifi|er [mɔdifje], *v.tr.* **1.** To modify (statement); to alter, change (plan). *Nau: M. la route,* to alter course. **2.** *Gram:* To qualify, modify (the verb). *a.* **-able.**

modillon [mɔdijɔ̃], *s.m.* *Arch:* Modillion.

modique [mɔdik], *a.* Moderate, reasonable (cost, charge); slender (income).

modiquement [mɔdikmɑ̃], *adv.* At a low price; at small cost.

modiste [mɔdist], *s.f.,* occ. *m.* Milliner, modiste.

modulation [mɔdylasjɔ̃], *s.f.* **1.** *Mus:* Modulation, transition. **2.** Modulation, inflexion (of the voice).

module [mɔdyl], *s.m.* **1.** (*a*) *Arch: Hyd: Num:* Module. (*b*) Standard, unit (of length, etc.). **2.** *Mth: Mec:* Modulus. *M. d'élasticité,* modulus of elasticity; Young's modulus.

moduler [mɔdyle], **1.** *v.tr.* To modulate (one's voice). **2.** *v.i. Mus:* To modulate.

moelle [mwal], *s.f.* **1.** Marrow (of bone). *Anat:* Medulla. **Os à moelle,** marrow-bone. *F:* Il n'a pas de moelle dans les os, he has got no backbone. *Anglais jusqu'à la moelle des os,* English to the backbone. *Glacé jusqu'à la m. (des os),* frozen to the bone, to the marrow. *Corrompu jusqu'à la m.,* rotten to the core. *Discours plein de m.,* pithy, marrowy, discourse. *Anat:* Moelle allongée, medulla oblongata. S.a. ÉPINIÈRE. **2.** *Bot:* Pith.

moelleu|x, -euse [mwalø, -øːz], *a.* **1.** (*a*) Marrowy (bone). (*b*) *Bot:* Pithy. **2.** (*a*) Soft, velvety (to the touch); mellow (wine, voice); easy (motion). *Couleur moelleuse,* soft colour. (*b*) *s.m.* Softness (of colour); mellowness (of voice, etc.); ease (of motion). *adv.* **-sement.**

moellon [mwalɔ̃], *s.m.* Quarry-stone. *M. brut,* rubble(-stone). *M. d'appareil,* ashlar.

mœurs [mœrs], *s.f.pl.* Morals or manners (of people); customs (of country, epoch, etc.); habits (of animals). **Bonnes mœurs,** morality. *Avoir de bonnes m.,* avoir des mœurs, to have high principles. **Certificat de bonne vie et mœurs,** certificate of good character. **Gens sans mœurs,** unprincipled people. **Autres temps autres mœurs,** other times other ways.

mofette [mɔfet], *s.f. Geol:* Mofette. (*a*) Gasspring. (*b*) Choke-damp.

mohair [mɔɛːr], *s.m. Tex:* Mohair.

moi [mwa]. **1.** Stressed *pers.pron.* (*a*) (Subject) I. *C'est moi,* it is I; *F:* it's me. *Il est plus âgé que moi,* he is older than I. *Elle est invitée et moi aussi,* she is invited and so am I. *Moi, je veux bien,* for my part, I am willing. *Je l'ai fait moi-même,* I did it myself. (*b*) (Object) Me. *Il accuse mon frère et moi,* he accuses my brother and me. *A moi!* help! **De vous à moi,** between you and me. *Ce livre est à moi,* this book is mine, belongs to me. *Un ami à moi,* a friend of mine. *Ces vers ne sont pas de moi,* the verses are not mine. (*c*) (After imp.) (i) (acc.) *Laissez-moi tranquille,* leave me alone. (ii) (dat.) *Donnez-le-moi,* give it (to) me. **2.** *s.m.* Ego, self. *Culte du moi,* egoism.

moignon [mwaɲɔ̃], *s.m.* Stump (of amputated limb, etc.).

moindre [mwɛ̃ːdr], *a.* **1.** *Comp.* Less(er). *Question de m. importance,* question of less(er) importance, of minor importance. *Les gens moindres que soi,* people of less importance than oneself. *s.* **Choisir le moindre de deux maux,** to choose the lesser of two evils. **2.** *Sup.* **Le, la, moindre,** the least. *Pas la m. chance,* not the slightest, remotest, chance. *Le dernier, mais non le m.,* last but not least. *s.* **Le moindre d'entre nous,** the least of us. S.a. DÉFAUT 2.

moindrement [mwɛ̃drəmɑ̃], *adv.* (Usu. with neg.) Less. *Je ne suis pas m. atteint que vous,* I am just as badly hit as you are. **Le moindrement,** least. *Sans être le m. intéressé,* without being interested in the least.

moine [mwan], *s.m.* **1.** Monk, friar. *Prov:* **L'habit ne fait pas le moine,** it is not the cowl that makes the monk. **2.** (*a*) Bed-warmer. (*b*) Hot-water bottle. **3.** *Typ:* Friar.

moineau [mwano], *s.m. Orn:* Sparrow. *F:* Brûler, tirer, sa poudre aux moineaux, to waste one's shot. *P: C'est un vilain m.,* he's a dirty dog.

moinillon [mwanijɔ̃], *s.m. F:* Young monk; shaveling.

moins [mwɛ̃]. **1.** *adv.* (*a*) *Comp.* Less. *M. encore,* still less, even less. *Beaucoup m. long,* much shorter. *M. d'argent,* less money, not so much money. *M. d'hommes, d'occasions,* fewer men, not so many opportunities. *Plus on le punit m. il travaille,* the more he is punished the less he works. *Il travaille de moins en moins,* he is working less and less. *M. de dix francs,* less than ten francs. *F: Trois voitures, pas moins!* three cars, no less! *En m. de dix minutes,* within, under, ten minutes. *En m. de rien,* in less than no time. **Dix francs de moins,** (i) ten francs less; (ii) ten francs short, too little. *Prep.phr.* **A moins de,** unless, barring. *A m. d'accidents,* barring accidents. *A m. d'avis contraire,* unless I hear to the contrary. *A m. (que) de l'insulter . . . ,* short of insulting him. . . . **A moins que** + *sub.,* unless. *A m. que vous (ne) l'ordonniez,* unless you order it. **Rien moins que,** (ambiguous) (i) anything but; (ii) nothing less than. *Ce n'est rien m. qu'un héros,* (i) he is nothing less than a hero; (ii) he is anything but a hero. *Ce n'est rien (de) m. qu'un miracle,* it is nothing short of a miracle. **Non moins que,** as well as; quite as much as. *Il mérite des éloges, non m. que son frère,* he deserves praise quite as much as his brother. (*b*) *Sup.* **Le moins,** least. *Les élèves les m. appliqués,* the least industrious pupils. **Pas le moins du monde,** not in the least (degree); by no means. *s.neut.* **C'est bien le moins** (*qu'il puisse faire*), it is the least he can do. *Adv.phr.* **Du moins,** at least, that is to say, at all events. **Au moins,** at least (= not less than). **Avoir 10,000 francs de rentes (tout) au moins, à tout le moins, pour le moins,** to have 10,000 francs a year at (the very) least. *Vous compterez cela en moins,* you may deduct that. **2.** (*a*) *prep.* Minus, less. *Une heure m. cinq,* five minutes to one. *Six m. quatre égale deux,* six minus four equals two. *Ten : M. quinze à rien,* owe fifteen, love. (*b*) *s.m. Mth :* Minus sign.

moins-value [mwɛ̃valy], *s.f.* Depreciation; diminution, drop, in value.

moire [mwaːr], *s.f.* Moire; watered material. *M. de soie,* watered silk.

moir|er [mware], *v.tr.* To water, to moiré (silk, etc.). *s.m.* **-age.**
    moiré. **1.** *a. Tex :* Watered, moiré (silk, etc.). **2.** *s.m.* = MOIRURE.

moirure [mwaryːr], *s.f.* Watered effect; moiré.

mois [mwa], *s.m.* Month. (*a*) *Le onze du m. prochain,* the eleventh proximo, *F :* prox. *Du m. dernier,* ultimo, *F :* ult. *De ce m.,* instant, *F :* inst. *Au m. d'août,* in (the month of) August. **Louer qch. au mois,** to hire sth. by the month. (*b*) Month's wages or salary.

moise [mwaːz], *s.f. Carp :* Cross-piece, binding-piece, tie, tie-beam.

Moïse [mɔiːz]. **1.** *Pr.n.m. B.Hist :* Moses. **2.** *s.m.* Wicker cradle; basket cot.

moisir [mwaziːr]. **1.** *v.tr.* To mildew; to make (sth.) mouldy. **2.** *v.i. & pr.* To mildew; to go mouldy.
    moisi. **1.** *a.* Mouldy, mildewy (bread, etc.); musty, fusty (taste, smell). **2.** *s.m.* Mould, mildew. **Sentir le moisi,** to smell musty, fusty.

moisissure [mwazisyːr], *s.f.* **1.** Mildew; mould. **2.** Mouldiness, mustiness.

moisson [mwasɔ̃], *s.f.* **1.** (*a*) Harvest(ing) (of cereals). *Faire la m.,* to harvest, to win the harvest. (*b*) Harvest-time. **2.** (Cereal) crop.

moissonn|er [mwasɔne], *v.tr.* **1.** To reap (corn, field); to harvest, gather (cereal crops). *F : M. des lauriers,* to reap laurels. **2.** *Être moissonné dans la fleur de l'âge,* to be cut off in the prime of life. *s.m.* **-age.**

moissonneur, -euse [mwasɔnœːr, -øːz], *s.* **1.** Harvester, reaper. **2.** *s.f.* **Moissonneuse,** reaping-machine.

moite [mwat], *a.* Moist (brow, hand). (**Froid et**) **moite,** clammy.

moiteur [mwatœːr], *s.f.* Moistness (of hands, etc.). *M. froide,* clamminess.

moitié [mwatje]. **1.** *s.f.* Half. *Perdre la m. de son argent,* to lose half one's money. *Une bonne m.,* a good half, fully a half. **Couper qch. par (la) moitié,** to cut something into halves. *Prov :* **A moitié fait qui commence bien,** well begun is half-done. **Vendre qch. à moitié prix,** to sell sth. at half-price. *S'arrêter à m. chemin,* to stop half-way. **Moitié plus,** half as much again. **Plus grand de moitié,** (i) half as large again; (ii) occ. twice as large. *Réduit de m.,* reduced by half. **Se mettre de moitié avec qn dans qch.,** to go halves with s.o. in sth. *Être de m. avec qn,* to take share and share alike. *F :* **Ma (chère) moitié,**

my better half. *Adv.phr.* **A moitié,** half. *A m. mort,* half-dead. *A m. cuit,* half-cooked, half-baked. **2.** *adv.* **Moitié riant, moitié pleurant,** half laughing, half crying. *M. l'un, m. l'autre,* half and half.

moitir [mwatiːr], *v.tr.* To moisten (the skin); to make (sth.) damp or clammy.

Moka [mɔka]. **1.** *Pr.n. Geog :* Mocha. **2.** *s.m.* Mocha (coffee).

mol. See MOU.

molaire [mɔlɛːr], *a. & s.f.* Molar (tooth); *F :* grinder.

môle [moːl], *s.m.* Mole; (harbour) breakwater.

moléculaire [mɔlekylɛːr], *a.* Molecular.

molécule [mɔlekyl], *s.f.* Molecule.

molène [mɔlɛn], *s.f. Bot :* Mullein.

moleskine, molesquine [mɔlɛskin], *s.f.* Imitation leather; (enamelled) American cloth.

molestation [mɔlɛstasjɔ̃], *s.f.* Molestation.

molester [mɔlɛste], *v.tr.* To molest.

molet|er [mɔlte], *v.tr.* (**je molette; je moletterai**) To mill, knurl. *s.m.* **-age.**

molette [mɔlɛt], *s.f.* **1.** Small pestle; muller. **2.** (*a*) Serrated or embossed roller or wheel. *M. d'éperon,* rowel of a spur. **Clef à molette,** adjustable spanner. (*b*) Cutting-wheel (for glass, etc.). *Phot :* Trimmer (for prints). (*c*) *Hort :* Grass edging-iron.

mollah [mɔlla], *s.m.* Mullah, moolah.

mollasse [mɔlas], *a. F :* (*a*) Soft, flabby; spineless (character). (*b*) Slow, lazy. [MOL]

molle. See MOU.

mollement [mɔlmɑ̃], *adv.* (*a*) Softly. (*b*) Slackly, feebly; indolently.

mollesse [mɔlɛs], *s.f.* (*a*) Softness (of cushion); flabbiness (of muscle). (*b*) Want of vigour; slackness, lifelessness; woolliness (of style). **Sans mollesse,** briskly, smartly. (*c*) Indolence, effeminacy.

mollet, -ette [mɔlɛ, -ɛt]. **1.** *a.* Softish. **Pain mollet,** (breakfast or dinner) roll. S.a. ŒUF 1. **2.** *s.m.* Calf (of leg).

molleterie [mɔltri], *s.f.* Light sole-leather.

molletière [mɔltjɛːr], *a. & s.f.* (*a*) (**Bandes**) **molletières,** puttees. (*b*) *M. cycliste,* anklet.

molleton [mɔltɔ̃], *s.m.* (*a*) Soft thick flannel or cotton. *M. à drapeaux,* bunting. (*b*) Swansdown, swanskin.

molletonné [mɔltɔne], *a.* **1.** (Of cloth) With raised nap. **2.** Lined with swansdown.

mollir [mɔliːr]. **1.** *v.i.* (*a*) To soften; to become soft. (*b*) (Of rope, etc.) To slacken; to slack off; (of wind) to die down, to abate. *Les troupes mollissaient,* the troops were giving ground. **2.** *v.tr.* To slacken (rope); to ease (helm).

mollusque [mɔlysk], *s.m.* Mollusc.

molosse [mɔlɔs], *s.m.* Watch-dog; mastiff.

molybdène [mɔlibdɛn], *s.m. Ch :* Molybdenum.

môme [moːm], *s. m. & f. P :* Brat, kid, youngster.

moment [mɔmɑ̃], *s.m.* **1.** Moment. *Le m. venu . . .,* when the time had come. . . . **Un moment!** one moment! wait (a bit)! **Il est là en, à, ce moment,** he is there at the moment, just now, at present. *Il ne me faut rien* **pour le moment,** I don't need anything at the moment, in the meantime. *Sur le m. je ne sus que faire,* for a moment I was at a loss. **J'ai répondu sur le moment,** I answered on the spur of the moment. **Arriver au bon moment,** to arrive in the nick of time. **Par moments,** at times, now and again. *Cela peut arriver d'un moment à l'autre,* it may happen any minute. **A tout moment, à tous moments,** constantly. *Au m. donné,* at the appointed time. **Au moment de partir,** just as I, he, was starting. *Nous étions au m. de partir*, we were on the point of starting. *Jusqu'au m. où . . .*, until (such time) as. . . . *Conj.phr.* Du moment que . . ., (i) from the moment when . . . ; (ii) seeing that. . . . **2.** *Mec:* Moment (of force). **Moment d'inertie,** moment of inertia.

momentané [mɔmɑ̃tane], *a.* Momentary (effort, etc.) ; temporary (absence). *adv.* **-ment.**

momerie [mɔmri], *s.f.* Mummery.

momie [mɔmi], *s.f.* Mummy.

momification [mɔmifikasjɔ̃], *s.f.* Mummification.

momifier [mɔmifje], *v.tr.* To mummify.

mon, ma, mes [mɔ̃, ma, me], *poss.a.* (*Mon* is used instead of *ma* before *f.* words beginning with vowel or h 'mute.') My. *Mon ami, mon amie*, my friend. *Mon meilleur ami, ma meilleure amie*, my best friend. *C'est mon affaire à moi*, that's my (own) business. *Un de mes amis*, a friend of mine. *Mon père et ma mère, mes père et mère*, my father and mother. *Non, mon colonel*, no, sir.

monacal, -aux [mɔnakal, -o], *a.* Usu. *Pej:* Monac(h)al, monkish.

monade [mɔnad], *s.f. Phil: Biol: Ch:* Monad.

monandre [mɔnɑ̃:dr], *a. Bot:* Monandrous.

monarchie [mɔnarʃi], *s.f.* Monarchy.

monarchique [mɔnarʃik], *a.* Monarchic(al).

monarchiste [mɔnarʃist], *a. & s.* Monarchist.

monarque [mɔnark], *s.m.* Monarch.

monastère [mɔnastɛ:r], *s.m.* Monastery ; convent. *Église de m.*, minster.

monastique [mɔnastik], *a.* Monastic. *adv.* **-ment,** -ally.

monceau [mɔ̃so], *s.m.* Heap, pile.

mondain, -aine [mɔ̃dɛ̃, -ɛn], *a.* **1.** Mundane, worldly, earthly. *s.* Worldling. **2.** Fashionable (resort, etc.). *Réunion mondaine*, society gathering. *s.* Un mondain, a man about town. **Une mondaine,** a society woman.

mondanité [mɔ̃danite], *s.f.* **1.** Mundaneness, worldliness. **2.** *pl. Journ:* Social events ; society news.

monde [mɔ̃:d], *s.m.* **1.** World. (*a*) **Le monde entier,** the whole world. *Geog:* **Le nouveau monde,** the New World. **Mettre qn, qch., au monde,** to bring s.o., sth., into the world ; to give birth to s.o., sth. **Être au monde,** to be in the land of the living. **Être seul au monde,** to be alone in the world. **Il est encore de ce monde,** he is still alive. **Pour rien au monde,** not for the world, not on any account. **Faire tout au monde pour obtenir qch.,** to do the utmost possible to get sth. **Personne au monde,** no man alive. **Être le mieux du monde avec qn,** to be on the best of terms with s.o. S.a. MOINS I (*b*). **Vieux comme le monde,** (as) old as the hills. **Il revient du bout du monde,** he is just back from the ends of the earth. **Ainsi va le monde,** such is the way of the world. **Dans l'autre monde,** in the next world. S.a. RENVERSÉ I. (*b*) Society. *Le m. savant*, the world of science. *Le m. du ciné*, filmdom. **Le beau monde,** fashionable people, (fashionable) society. **Le grand monde,** high society. **Aller dans le monde,** to move in society. **Savoir son monde,** to be accustomed to move in polite circles. **Homme du monde,** man of the world, man of quality. **Le petit monde,** the lower classes. **2.** People. (*a*) *Peu de m.*, *pas grand m.*, not many people, not a large crowd. **Avoir du monde à dîner,** to have people, company, to dinner. **Il connaît son monde,** he knows the people he has to deal with. S.a. SE MOQUER. **Tout le monde,** everybody, everyone. *F:* **Tout le monde et son père,** all the world and his wife.

(*b*) *Comment va tout votre m.?* how are all your people, all your family? (*c*) Servants, men, hands. *Congédier tout son m.*, to dismiss all one's servants, one's staff. **3.** *Her:* Mound, orb.

monder [mɔ̃de], *v.tr.* To clean (grain, etc.) ; to hull (barley, etc.) ; to blanch (almonds) ; to stone (raisins).

mondial, -aux [mɔ̃djal, -o], *a.* World-wide (crisis, etc.). **Guerre mondiale,** world war.

monégasque [mɔnegask], *a. & s.* (Native) of Monaco.

monétaire [mɔnetɛ:r], *a.* Monetary. *Unité m. d'un pays*, currency of a country. *Questions monétaires*, (i) questions of currency ; (ii) questions of finance. **Presse monétaire,** minting press. S.a. AGENT I.

monétiser [mɔnetize], *v.tr.* To monetize ; to mint.

mongol, -ole [mɔ̃gɔl], *a. & s. Ethn:* Mongol, Mongolian.

mongolique [mɔ̃gɔlik], *a.* Mongolian.

moniteur, -trice [mɔnitœ:r, -tris], *s. Sch:* Monitor. *Mil:* Gymnastic instructor. *Sp:* Coach.

monitoire [mɔnitwa:r], *a.* Monitory.

monnaie [mɔnɛ], *s.f.* **1.** Money. **Pièce de monnaie,** coin. *M. légale*, legal tender ; currency. **Fausse monnaie,** counterfeit coinage. *F:* **Battre monnaie,** to raise the wind. **(Hôtel (de) la Monnaie,** the Mint. *F:* **Payer qn en monnaie de singe,** to let s.o. whistle for his money ; to bilk s.o. **2.** Change. *Petite m.*, small change. **Donner la monnaie de mille francs,** to give change for a thousand-franc note. *F:* **Rendre à qn la monnaie de sa pièce,** to pay s.o. (back) in his own coin. S.a. BLANC I. 2. **3.** *Bot:* **Monnaie du pape,** honesty ; satin-flower.

monnayer [mɔneje], *v.tr.* (je monnaie, je monnaye ; je monnaierai, je monnayerai) To coin, mint. *s.m.* **-age.**

monnayeur [mɔnejœ:r], *s.m.* Coiner, minter. **Faux monnayeur,** coiner, counterfeiter.

monobloc [mɔnɔblɔk], *a.inv.* (Of cylinders, etc.) Made in one piece ; cast solid.

monocarpien, -ienne [mɔnɔkarpjɛ̃, -jɛn], *a. Bot:* Monocarpous.

monochrome [mɔnɔkro:m], *a.* Monochromic, monochrome.

monocle [mɔnɔkl], *s.m.* Monocle ; (single) eye-glass.

monocoque [mɔnɔkɔk], *a.* Avion *m.*, boatseaplane ; monocoque.

monocotylédone [mɔnɔkɔtiledɔn], *'Bot:* **1.** *a.* Monocotyledonous. **2.** *s.f.* Monocotyledon.

monoculaire [mɔnɔkylɛ:r], *a.* Monocular (fieldglass, etc.). *Cécité m.*, blindness in one eye.

monocylindrique [mɔnɔsilɛ̃drik], *a.* Singlecylinder, one-cylinder (engine).

monogame [mɔnɔgam], *a.* Monogamous.

monogamie [mɔnɔgami], *s.f.* Monogamy.

monogramme [mɔnɔgram], *s.m.* Monogram.

monographie [mɔnɔgrafi], *s.f.* Monograph.

monolithe [mɔnɔlit], **1.** *a.* Monolithic. **2.** *s.m.* Monolith.

monologue [mɔnɔlɔg], *s.m.* Monologue.

monologuer [mɔnɔlɔge], *v.i.* To soliloquize ; to talk to oneself.

monomane [mɔnɔman], **monomaniaque** [mɔnɔmanjak]. **1.** *a.* Monomaniac(al). **2.** *s.* Monomaniac ; person of one idea.

monomanie [mɔnɔmani], *s.f.* Monomania, obsession.

monôme [mɔno:m], *s.m.* **1.** *Alg:* Monomial ; single term. **2.** Parade (of students) through the streets in single file.

monophasé [mɔnɔfaze], *a. El.E:* Monophase, single-phase, uniphase (current).
monoplace [mɔnɔplas], *a. & s.m.* Single-seater (car, aeroplane).
monoplan [mɔnɔplɑ̃], *s.m. Av:* Monoplane.
monopolaire [mɔnɔpolɛːr], *a.* Single-pole (telephone, etc.).
monopole [mɔnɔpɔl], *s.m.* Monopoly.
monopoliser [mɔnɔpolize], *v.tr.* To monopolize; to have the monopoly of (sth.).
monoprix [mɔnɔpri], *s.m.* One-price shop.
monorail [mɔnɔraːj], *a. & s.m.* Monorail.
monosépale [mɔnɔsepal], *a.* Monosepalous.
monosyllabe [mɔnɔsillab]. **1.** *a.* Monosyllabic. **2.** *s.m.* Monosyllable.
monosyllabique [mɔnɔsillabik], *a.* Monosyllabic.
monotone [mɔnɔtɔn], *a.* Monotonous (speech, etc.). *F:* Humdrum, dull (life).
monotonie [mɔnɔtɔni], *s.f.* Monotony.
monotrèmes [mɔnɔtrɛm], *s.m.pl. Z:* Monotremata, monotremes.
monotype [mɔnɔtip]. **1.** *a.* Monotypous. *Sp:* Voiliers monotypes, one-design sailing boats. **2.** *s.f. Typ:* Monotype (machine).
monovalent [mɔnɔvalɑ̃], *a. Ch:* Monovalent; univalent.
monseigneur [mɔ̃sɛɲœːr], *s.m.* **1.** (a) (Referring to prince) His Royal Highness; (to cardinal) his Eminence; (to duke, archbishop) his Grace; (to bishop) his Lordship. *Monseigneur, Mgr, l'évêque de . . .,* the Lord Bishop of. . . . *pl. Nosseigneurs.* (b) (Mode of address) Your Royal Highness; (to cardinal) your Eminence; (to duke, archbishop) your Grace; (to bishop) my Lord (Bishop), your Lordship. *pl. Messeigneurs.* **2.** *F:* Pince monseigneur (*inv.*), (burglar's) jemmy.
monsieur, *pl.* **messieurs** [m(ə)sjø, mɛsjø], *s.m.* **1.** (a) *Monsieur, M., Jules Durand,* Mr Jules Durand. *Messieurs, MM., Durand et Cie,* Messrs Durand and Co. *M. le duc, le comte, de . . .,* the Duke, the Earl, of. . . . *M. le duc, M. le comte,* his Grace, his Lordship. *Comment va monsieur votre oncle?* how is your uncle? (b) (To or of a boy) *Monsieur Jean, M. Jean Dupont,* Master John, Master John Dupont. (c) (Used alone) *Voici le chapeau de monsieur,* here is Mr Smith's hat. *Monsieur n'y est pas,* Mr Smith is not at home. **2.** (a) (In address) Sir; (to titled gentleman) your Grace, your Lordship, etc. *Bonsoir, messieurs,* good evening, gentlemen. *M. a sonné?* did you ring, sir? *Que prendront ces messieurs?* what will you have, gentlemen? (b) (In letter writing) (i) (To stranger) *Monsieur* (always written in full), Dear Sir. (ii) (Where appropriate) *Monsieur et cher Confrère, Monsieur et cher Collègue,* Dear Sir. (iii) (Implying some friendship) *Cher Monsieur,* Dear Mr Durand. **3.** Gentleman. *Deux messieurs que je ne connais pas,* two gentlemen whom I do not know. *F:* Faire le gros monsieur, to play, come, the heavy swell. *Un vilain monsieur,* a bad lot. [SIEUR]
monstre [mɔ̃ːstr]. **1.** *s.m.* (a) *Ter:* Monster, monstrosity. (b) *Myth:* Monster. *Les monstres marins,* the monsters of the deep. *F: M. d'ingratitude,* monster of ingratitude. **2.** *a.* Huge; colossal; monster (demonstration).
monstrueu|x, -euse [mɔ̃stryø, -øːz], *a.* Monstrous. **1.** Unnatural. *Ombre monstrueuse,* grisly shadow. **2.** Huge, colossal. **3.** Shocking, scandalous. *adv.* **-sement.**
mont [mɔ̃], *s.m.* Mount, mountain. *Le m. Sinaï,* Mount Sinai. *Par monts et par vaux,* up hill and

down dale. *Être toujours par monts et par vaux,* to be always on the move. *F:* Promettre monts et merveilles à qn, to promise s.o. wonders. *Passer les monts,* to cross the Alps.
montagnard, -arde [mɔ̃taɲaːr, -ard]. **1.** *a.* Mountain, highland (people, etc.). **2.** *s.* (a) Mountaineer, highlander. (b) *Fr.Hist:* Member of the *Montagne.*
montagne [mɔ̃taɲ], *s.f.* **1.** (a) Mountain. *Les montagnes d'Écosse,* the Highlands (of Scotland). *B:* Le Sermon sur la montagne, the Sermon on the Mount. *C'est la montagne qui accouche,* it's the mountain in labour. *Montagnes russes,* scenic railway; switchback. (b) Mountain region. *Passer l'été dans une station de montagne,* to spend the summer in a hill station. (c) Montagne de glace, iceberg. **2.** *Fr.Hist:* La Montagne, name given during the Revolution to the extremist party, who occupied seats in the higher part of the House.
montagneux, -euse [mɔ̃taɲø, -øːz], *a.* Mountainous, hilly.
montant [mɔ̃tɑ̃]. **1.** *a.* (a) Rising, ascending. *Chemin m.,* uphill road. *Marée montante,* rising tide, flood-tide. *Robe montante,* high-necked dress. *Col m.,* stand-up collar. *Rail:* Train, quai, montant, down train, down platform. (b) *Mil:* Garde montante, new guard, relieving guard. **2.** *s.m.* (a) Upright (of ladder, etc.); leg (of trestle); column, pillar (in machine); pole (of tent); stile (of door, window); post (of gate); riser (of stair). *Fb:* Les montants, the goal-posts. *P:* Un montant, a pair of trousers. (b) Total amount (of account). *J'ignore le m. de mes dettes,* I do not know what my debts amount to.
mont-de-piété, *s.m. A:* (Now *crédit municipal*) Pawn-office. *Mettre qch. au m.-de-p.,* to pawn sth.
monte [mɔ̃ːt], *s.f.* **1.** Rising, mounting. *Mouvement de m. et baisse,* up and down movement, rising and falling movement. **2.** Breeding season, mating season (of domestic animals). **3.** *Turf:* (a) Mounting (of horse). *Jockey qui a eu trois montes dans la journée,* jockey who has ridden three times during the day. (b) (Method of) riding, horsemanship. *Monte à l'obstacle,* jumping.
monte-charge, *s.m. inv.* Hoist; goods-lift.
monténégrin, -ine [mɔ̃tenegrɛ̃, -in], *a. & s. Geog:* Montenegrin.
monte-plats, *s.m.inv.* Dinner-lift, service-lift.
monter [mɔ̃te]. I. *v.i.* (Aux. usu. *être,* occ. *avoir*) **1.** (a) To climb (up), mount, ascend; to go upstairs. (Of bird) To soar. *Av:* To climb. *M. à, sur, un arbre,* to climb (up) a tree. *M. en haut d'une colline,* to mount, climb, go up, to the top of a hill. *M. se coucher,* to go (up) to bed. *Faire monter qn,* to call, ask, show, s.o. upstairs. *Montez chez moi,* come up to my room(s). *Mil:* Monter en ligne, to go up the line. *M. à l'assaut, F:* to go over the top. *Ten:* M. au filet, to come, go, up to the net. (b) To climb on, into (sth.). *M. sur une chaise,* to get on to a chair. *M. en chaire,* to ascend the pulpit. *S.a.* TRÔNE. Monter à cheval, (i) to mount, (ii) to ride. *Montez-vous (à cheval)?* do you ride? *F:* Monter sur ses grands chevaux,* to get on one's high horse. *M. à, en, bicyclette,* to ride a bicycle. *M. en voiture,* to get into the carriage. *Faire m. qn avec soi,* to give s.o. a lift. *M. à bord,* to go on board (a ship). *M. sur la scène,* to go on the stage. **2.** (a) (Of balloon, of the sun, etc.) To rise; (of prices, barometer, etc.) to rise, to go up; (of tide) to flow. *Les frais montent,* the costs are mounting up. *Frais montant à mille francs,* expenses

amounting to one thousand francs. **Faire monter les prix**, to raise the prices. *Empêcher les prix de m.*, to keep the prices down. *Le sang lui monte à la tête*, the blood rushes to his head. *Faire m. les larmes aux yeux de qn*, to bring tears to s.o.'s eyes. *F: Monter comme une soupe au lait*, to flare up; to fire up in a moment. (*b*) (Of road, etc.) To ascend, to climb. (*c*) (Of pers., etc.) *M. dans l'estime de qn*, to rise in s.o.'s estimation. *Faire m. qn dans l'estime de qn*, to raise s.o. in s.o.'s estimation.

II. **mont|er**, *v.tr.* **1.** To mount. (*a*) To climb (up), go up, ascend (hill, etc.). *M. un fleuve*, to go, sail, steam, up a river. (*b*) *Mil:* *M. la garde, sa faction*, (i) to mount guard; (ii) to go on guard. (*c*) To ride (horse). **2.** *Nau:* To man (boat). **3.** (*a*) To raise, carry up, take up, haul up. *M. du vin de la cave*, to fetch, bring up, wine from the cellar. *Vous me monterez de l'eau chaude à sept heures*, you will bring me up a can of hot water at seven. (*b*) *F:* **Se monter la tête**, to get excited. **Monter la tête à qn**, to work on s.o.'s feelings. *M. la tête à qn contre qn*, to set s.o. against s.o. **4.** (*a*) To set, mount (jewel); to mount (photo, fish-hook, etc.); to fit on (tyre); to set up, fit up, erect (apparatus, etc.); to hang (door); to fit out, equip (workshop, etc.); to assemble, erect (machine). *Se m. un ménage*, to set up house. *M. un magasin*, to set up, open, a shop. *Knitting:* *M. les mailles*, to cast on (the stitches). *M. un complot, un coup*, to hatch a plot. *P:* **Monter le coup à qn**, to deceive s.o., to take s.o. in. S.a. BATEAU. (*b*) *El.E:* To connect up, wire up (batteries, etc.). *s.m.* **-age**.

se monter. 1. To amount. *A combien se monte tout cela?* how much does all this come to? **2.** To equip oneself, fit oneself out (*en*, with).

monté, *a.* **1.** Mounted (soldier, etc.). **2.** (*a*) **Monté en couleur**, high in colour. (*b*) *F:* Il était monté, il avait la tête montée, he was worked up, his blood was up. **3.** Set (jewel); mounted (gun, etc.); equipped, fitted, appointed (ship, etc.). *Photographies non montées*, unmounted photographs. *Pièce mal montée*, badly produced play. *Cave, boutique, bien montée*, well-stocked cellar, shop. *F:* **Coup monté**, plot; *F:* put-up job.

montée, *s.f.* **1.** Rise. (*a*) Rising. *Mouvement de m.*, up motion. *Tuyau de montée*, uptake pipe; riser. (*b*) Uphill pull; climb. *Aut: Av:* **Essai de montée**, climbing test. *Vitesse en m.*, climbing speed; speed on a gradient. **2.** (*a*) Ascent, gradient, acclivity, slope (up). (*b*) Step (of stair).

monteur, -euse [mɔ̃tœːr, -øːz], *s.* Setter (of jewels); mounter (of pictures); stager, producer (of play). *Mec.E:* *etc:* Fitter, assembler.

monticule [mɔ̃tikyl], *s.m.* (*a*) Hillock. (*b*) Hummock (of ice).

mont-joie, *s.f.* **1.** Cairn; heap of stones. *pl. Des monts-joie.* **2.** *Hist:* (War-cry of the French armies) **Mont-joie Saint-Denis!** montjoy(e)!

montmartrois, -oise [mɔ̃martrwa, -waːz], *a. & s.* (Native, inhabitant) of the Montmartre quarter (of Paris).

montoir [mɔ̃twaːr], *s.m.* Mounting-block, horseblock. **Côté (du) montoir**, near side (of horse). **Côté hors (du) montoir**, off side.

montrable [mɔ̃trabl], *a.* Fit to be seen; presentable.

montre [mɔ̃ːtr], *s.f.* **1.** (*a*) Show, display. **Faire montre d'un grand courage**, to display great courage. *Faire qch. pour la'm.*, to do sth. merely for show. (*b*) (i) Shop-window, display-window. *Mettre qch. en m.*, to put sth. in the window.

(ii) Show-case. (iii) Show pipes (of organ). **2.** (*a*) Watch. *M. de poignet*, wrist-watch, wristlet-watch. *M. à double boîtier, à recouvrement*, hunter. *M. à remontoir*, keyless watch. **Montre marine**, chronometer. **Cela lui a pris dix minutes montre en main**, it took him ten minutes by the clock. (*b*) *Aut:* Clock.

montrer [mɔ̃tre], *v.tr.* To show. (*a*) To display, exhibit. *Il a montré un grand courage*, he showed, displayed, great courage. S.a. CORDE 1, DENT 1. (*b*) To point out. *M. qch. du doigt*, to point sth. out (with one's finger). *M. qn du, au, doigt*, to point s.o. out with one's finger; *esp.* to point the finger of scorn at s.o. *M. le chemin à qn*, to show s.o. the way. (*c*) *M. à qn à faire qch.*, to show, teach, s.o. how to do sth.

se montrer. (*a*) *Se m. au bon moment*, to appear at the right moment. *Le soleil se montra tout à coup*, the sun shone out, burst forth. (*b*) *Des taches brunes se montrent sur la peau*, brown marks appear, can be seen, on the skin. (*c*) *Pred.* *Il se montra prudent*, he showed prudence. *Il s'est montré bon prophète*, he proved a good prophet. *Il s'est montré très brave*, he exhibited, displayed, great bravery.

montreur, -euse [mɔ̃trœːr, -øːz], *s.* Showman, -woman (at fair, etc.). *M. de bêtes féroces*, exhibitor of wild beasts. *M. d'ours*, bear-leader.

montueux, -euse [mɔ̃tɥø, -øːz], *a.* Hilly.

montuosité [mɔ̃tɥozite], *s.f.* Hilliness.

monture [mɔ̃tyːr], *s.f.* **1.** Mount (horse, ass, camel, etc.); (saddle-)horse. **2.** Setting (of jewel); mount(ing) (of picture, fan, etc.); frame (of saw, umbrella, spectacles, etc.); stock (of gun, pistol); handle, guard (of sword); attachment (of mud-guard, etc.). **Lunettes sans monture**, rimless spectacles. **3.** Stock and equipment (of farm).

monument [mɔnymɑ̃], *s.m.* **1.** Monument, memorial. *M. funéraire*, monument (over a tomb). **2.** Public or historic building.

monumental, -aux [mɔnymɑ̃tal, -o], *a.* (*a*) Monumental. (*b*) *F:* Huge, colossal.

moquer (se) [sɔmɔke], *v.pr.* *Se m. de qn, de qch.*, to mock, make fun of, make game of, s.o., sth. *Vous vous moquez*, you're joking, you're not serious. **Se faire moquer de soi**, to get laughed at, to make a fool of oneself. **Il se moque du tiers comme du quart**, he doesn't care (a fig) for anybody or anything. **Je m'en moque comme de l'an quarante, comme de coin-tampon**, I don't care a rap, a straw, a fig, two hoots. *Vous vous moquez du monde!* you are joking, I presume! *C'est se m. du monde!* it is the height of impertinence!

moquerie [mɔkri], *s.f.* (*a*) Mockery, scoffing; ridicule, derision. (*b*) Piece of mockery; jeer.

moquette¹ [mɔket], *s.f.* Decoy bird.

moquette², *s.f.* *Tex:* Moquette.

moqueu|r, -euse [mɔkœːr, -øːz]. **1.** *a.* (*a*) Mocking, scoffing. *Rires moqueurs*, derisive laughter. (*b*) Given to mockery; waggish. **2.** *s.* Mocker, scoffer. **3.** *s.m.* Mocking-bird. *adv.* **-sement**.

moraillon [mɔrajɔ̃], *s.m.* Hasp, clasp (of lock).

moraine [mɔrɛn], *s.f.* *Geol:* Moraine.

moral, -aux [mɔral, -o]. **1.** *a.* (*a*) Moral; ethical (philosophy, etc.). *Science morale*, moral science; ethics. (*b*) Mental, intellectual, moral. *Facultés morales*, faculties of the mind. *Courage m.*, moral courage. *Certitude morale*, moral certainty. **2.** *s.m.* (*a*) (State of) mind. *Relever, remonter, le m. de, à, qn*, to raise s.o.'s spirits; to cheer s.o. up. *M. d'une armée, d'une école*, morale of an army, of a school. (*b*) Moral nature. *Son m. dévoyé*, his warped nature. *adv.* **-ement**.

morale [mɔral], *s.f.* **1.** (*a*) Morals. *Contraire à la m.*, immoral. (*b*) Ethics; moral science. *F:* Faire de la morale à qn, to read s.o. a lecture. **2.** Moral (of fable, story).

moralisateur, -trice [mɔralizatœːr, -tris]. **1.** *a.* (*a*) Moralizing (person). (*b*) Elevating, edifying. **2.** *s.* Moralizer.

moraliser[1] [mɔralize]. **1.** *v.i.* To moralize. **2.** *v.tr.* To lecture, sermonize (s.o.).

moraliser[2], *v.tr.* To raise the moral standard of (community).

moraliste [mɔralist], *s. m. & f.* Moralist.

moralité [mɔralite], *s.f.* **1.** (*a*) Morality; (good) moral conduct. *Certificat de moralité,* good-conduct certificate; *F:* reference, character. (*b*) Morals; honesty. **2.** Moral lesson; moral (of story). **3.** *Lit.Hist:* Morality(-play).

moratoire [mɔratwaːr]. **1.** *a.* *Jur:* Moratory (agreement, etc.); (payment) delayed by agreement. *Intérêts moratoires,* interest on over-due payments. **2.** *s.m.* = MORATORIUM.

moratorium [mɔratɔrjɔm], *s.m.* Moratorium.

morbide [mɔrbid], *a.* Morbid. *adv.* **-ment.**

morbidité [mɔrbidite], *s.f.* Morbidity, morbidness.

morbleu [mɔrblø], *int.* Euphemism for MORDIEU.

morceau [mɔrso], *s.m.* **1.** (*a*) Morsel, piece (of food). *M. de choix,* choice morsel. *Aimer les bons morceaux,* to like good things (to eat). *F:* Manger un morceau, to have a snack. *Ne faire qu'un morceau de qch.,* to make one mouthful of sth. *F:* Gober le morceau, to swallow the bait. *Mâcher les morceaux à qn,* to spoon-feed s.o. *Compter les morceaux à qn,* to keep s.o. on short commons; to stint s.o. (*b*) *M. de rôti,* cut off the joint. **2.** Piece (of soap, cloth, music, etc.); bit, scrap, fragment; lump (of sugar). *Sucre en morceaux,* lump sugar. *Mettre qch. en morceaux,* to pull sth. to pieces, to bits. *S'en aller en morceaux, tomber en morceaux,* to be falling to pieces.

morc|eler [mɔrsəle], *v.tr.* (je morcelle; je morcellerai) To cut up (sth.) into small pieces. *M. une propriété,* to break up an estate; to parcel out an estate. *s.m.* **-ellement.**

mordache [mɔrdaʃ], *s.f.* *Tls:* Clamp, claw (of vice); jaw, clip, grip, dog (of chuck).

mordacité [mɔrdasite], *s.f.* **1.** Corrosiveness. **2.** Mordancy, causticity, mordacity (of critic, etc.).

mordant [mɔrdɑ̃]. **1.** *a.* (*a*) Eating away; (of acid) corrosive. *Lime mordante,* file that has plenty of bite. (*b*) Mordant, biting, caustic, pungent (wit, speech, etc.). (*c*) Penetrating, piercing (sound). **2.** *s.m.* (*a*) (i) Corrosiveness (of acid); bite of file, etc.). (ii) Mordancy, pungency, *F:* snap (of wit, etc.); keenness, dash (of troops, etc.). (*b*) *Dy: etc:* Mordant. (*c*) Gold size. (*d*) *Mus:* Mordent.

mordicus [mɔrdikyːs], *adv.* *F:* Stoutly, with might and main, with tooth and nail. *Nier qch. m.,* to deny sth. stoutly. *Défendre m. son opinion,* to stick to one's guns.

mordienne [mɔrdjɛn], *int.* Euphemism for MORDIEU.

mordieu [mɔrdjø], *int.* (*a*) *A:* 'Sdeath! zounds! (*b*) Hang it! by jingo!

mordill|er [mɔrdije], *v.tr.* **1.** To nibble. **2.** (Of puppy, etc.) To pretend to bite. *s.m.* **-age.**

mordorer [mɔrdɔre], *v.tr.* To bronze (leather). **mordoré,** *a. & s.m.* Bronze (colour). *Souliers mordorés,* bronze shoes.

mordre [mɔrdr], *v.tr. & ind.tr.* **1.** To bite. (*a*) *F: Quel chien l'a mordu?* what's bitten him? *Se m. la langue,* to bite one's tongue. *Se mordre*

la langue d'avoir parlé, to regret bitterly having spoken. *Il s'en mord les pouces, les lèvres,* he bitterly repents it. *Se mordre les lèvres (pour ne pas rire),* to bite one's lips (in order not to laugh). *Se mordre les poings d'impatience,* to gnaw one's fingers with impatience. S.a. DOIGT 1. *Poet:* Mordre la poussière, to bite the dust. (Of horse) Mordre son frein, to champ the bit. (*b*) *Lime, vis, qui mord,* file, screw, that bites, that has a good bite. *Acide qui mord (sur) les métaux,* acid that bites, acts on, metals. *M. à, dans, une pomme,* to bite into, take a bite out of, an apple. *F: Il mord au latin,* he is shaping well at Latin. *Fish: Ça mord,* I've got a bite. S.a. APPÂT, GRAPPE I, HAMEÇON. (*c*) (Of cog-wheels) To catch, engage. **2.** *Engr:* Mordre une planche, faire mordre une planche, to etch a plate.

morelle [mɔrɛl], *s.f.* *Bot:* Nightshade, morel.

moresque [mɔresk], *a.* = MAURESQUE.

morfil [mɔrfil], *s.m.* Wire-edge (on tool).

morfiler [mɔrfile], *v.tr.* To remove the wire-edge from (tool). *Pierre à morfiler,* hone; oilstone.

morfondre [mɔrfɔːdr], *v.tr.* (Of wind, etc.) To chill (s.o.) to the bone.

se morfondre. (*a*) To be bored to death. (*b*) *Se m. à la porte de qn,* to stand shivering at s.o.'s door.

morganatique [mɔrganatik], *a.* Morganatic; *F:* left-handed (marriage). *adv.* **-ment, -ally.**

morgeline [mɔrʒəlin], *s.f.* *Bot:* **1.** Scarlet pimpernel. **2.** Chickweed.

morgue [mɔrg], *s.f.* **1.** Pride, haughtiness, arrogance. **2.** Mortuary, morgue.

moribond [mɔribɔ̃], *a.* Moribund, at death's door.

moricaud, -aude [mɔriko, -oːd]. **1.** *a.* Dark-skinned, dusky, swarthy. **2.** *s.* (*a*) Blackamoor. (*b*) *F:* Darky, black.

morigéner [mɔriʒene], *v.tr.* (je morigène; je morigénerai) To lecture (s.o.); to take (s.o.) to task; to talk seriously to (s.o.); to rate (s.o.) (*d'avoir fait qch.,* for doing sth.).

morille [mɔriːj], *s.f.* **1.** *Fung: Cu:* Morel. **2.** *pl.* Jewing (of domestic pigeon).

morion [mɔrjɔ̃], *s.m.* *Archeol:* Morion.

mormon, -on(n)e [mɔrmɔ̃, -ɔn], *a. & s.* Mormon; *s.* Latter-day Saint.

mormonisme [mɔrmɔnism], *s.m.* Mormonism.

morne[1] [mɔrn], *a.* Dejected; gloomy (silence); dull (weather, etc.); bleak, dreary, dismal. *adv.* **-ment.**

morne[2], *s.f.* *Archeol:* Coronal (of tilting-lance); morne.

morne[3], *s.m.* Bluff, hillock (in West Indies).

morné [mɔrne], *a.* **1.** (Of tilting-lance) Blunted, harmless. **2.** *Her:* Disarmed (lion, etc.); (lion) morné.

morose [mɔroːz], *a.* Morose, moody, surly (person); gloomy, forbidding (building, etc.).

morosité [mɔrozite], *s.f.* Moroseness, moodiness, surliness.

Morphée [mɔrfe]. *Pr.n.m. Myth:* Morpheus. *F:* Dans les bras de Morphée, in the arms of Morpheus.

morphine [mɔrfin], *s.f.* Morphia, morphine.

morphinisme [mɔrfinism], *s.m.* *Med:* Morphinism.

morphinomane [mɔrfinɔman], *a. & s.* Morphi(n)omaniac; morphia addict; *F:* drug-fiend.

morphinomanie [mɔrfinɔmani], *s.f.* Morphi(n)omania; the morphia habit, the drug habit.

morphologie [mɔrfɔlɔʒi], *s.f.* Morphology.

morphologique [mɔrfɔlɔʒik], *a.* Morphological.

mors [mɔːr], *s.m.* **1.** (*a*) *Tls:* Jaw, chap, chop (of vice). (*b*) *Bookb:* Joint. **2.** *Harn:* Bit. *M. de*

bride, curb-bit, bridle-bit. *M. de bridon*, snaffle. **Ronger son mors**, (i) (of horse) to champ the bit; (ii) *F:* (of pers.) to fret. **Prendre le mors aux dents**, (i) (of horse) to take the bit in its teeth; to bolt; (ii) *F:* (of pers.) to take the bit between one's teeth.

morse[1] [mɔrs], *s.m. Z:* Walrus, morse.

Morse[2]. *Pr.n.m. Tg:* Morse (alphabet, etc.).

morsure [mɔrsyːr], *s.f.* **1.** Bite. **2.** *Engr:* Biting.

mort[1], **morte** [mɔːr, mɔrt]. See MOURIR.

mort[2], *s.f.* **1.** Death. **Pâle comme la mort**, as pale as death. **Il n'y a pas eu mort d'homme**, (i) there was no taking of life; (ii) there were no casualties. **Mettre qn à mort**, to put s.o. to death. **Sentence, arrêt, de mort**, death sentence, sentence of death. **A mort les traîtres!** death to the traitors! *Blessé à m.*, mortally wounded. **Se donner la mort**, to take one's life; to make away with oneself. *F:* **Vous allez attraper la mort!** you'll catch your death (of cold, etc.). **Mourir de sa belle mort**, to die a natural death. **Avoir la mort sur les lèvres; être à deux doigts de la mort**, to be at death's door, on the verge of death. S.a. ARTICLE I. **Haïr qn à mort**, to entertain a deadly, a mortal, hatred of s.o. *La m. d'Arthur, Lit:* the passing of Arthur. **Faire une bonne mort**, to die in the faith. S.a. LIT I. **Il avait la mort dans l'âme**, he was sick at heart. **C'est entre nous à la vie, à la mort**, we would lay down our lives for each other. **2.** (*a*) *Bot:* **Mort au(x) loup(s)**, wolf's-bane. **Mort aux poules**, henbane. (*b*) **Mort aux rats**, rat-poison; *A:* ratsbane. **Mort aux mouches**, fly-poison.

mortadelle [mɔrtadɛl], *s.f.* Bologna sausage.

mortaise [mɔrtɛːz], *s.f.* Slot. (*a*) *Carp:* Mortise. **Assemblage à tenon et à mortaise**, (tenon and) mortise joint. (*b*) *M. de clavette*, keyway.

mortais|er [mɔrteze], *v.tr.* To slot, mortise. *s.m.* **-age.**

mortalité [mɔrtalite], *s.f.* Mortality. **1.** Mortal nature. **2.** Death rate. *Ins:* **Tables de mortalité**, mortality tables.

mort-bois, *s.m. For:* Underwood, brushwood; undesirable tree or shrub.

morte-eau [mɔrto], *s.f.*, **mortes-eaux** [mɔrt-(ə)zo], *s.f.pl.* Neap tide(s); neaps.

mortel, -elle [mɔrtɛl], *a.* Mortal. (*a*) Destined to die. *s. Un m.*, *une mortelle*, a mortal. (*b*) Fatal (wound, etc.). *Coup m.*, mortal blow, death blow. *Il fit une chute mortelle de 200 pieds*, he fell 200 feet to his death. (*c*) *F:* **Je l'ai attendu deux mortelles heures**, I waited two mortal hours for him. (*d*) Deadly (hatred, sin). *Ennemi m.*, mortal foe. *Poison m.*, deadly poison.

mortellement [mɔrtɛlmã], *adv.* Mortally, fatally (wounded, etc.). *Pécher m.*, to commit a mortal sin. *F: S'ennuyer m.*, to be bored to death. *M. ennuyeux*, deadly dull. *M. offensé*, mortally offended.

morte-saison, *s.f. Com: etc:* Dead season, slack season, off season. *pl. Des mortes-saisons.*

morticole [mɔrtikɔl], *s.m. F:* Doctor, sawbones.

mortier [mɔrtje], *s.m.* Mortar. **1.** (*a*) *Pilon et m.*, pestle and mortar. (*b*) *Artil: M. de tranchée*, trench-mortar. **2.** *Const: M. ordinaire*, lime mortar. *M. hydraulique*, hydraulic cement, hydraulic mortar. *M. liquide, clair*, grout(ing). *Planche à m.*, mortar-board. *F:* **Bâti à chaux et à mortier**, built to last for ever.

mortifiant [mɔrtifjã], *a.* Mortifying.

mortification [mɔrtifikasjɔ̃], *s.f.* **1.** Mortification. (*a*) Gangrene, necrosis. (*b*) *M. des passions*, mortification, chastening, of the passions. (*c*) Chagrin, vexation. (*d*) Rebuff, humiliation. **2.** *Cu:* Hanging (of game, etc.).

mortifier [mɔrtifje], *v.tr.* **1.** (*a*) To gangrene; to cause (limb, etc.) to mortify. (*b*) *Cu:* To hang (game, etc.). **2.** (*a*) To mortify (one's passions). (*b*) To mortify (s.o.); to hurt (s.o.'s) feelings.

mortifié, *a.* Mortified. **1.** Gangrened. **2.** Chagrined, vexed (*de*, at).

mort-né, -née, *a.* (*a*) Still-born (child, etc.). (*b*) *Projet m.-né*, abortive plan; plan foredoomed to failure. *pl. Mort-nés, -nées.*

mortuaire [mɔrtɥɛːr], *a.* Mortuary (urn, etc.); of death, of burial. **Drap mortuaire**, pall. **Acte, extrait, mortuaire**, death certificate. **Registre mortuaire**, register of deaths. **La maison mortuaire**, the house of the deceased. *Chambre m.*, death-chamber. **Dépôt mortuaire**, mortuary.

morue [mɔry], *s.f.* **1.** *Ich:* Cod. **Huile de foie de morue**, cod-liver oil. S.a. QUEUE-DE-MORUE.

morutier [mɔrytje], *s.m.* **1.** Cod-fishing boat; banker. **2.** Cod-fisher.

morvandais, -aise [mɔrvãdɛ, -ɛːz], **morvandeau, -elle, -eaux** [mɔrvãdo, -ɛl], *a. & s. Geog:* (Native) of the Morvan region (between Loire, Seine, and Saône).

morve [mɔrv], *s.f.* **1.** *Vet:* Glanders. **2.** Nasal mucus; *V:* snot.

morveux, -euse [mɔrvø, -øːz], *a.* **1.** *Vet:* Glandered. **2.** *F:* Snotty. *Prov:* **Qui se sent morveux se mouche**, if the cap fits wear it. **3.** *s.* (*a*) *P:* Child, brat. (*b*) *F:* Greenhorn, Johnny Raw.

mosaïque[1] [mɔzaik], *a. B.Hist:* Mosaic (law).

mosaïque[2], *s.f. Art: etc:* Mosaic. **Dallage en mosaïque**, mosaic flooring.

moscatelle [mɔskatɛl], *s.f. Bot:* (Tuberous) moschatel.

Moscou [mɔsku]. *Pr.n. Geog:* Moscow.

moscoutaire [mɔskutɛːr], *a.* (Government, etc.) of Moscow.

moscovite [mɔskɔvit], *a. & s. Geog:* Muscovite.

mosquée [mɔske], *s.f.* Mosque.

mot [mo], *s.m.* **1.** Word. **Répéter qch. mot pour mot**, to repeat sth. word for word. **Traduire mot à mot** [motamo], to translate word for word. **Prendre qn au mot**, to take s.o. at his word. **Sans mot dire, sans dire mot**, without (saying) a word. **Qui ne dit mot consent**, silence gives consent. **Ne pas souffler mot de qch.**, not to breathe a word about sth. **Dire deux mots à qn**, to have a word with s.o. **Dire, glisser, un mot pour qn**, to put in a word for s.o. S.a. TOUCHER I. 2. **Vous avez dit le mot!** you've hit it! **Avoir le dernier mot**, to have the last word. **Ignorer le premier mot de la chimie**, not to know the first thing about chemistry. **A ces mots . . .**, (i) so saying . . .; (ii) at these words. . . . **En d'autres mots**, in other words. **En un mot, en peu de mots, en quelques mots**, briefly, in a word, in a nutshell. **Au bas mot**, at the lowest estimate, at the lowest figure. **Gros mot**, coarse expression, foul word, *F:* swear word. *Le mot de l'énigme*, the key to the enigma. **Voilà le fin mot de l'affaire!** so that's what's at the bottom of it! *Avoir le mot de l'affaire*, to be in the secret, in the know. **Faire comprendre qch. à qn à mots couverts**, to give s.o. a hint of sth. *F:* **Donner le mot à qn**, to give s.o. his cue. *Mil:* **Mot de ralliement**, password. **Mot d'ordre**, countersign. **Mots croisés**, cross-words, cross-word puzzle. **Envoyer un (petit) mot à qn**, écrire un mot à qn, to drop s.o. a line. **Placer un mot, dire son mot**, to put in one's word; *F:* to chime in. **Tranchons le mot, vous refusez**, to put it bluntly, you refuse. **Mot historique**, historical saying. **Bon mot**, witty remark; witticism. **Faire des mots**, to be witty, to say smart things. **Avoir le mot pour rire,** to be fond of a joke. **2.** *Her:* Motto.

mot-clé, *s.m.* Key-word (of cipher).

motet [mɔtɛ], *s.m. Mus:* (i) Motet; (ii) anthem.

moteur, -trice [mɔtœːr, -tris]. **I.** *a.* (*a*) Motive, propulsive, driving (power, etc.). **Arbre moteur,** driving shaft, main shaft. *Cy:* **Roue motrice,** back wheel. *Véhicule à traction motrice,* motor vehicle. *Eau motrice,* water power. *I.C.E:* **Temps moteur,** power stroke. (*b*) *Anat:* Motory (nerve); motorial (excitement). **2.** *s.m.* (*a*) **Premier moteur dans un complot,** prime mover in a plot. (*b*) Motor, engine. *M. électrique,* electric motor. *M. à combustion interne, à explosion,* internal combustion engine. *M. à gaz,* gas engine. *M. à clapets sur le dessus,* overhead-valve engine. *M. sans soupapes,* sleeve-valve engine. *M. d'avion,* aeromotor. **Mu par moteur,** power-driven. **Moteur de lancement,** starting engine; *Aut:* self-starter. **3.** *s.f. Rail:* **Motrice,** (electric) motor carriage.

motif, -ive [mɔtif, -iːv]. **I.** *a.* Motive (cause, etc.). **2.** *s.m.* (*a*) Motive, incentive; reason. *M. de mécontentement,* cause, grounds, for discontent. **Avoir un motif pour faire qch.,** to have a motive in doing sth. *F:* **Courtiser qn pour le bon motif,** to court s.o. with honourable intentions. **Soupçons sans motif,** groundless suspicions. *Insulter qn sans m.,* to insult s.o. gratuitously. *Jur:* **Motifs d'un jugement,** grounds upon which a judgment has been delivered. (*b*) (i) *Art:* Motif. (ii) *Needlew:* Design, pattern, motif (for embroidery, etc.). *Dressm:* Ornament, trimming. (iii) *Mus:* Theme, motto, figure.

motilité [mɔtilite], *s.f.* Motility, motivity.

motion [mɔsjɔ̃], *s.f.* Motion, proposal. **Faire une motion,** to propose, bring forward, a motion; to move a proposal. *La m. fut adoptée,* the motion was carried.

motiver [mɔtive], *v.tr.* **I.** To state the reason for (refusal, etc.). *M. une décision sur qch.,* to base a decision on sth. **2.** (*a*) To motive, motivate (an action). (*b*) To justify, warrant, be the motive for (sth.). *La situation motive des craintes,* the situation gives cause for apprehension. **Refus motivé,** justifiable refusal. **Non motivé,** unjustified, unwarranted.

moto [mɔto], *s.f. F:* Motor bike.

motobatteuse [mɔtɔbatøːz], *s.f. Husb:* Motor thresher.

motoculteur [mɔtɔkyltœːr], *s.m. Agr:* Power-driven cultivator.

motoculture [mɔtɔkylty:r], *s.f.* Power agriculture.

motocycle [mɔtɔsikl], *s.m.,* **motocyclette** [mɔtɔsiklɛt], *s.f.* Motor (bi)cycle.

motocycliste [mɔtɔsiklist], *s.m.* Motor cyclist. *Mil:* Dispatch-rider.

motoglisseur [mɔtɔglisœːr], *s.m.* Speed-boat.

motogodille [mɔtɔgodiːj], *s.f.* Motorized sculling oar. *Bateau à m.,* boat with an out-board slung motor.

motorisé [mɔtɔrize], *a.* Fitted with a motor; motorized.

motrice. See MOTEUR.

mot-souche, *s.m.* Catchword (in catalogue, etc.). *pl.* **Des mots-souches.**

motte [mɔt], *s.f.* **I.** Mound (of windmill, etc.). *M. de taupe,* mole-hill. **2.** Clod, lump (of earth). *Hort:* Ball (left on roots of tree). *M. de gazon,* sod, turf. *M. de tourbe,* (turf of) peat. *M. à brûler,* (i) sod of peat; (ii) briquette (of spent tan, etc.). **Motte de beurre,** pat of butter.

mottereau [mɔtro], *s.m. Orn:* Sand-martin.

motteux [mɔtø], *s.m. Orn: Dial:* Wheatear, stonechat.

motus [mɔtyːs], *int.* Mum's the word!

mou[1], mol, *f.* **molle** [mu, mɔl]. **I.** *a.* (The masc. form **mol** is used before vowel or h 'mute') Soft (wax, tyre, etc.); slack (rope); weak, lifeless, soft, flabby; *F:* spineless (person); flabby, woolly, limp (style); feeble (attempt); lax (government); gentle, light (breeze); soft, close, muggy (weather). *Fromage mou,* soft cheese. *Homme mou au travail,* slacker. *Mou, mol, au toucher,* soft to the touch. *Reposant sur un mol (et doux) oreiller,* resting on a (soft and) downy pillow. *S.a.* CHIFFE. **2.** *s.m.* Slack (of rope, etc.). *Prendre le mou,* to take in the slack. (Of rope) *Prendre du mou,* to slacken.

mou[2], *s.m.* Lights, lungs (of slaughtered animal).

mouchard [muʃaːr], *s.m. F:* Sneak, informer; esp. police-spy. *U.S:* Stool-pigeon.

mouchard|er [muʃarde], *v.tr. F:* To spy on (s.o.). *Abs.* To spy. *s.m.* **-age.**

mouche [muʃ], *s.f.* **I.** Fly. *M. commune,* house-fly. *M. à viande,* blow-fly. *M. bleue (de la viande),* bluebottle. *M. à feu,* fire-fly. *M. à miel,* honey-bee. *S.a.* COCHE[1], PATTE 1. **Faire d'une mouche un éléphant,** to make a mountain out of a mole-hill. **On aurait entendu voler une mouche,** you could have heard a pin drop. **Prendre la mouche,** to fly into a temper; to take offence. **Quelle mouche vous pique?** what is the matter with you? **C'est une fine mouche,** he's a knowing card; she's a sly minx. *S.a.* GOBER. *Box:* **Poids mouche,** fly-weight. *Fish: Pêche à la m. sèche,* dry-fly fishing. **2.** (*a*) Spot, speck; stain (on garment, etc.). *Cost: A:* Patch (on face); beauty-spot. (*b*) Tuft of hair (on lower lip); chin tuft. (*c*) Bull's-eye (of target). **Faire mouche,** to score a bull. (*d*) *Fenc:* Covering of foil button; button (on sword). **3.** (*a*) River steamer (on the Seine). (*b*) *Navy:* Advice boat.

moucher [muʃe], *v.tr.* **I.** (*a*) To wipe (child's) nose. (*b*) *F:* To put (s.o.) in his place; to snub (s.o.); to tell (s.o.) off. **2.** (*a*) To snuff (candle). (*b*) To trim the frayed end of (rope).

se moucher, to wipe, blow, one's nose. *F:* **Il ne se mouche pas du pied,** he thinks no small beer of himself; he does things in great style. *S.a.* MORVEUX 2.

moucherolle [muʃrɔl], *s.f. Orn:* Fly-catcher.

moucheron[1] [muʃrɔ̃], *s.m.* Gnat, midge.

moucheron[2], *s.m.* Snuff (of candle).

moucheter [muʃte], *v.tr.* (je mouchette; je moucchetterai) **I.** To spot, speckle. *Mer mouchetée d'écume,* foam-flecked sea. **2.** *M. un fleuret,* to cover the button of a foil. *M. une épée,* to put a button on a sword-point.

moucheté, *a. Cheval m.,* flea-bitten horse. *Chat m.,* tabby cat. *Blé m.,* smutty wheat.

mouchette [muʃɛt], *s.f.* **I.** *pl.* (Pair of) snuffers. **2.** (*a*) *Arch:* Outer fillet (of drip-moulding). (*b*) *Tls:* Moulding-plane.

moucheture [muʃtyːr], *s.f.* Spot, speck, speckle, fleck.

moucheur [muʃœːr], *s.m. Th: A:* Candle-snuffer.

mouchoir [muʃwaːr], *s.m.* **I.** *M. de poche,* pocket handkerchief. *M. de tête,* kerchief. **2.** *Carp: etc:* Triangular wooden bracket. **En mouchoir,** obliquely; in triangular shape.

mouchure [muʃyːr], *s.f.* **I.** Nasal mucus. **2.** Snuff (of candle); fag-end (cut off rope).

moudre [mudr], *v.tr.* (*pr.p.* **moulant;** *p.p.* **moulu;** *pr.ind.* je **mouds,** il **moud,** n. **moulons,** ils **moulent;** *pr.sub.* je **moule;** *p.h.* je **moulus;** *fu.* je **moudrai**) To grind, mill (corn); to grind (coffee). *F: Moulu de coups,* black and blue.

moulu, *a.* (*a*) Ground, powdered. **Or moulu,** ormolu. (*b*) *F:* (i) Dead-beat, fagged out ; (ii) aching all over.

moue [mu], *s.f.* Pout. **Faire la moue,** to purse one's lips, to pout, to look sulky. *Faire une vilaine m.,* (i) to pull a wry face ; (ii) to scowl.

mouette [mwɛt], *s.f. Orn:* Gull, seamew.

mouf(f)ette [mufɛt], *s.f. Z:* Skunk.

moufle[1] [mufl], *s.f. or m.* **1.** *pl.* Mitts ; mufflers (gloves). *El.E:* Wiring gloves. **2.** *Mec.E:* (*a*) Pulley-block (with several sheaves) ; tackle-block. (*b*) (= PALAN) (Block and) tackle ; purchase.

moufle[2], *s.m.* (in *Ch:* often *f.*) *Ch: Cer:* Muffle. (**Four à**) **moufle,** muffle furnace.

mouflon [muflɔ̃], *s.m. Z:* Moufflon, wild sheep.

mouillage [muja:ʒ], *s.m.* **1.** (*a*) Moistening, damping. (*b*) (Fraudulent) watering (of wine). **2.** *Nau:* (*a*) Casting anchor ; anchoring. (*b*) Laying, mooring (of mine) ; putting down (of buoy). **3.** Anchorage ; mooring ground. **Être au mouillage,** to ride at anchor. *Prendre son m.,* to anchor. *M. forain,* open berth.

mouill|er [muje], *v.tr.* **1.** (*a*) To wet, moisten, damp. *M. du linge,* (i) to steep linen ; (ii) to damp, sprinkle, linen (for ironing). *Se m. les pieds,* to get one's feet wet. (*b*) To water down (wine). **2.** (*a*) *M. l'ancre,* to cast, drop, anchor. *M. un vaisseau,* to bring a ship to anchor. *Mouillez!* let go (the anchor) ! (*b*) To lay (mine) ; to put down (buoy). **3.** *Ling:* To palatalize (consonant). *s.m.* **-ement.**
  se mouiller, to become wet ; (of pers.) to get wet ; (of eyes) to fill with tears.
mouillé, *a.* **1.** Moist, damp, wet. *F: M. jusqu'aux os,* wet to the skin, wet through. *F:* **Poule mouillée,** softy, milksop. **2.** (Of ship) (Lying) at anchor ; moored.

mouillette [mujɛt], *s.f. Cu:* Sippet. S.a. ŒUF 1.

mouilleur [mujœːr], *s.m.* **1.** *Navy:* Mouilleur de mines, de filets, mine-layer, net-layer. **2.** (*a*) Damper (for stamps). (*b*) *Nau:* Tumbler (of anchor).

mouillure [mujy:r], *s.f.* **1.** *Typ: etc:* Damping, wetting. **2.** Damp-mark, -stain.

moulage[1] [mula:ʒ], *s.m.* Grinding, milling.

moulage[2], *s.m.* **1.** Casting, moulding. *M. à cire perdue,* lost wax process. **2.** *M. au plâtre, en plâtre,* plaster cast.

moul-ant, -ons, -ez, etc. See MOUDRE, MOULER.

moule[1] [mul], *s.m.* Mould ; matrix. *M. à gelée,* jelly mould. **Jeter qch. en moule,** to cast sth. *F: Fait au m.,* exquisitely proportioned.

moule[2], *s.f.* **1.** *Moll:* Mussel. **2.** *P:* (*a*) Fathead. (*b*) Lazy-bones.

moule-beurre, *s.m.inv.* Butter-print.

mouler [mule], *v.tr.* (*a*) To cast (statue) ; to found (iron). (*b*) To mould (statue). *F: Robe qui moule la taille,* dress that shows the shape of the figure. *Se m. sur qn,* to model oneself on s.o.
  moulé, *a.* *Acier m.,* moulded steel, cast steel. *F:* **C'est moulé!** it fits you like a glove ! **Écriture moulée,** copperplate handwriting. **Lettres moulées,** block letters.

mouleur [mulœːr], *s.m.* Caster, moulder.

moulin [mulɛ̃], *s.m.* Mill. (*a*) *M. à vent,* windmill. *F:* **Se battre contre des moulins à vent,** to tilt at windmills (like Don Quixote). *M. à eau,* water-mill. **Roue de moulin,** mill-wheel. **Constructeur de moulins,** millwright. *F:* **Faire venir l'eau au moulin,** to bring grist to the mill. (Of young woman) **Jeter son bonnet par-dessus les moulins,** to throw propriety to the winds. (*b*) *M.*

à minerai, ore-crusher. *M. à huile,* oil-crusher. (*c*) *M. à bras,* hand-mill. **Moulin à café,** coffee-mill. *F:* **Moulin à paroles,** (i) chatterbox ; (ii) wind-bag.

moulinet [mulinɛ], *s.m.* **1.** (*a*) Winch. (*b*) *Fish:* Reel. *M. à cliquet,* click-reel. **2.** Turnstile. **3.** (*a*) *Ind:* Paddle(-wheel). (*b*) *Hyd.E:* Current-meter. **4.** *Fenc:* Moulinet, twirl. **Faire des moulinets** (**avec sa canne**), to twirl one's stick.

moult [mult], *adv.* *A:* Much, greatly.

moulu, -s, -t, etc. See MOUDRE.

moulure [muly:r], *s.f.* (Ornamental) moulding.

moulurer [mulyre], *v.tr.* To cut a moulding on (sth.). *Profils moulurés,* mouldings.

mourant, -ante [murɑ̃, -ɑ̃ːt]. **1.** *a.* Dying. *D'une voix mourante,* (i) faintly ; (ii) *Iron:* like a dying duck. **Bleu mourant,** pale blue. **2.** *s.* Dying man or woman. *Les mourants,* the dying.

mourir [muri:r], *v.i.* (*pr.p.* mourant ; *p.p.* mort ; *pr.ind.* je meurs, il meurt, n. mourons, ils meurent ; *pr.sub.* je meure, nous mourions ; *p.h.* il mourut ; *fu.* je mourrai [murre]. Aux. *être*) To die. **Bien mourir,** (i) to die in the faith ; (ii) to meet death without flinching. *Il est mort hier,* he died yesterday. *M. de faim,* (i) to die of starvation ; (ii) *F:* to be starving. *M. de mort naturelle,* to die a natural death. *Au moment de m.,* in the hour of death. **Mourir martyr pour une cause,** to die a martyr in a cause. **Faire mourir qn,** to put s.o. to death. *F: Il me fera m.,* he will be the death of me. *Je mourais de peur,* I was frightened to death. **La presse était à mourir,** we were nearly crushed to death. **Ennuyer qn à mourir,** to bore s.o. to death. **Mourir d'envie de faire qch.,** to be dying to do sth. *Je mourais de rire,* I nearly died laughing. *C'est à m. de rire,* it's simply killing. S.a. FEU[2].
  se mourir, to be dying. (Thus used only in the *pres.* and *p.d.* of the indicative.) *Je sens que je me meurs,* I feel that I am dying. *La lampe se mourait,* the lamp was giving out.

mort, morte. **1.** *a.* (*a*) Dead (person, leaf, language, colour, etc.). *F:* **Mort et enterré,** dead and buried, dead and gone. *Prov:* **Morte la bête, mort le venin,** dead men tell no tales. *Cœur m. à l'affection,* heart dead to affection. *Sp:* **Ballon mort,** dead ball ; ball out of play. *Geog:* **La mer Morte,** the Dead Sea. (*b*) **Temps mort,** time wasted, idle period (in a movement). *Mec.E:* **Poids mort,** dead weight. *Mch:* **Point mort,** (i) dead centre (of piston-stroke) ; (ii) neutral position (of lever). *Aut:* **Mettre le levier au point m.,** to put the (gear) lever into neutral. *N.Arch:* **Œuvres mortes,** dead-works. (*c*) **Eau morte,** still, stagnant, water. *Morte eau* = MORTE-EAU. *Art:* **Nature morte,** still life. (*d*) **Balle morte,** spent bullet. **2.** *s.* Dead person ; deceased. *Les morts,* the dead, the departed. *Ecc:* **Jour, fête, des Morts,** All Souls' day. *L'office des morts,* the burial service. **Faire le mort,** (i) to sham dead ; (ii) to lie low. **Tête de mort,** death's head ; skull. **3.** *s.m. Cards:* Dummy. **Faire le mort,** to be dummy.

mouron [murɔ̃], *s.m.* *M. rouge, des champs,* scarlet pimpernel. *M. des oiseaux,* chickweed. *M. d'eau,* water pimpernel, brookweed.

mousquet [muskɛ], *s.m.* *A:* Musket.

mousquetade [muskətad], *s.f.* *A:* Volley (of musket-shots).

mousquetaire [muskəte:r], *s.m.* Musketeer. **Gants** (**à la**) **m.,** gauntlet gloves.

mousqueton [muskətɔ̃], *s.m.* **1.** *A:* Musketoon, blunderbuss. **2.** Snap-hook.

moussaillon [musaj̃ɔ], *s.m.* Young ship's boy.

mousse¹ [mus], *s.f.* **1.** Moss. *Couvert de m.*, moss-grown. *Lit de m.*, mossy bed. *Prov:* Pierre qui roule n'amasse pas mousse, a rolling stone gathers no moss. **2.** (*a*) Froth, foam (of beer, etc.); lather (of soap). (*b*) Whipped (chocolate or vanilla) cream; mousse. **3.** *Ch:* Mousse de platine, platinum sponge.

mousse², *s.m.* Ship's boy.

mousse³, *a.* Blunt (knife-blade, point, etc.). *A l'esprit m.*, blunt-witted.

mousseline [muslin], *s.f.* **1.** *Tex:* (*a*) Muslin. *M. de soie*, chiffon. (*b*) *Bookb:* Mull. **2.** (*a*) (Verre) mousseline, muslin-glass; mousseline. (*b*) Gâteau mousseline, sponge-cake. (*c*) Pommes (de terre) mousseline, mashed potatoes.

mousser [muse], *v.i.* To froth, foam; (of soapy water) to lather; (of wine) to sparkle or effervesce, *F:* to fizz. Faire mousser de la crème, to whip, whisk, mill, cream. *F:* Faire mousser qn, (i) to make s.o. flare up; (ii) to crack up s.o.; to puff s.o.

mousseron [musrɔ̃], *s.m.* Edible mushroom; esp. St George's agaric.

mousseux, -euse [musø, -øːz], *a.* **1.** Mossy. Rose mousseuse, moss-rose. S.a. AGATE. **2.** (*a*) Frothy, foaming. (*b*) Sparkling (wine).

mousson [musɔ̃], *s.f. Meteor:* Monsoon.

moussu [musy], *a.* Mossy; moss-grown. Rose moussue, moss-rose.

moustache [mustaʃ], *s.f.* (*a*) La m., les moustaches, the moustache. *F: M. à la gauloise*, walrus moustache. *F:* Vieille moustache, old soldier. (*b*) Whiskers (of cat).

moustachu [mustaʃy], *a.* Moustached; wearing a heavy moustache.

moustiquaire [mustikɛːr], *s.f.* Mosquito-net.

moustique [mustik], *s.m. Ent:* (*a*) Mosquito. (*b*) Gnat; sand-fly.

moût [mu], *s.m.* Must (of grapes); wort (of beer).

moutard [mutaːr], *s.m. F:* (*a*) Kid(die), urchin, *P:* nipper. (*b*) *Pej:* Brat.

moutarde [mutard], *s.f.* **1.** Mustard. (*a*) Graine de m., mustard-seed. (*b*) Farine de m., (flour of) mustard. *F:* C'est de la moutarde après dîner, it's too late to be of any use; it's a day after the fair. La moutarde lui est montée au nez, he lost his temper; *F:* he got his dander up. **2.** Gaz moutarde, mustard-gas.

moutardier [mutardje], *s.m.* **1.** Mustard-maker. *F:* Il se croit le premier moutardier du pape, he thinks no small beer of himself. **2.** Mustard-pot.

moutier [mutje], *s.m. A. & Dial:* = MONASTÈRE.

mouton [mutɔ̃], *s.m.* **1.** (*a*) Sheep. Peau de mouton, sheepskin. *Éleveur de moutons*, (i) sheep-farmer; (ii) wool-grower. *F:* Revenons à nos moutons, let us revert to the subject; let us get back to the point. Saut de mouton, (i) (of horse) buck; (ii) *Games:* = SAUTE-MOUTON. Faire le mouton, to make a back (at leap-frog). (*b*) *Bookb: etc:* Sheepskin. **2.** *Cu:* Mutton. *Côtelettes de m.*, mutton cutlets. **3.** *Civ.E: etc:* Ram, monkey (of pile-driver); head (of beetle, rammer); tup (of steam-hammer); drop-hammer. **4.** *pl. Nau:* White horses (on sea).

moutonnant [mutɔnɑ̃], *a.* (Of the sea) Covered with white horses.

moutonn|er [mutɔne]. **1.** *v.tr.* To frizz, curl (hair, etc.). **2.** *v.i.* (Of the sea) To break into white horses; to froth. *s.m.* **-ement.**

moutonné, *a.* Fleecy (cloud, sky). *Mer moutonnée*, sea with white horses. *Tête moutonnée*, frizzy, woolly, head of hair. *Geol: Roche moutonnée*, ice-smoothed rock, glaciated rock.

moutonneux, -euse [mutɔnø, -øːz], *a.* **1.** (Of

the sea) Foam-flecked; covered with white horses. **2.** (Of the sky) Fleecy.

mouture [mutyːr], *s.f.* **1.** Grinding, milling (of corn). **2.** Milling dues. *F:* Tirer d'un sac deux moutures, to get double profit out of sth. **3.** *Husb:* Maslin.

mouvant [muvɑ̃], *a.* Moving; mobile. *F:* Unstable, fickle, changeable. *Sable m.*, drift-sand. Sables mouvants, shifting sands; quicksand.

mouvement [muvmɑ̃], *s.m.* Movement. **1.** Motion. *M. en arrière*, backward motion. Rester sans mouvement, to stand motionless, stock-still. Faire un mouvement, to move. Mettre qch. en mouvement, imprimer un mouvement à qch., to put, set, sth. in motion; to start (engine). Se mettre en mouvement, to start off, move off. Se donner du mouvement, (i) to bustle about, to stir about; (ii) to take exercise. Être toujours en mouvement, to be always on the move. Petite ville sans m., lifeless, dull, little town. Guerre de mouvement, war of movement, open warfare. *Un m. audacieux leur livra le village*, a daring move put them in possession of the village. *Mec:* Quantité de mouvement, momentum (mv.), impulse. *M. acquis*, impressed motion. *M. perpétuel*, perpetual motion. *Mus: Presser, ralentir, le m.*, to quicken the time, to slow the time. **2.** (*a*) Change, modification. *M. de terrain*, undulation in the ground. *M. du marché*, market fluctuations. Être dans le mouvement, to be in the swim, abreast of the times, up to date. (*b*) Premier mouvement, first impulse. *M. d'humeur*, outburst of temper, of petulance. Faire qch. de son propre mouvement, to do sth. of one's own accord. Avoir un bon mouvement, to act on a kindly impulse. (*c*) Agitation, emotion. *M. de plaisir*, thrill, flutter, of pleasure. *M. populaire*, popular commotion; rising of the people. **3.** Traffic. *Rail: Mouvements des trains*, train arrivals and departures. Chef de mouvement, traffic manager. *Journ:* Mouvements des navires, shipping intelligence. **4.** Works, action, movement (of clock, etc.). *M. d'horlogerie*, clock-work.

mouvementer [muvmɑ̃te], *v.tr.* To enliven, animate (discussion, etc.).

mouvementé, *a.* 1. Animated, lively (discussion, etc.); thrilling (voyage, etc.); full of incident. *Endroit m.*, busy town or thoroughfare. *Vie mouvementée*, eventful life. **2.** *Terrain m.*, undulating ground.

mouvette [muvɛt], *s.f.* Wooden spoon; stirrer.

mouvoir [muvwaːr], *v.tr.* (*pr.p.* mouvant; *p.p.* mû, mue; *pr.ind.* je meus, il meut, n. mouvons, ils meuvent; *pr.sub.* je meuve, n. mouvions, ils meuvent; *p.h.* je mus (rare); *fu.* je mouvrai) **1.** *M. qch. de sa place*, to move sth. from its place. **2.** To drive, actuate (machine, etc.); to propel (ship, etc.). *Navire mû à la vapeur*, ship propelled by steam. *Mû par la colère, par l'intérêt*, moved by anger, prompted by interest.

se mouvoir, to move, stir.

moyen¹, -enne [mwajɛ̃, -ɛn]. **1.** *a.* (*a*) Middle. *Personne d'un âge m.*, middle-aged person. Le moyen âge [mwajɛnɑ:ʒ], the Middle Ages. *Coutumes du m. âge*, medi(a)eval customs. L'Orient moyen, the Middle East. *Sch: Cours m.*, intermediate course (in French, in algebra, etc.). *Gram:* Voix moyenne, middle voice. (*b*) Average, mean (pressure, speed, etc.). Le Français m., the average Frenchman. *Log:* Moyen terme, middle term. *F:* Prendre un moyen terme, to take a middle course. (*c*) Medium (quality, etc.). *De taille, grandeur, moyenne*, medium-sized, middle-sized. **2.** *s.f.* Moyenne. (*a*) Moyenne *proportionnelle*, geometrical mean. (*b*) Average. *Établir la movenne (des pertes, etc.)*, to average (the losses, etc.). **En moyenne**, on an average. (*c*) *Sch:* Pass-mark. *Travail au-dessus, au-dessous, de la moyenne*, work above, below, par. **moyen²**, *s.m.* Means. (*a*) *Le journal comme m. de réclame*, the newspaper as a vehicle, medium, for advertising. *Prov:* **La fin justifie les moyens**, the end justifies the means. **Employer les grands moyens**, to take extreme measures. **Au moyen de qch.**, by means of sth. **Faire qch. par ses propres moyens**, to draw upon one's own resources (to do sth.). **Y a-t-il moyen de le faire?** is it possible to do it? **Il n'y a pas moyen**, it can't be done; it is impossible. **Trouver (le) moyen de faire qch.**, to find a means, a way, to do sth. *Par aucun m. l'on ne peut . . .*, by no means is it possible to. . . . **Voies et moyens**, ways and means. **Dans la (pleine) mesure de mes moyens**, to the best, to the utmost, of my ability. *Enfant qui a des moyens*, bright, talented, child. *F:* **Enlever les moyens à qn**, to upset, disconcert, s.o. (*b*) *Vivre au delà de ses moyens*, to live beyond one's means. *Il a largement les moyens de bâtir*, he can well afford to build.

moyenâgeux, -euse [mwajɛnɑʒø, -øːz], *a. F:* Sham-medieval.

moyennant [mwajɛnɑ̃], *prep.* On a (certain) condition. *Louer qch. m. quinze francs par jour*, to hire sth. for, at (a charge of), fifteen francs a day. *Faire qch.* **moyennant finances**, to do sth. for a consideration. **Moyennant quoi . . .**, return for which, in consideration of which. . . . **Moyennant que** + *fu. ind.* or + *sub.*, provided that . . .; on condition that. . . .

moyennement [mwajɛnmɑ̃], *adv.* **1.** Moderately, fairly. **2.** On an average, on the average.

moyette [mwajɛt], *s.f. Agr:* Shock (of corn).

moyeu, -eux [mwajø], *s.m.* Nave, (pipe-)box (of cart-wheel, etc.); boss (of fly-wheel, propeller, etc.); hub (of bicycle-wheel).

mu [my], *s.m. Gr.Alph: Ph.Meas:* Mu.

mû. See MOUVOIR.

muabilité [mɥabilite], *s.f.* Mutability, instability.

muable [mɥabl], *a.* Changeable, mutable, unstable; fickle.

mucilage [mysilaːʒ], *s.m.* Mucilage, gum.

mucilagineux, -euse [mysilaʒinø, -øːz], *a.* Mucilaginous, viscous.

mucosité [mykozite], *s.f.* Mucus, mucosity.

mucus [mykyːs], *s.m. Physiol:* Mucus.

mue [my], *s.f.* **1.** (*a*) Moulting (of birds); shedding or casting of the coat, of the skin, of the antlers (of animals); sloughing (of reptiles). **Serin en mue**, moulting canary. (*b*) Moulting-time. (*c*) Feathers moulted; antlers, etc., shed; slough (of snakes). **2.** Breaking of the voice (at puberty). **3.** Mew (for hawks); coop (for hens).

muer [mɥe]. **1.** *v.tr. Le cerf mue sa tête*, the stag casts its antlers. **2.** *v.i.* (*a*) (Of bird) To moult; (of animal) to shed or cast its coat, its antlers; (of reptile) to slough; to cast its skin. (*b*) (Of voice) To break (at puberty).

mu|et, -ette¹ [mɥɛ, -ɛt]. **1.** *a.* Dumb, mute. (*a*) Unable to speak. *M. de naissance*, born dumb. *M. de colère*, speechless with anger. S.a. SOURD-MUET. (*b*) Unwilling to speak. **Rester muet**, to remain silent. **Muet comme un poisson**, (as) dumb, mute, as a fish. **Muet comme la tombe**, (as) silent as the grave. (*c*) Without word or sound. *Jeu m.*, dumb show. *Th: Rôle m.*, silent part. S.a. FILM. *Carte muette*, blank map. *Gram:*

Lettre muette, silent letter. *H muet(te)*, 'mute' h. **2.** *s.* Dumb person; mute. **3.** *s.f. Gram:* **Muette**, mute letter, unsounded letter. *adv.* **-ettement.**

muette², *s.f.* Hunting-box.

muézin [mɥezɛ̃], *s.m.* Muezzin.

mufle [myfl], *s.m.* **1.** Muffle; (hairless part of) muzzle (of ox, bison); nose, *F:* snout (of lion, etc.). **2.** *P:* (*a*) Face, mug. (*b*) Rotter, skunk, cad. **3.** *Bot: F:* **Mufle de veau, de bœuf,** antirrhinum, snapdragon.

muflerie [myfləri], *s.f. P:* **1.** Low-down ways; caddishness. **2.** Low-down trick.

muflier [myflie], *s.m. Bot:* Antirrhinum, snapdragon. *M. bâtard*, linaria.

muge [myːʒ], *s.m. Ich:* Mullet.

mug|ir [myʒiːr], *v.i.* (*a*) (Of cow) To low; (of bull) to bellow. (*b*) (Of sea, wind) To roar; to boom; to moan. *s.m.* **-issement.**

muguet [mygɛ], *s.m.* **1.** *Bot:* Lily of the valley. **2.** *Med:* Thrush. **3.** *A:* Gallant, dandy.

mugueter [myg(ə)te], *v.i.* (**je muguette; je muguetterai**) *A:* To flirt, to philander.

muid [mɥi], *s.m. A:* Large barrel; hogshead.

mulassier, -ière [mylasje, -jɛːr], *s.m.* **mulatier, -ière** [mylatje, -jɛːr]. **1.** *a.* **Jument mulassière**, mule-breeding mare. **2.** *s.m.* Breeder of mules.

mulâtre [mylɑːtr]. **1.** *a.* Mulatto, half-caste. **2.** *s.* (*f.* **mulâtre** or **mulâtresse**) Mulatto.

mule¹ [myl], *s.f.* (She-)mule. S.a. TÊTU.

mule², *s.f.* **1. (*a*) (Lady's quarterless) bedroom slipper; mule. (*b*) (The Pope's) slipper. **Baiser la mule du Pape**, to kiss the Pope's toe. **2.** Chilblain on the heel.

mulet¹ [mylɛ], *s.m.* (He-)mule. S.a. TÊTU.

mulet², *s.m. Ich:* Grey mullet.

muletier [myltje], *s.m.* Mule-driver, muleteer.

mulle [myl], *s.m. Ich:* Mullet. *M. barbu*, red mullet, surmullet.

mulot [mylo], *s.m.* Field-mouse.

multicolore [myltikɔlɔːr], *a.* Multi-coloured.

multifilaire [myltifilɛːr], *a.* Multi-wire (aerial).

multiflore [myltiflɔːr], *a. Bot:* Multiflorous, many-flowered.

multiforme [myltifɔrm], *a.* Multiform.

multimillionnaire [myltimiljɔnɛːr], *a. & s.* Multimillionaire.

multimoteur, -trice [myltimɔtœːr, -tris], *a. Av:* Multi-engined.

multipare [myltipaːr], *a.* Multiparous.

multiple [myltipl]. **1.** *a.* Multiple, manifold; multifarious (duties, etc.). *Aut:* **Trompe à sons multiples**, multitone horn. **2.** *s.m.* Multiple. **Le plus petit commun multiple**, the least common multiple, the L.C.M.

multiplex [myltiplɛks], *a.inv.* Multiplex (telegraphy).

multipliable [myltipliabl], *a.* Multipli(c)able.

multiplicande [myltiplikɑ̃ːd], *s.m. Mth:* Multiplicand.

multiplicateur, -trice [myltiplikatœːr, -tris]. **1.** *a.* Multiplying. *Engrenage m.*, step-up gear. **2.** *s.m. Mth: El:* Multiplier.

multiplicatif, -ive [myltiplikatif, -iːv], *a.* Multiplicative, multiplying.

multiplication [myltiplikasjɔ̃], *s.f.* **1.** Multiplication. **2.** *Mec.E:* Gear(-ratio); step-up, -down, (of gear). *Grande, petite, m.*, high, low, gear. *Mec:* **M. du levier**, leverage.

multiplicité [myltiplisite], *s.f.* Multiplicity; multifariousness (of duties, etc.).

multiplier [myltiplie], *v.tr. & i.* **1.** To multiply (*par*, by). **2.** *Mec.E:* **M. la vitesse de révolution**, to gear up.

se multiplier. (a) To multiply. *Les crimes se multiplient,* crime is on the increase. (b) To be here, there, and everywhere; to be in half a dozen places at once. *Se m. pour servir qn,* to do one's utmost in order to serve s.o.
multiplié, a. Multiplied, multiple; manifold, multifarious.
multipolaire [myltipɔlɛːr], a. Multipolar.
multitubulaire [myltitybylɛːr], a. *Mch:* Multitubular (boiler).
multitude [myltityd], s.f. Multitude (*de,* of); crowd; multiplicity (of books, etc.).
municipal, -aux [mynisipal, -o], a. Municipal. *Conseil municipal,* town-council. *Loi municipale,* bye-law. *La Garde municipale,* the military police (of Paris).
municipalité [mynisipalite], s.f. Municipality. (a) Incorporated town. (b) Town-council. (c) Town-hall.
munificence [mynifisɑ̃ːs], s.f. Munificence; bounty; bounteousness.
munificent [mynifisɑ̃], a. Munificent; bounteous, bountiful.
munir [myniːr], v.tr. To furnish, supply, fit, equip, provide (*de,* with). *Se m. de provisions,* to provide oneself with eatables.
munition [mynisjɔ̃], s.f. **1.** (i) Munitioning, (ii) provisioning (of an army). *Pain de munition,* ration bread. **2.** pl. (a) A: *Munitions de guerre,* munitions of war; ammunition. (b) Stores, supplies. *Munitions de bouche,* provisions.
munitionner [mynisjɔne], v.tr. (i) To munition, (ii) to furnish (army) with supplies.
muqueux, -euse [mykø, -øːz]. **1.** a. Mucous. **2.** s.f. Muqueuse, mucous membrane.
mur [myːr], s.m. Wall. *Mur de clôture,* enclosing wall. *Mur d'appui,* low wall. *Mur de refend,* partition(-wall). *Gros murs,* main walls. *Ne laisser que les quatre murs,* to leave only the four walls standing. *Mettre qn au pied du mur,* (i) to drive s.o. into a corner; (ii) to demand a 'yes' or 'no' from s.o. *Donner de la tête contre un mur,* to run one's head against a brick wall. *Fenc:* *Parer au mur,* to remain entirely on the defensive; to 'stonewall.'
mûr [myːr], a. Ripe; mellow (wine, etc.); mature (age, mind). F: *Habit mûr,* coat that has done its time, seen better days.
mûraie [myrɛ], s.f. Mulberry plantation.
muraille [myraːj], s.f. **1.** High defensive wall. *Les murailles de la ville,* the town walls. *Muraille de glace,* ice-barrier. *Hautes murailles douanières,* high tariff walls. **2.** Side (of ship).
mural, -aux [myral, -o], a. Mural. *Pendule murale,* wall-clock. *Carte murale,* wall-map. *Console murale,* wall-bracket.
mûre [myːr], s.f. **1.** Mulberry. **2.** *M. sauvage, de ronce,* blackberry, bramble-berry.
mûrement [myrmɑ̃], adv. With mature consideration.
murène [myrɛn], s.f. *Ich:* Muraena.
mur|er [myre], v.tr. To wall in (town); to wall up, block up, brick up (doorway). s.m. **-age.**
mûrier [myrje], s.m. *Bot:* **1.** Mulberry(-tree, -bush). **2.** *M. sauvage,* bramble, blackberry-bush.
mûrir [myriːr]. **1.** v.tr. To ripen, mature. *M. un abcès,* to bring an abscess to a head. *M. une question,* to give a question mature consideration. **2.** v.i. & occ. pr. To ripen; to mature; to come to maturity; (of fruit) to grow ripe; (of abscess) to come to a head.
murmure [myrmyːr], s.m. Murmur, murmuring; *M. d'un ruisseau,* babbling, purl, brawl, of a brook.

murmurer [myrmyre], v.tr. & i. To murmur. **1.** To grumble, to complain. *M. de qch.,* to murmur at sth. *M. entre ses dents,* to mutter. **2.** *M. un secret dans l'oreille de qn,* to murmur, whisper, a secret in s.o.'s ear. *Le ruisseau coule en murmurant,* the stream brawls, bickers, babbles, purls, wimples, over the stones.
mûron [myrɔ̃], s.m. **1.** Blackberry. **2.** Wild raspberry.
mu-s, -t, etc. See MOUVOIR.
musaraigne [myzarɛɲ], s.f. Shrew-mouse.
musard, -arde [myzaːr, -ard]. **1.** a. Dawdling, idling. **2.** s. Dawdler, idler, trifler.
musarder [myzarde], v.i. = MUSER.
musarderie [myzard(ə)ri], s.f. Dawdling, idling.
musc [mysk], s.m. **1.** Musk. **2.** Z: Musk-deer.
muscade [myskad], s.f. **1.** (Noix) muscade, nutmeg. *Fleur de muscade,* mace. **2.** Thimble-rigger's vanishing ball or pea. *Passez muscade!* hey presto!
muscadier [myskadje], s.m. *Bot:* Nutmeg-tree.
muscadin [myskadɛ̃], s.m. A: Dandy, fop.
muscardin [myskardɛ̃], s.m. Dormouse.
muscat [myska], a. & s.m. **1.** *Vit:* Muscat. (Raisin) muscat, muscat grape. (Vin) muscat, muscat wine, muscatel. **2.** Musk-pear.
muscle [myskl], s.m. Muscle. *Être tout nerfs et muscles,* to be all thew and sinew.
musclé [myskle], a. Muscular; sinewy, brawny.
musculaire [myskylɛːr], a. Muscular (system, tissue, strength). *Fibre m.,* muscle-fibre.
musculeux, -euse [myskylø, -øːz], a. Muscular, brawny (person, arm, etc.).
Muse [myːz], s.f. Muse. *Invoquer la Muse,* to call on one's Muse.
museau [myzo], s.m. (a) Muzzle, snout (of animal). (b) F: *Joli petit m.,* nice little phiz. *Se poudrer le m.,* to powder one's face. *Vilain m.,* ugly mug.
musée [myze], s.m. (a) Museum. (b) *Musée de peinture, d'objets d'art,* picture-gallery, art-gallery.
mus|eler [myzle], v.tr. (je muselle; je musellerai) To muzzle (dog, F: s.o.). s.m. **-ellement.**
muselière [myzəljɛːr], s.f. Dog muzzle.
mus|er [myze], v.i. To idle, dawdle; to moon about. s. **-eur, -euse.**
muserie [myzri], s.f. Trifling, idling.
muserol(l)e [myzrɔl], s.f. *Harn:* Nose-band.
musette [myzɛt], s.f. **1.** *Mus:* A: Musette (of the bagpipe type). (Nowadays) F: *Orchestre musette,* band with accordions. *Bal musette,* popular dancing-hall (with accordion band); = 'shilling hop.' **2.** (a) Musette-mangeoire, (horse's) nose-bag. (b) (School-boy's) satchel. *Mil: etc:* Haversack.
muséum [myzeɔm], s.m. Natural history museum.
musical, -aux [myzikal, -o], a. **1.** Musical (sound, evening, etc.). *L'art m.,* the art of music. **2.** Avoir l'oreille musicale, to have an ear for music, a musical ear. adv. **-ement.**
musicien, -ienne [myzisjɛ̃, -jɛn], a. & s. **1.** Musician. *Elle est bonne musicienne,* (i) she is very musical; (ii) she is a good player. **2.** Bandsman; member of the band, of the orchestra.
musicomane [myzikɔman], s. m. & f. Music-lover.
musique [myzik], s.f. **1.** Music. *Mettre des paroles en musique,* to set words to music. *Instrument de musique,* musical instrument. *Boîte à musique,* musical box. *M. de chambre,* chamber music. *Faire de la musique,* to make music; to have a musical evening; to go in for music. *S.a.* RÉGLÉ 2. **2.** Band. *Chef de musique,* bandmaster.

musiquette [myzikɛt], *s.f.* (*a*) Amateur music. (*b*) *M. publicitaire*, signature-tune (of band).

musoir [myzwa:r], *s.m.* Pier-, jetty-head.

musquer [myske], *v.tr.* To scent with musk.

musqué, *a.* **I.** (*a*) Musky; scented with musk. *Rose musquée, rosier m.*, musk-rose. (*b*) Affected, effeminate (poet, style, etc.). **2.** Bœuf musqué, musk-ox. Rat musqué, muskrat, musquash. Canard musqué, musk-duck, Muscovy duck.

mussif [mysif], *a.m.* Or mussif, mosaic gold, disulphide of tin.

mustang [mystã], *s.m.* Mustang.

musulman, -ane [myzylmã, -an], *a. & s.* Mussulman, Mohammedan, Moslem.

mut|able [mytabl], *a.* **I.** = MUABLE. **2.** *Jur:* Alienable. *s.f.* **-abilité.**

mutation [mytasjɔ̃], *s.f.* (*a*) Change, alteration. *Mus: Biol:* Mutation. (*b*) *Jur:* Change of ownership; transfer (of property). (*c*) Transfer (of personnel, *Fb:* of players).

mutilateur [mytilatœ:r], *s.m.* Mutilator. (*a*) Maimer. (*b*) Defacer.

mutilation [mytilasjɔ̃], *s.f.* (*a*) Mutilation, maiming (of person). (*b*) Defacement (of statue); mutilation (of book, statue).

mutiler [mytile], *v.tr.* (*a*) To mutilate, maim (s.o.). *Affreusement mutilé*, frightfully mangled. (*b*) To deface; to mutilate (book, statue).

mutilé, -ée, *a. & s.* Mutilés de guerre, war cripples; disabled ex-service men. *Il est m. du bras*, he has lost an arm.

mutin, -ine [mytɛ̃, -in], *a. & s.* **I.** (*a*) Insubordinate; disobedient, unruly, unbiddable (child). Faire le mutin, to be refractory. (*b*) Roguish, pert, saucy. **2.** *s.m.* Mutineer.

mutiner (se) [səmytine], *v.pr.* To rise in revolt; (of troops) to mutiny, to rebel; (of children) to be disobedient, unruly.

mutiné, **I.** *a.* Rebellious; mutinous (troops). **2.** *s.m.* Mutineer.

mutinerie [mytinri], *s.f.* **I.** (*a*) Unruliness, disobedience (of children). (*b*) Roguishness, pertness, archness. **2.** Rebellion; mutiny.

mutisme [mytism], *s.m.* Dumbness, muteness. Se renfermer dans le mutisme, to maintain a stubborn silence.

mutualité [mytɥalite], *s.f.* **I.** Mutuality, reciprocity. **2.** Mutual insurance. Société de mutualité, friendly society.

mutu|el, -elle [mytɥɛl], *a.* Mutual. **Société de secours mutuels**, mutual benefit society, friendly society. *adv.* **-ellement.**

mycologie [mikɔlɔʒi], *s.f. Bot:* Myc(et)ology.

myélo-méningite [mjelɔmenɛ̃ʒit], *s.f. Med:* Myelo-meningitis, spinal meningitis.

mygale [migal], *s.f.* Mygale; trap-door spider.

myodynie [mjɔdini], *s.f. Med:* Myalgia; muscular rheumatism.

myologie [mjɔlɔʒi], *s.f.* Myology.

myope [mjɔp], *a. & s.* Myopic (eye); shortsighted (person).

myopie [mjɔpi], *s.f.* Myopia; short-sightedness.

myosotis [mjɔzɔtis], *s.m. Bot:* Forget-me-not.

myriade [mirjad], *s.f.* Myriad.

myriamètre [mirjamɛtr], *s.m.* Myriametre; ten thousand metres.

myriapode [mirjapɔd], *s.m.* **Z:** Myriapod; *pl.* myriapoda.

Myrmidons [mirmidɔ̃], *s.m.pl. Gr.Myth:* Myrmidons. *F: A: Un myrmidon*, a little whippersnapper of a man.

myrrhe [mi:r], *s.f.* Myrrh.

myrtacé [mirtase]. *Bot:* **I.** *a.* Myrtaceous. **2.** *s.f.pl.* Myrtacées, myrtaceae, myrtles.

myrte [mirt], *s.m. Bot:* Myrtle. *M. des marais*, sweet gale, bog myrtle.

myrtille [mirtil, mirti:j], *s.f.* Bilberry.

mystère [mistɛ:r], *s.m.* **I.** Mystery. *On n'a jamais pénétré ce m.*, this mystery has never been fathomed. Faire grand mystère d'un événement, to be very reticent about an event. Je n'en fais pas mystère, I make no mystery, no secret, of it. **2.** *Lit.Hist:* Mystery-play. *M. de la Passion*, Passion-play.

mystérieu|x, -euse [misterjø, -ø:z], *a.* Mysterious; enigmatical; uncanny. *adv.* **-sement.**

mysticisme [mistisism], *s.m.* Mysticism.

mystifiable [mistifjabl], *a.* Dupable, gullible.

mystificateur, -trice [mistifikatœ:r, -tris]. **I.** *a.* Mystifying. **2.** *s.* Hoaxer, mystifier.

mystification [mistifikasjɔ̃], *s.f.* (*a*) Mystification. (*b*) Hoax; practical joke.

mystifier [mistifje], *v.tr.* (*a*) To mystify. (*b*) To hoax, fool, gull (s.o.); to play a practical joke on (s.o.); *F:* to pull (s.o.'s) leg.

mystique [mistik]. **I.** *a.* Mystic(al). **2.** *s.* Mystic. *adv.* **-ment,** -ally.

mythe [mit], *s.m.* Myth, legend.

mythique [mitik], *a.* Mythical.

mythologie [mitɔlɔʒi], *s.f.* Mythology.

mythologique [mitɔlɔʒik], *a.* Mythological.

mythologiste [mitɔlɔʒist], *s.m.,* **mythologue** [mitɔlɔg], *s.m.* Mythologist.

myxœdème [miksedɛm], *s.m.* Myxoedema.

myxomycètes [miksɔmisɛt], *s.m.pl. Fung:* Myxomycetes.

N

N, n [ɛn], *s.f.* (The letter) N, n.

n'. See NE.

na [na], *int. P:* (*a*) (= *ld!*) There now! (*b*) (Emphatic and defiant) *J'irai pas, na!* I'm not going, so there!

nabab [nabab], *s.m.* Nabob.

nable [nabl], *s.m. Nau:* **I.** Plug-hole (of small boat). **2.** (Bouchon de) nable, plug.

nabot, -ote [nabo, -ɔt]. **I.** *s.* Dwarf, midget. **2.** *a.* Dwarfish, tiny.

Nabuchodonosor [nabykɔdɔnɔzɔ:r]. *Pr.n.m.* Nebuchadnezzar.

nac|rat [nakara], *s.m. & a.inv.* Nacarat, orange-red.

nacelle [nasɛl], *s.f.* **I.** Skiff, wherry, dinghy. **2.** (*a*) *Aer:* Nacelle, car (of balloon); gondola (of airship); cockpit (of aeroplane). (*b*) Car (of transporter-bridge).

nacre [nakr], *s.f.* Mother of pearl.

nacrer [nakre], *v.tr.* To give a pearly lustre to (beads, etc.).

nacré, *a.* Nacreous, pearly (lustre, etc.).

nadir [nadi:r], *s.m. Astr:* Nadir.

nævus [nevy:s], *s.m.* Naevus, birth-mark, mole.

nage [na:ʒ], s.f. **1.** Rowing, sculling. **Banc de nage,** thwart. **Chef de nage,** stroke oarsman. **Donner la nage,** to set the stroke. **2.** (a) Swimming. **Se jeter, se mettre, à la nage,** to start to swim. *Traverser une rivière à la n.,* to swim across a river. *F:* **Être (tout) en nage,** to be bathed in perspiration. (b) Stroke (in swimming). *N.* (à l')*indienne,* over-arm stroke. *N.* **en grenouille,** breast-stroke. *N. sur le dos,* back-stroke. **3.** Rowlock.

nagée [naʒe], s.f. Stroke's length (in swimming or rowing).

nageoire [naʒwa:r], s.f. **1.** (a) Fin (of fish). (b) *P:* Arm (of pers.); *F:* fin. **2.** *Av:* Float; stabilizing sponson.

nager [naʒe], v.i. (je nageai(s); n. nageons) **1.** *Nau:* To row, to pull; to scull (double). *N. en arrière, à culer,* to back water. *N. plat,* to feather. **2,** To swim. (a) *N. à l'indienne,* to use the over-arm stroke. *N. debout,* to tread water. **Nager en pleine eau, dans les grandes eaux,** (i) to swim in deep water; (ii) *F:* to live in style, to indulge oneself. **Nager entre deux eaux,** (i) to swim under water; (ii) *F:* to trim; to run with the hare and hunt with the hounds. **Nager contre le courant,** to swim against the current. (b) (To float on or be submerged in liquid) *Le bois nage sur l'eau,* wood floats on water. *Légumes qui nagent dans le beurre,* vegetables swimming in butter. *N. dans l'abondance,* to be rolling in luxury. *N. dans la joie,* to be overjoyed.

nageur, -euse [naʒœ:r, -ø:z]. **1.** a. Swimming (bird, animal). **2.** s. (a) Swimmer. (b) *Nau:* Oarsman, rower.

naguère [nage:r], adv. (*Poet:* also **naguères**) Not long since, a short time ago, but lately; *A:* erstwhile.

naïade [najad], s.f. Naiad, water-nymph.

naï|f, -ïve [naif, -i:v], a. **1.** Artless, ingenuous, unaffected, naive. *Avoir un air n.,* to look innocent, artless. **2.** Simple-minded, guileless, unsophisticated, *F:* green. s. *Quel n.!* what a simpleton! adv. **-vement.**

nain, naine [nɛ̃, nɛn]. **1.** s. Dwarf; *F:* midget, pygmy. *Cards:* **Nain jaune,** Pope Joan. **2.** a. Dwarf(ish). *Palmier n.,* dwarf palm-tree.

naissain [nɛsɛ̃], s.m. (Oyster-, mussel-)brood; spat.

naissance [nɛsɑ̃:s], s.f. **1.** Birth. (a) *Muet de n.,* dumb from birth, born dumb. **Jour, fête, anniversaire, de naissance,** birthday. **Acte de naissance,** birth-certificate. **Lieu de naissance,** birth-place. **Donner naissance à un enfant,** to give birth to a child. (b) Descent, extraction. *De n. obscure,* of low birth, of low extraction. *De haute n.,* high-born. (c) *La n. du printemps,* the birth of spring. *La n. du jour,* dawn; the break of day. **Donner naissance à une rumeur,** to give rise to a rumour. **Prendre naissance,** (of rumour, etc.) to originate, arise. **2.** Root (of tongue, etc.); rise (of river). *Arch:* Spring (of pillar, arch). **Point de naissance,** point of origin.

naiss-ant¹, -ais, -e, etc. See NAÎTRE.

naissant² [nɛsɑ̃], a. New-born; dawning (day); nascent (beauty). *A l'aube naissante,* at break of day. *Barbe naissante,* incipient beard. *Ch:* A l'état naissant, nascent.

naître [nɛ:tr], v.i. (pr.p. naissant; p.p. né, née; pr. ind. je nais, il naît, n. naissons, ils naissent; pr.sub. je naisse; p.h. je naquis; fu. je naîtrai. Aux. être) (a) To be born; to come into the world. *Il naquit, est né, en 1880,* he was born in 1880. *Impers. Il naît dans cette ville cent enfants*

par mois, in this town a hundred children are born every month. **Encore à naître, as yet unborn.** **Être bien, mal, né,** to be well-, low-born. *F:* **Être né pour qch.,** to be cut out for sth. **Je l'ai vu naître,** I have known him from his birth. *Marie Dupont, née Lapointe,* Marie Dupont, maiden name Lapointe, née Lapointe. *F:* **Je ne suis pas né d'hier,** I was not born yesterday. S.a. COIFFÉ 1. (b) (Of hopes, fears) To be born, to (a)rise; to spring up. **Faire naître,** to give birth to, to give rise to, awaken (hope, suspicion); to arouse (suspicion). *Faire n. un sourire,* to provoke, call forth, a smile. **C'est le désir qui fait naître la pensée,** the wish is father to the thought. (c) (Of vegetation) To begin to grow; to spring up, come up. (d) (Of river, project, etc.) To originate, (a)rise; to spring into existence.

naïveté [naivte], s.f. **1.** (a) Artlessness, simplicity, ingenuousness, naïvety. (b) *F:* Greenness, guilelessness. **2.** Ingenuous remark.

naja [naʒa], s.m. Naja, cobra, hooded snake.

nanan [nanɑ̃], s.m. *F:* (In the nursery) Something nice (to eat).

Nankin [nɑ̃kɛ̃]. **1.** *Pr.n. Geog:* Nanking. **2.** s.m. & a. inv. Nankeen.

nansouk [nɑ̃zu(k)], s.m. *Tex:* Nainsook.

nantir [nɑ̃ti:r], v.tr. (a) *Jur:* To give security to, to secure (creditor). **Être nanti de gages,** to be in possession of, secured by, pledges. (b) *F:* *N. qn de qch.,* to provide s.o. with sth. *Se n. d'un parapluie,* to provide, arm, oneself with an umbrella.

nantissement [nɑ̃tismɑ̃], s.m. **1.** Pledging, bailment. **2.** Pledge, collateral security, cover. **Déposer des titres en nantissement,** to lodge stock as security.

napel [napɛl], s.m. *Bot:* Monk's-hood, wolf's-bane.

naphtaline [naftalin], s.f. Naphthaline; *F:* moth-balls.

naphte [naft], s.m. Naphtha; mineral oil.

Napoléon [napɔleɔ̃]. **1.** *Pr.n.m.* Napoleon. **2.** s.m. A: Twenty-franc piece.

napoléonien, -ienne [napɔleɔnjɛ̃, -jɛn], a. Napoleonic.

napolitain, -aine [napɔlitɛ̃, -ɛn], a. & s. Neapolitan.

nappage [napa:ʒ], s.m. Table linen.

nappe [nap], s.f. **1.** (a) Table-cloth. *Mettre, ôter, la n.,* to lay, remove, the cloth. (b) Cloth, cover. *N. d'autel,* altar-cloth. **2.** Sheet (of ice, fire). **Nappe d'eau,** (i) sheet of water; (ii) underground water-level.

napperon [naprɔ̃], s.m. (a) Napkin. *N. de plateau,* tray-cloth. *Petit n.,* doily. (b) Slip (to protect table-cloth). (c) Tea-cloth.

naqui-s, -t, etc. See NAÎTRE.

Narcisse [narsis]. **1.** *Pr.n.m.* Narcissus. **2.** s.m. *Bot:* Narcissus. *N. sauvage, des bois, des prés,* daffodil. *N. des poètes,* pheasant's-eye.

narcissique [narsisik], a. *Psy:* Narcissic.

narcissisme [narsisism], s.m. *Psy:* Narcissism.

narcomanie [narkɔmani], s.f. Drug mania.

narcose [narko:z], s.f. *Med:* Narcosis.

narcotique [narkɔtik], a. & s.m. *Med:* Narcotic; s.m. opiate.

narcotiser [narkɔtize], v.tr. To narcotize; *F:* to drug, dope.

nard [na:r], s.m. *Bot: Pharm:* Spikenard, nard.

nargileh [nargile], s.m. Narghile, hookah.

nargue [narg], s.f. Faire nargue à qn, to snap one's fingers at s.o. **Nargue de, pour . . .!** a fig for . . .! *N. du chagrin!* away with care!

narguer [narge], *v.tr.* To flout; to snap one's fingers at (s.o.).

narguilé [nargile], *s.m.* = NARGHILEH.

narine [narin], *s.f.* Nostril.

narquois, -oise [narkwa, -wa:z], *a.* Quizzing, bantering (tone, smile). *adv.* **-ement.**

narrateur, -trice [narratœ:r, -tris], *s.* Narrator, relater, teller (of story).

narratif, -ive [narratif, -i:v], *a.* Narrative.

narration [narrasjɔ̃], *s.f.* **1.** Narrating, narration. *Gram:* **Présent de** *n.*, historic present. **2.** Narrative, account (of event).

narrer [nare], *v.tr. Lit:* To narrate, relate.

narré, *s.m.* Recital, account (of events).

narval [narval], *s.m. Z:* Narwhal, unicorn-fish. *pl. Des narvals.*

nasal, -als, -aux [nazal, -o]. **1.** *a.* Nasal (bone, sound). **2.** *s.m. Archeol:* Nasal (of helmet). **3.** *s.f. Ling:* **Nasale,** nasal.

nasalement [nazalmã], *adv.* Nasally; *F:* with a twang.

nasaliser [nazalize], *v.tr.* To nasalize (sound).

nasalité [nazalite], *s.f.* Nasality, *F:* twang.

nasarde [nazard], *s.f. A:* Fillip, rap, on the nose. *F: A:* Essuyer une n., to receive a rebuff, a snub.

naseau [nazo], *s.m.* Nostril (of horse, ox).

nasillard [nazija:r], *a. Ton n.*, (nasal) twang; snuffle. *Parler d'une voix nasillarde,* to talk through one's nose.

nasiller [nazije], *v.i.* To speak through one's nose, with a twang; to snuffle.

nasse [nas], *s.f.* Bow-net, eel-pot, eel-buck; hoop-net (for birds); trap (for rats). *F:* **Tomber dans la nasse,** to fall into the trap.

natal, -als, -aux [natal, -o], *a.* **1.** Native (country). *Ville natale,* birth-place. **2.** Jour natal, birthday.

natalité [natalite], *s.f.* **1.** Birth-rate. **2.** Centre de natalité, maternity centre.

natation [natasjɔ̃], *s.f.* Swimming, natation.

natatoire [natatwa:r], *a. Z:* Natatory (organ, membrane). *Ich:* **Vessie natatoire,** swim(ming)-bladder, air-bladder.

nat|if, -ive [natif, -i:v]. **1.** *a.* Native. (*a*) *Je suis n. de Londres,* I am London born. (*b*) *Argent n.*, native silver. (*c*) Natural, inborn. *Bon sens n.*, mother wit. **2.** *s.m.pl.* **Natifs,** natives. *adv.* **-ivement.**

nation [nasjɔ̃], *s.f.* Nation. *Il est Italien de n.*, he is of Italian nationality. S.a. SOCIÉTÉ 2.

national, -aux [nasjɔnal, -o]. **1.** *a.* National. S.a. ROUTE 1. **2.** *s.m.pl.* Nationaux, nationals (of a country). *adv.* **-ement.**

nationaliser [nasjɔnalize], *v.tr.* To nationalize.

nationalisme [nasjɔnalism], *s.m.* Nationalism.

nationaliste [nasjɔnalist], *s. m. & f.* Nationalist.

nationalité [nasjɔnalite], *s.f.* **1.** Nationality. *Nau:* Acte de nationalité, (ship's) certificate of registry. **2.** Nation.

nativité [nativite], *s.f. Ecc: Astrol:* Nativity.

natte [nat], *s.f.* **1.** Mat, matting (of rush, straw). **2.** Plait, braid (of hair, of gold thread). *Porter des nattes (dans le dos),* to wear one's hair in plaits.

natt|er [nate], *v.tr.* **1.** To cover (room) with mats. **2.** To plait, braid (hair, straw). *s.m.* **-age.**

naturalisation [natyralizasjɔ̃], *s.f.* **1.** Natural-ization, nationalization. **2.** (*a*) N. d'animaux, taxidermy. (*b*) Preservation, mounting (of botanical specimen).

naturaliser [natyralize], *v.tr.* **1.** To naturalize, to nationalize. **2.** (*a*) To mount, stuff, set up (animal). (*b*) To mount (botanical specimen).

naturalisme [natyralism], *s.m. Lit: Art:* Naturalism.

naturaliste [natyralist]. **1.** *s.* (*a*) Naturalist. (*b*) Taxidermist. **2.** *a.* Naturalistic.

nature [naty:r], *s.f.* Nature. **1.** *Les lois de la n.*, the laws of nature. **Contre nature,** unnatural. *Plus grand que n.*, larger than life. *Peindre d'après n.*, to paint from nature, from life. **Nature morte,** still-life (painting). S.a. DETTE, TRIBUT. **2.** (*a*) Kind, constitution, character. *N. du climat, du sol,* nature of the climate, of the soil. **Faits de nature à nous étonner,** facts of a nature, of a kind, calculated, to astonish us. (*b*) Character, disposition, temperament. **Il est timide de nature; il est d'une nature timide,** he is naturally shy, is shy by nature. **Il tient cela de sa nature,** it comes to him by nature. **C'est une bonne nature,** he is of a kindly disposition. **3.** Kind. **Payer en nature,** to pay in kind. **4.** *a.inv.* Bœuf, pommes, nature, plain boiled beef, potatoes. **Café nature,** plain black coffee (without spirits).

naturel, -elle [natyrɛl]. **1.** *a.* Natural. (*a*) *Mort naturelle,* death from natural causes. *Enfant n.*, natural, illegitimate, child. *Penchant n.*, natural inclination. **De grandeur naturelle,** life-size. **Je trouve naturel que** + *sub.*, I find it reasonable that (s.o. should do sth.). (*b*) *Don n.*, natural, innate, gift. *Il lui est n. d'écrire en vers,* it comes natural to him to write in verse. (*c*) Natural, unaffected (person). *Réponse naturelle,* simple, straightforward, answer. *Alcool n.*, raw spirit. **2.** *s.m.* Native (of country). **3.** *s.m.* (*a*) Nature, character, disposition. *Avoir un heureux n.*, to have a happy disposition. *Prov:* **Chassez le naturel, il revient au galop,** what's bred in the bone will come out in the flesh. (*b*) **Se conduire avec naturel,** to behave with naturalness, with native ease. (*c*) *Voir les choses au n.*, to see things as they are.

naturellement [natyrɛlmã], *adv.* Naturally. **1.** By nature; by birth. **2.** Without affectation; unaffectedly. **3.** *Vous lui avez répondu?—Naturellement,* you answered him?—Of course (I did); naturally. *F: N. que je viendrai!* of course I'll come!

naufrage [nofra:ʒ, nɔ-], *s.m.* (Ship)wreck. **Faire naufrage,** to be shipwrecked. *Périr dans un n.*, to be lost at sea. *Échapper au n.*, to be saved from the wreck.

naufragé, -ée [nofraʒe]. **1.** *a.* (Ship)wrecked; castaway (crew). **2.** *s.* Castaway.

naufrageur [nofraʒœ:r, nɔ-], *s.m.* Wrecker.

nauséabond [nozeabɔ̃], *a.* Nauseous, nauseating, foul (smell, etc.); evil-smelling.

nausée [noze], *s.f.* (*a*) Nausea. (*b*) Seasickness. **Avoir des nausées,** to feel squeamish, sick. *Donner des nausées à qn,* to nauseate s.o.

nauséeux, -euse [nozeø, -ø:z], *a.* Nauseating; loathsome.

nautique [notik], *a.* Nautical. **Sports nautiques,** aquatic sports. *Carte n.*, (sea-)chart. *adv.* **-ment.**

nautonier [notɔnje], *s.m. A:* Pilot, mariner.

naval, -als [naval], *a.* Naval, nautical. *Armée navale,* fleet; naval force. *Combats navals,* sea-fights. *Architecture navale,* shipbuilding. *L'École navale,* the Naval College.

navarin [navarɛ̃], *s.m.* Mutton stew (with potatoes and turnips); haricot mutton.

navet [nave], *s.m.* **1.** Turnip. *N. de Suède,* swede. *P:* **Des navets!** nothing doing! **Il a du sang de navet,** (i) he is anaemic; (ii) he's a listless, slack, kind of fellow. **2.** *F:* Bad painting; daub.

navette[1] [navɛt], *s.f.* **1.** Incense-boat; incense-box. (*a*) Shuttle. *F:* **Faire la navette** *entre deux endroits,* (of vehicle) to ply (to and fro) between two places; (of pers.) to run backwards and forwards, to and fro. *Ligne de chemin de fer exploitée en n.*, railway line over which a shuttle service is run. (*b*) Netting needle.

navette², *s.f. Bot:* Rape. (Huile de) navette, rape(-seed) oil, colza oil.

navigabilité [navigabilite], *s.f.* **1.** Navigability (of river, etc.). **2.** Seaworthiness (of ship); airworthiness (of airship). *En (bon) état de n.*, seaworthy; airworthy.

navigable [navigabl], *a.* **1.** Navigable (river). **2.** Seaworthy; airworthy.

navigateur [navigatœ:r]. **1.** *s.m.* (*a*) Navigator (of ship, aeroplane). (*b*) Navigator; seafarer. **2.** *a.m.* Seafaring (people).

navigation [navigasjɔ̃], *s.f.* Navigation, sailing. *N. côtière*, coastal navigation. *N. plane, loxodromique*, plane sailing, Mercator's sailing. *N. sur l'arc de grand cercle, n. orthodromique*, great circle sailing. **Compagnie de navigation**, shipping company. **Permis de navigation**, ship's passport, sea-letter. *Terme de n.*, nautical term.

naviguer [navige]. **1.** *v.i.* (*a*) To sail, navigate. *N. au commerce*, to be in the merchant service. **With cogn. acc. Naviguer les mers**, to sail the seas. (*b*) *Vaisseau qui navigue bien*, ship that behaves well at sea. **2.** *v.tr.* To navigate (ship).

navire [navi:r], *s.m.* Ship, vessel. *N. à voiles*, sailing-ship. *N..à vapeur*, steamer. *N. de guerre*, warship. *N. marchand, de commerce*, merchantman. *N. école*, training-ship. *Les navires dans le port*, the shipping in the harbour.

navire-citerne, *s.m.* Tanker. *pl. Des navires-citernes.*

navire-gigogne, *s.m.* Mother ship (for seaplanes). *pl. Des navires-gigogne.*

navrant [nɑvrɑ̃], *a.* Heart-rending, heartbreaking.

navrer [navre], *v.tr.* To grieve (s.o.) most deeply; to cut (s.o.) to the heart.

   navré, *a.* Heart-broken; woe-begone (expression); cut to the heart; dreadfully sorry. *Avoir le cœur n. de qch.*, to be deeply grieved, broken-hearted, at sth.

nazaréen, -enne [nazareɛ̃, -ɛn], *a. & s. B.Hist:* Nazarene. *s.* Nazarite.

ne, n' [n(ə)], *neg.adv.* Not. **1.** For the use of *ne* (i) strengthened by *pas, point, goutte, mie, mot,* or (ii) in conjunction with *ni, guère, nullement, aucunement, jamais, plus; aucun, nul, personne, rien; que ... que*), see these words. **2.** Used alone (*i.e.* with omission of *pas*), chiefly in literary style, with *cesser, oser, pouvoir, savoir, importer,* and often as an archaism with other verbs. *Il ne cesse de parler*, he is for ever talking. *Je n'ose lui parler*, I dare not speak to him. *Je ne sais que faire*, I don't know what to do. *Je ne saurais vous le dire*, I cannot tell you. Always used without *pas* in the phr. **N'importe**, never mind, it doesn't matter. **3.** In the following constructions: (*a*) *Qui ne connaît cette œuvre célèbre?* who does not know that famous work? *Que ne ferait-il pour vous?* what would he not do for you? (*b*) *Je n'ai d'autre désir que celui de vous plaire*, I have no other desire than to please you. (*c*) *Il n'est pas si stupide qu'il ne vous comprenne*, he is not so stupid but that he understands you. (*d*) *Si je ne me trompe . . .*, unless I am mistaken. . . . (*e*) *Voilà six mois que je ne l'ai vu*, it is now six months since I saw him. (*f*) *Il n'y a personne à qui il ne se soit adressé*, there is no one whom he did not apply to. (*g*) *Il n'eut garde d'y aller*, he took good care not to go. *Qu'à cela ne tienne!* by all means! *Je n'ai que*

faire de votre aide, I don't need your help. **4.** Used optionally in literary style with a vague negative connotation. (*a*) (Expressions of fear) *Je crains qu'il (ne) prenne froid*, I am afraid he may catch cold, of his catching cold. (*b*) *Évitez, prenez garde, qu'on (ne) vous voie*, avoid being seen; take care not to be seen. *Peu s'en fallut qu'il ne tombât*, he nearly came a cropper. *Je ne nie pas que cela (ne) soit vrai*, I don't deny that it is true. *A moins qu'on (ne) vous appelle*, unless they call you. (*c*) (Comparison) *Il est plus vigoureux qu'il (ne) paraît*, he is stronger than he looks. *Il agit autrement qu'il ne parle*, he acts otherwise than he speaks.

né. See NAÎTRE.

néanmoins [neɑ̃mwɛ̃], *adv.* Nevertheless, none the less; for all that; yet; still.

néant [neɑ̃], *s.m.* **1.** Nothingness, nought, naught. **Sortir du néant**, to rise from obscurity. *Rentrer dans un éternel n.*, to return to everlasting nothingness. **Réduire qch. à néant**, to reduce sth. to nothing, to nought; to annihilate sth. **2.** *Adm:* **Néant**, (on income-tax return, etc.) 'none'; (on report-sheet, etc.) 'nothing to report,' 'nil.'

néapolitain, -aine [neapolitɛ̃, -ɛn], *a. & s.* = NAPOLITAIN.

nébulaire [nebylɛ:r], *a. Astr:* Nebular.

nébuleu|x, -euse [nebylø, -ø:z]. **1.** *a.* Nebulous. (*a*) Cloudy, hazy, misty (sky, view). (*b*) Turbid, cloudy (liquor, crystal). (*c*) Gloomy, clouded (brow). (*d*) Unintelligible, obscure (writer, theory). **2.** *s.f. Astr:* **Nébuleuse**, nebula. *adv.* **-sement.**

nébulosité [nebylozite], *s.f.* **1.** Nebulosity, nebulousness, haziness. **2.** Patch of mist, of haze.

nécessaire [nesesɛ:r]. **1.** *a.* Necessary, needful; requisite. *N. à, pour, qch.*, required for sth. *Se rendre n. à qn*, to make oneself indispensable to s.o. *Avoir l'argent n.*, to have the money required. *s.* **Faire le nécessaire**, to play the busybody. *Il n'est pas n. de . . .*, there is no need to. . . . *Est-il n. que je + sub.?* is it necessary that I should . . .? **Peu nécessaire**, needless, unnecessary. **2.** *s.m.* (*a*) Necessaries, the needful, the indispensable. *Le strict n.*, bare necessaries. **Faire le nécessaire**, to do what is necessary; to do the needful. (*b*) Outfit. *N. à ouvrage*, (i) workbox, work-basket; (ii) housewife. *N. de réparation*, repairing outfit. *N. de toilette*, dressing-case.

nécessairement [nesesɛrmɑ̃], *adv.* **1.** Necesssarily; of necessity. **2.** Inevitably, infallibly.

nécessité [nesesite], *s.f.* Necessity. *La dure n. me force à . . .*, dire necessity compels me to. . . . **De nécessité, de toute nécessité . . .**, necessarily, of necessity. . . . *Il est de toute n. de (faire qch.)*, it is essential to (do sth.). **Être dans la nécessité de faire qch.**, to be under the necessity of doing sth. *Mettre qn dans la n. de faire qch.*, to make it necessary for s.o. to do sth.; to put s.o. under the necessity of doing sth. **Faire qch. par nécessité**, to do sth. out of necessity. **Faire de nécessité vertu**, to make a virtue of necessity. **Agir sans nécessité**, to act unnecessarily. **Nécessité n'a point de loi**, necessity knows no law. *Les nécessités de la vie*, the necessaries of life. **Objets de première nécessité, de toute nécessité**, indispensable articles. *Denrées de première n.*, essential foodstuffs. **Selon les nécessités**, as circumstances (may) require. *F:* **Faire ses nécessités**, to relieve nature. *Être dans la n.* to be in want, in need, in straitened circumstances.

nécessiter [nesesite], *v.tr.* **1.** To necessitate, entail (sth.). *Cela nécessitera des négociations,* this will entail negotiations. **2.** *N. qn à faire qch.*, to oblige, force, s.o. to do sth.

nécessiteux, -euse [nesesitø, -øːz], *a.* Needy, in want, necessitous. *s.* **Les nécessiteux,** the needy, the destitute.

nécrologe [nekrɔlɔːʒ], *s.m.* Obituary list, death-roll.

nécrologie [nekrɔlɔʒi], *s.f.* Obituary notice.

nécrologique [nekrɔlɔʒik], *a.* Necrological. *Notice n.*, obituary notice.

nécromancie [nekrɔmɑ̃si], *s.f.* Necromancy.

nécromancien, -ienne [nekrɔmɑ̃sjɛ̃, -jɛn], *s.* Necromancer.

nécrophore [nekrɔfɔːr], *s.m. Ent:* Carrion-beetle, burying-beetle.

nécropole [nekrɔpɔl], *s.f.* Necropolis.

nécrose [nekroːz], *s.f.* **1.** *Med:* Necrosis. **2.** *Bot:* Canker (in wood).

nécroser [nekroze], *v.tr.* **1.** To cause necrosis in (bone). **2.** *Bot:* To canker.   **se nécroser. 1.** *Med:* To necrose, to necrotize. **2.** *Bot:* To become cankered.

nectaire [nɛktɛːr], *s.m. Bot:* Nectary, honey-cup.

nectar [nɛktaːr], *s.m. Myth: Bot:* Nectar.

nectarine [nɛktarin], *s.f.* Thin-skinned free-stone peach.

néerlandais, -aise [neɛrlɑ̃dɛ, -ɛːz]. **1.** *a.* Of the Netherlands; 'Dutch. **2.** *s.* Netherlander; Dutchman, Dutchwoman.

nef [nɛf], *s.f.* **1.** Nave (of church). *Nef latérale*, aisle. **2.** *A:* Ship. *Hist:* **La Blanche Nef**, the White Ship.

néfaste [nefast], *a.* Luckless, ill-omened, inauspicious; baneful. *Jour n.,* (i) *Rom.Ant:* day of mourning or *dies non*; (ii) ill-fated day, black-letter day; ill-starred, evil, day. *Influence n.*, baleful, baneful, influence.

nèfle [nɛfl], *s.f.* Medlar (fruit). *F:* **Avoir qch. pour des nèfles,** to get sth. dirt cheap. *P:* **Des nèfles!** (i) no fear! (ii) nothing doing!

néflier [neflje], *s.m.* Medlar(-tree).

négateur, -trice [nɛgatœːr, -tris]. **1.** *a.* Denying. **2.** *s.* Denier.

négatif, -ive [nɛgatif, -iːv]. **1.** *a.* Negative (answer, electricity). *Phot:* *Épreuve négative*, *s.m.* négatif, negative. *Dessin n.,* blue print. **2.** *s.f.* *Soutenir la négative*, to maintain, uphold, the negative. *adv.* **-ivement.**

négation [nɛgasjɔ̃], *s.f.* **1.** Negation, denial. **2.** *Gram:* Negative.

négligeable [negliʒabl], *a.* Negligible.

négligence [negliʒɑ̃ːs], *s.f.* **1.** Negligence; neglect (of s.o., of duty); carelessness, want of care. *N. à faire qch.,* (i) carelessness in doing sth.; (ii) remissness with regard to sth., to be done. *Négligences de style,* negligences of style. *Par négligence,* through an oversight.

négligent [negliʒɑ̃], *a.* **1.** Negligent, careless; neglectful (*de,* of). *Être n. à faire qch.,* to be careless, remiss, in doing sth. **2.** Indifferent, casual (tone). *adv.* **-emment.**

négliger [negliʒe], *v.tr.* (je négligeai(s); n. négligeons) To neglect. **1.** To take no care of (s.o., sth.); ;, to be neglectful of (duty, one's interest); to be careless of (dress, appearance). **2.** (*a*) To disregard (advice, decimals). (*b*) *N. de faire qch.,* to omit to do sth.; to leave sth. undone.   **se négliger,** to neglect one's person.

négligé. 1. *a.* (*a*) Neglected, unheeded (opportunity). (*b*) Careless, slovenly (dress, appearance). **2.** *s.m.* Undress; dishabille; négligé (gown); (lady's) morning wrap.

négoce [negɔs], *s.m.* **1.** Trade, trading, business.

Faire le négoce, to trade. **2.** (Unscrupulous) traffic(king).

négociable [negɔsjabl], *a. Com:* Negotiable, transferable (bond, bill, cheque). *s.f.* **-abilité.**

négociant, -ante [negɔsjɑ̃, -ɑ̃ːt], *s.* (Wholesale) merchant; trader. *N. en vins,* wine-merchant.

négociateur, -trice [negɔsjatœːr, -tris], *s.* Negotiator.

négociation [negɔsjasjɔ̃], *s.f.* **1.** Negotiation, negotiating. **En négociation,** under negotiation, in treaty. **Engager, entamer, des négociations,** to enter into, upon, negotiations; *Mil:* to parley. **2.** Transaction.

négocier [negɔsje]. **1.** *v.i.* *A:* To trade (*en,* in). **2.** *v.tr.* To negotiate (loan, bill, treaty).

nègre, négresse [nɛːgr, negrɛs]. **1.** *s.* (*a*) Negro, *f.* negress; black. **Parler petit nègre,** to talk trading French, 'pidgin' (with the blacks). *a.inv.* (*Couleur*) **tête de nègre,** nigger-brown. (*b*) *F:* Drudge; 'ghost' (of literary man); 'devil' (of barrister). **2.** *a.* (*f.* **nègre**) *La race nègre,* the negro race.

négrerie [negrəri], *s.f.* **1.** *A:* Slave compound; barracoon. **2.** Negro quarters.

négrier [negrie], *s.m.* **1.** Slave-trader. **2.** Slave-ship.

négrillon, -onne [negrijɔ̃, -ɔn], *s.* (Little) nigger-boy,-girl; *F:* piccaninny.

neige [nɛːʒ], *s.f.* Snow. **Neiges éternelles,** perpetual snow. *Il tombe de la n.,* it is snowing. **Rafale de neige,** snow-flurry; blizzard. **Amas de neige,** snow-drift. *Être bloqué par la n.,* to be snowed up, snow-bound. **Neige fondue,** (i) sleet, (ii) slush. **Boule de neige,** snowball. *Histoire qui fait boule de neige,* story that grows as it spreads. **Faire un bonhomme de neige,** to make a snow-man. *Blanc comme la n.,* snow-white. *S.a.* ANTAN. *Cu:* **Blancs d'œufs battus en neige,** whites of eggs beaten stiff. **Œufs à la neige,** floating islands. *Ind:* **Neige carbonique,** (carbonic acid) 'snow.'

neiger [neʒe], *v.impers.* (il neigeait) To snow.

neigeux, -euse [neʒø, -øːz], *a.* Snowy (peak, weather); snow-covered (roof, etc.).

nélombo, nélumbo [nelɔ̃bo], *s.m.* Egyptian lotus, Nile-lily.

nématode [nɛmatɔd], *s.m.* Nematode, thread-worm.

ne m'oubliez pas [nəmubliepɑ], *s.m.inv. Bot: F:* Forget-me-not.

nenni [nani], *adv. A:* (a) Not he! (b) Nay!

nénufar, nénuphar [nenyfar], *s.m. Bot:* Ne-nuphar, water-lily. *N. des étangs, n. jaune,* yellow pond-lily.

néo-classicisme [neoklasisism], *s.m.* Neo-classicism.

néographie [neografi], *s.f.* Reformed spelling.

néo-grec, *f.* **néo-grecque** [neogrɛk], *a.* Neo-Greek, modern Greek (literature, language).

néo-impressionnisme [neoɛ̃presjɔnism], *s.m. Art:* Post-impressionism.

néo-latin [neolatɛ̃], *a.* Neo-Latin. *Langues néo-latines,* Romance languages.

néolithique [neolitik], *a.* Neolithic.

néologisme [neolɔʒism], *s.m.* Neologism.

néon [neɔ̃], *s.m. Ch:* Neon. **Tube, lampe, au néon,** neon tube; neon glow-lamp.

néophyte [neofit], *s.m.* (a) Neophyte. (b) Beginner, tyro.

néo-Zélandais, -aise [neozelɑ̃dɛ, -ɛːz]. **1.** *a.* New Zealand (butter). **2.** *s.* New Zealander.

népérien, -ienne [neperjɛ̃, -jɛn], *a. Mth:* Napierian (logarithms).

néphrétique [nefretik], *néphritique* [nefritik].

27

1. *a.* Nephritic, renal (pain, colic). **2.** *s.* Sufferer from nephritis.

néphrite [nefrit], *s.f.* **1.** *Med:* Nephritis. *N. chronique*, Bright's disease. **2.** *Miner:* Nephrite, jade, green-stone.

népotisme [nepotism], *s.m.* Nepotism.

néréide [nereid], *s.f.* Nereid; sea-nymph.

nerf [nɛːr, nɛrf, *pl.* always nɛːr], *s.m.* **1.** Nerve. *Maladie de nerfs*, nervous complaint. *Attaque de nerfs*, (fit of) hysterics. *Avoir une attaque, une crise, de nerfs*, to go into hysterics. *F:* Avoir les nerfs agacés, à vif, to have one's nerves jangled, on edge. *Porter, donner, sur les nerfs à qn*, to get, jar, on s.o.'s nerves. *Elle a ses nerfs aujourd'hui*, she is in her tantrums again to-day. **2.** *F:* Sinew, tendon, ligament. *Nerfs d'acier*, thews of steel. *P:* Mets-y du nerf [nɛrf]! put some vim into it! *Caractère sans nerf*, weak, nerveless, character. *Manquer de n.*, to lack energy, stamina. **3.** (*a*) *Bookb:* Band, cord, slip. (*b*) *Arch:* Rib, fillet (of groin).

nerprun [nɛrprœ̃], *s.m. Bot:* Buckthorn.

nervation [nɛrvasjɔ̃], *s.f. Bot: etc:* Nervation.

nervé [nɛrve], *a. Bot:* Nervate, nervose.

nerver [nɛrve], *v.tr.* To stiffen. (*a*) To back (panel) with strips of canvas, etc. (*b*) To put a flange on (sth.). (*c*) To put bands on (book).

nerveusement [nɛrvøzmɑ̃], *adv.* **1.** Energetically. **2.** Impatiently, irritably; *F:* nervily. *Rire n.*, to laugh hysterically.

nerveux, -euse [nɛrvø, -øːz], *a.* **1.** Nervous (system, disease). *Centre n.*, nerve centre. *Prostration nerveuse*, nervous breakdown. **2.** Sinewy, wiry; vigorous, virile (style). *Moteur n.*, responsive engine. **3.** Excitable, highly-strung, *F:* 'nervy' (person). *Rire n.*, hysterical laugh.

nervi [nɛrvi], *s.m. F:* Gangster.

nervosisme [nɛrvozism], *s.m. Med:* Nervous diathesis; nervous predisposition.

nervosité [nɛrvozite], *s.f.* Irritability, state of nerves, state of fidgets.

nervure [nɛrvyːr], *s.f.* (*a*) Nervure, rib, vein (of leaf, insect-wing). (*b*) Branch (of mountain-group). (*c*) Flange, rib (on casting, etc.); gill (of radiator, etc.). *Carter à nervures*, stiffened crank-case. (*d*) Rib, fillet (of groin, etc.). *Plafond à nervures*, filleted ceiling. (*e*) *Bookb:* Rib, raised band (on back of book).

nescience [nɛssjɑ̃ːs], *s.f.* Nescience; state of ignorance.

n'est-ce pas [nɛspɑ], *adv.phr.* (Inviting assent) *Vous venez, n'est-ce pas?* you are coming, aren't you? *Vous viendrez, n'est-ce pas?* you will come, won't you? *Vous ne venez pas, n'est-ce pas?* you are not coming, are you? *Il en a, n'est-ce pas?* he has some, hasn't he? *Il n'en vend pas, n'est-ce pas?* he doesn't sell any, does he? *N'est-ce pas qu'il a de la chance?* isn't he lucky?

net, nette [nɛt], *a.* **1.** Clean, spotless (plate, etc.); flawless (stone); clear, sound (conscience). *F:* J'ai les mains nettes, my hands are clean; I had nothing to do with it. *Faire les plats nets, F:* to lick the platter clean. *Son cas n'est pas net*, his case is not above suspicion. *Rente nette de tout impôt*, income free of tax. *Cassure nette*, clean break. *Maison nette comme un sou neuf*, house as clean as a new pin. *Gaming:* Faire tapis net, to clear the board. S.a. CŒUR 2, MAISON 2. **2.** (*a*) Clear (sight, idea); distinct (print); plain (answer). *Division nette*, clear-cut division. *Contours nets*, sharp outlines. *Écriture nette*, fair hand. *Phot:* Image nette, sharp image. *s.m.* Mettre un devoir au net, to write a fair copy of an exercise. (*b*) *Poids net*, net weight.

3. *adv.* (*a*) Plainly, flatly, outright. *Refuser net*, to refuse point-blank; to give a flat refusal. *S'arrêter net*, to stop dead. (*b*) *Voir net*, (i) to see distinctly, clearly; (ii) *F:* to be clear-headed. *adv.* **-ttement.**

netteté [nɛt(ə)te], *s.f.* **1.** Cleanness (of mirror, wound); cleanliness (of body). Écrit avec netteté, neatly written. **2.** (*a*) Clearness (of vision, of object); sharpness (of image). (*b*) Flatness (of refusal).

nettoie-becs [nɛtwabɛk], *s.m. inv.* Probe, pricker (for acetylene jet, etc.).

nett|oyer [nɛtwaje], *v.tr.* (je nettoie; je nettoierai) (*a*) To clean; to scour (pan, deck); to swab (deck); to scour, screen (corn); to gin (cotton). *N. à grande eau*, to scour. *N. une pièce à fond*, to turn out a room. *N. à sec*, to dry-clean. (*b*) *F:* (Of burglar) *N. une maison*, to strip a house bare. (*c*) *Mil:* N. les tranchées, to clear the trenches (of remaining enemy, after attack); *F:* to mop up. (*d*) *F:* Il est rentré du club nettoyé (à sec), he came home from the club cleaned out. *s.m.* **-oyage.** *s.m.* **-oiement.**

nettoyeur, -euse [nɛtwajœːr, -øːz]. **1.** *a.* Cleaning (apparatus, etc.). **2.** *s.* Cleaner. *Ind:* Greaser, scrubber. *N. de fenêtres*, window-cleaner. **3.** *s.f.* Nettoyeuse, cleaning machine.

neuf[1], *num. a. inv. & s.m. inv.* Nine. **1.** *Card.a.* (At the end of the word-group [nœf]; before *ans* and *heures* [nœv]; otherwise before vowel sounds [nœf]; before a noun or adj. beginning with a consonant usu. [nœ, often [nœf]) *J'en ai neuf* [nœf], I have nine. *Il a neuf ans* [nœvɑ̃], he is nine years old. *Neuf francs* [nœfrɑ̃], nine francs. **2.** Ordinal uses, etc. (Always [nœf]) *Le neuf mai* [lənœfmɛ], the ninth of May. *Louis Neuf*, Louis the Ninth. *Ar:* Faire la preuve par neuf, to cast out the nines.

neuf[2], neuve [nœf, nœːv]. **1.** *a.* (*a*) (Shop-)new; new (thought, subject). A l'état (de) neuf, in new condition; as new. S.a. BATTANT I. 1, FLAMBANT. (*b*) *Pays n.*, new country. *La rue Neuve*, New Street. *N. aux affaires*, new to business. (*c*) *F:* Qu'est-ce qu'il y a de neuf? what is the news? **2.** *s.m.* Habillé de neuf, dressed in new clothes; *F:* in a new rig-out. *Meublé de neuf*, newly refurnished. Il y a du neuf, I have news for you. *Adv.phr.* A neuf. (i) Anew. (ii) *Remettre qch. à n.*, to make sth. like new, as good as new.

neurasthénie [nørasteni], *s.f.* Neurasthenia.

neurasthénique [nørastenik], *a. & s.* Neurasthenic.

neurotique [nørɔtik], *a. Med:* Neurotic.

neutralisation [nøtralizasjɔ̃], *s.f.* Neutralization, neutralizing (of country, acid).

neutraliser [nøtralize], *v.tr.* To neutralize (effort, country, acid).

neutralité [nøtralite], *s.f.* Neutrality. Garder la neutralité, to remain neutral.

neutre [nøtr], *a.* **1.** Neuter. *s.m.* Adjectif au neutre, adjective in the neuter. *Abeille n.*, neuter bee. **2.** Neutral (tint, nation; *Ch:* substance). *Mil:* La zone neutre, no-man's land. *s.m.* Droits des neutres, rights of neutrals.

neutron [nøtrɔ̃], *s.m. El:* Neutron.

neuvaine [nœvɛn], *s.f. Ecc:* Novena.

neuve. See NEUF[2].

neuvième [nœvjɛm]. **1.** *num. a. & s.* Ninth. **2.** *s.m.* Ninth (part). **3.** *s.f. Mus:* Ninth. *adv.* **-ment.**

névé [neve], *s.m. Geol:* Firn, névé; granular ice.

neveu, -eux [n(ə)vø], *s.m.* **1.** Nephew. *F:* Neveu

à la mode de Bretagne, first cousin once removed.
2. *pl. A: Nos neveux,* our descendants.

névralgie [nevralʒi], *s.f.* Neuralgia.

névralgique [nevralʒik], *a.* Neuralgic.

névrite [nevrit], *s.f.* Neuritis.

névropathe [nevrɔpat], *s.m. & f.* Neuropath.

névroptère [nevrɔptɛːr]. *Ent:* **1.** *a. & s.m.* Neuropteran. **2.** *s.m.pl.* Névroptères, neuroptera.

névrose [nevroːz], *s.f. Med:* Neurosis.

névrosé, -ée [nevroze], *a. & s. Med:* Neurotic, neurasthenic (patient).

newyorkais, -aise [nœjɔrkɛ, nju-, -ɛːz]. **1.** *a.* Of New York. **2.** *s.* New Yorker.

nez [ne], *s.m.* **1.** Nose. (*a*) **Parler du nez,** to speak through one's nose **Mener, conduire, qn par le bout du nez,** to lead s.o. by the nose. **Fourrer son nez partout,** to poke, thrust, one's nose into everything. **Cela lui pend au nez,** the same thing may happen to him any day. **Ton nez branle!** you're telling a lie! you're fibbing! **Faire un pied de nez à qn,** to make a long nose at s.o. *P:* **Je l'ai dans le nez,** I can't stand him. S.a. PIQUER 2, SAIGNER 1, VER 2. (*b*) Sense of smell; (of dogs) scent. **Avoir bon nez, le nez fin,** (i) to have a good nose, a keen sense of smell; (ii) *F:* to be shrewd, far-seeing. (*c*) *F:* **Nez à nez,** face to face. **Montrer son nez, le bout de son nez,** quelque part, to show one's face somewhere. **Regardez donc quel fil il fait,** do look at the face he's pulling. **Regarder qn sous le nez,** to look defiantly at s.o. **Faire qch. au nez de qn,** to do sth. under s.o.'s nose. **Fermer la porte au nez de qn,** to shut the door in s.o.'s face. **Rire au nez de qn,** to laugh in s.o.'s face. **Faire qch. à vue de nez,** to do sth. (i) at first sight, (ii) in a rough and ready way. **Se casser le nez,** (i) to find nobody at home; (ii) to come a cropper. (Of two persons) **Se manger le nez,** to quarrel. **2.** (Nose-shaped object) (*a*) Bow, nose, head (of ship, dirigible). **Vaisseau sur le nez,** ship (down) by the head, down by the bow(s). **Piquer du nez,** (of ship) to dive into it; *Av:* to nose-dive. (*b*) Nosing (of step). (*c*) *Av:* Nose-piece (of engine).

ni [ni], *conj.* (*Ne* is either expressed or implied) Nor, or. (*a*) *Ni moi (non plus),* nor I (either); neither do I. *Sans argent ni bagages,* without money or luggage. (*b*) *Il ne mange ni ne boit,* he neither eats nor drinks. *Il est parti sans manger ni boire,* he went off without (either) eating or drinking. (*c*) *Ni . . . ni,* neither . . . nor. *Je n'ai ni femme ni enfant,* I have neither wife nor child. *Ni l'un ni l'autre ne l'a vu,* neither (of them) saw it.

niable [niabl, nja-], *a.* Deniable.

niais, -aise [nie, njɛ, -ɛːz]. **1.** *a.* Simple, foolish; inane (smile). *Je ne suis pas assez n. pour . . .,* I know better than to. . . . **2.** *s.* Fool, simpleton. *Petite niaise!* you little silly! *adv.* **-ement.**

niaiserie [niezri, nje-], *s.f.* **1.** Silliness, foolishness. **2.** *Dire des niaiseries,* to talk nonsense.

Nicée [nise]. *Pr.n.f. A.Geog:* Nicaea. **Le symbole de Nicée,** the Nicene Creed.

niche¹ [niʃ], *s.f.* **1.** Niche, nook, recess (in wall, etc.). **2.** *N. à chien,* dog-kennel.

niche², *s.f. F:* Trick, prank.

niche-abri, *s.f. Mil:* Dug-out, funk-hole. *pl. Des niches-abris.*

nichée [niʃe], *s.f.* Nest(ful) (of birds); brood (of mice, puppies).

nicher [niʃe]. **1.** *v.i.* (*a*) (Of bird) To build a nest; to nest. (*b*) *F:* *Où nichez-vous?* where do

you hang out? **2.** *v.tr.* To put, lodge (in a nest or niche); to niche.

se nicher. (*a*) (Of bird) *Se n. dans un arbre,* to build its nest in a tree. *Maisonnette nichée dans un bois,* cottage nestling in a wood. *F:* *Je ne sais où (aller) me n.,* I don't know where to find a lodging. (*b*) To ensconce oneself (*dans,* in).

nicheur, -euse [niʃœːr, -øːz], *a.* Nest-building, nesting (bird).

nichoir [niʃwaːr], *s.m.* Breeding-cage, -coop.

nickel [nikɛl], *s.m. Ch:* Nickel.

nickel|er [nikle], *v.tr.* (**je nickelle; je nickellerai**) To nickel; to nickel-plate. *F:* **Avoir les pieds nickelés,** to sit tight, to refuse to budge. *s.m.* **-age.**

nickélifère [nikelifɛːr], *a.* Nickel-bearing.

nickelure [niklyːr], *s.f.* Nickelling.

Nicodème [nikodɛːm]. **1.** *Pr.n.m.* Nicodemus. **2.** *s.m. F:* Ninny; simpleton, simple Simon.

niçois, -oise [niswa, -waːz], *a. & s.* (Native) of Nice.

nicol [nikɔl], *s.m. Opt:* Nicol (prism).

Nicolas [nikɔla]. **1.** *Pr.n.m.* Nicholas. **2.** *s.m. F:* = NICODÈME 2.

nicotine [nikɔtin], *s.f. Ch:* Nicotine.

nictation [niktasjɔ̃], *s.f.,* **nictitation** [niktitasjɔ̃], *s.f.* Nictation, nictitation.

nictitant [niktitɑ̃], *a.* Nictitating (membrane).

nid [ni], *s.m.* **1.** Nest. *F:* **Trouver le nid vide,** to find the bird flown. **Trouver la pie au nid,** (i) to find exactly what one is looking for; (ii) *Iron:* to discover a mare's-nest. *F:* **Nid de poule,** pot-hole (in road). **A tout oiseau son nid est beau,** home is home, be it never so homely. *F:* **Écraser une révolte au nid,** to nip a rising in the bud. **Nid de brigands,** robbers' den, robbers' retreat. S.a. ABEILLE. **2.** (*a*) **Nid de mitrailleuses,** nest of machine-guns. (*b*) *Nau:* **Nid de pie, de corbeau,** crow's-nest.

nièce [njɛs], *s.f.* Niece. *F:* **Nièce à la mode de Bretagne,** first cousin once removed.

nielle¹ [njɛl], *s.f. Agr:* **1.** Purples (of wheat). **2.** *F:* Smut, blight (of wheat).

nielle², *s.f. Bot:* **1.** *N. des blés,* corn-cockle. **2.** = NIGELLE.

nielle³, *s.m. Metalw:* Niello; inlaid enamel-work.

nieller¹ [njɛle], *v.tr. Agr:* To smut, to blight.

niell|er², *v.tr.* To inlay with niello. *s.m.* **-age.**

nielleur [njɛlœːr], *s.m.* Niellist, niello-worker.

niellure [njɛlyːr], *s.f.* Niello-work.

nier [nie, nje], *v.tr.* To deny (fact, God). *Abs. L'accusé nie,* the accused denies the charge, pleads not guilty. *Je nie l'avoir vu,* I deny having seen him. *Je nie qu'il m'ait vu,* I deny that he saw me. *Il n'y a pas à le nier,* there is no denying it.

nigaud, -aude [nigo, -oːd]. (*a*) *s.* Simpleton, booby. *Mon grand n. de fils,* my great noodle of a son. (*b*) *a.* *Elle est un peu nigaude,* she is rather simple.

nigauderie [nigodri], *s.f. F:* **1.** Stupidity, simplicity. **2.** Piece of stupidity.

nigelle [niʒɛl], *s.f. Bot:* Nigella; love-in-a-mist.

nihilisme [niilism], *s.m. Phil: Pol:* Nihilism.

nihiliste [niilist]. **1.** *a.* Nihilist(ic). **2.** *s.* Nihilist.

Nil (le) [lənil]. *Pr.n.m. Geog:* The (river) Nile.

nilgau(t) [nilgo], *s.m. Z:* Nylghau, nilgai; blue bull. *pl. Des nilgau(t)s.*

nille [niːj], *s.f.* **1.** Loose handle (of crank, tool, etc.). **2.** Tendril (of vine).

nimbe [nɛ̃ːb], *s.m.* Nimbus, halo.

nimbé [nɛ̃be], *a.* Nimbed, nimbused (head, etc.). *Front n. d'une auréole de gloire,* brow haloed with glory.

nimbus [nɛbyːs], *s.m.* Nimbus; rain-cloud.
Ninon [ninɔ̃]. *Pr.n.f. Hist:* Ninon (de Lenclos). Cheveux à la Ninon, bobbed hair.
nipper [nipe], *v.tr. F:* To fit (s.o.) out (with clothes); to rig (s.o.) out.

se **nipper,** to fit or rig oneself out; to buy a trousseau.
nippes [nip], *s.f.pl.* **1.** Garments. **2.** Old clothes.
nique [nik], *s.f.* Faire la nique à qn, to make a long nose at s.o. Faire la nique à qch., to despise sth.; to snap one's fingers at sth.
nitouche [nituʃ], *s.f. F:* Sainte nitouche, little hypocrite. *C'est une sainte n.,* butter wouldn't melt in her mouth. *Un petit air de sainte n.,* a demure look. [N'Y TOUCHE]
nitrate [nitrat], *s.m. Ch:* Nitrate.
nitre [nitr], *s.m.* Nitre, saltpetre.
nitré [nitre], *a. Ch:* Nitrated. *Composé n.,* nitro-compound.
nitreux, -euse [nitrø, -øːz], *a. Ch:* Nitrous.
nitrière [nitriɛːr], *s.f.* **1.** Nitre-bed, saltpetre-bed. **2.** Nitre-works.
nitrifier [nitrifje], *v.tr. Ch:* To nitrify.
nitrique [nitrik], *a. Ch:* Nitric (acid).
nitrocellulose [nitrɔsɛlyloːz], *s.f. Exp:* Nitro-cellulose.
nitrogélatine [nitrɔʒelatin], *s.f. Exp:* Gelatine dynamite.
nitroglycérine [nitrɔgliserin], *s.f. Exp:* Nitro-glycerine.
niveau [nivo], *s.m.* Level. **1.** (Instrument) (a) N. à bulle d'air, air-, spirit-level. N. de maçon, à plomb, vertical level, plumb-level. *Phot:* Viseur à niveau, view-finder and level combined. (b) *Mch: etc:* N. d'eau, water-gauge. *Aut:* N. d'essence, petrol-gauge. **2.** (a) Le n. de l'eau, de la mer, the level of the water, of the sea; the water-level. N. des hautes eaux, des basses eaux, high water mark, low water mark. A franc niveau, dead level. Mettre qch. de niveau, à niveau, to level sth.; to bring sth. to a level. *El:* Ramener l'électrolyte (de l'accu) à niveau, to top up the battery. *Mch:* Indicateur du n. d'eau, tube de niveau, water-gauge, gauge-glass. *Rail:* Passage à niveau, level crossing. S.a. COURBE 2. (b) Niveau de vie, standard of living. N. des études dans une école, level, standard, of learning in a school. Être au niveau de qch., de qn, to be on a level, on a par, with sth., with s.o.
niveler [nivle], *v.tr.* (je nivelle; je nivellerai) **1.** To take the level of, to survey (ground). **2.** To level, to even up (ground, fortunes).

se **niveler,** to become level, to settle (down).
niveleur, -euse [nivlœːr, -øːz]. **1.** *a.* Levelling. **2.** *s.* Leveller.
nivellement [nivɛlmɑ̃], *s.m.* **1.** Surveying, contouring (of land). *Surv:* Repère de nivellement, bench-mark. **2.** Levelling.
nivôse [nivoːz], *s.m. Fr.Hist:* Fourth month of Fr. Republican calendar (Dec.-Jan.).
nobiliaire [nɔbiljɛːr], *a.* Nobiliary (rank, etc.). *La particule n.,* the nobiliary particle (i.e. de). Almanach nobiliaire, *s.m.* Nobiliaire, Peerage(-book, -list).
noble [nɔbl]. **1.** *a.* Noble. (a) Être n. de race, to be of noble descent, of noble birth. (b) Stately, lofty (air). *Th:* Père noble, heavy father. (c) High-minded, lofty (soul). **2.** *s.* Noble-(man), noblewoman. Les nobles, the nobility. *adv.* **-ment.**
noblesse [nɔblɛs], *s.f.* **1.** Nobility. (a) Noble birth. S.a. LETTRE 3. (b) Coll. La haute et la petite n., the nobility and gentry. **2.** Nobility, nobleness (of heart, behaviour).

noce [nɔs], *s.f.* **1.** (a) Wedding; wedding festivities. (b) Wedding-party. (c) *pl. A:* Marriage, nuptials. (Still usual in) Repas de noces, wedding feast. Voyage de noces, wedding-trip, honeymoon trip. Noces d'argent, d'or, silver, golden, wedding. Épouser qn en secondes noces, to marry for the second time. **2.** *F:* (a) Faire la noce, to be, go, on the spree. Usé par la n., worn out with riotous living. (b) Il n'avait jamais été à pareille noce, he was having the time of his life. Je n'étais pas à la noce, I was having a bad time.
nocer [nɔse], *v.i. F:* (je noçai(s); n. noçons) **1.** To feast. **2.** To go on the spree.
noceur, -euse [nɔsœːr, -øːz], *s. F:* (a) Reveller. (b) Fast liver; dissipated man, woman.
nocher [nɔʃe], *s.m. Poet:* Pilot, boatman.
nocif, -ive [nɔsif, -iːv], *a.* Injurious, noxious, nocuous (à, to).
nocivité [nɔsivite], *s.f.* Noxiousness.
noctambule [nɔktɑ̃byl]. **1.** *a.* Noctambulant. **2.** *s.* (a) Somnambulist, sleep-walker. (b) *F:* Night-prowler.
noctambulisme [nɔktɑ̃bylism], *s.m.* Noctambulism; sleep-walking.
noctuelle [nɔktɥɛl], *s.f.* Noctua; owlet-moth.
nocturne [nɔktyrn]. **1.** *a.* Nocturnal (visit, animal). *Bot:* Night-flowering. Attaque n., night attack. *Jur:* Bruit et tapage nocturne, disorder by night. **2.** *s.m.* (a) *Ecc:* Nocturn. (b) *Mus:* Nocturne.
nocturnement [nɔktyrnəmɑ̃], *adv.* By night.
nocuité [nɔkɥite], *s.f.* Noxiousness.
nodal, -aux [nɔdal, -o], *a.* Nodal (point, line).
nodosité [nɔdozite], *s.f.* **1.** Nodosity. **2.** Node, nodule (on tree trunk, gouty hand).
nodule [nɔdyl], *s.m. Geol: Med:* Nodule.
Noé [nɔe]. *Pr.n.m. B.Hist:* Noah. S.a. ARCHE[1].
Noël [nɔɛl], *s.m.* **1.** Christmas; yule(-tide). A la Noël, à Noël, at Christmas. Le jour de N., Christmas-day. La nuit, la veillée, de N., Christmas Eve. Bûche de Noël, yule-log. Arbre de Noël, Christmas-tree. Le Bonhomme Noël, Father Christmas, Santa Claus. *A:* Crier Noël, to shout Nowel. **2.** Un noël, a Christmas carol.
nœud [nø], *s.m.* **1.** (a) Knot. *Nau:* Hitch, bend. N. coulant, (i) slip-knot, running knot; (ii) noose. N. de grappin, n. anglais, fisherman's bend. N. droit, plat, reef-knot. S.a. BOULINE. Corde à nœuds, knotted rope. Faire son nœud de cravate, to knot one's tie. *F:* Les nœuds de l'amitié, the bonds, ties, of friendship. Trancher le nœud gordien, to cut the Gordian knot. (b) Le n. de la question, the crux of the matter. (c) *Cost:* Bow. Faire un n., to tie a bow. N. de diamants, diamond cluster. **2.** Node (of curve, orbit, oscillation). **3.** (a) Knot (in timber). (b) Node, joint (in stem of grass, etc.). (c) Nœud de la gorge, Adam's apple. **4.** N. de voies ferrées, railway junction. **5.** *Nau.Meas:* Knot. Filer, faire, tant de nœuds, to make, steam, do, so many knots. S.a. FILER I. 2.
noir, -e [nwaːr]. **1.** *a.* Black. (a) N. comme du jais, jet-black. Race noire, negro race. *Art:* Dessiner au crayon n., to work in black and white. (b) Dark, swarthy (complexion). (c) Dark (night, dungeon); gloomy (weather, thoughts). Il fait déjà noir, it is dark already. Il faisait noir comme dans un four, il faisait nuit noire, it was pitch dark. S.a. CHAMBRE 3. Avoir des idées noires, to be in the blues. S.a. HUMEUR 2. Ma bête noire, my pet aversion. Misère noire, dire poverty. *Th:* Four noir, dead failure. S.a. SÉRIE I. (d) Dirty, grimy (hands, linen). (e) Base, black (ingratitude); foul (deed); black (magic). *Prov:* Le

diable n'est pas si noir qu'on le dit, the devil is not as black as he's painted. **2.** *s.* Black man, woman; negro, negress. *Traite des noirs,* slave-trade. **3.** *s.m.* (*a*) Cheveux d'un noir de corbeau, raven-black hair. **Voir tout en noir,** to look at the dark side of everything. **Broyer du noir,** to be in the dumps; to have a fit of the blues. S.a. BLANC II. 1, POT 1. **Être vêtu (tout) de noir, être en noir,** to be dressed (all) in black, to be in mourning. (*b*) Bull's-eye (of target). *F :* **Mettre dans le noir,** to hit the mark. (*c*) *Avoir des noirs,* to have bruises; to be black and blue. (*d*) *N. animal,* bone-black, animal-black. *N. à fourneaux,* grate-polish. *N. de fumée,* lamp-black. (*e*) *P :* **Petit noir,** cup of black coffee. *Mil : P :* **Gros noir,** heavy shell. **4.** *s.f.* Noire. (*a*) (At roulette) *Jouer sur la noire,* to stake, play, on the black. (*b*) (In balloting) Black ball. (*c*) *Mus :* Crotchet.

noirâtre [nwarɑːtr], *a.* Blackish, darkish.

noiraud [nwaro], *a.* Swarthy.

noirceur [nwarsœːr], *s.f.* **1.** Blackness; darkness, gloominess (of weather, etc.); baseness (of soul); heinousness, foulness (of crime). **2.** Black spot; smudge; smut (on the face). **3.** Atrocity; base action. **4. Dire des noirceurs de qn,** to slander s.o.; to vilify s.o.

noirc|ir [nwarsiːr]. **1.** *v.i.* To grow, become, turn, black or dark; to darken. **2.** *v.tr.* (*a*) To blacken. *Se n. le visage,* to black one's face. *Se n. la barbe,* to dye one's beard black. *F :* **Noircir du papier,** to scribble. (*b*) To smut, grime, sully (sth.). (*c*) To darken, throw a gloom over (the sky, etc.). *s.m.* **-issement.**

  se noircir, to grow black, dark. *Cela s'est noirci à la fumée,* it has blackened in the smoke.

noircissure [nwarsisyːr], *s.f.* Black spot; smudge.

noise [nwaːz], *s.f. A :* Quarrelling. **Chercher noise à qn,** to try to pick a quarrel with s.o.

noisetier [nwaztje], *s.m.* Hazel-(tree, -bush).

noisette [nwazɛt]. **1.** *s.f.* Hazel-nut. **2.** *a.inv.* Hazel; nut-brown. *Beurre n.,* brown butter.

noix [nwa], *s.f.* **1.** Walnut. **2.** Nut. *N. d'Amérique, du Brésil,* Brazil nut. *N. de coco,* coco(a)-nut. *N. d'acajou,* cashew-nut. *N. vomique,* nux vomica. **Noix de terre,** pig-nut, ground-nut. *P :* **Excuses à la n.** (*de coco*), worthless excuses. **Vieille noix,** old chap, old bean. **3. Noix de gigot,** pope's eye (in leg of mutton). S.a. GÎTE[1] 3. **4.** *Tchn :* (*a*) Tumbler (of gun-lock). (*b*) Sprocket (of chain-wheel); grinder (of coffee-mill). (*c*) Cam-wheel. (*d*) Plug (of cock). (*e*) Drum-head (of capstan). (*f*) Whorl (of spindle).

nolage [nɔlaːʒ], *s.m.,* **nolis** [nɔli], *s.m.* **1.** Freighting (of ships). **2.** (Cost of) freight.

nolisateur [nɔlizatœːr], *s.m.* Freighter, charterer.

noliser [nɔlize], *v.tr.* To freight (ship).

nom [nɔ̃], *s.m.* **1.** Name. *Un homme du nom de Pierre,* a man called Peter. *Nom de famille,* surname. *Nom de baptême, petit nom,* Christian name. *Son nom de demoiselle,* her maiden name. *Être connu sous le nom de . . .,* to go by the name of. . . . *Nom de guerre,* stage-name; assumed name; (journalist's) pen-name. *Nom de théâtre,* stage-name. *Voyager sous un faux nom,* to travel under an alias. *Nom et prénoms,* full name. *F :* **Appeler les choses par leur nom,** to call a spade a spade. **Quelqu'un dont je tairai le nom,** someone who shall be nameless. **Impolitesse qui n'a pas de nom,** rudeness beyond words. *Ça n'a pas de nom!* it is unspeakable ! **Je le ferai ou j'y perdrai mon nom,** I'll do it or my name isn't (Jones). **Nom d'un nom!** *nom d'une pipe! nom d'un chien!* euphemisms for *nom de Dieu.*

Se faire un grand nom, to win fame, renown; to make, achieve, a name for oneself. *N'être maître que de nom,* to be master in name only. **Au nom de la loi,** in the name of the law. **Fait en mon nom,** done in my name, by my authority. **2.** *Gram :* Noun, substantive.

nomade [nɔmad]. **1.** *a.* Nomadic; wandering (tribe); migratory (bird); roving (instinct). **2.** *s.m.pl.* **Nomades,** wandering tribes; nomads.

nombre [nɔ̃ːbr], *s.m.* Number. **1.** (*a*) *N. entier,* whole number; integer. *Ecc :* **Nombre d'or,** golden number. (*b*) **Nombre de . . .,** bon nombre de . . ., un certain nombre de . . ., un assez grand nombre de . . .,** a number of, a good many. . . . *Un grand n., un petit n., d'entre nous,* many, few, of us. **Ils ont vaincu par le nombre,** they conquered by force of numbers. **Succomber sous le n.,** to be overpowered by numbers. **Sans nombre,** countless, numberless; without number. **Tout fait nombre,** every little helps. *Venez pour faire n.,* come and help to make a crowd. **Ils sont au nombre de huit,** they are eight in number. **Il est au nombre, du nombre, des élus,** he is one of the elect. **Mettre, compter, qn au nombre de ses intimes,** to number s.o. among one's friends. **Dans le nombre** *se trouvaient plusieurs étrangers,* among them were several strangers. **2.** *Gram :* Number. **3. Phrase qui a du nombre,** well-balanced sentence.

nombrer [nɔ̃bre], *v.tr.* To number, reckon.

nombreux, -euse [nɔ̃brø, -øːz], *a.* **1.** (*a*) Numerous. *Pendant de nombreuses générations,* for many generations. **Peu nombreux,** few (in number). *Réunion peu nombreuse,* small party. *Auditoire peu n.,* thin house. (*b*) Multifarious, manifold (duties, etc.). **2.** Harmonious, rhythmical, well-balanced (prose).

nombril [nɔ̃bri], *s.m.* **1.** (*a*) Navel. (*b*) Hilum, eye (of fruit). **2.** *Bot :* **Nombril de Vénus,** navel-wort.

nomenclature [nɔmɑ̃klatyːr], *s.f.* **1.** Nomenclature. **2.** List, catalogue.

nominal, -aux [nɔminal, -o], *a.* (*a*) **Appel nominal,** roll-call, call-over. *Faire l'appel n.,* (i) to call over (assembly); (ii) to array (jury). (*b*) Nominal (price, horse-power). **Valeur nominale,** face value (of shares, etc.). *adv.* **-ement.**

nominateur [nɔminatœːr], *s.m.* Nominator (à, to); presenter, patron (of living, etc.).

nominatif, -ive [nɔminatif, -iːv]. **1.** *a.* Etat **nominatif,** list of names; nominal roll. *Fin :* **Titres nominatifs,** registered securities. **2.** *a. & s.m. Gram :* Nominative (case). *Au n.,* in the nominative (case).

nomination [nɔminasjɔ̃], *s.f.* **1.** Nomination for an appointment. **2.** Appointment. **Recevoir sa nomination,** to be appointed (à un poste, to a post). *N. à un grade supérieur,* promotion.

nommément [nɔmemɑ̃], *adv.* **1.** (*a*) Namely; to wit. (*b*) Especially. **2.** *Mentionner qn n.,* to mention s.o. by name.

nommer [nɔme], *v.tr.* **1.** To name; to give a name to (s.o., sth.). *On le nomma Jean,* they named him John. *Jur :* **Le nommé Dupont,** (i) a man of the name of Dupont; (ii) the man Dupont. **2.** (*a*) To mention by name. *Il ne nomma personne,* he mentioned no names. *Un homme que je ne nommerai pas,* a man who shall be nameless. (*b*) **Nommer un jour,** to appoint a day. **A jour nommé,** on the appointed day. S.a. POINT[1] 3. **3.** To appoint, name (s.o. to an office or post). *Être nommé au grade de . . .,* to be promoted to the rank of. . . .

se nommer. I. To state one's name. **2.** To be called, named (John, etc.).

nomographie [nɔmɔgrafi], *s.f.* **I.** Nomography. **2.** *Mth:* Nomogram; graph of parallel lines.

non [nɔ̃], *adv.* No; not. **I.** *Vient-il?—Non,* is he coming?—No (, he's not, he isn't). *Fumez-vous?—Non,* do you smoke?—No, I don't. *Mais non!* dame non! mon Dieu non! que non! oh dear, no! no indeed! **Non pas!** not so! not at all! **Je pense que non,** I think not. *Je parie que non,* I bet it isn't. **Faire signe que non,** to shake one's head. *Il est respecté mais non pas aimé,* he is respected but not loved. *Qu'il vienne ou non . . .,* whether he comes or not. . . . **Non (pas) que je le craigne,** not that I fear him. *Non que je ne vous plaigne,* not but that I pity you; not that I don't pity you. *s.m.inv. Vingt oui et trente non,* twenty ayes and thirty noes. *Les non l'emportent,* the noes have it. **2.** *Non loin de la ville,* not far from the town. *Non sans raison,* not without reason. *Non seulement . . . mais encore . . .,* not only . . ., but also. . . . **3.** (In compound words) Non-, in-, un-. *E.g. Non-comparution,* non-appearance. *Pacte de non-agression,* non-aggression pact. *Non-cohésif,* incohesive. *Non-vérifié,* unverified.

non-acceptation [nɔ̃aksɛptasjɔ̃], *s.f. Com:* Non-acceptance; refusal (of goods).

non-activité [nɔ̃aktivite], *s.f.* Non-activity. *Mil:* **Mettre un officier en non-activité,** to put an officer on half-pay.

nonagénaire [nɔnaʒenɛ:r], *a. & s.* Nonagenarian.

nonante [nɔnɑ̃:t], *num.a. Dial:* Ninety.

non-arrivée [nɔ̃arive], *s.f.* Non-arrival.

nonce [nɔ̃:s], *s.m. N. du Pape,* Papal Nuncio.

nonchalance [nɔ̃ʃalɑ̃:s], *s.f.* Nonchalance, listlessness, unconcern. **Avec nonchalance,** listlessly.

nonchal|ant [nɔ̃ʃalɑ̃], *a.* Nonchalant, listless, unconcerned. *adv.* **-amment.**

nonciature [nɔ̃sjaty:r], *s.f.* **I.** Nunciature. **2.** Nuncio's residence.

non-combattant, *a. & s.m.* Non-combatant.

non-conducteur, -trice. *Ph:* **I.** *a.* Non-conducting. **2.** *s.m.* Non-conductor.

non-conformisme, *s.m. Ecc:* Nonconformity.

non-conformiste, *a. & s. Ecc:* Nonconformist.

non-disponibilité, *s.f.* Non-availability, un-availability.

non-disponible, *a.* Non-available, unavailable.

non-exécution [nɔ̃egzekysjɔ̃], *s.f.* Non-fulfilment (of agreement, etc.); non-performance.

non-existant [nɔ̃egzistɑ̃], *a.* Non-existent.

non-existence [nɔ̃egzistɑ̃:s], *s.f.* Non-existence.

non-intervention [nɔ̃ɛtɛrvɑ̃sjɔ̃], *s.f.* Non-intervention, non-interference.

non-interventionniste [nɔ̃ɛ̃tɛrvɑ̃sjɔnist], *a. & s. Pol:* Non-interventionist.

non-lieu, *s.m. Jur:* No true bill, no ground for prosecution. **Ordonnance de non-lieu,** nonsuit.

non-livraison, *s.f.* Non-delivery.

non-moi, *s.m. Phil:* Non-ego, not-I.

nonne [nɔn], *s.f.* Nun.

non-négociable, *a.* Unnegotiable (bill).

nonnette [nɔnɛt], *s.f.* **I.** *A:* Young nun. **2.** Small cake of iced gingerbread. **3.** *Orn:* Titmouse, tom-tit.

nonobstant [nɔnɔpstɑ̃]. **I.** *prep.* Notwithstanding. **Ce nonobstant,** this notwithstanding. **2.** *adv.* Nevertheless.

non-ouvré [nɔ̃uvre], *a.* Unworked, unwrought.

nonpareil, -eille [nɔ̃parɛj]. **I.** *a.* Peerless, matchless; unparalleled (patience, etc.).

2. *s.f.* **Nonpareille.** (*a*) Nonesuch (apple, etc.); nonpareil. (*b*) (Confectioner's) fancy ribbon. (*c*) *Typ:* Six-point type; nonpareil.

non-recevable, *a. Jur:* Demandeur non-recevable dans son action, petitioner declared to have no right of action.

non-recevoir, *s.m. Jur:* **Opposer une fin de non-recevoir** (*à une réclamation*), to put in a plea in bar (of a claim); to traverse (a claim).

non-réussite, *s.f.* Failure, unsuccess(fulness); miscarriage (of plan).

non-sens [nɔ̃sɑ̃:s], *s.m.* Meaningless sentence, translation, or action.

non-succès [nɔ̃syksɛ], *s.m.* Non-success, failure.

non-syndiqué, -ée. I. *a.* Non-union (workman). **2.** *s.* Non-unionist.

nonuple [nɔnypl], *a.* Ninefold. *s.m.* **Au nonuple,** ninefold.

non-valable, *a.* **I.** *Jur:* Invalid (clause, etc.). **2.** (Of ticket, etc.) Not available.

non-valeur, *s.f.* **I.** Object of no value; bad debt; worthless security; non-productive land. **2.** (*a*) Inefficient employee; *F:* passenger. (*b*) *Mil:* Non-fighter. **3.** Unproductivity. **Terres en non-valeur,** unproductive land.

nopal, -als [nɔpal], *s.m. Bot:* Nopal; cochineal cactus, cochineal fig.

nord [nɔ:r], *s.m.* No *pl.* **I.** North. **Au nord, dans le nord,** in the north. **Au nord de,** (to the) north of (country, etc.). **L'Étoile du nord,** the North Star. *Vent du n.,* northerly wind. **Le Chemin de fer du Nord,** the Northern Railway (of France). **La mer du Nord,** the North Sea. *L'Amérique du Nord,* North America. *Nau:* Chemin nord (*d'un vaisseau*), northing (of a ship). *F:* **Perdre le nord,** to lose one's bearings, to be all at sea. **2.** *a.inv.* North, northern. **Le pôle nord,** the North Pole. **Le Cap Nord,** the North Cape.

nord-est [nɔr(d)ɛst, *Nau:* nɔrɛ], *s.m.* **I.** North-east. **2.** North-east wind; north-easter.

nordique [nɔrdik], *a.* Nordic, Scandinavian.

nord-ouest [nɔr(d)wɛst, *Nau:* nɔrwa], *s.m.* **I.** North-west. **2.** North-west wind; north-wester, *F:* nor'wester.

noria [nɔrja], *s.f.* **I.** Chain-pump, bucket-chain, noria. **2.** Bucket-conveyor.

normal, -aux [nɔrmal, -o]. **I.** *a.* (*a*) Normal. **École normale,** normal school; teachers' training college. **L'École normale (supérieure),** *s.f. F:* **Normale,** the training college for the professoriate. (*b*) *Poids n.,* standard weight. *Échantillon n.,* average sample. · *Aux cotes normales,* of standard dimensions. *Vitesse normale,* fixed speed. (*c*) *Geom:* Perpendicular, normal (*à,* to). **2.** *s.f.* **Normale.** (*a*) *Geom:* Perpendicular, normal. (*b*) *Température au-dessus de la normale,* temperature above (the) normal. *Golf: Normale du parcours,* Colonel Bogey; bogey of the course. *Jouer contre la normale,* to play against bogey. *adv.* **-ement.**

normalien, -ienne [nɔrmaljɛ̃, -jɛn], *s.* Student at a normal school; *esp.* student of the *École normale supérieure, q.v.* under NORMAL **1.**

normaliser [nɔrmalize], *v.tr.* To normalize; to standardize.

normalité [nɔrmalite], *s.f.* Normality.

normand, -ande [nɔrmɑ̃, -ɑ̃:d], *a. & s.* **I.** Norman; of Normandy. **Les îles Normandes,** the Channel Islands. *F:* **Réponse normande,** non-committal, pawky, answer. **Répondre en Normand,** to give an evasive, equivocal, answer. **C'est un fin Normand,** he is a shrewd, canny, fellow. **A Normand Normand et demi,** set a

thief to catch a thief. **2.** *Hist:* (*a*) **Les Normands,** the Norsemen, the Northmen. (*b*) *La conquête normande,* the Norman conquest.
Normandie [nɔrmãdi], *Pr.n.f.* Normandy.
norme [nɔrm], *s.f.* Norm, standard. *N. de conduite,* rule of conduct. **Qui échappe à la norme,** abnormal.
Norvège [nɔrvɛːʒ]. *Pr.n.f.* Norway.
norvégien, -ienne [nɔrveʒjɛ̃, -jɛn]. **1.** *a. & s.* Norwegian. **2.** *s.m. Ling:* Norwegian. **3.** *s.f.* **Norvégienne,** round-stemmed rowing-boat.
nos [no], *poss.a.* See NOTRE.
nostalgie [nɔstalʒi], *s.f.* Nostalgia; home-sickness. *N. de la mer,* hankering after the sea.
nostoc [nɔstɔk], *s.m. Algae:* Nostoc, star-jelly.
nota [nɔta], *s.m.inv.* **1.** Marginal note; foot-note. **2.** *Nota bene, N.B.* [nɔtabene], please note.
notabilité [nɔtabilite], *s.f.* Notability. **1.** Nota-bleness. **2.** Person of distinction, of note.
notable [nɔtabl], *a.* Notable. **1.** Worthy of note; considerable. *Sans variation n.,* without appreciable change. **2.** Eminent, distinguished (person). *s.m.* Person of influence, of standing. *adv.* **-ment.**
notaire [nɔtɛːr], *s.m.* Notary (executes authentic deeds; deals with sales of real estate, with successions, with marriage contracts). *Scot:* Notary public. **Par-devant notaire,** before a notary. *F:* **C'est comme si le notaire y avait passé,** his word is as good as his bond.
notamment [nɔtamã], *adv.* (*a*) More parti-cularly; especially; in particular. (*b*) Among others. . . .
notarié [nɔtarje], *a. Jur:* See ACTE 2.
notation [nɔtasjɔ̃], *s.f.* Notation.
note [nɔt], *s.f.* **1.** Note, memorandum, memo, minute. *N. d'avis,* advice note. *Jeter quelques notes sur le papier,* to jot down a few notes. **Prendre note de qch., prendre qch. en note,** to note sth.; to take, make, a note of sth. **Prendre bonne note de qch.,** to take due note of sth. **2.** Annotation. *N. en bas de page,* foot-note. **3.** Notice. *Faire passer une n. dans les journaux,* to have a notice put in the papers. **4.** *Sch: etc:* Mark. *Bonne, mauvaise, n.,* good, bad, mark. *Notes trimestrielles,* quarterly report. **5.** *Mus:* Note. *Faire une fausse n.,* to play or sing a false note. **Donner la note,** (i) to sound the key-note, give the lead (to singers, etc.); (ii) *F:* to give the lead, to set the fashion. *F:* **Changer de note,** to alter one's tone, change one's tune. **Forcer la note,** (i) to exaggerate; (ii) to overdo it. *Discours dans la note voulue,* speech that strikes the right note. **6.** (Repute) **Un homme de note,** a man of note. **7.** Bill, account, invoice.
noter [nɔte], *v.tr.* **1.** To note; to take notice of (sth.). **Chose à noter,** thing worthy of notice. *F:* **Notez bien!** mark! mind you! S.a. INFAMIE I. **2.** To put down, jot down (sth.); to take, make, a note of (sth.). **3.** *Mus: N. un air,* to write down, take down, a tune.
noté, *a. Homme mal n.,* man of bad reputa-tion. *Être bien n.,* to be well reported on.
notice [nɔtis], *s.f.* **1.** Notice, account. **2.** Review (of a book).
notification [nɔtifikasjɔ̃], *s.f.* Notification, notice, intimation.
notifier [nɔtifje], *v.tr. N. qch. à qn,* to notify s.o. of sth.; to intimate sth. to s.o. *N. son consentement,* to signify one's consent.
notion [nɔsjɔ̃], *s.f.* Notion, idea. *Perdre la n. du temps,* to lose count of time. *Sch:* (As title of book) *Notions de Géographie,* Primer of Geo-graphy, First Steps in Geography.

notoire [nɔtwaːr], *a.* Well-known (fact); (fact) of common knowledge; manifest (injustice). *Il est n. que . . .,* it is notorious that. . . . *adv.* **-ment.**
notoriété [nɔtɔrjete], *s.f.* **1.** Notoriety, noto-riousness (of fact); repute (of person). **Avoir de la notoriété,** to be well-known. **2.** *Jur:* **Acte de notoriété,** identity certificate; attested affida-vit (in proof of death, etc.).
notre, *pl.* **nos** [nɔtr, no], *poss.a.* Our. *Nos père et mère,* our father and mother. *N. meilleur ami,* our best friend.
nôtre [noːtr]. **1.** *poss.a.* Ours. *Provinces re-devenues nôtres,* provinces that have become ours again. **2. Le nôtre, la nôtre, les nôtres.** (*a*) *poss.pron.* Ours; our own. *Il préfère vos tableaux aux nôtres,* he prefers your pictures to ours. (*b*) *s.m.* (i) Our own (property, etc.). (ii) *pl.* Our own (friends, etc.). *Est-il des nôtres?* is he one of us? *Vous serez des nôtres, n'est-ce pas?* you will join our party, won't you?
Notre-Dame, *s.f. Ecc:* Our Lady. **La (fête de) Notre-Dame,** the feast of the Assumption.
nouba [nuba], *s.f.* **1.** Algerian military band. **2.** (*a*) *P:* **Faire la nouba,** to be on the spree, to paint the town red. (*b*) *F:* **Elle entra avec toute sa nouba,** she came in with all her crowd.
noue[1] [nu], *s.f.* Marshy meadow, water-meadow.
noue[2], *s.f. Const:* (*a*) Valley-channel (of roof). (*b*) Gutter-tile.
nouer [nwe, nue], *v.tr.* **1.** To tie, knot. *N. ses cheveux, se n. les cheveux,* to tie up, fasten up, one's hair. *N. qch. dans qch.,* to tie up sth. in sth. **2.** *L'âge lui a noué les membres,* age has stiffened his joints. **3. Nouer conversation avec qn,** to enter into conversation with s.o. S.a. AMITIÉ I. **4.** *N. l'intrigue,* to bring the plot, the action, (of a play, novel) to a head. *Pièce bien nouée,* well-knit play. *s.m.* **-age.**
se nouer. 1. (Of cord, thread) To become knotted; to kink. **2.** *Le lierre se noue à l'arbre,* ivy clings to the tree. **3.** (*a*) (Of joints) To become anchylosed. (*b*) (Of broken bone) To knit. **4.** (Of fruit) To set, knit.
noué, *a.* **1.** (*a*) Rickety (child). *F:* **Esprit n.,** stunted mind. (*b*) *Articulations nouées,* stiff, anchylosed, joints. **2.** *Needlew:* **Point noué,** lock-stitch (made by sewing-machine).
noueux, -euse [nuø, -øːz], *a.* **1.** Knotty (string, wood); gnarled (stem, hands). **2.** Anchylosed (joints, etc.). **Rhumatisme noueux,** arthritic rheumatism.
nougat [nuga], *s.m.* Nougat.
nouilles [nuːj], *s.f.pl. Cu:* Ribbon vermicelli; noodle(s).
nouillettes [nujɛt], *s.f.pl. Cu:* Small noodles.
noumène [numɛn], *s.m. Phil:* Noumenon.
nounou [nunu], *s.f. F:* (In the nursery) Nanny.
nourrain [nurɛ̃], *s.m. Pisc:* Fry; young fish.
nourrice [nuris], *s.f.* **1.** (Wet-)nurse. *N. sèche,* dry-nurse. *Conte de nourrice,* nursery tale. *La mémoire est la n. du génie,* genius is fostered by memory. S.a. ÉPINGLE I. **2.** (Wet-)nursing. **Mettre, prendre, un enfant en nourrice,** to put out, take in, a child to nurse. *Avoir été changé en n.,* to have been changed in the cradle. **Enfant changé en nourrice,** changeling. **3.** *Tchn:* (*a*) Auxiliary tank, service-tank; feed-tank. (*b*) Feed-pipe, -pump.
nourricerie [nurisri], *s.f.* **1.** Baby-farm. **2.** Stock-farm. **3.** Silkworm rearing.
nourricier, -ière [nurisje, -jɛːr]. **1.** *a.* Nutri-tious, nutritive. **2.** *s.m.* (**Père**) **nourricier,** foster-father. *s.f.* (**Mère**) **nourricière,** foster-mother.

nourrir [nuriːr], *v.tr.* To nourish. **I.** (*a*) To suckle, nurse (infant). *N. un enfant au biberon,* to bring up a child by hand, on the bottle. (*b*) To bring up, nurture, rear (children); to fatten (cattle). **2.** (*a*) To feed (*de, avec,* with, on); to maintain (one's family); to board (workers, pupils). *Cinq cents francs par mois logé et nourri,* five hundred francs a month with board and lodging. (*b*) *Mus: N. le son,* to give fullness, body, volume, to the tone. **3.** To foster (plants, hatred); to harbour (thoughts); to cherish, entertain (hope). **4.** *Abs. Le lait nourrit,* milk is nourishing, nutritious.

se nourrir. I. *Se n. de lait,* to live, subsist, on milk. **2.** To keep oneself.

nourri, *a.* **I.** (*a*) Nourished, fed. *Mal nourri,* ill-fed, underfed. (*b*) *Rapport n. de faits,* report well furnished with facts, packed with facts. **2.** Rich, copious (style); broad, firm (line in drawing); full (tone, sound). *Acclamations nourries,* sustained applause. *Mil: Feu nourri,* well-sustained fire.

nourrissage [nurisaːʒ], *s.m.* Rearing, feeding (of cattle); nourishing (of crystal, etc.).

nourrissant [nurisɑ̃], *a.* Nourishing, nutritive, nutritious; substantial (food).

nourrisseur [nurisœːr], *s.m.* **I.** Stock-raiser. **2.** Feed-roll (of various machines).

nourrisson, -onne [nurisɔ̃, -ɔn], *s.* **I.** Baby at the breast; infant. **2.** Nurs(e)ling, foster-child, nurse-child.

nourriture [nurityːr], *s.f.* **I.** Feeding; suckling (of infant); nurture (of the mind). **2.** Food, nourishment, sustenance; provender (for cattle). *Priver qn de nourriture,* to starve s.o. *N. de l'esprit,* mental pabulum. **3.** Board, keep. *Avoir sa nourriture en argent,* to be on board wages.

nous [nu], *pers.pron.* **I.** (*a*) (Subject) We. (*b*) (Object) Us; to us. *Lisez-le-nous,* read it to us. *Il nous en a parlé,* he spoke to us about it. (*c*) (Reflexive) *Nous nous chauffons,* we are warming ourselves. (*d*) (Reciprocal) *Nous nous connaissons,* we know each other. **2.** *C'est nous qui sommes fautifs,* it is we who are to blame. *Nous autres Anglais,* we English. *Nous l'avons fait nous-mêmes,* we did it ourselves. *Un ami à nous,* a friend of ours. *Ce livre est à nous,* that book is ours, belongs to us. *Entre nous soit dit,* this is between ourselves. *F:* **Ce que c'est que de nous!** such is life!

nouure [nuyːr], *s.f.* **I.** Setting (of fruit). **2.** Rickets.

nouveau, -el, -elle, -eaux [nuvo, -ɛl], *a.* (The form *nouvel* is used before m. sing. nouns beginning with a vowel or *h* 'mute'; also occ. before *et*.) **I.** New (invention, play). *Sujet toujours n.,* ever new topic. *Vêtu à la nouvelle mode,* dressed in the newest fashion. *Habit n.,* coat of a new cut. *Il n'y a rien de nouveau,* there is nothing new, no news. *Sch: Les nouveaux* (*élèves*), the new boys. *s.m.* **J'ai appris du nouveau,** I have heard something new; I have some news. **C'est du nouveau!** that is news to me. **2.** (*a*) New, recent, fresh. *Vin n.,* new wine. *L'herbe nouvelle,* the young grass. (*b*) (With adv. function) Newly, recently. *Le nouvel arrivé, le nouveau venu, les nouveaux arrivés, les nouveaux venus,* the newcomer(s). **Nouveau riche,** upstart, *nouveau riche.* **3.** Another, a second, new, fresh, further, additional. *Un nouvel époux,* another husband. *Commencer un n. chapitre,* to begin a fresh chapter. *Un nouvel Attila,* a second Attila. *Jusqu'à nouvel ordre,* till further orders. *La nouvelle génération,* the rising generation.

La **nouvelle lune,** the new moon. *Le* **nouvel an,** the new year. **4.** **De nouveau,** again, afresh. **A nouveau,** anew, afresh. *Com:* **Solde à nouveau,** balance brought down, *carried* forward.

nouveau-né, -née, *a. & s.* New-born (child). *pl.* (*Des*) *nouveau-nés, -nées.*

nouveauté [nuvote], *s.f.* **I.** Newness, novelty. *Costume de haute nouveauté,* costume in the latest style. **2.** Change, innovation. *La n. répugne aux vieillards,* old people hate change. **3.** New invention, new publication, etc. **4.** *pl. Com:* Fancy articles, fancy goods, dry goods. *Marchand de nouveautés,* linen-draper. *Magasin de nouveautés,* (drapery and fancy goods) stores.

nouvel, -elle¹. See NOUVEAU.

nouvelle² [nuvɛl], *s.f.* **I.** (*a*) (Piece of) news. *Bonne, mauvaise, n.,* good, bad, news. *En voici la première nouvelle,* that's the first I hear of it. *Quelles nouvelles?* what is the news? *Journ:* **Dernières nouvelles,** latest intelligence. **Nouvelles à la main,** (i) wit and humour (column); (ii) social gossip. (*b*) *pl.* Tidings, news (of, about, s.o.). *Demander, (aller) prendre, des nouvelles de* (la santé de) *qn,* to inquire, ask, after s.o.('s health). *Envoyez-moi de vos nouvelles,* let me hear from you. *F:* **Vous m'en direz des nouvelles,** you will be astonished at it, delighted with it. **2.** *Lit:* Novelette; short story.

Nouvelle-Écosse. *Pr.n.f.* Nova Scotia.

Nouvelle-Galles du Sud. *Pr.n.f.* New South Wales.

Nouvelle-Guinée. *Pr.n.f.* New Guinea.

nouvellement [nuvɛlmɑ̃], *adv.* Newly, lately, recently.

Nouvelle-Orléans (la). *Pr.n.f.* New Orleans.

Nouvelle-Zélande. *Pr.n.f.* New Zealand.

nouvelliste [nuvelist], *s. m. & f.* **I.** Novelette writer, short-story writer. **2.** *Journ: F:* 'Par' writer, news-writer.

novateur, -trice [nɔvatœːr, -tris]. **I.** *a.* Innovating (mind, etc.). **2.** *s.* Innovator.

novembre [nɔvɑ̃ːbr], *s.m.* November. **En novembre,** in November. **Au mois de novembre,** in the month of November. **Le premier n.,** (on) the first of November, (on) November first.

novice [nɔvis]. **I.** *s.m. & f.* Novice (in convent); probationer (in profession); tiro, tyro; fresh hand (in trade). **2.** *a. Être n. à, dans, qch.,* to be new to sth., unpractised in sth.

noviciat [nɔvisja], *s.m.* Noviciate. (*a*) Period of probation (of professing nun or monk). (*b*) Apprenticeship (*à,* to). *Faire son noviciat,* (i) to go through one's noviciate; (ii) to serve one's apprenticeship.

noyade [nwajad], *s.f.* **I.** Drowning (fatality). **2.** *Fr.Hist:* (Collective) execution by drowning.

noyage [nwajaːʒ], *s.m. Nau: etc:* Flooding; scuttling. *Vanne de noyage,* flooding cock.

noyau, -aux [nwajo], *s.m.* **I.** Stone (of fruit); kernel. *Fruit à noyau,* stone-fruit. **2.** Nucleus (of atom, cell, comet, colony). *Pol:* **Noyau communiste,** communist cell. **3.** (*a*) Newel (of stairs). *Escalier à noyau plein,* winding stair. (*b*) Stem, shank (of bolt, screw). (*c*) Plug, key (of cock). (*d*) Hub (of wheel). (*e*) *El.E:* Core (of armature). (*f*) Core (of mould).

noyaut|er [nwajote], *v.tr.* **I.** To set up (communist) cells in (trade-union). **2.** *Metall:* To core (mould). *s.m.* **-age.**

noyer¹ [nwaje], *s.m. Bot:* Walnut(-tree or -wood). *N.* (*blanc*) *d'Amérique,* hickory.

noyer², *v.tr.* (**je noie; je noierai**) **I.** To drown (s.o.); to scuttle (ship); to sink (enemy fleet);

to swamp, deluge (the earth, etc.). *Yeux noyés de larmes*, eyes suffused with tears. *Leur faillite me noierait*, their failure would ruin me, *F*: would swamp me. **2.** (*a*) To flood (carburettor, etc.). (*b*) To countersink (screw); to drive (nail) in flush. **3.** *Fish*: *N. le poisson*, to play the fish. **se noyer.** (*a*) To drown oneself. (*b*) To be drowned. *Un homme qui se noie*, a drowning man. *F*: *Il est en train de se n.*, he is on the road to ruin. **noyé,** *a.* **1.** (*a*) (i) Drowned, (ii) drowning. *Secours aux noyés*, first aid for the drowned. (*b*) *Games*: **Boule noyée,** dead bowl. **2.** Flooded (bunker, carburettor); choked (engine). **3.** *Vis à tête noyée,* countersunk screw. **4.** *Roche noyée,* sunken rock. **5.** Blurred (outline).

nu [ny]. **1.** *a.* (*a*) Unclothed; naked (person); bare (shoulders, wire). *Art*: Nude (figure). **Nu comme un ver,** stark naked. NOTE. *Nu* before the noun that it qualifies is invariable and is joined to the noun by a hyphen. **Aller la tête nue, les pieds nus, les jambes nues, aller nu-tête, nu-pieds, nu-jambes,** to go bare-headed, barefooted, bare-legged. **Visible à l'œil nu,** visible to the naked eye. (*b*) Uncovered, plain, undisguised. *La vérité nue,* the plain, naked, truth. (*c*) Bare (country, tree, room). **2.** *s.m. Art*: (The) nude. *Des nus,* studies from the nude. **3.** (*a*) **Mettre qch. à nu,** to lay bare, expose, denude, uncover, strip, sth. *Mettre son cœur à nu,* to lay bare one's heart. (*b*) *Monter un cheval à nu,* to ride a horse bareback.

nuage [nɥaːʒ], *s.m.* Cloud. (*a*) *N. en queue de vache,* cirrus, mare's-tail. *Nuages pommelés,* mackerel sky. *Sans nuages,* cloudless (sky); unclouded (future); unalloyed (happiness). *Ciel couvert de nuages,* overcast sky. *Mil*: *Navy*: **Nuage artificiel,** smoke-screen. (*b*) Haze, mist (on mirror, before the eyes). (*c*) Gloom, shadow. *Il n'y a pas de bonheur sans nuages,* there is no such thing as perfect bliss. **Être, se perdre, dans les nuages,** to be (lost) in a brown study.

nuageu|x, -euse [nɥaʒø, -øːz], *a.* (*a*) Cloudy (weather); overcast (sky); clouded over. (*b*) Hazy (thought, ideas). *adv.* **-sement.**

nuance [nɥɑ̃ːs], *s.f.* Shade (of colour); hue. *Une n. de regret, d'amertume,* a touch, a tinge, a suggestion, of regret, of bitterness. *Il y a une n.,* there is a slight difference of meaning.

nuanc|er [nɥɑ̃se], *v.tr.* (je nuançai(s); n. nuançons) **1.** To blend, shade (colours) (*de,* with). **2.** To vary (tone, etc.); to express faint differences in (character, etc.). *Mus*: *N. son jeu,* to introduce light and shade into one's playing. *s.m.* **-ement.**

nubile [nybil], *a.* Marriageable, nubile.
nubilité [nybilite], *s.f.* Nubility.
nucléaire [nykleɛːr], *a.* Nuclear.
nucléé [nyklee], *a.* Nucleate(d) (cell, etc.).
nucléole [nykleɔl], *s.m.* Nucleolus, nucleole.
nudisme [nydism], *s.m.* Nudism.
nudiste [nydist], *s.m. & f.* Nudist.
nudité [nydite], *s.f.* **1.** (*a*) Nudity, nakedness. (*b*) Bareness (of rock, room). **2.** *Peindre des nudités,* to paint nude figures.
nue [ny], *s.f.* (*a*) *A. & Lit*: High cloud(s). (*b*) *pl.* Skies. *F*: **Porter, élever, qn (jusqu')aux nues,** to laud, praise, *F*: crack up, s.o. to the skies. **Se perdre dans les nues,** to lose oneself in the clouds. **Tomber des nues,** (i) to arrive unexpectedly; (ii) to be thunderstruck.
nuée [nɥe], *s.f.* (*a*) (Large) cloud, storm-cloud. (*b*) *Une n. d'insectes, de traits,* a cloud of insects, of arrows.

nuire [nɥiːr], *v.ind.tr.* (*pr.p.* nuisant; *p.p.* nui; *pr.ind.* je nuis, il nuit, ils nuisent; *pr.sub.* je nuise; *p.h.* je nuisis; *fu.* je nuirai) *N. à qn, à qch.,* to be hurtful, injurious, prejudicial, to s.o., to sth. *Il cherche à vous n.,* he is trying to injure you (in business, etc.). *Cela ne nuira en rien,* that will do no harm. *N. aux intérêts de qn,* to prejudice s.o.'s interests. *Ils se sont nui l'un à l'autre,* they each did each other harm. **Dans l'intention de nuire,** maliciously. S.a. ABONDANCE 1.

nuisibilité [nɥizibilite], *s.f.* Harmfulness, injuriousness, noxiousness.
nuisible [nɥizibl], *a.* Hurtful, harmful, noxious, detrimental, prejudicial (*à,* to). *Plantes nuisibles,* noxious plants. *adv.* **-ment.**
nuit [nɥi], *s.f.* Night. (*a*) *Cette n.,* (i) to-night; (ii) last night. *Passer la n. chez des amis,* to stay overnight with friends. *(Je vous souhaite une)* **bonne nuit,** (I wish you) good night. *Le bateau de n.,* the night boat. **Oiseau de nuit,** night-bird. *Art*: **Effet de nuit,** night-effect, night-piece. **Partir de nuit,** to depart by night. **Nuit et jour** [nɥiteʒuːr], night and day. *Je n'ai pas dormi de la nuit,* I did not close my eyes all night. **Les Mille et une Nuits,** the Arabian Nights. S.a. BLANC 4, CONSEIL 1. (*b*) Darkness. **Il commence à faire nuit, il se fait nuit,** night is falling; it is growing dark. *Il fait déjà n.,* it is dark already. **A la nuit tombante,** at nightfall, at dusk. **Après la tombée de la nuit, à (la) nuit close,** after dark. **Être surpris par la nuit,** to be, to find oneself, benighted.
nuitamment [nɥitamɑ̃], *adv.* By night.
nuitée [nɥite], *s.f.* **1.** Whole night. **2.** Night's work; night-shift.
nul, nulle [nyl]. **1.** (With *ne* expressed or understood) (*a*) *indef. a.* No; not one. *Nul espoir,* no hope. *Il n'a nulle cause de se plaindre,* he has no reason to complain. *Sans nulle vanité,* without any conceit. S.a. PART[1] 3. (*b*) *indef.pron.* No one; nobody. *Nul ne le sait,* no one knows. **2.** *a.* (*a*) Worthless (argument, effort). *Homme nul,* man of no account; nonentity. *Élève nul en histoire,* perfect duffer at history. (*b*) *Jur*: **Nul et de nul effet, nul et sans effet, nul et non avenu,** invalid; null and void. *Bulletin (de vote) nul,* spoilt paper. *Sp*: **Course nulle,** dead heat. **Faire match nul,** to draw a game. **Partie nulle,** drawn game; draw. (*c*) Non-existent (capital, etc.). *Mec*: *Tension nulle,* zero tension.
nullement [nylmɑ̃], *adv.* (With *ne* expressed or understood) Not at all. *Nous ne sommes n. surpris,* we are not in the least surprised. *Il n'est n. sot,* he is by no means a fool.
nullification [nyllifikasjɔ̃], *s.f.* Nullification.
nullifier [nyllifje], *v.tr.* To nullify, neutralize.
nullité [nyllite], *s.f.* **1.** Nullity, invalidity (of deed, marriage). **Frapper une clause de nullité,** to render a clause void. **2.** (*a*) Nothingness; non-existence (of means); *F*: emptiness (of mind). (*b*) Incompetence; incapacity. **3.** Non-entity. *C'est une n.,* he is a mere cipher.
nûment [nymɑ̃], *adv.* Frankly; without embellishments. [NU]
numéraire [nymerɛːr]. **1.** *a.* (Of coins) Legal. **Valeur numéraire,** legal-tender value. **2.** *s.m.* Metallic currency, specie, current coin. **Payer en numéraire,** to pay in cash.
numéral, -aux [nymeral, -o], *a. & s.m.* Numeral.
numérateur [nymeratœːr], *s.m. Mth*: Numerator.
numération [nymerasjɔ̃], *s.f. Ar*: Numeration. *N. décimale,* decimal notation.
numérique [nymerik], *a.* Numerical. *adv.* **-ment.**

numéro [nymero], *s.m.* (a) Number (of house, ticket, etc.). *La chambre n.* 20, room number 20. *Le dernier n. du programme*, the last item on the programme. *Tp: N. d'appel*, telephone number. *Mil: Navy: N. matricule*, official number (of man, of rating). *F: Mon parapluie numéro deux*, my second-best umbrella. *Un dîner numéro un*, an Aı dinner. *P: C'est un drôle de numéro!* he is a queer card, a queer fish! (b) Size (of stock sizes).

numérot|er [nymerɔte], *v.tr.* To number (street, etc.); to page, paginate (book). *Mil: Numérotez-vous (à partir de la droite)!* (from the right) number! S.a. ABATTIS 3. *s.m.* **-age.**

numéroteur [nymerɔtœːr], *s.m.* Numbering-machine, -stamp.

numismate [nymismat], *s.m.* Numismatist.

numismatique [nymismatik]. I. *a.* Numismatic. 2. *s.f.* Numismatics.

nummulaire [nymmylɛːr], *s.f. Bot:* Money-wort.

nuptial, -aux [nypsjal, -o], *a.* Nuptial, bridal. *Marche nuptiale*, wedding-march. *Anneau nuptial*, wedding-ring.

nuque [nyk], *s.f.* (a) Nape of the neck. (b) Poll (of horse).

nutria [nytria], *s.m. Com:* Nutria (fur).

nutritif, -ive [nytritif, -iːv], *a.* Nutritious, nourishing. *Valeur nutritive*, food-value.

nutrition [nytrisjɔ̃], *s.f.* Nutrition.

nyctalope [niktalɔp], *a.* Day-blind, nyctalopic.

nyctalopie [niktalɔpi], *s.f.* Day-blindness, nyctalopia.

nymphe [nɛ̃ːf], *s.f.* 1. Nymph. 2. *Ent:* Nympha, pupa, chrysalis.

nystagme [nistagm], *s.m.*, **nystagmus** [nistagmyːs], *s.m. Med:* Nystagmus.

O

O, o [o], *s.m.* (The letter) O, o.

ô [o], *int.* (Address or invocation) O! oh!

oasis [oazi(ː)s], *s.f.* Oasis.

obédience [ɔbedjãːs], *s.f. R.C.Ch:* Obedience.

obéir [ɔbeiːr], *v.ind.tr.* To obey. (a) *O. à qn*, to obey s.o.; to be obedient to s.o. *v.tr.* Faire obéir la loi, to enforce obedience to the law. *Se faire obéir*, to compel, enforce, obedience. *Il est obéi*, he is obeyed. (b) *O. à qch.*, to yield, submit, to sth. *O. à un ordre*, to comply with an order. *O. à la force*, to yield to force. (Of ship) *Obéir à la barre*, to answer the helm.

obéissance [ɔbeisãːs], *s.f.* (a) Obedience (à, to). (b) Dutifulness (to parents); submission (to lawful authority); allegiance (to king). *Être sous l'obéissance paternelle*, to be under paternal authority.

obéissant [ɔbeisã], *a.* Obedient, dutiful, biddable; docile (animal); submissive. "Votre très obéissant serviteur," 'your obedient servant.'

obèle [ɔbɛl], *s.m. Typ: Pal:* Obelus, obelisk.

obélisque [ɔbelisk], *s.m. Archeol:* Obelisk.

obérer [ɔbere], *v.tr.* (j'obère; j'obérerai) To involve (s.o.) in debt; to encumber, burden, (sth.) with debt.

obèse [ɔbɛːz], *a.* Obese, fat, corpulent, stout.

obésité [ɔbezite], *s.f.* Obesity, corpulence.

obier [ɔbje], *s.m.* Guelder-rose, snowball-tree.

obituaire [ɔbityɛːr], *a. & s.m. Ecc:* (Registre) obituaire, obituary (list); register of deaths.

objecter [ɔbʒɛkte], *v.tr.* To raise, interpose, (sth.) as an objection. *On a objecté que . . .,* the objection has been raised that. . . .

objectif, -ive [ɔbʒɛktif, -iːv]. 1. *a.* Objective. 2. *s.m.* (a) Aim, object(ive), end. (b) *Mil: Navy:* Target. 3. *s.m.* (a) *Opt:* Object-glass, objective (of microscope). (b) *Phot:* Lens. *O. composé*, compound lens. *O. lumineux*, fast lens.

objection [ɔbʒɛksjɔ̃], *s.f.* Objection. Faire, formuler, soulever, dresser, une objection, to object (à, to); to make, raise, an objection.

objectivité [ɔbʒɛktivite], *s.f.* Objectivity.

objet [ɔbʒɛ], *s.m.* 1. (a) Object, thing. *O. de luxe*, article of luxury. *O. d'art*, object of art. (b) *Gram:* Object, complement. *O. direct*, direct object. 2. Subject, (subject-)matter. Faire l'objet d'un entretien, to form the subject

of a conversation. 3. Object, aim, purpose (of action). *Dans cet objet*, with this end in view. *Remplir son objet*, to attain one's end. Sans objet, (i) aimless, purposeless; (ii) aimlessly.

objurgation [ɔbʒyrgasjɔ̃], *s.f.* Objurgation.

oblat [ɔbla], *s.m. Ecc:* Oblate; lay brother.

oblation [ɔblasjɔ̃], *s.f. Ecc:* Oblation, offering.

obligataire [ɔbligatɛːr], *s.m.* Bondholder, debenture-holder; holder of redeemable stock.

obligation [ɔbligasjɔ̃], *s.f.* 1. (a) (Moral) obligation; duty. *Je me sens dans l'o. de vous avertir que . . .,* I feel called upon, I feel compelled, to warn you that. . . . Faire honneur, manquer, à ses obligations, to meet, to fail to meet, one's obligations. *Je me vois dans l'o. de . . .,* I find myself constrained to. . . . *Ecc:* Fête d'obligation, day of obligation. (b) *O. du service militaire*, liability to military service. 2. *Jur:* Recognizance, bond. Contracter une obligation, to enter into an agreement. S.a. S'ACQUITTER 1. 3. Bond, debenture, redeemable stock. *O. au porteur*, bearer-bond. Porteur d'obligations, bondholder. 4. Obligation, favour. Avoir des obligations envers qn, to be under obligations to s.o.; to be beholden to s.o.

obligatoire [ɔbligatwaːr], *a.* Obligatory; compulsory (military service); binding (agreement).

obligeance [ɔbliʒãːs], *s.f.* Obligingness. Ayez, veuillez avoir, l'obligeance de . . ., be good enough to . . ., be so kind as to. . . .

oblige|ant [ɔbliʒã], *a.* Obliging; kind, civil. *C'est très o. de votre part*, it is very obliging of you. *adv.* **-amment.**

obliger [ɔbliʒe], *v.tr.* (j'obligeai(s); n. obligeons) 1. To oblige, constrain, bind, compel. *Votre devoir vous y oblige*, you are in duty bound to do it. *O. qn à, occ. de, faire qch.*, to compel, force, s.o. to do sth. (In the passive usu. *de*) *Être obligé de faire qch.*, to be obliged, bound, to do sth. 2. *O. qn*, to oblige s.o.; to do s.o. a favour. *Prov:* Qui oblige promptement oblige doublement, he gives twice who gives quickly.

s'obliger *à faire qch.*, to bind oneself, to undertake, to do sth.

obligé, -ée. 1. *a.* (a) Obliged, bound, compelled (*de faire qch.*, to do sth.). (b) Indispensable, necessary. (c) Inevitable; sure to happen. (d) Obliged; grateful (de, for). **Bien obligé!** much obliged! many thanks! **2. s.** Person under obligation; *Jur:* obligee.

oblique [ɔblik], a. (a) Oblique (line, *Gram:* case). (b) Slanting (stitch); skew (arch). **Regard oblique,** side-glance. (c) Indirect, crooked (means); underhand (behaviour); devious (ways).

obliquement [ɔblikmã], adv. (a) Obliquely, slantwise, aslant, diagonally. (b) Indirectly. (c) By underhand means.

obliquer [ɔblike], v.i. (a) To move in an oblique direction; to oblique; to edge (sur, vers, to). (b) To slant.

oblitérateur [ɔbliteratœ:r], s.m. Cancel (for stamps, etc.).

oblitération [ɔbliterasjɔ̃], s.f. Obliteration; cancelling (of stamps, etc.). **Cachet d'oblitération,** postmark.

oblitérer [ɔblitere], v.tr. (j'oblitère; j'oblitérerai) **I.** To obliterate. **2.** To cancel, deface (stamp). **3.** *Med:* To obstruct (duct).

oblong, -ongue [ɔblɔ̃, -ɔ̃:g], a. Oblong.

obnubilé [ɔbnybile], a. Overcast; clouded.

oboïste [ɔbɔist], s. m. & f. Oboist, oboe-player.

obole [ɔbɔl], s.f. A: (Greek) obolus; F: farthing. **L'obole de la veuve,** the widow's mite.

obscène [ɔpsɛ(:)n], a. Obscene; lewd.

obscénité [ɔpsenite], s.f. Obscenity; lewdness.

obscur [ɔpsky:r], a. **I.** Dark; gloomy (weather). **Il fait obscur,** (i) it is dark; (ii) the sky is overcast. **2.** Obscure. (a) Difficult to understand. (b) Indistinct, dim (horizon, etc.). (c) Unknown, lowly, humble (birth). adv. **-ément.**

obscurantisme [ɔpskyrãtism], s.m. Obscurantism.

obscuration [ɔpskyrasjɔ̃], s.f. *Astr:* Obscuration, occultation.

obscurcir [ɔpskyrsi:r], v.tr. To obscure. (a) To darken, cloud. (b) To dim (the sight, fame). **Yeux obscurcis par les larmes,** eyes dimmed with tears. (c) To fog (situation).

    s'obscurcir, to darken; to grow dark; to become, grow, obscure or dim. *Le ciel s'obscurcit,* the sky is clouding over.

obscurcissement [ɔpskyrsismã], s.m. (a) Obscuration; darkening; growing dimness (of sight, of the mind). (b) 'Black-out.'

obscurité [ɔpskyrite], s.f. Obscurity. (a) Darkness. (b) Unintelligibility; obscureness (of oracle, etc.). (c) Dimness (of the future, of the past). (d) *Vivre dans l'o.,* to live in obscurity. *Sortir de l'o.,* to become known.

obsédant [ɔpsedã], a. Haunting (memory); obsessing (thought).

obséder [ɔpsede], v.tr. (j'obsède; j'obséderai) (a) To beset (prince, minister). (b) To importune, worry (s.o.). (c) To obsess. *Obsédé d'une idée,* obsessed by an idea.

obsèques [ɔpsɛk], s.f.pl. Obsequies; funeral.

obséquieu|x, -euse [ɔpsekjø, -ø:z], a. Obsequious. adv. **-sement.**

obséquiosité [ɔpsekjozite], s.f. Obsequiousness.

observance [ɔpsɛrvã:s], s.f. Observance; (i) observing, keeping (of rule); (ii) rule observed.

observateur, -trice [ɔpsɛrvatœ:r, -tris]. **I.** s. (a) Observer (of nature, of enemy's movements, etc.). (b) Observer, keeper (of rules, laws). **2.** a. Observant, observing.

observation [ɔpsɛrvasjɔ̃], s.f. **I.** Observance, keeping (of laws, etc.). **2.** Observation. (a) **Poste d'o.,** observation post, look-out post. **Tenir qn en observation,** to keep s.o. under observation; *F:* to keep an eye on s.o. **Être en observation,** to be on the look-out, on the watch. S.a. BALLON I.

(b) Remark. *Faire une o.,* to let fall a remark. **Faire des observations à qn,** to find fault with, to admonish, s.o. (c) *Observations sur un auteur,* comment, notes, on an author.

observatoire [ɔpsɛrvatwa:r], s.m. **I.** *Astr:* Observatory. **2.** *Mil:* Observation post.

observ|er [ɔpsɛrve], v.tr. To observe. (a) To keep (to), to comply with, to adhere to (rules, laws). **Ne pas observer la loi, le dimanche,** to break the law, the sabbath. **Observer les distances,** to keep one's distance; *F:* to keep one's place. **Faire observer la loi,** to enforce obedience to the law. (b) To watch. *On nous observe,* we are being watched. *Observez votre langage,* keep a watch upon your tongue. *Je l'observais faire,* I watched him at it. (c) *Surv: etc:* O. un angle, to take, read, an angle. *O. le soleil,* to take a sight at the sun. (d) To note, notice. **Faire observer qch. à qn,** to draw s.o.'s attention to sth.; to call sth. to s.o.'s notice. *Comme le fait o. cet historien . . .,* as this historian points out. . . . a. **-able.**

    s'observer, to be circumspect, careful, cautious; to keep a watch upon one's tongue.

obsession [ɔpsesjɔ̃], s.f. Obsession ((i) by evil spirit, (ii) by idea).

obsidienne [ɔpsidjɛn], s.f., **obsidiane** [ɔpsidjan], s.f. *Miner:* Obsidian; *F:* volcanic glass.

obstacle [ɔpstakl], s.m. Obstacle (à, to); impediment, hindrance. **Avancer sans obstacle,** to advance unimpeded, unmolested. **Dresser, susciter, des obstacles à qn,** to put obstacles in s.o.'s way. **Faire obstacle à qch.,** to stand in the way of sth. **Mettre obstacle à qch.,** to prevent, oppose, stem. **Course d'obstacles,** (i) steeplechase; (ii) hurdle race, obstacle race.

obstétrique [ɔpstetrik]. **I.** a. Obstetric(al). **2.** s.f. Obstetrics.

obstination [ɔpstinasjɔ̃], s.f. Obstinacy, stubbornness; *F:* mulishness.

obstiner (s') [sɔpstine], v.pr. To show obstinacy. *S'o. à qch., à faire qch.,* to persist in sth., in doing sth. *S'o. au silence,* to remain stubbornly, obstinately, silent.

obstiné, a. Stubborn, self-willed, obstinate, mulish; dogged (resistance); persistent (cough, fever). adv. **-ment.**

obstructif, -ive [ɔpstryktif, -i:v], a. **I.** *Parl:* Obstructive. **2.** *Med:* Obstruent.

obstruction [ɔpstryksjɔ̃], s.f. Obstruction. **I.** Blocking. *Parl:* **Faire de l'obstruction,** to practise obstruction; *U.S:* to filibuster. **2.** *Med:* O. intestinale, stoppage of the bowels. **3.** *Tchn:* Choking; clogging.

obstruer [ɔpstrye], v.tr. To obstruct, block (street, the view); to choke (outlet).

    s'obstruer, to become blocked or choked.

obtempérer [ɔptãpere], v.ind.tr. (j'obtempère; j'obtempérerai) O. à une sommation, to obey a summons. *O. à une requête,* to accede to a request. *O. à un ordre,* to comply with an order.

obtenir [ɔptəni:r], v.tr. (Conj. like TENIR) To obtain, get (goods, permission); to secure (promise); to gain, procure (s.o.'s consent, etc.); to achieve (result). *Où cela s'obtient-il?* where is it obtainable? *O. qch. de qn,* to obtain, get, sth. from s.o. *J'ai obtenu de le voir,* I obtained, procured, permission to see him.

obtention [ɔptãsjɔ̃], s.f. Obtainment, obtaining.

obturateur, -trice [ɔptyratœ:r, -tris]. **I.** a. Obturating. **2.** s.m. Obturator; closing device. *Artil:* Breech-plug. *Mec.E:* Stop-valve, stopcock. *I.C.E:* Throttle. *Phot:* Shutter (of camera). *O. au diaphragme,* diaphragm-shutter.

O. de plaque, focal-plane shutter. *I.C.E: etc:* Obturateur de joint, gasket.

obturation [ɔptyrasjɔ̃], *s.f.* Obturation; closing (of cavity); stopping (of tooth).

obturer [ɔptyre], *v.tr.* To seal, obturate (aperture); to stop (tooth).

obtus, -use [ɔpty, -y:z], *a.* **1.** Blunt(ed) (point); rounded (leaf, etc.). **2.** Dull, obtuse (person). **3.** *Geom:* Obtuse (angle).

obus [ɔby(:s)], *s.m. Artil:* Shell. *O. de combat,* live shell. *O. à balles,* shrapnel. *O. toxique,* gas shell. S.a. BRISANT 1, FUSANT, PERCUTANT.

obusier [ɔbyzje], *s.m. Artil:* Howitzer.

obusite [ɔbyzit], *s.f. Med:* Shell-shock.

obvier [ɔbvje], *v.ind.tr. O. à qch.,* to obviate, prevent, sth.

oc [ɔk], *adv.* (In Old Provençal) Yes. *Ling:* La langue d'oc, the dialect(s) of the south of France. *Cf.* OÏL.

ocarina [ɔkarina], *s.m. Mus:* Ocarina.

occasion [ɔkazjɔ̃, -ka-], *s.f.* **1.** (*a*) Opportunity, occasion, chance. Saisir, prendre, l'occasion aux cheveux, to take time, occasion, by the forelock; to seize the opportunity. L'occasion fait le larron, opportunity makes the thief. Suivant l'occasion, as occasion arises. A l'occasion, when the opportunity offers. A la première occasion, at the first opportunity. (*b*) Bargain. Vente d'occasion, (bargain) sale. Marchandises d'occasion, job-lot. Livre, meubles, d'occasion, second-hand book, furniture. **2.** Occasion, juncture. *A plusieurs occasions,* on several occasions. En toute occasion, on all occasions. Agir suivant l'occasion, to act as the occasion requires. Pour l'occasion, for the nonce. A l'occasion, in case of need. A l'occasion de son mariage, on the occasion of his marriage. Par occasion, (i) by chance; (ii) now and then, occasionally. En pareille occasion, (i) in similar circumstances; (ii) on such an occasion. En cette occasion, at this juncture. **3.** Motive, reason, cause, occasion. Donner occasion à la médisance, to give occasion for scandal. *Différend à l'occasion de . . .,* dispute with regard to . . .

occasionnel, -elle [ɔkazjɔnɛl], *a.* Occasional; acting as a cause.

occasionnellement [ɔkazjɔnɛlmɑ̃], *adv.* Occasionally; on occasion.

occasionner [ɔkazjɔne, -ka-], *v.tr.* To occasion, cause; to give rise to (sth.).

occident [ɔksidɛ̃], *s.m.* West, occident. *Hist:* L'Empire d'Occident, the Western Empire.

occidental, -aux [ɔksidɑtal, -o], *a.* West(ern); occidental. Les Indes occidentales, the West Indies.

occipital, -aux [ɔksipital, -o], *a.* Occipital.

occiput [ɔksipyt], *s.m.* Occiput; *F:* back of the head.

occire [ɔksi:r], *v.tr. A:* To kill, to slay.

occlure [ɔkly:r], *v.tr.* (Conj. like CONCLURE, with *p.p.* occlus) To occlude.

occlusion [ɔklyzjɔ̃], *s.f.* **1.** *Ch:* Occlusion (of gases). **2.** *Surg:* (*a*) Closing (of the eyelids, etc.). (*b*) *O. intestinale,* obstruction, stoppage, of the bowels. **3.** *Mch:* Cut-off (of steam).

occlusionner [ɔklyzjɔne], *v.tr.* = OCCLURE.

occultation [ɔkyltasjɔ̃], *s.f. Astr:* Occultation.

occulte [ɔkylt], *a.* Occult; hidden (cause). *adv.* -ment.

occulter [ɔkylte], *v.tr. Astr:* To occult; to hide, cut off, (heavenly body) from view.

occultisme [ɔkyltism], *s.m.* Occultism.

occupant [ɔkypɑ̃], *a.* **1.** Occupying; in possession (of property, etc.). *s. Jur:* Premier occupant, occupier. **2.** *F:* That keeps one occupied.

occupation [ɔkypasjɔ̃], *s.f.* Occupation. **1.** Occupancy, possession (of house, etc.). Armée d'occupation, army of occupation. **2.** (*a*) Business, work, employment. *N'avoir pas d'o., être sans o.,* to be unemployed, out of work. Cela me donne de l'occupation, it gives me something to do. (*b*) Pursuit, profession, avocation.

occuper [ɔkype], *v.tr.* To occupy. **1.** (*a*) To inhabit, reside in (house, etc.). (*b*) *Mil:* To hold, take possession of (town, fort). (*c*) To fill, take up (time, space). (*d*) *O. un poste important,* to occupy, fill, an important post. *O. une chaire d'anglais,* to hold a professorship in English. **2.** To give occupation to (s.o., the mind). *O. vingt ouvriers,* to employ twenty workmen. *O. qn,* to give s.o. something to do.

s'occuper. 1. To keep oneself busy; to employ oneself. *S'o. à qch.,* to be busied with sth. **2.** *S'o. de qch.,* (i) to go in for, be interested in (photography, etc.); (ii) to apply one's thoughts to, to attend to, sth.; to busy oneself with sth. *Il s'occupe de trop de choses,* he has too many irons in the fire. *Nous allons maintenant nous o. de . . .,* we will now turn our attention to. . . . *Je m'en occuperai,* I shall see to it, see about it. *Qui s'occupe de ce qu'il dit?* who minds what he says? *Occupez-vous de ce qui vous regarde!* mind your own business! *S'o. de qn,* to attend to s.o.; to show s.o. attention.

occupé, *a.* **1.** Busy, engaged. *O. aux, des, préparatifs du départ,* engaged on, busy with, the preparations for departure. *Je suis o.,* I am busy. **2.** *Cette place est occupée,* this seat is engaged, taken. *Tp: Ligne occupée,* line engaged.

occurrence [ɔkyr(r)ɑ̃:s], *s.f.* Occurrence, event; emergency. En l'occurrence, in, under, the circumstances.

océan [ɔseɑ̃], *s.m.* Ocean. *F:* L'Océan, the Atlantic. *F: Un o. de blés,* a sea of corn.

océanide [ɔseanid], *s.f. Gr.Myth:* Oceanid; ocean nymph.

Océanie (l') [ɔseani]. *Pr.n.f. Geog:* The South Sea Islands.

océanique [ɔseanik], *a.* Oceanic. *Courants océaniques,* ocean currents.

océanographie [ɔseanɔgrafi], *s.f.* Oceanography.

ocelle [ɔsɛl], *s.m. Nat.Hist:* Ocellus; simple eye.

ocelot [ɔslo], *s.m.* Ocelot; tiger-cat; leopard-cat.

ocre [ɔkr], *s.f.* Ochre. *O. jaune,* brown haematite.

ocr|er [ɔkre], *v.tr.* To ochre. *Phot:* To back (plate). Plaque ocrée, backed plate. *s.m.* -age.

octaèdre [ɔktaɛ:dr]. **1.** *a.* Octahedral. **2.** *s.m.* Octahedron.

octaédrique [ɔktaedrik], *a.* Octahedral.

octante [ɔktɑ̃t], *num.a. Dial:* Eighty.

octave [ɔkta:v], *s.f. Mus: etc:* Octave.

octavo [ɔktavo]. **1.** *adv.* Eighthly. **2.** *s.m.* = IN-OCTAVO.

octobre [ɔktɔbr], *s.m.* October. En octobre, in October. Au mois d'octobre, in the month of October. Le premier o., (on) October (the) first; (on) the first of October.

octogénaire [ɔktɔʒenɛ:r], *a. & s.* Octogenarian.

octogonal, -aux [ɔktɔgɔnal, -o], *a.* Octagonal.

octogone [ɔktɔgɔn]. *Geom:* **1.** *a.* = OCTOGONAL. **2.** *s.m.* Octagon.

octosyllabe [ɔktɔsillab], **octosyllabique** [ɔktɔsillabik], *a.* Octosyllabic (word, verse).

octroi [ɔktrwa], *s.m.* **1.** Concession, grant(ing) (of favour). **2.** (*a*) Town dues, city toll. (*b*) Toll-house.

octr|oyer [ɔktrwaje], *v.tr.* (j'octroie; j'octroierai) To grant, concede, allow (à, to); to bestow (à, on). *F: S'o. des plaisirs*, to indulge in pleasures. *s.m.* **-oiement.**

octuor [ɔktyɔːr], *s.m. Mus:* Octet, octette.

octuple [ɔktypl], *a. & s.m.* Octuple, eightfold.

oculaire [ɔkylɛːr]. **I.** *a.* Ocular (demonstration). *Témoin oculaire*, eyewitness. **2.** *s.m.* (*a*) *Opt:* Eye-piece, ocular. (*b*) *Cin:* Finder (on camera).

oculiste [ɔkylist], *s.m.* Oculist.

odalisque [ɔdalisk], *s.f.*, Odalisque, odalisk.

ode [ɔd], *s.f. Lit:* Ode.

Odéon [ɔdeɔ̃], *s.m.* (*a*) *Gr.Ant:* Odeum. (*b*) *L'Odéon*, the Odeon theatre (in Paris).

odeur [ɔdœːr], *s.f.* **I.** Odour, smell; scent (of cigar, etc.). *Sans odeur*, scentless. *Bonne o.*, pleasant smell; fragrance. *Mauvaise o.*, bad smell; stench. *F: Être en bonne, mauvaise, odeur*, to be in good, in bad, odour or repute (*auprès de*, with). *Mourir en odeur de sainteté*, to die in (the) odour of sanctity. **2.** *Toil:* Perfume, scent.

odieu|x, -euse [ɔdjø, -øːz]. **I.** *a.* Odious; hateful (person, vice); heinous (crime). **2.** *s.m.* Odiousness, hatefulness (of an action); odium. *adv.* **-sement.**

odomètre [ɔdɔmɛtr], *s.m.* Hodometer, odometer; pedometer.

odorant [ɔdɔrɑ̃], *a.* Odorous, sweet-smelling.

odorat [ɔdɔra], *s.m.* (Sense of) smell. *Avoir l'o. fin*, to have a keen sense of smell.

odoriférant [ɔdɔriferɑ̃], *a.* = ODORANT.

Odyssée [ɔdise], *s.f.* (*a*) *Gr.Lit:* L'O., the Odyssey. (*b*) *F:* Odyssey, wanderings.

œdème [edɛm], *s.m. Med:* Oedema.

Œdipe [edip]. *Pr.n.m. Gr.Lit:* Oedipus.

œil, pl. yeux [œːj, jø], *s.m.* **I.** Eye. **Visible à l'œil nu**, visible to the naked eye. *Hôpital pour les maladies des yeux*, ophthalmic hospital. *Je n'ai pas fermé l'œil de la nuit*, I didn't sleep a wink all night. *Fermer les yeux sur qch.*, to wink, connive, at sth. *Ouvrir de grands yeux*, to open one's eyes wide ; to stare. *Ouvrir les yeux à qn*, to open s.o.'s eyes ; to enlighten s.o. *Il avait les yeux hors de la tête*, his eyes were starting from his head. *Regarder qn entre (les) deux yeux, dans le blanc des yeux*, to look s.o. full in the face. *F: Entre quatre(-z-)yeux, entre quat'z yeux*, between you and me. *Levez les yeux*, lift up your eyes ; look up. *Épouser une femme pour ses beaux yeux*, to marry a woman for her pretty face. *Il ne travaille pas pour les beaux yeux de personne*, he doesn't do anything for love. *Chose qui saute aux yeux*, thing that leaps to the eye. *Cela saute aux yeux*, it is obvious, as plain as a pikestaff. *Payer, demander, coûter, les yeux de la tête*, to pay, ask, cost, an exorbitant price. *Avoir du travail par-dessus les yeux*, to be up to one's eyes in work. *P: Je m'en bats l'œil*, I don't care a rap, a hoot. *S.a.* CREVER 2, DOIGT I, FROID I. 1. **2.** Sight, look, eye. *Cela charme les yeux*, it delights the eye. *Chercher qn des yeux*, to look about for s.o. *Suivre qn des yeux*, to watch s.o. *F: Il n'a pas les yeux dans sa poche*, he keeps his eyes skinned. *Aux yeux de Dieu*, in the sight of God. *Coupable aux yeux de la loi*, guilty in the eye of the law. *Avoir qch. sous les yeux*, to have sth. before one's eyes. *Mettre qch. sous les yeux de qn*, to put sth. before s.o. ; to bring sth. to s.o.'s notice. *Mesurer qch. à l'œil*, to measure sth. by eye. *P: Entrer à l'œil*, to get in free, gratis. *Repas à l'œil*, meals on tick. *Cela manque d'œil*, it doesn't look well, there's no style about it. *Ten: etc:* Avoir la balle dans l'œil, to have one's eye in. *Prov:* Loin des yeux, loin du cœur, out of sight, out of mind.

Avoir l'œil, to be observant, sharp-eyed. *Avoir l'œil sur qn*, to keep an eye on s.o. *Avoir l'œil à tout*, to see to everything. *Ayez l'œil ouvert, les yeux ouverts*, have your eyes about you ; keep your eyes skinned. *Avoir l'œil américain*, to keep one's eyes skinned. *Se consulter de l'œil*, to exchange glances. *A vue d'œil*, (i) visibly ; (ii) at a first glance. *Coup d'œil*, (i) view ; (ii) glance. *Reculer pour juger du coup d'œil*, to step back in order to see what it looks like. *D'un coup d'œil j'avais jugé la situation*, I had taken in the situation at a glance. *Du, au, premier coup d'œil*, at first sight. *Jeter un coup d'œil sur le journal*, to have a look at the paper. *Lancer un coup d'œil à qn*, to glance at s.o. ; to throw, dart, a glance at s.o. *Avoir du coup d'œil*, (i) to be sure-sighted ; (ii) to have good judgment. *Regarder qn d'un bon œil, d'un mauvais œil*, to look favourably, unfavourably, upon s.o. *Voir du même œil que qn*, to see eye to eye with s.o. *F: Faire de l'œil à qn*, (i) to give s.o. the glad eye ; (ii) to tip s.o. the wink. *Faire les yeux doux à qn*, to look lovingly, to make sheep's eyes, at s.o. *Faire les gros yeux à qn*, to look sternly, severely, reprovingly, at s.o. *Être très sur l'œil*, to be very strict. **3.** (*a*) Eye (of needle, hammer, anchor-shank, etc.); hole (of hinge); eye-splice (on rope). *Vis à œil*, eye-bolt. (*b*) *Les yeux du pain, du gruyère*, the holes in bread, in gruyère cheese. (*c*) *Yeux du bouillon*, specks of fat on soup. *Yeux d'une plante*, eyes, buds, of a plant. **4.** *Nau:* L'œil du vent, the wind's eye. **5.** (In *sg.* only) Lustre, gloss, sheen (of stuffs, precious stones). **6.** *Typ:* Face (of letter); *Lettre d'un autre œil*, wrong fount. **7.** *Œil de verre*, œil artificiel, glass eye.

œil-de-bœuf, *s.m.* **I.** (*a*) Bull's-eye ; small circular window. (*b*) (Round) wall-clock. **2.** *Bot:* White ox-eye, ox-eyed daisy. *pl. Des œils-de-bœuf*.

œil-de-chat, *s.m.* **I.** *Lap:* Cat's-eye, tiger-eye. **2.** *Bot:* Nicker-nut, bonduc-seed. *pl. Des œils-de-chat*.

œil-de-perdrix, *s.m.* (Soft) corn (between toes). *pl. Des œils-de-perdrix*.

œillade [œjad], *s.f.* Glance, ogle, leer. *Lancer une o. à qn*, to glance meaningly at s.o.

œillère [œjɛːr], *s.f.* **I.** Eye-tooth. **2.** (*a*) Blinker (of horse's harness). (*b*) Eye-bath.

œillet [œjɛ], *s.m.* **I.** Eyelet, eyelet-hole (of boot, sail, etc.). **2.** *Bot:* Pink. *O. des fleuristes*, clove-pink, carnation. *O. maritime*, sea-pink. *O. de poète*, sweet-william. *O. des prés*, ragged robin.

œilleton [œjtɔ̃], *s.m.* **I.** *Hort:* (*a*) Eye(-bud). (*b*) Sucker; offset, layer. **2.** (*a*) Eyepiece shade (of telescope). (*b*) Peep-hole (of rifle sight).

œillette [œjɛt], *s.f.* Oil-poppy, opium-poppy. *Huile d'œillette*, poppy(-seed) oil.

œsophage [ezɔfaːʒ], *s.m.* Oesophagus, gullet.

œstre [ɛstr], *s.m. Ent: Vet:* Oestrus, gad-fly, bot(t)-fly. *Larve d'œstre*, bot(t).

œtite [etit], *s.f. Miner:* Aetites, eagle-stone.

œuf [œf], *pl.* **œufs** [ø], *s.m.* **I.** (*a*) Egg. *Biol:* Ovum. *Œuf frais*, new-laid egg. *Cu: Œuf mollet, à la mouillette*, soft-boiled egg. *Œuf dur*, hard-boiled egg. *Œuf sur le plat*, egg fried in butter. *Œufs au lait*, custard. *S.a.* BROUILLÉ I, COQUE I, NEIGE. *En œuf*, egg-shaped. *F: Marcher sur des œufs*, to tread on delicate ground. *Il tondrait un œuf*, he would skin a flint. *Faire d'un œuf un bœuf*, to make a mountain out of a mole-hill. *Donner un œuf pour avoir un bœuf*, to throw out a sprat to catch a mackerel. *Tuer la poule aux œufs d'or*, to kill the goose that lays the golden eggs. *F:* Écraser, tuer, détruire, qch. dans l'œuf, to nip sth. in the bud. (b) *pl.* Eggs (of insect) ; spawn (of fish, etc.) ; (hard) roe (of fish). **Œufs de homard,** berry. **2. Œuf en faïence,** nest-egg. **Œuf à repriser,** darning-egg. **Œuf à thé,** tea infuser.

œufrier [œfrie], *s.m.* **1.** Egg-holder (for boiling eggs). **2.** Egg-stand (for the table).

œuvé [œve], *a.* Hard-roed (fish) ; berried (lobster).

œuvre [œːvr], *s.f.* **1.** (a) Work, working. *Il ne fait jamais o. de ses dix doigts,* he never does a hand's turn. **Faire œuvre d'ami,** to behave like a friend. **Mettre qn à l'œuvre,** to set s.o. to work. **Mettre qch. en œuvre,** (i) to use, avail oneself of, sth. ; to bring sth. into play ; (ii) to put (piece of work) in hand. **Mettre des diamants en o.,** to set diamonds. **Exécuteur des hautes œuvres,** executioner, hangman. **Faire de bonnes œuvres,** to do good works. **Il est fils de ses œuvres,** he is a self-made man. (b) **Œuvre de bienfaisance, de charité,** charitable society or institution. **2.** (Finished) work, production. **Œuvres d'un écrivain,** works of a writer. *Prov:* **A l'œuvre on connaît l'artisan,** a good workman is known by his chips. **3.** *Ecc:* Fabric fund. **4.** *Nau:* **Œuvres vives,** quick works ; vitals. **Œuvres mortes,** dead works ; topsides. **5.** *s.m.* In *sg.* only. (a) **Gros o. d'un bâtiment,** main walls, foundations, of a building. *L'o. de Molière, de Mozart,* the works of Molière, of Mozart (as a whole). (b) **Le Grand Œuvre,** the philosopher's stone. (c) *Adj.phr.* **Dans œuvre,** inside (measurements, etc.). S.a. HORS 3, HORS-D'ŒUVRE, PIED 2.

offensant [ɔfãsã], *a.* Offensive, insulting.

offense [ɔfãːs], *s.f.* **1.** Offence. *Faire une o. à qn,* to offend s.o. **2.** Transgression, sin, trespass. **3.** *Jur:* **Offense à la Cour,** contempt of Court.

offens|er [ɔfãse], *v.tr.* **1.** To offend (s.o.) ; to give offence to (s.o.). *F:* **Soit dit sans vouloir vous offenser,** with all due respect to you. **2.** (a) To be detrimental to, to injure (lungs, etc.). (b) To offend, to be offensive to, to shock (feelings, modesty). *O. la grammaire,* to offend against grammar. *s.m.* **-eur.**

s'offenser, to take offence (de, at).

offensé, -ée, *s.* Offended, injured, party.

offens|if, -ive [ɔfãsif, -iːv]. **1.** *a.* Offensive (war, weapon). **2.** *s.f.* *Mil:* **L'offensive,** the offensive. *adv.* **-ivement.**

offert, -erte. See OFFRIR.

offertoire [ɔfɛrtwaːr], *s.m.* *Ecc:* Offertory.

office [ɔfis]. **1.** *s.m.* (a) Office, functions, duty. **Faire office de secrétaire,** to act as secretary. *Adv.phr.* **D'office,** (i) officially ; (ii) as a matter of course, of routine ; automatically. *Publ:* **Exemplaire d'office,** copy (of book) sent for publicity. (b) Service. **Rendre un bon, un mauvais, office à qn,** to do s.o. a good, a bad, turn. *Accepter les bons offices de qn,* to accept the good offices of s.o. (c) Divine Service. *L'o. des morts,* the burial-service ; the Office for the Dead. **Livre d'office,** prayer-book. **Aller à l'office,** to go to church (esp. to Protestant service). *Manquer l'o.,* to miss church. (d) Bureau, office. *O. de publicité,* advertising agency. **2.** *s.f.* (a) (Butler's) pantry. (b) Servants' hall.

officiant [ɔfisjã], *a. & s.m.* Officiating (priest).

offici|el, -elle [ɔfisjɛl], *a.* Official (statement) ; formal (call, etc.). **A titre officiel,** officially, formally. **Le Journal Officiel,** *abs.* **l'Officiel** = the (official) Gazette. *adv.* **-ellement.**

officier[1] [ɔfisje], *v.i.* To officiate.

officier[2], *s.m.* Officer. **1.** *O. de l'état civil,*

municipal magistrate in charge of register ; registrar. *O. de justice,* law-officer. *O. ministériel* = NOTAIRE. *O. de paix,* police-officer or official. *O. du ministère public,* public prosecutor. **2.** (a) *Mil:* (Commissioned) officer. *O. supérieur,* field-officer. (b) *O. de marine, de la flotte,* naval officer. *O. de pont,* executive officer, deck-officer. *O. des équipages (de la flotte)* = warrant officer. *O. marinier,* petty officer. *O. de port,* harbourmaster. **3. Officier de la Légion d'honneur,** Officer of the Legion of Honour.

officieu|x, -euse [ɔfisjø, -øːz]. **1.** *a.* (a) Officious (envers, towards) ; over-obliging. (b) Unofficial, semi-official. *Journ:* **Note d'origine officieuse,** inspired paragraph. **A titre officieux,** unofficially. (c) Kindly-meant (advice, etc.). **2.** *s.* Busybody. *adv.* **-sement.**

officinal, -aux [ɔfisinal, -o], *a.* *Pharm:* Officinal (preparation) ; medicinal (plant).

officine [ɔfisin], *s.f.* **1.** (a) *Pharm:* Dispensary. (b) Chemist's shop. **2.** *F:* Den (of shady business) ; thieves' kitchen.

offrande [ɔfrãːd], *s.f.* *Ecc:* Offering. *Déposer son o. dans le tronc,* to place one's offering in the alms-box. *F:* **A chaque saint son offrande,** all the people concerned will have to be squared.

offrant [ɔfrã], *a. & s.m.* **Le plus offrant (et dernier enchérisseur),** the highest bidder.

offre [ɔfr], *s.f.* Offer, proposal ; tender (for contract). **Faire offre de qch.,** to offer sth. **Faire des offres de service à qn,** to offer to help s.o. **L'offre et la demande,** supply and demand.

offrir [ɔfriːr], *v.tr.* (*pr.p.* offrant ; *p.p.* offert ; *pr.ind.* j'offre, n. offrons ; *p.h.* j'offris ; *fu.* j'offrirai) To offer ; to offer up (sacrifice). *O. dix francs d'un objet,* (i) to offer, (ii) to bid, ten francs for an object. *O. un déjeuner à qn,* to stand s.o. a luncheon. *O. la main à qn,* to hold out one's hand to s.o. *O. de faire qch.,* to offer to do sth. *O. une résistance acharnée,* to put up a desperate resistance. *L'histoire en offre plusieurs exemples,* history affords several examples of it.

s'offrir. 1. (Of pers.) To offer oneself. *S'o. à faire qch.,* to offer, volunteer, to do sth. **2.** (Of thg) To offer itself, to present itself ; to offer. *Le spectacle qui s'offrit à mes yeux, à ma vue,* the sight that met, greeted, my eyes.

offusquer [ɔfyske], *v.tr.* **1.** *A:* To dazzle (the eyes). **2.** To offend, shock (s.o.).

s'offusquer, to take offence (de, at). *Il s'offusque d'un rien,* he is easily shocked.

ogival, -aux [ɔʒival, -o], *a.* Pointed, ogival, Gothic (style, arch).

ogive [ɔʒiːv], *s.f.* Ogee, ogive ; Gothic arch ; pointed arch. *Adj.phr.* **En ogive** = OGIVAL.

ogre, ogresse [ɔgr, ɔgrɛs], *s.* Ogre, ogress.

oh [o], *int.* Oh ! O !

ohé [oe], *int.* (a) Hi ! hullo ! (b) **Ohé du navire !** ship ahoy !

ohm [oːm], *s.m.* *El.Meas:* Ohm.

ohmique [omik], *a.* *El.E:* Ohmic (resistance).

oïdium [ɔidjɔm], *s.m.* Oidium, vine-mildew.

oie [wa], *s.f.* (a) Goose. *Oie sauvage, cendrée,* greylag (goose). *F:* **Ne faites pas l'oie,** don't be silly. **Marcher au pas de l'oie,** to do the goose-step. (b) **Jeu de l'oie,** the game of goose. S.a. CONTE I.

oign-ais, -is, etc. [waɲe, -i]. See OINDRE.

oignon [ɔɲɔ̃], *s.m.* **1.** (a) Onion. **Petits oignons,** (i) spring onions (ii) pickling onions. **Aux petits oignons,** (i) *Cu:* stewed with spring onions ; (ii) *P:* tip-top. **Se mettre en rang d'oignons,** to form up in a row. **Regretter les oignons d'Égypte,** to sigh for the flesh-pots of Egypt. (b) Bulb (of

tulip, etc.). **2.** (*a*) Hard corn (under sole of foot).
(*b*) Bunion. **3.** *A :* Watch, 'turnip.'

oïl [ɔil], *adv.* (In Old Fr.) Yes. *Ling :* La langue
d'oïl, the dialect(s) of northern France. *Cf.* oc.

oindre [wɛːdr], *v.tr.* (Conj. like CRAINDRE) **I.** To
oil ; to rub with oil. **2.** To anoint (king, etc.).
L'Oint du Seigneur, the Lord's Anointed.

oint, ointe [wɛ̃, ˌɛ̃t]. See OINDRE.

oiseau [wazo], *s.m.* **I.** *Oiseaux domestiques,
de basse-cour*, poultry. *Oiseaux de volière*, cage-
birds. Perspective à vue d'oiseau, bird's-eye
view. Être comme l'oiseau sur la branche, to
have no settled home ; to be unsettled. *F :* Mon
petit oiseau, dearie. *P :* *Regarde-moi cet o.-là !*
just look at that fellow ! *Vilain o.*, undesirable
individual ; bad lot. *Drôle d'o.*, queer customer.
S.a. AUGURE², VOL¹ **I. 2.** (Bricklayer's) hod.

oiseau-mouche, *s.m.* *Orn :* Humming-bird.
pl. Des oiseaux-mouches.

oiseler [wazle], *v.i.* (il oiselle ; il oisellera) To
go bird-catching.

oiselet [wazlɛ], *s.m.* Small bird.

oiseleur [wazlœːr], *s.m.* Fowler, bird-catcher.

oiselier [wazəlje], *s.m.* Bird-seller, bird-fancier.

oiseu|x, -euse [wazø, -øːz], *a.* **I.** Idle, lazy.
2. Idle, otiose ; trifling (question). *Conte o.*,
idle tale. *Épithète oiseuse*, otiose epithet.
adv. **-sement.**

ois|if, -ive [wazif, -iːv]. **I.** *a.* Idle. (*a*) *Talent o.*,
unapplied talent. (*b*) Lazy. **2.** *s.* (*a*) Unemployed (person). (*b*) Idler. *adv.* **-ivement.**

oisillon [wazijɔ̃], *s.m.* Fledgling. [OISEAU]

oisiveté [wazivte], *s.f.* Idleness. (*a*) Leisure.
(*b*) Sloth.

oison [wazɔ̃], *s.m.* **I.** Gosling. **2.** Ninny, noodle.

okapi [ɔkapi], *s.m.* *Z :* Okapi.

oléagineux, -euse [ɔleaʒinø, -øːz], *a.* Oleaginous. **I.** Oily. **2.** Oil-yielding. *Graines
oléagineuses*, oil seeds.

oléandre [ɔleɑ̃ːdr], *s.m.* *Bot :* Oleander.

oléiculture [ɔleikylty:r], *s.f.* **I.** Culture of the
olive. **2.** The olive-oil industry.

oléifère [ɔleife:r], *a.* Oil-producing, oleiferous.

olfactif, -ive [ɔlfaktif, -iːv], *a.* Olfactory, olfactive (nerve, cell).

olibrius [ɔlibriyːs], *s.m.* Braggart, swaggerer.

olifant [ɔlifɑ̃], *s.m.* *Mediev.Lit :* Oliphant ;
ivory (hunting-)horn.

oligarchie [ɔligarʃi], *s.f.* Oligarchy.

oligarchique [ɔligarʃik], *a.* Oligarchic(al).

olivacé [ɔlivase], *a.* Olivaceous, olive-green.

olivaie [ɔlivɛ], *s.f.* Olive-plantation, -grove.

olivâtre [ɔliva:tr], *a.* Olive-hued ; sallow.

olive [ɔliːv], *s.f.* **I.** (*a*) Olive. Huile d'olive, olive
oil. (*b*) *a.inv.* Olive-green. **2.** (*a*) Olive(-shaped
button) ; frog (of frogged coat). (*b*) (Olive-
shaped) knob or handle. (*c*) Olive-moulding.

oliverie [ɔlivri], *s.f.* Olive-oil factory.

olivette [ɔlivɛt], *s.f.* **I.** Olive-plantation, -grove.
2. Imitation pearl ; olivette.

olivier¹ [ɔlivje], *s.m.* Olive-tree or -wood.
B.Hist : Le Mont, le Jardin, des Oliviers, the
Mount, the Garden, of Olives. *F :* Se présenter
l'olivier à la main, to hold out the olive-branch.

Olivier². *Pr.n.m.* Oliver.

olographe [ɔlɔgraf], *a.* *Jur :* Holograph(ic)(will).

Olympe [ɔlɛ̃ːp]. *Pr.n.m.* (Mount) Olympus.
Les dieux de l'O., the Olympian gods.

olympiade [ɔlɛ̃pjad], *s.f.* *Gr.Ant :* Olympiad.

olympien, -ienne [ɔlɛ̃pjɛ̃, -jɛn], *a.* Olympian.

olympique [ɔlɛ̃pik], *a.* Olympic. Les jeux
olympiques, the Olympic games.

ombelle [ɔ̃bɛl], *s.f.* *Bot :* Umbel.

ombellé [ɔ̃bɛlle], *a.* *Bot :* Umbellate(d).

ombellifère [ɔ̃bɛllife:r]. *Bot :* **I.** *a.* Umbelliferous. **2.** *s.f.pl.* Umbelliferae, umbellifers.

ombelliforme [ɔ̃bɛlliform], *a.* *Bot :* Umbelli-
form, umbellar.

ombellule [ɔ̃bɛllyl], *s.f.* *Bot :* Umbellule,
umbellet.

ombilic [ɔ̃bilik], *s.m.* **I.** Navel. **2.** *Bot :* Hilum.
3. *Geom :* Umbilic(us) ; umbilical point.

ombilical, -aux [ɔ̃bilikal, -o], *a.* Umbilical.

omble [ɔ̃:bl], *s.m.* *Ich :* Char.

ombon [ɔ̃bɔ̃], *s.m.* Umbo (of shield) ; boss.

ombrage [ɔ̃bra:ʒ], *s.m.* **I.** Shade (of trees) ;
Poet : umbrage. **2.** Prendre ombrage de qch.,
(i) (of horse) to shy at sth. ; (ii) *F :* to take
offence, umbrage, at sth.

ombrager [ɔ̃braʒe], *v.tr.* (il ombrageait) (*a*) To
shade ; to protect (sth.) against the sun. (*b*) To
overshadow.

s'**ombrager**. **I.** (Of garden, etc.) To become
shady. **2.** *S'o. de qch.*, to shelter from, protect
oneself against (the sun, heat, etc.).

ombragé, *a.* Shaded, shady (path, spot).

ombrageu|x, -euse [ɔ̃braʒø, -øːz], *a.* **I.** Shy,
skittish (horse). **2.** Easily offended ; touchy ;
quick to take offence. *adv.* **-sement.**

ombre¹ [ɔ̃:br], *s.f.* **I.** Shadow. *Astr :* Umbra.
Projeter une o., to cast a shadow. Ombres
chinoises, shadow-theatre, galanty show. *Opt :
Geom :* *O. portée*, cast shadow. **2.** Shade. *Se
reposer à l'o. d'un mur*, to rest under, in, the
shade of a wall. Quarante degrés à l'ombre,
forty degrees in the shade. *F :* Mettre qn à
l'ombre, (i) to put s.o. out of harm's way ;
(ii) to put s.o. in prison ; (iii) to kill s.o. Faire
ombre à qn, to put s.o. in the shade ; to eclipse
s.o. *Une o. de contrariété sur son visage*, a shade
of annoyance on his face. **3.** Darkness. *Les
ombres de la nuit*, the shades of night. A l'ombre
de la nuit, under cover of darkness. **4.** (*a*) Ghost,
shade, shadowy figure. N'être plus que l'ombre
de soi-même, to be merely the shadow of one's
former self ; to be worn to a shadow. (*b*) *Vous
n'avez pas l'o. d'une chance*, you have not the
ghost of a chance. Lâcher la proie pour l'ombre,
to drop the substance for the shadow. (*c*) *A :* Simulacrum, pretence. Sous (l')ombre de . . .,
under the pretext, the cloak, of. . . . (*d*) *Rom.Ant :*
Umbra (brought by guest).

ombre², *s.f.* Terre d'ombre, umber.

ombre³, *s.m.* *Ich :* (*a*) Umber, grayling. (*b*) Ombre
chevalier = OMBLE.

ombrelle [ɔ̃brɛl], *s.f.* Parasol, sunshade.

ombrer [ɔ̃bre], *v.tr.* To shade (conservatory,
drawing) ; to darken (eyelids, etc.).

ombreux, -euse [ɔ̃brø, -øːz], *a.* Shady (grove).

Ombrie [ɔ̃bri]. *Pr.n.f. Geog :* Umbria.

omelette [ɔmlɛt], *s.f.* *Cu :* Omelet(te). *O. aux
fines herbes*, savoury omelet. *O. aux confitures*,
sweet omelet.

omettre [ɔmɛtr], *v.tr.* (Conj. like METTRE) To
omit, miss out, pass over ; to leave out (passage).
O. de faire qch., to fail, omit, neglect, to do sth.

omi-s, -t, etc. See OMETTRE.

omission [ɔmisjɔ̃], *s.f.* Omission. *Typ :* Signe
d'omission, caret.

omnibus [ɔmniby:s]. **I.** *s.m.* (Horse-)omnibus,
F : bus. *O automobile*, motor bus. *O. de famille*,
private bus, (railway) station bus. **2.** *a.inv.* Suitable for all cases. Train omnibus, slow train.

omnidiffusé [ɔmnidiffyze], *a.* *W.Tp :* Broadcast.

omnipotence [ɔmnipotɑ̃:s], *s.f.* Omnipotence.

omnipotent [ɔmnipotɑ̃], *a.* Omnipotent.

omniprésence [ɔmniprezɑ̃:s], *s.f.* Omnipresence.

omniprésent [ɔmniprezɑ̃], *a.* Omnipresent.

omnium [ɔmniɔm], *s.m.* **1.** *Com:* (In Fr.) General trading company. **2.** *Sp:* Open race.

omnivore [ɔmnivɔ:r]. **1.** *a.* Omnivorous. **2.** *s.m. Z:* Omnivore.

omoplate [ɔmɔplat], *s.f.* Shoulder-blade, scapula.

on [ɔ̃], *indef.pron.* (Often **l'on** [lɔ̃], esp. after a vowel sound) One, people, they, we, etc. *On attend* [ɔ̃natɑ̃] *le courrier,* we are waiting for the letters. *On ne sait jamais,* you, one, never can tell. *On dit que* . . ., they say, men say, it is said, that. . . . *On enfonça la porte,* the door was burst open. *On frappe,* there is a knock at the door. *Danse-t-on?* shall we dance? *On demande une bonne cuisinière,* wanted, a good cook. *On était au sept mars,* it was the seventh of March. *Quand on demande à une jeune fille d'être votre femme* . . ., when you ask a girl to be your wife. . . . NOTE: A pred. noun or adj. following *on* is fem. or pl. as the sense requires. *On n'est pas toujours jeune et belle,* you can't be young and beautiful for ever. *Ici on est égaux,* here we are all equal.

onagre[1] [ɔna:gr], *s.m.* Onager; wild ass.

onagre[2], *s.f. Bot:* Evening primrose.

once[1] [ɔ̃:s], *s.f. Meas:* Ounce.

once[2], *s.f. Z:* Ounce, snow-leopard.

oncial, -aux [ɔ̃sjal, -o], *a.* Uncial (letter, MS.).

oncle [ɔ̃:kl], *s.m.* Uncle. **Oncle à la mode de Bretagne,** (i) first cousin once removed; (ii) *F:* very distant relation.

oncques [ɔ̃:k], *adv. A:* (a) Ever. (b) (With *ne* expressed or understood) Never.

onction [ɔ̃ksjɔ̃], *s.f.* **1.** Oiling (of athlete, of machine, etc.). **2.** Unction. (a) Anointing. *Ecc:* **L'extrême onction,** the last Sacrament, extreme unction. (b) Unctuousness. **Prêcher avec onction,** to preach with unction.

onctueu|x, -euse [ɔ̃ktɥø, -ø:z], *a.* **1.** (a) Unctuous (to the touch). (b) Greasy, oily (surface). **2.** (a) Unctuous (sermon, etc.). (b) *Pej:* Oily (manner). *adv.* **-sement.**

onctuosité [ɔ̃ktɥozite], *s.f.* (a) Unctuousness. (b) *Pej:* Oiliness (of manner).

ondain [ɔ̃dɛ̃], *s.m. Agr:* Swath.

onde [ɔ̃:d], *s.f.* **1.** *Lit:* (i) Wave, billow; (ii) *Poet:* water, tide. *L'o. amère,* the briny ocean. **L'Onde noire,** the Styx. *F: Les ondes de la foule,* the surging of the crowd. **2.** (a) Wavy line. *Cheveux en ondes,* waved hair. (b) Corrugation. **3.** *Ph: O. sonore,* sound-wave. *O. lumineuse, calorifique,* light-wave, heat-wave. **Longueur d'onde,** wavelength. *Grandes, petites, ondes,* long, short, waves. *Ondes entretenues,* undamped, continuous, waves. *Ondes amorties,* damped waves.

ondé [ɔ̃de], *a.* Waved, undulating, wavy (surface); waved (hair); watered (silk).

ondée [ɔ̃de], *s.f.* Heavy shower; summer plump. *Temps à ondées,* showery weather.

ondemètre [ɔ̃dmɛtr], *s.m. El:* Wave-meter.

ondin, -ine [ɔ̃dɛ̃, -in], *s. Myth:* Water-sprite; *f.* undine, nix(ie).

on-dit [ɔ̃di], *s.m. inv.* Rumour, hearsay.

ondoiement [ɔ̃dwamɑ̃], *s.m.* **1.** Undulation; wavy motion. **2.** *Ecc:* Private baptism.

ondoyant [ɔ̃dwajɑ̃], *a.* **1.** Undulating, wavy, billowy; swaying (crowd). *Blé o.,* waving corn. **2.** Changeable, fluctuating (nature).

ondoyer [ɔ̃dwaje], *v.* (j'ondoie; j'ondoierai) **1.** *v.i.* To undulate wave, ripple; (of crowds, flames) to billow. **2.** *v.tr. Ecc:* To baptize privately (in emergency).

ondulant [ɔ̃dylɑ̃], *a.* Undulating (landscape); waving (corn); flowing (mane, drapery).

ondulateur [ɔ̃dylatœ:r], *s.m.* **1.** Hair-waver, hair-waving tongs. **2.** *W.Tg:* Undulator.

ondulation [ɔ̃dylasjɔ̃], *s.f.* **1.** (a) Undulation (of water, etc.); wave-motion. (b) Rise (and fall), undulation (in the ground). *Région à ondulations,* rolling country. **2.** *Hairdr:* Wave. *Se faire faire des ondulations,* to have one's hair waved.

ondulatoire [ɔ̃dylatwa:r], *a. Ph:* Undulatory. *Mouvement o.,* wave-motion.

onduler [ɔ̃dyle]. **1.** *v.i.* To undulate, ripple. **2.** *v.tr.* To wave (the hair); to corrugate (iron). **Se faire onduler,** to have one's hair waved.

ondulé. **1.** *a.* Undulating; wavy (hair); corrugated; ripple(-plate). *Route ondulée,* *F:* switch-back road. **2.** *s.m. Tex:* **Ondulé de laine,** ripple-cloth.

onduleux, -euse [ɔ̃dylø, -ø:z], *a.* Wavy, sinuous.

onéreu|x, -euse [ɔnerø, -ø:z], *a.* Onerous; burdensome (tax); heavy (expenditure). **A titre onéreux,** subject to payment; *Jur:* for valuable consideration. *adv.* **-sement.**

ongle [ɔ̃:gl], *s.m.* (Finger-)nail; claw (of animal); talon (of bird of prey). *Z:* Unguis. **Coup d'ongle,** scratch. **Se faire les ongles,** to trim one's nails. *F:* **Rogner les ongles à qn,** to cut s.o.'s claws. **Se ronger les ongles,** (i) to bite one's nails; (ii) *F:* to be restless, impatient. **Avoir les ongles crochus,** to be rapacious. **Donner sur les ongles à qn,** to rap s.o. over the knuckles. **Savoir qch. sur le bout des ongles,** to know sth. perfectly. **Français jusqu'au bout des ongles,** French to the finger-tips. S.a. BEC I, RUBIS.

onglée [ɔ̃gle], *s.f.* Tingling, aching (of fingerends). *J'ai l'o.,* my fingers are tingling with cold.

onglet [ɔ̃glɛ], *s.m.* **1.** (Embroideress's) thimble. **2.** Nail-hole (of penknife); fullering (of sword). **3.** *Bookb:* (a) Guard. (b) Binding-strip (for map, etc.). (c) Tab (of thumb-index or register). *Dictionnaire à onglets,* thumb-indexed dictionary. **4.** (a) Unguis (of petal). (b) *Z:* Nictitating membrane. **5.** *Carp:* Mitre. **Boîte à onglet,** mitre-box. *Assemblage à o.,* mitre-joint. **6.** *Geom:* Ungula (of sphere).

onglier [ɔ̃glie], *s.m.* **1.** Manicure-set. **2.** *pl.* Nail-scissors.

onguent [ɔ̃gɑ̃], *s.m.* Ointment, unguent, salve.

ongulé [ɔ̃gyle]. **1.** *a.* (a) Nail-shaped. (b) Hoofed, ungulate (animal). **2.** *s.m.pl. Z:* Ungulata.

onomatopée [ɔnɔmatɔpe], *s.f.* Onomatopoeia.

ont [ɔ̃]. See AVOIR.

ontogénèse [ɔ̃tɔʒenɛ:z], *s.f. Biol:* Ontogenesis.

ontologie [ɔ̃tɔlɔʒi], *s.f. Ph:* Ontology; metaphysics.

ontologique [ɔ̃tɔlɔʒik], *a.* Ontological.

onyx [ɔniks], *s.m. Miner:* Onyx.

onze [ɔ̃:z], *num. a. inv. & s.m. inv.* (The *e* of *le, de,* is not, as a rule, elided before *onze* and its derivatives) Eleven. *Onze chevaux,* eleven horses. *Nous n'étions que onze* [kaɔ̃:z], *nous n'étions qu'onze,* there were only eleven of us. *Le onze avril,* the eleventh of April. *Louis Onze,* Louis the Eleventh. *P:* **Prendre le train onze,** to go on Shanks's mare.

onzième [ɔ̃zjem]. **1.** *num. a. & s.* Eleventh. **2.** *s.m.* Eleventh (part). *adv.* **-ment.**

oolithe [ɔɔlit], *s.m.,* occ.*f. Miner: Geol:* Oolite.

oolithique [ɔɔlitik], *a.* Oolitic.

opacimètre [ɔpasimɛtr], *s.m. Phot:* Plate-tester.

opacité [ɔpasite], *s.f.* Opacity (of body); cloudiness (of liquid); denseness (of intellect).

opale [ɔpal]. **1.** *s.f.* Opal. **2.** *a.inv.* Opalescent.

opalescence [ɔpalessɑ̃:s], *s.f.* Opalescence.

opalescent [ɔpalɛssã], *a.* Opalescent.

opalin [ɔpalɛ̃], *a.* Opaline.

opaque [ɔpak], *a.* Opaque.

opéra [ɔpera], *s.m.* 1. Opera. **Grand opéra,** grand opera. *O. comique,* opera with spoken dialogue. *O. bouffe,* comic opera, musical comedy. 2. Opera-house.

opérable [ɔperabl], *a.* Operable (patient, tumour).

opérateur, -trice [ɔperatœːr, -tris], *s.* (*a*) (Machine-)operator. *Cin:* Camera-man. *O. de T.S.F.,* wireless operator. (*b*) *St.Exch:* O. à la hausse, operator for a rise; bull. *O. à la baisse,* operator for a fall; bear. (*c*) Operating surgeon; operator.

opératif, -ive [ɔperatif, -iːv], *a.* Operative.

opération [ɔperasjɔ̃], *s.f.* 1. Operation; working (of nature); process. 2. (*a*) *Opérations militaires,* military operations. (*b*) *Subir une o.,* to undergo an operation; *F:* to be operated on. *Faire l'o. de l'appendicite,* to operate for appendicitis. **Salle d'opération,** operating-theatre. S.a. TABLE I. 3. (Commercial) transaction; deal; speculation.

opératoire [ɔperatwaːr], *a.* 1. (Mode, etc.) of operation. 2. *Surg:* Operative. **Médecine opératoire,** surgery.

opercule [ɔperkyl], *s.m.* Cover, lid, cap. *Nat. Hist:* Operculum; gill-cover (of fish). *Nau: O. de hublot,* deadlight.

opérer [ɔpere], *v.tr.* (j'opère; j'opérerai) To operate. 1. To bring about, to effect. *La foi opère des miracles,* faith works miracles. *Mil: O. une retraite,* to effect a retreat. 2. (*a*) To carry out, perform (multiplication, *Ch:* synthesis, etc.). (*b*) *Surg: O. un malade, un appendice, un abcès,* to operate on, perform an operation on, a patient, an appendix, an abscess. **Se faire opérer,** to undergo, have, an operation. 3. *Abs.* (Of remedy) To work, act.
　s'opérer, to be wrought, to take place. *Le miracle s'est opéré tout seul,* the miracle came about of itself.

opéré, -ée, *s.* Patient (operated upon).

opérette [ɔperet], *s.f.* Operetta; musical comedy.

ophicléide [ɔfikleiːd], *s.m. Mus: A:* Ophicleide.

ophidien [ɔfidjɛ̃], *s.m.* Ophidian; *pl.* ophidia.

ophioglosse [ɔfjɔglɔs], *s.m. Bot:* Adder's-tongue.

ophite [ɔfit], *s.m. Miner:* Ophite, serpentine.

ophrys [ɔfris], *s.f. Bot:* Ophrys, arachnites. *O. abeille,* bee-orchis. *O. araignée,* spider-orchis.

ophtalmie [ɔftalmi], *s.f.* Ophthalmia.

ophtalmique [ɔftalmik], *a.* Ophthalmic.

ophtalmologie [ɔftalmɔlɔʒi], *s.f.* Ophthalmology.

ophtalmoscope [ɔftalmɔskɔp], *s.m. Med:* Ophthalmoscope.

opiacer [ɔpjase], *v.tr.* (j'opiaçai(s); n. opiaçons) To opiate; to mix with opium.

opiat [ɔpja], *s.m.* 1. Opiate, narcotic. 2. Toothpaste.

opimes [ɔpim], *a.f.pl.* **Dépouilles opimes,** spolia opima.

opinant [ɔpinã], *s.m.* Speaker, voter (in debate).

opiner [ɔpine], *v.i.* To opine; to be of opinion (que, that). *O. pour, contre, une proposition,* to vote for, against, a proposal. *O. de la tête,* to nod approval, to nod assent. S.a. BONNET 1.

opiniâtre [ɔpinjɑːtr], *a.* Obstinate. (*a*) Self-opinionated. (*b*) Self-willed, headstrong; stubborn (mule); mulish (person). (*c*) Persistent, unyielding (cough). *Résistance o.,* stout, dogged, resistance. *adv.* **-ment.**

opiniâtrer (s') [sɔpinjɑtre], *v.pr.* To remain stubborn, obstinate. *S'o. à faire qch.,* to persist stubbornly in doing sth.

opiniâtreté [ɔpinjɑtrəte], *s.f.* Obstinacy, stubbornness.

opinion [ɔpinjɔ̃], *s.f.* Opinion (*de,* of; *sur,* about); view, judgment. *L'o.* (*publique*), public opinion. *Partager l'o. de qn,* to agree with s.o. *Amener qn à son o.,* to bring s.o. round, over, to one's way of thinking. **Avoir bonne, mauvaise, opinion de qn,** to have a good, bad, opinion of s.o.; to think well, ill, of s.o. **Donner bonne opinion de sa capacité,** to make a good impression. **Aller aux opinions,** to put the matter to the vote.

opiomane [ɔpjɔman]. 1. *a.* Opium-eating, opium-smoking (person). 2. *s.* Opium-eater, -smoker; opium addict.

opium [ɔpjɔm], *s.m.* Opium.

opodeldoch [ɔpɔdeldɔk], *s.m. Pharm:* Opodeldoc, soap-liniment.

opossum [ɔpɔsɔm], *s.m. Z:* Opossum.

opportun, -une [ɔpɔrtœ̃, -yn], *a.* (*a*) Opportune, seasonable, timely. *Arriver en temps o.,* to arrive opportunely. (*b*) Expedient, advisable. *Il ne semble pas o. que + sub.,* it does not seem advisable that. . . . *adv.* **-ément.**

opportunisme [ɔpɔrtynism], *s.m.* Opportunism; time-serving.

opportuniste [ɔpɔrtynist]. 1. *a.* Time-serving. 2. *s.* Opportunist; time-server.

opportunité [ɔpɔrtynite], *s.f.* 1. (*a*) Opportuneness, seasonableness, timeliness. (*b*) Expediency, advisability (of project, etc.). 2. Favourable occasion; opportunity.

opposable [ɔpozabl], *a.* Opposable (à, to).

opposant [ɔpozã]. 1. *a.* Opposing, adverse (party, etc.). 2. *s.m.* Opponent.

opposer [ɔpoze], *v.tr.* 1. To oppose; to set (sth.) over against (sth.). *O. une glace à une fenêtre,* to set a mirror opposite a window. *O. une vigoureuse résistance,* to put up, offer, a vigorous resistance. 2. To compare, to contrast (à, with).
　s'opposer à qch., to oppose sth.; to be opposed to sth. *S'o. résolument à qch.,* to set one's face against sth. *Il n'y a pas de loi qui s'y oppose,* there is no law against it. *Rien ne s'oppose à votre succès,* nothing stands between you and success.

opposé. 1. *a.* (*a*) Opposed, opposing (armies, etc.); opposite (side, shore); contrary (interests, advice). *Angles opposés par le sommet,* vertically opposite angles. *Tons opposés,* contrasting colours. (*b*) *Être o. à une mesure,* to be opposed to a measure; to be against a measure. 2. *s.m.* The contrary, reverse, opposite (of sth.). **A l'opposé de . . .,** contrary to. . . .

opposite [ɔpozit], *s.m.* Opposite, contrary. **Maison à l'opposite de l'église,** house opposite to, facing, the church.

opposition [ɔpozisjɔ̃], *s.f.* 1. (*a*) Opposition. **Mettre opposition à qch.,** to oppose sth. **Agir en opposition avec un droit,** to act in contravention of a right. *Pol: Le parti de l'o.,* the opposition. *Com:* **Frapper d'opposition,** to stop payment of (cheque, etc.). (*b*) *Jur:* (i) = SAISIE-ARRÊT. *O. sur titre,* attachment against securities. (ii) *Mettre, former, o. à qch.,* to oppose, make an injunction against, sth. *Mettre o. à un mariage,* to enter a caveat to a marriage; *F:* to forbid the banns. 2. Contrariety, contrast, antithesis. **Par opposition à qch.,** as opposed to sth. *O. d'humeur,* incompatibility of temper. 3. *Astr:* Opposition (of planets).

oppresser [ɔprese], *v.tr.* To oppress. (*a*) To weigh down; to lie heavy on (the chest, conscience); to impede (respiration). *Malade oppressé,* breathless patient. (*b*) To deject, depress.

28

oppresseur [ɔprɛsœːr]. **I.** *s.m.* Oppressor. **2.** *a.m.* Oppressive, tyrannical.

oppress|if, -ive [ɔprɛsif, -iːv], *a.* Oppressive. *adv.* **-ivement.**

oppression [ɔprɛsjɔ̃], *s.f.* Oppression.

opprimant [ɔprimɑ̃], *a.* Oppressing, oppressive.

opprimer [ɔprime], *v.tr.* To oppress, crush (down) (a people).

opprimé, *a.* Oppressed, down-trodden.

opprobre [ɔprɔbr], *s.m.* Disgrace, shame, opprobrium. *Vivre dans l'o.,* to live in infamy.

optant, -ante [ɔptɑ̃, -ãːt], *a. & s.* (Person) exercising an option; optant.

optatif, -ive [ɔptatif, -iːv]. **I.** *a.* Optative. **2.** *s.m. Gram:* Optative (mood).

opter [ɔpte], *v.i. O. entre deux choses,* to choose, decide, between two things. *O. pour qch.,* to decide in favour of sth.; to choose sth.

opticien [ɔptisjɛ̃], *s.m.* Optician.

optimisme [ɔptimism], *s.m.* Optimism.

optimiste [ɔptimist]. **I.** *a.* Optimistic; sanguine. **2.** *s.* Optimist.

option [ɔpsjɔ̃], *s.f.* Option, choice (*entre, between*). **Souscrire des valeurs à option,** to buy an option on stock. *Demander une o. pour un sujet de film,* to ask for an option on the film rights of a book.

optique [ɔptik]. **I.** *a.* Optic (nerve); optical (illusion). *Télégraphie o.,* visual signalling. **2.** *s.f.* (a) Optics. *Instruments d'o.,* optical instruments. (b) *A:* Raree-show. (c) Optical system (of projector, etc.).

opulence [ɔpylãːs], *s.f.* Opulence, affluence. *Vivre dans l'o.,* to live in affluence. *Nager dans l'o.,* to be rolling in wealth. *F: L'o. de ses charmes,* her buxom figure.

opul|ent [ɔpylɑ̃], *a.* Opulent, rich, wealthy (person); affluent (circumstances); abundant (harvest). *adv.* **-emment.**

opuscule [ɔpyskyl], *s.m.* Short treatise; pamphlet, tract.

or¹ [ɔːr], *s.m.* Gold. *Chercheur d'or,* gold-digger. *Or en barres,* ingot gold; bullion. *F:* **C'est de l'or en barre,** it is as good as ready money. *Poudre d'or,* gold-dust. *Feuille d'or,* gold-foil, -leaf. **Obtenir qch. à prix d'or,** to obtain sth. at a ransom price. **Affaire d'or,** excellent bargain. *F:* Parler d'or, to speak words of gold. S.a. ÂGE 3.

or², *conj.* Now. *Or Barabbas était un brigand,* now Barabbas was a robber. **Or donc,** well then.

oracle [ɔraːkl], *s.m.* Oracle. *Style d'o.,* oracular style.

orage [ɔraːʒ], *s.m.* (Thunder-)storm. *Le temps est à l'o.,* it is thundery weather. *Il va faire de l'o.,* a storm is brewing.

orageu|x, -euse [ɔraʒø, -øːz], *a.* **I.** Stormy. *Discussion orageuse,* stormy discussion. **2.** Threatening, thundery (weather); lowering (sky). *adv.* **-sement.**

oraison [ɔrɛzɔ̃], *s.f.* **I. Oraison funèbre,** funeral oration. **2.** Orison, prayer. **Faire ses oraisons,** to say one's prayers. S.a. DOMINICAL I.

oral, -aux [ɔral, -o], *a.* **I.** *a.* Oral (examination); verbal (deposition). **2.** *s.m.* Oral examination, viva voce examination. *F: Rater l'o.,* to be ploughed in the oral, in the viva. *adv.* **-ement.**

orange [ɔrãːʒ], *s.f.* **I.** Orange. *O. amère,* bitter orange, Seville orange. *O. douce,* China orange. **Écorce d'orange,** orange-peel. **2.** *a.inv. Rubans orange,* orange(-coloured) ribbons.

orangé [ɔrãʒe], *a.* Orange(-coloured).

orangeade [ɔrãʒad], *s.f.* Orangeade.

orangeat [ɔrãʒa], *s.m.* Candied orange-peel.

oranger¹ [ɔrãʒe], *s.m.* Orange-tree. **Couronne de fleurs d'oranger,** wreath of orange-blossom. **Eau de fleur(s) d'oranger,** orange-flower water.

oranger², -ère [ɔrãʒe, -ɛːr], *s.* Orange-seller; orange-girl.

orangerie [ɔrãʒri], *s.f.* Orangery; (i) orange-grove; (ii) orange-greenhouse.

orang-outan(g) [ɔrãutã], *s.m. Z:* Orang-outang. *pl. Des orangs-outan(g)s.*

orateur [ɔratœːr], *s.m.* (With occ. *f.* oratrice [ɔratris]) **I.** Orator, speaker. **2.** Spokesman.

oratoire¹ [ɔratwaːr], *a.* Oratorical. *L'art o.,* (the art of) oratory; public speaking.

oratoire², *s.m.* Oratory; chapel (for private worship).

oratorio [ɔratɔrjo], *s.m. Mus:* Oratorio.

orbe¹ [ɔrb], *s.m.* Orb; globe; sphere; heavenly body.

orbe², *a.* **I. Mur orbe,** blind wall. **2.** *Surg:* **Coup orbe,** bruise, contusion.

orbite [ɔrbit], *s.m.* or *f.* **I.** Orbit (of planet, etc.). **2.** *Anat:* Socket, orbit (of the eye).

Orcades (les) [lezɔrkad]. *Pr.n.f.pl. Geog:* The Orkneys.

orcanette, -ète [ɔrkanɛt], *s.f. Bot:* Alkanet, dyer's bugloss.

orchestral, -aux [ɔrkɛstral, -o], *a.* Orchestral.

orchestration [ɔrkɛstrasjɔ̃], *s.f.* Orchestration, scoring.

orchestre [ɔrkɛstr], *s.m.* Orchestra. **Chef d'orchestre,** (i) conductor of the orchestra; (ii) bandmaster.

orchestrer [ɔrkɛstre], *v.tr.* To orchestrate, to score (opera, etc.).

orchidée [ɔrkide], *s.f.* **I.** Orchid. **2.** *pl.* Orchidées, orchid(ac)eae, orchids.

orchis [ɔrkis], *s.m. Bot:* Orchis; wild orchid.

ordalie [ɔrdali], *s.f. A:* Ordeal. *O. de l'eau, du feu,* ordeal by water, by fire.

ordinaire [ɔrdinɛːr]. **I.** *a.* Ordinary, usual, common, customary, average. **Peu ordinaire,** unusual, uncommon, out of the ordinary. **Fractions ordinaires,** vulgar fractions. **Vin ordinaire,** table wine. **Médecin ordinaire du roi,** physician in ordinary to the King. *Ambassadeur o.,* ordinary ambassador. **2.** *s.m.* (a) Wont, custom, usual practice. **Selon, à, son ordinaire,** as is his wont. **A l'ordinaire, d'ordinaire, pour l'ordinaire,** usually, as a rule. **Comme à l'ordinaire, comme d'ordinaire,** as usual. *Contre mon ordinaire, j'étais sorti,* contrary to my normal habit, I had gone out. (b) Ordinary standard. *Événement qui sort de l'o.,* uncommon occurrence. *Cela sort de l'o.,* it is out of the ordinary. (c) (i) Ordinary (meal); daily bill of fare. *Auberge où l'o. est excellent,* inn where the fare is excellent. (ii) *Mil:* (Company) mess. (d) *Ecc.* (*R.C.Ch.*): **L'Ordinaire (de la messe),** the Ordinary (of the mass). (e) *Ecc:* **L'Ordinaire,** the Ordinary, the diocesan bishop. *adv.* **-ment.**

ordinal, -aux [ɔrdinal, -o], *a.* Ordinal.

ordination [ɔrdinasjɔ̃], *s.f. Ecc:* Ordination.

ordonnance [ɔrdɔnãːs], *s.f.* **I.** Order, (general) arrangement (of building, etc.); disposition, grouping (of picture, etc.). **2.** (a) Enactment, order. *O. d'amnistie,* amnesty ordinance. *O. de police,* police regulation. (b) Judge's order, decision, or ruling. **3.** *Mil:* **Habit d'ordonnance,** uniform, regimentals. *Revolver d'o.,* regulation revolver. **Officier d'ordonnance,** aide-de-camp; *Navy:* flag-lieutenant. **4.** *Mil:* (a) Orderly. (b) *Occ. m.* Officer's servant; batman. **5.** *Med:* Prescription.

ordonnateur, -trice [ɔrdɔnatœːr, -tris], *s.* Director, arranger; organizer (of festivities). **ordonner** [ɔrdɔne], *v.tr.* **1.** (*a*) To arrange (sth.); to set (sth.) to rights. (*b*) *Mth:* To arrange (terms) in ascending or descending order. (*c*) *v.i. O. du sort de qn,* to dispose of s.o.'s fate. **2.** To order, command, direct. (*a*) *O. à qn de faire qch.,* to order s.o. to do sth. *On nous ordonna d'entrer, de sortir,* we were ordered in, out. (*b*) *O. une punition à qn,* to order s.o. to be punished. *Med: O. un remède à qn,* to prescribe a remedy for s.o. **3.** *Ecc:* To ordain (priest). **ordonné, -ée. 1.** *a.* (*a*) Orderly, well-ordered. (*b*) (Person) of regular habits; tidy. **2.** *s.f. Mth:* **Ordonnée,** ordinate. *Axe des ordonnées,* Y-axis. *adv.* **-ment.** **ordre** [ɔrdr], *s.m.* Order. **1.** *Ranger des mots par o.* alphabétique, to arrange words in alphabetical order. **Numéro d'ordre,** serial number. **Avec ordre,** methodically. **Sans ordre,** untidy, untidily; unmethodical, unmethodically. **En bon ordre,** (i) in (an) orderly fashion; (ii) in order; in proper trim. **Homme d'ordre,** orderly, methodical, man. **Mettre qch. en ordre,** (re)-**mettre de l'ordre dans qch.,** to set sth. in order, to rights; to tidy up (room). **Mettre ordre à ses affaires,** *mettre ses affaires en o.,* to put one's affairs in order; to settle one's affairs. **Mettre (bon) ordre à un abus,** to see that an abuse comes to an end; to put an abuse right. **2.** *Maintenir l'o. dans une ville,* to maintain order, discipline, in a town; to police a town. **Rappeler qn à l'ordre,** to call s.o. to order. **A l'ordre!** order! chair! *Jur:* **Ordre public,** law and order. *Délit contre l'o. public,* breach of the peace. *Troubler l'o.* (*public*), to disturb the peace. **3. Ordre du jour,** (i) agenda (of meeting); (ii) *Mil:* general orders, order of the day. *Questions à l'o. du jour,* (i) items of the agenda; (ii) *F:* questions of the day. **Passer à l'ordre du jour,** to proceed with the business of the day; to set aside a motion. *Mil:* **Cité à l'ordre (du jour)** = mentioned in despatches. **4.** (*a*) Order (of architecture, etc.); class, division, category. **De premier ordre,** first-class, first-rate. **Hôtel de troisième ordre,** third-rate hotel. *Renseignements d'o. privé,* enquiries of a private nature. **De l'ordre de . . . ,** ranging about. . . . *Fréquences de l'o. de* 200, frequencies ranging about 200. *Dans cet o. d'idées . . . ,* in connection with this. . . . (*b*) **Ordre religieux,** monastic order. **Ordre de chevalerie,** order of knighthood. (*c*) *pl. Ecc:* Holy Orders. **Recevoir les ordres,** to be ordained. (*d*) **L'Ordre de la Jarretière,** the Order of the Garter. *Porter tous ses ordres,* to wear all one's decorations, all one's orders. **5.** (*a*) Command, fiat; warrant. *O. par écrit,* written order. *O. d'exécution,* death-warrant. **Donner ordre à qn de faire qch.,** to order s.o. to do sth. *Je reçus l'o. de revenir,* I was ordered back. *Je reçus l'o. de partir pour l'étranger,* I was ordered abroad. **Donner des ordres à qn,** to give s.o. orders. **Par ordre, sur l'ordre, de qn,** by order of s.o. **Se mettre aux ordres de qn,** to put oneself at s.o.'s disposal. **"Toujours à vos ordres,"** 'yours obediently.' **Jusqu'à nouvel ordre,** until further orders; until further notice. (*b*) *Com:* **Payez à l'ordre de . . . ,** pay to the order of. . . . **Billet à ordre,** promissory note; bill payable to order. **ordure** [ɔrdyːr], *s.f.* **1.** (*a*) Dirt, filth, muck. (*b*) Excrement, dung, ordure. (*c*) Filthiness, lewdness. **2.** *pl.* Sweepings, refuse, rubbish. *Ordures ménagères,* household refuse. **Boîte,**

panier, bac, à ordures, refuse-bin, dust-bin. **"Défense de déposer des ordures,"** 'shoot no rubbish.' **ordurier, -ière** [ɔrdyrje, -jɛːr], *a.* Lewd, filthy (book, song); foul, scurrilous (language). **oréade** [ɔread], *s.f. Myth:* Oread; grotto or mountain nymph. **orée** [ɔre], *s.f. A:* Edge, verge, skirt (of a wood). **oreille** [ɔrɛːj], *s.f.* Ear. **1. Avoir mal à l'oreille, aux oreilles,** to have ear-ache. *Aux oreilles courtes,* short-eared. *A longues oreilles,* long-eared. **Baisser l'oreille, avoir l'oreille basse,** to be crestfallen. (Of horse) **Coucher les oreilles,** to set, lay, its ears back; to show signs of temper. *Tirer les oreilles à un gamin,* to pull, tweak, a boy's ears. *F:* **Il s'est fait tirer l'oreille,** he took a lot of coaxing. *Il ne s'est pas fait tirer l'o.,* he did not have to be asked twice. **Montrer le bout de l'oreille,** to show the cloven hoof. *Autant lui peut à l'oreille,* the same thing may very well happen to him any day. *Ils se sont pris par les oreilles,* they had a set-to. **Il a toujours l'oreille déchirée,** he's always in the wars. *Mil: Fendre l'o. à un cheval,* to clip a horse's ear (as a cast-mark). *F:* **Fendre l'oreille à qn,** to retire (officer, official, etc.). S.a. **DORMIR** I, **PUCE** I. **2. N'écouter que d'une oreille,** to listen absent-mindedly. *Dire, souffler, qch. à l'o. de qn,* to whisper sth. to s.o. *F:* **Dresser l'oreille, tendre l'oreille,** to prick up one's ears. **Être tout oreilles,** to be all ears, all attention. **Prêter l'oreille à qn,** to lend an ear to s.o. **Fermer l'oreille aux plaintes,** to be deaf to complaints. **Faire la sourde oreille,** to pretend not to hear; to turn a deaf ear. **Ça lui entre par une oreille et sort par l'autre,** it goes in at one ear and out at the other. **Les oreilles doivent lui tinter,** his ears must be tingling, burning. **Rebattre les oreilles à qn de qch.,** to din sth. in s.o.'s ears. **Être dur d'oreille, avoir l'oreille dure,** to be hard of hearing. **Avoir l'oreille juste, avoir de l'oreille,** to have a good ear, to have an ear for music. S.a. **CORNER** I. **3.** *Tchn:* Ear (of porringer); handle (of vase); lug, attachment, flange (of piece of machinery, etc.); palm (of anchor); wing (of thumb-screw). **Écrou à oreilles,** wing-nut. **Bergère à oreilles,** grandfather's chair. **Faire une oreille à une page,** to dog's-ear, turn down the corner of, a page. **4.** *Bot:* **Oreille d'ours,** bear's-ear, auricula. **Oreille de souris,** mouse-ear. **oreiller** [ɔreje], *s.m.* Pillow. **Prendre conseil de son oreiller,** to sleep over it. **oreillette** [ɔrejɛt], *s.f.* (*a*) Auricle (of the heart). (*b*) **Casquette à oreillettes,** cap with ear-flaps. **oreillon** [ɔrejɔ̃], *s.m.* **1.** Ear-flap (of cap, sou'-wester). **2.** *pl. Med:* **Oreillons,** mumps. **ore(s)** [ɔːr], *adv. A:* Now. **D'ores et déjà,** here and now. **orfèvre** [ɔrfɛːvr], *s.m.* Goldsmith; gold and silversmith. **orfèvré** [ɔrfevre], *a.* Worked, wrought (by the goldsmith). **orfèvrerie** [ɔrfevrəri], *s.f.* **1.** (*a*) Goldsmith's trade, craft, or work. (*b*) Goldsmith's shop. **2.** (*a*) (Gold, silver) plate. (*b*) Jewellery. **orfraie** [ɔrfrɛ], *s.f.* Osprey, sea-eagle, sea-hawk. *F:* **Pousser des cris d'orfraie,** to shriek at the top of one's voice. **organdi** [ɔrgɑ̃di], *s.m.* Organdi(e), book-muslin. **organe** [ɔrgan], *s.m.* **1.** (*a*) Organ (of sight, hearing, etc.). (*b*) *Les organes d'une machine,* the parts, components, of a machine. **2.** (*a*) Voice. *O. mâle et sonore,* strong, manly voice. (*b*) *Journal qui* *est l'o. d'un parti*, newspaper which is the organ, the mouthpiece, of a party. *Certains organes* . . ., a certain section of the press. . . . (c) Agent, means, medium ; instrument (of a government, etc.). *Par un nouvel o.*, by another means, through another agency.

organeau [ɔrgano], *s.m.* (a) Mooring-ring. (b) Anchor-ring.

organique [ɔrganik], a. Organic. adv. **-ment,** **-ally.**

organisateur, -trice [ɔrganizatœːr, -tris]. **I.** a. Organizing. **2.** s. Organizer.

organisation [ɔrganizasjɔ̃], *s.f.* **I.** Organizing. **2.** Organization. (a) Structure (of human body, etc.). *Être d'une frêle o.*, to have a feeble constitution. (b) (Organized) body (of workers, etc.).

organiser [ɔrganize], *v.tr.* To organize ; to arrange ; to get up (entertainment, contest) ; to set (business) on foot.

s'organiser, to get into working order, to get shipshape.

organisé, a. **I.** Organic (body, life). *Êtres organisés*, organic beings. **2.** Organized, constituted. *C'est une tête bien organisée*, he is level-headed.

organisme [ɔrganism], *s.m.* Organism. *Anat:* (The) system. *Un o. de fer*, an iron constitution.

organiste [ɔrganist], *s.m. & f. Mus:* Organist.

orge [ɔrʒ], s. Barley. **I.** *s.f. Grain d'o.*, barley-corn. **Toile (à) grain d'orge,** huckaback linen. S.a. GRAIN-D'ORGE. **Sucre d'orge,** barley-sugar. **2.** *s.m.* **Orge mondé,** hulled barley. **Orge perlé,** pearl-barley.

orgeat [ɔrʒa], *s.m.* Orgeat (syrup). *F:* **C'est une carafe d'orgeat,** he's a characterless individual.

orgelet [ɔrʒǝlɛ], *s.m.* Sty(e) (on the eye).

orgiaque [ɔrʒjak], a. Orgiastic, orgiac (frenzy).

orgie [ɔrʒi], *s.f.* (a) Orgy ; drunken feasting or feast. (b) *F:* Profusion (of gay flowers, etc.) ; riot (of colour).

orgue [ɔrg], *s.m.* **I.** (Also *Ecc:* s.f.pl. **orgues**) *Mus:* (a) Organ. *Un bel orgue, de belles orgues,* a fine organ. **Grand orgue,** (i) grand organ (in organ loft) ; (ii) great (organ) (as opposed to *positif, récit, q.v.*). **Orgue du chœur,** choir organ (located in choir). **Tenir l'orgue, les orgues,** to be, preside, at the organ. (b) **Orgue de salon,** American organ or harmonium. **2. Orgue de Barbarie,** barrel-organ, street-organ.

orgueil [ɔrgœːj], *s.m.* Pride, vaingloriousness, arrogance. **Crever d'orgueil,** to be bursting with pride. **Mettre son orgueil à faire qch.,** to take a pride in doing sth.

orgueilleu|x, -euse [ɔrgœjø, -øːz], a. Proud, vainglorious, arrogant. *Être o. de sa maison, de ses richesses,* to be house-proud, purse-proud. adv. **-sement.**

orient [ɔrjɔ̃], *s.m.* **I.** (a) Orient, East. *F:* **Génie à son orient,** rising, budding, genius. (b) **Le proche, l'extrême, Orient,** the Near, the Far, East. *Hist:* **L'Empire d'Orient,** the Byzantine Empire. **2.** Water, orient (of pearl).

orientable [ɔrjɑ̃tabl], a. Swivelling ; free to turn.

oriental, -ale, -aux [ɔrjɑ̃tal, -o]. **I.** a. Eastern, oriental. *Les Indes orientales,* the East Indies. **2.** s. *Les Orientaux,* the Orientals, the peoples of the East.

orientation [ɔrjɑ̃tasjɔ̃], *s.f.* **I.** Orientation. **Table d'orientation,** indicator on view-point showing the direction of various landmarks. **Perdre le sens de l'orientation,** to lose one's bearings. *Sch:* **O. professionnelle,** vocational guidance. **Roue d'orientation,** directing wheel (of windmill). *Navy:* **O. d'un canon,** training

of a gun. **A orientation libre** = ORIENTABLE. **2.** *O. d'une maison,* aspect of a house. *L'o. de la politique,* the trend of politics. *Nau: O. des voiles,* set, trim, of the sails.

orientement [ɔrjɑ̃tmɑ̃], *s.m.* **I.** Orienting (of building). **2.** (a) **Prendre un orientement,** to take a bearing. (b) *Nau:* = ORIENTATION 2.

orienter [ɔrjɑ̃te], *v.tr.* **I.** (a) To orient (building). (b) *O. des voiles,* to trim sails. *Navy: O. un canon,* to train a gun. *W.Tel:* **Antenne orientée,** directional aerial. (c) To direct, guide. **2.** *Surv:* (a) To take the bearings of (spot). (b) To set (map) by the compass.

s'orienter, to take, find, one's bearings.

orifice [ɔrifis], *s.m.* Aperture, opening, orifice. *Mch: Orifices d'admission,* intake ports.

oriflamme [ɔriflɑːm], *s.f. Hist:* Oriflamme.

originaire [ɔriʒinɛːr], a. **I.** Originating (de, from, in) ; native (de, of). **2.** Original ; foundation (member).

originairement [ɔriʒinɛrmɑ̃], adv. Originally ; at the beginning.

original, -aux [ɔriʒinal, -o], a. & s. **I.** Original (text, manuscript). **Copier qch. sur l'original,** to copy sth. from the original. **Savoir qch. d'original,** to know sth. at first hand. **2.** (a) Original (style, idea) ; inventive (genius) ; novel, fresh (idea). (b) *F:* Odd, queer, eccentric. **C'est un original,** he's a character.

originalement [ɔriʒinalmɑ̃], adv. (a) In original fashion. (b) In a novel manner. (c) Oddly, eccentrically.

originalité [ɔriʒinalite], *s.f.* (a) Originality. (b) Eccentricity, oddity.

origine [ɔriʒin], *s.f.* Origin. **I.** (a) Beginning. **Dès l'origine,** from the very beginning, from the outset. **A l'origine, dans l'origine,** originally ; in the beginning. *Mth: Surv:* (Point) **origine,** zero point. **2.** (a) Extraction (of person, nation). *Être d'o. illustre,* to be of noble descent, of noble birth. (b) Nationality. **3.** (a) Source, derivation. **Mots de même origine,** cognate words. *Tirer son o. de . . .,* to originate with, from. . . . *Post:* **Bureau d'origine,** (postal) office of dispatch. *Cust:* **Certificat d'origine,** certificate of origin. (b) *Mth: etc:* **Point d'origine,** point of origin (of curve).

origin|el, -elle [ɔriʒinɛl], a. Primordial, original. **Péché originel,** original sin. **Tache originelle,** inherited taint. adv. **-ellement.**

orignac [ɔriɲak], *s.m.,* **orignal** [ɔriɲal], *s.m. Z:* Moose ; (Canadian) elk. *pl. Des orignals.*

orillon [ɔrijɔ̃], *s.m.* Ear, lug, handle (of porringer, etc.).

orin [ɔrɛ̃], *s.m. Nau:* Buoy-rope.

oripeau [ɔripo], *s.m.* **I.** Tinsel, foil ; Dutch gold. **2.** *pl.* Tawdry finery, cheap finery.

orléaniste [ɔrleanist], a. & s. *Hist:* Orleanist ; supporter of the Orleans branch of the French monarchy.

ormaie [ɔrmɛ], *s.f.* Elm-grove.

orme [ɔrm], *s.m. Bot: etc:* Elm(-tree, -wood). *O. de montagne,* wych-elm. *F:* **Attendez-moi sous l'orme!** you may wait for me till doomsday !

ormeau [ɔrmo], *s.m. Bot:* (Young) elm.

orne [ɔrn], *s.m. Bot:* Manna-ash, flowering ash.

ornement [ɔrnǝmɑ̃], *s.m.* Ornament, adornment, embellishment. *Mus:* Notes of o., grace-notes. **Sans ornement,** unadorned. **Dessin d'ornement,** decorative drawing.

ornemental, -aux [ɔrnǝmɑ̃tal, -o], a. Ornamental, decorative.

ornementation [ɔrnǝmɑ̃tasjɔ̃], *s.f.* Ornamentation.

ornementer [ɔrnəmɑ̃te], *v.tr.* To ornament.

orner [ɔrne], *v.tr.* To ornament, adorn, embellish, decorate. *Robe ornée de galon d'or,* dress set off with gold braid.
  orné, *a.* Ornate (letter); ornate, florid (style).

ornière [ɔrnjɛːr], *s.f.* **I.** Rut. *F:* **Sortir de l'ornière,** to get out of the rut, of the beaten track. **2.** Groove (of tram-rail, etc.).

ornithologie [ɔrnitɔlɔ ̣i], *s.f.* Ornithology.

ornithologique [ɔrnitɔlɔ ̣ik], *a.* Ornithological.

ornithologiste [ɔrnitɔlɔ ̣ist], *s.m.* Ornithologist.

ornithor(h)ynque [ɔrnitɔrɛ̃ːk], *s.m.* *Z:* Ornithorhynchus, duck-billed platypus.

orobanche [ɔrɔbɑ̃ːʃ], *s.f.* *Bot:* Broom-rape, choke-weed.

orographie [ɔrɔgrafi], *s.f.* Orography.

oronge [ɔrɔ̃ː ̣], *s.f.* *Fung:* Orange-milk agaric.

orpailleur [ɔrpɑjœːr], *s.m.* Gold-washer.

Orphée [ɔrfe]. *Pr.n.m. Gr.Myth:* Orpheus.

orphelin, -ine [ɔrfəlɛ̃, -in], *s.* Orphan; *a.* orphan(ed). *O. de père,* fatherless (boy). *O. de mère,* motherless (boy).

orphelinat [ɔrfəlina], *s.m.* Orphanage; orphan-home.

orphéon [ɔrfeɔ̃], *s.m.* Male-voice choir.

orphéoniste [ɔrfeɔnist], *s.m.* Member of a choral society.

orphie [ɔrfi], *s.f.* *Ich:* Garfish, sea-pike.

orpiment [ɔrpimɑ̃], *s.m.* *Miner:* Orpiment; yellow arsenic.

orpin [ɔrpɛ̃], *s.m.* **I.** = ORPIMENT. **2.** *Bot:* Stone-crop.

orque [ɔrk], *s.f.* = ÉPAULARD.

Orsay [ɔrsɛ]. *F:* **Le Quai d'Orsay,** the French Foreign Office (situated on the Quai d'Orsay).

orseille [ɔrsɛːj], *s.f.* *Bot:* Orchil; dyer's moss.

orteil [ɔrtɛːj], *s.m.* Toe. **Gros orteil,** big toe.

orthochromatique [ɔrtɔkrɔmatik], *a.* *Phot:* Orthochromatic.

orthodoxe [ɔrtɔdɔks], *a.* (*a*) Orthodox. (*b*) Sound (opinion); conventional, correct (manner, etc.).

orthodoxie [ɔrtɔdɔksi], *s.f.* Orthodoxy.

orthodromique [ɔrtɔdrɔmik], *a.* **Navigation orthodromique,** great-circle sailing.

orthogonal, -aux [ɔrtɔgɔnal, -o], *a.* *Geom:* Orthogonal. *adv.* **-ement.**

orthographe [ɔrtɔgraf], *s.f.* Orthography, spelling. **Faute d'orthographe,** mistake in spelling, mis-spelling.

orthographie [ɔrtɔgrafi], *s.f.* Elevation plan (of building); orthographic projection.

orthographier [ɔrtɔgrafje], *v.tr.* To spell (word). *Mal o.,* to mis-spell (word).

ortie [ɔrti], *s.f.* Nettle. *O. brûlante,* stinging nettle. S.a. FROC.

ortier [ɔrtje], *v.tr.* To urticate (limb, etc.).

ortolan [ɔrtɔlɑ̃], *s.m.* *Orn:* Ortolan (bunting).

orvet [ɔrvɛ], *s.m.* Slow-worm, blind-worm.

orviétan [ɔrvjetɑ̃], *s.m.* *A:* Nostrum; quack medicine. *Marchand d'o.,* charlatan.

os [ɔs; *pl.* o], *s.m.* Bone. **N'avoir que la peau et les os,** to be nothing but skin and bone. *Os à moelle,* marrow-bone. **Gelé jusqu'à la moelle des os,** frozen to the marrow, to the bone. **Trempé jusqu'aux os,** soaked to the skin; wet through. **Il ne fera pas de vieux os,** he won't make old bones; he won't live long. **Il y laissera ses os,** he'll die there. S.a. CHAIR I.

oscillant [ɔsijɑ̃, ɔsilɑ̃], *a.* **I.** Oscillating; rocking (shaft). **2.** Fluctuating (market). **3.** *W.Tel:* Circuit o., oscillatory circuit.

oscillateur, -trice [ɔsil(l)atœːr, -tris]. **I.** *a.* Oscillating. *W.Tel:* Lampe oscillatrice, oscillating valve; oscillator. **2.** *s.m.* Oscillating coil.

oscillation [ɔsil(l)asjɔ̃], *s.f.* Oscillation. (*a*) Swing (of pendulum). *Ph: etc:* Oscillations amorties, entretenues, damped, sustained, oscillations. (*b*) Rocking (of boat). (*c*) *Mec.E:* Vibration.

oscillatoire [ɔsil(l)atwaːr], *a. Ph:* Oscillatory.

osciller [ɔsije, ɔsile], *v.i.* To oscillate. **I.** (Of pendulum) To swing; to sway; (of boat) to rock. **2.** (*a*) *O. entre deux opinions,* to waver between two opinions. (*b*) (Of market) To fluctuate.

osculateur, -trice [ɔskylatœːr, -tris], *a. Geom:* Osculatory, osculating (curve).

osculation [ɔskylasjɔ̃], *s.f. Geom:* Osculation.

oseille [ozɛːj, o-], *s.f. Bot:* Sorrel. **Sel d'oseille,** salts of sorrel. *P:* **La faire à l'oseille à qn,** to try to deceive s.o.

oser [oze], *v.tr.* To dare, venture. *Je n'ose pas, Lit:* je n'ose, le faire, I dare not do it; I am afraid to do it. *J'ose croire que . . . ,* I venture to think that. . . . **Si j'ose (le) dire,** if I may venture to say so.
  osé. *I. a.* Bold, daring. **Être trop osé,** to venture too far. **2.** *s.m.* Audaciousness.

oseraie [ozrɛ], *s.f.* Osier-bed.

oseur, -euse [ozœːr, -øːz], *a.* Daring, bold.

osier [ozje], *s.m.* Osier, water-willow. **Branche d'osier,** withy, withe. **Panier d'osier,** wicker-basket.

Osmanli [ɔsmɑ̃li], *s.m.* Osmanli; Ottoman.

osmium [ɔsmjɔm], *s.m. Ch:* Osmium.

osmonde [ɔsmɔ̃ːd], *s.f. Bot:* Osmund. *O. royale,* royal fern, water-fern.

osmose [ɔsmoːz], *s.f. Ph:* Osmose, osmosis.

osmotique [ɔsmɔtik], *a. Ph:* Osmotic (pressure).

ossature [ɔssatyːr], *s.f.* **I.** Frame, skeleton (of man or animal). **2.** Frame(work), carcass (of aeroplane, etc.); skeleton, ossature (of building).

osselet [ɔslɛ], *s.m.* **I.** Huckle-bone, knuckle-bone (of sheep). **Jouer aux osselets,** to play at knucklebones. **2.** *Les osselets de l'oreille,* the ossicles of the ear. **3.** *Vet:* Osselet (on fetlock, etc.).

ossements [ɔsmɑ̃, os-], *s.m.pl.* Bones, remains (of dead men or animals).

osseux, -euse [ɔsø, -øːz], *a.* Bony; osseous.

ossianique [ɔsjanik], *a.* Ossianic (literature).

ossicule [ɔssikyl], *s.m.* Small bone; ossicle.

ossification [ɔssifikasjɔ̃], *s.f. Med:* Ossification.

ossifier [ɔssifje], *v.tr.* To ossify.
  s'ossifier, (of tissue) to ossify; to harden.

ossu [ɔsy], *a. A:* Big-boned, raw-boned, bony.

ossuaire [ɔssɥɛːr], *s.m.* (*a*) Heap of bones. (*b*) Ossuary, charnel-house.

ostensible [ɔstɑ̃sibl], *a.* Fit to be seen; open, patent, to all.

ostensiblement [ɔstɑ̃sibləmɑ̃], *adv.* Openly, publicly.

ostensoir [ɔstɑ̃swaːr], *s.m. Ecc:* Monstrance, ostensory.

ostentation [ɔstɑ̃tasjɔ̃], *s.f.* Ostentation, show; (vain) display. **Faire ostentation de sa misère,** to make a parade of one's poverty. **Avec ostentation,** ostentatiously, showily. **Sans ostentation,** unostentatiously.

ostéologie [ɔsteɔlɔ ̣i], *s.f.* Osteology.

ostraciser [ɔstrasize], *v.tr.* To ostracize; to banish.

ostracisme [ɔstrasism], *s.m.* Ostracism. **Frapper qn d'ostracisme,** to ostracize s.o.

ostréiculteur [ɔstreikyltœːr], *s.m.* Breeder of oysters.

ostréiculture [ɔstreikyltyːr], *s.f.* Ostreiculture, oyster-breeding.

ostrogot(h), -ot(h)e [ɔstrɔgo, -ɔt]. *Hist:* **I.** *a.* (*a*) Ostrogothic. (*b*) *F: A:* Barbarous, crude, unpolished. **2.** *s.* (*a*) Ostrogoth, Eastern Goth. (*b*) *F :* *A :* Barbarian, goth, vandal.

otage [ɔtaːʒ], *s.m.* Hostage (*de*, for); *F :* guarantee, surety. **Prendre qn pour otage,** to take s.o. as hostage.

otalgie [ɔtalʒi], *s.f.* *Med :* Ear-ache, otalgia.

otarie [ɔtari], *s.f.* Otary, sea-lion, eared seal.

ôter [ote], *v.tr.* To remove, take away. (*a*) *O. le couvert, la nappe,* to remove the cloth; to clear away. *O. son pardessus,* to take off one's overcoat. *O. son chapeau à qn,* to raise one's hat to s.o. *Prov :* En avril, n'ôtez pas un fil, ne'er cast a clout till May be out. (*b*) *O. qch. à qn,* to take sth. away from s.o. (*c*) *O. qch. de qch.,* to take sth. away from sth. *Il me l'a ôté des mains,* he snatched it out of my hands. *Cela me l'a ôté tout à fait de l'esprit,* that put it entirely out of my head.

s'ôter, to remove oneself. *Otez-vous de là,* get out of the way.

otite [ɔtit], *s.f.* *Med :* Otitis.

otologie [ɔtɔlɔʒi], *s.f.* Otology.

ottoman, -ane [ɔt(t)ɔmɑ̃, -an]. **1.** *a.* & *s.* Ottoman. **2.** *s.f.* Ottomane, divan, ottoman.

ou [u], *conj.* Or. **1.** *Trois ou quatre fois par jour,* three or four times a day. *Entrez ou sortez,* either come in or go out. *Vous ou moi, nous lui en parlerons,* you or I shall speak to him about it. **2.** Ou ... ou ..., either ... or ... (*Often* strengthened with *bien*) *Ils exigeaient ou bien du blé ou bien de l'argent,* they demanded either corn or (else) money.

où [u], *adv.* **1.** *Interr.* Where? whither? *Où allez-vous?* where are you going? *Où en êtes-vous?* how far have you got with it? *Déposez-le n'importe où,* put it down anywhere. *D'où?* whence? where ... from? *D'où vient que ...?* how does it happen that ...? *Par où?* (by) which way? *Jusqu'où?* up to what point? how far? **2.** *Rel.* (*a*) Where. **Partout où** *il va,* wherever he goes. **Là où,** (there) where. *Vous trouverez ma pipe là où je l'ai laissée,* you will find my pipe where I left it. *D'où on conclut que ...,* from which one concludes that ... *La maison d'où je sors,* the house I have just come out of. (*b*) When. *Dans le temps où il était jeune,* in the days when he was young. (*c*) *La maison où il demeure,* the house in which he lives; the house he lives in. *Le rang où je suis parvenu,* the rank to which I have attained. **3.** (Concessive) *Où que vous soyez,* wherever you may be.

ouadi. See OUED.

ouaille [waːj], *s.f.* **1.** *B.Lit :* Sheep. **2.** *Le pasteur et ses ouailles,* the minister and his flock.

ouais [we], *int.* *A :* (Surprise) What! my word!

ouate [wat], *s.f.* (Usu. *la ouate*) (*a*) Wadding. (*b*) Cotton-wool. *O. hydrophile,* absorbent cotton-wool; medicated cotton-wool.

ouater [wate], *v.tr.* **1.** To wad; to pad; to line with wadding; to quilt. **2.** *F :* *O. ses pas,* to tread softly; to deaden one's footsteps.

ouaté, *a.* **1.** Wadded, padded; quilted (dressing-gown). **2.** *F :* Woolly, fleecy (cloud, snow); soft (footstep).

oubli [ubli], *s.m.* **1.** (*a*) Forgetting; forgetfulness. **Par oubli,** inadvertently; by, through, an oversight. (*b*) Oblivion. **Tomber dans l'oubli,** to sink, fall, into oblivion; to be forgotten. **2.** Omission, oversight.

oubliable [ubliabl], *a.* Forgettable.

oublie [ubli], *s.f.* Wafer (rolled into a cone).

oublier [ublie], *v.tr.* To forget. (*a*) *J'ai oublié son nom,* I have forgotten his name; his name has slipped out of my mind. *Faire oublier son*

passé, to live down one's past. *O. de faire qch.,* to forget to do sth. *On ne nous le laissera pas o.,* we shall never hear the last of it. (*b*) To overlook, neglect; to be unmindful of (sth.). *O. son devoir,* to neglect one's duty. *O. ses intérêts,* to be unmindful of one's interests.

s'oublier. **1.** To be unmindful of oneself. **2.** To forget one's manners; to forget oneself.

oubliette [ubliɛt], *s.f.* Usu. in *pl.* Oubliette; secret dungeon.

oublieux, -euse [ubliø, -øːz], *a.* Forgetful (*de*, o.). *O. de ma présence,* oblivious of my presence.

oued [wɛd], *s.m.* Watercourse, wadi (in the Sahara). *pl. Des ouadi* [wadi], *des oueds.*

Ouessant [wesɑ̃]. *Pr.n.m. Geog :* Ushant.

ouest [wɛst]. **1.** *s.m.* No *pl.* West. **Un vent d'ouest,** a westerly wind. **Le vent (d')ouest,** the west wind. **A l'ouest de qch.,** (to the) west, (to the) westward, of sth. **A l'ouest, dans l'ouest,** in the west. **Vers l'ouest,** westward. **2.** *a.inv. Côté o.,* western, west, side.

ouf [uf, ff], *int.* **1.** (Sigh of relief) Ah! ha! what a relief! **2.** (Indicating oppression) Phew!

oui [wi]. Yes. *A.* & *Lit :* Ay, yea. **1.** *adv. Vient-il?—Oui,* is he coming?—Yes (, he is). **Je crois que oui, qu'oui,** I think so. *Faire signe que oui,* to nod assent. **Oui-dà!** bless you, yes! yes, rather! *Nau :* Oui, commandant! aye, aye, sir! **2.** *s.m. inv. Deux cents oui et trois cents non,* two hundred ayes and three hundred noes.

ouï [wi, ui]. See OUÏR.

ouiche [wiʃ], *int.* (Denotes incredulity) *Ah o.!* pooh! don't you believe it!

ouï-dire [widiːr], *s.m. inv.* Hearsay. *Je ne le sais que par o.-d.,* I only know it from hearsay.

ouïe [wi], *s.f.* **1.** (Sense of) hearing; audition. *Avoir l'o. fine,* to be sharp of hearing. **A portée de l'ouïe,** within hearing (distance). **2.** (*a*) *pl.* Sound-holes (of violin). (*b*) Ear (of ventilator); inlet. **3.** *pl.* Gills (of fish).

oui-ja [wiʒ], *s.m. Psychics :* Ouija.

ouïr [wiːr, uiːr], *v.tr.* (Used in the *inf.*; in *p.p.* ouï and compound tenses; in oyant, oyez, *q.v.*; and occ. in *p.h.* j'ouïs, *fu.* j'ouïrai) *A :* (= ENTENDRE) To hear. *Nous avons ouï dire à notre père que ...,* we have heard our father say that ... *Jur :* O. les témoins, to hear the witnesses.

ouistiti [wistiti], *s.m. Z :* Wistiti, marmoset.

ouragan [uragɑ̃], *s.m.* Hurricane. **Entrer en ouragan dans une pièce,** to burst into a room.

Oural (l') [lural]. *Pr.n. Geog :* The Ural (river). **Les Monts Ourals,** the Ural Mountains.

ourdir [urdiːr], *v.tr.* **1.** To warp (linen, cloth). *Prov :* A toile ourdie Dieu envoie le fil, God helps those who help themselves. **2.** *F :* To hatch (plot); to weave (intrigue). *s.m.* **-issage**. *s.* **-isseur, -euse**.

ourdou [urdu], *s.m. Ling :* Urdu, Hindustani.

ourler [urle], *v.tr.* **1.** To hem. **Ourler à jour,** to hem-stitch. **2.** To lap-joint (metal edges).

s'ourler, (of waves) to comb; to show white horses.

ourlet [urlɛ], *s.m.* **1.** Hem. *O. à jour,* hem-stitched hem. **Point d'ourlet,** hemming. **2.** Edge (of crater); helix, rim (of ear). **3.** *Metalw :* Lap-joint.

ours, -e [urs], *s.* **1.** (*a*) *Z :* Bear, *f.* she-bear. *O. blanc,* polar bear. *O. grizzlé,* grizzly bear. **Combats d'ours,** bear-baiting. *Toys :* **Ours Martin,** ours en peluche, Teddy bear. *F :* **Ours mal léché,** unlicked cub; unmannerly fellow. *Il est un peu ours,* he is somewhat bearish. *Prov :* Il ne faut pas vendre la peau de l'ours avant de l'avoir tué, don't count your chickens before they

are hatched. S.a. PAVÉ I. (b) F: MS. that has
'gone the rounds.' 2. Astr: La Grande Ourse,
the Great Bear. La Petite Ourse, the Little Bear.
3. Bot: Raisin d'ours, cerise d'ours, bearberry.
oursin [ursɛ̃], s.m. 1. Sea-urchin, sea-hedgehog.
2. Mil: A: **Bonnet d'oursin,** bearskin.
ourson [ursɔ̃], s.m. Bear's cub.
oust(e) [ust], int. P: **Allez ouste!** out you get!
P: **hop it!**
outarde [utard], s.f. Orn: Bustard.
outil [uti], s.m. Tool, implement. **Machine-outil,**
machine-tool.
outillage [utija:ʒ], s.m. 1. Making or providing
of tools. 2. (a) Set of tools. (b) Gear, plant,
equipment.
outill|er [utije], v.tr. To equip, fit out, supply,
(a workman) with tools, (a factory) with plant.
s.m. **-ement.**
  outillé, a. Supplied, equipped, with tools,
with plant. **Être bien o. en livres,** to be well set
up with books.
outrage [utra:ʒ], s.m. Outrage; flagrant insult
(against morals, etc.). **Faire outrage aux convenances,** to commit an offence against propriety.
Jur: **Outrage à la justice,** contempt of court.
Faire (subir un) outrage à qn, to commit an
outrage against, on, s.o. Poet: L'o. des ans, the
ravages of time.
outrageant [utraʒɑ̃], a. Insulting (offer); scurrilous (accusation).
outrager [utraʒe], v.tr. (j'outrageai(s); n. ou-
trageons) 1. To insult; to attack scurrilously.
O. le bon sens, to fly in the face of common sense.
2. To outrage (nature, the law).
outrageu|x, -euse [utraʒø, -øːz], a. Insulting,
scurrilous. adv. **-sement.**
outrance [utrɑ̃:s], s.f. Excess. (Used esp. in)
A outrance, to the utmost, to the bitter end.
Guerre à outrance, war to the knife. Industrialisme d o., out and out industrialism. [OUTRE²]
outrancier, -ière [utrɑ̃sje, -jɛːr]. I. a. Carrying
things to extremes. 2. s. Extremist; F: out-
and-outer.
outre¹ [u:tr], s.f. Goatskin bottle: water-skin.
outre². I. prep. (a) Beyond. **Outre mesure,**
beyond measure; inordinately. Élaborer un
argument o. mesure, to over-labour, over-
elaborate, an argument. (b) In addition to.
Outre cette somme qu'il me redoit . . ., in addition
to that sum he still owes me. . . . **Outre cela
. . .,** in addition to that . . ., besides . . .,
moreover. . . . (c) pref: Ultra-. **Outremarin,**
ultramarine. 2. adv. (a) **Passer outre, aller outre,**
to go on, proceed further. Passer o. à une objection,
to disregard, to take no notice of, to overrule,
an objection. Passer o. à la loi, to set the law at
naught, at defiance. (b) **En outre,** besides, moreover, further(more); again; over and above.
J'ai, en o., deux neveux, I have, besides, two
nephews. (c) **Transpercer qn d'outre en outre,**
to run s.o. through (and through). (d) **En outre
de,** in addition to; besides. Conj.phr. **Outre que**
+ ind., apart from the fact that . . ., not to
mention the fact that . . .
outrecuidance [utrəkɥidɑ̃:s], s.f. Presumptuousness, bumptiousness.
outrecuidant [utrəkɥidɑ̃], a. Overweening,
presumptuous, bumptious.
outre-Manche, adv.phr. On the other side of,
across, the Channel.
outremer [utrəmeːr], s.m. 1. Lapis lazuli.
2. (Bleu d')outremer, ultramarine (blue).
outre-mer, adv.phr. Beyond the sea(s). **Commerce d'outre-mer,** oversea(s) trade.

outre-monts, adv.phr. Beyond the mountains.
D'outre-monts, tra(ns)montane.
outrepasser [utrəpase], v.tr. To go beyond (one's
goal, one's rights); to exceed (given orders).
O. ses pouvoirs, to override one's commission.
outrer [utre], v.tr. 1. To carry (sth.) to excess,
beyond reason; to exaggerate; to overdo.
2. To tire out, exhaust; to overstrain, founder
(a horse). 3. To provoke (s.o.) beyond measure.
  outré, a. (a) Exaggerated, extravagant,
overdone (praise). (b) Carried away by indignation. O. de colère, beside oneself with anger.
outre-Rhin, adv.phr. Beyond the Rhine.
D'outre-Rhin, transrhenane.
outre-tombe (d'), adv.phr. From beyond the
grave.
ouvertement [uvertəmɑ̃], adv. Openly, frankly;
avowedly.
ouverture [uverty:r], s.f. 1. (a) Opening (of
door, session, etc.). O. d'un testament, reading of
a will. O. d'hostilités, outbreak of hostilities. **Conférence d'ouverture,** opening lecture.
(b) **Faire des ouvertures à qn,** to make overtures
to s.o. (c) Mus: Overture. (d) Open state.
Heures d'o., business hours (of shop); visiting
hours (of museum, etc.). 2. (a) Opening, aperture (in wall, etc.); gap, break (in hedge).
Pratiquer une o. dans la porte, to cut a hole in
the door. (b) Width, span (of arch); spread (of
compass legs). El.E: O. d'induit, armature gap.
ouvrable [uvrabl], a. 1. Workable, tractable;
kindly (material). 2. Jour ouvrable, working day.
ouvrage [uvra:ʒ], s.m. Work. 1. (a) (Something
to do) **Être sans ouvrage,** to be unemployed.
Se mettre à l'ouvrage, to set to work. (b) Workmanship. 2. Piece of work; product. O. en prose,
prose work. Const: Les gros ouvrages, the main
walls. **Ouvrages de dames,** ladies' fancy-work.
Table, corbeille, boîte, à ouvrage, work-table,
-basket, -box. Êtes-vous content de votre o.? are
you pleased with your handiwork? S.a. ART 2.
ouvrager [uvraʒe], v.tr. (j'ouvrageai(s); n.
ouvrageons) Tchn: To work (metal); to figure
(brocade).
  ouvragé, a. = OUVRÉ.
ouvrant [uvrɑ̃]. 1. a. (a) Opening (panel, etc.).
(b) A: **A jour ouvrant,** at break of day. **A audience ouvrante,** at the opening of the session.
2. s.m. Leaf (of door, shutter).
ouvre-boîtes, s.m.inv. Tin-opener.
ouvre-gants, s.m.inv. Glove-stretcher.
ouvre-huîtres, s.m.inv. Oyster-knife.
ouvre-lettres, s.m.inv. Letter-opener.
ouvrer [uvre], v.tr. (a) To work (up) (wood,
metal). **Facile à o.,** tractable (material). (b) To
diaper (linen, cloth). (c) A: Ne pas o. le dimanche,
not to work on Sundays.
  ouvré, a. (a) Worked (timber); wrought
(iron). (b) Linge ouvré, diaper.
ouvreur, -euse [uvrœːr, -øːz], s. Opener.
Th: **Ouvreuse (de loges),** box-opener.
ouvrier, -ère [uvrie, -ɛːr]. 1. s. (a) Worker;
workman, workwoman; working man, craftsman,
mechanic, operative. O. de ferme, farm-labourer.
O. à la journée, journeyman, day-labourer. O. de
fabrique, mill-hand. (b) **Ouvrière,** (i) sempstress,
seamstress; (ii) factory-girl. **Première ouvrière,**
forewoman. (c) Il a été l'o. de sa fortune, he is a
self-made man. 2. a. (a) Les classes ouvrières, the
working classes. L'agitation ouvrière, labour
unrest. Le parti o., the labour party. Train o.,
workmen's train. **Association ouvrière,** co-
operative society. (b) Abeille ouvrière, worker
bee. S.a. CHEVILLE I.

ouvrir [uvri:r], *v.* (*pr.p.* ouvrant; *p.p.* ouvert; *pr.ind.* j'ouvre, n. ouvrons; *pr.sub.* j'ouvre; *imp.* ouvre, ouvrez; *p.h.* j'ouvris; *fu.* j'ouvrirai) **I.** *v.tr.* To open. (*a*) O. *les portes toutes grandes à qn,* to open the doors wide for s.o. O. *sa maison à qn,* to throw open one's house to s.o. O. *la porte aux abus,* to open the door to abuses. O. *un robinet, le gaz,* to turn on a tap, the gas. *El:* **Ouvrir le circuit,** to break, switch off, the current. O. *les rideaux,* to draw back the curtains. O. *le lit,* to turn down the bedclothes. **Ouvrir à qn,** to answer the door to s.o.; to let s.o. in. (*b*) **Ouvrir son cœur à qn,** to open one's heart, to unbosom oneself, to s.o. (*c*) To cut through, open up (wall, canal, mine); to cut (sth.) open. *S'o. un chemin à travers la foule,* to cut, push, one's way through the crowd. *Surg:* O. *un abcès,* to open, to lance, an abscess. (*d*) To begin; to set a-going. O. *un débat,* to open, start, a debate. O. *le bal,* to open the ball. O. *une liste,* to head a list. O. *une parenthèse,* (i) to open, begin, a parenthesis; (ii) to embark on a digression. O. *une école, une boutique,* to start a school, a shop. **Ouvrir boutique,** to set up shop. O. *la marche,* to lead the way. *Com:* O. *un compte chez qn,* to open an account with s.o. **2.** *v.i.* (*a*) *La scène ouvre par un chœur,* the scene opens with a chorus. (*b*) *Le salon ouvrait sur le jardin,* the drawing-room opened on (to), into, the garden. (*c*) *Les boutiques n'ouvrent pas les jours de fête,* the shops do not open on holidays.

s'ouvrir, to open. (*a*) *La porte s'ouvrit en coup de vent,* the door flew open. *Le bal s'ouvrit par une valse,* the ball opened, began, started, with a waltz. (*b*) (Of pers.) To become expansive; to open one's heart. **S'ouvrir à qn,** to talk freely, to unbosom, unburden, oneself, to s.o.

ouvert, a. Open. (*a*) *Porte grande ouverte,* wide-open door. *Plaie ouverte,* gaping wound. **Accueillir qn à bras ouverts,** to receive s.o. with open arms. **Faire qch. les yeux ouverts,** to do sth. with one's eyes open. *Fleur ouverte,* flower in bloom. *Fb:* **Jeu ouvert,** loose game. S.a. LIVRE². (*b*) **Ville ouverte,** open, unfortified, town. (*c*) *Bureaux ouverts de 10 heures à 5 heures,* offices open from 10 to 5. **Ouvert la nuit,** open all night. (*d*) *Caractère o.,* frank, open, nature. *Guerre ouverte,* open war(fare), open hostilities. S.a. CŒUR 2.

ouvroir [uvrwa:r], *s.m.* (*a*) Workroom (in convent). (*b*) (Charity) needlework school (for indigent young women). [OUVRER]

ovaire [ɔvɛ:r], *s.m. Anat: Bot:* Ovary.
ovale [ɔval]. **I.** *a.* Oval, egg-shaped. **2.** *s.m.* Oval.
ovalisation [ɔvalizasjɔ̃], *s.f. Mec.E:* Ovalization, wearing out of round (of cylinders).
ovaliser [ɔvalize], *v.tr.* To make oval; to ovalize; to wear out of round.
ovation [ɔvasjɔ̃], *s.f.* Ovation. **Faire une ovation à qn,** to give s.o. an ovation; to acclaim s.o.
ové [ɔve], *a.* Egg-shaped, ovate (fruit, etc.).
ovibos [ɔvibos], *s.m. Z:* Ovibos, musk-ox.
oviforme [ɔvifɔrm], *a.* Oviform, egg-shaped.
ovin [ɔvɛ̃]. *Husb:* **I.** *a.* **Race ovine,** ovine race. **2.** *s.m.pl.* **Ovins,** sheep.
ovipare [ɔvipa:r], *a. Z:* Oviparous.
ovoïde [ɔvɔid], *a.* Ovoid, egg-shaped.
ovule [ɔvyl], *s.m. Biol:* Ovule.
oxalate [ɔksalat], *s.m. Ch:* Oxalate.
oxalique [ɔksalik], *a. Ch:* Oxalic (acid).
oxhydrique [ɔksidrik], *a. Ch:* Oxyhydrogen, oxyhydric (blow-pipe, etc.). **Lumière oxhydrique,** lime-light.
oxyacétylénique [ɔksiasetilenik], *a.* Oxyacetylene (welding).
oxydable [ɔksidabl], *a.* (*a*) *Ch:* Oxidizable. (*b*) Liable to rust.
oxydant [ɔksidɑ̃], *s.m.* Oxidizer.
oxydation [ɔksidasjɔ̃], *s.f. Ch:* Oxidizing, oxidation.
oxyde [ɔksid], *s.m. Ch:* Oxide.
oxyder [ɔkside], *v.tr. Ch:* To oxidize.
s'oxyder, (i) to become oxidized; (ii) to rust.
oxygène [ɔksiʒɛn], *s.m. Ch:* Oxygen.
oxygéner [ɔksiʒene], *v.tr.* (il oxygène; il oxygénera) To oxygenate. **Eau oxygénée,** peroxide of hydrogen.
oxylithe [ɔksilit], *s.f.* Oxylith (for respiratory apparatus).
oxyton [ɔksitɔ̃], *a. Gr.Gram:* Oxytone (word).
oxyure [ɔksiy:r], *s.f. Med:* Oxyuris. O. *vermiculaire,* pin-worm.
oyant [wajɑ̃]. *A:* **I.** *a.* Hearing, listening. (*Cf.* OUÏR.) **2.** *s.m. Jur:* Auditor.
oyez [waje], *int. A: Adm: Jur:* Oyez ! oyes !
ozokérite [ɔzɔkerit], *s.f.,* occ. **ozocérite** [ɔzɔserit], *s.f. Miner:* Ozocerite, ozokerite; mineral wax; fossil wax.
ozone [ɔzɔn, -o:n], *s.m. Ch:* Ozone.
ozonisation [ɔzɔnizasjɔ̃], *s.f.* Ozonization.
ozoniser [ɔzɔnize], *v.tr.* To ozonize.
ozoniseur [ɔzɔnizœ:r], *s.m.* Ozonizer; ozone apparatus.

P

P, p [pe], *s.m.* (The letter) P, p.
pacage [paka:ʒ], *s.m.* **I.** Pasture(-land), pasturage. **2.** Pasturing, grazing. *Jur:* **Droit(s) de pacage,** common of pasture.
pacager [pakaʒe], *v.tr.* (je pacageai(s); n. pacageons) To pasture, graze (beasts or field).
pacane [pakan], *s.f. Bot:* Pecan-nut.
pacha [paʃa], *s.m.* Pasha, pacha.
pachyderme [paʃidɛrm, paki-]. *Z:* **I.** *a.* Pachydermatous, thick-skinned. **2.** *s.m.* Pachyderm.
pacificateur, -trice [pasifikatœ:r, -tris]. **I.** *a.* Pacifying; peace-making; pacificatory. **2.** *s.* Pacifier; peacemaker.
pacification [pasifikasjɔ̃], *s.f.* Pacification.

pacifier [pasifje], *v.tr.* To pacify (country); to appease, to calm.
se pacifier, to calm down.
pacifique [pasifik], *a.* (*a*) Pacific, peaceable. (*b*) Peaceful, quiet (reign, etc.). (*c*) **L'Océan Pacifique,** the Pacific Ocean.
pacifiquement [pasifikmɑ̃], *adv.* Peaceably, quietly, pacifically.
pacifisme [pasifism], *s.m. Pol:* Pacifism.
pacifiste [pasifist], *s.m. & f. Pol:* Pacifist.
pack [pak], *s.m.* **I.** (Ice-)pack (of the polar seas). **2.** *Fb:* Pack.
pacotille [pakɔti:j], *s.f.* (*a*) *A:* Goods taken on board by seamen or passengers for private sale.

(b) Marchandises de pacotille, shoddy goods, trumpery stuff. *Meubles, maison, de p.*, gimcrack furniture, jerry-built house.

pacte [pakt], *s.m.* Compact, pact, agreement; covenant. *P. à quatre*, four-power pact. **Pacte de famille**, family settlement. *Com:* **Pacte social**, articles of association.

pactiser [paktize], *v.i.* *P. avec l'ennemi*, to enter into a compact, to treat, with the enemy. *P. avec sa conscience*, to compound, to compromise, with one's conscience.

paf [paf]. **I.** *int.* *F:* Slap! bang! **2.** *a.inv.* *P:* Être paf, to be tipsy, screwed.

pagaie [page], *s.f.* Paddle (for canoe).

pagaïe [paga:j], *s.f.*, **pagaille** [paga:j], *s.f.* Esp. *Nau:* Disorder, hurry; clutter (of objects). **Faire de la pagaïe** (*en manœuvrant*), to be all at sixes and sevens. **En pagaille**, in disorder; at random. *Tout ramasser en p.*, to bundle everything up. *Tout était en p.*, everything was higgledy-piggledy.

paganisme [paganism], *s.m.* Paganism. **I.** Heathenism. **2.** Heathendom.

pagayer [pageje], *v.* (*je pagaie, je pagaye*) **I.** *v.i.* To paddle; to ply a paddle. **2.** *v.tr.* To paddle (canoe). *s.* **-eur, -euse.**

page¹ [pa:ʒ], *s.f.* Page (of book, etc.). *F:* **Être à la page**, to be (i) up to date, (ii) in the know. *Ne pas être à la p.*, to be behind the times. *Typ:* **Mettre en pages**, to make up. **Mise en pages**, making up; page-setting.

page², *s.m.* Page(-boy). **Être hors de page**, to be out of pagehood; to be no longer a boy; to be one's own master.

pagination [paʒinasjɔ̃], *s.f.* Paging, pagination.

paginer [paʒine], *v.tr.* To page, paginate.

pagne [paɲ], *s.m.* Loin-cloth, pagne.

pagnot [paɲo], *s.m.* *P:* Bed.

pagnoter (se) [səpaɲote], *v.pr.* *P:* To go to bed.

pagode [pagɔd], *s.f.* (a) Pagoda ((i) temple, (ii) coin). (b) (Nodding toy) mandarin. (c) **Manches pagodes**, pagoda sleeves.

paie [pɛ], *s.f.* = PAYE.

paiement [pɛmɑ̃], *s.m.* = PAYEMENT.

païen, -ienne [pajɛ̃, -jɛn], *a. & s.* Pagan, heathen.

paillard, -arde [paja:r, -ard]. **I.** *a.* Ribald, lewd, lascivious. *Regard p.*, sensual leer. *Chanson paillarde*, ribald song, bawdy song. **2.** (a) *s.m.* Dissolute rake; debauchee. (b) *s.f.* **Paillarde**, wanton. [PAILLE]

paillarder [pajarde], *v.i.* To live in debauch.

paillardise [pajardi:z], *s.f.* **I.** Lewdness. **2.** Ribald joke.

paillasse [pajas]. **I.** *s.f.* (a) Straw mattress, palliasse, pallet. (b) (Laboratory-)bench. **2.** *s.m.* (a) Clown, buffoon. *Tours de p.*, clowneries. (b) *F:* (Political) mountebank.

paillasserie [pajasri], *s.f.* Clownery.

paillasson [pajasɔ̃], *s.m.* Mat; door-mat.

paille [pɑ:j], *s.f.* **I.** Straw. (a) *Botte de p.*, truss of straw. *P. de litière*, loose straw. **Paille de riz**, **d'Italie**, rice straw. *Chapeau de p. d'Italie*, Leghorn (straw) hat. *Chaise de p.*, straw-bottomed chair. *F:* **Homme de paille**, man of straw; dummy. *Feu de paille*, flash in the pan. **Être sur la paille**, to be reduced to beggary. **Voir la paille dans l'œil du prochain**, to see the mote in one's brother's eye. **Tirer à la courte paille**, to draw lots; to draw straws. (b) *a.inv.* Straw-coloured. (c) *Cu:* **Pailles au parmesan**, cheese straws. **2.** **Menue paille**, **paille d'avoine**, chaff. **3.** **Paille de fer**, iron shavings (for scrubbing floors). **4.** Flaw (in gem, etc.).

pailler¹ [paje], *s.m.* (a) Farm-yard, straw-yard. (b) Straw-stack. (c) Dunghill. *F:* **Être sur son pailler**, to be on one's own dunghill.

pailler², *v.tr.* **I.** *Hort:* To protect with straw; to mulch. **2.** **Chaise paillée**, rush-, straw-bottomed chair. *s.m.* **-age.**

paillet [pajɛ], *s.m.* *Nau:* Mat. *P. d'abordage*, collision-mat. [PAILLE]

pailleter [pajte], *v.tr.* (je paillette; je pailletterai) To spangle.

pailleté, *a.* Spangled (*de*, with); pailletted.

paillette [pajɛt], *s.f.* **I.** Spangle, paillette. *F:* *P. d'esprit*, flash, spark, of wit. **2.** (a) Grain of gold-dust (in stream). (b) Flake (of mica, etc.). **3.** Flaw (in gem).

pailleux, -euse [pajø, -ø:z], *a.* **I.** Strawy (manure). **2.** Flawy (iron, glass).

paillis [pɑji], *s.m.* *Hort:* Mulch.

paillon [pajɔ̃], *s.m.* **I.** (Large) spangle. **2.** (Jeweller's) foil. **3.** Wisp of straw. **4.** Straw-case (for bottle).

paîment [pɛmɑ̃], *s.m.* = PAYEMENT.

pain [pɛ̃], *s.m.* **I.** Bread. *P. de seigle*, rye bread. *P. frais, p. rassis*, new bread, stale bread. *P. de ménage*, household bread. *P. grillé*, toast. **Pain d'épice**, gingerbread. *F:* **Acheter qch. pour une bouchée de pain**, to buy sth. for a mere song. **Il ne vaut pas le pain qu'il mange**, he is not worth his salt. **Manger son pain blanc le premier**, to begin with the cake. *S.a.* BÉNIT, PLANCHE I, SEC I. **Gagner son pain**, to earn one's bread, one's living. **Nul pain sans peine**, no reward without toil. **2.** Loaf. (a) *P. de quatre livres*, quartern loaf. **Petit pain**, (French) roll. *F:* *Ça se vend comme des petits pains*, it's selling like hot cakes. (b) **Pain de sucre**, sugar-loaf. *P. de savon*, *de cire*, cake of soap, of wax. **3.** **Pain à cacheter**, (sealing) wafer. *Ecc:* **Pain à chanter**, unconsecrated wafer. **4.** *P:* **Flanquer un pain à qn**, to give s.o. a blow, a punch, a biff.

pair [pɛ:r]. **I.** *a.* (a) Equal. **Hors de pair**, unrivalled, peerless. **De pair** (**avec**), on a par, on an equal footing (with). **Marcher de pair avec qn**, (i) to keep pace with s.o.; (ii) to emulate s.o. *Cela va de p. avec . . .*, it is on a par with. . . . (b) *Ar:* **Nombres pairs**, even numbers. *P. et impair*, odd and even. *Rail:* **Voie paire**, up line. **2.** *s.m.* (a) Equal, peer. **Traiter qn de pair à compagnon**, to treat s.o. as an equal. (b) *Les pairs du royaume*, the peers of the realm. (In Engl.) **La Chambre des Pairs**, the House of Lords. (c) (Of bird) Mate. **3.** *s.m.* (State of) equality; par. (a) *Fin:* **Pair du change**, par of exchange. *Au-dessous, au-dessus, du p.*, below par, above par. (b) **Institutrice au pair**, governess on mutual terms, with board and lodging but no salary; **governess au pair**.

paire [pɛ:r], *s.f.* Pair (of stockings, etc.); brace (of birds, of pistols). **Ces tableaux font la paire**, these pictures are a match.

pairesse [pɛrɛs], *s.f.* Peeress.

pairie [pɛri], *s.f.* Peerage.

paisible [pɛzibl], *a.* Peaceful, peaceable, quiet; untroubled. *adv.* **-ment.**

paître [pɛ:tr], *v.* (*pr.p.* paissant; *pr.ind.* je pais, il pait, n. paissons; *pr.sub.* je paisse; *fu.* je paîtrai; no *p.h.*; the *p.p.* pu is used only in the phr. shown under 2) **I.** *v.tr.* (a) To graze (cattle). (b) (Of animals) To feed upon (mast, etc.); to crop (grass). **2.** *v.i.* (Of animals) To feed; to graze, browse; to pasture. **Faucon qui a pu**, hawk that has fed. *F:* **Je l'ai envoyé paître**, I sent him packing. **Allez paître!** go to Jericho!

paix [pɛ], *s.f.* Peace. (a) **Faire la paix**, to make

peace. *Rester en p. avec un pays*, to remain at peace with a country. *En temps de p.*, in time(s) of peace. (*b*) *Observer, troubler, la paix*, to keep, to break, the peace. **Homme de paix**, man of peace. *S.a.* JUGE. (*c*) *La p. du tombeau*, the peacefulness of the grave. *P. à ses cendres!* peace to his ashes! **Vivre en paix**, to live in peace and quietness. **Laissez-moi en paix**, leave me alone. **Ne donner ni paix ni trêve à qn**, to give s.o. no peace. *P:* **Fiche-moi la paix!** don't bother me! shut up! **Paix!** hush! be quiet! *Sch:* cave!

pal [pal], *s.m.* **1.** Pale, stake. **Le supplice du pal**, impalement. **2.** *Her:* Pale. *pl.* Des pals, des paux.

palabre [palɑːbr], *s.f.* Palaver.

palabrer [palabre], *v.i.* To palaver.

palace [palas], *s.m.* Sumptuous hotel or cinema.

paladin [paladɛ̃], *s.m.* Paladin ; knight-errant.

palais[1] [palɛ], *s.m.* **1.** Palace (of king, etc.). **Le Palais Bourbon**, the Chamber of Deputies. **2. Palais de Justice**, law-courts. **Gens du palais**, lawyers. **Terme de palais**, law-term.

palais[2], *s.m.* Palate. (*a*) Roof of the mouth ; hard palate. **Voile du palais**, soft palate. (*b*) (Sense of) taste. **Avoir le palais fin**, to have a delicate palate.

palan [palɑ̃], *s.m.* Pulley-block, (purchase-)tackle.

palanche [palɑ̃ːʃ], *s.f.* Yoke, shoulder-piece (for carrying buckets).

palanque [palɑ̃ːk], *s.f.* Timber stockade.

palanquer [palɑ̃ke], *v.tr.* To stockade.

palanquin [palɑ̃kɛ̃], *s.m.* Palankeen, palanquin.

palastre [palastr], *s.m.* (*a*) Lock-plate (of lock). (*b*) Box (of lock). **Serrure à palastre**, rim-lock.

palatal, -aux [palatal, -o], *a.* Palatal. *s.f.* **Palatale**, palatal ; front consonant. *Voyelle palatale*, front vowel.

palatin, -ine [palatɛ̃, -in]. **1.** *a. & s. Hist:* Palatine. **Comte palatin**, Count Palatine. **2.** *a.* **Le Mont Palatin**, the Palatine Hill (in Rome). **3.** *s.f. Cost:* **Palatine**, palatine ; fur tippet. **Le Palatinat (le)** [ləpalatina]. *Pr.n. Hist:* The Palatinate.

pale[1] [pal], *s.f.* **1.** Stake, pale, paling (used for fences, etc.). **2.** Blade (of oar, propeller) ; vane (of fan, etc.). **Hélice à quatre pales**, four-bladed screw. **3.** Sluice(-gate).

pale[2], *s.f. Ecc:* Pall(a), chalice-cover.

pâle [pɑːl], *a.* Pale. *Lit:* Pallid. *A face p.*, pale-faced. **Pâle comme un linge, comme un mort, comme la mort**, as white as a sheet, as death ; deadly pale. *Un sourire p.*, a wan, bleak, smile. *adv.* **-ment**.

palefrenier [palfrənje], *s.m.* Groom, stableman, ostler.

palefroi [palfrwa], *s.m. A:* Palfrey.

paléographe [paleɔgraf], *s.m.* Pal(a)eographer.

paléographie [paleɔgrafi], *s.f.* Pal(a)eography.

paléolithique [paleɔlitik], *a.* Pal(a)eolithic.

paléontologie [paleɔ̃tɔlɔʒi], *s.f.* Pal(a)eontology.

paleron [palrɔ̃], *s.m.* Shoulder-blade, blade-bone (of horse, ox).

palet [palɛ], *s.m. Games:* **1.** Quoit. **Jouer aux palets**, to play at quoits. **2.** Metal disc used for playing at TONNEAU *q.v.*

paletot [palto], *s.m.* **1.** Overcoat, greatcoat. **2.** Coat.

palette [palɛt], *s.f.* **1.** (*a*) (Wooden) battledore ; (table-tennis) bat. **2.** (*a*) Blade (of oar) ; paddle, float-board (of paddle-wheel) ; dasher (of churn). **Roue à palettes**, paddle-wheel. (*b*) Vane (of rotary pump, etc.). **3.** (Painter's) palette. *Art:* **Faire, charger, sa palette**, to set the palette.

palétuvier [paletyvje], *s.m. Bot:* Mangrove.

pâleur [pɑlœːr], *s.f.* Pallor, pallidness, paleness.

pâlichon, -onne [pɑliʃɔ̃, -ɔn], *a. F:* Palish.

palier [palje], *s.m.* **1.** (*a*) *Arch:* Landing (of stairs) ; stair-head. *P. de repos*, demi-palier, half-landing. (*b*) Stage, degree. *Taxes imposées par paliers*, graduated taxation. **2.** (*a*) *Aut: Civ.E:* Level run, level stretch. **Vitesse en palier**, speed on the level, on the flat. (*b*) *Av:* Horizontal flight. **3.** *Mec.E:* (*a*) Pillow-block (bearing) ; plummer-block. *P. à billes*, ball-bearing. (*b*) Pedestal. *S.a.* BUTÉE I.

palière [paljɛːr], *a.f.* **Porte palière**, landing door. **Marche palière**, *s.f.* **palière**, top step.

palikare [palikaːr], *s.m. Gr.Hist:* Palikar.

palimpseste [palɛ̃psɛst], *a. & s.m.* Palimpsest.

palindrome [palɛ̃drɔm], *s.m.* Palindrome.

palinodie [palinɔdi], *s.f.* Recantation, retraction. **Chanter la palinodie**, to recant.

pâl|ir [pɑliːr]. **1.** *v.i.* To become pale, grow pale ; (of light, star) to grow dim, to pale ; (of colour) to fade. *F:* **Son étoile pâlit**, his star is on the wane. **Faire pâlir les mérites de qn**, to throw s.o.'s merits into the shade. **2.** *v.tr.* To make (s.o., sth.) pale ; to bleach (colours). *s.m.* **-issement**.

pâli, *a.* Wan, blanched (face, etc.).

palis [pali], *s.m.* Paling. **1.** (*a*) Picket-fence. (*b*) Enclosure (within picket-fence). **2.** *F:* Pale, stake, picket.

palissade [palisad], *s.f.* (*a*) Palisade, fence, paling. (*b*) Stockade. (*c*) (Street) hoarding.

palissad|er [palisade], *v.tr.* (*a*) To palisade ; to fence in, rail in ; to enclose. (*b*) To stockade. *s.m.* **-ement**.

palissandre [palisɑ̃ːdr], *s.m.* Brazilian rosewood.

palliatif, -ive [palljatif, -iːv], *a. & s.m.* Palliative.

palliation [palljasjɔ̃], *s.f.* Palliation.

pallier [palje], *v.tr.* To palliate.

palmarès [palmarɛːs], *s.m. Sch:* Prize-list, honours list.

palme [palm], *s.f.* **1.** *A:* (= PALMIER) Palm (-tree). *Huile, vin, de p.*, palm-oil, -wine. **2.** Palm (-branch). **Remporter la palme**, to bear the palm. **Décerner la palme à qn**, to assign the palm to s.o. *P. du martyre*, crown of martyrdom. **Recevoir les palmes (académiques)**, to be decorated by the Ministry of Public Instruction.

palmé [palme], *a.* **1.** Palmate (leaf). **2.** Web-footed. **Pied palmé**, webbed foot.

palmeraie [palmərɛ], *s.f.* Palm-grove.

palmette [palmɛt], *s.f.* **1.** *Bot:* Dwarf fan-palm. **2.** Palm-leaf (moulding) ; palmette.

palmier [palmje], *s.m.* Palm-tree. **Huile, beurre, de palmier**, palm-oil, -butter.

palmipède [palmipɛd], *a. & s.m.* Palmiped.

palmiste [palmist], *a. & s.m.* (Chou) palmiste, (i) cabbage-palm, cabbage-tree, palmetto ; (ii) palm-cabbage.

palombe [palɔ̃ːb], *s.f.* Ring-dove, wood-pigeon.

palonnier [palɔnje], *s.m.* (*a*) *Veh:* Swingle-bar, whipple-tree. (*b*) *Av:* Rudder-bar, swing-bar. (*c*) *Mec.E:* Compensation bar, rocking lever.

pâlot, -otte [pɑlo, -ɔt], *a. F:* Palish (child) ; peaky (look).

palourde [palurd], *s.f. Moll:* Clam.

palpa|ble [palpabl], *a.* Palpable. **1.** Tangible. **2.** Obvious, plain (truth) ; palpable (error). *s.f.* **-bilité**. *adv.* **-blement**.

palpe [palp], *s.f.* Palpus, palp, feeler (of insect) ; barbel (of fish).

palper [palpe], *v.tr.* To feel ; to examine (sth.) by feeling ; *Med:* to palpate. *F:* **Palper (de l'argent)**, to receive money, one's pay.

se palper. *P:* **Tu peux te palper!** don't you wish you may get it!

palpitant [palpitɑ̃], a. Palpitating, throbbing, quivering. *Roman p. d'intérêt*, thrilling novel.

palpitation [palpitasjɔ̃], s.f. Palpitation. *Être sujet à des palpitations*, to be subject to palpitation.

palpiter [palpite], v.i. To palpitate. (a) (Of pulse, eyelid) To flutter; (of limb) to quiver. (b) (Of heart) To throb; F: to go pit-a-pat. (c) To thrill (with pleasure, fear).

palsambleu [palsɑ̃blø], int. A: (Softened form of *Par le sang de Dieu*) 'Od's blood !

paltoquet [paltɔkɛ], s.m. F: Whipper-snapper; mere nobody.

paludéen, -enne [palydeɛ̃, -ɛn], a. Paludal. (a) *Plante paludéenne*, marsh plant. (b) **Fièvre paludéenne**, malaria; swamp-fever; ague.

paludisme [palydism], s.m. Med: (Im)paludism, malaria.

palustre [palystr], a. Paludous (plant, etc.); swampy (ground).

pâmer [pɑme], v.i. & pr. To swoon; to faint (away). F: (Se) **pâmer de rire**, to die with laughter. *Se p. d'admiration*, to be in raptures (*sur*, over). **Se pâmer de joie, d'aise**, to be over-joyed, delighted.
   pâmé, a. In a swoon. **Tomber pâmé**, to swoon, to faint away. S.a. CARPE.

pâmoison [pɑmwazɔ̃], s.f. Swoon; fainting fit. *Tomber en pâmoison*, to swoon; to faint away.

pampas [pɑ̃pɑ(s)], s.f.pl. Pampas (of S. America). *Herbe des pampas*, pampas-grass.

pamphlet [pɑ̃flɛ], s.m. (Usu. scurrilous) pamph-let; lampoon.

pamphlétaire [pɑ̃fletɛːr], s.m. Pamphleteer, lampooner.

pamplemousse [pɑ̃pləmus], s.m. or f. (a) Bot: Shaddock. (b) Grape-fruit.

pampre [pɑ̃ːpr], s.m. **1.** Vine-branch (with leaves). **2.** Arch: Art: Pampre.

pan¹ [pɑ̃], s.m. **1.** Skirt, flap (of garment); free end (of tie). *Saisir qn par le pan de son habit*, to catch hold of s.o. by the coat-tails. **2.** Section, piece, surface. *Pan de mur*, bare wall, piece of wall. *Pan de bois*, timber framing, wooden parti-tion. F: *Pan de ciel*, bit, patch, of sky. **3.** Face, side (of building, etc.). *Tour à huit pans*, octa-gonal tower. *Écrou à six pans*, hexagonal nut. **A pans coupés**, with the corners off.

Pan². Pr.n.m. Myth: Pan. **Flûte de Pan**, Pan's pipe.

pan³, int. **1.** Bang ! bif(f) ! **2.** *Un pan pan à la porte*, a rat-tat at the door.

panacée [panase], s.f. Panacea.

panache [panaʃ], s.m. **1.** (a) Plume, tuft (of waving feathers). F: *Avoir son panache*, to be tipsy, slightly elevated. *P. de fumée*, wreath of smoke. (b) F: **Faire panache**, (of rider) to be pitched over the horse's head, F: to take a header; (of cyclist) to be pitched over the handle-bars; (of motor car, aeroplane) to turn over, to capsize. (c) F: *Il a du panache*, he has an air about him. **2.** Arch: Panache (of penden-tive). **3.** Hort: Stripe, variegation.

panach|er [panaʃe], v.tr. **1.** To plume (helmet). **2.** Hort: To variegate (with different colours). s.m. **-age**.
   se panacher. 1. To put on plumes, fine feathers. **2.** (Of flowers) To become variegated.
   panaché, a. **1.** Plumed (helmet, bird). **2.** Parti-coloured, variegated (bird, flower). *Foule panachée*, motley crowd. *Salade panachée*, mixed salad. *Glace panachée*, mixed ice.

panade [panad], s.f. Bread and butter boiled to a pulp; panada. P: **Être dans la panade**, (i) to be in the soup, in a fix; (ii) to be in want.

panais [panɛ], s.m. Parsnip.

Panam(e) [panam]. Pr.n.m. P: Paris.

Panama [panama]. **1.** Pr.n.m. Panama. **Bois de Panama**, quillai(a) bark. **2.** s.m. Panama hat; fine-straw hat.

panard [panaːr], a. inv. in f. (Of horse) With out-turned feet; knock-kneed; cow-hocked.

panaris [panari], s.m. Med: Whitlow.

panca [pɔ̃ka], s.m. Punkah. **Tireur de panca**, punkah-boy, punkah-wallah.

pancarte [pɑ̃kart], s.f. **1.** Placard, bill; (show-) card. **2.** Jacket (for documents, etc.).

panchromatique [pɑ̃krɔmatik], a. Phot: Pan-chromatic (plate).

pancréas [pɑ̃kreɑːs], s.m. Anat: Pancreas.

pancréatique [pɑ̃kreatik], a. Pancreatic (juice).

pandit [pɑ̃di], s.m. Pundit.

Pandore¹ [pɑ̃dɔːr]. Pr.n.f. Gr.Myth: Pandora. *Le coffret de Pandore*, Pandora's box.

pandore², s.m. P: = GENDARME. (From the hero of the popular song by Nadaud.)

panégyrique [paneʒirik]. **1.** s.m. Panegyric, encomium. **2.** a. Panegyric(al).

panégyriste [paneʒirist], s.m. Panegyrist.

paner [pane], v.tr. **1.** To cover (meat, fish) with bread-crumbs; to fry (chop, etc.) in bread-crumbs. **2.** **Eau panée**, toast-water.

panerée [panre], s.f. Basketful.

paneterie [pantri], s.f. (a) Bread-pantry. (b) Bread-store (in barracks, school).

panetier [pantje], s.m. B: Nau: Baker.

panetière [pantjɛːr], s.f. **1.** (Shepherd's) scrip. **2.** Sideboard, dresser.

pangermanisme [pɑ̃ʒermanism], s.m. Pan-Germanism.

panic [panik], s.m. Panic-grass; millet.

panicule [panikyl], s.f. Bot: Panicle.

panier [panje], s.m. **1.** Basket. *Gros p.*, hamper. *P. à papier*, waste-paper basket. *P. à ouvrage*, work-basket. *P. à provisions*, (i) shopping-basket; (ii) luncheon-basket. *Rail:* **Panier-repas**, luncheon-basket (containing a cold lunch). **Panier à salade**, (i) (wire) salad washer; (ii) P: prison van, Black Maria. F: **C'est un panier percé**, he is a spendthrift. S.a. ANSE 1. *P. de fruits*, basket(ful) of fruit. **2.** (Wicker) governess-cart; pony-carriage. **3.** A.Cost: Pannier; hoop-petticoat. **4.** Beehive.

panifiable [panifjabl], a. **Céréales panifiables**, bread-stuffs; bread crops.

paniquard [panikaːr], s.m. F: Scare-monger.

panique [panik]. **1.** a. Panic (terror). **2.** s.f. Panic, scare; stampede. *Pris de p.*, panic-stricken. *Sujet à la panique*, F: panicky. *Semeur de panique*, panic-monger, scare-monger.

panne¹ [pan], s.f. **1.** (a) Tex: Panne, plush. (b) (Hog's) fat; lard. (c) *P. de nuages*, bank of clouds. (d) A: Rag(s). F: **Tomber dans la panne**, to fall into poverty; to come on hard times. **2.** Th: Small part, insignificant part.

panne², s.f. **1.** Nau: **En panne**, hove to. **En panne sèche**, hove to under bare poles. **(Se) mettre en panne, prendre la panne**, to heave to, to bring to. **2.** Breakdown, mishap; hold-up (on the Underground); failure (of electric light). *P. de la machine, du moteur*, engine trouble, engine failure. *I.C.E: P. d'allumage*, ignition trouble. **Panne sèche**, failure of engine through shortage of petrol. **Avoir une panne, rester en panne**, to break down, to have engine trouble. *Rester en p. devant une difficulté*, to stick at a difficulty. F: **Laisser qn en panne**, to leave s.o. in the lurch.

panne³, *s.f. Const:* (a) Purlin (of roof). (b) Pantile.

panne⁴, *s.f.* Pane, *U.S:* peen (of hammer). *P. fendue,* claw (of hammer).

panné [pane], *a. P:* Stony-broke ; penniless.

panneau [pano], *s.m.* **1.** Snare, net (for game). *F:* Tendre un panneau à qn, to set a snare for s.o. Tomber, donner, dans le panneau, to fall, walk, into the net, into the trap. **2.** Panel. *Porte à panneaux,* panelled door. *Diviser un mur en panneaux,* to panel a wall. *Aer:* Panneau de déchirure, ripping panel (of balloon). **3.** Board(s), *e.g.* sandwich-man's board. *P. à affiches,* advertisement hoarding. *Nau:* P. d'écoutille, hatch-cover. *Fermer le p.,* to close down the hatch. *L'entrée des panneaux,* the hatchway. *Condamner les panneaux,* to cover and secure the hatches. *Nous avons des marchandises dans trois panneaux,* we have cargo in three holds. *Navy:* Panneau de dragage, (mine-sweeping) kite. **4.** *Av:* Ground strip-signal. **5.** Glass frame (for seeds).

panneau-réclame, *s.m.* Advertisement hoarding. *pl. Des panneaux-réclame.*

panneauter [panote], *v.tr.* **1.** (a) To net, snare (game). (b) *Abs.* To poach. **2.** To panel.

panneauteur [panotœ:r], *s.m.* Poacher.

panneton [pantɔ̃], *s.m.* **1.** Web, bit (of key). **2.** *P. d'espagnolette,* window-catch.

panonceau [panõso], *s.m.* Escutcheon-sign (over office of *avoué, notaire*).

panoplie [panɔpli], *s.f.* **1.** (a) Panoply ; full suit of plate armour. (b) *Toys:* Soldier's outfit (for child). **2.** (Wall-)trophy.

panorama [panɔrama], *s.m.* Panorama.

panoramique [panɔramik], *a.* Panoramic.

pansage [pɑ̃sa:ʒ], *s.m.* Grooming (of horses). *Mil:* 'Stables.' *Effets de p.,* grooming kit.

panse [pɑ̃:s], *s.f.* **1.** (a) *F:* Belly. *Grosse p.,* paunch, pot-belly. (b) Paunch, first stomach (of ruminant). **2.** Belly, bulge of (bottle, vase).

pansement [pɑ̃smɑ̃], *s.m. Med:* **1.** (Action of) dressing (a wound). *Faire un p.,* to apply a dressing. *Mil:* Paquet de pansement, first-aid field-outfit. *Trousse de p.,* surgical dressing-case. **2.** Dressing. *Après l'application d'un premier p.,* after a first dressing has been applied.

panser [pɑ̃se], *v.tr.* **1.** To groom, rub down (horse). **2.** To dress (wound) ; to tend (wounded man).

panslavisme [pɑ̃slavism], *s.m.* Pan-slavism.

pansu [pɑ̃sy], *a. F:* Big-bellied, pot-bellied.

pantagruélique [pɑ̃tagryelik], *a.* Pantagruelic (repast, etc.).

Pantalon [pɑ̃talɔ̃]. **1.** *Pr.n.m.* Pantaloon (in Italian comedy). **2.** *s.m. Cost:* (a) (Pair of) trousers ; *P:* bags. *P. blanc, p. de coutil,* ducks. (b) (Woman's) drawers or knickers.

pantalonnade [pɑ̃talɔnad], *s.f.* (a) *Th.Hist:* Knock-about turn by Pantaloon and others ; pantaloonery. (b) *A:* Sham demonstration of joy, grief, etc. ; piece of humbug.

pantelant [pɑ̃tlɑ̃], *a.* (a) Panting. (b) *Corps encore pantelants,* bodies still quivering, still warm.

panteler [pɑ̃tle], *v.i.* (il pantelle) To pant.

pantène, pantenne [pɑ̃ten], *s.f.* **1.** Draw-net. **2.** Wicker tray. **3.** En pantenne. (a) (Of ships, convoy) In disorder. (b) *Vergues en p.,* yards apeak (as sign of mourning).

panthéisme [pɑ̃teism], *s.m.* Pantheism.

panthéiste [pɑ̃teist]. **1.** *a.* Pantheistic(al). **2.** *s.* Pantheist.

panthéon [pɑ̃teɔ̃], *s.m.* Pantheon.

panthère [pɑ̃te:r], *s.f. Z:* Panther.

pantin [pɑ̃tɛ̃], *s.m. Toys:* Jumping-jack. *F:* (Of man) Nonentity ; mere puppet. *P. politique,* political jumping-jack.

pantographe [pɑ̃tɔgraf], *s.m.* **1.** *Draw:* Pantograph. **2.** (Any) lazy-tongs device. Esp. *El.E:* Pantagraph (of trolley-bus).

pantois [pɑ̃twa], *a. F: A:* Amazed, nonplussed, flabbergasted.

pantomime¹ [pɑ̃tɔmim], *s.m. Th:* Pantomime (actor) ; dumb-show actor.

pantomime², *s.f.* (a) Dumb-show performance ; pantomime. (b) Dumb show ; significant play of features.

pantouflard [pɑ̃tufla:r], *s.m. F:* Man who loves his slippered ease ; stay-at-home.

pantoufle [pɑ̃tufl], *s.f.* **1.** Slipper. En pantoufles, (i) in one's slippers ; (ii) free and easy. *F:* Raisonner comme une pantoufle, to talk nonsense, to talk through one's hat. **2.** *Hyg:* Slipper bed-pan.

Pantruchard, -arde [pɑ̃tryʃa:r, -ard], *s. P:* Parisian.

Pantruche [pɑ̃tryʃ]. *Pr.n. P:* Paris.

panure [pany:r], *s.f. Cu:* Bread-crumbs.

Panurge [panyrʒ]. *Pr.n.m.* Panurge. (Character in *Pantagruel,* by Rabelais.) *F:* Ce sont les moutons de Panurge, they follow one another like sheep ; they are led like sheep.

paon [pɑ̃], *s.m.* **1.** Peacock. *F:* Pousser des cris de paon, to screech like a peacock. Se parer des plumes du paon, to strut in borrowed plumes. **2.** Peacock-butterfly.

paonne [pan], *s.f. Orn:* Peahen.

paonneau [pano], *s.m. Orn:* Pea-chick.

paonner [pane], *v.i. F:* To strut ; to preen oneself.

papa [papa], *s.m. F:* Papa, dad(dy). Bon papa, grandpapa, grand-dad. Faire qch. à la papa, to do sth. in a leisurely fashion. *Aut:* Aller à la papa, to potter along. S.a. FILS 1.

papal, -aux [papal, -o], *a.* Papal.

papauté [papote], *s.f.* Papacy.

pape [pap], *s.m. Ecc:* Pope.

papegai [papɡɛ], *s.m. A:* Popinjay.

papelard, -arde [papla:r, -ard]. **1.** *s.* Sanctimonious person. **2.** *a.* Sanctimonious, canting.

paperasse [papras], *s.f.* Usu. *pl.* (a) Official papers ; old archives. (b) Red tape. [PAPIER]

paperasser [paprase], *v.i.* **1.** To go through old papers. **2.** To be for ever scribbling.

paperasserie [paprasri], *s.f.* **1.** Accumulation of old papers. **2.** *F:* Red-tapism.

paperassier, -ière [paprasje, -jɛ:r], *a.* (a) Fond of scribbling, of accumulating notes. (b) Fond of red tape.

papesse [papɛs], *s.f.* La papesse Jeanne, Pope Joan.

papeterie [paptri], *s.f.* **1.** (a) Paper-making. (b) Paper-mill, paper-factory. (c) Paper trade. **2.** (a) Bookselling and stationery business. (b) Stationer's shop.

papetier, -ière [paptje, -jɛ:r], *s.* (a) Paper-maker, -manufacturer. (b) Stationer.

papier [papje], *s.m.* Paper. **1.** (a) *P. vergé,* laid paper. *P. de Chine, p. de riz,* rice-paper. *P. du Japon,* Japanese vellum. *P. à cigarettes,* cigarette paper. *P. de soie,* tissue-paper. *P. gris,* brown paper. *P. buvard,* blotting-paper. *P. couché,* surface-coated paper, art paper. *P. de verre,* glass-paper or sandpaper. S.a. PARCHEMIN 2, PELURE. (b) *P. pour écrire,* papier à lettres, note-paper. *P. deuil,* black-edged paper. *P. d'impression,* printing-paper. *P. de journal,* news-print. *P. calque*, tracing-paper. *P. à dessin*, drawing-paper. *P. d'emballage*, packing paper, wrapping paper. *P. à tapisser, p. tenture, p. peint*, wall-paper. *P. hygiénique en rouleau*, toilet-roll. *F:* **Figure de papier mâché**, mealy, washed-out, face. **2.** Document, paper. *(a) Papiers domestiques*, private papers, family papers. *Papiers d'une affaire*, documents relating to a case. **Être bien, mal, dans les papiers de qn**, to be in s.o.'s good, bad, books. *Vieux papiers*, waste paper. *(b) Com: Jur: P. timbré, p. libre*, stamped, unstamped, paper. *(c) Com:* Bill(s). *P. à longue échéance*, long-dated bill(s). *(d) pl. Adm:* Papers (passport, identification certificate, etc.). *Faire viser ses papiers*, to have one's papers viséd. *Papiers de bord*, ship's papers. **3. Papier d'étain, d'argent**, lead-foil, tinfoil.

papier-cuir, *s.m.* Leatherette.

papier-monnaie, *s.m.* Paper money, paper currency.

papilionacées [papiljɔnase], *s.f.pl. Bot:* Papilionaceae; pea-flowers.

papillaire [papillɛr], *a. Anat: etc:* Papillary.

papille [papiːj], *s.f. Anat: Bot:* Papilla.

papillon [papijɔ̃], *s.m.* **1.** Butterfly. **Papillon de nuit**, moth. *F:* **Papillons noirs**, dark, gloomy, thoughts. *Cost:* **Nœud papillon**, butterfly bow. **2.** *(a)* Inset (in book). *(b)* Leaflet. *(c)* Fly-bill (poster). *(d)* Inset map (in corner of large map). *(e)* Rider (to document). **3.** *Tchn: (a)* Butterfly-valve, throttle-valve. *Aut:* Disc-type throttle. *(b)* Thumb-screw; wing-nut. *(c)* Bat's-wing gas-burner.

papillonn|er [papijɔne], *v.i.* To flutter (about), to flit about (like a butterfly). *s.m.* **-age.**

papillote [papijɔt], *s.f.* **1.** Curl-paper; *P:* cracker. **Être en papillotes**, to have one's hair in curl-papers. **Fer à papillotes**, curling-tongs. **2.** Twist of paper; frill (round knuckle of ham). **3.** *Cu:* Buttered paper (for cooking chops, etc.).

papillotement [papijɔtmɑ̃], *s.m.* **1.** Dazzle. **2.** *Cin:* Flickering.

papillot|er [papijɔte]. **I.** *v.i. (a)* (Of eyes) To blink; *(of light)* to blink, twinkle. *Cin:* To flicker. *(b)* To dazzle; to glitter. *(c) Typ:* To mackle, slur. **2.** *v.tr.* To put (hair) into curl-papers. *s.m.* **-age.**

papiste [papist]. **I.** *s.m. & f.* Papist. **2.** *a. Pej:* Papistic(al); popish.

papotage [papotaːʒ], *s.m.* Idle talk; chatter.

papoter [papote], *v.i. F:* To gossip; to talk about nothings.

papule [papyl], *s.f.* Papula, papule; pimple; weal (of urticaria).

papyracé [papirase], *a.* Papyraceous, papery.

papyrus [papiryːs], *s.m.* Papyrus.

pâque [pɑːk]. **I.** *s.f.* (Jewish) Passover. **Manger la pâque**, to eat the Passover. **2.** *(a) s.m.* Usu. spelt **Pâques**, Easter. **A Pâque(s) prochain**, next Easter. *F:* **A Pâques ou à la Trinité**, to-morrow come never. *Bot:* **Fleur de Pâques**, pasque-flower. *(b)* **Pâques**, *s.f.pl.* **Faire ses pâques**, to take the Sacrament at Easter. **Pâques fleuries**, Palm Sunday. **Pâques closes**, Low Sunday.

paquebot [pakbo], *s.m.* (Steam-)packet; liner; (passenger and mail) steamer.

pâquerette [pɑkrɛt], *s.f. Bot:* Daisy.

paquet [pakɛ], *s.m.* **1.** Parcel, package, bundle, packet. *P. de livres*, parcel of books. *P. de cartes*, pack of cards. **Mettre des livres en paquet**, to parcel up books. *Typ: P. de composition*, parcel of type; 'take.' *F:* **Faire son paquet, ses paquets**, to pack up one's traps; to pack up. **Donner son paquet à qn**, to give s.o. the sack.

Paquet de sottises, pack of nonsense. **Quel paquet!** (i) what a frump! what a dowdy! (ii) what a clumsy lout! **2.** *Nau:* **Paquet de mer**, heavy sea, green sea.

paquetage [paktaːʒ], *s.m.* **1.** Parcelling; baling. **2.** (Soldier's) pack.

paqueter [pakte], *v.tr.* (je paquette; je paquetterai) To do (sth.) up into a parcel, into parcels; to parcel (sth.) up; to bale.

paqueteur [paktœr], *s.m.* Packer.

par [par], *prep.* **1.** *(a)* (Of place) *On y arrive par un escalier*, the place is reached by (means of) a stair. *Jeter qch., regarder, par la fenêtre*, to throw something, to look, out of the window. **Par mer et par terre**, by land and sea. **Par monts et par vaux**, over hill and dale. **Il court par les rues**, he runs about the streets. **Par tout le pays**, all over the country. *Par latitude* 10° *nord*, in latitude 10° north. **Venez par ici, allez par là**, come this way, go that way. *Par où a-t-il passé?* which way did he go? S.a. DERRIÈRE 2, DEVANT 2. *(b)* (Of time) *Par un jour d'hiver*, on a winter's day. *Par le froid qu'il fait*, in this cold weather. *Par temps de brume*, in foggy weather. *Par le passé*, in the past. *Je l'ai averti par trois fois*, I warned him three times. **2.** *(a)* (Agent) (i) (With a passive verb) *Il a été puni par son père*, he was punished by his father. *Accablé par l'inquiétude*, overcome by, with, anxiety. (ii) (With an active verb) **Faire qch. par soi-même**, to do sth. unaided. *Je l'ai appris par les Smith*, I heard of it through, from, the Smiths. *Faire faire qch. par qn*, to have sth. done by s.o. *(b)* (Means, instrument) *Réussir par l'intrigue*, to succeed through intrigue. *Attacher qch. par une chaîne*, to fasten sth. by means of, with, a chain. *Conduire qn par la main*, to lead s.o. by the hand. *Envoyer qch. par la poste*, to send sth. by post, through the post. *Dame remarquable par sa beauté*, lady remarkable for her beauty. *Appeler qn par son nom*, to call s.o. by his name. *(c)* (Redundant) *Vous êtes par trop aimable*, you are far too kind. *Examiner, juger, qch. par soi-même*, to examine, judge, sth. (for) oneself. **3.** (Cause, motive) *J'ai fait cela par amitié, par respect, pour vous*, I did it out of friendship, out of respect, for you. **Par pitié!** for pity's sake! *Faire qch. par pitié*, to do sth. out of pity. *Par hasard*, by chance. *Par bonheur*, by good fortune. **4.** (Distributive) *Par ordre alphabétique*, in alphabetical order. *Entrer deux par deux*, to come in two by two, by twos, in twos. *Trois fois par jour*, three times a day. *Mille francs par an*, a thousand francs a year, per annum. *Gagner tant par semaine*, to earn so much per week, so much a week. *On les a par douzaines*, they are to be had by the dozen. **5. Par** + *inf. Commencer, débuter, finir, achever, terminer, par faire qch.*, to begin, end, by doing sth. **6. Par-ci par-là**, (i) hither and thither; (ii) now and then. *C'est Charles par-ci, Charles par-là*, it's Charles here and Charles there. **De par le monde** *on trouverait . . .*, somewhere in the world one would find. . . . **De par le Roi**, by order of the King, in the name of the King. **De par la façon** *dont il s'y prend, on voit bien que . . .*, from his way of setting about it, one can see that. . . .

parabole [parabɔl], *s.f.* **1.** Parable. **Parler en, par, paraboles**, to speak in parables. **2.** *Geom:* Parabola.

parabolique [parabɔlik], *a.* Parabolic(al).

paracentrique [parasɑ̃trik], *a.* Paracentric.

parach|ever [paraʃve], *v.tr.* (Conj. like ACHEVER) To complete; to finish (sth.) off; to perfect. *s.m.* **-èvement.**

parachute [paraʃyt], *s.m.* **1.** *Aer:* Parachute. **2.** *P. de mine*, safety device (of pit-shaft cage).
parachutiste [paraʃytist], *s.m. & f.* Parachutist.
parade[1] [parad], *s.f.* **1.** *Mil:* Parade (for guard, etc.); guard-mounting. **Faire la parade,** to parade. **Marcher au pas de parade,** to march as if on parade. *Navy:* **Faire parade,** to dress ship. **2.** (i) Parade, show, ostentation; (ii) pomp and circumstance. **Faire parade de ses bijoux,** to display, show off, one's jewels. **Patriotisme de parade,** showy patriotism. **Habits de parade,** full-dress clothes. **Lit de parade,** bed for lying-in state.
parade[2], *s.f.* *Fenc:* *Box:* Parry. **Être prompt à la parade,** (i) to be quick at parrying ; (ii) *F:* to be sharp at repartee.
parader [parade], *v.i.* **1.** *Mil:* To parade ; to go on parade. **2.** To make a display ; to promenade ; to strut about ; to show off.
paradigme [paradigm], *s.m.* *Gram:* Paradigm.
paradis [paradi], *s.m.* Paradise. **1.** **Le Paradis terrestre,** the Earthly Paradise, the Garden of Eden. **2.** **Aller en paradis,** to go to heaven, to paradise. *F:* **C'est le paradis sur terre,** it is heaven on earth, an earthly paradise. *F:* **Il ne l'emportera pas en paradis,** I'll be even with him yet. *Th:* *F:* **Le paradis,** the gallery, the gods. *Orn:* **Oiseau de paradis,** bird of paradise.
parados [parado], *s.m.* *Fort:* Parados.
paradoxal, -aux [paradɔksal, -o], *a.* Paradoxical. *adv.* **-ement.**
paradoxe [paradɔks], *s.m.* Paradox.
parafe [paraf], *s.m.* (*a*) Paraph ; flourish (following signature). (*b*) Initials (of one's name).
parafer [parafe], *v.tr.* To put one's initials to, to initial (document).
paraffine [parafin], *s.f.* *Ch:* Paraffin ; *Com:* paraffin wax. *Pharm:* **Huile de paraffine,** liquid paraffin.
parafoudre [parafudr], *s.m.* *El.E:* (*a*) Lightning-arrester, lightning-protector (for electrical apparatus). (*b*) Safety-gap, spark-arrester (of magneto, etc.). (*c*) Spark-gap discharger.
parage[1] [paraːʒ], *s.m.* Birth, descent. **De haut parage,** of high degree, of high lineage.
parage[2], *s.m.* (*a*) Paring, trimming (of iron, etc.). (*b*) *Tex:* Dressing, sizing (of cloth).
parages [paraːʒ], *s.m.pl.* *Nau:* Localities (of the ocean) ; latitudes, regions. *F:* **Que fait-il dans, en, ces parages?** what is he doing in these parts?
paraglace [paraglas], *s.m.* *Nau:* Ice-fender.
paragraphe [paragraf], *s.m.* **1.** Paragraph (section of page, of column). **2.** Section mark ; paragraph.
paragrêle [paragrɛːl], *a.inv. & s.m.* (Canon) **paragrêle,** gun discharged against hail-clouds ; cloud-cannon.
paraître [parɛːtr], *v.i.* (*pr.p.* paraissant ; *p.p.* paru ; *pr.ind.* je parais, il paraît, n. paraissons ; *p.h.* je parus ; *fu.* je paraîtrai) To appear. **1.** (*a*) To make one's appearance ; (of land, ship) to heave in sight, to come up ; (of star, moon) to come out ; (of actor) to come on. *Le jour commençait à p.,* the day was dawning. (*b*) (Of book, etc.) To be published, to come out. **Faire paraître un livre,** to publish, bring out, a book. **"Sur le point de paraître,"** 'just ready.' **"Vient de paraître,"** 'just out,' 'just published.' **2.** (*a*) To be visible, apparent. *Cette tache paraît à peine,* the stain hardly shows. **Laisser paraître ses sentiments,** to show, betray, one's feelings. **Faire paraître qch.,** to show, display, sth. ; to bring sth. to light. (*b*) **Chercher à paraître,** to show off ; to make a display. (*c*) *Impers.* **Il y paraît,** that is

easy to see ; that is quite apparent. *Je suis très mal.*—Il n'y paraît pas, I am very ill.—You don't look it, one would not have thought it. **Sans qu'il y paraisse,** without its being apparent. **3.** To seem, to look. (*a*) *Il paraît triste,* he looks sad. *Elle paraissait avoir vingt ans,* she seemed, appeared, to be about twenty. *Elle paraît son âge,* she looks her age. (*b*) *Impers:* *Il paraît qu'elle fait des vers,* it seems she writes poetry. *Il me paraît que . . .,* it seems to me, it strikes me, that. . . . **A ce qu'il paraît,** (i) apparently, as it would appear . . .; (ii) apparently so, it would seem so. **A ce qu'il me paraît,** as far as I can judge. *Il paraît que oui,* so it appears.
parallactique [parallaktik], *a.* *Astr:* Parallactic.
parallaxe [parallaks], *s.f.* *Astr:* *etc:* Parallax.
parallèle [parallɛl]. **1.** *a. & s.f.* *Geom:* Parallel (*à,* to, with). **2.** *s.m.* (*a*) Parallel, comparison. **Mettre qn en parallèle avec qn,** to compare s.o. with s.o. *Établir un p. entre . . . et . . .,* to draw a parallel between . . . and. . . . *El:* **Piles en parallèle,** batteries in parallel, in multiple. (*b*) *Geog:* Parallel (of latitude).
parallèlement [parallɛlmã], *adv.* In a parallel direction (*à,* to, with).
parallélépipède [parallelepipɛd], *s.m.* *Geom:* Parallelepiped.
parallélisme [parallelism], *s.m.* Parallelism.
parallélogramme [parallelɔgram], *s.m.* Parallelogram.
paralogisme [paralɔʒism], *s.m.* *Log:* Paralogism, fallacy.
paralysant [paralizã], **paralysateur, -trice** [paralizatœːr, -tris], *a.* Paralysing.
paralyser [paralize], *v.tr.* To paralyse. *Paralysé des deux jambes,* paralysed in both legs. *Lois qui paralysent l'industrie,* laws that cripple industry.
paralysie [paralizi], *s.f.* *Med:* Paralysis, *A:* palsy. *P. progressive,* creeping paralysis. **Tomber en paralysie,** to have a paralytic stroke, *F:* a seizure.
paralytique [paralitik], *a. & s.* *Med:* Paralytic.
paramètre [paramɛtr], *s.m.* *Mth:* Parameter.
parangon [parãgɔ̃], *s.m.* **1.** Paragon. (*a*) Pattern, model, type (of beauty, chivalry). (*b*) Precious stone without blemish. **2.** *Typ:* **Gros parangon,** double pica. **Petit parangon,** two-line long primer.
parangonner [parãgɔne], *v.tr.* *Typ:* To justify (type, lines).
parapet [parapɛ], *s.m.* Parapet ; breastwork.
paraphe [paraf], *s.m.* = PARAFE.
parapher [parafe], *v.tr.* = PARAFER.
paraphrase [parafraːz], *s.f.* *Lit:* Paraphrase. *F:* **Sans tant de paraphrases,** without so much circumlocution.
paraphraser [parafraze], *v.tr.* (*a*) To paraphrase. (*b*) To expand, amplify (story, speech).
paraphrastique [parafrastik], *a.* Paraphrastic.
paraplégie [parapleʒi], *s.f.* *Med:* Paraplegia.
parapluie [paraplɥi], *s.m.* **1.** Umbrella. **2.** (Driver's) waterproof coat.
parasitaire [parazitɛːr], *a.* **1.** Parasitic (disease). **2.** *W.Tel:* **Effet parasitaire,** interference.
parasite [parazit]. **1.** *s.m.* (*a*) Parasite, hanger-on, sponger. (*b*) *Biol:* Parasite. **2.** *a.* Parasitic (insect, plant). *El:* **Circuit des courants parasites,** eddy-current circuit. *W.Tel:* **Bruits parasites,** *s.m.pl.* **parasites,** strays, x's, interference.
parasitaire [parazitik], *a.* Parasitical.
parasitisme [parazitism], *s.m.* Parasitism.
parasol [parasɔl], *s.m.* **1.** Parasol, sunshade. **2.** *Aut:* Visor (over wind-screen).
parasoleil [parasɔlɛj], *s.m.* (*a*) Sunshade (of telescope). (*b*) *Phot:* Lens-shade, lens-hood.

paratonnerre [paratɔnɛːr], *s.m.* Lightning-conductor, -rod.

paratyphoïde [paratifɔid], *a. & s.f. Med:* Paratyphoid (fever).

paravane [paravan], *s.m. Navy:* Paravane.

paravent [paravɑ̃], *s.m.* Draught-screen, folding-screen.

paraverse [paravɛrs], *s.m. Cost:* Light-weight waterproof.

parbleu [parblø], *int.* (Attenuated form of PARDIEU) Why, of course ! to be sure ! rather !

parc [park], *s.m.* **I.** Park. *P. d'agrément*, pleasure grounds. **2.** *P. pour autos*, car-park, parking-place. *P. pour chevaux*, paddock. *P. à bestiaux, à moutons*, cattle-pen, sheep-fold. *P. à huîtres*, oyster-bed. *P. d'artillerie*, artillery-park. *P. à munitions*, ammunition-depot. *P. aérostatique*, balloon-park. *Mil: P. des prisonniers*, prisoners' cage.

parcage [parkaːʒ], *s.m.* Parking (of cars); enclosing, penning (of cattle); folding (of sheep); laying down (of oysters). *Aut: "P. interdit,"* 'no parking.'

parcellaire [parsɛlɛːr], *a.* Divided into small portions, into parcels (of land).

parcelle [parsɛl], *s.f.* Small fragment; particle (of gold); plot, patch (of land). *Pas la moindre p. de jugement*, not a scrap of common sense.

parcell|er [parsɛle], *v.tr.* To divide into lots; to portion out (inheritance, etc.). *s.m.* **-ement.**

parce que [pars(ə)kə], *conj.phr.* Because.

parchemin [parʃəmɛ̃], *s.m.* **I.** (*a*) Parchment. *Bookb:* Vellum. *F:* **Visage de parchemin,** wizened, shrivelled, countenance. (*b*) *pl.* Title-deeds, titles of nobility; diplomas. **2. Papier parchemin,** vegetable parchment, parchment-paper.

parcheminer (se) [səparʃəmine], *v.pr.* To shrivel up; to become shrivelled.

parcheminé, *a.* Parchment-like, dried (skin).

par-ci par-là. See CI¹, PAR 6.

parcimonie [parsimɔni], *s.f.* Parsimony, stinginess.

parcimonieu|x, -euse [parsimɔnjø, -øːz], *a.* Parsimonious; stingy, niggardly. *P. de louanges*, chary, sparing, of praise. *adv.* **-sement.**

parcourir [parkuriːr], *v.tr.* (Conj. like COURIR) **I.** To travel through, go over, traverse (piece of country). *P. toutes les rues de la ville*, to wander, ramble, through every street in the town. *P. une distance de plusieurs lieues*, to cover a distance of several leagues. *Un frisson me parcourut*, a shiver went through me. *P. les mers*, to sail the seas. **2.** To examine (cursorily). *P. qch. des yeux, du regard*, to run, cast, one's eye over sth. *P. un livre*, to glance, skim, through a book. *Son regard parcourut l'horizon*, his eyes swept the horizon.

parcours [parkuːr], *s.m.* **I.** (*a*) Distance covered; length, run (of a pipe-line); length of stroke (of piston). (*b*) Route (of procession, omnibus, etc.); course (of river, etc.). *Rail:* **Avoir libre .parcours sur un réseau,** to have running rights over a system. (*c*) *Golf:* Course, links. *Sp:* Circuit, course. **2.** Run, trip (of locomotive, etc.).

par-dessous, *prep. & adv.* Under, beneath, underneath. *J'ai passé p.-d.*, I crept under it.

par-dessus, *prep. & adv.* Over (the top of). *Jeter qch. p.-d. bord*, to throw sth. overboard. **Par-dessus le marché,** into the bargain. *J'ai sauté p.-d.*, I jumped over it.

pardessus [pardəsy], *s.m.* Overcoat, greatcoat, top-coat.

par-devant, *prep. Jur:* In front of; before.

Signé p.-d. (*le*) *notaire*, signed in the presence of the notary.

pardi [pardi], *int. Dial: =* PARBLEU.

pardieu [pardjø], *int.* Usu. attenuated to PARBLEU, *q.v.*

pardon [pardɔ̃], *s.m.* Pardon. (*a*) Forgiveness (of an offence). **Je vous demande pardon,** I beg your pardon (*de*, for). *P. de vous avoir retenu*, I am sorry to have kept you. **Pardon?** I beg your pardon? (*b*) *Jur:* Remission of a sentence. (*c*) *Ecc:* (In Brittany) (Local processional) pilgrimage. (*d*) *pl.* Papal indulgences.

pardonn|er [pardɔne], *v.tr.* To pardon, forgive. (*a*) *Pardonnez la liberté que je prends*, pardon, excuse, the liberty I am taking. (*b*) *P. à qn*, to pardon s.o. **Dieu me pardonne !** God forgive me ! **La mort ne pardonne (à) personne,** death spares no one. **Pardonnez-moi,** excuse me. *F:* **Vous êtes tout pardonné,** please don't mention it. *a.* **-able.**

pare-boue, *s.m.inv.* Dash-board (of carriage); mudguard (of motor car, bicycle).

pare-brise, *s.m.inv. Aut: etc:* Wind-screen.

pare-choc(s), *s.m.inv. Aut:* Fender; bumper.

pare-éclats, *s.m.inv. Mil:* Splinter-proof shield. *a. Navy: Pont p.-é.*, splinter-deck.

pare-étincelles, *s.m.inv.* (*a*) Fire-guard. (*b*) *Rail: etc:* Spark-arrester, spark-catcher.

pare-fumée, *s.m.inv.* Smoke-shield (in roof of station). *a.* **Casque pare-fumée,** smoke-helmet.

parégorique [paregɔrik], *a. & s.m. Pharm:* Paregoric.

pare-gouttes, *s.m.inv.* Splash-guard, oil-guard.

pareil, -eille [parɛːj]. **I.** *a.* (*a*) Like, alike; similar (*à*, to). *En voici un tout p.*, here is one exactly like it. **Toutes choses pareilles,** all things being equal. (*b*) (Of time) Same, identical. **L'an dernier à pareil jour,** this day last year. (*c*) Such; like that. **En pareil cas,** in any such emergency; in such cases. *Avez-vous jamais entendu chose pareille!* did you ever hear of such a thing ! **2.** *s.* (*a*) *Mes pareils*, my equals, my peers. *Lui et ses pareils*, he and people like him; he and his like. (*b*) Equal, fellow, match. **De longtemps on ne verra pas son pareil,** it will be long before we see his like. *Il n'a pas son p. pour le travail*, *F:* he's a beggar for work. **Sans pareil,** peerless, matchless; unequalled. **Méchanceté sans pareille,** unparalleled wickedness. **3.** *s.f.* **La pareille,** the like. **Rendre la pareille à qn,** to give s.o. tit for tat; to pay s.o. back in his own coin.

pareillement [parɛjmɑ̃], *adv.* **I.** In like manner. **2.** Also; likewise. **A vous pareillement!** the same to you ! *Et moi p.*, and so do I (so am I, so shall I).

pare-jambes, *s.m.pl.* Leg-shields.

pare-lumière, *s.m.inv. Aut:* Anti-dazzle shield.

parement [parmɑ̃], *s.m.* **I.** (*a*) Adorning. (*b*) Dressing (of stone, etc.). **2.** (*a*) Ornament, adornment; decoration, ornamentation (of façade, etc.). (*b*) Cuff (of sleeve); (cuff or collar) facing. *pl.* Facings (of coat, uniform). **3.** *Const:* Face, facing (of wall); (dressed) face (of stone). **4.** Kerb-stone.

pare-mines, *s.m.inv.* Mine-sweeping device.

parent, -ente [parɑ̃, -ɑ̃ːt], *s.* **I.** *s.m.pl.* (*a*) Parents; father and mother. *Sans parents*, parentless. (*b*) Forefathers, forbears. **2.** Relative, connection; kinsman, kinswoman; (blood) relation. *Son plus proche p.*, his next of kin. *P. par alliance*, relation by marriage.

parentage [parɑ̃taːʒ], *s.m.* **I.** Parentage, birth, lineage. **2.** *Coll.* Kindred, family, relations.

parenté [parãte], s.f. **1.** Kinship, relationship; consanguinity. Être de même parenté, to be of the same kith and kin. **2.** Coll. = PARENTAGE 2.

parenthèse [parãtɛːz], s.f. Parenthesis; (i) digression; (ii) Typ: bracket. Entre parenthèses, in parentheses. F: Soit dit par parenthèse, entre parenthèses, be it said parenthetically, by the way.

pare-pierres, s.m.inv. Aut: Stone-guard.

pare-poussière, s.m.inv. **1.** (a) Dust-coat. (b) (Lady's) motor-veil. **2.** Aut: etc: Dust-guard; dust-cap (of valve, etc.).

parer[1] [pare], v.tr. **1.** To prepare; to dress, trim (meat, castings); to pare (hoof, leather). Nau: To clear (cable, anchor). **2.** To adorn, embellish, deck out (de, with).
se parer, to adorn oneself. Se p. de sa plus belle robe, to deck oneself out in one's finest dress. Se p. d'un faux titre, to parade a false title.
paré, a. **1.** Nau: (Qu'on soit) paré! (make) ready! P. à virer! ready about! On est paré! aye, aye, sir! **2.** Adorned, bedecked. Parée d'une jolie broche, wearing a pretty brooch. Parée de tous ses atours, wearing all her finery; F: dressed up to the nines. S.a. BAL 1.

parer[2]. **1.** v.tr. (a) To avoid, ward off; to fend off (collision). P. un cap, to clear, double, a headland. P. un grain, to steer clear of a squall. (b) To parry, ward off (blow, thrust). **2.** v.ind.tr. P. à qch., to provide, guard, against sth.; to avert (accident); to obviate (difficulty). On ne peut pas parer à tout, one cannot guard against everything; accidents will happen. Nau: P. à un grain, to prepare to meet a squall.

pare-soleil, s.m. inv. **1.** Sunshade (of telescope). **2.** Aut: Visor.

paresse [parɛs], s.f. (a) Laziness, idleness, sloth. Par pure paresse, out of sheer laziness. (b) Sluggishness (of mind, of the liver).

paresser [parɛse], v.i. To idle; to take one's ease; F: to laze.

paresseu|x, -euse [parɛsø, -øːz]. **1.** a. (a) Lazy, idle, slothful. P. à apprendre ses leçons, lazy over his lessons. (b) Sluggish (liver, bowels); slow-acting (spring, balance). **2.** s. Lazy person; sluggard; F: lazy-bones. **3.** s.m. Z: Ai, three-toed sloth. adv. -sement.

pare-torpilles, s. m. & a. inv. (Filet) pare-torpilles, torpedo-net.

parfaire [parfɛːr], v.tr. (Conj. like FAIRE; used chiefly in inf. and p.p.) To finish off, perfect, round off (one's work, etc.); to make up (a sum).

parfait [parfɛ]. **1.** a. Perfect. (a) Faultless, flawless. En ordre p., in perfect order, F: in apple-pie order. F: C'est parfait! excellent! F: that's fine! Mus: Accord parfait, perfect chord. (b) Complete, thorough. Un p. orateur, a finished speaker. F: Un p. imbécile, an out-and-out idiot. **2.** s.m. Gram: Verbe au parfait, verb in the perfect tense.

parfaitement [parfɛtmã], adv. **1.** (a) Perfectly; to perfection. (Of a hotel) On y est p., one is thoroughly comfortable there. (b) Completely, thoroughly. Je comprends p., I quite understand. Être p. maître d'un jeu, to be a perfect master of a game. **2.** (Emphatic answer) That is so; quite so; certainly; exactly.

parfois [parfwa], adv. Sometimes, at times, occasionally, now and then.

parfum [parfœ̃], s.m. Perfume. **1.** Fragrance, sweet smell, scent (of flower). **2.** Toil: Scent.

parfumer [parfyme], v.tr. To scent (one's handkerchief, etc.). Elle se parfume trop, she uses too much scent. L'air parfumé du soir, the balmy evening air.

parfumerie [parfymri], s.f. Perfumery.

parfumeur, -euse [parfymœːr, -øːz], s. Perfumer.

parhélie [pareli], s.m. Parhelion, mock sun (i▪ solar halo); sun-dog.

pari [pari], s.m. **1.** Bet, wager. Faire, offrir, u▪ pari, to make a bet; to lay a bet, a wager. Tenir soutenir, un pari, to take (up) a bet. **2.** Betting Pari mutuel, pari mutuel; totalizator system.

paria [parja], s.m. Pariah.

parier [parje], v.tr. To bet, to wager, to lay P. cent contre un, to bet, lay, a hundred to one P. à l'égalité, to lay even odds. P. sur, pour, u▪ cheval, to back a horse. P. gros, to bet heavily Il y a (gros) à parier que . . ., it is long odd that. . . .

pariétaire [parjetɛːr], s.f. Bot: (Wall-)pellitory

pariétal, -aux [parjetal, -o], a. Parietal (bone etc.); mural (painting).

parieur, -euse [parjœːr, -øːz], s. Better punter; backer.

Paris [pari]. Pr.n.m. Geog: Paris. Premiè Paris, leading article (in a Paris newspaper) Articles de Paris, fancy goods. A: Monsieu de Paris, the public executioner.

parisette [parizɛt], s.f. Bot: P. à quatre feuilles herb Paris, (herb) true-love.

parisien, -ienne [parizjɛ̃, -jɛn], a. & s. Parisian s.f. also Parisienne.

parisyllabe [parisillab], **parisyllabiqu▪** [parisillabik], a. Parisyllabic.

parité [parite], s.f. Parity. **1.** Equality (of rank value). Il n'y a pas de p. entre ces deux cas, th▪ two cases are not on all fours. Fin: P. de change equivalence of exchange. Change à (la) parité exchange at par. **2.** Mth: Evenness (of numbers)

parjure[1] [parʒyr], s.m. Perjury; (i) false swear ing (as a moral offence); false oath; (ii) violatio▪ of one's oath.

parjure[2]. **1.** a. Perjured, forsworn. **2.** s. Perjure (who has violated his oath).

parjurer (se) [səparʒyre], v.pr. To forswea▪ oneself, to perjure oneself; to be guilty of commit, perjury (before God).

parlant [parlã], a. Speaking; talking (creature voice). S.a. FILM. F: Portrait p., speakin▪ likeness. Peu p., reticent, silent.

parlement [parləmã], s.m. Parliament. (a) Fr Hist: High judicial court (in Paris and in eac▪ province). (b) (Modern times) Legislativ▪ assembly. Les Palais du Parlement, the House▪ of Parliament (in England).

parlementaire[1] [parləmãtɛːr], a. Parliamentary Expression peu p., unparliamentary expression.

parlementaire[2]. **1.** s.m. (a) Mil: Bearer o▪ flag of truce. (b) Navy: (Vaisseau) parlemen taire, cartel(-ship). **2.** a. Drapeau parlementaire flag of truce.

parlement|er [parləmãte], v.i. To parley, t▪ hold a parley (avec, with). s.m. -age.

parler [parle]. I. v.i. To speak, talk. **1.** (a) P haut, to talk loud. P. bas, to speak in a low voice P. entre ses dents, to mumble. P. à l'oreille de qʳ to whisper to s.o. S'enrouer à force de parler, t▪ talk oneself hoarse. Celui qui a parlé le premier le dernier, the first, last, speaker. (b) Parlez-vou▪ sérieusement? are you in earnest? Laissez-le p. let him have his say. Parler pour parler, to tal▪ for talking's sake. Parlons peu et parlons bien let us be brief but to the point. Parler pour n▪ rien dire, F: to talk through one's hat; to tal▪ drivel, bosh. Pour parler franc . . ., to put i▪ bluntly . . ., to speak candidly. . . . Génerale ment parlant, generally speaking. Savoir ce qu▪

parler veut dire, to be able to take a hint. Faire parler qn, to loosen s.o.'s tongue. *On parlait très peu au déjeuner*, there was very little talking over breakfast. Façon de parler, (i) way of speaking ; (ii) manner of speech. Voilà ce qui s'appelle parler! *P:* tu parles! now you're talking! (c) *P. à qn*, to talk to, to converse with, s.o. Elle a trouvé à qui parler, she has met her match, has caught a Tartar. *Nous ne nous parlons pas à présent*, we are not on speaking terms at present. *Nau: P. à un navire*, to speak a ship. (d) *P. de qn, de qch.*, to mention, to refer to, s.o., sth. *Il n'en parle jamais*, he never refers to it. *Est-ce de moi que vous parlez?* do you mean me? *Je sais qu'on parlait de moi*, I know they were discussing me. *Nous en parlerons après déjeuner*, we can talk it over after lunch. N'en parlons plus, let us say no more about it. Cela ne vaut pas la peine d'en parler, it isn't worth mentioning. Entendre parler de qn, de qch., to hear of, about, s.o., sth. *Mon père ne veut pas en entendre p.*, father won't hear of it. *C'est la première fois que j'en entends p.*, this is the first I have heard of it. Faire parler de soi, (i) to get talked about ; (ii) to get a bad name. *On ne parle que de cela*, it is the (common) talk of the place, of the town. *P. de choses et d'autres*, to talk on indifferent matters. Sans parler de . . ., to say nothing of . . ., not to mention . . ., let alone. . . . *P:* Tu parles d'une chance! talk about luck! (e) *P. pour, contre, qn*, to speak for, against, s.o. 2. (a) Parler français, (i) to talk, speak, French ; (ii) to speak plainly intelligibly. *L'anglais se parle partout*, English is spoken everywhere. (b) Parler affaires, parler boutique, to talk business, to talk shop.

II. parler, *s.m.* (Way of) speaking ; speech, language. *P. populaire*, popular speech. *P. irlandais*, Irish brogue.

parlé. 1. *a.* Spoken (language, word). S.a. FILM, JOURNAL 2. 2. *s.m.* Patter (in song) ; spoken part (in opera).

parleur, -euse [parlœːr, -øːz]. 1. *s.* (a) Talker, speaker. *F: C'est un beau p.*, he is very glib of the tongue. (b) *W.Tel:* Announcer. 2. *s.m. Tg:* Sounder. S.a. HAUT-PARLEUR.

parloir [parlwaːr], *s.m.* Parlour (of school, convent).

parlot(t)e [parlɔt], *s.f.* 1. (a) (Legal) debate ; moot. (b) (Legal) debating society. 2. *F:* (a) *P. en plein air*, open-air discussion, debate. (b) Talk, gossip.

parmesan, -ane [parmǝzã, -an]. 1. *a. & s.* Parmesan. 2. *s.m.* Parmesan (cheese).

parmi [parmi]. 1. *prep.* Amóng(st), amid(st). *Cela ne se fait pas p. nous*, it is not done with us, in our circle. *P. le silence de la nuit*, amid the silence of the night. 2. *adv. Il y en a de bons p.*, there are good ones among them.

Parnasse (le) [lǝparnɑːs]. *Pr.n.* 1. (a) Parnassus. (b) *Fr.Lit.Hist:* The Parnassian School (of poetry, from 1860). 2. *Bot:* Gazon du Parnasse, grass of Parnassus.

parnassien, -ienne [parnasjɛ̃, -jen]. 1. *a.* Parnassian. 2. *s.m.* Member of the Parnassian School (of French poetry).

parodie [parɔdi], *s.f.* Parody ; skit (de, upon).

parodier [parɔdje], *v.tr.* To parody, to burlesque ; to take (s.o.) off.

parodiste [parɔdist], *s.m.* Parodist.

paroi [parwa], *s.f.* 1. (a) Partition-wall (between rooms). (b) Wall (of rock, cylinder) ; casing, wall, shell (of boiler) ; wall, crust (of horse's hoof). 2. Inner surface (of vase, etc.) ; lining (of tunnel) ; coat(ing) (of the stomach).

29

paroisse [parwas], *s.f.* 1. Parish. 2. Parish church.

paroissial, -aux [parwasjal, -o], *a.* Parochial. *L'église paroissiale*, the parish church.

paroissien, -ienne [parwasjɛ̃, -jen]. 1. *a.* Parochial. 2. *s.* Parishioner. 3. *s.m.* Prayer-book.

parole [parɔl], *s.f.* 1. (Spoken) word ; utterance, remark. *Ne prononcer aucune p.*, to say not a single word, to pass no remark. *Romance sans paroles*, song without words. *Perdre le temps en paroles*, to waste time talking. *Cette p. le piqua*, this remark went home. *Belles paroles*, fair words. 2. Promise, word ; *Mil:* parole. Donner sa parole, to pass one's word. Tenir (sa) parole, to keep one's promise, one's word. Manque de parole, breach of faith. Manquer à sa parole, to break one's word ; *Mil:* to break one's parole. Rendre sa parole à qn, to release s.o. from his promise. Ma parole! parole d'honneur! upon my word (of honour)! Croire qn sur parole, to take a person's word. Prisonnier sur parole, prisoner on parole. 3. Speech, speaking. (a) Delivery. *Avoir la p. embarrassée*, to have an impediment in one's speech. *Avoir la p. facile*, to be an easy, ready, speaker. Perdre la parole, to lose the power of speech. (b) Adresser la parole à qn, to speak to s.o. ; to address s.o. Couper la parole à qn, to interrupt s.o. Porter la parole (*pour ses collègues*), to act as spokesman (for one's colleagues). Prendre la parole, to begin to speak ; to take the floor. Avoir la parole, to have the floor. *La p. est à M. X*, I will now call on Mr X. Demander la parole, to request leave to speak. *Cards:* Passer parole, to pass ; to leave the call to one's partner.

parotide [parɔtid], *a. & s.f.* Parotid (gland).

paroxysme [parɔksism], *s.m.* Paroxysm (of rage, laughter, etc.). Être au paroxysme de la colère, to be in a towering rage.

parpaillot, -ote [parpajo, -ɔt], *s. Pej: A:* (a) Calvinist. (b) Heretic ; unbeliever.

parpaing [parpɛ̃], *s.m. Const:* Parpen ; bondstone ; through-stone. Mur de parpaing, parpen wall.

parquer [parke], *v.tr.* To pen (cattle) ; to fold (sheep) ; to put (horse) in paddock ; to park (artillery, motor cars, etc.) ; to bed (oysters).

Parques [park]. *Pr.n.f.pl. Myth:* The Parcae, the Fates.

parquet [parke], *s.m.* 1. (a) *Jur:* (i) Well of the court ; (ii) public prosecutor's room. Membres du parquet, public prosecutor and his deputies. Déposer une plainte au parquet, to lodge a complaint in court. (b) *St.Exch:* Le Parquet = the Ring, the official market. 2. (a) Floor, flooring. *P. ciré*, waxed floor, polished floor. (b) (Wooden) backing (of painting). *Phot:* Parquet réversible, reversing back. (c) *Nau: P. de chargement*, dunnage. *P. de chaufferie*, stokehold platform.

parquetage [parkǝtaːʒ], *s.m.* 1. (a) Laying of floors. (b) Flooring, floor. 2. Parquetry.

parquet|er [parkǝte], *v.tr.* (je parquette; je parquetterai) (a) To lay a floor in (room, etc.). (b) To parquet. *s.m.* -eur.

parqueterie [parkǝtri], *s.f.* Laying of floors. *P. en mosaïque*, (i) inlaying ; (ii) inlaid floor.

parrain [parɛ̃], *s.m.* (a) Godfather, sponsor. Être p., to stand godfather (de, to). (b) Proposer (of new member for club, etc.) ; sponsor.

parricide[1] [parisid]. 1. *s. m. & f.* Parricide. 2. *a.* Parricidal.

parricide[2], *s.m.* (Crime of) parricide.

pars [paːr]. See PARTIR.

parsemer [parsǝme], *v.tr.* (Conj. like SEMER) To

strew, sprinkle (*de*, with). *Ciel parsemé d'étoiles*, sky studded, spangled, with stars. *La contrée est parsemée de fermes*, the country-side is dotted with farms. *Barbe parsemée de gris*, beard shot with grey.

parsi, -e [parsi], *a. & s. Rel.H :* Parsee.

part[1] [paːr], *s.f.* **1.** Share, part, portion. (*a*) *Diviser un gâteau en plusieurs parts*, to share out a cake. S.a. FEU[1] **1**, LION. *Vous lui faites la p. trop belle*, you favour him unduly. *Avoir une p. dans les bénéfices*, to have a share, an interest, in the profits ; to share in the profits. *Avoir sa bonne p. d'éloges*, to come in for one's full meed of praise. **Mettre qn de part** (*dans une affaire*), to give s.o. a share in the profits. **Mettre qn de part à demi**, to go half-shares with s.o. S.a. HÉRITAGE. (*b*) **Pour ma part . . .**, as for me . . ., as far as I am concerned . . ., (speaking) for myself. . . . (*c*) **Prendre qch. en bonne part, en mauvaise part**, to take sth. in good part, in bad part. **2.** Share, participation. **Avoir part à qch.**, to have a hand, a share, in sth. *F :* **Avoir part au gâteau**, to have a finger in the pie. **Prendre part à qch.**, to take (a) part in, to join in, to be a party to, sth. ; to share in sth. *Prendre p. à une cérémonie*, to assist at a ceremony. *Prendre p. à la conversation, aux rires*, to join in the conversation, in the laughter. *Je n'y ai pris aucune p.*, I had neither part nor lot in it. **Faire part de qch. à qn**, to inform, advise, s.o. of sth. ; to acquaint s.o. with sth. **Billet, lettre, de faire part**, card, notice (announcing a wedding, death, etc.) ; intimation (of wedding, etc.). S.a. FAIRE-PART. **Faire la part de qch.**, to take sth. into consideration. **Faire la part des circonstances**, to take circumstances into account. **3.** **Savoir, tenir, qch. de bonne part**, to have it from a reliable source, on good authority. **Nulle part**, nowhere. **Autre part**, elsewhere, somewhere else. **Nulle autre part**, nowhere else. **Courir de part et d'autre**, to run here and there. **Faire des concessions de part et d'autre**, to make concessions on both sides. *De toutes parts*, on all sides, on all hands. *Ils viennent de toutes parts*, they come from all quarters. **De part en part**, through and through. **D'une part . . .**, on the one hand. . . . **D'autre part . . .**, on the other hand . . . ; then again. . . . S.a. QUELQUE PART. **Je viens de la part de . . .**, I come on the part of. . . . *Dites-lui de ma part que . . .*, tell him from me that. . . . *C'est une insolence de sa p.*, it is a piece of insolence on his part. **4.** **A part**, apart, separately. *Prendre qn à p.*, to take, draw, s.o. aside. *Mettre de l'argent à p.*, to put money by, aside. *Plaisanterie à p.*, joking apart. *Emballage à p.*, packing extra. **Et à part lui?** who besides him? **A part moi . . .**, in my own heart. . . . *Th :* **Mots prononcés à part**, words spoken aside. **A part quelques exceptions**, with a few exceptions. *A p. quelques pages . . .*, except for a few pages. . . .

part[2]. See PARTIR.

partage [partaːʒ], *s.m.* **1.** Division. (*a*) Sharing, allotment, apportionment (of spoils, etc.). *Jur :* Partition (of real property). **Faire le partage de qch.**, to divide, share out, sth. (*b*) *P. d'un pays*, partition of a country. **Il y a partage d'opinions**, opinions are divided. *Geog :* **Ligne de partage des eaux**, watershed ; *U.S :* divide. **2.** Share, portion, lot. **Avoir qch. en partage**, to receive (a house, etc.) as one's share. **Tomber, échoir, en partage à qn**, to fall to s.o.'s share, to s.o.'s lot.

partag|er [partaʒe], *v.tr.* (je **partageai(s)**; n. **partageons**) **1.** To divide. (*a*) To parcel out, to apportion (property, etc.) ; to share out (loot,

etc.). (*b*) *Fleuve qui partage le pays en deux*, river that divides, cuts, the country into two. **Être partagés d'opinion sur qch.**, to be divided in opinion over sth. **Partager le différend** (par la moitié), to split the difference ; to compromise. **2.** (*a*) *P. qch. avec qn*, to share sth. with s.o. ; to go halves, to go shares, in sth. with s.o. *Ils se partagent les bénéfices*, they share the profits between them. *P. le même sort*, to fare and share alike. *P. les idées de qn*, to agree with s.o.'s views. *Amour partagé*, requited love. *Golf :* **Trou partagé**, halved hole. (*b*) *v.i. P. dans une succession*, to share in, have a share in, a succession. **3.** **Être bien, mal, partagé**, to be well, ill, provided for. *a.* **-eable.**

se partager, to divide ; (of river) to branch.

partance [partɑ̃ːs], *s.f. Nau :* Departure. Esp. **Navire en partance**, ship about to sail, outward bound. **Pavillon de partance**, Blue Peter. **En partance pour Bordeaux**, bound for Bordeaux.

partant[1] [partɑ̃], *adv.* Consequently, therefore.

partant[2]. **1.** *a.* Departing. **2.** *s.m.pl.* Les partants, (i) the departing guests, etc. ; (ii) *Turf : etc :* the starters.

partenaire [partənɛːr], *s.m. Games : Sp : Danc :* Partner.

parterre [partɛːr], *s.m.* **1.** Flower-bed. **2.** *Th :* **Le parterre**. (i) The pit ; the area (of concert-hall). *F :* **Prendre un billet de parterre**, to come a cropper. (ii) The audience (in the pit).

parthe [part], *a. & s.* Parthian. *F :* **Lancer, décocher, la flèche du Parthe**, to let fly a Parthian shaft.

parti [parti], *s.m.* **1.** Party. *Guerre de partis*, party warfare. *Esprit de p.*, party spirit. **Prendre parti pour, contre, qn**, to side with, against, s.o. **Prendre, épouser, le parti de qn**, to take s.o.'s side, s.o.'s part. **Être, se ranger, du parti de qn**, to side with s.o. **2.** (Marriageable person) **C'est un bon parti**, he, she, is a good match ; he is a very eligible parti. **3.** Decision, choice, course. *Hésiter entre deux partis*, to hesitate between two courses (of action). **Prendre (un) parti**, to come to a decision, to make up one's mind. *Mon p. est pris*, my mind is made up. **En prendre son parti**, to resign oneself to the inevitable ; to make the best of it. **Prendre le parti de faire qch.**, to decide, resolve, to do sth. **Parti pris**, (i) set purpose ; (ii) rank obstinacy (of opinion) ; bias ; prejudice. **De parti pris**, deliberately ; of set purpose. **4.** Advantage, profit. **Tirer parti de qch.**, to make use of sth. ; to turn sth. to account. *Tirer le meilleur p. de qch.*, to turn sth. to the best account. **5.** *F :* **Faire un mauvais parti à qn**, (i) to ill-treat s.o. ; to knock s.o. about ; (ii) to kill s.o.

partial, -aux [parsjal, -o], *a.* Partial (judge) ; bias(s)ed, unfair (critic). *adv.* **-ement.**

partialité [parsjalite], *s.f.* Partiality (*envers*, for, to) ; bias, unfairness.

participant, -ante [partisipɑ̃, -ɑ̃ːt], *s.* Participant ; participator (*de*, in).

participation [partisipasjɔ̃], *s.f.* **1.** Participation. **Cela s'est fait sans ma participation**, I had no hand in it, no share in it. **2.** *Com :* Share, interest (*à*, in). *P. aux bénéfices*, profit-sharing. **Compte en participation**, joint account.

participe [partisip], *s.m. Gram :* Participle.

participer [partisipe], *v.i.* **1.** **Participer à qch.** (*a*) To participate, have a share, an interest, in (profits, etc.). (*b*) To take a hand in, to be a party to (plot, etc.) ; to share in, take (a) part in (work, etc.). **2.** **Participer de qch.**, to partake of, have some of the characteristics of, sth.

participial, -aux [partisipjal, -o], *a.* Participial.

particularisation [partikylarizasjɔ̃], *s.f.* Particularization, particularizing.

particulariser [partikylarize], *v.tr.* **1.** To particularize. **2.** To specify (details); to give particulars, details, of (sth.). *se* **particulariser,** to distinguish oneself from others (*par*, through).

particularité [partikylarite], *s.f.* **1.** Particularity. (*a*) Particular nature (of sth.). (*b*) Detail, circumstance, particular. **2.** Peculiarity. (*a*) Peculiar nature (of sth.). (*b*) Characteristic.

particule [partikyl], *s.f.* **1.** Particle, F: atom. **2.** *Gram:* Particle. *La p. nobiliaire,* the nobiliary particle (the prep. *de*, indicating that a name derives from landed property).

particulier, -ière [partikylje, -jɛːr].' **1.** *a.* (*a*) Particular, special. (On passport) *Signes particuliers,* special peculiarities. (*b*) Peculiar characteristic. *Attitude qui lui est particulière,* attitude (that is) peculiar to him, characteristic of him. (*c*) Unusual, uncommon, peculiar. *Voilà qui est p.!* well, that's odd! that's peculiar! (*d*) Private (room, life, lesson, etc.); personal (account). *Secrétaire p.,* private secretary; confidential clerk. *Entrée particulière,* separate, private, entrance. *J'ai des raisons particulières pour le désirer,* I have my own (private) reasons, reasons of my own, for wishing it. *A titre particulier,* in a private capacity. **2.** *s.* Private person, private individual. *Agir en tant que particulier, en* (*qualité de*) *simple particulier,* to act merely as a private individual. *Quel drôle de particulier!* what a queer stick! **3.** *s.m.* Il est très aimable dans le particulier, he is very pleasant in his own home. *Notez en particulier que . . .,* notice particularly that. . . . *Recevoir qn en particulier,* to receive s.o. privately. *En mon particulier,* in my own mind; on my own account.

particulièrement [partikyljɛrmã], *adv.* (*a*) Particularly, (e)specially. (*b*) Peculiarly, uncommonly. (*c*) *Raconter qch. plus p.,* to recount sth. in greater detail. (*d*) Intimately.

partie [parti], *s.f.* **1.** Part (of a whole). *La plus grande p. du chemin,* most of the way. *Une bonne p. du papier est avariée,* a good deal of the paper is damaged. *Les parties du corps,* the parts of the body. *Gram: Parties du discours,* parts of speech. *En partie, partly; in part. En grande partie, largely; to a great extent. Faire partie de qch.,* to be or form a part of sth. *Je ne fais plus p. de ce cercle,* I don't belong to this club any longer. *Faire p. du bureau,* to be on the committee. *Vendre qch. par parties,* to sell sth. in 'ots. *Tenue des livres en partie double,* double entry book-keeping. *Dans quelle p. êtes-vous?* what is your line (of business)? *Chant à trois parties,* three-part song. *Parties d'orchestre,* orchestral parts. **2.** (*a*) Party. *Partie de plaisir,* pleasure party; picnic, outing. *La vie n'est pas une p. de plaisir,* life is not a picnic. *Voulez-vous être de la partie?* will you join us? *Dîner en partie fine,* to dine in intimate tête-à-tête. *S.a.* CARRÉ I. (*b*) Game, match. *P. de cricket,* cricket match. *Faire une p. de cartes, d'échecs,* to have a game of cards, of chess. *Partie nulle,* drawn game; (in racing) dead heat. *Gagner la p.,* to win the game or the match. *F: Vous avez la partie belle,* now's your chance! *Se mettre de la partie,* to take a hand, to join in. **3.** *Jur:* Party (to dispute, etc.). (*a*) *P. en cause,* party to the case. *La p. lésée,* the injured party. *Entendre les avocats des deux parties,* to hear counsel on both sides. *F: Avoir affaire à forte partie,* to have a powerful opponent to deal with. *F: Prendre qn à partie (d'avoir fait qch.),* to take s.o. to task, to call s.o. to account (for doing sth.). (*b*) (Of barrister) *Ma p.,* my client.

partiel, -elle [parsjɛl], *a.* Partial, incomplete. *Paiement p.,* part payment.

partiellement [parsjɛlmã], *adv.* Partially, partly, in part.

partir [partiːr], *v.* (*pr.p.* partant; *p.p.* parti; *pr.ind.* je pars, il part, ils partent; *pr.sub.* je parte; *p.h.* je partis; *fu.* je partirai) **1.** *v.tr. A:* To divide, part. *S.a.* MAILLE². **2.** *v.i.* (Aux. *être*) (*a*) To depart, leave, start; to set out; to go off; to go away; (of ship) to sail away; (of ship, train) to steam away; (of train) to steam off; (of pers.) to walk off, walk away; (of horseman) to ride off. *Je pars d'ici,* I am going away from here. *Je pars de la maison à huit heures,* I leave home at eight o'clock. *Nous partons demain,* we leave, start, to-morrow. *Sp: Partez!* go! *P. de ce monde,* to depart this life. *P. au galop,* to set off at a gallop, to gallop away. *Partir comme une flèche, comme un trait,* to be off, go off, like a shot. *Nous voilà partis,* off we go! *F:* now we're off! *Son livre est bien parti,* his book has made a good start. *Aut: Le moteur est parti au premier appel,* the engine started at the first touch (of the switch). *F: Être un peu parti,* to be slightly tipsy, slightly elevated. (*b*) (Of button, paint, etc.) To come off; (of cable) to part, to give way; (of gun) to go off. *P. d'un éclat de rire, p. de rire,* to burst out laughing. (*c*) To emanate, spring, proceed (from). *Il est parti de rien,* he rose from nothing. (*d*) *A partir d'aujourd'hui,* from this day forward, from to-day (onwards). *A p. du quinze,* on and after the 15th. **3.** Faire partir. (*a*) To send off, dispatch (troops). (*b*) To remove (stain). (*c*) To fire, discharge, let off (gun); to let off, set off (fireworks); to touch off (mine); to set going (the engine).

partisan, -ane [partizã, -an]. **1.** *s.* Partisan, follower; upholder, supporter (of custom, etc.). *P. de la manière forte,* believer in the strong hand. **2.** *s.m. Mil:* Guer(r)illa soldier. *Guerre de partisans,* guer(r)illa warfare.

partitif, -ive [partitif, -iv], *a. Gram:* Partitive.

partition [partisjɔ̃], *s.f.* **1.** *Her:* Quarter (of shield). **2.** *Mus:* Score. *P. d'orchestre,* full score.

partout [partu]. *adv.* (*a*) Everywhere; on all sides. *En tout et partout,* at all times and in all places. *Partout où . . .,* wherever. . . . *P ailleurs,* anywhere else. *Souffrir de partout,* to feel pain, to be sore, all over. (*b*) All; all together. *Ten: Quatre jeux p.,* four all. *Nau:* (To boat crew) *Sciez p.!* back together!

parturition [partyrisjɔ̃], *s.f.* Parturition.

paru, -s, -t, etc. See PARAÎTRE.

parure [paryːr], *s.f.* **1.** Ornamenting, adorning. *La beauté sans parure,* beauty unadorned. **2.** (*a*) Dress, finery. (*b*) Ornament, head-dress. (*c*) Set of jewellery, of underclothes, etc.). **3.** Parings (of leather); trimmings (of meat).

parution [parysjɔ̃], *s.f.* Appearance, publication (of book). *Dès p.,* as soon as published.

parvenir [parvəniːr], *v.i.* (Conj. like VENIR. Aux. *être*) **1.** *P. à un endroit,* to arrive at, to reach, a place. *Votre lettre m'est parvenue,* your letter has reached me, has (duly) come to hand. *Faire parvenir qch. à qn,* to send, to forward, sth. to s.o. **2.** (*a*) To attain, reach; to succeed. *P. à la dignité de maréchal,* to attain (to) the dignity of field-marshal. *P. à faire qch.,* to manage to do sth. *Il parvint à s'échapper,* he succeeded in escaping, he made good his escape. (b) *Abs.* To succeed in life.

parvenu, -ue, *s.* Parvenu, upstart. *Les parvenus,* the newly rich.

parvis [parvi], *s.m.* Parvis, square (in front of a church). *Poet:* Les célestes parvis, the courts of heaven.

pas[1] [pɑ], *s.m.* 1. Step, pace, stride. (*a*) Mesurer une distance au pas, to pace off a distance. Pas à pas, step by step, little by little. A chaque pas, at every step, at every turn. Marcher à pas comptés, to walk with measured tread. Allonger le pas, to step out. Hâter, presser, le pas, to quicken one's pace. J'y vais de ce pas, I am going at once. Porter, diriger, ses pas vers un endroit, to proceed, to wend one's way, to bend one's steps, towards a place. Aller, marcher, à grands pas, to stride, stalk, along. Marcher à petits pas, (i) (of child) to toddle (along) ; (ii) to take mincing steps. Faux pas, (i) slip, stumble ; (ii) (social) blunder. *Faire un faux pas,* (i) to stumble ; (ii) to blunder, to make a *faux pas.* Il n'y a que le premier pas qui coûte, only the beginning is hard. Faire un pas, to take a step. C'est déjà un grand pas de fait, that is a long step forward, a great step forward. Avoir, prendre, le pas sur qn, (i) to have, take, precedence of s.o. ; (ii) to put s.o. into the background. Il demeure à deux pas d'ici, he lives a few steps away, within a stone's throw from here. S.a. CENT 1, CLERC 2. (b) Au pas, at a walking pace. *Aut:* Avancer au pas, to go dead slow. *Pas de valse,* waltz step. Pas seul, solo dance. Pas accéléré, redoublé, quick step, quick march. Avancer au pas gymnastique, to advance at the double. "Pas de route!" 'march at ease!' Marquer le pas, to mark time. Perdre le pas, to fall out of step. Marcher au pas, to march in step. Marcher du même pas que qn, to keep pace with s.o. S.a. CADENCÉ, ROMPRE 1. 2. Footprint, foot-mark. Marcher sur les pas de qn, (i) to follow in s.o.'s footprints, in s.o.'s tracks ; (ii) *F:* to follow in s.o.'s footsteps. 3. Step (of stair) ; threshold (of door). Le pas de la porte, the door-step. 4. Passage ; (mountain) pass ; strait. Le Pas de Calais, the Straits of Dover. Mauvais pas, tight corner, awkward situation. Tirer qn d'un mauvais pas, to get s.o. out of a hole, out of a fix. Sauter le pas, to take the plunge, to cross the Rubicon. 5. Pitch (of screw, propeller) ; thread (of screw).

pas[2], *neg.adv.* 1. Not. *Je ne sais pas,* I don't know. *Je ne l'ai pas encore vu,* I have not seen him vet. Pas du tout, not at all, by no means Pourquoi pas? why not? Pas moi, not I. *Nous marchons peu ou pas,* we walk little or not at all. *F:* Pas (vrai)? = N'EST-CE PAS? *Affaibli mais non pas découragé,* weakened but not discouraged. *Non pas!* not at all! *Des lilas pas fleuris,* lilac not vet in bloom. 2. Pas un. (*a*) *Pas un mot ne fut dit,* not a word was spoken. (*b*) *Il connaît Paris mieux que pas un,* he knows Paris better than anyone. 3. Pas mal de, see MAL[3].

pascal, -aux [paskal, -o], *a.* Paschal (lamb).

pasquinade [paskinad], *s.f.* Pasquinade, lampoon.

passable [pɑsabl], *a.* Passable, tolerable, pretty good, fair ; so so. adv. **-ment.**

passage [pɑsɑːʒ], *s.m.* Passage. 1. Crossing (of sth.) ; passing over, through, across ; going past (a place). (*a*) *La rivière est de p. facile,* the river is easy to cross. *Chacun sourit sur son p.,* everyone smiles as he passes, as he goes by. Guetter le passage de qn, to waylay s.o. ; to lie in wait for s.o. Livrer passage à qn, to allow s.o.

to pass. P. de Vénus (sur le disque du soleil) transit of Venus. Oiseau de passage, bird o passage. Droit de passage, right of way. "Pas sage interdit au public," 'no thoroughfare.' Êtr de passage dans une ville, to be only passin through a town. *Mus:* Note de passage, passin note. *El:* P. du courant, flow of the current (b) *Nau:* Payer son p., to pay for one's passage Bateau de passage, ferry-boat. (c) P. du jour la nuit, transition, change, from day to nigh (d) *Metall:* Pass (through rolling-mill) 2. (*a*) Way, way through, thoroughfare. *Nau* Channel. P. dans les montagnes, mountain pass Se frayer un p., to force a way through. Barre le passage à qn, to stand in s.o.'s way. (b) *Arcad* (with shops on either side). (c) *Rail:* Passage niveau, level crossing. (d) Outlet (of pipe) water-way (of tap). (*e*) Crossing. See CLOUTER 1 3. Passage (in book, in musical composition).

passager, -ère [pɑsaʒe, -ɛːr]. 1. *a.* (*a*) Oiseau d migratory bird, bird of passage. (b) Fleeting short-lived, transitory (beauty, etc.) ; momentar (pain, etc.). 2. *s.* Passenger (by sea or air).

passant, -ante [pɑsɑ̃, -ãːt]. 1. *a.* (Of road Through which there is much traffic ; busy 2. *s.* Passer-by. 3. *s.m.* (*a*) *Harn:* Keeper (b) *Sm.a.* Frog (for scabbard).

passation [pɑsasjɔ̃], *s.f.* Drawing up, signing (c agreement).

passavant [pɑsavɑ̃], *s.m.* 1. *Nau:* (Fore-and aft) gangway. 2. *Cust:* Permit.

passe [pɑːs], *s.f.* 1. (*a*) Passing, passage (o birds, etc.). (b) Permit ; pass. P: de chemin d fer, (free) railway pass. Mot de passe, password (c) P. magnétique, mesmeric pass. (d) *Fb:* P. e avant, forward pass. (*e*) *Metalw:* Cu. (o lathe). 2. (*a*) *Fenc:* Pass, thrust. (b) Passe d'armes, passage of arms. 3. *Nau:* Pass, fairway P. étroite, narrows. Vous êtes en bonne passe it is all plain sailing ; you are in a strong position Être en (bonne) passe de . . ., to be in a fai way to. . . . Être en mauvaise passe, to be in tight corner.

passe-bouillon, *s.m.inv.* Soup-strainer.

passe-cordon, *s.m.* Bodkin. *pl. Des passe cordons.*

passe-coude, *s.m.* Elbow-glove. *pl. Des passe coudes.*

passe-debout, *s.m.inv. Cust:* Transire.

passe-droit, *s.m.* Injustice ; illegitimate favour unfair promotion. *pl. Des passe-droits.*

passe-lacet, *s.m.* Bodkin. *pl. Des passe-lacets.*

passe-lait, *s.m.inv.* Milk-strainer.

passement [pɑsmɑ̃] *s.m.* (Gold, silk) lace (fo clothes) ; braid, braiding (for furniture).

passementer [pɑsmɑ̃te], *v.tr.* To trim (garment etc., with passementerie.

passementerie [pɑsmɑ̃tri], *s.f.* Passementerie trimmings.

passementier, -ière [pɑsmɑ̃tje, -jɛːr], *s.* Deale in passementerie

passe-montagne, *s.m.* Cap-comforter ; Bala klava helmet. *pl. Des passe-montagnes.*

passe-partout, *s.m.inv.* 1. (*a*) Master-key pass-key. (b) Latch-key. 2. (*a*) Cross cut saw (b) Compass-saw. 3. *Phot: etc:* (*a*) Slip(-in mount. Album passe-partout, slip-in album (b) Passe-partout (frame).

passe-passe, *s.m.* No pl. Legerdemain, sleigh of hand, jugglery. Esp. Tour de passe-passe conjuring trick.

passe-plats, *s.m.inv.* Service-hatch.

passepoil [pɑspwal], *s.m.* Braid, piping (fo garments).

passeport [paspɔːr], *s.m.* (*a*) *Adm:* Passport. (*b*) *Nau:* Sea-pass, sea-letter.

passe-purée, *s.m.inv.* Potato-masher.

passer [pɑse]. I. *v.i.* **1.** (Aux. *avoir* or *être*) To pass; to go past; to go (on, by, along); to proceed. *P. sur un pont,* to cross (over) a bridge. *Il est passé, a passé, devant la boutique,* he went by, went past, the shop. *L'auto lui a passé sur les jambes,* the car ran over his legs. *La bouteille passe de main en main,* the bottle passes round. **Faire passer les gâteaux,** to hand round the cakes. *Par où est-il, a-t-il, passé?* which way did he go? *Je ne peux pas p.,* I can't get by. "**On ne passe pas,**" 'no thoroughfare.' "**Défense de passer sous peine d'amende,**" 'trespassers will be prosecuted.' "**Laissez passer,**" 'admit bearer.' *P. à l'ennemi,* to go, pass, over to the enemy. *Passons à la salle à manger,* let us proceed to the dining-room. *P. sur une faute,* to pass over a mistake. **En passant,** by the way. *Une fois en passant,* once in a while. *Remarque en passant,* passing, casual, remark. *Dire qch. en passant,* to mention sth. casually. *(Ceci) soit dit en passant,* (be it said) by the way, in passing. *Passons à autre chose,* (i) let us pass on to other matters; (ii) let us change the subject. *Aut: P. en deuxième vitesse,* to change into second gear. *P. à la postérité,* to go down to posterity. *Glose qui a passé dans le texte,* gloss that has slipped into the text. *La route passe tout près du village,* the road runs quite close to the village. *Cela m'est passé de l'esprit,* it has quite slipped my memory. *Mon dîner ne passe pas,* my dinner won't go down. *Passez par la fenêtre,* go, get, through the window. *Faire passer un tuyau à travers le mur,* to run a pipe through the wall. *Il faut que le café passe très lentement,* coffee must percolate, filter, very slowly. (With cogn. acc.) **Passer son chemin,** to go one's way. *Passez votre chemin!* (i) pass along, pass on! (ii) begone! S.a. DEBOUT 1. **2.** (Aux. *être*) *P. chez qn,* to call on s.o. *Entrer en passant,* to drop in. *Est-ce que le facteur est passé?* has the postman been? **3.** (Aux. *avoir*) (*a*) To undergo, pass through. *J'ai passé par là,* I have gone through it. **Il a dû en passer par là;** il a dû y passer, he had to put up with it. (*b*) **Il la fait passer par où il veut,** he makes her do anything he wants. **4.** (Aux. *avoir*) To pass away. (*a*) To disappear, to cease. *La douleur a passé,* the pain has passed off, has gone. *P. de mode,* to pass out of fashion. *Couleurs qui passent,* colours that fade, go off. *Il faut laisser p. l'orage,* we must let the storm blow over. (*b*) (Of time) To elapse, to go by. *Les années qui passent,* the fleeting years. *A mesure que les années passent,* as the years go by. *Comme le temps passe (vite)!* how (quickly) time flies! **Faire passer le temps,** to pass the time. **5.** (= TRÉPASSER) (Aux. *avoir* or *être*) To die. *Il est, il a, passé dans mes bras,* he passed away in my arms. **6.** *Pred.* (*a*) (Aux. *avoir* or *être*) To become. *P. femme,* to grow into a woman. *P. capitaine,* to be promoted captain. (*b*) (Aux. *avoir*) To be considered, to pass for. *P. pour riche,* to be accounted rich. *P. pour avoir fait qch.,* to be credited with having done sth. *P. pour exact,* (i) (of pers.) to have a name for punctuality; (ii) (of fact) to be supposed to be correct. **Se faire passer pour . . . ,** to give oneself out to be . . . , to pass oneself off as, for. . . . *Se faire p. pour Français,* to pose as a Frenchman. **7.** (Aux. *avoir*) To be accepted, to pass muster. *La loi a passé,* the bill has been carried, *F:* has gone through. *Cela peut p.,* it will pass muster. *Monnaie qui ne passe plus,* coinage that is no longer current.

Qu'il revienne demain, **passe encore,** if he returns to-morrow, well and good. **Cela ne passe pas,** that won't do. **Enfin, passe pour lui!** well, that's all right as far as he is concerned. **8.** (Aux. *avoir*) *Jur:* (Of lawsuit) *P. en jugement,* to come up for judgment. *L'affaire passera en janvier, demain,* the case will be heard in January, comes on to-morrow.

II. **passer,** *v.tr.* **1.** To pass, traverse, cross, go over (bridge, river, sea). *Vous avez passé la maison,* you have gone past the house. **2.** (*a*) To carry across; to ferry (goods, passengers) over. *Voulez-vous me p.?* will you ferry me across? *P. des marchandises en fraude,* to smuggle in goods. (*b*) *P. qch. à qn,* to hand sth. to s.o. *Veuillez me p. l'eau,* please pass me the water. *P. une nouvelle,* to hand on news. *Faire p. une lettre à son adresse,* to forward a letter. *P. une commande,* to place an order. *Fb: P. le ballon,* to pass the ball. (*c*) *P. une éponge sur le tableau,* to pass a sponge over the blackboard. *Se p. la main dans les cheveux,* to run one's fingers through one's hair. *P. sa tête par la fenêtre,* to put in (or out) one's head at the window. *P. une chemise,* to slip on a shirt. (*d*) *P. un couteau à la meule,* to grind, sharpen, a knife. *P. un dessin à l'encre,* to ink in a drawing. *P. un déserteur par les armes,* to shoot a deserter. **3.** To pass, spend (time, one's life). *P. son temps à faire qch.,* to spend one's time (in) doing sth. *Leur lune de miel se passa à Naples,* their honeymoon was spent in Naples. *F:* **Se la passer douce,** to have an easy time, to take it easy. **4.** To pass, go beyond, exceed, surpass. *Cela passe ma capacité,* that is beyond my powers. *Cela passe la mesure, les bornes,* that is going too far. *F:* **Cela me passe,** it passes my comprehension. *Le vieux ne passera pas l'hiver,* the old man won't live through the winter. *Prov:* **Contentement passe richesse,** content is better than wealth. **5.** To pass over. (*a*) To excuse, pardon (fault, etc.). *Je vous passe cela,* I grant you that. *P. une fantaisie à qn,* to indulge, humour, s.o.'s fancy. (*b*) To omit, leave out. **Passer qch. sous silence,** to pass over sth. in silence. (*c*) *Cards: etc: P. son tour,* *Abs.* **passer,** to pass. **6.** (*a*) *Jur:* **Passer un accord,** to conclude an agreement. *P. un contrat,* to enter into, sign, a contract. *Book-k:* **Passer écriture d'un article,** to post an entry. (*b*) *P. une loi,* to pass a law. (*c*) *P. un examen,* (i) to sit for, (ii) to pass, get through, an examination. **7.** To strain (liquid); to percolate (coffee).

se passer. 1. To happen; to take place. *Que se passe-t-il? qu'est-ce qui se passe?* what is going on? *F:* what's up? *Est-ce que la cérémonie s'est bien passée?* did the ceremony go off all right? **2.** (*a*) To pass away, to cease; (of time) to elapse, go by. *Il faut que jeunesse se passe,* youth will have its fling. **Cela ne se passera pas ainsi,** I shall not let it rest at that. (*b*) To fade, decay, wither. **3. Se passer de qch.,** to do without, to dispense with, sth. *Je ne peux pas m'en p.,* I can't do without it.

passé. 1. *a.* (*a*) Past; gone by. *La semaine passée,* last week. *Il a quarante ans passés,* he is over forty. S.a. MAÎTRE 1. *L'orage est p.,* the storm is over. (*b*) Faded. **2.** *s.m.* Le passé. (*a*) The past; former times. **Comme par le passé,** as in the past, as hitherto. **Oublions le passé,** let bygones be bygones. (*b*) *Gram:* **Verbe au passé,** verb in the past tense. (*c*) **Broderie au passé,** satin-stitch embroidery. **3.** *prep.* Passé, beyond. **Il est passé quatre heures,** it is, has, gone four. *P. cette date . . . ,* after this date. . . .

passereau [pɑsro], *s.m.* Sparrow.

passerelle [pɑsrɛl], *s.f.* **1.** Foot-bridge. **2.** *Nau :* La passerelle de commandement, the bridge. *P. de service,* gangway. [PASSER]

passe-rose, *s.f. Bot :* Hollyhock, rose-mallow. *pl Des passe-rose(s).*

passe-temps, *s.m.inv.* Pastime, diversion.

passe-thé, *s.m.inv.* Tea-strainer.

passeur, -euse [pɑsœːr, -øːz], *s.* Ferryman, ferrywoman.

passible [pasibl], *a.* Liable (*de,* to, for). *P. d'une amende,* liable to a fine.

pass|if, -ive [pasif, -iːv]. **1.** *a.* (*a*) Passive (obedience, etc.). *Gram : Voix passive,* passive voice. (*b*) *Com :* Dettes passives, debts due by us ; liabilities. **2.** *s.m.* (*a*) *Gram :* Passive (voice). (*b*) *Com :* Liabilities. *adv.* **-ivement.**

passim [pasim], *Lt. adv.* Passim.

passion [pɑsjɔ̃], *s.f.* **1.** La Passion, the Passion (of Christ). Semaine de la Passion, Passion Week. *Bot :* Fleur de la Passion, passion-flower. **2.** *P. pour la musique,* passion for music. Aimer qn à la passion, to be passionately in love with s.o. La *p. de la vérité,* a passion for truth. Avoir la passion de faire qch., to be passionately fond of doing sth. Parler avec passion, sans passion, to speak passionately, dispassionately.

passionnant [pɑsjɔnɑ̃], *a.* Entrancing, thrilling.

passionnel, -elle [pɑsjɔnɛl], *a.* Pertaining to the passions. Crime passionnel, love tragedy ; crime due to jealousy.

passionner [pɑsjɔne], *v.tr.* To impassion ; to excite (s.o.) with passion. Le sport le passionne, he is passionately fond of sport. *Livre qui passionne,* book that grips you.

se passionner *de, pour, qch.,* to conceive a passion for sth.

passionné, *a.* Passionate, impassioned, ardent. *P. de, pour, qn,* passionately fond of, doting on, s.o. *P. contre qch.,* deeply prejudiced against sth. *s. Un p. de musique,* a music enthusiast. *adv.* **-ment.**

passivité [pasivite], *s.f.* Passivity.

passoire [pɑswaːr], *s.f. Cu :* Strainer. *P. à légumes,* colander. [PASSER]

pastel [pastɛl], *s.m.* Pastel. **1.** *Bot :* Woad. **2.** *Art :* (*a*) Crayon. (*b*) Pastel drawing.

pastèque [pastɛk], *s.f.* Water-melon.

pasteur [pastœːr], *s.m.* **1.** Shepherd. *Peuple p.,* pastoral people. **2.** Pastor ; (protestant) minister.

pasteuriser [pastœrize], *v.tr.* To Pasteurize, to sterilize (milk, etc.).

pastiche [pastiʃ], *s.m.* **1.** *Art : Mus :* Pasticcio. **2.** *Lit :* (*a*) Pastiche, imitation. (*b*) Parody.

pasticher [pastiʃe], *v.tr. Art : etc :* (*a*) To imitate, copy (the style of s.o.). (*b*) To parody.

pastille [pastiːj], *s.f.* **1.** Lozenge, jujube. *Pastilles de chocolat,* chocolate buttons or drops. **2.** Rubber patch (for inner tube of tyre). **3.** *P. microphonique,* capsule (of transmitter).

pastoral, -aux [pastɔral, -o]. **1.** *a.* Pastoral. *Anneau p.,* episcopal ring. **2.** *s.f.* Pastorale. (*a*) Pastoral (play, poem). (*b*) (Bishop's) pastoral (letter). *adv.* **-ement.**

pastorat [pastɔra], *s.m.* Pastorate.

pastoureau, -elle [pasturo, -ɛl]. **1.** *s.* Poet : Shepherd-lad, -lass. **2.** *s.f.* Pastourelle, pastoral (poem).

pat [pat], *s.m. inv. Chess :* Stalemate. *a.inv.* Faire pat son adversaire, to stalemate one's opponent.

patache [pataʃ], *s.f. F :* Ramshackle conveyance ; shandrydan.

patachon [pataʃɔ̃], *s.m.* (*a*) *A :* Stage-cart driver. (*b*) *P :* Mener une vie de patachon, to lead a rollicking life, a wild life.

patapouf [patapuf]. **1,** *int.* Flop ! Faire p., to fall flop. **2.** *s.m. F : Gros p.,* fat lump of a man.

pataquès [patakɛs], *s.m. F :* Faulty liaison (betraying illiteracy) ; bloomer.

patarafe [pataraf], *s.f. F :* Scrawl.

patate [patat], *s.f.* **1.** Batata ; sweet potato. **2.** *P :* Potato ; *P :* spud.

patati [patati]. *F :* Et patati et patata, and so forth and so on.

patatras [patatrɑ], *int. F :* Crash !

pataud, -aude [pato, -oːd], *a. & s.* Clumsy, loutish, lumpish (person).

pataug|er [patoʒe], *v.i.* (je pataugeai(s) ; n. pataugeons) (*a*) To splash and flounder in the mud. (*b*) *F :* To flounder (in a speech, in viva voce exam.). (*c*) To paddle, to wade (in sea, etc.). *s.m.* **-eage.** *s.* **-eur, -euse.**

patch [patʃ], *s.m.* Patch (for tyre).

patchouli [patʃuli], *s.m. Bot : Toil :* Patchouli.

pâte [pɑt], *s.f.* **1.** Paste. (*a*) *P. à pain,* dough. *Pâtes d'Italie,* Italian paste. *F :* Être de la pâte dont on fait les héros, to be of the stuff that heroes are made of. Mettre la main à la pâte, to take a hand in the work oneself. C'est une bonne pâte (d'homme), he's a good sort. (*b*) *Toil :* *P. d'amandes,* almond-cream. *P. dentifrice,* toothpaste. *P. à polycopier,* hectograph jelly. Pâte de bois, wood-pulp. Pâte de carton, papier mâché. *Art :* Peindre en pleine pâte, to paint with a full brush. **2.** *Typ :* (Printer's) pie. **3.** Cramming. Vivre comme un coq en pâte, to live like a fighting cock.

pâté [pate], *s.m.* **1.** (*a*) (Meat or fish) pie. *F :* Quel gros pâté que ce petit! what a fat little boy ! (*b*) *P. en terrine,* potted pâté (of foie gras). *P. de cochon,* brawn. **2.** Block (of houses) ; clump (of trees). **3.** Blot, blob (of ink).

pâtée [pate], *s.f.* Mash (for poultry) ; dogs', cats', food.

patelin[1], -ine [patlɛ̃, -in]. (*a*) *a.* Smooth-tongued, smooth-spoken, mealy-mouthed ; glib. (From the 15th cent. farce *Maistre Pierre Pathelin.*) *Voix pateline,* wheedling voice. *Excuses patelines,* humbugging excuses. (*b*) *s.* Smooth-tongue, wheedler.

patelin[2], *s.m. P :* **1.** (*a*) Native village or farm. (*b*) Man from the same village (as myself, etc.). **2.** Small locality.

patelinage [patlinaːʒ], *s.m.* Smooth words ; blarney ; humbug.

patelle [patɛl], *s.f.* **1.** *Archeol :* Patella. **2.** Limpet, barnacle.

patène [patɛn], *s.f. Ecc :* Paten.

patenôtre [patnoːtr], *s.f.* **1.** (*a*) Paternoster, Lord's prayer. (*b*) *F :* Prayer. (*c*) *pl. F :* Beads, rosary. Dire ses patenôtres, (i) to tell one's beads ; (ii) to say one's prayers. **2.** Paternoster pump ; noria.

patent [patɑ̃], *a.* (*a*) Patent ; open to all. Lettres patentes, (letters) patent. (*b*) Obvious, evident.

patentable [patɑ̃tabl], *a.* (Trade, etc.) subject to a licence, requiring a licence.

patente [patɑ̃ːt], *s.f.* **1.** (*a*) Licence (to exercise a trade or profession). Se faire inscrire à la patente, to take out a licence. (*b*) Tax. Payer patente, to be duly licensed. **2.** *Nau :* Patente de santé, bill of health.

patenter [patɑ̃te], *v.tr.* To license.

patenté, -ée, *a.* Licensee ; licensed dealer.

pater [patɛːr], *s.m.inv.* The Lord's prayer. Dire cinq pater, to say five paternosters.

patère [patɛːr], *s.f.* (*a*) Hat-peg, coat-peg. (*b*) Curtain-hook (for looping up the curtain).

paterne [patɛrn], *a.* Benevolent, soft-spoken ; smooth (tone).

patern|el, -elle [paternɛl], *a.* Paternal. (*a*) *Du côté p.,* on the father's side. *s.m. P :* **Le paternel,** the pater. (*b*) Fatherly, kindly (tone, advice). *adv.* **-ellement.**

paternité [patɛrnite], *s.f.* Paternity, fatherhood. *F : Revendiquer la p. d'un livre,* to claim the authorship of a book.

pâteux, -euse [patø, -øːz], *a.* (*a*) Pasty, clammy ; doughy (bread). *Langue pâteuse,* coated tongue. (*b*) Thick, dull (voice) ; muddy (ink). (*c*) (Of gem) Cloudy, milky.

pathétique [patetik]. **1.** *a.* Pathetic, moving, touching. **2.** *s.m.* Pathos. *adv.* **-ment,** -ally.

pathologie [patɔlɔʒi], *s.f.* Pathology.

pathologique [patɔlɔʒik], *a.* Pathological.

pathologiste [patɔlɔʒist], *s.m.* Pathologist.

pathos [patɔs], *s.m.* Affected pathos ; bathos.

patibulaire [patibylɛːr], *a.* Relating to the gallows. **Fourches patibulaires,** gibbet. **Avoir une mine patibulaire,** to wear a hang-dog look.

patience¹ [pasjɑ̃ːs], *s.f.* **1.** Patience, long-suffering. *Avoir de la p.,* **prendre patience,** to have patience, to be patient. **Prendre qch. en patience,** to bear sth. patiently ; to put up with sth. **Attendre avec patience,** to wait patiently. *Ma p. est à bout,* **je suis à bout de patience,** my patience is exhausted. **Faire perdre patience à qn,** to put s.o. out of patience. **Jeu de patience,** puzzle ; esp. jig-saw puzzle. **2.** *Mil :* Button-stick.

patience², *s.f. Bot :* Patience-dock.

pati|ent, -ente [pasjɑ̃, -ɑ̃ːt]. **1.** *a.* Patient. (*a*) Enduring, long-suffering. (*b*) Forbearing. **2.** *s.* (*a*) Condemned man (about to be executed). (*b*) Patient (in surgical case). *adv.* **-emment.**

patienter [pasjɑ̃te], *v.i.* To exercise patience.

patin [patɛ̃], *s.m.* **1.** *A :* Patten (foot-gear). **2.** (*a*) Skate. *Patins à roulettes,* roller skates. (*b*) Runner (of sledge) ; skid (of aeroplane). **3.** (*a*) (Drag-)shoe, skid(-pan) (of wheel). (*b*) Shoe (of brake).

patine [patin], *s.f.* Patina (on ancient bronzes).

patin|er¹ [patine], *v.i.* **1.** To skate. **2.** (Of wheel) To skid ; (of belt) to slip. *s.m.* **-age.**

patiner², *v.tr.* To give a patina to (bronze). **patiné,** *a.* Patinated (bronze).

patinette [patinɛt], *s.f.* Scooter.

patineur, -euse [patinœːr, -øːz], *s.* Skater.

patinoire [patinwaːr], *s.f.* Skating-rink.

pâtir [patiːr], *v.i.* To suffer (for others) ; to suffer in health.

pâtis [pati], *s.m.* Grazing-ground, pasture.

pâtisserie [patisri], *s.f.* **1.** (*a*) Pastry. (*b*) *pl.* Cakes. **2.** Pastry-making. **3.** Cake-shop ; tea-rooms.

pâtissier, -ière [patisje, -jɛːr], *s.* **1.** Pastry-cook. **2.** Tea-room proprietor.

patois [patwa], *s.m.* (*a*) Patois ; provincial dialect. (*b*) *F :* Jargon, lingo.

patoiser [patwaze], *v.i.* To speak in patois.

patouiller [patuje]. **1.** *v.i.* To splash, flounder (in the mud). **2.** *v.tr. P :* To paw (s.o., sth.). ·

patraque [patrak]. **1.** *s.f.* (*a*) Worn-out machine. (*b*) *F :* Chronic invalid ; old crock. **2.** *a. F :* Out of sorts ; seedy.

pâtre [paːtr], *s.m.* Herdsman ; *occ.* shepherd.

patriarcal, -aux [patriarkal, -o], *a.* Patriarchal. *adv.* **-ement.**

patriarche [patriarʃ], *s.m.* Patriarch.

patricien, -ienne [patrisjɛ̃, -jɛn], *a. & s. Rom. Hist :* Patrician.

patrie [patri], *s.f.* One's native land or country ; fatherland. **Mère patrie,** mother country.

patrimoine [patrimwan], *s.m.* Patrimony, heritage.

patrimonial, -aux [patrimɔnjal, -o], *a.* Patrimonial.

patriote [patriɔt]. **1.** *a.* Patriotic (person). **2.** *s.* Patriot.

patriotique [patriɔtik], *a.* Patriotic (song, speech). *adv.* **-ment,** -ally.

patriotisme [patriɔtism], *s.m.* Patriotism.

patron, -onne [patrɔ̃, -ɔn], *s.* **1.** (*a*) Patron, patroness ; protector, protectress. (*b*) Patron saint. **2.** (*a*) Master, mistress (of house) ; employer (of labour) ; chief, head, owner (of firm) ; proprietor (of hotel). (*b*) *Nau :* Skipper, master (of small vessel) ; coxswain (of boat crew). **3.** *s.m.* (*a*) Pattern (for dress) ; model. (*b*) Template, templet. **Patron ajouré,** stencil(-plate).

patronage [patrɔnaːʒ], *s.m.* **1.** (*a*) Patronage, support. (*b*) *Ecc :* Advowson. **2.** (*a*) (Church) club (for young people) ; guild. (*b*) Headquarters of church guild.

patronal, -aux [patrɔnal, -o], *a.* **1.** Pertaining to the patron saint. **Fête patronale,** patronal festival. **2.** Pertaining to employers. *Syndicat p.,* employers' association.

patronat [patrɔna], *s.m.* **1.** *Rom.Ant : etc :* Patronate, protection. **2.** Body of employers.

patron-jaquet [patrɔ̃ʒakɛ], *s.m.,* **patron-minet** [patrɔ̃minɛ], *s.m.* **Dès (le) patron-jaquet, -minet,** at early dawn, at peep of day.

patronner¹ [patrɔne], *v.tr.* To stencil.

patronner², *v.tr.* To patronize, support (hospital, charity ball, etc.).

patronnesse [patrɔnɛs], *a. & s.f.* (*Dame) p.,* patroness.

patronymique [patrɔnimik], *a.* Patronymic. **Nom patronymique,** surname.

patrouille [patruːj], *s.f.* Patrol. *Chef de p.,* patrol leader. **Aller en patrouille, faire la patrouille,** to go on patrol ; to patrol.

patrouiller [patruje], *v.i.* To patrol.

patrouilleur [patrujœːr], *s.m.* Member of a patrol. *Navy :* Patrol-boat, patrol-ship.

patte [pat], *s.f.* **1.** Paw (of lion, cat, dog) ; foot (of bird) ; leg (of insect). *F :* **Pattes de mouche,** cramped handwriting ; scrawl. **Pattes d'araignée,** (i) long thin fingers ; (ii) scrawling writing ; (iii) *Mec.E :* oil-grooves, grease-channels (of bearing). **Marcher, aller, à quatre pattes,** to go on all fours, on one's hands and knees. **Animaux à quatre pattes,** four-footed animals. **Faire patte de velours,** (of cat) to draw in its claws. **Coup de patte,** scratch, claw, pat. **Tenir qn sous sa patte,** to have s.o. at one's mercy. **Tomber sous la patte de qn,** to fall into s.o.'s clutches. **A bas les pattes !** (i) (to dog) down, sir ! (ii) *F :* hands off ! (Of dog, etc.) **A toutes pattes,** at full speed. *S.a.* BLANC I. 3, GRAISSER I. **2.** Foot (of wine-glass). **3.** Flap (of pocket, of envelope). **4.** Holdfast, clamp, clip, fastening. *Cy : P. de tension,* chain-adjuster. **5.** Fluke, palm (of anchor) ; claw (of grapnel). **6.** Tab, strap (on garment). *Pattes d'épaule,* shoulder-straps.

patte-d'araignée, *s.f. Bot :* Love-in-the-mist.

patte-de-lièvre, *s.f. Bot :* Hare's-foot trefoil.

patte-d'oie, *s.f.* **1.** Cross-roads ; goose-foot. **2.** Crow's-foot (wrinkle). **3.** *Bot :* Chenopodium, goose-foot. *pl. Des pattes-d'oie.*

patte-fiche, *s.f.* Holdfast. *pl. Des pattes-fiches.*

patte-pelu(e), *s. m. & f. F :* Sneak, pussyfoot.

pattu [paty], *a. F :* **1.** Large-pawed (dog). **2.** Feather-legged (hen, pigeon). [PATTE]

pâturage [patyraːʒ], *s.m.* **1.** Grazing. **2.** (*a*) Pasture, grazing-ground ; sheep-walk, -run. (*b*) *pl.* Pasture-land.

pâture [pɑty:r], *s.f.* **I.** Food, feed, fodder (of animals). *P. intellectuelle*, mental pabulum. **2.** Pasture. **Mettre les chevaux eu pâture**, to turn the horses out to grass.

pâturer [pɑtyre], **I.** *v.i.* To graze, to feed. **2.** *v.tr.* (Of cattle) To graze (on) (meadow).

pâturin [pɑtyrɛ̃], *s.m. Bot:* Meadow-grass.

paturon [pɑtyrɔ̃], *s.m.* Pastern (of horse).

paume [po:m], *s.f.* **I.** (a) Palm (of hand). (b) Hand (as a measure of horses). **2.** (Jeu de) **paume.** (i) Tennis. (*N.B.* Not lawn-tennis.) (ii) Tennis-court. *Fr.Hist:* **Le Serment du Jeu de Paume**, the Oath of the Tennis-Court (1789).

paumelle [pomɛl], *s.f.* **I.** (Sail-maker's) palm. **2.** (a) Plate (of door-hinge). (b) Door-hinge.

paumer [pome], *v.tr. P:* **I.** To smack, slap (s.o.'s face). **2.** To nab, cop (thief).

paumure [pomy:r], *s.f.* Palm (of deer's antlers).

paupérisme [poperism], *s.m.* Pauperism.

paupière [popjɛːr], *s.f.* Eyelid. *Fermer la p. d qn*, to close s.o.'s eyes (as a last duty).

paupiette [popjɛt], *s.f. Cu:* (Meat-)olive.

pause [po:z], *s.f.* **I.** Pause. *Ind:* Meal interval. **Faire une pause**, to pause; to stop. **2.** *Mus:* (i) Rest, pause. (ii) Semibreve rest. (iii) Bar rest.

pauvre [po:vr]. **I.** *a.* Poor. (a) Needy, in want, penurious; scant(y) (vegetation). *Un homme p.*, a poor, an indigent, man. *P. en esprit*, poor in spirit. *P. d'esprit*, dull-witted. **Pauvre comme un rat d'église**, poor as a church mouse. *Minerai p. en métal*, ore poor in metal. *Aut: Mélange p.*, weak mixture. (b) Unfortunate. *Le p. homme! poor fellow! P. de moi!* poor me! (c) Wretched, mean; sorry (horse); shabby (furniture). *P. excuse*, lame, paltry, excuse. *De pauvres vers*, sorry verses. **2.** *s.* (a) Poor man, poor woman. *Adm:* Pauper. **Ayez pitié des pauvres**, pity the poor. *Th:* **Droit des pauvres**, entertainment tax. (b) Beggar. *adv.* **-ment.**

pauvresse [povrɛs], *s.f.* (a) Poor woman. *Adm:* Pauper. (b) Beggar-woman.

pauvret, -ette [povre, -ɛt], *s. F: Le p., la pauvrette*, the poor little thing.

pauvreté [povrəte], *s.f.* **I.** (a) Poverty, indigence, want. *P. en céréales*, lack of cereal crops (in a region). (b) Poorness (of language); baldness (of style). **2.** *N'écrire que des pauvretés*, to write poor stuff.

pavage [pava:ʒ], *s.m.* **I.** (Action of) paving. **2.** Pavement.

pavaner (se) [səpavane], *v.pr.* To strut (about); to peacock (about).

pavement [pavmã], *s.m.* (Ornate) pavement.

paver [pave], *v.tr.* To pave. *Rue pavée en bois*, wood-paved street.

pavé, *s.m.* **I.** (a) Paving-stone, paving-block. *F:* **C'est le pavé de l'ours** (allusion to La Fontaine's fable), (i) 'save me from my friends!' (ii) it is like breaking a butterfly on the wheel. (b) Slab (of gingerbread). **2.** (a) Pavement. (b) Paved road, carriage road, highway. (c) *A:* Paved sides of (unpaved) thoroughfare; footway. **Prendre le haut du pavé**, (i) to walk on the wall side of the pavement; (ii) *F:* to lord it. **Céder le haut du pavé à qn**, to give way to s.o. (d) *F:* **Battre le pavé**, (i) to loaf about the streets, about town; (ii) to tramp the streets in search of work. **Être sur le pavé**, (i) to be homeless, on the streets; (ii) to be out of work.

paveur [pavœ:r], *s.m.* Paver, paviour.

Pavie [pavi]. **I.** *Pr.n.f. Geog:* Pavia. **2.** *s.f.* Clingstone (peach).

pavillon [pavijɔ̃], *s.m.* **I.** Pavilion. (a) *A:* Tent. (b) Detached building. *P. d'entrée (d'une propriété)*, gate-lodge. *P de jardin*, summer-house. *P. de chasse*, shooting-lodge; (hunting-)box. *P. de golf*, golf-pavilion, club-house. **2.** (a) Horn (of gramophone, etc.); bell (of trumpet); mouth (of funnel); ear-piece or mouth-piece (of telephone). (b) *P. de l'oreille*, external ear. **3.** *Nau:* Flag, colours. *P. couplé*, waft. *P. de départ, p. de partance*, Blue Peter. *P. noir, de pirate*, jolly Roger; black flag. *P. de poupe*, ensign. *P. de détresse*, flag of distress. *Hisser, arborer, son p.*, to hoist one's colours. *Montrer son p.*, to show, display, one's colours. *Amener, baisser, son* **pavillon**, to strike one's flag. **Clouer son pavillon**, to nail one's colours to the mast. *S.a.* BATTRE I.

pavois [pavwa], *s.m.* **I.** *Archeol:* (Body-)shield; pavis(e). **2.** *Nau:* (a) Bulwark. (b) *Coll.* Flags (for dressing ship). **Mettre, hisser, le grand pavois**, to dress ship over all.

pavoiser [pavwaze], *v.tr.* (a) *Nau:* To dress (ship). *Abs.* To dress ship. (b) *F:* To deck (house, etc.) with flags; to put out bunting. *s.m.* **-ement.**

pavot [pavo], *s.m. Bot:* Poppy. **Tête de pavot**, poppy-head. **Graine(s) de pavot**, poppy-seed.

payable [pɛjabl], *a.* Payable. *P. à vue, à l'ordre*, payable at sight, to order.

payant, -ante [pɛjã, -ãt]. **I.** *a.* (a) Paying (pupil, etc.) (b) Charged for. *"Toutes les places sont payantes,"* 'no free seats.' *"Entrée payante,"* 'no free admission.' *Pont p.*, toll-bridge. **2.** *s.* Payer.

paye [pɛ:j], *s.f.* **I.** Pay (of soldiers); wages (of workmen). **Demi-paye**, half-pay. **2.** Payment. **Jour de paye**, pay-day. **Faire la paye**, to pay out the wages. **3.** *F:* **C'est une mauvaise paye**, he is a bad payer, a slow payer.

payement [pɛjmã], *s.m.* Payment; discharge (of debt). *Gros p.*, heavy disbursement. *P. d'avance*, prepayment. *P. contre livraison*, cash on delivery; C.O.D. *P. à termes, par acomptes*, instalments.

payer [pɛje], *v.tr.* (je paye, je paie; je payerai, je paierai) (a) **Payer qn**, to pay s.o. *P. qn de ses services*, to (re)pay s.o. for his services. *Trop payé, trop peu payé*, overpaid, underpaid. *F:* **Payer qn de la même monnaie**, to pay s.o. back in his own coin. *Il me paie d'ingratitude*, he requites me with ingratitude. **Payer qn de paroles, de mots**, to put s.o. off with fine words. **Payer de sa personne**, (i) to risk one's own skin; (ii) to take a personal share in the work. **Payer d'audace**, to take the risk. **Payer d'effronterie**, to brazen it out; to put a bold face on it. (b) To pay, discharge, settle (debt). **Payer rubis sur l'ongle**, to pay on the nail. *P. un effet*, to honour a bill. *S.a.* DETTE. (c) To pay for (sth.). *P. qch. à qn*, to pay s.o. for sth. *Je le lui ai payé cent francs*, I paid him a hundred francs for it. *P. un dîner à qn*, to stand s.o. a dinner. *Je me suis payé une glace*, I treated myself to an ice. **Se payer la figure, la tête, de qn**, to make fun of s.o.; to take a rise out of s.o. *P:* **S'en payer**, to have a good time. **Port payé**, carriage-paid, post-paid. *Il a payé sa témérité de sa vie*, he paid for his rashness with his life. *Cela ne se paie pas*, money cannot buy it. *Faire p. ses méfaits à qn*, to bring s.o. to account. **Vous me le paierez!** you shall smart for this! *Je suis payé pour le savoir*, I have learnt it to my cost. *Je l'ai payé cher*, I paid dearly for it (*i.e.* for my rashness, etc.).

payeur, -euse [pɛjœ:r, -ø:z], *s.* **I.** Payer. **2.** Disbursing official *Mil:, Navy:* Paymaster. *Bank:* Teller.

pays¹ [pe(j)i], *s.m.* Country. *(a)* Land. *Visiter des p. étrangers*, to visit foreign lands. *Les p. chauds*, the tropics. *P: Un petit pays chaud, a little native of warmer climes, a little nigger boy. Battre du pays*, to roam about. *Il a vu du pays*, he has travelled (about) a great deal. *(b)* Region, district, locality. *Vous n'êtes donc pas de ce p.?* so you don't belong to these parts? **Pays perdu**, out-of-the-way place. *F:* **Être en pays de connaissance**, to be among friends. *Denrées du p.*, home(-grown) produce. **Vin du pays**, local wine. *(c) P. de montagne(s)*, hill country. *pl. P. bas*, lowlands. *S.a.* PAYS-BAS. *(d)* Native land; home. **Avoir le mal du pays**, to be homesick. *F:* **Il est bien de son pays!** well, he is green !

pays², **payse** [pe(j)i, pe(j)iːz], *s. F:* Fellow-countryman, -woman. *Nous sommes p.*, we are from the same parts, from the same village.

paysage [peizaːʒ], *s.m.* **1.** Landscape; scenery. **2.** *Art:* Landscape(-painting). *F:* **Cela fait bien dans le paysage**, it works well in the picture.

paysagiste [peizaʒist], *s.m.* Landscape-painter.

paysan, -anne [peizɑ̃, -an], *s. & a.* Peasant, rustic. *Les paysans*, the peasantry. *Faire qch.* **à la paysanne**, to do sth. country-fashion.

paysannerie [peizanri], *s.f.* **1.** *Coll.* Peasant people; peasantry. **2.** *A:* Story of peasant life.

Pays-Bas (les). *Pr.n.m.* The Netherlands.

payse. See PAYS².

péage [peaːʒ], *s.m.* **1.** Toll. **Barrière de péage**, turnpike, *A:* toll-bar. **Pont à péage**, toll-bridge. **2.** Toll-house.

péager, -ère [peaʒe, -ɛːr], *s.* Toll-collector.

péan [peɑ̃], *s.m.* Paean; song of triumph.

peau [po], *s.f.* **1.** Skin. *A même la p.*, next to the skin. *Beauté à fleur de p.*, skin-deep beauty. *Prendre qn par la p. du cou*, to take s.o. by the scruff of the neck. **Faire peau neuve**, (i) (of snake) to cast its slough, its skin; (ii) *F:* to turn over a new leaf. **Ne pas tenir dans sa peau**, to be bursting with pride, with joy. **Il mourra dans la peau d'un imbécile**, he'll be a fool as long as he lives. *Je ne voudrais pas être dans sa p.*, I should not like to be in his shoes. **Risquer sa peau**, to risk one's life. **Sauver sa peau**, to save one's bacon. **Craindre pour sa peau**, to fear for one's skin. *P:* **Avoir la peau courte**, to be lazy. **Avoir qn dans la peau**, to be infatuated with s.o. **Travailler pour la peau**, to work for love, for nothing; to have all one's trouble for nothing. **La peau!** nothing doing ! **Vieille peau**, old hag. **2.** *(a)* Pelt, fell, fur (of. animal); hide (of bullock). *P. de lapin*, rabbit skin. *(b)* (Leather) *P. de cheval*, horse-hide. *P. de mouton*, sheepskin. *P. de chevreau*, kid. *P. de daim*, buckskin. *P. de veau*, box-calf. *P. de requin*, shagreen. *P. de taupe*, moleskin (fur). *(c) P. de tambour*, (i) drum parchment; (ii) drum-head. **3.** Peel, skin (of fruit). **4.** Coating; film, skin (of boiled milk).

Peau-Rouge, *s.m.* Red Indian, redskin. *pl. Des Peaux-Rouges.*

peausserie [posri], *s.f.* **1.** Skin dressing. **2.** Skins.

peaussier [posje], *s.m.* *(a)* Skin-dresser. *(b)* Fellmonger.

pécari [pekari], *s.m. Z:* Peccary; Mexican hog.

peccable [pɛkkabl], *a.* Peccable; liable to sin.

peccadille [pɛkkadiːj], *s.f.* Peccadillo.

pêche¹ [peːʃ], *s.f.* Peach.

pêche², *s.f.* **1.** Fishing. *P. des truites*, trout-fishing. *P. à la sardine*, sardine-fishing. *P. à la ligne*, angling. *P. à la mouche*, fly-fishing. *La p. des perles*, pearl-fishing. **Aller à la pêche**, to go fishing. **2.** Catch. *B:* **La pêche miraculeuse**,

the miraculous draught of fishes. **3.** Fishery. *Grande p.*, high-sea fishery. *P. à la drague*, trawling.

péché [peʃe], *s.m.* Sin; trespass, transgression. *Les péchés capitaux*, the deadly sins. *F:* **Laid comme les sept péchés**, as ugly as sin. *F:* **Pour mes péchés, je fus nommé à . . .**, for my sins, I was appointed to. . . . *Son p. mignon, d'habitude*, his besetting sin. *Péchés de jeunesse*, indiscretions of youth.

pécher [peʃe], *v.i.* (je pèche; je pécherai) To sin. *P. contre la politesse*, to offend against the laws of courtesy. *Il pèche par trop de timidité*, his fault is his excessive shyness. *P. par excès, par défaut*, to exceed, fall short of, what is required. *Prov:* **Qui perd pèche**, the loser is always in the wrong.

pêcher¹ [peʃe], *s.m.* Peach-tree.

pêcher², *v.tr.* **1.** *(a)* To fish for (trout, etc.). *P. à la ligne*, to angle (with rod and line). *P. un câble*, to sweep for a cable. *P. des perles*, to dive for pearls. *P. la baleine*, to hunt whales. *P. des compliments*, to fish for compliments. *(b)* **Pêcher au plat**, to dig one's fork or spoon into the dish. **2.** *P. une truite*, to catch a trout. *P. un cadavre*, to fish up a dead body. *F:* **Où avez-vous pêché cela?** where did you get hold of that?

pécheresse. See PÉCHEUR.

pêcherie [peʃri], *s.f.* Fishery, fishing-ground.

pécheur, pécheresse [peʃœːr, peʃrɛs]. **I.** *s.* Sinner, offender, transgressor. **2.** *a.* Sinning.

pêcheur, -euse [peʃœːr, -øːz], *s.* **I.** Fisher; fisherman -woman. *P. à la ligne*, angler. *P. de baleines*, whaler. *P. de perles*, pearl-diver. **2.** *s.m.* Fishing-smack, -boat.

pécore [pekɔːr], *s.f. A:* *(a)* Creature, animal. *(b) F:* (Of woman) Goose; silly girl.

pecque [pɛk], *s.f. A:* Ignorant and pert young woman.

pectiné [pɛktine], *a. Nat.Hist:* Pectinate(d); comb-shaped; ctenoid.

pectoral, -aux [pɛktɔral, -o]. **I.** *a.* Pectoral (muscle, etc.). *Pastille de pâte pectorale*, cough-lozenge. **2.** *s.m.* Pectoral, breast-plate.

péculat [pekyla], *s.m.* Peculation, embezzlement.

péculateur [pekylatœːr], *s.m.* Peculator; embezzler.

pécule [pekyl], *s.m.* *(a)* Savings, store of money; nest-egg. *(b)* Earnings (of convict). *(c) Mil:* Gratuity (on discharge).

pécuniaire [pekynjɛːr], *a.* Pecuniary. **Intérêt pécuniaire**, (i) money interest; (ii) insurable interest. **Peine pécuniaire**, fine. *adv.* **-ment**.

pédagogie [pedagɔʒi], *s.f.* Pedagogy, pedagogics.

pédagogique [pedagɔʒik], *a.* Pedagogic(al). *adv.* **-ment**, -ally.

pédagogue [pedagɔg], *s. m. & f.* Pedagogue; *esp. Pej:* pedant.

pédale [pedal], *s.f.* **I.** Pedal (of piano, organ, cycle); treadle (of lathe, etc.). *Frein à p.*, foot-brake. *P. d'embrayage*, clutch-pedal. *Organ:* *P. expressive*, swell-pedal. *Piano:* *Petite p.*, soft pedal. *Grande p.*, loud pedal. **2.** *Mus:* Pedal (-note).

pédaler [pedale], *v.i.* To pedal. *(a)* To work a treadle. *(b)* To cycle, *F:* to bike.

pédalier [pedalje], *s.m.* **I.** Crank-gear (of cycle, etc.). **2.** Pedal-board (of organ); pedalier.

pédant, -ante [pedɑ̃, -ɑ̃ːt]. **I.** *s.* Pedant. **2.** *a.* Pedantic.

pédanterie [pedɑ̃tri], *s.f.* Pedantry.

pédantisme [pedɑ̃tism], *s.m.* = PÉDANTERIE.

pédard [pedaːr], *s.m. P:* Road-hog (cyclist); scorcher.

pédestre [pedɛstr], *a.* Pedestrian.

pédicelle [pedisɛl], *s.m. Bot:* Pedicel, pedicle.
pédiculaire [pedikylɛːr]. **I.** *a.* Pedicular, lousy. *Maladie p.,* phthiriasis. **2.** *s.f. Bot:* Lousewort.
pédicule [pedikyl], *s.m. Biol:* Pedicle.
pédicure [pedikyːr], *s. m. & f.* Chiropodist.
pégamoïd [pegamɔid], *s.m.* Pegamoid.
Pégase [pegaːz]. *Pr.n.m.* Pegasus. *F:* Enfourcher Pégase, to mount one's Pegasus.
pègre [pɛːgr], *s.f. P:* Thieves (as a class). *La haute p.,* the mobsmen, the swell mob.
peigne [pɛɲ], *s.m.* **I.** Comb. *P. fin,* tooth-comb. Donner un coup de peigne à qn, to run the comb through s.o.'s hair. S.a. SALE I. **2.** (*a*) (i) Card (for wool); gill, hackle (for hemp). (ii) *P. de métier à tisser,* reed. (*b*) *P. à fileter,* screw-chasing tool. **3.** *Moll:* Pecten; comb(-shell); scallop. **4.** Comb (of escalator).
peign-e, -ons, etc. See PEINDRE and PEIGNER.
peign|er [pɛɲe], *v.tr.* **I.** (*a*) To comb (out) (the hair, etc.). (*b*) *P:* To thrash, drub, dress (s.o.) down. **2.** (*a*) To card, comb (wool); to hackle (hemp). (*b*) To chase (screw-thread). *s.m.* **-age.**
se peigner. I. To comb, do, one's hair. **2.** *P:* (Esp. of women) To fight; to have a set-to.
peigné, *a. Bien p.,* well-groomed (person); trim (garden). *Mal p.,* unkempt, slatternly; tousled (hair). *s.* Une mal peignée, a slattern.
peignée, *s.f.* **I.** Cardful (of wool, flax). **2.** *P:* Thrashing, drubbing, dressing-down.
peigneur, -euse [pɛɲœːr, -øːz]. *Tex:* **I.** *s.* Woolcomber. **2.** *s.f.* Peigneuse. (*a*) Wool-combing machine. (*b*) Hackling-machine.
peignoir [pɛɲwaːr], *s.m.* (Lady's) dressing-gown; morning wrapper. *P. de bain,* bathing-wrap.
peignures [pɛɲyːr], *s.f.pl.* Combings.
peindre [pɛ̃ːdr], *v.tr. (pr.p.* peignant; *p.p.* peint; *pr.ind.* je peins, il peint, n. peignons; *p.h.* je peignis; *fu.* je peindrai) To paint. **I.** To cover, coat, (sth.) with paint. *P. qch. en vert,* to paint sth. green. *P. une carte,* to colour a map. Papiers peints, wall-papers. Vitraux peints, stained-glass windows. **2.** To portray, represent (in colours). *P. un coucher de soleil,* to paint a sunset. *P. à l'huile, à l'aquarelle,* to paint in oils, in water colour. *F:* Elle est à peindre, she is a perfect picture. Se faire peindre, to have one's portrait painted. *F:* Peindre tout en beau, to paint everything in rosy colours. *Sa douleur ne saurait se p.,* his grief is indescribable. *Cette action le peint bien,* that action is typical of him, displays him to a T.
peine [pɛn], *s.f.* **I.** Punishment, penalty. *P. capitale,* capital punishment. *La p. de mort,* the death penalty. *Sous p. de mort,* on pain of death. Ames en peine, souls in Purgatory. Errer comme une âme en peine, to wander about like a lost soul. **2.** (*a*) Sorrow, affliction. Faire de la peine à qn, to grieve, vex, distress, s.o. Nous apprenons avec peine que . . ., we are sorry, grieved, to hear that. . . . Cela fait peine à voir, it is painful to behold. Être en peine de qn, to be uneasy, anxious, about s.o. (*b*) Être dans la peine, to be in want, in trouble, in distress. **3.** Pains, trouble. Prendre, se donner, de la peine pour faire qch., to take trouble, take pains, to do sth. Ne pas ménager sa peine, to spare no trouble. Donnez-vous la peine de vous asseoir, pray take a seat. C'est peine perdue, it is labour lost. En être pour sa peine, to have one's labour for one's pains. Cela vaut la peine d'essayer, it is worth trying. Cela n'en vaut pas la peine, it is not worth the trouble, not worth while. *Iron:* C'était bien la peine de venir! we might as well have stayed

at home! Homme de peine, common labourer, odd-job man. Mourir à la peine, to die in harness. **4.** Difficulty. J'ai eu toutes les peines du monde à le trouver, I had the utmost difficulty in finding it. J'ai peine à croire que + *sub.,* it is difficult for me to believe that. . . . Ne jamais être en peine de trouver une excuse, never to be at a loss to find an excuse. Avec peine, à grand'peine, with (great) difficulty. **5.** A peine, hardly, barely, scarcely. *C'est à p. si je le connais,* I hardly know him. *A p. étions-nous sortis qu'il se mit à pleuvo.r,* hardly had we gone out when the rain began.
peiner [pɛne]. **I.** *v.tr.* (*a*) To pain, grieve, vex, distress (s.o.). *Impers. Il me peine beaucoup de . . .,* it gives me much pain to. . . . (*b*) To fatigue. *Métier qui peine beaucoup,* strenuous profession. **2.** *v.i.* To toil, labour, drudge. *Aut: Le moteur peine,* the engine is labouring.
pein-s, -t. See PEINDRE.
peintre [pɛ̃ːtr], *s.m.* Painter. **I.** (*Artiste*) *p.,* artist. *Une femme p.,* a woman artist. *P. de portraits,* portrait-painter, portraitist. **2.** *P. en bâtiment(s), p. décorateur,* house-painter. *Th: P. décorateur,* scene-painter.
peinture [pɛ̃tyːr], *s.f.* **I.** (Action, art, of) painting. (*a*) Faire de la peinture, to paint. *P. à l'huile,* oil-painting. *P. à l'aquarelle,* water-colour painting. (*b*) *P. en bâtiments,* house-painting. (*c*) *P. de mœurs,* portrayal of manners, of customs. **2.** Picture, painting. **3.** Paint, colour. "Attention à la peinture!" 'wet paint'; 'mind the paint!'
peinturer [pɛ̃tyre], *v.tr.* (*a*) To cover (wall, etc.) with a coat of paint. (*b*) *F:* To bedaub. *Abs.* To paint daubs.
peinturlurer [pɛ̃tyrlyre], *v.tr. F:* To paint (building, etc.) in all the colours of the rainbow; to daub (with colour).
péjoratif, -ive [peʒɔratif, -iːv], *a. & s.m.* Pejorative (suffix, etc.); disparaging, depreciatory.
Pékin [pekɛ̃]. **I.** *Pr.n.m. Geog:* Pekin(g). **2.** *s.m.* (*a*) *Tex:* Pekin (fabric). (*b*) *Mil: F:* Civilian. Être en pékin, to be in mufti.
pelade [pəlad], *s.f.* Alopecia, fox-evil, pelade.
pelage [pəlaːʒ], *s.m.* Coat, wool, fur (of animal).
pélagien, -ienne [pelaʒjɛ̃, -jɛn], *a.* Pelagian; deep-sea (animal, plant).
pélagique [pelaʒik], *a.* Pelagic, pelagian (fauna).
pélargonium [pelargɔnjɔm], *s.m. Bot:* Pelargonium; (i) stork's-bill; (ii) *F:* geranium.
pêle-mêle [pɛlmɛl]. **I.** *adv.* Pell-mell; (i) higgledy-piggledy; (ii) promiscuously; (iii) helter-skelter. **2.** *s.m. inv.* Jumble, medley, confusion.
peler[1] [p(ə)le], *v.tr.* (je pèle; je pèlerai) To unhair, depilate (hide).
se peler, (of animal) to lose its hair; (of skin) to grow bare.
pelé, *a.* Bald; bare, hairless. *F:* Il n'y avait que quatre pelés et un tondu, there was only a handful of nobodies.
peler[2]. **I.** *v.tr.* To peel, skin (vegetable, fruit); to peel off (bark). **2.** *v.i. & pr.* (Of animal) To peel; (of skin) to peel off.
pèlerin, -ine [pɛlrɛ̃, -in]. **I.** *s.* Pilgrim. **2.** *s.f.* Pèlerine. (*a*) (Woman's) cape or mantle; pelerine. (*b*) (Man's) hooded cape. (*c*) *Moll:* Scallop.
pèlerinage [pɛlrinaːʒ], *s.m.* **I.** Pilgrimage. Aller en pèlerinage, faire un pèlerinage, to go on a pilgrimage. **2.** Place of pilgrimage.
pélican [pelikɑ̃], *s.m. Orn:* Pelican. **2.** *Tls:* (Bench) holdfast.
pelisse [p(ə)lis], *s.f.* Pelisse; fur-lined cloak.
pellagre [pɛlaːgr], *s.f. Med:* Pellagra.
pelle [pɛl], *s.f.* **I.** Shovel, scoop. (*a*) *P. à charbon,*

coal-scoop, -shovel. **Ramasser qch. à la pelle,** to shovel sth. up. *Enlever qch. à la p.,* to shovel sth. away. *F:* **Ramasser une pelle,** to have a spill (off a cycle); to come a cropper. (*b*) *P. à vapeur,* steam shovel. **2.** (Child's) spade (at seaside). **3.** Blade (of oar).

pelle-bêche, *s.f. Mil:* Entrenching-tool. *pl. Des pelles-bêches.*

pelletée [pɛlte], *s.f.* Shovelful, spadeful.

pellet|er [pɛlte], *v.tr.* (**je pellette** [pɛlt]; **je pelletterai** [pɛltre]) To turn (with a shovel); to shovel (corn, etc.). *s.m.* **-age.** *s.m.* **-eur.**

pelleterie [pɛltri], *s.f.* **I.** *Coll.* Fur-skins, peltry. **2.** Fur-trade, furriery.

pelletier, -ière [pɛltje, -jɛːr], *s.* Furrier.

pelliculaire [pɛllikylɛːr], *a.* Pellicular. *El:* **Effet pelliculaire,** skin effect, Kelvin effect.

pellicule [pɛllikyl], *s.f.* **I.** (*a*) Pellicle; thin skin; skin (on boiled milk, etc.); film (of ice, of oil). (*b*) Skin of the grape, grape-skin. (*c*) *Phot:* Film. *P. en bobine,* roll-film. **2.** *pl.* Scurf, dandruff.

pelliculeux, -euse [pɛllikylø, -øːz], *a.* Scurfy.

pellucide [pɛllysid], *a.* Pellucid, limpid.

pelote [plɔt], *s.f.* **I.** Ball, clew (of wool); ball (of string); wad (of cotton wool). **Mettre de la laine en pelote,** to ball wool; to wind wool into a ball. *P. à épingles,* pincushion. *F:* **Faire sa (petite) pelote,** to make one's pile. **Avoir les nerfs en pelote,** to be nervy; to have one's nerves in a tangle. **2.** Blaze, star (on horse's forehead). **3.** *P. digitale,* pad (on the foot of certain animals). **4.** *Games:* Pelote basque, pelota. **5.** *Mil: P:* **La pelote,** the defaulters' squad.

pelot|er [plɔte]. **I.** *v.tr.* (*a*) To wind (wool, string) into a ball. (*b*) *F:* To handle (s.o.) roughly; to maul (s.o.) about. (*c*) *P:* To paw, cuddle (a woman); to flatter (s.o.). **2.** *v.i.* (In tennis, etc.) To knock the balls about. *s.m.* **-age.**

peloton [plɔtɔ̃], *s.m.* **I.** Ball, clew (of wool, etc.). **2.** Group (of people); cluster (of caterpillars). *Rac:* **Le peloton,** the main body (of runners); 'the bunch.' **3.** *Mil:* (*a*) Half-company (of infantry); troop (of cavalry). (*b*) Squad, party. *P. de punition,* punishment squad.

pelotonner [plɔtɔne], *v.tr.* To wind (wool, string) into a ball.

    se pelotonner. I. To curl up (into a ball); to coil or roll oneself up. **2.** (*a*) To gather into groups. (*b*) To huddle, crowd, together. (*c*) (Of bees) To cluster.

pelouse [pluːz], *s.f.* Lawn; plot (of grass); green(sward). *Golf: P. d'arrivée,* (putting-)green. *Turf:* **La Pelouse,** the public enclosures.

pelu [pəly], *a.* Hairy.

peluche [plyʃ], *s.f. Tex:* Plush; shag.

pelucher [plyʃe], *v.i.* (Of worn material) To become fluffy; to shed fluff.

    peluché, *a.* Shaggy, nappy (material).

pelucheux, -euse [plyʃø, -øːz], *a.* **I.** Shaggy. **2.** Fluffy; downy (fruit).

pelure [plyːr], *s.f.* Peel, skin (of apple, onion); paring (of vegetables); rind (of cheese). **Papier pelure,** foreign note-paper, pelure-paper.

pelvien, -ienne [pɛlvjɛ̃, -jɛn], *a. Anat:* Pelvic.

pelvis [pɛlvis], *s.m. Anat:* False pelvis.

pénal, -als, -aux [penal, -o], *a.* Penal (code). **Clause pénale,** penalty clause (in contract).

pénalisation [penalizasjɔ̃], *s.f. Sp:* Penalization.

pénalité [penalite], *s.f. Jur: Sp:* Penalty.

pénates [penat], *s.m.pl.* Penates; household gods. *F:* **Revoir ses pénates,** to return home.

penaud [pəno], *a.* Crestfallen, chapfallen, shame-faced. *D'un air p.,* sheepishly.

penchant [pɑ̃ʃɑ̃]. **I.** *a.* (*a*) Sloping, inclined, leaning (wall, tower). (*b*) Tottering (empire); declining (power). **2.** *s.m.* (*a*) Slope, declivity. *Le p. de la colline,* the hillside. *Être sur le p. de sa ruine,* to be on the brink, verge, of ruin. (*b*) *P. à, pour, vers, qch.,* inclination to, propensity for, tendency to, sth.; leaning towards sth. *Avoir un p. au mysticisme,* to have a bent towards mysticism. *Avoir un p. pour qn,* to be rather fond of s.o.

penchement [pɑ̃ʃmɑ̃], *s.m.* **I.** Leaning (of wall, etc.). **2.** Stoop, bend.

pencher [pɑ̃ʃe], *v.* To incline, bend, lean. **I.** *v.tr. P. une cruche,* to tilt a jug. *P. la tête en avant,* to bend, lean, forward. **2.** *v.i.* To lean (over). *Mur qui penche,* leaning wall. **Faire pencher la balance,** to turn the scale. *Terrain qui penche,* ground on the slope. *P. à, vers, l'indulgence,* to incline to(wards) indulgence.

    se pencher, to incline, bend, stoop. *Se p. en avant,* to bend forward. *Se p. (en), (au), dehors,* to lean out. *Se p. à, par, la fenêtre,* to lean out of the window.

    penché, *a.* **I.** Leaning. *F:* **Prendre des airs penchés,** to stand or recline like a drooping lily. **2.** Stooping. *Il marche p.,* he walks with a stoop.

pendable [pɑ̃dabl], *a.* (*a*) That deserves hanging. **Cas pendable,** hanging matter. (*b*) *F:* Outrageous, abominable (trick, etc.).

pendaison [pɑ̃dɛzɔ̃], *s.f.* (Death by) hanging.

pendant [pɑ̃dɑ̃]. **I.** *a.* **I.** Hanging, pendent. *Joues pendantes,* flabby, baggy, cheeks. *Oreilles pendantes,* flap-ears, lop-ears. **2.** Pending, undecided (lawsuit); in suspense, in abeyance.

    II. pendant, *s.m.* **I.** Pendant. **Pendant d'oreille,** ear-pendant, -drop. **2.** Match, fellow, pendant (of picture, etc.). **Ces deux tableaux (se) font pendant,** these two pictures make a pair.

    III. pendant, *prep.* During. *Restez là p. quelques minutes,* stay there for a few minutes. *Conj. phr.* **Pendant que,** while, whilst.

pendard, -arde [pɑ̃daːr, -ard], *s. F:* Rascal, gallows-bird, rogue; *f.* hussy. [PENDRE]

pendeloque [pɑ̃dlɔk], *s.f.* (*a*) *pl.* Pendants; drops, crystals (of chandelier). (*b*) Ear-drop. (*c*) *F:* (Torn) shred (of cloth).

pendentif [pɑ̃dɑ̃tif], *s.m.* **I.** *Arch:* Pendentive. **En pendentif,** hanging. **2.** (*a*) Pendant (worn round the neck). (*b*) (Electric) pendant.

penderie [pɑ̃dri], *s.f.* Hanging-wardrobe, -closet.

pendiller [pɑ̃dije], *v.i.* To dangle.

pendre [pɑ̃ːdr]. **I.** *v.tr.* (*a*) To hang (sth.) up. *S.a.* CRÉMAILLÈRE I. *F:* **Il est toujours pendu à mes côtés,** he follows me about everywhere. (*b*) To hang (on the gallows). *Prov:* **Le bruit pend l'homme,** give a dog a bad name and hang him. **Dire pis que pendre de qn,** to say everything that is bad about s.o. **Je veux être pendu si . . . ,** I'll be hanged if . . . **2.** *v.i.* To hang. *Vos cheveux pendent,* your hair is hanging down.

    se pendre *à qch.,* to hang on, cling, to sth.

    pendu. I. *a.* Hanged, hung; hanging (*à,* from). *S.a.* LANGUE I. **2.** *s.* One who has been hanged or who has hanged himself.

pendule [pɑ̃dyl]. **I.** *s.m.* (*a*) Pendulum. (*b*) Balancer (of torpedo). **2.** *s.f.* Clock, timepiece. *P. à coucou,* cuckoo-clock.

pendulette [pɑ̃dylɛt], *s.f.* Small clock.

pêne [pɛːn], *s.m.* Bolt (of lock); latch.

pénétrabilité [penetrabilite], *s.f.* Penetrability.

pénétrable [penetrabl], *a.* Penetrable.

pénétrant [penetrɑ̃], *a.* Penetrating; sharp (point); piercing (wind); pervasive, obtrusive, searching (smell); subtle (scent); searching, keen (glance); discerning (person); shrewd (mind); (mind) of deep insight. *Plaie pénétrante,* perforating wound.

pénétration [penɛtrasjɔ̃], *s.f.* (*a*) Penetration (of bullet). (*b*) Penetration, insight; acuteness (of mind); acumen, shrewdness.

pénétrer [penetre], *v.* (je **pénètre**; je **pénétrerai**) To penetrate. **1.** *v.i.* To enter. *La baïonnette pénétra jusqu'au poumon,* the bayonet penetrated to the lung. *Un cambrioleur a pénétré dans la maison,* a burglar broke into the house. *L'eau avait pénétré partout,* the water had got in everywhere. **2.** *v.tr.* (*a*) *La balle pénétra l'os,* the bullet penetrated, pierced, the bone. *P. un secret,* to fathom a secret. *P. la pensée, les intentions, de qn,* to see through s.o. (*b*) *P. qn d'une idée,* to imbue, possess, s.o. with an idea. *Votre lettre m'a pénétré de douleur,* your letter has filled me with grief.

se pénétrer. (*a*) To become impregnated (*de,* with). (*b*) To become imbued, pervaded (*de,* with). *Il faut bien se p. que . . .,* we must get it thoroughly into our minds that. . . . *D'un ton pénétré,* in a voice full of conviction. *D'un air pénétré,* with an earnest air.

pénible [penibl], *a.* **1.** Laborious, hard, toilsome (task); laboured, heavy (breathing); arduous, rough (road). **2.** Painful, distressing. *P. à voir,* painful to behold. *adv.* **-ment.**

péniche [peniʃ], *s.f. Nau:* **1.** *A:* Pinnace, shallop. **2.** Canal-boat; coal-barge; lighter.

péninsulaire [penɛ̃sylɛ:r], *a.* Peninsular.

péninsule [penɛ̃syl], *s.f.* Peninsula.

pénitence [penitɑ̃:s], *s.f.* **1.** Penitence, repentance. **2.** Penance. **Faire pénitence,** to do penance (*de,* for). *F:* **Mettre un enfant en pénitence,** to put a child in the corner. *Il est en p.,* he is in disgrace.

pénitencier [penitɑ̃sje], *s.m.* **1.** *Ecc:* Penitentiary (priest). **2.** (*a*) Penitentiary; reformatory prison. (*b*) Convict station.

pénitent, -ente [penitɑ̃, -ɑ̃:t], *a. & s.* Penitent. **pénitentiaire** [penitɑ̃sjɛ:r], *a.* Penitentiary (system). **Maison pénitentiaire,** penitentiary. S.a. COLONIE.

penne [pɛn], *s.f.* (*a*) Quill(-feather). (*b*) Feather (of arrow).

penné [pɛnne], *a.* = PINNÉ.

pennon [pɛnɔ̃], *s.m.* Pennon.

pénombre [penɔ̃:br], *s.f.* (*a*) Penumbra. (*b*) Half-light, semi-darkness.

pensant [pɑ̃sɑ̃], *a.* Thinking (man, woman). **Bien pensant,** orthodox, right-thinking. **Mal pensant,** (i) unorthodox; (ii) uncharitable.

pensée¹ [pɑ̃se], *s.f. Bot:* Pansy.

penser [pɑ̃se], *v.* To think. **1.** *v.ind.tr.* Penser à qn, à qch., to think of s.o., sth. *A quoi pensez-vous?* (i) what are you thinking about? (ii) how could you (think of such a thing)! **Je l'ai fait sans y penser,** I did it without thinking. **(Y) pensez-vous!** what an idea! **Vous n'y pensez pas!** you don't mean it! **N'y pensez plus,** forget all about it. **Ah, j'y pense!** by the way! **Rien que d'y penser,** *mon sang bout,* the mere thought (of it) makes my blood boil. *P. à faire qch.,* (i) to think of doing sth.; (ii) to remember to do sth. **Faire penser qn à qch.,** to remind s.o. of sth. **Faites-moi penser à lui écrire,** remind me to write to him. **2.** *v.i.* Manière de penser, attitude of mind. *Je pense comme vous,* I agree with you. **Voilà ma façon de penser,** that is my way of thinking. *Pensez donc!* just fancy! **3.** *v.tr.* (*a*) Penser qch., (i) to think sth.; (ii) to imagine, picture, sth. **Je le pensais bien,** I thought as much. **Je pense que oui, que non,** I think so,

I think not. *Pensez si j'étais furieux,* you can imagine how angry I was. *Je ne savais plus que p.,* I was absolutely nonplussed. (*b*) *Pred. Je ne pense fou,* I consider him crazy. (*c*) **Penser qch. de qn, de qch.,** to think sth. of s.o., of sth. *P. du bien, du mal, de qn,* to think well, ill, of s.o. (*d*) **Penser faire qch.** (i) To expect to do sth. *Je pense le voir demain,* I have hopes of seeing him to-morrow. (ii) (= FAILLIR) *Il a pensé se noyer,* he was nearly drowned, he had a narrow escape from drowning. *J'ai pensé mourir de rire,* I nearly died with laughter.

pensée², *s.f.* **1.** Thought. *Absorbé, perdu, dans ses pensées,* lost in thought. *Se représenter clairement qch. par la p.,* to have a clear idea of sth. **Il me vint dans la pensée que . . .,** the thought occurred to me that. . . . **Entrer dans la pensée de qn,** to understand what is in s.o.'s mind. **Libre pensée,** free-thought. **2.** Intention. *Changer de p.,* to change one's mind.

penseur, -euse [pɑ̃sœːr, -øːz], *s.* Thinker. **Libre penseur,** free-thinker. *a. L'homme p.,* the thinking man.

pens|if, -ive [pɑ̃sif, -iːv], *a.* Thoughtful, pensive (person); abstracted (air). *adv.* **-ivement.**

pension [pɑ̃sjɔ̃], *s.f.* **1.** Pension, allowance. *P. de retraite,* retiring pension; *F:* pension. *P. viagère,* life annuity. *P. alimentaire,* allowance for board; *Jur:* alimony. **2.** (*a*) Payment for board (and lodging). **Être en pension, prendre pension, chez qn,** to board with s.o. **Pension et chambre,** board and residence. **Cheval en pension,** horse at livery(-stable). (*b*) **Pension de famille, pension bourgeoise,** residential hotel; boarding-house. **3.** (*a*) Boarding-school fees. (*b*) (Private) boarding-school. **Mettre un enfant en pension,** to send a child to a boarding-school.

pensionnaire [pɑ̃sjɔnɛːr], *s.m. & f.* **1.** Boarder ((i) in boarding-house, (ii) in school); guest (in hotel); inmate (of mental hospital). *Prendre, avoir, des pensionnaires,* to take in boarders, paying guests. S.a. DEMI-PENSIONNAIRE..

pensionnat [pɑ̃sjɔna], *s.m.* **1.** (Private) boarding-school. **2.** Hostel (attached to girls' *lycée*).

pensionner [pɑ̃sjɔne], *v.tr.* To pension.

pensum [pɛ̃sɔm], *s.m. Sch:* Imposition.

pentaèdre [pɛ̃taɛdr], *Geom:* **1.** *a.* Pentahedral. **2.** *s.m.* Pentahedron.

pentagonal, -aux [pɛ̃tagɔnal, -o], *a.* Pentagonal.

pentagone [pɛ̃tagɔn], **1.** *a.* Pentagonal. **2.** *s.m.* Pentagon.

pentamètre [pɛ̃tamɛtr], *s.m. Pros:* Pentameter.

pentane [pɛ̃tan], *s.m. Ch:* Pentane.

pentasyllabe [pɛ̃tasillab], *a.* Pentasyllabic.

Pentateuque (le) [ləpɛ̃tatøːk], *s.m. B:* The Pentateuch.

pentavalent [pɛ̃tavalɑ̃], *a. Ch:* Pentavalent, quinquivalent.

pente [pɑ̃ːt], *s.f.* (*a*) Slope, incline gradient. *P. ascendante,* slope up, up grade. *P. descendante,* slope down, down grade. (Of ground) Aller en pente, to slope (down); to shelve. *Civ.E: P. naturelle de talus, d'éboulis,* angle of repose; natural slope; talus. *P. d'un toit,* pitch of a roof. *Hyd.E: P. d'une rivière,* fall of a river. *Rail:* Lignes à forte pente, steep gradients. *Aut:* Indicateur de pente, gradient-meter, inclinometer. (*b*) Bent, inclination, propensity (*à,* for).

Pentecôte [pɑ̃tkoːt], *s.f.* (*a*) Whitsun(tide); Pentecost; **Dimanche de la Pentecôte,** Whit-Sunday.

pent(h)ode [pɛ̃tɔd], *s.f. W.Tel:* Three-grid tube.

penture [pɑ̃tyːr], *s.f.* Strap-hinge (of door, etc.)

P. et gond, hook and hinge. *pl. Nau:* Pentures *du gouvernail*, rudder-bands, -braces.

pénultième [penyltjɛm], *a. & s.f.* Penultimate; last but one.

pénurie [penyri], *s.f.* (a) Scarcity, shortage (of money, etc.); lack (of words). (b) Poverty.

pépère [pepɛ:r]. *P:* **I.** *s.m.* (a) Quiet old fellow. (b) Territorial soldier. **2.** *a.* Pleasant, comfortable, snug (job); tip-top, first-rate.

pépette, pépète [pepet], *s.f. P:* Money, *P:* brass, dibs.

pépie [pepi], *s.f.* Pip (disease of the tongue of fowls). Hence *F:* **Avoir la pépie,** to have a perpetual thirst.

pépiler [pepje], *v.i.* (Of birds) To cheep, chirp, peep. *s.m.* **-ement.**

pépin[1] [pepɛ̃], *s.m.* Pip (of apple); stone (of grape).

pépin[2], *s.m. P:* (Gingham) umbrella; *F:* gamp.

Pépin[3]. *Pr.n.m. Hist:* Pepin, Pippin.

pépinière [pepinjɛ:r], *s.f. Hort:* Seed-bed; nursery. [PÉPIN[1]]

pépiniériste [pepinjerist], *s.m.* Nurseryman, nursery gardener.

pépite [pepit], *s.f.* Nugget (of gold).

pepsine [pepsin], *s.f. Physiol: Ch:* Pepsin.

peptone [pɛptɔn], *s.f. Physiol: Ch:* Peptone.

peptoniser [pɛptɔnize], *v.tr.* To peptonize.

péquin [pekɛ̃], *s.m.* = PÉKIN 2 (b).

pérambulation [perɑ̃bylasjɔ̃], *s.f.* Perambulation.

percale [pɛrkal], *s.f.* Cotton cambric; percale.

percaline [pɛrkalin], *s.f. Tex:* Percaline. *Dre sm: etc:* Glazed lining; calico.

perçant [pɛrsɑ̃], *a.* Piercing, penetrating (eyes, sound); keen, sharp (wits); shrill (voice); biting (wind). **A la vue perçante,** keen-sighted.

perce [pɛrs], *s.f.* **I.** *Tls:* Borer, drill, punch. **2.** Barrique **en perce,** broached cask. **Mettre un fût, le vin, en perce,** to broach a cask, the wine.

perce-bois, *s.m. inv. Ent:* Wood-borer; (in ships) teredo.

perce-feuille, *s.f. Bot:* Hare's-ear.

perce-muraille, *s.f. Bot:* Wall-pellitory.

perce-neige, *s. m. or f. inv. Bot:* Snowdrop.

perce-oreille, *s.m. Ent:* Earwig. *pl. Des perce-oreilles.*

perce-pierre, *s.f. Bot:* **I.** Samphire. **2.** (White, meadow) saxifrage.

percepteur, -trice [pɛrsɛptœ:r, -tris]. **I.** *a.* Perceiving, discerning. **2.** *s.* (a) Tax-collector (b) Bus or tram conductor.

perceptible [pɛrsɛptibl], *a.* **I.** Perceptible (*à*, by, to); discernible. *P. à l'oreille,* audible. **2.** Collectable, collectible (tax). *adv.* **-ment.**

perceptif, -ive [pɛrsɛptif, -i:v], *a.* Perceptive.

perception [pɛrsɛpsjɔ̃], *s.f.* **I.** Perception. **2.** (a) Collection, receipt (of taxes, rent); levying (of taxes). **(Bureau de) perception,** tax-collector's office. (b) Collectorship.

perlcer [pɛrse], *v.* **(je perçai(s); n. perçons) I.** *v.tr.* (a) To pierce, to go through (sth.). *Vous me percez les oreilles,* you are deafening me. *P. un abcès,* to lance an abscess. *P. qn d'un coup d'épée,* to run s.o. through. *Le soleil perce les nuages,* the sun breaks through the clouds. *P. le cœur à qn,* to cut s.o. to the heart. *P. l'avenir,* to foresee the future. *P. un secret,* to penetrate a secret. *P. la foule,* to break through the crowd. S.a. DENT I. (b) To perforate; to make a hole, an opening, in (sth.); to sink (well). *P. un tonneau,* to broach, tap, a cask. *P. une porte dans un mur,* to make, let in, a door in a wall. (c) *P. un trou,* to drill, bore, a hole. *P. un tunnel dans une montagne,* to drive a tunnel through a mountain. **2.** *v.i.* To pierce; **to come, break, through.** *Ses dents*

percent, he is cutting his teeth. *L'abcès a percé,* the abscess has burst. *La vérité perce tôt ou tard,* truth will out. *s.m.* **-çage.** *s.m.* **-cement.**

percé, *a.* (a) Pierced; holed. **Percé de vers,** worm-eaten. S.a. PANIER I. (b) (Of garment) In holes; (coat) out at elbows; (trousers) torn in the seat.

percée, *s.f.* **I.** (a) Cutting (in a forest); break (in hedge); glade; vista. *Faire une p. dans un bois,* to make an opening in, cut a passage through, a wood. (b) Window or door) opening (in wall). **2.** *Mil:* Break-through. **Faire une percée,** to break through. **3.** *Metall:* (i) Tapping (of blast-furnace); (ii) tap-hole.

perceur, -euse [pɛrsœ:r, -ø:z]. **I.** *s.* Borer; driller (of rivet-holes); puncher (of sheet metal). **2.** *s.f.* **Perceuse,** drilling-machine. *Perceuse à main,* hand-drill.

percevable [pɛrsəvabl], *a.* **I.** Perceivable. **2.** Leviable (tax).

percevoir [pɛrsəvwa:r], *v.tr.* (*pr.p.* **percevant;** *p.p.* **perçu;** *pr.ind.* **je perçois, n. percevons, ils perçoivent;** *pr.sub.* **je perçoive, n. percevions;** *p.h.* **je perçus;** *fu.* **je percevrai**) **I.** To perceive, discern. *P. un bruit,* to hear, catch, a sound. **2.** To collect, gather, levy (taxes).

perche[1] [pɛrʃ], *s.f.* **I.** (Thin) pole. *Perches à houblon,* hop-poles. **Saut à la perche,** pole-jump(ing). *F:* **Grande perche,** tall, lanky individual, esp. woman. **Conduire un bateau à la perche,** to pole, punt, a boat. *F:* **Tendre la perche à qn,** to hold out a hand to s.o. (in difficulties). **2.** *Meas: A:* Perch, rod, pole.

perche[2], *s.f. Ich:* Perch.

percher [pɛrʃe], *v.i.* (Of birds) To perch, roost. *Poules perchées,* roosting hens. *F: Où perchez-vous?* where do you hang out?

se percher, (Of bird) *Se p. sur une branche,* to alight, perch, on a branch.

percheron, -onne [pɛrʃərɔ̃, -ɔn], *a. & s. Geog:* (Native) of the Perche region. *Cheval p., s.m.* **percheron,** strong draught-horse bred in the Perche region; Percheron.

percheur, -euse [pɛrʃœ:r, -ø:z], *a.* Perching, roosting (bird, fowl).

perchlorate [pɛrklɔrat], *s.m. Ch:* Perchlorate.

perchlorique [pɛrklɔrik], *a. Ch:* Perchloric.

perchlorure [pɛrklɔry:r], *s.m. Ch:* Perchloride. *P. de fer,* ferric chloride.

perchoir [pɛrʃwa:r], *s.m.* (Bird's) perch, roost.

perclus [pɛrkly], *a.* Stiff-jointed, anchylosed (limb, person). *F: P. de rhumatismes,* crippled with rheumatism.

perçoir [pɛrswa:r], *s.m. Tls:* (a) Punch, borer, broach. (b) Awl, gimlet.

perçoi-s, -t, -ve, etc. See PERCEVOIR.

percolateur [pɛrkɔlatœ:r], *s.m.* Percolator.

perçu, -s, -t, etc. See PERCEVOIR.

percussion [pɛrkysjɔ̃], *s.f.* (a) Percussion, impact. (b) Sounding (by percussion); percussion. (c) *Mus:* **Instruments de, à, percussion,** percussion instruments.

percutant [pɛrkytɑ̃], *a.* Percussive. *Artil:* **Fusée percutante,** percussion fuse. *Obus p.,* percussion-fuse shell.

percuter [pɛrkyte], *v.tr.* (a) To strike, tap (sth.) lightly and sharply. (b) *Med:* To sound (chest) by percussion; to percuss.

percuteur [pɛrkytœ:r], *s.m.* Striker, hammer (of gun, of fuse); needle (of rifle).

perdable [pɛrdabl], *a.* Losable.

perdant, -ante [pɛrdɑ̃, -ɑ̃:t]. **I.** *a.* Losing. Esp. Billet perdant, blank (ticket, at lottery). **2.** *s.* Loser.

perdition [pɛrdisjɔ̃], *s.f.* **1.** *Ecc:* Perdition. **2.** *Nau:* Navire en perdition, ship (i) in distress, (ii) breaking up, sinking.

perdre [pɛrdr], *v.tr.* **1.** To ruin, destroy. *A. & Lit:* Perdre qn d'honneur, to disgrace, dishonour, s.o. Perdre qn de réputation, to ruin s.o.'s good name. **2.** To lose. Perdre la partie, to lose the game. Perdre la raison, to lose one's reason. Faire perdre une habitude à qn, to break s.o. of a habit. Cela se perd facilement, it is easily lost. Vous ne perdrez rien pour attendre, you will lose nothing by waiting. *P. son chemin,* to lose one's way. Perdre son temps, to waste (one's) time. *P. du temps,* to lose time. *Sans p. de temps,* without loss of time. Perdre pied, terre, to lose one's footing, to get out of one's depth (in bathing, etc.). S.a. FOND 1, LATIN 2, TÊTE 2, VUE 1. **3.** *Abs.* (a) Vous n'y perdrez pas, you won't lose by it. (b) *Fût qui perd,* cask that is leaking. (c) *Le grain perd en vieillissant,* grain loses in value, deteriorates, with age. *P. dans l'estime de qn,* to fall in s.o.'s estimation. (d) *P. sur ses concurrents,* to fall behind; to drop behind.

se perdre. 1. To be lost. (a) *Le navire se perdit corps et biens,* the ship was lost with all hands. (b) *Se p. dans la foule,* to vanish, disappear, in the crowd. *Usage qui se perd,* custom that is falling into disuse. Être perdu dans ses pensées, to be wrapped, lost, in thought. (c) (Of power, etc.) To be wasted, to run to waste; (of liquid) to leak away, to escape. **2.** To lose one's way. *F:* Ma tête s'y perd, je m'y perds, I can't make head or tail of it.

perdu, *a.* **1.** Ruined. *P. de dettes,* over head and ears in debt. *Ame perdue,* lost soul. **2.** Lost. Peine perdue, wasted, lost, labour. A mes heures perdues, in my spare time. Sentinelle perdue, advanced sentry. *Petit trou p.,* little out-of-the-way place. *Mec:* Mouvement perdu, idle motion. **3.** A corps perdu, recklessly. Se jeter à corps p. dans la mêlée, to hurl oneself into the fray.

perdreau [pɛrdro], *s.m.* Young partridge.

perdrix [pɛrdri], *s.f.* Partridge. *P. rouge,* red-legs. *P. de neige,* ptarmigan. *Compagnie de p.,* covey of partridges. S.a. ŒIL-DE-PERDRIX.

père [pɛr], *s.m.* **1.** Father. De père en fils, from father to son. M. Dupont père, Mr Dupont senior. *Prov:* Tel père tel fils, like father like son. *P. de famille,* paterfamilias. *Jur:* Bon père de famille, prudent administrator (of family wealth). Valeurs de père de famille, gilt-edged securities. *Th:* Père noble, heavy father. Nos pères, our forefathers. *F:* Le père Jean, old John. **2.** *Ecc:* Father. *P. spirituel,* father confessor. Le Saint-Père, the Holy Father, the Pope. *Un p. carme,* a Carmelite father.

pérégrination [peregrinasjɔ̃], *s.f.* Peregrination.

péremption [perɑ̃psjɔ̃], *s.f. Jur:* Time-limitation (in a suit).

péremptoire [perɑ̃ptwaːr], *a.* **1.** (a) Peremptory (tone). (b) Unanswerable, decisive (argument). **2.** *Jur:* Délai p., strict time-limit. *adv.* -ment.

pérennité [perennite], *s.f.* Perenniality.

péréquation [perekwasjɔ̃], *s.f.* Equalisation (of taxes, salaries); standardizing (of charges).

perfectible [pɛrfɛktibl], *a.* Perfectible.

perfection [pɛrfɛksjɔ̃], *s.f.* Perfection. En perfection, à la perfection, to perfection; perfectly.

perfectionnement [pɛrfɛksjɔnmɑ̃], *s.m.* **1.** Perfecting; improving. Brevet de p., patent relating to improvements. **2.** Apporter des perfectionnements à qch., to improve sth.

perfectionner [pɛrfɛksjɔne], *v.tr.* **1.** To perfect. **2.** To improve (machine, method).

se perfectionner *dans qch.,* to improve one's knowledge of (language, science, etc.).

perfide [pɛrfid], *a.* Treacherous (envers, to); perfidious; false-hearted. *adv.* -ment.

perfidie [pɛrfidi], *s.f.* **1.** Treachery, perfidy, perfidiousness; false-heartedness. **2.** Treacherous act. Faire une p. à qn, to play s.o. false.

perforant [pɛrfɔrɑ̃], *a.* Perforating, perforative. *Obus p.,* armour-piercing shell.

perforateur, -trice [pɛrfɔratœːr, -tris]. **1.** *a.* Perforative, perforating. **2.** *s.m.* Perforator; drill, punch. **3.** *s.f.* Perforatrice, drilling-machine.

perforation [pɛrfɔrasjɔ̃], *s.f.* Perforation. **1.** (a) Boring or drilling. (b) Puncturing (of tyre, etc.). **2.** Hole, puncture.

perforer [pɛrfɔre], *v.tr.* **1.** To perforate; to bore (through), to drill (material); to punch (leather, etc.). Bande perforée, music-roll (of piano-player). **2.** To puncture (tyre). *s.m.* -age.

performance [pɛrfɔrmɑ̃ːs], *s.f. Sp:* Performance (in race, etc.).

péri [peri], *s. m. & f.* (Oriental) peri; genie; fairy.

périanthe [perjɑ̃ːt], *s.m. Bot:* Perianth.

péricarde [perikard], *s.m. Anat:* Pericardium.

péricarpe [perikarp], *s.m. Bot:* Pericarp.

périclitant [periklitɑ̃], *a.* Unsound, shaky (business, undertaking).

péricliter [periklite], *v.i.* (Of undertaking) To be in danger, in jeopardy. Faire péricliter une entreprise, to jeopardize an undertaking.

périgée [periʒe], *s.m. Astr:* Perigee.

périgourdin, -ine [perigurdɛ̃, -in], *a. & s.* (Native) of Périgord.

périhélie [perieli], *s.m. Astr:* Perihelion.

péril [peril], *s.m.* Peril, danger; risk, hazard. Au péril de sa vie, at the risk of his life, in peril of his life. En péril, in jeopardy, in peril. Mettre qch. en p., to imperil, jeopardize, sth. *Ins:* Péril de mer, risk and peril of the seas. S.a. DEMEURE 1.

périlleu|x, -euse [perijø, -øːz], *a.* Perilous, hazardous. S.a. SAUT 1. *adv.* -sement.

périmer [perime], *v.i. Jur:* To lapse; to become out of date.

périmé, *a.* **1.** *Jur:* Barred by limitation. **2.** Out-of-date (coupon, method); expired (bill); (ticket) no longer available; lapsed (money order, ticket).

périmètre [perimɛtr], *s.m.* (a) Perimeter, periphery. (b) Area, sphere (of influence).

périnée [perine], *s.m. Anat:* Perineum.

période [perjɔd]. **1.** *s.f.* (a) Period (of recurring phenomenon, or cycle). Nombre de périodes par seconde, frequency (of oscillation). (b) Period of time; age, era. Longue p. de pluie, long spell of rain. (c) *Gram: Rh:* Period; complete sentence. **2.** *s.m. Lit:* Le plus haut période (de la gloire, de l'éloquence), the highest point, pitch, degree, the height, acme of glory, of eloquence).

périodicité [perjɔdisite], *s.f.* Periodicity.

périodique [perjɔdik]. **1.** *a.* Periodical; recurring (at regular intervals); intermittent. Fraction périodique, recurring decimal. **2.** *s.m.* Periodical (publication). *adv.* -ment.

périoste [perjɔst], *s.m. Anat:* Periosteum.

péripatéticien, -ienne [peripatetisjɛ̃, -jɛn], *a. & s. péripatétique* [peripatetik], *a. A.Phil:* Peripatetic.

péripétie [peripesi], *s.f.* **1.** Sudden change of fortune. **2.** *pl.* Vicissitudes; ups and downs (of life); mishaps; adventures.

périphérie [periferi], *s.f.* **1.** Periphery; circumference; girth (of parcel). **2.** Outskirts (of town).

périphérique [periferik], *a.* Peripheral.

périphrase [perifrɑːz], *s.f. Gram*: Periphrasis, periphrase.

périphrastique [perifrastik], *a.* Periphrastic.

périr [periːr], *v.i.* (Aux. *avoir*) To perish, to die (unnaturally); to be destroyed; (of ship) to be wrecked, lost. *P. de sa propre main,* to die by one's own hand. **Faire périr qn,** to kill s.o.; to put s.o. to death. *F: P. d'ennui,* to be bored to death. *Son nom ne périra pas,* his name will live on. *P. victime de son devoir,* to fall a victim to duty.

périscope [periskɔp], *s.m.* Periscope.

périscopique [periskɔpik], *a.* Periscopic (lens).

périssable [perisabl], *a.* Perishable.

périssoire [periswaːr], *s.f.* (Single-seater river-) canoe. **Faire de la périssoire,** to go in for canoeing.

péristaltique [peristaltik], *a. Physiol*: Peristaltic, vermicular (motion).

péristyle [peristil], *s.m. Arch*: Peristyle. *Ecc*: Cloisters.

péritoine [peritwan], *s.m. Anat*: Peritoneum.

péritonite [peritɔnit], *s.f. Med*: Peritonitis.

perle [pɛrl], *s.f.* **1.** Pearl. *P. fine,* real pearl. *Fil de perles* string of pearls. **Nacre de perle,** mother-of-pearl. *F: Jeter des perles devant les pourceaux,* to cast pearls before swine. *Ma nouvelle bonne est une p.,* my new maid is a treasure. **Blanc de perle,** pearl white. **2.** Bead (of glass, etc.). *Perles de rosée,* beads of dew.

perler [pɛrle]. **1.** *v.tr.* (*a*) To pearl (barley); to husk (rice). *Orge perlé,* pearl barley. (*b*) To execute (work) to perfection. **2.** *v.i.* (*a*) (Of tears, sweat) To form in beads. (*b*) (Of sugar) To bead.

perlé, *a.* **1.** (*a*) Resembling pearls; pearly (teeth). *El: Accumulateur p.,* milky accumulator. (*b*) Set with pearls. (*c*) Adorned with beads; beaded. (*d*) *F: Rires perlés,* rippling laughter. **2.** Tastefully done; well-finished. **C'est perlé,** it's perfect. S.a. GRÈVE **2.**

perlimpinpin [pɛrlɛ̃pɛ̃pɛ̃], *s.m.* **Poudre de per-limpinpin,** (any) quack powder, wonder-working powder; bunkum.

perlot [pɛrlo], *s.m. P:* Tobacco, *P:* baccy.

permanence [pɛrmanɑ̃ːs], *s.f.* **1.** Permanence. **Assemblée en permanence,** permanent assembly. *Être attaché en p. à une maison,* to be permanently attached to a firm. **2.** Building, room, etc., always open to the public. *P. de police,* police station open night and day.

permanent [pɛrmanɑ̃]. **1.** *a.* Permanent; standing (order, army); abiding (peace). *Cin:* **Spectacle permanent,** continuous performance. **2.** *s.f. Hairdr:* **Permanente,** permanent wave.

permanganate [pɛrmɑ̃ganat], *s.m. Ch:* Permanganate.

perméabilité [pɛrmeabilite], *s.f. Ph:* Permeability, perviousness.

perméable [pɛrmeabl], *a.* Permeable, pervious (*à,* to); porous.

permettre [pɛrmɛtr], *v.tr.* (Conj. like METTRE) To permit, allow. *P. qch. à qn,* to allow s.o. sth. *On ne me permet pas le vin,* I am not allowed wine. *P. à qn de faire qch.,* to allow s.o. to do sth.; to let s.o. do sth.; to give s.o. leave to do sth. *Mes moyens ne me le permettent pas,* I cannot afford it. **Qu'il me soit permis de . . . ,** I beg to. . . . *Est-il permis d entrer?* may I come in? *S'il est permis de s'exprimer ainsi,* if one may say so. **Permis à vous de ne pas me croire,** you are at liberty to believe me or not. **Il se croit tout permis,** he thinks he can do anything he likes. *Permettez que je vous dise . . . ,* allow me to tell you. . . . **Permettez!** excuse me! allow me! not so fast! **Vous permettez?** may I? *Si le*

temps le permet, weather permitting. *Cela ne permet pas de doute,* it admits of no doubt. *Se p. un cigare,* to indulge in a cigar. *Il se permet bien des choses,* he takes a good many liberties. *Se p. de faire qch.,* to make bold to do sth.

permis. 1. *a.* Allowed, permitted, lawful, allowable, permissible. **2.** *s.m.* Permit, permission. *P. de chasse,* shooting-licence; game-licence. *P. de séjour,* permission to reside = certificate of registration. *Aut: P. de conduire,* driving-licence. *P. de circulation,* car-licence.

permission [pɛrmisjɔ̃], *s.f.* (*a*) Permission, leave. **Avec votre permission,** with your leave, by your leave. *Demander, donner, la p. de faire qch.,* to ask, to give, permission to do sth. (*b*) *Mil: Navy:* Leave of absence (for so many days); short leave. *En permission,* (i) on leave; (ii) on pass.

permissionnaire [pɛrmisjɔnɛːr], *s.m.* Soldier, person, on (short) leave. *Navy:* Liberty man.

permutable [pɛrmytabl], *a.* Permutable, interchangeable.

permutation [pɛrmytɑsjɔ̃], *s.f.* **1.** Exchange of posts. **Prendre un nouveau poste par permutation,** to exchange into a new post. **2.** *Mth:* Permutation.

permutatrice [pɛrmytatris], *s.f. El.E:* Rectifying commutator; rectifier (of alternating current).

permuter [pɛrmyte], *v.tr.* **1.** (*a*) To exchange (post) (*avec qn,* with s.o.). *Abs.* To exchange posts (with colleague). (*b*) *El.E:* To change over (by switching). **2.** *Mth:* To permute.

pernicieu|x, -euse [pɛrnisjø, -øːz], *a.* Pernicious, injurious, hurtful; baneful, baleful (influence). *adv.* **-sement.**

péroné [perɔne], *s.m. Anat:* Fibula, splint-bone.

péronnelle [perɔnɛl], *s.f. F: A:* Pert hussy, saucy woman.

péroraison [perɔrɛzɔ̃], *s.f.* Peroration.

péror|er [perɔre], *v.i.* To hold forth; to speechify. *s.* **-eur, -euse.**

Pérou (le) [ləpəru]. *Pr.n.m. Geog:* Peru. *F:* **Ce n'est pas le Pérou,** it is not highly paid.

peroxyde [pɛrɔksid], *s.m. Ch:* Peroxide.

perpendiculaire [pɛrpɑ̃dikylɛːr]. **1.** *a.* Perpendicular (*à, sur,* to); plumb, upright. **2.** *s.f.* (*a*) *Abaisser une p.,* to drop, draw, a perpendicular (*à, sur,* to). (*b*) *Surv:* Offset. *adv.* **-ment.**

perpendicularité [pɛrpɑ̃dikylarite], *s.f.* Perpendicularity, uprightness.

perpétration [pɛrpetrasjɔ̃], *s.f.* Perpetration.

perpétrer [pɛrpetre], *v.tr.* (je perpètre; je perpétrerai) To perpetrate (crime, etc.).

perpétuation [pɛrpetɥasjɔ̃], *s.f.* Perpetuance, perpetuation.

perpétu|el, -elle [pɛrpetɥɛl], *a.* (*a*) Perpetual, everlasting; (imprisonment) for life. *Le mouvement p.,* perpetual motion. (*b*) *F:* Constant, endless (strife, chatter). *adv.* **-ellement.**

perpétuer [pɛrpetɥe], *v.tr.* To perpetuate.

se perpétuer, to endure, to become established.

perpétuité [pɛrpetɥite], *s.f.* Perpetuity; endlessness. **A perpétuité,** in perpetuity, for ever; (penal servitude) for life.

perpignan [pɛrpiɲɑ̃], *s.m.* **1.** Nettle-tree. **2.** (Nettle-tree) stock, handle (of whip); whip.

perplexe [pɛrplɛks], *a.* **1.** Perplexed, puzzled. **2.** Perplexing (situation).

perplexité [pɛrplɛksite], *s.f.* Perplexity.

perquisition [pɛrkizisjɔ̃], *s.f. Jur:* Thorough search or inquiry. **Mandat de perquisition,** search-warrant. **Faire une perquisition chez qn,** to search s.o.'s premises.

perquisitionner [pɛrkizisjɔne], *v.i. Jur:* To make, conduct, a search (in premises, etc.).
perré [pɛre], *s.m. Civ.E:* Stone facing (of embankment); dry wall.
perron [pɛrɔ̃], *s.m.* (Flight of) steps (before building); perron.
perroquet [pɛrɔke], *s.m.* 1. Parrot. *P:* Étrangler un perroquet, to drink a glass of absinthe. 2. *Nau:* Topgallant (sail). Mât de perroquet, topgallant mast.
perruche [pɛryʃ], *s.f.* 1. *Orn:* (a) Parakeet. (b) Hen-parrot. 2. *Nau:* Mizzen topgallant sail.
perruque [pɛryk], *s.f.* Wig. *P. à marteaux,* bob-wig. Tête à perruque, barber's block. *F:* Vieille perruque, old fog(e)y, old fossil.
perruquier, -ière [pɛrykje, -jɛːr], *s.* (a) Wig-maker. (b) *A:* Hairdresser, barber.
pers [pɛːr], *a.* Sea-green or grey. Minerve aux yeux pers, grey-eyed Minerva.
persan, -ane [pɛrsã, -an]. 1. *a. & s.* Persian. 2. *s.m. Ling:* Persian.
Perse [pɛrs]. 1. *Pr.n.f.* Persia. Tapis de Perse, Persian rug or carpet. 2. *a. & s. A.Geog:* Persian. 3. *s.f. Tex:* Chintz.
persécuter [pɛrsekyte, *v.tr.* (a) To persecute. (b) *F:* To importune, harass, pester.
persécuteur, -trice [pɛrsekytœːr, -tris], *s.* Persecutor.
persécution [pɛrsekysjɔ̃], *s.f.* (a) Persecution. (b) *F:* Importunity, dunning.
persévérance [pɛrseverãːs], *s.f.* Perseverance (à faire qch., in doing sth.); doggedness of purpose.
persévérant [pɛrseverã], *a.* Persevering, steadfast; dogged (work).
persévérer [pɛrsevere], *v.i.* (je persévère; je persévérerai) 1. To persevere (dans, in). *P. dans le bien, à faire le bien,* not to be weary in well-doing. 2. La fièvre persévère, the fever persists.
persicaire [pɛrsikɛːr], *s.f. Bot:* Persicaria, lady's-thumb.
persienne [pɛrsjɛn], *s.f.* Venetian shutter; slatted shutter; persienne.
persiflage [pɛrsiflaːʒ], *s.m.* (Ill-natured) banter; persiflage.
persifler [pɛrsifle], *v.tr.* To banter, rally (ill-naturedly). [SIFFLER]
persifleur, -euse [pɛrsiflœːr, -øːz]. 1. *s.* Banterer; persifleur. 2. *a.* Bantering; supercili-ously ironical.
persil [pɛrsi], *s.m. Bot:* Parsley.
persillé [pɛrsije], *a.* 1. Blue-moulded (cheese). 2. (Of meat) Marbled.
persique [pɛrsik], *a.* (Ancient) Persian. *Geog:* Le Golfe Persique, the Persian Gulf.
persistance [pɛrsistãːs], *s.f.* Persistence, persistency (à faire qch., in doing sth.). 1. Doggedness. Avec persistance, persistently, doggedly. 2. Continuance (of fever, etc.).
persistant [pɛrsistã], *a.* Persistent. 1. Dogged (efforts, etc.). 2. Lasting, enduring.
persister [pɛrsiste], *v.i.* To persist. 1. *P. à faire qch.,* to persist in doing sth. *Il y persiste,* he persists in it; he sticks to it; he adheres to it. 2. La fièvre persiste, the fever pursues its course.
personnage [pɛrsɔnaːʒ], *s.m.* Personage. (a) Person of rank, of distinction. Être un p., to be somebody, *F:* to be a big gun. (b) *Pej:* Person, individual. *C'est un triste p.,* he is a sorry specimen. (c) *Lit:* Character (in play, in novel). Les personnages, the dramatis personae.
personnalité [pɛrsɔnalite], *s.f.* Personality. 1. Individuality; individual characteristics. 2. Person, personage. Toutes les personnalités

de la ville, all the big people in the town. 3. *pl.* Dire des personnalités à qn, to make personal, offensive, remarks to s.o.
personne [pɛrsɔn]. 1. *s.f.* Person. (a) Individual. La p. dont je vous ai parlé, the person whom I mentioned to you. Une tierce p., a third party. Jeune personne, young lady. Les grandes personnes, the grown-ups. Être bonne personne, to be a good sort. *Jur:* Personne morale, civile, juridique, body corporate, corporate body; artificial person. (b) Own self. Je parle à ma personne, I am talking to myself. En personne, in person; personally. *Il est la bonté en p.,* he is kindness itself. *C'est l'avarice en p.,* he is avarice personified. (c) Sa p. me plaît, I like his personal appearance, his looks. Elle est bien faite de sa p., she is a fine figure of a woman. (d) *Gram:* Écrire à la troisième p., to write in the third person. 2. *pron.indef.m.inv.* (a) Anyone, anybody (with vaguely implied negation. *Cf.* QUELQU'UN). Connaissez-vous p. qui puisse m'aider? I suppose you don't know of anyone who can assist me? Il s'y connaît comme personne, nobody is more expert at it than he is. Il travaille plus fort que p., he works harder than anyone. (b) (With ne expressed or understood) No one; nobody. *P. n'est venu,* nobody has come. Qui est là? —Personne, who is there?—No one. Il n'y a p. de blessé, there is no one wounded. Personne (d')autre n'était à bord, there was no one else on board. Sans nommer p., without mentioning any names.
personn|el, -elle [pɛrsɔnɛl]. 1. *a.* (a) Personal (letter, business, pronoun, mood). Strictement p., not transferable (ticket, pass). (b) Maîtrise personnelle, self-mastery, self-control. 2. *s.m.* (a) Personnel, staff; hands (of farm, etc.); (hotel) servants. Faire partie du p. de . . ., to be on the staff of. . . . Manquer de p., to be under-staffed, short-handed. (b) *Navy:* Complement. *adv. -ellement.*
personnification [pɛrsɔnifikasjɔ̃], *s.f.* (a) Personification. (b) Impersonation.
personnifier [pɛrsɔnifje], *v.tr.* (a) To personify. (b) To impersonate.
perspectif, -ive [pɛrspɛktif, -iːv]. 1. *a.* Perspective (plan). 2. *s.f.* Perspective. (a) *Art:* (Linear) perspective. Perspective à vol d'oiseau, bird's-eye view. (b) Outlook, view, prospect. Avoir qch. en perspective, to have sth. in view, in prospect. (c) Une longue perspective de hêtres, a long vista of beech-trees.
perspicace [pɛrspikas], *a.* Perspicacious, shrewd.
perspicacité [pɛrspikasite], *s.f.* Perspicacity, insight, acumen, shrewdness.
persuadant [pɛrsɥadã], *a.* Persuasive, engaging; convincing (argument).
persuader [pɛrsɥade], *v.tr.* 1. *P. qch. à qn,* to persuade s.o. of sth.; to make s.o. believe sth. Ils se sont persuadé que + ind., they have got it into their heads that. . . . 2. *P. m,* to persuade, convince, s.o. (de qch.) Se laisser persuader à la raison, to allow oneself to be convinced. 3. *P. à qn de faire qch.,* to induce s.o., to prevail upon s.o., to do sth.
persuadé, *a.* Persuaded, convinced sure (de, of; que, that).
persuas|if, -ive [pɛrsɥazif, -iːv], *a.* Persuasive (manner); convincing (language). *adv. -ivement.*
persuasion [pɛrsɥazjɔ̃], *s.f.* 1. Persuasion. 2. Conviction, belief. Je suis dans la p. qu'il a tort, I am convinced that he is wrong.
persulfate [pɛrsylfat], *s.m. Ch:* Persulphate.

perte [pɛrt], *s.f.* **I.** Ruin, destruction. *Il court à sa p.*, he is heading for disaster. *Nau:* *P. corps et biens*, loss of vessel with all hands. **2.** Loss. Profits et pertes, profit and loss. *Vendre qch. à perte*, to sell sth. at a loss. **Être en perte**, to be out of pocket. **Perte sèche**, dead loss. *Courir à perte d'haleine*, to run oneself out of breath. S,a. VUE I. *P. de temps*, waste of time. **Parler en pure perte**, to talk to no purpose. **3.** Loss, leakage. *P. de chaleur*, loss of heat. *El.E:* *P. à la terre*, earth leakage. *P. de charge*, drop in voltage.

pertinemment [pɛrtinamɑ̃], *adv.* **I.** Pertinently. **2.** *J'en parle p.*, I speak with knowledge.

pertinence [pɛrtinɑ̃:s], *s.f.* Pertinence, pertinency, appositeness, relevance.

pertinent [pɛrtinɑ̃], *a.* Pertinent, apposite; relevant (*d*, to).

pertuis [pɛrtɥi], *s.m.* **I.** *A:* Hole, opening. **2.** Sluice. **3.** (*a*) Narrows (of a river). (*b*) Strait(s), channel. (*c*) (In the Jura) Pass.

pertuisane [pɛrtɥizan], *s.f.* *Archeol:* Partisan, halberd.

perturbateur, -trice [pɛrtyrbatœ:r, -tris]. **I.** *a.* Disturbing, upsetting. **2.** *s.* Disturber, upsetter. *P. de la paix*, disturber of the peace.

perturbation [pɛrtyrbasjɔ̃], *s.f.* (*a*) Perturbation; agitation of mind. (*b*) *P. magnétique*, magnetic disturbance. **Perturbations atmosphériques**, atmospheric disturbances; *W.Tel:* atmospherics.

pervenche [pɛrvɑ̃:ʃ], *s.f.* *Bot:* Periwinkle.

pervers [pɛrvɛ:r], *a.* Perverse, depraved. *Goûts p.*, vicious tastes. *Conseil p.*, evil counsel. *s.* **Les pervers**, evil-doers. *adv.* **-ement.**

perversion [pɛrvɛrsjɔ̃], *s.f.* Perversion.

perversité [pɛrvɛrsite], *s.f.* Perversity.

pervert|ir [pɛrvɛrti:r], *v.tr.* To pervert, to corrupt. *s.m.* **-issement.** *s.* **-isseur, -euse.** **se pervertir**, to become depraved; to grow vicious.

pesage [pəza:ʒ], *s.m.* **I.** Weighing. *Bureau de p.*, weigh-house. **2.** *Turf:* (*a*) Weighing in. (*b*) Weighing-in room. (*c*) Paddock.

pes|ant [pəzɑ̃]. **I.** *a.* (*a*) Heavy, weighty; ponderous, clumsy (style); sluggish (mind). **Marcher à pas pesants**, to walk heavily. *Entrer, sortir, à pas pesants*, to lumber in, out. (*b*) *Ph:* Ponderable (gas, etc.). **2.** *s.m.* *Cela vaut son pesant d'or*, it is worth its weight in gold. *adv.* **-amment.**

pesanteur [pəzɑ̃tœ:r], *s.f.* **I.** Weight. *Ph:* Gravity. *P. spécifique*, specific gravity. **2.** (*a*) Heaviness. (*b*) Dullness, sluggishness (of mind).

pèse-acide, *s.m.* Acidimeter.

pèse-alcool, *s.m.* Alcoholometer.

pèse-bébé, *s.m.* Baby-weighing machine.

pesée [pəze], *s.f.* **I.** (*a*) Weighing. *Faire la p. de qch.*, to weigh sth. (*b*) Amount weighed at one time. **2.** Force, leverage, effort. *Exercer des pesées sur une porte*, to bring a crow-bar to bear upon a door.

pèse-lait, *s.m.inv.* Lactometer, milk-tester.

pèse-lettre(s), *s.m.* Letter-balance.

peser [pəze], *v.* (je pèse; je pèserai) **I.** *v.tr.* To weigh (parcel, etc.). *P. ses paroles*, to weigh one's words. *Sp:* **Se faire peser**, to weigh in. **2.** *v.i.* (*a*) To weigh; to be heavy. *Paquet qui pèse deux livres*, parcel weighing two pounds. *Cet impôt pèse lourdement sur les commerçants*, this tax presses heavily on tradesmen. *Un silence pesait sur l'assemblée*, a heavy silence hung, brooded, over the meeting. *Le temps lui pèse*, time hangs on his hands. *Sa responsabilité lui pèse*, he feels the weight of his responsibility. (*b*) *P. sur un*

levier, to bear on a lever. *P. sur un mot*, to lay stress on a word.

peseur, -euse [pəzœ:r, -ø:z], *s.* Weigher.

pèse-vin [pɛzvɛ̃], *s.m.inv.* Oenometer.

peson [pəzɔ̃], *s.m.* *P. à ressort*, spring-balance. *P. à contrepoids*, steelyard.

pesse [pɛs], *s.f.*, **pessereau** [pɛsro], *s.m.* *Bot:* Horse-tail, equisetum.

pessimisme [pɛsimism], *s.m.* Pessimism.

pessimiste [pɛsimist]. **I.** *a.* Pessimistic. **2.** *s.* Pessimist; *F:* croaker.

peste [pɛst], *s.f.* Plague, pestilence. *F:* **Fuir qn comme la peste**, to shun, avoid, s.o. like the plague. *Peste!* bless my soul! *A. & Lit:* **Peste (soit) du vieux fou!** a plague on the old fool!

pester [pɛste], *v.i.* *F:* *P. contre qn*, to storm, curse, at s.o.

pestifère [pɛstifɛ:r], *a.* Pestiferous, pestilential.

pestiféré, -ée [pɛstifere], *a. & s.* Plague-stricken.

pestilentiel, -elle [pɛstilɑ̃sjɛl], *a.* Pestilential.

pet [pɛ], *s.m.* **I.** Breaking of wind. *Faire un pet*, to break wind. **2.** *Cu:* **Pet de nonne**, fritter.

pétale [petal], *s.m.* *Bot:* Petal.

pétarade [petarad], *s.f.* (*a*) Crackling (of fireworks); promiscuous firing (of arms). (*b*) *Aut:* (i) Popping back (in carburettor); (ii) back-fire.

pétarader [petarade], *v.i.* (*a*) To emit a succession of bangs. (*b*) *I.C.E:* (Of engine) To pop back.

pétard [peta:r], *s.m.* **I.** (*a*) *Mil:* *A:* Petard. (*b*) *Min:* Shot, blast. (*c*) *Rail:* Detonator; fog-signal. (*d*) (Firework) cracker. **2.** *F:* Sensational piece of news.

pétarder [petarde]. **I.** *v.tr.* To blow up (gate) with a petard; to blast (rock). **2.** *v.i.* *I.C.E:* To back-fire. **3.** *v.i.* *P:* To kick up a row.

pétaudière [petodjɛ:r], *s.f.* *F:* *A:* Disorderly meeting; regular bear-garden.

pet-en-l'air [petɑ̃lɛ:r], *s.m.inv.* (Man's) short indoor jacket.

péter [pete], *v.i.* (je pète; je péterai) **I.** To break wind. **2.** To crackle; (of cork, etc.) to pop.

pétillant [petijɑ̃], *a.* Crackling (fire); semi-sparkling (wine); sparkling (eyes, wit).

pétill|er [petije], *v.i.* (Of burning wood) To crackle; (of champagne) to sparkle, fizz, bubble; (of eyes) to sparkle. *P. de joie*, to bubble over with joy. *Livre qui pétille d'esprit*, book sparkling with wit. *s.m.* **-ement.**

pétiole [pesjɔl], *s.m.* *Bot:* Petiole, leaf-stalk.

petiot, -ote [pətjo, -ɔt], *a. & s.* *F:* Tiny, wee (child); little chap. *Ma petiote*, my little girl.

petit, -ite [pəti, -it], *a.* Small, little. **I.** (*a*) *Un p. homme*, a little man. *C'est un homme p.*, he is small, short. *Une toute petite maison*, a tiny little house. **En petit**, on a small scale; in miniature. **Petit à petit**, little by little, bit by bit. *F:* **Se faire tout petit**, (i) to make oneself as inconspicuous as possible; (ii) to humble oneself (*devant*, before). (*b*) *Les petits talents*, the lesser talents. *Les petits prophètes*, the minor prophets. *Sch:* **Les petites classes**, the lower forms. *Petite guerre*, sham fight. *Com:* **Petite caisse**, petty cash. **2.** Insignificant, unimportant, petty. *P. négociant*, petty tradesman, small tradesman. *La petite propriété*, small holdings. *Ce n'est pas une petite affaire!* it is no small matter! *Les petites gens*, s. **les petits**, humble folk; common folk. **Petit prince**, petty prince. S.a. BIÈRE[1]. **3.** Mean, petty, paltry (spirit). **4.** (*P. enfant*, little child; infant. **Le petit Jésus**, the infant Jesus. *P. chien, chat*, pup, kitten. *Un p. Anglais*, an English boy. *Les petits Dupont sont invités*, the Dupont children are invited. (*b*) *s.* Little boy, little girl, little one. *Pauvre petit(e)*, poor little chap, poor little thing.

(c) *s.m.* Les *petits des animaux*, the young of animals. *Les petits d'un chien, d'un chat, d'un lion, d'un loup*, a dog's pups, a cat's kittens, a lion's whelps, a wolf's cubs. **Faire des petits**, (of animals) to bring forth young ; (of bitch) to pup ; (of lion) to whelp ; (of sow) to farrow ; (of cat) to kitten ; (of wolf) to cub.

petit-cheval, *s.m. Mch:* Donkey-engine.

petit-cousin, petite-cousine, *s.* Second cousin. *pl. Des petit(e)s-cousin(e)s.*

petite-fille, *s.f.* Grand-daughter. *pl. Des petites-filles.*

petitement [p(ə)titmã], *adv.* (a) To a limited extent; in small quantities. (b) Poorly, meanly, pettily. *Se venger p.*, to take a mean revenge.

petite-nièce, *s.f.* Grand-niece. *pl. Des petites-nièces.*

petitesse [pətites], *s.f.* **1.** (a) Smallness, littleness, diminutiveness ; slenderness (of figure). (b) Meanness, pettiness, paltriness. *P. d'esprit,* narrow-mindedness. **2.** *Faire des petitesses,* to do mean, shabby, things.

petit-fils, *s.m.* Grandson. *pl. Des petits-fils.*

petit-gris, *s.m.* **1.** *Z:* Miniver. **2.** Squirrel (fur).

pétition [petisjɔ̃], *s.f.* (a) Petition, memorial. *Faire droit à une p.*, to grant a petition. (b) *Log:* **Pétition de principe,** petitio principii. *Faire une p. de principe,* to beg the question.

pétitionnaire [petisjɔnɛːr], *s.m. & f.* Petitioner.

pétitionner [petisjɔne], *v.i.* To petition.

petit-lait, *s.m.* Whey.

petit-maître, *s.m. A:* Fop, coxcomb. *pl. Des petits-maîtres.*

petit-neveu, *s.m.* **1.** Grand-nephew. **2.** *pl. Nos petits-neveux,* our descendants.

petits-enfants, *s.m.pl.* Grand-children.

pétoire [petwaːr], *s.f.* Pop-gun. [PÉTER]

peton [pətɔ̃], *s.m. F:* (In nursery speech) Tiny foot; tootsy-wootsy. [PIED]

pétoncle [petɔ̃kl], *s.m. Moll:* Scallop.

pétrel [petrɛl], *s.m. Orn:* Petrel. *P. des tempêtes,* stormy petrel.

pétrification [petrifikasjɔ̃], *s.f.* Petrifaction.

pétrifier [petrifje], *v.tr.* To petrify. *F: Pétrifié de peur,* petrified, paralysed, with fear.

  se pétrifier, to turn into stone ; to petrify.

pétrin [petrɛ̃], *s.m.* Kneading-trough. *F: Se mettre dans le pétrin,* to get into trouble, into a mess, into a fix. **Être dans le pétrin,** to be in a hole, in a tight corner, *P:* in the soup.

pétr|ir [petriːr], *v.tr.* To knead (dough, bread) ; to knead, pug, shape, mould (clay) ; to mould, shape (a person's character). *F: Un homme pétri d'amour-propre,* a man eaten up with self-conceit. *s.m.* **-issage.** *s.* **-isseur, -euse.**

pétrole [petrɔl], *s.m.* Petroleum ; mineral oil. *P. brut,* crude petroleum. *P. lampant,* paraffin oil, lamp-oil, *U.S:* kerosene. **Moteur à pétrole,** (heavy-)oil engine.

pétrol|er [petrɔle], *v.tr.* **1.** To kindle, to set fire to, (sth.) with paraffin oil. **2.** To oil (pools) against mosquitoes. *s.m.* **-age.**

pétroleur, -euse [petrɔlœːr, -øːz], *s.* Incendiary (who uses paraffin).

pétrolier, -ière [petrɔlje, -jɛːr]. **1.** *a. L'industrie pétrolière,* the mineral-oil industry. **2.** *a. & s.m.* (Navire, cargo) **pétrolier,** tank steamer ; tanker.

pétrolifère [petrɔlifɛːr], *a.* Oil-bearing. *Gisement* **pétrolifère,** oil-field.

pétulance [petylɑ̃ːs], *s.f.* Liveliness, irrepressibleness (of spirits) ; friskiness (of horse).

pétulant [petylɑ̃], *a.* Lively, irrepressible ; frisky.

pétunia [petynja], *s.m. Bot:* Petunia.

peu [pø]. **I.** *adv.* (a) Little. **Peu ou point,** little or not at all. *Peu de viande,* not much meat. *Si peu qu'il pleuve cela gâtera les foins,* however little it rains it will spoil the hay. **Pour peu que,** see POUR 3 (c). *Ce n'est pas peu dire,* that's saying a good deal. **Quelque peu,** to a slight extent. *Quelque peu surpris,* somewhat surprised. **Tant soit peu,** see TANT 1. **Peu de chose,** (very) little, not much. *J'ai peu de chose de neuf à vous dire,* I have little to tell you that is new. **Pour si peu de chose,** for so small a matter. S.a. PRÈS 2. (b) Few. *Peu de gens,* few people. **En peu de mots,** in a few words. **Peu d'entre eux,** few of them. (c) Not very ; un-. *Peu utile,* not very useful. *Peu intelligent,* unintelligent, not over-intelligent. *Peu soucieux,* heedless. *Peu honnête,* dishonest. *Peu en situation,* inappropriate. *Peu profond,* shallow. *Peu abondant,* scarce. **2.** *s.m.* (a) Little, bit. **Donnez-m'en si peu que rien,** give me the least little bit. *Son peu d'éducation,* his lack of learning. **Homme de peu,** low-born fellow. *Il a un peu moins, un peu plus, de quarante ans,* he is something under, over, forty. *Un peu de vin,* a little wine. *Encore un peu,* a little more, a few more. *F:* Ça, c'est un peu fort! that's rather too much of a good thing ! *Mais pourquoi,* je vous demande un peu! but why, I ask you ! *Un tout petit peu,* a tiny bit. *Pour un peu on eût crié,* we very nearly shouted. *Écoutez un peu,* just listen. *F:* **Excusez du peu** is that all ? nothing less ? *P:* **Un peu !** you bet ! rather ! **Peu à peu,** little by little, bit by bit. (b) (Of time) *Restez encore un peu,* stay a little (while) longer. **Peu après,** shortly after. **Sous peu, dans peu, avant peu, d'ici peu,** before long, ere long. **Depuis peu,** lately.

peuh [pø], *int.* Pooh !

peuplade [pœplad], *s.f.* Small tribe.

peuple [pœpl], *s.m.* People. **1.** Nation. *Le p. français,* the French people. **2.** **Le peuple,** the multitude, the uneducated classes, the masses. **Les gens du peuple ;** le petit, menu, bas, **peuple,** the common people, the lower classes. *a.inv. Des expressions peuple,* plebeian expressions.

peuplement [pœpləmã], *s.m.* **1.** Peopling (of place) ; stocking (of fish-pond, etc.). **Colonie de peuplement,** settlement. **2.** *For:* Plantation.

peupler [pœple]. **1.** *v.tr.* To people, populate (country) ; to stock (fish-pond, etc.). *Rues peuplées de monde,* streets thronged with people. **2.** *v.i.* To multiply, to breed.

  se peupler, to become peopled, populous.

peuplier [pœplie], *s.m.* Poplar.

peur [pœːr], *s.f.* Fear, fright, dread. **Avoir peur,** to be, feel, frightened. *Avoir p. du chien,* to be frightened, afraid, of the dog. *J'ai p. de vous gêner,* I fear I might be in your way. **N'ayez pas peur!** do not be afraid. *J'en ai bien p.,* I'm afraid it is so. **J'ai peur qu'il (ne) soit en retard,** (i) I am anxious lest he should be late ; (ii) I fear he may be late. **Prendre peur,** to take fright. *F:* **Avoir la peur au ventre, avoir une peur bleue,** to be in a blue funk, to be scared to death. *Avoir une p. bleue de qn,* to go in terror of s.o. **En être quitte pour la peur,** to get off with a fright. **Faire peur à qn,** to frighten s.o. ; to give s.o. a fright. **Être laide à faire peur,** to be frightfully ugly. **Sans peur,** fearless, fearlessly. **De peur de,** for fear of (sth.). **De peur que ... (ne) + sub.,** lest ; for fear that. *De p. que vous (ne) tombiez,* lest you should) fall.

peureu|x, -euse [pœrø, -øːz], *a.* Timorous ; easily frightened ; nervous ; timid (nature) ; shy, skittish (horse). *adv.* **-sement.**

peut [pø]. See POUVOIR.

peut-être [pøtɛːtr], *adv.* Perhaps, maybe, possibly. *P.-ê. que oui, p.-ê. que non,* perhaps so, perhaps not. *P.-ê. bien qu'il viendra,* he will very possibly come.

peuvent [pœːv], **peux** [pø]. See POUVOIR.

phagocyte [fagɔsit], *s.m. Biol:* Phagocyte.

phalange [falɑ̃ːʒ], *s.f.* **1.** (*a*) *Gr.Ant: Mil:* Phalanx. (*b*) *F:* Host, army. **2.** *Anat:* Phalanx; finger-joint, toe-joint.

phalangette [falɑ̃ʒɛt], *s.f.* Ungual phalanx, top joint (of finger, toe); third phalanx.

phalène [falɛn], *s.f. Ent:* Phalaena, moth.

phanérogame [fanerɔgam]. *Bot:* **1.** *a.* Phanerogamic, phanerogamous. **2.** *s.f.* Phanerogam.

phantasme [fɑ̃tasm], *s.m. Med:* Phantasm.

pharamineux, -euse [faraminø, -øːz], *a. P:* Amazing, phenomenal, colossal. ▪

pharaon [faraɔ̃], *s.m.* **1.** Pharaoh. **2.** *Cards:* Faro.

phare [faːr], *s.m.* **1.** Lighthouse. *P. à éclats,* flashing light. *P. flottant,* light-ship. **2.** Beacon. *Av: P. d'atterrissage,* landing light. *P. de ligne,* airway beacon. **3.** *Aut: etc:* Head-light, headlamp. *Baisser les phares,* (i) to dip, (ii) to dim, the head-lights. **4.** *W.Tel: P. radio-goniométrique,* wireless direction-finding station.

phare-code, *s.m. Aut:* Non-dazzle head-light. *pl. Des phares-code.*

pharisaïque [farizaik], *a.* Pharisaic(al). *adv.* **-ment,** -ally.

pharisien [farizjɛ̃], *s.m.* Pharisee.

pharmaceutique [farmasøtik]. **1.** *a.* Pharmaceutic(al). **2.** *s.f.* Pharmaceutics.

pharmacie [farmasi], *s.f.* **1.** Pharmacy, dispensing. **2.** (*a*) Pharmacy; chemist's and druggist's shop. (*b*) Dispensary. **3.** (Armoire à) pharmacie, medicine-chest.

pharmacien, -ienne [farmasjɛ̃, -jɛn], *s.* (Pharmaceutical) chemist; druggist.

pharmacopée [farmakɔpe], *s.f.* Pharmacopoeia.

pharyngien, -ienne [farɛ̃ʒjɛ̃, -jɛn], *a. Anat:* Pharyngeal.

pharyngite [farɛ̃ʒit], *s.f. Med:* Pharyngitis.

pharynx [farɛ̃ːks], *s.m. Anat:* Pharynx.

phase [faːz], *s.f.* Phase. **1.** Phasis (of moon, etc.). **2.** (*a*) Stage, period (of an illness, etc.). (*b*) *El.E:* Transformateur de phase, phase transformer. *Décalage de phase,* difference of phase. *En phase,* in phase, in step. *Hors de phase, décalé en phase,* out of parallel, out of phase.

phasé [faze], *a. El.E:* Phased.

phaséole [fazeɔl], *s.f. Bot:* Haricot bean.

phénacétine [fenasetin], *s.f. Med:* Phenacetin.

Phénicie [fenisi]. *Pr.n.f. A.Geog:* Phoenicia.

phénicien, -ienne [fenisjɛ̃, -jɛn], *a. & s.* Phoenician.

phénique [fenik], *a.* Carbolic (acid).

phéniquer [fenike], *v.tr.* To carbolize.
  phéniqué, *a.* Carbolic (lotion, etc.). *Gaze phéniquée,* carbolated gauze.

phénix [feniks], *s.m.* (*a*) *Myth:* Phoenix. (*b*) *F:* Paragon; Admirable Crichton.

phénol [fenɔl], *s.m.* (*a*) *Ch:* Phenol; phenyl alcohol. (*b*) *Com:* Carbolic acid.

phénoménal, -aux [fenɔmenal, -o], *a.* Phenomenal; *F:* prodigious, amazing. *adv.* **-ement.**

phénomène [fenɔmɛn], *s.m.* Phenomenon. (*a*) *Les phénomènes de la nature,* the phenomena of nature. (*b*) Freak (of nature).

philanthrope [filɑ̃trɔp], *s.m.* Philanthropist.

philanthropie [filɑ̃trɔpi], *s.f.* Philanthropy.

philanthropique [filɑ̃trɔpik], *a.* Philanthropic(al).

philanthropisme [filɑ̃trɔpism], *s.m.* Philanthropism.

philatélie [filateli], *s.f.,* **philatélisme** [filatelism], *s.m.* Philately, stamp-collecting.

philatélique [filatelik], *a.* Philatelic.

philatéliste [filatelist]. **1.** *s. m. & f.* Philatelist, stamp-collector. **2.** *a.* Philatelic.

Philémon [filemɔ̃]. *Pr.n.m. Gr.Lit:* Philemon. *F:* Ils sont comme Philémon et Baucis, they're just like Darby and Joan.

philharmonique [filarmɔnik], *a.* Philharmonic.

Philippe [filip]. *Pr.n.m.* Philip. *Hist:* Philippe le Bel, Philip the Fair (of France).

philippique [filipik], *s.f.* Philippic (oration).

philistin, -ine [filistɛ̃, -in], *a. & s.* Philistine.

philistinisme [filistinism], *s.m.* Philistinism; vulgarity of taste.

philologie [filɔlɔʒi], *s.f.* Philology.

philologique [filɔlɔʒik], *a.* Philological. *adv.* **-ment.**

philologue [filɔlɔg], *s.m.* Philologist.

philosophale [filɔzɔfal], *a.f. A:* La pierre philosophale, the philosopher's stone.

philosophe [filɔzɔf]. **1.** *s. m. & f.* Philosopher, sage. **2.** *a.* Philosophical.

philosopher [filɔzɔfe], *v.i.* To philosophize.

philosophie [filɔzɔfi], *s.f.* Philosophy.

philosophique [filɔzɔfik], *a.* Philosophical. *adv.* **-ment.**

philtre [filtr], *s.m.* (Love) philtre.

phlébite [flebit], *s.f. Med:* Phlebitis.

phlébotomie [flebɔtɔmi], *s.f.* Phlebotomy.

phlogistique [flɔʒistik]. *A.Ch:* **1.** *a.* Phlogistic. **2.** *s.m.* Phlogiston.

phlox [flɔks], *s.m. Bot:* Phlox.

phlyctène [flikten], *s.f. Med:* Vesicle, pimple, (water-)blister, bleb.

phobie [fɔbi]. **1.** *s.f. Med:* Phobia; morbid fear. *F: Avoir une p. du téléphone,* to live in daily dread of the telephone. **2.** *s.suff.f.* Anglophobie, Anglophobia. *Claustrophobie,* claustrophobia.

phonéticien [fɔnetisjɛ̃], *s.m.* Phonetician.

phonétique [fɔnetik]. **1.** *a.* Phonetic (writing, etc.). **2.** *s.f.* Phonetics. *adv.* **-ment,** -ally.

phonique [fɔnik], *a.* Phonic; acoustic. *Signal p.,* sound signal. *Tp:* Appel phonique, buzzer.

phonogramme [fɔnɔgram], *s.m. Cin: etc:* Sound-record.

phonographe [fɔnɔgraf], *s.m.* (*a*) Phonograph. (*b*) *P. à disques,* gramophone.

phonographie [fɔnɔgrafi], *s.f.* **1.** Phonography; phonetic spelling. **2.** Gramophone recording.

phonolite [fɔnɔlit], *s.f.* Clinkstone, phonolite.

phonologie [fɔnɔlɔʒi], *s.f. Ling:* Phonology.

phonologique [fɔnɔlɔʒik], *a.* Phonologic(al).

phoque [fɔk], *s.m. Z:* Seal. *Pêche des phoques,* seal-fishing; sealing.

phosgène [fɔsʒɛn], *s.m. Ch:* Phosgene (gas).

phosphate [fɔsfat], *s.m. Ch: Agr:* Phosphate. *P. de chaux,* calcium phosphate.

phosphaté [fɔsfate], *a. Ch:* Phosphatic, phosphated.

phosphène [fɔsfɛn], *s.m.* **1.** *Physiol:* Phosphene. **2.** *Ent:* Fire-fly.

phosphore [fɔsfɔːr], *s.m. Ch:* Phosphorus. *P. blanc,* yellow phosphorus.

phosphorer [fɔsfɔre], *v.tr.* To phosphorate.
  phosphoré, *a.* **1.** Phosphorated. *Allumettes phosphorées,* phosphorus matches. **2.** *Ch:* Phosphuretted (hydrogen).

phosphorescence [fɔsfɔrɛssɑ̃ːs], *s.f.* Phosphorescence. *Luire par phosphorescence,* to phosphoresce.

phosphorescent [fɔsfɔrɛssã], a. Phosphorescent.
phosphoreux [fɔsfɔrø], a.m. Ch: Phosphorous.
phosphorique [fɔsfɔrik], a. Ch: Phosphoric.
phosphure [fɔsfy:r], s.m. Ch: Phosphide.
phosphuré [fɔsfyre], a. Ch: Phosphuretted.
photo [fɔto], s.f. F: (= PHOTOGRAPHIE) Photograph, F: photo.
photocalque [fɔtɔkalk], s.m. Ind: Prototype (from tracing); blue print.
photochimie [fɔtɔʃimi], s.f. Photochemistry.
photo-électrique, a. Ph: Photo-electric (cell).
photogénique [fɔtɔʒenik], a. 1. Actinic. 2. Cin: Être p., to photograph well; to have a film face.
photographe [fɔtɔgraf], s.m. Photographer.
photographie [fɔtɔgrafi], s.f. 1. Photography. Faire de la p., to go in for photography. 2. Photograph, F: photo.
photographier [fɔtɔgrafje], v.tr. To photograph; to take a photograph of (sth.). Se faire photographier, to have one's photo(graph) taken.
photographique [fɔtɔgrafik], a. Photographic. S.a. APPAREIL 2. adv. **-ment**, -ally.
photograveur [fɔtɔgravœ:r], s.m. Photo-engraver, process-engraver; block-maker.
photogravure [fɔtɔgravy:r], s.f. Photo-engraving; photogravure (process or print).
photolithographe [fɔtɔlitɔgraf], s.m. Photolithographer.
photolithographie [fɔtɔlitɔgrafi], s.f. 1. Photolithography. 2. Photolithograph.
photolyse [fɔtɔli:z], s.f. Biol: Bot: Photolysis.
photomécanique [fɔtɔmekanik], a. Photomechanical.
photomètre [fɔtɔmɛtr], s.m. Photometer.
photométrie [fɔtɔmetri], s.f. Photometry.
photomicrographie [fɔtɔmikrɔgrafi], s.f. 1. Photomicrography. 2. Photomicrograph.
photopoudre [fɔtɔpu:dr], s.f. Phot: Flashlight powder.
photosphère [fɔtɔsfɛ:r], s.f. Astr: Photosphere.
phototélégraphie [fɔtɔtelegrafi], s.f. 1. Phot: Telephotography. 2. Tg: Phototelegraphy.
photothérapie [fɔtɔterapi], s.f. Phototherapy; light-cure.
photothérapique [fɔtɔterapik], a. Med: Phototherapeutic. Bain p., light-bath.
phototype [fɔtɔtip], s.m. Phot.Engr: 1. Phototype. 2. Collotype (print).
phototypie [fɔtɔtipi], s.f. Collotype (process).
phototypographie [fɔtɔtipɔgrafi], s.f. Phototypography; half-tone reproduction.
phrase [fra:z], s.f. 1. Sentence. F: Faire des phrases, faire de grandes phrases, to speak in flowery language. Parler sans phrase, to speak straight out, without mincing matters. Membre de phrase, phrase. 2. Mus: Phrase.
phraséologie [frazeɔlɔʒi], s.f. Phraseology.
phraser [fraze]. 1. v.i. = Faire des phrases, q.v. under PHRASE 1. 2. v.tr. Mus: etc: To phrase.
phraseur, -euse [frazœ:r, -ø:z], s.t. F: Phrasemonger.
phrénologie [frenɔlɔʒi], s.f. Phrenology.
phrénologique [frenɔlɔʒik], a. Phrenological.
phrénologiste [frenɔlɔʒist], s.m. Phrenologist.
phrygane [frigan], s.f. Ent: Phryganea; esp. caddis-fly, may-fly. Larve de phrygane, caddis-worm.
phrygien, -ienne [friʒjɛ̃, -jɛn], a. & s. A.Geog: Phrygian. Bonnet phrygien, Phrygian cap (as emblem of liberty).
phtisie [ftizi], s.f. Med: Phthisis; (pulmonary) consumption.

phtisique [ftizik]. Med: 1. a. Phthisical, consumptive. 2. s. Consumptive.
phylactère [filaktɛ:r], s.m. Phylactery.
phylloxéra [fillɔksɛra], s.m. Ent: Phylloxera.
physicien, -ienne [fizisjɛ̃, -jɛn], s. Physicist; natural philosopher.
physico-chimie, s.f. Physical chemistry.
physiologie [fizjɔlɔʒi], s.f. Physiology.
physiologique [fizjɔlɔʒik], a. Physiological. Bio-Ch: Solution physiologique, normal saline solution. adv. **-ment**.
physiologiste [fizjɔlɔʒist], s.m. Physiologist.
physionomie [fizjɔnɔmi], s.f. Physiognomy; cast of features; face, countenance; (of thg) appearance, aspect. Il manque de p., his face lacks character. Jeu de physionomie, play of features. Région qui a une p. particulière, region with a character of its own.
physionomiste [fizjɔnɔmist], s. m. & f. Physiognomist; good judge of faces.
physique [fizik]. 1. a. Physical. (a) Douleur p., bodily pain. Force p., physical strength. (b) Chimie p., physical chemistry. 2. s.f. Physics; natural philosophy. Appareil de physique, (piece of) physical apparatus. 3. s.m. Physique (of person). Th: Il a le physique de l'emploi, he looks the part. Comment est-il au physique? what is he like to look at?
physiquement [fizikmɑ̃], adv. Physically, materially.
phytophage [fitɔfa:ʒ], a. Phytophagous; plant-eating.
pi [pi], s.m. Gr.Alph: Pi.
piaculaire [pjakylɛ:r], a. Piacular, expiatory.
piaffe [pjaf], s.f. F: A: Ostentation, show. Faire de la piaffe, to swagger.
piaffer [pjafe], v.i. 1. A: To swagger; to show off. 2. (Of horse) (a) To paw the ground. (b) To prance. s.m. **-ement**.
piaffeur, -euse [pjafœ:r, -ø:z], a. & s. Mettlesome (horse); high-stepper.
piaillard, -arde [pjɑja:r, -ard], a. & s. Cheeping (bird); squalling, mewling (child).
piailler [pjɑje], v.i. (Of small birds) To cheep; (of children) to squall, squeal. s. **-eur, -euse**.
piaillerie [pjɑjri], s.f. Continuous cheeping (of birds); squalling, squealing (of children).
pianiste [pjanist], s. m. & f. Pianist.
piano¹ [pjano], s.m. Piano, pianoforte. P. à queue, grand piano. P. à demi-queue, baby-grand (piano). P. droit, vertical, upright piano. Piano mécanique, (i) (à rouleau) piano-player (instrument), player-piano; (ii) (à cylindre) (street) piano-organ. Jouer du piano, to play the piano.
piano², adv. Mus: Piano, softly.
pianola [pjanɔla], s.m. Pianola.
pianoter [pjanɔte], v.i. F: To strum (on piano). s.m. **-age**. s. **-eur, -euse**.
piastre [pjastr], s.f. Num: Piastre.
piaulard [pjolɑ:r], a. F: Peeping, cheeping (chicken); whimpering, whining (child).
piauler [pjole], v.i. (Of chicks) To peep, cheep; (of children) to whine, whimper. s.m. **-ement**.
piaulis [pjoli], s.m. F: Cheeping, squeaking (of birds).
pibroch [pibrɔk], s.m. 1. Pibroch. 2. Bagpipe.
pic¹ [pik], s.m. 1. Pick, pickaxe. Pic de tailleur de pierre, stone-dressing pick. Pic à main, miner's pick. Pic à air comprimé, pneumatic pick. Pic à tranche, mattock. 2. Cards: Pique (at piquet). 3. (Mountain-)peak. Adv.phr. A pic, perpendicular(ly), sheer. Sentier à pic, precipitous path. Côte à pic, bluff coast. Promontoire à pic, bold headland; bluff. F: Arriver, tomber, à pic, to

come, happen, in the nick of time. **4.** *Nau:* (a) Peak (of sail, of gaff). **Drisse de pic,** peak-halyard. (b) **L'ancre est à pic,** the anchor is apeak.

pic², *s.m. Orn:* Woodpecker.

picard, -arde [pikaːr, -ard], *a. & s.* (Native) of Picardy.

Picardie [pikardi]. *Pr.n.f. Geog:* Picardy.

pichenette [piʃnɛt], *s.f. F:* Fillip, flip, flick (of the finger).

pichet [piʃe], *s.m.* Pitcher (for wine or cider).

picholine [pikɔlin], *s.f. Cu:* Pickled olive.

pick-up [pikœp], *s.m.* (Gramophone) pick-up, reproducer.

picorée [pikɔre], *s.f.* (a) Pilfering (of fruit, etc.). (b) (Of birds) **Aller à la picorée,** to go in search of food.

picorier [pikɔre]. **1.** *v.i.* (a) (Of bird, etc.) To forage ; to pick, scratch about, for food. (b) To pilfer. **2.** *v.tr.* To pilfer (fruit, etc.). *s.m.* **-eur.**

picot [piko], *s.m.* **1.** (a) Splinter (of wood). (b) Barb, point. **2.** Pick-hammer. **3.** Wedge. **4.** *Needlew: Lacem:* Picot.

picotement [pikɔtmɑ̃], *s.m.* Pricking, tingling, smarting (sensation).

picoter [pikɔte], *v.tr.* **1.** (a) To prick tiny holes in (sth.). *Picoté de petite vérole,* pitted with smallpox. (b) (Of bird) To peck, peck at (fruit, etc.). (c) *Fumée qui picote les yeux,* smoke that stings the eyes, that makes the eyes smart. *P. son cheval,* to prick one's horse lightly (with the spur). **2.** To picot, to put picots on (piece of lace, etc.). **3.** *v.i.* To smart, tingle. *J'ai les yeux qui me picotent,* my eyes are smarting.

picotin [pikɔtɛ̃], *s.m.* Peck, feed (of oats).

picrate [pikrat], *s.m. Ch:* Picrate.

picrique [pikrik], *a. Ch:* Picric (acid).

Pictes [pikt], *s.m.pl. Ethn: Hist:* Picts.

pictural, -aux [piktyral, -o], *a.* Pictorial ; worthy of an artist's brush. *adv.* **-ement.**

pic-vert [piveːr], *s.m. Orn:* Green woodpecker. *pl. Des pics-verts.*

pie¹ [pi]. **1.** *s.f. Orn:* Magpie. *F:* **Larron comme une pie,** as thievish as a magpie. S.a. JASER, NID 1, 2. **2.** (a) *s. m. or f.* Piebald horse. (b) *a.,* often *inv.* Piebald.

pie², *a.f. A:* Pious, charitable. **Œuvre(s) pie(s),** charitable deed(s), good works.

Pie³. *Pr.n.m.* Pius.

pièce [pjɛs], *s.f.* **1.** Piece (as a whole). (a) **Pièce de bétail, de gibier,** head of cattle, of game. *P. de blé,* corn-field. *P. d'eau,* sheet of water ; ornamental lake. *P. de vin,* barrel, cask, of wine. **Vin en pièce,** wine in the cask, in the wood. **Pièce de monnaie,** coin. *P. de dix francs,* ten-franc piece. **Donner la pièce à qn,** to give s.o. a tip. *P. d'étoffe,* roll of material. *Cu: Pyr:* **Pièce montée,** set piece. S.a. RÉSISTANCE 2. *Ils coûtent mille francs p.,* they cost a thousand francs apiece. **Ils se vendent à la pièce,** they are sold singly, in ones. **Travailler à la pièce, aux pièces,** to do piece-work. **Pièce d'artillerie,** piece of ordnance ; gun. **Grosse pièce,** heavy gun. **Pièce de bord,** naval gun. *F:* **C'est une bonne pièce,** he's a decent fellow. (b) *Jur:* **Pièces d'un procès,** documents in a case. S.a. CONVICTION 2, JUSTIFICATIF. (c) **Pièce de théâtre,** play. *Monter une p.,* to put on a play ; to cast a play. *F:* **Jouer une pièce à qn, faire pièce à qn,** to play a trick or a joke on s.o. (d) **Pièce moulée,** moulding ; (plaster, etc.) *cast. Metall:* **Pièce coulée,** casting. **Grosses pièces,** heavy castings. *P. estampée,* punched piece. **Tout d'une pièce,** all of a piece. *F: Homme tout d'une p.,* man cast in a simple mould. **2.** Piece (as part of a whole). (a) *P. de*

bœuf, joint of beef. *Pièces d'une machine, d'une horloge,* parts of a machine, of a clock. *P. de rechange,* spare part. **Être armé de toutes pièces,** to be fully armed, armed at all points. *F:* **Créer une armée de toutes pièces,** to create an army out of nothing. (b) *Games:* (Chess-)piece ; (draughts)man. (c) Room (in house). (d) Patch. **Mettre, poser, une p. à un vêtement,** to patch a garment. (e) *Her:* Piece, ordinary, charge. **Pièce honorable,** honourable ordinary. **3.** Fragment, bit. **Fait de pièces et de morceaux,** made of shreds and patches, of odds and ends. **Vêtements en pièces,** tattered garments. **Mettre qch. en pièces,** to break sth. into fragments ; to break sth. to pieces ; to tear (garment, etc.) to pieces. **Pièce à pièce,** bit by bit, piece by piece.

piécette [pjesɛt], *s.f.* **1.** Small coin. **2.** Short play ; curtain-raiser.

pied [pje], *s.m.* **1.** (a) Foot (of man, of hoofed animal). *Il n'avait pas de souliers aux pieds,* he had no shoes to his feet. *Se jeter aux pieds de qn,* to throw oneself at s.o.'s feet. *F:* **Partir du pied gauche,** to make a good start. *Se lever du p. gauche,* to get out of bed on the wrong side. **De la tête aux pieds, de pied en cap** [dɔpjetɑ̃kap], from head to foot, from top to toe. *Frapper du p.,* to stamp one's foot. **Faire des pieds et des mains pour . . . ,** to do one's utmost, to move heaven and earth, in order to. *. . .* **Mettre pied à terre** [pjeataːr], to alight (from carriage) ; to dismount (from horse) ; to step ashore, to land (from boat). **Marcher sur les pieds de qn,** to tread on s.o.'s toes. **Avoir bon pied, bon œil,** to be hale and hearty. **Avoir toujours un pied en l'air,** to be always on the go. *F:* **Lever le pied,** to make oneself scarce. **Faire qch. au pied levé,** to do sth. off-hand, at a moment's notice. **Il ne peut pas mettre un pied devant l'autre,** (he is so weak that) he can hardly crawl. **Valet de pied,** footman, *F:* flunkey. *F:* **Avoir les pieds chauds,** to be in clover. **Coup de pied,** kick. **Chasser qn à coups de pied,** to kick s.o. out. **Enfoncer la porte à coups de pied,** to kick the door in. **C'est le coup de pied de l'âne,** that is the most unkindest cut of all. *Rugby Fb:* **Coup de pied tombé,** drop-kick. *Cu: P. de veau, p. de cochon,* calf's foot, pig's trotter. S.a. BOT, CHAUSSURE, DANSER 1, ÉPINE 2, FOULER 1, FOURCHU, JOINT 1, PLAT 2. *Achille aux pieds légers,* swift-foot(ed) Achilles. *Un poney au p. sûr,* a sure-footed pony. **A pied,** on foot, walking. **Voyageur à pied,** pedestrian. *Excursionnistes à p.,* hikers. **Aller à pied,** to walk. *Faire deux lieues à p.,* to walk five miles. *Vous en avez pour vingt minutes à p.,* you can walk it in twenty minutes. **Course à pied,** foot-race, running-match. **Mettre un jockey, P:** un employé, à pied, to suspend a jockey ; to dismiss, *F:* to sack, an employee. **Sur pied,** afoot, standing, on one's legs. **Récolte sur pied,** standing crop. *Remettre qn sur p.,* (i) to restore s.o. to health, (ii) (in business) to set s.o. up, on his feet, again. **Portrait en pied,** full-length portrait. *Mil:* **L'arme au pied,** with arms at the order. (b) Footing, foothold. **Perdre pied,** to lose one's foothold ; to get out of one's depth (in bathing). **Le pied me manqua,** I lost my footing. **Tenir pied,** to stand fast. **Tenir pied à qn,** to stand up to s.o. **Prendre pied,** (i) to get a footing, a foothold ; (ii) to take root. **Armée sur pied de guerre,** army on a war footing. **Être sur un bon pied avec qn,** *F:* to be well in with s.o. *Établir une maison sur un grand p.,* to set up house or to open a business on a large scale. **Payer qn sur le pied de . . . ,** to pay s.o. at the rate of. *. . .*

S.a. FERME¹ I, GRUE I, LÂCHER I, MARIN I. (c) Foot-print, track (of animal). Typ: Pied de mouche, paragraph mark. 2. (a) Foot (of stocking, tree); foot, base (of column, wall, mountain). (Of wall) Avoir du pied, to have batter. Donner plus de p. à une échelle, to give more slope to a ladder. S.a. LETTRE 2 Civ.E: Const: A pied d'œuvre, on site. F: Reprendre un travail à p. d'œuvre, to start again from the very beginning. (b) Leg (of chair, piano, etc.); stem, foot (of glass). (c) P. de céleri, de laitue, head of celery, of lettuce. (d) Stand, rest (for telescope, camera, etc.). P. de lampe, lamp-stand. Laund: Pied à manches, sleeve-board. (e) Nau: Step, heel (of mast). (f) Bookb: Tail (of book). 3. (a) Meas: Foot. Long de trois pieds six pouces, three foot six in length. Pied carré, square foot. F: Donnez-lui un pied, il en prendra quatre, give him an inch and he will take an ell. F: C'est un Napoléon au petit pied, he's quite a miniature Napoleon. Pied à pied [pjeapje], foot by foot, step by step. (b) Foot-rule. Pied à coulisse, (i) calliper-square; (ii) (shoemaker's) size-stick. 4. Pros: (Metrical) foot.

pied-à-terre [pjɛtatɛːr], s.m.inv. (Small) occasional lodging, shooting-box, pied-à-terre.

pied-d'alouette, s.m. Larkspur, delphinium.

pied-de-biche, s.m. **1.** Bell-pull. **2.** (a) Nail-extractor, nail-claw. (b) Crow-bar, spike-bar. **3.** Cabriole leg (of chair, etc.). pl. Des pieds-de-biche.

pied-droit, piédroit [pjedrwa], s.m. **1.** Civ.E: Pier (of arch). **2.** Arch: (a) Engaged pier. (b) Jamb, pier (of window, etc.). pl. Des pieds-droits, piédroits.

piédestal, -aux [pjedɛstal, -o], s.m. Pedestal.

piédouche [pjeduʃ], s.m. Small pedestal.

pied-tonne, s.m. Mec.Meas: Foot-ton. pl. Des pieds-tonnes.

piège [pjɛːʒ], s.m. Trap, snare. P. à loups, man-trap. Armer, dresser, tendre, un p., to set a trap (à, for). Prendre un animal au p., to trap an animal. Attirer l'ennemi dans un p., to ambush the enemy. Donner, tomber, dans le piège, se prendre au piège, to walk, fall, into the trap.

piégler [pjeʒe], v.tr. (je piège ; je piégeai(s); je piégerai) To trap (beast). s.m. -cage. s.m. -eur.

pie-grièche [pigrieʃ], s.f. **1.** Orn: Shrike. **2.** F: Shrew (of a woman). pl. Des pies-grièches.

pie-mère [pimɛːr], s.f. Anat: Pia mater.

pierraille [pjerɑːj], s.f. Broken stones; rubble; ballast; road metal.

pierre¹ [pjɛːr], s.f. Stone. (a) P. de taille, free-stone, ashlar. Poser la première pierre, to lay the foundation stone. P. calcaire, limestone. P. à plâtre, gypsum. Ouvrage en p., stone-work. Ne pas laisser pierre sur pierre, not to leave a stone standing. Pierre milliaire, milestone. P. à aiguiser, à repasser, whetstone, grindstone. P. à huile, oilstone, hone. Pierre à briquet, à feu, flint, strike-a-light. P. à fusil, gun-flint. Pierre de touche, touchstone. P. précieuse, precious stone; gem. Pierre d'achoppement, stumbling-block. Avoir un cœur de pierre, to have a heart of stone. Assaillir qn à coups de pierres, to pelt s.o. with stones. F: Jeter la pierre à qn, to cast a stone at s.o.; to accuse s.o. C'est une pierre dans votre jardin, that's a dig at you. Faire d'une pierre deux coups, to kill two birds with one stone. L'âge de la p. taillée, the palaeolithic age. S.a. ÂGE 3. Prov: Pierre qui roule n'amasse pas mousse, a rolling stone gathers no moss. (b) Med: Stone, calculus.

Pierre². Pr.n.m. Peter. F: Découvrir saint

Pierre pour couvrir saint **Paul,** to rob Peter to pay Paul.

pierreries [pjɛr(ə)ri], s.f.pl. Precious stones, jewels, gems.

pierrette¹ [pjɛrɛt], s.f. Small stone ; pebble.

pierrette², s.f. **1.** Th: Pierrette. **2.** Orn: F: Hen-sparrow.

pierreux, -euse [pjɛrø, -øːz], a. (a) Stony (ground); gravelly (bed of river); gritty (pear). (b) Med: (i) Calculous (formation); (ii) (patient) suffering from calculus.

Pierrot [pjɛro]. **1.** Pr.n.m. F: Peterkin. **2.** s.m. (a) Th: Pierrot, clown. (b) Orn: F: Sparrow.

piété [pjete], s.f. (a) Affectionate devotion. P. filiale, filial reverence or dutifulness. (b) Piety, godliness. Articles de piété, devotional articles.

piétin|er [pjetine]. **1.** v.tr. To trample, stamp, on (sth.); to trample (sth.) down ; to tread (sth.) under foot. Ind: P. l'argile, to tread the clay. **2.** v.i. P. sur place, to mark time. P. de rage, to dance with rage. P. sur le feu pour l'éteindre, to stamp out the fire. s.m. **-ement.**

piétisme [pjetism], s.m. Rel.H: Pietism.

piéton [pjetɔ̃], s.m. Pedestrian. Sentier pour piétons, a. sentier piéton, footpath.

piètre [pjɛtr], a. F: Wretched, poor (coat, meal); lame, paltry (excuse). adv. **-ment.**

pieu¹, -eux [pjø], s.m. **1.** Stake, post. F: Raide comme un pieu, as stiff as a post. **2.** Civ.E: Pile. Enfoncer, battre, un p., to drive (in) a pile.

pieu², s.m. P: Bed ; P: kip. Se mettre au pieu, to get into bed ; P: to kip down.

pieuvre [pjœːvr], s.f. Octopus, devil-fish, poulpe.

pieu|x, -euse [pjø, -øːz], a. (a) Reverent, A: pious. (b) Pious, godly. Legs pieux, charity bequest. adv. **-sement.**

piézomètre [pjezɔmɛtr], s.m. Ph: Piezometer.

pif¹ [pif], int. Pif, paf! (exchange of sharp blows, of revolver shots, etc.) bang, bang!

pif², s.m. P: Large nose ; P: conk.

piffrer (se) [səpifre], v.pr. P: To guzzle, gorge.

pige [piːʒ], s.f. **1.** Measuring-rod. Aut: P. de niveau d'huile, dip-stick. **2.** Typ: 'Take' (of copy). **3.** P: Faire la pige à qn, to outdo s.o.

pigeon, -onne [piʒɔ̃, -ɔn], s. **1.** Pigeon. P. mâle, femelle, cock-pigeon, hen-pigeon. P. bleu, stock-dove. P. ramier, ring-dove, wood-pigeon. P. à capuchon, jacobin. P. tambour, tambourine-pigeon. P. voyageur, carrier-pigeon, homing pigeon. P. homer. S.a. BOULANT I, CULBUTANT, GORGE-DE-PIGEON. P. artificiel, clay pigeon. **2.** F: Greenhorn, gull, pigeon.

pigeonneau [piʒɔno], s.m. **1.** Young pigeon; squab. **2.** F: Gull, dupe.

pigeonnier [piʒɔnje], s.m. Pigeon-house, dove-cot(e).

piger [piʒe], v.tr. (je pigeai(s); n. pigeons) **1.** P: (a) To look at (sth.). Pige-moi ça! just look at that! (b) To catch (cold, thief, etc.). Se faire piger, to get nabbed, collared. Piges-tu la combine? do you twig their little game? **2.** Games: To measure the distance of opposing bowls.

pigment [pigmɑ̃], s.m. Pigment.

pigmentaire [pigmɑ̃tɛːr], a. Pigmentary.

pigmentation [pigmɑ̃tasjɔ̃], s.f. Pigmentation.

pigmenté [pigmɑ̃te], a. Pigmented.

pigne [piɲ], s.f. (a) Pine-, fir-cone. (b) = PIGNON².

pignocher [piɲɔʃe], v.tr. F: **1.** To pick at (one's food). **2.** To paint with little niggling strokes.

pignon¹ [piɲɔ̃], s.m. **1.** Gable, gable-end. F: Avoir pignon sur rue, to have a house of one's own ; to own houses. **2.** Mec.E: Pinion. P. de chaîne, sprocket-wheel, chain-sprocket (of motor cycle, etc.). *Grand p.*, front chain-wheel (of bicycle). *Aut:* P. *de boîte de vitesses*, gear pinion. P. *d'angle*, bevel wheel.

pignon², *s.m. Bot:* Pine-seed, -kernel.

pignouf [piɲuːf], *s.m. P:* **1.** Cad. **2.** Stingy fellow.

pilaf [pilaf], *s.m. Cu:* Pilau, pilaw, pilaff.

pilaire [pilɛːr], *a.* = PILEUX.

pilastre [pilastr], *s.m.* Pilaster. P. *d'escalier*, newel.

pile¹ [pil], *s.f.* **1.** Pile; heap (of coins, books); stack (of wood). **Mettre en pile,** to heap, to stack, to pile up. **2.** Pier (of bridge). **3.** *El:* Battery. Élément de pile, cell. P. *sèche,* dry cell. P. *de rechange*, refill (for torch).

pile², *s.f.* Beating-trough, -engine, stamping-trough (for paper, etc.) *F:* **Flanquer une pile à qn,** to give s.o. a thrashing.

pile³, *s.f.* Reverse (of coin). **Pile ou face,** heads or tails. S.a. CROIX I.

pil|er [pile], *v.tr.* To pound; to crush, bruise (in mortar, etc.); to grind (almonds); to stamp, beat (skins). **Poivre pilé,** ground pepper. *s.m.* **-age.** *s.* **-eur, -euse.**

pilet [pile], *s.m. Orn:* Pintail (duck).

pileux, -euse [pilø, -øːz], *a.* Pilose, pilous, hairy. S.a. BULBE 2.

pilier [pilje], *s.m.* Pillar, column, post; shaft (of column). *F:* **Un pilier d'église,** a pillar, a strong supporter, of the Church. P. *d'estaminet, de cabaret*, public-house loafer, bar-lounger.

pilifère [pilifɛːr], *a. Bot:* Piliferous.

pillage [pijaːʒ], *s.m.* (*a*) Pillage, looting. **Mettre une ville au pillage,** to sack a town. (*b*) *F:* Pilfering, filching.

pillard, -arde [pijaːr, -ard]. **1.** *a.* (*a*) Pillaging. (*b*) Thieving, pilfering. **2.** *s.* (*a*) Pillager, looter, plunderer. (*b*) Pilferer.

piller [pije], *v.tr.* **1.** (*a*) To pillage, plunder, loot, sack, ransack. (*b*) P. *un auteur*, to plagiarize, steal from, an author. **2.** (Of dog) To attack, worry (person, sheep). **Pille! pille!** at him!

pilleur, -euse [pijœːr, -øːz]. **1.** *a.* Given to plunder; pilfering (servant). **2.** *s.* Pillager. P. *d'épaves*, wrecker.

pilon [pilɔ̃], *s.m.* **1.** (*a*) Pestle. (*b*) Earth-rammer, punner. (*c*) (Ore-crushing) stamp. (*d*) Steam hammer. S.a. MARTEAU-PILON. **Mettre un livre au pilon,** to pulp a book. **2.** *F:* (*a*) Drumstick (of fowl). (*b*) Wooden leg. [PILER]

pilonn|er [pilɔne]. **1.** *v.tr.* To pound (drugs, etc.); to pulp (paper, etc.); to ram, beat, pun (earth, concrete, etc.); to stamp (ore). **2.** *v.i.* (*a*) *F:* To work hard to slog. (*b*) *Aut:* (Of engine) To knock. *s.m.* **-age.**

pilori [pilɔri], *s.m.* Pillory. **Mettre au pilori** = PILORIER.

pilorier [pilɔrje], *v.tr.* To pillory (s.o.); to put (s.o.) in the pillory.

pilot [pilo], *s.m.* **1.** *Civ.E:* Pile. P. *de pont*, bridge pile. **2.** Heap of salt (in salt-pans).

pilotage¹ [pilotaːʒ], *s.m.* Pile-driving.

pilotage², *s.m Nau: Av:* (*a*) Pilotage, piloting. *Av:* **École de pilotage,** flying-school. (*b*) (Frais de) pilotage, pilotage (dues).

pilote [pilɔt], *s.m.* **1.** *Nau: Av:* Pilot. P. *hauturier,* deep-sea pilot. P. *côtier, p. lamaneur,* coast pilot, in-shore pilot. P. *aviateur,* air pilot. *a.* **Bateau pilote,** pilot-boat. **Ballon pilote,** pilot-balloon. **2.** *Ich:* Pilot-fish.

piloter¹ [pilɔte], *v.tr. Civ.E:* To drive piles into (sand, etc.).

piloter², *v.tr.* To pilot (ship, aeroplane); to fly (aeroplane).

pilotis [pilɔti], *s.m. Civ.E:* Piling. P. *de support,* pile foundation.

pilou [pilu], *s.m.* Flannelette, cotton flannel, Canton flannel.

pilule [pilyl], *s.f. Pharm:* Pill. *F:* **Prendre la pilule,** to meet with a rebuff. **Avaler la pilule,** to swallow the pill. S.a. DORER I.

pimbêche [pɛ̃bɛʃ], *s.f. F:* Uppish and disagreeable woman; *F:* old cat.

piment [pimɑ̃], *s.m.* Pimento, capsicum. *Cu:* Red pepper.

pimenter [pimɑ̃te], *v.tr. Cu:* To season (sth.) with red pepper. *F:* P. *son récit*, to give spice to one's story.

pimenté, *a.* Highly spiced.

pimpant, *a.* Smart, spruce.

pimprenelle [pɛ̃prənɛl], *s.f. Bot:* Burnet, bloodwort. P. *aquatique*, brookweed.

pin [pɛ̃], *s.m.* Pine(-tree), fir(-tree). P. *d'Écosse*, Scotch pine, Scotch fir. Pin *sylvestre, suisse,* Norway pine. **Pin pignon, pin (en) parasol,** stone-pine, parasol pine. *Pin de montagne,* silver pine, white pine. *Pin de Virginie,* scrub-pine. **Pomme de pin,** fir-cone, pine-cone.

pinacle [pinakl], *s.m.* Pinnacle; ridge ornament. *F:* **Porter qn au pinacle; mettre qn sur le pinacle,** to extol s.o.; to praise s.o. to the skies.

pinard [pinaːr], *s.m. P:* Wine.

pinastre [pinastr], *s.m. Bot:* Pinaster, sea-pine.

pinçage [pɛ̃saːʒ], *s.m. Hort:* (*a*) Pinching off, nipping off (of buds). (*b*) Topping.

pince [pɛ̃ːs], *s.f.* **1.** Grip, hold (of tool, hand, etc.). **Avoir bonne pince,** to have a strong grip. **2.** Holder, gripper. (*a*) Pincers, pliers, nippers; (smith's) tongs. *Surg:* Forceps. *Petites pinces,* tweezers. *Pince(s) coupante(s),* cutting pliers; wire-nippers. P. *à gaz, de plombier,* gas-pliers. P. *à sucre,* sugar-tongs. *Fish:* P. *à dégorger,* gag. *Surg:* P. *hémostatique,* artery clip. (*b*) (Paper-, bicycle-, suspenders-)clip. P. *à linge,* clothes-peg, -pin. *El:* P. *pour fils,* terminal clamp. (*c*) Crowbar, tommy-bar. **Pince monseigneur,** (burglar's) jemmy. **3.** (*a*) Claw, nipper (of crab, etc.). P: **Serrer la p. à qn,** to shake hands with s.o. (*b*) Toe, point (of horse's hoof or shoe). **4.** Pleat (in garment); dart.

pinceau [pɛ̃so], *s.m.* **1.** (*a*) (Artist's) paint-brush. **Coup de pinceau,** stroke of the brush. P. *vaporisateur*, air-brush, aerograph. P. *à barbe,* shaving-brush. **2.** *Opt:* P. *lumineux,* pencil of light. *Ph:* P. *sonore,* sound-beam.

pince-feuilles, *s.m.inv.* Paper-clip, -clamp.

pincement [pɛ̃smɑ̃], *s.m.* **1.** Pinching, nipping. **2.** Plucking (of strings of guitar). **3.** = PINÇAGE. **4.** *Aut:* Toe-in (of front wheels).

pince-nez, *s.m.inv.* Eye-glasses, pince-nez.

pince-notes, *s.m.inv.* = PINCE-FEUILLES.

pince-oreille, *s.m. F:* Earwig. *pl.* **Des pince-oreilles.**

pincer [pɛ̃se], *v.tr.* (je pinçai(s); n. pinçons) **1.** To pinch, nip. (*a*) *Il lui pinça la joue,* he pinched her cheek. *F: Le froid pince,* there's a nip in the air. S.a. LÈVRE I. (*b*) *Hort:* (i) To nip off (buds); (ii) to top (plant). (*c*) *Aut:* **Faire pincer les roues avant,** to toe in the front wheels. (*d*) *Mus:* To pluck (strings of harp, etc.). **Pincer de la harpe,** to play, touch, the harp. **2.** To grip, hold fast (with pincers, etc.). *Nau:* P. *le vent,* to hug the wind. *F:* P. *un voleur,* to catch a thief. **Se faire pincer,** to get pinched, nabbed. *P:* **En pincer pour qn,** to be gone on s.o.

pincé. **1.** *a.* Affected, supercilious, prim. *Sourire p.,* tight-lipped smile; wry smile. **2.** *s.m. Mus:* Pizzicato.

pincée, *s.f.* Pinch (of snuff, etc.).

pince-sans-rire, *s.m.inv.* F: Man of dry (and mischievous) humour.

pincette [pɛ̃sɛt], *s.f.* Usu. *pl.* (a) Tweezers, nippers. (b) (Fire-)tongs ; pair of tongs.

pinçon [pɛ̃sɔ̃], *s.m.* **1.** Mark, bruise (left by a pinch). **2.** Toe-clip (of horse-shoe).

pinéal, -aux [pineal, -o], *a. Anat:* Pineal (gland).

pinède [pinɛd], *s.f. Dial:* (In S. of Fr.) Pine-tract, pine-land.

pineraie [pinrɛ], *s.f.* Pine-plantation ; pinetum.

pingouin [pɛ̃gwɛ̃], *s.m. Orn:* Auk.

pingouinière [pɛ̃gwinjɛ:r], *s.f.* Auk rookery.

pingre [pɛ̃:gr]. **1.** *a.* Stingy, miserly, niggardly. **2.** *s.m.* Skinflint.

pingrerie [pɛ̃grəri], *s.f. F:* Stinginess, niggardliness.

pinière [pinjɛ:r], *s.f.* Pine-wood, fir-plantation.

pinné [pinne], *a. Nat.Hist:* Pinnate(d), pennate.

pinnule [pinnyl], *s.f.* **1.** *Nat.Hist:* Pinnule. **2.** Sight-vane, sight (of alidade, sextant).

pinson [pɛ̃sɔ̃], *s.m. Orn:* Finch. *P. vulgaire,* chaffinch. S.a. GAI I.

pintade [pɛ̃tad], *s.f.* (a) Guinea-fowl. *P. mâle,* guinea-cock. (b) *F:* Stuck-up, pretentious, woman.

pintadeau [pɛ̃tado], *s.m. Orn:* Guinea-poult.

pinte [pɛ̃:t], *s.f. Meas: A:* (French) pint (nearly = English quart). *F: Se faire une pinte de bon sang,* to laugh loud and long.

pinter [pɛ̃te], *v.i. & tr. P:* To swill (beer, wine) ; to booze.

pioche [pjɔʃ], *s.f.* **1.** Pickaxe, pick, mattock. **Donner les premiers coups de pioche,** to break ground. **2.** *F:* (Hard) work.

pioch|er [pjɔʃe], *v.tr.* (a) To dig (with a pick) ; to pick. (b) *F:* To grind, swot, mug, at (sth.). *s.m.* **-age.**

piocheur, -euse [pjɔʃœ:r, -ø:z]. **1.** *s.m.* Pickman, digger, navvy. **2.** *s.m. & f. F:* Hard worker ; swot, swotter. **3.** *s.f.* Piocheuse, steam-digger, (steam-)navvy. *Piocheuse-défonceuse,* excavator.

piolet [pjɔlɛ], *s.m.* Piolet ; ice-axe.

pion [pjɔ̃], *s.m.* **1.** *Sch: F:* Usher ; junior master. **2.** (a) *Chess:* Pawn. (b) *Draughts:* Piece, man. S.a. DAMER I.

pionc|er [pjɔ̃se], *v.i.* (je pionçai(s) ; n. pionçons) *P:* To sleep, to snooze. *s.* **-eur, -euse.**

pionnier [pjɔnje], *s.m.* Pioneer. **Faire œuvre de** pionnier, to break new ground.

pioupiou [pjupju], *s.m. P: A:* (Foot-)soldier.

pipe [pip], *s.f.* Pipe. **1.** Tube. **2.** Large cask (for wine, spirits) ; pipe. **3.** Tobacco-pipe. *P. de bruyère,* briar pipe. *P. de terre,* clay pipe. *F: Mettez ça dans votre p.!* put that in your pipe and smoke it ! **Terre de pipe,** pipe-clay. *Passer qch. à la terre de p.,* to pipe-clay sth.

pipeau [pipo], *s.m.* **1.** *Mus:* (Reed-)pipe ; shepherd's pipe. *P. de chasse,* bird-call. **2.** *pl.* Limed twigs (to snare birds) ; snare.

pipée [pipe], *s.f.* Bird-snaring, bird-catching. *Prov:* **On ne prend pas les vieux merles à la pipée,** you can't catch old birds with chaff.

pipelet, -ette [piplɛ, -ɛt], *s. P:* (In Paris) Concierge, door-keeper. (From the character in Eugène Sue's *Mystères de Paris.*)

piper [pipe]. **1.** *v.i. A:* (Of small birds) To peep, cheep. **2.** *v.tr.* (a) To lure (birds by means of bird-calls.) *F:* **Piper qn,** to dupe, decoy, trick, s.o. **Se faire piper,** to get caught. (b) *P.* **les dés,** to load, cog, dice. *P. une carte,* to mark a card.

pipette [pipɛt], *s.f.* (a) *Ch: etc:* Pipette. (b) *P. tâte-vin,* plunging-siphon ; wine-taster.

pipi¹ [pipi], *s.m. F:* (In the nursery) **Faire pipi,** to piddle.

pipi², pipit [pipit], *s.m. Orn:* Pipit. *P. farlouse,* meadow-pipit, -titlark.

pipistrelle [pipistrɛl], *s.f. Z:* (Small) bat.

piquant [pikɑ̃]. **1.** *a.* Pricking (weapon) ; stinging (nettle) ; pungent (odour) ; tart, biting (wine) ; sharp, biting, cutting (remark, wind) ; racy (anecdote) ; piquant (beauty, appearance). *Cu: Sauce piquante,* sharp sauce. **2.** *s.m.* Point, zest, pith (of story) ; pointedness, pungency (of style) ; bite (of beverage, etc.). **3.** *s.m.* Prickle, sting (of plant) ; quill, spine (of porcupine) ; spike (of barbed wire).

pique¹ [pik]. **1.** *s.f.* (a) Pike. **Bois de pique,** pikestaff. (b) (Pointed) tip (of alpenstock, etc.). **2.** *s.m. Cards:* Spade(s). **Jouer pique,** to play a spade ; to play spades. S.a. AS¹ I.

pique², *s.f.* Pique, ill-feeling. **Par pique,** out of spite, in a pique.

pique-assiette, *s.m.inv. F:* Sponger, parasite.

pique-feu, *s.m.inv.* Fire-rake ; pricker.

pique-nique [piknik], *s.m.* Picnic. **Faire un pique-nique,** to go for a picnic ; to picnic. *pl. Des pique-niques.*

pique-niquer [piknike], *v.i.* To picnic.

pique-notes, *s.m.inv.* (Bill-)file, spike-file.

piqu|er [pike], *v.tr.* **1.** (a) To prick, sting ; (of flea) to bite. *Être piqué par une guêpe,* to be stung by a wasp. *P. un cheval de l'éperon,* to prick, spur, a horse. **Piquer des deux,** to clap spurs to one's horse. *P. les bœufs,* to goad the oxen. *P. qn d'honneur,* to put s.o. on his mettle. *La fumée pique les yeux,* the smoke makes the eyes smart. *Vent qui pique,* biting wind. S.a. MOUCHE. (b) *Med: P. qn à la morphine,* to give s.o. a hypodermic injection of morphia. (c) To nettle, pique, offend (s.o.). *P. qn au vif,* to cut s.o. to the quick. *P. la jalousie de qn,* to arouse s.o.'s jealousy. **2.** (a) *P. une surface,* to eat into, to pit, a surface. (b) *P. un moellon,* to dress a stone. *P. une chaudière,* to scale, chip, a boiler. *P: Se piquer le nez,* to tipple. **3.** *Nau: Piquer l'heure,* to strike the hour. **4.** (a) To prick, puncture (sth.) ; to quilt (counterpane). *P. du cuir,* to stitch leather. **Piquer dans l'assiette de qn,** (i) to steal from s.o.'s plate ; (ii) to sponge on s.o. *Fish: P. un poisson,* to strike a fish. (b) To prick off (name on a list). *Sch: P: Piquer une bonne note,* to get a good mark. **5.** To stick, insert (sth. into sth.). **6.** (a) **Piquer une tête,** to take a header ; to dive. (Of ship) **Piquer de l'avant,** to go down by the bows. *Av: P. de haut sur un ennemi,* to dive down on an enemy. S.a. NEZ 2. (b) *Nau: P. sur une île,* to head for an island. **7.** *P: Piquer un soleil,* **un fard,** to blush. S.a. LAÏUS. *s.m.* **-age.**

se piquer. 1. (a) To prick oneself. (b) *F:* To be addicted to morphia. **2.** To take offence, to become nettled. **3.** *Se piquer de qch., de faire qch.,* to pride oneself, plume oneself, on sth., on doing sth. *Se p. de littérature,* to have pretensions to literary taste. **4.** *Se piquer au jeu,* to get excited over the game ; to be stimulated by opposition. *Je m'étais piqué au jeu,* I was on my mettle. **5.** *Se p. pour qn,* to take a fancy to s.o. **6.** To become spotted (with rust, etc.) ; (of metal) to pit ; (of wood) to become worm-eaten ; (of clothes, etc.) to become moth-eaten.

piqué, a. 1. (a) Quilted ; padded (door). (b) *s.m.* Quilting, piqué. **2.** *Cu:* Larded (meat). **3.** Worm-eaten ; (damp-, dust-, mould-)spotted ; foxed (engraving) ; pitted (metal). *P. des mouches,* fly-spotted. *Ciel p. d'étoiles,* sky studded with stars. **Vêtement piqué des vers,** moth-eaten garment. *P:* Être piqué, to be dotty. *Gens au cerveau p.*, crack-brained people. **4.** Sour (wine). **5.** *Mus:* Staccato (notes). **6.** *Av:* Descente piquée, *s.m.* piqué, vertical dive; nose-dive. Descendre en p., to nose-dive. *Golf: Approche piquée*, short approach.

piquet[1] [pikɛ], *s.m.* **1.** (a) Peg, stake, post. *P. de tente*, tent-peg. Attacher les chevaux au piquet, to tether, picket, the horses. *Croquet: Toucher le p. final*, to peg out. (b) *P. de fleurs*, cluster of (millinery) flowers. **2.** *Mil:* Picket. Être de piquet, to be on picket. *Piquets de grève*, strike pickets.

piquet[2], *s.m. Cards:* Piquet. **Faire un piquet**, to play a hand at piquet.

piquet|er [pikte], *v.tr.* (Je piquette; je piquetterai) **1.** To peg out, stake out (claim, camp). **2.** To picket (approaches to works, etc.). **3.** To spot, dot. *Piqueté de noir*, dotted with black. *s.m.* **-age.**

piquette [pikɛt], *s.f.* **1.** *Wine-m:* Second wine. **2.** *F:* (Unpretentious) local wine.

piqueur, -euse [pikœːr, -øːz], *s.* **1.** (a) *Ven:* Whipper-in, huntsman. (b) Stud-groom. (c) Outrider. **2.** *Ind:* (a) (Leather-)stitcher. *Piqueur, piqueuse, en bottines*, shoe-stitcher. (b) *Piqueuse à la machine*, sewing-woman. **3.** *Min: etc:* Hewer, pickman. **4.** *Rail:* Foreman platelayer.

piqûre [pikyːr], *s.f.* **1.** (a) Prick, sting, bite (of insect). *P. d'épingle*, pin-prick. *P. de puce*, flea-bite. (b) Subcutaneous injection, hypodermic injection. *P. de morphine, F:* shot of morphia. **2.** Puncture, small hole; pit (in metal). *P. de vers*, worm-hole; moth-hole. **3.** (a) *Bookb: P. métallique*, stabbing. (b) *Publ:* (Stabbed) pamphlet. **4.** Spot, speck (of rust, mould); foxing (of paper). *P. de mouches*, fly-speck.

pirate [pirat], *s.m.* (a) Pirate. (b) *F:* Plagiarist.

pirater [pirate], *v.i.* (a) To practise piracy. (b) *F:* To pirate, plagiarize.

piraterie [piratri], *s.f.* **1.** Piracy. **2.** Act of piracy.

pire [piːr], *a.* **1.** *Comp.* Worse. (a) *Tomber d'un mal dans un pire*, to jump out of the frying-pan into the fire. *Prov:* Il n'est pire eau que l'eau qui dort, still waters run deep. (b) (Often = PIS) *Cela serait pire*; ce qui est pire; rien de pire; see PIS[1] **1** (b). **2.** *Sup.* Le pire, the worst. (a) *Exposé aux pires dangers, aux pires injures*, exposed to the direst dangers, to the foulest insults. (b) (= PIS) *Mettre les choses au pire; prendre les choses au pire*; see PIS[2] **2.**

Pirée (le) [lɔpire]. *Pr.n.m. Geog:* The Piraeus.

piriforme [piriform], *a.* Pear-shaped, pyriform.

pirogue [pirog], *s.f.* **1.** Pirogue; (dug-out) canoe. **2.** Canoe.

pirouette [pirwɛt], *s.f.* **1.** Whirligig (toy). **2.** *Danc: Equit:* Pirouette. **Faire la pirouette**, (i) to pirouette; (ii) *F:* to reverse one's opinions; to face right-about.

pirouetter [pirwɛte], *v.i.* To pirouette.

pis[1] [pi], *s.m.* **1.** Udder, dug (of cow). **2.** *Geog:* Pap (of mountain).

pis[2], *adv.* (Used chiefly in a number of set phrases. The usu. form is *plus mal.*) **1.** *Comp.* Worse. (a) *Pis que tout cela*, worse than all that. *Il y a pis*, there is, are, worse. **Mettre qn à faire pis, à pis faire**, to challenge s.o. to do his worst. *C'est à qui pis fera*, they are each trying to behave worse than the other. **De pis en pis**, worse and worse. *Aller de mal en pis*, to go from bad to worse. S.a. ALLER II. 2, TANT 1. (b) *Cela serait encore pis*, that would be worse still. *Ce qui est pis . . .*, what is worse. . . . *Et qui pis est . . .*, and what is worse. . . . *Rien de pis*, nothing

worse. *Le malade est pis*, the invalid is worse. *Pour ne pas dire pis*, to say no more. *Il a fait tout cela et pis*, he did all that and something even worse. **2.** *Sup.* Le pis, (the) worst. *Ce qu'il y a de pis*, (i) what is worst; (ii) the worst there is. **Faire de son pis**, to do one's worst. **Mettre les choses au pis**, to suppose, assume, the worst. **Prendre les choses au pis**, to put the worst face on things.

pis-aller [pizale], *s.m.inv.* Last resource; make-shift. S.a. ALLER II. 2.

pisciculteur [pissikyltœːr], *s.m.* Pisciculturist.

pisciculture [pissikyltyːr], *s.f.* Pisciculture.

piscine [pissin], *s.f.* **1.** *Ant:* (a) Fish-pond. (b) Bathing-pond. **2.** *Ecc:* Piscina. **3.** Public swimming-bath; public baths.

pisé [pize], *s.m. Const:* Pisé; puddled clay.

pissat [pisa], *s.m.* Urine (of animals).

pissenlit [pisãli], *s.m. Bot:* Dandelion.

piss|er [pise], *v.i.* (Not in polite use) To make water. (With cogn. acc.) *P. du sang*, to pass blood with the urine. *s.m.* **-ement.**

pissoir [piswaːr], *s.m. F:* Urinal.

pissotière [pisɔtjɛːr], *s.f. F:* (Public) urinal.

pistache [pistaʃ], *s.f.* (a) Pistachio(-nut). (b) *P. de terre*, peanut, ground nut.

pistachier [pistaʃje], *s.m.* Pistachio-tree.

piste [pist], *s.f.* **1.** (a) Running-track; race-track. *P. cyclable*, bicycle-track. **Piste cavalière**, (i) riding-track; (ii) bridle-path. *P. d'autodrome*, speedway. **Courses de piste**, track-racing. **Tour de piste**, lap. (b) Racecourse. (c) *P. de patinage*, skating-rink. *P. de toboggan*, toboggan-run. *Av:* La p. d'envol, the tarmac. (d) *Cin:* Piste sonore, sound-track (of talking film). **2.** *Ven:* Track, trail, scent. **Suivre un lièvre à la piste**, to track, trail, a hare. *F:* Être à la piste de qn, to be on the track of s.o. **Fausse piste**, false trail. **Faire fausse piste**, to be on the wrong track.

pist|er [piste], *v.tr.* (a) To track (hare). *P. qn*, to shadow s.o. (b) *P. des clients*, (i) to keep track of, (ii) to tout for, customers. *s.m.* **-age.**

pisteur [pistœːr], *s.m.* (a) Tracker; esp. police spy. (b) Hotel tout.

pistil [pistil], *s.m. Bot:* Pistil.

pistolet [pistɔlɛ], *s.m.* **1.** (a) Pistol; *U.S:* gun. *Pistolets de combat*, duelling pistols. **Coup de pistolet**, pistol-shot. *F:* C'est un drôle de pistolet, he's a queer customer. (b) *Artil: P. de tir*, firing-pistol. (c) *P. à peinturer, p. vaporisateur*, spray-gun; air-brush. **2.** *Draw:* French curve. **3.** *Nau:* (a) *P. d'embarcation*, davit. (b) *P. d'amure*, bumpkin.

piston [pistɔ̃], *s.m.* **1.** (a) *Mch:* Piston. **Tête de piston**, crosshead. (b) Sucker (of pump); plunger (of force-pump); ram (of hydraulic press). (c) *F:* Avoir du piston, to have friends at court, to be well backed. **Il est arrivé à coups de piston**, he succeeded through backstairs influence. **2.** *Mus:* (a) Valve (of saxhorn, etc.). (b) Cornet à pistons, *F:* piston, cornet. **3.** Spring-stud (releasing camera front, etc.).

pistonn|er [pistɔne], *v.tr. F:* To back, recommend (s.o.); *F:* to push (s.o.). *s.m.* **-age.**

pitance [pitãːs], *s.f.* (a) (Monk's) allowance (of food). (b) *F:* Se faire une maigre pitance, to eke out a living.

pitchpin [pitʃpɛ̃], *s.m.* Pitch-pine.

piteu|x, -euse [pitø, -øːz], *a.* Piteous, woeful, pitiable. *Faire piteuse mine*, to look crestfallen. *Faire piteuse figure*, to cut a sorry figure. *adv.* **-sement.**

pithécanthrope [pitɛkãtrɔp], *s.m.* Pithecanthrope; *F:* (the) 'missing link.'

pitié [pitje], *s.f.* Pity, compassion. **Avoir pitié de qn,** to have mercy, pity, on s.o. **Prendre pitié de qn, prendre qn en pitié,** to take pity on s.o. **Sans pitié,** pitiless(ly), merciless(ly), ruthless(ly). **Par pitié,** for pity's sake ; out of pity. **Regarder qn d'un œil de pitié,** to look compassionately at s.o. **Faire pitié,** to arouse pity, compassion. *Il me faisait p.,* I felt sorry for him. *C'est p. qu'il soit resté seul,* it is sad that he should have remained alone. **C'est à faire pitié!** it is pitiful! **Quelle pitié!** (i) what a pity! (ii) what a sorry sight!

piton [pitɔ̃], *s.m.* **I.** (Metal) eye, eye-bolt. *P. à vis,* screw-eye ; screw-ring. *P. à boucle,* ring-bolt. **2.** Peak (of mountain).

pitoyable [pitwajabl], *a.* (*a*) Pitiable, pitiful, piteous ; wretched (health). (*b*) Paltry, despicable, wretched (excuse, etc.). *adv.* **-ment.**

pitre [piːtr], *s.m.* **I.** Clown (of travelling show). **2.** *F: Pej:* Clown, buffoon.

pitrerie [pitrəri], *s.f. F:* Piece of clownery ; foolery, buffoonery.

pittoresque [pitɔresk]. **I.** *a.* (*a*) Picturesque, quaint. (*b*) Pictorial (magazine). **2.** *s.m.* Picturesqueness. *adv.* **-ment.**

pituitaire [pitɥiteːr], *a.* Pituitary (gland).

pituite [pitɥit], *s.f.* **I.** (*a*) Gastric catarrh. (*b*) Water-brash. **2.** Phlegm ; mucus.

pivert [piveːr], *s.m.* = PIC-VERT.

pivoine [pivwan], *s.f.* Peony.

pivot [pivo], *s.m.* **I.** Pivot, pin, axis ; swivel ; fulcrum (of lever). *P. à rotule,* ball-pivot. **A pivot,** pivoted, swivelling ; revolving (crane). *Canon à p.,* swivel-gun. S.a. AGENT 2. **2.** *Bot:* Tap-root.

pivotant [pivotɑ̃], *a.* **I.** Pivoting. (*a*) Swivelling ; slewing (crane, etc.). (*b*) *Mil:* Wheeling (wing, movement). **2.** *Bot:* Tap-rooted (plant). *Racine pivotante,* tap-root.

pivot|er [pivote], *v.i.* **I.** (*a*) To pivot ; to turn, hinge (*sur,* upon) ; to swivel, revolve. **Faire pivoter qch.,** to slew sth. round. *F: P. sur ses talons,* to turn on one's heels. (*b*) *Aut:* To slew round. **2.** (*a*) (Of troops) To wheel ; to change front. **Faire pivoter un escadron,** to wheel a squadron. (*b*) *F:* To do drill movements. (*c*) To turn about aimlessly ; to waste one's time. *s.m.* **-ement.**

piz [pi], *s.m. Geog:* Pap (of mountain).

placabilité [plakabilite], *s.f.* Placability.

placable [plakabl], *a.* Placable, forgiving.

placage [plakaːʒ], *s.m.* **I.** Veneering (of wood). **Bois de placage,** veneer. **2.** Plating (of metal). *P. au chrome,* chromium plating. [PLAQUER]

placard [plakaːr], *s.m.* **I.** Wall-cupboard. **2.** Poster, bill, placard. *P. officiel,* public notice. **3.** *Typ:* Épreuve en placard, slip-proof, galleyproof. **4.** (*a*) Patch (on sail). (*b*) Panel (of door).

placarder [plakarde], *v.tr.* **I.** (*a*) To stick (a bill) on a wall ; to post up (a bill). (*b*) *P. un mur,* to stick bills on a wall ; to placard a wall with posters. **2.** *Nau:* To patch (sail).

placardeur [plakardœːr], *s.m.* Bill-sticker.

place [plas], *s.f.* Place. **I.** (*a*) Position. *Changer sa chaise de p.,* to shift one's chair. **Mettre qch. en place,** to place sth. in position. S.a. MISE I. *Remettez vos livres à leur p.,* put your books away. *F:* **Remettre qn à sa place,** to put s.o. in his place ; to sit on, snub, s.o. **A vos places!** take your places, your seats! **Il ne peut pas rester en place,** he can't keep still. **Son nom a pris place dans l'histoire,** his name has found a place in history. (*b*) Stead. **Je viens à la place de mon père, au lieu et place de mon père,** I come instead of my father, in my father's place. **A votre place, je . . .,** in your place, if I were you, I . . . . (*c*) **Faire place à qch.,** to give place to sth. (*d*) *Occuper beaucoup de p.,* to take up a great deal of room. **Faire place à qn,** to make room, make way, for s.o. **(Faites) place!** stand aside! make way! **Place aux dames!** ladies first! **2.** (*a*) Seat. *Restez à votre p.,* keep your seat. *Il n'y avait pas une p.,* there wasn't a seat to be found, to be had. *Th:* **Petites places,** cheap seats. **Place d'honneur,** place, seat, of honour. *Voiture à deux, à quatre, places,* carriage to hold two, four ; *Aut:* two-seater, four-seater. *Prix des places,* (i) fares ; (ii) prices of admission. **Payer place entière,** to pay (i) full fare, (ii) full price. (*b*) Situation, office, post ; *F:* job. *Perdre sa p.,* to lose one's job, one's berth. (Of servant) **Être en place,** to be in a situation, in service. **Être sans place,** to be out of a situation, *F:* out of a job. **3.** Locality, spot. (*a*) **Place publique,** public square, market-place. **Place d'armes,** drillground, parade-ground. *P. de voitures,* cab-stand. **Voiture de place,** hackney-carriage. **Automobile de place,** motor car plying for hire. **Sur place,** on the spot. *Personnel engagé sur p.,* staff engaged locally. **Rester sur place,** to be left on the field (dead or wounded). (*b*) **Place marchande,** tradingtown, market-town. **Jour de place,** market-day. **Avoir du crédit sur la place,** to be a sound man. **Faire la place,** to canvass for orders. (*c*) *Mil:* **Place forte, de guerre,** fortress ; fortified town.

placement [plasmɑ̃], *s.m.* **I.** (*a*) Placing ; investing (of money). **Bureau de placement,** employment bureau ; (servants') registry office. (*b*) Sale, disposal (of goods). **2.** Investment. **Faire des placements,** to invest money, to make investments. *P. avantageux,* good investment.

placer [plase], *v.tr.* (je plaçai(s); ns. plaçons) To place. **I.** (*a*) To put, set (in a certain place) ; to find a place, places, for (spectators, etc.). *Vous êtes mieux placé que moi pour en juger,* you are in a better position to judge. *P. qn sur le trône,* to set s.o. on the throne. *P. un soldat en sentinelle,* to post a soldier on sentry duty. *Confiance mal placée,* misplaced confidence. *F: Il a le cœur bien placé,* his heart is in the right place. (*b*) To find a post, a situation, for (s.o.). *Gens bien placés,* people of good position. **Fille difficile à placer,** daughter difficult to marry, to settle. (*c*) To invest (money). **2.** (*a*) To sell, dispose of (goods). (*b*) *P. son affection sur qn,* to set, bestow, one's affections on s.o.

se placer. I. To take one's seat, one's place ; to take up one's position, one's stand. *Dites-moi où me p.,* tell me what seat to take. **2.** To obtain a situation, a post, a job. *Se p. comme domestique,* to go into service.

placé, *a. Turf:* Placed (horse). *Non placé,* unplaced (horse) ; 'also ran.'

placet [plase], *s.m. A:* Petition, address.

placeur, -euse [plasœːr, -øːz], *s.* **I.** Manager of an employment agency. **2.** *Com:* Placer, seller. **3.** Steward (at public meetings).

placide [plasid], *a.* Placid, good-tempered ; calm, unruffled (temper). *adv.* **-ment.**

placidité [plasidite], *s.f.* Placidity.

placier [plasje], *s.m.* Town-traveller ; agent, canvasser ; *U.S:* drummer. [PLACE]

plafond [plafɔ̃], *s.m.* **I.** Ceiling. *P. vitré,* glazed roof. *Tableau exposé au p.,* skied picture. S.a. ARAIGNÉE I. **2.** Maximum attainable or permissible. (*a*) *Fixer un p. à un budget,* to fix an extreme limit for a budget. (*b*) Ceiling (of aeroplane). **Valeur de plafond,** maximum flying height. (*c*) *Cards:* (i) 'Above the line' (on bridge-scorer); (ii) (form of) contract bridge; plafond.

plafonnage [plafɔnaːʒ], *s.m.* Ceiling-work.

plafonner [plafɔne]. **I.** *v.tr.* To ceil (room). **2.** *v.i. Av:* To fly at the ceiling.

plafonnier [plafɔnje], *s.m.* Ceiling-light ; (electric) ceiling fitting. *Aut:* Roof-light, -lamp.

plage [plaːʒ], *s.f.* **I.** (*a*) Beach, shore. *Jouer sur la p.*, to play on the sands. (*b*) Seaside resort, watering-place. **2.** *Navy:* Freeboard deck (of battleship). *P. arrière*, quarter-deck. **3.** *W.Tg: P. d'écoute (d'un appareil)*, limits within which tuning is possible.

plagiaire [plaʒjɛːr], *a. & s.m.* Plagiarist.

plagiarisme [plaʒjarism], *s.m.* (Habitual) plagiarism.

plagiat [plaʒja], *s.m.* Plagiarism, plagiary. *Faire un p. à un auteur, F:* to lift a passage from an author.

plagier [plaʒje], *v.tr.* To plagiarize.

plaid [plɛ], *s.m.* Travelling-rug.

plaidant [plɛdɑ̃], *a. Jur:* Pleading (counsel). *Les parties plaidantes*, the litigants.

plaider [plɛde], *v.tr.* To plead (a cause); to allege (sth.) in plea. *P. pour qn*, to plead in favour of s.o. (*auprès de*, with). *La cause s'est plaidée hier*, the case was heard, came on, yesterday. *P. la jeunesse de l'accusé*, to plead the prisoner's youth. *F:* **Plaider le faux pour savoir le vrai**, to make a false allegation in order to get at the truth.

plaideur, -euse [plɛdœːr, -øːz], *s.* Litigant, suitor.

plaidoirie [plɛdwari], *s.f.* **I.** Pleading. **2.** Counsel's speech.

plaidoyer [plɛdwaje], *s.m. Jur:* Address to the Court; speech for the defence.

plaie [plɛ], *s.f.* **I.** Wound, sore. *P. profonde*, deep-seated wound. *F:* **Rouvrir d'anciennes plaies**, to open old sores. **Ne demander que plaies et bosses**, to be always ready for a row. *P. sociale*, social evil. **2.** Affliction, evil. *Les dix plaies d'Égypte*, the ten plagues of Egypt.

plaignant, -ante [plɛɲɑ̃, -ɑ̃ːt], *s.* Plaintiff; prosecutor, *f.* prosecutrix; complainant.

plaign-e, -es, etc. See PLAINDRE.

plain [plɛ̃], *a. A:* Even. (Still used in) **Velours plain**, plain velvet. **En plaine campagne**, in (the) open country. S.a. PLAIN-PIED.

plain-chant, *s.m. Mus:* Plainsong, plain-chant.

plaindre [plɛ̃ːdr], *v.tr.* (*pr.p.* plaignant; *p.p.* plaint; *pr.ind.* je plains, il plaint, n. plaignons; *p.h.* je plaignis; *fu.* je plaindrai) To pity. *Il est fort à p.*, he is greatly to be pitied.

se plaindre, to complain. *Se p. de qn, de qch.*, to complain of, about, to find fault with, s.o., sth. *Il n'y a pas de quoi vous p.*, *vous n'avez pas à vous p.*, you have nothing to complain of; you needn't grumble.

plaine [plɛn], *s.f.* Plain; flat open country.

plain-pied, *s.m.* **I.** Suite of rooms on one floor. **2.** *Adv.phr.* **De plain-pied**, on one floor, on a level. *Salon de p.-p. avec le jardin*, drawing-room on a level with the garden. *F:* *Affaire qui va de p.-p.*, business that progresses smoothly.

plain-s, -t. See PLAINDRE.

plainte [plɛ̃ːt], *s.f.* **I.** Moan, groan. **2.** (*a*) Complaint. (*b*) *Jur:* Indictment, complaint. **Porter plainte**, **dresser plainte**, **déposer une plainte**, **contre qn**, to lodge a complaint against s.o. (*auprès de*, with); to bring an action against s.o. *P. en diffamation*, action for libel.

plaintif, -ive [plɛ̃tif, -iːv], *a.* (*a*) Plaintive, doleful (tone). (*b*) Querulous. *adv.* **-ivement.**

plaire [plɛːr], *v.ind.tr.* (*pr.p.* plaisant; *p.p.* plu ·

pr.ind. je plais, il plaît, n. plaisons, ils plaisent; *pr.sub.* je plaise; *p.h.* je plus; *fu.* je plairai) *P. à qn*, to please s.o.; to be agreeable to s.o. *Cet homme me plaît*, I like this man. *Chercher à p. à qn*, to lay oneself out to please s.o. *Elle ne lui plaît pas*, he is not attracted to her; he does not care for her. *Je le ferai si cela me plaît*, I shall do it if I please, if I choose. **Cela vous plaît à dire**, you are saying that for fun; you are joking. *Impers.* **S'il vous plaît**, (if you) please. *Vous plairait-il de nous accompagner?* would you like to come with us? **Plaît-il?** I beg your pardon? what did you say? **Comme il vous plaira**, as you like (it). **Plaise à Dieu qu'il vienne!** God grant, please God, that he may come! **A Dieu ne plaise (que)**, God forbid (that). **Plût au ciel, plût à Dieu, que . . .!** would to heaven that . . .!

se plaire, to take pleasure; to be pleased, be happy. *Je me plais beaucoup à Paris*, I enjoy Paris. *Il ne se plaît pas dans son nouvel entourage*, he is unhappy in his new surroundings. *Ils se sont plu à me tourmenter*, they took pleasure in teasing me. *La vigne se plaît sur les coteaux*, the vine thrives, does well, on hill-sides.

plaisance [plɛzɑ̃ːs], *s.f.* (*a*) *A:* Pleasure. (*b*) **Bateau de plaisance**, pleasure-boat. **Maison de plaisance**, country-seat.

plaisant [plɛzɑ̃]. **I.** See PLAIRE. **2.** *a.* (*a*) Funny, amusing, droll. (*b*) (Always before the noun) Ridiculous, absurd, ludicrous (person, answer). **3.** *s.m.* Wag, joker. *Des mauvais plaisants*, practical jokers. *adv.* **-amment.**

plaisanter [plɛzɑ̃te]. **I.** *v.i.* To joke, jest; to speak in jest. **Je ne plaisante pas**, I am serious, in earnest. **Dire qch. en plaisantant**, to say sth. in jest. **Vous plaisantez!** you are joking! you don't mean it! *C'est un homme avec qui on ne plaisante pas*, he is not a man to be trifled with. *Il ne plaisante pas là-dessus*, he takes such matters seriously. **2.** *v.tr.* To chaff, banter (s.o.) (*sur*, about); to poke fun at (s.o.).

plaisanterie [plɛzɑ̃tri], *s.f.* Joke, jest; joking, jesting. *Faire des plaisanteries*, to crack jokes. *Faire des plaisanteries à qn*, to play pranks, tricks, on s.o. *Une mauvaise p.*, a silly joke. **Tourner une chose en plaisanterie**, to laugh a thing off. **Entendre la plaisanterie**, to know how to take a joke. **Par plaisanterie**, for fun, for a joke.

plaisir [plɛziːr], *s.m.* Pleasure. **I.** Delight. **Faire plaisir à qn**, to please s.o. *Cela m'a fait p. de le revoir*, it gave me great pleasure to see him again. *Cela me fait p. qu'il vienne*, I am very pleased that he is coming. **Cela fait plaisir à voir**, it is pleasant to see, to look upon. **Faire à qn le plaisir de . . .**, to do s.o. the favour of. . . . *Je me ferai un p. de vous accompagner*, it will be a pleasure to go with you. **Au plaisir de vous revoir**, good-bye; I hope we shall meet again. **Prendre (du) plaisir à qch.** to take pleasure in sth.; to enjoy sth. **Avoir plaisir à faire qch.**, to take pleasure in doing sth. **A votre bon plaisir**, (i) at your convenience; (ii) at your discretion. **Avec plaisir!** with pleasure! **A plaisir**, (i) wantonly, without cause; (ii) ad lib. **C'est par plaisir que vous faites cela?** are you doing that because you like it, for the fun of the thing? **Parler pour le plaisir de parler**, to talk for talking's sake. **2.** (*a*) Amusement, enjoyment. **Argent pour menus plaisirs**, pocket-money. **Jouer aux cartes pour le plaisir**, to play cards for love. **Train de plaisir**, excursion train. **Partie de plaisir**, pleasure-trip, pleasure-party: picnic, outing. (*b*) *Le p.*, *les plaisirs*, dissipation. *Vie de plaisirs*, gay life. **3.** = OUBLIE.

plan¹ [plɑ̃]. **1.** *a.* Even, plane, level, flat (ground, surface). **2.** *s.m.* (a) Plane. **Plan incliné,** inclined plane. *Opt:* P. *focal,* focal plane. (b) *Av:* Aerofoil; wing. P. *supérieur,* upper wing or plane. P. *fixe,* tail-plane. (c) **Premier plan,** (i) *Art:* foreground; (ii) *Th:* down-stage. **Second plan,** middle ground. *Reléguer qn au second p.,* to put s.o. into the background. *Un artiste du premier p.,* an artist of the first rank. S.a. ARRIÈRE-PLAN. *Cin:* **Premier plan, gros plan,** close-up.

plan², *s.m.* Plan. (a) Drawing; draught, draft (of construction). P. *cadastral,* cadastral survey. P. *horizontal,* ground-plan. *Tracer un p.,* to draw a plan. **Lever les plans d'une région,** to survey a district. (b) *El.E:* P. *de pose,* wiring diagram. (c) Scheme, project, design. P. *de campagne,* plan of campaign. P. *d'études,* programme of studies; curriculum. *Dresser un p.,* to draw up a plan. P. *d'ensemble,* general plan. **Sans plan arrêté,** following no preconceived plan.

plan³, *s.m.* (= PLANT) **Laisser qn en plan,** to leave s.o. in the lurch.

planche [plɑ̃:ʃ], *s.f.* **1.** (a) Board, plank. P. *à dessin,* drawing-board. P. *à repasser,* ironing-board. *Veh:* P. *garde-crotte,* splash-board, dash-board. *Aut:* **Planche de bord, planche tablier,** instrument-board dash-board. *F:* **C'est ma planche de salut,** it's my sheet-anchor, my last hope. **Faire la planche à qn,** to smooth the way for s.o. *Com:* *Nau:* **Jours de planche,** lay days. *Th:* *F:* **Monter sur les planches,** to go on the stage. **Brûler les planches,** to act with fire. *Nau:* *A:* **Passer à la planche,** to walk the plank. *Nau:* P. *de débarquement,* gang-plank. *Swim:* **Faire la planche,** to float, swim, on one's back. (b) Shelf (of cupboard, etc.). *F:* **Avoir du pain sur la planche,** to have money put by. (c) (At the seaside) **Les planches,** the broad walk (on the sand). **2.** *Art:* *Engr:* (i) (Metal) plate, block (for printing, etching, etc.). (ii) (Printed) plate, (wood)cut, engraving. **3.** (a) *Agr:* Land (i.e. space between water-furrows). (b) (Rectangular) flower-bed.

planchéier [plɑ̃ʃeje], *v.tr.* (a) To board (partition); to board over, plank over (deck). (b) To floor (room).

plancher [plɑ̃ʃe], *s.m.* (a) (Boarded) floor. *F:* **Le plancher des vaches,** terra firma. (b) Planking (of deck); floor-plates (of engine-room); flooring (of trench). *Aut:* *Av:* Floor-board. (c) Roadway, road-covering (of bridge). (d) *Hyd.E:* Bottom (of lock).

planchette [plɑ̃ʃet], *s.f.* **1.** Small plank or board; *Phot:* (lens) panel. **2.** *Surv:* Plane-table. **3.** *Psychics:* Planchette.

plançon [plɑ̃sɔ̃], *s.m.* *Hort:* (a) Sapling. (b) Set, slip (for planting).

plancton [plɑ̃ktɔ̃], *s.m.* *Biol:* Plankton.

plane¹ [plan], *s.m.* *Bot:* Plane-tree. **Faux plane,** sycamore, great maple.

plane², *s.f.* *Tls:* (a) Drawing-knife. (b) Turning-chisel, planisher.

plan|er¹ [plane], *v.tr.* **1.** To smooth, make even; to plane or shave (wood). **2.** To planish (metal). *s.m.* **-age.**

plané¹, *s.m.* Rolled gold; gold casing.

plan|er², *v.i.* **1.** (a) (Of bird) To soar; to hover; (of balloon) to float. (b) *Av:* To glide; to volplane. **2.** (a) (Of mist, etc.) To hover. (b) To look down (from the air, from on high) (*sur, upon*). *s.m.* **-ement.**

plané², *a.* & *s.m.* *Av:* Gliding. **Vol plané,**
glide; gliding flight; volplane. *Descendre en vol p.,* to volplane down.

planétaire [planete:r]. **1.** *a.* (a) Planetary (system). (b) *Mec.E:* **Engrenage planétaire,** (sun-and-)planet gear. **2.** *s.m.* Planetarium, orrery.

planète [planet], *s.f.* *Astr:* Planet.

planeur¹ [planœ:r], *s.m.* Planisher (of metals).

planeur², *s.m.* *Av:* Glider; sail-plane.

planimètre [planimetr], *s.m.* Planimeter; surface integrator.

planisphère [planisfe:r], *s.m.* Planisphere.

planking [plɑ̃ŋkiŋ], *s.m.* *Sp:* Surf-riding.

planquer (se) [səplɑ̃ke], *v.pr.* **1.** To take cover. **2.** To lie flat.

plant [plɑ̃], *s.m.* **1.** (a) (Nursery) plantation (of trees, bushes). (b) P. *de choux,* cabbage-patch. **2.** Sapling, set, slip. *Jeunes plants,* seedlings.

plantage [plɑ̃ta:ʒ], *s.m.* **1.** Planting. **2.** Patch of ground under cultivation.

plantain [plɑ̃tɛ̃], *s.m.* *Bot:* Plantain (genus *Plantago*).

plantation [plɑ̃tasjɔ̃], *s.f.* **1.** Planting (of seeds, flowers). **2.** (Sugar-, tea-)plantation. P. *d'oranges,* orange-grove.

plante¹ [plɑ̃:t], *s.f.* Sole (of the foot).

plante², *s.f.* Plant. P. *potagère,* herb or vegetable. P. *marine,* seaweed. P. *à fleurs,* flowering plant. **Le Jardin des Plantes,** the Botanical Gardens.

planter [plɑ̃te], *v.tr.* **1.** To plant, set (seeds, flowers). **2.** To fix, set (up). P. *un pieu dans le sol,* to drive a stake into the ground; to set a stake. P. *une échelle contre le mur,* to fix, set, a ladder against the wall. P. *sa tente,* to pitch one's tent. *F:* P. *son chapeau sur la tête,* to stick one's hat on one's head. *F:* **Planter là qn,** to leave s.o. in the lurch. *Elle l'a planté là,* she (has) jilted him. *Ne la laissez pas plantée là,* don't leave her standing there.

se planter, to stand, take one's stand (firmly). *Se p. sur ses jambes,* to take a firm stand.

planteur [plɑ̃tœ:r], *s.m.* (a) Planter, grower (of vegetables). (b) Planter, settler (in new colony).

plantigrade [plɑ̃tigrad], *a.* & *s.m.* *Z:* Plantigrade.

plantoir [plɑ̃twa:r], *s.m.* *Tls:* *Hort:* Dibble.

planton [plɑ̃tɔ̃], *s.m.* *Mil:* Orderly. **Être de planton,** to be on orderly duty.

plantureu|x, -euse [plɑ̃tyrø, -ø:z], *a.* **1.** Copious, abundant; lavish (meal). **2.** Rich, fertile (countryside). *adv.* **-sement.**

planure [plany:r], *s.f.* (Wood-)shaving(s).

plaquage [plaka:ʒ], *s.m.* **1.** *Rugby Fb:* Tackle. **2.** *P:* Chucking, forsaking (esp. of lover).

plaque [plak], *s.f.* **1.** (a) Plate, sheet (of metal); slab (of marble). P. *de cheminée,* fire-back. *Cu:* P. *chauffante,* hot plate. P. *de blindage,* armour(ed) plate. *Tp:* P. *vibrante,* vibrating diaphragm. (b) *Plaque(s) de fondation, de fond,* bed-plate. P. *tournante,* turn-table. (c) *El:* P. *d'accumulateur,* accumulator plate. P. *empâtée, tartinée,* pasted plate. P. *à grillage,* grid plate. (d) *W.Tel:* Plate, anode. *Tension de p.,* plate or anode voltage. (e) **Plaque photographique,** photographic plate. **2.** (a) (Ornamental) plaque. P. *commémorative,* (votive) tablet. (b) P. *de porte,* door-plate, name-plate. **3.** Badge. P. *d'identité* number plate; (soldier's) identity disc. P. *d'un ordre,* star of an order. *Aut:* P. *matricule, p. de police,* number plate. **4.** P. *de gazon,* sod. **5.** P. *sanguine,* red blood-disc.

plaquemine [plakmin], *s.f.* *Bot:* Persimmon.

plaqueminier [plakminje], *s.m.* **1.** P. *ébénier,* ebony(-tree). **2.** P. *de Virginie,* persimmon(-tree).

plaquer ̣plake], *v.tr.* **1.** (*a*) To veneer (wood); to plate (metal); to flash (glass); to lay on (plaster). *Plaqué de sang, de.boue,* caked with blood, with mud. *F: P. un soufflet à qn,* to smack s.o.'s face. *Se p. les cheveux sur le front,* to plaster one's hair down on one's forehead. *P. son chapeau sur ses oreilles,* to pull, cram, one's hat down over one's ears. (*b*) *Rugby Fb:* To tackle, bring down (opponent). (*c*) *Mus:* P. *un accord,* to strike (and hold) a chord. **2.** *P:* To abandon, forsake (s.o.); to give (s.o.) the chuck. **Tout plaquer,** to chuck everything up.
  se plaquer. 1. *Se p. contre le sol, contre un mur,* to lie flat on the ground, to flatten oneself against a wall. *F: Se p. par terre,* to fall at full length. **2.** *Av:* To pancake.
  plaqué, *a. & s.m.* **1.** (**Métal**) **plaqué,** plated metal, plated goods; electro-plate. **2.** (**Bois**) **plaqué,** veneered wood.
plaquette [plaket], *s.f.* **1.** Plaquette, small plate (of metal, etc.). **2.** Thin booklet; brochure.
plaqueur [plakœ:r], *s.m.* **1.** (*a*) Plater (of metal). (*b*) Veneerer. **2.** *Fb:* Tackler.
plasticine [plastisin], *s.f.* Plasticine.
plasticité [plastisite], *s.f.* Plasticity.
plastique [plastik]. **1.** *a.* Plastic. *F: Aux formes plastiques,* buxom. **2.** *s.f.* (*a*) Plastic art; art of modelling. (*b*) *Danseuse d'une belle p.,* dancer with a beautifully modelled figure.
plastron [plastrɔ̃], *s.m.* **1.** Breast-plate (of cuirass). **2.** *Mec.E:* Drill-plate. **3.** (*a*) (Fencer's) plastron, pad. (*b*) *F:* Butt, target (of jokes). **4.** *Cost:* (*a*) (Woman's) bodice-front, modesty-front. (*b*) *P. de chemise,* (man's) shirt-front.
plastronn|er [plastrɔne], *v.i. F:* To throw out one's chest; to pose, strut, attitudinize; to swagger. *s.m.* **-eur.**
plat [pla]. **1.** *a.* (*a*) Flat, level. *Soulier p.,* low-heeled shoe. **Avoir la poitrine plate, le pied plat,** to be flat-chested, flat-footed. *Mer plate,* smooth sea. *Calme p.,* dead calm. **Vis à tête plate,** screw with countersunk head. **Vaisselle plate,** (solid) gold plate or silver plate. S.a. COUTURE 2, RIME. (*b*) Mean, dull, insipid, tame. *Style p.,* commonplace style. *Vin p.,* dull, flat, wine. **C'est un plat personnage,** he's a contemptible fellow. *Faire de plates excuses,* to make (i) a complete apology, (ii) paltry excuses. *s.m.* **Faire du plat à qn,** to toady (to) s.o. (*c*) **A plat,** flat. *Pierres à p.,* stones laid flat. **Tomber à plat** (ventre), to fall flat on one's face. *La pièce est tombée à p.,* the play fell flat. *Pneu à p.,* flat tyre. *Accu à p.,* accumulator run down. *F:* (Of athlete, etc.) **Être à plat,** to be exhausted; to be cooked. *Av: Descendre à p.,* to pancake (to the ground). **2.** *s.m.* (*a*) Flat (part) (of hand etc.); blade (of oar); face (of hammer). *Bookb:* **Plats,** boards, sides. *Plats toile,* cloth boards. *Sp:* **Le plat,** flat racing. (*b*) *Cu:* Dish (container or contents). S.a. ŒUF 1. *F:* **Mettre les petits plats dans les grands,** to make a great spread. **Mettre les pieds dans le plat,** to put one's foot in it; to blunder. **Il nous a donné, servi, un plat de son métier,** he played us one of his tricks. *Navy:* **Faire plat avec . . .,** to mess with. . . . **Camarade de plat,** messmate. (*c*) *Cu:* Course (at dinner, etc.). S.a. JOUR 3. (*d*) *P. de quête,* collection-plate.
platane [platan], *s.m. Bot:* Plane-tree.
plat-bord, *s.m. Nau:* Gunwale, gunnel. *pl. Des plats-bords.*
plateau [plato], *s.m.* **1.** (*a*) Tray. *P. à thé,* tea-tray. *P. d'argent,* silver salver. (*b*) Pan, scale (of balance). **2.** *Geog:* Plateau, table-land. *P. continental,* continental shelf. **3.** Platform.

(*a*) *Artil:* P. *chargeur,* loading-platform. (*b*) *Th:* 'Floor' (of the stage). *P. tournant,* revolving stage. **4.** (*a*) Disc, plate; chuck, face-plate (of lathe). *Aut:* P. *d'embrayage,* clutch-plate. *P. d'excentrique,* eccentric sheave. *P. tourne-disques,* turn-table (of gramophone). (*b*) Base-plate (of theodolite); bed-plate (of machine-tool). (*c*) *P. d'assemblage,* coupling flange. **Assemblage à plateaux,** flanged coupling. (*d*) *El: P. d'annonciateur,* annunciator disc (of bell). (*e*) *Mus:* Key (of Boehm flute, etc.).
plate-bande, *s.f.* **1.** (*a*) Grass border. (*b*) Flower-bed. **2.** *Arch:* (i) Flat arch; (ii) flat moulding; lintel course. **3.** Metal strap; ring (on gun). *pl. Des plates-bandes.*
platée [plate], *s.f. F:* Dishful (of food, etc.).
plate-forme, *s.f. F:* **1.** Platform (of motor bus, etc.); flat roof (of house); foot-plate (of locomotive). *Artil:* Gun-platform. *P.-f. tournante,* gun turn-table. *Rail: P.-f. roulante,* open truck. **2.** *Pol:* Platform (= declaration of policy of party). *pl. Des plates-formes.*
plate-longe, *s.f. Harn:* (*a*) Kicking-strap. (*b*) Leading-rein. *pl. Des plates-longes.*
platement [platmã], *adv.* Flatly. (*a*) Dully, prosaically. (*b*) Contemptibly, meanly.
plat-fond, *s.m.* Well (of boat).
platine[1] [platin], *s.f.* Plate (of lock, watch); lock (of fire-arm); platen (of printing press, of typewriter); stage (of microscope).
platine[2], *s.m.* Platinum. **Mousse, éponge, de platine,** platinum sponge. *P. laminé,* platinum foil.
platin|er [platine], *v.tr.* To platinize; to plate with platinum. *El.E:* **Grain platiné,** platinum point (of make-and-break). *s.m.* **-age.**
platitude [platityd], *s.f.* **1.** (*a*) Flatness, dullness (of style, etc.); vapidity (of style). (*b*) Contemptibleness (of conduct). **2.** (*a*) Commonplace remark; platitude. *Débiter des platitudes,* to platitudinize. (*b*) **Faire des platitudes à qn,** to fawn and cringe to s.o.
Platon [platɔ̃]. *Pr.n.m.* Plato.
platonicien, -ienne [platɔnisjɛ̃, -jɛn]. **1.** *a.* Platonic (school, philosopher). **2.** *s.* Platonist.
platonique [platɔnik], *a.* Platonic (love).
plâtrage [platra:ʒ], *s.m.* Plastering; plaster-work.
plâtras [platrɑ], *s.m.* Debris of plaster-work; rubbish.
plâtre [plɑ:tr], *s.m.* **1.** (*a*) Plaster. *P. de moulage,* plaster of Paris. **Pierre à plâtre,** gypsum. *Enduire qch. de p.,* to plaster sth. over. S.a. BATTRE 1. (*b*) *pl.* Plaster-work (in house, etc.); pargeting. *F:* Essuyer les plâtres, to be the first occupant of a house. **2.** Plaster cast.
plâtrer [platre], *v.tr.* **1.** (*a*) To plaster (wall, ceiling); to plaster up (hole, crack). *F: Se p. le visage,* to paint one's face. (*b*) *F:* To plaster up, hide (defect); to smooth over, patch up (a quarrel). **2.** (*a*) To plaster, to gypsum (field). (*b*) To plaster (wine).
plâtrière [platriɛ:r], *s.f.* **1.** Gypsum-quarry; chalk-pit. **2.** Plaster-kiln.
plat-ventre, *s.m. inv. Swim: F:* Belly-flop.
plausibilité [plozibilite], *s.f.* Plausibility (of statement).
plausible [plozibl], *a.* Plausible (statement). *adv.* **-ment.**
plèbe [plɛb], *s.f.* The plebs; the lower orders, the common people.
plébéien, -ienne [plebejɛ̃, -jɛn], *a. & s.* Plebeian.
plébiscite [plebissit], *s.m.* Plebiscite; referendum.

plectre [plɛktr], *s.m. Mus:* Plectrum.
pléiade [plejad], *s.f. Astr: Lit:* Pleiad.
plein [plɛ̃]. **I.** *a.* Full (*de*, of). (*a*) Filled, replete (*de*, with). *Bouteille pleine*, full bottle. *Pleine bouteille*, bottleful. *Joues pleines*, full, plump, cheeks. **Plein comme un œuf**, full as an egg. *F:* Être plein, to be drunk; *P:* to have a skinful. *Th: Salle pleine à étouffer*, house crammed to suffocation. *J'ai le cœur p.*, my heart is full. (*b*) (Of animal) Big (with young). *Jument, brebis, pleine*, mare in foal, ewe with lamb. (*c*) Complete, entire, whole. *Pleine lune*, full moon. *Pleine mer*, (i) high tide; (ii) the high sea(s). *Reliure pleine peau*, full leather binding. *Plein pouvoir*, full power; *Jur:* power of attorney. **De plein gré**, of one's own free will. S.a. FOUET 2. (*d*) Solid (tyre, axle, etc.). *Table en acajou p.*, solid mahogany table. (*e*) **En plein** *visage*, full, right, in the face. *En p. hiver*, in the depth, the middle, of winter. *En p. air*, in the open; al fresco. *En p. jour*, (i) in broad daylight; (ii) publicly. *En pleine nuit*, at dead of night. *En pleine mer*, in the open sea, on the high sea(s). *En p. tribunal*, in open court. *En p. travail*, in the thick of the (his) work. *Être en p. travail*, to be (i) hard at work, (ii) (of factory, etc.) in full swing. (*f*) *Respirer* **à pleine poitrine, à pleins poumons**, to breathe deep. *Boire à p. verre*, to drink deep. *Crier à pleine gorge*, to shout at the top of one's voice. *A pleines voiles*, with all sails set; under full sail. S.a. MAIN I. (*g*) *adv. Il avait des larmes* **plein les yeux**, his eyes were full of tears. *Avoir de l'argent p. les poches*, to be flush of money. *S'arrêter p. au milieu de la place*, to stop in the very middle of the square. *P:* **Tout plein**, very, very much. *Elle est mignonne tout p.*, she's awfully sweet. **Tout plein de gens**, any amount of people. *Nau:* **Porter plein**, to keep her full. **Près et plein**, full and by. **2.** *s.m.* (*a*) Plenum; fully occupied space. **Mettre dans le plein**, to hit the bull's-eye. *Mch:* **Faire le plein des chaudières**, to fill the boilers; to fill up. *Aut:* **Faire le p. d'essence**, to fill up with petrol. (Of ship) **Avoir son plein**, to be fully laden. (*b*) Full (extent, height, etc.). *La lune est dans son p.*, the moon is at the full. **Le plein** (*de la mer*), high tide. (Of tide) **Battre son plein**, to be at the full. *F: La saison bat son p.*, the season is in full swing. (*c*) **En plein dans le centre**, full, right, in the middle. (*d*) Downstroke (in writing). *Typ:* Thick stroke.
pleinairiste [plɛnɛrist], *s.m. & f.* Fresh-air fiend.
pleinement [plɛnmɑ̃], *adv.* Fully, entirely, quite.
plein-vent [plɛ̃vɑ̃], *s.m.inv.* **I.** Hardy fruit-tree. **2.** Isolated tree.
pléistocène [pleistɔsɛn], *a. & s.m. Geol:* Pleistocene.
plénière [plenjɛːr], *a.f.* Full, complete, absolute (liberty); plenary (court, indulgence).
plénipotentiaire [plenipɔtɑ̃sjɛːr], *a. & s.m.* (*a*) Plenipotentiary. (*b*) *s.m.* Authorized agent.
plénitude [plenityd], *s.f.* Plenitude, fullness (of time, power); completeness (of victory).
pléonasme [pleɔnasm], *s.m.* Pleonasm. **Par pléonasme**, pleonastically.
pléonastique [pleɔnastik], *a.* Pleonastic.
plésiosaure [plezjɔsɔːr], *s.m.* Plesiosaurus.
plet [plɛ], *s.m.* Fake. (single) turn (of coil of rope).
pléthore [pletɔːr], *s.f.* (*a*) *Med:* Plethora. (*b*) *F:* Superabundance, plethora.
pléthorique [pletɔrik], *a.* (*a*) *Med:* Full-blooded, plethoric. (*b*) *F:* Superabundant.
pleur [plœːr], *s.m. Lit:* Usu. *pl.* Tear. *Verser des pleurs*, to shed tears. **Fondre en pleurs**, to

dissolve into tears. **Cessez vos pleurs**, dry your tears. **Être tout en pleurs**, to be bathed in tears.
pleural, -aux [plœral, -o], *a. Anat:* Pleural.
pleurard, -arde [plœraːr, -ard]. **I.** *a.* Whimpering, fractious (child); whining, tearful (voice). **2.** *s.* Whimperer.
pleurer [plœre]. **I.** *v.tr.* To weep, mourn, for (s.o., sth.); to bewail. *Mourir sans être pleuré*, to die unmourned, unwept. **2.** *v.i.* (*a*) To weep, to shed tears, to cry (*sur*, over; *pour*, for). *P. de joie*, to weep for joy. **Pleurer à chaudes larmes**, to cry bitterly. *S'endormir en pleurant*, to cry oneself to sleep. **Pleurer misère**, to cry poverty. (*b*) (Of the eyes) To water, to run. *Robinet qui pleure*, dripping tap.
pleureries [plœr(ə)ri], *s.f.pl.* Snivelling, whining.
pleurésie [plœrezi], *s.f. Med:* Pleurisy.
pleurétique [plœretik]. **I.** *a.* Pleuritic (pain). **2.** *s.* Pleurisy patient.
pleureur, -euse [plœrœːr, -øːz]. **I.** *s.* (*a*) One who weeps; whimperer. (*b*) Mute; hired mourner. **2.** *a.* Weeping, whimpering, tearful. **Saule pleureur**, weeping willow.
pleurnich|er [plœrniʃe], *v.i.* To whimper, whine, snivel, grizzle. *s.m.* **-ement.** *s.f.* **-erie.** *a. & s.* **-eur, -euse.**
pleutre [pløːtr], *s.m. F:* (*a*) Cad; contemptible fellow; outsider. (*b*) Coward.
pleutrerie [pløtrəri], *s.f.* Caddish trick; piece of ill-breeding; piece of cowardice.
pleuviner [plœvine], *v.impers. F:* To drizzle.
pleuvoir [plœvwaːr], *v.* (*pr.p.* pleuvant; *p.p.* plu; *pr.ind.* il pleut, ils pleuvent; *p.h.* il plut; *fu.* il pleuvra) To rain. **I.** *v. impers.* **Il pleut à verse,** *F:* à seaux, it is raining hard, fast; it is pouring (with rain). *Il pleut à petites gouttes*, is drizzling. *F: Il pleuvait des coups*, blows fell thick and fast. **Faire pleuvoir des coups sur qn,** to rain, shower, blows, on s.o. **2.** *Occ. v. pers. Les invitations lui pleuvent de tous les côtés*, invitations are pouring in on him.
plèvre [plɛːvr], *s.f. Anat:* Pleura.
plexus [plɛksys], *s.m. Anat:* Plexus.
pleyon [plɛjɔ̃], *s.m.* **I.** *Arb:* Shoot trained back. **2.** Withe; osier tie.
pli [pli], *s.m.* **I.** (*a*) Fold, pleat. *Pli creux, double pli*, box-pleat. *Pli inverti*, inverted pleat. *Petit pli*, tuck. *Jupe en plis d'accordéon*, accordion-pleated skirt. **Faire des plis à une robe,** to pleat a dress. *Faire un pli à une page*, to turn down a page. *Hairdr:* **Mise en plis**, setting (the hair). (*b*) Wrinkle, pucker. **Front en plis**, puckered brows. *Pli de terrain*, fold of the ground. (Of garment) **Faire des plis**, to pucker, wrinkle. (*c*) Crease. *Pantalon bien marqué d'un pli*, well-creased trousers. **Faux pli**, (unintentional) crease. **2.** Bend (of the arm, leg). **3.** (*a*) Cover, envelope (of letter). **Sous pli séparé**, under separate cover. **Nous vous l'envoyons sous ce pli**, we send it you herewith. (*b*) Letter, note. *Navy:* *Pli cacheté*, sealed orders. **4.** *Cards:* *Faire un pli*, to take a trick.
pliable [pliabl], *a.* That may be folded; pliable, flexible. *Canot p.*, folding boat.
pliant [pliɑ̃]. **I.** *a.* (*a*) Pliant, flexible; docile, tractable. (*b*) Folding (chair, bed); collapsible. *Pied p.*, folding tripod. **2.** *s.m.* Folding chair or stool; camp-stool.
plie [pli], *s.f. Ich:* Plaice.
pli|er [plie]. **I.** *v.tr.* (*a*) To fold, fold up; to strike (tent); to furl (sail). S.a. BAGAGE I. (*b*) (= PLOYER) To bend (bough, cane). *P. les reins*, to stoop. *P. le genou*, to bend the knee.

(c) *P. qn à la discipline*, to bring s.o. under discipline. *P. un cheval*, to break a horse. *F:* **Être plié au métier**, to be broken in. **2.** *v.i.* (a) To bend. *Mieux vaut p. que rompre*, better bend than break. (b) To submit, yield; (of troops in battle) to give way. *Tout plie devant lui*, he carries all before him. *s.m.* **-age.**

se **plier** *aux circonstances, à la discipline*, to yield, bow, submit, to circumstances; to conform to discipline. *Se p. aux lois*, to obey the law.
plieur, -euse [pliœ:r, -ø:z], *s.* **1.** Folder. **2.** *s.f.* **Plieuse,** folding machine.
Pline [plin]. *Pr.n.m. Lt.Lit:* Pliny.
plinthe [plɛ̃:t], *s.f.* **1.** Plinth (of column). **2.** Skirting-board (of room); plinth.
plioir [pliwa:r], *s.m.* **1.** *Bookb:* Folder; paper-knife. **2.** Winder (for fishing-line).
plissement [plismɑ̃], *s.m.* **1.** Pleating; corrugation. **2.** Crumpling; puckering; crinkling. *Geol:* Flexure (of strata).
pliss|er [plise]. **1.** *v.tr.* (a) To pleat, kilt (skirt, etc.). (b) To crease, crumple; to crinkle (paper); to corrugate (metal). *P. les yeux*, to screw up one's eyes. **2.** *v.i. & pr.* (a) To have folds, creases, pleats. (b) To crease, crumple, pucker. *s.m.* **-age.** *s.* **-eur, -euse.**
pliure [pliy:r], *s.f. Bookb:* **1.** Folding. **2.** Folding-room.
ploc [plɔk], *s.m.* **1.** Hair (from cow, dog). **2.** Waste wool. **3.** *Nau:* Sheathing-felt, caulking-felt.
ploiement [plwamɑ̃], *s.m.* Folding, bending. *Mil:* Ployment (from line to column).
plomb [plɔ̃], *s.m.* **1.** Lead. *P. laminé, en feuilles*, sheet lead. *Tuyau de p.*, lead(en) pipe. *Papier de p.*, lead-foil. **Blanc de plomb,** white lead. S.a. MINE¹ 2. *F:* **Sommeil de plomb,** heavy sleep. *Ciel de p.*, leaden, grey, sky. **N'avoir pas de plomb dans la tête,** to lack ballast. **2.** *Ven:* Shot. **Petit, menu, plomb,** small shot, bird shot. **Gros plomb,** buck-shot. **3.** *pl.* (a) (Housemaid's) sink. (b) Lead roof. **Les plombs,** the leads. **4.** (a) Lead (weight). *Nau:* Jeter, lancer, le plomb de sonde, to heave the lead. (b) **Fil à plomb,** plumb-line. **A plomb,** upright, vertical(ly). **5.** Lead stamp; seal. **6.** *El.E:* **Plomb fusible, de sûreté,** fuse, cut-out. **Faire sauter les plombs,** to blow the fuses.
plombagine [plɔ̃baʒin], *s.f.* Black lead; graphite, plumbago.
plomb|er [plɔ̃be], *v.tr.* **1.** (a) To cover, sheathe, (sth.) with lead. (b) To weight (sth.) with lead. (c) *Cer:* To glaze. **2.** To give a leaden, livid, hue to (complexion, sky). **3.** *Dent:* To stop, fill (tooth). **4.** *P. un mur*, to plumb a wall. **5.** *Cust:* To seal; to affix leads to (waggon). *s.m.* **-age.**
se **plomber,** (of sky, complexion) to take on a leaden hue.
plombé, *a.* **1.** Leaded; lead-covered (roof). S.a. CANNE 2. **2.** Leaden. murky (sky); livid (complexion).
plomberie [plɔ̃bri], *s.f.* **1.** Plumbing. **2.** (a) Lead-works. (b) Plumber's shop.
plombier [plɔ̃bje], *s.m.* (a) Worker in lead. (b) Plumber.
plongeant [plɔ̃ʒɑ̃], *a.* Plunging (fire). *Vue plongeante*, view from above.
plongeoir [plɔ̃ʒwa:r], *s.m.* Diving-board.
plongeon [plɔ̃ʒɔ̃], *s.m.* **1.** *Orn:* Diver, loon. **2.** Plunge, dive (of swimmer). *P. de haut vol*, high dive. **Faire le plongeon,** (i) to dive; (ii) *F:* to take the plunge.
plonger [plɔ̃ʒe], *v.* (je plongeai(s); n. plongeons) **1.** *v.i.* To plunge. (a) To dive; to take a header.

F: *P. dans sa poche pour y prendre des sous*, to dive into one's pocket for pennies. (b) To become immersed; (of submarine) to submerge; (of angler's float) to bob under. (c) *Les murs plongent dans le fossé*, the walls run down into the moat. (d) *Nau:* (Of ship) *P. du nez*, to pitch. (e) (Of coal-seam) To dip. **2.** *v.tr.* To plunge, immerse (s.o., sth., in liquid); to quench (steel, etc.). *P. la main dans sa poche*, to thrust one's hand, *F:* to dive, into one's pocket.
se **plonger,** to immerse oneself (*dans*, in). *Se p. dans le plaisir*, to give oneself up completely to pleasure. *Se p. dans le vice, dans le sang*, to wallow in vice, in blood. *Plongé dans ses pensées*, immersed, lost, in thought.
plongée, *s.f.* **1.** (a) Plunge, dive. (b) Submergence, submersion (of submarine). (Of submarine) **Effectuer sa plongée,** to submerge. **Vitesse en plongée,** speed submerged. **2.** Dip. slope (of ground).
plongeur, -euse [plɔ̃ʒœ:r, -ø:z]. **1.** *a.* Diving (bird). **2.** *s.m.* (a) Diver. **Agents plongeurs,** riverside police. **Cloche à plongeurs,** diving-bell. (b) Washer-up, bottle-washer (in restaurant). (c) *Orn:* Diving-bird. (d) Plunger (of pump).
plosive [plozi:v], *s.f. Ling:* Plosive (consonant).
plot [plo], *s.m.* **1.** *El:* (Contact) stud. *Lampe à un p.*, single-contact bulb. **2.** *Aut:* *P. de démarrage*, foot-starter stud.
ploutocrate [plutɔkrat], *s.m.* Plutocrat.
ploutocratie [plutɔkrasi], *s.f.* Plutocracy.
ployable [plwajabl], *a.* Pliable, flexible.
ploy|er [plwaje], *v.* (je ploie; je ploierai) **1.** *v.tr.* To bend (branch, the knee); *Mil:* to ploy (troops). **2.** *v.i.* To bow (under yoke, burden). *P. devant l'ennemi*, to give way before the enemy. *s.m.* **-age.**
plu [ply]. See PLAIRE and PLEUVOIR.
pluie [plɥi], *s.f.* Rain. (a) *P. battante, torrentielle*, pouring rain, pelting rain, downpour. *P. d'orage*, thunder rain or shower. *P. fine*, drizzle. *Goutte de p.*, raindrop. **Le temps est à la pluie**, it looks like rain. **Temps de pluie**, rainy, wet, weather. *Jour sans p.*, rainless day. **Être sous la pluie**, to be in the rain. "Craint la pluie," 'to be kept dry.' **Parler de la pluie et du beau temps**, to talk about the weather, of nothing in particular. *Prov:* **Après la pluie le beau temps**, every cloud has a silver lining. *F:* **Faire la pluie et le beau temps**, to be all-powerful; to rule the roost. (b) **Pluie d'or**, (i) shower of gold; (ii) *Pyr:* golden rain. **Douche en pluie**, shower-bath.
plumage [plyma:ʒ], *s.m.* Plumage, feathers.
plumard [plyma:r], *s.m. P:* Bed.
plumasserie [plymasri], *s.f.* Feather-trade.
plume [plym], *s.f.* **1.** (a) Feather. **Oiseau sans plumes**, callow, unfledged, bird *F:* **Arracher à qn une plume de l'aile**, to pluck a feather out of s.o.'s wing; to deprive s.o. of some important advantage. **Il y a laissé des plumes**, he did not get away unscathed. **Jeter la plume au vent**, to take a decision by spinning a coin; to toss up. *Prov:* **La belle plume fait le bel oiseau**, fine feathers make fine birds. *Box:* **Poids plume**, feather-weight. (b) *Coll.* **La p. d'un oreiller**, the feathers of a pillow. S.a. LIT 2. **2.** Pen. *P. d'oie*, quill (pen). *P. d'acier*, steel nib. *P. à dessin*, drawing-pen. **Dessin à la plume**, pen-and-ink drawing. **Trait de plume**, stroke of the pen. **Guerre de plume**, paper war. **Prendre la plume** (en main), **mettre la main à la plume**, to take pen in hand; to put, set, pen to paper. **Tenir la plume pour qn**, to act as amanuensis to s.o.
plumeau [plymo], *s.m.* Feather-duster; whisk.

P: Un vieux plumeau, an old stick-in-the-mud.

plumer [plyme]. **1.** *v.tr.* To pluck (poultry); *F:* to fleece (s.o.). **2.** *v.i. Row:* To feather.

plumet [plymɛ], *s.m.* (a) Plume (of helmet, etc.). *P:* **Avoir son plumet,** to be slightly elevated (with drink), a little glorious. (b) Ostrich feather (as head ornament).

plumetis [plymti], *s.m. Needlew:* Satin-stitch.

plumeux, -euse [plymø, -øːz], *a.* Feathery.

plumier [plymje], *s.m.* (a) Pen-tray. (b) Pen-box.

plumitif [plymitif], *s.m.* **1.** *Jur:* Minute-book (of clerk of court). **2.** *F:* Quill-driver, pen-pusher.

plupart (la) [laplypaːr], *s.f.* The most; the greatest or greater part or number. *La p. des hommes croient . . .,* most men, the generality of men, believe. . . . *La p. des citoyens,* the main body, the bulk, of the citizens. *La p. d'entre eux,* most of them. **La plupart du temps,** most of the time; in most cases; generally. *Pour la plupart,* for the most part; mostly.

plural, -aux [plyral, -o], *a.* Plural (vote).

pluralité [plyralite], *s.f.* (a) Plurality, multiplicity. *P. de bénéfices,* pluralism. (b) Élu à la p. des voix, elected by a majority.

pluriel, -elle [plyrjɛl], *a. & s.m. Gram:* Plural. **Au pluriel,** in the plural.

plus¹ [ply]. **1.** *adv.* (a) More. *Ils sont plus nombreux,* they are more numerous. *Il est plus grand que moi,* he is taller than I. *Je ne suis pas plus grand que lui,* I am no taller than he (is). *Il a plus de patience que moi,* he has more patience than I. *Deux fois plus grand,* twice as large. *Je gagne plus que vous,* I earn more than you. *Plus qu'à moitié, plus d'à moitié,* more than half (done, etc.). *Pendant plus d'une heure,* for over an hour. *La maladie pas plus que les obstacles,* non plus que les obstacles, *ne put le vaincre,* neither disease nor difficulties could vanquish him. *Plus de dix hommes,* more than, over, ten men. **Plus loin,** farther on. **Plus tôt,** sooner. **Pour ne pas dire plus,** to say the least. **Plus . . . (et) plus . . .,** the more . . . the more. . . . **Plus on est de fous plus on rit,** the more the merrier. *Plus je lis moins je retiens,* the more I read the less I remember. **Et qui plus est** [plyzɛ] . . ., and what is more . . ., moreover. . . . **Il y en a tant et plus,** there is any amount of it. S.a. AUTANT 4. (b) (Le) plus, most. *La plus belle dame,* the most beautiful lady. *C'est à trente ans qu'elle a été le plus belle,* she was at her best at thirty. S.a. LE¹ 2. *Une ascension des plus hasardeuses,* a most perilous ascent. **C'est tout ce qu'il y a de plus simple,** nothing could be simpler. (c) **Ne . . . plus** (with negative expressed or understood), no more, no longer, not again. *Je ne veux plus de cela,* I want no more of that. *Je ne la verrai plus,* I shall never see her again. **Il n'est plus,** he is no more; he is dead. *Je n'ai plus d'argent,* I have no money left. **Sans plus attendre,** without waiting any longer. **Plus de doute,** there is no more doubt about it. **Plus de potage, merci,** no more soup, thank you. **Plus rien,** nothing more. **Plus que dix minutes!** only ten minutes left! (d) **Non plus,** (not) either. *Je n'en ai pas non plus,* I have not any either. **Ni moi non plus,** neither do I, did I, shall I, can I, etc. **Jamais non plus** *je n'avais songé à . . .,* nor had I ever thought of. . . . *Vous n'en avez guère non plus,* you have not got much either. (e) (Often [plys]) Plus, also, besides, in addition. *Sept plus neuf plus un,* seven plus nine plus one. *Cent francs d'amende, plus les frais,* a hundred francs' fine, and costs. *Golf: Plus quatre*

[plyskatr], plus four. (f) De plus, more. *Une journée de plus,* one day more. *Rien de plus, merci,* nothing besides, nothing else, thank you. De **plus en plus,** more and more. *De plus en plus froid,* colder and colder. **En plus,** in addition; (i) into the bargain, (ii) extra. *Le vin est en plus,* wine is extra. **En plus de** *ce qu'il me doit,* over and above what he owes me. **Plus ou moins** [plyzumwɛ̃], more or less. Ni plus ni moins, neither more nor less. **2.** *s.m.* (a) More. **Qui peut le plus peut le moins,** he who can do more can do less. **Sans plus,** (just that and) nothing more. *Sans plus il les mit à la porte,* without more ado he turned them out of doors. (b) Most. *Faites le plus que vous pourrez,* do the most you can. **Au plus, tout au plus,** at (the very) most, at the utmost, at the best. **C'est tout au plus s'il est midi,** it is twelve o'clock at the latest, at the outside. (c) *Alg:* Plus (sign). (d) *Golf:* **Le plus** [laplyːs], the odd.

plus². See PLAIRE.

plusieurs [plyzjœːr], *a. & pron.pl.* Several. *P. personnes l'ont remarqué,* a number of persons noticed it. *De p. manières,* in more ways than one. *J'en ai p.,* I have several. **Un ou plusieurs,** one or more.

plus-que-parfait [plyskəparfɛ], *s.m. Gram:* Pluperfect (tense).

pluss-e, -es, etc. See PLAIRE.

plus-value [plyvaly], *s.f.* **1.** Increase in value; increment value, appreciation (of land, etc.); surplus, excess yield (of tax, etc.). *Les recettes présentent une p.-v. de . . .,* the receipts show an increase of. . . . **2.** Extra payment. *pl. Des plus-values.*

plut, plût [ply]. See PLAIRE and PLEUVOIR.

plutôt [plyto], *adv.* (a) Rather, sooner. *P. la mort que l'esclavage,* sooner death than slavery. *P. souffrir que mentir,* it is better to suffer than to lie. *Il récite p. qu'il ne chante,* he recites rather than sings. (b) Rather; on the whole. *Il faisait p. froid,* the weather was cold if anything.

pluvial¹, -aux [plyvjal, -o], *a.* Pluvial; rainy (season). *Eau pluviale,* rain-water.

pluvial², -aux [plyvjal, -o], *s.m. Ecc:* Cope.

pluvier [plyvje], *s.m. Orn:* Plover.

pluvieux, -euse [plyvjø, -øːz], *a.* Rainy (season); wet (weather).

pluviner [plyvine], *v.impers. F:* To drizzle.

pluviographe [plyvjɔgraf], *s.m.* Recording rain-gauge.

pluviomètre [plyvjɔmɛtr], *.m.* Rain-gauge. pluviometer.

pluviôse [plyvjoːz], *s.m. Fr. Hist:* Fifth month of the Republican calendar (Jan.-Feb.).

pluviosité [plyvjozite], *s.f. Meteor:* Rainfall.

pneu [pnø], *s.m. F:* **1.** (Pneumatic) tyre (of motor car, bicycle). *P. à tringles,* wired tyre. S.a. BALLON 1. **2.** = PNEUMATIQUE 2 (b). *pl. Des pneus.*

pneumatique [pnømatik]. **1.** *a.* Pneumatic; air-(pump, etc.). **2.** *s.m.* (a) Pneumatic tyre. S.a. PNEU 1. (b) (In Paris) Express letter (transmitted by pneumatic tube).

pneumonie [pnømɔni], *s.f.* Pneumonia.

pneumopleurésie [pnømɔplœrezi], *s.f.* Pleuro-pneumonia.

pochade [pɔʃad], *s.f.* Rapid sketch.

pochard, -arde [pɔʃaːr, -ard]. *P:* **1.** *s.* Drunkard, boozer. **2.** *a.* Drunken, *P:* boozy.

pocharder (se) [səpɔʃarde], *v.pr.* To get tipsy, fuddled; to booze.

poche¹ [pɔʃ], *s.f.* **1.** Pocket. *P. de poitrine,* breast-pocket. *P. de côté,* side-pocket. **Couteau**

de poche, pocket-knife. **Carnet de poche**, pocket-book. **Argent de poche**, pocket-money. **Avoir la poche vide**, to be penniless. **Avoir toujours la main à la poche**, to be always paying out. **J'y suis de ma poche**, I am out of pocket by it. *Mettre qch. dans sa p.*, to pocket sth. F: **Mettez ça dans votre poche (et votre mouchoir dessus)**, put that in your pipe and smoke it. **Connaître qch. comme le fond de sa poche**, to know sth. intimately, through and through. **Il n'a pas sa langue dans sa poche**, he has plenty to say for himself. **2.** (*a*) Bag, pouch, sack. F: **Acheter chat en poche**, to buy a pig in a poke. **Poche d'air**, (i) *Av:* air-pocket; (ii) *Hyd.E:* air-lock. (*b*) *Biol: Med:* Sac. **3.** (*a*) *Pantalon qui fait des poches aux genoux*, trousers that are baggy at the knees. (*b*) *Poches sous les yeux*, pockets, pouches, under the eyes.

poche², *s.f.* Ladle. *P. à couler*, casting-ladle.

pocher¹ [pɔ̰ʃe]. **1.** *v.tr. Cu:* To poach (eggs). F: **Pocher l'œil à qn**, to black s.o.'s eye. *Œil poché*, black eye. **2.** *v.i.* (Of clothes) To pucker; to get baggy.

pocher², *v.tr.* **1.** To dash off (sketch). **2.** To stencil (design).

pochetée [pɔʃte], *s.f.* **1.** Pocketful. **2.** *P:* Duffer.

pochette [pɔʃet], *s.f.* **1.** (*a*) Small pocket; pouch; handbag. (*b*) Pocket-case (of mathematical instruments). (*c*) *Phot:* **P. de papier**, packet of paper. (*d*) **P. de papeterie**, compendium. **P. d'allumettes**, book of matches. **2.** *Ven:* Purse-net. **3.** Pocket-violin; *A:* kit. **4.** Fancy handkerchief.

pochoir [pɔʃwaːr], *s.m.* Stencil(-plate). **Passer qch. au pochoir**, to stencil sth.

pochon [pɔʃɔ̃], *s.m.* **1.** Stencil-brush. **2.** *P:* (*a*) Black eye. (*b*) Blow, F: 'sock,' in the eye.

podagre [pɔdagr]. **1.** *s.f.* Podagra, gout (in the feet). **2.** *a. & s.* Podagrous, gouty (person).

poêle¹ [pwaːl, pwal], *s.f.* Frying-pan. F: **Sauter de la poêle dans le feu, dans la braise**, to jump out of the frying-pan into the fire.

poêle², *s.m.* **1.** *Ecc:* Canopy (held over the Sacrament in procession). **2.** (Funeral-)pall. **Porteurs des cordons du poêle**, pall-bearers.

poêle³, *s.m.* Stove. *P. à feu continu*, slow-combustion stove. *P. à gaz*, gas-stove. **P. de cuisine**, cooking-range; cooker.

poêlée [pwale], *s.f.* Panful.

poêlette [pwalet], *s.f.* Small frying-pan.

poêlier [pwalje], *s.m.* (*a*) Dealer in stoves. (*b*) Stove-setter.

poêlon [pwalɔ̃], *s.m.* Small (earthenware or metal) saucepan; casserole.

poème [pɔɛm], *s.m.* Poem.

poésie [pɔezi], *s.f.* **1.** Poetry. **2.** Poem; piece of poetry.

poète [pɔɛt]. **1.** *s.m.* Poet. **2.** *a.* **Femme p.**, *s.f.* **poétesse**, woman poet; poetess.

poétique [pɔetik]. **1.** *a.* (*a*) Poetic (muse, licence). *L'art p.*, the art of poetry. (*b*) Poetical (works, passage). **2.** *s.f.* Poetics. *adv.* **-ment**, -ally.

poétiser [pɔetize], *v.tr.* To poet(ic)ize.

pognon [pɔɲɔ̃], *s.m. P:* Money; *P:* dibs, oof.

poids [pwɑ], *s.m.* Weight. **1.** (*a*) Heaviness. *Appuyer de tout son p. sur qch.*, to lean on sth. with the whole of one's weight. **Vendre au poids**, to sell by weight. *Le p. n'y est pas*, this is short weight. **Faire bon poids**, to give good weight. **Ajouter qch. pour faire le poids**, to throw sth. in as a make-weight. *Ch:* **Poids atomique**, atomic weight. *Ph:* **Poids spécifique**, specific weight. *Box:* **P. coq**, bantam-weight. **P. lourd**, heavy-weight. **P. moyen**, middle weight. **P. mouche**,

fly-weight. *S.a.* PLUME 1. (*b*) Importance. *Son opinion a du p.*, his opinion carries weight. **Gens de poids**, people of weight, of consequence. **2.** *Poids et mesures*, weights and measures. F: **Avoir deux poids et deux mesures**, to have one law for the rich and another for the poor. *Les p. d'une horloge*, the weights of a clock. **3.** Load, burden. **P. utile**, live weight; useful load. **P. mort**, dead weight, dead load. **P. de charge**, load (of valve, etc.). *Mec.E:* **P. du cheval**, weight per horse-power. F: *Le p. des impôts*, the burden of taxation.

poign|ant [pwaɲɑ̃], *a.* Poignant; heart-gripping. **Spectacle p.**, (i) agonizing, (ii) thrilling, sight. *adv.* **-amment**.

poignard [pwaɲaːr], *s.m.* (*a*) Dagger, poniard. **Coup de poignard**, stab. *Donner un coup de p. à qn*, to stab s.o. (*b*) Dirk.

poignarder [pwaɲarde], *v.tr.* To stab (s.o.).

poigne [pwaɲ], *s.f.* Grip, grasp. **Un homme à poigne, de poigne**, a strong, energetic, man. **Montrer de la poigne**, to show energy.

poignée [pwaɲe], *s.f.* **1.** (*a*) Handful. **A poignées**, in handfuls; by the handful. **P. d'hommes**, handful, small number, of men. (*b*) **Poignée de main**, handshake. *Donner une p. de main à qn*, to shake hands with s.o. **2.** Handle (of door, cycle); grasp (of oar); hilt (of sword); grip (of pistol); haft (of tool). **3.** Hank (of thread, etc.).

poignet [pwaɲɛ], *s.m.* **1.** Wrist. **Faire qch. à la force du poignet**, to do sth. by sheer strength of arm; by sheer hard work. **2.** (*a*) Wristband (of shirt). (*b*) Cuff (of garment).

poil [pwal], *s.m.* **1.** (*a*) (Of animal) Hair, fur. **P. de chameau**, camel's hair. *A p. long*, long-haired, shaggy. *P:* **Coucher le poil à qn**, to soft-sawder s.o. **Monter à poil**, to ride (a horse) bareback. *P:* **Tomber sur le poil à qn**, to 'go for' s.o. *S.a.* BÊTE 1. (*b*) Coat (of animals). *Cheval d'un beau p.*, sleek horse. **Chien au p. rude**, wire-haired dog. (*c*) Nap (of cloth); pile (of velvet). **Velours à trois poils**, three-pile velvet. *S.a.* BRAVE 1. (*d*) *Poils d'une brosse*, bristles of a brush. (Of pers.) Hair (on the body). **Homme à poil**, (i) hairy man; (ii) *F:* man of vigour, of energy. *Sans p. au menton*, beardless. **Poils follets**, down. *F:* **A poil**, naked. *Se mettre à p.*, to strip to the skin. *P:* **Avoir un poil (dans la main)**, to be work-shy. **3.** (Of plants) Down.

poilu [pwaly]. **1.** *a.* (*a*) Hairy, shaggy. (*b*) Nappy (material). (*c*) *Nat.Hist:* Pilose. **2.** *s.m. F:* Man of mettle; esp. French soldier.

poinçon¹ [pwɛ̃sɔ̃], *s.m.* **1.** (*a*) (Engraver's) point; chasing-chisel. (*b*) Awl, bradawl; (embroiderer's) piercer, pricker; (sailmaker's) stabber. **2.** (*a*) (Perforating) punch. **(Coup de) poinçon sur un billet**, punch-hole in a ticket. (*b*) Die, stamp. *P. à chiffrer*, number-punch. (*c*) Stamped mark. **P. de contrôle**, hall-mark. **3.** *Const:* (*a*) King-post. (*b*) Scaffolding-pole.

poinçon², *s.m.* Large cask; puncheon.

poinçonn|er [pwɛ̃sɔne], *v.tr.* **1.** (*a*) To prick, bore. (*b*) To punch. **2.** (*a*) To punch, clip (ticket, etc.). (*b*) To stamp, to hall-mark. *s.m.* **-age**. *s.m.* **-eur**.

poinçonneuse [pwɛ̃sɔnøːz], *s.f.* Stamping-, punching-machine; ticket-punch.

poindre [pwɛ̃ːdr], *v.i.* (*pr.p.* **poignant**; *p.p.* **point**; *pr.ind.* **il point, ils poignent**; *p.h.* **il poignit**; *fu.* **il poindra**. Used esp in *infin.*, *pr.ind.* and *fu.*) (Of daylight) To dawn, break; (of plants) to come up, sprout, spear. (Of ship) *P. à l'horizon*, to heave in sight. F: *Je sens p. un rhume*, I feel a cold coming on.

poing [pwɛ̃], s.m. Fist. *Poings nus*, naked fists, bare knuckles. *Sabre, revolver, au poing*, sword, revolver, in hand. *Serrer les poings*, to clench one's fists. **Menacer qn du poing**, to shake one's fist at s.o. **Dormir à poings fermés**, to sleep soundly, like a log. **Coup de poing**, blow given with the fist; punch. S.a. COUP-DE-POING. *Il tomba sur eux à coups de p.*, he went for them with his fists. **Faire le coup de poing**, to use one's fists.

point¹ [pwɛ̃], s.m. **1.** Hole (in strap). **2.** (a) Stitch. *P. droit, p. devant*, running stitch. *P. arrière*, back-stitch. *P. de piqûre*, (i) back-stitch; (ii) (on machine) lock-stitch. *P. de reprise*, darning-stitch. *P. noué*, knot-stitch. **Faire un point à un vêtement**, to put a few stitches in a garment. *Provs:* **Un point à temps en épargne cent**, a stitch in time saves nine. **Faute d'un point Martin perdit son âne**, for want of a nail the shoe was lost. (b) (Needle-)point lace. (c) **Point de côté**, stitch in one's side. **3.** Point. (a) (In time) **Le point du jour**, daybreak, the peep of day. **Être sur le point de faire qch.**, to be on the point of doing sth. **Sur le point de mourir**, at, on, the point of death. **Arriver à point nommé, juste à point**, to arrive in the nick of time. *Prov:* **Tout vient à point à qui sait attendre**, all things come to him who waits. (b) (In space) **Point de départ**, starting-point. **Point de chute**, (place of) fall. **Point de vue**, (i) point of view; (ii) view-point. *Mil:* **P. de ralliement**, rallying point, alarm post. **Point d'appui**, (i) base of operations, point d'appui; *Navy:* outlying station; (ii) *Mec:* fulcrum (of lever); purchase. **Au point, Opt:** in focus; *I.C.E:* in tune. **Mettre au point**, to focus (lens, image); to adjust (opera-glasses); to perfect (invention); *I.C.E:* to tune (engine). *La question n'est pas encore mise au p.*, the question is not yet ready for discussion. *Mettre un article au p.*, to put, *F:* lick, an article into shape. *F:* **Mise au point d'une question**, restatement of a question. (c) *Nau:* **P. de voile**, clew, corner, of a sail. **4.** (a) Point, dot, tick; punctuation mark. **Mettre les points sur les i**, (i) to dot one's i's; (ii) *F:* to make one's meaning perfectly plain; not to mince words (with s.o.). **Point (final)**, full stop. **Deux points**, colon. **Point et virgule**, semicolon. *P. d'interrogation*, question mark. *P. d'exclamation*, note of exclamation. *Tg:* **Points et traits**, dots and dashes (of Morse alphabet). *Faire un p. en face d'un nom*, to tick off a name. (b) *Mus:* **Noire suivie d'un p.**, dotted crotchet. **Point d'orgue**, pause, fermata. (c) *Nau:* **Faire le point**, (i) to take (the ship's) bearings; (ii) to prick the chart. *P. estimé*, dead reckoning. *P. observé*, position by observation. (d) *Games:* Point, score. *Marquer les points*, to keep the score. *Box:* **Gagner aux points**, to win on points. **Rendre des points à qn**, to give s.o. points; to be more than a match for s.o. (e) *Sch:* Mark. *Mauvais p.*, bad mark. (f) *Typ:* Point. *Caractères de huit points*, eight-point type. (g) Speck, spot, dot. *Le navire n'est qu'un p. à l'horizon*, the ship is a mere speck on the horizon. **5.** (a) Point, stage, degree, extent. *P. d'ébullition*, boiling-point. *P. d'éclair*, flash-point. *P. de fusion*, melting-point. *Jusqu'à un certain p.*, to a certain extent; in some degree. *Au p. où en sont les choses*, as matters stand. **A ce point que, à tel point que, au point que . . .**, to such a pass, so much so, that. . . . **Au dernier point**, to, in, the last degree. (b) **En bon point**, in good condition, in good fettle. **Le commerce est en mauvais point**, trade is in a bad way. (c) **A point**, in the right

condition. *Viande cuite à p.*, meat done to a turn. **6.** Point, particular. *Le p. capital*, the main point. *Le grand p. c'est de . . .*, the great thing is to. . . . **C'est là le point**, that's the point. **Mettre son point d'honneur à ne pas céder**, to make it a point of honour not to yield. **Équiper un homme de tout point**, to equip a man at all points. **Exécuter un ordre de point en point**, to execute an order exactly, to the letter.

point², adv. A: Dial: Lit: = PAS² (often with an affectation of archaism). **Peu ou point**, little or not at all. *Le connaissez-vous?*—**Point!** do you know him?—Not at all.

pointe [pwɛ̃t], s.f. **1.** (a) Point (of pin, sword, etc.); tip, head (of arrow, lance); nose (of bullet); toe (of shoe); top (of spire). **Pointe d'aiguille**, (i) needle-point; (ii) *Rail:* point of a switch-blade. *P. d'une épigramme*, point, sting, of an epigram. **Coup de pointe**, thrust. **A la pointe de l'épée**, at the point of the sword. *P. d'asperge*, asparagus tip. **En pointe**, tapering; pointed. *Aller en p.*, to taper. *Tailler en p.*, to point (stick, pencil). **Marcher, se tenir, sur la pointe des pieds**, to walk, stand, on tiptoe. *Mth: El.E: etc: P. d'une courbe, d'une charge*, peak of a curve, of a load. *Ind: Rail:* **Heures de pointe**, peak hours, busy hours, rush hours. (b) *Mil:* Point (of advanced guard). **Faire une pointe**, to push a small force far in advance of main army. *F:* **Pousser une pointe jusque chez un ami**, to go as far as a friend's house. *Navy:* **Tir en pointe**, firing ahead. (c) *Row:* **Aviron de pointe**, oar (as opposed to scull). **Ramer, nager, en pointe**, to row (as opposed to sculling). **Huit de pointe**, eight-oared boat. (d) **Pointe du jour**, daybreak. **Pointe de douleur**, twinge of pain. *P. d'ironie*, touch of irony. *P. de vanille*, flavour, dash, of vanilla. *Sp:* **Pointe de vitesse**, spurt, sprint. (e) *A:* Witty phrase; conceit; quip. **2.** *Geog:* Pointe de terre, foreland, head(land); cape; spit, tongue (of land). **3.** *Tls:* **Pointe carrée**, bradawl. *P. à tracer*, scriber. **Pointe sèche**, (etcher's) point; etching-needle. S.a. POINTE-SÈCHE. **4.** **Pointe de Paris**, wire nail, French nail. **5.** *Med:* Pointes de feu, ignipuncture. **6.** (a) (Triangular) napkin, diaper (for infant). (b) Kerchief or fichu. (c) *Nau:* Gore (of sail).

pointeau [pwɛ̃to], s.m. **1.** *Tls:* Centre-punch. **2.** (a) Needle, float-spindle (of carburettor). *Agir sur le p.*, to tickle the carburettor. (b) *P. de soupape (de pneu)*, valve-needle.

point|er¹ [pwɛ̃te], v.tr. **1.** (a) To check, tick off, prick off (names on list); to scrutinize (votes, etc.). *Nau:* To prick (the chart). (b) *Mus:* **Note pointée**, dotted note. (c) *Ind:* *P. à l'arrivée, au départ*, to clock on, clock off. **2.** To point, level, train (telescope, etc.); to aim, lay (gun); to train (searchlight) (*sur*, on). s.m. **-age**.

pointer². **1.** v.tr. (a) To thrust, point, stab (with sword, etc.). (b) To point (needle); to sharpen (pencil). (c) (Of horse) *P. les oreilles*, to prick up its ears. **2.** v.i. To appear; (of plant) to sprout, to spear; (of wind) to rise; (of bird) to soar; (of horse) to rear; (of steeple) to jut upwards.

pointe-sèche, s.f. Dry-point etching. *pl. Des pointes-sèches.*

pointeur [pwɛ̃tœ:r], s.m. **1.** Checker; tallyman, timekeeper; (billiard-)marker, scorer. **2.** *Artil:* Gun-layer. **3.** Chien pointeur, pointer.

pointill|er¹ [pwɛ̃tije], v.tr. **1.** To dot. **2.** *Engr:* To stipple. s.m. **-age¹**.

pointillé. 1. *a.* Dotted (line); stippled (engraving); *Tex:* pin-head (cloth). **2.** *s.m.* (a) Dotted line. (b) Stippling; stippled engraving.

pointill|er². 1. *v.i.* (a) To cavil, bicker (over trifles). (b) To split hairs. **2.** *v.tr.* To plague; to annoy (s.o.) with pinpricks. *s.m.* **-age².**

pointillerie [pwɛ̃tijri], *s.f.* **1.** Captiousness. **2.** Hair-splitting.

pointilleu|x, -euse [pwɛ̃tijø, -øːz], *a.* **1.** Captious (person); carping (critic); touchy (person). **2.** (a) Particular (*sur*, about); fastidious (as to). (b) Finical (person). *adv.* **-sement.**

pointu [pwɛ̃ty], *a.* (a) Sharp-pointed. *Oreilles pointues,* pointed ears; prick-ears. *Chapeau p.,* sugar-loaf hat. (b) Angular, touchy (disposition); shrill (voice). S.a. RIRE I. 1.

pointure [pwɛ̃tyːr], *s.f.* Size (in boots, gloves, collars, etc.). *J'ai six de p.,* I take sixes.

poire [pwaːr], *s.f.* **1.** Pear. *F:* **Entre la poire et le fromage,** 'over the walnuts and wine.' **Garder une poire pour la soif,** to put something by for a rainy day. **Couper la poire en deux,** to compromise, to split the difference. S.a. ANGOISSE. **2.** (Pear-shaped) bulb (of camera shutter, horn, etc.); pear-switch (of electric light). *P. à poudre,* powder-flask. **3.** *P:* (a) Head, nut; phiz. (b) Mug, juggins, easy mark. (c) **Faire sa poire,** to fancy oneself, to put on side.

poiré [pware], *s.m.* Perry.

poireau [pwaro], *s.m.* **1.** (a) Leek. (b) *P:* Simpleton. **2.** *F:* Wart.

poireauter [pwarote], *v.i. P:* To be kept waiting; to cool one's heels.

poirée [pware], *s.f.* White beet.

poirier [pwarje], *s.m.* (a) Pear-tree. (b) Pear-tree wood.

pois [pwa], *s.m.* **1.** Pea. *P. chiche,* chick-pea. *P. carrés,* marrowfats. *P. de senteur,* sweet pea. *F:* **La fleur des pois,** the pick of the bunch. **2.** *Cu:* **Petits pois, pois verts,** green peas. *P. cassés,* split peas. **Purée de pois,** (i) thick pea-soup; (ii) pease-pudding. **3.** *Cravate bleue à pois blancs,* blue tie with white spots. *Étoffe à p.,* spotted material.

poison [pwazɔ̃], *s.m.* Poison.

poissard, -arde [pwasaːr, -ard]. **1.** *a.* Vulgar, low; 'Billingsgate' (language). **2.** *s.f.* **Poissarde,** fishwife. **Langage de poissarde,** 'Billingsgate.'

poisse [pwas], *s.f. P:* Bad luck. *Jour de p.,* bad day (at races, etc.). *Être dans la p.,* to be hard up, stony-broke. [POISSER]

poisser [pwase], *v.tr.* **1.** To pitch; to coat (sth.) with cobbler's wax. *Fil poissé,* waxed thread. **2.** (a) To make (hands, etc.) sticky (with jam, etc.). (b) *Abs.* (Of substance) To be sticky.

poisseux, -euse [pwasø, -øːz], *a.* Sticky.

poisson [pwasɔ̃], *s.m.* **1.** Fish. *P. d'eau douce,* fresh-water fish. *P. rouge,* gold-fish. *F:* **Poisson d'avril,** First of April hoax. S.a. AVRIL. **Être comme le poisson dans l'eau,** to be in one's element. **Être comme un poisson sur la paille,** to be like a fish out of water. **Les gros poissons mangent les petits,** (i) might overcomes right; (ii) the big traders cut out the small. S.a. CHAIR 2. **2.** *Ent:* **Poisson d'argent, petit poisson d'or,** bristle-tail.

poisson-lune, *s.m.* Sunfish, moon-fish. *pl. Des poissons-lunes.*

poissonnaille [pwasonaːj], *s.f.* Small fry.

poissonnerie [pwasonri], *s.f.* Fish-market or fish-shop.

poissonneux, -euse [pwasonø, -øːz], *a.* (Of river) Full of fish, abounding with fish.

poissonnier, -ière [pwasɔnje, -jɛːr]. **1.** *s.* Fishmonger, fishwife. **2.** *s.f.* **Poissonnière,** fish-kettle.

poitevin, -ine [pwatvɛ̃, -in], *a. & s. Geog:* (Native) of (i) Poitou, (ii) Poitiers.

poitrail [pwatraːj], *s.m.* **1.** (a) *Const:* Breast-summer. (b) *Tls:* Breast-piece (of a breast-drill). **2.** (a) Breast (of horse). (b) *Harn:* Breast-strap, breast-plate.

poitrinaire [pwatrinɛːr], *a. & s.* Consumptive.

poitrine [pwatrin], *s.f.* **1.** Chest. *Rhume de p.,* cold on the chest. *S'en aller de la p.,* to be dying of consumption. **Chanter à pleine poitrine,** to sing lustily, at the top of one's voice. *Mus: Voix de p.,* chest voice. **2.** (a) Breast, chest; (of woman occ.) bosom. *Tour de p.,* chest measurement. *Dans l'eau jusqu'à la p.,* breast-deep, breast-high, in water. (b) *Cu:* Breast (of veal); brisket (of beef).

poivrade [pwavrad], *s.f. Cu:* High-seasoned dressing (for calf's head, etc.).

poivre [pwaːvr], *s.m.* Pepper. *P. de Cayenne,* Cayenne pepper, red pepper. *Grain de p.,* peppercorn. *Livre qui manque de p.,* book that lacks 'pep.' *a.inv.* **Poivre et sel,** pepper-and-salt (colour); grizzly, iron-grey (hair).

poivrer [pwavre], *v.tr.* To pepper; to season with pepper. *F: P. ses écrits,* to pepper, spice, one's writings (with licentiousness, etc.). *P. l'addition, une note (d'hôtel), F:* to stick it on.

poivré, *a.* Peppery (food); pungent (smell); caustic (speech); spicy (tale); stiff (price).

poivrier [pwavrie], *s.m.* **1.** Pepper-plant. **2.** Pepper-box.

poivrière [pwavriɛːr], *s.f.* **1.** Pepper-plantation. **2.** (a) Pepper-box, pepper-castor. (b) *A:* (Small overhanging) watch-turret; *F:* pepper-box.

poivron [pwavrɔ̃], *s.m.* Jamaica pepper; allspice.

poivrot [pwavro], *s.m. P:* Drunkard, boozer.

poix [pwa], *s.f.* (a) (Pine-)pitch; cobbler's wax. *P. sèche,* resin. (b) *P. liquide,* tar. *P. de Judée,* asphalt. **Enduire de poix,** to pitch; to wax.

polaire [polɛːr], *a.* Polar. **L'étoile polaire, s. la polaire,** the pole-star. *El:* **Pièce polaire,** pole-piece.

polarimètre [polarimɛtr], *s.m. Ph:* Polarimeter.

polarisateur, -trice [polarizatœːr, -tris]. *Ph:* **1.** *a.* Polarizing (prism, current). **2.** *s.m.* Polarizer.

polarisation [polarizasjɔ̃], *s.f.* Polarization, polarizing (of light; *El:* of electrodes). *W.Tel:* **Polarisation de grille,** grid-bias. *P. négative de grille,* negative grid-voltage.

polariscope [polariskop], *s.m.* Polariscope.

polariser [polarize], *v.tr.* To polarize.

polariseur [polarizœːr], *s.m. Opt:* Polarizer.

polarité [polarite], *s.f.* Polarity.

polatouche [polatuʃ], *s.m. Z:* Flying-squirrel, flying phalanger.

polder [poldɛːr], *s.m.* (In Holland) Polder; sunk meadow.

pôle [poːl], *s.m.* Pole. *Le p. nord,* the North Pole. *El:* **Pôles de même nom,** like poles. *Pôles de noms contraires,* opposite, unlike, poles.

polémique [polemik]. **1.** *a.* Polemic(al). **2.** *s.f.* Polemic, controversy.

polémiste [polemist], *s.m.* Controversialist, polemist.

poli [poli], *a.* See POLIR.

police¹ [polis], *s.f.* **1.** Policing. **Faire la police,** to keep order. *P. des mers,* policing of the seas. **Tribunal de simple police,** police-court. S.a. CORRECTIONNEL. (At hotel) **Feuille, fiche, de police,** police-form (to be filled in by travellers). *Mil:* **Salle de police,** guard-room. S.a. BONNET 1. **2.** Police. **Officier de police** = high constable.

La p. est à vos trousses, the police are after you. **Remettre qn entre les mains de la police**, to give s.o. in charge. S.a. AGENT 2, COMMISSAIRE, PRÉFET 2, SECRET¹, SÛRETÉ I.

police², *s.f.* (*a*) (Insurance) policy. *P. d'assurance sur la vie*, life-insurance policy. *Prendre une p.*, to take out a policy. (*b*) *Com:* **P. de chargement**, bill of lading. (*c*) *P. mixte (force et lumière)*, electricity all-in agreement.

policer [pɔlise], *v.tr.* (je poliçai(s); n. poliçons) To bring (country) under orderly government; to organize (country); to civilize.

polichinelle [pɔliʃinɛl], *s.m.* **1.** Punch, punchinello. **Théâtre de polichinelle** = Punch and Judy show. *F:* **Secret de polichinelle**, open secret. **2.** *F:* Buffoon; (political) jumping jack. **3.** *F:* Scapegrace.

policier, -ière [pɔlisje, -jɛːr]. **1.** *a.* *Ordonnance policière*, police regulation. **Roman policier**, detective novel. **2.** *s.m.* Policeman; detective.

policlinique [pɔliklinik], *s.f.* (*a*) Out-patients' department (of hospital); policlinic. (*b*) Dispensary.

poliment [pɔlimɑ̃], *adv.* Politely, civilly.

poliomyélite [pɔljɔmjelit], *s.f.* *Med:* Poliomyelitis, esp. infantile paralysis.

pol|ir [pɔliːr], *v.tr.* **1.** To polish; to burnish, buff (metal). *Poli par l'usage*, shiny with use. *Se p. les ongles*, to buff one's nails. **2.** To polish, refine (the mind, manners). *s.m.* **-issage**.

poli. 1. *a.* (*a*) Polished; buffed; burnished; bright (steel); glossy, sleek (coat of animal). (*b*) Polished, elegant (style, writer). (*c*) Polite, civil, urbane. *Être très p. avec qn*, to be very polite, very courteous, to s.o. **2.** *s.m.* Polish, gloss.

polisseur, -euse [pɔlisœːr, -øːz]. **1.** *s.* Polisher; (sword) furbisher; (gem) cutter. **2.** *s.f.* **Polisseuse**, polishing-machine.

polissoir [pɔliswaːr], *s.m.* *Tls:* Polisher, burnisher; buff-stick, -wheel. *Toil:* Nail-polisher; buffer.

polisson, -onne [pɔlisɔ̃, -ɔn]. **1.** *s.* (*a*) Naughty child; scapegrace; rascal, scamp. (*b*) Depraved person; thorough rascal. **2.** *a.* *Enfant p.*, child precocious in vice. *Propos polissons*, smutty talk. *Regard p.*, leer.

polissonner [pɔlisɔne], *v.i.* **1.** (Of children) To run the streets. **2.** To be lewd (in word or act).

polissonnerie [pɔlisɔnri], *s.f.* **1.** (Child's) mischievousness. **2.** (*a*) Depravity. (*b*) Lewd act; smutty joke.

polissure [pɔlisyːr], *s.f.* **1.** Polishing. **2.** Polish.

politesse [pɔlitɛs], *s.f.* Politeness; good manners, good breeding; civility, courtesy, urbanity. **Faire des politesses à qn**, to show s.o. civility. **Faire échange de politesses**, to exchange compliments. **Brûler la politesse à qn**, (i) to fail to keep an appointment with s.o.; (ii) not to wait for s.o.; to take French leave. *Aut:* **P. de la route**, road manners.

politicien, -ienne [pɔlitisjɛ̃, -jɛn], *s.* Usu. *Pej:* Politician.

politique [pɔlitik]. **1.** *a.* (*a*) Political. **(Homme) politique**, politician. **Le corps politique**, the body politic. S.a. ÉCONOMIE I. (*b*) Politic, prudent, shrewd; diplomatic (answer, conduct). **2.** *s.f.* (*a*) Policy. *P. intérieure, extérieure*, home policy, foreign policy. (*b*) Politics. *Se lancer dans la p.*, to go into politics.

politiquement [pɔlitikmɑ̃], *adv.* (*a*) Politically. (*b*) Shrewdly, prudently.

polka [pɔlka], *s.f.* *Danc:* Polka.

polk|er [pɔlke], *v.i.* To dance the polka. *s.* **-eur, -euse**.

pollen [pɔllɛn], *s.m.* *Bot:* Pollen.

pollinisation [pɔllinizasjɔ̃], *s.f.* *Bot:* Pollination, fertilization.

polluer [pɔllɥe], *v.tr.* To pollute, defile.

pollution [pɔllysjɔ̃], *s.f.* Pollution, defilement.

polo [pɔlo], *s.m.* **1.** Polo. **2.** *Cost:* Polo jumper.

polochon [pɔlɔʃɔ̃], *s.m.* *P:* Bolster. *Combat à coups de polochons*, pillow-fight.

Pologne [pɔlɔɲ]. *Pr.n.f.* Poland.

polonais, -aise [pɔlɔnɛ, -ɛːz]. **1.** (*a*) *a.* Polish. (*b*) *s.* Pole. **2.** *s.m. Ling:* Polish. **3.** *s.f. Cost: Danc: Mus:* **Polonaise**, polonaise.

poltron, -onne [pɔltrɔ̃, -ɔn]. **1.** *a.* Easily frightened; timid; *F:* chicken-hearted. **2.** *s.* Poltroon, milksop.

poltronnerie [pɔltrɔnri], *s.f.* Poltroonery, timidity.

polyandrie [pɔljɑ̃dri], *s.f.* **1.** *Anthr:* Polyandry. **2.** *Bot:* Polyandria.

polyanthe [pɔljɑ̃ːt], *a. Bot:* Polyanthous.

polychroïsme [pɔlikrɔism], *s.m. Cryst:* Polychroism, pleochroism.

polychrome [pɔlikrɔm, -oːm], *a.* Polychrome, polychrom(at)ic.

polycopier [pɔlikɔpje], *v.tr.* To manifold; (i) to (hecto)graph; to jellygraph; (ii) to stencil, to cyclostyle.

polyèdre [pɔljɛdr]. *Geom:* **1.** *a.* Polyhedral. **2.** *s.m.* Polyhedron.

polygame [pɔligam]. **1.** *a.* Polygamous. **2.** *s.* Polygamist.

polygamie [pɔligami], *s.f.* Polygamy.

polyglotte [pɔliglɔt], *a. & s.* Polyglot.

polygonal, -aux [pɔligɔnal, -o], *a.* Polygonal.

polygone [pɔligɔn]. **1.** *a.* Polygonal. **2.** *s.m.* (*a*) *Geom:* Polygon. (*b*) *Artil:* Experimental range, shooting-range.

polymère [pɔlimɛːr], *a. Ch:* Polymeric.

polymérie [pɔlimeri], *s.f. Ch:* Polymerism.

polymorphe [pɔlimɔrf], *a. Biol: Ch:* Polymorphous, polymorphic, pleomorphic.

Polynésie [pɔlinezi], *Pr.n.f. Geog:* Polynesia.

polynésien, -ienne [pɔlinezjɛ̃, -jɛn], *a. & s. Geog:* Polynesian.

polynôme [pɔlinoːm], *s.m. Alg:* Polynomial.

polype [pɔlip], *s.m.* **1.** *Coel:* Polyp. **2.** *Med:* Polypus.

polypétale [pɔlipetal], *a. Bot:* Polypetalous.

polyphasé [pɔlifaze], *a. El.E:* Polyphase, multiphase (current).

polypode [pɔlipɔd]. **1.** *a. & s.m. Z:* Polypod. **2.** *s.m. Bot:* Polypodium.

polysoc [pɔlisɔk], *s.m. Agr:* Multiple plough, gang-plough.

polysyllabe [pɔlisillab]. **1.** *a.* Polysyllabic (word). **2.** *s.m.* Polysyllable.

polysyllabique [pɔlisillabik], *a.* Polysyllabic.

polytechnicien [pɔliteknisjɛ̃], *s.m.* Student at the *École polytechnique*.

polytechnique [pɔliteknik], *a.* Polytechnic. S.a. ÉCOLE I.

polyvalence [pɔlivalɑ̃ːs], *s.f. Ch:* Polyvalency, multivalency.

polyvalent [pɔlivalɑ̃], *a. Ch:* Polyvalent, multivalent.

pomiculteur [pɔmikyltœːr], *s.m.* Orchardist.

pommade [pɔmad], *s.f.* Pomade, pomatum. *P:* **Passer de la pommade à qn**, to flatter s.o.; to butter s.o. up. (*b*) Ointment (for skin troubles).

pommader [pɔmade], *v.tr.* To pomade.

pomme [pɔm], *s.f.* **1.** (*a*) Apple. *P. à, au, couteau*, eating apple, dessert apple. *P. sauvage*, crabapple. *Compote de pommes*, (i) stewed apples; (ii) apple-sauce. *Anat:* **Pomme d'Adam**, Adam's apple. (b) Pomme de terre, potato. *Purée de pommes de terre*, mashed potatoes. **Bifteck aux pommes**, steak and chips. *P:* **Aux pommes**, first rate, A1. (c) **Pomme épineuse**, thorn-apple, datura stramonium. (d) **Pomme de chêne**, oak-apple. **Pomme de pin**, fir-cone, pine-cone. **2.** (a) Knob (of bedstead, walking-stick); head (of cabbage, lettuce). *Canne à p. d'or*, gold-headed stick. **Pomme d'arrosoir**, rose of a water-ing-can. (b) *Nau:* Truck (of mast).

pommeau [pɔmo], *s.m.* Pommel (of sword); butt (of fishing-rod). *Canne à p.*, knobstick.

pommeler (se) [sɔpɔmle], *v.pr.* (il se pommelle; il se pommellera) **1.** (Of sky) To become dappled with small clouds. **2.** (Of horse) To turn grey. **pommelé**, *a.* Dappled, mottled. *Ciel p.*, mackerel sky. S.a. NUAGE.

pommer [pɔme], *v.i. & pr.* (Of cabbage, etc.) To form a head, to loaf; (of lettuce) to cabbage. **pommé**, *a.* (a) (Of lettuce, etc.) Well rounded. **Chou pommé**, white-heart cabbage. *Choux bien pommés*, fine heads of cabbage. (b) *P:* Complete, utter, absolute, downright (fool, blunder, etc.). **En voilà des pommés!** these are whoppers!

pommeraie [pɔmrɛ], *s.f.* Apple-orchard.

pommette [pɔmɛt], *s.f.* **1.** Knob; ball ornament. **2.** Cheek-bone. *Petite vieille aux pommettes rouges*, little apple-cheeked old woman. [POMME]

pommier [pɔmje], *s.m.* Apple-tree. *P. sauvage*, crab(-apple) tree.

pompe¹ [pɔ̃:p], *s.f.* Pomp, ceremony, display. **Pompe funèbre**, obsequies, funeral. **Entrepreneur de pompes funèbres**, undertaker.

pompe², *s.f.* **1.** Pump. (a) *P. aspirante*, suction-pump. *P. (re)foulante*, force-pump. **Épuiser l'eau à la pompe**, to pump out the water. **Pompe à feu, pompe à incendie, pompe d'incendie**, fire-engine. *Ind: Mch: P. alimentaire, p. d'alimentation*, feed-pump, donkey-pump. *Eau de p.*, pump water. *F:* **Château la Pompe**, Adam's ale. (b) **Pompe à air**, air-pump. *P. à pneus*, tyre-inflator. (c) **Pompe à vide**, *p. pneumatique*, vacuum air-pump. (d) **Pompe à graisse**, grease-gun. **2.** (a) Slide (of trombone). (b) *P. d'accord*, tuning-slide (of wind-instrument). **3.** Serrure à pompe, Bramah lock. **Couteau à pompe**, Norwegian knife.

Pompée [pɔ̃pe]. *Pr.n.m. A.Hist:* Pompey.

Pompéi [pɔ̃pei]. *Pr.n.f. A.Geog:* Pompeii.

pomp|er [pɔ̃pe]. **1.** *v.tr.* To pump; to suck up, suck in (liquid). **2.** *v.i.* (Of engine, governor) To hunt. *s.m.* **-age.**

pompette [pɔ̃pɛt], *a. F:* Tipsy, screwed.

pompeu|x, -euse [pɔ̃pø, -øːz], *a.* Pompous. **1.** Stately (procession). **2.** High-flown, high-falutin; high-sounding (praise). *adv.* **-sement.**

pompier [pɔ̃pje], *s.m.* (a) Fireman. S.a. SAPEUR-POMPIER. (b) *F:* Conventionalist; uninspired writer or artist. *a.m.* Conventional, uninspired, traditional (style, art). [POMPE²]

pompon [pɔ̃pɔ̃], *s.m.* **1.** Pompon; tuft. *F:* **A lui le pompon**, he is easily first; *P:* he takes the bun. *P:* **Avoir son pompon**, to be tipsy. S.a. ROSE 1. **2.** Powder-puff.

pomponner [pɔ̃pɔne], *v.tr.* To adorn, bedizen (s.o.); to elaborate (one's style). **se pomponner**, to smarten oneself up, to titivate.

ponce [pɔ̃:s], *s.f.* **1.** (Pierre) ponce, pumice-stone. **2.** *Draw:* (a) Pounce. (b) Pouncing bag.

ponceau¹ [pɔ̃so], *s.m.* Culvert.

ponceau². **1.** *s.m.* Corn-poppy. **2.** *s.m. & a.inv.* Poppy-red, flaming red.

Ponce Pilate [pɔ̃spilat]. *Pr.n.m. B.Hist:* Pontius Pilate.

pon|cer [pɔ̃se], *v.tr.* (je ponçai(s); n. ponçons) **1.** To pumice; to sandpaper; to rub down (paint). **2.** *Leath:* To stone (a skin). **3.** *Draw:* To pounce. *s.m.* **-çage.**

poncho [pɔ̃tʃo], *s.m. Cost:* Poncho.

poncif [pɔ̃sif], *s.m.* **1.** *A:* Pouncing pattern; pounced drawing. **2.** *F:* (a) Conventional piece of work; stereotyped plot, effect; hackneyed effect. (b) Conventionalism.

ponction [pɔ̃ksjɔ̃], *s.f. Surg:* Puncture; tapping (of lung); pricking (of blister).

ponctionner [pɔ̃ksjɔne], *v.tr. Surg:* To puncture; to tap (lung, patient); to prick (blister).

ponctualité [pɔ̃ktɥalite], *s.f.* Punctuality.

ponctuation [pɔ̃ktɥasjɔ̃], *s.f.* Punctuation.

ponctu|el, -elle [pɔ̃ktɥɛl], *a.* **1.** Punctual (*dans, en,* in). **2.** Source ponctuelle de chaleur, pin-point flame. *adv.* **-ellement.**

ponctuer [pɔ̃ktɥe], *v.tr.* To punctuate, point (sentence); to emphasize, accentuate (one's words in speaking). **ponctué**, *a.* **1.** Punctuated. **2.** Dotted (line); spotted (leaf, etc.).

pondaison [pɔ̃dɛzɔ̃], *s.f.* **1.** Laying (of eggs). **2.** Egg-laying time.

pondérable [pɔ̃derabl], *a.* Ponderable, weighable.

pondérateur, -trice [pɔ̃deratœːr, -tris], *a.* Balancing; preserving the balance. *Éléments pondérateurs du marché*, stabilizing factors of the market.

pondération [pɔ̃derasjɔ̃], *s.f.* Ponderation. (a) Equipoise. (b) *Art:* Proper balance (of parts). (c) Level-headedness; coolness.

pondérer [pɔ̃dere], *v.tr.* (je pondère; je pondérerai) To balance (powers, etc.). **pondéré**, *a.* Well-balanced (mind); cool, level-headed (person).

pondeur, -euse [pɔ̃dœːr, -øːz], *a. & s.* (Egg-)laying. **Poule pondeuse**, laying hen. **Bonne pondeuse**, good layer.

pondoir [pɔ̃dwaːr], *s.m.* **1.** Laying-place (for hens); nest-box. **2.** Ovipositor (of insect).

pondre [pɔ̃:dr], *v.tr.* (a) To lay (eggs); *abs.* to lay. **Œuf frais pondu**, new-laid egg. (b) *F:* (Of writer) To bring forth, produce, be delivered of (poem, etc.).

poney [pɔnɛ, pɔne], *s.m.* Pony.

pongée [pɔ̃ʒe], *s.m. Tex:* Pongee.

pont¹ [pɔ̃], *s.m.* **1.** (a) Bridge. *P. pour piétons*, foot-bridge. *P. en encorbellement*, *p. à consoles*, cantilever bridge. *P. suspendu*, suspension-bridge. *P. tournant*, *p. pivotant*, swing-bridge. *P. à bascule*, (i) drawbridge; (ii) weigh-bridge. *P. volant*, flying-bridge. *P. de bateaux*, pontoon-bridge. S.a. TRANSBORDEUR. *Adm:* **Les ponts et chaussées**, the Department of civil engineering; the Highways Department. *F:* **Jour de pont**, working day intervening between a Sunday and a public holiday, and also taken as a holiday. **Faire le pont**, to take the intervening working day(s) off. *Pont aux ânes* [pɔ̃tozaːn], *pons asinorum.* (b) *Ind:* Platform, stage, bridge. *P. à chariots culbuteurs*, tipping-stage. (c) **Pont roulant** (overhead) crane runway; gantry. (d) *El.E: P. de Wheatstone*, Wheatstone's bridge. **2.** Deck (of ship). *Monter sur le p.*, to go, come, on deck. *Être sur le p.*, to be on deck. *P. à coffre*, well-deck. **Faux pont**, orlop-deck. *P. des gaillards*, upper deck. *A: Navire à deux, trois, ponts*, two-, three-decker. *Com:* **Sur pont**, free on board; f.o.b. **3.** *Mec.E:* Live axle. *Aut:* Pont arrière, rear-axle (and drive); final drive. **4.** *Cost:* Culotte à pont, full-fall trousers. **5.** Couper dans le pont, (i) *Cards:* to cut the pack at the bridge; (ii) *P:* to walk into the trap.

Pont² (le). *Pr.n.m. A.Geog:* **1.** The (Kingdom of) Pontus. **2.** Le Pont-Euxin, the Euxine, the Black Sea.

pont-abri, *s.m.* Shelter-deck, awning-deck.

ponte¹ [pɔ̃:t], *s.f.* (*a*) Laying (of eggs). (*b*) The eggs laid. [PONDRE]

ponte², *s.m. Gaming:* Punter.

ponté [pɔ̃te], *a.* Decked (boat). **Non ponté,** open (boat).

pontet [pɔ̃tɛ], *s.m.* **1.** (*a*) Trigger-guard. (*b*) Scabbard-catch (of bayonet). **2.** Saddle-bow.

pontife [pɔ̃tif], *s.m.* Pontiff. **Le souverain Pontife,** the sovereign pontiff; the Pope. *F: Les pontifes,* the pundits (of literature, etc.).

pontifical, -aux [pɔ̃tifikal, -o], *a. & s.m.* Pontifical. *adv.* **-ement.**

pontificat [pɔ̃tifika], *s.m.* Pontificate.

pontifier [pɔ̃tifje], *v.i.* To pontificate. (*a*) To officiate as a pontiff. (*b*) *F:* To lay down the law; to be Sir Oracle.

pont-levis, *s.m.* Drawbridge (of castle).

Pont-Neuf, *s.m.* Famous old bridge in Paris. *F:* Se porter comme le Pont-Neuf, to be as fit as a fiddle.

Pontoise [pɔ̃twa:z]. *Pr.n.* Pontoise (near Paris). *F:* Vous revenez de Pontoise, you've been wool-gathering!

ponton [pɔ̃tɔ̃], *s.m.* **1.** *A:* Hulk; prison-ship. **2.** *Mil:* Section of pontoon-bridge. **3.** (*a*) *Nau:* P. à mâture, sheer-hulk. (*b*) P. d'incendie, fire-float. **4.** (Floating) landing-stage. **5.** *Aut:* P. de visite, garage repair ramp.

pontonnier [pɔ̃tɔnje], *s.m.* **1.** *Mil:* Pontoneer, pontonier. **2.** (Bridge, ferry) toll-collector. **3.** Landing-stage attendant.

pont-promenade, *s.m. Nau:* Promenade-deck.

pope [pɔp], *s.m. Ecc:* Pope (of the Greek church).

popeline [pɔplin], *s.f. Tex:* Poplin.

popote [pɔpɔt], *s.f. F:* (*a*) (Child's word for) soup. **Faire la popote,** to do the cooking. (*c*) Kitchen or meal-room; cook-shop. *Mil:* P. des officiers, officers' (field-)mess. **Faire p. ensemble,** to mess together.

populace [pɔpylas], *s.f.* Populace, rabble, riff-raff.

populacier, -ière [pɔpylasje, -jɛ:r], *a.* Of the rabble; common, low.

populage [pɔpyla:ʒ], *s.m.* Marsh marigold.

populaire [pɔpylɛ:r], *a.* Popular. (*a*) Intended for the people. Places populaires, cheap seats. (*b*) Of the people. Expression p., vulgar, popular, expression. Chanson p., (i) folk-song; (ii) street song. (*c*) Se rendre p., to make oneself popular. *adv.* **-ment.**

populariser [pɔpylarize], *v.tr.* To popularize (an idea); to make (s.o.) popular. *s.f.* **-ation.**

popularité [pɔpylarite], *s.f.* Popularity.

population [pɔpylasjɔ̃], *s.f.* Population.

populeux, -euse [pɔpylø, -ø:z], *a.* Populous.

populo (le) [ləpɔpylo], *s.m. F:* The common people; the rabble.

poquet [pɔkɛ], *s.m. Agr: Hort:* Seed-hole.

porc [pɔ:r], *s.m.* **1.** Pig. **Gardeur de porcs,** swine-herd. **Peau de porc,** pigskin. *F:* Être comme un porc à l'auge, to be in clover. *F:* (Of pers.) C'est un p., he's a swine. **2.** *Cu:* Pork. Côtelette de p., pork chop.

porcelaine [pɔrsəlɛn], *s.f.* **1.** Cowrie, porcelain-shell. **2.** *Cer:* Porcelain, china(ware). P. de Chine, china. P. de Saxe, Dresden china.

porcelainier, -ière [pɔrsəlɛnje, -jɛ:r]. **1.** *a.* Industrie porcelainière, china industry. **2.** *s.m.* Porcelain manufacturer.

porcelet [pɔrsəlɛ], *s.m.* **1.** Young pig; piglet. **2.** Wood-louse.

porc-épic [pɔrkepik], *s.m.* Porcupine. *pl. Des porcs-épics* [pɔrkepik].

porche [pɔrʃ], *s.m.* Porch.

porcher, -ère [pɔrʃe, -ɛ:r], *s.* Swine-herd, -maiden.

porcherie [pɔrʃəri], *s.f.* Piggery; pigsty; pig farm.

porcine [pɔrsin], *a.f.* Porcine; pig-(breeding).

pore [pɔ:r], *s.m.* Pore (of skin, plant, stone).

poreux, -euse [pɔrø, -ø:z], *a.* Porous.

porion [pɔrjɔ̃], *s.m. Min:* (In N. of Fr.) Over-man.

pornographie [pɔrnɔgrafi], *s.f.* Pornography.

porosité [pɔrozite], *s.f.* Porosity, porousness.

porphyre [pɔrfi:r], *s.m.* **1.** Porphyry. **2.** *Pharm:* Porphyry muller.

porque [pɔrk], *s.f. N.Arch:* Rider, web-frame.

port¹ [pɔ:r], *s.m.* **1.** Harbour, haven, port. P. de, d, marée, tidal harbour. Entrer dans le p., to enter harbour. Entrer au port, to come into port. Quitter le port, to leave port; to clear the harbour. Arriver à bon port, to come safe into port; to arrive safely. **Droits de port,** harbour dues. Capitaine de port, harbour-master. **2.** (*a*) Port (-town). **Port de mer,** seaport. P. militaire, de guerre, naval port, naval base. P. d'armement, port of registry (of merchant ship). *Navy:* P. d'attache, home port. (*b*) Port aérien, air-port.

port², *s.m.* **1.** (*a*) (Act of) carrying. **Permis de port d'armes,** permit for carrying fire-arms. *Mil:* Se mettre au port d'armes, to shoulder arms. (*b*) Wearing (of uniform, etc.); manner of carrying (sword, etc.). **2.** Cost of transport; porterage, carriage (of goods); postage (of parcel, letter); charge for delivery (of telegram). **Port payé, perçu; franc de port,** carriage paid, postpaid. **En port dû,** carriage forward. **3.** Bearing, gait, carriage (of person). **4.** *Nau:* Burden (of ship). **5.** *Mus:* Port de voix, glide, portamento.

portable [pɔrtabl], *a.* **1.** Portable (burden). **2.** Wearable, presentable (garment, etc.).

portage [pɔrta:ʒ], *s.m.* **1.** (*a*) Porterage, conveyance, transport (of goods). **Frais de portage,** porterage. (*b*) Portage; conveying of a boat across land between navigable waters. **2.** *Mec.E:* (i) Bearing, (ii) journal (of machine part).

portail [pɔrta:j], *s.m.* Portal (of church, etc.). *pl. Des portails.*

portance [pɔrtɑ̃:s], *s.f. Av:* Lift (per unit area).

portant [pɔrtɑ̃]. **1.** *a.* (*a*) Bearing, carrying (part of machine, etc.). **A bout portant,** see BOUT¹ 2. S.a. SURFACE. (*b*) Être bien portant, to be in good health. **Mal portant,** in bad health; ailing. **2.** *s.m.* (*a*) Supporter, stay, strut. (*b*) (Lifting-) handle (of trunk). (*c*) Armature, keeper (of magnet). (*d*) Tread (of a wheel).

portatif, -ive [pɔrtatif, -i:v], *a.* Portable; easily carried. Dictionnaire p., pocket dictionary. **Peu portatif,** bulky, unwieldy.

porte [pɔrt], *s.f.* **1.** (*a*) Gateway, doorway, entrance. Portes d'une ville, gates of a town. Arriver à porte(s) ouvrante(s), fermante(s), to arrive at the opening, at the closing, of the gates. P. cochère, charretière, carriage entrance, gateway. *Hist:* La Porte ottomane, la sublime Porte, the (Sublime) Porte, the Turkish Government. (*b*) P. de visite, inspection-door, manhole-door. *Min:* P. d'aérage, air-gate, trap(-door). P. d'écluse, water-gate, lock-gate. **2.** Door. P.

d'entrée, entrance door, front door, street door.
P. à deux battants, folding door. *P de derrière,*
de service, back door. *P. battante,* swing-door.
P. vitrée, glass door. *Aller ouvrir la p.,* to answer
the door. **Faire la porte,** (i) to keep the door (at
monastery); (ii) to tout at the shop door.
F: **Agir à porte close, à portes ouvertes,** to act
secretly, publicly. *Trouver porte close,* (i) to find
nobody at home; (ii) to be denied the door.
Jeter qn à la porte, (i) to turn s.o. out (of doors);
(ii) to throw s.o. out; (iii) to fire, sack, s.o. **Nous**
demeurons porte à porte, we live next door to
each other. **Demander la porte,** to call to the
concierge to open the door. **Refuser la porte à**
qn, to refuse s.o. admission. **Il faut qu'une porte**
soit ouverte ou fermée, there can be no middle
course. **Défendre sa porte,** (i) to be 'not at home';
(ii) *Sch:* to sport one's oak. **Écouter aux portes,**
to eavesdrop. **3.** Eye (of hook and eye). S.a.
AGRAFE 1. **4.** *pl.* Gorge, defile, pass.
porte-adresse, *s.m.inv.* Luggage-label holder.
porte-à-faux, *s.m.* Overhang. **En porte-à-faux,**
overhanging, overhung.
porte-affiches, *s.m.inv.* Advertisement-board;
notice-board.
porte-aiguilles, *s.m.inv.* Needle-case.
porte-allumettes, *s.m.inv.* Match-holder.
porte-amarre, *s.m.inv.* Life-saving (rocket)
apparatus. *Fusée p.-a.,* life-saving rocket.
porte-ampoule, *s.m.inv.* (Electric) lamp-holder,
bulb-holder.
porte-avions, *s.m.inv.* *Navy:* Aircraft carrier.
porte-bagages, *s.m.inv.* *(a)* Luggage-rack.
(b) Aut: Luggage-carrier; luggage-grid.
porte-balais, *s.m.inv.* *El.E:* Brush-holder (of
dynamo).
porteballe [pɔrtəbal], *s.m.* Packman, pedlar.
porte-bijoux, *s.m.inv.* Jewel-stand.
porte-billets, *s.m.inv.* (Bank-)note case.
porte-bonheur, *s.m.inv.* **1.** Charm, amulet,
mascot. **2.** Bangle.
porte-bouteille, *s.m.* Bottle-stand; coaster.
pl. Des porte-bouteilles.
porte-bouteilles, *s.m.inv.* Bottle-rack; wine-bin.
porte-carte, *s.m.* *Av: Mil:* Map-case, map-
holder. *pl. Des porte-cartes.*
porte-cartes, *s.m.inv.* *(a)* (Visiting-)card case.
(b) Card-tray.
porte-chapeau, *s.m.* Hat-peg. *pl. Des porte-*
chapeaux.
porte-chapeaux, *s.m.inv.* Hat-stand.
porte-cigare, *s.m.* Cigar-holder. *pl. Des*
porte-cigares.
porte-cigares, *s.m.inv.* Cigar-case.
porte-cigarette, *s.m.* Cigarette-holder. *pl. Des*
porte-cigarettes.
porte-cigarettes, *s.m.inv.* Cigarette-case.
porte-clefs, *s.m.inv.* **1.** Turnkey, prison
warder. **2.** Key-ring.
porte-copie, *s.m.inv.* *Typewr:* Copy-holder.
porte-couteau, *s.m.inv.* Knife-rest.
porte-crayon, *s.m.inv.* **1.** Pencil-case. **2.** *Art:*
Portcrayon.
porte-croix, *s.m.inv.* Cross-bearer.
porte-drapeau, *s.m.inv.* *Mil:* Colour-bearer.
porte-épée, *s.m.inv.* Sword-knot, frog.
porte-épingles, *s.m.inv.* Pin-tray.
porte-étendard, *s.m.inv.* Standard-bearer (in
cavalry).
porte-étiquette, *s.m.inv.* (Leather) luggage-
label.
porte-étriers, *s.m.inv.* Stirrup-strap.
portefaix [pɔrtəfɛ], *s.m.* Porter; esp. (i) street-
porter, (ii) dock hand.

porte-fenêtre, *s.f.* French window. *pl. Des*
portes-fenêtres.
portefeuille [pɔrtəfœːj], *s.m.* **1.** Portfolio.
F: **Avoir des vers en portefeuille,** to have poems
in MS., unpublished. **Ministre sans portefeuille,**
minister without portfolio. **2.** *(a)* Pocket-book;
letter-case. *F:* **Lit en portefeuille,** apple-pie bed.
(b) Com: Bill-case, wallet. **Effets en portefeuille,**
bills in hand; holdings.
porte-flambeau, *s.m.inv.* *(a)* Torch-bearer.
(b) A: Linkman, link-boy.
porte-fleurs, *s.m.inv.* *Aut:* Flower-holder.
porte-fusain, *s.m.inv.* *Art:* Portcrayon.
porte-fût(s), *s.m.inv.* Barrel-stand; gantry.
porte-greffe, *s.m.inv.* *Hort:* Stock.
porte-lance, *s.m.inv.* *Mil:* Lance-bucket.
porte-lanterne, *s.m.inv.* *Cy:* Lamp-bracket.
porte-lettres, *s.m.inv.* Letter-case.
porte-livres, *s.m.inv.* Book-rest.
porte-malheur, *s.m.inv.* Bringer of ill-luck;
F: Jonah; bird of ill omen.
portemanteau [pɔrtmɑ̃to], *s.m.* **1.** *A:* Portmanteau. **2.** Coat(-and-hat)-rack, -stand.
porte-masse, *s.m.inv.* Mace-bearer.
porte-menu, *s.m.inv.* Menu-holder.
porte-mine, *s.m.inv.* Pencil-case. *P.-m. à vis,*
propelling pencil.
porte-monnaie, *s.m.inv.* Purse.
porte-montre, *s.m.inv.* Watch-stand.
porte-mousqueton, *s.m.inv.* **1.** Carbine-swivel
(on bandolier). **2.** Snap-hook (on watch-chain).
porte-musique, *s.m.inv.* Music-case, -carrier;
music folio.
porte-objectifs, *s.m.inv.* **1.** *Phot:* Lens-panel.
2. Nose-piece (of microscope).
porte-objet, *s.m.inv.* (i) Object-slide, (ii) stage
(of microscope).
porte-outil(s), *s.m.inv.* Tool-holder (of
machine-tool); slide-rest (of lathe).
porte-parapluies, *s.m.inv.* Umbrella-stand.
porte-parole, *s.m.inv.* Spokesman, *F:* mouthpiece (of deputation, etc.).
porte-phare, *s.m.inv.* *Aut:* Head-lamp
bracket.
porte-pipes, *s.m.inv.* Pipe-rack.
porte-plaque, *s.m.* **1.** *Phot:* Plate-carrier.
2. *Aut:* Number-plate bracket. *pl. Des porte-*
plaques.
porte-plat, *s.m.* Dish-stand. *pl. Des porte-plats.*
porte-plume, *s.m.inv.* Penholder; pen. *P.-p.* (à)
réservoir, fountain-pen.
porte-queues, *s.m.inv.* *Bill:* Cue-rack.
porter [pɔrte]. **1.** *v.tr.* To carry. *(a)* To bear,
support (burden). *P. qn en triomphe,* to carry
s.o. shoulder high. *La lettre porte la date du deux*
juin, the letter bears the date of the second of
June. *F: Il porte bien son vin,* he carries his
liquor well. *Elle porte bien son âge,* she wears
well, she does not look her age. *L'un portant*
l'autre . . ., taking one thing with another. . . .
Croyez-vous que la glace porte? do you think the
ice is bearing? *Ces abus portent en eux leur*
propre châtiment, these abuses carry their own
punishment. *F: Il ne le portera pas loin!* I'll
be even with him yet! *(b)* To carry (sth.) on one
habitually; to wear (garment, etc.). *P. une*
bague, une moustache, to wear a ring, a moustache.
Le bleu se porte beaucoup cette année, blue is being
much worn this year. *P. des cicatrices,* to bear
scars. *P. un nom illustre,* to bear an illustrious
name. **Porter la tête haute,** to carry one's head
high. *F:* **Le porter haut,** to think no small beer
of oneself. *Mil:* **Portez armes!** shoulder arms!
(Of ship) **Porter tout dessus,** to have all sails set.

(c) To carry, convey, take (sth. somewhere). *P. qch. dans la maison, p. qch. dehors,* to carry sth. in, out. *P. une lettre à la poste,* to take a letter to the post. *P. le lait à domicile,* to deliver milk at the door. *Il porta le verre à ses lèvres,* he lifted, raised, set, the glass to his lips. *P. qn en terre,* to carry s.o. to his grave. *Courant qui porte au sud,* current that sets to the south. (d) Porter un coup à qn, porter la main sur qn, to deal, aim, strike, a blow at s.o.; to strike s.o.; to lay a hand on s.o. *Abs. Fusil qui porte à mille mètres,* rifle that carries a thousand yards. *P. ses regards sur qn,* to cast one's eye on s.o. *P. un différend devant un tribunal,* to bring a dispute before a court. *P. une accusation contre qn,* to bring, lay, a charge against s.o. *P. qch. à la connaissance de qn,* to bring sth. to s.o.'s knowledge. (e) To inscribe, enter. *P. une position sur une carte,* to mark, show, a position on a chart. *Portez cela à mon compte,* put that down to me, to my account. *Book-k: P. un article au grand-livre,* to post an item (in the ledger). *P. qn déserteur,* to declare s.o. a deserter. *P. qn manquant à l'appel,* to report s.o. absent from roll-call. **Se faire porter malade,** to report sick. (f) To induce, incline, prompt. *Tout me porte à croire que . . .,* everything leads, inclines, me to believe that. . . . (g) To produce, bring forth. *P. des fruits,* to bear fruit. *Terres qui portent du blé,* grain-bearing lands. *Argent qui porte intérêt,* money that bears, brings in, interest. *Cela vous portera bonheur,* that will bring you luck. *Prov:* **La nuit porte conseil,** seek counsel from your pillow; sleep on it. (h) *P. la température à* 100°, to raise the temperature to 100°. *P. la production au maximum,* to raise production to a maximum. (i) To entertain (affection, respect, for s.o.). *Par la tendresse que je vous porte,* by the love I bear you. (j) To declare, state. *Le rapport ne porte rien de tout cela,* nothing of the kind is mentioned in the report. *Mil: La décision porte que . . .,* it is stated in orders that. . . . **Porter témoignage,** to bear witness. **2.** *v.i.* (a) To rest, bear. *Tout le poids porte sur cette poutre,* all the weight bears on this beam. *La discussion porte toujours sur le même sujet,* the discussion always turns on the same subject. *La perte a porté sur nous,* we had to stand the loss. (b) To hit, reach (a mark). *Aucun des coups de feu ne porta,* none of the shots took effect. *Chaque coup, chaque mot, porte,* every shot, every word, tells. *Vin qui porte à la tête,* wine that goes to the head. *Sa voix porte bien,* his voice carries well. *Ce bruit me porte sur les nerfs,* the noise gets on my nerves. *Sa tête a porté sur le trottoir,* his head hit, knocked, struck, against the pavement. (c) *Nau:* (Of sail) To fill, draw. **Portez plein!** keep her full! (d) *Nau:* **Laisser porter,** to bear away. *Laisser p. sur un vaisseau,* to bear down upon, to run down, a ship.

se porter. 1. To betake oneself, repair, proceed (to a place). *Se p. au secours de qn,* to go to s.o.'s help. *La foule se porta vers les hauteurs,* the crowd made for the heights. *Se p. à des voies de fait,* to commit acts of violence. **2. Se bien porter, se porter à merveille,** to be in good health; to enjoy the best of health. **Comment vous portez-vous?** how are you? how do you do? *Je ne m'en porte pas plus mal,* I am none the worse for it. **3.** *Se p. candidat,* caution, to offer oneself, stand, as candidate, as surety.

porté, a. (a) Inclined, disposed. *Être p. à l'indulgence,* to be inclined to indulgence. *Être p. à la colère,* to be prone to anger. *P. à faire qch.,* inclined to do sth.; given to doing sth.

P. pour qn, fond of s.o. *Être p. sur la bouche,* to be fond of nice things to eat. (b) *Ombre portée,* projected shadow.

portée, *s.f.* **1.** (a) Bearing (of beam); span (of roof or bridge). (b) *Nau: P. en lourd, en poids,* dead-weight (capacity). **2.** (a) Litter, brood (of animals); farrow (of pigs). (b) *Mec.E:* Bearing surface. *Portées d'un arbre,* (main) journals. (c) Boss (on shaft, etc.). (d) *Mus:* Stave. **3.** (a) Reach (of arm); reach, radius (of crane-jib); range (of gun, of wireless station); scope (of treaty); compass (of voice). *Canon à longue portée,* long-range gun. *A courte, petite, portée,* at short range. *A (la) portée de la main,* (i) within (hand-)reach; ready, convenient, to hand; (ii) within striking distance. *A p. de fusil, de canon,* within range. *A p. de la voix,* within call. *A p. d'oreille,* within ear-shot. **Hors de portée,** out of reach; out of range. **Hors de ma portée,** (i) beyond my reach; (ii) beyond the compass of my voice; (iii) beyond my understanding. *W.Tel:* **Poste émetteur de grande p.,** high-power station. (b) Bearing, full significance (of a statement). *Il ne se rendait pas compte de la p. de ces paroles,* he did not realize the full implications of these words. *Affirmation d'une grande p.,* statement of far-reaching effect; weighty statement.

porte-respect, *s.m.inv.* **1.** *F:* Person of imposing appearance. **2.** Weapon (for self-defence); life-preserver.

porte-rôties, *s.m.inv.* Toast-rack.

porte-sabre, *s.m.inv.* Sword-frog.

porte-serviette(s), *s.m.inv.* Towel-horse, towel-rail, towel-airer. *Rouleau p.-s.,* towel-roller.

porteur, -euse [pɔrtœːr, -øːz]. **I.** *s.* (a) Porter, carrier, bearer. *P. d'eau,* water-carrier. *P. de nouvelles,* bearer, bringer, of news. *P. d'une lettre,* bearer of a letter. S.a. CHAISE 2. *Com: P. d'un chèque,* bearer, endorsee, payee, of a cheque. *P. de titres,* holder of stock; stockholder. *P. d'actions,* shareholder. **Payable au porteur,** payable to bearer. **Effets au porteur,** bearer stock(s). *Med:* Porteur de germes, germ carrier, *F:* carrier. (b) *Essieu porteur,* bearing axle. *Câble p.,* suspension cable. *W.Tel:* **Onde porteuse,** carrier wave. **2.** *s.m. Rail:* Sleeper.

porte-valve, *s.m.inv. W.Tel:* Valve-holder.

porte-veine, *s.m.inv.* = PORTE-BONHEUR.

porte-vent, *s.m.inv.* Air-duct. **1.** Wind-trunk (of organ). **2.** *Metall:* Blast-pipe, -main. **3.** *Aer:* Trousers (of kite-balloon).

porte-verge, *s.m.inv.* Verger, beadle.

porte-vêtement(s), *s.m.inv.* Coat-, skirt-, dress-hanger.

porte-voix, *s.m.inv.* **1.** Speaking-tube. **2.** Speaking-trumpet; megaphone.

portier, -ière¹ [pɔrtje, -jɛːr], *s.* (a) Porter, door-keeper, janitor. (b) Gate-keeper. (c) *Fb:* Goal-keeper.

portière², *s.f.* **1.** Door (of carriage, car, railway-carriage). **2.** Door-curtain; portière.

portière³, *s.f.* **1.** Raft, cut (of pontoon-bridge). **2.** *Portières de dames (d'un canot),* (rowlock) poppets. [PORTER]

portillon [pɔrtijɔ̃], *s.m.* Wicket(-gate); kissing-gate. *Rail:* Side-gate (at level crossing). *P. d'accès,* ticket barrier.

portion [pɔrsjɔ̃], *s.f.* Portion, share, part. *P. de viande,* (in restaurant) portion, helping, of meat. S.a. CONGRU.

portionner [pɔrsjɔne], *v.tr.* **1.** To portion out. **2.** To apportion (prize-money, etc.).

portique [pɔrtik], *s.m.* **1.** (a) Portico, porch. (b) *Fb: P. du but,* goal-mouth. (c) *Rail:* Awning (over platforms). **2.** Portique roulant, grue à portique, travelling gantry crane.

portland [pɔrtlɑ̃(:d)], *s.m.* Portland cement.

Porto [pɔrto]. **1.** *Pr.n. Geog:* Oporto. **2.** *s.m.* (Also **vin de Porto**) Port (wine).

portrait [pɔrtrɛ], *s.m.* **1.** Portrait, likeness. *P. en pied, en buste,* full-length, half-length, portrait. *Faire le p. de qn,* to make, paint, a portrait of s.o.; to draw a likeness of s.o. *F:* **C'est le portrait vivant de son père,** he is the living image of his father. *P. littéraire,* character-sketch. **2.** **L'art du portrait,** the art of portraiture.

portraitiste [pɔrtrɛtist], *s.m.* Portrait-painter.

portugais, -aise [pɔrtygɛ, -ɛːz]. **1.** *a. & s.* Portuguese. **2.** *s.m. Ling:* Portuguese. **3.** *s.f.* Portugaise, Portuguese oyster.

pose [poːz], *s.f.* **1.** (*a*) = POSAGE. *P. de câbles sous-marins,* cable-laying. (*b*) *Mil:* Posting, stationing (of sentry, guard). **2.** (*a*) Pose, attitude, posture. *Prendre une p.,* to assume a pose, to strike an attitude. **Faire, donner, des heures de pose,** to sit (as model) for painters. *Golf: P. d'une balle,* lie of a ball. (*b*) Posing, affectation; posturing, attitudinizing. **Sans pose,** unaffected(ly). **3.** *Phot:* (*a*) (Time of) exposure. *P. instantanée,* instantaneous exposure; snapshot. **Manque de pose,** under-exposure. (*b*) Time-exposure.

pose-cigare(s), *s.m.inv.* Cigar-rest.

pose-mines, *a.inv.* Navire pose-mines, mine-layer.

pose-plumes, *s.m.inv.* Pen-rack, pen-tray.

pos|er [poze]. **1.** *v.i.* (*a*) To rest, lie (on sth.). (*b*) To pose (as artist's model); to sit (for one's portrait). *P. pour le buste, v.tr.* **poser le buste,** to sit for the bust. *F:* **Faire poser qn,** to keep s.o. waiting. *Je ne pose pas pour un savant,* I do not lay claim to learning. (*c*) *F:* To pose, attitudinize; *F:* to put on side. **2.** *v.tr.* (*a*) To place, put, set, lay (sth. somewhere). *P. un livre sur la table,* to lay down, place, a book on the table. *P. son chapeau,* to put, lay, down one's hat. *P. les armes,* to lay down one's arms. *P. un chiffre,* to put down a number. *P. un soldat en sentinelle,* to post a soldier as sentry. **Poser une question à qn,** to put, propound, a question to s.o. *P. un problème,* to set a problem (*à,* to). *P. une règle de conduite,* to lay down a rule of conduct. *Jur:* **Je pose en fait que** + *ind.,* I submit that. . . . (*b*) To put up, fix (up) (curtain, etc.); to hang (bell); to lay (bricks, carpet, foundation stone); to set (stones, rivets, boiler); to fit (a watch-glass, lens). S.a. QUILLE². *F:* **Poser qn,** to establish s.o.'s reputation (as an author, etc.). (*c*) To suppose, admit, grant. **Posons le cas que cela soit,** let us suppose that to be the case. *Cela posé . . .,* granting this . . ., this being granted. . . . (*d*) *P. un modèle,* to pose a model, to arrange a model in a pose. (*e*) *Mus:* *Bien p. la voix,* to pitch one's voice correctly. *s.m.* **-age.**

se poser. 1. (Of bird) To settle, alight (*sur,* on); (of aviator) to land. **2.** *Se p. dans le monde,* to establish a position in society. **3.** *Se p. en, comme, réformateur,* to set (oneself) up as a reformer.

posé, *a.* **1.** Sitting (bird). **2.** Staid, grave, sedate (person); steady (bearing, etc.); sober (mien). **Écrire à main posée,** to write slowly, carefully. *Voix posée,* calm, even, steady, voice. *adv.* **-ment.**

poseur, -euse [pozœːr, -øːz]. **1.** *s. Tchn:* Layer (of cables, etc.). *P. de sonnettes,* bell-hanger. *Rail: P. de rails, de voie,* plate-layer. *P. d'affiches,* bill-sticker. *Navy: P. de mines,* mine-layer.

2. *a. & s.* (Person) who poses; attitudinizer. *Elle est un peu poseuse,* she is rather affected.

posit|if, -ive [pozitif, -iːv]. **1.** *a.* (*a*) Positive, actual, real (fact, etc.). **C'est positif,** that's so; it's a positive fact. (*b*) *Alg: El: Phot:* Positive (number, pole, print). (*c*) Practical, unsentimental, matter-of-fact (person). **2.** *s.m.* (*a*) *Mus:* Choir-organ (of full organ). (*b*) *Phot:* **Positif pour projection,** lantern-slide. *adv.* **-ivement.**

position [pozisjɔ̃], *s.f.* Position. **1.** (of house), site (of house, town); position (of ship at sea). *Mth:* **Appliquer la règle de fausse position,** to proceed by trial and error. (*b*) Posture, attitude. *Golf:* Stance. (*c*) Tactical position. *P. masquée,* position behind cover. *Acculé dans une mauvaise p.,* driven into a corner. *F:* **Prendre position (sur une question),** to adopt a definite position regarding a matter. (*d*) Condition, circumstances. *P. sociale,* social standing, position, or status. *Il est dans une meilleure p. où il est,* he is better off where he is. **Être en position de faire qch.,** to be in a position to do sth. **2.** Post, situation, appointment; *F:* job.

positivisme [pozitivism], *s.m.* (*a*) *Phil:* Positivism. (*b*) Materialism. (*c*) Matter-of-factness.

positiviste [pozitivist], *a. & s. Phil:* Positivist.

possédant, -ante [pɔsedɑ̃, -ɑ̃ːt], *a. & s.* Les **possédants, les classes possédantes,** the propertied classes.

posséder [pɔsede], *v.tr.* (**je possède;** **je posséderai**) To be in possession of (sth.). (*a*) To possess, own; to enjoy the possession of (sth.); to have, to be possessed of (sth.). *P. un titre,* to hold a title. *P. l'oreille de qn,* to have a person's ear. (*b*) To have a thorough knowledge of, be master of (subject). (*c*) To curb, control (one's tongue, etc.). **Posséder son âme en paix,** to possess one's soul in peace. (*d*) *Quel démon le possède?* what devil possesses him? *Tous étaient possédés de la même illusion,* they all laboured under the same delusion.

se posséder, to possess oneself; to contain oneself. *Il ne se possédait plus de joie,* he was beside himself with joy.

possédé, -ée. 1. *a.* Possessed (*de,* by, of); infatuated, dominated (by passion, etc.). *Être p. du démon,* to be possessed of the devil. **2.** *s.* Person possessed; madman, maniac.

possesseur [pɔsesœːr], *s.m.* Possessor, owner; occupier.

possessif, -ive [pɔsesif, -iːv], *a. & s.m. Gram:* Possessive.

possession [pɔsesjɔ̃], *s.f.* **1.** Possession. **Être en possession de qch.,** to be in possession of sth., to be possessed of sth. **Entrée en p. d'un patrimoine,** accession to an estate. **Prendre possession de qch.,** to take possession of sth.; to take over (authority); to assume (power). **Rentrer en p. de qch.,** to regain possession of sth.; to recover sth. *Prov:* **Possession vaut titre,** possession is nine points of the law. **2.** Property, estate; in *pl.* possessions. **3.** Possession (by evil spirit).

possibilité [pɔsibilite], *s.f.* Possibility; feasibility (of a plan). *Voir la p. de faire qch.,* to see one's way to do sth.

possible [pɔsibl]. **1.** *a.* Possible. *Tous les détails possibles,* every possible detail. *Dans la plus large mesure p.,* as far as possible. *Faites toute la diligence p.,* make all the haste you can. *Cela ne m'est pas p.,* it is beyond my power. *Est-il p. de faire des fautes pareilles!* how can people make such mistakes! **C'est bien possible,** it is quite possible, quite likely. **Aussitôt que possible,** as soon as possible. *Corr: Le plus tôt qu'il vous sera p.,* at your earliest convenience. **Pas possible! you don't say so! well, I never! not really! 2.** *s.m.* **Dans la mesure du possible,** as far as possible. **Faire tout son possible pour . . .,** to do all one can, to do one's utmost, to make every endeavour, to try one's hardest, to. . . . **Scrupuleux au possible,** scrupulous to a degree.

postal, -aux [pɔstal, -o], *a.* Postal (service, etc.). *Caisse d'épargne postale,* post office savings-bank. S.a. CARTE 3, COLIS 1.

postdater [pɔstdate], *v.tr.* To post-date, to date forward (cheque, etc.).

poste[1] [pɔst], *s.f.* **1.** *A:* Post, relay (of horses). **Chevaux de poste,** post-horses. **Maître de poste,** postmaster. S.a. CHAISE 2. **Aller, voyager, en poste,** to travel post. *F:* **Aller un train de poste, courir la poste,** to go post-haste. **2.** *(a)* **Les Postes et Télégraphes,** the Postal and Telegraph Service. *P. aux lettres,* letter post. **Mettre une lettre à la poste,** to post a letter. *Par p. aérienne,* by air-mail. **Directeur des Postes,** Postmaster General. *(b)* Post office. **Petite poste,** (i) district post office; (ii) *Journ:* 'answers to correspondents.' **Bureau de(s) poste(s),** post office. S.a. BON II, RECEVEUR 2, RESTANT I.

poste[2], *s.m.* **1.** Post, station. *(a) Mil:* **La sentinelle était à son p.,** the sentry was at his post. **Poste avancé,** advanced post; outpost. *F:* **Il est toujours solide au poste,** he is still going strong. *P. de mouillage,* anchoring berth. *P. d'amarrage,* mooring berth; moorings. *Navy:* **Postes de combat,** action stations. *(b) Navy:* **P. des aspirants,** gun-room. *P. des maîtres,* warrant-officers' wardroom. *P. d'équipage,* sailors' quarters; (in merchant service) forecastle. *Av:* **P. du pilote,** pilot's cockpit. *Nau:* **Mettre les ancres à poste,** to stow the anchors. *(c) P. d'incendie,* (i) firestation; (ii) hydrant. **Poste de police,** (i) police station, *F:* lock-up; (ii) *Mil:* guard-room. **Conduire qn au poste,** to run s.o. in. *Mil: P. d'écoute,* listening-station. *Navy:* **P. de commandement,** control-room. *(d) P. téléphonique,* telephone-station. *W.Tel: P. émetteur,* (i) sending-out station; (ii) broadcasting station. **"Ici poste de Toulouse,"** 'Toulouse calling.' *(e) P. téléphonique,* telephone set. *P. récepteur,* receiving set. **Entrée de poste,** telephone lead-in. **Ligne à postes groupés,** party line. *W.Tel: P. (portatif) de T.S.F.,* (portable) wireless set. *P. à accus,* battery set. S.a. ESSENCE 2. **2.** Post, place, appointment, *F:* berth. **Occuper un p. élevé,** to hold a high appointment, a high position. **3.** *Book-k:* Entry (in books).

poster [pɔste], *v.tr.* To post, set (sentry, etc.); to station (men).

se poster, to take up a position; to take one's stand.

postérieur [pɔsterjœːr]. **1.** *a.* Posterior. *(a)* (Of time) Subsequent (*à,* to); later. *(b)* (Of place) Hinder, hind. **Partie postérieure de la tête,** back of the head. **2.** *s.m. F:* Posterior(s); buttocks; *F:* bottom, backside.

postérieurement [pɔsterjœrmã], *adv.* Subsequently (*à,* to); at a later date.

postérité [pɔsterite], *s.f.* Posterity. *(a)* Descendants. **Laisser postérité,** to leave issue. *(b)* Generations yet unborn.

postes [pɔst], *s.f.pl. Arch:* Vitruvian scroll.

posthume [pɔstym], *a.* Posthumous. *adv.* **-ment.**

postiche [pɔstiʃ]. **1.** *a.* False (hair, moustache, etc.). *Dent p.,* false tooth. *Perle p.,* sham, imitation, pearl. *Canon p.,* dummy gun. **2.** *s.m.* *(a)* Piece of false hair. *(b)* Wig.

postier, -ière [pɔstje, -jɛːr]. **1.** *s.* Post-office employee. **2.** *s.m.* Post-horse.

postillon [pɔstijɔ̃], *s.m.* **1.** Postilion. **2.** Messenger (sent up the line of a kite). *P:* **Envoyer des postillons,** to sputter, splutter, in speaking.

postscolaire [pɔstskɔleːr], *a.* (i) After-school, (ii) post-graduate (instruction); continuation (class).

post-scriptum [pɔstskriptɔm], *s.m.inv.* Postscript; P.S.

postulant, -ante [pɔstylã, -ãːt], *s.* *(a)* Candidate, applicant (for post). *(b) Ecc:* Postulant.

postulat [pɔstyla], *s.m.* Postulate, assumption. **Admettre qch. en postulat,** to postulate sth.; to assume sth.

postuler [pɔstyle]. **1.** *v.tr.* To solicit, ask for, apply for (situation). **2.** *v.i.* (Of lawyer) To conduct a suit.

posture [pɔstyːr], *s.f.* **1.** Posture, attitude. **2.** Position. *Être en p. de faire qch.,* to be in a position, in a situation, to do sth.

pot [po], *s.m.* **1.** Pot, jug, can, jar. *Pot d'étain,* pewter tankard. *Pot de confiture,* pot of jam. *Pot à bière,* beer mug. *Pot de chambre,* chamberpot. **Pot de fleurs,** pot of flowers. **Pot à fleurs,** flower-pot. **Pot à eau** [pɔtao], water-jug, ewer. **Pot à lait** [pɔtalɛ], **le pot au lait** [pɔtɔlɛ], milk-jug, milk-can. **Pot pourri,** *Mus: etc:* pot-pourri, medley; *Perfumery:* pot-pourri. **Mettre en pot,** to pot (plant, meat, etc.). *F:* **Payer les pots cassés,** to pay the piper; to stand the racket. **Dîner à la fortune du pot,** to take pot-luck. **Le feu est au pot,** the fat is in the fire. **C'est le pot de terre contre le pot de fer,** he is up against more than his match. *Nau:* **Le pot au noir,** (i) the pitch-pot; (ii) the doldrums. *F:* **C'est le pot au noir,** it's a hopeless tangle. S.a. ANSE 1, ROSE 1, TOURNER 2. **2. Pot d'échappement,** (i) *Mch:* exhaust-tank; (ii) *I.C.E:* silencer, muffler.

potable [pɔtabl], *a.* **1.** Drinkable; fit to drink. **Eau potable,** drinking water. **2.** *F:* Fair; good enough. *Travail p.,* tolerably good work.

potache [pɔtaʃ], *s.m. Sch: F:* Schoolboy (attending *collège* or *lycée*).

potage [pɔtaːʒ], *s.m.* Soup. *F:* **J'ai reçu cent francs pour tout potage,** I got only a hundred francs all told; all I received was a hundred francs. [POT]

potager, -ère [pɔtaʒe, -ɛːr]. **1.** *a.* Of, for, the pot; for cooking. **Herbes potagères,** pot-herbs. **Plante potagère,** vegetable. **Jardin potager,** kitchen-garden. **2.** *s.m.* Kitchen-garden.

potamot [pɔtamo], *s.m. Bot:* Pondweed.

potard [pɔtaːr], *s.m. P:* Apothecary, chemist.

potasse [pɔtas], *s.f.* *(a) Ch:* Potash. *Chlorate de p.,* potassium chlorate. *(b) Com:* (Impure) potassium carbonate.

potasser [pɔtase], *v.tr. & i. Sch: F:* To swot, grind, at (sth.); to mug up (subject). *P. un examen,* to swot up for an examination.

potasseur [pɔtasœːr], *s.m. Sch: F:* Swotter.

potassium [pɔtasjɔm], *s.m. Ch:* Potassium.

pot-au-feu [pɔtofø], *s.m.inv.* **1.** Soup-pot, stock-pot. **2.** Beef-broth. **3.** Boiled beef with vegetables out of the pot. **4.** *a.inv.* Plain, homely, commonplace (matter or person).

pot-de-vin [pɔdvɛ̃], *s.m. F:* **1.** Douceur, gratuity. **2.** *(a)* Bribe. *(b)* Hush-money. *pl. Des pots-de-vin.*

pote [pɔt], *a.f. F:* (Of the hand) Big, swollen; clumsy.

poteau [pɔto], *s.m.* **1.** Post, pole, stake. *Min:* Pit-prop. *P. de réverbère,* lamp-post. *P. télégraphique,* telegraph-pole. *Sp: P. de départ,* starting-post. (Of horse) **Rester au poteau, to refuse to leave the post.** *P. d'arrivée,* winning-post. **Se faire battre sur le poteau, to be beaten on the post.** S.a. INDICATEUR 1. **2.** *P:* Chum, pal.

poteau-frontière, *s.m.* Frontier-post. *pl. Des poteaux-frontière.*

potée [pote], *s.f.* **1.** (a) Potful, jugful. (b) *F:* Swarm (of children, etc.). *J'en ai une p.,* I have quite a lot. **2.** Putty powder.

potelé [potle], *a.* Plump and dimpled (arm, etc.); chubby (cheek, child).

potelet [potlε], *s.m.* Small post, strut, or prop.

potence [potā:s], *s.f.* **1.** Gallows, gibbet. **Mettre, attacher, qn à la potence, to hang s.o. on the gallows.** *Échapper à la p.,* to cheat the gallows. S.a. GIBIER. **2.** (a) Support, arm, cross-piece, bracket; jib (of crane). *Cy:* Stem (of handle-bar). **En potence,** T-shaped. (b) (Hoisting) derrick. *Artil:* Loading davit. (c) Fork (of incandescent mantle).

potentat [potāta], *s.m.* Potentate.

potenti|el, -elle [potāsjεl]. **1.** *a.* Potential. **2.** *s.m.* (a) Potentialities (of a country, etc.). (b) *El:* Potential. *W.Tel:* P. de grille, grid potential. (c) *Gram:* Potential (mood). *adv.* **-ellement.**

potentille [potāti:j], *s.f. Bot:* Potentilla, cinque-foil. *P. ansérine,* goose-grass.

potentiomètre [potātjometr], *s.m. El:* Potentio-meter. *Cin:* Fader (of sound).

poter [pote], *v.tr. Golf:* (a) To put(t) (ball). (b) *Abs.* To hole out.

poterie [potri], *s.f.* **1.** (a) Pottery works. (b) Potter's workshop. (c) Potter's art. **2.** Pottery. *P. de grès,* stoneware. *P. de Delft,* delft. **3.** *P. d'étain,* pewter (ware).

poterne [potεrn], *s.f.* Postern (gate).

potiche [potiʃ], *s.f.* (Large) vase, esp. of Chinese or Japanese porcelain.

potier, -ière [potje, -jε:r], *s.* **1.** Potter. **2.** *P. d'étain,* pewterer.

potin[1] [potε̃], *s.m.* (a) Pinchbeck (metal). (b) Pewter; white metal. *P. jaune,* brass.

potin[2], *s.m. F:* **1.** (a) Piece of gossip. (b) *pl.* Gossip, tittle-tattle. **2. Faire du potin, to make a fuss or to kick up a row.**

potin|er [potine], *v.i. F:* To tittle-tattle, gossip. *s.m.* **-age.**

potinier, -ière [potinje, -jε:r]. *F:* **1.** *a.* Gos-sipy. **2.** *s.* Gossip(er), scandal-monger.

potion [posjɔ̃], *s.f. Med:* Potion, draught.

potiron [potirɔ̃], *s.m.* Pumpkin.

pou, *pl.* **poux** [pu], *s.m.* **1.** (a) Louse, *pl.* lice. *Œuf de pou,* nit. (b) *Pou de mouton,* sheep-tick. **2. Pou de mer,** sea-louse.

pouah [pwa], *int.* Faugh! ugh!

poubelle [pubεl], *s.f.* (Regulation pattern) dust-bin, refuse-bin. *F:* **Éplucheur de poubelles,** bin-raker, rag-picker.

pouce [pu:s], *s.m.* **1.** (a) Thumb. *F:* **Donner un coup de pouce à qch.,** (i) to give sth. a push; to shove sth. on; (ii) to deflect the course of (justice, etc.); (iii) *P:* to strangle, throttle (s.o.). **Donner le coup de pouce à qch.,** to give the finishing touches to sth. **Manger sur le pouce,** to take a snack. **Tourner ses pouces,** to twiddle, twirl, one's thumbs. **Serrer les pouces à qn,** (i) *A:* to apply the thumb-screw to s.o.; (ii) *F:* to put on the screw; to torment s.o. (into a confession). **Mettre les pouces,** to give in; to knuckle under. **Et le pouce, and something besides, and a bit over.** *Sch: P:* **Pouce! pax!** S.a. MORDRE 1. (b) Big toe. **2.** *A:* Inch.

Poucet [pusε]. **1.** *Pr.n.m.* **Le Petit Poucet,** Hop-o'-my-thumb, Tom Thumb. **2.** *s.m.* Cam lever.

poucettes [pusεt], *s.f.pl.* **1.** Thumb-cuffs, -fetters. **2.** *A:* Thumb-screw (instrument of torture). **Mettre les poucettes à qn, to put on, tighten, the screw.**

poucier [pusje], *s.m.* **1.** Thumb-stall. **2.** Thumb-piece (of door-latch).

pou-de-soie [putswa], *s.m. Tex:* Poult-de-soie; grained taffeta.

pouding [pudiŋ, -dε̃(:g)], *s.m.* Pudding, esp. suet pudding with raisins, or plum-pudding.

poudingue [pudε̃:g], *s.m. Miner:* Conglomerate, pudding-stone.

poudre [pu:dr], *s.f.* **1.** *A:* Dust. *F:* **Poudre aux yeux,** bluff. *Jeter de la p. aux yeux de qn,* to throw dust in s.o.'s eyes; to bluff s.o. **2.** Powder. *P. d'or,* gold-dust. *P. à lever,* baking-powder. *P. dentifrice,* tooth-powder. **Réduire qch. en poudre,** (i) to pulverize sth.; (ii) to smash sth. **to smithereens.** *Café en p.,* ground coffee. *P. vermifuge,* worm-powder. S.a. PERLIMPINPIN, PYRÈTHRE. **Poudre de riz,** toilet-powder, face-powder. *Elle met de la p.,* she powders (her face). **3.** (Generic term for) explosive (including gun-powder, cordite, dynamite, etc.). *P. de chasse,* sporting powder. *P. à canon,* gunpowder. **Tirer à poudre, to fire blank cartridge. Poudre-coton,** gun-cotton. *F:* **Être vif comme la poudre, to be very excitable.** *La nouvelle se répandit comme une traînée de p.,* the news spread like wildfire. **Il n'a pas inventé la poudre,** he won't set the Thames on fire.

poudre-éclair, *s.f. Phot:* Flash-powder.

poudr|er [pudre], *v.tr.* To powder; to sprinkle with powder; to dust on (flour, etc.). *Se p.,* to powder one's face, hair, etc. **Feuilles à poudrer,** papier-poudré. *s.m.* **-age.**

poudrerie [pudrəri], *s.f.* (Gun)powder-factory.

poudrette [pudrεt], *s.f.* Powdered night-soil (for manure).

poudreux, -euse [pudrø, -ø:z], *a.* Dusty.

poudrier [pudrie], *s.m.* Powder-box; compact.

poudrière [pudriε:r], *s.f.* **1.** Powder-flask, powder-horn. **2.** Powder-magazine. **3.** = POU-DRERIE.

poudrin [pudrε̃], *s.m.* Spindrift. [POUDRE]

poudroiement [pudrwamā], *s.m.* Dusty condi-tion; clouds of dust (on road, etc.).

poudroyant [pudrwajā], *a.* Dusty (road).

poudroyer [pudrwaje], *v.* (il poudroie; il pou-droiera) **1.** *v.tr.* To cover (sth.) with dust. **2.** *v.i.* To form clouds of dust.

pouf [puf]. **1.** *int.* (a) Plop! flop! plump! wallop! (b) (Denoting relief, oppressive heat, etc.) Phew! **2.** *s.m.* (a) Puff; inflated advertise-ment. (b) *Furn:* Pouf; humpty; dumpy; tuffet. (c) *Cost:* A: Bustle.

pouffant [pufā], *a. F:* Excruciatingly funny.

pouff|er [pufe], *v.i. & pr.* (Se) p. (de rire), to burst out laughing, to guffaw; to bubble over with laughter. *s.m.* **-ement.**

pouillerie [pujri], *s.f.* **1.** Abject poverty. **2.** (a) Filthy place, lousy hole. (b) (In hospital) Stripping-room. [POU]

pouilleux, -euse [pujø, -ø:z], *a.* **1.** Lousy, verminous. **2.** *F:* Miserable; abjectly poor. *Geog:* **La Champagne pouilleuse,** the barren regions of Champagne. [POU]

pouillot[1] [pujo], *s.m. Orn:* Willow-warbler.

poulailler[1] [pulaje], *s.m.* (a) Hen-house, hen-roost. (b) *Th: F:* (Top) gallery; 'the gods.'

poulailler[2], **-ère** [pulaje, -ε:r], *s.* Poulterer.

poulain [pulɛ̃], *s.m.* **1.** (*a*) Colt, foal. (*b*) *Box:* Trainee. **2.** *Furs:* Pony-skin. **3.** Skid (for unloading barrels).

poulaine [pulɛn], *s.f. Nau:* (*a*) (Ship's) head. (*b*) *pl.* Latrines (for crew); *F:* the 'heads.'

poularde [pulard], *s.f. Cu:* (Table-)fowl.

poule [pul], *s.f.* **1.** (*a*) Hen. *Cu:* Fowl. **Poule au pot,** boiled fowl. **Ma petite poule!** my dear! my pet! **Lait de poule,** (non-alcoholic) egg-flip, egg-nog. *F:* **Quand les poules auront des dents,** when pigs (begin to) fly. S.a. CHAIR 1, MOUILLÉ 1. (*b*) *P. d'eau,* moor-hen, marsh-hen. *P. de Guinée,* guinea-fowl, -hen. *P. d'Inde,* turkey-hen. **2.** (*a*) (At games) Pool. (*b*) (At races) Sweepstake.

poulet [pulɛ], *s.m.* **1.** (*a*) Chicken, chick. (*b*) *Cu:* Chicken. **2.** *A:* (Witty, playful, or amorous) letter (to lady).

poulette [pulɛt], *s.f.* **1.** Young hen; pullet. **2.** *F:* Girl, lass, lassie. **3.** *Cu:* **Sauce (à la) poulette,** German sauce (with chopped parsley).

pouliche [puliʃ], *s.f.* Filly.

poulie [puli], *s.f.* **1.** Pulley; (i) sheave, (ii) block. *P. simple, double,* single block, double block. S.a. GRADIN 2. **2.** (Belt-)pulley; driving-wheel.

pouliner [puline], *v.i.* (Of mare) To foal.

poulinière [pulinjɛːr], *a.f. & s.f.* (**Jument**) **poulinière,** brood-mare. [POULAIN]

pouliot¹ [puljo], *s.m. Bot:* Pennyroyal.

pouliot², *s.m.* Windlass (on dray, etc.).

poulpe [pulp], *s.m. Moll:* Octopus.

pouls [pu], *s.m. Physiol:* Pulse. **Tâter le pouls à qn,** (i) to feel s.o.'s pulse; (ii) *F:* to sound s.o.'s intentions. **Se tâter le pouls,** to reflect; to consider well.

poumon [pumɔ̃], *s.m.* Lung. **Respirer à pleins poumons,** to draw a deep breath. **Crier à pleins poumons,** to shout at the top of one's voice.

poupard [pupaːr]. **1.** *s.m.* (*a*) Baby in long clothes. (*b*) Baby-doll. **2.** *a.* Chubby (as a baby). *Physionomie pouparde,* baby face.

poupart [pupaːr], *s.m.* Edible crab.

poupe [pup], *s.f. Nau:* Stern, poop. **Avoir le vent en poupe,** (i) to have the wind aft; (ii) *F:* to be favoured by fortune; to be forging ahead.

poupée [pupe], *s.f.* **1.** Doll. *Maison de p.,* doll's house. *Jouer à la p.,* to play with dolls. **2.** (*a*) Puppet. (*b*) (Tailor's) dummy; (milliner's) block. **3.** *F:* Bandaged finger. **4.** Headstock, poppet(-head) (of lathe). **5.** *Nau:* Belaying-pin.

poupin, -ine [pupɛ̃, -in], *a.* Rosy(-cheeked). *Visage p.,* baby face.

poupon, -onne [pupɔ̃, -ɔn], *s. F:* Baby.

pouponnière [pupɔnjɛːr], *s.f.* Day-nursery.

pour [puːr]. I. *prep.* For. **1.** (*a*) Instead of. *Allez-y pour moi,* go in my stead. **Traduire mot pour mot,** to translate word for word. *Agir pour qn,* to act on s.o.'s behalf. (*b*) *Il me veut pour femme,* he wants me for, as, his wife. *Tenir qn pour fou,* to regard s.o. as a madman. *Laisser qn pour mort,* to leave s.o. for dead. *F:* **C'est pour de bon, pour de vrai,** I am in earnest. (*c*) (Direction) *Je pars pour la France,* I am starting for France. *Bon pour les pauvres,* good to the poor. (*d*) (i) (Time) *Je vais en Suisse pour quinze jours,* I am going to Switzerland for a fortnight. *Pour toujours,* for ever. *Il sera ici pour quatre heures,* he will be here by four o'clock. (ii) *J'en ai pour huit jours,* it will take me a week. *Trois coups pour deux sous,* three shies a penny. *Pour deux francs de chocolat,* two francs' worth of chocolate. *Être pour beaucoup, pour peu, dans une affaire,* to count for much, for little, in a business. S.a. MOINS 1. (*e*) (Purpose) *Je suis ici pour affaires,* I am here on business. *Vêtements pour hommes,* garments for men. *J'épargne pour quand je serai vieux,* I am saving for my old age. *C'est pour cela qu'il est venu,* that is why he came. (*f*) Because of, for the sake of. *Pour l'amour de Dieu,* for heaven's sake. *Faites-le pour moi,* do it for my sake. *J'avais peur pour lui,* I was nervous on his account. *Mourir pour sa patrie,* to die for one's country. *L'art pour l'art,* art for art's sake. *Pour la forme,* for form's sake. **Beaucoup de bruit pour rien,** much ado about nothing. (*g*) In favour of. *Parler pour qn,* to speak in favour of s.o. *Adv.* **Moi, je suis pour,** I am in favour of it. *Le vote est pour,* the ayes have it. **Parler pour et contre,** to speak for and against. (*h*) With regard to. *Pour mon compte,* for my part; as far as I am concerned. **Pour ce qui est de . . .,** as concerns . . ., as regards . . ., with regard to. . . . *Pour (ce qui est de) moi . . .,* as for me . . ., for my part. . . . *Pour moi, je veux bien,* personally, I am willing. *F:* **Pour de la chance, c'est de la chance,** you are in luck and no mistake. (*i*) For lack of. *Pour un moine l'abbaye ne chôme pas,* for want of one monk the abbey does not stand idle. (*j*) *Dix pour cent,* ten per cent. **2. Pour +** *inf.* (*a*) (In order) to. *Il faut manger pour vivre,* one must eat to live. **Pour ainsi dire,** so to speak. *Il s'en va pour ne jamais revenir,* he is going away for good. (*b*) (After *assez, trop*) *Être trop faible pour marcher,* to be too weak to walk. (*c*) Considering. *Il est bien ignorant pour avoir étudié si longtemps,* he is very ignorant considering the long time he has studied. (*d*) Although. *Pour être petit il n'en est pas moins brave,* though small he is none the less brave. *Nous ne perdrons rien pour attendre,* we shall lose nothing by waiting. (*e*) Because of. *Je le sais pour l'avoir vu,* I know it through having seen it. *Il est mort pour avoir trop travaillé,* he died of overwork. (*f*) Of a nature to. *Cela n'est pas pour me surprendre,* that does not come as a surprise to me. *Cette amitié n'était pas pour lui plaire,* this friendship was not to his liking. (*g*) *F:* **Être pour partir,** to be about to start. **3.** (*a*) **Pour que +** *sub.,* in order that. *Je vous dis cela pour que vous soyez sur vos gardes,* I am telling you that in order that you may be on your guard. *Il est trop tard pour qu'elle sorte,* it is too late for her to go out. *F:* **Pour ne pas que +** *sub.* *Mettez-le là, pour ne pas qu'on l'oublie,* put it there so that it won't be forgotten. (*b*) (Concessive) **Pour (+** *adj.* or *sb.*) **que +** *sub.,* however, although. *Cette situation, pour terrible qu'elle soit,* this situation, terrible though it may be. (*c*) **Pour peu que +** *sub.,* if only, if ever. *Pour peu que vous hésitiez vous êtes flambé,* if you hesitate but a moment, if you hesitate at all, it is all up with you.

II. **pour,** *s.m.* Peser le pour et le contre, to weigh the pros and cons. *Entendre le pour et le contre,* to hear both sides.

pourboire [purbwaːr], *s.m.* Tip, gratuity. *Donner un p. au porteur,* to tip the porter.

pourceau [purso], *s.m.* Hog, pig, swine. **Jeter des perles aux pourceaux,** to cast pearls before swine.

pour-cent, *s.m.* Percentage; rate per cent.

pourcentage [pursɑ̃taːʒ], *s.m.* Percentage; amount per cent; rate (of interest).

pourchass|er [purʃase], *v.tr.* To pursue, to follow hot on the track of (game, etc.). *P. un débiteur,* to dun, harry, a debtor. *P. un emploi, F:* to be after a job. *s.m.* **-eur.**

pourfendeur [purfɑ̃dœːr], *s.m.* **Pourfendeur de géants,** swashbuckler, swaggerer.

pourfendre [purfɑ̃ːdr], *v.tr. A:* To cleave in twain.

pourlécher [purleʃe], *v.tr.* (je pourlèche; je pourlécherai) **1.** Se pourlécher les babines, to lick one's chops. **2.** *F:* To polish up, finish with care (verses, sketch).

pourparlers [purparle], *s.m.pl.* (a) *Mil:* Parley. (b) Diplomatic conversation; pourparlers. Entrer en pourparlers, entamer des pourparlers, to enter on, enter into, negotiations (*avec*, with).

pourpier [purpje], *s.m. Bot:* Purslane.

pourpoint [purpwɛ̃], *s.m. Cost: A:* Pourpoint, doublet.

pourpre [purpr]. **1.** *s.f.* (a) Purple (dye) (of the ancients). (b) Royal or imperial dignity. Né dans la pourpre, born in the purple. **2.** *s.m.* (a) Crimson; rich red. Le *p.* lui monta au visage, he turned crimson, he flushed up. (b) *Her:* Purpure. (c) *Med:* Purpura, *F:* purples. **3.** *a.* Crimson.

pourpré [purpre], *a.* Purple or crimson.

pourquoi [purkwa], *adv. & conj.* Why? Pourquoi faire? what for? Pourquoi cela? why so? Mais *p.* donc? what on earth for? ·Voilà *p.*, that's (the reason) why. Pourquoi pas? pourquoi non? why not? *P:* Demandez-moi pourquoi, ask me another! C'est pourquoi, therefore; wherefore.

pourrir [puri:r]. **1.** *v.i.* To rot, decay; to become rotten; to go bad; (of egg) to addle. Faire pourrir, to rot (wood, etc.). **2.** *v.tr.* To rot.
  se pourrir, to go bad; (of egg) to addle.

pourri, *a.* Rotten; rotted (wood); putrid (flesh). *F:* Il est pourri de vices, he is rotten to the core. P. *d'orgueil*, eaten up with self-conceit. S.a. BOURG 2, TERRE 4.

pourriture [purity:r], *s.f.* **1.** Rotting, rot, decay. Pourriture sèche (*du bois*), dry rot. Pourriture d'hôpital, hospital gangrene. En pourriture, putrescent, rotting. **2.** Rottenness.

poursuite [pursɥit], *s.f.* **1.** Pursuit; chase (of enemy ship); tracking (of criminal). Être à la poursuite de qch., to be in pursuit of sth. Se mettre, s'élancer, à la poursuite de qn, to set off in pursuit of s.o.; to chase after s.o. **2.** Usu. pl. *Jur:* Lawsuit, action; prosecution; suing (of debtor). Engager, entamer, intenter, commencer, exercer, des poursuites (judiciaires) contre qn, to take, institute, proceedings, to take (legal) action, against s.o.

poursuivant, -ante [pursɥivã, -ã:t], *s.* (a) Plaintiff, prosecutor. (b) *Her:* Poursuivant d'armes, poursuivant (at arms).

poursuivre [pursɥi:vr], *v.tr.* (Conj. like SUIVRE) **1.** To pursue; to go after, make after (s.o., an animal); to chase. Ce songe me poursuit, that dream haunts me. Poursuivi par la guigne, dogged by ill-luck. **2.** P. *qn en justice*, to prosecute s.o.; to sue (debtor); to proceed against s.o. **3.** To pursue, continue, proceed with, go on with (story, etc.). P. un travail, to carry on a work. P. un avantage, to follow up an advantage; to press an advantage. Les préparatifs se poursuivent, preparations are going on. Abs. Poursuivez, go on; continue (your story).

pourtant [purtã], *adv.* Nevertheless, however, still, (and) yet. . . .

pourtour [purtu:r], *s.m.* Periphery, circumference, compass (of building). P. *d'une cathédrale*, precincts of a cathedral. Mur de *p.*, enclosure wall (of prison, town).

pourvoi [purvwa], *s.m. Jur:* (a) Appeal. (b) P. en grâce, petition for mercy. [POURVOIR]

pourvoir [purvwa:r], *v.* (*pr.p.* pourvoyant; *p.p.* pou~vu; *pr.ind.* je pourvois, n. pourvoyons; *pr.sub.* je pourvoie; *p.h.* je pourvus; *fu.* je pourvoirai) To provide. **1.** *v.ind.tr.* P~ aux besoins de qn, to provide for the wants of s.o.

P. aux frais, to defray the cost. P. à un emploi, to fill (up) a post. On n'y a pas pourvu, no provision has been made for it. **2.** *v.tr.* (a) P. qn de qch., to supply, provide, furnish, equip, s.o. with sth. Se p. d'argent, to provide oneself with money. P. qn d'une charge, to invest s.o. with, appoint s.o. to, an office. Pourvoir sa fille, to settle one's daughter. (b) To equip, fit (de, with).
  se pourvoir. *Jur:* (a) Se p. en cassation, to lodge an appeal with the Supreme Court. (b) Se p. en grâce, to petition for mercy.

pourvu que, *conj.phr.* Provided (that); so long as. *F:* Pourvu qu'il ne fasse pas de gaffes! I only hope he won't make any blunders!

pourvoyeur, -euse [purvwajœ:r, -ø:z], *s.* Purveyor, provider; contractor; caterer.

poussa(h) [pusa], *s.m.* (a) (Toy) tumbler, tumble-over. (b) *F:* Pot-bellied individual.

pousse [pus], *s.f.* **1.** Growth (of leaves, hair, feathers). P. des dents, cutting of teeth. **2.** Young shoot, sprout.

pousse-café, *s.m.inv. F:* (Glass of) liqueur (after coffee); 'chaser.'

pousse-cailloux, *s.m.inv. P:* Infantryman, foot-slogger.

pousse-pousse [puspus], *s.m. inv.* **1.** (a) Jin-ricksha, rickshaw. (b) Child's go-cart. **2.** Rickshaw-man.

pousser [puse]. **1.** *v.tr.* (a) To push, shove, thrust. Ne poussez pas! don't push! don't shove! P. qn du coude, to nudge s.o. (Of wind) P. un navire à la côte, to blow a ship ashore. P. le verrou, to shoot the bolt. P. la porte, to push the door to. *F:* Montez; je vais vous pousser un bout, get in; I'll give you a lift. *Boating:* Pousser du fond, to punt. (b) To drive, impel, urge. P. qn à faire qch., to egg s.o. on, to induce s.o., to do sth. Poussé par la pitié, prompted by pity. Poussé par la nécessité, under the pressure of necessity. (c) To push on, urge forward (piece of work); to elaborate (ornamentation, etc.). P. une attaque à fond, to push, thrust, drive, an attack home. P. une promenade jusqu'à la ville, to extend a walk as far as the town. P. la guerre jusqu'au bout, to carry the war to its conclusion. P. la vente, to push the sales. P. un cheval, (i) to urge on a horse; (ii) to try a horse's mettle. P. un écolier, to push on a pupil. S.a. BOUT 1. *Mch:* P. les feux, to raise steam, to stoke up. El: P. une lampe, to over-run a lamp. (d) (Of trees, etc.) To put forth, shoot forth, shoot out (leaves, roots). (e) To utter (cry), to heave, fetch (sigh). **2.** *v.i.* (a) To push. P. à la roue, to put one's shoulder to the wheel. (b) To push on, push forward, make one's way (to a place). (c) (Of plants, etc.) To grow, shoot, burgeon; (of hair, nails) to grow. Laisser pousser sa barbe, to grow a beard. Les dents commencent à lui p., he is beginning to cut his teeth. Tous ces enfants poussent, all these children are shooting up.
  se pousser, to push oneself forward; to make one's way; to shove, elbow, one's way to the front.

poussé, *a.* Elaborate (ornamentation, etc.); deep, searching (study). Cliché trop *p.*, over-developed negative. *I.C.E:* Moteur poussé, high-efficiency engine.

poussée, *s.f.* **1.** (a) Thrust. P. latérale d'une voûte, lateral thrust of an arch. (b) P. du vent, wind-pressure. Centre de poussée, centre of pressure. (c) Buoyancy (of liquid). Force de poussée, upward thrust. Centre de poussée, centre of buoyancy. (d) Lift (of balloon). **2.** (a) Pushing, pressure (of crowd). (b) *Com:*

Forte p. en hausse, strong upward tendency (of the market). **3.** Push, shove. *Fb: P. irrégulière*, foul. *Écarter qch. d'une poussée*, to push, shove, sth. aside. **4.** (a) Sprouting, growth. *P. de boutons*, outbreak of pimples. (b) *P. de la sève*, rising of the sap. **5.** *P. de fièvre*, bout of fever.

poussette [pusɛt], *s.f.* **1.** (Game of) push-pin. **2.** *F:* = POUSSE-POUSSE I (b).

poussier [pusje], *s.m.* Coal-dust; slack.

poussière [pusjɛːr], *s.f.* **1.** Dust. *Enlever la p. des meubles*, to dust the furniture. *S'en aller en poussière*, to crumble into dust. *Réduire qch. en poussière*, (i) to reduce sth. to dust; (ii) to smash sth. to atoms. *Mordre la poussière*, to bite the dust. *S.a.* ASPIRATEUR 2. **2.** *Poussière d'eau*, (fine) spray; spindrift.

poussiéreux, -euse [pusjerø, -øːz], *a.* **1.** Dust-like. **2.** Dusty.

poussif, -ive [pusif, -iːv], *a.* (a) Broken-winded (horse). (b) *F:* Wheezy, short-winded (person).

poussin [pusɛ̃], *s.m.* (a) Chick. (b) *Cu:* Spring chicken.

poussinière [pusinjɛːr], *s.f.* (a) Chicken-coop. (b) Incubator.

poussoir [puswaːr], *s.m.* Push-button, -piece (of electric bell, repeater watch); thumb-piece. *P. de soupape*, push-rod of a valve. *P. à ressort*, trigger.

poutre [puːtr], *s.f.* **1.** (Wooden) beam; balk. *P. de faîte*, ridge-piece, roof-tree. *P. de plancher*, ceiling joist. **2.** Girder. *P. à âme pleine*, plate-girder. *P. armée*, trussed girder.

poutrelle [putrɛl], *s.f.* Small beam or girder. *Av:* Spar (of wing).

pouvoir [puvwaːr]. **I.** *v.tr.* (*pr.p.* pouvant; *p.p.* pu; *pr.ind.* je puis or je peux (always puis-je [pɥiːʒ]), tu peux, il peut, n. pouvons, ils peuvent; *pr.sub.* je puisse, n. puissions; *p.d.* je pouvais; *p.h.* je pus; *fu.* je pourrai [pure]) **1.** To be able; 'can.' *Je ne puis (pas) le faire*, I cannot do it; I am unable to do it. *Cela ne peut (pas) se faire*, it cannot be done. *Comment a-t-il pu dire cela?* how could he say that? *Il aurait pu le faire s'il avait voulu*, he could have done it if he had wanted to. *J'ai fait toutes les démarches que j'ai pu*, I took every step that I possibly could. *J'ai pu le revoir*, I managed to see him again. *Je n'y puis rien*, I cannot help it. *On n'y peut rien*, (i) it can't be helped; (ii) there is nothing that can be done. *Il a été on ne peut plus grossier*, he was most rude. *Il travaille on ne peut mieux*, he could not work better. *N'en plus pouvoir*, to be tired out, exhausted. *Les chevaux n'en peuvent plus*, the horses are spent. *S.a.* MAIS I. *Sauve qui peut*, every man for himself. *On ne peut pas ne pas l'admirer*, one cannot but admire him. *Je viendrai aussitôt que je pourrai*, I will come as soon as I can. *v.pr. Si cela se peut, si faire se peut*, if it can be done; if possible. **2.** 'May.' (a) To be allowed. *Vous pouvez partir*, you may go. *Puis-je entrer?* may I, shall I, come in? (b) (Optative) *Puissiez-vous dire vrai!* may what you say be true! **3.** To be possible, probable. *Cela peut (bien) être, v.pr. cela se peut (bien)*, it may be; it is quite possible; may be! possibly! *La porte a pu se fermer toute seule, la porte peut s'être fermée toute seule*, the door may have closed of itself. *La chose aurait pu arriver plus tôt*, it might have happened sooner. *Il pouvait avoir dix ans*, he may, might, have been ten. *Advienne que pourra*, come what may. *v.pr. Il peut se faire, il peut arriver, que + sub.*, it may be, may happen, that . . .

II. pouvoir, *s.m.* Power. **1.** (a) Force, means. *Il n'est pas en mon pouvoir de . . .*,

it is not within my power to. . . . *Je vous aiderai de tout mon pouvoir*, I will do all I possibly can to help you. *En dehors de mon pouvoir*, beyond my power. (b) *Ch: Ph:* Pouvoir éclairant, illuminating power. *P. calorifique*, heating value. *P. radiant*, radiating capacity. **2.** Influence, sway. *Avoir un p. absolu sur qn*, to hold complete sway over s.o. *Tomber au p. de l'ennemi*, to fall into the hands of the enemy. *Être au pouvoir de qn*, to be in s.o.'s power. **3.** (a) *P. paternel*, paternal authority. (b) Competency, warrant, power. *En dehors de mes pouvoirs*, not within my competence; not within my sphere. *Agir en dehors de ses pouvoirs*, to act *ultra vires*. (c) *Ambitionner le p.*, to aim at power. *Prendre le pouvoir*, (i) to assume power; (ii) to take office. *Le parti au pouvoir*, the party in power. *Le quatrième pouvoir*, the fourth estate, the Press. **4.** *Jur:* Power of attorney; procuration. *Avoir, recevoir, plein(s) pouvoir(s) pour agir*, to have full powers, to be (fully) empowered, to act. *Se présenter sans pouvoirs réguliers*, to come without full credentials. *S.a.* FONDÉ 2.

pouzzolane [puzɔlan], *s.f.* Pozzolana.

pragmatique [pragmatik], *a.* Pragmatic. *adv.* **-ment**, -ally.

pragmatisme [pragmatism], *s.m.* Pragmatism.

prairial [prɛrjal], *s.m. Fr.Hist:* Ninth month of Fr. Republican calendar (May-June).

prairie [prɛri], *s.f.* (a) Meadow. (b) Grass-land.

praline [pralin], *s.f.* Burnt almond; praline.

praliner [praline], *v.tr. Cu:* To brown (almonds, etc.) in sugar.

praticabilité [pratikabilite], *s.f.* Practicability, practicableness; feasibility, feasibleness.

praticable [pratikabl], *a.* **1.** Practicable. (a) Feasible (plan, idea). (b) Passable, negotiable (road, ford). (c) *Th:* Practicable (door, window). **2.** Sociable; easy to get on with.

praticien [pratisjɛ̃], *s.m.* (a) (Legal, medical) practitioner. (b) Practical man; expert. (c) *Art:* Sculptor's rougher-out.

pratiquant [pratikɑ̃], *a. Catholique p.*, practising Catholic; Catholic who partakes of the sacrament.

pratique[1] [pratik], *a.* **1.** Practical, useful (method, article). *Sens p.*, practical common sense. **2.** Experienced (person). *adv.* **-ment**.

pratique[2], *s.f.* **1.** Practice; application (of theory). *Mettre qch. en pratique*, to put sth. into practice; to apply (system). *C'est de pratique courante*, it is the usual practice; it is quite usual. **2.** (a) Practice, experience. *P. du théâtre*, theatrical experience. *Perdre la pratique de qch.*, to lose the knack of sth.; to get out of practice. *Êtes-vous dans la p. des affaires?* are you a practical business man? (b) *Jur:* Practice (of the law). *Terme de pratique*, legal term. (c) *Avoir des pratiques avec l'ennemi*, to have dealings with the enemy. *Il avait vécu dans la p. des employés de ministères*, he had associated with civil servants. **3.** *Pratiques religieuses*, religious observances. *Pratiques clandestines*, underhand practices. **4.** Custom, business (of tradesman). (Of customer) *Donner sa p. à qn*, to give s.o. one's custom. **5.** (Tradesman's) customer. **6.** *Jur:* Libre pratique, free exercise (of one's religion). *Nau:* Avoir libre pratique, to be out of quarantine. **7.** (Puppet-showman's) squeaker.

pratiquer [pratike], *v.tr.* **1.** To practise (rules, virtues); to employ, use. *Voilà comment cela se pratique ici*, that is how it is usually done here. *P. les conseils de qn*, to put into practice s.o.'s advice. *Médecin qui pratique dans cette ville,* doctor who practises in this town. *Il ne pratique plus,* he is no longer in practice. *Com: Les cours pratiqués,* the ruling prices. **2.** *P. un escalier dans l'épaisseur d'un mur,* to contrive, cut, a stair in, to work a stair into, the thickness of a wall. *P. une ouverture dans un mur,* to make an opening in a wall. **3.** To frequent; to associate with (s.o.). *J'ai pratiqué le monde,* I have lived in the world.

pratiqué, *a.* Accustomed, trained (*à,* to).

pré [pre], *s.m.* Meadow. *A :* Aller **sur le pré,** to fight a duel. S.a. SALÉ I.

préalable [prealabl]. **I.** *a.* (*a*) Previous (*à,* to). Réclamer, poser, la question préalable, to call for, to move, the previous question. (*b*) Preliminary (agreement). **2.** *s.m.* **Au préalable,** to begin with, as a preliminary. *adv.* **-ment.**

préambule [preãbyl], *s.m.* Preamble (*de,* to).

préamplificateur [preãplifikatœːr], *F :* **préampli,** *s.m.* *El.E :* *Cin :* First-stage (sound) amplifier; preamplifier.

préau [preo], *s.m.* (*a*) (Court)yard (esp. of prison); playground (of school). (*b*) (Covered) ambulatory (round playground).

préavis [preavi], *s.m.* Previous notice.

prébende [prebãːd], *s.f.* *Ecc :* Prebend.

prébendier [prebãdje], *s.m.* *Ecc :* Prebendary.

précaire [prekeːr], *a.* (*a*) Precarious (tenure, etc.). (*b*) Delicate (health); precarious (state of health). *adv.* **-ment.**

précaution [prekosjɔ̃], *s.f.* **I.** Precaution. *Prendre des précautions,* to take precautions (*pour,* for). *Mesures de p.,* precautionary measures. **2.** Caution, wariness; care. **Avec précaution,** cautiously; warily.

précautionner [prekosjɔne], *v.tr.* To warn, caution (*contre,* against). *se précautionner contre qch.,* to take precautions, to guard, against sth.

précautionneu|x, -euse [prekosjɔnø, -øːz], *a.* Cautious, wary, precautious; careful. *adv.* **-sement.**

précédemment [presedamã], *adv.* Previously, already, before.

précédence [presedãːs], *s.f.* Precedence (*de,* of); priority.

précédent [presedã]. **I.** *a.* Preceding, previous, former. *Le jour p.,* the day before, the previous day. **2.** *s.m.* Precedent. *Créer un p.,* to create, set, a precedent. **Fait sans précédents,** unprecedented occurrence.

précéder [presede], *v.tr.* (Conj. like CÉDER) **I.** To precede, to go before. *La musique précède les troupes,* the band marches in front of the troops. *La page qui précède,* the preceding page, the page before. *Ce qui précède,* the foregoing. **2.** *P. qn (en dignité),* to have precedence of s.o.

précepte [presept], *s.m.* Precept.

précepteur, -trice [preseptœːr, -tris], *s.* Family tutor; (private) teacher; *f.* governess.

préceptoral, -aux [preseptɔral, -o], *a.* Tutorial.

précession [presesjɔ̃], *s.f.* *Astr :* Precession.

prêche [preʃ], *s.m.* Protest.Rel : Sermon.

prêche-malheur, *s. m. & f. inv.* Prophet(ess) of evil; *F :* croaker.

prêcher [preʃe], *v.tr.* **I.** (*a*) To preach (the Gospel, etc.) (*à,* to). *P. l'économie,* to preach, extol, economy. **Prêcher d'exemple,** to practise what one preaches. S.a. DÉSERT[2], SAINT 2. (*b*) *P. à qn de faire qch.,* to exhort s.o. to do sth. **2.** To preach (s.o.); to exhort. *F :* **Prêcher un converti,** to preach to the converted.

prêcheur, -euse [preʃœːr, -øːz]. **I.** *a.* (*a*) Preaching (friar). (*b*) *F :* Sermonizing, preachy (person). **2.** *s. F :* Sermonizer, preacher.

précieu|x, -euse [presjø, -øːz]. **I.** *a.* (*a*) Precious. (*b*) Valuable (advice, help, time) (*à,* to). (*c*) Affected, mannered (style). **2.** *s.m.* = PRÉCIOSITÉ. **3.** *s.f.* *Fr.Lit.Hist :* Précieuse, Précieuse. *adv.* **-sement.**

préciosité [presjozite], *s.f.* (*a*) Preciosity; concettism. (*b*) Affectation, affectedness.

précipice [presipis], *s.m.* (*a*) Precipice. (*b*) Beetling height.

précipitable [presipitabl], *a.* *Ch :* Precipitable.

précipitamment [presipitamã], *adv.* Precipitately, headlong. *Entrer, sortir, monter, descendre, p.,* to rush or hurry in, out, up, down. *Agir trop p.,* to be too precipitate.

précipitant [presipitã], *s.m.* *Ch :* Precipitant; precipitating agent.

précipitation [presipitasjɔ̃], *s.f.* **I.** Precipitancy, violent hurry, hot haste. **Sortir avec précipitation,** to hurry, hasten, out. **2.** (*a*) *Ch :* *Ph :* Precipitation. (*b*) *Meteor :* Precipitation, esp. rain.

précipiter [presipite], *v.tr.* **I.** (*a*) To precipitate; to throw down, hurl down. *P. un peuple dans la guerre,* to rush, precipitate, a people into war. (*b*) *Ch :* To precipitate (a substance). *v.i.* (Of substance) To form a precipitate. **2.** To hurry, hasten, precipitate (departure, etc.). *Ne précipitons rien,* let us not be over-hasty. *se précipiter.* **I.** To dash, to rush headlong, to make a rush (*sur,* at, upon). **2.** *Ch :* To precipitate, to be precipitated.

précipité. **I.** *a.* Precipitate; hasty; hurried, headlong (flight); abrupt (departure). *S'avancer à pas précipités,* to hasten forward, to hasten up. **2.** *s.m.* *Ch :* etc : Precipitate.

précis [presi]. **I.** *a.* Precise, exact, accurate, definite; unambiguous. *Exiger d'une façon précise que . . .,* to call definitely for. . . . *A deux heures précises,* at two o'clock precisely. *Je suis parti sans raison précise,* I left for no definite reason. *En termes p.,* in distinct terms. **2.** *s.m.* Abstract, summary, précis; epitome. **Précis d'histoire de France,** short history of France.

précisément [presizemã], *adv.* (*a*) Precisely, exactly. (*b*) *C'est p. l'homme que je cherche,* he is just the man I am looking for.

préciser [presize], *v.tr.* (*a*) To specify; to state (sth.) precisely. *P. des règles de procédure,* to specify rules of procedure. *P. les détails,* to go further into detail. **Sans rien préciser,** (i) without going into details, (ii) without pinning oneself down to anything. (*b*) *Abs.* To be precise, explicit.

précision [presizjɔ̃], *s.f.* **I.** Precision, preciseness, exactness, accuracy. *P. de tir,* accuracy of fire. *Instruments de p.,* precision instruments. **2.** *Donner, apporter, des précisions sur qch.,* to give precise details about sth. **Demander des précisions sur qch.,** to ask for full particulars regarding sth.

précité [presite], *a.* Aforesaid; above-mentioned.

précoce [prekɔs], *a.* Precocious; early, forward (fruit). *adv.* **-ment.**

précocité [prekɔsite], *s.f.* Precocity; precociousness; forwardness (of season).

préconception [prekɔ̃sepsjɔ̃], *s.f.* Preconception; prejudice.

préconcevoir [prekɔ̃savwaːr], *v.tr.* (Conj. like CONCEVOIR) To preconceive.

préconiser [prekɔnize], *v.tr.* To (re)commend, praise; to advocate (course of action).

préconnaissance [prekɔnesãːs], *s.f.* Foreknowledge, precognition.

préconscient [prekɔ̃sjã], *s.m.* Fore-conscious.

précurseur [prekyrsœ:r]. **1.** s.m. Precursor, forerunner; harbinger (of spring). **2.** a.m. Precursory; premonitory (sign).

prédécéder [predesede], v.i. (Conj. like DÉCÉDER) To die first.

prédécès [predesɛ], s.m. Predecease.

prédécesseur [predesɛsœ:r], s.m. Predecessor.

prédestination [predɛstinasjɔ̃], s.f. Predestination.

prédestiner [predɛstine], v.tr. To predestinate, predestine, foredoom (à, to).

prédétermination [predetɛrminasjɔ̃], s.f. Predetermination.

prédéterminer [predetɛrmine], v.tr. To predetermine.

prédicat [predika], s.m. Gram: Log: Predicate.

prédicateur [predikatœ:r], s.m. Preacher.

prédicatif, -ive [predikatif, -i:v], a. Gram: Predicative.

prédication [predikasjɔ̃], s.f. **1.** Preaching. **2.** Sermon.

prédiction [prediksjɔ̃], s.f. Prediction. **1.** Predicting, foretelling. **2.** Forecast.

prédilection [predilɛksjɔ̃], s.f. Predilection, partiality, fondness (pour, for). Auteur de prédilection, favourite author.

prédire [predi:r], v.tr. (Conj. like DIRE except pr. ind. & imp. (v.) prédisez) To predict, prophesy, foretell, forecast.

prédisposer [predispoze], v.tr. To predispose (à, to). P. qn contre qn, to prejudice, bias, s.o. against s.o.

prédisposition [predispozisjɔ̃], s.f. **1.** Predisposition (à, to). P. à l'arthrite, arthritic diathesis. P. au vice, propensity to vice. P. aux accidents, proneness to accidents. **2.** Predisposition (en faveur de, in favour of); prejudice, bias (contre, against).

prédominance [predɔminɑ̃:s], s.f. Predominance, prevalence.

prédominant [predɔminɑ̃], a. Predominant, predominating, prevailing, prevalent.

prédominer [predɔmine]. **1.** v.i. To predominate, prevail; to have the upper hand (sur, over). **2.** v.tr. L'intérêt prédomine tout, interest always comes first.

prééminence [preeminɑ̃:s], s.f. Pre-eminence.

prééminent [preeminɑ̃], a. Pre-eminent.

préemptif, -ive [preɑ̃ptif, -i:v], a. Pre-emptive.

préemption [preɑ̃psjɔ̃], s.f. Pre-emption.

préétablir [preetabli:r], v.tr. To pre-establish.

préétabli, a. Pre-established; pre-ordained.

préexistant [preɛgzistɑ̃], a. Pre-existent.

préexistence [preɛgzistɑ̃:s], s.f. Pre-existence.

préexister [preɛgziste], v.i. To pre-exist; to be pre-existent (à, to).

préface [prefas], s.f. **1.** Preface, foreword (à, de, to). **2.** Ecc: Preface.

préfacer [prefase], v.tr. To write a preface to, for (a work).

préfectoral, -aux [prefɛktɔral, -o], a. Prefector(i)al; of the prefect.

préfecture [prefɛkty:r], s.f. **1.** Rom.Ant: (a) Prefectship. (b) Prefecture. **2.** Fr.Adm: Prefecture. **3.** La Préfecture de police, the headquarters of the (Paris) police. **4.** Préfecture maritime, port-admiral's head-quarters.

préférable [preferabl], a. Preferable (à, to); more advisable; better. adv. -**ment.**

préférence [preferɑ̃:s], s.f. Preference. De préférence à, in preference to. Donner, accorder, la préférence à qn, to give s.o. preference (sur, over). Tarif de préférence, preferential tariff.

Droits de p., priority rights. Actions de préférence, preference shares, preferred shares.

préférer [prefere], v.tr. (je préfère; je préférerai) To prefer (à, to); to like better. Je préférerais que vous veniez, I would rather (that) you came. Il préféra mourir que de se rendre, he preferred death to surrender.

préféré, -ée, a. & s. Favourite.

préfet [prefɛ], s.m. **1.** Rom.Ant: Fr.Adm: Prefect. **2.** Le préfet de police, the prefect, chief commissioner, of the Paris police. **3.** Préfet maritime, port-admiral. **4.** Sch: Préfet des études, vice-principal.

préfète [prefɛt], s.f. F: The prefect's wife.

préfixe [prefiks], s.m. (a) Gram: Prefix. (b) Code letter.

préfixer [prefikse], v.tr. **1.** To fix, settle, (date) beforehand. **2.** To prefix (a particle to the verb).

préhenseur [preɑ̃sœ:r], a.m. Prehensile.

préhension [preɑ̃sjɔ̃], s.f. Prehension, gripping.

préhistoire [preistwa:r], s.f. Prehistory.

préhistorique [preistɔrik], a. Prehistoric.

préjudice [preʒydis], s.m. Prejudice, detriment; (moral) injury; wrong, damage; Jur: tort. Porter, faire, préjudice à qn, to inflict injury, loss, on s.o. Au préjudice de qn, to the prejudice, detriment, of s.o. Sans préjudice de . . ., without prejudice to. . . .

préjudiciable [preʒydisjabl], a. Prejudicial, injurious, detrimental (à, to). Jur: Tortious.

préjudicier [preʒydisje], v.i. To be detrimental, prejudicial (à, to).

préjuger [preʒyʒe], v.tr. (Conj. like JUGER) To prejudge. Autant qu'on peut p., as far as one can judge beforehand.

préjugé, s.m. **1.** Jur: Precedent (in law). **2.** Presumption. Les préjugés sont contre lui, appearances are against him. **3.** Prejudice, preconception, prepossession; pl. antiquated notions. Avoir un p. pour, vers, qch., to have a bias towards sth. Gens à préjugés, prejudiced people. Gens sans préjugés, unprejudiced people.

prélart [prela:r], s.m. Nau: etc: Tarpaulin.

prélasser (se) [səprelase], v.pr. F: **1.** To put on all the importance of a prelate; P: to do the heavy. **2.** Se p. dans un fauteuil, to loll in an arm-chair; to take one's ease in an arm-chair.

prélat [prela], s.m. Prelate.

prélature [prelaty:r], s.f. Prelature, prelacy.

prêle [prɛl], s.f. Bot: Horse-tail.

prélèvement [prelɛvmɑ̃], s.m. **1.** Deduction in advance; setting apart. P. d'échantillons, sampling. Med: P. de sang, taking of blood (for a test). P. sur le capital, sur la fortune, capital levy. **2.** (a) Sample. (b) Amount deducted.

prélever [prelve], v.tr. (Conj. like LEVER) To deduct, set apart, (portion) in advance. P. la dîme, to levy the tithes. P. une commission de deux pour cent, to deduct a commission of two per cent. P. un échantillon, to take, cut off, a sample.

préliminaire [prelimine:r]. **1.** a. Preliminary. **2.** s.m.pl. Les préliminaires de (la) paix, the preliminaries to peace, the peace preliminaries. adv. -**ment.**

prélude [prelyd], s.m. Prelude (de, à, to).

préluder [prelyde], v.i. **1.** Mus: To prelude. **2.** F: Préluder à qch., to serve as prelude to sth.

prématuré [prematyre], a. Premature, untimely. S.a. ALLUMAGE. adv. -**ment.**

préméditation [premeditasjɔ̃], s.f. Premeditation. Avec préméditation, deliberately; Jur: with malice aforethought, with malice prepense.

préméditer [premedite], v.tr. To premeditate. De dessein prémédité, of set purpose; designedly.

Insulte préméditée, deliberate insult, studied insult.

prémices [premis], *s.f.pl.* First fruits.

premier, -ière [prəmje, -jɛːr], *a.* First. **1.** (*a*) *Le p. jour du mois*, the first day of the month. *Le p. janvier*, the first of January. *Les trois premières années*, the first three years. *Première éducation*, early education. **Dans les premiers temps**, at first. **En premier (lieu)**, in the first place; firstly. **Dès le premier jour**, from the outset. **Au premier jour**, at the first opportunity. **Du premier coup**, at the first attempt. *Arriver le p.*, to arrive first. *Sp:* **Arriver bon premier**, to come in an easy first. *Être le p. à faire qch.*, to be first to do sth. **Les premiers venus**, the first comers. *F:* **Le premier venu vous dira cela**, anyone will tell you that. **Ce n'est pas le premier venu**, he isn't just anybody. *F:* **Il n'a pas le premier sou**, he hasn't a single penny (of the sum required). *Nau:* **P.** *voyage*, maiden trip of ship). *St.Exch:* **Premier cours**, opening price. **Frais de premier établissement**, initial expenses. *Aut:* **Première vitesse**, bottom gear. (*b*) *Sens p. d'un mot*, original meaning of a word. *Cause première d'un malheur*, primary cause of a misfortune. *Com:* **Matières premières**, raw materials. **2. Demeurer au premier**, to live on the first floor; *F:* to live one stair up. *Journ:* **Premier (article)**, leading article. *S.a.* PREMIER-PARIS. **Premier plan**, foreground. *Th:* **Les premières (loges)**, the first-tier boxes. **3.** *Au p. rang*, in the first rank. **Le tout premier**, the foremost. *Au tout p. rang*, in the foremost rank. **Premier ministre**, Prime Minister, Premier. **P.** *commis*, principal clerk. *Navy:* **P.** *maître*, chief petty officer. **Capitaine en premier**, senior captain. *Travail de première urgence*, work of immediate urgency. *Billet de première classe*, first-class ticket. **Monter en première**, to travel first (class). *S.a.* SOLDAT. *Mth:* **Nombres premiers**, prime numbers. *Nombres premiers entre eux*, incommensurable numbers. *Th:* **Premier rôle**, leading part; *F:* lead. **Première danseuse**, leader of the ballet. *S.a.* JEUNE-PREMIER. **4.** *Sch:* (Classe de) première, sixth form.

première [prəmjɛːr], *s.f.* **1.** *Dressm:* Forewoman. **2.** *Th:* First performance; first-night (of play). **3.** *Com:* **Première de change**, first of exchange.

premièrement [prəmjɛrmɑ̃], *adv.* First, firstly, in the first place.

premier-né, première-née [prəmjene, prəmjerne], *a. & s.* First-born.

premier-Paris [prəmjepari], *s.m.* Leading article (in Paris newspapers).

prémisse [premis], *s.f. Log:* Premise, premiss.

prémonition [premonisjɔ̃], *s.f.* Premonition.

prémunir [premyniːr], *v.tr.* **P.** *qn contre qch.*, (i) to caution, forewarn, s.o., to put s.o. on his guard, against sth.; (ii) to secure s.o. against sth. **se prémunir**, to provide oneself (*de*, with; *contre*, against).

prenable [prənabl], *a.* **1.** Seizable; pregnable (town or fort). **2.** Corruptible; open to a bribe.

prenant, -ante [prənɑ̃, -ɑ̃ːt]. **1.** *a.* (*a*) *Fin:* **Partie prenante**, payee. (*b*) **Queue prenante**, prehensile tail. (*c*) *Glu prenante*, sticky bird-lime. (*d*) Engaging (voice). **2.** *s.* Taker (of bet).

prénatal [prenatal], *a.* (The masc. pl. is *prénatals* or *prénataux*) Prenatal, ante-natal.

prendre [prɑ̃ːdr], *v.* (*pr.p.* **prenant**; *p.p.* **pris**; *pr.ind.* je **prends**, il **prend**, n. **prenons**, ils **prennent**; *pr.sub.* je **prenne**, n. **prenions**; *p.h.* je **pris**, n. **primes**; *fu.* je **prendrai**) **I.** *v.tr.* To take. (*a*) To take (up), to take hold of, lay hold of (sth.). **P.** *les armes*, to take up arms. **P.** *brusquement*

qch., to snatch sth. **P.** *qch. dans ses bras, entre ses mains*, to clasp sth. **P.** *qn par les cheveux*, to grasp s.o. by the hair. *F:* **Je sais comment le prendre**, I know (i) how to manage him, (ii) how to cajole him. **P.** *qch. dans un tiroir*, to take something out of a drawer. **P.** *qch. sur la table*, to take sth. from the table. *F:* **Où avez-vous pris cela?** where did you get that idea? *Je la pris dans mes bras*, I took her in my arms. *Vêtement qui prend (bien) la taille*, close-fitting garment. (*b*) **P.** *qch. à sa charge*, to take charge of, take care of, sth. *S.a.* CHARGE 4. **P.** *des pensionnaires*, to take in boarders. **P.** *qch. sur soi*, to assume responsibility for sth. **P.** *sur soi de faire qch.*, to take it upon oneself to do sth. **P.** *qn au sérieux*, to take s.o. seriously. *Vous avez mal pris mes paroles*, you took me up wrong. *S.a.* CŒUR 2. (*c*) **Prendre qch. à qn**, to take sth. from s.o. *La mort lui a pris son fils*, death has deprived him of his son. *Cela me prend tout mon temps*, it takes (up) all my time. *Mon temps est entièrement pris*, I haven't a free minute. *F:* **C'est autant de pris sur l'ennemi**, that is so much to the good. *J'ai dû p. sur mes réserves*, I had to draw on my reserves. (*d*) *Prenez ce que je vous offre*, take what I offer you. **C'est à prendre ou à laisser**, (you may) take it or leave it. **A tout prendre**, (up)on the whole; everything considered. **A bien prendre les choses . . .**, rightly speaking. **. . .** *Prenons qu'il en soit ainsi*, let us take it that such is the case. *F:* **En prendre à son aise**, to take it easy. *Il en prend trop à son aise*, he is really too casual. **Le prendre de haut**, to put on airs, to show arrogance. *Prenez-le sur un autre ton!* please alter your tone! **2.** To take, seize, catch, capture. (*a*) **P.** *une ville d'assaut*, to take a town by assault. **P.** *un poisson, un voleur*, to catch a fish, a thief. **Tel est pris qui croyait prendre**, it's a case of the biter bit. **Se faire prendre**, to get caught. **Se laisser prendre**, to let oneself be caught. *Il s'y laissa p.*, he fell into the trap. **P.** *qn à voler*, to catch s.o. stealing. **P.** *qn à mentir*, to catch s.o. in a lie. *Je vous y prends!* I have caught you (in the act)! **Que je vous y prenne!** let me catch you at it! **On ne m'y prendra pas!** I know better! *S.a.* FAIT² 1. *Il se prit le pied contre une racine et tomba*, he caught his foot on a root and fell. *Elle fut prise d'une crise de larmes*, she broke into tears. (*b*) *Le vin lui (or le) prit à la tête*, the wine went to his head. *L'envie lui prend de partir*, he is seized with a desire to go away. *Si jamais l'envie vous en prenait*, if ever you should feel so inclined. *Il lui prend des lubies impossibles*, he is subject to extraordinary whims. **Qu'est-ce qui lui prend?** what's up with him now? **Bien lui en prit**, it was lucky for him that he did. **3.** (*a*) *Je passerai vous p. à votre hôtel*, I shall call for you at your hotel. (Of train) **P.** *des voyageurs*, to take up passengers. (Of boat) **P.** *des marchandises*, to take in cargo. (*b*) **P.** *une chambre*, to take a room. **P.** *des billets*, to take, book, tickets. **P.** *un billet direct pour Londres*, to book through to London. **P.** *des renseignements*, to make inquiries. **P.** *un ouvrier*, to engage, take on, a workman. (*c*) **P.** *qn comme secrétaire*, to engage s.o. as (one's) secretary. **P.** *qn pour exemple*, to take s.o. as an example. (*d*) **P.** *une personne pour une autre*, to take, mistake, one person for another. *Il se faisait p. pour un colonel*, he passed himself off as a colonel. (*e*) **P.** *des aliments*, to take food. **P.** *un remède*, to take medicine, a remedy. **P.** *un bain*, to take a bath. (*f*) **P.** *une maladie*, to take an illness. **P.** *des habitudes*, to acquire habits. (*g*) **P.** *un air de fête*, to assume a holiday appearance. *Les arbres*

32

prennent une couleur d'automne, the trees take on autumn tints. *P. un air innocent*, to put on an innocent air. *P. du poids*, to put on weight. (*h*) **Prendre de l'âge**, to be getting on in years. **4.** *P. le train, le bateau*, to take the train, the boat. *Prenez une chaise*, take a chair. *P. à travers champs*, to strike across the fields. *Aut: P. un virage*, to take a corner. *Abs.* "**Prendre à gauche**," 'bear left'; 'fork left.' *Nau:* **Prendre le large**, to take to the open sea. *Le cheval prit le trot*, the horse broke into a trot. S.a. LIT I.

II. prendre, *v.i.* **I.** (*a*) (Of mortar) To set; (of jelly) to set, to congeal; (of milk) to curdle. (*b*) To freeze. (*c*) (Of pump) To get choked, fouled up; (of engine) to seize, to jam. (*d*) *Cu:* To catch (in the pan). **2.** *Le feu a pris*, the fire has taken, has caught. *Le vaccin a pris*, the vaccine has taken (effect). *Cette mode a pris*, this fashion has caught on. *F: Ce truc-là prend toujours*, that trick is always successful. *Ça ne prend pas! it's no go!* it won't wash! you can't bamboozle me!

se prendre. I. (*a*) To catch, to be caught. *Son manteau se prit dans la porte, à un clou*, her cloak (got) caught in the door, on a nail. (*b*) **Se prendre d'amitié pour qn**, to take a liking, conceive a friendship, for s.o. **2. Se prendre à qch.**, to cling to, grasp at, sth. *Ne savoir où se p.*, not to know what to clutch at. **3. Se prendre à pleurer, à rire**, to begin to weep, to laugh. **4. S'en prendre à qn**, to attack, blame, s.o.; to cast, lay, the blame (up)on s.o. **5. S'y prendre.** *Il sait comment s'y p.*, he knows how to go about it, how to set about it, how to manage it. *S'y p. maladroitement*, to bungle. *Il s'y prend bien*, he sets about it in the right way. **S'y prendre à deux fois**, to make two attempts (before succeeding).

pris, *a.* **I.** Engaged, occupied. *Je suis très p. ce matin*, I am very busy, very much taken up, this morning. **2. Être bien pris (dans sa taille)**, to be well-proportioned, well set up. **3. Pris de vin, de boisson**, the worse for drink. **Pris de colère**, in a passion. *P. de remords*, smitten with remorse.

preneur, -euse [prənœːr, -øːz]. **I.** *s.* Taker. (*a*) *P. de tabac*, snuff taker. (*b*) *P. de rats*, rat-catcher. (*c*) Buyer, purchaser; payee (of cheque); taker (of bill). (*d*) Lessee, leaseholder. (*e*) *Turf:* *Les preneurs*, the takers of odds. **2.** *a.* Buying, purchasing.

prénom [prenɔ̃], *s.m.* First name; Christian name.

prénommé [prenɔme], *a.* Above-named.

préoccupation [preɔkypasjɔ̃], *s.f.* **I.** Pre-occupation, abstractedness; absence of mind. **2.** (= souci) (*a*) *Ma seule p. a été d'assurer . . .*, my only care, concern, study, has been to ensure. . . . (*b*) Anxiety. *Préoccupations matérielles*, material cares. **3.** Preoccupation, pre-occupancy (of house, etc.).

préoccuper [preɔkype], *v.tr.* To preoccupy, engross (s.o.). *Elle a quelque chose qui la préoccupe*, she has something on her mind. *Sa santé me préoccupe*, I am anxious about his health.

se préoccuper *de qch.*, to give one's attention, to attend, see, to a matter.

préoccupé, *a.* **I.** Preoccupied, taken up (*de*, with). **2.** *Répondre d'un ton p.*, to answer absent-mindedly.

préopinant, -ante [preɔpinɑ̃, -ɑ̃:t], *s.* Previous speaker.

préopiner [preɔpine], *v.i.* To speak or vote first.

préordonné [preɔrdɔne], *a.* Preordained.

préparateur, -trice [preparatœːr, -tris], *s.* **I.** Preparer, mixer (of drug, etc.). **2.** Assistant

(in laboratory); demonstrator. **3.** Tutor; *F:* coach.

préparatifs [preparatif], *s.m.pl.* Preparations (*de*, for). **Faire ses préparatifs de départ**, to prepare for departure. (In sg.) **Sans aucun préparatif**, without any preparation.

préparation [preparasjɔ̃], *s.f.* **I.** Preparation, preparing (*à*, for). **Parler sans préparation**, to speak extempore. *Annoncer une nouvelle sans p.*, to blurt out a piece of news. **2.** *P. anatomique*, anatomical preparation; specimen.

préparatoire [preparatwaːr], *a.* Preparatory.

préparer [prepare], *v.tr.* **I.** (*a*) To prepare; to make ready, get ready (meal, etc.). (*b*) *Ind:* To dress (raw material). **2. Préparer qn à qch.**, (i) to prepare, (ii) to fit, train, s.o. for sth. **3.** *P. un examen*, to prepare, read, for an examination.

se préparer. I. *De grands événements se préparent*, great events are preparing. *Un orage se prépare*, a storm is brewing. *Il se prépare quelque chose*, there is something afoot. **2.** *Se p. à, pour, un voyage*, to get ready for a journey. *Se p. à partir*, to make ready to depart.

prépondérance [prepɔ̃derɑ̃:s], *s.f.* Preponderance (*sur*, over).

prépondérant [prepɔ̃derɑ̃], *a.* Preponderant, preponderating. **Voix prépondérante**, casting vote. *Jouer un rôle p.*, to play a leading part.

préposer [prepoze], *v.tr.* *P. qn à une fonction*, to appoint s.o. to an office.

préposé, -ée, *s.* **I.** Official in charge, super-intendent (*à*, of). *Rail: La préposée (à la librairie)*, the bookstall-keeper. **2.** *Jur:* Commettant et préposé, principal and agent.

prépositif, -ive [prepozitif, -iːv], *a.* *Gram:* Prepositive; prepositional (phrase).

préposition [prepozisjɔ̃], *s.f.* *Gram:* Preposition.

prépotence [prepotɑ̃:s], *s.f.* Prepotency.

prépuce [prepys], *s.m.* *Anat:* Prepuce, foreskin.

prérogative [prerɔgatiːv], *s.f.* Prerogative. *P. parlementaire*, parliamentary privilege.

près [prɛ]. **I.** *adv.* Near. *Il demeure ici près, tout près*, he lives quite near, close by, near by. **Plus près**, nearer. **2.** *Adv.phr.* A . . . près. *A cela près*, save on that point; with that exception. *A ce détail près*, save in this particular. *A peu d'exceptions près*, with (a) few exceptions. *Il devinerait votre poids à un milligramme près*, he would guess your weight to a grain. *Nous n'en sommes pas à un ou deux jours près*, a day or two more or less doesn't matter. **A cela près que . . .**, except that. . . . *Un chef-d'œuvre à peu de chose près*, little short of a masterpiece. **A peu près**, (i) nearly, about, approximately; (ii) *s.m.inv.* approximation; rough estimate. *Il lui tint à peu près ce langage*, he spoke to him more or less in the following terms. *Il était à peu près certain que . . .*, it was fairly, tolerably, certain that. . . . *Je n'aime pas les à peu près*, I don't like loose answers. *Calculer une somme par à peu près*, to make a rough reckoning of a sum. *Le mieux équipé à beaucoup près*, by far the best equipped. *Ce n'est pas à beaucoup près la somme qu'il me faut*, that's nothing like, nowhere near, the sum I require. **Au plus près**. (i) To the nearest point. (ii) *Nau: Courir au plus près*, to sail on a wind; to sail close-hauled. **De près**, close, near; from close to. *Tirer de près*, to fire at close range. *Rasé de près*, close-shaved. *Examiner qch. de près*, to examine sth. closely. *Suivre qn de près*, to follow hard, close, (up)on s.o. **Il n'y regarde pas de si près**, he is not so particular as all that. **3.** *Prep.phr.* **Près de qn**, near, close to, s.o. *Près de là*, near by.

Assis tout près du feu, seated close by the fire. *Courir près du vent*, to sail close to the wind. *Il est près de midi*, it is nearly, close on, twelve. *Il y a près de dix ans*, nearly ten years ago ; close on ten years ago. *Près de partir*, on the point of starting ; about to start.

présage [preza:ʒ], *s.m.* Presage, portent, foreboding. **Mauvais présage**, bad omen. **Oiseau de sinistre présage**, bird of ill omen.

présager [prezaʒe], *v.tr.* (**je présageai(s)** ; n. **présageons**) To presage. **1.** To (fore)bode, portend, betoken. *Cela ne présage rien de bon*, it bodes no good. **2.** To predict, to augur.

pré-salé, *s.m.* (i) Salt-meadow sheep ; (ii) salt-meadow mutton. *pl. Des prés-salés.*

presbyte [prezbit], *a.* Long-sighted.

presbytère [prezbite:r], *s.m.* R.C.Ch: Presbytery. *Protest.Ch:* Parsonage, vicarage, rectory ; (Scottish) manse.

presbytérien, -ienne [prezbiterjɛ̃, -jen], *a. & s.* Presbyterian.

prescience [presjɑ̃:s, press-], *s.f.* Prescience, foreknowledge (*de*, of).

prescient [presjɑ̃, press-], *a.* Prescient (*de*, of).

prescription [preskripsjɔ̃], *s.f.* **1.** *Jur:* Prescription. **Invoquer la prescription**, to raise a defence under the statute of limitations. **2.** (*a*) *Med:* Direction(s) (for treatment). (*b*) Regulation(s). *Contraire aux prescriptions*, contrary to regulations.

prescrire [preskri:r], *v.tr.* (Conj. like ÉCRIRE) **1.** To prescribe, ordain, lay down (rule of conduct, etc.) ; to stipulate (for quality, etc.) ; to prescribe (remedy) (*à*, to). **Dans le délai prescrit**, within the prescribed time. *A la date prescrite*, on the date fixed. **2.** *Jur:* To prescribe ; to bar by the statute of limitations. *Chèque prescrit*, stale cheque.

préséance [preseɑ̃:s], *s.f.* Precedence (*sur*, of) ; priority (*sur*, of). **Avoir la préséance sur qn**, to take precedence of s.o.

présence [prezɑ̃:s], *s.f.* Presence. (*a*) *Je désire sa p. ici*, I desire his attendance here. *Il ignore votre p.*, he does not know that you are here. **Faire acte de présence**, to enter an appearance ; *F:* to show up. *Sch: Régularité de p.*, regular attendance. *Ind:* Feuille de p., time-sheet. **En présence**, face to face ; in view of one another. *Mettre les deux parties en p.*, to bring the parties together. **En présence de la mort**, in the presence of death. *Cela s'est fait en ma p.*, it was done in my sight. (*b*) **Présence d'esprit**, presence of mind.

présent[1] [prezɑ̃], *a.* Present. (*a*) *Les personnes présentes*, those present. *Cela m'est toujours p. à l'esprit*, it is always present to my mind. *Il n'est pas p. à ce que je dis*, he is not attending to what I say. **La présente** (**lettre**), the present letter, this letter. *Jur:* **Par la présente**, hereby ; by these presents. *Le temps p.*, s.m. **le présent**, the present (time) ; *Gram:* the present (tense). **Pour le présent**, for the present, for the time being. **A présent**, just now. **Jusqu'à présent**, up to the present ; as yet. **Dès à présent**, (i) (even) now ; (ii) from now on, henceforth. **A présent que** . . . , now that . . . . (*b*) **Esprit présent**, alert mind, quick mind ; ready wit.

présent[2], *s.m.* Present, gift. *P. de noces*, wedding-present. **Faire présent de qch. à qn**, **donner qch. en présent à qn**, to make a present of sth. to s.o.

présentable [prezɑ̃tabl], *a.* *F:* Presentable. *Je ne suis pas p.*, I am not fit to be seen.

présentateur, -trice [prezɑ̃tatœ:r, -tris], *s.* (*a*) Presenter (of a bill) ; introducer, presenter (of a person). (*b*) *Ecc:* Patron (of a living).

présentation [prezɑ̃tasjɔ̃], *s.f.* **1.** (*a*) Presentation

(of bill, play). *Com:* **Payable à présentation**, payable on demand, on presentation. (*b*) Appearance. **Livre de bonne présentation**, well-produced book. **2.** (Formal) introduction (*à qn*, to s.o.) ; presentation (at court). **Lettre de présentation**, letter of introduction.

présentement [prezɑ̃tmɑ̃], *adv.* At present.

présenter [prezɑ̃te], *v.tr.* **1.** To present, offer. (*a*) *P. qch. à qn*, to present s.o. with sth. ; to present sth. to s.o. *P. sa main à qn*, to hold out one's hand to s.o. *P. une excuse à qn*, to offer an apology to s.o. *P. son passeport*, to produce, exhibit, one's passport. *Mil:* **Présenter les armes**, to present arms. *P. un revolver à qn*, to point a revolver at s.o. (*b*) *Il me présenta tous les faits*, he put, laid, before me all the facts of the case ; he stated all the facts. *P. des conclusions*, to bring up, submit, conclusions (at a meeting). *P. un projet de loi*, to bring in, to introduce, a bill. *Son travail est bien présenté*, his work is well set out. *L'ouvrage est bien présenté*, the general get-up of the volume is attractive. **2.** **Présenter qn à qn**, to present, introduce, s.o. to s.o.

se présenter. **1.** *Une occasion se présente* (*de faire qch.*), an opportunity presents itself, offers, occurs (for doing sth.). *Si le cas se présente*, if the case arises, occurs. *Attendre que quelque chose se présente*, to wait for something to turn up. *La chose se présente bien*, the matter looks promising. **2.** To present oneself ; *Mil: etc:* to report oneself. *Se p. à, pour, un examen*, to go in for, go up for, sit for, an examination. *Se p. chez qn*, to call on, wait upon, s.o. *Se p. à qn*, to introduce oneself to s.o. *Se p: aux élections*, to stand at the elections. *Il se présente bien*, he is a man of good address ; he makes a good appearance.

préservateur, -trice [prezervatœ:r, -tris], *a.* Preserving, preservative (*de*, from).

préservatif, -ive [prezervatif, -i:v], *a. & s.m.* Preservative ; preventive (*contre*, of) ; protective.

préservation [prezervasjɔ̃], *s.f.* Preservation, protection (of crops, etc.).

préserver [prezerve], *v.tr.* To preserve, to protect (*de*, from). **Le ciel m'en préserve!** heaven forbid ! *"A préserver de l'humidité,"* 'to be kept dry.'

présidence [prezidɑ̃:s], *s.f.* **1.** (*a*) Presidency. (*b*) Chairmanship. (*c*) Board (of a company). **2.** President's house.

président, -ente [prezidɑ̃, -ɑ̃:t], *s.* **1.** President. **2.** Chairman, -woman (of a meeting). **Être élu président**, to be voted into the chair.

présidentiel, -elle [prezidɑ̃sjel], *a.* Presidential. *Prendre possession du fauteuil p.*, to take the chair.

présider [prezide], *v.tr. & i.* (*a*) *P. un conseil*, to preside over a council. (*b*) To preside, to be in the chair, to take the chair. *P.* (*à*) *une réunion*, to preside at, over, a meeting.

présompt|if, -ive [prezɔ̃ptif, -i:v], *a.* Presumptive. **Héritier présomptif**, heir presumptive, esp. heir apparent. *adv.* **-ivement.**

présomption [prezɔ̃psjɔ̃], *s.f.* **1.** Presumption ; presumptive evidence. *Ins: Il y a p. de perte*, the ship is a presumptive loss. **2.** Presumption, presumptuousness.

présomptueu|x, -euse [prezɔ̃ptɥø, -ø:z], *a.* Presumptuous, presuming, overweening. *s. Un jeune p.*, a presumptuous youth. *adv.* **-sement.**

presque [presk], *adv.* (Final *e* is elided only in *presqu'île*) **1.** (*a*) Almost, nearly. *Je les ai p. tous*, I have nearly all of them. (*b*) *J'en ai la presque-certitude*, I am almost certain of it. **2.** (With negative) Scarcely, hardly. **Presque jamais**, hardly ever. **Presque rien**, scarcely anything.

next to nothing. **Presque personne,** hardly any-one.

presqu'île [prɛskil], *s.f.* Peninsula.

pressant [prɛsɑ̃], *a.* Pressing, urgent (need, etc.). **En termes pressants,** in pressing terms. **Cas pressant,** urgent case.

presse [prɛ:s], *s.f.* **1.** Press, pressing-machine. (*a*) *P. hydraulique à estamper,* drop-forging press. *P. mécanique,* power-press. *P. à vis,* screw-press. **Travailler le métal à la presse,** to stamp metal. *P. à copier,* letter-press, copying-press. (*b*) *P. à imprimer, d'imprimerie,* printing-press. *P. rota-tive,* rotary press. **Livre sous presse,** book in the press. **Prêt à mettre sous presse,** ready for press. (*c*) *Bookb:* **P. à rogner,** guillotine; plough. **2.** Press, newspapers. **Avoir une bonne, mau-vaise, presse,** to have a good, bad, press. *Publ:* **Service de presse,** press copies. **3.** (*a*) Pressure, congestion (in a crowd); press, crowd, throng. *Fendre la p.,* to force one's way through the crowd. (*b*) *A:* (i) Impressment (of men for the navy). (ii) Press-gang. **4.** (*a*) Haste, urgency. **Il n'y a pas de presse,** there is no hurry. (*b*) *P. des affaires,* pressure of business. **Moments de presse,** rush hours.

presse-citron(s), *s.m.inv.* Lemon-squeezer.

presse-étoupe, *s.m.inv. Mch:* Stuffing-box, packing-box (and gland).

pressentiment [presɑ̃timɑ̃], *s.m.* Presentiment, forewarning; foreboding.

pressentir [presɑ̃ti:r], *v.tr.* (Conj. like SENTIR) **1.** To have a presentiment, a foreboding, of (sth.). **Faire, laisser, pressentir qch.,** to forebode, fore-shadow, portend, sth. *Faire p. qch. à qn,* to give s.o. an inkling of sth. **2.** *P. qn* (*sur qch.*), to sound s.o. (on sth.).

presse-pantalon, *s.m.* Trouser-press, trouser-stretcher. *pl. Des presse-pantalon(s).*

presse-papiers, *s.m.inv.* Paper-weight.

presse-purée, *s.m.inv.* Potato-masher.

press|er [prese], *v.tr.* To press. **1.** To squeeze (lemon, etc.). *Metalw:* **P. à froid,** to cold-press. *P. du raisin, des pommes,* to press grapes, apples. *P. qn contre, sur, son cœur,* to press, clasp, fold, s.o. to one's heart. **P. les rangs,** to close up the ranks. **2.** To press (upon); to beset. *Pressé par ses créanciers,* hard pressed, dunned, by his creditors. *P. l'ennemi,* to press hard upon the enemy. *P. qn de questions,* to ply s.o. with questions; to question s.o. closely. *P. qn de faire qch.,* to press, urge, s.o. to do sth. **3.** To hurry, push, (s.o.) on. *P. le pas,* to hasten one's steps; to quicken one's pace. *P. le départ de qn,* to hasten, hurry on, s.o.'s departure. *Qu'est-ce qui vous presse?* why are you in such a hurry? *F:* what's your hurry? *Abs. Le temps presse,* time presses. *L'affaire presse,* the matter is urgent. **Il n'y a rien qui presse; rien ne presse;** *F:* **ça ne presse pas,** there is no hurry. *s.m.* **-age.**

se presser. 1. To press, crowd, throng. *On se presse à ses jours de réception,* people throng at her at-homes. **2.** To hurry, make haste. **Pressez-vous!** look sharp! hurry up! **Répondre sans se presser,** to answer deliberately, leisurely.

pressé, *a.* **1.** (*a*) Pressed, crowded, close together. **En rangs pressés,** in serried ranks. (*b*) Compressed. *Pièce pressée,* pressing. **2.** (*a*) Pressed, hurried; in a hurry. *Je suis très p.,* I am in a great hurry. (*b*) *P. d'argent,* pressed for money. (*c*) Pressing, urgent (work). *Ce n'est pas p.,* there's no hurry. *s.m.* **Courir au plus pressé,** to attend to the most pressing thing(s) first.

pression [presjɔ̃], *s.f.* Pressure. (*a*) *P. en colonne d'eau,* hydraulic head. **Vérificateur de pression,**

pressure-gauge (for tyres). *Mch:* **Machine à haute, basse, pression,** high-, low-pressure engine. **Mettre (la chaudière) sous pression,** to get up steam. (*b*) *El.E:* Tension. (*c*) **Vis de pression,** binding-screw. (*d*) *Exercer une p. sur qn,* to bring pressure to bear on s.o.

pressoir [preswa:r], *s.m.* **1.** (*a*) Wine-press, cider-press, oil-press. (*b*) Press-house, -room. **2.** Push-button.

pressur|er [presyre], *v.tr.* **1.** (*a*) To press (grapes for wine). (*b*) To press out (the juice). **2.** *F:* To squeeze, grind down, extort money from (s.o.). *s.m.* **-age.**

prestance [prestɑ̃:s], *s.f.* Fine presence, martial bearing. *Avoir une belle p.,* to have a fine presence.

prestation [prestasjɔ̃], *s.f.* **1.** Prestation (of dues); furnishing, loan(ing) (of money). **2.** Pres-tation de serment, taking the oath. *Hist:* **P. de foi,** oath of fealty. **3.** *Mil:* Prestations, allow-ances. **4.** *Ins:* Benefit.

preste [prest], *a.* Quick, sharp, nimble; alert. *Être p. à la réplique,* to be smart at repartee. **Avoir la main preste,** to be free with one's hands. *adv.* **-ment.**

prestesse [prestes], *s.f.* Quickness, alertness.

prestidigitateur [prestidiʒitatœ:r], *s.m.* Con-jurer.

prestidigitation [prestidiʒitasjɔ̃], *s.f.* Con-juring, legerdemain, sleight of hand. **Tour de prestidigitation,** conjuring trick.

prestige [presti:ʒ], *s.m.* **1.** Marvel. **Qui tient du prestige,** marvellous. **2.** Glamour (of a name, etc.). *Le p. de son éloquence,* the magic of his eloquence. **3.** Prestige; high reputation. **Sans prestige,** undistinguished.

prestigieux, -euse [prestiʒjø, -ø:z], *a.* Mar-vellous, wondrous, amazing (dexterity, etc.).

présumable [prezymabl], *a.* Presumable (*de la part de qn,* of s.o.).

présumer [prezyme], *v.tr.* To presume. **1.** *P. qn innocent,* to presume, assume, s.o. to be innocent. *Le coupable présumé, le présumé coupable,* the supposed culprit. *Le voleur, l'assassin, présumé,* the alleged thief, murderer. **Il est à présumer, on présume, qu'il est mort,** the presumption is that he is dead. **2.** (*a*) *P. de faire qch.,* to presume to do sth. (*b*) **Trop présumer de soi,** to presume too much; to show presumption. *Trop p. de ses forces,* to over-estimate, overrate, one's strength.

présupposer [presypoze], *v.tr.* To presuppose; to take (sth.) for granted.

présure [prezy:r], *s.f.* Rennet.

prêt¹ [prɛ], *a.* Ready, prepared. *P. à servir,* ready for use. *Elle est prête à tout,* she is ready, game, for anything. *P. à partir,* ready to start. *Tenez-vous p.,* hold yourself in readiness.

prêt², -s *s.m.* **1.** Loan. *Cent francs de p.,* a loan of a hundred francs. *P. à terme,* loan at notice. *P. à court terme,* short loan. *P. d'honneur,* loan on trust. *Caisse de prêts,* loan bank. *P. sur gage,* loan against security. **Prêts au jour le jour,** money at call; call money. **A titre de prêt,** as a loan. **2.** Advance (on wages); (soldier's) pay.

prétantaine [pretɑ̃ten], *s.f.* **Courir la prétan-taine,** to gad about.

prétendant, -ante [pretɑ̃dɑ̃, -ɑ̃:t], *s.* **1.** Appli-cant, candidate (*à,* for); claimant; pretender (to a throne). **2.** *s.m.* Suitor, wooer.

prétendre [pretɑ̃:dr], *v.tr.* **1.** To claim; to require. (*a*) *A:* **Prétendre part à qch.,** to claim a share in sth. (*b*) *Que prétendez-vous de moi?* what do you require of me? *Je prétends que vous m'obéissiez,* I claim obedience from you; I mean

you to obey me. *Prétendez-vous me faire la loi?* do you pretend to dictate to me? **2.** To maintain, assert. **A ce qu'on prétend**, as is asserted, as report will have it. *On le prétend fou*, they make him out to be mad. *Se p. parent de qn*, to claim kinship with s.o. **3.** *v.ind.tr.* **Prétendre à qch.**, to lay claim to sth. *P. aux honneurs*, to aspire to honours. *P. à la main de qn*, to seek s.o. in marriage.
prétendu, -ue. I. *a.* Alleged, would-be. *P. voleur*, alleged thief. *Un p. baron*, a self-styled, bogus, baron. *Prétendus progrès*, so-called improvements. **2.** *s.* **Mon prétendu, ma prétendue**, my intended.
prête-nom, *s.m.* Person who lends his name; figure-head, man of straw. *pl. Des prête-noms*.
prétentieu|x, -euse [pretɑ̃sjø, -øːz], *a.* Pretentious, showy; highfalutin (style). *s. Un jeune p.*, *F*: a conceited puppy. *adv.* **-sement.**
prétention [pretɑ̃sjɔ̃], *s.f.* (*a*) Pretension, claim (*à*, to). *Je n'ai pas la p. de remporter le prix*, I don't for a moment suppose that I shall get the prize. (*b*) **Homme à prétentions**, pretentious man. **Homme sans prétentions**, unassuming man.
prêter [prete], *v.tr.* **I.** To lend. (*a*) *P. qch. à qn*, to lend sth. to s.o. *P. sur gages*, to lend against security. (*b*) *P. son appui à qn*, to lend, give, s.o. one's support. **Prêter la main à qn**, to lend s.o. a hand; to assist s.o. **Prêter l'oreille**, to lend one's ear; to give ear. **Prêter attention**, to pay attention. **Prêter serment**, to take the oath; to be sworn. *P. le flanc à l'ennemi*, to expose, offer, one's flank to the enemy. **2.** To attribute, ascribe (*à*, to). *On me prête des discours dont je suis innocent*, I am credited with speeches of which I am innocent. **3.** *Abs.* (*a*) (Of gloves, cloth, etc.) To stretch, to give. (*b*) *C'est un sujet qui prête*, the subject is full of possibilities. **4.** *v.ind.tr.* *Privilège qui prête aux abus*, privilege that lends itself to abuses, that gives rise to abuses.
se prêter. I. To lend oneself, to be a party (*à*, to). *Se p. à un accommodement*, to consent to, fall in with, an arrangement. **2.** *Se p. au plaisir*, to indulge in pleasure. **3.** *Sujet qui se prête à des développements variés*, subject that lends itself to a varied treatment.
prêté, *s.m.* **Un prêté rendu, un prêté pour un rendu**, tit for tat; a Roland for an Oliver.
prétérit [preterit], *s.m.* *Gram:* Preterite (tense).
préteur [pretœːr], *s.m.* *Rom.Hist:* Praetor.
prêteur, -euse [pretœːr, -øːz]. **I.** *s.* Lender. **Prêteur sur gages**, pawnbroker. **2.** *a.* (*a*) Disposed to lending. (*b*) *Banque prêteuse*, lending bank.
prétexte¹ [pretekst], *s.m.* Pretext, excuse, plea. *Ce n'était qu'un p.*, it was only a blind. **Prendre, tirer, prétexte de qch. pour faire qch.**, to make a pretext of sth. for doing sth. **Sous prétexte de . . .**, on pretext, on a plea, of . . . *Il sortit sous p. de mettre une lettre à la poste*, he went out ostensibly to post a letter. **Sous aucun prétexte**, not on any account.
prétexte², *a. & s.f.* *Rom.Ant:* (Toga) praetexta.
prétexter [pretekste], *v.tr.* To allege as a pretext; to pretext. *P. la fatigue*, to plead fatigue.
prétoire [pretwaːr], *s.m.* (*a*) *Rom.Ant:* Praetorium. (*b*) *Jur:* (Floor of the) court.
prétorien, -ienne [pretorjɛ̃, -jɛn], *a. & s.m.* *Rom.Ant:* Praetorian.
prêtre [preːtr], *s.m.* Priest. **Grand prêtre**, high priest.
prêtresse [pretres], *s.f.* Priestess.
prêtrise [pretriːz], *s.f.* Priesthood. **Recevoir la prêtrise**, to take (holy) orders.

préture [pretyːr], *s.f.* *Rom.Hist:* Praetorship.
preuve [prœːv], *s.f.* Proof, evidence, token. (*a*) **En preuve**, as a proof. **Faire la preuve de qch.**, to prove sth. *S.a.* NEUF¹ 2. **Faire preuve d'intelligence**, to give proof of, to show, display, intelligence. **Faire ses preuves**, to prove oneself; to show one's mettle. (*b*) *Jur:* *Le soin, l'obligation, de faire la p.*, the onus of proof, the burden of proof. *P. directe*, direct evidence. *P. indirecte*, circumstantial evidence. *Preuves testimoniales*, (witnesses') evidence.
preux [prø]. *A:* **I.** *a.m.* Gallant, valiant, doughty. **2.** *s.m.* Valiant knight; champion.
prévaloir [prevalwaːr], *v.i.* (Conj. like VALOIR, except *pr.sub.* **je prévale**) To prevail. **Faire prévaloir son droit**, to make good one's right.
se prévaloir de *qch.* (*a*) To avail oneself, take advantage, of sth. *Se p. d'un droit*, to exercise a right. (*b*) To presume on (one's birth, wealth).
prévaricateur, -trice [prevarikatœːr, -tris]. **I.** *a.* Unjust, dishonest (judge, etc.). **2.** *s.* Unjust judge; betrayer of his trust.
prévarication [prevarikasjɔ̃], *s.f.* Breach of trust; maladministration; jobbery.
prévariquer [prevarike], *v.i.* (Of judge, etc.) To depart from justice; to betray one's trust.
prévenance [prevnɑ̃ːs], *s.f.* **I.** (Kind) attention; kindness. **2.** **Avoir des prévenances pour qn**, to be attentive to s.o.
prévenant [prevnɑ̃], *a.* **I.** Kind, attentive, considerate (*envers*, to). **2.** Pleasing, prepossessing.
prévenir [prevniːr], *v.tr.* (Conj. like VENIR) **I.** (*a*) To forestall, anticipate (s.o., s.o.'s desires). (*b*) To prevent, ward off (illness, danger); to avert (accident). *Prov:* **Mieux vaut prévenir que guérir**, prevention is better than cure. **2.** To predispose to bias. *P: qn en faveur de qn*, to prepossess s.o. in favour of s.o. *P. qn contre qn*, to prejudice s.o. against s.o., to set s.o. against s.o. **3.** To inform, apprise, forewarn. *P. qn de qch.*, to give s.o. notice of sth. *On m'avait prévenu que la police était à mes trousses*, I had been warned that the police were after me. *Vous auriez dû m'en p.*, you ought to have told me of it beforehand.
prévenu, -ue. I. *a.* Prejudiced, prepossessed, bias(s)ed. **2.** *Jur:* (*a*) *a.* **Prévenu de vol**, accused of, charged with, theft. (*b*) *s.* **Le prévenu, la prévenue**, the prisoner, the accused.
préventif, -ive [prevãtif, -iːv], *a.* **I.** Preventive (medicine). **A titre préventif**, preventively. *Exercer un effet p.*, to act as a deterrent. *Cards:* **Ouverture préventive**, pre-emptive bid; shut-out bid. **2.** *Jur:* **Détention préventive**, detention on suspicion.
prévention [prevãsjɔ̃], *s.f.* **I.** Prepossession (*en faveur de*, in favour of); prejudice, bias (*contre*, against). **Observateur sans prévention**, unprejudiced, unbias(s)ed, observer. **2.** *Jur:* Imprisonment on suspicion. **Être en état de prévention**, to be in custody, in confinement under remand.
prévi-s, -t, etc. See PRÉVOIR.
prévision [previzjɔ̃], *s.f.* Forecasting or forecast; prevision. *P. du temps*, weather forecast(ing). *Prévisions budgétaires*, estimates. **Selon toute prévision**, in all likelihood. **Contre toute prévision**, contrary to all expectations. **En prévision de qch.**, in the expectation, in anticipation, of sth. *Dépasser les prévisions*, to exceed all expectation.
prévoir [prevwaːr], *v.tr.* (Conj. like VOIR except *fu.* and *condit.* **je prévoirai, je prévoirais**) **I.** To

foresee, forecast, gauge (events, the future). **Faire prévoir qch., laisser prévoir qch.,** to foreshadow sth. **2.** To take measures beforehand; to provide for (sth.). *Dépenses prévues au budget,* expenses provided for in the budget. **On ne peut pas tout prévoir,** one cannot provide for everything. *Article qui prévoit un cas,* clause under which a case is dealt with. *Chiffre prévu pour les dépenses,* estimate of expenditure. *Vitesse prévue (d'un vapeur, etc.),* designed speed. *Charge prévue,* rated load; specified load.

prévôt [prevo], *s.m.* (*a*) *Jur:* Provost. (*b*) *Mil:* Assistant provost-marshal. **Grand prévôt,** provost-marshal. (*c*) *Fenc: P. de salle,* assistant fencing-master.

prévôté [prevote], *s.f.* **1.** *Hist:* Provostship. **2.** *Mil:* Military police establishment.

prévoyance [prevwajã:s], *s.f.* Foresight, forethought, precaution. **Prévoyance sociale,** state insurance. **Fonds de prévoyance,** reserve fund. **Société de prévoyance,** provident society.

prévoyant [prevwajã], *a.* Provident; foreseeing; far-sighted (administration).

prie-Dieu [pridjø], *s.m.inv.* Kneeling-chair, prayer-stool.

prier [prie], *v.tr.* **1.** To pray. *Je prie Dieu qu'il en soit ainsi,* I pray God that it may be so. *P. pour qn,* to pray for s.o. **2.** To ask, beg, request, beseech. *P. qn de faire qch.,* to ask, beg, s.o. to do sth. *P. qn d'entrer,* to ask s.o. in. *P. qn de sortir,* (i) to show s.o. the door; (ii) to call s.o. out. *Dites-moi, je vous prie,* pray tell me; tell me, please. **Je vous en prie!** oh do! do, please! **Se faire prier,** to require much pressing. **3.** *P. qn à dîner,* to invite s.o. to dinner. *Être prié chez qn,* to be invited by s.o.

prié, *a.* (*a*) Invited (guest). (*b*) **Dîner prié,** formal dinner, set dinner.

prière [priε:r], *s.f.* **1.** Prayer. **Faire, dire, ses prières,** to say one's prayers. **Faire la prière,** to offer prayer; to pray (in common). **Se mettre en prières,** to kneel down and pray. **Être en prières,** to be at prayers. *P. avant le repas,* grace. **2.** Request, entreaty. *Être accessible aux prières,* to be open to entreaty. **Faire qch. à la prière de qn,** to do sth. at s.o.'s request, by the desire of s.o. **"Prière de ne pas fumer,"** 'please do not smoke.'

prieur, -eure [priœ:r], *s.* *Ecc:* Prior, prioress.

prieuré [priœre], *s.m.* **1.** Priory. **2.** Priorship.

primaire [primε:r], *a.* Primary (education, school). **El:** *Courant p.,* primary current, inducing current.

primat [prima], *s.m.* *Ecc:* Primate.

primates [primat], *s.m.pl.* *Z:* Primates.

primauté [primote], *s.f.* **1.** *Ecc: etc:* Primacy. **2.** (*a*) Priority. (*b*) Lead (at cards, etc.).

prime¹ [prim]. **1.** *a.* (*a*) *A:* First. (Still used in) **De prime abord,** to begin with; at first. **De prime saut,** (i) on the first impulse; (ii) at the first attempt, at once. **Dans ma prime jeunesse,** in my earliest youth. (*b*) *Mth:* N prime, n prime, n'. **2.** *s.f.* *Ecc: Fenc:* Prime. **Chanter prime,** to sing the Prime.

prime², *s.f.* **1.** (*a*) Premium. **Faire prime,** to be at a premium. (*b*) *St.Exch:* **Marché à prime,** (i) option (bargain); (ii) option market. **2.** (*a*) Bounty, subsidy, bonus. *Mil: P. de démobilisation,* gratuity on demobilization. (*b*) *Com:* Gift (on presentation of so many coupons); free gift.

primer¹ [prime], *v.tr.* To excel, surpass; to take precedence of, take the lead of (s.o., sth.). S.a. FORCE I. *Abs.* **Primer par, en, qch.,** to excel, take the lead, in sth.

primer², *v.tr.* **1.** To award a prize to (cattle at show, etc.). *Taureau primé,* prize bull. **2.** To give or award a bounty, a bonus, to (s.o., sth.). *Industrie primée,* subsidized, bounty-fed, industry.

primerose [primro:z], *s.f.* Hollyhock.

prime-saut, primesaut [primso], *s.m.* First impulse. **De prime-saut,** see PRIME¹ I.

prime-sautier, -ière [primsotje, -jε:r], *a.* Impulsive, spontaneous; ready, quick.

primeur [primœ:r], *s.f.* **1.** Newness, freshness. *Avoir la p. d'une nouvelle,* to be the first to hear a piece of news. **2.** *Cultiver des primeurs,* to grow early vegetables.

primevère [primvε:r], *s.f.* *Bot:* Primula. *P. à grandes fleurs,* primrose or oxlip. *P. commune,* cowslip.

primitif, -ive [primitif, -i:v], *a.* Primitive. **1.** (*a*) Primeval, original, earliest. *Gram: Temps primitifs,* primary tenses. *Opt: Couleurs primitives,* primary colours. *s.m. Art:* **Les primitifs,** the primitives; the early masters. (*b*) First, original. *La question primitive,* the original question. **2.** Primitive, crude (method, customs). *adv.* **-ivement.**

primo [primo], *adv.* Firstly; in the first place.

primogéniture [primɔʒenity:r], *s.f.* Primogeniture.

primordial, -aux [primɔrdjal, -o], *a.* (*a*) Primordial. *Nécessité primordiale,* prime necessity. (*b*) *F:* Of prime importance. (*c*) Primeval. *adv.* **-ement.**

primulacées [primylase], *s.f.pl.* Primulaceae.

prince [prε̃s], *s.m.* Prince. *P. royal, impérial,* crown prince. **Le prince des ténèbres,** the prince of darkness. **Il est bon prince,** he is a decent fellow; he is open-handed.

princeps [prε̃sεps], *a.inv.* **Édition princeps,** first edition.

princesse [prε̃sεs], *s.f.* Princess. *P. royale,* princess royal. *P:* **Aux frais de la princesse,** at the expense of the State; buckshee.

princier, -ière [prε̃sje, -jε:r], *a.* Princely.

principal, -aux [prε̃sipal, -o]. **1.** *a.* Principal, chief, leading (person, thing). *Associé p.,* senior partner. *But p.,* main object, chief object. **2.** *s.m.* (*a*) Principal, chief; headmaster, head (of school); chief partner, senior partner (of a firm). (*b*) Principal thing, chief thing, main point. *Le p. est de réussir,* the great thing is to succeed. (*c*) *Com:* Principal; capital sum. *adv.* **-ement.**

principauté [prε̃sipote], *s.f.* Principality.

principe [prε̃sip], *s.m.* Principle. **1.** **Aboutir à un accord de principe,** to reach a general agreement on fundamentals. *P. de nos actions,* mainspring of our actions. **Dans le principe,** in the beginning. **Dès le principe,** from the outset. **2.** *Les principes de la géométrie,* the principles of geometry. **Poser qch. en principe,** to lay down sth. as a principle. **3.** *Ch: P. gras, amer, actif,* fatty, bitter, active, principle or constituent. **4.** Rule of conduct. **Par principe,** on principle. **En principe . . . ,** as a rule. . . . **Avoir pour principe de se lever tard,** to make it a matter of principle to get up late. **Homme sans principes,** unprincipled man.

printanier, -ière [prε̃tanje, -jε:r], *a.* Vernal; spring (season, flowers). [PRINTEMPS]

printemps [prε̃tã], *s.m.* Spring, springtime. **Au printemps,** in (the) spring.

priorité [priorite], *s.f.* Priority. *Droits de p.,* priority rights. *Réclamer la p.,* to claim the right to speak first. **Actions de priorité,** preference shares. *Aut:* **Route de priorité,** major road.

pri-s, -t, etc. See PRENDRE.

prise [priːz], *s.f.* **1.** Hold, grasp, grip. (*a*) Trouver prise à qch., to get a grip, a hold, of sth. Avoir prise sur qn, to have a hold on, over, s.o. Lâcher prise, to lose one's hold ; to let go. Donner prise à la calomnie, to give a handle to, for, calumny. (*b*) Être aux prises avec qn, to be at grips with s.o. En venir aux prises, to come to grips. Mettre les gens aux prises, to set people by the ears. *Mettre aux prises des intérêts*, to bring interests into conflict. S.a. BEC 2. (*c*) *Mec.E:* Engagement, mesh(ing). En prise, in gear, engaged. Mettre en prise, to engage. En prise directe sur le moteur, coupled direct to the motor. *Aut:* Vitesse en p. directe, speed on direct drive. Hors de prise, out of gear. **2.** Solidification, congealing, setting. (Of cement) Faire prise, to set. **3.** (*a*) Taking ; capture. *Jur:* Prise de corps, arrest. (*b*) P. de colis à domicile, collection of parcels. (*c*) Prise de vues, taking of photographs ; *Cin:* shooting. (*d*) *Nau:* Prize. Être de bonne prise, to be (*a*) lawful prize. Part de prise, prize-money. Cour des prises, prize court. **4.** (Thing taken) (*a*) P. de poisson, catch of fish. (*b*) P. de quinine, dose of quinine. Prise de tabac, pinch of snuff. P. de minerai, sample of ore. **5.** Prise d'air, (i) ventilation aperture ; (ii) *I.C.E:* air-intake. Prise d'eau, (i) intake of water ; (ii) cock, tap, valve ; fire-hydrant ; (iii) water-catchment. P. de gaz latérale, down-comer, downtake (in blast-furnace). Prise de vapeur, steam-cock, steam-valve, injection-cock. *El:* Prise de courant, (wall-)plug, point ; current collector (of trolley). P. médiane, centre tap (of coil or transformer). P. de terre, earth connection. Faire une prise à une rivière, *El.E:* sur un câble, to tap a river, a cable.

priser[1] [prize], *v.tr.* To snuff (sth.) up. *Abs.* To take snuff, to snuff. Tabac à priser, snuff.

priser[2], *v.tr.* (*a*) To appraise, value (goods). (*b*) To set a (high) value on (sth.) ; to prize, value. **prisée**, *s.f.* Valuation (of goods) ; appraisement (before auction).

priseur[1], **-euse** [prizœːr, -øːz], *s.* Snuff-taker.

priseur[2], *s.m.* (Commissaire-)priseur, official valuer ; appraiser (of goods) ; auctioneer.

prismatique [prismatik], *a.* Prismatic.

prisme [prism], *s.m.* Prism. Jumelle(s) à prismes, prism(atic) binoculars.

prison [prizɔ̃], *s.f.* **1.** Prison, gaol, jail. Aller en prison, to go to prison, to jail. S'échapper, s'évader, de prison, to break prison. **2.** Imprisonment. Faire de la prison, garder la prison, *F:* tirer de la prison, to be in prison ; *F:* to do time, to do one's stretch. *Mil:* Trois jours de p., three days' cells.

prisonnier, -ière [prizɔnje, -jɛːr]. **1.** *s.* Prisoner. Faire qn prisonnier, to take s.o. prisoner. Se constituer prisonnier, to give oneself up. **2.** *a.* Imprisoned, captive.

privatif, -ive [privatif, -iːv], *a.* *Gram:* Privative.

privation [privasjɔ̃], *s.f.* **1.** Deprivation. P. de la vue, loss of sight. **2.** Privation, hardship. Vivre de privations, to live in privation, in want.

privautés [privote], *s.f.pl.* (Undue) familiarity. Prendre des privautés avec qn, to take liberties with s.o.

privé [prive]. **1.** *a.* (*a*) Private (individual, enterprise, etc.). *Se réunir en séance privée*, to sit in private. (*b*) Le Conseil privé, the Privy Council. (*c*) Tame (animal). **2.** *s.m.* (*a*) Connaître qn au privé, to know s.o. in private life. (*b*) Privy, water-closet. *adv.* **-ment.**

priver [prive], *v.tr.* P. qn de qch., to deprive s.o.

of sth. Je ne vous en prive pas? can you spare it? *Privé de tout espoir*, bereft of all hope. **se priver** de qch., to do without sth. ; to deny oneself sth. *Se p. pour ses enfants*, to deny, stint, oneself for one's children.

privilège [privilɛːʒ], *s.m.* **1.** Privilege. (*a*) C'est là un p. de la vieillesse, that is a prerogative of old age. Jouir du privilège de faire qch., to be privileged to do sth. ; to enjoy the privilege of doing sth. *F:* Il a le privilège de me déplaire, I have a particular dislike for him. (*b*) Licence, grant. P. d'une banque, bank charter. **2.** Preferential right ; preference. P. de créancier, creditor's preferential claim.

privilégier [privileʒje], *v.tr.* To privilege ; to license ; to grant a charter to (bank, etc.). **privilégié**, *a.* (*a*) Privileged. (*b*) Licensed. Banque privilégiée, chartered bank. (*c*) Créancier p., preferential creditor. Action privilégiée, preference share.

prix [pri], *s.m.* **1.** (*a*) Value, worth, cost. A tout prix, at all costs. Faire qch. à prix d'argent, to do sth. for money. Se vendre à prix d'or, (i) to sell oneself for gold ; (ii) (of goods) to fetch huge prices. A aucun prix, not on any terms, not at any price. Au prix de, (i) at the price of ; (ii) in comparison with. *Attacher beaucoup de p. à qch.*, to set a high value (up)on sth. ; to set great store by sth. Tenir qch. en haut prix, to prize sth. highly. (*b*) Price. Acheter qch. à bas prix, à juste prix, to buy sth. at a low price, at a fair price. P. de vente, selling price. P. au comptant, cash price. P. courant, current price, market price. P. initial, prime cost. Au p. coûtant, au p. de revient, at cost price. Faire un prix à qn, to quote a price to s.o. Articles de prix, expensive goods. Coûter un prix fou, to cost no end of money. C'est hors de prix, the price is prohibitive. N'avoir pas de prix, to be priceless. Mettre à prix la tête de qn, to set a price on s.o.'s head. Mise à prix d'un domaine, upset price of an estate. (*c*) Charge. P. d'un port de lettre, charge for postage. P. d'un trajet, du voyage, fare. **2.** Reward, prize. Remporter le prix, to carry off the prize. Le Prix Nobel, the Nobel Prize. Distribution des prix, prize-giving. Livre de prix, prize-book.

prix-courant, *s.m.* Price-list ; catalogue. *pl.* Des prix-courants.

probabilité [probabilite], *s.f.* Probability, likelihood. Selon toute probabilité, in all likelihood. *Journ:* Probabilités pour aujourd'hui, to-day's weather forecast.

probable [probabl], *a.* Probable, likely. Peu probable, improbable, unlikely. *Il est peu p., n'est pas p., qu'elle vienne*, she is not likely to come. C'est plus que probable, it is more than likely. *adv.* **-ment.**

probant [probɑ̃], *a.* *Jur:* Probative, convincing, conclusive (evidence, etc.).

probation [probasjɔ̃], *s.f.* *Ecc:* Probation.

probe [prob], *a.* Honest, upright.

probité [probite], *s.f.* Probity, integrity.

problématique [problematik], *a.* Problematical ; questionable (mode of life). *adv.* **-ment.**

problème [problɛm], *s.m.* Problem. *Sch:* Faire des problèmes, to do sums.

procédé [prosede], *s.m.* **1.** Proceeding, dealing, conduct. *Procédés honnêtes*, (i) courteous behaviour ; (ii) square dealing. *Échange de bons procédés*, exchange (i) of courtesies, of civilities, (ii) of friendly services. **2.** Process ; method (of working). P. de travail, operating process. **3.** Tip (of billiard cue).

procéder¹ [prɔsede], *v.i.* (Conj. like CÉDER) To proceed. (*a*) *P. avec méthode*, to proceed methodically. *P. à une enquête*, to institute, initiate, an enquiry. (*b*) *Jur:* **Procéder contre qn**, to take proceedings against s.o.

procéder², *v.i.* To proceed (*de*, from); to originate (*de*, in). *Sa maladie procède de l'intempérie du climat*, his illness proceeds from the inclemency of the climate.

procédure [prɔsedy:r], *s.f. Jur:* **1.** Procedure. *Terme de p.*, law term. **2.** Proceedings.

procès [prɔse], *s.m.* **1.** Proceedings at law; action at law; cause, case. **Procès civil**, lawsuit. **Procès criminel**, (criminal) trial. **Intenter un procès à qn**, (i) to institute proceedings against s.o.; to sue s.o.; (ii) to prosecute s.o. **Être en procès avec qn**, to be at law with s.o. *Intenter un p. en divorce à qn*, to institute divorce proceedings against s.o. *Perdre un p.*, to fail in a suit. *Sans autre forme de procès*, without further ceremony, without further ado; out of hand. **2.** *Anat:* Process.

processif, -ive [prɔsesif, -iːv], *a.* **1.** Litigious. **2.** *Formes processives*, forms of legal procedure.

procession [prɔsesjɔ̃], *s.f.* Procession. **Aller en procession**, to go, walk, in procession.

processionn|el, -elle [prɔsesjɔnɛl], *a.* Processional (hymn, march). *adv.* **-ellement.**

processionner [prɔsesjɔne], *v.i.* To go, walk, in procession.

processus [prɔsesyːs], *s.m.* **1.** *Anat:* Process. **2.** Method, process. *Le p. est toujours le même*, the method of operation, the process, is always the same.

procès-verbal, *s.m.* **1.** (Official) report; proceedings, minute(s) (of meeting); record (of evidence, etc.). *Dresser p.-v.*, to draw up a report; to report. *Registre des procès-verbaux*, minute-book. **2.** Policeman's report (against s.o.). *Dresser le p.-v. d'un délit; dresser un p.-v. à qn*, to take down the particulars of a minor offence; *F:* to take s.o.'s name and address.

prochain [prɔʃɛ̃]. **1.** *a.* (*a*) Nearest (village, etc.). *Cause prochaine*, proximate cause, immediate cause. (*b*) Next. *Dimanche prochain*, (i) next Sunday; (ii) on Sunday next. *Com:* *Fin prochain*, at the end of next month. *Le p. numéro*, the next number (of periodical). (*c*) Near at hand. (i) *Une auberge prochaine*, a neighbouring inn. (ii) *Son p. départ, son départ p.*, his approaching, impending, departure. *L'arrivée prochaine de la police*, the impending arrival of the police. *Dans un avenir p.*, in the near future; before long, ere long. **2.** *s.m.* Neighbour, fellow-creature, fellow-being.

prochainement [prɔʃɛnmɑ̃], *adv.* Shortly, soon; at an early date.

proche [prɔʃ]. **1.** *adv.* Near. **Il demeure ici proche**, he lives close to here. **Tout proche**, close at hand. *De proche en proche*, step by step; by degrees. *Il loge proche (de) l'église*, he lodges near the church. *P. de mourir*, near death; nigh unto death. *P. de la ruine*, on the verge of ruin. **2.** *a.* Near, neighbouring. *La ville la plus p.*, the nearest town. *L'heure est p.*, the hour is at hand. *Ses proches (parents)*, his near relations; his next of kin. *Geog:* **Le Proche Orient**, the Near East.

proclamation [prɔklamasjɔ̃], *s.f.* Proclamation.

proclamer [prɔklame], *v.tr.* To proclaim, declare, publish. *P. le résultat du scrutin*, to declare the poll. *On proclama que . . .*, it was given out that. . . . **Proclamer qn roi**, to proclaim s.o. king.

proclitique [prɔklitik], *a. & s.m. Ling:* Proclitic.

procréateur, -trice [prɔkreatœːr, -tris]. **1.** *a.* Procreative. **2.** *s.* Procreator.

procréation [prɔkreasjɔ̃], *s.f.* Procreation, begetting.

procréer [prɔkree], *v.tr.* To procreate, to beget.

procurable [prɔkyrabl], *a.* Procurable, obtainable.

procurateur [prɔkyratœːr], *s.m. Hist:* Procurator.

procuration [prɔkyrasjɔ̃], *s.f.* Procuration, proxy, power of attorney. *Agir par procuration*, to act by procuration, by proxy. **Donner la procuration à qn**, to confer powers of attorney on s.o.

procurer [prɔkyre], *v.tr. P. qch. à qn*, to procure, obtain, get, sth. for s.o. *Se p. de l'argent*, to raise, obtain, find, money. *Où peut-on se p. ce livre?* where is that book to be had, obtained? **Impossible à se procurer**, unobtainable.

procureur, procuratrice [prɔkyrœːr, prɔkyratris], *s.* **1.** Procurator, proxy. **2.** *s.m.* Attorney (at law). **Procureur de la République** = public attorney, public prosecutor. **Procureur général** = Attorney General.

prodigalité [prɔdigalite], *s.f.* Prodigality, lavishness; extravagance.

prodige [prɔdiːʒ], *s.m.* Prodigy, wonder, marvel. *C'est un prodige*, (i) he is a prodigy; (ii) it is something prodigious. **Faire des prodiges**, to do, work, wonders; to perform prodigies. *a.* **Enfant prodige**, infant prodigy.

prodigieu|x, -euse [prɔdiʒjø, -øːz], *a.* Prodigious, stupendous. *adv.* **-sement.**

prodigue [prɔdig]. **1.** *a.* (*a*) Prodigal, lavish, unsparing (*de*, of). *P. d'excuses*, profuse in apologies. *Être p. de son argent*, to spend lavishly. (*b*) Prodigal, wasteful, spendthrift, thriftless. *B:* **L'enfant prodigue**, the Prodigal Son. **2.** *s.* Prodigal, spendthrift, squanderer.

prodiguer [prɔdige], *v.tr.* **1.** To be prodigal, lavish, of (sth.). *P. qch. à qn*, to lavish sth. on s.o. *P. sa santé*, to be unsparing of one's health. **2.** To waste, squander.

se prodiguer. **1.** To lay oneself out to please. **2.** *Se p. en éloges*, to be lavish of praise.

prodrome [prɔdroːm], *s.m.* Prodrome (*de*, to); premonitory symptom (of disease); preamble (to a treatise).

producteur, -trice [prɔdyktœːr, -tris]. **1.** *a.* Productive (*de*, of); producing. *Ind:* *Appareil p.*, generating apparatus. **2.** *s.* Producer.

productible [prɔdyktibl], *a.* Producible.

productif, -ive [prɔdyktif, -iːv], *a.* Productive.

production [prɔdyksjɔ̃], *s.f.* **1.** Production. (*a*) Exhibiting. *Cin:* Directeur de productions, producer. *Jur:* *P. des pièces*, exhibition of documents. (*b*) Producing; generation (of electricity, etc.). *Ralentir la p.*, to slow down production, to reduce the output. **2.** (*a*) Product. *P. du génie*, work of genius. (*b*) Yield (of mine, etc.); output (of factory).

productivité [prɔdyktivite], *s.f.* Productivity, productiveness; productive capacity.

produire [prɔduiːr], *v.tr.* (*pr.p.* produisant; *p.p.* produit; *pr.ind.* je produis, n. produisons; *p.h.* je produisis; *fu.* je produirai) **1.** To produce, bring forward, adduce (evidence, etc.). **2.** To produce, yield; to bear (fruit). *Argent qui produit de l'intérêt*, money that yields interest. *P. de la chaleur*, to generate heat. **3.** To produce, bring about (result, effect). *P. une impression favorable*, to create a favourable impression.

se produire. **1.** *Se p. (dans le monde)*, to come forward; to make one's way (in society).

2. To occur, happen, arise; to take place; to come into being. *Il pourrait se p. des incidents,* incidents might arise.

produit, *s.m.* **1.** (*a*) Product. *P. naturel,* natural produce. *P. manufacturé,* manufactured article. *P. secondaire,* by-product. (*b*) *P. d'une vente,* proceeds of a sale. *Com: Le p. de la journée,* the day's takings, receipts. **2.** *Mth:* Product (of multiplication).

proéminence [prɔeminɑ̃:s], *s.f.* **1.** Prominence. **2.** Protuberance.

proéminent [prɔeminɑ̃], *a.* Prominent projecting, protuberant.

profanateur, -trice [prɔfanatœ:r, -tris], *s.* Profaner, desecrator.

profanation [prɔfanasjɔ̃], *s.f.* Profanation, desecration.

profane [prɔfan]. **1.** *a.* Profane. (*a*) Secular. (*b*) Unhallowed, ungodly. (*c*) Impious, sacrilegious. **2.** *s.* Uninitiated person; layman; *F:* outsider. *Les profanes,* the laity.

profaner [prɔfane], *v.tr.* **1.** To profane; to desecrate (church, etc.); to violate (a grave). **2.** To misuse, degrade (one's talent).

proférer [prɔfere], *v.tr.* (je profère; je proférerai) To utter. *Sans p. un mot,* without a word. S.a. BLASPHÈME.

profès, -esse [prɔfɛ, -ɛs], *a. & s. Ecc:* Professed (monk, nun).

professer [prɔfese], *v.tr.* **1.** To profess (religion, opinion). **2.** To profess, to teach, to be a professor of (science, etc.); to exercise (a calling).

professeur [prɔfesœ:r], *s.m.* **1.** Professor (at a university); teacher, master or mistress (in a *lycée* or *collège*). *Elle est p. de piano,* she teaches the piano. **2.** Professor (of a faith).

profession [prɔfesjɔ̃], *s.f.* **1.** *P. de foi,* profession of faith. *Ecc:* Faire profession (*dans un ordre*) to make one's profession (in an order). **2.** Occupation, calling, business, trade. *P. libérale,* profession. *Menuisier de p.,* carpenter by trade.

professionnalisme [prɔfesjɔnalism], *s.m. Sp:* Professionalism.

professionnel, -elle [prɔfesjɔnɛl]. **1.** *a.* Professional; vocational (training, etc.). **2.** *s.* Esp. *Sp:* Professional.

professoral, -aux [prɔfesɔral, -o], *a.* Professorial.

professorat [prɔfesɔra], *s.m.* **1.** (*a*) Professorship. (*b*) Mastership, mistress-ship (in *lycée* or *collège*). **2.** *Coll.* Professoriate; body of teachers.

profil [prɔfil], *s.m.* **1.** Profile, side-face. *Dessiner qn de profil,* to draw s.o. in profile. **2.** Contour, outline, section. *P. en long,* longitudinal section. *P. en travers,* cross-section.

profiler [prɔfile], *v.tr.* **1.** To profile; to draw (sth.) in section. **2.** To cut, to machine, (sth.) to a special shape; to shape (a piece). *s.m.* **-age.**
profilé, *a.* **1.** Stream-lined. **2.** **Fer profilé,** sectional iron, iron section. *s.m. Profilés en acier,* steel sections; sectional steel.
profilée, *s.f.* Side-view (of object). *Toute une p. d'arcs,* a long range of arches.

se profiler, to stand out in profile, to be outlined, to be silhouetted (*à, sur, contre,* on, against).

profit [prɔfi], *s.m.* Profit, benefit. **Profits et pertes,** profit and loss. **Faire (son) profit de qch.,** to profit by sth. **Vendre à profit,** to sell at a profit. **Mettre qch. à profit,** to turn sth. to account. **Tirer profit de qch.,** (i) to reap advantage from sth.; (ii) to make use of sth. *Travail sans profit,* unprofitable, profitless, work. **Au profit de,** on behalf of, for the benefit of (s.o.).

profitable [prɔfitabl], *a.* Profitable, advantageous (*à,* to). *adv.* **-ment.**

profiter [prɔfite], *v.i.* **1.** (*a*) *P. de qch.,* to take advantage of sth.; to turn sth. to account. *P. de l'occasion,* to improve the occasion. (*b*) *P. sur une vente,* to make a profit on a sale. **2.** *P. à qn,* to profit s.o.; to be profitable to s.o. **Faire profiter son argent,** to lay out one's money to advantage S.a. ACQUÉRIR. **3.** (Of child, etc.) To thrive, grow.

profiteur [prɔfitœ:r], *s.m. F:* Profiteer.

profond [prɔfɔ̃]. **1.** *a.* (*a*) Deep. *Puits p. de six mètres,* well six yards deep. *Voix profonde,* deep voice. *Peu profond,* shallow. (*b*) Deep-seated; underlying, ultimate (cause). *Anat:* **Vaisseau profond,** profunda. (*c*) Profound (wisdom scholarship); deep, sound (sleep). *P. scélérat,* downright, utter, scoundrel. **2.** *adv.* **Creuser profond,** to dig deep. **Retentir profond,** to give a hollow sound. **3.** *s.m.* **Au plus profond de mon cœur,** in the depths of my heart, in my heart of hearts. *Au plus p. de la nuit,* at dead of night, in the dead of night. **4.** *s.f. P:* Profonde, pocket. *adv.* **-ément.**

profondeur [prɔfɔ̃dœ:r], *s.f.* **1.** Depth. *Avoir dix pieds de p.,* to be ten foot deep, ten feet in depth. *Peu de profondeur,* shallowness. **2.** *La p. de son savoir,* the profoundness, profundity, depth, of his knowledge.

profus [prɔfy], *a.* Profuse. *adv.* **-ément.**

profusion [prɔfyzjɔ̃], *s.f.* Profusion, profuseness. (*a*) Abundance. **Avoir tout à profusion,** to have everything in profusion. (*b*) Lavishness.

progéniture [prɔʒenity:r], *s.f.* Progeny, progeniture, offspring.

prognathe [prɔgnat], *a. Anthr:* Prognathous, prognathic (pers.); undershot (jaw).

prognathisme [prɔgnatism], *s.m.* Prognathism.

pronostique [prɔgnɔstik], *a. Med:* Prognostic.

programme [prɔgram], *s.m.* Programme (of concert, etc.); *Pol:* platform (of a party). *P. d'un cours,* syllabus of a course. *Sch: P. d'études,* curriculum. *Les auteurs du p.,* the set books.

progrès [prɔgrɛ], *s.m.* Progress. (*a*) *Le mal fait du p.,* the disease is making progress, is making headway. (*b*) Advancement, improvement (of pupil). *Faire des p. dans ses études,* to make progress, to get on, in one's studies. *La science a réalisé de sérieux p.,* science has made great strides. *Ami du p.,* progressive.

progresser [prɔgrese], *v.i.* (*a*) To progress, advance; to make headway. (*b*) To improve.

progressif, -ive [prɔgresif, -i:v], *a.* Progressive. (*a*) Forward (movement). (*b*) Gradual (growth). **Impôt progressif,** graduated tax. *adv.* **-ivement.**

progression [prɔgresjɔ̃], *s.f.* **1.** Progress(ion); moving forward; advancement. **2.** *P. arithmétique,* arithmetical progression. *Mus: P. harmonique,* harmonic progression.

prohiber [prɔibe], *v.tr.* To prohibit, forbid. *P. à qn de faire qch.,* to prohibit s.o. from doing sth. *P. le tabac à qn,* to forbid s.o. tobacco. *Marchandises prohibées,* prohibited goods. *Temps prohibé,* close season (for hunting, fishing).

prohibitif, -ive [prɔibitif, -i:v], *a.* **1.** Prohibitory (law). **2.** Prohibitive (price).

prohibition [prɔibisjɔ̃], *s.f.* Prohibition.

proie [prwa], *s.f.* Prey; *Ven:* quarry. **Oiseau de proie,** bird of prey. *Devenir la p. de qn, de qch.,* to become the prey of s.o., sth. **Être en proie aux remords,** to be a prey to remorse. *Être en p. à une violente émotion,* to be under a violent emotion. **Tomber en proie à . . .,** to fall a prey to. . . .

projecteur [prɔʒɛktœ:r], *s.m.* **1.** (*a*) Projection apparatus; *F:* magic lantern; *Cin:* picture projector. (*b*) Searchlight, projector. (*c*) *Aut:* Headlight. *P. orientable*, spot-light. *Av: P. d'atterrissage*, landing flood-light. **2.** *Mil: P. de flammes*, flame projector.

projectile [prɔʒɛktil], *a. & s.m.* Projectile; missile.

projection [prɔʒɛksjɔ̃], *s.f.* Projection. **1.** (*a*) Throwing up, out (of liquids, etc.). (*b*) **Lanterne à projection**, (i) motion-picture projector; (ii) lecture-lantern. *Conférence avec projections*, lecture with lantern slides or films. (*c*) Beam (of light). **2.** *Mth: Arch:* Projection, plan. *P. horizontale*, ground-plan.

projet [prɔʒɛ], *s.m.* (*a*) Project, plan; scheme. *Former, accomplir, un p.*, to form, carry out, a project. **Homme à projets**, planner, schemer. **Avoir des projets sur qn**, to have designs on s.o. (matrimonially). (*b*) Plan (of building, etc.); (first) sketch; preliminary design. *P. de contrat*, draft agreement. **Projet de loi**, (draft) bill. **Bâtiment en projet**, projected building.

projeter [prɔʒte, -ʃte], *v.tr.* (Conj. like JETER) To project. **1.** To throw; to cast (shadow); to flash (beam of light). *L'explosion les projeta au loin*, the explosion hurled them, flung them, far and wide. **2.** To plan, contemplate (departure).
  se projeter, to project, stand out; (of cliff) to jut out. *Une ombre se projeta sur le mur*, a shadow was cast on the wall.

prolétaire [prɔletɛ:r], *a. & s.m.* Proletarian.

prolétariat [prɔletarja], *s.m.* **1.** Proletarianism. **2.** *Coll.* The proletariate.

prolifération [prɔliferasjɔ̃], *s.f.* Proliferation.

prolifère [prɔlifɛ:r], *a. Nat.Hist:* Proliferous.

prolifique [prɔlifik], *a.* Prolific.

prolixe [prɔliks], *a.* Prolix, verbose, wordy.

prolixité [prɔliksite], *s.f.* Prolixity; verbosity.

prologue [prɔlɔg], *s.m.* Prologue (*de*, to).

prolongation [prɔlɔ̃gasjɔ̃], *s.f.* Prolongation (in time); protraction; lengthening (of stay); extension (of leave). *Fb: Jouer les prolongations*, to play extra time.

prolonge [prɔlɔ̃:ʒ], *s.f. Artil:* **1.** Prolonge, trail-rope. **2.** Ammunition waggon.

prolongement [prɔlɔ̃ʒmɑ̃], *s.m.* Prolongation (in space); lengthening, extension (of wall, railway, etc.).

prolonger [prɔlɔ̃ʒe], *v.tr.* (je prolongeai(s); n. prolongeons) To prolong; to protract, extend; to draw out, spin out (discourse, etc.). *Visite très prolongée*, protracted call. *Mth: P. une droite*, to produce a line.
  se prolonger, to be prolonged; to continue, extend.

prolongé, *a.* **1.** Long(-continued); of long continuance; prolonged (absence); long-drawn (sigh). **2.** Prolate (ellipsoid).

promenade [prɔmnad], *s.f.* **1.** (*a*) Walking (as exercise). (*b*) Stroll, outing. **Faire une promenade (à pied)**, to go for a walk; to have a walk. *F: Ce n'est qu'une promenade*, it is only a short walk; it is no distance (away). **Faire une promenade à cheval, à bicyclette**, to go for a ride (on horseback); for a bicycle ride. *P. en voiture*, drive. *P. en bateau*, row, sail. *P. en auto*, motor run. **Être en promenade**, to be out walking; to be out for a walk, for a drive, for a spin, etc. **Faire faire une promenade à qn**, to take s.o. for a walk, for an outing. **Promenade militaire**, route march. **2.** (Place for walking) Promenade, (public) walk.

promener [prɔmne], *v.tr.* (je promène; je promènerai) **1.** (*a*) To take (s.o.) (out) for a walk,

for a drive, etc. (*b*) To take, lead, (s.o.) about. *P. un chien*, to exercise a dog. **2.** *P. sa main sur qch.*, to pass, run, one's hand over sth. *P. ses yeux sur qch.*, to cast one's eyes over sth.
  se promener. **1.** To walk; to go for a walk, for a drive, for a ride. **Mener promener les enfants**, to take the children out for a walk. *F:* **Envoyer promener qn**, to send s.o. to the right-about, about his business; to send s.o. packing. **Allez vous promener!** away with you! *Il laisse p. ses affaires de tous les côtés*, he leaves his things all over the place. **2.** *Ses yeux se promenaient sur la foule*, his eyes wandered over the crowd.

promeneur, -euse [prɔmnœ:r, -ø:z], *s.* **1.** (*a*) Walker, pedestrian; rambler, hiker. (*b*) Promenader. **2.** *P. de touristes*, tourists' guide.

promenoir [prɔm(ə)nwa:r], *s.m.* Promenade; lounge (of music-hall); lobby (of law-courts).

promesse [prɔmɛs], *s.f.* Promise, assurance. **Tenir sa promesse**, to keep one's promise. **Manquer à sa promesse**, to break one's promise.

prometteur, -euse [prɔmɛtœ:r, -ø:z], *a. & s.* **1.** (Person) quick to promise. **2.** Promising, attractive (invitation); full of promise.

promettre [prɔmɛtr], *v.tr.* (Conj. like METTRE) **1.** (*a*) *P. qch. à qn*, to promise s.o. sth.; to promise sth. to s.o. *P. à qn de faire qch.*, to promise s.o. to do sth. *F: Je vous promets qu'on s'est amusé!* you bet we had a good time! *Prov:* **Promettre et tenir sont deux**, saying and doing are different things. (*b*) *Se p. qch.*, to promise oneself sth.; to set one's hopes, one's mind, on sth. *F:* **Je m'en promets**, I am looking forward to having a good time. **2.** *Le temps promet de la chaleur*, it promises to be warm. *Il promet d'éclipser tous ses rivaux*, he bids fair to eclipse all his rivals. *Abs. Les vignes promettent*, the vines look promising.

promis, *a.* (*a*) **La Terre promise**, Promised Land. (*b*) Promised (in marriage); engaged.

promiscuité [prɔmiskɥite], *s.f. Pej:* Promiscuity.

promontoire [prɔmɔ̃twa:r], *s.m.* Promontory; headland, cape.

promoteur, -trice [prɔmɔtœ:r, -tris]. **1.** *a.* Promoting. **2.** *s.* Promoter, originator (*de*, of).

promotion [prɔmɔsjɔ̃], *s.f.* **1.** (*a*) Promotion, preferment. *P. à l'ancienneté*, promotion by seniority. (*b*) List of promotions, of appointments. **2.** *Coll.* Persons promoted. *Sch:* Batch (of schoolboys) promoted. **Camarade de promotion**, class-mate. *Le premier de sa p.*, the first of his year.

prompt [prɔ̃], *a.* Prompt, quick, ready; hasty. *Esprit p.*, quick mind or ready wit. *Être d'humeur prompte*, to be hasty-tempered. **Prompt à la colère**, **à se fâcher**, quick to anger. *adv.* **-ement**.

promptitude [prɔ̃tityd], *s.f.* Promptitude, promptness; quickness, alertness. *Avec toute la p. possible*, with all possible dispatch.

promu [prɔmy], *a.* Promoted, raised (*à*, to).

promulgation [prɔmylgasjɔ̃], *s.f.* Promulgation.

promulguer [prɔmylge], *v.tr.* To promulgate (law); to publish; to issue (decree).

pronation [prɔnasjɔ̃], *s.f.* Prone position; pronation. **En pronation**, prone.

prône [pro:n], *s.m. Ecc:* Sermon, homily.

prôner [prone], *v.tr.* **1.** *A:* To preach to (congregation). **2.** *F:* To extol, crack up, cry up (s.o., sth.); to puff, boost (sth.).

pronom [prɔnɔ̃], *s.m. Gram:* Pronoun.

pronominal, -aux [prɔnɔminal, -o], *a. Gram:* Pronominal. *adv.* **-ement.**

ononçable [pronõsabl], *a.* Pronounceable.

ononcer [pronõse], *v.tr.* (je prononçai(s); n. rononçons) To pronounce. **I.** (a) *Sans p. un ot,* without a word. *J'entendis p. mon nom,* I eard my name (mentioned). *Il ne faut jamais p. on nom,* you must never mention him, never tter his name. (b) *P. un discours,* to deliver, nake, a speech. *Jur: P. une sentence,* to pass, eliver, a sentence; to pronounce sentence. *Abs.* *. en faveur de qn,* to decide, declare, in favour f s.o. *P. sur une question,* to adjudge, adjudicate, question. S.a. vœu 1. **2.** *Mot difficile à p.,* word hard to pronounce. **Mal prononcer un mot,** o mispronounce a word.

se prononcer, to declare, pronounce, ex-ress, one's opinion or decision; to make a ecision.

prononcé. I. *a.* Pronounced, decided, well-)marked (feature, etc.). *Courbe prononcée,* harp curve. *Accent étranger très p.,* marked oreign accent. *Peu p.,* faint. **2.** *s.m.* (a) *Jur:* Decision. (b) Delivering (of decision).

ononciation [pronõsjasjõ], *s.f.* **I.** Delivery of speech); bringing in (of verdict); passing of sentence). **2.** Pronunciation. *Défaut de p.,* aulty articulation. *Faute de p.,* mispronunciation.

ronostic [pronostik], *s.m.* **I.** Prognostic(ation). *. du temps, des courses,* weather forecast, racing orecast. **2.** *Med:* Prognosis.

ronostiqu|er [pronostike], *v.tr.* **I.** To prog-nosticate, to forecast. **2.** *Med:* To prognose. *P. au plus grave,* to anticipate, expect, the worst. *.m.* **-eur.**

ropagande [propagã:d], *s.f.* Propaganda. ublicity. *Com:* **Faire de la propagande,** to dvertise.

ropagateur, -trice [propagatœ:r, -tris]. **I.** *a.* Propagating, propagative. **2.** *s.* Propagator, spreader (of news, disease, etc.).

ropagation [propagasjõ], *s.f.* (a) Spread(ing), propagation. *Ph: P. des ondes,* wave propagation. b) *P. d'une espèce,* propagation of a species.

ropager [propaʒe], *v.tr.* (je propageai(s); n. ropageons) To propagate; to spread (abroad).

se propager. I. (a) (Of disease, etc.) To spread. (b) (Of sound, light) To be propagated. **2.** (Of living creatures) To propagate, reproduce.

ropension [propãsjõ], *s.f* Propensity ten-dency, inclination (à, to).

rophète, prophétesse [profe:t, profetes], *s.* a) Prophet, seer; *f.* prophetess. (b) *P. de mal-heur,* prophesier of evil. *Il s'est montré bon p.,* he proved a true prophet.

rophétie [profesi], *s.f.* Prophecy. **I.** Prophesy-ing. **2.** Prophetic utterance.

rophétique [profetik], *a.* Prophetic(al). *adv.* **-ment,** -ally.

rophétiser [profetize], *v.tr.* (a) To prophesy. (b) To foretell (the weather, etc.).

rophylactique [profilaktik], *a. & s.m.* Pro-phylactic.

rophylaxie [profilaksi], *s.f.* Prophylaxis.

ropice [propis], *a.* (a) Propitious (à, to); auspi-cious; favourable. **Né sous une étoile propice,** born under a lucky star. **Peu propice,** (i) unpro-pitious; (ii) inauspicious (moment).

ropitiation [propisjasjõ], *s.f.* Propitiation.

ropitiatoire [propisjatwa:r], *a.* Propitiatory.

ropolis [propolis], *s.f.* Propolis, bee-glue.

roportion [proporsjõ], *s.f.* **I.** Proportion, ratio, percentage. *Varier en p. directe, en p. inverse,* to vary in direct ratio, in inverse ratio. **A proportion,** **en proportion (de),** in proportion, proportionately (to). **A proportion que** + *ind.,* in proportion

as. . . . **Hors de (toute) proportion avec . . .,** out of (all) proportion to. . . . **Défaut de pro-portion,** disproportion (*entre,* between). **Toute(s) proportion(s) gardée(s),** due allowance being made. **2.** *pl.* Size. *Salle de vastes proportions,* hall of great size, of huge proportions.

proportionn|el, -elle [proporsjonɛl]. **I.** *a.* Pro-portional (à, to). *Inversement p.,* in inverse ratio (à, to). *Cust:* **Droit proportionnel,** ad valorem duty. **2.** *s.f. Mth:* **Moyenne proportionnelle** *entre a et b,* mean proportional between a and b. *adv.* **-ellement.**

proportionner [proporsjone], *v.tr. P. qch. à, avec, qch.,* to proportion, adjust, adapt, sth. to sth. *Se p. à ses auditeurs,* to adapt oneself to one's audience.

proportionné, *a.* **I.** *Bien p.,* well-propor-tioned (body). **2.** Proportionate, suited (à, to).

propos [propo], *s.m.* **I.** Purpose, resolution. S.a. DÉLIBÉRÉ 1. **2.** Subject, matter. **A ce propos,** talking of this; in this connection. **A tout propos,** at every turn. **A tout propos, et sans propos,** in season and out of season. *Dire qch.* **à propos,** to say sth. to the point, to the purpose. *Mot jeté à p.,* timely word. *Remarque faite à p.,* apposite remark. *Faire qch. à p.,* to do sth. at the right moment, opportunely. *Arriver fort à p.,* to arrive in the nick of time. *Juger à p. de . . .,* to think or deem it fitting, opportune, advisable, to. . . . **A propos,** *avez-vous lu ce livre?* by the way, that reminds me, have you read this book? **Mal à propos,** at the wrong moment, inoppor-tunely. **Hors de propos,** ill-timed or irrelevant (remark, etc.); (observation) out of place. **A propos de,** with regard to, in connection with (sth.). *A p. de rien,* for nothing at all, for no earthly reason. **A propos de quoi? à quel propos?** on what account? in what connection? S.a. À-PROPOS, BOTTE[2] 1. **3.** Utterance, remark; *pl.* talk, gossip, tittle-tattle. *Des p. de table,* table-talk. **Changer de propos,** to change the subject. **Entrer en propos avec qn,** to enter into conversation with s.o.

proposable [propozabl], *a.* Worthy to be brought forward for consideration.

proposant [propozã], *s.m.* (Protestant) student in divinity.

propos|er [propoze], *v.tr.* To propose (plan); to propound (theory). *P. un amendement,* to move an amendment. *P. qn comme modèle,* to set up, hold up, s.o. as a model. *P. qn pour un emploi,* to propose s.o., put s.o. forward, recom-mend s.o., for a post. *P. un candidat,* to put up, put forward, a candidate. *P. que l'on fasse qch.,* to propose, move, that sth. be done. *P. à qn de faire qch.,* to propose to s.o. to do sth. *s.* **-eur,** **-euse.**

se proposer. I. To offer oneself, to come forward (as secretary, etc.). **2.** *Se proposer qch.,* to intend sth.; to have sth. in view. *Se p. de faire qch.,* to purpose, mean, to do sth.

proposition [propozisjõ], *s.f.* **I.** Proposal, proposition. **Faire une proposition,** to make a proposal; (in an assembly) to put a motion. *Mettre une p. aux voix,* to put a motion to the vote. *P. de mariage,* proposal of marriage. **2.** (a) *Log: Mth: etc:* Proposition. (b) *Gram:* Clause.

propre [propr]. **I.** *a.* (a) Proper. *Signification p. d'un mot,* proper meaning of a word. *Aller en* **propre personne,** to go in person; to go person-ally. *Il me dit en propres termes que . . .,* he told me in so many words that. . . . *Ce sont là ses propres paroles,* these are his very words.

(b) Peculiar (à, to). *Une façon de marcher à lui p.*, a gait peculiar to him. (c) *Ph:* Vibration p., natural beat. (d) Own. *Faire qch. de son p. mouvement*, to do sth. of one's own accord. *Ses idées lui sont propres*, his ideas are his own. *Voir avec ses propres yeux*, to see with one's own eyes. *Je le lui ai remis en main p.*, I delivered it into his own hands. (e) Appropriate, proper, fit(ting). *P. à qch.*, adapted, fitted, suited, to, for, sth. *Exercice p. à aiguiser l'intelligence*, exercise calculated to sharpen the wits. **Propre à tout**, fit for anything. **Propre à rien**, good for nothing. **Être mal propre à faire qch.**, to be ill-fitted to do sth. *Prov:* **Qui est propre à tout n'est propre à rien**, a Jack of all trades is master of none. (f) Neat, clean. *Propre comme un sou neuf*, as clean as a new pin. *F:* **Nous voilà propres!** we're in a nice mess! (g) *Le chat est très p.*, the cat is a very cleanly animal. **2.** *s.m.* (a) Property, attribute. *Le p. de cette nation . . .*, the characteristic of this nation. . . . (b) *Employer un mot au p.*, to use a word in its literal sense. (c) *Avoir qch. en propre*, to possess sth. in one's own right.

proprement [prɔprəmã], *adv.* **1.** Properly, appropriately. **Proprement dit**, properly so called **2.** (a) Cleanly, neatly, nicely; in a cleanly manner. (b) *F:* Well, efficiently. *Assez p.*, tolerably well.

propret, -ette [prɔprɛ, -ɛt], *a. F:* Neat, tidy.

propreté [prɔprəte], *s.f.* Cleanliness; cleanness, neatness, tidiness.

propriétaire [prɔprietɛːr], *s.m. & f.* **1.** Proprietor, proprietress; owner. *Se rendre p. de qch.*, to acquire sth. *P. foncier*, (i) ground landlord; (ii) landed proprietor, landowner. *Être p.*, (i) to be a man of property; (ii) to have a house of one's own. **2.** Landlord, landlady

propriété [prɔpriete], *s.f.* **1.** (a) Proprietorship, ownership **Nue propriété**, bare ownership. **Titres de propriété**, title-deeds. **Propriété littéraire**, literary property; copyright. *P. industrielle*, patent rights. (b) Property, estate; holding. *P. foncière*, landed property, landed estate. **2.** Property, characteristic, peculiar quality. *Les propriétés de la matière*, the properties of matter. **3.** Propriety, correctness (of language, etc.).

proprio [prɔprio], *s.m. P:* = PROPRIÉTAIRE.

propulser [prɔpylse], *v.tr.* To propel.

propulseur [prɔpylsœːr]. **1.** *a.m.* Propelling, propellent, propulsive. **2.** *s.m.* Propeller. *P. à hélice*, screw-propeller.

propulsif, -ive [prɔpylsif, -iːv], *a.* Propulsive, propelling.

propulsion [prɔpylsjɔ̃], *s.f.* Propulsion, propelling; impulsion, impelling; driving, drive.

propylée [prɔpile], *s.m. Gr.Ant:* Propylaeum. **Les Propylées**, the Propylaea.

prorata [prɔrata], *s.m.inv.* Proportional part. *Payement au prorata*, payment pro rata. *Au prorata de*, in proportion to.

prorogation [prɔrɔgasjɔ̃], *s.f.* **1.** Prorogation (of parliament). **2.** Esp. *Jur:* Extension of time.

proroger [prɔrɔʒe], *v.tr.* (je prorogeai(s); n. prorogeons) **1.** To prorogue, adjourn (parliament). **2.** To extend (time-limit).

prosaïque [prɔzaik], *a.* Prosaic(al); commonplace. *adv.* **-ment**, -ally.

prosateur, -trice [prɔzatœːr, -tris], *s.* Prose-writer

proscription [prɔskripsjɔ̃], *s.f.* (a) Proscription; banishment, outlawry. (b) *F:* Tabooing.

proscrire [prɔskriːr], *v.tr.* (Conj. like ÉCRIRE) (a) To proscribe, outlaw, banish. *F: P. qn d'une*

société, to proscribe, ostracize, s.o. from a socie' (b) *F:* To taboo (a practice).

proscrit, -ite. 1. *a.* Proscribed. **2.** *s. P* script, outlaw.

prose [proːz], *s.f.* Prose. *F:* **Vous faites de prose sans le savoir**, you are doing just the rig thing (though you don't know it). (Fro Molière's *Le Bourgeois Gentilhomme*.)

prosecteur [prɔsɛktœːr], *s.m. Sch:* Prosecto demonstrator (in anatomy).

prosélyte [prɔzelit], *s. m. & f.* Proselyte.

prosélytisme [prɔzelitism], *s.m.* Proselytism.

proser [proze], *v.i.* To prose; to write, d course, prosily.

prosodie [prɔzɔdi], *s.f.* Prosody.

prospecter [prɔspɛkte], *v.tr. Min:* To prospect

prospecteur [prɔspɛktœːr], *s.m.* Prospector.

prospectus [prɔspɛktyːs], *s.m.* **1.** Prospectu **2.** Handbill.

prospère [prɔspɛːr], *a.* **1.** Favourable (à, to); kir (weather). **2.** Prosperous, thriving, flourishing.

prospérer [prɔspere], *v.i.* (je prospère; n. pro pérerai) To prosper, thrive; to do well.

prospérité [prɔsperite], *s.f.* Prosperity, pro perousness. *Com:* **Vague de prospérité**, boom.

prosternation [prɔsternasjɔ̃], *s.f.*, **prosterne ment** [prɔsternamɑ̃], *s.m.* (a) Lying prone prostration. (b) *F:* Grovelling, kotowing. *Ass de prosternations!* enough bowing and scraping

prosterner (se) [səprɔsterne], *v.pr.* (a) T prostrate oneself (*devant*, before); to bow dow (*devant*, to, before). (b) *F:* To grovel, to kotov

prosterné, *a.* Prostrate, prone.

prostituer [prɔstitɥe], *v.tr.* To prostitute (pe son, talent).

se prostituer, to prostitute oneself.

prostituée, *s.f.* Prostitute.

prostitution [prɔstitɥsjɔ̃], *s.f.* Prostitution.

prostration [prɔstrasjɔ̃], *s.f.* Prostration. **1.** Ly ing prone. **2.** Exhaustion. *P. nerveuse*, nervou break-down.

prostré [prɔstre], *a.* Prostrate(d); exhausted.

protagoniste [prɔtagɔnist], *s.m.* Protagonist.

protane [prɔtan], *s.m. Ch:* Methane.

prote [prɔt], *s.m. Typ:* Foreman, overseer.

protecteur, -trice [prɔtɛktœːr, -tris]. **1.** *s.* (e Protector, protectress. (b) Patron, patroness (c art, etc.). **2.** *s.m.* Shield; guard (for machine tool, etc.). **3.** *a.* (a) Protecting. **Société protec trice des animaux**, Society for the Prevention c Cruelty to Animals. (b) Patronizing (tone, etc. (c) Protective (device, tariff)

protection [prɔtɛksjɔ̃], *s.f.* **1.** Protection (contr from). *Dispositif de p.*, safety device, protectiv device. **2.** Patronage, influence. **Prendre qn sou sa protection**, to take s.o. under one's protectior *F:* under one's wing. **Avoir de la protection**, t have a friend at court.

protectionnisme [prɔtɛksjɔnism], *s.m. Pol.Ec* Protection(ism).

protectorat [prɔtɛktɔra], *s.m.* Protectorate.

Protée [prɔte], *Pr.n.m. Myth:* Proteus.

protéen, -enne [prɔtɛɛ̃, -ɛn], *a.* Protean.

protège-aile, *s.m. Av:* Wing-skid. *pl.* D *protège-ailes.*

protège-cheville, *s.m.inv. Fb:* Ankle-pad.

protège-jambes, *s.m.inv.* Leg-shield.

protège-oreilles, *s.m.inv.* Scrum-cap; ea protector.

protéger [prɔteʒe], *v.tr.* (je protège, n. protè geons; je protégeai(s); je protégerai) To protec **1.** To shelter, shield, guard (*contre*, agains from). *Se p. de qch.*, to guard against sth. **2.** T patronize; to be a patron of (arts, etc.).

protégé, -ée, *s.* (*a*) Protégé, *f.* protégée. (*b*) Dependant.

protège-radiateur, *s.m.inv.* *Aut:* Stoneguard (of radiator).

protège-tympan, *s.m.inv.* Ear-protector.

protège-vue, *s.m.inv.* Eye-shade.

protéiforme [prɔteifɔrm], *a.* Infinitely variable; Protean.

protéine [prɔtein], *s.f.* *Ch:* Protein.

protestant, -ante [prɔtɛstɑ̃, -ɑ̃:t], *a.* & *s.* Protestant.

protestantisme [prɔtɛstɑ̃tism], *s.m.* Protestantism.

protestataire [prɔtɛstatɛ:r], *s. m.* & *f.*, protestateur, -trice [prɔtɛstatœ:r, -tris], *s.* Protester, objector.

protestation [prɔtɛstasjɔ̃], *s.f.* 1. Protestation, asseveration. *Faire une p. de son innocence*, to make a protestation of innocence. 2. Protest. *Élever des protestations énergiques*, to raise a strong protest. Réunion de protestation, indignation meeting.

protester [prɔtɛste]. 1. *v.tr.* (*a*) To protest, asseverate. *Il proteste n'avoir rien fait de pareil*, he vows, swears, that he did no such thing. (*b*) *Com:* P. un billet, to protest a bill. 2. *v.i.* (*a*) *P. de son innocence*, to protest one's innocence. (*b*) *P. contre qch.*, to protest, make a protest, against sth.; to challenge (a statement).

protêt [prɔtɛ], *s.m.* *Com:* *Jur:* Protest. Lever protêt, to make a protest. *Lever p. d'un effet*, to protest a bill.

prothèse [prɔtɛ:z], *s.f.* Prosthesis (of artificial limb, of eye, etc.). *P. dentaire*, dental prosthesis.

protocolaire [prɔtɔkɔlɛ:r], *a.* Pertaining to State etiquette.

protocole [prɔtɔkɔl], *s.m.* 1. Protocol. (*a*) Correct form of procedure. (*b*) Ceremonial. 2. *F:* Formalities, social conventions; etiquette. *Soucieux du p.*, punctilious.

protoplasma [prɔtɔplasma], *s.m.*, protoplasme [prɔtɔplasm], *s.m.* *Biol:* Protoplasm, cell-body.

prototype [prɔtɔtip], *s.m.* Prototype.

protoxyde [prɔtɔksid], *s.m.* *Ch:* Protoxide, monoxide. Protoxyde d'azote, nitrous oxide.

protozoaire [prɔtɔzɔɛ:r], *s.m.* *Z:* Protozoan. Les protozoaires, the protozoa.

protubérance [prɔtyberɑ̃:s], *s.f.* Protuberance; (solar) prominence; knob (on stick). *Anat:* Protubérances du crâne, bumps of the cranium.

protubérant [prɔtyberɑ̃], *a.* Protuberant.

prou [pru], *adv.* *A:* Much; many. (Still used in) Peu ou prou, more or less; not much; not many. Ni peu ni prou, not at all; none at all.

proue [pru], *s.f.* Prow, stem, bows (of ship).

prouesse [prues], *s.f.* 1. Prowess, valour. 2. Faire des prouesses, to perform feats of valour, doughty deeds.

prouver [pruve], *v.tr.* 1. To prove (fact). *P. le bien-fondé d'une réclamation*, to substantiate a claim; to make good one's claim. *P. une accusation contre qn*, to bring a charge home to s.o. *F:* Prouver clair comme le jour que . . .*, to make it as clear as daylight that. . . . 2. *P. sa capacité*, to give proof, show proof, of (one's) capacity. *a.* -able.

provenance [prɔvnɑ̃:s], *s.f.* 1. Source, origin. *De p. anglaise*, of English origin. *Train en p. du Midi*, train from the South. 2. Produce, product(ion). *Les provenances des colonies*, colonial produce.

provençal, -aux [prɔvɑ̃sal, -o]. 1. *a.* & *s.* Provençal; of Provence. 2. *s.m.* *Ling:* Provençal.

provende [prɔvɑ̃:d], *s.f.* Provender, fodder.

provenir [prɔvni:r], *v.i.* (Conj. like VENIR) To proceed, result, arise, come (*de*, from); to originate (*de*, in). *Les enfants provenant, provenus, de ce mariage*, the children issuing from this marriage.

proverbe [prɔvɛrb], *s.m.* Proverb. Passer en proverbe, to become a proverb; to become proverbial.

proverbial, -aux [prɔvɛrbjal, -o], *a.* Proverbial. *adv.* -ement.

providence [prɔvidɑ̃:s], *s.f.* Providence. Aller contre la providence, to fly in the face of providence.

providentiel, -elle [prɔvidɑ̃sjɛl], *a.* Providential. *adv.* -ellement.

provigner [prɔviɲe], *v.tr.* To layer (vine). *s.m.* -age.

province [prɔvɛ̃:s], *s.f.* 1. *A.Adm:* Province. 2. La Province, the provinces, the country. Vivre en province, to live in the country. Vie de province, provincial life. Il est bien de sa province, he's a regular provincial.

provincial, -aux [prɔvɛ̃sjal, -o], *a.* Provincial; countrified (manners). 2. *s.* Provincial.

provincialisme [prɔvɛ̃sjalism], *s.m.* Provincialism; esp. word or phrase peculiar to a province.

proviseur [prɔvizœ:r], *s.m.* Head-master (of a lycée).

provision [prɔvizjɔ̃], *s.f.* 1. Provision, store, stock, supply. Faire provision de charbon, to lay in a stock of coal. Aller aux provisions, to go marketing. Sac à provisions, shopping-bag. *Provisions de guerre*, munitions. 2. *Jur:* Jugement par provision, provisional judgment. 3. *Com:* Funds, cover, reserve, margin. *Verser une p., des provisions; verser une somme par p.*, to pay in a sum as a security; to pay a deposit.. Faire provision pour une lettre de change, to provide for a bill. Insuffisance de provision, insufficient funds (to meet cheque, etc.).

provisoire [prɔvizwa:r], *a.* Provisional; acting (manager, etc.); temporary. *Nommé à titre provisoire*, appointed provisionally. *Dividende p.*, interim dividend. *adv.* -ment.

provisorat [prɔvizɔra], *s.m.* Head-mastership (of a lycée).

provocant [prɔvɔkɑ̃], *a.* Provocative. 1. Aggressive. 2. Tantalizing, alluring, lascivious (smile).

provocateur, -trice [prɔvɔkatœ:r, -tris]. 1. *a.* Provocative. Agent provocateur, agent provocateur. 2. *s.* (*a*) Aggressor. (*b*) Instigator.

provocatif, -ive [prɔvɔkatif, -i:v], *a.* Provocative.

provocation [prɔvɔkasjɔ̃], *s.f.* 1. Provocation. *Lancer des provocations à qn*, to hurl defiance at s.o. P. en duel, challenge to a duel. 2. Instigation. *P. au crime*, inciting to crime.

provoquer [prɔvɔke], *v.tr.* 1. To provoke. P. qn en duel, to challenge s.o. to a duel. 2. To induce, instigate. *P. qn au crime*, to instigate s.o. to crime. 3. To cause, bring about. *P. un appel d'air*, to create a draught. *P. la sueur*, to induce perspiration. *P. une explosion*, to give rise to, to cause, an explosion. S.a. INCENDIE. *P. la curiosité de tous*, to arouse universal curiosity. *P. la gaieté*, to cause, provoke, mirth. *P. un sourire*, to raise a smile. *P. des commentaires*, to give rise to comments.

proxénète [prɔksenɛt], *s. m.* & *f.* Procurer, procuress; pander; white-slaver.

proximité [prɔksimite], *s.f.* 1. Proximity, nearness, propinquity. A proximité, near at hand,.

close by. **A proximité de** . . ., close to. . . . **2. Proximité du sang,** proximity of blood.
proyer [prwaje], *s.m. Orn:* (Bruant) proyer, bunting.
prude [pryd]. **1.** *a.* Prudish. **2.** *s.f.* Prude.
prudence [prydã:s], *s.f.* Prudence, carefulness. *Agir avec p.,* to use discretion. *Prov:* **Prudence est mère de sûreté,** 'safety first !'
prud|ent [prydã], *a.* Prudent, discreet ; advisable. *adv.* **-emment.**
pruderie [prydri], *s.f.* Prudery, prudishness.
prud'homme [prydɔm], *s.m.* **1.** *A:* Man of experience and integrity. **2.** *Ind:* **Conseil des prud'hommes,** conciliation board.
Prudhomme (Joseph) [ʒozɛfprydɔm]. *Pr.n.m.* Personification of the pompous and empty-headed bourgeois.
pruine [prɥin], *s.f.* Bloom (on fruit).
prune [pryn], *s.f.* Plum. *P. de damas,* damson. *P. de Reine-Claude,* greengage. *F:* **Ce n'est pas pour des prunes que** . . ., it is not for nothing that. . . . *a.inv.* **Des rubans prune,** plum-coloured ribbons.
pruneau [pryno], *s.m.* **1.** Prune, dried plum. **2.** *P:* (a) Bruise(-mark) ; black eye. (b) (Rifle-) bullet.
prunelle [prynɛl], *s.f.* **1.** *Bot:* (a) Sloe. (b) Prunella, self-heal. **2.** Pupil, apple (of the eye). *F:* **Chérir qn comme la prunelle de ses yeux,** to cherish s.o. like the apple of one's eye. **Jouer de la prunelle,** to ogle. **3.** *Tex:* Prunella.
prunellier [prynɛlje], *s.m.* Blackthorn, sloe-tree.
prunier [prynje], *s.m.* Plum-tree.
Prusse [prys]. *Pr.n.f. Geog:* Prussia. **Bleu de Prusse,** Prussian blue.
prussiate [prysjat], *s.m. Ch:* Prussiate, cyanide.
prussien, -ienne [prysjɛ̃, -jɛn], *a. & s.* Prussian.
prussique [prysik], *a. Ch:* Prussic (acid).
psalmiste [psalmist], *s.m.* Psalmist.
psalmodie [psalmɔdi], *s.f.* **1.** (a) *Ecc:* Intoning. (b) *F:* Singsong, droning. **2.** Intoned psalm.
psalmodier [psalmɔdje]. **1.** *v.i.* To intone, to chant ; to psalmodize. **2.** *v.tr.* To intone (office, etc.) ; *F:* to recite (sth.) in a singsong manner.
psaltérion [psalterjɔ̃], *s.m.* Psaltery.
psaume [pso:m], *s.m.* Psalm.
psautier [psotje], *s.m.* Psalter, psalm-book.
pseud(o)- [psød(ɔ)], *pref.* Pseud(o)-.
pseudo-archaïque, *a.* Pseudo-archaic.
pseudo-membrane, *s.f. Med:* Pseudomembrane, false membrane.
pseudonyme [psødɔnim]. **1.** *a.* Pseudonymous. **2.** *s.m.* Pseudonym ; assumed name.
psitt [pst], *int.* Hist ! here !
psittacisme [psittasism], *s.m.* Psittacism, parrotry.
psittacose [psittako:z], *s.f. Med:* Psittacosis ; parrot disease.
psoque [psɔk], *s.m. Ent:* Psocus, book-louse.
psore [psɔ:r], *s.f.,* **psora** [psɔra], *s.f. Med:* Psora, itch.
pst(t) [pst], *int.* = PSITT.
psychanalyse [psikanali:z], *s.f.* Psycho-analysis.
psychanalyste [psikanalist], *s.m.* Psycho-analyst.
Psyché [psiʃe]. **1.** *Pr.n.f. Gr.Myth:* Psyche. **2.** *s.f.* Cheval-glass, swing-mirror.
psychiatre [psikja:tr], *s.m.* Mind-healer.
psychiatrie [psikjatri], *s.f.* Psychiatry ; mind-healing.
psychique [psiʃik], *a.* Psychic(al).
psychoanalyse [psikɔanali:z], *s.f.* = PSYCHANALYSE.
psychologie [psikɔlɔʒi], *s.f.* Psychology.

psychologique [psikɔlɔʒik], *a.* Psychological. *F:* **Le moment psychologique,** the psychological moment. *adv.* **-ment.**
psychologiste [psikɔlɔʒist], *s.m.,* **psychologue** [psikɔlɔg], *s.m.* Psychologist.
psychonévrose [psikɔnevro:z], *s.f.* Psycho-neurosis.
psychose [psiko:z], *s.f. Med:* Psychosis. **Psychose traumatique,** shell-shock.
psychothérapeutique [psikɔterapøtik]. **1.** *a.* Psycho-therapeutic. **2.** *s.f.* Psycho-therapeutics.
psychothérapie [psikɔterapi], *s.f.* Psycho-therapy.
psychromètre [psikrɔmɛtr], *s.m. Meteor:* Psychrometer.
ptérodactyle [pterɔdaktil], *s.m.* Pterodactyl.
Ptolémée [ptɔleme]. *Pr.n.m. A.Hist:* Ptolemy. *Astr: Système de P.,* Ptolemaic system.
pu. See POUVOIR and PAÎTRE.
puant [pɥã], *a.* Stinking, ill-smelling, noisome. *F: Personnage p.,* (i) offensive person ; (ii) individual eaten up with self-conceit. *Ch: F: Gaz p.,* hydrogen sulphide.
puanteur [pɥãtœ:r], *s.f.* Stench ; foul smell.
pubère [pybɛ:r], *a.* Pubescent ; who has arrived at puberty.
puberté [pybɛrte], *s.f.* Puberty.
pubescent [pybɛssã], *a.* Pubescent, downy.
public, -ique [pyblik]. **1.** *a.* Public ; open (meeting). **La chose publique,** the common weal, the public welfare. *Travailler pour le bien p.,* to work for the common good. **Force publique,** (civil) police. **La Dette publique,** the National Debt. *Jur:* **Marché public,** market overt. *Adm:* **Le Ministère public,** the public prosecutor. **2.** *s.m.* **Le public,** the public, the people. *Le grand p.,* the general public. **En public, in public,** publicly.
publicain [pyblikɛ̃], *s.m. Rom.Hist:* Tax-gatherer. *B:* Publican.
publication [pyblikasjɔ̃], *s.f.* Publication. **1.** Publishing. (a) Issue (of an order). *P. de vente aux enchères,* notice of sale by auction. (b) Bringing out (of a book). **2.** Published work. *P. périodique,* periodical.
publiciste [pyblisist], *s.m.* Publicist.
publicité [pyblisite], *s.f.* Publicity, advertising. **Faire de la publicité,** to advertise. **Agent de publicité,** advertising agent. *Exemplaires de p.,* press copies.
publi|er [pyblie], *v.tr.* To publish. **1.** To make known ; to proclaim. *P. un ordre,* to issue an order. **2.** To bring out (book). *a.* **-able.**
publiquement [pyblikmã], *adv.* Publicly ; in public ; openly.
puce [pys]. **1.** *s.f.* Flea. **Piqûre de puce,** flea-bite. *F:* **Avoir la puce à l'oreille,** to be uneasy, suspicious. **Mettre la puce à l'oreille à qn,** to awaken s.o.'s suspicions. S.a. HERBE 4, SECOUER 1. **2.** *a.inv.* Puce(-coloured).
pucelle [pysɛl], *s.f.* Maid(en), virgin. *Hist:* **La Pucelle d'Orléans,** the Maid of Orleans.
puceron [pysrɔ̃], *s.m.* Plant-louse, green-fly.
pudd|ler [pydle], *v.tr. Metall:* To puddle. *s.m.* **-age.** *s.m.* **-eur.**
pudeur [pydœ:r], *s.f.* Modesty ; sense of decency. **Sans pudeur,** unblushing(ly), shameless(ly). **Rougir de pudeur,** to blush for shame.
pudibond [pydibɔ̃], *a.* Easily shocked ; prudish.
pudibonderie [pydibɔ̃dri], *s.f.* False modesty ; prudishness.
pudique [pydik], *a.* Modest ; chaste.
pudiquement [pydikmã], *adv.* Modestly ; with natural delicacy.

puer [pɥe], *v.i.* To stink, smell. **Puer l'ail,** to smell, stink, of garlic.

puériculture [pɥerikylty:r], *s.f.* Rearing of children; child welfare.

puéril [pɥeril], *a.* Puerile, childish. *adv.* **-ement.**

puérilité [pɥerilite], *s.f.* Puerility.

puffin [pyfɛ̃], *s.m. Orn:* Shearwater.

puffisme [pyfism], *s.m.* Puffery, puffing; *U.S:* boosting.

puffiste [pyfist], *s.m.* Puffer; writer of puffs; *U.S:* booster.

pugilat [pyʒila], *s.m.* Pugilism, boxing.

pugiliste [pyʒilist], *s.m.* Pugilist, boxer.

puîné, -ée [pɥine], *a.* Younger (brother or sister).

puis¹, puisse [pɥi, pɥis]. See POUVOIR.

puis², *adv.* (*a*) Then, afterwards, next. (*b*) Besides. **Et puis,** (i) and then; (ii) moreover; and besides. **Et puis après?** (i) what then? what next? (ii) *P:* what about it?

puisard [pɥiza:r], *s.m.* Sunk draining trap; cesspool. *Min: Mch:* Sump.

puisatier [pɥizatje], *s.m.* **1.** (*a*) Well-sinker. (*b*) *Min:* Shaft-sinker. **2.** *Min:* Sumpman.

puis|er [pɥize], *v.tr.* (*a*) To draw (water) (*à, dans,* from). *F:* **Il n'y a qu'à y puiser,** you have only to put out your hand. (*b*) *P.* **une idée chez un** *auteur,* to take, derive, an idea from an author. *Abs.* **Puiser à la source,** aux sources, to go to the source, to the fountain-head. [PUITS] *s.m.* **-age.** *s.m.* **-ement.**

puisette [pɥizet], *s.f.* Ladle, scoop.

puisoir [pɥizwa:r], *s.m. Ind:* Ladle. [PUISER]

puisque [pɥisk(ə)], *conj.* (**Puisqu'** before *il(s),* *elle(s), on, en, un(e),* and to-day frequently before any initial vowel) Since, as, seeing that. *Je le ferai, puisqu'il le faut,* I shall do it, since I must. *F:* **Puisque je te dis que je l'ai vu!** but I tell you I saw it!

puissance [pɥisɑ̃:s], *s.f.* Power. **1.** Force (of habit); strength (of the wind). *P. d'une machine,* power of an engine. *Mec:* **Puissance vive,** kinetic energy ($\frac{1}{2}mv^2$). *P.* **en chevaux,** horse-power. *P. au frein,* brake-power. *P. fiscale d'une auto,* Treasury rating of a car. **A toute puissance,** at full power. S.a. MASSIQUE. *W.Tel:* **Poste émetteur de haute puissance,** high-power wireless station. **Lampe de puissance,** power valve. *Mth:* *P. d'un nombre,* power of a number. *Élever un nombre à la nième p.,* to raise a number to the nth (power). **2.** Sway, authority. **Avoir qn en sa puissance,** to have s.o. in one's power. **Être en puissance de mari,** to be under a husband's control. *P. paternelle,* paternal authority. **3.** *Les puissances européennes,* the European Powers. **4. En puissance,** in posse, potential(ly).

puiss|ant [pɥisɑ̃]. **1.** *a.* (*a*) Powerful, mighty, strong. *Homme p.,* man. *Puissante machine,* powerful machine. (*b*) *Remède p.,* potent remedy. *En p. relief,* in bold relief. **2.** *s. Les puissants de la terre,* the mighty ones of the earth. S.a. TOUT-PUISSANT. *adv.* **-amment.**

puits [pɥi], *s.m.* **1.** Well, hole. *P. de sondage,* boring. *P. artésien,* artesian well. *P. à ciel ouvert,* open well. *Eau de p.,* well-water. *P. absorbant,* *p. perdu,* cesspool. *F:* **C'est un puits de science,** he is a fount of knowledge. S.a. JAILLISSANT. **2.** (*a*) Shaft, pit (of mine). *P. d'aérage,* air-shaft. *P. d'extraction,* winding-shaft. (*b*) *Ind:* *P. de montage,* erecting pit.

pullulation [pyllylasjɔ̃], *s.f.,* **pullulement** [pyllylmɑ̃], *s.m.* (*a*) Pullulation, rapid multiplication (of animals, etc.). (*b*) *F:* Swarming.

pulluler [pyllyle], *v.i.* To pullulate. (*a*) To multiply rapidly. (*b*) To be found in profusion; to swarm.

pulmonaire [pylmɔnɛ:r]. **1.** *a.* Pulmonary, pulmonic. *Congestion p.,* congestion of the lungs. **2.** *s.f. Bot:* Lungwort.

pulpe [pylp], *s.f.* **1.** Pulp. **Réduire qch. en pulpe,** to reduce sth. to a pulp; to pulp sth. **2.** Pad (of finger or toe).

pulper [pylpe], *v.tr.* To pulp.

pulpeux, -euse [pylpø, -ø:z], *a.* Pulpy; pulpous.

pulsatif, -ive [pylsatif, -i:v], *a.* Pulsatory; throbbing (pain).

pulsatille [pylsati:j], *s.f. Bot:* Pulsatilla, pasque-flower.

pulsation [pylsasjɔ̃], *s.f.* Pulsation. **1.** Throbbing; beating (of the heart, etc.). **2.** Throb; (heart-)beat.

pulsatoire [pylsatwa:r], *a.* Pulsatory.

pulvérisable [pylverizabl], *a.* (*a*) Pulverizable. (*b*) (Liquid) that may be sprayed or atomized.

pulvérisateur [pylverizatœ:r], *s.m.* (*a*) Pulverizer. (*b*) Atomizer; sprayer, vaporizer.

pulvérisation [pylverizasjɔ̃], *s.f.* (*a*) Pulverization, crushing. (*b*) Atomization, spraying (of liquids).

pulvériser [pylverize], *v.tr.* (*a*) To pulverize; to grind, reduce, (substance) to powder. *F:* *P.* *qn,* to pulverize s.o.; to knock s.o. into a cocked hat. (*b*) To spray, atomize (liquid). *I.C.E:* *P. l'essence,* to atomize the petrol.

pulvérulent [pylverylɑ̃], *a.* Pulverulent, powdery.

puma [pyma], *s.m. Z:* Puma, cougar.

pûmes [pym]. See POUVOIR.

punaise [pynɛ:z], *s.f.* **1.** *Ent:* Bug. *P. des lits,* bed-bug, house-bug. **2.** Drawing-pin.

punch [pɔ̃:ʃ], *s.m.* Punch. **Bol à punch,** punch-bowl.

punique [pynik], *a. Hist:* Punic (war, etc.). **Foi punique,** Punic faith; treachery.

pun|ir [pyni:r], *v.tr.* To punish; to avenge (crime). *P. qn de mort, de prison,* to punish s.o. with death, with imprisonment. **Être puni par où l'on a péché,** to be justly punished for one's sins. *Mil: Homme puni,* defaulter. *a.* **-issable.** *s.* **-isseur, -euse.**

punition [pynisjɔ̃], *s.f.* **1.** Punishing; punishment. **Donner une punition à qn,** to inflict a punishment, a penalty, on s.o. **Par, pour, punition,** for, by way of, punishment; as a punishment. **2.** *Games:* Forfeit.

pupe [pyp], *s.f. Ent:* **1.** Pupa-case. **2.** Pupa, chrysalis.

pupille¹ [pypil]. **1.** *s. m. & f.* (*a*) *Jur:* Ward. (*b*) Child in orphanage; boy on training-ship, etc. **2.** *s.f.* **Enfant en pupille,** child in pupilage.

pupille², *s.f.* Pupil, *F:* apple (of the eye).

pupitre [pypi:tr], *s.m.* **1.** Desk. *P. à musique,* music-stand, -desk. **2.** (Wine-bottle) rack. **3.** *Mus:* Group (of instruments). **Chef de pupitre,** leader (of a group).

pur [py:r], *a.* Pure. **1.** *Or pur,* pure gold. *Vin pur,* wine without water. *Liquide pur de tout mélange,* liquid free from all admixture. *Pur hasard,* pure chance, mere chance. *La pure vérité,* the simple, plain, honest, unvarnished, truth. *Pur coquin,* downright rogue. *Par pure malice,* out of pure, sheer, malice. S.a. SANG 2. **2.** (Free from taint) *Air pur,* pure air. *Ciel pur,* clear sky. *Conscience pure,* clear conscience. *adv.* **-ement.**

purée [pyre], *s.f. Cu:* (*a*) Mash. *P. de pommes de terre,* mashed potatoes. (*b*) Thick soup; purée.

P: Être dans la purée, to be down on one's luck ; to be in the soup.

purent [pyːr]. See POUVOIR.

pureté [pyrte], *s.f.* Purity ; pureness ; clearness (of the sky).

purgatif, -ive [pyrgatif, -iːv], *a. & s.m. Med:* Purgative.

purgation [pyrgasjɔ̃], *s.f.* Purging, purgation.

purgatoire [pyrgatwaːr], *s.m. Theol:* Purgatory.

purge [pyrʒ], *s.f.* **1.** (*a*) Purge, purgative. (*b*) Disinfection (of goods). (*c*) *Tex:* Cleaning (of silk thread). **2.** *Mch:* Blow-off, draining. Robinet de purge, blow-off cock, drain-cock. **3.** Paying off, redemption (of mortgage).

purger [pyrʒe], *v.tr.* (je purgeai(s) ; n. purgeons) To purge, clean, cleanse, clear. (*a*) *P. un malade,* to purge a patient. *P. les intestins,* to clear out the bowels. (*b*) *P. l'or,* to refine gold. *P. un pays de voleurs,* to rid a country of bandits. (*c*) *P. ses terres de dettes,* to clear, disencumber, one's estate of debt. *Se p. d'une accusation,* to clear oneself of an accusation. *P. une hypothèque,* to redeem, pay off, a mortgage. *Nau: P. la quarantaine,* to clear one's quarantine. S.a. CONDAMNATION 1. (*d*) *Mch:* To blow off, blow out, drain (cylinder, etc.).
    se purger, to take a purgative ; *F:* to take medicine.

purificateur, -trice [pyrifikatœːr, -tris]. **1.** *a.* Purifying, cleansing. **2.** *s.* Purifier, cleanser.

purification [pyrifikasjɔ̃], *s.f.* Purification ; cleansing (of the blood, etc.).

purifier [pyrifje], *v.tr.* To purify, cleanse ; to sweeten (air, water) ; to refine (metal).
    se purifier, to become pure ; to purify.

purin [pyrɛ̃], *s.m.* Liquid manure. Fosse à purin, manure pit or sump.

purisme [pyrism], *s.m.* Purism (of language).

puriste [pyrist]. **1.** *s.m.* Purist. **2.** *a.* Puristical.

puritain, -aine [pyritɛ̃, -ɛn], *s.* Puritan.

puritanisme [pyritanism], *s.m.* Puritanism.

purotin, -ine [pyrotɛ̃, -in], *s. P:* Hard-up, impecunious, person. [PURÉE]

purpurin [pyrpyrɛ̃], *a.* (*a*) (Approaching to) crimson. (*b*) Purplish.

pur-sang, *s.m.inv.* Thoroughbred (horse, dog).

purulence [pyrylɑ̃ːs], *s.f. Med:* Purulence, purulency.

purulent [pyrylɑ̃], *a. Med:* Purulent. Foyer purulent, abscess.

pus[1] [py], *s.m. Med:* Pus, matter.

pus[2]. See POUVOIR.

pusillanime [pyzillanim], *a.* Pusillanimous ; faint-hearted.

pusillanimité [pyzillanimite], *s.f.* Pusillanimity ; faint-heartedness.

puss-e, -ent [pys]. See POUVOIR.

pustule [pystyl], *s.f.* Pustule ; *F:* pimple.

put [py]. See POUVOIR.

putat.if, -ive [pytatif, -iːv], *a.* Putative, supposed, presumed. *adv.* **-ivement.**

pûtes [pyt]. See POUVOIR.

putois [pytwa], *s.m.* Polecat, fitchet. *P. d'Amérique,* skunk.

putréfactif, -ive [pytrɛfaktif, -iːv], *a.* Putrefactive.

putréfaction [pytrɛfaksjɔ̃], *s.f.* Putrefaction.

putréfier [pytrefje], *v.tr.* To putrefy.
    se putréfier, to putrefy ; to become putrid.

putrescence [pytrɛssɑ̃ːs], *s.f.* Putrescence.

putrescent [pytrɛssɑ̃], *a.* Putrescent.

putrescible [pytrɛssibl], *a.* Putrescible.

putride [pytrid], *a.* Putrid, tainted. *Fermentation p.,* putrefactive fermentation.

puy [pɥi], *s.m. Dial:* (In Auvergne) Peak.

pygargue [pigarg], *s.m. Orn:* Sea-eagle, erne.

pygmée [pigme], *s. m. & f.* Pygmy.

pyjama [piʒama], *s. m.* Pyjamas. *Un p.,* a suit of pyjamas.

pylône [piloːn], *s.m.* **1.** Pylon (of Egyptian temple). **2.** Pylon(e) ; tower (conveying electric power, etc.) ; lattice-mast (supporting telegraph-wires, etc.). Grue à pylône, tower-crane.

pylore [piloːr], *s.m. Anat:* Pylorus.

pyorrhée [pjore], *s.f. Med:* Pyorrhea.

pyracanthe [pirakɑ̃ːt], *s.f. Bot:* Pyracanth ; evergreen thorn.

pyrale [piral], *s.f. Ent:* Pyralis ; *F:* meal-moth, bee-moth.

pyramidal, -aux [piramidal, -o], *a.* Pyramidal. *F: Succès p.,* tremendous, colossal, success.

pyramide [piramid], *s.f.* Pyramid.

pyrénéen, -enne [pireneɛ̃, -ɛn], *a.* Pyrenean.

Pyrénées (les) [lepirene]. *Pr.n.f.pl. Geog:* The Pyrenees.

pyrèthre [pirɛtr], *s.m. Bot:* (*a*) Feverfew ; *Pharm:* pyrethrum. (*b*) Pellitory of Spain. Poudre de pyrèthre, pyrethrum-powder, insect-powder.

pyrex [pirɛks], *s.m. Glassm:* Pyrex.

pyrexie [pireksi], *s.f.* Pyrexia, feverishness.

pyrite [pirit], *s.f.* (Iron) pyrites. *P. de cuivre,* copper pyrites.

pyriteux, -euse [piritø, -øːz], *a.* Pyritic, pyritous.

pyrogallique [pirɔgallik], *a. Ch:* Pyrogallic. *Acide p., F:* pyro.

pyrogravure [pirɔgravyːr], *s.f.* Poker-work.

pyromètre [pirɔmɛtr], *s.m.* Pyrometer.

pyrotechnie [pirɔtɛkni], *s.f.* Pyrotechnics.

pyrotechnique [pirɔtɛknik], *a.* Pyrotechnic(al).

pyrrhique [pirrik], *a. & s.f.* Pyrrhic (dance).

Pythagore [pitagoːr]. *Pr.n.m. Gr.Phil:* Pythagoras. La table de Pythagore, the multiplication table.

pythie [piti], *s.f. Gr.Rel:* Pythoness.

python [pitɔ̃], *s.m. Gr.Ant: Myth: Z:* Python.

pythonisse [pitɔnis], *s.f.* Pythoness.

pyxide [piksid], *s.f.* **1.** *Z:* Pyxis. **2.** *Bot:* Pyxidium, pyxis.

Q

Q, q [ky], *s.m.* (The letter) Q, q.

quadragénaire [kwadraʒenɛːr], *a. & s.* Quadragenarian.

Quadragésime [kwadraʒezim], *s.f. Ecc:* (Le dimanche de) la Quadragésime, Quadragesima Sunday) ; the first Sunday in Lent.

quadrangulaire [kwadrɑ̃gylɛːr], *a.* Quadrangular, four-angled.

quadrant [k(w)adrɑ̃], *s.m. Mth:* Quadrant.

quadrat [k(w)adra], *s.m.* = CADRAT.

quadratique [kwadratik], *a.* **1.** *Mth:* Quadratic. **2.** *Cryst:* Quadratic, tetragonal.

quadrature [kwadraty:r], *s.f.* Quadrature; squaring (esp. of the circle). *F:* **Chercher la quadrature du cercle,** to try to square the circle; to attempt the impossible. **Marées de quadrature,** neap tides, *F:* neaps.

quadriennal, -aux [kwadriɛnnal, -o], *a.* Quadrennial. **1.** Lasting for four years. **2.** Occurring every four years.

quadrifide [kwadrifid], *a.* Quadrifid, four-cleft.

quadrifolié [kwadrifɔlje], *a.* Quadrifoliate.

quadrige [kwadri:ʒ], *s.m. Rom.Ant:* Quadriga.

quadrijumeaux [kwadriʒymo], *a.m.pl. Anat:* **Tubercules quadrijumeaux,** the quadrigeminal bodies (of the brain).

quadrilatéral, -aux [kwadrilateral, -o], *a.* Quadrilateral, four-sided.

quadrilatère [kwadrilate:r], *s.m.* Quadrilateral.

quadrillage [kwadrija:ʒ], *s.m.* **1.** Cross-ruling, squaring (of paper, map). **2.** (Pattern of) squares; chequer-work.

quadrille [kwadri:j], *s.m.* Quadrille (dance, air); set of quadrilles.

quadriller [kwadrije], *v.tr.* To rule in squares; to cross-rule.

quadrillé, *a.* Squared, cross-ruled; checked, chequered. *Carte quadrillée,* grid map.

quadrillion [k(w)adriljɔ̃, -ijɔ̃], *s.m.* A thousand billions (10¹⁵); *U.S:* quadrillion.

quadrimoteur, -trice [kwadrimɔtœ:r, -tris], *a. Av:* Four-engined.

quadrisyllabe [kwadrisillab], *s.m.* Quadrisyllable.

quadrisyllabique [kwadrisillabik], *a.* Quadrisyllabic.

quadrumane [kwadryman]. **1.** *a.* Quadrumanous, four-handed. **2.** *s.m.* Quadrumane.

quadrupède [kwadrypɛd]. **1.** *a.* Four-footed. **2.** *s.m.* Quadruped.

quadruple [kwadrypl], *a. & s.m.* Quadruple, fourfold. *Être payé au q.,* to be repaid fourfold.

quadrupler [kwadryple], *v.tr. & i.* To quadruple; to increase fourfold.

quai [ke], *s.m.* (*a*) Quay, wharf, pier. **Propriétaire de quai.** wharfinger. **A quai,** alongside the quay. *Amener un vaisseau à q.,* to berth a ship. (*b*) Embankment (along river). *F:* **Le Quai d'Orsay,** the French Foreign Office. (*c*) *Rail:* Platform. **Le train est à quai,** the train is in. *Sur quel q. part le train?* from what platform does the train leave?

quaiche [kɛʃ], *s.f. Nau:* Ketch.

qualifiable [kalifjabl], *a.* That may be characterized (*de,* as). **Conduite peu qualifiable,** unwarrantable conduct.

qualificatif, -ive [kalifikatif, -i:v], *a.* Qualifying, qualificative (adjective, etc.); epithet (adjective).

qualification [kalifikasjɔ̃], *s.f.* **1.** (*a*) *Q. de faussaire,* calling s.o. a forger. (*b*) *Gram:* Qualifying (of noun, etc.). (*c*) *Fin:* Qualifying (by acquisition of shares). **2.** Designation, name, title. *S'attribuer la q. de colonel,* to call oneself a colonel.

qualifier [kalifje], *v.tr.* **1.** To style, call, term, qualify. *Q. qn de son titre, de son grade,* to address or designate s.o. by his correct title. *F: Q. qn de charlatan, de menteur,* to call s.o. a quack, a liar. *Conduite qu'on ne saurait q.,* unspeakable conduct. **2.** *Gram:* To qualify.

se qualifier. 1. *Se q. colonel,* to call, style, oneself colonel. **2.** *Se q. pour une fonction,* to qualify for an office.

qualifié, *a.* (*a*) *Q. pour faire qch.,* qualified to do sth. **Ouvriers qualifiés,** skilled workmen.

(*b*) **Personne qualifiée,** (i) qualified person; (ii) person of quality, of rank, of standing. (*c*) *Jur:* **Crime qualifié,** aggravated crime.

qualitatif, -ive [kalitatif, -i:v], *a. Ch:* **Analyse qualitative,** qualitative analysis.

qualité [kalite], *s.f.* **1.** Quality. (*a*) Degree of excellence. *Article de bonne q.,* good(-quality) article. *Vin de première q.,* choice wine. (*b*) Excellence. **Personne qui a beaucoup de qualités,** person who has many good qualities. **2.** Quality, property (of sth.). *Qualités fébrifuges,* antifebrile properties. **3.** Qualification, capacity, profession, occupation. *Décliner ses titres et qualités,* to enumerate one's titles and qualifications; to introduce oneself. *Il nous révéla sa q. de prêtre,* he disclosed the fact that he was a priest. **En qualité de page,** to serve as a page. *Agir en q. de tuteur,* to act in one's capacity as guardian. **Avoir qualité pour agir,** to be qualified, entitled, to act; to have authority to act. **4.** Title, rank. **Gens de qualité,** people of quality.

quand [kɑ̃]. When. **1.** *conj.* (*a*) *Je lui en parlerai q. je le verrai,* I'll mention it to him when I see him. *F:* **Quand je vous le disais!** didn't I tell you so! (*b*) **Quand (même).** (i) Even if, even though, although. *Q. il me l'affirmerait je n'en croirais rien,* even if he asserted it I wouldn't believe it. (ii) **Je le ferai quand même,** I'll do it all the same, notwithstanding, in spite of all. (*c*) *F:* **Ça ne m'étonnerait pas quand il pleuvrait,** I shouldn't wonder if it rained. **2.** *adv. Q. viendra-t-il?* when will he come? **N'importe quand,** no matter when; at any time. **Jusqu'à quand serez-vous à Paris?** till when, how long, will you be in Paris? **Depuis quand êtes-vous à Paris?** how long, since when, have you been in Paris? **A quand** *la noce?* when is the wedding to be? **De quand** *est ce journal?* what is the date of this paper?

quant¹ [kɑ̃], *a.* (Used in the phr.) **Toutes et quantes fois que . . . .,** whenever . . .; every time that. . . .

quant² [kɑ̃t], *adv.* (Always followed by *à*) **Quant à qn, à qch.,** as to, as for, as regards, with respect to, with regard to, s.o., sth. *Q. à moi,* for my part, as for me.

quant-à-moi, *s.m. inv.,* **quant-à-soi,** *s.m.inv.* Dignity, reserve. **Se mettre, se tenir, sur son quant-à-moi, sur son quant-à-soi; prendre, tenir, garder, son quant-à-soi,** to stand on one's dignity; to be stand-offish; to keep oneself to oneself.

quantième [kɑ̃tjɛm], *s.m.* Day of the month.

quantita|if, -ive [kɑ̃titatif, -i:v], *a.* **1.** *Ch:* **Analyse quantitative,** quantitative analysis. **2.** *Gram:* **Adjectif quantitatif,** adjective of quantity. *adv.* **-ivement.**

quantité [kɑ̃tite], *s.f.* Quantity. *Q. d'eau tombée,* rainfall. S.a. MOUVEMENT 1. *El.E: Couplage en q.,* connection in parallel, in quantity. **En quantité,** in quantity, in abundance. *Par quantités considérables,* in large quantities. *Par petites quantités,* in small amounts. **Quantité de gens,** a lot of people, lots of people. **Venez pour faire quantité,** come along to help to make up a crowd.

quantum [kwɑ̃tɔm], *s.m.* **1.** *Ch: Mth: Ph:* Quantum. **La doctrine des quanta,** the quantum theory. **2.** Amount, proportion. *Fixer le q. des dommages-intérêts,* to fix the amount of damages; to assess the damages.

quarantaine [karɑ̃tɛn], *s.f.* **1.** (About) forty, some forty; some two score. **Approcher de la quarantaine,** to be getting on for forty. **2.** Quarantine. **Mettre un vaisseau, des passagers, en**

quarantaine, to quarantine a ship, passengers. *Pavillon de quarantaine,* quarantine flag. *F:* Mettre qn en quarantaine, to send s.o. to Coventry.

quarante [karɑ̃:t], *num.a.inv. & s.m.inv.* Forty. *Au chapitre q. de . . .,* in the fortieth chapter of. . . . **Les Quarante,** the Forty, the French Academy. *F:* Je m'en fiche comme de l'an quarante, I don't care a rap. S.a. SE MOQUER.

quarantenaire [karɑ̃tnɛːr], *a.* Lasting for forty years; of forty years.

quarantième [karɑ̃tjɛm], *num.a. & s.m.* Fortieth.

quart¹ [kaːr], *a. (a) A:* Fourth. *Un q. voleur survint,* a fourth robber arrived. *s.m.* **Le tiers et le quart,** see TIERS 2. *(b) Med:* **Fièvre quarte,** quartan ague.

quart², *s.m.* **I.** Quarter, fourth part. *Donner un q. de tour à une vis,* to give a screw a quarter turn. *Com:* Remise du q., discount of 25%. *F:* **Dans un petit quart d'heure,** in a few minutes. **Pour le quart d'heure,** for the time being; for the moment. *F:* **Passer un mauvais quart d'heure,** to have a trying moment. **Le quart d'heure de Rabelais,** the hour of reckoning. *Trois quarts,* three quarters. *F:* **Les trois quarts du temps,** most of the time, more than half the time. **Être aux trois quarts ivre,** *F:* to be three sheets in the wind, to be half-seas over. **Il est deux heures et quart,** **deux heures un quart,** it is a quarter past two. **Il est deux heures moins le quart,** **moins un quart,** it is a quarter to two. **L'horloge a sonné le quart,** the quarter has struck. *Arch:* **Quart de rond,** quarter round; ovolo. **Quart de cercle,** quadrant. **2.** *Nau:* **Quart de vent,** point of the compass (= 11° 15'). *Nord-est q. est,* north-east by east. *Changer la route de deux quarts vers l'est,* to alter (the) course two points to the east. **3.** *(a) Nau:* Watch. **Petit quart,** dog-watch. **Être de quart,** to be on watch. **Faire le quart,** to keep watch. S.a. BATTRE 1. **L'officier de quart,** the officer of the watch. **Faire bon quart,** to keep a good look-out. *(b) Mil:* Portion of a unit on duty. **Officier de quart,** officer on duty. **4.** *Mil:* Drinking vessel, mug (holding a quarter of a litre).

quarte [kart], *s.f.* **I.** *Mus:* Fourth. **2.** *Fenc:* Parer en q., to parry in carte.

quarteron, -onne [kart(ə)rɔ̃, -ɔn], *a. & s. Ethn:* Quadroon.

quartier [kartje], *s.m.* **I.** Fourth part. Bois de quartier, quartered logs. *Q. de la lune,* quarter of the moon. *Cu:* Q. d'agneau, quarter of lamb. *Her:* Quartiers de l'écusson, quarterings of the escutcheon. **2.** Part, portion. *Mettre qch. en quartiers,* to tear sth. to pieces. *Q. de terre,* plot of land. *Q. de chevreuil,* haunch of venison. *Q. d'un cheval,* horse's quarters. **3.** *(a)* District, neighbourhood; ward (of town). *Les bas quartiers,* the slums. *Bureau de q.,* branch office (of bank, etc.); branch post office. S.a. LATIN 1. *(b) Nau:* De quel q. vient le vent? from what quarter is the wind blowing? *(c) Mil:* Rentrer au q., to return to quarters, to barracks. *Prendre ses quartiers d'hiver,* to go into winter quarters. **Quartier général,** headquarters. *Grand Q. général,* General Headquarters. **4.** Faire, donner, quartier à qn, to grant, give, s.o. quarter. *Demander q.,* to ask for quarter; to cry quarter.

quartier-maître, *s.m.* **I.** *Mil: A:* Quartermaster. **2.** *Navy:* Leading seaman. *pl.* Des quartier(s)-maîtres.

quarto [kwarto], *adv.* **I.** Fourthly. **2.** See IN-QUARTO.

quartz [kwarts], *s.m.* Quartz, rock-crystal.

quartzeux, -euse [kwartsø, -øːz], *a.* Quartzy.

quasi¹ [kazi], *s.m. Cu:* Chump-end (of loin).

quasi², *adv.* Quasi, almost. *Q. aveugle,* all but blind. *Je n'ai q. rien senti,* I felt scarcely anything. **Une quasi-amitié,** a sort of friendship, a quasi-friendship. *J'en ai la q.-certitude,* I am all but certain of it.

quasi-délit, *s.m. Jur:* Technical offence. *pl. Des quasi-délits.*

quasiment [kazimɑ̃], *adv. F:* Almost, as it were, as one might say; to all intents and purposes. *Q. guéri,* as good as cured.

Quasimodo [kazimɔdo], *s.f. Ecc:* Low Sunday. *Le lundi de (la) Q.,* Low Monday.

quassia [kwasja], *s.m.* **I.** = QUASSIER. **2.** Quassia; quassia chips.

quassier [kwasje], *s.m.* Quassia(-tree).

quaternaire [kwatɛrnɛːr], *a. Quat.:nary.*

quatorze [katɔrz], *num. a. inv. & s.m. inv.* Fourteen. Louis Quatorze, Louis the Fourteenth. *Le q. juillet,* the fourteenth of July. S.a. MIDI 1.

quatorzième [katɔrzjɛm]. **I.** *num. a. & s.* Fourteenth. **2.** *s.m.* Fourteenth (part).

quatrain [katrɛ̃], *s.m. Pros:* Quatrain.

quatre [katr], *num.a.inv. & s.m.inv.* Four. *Hist:* **Henri Quatre,** Henry the Fourth. *Le q. août,* the fourth of August. **A quatre pattes,** on all fours. **Conduire à quatre,** to drive four-in-hand. *Pain de q. livres,* quartern loaf. **Par quatre,** in fours. **Se mettre par quatre,** to form fours. *F:* Un de ces quatre matins, one of these days; sometime soon. Il demeure à quatre pas (d'ici), he lives close by. **Ménager ses quatre sous,** to be careful of one's small savings. **Maison exposée aux quatre vents du ciel,** house exposed to the four winds of heaven. **Clair comme deux et deux font quatre,** as clear as daylight. **Manger comme quatre,** to eat voraciously. **Se mettre en quatre pour faire qch.,** to do one's utmost to accomplish sth. Il se mettrait en quatre pour vous, he would do anything for you. Je me tenais à quatre pour ne pas rire, it was all I could do to keep from laughing. S.a. CHEMIN 1, CHEVEU 1, JEUDI, MARCHAND 1, ŒIL 1, TIRER I. 2, TRAVAILLER 2, VÉRITÉ 2, VOLONTÉ 2.

Quatre-Cantons. *Pr.n.* **Le lac des Quatre-Cantons,** the Lake of Lucerne.

quatre-épices, *s.f. Bot:* Fennel-flower.

quatre-mâts, *s.m. inv.* Four-masted ship.

quatre-saisons, *s.f. inv.* Variety of strawberry.

Quatre-Temps, *s.m.pl. Ecc:* Ember-days.

quatre-vingt-dix, *num.a. & s.m.* Ninety.

quatre-vingtième, *num.a. & s.m.* Eightieth.

quatre-vingts [katrəvɛ̃], *num.a. & s.m.* (Omits the final s when followed by another *num.a.* or when used as an ordinal) Eighty. *Quatre-vingt-un* [katrəvɛ̃œ̃], eighty-one. *Quatre-vingt-onze* [katrəvɛ̃:z], ninety-one.

quatrième [katriɛm]. **I.** *num. a. & s.* Fourth. **2.** *s.m.* Fourth (part).

quatrillion [k(w)atriljɔ̃], *s.m.* = QUADRILLION.

quatuor [kwatɥɔːr], *s.m.* Quartet(te), quatuor.

quayage [keja:ʒ], *s.m.* Quayage, wharfage.

que¹ [k(ə)], *rel.pron.* (Of pers.) That, whom; (of thg) that, which; (in the neut.) which, what. **I.** (Subject) *A:* (Still found in) Advienne que pourra, come what may. *Faites ce que bon vous semble,* do as you think fit. **2.** (Pred.) *Pauvre malheureux que je suis!* poor wretch that I am! *Menteur que tu es!* you liar! *Couvert qu'il était de poussière,* covered with dust as he was. *Purs mensonges que tout cela!* that's all a pack of lies! *(C'est un) drôle de garçon que Pierre,* he's a queer fish, is Peter. *C'est une belle maison que la vôtre,* yours is a fine house. **3.** (Object) (a) *L'homme que vous voyez,* the man whom, that, you see. *Les livres que vous avez achetés,* the books you have bought. *C'est le seul de ses romans que je lise avec plaisir,* it is the only novel of his that I read with pleasure. *Il n'est venu personne que je sache,* no one has come that I know of. (b) (In the construction **C'est . . . que. . . .**) *C'est vous que j'ai vu hier?* was it you I saw yesterday? *C'est la plus âgée que nous préférons,* we like the eldest best. **4.** (Adv. use) *Pendant les dix mois qu'il languit encore,* during the ten months that he continued to languish. *Les jours qu'il fait chaud,* on (the) days when it is warm. *Les trois ans que j'ai habité à Paris,* the three years (during which) I lived in Paris. *Je le ferai coûte que coûte,* I shall do it cost what it may. **5. Ce que.** See CE[1] 3.

que², *interr. pron. neut.* What? **1.** (Object) *Que voulez-vous?* what do you want? *Qu'a répondu Pierre?* what did Peter answer? *Qu'y a-t-il à voir dans cette ville?* what is there to be seen in this town? *Que faire?* what's to be done? *Que dire?* what could I say? *Dites-moi que faire,* tell me what to do. **2.** (a) (Logical subject) *Qu'est-il arrivé? que s'est-il passé?* what has happened? (b) (Pred.) *Qu'êtes-vous?* what are you? *Qu'est-ce* [kɛːs]? what is it? *Que devenir?* what was to become of us? S.a. QU'EST-CE QUE, QU'EST-CE QUI. **3.** (Adv. use) (a) (= POURQUOI) *Que ne le disiez-vous?* why didn't you say so? (b) (Exclamatory) (i) (= COMME) *Qu'il est beau!* how handsome he is! *Que c'est bien vrai!* how true! (ii) (= COMBIEN) *Que de déceptions!* how many disappointments! *Que de gens!* what a lot of people!

que³, *conj.* That; but (that); lest. **1.** *Je vois qu'il me trompe,* I see (that) he is deceiving me. *Je ne doute pas qu'il (ne) consente,* I do not doubt but (that) he will consent. *Je désire qu'il vienne,* I want him to come. *Je pense que non,* I think not. **2.** (a) (Imperative or optative) *Qu'elle entre!* let her come in! *Dieu dit: Que la lumière soit,* God said : Let there be light. *Que je vous y reprenne!* just let me catch you at it again! (b) (Hypothetical) *Que la machine vienne à s'arrêter et il y aura un accident,* let the machine stop and there will be an accident. (c) (i) (**Soit) que . . . ou (soit) que.** *Qu'il pleuve ou qu'il fasse du vent,* whether it rains or blows. (ii) **Que . . . ou non.** *Que tu le veuilles ou non,* whether you wish it or not. **3.** (a) (Linking up two verbs in the future-in-the-past) *Il l'affirmerait que je ne le croirais pas,* even though he affirmed it, I would not believe it. (b) **Que . . . ne,** after negative clause. *Il ne se passe jamais une année qu'il ne nous écrive,* a year never goes by but he writes to us. **4.** Equivalent to *afin que, alors que, avant que, depuis que, puisque, sans que, tant que,* etc. *Approchez qu'on vous entende,* come nearer that we may hear you. *Je ne le quitterai pas que l'affaire ne soit terminée,* I will not leave him till the matter is concluded. *Il y a trois jours que je ne l'ai vu,* it is three days since I saw him. **5.** (To avoid repetition of conj.) *Quand il entrera et qu'il vous trouvera ici,* when he comes in and finds you here. *Quoiqu'il pleuve et qu'il fasse froid,* although it is rainy and cold. *Si on vient et qu'on veuille me consulter,* if anyone comes and wants to consult me. **6. A ce que, de ce que.** *Je ne m'attendais pas à ce qu'on entrât,* I did not expect anyone to enter. *On s'alarmait de ce qu'il ne reparaissait pas,* alarm was felt at his failure to appear again. **7.** (In comparison) *Aussi grand que moi,* as tall as I (am). *Plus fort que son frère,* stronger than his

brother. *J'ai un autre parapluie que celui-là,* I have another umbrella besides that one. *Vous écrivez plus correctement que vous (ne) parlez,* you write more correctly than you speak. **8.** (a) **Ne . . . que,** only. *Il n'a qu'une jambe,* he has only one leg. *Il n'a fait qu'entrer et sortir,* F: he just popped in and out again. *Je n'ai fait que le toucher,* I only touched it. *Il n'y a que lui qui le sache,* no one else but he knows about it. *Je ne sais que vous capable de l'entreprendre,* I don't know anyone but you that is fit to undertake it. *Il ne fait que de sortir,* he has only just gone out. *Il n'est arrivé que trop vite,* he came all too soon. *Il n'y avait que lui à ne pas paraître ému,* he was the only person to appear unmoved. (With *ne* understood) *Il me faudrait un million de francs.* —*Que cela!* I should require a million francs.—Is that all (= only that)! *C'est vrai, n'est-ce pas?* —*Que trop vrai,* it's true, isn't it?—Only too true. (b) **Sans . . . que.** *J'étais sans ami que mon chien,* I had no friend but my dog. (c) **Ne . . . pas que,** not only. *Il n'y a pas que lui qui le sache,* he is not the only one who knows it. *L'homme ne vit pas que de pain,* man does not live by bread alone. (d) **Ne . . . plus, jamais, guère, que.** *Il ne me reste plus que vingt francs,* I have only twenty francs left. *Plus que dix minutes!* only ten minutes left! *Je ne bois jamais que de l'eau,* I never drink anything but water. (e) **Ne . . . pas plus tôt . . . que, à peine . . . que.** *Il n'eut pas plus tôt paru qu'on l'assaillit de questions,* no sooner did he appear than questions were showered upon him. *A peine était-il rentré que le téléphone retentit,* he had scarcely come in when the telephone bell rang. **9.** *Lit:* **Que si,** if. *Que si vous savez la vérité, il est de votre devoir de la révéler,* if you know the truth, it is your duty to reveal it. **10.** *F:* **Ah!** que non ! que si ! ah ! surely not ! surely yes ! *Que non pas!* not at all ! **11.** (Intensive) *F:* *Ton chapeau est dans un état, que c'est une horreur!* your hat is in a terrible state !

quel, quelle [kɛl], *a. & pron.* What, which. **1.** (Correlative) *Quel que soit le résultat, je le ferai,* whatever the result may be, I will do it. *Quelle que soit mon affection pour vous,* however great my affection for you; much as I love you. *Quels que soient ces hommes,* whoever these men may be. S.a. TEL 2. **2.** (Interrogative) *Quelle réponse a-t-il faite?* what reply did he make? *Quelle heure est-il?* what is the time? what o'clock is it? *Dites-moi quelle heure il est,* tell me the time. *Quel livre avez-vous pris?* what, which, whose, book did you take? *Avec quel argent?* with whose money? *Quel homme?* which man? *Je ne sais quel auteur a dit . . .,* some author or other has said. . . . *Mettez-moi à n'importe quelle table,* put me at any table you like. *Quels sont ces messieurs?* who are these gentlemen? **3.** (Exclamatory) *Quel homme!* what a man ! *Quelle bonté!* how kind !

quelconque [kɛlkɔ̃:k], *a.* **1.** Any (whatever). *Un cercle passant par trois points quelconques,* a circle passing through any three points. *Les proportions des éléments sont absolument quelconques,* the elements may be in any proportions. **2.** *Un q. général X,* some general X or other. *Répondre d'une façon q.,* to make some sort of reply. **3.** *F: C'est un homme très q.,* he is a very ordinary, commonplace, kind of man.

quellement [kɛlmɑ̃], *adv.* See TELLEMENT.

quelque [kɛlk(ə)]. **1.** *a.* (a) Some, any. *Il arrivera q. jour,* he will arrive some day. *Adressez-vous à q. autre,* apply to someone else. (b) Some, some little, a few. *Pendant q. temps*, for some time, for a brief period. *Il y a quelques jours*, a few days ago, some days ago. *Leurs quelques minutes d'entretien*, their few minutes of conversation. *Cent et quelques mètres*, a hundred odd yards. (*c*) (Correlative to *qui, que* + *sub.*) **Quelque . . . qui, que**, whatever, whatsoever. **Quelque chose qu'il vous ait dite**, whatever (thing) he said to you. (Cp. QUELQUE CHOSE.) *Sous q. prétexte que ce soit*, under any pretext whatever. *Tout traité de q. nature qu'il soit*, every treaty of whatsoever character. **2.** *adv.* (*a*) Some, about. *Quelque dix ans*, some, about, ten years. *Les quelque mille francs qu'il m'a prêtés*, the thousand francs or so that he lent me. (*b*) **Quelque . . . que**, however. *Q. grandes que soient ses fautes*, however great his faults may be.

quelque chose [kɛlkəʃoːz], *indef. pron. m. inv.* Something, anything. *Quelque chose me dit qu'il viendra*, something tells me he will come. *Avez-vous quelque chose à dire?* have you anything to say? *Quelque chose de nouveau, d'autre*, something new, something else. *F:* **Il a quelque chose**, there's something the matter with him. **Il y a quelque chose**, there's something up, something the matter. *Cela m'a fait quelque chose*, I felt it a good deal.

quelquefois [kɛlkəfwa], *adv.* Sometimes; now and then.

quelque part [kɛlkəpaːr], *adv.* **1.** Somewhere. **2.** (Correlative to *que* + *sub.*) *Quelque part qu'il fouillât, rien de suspect*, wherever he rummaged he found nothing suspicious.

quelques-uns, -unes [kɛlkəzœ̃, -yn], *indef. pron. pl.* See QUELQU'UN 1.

quelqu'un, quelqu'une [kɛlkœ̃, kɛlkyn], *indef. pron.* **1.** *m. & f.* One (or other). *Quelqu'une de ces dames va s'en occuper*, one of the ladies will see to it. *Quelques-uns des magasins*, some of the shops. *J'ai lu quelques-unes des lettres*, I have read a few of the letters. *Quelques-un(e)s d'entre nous*, a few of us. **2.** *m.* Someone, somebody; anyone, anybody. *Quelqu'un me l'a dit*, someone told me so. *Est-il venu quelqu'un?* has anybody come? *Com: Quelqu'un! shop! Quelqu'un de plus*, someone extra. *Quelqu'un d'autre*, someone else. *Y a-t-il eu quelqu'un de blessé?* was anyone wounded? *F: Elle se croit quelqu'un*, she thinks she is somebody.

quémand|er [kemɑ̃de]. **1.** *v.i.* To beg (from door to door). **2.** *v.tr. Q. qch. à qn*, to beg for, solicit, sth. from s.o. *s.* **-eur, -euse.**

qu'en-dira-t-on (le) [ləkɑ̃diratɔ̃], *s.m.inv.* What people will say; gossip; Mrs Grundy.

quenelle [kənɛl], *s.f.* Fish or forcemeat ball; quenelle.

quenotte [kənɔt], *s.f. F:* (In nursery) Tooth.

quenouille [kənuːj], *s.f.* **1.** Distaff. **2.** Quenouille-trained fruit-tree. **3.** Bed-post. **4.** *Bot:* Cat's-tail, bulrush.

querelle [kərɛl], *s.f.* Quarrel, dispute. **Chercher querelle à qn,** to try to pick a quarrel with s.o. *Avoir une q. avec qn*, to have a quarrel, an altercation, a row, with s.o. *Être en q. avec qn*, to be at variance, at loggerheads, with s.o. **Querelle d'Allemand,** trumped-up quarrel. *Q. d'amoureux*, lovers' tiff. **Familles en querelle ouverte,** families at open feud. **Épouser la querelle de qn,** to take up s.o.'s quarrel, s.o.'s cause.

quereller [kərɛle], *v.tr. Q. qn*, to quarrel with s.o. *Aimer à q.*, to be fond of wrangling.

se quereller, to quarrel, wrangle; to have words, to fall out (*avec*, with).

querelleur, -euse [kərɛlœːr, -øːz]. **1.** *s.* Quarreller, wrangler; *f.* scold. **2.** *a.* Quarrelsome.

querir, quérir [kəriːr, keriːr], *v.tr.* (Used after the verbs *aller, venir, envoyer*) *Aller q. qn*, to go and fetch s.o. (esp. the police). *Envoyer q. main forte*, to send for the police.

qu'est-ce que [kɛskə], *interr. pron.* What? *Qu'est-ce que vous voulez?* what do you want? *Qu'est-ce que la grammaire?* what is grammar? *F:* **Qu'est-ce que c'est que** *cet homme-là!* what ever is that man! **Qu'est-ce que c'est que ça?** what's that? *F: Qu'est-ce que vous êtes de personnes ici?* how many are there of you here?

qu'est-ce qui [kɛski], *interr. pron.* (Used as subject) **1.** What? *Qu'est-ce qui est arrivé?* what has happened? **2.** *F:* (= QUI EST-CE QUI) Who?

question [kɛstjɔ̃], *s.f.* **1.** (*a*) Question, query. **Faire, poser, adresser, une question à qn,** to put a question to s.o. ; to ask s.o. a question. *Presser qn de questions*, to press, ply, s.o. with questions. **Son adhésion ne fait pas question,** there is no doubt, no question, of his adherence. **Mettre qch. en question,** to question sth. ; to challenge (statement, s.o.'s honour). (*b*) Question, matter, point, issue. **Poser une question,** to state a question, an issue. **L'affaire, la personne, en question,** the matter, the person, in question. *C'est une simple q. de temps*, it is simply a matter of time. *Ce n'est pas là la q.*, that is not the point. **C'est là la question,** that is the question. *Sortir de la q.*, to wander from the point. *Rappeler qn à la q.*, to call s.o. to order. *Après le premier chapitre il n'est plus q. de lui*, after the first chapter no further mention is made of him. (*c*) *Jur:* (Point at) issue. *Q. de fait, de droit*, issue of fact, of law. **2.** *Hist:* Question ; judicial torture; the rack. **Appliquer la question à qn, mettre qn à la question,** to put, submit, s.o. to the question, to the rack; to torture s.o.

questionnaire [kɛstjɔnɛːr], *s.m.* List, set, of questions ; questionnaire.

questionner [kɛstjɔne], *v.tr.* To question (s.o.) ; to ask (s.o.) questions.

questionneur, -euse [kɛstjɔnœːr, -øːz], *a. & s.* Inquisitive (person).

quête [kɛːt], *s.f.* **1.** (*a*) Quest, search. **Se mettre en quête de qch.,** to set out, go, in quest of sth. (*b*) *Ven:* Tracking, scenting ; quartering. **2.** *Ecc: etc:* Collection. **Faire la quête,** to take up the collection ; (in an emergency) to pass round the hat.

quêter [kɛte], *v.tr.* (*a*) To collect (alms, etc.). *Abs.* To take up the collection. (*b*) *F: Q. des compliments*, to fish, angle, for compliments.

quêteur, -euse [kɛtœːr, -øːz], *s.* Alms-collector. *Ecc:* Taker of the collection.

queue [kø], *s.f.* **1.** Tail. *Couper la q. à un cheval*, to dock a horse, a horse's tail. *Cheval à q. écourtée*, bobtail (horse). *Q. de renard*, fox's brush. *Q. de rat*, rat-tail. *S.a.* QUEUE-DE-RAT. **Queue de poisson,** (i) fish-tail ; (ii) *Aut: F:* wail-wobble (on greasy road). *F:* (Of play, novel) **Finir en queue de poisson,** to fizzle out. *Sans q.*, tailless. **À la queue gît le venin,** the sting is in the tail. *Il s'en retourna la q. entre les jambes*, he departed with his tail between his legs. *S.a.* DIABLE 1, NUAGE, SERRER 2. **2.** Tail (of comet, kite) ; trail (of meteor) ; stem (of crotchet or quaver) ; handle (of pan) ; stalk (of fruit, flower) ; shank (of button) ; pin (of brooch) ; tail-piece (of violin) ; train (of dress) ; end (of a piece of stuff) ; pigtail, queue (of hair) ; fang, tang, shank (of tool) ; tail-planes (of aeroplane) ; rudder, tail (of windmill). **Bouton à queue,**

shanked button. **Habit à queue,** swallow-tail coat. **Piano à queue,** grand piano. **3.** (*a*) (Tail-) end, fag-end (of a procession, etc.). Venir en queue (*du cortège*), to bring up the rear. *Être à la q. de la classe,* to be at the bottom of the class. (*b*) *Mil:* Rear (of army). *Navy: Colonne de q.,* rear column. **4.** Queue, file (of people). **Faire (la) queue,** to form a queue; to queue up. **A la queue leu leu,** see LEU. **5.** *Bill:* (*a*) Cue. (*b*) **Fausse queue.** miscue. **Faire fausse queue,** to miscue.

queue-d'aronde, *s.f. Carp:* Dovetail. *Assemblage à q.-d'a.,* dovetailing. *A q.-d'a.,* dovetailed.

queue-de-chat, *s.f.* **1.** Cat-o'-nine-tails. **2.** Mare's-tail (cloud); cirrus. *pl. Des queues-de-chat.*

queue-de-morue, *s.f.* **1.** (**Habit à**) **queue-de-morue,** swallow-tail coat; *F:* swallow-tail(s). **2.** (Painter's) flat brush.

queue-de-rat [kødra], *s.f.* **1.** *Tls:* (*a*) Rat-tail, rat-tailed file. (*b*) Reamer. **2.** Small wax taper. **3.** *Vet:* Rat-tail (of horse). *pl. Des queues-de-rat.*

queut|er [køte], *v.i. Bill: etc:* To push the ball; to play a push-stroke. *Coup queuté,* push-stroke. [QUEUE] *s.m.* **-age.**

queux [kø], *s.m.* (Used only in) *A. & Hum:* **Maître queux,** cook, chef.

qui¹ [ki], *rel. pron.* **1.** (Subject) Who, that; (of thg) which, that. (*a*) *Phrases qui ne sont pas françaises,* sentences that are not French. *Notre Père qui êtes aux cieux,* our Father which art in heaven. *Il y a peu de gens qui sachent cela,* there are few people who know that. *Il n'y a personne qui ne comprenne cela,* there is no one but understands that. *Je le vois qui vient,* I see him coming. *J'ai le cœur qui m'étouffe,* I feel like choking. *C'est une simple farce, et qui est médiocre,* it is a mere farce and a poor one. (*b*) (In the construction* C'est . . . qui . . .*) *C'est la plus âgée qui a répondu,* it was the eldest who answered. **2.** (*a*) (= *celui qui*) *Qui vivra verra,* he who lives will see. *Tout vient à point à qui sait attendre,* all things come to him who waits. *Sauve qui peut,* every man for himself. (*b*) (= *ce qui*) *Qui plus est,* what is more. *Qui pis est,* what is worse. (*c*) **Ce qui.** See CE¹ 3. **3.** (After prep.) Whom; occ. which. (*a*) *Voilà l'homme à qui je pensais, de qui je parlais,* there is the man of whom I was thinking, speaking. *Il cherche quelqu'un avec qui jouer,* he is looking for someone to play with. *Le champ sur qui tombait la nuit,* the field on which night was falling. (*b*) (Without antecedent) *Adressez-vous à qui vous voudrez,* apply to whom you please, to anyone you please. *On se dispersa, qui d'un côté, qui d'un autre,* we scattered, some going one way, some the other. **4.** (*a*) **Qui que,** who(so)ever, whom(so)ever. *Qui que vous soyez, parlez,* whoever you are, speak. (*b*) **Qui que ce soit,** anyone (whatever). *Je défie qui que ce soit de . . . ,* I challenge anyone to. . . . *Je n'ai trouvé qui que ce soit,* I found no one whatever.

qui², *interr.pron.m.sg.* **1.** Who? whom? (*a*) *Qui a dit cela?* who said that? *Qui désirez-vous voir?* whom do you wish to see? *Qui vient à la réunion?* who is coming, who are coming, to the meeting? *A qui est ce canif?* whose is this knife? *De qui êtes-vous fils?* whose son are you? *Pour qui est ce livre?* *F:* who is that book for? *Qui d'autre?* who(m) else? *C'était à qui l'aiderait,* they vied with each other in helping him. *F: Il est là.—Qui ça? Qui donc?* he is there.—Who? (*b*) (= LEQUEL) *Qui des deux a raison?* which of the two is right? **2.** (= QU'EST-CE QUI) *Qui t'amène si matin?* what brings you so early?

quia (à) [akɥia], *adv.phr.* **Être à quia,** to be nonplussed, in a quandary.

Quichotte, Don [dɔ̃kiʃɔt]. *Pr.n.m. Span.Lit:* Don Quixote. *Agir en Don Q.,* to act quixotically.

quiconque [kikɔ̃:k], *indef. pron. m. sg.* **1.** Who(so)ever; anyone who. **2.** (= *qui que ce soit*) *Il m'aidera mieux que q.,* he will help me better than anyone (else). *Pas un mot de cela à q.,* not a word of that to anybody.

quidam [kɥidam, kidɑ̃], *s.m.* (*a*) *Jur:* Person (name unknown). (*b*) *F: Survint un q.,* someone, an individual, appeared.

qui est-ce que [kieskə], *interr. pron.* Whom?

qui est-ce qui [kieski], *interr. pron.* Who?

quiétude [kɥietyd, kje-], *s.f.* Quietude.

quignon [kiɲɔ̃], *s.m.* Chunk, hunch, hunk (of bread).

quille¹ [ki:j], *s.f.* (*a*) Ninepin, skittle(-pin). *F:* **Droit comme une quille,** as straight as a ramrod. **Jeu de quilles,** (i) set of ninepins, of skittles; (ii) skittle-alley. **Être reçu comme un chien dans un jeu de quilles,** to be treated as an intruder, to be given a cold welcome. (*b*) *P: Il ne tient pas sur ses quilles,* he is shaky on his pins. **Jouer des quilles,** to run hard, to skedaddle.

quille², *s.f.* Keel. **Poser la quille d'un vaisseau,** to lay down a ship. S.a. DÉRIVE.

quillon [kijɔ̃], *s.m.* **1.** Cross-bar, cross-guard (of sword). **2.** Piling-pin (of Lebel rifle).

quinaud [kino], *a. A:* Abashed, confused. **Rester quinaud,** to look foolish.

quincaillerie [kɛ̃kajri], *s.f.* **1.** Hardware, ironmongery, small-wares. **2.** Hardware business or shop.

quincaillier [kɛ̃kaje], *s.m.* Hardware merchant; ironmonger.

quinconce [kɛ̃kɔ̃:s], *s.m.* Quincunx. *Arbres en q.,* trees planted in alternate rows. **Rivetage en quinconce,** staggered riveting, zigzag riveting.

quinine [kinin], *s.f.* Quinine; sulphate of quinine.

quinquagénaire [kɥɛ̃kwaʒenɛ:r], *a. & s.* Quinquagenarian.

quinquennal, -aux [kɥɛ̃kɥennal, -o], *a.* Quinquennial; five-year (plan, etc.).

quinquet [kɛ̃kɛ], *s.m.* Argand lamp.

quinquina [kɛ̃kina], *s.m.* Cinchona, quinquina (bark, tree); Peruvian bark.

quint [kɛ̃], *a. A:* Fifth. *Charles-Quint,* Charles the Fifth (of Germany).

quintaine [kɛ̃tɛn], *s.f. A:* Quintain. **Courir la quintaine,** to tilt at the quintain.

quintal, -aux [kɛ̃tal, -o], *s.m. Meas:* **1.** *A:* Quintal; hundredweight. **2.** Quintal métrique = 100 kilogrammes.

quinte [kɛ̃:t], *s.f.* **1.** *Mus:* Fifth, quint. **Fausse quinte,** diminished fifth. **2.** (At piquet) Quint. *F:* **Renvoyer qn de quinte en quatorze,** to drive s.o. from pillar to post. **3.** *Fenc:* Quint(e). **4.** (*a*) **Quinte de toux,** fit of coughing. (*b*) *F:* Caprice, crotchet; fit of ill-temper.

quintessence [kɛ̃tessɑ̃:s], *s.f.* Quintessence.

quintessencié [kɛ̃tessɑ̃sje], *a.* Quintessential; sublimated (thoughts).

quintette [k(ɥ)ɛ̃tɛt], *s.m. Mus:* Quintet(te).

quinteux, -euse [kɛ̃tø, -ø:z], *a. F:* Capricious, crotchety (person); restive, jibbing (horse).

quintillion [kɥɛ̃tiljɔ̃], *s.m.* Trillion (10¹⁸); *U.S:* quintillion.

quintuple [k(ɥ)ɛ̃typl], *a. & s.m.* Quintuple, fivefold. *Être payé au q.,* to be repaid fivefold.

quintupler [k(ɥ)ɛ̃typle], *v.tr. & i.* To quintuple; to increase fivefold.

quinzaine [kɛ̃zɛn], *s.f.* **1.** (About) fifteen, some

fifteen. **2.** Fortnight. *Dans la q.*, within a fortnight.

quinze [kɛ̃:z], *num. a. inv. & s.m. inv.* **I.** Fifteen. **Louis Quinze**, Louis the Fifteenth. *Le q. mai*, (on) the fifteenth of May. *Ten :* **Quinze à**, fifteen all. **2. Quinze jours**, a fortnight. **D'aujourd'hui en quinze**, this day fortnight. *Tous les q. jours*, once a fortnight ; fortnightly.

Quinze-Vingts [kɛ̃zvɛ̃]. **I.** *Pr.n.m.* **Les Quinze-Vingts**, the Hospital for the blind (originally 300) in Paris. **2.** *s.m.* **Un quinze-vingt(s)**, an inmate of this hospital.

quinzième [kɛ̃zjɛm]. **I.** *num. a. & s.* Fifteenth. **2.** *s.m.* Fifteenth (part). *adv.* **-ment**.

quiproquo [kiprɔko], *s.m.* Mistake (taking of one thing for another) ; misunderstanding. *Il y a eu q.*, (i) we misunderstood each other ; (ii) I took you for someone else.

quittance [kitɑ̃:s], *s.f. Com :* Receipt, discharge. *Q. pour solde*, receipt in full. **Donner quittance à qn**, (i) to give s.o. a receipt in full ; (ii) *F :* to forgive s.o.

quitte [kit], *a.* **I.** Free, quit, rid (*de*, of) ; discharged (*de*, from). *Être q. de dettes*, to be out of debt. *Nous sommes quittes*, I am quits with you. **Tenir qn quitte de qch.**, to release s.o. from, let s.o. off, sth. **En être quitte pour, avec, qch.**, to get off, come off, be let off, with sth. *Il en a été q. pour la peur*, he got off with a fright. **2.** *Inv.* Je **le ferai quitte à être grondé**, I'll do it and chance the scolding. *J'abandonne ce travail, q. à le reprendre plus tard*, I am giving up this work, but may perhaps resume it later. **Nous voilà quitte à quitte**, now we're quits, square. **Jouer quitte ou double**, to play double or quits.

quitter [kite], *v.tr.* **I.** **Quitter la partie**, to throw up one's cards ; to throw up the sponge. **2.** To leave, quit (place, person) ; to vacate (office). *Q. le lit*, to leave one's bed. *Q. ses habits*, to take off, lay aside, one's clothes. **Quitter le droit chemin**, to swerve from the straight path, from the path of duty. (Of train) **Quitter les rails**, to jump the metals. *Nau :* **Q. la jetée, le quai**, to cast off. *Q. le service*, to leave, quit, the service. *Q. les affaires*, to retire from business. *Q. ses mauvaises habitudes*, to leave off, give up, one's bad habits. *Q. ce monde*, to depart this life. *Ne le quittez pas des yeux*, do not let him out of your sight. *Ils se sont quittés bons amis*, they parted good friends. *Tp :* **Ne quittez pas (l'écoute) !** hold the line !

quitus [kɥity:s], *s.m. Com :* Auditor's final discharge ; receipt in full.

qui-vive [kivi:v], *s.m.inv. Mil :* Sentry's challenge. *F :* **Être sur le qui-vive**, to be on the qui vive, on the alert. S.a. VIVRE I.

quoi[1] [kwa], *rel. pron.* What. **I.** (*a*) *C'est ce à quoi je m'attendais*, that is what I was expecting. *Ce sur quoi l'on discute*, what is being discussed ; the matter under discussion. *C'est en quoi vous vous trompez*, that is where you are wrong. (*b*) (= LEQUEL, LAQUELLE) *Il a bien autre chose à quoi penser !* he has something else to think about ! *Un autre fait, à quoi vous n'avez pas pris garde*, another fact, which you have left out of consideration. **2. De quoi.** *Il a de quoi vivre*, he has enough to live on. *F :* **Il a de quoi**, he is well off, comfortably off. *Il y a de quoi vous faire enrager*, it's enough to drive you mad. *Il n'y a pas de quoi chanter victoire*, there's no occasion to crow. **Il n'y a pas de quoi**, pray don't mention it. *Avez-vous de quoi écrire?* have you anything to write with? *Il faut trouver de quoi allumer du feu*, we must find something to light the fire with. **3. Sans quoi.** *Travaille, sans quoi tu ne mangeras pas*, work, otherwise you shall not eat. **4.** *F :* **Comme quoi.** *Montrer comme quoi la chose est possible*, to show that the thing is possible. **5. Quoi qui, quoi que.** (*a*) *Quoi qui survienne. restez calme*, whatever comes of it, keep calm, *Quoi qu'il en soit*, however that may be ; be that as it may. (*b*) **Quoi que ce soit**, (i) anything (whatever) ; (ii) whatever it may be. *Puis-je vous être utile en quoi que ce soit?* can I be of use to you in anything? *Avez-vous dit quoi que ce soit?* did you say anything at all?

quoi[2], *interr. pron.* What? (*a*) (Subject) *Qui ou quoi vous a donné cette idée?* who or what gave you that idea? *Quoi d'autre?* what else? *Quoi de nouveau?* what news? *Eh bien! quoi?* well, what about it? (*b*) (Object) *Vous désirez quoi?* what is it you want? *Les journaux ne savent quoi inventer*, the papers are always inventing new lies. **Un je ne sais quoi**, an indescribable something. S.a. IMPORTER[2] 2. (*c*) (After prep.) *De quoi parlez-vous?* what are you talking about? *À quoi pensez-vous?* what are you thinking of? *À quoi bon (faire qch.)?* what's the use, the good (of doing sth.)? *En quoi est-ce? c'est en quoi?* what is it made of?

quoique [kwak(ə)], *conj.* Usu. + sub. (Al)though. (*a*) *Quoiqu'il soit pauvre il est généreux*, although he is poor he is generous. (*b*) (With ellipsis of verb) *Je suis heureux quoique garçon*, I am happy though a bachelor.

quolibet [kɔlibɛ], *s.m.* Gibe. *Poursuivre qn de quolibets*, to gibe, jeer, at s.o.

quote-part [kɔtpa:r], *s.f.* Share, quota, portion.

quotidien, -ienne [kɔtidjɛ̃, -jɛn]. **I.** *a.* Daily, everyday ; of daily occurrence. **La vie quotidienne**, everyday life. **Notre pain quotidien**, our daily bread. **2.** *s.m.* **Les quotidiens**, the daily papers, the dailies.

quotidiennement [kɔtidjɛnmɑ̃], *adv.* Daily.

quotient [kɔsjɑ̃], *s.m.* **I.** *Mth :* Quotient. **2.** *Q. électoral*, electoral quota.

quotité [kɔtite], *s.f.* Amount of share ; quota. *Jur :* **Q. disponible**, disposable portion of estate.

quott|er [kote], *v.i. Mec.E :* (Of gearing) To engage, catch. *s.m.* **-ement**.

R

R, r [ɛːr], *s.f.* (The letter) R, r. *Rouler ses r*, to roll one's r's.

rabâchage [rabɑʃa:ʒ], *s.m.*, **rabâchement** [rabɑʃmɑ̃], *s.m.* Wearisome reiteration (of words) ; twaddle, drivel.

rabâcher [rabɑʃe]. **I.** *v.i.* To be everlastingly repeating the same thing ; to talk twaddle. **2.** *v.tr.* *Ils rabâchent toujours la même chose*, they are for ever harping on the same string.

rabâcheur, -euse [rabɑʃœːr, -øːz], *s.* Twaddler, driveller.

rabais [rabɛ], *s.m.* Reduction (in price) ;

allowance, rebate, discount. **Vendre qch. au rabais,** to sell sth. at a reduced price. **Vente au grand rabais,** sale at greatly reduced prices.

rabaiss|er [rabɛse], *v.tr.* **1.** To lower (veil, voice); to reduce, lower (price). **2.** (*a*) To depreciate, disparage, belittle (person, talent). (*b*) To humble (s.o., s.o.'s pride). **3.** To cut back (tree, plant). *s.m.* **-ement.**

rabaisseur [rabɛsœːr], *s.m.* Disparager, depreciator.

raban [rabã], *s.m. Nau:* (*a*) (Small) rope. *Rabans de ferlage, de ris,* gaskets. (*b*) *R. de cabestan,* swifter. (*c*) Lashing (of hammock).

rabat [raba], *s.m.* Bands (of clerical costume); turned-down piece; flap (of handbag).

rabat-joie, *s.m. & f. inv.* Kill-joy, spoil-sport.

rabattable [rabatabl], *a.* That can be folded back. *Aut: Coupé à capote r.,* drop-head coupé.

rabatteur, -euse [rabatœːr, -øːz], *s.* **1.** Hotel tout. **2.** *s.m. Ven:* Beater.

rabatt|re [rabatr], *v.tr.* (Conj. like BATTRE) **1.** To fold (sth.) back; to bring (sth.) down (to a lower level); to shut down (lid); to lower, pull down (one's veil); to turn down (one's collar); to tilt back (seat of a car). *R. une couture,* (i) to fell a seam; (ii) to press down, flatten, a seam. *R. le bord d'une tôle,* to flange a plate, to turn over the edges of a plate. *Porte rabattue contre la paroi,* door folded back to the wall. *Le vent rabat la fumée,* the wind beats down the smoke. **2.** To reduce, lessen, diminish. (*a*) *Com: R. tant du prix,* to take so much off the price. *Je n'en rabattrai pas un sou,* I won't take a halfpenny less for it. (*b*) *R. l'orgueil de qn,* to lower, take down, humble, s.o.'s pride. *R. de ses prétentions,* **en rabattre,** to climb down, to draw in one's horns. (*c*) *Hort:* To cut back (tree). (*d*) *Knitting:* **Rabattre les mailles,** to cast off. **3.** *R. le gibier,* (i) to beat up the game; (ii) to head back the game. *R. les flammes,* to beat back the flames. *F: R. des clients,* to beat up customers. **4.** *v.i. Il faut r. à droite,* you must turn off, bear, to the right. *s.m.* **-age.** *s.m.* **-ement.**

se rabattre. 1. *Table qui se rabat,* folding-, flap-table. **2.** (*a*) *L'armée se rabattit sur la ville,* the army fell back upon the town. (*b*) *Se r. sur qch.,* to fall back upon a course of action.

rabbin [rabɛ̃], *s.m.* (Voc. case **rabbi**) *Jew.Rel:* Rabbi. *Grand r.,* Chief Rabbi.

rabelaiserie [rablɛzri], *s.f.* **1.** Rabelaisianism. **2.** Rabelaisian joke; broad joke.

rabelaisien, -ienne [rablɛzjɛ̃, -jɛn], *a.* Rabelaisian, broad (humour).

rabes [rab], *s.f.pl. R. de morue,* salted cod-roe.

rabiau, rabiot [rabjo], *s.m. Mil: P:* **1.** (*a*) Surplus of food (after distribution of rations); buckshee. (*b*) Illicit profits. **2.** Extra work; overtime.

rabibocher [rabiboʃe], *v.tr. F:* To tinker up, patch up (sth.); to make it up between (two people).

se rabibocher, to become reconciled, to make it up again.

rabique [rabik], *a. Med:* Rabic (virus, animal).

râble¹ [rɑːbl], *s.m.* Back (of hare, etc.); *Cu:* saddle (of hare).

râble², *s.m. Tls:* Fire-rake.

râblé [rɑble], *a.* Broad-backed, strong-backed; strapping (fellow).

rabonnir [raboniːr]. **1.** *v.tr.* To improve (wine). **2.** *v.i.* (Of wine, etc.) To improve; to get better.

rabot [rabo], *s.m. Tls:* Plane. *R. à languette,* grooving-plane. **Fer de rabot,** plane-iron. **Fût de rabot,** plane-stock. *Passer le r. sur une planche,* to run the plane over a plank.

rabot|er [rabɔte], *v.tr.* (*a*) To plane (wood). (*b*) To file down (horse's hoof). *F:* **Raboter son style,** to polish one's style. *s.m.* **-age.** *s.m.* **-ement.**

raboteuse¹ [rabɔtøːz], *s.f.* Planing-machine.

raboteux, -euse² [rabɔtø, -øːz], *a.* **1.** Rough, uneven. *Bois r.,* knotty wood. *Chemin r.,* rough, bumpy, road. **2.** Unpolished, rugged (style).

rabougrir [rabugriːr]. **1.** *v.tr.* To stunt the growth of (sth.). **2.** *v.i. & pr.* To become stunted.

rabougri, *a.* Stunted, ill-thriven.

rabougrissement [rabugrismã], *s.m.* Stuntedness; scragginess (of vegetation).

rabouter [rabute], **raboutir** [rabutiːr], *v.tr.* To join end to end. *s.m.* **-issage.**

rabrouer [rabrue], *v.tr.* To scold, snub; to jump down (s.o.'s) throat.

rabroueur, -euse [rabruœːr, -øːz], *s.* Surly fellow; *f.* scold.

racage [rakaːʒ], *s.m. Nau:* Parrel, parral.

racaille [rakɑːj], *s.f.* **1.** Rabble, riff-raff. **2.** (Of thgs) Trash, rubbish.

raccastillage [rakastijaːʒ], *s.m. Nau:* Repairs to upper works.

raccommodage [rakɔmɔdaːʒ], *s.m.* **1.** Mending, repairing; darning (of stockings). **2.** Mend, repair, darn.

raccommodement [rakɔmɔdmã], *s.m.* Reconciliation; making up (of a quarrel).

raccommod|er [rakɔmɔde], *v.tr.* **1.** To mend, repair; to darn (stocking). **2.** To reconcile, to make it up between (two persons). *a.* **-able.** *s.* **-eur, -euse.**

se raccommoder (*avec qn*), to make it up (with s.o.); to become friends again.

raccord [rakɔːr], *s.m.* **1.** *Tp: etc:* Linking up (of subscribers). **2.** (*a*) Join (in a building, a picture, etc.). *Faire des raccords dans un roman,* to join up parts of a novel. (*b*) *Mec.E:* Joint, coupling, connection. *R. à vis,* union-nut joint. *El.E: R. de lampe,* lamp-adapter, lamp-connector. **Bouchon de raccord,** adapter-plug.

raccordement [rakɔrdəmã], *s.m.* **1.** Joining, adjusting, linking up. **Pièces de raccordement, making-up lengths.** *El.E:* **Boîte de raccordement,** connecting-box (for cables). *Rail:* **Voie de raccordement,** junction-line, loop-line. **2.** Junction; lead (from chamber of gun to bore); neck (of cartridge-case). *El.E:* Connection (of telephone cables). *Faux r.,* wrong connection.

raccorder [rakɔrde], *v.tr.* (*a*) To join, connect, unite, couple; to link up (*avec,* with). (*b*) To bring (parts) into line; to make (parts) flush.

se raccorder, to fit together.

raccourc|ir [rakursiːr]. **1.** *v.tr.* (*a*) To shorten; to take up (sleeve); to reduce the length of (sth.). **Raccourcir son bras,** to draw up one's arm. *R. son chemin,* to take a short cut. (*b*) To abridge, curtail; to cut (speech) short. (*c*) *Art:* To foreshorten. **2.** *v.i. & pr.* To grow shorter; to shorten; to shrink. *Les jours (se) raccourcissent,* the days are drawing in. *s.m.* **-issement.**

raccourci. 1. *a.* Shortened; short, squat; abridged (plan); bobbed (hair); oblate (ellipsoid). *F:* **Tomber à bras raccourci(s) sur qn,** to give s.o. a good pummelling; to pitch into s.o. **2.** *s.m.* (*a*) Abridgment, epitome. (*b*) *Art:* Foreshortening. *Bras en r.,* foreshortened arm. (*c*) Short cut (to a place).

raccoutr|er [rakutre], *v.tr.* (*a*) To mend, repair, the garments of (s.o.). (*b*) To mend, repair (garment). *s.m.* **-age.** *s.* **-eur, -euse.**

raccoutumer (se) [sərakutyme], *v.pr.* To re-accustom oneself, to get reaccustomed (*à,* to).

raccroc [rakro], *s.m.* (*a*) *Bill:* Fluke; lucky stroke. **Coup de raccroc,** fluky shot or stroke. (*b*) **Visiteurs de raccroc,** chance visitors.

raccrocher [rakrɔʃe], *v.tr.* **1.** To hook up, hang up, (sth.) again. *Tp:* R. (*l'appareil*), to hang up the receiver; to ring off. **2.** *F:* To recover (sth.); to lay hold of (sth.) again; to get hold of (s.o.) again.
  se raccrocher. 1. *Se r. à qch.,* to clutch hold of sth.; to catch on to sth. **2.** *F:* To recover one's losses.

race [ras], *s.f.* Race. **1.** Ancestry or descent; strain. *De r. noble,* of noble race, of noble strain. **Ne point laisser de race,** to leave no descendants. **Minorités de race,** racial minorities. **2.** Stock, breed. *La r. blanche,* the white race. *Améliorer, croiser, les races,* to improve, to cross, the breeds. **Chien de (pure) race, qui a de la race,** pure-bred dog; pedigree dog. *Cheval de r.,* thoroughbred horse. *R. croisée,* cross-breed. *Prov:* **Bon chien chasse de race,** what's bred in the bone comes out in the flesh. *F:* **Il chasse de race,** he is a chip of the old block; it runs in his blood.

racé [rase], *a.* (Of horse, dog, etc.) Thorough-bred; true to race, true to stock.

racème [rasɛm], *s.m. Bot:* Raceme.

rachat [raʃa], *s.m.* (*a*) Repurchase, buying back; buying in (of goods); redemption (of annuity). *Theol:* Atonement. (*b*) *Ins:* Surrender (of policy). **Valeur de rachat,** surrender value. (*c*) *R. des bans* (*de mariage*), marriage licence.

rachetable [raʃtabl], *a.* Redeemable (stock); atonable (sin).

rachet|er [raʃte], *v.tr.* (Conj. like ACHETER) **1.** (*a*) To repurchase; to buy (sth.) back. *Com:* To buy (sth.) in. (*b*) To redeem (debt, annuity). *R. ses péchés,* to atone for one's sins. *R. son honneur,* to retrieve one's honour. *R. son passé,* to atone for one's past. (*c*) *Ins:* To sur-render (policy). (*d*) To ransom (prisoner). **2.** To make a further purchase of (sth.). *s.* **-eur, -euse.**

rachidien, -ienne [raʃidjɛ̃, -jɛn], *a. Anat:* Rachidian (bulb, canal).

rachitique [raʃitik], *a. & s.* Rachitic; *F:* rick-ety (child).

rachitisme [raʃitism], *s.m.* Rachitis, *F:* rickets.

racinage [rasinaːʒ], *s.m.* **1.** *Coll.* (Edible) roots. **2.** *Tex:* Walnut dye. **3.** *Bookb:* Tree-marbling.

racinal, -aux [rasinal, -o], *s.m.* (Foundation) beam, sleeper; main sill (of sluice); sole (of crane).

racine [rasin], *s.f.* **1.** (*a*) Root (of plant, hair, etc.). *De vieilles racines de dents,* old stumps (of teeth). **Jeter, pousser, des racines,** to throw out roots, to strike root. **Prendre racine,** to take root. **Couper le mal dans sa racine,** to strike at the root of the evil. (*b*) *Mth:* **Racine carrée, cubique,** square root, cube root. **2.** *Fish:* **Racine anglaise,** silkworm gut; silk gut.

raciné [rasine], *a. Bookb:* Marbled. *Veau r.,* marbled calf or tree-calf.

racle [raːkl], *s.f. Tls:* Scraper.

racl|er [rakle], *v.tr.* To scrape (skin, carrot, etc.). *R. une allée,* to rake a walk. *F:* **Racler du violon,** to scrape, saw, on the fiddle. *Vin qui racle le gosier,* wine that rasps the throat. *Se r. la gorge,* to clear one's throat. *La police les a raclés,* the police made a clean sweep of them. *s.m.* **-age.**

raclée, *s.f. F:* Hiding, licking, drubbing. **Administrer une raclée à qn,** to give s.o. a thrashing, a trouncing; to dust s.o.'s jacket.

raclette [raklɛt], *s.f. Tls:* (*a*) Scraper. (*b*) *Phot: etc:* Squeegee. (*c*) *Hort:* Hoe.

racleur, -euse [raklœːr, -øːz]. **1.** *s.* (Pers.) Scraper. **2.** *s.m. I.C.E:* (Segment) **racleur d'huile,** scraper-ring.

racloir [raklwaːr], *s.m.* (*a*) Scraper, scraping-tool. (*b*) (Cooper's) hoop-shave. (*c*) (Street orderly's) squeegee.

racloire [raklwaːr], *s.f.* **1.** Strickle, strike. **2.** *Tls:* Spokeshave. **3.** Tongue scraper.

raclure [raklyːr], *s.f.* Scrapings.

racol|er [rakɔle], *v.tr.* (*a*) To recruit (men for the army or navy). (*b*) *A:* To crimp, impress (men). (*c*) *F:* **R. des partisans,** to enlist sup-porters. *s.m.* **-age.**

racoleur [rakɔlœːr], *s.m.* (*a*) Recruiting-sergeant. (*b*) *A:* Crimp. (*c*) Hired tout.

racontage [rakɔ̃taːʒ], *s.m.* **1.** Telling, recounting. **2.** Story; piece of gossip. *Racontages,* tittle-tattle; idle talk.

racontar [rakɔ̃taːr], *s.m. F:* = RACONTAGE 2. *Ce n'est que des racontars,* it's nothing but ill-natured gossip.

raconter [rakɔ̃te], *v.tr.* To tell, relate, narrate, recount. *R. de longues histoires,* to spin long yarns. *Il vous en raconte,* he is drawing the long bow. *R. au long une histoire,* to unfold a tale. *Je vous raconterai cela plus tard,* I shall tell you all about it later. *Qu'est-ce qu'il raconte là?* what ever is he talking about?

raconteur, -euse [rakɔ̃tœːr,-øːz]. **1.** *s.* (*a*) (Story-) teller, narrator. (*b*) (Public entertainer) Racon-teur, raconteuse. **2.** *a.* Garrulous.

racorn|ir [rakɔrniːr], *v.tr.* To make (sth.) hard or tough (as horn). *Se r. les mains,* to make one's hands horny. *s.m.* **-issement.**
  se racornir, to grow horny, hard, or tough; to harden; to shrivel up.

racquitter (se) [sərakite], *v.pr.* To recoup oneself; to retrieve one's losses.

rade [rad], *s.f. Nau:* Roadstead, roads. **En rade,** in the roads. **Mettre un navire en rade,** to lay up a ship. *R. foraine, ouverte,* open road-stead.

radeau [rado], *s.m.* Raft.

radiaire [radjɛːr]. **1.** *a. Nat.Hist:* Radiate(d). **2.** *s.m.* **Les radiaires,** the radiata.

radian(t)[1] [radjã], *s.m. Mth:* Radian.

radiant [radjã]. **1.** *a.* Radiant (heat, etc.). **Pouvoir r.,** radiating capacity. **2.** *s.m. Astr:* Radiant (point).

radiateur, -trice [radjatœːr, -tris]. **1.** *a.* Radi-ating. **2.** *s.m.* Radiator. (*a*) *R. à eau chaude,* hot-water radiator. *R. électrique,* electric fire or radiator. (*b*) *I.C.E: etc:* (Cooling) radiator. *R. soufflé,* fan-cooled radiator.

radiation[1] [radjasjɔ̃], *s.f.* (*a*) Erasure, striking out, crossing out; cancellation (of debt). (*b*) Strik-ing off the roll; disbarment (of barrister); striking off (of solicitor).

radiation[2], *s.f. Ph:* Radiation.

radical, -aux [radikal, -o], *a. & s.m. Alg: Pol: etc:* Radical. *Mth:* **Signe radical,** root-sign. *adv.* **-ement.**

radicalisme [radikalism], *s.m. Pol:* Radicalism.

radicelle [radisɛl], *s.f. Bot:* Radicle, rootlet.

radicivore [radisivɔːr], *a. Ent: Z:* Root-eating; rhizophagous.

radiculaire [radikylɛːr], *a. Bot:* Radicular.

radicule [radikyl], *s.f. Bot:* Radicle.

radié [radje], *a. Nat.Hist:* Radiate(d), rayed.

radier[1] [radje], *s.m. Civ.E:* Frame, floor, bed; sill (of lock-gate); apron (of dock). *R. de fonda-tion,* foundation-raft.

radier², *v.tr.* To erase; to strike (sth.) out; to strike (sth.) off, cross (sth.) off (a list, etc.).

radier³, *v.i.* To radiate, to beam.

radieux, -euse [radjø, -ø:z], *a.* Radiant; dazzling (sky); beaming (with joy).

radifère [radifɛ:r], *a.* Miner: Radiferous; containing radium.

radiner [radine], *v.i.* P: To come (back); to turn up. Mil: To reach camp, billets.

radio [radjo]. **I.** *s.m.* F: (a) Wireless message; radio. (b) Av: Nau: Wireless operator; F: 'sparks.' **2.** *s.f.* F: (a) Wireless telegraphy or telephony; 'wireless.' Annonce par r., broadcast message or advertisement. Parler à la r., F: to be on the air. (b) X-rays. Passer qn à la r., to X-ray s.o.

radio-actif, -ive, *a.* Ph: Radio-active.

radio-activité, *s.f.* Ph: Radio-activity.

radio-concert, *s.m.* Wireless concert.

radiodermite [radjodɛrmit], *s.f.* Med: X-ray dermatitis.

radiodiffuser [radjodiffyze], *v.tr.* W.Tel: To broadcast.

radio-diffusion, *s.f.* W.Tel: Broadcasting. Poste de r.-d., broadcasting station.

radio-émission, *s.f.* **I.** Broadcasting. **2.** Broadcast.

radiogoniomètre [radjogonjomɛtr], *s.m.* Directional receiving-apparatus, direction-finder, radiogoniometer.

radiogoniométrie [radjogonjometri], *s.f.* Location, direction-finding (by wireless).

radiogramme [radjogram], *s.m.* Radiogram. **I.** X-ray photograph. **2.** Wireless message.

radiographie [radjografi], *s.f.* **I.** Radiography, X-ray photography. **2.** = RADIOGRAMME I.

radiographier [radjografje], *v.tr.* To radiograph.

radiographique [radjografik], *a.* Radiographic. Examen r., X-ray examination.

radiologie [radjoloʒi], *s.f.* X-ray treatment; radiology.

radiologique [radjoloʒik], *a.* Radiological. Équipage r., X-ray outfit.

radiophare [radjofa:r], *s.m.* Wireless beacon.

radio-reportage, *s.m.* Broadcasting (of news); running commentary (on a match).

radioscopie [radjoskopi], *s.f.* Radioscopy.

radioscopique [radjoskopik], *a.* Examen radioscopique, X-ray examination.

radiotélégramme [radjotelegram], *s.m.* Wireless telegram.

radiotélégraphie [radjotelegrafi], *s.f.* Wireless telegraphy, radio-telegraphy.

radiotélégraphique [radjotelegrafik], *a.* Wireless (message, station).

radiothérapie [radjoterapi], *s.f.* X-ray treatment; radio-therapy.

radis [radi], *s.m.* Radish. P: Ne pas avoir un radis, to be without a penny, P: to be stony-broke.

radium [radjom], *s.m.* Radium.

radius [radjy:s], *s.m.* Anat: Radius.

radotage [radota:ʒ], *s.m.* Twaddle; drivelling nonsense. Tomber dans le r., to fall into one's dotage. Ce sont là des radotages, these are the ramblings of old age.

radoter [radote], *v.i.* To talk (drivelling) nonsense; to drivel.

radoteur, -euse [radotœ:r, -ø:z], *s.* Dotard.

radoub [radu], *s.m.* Nau: Repair, refitting, graving (of ship). Navire en radoub, ship under repair, in dry dock. Bassin, forme, de radoub, graving-dock, dry dock.

radoub|er [radube], *v.tr.* (a) To repair the hull of (ship); to dry-dock (ship). (b) To mend, repair (net, etc.). *s.m.* **-age.** *s.m.* **-eur.**

radouc|ir [radusi:r], *v.tr.* To calm, soften; to make (s.o.'s temper) milder; to mollify (s.o.). *s.m.* **-issement.**

se radoucir. I. (Of s.o.'s mood, etc.) To grow softer, to soften down. **2.** (Of weather) To grow milder.

rafale [rafal], *s.f.* (a) Squall; strong gust, blast (of wind). Vent à rafales, gusty wind. Temps à rafales, squally weather. S.a. NEIGE. (b) Burst of gun-fire.

rafalé [rafale], *a.* **I.** (Of ship) Disabled by a squall. **2.** F: (Of pers.) Cleaned out; down and out.

rafferm|ir [rafɛrmi:r], *v.tr.* **I.** To harden (once more); to make (sth.) firm(er). **2.** (a) To confirm, strengthen (s.o.'s authority); to fortify, reinforce, restore (courage); to steady (prices, s.o.'s nerves). (b) R. un poteau, to firm up a post. *s.m.* **-issement.**

se raffermir. I. (a) (Of ground, muscle) To harden. (b) Sa santé s'est raffermie, his health has improved. **2.** Son autorité, son crédit, se raffermit, he is recovering his authority, his credit.

raffinement [rafinmã], *s.m.* **I.** = RAFFINAGE. **2.** (Over-)refinement; affectedness.

raffin|er [rafine], *v.tr.* To refine. Abs. Il raffine sur le point d'honneur, he is punctilious on the point of honour. Vous raffinez, you are being too subtle. *s.m.* **-age.**

se raffiner, to become, grow, refined.

raffiné, *a.* (a) Refined (sugar, etc.). (b) Subtle, clever (mind, etc.). (c) Refined, delicate, nice (taste). Friandises raffinées, choice dainties.

raffinerie [rafinri], *s.f.* (Sugar-)refinery.

raffineur, -euse [rafinœ:r, -ø:z], *s.* **I.** (Sugar-)refiner. **2.** Person who affects nicety or subtlety in thought or language.

raffol|er [rafole], *v.i.* R. de qch., de qn, to be excessively fond of, to dote upon, to be infatuated with, sth., s.o. *s.m.* **-ement.**

raffût [rafy], *s.m.* P: Noise, row, shindy.

raffûter [rafyte], *v.tr.* To (re)sharpen (tool).

rafiau [rafjo], *s.m.* Nau: (a) Skiff (with lateen sail). (b) F: Vieux r., old tub.

rafistol|er [rafistole], *v.tr.* F: To patch up, tinker up (sth.). *s.m.* **-age.**

rafle [ra:fl], *s.f.* (a) (i) Clean sweep (by burglars, etc.). (ii) Swag. (b) Looting raid; foray. (c) Round-up, raid, comb-out (by the police).

rafler [rafle], *v.tr.* (a) To sweep off, carry off (contents of a house, etc.). (b) (Of police) To round up (criminals).

rafraîchir [rafreʃi:r], *v.tr.* **I.** To cool, refresh; to air (a room). **2.** (a) To freshen up, revive (colour, painting); to do up, renovate (picture); to touch up (edged tool); to recut (groove). Rafraîchir les cheveux à qn, to trim, clip, s.o.'s hair. (b) R. la mémoire à qn, to refresh s.o.'s memory. R. son anglais, to rub up, brush up one's English.

se rafraîchir. I. (Of weather) To grow, turn, cooler. **2.** To refresh oneself; to have sth. to drink; to take some refreshment. **3.** (Of troops) To rest.

rafraîchissant [rafreʃisã]. **I.** *a.* Refreshing, cooling. **2.** *a. & s.m.* Med: Laxative.

rafraîchissement [rafreʃismã], *s.m.* **I.** (a) Cooling. (b) Freshening up (of picture); reviving (of colour). (c) Refreshing; rubbing up, brushing up (of one's knowledge). Sch: Cours de

rafraîchissement, refresher course. **2.** *pl.* Refreshments (at a dance, etc.).

ragaillardir [ragajardiːr], *v.tr.* *F:* To cheer (s.o.) up ; *F:* to buck (s.o.) up.

se ragaillardir, to cheer up ; *F:* to buck up.

rage [raːʒ], *s.f.* **1.** (Canine) madness ; rabies. **2.** Rage, fury. **La tempête fait rage,** the storm is raging. *F:* **Cela fait rage,** it is quite the rage, all the rage. **Avoir la rage du jeu,** to have a passion for gaming. *R. d'écrire,* mania for writing. **Aimer qn à la rage,** to love s.o. to distraction. **Rage de dents,** paroxysm of toothache.

rager [raʒe], *v.i.* (je rageai(s) ; n. rageons) *F:* To rage ; to be in a rage ; to (fret and) fume. *Ça me fait r. de voir ça!* it makes me wild, *P:* it gets my goat, to see it !

rageu|r, -euse [raʒœːr, -øːz], *a.* Passionate, choleric, violent-tempered ; waspish (tone, retort). *adv.* **-sement.**

ragot¹, -ote [rago, -ɔt]. **I.** *a. & s.* (a) Stumpy, squat, stocky (person). (b) Stocky, cobby (horse). **2.** *s.m. Veh:* Shaft-hook, breeching-hook.

ragot², *s.m.* *F:* **1.** Piece of (ill-natured) gossip. **2.** *pl.* Gossip, tittle-tattle.

ragoût [ragu], *s.m.* **1.** Stew, ragout. *R. de mouton,* stewed mutton. **(Faire) cuire qch. en ragoût,** to stew sth. **2.** Spice, savour, relish. *Avec la faim pour r.,* with hunger for a relish.

ragoûtant [ragutã], *a.* Tempting, inviting. **Peu ragoûtant,** not very tempting.

ragoûter [ragute], *v.tr.* To revive the appetite of (invalid, etc.).

se ragoûter, to recover one's appetite. *Se r. à la vie,* to take a fresh interest in life.

ragrafer [ragrafe], *v.tr.* To hook (up), do up, (dress, belt) again.

ragré|er [ragree], *v.tr.* **1.** *Nau:* To re-rig (a ship). **2.** To clean down (brickwork) ; to clean up (joint, etc.). *s.m.* **-ement.**

raguer [rage], *v.tr.* To chafe, rub (a rope). *Nau: R. le fond,* to be in shoal water ; (of anchor) to drag.

rahat loukoum [raatlukum], *s.m.* Turkish delight.

raid [rɛd], *s.m.* **1.** *Mil:* Raid. *R. aérien,* air-raid. **2.** Long-distance run (in a car) ; long-distance flight.

raide [rɛd]. **I.** *a.* (a) Stiff ; tight, taut (rope). **Mettre un câble au raide,** to take up the slack in a cable. *Cheveux raides,* straight and wiry hair. (b) *Vol r.,* swift and straight flight. **Coup raide comme une balle,** lightning blow, stinging blow ; stinger. (c) Stiff, starchy (manner) ; inflexible, unbending, unyielding (character). (d) Steep (stair, incline) ; abrupt (hill, path). (e) *F:* **Ça, c'est un peu raide!** that's a bit stiff, a bit thick ! **Il en raconte de raides,** he tells some stiff yarns. **Il en a vu de raides,** he's had some queer experiences. *P:* **Boire du raide,** to drink raw spirits, neat spirits. **2.** *adv.* (a) **Filer raide,** to go at a spanking rate ; to scorch along. *Boire r.,* to drink hard. *Frapper r.,* to strike hard. (b) **Tuer qn raide,** to kill s.o. outright, on the spot. **Tomber raide mort,** to fall stone-dead. *adv.* **-ment.**

raideur [rɛdœːr], *s.f.* **1.** Stiffness ; tightness (of rope). **Donner plus de raideur à qch.,** to stiffen sth. **2.** Stiffness, starchiness (of manner) ; inflexibility (of character) ; severity. *Répondre avec raideur,* to answer (i) stiffly, (ii) in an overbearing manner. **3.** Steepness, abruptness. **4.** *Lancer une pierre avec r.,* to throw a stone hard.

raidillon [rɛdijõ], *s.m.* (Short and steep) rise (in a road) ; abrupt path.

raid|ir [rɛdiːr], *v.tr.* (a) To stiffen ; to tighten,

tauten (rope, etc.) ; to haul (rope) taut. (b) *R. qn,* to make s.o. obdurate, intractable. (b) *R. sa volonté, ses forces,* to stiffen one's will ; to brace oneself. *s.m.* **-issement.**

se raidir. 1. To stiffen, to grow stiff ; (of cable) to grow taut. **2.** *Se r. contre le malheur,* to steel, harden, brace, oneself against misfortune.

raidisseur [rɛdisœːr], *s.m.* *Tchn:* Wire-strainer ; counter-brace. *a. Hauban r.,* straining-tie or -stay.

raie¹ [rɛ], *s.f.* **1.** Line, stroke (on paper). *Passer une r. sur un mot,* to strike out a word. **2.** (a) Streak, stripe (on skin of animal) ; streak (in marble) ; stripe (on stuffs). (b) *Opt:* **Raies noires du spectre,** spectrum-lines. **3.** Parting (of the hair). **4.** (i) Furrow ; (ii) ridge (between furrows).

raie², *s.f.* *Ich:* Ray, skate. *R. bouclée,* thornback.

raifort [rɛfɔːr], *s.m.* Horse-radish.

rail [rɑːj, raːj], *s.m.* Rail. (Of train) *Sortir des rails,* to jump the metals ; to derail. *R. conducteur, r. de contact,* live rail (of electric railway).

railler [rɑje], *v.tr.* To laugh at, jeer at, make game of (s.o.). *R. qn de qch.,* to banter, chaff, s.o. about sth. *Abs. Je ne raille point,* I am not joking.

se railler *de qn, de qch.,* to make game of, poke fun at, mock at, scoff at, s.o., sth.

raillerie [rɑjri], *s.f.* Raillery, banter, chaff. **Il n'entend pas raillerie,** he cannot take a joke. *Il n'entend pas r. là-dessus,* he is very touchy on that point.

railleu|r, -euse [rɑjœːr, -øːz]. **I.** *a.* Bantering, scoffing, mocking. **2.** *s.* Banterer, scoffer. *adv.* **-sement.**

rainer [rɛne], *v.tr.* To groove, flute ; to slot.

rainette [rɛnɛt], *s.f.* **1.** Tree-frog. **2.** Rennet, pippin (apple). *R. grise,* russet.

rainure [rɛnyːr], *s.f.* Groove, channel, furrow, slot, rabbet. *R. de clavette,* key-way. **A rainure(s),** grooved, slotted ; fluted.

raiponce [rɛpõːs], *s.f.* *Bot:* *Cu:* Rampion.

rais [rɛ], *s.m.* Spoke (of wheel) ; rowel (of spur).

raisin [rɛzɛ̃], *s.m.* **1.** Le raisin, du raisin, grapes. **Un raisin,** a (variety of) grape. **Grappe de raisin,** bunch of grapes. **Grain de raisin,** grape. **Raisins secs,** raisins. *Raisins de Corinthe,* (dried) currants. *Raisins de Smyrne,* sultanas. S.a. FIGURE 1. **2.** *F:* Lip-stick. **3.** *Bot:* Raisin de loup, black nightshade. **4.** *Paperm:* Grand raisin = royal.

raisiné [rezine], *s.m.* Fruit preserved in grape juice ; raisiné.

raison [rɛzõ], *s.f.* **1.** Reason, motive, ground (de, for). *Pour une r. ou une autre . . . ,* for one reason or another. . . *Demander la r. de qch.,* to ask the reason for, of, sth. *Ce n'est pas une r.,* that doesn't follow. *Pour des raisons personnelles,* on personal grounds. **Pas tant de raisons!** don't argue so much ! **Sans raison,** without reason, groundlessly, needlessly. *Absent pour r. de santé,* absent on account of ill health. *En r. de son âge,* by reason of his age. *En r. d'un deuil récent,* owing to a recent bereavement. **A plus forte raison . . .,** with greater reason . . . ; all the more. . . **Raison de plus,** all the more reason. **Raison d'être de qch.,** reason, object, justification, of sth. *La r. pour laquelle il est venu,* the reason why he came. **2.** Reason (= faculty of reasoning). **Il n'a plus sa raison,** his mind is unhinged, deranged. *Il n'a pas toute sa r.,* he is not quite in his right mind. **Ramener qn à la raison,** to bring s.o. to his senses. **Avoir toute sa raison,** to be in possession of one's reason. **Vous perdez la raison!** have you taken leave of your senses ? *Manque de r.,* irrationality. **Mettre qn à la raison,** to bring s.o. to his senses. **La Mégère mise à la**

raison, the Taming of the Shrew. **Parler raison,** to talk sense. **Entendre raison,** to listen to reason. **Faire entendre raison à qn,** to bring s.o. to reason. **Rendre raison de qch.,** to give an explanation of sth. ; to explain sth. ; to account for sth. *Cf.* 4. **Sans rime ni raison,** without rhyme or reason. **L'âge de raison,** years of discretion. **Mariage de raison,** marriage of convenience. **3.** Reason, justification. **Avoir raison,** to be right. *Avoir r. de faire qch.,* to be justified, right, in doing sth. **Donner raison à qn,** (i) to declare, admit, that s.o. is right ; (ii) to declare s.o. to be in the right. *On lui a demandé r. de sa conduite,* he has been called upon to account for his conduct. **Se faire une raison,** to accept the inevitable, to make the best of a bad job. **Avec raison,** rightly. *S.a.* TORT 1. **Boire plus que de raison,** to drink to excess, more than one ought. **Comme de raison,** as in reason, as one might expect. **4.** Satisfaction, reparation. **Demander raison d'un affront,** to demand satisfaction for an insult. **Faire raison à qn,** (i) to give s.o. satisfaction (by accepting his challenge to a duel) ; (ii) to answer s.o.'s toast. **Se faire raison à soi-même,** to take the law into one's own hands. **Rendre raison de qch.,** to give satisfaction for sth. *Cf.* 2. **Avoir raison de qn, de qch.,** to overcome, get the better of, get the upper hand of, s.o., sth. **5.** *Com:* **Raison sociale,** name, style (of a firm) ; trade name. **6.** *Mth:* **Raison géométrique, arithmétique,** geometrical ratio, arithmetical ratio. **Le poids est en raison directe du volume,** the weight is directly proportional to the volume. *Travail payé à raison de deux francs l'heure,* work paid at the rate of two francs an hour.

raisonnable [rɛzɔnabl], *a.* Reasonable. **1.** Rational. *Voyons, soyez r.,* come, be reasonable. **2.** (*a*) According to reason. *Il est r. qu'il soit récompensé,* it is only reasonable, only fair, that he should be rewarded. (*b*) Adequate. *adv.* **-ment.**

raisonnement [rɛzɔnmɑ̃], *s.m.* (*a*) Reasoning. *Homme de r. juste,* man of sense. (*b*) (Line of) argument. *Pas de raisonnements !* don't argue !

raisonner [rɛzɔne]. **1.** *v.i.* (*a*) To reason (*sur,* about, upon) ; to argue (*sur,* about). (*b*) *F:* To argufy. **Ne raisonnez pas tant,** don't be so argumentative. (*c*) *Nau:* **R. avec les autorités du port,** to show the ship's papers (on entering port). **2.** *v.tr.* (*a*) **R. ses actions,** to consider, study, one's actions. (*b*) **R. qn,** to reason with s.o. *Il faut vous r.,* you must try to be reasonable.

    raisonné, *a.* Reasoned (analysis, argument). *Com:* **Catalogue raisonné,** descriptive catalogue.

raisonneur, -euse [rɛzɔnœːr, -øːz]. **1.** *a.* (*a*) Reasoning, rational. (*b*) Contradictious, argumentative. **2.** *s.* (*a*) Reasoner, arguer. (*b*) *F:* Argufier.

rajeun|ir [raʒœniːr]. **1.** *v.tr.* (*a*) To rejuvenate ; to make (s.o.) young again. *Ce chapeau la rajeunit de dix ans,* this hat makes her look ten years younger. (*b*) To renovate ; to revive (a word). **2.** *v.i.* To grow young again ; to get younger. *s.m.* **-issement.**

rajouter [raʒute], *v.tr.* To add (sth.) ; to add more of (sth.).

rajust|er [raʒyste], *v.tr.* To readjust ; to set (sth.) to rights. **R. sa cravate,** to set one's tie straight. *s.m.* **-ement.**

    se rajuster, to put one's clothes straight.

râle¹ [rɑːl], *s.m.* *Orn:* Rail. **R. des genêts,** landrail, corncrake. **R. d'eau,** brook ouzel.

râle², *s.m.* Rattle (in the throat). **Le râle** (*de la mort*), the death-rattle.

ralent|ir [ralɑ̃tiːr], *v.tr. & i.* To slacken, slow down, slow up (one's pace, etc.). **R. l'allure,** to

slacken the pace. **"Ralentir !"** 'drive slowly !' *Nau:* **R. les feux,** to bank the fires. **R. la marche,** to reduce speed. *s.m.* **-issement.**

    se ralentir, (of movements) to slow up, slow down ; (of zeal) to abate, relax.

    ralenti. **1.** *a.* Slow(er). *Au trot r.,* at a slow trot. **2.** *s.m.* Slow motion. **Film tourné au ralenti,** slow-motion picture. **Mettre le moteur au ralenti,** to throttle down the engine. *Aut:* **Prendre un virage au grand r.,** to take a corner dead slow. *Aut:* (Of engine) **Prendre le r.,** to slow down. **Tourner au r.,** to idle ; to tick over.

râler [rɑle], *v.i.* To rattle (in one's throat) ; to be at one's last gasp. *F:* **R. de colère,** to fume.

ralingue [ralɛ̃ːg], *s.f.* *Nau:* **1.** (*a*) Bolt-rope (of sail). (*b*) Awning-rope. **2. Tenir les voiles en ralingue,** to keep the sails shivering.

ralinguer [ralɛ̃ge]. *Nau:* **1.** *v.tr.* To rope (a sail). **2.** *v.i.* (Of the sails) To shiver, to shake in the wind. **Faire ralinguer les voiles,** to shiver, shake, the sails.

ralliement, *A:* **ralliment** [ralimɑ̃], *s.m.* Rally(ing), assembly (of troops, etc.). **Mot de ralliement,** password.

rallier [ralje], *v.tr.* **1.** (*a*) To rally, assemble (troops, ships). (*b*) *Mil: Nau:* To rejoin (unit, ship). (*c*) *Nau:* **R. la terre,** to stand in for land. **2.** To rally, to win (s.o.) over, to bring (s.o.) round (to a party, etc.).

    se rallier. **1.** (*a*) (Of troops, ships, etc.) To rally. (*b*) *Nau:* **Se r. à terre,** to hug the shore. **2.** *Se r. à un parti,* to rally to, throw in one's lot with, join, a party.

rallonge [ralɔ̃ːʒ], *s.f.* (*a*) Extension-piece (of lifting-jack, etc.) ; eking-piece, lengthening-piece. (*b*) Extra leaf, extension leaf (of table).

rallong|er [ralɔ̃ʒe], *v.tr.* (je rallongeai(s) ; n. rallongeons) To lengthen ; to make longer ; to let down (a skirt). *S.a.* SAUCE 1. *s.m.* **-ement.**

rallumer [ralyme], *v.tr.* To relight (lamp, fire) ; to rekindle (fire) ; to revive (anger, etc.).

    se rallumer, to rekindle ; to light up again ; to blaze up again ; (of anger, etc.) to revive.

rallye [rali], *s.m.* *Sp.* (*Aut.*): Race-meeting.

rallye-paper [ralipepœːr], *s.m.* Paper-chase.

ramage [ramaːʒ], *s.m.* **1.** Floral design. **2.** (*a*) Song, warbling (of birds). (*b*) *F:* Prattle.

ramas [ramɑ], *s.m.* *F:* (*a*) Heap, pile, collection (of old clothes, etc.) ; scratch collection (of articles). (*b*) Set, pack (of thieves, etc.).

ramasse-couverts, *s.m.inv.* Plate-basket, cutlery-basket.

ramasse-miettes, *s.m.inv.* Crumb-tray, -scoop.

ramasse-poussière, *s.m.inv.* Dust-pan.

ramass|er [ramase], *v.tr.* **1.** To gather (sth.) together (in a mass). **R. à la pelle,** to shovel up. **R. toutes ses forces,** to gather, muster, all one's strength. **2.** To collect, gather (different things). **R. les cartes,** to gather up the cards. **R. de l'argent,** to scrape money together ; *F:* to make one's pile. *P:* **Se faire ramasser,** to be run in (by the police). **3.** *R. son mouchoir,* to pick up one's handkerchief. *Rugby:* **R. le ballon,** to gather the ball. *F:* **Ramasser une bûche,** to come a cropper. *s.m.* **-age.** *s.m.* **-ement.** *s.* **-eur, -euse.**

    se ramasser. **1.** To collect, gather (into a crowd). **2.** (*a*) (Of animal) To double up ; to roll itself up. (*b*) (Of pers.) To gather oneself (for an effort) ; (of tiger) to crouch (for a spring). **3.** To pick oneself up (after a fall).

    ramassé, *a.* **1.** Thick-set, stocky, squat (person) ; stocky, cobby (horse). **2.** Compact (machine, style).

ramassis [ramɑsi], *s.m.* *F:* = RAMAS.

rame¹ [ram], s.f. (a) Stick, prop (for peas, etc.). (b) = RAMEAU I (b).

rame², s.f. Oar, scull. *Embarcation à huit rames,* eight-oared boat. *Aller à la rame,* to row. *Faire force de rames,* to row hard. *Faire fausse rame,* to catch a crab.

rame³, s.f. **I.** Ream (of paper). **2.** (a) String, tow (of barges). (b) *Rail: R. de wagons,* (i) lift of carriages, of trucks; (ii) made-up train. *Collision entre deux rames du Métro,* collision between two Underground trains.

rameau [ramo], s.m. **I.** (a) (Small) branch, bough, twig (of tree). (b) *Ecc:* (Processional) palm. *Le dimanche des Rameaux,* Palm Sunday. (c) pl. Antlers (of stag). **2.** Branch, subdivision (of science, family).

ramée [rame], s.f. **I.** Green boughs; arbour. **2.** Small wood, leafage.

ramener [ramne], v.tr. (Conj. like MENER) **I.** To bring (s.o., sth.) back (again). *R. qn chez lui en voiture,* to drive s.o. home. *R. qn à terre,* to bring s.o. off (from a vessel). *R. un malade à la vie,* to bring a patient round. *R. la conversation sur un sujet,* to lead the conversation back to a subject. *R. ses pensées en arrière,* to cast one's thoughts back. *R. tout à un seul principe,* to reduce everything to a single principle. *Mth: R. une fraction à sa plus simple expression,* to reduce a fraction to its simplest terms. *Aut: R. le compteur à zéro,* to reset the speedometer to o. *R. son chapeau sur ses yeux,* to pull down, draw down, one's hat over one's eyes. *R. le poing,* to draw back one's fist. *Equit: R. un cheval,* to rein in a horse. **2.** *R. un autre à son opinion,* to bring s.o. over, round, to one's opinion (again). **3.** *R. la paix,* to restore peace. *R. le courage de qn,* to put fresh courage into s.o.; to revive s.o.'s courage.

ramequin [ramkɛ̃], s.m. *Cu:* Ramekin.

ramer¹ [rame], v.tr. To stick, prop, stake (peas).

ramer², v.i. To row; to pull (at the oar). *R. en couple,* to scull. Cp. NAGER I.

ramer³, v.i. (Of stag) To grow its horns. *Ven: Her:* Cerf ramé, stag attired.

rameur, -euse¹ [ramœːr, -øːz], s. Rower; oarsman, oarswoman. *R. de couple,* sculler.

rameux, -euse² [ramø, -øːz], a. Ramose, branched.

ramie [rami], s.f. Ramie, ramee, grass-cloth plant. *Toile de ramie,* grass-cloth.

ramier [ramje], a.m. & s.m. *Orn:* (Pigeon) ramier, ring-dove, wood-pigeon.

ramification [ramifikasjɔ̃], s.f. Ramification. (a) Branching. (b) Branch.

ramifier (se) [səramifje], v.pr. To ramify, branch out; to divide.

ramille [ramiːj], s.f. **I.** Twig. **2.** pl. Small-wood.

ramoindrir [ramwɛ̃driːr], v.tr. To diminish, lessen.

ramollir [ramɔliːr], v.tr. **I.** To soften (wax, etc.). **2.** To enervate, weaken. *se ramollir,* to soften; to grow soft. *Son cerveau se ramollit,* he has softening of the brain. *F: Il se ramollit,* he is getting soft(-witted). **ramolli, -ie.** *F:* **I.** a. Soft-witted, soft-headed. **2.** s. Dodderer.

ramollissement [ramɔlismɑ̃], s.m. Softening. *Ramollissement du cerveau,* softening of the brain.

ramollot [ramɔlo], s.m. *P:* Un vieux r., an old dug-out; an old dodderer.

ramonage [ramɔnaːʒ], s.m. Chimney-sweeping.

ramoner [ramɔne], v.tr. To sweep (chimney); to rake out (flue); to clear (fire-tubes).

ramoneur [ramɔnœːr], s.m. Chimney-sweeper; sweep.

rampant [rɑ̃pɑ̃], a. **I.** *Her:* Lion rampant, lion rampant. *Arch:* Voûte, arche, rampante, rampant arch or vault. **2.** (a) Creeping; crawling. (b) Grovelling, cringing.

rampe [rɑ̃ːp], s.f. **I.** A: Flight of stairs. **2.** (a) Slope, rise, incline (of hill); pitch (of roof). (b) *Civ.E:* Gradient, up grade. *Aut: Vitesse en r.,* speed when hill-climbing. (c) *Civ.E: Fort:* Ramp. *R. d'accès d'un pont,* approach-ramp of a bridge. **3.** Banisters, hand-rail (of stair). *P: Lâcher la rampe,* to die. **4.** (a) *Th:* (i) Rail (in front of stage). (ii) Footlights, float(s). *F: La pièce n'a pas passé la rampe,* the play failed to get across. *F: Être sous les feux de la rampe,* to be in the limelight. (b) *Av: R. lumineuse d'atterrissage,* illuminated landing-ramp.

ramper [rɑ̃pe], v.i. To creep, crawl; (of plant) to creep, trail. *Entrer, sortir, en rampant,* to crawl in, out. *F: R. devant les grands,* to truckle, cringe, to the great; to grovel before the great. *Style qui rampe,* uninspired, prosy, style. s.m. **-ement.**

ramure [ramyːr], s.f. **I.** Branches, boughs, foliage. **2.** Antlers (of stag).

rancart [rɑ̃kaːr], s.m. (Used in) Mettre qch., qn, au rancart, to cast sth. aside; to retire (officer, official). *F: Elle est au r.,* she's on the shelf.

rance [rɑ̃ːs], a. Rancid, rank (butter, oil). s.m. *Sentir le rance,* to smell rancid.

ranch [rɑ̃ːʃ], s.m. Ranch. *Exploiter un r.,* to ranch.

rancidité [rɑ̃sidite], s.f. Rancidity, rancidness.

rancir [rɑ̃siːr], v.i. To become, grow, rancid. s.m. **-issement.**

rancœur [rɑ̃kœːr], s.f. Rancour; bitterness (of mind).

rançon [rɑ̃sɔ̃], s.f. Ransom. *Mettre qn à rançon,* to hold s.o. to ransom.

rançonner [rɑ̃sɔne], v.tr. (a) To hold (s.o., town) to ransom; to exact a ransom from (s.o.); to ransom (s.o.). (b) *F:* To fleece (customer). s.m. **-ement.**

rancune [rɑ̃kyn], s.f. Rancour, spite, malice, grudge. *Sentiment de r.,* feeling of pique. *Garder rancune à qn,* avoir de la rancune contre qn, to harbour resentment against s.o.; to bear s.o. a grudge (d'avoir fait qch., for having done sth.). *Je ne lui garde pas de r.,* I bear him no malice. *Par rancune,* out of spite. *Sans rancune,* (i) without malice, without ill-feeling; (ii) let bygones be bygones.

rancunier, -ière [rɑ̃kynje, -jɛːr], a. Grudge-bearing, vindictive, rancorous, spiteful.

randonnée [rɑ̃dɔne], s.f. **I.** *Ven:* Circuit (made by hunted game). **2.** *Aut: Cy:* Outing, run, trip, excursion; *Cy:* long road-race. *Être en randonnée,* (i) to be touring; (ii) to be out for a good long run.

rang [rɑ̃], s.m. **I.** (a) Row, line (of trees, columns, etc.). *R. de tricot,* row, round, of knitting. *R. d'oignons,* row of onions. S.a. OIGNON I. *Th: Loge de premier r.,* first-tier box. *Premier r. des fauteuils d'orchestre,* first row of the stalls. (b) *Mil:* Rank (= row in line abreast). *Par rangs de quatre,* four abreast. *Sur deux rangs!* form two deep! *Se mettre en rangs,* former les rangs, to fall in. *Rompre les rangs,* to disperse; *Mil:* to dismiss. *Serrer les rangs,* to close the ranks; to close up. *En rangs serrés,* in close order, *Lit:* in serried ranks. *Quitter son rang,* les rangs, to fall out; to break rank. *Sortir du rang,* (i) to rise from the ranks; (ii) *F:* to get out of the ruck, to make one's name. (c) *Se mettre sur les rangs,* to enter the lists, to come forward (as a candidate). **2.** (a) Rank; station (in life). **Avoir rang de colonel,** to hold the rank of colonel. F: De premier rang, first-class, first-rate, A1. **Arriver au premier rang,** to come to the front. **Par rang d'âge, de taille,** according to age, height. **Prendre rang, avoir rang, avant, après, qn,** to rank before, after, s.o. (b) **Rang social,** social status.

rang|er [rɑ̃ʒe], v.tr. (je rangeai(s); n. rangeons) **1.** To arrange; to set (books, etc.) in rows; to draw up (troops). **2.** (a) To put (sth.) away; to put (sth.) back in its place; to stow away, tidy away (objects). (b) R. la foule, to keep the crowd back, in its place. **3.** (a) To arrange, tidy; to put, set, (things) to rights, in order. (b) Le mariage l'a rangé, marriage has made him settle down. **4.** R. qn parmi les grands écrivains, to rank, set, range, s.o. amongst the great writers. **5.** R. une ville sous sa puissance, to bring a town under one's power. **6.** Nau: **Ranger la terre, la côte,** to range the land; to hug the coast. s.m. **-ement.**

se ranger. 1. To draw up, line up. (Of car) Se r. le long du trottoir, to pull up at the kerb. Nau: Se r. à quai, to berth. **2.** Se r. du côté de qn, to take sides, to side, with s.o. Se r. à l'opinion de qn, to fall in with, come over to, s.o.'s opinion. **3.** Se r. (de côté), to get out of the way; to stand aside. On se rangea pour nous laisser passer, they stood aside to make room for us. **4.** Il s'est rangé, (i) he has steadied down, settled down; (ii) he has got married.

rangé, a. **1.** Bataille rangée, pitched battle. **2.** Tidy, orderly, well-ordered. **3.** Steady (person); (man) of regular habits.

rangée, s.f. Row, line (of persons, trees); tier (of seats); array (of figures).

rani [rani], s.f. Ranee.

ranimer [ranime], v.tr. To revive; to put new life into (s.o.); to restore (fainting person) to consciousness, to life; to stir up (the fire). R. la colère, l'espoir, l'amour, de qn, to reawaken, rekindle, s.o.'s anger, hope, love. R. l'assemblée, to put fresh life into the meeting.

se ranimer, to revive; to come to life again; (of fire) to burn up.

ranz [rɑ̃(ːs)], s.m. **Ranz des vaches, ranz-des-vaches** (Swiss pastoral melody).

Raoul [raul]. Pr.n.m. Ralph.

raout [raut], s.m. (Social) party; reception.

rapace [rapas], a. **1.** Rapacious, predaceous. s.m.pl. Z: **Les rapaces,** the raptores; birds of prey. **2.** Rapacious, grasping (person).

rapacité [rapasite], s.f. Rapacity; rapaciousness.

rapapilloter [rapapijɔte], v.tr. P: To reconcile (persons).

se rapapilloter, to make it up.

rapatriement [rapatrimɑ̃], s.m. Repatriation.

rapatrier [rapatrie], v.tr. To repatriate; to send (s.o.) home (from abroad).

râpe [rɑːp], s.f. Rasp. (a) R. à muscade, nutmeg-grater. (b) Rough file.

râp|er [rɑpe], v.tr. **1.** To rasp (wood); to grate (sugar, nutmeg); to grind (snuff). **2.** To wear (garment) threadbare. s.m. **-age.**

râpé, a. (a) Grated; rasped. (b) Worn out, threadbare. **Avoir l'air râpé,** to look shabby, seedy, out-at-elbows.

rapetass|er [raptase], v.tr. F: To patch up, do up (garment); to cobble (shoe); to botch up (literary work). s.m. **-age.** s.m. **-eur.**

rapetiss|er [raptise]. **1.** v.tr. To make (sth.) smaller; to shorten (garment); to shrink (stuff).

Sa maison rapetisse les autres, his house dwarfs the others. Se r. pour monter dans la voiture, to stoop in order to get into the car. **2.** v.i. & pr. To shorten; to become shorter, smaller; to shrink. Les jours (se) rapetissent, the days are drawing in. [PETIT] s.m. **-ement.**

raphia [rafja], s.m. Raphia(-grass), raffia.

rapiat, -ate [rapja, -at]. F: **1.** a. Stingy, avaricious. **2.** s. Miser, skinflint, hunks.

rapide [rapid]. **1.** a. (a) Rapid, swift, fast. **Rapide comme la pensée,** as swift as thought. La r. conclusion des négociations, the speedy conclusion of the negotiations. **Fusil à tir rapide,** quick-firing rifle. (b) Steep, rapid (slope). **2.** s.m. (a) Rapid (in river). (b) Express (train), fast train. adv. **-ement.**

rapidité [rapidite], s.f. (a) Rapidity, swiftness. (b) Steepness (of slope).

rapiéçage [rapjesaːʒ], s.m. **1.** = RAPIÈCEMENT. **2.** Patchwork.

rapi|écer [rapjese], v.tr. (je rapièce; je rapiècerai) To piece, patch (garment, etc.). s.m. **-ècement.**

rapière [rapjɛːr], s.f. A: Rapier. **Traîneur de rapière,** swashbuckler.

rapin [rapɛ̃], s.m. F: **1.** Art student. **2.** Dauber, daubster.

rapine [rapin], s.f. Lit: (a) Rapine, pillage, depredation. (b) Graft.

rapiner [rapine], v.tr. & i. (a) To pillage; to commit depredations. (b) To practise graft.

rapinerie [rapinri], s.f. = RAPINE.

raplapla(t) [raplapla], a.inv. F: **1.** Commonplace, trite. **2.** Without energy, washed out.

rappareill|er [rapareje], v.tr. To match, complete (set of china). s.m. **-ement.**

rapparier [raparje], v.tr. To match, complete (a pair); to pair (two things).

rappel [rapɛl], s.m. **1.** (a) Recall. **Lettres de rappel,** letters of recall. Ven: R. des chiens, calling off of the hounds. (b) Com: Calling in (of sum advanced). (c) R. à l'ordre, call(ing) to order. (d) Recall to the colours (of reservists); (re)call (of actor). **2.** Art: **Rappel de lumière,** high light (in picture). **3.** (a) Com: R. de compte, d'échéance, reminder of account due, of due date. (b) R. de traitement, back pay. **4.** Jur: Repeal, recall (of decree). **5.** Mec.E: (a) **Vis de rappel,** adjusting screw. R. de l'usure, taking up of the wear. (b) Ressort de r., return-spring, drawback-spring. Typewr: Rappel de chariot, (i) return of carriage; (ii) back-spacer. **6.** Mil: **Battre le rappel,** to call, beat, to arms.

rappeler [raple], v.tr. (Conj. like APPELER) **1.** (a) To recall (s.o.); to call, summon, (s.o.) back. R. un acteur, to call for, recall, an actor. R. son chien, to call off one's dog. (b) **Rappeler qn à l'ordre,** to call s.o. to order. R. qn à son devoir, to recall s.o. to the paths of duty. (c) R. son courage, to summon up one's courage anew. **2.** To call back, recall, (sth.) to mind. R. qch. à qn, to recall sth. to s.o.; to remind s.o. of sth. Vous me rappelez mon oncle, you remind me of my uncle. **Rappelez-moi à son bon souvenir,** remember me kindly to him. **3.** R. un décret, to repeal, recall, a decree. **4.** Mec.E: (a) To draw back (part, etc.). Typewr: **Rappeler le chariot,** (i) to return the carriage; (ii) to back-space. (b) R. l'usure, to take up the wear.

se rappeler qch., to recall, recollect, remember, sth.; to call sth. to mind. Je ne me le rappelle pas, I do not remember it. **Se rappeler (d')avoir promis** qch., to recollect, remember, having promised sth.

rappliquer [raplike]. **1.** v.tr. To re-apply

(poultice, etc.). **2.** *v.i. P:* To come back. *R. à la maison*, to make tracks for home.

rapport [rapɔːr], *s.m.* I. **1.** Return, yield, profit. **Être en plein rapport**, to be in full yield; (of land) to be in full productiveness. *Emploi d'un bon r.*, profitable employment. **Maison de rapport**, block of flats; tenement. **2.** (*a*) (Official) report. *R. financier*, treasurer's report. *Nau:* Rapport de mer, ship's protest; master's (sworn) report. (*b*) Report, account, statement. *F:* Faire des rapports, to tell tales (out of school). **3.** (*a*) Terres de rapport, made ground, artificial soil. (*b*) Pièces de rapport, (i) built-up parts (of machinery, etc.); (ii) inlaid pieces, mosaic work.

II. **rapport. 1.** Relation, connection (*avec*, with). *Sans r. avec le sujet*, without any bearing on the subject. **Avoir rapport à qch.**, to relate, refer, to sth. **En rapport avec qch.**, in keeping with sth., in harmony with sth.; consonant with (dignity). **Par rapport à qch.**, (i) with regard to sth.; with respect to sth.; in relation to sth.; (ii) in comparison with, compared with, sth. **Sous le rapport de qch.**, with regard to, with respect to, sth.; in respect of sth. *Sous tous les rapports*, in all respects, in every respect. **2.** *Mth:* Ratio, proportion. *R. d'engrenage*, gear-ratio. **3.** Relations, intercourse (between persons). **Mettre qn en rapport avec qn**, to bring s.o. into contact, put s.o. in touch, with s.o. **Avoir des rapports avec qn**, to be in touch, in relation, with s.o. *Avoir de bons rapports avec qn*, to be on good terms with s.o.

rapportable [rapɔrtabl], *a.* **1.** *Tchn:* Pièces rapportables, parts that fit together. **2.** Referable, attributable (*à*, to).

rapportage [rapɔrtaːʒ], *s.m.* **1.** Talebearing. **2.** Underhand report.

rapporter [rapɔrte], *v.tr.* **1.** To bring back; (of dog) to retrieve (game). **2.** To bring in, bear, yield, produce. *Placement qui rapporte cinq pour cent*, investment that brings in, returns, five per cent. *Cela ne rapporte rien*, it doesn't pay. **3.** (*a*) *R. un fait*, to report, relate, a fact. (*b*) *v.i. R. sur un projet*, to report, present a report, on a plan. (*c*) *Sch: F:* To tell tales. **4.** *R. qch. à une cause*, to ascribe sth. to a cause. *R. un événement à une époque*, to assign, refer, an event to a period. *R. tout à soi, à ses intérêts*, to have nothing but one's selfish interests in view. **5.** *Book-k: R. un article*, to post an item. **6.** To rescind, revoke (decree, etc.); to withdraw (order); to call off (strike). **7.** *Surv: R. un angle*, to plot, set off, lay off, an angle.

se rapporter. 1. (*a*) To agree, tally (*avec*, with). (*b*) To fit together. **2.** To refer, relate (*à*, to); to have reference (to). *Les documents qui se rapportent à l'affaire*, the relevant documents. **3.** S'en rapporter à qn, to rely on s.o. *Je m'en rapporte à vous*, (i) I take your word for it; (ii) I leave it to you.

rapporté, *a.* **1.** *Terre rapportée*, made ground. **2.** (*a*) Built-up (machine); compound (girder). (*b*) *Étau à mâchoires rapportées*, vice with detachable jaws, with inserted jaws. *Moteur à culasse rapportée*, engine with detachable head. (*c*) Pièces rapportées, inlaid work, mosaic work.

rapporteur, -euse [rapɔrtœːr, -øːz], *s.* **1.** Talebearer, sneak. **2.** *s.m.* Reporter, recorder; chairman (of committee); judge advocate (at court martial). **3.** *s.m. Mth:* Protractor.

rapprendre [raprɑ̃ːdr], *v.tr.* (Conj. like PRENDRE) **1.** To learn (sth.) (over) again. **2.** To teach (sth.) again (*à*, to).

rapprochement [raprɔʃmɑ̃], *s.m.* **1.** Bringing together; reconciling (of two persons); putting together, comparing (of facts, ideas). **2.** Nearness, proximity, closeness. **3.** Coming together; reconciliation; rapprochement.

rapprocher [raprɔʃe], *v.tr.* **1.** To bring (sth.) near again. **2.** (*a*) To bring (objects) nearer, closer together. *R. les lèvres d'une plaie*, to draw together, join, unite, the lips of a wound. *R. qch. de qch.*, to bring sth. nearer to sth. *R. une chaise du feu*, to draw up a chair to the fire. (*b*) To bring together; to create a fellowship between (two persons). **3.** *R. des faits, des idées*, to put together, to compare, facts, ideas.

se rapprocher de qch., to draw near(er) to sth. *Se r. de la vérité*, to approximate to the truth. *La France et l'Espagne s'étaient rapprochées*, a rapprochement had taken place between France and Spain.

rapproché, *a.* (*a*) Near (in space or time) (*de*, to). *Yeux rapprochés*, close-set eyes. *Navy: Combat r.*, close action. (*b*) *Espèces rapprochées*, closely related species.

rapsode [rapsɔd], *s.m.* Rhapsode, rhapsodist.

rapsodie [rapsɔdi], *s.f.* Rhapsody.

rapt [rapt], *s.m., Jur:* Abduction of a minor.

râpure [rɑpyːr], *s.f.* Raspings; gratings.

raquette [raket], *s.f.* **1.** *Games:* Racket, racquet. *Aut: F:* Coups de raquette, jars, back-lash; bumping (off the springs). **2.** Regulating lever (of watch). **3.** Snow-shoe. **4.** Prickly-pear, nopal.

rare [rɑːr], *a.* **1.** Rare. *Visites rares (et éloignées)*, visits few and far between. *Une des rares personnes qui . . .*, one of the few people who . . . **Se faire rare**, to be seldom seen. *Il est r. qu'on le voie*, he is seldom seen. **2.** (*a*) Rare, uncommon, exceptional (merit, beauty). *Courage r.*, rare courage, singular courage. (*b*) Unusual (occurrence). **3.** Thin, sparse, scanty (hair, etc.). **4.** *Ph:* Rare (atmosphere). *adv.* **-ment.**

raréfaction [rarefaksjɔ̃], *s.f.* (*a*) Rarefaction (of gas, air). (*b*) Depletion (of supplies); growing scarcity (of labour, of money).

raréfier [rarefje], *v.tr.* (*a*) *Ph:* To rarefy. (*b*) To deplete; to make (sth.) scarce.

se raréfier, to become scarce.

rareté [rarte], *s.f.* **1.** (*a*) Rarity, tenuity (of gas, etc.). (*b*) Scarceness, scarcity, dearth. (*c*) Singularity, unusualness (of phenomenon). **2.** (*a*) Cabinet de raretés, cabinet of rarities, of curiosities. (*b*) Rare occurrence.

rarissime [rarisim], *a. F:* Exceedingly rare; very unusual.

ras¹ [rɑ]. **1.** *a.* (*a*) Close-cropped (hair); close-shaven (beard, chin); short-napped (velvet). *Couper ras les cheveux*, to crop the hair short, close. *A poil ras*, (i) short-haired (dog); (ii) smooth, short-napped (cloth). (*b*) Bare, blank. *En rase campagne*, in the open country. **Faire table rase de qch.**, to make a clean sweep of sth. *Sa mémoire est une table rase*, his memory is a complete blank. (*c*) *Mesure rase*, full measure but not heaped; stricken measure (of corn, etc.). *Verser du vin à qn à ras bord*, to fill s.o.'s glass to the brim. (*d*) *Écueil ras*, reef awash. **2.** *s.m.* (*a*) Reef awash; spit. (*b*) **A, au, ras de**, (on a) level with, flush with. *Voler au ras du sol*, to skim (along) the ground.

ras², *s.m.* = RAZ.

rasade [rɑzad], *s.f.* Brim-full glass of wine, etc.); bumper. *Se verser une r.*, to fill one's glass. [RAS¹]

rasant [rɑzɑ̃], *a.* **1.** Vol rasant, flight that skims the ground. *Mil:* Tir rasant, grazing fire.

2. F: Boring, tiresome (person); prosy, dull (speech).

rascasse [raskas], s.f. Ich: Hog-fish.

rase-mottes, s.m. Av: Vol à rase-mottes, hedge-hopping.

ras|er [rɑze], v.tr. **1.** (a) To shave; to shave off (moustache); to shear (cloth). Se faire raser, to have, get, a shave. (b) F: To bore (s.o.). **2.** To raze (building) to the ground. **3.** (a) To graze, brush, skim (over) (surface). L'hirondelle rase le sol, the swallow skims the ground. (b) Raser la côte, le mur, to hug the shore, the wall. s.m. -age. s.m. -ement.
  se raser. 1. (a) To shave. (b) F: To be bored. **2.** Ven: (Of game) To squat.

raseur, -euse [rɑzœːr, -øːz], s. **1.** Shaver. **2.** F: Bore.

rasoir [rɑzwaːr], s.m. Razor. Rasoir de sûreté, américain, safety razor. Pierre à rasoir, hone. Cuir à rasoir, strop. F: Quel rasoir! what a bore!

rassasiant [rasɑzjɑ̃], a. (a) Satisfying (meal). (b) Satiating, filling (food).

rassasiement [rasɑzimɑ̃], s.m. **1.** Satisfying (of hunger). **2.** Satiety, surfeit.

rassasier [rasɑzje], v.tr. **1.** To satisfy (hunger, passion). R. qn, to satisfy s.o., s.o.'s hunger. R. son regard à contempler qch., to feast one's eyes on sth. **2.** To sate, satiate, surfeit, cloy (de, with).
  se rassasier, to eat one's fill; to glut, gorge, oneself (de, with).

rassemblement [rasɑ̃bləmɑ̃], s.m. **1.** Assembling, collecting, gathering. Mil: Fall-in. Sonner le r., to sound the assembly. **2.** Assemblage, crowd.

rassembler [rasɑ̃ble], v.tr. To assemble, muster (troops, etc.); to collect, gather together, get together (persons, things). R. toutes ses forces, to muster, summon up, all one's strength.
  se rassembler, to assemble, to come together, to flock together. Mil: To fall in, to muster.

rasseoir [raswaːr], v.tr. (Conj. like ASSEOIR) **1.** To reseat (s.o.). **2.** To settle, compose (one's ideas).
  se rasseoir. 1. To sit down again; to resume one's seat. Rasseyez-vous, take your seats again. **2.** A: To calm down.

rassis, a. (a) Settled, staid, sedate (disposition). Personne de sens rassis, person of sane, well-balanced, judgment. (b) Pain rassis, stale bread.

rassér|éner [raserene], v.tr. (je rassérène; je rassérénerai) **1.** To clear (up) (the weather). **2.** To restore (s.o.'s) equanimity. s.m. -ènement.
  se rasséréner. 1. (Of weather) To clear (up). **2.** (Of pers.) To recover one's equanimity, one's spirits; to brighten up. Son front se rasséréna, his brow cleared.

rassied [rasje], **rassis** [rasi]. See RASSEOIR.

rassortiment [rasɔrtimɑ̃], s.m. Com: **1.** Restocking. **2.** New stock.

rassortir [rasɔrtiːr], v.tr. (Conj. like ASSORTIR) Com: To restock (goods or shop).
  se rassortir, to lay in a new stock (en, of).

rassurer [rasyre], v.tr. **1.** To reassure, cheer, hearten. **2.** To stay, strengthen (wall).
  se rassurer, to get over one's apprehensions, one's misgivings; to feel reassured. Rassurez-vous (là-dessus), make yourself easy, set your mind at ease, at rest (on that point).

rastaquouère [rastakweːr], s.m., P: **rasta** [rasta], s.m. Flashy (South-American) adventurer.

rat [ra], s.m. **1.** (a) Rat. Rat des champs, field-mouse. Rat surmulot, brown rat. Rat d'égout, sewer-rat. Mort aux rats, rat-poison. Preneur de rats, rat-catcher. F: Avoir un rat, des rats, dans la tête, to have a bee in one's bonnet. P: Être rat, to be stingy, miserly. S.a. CHAT 1, QUEUE-DE-RAT. (b) Rat musqué, musk-rat, musquash. Rat d'eau, water-vole. **2.** (Of persons, used contemptuously) Rat de cave, (i) exciseman; also (ii) wax-taper (sold coiled or folded). Rat d'église, (i) devout attender at church services; (ii) minor church official. S.a. GUEUX 2. Rat d'hôtel, flashy hotel thief. Rat d'Opéra, young ballet-girl.

rata [rata], s.m. Mil: P: = RATATOUILLE. Rata aux choux, bubble-and-squeak.

ratafia [ratafja], s.m. Ratafia (liqueur).

rataplan [rataplɑ̃], s.m. Rat-tat, rub-a-dub (of a drum).

ratatin|er [ratatine], v.tr. & pr. To shrivel (up); to shrink; to dry up; (of parchment) to crinkle up. Petite vieille ratatinée, wizened little old woman. s.m. -ement.

ratatouille [ratatuːj], s.f. P: Stew, skilly.

rate¹ [rat], s.f. Anat: Spleen. F: Épanouir, dilater, désopiler, la rate de qn, to make s.o. shake with laughter. Ne pas se fouler la rate, to take things easy.

rate², s.f. She-rat.

râteau [rɑto], s.m. **1.** Tls: (a) Rake. (b) Nau: Râteau de pont, squeegee. (c) Toil: Big-toothed comb; rake. **2.** Bill: (Cue-)rest.

râteler [rɑtle], v.tr. (je râtelle; je râtellerai) **1.** To rake up (hay, etc.). **2.** = RATISSER.

râtelier [rɑtəlje], s.m. **1.** Rack (in a stable). F: Manger à deux râteliers, (i) to have two strings to one's bow; (ii) to have a foot in both camps. **2.** R. d'armes, à outils, à pipes, arm-rack, tool-rack, pipe-rack. **3.** (a) (Upper or lower) row of teeth. (b) F: Set of false teeth; denture.

râtelures [rɑtlyːr], s.f.pl. Rakings.

rater [rate]. **1.** v.i. (a) (Of gun) To miss fire, misfire; to fail to go off. (b) (Of motor engine) To misfire. (c) (Of enterprise, etc.) To fail; to miscarry. **2.** v.tr. (a) R. son coup, to miss one's shot, to miss the mark; Golf: to foozle one's shot. R. un lièvre, to miss a hare. (b) F: R. une affaire, to fail in an affair. R. son train, to miss one's train.

raté, -ée. 1. a. Miscarried, ineffectual. Coup raté, (i) shot that has missed the mark, (ii) misfire, (iii) Golf: foozled shot. Av: Atterrissage r., bad landing. **2.** s. (Of pers., esp. of writer, artist, actor) Failure. **3.** s.m. Misfire (of gun, etc.; I.C.E: of engine). S.a. ALLUMAGE.

ratiboiser [ratibwaze], v.tr. P: **1.** R. qch. à qn, to do s.o. out of sth. **2.** To fleece (s.o.); to clean (s.o.) out.

ratier [ratje], a. & s.m. (Chien) ratier ratter.

ratière [ratjɛːr], s.f. Rat-trap.

ratificatif, -ive [ratifikatif, -iːv], a. Ratifying.

ratification [ratifikasjɔ̃], s.f. Ratification, confirmation, approval (of a decision, etc.).

ratifier [ratifje], v.tr. To ratify (treaty, etc.); to confirm, approve (decision).

ratine [ratin], s.f. Tex: Frieze, ratteen, petersham.

ration [rasjɔ̃], s.f. Ration(s), allowance; (horse's) feed. R. réduite, diminuée, short ration. Mettre qn à la ration, to put s.o. on short allowance, on short rations; to ration s.o.

rationaliser [rasjɔnalize], v.tr. To rationalize.

rationn|el, -elle [rasjɔnɛl], a. Rational. Mécanique rationnelle, theoretic mechanics, pure mechanics. adv. -ellement.

rationn|er [rasjɔne], *v.tr.* To ration; to ration (out) (bread). *F:* R. *l'avoine à ses chevaux*, to stint one's horses of oats. *s.m.* **-ement.**

ratiss|er [ratise], *v.tr.* **1.** (*a*) To rake. (*b*) To hoe; to scuffle (path). (*c*) To scrape (skins, etc.). **2.** (At casino) R. *les mises*, to rake in the stakes. *F: La police les a ratissés*, the police nabbed the lot. *s.m.* **-age.**

ratissoire [ratiswaːr], *s.f. Tls:* (*a*) Hoe, scuffle. (*b*) Light rake. (*c*) Scraper.

ratissure [ratisyːr], *s.f.* Raking(s), scraping(s).

raton [ratɔ̃], *s.m.* Little rat. S.a. BERTRAND.

rattach|er [rataʃe], *v.tr.* **1.** To fasten, tie (up), (sth.) again; to refasten, retie. **2.** (*a*) *Les liens qui vous rattachent à la famille*, the ties that bind one to the family. (*b*) To link up, connect (one question with another). *s.m.* **-age.**
  se rattacher *à qch.* **1.** To be fastened to sth. **2.** To be connected with sth. *En ce qui se rattache à . . .*, with regard to. . . .

ratteindre [ratɛ̃ːdr], *v.tr.* (Conj. like ATTEINDRE) **1.** To retake, recapture. **2.** To overtake (s.o.); to catch up with (s.o.).

ratteler [ratle], *v.tr.* (Conj. like ATTELER) To reharness.

rattrapage [ratrapaːʒ], *s.m. Mec.E:* R. *de jeu, d'usure*, taking up of play, of wear.

rattraper [ratrape], *v.tr.* **1.** To recapture; to catch (s.o.) again. *F:* On ne m'y rattrapera pas! you won't catch me doing that again! *Je vous rattraperai!* I'll get my own back on you! **2.** To overtake; to catch (s.o.) up. **3.** To recover (one's money, one's health). R. *le temps perdu*, to make up for lost time. **4.** *Mec.E:* R. *l'usure*, to take up the wear.
  se rattraper. 1. *Se r. d une branche*, to steady oneself, to save oneself, by catching hold of a branch. **2.** *Se r. de ses pertes*, to make good one's losses; to recoup oneself.

rature [ratyːr], *s.f.* **1.** Erasure: **2.** Scraping(s).

ratur|er [ratyre], *v.tr.* **1.** To erase, scratch out, cross out (word). **2.** To scrape (parchment, etc.). *s.m.* **-age.**

raucité [rosite], *s.f.* Raucity; hoarseness.

rauque [roːk], *a.* Hoarse, raucous, rough, harsh, raw (voice, etc.).

ravage [ravaːʒ], *s.m.* Usu. *pl.* Havoc, devastation, ravages. *Faire des ravages*, to work havoc.

ravag|er [ravaʒe], *v.tr.* (*je ravageai(s)*; *n.* ravageons) To ravage, devastate; to lay (country) waste; to make havoc of, play havoc with (sth.). *Les régions ravagées*, the devastated regions. *Face ravagée*, (i) face pitted by smallpox; (ii) face on which life has left its mark. *s.m.* **-ement.** *s.* **-eur, -euse.**

raval|er [ravale], *v.tr.* **1.** To swallow (sth.) again; to swallow (sth.) down; to choke down (sob). *F:* Ravaler ses paroles, (i) to resist the temptation to speak; to check oneself; (ii) to retract a statement. **2.** (*a*) R. *qn au niveau des bêtes*, to reduce s.o. to the level of the beasts. (*b*) To take (s.o.) down; to snub, slight (s.o.). **3.** *Const:* (*a*) To re-dress, resurface (stonework). (*b*) To rough-cast. *s.m.* **-ement.**
  se ravaler, to degrade, lower, debase, oneself.

ravaudage [ravodaːʒ], *s.m.* **1.** Mending (of clothes); darning (of stockings). **2.** Mend; darn.

ravaud|er [ravode], *v.tr.* To mend, patch (clothes); to darn (stockings). *s.* **-eur, -euse.**

rave [raːv], *s.f. Bot:* Rape, coleseed.

ravier [ravje], *s.m.* **1.** Radish-dish, hors-d'œuvres dish. **2.** Turnip silo.

ravigote [ravigɔt], *s.f. Cu:* Ravigote sauce.

ravigoter [ravigɔte], *v.tr. F:* To revive, refresh; *F:* to buck (s.o.) up.
  se ravigoter, to revive; to recover one's good spirits; *F:* to perk up.

ravin [ravɛ̃], *s.m.* Ravine, gully.

ravin|er [ravine], *v.tr.* (Of storm torrents) To gully, hollow out, channel (the ground); to furrow, cut up (roads). *s.m.* **-ement.**

ravir [raviːr], *v.tr.* **1.** To ravish, carry off (s.o.). R. *qch. à qn*, to rob s.o. of sth.; to steal sth. from s.o. **2.** To ravish, enrapture, delight (s.o.). *Être habillée à ravir*, to be ravishingly, bewitchingly, dressed.

ravi, *a.* **1.** Entranced, enraptured. **2.** *F:* Delighted (*de*, with); overjoyed (*de*, at). R. *de joie*, overjoyed. *Je suis r. de vous voir*, I am delighted to see you. *D'un air r.*, delightedly.

raviser (se) [sɔravize], *v.pr.* To change one's mind; to think better of it.

raviss|ant [ravisɑ̃], *a.* Entrancing, bewitching; ravishing, delightful. *adv.* **-amment.**

ravissement [ravismɑ̃], *s.m.* **1.** Carrying off, ravishing. **2.** Rapture, ecstasy, delight.

ravisseur [ravisœːr], *s.m.* Ravisher. (*a*) Plunderer. (*b*) Abductor (of a woman). (*c*) R. *d'enfant*, kidnapper.

ravitaillement [ravitajmɑ̃], *s.m.* Revictualling; provisioning (*en*, with). R. *en munitions*, ammunition supply. *Service du ravitaillement* = Army Service Corps.

ravitailler [ravitaje], *v.tr.* To revictual, to provision (*en*, with); to supply (place) with fresh provisions, ammunition, etc.
  se ravitailler. *Nau:* To take in fresh supplies; to revictual.

ravitailleur [ravitajœːr], *s.m.* **1.** Carrier (of ammunition, etc.). **2.** Supply-ship, store-ship. R. *d'aviation*, aircraft tender.

raviv|er [ravive], *v.tr.* **1.** To revive (fire, hope, pain). **2.** To brighten up, to touch up (colour, etc.); to clean, file up (surfaces to be soldered). *Raviver une plaie*, to re-open an old sore. *s.m.* **-age.**
  se raviver, (of hope, fire) to revive.

ravoir [ravwaːr], *v.tr.* (Used only in the inf.) To get (sth.) back again; to recover (sth.).

ray|er [reje], *v.tr.* (*je raie, je raye*; *je raierai, je rayerai*) **1.** (*a*) To scratch (glass, etc.); to score (cylinder). (*b*) To rule, line (paper). (*c*) To stripe, streak (fabric). (*d*) To rifle (gun). **2.** To strike out, expunge (word); to remove s.o.'s name (*de*, from). *Mil:* R. *qn des contrôles*, to strike s.o. off the strength. *s.m.* **-age.**

rayère [rejɛːr], *s.f.* **1.** *Arch:* Dream-hole. **2.** Head-race (of overshot wheel); flume, leat.

rayon[1] [rejɔ̃], *s.m.* **1.** (*a*) Ray (of light, hope); beam (of light). R. *de lune*, moonbeam. *Ph: Rayons X*, X-rays. (*b*) Rayon visuel, line of sight. **2.** Radius (of a circle). R. *d'action d'un avion*, radius of action of an aeroplane. S.a. VECTEUR. **3.** (*a*) Spoke, arm (of wheel). (*b*) *Étoile à cinq rayons*, five-point star.

rayon[2], *s.m. Hort:* Drill; (small) furrow (for planting seed); row (of onions).

rayon[3], *s.m.* **1.** Rayon de miel, honeycomb. **2.** (*a*) Shelf (of cupboard, etc.). (*b*) Department (in shop). Chef de rayon, head or buyer of a department; shop-walker.

rayonnant [rɛjɔnɑ̃], *a.* (*a*) *Ph:* Radiant (heat); radiating, radiative (power). (*b*) Radiant, beaming (face); (face) wreathed in smiles.

rayonne [rɛjɔn], *s.f. Tex:* Rayon; artificial silk.

rayonnement [rɛjɔnmɑ̃], *s.m.* (*a*) *Ph:* Radiation. (*b*) Radiance, effulgence.

rayonner[1] [rɛjɔne], *v.i.* (*a*) *Ph:* To radiate. *W.Tel: R. dans l'antenne*, to howl. (*b*) To beam, shine. *Il rayonnait de joie*, he was radiant, beaming, with joy.

rayonner[2], *v.tr. Hort:* To drill, furrow.

rayure [rɛjy:r], *s.f.* **1.** (*a*) Stripe, streak. A **rayures**, striped. (*b*) Scratch, score. (*c*) Groove. *Sm.a:* Rifling. **2.** (*a*) Striking out, expunging (of conviction). (*b*) Erasure.

raz [rɑ], *s.m.* Strong current (in estuary); race. *Raz de marée*, (i) tide-race; bore; (ii) tidal wave.

razzia [ra(d)zja], *s.f.* (*a*) Incursion, raid, foray, razzia. (*b*) *F:* (Police) raid.

razzier [ra(d)zje], *v.tr.* To raid.

ré [re], *s.m. inv. Mus:* (*a*) (The note) D. (*b*) The D string (of violin, etc.).

réa [rea], *s.m. Mec.E:* Sheave; pulley-wheel.

réabonnement [reabɔnmã], *s.m.* Renewal of subscription (*à*, to).

réabonner [reabɔne], *v.tr.* To renew (s.o.'s) subscription (*à*, to).
  se réabonner, to renew one's subscription.

réabsorber [reapsɔrbe], *v.tr.* To reabsorb.

réaccoutumer [reakutyme], *v.tr.* To re-accustom (*à*, to).

réactance [reaktã:s], *s.f. El.E:* Reactance, *F:* choking. S.a. BOBINE I.

réactif, -ive [reaktif, -i:v]. **1.** *a. Ch: etc:* (*a*) Reactive. **Papier réactif,** test-paper. (*b*) *W.Tel:* Regenerative. **2.** *s.m. Ch:* Reagent.

réaction [reaksjɔ̃], *s.f.* **1.** Reaction; kick (of rifle). **2.** *W.Tel:* Regeneration. *R. intempestive, dans l'antenne,* howling. S.a. BOBINE I.

réactionnaire [reaksjɔne:r], *a. & s. Pol:* Reactionary.

réactivité [reaktivite], *s.f. Ch:* Reactivity.

réaffirmer [reafirme], *v.tr.* To reaffirm.

réagir [reaʒi:r], *v.i.* To react (*sur*, upon).

réalés|er [realeze], *v.tr.* (Conj. like ALÉSER) *Metalw:* To rebore. *s.m.* **-age.**

réalgar [realgar], *s.m.* Realgar; red arsenic.

réalisable [realizabl], *a.* Realizable; workable.

réalisation [realizasjɔ̃], *s.f.* Realization; carrying into effect, carrying out (of a plan); selling out (of shares).

réaliser [realize], *v.tr.* To realize. **1.** To effect, carry into effect, carry out, work out (plan). **2.** To sell out (shares); to realize (one's assets). **3.** (As an Anglicism) = *se rendre compte de (qch.). Ils ne réalisent pas que . . .,* they do not realize that. . . .
  se réaliser, (of projects, etc.) to be realized; to materialize; (of prediction) to come true.

réalisme [realism], *s.m.* Realism.

réaliste [realist]. **1.** *a.* Realistic. **2.** *s.* Realist.

réalité [realite], *s.f.* Reality. **En réalité,** in reality, really, actually, as a matter of fact.

réapparaître [reapare:tr], *v.i.* (Conj. like APPARAÎTRE. Aux. usu. *être*) To reappear.

réapparition [reaparisjɔ̃], *s.f.* Reappearance.

réapprendre [reaprã:dr], *v.tr.* (Conj. like APPRENDRE) = RAPPRENDRE.

réapprovisionner [reaprɔvizjɔne], *v.tr.* To revictual; to replenish (s.o.'s) supplies (*en*, of); to restock (shop) (*en*, with).

réargenter [rearʒãte], *v.tr.* To resilver, replate.

réarm|er [rearme], *v.tr.* **1.** (*a*) *Mil:* To rearm. (*b*) To recock (gun). **2.** *Nau:* To refit, recommission; to put (vessel) into commission again. *s.m.* **-ement.**

réarrim|er [rearime], *v.tr. Nau:* To restow (cargo). *s.m.* **-age.**

réassurance [reasyrã:s], *s.f.* Reinsurance, reassurance (of a risk). *Effectuer une r.,* to lay off a risk.

réassur|er [reasyre], *v.tr.* To reinsure, reassure (a risk). *s.m.* **-eur.**

rébarbatif, -ive [rebarbatif, -i:v], *a.* Grim, forbidding (face, aspect); surly (humour); crabbed (style).

rebâtir [rɑbɑti:r], *v.tr.* To rebuild.

rebattre [rɑbatr], *v.tr.* (Conj. like BATTRE) **1.** (*a*) To beat, hammer, (sth.) again. (*b*) To reshuffle (cards). **2.** *F:* **Rebattre les oreilles à qn de qch.,** to say the same thing over and over again; to din sth. into s.o.'s ears. *J'en ai les oreilles rebattues,* I hear of nothing else.
  rebattu, *a.* (*a*) **Sentier rebattu, les vieux sentiers rebattus,** the beaten track. (*b*) Hackneyed.

rebelle [rɑbɛl]. **1.** *a.* Rebellious; stubborn, obstinate (fever, etc.). *R. à la loi, à toute discipline,* unamenable to law, to discipline. *Matière r.,* unworkable material. *Minerai r.,* refractory ore. **2.** *s.* Rebel.

rebeller (se) [sərəbɛle], *v.pr.* To rebel, to rise, to revolt (*contre*, against).

rébellion [rebɛljɔ̃], *s.f.* Rebellion, rising, revolt.

rebéquer (se) [sərəbeke], *v.pr.* (je me rebèque; je me rebéquerai) *F:* To answer back. [BEC]

rebiffer (se) [sərəbife], *v.pr. F:* To bristle up, bridle up (in protest); to kick over the traces. **Faire rebiffer qn,** to get s.o.'s back up.

rebobiner [rɑbɔbine], *v.tr.* To rewind (coil).

reboire [rɑbwa:r], *v.tr.* (Conj. like BOIRE) To drink again. *Jamais je ne reboirai de ce vin,* I shall never touch that wine again.

reboisement [rɑbwazmã], *s.m.* (Re)afforestation; retimbering.

reboiser [rɑbwaze], *v.tr.* To (re)afforest; to retimber (land).

rebond [rɑbɔ̃], *s.m.* Rebound, bounce (of ball).

rebondi [rɑbɔ̃di], *a.* Rounded, chubby (cheeks); plump (body). *Femme aux formes rebondies,* buxom woman. *Bourse rebondie,* well-filled purse.

rebond|ir [rɑbɔ̃di:r], *v.i.* (*a*) To rebound; (of ball) to bounce. (*b*) (Of torrent, etc.) To surge. *s.m.* **-issement.**

rebord [rɑbɔ:r], *s.m.* **1.** Edge, border, rim; hem (of garment); lip (of cup); helix (of the ear); ledge. **2.** (Of sheet metal, etc.) Raised edge; flange. **A rebord, flanged.**

reborder [rɑbɔrde], *v.tr.* **1.** (*a*) To put a new edging or border to (sth.); to re-hem (garment). (*b*) To reflange. **2.** *R. qn dans son lit,* to tuck s.o. in again.

rebotter (se) [sərəbɔte], *v.pr.* To put on one's boots again.

reboucher [rɑbuʃe], *v.tr.* To stop, block, (sth.) up again; to recork (bottle). *s.m.* **-age.**

rebours [rɑbu:r], *s.m.* Wrong way (of the grain, of the nap); contrary, reverse. *Adv.phr.* **A rebours, au rebours,** against the grain, against the hair, the wrong way, backwards. **Prendre tout à rebours,** to take everything the wrong way, to misconstrue everything. **Prendre à rebours une rue à sens unique,** to enter a one-way street at the wrong end. **A, au, rebours de,** contrary to.

reboutage [rɑbuta:ʒ], *s.m.,* **reboutement** [rɑbutmã], *s.m.* Bone-setting.

rebouter [rɑbute], *v.tr.* (Of bone-setter) To set (broken limb, etc.).

rebouteur [rɑbutœ:r], *s.m.* Bone-setter.

reboutonner [rɑbutɔne], *v.tr.* To rebutton; to button up again.

rebrousse-poil (à), *adv.phr. Brosser un chapeau à r.-p.,* to brush a hat against the nap, the wrong way.

rebrouss|er [rɑbruse], *v.tr.* **1.** (*a*) To turn up,

brush up (hair, nap). (*b*) To grain, board (leather); to nap (cloth). **2.** (*a*) **Rebrousser chemin,** to retrace one's steps, to turn back. **Faire rebrousser chemin à qn,** to head s.o. off. (*b*) *v.i.* (Of path, etc.) To turn back; (of curve) to retrogress. *s.m.* **-ement.**
rebuffade [rəbyfad], *s.f.* Rebuff; snub.
rébus [rebyːs], *s.m.* (*a*) Picture puzzle; rebus. (*b*) Punning riddle.
rebut [rəby], *s.m.* (*a*) Casting out, scrapping. (*b*) Thing scrapped. **Papier de rebut,** waste paper. *Ind:* **Pièces de r.,** **les rebuts,** rejects; *F:* throw-outs. *Marchandises de r.,* rubbishy goods; trash. **Mettre qch. au rebut,** to throw sth. away; to scrap (machinery); to reject (casting). *Post:* **Bureau des rebuts,** dead-letter office. S.a. LETTRE 3. *F:* **Rebut de la société,** (i) waster; (ii) *Coll.* sweepings of society; riff-raff.
rebutant [rəbytɑ̃], *a.* **1.** Tiresome, irksome; deadly dull; tedious (conversation). **2.** Brusque, overbearing (manner).
rebuter [rəbyte], *v.tr.* **1.** To rebuff. **2.** *Jur:* To disallow (document, evidence). **3.** To dishearten, discourage. *Ce travail se rebute,* they find the work deadly dull.
se rebuter, to become discouraged, disheartened. *Se r. devant un obstacle,* to balk at a difficulty.
récalcitrance [rekalsitrɑ̃ːs], *s.f.* Recalcitrance.
récalcitrant [rekalsitrɑ̃], *a.* Recalcitrant, refractory (person, horse).
recaler[1] [rəkale], *v.tr.* *F:* To set (s.o.) up again; to put new life into (s.o.).
recaler[2], *v.tr.* *F:* To plough, pluck (s.o. in an examination).
recaoutchout|er [rəkautʃute], *v.tr.* To rerubber (material); to retread (tyre). *s.m.* **-age.**
récapitulatif, -ive [rekapitylatif, -iːv], *a.* Recapitulatory.
récapitulation [rekapitylasjɔ̃], *s.f.* (*a*) Recapitulation; summing up. (*b*) Summary, résumé.
récapituler [rekapityle], *v.tr.* To recapitulate; to sum up (proceedings).
recel [rəsɛl], *s.m.,* **recélé** [rəsele], *s.m.,* **recèlement,** [rəsɛlmɑ̃], *s.m.* *Jur:* **1.** Receiving and concealing (of stolen goods). **2.** Concealment (of child, of part of estate of deceased person); harbouring (of criminal).
recéler [rəsele], *v.tr.* (je recèle) je recélerai) *Jur:* **1.** To receive (stolen goods). **2.** (*a*) To conceal (child, part of estate of deceased person); to harbour (criminal). (*b*) *F:* *La terre recèle de grands trésors,* great treasures lie hidden within the earth.
receleur, -euse [rəslœːr, -øːz], *s.* *Jur:* Receiver (of stolen goods); *F:* fence.
récemment [resamɑ̃], *adv.* Recently, lately.
recensement [rəsɑ̃smɑ̃], *s.m.* (*a*) *Adm:* Census; return (of population). *Faire un r.,* to take a census. (*b*) *Com:* Checking of (of accounts). (*c*) Counting (of votes).
recenser [rəsɑ̃se], *v.tr.* (*a*) To take the census of (a town, etc.). (*b*) To check off (goods). (*c*) To count (votes).
recenseur [rəsɑ̃sœːr], *s.m.* (*a*) Census-taker; enumerator. (*b*) Teller (of votes).
recension [rəsɑ̃sjɔ̃], *s.f.* Recension (of text).
récent [resɑ̃], *a.* Recent, late (event).
recep|er [rəsəpe], **recéper** [rəsepe], *v.tr.* (je recèpe; je recéperai) To cut down, cut back (tree, vine-stock). *s.m.* **-age.**
récépissé [resepise], *s.m.* (*a*) (Acknowledgment of) receipt. (*b*) Acknowledgment (of complaint).

réceptacle [resɛptakl], *s.m.* **1.** Receptacle; repository. **2.** Collector (of waters, steam). **3.** *Bot:* Receptacle, torus.
récepteur, -trice [resɛptœːr, -tris]. **1.** *a.* Receiving. *Tg:* *Tp:* **Appareil récepteur,** receiving apparatus. *W.Tel:* **Poste récepteur,** (i) receiving station, (ii) receiving set. **2.** *s.m.* (*a*) Driven part (of machine). (*b*) *Tg:* *etc:* Receiver. *Tp:* **Décrocher le r.,** to lift the receiver. **3.** *s.f.* *El.E:* Réceptrice, dynamo driven as a motor.
réception [resɛpsjɔ̃], *s.f.* **1.** (*a*) Receipt (of letter, order, etc.). **Accuser réception de qch.,** to acknowledge receipt of sth. **Avis de réception, accusé de réception,** advice of delivery; acknowledgment of receipt. (*b*) Taking delivery (of goods); acceptance (by inspector); taking over (of machine, etc.). **2.** (*a*) Reception (of candidate by learned body, etc.). (*b*) *Th:* Acceptance (of new play for performance). **3.** (*a*) Welcome. **Faire une bonne réception à qn,** to welcome s.o. warmly. (*b*) Reception (at court, etc.); levee, drawing-room (at court). (*c*) At-home. **Jour de réception, at-home day. 4.** *Tg:* *Tp:* Receiving, reception. *W.Tel:* **Appareil, poste, de r.,** receiving set. **5.** (Hotel) receiving desk or office.
réceptionnaire [resɛpsjɔnɛːr], *a. & s.* *Com:* *Ind:* **1.** Receiving (clerk, agent). **2.** Consignee, receiver (of goods).
recette [rəsɛt], *s.f.* **1.** Receipts, returns. *Th:* *etc:* Takings. *Sp:* Gate-money. (Of play, film) **Faire recette,** to be a draw. **2.** (*a*) Collection (of bills by bank messenger). **Faire la recette** (*des traites*), to collect moneys due. (*b*) Receiving; receipt (of stores). **Prendre qch. en recette,** to accept (delivery of) sth. **Essais de recette,** acceptance trials (of ship, etc.). **3.** *Adm:* (*a*) Receivership, collectorship of rates and taxes. (*b*) Receiver's office, collector's office. **4.** (*a*) *Cu:* Recipe, receipt (for dish). (*b*) *Recettes de métier,* tricks, dodges, of the trade.
recevable [rəsəvabl], *a.* **1.** *Jur:* (*a*) Admissible (evidence, etc.); allowable. *Excuse non recevable,* inadmissible excuse. (*b*) (Goods) in sound condition and fit for acceptance. **2.** *Être r. à faire qch.,* to be entitled to do sth.
receveur, -euse [rəsəvœːr, -øːz], *s.* **1.** Receiver (of sth.); addressee (of telegram). **2.** (*a*) **Receveur des Finances,** district collector (of taxes). **R. des Postes** (*et Télégraphes*), postmaster. (*b*) Conductor (of bus or tramcar). (*c*) *Th:* **Receveuse,** attendant; programme girl.
recevoir [rəsəvwaːr], *v.tr.* (*pr.p.* **recevant;** *p.p.* **reçu;** *pr.ind.* je reçois, n. recevons, ils reçoivent; *pr.sub.* je reçoive, n. recevions; *p.h.* je reçus; *fu.* je recevrai) **1.** (*a*) To receive, get (letter, salary, etc.). *R. qch. de qn,* to receive sth. from s.o. *Corr:* *Nous avons bien reçu votre lettre,* we are in receipt of your letter. (*b*) To receive (punishment, reward); to meet with (insults); to incur (blame). **2.** (*a*) To receive, welcome (s.o.). (*b*) To receive, entertain (friends). *Abs.* To hold a reception, a levee, an at-home. *Elle ne reçoit pas aujourd'hui,* she is not at home to-day. (*c*) (At hotel) *Pouvez-vous nous r.?* can you take us in? *Elle reçoit des pensionnaires,* she takes in boarders. (*d*) *Être reçu à un examen,* to pass an examination. *Être reçu premier,* to come out first. *Être reçu avocat,* to be admitted to the bar. *Être reçu médecin,* to qualify as a doctor. *Nau:* *Être reçu capitaine,* to get one's captain's certificate. (*e*) *Être reçu à faire qch.,* to be authorized, free, to do sth. **3.** (*a*) *R. de l'eau dans un vase,* to catch water in a vessel. *Il reçut la balle dans sa main,* he caught the ball in his

hand. (b) To accept, admit (opinion, excuse). "*Recevez mes respects,*" 'respectfully yours.'

recu. **1.** *a.* Received, accepted, recognized (opinion, custom). **2.** *s.m.* (a) Receipt, voucher (for goods, money). (b) *Au reçu de votre lettre,* on receipt of your letter. *Payer au reçu,* to pay on delivery.

rechange [rəʃɑ̃:ʒ], *s.m.* Replacement. *Avoir du linge de rechange,* to have (with one) a change of linen. *Pièces de rechange, Abs.* rechanges, spare parts, spares. *Batterie de r.* (*pour lampe*), refill (for torch).

rechanger [rəʃɑ̃ʒe], *v.tr.* (Conj. like CHANGER) To change or exchange (sth.) again.

rechap|er [rəʃape], *v.tr.* To retread (pneumatic tyre). *s.m.* **-age.**

réchapper [reʃape]. **1.** *v.i.* (Aux. *avoir* or *être*) *R. d'un péril, d'une maladie,* to escape from a peril ; to recover from, get over, a dangerous illness. *Il a réchappé du naufrage,* he was saved from the wreck. *Il n'en réchappera pas,* it is all up with him. **2.** *v.tr.* F: To rescue, save (s.o.) (*de,* from).

réchappé, *s.m. Les réchappés,* those who have escaped, those saved (from an explosion, etc.) (*Cf* RESCAPÉ, more usual to-day.) *F:* **Réchappé de potence,** gallows-bird.

recharg|er [rəʃarʒe], *v.tr.* (Conj. like CHARGER) **1.** (a) To recharge (accumulator). (b) To reload (waggon, gun) ; to relade (ship) ; to make up (the fire). **2.** To remetal (road) ; to reballast (railway track). *s.m.* **-ement.**

rechasser [rəʃase], *v.tr.* **1.** To drive back (the ball). **2.** To hunt out, beat up (s.o.).

réchaud [reʃo], *s.m.* (a) Small portable stove. *R. à gaz à un feu,* gas-ring. *Réchaud-four,* gas-cooker. (b) Hot-plate, plate-warmer, dish-heater, chafing-dish.

réchauff|er [reʃofe], *v.tr.* **1.** To reheat ; to warm (sth.) up again ; to make (sth.) hot again. *Voilà qui vous réchauffera,* that will warm you up. *F:* **Réchauffer un serpent dans son sein,** to nourish a viper in one's bosom. **2.** *R. une vieille histoire,* to revive an old story. **2.** *R. le zèle de qn,* to rekindle, stir up, s.o.'s zeal. *F: R. le cœur à qn,* to comfort s.o. ; to put new heart into s.o. *s.m.* **-age.** *s.m.* **-ement.**

se réchauffer, to warm oneself at the fire, by exercise). *Je ne pouvais pas me r.,* I couldn't get warm.

réchauffé, *s.m.* (a) Warmed-up dish or food. (b) *F:* Rehash (of old literature) ; stale news.

réchauffeur [reʃofœ:r], *s.m.* Heating or warming device. *Mch:* Reheater, feed(-water) heater.

rechausser [rəʃose], *v.tr.* **1.** To put (s.o.'s) shoes or boots on again (for him). (b) To fit (s.o.) with new boots. **2.** (a) To underpin (structure). (b) To bank up the foot of (tree, etc.).

se rechausser, to put one's shoes, one's shoes and stockings, on again.

rêche [rɛʃ], *a.* Harsh, rough (surface, wine, humour). *Esprit r., caractère r.,* crabbed, cross-grained, nature.

recherche [rəʃɛrʃ], *s.f.* **1.** (a) Quest, search, pursuit. *R. des plaisirs,* pleasure-seeking. *Être à la recherche de qn,* to be in search of s.o. *Se mettre à la r. de qn,* to set out in quest of s.o. *El.E: R. de dérangements,* locating of faults. (b) Research. *Faire des recherches sur qch.,* to make researches into sth. ; to inquire into sth. *Se livrer, procéder, à des recherches,* to engage in research. (c) Searching. *Nau:* Droit de recherche, right of search (at sea). **2.** Affectation,

studied refinement, studied elegance. *Style sans recherche,* unlaboured, unaffected, style.

rechercher [rəʃɛrʃe], *v.tr.* (a) To search for, search into, inquire into (causes, etc.). *Ind: etc: R. un dérangement,* to try to locate a fault. *Homme recherché par la police,* man wanted by the police. (b) To seek (after), to try to obtain (favours, etc.) ; to court (praise). *R. une femme en mariage,* to court, woo, a woman. *Recherchée en mariage par . . .,* sought in marriage by. . . .

recherché, *a.* **1.** *Article très r.,* article in great request, in keen demand. *Article peu r.,* article in limited demand. **2.** Choice, select, elaborate (dress, etc.). **3.** Studied, strained, affected, mannered (style, expression).

rechignement [rəʃiɲmɑ̃], *s.m.* **1.** Crabbedness, sourness. **2.** *R. devant la besogne,* jibbing at the work.

rechigner [rəʃiɲe], *v.i. F:* To jib ; to look sour (when asked to do sth.). *Faire qch. en rechignant, sans rechigner,* to do sth. with a bad grace, with a good grace. *R. devant la besogne,* to jib, ba(u)lk, at the work. *R. à faire qch.,* to jib at doing sth.

rechigné, *a.* Sour-tempered, sour-faced.

rechute [rəʃyt], *s.f.* **1.** *Med:* Relapse, set-back. **2.** *R. dans le péché,* relapse into sin ; backsliding.

rechuter [rəʃyte], *v.i.* **1.** *Med:* To have a relapse, a set-back. **2.** To backslide.

récidive [residi:v], *s.f.* **1.** Repetition of an offence ; relapse (into crime). **2.** Recurrence (of a disease).

récidiver [residive], *v.i.* **1.** To repeat an offence ; to relapse into crime. **2.** (Of disease) To recur.

récidiviste [residivist], *s. m. & f.* Recidivist, habitual criminal ; *F:* old lag.

récif [resif], *s.m.* Reef. *R. sous-marin,* submerged reef. *R. de corail, corallien,* coral reef.

récipient [resipjɑ̃], *s.m.* (a) Container, vessel, receptacle. *Ch:* (i) Bell-jar, (ii) pressure-flask. (b) Receiver (of air-pump, of a retort). (c) Cistern.

réciprocité [resiprosite], *s.f.* Reciprocity.

réciproque [resiprɔk]. **1.** *a.* (a) Reciprocal, mutual (benefits, love, etc.). (b) Reciprocal (verb, pronoun, terms) ; convertible (terms) ; inverse (ratio). *Geom:* Converse (propositions). *Mec:* Reversible (motion). **2.** *s.f.* (a) *Rendre la réciproque à qn,* to give s.o. back the like ; to be even with s.o. (b) *Log: Geom:* Converse. *Mth:* Reciprocal. *adv.* **-ment.**

récit [resi], *s.m.* **1.** Narration, narrative ; account, recital, relation (of events). *Faire un r. exact de qch.,* to give an exact account of sth. **2.** *Mus:* (a) Solo (in a concerted piece). (b) Swell-box (of organ) ; swell-organ. [RÉCITER]

récitant, -ante [resitɑ̃, -ɑ̃:t], *a. & s. Mus:* (a) Solo (voice, instrument). (b) (In oratorio) Narrator.

récitateur, -trice [resitatœ:r, -tris], *s.* Reciter.

récitatif [resitatif], *s.m. Mus:* Recitative.

récitation [resitasjɔ̃], *s.f.* Recitation, reciting.

réciter [resite], *v.tr.* (a) To recite (poem, etc.). (b) *Sch: R. les leçons,* to say the lessons. *Faire réciter les leçons,* to hear the lessons.

réclamant, -ante [reklɑmɑ̃, -ɑ̃:t], *s.* (a) Complainer. (b) *Jur:* Claimant.

réclamation [reklɑmasjɔ̃], *s.f.* (a) Complaint ; objection, protest. (b) *Jur:* Claim, demand.

réclame [reklɑ:m], *s.f.* (a) Advertising ; publicity. *Faire de la réclame,* to advertise ; to puff one's goods. (b) (Puffing) advertisement ; *F:* puff. (c) (Advertisement) sign. *R. lumineuse,* illuminated sign.

réclam|er [reklɑme]. **I.** *v.i.* To complain ; to lodge a complaint. *R. contre qch.*, to protest against sth. ; to appeal against (a decision). **2.** *v.tr.* (*a*) To lay claim to (sth.) ; to claim (sth.). *R. son droit*, to claim one's right. **Dividende non réclamé**, unclaimed dividend. *Turf :* **Course à réclamer,** selling race. (*b*) To claim (sth.) back ; to demand (sth.) back. *R. de l'argent à qn,* to dun s.o. (*c*) To crave, beg, for (sth.). *Je réclame votre indulgence*, I crave, beseech, entreat, your indulgence. (*d*) To call for (s.o., sth.). *R. qch. à grands cris*, to call (out) for, to clamour for, sth. (*e*) *R. qch. de qn*, to require sth. of s.o. *Plante qui réclame des soins continuels*, plant that calls for, demands, continual care. *s.* **-eur, -euse.**
se réclamer *de qn*, to appeal to s.o. ; to call s.o. to witness ; to quote s.o. as one's authority (for a statement).

reclasser [rəklɑse], *v.tr.* To regroup, rearrange, redistribute.

reclouer [rəklue], *v.tr.* To nail (sth.) (up) again.

reclus, -use [rəkly, -yːz], *s.* Recluse.

réclusion [reklyzjɔ̃], *s.f.* **I.** Reclusion, seclusion, retirement. **2.** *Jur :* Solitary confinement with hard labour.

récognitif, -ive [rekɔgnitif, -iːv], *a.* Recognitory, recognitive.

récognition [rekɔgnisjɔ̃], *s.f. Phil :* Recognition.

recoiffer [rəkwafe], *v.tr. R. qn*, to dress, to do (up), s.o.'s hair again.
se recoiffer. **I.** To dress, do (up), one's hair again. **2.** To put on one's hat again.

recoin [rəkwɛ̃], *s.m.* Nook, recess. **Coins et recoins,** nooks and corners.

reçoi-s, -t, -vent [rəswa, -waːv]. See RECEVOIR.

récol|er [rekɔle]; *v.tr. Jur :* To verify, check, re-examine (accounts) ; to check (inventory). *s.m.* **-ement.**

recollement [rəkɔlmɑ̃], *s.m.* **I.** = RECOLLAGE. **2.** Setting, knitting (of broken bone).

recoll|er [rəkɔle], *v.tr.* To paste, glue, (sth.) together again. *s.m.* **-age.**
se recoller, (of broken bone) to knit ; (of wound) to heal.

récollet, -otte [rekɔlɛ, -ɛt], *s. Rel.H :* Recollect (friar or nun).

récolte [rekɔlt], *s.f.* **I.** (*a*) Harvesting (of grain) ; vintaging (of grapes). *Faire une r.*, to win a crop. (*b*) Collecting, gathering (of documents, etc.). **2.** Harvest, crop(s). *R. sur pied*, standing crop. *Rentrer la r.*, to get in, gather in, the harvest, the crops.

récolter [rekɔlte], *v.tr.* **I.** To harvest ; to gather in, get in, win (crop). **2.** To collect, gather (documents, anecdotes, etc.).

recommandable [rəkɔmɑ̃dabl], *a.* **I.** (*a*) Worthy of commendation ; (of pers.) estimable, respectable. (*b*) (Of hotel, etc.) To be recommended ; recommendable. **2.** Advisable.

recommandation [rəkɔmɑ̃dasjɔ̃], *s.f.* **I.** Recommendation, recommending. (**Lettre de**) **recommandation,** (i) letter of recommendation, of introduction ; (ii) testimonial. **2.** Advice, injunction. **3.** Registration (of letter or parcel).

recommander [rəkɔmɑ̃de], *v.tr.* **I.** (*a*) *R. qn à ses amis*, to (re)commend s.o. to one's friends. (*b*) *R. son âme à Dieu*, to commend one's soul to God. (*c*) *R. qch. à l'attention de qn*, to call s.o.'s attention to sth. **2.** *R. la prudence à qn*, to enjoin prudence on s.o. *R. à qn de faire qch.*, to recommend, enjoin, s.o. to do sth. *Je vous recommande de . . .,* I strongly advise you to. . . . **3.** To register (letter or parcel).
se recommander. **I.** *Se r. à qn, à la bonté*

de qn, to commend oneself to s.o., to s.o.'s good graces. **2.** *Se r. de qn*, to give s.o. as a reference.

recommencer [rəkɔmɑ̃se], *v.* (*je* **recommençai(s)** ; *n.* **recommençons**) **I.** *v.tr.* To recommence ; to begin, start, (sth.) again. *R. sa vie*, to start life afresh. **2.** *v.i.* To do it again ; to begin again ; to start afresh. **Le, voilà qui recommence!** he's at it again ! **Recommencer de plus belle,** to begin again more vigorously, harder, worse, than ever.

récompense [rekɔ̃pɑ̃ːs], *s.f.* (*a*) Recompense, reward. **En récompense, pour récompense, de vos services,** as a reward for your services, in return for your services. (*b*) (At prize show, etc.) *Distribution des récompenses*, giving out of the awards, of the prizes.

récompenser [rekɔ̃pɑ̃se], *v.tr.* To reward, recompense (person, action) ; to requite (services). *R. qn de qch.*, to reward s.o. for sth.

recomposer [rəkɔ̃poze], *v.tr.* **I.** *Ch :* To recompose, recombine (elements). **2.** *Typ :* To reset (matter).

réconciliable [rekɔ̃siljabl], *a.* Reconcilable.

réconciliateur, -trice [rekɔ̃siljatœːr, -tris], *s.* Reconciler.

réconciliation [rekɔ̃siljasjɔ̃], *s.f.* Reconciliation. *Amener une r. entre deux personnes*, to bring about a reconciliation, to heal the breach, between two people.

réconcilier [rekɔ̃silje], *v.tr.* To reconcile ; to make it up between (persons).
se réconcilier. **I.** *Se r. à, avec, qn*, to make it up with s.o. *Se r. avec Dieu*, to make one's peace with God. **2.** To become friends again ; *F :* to make it up.

reconduire [rəkɔ̃dɥiːr], *v.tr.* (Conj. like CONDUIRE) (*a*) To escort, see, (s.o.) home ; to accompany, take, bring, (s.o.) back (to a place). *Je vais vous r. jusqu'à la gare*, I will see you to the station. (*b*) To see, show, (s.o.) out ; to accompany (s.o.) to the door.

reconduite [rəkɔ̃dɥit], *s.f.* (*a*) Seeing (of s.o.) home ; accompanying, escorting, bringing, taking, (of s.o.) back (to a place). **Faire un bout de reconduite à qn,** to see s.o. so far on the way. (*b*) Showing out (of s.o.).

réconfort [rekɔ̃fɔːr], *s.m.* Comfort. (*a*) Consolation. *Quelques paroles de r.*, a few words of comfort. (*b*) Stimulant.

réconfortant [rekɔ̃fɔrtɑ̃]. **I.** *a.* (*a*) Strengthening, stimulating ; tonic (medicine). (*b*) Comforting, cheering (words, letter). **2.** *s.m.* Tonic, stimulant ; *F :* pick-me-up.

réconforter [rekɔ̃fɔrte], *v.tr.* **I.** To strengthen, fortify, refresh (s.o.). **2.** To comfort ; to cheer (s.o.) up.
se réconforter. **I.** To take refreshment. **2.** To cheer up.

reconnaissable [rəkɔnɛsabl], *a.* Recognizable (à, by, from, through). *Il n'est plus r.*, you wouldn't know him again.

reconnaissance [rəkɔnɛsɑ̃ːs], *s.f.* **I.** Recognition (of s.o., of sth.). *Sourire de r.*, smile of recognition. **2.** (*a*) Recognition, acknowledgment (of promise, debt) ; avowal, admission (of a lapse). (*b*) **Donner une reconnaissance à qn,** to give s.o. an I.O.U. **Reconnaissance du mont-de-piété,** pawn-ticket. **3.** (*a*) Reconnoitring. *Av :* **Appareil de reconnaissance,** reconnaissance machine. *R. du littoral*, charting of the coast. (*b*) Reconnaissance. **Faire une reconnaissance, aller en reconnaissance,** to reconnoitre. **4.** (*a*) Gratitude, gratefulness. **Témoigner de la reconnaissance à qn,** to show gratitude to s.o.

Aveo reconnaissance, gratefully. (b) R. de, pour, la bonté de Dieu, thankfulness for the kindness of God.

reconnaissant [rəkɔnɛsã], a. (a) Grateful (envers, to; de, for). Être r. à qn de qch., to be grateful, obliged, beholden, to s.o. for sth. (b) Thankful (de, for).

reconnaître [rəkɔnɛːtr], v.tr. (Conj. like CONNAÎTRE) **1.** To recognize; to know (s.o.) again. Nau: **Reconnaître la terre**, to sight land, to make land. R. qn à sa démarche, à sa voix, to recognize, know, tell, s.o. by his walk, by his voice. **Se faire reconnaître de qn**, to make oneself known to s.o. Gaz qui se reconnaît à son odeur, gas recognizable by its smell. F: **Je vous reconnais bien là!** that's just like you! **2.** (a) To recognize, acknowledge (truth, right, etc.); to acknowledge, admit, avow (mistake). D'abord on refusa de le r., at first they would have nothing to say to him. **Faire reconnaître qn pour chef**, to proclaim s.o. chief. R. qch. pour vrai, to allow sth. to be true. Reconnu pour, comme, incorrect, admittedly incorrect. (b) To own, acknowledge (a child). **3.** To reconnoitre, explore (the ground, etc.). **4.** R. une faveur, to be grateful for a favour.

se reconnaître. 1. Se r. vaincu, to own oneself beaten, to acknowledge defeat. **2.** (a) To collect oneself, one's thoughts. (b) To get one's bearings. **C'est à ne pas s'y reconnaître**, it is extremely confusing. Je ne m'y reconnais plus, I am quite at sea.

reconquérir [rəkɔ̃keriːr], v.tr. (Conj. like CONQUÉRIR) To regain, recover (province); to regain (s.o.'s esteem).

reconquête [rəkɔ̃kɛːt], s.f. Reconquest.

reconstituant [rəkɔ̃stituɑ̃], a. & s.m. Med: Reconstituent, restorative, tonic.

reconstituer [rəkɔ̃stitɥe], v.tr. **1.** To reconstitute (an administration, a crime, etc.); to restore (devastated regions, etc.). **2.** To restore (s.o.'s health).

se reconstituer, to build up one's strength again.

reconstitution [rəkɔ̃stitysjɔ̃], s.f. Reconstitution, reconstruction.

reconstruction [rəkɔ̃stryksjɔ̃], s.f. Reconstruction, rebuilding.

reconstruire [rəkɔ̃strɥiːr], v.tr. (Conj. like CONSTRUIRE) To reconstruct, rebuild.

reconvention [rəkɔ̃vɑ̃sjɔ̃], s.f. Jur: Counterclaim; cross-action.

reconventionnel, -elle [rəkɔ̃vɑ̃sjɔnɛl], a. Jur: Demande reconventionnelle, counter-claim.

recopier [rəkɔpje], v.tr. To recopy; to copy (over) again; to take another copy of (sth.).

recoquiller [rəkɔkije], v.tr. To curl (sth.) up; to cockle, shrivel (sth.). Pages recoquillées, dog'seared pages. s.m. **-ement.**

se recoquiller, to curl up, cockle, shrivel.

record [rəkɔːr], s.m. **1.** Sp: etc: Record. Battre le r., to beat the record. Détenir le r., to hold the record. **2.** Ind: Peak output.

recorder[1] [rəkɔrde], v.tr. (a) Th: R. un rôle, to con a part, to go over a part. (b) F: Recorder sa leçon à qn, to put a person up to what he has to say.

recorder[2], v.tr. **1.** To rope up (bale) again; to retie (packet). **2.** To restring (racquet).

recors [rəkɔːr], s.m. Jur: A: Bailiff's man. F: **Les recors de la justice**, the minions of the law.

recoucher (se) [sərəkuʃe], v.pr. To go to bed again, to go back to bed. Se r. par terre, to lie down (on the ground) again.

recoudre [rəkudr], v.tr. (Conj. like COUDRE) To sew (garment) up again; to sew (button) on again.

recoupement [rəkupmã], s.m. **1.** (a) Stepping (of embankment, of foot of wall). (b) Batter (of stepped wall). **2.** (a) Surv: Countersection. (b) Cross-checking.

recouper [rəkupe], v.tr. **1.** (a) To cut (sth.) again. (b) To cut again (at cards). (c) To step (wall). **2.** To blend (wines, etc.).

recourber [rəkurbe], v.tr. To bend (down, back, round).

se recourber, to bend, to curl.

recourbé, a. Bent, curved; bent back; reflexed. Poignée recourbée, crook handle.

recourir [rəkuriːr], v.i. (Conj. like COURIR) **1.** (a) To run again. (b) R. jusque chez soi, to run back home (for sth.). **2.** (a) R. à qn, à l'aide de qn, to call in s.o.'s aid, to have recourse to s.o.; to resort to (money-lender). R. à qch., to have recourse to sth.; to resort to (stratagem, etc.). R. à la violence, to resort, proceed, to violence. R. aux armes, to appeal to arms. (b) Jur: R. en cassation, to appeal. R. en grâce, to petition for a reprieve.

recours [rəkuːr], s.m. (a) Recourse, resort, resource. **En dernier recours**, as a last resort. **Avoir recours à qn** = recourir à qn. (b) Jur: R. en cassation, appeal. R. en grâce, petition for reprieve. N'avoir aucun r. contre qn, (i) to have no claim whatever on s.o.; (ii) to have no remedy at law.

recouvrement[1] [rəkuvrəmã], s.m. **1.** (a) Recovery (of health, etc.). (b) Collection (of debts, bill, etc.). **Faire un recouvrement**, to recover, collect, a debt. **2.** pl. Outstanding debts.

recouvrement[2], s.m. **1.** Re-covering, covering again. **2.** (a) Covering. (b) Cover. (c) Overlapping; lap (of slates, etc.). **A recouvrement**, lapped, lap-jointed. Poser des planches à r., to lap boards. Planches à r., weather boarding. Joint à r., lap-joint.

recouvr|er [rəkuvre], v.tr. **1.** To recover, retrieve (one's freedom, one's property); to regain (health, freedom). **2.** To recover, collect (debts). a. **-able.**

recouvrir [rəkuvriːr], v.tr. (Conj. like COUVRIR) **1.** To re-cover (umbrella, roof). **2.** (a) To cover (sth.) (over); to cap (sth.) (de, with). Ces fictions recouvrent un fait, under these fictions rests a fact. (b) To cover, mask, hide (faults). **3.** To (over)lap.

se recouvrir, (of the sky) to cloud over, to become overcast.

récréatif, -ive [rekreatif, -iːv], a. Entertaining, amusing (occupation); recreative. Lecture(s) récréative(s), light reading.

récréation [rekreasjɔ̃],s.f. Recreation. **1.** Amusement; relaxation. **2.** Sch: Playtime, playhour; 'break.' Cour de récréation, playground. Enfants en récréation, children at play.

recréer [rəkree], v.tr. To recreate; to create or establish (sth.) anew.

récréer [rekree], v.tr. **1.** To enliven, refresh (the mind, etc.); to please (the eye). **2.** To divert, amuse, entertain.

se récréer, to take some recreation, some diversion.

recrép|ir [rəkrepiːr], v.tr. (a) To rough-cast anew; to replaster; to repoint (wall, etc.). (b) F: To patch up (s.o., sth.). R. son visage, to do up one's face. s.m. **-issage.**

récrier (se) [sərekrie], v.pr. **1.** Se r. d'admiration, to exclaim, cry out, in admiration. **2.** Se r.

contre, sur, qch., to exclaim, cry out, expostulate, protest, against sth.
récrimination [rekriminasjɔ̃], *s.f.* Recrimination.
récriminatoire [rekriminatwa:r], *a.* Recriminatory.
récriminer [rekrimine], *v.i.* To recriminate.
récrire [rekri:r], *v.tr.* (Conj. like ÉCRIRE) **1.** To rewrite; to write (sth.) over again; (i) to make a fresh copy, (ii) to recast, put into new shape. **2.** *Abs.* To write (to s.o.) again.
recroqueviller (se) [sərəkrɔkvije], *v.pr.* (*a*) To shrivel (up) (with the heat); to curl up; to cockle; to crumple up; (of flower) to wilt. (*b*) (Of fingers) To curl in, to clench (with rheumatism). **recroquevillé,** *a.* (*a*) Shrivelled, curled up, cockled (leaf, parchment, etc.). (*b*) (Fingers) clenched, knotted (by rheumatism).
recru [rəkry], *a.* *A:* Recru de fatigue, tired out; dead tired.
recrudescence [rəkrydɛssɑ̃:s], *s.f.* Recrudescence; renewed outbreak (of fire, etc.). *R. du froid,* new spell of cold weather.
recrue [rəkry], *s.f.* Recruit; *F:* new member, fresh adherent (of party, etc.).
recruter [rəkryte], *v.tr.* To recruit (regiment, party); to bring (regiment) up to strength; to enlist, beat up (supporters). *s.m.* **-ement.**
recruteur [rəkrytœ:r], *a.* Sergent recruteur, recruiting sergeant.
recta [rɛkta], *adv.* *F:* (To pay) on the nail; (to arrive) punctually.
rectal, -aux [rɛktal, -o], *a.* *Anat:* Rectal.
rectangle [rɛktɑ̃:gl]. **1.** *a.* Right-angled. **2.** *s.m.* Rectangle.
rectangulaire [rɛktɑ̃gylɛ:r], *a.* Rectangular.
recteur, -trice [rɛktœ:r, -tris]. **1.** *s.m.* (*a*) Rector, vice-chancellor (of university). (*b*) *Ecc:* Parish priest (in Brittany). **2.** *a.* *Orn:* Penne rectrice, *s.f.* rectrice, tail-feather, rectrix.
rectificateur [rɛktifikatœ:r], *s.m.* (*a*) *Dist:* etc: Rectifier. (*b*) *El:* R. de courants, current rectifier.
rectificatif, -ive [rɛktifikatif, -i:v], *a.* Rectifying.
rectification [rɛktifikasjɔ̃], *s.f.* **1.** Straightening. **2.** (Re)adjustment; correction (of prices, etc.); adjustment (of optical apparatus); truing (of work on lathe). **3.** Rectifying, re-distillation. **4.** *R. de courants alternatifs,* rectification of alternating currents.
rectifier [rɛktifje], *v.tr.* **1.** To straighten. *Mil:* R. l'alignement, to dress the ranks. **2.** To rectify, correct (error); to amend (account); to put (mistake) right; to reform, correct (habit); to adjust (instrument); to true up (work on the lathe). **3.** To rectify, re-distil. *Pétrole non rectifié,* crude petroleum. *a.* **-able.**
rectiligne [rɛktiliɲ], *a.* Rectilinear; linear (movement).
rectilinéaire [rɛktilineɛ:r], *a.* *Phot:* Rapid rectilinear (lens).
rectitude [rɛktityd], *s.f.* **1.** Straightness (of line). **2.** Rectitude. (*a*) Correctness, rightness (of judgment). (*b*) Uprightness, integrity.
recto [rɛkto], *s.m.* Recto, right-hand side (of page); view side (of picture postcard).
rectorat [rɛktɔra], *s.m.* Rectorship, rectorate; vice-chancellorship.
rectum [rɛktɔm], *s.m.* *Anat:* Rectum.
reçu [rəsy]. See RECEVOIR.
recueil [rəkœ:j], *s.m.* Collection, compilation (of poems, laws, etc.); miscellany. *R. de morceaux choisis,* selection, anthology. *R. de locutions,* phrase-book.

recueillement [rəkœjmɑ̃], *s.m.* Self-communion, meditation, contemplation. *R. d'esprit,* composure.
recueillir [rəkœji:r], *v.tr.* (Conj. like CUEILLIR) **1.** (*a*) To collect, gather. *R. les miettes,* to gather up the crumbs. *R. des renseignements,* to obtain, pick up, information. (*b*) *R. ses forces,* to collect, gather, all one's strength. (Of apparatus) *R. les sons,* to pick up sounds. **2.** (*a*) To garner, get in, gather (crops); to recover (by-products). (*b*) *R. un héritage,* to inherit. (*c*) *R. les suffrages,* to be elected, to win the election. **3.** To take in, to shelter (pilgrim, someone in need). *R. un orphelin,* to give an orphan a home.
se recueillir, to collect oneself, one's thoughts; to commune with oneself; to retire within oneself.
recueilli, *a.* Collected, meditative, contemplative, rapt (person, frame of mind).
recuire [rəkɥi:r], *v.tr.* (Conj. like CUIRE) **1.** To cook, bake, (sth.) (over) again. **2.** *Tchn:* To reheat; to temper (steel); to anneal (glass); to reboil (syrup). *R. après trempe,* to draw, let down, the temper (of tool).
recuit, -ite. 1. *a.* Annealed. **2.** *s.m.* Recuit, *s.f.* recuite, reheating; tempering (of steel); annealing (of glass); reboiling (of syrup).
recul [rəkyl], *s.m.* **1.** Retirement, recession (of sea-water, etc.); backing (of horse); set-back (in business, in health). Mouvement de recul, backward movement. *Bill:* Effet de recul, screw-back. **2.** (*a*) Recoil (of cannon); kick (of rifle). (*b*) *Nau:* Slip (of propeller). **3.** Room to move back. *Statue qui manque de r.,* statue that cannot be viewed in proper perspective.
reculade [rəkylad], *s.f.* (*a*) Backward movement, falling back, retreat; backing (of carriage). (*b*) *F:* (In debate, etc.) Une honteuse r., a miserable climb-down.
reculement [rəkylmɑ̃], *s.m.* **1.** Backing. **2.** Moving back; postponement (of an event). **3.** Breeching, breech-band (of harness).
reculer [rəkyle]. **1.** *v.i.* To move back, step back, draw back, recede; to fall back, to retreat; (of horse) to back; (of car) to run back(wards); (of gun) to recoil; (of rifle) to kick. Faire reculer qn, to make s.o. fall back. *Faire r. un cheval,* to back a horse. *Ses affaires ont reculé,* his business has had a set-back. Il n'y a plus moyen de reculer, there is no going back. *R. devant qch.,* to draw back, shrink, from sth.; to recoil, flinch, before sth. Ne reculer devant rien, to shrink from nothing; *F:* to stick at nothing. S.a. SAUTER I. **2.** *v.tr.* (*a*) To move (s.o., sth.) back. *R. un cheval,* to rein back, to back, a horse. (*b*) To postpone, defer, put off (payment, marriage).
se reculer. 1. To draw back; to step back, to move back. **2.** *Le retour du roi se recule toujours,* the King's return becomes more and more remote.
reculé, *a.* Distant, remote (time, place). *Dans un avenir r.,* in a distant, remote, future.
reculée, *s.f.* Backing-space, backing-room.
reculons (à) [arəkylɔ̃], *adv.phr.* Marcher à reculons, to walk backwards. *Sortir à r.,* to go out backwards, to back out.
récupérateur [rekyperatœ:r], *s.m.* *Ind:* *Artil:* Recuperator.
récupération [rekyperasjɔ̃], *s.f.* **1.** (*a*) Recuperation, recovery (of debt). (*b*) *Ind:* Recovery (of waste products). **2.** Recoupment (of losses). **3.** Recovery (from ill-health).
récupérer [rekypere], *v.tr.* (je récupère; je récupérerai) **1.** To recover (debt, waste products). **2.** To retrieve, recoup (a loss). *a.* **-able.**

se récupérer. 1. To recuperate, recover (from ill-health). **2.** *Se r. de ses pertes*, to recoup one's losses.

récur|er [rekyre], *v.tr.* To scour, clean (pots and pans). *s.m.* **-age.**

récurrence [rekyrrãːs], *s.f.* Recurrence.

récurrent [rekyrrã], *a.* Recurrent.

récusable [rekyzabl], *a. Jur:* Challengeable, exceptionable, untrustworthy (witness).

récusation [rekyzasjɔ̃], *s.f.* **1.** *Jur: R. de témoin*, exception to, objection to, a witness. *R. de témoignage*, impugnment of evidence. **2.** Disclaimer.

récuser [rekyze], *v.tr.* To challenge, take exception to, object to (witness) ; to impugn (evidence).

se récuser, to decline to give an opinion ; to declare oneself incompetent to judge.

rédacteur, -trice [redaktœːr, -tris], *s.* **1.** Writer, drafter (of deed, etc.). **2.** Member of the staff (of a newspaper or periodical). **Rédacteur en chef,** editor.

rédaction [redaksjɔ̃], *s.f.* **1.** (*a*) Drafting, drawing up, wording, writing (of deed, etc.). (*b*) Editing (of journal). (*c*) *Sch:* Composition. **2.** (*a*) Editorial staff. (*b*) (Newspaper) office(s).

redan [rədã], *s.m.* **1.** *Fort:* Redan. **2.** Step (in gable, etc.). *Hydroplane à redans multiples*, multistepped hydroplane. (Of hydroplane) *Courir sur le r.*, to plane along the water.

reddition [rɛdisjɔ̃], *s.f.* **1.** Surrender (of town, of ship). **2.** Rendering (of account).

redemander [rədmãde], *v.tr.* **1.** To ask for (sth.) again ; to ask for more of (sth.), for a second helping of (sth.). **2.** To ask for (sth.) back (again).

rédempteur, -trice [redãptœːr, -tris]. **1.** *a.* Redeeming. **2.** *s.* Redeemer.

rédemption [redãpsjɔ̃], *s.f.* Redemption, redeeming.

redent [rədã], *s.m. Gothic Arch:* Foliated cusp.

redescendre [rədɛsãːdr]. **1.** *v.i.* (*a*) To come, go, down again. (*b*) *Nau:* (Of the wind) To back. **2.** *v.tr.* (*a*) To take (picture, etc.) down again ; to let (s.o.) down again (with a rope) ; to bring (sth.) down again. (*b*) *R. l'escalier*, to come down the stairs again.

redevable [rədvabl], *a. Être r. de qch. à qn*, to be indebted, beholden, to s.o. for sth. ; to owe (one's life, etc.) to s.o.

redevance [rədvãːs], *s.f.* (*a*) Rent; rental. (*b*) Dues. (*c*) *Redevances d'auteur*, author's royalties. (*d*) Tax (on wireless sets, etc.). (*e*) Fee.

redevenir [rədvəniːr], *v.i.* (Conj. like DEVENIR) To become (sth., s.o.) again. *R. jeune*, to grow young again.

redevoir [rəd(ə)vwaːr], *v.tr.* (Conj. like DEVOIR) To owe a balance of (a sum on an account, etc.).

redû, *s.m.* Balance due.

rédhibitoire [redibitwaːr], *a. Jur:* **Vice rédhibitoire,** redhibitory defect (in horse, etc.) ; latent defect that makes a sale void.

rédiger [rediʒe], *v.tr.* (**je rédigeai(s)**; n. **rédigeons**) **1.** To draw up, draft, word (agreement, letter, etc.) ; to write (article). *A l'heure où le présent article est rédigé*, at the time of writing. **2.** To edit (journal, etc.).

rédimer [redime], *v.tr.* To redeem ; to buy (s.o.) off.

se rédimer *de qch.*, to redeem, exempt, oneself from sth.

redingote [rədɛ̃gɔt], *s.f.* Frock-coat.

redire [rədiːr], *v.tr.* (Conj. like DIRE) **1.** To tell, say, (sth.) again ; to repeat. **2.** *Trouver à redire à qch.*, to take exception to sth. ; to find fault

with sth. *Il n'y a rien à redire à cela*, there is nothing to be said against that.

redite, *s.f.* (Useless) repetition.

redoi-s, -t, -vent [rədwa, -waːv]. See REDEVOIR.

redondance [rədɔ̃dãːs], *s.f.* Redundance, redundancy.

redondant [rədɔ̃dã], *a.* Redundant ; pleonastic.

redonder [rədɔ̃de], *v.i.* (*a*) To be redundant. (*b*) To be in excess ; to superabound (*de*, in).

redonner [rədɔne]. **1.** *v.tr.* (*a*) To give (sth.) again, anew. *On redonne "Hamlet,"* 'Hamlet' is on again. (*b*) To give more of (sth.). (*c*) To give (sth.) back ; to restore, return. **2.** *v.i.* (*a*) *R. dans un piège*, to fall into a trap again. (*b*) *Le froid redonne*, the cold has set in again. (*c*) *La cavalerie redonna*, the cavalry charged again.

redoublement [rədubləmã], *s.m.* **1.** Redoubling (of joy, zeal). **2.** *Ling:* Reduplication. **3.** *Mus:* Doubling (of note in chord).

redoubler [rəduble]. **1.** *v.tr.* (*a*) To redouble, increase (dose, s.o.'s fears). (*b*) *Sch:* Redoubler une classe, to stay in a form a second year. (*c*) To reline (a dress). **2.** *v.i.* To redouble. *R. de zèle*, to redouble one's zeal.

redoublé, *a. Rime redoublée*, double rime. **Battre qn à coups redoublés,** to belabour s.o. soundly. S.a. PAS¹ 1.

redoutable [rədutabl], *a.* Redoubtable, formidable ; dangerous (*à*, to).

redoute [rədut], *s.f.* **1.** *Fort:* Redoubt. **2.** Gala evening (at dancing-hall).

redouter [rədute], *v.tr.* To dread, fear (s.o., sth.) ; to hold (s.o., sth.) in awe. *R. d'apprendre qch.*, to dread hearing of sth. *R. que . . . (ne) + sub.*, to be apprehensive lest. . . .

redresse [rədrɛs], *s.f.* **1.** *Nau:* **Palans de redresse,** righting tackle. **2.** *P:* Être à la redresse, to be clever, knowing, cute.

redressement [rədrɛsmã], *s.m.* **1.** (*a*) Re-erecting ; setting up again (of fallen object). (*b*) Righting (of a boat). (*c*) *Opt:* Erecting of inverted image. **2.** (*a*) Straightening ; truing (of a surface). *R. économique*, economic recovery. (*b*) *El.E:* Rectifying (of alternating current). **Valve de redressement,** rectifying valve. *Poste de r.*, rectifier station. (*c*) Rectification, righting, amendment (of wrong, mistake).

redresser [rədrɛse], *v.tr.* **1.** (*a*) To re-erect ; to set (sth.) upright again. (*b*) To right (boat). (*c*) *Av: R. l'avion*, to pull on the joy-stick. (*d*) *Opt:* To erect (inverted image). **2.** (*a*) To straighten (out) (path, bent wood) ; to true (surface). (*b*) *R. la tête*, (i) to hold up one's head ; to look up ; (ii) (with indignation) to bridle up. (*c*) *El.E:* To rectify (alternating current). (*d*) To redress, to right (wrong, grievance) ; to rectify (mistake).

se redresser, (*a*) *Se r. sur son séant*, to sit up again. (*b*) (Of boat) To right. **2.** (*a*) To draw oneself up, to hold one's head high. (*b*) To bridle up. **3.** *Av:* To flatten out (after a dive).

redressé, *a.* Erect.

redresseur, -euse [rədrɛsœːr,-øːz]. **1.** *s.* Righter (of wrongs, etc.). Esp. *F:* **Redresseur de torts,** knight-errant. **2.** *s.m. El.E:* Rectifier (of alternating current). **3.** *a. Dispositif r.*, (i) *El.E:* rectifying device ; (ii) *Opt:* erecting device.

réducteur, -trice [redyktœːr, -tris]. **1.** *a.* Reducing. **2.** *s.m.* Reducer ; reducing agent.

réductible [redyktibl], *a.* Reducible.

réduction [redyksjɔ̃], *s.f.* **1.** (*a*) Reduction ; cutting down (of expenditure). *Échelle de r.*, reducing scale. **Réduction à l'absurde,** *reductio ad absurdum. R. de peine*, mitigation of penalty.

R. à un grade inférieur, Mil : reducing (of a man) ; *Navy :* disrating. (*b*) *Surg :* Setting, reducing (of a fracture). (*c*) Gearing down (of machinery) ; gear ratio ; stepping down (of voltage). (*d*) *Ch :* Reduction. (*e*) Conquest (of a province) ; capture by siege, reduction (of a town). **2.** (*a*) *Réductions de salaires,* cuts in wages. (*b*) *Mus : R. pour piano,* short score.

réduire [redɥiːr], *v.tr.* (*pr.p.* réduisant ; *p.p.* réduit ; *pr.ind.* je réduis, n. réduisons ; *p.h.* je réduisis ; *fu.* je réduirai) **1.** (*a*) To reduce (pressure, speed, price). *Billets à prix réduits,* cheap tickets. *R. ses dépenses,* to cut down one's expenses. **Édition réduite,** abridged edition. *R. une dissolution,* to boil down a solution. *R. un homme à un grade inférieur, Mil :* to reduce a man ; *Navy :* to disrate a man. *El.E : R. la tension,* to step down the voltage. (*b*) *R. du grain en farine,* to reduce grain to flour. *R. qch. en miettes,* to crumble sth. up ; *F :* to pound sth. to atoms. (*c*) *Ch : R. un oxyde,* to reduce an oxide. (*d*) *R. deux fractions au même dénominateur,* to reduce two fractions to a common denominator. **2.** (*a*) *R. qn à la misère, au désespoir,* to reduce s.o. to poverty ; to drive s.o. to despair. *J'en suis réduit à mendier,* I am reduced to begging. (*b*) *R. une ville,* to reduce a town. **3.** *Surg :* To reduce (fracture, dislocation).

se réduire. 1. *Se r. au strict nécessaire,* to confine oneself to what is strictly necessary. **2.** *Voilà où se réduit votre argument,* that is what your argument amounts to, comes to. *Se r. en poussière,* to crumble into dust. *La sauce s'est réduite,* the sauce has boiled down. **Faire réduire un sirop,** to boil down a syrup.

réduit [redɥi], *s.m.* **1.** Retreat ; nook. *Un misérable r.,* a wretched hovel. **2.** *Fort :* Keep, redoubt.

réédifier [reedifje], *v.tr.* To rebuild.

rééditer [reedite], *v.tr.* To republish.

réédition [reedisjɔ̃], *s.f.* Re-issue (of book, etc.) ; republication.

rééducation [reedykasjɔ̃], *s.f. Med :* Re-education (of nerve-centres after paralysis, etc.).

réel, -elle [reɛl]. **1.** *a.* (*a*) Real, actual. (*b*) *Com :* Offre réelle, offer in cash. (*c*) *Jur :* Of real estate. **2.** *s.m.* Le réel, the real ; reality.

réélection [reelɛksjɔ̃], *s.f.* Re-election.

rééligible [reeliʒibl], *a.* Re-eligible.

réélire [reeliːr], *v.tr.* (Conj. like ÉLIRE) To re-elect.

réellement [reelmɑ̃], *adv.* Really, in reality, actually.

réexpédier [reɛkspedje], *v.tr.* To send on, to (re)forward (sth.) ; to retransmit (telegram).

réexporter [reɛkspɔrte], *v.tr.* To re-export.

refaçonner [rəfasɔne], *v.tr.* To remake, re-fashion.

réfaction [refaksjɔ̃], *s.f.* **1.** *Com :* Allowance, reduction, rebate. **2.** Repairs (to property).

refaire [rəfɛːr], *v.tr.* (Conj. like FAIRE) **1.** To remake ; to do (work) again ; to make (journey) again ; to recast (a sentence). *R. sa malle,* to pack up again. *C'est à r.,* it will have to be done (over) again. **Si c'était à refaire . . .,** if I had to do it again. . . . **2.** To repair ; to recruit, recover (one's health). **3.** *P :* (*a*) To dupe, do, diddle (s.o.) ; to take (s.o.) in. *Être refait, P :* to be done brown. (*b*) *R. qch. à qn,* to rob s.o. of sth.

se refaire. 1. (*a*) To recover one's health ; to recuperate ; *F :* to pick up again. (*b*) To refresh the inner man. **2.** To retrieve one's losses.

refasse, etc. See REFAIRE.

réfection [refɛksjɔ̃], *s.f.* **1.** Remaking ; rebuilding ; repairing ; restoration ; doing up. *Route en r.,* road 'up.' **2.** Restoration to health and strength. **3.** (In convent) = REPAS.

réfectoire [refɛktwaːr], *s.m.* Refectory, dining-hall (in monastery, school).

refend [rəfɑ̃], *s.m.* Bois de refend, wood in planks. **Pierre de refend,** corner stone. S.a. MUR.

refendre [rəfɑ̃ːdr], *v.tr.* To split, cleave (slates) ; to slit (leather) ; to rip (timber).

référence [referɑ̃ːs], *s.f.* **1.** Reference, referring. *Nau :* Position de référence, reference position. **2.** (Servant's) reference ; recommendation.

référendaire [referɑ̃deːr], *s.m. Jur :* Chief clerk (of commercial court).

référendum [referɛ̃dɔm], *s.m.* Referendum.

référer [refere], *v.* (je réfère ; je référerai) **1.** *v.tr.* To refer, ascribe (qch. à qch., sth. to sth.). **2.** *v.i. R. à qn d'une question,* to refer a matter to s.o. *En r. à la cour,* to submit the case to the court.

se référer. 1. *Se r. à qch.,* to refer to sth. **2.** *Se r. à qn,* to ask s.o.'s opinion. *S'en r. à qn, à l'avis de qn,* to refer the matter to s.o., to s.o.'s decision.

référé, *s.m. Jur :* Summary procedure. **Ordonnance de référé,** provisional order, injunction.

refermer [rəfɛrme], *v.tr.* To reclose ; to shut, close, (door) again ; to close up (grave) again.

se refermer, to close again ; (of wound) to close up, to heal.

refiler [rəfile], *v.tr. P : R. qch. à qn,* (i) to palm off sth. (up)on s.o. ; (ii) to give s.o. sth.

refi-s, -t, etc. See REFAIRE.

réfléchir [refleʃiːr]. **1.** *v.tr.* To reflect, to throw back (light, sound) ; to reverberate (sound). **2.** *v.i. R. sur, à, qch.,* to reflect on sth. ; to ponder, consider, weigh, sth. ; to turn sth. over in one's mind. *Réfléchissez avant d'agir,* think well before you act. *Réfléchissez donc !* do consider ! **Donner à réfléchir à qn,** to give s.o. food for thought, cause for reflection. **Parler sans réfléchir,** to speak without thinking, hastily.

se réfléchir. 1. To curl back. **2.** To be reflected ; (of sound) to reverberate.

réfléchi, a. 1. Reflective, thoughtful, serious-minded ; deliberate, considered (action, opinion) ; premeditated (crime). *Opinion peu réfléchie,* inconsiderate, hasty, opinion. **Tout réfléchi . . .,** everything considered . . ., after due considera-tion. . . . **2.** Reflexive (verb, pronoun).

réfléchissement [refleʃismɑ̃], *s.m.* Reflection, reflecting (of light, sound).

réflecteur [reflɛktœːr]. **1.** *a.m.* Reflecting (mirror). **2.** *s.m.* Reflector ; reflecting mirror or telescope.

reflet [rəflɛ], *s.m.* Reflection ; reflected light or image. *Chevelure à reflets d'or,* hair with glints of gold. *R. des glaces,* ice-blink. *Reflets irisés,* play of (iridescent) colours.

refléter [rəflete], *v.tr.* (il reflète ; il reflétera) To reflect, send back, throw back (light, colour).

refleur|ir [rəflœriːr], *v.i.* **1.** To flower, blossom, again. **2.** To flourish anew. **Faire refleurir les arts,** to revive the arts. *s.m.* **-issement.**

réflexe [reflɛks]. **1.** *a.* Reflex (action). **2.** *s.m. Physiol :* Reflex. *Med : R. du genou,* knee-jerk.

réflexion [reflɛksjɔ̃], *s.f.* **1.** Reflection, reflexion (of image, light). *Angle de r.,* angle of reflection. **2.** Reflection, thought. *Être plongé dans ses réflexions,* to be deep in thought. **Agir sans réflexion,** to act rashly, inconsiderately. *Cela mérite r.,* it is worth thinking over. *Cela exige*

la r., it requires consideration. **(Toute) réflexion faite . . ., à la réflexion . . .,** on thinking it over . . ., everything considered . . .; when you come to think of it. . . .
refluer [rəflye], *v.i.* (*a*) To flow back; (of the tide) to ebb. (*b*) (Of invading horde) To fall back, to surge back. (*c*) *L'eau reflua sur la berge,* the water washed up on to the bank.
reflux [rafly], *s.m.* (*a*) Reflux, flowing back; ebb(ing) (of tide); ebb-tide. **Le flux et le reflux,** the ebb and flow. (*b*) Surging back.
refondre [rəfɔ̃:dr], *v.tr.* **1.** To remelt; to recast (metal, a bell); to recoin, remint (money). **2.** To recast, remodel (poem).
refonte [rafɔ̃:t], *s.f.* **1.** Recasting, remelting; recoinage (of money). **2.** Recasting (of treatise, etc.); remodelling, reorganization (of factory).
réformateur, -trice [reformatœːr, -tris]. **1.** *a.* Reforming. **2.** *s.* Reformer.
réformation [reformasjɔ̃], *s.f.* Reformation.
réforme [refɔrm], *s.f.* **1.** Reformation, reform (of abuses, of the calendar). **École de réforme,** reformatory. *Rel.H:* **La Réforme,** the Reformation. **2.** (*a*) *Mil:* *Navy:* (i) Discharge; invaliding out of the service; (ii) cashiering, dismissal from the service; (iii) casting (of horses). **Chevaux de réforme,** cast horses. (*b*) *Ind:* *R. du matériel,* scrapping of the plant.
reformer [rəfɔrme], *v.tr.* To form again, to re-form.
réformer [reforme], *v.tr.* **1.** (*a*) To reform, amend (one's conduct, the laws). (*b*) To retrench (expenditure). **2.** *Jur:* To reverse (a decision). **3.** (*a*) (i) To discharge (soldier) as unfit; to retire (officer); (ii) to dismiss (officer) from the service; to cashier; (iii) to cast (horse). (*b*) *Ind:* To scrap (the plant). *a.* **-able.**
　se réformer, to reform, to mend one's ways.
　réformé, -ée, *s.* (*a*) Protestant. (*b*) Man invalided out of the service. **Réformés de guerre avec invalidité,** disabled ex-service-men.
refoulant [rəfulɑ̃], *a.* **Pompe refoulante,** force-pump.
refoulement [rəfulmɑ̃], *s.m.* **1.** (*a*) Pressing back; driving back, forcing back; driving in or out (of pin, bolt); backing (of train); tamping (of earth). (*b*) *Hyd.E:* (i) Delivery, output (of pipe). (ii) Lift (of pump). (iii) Back-flow. **2.** *Psy:* (Unconscious) repression, suppression (of desires); suppressed desire.
refouler [rəfule], *v.tr.* To drive back, force back, press back; to compress (gas); to drive in or out (bolt, pin); to back (train); to tamp (earth, etc.). *R. l'ennemi,* to drive back the enemy. *R. ses sentiments,* to repress one's feelings. *R. ses larmes,* to force back, keep back, one's tears. *Psy:* *R. un instinct dans l'inconscient,* to drive back an instinct into the unconscious; to repress an instinct.
refouloir [rəfulwaːr], *s.m.* (*a*) Tamping-tool. (*b*) *Artil:* Rammer.
réfractaire [refraktɛːr]. **1.** *a.* (*a*) Refractory, contumacious, rebellious, insubordinate. *R. à la loi,* unwilling to accept the law. (*b*) Refractory (ore); fire-proof (brick, clay). (*c*) *R. aux acides,* acid-proof. *R. au poison,* proof against poison. **2.** *s.* Refractory person; defaulter.
réfracter [refrakte], *v.tr.* To refract, bend (rays).
　se réfracter, (of rays) to be refracted, to suffer refraction.
réfracteur [refraktœːr], *s.m.* Refractor; refracting telescope.
réfraction [refraksjɔ̃], *s.f.* *Ph:* Refraction. **Index de réfraction,** refractive index.

réfractomètre [refraktɔmɛtr], *s.m.* *Ph:* Refractometer.
refrain [rəfrɛ̃], *s.m.* **1.** Refrain, burden (of a song). *F:* *Chanter de vieux refrains,* to sing old songs, old ditties. *F:* **C'est le refrain (de la ballade),** it's the same old story. **2.** **Refrain en chœur,** chorus.
réfranger [refrɑ̃ʒe], *v.tr.* = RÉFRACTER.
réfrangible [refrɑ̃ʒibl], *a.* *Ph:* Refrangible.
refr|éner [rafrene], *v.tr.* (je refrène; je refrénerai) To curb, bridle, restrain; to control (a passion). *s.m.* **-ènement.**
réfrigérant [refriʒerɑ̃]. **1.** *a.* Refrigerating, cooling; freezing (mixture). **2.** *s.m.* (*a*) Refrigerator, condenser (of still). (*b*) *Ind:* Cooling-tower; cooler.
réfrigération [refriʒerasjɔ̃], *s.f.* Refrigeration, cooling; chilling (of meat).
réfrigérer [refriʒere], *v.tr.* (je réfrigère; je réfrigérerai) To refrigerate, cool. *Viande réfrigérée,* chilled meat.
réfringent [refrɛ̃ʒɑ̃], *a.* *Ph:* Refringent, refractive, refracting.
refrogner [rəfrɔɲe], *v.tr.* = RENFROGNER.
refroidir [rəfrwadiːr]. **1.** *v.tr.* To cool, chill; to damp (sympathy); to dash (s.o.'s enthusiasm). *Moteur refroidi par l'air,* air-cooled engine. **2.** *v.i.* & *pr.* (*a*) To grow cold; to cool down, off. *Le temps s'est refroidi,* it is colder. (*b*) *Med:* **Se refroidir,** to catch a chill.
refroidissement [rəfrwadismɑ̃], *s.m.* **1.** Cooling (down). *Moteur à r. d'eau,* water-cooled engine. *R. du temps,* fall in temperature. **2.** *Med:* **Attraper un refroidissement,** to catch a chill.
refuge [rəfyːʒ], *s.m.* **1.** Refuge; shelter (for the poor); house of refuge; (bird) sanctuary. **2.** (Street) refuge, street island. **3.** *Dieu est mon r.,* God is my refuge.
réfugier (se) [sərefyʒje], *v.pr.* To take refuge; to find shelter (*chez qn,* with s.o.). *Se r. dans les mensonges,* to take refuge in lying; to fall back on lies.
　réfugié, -ée, *s.* Refugee.
refus [rəfy], *s.m.* Refusal. *Essuyer un r.,* to meet with a refusal. *R. d'obéissance,* (i) insubordination; (ii) *Jur:* contempt of court. **Ce n'est pas de refus,** I can't say no to that; I accept gladly. *Tchn:* *Enfoncer un pilot* **(jusqu')à refus** (*de mouton*), to drive a pile home.
refus|er [rəfyze], *v.tr.* **1.** (*a*) To refuse, decline (sth.); *F:* to turn down (offer). *R. qch. d'un geste,* to wave sth. away. *R. qch. à qn,* to refuse, deny, s.o. sth. *R. tout talent à qn,* to deny that s.o. has any talent. *R. la porte à qn,* to deny s.o. admittance. *R. tout net,* to give a flat refusal, to refuse point-blank. *R. de faire qch.,* to refuse to do sth. (*b*) (Of horse) To refuse, to ba(u)lk. (*c*) (Of ship) Not to obey the helm. **2.** (*a*) To reject (a man for military service); to turn (a man) down. *Sch:* **Refuser un candidat,** to refuse, fail, *F:* plough, pluck, a candidate. *Être refusé,* to fail; *F:* to get plucked, ploughed. (*b*) *Th:* *etc:* *R. du monde,* to turn people away. **3.** *v.i.* Ne *r. à aucune besogne,* to shrink from no work, from no task. *s.* **-eur, -euse.**
　se refuser *à qch.,* to object to, to set one's face against, demur to, sth. *Se r. à l'évidence,* to shut one's eyes to the evidence. *Se r. à faire qch.,* to refuse, decline, to do sth.
　refusé, *a.* Refused, rejected. *Post:* *Lettre refusée,* blind letter.
réfutateur, -trice [refytatœːr, -tris], *s.* Refuter.
réfutation [refytasjɔ̃], *s.f.* Refutation.
réfut|er [refyte], *v.tr.* To refute, confute (theory); to disprove (statement). *a.* **-able.**

regagner [rəgɑɲe], *v.tr.* **1.** (*a*) To regain, recover. *R. qn,* to win s.o. back. (*b*) To recover, win back (money, etc.). *R. le temps perdu,* to make up for lost time. **2.** To get back to (a place) ; to reach (a place) again ; to regain (the shore). *R. son foyer,* to return to one's home.

regain [rəgɛ̃], *s.m.* **1.** *Agr:* Aftermath, after-growth, aftercrop. **2.** Renewal (of youth, beauty, etc.). *R. d'activité,* recrudescence of activity. *R. de vente,* revival of sales.

régal [regal], *s.m.* (*a*) Feast ; *F:* good tuck-in, blow-out. (*b*) Exquisite dish ; treat. *pl. Des régals.*

régalade [regalad], *s.f. F:* (*a*) Regaling, treating (of s.o.). (*b*) Treat.

régale [regal], *a.f. Ch:* Eau régale, aqua regia.

régaler [regale], *v.tr.* To entertain, feast (one's friends). *C'est moi qui régale,* I'm standing treat. **se régaler,** to feast (*de,* on) ; to treat oneself (*de,* to). *On s'est bien régalé,* we did ourselves well.

regard [rəgaːr], *s.m.* **1.** Look, glance, gaze. *R. de côté, en coulisse,* sidelong glance. *R. terne, vitreux,* glassy stare. Yeux sans regard, dull, lack-lustre, eyes. *Jeter un r. à qn,* to give s.o. a look ; to catch s.o.'s eye. *Jeter un r. sur qch.,* to cast a glance at, over, sth. Chercher qn du regard, to look round for s.o. *Détourner le r.,* to look away, to avert one's eyes (*de,* from). Promener ses regards sur qch., (i) to let one's eyes roam over sth. ; (ii) to eye, scan, sth. *R. appuyé,* stare. Caché aux regards, out of sight ; hidden from view. Attirer le(s) regard(s), to draw the eye ; to be conspicuous. En regard de qch., opposite, facing, sth. Au regard de qch., in comparison with sth., compared with sth. **2.** Inspection hole. (*a*) Man-hole (of sewer, etc.) ; draught-hole (of furnace). (*b*) Sight-hole, peep-hole ; observation aperture.

regardant, -ante [rəgardɑ̃, -ɑ̃ːt]. **1.** *a.* (*a*) Close (-fisted), stingy. (*b*) Particular (*pour,* about) ; careful (housewife). **2.** *s.* Onlooker, spectator.

regarder [rəgarde], *v.tr.* **1.** (*a*) *Pred.* To regard, consider. *R. qch. comme un crime,* to regard, look on, sth. as a crime. (*b*) *Ne r. que ses intérêts,* to consider only one's interest. (*c*) *v.ind.tr. R. à qch.,* to pay attention to sth. ; to be particular about sth. *Sans r. à la dépense,* regardless of expense. Y bien regarder, y regarder à deux fois, avant de faire qch., to consider a matter carefully ; to think twice before doing sth. *Je n'y regarde pas de si près,* I am not so very particular. *A y r. de près . . .,* on close inspection. . . . (*d*) (Of thg) To concern, regard (s.o.). Cela me regarde, that is my business. Cela ne vous regarde pas, that is no concern of yours, that is none of your business. En ce qui regarde . . ., as regards. . . . **2.** To look at (sth., s.o.). *R. qn dans les yeux,* to look s.o. in the eyes. *R. qn fixement,* to stare at s.o. *R. qn de travers,* to look askance at s.o. *R. qn avec méfiance,* to eye s.o. suspiciously. *R. qn en face,* to look s.o. in the face. Se faire regarder, to attract attention ; to make oneself conspicuous. *R. qn faire qch.,* to watch s.o. doing sth. *R. à la fenêtre,* to look in at the window. *R. par la fenêtre,* to look out of the window. *R. à sa montre,* to look at the time (by one's watch). Regarder en arrière, to look back. Puis-je regarder? may I have a look? **3.** To look on to (sth.) ; to face, front (the sea, etc.). *Fenêtre qui regarde sur le jardin,* window that looks on to the garden.

regarnir [rəgarniːr], *v.tr.* To regarnish ; to refill (one's purse) ; to re-stock (larder) ; to re-cover (furniture) ; to retrim (dress).

régate [regat], *s.f.* **1.** Regatta. *R. à voiles,* yacht-races. *R. à rames, à l'aviron,* boat-races.

2. (*a*) (Narrow) sailor-knot tie. (*b*) (Boating) straw-hat ; boater.

regel [rəʒel], *s.m.* Renewed frost.

regeler [rəʒle], *v.tr. & i.* (il regèle ; il regèlera) To freeze (sth.) again. *Impers. Voilà qu'il regèle,* it is freezing again.

régence [reʒɑ̃ːs], *s.f.* Regency. *Hist:* La Régence, the Regency (of Philip of Orleans (1715-1723)). *a.inv.* Des mœurs Régence, profligacy (reminiscent of the *Régence* period).

régénérateur, -trice [reʒeneratœːr, -tris]. **1.** *a.* Regenerating, regenerative. **2.** *s.* Regenerator. **3.** *s.m.* (*a*) *Ind:* Regenerating plant ; regenerative furnace. (*b*) Hair-restorer.

régénération [reʒenerasjɔ̃], *s.f.* **1.** Regeneration. **2.** Reclamation (of land).

régénérer [reʒenere], *v.tr.* (je régénère ; je régénérerai) To regenerate.

régent, -ente [reʒɑ̃, -ɑ̃ːt], *s.* **1.** Regent. **2.** Governor (of the Bank of France).

régenter [reʒɑ̃te], *v.tr. F:* To domineer over, dictate to (s.o.).

régicide¹ [reʒisid], *s.m.* Regicide.

régicide², *s.m.* Regicide (as a crime).

régie [reʒi], *s.f.* **1.** *Jur: etc:* Administration, stewardship (of property, etc.) ; management, control. En régie, in the hands of trustees, or under State supervision. Régie du dépôt légal, copyright department. **2.** (*a*) Régie des impôts indirects, excise(-administration). (*b*) Excise-office. *Employé de la r.,* exciseman.

regimbement [rəʒɛ̃bmɑ̃], *s.m.* Refractoriness ; *F:* kicking (*contre,* against).

regimber [rəʒɛ̃be], *v.i.* (Of horse, *F:* of pers.) To kick (*contre,* at, against) ; to jib, to ba(u)lk (*contre,* at).

regimbeur, -euse [rəʒɛ̃bœːr, -øːz], *a. & s.* Refractory (person, mule) ; recalcitrant.

régime [reʒim], *s.m.* **1.** Form of government or of administration ; regime. *Le r. du travail,* the organization of labour. *Jur:* Mariée sous le r. dotal, married under the dotal system. *Le r. actuel,* the present order of things. *Fr.Hist:* L'ancien régime, the old regime (the system of government in France before 1789). **2.** (*a*) Normal operation, normal running (of engine, motor, etc.). *R. de marche normal,* normal working conditions. Vitesse de régime, rated speed ; working speed. *El.E: R. de chargement (d'un accumulateur),* rate of charging. (*b*) Flow, regime (of watercourse). **3.** *Med:* Regimen, diet. *R. lacté,* milk diet. Être au régime, to be on (a) diet. **4.** *Gram:* Object. Cas régime, objective case. **5.** Bunch, cluster (of dates) ; stem (of bananas).

régimenter [reʒimɑ̃te], *v.tr.* *Mil:* Regiment. *F: Ça ne se faisait pas comme ça au r.,* that wasn't the way in the army.

régimentaire [reʒimɑ̃tɛːr], *a.* Regimental.

région [reʒjɔ̃], *s.f.* Region, territory ; area. *Les régions polaires,* the polar regions. *Anat:* La r. lombaire, the lumbar region. *Magn: R. attractive,* field of attraction.

régional, -ale, -aux [reʒjɔnal, -o]. **1.** *a.* Regional, local. Concours régional, (regional) agricultural show or cattle-show. **2.** *s.f.* Régionale, provincial branch (of an association).

régionalisme [reʒjɔnalism], *s.m.* Regionalism.

régir [reʒiːr], *v.tr.* (*a*) To govern, rule ; to manage (estate) ; to direct (undertaking). (*b*) *Gram:* To govern (case, noun).

régisseur [reʒisœːr], *s.m.* Manager ; agent, steward ; (farm) bailiff. *Th:* Stage-manager.

registre [rəʒistr], *s.m.* **1.** Register ; account-book ; minute-book. Tenir registre des événements, to take note of events. *Adm: Les registres de l'état civil*, the registers of births, marriages, and deaths. *Breed: R. des chevaux*, stud-book. *R. d'une machine*, log-book of a machine. **2.** *Mus:* Register; (i) compass, (ii) tone quality. **3.** (*a*) *R. d'aérage*, ventilation flap. *R. de cheminée*, register, damper (of furnace or chimney). (*b*) *Mch:* Regulator-lever, throttle(-valve). (*c*) Draw-stop (of organ).

réglable [reglabl], *a.* Adjustable.

réglage [regla:ʒ], *s.m.* **1.** Ruling (of paper). **2.** (*a*) Regulating, adjusting, adjustment, setting (of apparatus); rating (of chronometer). *Vis de réglage*, set screw, adjusting screw. *R. de la vitesse*, speed control. *Artil: R. du tir*, *tir de réglage*, ranging. (*b*) *W.Tel:* Tuning. *Réglages*, dial readings. *Changer de r.*, to switch over to another station.

règle [regl], *s.f.* **1.** (*a*) Rule, ruler; straight-edge. *R. divisée*, scale. *R. à calcul*, slide-rule. (*b*) *Surv:* Measuring-rod. **2.** Rule (of conduct, grammar, arithmetic). *Ecc: R. d'un ordre*, rule of an order. *Nau: Règles de la route de mer*, the rule of the road (at sea). *Règles d'un jeu*, rules, laws, of a game. *Com:* **Pour la bonne règle . . .**, for order's sake. . . . *Se faire une règle de se coucher de bonne heure*, to make it a rule to go to bed early. **Mettre qch. en règle**, to put sth. in order. **Tout est en règle**, everything is in order; *F:* everything is O.K. **Reçu en règle**, formal receipt. *F:* **Bataille en règle**, regular set-to, stand-up fight. **En règle générale**, as a general rule. **Agir dans les règles**, to act according to rule. S.a. EXCEPTION I. **3.** Prendre qn pour règle, to take s.o. as a guide, as an example.

règlement [regləmã], *s.m.* **1.** Settlement, adjustment (of account, etc.). **2.** Regulation(s); statutes. **Règlements de police**, by(e)-laws. **3.** *Se faire un r. de vie*, to adopt a rule of life.

réglementaire [regləmãte:r], *a.* Regular, statutory, prescribed. *Nau: Les feux réglementaires*, the regulation lights.

réglementairement [regləmãtermã], *adv.* In the regular, prescribed, manner.

réglementation [regləmãtasjõ], *s.f.* **1.** Making of rules. **2.** Regulating, regulation. *R. de la natalité*, birth-control.

réglementer [regləmãte], *v.tr.* To regulate; to make rules for (sth.).

régler [regle], *v.tr.* (je règle; je réglerai) **1.** To rule (paper, etc.). **2.** (*a*) To regulate, order (one's life, etc.). *R. sa journée*, to make one's plans for the day. *Mil: R. le tir*, to range. (*b*) To regulate, adjust, set (mechanism); to adjust (compass); to rate (chronometer). *R. sa montre*, to set one's watch right. *I.C.E: R. l'allumage, les soupapes*, to time the ignition, the valves. (*c*) *Nau: R. les quarts*, to set the watches. **3.** (*a*) To settle (question, account). *Com: R. les livres*, to close, balance, the books. S.a. COMPTE (*c*). (*b*) *R. ses affaires*, to set one's affairs in order.

se régler *sur qn, sur qch.*, to take pattern by s.o.; to take s.o. as an example; to go by sth.

réglé, *a.* **1.** Ruled (paper). **2.** Regular; steady, methodical (person, life, habits). *A des heures réglées*, at set, stated, hours. *Nau:* Vent réglé, trade wind. *F:* **C'est réglé comme du papier à musique**, it is like the laws of the Medes and Persians.

réglet [regle], *s.m.* (*a*) *Arch:* Reglet. (*b*) Carpenter's rule.

réglette [reglet], *s.f.* **1.** Small rule, scale. **2.** Slider (of a slide-rule). **3.** Strip (of metal).

réglette-jauge, *s.f. Aut:* Dip-rod, dip-stick.

réglisse [reglis], *s.f.* Liquorice. **Bâton de réglisse**, Spanish liquorice.

réglure [regly:r], *s.f.* Ruling (of or on paper).

règne [reɲ], *s.m.* **1.** (Vegetable, animal) kingdom. **2.** Reign (of a king); sway (of fashion). **Sous le règne de Louis XI**, in the reign of Louis XI.

régn|er [reɲe], *v.i.* (je règne; je régnerai) **1.** (Of monarch) To reign, rule; to hold sway (*sur*, over); (of conditions) to prevail, to be prevalent. *R. en maître*, to reign supreme. *Le calme règne*, calm prevails. **2.** *Une galerie règne le long du bâtiment*, a gallery runs, extends, along the building. *a.* -ant.

regommer [regɔme], *v.tr.* To retread (tyre).

regonfl|er [regõfle], *v.tr.* To reinflate (balloon); to pump up (tyre). *s.m.* -ement.

regorgeant [regɔrʒã], *a.* Overflowing, abounding (*de*, with); *F:* cram-full (*de*, of).

regorger [regɔrʒe], *v.* (je regorgeai(s); n. regorgeons) **1.** *v.i.* (*a*) To overflow, run over; to brim over. (*b*) To abound (*de*, in); to be glutted (*de*, with). *Les trains regorgent de gens*, the trains are packed with people. *Les rues regorgeaient de monde*, the streets were crowded, teeming, swarming, with people. *Sa maison regorge de livres*, his house is cram-full of books. *Il regorge de santé*, he is bursting with health. (*c*) (Of water) To flow back (up a drain, etc.). **2.** *v.tr.* To bring up, regurgitate (food). *F: Faire r. à qn ce qu'il a volé*, to make s.o. disgorge what he has stolen.

regoûter [regute], *v.tr. & i.* (*a*) *R. à, de, qch.*, to have another taste of sth. (*b*) *R. la vie*, to enjoy life again.

regrat [regra], *s.m.* Huckstering.

regratter [regrate], **1.** *v.tr. Const:* To scrape, rub down (wall). **2.** *v.i.* To huckster.

regratterie [regratri], *s.f.* **1.** Huckstery, huckstering. **2.** Huckster's wares.

regrattier, -ière [regratje, -je:r], *s.* Huckster; hucksterer, hucksteress.

régressif, -ive [regresif, -i:v], *a.* Regressive. *Biol: Forme régressive*, throw-back.

régression [regresjõ], *s.f.* **1.** Regression; recession (of sea from the coast). **2.** *Biol:* (*a*) Retrogression. (*b*) Throw-back. **3.** Drop (in sales).

regret [regra], *s.m.* Regret (*de*, of, for). **Avoir du regret**, to feel regret. **Avoir regret de qch.**, to regret sth. **J'ai regret à vous quitter**, I am lo(a)th to leave you. **J'ai le regret de vous annoncer que . . .**, I regret to have to inform you that. . . . **Faire qch. à regret**, to do sth. with regret, regretfully, with reluctance, reluctantly. **A mon (grand) regret . . .**, to my (great) sorrow, (much) to my regret. . . . *Le r. de la patrie*, home-sickness.

regrettable [regretabl], *a.* Regrettable; unfortunate (mistake). *adv.* -ment.

regretter [regrete], *v.tr.* **1.** To regret. *R. d'avoir fait qch.*, to regret, be sorry for, having done sth. *Je regrette qu'il soit parti si tôt*, I regret, am sorry, that he left so early. **Je regrette!** (I'm) sorry! **2.** *R. un absent*, to miss an absent friend. *R. son argent*, to wish one had spent one's money back.

régularisation [regylarizasjõ], *s.f.* Regularization, regularizing; putting in order.

régulariser [regylarize], *v.tr.* To regularize; to put (sth.) in order; to equalize (dividends, etc.).

régularité [regylarite], *s.f.* (*a*) Regularity (of features, of habits). (*b*) Steadiness, evenness (of motion). **Épreuve de régularité**, reliability trial. (*c*) Equability (of temper). (*d*) Punctuality.

régulateur, -trice [regylatœ:r, -tris]. **I.** *a.* Regulating, regulative. **Soupape régulatrice**, governor-valve. **2.** *s.m.* Regulator, governor (of watch, arc-light, etc.); balance-wheel (of watch); ball governor (of engine); throttle-valve. *Typewr:* R. *de marges,* marginal stop.

régulation [regylasjɔ̃], *s.f. Nau:* Regulation, readjustment (of compass).

régule [regyl], *s.m. Mec.E:* White metal, antifriction metal.

réguli|er, -ère [regylje, -ɛːr]. **I.** *a.* (*a*) Regular (features, habits, etc.). *Quittance régulière,* receipt in due form. *Gram:* Verbe régulier, regular verb. (*b*) Steady (pulse); even (motion); orderly (life); punctual. (*c*) *Humeur régulière,* equable temper. **2.** *a. & s.m.* Regular (priest, soldier). **Troupes régulières,** regular troops; regulars. *adv.* **-èrement.**

régurgiter [regyrʒite], *v.tr.* To regurgitate.

réhabilitation [reabilitasjɔ̃], *s.f.* Rehabilitation; recovery of civil rights; discharge (of bankrupt).

réhabiliter [reabilite], *v.tr.* To rehabilitate (s.o.); to discharge (bankrupt). R. *qn dans ses droits,* to reinstate s.o. in his rights.

se réhabiliter, to rehabilitate oneself; to obtain one's discharge (after bankruptcy); to re-establish one's good name.

réhabituer [reabitɥe], *v.tr.* To reaccustom.

rehauss|er [roose], *v.tr.* **I.** (*a*) To raise; to make (construction) higher. (*b*) R. *les monnaies,* to appreciate the coinage. R. *le prix du pain,* to raise the price of bread. **2.** To heighten, enhance, set off (colour, complexion); to touch up (a colour). R. *un détail,* to accentuate a detail. *s.m.* **-ement.**

reillère [rɛjɛːr], *s.f.* = RAYÈRE 2.

réimportation [reɛ̃pɔrtasjɔ̃], *s.f.* **I.** Reimportation. **2.** Reimport.

réimporter [reɛ̃pɔrte], *v.tr.* To reimport.

réimpression [reɛ̃presjɔ̃], *s.f.* **I.** Reprinting. **2.** Reprint, reimpression.

réimprimer [reɛ̃prime], *v.tr.* To reprint.

Reims [rɛ̃s]. *Pr.n.m. Geog:* Rheims.

rein [rɛ̃], *s.m.* **I.** *Anat:* Kidney. **2.** *pl.* Loins, back. **La chute, le creux, des reins,** the small of the back. **Se casser les reins,** to break one's back. **Mal de reins,** lumbago. **Ceindre ses reins,** to gird (up) one's loins. **Il a les reins solides,** (i) he has a strong back, he is a sturdy fellow; (ii) *F:* he is a man of substance. S.a. ÉPÉE.

réincorporer [reɛ̃kɔrpɔre], *v.tr.* To reincorporate; to re-embody.

reine [rɛn], *s.f.* **I.** (*a*) Queen. *La r. Anne,* Queen Anne. *Por de r.,* queenly bearing. (*b*) R. *des abeilles,* queen-bee. (*c*) *Chess: etc:* = DAME[1] 2 (*b*). **2.** *F:* *La r. du bal,* the belle of the ball.

reine-Claude [rɛnglɔːd, -klɔːd], *s.f.* Greengage. *pl.* *Des reines-Claude.*

reine-marguerite, *s.f. Bot:* China-aster. *pl.* *Des reines-marguerites.*

réinhumation [reinymasjɔ̃], *s.f.* Reinterment.

réinhumer [reinyme], *v.tr.* To reinter.

réinstallation [reɛ̃stalasjɔ̃], *s.f.* Reinstalment.

réinstaller [reɛ̃stale], *v.tr.* To reinstall.

se réinstaller, to settle down again.

réintégration [reɛ̃tegrasjɔ̃], *s.f.* **I.** Reinstatement, restoration. **2.** R. *de domicile,* resumption of residence.

réintégrer [reɛ̃tegre], *v.tr.* (Conj. like INTÉGRER) **I.** R. *qn (dans ses fonctions),* to reinstate s.o.; to restore s.o. to his position. R. *des employés,* to re-engage employees. **2.** R. *son domicile,* to resume possession of one's domicile; to return to one's home.

réitératif, -ive [reiteratif, -iːv], *a.* Reiterative. *Sommation réitérative,* second summons.

réitération [reiterasjɔ̃], *s.f.* Reiteration.

réitérer [reitere], *v.tr.* (je réitère; je réitérerai) To reiterate, repeat.

reître [rɛːtr], *s.m. Hist:* Reiter (German mercenary).

rejaill|ir [rəʒajiːr], *v.i.* (Of water, blood) To spirt back, to gush out (*sur,* upon); to spirt up, out; to spout (up, out); (of light) to be reflected, to flash or glance back. *La honte en rejaillira sur vous,* the disgrace will be yours, will fall on you. *s.m.* **-issement.**

rejet [rəʒɛ], *s.m.* **I.** (*a*) Throwing out; throwing up; casting up. (*b*) Material thrown out; spoil-earth. (*c*) *Geol:* Throw (of fault). **2.** Rejection (of proposal, etc.). **3.** *Ap:* Cast, afterswarm (of bees). **4.** *Hort:* Shoot.

rejéteau [rəʒeto], *s.m.* (*a*) Drip-moulding; flashing-board (of door, etc.). (*b*) *Av:* Drip-flap.

rejeter [rəʒ(ə)te], *v.tr.* (Conj. like JETER) **I.** (*a*) To throw, fling, (sth.) back; to return (ball). R. *l'ennemi,* to hurl, fling, back the enemy. (*b*) To throw up, cast up. **2.** To transfer. (*a*) R. *la faute sur d'autres,* to shift, cast, lay, the blame on others. R. *un crime sur quelqu'un d'autre,* to lay a crime at someone else's door. (*b*) To carry on (word to next line). **3.** To reject, set at naught, set aside; to refuse to acknowledge (s.o.). R. *une offre,* to reject, dismiss, an offer. R. *un projet de loi,* to throw out a bill. **4.** *Arb:* To throw out (new shoots).

se rejeter. I. To fall back (*sur,* on). *Se r. sur les circonstances,* to lay the blame on circumstances. **2.** *Se r. en arrière,* to leap, dart, spring, back(wards).

rejeton [rəʒtɔ̃], *s.m.* **I.** Shoot, sucker (of plant). **2.** Scion, descendant, offspring (of a family).

rejetonner [rəʒtɔne], *v.i.* (Of plant) To sucker.

rejoindre [rəʒwɛ̃ːdr], *v.tr.* (Conj. like JOINDRE) **I.** To rejoin, reunite; to join (things, persons) (together) again. **2.** R. *qn,* to rejoin, overtake, s.o.; to catch s.o. up (again). R. *son régiment,* to rejoin one's regiment.

se rejoindre. I. To meet. **2.** To meet again.

rejouer [rəʒwe], *v.tr.* To replay (match, etc.); to play off (a draw); to play (piece of music) again; to act (a play) again.

réjouir [reʒwiːr], *v.tr.* (*a*) To delight, gladden (s.o.). R. *l'œil,* to delight the eye. (*b*) R. *la compagnie,* to amuse, divert, entertain, the company.

se réjouir. I. To rejoice (*de,* at, in); to be glad (*de,* of); to be delighted (*de,* at). *Je me réjouis de le revoir,* I am delighted to see him again. **2.** To make merry. *Laissons r. le monde,* we must allow people to enjoy themselves.

réjoui, *a.* Jolly, joyous, cheerful, cheery. *s. F:* *Un gros réjoui,* a jovial fellow.

réjouissance [reʒwisãːs], *s.f.* **I.** Rejoicing. *Des réjouissances publiques,* public rejoicings. **2.** *Com:* Make-weight (in bones, added to meat sold).

réjouissant [reʒwisã], *a.* **I.** Cheering, heartening. **2.** Mirth-provoking, diverting.

relâchant [rəlɑʃã], *a.* Relaxing; *Med:* laxative.

relâche [rəlɑːʃ]. **I.** *s.m.* (*a*) Slackening. (*b*) Relaxation, respite, rest (from regular work); breathing space. **Travailler sans relâche,** to work without respite. (*c*) *Th:* Il y a relâche ce soir, there is no performance this evening. (On bills) "Relâche," 'Closed.' **2.** *s.f. Nau:* (*a*) Call; putting in. **Faire relâche à un port, faire une relâche,** to call at, put into, a port. **Relâche forcée,** putting in through stress of weather. *En r. forcée,* storm-bound. (*b*) Port of call.

relâchement [rəlɑʃmã], *s.m.* (*a*) Relaxing, slackening. (*b*) Falling off (of discipline, of zeal);

abatement (of severe weather); looseness (of the bowels); looseness, laxity (of morals, conduct). (c) Relaxation (from work).

relâcher [rəlɑʃe]. **I.** *v.tr.* (a) To loosen, slacken, ease (cord, etc.). (b) To relax (discipline, morals); to abate (one's zeal); to loosen (the bowels). **2.** *v.tr.* *R. un prisonnier, un oiseau,* to release a prisoner, a bird; to set a prisoner at liberty; to let a bird go. *Relâché sous caution,* let out on bail. **3.** *v.i. Nau:* To put into port.

se relâcher. I. To slacken; (of shoe-lace) to get loose; (of fever) to abate; (of pers.) to become slack; (of zeal) to flag, to abate, to fall off; (of affection) to grow less; (of morals) to grow lax, loose. **2.** (Of the weather) To grow milder; (of pain) to grow less acute.

relâché, *a.* Relaxed; slack (rope, etc.); loose, lax (conduct); loose (bowels).

relais[1] [rəlɛ], *s.m.* Sand-bank (along a river); sand-flats (along the shore); silt, warp.

relai(s)[2], *s.m.* **I.** (a) Relay (of horses, of persons); shift (of workmen). *Chevaux de relais,* relay horses. *Travail sans r.,* unrelieved spell of work. *Sp:* *Course de relais, à relais,* relay race. (b) Stage, posting-house, relay station. *Aut:* *R. d'essence,* (re)filling station. **2.** *El.E:* (a) Relay (battery). (b) Relay station.

relancer [rəlɑ̃se], *v.tr.* (Conj. like LANCER) **I.** To throw, cast, (sth.) again or back. *Ten:* To return (the ball). **2.** (a) *Ven:* To start (the quarry) again. (b) *F:* *Aller r. qn,* to hunt out s.o.; to go and badger s.o. (c) *Aut:* *R. le moteur,* to restart the engine. (d) *Cards:* (Bridge) To raise the bid.

relanceur, -euse [rəlɑ̃sœːr, -øːz], *s.* *Ten:* Striker(-out).

relaps, -e [rəlaps], *a. & s.* Relapsed (heretic); backslider. S.a. LAPS[2].

relater [rəlate], *v.tr.* To relate, state (facts).

relat|if, -ive [rəlatif, -iːv], *a.* (a) Relative (value, pronoun). *Mus:* Tons relatifs, related keys. (b) *Questions relatives à un sujet,* questions relating to, connected with, a matter. (c) *Période de repos r.,* period of comparative rest. *adv.* **-ivement.**

relation [rəlasjɔ̃], *s.f.* Relation. **I.** *Les relations humaines,* human intercourse. **Entamer des relations, se mettre, entrer, en relations, avec qn,** to enter into relations, get into touch, with s.o. *Être en r. avec qn,* to be in communication, in touch, with s.o. *Être en relations suivies,* to hear regularly from one another. *Être en relations d'amitié avec qn,* to be on friendly terms with s.o. *Être en relations d'affaires avec qn,* to have business relations, to have dealings, with s.o. *Tp:* *Être mis en r. avec qn,* to be put through to s.o. **Il a de belles relations,** (i) he is well connected; (ii) he has influential friends. *R. entre la cause et l'effet,* relation, connection, between cause and effect. *R. étroite entre deux faits,* close connection between two facts. *R. entre Paris et Lille,* service of trains between Paris and Lille. *Relations directes,* through connections. *Anat:* *Relations de deux organes,* relative positions of two parts. **2.** Account, report, narrative, statement. *Faire la relation de qch.,* to give an account of sth.

relationné [rəlasjɔne], *a.* *Être très bien r.,* (i) to be very well connected; (ii) to be in touch with all the best people.

relativité [rəlativite], *s.f.* Relativity.

relaxation [rəlaksasjɔ̃], *s.f.* (a) Reduction (of a sentence). (b) Release, discharge (of prisoner).

relaxer [rəlakse], *v.tr.* *Jur:* To release, set at large (prisoner).

relayer [rəleje], *v.* (je relaie, je relaye; je relaierai, je relayerai) **I.** *v.i.* To relay; to change horses.

2. *v.tr.* (a) To relay, relieve, take turns with (s.o.). (b) To relay (telephonic message, etc.).

se relayer, to relieve one another; to take (it in) turns; *Ind:* to work in shifts.

relégation [rəlegasjɔ̃], *s.f.* Relegation (to a penal colony); transportation for life.

reléguer [rəlege], *v.tr.* (Conj. like LÉGUER) To relegate. (a) To transport (convict). (b) *F:* *R. un tableau au grenier,* to relegate, consign, a picture to the attic.

relégué, *s.m.* Convict (sentenced to transportation).

relent [rəlɑ̃], *s.m.* Musty smell or taste; unpleasant smell (of stale beer, etc.).

relevage [rəlvaːʒ], *s.m.* **I.** Raising, lifting; salving (of submarine). **2.** *Post:* Collection (of the letters).

relevailles [rəlvaːj], *s.f.pl.* Churching (of a woman after childbirth). *Faire ses relevailles,* to be churched.

relevant [rəlvɑ̃], *a.* Dependent, depending (de, on); within the jurisdiction (de, of).

relève [rəlɛːv], *s.f.* **I.** Relief (of troops, sentry); changing (of the guard). *Troupes de r., F:* la **relève,** relieving troops; draft of reliefs. **2.** *R. des blessés,* picking up of the wounded.

relèvement [rəlɛvmɑ̃], *s.m.* **I.** (a) Raising up or again, setting up again (of fallen object). (b) Picking up (of object); *Mil:* collection (of the wounded). (c) Re-establishment, restoration, retrieval (of fortunes); recovery, revival (of business); increase (of wages); raising (of tariff, tax). **2.** *Com:* Statement. **3.** Relieving (of sentry). **4.** *Nau:* *Surv:* Bearing (by compass); resection. *Faire, prendre, un r.,* to take a bearing; to take the bearings (of a coast, etc.). **Porter un relèvement** *sur la carte,* to prick a bearing on the chart; to lay off a bearing. S.a. COMPAS 2. **5.** Rise (in temperature). **6.** *Geol:* Upcast (fault).

relever [rəlve], *v.* (Conj. like LEVER) **I.** *v.tr.* **I.** (a) To raise, lift, set, (sth.) up again; to set (s.o.) on his feet again; to rebuild (wall); to right (ship). (b) To pick up (object, from the ground). **Relever le gant,** to pick up the gauntlet; to accept the challenge. (c) To raise (to a greater height); to turn up (one's collar); to tuck up (one's skirt). *R. sa moustache,* to turn up one's moustache. *R. ses lunettes sur son front,* to push up one's spectacles. *R. la tête,* to hold one's head high; to look up. *R. les salaires, les prix,* to raise, increase, wages, prices. *R. un navire coulé,* to refloat, raise, a sunken ship. **2.** (a) To call attention to (sth.). *R. les fautes d'un ouvrage,* to point out, criticize, the defects of a work. *R. une affirmation,* to challenge a statement. (b) *R. qn,* to take s.o. up sharply. **3.** (a) To bring into relief; to enhance, heighten, set off (colour, etc.). (b) *Cu:* To season, to add condiments to (sauce, etc.). **4.** To relieve (troops, a sentry); to take s.o.'s place (at a duty); to take over (a trench). **5.** *R. qn de ses vœux,* to release s.o. from his vows. *R. qn de ses fonctions,* to relieve s.o. of his office. **6.** *Com: etc:* To make out (account); to read (gas-meter). **7.** *Nau:* To take the bearing(s) of (land). *Surv:* *R. un terrain,* to survey, plot, land.

II. relever, *v.i.* **I.** *R. de maladie,* to have only just recovered from an illness. **2.** *R. de qn,* to be dependent on, answerable to, responsible to, s.o.

se relever. I. To rise to one's feet (again); to get up from one's knees. **2.** (Of trade, courage) To revive. *Les affaires se relèvent,* business is looking up. **3.** (a) To rise again (in public estimation). (*b*) Se *r. de qch.*, to recover from sth. *Il ne s'en relèvera pas,* he will never get over it.

relevé. I. *a.* (*a*) Raised, erect; turned up (collar, sleeve). (*b*) Exalted, high (position); noble (sentiment); lofty (style). (*c*) Highly-seasoned (sauce). **2.** *s.m.* (*a*) Abstract, summary, account, statement. *R. de consommation du gaz,* gas-meter reading. *R. des naissances,* table, summary, of births. *Relevés officiels,* official returns. *Com: R. de compte,* statement (of account). (*b*) Survey (of land). (*c*) *Cu :* Next course after the soup ; remove.

relevée, *s.f. A. & Adm :* Afternoon. A une heure de relevée, at one p.m.

relief [rəljef], *s.m.* **I.** *Sculp :* Relief, relievo. Carte en relief, relief map, raised map. *F :* **Mettre qch. en relief, donner du relief à qch.,** to throw sth. into relief ; to set off (beauty, etc.). *Position très en r.,* very prominent position. S.a. BAS-RELIEF, HAUT-RELIEF. **2.** *pl. A :* Scraps (from the table).

relier [rəlje], *v.tr.* **I.** To bind, tie, again. **2.** (*a*) To connect, bind, join, couple (things, persons). *El : R. à la terre,* to connect to earth. (*b*) To bind (book). *Relié en veau,* bound in calf.

relieur [rəljœːr], *s.m.* (Book)binder.

religieu|x, -euse [rəliʒjø, -øːz]. **I.** *a.* Religious ; sacred (music) ; scrupulous (care). **2.** *s.* Religious. (*a*) *m.* Monk, friar. (*b*) *f.* Nun. *adv.* **-sement.**

religion [rəliʒjɔ̃], *s.f.* (*a*) Religion. Avoir de la **religion,** to be religious. **Mourir en religion,** to die in the faith. **Entrer en religion,** to enter into religion, to take the vows. **Les guerres de religion,** the wars of religion. (*b*) **Se faire une religion de qch.,** to make a religion of sth. ; to make sth. a point of conscience. **Forfaire à la religion du serment,** to violate the sanctity of the oath.

relimer [rəlime], *v.tr.* To file (sth.) again ; to polish up (one's style).

reliquaire [rəlikɛːr], *s.m.* Reliquary, shrine.

reliquat [rəlika], *s.m.* (*a*) Remainder, residue ; unexpected balance. (*b*) After-effects, dregs (of an illness).

relique [rəlik], *s.f.* Relic (of saint). **Garder qch. comme une relique,** to treasure sth.

relire [rəliːr], *v.tr.* (Conj. like LIRE) To re-read ; to read (sth.) (over) again.

reliure [rəljyːr], *s.f.* **I.** Bookbinding. *Atelier de r.,* bindery. **2.** Binding (of book). *R. anglaise, en toile,* cloth binding. *R. amateur,* library binding. S.a. DEMI-RELIURE.

relouer [rəlue], *v.tr.* **I.** To relet (house). **2.** To take a new lease of (house). **3.** To sub-let.

reluctance [rəlyktãːs], *s.f. El :* Reluctance.

reluctivité [rəlyktivite], *s.f. El :* Reluctivity.

reluire [rəlɥiːr], *v.i.* (Conj. like LUIRE) To shine (by reflected light) ; to glitter, glisten, gleam. *Prov :* **Tout ce qui reluit n'est pas or,** all is not gold that glitters. **Brosse à r.,** polishing brush (for shoes).

reluisant [rəlɥizã], *a.* Shining, glittering ; glossy ; well-groomed (horse).

reluqu|er [rəlyke], *v.tr. F :* **I.** To eye, ogle (s.o.). **2.** To have an eye on, to covet (sth.). *s.* **-eur, -euse.**

remâcher [rəmɑʃe], *v.tr.* (*a*) To chew (sth.) again. (*b*) *F :* To ruminate on, over (sth.) ; to turn (sth.) over in one's mind.

remaill|er [rəmaje], *v.tr.* To mend the meshes of, to re-mesh (net) ; to mend a ladder in (stocking). *s.m.* **-age.**

remanence [rəmanãːs], *s.f.* Remanence ; retentivity ; residual magnetism.

remanent [rəmanã], *a.* Residual (magnetism).

remaniement, remaniment [rəmanimã], *s.m.* **I.** = REMANIAGE. **2.** Alteration, modification, change. *Apporter des remaniements à un travail,* to alter, recast, a work.

remani|er [rəmanje], *v.tr.* (*a*) To rehandle (material). *Typ :* To overrun (matter). (*b*) To recast, reshape, alter, adapt (literary work, etc.). *s.m.* **-age.** *s.* **-eur, -euse.**

remari|er [rəmarje], *v.tr.* To remarry (one's daughter). *s.m.* **-age.**

se remarier, to remarry ; to marry again, a second time.

remarquable [rəmarkabl], *a.* (*a*) Remarkable, noteworthy (*par,* for) ; distinguished (*par,* by) ; prominent. **Chose remarquable,** *il était à l'heure,* for a wonder he was in time. (*b*) Strange, astonishing. *adv.* **-ment.**

remarque [rəmark], *s.f.* **I.** Remark. *Faire une r.,* to make, pass, a remark. *Faire la r. que . . .,* to remark that. . . . *Digne de remarque,* noteworthy. **2.** *Nau :* Landmark, beacon.

remarquer [rəmarke], *v.tr.* **I.** To re-mark ; to mark (linen) again. **2.** (*a*) To remark, notice, observe, note (sth.). **Faire remarquer qch. à qn,** to point sth. out to s.o. ; to call s.o.'s attention to sth. (*b*) *R. qn dans la foule,* to notice, distinguish, s.o. in the crowd. **Se faire remarquer,** to attract attention ; to make oneself conspicuous.

remâter [rəmɑte], *v.tr.* To remast (ship).

remball|er [rãbale], *v.tr.* To repack, re-bale (goods). *s.m.* **-age.**

rembarqu|er [rãbarke]. **I.** *v.tr.* To re-embark ; to re-ship (goods). **2.** *v.i. & pr.* (*a*) To re-embark, to go on board again. (*b*) To go to sea again. *s.m.* **-ement.**

rembarrer [rãbare], *v.tr.* (*a*) To snub (s.o.) ; to put (s.o.) in his place. (*b*) To go for (s.o.) ; to jump down (s.o.'s) throat ; *F :* to tell (s.o.) off.

remblai [rãblɛ], *s.m. Civ.E :* **I.** = REMBLAYAGE. **2.** Filling material ; earth. **3.** Embankment, mound, bank. **Route en remblai,** embanked road.

remblay|er [rãblɛje], *v.tr.* (je remblaie, je remblayerai, je remblayerai) *Civ.E :* (*a*) To fill (up), pack (sunk part of ground, etc.). (*b*) To embank, to bank (up) (road, railway line). *s.m.* **-age.**

rembobinage [rãbɔbinaːʒ], *s.m. Typewr :* Rewinding (of the ribbon).

remboît|er [rãbwate], *v.tr.* **I.** To re-case (book). *s.m.* **-age. 2.** (*a*) To reassemble ; to fit (pieces) together again. (*b*) *Surg :* To set (bone in its socket). *s.m.* **-ement.**

rembourr|er [rãbure], *v.tr.* To stuff, pad, upholster (chair, mattress). *s.m.* **-age.**

remboursement [rãbursəmã], *s.m. Com : Fin :* Reimbursement, repayment, refunding ; redeeming, redemption (of annuity, etc.). **Livraison contre remboursement,** payment on delivery, cash on delivery, *F :* C.O.D.

rembours|er [rãburse], *v.tr.* **I.** To repay, refund (expenses, etc.) ; to redeem, pay off (annuity, bond) ; to return (loan). **2.** *R. qn de qch.,* to reimburse, repay, s.o. for sth. *a.* **-able.**

rembrunir [rãbryniːr], *v.tr.* **I.** To make dark(er) ; to darken (sth.). **2.** To cast a gloom over (the company) ; to make (s.o.) sad.

se rembrunir, (of the sky) to cloud over, to grow dark. *Son front se rembrunit,* his brow darkened.

rembucher [rãbyʃe], *v.tr. Ven :* To drive (stag) to cover, to covert.

se **rembucher,** (of stag) to return to cover(t).
remède [rəmɛd], *s.m.* Remedy, cure (*pour,
contre,* for). *F:* R. *de bonne femme,* old wives'
remedy. *R. de charlatan,* nostrum. **(Ap)porter
remède à un mal,** to remedy an evil. *Le r. est
pire que le mal,* the cure is worse than the evil.
Aux grands maux les grands remèdes, desperate
ills call for desperate remedies. **C'est sans
remède,** it is past, beyond, remedy; it can't be
helped. *Il n'y a pas de r.,* there is no help for it.
remédiable [rəmedjabl], *a.* Remediable.
remédier [rəmedje], *v.ind.tr. R. à qch.,* to
remedy sth. *R. à un mal,* to cure an evil; to put
a trouble right.
remêler [rəmɛle], *v.tr.* To mix again; to
re-shuffle (cards).
remémoratif, -ive [rəmemɔratif, -iːv], *a.* Commemorative (festival, etc.).
remémorer [rəmemɔre], *v.tr. R. qch. à qn,* to
remind s.o. of sth. *Se r. qch.,* to remember sth.;
to call sth. to mind.
remerciement, remercîment [rəmɛrsimɑ̃],
s.m. Thanks, acknowledgment. **Faire ses remerciements à qn,** to thank s.o. **Se confondre en
remerciements,** to thank s.o. effusively. *Voter des
remerciements à qn,* to pass a vote of thanks to s.o.
remercier [rəmɛrsje], *v.tr.* **1.** (*a*) *R. qn de qch.,*
to thank s.o. for sth. *Je vous remercie de . . .,*
thank you very much for. . . . (*b*) To decline.
Du café?—Je vous remercie, have some coffee?
—No, thank you. **2.** To dismiss, discharge
(employee).
réméré [remere], *s.m.* **Faculté de réméré,** option
of repurchase. **Vente à réméré,** sale with privilege
of repurchase.
remettant, -ante [rəmɛtɑ̃, -ɑ̃ːt], *s.* Sender (of
money).
remetteur, -euse [rəmɛtœːr, -øːz]. **1.** *a.* Remitting (bank, etc.). **2.** *s.* = REMETTANT.
remettre [rəmɛtr], *v.tr.* (Conj. like METTRE)
1. To put, set, (sth.) back (again). (*a*) *R. son
chapeau, son habit,* to put one's hat, one's coat,
on again. *R. un livre à sa place,* to put a book
back in its place. *F:* **Remettre qn à sa place,** to
put s.o. in his place; to snub s.o. *R. qn sur le
trône,* to restore s.o. to the throne. *Fb: R. le
ballon en jeu,* to throw in the ball. *Ten:* **Balle à
remettre,** let ball. *Remettez cela!* put that away!
Remettre un os, to set a bone. *R. qch. en usage,*
to bring sth. into use again. *R. en état,* to repair,
to overhaul. S.a. NEUF² *R. en marche,* to restart
(engine, etc.). (*b*) *R. l'esprit de qn,* to calm,
compose, s.o.'s mind. **Remettre qn sur pied,** to
restore s.o. to health. *(Se) remettre qn,* to
recall, recollect, s.o. *Vous ne me remettez pas?*
don't you remember me? (*d*) **Remettre bien
ensemble** *des personnes brouillées,* to bring together, to reconcile, persons at variance. *Se r.
bien ensemble,* to make it up again. **2.** (*a*) *R. une
dépêche à qn,* to deliver, hand, a telegram to s.o.
R. de l'argent à qn, to remit money to s.o. *R. un
prisonnier à la justice,* to hand over a prisoner to
justice. *R. son âme à Dieu,* to commit one's soul
to God. (*b*) *R. une charge,* to hand over one's
duties (to s.o. else); to demit office. **3.** *R. une
peine, des péchés,* to remit a penalty, sins. *R. une
offense à qn,* to pardon, forgive, s.o. an offence.
4. To postpone. *R. une affaire au lendemain,* to
put off, defer, a matter till the morrow. *R. une
cause à huitaine,* to adjourn, remand, a case for a
week. *Chess: etc:* **Partie remise,** drawn game.
F: **C'est partie remise,** it is only a pleasure
deferred. **5.** *P:* **Remettons ça,** let's have another
try, let's begin again. *Remettez ça!* as you were!

se **remettre.** **1.** (*a*) *Se r. au lit,* to go back
to bed. *Se r. en route,* to start off on one's way
again. *Le temps se remet au beau,* Abs. *le temps se
remet,* the weather is clearing up. (*b*) *Se r. au
travail, à travailler,* to start work again; to
resume one's work. *Se r. à pleurer,* to start
crying again. **2.** *Se r. d'une maladie,* to recover
from, get over, an illness. **Remettez-vous!** calm
yourself! *Voyons, remettez-vous!* come, pull
yourself together! **3.** **S'en remettre à qn** (*de qch.*),
to rely on s.o. (for sth.); to leave it to s.o.
réminiscence [reminisɑ̃ːs], *s.f.* Reminiscence.
remise [rəmiːz], *s.f.* **1.** (*a*) Putting back (of sth.
into its place). *Fb:* **Remise en jeu,** throw-in.
(*b*) *R. en état,* repairing, overhauling. *R. en
marche,* restarting. **2.** (*a*) Delivery (of letter,
parcel); remitting (of money). *Payable contre r.
du coupon,* payable on presentation of the coupon.
(*b*) Remission (of penalty, tax). **Faire remise
d'une dette,** to remit, cancel, a debt. **3.** *Com:*
(*a*) Remittance. **Faire une remise à qn,** to send
s.o. a remittance. (*b*) Discount, rebate, allowance.
Faire une remise sur un article, to allow a
discount, make a reduction, on an article.
4. *A:* Postponement. (Still so used in) *Je
partirai demain* **sans remise,** I shall start to-
morrow without fail. **5.** (*a*) Coach-house.
Voiture de remise, hired carriage, livery carriage.
(*b*) *R. de locomotives,* engine-shed. [REMETTRE]
remis|er [rəmize], *v.tr.* **1.** To put up (vehicle);
to put (vehicle) in the coach-house; to put
(engine) in the shed. (Of cabman) **Aller remiser,**
to go back to the stables, to the garage (for the
night). **2.** *F:* To superannuate (s.o.). *s.m. -age.*
se **remiser,** (of winged game) to alight, to
take cover.
rémissible [remisibl], *a.* Remissible.
rémission [remisjɔ̃], *s.f.* **1.** Remission (of sin,
debt). **Sans rémission,** (i) unremitting(ly),
(ii) relentless(ly). **2.** *Med:* Remission, abatement
(of fever).
remmener [rɑ̃mne], *v.tr.* (Conj. like MENER) To
lead (s.o., cart) away (again). *Il fut remmené en
prison,* he was taken back to prison. [EMMENER]
remontant [rəmɔ̃tɑ̃]. **1.** *a.* (*a*) Ascending.
(*b*) Stimulating, strengthening, tonic (drink, etc.).
2. *s.m.* Tonic; *F:* pick-me-up.
remonte [rəmɔ̃ːt], *s.f.* **1.** Ascent (of salmon)
from sea to river. **2.** *Mil:* Remounting (of
cavalry). **Cheval de remonte,** remount.
remont|er [rəmɔ̃te]. **1.** *v.i.* (Aux. usu. *être,* occ.
avoir) (*a*) To go up again. *R. à, dans, sa chambre,*
to go up to one's room again. *R. sur le trône,* to
re-ascend the throne. *R. à cheval, sur son cheval,*
to remount one's horse. *R. vers la source de la
rivière,* to proceed, sail up, row up, towards the
source of the river. *R. sur l'eau,* to come (up) to
the surface again. *F:* (Of pers.) *Ses actions
remontent,* his fortunes are on the rise. (*b*) To go
back. *R. plus haut,* to go further back. *R. à la
cause de qch.,* to go back to the cause of sth.
Il fait r. sa famille à la Conquête, he traces back
his family to the Conquest. (*c*) *Nau:* (Of the
tide) To flow. **2.** *v.tr.* (*a*) To re-ascend; to climb
up, go up, (hill, stairs) again. *R. la rue,* to go
(walk, drive, ride) up the street. (*b*) To take,
carry, raise, (sth.) up. *R. ses chaussettes,* to pull
up one's socks. *R. son pantalon,* to hitch up one's
trousers. (*c*) To remount (cavalry). (*d*) To wind
(up) (clock, spring). *R. le courage de qn,
F:* **remonter qn,** to revive s.o.'s courage; to
cheer, *F:* buck, s.o. up. *Voilà qui vous remonte!
F:* that's a rare pick-me-up! (*e*) To refit; to
reassemble (mechanism, etc.); to restring

(violin, etc.); to remount (map). (*f*) *R. une ferme, un magasin,* to restock a farm, a shop. *R. sa garde-robe,* to replenish one's wardrobe. (*g*) *Th:* To put (a play) on again. *s.m.* **-age.**
  se remonter. 1. To recover one's strength, one's spirits. **2.** *Se r. de qch.,* to take in a fresh supply of sth.
  remontée, *s.f.* Climb (after descent).

remontoir [rəmɔ̃twaːr], *s.m.* **1.** Winder, button (of keyless watch). *Montre à r.,* stem-winder. **2.** (Watch-, clock-)key.

remontrance [rəmɔ̃trãːs], *s.f.* Remonstrance. Faire des remontrances à qn, to remonstrate with s.o.

remontrer [rəmɔ̃tre], *v.tr.* **1.** To show, demonstrate, (sth.) again. **2.** (*a*) *R. à qn sa faute, son devoir,* to point out to s.o. his error, his duty. (*b*) **En remontrer à qn,** to give advice to s.o.; to remonstrate with s.o. S.a. GROS-JEAN.

rémora [remɔra], *s.m.* Remora, sucking-fish.

remordre [rəmɔrdr]. **1.** *v.tr.* To bite again. **2.** *v.i. R. à qch.,* to have another bite or another go at sth. *F:* **Remordre à l'hameçon,** to be taken in again by the same trick.

remords [rəmɔːr], *s.m.* Remorse, self-reproach, compunction. *Un r.,* a twinge of remorse. Éprouver du, des, remords d'avoir fait qch., to be smitten with remorse, to feel remorse, at having done sth. Atteint de remords, bourrelé de remords, conscience-stricken. Sans remords, remorseless(ly).

remorque [rəmɔrk], *s.f.* **1.** Towing. Prendre un vaisseau, une auto, à la remorque, to take a ship, a car, in tow. *Sortir du port à la r.,* to be towed out of harbour. **2.** Tow-line, -rope. **3.** (*a*) Tow; vessel towed. (*b*) *Veh:* Trailer. Voiturette remorque, trailer-car. (*c*) *Rail:* Rame remorque, slip-portion.

remorqu|er [rəmɔrke], *v.tr.* To tow (ship or car); to trail (trailer); to pull, draw, haul (train). *s.m.* **-age.**

remorqueur, -euse [rəmɔrkœːr, -øːz]. **1.** *s.m.* Tug-boat; tug. *R. à vapeur,* steam-tug. **2.** Remorqueur or remorqueuse, traction-engine; tractor.

remoudre [rəmudr], *v.tr.* (Conj. like MOUDRE) To regrind (corn, coffee).

rémoudre [remudr], *v.tr.* (Conj. like MOUDRE) To resharpen; to regrind (tool).

rémoulade [remulad], *s.f. Cu:* Sharp sauce.

rémouleur [remulœːr], *s.m.* (Knife-and-scissors-) grinder.

remous [rəmu], *s.m.* Eddy (water or wind); wash (of ship); swirl (of the tide); backwash. *R. de courant,* eddy-current.

rempaill|er [rɑ̃paje], *v.tr.* To re-seat, re-bottom (rush-bottomed chair). *s.m.* **-age.**

rempailleur, -euse [rɑ̃pajœːr, -øːz], *s.* Chair-bottomer, chair-mender.

rempart [rɑ̃paːr], *s.m.* Rampart. *F: Le r. de nos libertés,* the bulwark of our liberties.

rempiéter [rɑ̃pjete], *v.tr.* (je rempiète; je rempiéterai) To re-foot, new-foot (stockings).

rempiler [rɑ̃pile], *v.i. P:* To re-engage for military service.
  rempilé, *s.m. P:* Re-engaged sergeant.

remplaçable [rɑ̃plasabl], *a.* Replaceable.

remplaçant, -ante [rɑ̃plasɑ̃, -ɑ̃ːt], *s.* Substitute (in team, etc.); locum tenens (of doctor, etc.).

remplacement [rɑ̃plasmɑ̃], *s.m.* Replacing, replacement; substitution. En remplacement de qch., in the place of sth.; as a substitute for sth.; in lieu of sth. De remplacement, refill (battery, pencil-lead, etc.); spare (tyre, man).

remplacer [rɑ̃plase], *v.tr.* (Conj. like PLACER) **1.** To take, fill, the place of, to serve as substitute for, to do duty for (s.o., sth.); to deputize for (s.o.). **2.** (*a*) To replace (s.o., sth.). *Employé difficile à r.,* clerk difficult to replace. *R. qch. par qch.,* to put sth. in the place of sth.; to replace sth. by sth. (*b*) To supersede (official).

remplage [rɑ̃plaːʒ], *s.m.* Rubble filling (within wall); backing.

rempli [rɑ̃pli], *s.m.* Tuck (in a dress).

remplier [rɑ̃plie], *v.tr.* To make, put, a tuck in (garment).

rempl|ir [rɑ̃pliːr], *v.tr.* **1.** (*a*) To fill up or refill (*de,* with); to fill in (gap, space). *Cela a rempli mon temps,* it occupied, took up, all my time. *R. une place,* to fill, occupy, a situation. *R. les fonctions de . . .,* to serve in the capacity of. . . . (*b*) To sew over, to darn (hole). **2.** *Les étrangers remplissaient la ville,* the strangers filled the town. *R. l'air de ses cris,* to fill the air with one's cries. **3.** To fill up, fill in, complete (a form, etc.). **4.** To fulfil (expectation, etc.). *R. les instructions de qn,* to carry out s.o.'s instructions. *R. le but,* to serve, answer, the purpose. *R. son devoir,* to do, perform, one's duty. *Th: R. un rôle,* to fill a part. *s.m.* **-issage.**
  se remplir, to fill.

remplumer (se) [sərɑ̃plyme], *v.pr.* **1.** (Of bird) To get new feathers. **2.** *F:* (Of pers.) (*a*) To put on flesh again. (*b*) To pick up again; to recover one's (fallen) fortunes.

remporter [rɑ̃pɔrte], *v.tr.* **1.** To carry, take, (sth.) back or away. **2.** To carry off, bear away (prize); to achieve (success); to win, reap, gain (victory, advantage) (*sur,* over). *R. la première place,* to obtain first place.

rempot|er [rɑ̃pɔte], *v.tr.* To repot (plant). *s.m.* **-age.**

remuant [rəmɥɑ̃], *a.* Restless, bustling; turbulent.

remue-ménage, *s.m.inv.* Stir, bustle, hullabaloo. *Il y eut un grand r.-m.,* there was a great to-do, a great stir.

remuement, remûment [rəmymɑ̃], *s.m.* **1.** Moving, stirring. **2.** Stir, disturbance.

remu|er [rəmɥe]. **1.** *v.tr.* To move (one's head); to move, shift (a piece of furniture); to stir (one's coffee); to turn up, turn over (the ground). *R. les masses,* to stir up, rouse, the masses. *F:* **Remuer ciel et terre,** to move heaven and earth, to leave no stone unturned. *R. beaucoup d'argent,* to handle a lot of money. *R. qn, le cœur de qn,* to stir, move, s.o., s.o.'s heart. **2.** *v.i.* (*a*) To move, stir, budge. (To child) *Ne remue pas tout le temps!* don't fidget! (*b*) *Dent qui remue,* loose tooth. *s.m.* **-age.**
  se remuer, to move, stir; to bustle about; to bestir oneself. **Remuez-vous un peu!** look sharp! look alive!

remueur, -euse [rəmɥœːr, -øːz]. **1.** *a.* Active, bustling. **2.** *s.* Mover; shifter (of furniture, etc.); stirrer-up (of trouble, etc.). *Remueurs d'affaires,* go-ahead business men; *F:* hustlers. **3.** *s.m.* Stirrer; stirring device.

rémunérateur, -trice [remyneratœːr, -tris]. **1.** *a.* Remunerative; paying, profitable. Peu rémunérateur, unremunerative. **2.** *s.* Remunerator, rewarder.

rémunération [remynerasjɔ̃], *s.f.* Remuneration, payment (*de,* for); consideration (for services rendered).

rémunér|er [remynere], *v.tr.* (je rémunère; je rémunérerai) To remunerate. **1.** To reward (s.o.). **2.** To pay for (services).

renâcl|er [rənɑkle], *v.i.* (*a*) (Of horse) To snort ; (of pers.) to sniff, snort. (*b*) *F:* To show reluctance (in doing sth.) ; to hang back. **Renâcler à la besogne,** to shirk one's job ; to be work-shy. *s.m.* **-eur.**

renaissance [rənɛsɑ̃:s], *s.f.* (*a*) Rebirth. (*b*) *R. des lettres,* revival of letters. *R. du printemps,* reappearance of spring. *Art: Lit:* **La Renaissance,** the Renaissance.

renaissant [rənɛsɑ̃], *a.* Renascent ; reviving.

renaître [rənɛːtr], *v.i.* (Conj. like NAÎTRE, but *p.p.* rené and comp. tenses are not in use, and *p.h.* je renaquis is rare) **1.** To be born again. *R. à l'espérance,* to feel one's hopes reviving. *R. à la vie,* to take on a new lease of life. **2.** To reappear ; (of plants) to spring up again ; (of hope, of the arts) to revive. **Faire renaître les espérances de qn,** to revive s.o.'s hopes.

rénal, -aux [renal, -o], *a. Anat: Med:* Renal. *Calcul r.,* stone in the kidneys.

renaqui-s, -t [rənaki]. See RENAÎTRE.

renard [rənaːr], *s.m.* (*a*) Fox. *La chasse au r.,* fox-hunting. *Lit:* **Maître renard,** Reynard (the Fox). *F:* **C'est un fin renard,** he's a sly dog, a sly fox. S.a. MARTRE. (*b*) *Ind: P:* Strike-breaker, *F:* blackleg.

renarde [rənard], *s.f. Z:* Vixen, she-fox.

renardeau [rənardo], *s.m.* Fox-cub.

rencaiss|er [rɑ̃kɛse], *v.tr.* **1.** To put (plants) in boxes or tubs again ; to re-box (orange-trees). **2.** To receive back (money) ; to have (money) refunded. *s.m.* **-age.** *s.m.* **-ement.**

renchaîner [rɑ̃ʃɛne], *v.tr.* To chain (dog, etc.) up again.

renchérir [rɑ̃ʃeriːr], *v.i.* (*a*) (Of goods) To get dearer ; to advance, increase, rise, in price. (*b*) (Of pers.) *R. sur qn,* (i) to outbid s.o. ; (ii) to outdo s.o. ; to go one better than s.o.
  renchéri, -ie, *a. & s. F:* Particular, fastidious, over-nice. **Ne faites pas tant le renchéri,** (i) don't be so fastidious ; (ii) don't put on such airs.

renchérissement [rɑ̃ʃerismɑ̃], *s.m.* Rise, advance, in price.

renchérisseur, -euse [rɑ̃ʃerisœːr, -øːz], *s.* (*a*) Outbidder. (*b*) Outdoer.

rencogner [rɑ̃kɔɲe], *v.tr. F:* To push, drive, (s.o.) into a corner.
  se rencogner *dans un angle,* to retreat into, to ensconce oneself in, a corner.

rencontre [rɑ̃kɔ̃ːtr], *s.f.* **1.** (*a*) Meeting, encounter. **Faire la rencontre de qn, faire une rencontre,** to meet, fall in with, s.o. **Aller, venir, à la rencontre de qn,** to go, come, to meet s.o. *Faire une mauvaise r.,* to have a nasty (wayside) experience. *Un bibelot de r.,* a curio that I came across, that I picked up. *Connaissance de r.,* chance acquaintance. (*b*) *R. de deux automobiles,* collision of two motor cars. (*c*) *R. de pétrole,* strike, striking, of oil. **2.** Encounter (of adversaries) ; duel ; skirmish ; brush (with the enemy). **3.** Occasion, conjuncture. *Cela vous servira en toute rencontre,* that will serve you on every occasion.

rencontrer [rɑ̃kɔ̃tre], *v.tr.* **1.** To meet, to fall in with (s.o.) ; to come upon, to light upon (sth.) ; to chance upon (an old friend) ; to run across (s.o.). *R. l'ennemi,* to encounter the enemy. *R. les yeux de qn,* to meet s.o.'s glance. *R. un obstacle,* to encounter a difficulty. *R. un indice,* to hit upon a clue. *Abs.* **Vous avez bien rencontré, vous avez rencontré juste,** you have guessed right. **2.** *R. un argument,* to refute an argument.

se rencontrer. 1. (*a*) To meet. (*b*) To collide ; (of ships) to run foul of one another. (*c*) To occur, to be met with. **Comme cela se rencontre!** how things do happen! **2.** (Of ideas) To agree, tally.

rendement [rɑ̃dmɑ̃], *s.m.* **1.** (*a*) Produce, yield (of ground, tax, etc.) ; return, profit (of transaction). *Actions à gros r.,* shares that bear high interest. (*b*) Output (of works, mine). **Travailler à plein rendement,** to work to full output. (*c*) *Mec.E:* **R. utile,** efficiency (of a machine). **Machine à bon rendement,** high-efficiency machine. **2.** *Rac:* **Rendement de temps,** time allowance ; time handicap.

rendez-vous [rɑ̃devu], *s.m.inv.* Rendezvous. **1.** Appointment. **Donner rendez-vous, fixer un rendez-vous, à qn,** to make, fix, an appointment with s.o. ; to arrange to meet s.o. **Prendre rendez-vous avec qn pour trois heures,** to arrange to meet s.o. at three o'clock. **2.** Place of meeting ; trysting-place (of lovers) ; resort, haunt.

rendormir [rɑ̃dɔrmiːr], *v.tr.* (Conj. like DORMIR) To send, lull, (s.o.) to sleep again.
  se rendormir, to go to sleep again ; to drop off to sleep again.

rendosser [rɑ̃dose], *v.tr. R.* son habit, to put one's coat on again. *F: R. l'uniforme,* to don one's uniform again, to return to military life.

rendre [rɑ̃ːdr], *v.tr.* **1.** (*a*) To give back, return, restore ; to repay, pay back (money). *R. son salut à qn,* to return s.o.'s bow or salute. *R. qn à la santé, à la liberté,* to restore s.o. to health, to liberty. *R. la monnaie d'une pièce de cinq francs,* to give change for a five-franc piece. S.a. MONNAIE 2. **Rendre le bien pour le mal,** to return good for evil. *F:* **Je le lui rendrai!** I'll be even with him yet! (*b*) To render, give. **Rendre hommage à qn,** to render, do, pay, homage to s.o. S.a. HONNEUR 3. **Rendre grâce à qn,** to give, render, thanks to s.o. **Rendre service à qn,** to render, do, s.o. a service. **Rendre la justice,** to dispense, administer, justice. S.a. JUSTICE 1. **Rendre compte de qch.** See COMPTE. (*c*) To yield (produce, etc.) ; (of flower) to give out (scent) ; (of musical instrument) to give forth, emit (sound) ; (of land, taxes, etc.) to give, produce, yield (so much). **Terre qui ne rend pas,** land that yields no return ; unproductive land. (*d*) *Abs.* (Of rope) To stretch. **2.** To convey, deliver. *R. des marchandises à destination,* to deliver goods. *Rendu à bord,* delivered on board. **3.** (*a*) To bring up, throw up (food) ; *Abs.* to vomit. **Rendre l'âme, la vie,** to breathe one's last, to give up the ghost. S.a. GORGE 3. (*b*) *Jur: R. un arrêt,* to issue, pronounce, a decree. *R. un jugement,* to deliver a judgment. **4.** To render up, give up, surrender, yield (fortress). **Rendre les armes,** to surrender one's arms. **Rendre son âme à Dieu,** to commit one's soul to God. **5.** To reproduce, render, express. *R. l'aspect de qch.,* to render the appearance of sth. *R. le sens de l'auteur,* to express, convey, the author's meaning. **6.** *Pred. Le homard me rend malade,* lobster makes me ill. *Il se rend ridicule,* he is making himself ridiculous.

se rendre. 1. *Se r. dans un lieu,* to betake oneself, proceed, repair, to a place ; to make one's way to a place. *Se r. en toute hâte à un endroit,* to make all speed to a place. *Se r. chez qn,* to call on s.o. **Se rendre à une assignation,** to keep an appointment. **2.** (*a*) To surrender ; to give in, to yield. *Se r. prisonnier,* to give oneself up. **Rendez-vous!** hands up! (*b*) **Se rendre à la raison,** to yield to reason.

35

rendu. 1. *a.* **Rendu (de fatigue),** exhausted, done up, dead-beat. **2.** *s.m.* (*a*) *Art:* Rendering (of subject). *R. exact des couleurs,* right reproduction of colour. (*b*) *Com:* Returned article ; return.

rêne [rɛn], *s.f.* Usu. *pl.* Rein. *Fausses rênes,* bearing-rein, check-rein. *Rênes de bride,* bit reins. **A bout de rênes,** with reins slack. **Lâcher les rênes,** to slacken the reins ; to give a horse his head. *F:* **Prendre, tenir, les rênes du gouvernement,** to assume, hold, the reins of government.

renégat, -ate [rənega, -at], *s.* Renegade, turncoat.

rêner [rene], *v.tr.* **1.** To put the reins on (horse). **2.** To rein in (horse).

renfaît|er [rɑ̃fete], *v.tr.* To new-ridge, repair (roof). *s.m.* **-age.**

renferm|er [rɑ̃fɛrme], *v.tr.* **1.** To shut up, lock up, again. **2.** (*a*) To shut, lock, (sth., s.o.) up. *R. un fou,* to shut up, confine, a madman. (*b*) *Se r. dans ses instructions,* to confine oneself to one's instructions. **3.** To contain, comprise, include, enclose. *Livre qui renferme des idées nouvelles,* book that contains new ideas. *Le crâne renferme le cerveau,* the skull encloses the brain. *s.m.* **-ement.**

se renfermer *dans le silence, en soi-même,* to withdraw into silence, into oneself.

renfermé. 1. *a.* Uncommunicative, close (person). **2.** *s.m.* **Odeur de renfermé,** close smell, fusty smell. **Sentir le renfermé,** to smell stuffy.

renflammer [rɑ̃flɑme], *v.tr.* To rekindle.

se renflammer, to take fire again ; to flare up, blaze up. *F:* *Son cœur se renflamma,* his love rekindled.

renflement [rɑ̃fləmɑ̃], *s.m.* **1.** Swelling, bulging. **2.** Bulge, boss ; swell (of gun).

renfler [rɑ̃fle], *v.tr. & i.* To swell (out) ; to enlarge, to (re)inflate.

renflé, *a.* Swelling (pillar, etc.) ; (pillar) with entasis ; ventricose (shell) ; bluff-bowed (ship).

renflou|er [rɑ̃flue], *v.tr.* **1.** To refloat, set afloat (stranded ship). **2.** To reinflate, top up (balloon). *s.m.* **-age.** *s.m.* **-ement.**

renfoncement [rɑ̃fɔ̃smɑ̃], *s.m.* **1.** Knocking in (of sth.) again ; driving in (of sth.) deeper. **2.** (*a*) Hollow, recess, cavity, dent. (*b*) *Typ:* Indention, indentation (of line).

renfoncer [rɑ̃fɔ̃se], *v.tr.* (Conj. like ENFONCER) **1.** To knock in, drive in ; to drive (sth.) further in. **Renfoncer son chapeau,** (i) to pull down one's hat ; (ii) to bash in one's hat. **Renfoncer ses armes,** to choke back one's tears. **2.** (*a*) To recess, set back (façade, etc.). (*b*) *Typ:* To indent (line).

renfoncé, *a.* Deep-set ; sunken (eyes).

renfor|cer [rɑ̃fɔrse]. **1.** *v.tr.* (Conj. like FORCER) (*a*) To reinforce (garrison, etc.). (*b*) To strengthen, reinforce, stiffen, brace (wall, beam) ; to truss (girder, etc.) ; to back (map). *Citer des faits pour r. son dire,* to quote facts to back up one's assertion. (*c*) To reinforce, magnify (sound) ; to intensify (colour, *Phot:* negative or print). **2.** *v.i.* (Of wind) To grow stronger. *s.m.* **-çage.** *s.m.* **-cement.**

se renforcer, to grow stronger, more vigorous ; to gather strength.

renforcé, *a.* Stout, strong (cloth, etc.) ; reinforced, trussed (girder) ; thickset (horse). *F:* **Sot renforcé,** downright, arrant, fool.

renfort [rɑ̃fɔːr], *s.m.* **1.** Reinforcement(s) ; fresh supply (of troops, etc.). **Cheval de renfort,** extra horse, trace-horse. **En renfort,** in support. *F:* **Pour renfort de potage,** to make matters worse. **2.** Strengthening piece ; reinforce (of gun) ; stiffener, backing. **Plaque, tôle, de renfort,** stiffening plate. **Tenon à renfort,** tusk tenon.

renfrogn|er [rɑ̃frɔɲe], *v.tr. R. sa mine, son front,* to knit one's brows ; to scowl. *s.m.* **-ement.**

se renfrogner, to frown, scowl ; to look glum.

renfrogné, *a.* Frowning (face) ; sullen, crabbed (person) ; glum (look).

rengag|er [rɑ̃gaʒe], *v.tr.* (Conj. like ENGAGER) **1.** (*a*) To re-engage ; to engage (s.o.) again ; to renew (combat). (*b*) *v.i.* To re-enlist. **2.** To pledge, pawn, (sth.) again. *s.m.* **-ement.**

se rengager, to re-enlist, rejoin.

rengagé, *a. & s.m.* Re-enlisted (usu. N.C.O.).

rengaine [rɑ̃gɛːn], *s.f. F:* **Vieille rengaine,** (i) old refrain ; (ii) old story ; threadbare story. *C'est toujours la même r., la vieille r.,* it's always the same old story.

rengainer [rɑ̃gene], *v.tr.* To sheathe, put up (one's sword). *F:* **Rengainer son compliment,** to shut up, to say no more.

rengorgement [rɑ̃gɔrʒəmɑ̃], *s.m.* Strut (of peacock) ; swagger.

rengorger (se) [sərɑ̃gɔrʒe], *v.pr.* (Conj. like ENGORGER) To strut, swagger ; to give oneself airs.

reniement, renîment [rənimɑ̃], *s.m.* **1.** Disowning (of friend) ; repudiation (of opinion) ; denial (of Christ). **2.** (*a*) Disavowal (of action). (*b*) Abjuration (of one's faith).

renier [rənje], *v.tr.* **1.** To disown (friend, opinion) ; to repudiate (opinion) ; to deny (Christ). *F: R. Dieu,* to utter a profane oath ; *F:* to swear. **2.** (*a*) To disavow (action). (*b*) To abjure (one's faith). **Chrétien renié,** renegade.

reniflage [rənifla:ʒ], *s.m. I.C.E:* Popping back.

reniflard [rənifla:r], *s.m.* **1.** (*a*) Sniffing-valve ; air-valve, blow-valve (of steam boiler). (*b*) = RENIFLEUR 2. **2.** Strainer, rose (of pump).

reniflement [rənifləmɑ̃], *s.m.* (*a*) Sniffing, snuffling, snorting. (*b*) Snivelling. **2.** Sniff, snort.

renifler [rənifle]. **1.** *v.i.* (*a*) To sniff, snort, snuffle. *R. sur qch.,* to sniff at, turn up one's nose at, sth. (Of horse) **Renifler sur l'avoine,** to be off his feed. (*b*) To snivel. (*c*) *I.C.E:* To pop back. **2.** *v.tr.* (*a*) To sniff (up) (sth.). (*b*) To sniff, smell (flower).

renifleur, -euse [rəniflœːr, -øːz], *s.* **1.** Sniffer. **2.** *s.m. I.C.E:* Breather(-pipe).

reniv|eler [rənivle], *v.tr.* (Conj. like NIVELER) To relevel (sth.) again ; to re-level ; to top up (accumulator). *s.m.* **-ellement.**

renne [rɛn], *s.m. Z:* Reindeer.

renom [rənɔ̃], *s.m.* Renown, fame. **En renom,** renowned, famed, well known. **Se faire un mauvais renom,** to get a bad name.

renommer [rənɔme], *v.tr.* **1.** To re-elect, re-appoint. **2.** *A:* **Se faire renommer,** to make oneself renowned, famous.

renommé, *a.* Renowned, famed, celebrated.

renommée, *s.f.* **1.** (*a*) Renown, fame ; good name. *Prov:* **Bonne renommée vaut mieux que ceinture dorée,** a good name is better than riches. (*b*) *Connaître qn de r.,* to know s.o. by repute. **2.** Rumour, report. Esp. *Jur:* (Preuve par) **commune renommée,** hearsay evidence ; common report.

renonce [rənɔ̃:s], *s.f. Cards:* **1.** Renounce ; inability to follow suit. **Avoir une renonce à cœur,** to be short of hearts. **2. Fausse renonce,** revoke. *Faire une r.,* to revoke.

renoncement [rənɔ̃smɑ̃], *s.m.* **1.** Renouncing, renouncement (*à,* of). **2.** (*a*) Self-denial. (*b*) Renunciation.

renoncer [rənɔ̃se], *v.* (je renonçai(s); n. renon-
çons) **1.** *v.ind.tr.* (*a*) R. *à qch.*, to renounce, give
up, forgo, sth. R. *à faire qch.*, (i) to forgo doing
sth.; (ii) to give up, drop, the idea of doing sth.
R. *à un droit*, to waive a right. R. *à une réclamation, à une prétention*, to renounce, withdraw,
waive, a claim. **Renoncer à la lutte**, to give up
the struggle; *F:* to throw up the sponge.
Y renoncer, to abandon the attempt or the idea;
to give it up (as a bad job). (*b*) R. *à ses dieux,
à sa religion*, to renounce one's gods, to abnegate
one's religion. (*c*) (At cards) (i) To renounce, to
fail to follow suit; (ii) to revoke. **2.** *v.tr.* R. *sa
foi*, to renounce, abnegate, one's faith. R. *sa
patrie*, to renounce one's country.

renonciateur, -trice [rənɔ̃sjatœːr, -tris], *s.*
1. *Jur:* Releasor. **2.** Renouncer.
renonciation [rənɔ̃sjasjɔ̃], *s.f.* **1.** *Jur:* R. *à un
droit*, renunciation, waiver, of a right. **2.** Renunciation, abnegation.
renoncule [rənɔ̃kyl], *s.f. Bot:* Ranunculus;
buttercup. R. *langue*, spearwort. R. *double*,
bachelor's buttons.
renouée [rənwe], *s.f. Bot: F:* Polygonum,
knot-grass; hogweed.
renouer [rənwe], *v.tr.* (*a*) To tie (up), knot,
(sth.) again. (*b*) To renew, resume (conversation,
etc.). **Renouer** (amitié) **avec qn**, to renew one's
friendship, an intimacy, with s.o. *s.m.* **-ement.**
renouveau [rənuvo], *s.m.* (*a*) *A. & Lit:* Spring-
tide; spring (of the year). (*b*) *F:* R. *de jeunesse,
d'amour*, renewal of youth, renewed love.
renouvelable [rənuvlabl], *a.* Renewable.
renouveler [r(ə)nuvle], *v.tr.* (je renouvelle;
je renouvellerai) **1.** (*a*) To renew or renovate
(one's wardrobe, etc.). R. *l'air d'une salle*, to air
a room. (*b*) R. *sa maison, son service*, to make a
complete change of servants. R. *son personnel*, to
renew one's staff. (*c*) R. *la face du pays*, to alter
the whole appearance of the country. **2.** To
renew (promise, alliance, etc.); to revive
(custom). **Renouveler connaissance avec qn**, to
renew acquaintance with s.o. *Com:* R. *une
commande*, to repeat an order. **Commandes
renouvelées**, repeat orders. **3.** *v.i.* (*a*) La lune
vient de r., the moon is new. (*b*) R. *de zèle*, to
act with renewed zeal. *s.m.* **-ellement.**
se renouveler. 1. To be renewed. **2.** To
recur; to happen again.
rénovateur, -trice [renɔvatœːr, -tris]. **1.** *a.* Renovating. **2.** *s.* Renovator, restorer.
rénovation [renɔvasjɔ̃], *s.f.* **1.** Renovation,
restoration (of morals); (religious) revival.
2. Renewing, renewal (of a vow, *Jur:* of a
title).
rénover [renɔve], *v.tr.* **1.** To renovate, restore
(morals, etc.). **2.** *Jur:* To renew (a title).
renseignement [rãsɛɲmã], *s.m.* (Piece of)
information, (piece of) intelligence; indication.
Donner des renseignements sur qch., to give
information, particulars, on, about, regarding,
sth. **Prendre des renseignements sur qch.**, to
make inquiries about sth.; to inquire about sth.
Aller aux renseignements, to make inquiries.
Prendre un domestique sans renseignements, to
engage a servant without references. **Bureau de
renseignements**, information bureau, inquiry
office. *Pour plus amples renseignements s'adresser
à . . .*, for further information, for further particulars, apply to. . . . *Mil: etc:* **Service de(s)
renseignements**, intelligence (service or department).
renseigner [rãsɛɲe], *v.tr.* R. *qn sur qch.*, to
inform s.o., give s.o. information, about sth.

On vous a mal renseigné, you have been misinformed. **Par qui vous êtes-vous fait renseigner?**
from whom did you seek information?
se renseigner *v.pr.*, to make inquiries,
find out, about sth.; to inquire, ask, about sth.
rente [rãːt], *s.f.* **1.** *Pol.Ec:* Revenue, rent. R.
foncière, ground rent. **2.** Usu. *pl.* (Unearned)
income. *Avoir cent mille francs de rente(s)*, to
have a private income of a hundred thousand
francs. *Vivre de ses rentes*, to live on one's private means. **3.** Annuity, pension, allowance.
Rente viagère, life annuity. *Faire une r. de mille
francs à qn*, to allow s.o. a thousand francs a year.
4. Rente(s) (sur l'État), (government) stock(s),
bonds. **Rentes consolidées**, consolidated funds,
F: consols.
renter [rãte], *v.tr.* (*a*) To assign a yearly income
to (s.o.). (*b*) To endow (school, etc.).
renté, *a.* (*a*) Endowed (hospital, etc.).
(*b*) (Person) of independent means.
rentier, -ière [rãtje, -jɛːr], *s.* **1.** (*a*) *Fin:* Stockholder, fund-holder. (*b*) Annuitant. (*c*) *Pol.Ec:*
Rentier. **2.** *F:* Person of independent means.
Petit rentier, small investor.
rentoiler [rãtwale], *v.tr.* To reline (cuff); to
remount (map); to back (a painting). *s.m.* **-age.**
rentraire [rãtrɛːr], *v.tr.* (*p.p.* rentrait; no other
parts) **1.** To fine-draw (seam). **2.** = STOPPER.
s.m. **-ayage.**
rentraiture [rãtrɛtyːr], *s.f.* Fine-drawn seam.
rentrant, -ante [rãtrã, -ãːt]. **1.** *a.* Re-entrant
(angle). **2.** *s.* New player. *Cards:* Cutter in.
3. *s.m.* Recess (in wall).
rentrer [rãtre]. **I.** *v.i.* (Aux. être) **1.** (*a*) To
re-enter; to come, go, in again. R. *dans sa
chambre*, to return to, go back into, one's room.
Nau: R. *au port*, to return, put back, to port.
R. *en faveur*, to return to favour. R. *dans ses droits*,
to recover one's rights. R. *dans ses avances*, to
recover money advanced. *Faire r. qn dans l'ordre*,
to reduce s.o. to order again. (Of actor) R. *en
scène*, to come on again. *Macbeth rentre*, re-enter
Macbeth. *F:* **Rentrer en danse, en lice**, to return
to the fray. (*b*) To return home, come home,
come in again. *Il est l'heure de r.*, it is time we
went home. R. *dîner*, to go home to dinner.
Faire rentrer les enfants, to call the children in.
(*c*) (Of law-courts, etc.) To re-open, to resume;
(of Parliament) to reassemble; (of schoolboy) to
return to school. (Of official) R. *en fonction(s)*,
to resume duty, to resume his duties. (*d*) *Faire
r. qch. dans sa boîte*, to get sth. back into its box.
(*e*) (Of money, etc.) To come in. **Faire rentrer
ses fonds**, to call in one's money. **2.** (Intensive
form of *entrer*) (*a*) To enter, go in. *Cards:* To
cut in. R. *en soi-même*, to retire within oneself;
to examine one's conscience. *P:* **Rentrer dedans
à qn**, to pitch into s.o. *S.a.* COQUILLE 1. (*b*) *Tubes
qui rentrent les uns dans les autres*, tubes that fit
into one another. *F:* **Les jambes me rentrent
dans le corps**, I am too tired to stand. (*c*) *Cela ne
rentre pas dans mes fonctions*, that does not fall
within my province. (*d*) *Typ:* **Faire rentrer une
ligne**, to indent a line.
II. rentrer, *v.tr.* To take in, bring in, get
in, draw in, pull in (sth.); to put away (instrument); to heave in, haul in (rope); to haul
down (the colours); to lay in, ship, unship (the
oars). R. *une embarcation*, to get in, haul up, a
boat. R. *la récolte*, to gather in the harvest.
Qui va r. les chaises? who's going to carry in the
chairs? R. *sa chemise*, to tuck in one's shirt.
rentré, *a.* **1.** Hollow, sunken (eyes, cheeks).
2. Checked, suppressed (feelings, laughter).

rentrée, *s.f.* **1.** (*a*) Return, home-coming. *Mus:* R. *du motif principal,* re-entry of the original theme. (*b*) Re-opening (of schools, law-courts); reassembly (of Parliament). *Sch:* La rentrée des classes, the beginning of term. **2.** (*a*) Taking in, encashment (of money); getting in, collection (of taxes). Opérer une rentrée, to collect a sum of money. *J'attends des rentrées,* I am expecting to receive payments. (*b*) Ingathering, getting in (of crops). **3.** Coming in. **4.** *Fb:* R. en touche, throw-in.

renversant [rɑ̃vɛrsɑ̃], *a.* *F:* Astounding, staggering (news, etc.); stunning (hat).

renverse [rɑ̃vɛrs], *s.f.* **1.** *Nau:* Turn (of tide); change round (of the wind). **2.** Tomber à la renverse, (i) to fall backwards; (ii) *F:* to be bowled over (by piece of news).

renversement [rɑ̃vɛrsəmɑ̃], *s.m.* **1.** (*a*) Reversal, inversion (*Opt:* of image; *Log:* of proposition). (*b*) *Mch:* Renversement de la vapeur, reversing (of engine). *Mécanisme de r.,* reversing gear. (*c*) Turn(ing) (of the tide); backing (of the wind). **2.** Overthrow; overturning, upsetting. Charrette à renversement, tip-up cart. *Mec:* Couple de renversement, torque.

renvers|er [rɑ̃vɛrse]. **1.** *v.tr.* (*a*) To reverse, invert (*Opt:* image; *Log:* proposition). *Mus:* To invert (interval). R. un levier, to throw over a lever. Renverser la marche, *Mch:* to reverse (the engine); *Aut:* to go into reverse. *F:* Renverser les rôles, to turn the tables on s.o. (*b*) To turn upside down. *Com:* "Ne pas renverser," 'this side up.' *F:* Tout renverser, to turn everything topsy-turvy. Renverser l'esprit à qn, to send s.o. out of his wits. (*c*) To knock over; to throw down; to overturn, upset (pail); to spill (liquid). *F:* Une odeur à vous renverser, a smell fit to knock you down. (*d*) To overthrow (government, theory, etc.). (*e*) *F:* To astound, astonish, amaze. **2.** *v.i.* To overturn, upset, to capsize. *a.* -able. *s.* -eur, -euse.

se renverser, to fall over, fall down; to upset, overturn; to capsize. Se renverser sur sa chaise, (i) to lean back, loll back, in one's chair; (ii) to tilt one's chair back.

renversé, *a.* **1.** Inverted, reversed. *Cu:* Crème renversée, custard mould. *F:* C'est le monde renversé! it is preposterous! **2.** Il avait le visage renversé, he looked very much upset.

renvoi [rɑ̃vwa], *s.m.* **1.** Return(ing), sending back (of goods); throwing back (of ball); reverberation (of sound); reflecting (of light). *Rugby Fb:* Kick-out (from the 25-line). *Ten:* Return. **2.** Dismissal (of servant); discharge (of troops). **3.** Putting off, postponement; adjournment (of debate). **4.** Referring, reference (of a matter to some authority). **5.** (*a*) *Typ:* Reference (mark). (*b*) Caret; insertion mark. R. en marge, marginal alteration. (*c*) *Mus:* Repeat (mark). **6.** *Mec.E:* (*a*) Renvoi de mouvement, counter-gear(ing). Arbre de renvoi, countershaft, lay shaft. *Levier de r.,* (i) reversing lever; (ii) bell-crank lever. (*b*) Pulley. **7.** *Med:* Eructation, belch. *F:* (Of food) Donner des renvois, to repeat. **8.** Backwater (of sea). Renvoi de vent, eddy-wind. R. de courant, cross-current.

renvoler (se) [sərɑ̃vɔle], *v.pr.* To fly away again.

renvoyer [rɑ̃vwaje], *v.tr.* (Conj. like ENVOYER) **1.** To send back; to return (sth.); to throw back, re-echo, reverberate (sound); to reflect (heat, light). *F:* Être renvoyé de Caïphe à Pilate, to be driven from pillar to post. S.a. BALLE[1] 1. **2.** (*a*) To send turn, (s.o.) away.

Jur: To discharge (defendant). R. des troupes dans leurs foyers, to dismiss troops. *F:* Renvoyer qn bien loin, to send s.o. packing; to send s.o. about his business. *Jur:* Le plaideur de sa demande, to nonsuit the plaintiff. (*b*) To dismiss, *F:* sack (servant, etc.); to expel (boy from school). **3.** To put off, postpone, defer, adjourn (a matter). **4.** To refer. R. un projet à une commission, to send a bill to a committee. Les numéros renvoient aux notes, the numbers refer to the notes.

réorganisation [reɔrganizasjɔ̃], *s.f.* Reorganization.

réorganiser [reɔrganize], *v.tr.* To reorganize.

réouverture [reuvɛrtyr], *s.f.* Reopening (of theatre, etc.); resumption.

repaire [rəpɛr], *s.m.* Den; lair (of wild beasts); nest (of pirates); haunt (of criminals).

repaître [rəpɛtr], *v.tr.* (*pr.p.* repaissant; *p.p.* repu; *pr.ind.* je repais, il repaît, n. repaissons; *pr.sub.* je repaisse; *p.h.* je repus; *fu.* je repaîtrai) (*a*) To feed (animal). (*b*) R. qn d'espérances, to feed s.o. on hopes. R. ses yeux de (la vue de) qch., to feast one's eyes on (the sight of) sth.

se repaître. (*a*) To eat one's fill. (*b*) Se r. de qch., to feed on, eat one's fill of, sth.; to batten, raven, on sth. *F:* Se r. de sang, to wallow in blood. Se r. de chimères, to feed one's mind on fancies.

repu, *a.* Satiated, full; sated.

répandre [repɑ̃dr], *v.tr.* **1.** To pour out; to spill, drop, shed. R. des larmes, son sang, to shed tears, one's blood. **2.** To spread, diffuse, scatter (light); to give off, give out (heat, scent); to strew (flowers); to sprinkle (sand). R. une forte odeur, to give off a strong smell. R. la terreur, to spread terror. R. une nouvelle, to spread, circulate, broadcast, a piece of news. **3.** To scatter, distribute, lavish (money, alms).

se répandre. 1. (Of pers.) (*a*) Se r. dans le monde, to go a great deal into society. (*b*) Se r. en un long discours, en invectives, to launch into a long speech, into abuse. Se r. en excuses, to apologize profusely. Se r. en menaces, to pour out threats. **2.** (*a*) (Of liquid) To spill; to run over. (*b*) To spread. L'odeur s'en répand partout, the smell of it spreads everywhere. Sa chevelure se répandit sur ses épaules, her hair came down over her shoulders. Cette opinion se répand, this opinion is gaining ground, is spreading. *Impers.* Il s'est répandu que . . ., the rumour has spread, has gone abroad, that. . .,

répandu, *a.* **1.** (Of thg) Wide-spread, widely distributed, prevalent, in general use. Opinion répandue, generally received opinion. **2.** (Of pers.) Widely known, much in evidence.

reparaître [rəparɛtr], *v.i.* (Conj. like PARAÎTRE. Aux. usu. *avoir*) To reappear; to make one's appearance again; *F:* to turn up again.

réparateur, -trice [reparatœr, -tris]. **1.** *a.* Repairing, restoring; refreshing (sleep). **2.** *s.* Repairer, mender.

réparation [reparasjɔ̃], *s.f.* Reparation. **1.** Repairing. Être en réparation, to be under repair. Route en r., road 'up' (for repairs). Faire des réparations, to make repairs. Réparations d'entretien, keeping in repair. S.a. LOCATIF[1]. **2.** Atonement, amends, redress. En réparation d'un tort, in reparation of, in atonement for, a wrong. R. par les armes, duel. S.a. HONNEUR I. *Jur:* R. légale, legal redress. Réparation civile, compensation. *Fb:* Coup de pied de réparation, penalty kick.

répar|er [repare], *v.tr.* **1.** To repair, mend; to overhaul (machine); to refit (ship). R. ses forces, to restore, recruit, one's strength. *R. ses pertes,* to retrieve, make good, one's losses. *La maison a besoin d'être réparée,* the house needs putting in repair. **2.** To make atonement, make amends, for (misdeed); to rectify (mistake); to put (mistake) right. *R. un tort, un dommage,* to redress a wrong, an injury. *R. les dégâts,* to make good the damage. *R. le mal,* to undo the mischief. *a.* **-able.**

reparler [rəparle], *v.i.* *R. de qch.,* to speak about sth. again. *R. à qn,* to speak to s.o. again.

repartir [rəparti:r], *v.i.* (Conj. like PARTIR) **I.** (Aux. *être*) To set out again, go off again, start (out) again. *Je repars pour Paris,* I am off to Paris again. **2.** (Aux. *avoir*) To retort, reply.

repartie, *s.f.* Repartee; retort, rejoinder (*à,* to). **Avoir l'esprit de repartie, avoir la repartie prompte,** to be quick at repartee.

répart|ir [rəparti:r], *v.tr.* (je répartis, n. répartissons) **I.** To distribute, divide, share out (*entre, amongst*). *R. un dividende,* to distribute a dividend. *Charge uniformément répartie,* evenly distributed load. **2.** To apportion, assess (taxes); to allot, allocate (shares). *a.* **-issable.**

répartiteur [rəpartitœ:r], *s.m.* Distributor, apportioner. *Mil:* Billet master. *Nau:* Adjuster, stater (of average). *Adm:* (Commissaire) **répartiteur,** assessor of taxes.

répartition [rəpartisjɔ̃], *s.f.* **I.** Distribution; dividing up (of work); sharing out (of expenses); adjudication (of bankrupt's debts). **2.** Apportionment, allocation (of land); allotment (of shares); assessment (of taxes).

repas [rəpɑ], *s.m.* Meal, repast; (of horse) feed, feeding. **Repas de noce,** wedding breakfast or banquet. **Faire un repas,** to have, take, a meal. *Léger r., petit r.,* light meal; snack; quick lunch. *Aux heures de r.,* at meal times. *Prendre ses r. chez qn,* to board with s.o.

repass|er [rəpɑse]. **I.** *v.i.* (Aux. usu. *être*) To repass; to pass (by) again, go by again. *R. chez qn,* to call on s.o. again. *R. en Angleterre,* to cross over to England again. **Une idée me repasse dans l'esprit,** an idea keeps running through my mind. **2.** *v.tr.* (*a*) To repass; to pass by, pass over, cross (over), (sth.) again. (*b*) To go over, look over, (sth.) (again). *R. qch. dans son esprit,* to go over sth. in one's mind. *R. une leçon, un rôle,* to go over a lesson, a part. (*c*) To convey over again. *Le batelier nous repassera,* the boatman will take us back. *R. un plat à qn,* to pass s.o. a dish again. *Repassez-moi cette lettre,* let me see that letter again. *F:* **Repasser une fausse pièce à qn,** to palm off a bad coin on s.o. (*d*) To sharpen, whet, grind (knife, tool); to strop (razor). (*e*) To iron (clothes). **Fer à repasser,** flat-iron, laundry iron. **Planche à repasser,** ironing board. (*f*) *R. une allée,* to rake (over) a path. *s.m.* **-age.**

repasseur, -euse [rəpasœ:r, -ø:z], *s.* **I.** *Ind:* Finisher. **2.** *s.m.* Grinder (of knives, etc.). **3.** *s.f.* Repasseuse, ironer (person or machine).

repav|er [rəpave], *v.tr.* To repave. *s.m.* **-age.**

repêch|er [rəpeʃe], *v.tr.* (*a*) To fish (sth.) up (again), out (again); to pick up (torpedo). (*b*) *F:* To rescue, *F:* to fish out (drowning man). **Repêcher un candidat à l'oral,** to give a candidate a chance of scraping through at the *viva voce.* *Ceux qui ont échoué au mois de juillet peuvent se r. en octobre,* those who failed in July get a second chance in October. *s.m.* **-age.**

repeindre [rəpɛ̃:dr], *v.tr.* (Conj. like PEINDRE) **I.** To repaint; to paint (sth.) again. **2.** *Se r. un*

événement passé, to recall to mind, to revisualize, a past event.

repenser [rəpɑ̃se], *v.i.* To think again (*à,* of, about). *Je n'y ai pas repensé,* (i) I did not give it another thought; (ii) I forgot all about it.

repentant [rəpɑ̃tɑ̃], *a.* Repentant.

repentir (se) [sərəpɑ̃ti:r]. **I.** *v.pr.* (pr.p. se repentant; *p.p.* repenti; *pr.ind.* je me repens, il se repent; *pr.sub.* je me repente; *p.h.* je me repentis; *fu.* je me repentirai) *Se r. de qch.,* to repent, rue, sth.; to be sorry for sth. *Se r. d'avoir fait qch.,* to repent having done sth. **Faire repentir qn,** to make s.o. repent. **II. repentir,** *s.m.* Repentance. **repenti, -ie,** *a. & s.* Repentant. Esp. **(Fille) repentie,** Magdalen(e). *Les justes et les repentis,* the righteous and the repentant.

repercer [rəpɛrse], *v.tr.* (Conj. like PERCER) To pierce, bore, perforate, (sth.) again.

répercussion [rəpɛrkysjɔ̃], *s.f.* Repercussion. (*a*) Back-lash (of an explosion); reverberation (of sound). (*b*) Consequential effects (of an action).

répercuter [rəpɛrkyte], *v.tr.* To reverberate, reflect back (sound); to reflect (light, heat). **se répercuter. I.** To reverberate. **2.** To have repercussions.

reperdre [rəpɛrdr], *v.tr.* To lose again. **se reperdre,** to lose one's way again.

repère [rəpɛ:r], *s.m.* (*a*) Reference (to datum line). *Surv:* **Ligne de repère,** datum line. **Point de repère,** reference mark, guide mark, adjusting mark (on instrument); landmark; *Surv:* bench-mark. *F:* **Les points de repère dans la vie,** the landmarks in one's life. S.a. NIVELLEMENT I. (*b*) *Aut:* Wing indicator. **repér|er** [rəpere], *v.tr.* (je repère; je repérerai) **I.** (*a*) To mark (instrument) with guide marks or reference marks. *W.Tel:* To log (station). (*b*) To adjust, fix, set, (instrument) by guide marks, by reference marks. **2.** *Artil:* To locate, *F:* to spot (gun, etc.). *R. le point de chute d'un obus,* to mark the fall of a shell. *F:* **Il m'a repéré de sa loge,** he spotted me from his box. *s.m.* **-age. se repérer,** to take one's bearings.

répertoire [rəpɛrtwa:r], *s.m.* **I.** Index, table, list, catalogue. *R. à onglets,* thumb-index, thumb-register. *R. d'adresses,* (i) directory; (ii) address-book. **2.** Repertory, repository (of information). **3.** *Th:* Repertoire, repertory. **Pièce de, du, répertoire,** stock piece.

répertorier [rəpɛrtɔrje], *v.tr.* **I.** To index (file, etc.); to make a reference table for (sth.). **2.** To index (item); to enter (item) in the index.

répéter [repete], *v.tr.* (je répète; je répéterai) (*a*) To repeat; to say or do (sth.) (over) again. *Chose qui se répète souvent,* thing that happens over and over again. *Cela ne se répétera pas,* it will not occur again. S.a. COMPAS 2. **Je ne me le ferai pas répéter,** I shall not require to be told twice. (*b*) *Th:* To rehearse (play). **se répéter. I.** (Of pers.) To repeat oneself. **2.** (Of decimal fractions) To repeat, recur.

répétiteur, -trice [repetitœ:r, -tris], *a. & s.* (*a*) **(Maître) répétiteur, (maîtresse) répétitrice,** assistant-master, assistant-mistress (in charge of preparation time). (*b*) Private tutor; coach. (*c*) *Th:* Chorus master.

répétition [repetisjɔ̃], *s.f.* **I.** (*a*) Repetition. **Fusil à répétition,** repeating rifle. **Montre à répétition,** repeater (watch). (*b*) Reproduction, duplicate, replica. **2.** (*a*) *Th:* Rehearsal (of play). *R. générale,* dress rehearsal. (*b*) (Band or choral) practice. **3.** *Sch:* (Coach's) lesson. *Donner des répétitions,* to give private lessons.

repeupl|er [rəpœple], *v.tr.* To repeople (country); to réstock (river, pond); to replant (wood). *s.m.* **-ement.**

repincer [rapɛ̃se], *v.tr.* (Conj. like PINCER) *P:* To catch (s.o.) again. *On ne m'y repincera pas!* I shan't be caught doing it again!

repiqu|er [rəpike]. **I.** *v.tr.* (a) To prick, pierce, (sth.) again. (b) *Civ.E:* To mend, repair (road). (c) To restitch. (d) *Hort:* To prick out, thin out (seedlings). **2.** *v.i.* (a) *R. au plat,* to have a second helping. *P:* **Repiquer au truc,** to begin again; to re-enlist. (b) *Nau:* **R.** *dans le vent,* to haul the wind again. *s.m.* **-age.**

répit [repi], *s.m.* Respite; breathing-space. *Com:* **Jours de répit,** days of grace. **Souffrir sans répit,** to have no respite from pain.

replac|er [rəplase], *v.tr.* (Conj. like PLACER) (a) To replace; to put (sth.) back in its place. (b) To reinvest (funds). *s.m.* **-ement.**
  se replacer, to go into service again.

replant|er [rəplɑ̃te], *v.tr.* To replant. *F:* *Jamais je ne replanterai les pieds chez lui,* I shall never set foot in his house again. *s.m.* **-age.**

replâtrage [rəplɑtra:ʒ], *s.m.* **I.** (a) Replastering. (b) *F:* Tinkering up, patching up. **2.** (a) Superficial repair. (b) *F:* Patched-up peace.

replâtrer [rəplɑtre], *v.tr.* **I.** To replaster (wall). **2.** *F:* To patch up, tinker up (sth. radically unsound); to patch up (quarrel).

replet, -ète [rəplɛ, -ɛt], *a.* Stoutish, *F:* podgy (person). *Petit homme r.,* dumpy little man.

réplétion [replesjɔ̃], *s.f.* **I.** (a) Repletion. (b) Surfeit (of food). **2.** Corpulence.

repli [rəpli], *s.m.* **I.** Fold, crease (in cloth, etc.). *Les plis et les replis du cœur,* the innermost recesses of the heart. **2.** Winding, meander, bend (of river); coil (of rope, or serpent). **3.** *Mil:* Falling back, withdrawal.

repli|er [rəplie], *v.tr.* To fold (sth.) up (again); to coil (sth.) up; to turn (sth.) back; to turn in, tuck in (edge). *R. un parapluie,* to fold up, close, an umbrella. *a.* **-able.** *s.m.* **-ement.**
  se replier. **I.** (a) (Of object) To fold up, turn back; (of serpent) to coil up. (b) (Of stream, path) To wind, turn, twist, bend; (of stream) to meander. **2.** *Se r. sur soi-même,* to retire within oneself. **3.** *Mil:* (a) (Of outposts) To withdraw. (b) (Of troops in combat) To give ground; to fall back.

réplique [replik], *s.f.* **I.** Retort, rejoinder; pat answer. **Avoir la réplique prompte,** to be ready with an answer. **Argument sans réplique,** unanswerable argument; *F:* clincher. **2.** *Th:* Cue. **Donner la réplique à qn,** (i) to give s.o. his cue; (ii) *F:* to play up to s.o.; (iii) to answer s.o. back. **3.** *Art:* Replica. **4.** *Cin:* Retake (of a scene).

répliquer [replike], *v.i.* To retort, rejoin; to answer back. *R. à qn,* to answer s.o. back.

replonger [rəplɔ̃ʒe], *v.* (Conj. like PLONGER) **I.** *v.tr.* To plunge, dip, immerse, (sth.) again; to replunge (sth.) (*dans,* into). **2.** *v.i.* To dive in again.
  se replonger *dans l'étude,* to immerse oneself once more in study.

repol|ir [rəpɔli:r], *v.tr.* To repolish; to reburnish (metal); to rub up (spoon). *s.m.* **-issage.**

répondant [repɔ̃dɑ̃], *s.m.* **I.** *Ecc:* Server (at mass). **2.** *Jur:* Surety, security, referee, guarantor.

repondre [rəpɔ̃:dr], *v.tr.* To lay (eggs) again.

répondre [repɔ̃:dr]. **I.** *v.tr.* To answer, reply, respond. *Je n'ai rien répondu,* I answered nothing. *Qu'avez-vous à r.?* what have you to say in reply? *Il répondit n'en rien*

savoir, he answered that he knew nothing about it. *Ecc:* **Répondre la messe,** to make, the responses at Mass. **2.** *v.ind.tr.* **R.** *à une question,* to answer a question. *R. à l'appel,* to answer the roll, to answer one's name. *R. à une demande,* to comply with, fall in with, a request. *R. à l'amour de qn,* to respond to, return, s.o.'s love. *Ne pas r. aux avances de qn,* to fail to respond to s.o.'s advances. S.a. NORMAND **I.** **3.** *v.ind.tr.* To answer, correspond to, *F:* come up to (a standard, etc.). *Cela ne répond pas à mes besoins,* it does not meet, answer, my requirements. *R. à l'attente de qn,* to come up to s.o.'s expectation. *Ne pas r. à l'attente,* to fall short of expectation. **4.** *v.i.* *R. de qn, de qch.,* to answer for s.o., for sth.; to be answerable, accountable, responsible, for s.o., for sth. *Il va revenir,* **je vous en réponds,** he will come back, I'll be bound, (you may) take my word for it. *F:* *Je vous en réponds!* you bet! rather!

répons [repɔ̃], *s.m. Ecc:* Response.

réponse [repɔ̃:s], *s.f.* (a) Answer, reply. **Avoir, trouver, réponse à tout,** to have, find, an answer for everything; never to be at a loss for an answer. **Rendre réponse à qn,** to return s.o. an answer; to reply to s.o. **Argument sans réponse,** unanswerable argument. **Pour toute réponse,** *elle éclata en sanglots,* her only answer was to break into sobs. *Post:* **Réponse payée,** reply paid. S.a. NORMAND **I.** (b) Response (to an appeal). (c) Responsiveness, response (to stimulus).

repopulation [rəpɔpylasjɔ̃], *s.f.* Repopulation, repopulating; restocking (of river).

report [rəpɔ:r], *s.m.* **I.** *Com:* Book-k: (a) Carrying forward, bringing forward. (b) Amount carried forward; carry-forward, carry-over. (c) Posting (of journal entries). **2.** *St.Exch:* Contango(ing), continuation. **Taux de report,** contango rate. **3.** *Phot:* Lith: Transfer. **Papier à report,** transfer paper.

reportage [rəpɔrta:ʒ], *s.m. Journ:* **I.** Reporting. **2.** (Newspaper) report. **3.** Set of contributed articles on a topical subject. **4.** *W.Tel:* Running commentary (on a match, etc.).

reporter[1] [rəpɔrte], *v.tr.* **I.** To carry back; to take (sth.) back (*à,* to). **2.** (a) *R. qch. à plus tard,* to postpone, defer, sth. until later, to a later date. (b) *Com:* Book-k: To carry forward, bring forward, carry over (total). **A reporter,** carried forward. (c) *St.Exch:* To continue, contango; to carry over. **3.** *Lith:* Phot: To transfer.
  se reporter. **I.** *Se r. à un document,* to refer to a document. **"Se reporter à ..,"** 'the reader is referred to. ...' **2.** *Se r. au passé,* to look back to the past.

reporter[2] [rəpɔrtœːr, -tɛːr], *s.m.* Reporter.

repos [rəpo], *s.m.* **I.** (a) Rest, repose. **Se donner, prendre, du repos,** to take a rest. **En repos,** at rest. **Le repos éternel,** the last sleep. **Le champ de repos,** the churchyard. **Être au repos,** (i) (of soldier) to be standing at ease; (ii) (of machine) to be out of gear; (of boiler) to be laid off, standing by; (iii) (of gun) to be at half-cock. **Terre au repos,** fallow land. *Mil:* **En repos, repos!** stand at ease! (b) Pause, rest (in a verse). **2.** Peace, tranquillity (of mind). *Être en r. au sujet de qn,* not to be anxious about s.o. **Valeur de tout repos,** perfectly safe investment; gilt-edged security. **3.** Resting-place; landing (on stair).

reposant [rəpozɑ̃], *a.* Restful (spot, occupation); refreshing (sleep).

repose-pied(s) [rəpozpje], *s.m.inv.* Foot-rest (of motor cycle).

reposer [rəpoze]. I. *v.tr.* **1.** (*a*) To put, place, lay, set, (sth.) back (in its place); to replace. *Mil:* Reposer l'arme, to return to the 'order' (from the 'slope'); to order arms. (*b*) *Rail:* To re-lay (track). **2.** (*a*) *R. ses regards sur qch.*, to let one's glance rest on sth. (*b*) *R. sa tête sur un coussin*, to rest one's head on a cushion. *R. l'esprit*, to rest, refresh, the mind. *Couleur qui repose les yeux*, colour that is restful to the eyes. **II. reposer,** *v.i.* To lie, rest. *Le corps reposait sur son lit de parade*, the body was lying in state. *Ici repose . . .*, here lies (buried). . . . *Le commerce repose sur le crédit*, commerce rests on, is based upon, credit. *Bruit qui ne repose sur rien*, groundless report, unfounded report. **se reposer. 1.** To alight, settle, again. *L'oiseau se reposa sur la branche*, the bird settled on the bough again. **2.** (*a*) To rest, repose; to take a rest. Faire reposer ses chevaux, to rest one's horses. *Laisser r. une terre*, to let a piece of ground lie fallow. S.a. LAURIER. (*b*) *Se r. sur qn*, to rely upon, put one's trust in, s.o. (*c*) (Of liquid) To settle. **reposé,** *a.* **1.** Rested, refreshed (look, etc.); fresh (complexion). **2.** Quiet, calm. A tête reposée, (i) deliberately, coolly; (ii) at leisure. **reposoir** [rəpozwaːr], *s.m.* Resting-place. (*a*) *A:* Wayside shelter. (*b*) *Ecc:* Station, temporary altar (when the host is carried in procession).

repoussant [rəpusɑ̃], *a.* Repulsive, repellent, loathsome.

repousse [rəpus], *s.f.* **1.** Growing again. **2.** Fresh growth (of hair, etc.).

repoussement [rəpusmɑ̃], *s.m.* **1.** Repulse (of person); rejection, voting down (of motion); rejection (of idea). **2.** Recoil, kick (of fire-arm). **3.** Dislike, disinclination. *Éprouver du r. à faire qch.*, to dislike the idea of doing sth.

repousser [rəpuse]. **1.** *v.tr.* (*a*) To push back, push away, drive off, thrust aside, repulse, repel. *R. un assaut*, to repulse, repel, beat off, an attack. *R. une offre*, to reject, decline, an offer. *R. la tentation*, to thrust aside temptation. *R. qn, les avances de qn*, to spurn s.o., s.o.'s advances. *R. une accusation*, to deny a charge. *R. un projet de loi*, to throw out a bill. *R. une mesure*, to reject, vote down, a measure. *R. un rivet*, to drive out a rivet. (*b*) *R. une conférence à plus tard*, to postpone a conference. (*c*) To be repellent to (s.o.); to repel. (*d*) *Tchn:* To emboss (leather); to chase (metal); to work (metal) in repoussé. (*e*) (Of fire-arm) To recoil, kick. **2.** (*a*) *v.tr.* (Of tree, plant, etc.) To throw out (branches, shoots) again. (*b*) *v.i.* (Of tree, plant) To shoot (up) again, spring (up) again, sprout again.

repoussé. 1. *a.* Chased; embossed; repoussé (work). **2.** *s.m.* Chasing, embossing; repoussé.

repoussoir [rəpuswaːr], *s.m.* **1.** *Tls:* (*a*) Drift (-bolt). (*b*) Embossing-punch. **2.** *Hyd.E:* Fender pile. **3.** Set-off, foil (to s.o.'s beauty).

répréhensible [repreɑ̃sibl], *a.* Reprehensible. *adv.* -ment.

répréhension [repreɑ̃sjɔ̃], *s.f.* Reprehension.

reprendre [rəprɑ̃ːdr], *v.* (Conj. like PRENDRE) **I.** *v.tr.* (*a*) To take again, retake, recapture. *R. une ville à, sur, l'ennemi*, to retake, recapture, a town from the enemy. (*b*) *R. du pain*, to take, have, some more bread. *R. les armes*, to take up arms again. *J'ai repris mon pardessus d'hiver*, I have gone back to my winter overcoat. *R. sa place*, to resume one's seat. *La fièvre l'a repris*, he has (had) another bout of fever. *R. ses esprits, ses sens*, to recover consciousness; to come to. Reprendre froid, to catch cold again. *F: On ne*

m'y reprendra plus, you won't catch me at it again. (*c*) To take back (a gift); to re-engage (a servant); to retract (a promise). (*d*) To resume, take up again (conversation). *R. une tâche*, to return to a task. *R. ses habitudes*, to resume one's habits. *R. les travaux*, to restart work; to resume operations. *R. l'affaire à son origine*, to go back to the beginning (of the matter). *R. les faits de plus haut*, to go further back into the matter. *R. du goût pour qch.*, to recover one's taste for sth. Reprendre le chemin, to take (to) the road again. Reprendre la mer, to put out to sea again. *Th:* Reprendre une pièce, to revive a play. *R. des forces*, to regain strength. *R. courage*, to take courage again. S.a. HALEINE. Reprendre le dessus, to get the upper hand again. Reprendre la parole, (i) to find one's tongue again; (ii) to resume, go on. *Abs. Oui, madame, reprit-il*, yes, madam, he replied. *Il reprit après un instant*, he went on again after a moment. Reprendre un mur en sous-œuvre, to underpin a wall. (*e*) To reprove, chide, admonish. *Son affirmation était fausse et je le repris aussitôt*, his statement was false and I took him up at once. **2.** *v.i.* (*a*) To recommence, return, revive. *Le froid a repris*, cold weather has set in again. *Cette mode reprend*, this fashion is coming in again. *Le malade reprend*, the patient is recovering, is picking up again. *Les affaires reprennent*, business is improving. *Aut:* (Of engine) *R. vivement*, to pick up smartly. (*b*) (Of liquid) To freeze, set, again. (*c*) (Of plant) To take root again.

se reprendre. 1. To recover oneself, to pull oneself together. *Se r. à un cordage*, to save oneself by grabbing a rope. **2.** To correct oneself (in speaking). **3.** *Se r. à espérer, à pleurer*, to begin to hope, to cry, again. Se reprendre à la vie, to take a new lease of life. **4.** S'y reprendre à plusieurs fois (*pour faire qch.*), to make several attempts; to have several goes at sth.

repris, -ise[1], *s.* Repris de justice, habitual criminal; old offender; *F:* old lag.

reprise[2], *s.f.* **1.** (*a*) (i) Retaking, recapture, recovery (of position, etc.). (ii) Ship recaptured. (*b*) Taking over (of fittings, etc., with house). (*c*) *Com: R. des invendus*, taking back of unsold goods or copies. **2.** (*a*) Resumption, renewal (of negotiations). *R. d'une pièce*, revival of a play. (*b*) *R. du froid*, new spell of cold. *R. des affaires*, recovery, revival, of business. (*c*) *I.C.E:* Pick-up, acceleration (of engine). (*d*) (One of several stages) *Box:* Round. *Fenc:* Bout. *Fb:* Second half (of game). Faire qch. par reprises, to do sth. in successive stages. A plusieurs reprises, (i) repeatedly; (ii) on several occasions. (*e*) *Mus:* (i) Repetition (in singing, playing). Points de reprise, double bars (in a piece of music). Chanson à reprises, catch (song). (ii) Re-entry (of subject in fugue). **3.** (*a*) *Needlew:* (i) Darning, mending; (ii) darn. Point de reprise, darning stitch. Reprise perdue, fine-drawn mend. (*b*) *Const: R. en sous-œuvre*, underpinning. **4.** Car, etc., taken in part exchange.

représailles [rəprezaːj], *s.f.pl.* Reprisals, retaliation. User de représailles, to make reprisals; to retaliate (*envers*, upon).

représentant, -ante [rəprezɑ̃tɑ̃, -ɑ̃ːt]. **I.** *a.* Representative. **2.** *s.* (*a*) Representative (of the people). (*b*) *Com:* (i) Agent; (ii) traveller.

représentatif, -ive [rəprezɑ̃tatif, -iːv], *a.* Representative.

représentation [rəprezɑ̃tasjɔ̃], *s.f.* **1.** (*a*) *Pol: Jur:* Representation. *R. proportionnelle*, proportional representation. (*b*) *Com:* Agency. *Avoir*

la r. exclusive de . . ., to be sole agents for. . . .
2. *Jur:* Production, exhibition (of documents).
3. *Th:* Performance (of a play). **Troupe en
représentation,** company on tour. **Droits de
représentation,** dramatic fees. **4.** *Adm:* (Official)
state, display ; dignity (of state official). **Frais
de représentation,** expenses of official entertainment. *F:* **Être toujours en représentation,** to be
always showing off. **5.** Remonstrance, protest.
Faire des représentations à qn, to make representations to s.o. ; to remonstrate with s.o.
représenter [rəprezɑ̃te], *v.tr.* **1.** (*a*) To present
(sth.) again. (*b*) To reintroduce (s.o.). **2.** *Jur:*
To produce, exhibit (documents). *R. son passeport,* to show one's passport. **3.** To represent.
(*a*) To depict, portray. *Tableau représentant un
moulin,* picture representing a mill. *Représentez-
vous mon étonnement,* picture (to yourself) my
astonishment. (*b*) To represent, stand for, act
for (s.o.). **Se faire représenter,** to appoint, send,
a representative, a deputy, a proxy. *R. une
circonscription,* to sit for a constituency. *Nous
représentons la maison X,* we are agents for
Messrs X. (Of advocate) *R. qn en justice,* to
appear for s.o. **4.** *Th:* (*a*) To perform, act (a
play). (*b*) To act, personate (part) ; to take the
part of (M. Perrichon, etc.). **5.** *R. qch. à qn,* to
represent, point out, sth. to s.o. **6.** *Abs.* (*a*) To
have a good presence. **C'est un homme qui
représente (bien),** he is a man of good presence
and address. (*b*) To maintain the dignity of one's
(official) position ; to make some show.
se représenter. 1. (Of pers.) (*a*) To present
oneself anew ; to offer oneself again as a candidate. (*b*) To reappear ; to turn up again. (*c*) (Of
an occasion) To occur again ; to recur. **2.** *Pred.*
Se r. comme acteur, comme officier, to represent,
describe, oneself as an actor, as an officer.
répressif, -ive [represif, -iːv], *a.* Repressive.
répression [represjɔ̃], *s.f.* Repression.
réprimable [reprimabl], *a.* Repressible.
réprimandable [reprimɑ̃dabl], *a.* Deserving of
reproof, of censure.
réprimande [reprimɑ̃d], *s.f.* Reprimand, reproof ; *F:* talking-to.
réprimand|er [reprimɑ̃de], *v.tr.* To reprimand,
reprove ; to take (s.o.) to task ; *F:* to talk to
(s.o.). *s.* **-eur, -euse.**
réprimer [reprime], *v.tr.* To repress. (*a*) To
check, curb (desire, etc.) ; to strangle (sneeze).
(*b*) To quell, put down (revolt).
repris, reprise [rəpri, -iːz]. See REPRENDRE.
repris|er [rəprize], *v.tr.* To mend, darn (stock-
ings, etc.). **Boule, œuf, à repriser,** darning-ball,
-egg. *s.m.* **-age.** *s.f.* **-euse.**
reprit [rəpri]. See REPRENDRE.
réprobateur, -trice [reprɔbatœːr, -tris], *a.*
Reproachful ; reproving.
réprobation [reprɔbasjɔ̃], *s.f.* Reprobation.
reproche [rəprɔʃ], *s.m.* **1.** Reproach. *Mériter des
reproches,* to deserve blame, censure. **Faire des
reproches à qn,** to reproach, upbraid, s.o. (*au
sujet de,* about). **Ton de reproche,** reproachful,
reproving, tone. **Vie sans reproche,** blameless
life. **Qui n'est pas à l'abri du reproche,** not
beyond reproach. **2.** *Jur:* **Témoin sans reproche,**
unimpeachable witness.
reproch|er [rəprɔʃe], *v.tr.* **1.** To reproach,
upbraid. *R. ses fautes à qn,* to reproach s.o. with
his faults. *On lui reproche la moindre peccadille,*
he is taken to task for the merest trifle. **Je n'ai
rien à me reprocher,** I have nothing to reproach
myself with, to blame myself for. **2.** *R. un
plaisir, un succès, à qn,* to grudge s.o. a pleasure,

a success. **Reprocher les morceaux à qn,** to
grudge s.o. every bite he eats. **3.** *Jur:* To
take exception to (a witness, evidence). *a.* **-able.**
reproducteur, -trice [rəprɔdyktœːr, -tris].
1. *a.* Reproductive (organ, etc.). **2.** *s.m.* Animal
kept for breeding purposes. *R. d'élite,* pedigree
sire. **3.** *s.m.* Reproducer (of phonograph).
reproductif, -ive [rəprɔdyktif, -iːv], *a.* Reproductive.
reproduction [rəprɔdyksjɔ̃], *s.f.* **1.** Reproduction. **2.** Copy.
reproduire [rəprɔdɥiːr], *v.tr.* (Conj. like PRO-
DUIRE) To reproduce.
se reproduire. 1. (Of events) To recur ; to
happen again. **2.** To reproduce, breed, multiply.
réprouver [repruve], *v.tr.* To reprobate (crime) ;
to reject (doctrine) ; to disapprove of (s.o., sth.).
réprouvé, -ée, *s.* Outcast (of society) ;
reprobate.
reps [rɛps], *s.m. Tex:* Rep(s), repp.
reptile [reptil], *s.m. & a.* Reptile.
repu, -s, -t, etc. [rəpy]. See REPAÎTRE.
républicain, -aine [repyblikɛ̃, -ɛn], *a. & s.*
Republican.
républicanisme [repyblikanism], *s.m.* Republicanism.
republier [rəpyblie], *v.tr.* To republish.
république [repyblik], *s.f.* (*a*) Republic.
(*b*) Commonwealth, community (of letters, etc.).
répudiable [repydjabl], *a.* Repudiable.
répudiation [repydjasjɔ̃], *s.f.* **1.** Repudiation (of
wife, debt). **2.** Renunciation (of succession).
répudier [repydje], *v.tr.* **1.** To repudiate (wife,
opinion). **2.** *Jur:* To renounce (succession).
répugnance [repyɲɑ̃ːs], *s.f.* **1.** Repugnance.
(*a*) Dislike (*pour,* to, of, for) ; aversion (*pour,* to,
from, for). (*b*) Loathing (*pour,* of, for). **2.** *R. à
faire qch.,* reluctance to do sth. **Faire qch. avec
répugnance,** to do sth. reluctantly.
répugnant [repyɲɑ̃], *a.* **1.** Repugnant, loathsome (*à,* to). **2.** *Occ.* Reluctant, loath (*à faire
qch.,* to do sth.).
répugner [repyɲe], *v.i.* **1.** *R. à qch.,* to feel
repugnance to, to revolt at, sth. *R. à faire qch.,*
to feel reluctant, lo(a)th, to do sth. **2.** (Of thg,
pers.) *R. à qn,* to be repugnant, distasteful, to
s.o. *Impers. Il me répugne de le faire,* it is repugnant to me, I am reluctant, to do it ; I loathe
doing it.
répulsif, -ive [repylsif, -iːv], *a.* Repulsive.
répulsion [repylsjɔ̃], *s.f.* Repulsion. *Inspirer de
la r. à qn,* to be repellent to s.o.
réputation [repytasjɔ̃], *s.f.* Reputation, repute.
Jouir d'une bonne réputation, to bear a good
character. *Cela a fait sa r.,* it made his name.
Avoir la r. d'être riche, to be reputed wealthy.
Sa r. de chirurgien, his reputation as a surgeon.
Se faire une réputation, to make a name for
oneself. *Avoir la r. de médecin habile,* to have
the name of (being) a skilful doctor. *Connaître
qn de r.,* to know s.o. by reputation, by repute.
Perdre qn de réputation, to ruin s.o.'s reputation,
s.o.'s character.
réputer [repyte], *v.tr.* To repute, consider,
deem, think. *On les réputait riches,* they were
thought, deemed, to be rich. **Se réputer heureux,**
to consider, esteem, oneself happy. *L'intention
est réputée pour le fait,* we take the will for the deed.
réputé, -ée, *a.* Well-known (expert) ; (doctor)
of repute. *R. par qch.,* well known for sth.
requérable [rəkerabl], *a.* Demandable.
requérant, -ante [rəkerɑ̃, -ɑ̃ːt], *s. Jur:* Plaintiff,
petitioner, applicant.

requérir [rəkeri:r], *v.tr.* (Conj. like ACQUÉRIR)
1. (*a*) *A: Venir r. qn,* to come for s.o. *On me requit de l'aller trouver,* I was asked to go to him. (*b*) To ask for (sth.); to solicit (a favour). *R. la présence de qn,* to ask, beg, s.o. to attend. 2. (*a*) **Requérir aide et assistance,** to demand assistance. *R. qn,* to call upon s.o. to give assistance. (*b*) *R. qn de faire qch.,* to call upon, summon, s.o. to do sth.
  requis, *a.* Required, requisite, necessary.
requête [rəkɛ:t], *s.f.* Request, suit, petition. *Adresser une requête à qn,* to petition s.o. *A la requête de . . .,* at the suit of. . . .
requiem [rekɥiɛm], *s.m. Ecc:* **Messe de requiem,** requiem mass; requiem.
requin [rəkɛ̃], *s.m.* 1. *Ich:* Shark. **Peau de requin,** shagreen. 2. *F:* Shark, swindler.
requinqu|er [rəkɛ̃ke], *v.tr. P:* ·(*a*) To repair; to put (sth.) to rights. (*b*) To smarten (s.o.) up; to rig (s.o.) out anew. *s.m.* **-age.**
  se requinquer. 1. To smarten, spruce, oneself up; to renew one's wardrobe. 2. To recover, pick up (after illness).
requis [rəki]. See REQUÉRIR.
réquisition [rekizisjɔ̃], *s.f.* (*a*) Requisitioning, commandeering. (*b*) Requisition, levy. **Mettre en réquisition,** to requisition. (*c*) Requisition, demand. **Agir sur, à, la réquisition de qn,** to act on s.o.'s requisition.
réquisitionn|er [rekizisjɔne], *v.tr.* To requisition; to commandeer (provisions, etc.); to impress (men of fighting age). *s.m.* **-ement.**
réquisitoire [rekizitwa:r], *s.m.* (Public Prosecutor's) charge, indictment.
rescapé, -ée [rɛskape], *a. & s.* (Person) rescued; survivor (of disaster). *F: Heures rescapées,* hours saved.
rescinder [rɛssɛ̃de], *v.tr. Jur:* To rescind, annul.
rescision [rɛssizjɔ̃], *s.f.* Rescission, annulment.
rescousse [rɛskus], *s.f. A:* Rescue. (Still used in) **Aller à la rescousse de qn,** to go to s.o.'s rescue.
rescrit [rɛskri], *s.m. Ecc: etc:* Rescript.
réseau [rezo], *s.m.* 1. (*a*) *A:* Net; (spider's) web. *F:* **Le réseau du crime,** the fabric of law. (*b*) Netting, network (for lace). (*c*) *Cost:* Hairnet. (*d*) *Arch:* Tracery. (*e*) *Anat:* Plexus (of nerves). (*f*) *Opt:* Diffraction grating. 2. (*a*) Network, system (of roads, railways, etc.). *R. fluvial,* river system. *El.E: R. de distribution de ville,* town mains. (*b*) *Mil: Réseau(x) de fil de fer,* wire entanglements.
résection [resɛksjɔ̃], *s.f. Surg:* Resection (of bone).
réséda [rezeda], *s.m. Bot:* Mignonette.
réséquer [reseke], *v.tr.* (je résèque; je réséquerai) *Surg:* To resect (bone).
réservation [rezɛrvasjɔ̃], *s.f.* Reservation. **Réservation faite de tous mes droits,** without prejudice to my rights.
réserve [rezɛrv], *s.f.* 1. (*a*) Reserving, reservation. **Réserve de places,** reservation, booking, of seats. (*b*) Reserve. **En réserve,** in reserve. **Mettre qch. en réserve,** to reserve sth.; to lay sth. by. **Mettre un navire en réserve,** to put a ship out of commission. **Officier de réserve,** reserve officer. **Fonds de réserve,** reserve fund. **Pièces de réserve,** spare parts. *Nau: Soute de r.,* spare bunker. *Ecc:* **La sainte Réserve,** the Reservation (of the Sacrament). 2. (*a*) *Apporter une r. à un contrat,* to enter a reservation in respect of an agreement. **A la réserve de . . .,** except for . . ., with the reservation of. . . . **A la réserve que + ind.,** except that. . . . **Sous (la) réserve de qch.,** subject to, contingent on, sth. *Jur:* **Sous réserve,** without prejudice. **Sous**

toutes réserves, without committing, oneself. **Sans réserve,** without reservation; unreservedly. *Éloges sans r.,* unqualified praise. (*b*) Reserve, guardedness, caution (in speech); coyness. **Se tenir sur la réserve,** to be reserved; to be on one's guard. 3. (*a*) Reserve (of provisions, etc.). *Mil: Navy:* Reserve (of men). (*b*) *Jur:* **Réserve légale,** portion (of inheritance) that must devolve upon the heirs. (*c*) *For: Ven:* Preserve.
4. *Engr: Dy: etc:* Resist.
réserver [rezɛrve], *v.tr.* (*a*) To reserve; to set (sth.) aside; to put, lay, (sth.) by; to save (sth.) up; to keep (sth.) back; to keep (sth.) in store. *R. une place à qn,* to reserve a seat for s.o. *R. une danse à qn,* to save a dance for s.o. **Tous droits réservés,** all rights reserved. **Pêche réservée,** fishing preserve. *Se r. de faire qch.,* to reserve the right to do sth. *Ecc:* **Cas réservé,** reserved sin. (*b*) To set apart (sum for a purpose, etc.).
  se réserver *pour qch.,* to reserve oneself, save oneself, hold back, wait, for sth.
  réservé, *a.* Reserved. (*a*) Guarded, cautious. (*b*) Shy; (of woman) coy. (*c*) Stand-offish.
réserviste [rezɛrvist], *s.m. Mil:* Reservist.
réservoir [rezɛrvwa:r], *s.m.* 1. (*a*) Reservoir. (*b*) (Fish-)pond or tank. 2. (*a*) Tank, well, cistern, container. *R. à mazout,* oil-fuel tank. *R. à gaz,* gas-holder, gasometer. (*b*) *I.C.E: R. d'essence,* petrol-tank. *R. en charge,* gravity feedtank. *Mch: R. de vapeur,* steam-chamber, steam-space. *Min: R. à minerai,* ore-bin, ore-bunker. *S.a.* PORTE-PLUME.
résidence [rezidɑ̃:s], *s.f.* Residence. 1. Residing. *Lieu de r.,* place of abode. 2. Dwelling-place, abode. *Changer de r.,* to remove; *F:* to shift one's quarters.
résident [rezidɑ̃], *s.m.* Resident (diplomatic) minister or agent.
résider [rezide], *v.i.* 1. To reside, dwell, live (*à, dans,* at, in). 2. *Toute la difficulté réside en ceci,* all the difficulty rests, lies, consists, in this.
résidu [rezidy], *s.m.* 1. Residue, residuum. *Résidus urbains,* town refuse. 2. (*a*) *Mth:* Residue (of a function). (*b*) *Com: R. de compte,* amount still owing; balance.
résiduel, -elle [rezidɥɛl], *a.* Residual.
résignation [reziɲasjɔ̃], *s.f.* Resignation. 1. Handing over, giving up (of a living, etc.). 2. Submissiveness (to God); resignedness.
résigner [reziɲe], *v.tr.* To resign (a possession, etc.); to give (sth.) up (*à, to*). *R. son âme à Dieu,* to commit one's soul to God. *R. un bénéfice,* to resign a living.
  se résigner (*à qch., à supporter qch.*), to resign oneself, to submit (to sth., to enduring sth.).
  résigné, -ée, *a. & s.* Resigned (*à, to*); meek, uncomplaining.
résiliation [reziljasjɔ̃], *s.f.* Cancellation, annulment, termination (of contract).
résilience [reziljɑ̃:s], *s.f. Mec:* Resilience.
résili|er [rezilje], *v.tr.* To annul, cancel, terminate (agreement). *a.* **-able.**
résille [rezi:j], *s.f.* 1. Hair-net. 2. Cames (of stained-glass window).
résine [rezin], *s.f.* Resin.
résiner [rezine], *v.tr.* 1. To resin; to dip in resin. 2. To tap (fir-trees) for resin.
résineux, -euse [rezinø, -ø:z], *a.* Resinous.
résinifère [rezinifɛ:r], *a.* Resin-producing (tree).
résipiscence [resipissɑ̃:s], *s.f.* Resipiscence. *Venir à résipiscence,* to show repentance, to return to a better mind.
résistance [rezistɑ̃:s], *s.f.* Resistance. 1. (*a*) Opposition (*à,* to). **Faire (de la) résistance,** to offer

resistance. (b) *El.E*: **Caisse, boîte, de résistance,** resistance box. *R. à curseur,* rheostat. *W.Tel*: *R. de fuite de la grille,* grid-leak. **2.** (*a*) Strength, toughness (of materials). *R. à la flexion,* bending-strength. *R. à la traction,* tensile strength. *R. au choc,* impact resistance. **Limite de résistance,** yield point. *Acier à haute r.,* high-resistance steel. (b) Staying power, stamina, endurance (of pers. or animal). **Pièce de résistance,** (i) principal dish, substantial dish; (ii) principal feature.

résistant [rezistã], *a.* Resistant; strong, stout (material). *Couleur résistante,* fast colour. *R. à l'acide,* acid-proof.

résister [reziste], *v.ind.tr.* To resist. (*a*) *R. à qn, à la justice,* to offer resistance to s.o., to the law. (b) *R. à qch.,* to withstand (pain, temptation, etc.); to hold out against (attack); to take, support (a stress). (*c*) *Ces couleurs ne résistent pas,* these colours are not fast, do not stand.

résolu, -s, -t, etc. [rezɔly]. See RÉSOUDRE.

résoluble [rezɔlybl], *a.* **1.** Solvable (problem). **2.** Annullable, terminable (contract).

résolument [rezɔlymã], *adv.* Resolutely, determinedly.

résolution [rezɔlysjɔ̃], *s.f.* **1.** (*a*) Resolution (of substance, of dissonance); solution (of problem). (b) Termination, annulment (of agreement); cancelling (of sale). **2.** Resolution, determination. (*a*) Resolve. **Prendre la résolution de faire qch.,** to resolve upon doing sth., to determine to do sth. (b) Resoluteness. (*c*) **Prendre, adopter, une résolution,** (of meeting) to pass, carry, adopt, a resolution.

résonance [rezɔnã:s], *s.f.* **1.** Resonance. *Mus*: *Caisse de r.,* sound-box, -chest. **2.** *W.Tel*: **Mettre le poste en résonance,** to tune the set; to tune in.

résonnement [rezɔnmã], *s.m.* Resounding, resonance, reverberation.

résonn|er [rezɔne], *v.i.* To resound, re-echo, reverberate; *F*: (of metal, etc.) to ring, clang, clank; (of string) to twang. *Le timbre électrique résonna,* the electric bell rang, sounded. *a.* **-ant.**

résorber [rezɔrbe], *v.tr. Med*: To resorb, reabsorb.

résorption [rezɔrpsjɔ̃], *s.f. Med*: Resorption.

résoudre [rezu:dr], *v.tr.* (*pr.p.* **résolvant;** *p.p.* (i) **résolu,** (ii) *Ph*: **résous, -oute;** *pr.ind.* **je résous,** il résout, n. résolvons; *p.h.* je résolus; *fu.* je résoudrai) **1.** (*a*) *R. qch. en qch.,* to resolve, dissolve, break up, sth. into sth. *La vapeur que le froid avait résoute en eau,* the steam that the cold had resolved into water. (b) *Jur*: To annul, cancel, terminate (contract). **2.** To resolve, clear up (a difficulty); to solve (equation); to work out (problem); to settle (a question). *Mus*: *R. une dissonance,* to resolve a discord. **3.** (*a*) *A*: *R. qn à faire qch.,* to induce, persuade, prevail upon, s.o. to do sth. (b) *On a résolu la guerre,* war has been decided upon. *R. de partir,* to resolve on going, to decide to go.

se résoudre. 1. *Se r. en qch.,* to resolve, dissolve, into sth. **2.** *Se r. à faire qch.,* to make up one's mind to do sth., to bring oneself to do sth. *Il faut nous y r.,* we must do it, accept it (however reluctantly).

résolu, *a.* **1.** Resolute, determined (person). **2.** *R. à faire qch.,* resolved, determined, to do sth.

respect [rɛspɛ], *s.m.* Respect, regard. *Avoir le r. des lois,* to respect the law. **Parler avec respect,** to speak respectfully. **Respect de soi,** self-respect. **Respect humain** [rɛspɛkymɛ̃], deference to public opinion; common decency. *Faire qch. par r. pour qn,* to do sth. out of respect for s.o.,

out of regard for s.o. *Manquer de r. à, envers, qn,* to be disrespectful to s.o. **Tenir qn en respect,** (i) to keep s.o. at a respectful distance, at arm's length; (ii) to hold s.o. in check; (iii) to keep s.o. in awe. **Sauf le respect que je vous dois, sauf votre respect,** with all due respect, with all due deference. **Rendre ses respects à qn,** to pay one's respects to s.o.

respectabilité [rɛspɛktabilite], *s.f.* Respectability.

respectable [rɛspɛktabl], *a.* **1.** Respectable; worthy of respect. **2.** *F*: *Nombre r. de . . .,* fair number of. . . . *adv.* **-ment.**

respecter [rɛspɛkte], *v.tr.* To respect, have regard for (s.o.). *R. la loi, une décision,* to abide by the law, by a decision. **Faire respecter la loi,** to enforce the law. *Un homme qui se respecte,* a self-respecting man. *Je me respecte trop pour faire cela,* I am above doing that.

respect|if, -ive [rɛspɛktif, -i:v], *a.* Respective. *adv.* **-ivement.**

respectueu|x, -euse [rɛspɛktɥø, -ø:z], *a.* Respectful (*envers,* to, towards); dutiful (child). *R. des lois,* respectful of the law; law-abiding. *adv.* **-sement.**

respirable [rɛspirabl], *a.* Respirable, breathable.

respirateur [rɛspiratœ:r], *s.m. Med*: Respirator.

respiration [rɛspirasjɔ̃], *s.f.* Respiration, breathing. **Couper la respiration à qn,** (i) to wind s.o.; (ii) *F*: to take s.o.'s breath away. *Avoir la r. coupée,* (i) to be short of breath; (ii) to be flabbergasted.

respiratoire [rɛspiratwa:r], *a.* Respiratory. **Casque respiratoire,** (fireman's) smoke-helmet.

respirer [rɛspire]. **1.** *v.i.* To breathe. *R. longuement,* to draw a long breath. *"N'est-ce que cela?" Je respirai,* "Is that all?" I breathed again. *Laissez-moi r.,* let me take breath. **2.** *v.tr.* (*a*) To breathe (in); to inhale. *Aller r. un peu d'air,* to go for a breather. (b) *R. la vengeance,* to breathe (out, forth) vengeance. *Ici tout respire la paix,* here everything breathes, betokens, peace.

resplendir [rɛsplãdi:r], *v.i.* To be resplendent, to shine, to glitter. *F*: *R. de santé,* to glow with health.

resplendissant [rɛsplãdisã], *a.* Resplendent, shining; dazzling. *Visage r. de santé,* face glowing, aglow, with health.

responsabilité [rɛspɔ̃sabilite], *s.f.* Responsibility; liability (*de,* for). *R. des patrons,* employers' liability. **Accepter une r.,** to assume, accept, a responsibility. **Engager la r. de qn,** to involve s.o.'s responsibility. **Engager sa r. personnelle,** to assume personal responsibility. **Faire qch. sous sa (propre) r.,** to do sth. on one's own responsibility. *R. civile,* civil liability.

responsable [rɛspɔ̃sabl], *a.* Responsible, accountable, answerable (*envers,* to; *devant,* before). *R. pour ses serviteurs,* answerable for one's servants. **Tenir qn r. de qch.,** to hold s.o. responsible for sth. *Être r. du dommage,* to be liable for the damage.

resquilleur, -euse [rɛskijœ:r, -ø:z], *s. F*: Uninvited guest; gate-crasher.

ressac [rəsak], *s.m. Nau*: **1.** Underset, undertow. **2.** Surf.

ressaisir [rəsɛzi:r], *v.tr.* To seize again; to recapture.

se ressaisir. 1. To regain possession of oneself; to regain one's self-control; *F*: to pull oneself together. **2.** To recover one's balance (after stumbling).

ressass|er [rəsase], *v.tr.* (*a*) To re-sift. (b) *F*: **Toujours ressasser la même histoire,** to be for ever going back over, harking back to, the same old story. *s.m.* **-age.**

ressaut [rəso], *s.m.* **1.** (a) *Arch:* Projection. *Mec.E:* Swell, lug. *R. d'un projectile,* shoulder of a projectile. *Faire ressaut,* to project. (b) Sharp rise (in the ground). **2.** *Equit:* Rise (in the saddle).

ressauter [rəsote], *v.i.* = TRESSAUTER.

resseller [rəsɛle], *v.tr.* To re-saddle (horse, etc.).

ressemblance [rəsɑ̃blɑːs], *s.f.* Resemblance, likeness. *Avoir, offrir, de la r. avec qn,* to bear, show, a resemblance to s.o.

ressemblant [rəsɑ̃blɑ̃], *a.* Like, alike. *Portrait bien r.,* good likeness.

ressembler [rəsɑ̃ble], *v.ind.tr. R. à qn, à qch.,* to resemble, to be like, to look like, s.o., sth. *Il n'y eut rien qui ressemblât à une émeute,* there was no approach to a riot. *Cela ne vous ressemble pas du tout,* F: it isn't a bit like you. *Cela ne ressemble à rien,* it's like nothing on earth.

se ressembler, to be (a)like. F: *Ils se ressemblent comme deux gouttes d'eau,* they are as like as two peas. S.a. S'ASSEMBLER.

ressentiment [rəsɑ̃timɑ̃], *s.m.* Resentment (*de,* at; *contre,* against).

ressentir [rəsɑ̃tiːr], *v.tr.* (Conj. like SENTIR) (a) To feel (pain, emotion). *R. de l'affection pour qn,* to be fond of s.o. (b) To resent (an injury). (c) To feel, experience (shock).

se ressentir *d'un accident,* to feel the effects of an accident.

resserre [rəsɛːr], *s.f.* **1.** (a) Storage; safe keeping. (b) Holding up (of food-stuffs, etc.). **2.** (a) Storage yard or shed; store-room. (b) Secret niche. (c) (Garden) tool-shed.

resserrement [rəsɛrmɑ̃], *s.m.* **1.** Contracting, contraction, tightening, narrowing. *Med:* Costiveness, constipation. **2.** Tightness, scarceness (of money); heaviness, oppression (of heart).

resserrer [rəsɛre], *v.tr.* **1.** To put (sth.) away again; to lock up again. **2.** To contract, restrain, confine, close up, constrict. *R. un récit,* to condense, compress, a story. **3.** To tie (up) again; to draw (sth.) closer, tighter; to tighten.

se resserrer. 1. To contract, shrink; to become tighter. **2.** To retrench; to curtail one's expenses.

resserré, *a.* Narrow, confined, cramped, shut in.

resservir [rəsɛrviːr], *v.tr. & i.* (Conj. like SERVIR) To serve again; to be used again.

ressort[1] [rəsɔːr], *s.m.* **1.** (a) Elasticity, springiness. *Faire ressort,* to be elastic, springy; to spring back, fly back. *Avoir du ressort,* to be resilient; (of pers.) to be full of buoyancy. (b) Spring. *Tp:* Spring-band (of head-phones). *R. en spirale, à boudin,* spiral spring, coil-spring. *R. à feuilles, à lames,* laminated spring, leaf-spring. *Grand r., r. moteur,* mainspring. *Suspendu à ressorts,* sprung. *Sans ressorts,* unsprung. *Faire ressort,* to act as a spring. F: *Faire jouer tous les ressorts,* to pull all the strings, to leave no stone unturned. *L'intérêt est un puissant r.,* interest is a powerful motive. **2.** *Jur:* (a) Province, scope, competence; (extent of) jurisdiction. *Être du ressort de la cour,* to be, fall, within the competence of the court. (b) *Jugement en premier r.,* judgment with possibility of appeal. *En dernier ressort,* (i) without appeal; (ii) F: in the last resort.

ressort[2]. See RESSORTIR.

ressortir [rəsɔrtiːr], *v.i.* (Conj. like SORTIR, except in 3) **1.** (a) (Aux. *être*) To come, go, out again. (b) *v.tr. R. les chaises,* to bring out the

chairs again. **2.** (Aux. usu. *être*) (a) To stand out (in relief); to be evident. *Faire ressortir des couleurs,* to bring out, set off, colours. *Faire r. un fait,* to emphasize a fact. *Faire r. le sens de qch.,* to bring out the meaning of sth. (b) To result, follow (*de,* from). *Comme il ressort de la lettre ci-jointe,* as appears from the enclosed letter. **3.** (Aux. *avoir*) (*pr.p.* ressortissant; *pr.ind.* il ressortit; *p.d.* il ressortissait) (a) *Jur: R. à qn, à qch.,* to be under the jurisdiction of, to be amenable to (a court, a country). *Ces affaires ressortissent à la justice de paix,* these cases belong to, come before, a conciliation court. (b) *Concepts qui ressortissent à la géométrie,* concepts that belong to geometry.

ressortissant [rəsɔrtisɑ̃]. **1.** *a.* Under the jurisdiction (*à,* of). **2.** *s.m. Les ressortissants d'un pays,* the nationals of a country.

ressouder [rəsude], *v.tr.* To resolder or reweld.

se ressouder, (of bone) to knit again, to join again.

ressource [rəsurs], *s.f.* Resource. **1.** (a) Resourcefulness. (b) *Ville de ressource,* well-supplied town. *Être ruiné sans ressource,* to be irretrievably ruined. **2.** Expedient, shift. *Avoir mille ressources,* to be full of expedients. *Faire ressource de tout,* to turn all one's possessions into ready cash. *En dernière ressource . . .,* in the last resort. . . . **3.** *pl.* Resources, means. *Être à bout de ressources,* to be at the end of one's resources, F: on one's last legs. *Être sans ressources,* to be penniless. *Ressources personnelles,* private means. **4.** *Av:* Flattening out.

ressouvenance [rəsuvnɑ̃ːs], *s.f. A. & Lit:* Recollection, remembrance.

ressouvenir [rəsuvniːr]. I. *v.* (Conj. like VENIR) To remember (again). **1.** *v.impers. A: Il me ressouvient de . . .,* I have a distant memory of. . . . **2.** *v.pr. Se r. de qch.,* to remember sth. (from long ago). *Faire ressouvenir qn de qch.,* to remind s.o. of sth.

II. **ressouvenir,** *s.m.* Remembrance.

ressu|er [rəsɥe], *v.i.* **1.** (Of walls, etc.) To sweat. **2.** *Faire ressuer,* to sweat, roast (lead and silver ore). *s.m.* **-age.**

ressusciter [resysite]. **1.** *v.tr.* (a) To resuscitate; to restore (s.o.) to life; to raise (the dead). (b) F: To revive (quarrel, fashion). **2.** *v.i.* To resuscitate, revive, come to life again. *Ressuscité d'entre les morts,* risen from the dead.

restant, -ante [restɑ̃, -ɑ̃ːt]. **1.** *a.* (a) Remaining, left. (b) *Poste restante,* 'to be (held till) called for.' **2.** *s.* Remaining person, person left behind. **3.** *s.m.* (= RESTE) Remainder, rest. *Com: R. d'un compte,* balance of an account. *Quelques restants de nourriture,* a few remnants of food.

restaurant [restorɑ̃]. **1.** *a.* Restoring, restorative (food). **2.** *s.m.* (a) Restorative. (b) Restaurant, eating-house.

restaurateur, -trice [restoratœːr, -tris], *s.* **1.** Restorer (of monument, etc.). **2.** *s.m.* Keeper of a restaurant.

restauration [restorasjɔ̃], *s.f.* Restoration (of building, dynasty, finances); restoring, re-establishment (of discipline).

restaurer [restore], *v.tr.* (a) To restore (building, one's health, etc.); to re-establish (discipline). (b) To refresh (s.o.).

se restaurer. (a) To take refreshment, to refresh one's inner man. (b) To feed up (after illness); to recruit.

reste [rɛst], *s.m.* **1.** Rest, remainder, remains. *Elle a des restes de beauté,* she still has traces of beauty. F: *Jouir de son reste,* to make the most of what is left, of one's remaining time. Être en reste, to be in arrears, behindhand. Jouer son reste, to play'one's last stake. *F:* Donner son reste à qn, to finish s.o. off, to settle s.o. Ne pas demander son reste, to have had enough of it; to decamp. Et le reste, and so on; and so forth. *Ar:* Division sans reste, division with no remainder. De reste, left (over); over and above. Avoir de l'argent de reste, to have money and to spare. Je sais de reste *quelle patience cela exige,* I know only too well what patience it requires. Au reste, du reste, besides, moreover. **2.** *pl.* (*a*) Remnants, remains; leavings, scraps (of a meal). (*b*) *Com:* Left-overs. (*c*) Restes mortels, mortal remains.

rester [reste], *v.i.* (Aux. *être*) To remain. **I.** To be left. *Le seul espoir qui nous reste,* our only remaining hope. *Il me reste cinq francs,* I have five francs left. *Il reste beaucoup à faire,* much remains to be done. (Il) reste à savoir si . . ., it remains to be seen whether. . . . **2.** (*a*) To stay, remain behind. (Of thg) *R. à la même place,* to remain in the same place. *Il restait là à me regarder,* he remained, sat, stood, there looking at me. *R. au lit,* to stay, keep, in bed. *R.* (*à*) *dîner,* to stay to dinner. En rester là, to stop at that point; to proceed no further. *Où en sommes-nous restés* (*de notre lecture, etc.*)? where did we leave off? (*b*) *Pred.* R. tranquille, calme, to keep still, calm. *R. bien avec qn,* to keep on good terms, to keep in, with s.o. **3.** (Aux. may be *avoir*) To stay, dwell. *J'ai resté trois mois à Paris,* I stayed in Paris for three months.

restitu|er [restitɥe], *v.tr.* **I.** (*a*) To restore (building, text, etc.). (*b*) *Jur:* To reinstate, rehabilitate (s.o.). **2.** To restore (*à,* to); to hand (sth.) back, over; to return, refund (money); to make restitution of (sth.). **3.** *Surv:* To plot (district, with stereoautograph). *a.* **-able.**

restituteur [restitytœ:r], *s.m.* **I.** Restorer (of mutilated text). **2.** *Surv:* Plotter (with stereoautograph).

restitution [restitysjɔ̃], *s.f.* **I.** Restoration (of text, building). **2.** Restitution.

restreindre [restrɛ̃:dr], *v.tr.* (*pr.p.* restreignant; *p.p.* restreint; *pr.ind.* je restreins, il restreint, n. restreignons; *p.h.* je restreignis; *fu.* je restreindrai) To restrict; to curtail (expenses). *R. ses désirs,* to limit one's desires.

se restreindre. I. To cut down expenses; to retrench. **2.** *Se r. au strict nécessaire,* to limit oneself to essential necessities. *Se r. à faire qch.,* to limit oneself to doing sth.

restreint, *a.* Restricted, limited. Édition à tirage restreint, limited edition.

restrictif, -ive [restriktif, -i:v], *a.* Restrictive (term); limitative (clause).

restriction [restriksjɔ̃], *s.f.* Restriction; limitation (of authority). **Restriction mentale,** mental reservation. *Consentir* sans restriction, to consent unreservedly.

restringent [restrɛ̃ʒɑ̃], *a. & s.m.* Astringent.

résultant, -ante [rezyltɑ̃, -ɑ̃:t]. **I.** *a.* Resultant; resulting (*de,* from); consequent (*de,* upon). **2.** *s.f. Mec: Mth:* Résultante, resultant.

résultat [rezylta], *s.m.* Result, outcome. *Donner des résultats,* to yield results. *Traitement* sans résultat, ineffectual, ineffective, treatment. *Sp:* Match sans résultat, draw.

résulter [rezylte], *v.i.* (Used only in the third pers. Aux. usu. *être*) To result, follow, arise (*de,* from). *Qu'en est-il résulté?* what was the result of it? what came of it? *Il en est résulté beaucoup de mal,* much harm resulted from this. *Il en résulte que* + *ind.,* consequently. . . .

résumer [rezyme], *v.tr.* To summarize; to give a summary of (sth.); to sum up (an argument).

se résumer, to sum up (what one has said).

résumé, *s.m.* Summary, abstract, epitome; résumé, abridgement. *Jur:* R. des débats, summing up. En résumé, in short, to sum up, in brief.

résurrection [rezyrɛksjɔ̃], *s.f.* **I.** Resurrection. **2.** Revival (of the arts, etc.).

retable [rətabl], *s.m.* Retable, reredos, altarpiece.

rétabl|ir [retabli:r], *v.tr.* To re-establish, restore, set up again. (*a*) *R. l'ordre,* to restore public order. *R. sa position,* (i) to retrieve one's position; (ii) to regain the upper hand. *R. sa santé,* to recover one's health. (*b*) *R. un texte,* to restore a text. (*c*) To reinstate (official); to bring (a law) into force again. *s.m.* **-isseur.**

se rétablir. I. (*a*) To recover; to get well again. *Je me sens bien rétabli,* I feel quite myself again. (*b*) *L'ordre se rétablit,* public order is being restored. **2.** *Se r. dans les bonnes grâces de qn,* to re-establish oneself in s.o.'s good graces.

rétablissement [retablismɑ̃], *s.m.* **I.** Re-establishment; restoration (of order, of building); reinstatement (of an official); retrieval (of fortune). **2.** Recovery (after illness).

retailler [rətaje], *v.tr.* To cut (sth.) again; to recut (file, etc.); to re-sharpen (pencil).

rétam|er [retame], *v.tr.* **I.** To re-tin. **2.** To re-silver (mirror). *s.m.* **-age.**

rétameur [retamœ:r], *s.m.* Travelling tinman; *F:* tinker.

retap|er [rətape], *v.tr. F:* **I.** (*a*) To do up (hat, dress); to straighten (bed); to touch up or recast (speech, play); to buck (s.o.) up. *F:* Se retaper le moral, to buck up. (*b*) *Se r. les cheveux,* to fluff out one's hair; to put one's hair straight. **2.** *P:* To plough, pluck (candidate). *s.m.* **-age.**

se retaper. *F:* = SE RÉTABLIR I (*a*).

retard [rəta:r], *s.m.* (*a*) Delay, slowness; backwardness (of harvest, of child). Agir sans retard, to act without delay. Le train a du retard, the train is behind time. *Apporter du r. à* (*faire*) *qch.,* to be slow, behindhand, to delay, in doing sth. En retard, late, behindhand. Mettre qn en retard, to make s.o. late. Être en retard, (i) to be late, behind one's time; (ii) to be behindhand, in arrears. En r. de dix minutes, ten minutes late. *Moisson en r.,* backward harvest. *Les élèves en r.,* the backward boys. *Être en r. sur son siècle,* to be behind the times. *Votre montre a dix minutes de r.,* your watch is ten minutes slow. (*b*) *Tchn:* Retardation. *R. diurne de la marée,* lag of the tides. *Mch:* R. à l'admission, retarded admission, late admission. *El:* R. d'aimantation, magnetic lag.

retardataire [rətardata:r]. **I.** *a.* (*a*) Late, behind time; behindhand, in arrears. (*b*) Backward (pupil, etc.). **2.** *s.* (*a*) Late-comer. (*b*) Loiterer; laggard. (*c*) Tenant in arrears.

retardateur, -trice [rətardatœ:r, -tris]. **I.** *a.* Retarding. **2.** *s.m. Phot:* Restrainer.

retardation [rətardasjɔ̃], *s.f. Mec:* Retardation.

retard|er [rətarde]. **I.** *v.tr.* (*a*) To retard, delay (s.o., sth.); to make (s.o.) late. (*b*) To delay, put off (an event). (*c*) *R. la pendule,* to put back, set back, the clock. **2.** *v.i.* (*a*) To be late, slow, behindhand. *L'horloge retarde,* the clock (i) loses (time), (ii) is slow. *F: Il retarde sur son siècle,* he is behind the times. (*b*) (Of tides, etc.) To lag. *s.m.* **-ement.**

retâter [rətate]. **I.** *v.tr.* (*a*) To touch, feel, (sth.) again. (*b*) *F:* To sound (s.o.) again (*sur une affaire,* on a matter). **2.** *v.ind.tr. R. de qch.,* to try, taste, sth. again. *F:* **Retâter de la prison,** to go to prison again; *F:* to do another stretch.

reteindre [rətɛ̃:dr], *v.tr.* (Conj. like TEINDRE) To redye.

retendre [rətɑ̃:dr], *v.tr.* **1.** To stretch (sth.) again; to reset (trap); to spread (sail) again. **2.** To hold out (one's hand, etc.) again.

retenir [rətni:r], *v.tr.* (Conj. like TENIR) **1.** (*a*) To hold (s.o., sth.) back; to keep back (s.o. from falling, etc.); to detain. *R. qn,* (i) to keep hold of s.o.; (ii) to detain, delay, s.o. *R. l'attention,* to hold, arrest, the attention. *R. qn au lit,* to keep s.o. in bed, to confine s.o. to bed. *On m'a retenu pour ce soir,* I am booked for this evening. *Retenir qn prisonnier,* to keep s.o. prisoner. *Il ne faut pas que je vous retienne, je ne vous retiens pas,* I must not detain you, don't let me keep you. *Nau: Retenu par les glaces, par la marée,* ice-bound, tide-bound. (*b*) To hold (sth.) in position; to secure (sth.). *R. l'eau,* (i) to impound water; (ii) to be watertight. **2.** To retain. (*a*) *R. les gages d'un domestique,* to hold back, withhold, a servant's wages. *R. qch. par cœur,* to remember sth. by heart. *R. son accent anglais,* to retain one's English accent. (*b*) To engage (a servant); to reserve, book (a seat). (*c*) *Ar: Je pose deux et je retiens cinq,* I put down two and carry five. **3.** To restrain, curb, check (one's anger, etc.). *R. un cri,* to stifle a cry. *R. son haleine,* to hold one's breath. *R. ses larmes,* to keep back, hold back, one's tears. *R. sa langue,* to put a curb on one's tongue. *R. qn de faire qch.,* to restrain s.o. from doing sth.

se retenir. 1. *Se r. à qch.,* to catch hold of, cling to, sth. **2.** To restrain, control, contain, oneself; to hold oneself in. *Se r. de faire qch.,* to refrain from doing sth.

retenu, *a.* Prudent, circumspect, cautious.

retenue, *s.f.* **1.** (*a*) Withholding, deduction, docking (of pay, etc.). **Faire une retenue de 5% sur les salaires,** to stop, deduct, 5% from the wages. (*b*) Sum kept back. (*c*) *Ar:* Carry over. **2.** *Sch:* Detention, keeping in. *Mil:* Confinement (to barracks). *Mettre un élève en r.,* to keep a pupil in. **3.** Reserve, discretion; modesty (in bearing); restraint (in one's words). **4.** (*a*) Holding back. *Clapet, soupape, de r.,* back-pressure valve, non-return valve. (*b*) Damming (of water). (*c*) Holding up, staying (of flagstaff, etc.). (*d*) Holding down. **5.** Dam; reservoir (for town supply). **6.** *Retenues de mât d'antenne,* stays of an aerial mast. **7.** *R. d'air,* air-pocket (in pipe).

rétention [retɑ̃sjɔ̃], *s.f.* **1.** *Med:* Retention (of urine, bile). **2.** *Jur:* Retaining (of pledge). **3.** *Ar:* Carrying (of a figure).

retentir [rətɑ̃ti:r], *v.i.* To (re)sound, echo, ring, reverberate. *Choc qui retentit dans tout l'organisme,* shock that causes repercussion throughout the organism.

retentissant [rətɑ̃tisɑ̃], *a.* Resounding, ringing, loud (voice, noise). *Discours r.,* speech that excited world-wide interest.

retentissement [rətɑ̃tismɑ̃], *s.m.* Resounding sound or noise; reverberation; repercussion (of an event, etc.). *Discours qui a eu un grand r.,* speech that excited universal interest. *Avoir peu de r.,* to create little stir, to pass almost unnoticed.

réticence [retisɑ̃:s], *s.f.* Reticence, reserve. *Jur:* Non-disclosure, concealment.

réticulaire [retikylɛ:r], *a.* Reticular.

réticulation [retikylasjɔ̃], *s.f.* Reticulation.

réticule [retikyl], *s.m.* **1.** Reticule, hand-bag. **2.** Reticle, cross-wires, cross-hairs (of optical instrument).

réticulé [retikyle], *a.* Reticulate(d).

rétif, -ive [retif, -i:v], *a.* Restive, stubborn, disobedient.

rétiforme [retifɔrm], *a.* Retiform, netlike.

rétine [retin], *s.f.* *Anat:* Retina.

retirable [rətirabl], *a.* Withdrawable.

retiration [rətirasjɔ̃], *s.f.* *Typ:* Printing of verso, backing up, perfecting. **Presse à retiration,** perfecting machine.

retirer [rətire], *v.tr.* **1.** (*a*) To pull, draw, (sth., s.o.) out; to withdraw (sth.). *R. un enfant du collège,* to take a child away from school. *R. des marchandises de la douane,* to take goods out of bond; to clear goods. *R. son habit,* to take off one's coat. (*b*) *R. qn chez soi,* to give shelter to s.o.; to make a home for s.o. (*c*) *R. un profit de qch.,* to derive, draw, a profit from sth.; to reap a benefit from sth. (*d*) To extract (oil from shale). **2.** (*a*) *R. qch. à qn,* to withdraw sth. from s.o.; to take, snatch, sth. back from s.o. *R. sa faveur à qn,* to withdraw one's favour from s.o. *R. sa main,* to draw one's hand away. *R. une arme à un enfant,* to take a weapon away from a child. (*b*) *R. sa parole, sa promesse,* to take back, recall, withdraw, one's word. *R. sa candidature,* to withdraw one's candidature; to stand down. **3.** To reprint (book).

se retirer. 1. (*a*) To retire, withdraw. *Se r. dans sa chambre,* to retire to one's bedroom. *Se r. de la lutte, du combat,* to retire from the field; to withdraw from the fight. (Of candidate) *Se r. en faveur de qn,* to stand down. (*b*) *Se r. des affaires,* to retire (from business); to give up business. **2.** (Of waters) To fall, subside; (of sea) to recede; (of tide) to ebb.

retiré, *a.* (*a*) Retired, remote (place). (*b*) *Vivre r.,* to live in retirement.

rétivité [retivite], *s.f.* Obstinacy, mulishness.

retombant [rətɔ̃bɑ̃], *a.* Drooping; pendent.

retomber [rətɔ̃be], *v.i.* (Aux. usu. *être*) **1.** To fall (down) again. *R. dans le vice, la misère,* to relapse into vice, into poverty. *R. malade,* to fall ill again. *R. dans l'oubli,* to sink into oblivion again. **2.** To fall (back). *R. sur sa chaise,* to sink back, drop back, into one's chair. *Laisser r. ses bras, son regard,* to drop one's arms, one's eyes. *Faire r. la faute sur qn,* to lay the blame on s.o. *F: Tout ça retombera sur moi,* it'll all come down on me. *F:* **Retomber sur ses pieds,** to fall on one's feet. **3.** To hang down. *Ses cheveux lui retombaient sur le cou,* her hair fell about her neck.

retoquer [rətɔke], *v.tr.* *F:* To plough, pluck (candidate at an examination).

retord|re [rətɔrdr], *v.tr.* **1.** To wring out (the washing) anew. **2.** *Tex:* To twist (thread, yarn, silk). **Métier à retordre,** twisting mill. *F: Il vous donnera du fil à retordre,* he will give you trouble, you have your work cut out with him. *s.m.* **-age.** *s.* **-eur, -euse.**

rétorquer [retɔrke], *v.tr.* (*a*) To retort. (*b*) To cast back, hurl back (accusation).

retors, -orse [rətɔ:r, -ɔrs], *a.* **1.** *Tex:* Twisted (thread, silk). **2.** Crafty, wily, intriguing (person); pettifogging, rascally (lawyer).

retouche [rətuʃ], *s.f.* (*a*) Slight alteration (à, in); retouching (à, of). *Art:* Retouch (to painting, to engraved plate). *Faire des retouches à un travail,* to retouch a piece of work. (*b*) *Phot:* Retouching.

retoucher [rətuʃe], *v.tr.* To retouch, touch up, improve (photograph, etc.).

retoucheur, -euse [rətuʃœ:r, -ø:z], *s.* **1.** *Phot:* Retoucher. **2.** *s.f. Dressm:* **Retoucheuse,** finisher.

retour [rətu:r], *s.m.* **1.** (*a*) Twisting, winding.

Tours et retours, twists and turns. (b) Turn (of rope); lead (of tackle). (c) Turn, vicissitude, reversal (of fortune, opinion); revulsion (of feeling). **Retour de conscience,** qualms of conscience. **Faire un retour sur soi-même,** to indulge in serious reflexions on one's conduct. **Faire un retour sur le passé,** to look back upon the past. (d) Recurrence (of fever, etc.). **2.** Return, going back, coming back. *Biol:* **R. à un type,** reversion to a type. **Être sur son retour,** to be on the point of returning. **Dès mon retour,** as soon as I am back. **A mon retour,** on my return. **Être de retour,** to be back (again). *F:* **Un journaliste retour de Paris,** a reporter just back from Paris. **Être sur le retour,** to be past middle age, past one's prime. **Partir sans retour,** to depart for ever. **Être perdu sans retour,** to be irretrievably lost. *Aut:* **Retour de manivelle,** back-fire kick. *El.E:* **Retour par la terre,** earth return; earth circuit. *Mil:* **Retour offensif,** counter-attack. *Post:* **Par retour du courrier,** by return of post. *Rail:* **Billet de retour,** return ticket. **Coupon de r.,** return half. **Train de r.,** up train. S.a. ALLER II. 1, FLAMME[1] 1. **3.** (a) *Com:* Return (of goods). *Territoires qui ont fait r. à la France,* territories returned to France. (b) *Jur:* Reversion (of an estate). (Of estate) **Faire retour à un ascendant,** to revert to an ascendant. **4.** Return (for a kindness, service, etc.). **Payer qch. de retour,** to requite sth.; to reciprocate (feeling). **En retour de . . .,** in return for . . ., in exchange for. . . . *A beau jeu beau retour,* one good turn deserves another. *Sp:* **Match retour,** return match.

retourne [rəturn], *s.f.* *Cards:* Turned-up card, turn-up.

retourn|er [rəturne]. **I.** *v.tr.* (a) To turn (a skin, etc.) inside out. **Retourner un habit,** (i) to turn a coat inside out; (ii) *Tail:* to turn a coat. S.a. VESTE. (b) To turn (sth.) over; to turn (sth.) up, down, back. **R. le sol,** to turn over the soil. **R. une idée,** to turn over, revolve, an idea. **R. le foin, une omelette,** to turn the hay, an omelette. **R. une carte,** to turn up a card. *F:* **Cela m'a retourné les sangs,** it gave me quite a turn. (c) To turn (sth.) round. **R. la tête,** to turn one's head; to look round. **R. un argument contre qn,** to turn an argument round on s.o. **R. les rires contre qn,** to turn the laughter against s.o. **R. une situation,** to reverse a situation. **2.** *v.tr.* **R. qch. à qn,** to return sth. to s.o.; to give, send, sth. back to s.o. **3.** *v.i.* (Aux. *être*) (a) To return; to go back (*cf.* REVENIR = to come back); to drive, ride, sail, walk, back. **R. en toute hâte,** to hasten back. *Ne retournons pas sur le passé,* we won't go back to the past. **Retourner en arrière,** (i) to turn back, go back; (ii) to retrograde. *F:* **N'y retournez plus,** don't you do it again. *Biol:* **R. à un type,** to revert to a type. (b) (Of a crime, etc.) **R. sur qn,** to recoil upon s.o.; to come home to roost. **4.** *Impers.* **De quoi retourne-t-il?** (i) *Cards:* what is the turn-up? what are trumps? (ii) *F:* what is it all about? what's up? *s.m.* **-ement.**

se retourner. I. (a) To turn (round); to turn over. *Je sentais mon estomac se r.,* I felt my stomach heaving. *F:* **Avoir le temps de se retourner,** to have time to look round. **Il sait se retourner,** he is never at a loss. (b) To turn round, to look round, to look back. (c) To round (*contre qn,* on s.o.). **2.** To turn round, veer (in one's opinion). **3.** *F:* **S'en retourner** (*à un endroit*), to return, go back (to a place).

retracer [rətrase], *v.tr.* (Conj. like TRACER.) **I.** To retrace (a line); to trace (sth.) again.

2. To recall. *Tout ici me retrace ma jeunesse,* everything here recalls my youth to me.

rétractation [retraktasjɔ̃], *s.f.* (a) Retractation, recantation. (b) *Jur:* Rescinding (of decree).

rétracter[1] [retrakte], *v.tr.* To retract, to draw in (claws, etc.).

rétracter[2], *v.tr.* To retract; to withdraw, recant; *F:* to go back on (opinion, etc.). **R. ses paroles,** *F:* to eat one's words. *Jur:* **R. un arrêt,** to rescind, retract, a decree.

se rétracter. (a) To retract, recant. (b) To withdraw a charge.

rétractile [retraktil], *a.* Retractile (organ, etc.).

retrait [rətrɛ], *s.m.* **I.** (a) Shrinkage, shrinking (of wood, etc.). **Caler une frette à retrait,** to shrink on a ring. (b) Retirement (of the waters). **2.** (a) Withdrawal (of order, of troops, etc.); cancelling (of licence); calling off (a strike). **Mettre qn en retrait d'emploi,** to retire s.o. (from his employment). (b) Redemption, repurchase (of estate, etc.). **3.** Recess (in wall); step (of seaplane float). **En retrait,** recessed (shelves, etc.); sunk (panel). **Maison en r.,** house standing back, set back (from the alignment). *Typ:* **Ligne en r.,** indented line.

retraite [rətrɛt], *s.f.* **I.** (a) *Mil:* *Navy:* Retreat, withdrawal, retirement. **Battre en retraite,** to beat a retreat; to retire. (b) *Navy:* **En retraite,** on the quarter. **Pièce de retraite,** stern-chaser (gun); after gun. **En ordre de retraite,** in retiring order. **2.** Tattoo. **Battre, sonner, la retraite,** to beat, sound, the tattoo. *Navy:* **Coup de canon de retraite,** evening gun. **Retraite aux flambeaux,** torchlight tattoo. **3.** (a) Retirement (from active life). **R. par limite d'âge,** superannuation. **Pension de retraite,** retiring pension; *Mil:* retired pay. **Caisse de retraite,** superannuation fund. **Retraite de vieillesse,** old-age pension. **Être en retraite,** to be on the retired list. **Mettre qn à la retraite,** to pension off, superannuate, s.o. S.a. MISE 1. (b) *Ecc:* Retreat. (c) Vivre dans la retraite, to live in retirement. **4.** (a) Retreat; place of retirement. (b) (Place of) shelter; refuge; lair, haunt (of wild beasts).

retraiter [rətrɛte], *v.tr.* To pension (s.o.) off; to retire, superannuate (s.o.). *Soldat retraité,* (army) pensioner.

retranchement [rətrɑ̃ʃmɑ̃], *s.m.* **I.** Cutting off; stopping (of ration, etc.); docking (of pension); excision (of a word). **2.** *Mil:* Retrenchment, entrenchment. *F:* **Forcer qn dans ses (derniers) retranchements,** not to leave s.o. a leg to stand on.

retrancher [rətrɑ̃ʃe], *v.tr.* **I.** (a) **R. qch. de qch.,** to cut off sth. from sth. **R. un passage d'un livre,** to cut, strike, a passage out of a book. (b) **R. qch. à qn,** to dock s.o. of sth. **R. le superflu,** to cut out everything that is not necessary. **2.** *Mil:* To entrench, fortify (post).

se retrancher. I. To retrench; to curtail one's expenses. **2.** *Mil:* To entrench oneself.

retranché, *a.* *Mil:* **Camp retranché,** entrenched camp; fortified area; fortress.

retransmettre [rətrɑ̃smetr], *v.tr.* (Conj. like METTRE) To retransmit.

retransmission [rətrɑ̃smisjɔ̃], *s.f.* *W.Tel:* Retransmission.

retraverser [rətraverse], *v.tr.* To recross.

rétréc|ir [retresi:r]. **I.** *v.tr.* (a) To narrow (a street, the mind); to contract, straiten; to shrink (garment); to waist (pipe). (b) To take in (garment). **2.** *v.i.* & *pr.* To contract; to narrow, to grow narrow. *s.m.* **-issement.**

rétréci, *a.* Narrow, contracted, restricted. *Esprit r.,* narrow mind.

retrempe [rətrɑ̃:p], *s.f.* Retempering (of steel).

retremper [rətrɑ̃pe], *v.tr.* **I.** To soak, steep, again. **2.** (*a*) To retemper (steel, etc.). (*b*) *F:* To tone, brace, (s.o.) up ; to reinvigorate (s.o.).
se retremper, to get toned up, braced up ; to recruit ; to acquire new strength.

rétribuer [retribɥe], *v.tr.* To remunerate, pay (employee, service). *s.m.* **-teur.**

rétribution [retribysjɔ̃], *s.f.* Remuneration, reward ; salary. **Fonctions sans rétribution,** unsalaried office ; honorary duties.

rétro [retro], *s.m. F:* **I.** *Bill:* Pull-back, screw-back (stroke). **2.** *Aut:* **Bruits de rétro,** overrun noises.

rétroactif, -ive [retroaktif, -i:v], *a.* Retroactive, retrospective (law, etc.). *adv.* **-ivement.**

rétroaction [retroaksjɔ̃], *s.f.* **I.** Retroaction. **2.** *El.E:* W.*Tel:* Feed-back.

rétroactivité [retroaktivite], *s.f.* Retroactivity, retrospective effect (of law, etc.).

rétrocéder [retrosede], *v.tr.* (Conj. like CÉDER) *Jur:* To retrocede, reassign (right, etc.).

rétrocession [retrosesjɔ̃], *s.f. Jur:* Retrocession, reconveyance.

rétrogradation [retrogradasjɔ̃], *s.f.* **I.** *Astr:* Retrogradation, retrogression. **2.** Reduction (of N.C.O.) to lower rank.

rétrograde [retrograd], *a.* Retrograde, backward, reversed (motion). *Bill:* **Effet r.,** pull-back, screw-back.

rétrograder [retrograde]. **I.** *v.i.* To retrogress ; to move backwards, to go back. **2.** *v.tr.* To reduce (N.C.O.) to a lower rank.

rétrogressif, -ive [retrogresif, -i:v], *a.* Retrogressive.

rétrogression [retrogresjɔ̃], *s.f.* Retrogression.

rétropédaler [retropedale], *v.i.* To back-pedal. *s.m.* **-age.**

rétrospectif, -ive [retrospektif, -i:v], *a.* Retrospective. *adv.* **-ivement.**

retrousser [rətruse], *v.tr.* To turn up, roll up (one's sleeves, etc.); to tuck up (one's skirt) ; to turn up, twist up (one's moustache) ; to curl up (one's lip) ; to cock (one's hat). **Nez retroussé,** snub nose ; turned-up nose.

retrouver [rətruve], *v.tr.* (*a*) To find (sth., s.o.) (again) ; to meet (with) (sth., s.o.) again ; to rediscover (sth.). **R.** *son chemin,* to find one's way again. **R.** *ses forces,* to regain one's strength. (*b*) **Aller retrouver qn,** to go and join s.o. **Je vous retrouverai ce soir,** I shall see you again this evening. *a.* **-able.**
se retrouver. I. *Se r. dans la même position,* to find oneself once again in the same position. **2.** To find one's bearings. **Je ne puis m'y retrouver!** I can't make it out! **3.** To recover oneself ; to collect one's wits. **4.** To meet again. *Comme on se retrouve!* how people do run across one another! how small the world is!

rétroviseur [retrovizœ:r], *s.m. Aut:* Driving mirror, rear-view mirror.

rets [rɛ], *s.m. Ven: A. & L.* Net. *F:* **Prendre qn dans ses rets,** to catch s.o. in one's toils.

réunion [reynjɔ̃], *s.f.* Reunion. **I.** Bringing together, reuniting ; junction, joining up again ; connecting. **2.** (*a*) Coming together. **Droit de réunion,** right of public meeting. **Salle de réunion,** assembly room. (*b*) Assembly, gathering, meeting. **R.** *publique,* public meeting. (*c*) Social gathering.

réunir [reyni:r], *v.tr.* To (re)unite ; to join (things) together. **R.** *une armée,* to raise an army. **R.** *les eaux,* to collect the water.
se réunir. (*a*) To meet ; to gather together.

(*b*) (Of banks, etc.) To amalgamate ; (of churches) to unite. **Se r.** *contre qn,* to join forces against s.o. **Se r.** *pour faire qch.,* to join together to do sth.

réussir [reysi:r]. **I.** *v.i.* (*a*) *A:* To result, issue (well or ill). **Cela lui a mal réussi,** it turned out badly for him. (*b*) **R.** *dans qch.,* to succeed, be successful, at, in, sth. **R.** *à faire qch.,* to succeed in doing sth. **Ne pas réussir,** to fail. **Tout lui réussit,** he is successful in everything. (*c*) *La pièce a réussi,* the play is a success, has taken on. (*d*) (Of plant) To thrive. **2.** *v.tr.* To make a success of (sth.). **Je n'ai pas réussi le coup,** I didn't bring it off. *Cards:* **R.** *son contrat,* to make one's contract.

réussi, *a.* Successful ; successfully done. **Mal réussi,** badly done ; spoilt.

réussite [reysit], *s.f.* **I.** Issue, result, upshot. **Bonne réussite,** happy issue. **Mauvaise réussite,** ill-success. **2.** Success ; successful result. **3.** *Cards:* Patience. **Faire une réussite,** to work out, *F:* to do, a patience.

revaloir [rəvalwa:r], *v.tr.* (Conj. like VALOIR ; used chiefly in the *fu.*) To return, pay back, (esp. evil) in kind. **Je vous revaudrai cela!** (i) I'll be even with you yet! (ii) I shall do as much for you another time.

revanche [rəvɑ̃:ʃ], *s.f.* **I.** Revenge. (*a*) **Prendre sa revanche sur qn,** to take one's revenge on s.o. ; *F:* to get even with s.o. (*b*) *Games:* **Jouer la revanche,** to play the return match or game. **2.** Requital ; return service. **En revanche,** (i) in return, in compensation ; (ii) on the other hand. *S.a.* CHARGE 5.

revancher (se) [sərəvɑ̃ʃe], *v.pr.* To have one's revenge ; to give as good as one gets.

rêvasser [revase], *v.i.* **I.** To dream of one thing and another. **2.** To muse (*d*, on) ; to indulge in day-dreaming ; to be wool-gathering. *s.* **-eur, -euse.**

rêvasserie [revasri], *s.f.* **I.** Musing, day-dreaming. **2.** *pl.* Day-dreams, idle musings.

rêve [rɛ:v], *s.m.* **I.** Dream. **Faire un rêve,** to have a dream. **2.** Day-dream. **C'est le rêve!** it is everything one could desire ; it is ideal.

revêche [rəvɛʃ], *a.* **I.** Harsh, rough (cloth, wine) ; (stone, wood) difficult to work. **2.** Crabbed, cross-grained, cantankerous.

réveil [revɛj], *s.m.* **I.** (*a*) Waking, awakening. **A mon r., je me souvins . . .,** on waking, I remembered. . . . *F:* **Avoir un fâcheux réveil,** to have a rude awakening. (*b*) *Mil:* **Sonner le réveil,** to sound reveille. **2.** Alar(u)m(-clock).

réveille-matin, *s.m. inv.* = RÉVEIL 2.

réveiller [revɛje], *v.tr.* **I.** To awake, awaken, wake, waken (s.o.) ; to wake (s.o.) up ; to rouse (s.o.). **Ne réveillez pas le chat qui dort,** let sleeping dogs lie. **2.** To awaken, stir up, rouse (feelings, memories).
se réveiller. I. To awake ; to wake (up). *Se r. célèbre,* to wake up to find oneself famous. *S.a.* SURSAUT. **2.** (Of feelings) To be awakened, roused, stirred up ; to revive.

réveillon [revɛjɔ̃], *s.m.* Midnight supper (esp. after midnight mass on Christmas Eve, and on New Year's Eve). **Faire réveillon** = RÉVEILLONNER.

réveillonner [revɛjone], *v.i.* To take part in a *réveillon* ; to see the New Year in.

révélateur, -trice [revelatœ:r, -tris]. **I.** *a.* Revealing, tell-tale (sign, etc.). *S.a.* BAIN 2. **2.** *s.* Revealer, discoverer (of plot, etc.). **3.** *s.m.* (*a*) *Phot:* Developer. (*b*) Detector (of leakages, etc.).

révélation [revelasjɔ̃], *s.f.* **I.** Revelation, disclosure ; betrayal (of one's ignorance). *F:* **Ce**

fut une révélation! that was an eye-opener!
2. *Theol:* Revelation.

révéler [revele], *v.tr.* (je révèle; je révélerai)
1. (*a*) To reveal, disclose; *F:* to let out (secret).
(*b*) To show; to betoken (kindness); to betray, reveal (faults). **2.** *Phot:* To develop (plate, image).
se révéler. 1. (*a*) To reveal oneself, one's character. (*b*) To come to the front. **2.** To be revealed; to come to light.

revenant [rəvnã]. **1.** *a.* Pleasing, prepossessing (face, manners). **2.** *s.m.* Ghost. *Histoire de revenants,* ghost-story. [REVENIR]

revendeur, -euse [rəvãdœːr, -øːz], *s.* (*a*) Retailer, middleman. (*b*) Second-hand dealer.

revendication [rəvãdikasjɔ̃], *s.f.* **1.** Claiming.
2. Claim, demand. **Action en revendication,** action for recovery of property.

revendiquer [rəvãdike], *v.tr.* (*a*) To claim, demand; to assert (one's rights). (*b*) *R. une responsabilité,* to assume a responsibility.

revendre [rəvãːdr], *v.tr.* To resell; to sell (sth.) again. *F:* **Avoir de qch. à revendre,** to have enough and to spare of sth.

revenez-y [rəvnezi], *s.m.inv. F:* **1.** Going back, return (to a habit, etc.); repetition. *Un r.-y de tendresse,* a return, renewal, of affection. **2.** Appetizing dish.

revenir [rəvniːr], *v.i.* (Conj. like VENIR. Aux. *être*) **1.** To return; to come back, come again; to walk, ride, drive, sail, fly, back. *R. à la hâte,* to hasten, hurry, back. *On revient au chemin de fer,* we are coming back, reverting, to travel by rail. *Je suis revenu par chemin de fer,* I came back by rail. *L'herbe reviendra,* the grass will grow again. **Esprit qui revient,** ghost that walks. *Impers. Il revient (des esprits) dans le château,* the castle is haunted. **Revenir sur ses pas,** to retrace one's steps, to turn back. **Revenir sur une promesse,** to go back on a promise. *Cette question est revenue sur l'eau,* this question has come up, cropped up, again. *R. sur un sujet,* to hark back to a subject. **Il n'y a pas à y revenir,** there is no going back on it, the question cannot be reopened. *S.a.* CHARGE 8, MOUTON I, PONTOISE.
2. Revenir à qn. (*a*) To return, come back, to s.o. *La mémoire me revient,* my memory is coming back. *Il me revient encore dix francs,* I have still ten francs to get. *Honneur qui me revient,* honour that falls to me by right. *A chacun ce qui lui revient,* to each one his due. (*b*) *Son visage, son nom, me revient,* I am beginning to recall his face, his name. *Votre nom ne me revient pas,* I can't think of your name. *Il me revient que . . .,* it comes back to my mind that. . . .
(*c*) *Son visage ne me revient pas,* I don't like his looks. (*d*) *Impers. Il me revient que vous dites du mal de moi,* I hear that you are speaking ill of me.
3. (*a*) *R. de ses craintes, d'une maladie,* to get over one's fears, an illness. *R. d'une théorie,* to abandon a theory. *R. d'une erreur,* to realize one's mistake. *Être revenu de qch.,* to have lost one's infatuation for sth. *Vous en reviendrez,* you'll get over it. **Je n'en reviens pas!** I can't get over it! **En revenir d'une belle,** to have had a narrow escape. **Il revient de loin,** he has been at death's door. **Revenir à soi,** to recover consciousness; *F:* to come round, to come to. (*b*) *Cu:* **Faire revenir,** to brown (in a pan). **4. En revenir à qch.,** y revenir, to revert, hark back, to sth. *Il y revient toujours,* he keeps coming back to it.
5. (*a*) To cost. *Sa maison lui revient à 50.000 francs,* his house has cost him 50,000 francs.
(*b*) To amount. *Cela revient au même,* it amounts, comes, to the same thing.

s'en revenir, *F:* to return; to wend one's way back.

revenu, *s.m.* **1.** Income (of pers.); revenue (of the State). **Impôt sur le revenu,** income-tax.
2. *Com:* (i) Yield (of investment); (ii) *pl.* incomings. **3.** *Metall:* Drawing the temper (of steel). **Couleur de revenu,** tempering colour.

revente [rəvãːt], *s.f.* Resale. **Objet de revente,** second-hand article.

rêver [reve]. **1.** *v.i.* To dream. (*a*) *R. de qch.,* to dream (in one's sleep) about sth. (*b*) *R. à, sur, qch.,* to muse on, ponder over, sth. *R. creux,* to day-dream. (*c*) **Rêver tout éveillé,** to be full of idle fancies. *Vous rêvez!* you are dreaming!
2. *v.tr.* To dream (of sth.). *F:* **Vous l'avez rêvé!** you must have dreamt it! *Il rêvait de faire un long voyage,* he longed to go for a long voyage.

réverbération [reverberasjɔ̃], *s.f.* Reverberation.

réverbère [reverbɛːr], *s.m.* **1.** Reverberator, reflector (of heat). **Four à réverbère,** reverberatory furnace. **2.** (*a*) Reflector, reflecting mirror. (*b*) Street-lamp.

réverbérer [reverbere], *v.* (il réverbère; il réverbérera) To reverberate. **1.** *v.tr.* To reflect, throw back (heat, light). **2.** *v.i.* To be reverberated, reflected.

reverdir [rəverdiːr]. **1.** *v.i.* (Of plants) To grow green again; *F:* (of pers.) to grow young again.
2. *v.tr. Le printemps reverdit les champs,* spring makes the fields green again. *s.m.* **-issement.**

révéremment [reveramã], *adv.* Reverently.

révérence [reverãːs], *s.f.* **1.** (*a*) Reverence (*envers, pour,* for). *A:* **Sauf révérence,** saving your reverence. (*b*) *A:* (To ecclesiastic) **Votre Révérence,** your Reverence. **2.** Bow or curtsey. **Faire la révérence à qn;** tirer sa révérence à qn, to bow to s.o.; to drop s.o. a curtsey. **Tirer sa révérence à la compagnie,** to bow oneself out.

révérenciel, -elle [reverãsjɛl], *a.* Reverential (respect or awe).

révérencieu|x, -euse [reverãsjø, -øːz], *a.* Overpolite, fussily ceremonious (person); ceremonious (compliment). *adv.* **-sement.**

révérend, -ende [reverã, -ãːd], *a. Ecc:* Reverend. **Très révérend,** very reverend.

révérer [revere], *v.tr.* (je révère; je révérerai) To revere; to reverence.

rêverie [revri], *s.f.* Reverie; dreaming, musing.

revernir [rəverniːr], *v.tr.* To revarnish.

reverr-ai, -as, etc. [rəvere, -a]. See REVOIR.

revers [rəveːr], *s.m.* **1.** (*a*) Reverse (side) (of coin); wrong side (of stuff); other side (of page). *R. de la main,* back of the hand. **Donner un revers de main à qn,** to deal s.o. a back-handed blow. **Coup de revers,** (i) *Ten:* back-hand stroke; (ii) *Fenc:* reverse. **Prendre une position à revers,** to take a position in reverse, in the rear. (*b*) Facing, lapel, revers (of coat, etc.); turn-over (of stocking). **Bottes à revers,** top-boots. **2.** Reverse (of fortune). **Essuyer un revers,** to suffer a reverse, a set-back.

reverser [rəverse], *v.tr.* **1.** (*a*) To pour (sth.) out again. *Il me reversa à boire,* he poured me out another glass. (*b*) To pour (sth.) back. **2.** To shift (blame, responsibility) (*sur,* on to).

réversible [reversibl], *a.* **1.** Reversible; reversing (back of camera). **2.** *Jur:* Revertible (*d, sur,* to).

réversion [reversjɔ̃], *s.f.* Reversion (*à, to*).

revêtement [rəvɛtmã], *s.m.* Facing, coating, casing, sheathing. *Join:* Veneer. *Fort:* Revetment. *Câble à r. en caoutchouc,* rubber-covered cable. *R. calorifuge*, lagging (of boiler). *Civ.E:* **Mur de revêtement**, revetment wall.

revêtir [rəvetiːr], *v.tr.* (Conj. like VÊTIR) **1.** To clothe again ; to reclothe. **2.** (*a*) To clothe, dress. *R. qn de qch.*, to dress, clothe, s.o. in sth. ; to invest s.o. (with a dignity). *Pièce revêtue de votre signature*, document bearing your signature. *Revêtu de verdure*, verdure-clad. (*b*) *Const: etc:* To face, coat, case, sheathe ; to lag (boiler). *Murs revêtus de boiseries*, walls lined with panelling ; panelled walls. **3.** *R. un habit, un uniforme*, to don, put on, a coat, a uniform. *R. la forme humaine*, to assume human shape.

se revêtir. 1. To put on one's clothes again. **2.** *Se r. de qch.*, to clothe oneself in sth., to put on sth. ; to assume (a dignity).

êveur, -euse [rɛvœːr, -øːz]. **1.** *a.* Dreaming, dreamy, musing. **D'un air rêveur**, dreamily, musingly. **2.** *s. F:* Dreamer ; wool-gatherer.

êveusement [rɛvøzmɑ̃], *adv.* Dreamily.

evidage [rəvidaːʒ], *s.m.* **1.** Re-emptying. **2.** *Com:* Knock-out (after auction sale).

evider [rəvide], *v.tr.* **1.** To re-empty. **2.** *Com:* To knock-out (after auction sale).

evien-s, -t, etc. See REVENIR.

evient [rəvjɛ̃], *s.m.* **1.** (Prix de) **revient**, cost price, prime cost. **2.** *Metalw:* Drawing the temper ; tempering.

evin-s, -t, etc. See REVENIR.

evirement [rəvirmɑ̃], *s.m.* **1.** Sudden change (of fortune) ; revulsion (of feeling). **2.** *Com:* Transfer, making over (of a debt).

evi-s, -t, etc. See REVIVRE and REVOIR.

revis|er [rəvize], **réviser** [revize], *v.tr.* **1.** (*a*) To revise (text, etc.). (*b*) To audit (accounts). (*c*) *Jur:* To reconsider (sentence). **2.** To examine, inspect (sth.) (again) ; to overhaul, go over (motor car). **Voiture révisée**, reconditioned car. *a.* **-able.**

reviseur [rəvizœːr], **réviseur** [revizœːr], *s.m.* Reviser, examiner ; auditor. *Typ:* Proof-reader.

revision [rəvizjɔ̃], **révision** [revizjɔ̃], *s.f.* **1.** (*a*) Revision (of list, account). *Typ:* Proof-reading. (*b*) Audit(ing) (of accounts). (*c*) Reconsideration (of sentence). **2.** Inspection, testing (of boilers, etc.) ; overhaul(ing) (of motor car, etc.) ; medical examination (of recruits). *Mil:* **Conseil de revision**, (i) military appeal court ; (ii) recruiting board.

revisser [rəvise], *v.tr.* To screw up, tighten up.

revivifier [rəvivifje], *v.tr.* To revivify, revive.

revivre [rəviːvr], *v.i.* (Conj. like VIVRE) (*a*) To live again ; to come to life again ; to revive. **Faire r. une coutume**, to revive a custom. (*b*) (With cogn. acc.) To relive (the past).

révocable [revɔkabl], *a.* **1.** Revocable. **2.** Removable (official) ; subject to dismissal.

révocation [revɔkasjɔ̃], *s.f.* **1.** Revocation (of will) ; repeal (of edict) ; rescinding, countermanding. **2.** Removal, dismissal (of an official).

révocatoire [revɔkatwaːr], *a.* Revocatory.

revoici [rəvwasi], *prep. F:* **Me revoici!** here I am again !

revoilà [rəvwala], *prep. F:* **Le revoilà!** there he is again !

revoir [rəvwaːr], *v.tr.* (Conj. like VOIR) **1.** To see (s.o., sth.) again ; to meet (s.o.) again. *s.m.inv.* **Au revoir**, good-bye (for the present). *Ce furent ces au revoir sans fin*, endless good-byes were spoken. **2.** To revise, re-examine ; to look over (accounts, manuscript) ; to read (proofs).

revue, *s.f.* **1.** Review, survey, inspection ; *Mil:* muster inspection. **Passer les troupes en revue ; faire la revue des troupes**, to review,

inspect, the troops. (Of troops) **Passer en revue,** to be reviewed, inspected. **2.** (*a*) Review, magazine. (*b*) *Th:* Revue. **3.** *F:* **Nous sommes de revue,** we shall meet again.

revoler [rəvɔle], *v.i.* **1.** To fly again. **2.** To fly back (*à*, to).

revolin [rəvɔlɛ̃], *s.m. Nau:* **1.** Eddy-wind. **2.** Back current ; eddy.

révoltant [revɔltɑ̃], *a.* Revolting, sickening, shocking ; outrageous (behaviour).

révolte [revɔlt], *s.f.* Revolt, rebellion ; mutiny.

révolter [revɔlte], *v.tr.* To arouse (s.o.'s) indignation ; to revolt (s.o.). *Ses procédés me révoltent,* his business methods disgust me. *Ce spectacle m'a révolté,* I was shocked at the sight.

se révolter, to revolt, rebel (*contre*, against). *Mil: Navy:* To mutiny.

révolté, -ée, *s.* Rebel, insurgent. *Mil: Navy:* Mutineer.

révolu [revɔly], *a.* (Of time) Completed. **Avoir quarante ans révolus,** to have completed one's fortieth year. *Quand le temps sera r.,* in the fullness of time.

révolution [revɔlysjɔ̃], *s.f.* Revolution ; upheaval ; revulsion (of feeling). *Hist:* **La Révolution,** the Revolution (of 1789).

révolutionnaire [revɔlysjɔnɛːr]. (*a*) *a. & s.* Revolutionary. (*b*) *s.* Revolutionist.

révolutionner [revɔlysjɔne], *v.tr.* (*a*) To revolutionize (a country, etc.). (*b*) *F:* To give (s.o.) quite a turn.

revolver [revɔlvɛːr], *s.m.* **1.** Revolver, *U.S:* gun. *R. à six coups, F:* six-shooter. **2.** (*a*) (**Porte-outils**) revolver, revolving tool-holder ; turret, capstan (of lathe). (*b*) Revolving nose-piece (of microscope).

revomir [rəvɔmiːr], *v.tr.* To vomit up ; to throw up (food).

révoquer [revɔke], *v.tr.* **1.** (*a*) To revoke, repeal, rescind (decree) ; to countermand (an order). (*b*) *R. qch. en doute,* to call sth. in question ; to question (statement). **2.** To dismiss (official) ; to recall (ambassador).

revu, revue [rəvy]. See REVOIR.

révulsif, -ive [revylsif, -iv], *a. & s.m. Med:* Revulsive ; counter-irritant.

révulsion [revylsjɔ̃], *s.f. Med:* Revulsion.

rez [re, rɛ], *prep. A:* (Also **A rez de**) (On a) level with ; even with. **Voler rez terre, à rez de terre,** to skim the ground.

rez-de-chaussée [redʃose], *s.m.inv.* (*a*) Ground level, street level. (*b*) Ground-floor, *U.S:* first floor (of house) ; ground-floor flat.

rhabill|er [rabije], *v.tr.* **1.** To repair, overhaul, mend ; to put (watch) in order. **2.** (*a*) To reclothe (s.o.). (*b*) To dress (s.o.) again. *s.m.* **-age.**

se rhabiller. (*a*) To put on one's clothes again. (*b*) To buy a new outfit.

rhabilleur [rabijœːr], *s.m.* **1.** Repairer ; esp. clock and watch repairer. **2.** *F:* Bone-setter.

rhabituer [rabitɥe], *v.tr. R. qn à qch.*, to reaccustom, reinure, s.o. to sth.

se rhabituer, to become reaccustomed, reinured (*à*, to).

rhénan, -ane [renɑ̃, -an]. **1.** *a.* Rhenish, (of the) Rhine. **2.** *s.* Rhinelander.

rhéostat [reɔsta], *s.m. El:* Rheostat ; variable resistance. *R. de démarrage,* starting rheostat ; starter (of electric motor).

rhéteur [retœːr], *s.m.* **1.** Rhetor. **2.** *F: Pej:* Mere talker.

rhétique [retik], *a.* **Les Alpes rhétiques,** the Rhaetian Alps.

rhétoricien [retɔrisjɛ̃], *s.m.* Rhetorician.
rhétorique [retɔrik], *s.f.* (a) Rhetoric. (b) *Sch:* A: **Classe de rhétorique** (now *classe de première*) = top classical form. **Faire sa rhétorique,** to study for the first part of the *baccalauréat* examination.
Rhin (le) [lərɛ̃]. *Pr.n.m. Geog:* The Rhine.
rhingrave [rɛ̃graːv], *s.m. Hist:* Rhinegrave.
rhinocéros [rinɔserɔs], *s.m.* Rhinoceros.
rhizome [rizoːm], *s.m. Bot:* Rhizome.
rhodanien, -ienne [rɔdanjɛ̃, -jɛn], *a. Geog:* Of the Rhone.
rhodium [rɔdjɔm], *s.m. Ch:* Rhodium.
rhododendron [rɔdɔdɛ̃drɔ̃], *s.m. Bot:* Rhododendron; rose-bay.
rhombe [rɔ̃ːb], *s.m.* (a) *Cryst:* Rhomb. (b) *Geom:* Rhombus.
rhomboèdre [rɔ̃bɔɛdr], *s.m.* Rhombohedron.
rhomboïde [rɔ̃bɔid], *s.m. & a.* Rhomboid.
rhubarbe [rybarb], *s.f. Bot: Pharm:* Rhubarb. *Prov:* **Passez-moi la rhubarbe et je vous passerai le séné,** claw me and I'll claw thee; you scratch my back and I'll scratch yours.
rhum [rɔm], *s.m.* Rum.
rhumatisant, -ante [rymatizɑ̃, -ɑ̃ːt], *a. & s.* Rheumatic (subject); *F:* rheumaticky (person).
rhumatismal, -aux [rymatismal, -o], *a.* Rheumatic (pain, fever).
rhumatisme [rymatism], *s.m.* (a) Rheumatism. S.a. NOUEUX 2. (b) *pl. F:* **Être perclus de rhumatismes,** to be crippled with rheumatism, *F:* with the rheumatics.
rhume [rym], *s.m. Med:* Cold. **Gros r.,** heavy cold. **R. de poitrine,** cold on the chest. **R. de cerveau,** cold in the head. *P:* **Prendre qch. pour son rhume,** to get hauled over the coals.
ri [ri]. See RIRE.
riant, *a.* **1.** Smiling (face, etc.). **2.** Cheerful, agreeable, pleasant (prospect).
ribambelle [ribɑ̃bɛl], *s.f. F:* Usu. *Pej:* Long string (of animals, insults). Esp. **R. d'enfants,** swarm, whole lot, of brats.
ribaud, -aude [ribo, -oːd], *a. & s. A:* Ribald.
ribauderie [ribodri], *s.f. A:* Ribaldry.
ribler [rible], *v.tr.* To true up, dress (millstone).
riblons [riblɔ̃], *s.m.pl.* (Iron or steel) scrap; swarf.
ribord [riboːr], *s.m. N.Arch:* Bottom planking.
ribote [ribɔt], *s.f. F:* Drunken bout. **Faire (la) ribote,** to booze; to have a drinking bout. **Être en ribote,** (i) to be tipsy; (ii) to be on the spree.
riboter [ribɔte], *v.i. F:* = *Faire la ribote.*
riboteur, -euse [ribɔtœːr, -øːz], *s. F:* Toper, boozer.
ribouis [ribwi], *s.m. P:* (a) Boot or shoe. (b) Cobbler.
ricanement [rikanmɑ̃], *s.m.* Unpleasant, sneering, or derisive laugh. *pl.* Derisive laughter.
ricaner [rikane], *v.i.* To laugh unpleasantly, derisively; to indulge in mocking, sneering, laughter.
ricaneur, -euse [rikanœːr, -øːz]. **1.** *a.* Derisive (air, etc.). **2.** *s.* Sneerer, derider.
richard [riʃaːr], *s.m. F:* Moneyed man.
riche [riʃ], *a.* **1.** Rich, wealthy, well-off. **Être r. à millions,** to be worth millions. **R. d'espérances,** rich in hope. **Pays r. en blé,** country rich in corn. S.a. FAIRE III. 3, NOUVEAU 2. *B:* **Le mauvais riche,** Dives. **2.** Valuable; handsome (gift). **Faire un r. mariage,** to marry into a wealthy family. *Com:* **Article r.,** superior article. **3.** *F:* **Une r. idée,** a topping idea. **Rater une r. occasion,** to miss a rare occasion. *adv.* **-ment.**
richesse [riʃɛs], *s.f.* **1.** Wealth. (a) **R. en matières**

premières, wealth in raw materials. (b) **Riches**
2. Richness; fertility (of soil); exuberance (o vegetation); sumptuousness (of furniture).
richissime [riʃisim], *a. F:* Extremely rich rolling in money.
ricin [risɛ̃], *s.m.* Castor-oil plant. **Huile de ricin** castor oil.
ricocher [rikɔʃe], *v.i.* (a) To rebound; to glance off. (b) (Of bullet, etc.) To ricochet.
ricochet [rikɔʃɛ], *s.m.* (a) Rebound. **Faire des ricochets** (*sur l'eau*), to make ducks and drakes (b) Ricochet. *Artil:* **Tir à ricochet,** ricochet fire
rictus [rikty:s], *s.m.* **1.** Rictus. **2.** Grin.
ride¹ [rid], *s.f.* **1.** Wrinkle (on the face). *Fron* **creusé de rides profondes,** deeply lined brow. *Fron* **sans rides,** smooth, unwrinkled, brow. **2.** Rippl (on water, sand); ridge (on sand).
ride², *s.f. Nau:* (Shroud) lanyard.
rideau [rido], *s.m.* **1.** Screen, curtain (of trees etc.). *Mil: Navy:* **R. de fumée,** smoke-screen **2.** (a) Curtain. **Garni de rideaux,** hung with curtains; curtained (bed). **Tirer les rideaux,** to draw the curtains. *F:* **Tirer le rideau sur . . .** to draw a veil over. . . . (b) *Th:* (Drop-curtain. **R. d'entr'acte,** act-drop. **Rideau à huit heures précises,** the curtain rises at eight sharp S.a. LEVER II. 2. (c) **R. de cheminée,** register of a fire-place. **Classeur à r.,** roll-shutter cabinet *Phot:* **R. de châssis,** dark-slide shutter.
ridelle [ridɛl], *s.f.* Rack, rail (of cart). **Fausse** *ridelles,* (cart-)ladders.
rider [ride], *v.tr.* **1.** (a) To wrinkle, line (fore-head, etc.); to shrivel (skin). (b) To corrugate flute, rib (metal). **2.** To ripple, ruffle (the water) **se rider.** **1.** To wrinkle; (of forehead, etc.) to become lined; (of apple) to shrivel up. **2.** (Of water) To ripple.
· **ridé,** *a.* **1.** Wrinkled. *Bot:* Rugose, rugous **Pomme ridée,** shrivelled apple. **2.** Ribbed, cor-rugated, fluted. **Tôle ridée,** corrugated iron.
ridicule [ridikyl]. **1.** *a.* Ridiculous, laughable ludicrous. **2.** *s.m.* (a) Ridiculousness, absurdity **C'est d'un r. achevé,** it is perfectly ridiculous. **Tomber dans le ridicule,** to make oneself ridicu-lous. **Tourner qn en ridicule,** to hold s.o. up to ridicule; to poke fun at s.o. (b) Ridicule. **S'exposer au r.,** to lay oneself open to ridicule. (c) Ridiculous habit or touch. **Se moquer des ridicules de qn,** to laugh at s.o.'s ridiculous ways, at s.o.'s little absurdities. *adv.* **-ment.**
ridiculiser [ridikylize], *v.tr.* To ridicule.
rien [rjɛ̃]. **I.** *pron. indef. m.* **1.** Anything. (In questions *rien* is preferred to *quelque chose* when a negative answer is expected. *Cf.* AUCUN) **Y a-t-il rien de plus triste?** is there anything more depressing? **2.** Nothing, not anything. (a) (With *ne* expressed) **Rien ne l'intéresse,** nothing interests him. **Je n'ai rien à faire,** I have nothing to do. **Il n'y a rien à faire,** there is nothing to be done; it can't be helped. **Il ne faut rien lui dire,** he must not be told anything. **Il n'est rien de tel que de se bien porter,** there is nothing like health. **Il ne vous faut rien d'autre,** is there nothing else? do you require anything else? **Cela ne fait rien,** that doesn't matter, it makes no difference. **Si cela ne vous fait rien,** if you have no objection, if you don't mind. **Comme si de rien n'était,** as if nothing had happened. **Il n'en est rien!** nothing of the kind! **Je n'en ferai rien,** I shall do nothing of the sort, nothing of the kind. **N'être pour rien dans une affaire,** to have no hand in a matter. *F:* **Il ne sait rien de rien,** he knows nothing at all. S.a. MOINS 1, MONDE 1. (b) (With *ne* under-stood) **Que faites-vous?—Rien, presque rien,**

what do you do?—Nothing, hardly anything. **Rien du tout,** nothing at all. **Venir à rien,** to come to nothing. **Parler pour rien,** to waste one's breath. *Merci, madame.*—*De rien, monsieur,* thank you, madam.—Please don't mention it. **En moins de rien,** in less than no time. **Une affaire de rien (du tout),** an insignificant matter. **Un (homme de) rien du tout,** a man of no account; a nobody. *Ten:* **Quinze à rien,** fifteen love. *(c) Il est inutile de rien dire,* you needn't say anything. *Sans rien faire,* without doing anything. *(d)* **Rien que,** nothing but, only, merely. *Rien que ce silence le condamne,* his silence alone is sufficient proof against him. *Il tremblait rien qu'en le racontant,* only, merely, to tell of it made him tremble. *(e)* (With *ne* . . . *pas*) *On ne peut pas vivre de rien,* you can't live on nothing. *Ce n'est pas rien!* that's something! *Ce n'est pas pour rien que* . . ., it is not without good reason that. . . . **3.** *P:* (Intensive) **Elle est rien chic!** she isn't half smart! **II. rien,** *s.m.* **1.** Trifle; mere nothing. *Se piquer d'un rien,* to take offence at the slightest thing. *S'amuser à des riens,* to trifle. *Il le fera en un rien de temps,* he'll do it in no time. **2.** Just a little. *Donnez-moi un rien de fromage,* give me just a taste of cheese.

rieur, -euse [rjœːr, -øːz]. **1.** *a.* Laughing; fond of laughter. **2.** *s.* Laugher. **Avoir les rieurs de son côté,** to have the laugh on one's side.

riflard¹ [riflaːr], *s.m. Tls:* **1.** Coarse file (for metals); riffler. **2.** Paring chisel. **3.** Jack-plane. **4.** Plastering trowel.

riflard², s.m. *F:* Umbrella; *F:* brolly, gamp.

rifler [rifle], *v.tr. (a)* To plane. *(b)* To pare. *(c)* To file.

rigide [riʒid], *a.* Rigid; tense (muscle, etc.); cast-iron (etiquette); fixed (axle). *adv.* **-ment.**

rigidité [riʒidite], *s.f.* Rigidity; stiffness; tenseness. *R. cataleptique,* cataleptic rigor. *R. cadavérique,* rigor mortis.

rigodon [rigɔdɔ̃], *s.m.* **1.** *Danc: A:* Rigadoon. **2.** *Mil:* **Faire un rigodon,** to score a bull's-eye.

rigolade [rigɔlad], *s.f. P:* Fun; lark, spree.

rigole [rigɔl], *s.f.* Drain, furrow-drain, trench, gutter, channel.

rigoler [rigɔle], *v.i. P: (a)* To laugh. *(b)* To have some fun, to enjoy oneself.

rigoleur, -euse [rigɔlœːr, -øːz]. **1.** *a.* Fond of fun. **2.** *s. (a)* Laugher. *(b)* Jolly chap; joker.

rigollot [rigɔlo], *s.m. Pharm:* **(Papier) rigollot,** mustard-leaf, -plaster.

rigolo, -ote [rigɔlo, -ɔt]. *P:* **1.** *a. (a)* Comical, laughable, funny. *Ce n'est pas r.,* it's no joke. *(b)* Surprising, queer. **2.** *s.* Wag, joker. **3.** *s.m.* Revolver or pistol.

rigorisme [rigɔrism], *s.m.* Rigorism, strictness.

rigoriste [rigɔrist]. **1.** *a.* Rigorous; strict (code of morals). **2.** *s.* Rigorist; rigid moralist.

rigoureux, -euse [rigurø, -øːz], *a.* Rigorous. **1.** Severe, harsh; hard (winter). **2.** Strict. *Observer une neutralité rigoureuse,* to observe strict neutrality. *adv.* **-sement.**

rigueur [rigœːr], *s.f.* **1.** Rigour, harshness, severity. *Les rigueurs du sort,* the hardships of fate. **Prendre des mesures de rigueur,** to take rigorous, severe, measures. **User de rigueur** *avec qn,* to be severe with, hard on, s.o. **Tenir rigueur à qn,** to refuse to relent towards s.o. **2.** Strictness. *La r. d'un raisonnement,* the closeness, exactness, of a piece of reasoning. (Of thg) **Être de rigueur,** to be indispensable, compulsory, obligatory. *L'habit n'est pas de r.,* evening dress is optional. **A la rigueur,** (i) rigorously, strictly; (ii) if need

be, if really necessary. *A la r. on peut se servir de* . . ., at a pinch one may use. . . .

rillettes [rijɛt], *s.f.pl.* Potted mince (of pork).

rillons [rijɔ̃], *s.m.pl. Cu:* Greaves.

rimailler [rimɑje], *v.i. F:* To string rhymes together.

rimailleur [rimɑjœːr], *s.m. F:* Rhymester.

rime [rim], *s.f. Pros:* Rhyme. *Rimes plates, suivies,* alternate masculine and feminine couplets; couplet rhymes. *Rimes croisées, alternées,* alternate rhymes. *Dictionnaire de rimes,* rhyming dictionary. *F:* **Sans rime ni raison,** without rhyme or reason.

rimer [rime]. **1.** *v.tr.* To versify; to put (tale, etc.) into rhyme. **2.** *v.i. (a)* (Of word) To rhyme (*avec,* with; *à,* to). *F:* **Cela ne rime à rien,** there's no sense, neither rhyme nor reason, in it. *(b)* (Of pers.) To rhyme, to write verse.

rimeur [rimœːr], *s.m.* Rhymer, rhymester.

rinceau [rɛ̃so], *s.m.* **1.** *Arch:* Foliated scroll. **2.** (Curtain) loop-hook.

rince-bouche, s.m.inv., rince-doigts, s.m.inv. Finger-bowl.

rincer [rɛ̃se], *v.tr.* (je rinçai(s); n. rinçons) To rinse (clothes); to rinse out (glass). *P:* **Se rincer le gosier, la dalle,** to wet one's whistle. *s.m.* **-çage.**

rincée, s.f. *P:* Drubbing, thrashing.

rinçure [rɛ̃syːr], *s.f.* Rinsings, slops.

ringard [rɛ̃gaːr], *s.m.* (Furnace) fire-iron, poker, slice-bar, pricker.

ripaille [ripɑːj], *s.f. F:* Feasting, carousal. **Faire ripaille,** to feast, carouse.

ripailler [ripɑje], *v.i. F:* To feast, carouse, revel. *s.* **-eur, -euse.**

ripatonner [ripatɔne], *v.tr. P:* To mend; to patch (sth.) up; to botch (sth.) up.

ripatons [ripatɔ̃], *s.m.pl. P:* **1.** Feet. **2.** Boots.

ripe [rip], *s.f. Tls: Sculp: etc:* Scraper.

riper [ripe]. **1.** *v.tr.* To scrape, polish (stone). **2.** *v.tr. (a)* To slip (chain on capstan, etc.). (Of) To slide along, to shift (load). **3.** *v.i. (a)* (Of hawser) To scrape, rub. *(b)* (Of wheels) To skid. *s.m.* **-age.**

ripolin [ripɔlɛ̃], *s.m.* Ripolin enamel.

ripopée [ripɔpe], *s.f. F:* Slops; lap; heel-taps (of wine); hash-up (of old theories).

riposte [ripɔst], *s.f.* Riposte. **1.** *Box: Fenc:* Counter. **2.** *(a)* Retort. *(b)* Counterstroke.

riposter [ripɔste], *v.i.* **1.** *Box: Fenc:* To riposte, counter. **2.** To retort.

ripuaire [ripɥɛːr], *a. & s.* Ripuarian.

riquiqui [rikiki], *s.m. F:* **1.** *(a)* The little finger. *(b)* Undersized person. **2.** Brandy (of poor quality). *Un petit verre de r.,* a little drop of spirits.

rire [riːr]. **1.** *v.i.* (*pr.p.* riant; *p.p.* ri; *pr.ind.* je ris, n. rions, ils rient; *pr.sub.* je rie; *p.h.* je ris; *fu.* je rirai) **1.** To laugh. **Se tenir les côtes de rire,** **rire comme un bossu,** to be convulsed with laughter, to shake with laughter. *R. bruyamment,* to guffaw. *R. en soi-même,* *r. tout bas,* to laugh to oneself; to chuckle. *R. faux, pointu,* to force a laugh. *R. bêtement,* (i) to haw-haw, (ii) to giggle, titter. *S.a.* ANGE I, BARBE¹ I, CAPE I, DENT I, ÉCLAT I, ÉCLATER 2, etc. *Il a ri (jusqu')aux larmes,* he laughed till he cried. *C'était à mourir de rire,* *P:* **à crever de rire,** it was killingly funny. **Ne pas avoir le cœur à rire,** not to be in a laughing mood. **Il n'y a pas de quoi rire,** it is no laughing matter. **Rire de qn,** to laugh at s.o. **Rire d'une histoire,** to laugh over a story. *Prov:* **Tel qui rit vendredi dimanche pleurera,** laugh on Friday, cry on Sunday. **Rira bien qui rira le dernier,** he laughs longest who laughs last. *S.a.* NEZ I. **2.** To jest, joke. **Vous voulez rire !** you are joking ! *Prendre qch. en riant,* to laugh sth. off. **Pour rire,** for fun, for a joke. *Journal pour rire,* comic paper. **Roi pour rire,** sham king. *Soldats pour r.,* make-believe soldiers. **Je l'ai fait histoire de rire,** I did it for a joke, for fun. S.a. MOT 1. **3.** (a) *R. à qn,* to greet s.o. with a smile. (b) To be favourable, propitious (*à,* to). *La fortune lui rit,* fortune smiles on him.

se rire. (a) *Se rire de qn,* to laugh at, mock at, s.o. (b) *Se r. de qch.,* to make light of sth. II. **rire,** *s.m.* (a) Laughter, laughing. **Éclat de rire,** burst of laughter. **Il eut un court éclat de rire,** he gave a short laugh. **Avoir un accès de fou rire,** to be overcome with uncontrollable laughter. (b) **Un rire,** a laugh. *Il eut un r. d'incrédulité,* he laughed incredulously.

ris¹ [ri], *s.m. A. & Poet :* Laugh, laughter.

ris², *s.m. Nau :* Reef (in sail). **Prendre un ris,** to take in a reef. **Voile au bas ris,** close-reefed sail. **Larguer un ris,** to shake out a reef.

ris³, *s.m. Cu :* Ris de veau, **d'agneau,** sweetbread.

risée [rize], *s.f.* **1.** (a) Jeer, mockery. (b) Laughing-stock, butt. **2.** *Nau :* Light squall.

risette [rizɛt], *s.f.* (Child's) pretty laugh or smile. **Fais (la) risette à papa !** now smile to daddy !

risible [rizibl], *a.* Ludicrous, laughable (mistake). *adv.* **-ment.**

risque [risk], *s.m.* Risk. *Courir un r.,* to run, incur, a risk. **A tout risque,** at all hazards. *Vous le faites* **à vos risques et périls,** you do it at your own risk. **Au risque de sa vie,** at the risk, peril, of his life. *Ins :* Police **tous risques,** all-in policy. **Risques de guerre,** war-risks.

risquer [riske], *v.tr.* To risk, venture, chance. *R. sa vie,* to risk one's life. *Je ne veux rien r.,* I am not taking any risks, any chances. *Prov :* Qui **ne risque rien n'a rien,** nothing venture, nothing have. **Risquer le coup,** to chance it. *a.* **-able.**

se risquer, to take a risk ; to take risks. *Se r. à faire qch.,* to venture, to make bold, to do sth.

risqué, *a.* Risky.

risque-tout, *s.m.inv.* Desperado, dare-devil.

rissole [risol], *s.f. Cu :* Rissole.

rissoler [risole], *v.tr. Cu :* To brown.

ristourne [risturn], *s.f.* Refund ; return (of amount overpaid) ; rebate.

ristourner [risturne], *v.tr.* To refund, return (amount overpaid).

rit, rite [rit], *s.m.* (The *pl.* is always *rites*) Rite.

ritournelle [riturnɛl], *s.f. Mus :* Ritornelle. *F :* **C'est toujours la même ritournelle,** he's always harping on the same string.

ritualisme [ritɥalism], *s.m. Ecc :* Ritualism.

ritualiste [ritɥalist]. **1.** *a.* Ritualistic. **2.** *s.* Ritualist ; *Pej :* ceremonialist.

rituel, -elle [ritɥɛl]. **1.** *a.* Ritual. **2.** *s.m.* Ritual.

rivage [riva:ʒ], *s.m.* Bank, side (of river) ; shore, strand (of lake, sea) ; waterside. [RIVE]

rival, -ale, -aux [rival, -o], *a. & s.* Rival. **Sans rival,** unrivalled.

rivaliser [rivalize], *v.i. R. avec qn,* (i) to rival s.o. ; (ii) to compete, vie, with s.o. ; to emulate s.o. *Il peut r. avec les meilleurs,* he can hold his own, compare, with the best. *R. d'efforts avec qn,* to vie with s.o.

rivalité [rivalite], *s.f.* Rivalry, emulation.

rive [ri:v], *s.f.* **1.** Bank (of river) ; shore (of lake) ; waterside ; skirt (of a wood). (Of the Seine) **La rive droite, gauche,** the north, south, side. **2.** *Tchn :* Edge, edging ; border (of horseshoe).

rivelaine [rivlɛn], *s.f. Tls : Min :* Pick.

river [rive], *v.tr.* (a) To rivet. (b) To clinch

(nail). *F :* **River son clou à qn,** (i) to give s.o. a clincher ; (ii) to give s.o. a piece of one's mind

riverain, -aine [rivrɛ̃, -ɛn]. **1.** *a.* (a) Riparian riverside, waterside, riverain (owner, property etc.). (b) Bordering on a road, on a wood, etc. wayside (property, etc.). **2.** *s.* (a) Riverside resident. (b) Borderer (upon a road, etc.).

rivet [rivɛ], *s.m.* (a) Rivet. *Assemblage à rivets* riveted joint. (b) Clinch.

riveter [rivte], *v.tr.* (je rivette ; je rivetterai) To rivet. *s.m.* **-age.** *s.m.* **-eur.**

rivière [rivjɛ:r], *s.f.* **1.** River, stream. S.a. RUISSEAU 1. **2.** *Geog :* **La Rivière (de Gênes),** the Riviera. **3.** **Rivière de diamants,** diamond rivière. **4.** *Needlew :* Open-work, hem-stitch.

rivoir [rivwa:r], *s.m.* Riveting-hammer.

rivure [rivy:r], *s.f.* **1.** Riveting. **2.** (a) Rivet(ed) joint. (b) Rivet head. **3.** (a) Pin-joint (b) Hinge-pin.

rixe [riks], *s.f.* Brawl, scuffle, affray.

riz [ri], *s.m.* Rice. *Riz en paille,* paddy. *Riz décortiqué,* husked rice. **Eau de riz,** rice-water. *Cu :* **Riz au lait** [rjolɛ], rice pudding. **Gâteau de riz,** rice shape. S.a. PAPIER 1, POUDRE 2.

rizière [rizjɛ:r], *s.f.* Rice-plantation ; rice-swamp

robe [rɔb], *s.f.* **1.** (a) (Lady's) dress, gown, frock. *R. du soir,* evening dress. *R. de ville,* walking dress. (b) **Robe de chambre,** dressing-gown ; (lady's) wrapper. **Pommes de terre en robe de chambre,** potatoes in their jackets (c) (Long) robe, gown (of lawyer, etc.). **Les gens de robe ; la robe,** the legal profession. **2.** (a) Skin (of onion, sausage, etc.) ; husk (of bean) ; outer leaf (of cigar). (b) Coat (of horse, dog).

robin [rɔbɛ̃], *s.m. F :* Gentleman of the robe ; lawyer.

robinet [rɔbinɛ], *s.m.* (Stop-)cock ; tap, faucet, spigot. *R. à flotteur,* ball-cock. *Mch : R. d'extraction,* blow-off cock. *Ouvrir, fermer, le r.,* to turn on, turn off, the tap, the gas, the water, etc. *Tourner le r.,* to turn (on, off) the tap.

robinetier [rɔbinetje], *s.m.* Brass-founder and finisher ; brass-smith.

robinier [rɔbinje], *s.m. Bot :* False acacia.

robre [rɔbr], *s.m. Cards :* Rubber.

robuste [rɔbyst], *a.* Robust ; sturdy (child) ; stout (faith) ; hardy (plant) ; strongly built (bicycle). *adv.* **-ment.**

robustesse [rɔbystɛs], *s.f.* Robustness, sturdiness, hardiness ; strength.

roc [rɔk], *s.m.* Rock. *Bâti sur le roc,* built on rock.

rocaille [rɔka:j], *s.f.* (a) Rock-work. **Jardin de rocaille,** rockery ; rock-garden. (b) Rubble.

rocailleux, -euse [rɔkajø, -ø:z], *a.* (a) Rocky, pebbly, stony. (b) *F :* Rugged, harsh (style).

roche [rɔʃ], *s.f.* Rock, boulder. **Roche de fond,** bed-rock. *Terrain de r.,* hard, rocky, soil. *F :* **Clair comme de l'eau de roche,** clear as crystal. **Avoir un cœur de roche,** to have a heart of stone. **Homme de la vieille roche,** man of the good old stock, of the old school. **Il y a quelque chose sous roche,** there is something in the wind. S.a. ANGUILLE 1, CRISTAL 1.

rocher [rɔʃe], *s.m.* Rock (high and pointed) ; crag. *Côte hérissée de rochers,* rock-bound coast. *Le r. de Gibraltar,* the rock of Gibraltar. *R. branlant,* rocking stone, logan-stone. **Ferme comme un rocher,** firm as a rock.

rochet¹ [rɔʃe], *s.m.* Ratchet. **Roue à rochet,** ratchet-wheel.

rochet², *s.m. Ecc.Cost :* Rochet.

rocheux, -euse [rɔʃø, -ø:z], *a.* Rocky, stony. **Les montagnes Rocheuses,** the Rocky Mountains, *F :* the Rockies.

rococo [rɔkɔko]. **1.** *a.inv.* (*a*) Rococo; in the French XVIII century style. (*b*) *F*: Antiquated, old-fashioned. **2.** *s.m.* **Le rococo,** rococo, baroque.

rodage [rɔdaːʒ], *s.m.* Grinding. **1.** Lapping, polishing (of shaft, gem); grinding in (of glass stopper, of valve). *Aut*: **"En rodage,"** 'running in.' **2.** Wearing (of parts).

roder [rɔde], *v.tr.* To grind. (*a*) To lap, polish; to grind in (glass stopper, valve). **Poudre à roder,** abradant. (*b*) *Moteur encore mal rodé,* engine not yet run in.

rôder [rode], *v.i.* **1.** To prowl; to be on the prowl. *R. les rues,* to prowl about the streets. **2.** (Of ship) *R. sur son ancre,* to veer at anchor.

rôdeur, -euse [rodœːr, -øːz]. **1.** *a.* Prowling. **2.** *s.* Prowler. *R. de grève,* riverside loafer.

rodoir [rɔdwaːr], *s.m.* Grinding-tool.

rodomont [rɔdɔmɔ̃]. **1.** *Pr.n.m. Lit*: Rodomont (in Ariosto's *Orlando Furioso*). **2.** *s.m. A*: Swashbuckler, braggart, swaggerer, blusterer.

rodomontade [rɔdɔmɔ̃tad], *s.f.* Rodomontade; *pl.* bluster, braggadocio, swagger.

Rogations [rɔgasjɔ̃], *s.f.pl. Ecc*: Rogation-days.

rogatons [rɔgatɔ̃], *s.m.pl.* Scraps (of food); odds and ends; broken meat.

Roger [rɔʒe]. *Pr.n.m.* Roger. **Un Roger Bontemps,** a happy-go-lucky fellow, a jovial soul.

rogne [rɔɲ], *s.f. P*: **Être en rogne,** to be cross, in a temper.

rogn|er [rɔɲe], *v.tr.* To clip, trim, pare. *R. les tranches,* to cut, trim, the edges (of a book). *F*: **Rogner les ailes à qn,** to clip s.o.'s wings. **Rogner les morceaux à qn,** to cut down s.o.'s allowance or profits. S.a. ONGLE 1. *s.m.* **-age.** *s.m.* **-ement.** *s.* **-eur, -euse.**

rognoir [rɔɲwaːr], *s.m.* Paring-tool.

rognon [rɔɲɔ̃], *s.m.* **1.** *Cu*: Kidney (of animals). **2. Rognon de silex,** flint-nodule, kidney-stone.

rognonn|er [rɔɲɔne], *v.i. P*: To grumble, growl; to grouse. *s.m.* **-ement.**

rognures [rɔɲyːr], *s.f.pl.* Cuttings, clippings, parings; trimmings; scraps.

rogomme [rɔgɔm], *s.m. F*: Spirits, liquor. **Voix de rogomme,** husky voice (of a drunkard).

rogue¹ [rɔg], *a.* Arrogant, haughty (voice).

rogue², *s.f. Fish*: Salted cod-roe (used as bait).

roi [rwa], *s.m.* King. *Les rois de France,* the kings of France, the French kings. **De par le roi,** in the King's name. **Morceau de roi,** dish fit for a king. *La maison du roi,* the royal household. **Jour, fête, des Rois,** Twelfth-day. **Veille des Rois,** Twelfth-night. **Faire les Rois,** to celebrate, keep, Twelfth-night, the Epiphany. **Gâteau, galette, des Rois,** Twelfth-cake. *Cards*: *Le roi de trèfle,* the king of clubs. *Chess*: *Le roi,* the king.

roide [red], *a.,* **roideur** [redœːr], *s.f.,* **roidir** [rediːr], *v.tr.* See RAIDE, RAIDEUR, RAIDIR.

roitelet [rwatlɛ], *s.m.* **1.** Petty king. **2.** *Orn*: (Golden-crested or fire-crested) wren.

rôle [roːl], *s.m.* **1.** (*a*) Roll (of parchment, etc.). (*b*) *Jur*: Roll (of court); list; register. *Mil*: Roster. **A tour de rôle,** in turn, by turns, in rotation. *Faire qch. à tour de r.,* to take turns in doing sth. *Nau*: *R. de l'équipage,* list of the crew; muster-roll. **2.** *Th*: Part, rôle. **Premier** *r.,* leading part; leading man; leading lady. **Assigner un rôle à qn,** to cast s.o. for a part. **Distribution des rôles,** (i) casting, (ii) cast (of the play). *Jouer un r. important dans une affaire,* to play, take, a prominent part in an affair. **Sortir de son rôle,** (i) to go beyond one's part; (ii) to take too much upon oneself.

rollier [rɔlje], *s.m. Orn*: Roller.

romain, -aine¹ [rɔmɛ̃, -ɛn]. **1.** *a. & s.* Roman. **2.** *s.m. Typ*: Roman type. **3.** *s.f.* **Romaine,** cos lettuce.

romaine², *s.f.* Steelyard. S.a. BALANCE 1, BASCULE 1.

roman¹ [rɔmɑ̃], *s.m.* **1.** (*a*) Novel. *R. policier,* detective novel. *F*: *R. à deux sous,* penny dreadful. (*b*) *L'histoire de notre rencontre est tout un r.,* the story of our meeting is quite a romance. (*c*) **Le roman, les romans,** (prose) fiction. **2.** *Mediev.Lit*: Romance. **Le Roman de la Rose,** the Romaunt of the Rose.

roman², -ane [rɔmɑ̃, -an], *a. & s.m.* **1.** *Ling*: Romance, Romanic. **2.** *Arch*: Romanesque; (in Eng.) Norman.

romance [rɔmɑ̃ːs], *s.f. Mus*: (Sentimental) song, drawing-room ballad.

romancier, -ière [rɔmɑ̃sje, -jɛːr], *s.* Novelist.

romand [rɔmɑ̃], *a. Geog*: **La Suisse romande,** French Switzerland.

romanesque [rɔmanɛsk], *a.* Romantic (idea, etc.). *adv.* **-ment.**

roman-feuilleton, *s.m. Journ*: Serial (story). *pl. Des romans-feuilletons.*

romanichel, -elle [rɔmaniʃɛl], *s.* (*a*) Gipsy, romany. (*b*) Vagrant.

romaniste [rɔmanist], *s.m.* **1.** *Ecc*: Romanist. **2.** *Ling*: Student of the Romance languages.

romantique [rɔmɑ̃tik]. **1.** *a.* Romantic; belonging to the Romantic school of literature. **2.** *s.* Romanticist. S.a. CLASSIQUE 3.

romantisme [rɔmɑ̃tism], *s.m. Lit.Hist*: Romanticism.

romarin [rɔmarɛ̃], *s.m. Bot*: Rosemary.

Rome [rɔm]. *Pr.n.f. Geog*: Rome. *Prov*: **Tout chemin mène à Rome,** all roads lead to Rome. **A Rome il faut vivre comme à Rome,** when at Rome you must do as the Romans do.

rompre [rɔ̃ːpr], *v.* (*pr.ind.* **je romps, il rompt, ils rompent**) **1.** *v.tr.* To break. (*a*) To break in two (with an effort); to snap (stick, bough). *Se r. le cou,* to break one's neck. S.a. LANCE 1. (*b*) To disrupt. *R. un chemin,* to break up a road. (Of stream) *R. ses digues,* to burst its banks. *Se r. une artère,* to burst, rupture, an artery. **Applaudir à tout rompre,** to bring down the house. *F*: **Rompre la tête, les oreilles, à qn,** (i) to make a deafening noise; (ii) to drive s.o. crazy (with questions, etc.). **Se rompre la tête,** to cudgel one's brains. *Mil*: **Rompre le pas,** to break step. **Rompez!** dismiss! S.a. GLACE 1, RANG 1. (*c*) *R. le silence,* to break the silence. *R. une promesse,* to break a promise. S.a. BAN 2. (*d*) *R. un coup, un choc,* to deaden the force of a blow, to deaden a shock. (*e*) *R. un mariage, une conversation,* to break off an engagement, a conversation. *R. un tête-à-tête,* to interrupt a private conversation. *R. un marché,* to call off a deal. *El*: *R. un circuit,* to break, open, a circuit. (*f*) *R. l'équilibre,* to upset the equilibrium, the balance. **Rompre les chiens,** (i) to call off the hounds; (ii) *F*: to change the subject; (iii) *F*: to put an end to the conversation. (*g*) *R. un cheval,* to break in a horse. *R. qn à la discipline, aux affaires,* to break s.o. in to discipline, to train s.o. to business. *R. qn à la fatigue,* to inure s.o. to fatigue. **2.** *v.i.* (*a*) To break (off, up, asunder). *R. avec qn,* to break with s.o. *R. avec une habitude,* to break (off) a habit. S.a. VISIÈRE 1. (*b*) (Of troops) *R. devant l'ennemi,* to break before the enemy. (*c*) *Box: Fenc*: To give ground, to step back.

se rompre. 1. To break (asunder); (of branch) to snap, break off; (of ice) to break (up).

2. *Se r. à qch.*, to break oneself in to sth.; to accustom oneself to sth. **rompu,** *a.* (*a*) Broken. **Être rompu de fatigue,** to be worn out, tired out. *S.a.* BÂTON I, JAMBE I. (*b*) Broken in. *Être r. aux affaires,* to be experienced in business.

romsteck [rɔmstɛk], *s.m. Cu:* Rump-steak.

ronce [rɔ̃:s], *s.f.* **I.** *Bot:* Bramble; blackberry-bush. **2.** *F:* Thorns. **Ronce(s) artificielle(s),** barbed wire. **3.** Curl (in grain of wood). *R. de noyer,* bur-walnut.

ronce-framboise, *s.f.* Loganberry. *pl. Des ronces-framboises.*

ronceux, -euse [rɔ̃sø, -ø:z], *a.* **I.** Brambly. **2.** *Acajou r.,* figured mahogany.

ronchon [rɔ̃ʃɔ̃], *a. & s. inv. in f. F:* Grumbler. *Elle est ronchon,* she is something of a scold.

ronchonn|er [rɔ̃ʃɔne], *v.i.* **I.** *F:* To grumble, grouse. **2.** *W.Tel:* To hum. *s.m.* **-ement.**

ronchonneur, -euse [rɔ̃ʃɔnœ:r, -ø:z], *s. F:* Grumbler; *f.* scold.

rond, ronde [rɔ̃, rɔ̃:d]. **I. I.** *a.* (*a*) Round (table, etc.); rounded (arm); plump (figure). **Bourse ronde,** well-lined purse. *adv.* (Of wheel) **Tourner rond,** to run true. (*b*) *Voix ronde,* full voice. *En chiffres ronds,* in round figures. *Compte r.,* round sum, even money. *F:* **Homme tout rond,** straightforward, bluff, man. *Il est r. en affaires,* he does a straight deal. **2.** *s.m.* (*a*) Round, ring, circle. **Le chat se met en rond,** the cat curls up, coils itself up. **Danser en rond,** to dance in a ring. *S.a.* EMPÊCHEUR. **Rond de serviette,** napkin ring. (*b*) *Disc. Mec.E:* Washer. *R. de pain, de saucisson,* slice, round, of bread, of sausage. *R. de beurre,* pat of butter. **Rond de cuir,** (round leather) chair cushion. *S.a.* ROND-DE-CUIR. *P:* **Il n'a pas un rond,** he hasn't a brass farthing. **II. ronde,** *s.f.* **I.** (*a*) Round (dance). (*b*) *Mil:* etc:* Round(s); (of policeman) beat. **Faire la ronde,** to go the rounds. *A: La r. de nuit,* (i) the watch patrol; (ii) the watch. (*c*) Round-hand (writing). (*d*) *Mus:* Semibreve. **2. A la ronde,** around. *A dix lieues à la r.,* for thirty miles round. **(Faire) passer le vin à la ronde,** to pass the wine round, to hand round the bottle. *Boire à la r.,* to drink in turn.

rond-de-cuir, *s.m. F:* (*a*) Clerk (esp. in Government service). (*Cf.* ROND 2) *Vieux r.-de-c.,* old stick-in-the-mud. (*b*) Bureaucrat. *pl. Des ronds-de-cuir.*

rondeau [rɔ̃do], *s.m.* **I.** *Fr.Lit:* Rondeau. **2.** *Mus:* Rondo.

rondelet, -ette [rɔ̃dlɛ, -ɛt], *a.* Roundish, plumpish (person). *Somme rondelette,* nice, tidy, little sum.

rondelle [rɔ̃dɛl], *s.f.* **I.** Small round; disc (of cardboard, etc.); slice (of gherkin). **Rondelle fusible,** fusible plug (of boiler). **2.** (*a*) Ring. (*b*) Washer. *R. à ressort,* spring washer.

rondement [rɔ̃dmã], *adv.* (*a*) Roundly, briskly, promptly, smartly. *Mener r. les choses,* to hustle things on. (*b*) *Il nous a dit r. que . . .,* he told us straight that. . . .

rondeur [rɔ̃dœ:r], *s.f.* **I.** Roundness, rotundity; fullness (of shape); *pl.* rounded forms or lines. **2.** Frankness, outspokenness.

rondin [rɔ̃dɛ̃], *s.m.* (*a*) (Round) billet; log (of firewood). *Chemin de rondins,* corduroy road. (*b*) Thick stick; cudgel.

rond-point, *s.m.* Circus (where several roads meet). *pl. Des ronds-points.*

ronflant [rɔ̃flã], *a.* **I.** Snoring. **2.** (*a*) Rumbling, booming, humming, whirring, throbbing (noise).

(*b*) *Voix ronflante,* booming voice. *Titres ronflants,* sonorous titles. *Tirade ronflante,* high-sounding tirade.

ronflement [rɔ̃fləmã], *s.m.* **I.** (*a*) Snoring. (*b*) Snore. **2.** Rumbling, booming, humming, whirring. *W.Tel:* Buzzing; hum (in loud-speaker).

ronfler [rɔ̃fle], *v.i.* **I.** To snore. **2.** (Of wind, fire, etc.) To roar; (of organ) to boom; (of top) to hum; (of engine) to whirr.

ronfleur, -euse [rɔ̃flœ:r, -ø:z], *s.* Snorer.

rongeant [rɔ̃ʒã], *a.* (*a*) Corroding; rodent (ulcer). (*b*) Gnawing, carking (care).

ronger [rɔ̃ʒe], *v.tr.* (je rongeai(s); n. rongeons) **I.** To gnaw, nibble. *R. un os,* (of dog) to gnaw a bone; (of pers.) to pick a bone. *Se ronger le cœur,* to eat, fret, one's heart out. *S.a.* FREIN I, ONGLE I, VER 2. **2.** (Of acid, etc.) To corrode; to pit, to eat away (metal); (of the sea) to erode (coast). *F:* **Être rongé de chagrin,** to be consumed, tormented, with grief.

rongeur, -euse [rɔ̃ʒœ:r, -ø:z]. **I.** *a.* Rodent, gnawing (animal); rodent (ulcer). *F:* **Soucis rongeurs,** carking care. *S.a.* VER 2. **2.** *s.m. Z:* Rodent.

ronron [rɔ̃rɔ̃], *s.m.* **I.** Purr(ing). **Faire ronron,** to purr. **2.** *F:* Hum, whirr.

ronronn|er [rɔ̃rɔne], *v.i.* (*a*) To purr. (*b*) *Mch: W.Tel:* To hum. *a.* **-ant.** *s.m.* **-ement.**

roquefort [rɔkfɔ:r], *s.m.* Roquefort cheese.

roquer [rɔke], *v.i.* **I.** *Chess:* To castle. **2.** *Croquet:* To (loose-)croquet (the ball).

roquet [rɔkɛ], *s.m.* (*a*) Pug-dog. (*b*) Cur, mongrel.

roquette [rɔkɛt], *s.f. Bot:* Rocket.

rorqual [rɔrkwal], *s.m. Z:* Rorqual; finback.

rosace [rozas], *s.f.* (*a*) Rose(-window), wheel-window. (*b*) *R. de plafond,* ceiling-rose; rosette.

rosacé [rozase]. *Bot:* **I.** *a.* Rosaceous. **2.** *s.f.pl.* **Rosacées,** rosaceae.

rosaire [rozɛ:r], *s.m. Ecc:* Rosary. **Dire le rosaire,** to tell one's beads.

rosâtre [rozɑ:tr], *a.* Pinkish.

rosbif [rɔsbif], *s.m.* Roast beef.

rose [ro:z]. **I.** *s.f. Bot:* Rose. (*a*) *R. mousseuse,* moss rose. *R. pompon,* fairy rose. *R. sauvage,* wild rose, dog-rose. **Eau de rose,** rose-water. **Essence de roses,** attar of roses. *F:* **Lèvres de rose,** rosy lips. **Tout n'est pas rose(s) dans ce monde,** life is not a bed of roses. **(Il n'est) pas de rose sans épines,** no rose without a thorn. **Découvrir le pot aux roses** [potoro:z], to find out the secret. (*b*) **Rose trémière,** hollyhock. **Bois de rose,** tulip-wood. **2.** (*a*) *a.* Pink (dress); rosy (complexion). (*Inv.* in compounds) *Des rubans rose pivoine,* peony-red ribbons. (*b*) *s.m.* Rose (colour); pink. *F:* **Voir tout en rose,** to see everything through rose-coloured spectacles. **3.** *s.f.* (*a*) *Arch:* Rose-window. (*b*) *Nau:* **Rose des vents,** compass-card; mariner's card. (*c*) *Lap:* Rose (diamond).

roseau [rozo], *s.m. Bot:* Reed. *R. des sables,* beach-grass. *F:* **S'appuyer sur un roseau,** to lean on a broken reed.

rosée [roze], *s.f.* Dew. *Goutte de r.,* dewdrop. **Couvert, humecté, de rosée,** dewy. *Ph:* **Point de rosée,** dew-point.

roséole [rozeɔl], *s.f. Med:* Roseola. *R. épidémique,* German measles.

roser [roze], *v.tr.* To rose; to make (sth.) pink, rosy.

rosé, *a.* Roseate, rosy. *S.a.* VIN.

roseraie [rozrɛ], *s.f.* Rosery; rose-garden.

rosette [rozɛt], *s.f.* **I.** (*a*) Bow (of ribbon). (*b*) Rosette (of the Legion of Honour). **2.** (*a*) Red

ink. (b) Red chalk. **3.** (Cuivre de) **rosette**, rose-copper. **4.** Clout nail.

rosier [rozje], s.m. Rose-tree, rose-bush.

rosière [rozjɛːr], s.f. Maiden to whom is awarded the wreath of roses (and a small dowry) for virtuous conduct. (Le couronnement de la Rosière is an annual event in certain French villages.)

rosir [roziːr], v.i. To become, turn, rosy; to blush; to go pink.

rosse [rɔs]. **1.** s.f. (a) F: Sorry steed; screw. (b) P: Objectionable, ill-natured, person; 'beast.' **2.** a. P: Objectionable, ill-natured; nasty (person, song, etc.); low-down (trick).

rosser [rɔse], v.tr. F: To give (s.o.) a beating, a thrashing.

rossée, s.f. P: Beating, thrashing.

rosserie [rɔsri], s.f. P: **1.** Nastiness, scurviness (of conduct, of speech). **2.** (a) Nasty, scurvy, trick. (b) Nasty story, scurrilous expression. (c) Spiteful, catty, remark.

rossignol [rɔsiɲɔl], s.m. **1.** Nightingale. **2.** Picklock, skeleton-key. **3.** F: Old unsaleable article (in shop); piece of junk.

rossinante [rɔsinãːt], s.f. F: Rosinante, old worn-out hack. (From Don Quixote's horse.)

rossolis¹ [rɔsɔli], s.m. Bot: Sundew, drosera.

rossolis², s.m. Rosolio (cordial).

rostral, -aux [rɔstral, -o], a. Rostral. Rom.Ant: **Couronne rostrale**, rostral crown.

rostre [rɔstr], s.m. Bot: Z: Rostrum. Rom.Ant: **Les rostres**, the Rostra.

rot [ro], s.m. P: Belch; eructation.

rôt [ro], s.m. A: (a) Roast (meat). (b) Roast meat course.

rotang [rɔtɑ̃], s.m. Bot: = ROTIN¹ **1.**

rotatif, -ive [rɔtatif, -iːv]. **1.** a. Rotary (pump, etc.). **2.** s.f. Rotative, rotary printing-press.

rotation [rɔtasjɔ̃], s.f. Rotation. Mouvement de r., rotary motion. **Axe de rotation**, axis of rotation. **Pièce à rotation**, revolving part. **Corps en rotation**, rotating body.

rotatoire [rɔtatwaːr], a. **1.** Mec: Rotatory; rotative. **2.** Ph: Rotary (polarization).

roter [rɔte], v.i. To belch; to bring up wind.

rotifère [rɔtifɛːr], s.m. Biol: Rotifer. pl. Rotifera.

rotin¹ [rɔtɛ̃], s.m. **1.** Bot: Rattan. **Sièges en rotin**, cane chairs. **2.** Rattan walking-stick.

rotin², s.m. P: Penny. Il n'a pas un rotin, he hasn't a penny-piece.

rôt|ir [rɔtiːr, rɔ-]. **1.** v.tr. (a) To roast (meat); to toast (bread). **Porc rôti**, roast pork. **Pain rôti**, toast. (b) F: (Of the sun) To scorch, dry up (grass, etc.). **2.** v.i. To roast; to toast; to scorch. s.m. **-issage.**

rôti, s.m. (a) Roast (meat). **R. de mouton**, roast mutton. (b) Roast meat course.

rôtie, s.f. Round of toast. **Rôties beurrées**, buttered toast. **Rôtie à l'anglaise**, Welsh rabbit.

rôtisserie [rotisri], s.f. A: Cook-shop.

rôtisseur, -euse [rotisœːr, -øːz], s. A: Cook-shop proprietor.

rôtissoire [rotiswaːr], s.f. Dutch oven.

rotonde [rɔtɔ̃ːd], s.f. **1.** Rotunda; circular hall. Rail: Engine shed. **2.** (Lady's long sleeveless) cloak.

rotondité [rɔtɔ̃dite], s.f. Rotundity. **1.** Roundness; stoutness. **2.** Rounded part.

rotor [rɔtɔːr], s.m. Rotor (of dynamo, turbine).

rotule [rɔtyl], s.f. **1.** Knee-cap; patella. **2.** Mec.E: Knee-joint; ball-and-socket joint. Aut: **R. de direction**, steering-knuckle.

roture [rɔtyːr], s.f. **1.** Commoner's condition. **2.** Coll. Commonalty, commons.

roturier, -ière [rɔtyrje, -jɛːr]. **1.** a. Of the common people. **2.** s. (a) Commoner. Les roturiers, the commonalty. (b) Self-made man.

rouable [rwabl], s.m. Fire-rake.

rouage [rwaːʒ], s.m. **1.** Wheels, wheelwork. **Rouage(s) d'une montre**, works, train of wheels, of a watch. **2.** (Toothed) wheel, gear-wheel.

rouan, -anne [rwɑ̃, -an], a. Roan (horse, cow).

roublard, -arde [rublaːr, -ard], a. & s. F: Foxy, wily, artful (person).

roublarder [rublarde], v.i. P: To finesse; to cheat.

roublardise [rublardiːz], s.f. P: **1.** Cunning, foxiness, craftiness. **2.** Piece of trickery.

rouble [rubl], s.m. Num: Rouble.

roucoul|er [rukule], v.i. To coo. a. **-ant.** s.m. **-ement.**

roue [ru], s.f. Wheel. (a) Voiture à quatre roues, four-wheeled carriage; F: four-wheeler. F: **Cinquième roue à un carrosse**, entirely useless person or thing. **Pousser à la roue**, to put one's shoulder to the wheel. **Sans roues**, wheelless. **Faire la roue**, (i) (of peacock, etc.) to spread (out) its tail; (ii) to strut, swagger; (iii) to turn cart-wheels. S.a. BÂTON **1.** (b) Mec.E: **R. à aile, r. volante**, fly-wheel. **R. dentée, r. d'engrenage**, cog-wheel, gear-wheel. **R. d'angle**, bevel wheel, mitre wheel. **R. de courroie**, belt pulley. **R. folle**, décalée, loose wheel, idle wheel. **R. à patin**, caterpillar wheel. (c) **R. à eau, r. hydraulique**, water-wheel. **R. de moulin**, mill-wheel. **R. en dessus, r. à augets**, overshot wheel. **R. en dessous, r. à aubes**, undershot wheel. (d) N. Arch: **R. à aubes**, paddle-wheel. (e) Nau: **R. du gouvernail**, steering-wheel, 'the wheel.'

rouelle [rwel], s.f. Round slice (of lemon); round (of beef). **R. de veau**, fillet of veal. S.a. SÉTON **1.**

rouennerie [rwanri], s.f. Tex: Printed cotton goods (originally of Rouen).

rouer [rwe], v.tr. (a) A: To break (s.o.) upon the wheel. (b) F: **Rouer qn de coups**, to beat s.o. black and blue.

roué, -ée. 1. s.m. Rake, profligate; roué. **2.** a. & s. Cunning, sly, artful (person).

rouerie [ruri], s.f. **1.** Piece of trickery of knavery; piece of sharp practice. [ROUÉ]

rouet [rwe], s.m. **1.** Spinning-wheel. **2.** Sheave; pulley-wheel. **3.** A: Wheel-lock (of gun).

rouf [ruf], s.m. = ROUFLE.

rouflaquette [ruflaket], s.f. P: Lovelock; Newgate knocker.

roufle [rufl], s.m. (a) Deck-house (of ship). (b) Cuddy (of barge).

rouge [ruːʒ]. **1.** a. Red. (a) **Fer rouge**, red-hot iron. **Être rouge de honte**, to be red, blushing, with shame. **Devenir r. comme une pivoine**, to turn as red as a peony. **Le chapeau rouge**, the cardinal's (red) hat. **Le drapeau rouge**, the red flag. S.a. COQ **1**, ÉCREVISSE **1**, PEAU-ROUGE. adv. **Se fâcher tout rouge**, to lose one's temper completely. **Voir rouge**, to see red. (b) (Inv. in compounds) Rouge sang, blood-red. **Des rubans rouge cerise**, cherry-red ribbons. S.a. CAROTTE **1.** **2.** s.m. (a) Red. **Porter le fer au rouge**, to make the iron red-hot. **Rouge-blanc**, white heat. (b) Rouge. **Mettre du rouge**, to rouge (oneself). **Bâton de rouge**, lipstick.

rougeâtre [ruʒɑːtr], a. Reddish.

rougeaud, -eaude [ruʒo, -oːd], a. & s. Red-faced (person).

rouge-gorge, s.m. (Robin) redbreast. pl. Des rouges-gorges.

rougeole [ruʒɔl], s.f. (a) Med: Measles. **R. bénigne**, German measles. (b) Vet: Sheep-pox.

rougeoy|er [ruʒwaje], *v.i.* (il **rougeoie**; il **rougeoiera**) (Of thg) (*a*) To turn red. (*b*) To glow; to emit a lurid glow. *a.* **-ant.**

rouge-queue, *s.m. Orn:* Redstart. *pl. Des rouges-queues.*

rouget [ruʒɛ], *s.m.* (*a*) *Bot: F:* Cow-wheat. (*b*) *Ent: F:* Harvest-bug; harvester. (*c*) *Ich: F:* (i) Red mullet, (ii) surmullet, (iii) gurnard.

rougeur [ruʒœ:r], *s.f.* **1.** Redness. **2.** Blush, flush. **3.** Red spot, blotch (on the skin).

rougir [ruʒi:r]. **1.** *v.tr.* (*a*) To redden; to turn (sth.) red. *Eau rougie,* water with a little red wine. (*b*) To bring (metal) to a red heat. *R. le fer au blanc,* to make iron white-hot. (*c*) To flush (the face). **2.** *v.i.* (*a*) To redden, to turn red. (*b*) *Faire rougir un métal,* to heat a metal red-hot. (*c*) (Of pers.) To turn, go, red; to colour; to blush; to flush (up). *R. de qch.,* to be ashamed of sth. *Faire rougir qn,* to put s.o. to the blush; to put s.o. to shame. *R. de colère,* to flush with anger.

rouille [ru:j], *s.f.* **1.** Rust. *Acier sans rouille,* rustless steel. *Tache de rouille,* iron-mould. **2.** *Agr:* Rust, mildew, blight.

rouiller [ruje], *v.tr.* **1.** To rust. **2.** To mildew, blight (plant).
se rouiller. 1.(*a*) To rust (up). (*b*) *F:* Laisser rouiller ses connaissances, to allow one's knowledge to rust. **2.** (Of plant) To become mildewed.
rouillé, *a.* **1.** (*a*) Rusted, rusty. (*b*) *Sp: etc:* Out of practice. **2.** Mildewed.

rouilleux, -euse [rujø, -ø:z], *a.* Rust-coloured; rusty (black, etc.).

rouillure [rujy:r], *s.f.* **1.** Rustiness. **2.** (Of plants) Rust, blight.

rou|ir [rwi:r]. **1.** *v.tr.* To steep, ret (flax). **2.** *v.i.* (Of flax) To steep, ret. *s.m.* **-issage.**

roui, *s.m.* **1.** Retting, steeping (of flax). **2.** *F:* Sentir le roui, to taste of dish-water.

roukerie [rukri], *s.f.* Rookery (colony of rooks, penguins, seals, etc.).

roulade [rulad], *s.f.* **1.** *Faire une roulade,* to roll downhill. **2.** *Mus:* Roulade, run. **3.** *Cu:* (*a*) Beef olive. (*b*) Jam roll.

roulage [rula:ʒ], *s.m.* **1.** (*a*) Rolling (esp. of ploughed land). (*b*) Easy running (of vehicle). **2.** Carriage, cartage (of goods); haulage (of coal). *Cheval de roulage,* cart-horse, draught-horse. S.a. ENTREPRISE 1. **3.** Road traffic.

roulant [rulɑ̃], *a.* **1.** (*a*) Rolling; sliding (door); moving (staircase); travelling (crane). *Rail: Matériel roulant,* rolling-stock. S.a. FEU¹ 3. (*b*) Smooth. *Chemin bien r.,* good carriage road, easy(-running) road. **2.** *Com: Affaire roulante,* going concern. *Fonds roulant,* working capital. **3.** *P:* Side-splitting, killing (sight, joke).

rouleau [rulo], *s.m.* **1.** Roller. (*a*) *Roulements à rouleaux,* roller-bearings. (*b*) *R. compresseur, r. à vapeur,* steam-roller. *Passer le gazon au rouleau,* to roll the grass. (*c*) *R. porte-serviettes,* towel-roller. *Typewr: R. porte-papier,* platen; cylinder. *Carte sur rouleau,* roller-map. *Store sur r.,* roller-blind. (*d*) *Typ:* (Ink) roller. *Phot:* (Roller-)squeegee. **2.** (*a*) Roll (of paper, etc.); roll, web (of news-print); coil, spool (of cinematograph film); coil (of rope). *F: Je suis au bout de mon rouleau,* I am at the end of my tether, at my wits' end. *Tabac en rouleau,* twist tobacco. (*b*) Roller-blind.

roulement [rulmɑ̃], *s.m.* **1.** (*a*) Rolling. *Av: R. sur le sol,* taxying. *Bande de roulement,* tread (of tyre). (*b*) Running, working (of machine, etc.). **2.** Rumbling (of waggon, of thunder); rattle (of carriage); roll(ing) (of drum). **3.** *Mec.E:* Bearing. *R. à billes,* ball-bearing. *Voie, chemin, de roulement (pour billes),* ball-race. S.a. BAGUE 2. **4.** (*a*) *Com: R. de fonds,* circulation of capital. S.a. FONDS 3. (*b*) Alternation, taking turns (in duties); rotation-roll. *Par roulement,* in rotation.

rouler [rule]. **1.** *v.tr.* (*a*) To roll (cask, etc.) (along). *R. les yeux,* to roll one's eyes. *R. un projet dans sa tête,* to revolve, turn over, a plan in one's mind. *Min: R. le charbon,* to haul the coal. *Golf: Coup roulé,* putt. S.a. BOSSE 1, CARROSSE. (*b*) *F: Rouler qn,* (i) to take s.o. in, to do s.o.; (ii) to beat, lick, s.o. (*c*) To roll up (map); to collar (meat, fish). *R. une cigarette,* to roll a cigarette. (*d*) To roll (the lawn). (*e*) *R. les r,* to roll one's r's. (*f*) *R. qn dans une couverture,* to roll, wrap, s.o. up in a blanket. **2.** *v.i.* (*a*) To roll (over, along). *R. sur une pente,* to roll down a slope. *R. en voiture,* to drive, *F:* to bowl along, in a carriage. *Av: R. sur le sol,* to taxi. *F: Rouler sur l'or et sur l'argent,* to be rolling in money. *La conversation roulait sur le sport,* the talk ran, turned, upon sport. *Tout roule sur lui,* everything turns upon him. *R. dans tous les pays, r. par le monde,* to rove, roam, in every land; to knock about the world. *Prov: Pierre qui roule n'amasse pas mousse,* a rolling stone gathers no moss. (*b*) (Of thunder) To roll, rumble. (*c*) *Auto qui roule bien,* car that runs well. *Auto très peu roulée,* car with very small mileage. (*d*) *Nau:* (Of ship) To roll. *Rouler à faire cuiller,* to roll gunwale under. (*e*) To rotate, to take turns (in the performance of a duty, etc.).
se rouler. (*a*) To roll, to turn over and over (in the grass, etc.). (*b*) *Le hérisson se roule en boule,* the hedgehog rolls up into a ball.

roulée, *s.f. P:* Thrashing, licking.

roulette [rulɛt], *s.f.* **1.** (*a*) Caster; roller; small wheel. *Patins à roulettes,* roller-skates. *F: Ça va comme sur des roulettes,* things are going like clockwork. (*b*) *Tls:* Pricking-wheel; tracing wheel. (*c*) (Spring) tape-measure. **2.** (Game of) roulette.

rouleur [rulœ:r], *s.m.* **1.** Haulage-man. **2.** Workman who never remains long on the same job; rolling stone. *F: R. de cabarets,* pub-crawler. **3.** *Nau:* Ship that rolls heavily.

roulier [rulje], *s.m.* Carter, waggoner; carrier.

roulis [ruli], *s.m. Nau:* Rolling. *Coup de roulis,* roll, lurch.

roulotte [rulɔt], *s.f.* House on wheels; caravan; esp. gipsies' caravan.

roulure [ruly:r], *s.f.* **1.** Rolled edge. **2.** Cupshake (in timber).

roumain, -aine [rumɛ̃, -ɛn], *a. & s.* Rumanian.

Roumanie [rumani]. *Pr.n.f. Geog:* Rumania.

roupie¹ [rupi], *s.f. Num:* Rupee.

roupie², *s.f.* Drop (at end of nose).

roupill|er [rupije], *v.i. P:* To sleep; *F:* to snooze. *s.* **-eur, -euse.**

roupillon [rupijɔ̃], *s.m. P:* Nap, snooze.

rouquin, -ine [rukɛ̃, -in], *a. & s. P:* Red-haired, carroty-haired. *s.* Ginger, Carrots.

rouspétance [ruspetɑ̃:s], *s.f. P:* Resistance; refractoriness (esp. to the police). *Faire de la rouspétance,* to be obstreperous.

rouspéter [ruspete], *v.i. (je rouspète; je rouspéterai) P:* To resist, protest; to show fight; to be refractory (to the police).

rouspéteur [ruspetœ:r], *s.m. P:* Refractory street-prisoner; quarrelsome fellow.

roussâtre [rusɑ:tr], *a.* Reddish (hair).

rousse [rus]. See ROUX.

rousselet [ruslɛ], *s.m.* Russet pear.

ousserolle [rusrɔl], *s.f. Orn:* Sedge-warbler.

ousseur [rusœːr], *s.f.* Redness (of hair, etc.). **Tache de rousseur**, freckle. *Couvert de taches de r.*, freckled.

oussin[1] [rusɛ̃], *s.m.* Cob; plough-horse.

oussin[2], *s.m. P:* Policeman; police-spy.

ouss|ir [rusiːr]. **I.** *v.tr.* (a) To turn (sth.) russet or brown; to redden. *Cu:* To brown (meat). (b) To scorch, singe (linen). **2.** *v.i.* (a) To turn brown; to redden. (b) *Cu:* **Faire roussir du beurre,** une sauce, to brown butter, a sauce. (c) To singe; to get scorched. *s.m.* **-issement.**

roussi. I. *a.* Browned; scorched. **2.** *s.m.* **Cela sent le roussi,** there is a smell of something burning. *F:* (Of pers., opinions) **Sentir le roussi,** to be in danger of burning at the stake; to smack of heresy.

oute [rut], *s.f.* **I.** Road(way), path, track. **Grande route, route nationale,** main road, high-road, highway. *R. départementale,* secondary road. *R. vicinale, cantonale,* local road. *R. muletière,* mule-track. *R. à barrière,* turnpike. **2.** Route, course, way. *R. de mer,* sea route. *R. de terre,* overland route. *Montrer la r. à qn,* to show s.o. the way. *Barrer la r. à qn,* to bar s.o.'s way. **Se mettre en route,** to start on one's way, to set out; *Nau:* to get under way. **Être en route,** to be on the way. **Frais de route,** travelling expenses. **En route!** (i) let us be off! (ii) off you go! **Faire route avec qn,** to travel with s.o. *Mil:* **Chanson de route,** marching song. S.a. FAUX[1] I. 3. *Navire en r. pour l'étranger,* ship outward bound. *Nau:* **Tracer la route,** to set the course (on the chart). **Faire route,** (i) to go ahead; (ii) to steer the course. *Faire r. au sud,* to steer south. **Route commerciale,** trade route. S.a. FEUILLE 3. **3. Mettre des travaux en route,** to start operations. *Mettre en r. le moteur,* to start (up) the engine.

outier[1], **-ière** [rutje, -jɛːr], *a. & s.* (a) *Nau:* (**Livre**) **routier,** track-chart. (b) **Carte routière,** road-map. (c) **Voie routière,** highway, carriage-way. (d) (**Bicyclette**) **routière,** roadster. (*Locomotive*) *routière,* traction-engine, road-engine. *Transports routiers,* road transport. (e) *s.m. Cy: Rac:* (Of pers.) Road racer.

outier[2], *s.m. Mil: A:* Mercenary. *F:* **Vieux routier,** old campaigner; old stager.

routine [rutin], *s.f.* (a) Routine. (b) Routinism. **Faire qch. par routine,** (i) to do sth. by rule of thumb; (ii) to do sth. out of sheer habit.

routinier, -ière [rutinje, -jɛːr]. **I.** *a.* (a) Routine (duties). (b) (Person) who follows a routine. **2.** *s.* Routinist.

rouvrir [ruvriːr], *v.* (Conj. like OUVRIR) **I.** *v.tr.* To reopen. **2.** *v.i.* (Of theatre) To reopen.

se rouvrir, (of door, wound, etc.) to open again; to reopen.

roux, rousse [ru, rus]. **I.** (a) *a.* (Russet-)red, (reddish-)brown; (of hair) red, *F:* carroty. *Cu:* **Beurre roux,** brown(ed) butter. S.a. LUNE I. (*Inv.* in compounds) *Chevelure blond roux,* sandy hair. (b) *s.* Red-haired, sandy-haired, person. **2.** *s.m.* (a) Russet, reddish-brown (colour). (b) *Cu:* Brown sauce; browning. **3.** *s.f. P:* **La rousse,** the police.

royal, -aux [rwajal, -o], *a.* Royal, regal, kingly. **Prince royal,** crown prince. *adv.* **-ement.**

royalisme [rwajalism], *s.m.* Royalism.

royaliste [rwajalist], *a. & s.* Royalist.

royaume [rwajoːm], *s.m.* Kingdom, realm. **Le Royaume-Uni,** the United Kingdom. **Le royaume des cieux,** the kingdom of heaven.

royauté [rwajote], *s.f.* Royalty; kingship.

ru [ry], *s.m. Dial:* Channel, water-course.

ruade [rɥad], *s.f.* Lashing out, fling out (of horse). **Allonger une ruade,** to lash out (à, at). [RUER]

ruban [rybɑ̃], *s.m.* **I.** (a) Ribbon, band. *R. de chapeau,* hatband. **Le ruban rouge,** the red ribbon (of the Legion of Honour). (b) *R. de fil,* tape. **Mètre à ruban, en ruban,** measuring-tape. *Rac:* **Les rubans,** the tapes (at starting-gate). *Typewr:* *R. encreur,* inking ribbon. *El:* **Fil sous ruban,** taped wire. **2.** Metal strip. *R. d'acier,* steel band. **Fer à ruban,** hoop-iron. *Tls:* **Scie à ruban,** band-saw. *R. d'un frein,* brake-band. **3.** *Ind:* **R. roulant, transporteur,** belt conveyor.

rubaner [rybane], *v.tr.* **I.** (a) To trim (sth.) with ribbons. (b) To tape (wire). **2.** To cut into strips.

rubané, *a.* **I.** *Nat.Hist:* etc: Striped. **2. Canon rubané,** strip-wound gun-barrel.

rubéfiant [rybefjɑ̃], *a. & s.m.* Rubefacient.

rubéroïde [rybɛrɔid], *s.m. Const:* Rubberoid.

rubicond [rybikɔ̃], *a.* Rubicund, florid.

rubis [rybi], *s.m.* Ruby. *R. balais,* balas ruby. *R. de Bohême,* rose quartz. **Montée sur rubis,** jewelled (watch). *F:* **Faire rubis sur l'ongle,** to drink supernaculum, to the last drop. **Payer rubis sur l'ongle,** to pay to the last farthing.

rubrique [rybrik], *s.f.* **I.** Red chalk, red ochre, ruddle. **2.** (a) *Ecc: Jur:* Rubric. (b) Imprint (of book). (c) *Journ:* etc: Heading; item. *Il tient la r. de la Mode au Figaro,* he writes the Fashions column in the Figaro.

ruche [ryʃ], *s.f.* **I.** (Bee-)hive. *R. en paille,* bee skep. *R. démontable,* frame-hive. *F:* **Ruche d'industrie,** regular (bee-)hive of industry. **2.** *Needlew:* Ruche, ruching.

rucher[1] [ryʃe], *s.m.* Apiary.

rucher[2], *v.tr. Needlew:* To ruche; to quill.

rude [ryd], *a.* **I.** (a) Uncouth, unpolished, primitive; untaught (people). (b) Rough (skin, wine, etc.); stiff, hard (brush); harsh, grating (voice); rugged (path). S.a. ESPRIT 3. **2.** (a) Hard, arduous, severe. *Temps rudes,* hard times. *R. épreuve,* severe trial. *R. tâche, tâche r.,* stiff, arduous, task. *Coup r.,* heavy blow. *R. montée,* stiff, steep, climb. (b) Gruff, ungracious, brusque (voice or manner). **3.** *F:* (Intensive) *R. appétit,* hearty appetite. *R. adversaire,* tough opponent. *Faire une r. gaffe,* to make a dreadful blunder. *adv.* **-ment.**

rudement [rydmɑ̃], *adv.* **I.** (a) Roughly, harshly, severely. (b) Roughly, coarsely. **2.** *F:* (Intensive) *Je suis r. fatigué,* I am awfully tired.

rudenté [rydɑ̃te], *a. Arch:* Cabled (column).

rudesse [rydɛs], *s.f.* **I.** Uncouthness, primitiveness (of savages, etc.). **2.** Roughness, ruggedness; coarseness (of material); harshness (of voice). **3.** (a) Severity (of winter, task). (b) Abruptness, bluntness, gruffness (envers, towards). **Traiter qn avec rudesse,** to browbeat s.o.

rudiment [rydimɑ̃], *s.m.* **I.** *Biol:* Rudiment (of a thumb, of a tail). **2.** *pl.* Rudiments (of knowledge).

rudimentaire [rydimɑ̃tɛːr], *a.* Rudimentary.

rud|oyer [rydwaje], *v.tr.* (je rudoie; je rudoierai) To treat (s.o.) roughly. (a) To browbeat, bully. (b) To knock (s.o.) about. *R. un cheval,* to be rough with a horse. *s.m.* **-oiement.**

rue[1] [ry], *s.f.* Street, thoroughfare. **La grande rue, la grand'rue,** the high street, the main street. *Le peuple descendit dans la rue,* the street-fighting began. **Histoire vieille comme les rues,** story as old as the hills. **Courir les rues,** (i) to run about the streets; (ii) (of news) to be common talk.

rue[2], *s.f. Bot:* Rue. *Rue odorante,* common rue.

ruelle [rɥɛl], *s.f.* **1.** Lane, by-street, alley. **2.** (*a*) Space between the bedside and the wall; ruelle. (*b*) *A:* Literary clique or coterie. [RUE¹]

ru|er [rɥe], *v.i.* (*a*) (Of animal) To kick, to fling out, to lash out. (*b*) (Of gun-carriage) To jump (on recoil). *a. & s.* **-eur, -euse.**

   se ruer *sur qn, sur qch.*, to hurl, fling, oneself at s.o., at sth.

   ruée, *s.f.* Rush, onrush. *Hist: La r. sur Verdun,* the onslaught on Verdun.

rugine [ryʒin], *s.f. Surg:* Xyster. *Dent:* Scaler.

ruginer [ryʒine], *v.tr.* To scrape (bone); to scale (teeth).

rug|ir [ryʒiːr], *v.i.* To roar; (of wind) to howl. *a.* **-issant.**

rugissement [ryʒismã], *s.m.* **1.** Roaring (of lion); howling (of storm). **2.** Roar.

rugosité [rygozite], *s.f.* **1.** Rugosity, ruggedness, roughness. **2.** Wrinkle, corrugation.

rugueux, -euse [ryg∅, -∅:z]. **1.** *a.* (*a*) Rugose; rugged, rough; gnarled (tree). (*b*) Wrinkled. corrugated. **2.** *s.m. Artil:* Percussion pin (of fuse).

ruine [rɥin], *s.f.* Ruin. **1.** (*a*) Downfall; decay (of building, etc.). **Tomber en ruine(s),** to fall in(to) ruin(s). *Tout tombe en r.,* everything is going to (w)rack and ruin. (*b*) Downfall (of pers., society). **Aller, courir, à la ruine,** to be on the road to ruin. *Ce sera sa r.,* it will be the ruin, the ruination, of him. **C'est la ruine,** it's all up with me. **2.** (Usu. in *pl.*) Ruins.

ruiner [rɥine], *v.tr.* To ruin, destroy; to blast (reputation). *Se r. la santé,* to ruin one's health. *Ces pertes le ruinèrent,* these losses broke him, ruined him.

   se ruiner. 1. To ruin oneself. **2.** (Of thg) To fall, go, to ruin.

ruineux, -euse [rɥin∅, -∅:z], *a.* Ruinous.

ruisseau [rɥiso], *s.m.* **1.** (*a*) Brook; (small) stream. *Prov:* **Les petits ruisseaux font les grandes rivières,** many a little makes a mickle. (*b*) Stream (of blood, etc.). **2.** (Street) gutter, runnel, kennel. *F: Calomnie ramassée dans le r.,* slander picked up in the gutter.

ruiss|eler [rɥisle], *v.i.* (il ruisselle; il ruissellera) **1.** (Of liquid) (*a*) To stream (down), run (down). (*b*) To trickle. **2.** (Of surface) To run, to drip, to trickle. *a.* **-elant.** *s.m.* **-ellement.**

ruisselet [rɥislɛ], *s.m.* Brooklet, streamlet, rill.

rumb [rõ:b], *s.m. Nau:* Ligne de rumb, rhumb line.

rumeur [rymœːr], *s.f.* **1.** (*a*) Confused or distant murmur; hum (of traffic). (*b*) Din, clamour. **Tout est en rumeur,** everything is in an uproar. **2.** Rumour, report. *La r. court que . . .,* it is rumoured that. . . .

ruminant [ryminã], *a. & s.m. Z:* Ruminant.

rumination [ryminasjõ], *s.f.* Rumination, ruminating.

ruminer [rymine], *v.tr.* **1.** *Abs.* (Of animal) T ruminate; to chew the cud. **2.** *F: R. une ide* to ruminate about, on, over, an idea; to pond an idea.

runes [ryn], *s.f.pl.* Runes.

runique [runik], *a.* Runic (letters, verse).

ruolz [rɥɔls, ryɔls], *s.m.* Electroplated ware.

rupestre [rypɛstr], *a. Bot:* Rupestral, rup strine; rupicolous.

rupin, -ine [rypɛ̃, -in], *a. P:* Fine, first-rat *s.m.* **Les rupins,** the swells, nobs, toffs.

rupteur [ryptœːr], *s.m. El.E: I.C.E:* Contac breaker, circuit-breaker.

rupture [ryptyːr], *s.f.* Breaking, ruptur (*a*) Breaking down (of beam); bursting (of dam (*b*) Breaking (in two); rupture (of blood-vesse of ligament); fracture (of bone); parting (c hawser). (*c*) Breaking up. **Obus de ruptur** armour-piercing shell. *R. de l'équilibre,* upsettin of the equilibrium. (*d*) Breaking off, breach discontinuance. *R. des négociations,* breaking o of negotiations. *R. de contrat,* breach of contrac **État en rupture de pacte,** covenant-breakin state. S.a. BAN 2. *El.E: R. du circuit,* breakin of the circuit; break in the circuit.

rural, -aux [ryral, -o], *a.* Rural. *Chemin r* country lane. *adv.* **-ement.**

ruse [ry:z], *s.f.* Ruse, trick, wile, dodge. *Obten qch. par r.,* to obtain sth. by trickery, by guile.

ruser [ryze], *v.i.* To use craft, trickery.

   rusé, -ée, *a.* Artful, crafty, sly, astute wily. *s. La petite rusée,* the little slyboots.

russe [rys], *a. & s.* Russian.

Russie [rysi]. *Pr.n.f. Geog:* Russia. S.a. CUIR

russifier [rysifje], *v.tr.* To Russify, Russianize.

rustaud, -aude [rysto, -o:d]. **1.** *a.* Boorish uncouth. **2.** *s.* Boor; bumpkin. [RUSTRE]

rusticité [rystisite], *s.f.* **1.** Rusticity. **2.** (*a*) Pr mitiveness, simplicity (of machine, etc.). (*b*) Har diness (of plant).

rustique [rystik], *a.* (*a*) Rustic. (*b*) Hard (plant); robust (engine). *adv.* **-ment,** -ally.

rustre [rystr]. **1.** *a.* Boorish, clownish, loutish **2.** *s.m.* Boor, churl, lout; bumpkin.

rustrerie [rystrəri], *s.f.* Boorishness.

rut [ryt], *s.m.* (Of animals) Rut(ting).

rutabaga [rytabaga], *s.m.* Swedish turnip swede.

Ruthène [rytɛn], *a. & s.* Ruthenian; Littl Russian.

rutilance [rytilãːs], *s.f.* Glow(ing) (of colour).

rutilant [rytilã], *a.* Glowing red, rutilant gleaming.

rutiler [rytile], *v.i.* To glow; to gleam red.

rythme [ritm], *s.m.* Rhythm.

rythmer [ritme], *v.tr.* To put rhythm into (motion).

   rythmé, *a.* Rhythmed; rhythmic(al).

rythmique [ritmik], *a.* Rhythmic(al).

S

S, s [ɛs], *s.f.* (The letter) S, s. **Sentier en s,** winding path. *S de suspension,* S(-shaped) hook.

s'. See SE.

sa [sa], *a.poss.f.* See SON¹.

sabbat [saba], *s.m.* **1.** (Jewish) Sabbath. *Observer, violer, le s.,* to keep, break, the Sabbath. **2.** (Witches') sabbath, midnight revels. *F:* **Faire**

un **sabbat de tous les diables,** to make frightful row.

sabbatique [sabatik], *a.* Sabbatic(al) (year, etc)

sabelle [sabɛl], *s.f. Ann:* Sabella.

sabin, -ine¹ [sabɛ̃, -in], *a. & s. A. Hist:* Sabine **L'enlèvement des Sabines,** the rape of the Sabine women.

sabine², *s.f. Bot:* Savin(e).

sabir [sabiːr], *s.m.* Lingua franca (in the Levant).

sable¹ [saːbl], *s.m.* **1.** Sand. *Sables boulants, mouvants,* quicksands. *Nau: Fond de s.;* sandy bottom. *F:* **Avoir du sable dans les yeux,** to be sleepy. **Le marchand de sable a passé,** the sandman has gone by. S.a. CHAUX. **2.** *Med:* Gravel. **3.** **Sable de fer,** fine iron filings. **4.** **Horloge de sable,** sand-glass, hour-glass.

sable², *s.m.* **1.** Sable (fur). **2.** *Her:* Sable, black.

sabl|er [sable], *v.tr.* **1.** To sand, gravel (path). **2.** *F:* To swig, toss off (champagne, etc.). **3.** To sand-blast (casting). *s.m.* **-age.** **sablé.** **1.** *a.* Sanded, gravelled (path). **2.** *s.m. Cu:* (Sort of) shortbread.

sableux, -euse [sablø, -øːz], *a.* Sandy.

sablier [sablie], *s.m.* **1.** Sand dealer. **2.** Sand-box (holding sand for drying ink). **3.** Sand-glass, hour-glass. *Cu:* Egg-timer.

sablière¹ [sabliɛːr], *s.f.* **1.** Sand-pit, gravel-pit. **2.** Sand-box (of locomotive).

sablière², *s.f.* **1.** (Lengthwise) beam, stringer, templet; wall-plate (of roof-truss). **2.** *Nau: S. de lancement,* sliding-way.

sablon [sablɔ̃], *s.m.* Scouring sand.

sablonner [sablɔne], *v.tr.* To scour with sand.

sablonneux, -euse [sablɔnø, -øːz], *a.* Sandy (shore, plain); gritty (fruit).

sablonnier [sablɔnje], *s.m.* Sand dealer.

sablonnière [sablɔnjɛːr], *s.f.* Sand-pit.

sabord [sabɔːr], *s.m. Nau:* Port(-hole). *S. de charge,* cargo door. **Faux sabord,** deadlight.

sabord|er [sabɔrde], *v.tr. Nau:* To scuttle (ship). *s.m.* **-ement.**

sabot [sabo], *s.m.* **1.** (a) Wooden shoe; clog, sabot. *F:* **Je vous entends venir avec vos gros sabots,** it's easy to see what your little game is. **Baignoire en sabot,** slipper-bath. (b) *P:* Any bad, worn out, or antiquated article; old tub (of a ship); ramshackle old motor car. **2.** Hoof (of horse, etc.). **3.** *Tchn:* Shoe, sabot (of pile, lance). *S. d'enrayage,* drag, skid (of wheel). *S. d'arrêt,* scotch. *S. de frein,* brake-block, brake-shoe. **4.** Whip(ping)-top. S.a. DORMIR 1. **5.** *Bot:* **Sabot de Vénus,** lady's-slipper. **6.** *Tls:* Curved plane.

sabotage [sabotaːʒ], *s.m.* **1.** Sabot-making. **2.** (a) Scamping, botching (of work). (b) Sabotage, malicious destruction (of machinery); rattening.

saboter [sabote], *v.tr.* **1.** (a) *Tchn:* To shoe (a pile). (b) *Rail:* To chair (sleeper). **2.** To botch, bungle, scamp (a piece of work); to do wilful damage to (machinery, etc.); to sabotage (a job).

saboterie [sabotri], *s.f.* Sabot factory.

saboteur, -euse [sabotœːr, -øːz], *s. F:* **1.** Bungler, botcher. **2.** Perpetrator of acts of sabotage; rattener.

sabotier [sabotje], *s.m.* Maker of sabots.

sabotière [sabotjɛːr], *s.f.* Clog-dance.

saboul|er [sabule], *v.tr. F:* To haul (s.o.) over the coals; to give (s.o.) a wigging. *s.m.* **-age.**

sabre [saːbr], *s.m.* **1.** Sabre; (cutting) sword. **Coup de sabre,** sabre cut. **Sabre au clair,** (i) drawn sword; (ii) with drawn swords. **Sabre de bois,** (i) (Harlequin's) lath; (ii) (as a mild oath) = SACRISTI! **2.** *Ich:* Sword-fish.

sabrer [sabre], *v.tr.* **1.** (a) To sabre; to cut down (s.o.) with the sword. (b) *F:* To make drastic cuts in (a MS., a play). **2.** *F:* To botch, scamp (work).

sabretache [sabrətaʃ], *s.f. Mil:* Sabretache.

sabreur [sabrœːr], *s.m.* **1.** Dashing cavalry officer (but no strategist). **2.** *F:* **Sabreur de besogne,** slap-dash worker.

sac¹ [sak], *s.m.* **1.** (a) Sack, bag, pouch. *Sac de, en, papier,* paper bag. *Sac à blé,* corn-sack. *Sac à main,* hand-bag. *Sac à ouvrage,* work-bag. *Sac à outils,* tool-bag or -wallet. *Sac de nuit, de voyage,* travelling-bag, carpet-bag. *Sac touriste,* knapsack, rucksack. **Course en sacs,** sack-race. *Mil:* **Sac d'ordonnance,** (soldier's) pack, knapsack, or kitbag. *Sac de couchage,* sleeping-bag. *Sac à fourrages,* nose-bag. *F:* **Sac percé,** spendthrift. **Sac à vin,** toper, boozer. **Homme de sac et de corde,** thorough-paced scoundrel; gallows-bird. *P:* **Avoir le sac,** to be rich. *F:* **Prendre qn la main dans le sac,** to catch s.o. red-handed. **Vider son sac,** to unbosom oneself. **Mettez ça dans votre sac!** put that in your pipe and smoke it! **L'affaire est dans le sac,** it's as good as settled. **Sac à papier!** hang it all! (b) *Av: Sac à vent,* wind-cone. **2.** Sackcloth. **Sous le sac et la cendre,** in sackcloth and ashes.

sac², *s.m.* Sacking, pillage. **Mettre à sac une ville,** to sack a town.

saccade [sakad], *s.f.* Jerk, start, jolt. **Par saccades,** in jerks; by fits and starts.

saccader [sakade], *v.tr.* To jerk (a horse's rein). **saccadé,** *a.* Jerky, abrupt (movement, style). *D'une voix saccadée,* in a jerky, staccato, voice.

saccag|er [sakaʒe], *v.tr.* (je saccageai(s); n. saccageons) (a) To sack, pillage (town); to ransack (house, etc.). (b) To throw (room, etc.) into disorder, into confusion. *s.m.* **-ement.**

saccharifier [sakkarifje], *v.tr.* To saccharify.

saccharimètre [sakkarimɛtr], *s.m.* Saccharimeter.

saccharine [sakkarin], *s.f.* Saccharin(e).

sacerdoce [saserdɔs], *s.m.* **1.** Priesthood; ministry. **2.** *Coll.* The priesthood.

sacerdotal, -aux [saserdɔtal, -o], *a.* Sacerdotal; priestly (garb, caste). S.a. VÊTEMENT.

sach-e, -es, etc. See SAVOIR.

sachée [saʃe], *s.f.* Sackful, bagful.

sachet [saʃe], *s.m.* **1.** Small bag. *Artil:* Cartridge-bag. **2.** **Sachet à parfums,** sachet.

sacoche [sakɔʃ], *s.f.* **1.** (a) Satchel, wallet. (b) *Mil:* Saddlebag. **2.** Wallet (of cyclist). *Aut:* Tool-bag.

sacquer [sake], *v.tr.* = SAQUER².

sacrament|el, -elle [sakramɑ̃tɛl], *a.* (a) *Ecc:* Sacramental. (b) *F:* Decisive, binding. adv. **-ellement.**

sacre¹ [sakr], *s.m.* Anointing, coronation (of king); consecration (of bishop).

sacre², *s.m.* (a) *Orn:* Saker. (b) *F: A:* Miscreant; bandit. *A:* **Jurer comme un sacre,** to swear like a trooper.

sacrebleu [sakrəblø], *int.* = SACREDIEU.

Sacré-Cœur [sakrekœːr], *s.m. Ecc:* **Fête du Sacré-Cœur,** feast of the Sacred Heart of Jesus.

sacredieu [sakrədjø], **sacredieu** [sakrədjø], *int.* (Profane) Confound it! damn (it)!

sacrement [sakrəmɑ̃], *s.m. Ecc:* (a) Sacrament. **Le saint Sacrement** (*de l'autel*), the Blessed Sacrament. *S'approcher des sacrements,* to partake of the Sacrament. (b) *F:* The marriage tie.

sacrer [sakre], **1.** *v.tr.* To anoint, crown (king); to consecrate (bishop). *S. qn roi,* to crown s.o. king. **2.** *v.i. F:* To curse and swear. **sacré,** *a.* **1.** Holy (scripture); sacred, consecrated (vessel, etc.). *Les ordres sacrés,* holy orders. *F:* **Avoir le feu sacré,** to be filled with the sacred fire. *s.m.* **Le sacré et le profane,** things sacred and profane. **2.** Sacred, inviolable (trust, law). **3.** (Profane, often epith s—) 'Confounded,' 'cursed,' 'damned.' *S— imbécile!* you d—d fool! **4.** *Anat:* Sacral (region).

sacret [sakrɛ], *s.m. Orn:* Sakeret.
sacrificateur, -trice [sakrifikatœːr, -tris], *s.* Sacrificer.
sacrificatoire [sakrifikatwaːr], *a.* Sacrificial.
sacrifice [sakrifis], *s.m.* Sacrifice. *Offrir un s.*, to offer up a sacrifice. **Offrir qch. en sacrifice,** to offer up sth. as a sacrifice. *Ecc:* **Le saint sacrifice,** the celebration of mass.
sacrifier [sakrifje], *v.tr.* (*a*) To sacrifice (victim); to offer (sth.) in sacrifice. *F: S. à la mode,* to conform to fashion. *S. des marchandises,* to sell goods at a sacrifice. (*b*) To sacrifice, give up (time, money, etc.) (*à,* to). *S. sa vie,* to lay down one's life.
sacrilège¹ [sakrilɛːʒ], *s.m.* Sacrilege.
sacrilège², *a. & s.* Sacrilegious (person). *adv.* **-ment.**
sacripant [sakripɑ̃], *s.m.* Rascal, scoundrel.
sacristain [sakristɛ̃], *s.m.* Sacristan; sexton.
sacristi [sakristi], *int.* **1.** The devil! hang it! **2.** Good Lord!
sacristie [sakristi], *s.f. Ecc:* **1.** Sacristy, vestry. **2.** Church-plate and vestments.
sacristine [sakristin], *s.f.* Vestry-nun, sacristine.
sacro-saint [sakrɔsɛ̃], *a.* Sacrosanct.
sacrum [sakrɔm], *s.m. Anat:* Sacrum.
sadique [sadik], *a.* Sadistic.
sadisme [sadism], *s.m.* Sadism.
sadiste [sadist], *s. m. & f.* Sadist.
saducéen [sadyseɛ̃], *s.m. Rel.H:* Sadducee.
safran¹ [safrɑ̃], *s.m.* **1.** *Bot:* Saffron, crocus. **2.** *a.inv. Gants safran,* saffron(-coloured) gloves.
safran², *s.m. Nau: S. du gouvernail,* back-piece, cheek, of the rudder.
safranine [safranin], *s.f. Ch: Ind:* Safranin.
saga [saga], *s.f. Scand.Lit:* Saga.
sagace [sagas], *a.* Sagacious, shrewd. *adv.* **-ment.**
sagacité [sagasite], *s.f.* Sagacity, shrewdness.
sagaie [sagɛ], *s.f.* Assegai.
sage [saːʒ], *a.* **1.** Wise. *s.m.* **Les sept Sages,** the Seven Sages; the Seven Wise Men. **2.** Judicious, wise (policy, etc.); discreet (behaviour). *Les esprits sages,* sensible people. **Politique peu sage,** unwise policy. **3.** Well-behaved, well-conducted; good (child); quiet, docile (animal); well-mannered (horse). **Sois sage!** be a good child! be good! **Sage comme une image,** as good as gold. *adv.* **-ment.**
sage-femme, *s.f.* Midwife. *pl. Des sages-femmes.*
sagesse [saʒɛs], *s.f.* **1.** (*a*) Wisdom. (*b*) Prudence, discretion. **Dent de sagesse,** wisdom tooth. **2.** Steadiness, good behaviour; quietness (of horse). *Sch:* **Prix de sagesse,** good-conduct prize.
sagittaire [saʒittɛːr]. **1.** *s.m. Rom.Ant:* Archer. *Astr:* Sagittarius. **2.** *s.f. Bot:* Sagittaria, arrow-head.
sagou [sagu], *s.m.* Sago.
sagouin [sagwɛ̃], *s.m.* **1.** *Z:* Squirrel-monkey. **2.** *F:* (*f.* **sagouine**) Sloven; slovenly, dirty (fellow); *f.* slattern, slut.
sagoutier [sagutje], *s.m. Bot:* Sago-palm.
saignant [sɛɲɑ̃], *a.* **1.** Bleeding, raw (wound). **2.** *Cu:* Raw, underdone, red (meat).
saign|er [sɛɲe]. **1.** *v.i.* To bleed. *S. du nez,* (i) to bleed at, from, the nose; (ii) *P:* to funk, to show the white feather. *Le cœur m'en saigne,* it makes my heart bleed. **2.** *v.tr.* (*a*) To bleed; (i) *Med:* to draw, let, blood from (s.o.); (ii) *F:* to extort money from (s.o.). **Saigner un animal,** *F:* qn, **à blanc,** to bleed an animal, *F:* s.o., white. **Se saigner aux quatre membres pour qn,** to make every sacrifice for s.o. (*b*) To tap (gum-tree, stream). *s.m.* **-ement.**

saignée, *s.f.* **1.** *Med:* Bleeding, blood letting. *F: S. continuelle,* constant drain (on one's resources). **2.** Bend of the arm. **3.** (*a*) (Drainage) trench, ditch. (*b*) Cut, groove (for oil, etc.). (*c*) *El.E: Conducteur à saignées* tapped conductor.
saigneux, -euse [sɛɲø, -øːz], *a.* Bloody. **Bou** **saigneux,** scrag-end (of mutton, etc.).
saillant [sajɑ̃]. **1.** *a.* (*a*) *Her:* Salient. (*b*) Pro jecting, jutting out. *Pommettes saillantes,* promi nent cheek-bones. *Dents saillantes,* buck-teeth (*c*) Salient, outstanding. **2.** *s.m. Mil:* Salient.
saillir [sajiːr], *v.i.* **1.** (*pr.p.* **saillissant;** *p.p.* **sailli** *pr.ind.* **je saillis,** n. **saillissons;** *fu.* **je saillirai)** (O liquid) To gush out, spurt out, spirt out; (o besieged troops) to (make a) sally. **2.** (Used only in *pr.p.* **saillant;** *p.p.* **sailli;** *pr.ind.* **il saille, il** **saillent;** *fu.* **il saillera)** To jut out, stand out *Les traits qui le font s. dans la foule,* characteristic that make him stand out in the crowd.
saillie, *s.f.* **1.** (*a*) Spurt, spirt; spring bound. **Avancer par bonds et saillies,** to advanc by leaps and bounds. *S. de sang,* spurt, issue, o blood. (*b*) *Mil:* Sally. (*c*) *F:* Sally; flash of wit **2.** Protrusion; projection, ledge. **Pierre er** saillie, projecting stone. *Fenêtre en s.,* bay window. *S. du mollet,* swell of the calf. **Faire** saillie, to project, jut out.
sain, saine [sɛ̃, sɛn], *a.* (*a*) Healthy, hale (per son); sound (fruit, timber); sound, sane (judgment); wholesome (food). **Sain et sauf** safe and sound. *Jur:* **Sain d'esprit,** of sound mind, sound in mind. **Avoir le corps sain,** to be sound in wind and limb. (*b*) *Nau:* Clear, safe (coast, anchorage); fair (channel). *adv.* **-ement**
sainbois [sɛ̃bwɑ], *s.m. Bot:* Spurge-flax.
saindoux [sɛ̃du], *s.m.* Lard.
sainfoin [sɛ̃fwɛ̃], *s.m. Bot: Agr:* Sainfoin.
saint, sainte [sɛ̃, sɛːt]. **1.** *a.* (*a*) Holy. (*a*) *La Sainte* Église, the Holy Church. *Les Saintes Écritures* Holy Writ. *La Semaine sainte,* Holy Week (*b*) Saintly, godly (person, life). (*c*) *Terre sainte* hallowed, consecrated, ground. **La Terre Sainte** the Holy Land. *F:* **Toute la sainte journée,** the whole blessed day. (*d*) Saint. *L'église Saint-Pierre* St Peter's (church). *La Sainte-Catherine,* Sain Catherine's day. **2.** *s.* Saint. **Fête de saint** saint's day. *Ecc:* **Mettre qn au nombre des** saints, to canonize s.o. *F:* **Prendre un air de** petit saint, to put on a saintly air. **Chacun prêche** pour son saint, everyone has an eve to his own interest. **Ne savoir plus à quel saint se vouer,** to be at one's wits' end. **A chaque saint sa c andelle,** honour where honour is due. **3.** *s.m.* **Le Saint des** Saints, the Holy of Holies.
Saint-Barthélemy (la) [lasɛ̃bartɛlmi], *s.f* (i) St Bartholomew's Day; (ii) the Massacre of St Bartholomew (1572).
saint-bernard, *s.m.inv.* St Bernard (dog).
saint-crépin, *s.m.* No *pl. F:* (*a*) Shoemaker's tools. (*b*) **Porter tout son saint-crépin sur son** dos, to carry all one's worldly goods on one's back
Saint-Cyr [sɛ̃siːr]. *Pr.n.m.* Saint-Cyr military school (infantry and cavalry).
Saint-Cyrien [sɛ̃sirjɛ̃], *s.m.* Cadet training at Saint-Cyr. *pl. Des Saint-Cyriens.*
Saint-Domingue [sɛ̃dɔmɛ̃ːg]. *Pr.n.m.* Santo Domingo.
Sainte-Hélène. *Pr.n. Geog:* Saint Helena.
Saint-Elme [sɛ̃tɛlm]. *Pr.n.m.* Feu de Saint-Elme, corposant, Saint-Elmo's fire.
Saint-Esprit [sɛ̃tɛspri]. *Pr.n.m.* **Le Saint-** Esprit, the Holy Ghost.
sainteté [sɛ̃təte], *s.f.* Holiness, saintliness,

sanctity (of a vow). *Ecc*: **Sa, Votre, Sainteté, His, Your, Holiness** (the Pope).

saint-frusquin [sɛ̃fryskɛ̃], *s.m.* No *pl.* *P*: All the worldly goods (of a person). **Et tout le saint-frusquin**, and the whole caboodle.

Saint-Glinglin [sɛ̃glɛ̃glɛ̃]. (Used in) *F*: **Jusqu'à la Saint-Glinglin**, for ever more. **A la Saint-Glinglin**, to-morrow come never.

Saint-Jean (la), *s.f.* Midsummer Day.

Saint-Jean d'Acre. *Pr.n. Geog*: Acre.

Saint-Laurent (le). *Pr.n.m. Geog*: The Saint Lawrence (river).

Saint-Martin (la), *s.f.* Saint Martin's day; Martinmas. *F*: **Été de la Saint-Martin,** Saint Martin's summer.

Saint-Michel (la), *s.f.* Michaelmas.

Saint-Père (le), *s.m.* The Holy Father, the Pope.

Saint-Siège (le), *s.m.* The Holy See.

Saint-Sylvestre (la), *s.f.* New-year's eve.

sais [sɛ]. See SAVOIR.

saisie-arrêt [seziarɛ], *s.f. Jur*: Attachment, garnishment. **Ordonnance de saisie-arrêt,** garnishee order. *pl. Des saisies-arrêts.*

saisir [sezi:r], *v.tr.* **I.** To seize. (*a*) To grasp; to grab; to lay hold, take hold, catch hold, of (s.o., sth.). *Jur*: *S. qn au corps*, to apprehend s.o. *S. un prétexte*, to seize upon a pretext. *La peur le saisit*, fear gripped him; he took fright. *Être saisi (d'étonnement)*, to be startled, staggered. (*b*) *Jur*: To seize, attach (real estate); to distrain upon (goods); to attach (ship). **Faire saisir qn,** *F*: to sell s.o. up. (*c*) *Nau*: To stow, secure, lash (the anchors, the boats). (*d*) To perceive, discern, apprehend. *Je ne saisis pas*, I don't quite get the idea. **2.** *Jur*: (*a*) *S. qn d'un héritage*, to vest s.o. with an inheritance. (*b*) *S. un tribunal d'une affaire*, to refer a matter to a court.

se saisir *de qn, de qch.*, to possess oneself of, to seize upon, s.o., sth.; to lay hands on sth.

saisi, *s.m. Jur*: Distrainee.

saisie, *s.f.* (*a*) Seizure (of contraband goods). (*b*) *Jur*: Distraint, execution. *Nau*: Embargo. *S. immobilière*, attachment of real property. *S. pour loyer*, distress. *S. d'une hypothèque*, foreclosure of a mortgage.

saisissable [sezisabl], *a.* **I.** Perceptible, distinguishable. **2.** *Jur*: Distrainable, attachable.

saisissant [sezisã], *a.* (*a*) Piercing, nipping (cold). (*b*) Startling, striking (resemblance); gripping, thrilling (spectacle).

saisissement [sezismã], *s.m.* Seizure. (*a*) Sudden chill. (*b*) Surprise, thrill. (*c*) Shock. *Il mourut de s.*, he died of the shock; the shock killed him.

saison [sezɔ̃], *s.f.* **I.** Season. *Les quatre saisons,* the four seasons. S.a. MARCHAND I. *La belle s.*, the summer months. *La s. des semailles,* sowing time. **Fruits en pleine saison,** fruit in its prime. **La saison bat son plein,** it is the height of the season. S.a. MORTE-SAISON. **De saison,** (i) in season, seasonable; (ii) timely. *Les huîtres sont hors de saison,* oysters are out of season. **Propos hors de saison,** ill-timed, inopportune, remarks. **2. Saison thermale,** spell of treatment at a watering-place.

saisonnier, -ière [sezɔnje, -jɛːr], *a.* Seasonal.

sait [sɛ]. See SAVOIR.

sajou [saʒu], *s.m. Z*: Sajou, sapajou (monkey).

salacité [salasite], *s.f.* Salaciousness, salacity.

salade¹ [salad], *s.f.* (*a*) Salad. *Faire la s.*, to mix the salad. S.a. PANIER I. (*b*) **Salade de fruits,** fruit salad. **Salade russe,** (i) Russian salad; (ii) *F*: jumble, miscellany, hotchpotch. *F*: **Mettre tout en salade,** to jumble everything up.

salade², *s.f. Archeol*: Sallet (helmet).

saladier [saladje], *s.m.* Salad-bowl.

salaire [salɛːr], *s.m.* Wage(s). **I.** Pay (of manual worker). *S. de base,* base rate. *Prov*: **Toute peine mérite salaire,** the labourer is worthy of his hire. **2.** Reward, recompense, retribution.

salaison [salezɔ̃], *s.f.* **I.** Salting; curing (of bacon). **2.** *pl.* Salt provisions.

salamalec [salamalɛk], *s.m. F*: Salaam. *Faire des salamalecs,* to bow and scrape.

salamandre [salamɑ̃:dr], *s.f.* **I.** (*a*) Salamander. (*b*) *S. aquatique,* newt. **2.** Slow-combustion stove.

salanque [salɑ̃:k], *s.f.* Salt-marsh, salt-pans.

salant [salɑ̃], *a.m.* **Marais salant,** salt-marsh, salt-pans, saltern, saline.

salariat [salarja], *s.m.* **I.** Wage-earning. **2.** *Coll.* The wage-earning classes.

salarier [salarje], *v.tr.* To pay a wage to (s.o.).
    salarié, -ée. **I.** *a.* (*a*) Wage-earning. (*b*) Paid (work). **2.** *s.* Wage-earner.

salaud, -aude [salo, -o:d], *s. P*: (*a*) Sloven; dirty fellow; *f.* slut. (*b*) Dirty dog; skunk.

sale [sal], *a.* Dirty. **I.** (*a*) Unclean, filthy; soiled (linen). **Sale comme un peigne,** filthy. *Couleur s.*, dull, dingy, dirty, colour. (*b*) Offensive, nasty (word). **2.** *F*: (Always before the noun) *S. individu,* s. *type,* rotter. *S. coup,* (i) nasty blow; (ii) low, dirty, trick. *S. temps,* (i) *Nau*: foul weather; (ii) *F*: beastly weather. *adv.* **-ment.**

saler [sale], *v.tr.* To salt. **I.** (*a*) To season (sth.) with salt. (*b*) *F*: To charge exorbitantly for (sth.); to fleece (customers). *S. la note,* to stick it on (to the bill). **2.** To salt, pickle; to cure (bacon); to corn (beef). **3.** *P*: *S. une mine,* to plant, salt, a mine. [SEL]

salé, *a.* **I.** Salt (fish, etc.); salted (almonds). *Eau salée,* (i) salt water; (ii) brine. *Le potage est trop s.*, the soup is too salt(y). *Husb*: **Prés salés,** saltings. S.a. PRÉ-SALÉ. *s.m.* **Petit salé,** pickled pork. **2.** *F*: Keen, biting (epigram, etc.). (*b*) Broad, spicy (tale, joke). **En raconter de salées,** to tell highly seasoned stories. (*c*) *F*: Exorbitant, stiff (price); stiff (sentence).

saleté [salte], *s.f.* **I.** (*a*) Dirtiness, filthiness. (*b*) Dirt, filth. (*c*) Piece of dirt. (*d*) Trashy goods; trash, rubbish. **2.** (*a*) Nastiness, obscenity; beastliness (of mind). (*b*) Nasty, coarse, remark or jest. (*c*) Dirty trick. [SALE]

saleur [salœːr], *s.m.* Salter, dry-curer.

salicoque [salikɔk], *s.f.* *Crust*: (Grande crevette) **salicoque,** palaemon, *F*: prawn.

salicorne [salikɔrn], *s.f. Bot*: Saltwort.

salicylate [salisilat], *s.m. Ch*: Salicylate.

salicylique [salisilik], *a.m. Ch*: Salicylic.

salière [saljɛːr], *s.f.* **I.** (*a*) Salt-cellar. (*b*) (Kitchen) salt-box. **2.** (*a*) Eye-socket (of horse). (*b*) Hollow above the collar-bone (when conspicuous in woman); salt-cellar. [SEL]

saligaud [saligo], *s.m. P*: = SALAUD.

salignon [saliɲɔ̃], *s.m.* Cake of salt.

salin, -ine [salɛ̃, -in], **I.** *a.* Saline, briny; salty. **2.** *s.m.* Salt-marsh. **3.** *s.f.* Saline. (*a*) Salt-works, salt-pan. (*b*) Rock-salt mine.

salinage [salina:ʒ], *s.m.* **I.** Salt-mine; salt-marsh; salt-works. **2.** Saturated solution of salt.

salinier [salinje], *s.m.* (*a*) Salt-mine owner. (*b*) Salt merchant; salter.

salinité [salinite], *s.f.* Saltness, salinity.

salique [salik], *a. Hist*: Salic (law).

salir [sali:r], *v.tr.* To dirty, soil; to besmirch, defile, sully (the imagination). *Étoffe qui se salit facilement,* material that soils easily. *S. sa* *réputation*, to sully, tarnish, one's good name. S.a. BLASON. [SALE]

se salir. 1. To get dirty, soiled. **2.** To soil, dirty, one's clothes; to sully one's reputation.

salissant [salisɑ̃], *a.* **1.** *Travail s.*, dirty, messy, work. **2.** Easily soiled (material, etc.).

salisson [salisɔ̃], *s.f.* *F:* Dirty, untidy, little girl.

salissure [salisy:r], *s.f.* Stain; dirty mark.

salivaire [salivɛ:r], *a.* Salivary (gland, etc.).

salivation [salivasjɔ̃], *s.f.* *Med:* Salivation.

salive [sali:v], *s.f.* Saliva, spittle. *F:* **Perdre sa salive,** to waste one's breath.

saliver [salive], *v.i.* To salivate.

salle [sal], *s.f.* **1.** Hall; (large) room. *S. commune,* living-room. **Salle à manger,** dining-room. *S. des festins,* banqueting-hall. *S. de bain,* bathroom. *S. d'études,* schoolroom. *S. de conférences,* lecture-room. *S. d'expériences,* laboratory. *S. d'hôpital,* hospital ward. *S. d'opérations,* operating theatre. *S. de ventes,* sale-room. *S. d'audience,* court-room. *Les salles du Louvre,* the galleries of the Louvre. *S. d'attente,* waiting-room. **Salle des pas perdus,** waiting-hall (of law-courts, etc.); lobby (of Houses of Parliament). *S. des machines,* engine-house, -room. *Mil:* *S. de police,* guardroom. S.a. ARME 1, ASILE. **2.** *Th:* *etc:* Auditorium, 'house.' *Toute la s. applaudit,* the whole house, the whole audience, applauded.

salmigondis [salmigɔ̃di], *s.m.* **1.** *Cu:* Salmagundi, hotchpotch. **2.** *F:* Medley, miscellany.

salmis [salmi], *s.m.* *Cu:* Salmi; ragout (of roasted game).

saloir [salwa:r], *s.m.* **1.** Salting-tub. **2.** *Cu:* Saltsprinkler.

Salomon [salɔmɔ̃]. *Pr.n.m.* Solomon. S.a. SCEAU.

salon [salɔ̃], *s.m.* (a) Drawing-room. *Petit s.,* morning-room. Jeux de salon, parlour-games. S.a. COMÉDIE 1. Fréquenter les salons, to move in fashionable circles. (b) Saloon, cabin (in ship); saloon-car (in train). (c) *S. de thé,* tea-room(s). *S. de coiffure,* hairdressing-saloon. *S. de modiste,* milliner's showroom. (d) **Le Salon,** the Salon (annual art exhibition in Paris). *Le S. de l'automobile,* the (French) Motor Show.

salope [salɔp], *s.f.* *P:* Slattern, slut. [SALE]

saloper [salɔpe], *v.tr.* *P:* To botch (work).

saloperie [salɔpri], *s.f.* *P:* **1.** (a) Filthiness, filth. (b) Trashy goods; trash, rubbish. **2.** (a) Faire une saloperie à qn, to play a dirty trick on s.o. (b) *Dire des saloperies,* to talk smut.

salopette [salɔpɛt], *s.f.* (a) (Workman's, child's) overall(s). (b) (Engineer's) dungarees.

salpêtre [salpɛ:tr], *s.m.* Saltpetre, *F:* nitre.

salpêtrière [salpetrie:r], *s.f.* **1.** Saltpetre-works. **2.** La Salpêtrière, home for aged and mentally afflicted women (in Paris).

salse [sals], *s.f.* *Geol:* Salse; mud volcano.

salsepareille [salsparɛ:j], *s.f.* *Bot:* Sarsaparilla.

salsifis [salsifi], *s.m.* *Bot:* Cu: Salsify.

saltimbanque [saltɛ̃bɑ̃:k], *s.m.* **1.** Member of travelling circus; showman. **2.** *F:* Mountebank, charlatan, humbug.

salubre [saly:br], *a.* Salubrious, healthy (air, climate); wholesome (food). adv. **-ment.**

salubrité [salybrite], *s.f.* Salubrity, salubriousness, healthiness (of climate); wholesomeness (of food). *S. publique,* public health; sanitation.

saluer [salɥe], *v.tr.* (a) To salute; to bow to (s.o.). *S. qn de la main,* (i) to wave to s.o.; (ii) to touch one's hat to s.o. *Il sortit en saluant,* he bowed himself out. *Passer qn sans le s.,* to cut s.o. *Nau:* *S. du pavillon,* Abs. **saluer,** to dip the flag, Abs. to dip. *S. de vingt coups,* to fire a salute of

twenty guns. (b) To greet, to hail. *Saluez-le de ma part,* give him my kind regards. "J'ai (bien) l'honneur de vous saluer," 'I am yours very truly.' *S. qn roi,* to hail, acclaim, s.o. king.

salure [saly:r], *s.f.* Saltness, salinity; tang (of the sea air). [SALER]

salut [saly], *s.m.* **1.** (a) Safety. **Le salut public,** public welfare, public well-being. **Port de salut,** haven of refuge. S.a. PLANCHE 1. (b) Salvation. Faire son **salut,** to find salvation. *Travailler à son s.,* to work out one's own salvation. **L'Armée du Salut,** the Salvation Army. **2.** (a) Bow, salutation, greeting. **Adresser un salut à qn,** (i) to bow to s.o.; (ii) to lift one's hat to s.o. *Adresser de la tête, de la main, un s. à qn,* to nod to s.o.; to wave to s.o. **Salut, Marie!** *pleine de grâce,* hail Mary! full of grace. **Salut à tous!** (i) greeting(s) to all! (ii) *F:* hullo, everybody! S.a. ENTENDEUR. (b) *Mil:* *etc:* Salute. *Faire le s. militaire,* to salute. *S. du drapeau,* lowering of the colour. *Nau:* *S. du pavillon,* dipping of the flag. **3.** *Ecc:* Evening service (in honour of the Host).

salutaire [salytɛ:r], *a.* Salutary, wholesome, beneficial, beneficent. adv. **-ment.**

salutation [salytasjɔ̃], *s.f.* Salutation, greeting; bow, salute. "*Salutations à votre famille,*" 'kind regards to your family.' "*Agréez mes salutations très respectueuses,*" 'I remain yours respectfully.' S.a. ANGÉLIQUE 1, EMPRESSÉ.

salutiste [salytist], *s. m. & f.* Salvationist; member of the Salvation Army.

salve [salv], *s.f.* Salvo. **Lancer, tirer, une salve,** to fire a salvo, a salute. *F:* *S. d'applaudissements,* round, burst, of applause.

samare [sama:r], *s.f.* *Bot:* Samara, key, winged seed (of ash, sycamore).

samaritain, -aine [samaritɛ̃, -ɛn], *a. & s.* *B:* Samaritan. *La Samaritaine,* the woman of Samaria.

samedi [samdi], *s.m.* Saturday. **Le Samedi saint,** (the) Saturday before Easter.

samole [samɔl], *s.m.* *Bot:* Water-pimpernel.

samouraï [samurai], *s.m.* *Jap.Hist:* Samurai.

samovar [samɔva:r], *s.m.* Samovar.

sampan(g) [sɑ̃pɑ̃], *s.m.* Sampan.

sanatorium [sanatɔrjɔm], *s.m.* Sanatorium; convalescent home.

sancir [sɑ̃si:r], *v.i.* *Nau:* To founder head down.

sanctificateur, -trice [sɑ̃ktifikatœ:r, -tris]. **1.** *a.* Sanctifying. **2.** *s.* Sanctifier.

sanctification [sɑ̃ktifikasjɔ̃], *s.f.* (a) Sanctification. (b) *S. du dimanche,* keeping of the Sabbath (-day); observance of the Sabbath.

sanctifier [sɑ̃ktifje], *v.tr.* To sanctify; to make holy; to hallow. *Que Votre nom soit sanctifié,* hallowed be Thy Name. *S. le dimanche,* to observe the sabbath. adv. **-ant.**

sanction [sɑ̃ksjɔ̃], *s.f.* Sanction. **1.** Approbation. *S. royale,* royal assent. **2.** **Sanction (pénale),** penalty; vindicatory or punitive sanction; coercive weapon.

sanctionner [sɑ̃ksjɔne], *v.tr.* To sanction. **1.** To approve, ratify. *Sanctionné par l'usage,* sanctioned by custom. **2.** (a) To sanction, attach a penalty to (decree). (b) To penalize (an offence).

sanctuaire [sɑ̃ktɥɛ:r], *s.m.* (a) Sanctuary, penetralia. (b) *F:* Sanctum, den.

sandale [sɑ̃dal], *s.f.* (a) Sandal. (b) Fencing-shoe, gymnasium-shoe; sand-shoe, plimsoll.

sandaraque [sɑ̃darak], *s.f.* (Gum) sandarac.

sandow [sɑ̃dof], *s.m.* **1.** *Gym:* Chest-expander. **2.** *Av:* *etc:* Rubber extensible spring; rubber shock-absorber.

sandwich [sɑ̃dwitʃ], *s.m.* Sandwich. *F:* **Homme**

sandwich, sandwich-man. *P:* **Faire sandwich,** to play gooseberry.

sang [sɑ̃], *s.m.* **1.** Blood; *Poet:* gore. **Coup de sang,** apoplectic fit; *F:* stroke. **Yeux injectés de sang,** bloodshot eyes. *Répandre, verser, le s.,* to shed blood. **Effusion de sang,** (i) bleeding, (ii) bloodshed. **Écoulement de sang,** bleeding, haemorrhage. **Souillé de sang,** bloodstained. **Avoir le sang chaud,** to be quick-tempered. *F:* **Cela me glace le sang,** it makes my blood run cold. **Se faire du mauvais sang, se manger le(s) sang(s),** to fret (and fume); to worry. **Se faire du bon sang,** (i) to laugh heartily; (ii) to enjoy oneself, to enjoy life. **Son sang soit sur lui,** his blood be on his own head. **Suer sang et eau** [săkeo], to toil and moil. **Conte à tourner les sangs,** blood-curdling tale. *P:* **Bon sang (de bon sang)!** hang it! **Bon sang d'imbécile!** you idiot! S.a. NAVET 1. **2.** (*a*) Blood, race, lineage. **Cheval de sang,** blood-horse. **Cheval pur sang,** full-bred horse; thoroughbred (horse). **Cheval demi-sang,** half-bred horse; half-bred. *Prov:* **Bon sang ne peut mentir,** blood, breed, will tell. (*b*) Blood, kinship, relationship. **Les liens du sang,** the tie of kindred. *Son propre s.,* one's own flesh and blood. **Prince du sang,** prince of the blood.

sang-froid, *s.m.* No *pl.* Coolness, composure. **Garder, conserver, son sang-froid,** (i) to keep cool (and collected); (ii) to keep one's temper. **Perdre son sang-froid,** to lose one's self-control, one's self-possession, one's temper. **De sang-froid,** deliberately.

sanglade [sɑ̃glad], *s.f.* Cut (with a whip); lash.

sanglant [sɑ̃glɑ̃], *a.* **1.** Bloody; blood-stained; (face) covered with blood; *Poet:* gory. **2.** (*a*) Cruel, cutting (reproach); scathing (criticism). (*b*) **Affront sanglant,** deadly affront.

sangle [sɑ̃:gl], *s.f.* Strap, band, webbing. *S. de selle,* (saddle-)girth. **Lit de sangle,** camp-bed, trestle-bed. *Aut: Rail: S. de frein,* check-strap.

sangler [sɑ̃gle], *v.tr.* **1.** To girth (horse); to strap (parcel, etc.). **2.** To thrash, lash (s.o.).
se sangler, to lace oneself tight.

sanglier [sɑ̃glje], *s.m.* Wild boar.

sanglot [sɑ̃glo], *s.m.* Sob. *Pousser un s.,* to give a sob. *Elle pleurait à gros sanglots,* she was sobbing her heart out.

sangloter [sɑ̃glɔte], *v.i.* To sob. *a.* **-ant.**

sangsue [sɑ̃sy], *s.f.* (*a*) *Ann:* Leech. (*b*) *F:* Leech, blood-sucker, extortioner.

sanguin, -ine [sɑ̃gɛ̃, -in]. I. *a.* **1.** *Émission sanguine,* flow of blood. *Les vaisseaux sanguins,* the blood-vessels. **2.** Full-blooded, sanguineous.
II. **sanguine,** *s.f.* **1.** (*a*) Red hematite, red chalk. (*b*) Drawing in red chalk. **2.** Bloodstone. **3.** Blood-orange.

sanguinaire [sɑ̃gine:r], *a.* Sanguinary; blood-thirsty (man); bloody (fight).

sanguinelle [sɑ̃ginɛl], *s.f. Bot:* Dogwood.

sanguinolent [sɑ̃ginɔlɑ̃], *a.* Sanguinolent; tinged with blood.

sanicle [sanikl], *s.f.,* **sanicule** [sanikyl], *s.f. Bot:* Sanicle.

sanie [sani], *s.f. Med:* Sanies, pus, *F:* matter.

sanieux, -euse [sanjø, -ø:z], *a. Med:* Sanious.

sanitaire [sanite:r], *a.* Sanitary. *Matériel s.,* medical stores. *Train s.,* hospital train. *Avion s.,* ambulance aeroplane.

sans [sɑ̃], *prep.* **1.** (*a*) Without. *Il est revenu sans un sou,* he came back without a penny. *Il arriva sans argent ni bagages,* he arrived without either money or luggage. *Sans faute,* without fail. **Sans plus,** nothing more. *Sans parler,* without speaking.

Cela va sans dire, (it is a matter) of course. *Sans mentir . . .,* to tell the truth. . . . *Vous n'êtes pas sans le connaître,* you cannot but know him. **Non sans difficulté,** not without trouble. *Com:* (On bill of exchange) "*Sans frais,*" "*sans protêt,*" 'no expenses.' *Conj.phr.* **Sans que** + *sub.,* without it + *ger. Sans que nous le sachions,* without our knowing it. (*b*) -less, -lessly. *Homme sans peur,* fearless man. *Agir sans peur,* to act fearlessly. *Être sans le sou,* to be penniless. (*c*) Un-. *Plaintes sans fin,* unending complaints. *Sans hésiter,* unhesitatingly. **2.** But for; were it not for. *Sans vous je ne l'aurais jamais fait,* but for you I should never have done it. **Sans cela, sans quoi,** otherwise, else, had it not been for that.

sans-cœur, *s.m. & f.inv. F:* Heartless person.

sanscrit, -ite [sɑ̃skri, -it], *a. & s.m. Ling:* Sanskrit.

sans-culotte, *s.m. Hist:* (Fr. Revol.) Sansculotte, extreme republican. *pl. Des sans-culottes.*

sans-façon. **1.** *s.m.* (*a*) Homeliness, straightforwardness (of speech, etc.). (*b*) = SANS-GÊNE 1. **2.** (*a*) *a.inv.* Homely. (*b*) *s.m. & f.inv.* Homely person. **3.** = SANS-GÊNE 2.

sans-fil, *s.inv.* **1.** *s.f.* Wireless (telegraphy). **2.** *s.m.* (Dépêche par) sans-fil, wireless message; marconigram.

sans-filiste, *s. m. & f.* **1.** Wireless enthusiast, listener-in. **2.** Wireless operator.

sans-gêne. **1.** *s.m.* (Offensive) off-handedness, over-familiarity; *F:* cheek. **2.** (*a*) *a.inv.* Unceremonious. (*b*) *s. m. & f. inv.* Unceremonious person; cool customer.

sans-le-sou, *s.m.pl.* (The) penniless, destitute.

sans-logis, *s.m./f.* (The) homeless.

sansonnet [sɑ̃sɔnɛ], *s.m. Orn:* Starling.

sans-patrie, *s. m. & f. inv.* Stateless person.

sans-souci, *s.inv.* **1.** *s. m. & f.* Easy-going, care-free, individual. **2.** *s.m.* Unconcern; insouciance.

sans-travail, *s.m.pl.* (The) unemployed, (the) workless.

santal, -als, -aux [sɑ̃tal, -o], *s.m.* Sandal(wood).

santé [sɑ̃te], *s.f.* Health; well-being. **Être en bonne santé,** to be well, to enjoy good health. *F:* **Crever de santé,** to be bursting with health. *S. de fer,* iron constitution. *Avoir une s. faible,* to suffer from weak health, to be delicate. *Air plein de s.,* healthy look. **Respirer la santé,** to look the picture of health. S.a. MAISON 1. **Le service de (la) santé,** *Mil:* the medical service; *Nau:* the quarantine service. **Bureau de santé,** (i) board of health; (ii) health-officer's office. **Officier de santé,** (i) *Nau:* health officer (of port); (ii) *A:* medical practitioner authorized to practise without a degree. S.a. PATENTE 2, RAISON 1. **Boire à la santé de qn, porter la santé de qn,** (i) to drink to s.o.'s health; (ii) to pledge s.o. *F:* **A votre santé!** good health! *P:* **Vous en avez une santé!** I like your cheek!

santoline [sɑ̃tɔlin], *s.f. Bot:* Lavender-cotton.

sanve [sɑ̃:v], *s.f. Bot:* Charlock; wild mustard.

saoul [su], **saouler** = SOÛL, SOÛLER.

sapajou [sapaʒu], *s.m. Z:* Sapajou.

sape [sap], *s.f.* Undermining. *Mil:* Sap(ping). *Exécuter une s.,* to drive a sap. **Travail en sape,** sapping.

sapèque [sapɛk], *s.f. Num:* (China) Sapeke, cash.

saper [sape], *v.tr.* To sap, undermine. *s.m.* **-ement.**

saperlotte [saperlɔt], **saperlipopette** [saperlipɔpɛt], *int. F:* = SAPRISTI.

sapeur [sapœ:r], *s.m. Mil:* Sapper; pioneer.

sapeur-aérostier, *s.m. Mil:* Soldier of a

balloon unit; balloon man. *pl. Des sapeurs-aérostiers.*

sapeur-pompier, *s.m.* Fireman. *Les sapeurs-pompiers,* the fire-brigade.

sapeur-télégraphiste, *s.m. Mil:* Telegraph-operator. *Les sapeurs-télégraphistes,* the signal corps; *F:* signals.

saphène [safɛn], *s.f. Anat:* Saphena (vein).

saphique [safik], *a. Pros:* Sapphic (stanza, etc.).

sapide [sapid], *a.* Sapid, savoury, palatable.

sapidité [sapidite], *s.f.* Sapidity; savouriness.

sapience [sapjɑ̃:s], *s.f. A:* Sapience, wisdom.

sapin [sapɛ̃], *s.m.* **I.** (*a*) Fir(-tree). *S. argenté, blanc,* silver fir, Swiss pine. *S. du Nord,* Scotch fir. Faux sapin, pitch-pine. (*b*) (**Bois de**) **sapin,** deal. **2.** *P:* (*a*) Cab, four-wheeler. (*b*) Coffin. **Toux qui sent le sapin,** churchyard cough.

sapine [sapin], *s.f.* (*a*) Fir plank; deal board. (*b*) Fixed scaffolding.

sapinette [sapinɛt], *s.f.* **I.** *Bot:* (Hemlock) spruce. **2.** Spruce beer.

sapinière [sapinjɛ:r], *s.f.* Fir-plantation; pine-tum.

saponacé [saponase], *a.* Saponaceous, soapy.

saponaire [saponɛ:r], *s.f. Bot:* Soapwort.

saponifier [saponifje], *v.tr.* To saponify.

sapristi [sapristi], *int.* Mild form of SACRISTI.

saquer[1] [sake], *v.tr.* To jerk (heavy body) along.

saquer[2], *v.tr. P:* To sack (s.o.); to give (s.o.) the sack; to fire (s.o.).

sarabande [sarabɑ̃:d], *s.f. Danc: Mus:* Sara-band.

sarbacane [sarbakan], *s.f.* (*a*) Blow-tube, -pipe; (child's) pea-shooter. (*b*) *Glassm:* Blow-pipe.

sarcasme [sarkasm], *s.m.* (Piece of) sarcasm; taunt, gibe.

sarcastique [sarkastik], *a.* Sarcastic.

sarcelle [sarsɛl], *s.f. Orn:* Teal.

sarcl|er [sarkle], *v.tr.* **I.** To clean (a field); to weed (garden); to hoe (turnips). **2.** To hoe up (weeds). *s.m.* **-age.**

sarcleur, -euse [sarklœ:r, -ø:z]. **I.** *s.* Weeder. **2.** *s.f.* Sarcleuse, weeding-machine.

sarcloir [sarklwa:r], *s.m.* (Weeding-)hoe; spud.

sarcologie [sarkɔlɔʒi], *s.f.* Sarcology.

sarcomateux, -euse [sarkɔmatø, -ø:z], *a. Med:* Sarcomatous.

sarcome [sarko:m], *s.m. Med:* Sarcoma.

sarcophage [sarkɔfa:ʒ], *s.m.* Sarcophagus.

sarcopte [sarkɔpt], *s.m. Ent:* Itch-mite.

sarcose [sarko:z], *s.f. Physiol:* Sarcosis.

Sardaigne [sardɛɲ]. *Pr.n.f. Geog:* Sardinia.

sarde [sard], *a. & s. Geog:* Sardinian.

sardine [sardin], *s.f.* **I.** (*a*) *Ich:* Pilchard. (*b*) *Com:* Sardine. **2.** *Mil: F:* N.C.O.'s stripe.

sardinerie [sardinri], *s.f.* Sardine curing and packing establishment.

sardinier, -ière [sardinje, -jɛ:r]. **I.** *s.* (*a*) Sardine fisher. (*b*) Sardine curer. **2.** *s.m.* (*a*) Sardine-net. (*b*) Sardine-boat.

sardonique [sardɔnik], *a.* Sardonic (smile, grin).

sargasse [sargas], *s.f.* Sargasso, gulf-weed. *Geog:* **La mer des Sargasses,** the Sargasso Sea.

sarigue [sarig], *s.m.* (The female is **la sarigue**) *Z:* Sarigue; (South American) opossum.

sarment [sarmɑ̃], *s.m.* (*a*) Vine-shoot. (*b*) Climbing stem; bine.

sarmenteux, -euse [sarmɑ̃tø, -ø:z], *a.* (*a*) Sarmentous. **Rosier sarmenteux,** rambler. (*b*) Vigne sarmenteuse, climbing vine.

sarrasin, -ine [sarazɛ̃, -in]. **I.** *Hist:* (*a*) *a.* Sara-cenic, Saracen. (*b*) *s.* Saracen. **2.** *s.m. Agr:* Buckwheat; Saracen corn.

sarrau, *pl.* **-s, -x** [saro], *s.m.* Overall, smock.

Sarre (la) [lasa:r]. *Pr.n.f. Geog:* (i) The (river) Saar; (ii) the Saar Basin.

Sarrebruck [sarbryk]. *Pr.n.m. Geog:* Saar-brücken.

sarriette [sarjɛt], *s.f. Bot:* Savory.

sas[1] [sɑ], *s.m.* Sieve, bolter, screen, riddle. **Passer qch. au sas,** to sift, bolt, sth.

sas[2], *s.m.* (*a*) *Hyd.E:* Lock-chamber; coffer (*b*) Lock. (*c*) Flooding-chamber (of submarine).

sassafras [sasafra(s)], *s.m. Bot:* Sassafras.

sasse [sɑ:s], *s.f. Nau:* Bailing-scoop, bailer.

sass|er[1] [sɑse], *v.tr.* (*a*) To sift, bolt, screen (flour); to winnow (grain); to jig (ore) (*b*) *F:* **Sasser (et ressasser),** to sift, scrutinize (evidence); to go over (a matter) again and again. *s.m.* **-age**[1].

sass|er[2], *v.tr.* To pass (a boat) through a lock to lock (a boat). *s.m.* **-age**[2].

sasseur, -euse [sɑsœ:r, -ø:z]. **I.** *s.* (Pers.) Sifter winnower. **2.** *s.m.* Sifting machine; winnower.

Satan [satɑ̃]. *Pr.n.m.* Satan; the Fiend.

satané [satane], *a. F:* (Intensive) Devilish confounded. *S. temps!* beastly weather! *C'est un s. menteur,* he's the deuce of a liar.

satanique [satanik], *a.* Satanic; fiendish (cruelty); diabolical (idea). *adv.* **-ment,** -ally

satellite [satɛllit], *s.m.* (*a*) Satellite, henchman. (*b*) *Astr:* Satellite; secondary planet. (*c*) *Tchn* Planet-wheel. **Engrenage à satellites,** (sun-and-planet gear.

satiété [sasjete], *s.f.* Satiety; surfeit. **Mange. jusqu'à satiété,** to eat to repletion.

satin [satɛ̃], *s.m.* **I.** *Tex:* Satin. *F: Une peau de s.,* a smooth and delicate skin. **2.** (*a*) Bois de satin, satin-wood. (*b*) *Bot:* **Satin blanc,** honesty satin-flower.

satin|er [satine], *v.tr.* (*a*) To satin, give a glossy surface to (material); to surface (paper) (*b*) *Phot:* To burnish, enamel (print). *s.m.* **-age.**

satinette [satinɛt], *s.f. Tex:* Sateen, satinet(te).

satineur, -euse [satinœ:r, -ø:z]. **I.** *s.* Satiner glazer. **2.** *s.f.* **Satineuse,** satining-machine glazing-machine.

satire [sati:r], *s.f.* **I.** Satire (*contre,* (up)on) **Trait de satire,** epigram. **2.** Satirizing.

satirique [satirik]. **I.** *a.* Satiric(al). **2.** *s.m* Satirist. *adv.* **-ment,** -ally.

satiriser [satirize], *v.tr.* To satirize.

satisfaction [satisfaksjɔ̃], *s.f.* **I.** Satisfaction gratification. **Donner de la satisfaction à qn,** to give s.o. cause for satisfaction. **Donner satisfaction aux vœux de qn,** to satisfy s.o.'s desires **2.** Reparation, amends (*pour, de,* for). *Theol* Atonement (for). **Demander satisfaction (d'une offense),** to demand satisfaction for an offence to challenge s.o.

satisfaire [satisfɛ:r], *v.* (Conj. like FAIRE) T satisfy. **I.** *v.tr.* (*a*) To content; to give satisfaction to (s.o.). *S. le désir de qn,* (i) to meet, grant (ii) to carry out, (iii) to gratify, s.o.'s wish. *S l'attente de qn,* to answer, come up to, s.o.' expectations. (*b*) To make amends to (s.o.) **2.** *v.ind.tr.* **Satisfaire à qch.,** to satisfy (honour) to answer, meet (condition, objection); to fulfil carry out (duty).

　satisfait, *a.* Satisfied, contented (*de,* with) *Je n'en suis pas s.,* I am not pleased with it. **Ma satisfait,** dissatisfied (*de,* with).

satisfaisant [satisfəzɑ̃], *a.* Satisfying, satis factory. **Peu satisfaisant,** unsatisfactory.

satur|able [satyrabl], *a.* Saturable. *s.f.* **-abilité**

saturation [satyrasjɔ̃], *s.f.* Saturation.

saturer [satyre], *v.tr.* To saturate.

　se saturer, to become saturated (*de,* with).

saturnales [satyrnal], *s.f.pl. Rom Ant. & F:* Saturnalia.

saturnin [satyrnɛ̃], *a.* Saturnine. **1.** *Intoxication saturnine,* lead-poisoning. **2.** *A:* Gloomy (disposition).

saturnisme [satyrnism], *s.m.* Lead-poisoning.

satyre [sati:r], *s.m.* Satyr.

satyrique [satirik], *a. Gr.Ant:* Satyric (drama).

sauce [so:s], *s.f.* **1.** Sauce. *S. blanche,* white sauce, melted butter. S.a. MAÎTRE 1, PIQUANT. **Rallonger la sauce,** (i) to thin out the sauce; (ii) *F:* to pad out a book. *Prov:* **Il n'est sauce que d'appétit,** hunger is the best sauce. *F:* **Accommoder un même sujet à toutes les sauces,** to dish up the same subject in every shape. **Gâter la sauce,** to spoil the whole business. *Av: Aut: F:* **Mettre toute la sauce,** to give full throttle; *P:* to step on the gas. **2.** *Draw:* Soft black crayon.

saucer [sose], *v.tr.* (je sauçai(s); n. sauçons) **1.** (*a*) To dip, sop, (one's bread) in the sauce. (*b*) To souse, drench (sth. in a liquid). **2.** *F:* To give (s.o.) a blowing-up.

saucée, *s.f. P:* **1.** (*a*) Downpour. (*b*) *Recevoir une s.,* to get a wetting, a soaking. **2.** Scolding, dressing-down, blowing-up.

saucière [sosjɛ:r], *s.f.* Sauce-boat.

saucisse [sosis], *s.f.* **1.** (*a*) ('Fresh' or 'wet') sausage. (*b*) *P:* Fat-head, duffer. **2.** *Mil: F:* Observation balloon, sausage balloon.

saucisson [sosisɔ̃], *s.m.* **1.** (Large 'dry') sausage. **2.** (*a*) *Exp:* Powder-hose; saucisse. (*b*) *Mil:* (Long) tascine. **3.** *Av: F:* Aerial torpedo.

sauf¹, sauve [sof, so:v], *a.* Safe, unscathed, unhurt. *L'honneur est s.,* honour is saved. **S'en tirer la vie sauve,** to get off with a whole skin. *Ils obtinrent la vie sauve,* they obtained an assurance that their lives would be spared. S.a. SAIN.

sauf², *prep.* Save, but, except. *Il est indemne s. une écorchure au bras,* he is unhurt except for a grazed arm. **Sauf correction,** subject to correction. **Sauf votre respect,** saving your presence. **Sauf avis contraire de votre part, sauf contre-ordre,** unless I hear to the contrary. *S. de rares exceptions,* with very few exceptions. **Sauf accidents, sauf imprévu,** barring accidents. **Sauf erreur ou omission,** errors and omissions excepted. **Je consens, sauf à revenir sur ma décision,** I consent, reserving the right to reconsider my decision. *Conj.phr.* **Sauf que +** *ind.,* except that. *Tout se passa bien s. que la mariée arriva en retard,* everything went off well, except that the bride turned up late.

sauf-conduit, *s.m.* Safe-conduct; pass. *pl. Des sauf-conduits.*

sauge [so:ʒ], *s.f. Bot: Cu:* Sage. *S. sauvage, s. des prés,* meadow sage.

saugrenu [sogrəny], *a.* Absurd, preposterous, ridiculous (question, answer).

saulaie [solɛ], *s.f.* Willow-plantation.

saule [so:l], *s.m. Bot:* Willow. *S. pleureur,* weeping willow.

saulée [sole], *s.f.* Row of willows.

saumâtre [somɑ:tr], *a.* Brackish, briny.

saumon [somɔ̃], *s.m.* **1.** Salmon. *a.inv. Rubans saumon,* salmon-pink ribbons. **2.** *Metall:* Ingot (of tin, etc.); pig (of lead, etc.). *S. de fonte,* pig-iron; *Nau:* kentledge.

saumoné [somɔne], *a.* **Truite saumonée,** salmon-trout.

saumoneau [somɔno], *s.m.* Young salmon; parr.

saumure [somy:r], *s.f.* Pickling brine; pickle.

saunier [sonje], *s.m.* Salt-maker.

saupoudrier [sopudre], *v.tr.* To sprinkle, powder, dust, dredge (*de,* with). *S. un gâteau de sucre,* to dust a cake with sugar. *F: S. un discours de citations latines,* to sprinkle, interlard, a speech with Latin quotations. [SEL] *s.m.* **-age.**

saupoudroir [sopudrwa:r], *s.m.* Dredger, castor; sugar-sifter.

saur [so:r], *a.m.* **Hareng saur,** (smoked and salted) red herring.

saur-ai, -as, etc. See SAVOIR.

saure [so:r]. *a.* Yellowish-brown. (*a*) **Jument saure,** sorrel mare. (*b*) **Faucon saure,** red hawk.

saurer [sore], *v.tr.* To cure, bloat, kipper (herrings).

saurien [sɔrjɛ̃], *a. & s.m. Rept:* Saurian.

saut [so], *s.m.* **1.** (*a*) Leap, jump, vault. **Au saut du lit,** on getting out of bed. **Faire un saut,** to take a leap. **Franchir un fossé de plein saut,** to clear a ditch at one bound. **Avancer par sauts et par bonds,** to skip, hop, along. *Travailler par sauts et par bonds,* to work by fits and starts. **Saut périlleux,** somersault. *F:* **Faire le s.** (périlleux), to take the plunge. *Sp: S. en longueur, en hauteur,* long jump, high jump. *S. de pied ferme, sans élan,* standing jump. S.a. JOINT 1. *S. à la perche,* pole-jump. *S. d'obstacles,* obstacle jumping; hurdling S.a. CARPE, MOUTON 1. (*b*) *S. de température,* sudden rise, jump, of temperature. *S. d'un cordage,* surge, jerk, of a rope. **2.** (Water-) fall. *Le s. du Niagara,* the Niagara Falls. **3.** **Saut de loup,** ha-ha, sunk fence.

saut-de-lit, *s.m.* **1.** (Bedside) rug. **2.** Morning wrap, dressing-gown. *pl. Des sauts-de-lit.*

saute [so:t], *s.f.* Jump (in temperature, price). Esp. *Nau:* **Saute de vent,** shift, change, of wind.

saute-mouton, *s.m. Games:* Leap-frog.

sauter [sote]. **I.** *v.i.* (Aux. *avoir*) (*a*) To jump, leap, skip. *S. de joie,* to jump, leap, for joy. *S. à la perche,* to pole-vault. S.a. CORDE 1. *S. à bas de son lit,* to jump, hop, out of bed. *S. à cheval,* to vault on to one's horse. *S. à terre,* (i) to jump down; (ii) (of rider) to dismount. *S. au collet, à la gorge, de qn,* to fly at s.o., to fly at s.o.'s throat. *S. au cou de qn,* to fling one's arms round s.o.'s neck. **Reculer pour mieux sauter,** to step back in order to have a better take-off. *F:* **Sauter au plafond,** to jump out of one's skin (with astonishment, etc.). *S. sur une offre,* to leap, jump, at an offer. (*b*) (Of mine) To explode; (of magazine, ship) to blow up; (of bank, etc.) to go smash; (of ministry) to fall; (of business) to go bankrupt, to fail; (of button, rivet-head) to come off, fly off; (of rivet) to start; *El.E:* (of fuse) to blow out. (*c*) *Nau:* (Of wind) To change, shift; to chop round; to veer. (*d*) **Faire sauter,** to make (s.o., sth.) jump; to blast (rock); to blow up (magazine, bridge, etc.); to explode (mine); to burst (boiler). **Faire sauter une serrure,** to burst a lock. **Faire s. le bouchon,** to pop the cork (of a bottle). **Se faire sauter,** to blow up one's ship. **Se faire sauter la cervelle,** to blow one's brains out. *Gaming:* **Faire sauter la banque,** to break the bank. *El.E:* **Faire s. les plombs,** to blow the fuses. S.a. COUPE² 2. **2.** *v.tr.* (*a*) To jump (over), leap over, clear (ditch, etc.). (*b*) To skip (pages in reading); to leave out (line in copying); to drop (a stitch). *S. une danse,* to sit out a dance. (*c*) To toss (in the air); to ted (hay).

sauté, *a.* **Pommes de terre sautées,** sauté potatoes, jumped potatoes.

sauterelle [sotrɛl], *s.f.* **1.** Grasshopper. **Grande sauterelle d'Orient,** locust. **2.** *Const:* etc: (Shifting) bevel, bevel square.

37

sauterie [sotri], *s.f.* **I.** Jumping, hopping. **2.** Cinderella (dance) ; hop.

sauternes [sotɛrn], *s.m.* (Also **vin de Sauternes**) Sauterne (wine).

saute-ruisseau, *s.m.inv.* (Office) errand-boy.

sauteur, -euse [sotœːr, -øːz]. **I.** *a.* Leaping, jumping (insect, etc.). **2.** *s.* (*a*) Leaper, jumper ; bucking horse. (*b*) *F:* Weather-cock (politician) ; trimmer.

sautill|er [sotije], *v.i.* (*a*) To hop (like a sparrow) ; to skip, jump (about). (*b*) *F:* To jump from one thing to another (in conversation). *s.m.* **-age.** *s.m.* **-ement.**

sautoir [sotwaːr], *s.m.* **I.** (*a*) St Andrew's Cross ; *Her:* saltire. **En sautoir,** crosswise ; in saltire. *Porter un baudrier en s.,* to wear a belt crosswise, over the shoulder. (*b*) (Woman's) watch-guard ; long neck chain. (*c*) Kerchief (worn over the shoulders). **2.** *Cu:* (Shallow) pan (for jumping potatoes). **3.** Jumping-bar, hurdle.

sauvage [sovaːʒ]. **I.** *a.* (*a*) Savage, uncivilized, rude (people, life) ; wild, untamed (beast) ; barbarous, brutal (custom). *Chat s.,* wild cat. *Lieu s.,* wilderness. (*b*) *Rac:* **Cheval sauvage,** loose horse. (*c*) Averse to society ; unsociable ; shy ; coy (maiden). **2.** *s.* (With *f.* **sauvage** or *F:* **sauvagesse**) (*a*) Savage. (*b*) Unsociable person. *adv.* **-ment.**

sauvageon [sovaʒɔ̃], *s.m.* (*a*) Wild stock (for grafting). (*b*) Wilding, seedling.

sauvagerie [sovaʒri], *s.f.* **I.** (State of) savagery, savageness. **2.** Unsociability.

sauvagesse [sovaʒɛs]. See SAUVAGE 2.

sauvagin, -ine [sovaʒɛ̃, -in]. **I.** *a.* Fishy (taste, smell). **2.** *s.f.* Sauvagine. (*a*) Coll. Waterfowl. (*b*) *Com:* Common pelts.

sauvegarde [sovgard], *s.f.* **I.** Safeguard, safe-keeping. *Sous la s. de qn,* under s.o.'s protection. **Clause de sauvegarde,** saving clause. **2.** Safe-conduct. **3.** Body-guard. **4.** *Nau:* Life-line, man-rope.

sauvegarder [sovgarde], *v.tr.* To safeguard, protect. *S. les apparences,* to save appearances.

sauve-qui-peut, *s.m.inv.* Stampede, helter-skelter flight, headlong flight.

sauv|er [sove], *v.tr.* **I.** (*a*) To save, rescue, deliver (s.o.). *Dieu sauve le roi!* God save the King! *S. les apparences, les dehors,* to save, preserve, appearances. (*b*) To salve (ship, goods). **2.** *A:* To conceal, palliate (faults). *a.* **-able.**

se sauver. **I.** (*a*) *Se s. d'un péril,* to escape, make one's escape, from a danger. **Sauve qui peut!** every man for himself! *S.a.* SAUVE-QUI-PEUT. (*b*) To take refuge (in church). (*c*) *Vendre à bas prix et se s. sur la quantité,* to sell at a low price and recoup oneself by large sales. **2.** (*a*) To run away, to be off, *F:* to clear out. *Se s. à toutes jambes, F:* to cut and run, to skedaddle. (*b*) (Of liquid) To boil over.

sauvetage [sovtaːʒ], *s.m.* (*a*) Life-saving ; rescue (from fire or drowning). **Appareil de sauvetage,** life-saving apparatus. **Ceinture de sauvetage,** life-belt. **Bouée de sauvetage,** life-buoy. **Canot, bateau, de sauvetage,** lifeboat. **Échelle de sauvetage,** fire-escape. (*b*) Salvage, salving (of ship, goods). **Société de sauvetage,** salvage company.

sauveteur [sovtœːr], *s.m.* (*a*) Rescuer, life-saver. (*b*) Lifeboatman. (*c*) Salvor, salvager.

sauveur [sovœːr], *s.m.* Saver, preserver, deliverer. *Theol:* **Le Sauveur,** the Saviour, the Redeemer.

savamment [savamɑ̃], *adv.* (*a*) Learnedly. (*b*) Knowingly, wittingly.

savane [savan], *s.f.* Savanna(h).

savant, -ante [savɑ̃, -ɑ̃ːt]. **I.** *a.* (*a*) Learned (en, in) ; erudite, scholarly, well-informed. (*b*) Skilful, clever, able. **Chien savant,** performing dog. (*c*) Knowing. **2.** *s.* Scientist ; scholar.

savarin [savarɛ̃], *s.m.* *Cu:* Savarin (round cake with hollow centre, moistened with rum).

savate [savat], *s.f.* **I.** Old, worn-out, shoe. *F:* **Traîner la savate,** (i) to go slipshod ; (ii) to be down at heel. **En savates,** down at heel ; slipshod (person). **2.** Foot boxing, French boxing. *Tirer la savate,* to go in for foot boxing.

saveter [savte], *v.tr.* (The forms **je savette, je savetterai** are never used) *F:* To botch, bungle.

savetier [savtje], *s.m.* **I.** Cobbler. **2.** *F:* Botcher, bungler. [SAVATE]

saveur [savœːr], *s.f.* **I.** Savour, taste, flavour. **Plein de saveur,** full-flavoured. **Sans saveur,** tasteless, insipid. **2.** Pungency (of style, story).

Savoie [savwa]. *Pr.n.f.* *Geog:* Savoy. **S.a.** BISCUIT 1.

savoir [savwaːr]. **I.** *v.tr.* (*pr.p.* **sachant**; *p.p.* **su**; *pr.ind.* **je sais, il sait, n. savons, ils savent**; *pr.sub.* **je sache, n. sachions** ; *imp.* **sache, sachons, sachez**; *p.d.* **je savais** ; *p.h.* **je sus**; *fu.* **je saurai**) To know. **I.** *S. qch. par cœur,* to know sth. by heart. *S. sa leçon,* to know one's lesson. *S. son monde,* to know how to behave in company. *Il en sait plus d'une,* he knows a thing or two. *Prov:* **Savoir c'est pouvoir,** knowledge is power. **2.** To be aware of (sth.). (*a*) *Savez-vous qu'il est midi?* do you know, are you aware, that it is twelve o'clock? **Je (le) sais bien!** I know! *Ce n'est pas bien,* **tu sais!** it isn't right, you know! **Vous ne savez pas!** *nous allons nous cacher . . .,* I'll tell you what, let us hide. . . . **Je n'en sais rien,** I know nothing about it ; I don't know, I cannot tell. **Je n'en sais trop rien, je ne sais trop,** I am not very sure. *Vous en savez plus long que moi,* you know more (about it) than I do. *S.a.* LONG 2. (In careful speech) *Je ne sais,* I do not know, *Lit:* I know not. **Sans le savoir,** unwittingly, unconsciously. **Pas que je sache,** not that I know of, not that I am aware of. **(Pour) autant que je sache,** (i) to the best of my knowledge, as far as I know ; (ii) for aught I know. **La question est de savoir si elle viendra,** the question is whether she will come. **On ne sait jamais,** one never knows ; you never can tell. **Si jeunesse savait!** if youth but knew! (*b*) **Je ne sache pas** *l'avoir froissée,* I am not aware of having offended her. *Je ne sache pas qu'on vous y ait autorisé,* I am not aware that you have been allowed to do so. (*c*) *Je la sais intelligente,* I know her to be intelligent. *Je vous savais à Paris,* I knew you were in Paris. (*d*) (With dat.) *Je lui savais une grande fortune,* I knew him to be wealthy. (*e*) *Je ne sais (pas) où le trouver,* I don't know where to find him. **Ne savoir que faire, que dire,** to be at a loss what to do, what to say. **Sachez que . . .,** I would have you know that. . . . **3.** (*a*) *On a su la nouvelle à quatre heures, la nouvelle s'est sue à quatre heures,* the news came out, became known, at four o'clock. *La nouvelle se sait déjà,* the news is already known. *Tout se sait tôt ou tard,* everything gets known sooner or later. *Il n'en a rien su,* he never knew of it. **C'est à savoir,** that remains to be seen. **Reste à savoir si . . .,** it remains to be seen whether. . . . *Je voudrais bien s. pourquoi,* I wonder why. **Il n'a voulu rien savoir,** he wouldn't hear of it. (*b*) **Faire savoir qch. à qn,** to let s.o. know sth. ; to inform s.o. of sth. **On fait savoir que . . .,** notice is hereby given that. . . . (*c*) (A) **savoir,** to wit, namely, viz., that is to say. **4.** To know how, to be able (to do sth.). *Savez-vous nager?* can you swim? *Elle ne sait rien faire*, she is quite untrained. *Je crois que je saurai le faire*, I think I can manage it. S.a. VIVRE I. **2. Je ne saurais** *dire pourquoi*, I cannot say, have no idea, why. (Polite refusal) *Je ne saurais permettre cela*, I cannot allow that. **5.** (Un) je ne sais qui *nous a écrit*, we have had a letter from someone or other, from some individual. *Un* je ne sais quoi *de déplaisant*, an indefinable something that displeases. *Elle a lu* je ne sais quoi, she has read some rubbish or other. *Il est mort de* je ne sais quelle maladie, he died of some disease or other. **Je suis tout** je ne sais comment, I feel so queer. S.a. COMBIEN 2. *Des robes, des chapeaux, que* sais-je! dresses, hats, and goodness knows what else! *Il a des amis,* **Dieu sait!** he has friends in plenty, God knows! **II. savoir,** *s.m.* Knowledge, learning, scholarship.   **su,** *s.m.* Knowledge. (In the phr.) **Au su de . . .**, to the knowledge of. **. . . A mon vu et su,** to my certain knowledge.

savoir-faire, *s.m.* Ability, tact; *F:* gumption.

savoir-vivre, *s.m.* Good manners, good breeding, knowledge of the world. **Manque de savoir-vivre,** ill-breeding. *N'avoir pas de s.-v.*, to have no manners.

savoisien, -ienne [savwazjɛ̃, -jɛn], *a. & s. Geog:* Savoyard; of Savoy.

savon [savɔ̃], *s.m.* **1.** Soap. **Pain de savon,** cake of soap. *S. à barbe*, shaving-soap. *S. de Marseille*, yellow soap. S.a. MARBRÉ 1. **Eau de savon,** soap-suds. **Bulle de savon,** soap-bubble. **Fabricant de savon,** soap-boiler. *F:* **Donner, flanquer, un savon à qn,** to give s.o. a good dressing-down; to haul s.o. over the coals. *Recevoir un s.*, to catch it. **2. Pierre de savon,** soapstone; steatite.

savonnage [savɔnaːʒ], *s.m.* Soaping, washing. **Faire un petit savonnage,** to do a little washing.

savonner [savɔne], *v.tr.* To soap; to wash (clothes, etc.) in soap and water. *Se s. le menton*, to lather one's chin.

savonnerie [savɔnri], *s.f.* **1.** Soap-works. **2.** Soap-trade.

savonnette [savɔnɛt], *s.f.* **1.** Cake of toilet-soap. **2.** Shaving-brush. **3.** (Montre à) savonnette, hunter (watch).

savonneux, -euse [savɔnø, -øːz], *a.* **1.** Soapy. **2. Terre savonneuse,** fuller's earth.

savonnier, -ière [savɔnje, -jɛːr]. **1.** (a) *a. Industrie savonnière*, soap-industry. (b) *s.m.* Soap-boiler **2.** *s.m.* Soapberry(-tree).

savourer [savure], *v.tr.* To relish, enjoy (one's food, cup of coffee); *F:* to roll (sth.) over one's tongue. *S. un spectacle, sa vengeance*, to gloat over a sight, one's revenge.

savoureusement [savurøzmɑ̃], *adv.* **1.** With relish, with gusto. **2.** *Mets préparé s.*, dish prepared in a tasty way.

savoureux, -euse [savurø, -øːz], *a.* Savoury, tasty (dish); racy (anecdote). **Peu savoureux,** unsavory.

savoyard, -arde [savwajaːr, -ard]. **1.** *a. & s. F:* = SAVOISIEN. **2.** *s.m. A:* Petit savoyard, little chimney-sweep; climbing-boy.

Saxe [saks]. *Pr.n.f.* Saxony. *Porcelaine de Saxe,* Dresden china.

saxhorn [saksɔrn], *s.m. Mus:* Saxhorn. *S. basse*, euphonium.

saxifrage [saksifraːʒ], *s.f. Bot:* Saxifrage.

saxophone [saksɔfɔn], *s.m.* Saxophone.

saynète [sɛnɛt], *s.f. Th:* Playlet, sketch, comedietta.

sbire [zbiːr], *s.m.* **1.** Sbirro. **2.** *F:* Myrmidon (of the law).

scabieux, -euse [skabjø, -øːz]. **1.** *a.* Scabby, scabious (eruption, etc.). **2.** *s.f. Bot:* Scabieuse, scabious.

scabreux, -euse [skabrø, -øːz], *a.* **1.** Difficult, risky, ticklish (work). **2.** Indelicate (allusion); delicate (question); improper, scabrous (tale, conduct).

scaferlati [skaferlati], *s.m.* Cut tobacco (of the French State factories).

scalène [skalɛn], *a.* Scalene (triangle).

scalpe [skalp], *s.m.* Scalp (as a war trophy).

scalpel [skalpɛl], *s.m. Surg:* Scalpel.

scalper [skalpe], *v.tr.* To scalp (an enemy).

scammonée [skamɔne], *s.f. Bot:* Scammony.

scandale [skɑ̃dal], *s.m.* Scandal; (cause of) shame. *C'est un s.*, it's disgraceful. *Faire un s., causer du s.*, to create a scandal. **Livre qui fait scandale,** book that is shocking the public. *Éviter le s.*, to avoid public exposure.

scandaleu|x, -euse [skɑ̃dalø, -øːz], *a.* Scandalous, shameful, disgraceful; glaring (abuse). *adv.* **-sement.**

scandaliser [skɑ̃dalize], *v.tr.* To scandalize.   **se scandaliser,** to be scandalized (de, at).

scander [skɑ̃de], *v.tr.* To scan (verse). *Mus:* To mark, stress (a phrase). *F:* To punctuate (one's words, actions). *Marche scandée*, measured, rhythmical, tread.

scandinave [skɑ̃dinaːv], *a. & s.* Scandinavian.

Scandinavie [skɑ̃dinavi]. *Pr.n.f.* Scandinavia.

scandix [skɑ̃diks], *s.m. Bot:* Scandix, *F:* shepherd's-needle.

scansion [skɑ̃sjɔ̃], *s.f.* Scansion, scanning.

scaphandre [skafɑ̃ːdr], *s.m.* Diving-suit.

scaphandrier [skafɑ̃drie], *s.m.* Diver (in diving-suit).

scapulaire [skapylɛːr]. **1.** *s.m. Ecc:* Scapular, scapulary. **2.** *a. Anat:* Scapular (artery).

scarabée [skarabe], *s.m.* **1.** (Scarabaeid) beetle. *S. pilulaire*, scarabaeus. **2.** *Egypt.Ant:* Scarab.

scare [skaːr], *s.m. Ich:* Scarus; parrot-fish.

scarificateur [skarifikatœːr], *s.m.* (a) *Agr:* Scarifier. (b) *Surg:* Scarificator.

scarification [skarifikasjɔ̃], *s.f.* Scarification.

scarifi|er [skarifje], *v.tr. Agr: Surg:* To scarify. S.a. VENTOUSE 1. *s.m.* **-age.**

scarlatine [skarlatin], *a. & s.f. Med:* (**Fièvre**) scarlatine, scarlet fever, scarlatina.

scarole [skarɔl], *s.f.* = ESCAROLE.

scatologie [skatɔlɔʒi], *s.f.* (a) Scatological humour or literature. (b) Taste for filthy literature.

scatologique [skatɔlɔʒik], *a.* Scatological.

sceau [so]. *s.m.* Seal. (a) *S. te l'État*, State seal. **Mettre, apposer, son sceau à un document,** to affix, set, put, one's seal to a document. **Sous le sceau du secret,** under the seal of secrecy. *S. du génie*, mark, stamp, of genius. *Adm:* Les Sceaux = the Great Seal. S.a. GARDE[1] 1. (b) *Bot:* Sceau de Salomon, Solomon's-seal.

scélérat, -ate [selera, -at], **1.** *a.* (a) Wicked, villainous. (b) Crafty, cunning. **2.** *s.* (a) Scoundrel, villain. (b) Cunning scoundrel. *F:* Petite scélérate! you little jade! *adv.* **-ement.**

scélératesse [seleratɛs], *s.f.* **1.** (a) Wickedness, villainy. (b) Low cunning. **2.** Wicked action or piece of low cunning.

scell|er [sele], *v.tr.* **1.** (a) To seal (letter, etc.); to seal up (test tube). *Jur:* To affix an official seal to (box, door). **Sceller en cire rouge,** sealed with red wax. **Signé et scellé par moi,** given under my hand and seal. (b) *F:* To ratify, confirm (privilege, friendship); to seal (alliance, etc.). *s.m.* -**age**. **2.** *Const:* To bed, fasten, fix in (post, iron bar, etc.); to plug (nail in wall, etc.). *s.m.* -**ement**.

scellé. **1.** *a.* Sealed; under seal. **2.** *s.m.* (Imprint of official) seal. **Apposer les scellés** (*à un meuble*), **mettre** (*un meuble*) **sous le scellé**, to affix the seals (to desk, etc.). **Lever les scellés**, to remove the seals. **Bris de scellé(s)**, breaking of seals.

scénario [sɛnarjo], *s.m. Th:* Scenario.

scène [sɛn], *s.f. Th:* **1.** Stage. **Entrer en scène**, to appear, come on. **Mettre en scène**, to stage. **Mise en scène**, (i) staging, production; (ii) (stage-) setting (of a play). **L'art de la mise en scène**, stage-craft. **Metteur en scène**, producer. **Quitter la scène**, to give up the stage. **2.** Scene. (*a*) Scene of action. **La scène se passe à Paris**, the action takes place in Paris. (*b*) *Troisième s. du second acte*, scene three of act two. (*c*) *Ce fut une s. pénible*, it was a painful scene. *Scènes de la vie des camps*, scenes from camp life. (*d*) *F:* Angry discussion; row. *Scènes de famille*, family wrangles. **Faire une scène**, to make a scene.

scénique [senik], *a.* Scenic; theatrical; of the stage. **Indications scéniques**, stage directions.

scepticisme [sɛptisism], *s.m.* Scepticism.

sceptique [sɛptik]. **1.** *a.* Sceptical. **2.** *s.* Sceptic. *adv.* -**ment**.

sceptre [sɛptr], *s.m.* Sceptre. *F:* **Sous un sceptre de fer**, under iron despotism.

schabraque [ʃabrak], *s.f. Mil:* Shabrack.

schah [ʃa], *s.m.* Shah.

schako [ʃako], *s.m.* Shako.

schampooing [ʃãpwɛ̃], *s.m.* Hair-wash, shampoo.

schelling [ʃ(ə)lɛ̃], *s.m.* Shilling.

schéma [ʃema, ske-], *s.m.* Diagram; (sketch-) plan. *El.E: S. des connexions*, wiring diagram.

schématique [ʃematik, ske-], *a.* Schematic; diagrammatic. *Coupe s.*, diagrammatic section. *Dessin s.*, diagram, draft. *adv.* -**ment**, -al**ly**.

schibboleth [ʃibɔlɛt], *s.m. B.Hist. & F:* Shibboleth.

schismatique [ʃismatik], *a. & s.* Schismatic.

schisme [ʃism], *s.m.* Schism.

schiste [ʃist], *s.m. Geol:* Schist, shale. **Huile de schiste**, shale-oil.

schisteux, -euse [ʃistø, -ø:z], *a. Geol:* Schistose, schistous. *Houille schisteuse*, slaty coal.

schizophrène [skizɔfrɛn], *a.* Schizophrenic.

schizophrénie [skizɔfreni], *s.f.* Schizophrenia.

schlague (la) [laʃlag], *s.f. Mil: A:* Flogging.

schlinguer [ʃlɛ̃ge], *v.i. P:* To stink.

schlitte [ʃlit], *s.f.* Wood-sledge (for transporting lumber down the mountain-side); *U.S:* dray.

schlitter [ʃlite], *v.tr.* To transport (lumber) on a *schlitte. s.m.* -**age**.

schlitteur [ʃlitœ:r], *s.m.* Lumber-man.

schnaps [ʃnaps], *s.m. F:* Brandy, spirits.

schnick [ʃnik], *s.m. P:* (Inferior) brandy, spirits.

sciant [sjã], *a. P:* Boring, tiresome.

sciatique [sjatik]. **1.** (*a*) *a.* Sciatic (nerve, etc.). (*b*) *s.m.* Sciatic nerve. **2.** *s.f. Med:* Sciatica.

scie [si], *s.f.* **1.** Saw. *S. à main*, hand-saw. *S. mécanique*, power-saw, sawing-machine. *S. à ruban*, band-saw. *S. à chantourner*, compass-saw, scroll-saw. *S. à araser*, *s. à tenon*, tenon-saw. *S. à découper*, fret-saw. *S. à refendre*, rip-saw. *S. à métaux*, hack-saw. **Trait de scie**, saw-cut; kerf. *Bot:* **En dents de scie**, serrate. *Games:* Jeu de la scie, cat's-cradle. **2.** *Ich:* **Scie de mer**, saw-fish. **3.** *P:* (*a*) Bore, nuisance. **Quelle scie!** what a nuisance! **Monter une scie à qn**, to play the same practical joke on s.o. again

and again. (*b*) Catch-phrase (of comic song); catchword, gag.

sciemment [sjamã], *adv.* Knowingly, wittingly.

science [sjɑ̃:s], *s.f.* **1.** Knowledge, learning, skill. *Il vous égale en s.*, he is your equal in learning. **Être un puits de science**, to be a well of learning. *B:* **L'arbre de la science du bien et du mal**, the tree of knowledge of good and evil. **2.** Science. *Étudier les sciences*, to study science. **Hommes de science**, scientists.

sciène [sjɛn], *s.f. Ich:* Sciaena.

scientifique [sjãtifik], *a.* Scientific. *adv.* -**ment**, -al**ly**.

scientiste [sjãtist], *s.m.* **Scientistes chrétiens**, Christian scientists.

scier[1] [sje], *v.tr.* **1.** To saw. *S. de long*, to rip. *F:* **Scier le dos à qn**, to bore s.o. stiff. **2.** To saw off (branch, etc.). *s.m.* -**age**.

scier[2], *v.i. Row:* To back water, back the oars.

scierie [siri], *s.f.* Saw-mill, saw-yard.

scieur [sjœ:r], *s.m.* Sawyer. *S. de long*, (pit-) sawyer.

scille [sil], *s.f.* (*a*) Squill. (*b*) *Pharm:* Squills.

scinder [sɛ̃de], *v.tr.* To divide, split up (question). *s.m.* -**ement**.

se scinder, (of political party) to divide, split.

scintillant [sɛtijã, -tillã], *a.* Scintillating; twinkling (star, *Nau:* light); sparkling (wit).

scintillation [sɛtijasjɔ̃, -tilla-], *s.f.* Scintillation, sparkling; twinkling (of star). *Cin:* Flicker(ing).

scintiller [sɛtije, -tille], *v.i.* To scintillate; to sparkle; (of star) to twinkle. *Cin:* To flicker. *s.m.* -**ement**.

scion [sjɔ̃], *s.m.* **1.** *Hort:* Scion, shoot. **2.** Top (-piece), tip (of fishing-rod).

scissile [sissil], *a.* Scissile (rock).

scission [sissjɔ̃], *s.f.* Scission, division, cleavage, split (in party, etc.); secession. **Faire scission**, to secede.

scissionnaire [sissjɔnɛ:r]. **1.** *a.* Seceding. **2.** *s.* Seceder.

scissipare [sissipa:r], *a. Biol:* Fissiparous.

sciure [sjy:r], *s.f.* **Sciure de bois**, sawdust. [SCIER]

scléreux, -euse [sklerø, -ø:z], *a. Med:* Sclerous, sclerosed, hard (tissue).

sclérose [sklero:z], *s.f. Med:* Sclerosis.

scléroser [skleroze], *v.tr. Med:* To harden. **sclérosé**, *a.* Sclerosed.

sclérotique [sklerɔtik]. *Anat:* **1.** *a.* Sclerotic. **2.** *s.f.* Sclerotic, sclera (of the eye).

scolaire [skɔlɛ:r], *a. Vie s.*, school life. *Réformes scolaires*, school reforms. **Année scolaire**, school year, academic year. **Livre scolaire**, school-book.

scolastique [skɔlastik]. **1.** *a.* Scholastic (philosophy). **2.** *s.m.* Schoolman, scholastic. **3.** *s.f.* Scholasticism.

scoliaste [skɔljast], *s.m.* Scholiast.

scolopendre[1] [skɔlɔpɑ̃:dr], *s.f. Myr:* Scolopendra, centipede.

scolopendre[2], *s.f. Bot:* Hart's-tongue.

scombre [skɔ̃:br], *s.m. Ich:* Mackerel, scomber.

scons(e) [skɔ̃:s], *s.m. Com:* Skunk (fur).

scops [skɔps], *s.m. Orn:* Scops owl.

scorbut [skɔrby], *s.m. Med:* Scurvy.

scorbutique [skɔrbytik], *a. & s. Med:* Scorbutic, scurvied.

scorie [skɔri], *s.f.* Usu. *pl. Metall:* Slag, cinders, scoria; (iron) dross. *Scories vitreuses*, clinker. *S. de forge*, hammer scale.

scorpène [skɔrpɛn], *s.f. Ich:* Scorpion-fish.

scorpion [skɔrpjɔ̃], *s.m.* (*a*) *Arach:* Scorpion. (*b*) *Astr:* **Le Scorpion**, Scorpio.

scorsonère [skɔrsɔnɛ:r], **scorzonère** [skɔrzɔnɛ:r], *s.f. Bot:* Scorzonera; black salsify.

scotie [skɔsi], *s.f. Arch:* Scotia (of pillar).
scoutisme [skutism], *s.m.* (*a*) Boy-scout movement. (*b*) Boy-scouting.
scratch [skratʃ], *s.m. Sp:* **1.** Scratch. **Partir scratch**, to start (at) scratch. **2.** Scratch-man, scratch-player.
scribe [skrib], *s.m.* (*a*) *Jew.Hist:* Scribe. (*b*) Copyist, *F:* quill-driver.
scriptural, -aux [skriptyral, -o], *a.* Scriptural.
scrofulaire [skrɔfylɛːr], *s.f. Bot:* Figwort.
scrofule [skrɔfyl], *s.f. Usu. pl. Med:* Scrofula.
scrofuleux, -euse [skrɔfylø, -øːz], *a.* Scrofulous.
scrupule [skrypyl], *s.m.* **1.** Scruple (weight). **2.** Scruple, (conscientious) doubt (*sur*, about). **Sans scrupules,** unscrupulous. **Se faire (un) scrupule de faire qch.,** avoir des scrupules à faire qch., to have scruples about doing sth.; to scruple to do sth. *Avoir le s. de l'exactitude*, to make a point of accuracy. **Exact jusqu'au scrupule,** scrupulously accurate.
scrupuleu|x, -euse [skrypylø, -øːz], *a.* Scrupulous (*sur*, about, over). **Peu scrupuleux,** unscrupulous. *S. à remplir ses devoirs*, punctilious in the performance of one's duties. *adv.* **-sement.**
scrutateur, -trice [skrytatœːr, -tris]. **1.** *a.* Searching (mind, look); scrutinizing. **2.** *s.* (*a*) Scrutinizer, scrutator. (*b*) Teller, scrutineer (of a ballot or poll).
scruter [skryte], *v.tr.* To scrutinize; to scan; to examine closely. *S. le visage de qn*, to scan s.o.'s face. *S. qn du regard*, to give s.o. a searching look.
scrutin [skrytɛ̃], *s.m.* **1.** Poll. *S. d'arrondissement*, constituency poll. *S. de liste*, voting for several members (out of a list). **Bureau de scrutin,** polling-booth. *Dépouiller le s.*, to count the votes. **2.** **Tour de scrutin,** ballot. **Voter au scrutin,** to ballot. *Élire qn au s.*, to ballot for s.o. **3.** Voting. **Procéder au scrutin,** to take the vote; (in Engl. Parliament) to divide.
scrutiner [skrytine], *v.i.* (*a*) To poll, vote. (*b*) To ballot.
sculpt|er [skylte], *v.tr.* To sculpture, to carve (*dans*, out of). *s.m.* **-age.**
sculpteur [skyltœːr], *s.m.* Sculptor. **Femme sculpteur,** woman sculptor; sculptress. *S. sur bois*, wood-carver.
sculptural, -aux [skyltyral, -o], *a.* Sculptural (art); statuesque (figure).
sculpture [skyltyːr], *s.f.* Sculpture. *S. sur bois*, wood-carving.
scutellaire [skytɛlɛːr], *s.f. Bot:* Scutellaria; skull-cap.
scutelle [skytɛl], *s.f. Nat.Hist:* Scutellum.
scutiforme [skytiform], *a.* Scutiform, shield-shaped.
scutum [skytɔm], *s.m. Rom.Ant:* Z: Scutum.
Scylla [silla]. *Pr.n.m. Myth:* Scylla. S.a. CHARYBDE.
scythe [sit], *a. & s. A.Geog:* Scythian.
Scythie [siti]. *Pr.n.f. A.Geog:* Scythia.
se, before a vowel sound **s'** [s(ə)], *pers. pron. acc. & dat.* **1.** (*a*) (Reflexive) Oneself; himself, herself, itself, themselves. *Se flatter*, to flatter oneself. *Elle s'est coupée au doigt, s'est coupé le doigt*, she has cut her finger. (*b*) (Reciprocal) Each other, one another. *Se nuire (l'un à l'autre)*, to hurt one another. *Il est dur de se quitter*, it is hard to part. **2.** (Giving passive meaning to active vbs) *La clef s'est retrouvée*, the key has been found. *Cet article se vend partout*, this article sells, is sold, everywhere. **3.** (In purely pronom. conjugation) See S'EN ALLER, SE BATTRE, SE DÉPÊCHER, SE FÂCHER, etc. NOTE. *Se* is often omitted before

an infinitive dependent on *faire, laisser, mener, envoyer, voir. E.g:* Faire taire *les enfants*. **Faire envoler** *les oiseaux*. **Mener promener** *les enfants*. Envoyer coucher *les enfants*. *Nous avons vu lever le soleil*.
séance [seɑ̃ːs], *s.f.* **1.** **Prendre séance,** to take one's seat (at a council table). **Avoir séance à un conseil,** to have a seat on a committee or board. **2.** Sitting, session, meeting. (Of parliament) **Être en séance,** to be sitting, in session. **Déclarer la séance ouverte,** to open the meeting. **Lever la séance,** (i) to dissolve the meeting, to leave the chair; (ii) to adjourn. **Tenir une séance publique,** to have, hold, an open meeting. **En séance publique,** at an open meeting. S.a. TENANT 1. **3.** Performance (at cinema, etc.). **Séance de spiritisme,** seance. **4.** Sitting (for one's portrait, etc.). *Peindre un portrait en une s.*, to paint a portrait at one sitting. [SEOIR]
séant [seɑ̃]. **I.** See SEOIR.
II. **séant,** *a.* **1.** (*a*) Sitting; in session. (*b*) *s.m.* **Se mettre, se dresser, sur son séant,** to sit up (in bed). *Tomber sur son s., F:* to fall on one's behind. **2.** Becoming (*à*, to); fitting, proper, seemly. *Il n'est pas s. qu'elle sorte seule*, it is not proper that she should go out alone.
seau [so], *s.m.* Pail, bucket. *S. à incendie*, fire-bucket. *S. à charbon*, coal-scuttle. *S. de toilette, de ménage*, slop-pail. *S. à biscuits*, biscuit-barrel.
sébacé [sebase], *a.* Sebaceous (gland).
sébile [sebil], *s.f.* Wooden bowl. **Tendre la sébile,** to beg.
sec, sèche [sɛk, sɛʃ]. **I.** *a.* **1.** (*a*) Dry. *Temps sec*, dry weather. **Avoir la gorge sèche,** *F:* avoir le gosier sec, to be thirsty; to feel dry. *Gorge sèche*, parched throat. **Mettre un enfant au pain sec et à l'eau,** to put a child on bread and water. *Traverser un torrent à pied sec*, to cross a torrent dry-shod. *F:* **Sec comme une allumette,** bone-dry. *Adm:* **Le régime sec, the dry regime;** prohibition. *Adv.* **Boire sec,** (i) to drink one's wine or spirits neat; (ii) to drink hard. S.a. NOURRICE 1, POINTE 3, VENTOUSE 1. (*b*) Dried (cod, raisins); seasoned, matured (wood, cigar); dry (wine). S.a. FRUIT[1]. *Adv.* **Brûler sec,** to burn like tinder. (*c*) **Argent sec,** hard cash. **Perte sèche,** dead loss. (*d*) *Cards:* **Roi sec,** unguarded king. **2.** (*a*) Spare, gaunt (person); lean (figure, horse). **Sec et nerveux,** wiry. (*b*) Sharp, dry, curt (answer); incisive (tone). **Donner un coup sec à qch.,** to give sth. a sharp blow or tap. **Casser qch. d'un coup sec,** to break sth. with a snap. *Mine sèche*, sour face. *Un merci tout sec*, a bare thank you. *Adv.* **Parler sec,** not to mince one's words, to rap out one's words. (*c*) Unsympathetic, unfeeling (heart, etc.). *Adv.* **Rire sec,** to give a harsh, dry, laugh. (*d*) Barren; meagre, dry, bald (narrative, etc.). (*e*) *Cards: etc:* **Partie sèche,** one game (without revenge). **On va faire un écarté en cinq sec,** we'll have one game at écarté. *F:* **Faire qch. en cinq sec,** to do sth. in a jiffy, in less than no time. *Cf.* LIÉ 4. (*f*) *Nau:* **Vergue sèche,** bare yard. **3.** *Adv.phr.* **A sec,** (i) dry, (ii) dried up, (iii) *P:* hard-up, on the rocks. **Mettre une mare à sec,** to drain a pond. **Navire à sec,** ship aground, high and dry. (Of ship) **Filer, courir, fuir, à sec (de toile),** to run, scud, under bare poles.
II. **sèche,** *s.f. P:* **1.** Cigarette; *P:* fag, gasper. **2.** *Sch:* **Piquer une sèche,** to get a nought (in an exam).
sécable [sekabl], *a.* Sectile, divisible.
sécant, -ante [sekɑ̃, -ɑ̃ːt]. *Geom:* **1.** *a.* Secant, cutting (line, surface). **2.** *s.f.* **Sécante,** secant.

sécateur [sɛkatœ:r], *s.m.* Pruning-scissors, -shears.

seccotine [sɛkɔtin], *s.f.* Seccotine. *Recollé à la s.*, seccotined together again.

sécession [sesɛsjɔ̃], *s.f.* Secession. *Faire sécession*, to secede (*de*, from).

sécessionniste [sesɛsjɔnist], *a. & s.* Secessionist.

sèche [sɛʃ]. See SEC.

sèchement [sɛʃmɑ̃], *adv.* 1. Curtly, tartly. 2. *Peindre s.*, to paint with a hard touch. *Traiter un sujet s.*, to treat a subject baldly.

séch|er [seʃe], *v.* (je sèche; je sécherai) 1. *v.tr.* (*a*) To dry (up). *S. ses larmes*, to dry one's tears. *Séché au soleil*, sun-dried. *S. le houblon au four*, to kiln the hops. (*b*) *Sch: P: S. un candidat*, to fail an examinee. (*c*) *Sch: P: S. une conférence*, to cut a lecture. 2. *v.i.* To dry. *Faire sécher du linge*, to dry clothes. *F: S. d'ennui*, to be consumed with boredom. **Sécher sur pied**, (i) (of plant) to wilt, to wither away; (ii) (of pers.) to be pining away. *s.m.* -**age**.
se sécher. 1. To dry oneself, one's clothes (at the fire, etc.). 2. (Of stream, etc.) To dry up.

sécheresse [seʃrɛs], *s.f.* 1. (*a*) Dryness. (*b*) Drought. 2. (*a*) Leanness, spareness (of the figure). (*b*) Curtness (of manner). (*c*) Coldness, unfeelingness (of heart). (*d*) Barrenness, meagreness, baldness (of style).

sécherie [seʃri], *s.f.* Drying-room, -ground.

sécheur [seʃœ:r], *s.m.* Drying apparatus; drier.

sécheuse [seʃø:z], *s.f.* Steam drier.

séchoir [sɛʃwa:r], *s.m.* *Tchn:* 1. Drying-place, -room, -loft, -ground. *S. à houblon*, oast-house. 2. (*a*) Drying apparatus; desiccator; steam drier. (*b*) Clothes-horse, towel-rail.

second, -onde [səgɔ̃, zgɔ̃, -ɔ̃:d]. 1. *a.* Second. *En second lieu*, in the second place. *Habiter au second (étage)*, to live on the second floor. *Sans second*, matchless, peerless. *Com: S. associé*, junior partner. *Sp:* Finir bon second derrière (un tel), to run a good second to (so and so). S.a. MAIN 1, PLAN[1] 2. *Ouvrage de s. ordre*, inferior piece of work. *Mth: n seconde*, n double dash (n″). 2. *s.m.* Principal assistant; second (in command). *Nau:* First mate, first officer, chief officer (of ship). **Commander en second**, to be second in command. *Navy:* **Second maître**, petty officer. 3. *s.f.* Seconde. (*a*) *Typ:* Second proof; revise. *Rail: etc:* *Voyager en seconde*, to travel second (class). *Sch:* (Classe de) seconde = fifth form (of upper school). (*b*) Second (of time, arc, angle). *Je reviens dans deux secondes*, I'll be back in two seconds, *F:* in two ticks.

secondaire [səgɔ̃dɛ:r, zgɔ̃-], *a.* 1. Secondary (planet, etc.). 2. Subordinate; of minor importance. *Th:* **Intrigue secondaire**, by-plot. 3. *s.m. El.E:* Secondary winding.

seconder [səgɔ̃de, zgɔ̃-], *v.tr.* 1. To second, back up, support (s.o.). 2. To forward, further, promote (s.o.'s interests, etc.).

secou|er [səkwe], *v.tr.* 1. (*a*) To shake (tree, one's head). *Navire secoué rudement par le vent*, ship buffeted by the wind. (*b*) *S. l'indifférence, l'énergie, de qn, F: s. qn*, to shake up, rouse (lethargic pupil, etc.). *P:* **Secouer les puces à qn**, to dust s.o.'s jacket, to give s.o. a good drubbing. 2. (*a*) To shake down (fruit). (*b*) *Secouer le joug*, to shake off the yoke. *F:* **Secouer la poussière de ses pieds, de ses souliers**, to shake the dust from one's feet. *s.m.* -**age**.
se secouer. (*a*) To shake oneself. (*b*) To bestir oneself.

secourable [səkurabl], *a.* 1. Helpful; willing to help. *S. aux pauvres*, ready to help the poor. *Tendre une main s. à qn*, to lend s.o. a helping hand. 2. *Place s. par mer*, place relievable by sea.

secourir [səkuri:r], *v.tr.* (Conj. like COURIR) To succour, help, aid.

secourisme [səkurism], *s.m.* First-aid practice.

secouriste [səkurist], *s.m. & f.* Member of a first-aid association; voluntary ambulance worker.

secours [s(ə)ku:r], *s.m.* Help, succour, relief, aid assistance. **Crier au secours**, to call for help. *Au secours!* help! **Porter, prêter, secours à qn**, to give, lend, assistance to s.o. *Med:* **Premiers secours**, first aid. **Société de secours**, first-aid association. **Demander (du) secours**, to ask for help. **Aller, se porter, au secours de qn**, to go to s.o.'s aid. **Rendre secours à qn**, to come to s.o.'s help. *Adm:* **Secours aux pauvres**, assistance of the poor. *S. à domicile*, outdoor relief. **Le secours aux enfants**, child-welfare work. **Société de secours mutuels**, benefit society, friendly society. **Sortie, porte, de secours**, emergency exit. *Aut:* **Roue de secours**, spare wheel. *Av:* **Terrain de secours**, emergency landing-ground. *Ecc:* **Chapelle de secours**, chapel of ease. **Machine de secours**, stand-by engine. *Mil:* **Troupes de secours**, relief troops. *Rail:* **Convoi de secours**, break-down train.

secousse [səkus], *s.f.* Shake, shaking; jolt, jerk; shock. **Imprimer une (brusque) secousse à qch.**, to jolt sth.; to make (table, etc.) jump. *Se dégager d'une s.*, to jerk, shake, oneself free. *Respirer par secousses pénibles*, to breathe in painful gasps. *S. universelle*, world commotion. *Ind:* **Tamis à secousses**, jigging-sieve. *Physiol:* *S. musculaire*, (muscle) jerk.

secret[1], -ète [səkrɛ, -ɛt], *a.* Secret; hidden (feelings). **Influence secrète**, secret or backstair influence. **Fonds secrets**, secret-service funds. **La (police) secrète** the Criminal Investigation Department, *F:* the C.I.D.

secret[2], *s.m.* 1. Secret. **Garder le secret au sujet de qch.**, to keep sth. secret. **Mettre qn dans le secret**, to let s.o. into the secret. **Être dans le secret**, to be in the secret, *F:* in the know. **N'avoir point de secret pour qn**, to have no secrets from s.o. **Faire jouer le secret**, to touch, press, the secret spring. S.a. POLICHINELLE 1. 2. Secrecy, privacy. **Dire qch. à qn sous le secret, en grand secret**, to tell s.o. sth. under pledge of secrecy, as a great secret. **En secret**, in secrecy, in secret, privily, privately. 3. **Mettre qn au secret**, to put s.o. in solitary confinement.

secrétaire [səkretɛ:r]. 1. *s.m. & f.* Secretary, amanuensis. *Journ:* *S. de la Rédaction*, sub-editor. *S. de la mairie*, town clerk; clerk to the parish council. 2. *s.m. Orn:* Secretary-bird. 3. *s.m.* Writing-desk; secretaire.

secrétariat [səkretarja], *s.m.* 1. Secretaryship. 2. Secretary's office; secretariat.

secrètement [səkrɛtmɑ̃], *adv.* Secretly, covertly; in secret.

sécréter [sekrete], *v.tr.* (il sécrète; il sécrétera) (Of gland) To secrete.

sécréteur, -trice, occ. **-euse** [sekretœ:r, -tris, -ø:z], *a.* Secreting, secretory (gland, etc.).

sécrétion [sekresjɔ̃], *s.f. Physiol:* Secretion.

sectaire [sɛktɛ:r], *s. m. & f.* Sectary, sectarian.

sectateur, -trice [sɛktatœ:r, -tris], *s.* Follower, votary, member (of a sect).

secte [sɛkt], *s.f.* Sect. **Faire secte**, to win adherents. **Ils font secte à part**, they form a party of their own.

secteur [sεktœːr], *s.m.* **1.** (*a*) *Astr: Geom:* Sector. (*b*) *Mec.E:* S. denté, toothed segment. Vis sans fin et secteur, worm and segment. *Aut: Nau:* S. du gouvernail, steering-quadrant. **2.** (*a*) District area (served by utility works); *El.E:* local supply circuit. Brancher sur le secteur, to take one's power from the mains. (*b*) S. de surveillance, (policeman's) beat. (*c*) *Mil:* Sector.

section [sεksjɔ̃], *s.f.* **1.** Section, cutting. **2.** Section (of chapter, building); branch (of a department); platoon (of infantry); subdivision (of fleet). **3.** *Geom:* Sections coniques, conic sections. Point de section, point of intersection. **4.** Stage (on bus or tramway route).

sectionner [sεksjone], *v.tr.* **1.** To divide (district) into sections. **2.** (*a*) To cut (off), sever. (*b*) To cut (cake) into pieces.

séculaire [sekylεːr], *a.* **1.** Occurring once in a hundred years; secular. **2.** Century-old (tree, monument).

sécularisation [sekylarizasjɔ̃], *s.f.* Secularization; conversion (of church) to secular uses; deconsecration.

séculariser [sekylarize], *v.tr.* To secularize; to convert (church property) to secular uses; to deconsecrate (church).

séculier, -ière [sekylje, -jεːr]. **1.** *a.* (*a*) Secular (clergy, jurisdiction). Le bras s., the secular arm. (*b*) Laïc. **2.** *s.* Layman, -woman.

secundo [sekɔ̃do]. *Lt.adv.* Secondly; in the second place.

sécurité [sekyrite], *s.f.* **1.** Security, secureness. Être en sécurité contre le danger, to be secure against, from, danger. *Ind:* S. du fonctionnement, reliability, dependability (of machinery). **2.** Safety. Dispositif de sécurité, safety device. Coefficient de s., safety factor.

sédatif, -ive [sedatif, -iːv], *a. & s.m. Med:* Sedative.

sédentaire [sedɑ̃tεːr], *a.* **1.** Sedentary (occupation). **2.** Fixed, stationary; non-mobile (troops); non-migrant (bird).

sédentarité [sedɑ̃tarite], *s.f.* Sedentariness; sedentary life.

sédiment [sedimɑ̃], *s.m.* Sediment, deposit.

sédimentaire [sedimɑ̃tεːr], *a.* Sedimentary (stratum, etc.); sedimental (matter).

séditieu|x, -euse [sedisjø, -øːz]. **1.** *a.* (*a*) Seditious. Tenir des propos séditieux, to talk treason. (*b*) Mutinous, rebellious. **2.** *s.m.* Mutineer. *adv.* **-sement.**

sédition [sedisjɔ̃], *s.f.* Sedition; mutiny. Être en sédition, to be in revolt.

séducteur, -trice [sedyktœːr, -tris]. **1.** *s.* (*a*) Tempter, beguiler, enticer, inveigler. (*b*) *s.m.* Seducer. **2.** *a.* Tempting, enticing, seductive.

séductible [sedyktibl], *a.* Seducible.

séduction [sedyksjɔ̃], *s.f.* **1.** Seduction; enticement; leading astray; subornation (of witness). **2.** Charm, seductiveness.

séduire [sedɥiːr], *v.tr.* (*pr.p.* séduisant; *p.p.* séduit; *pr.ind.* je séduis, il séduisons, ils séduisent; *pr.sub.* je séduise; *p.h.* je séduisis; *fu.* je séduirai) **1.** To seduce; to lead astray; to beguile; to bribe, suborn (witness). **2.** To fascinate, captivate, lure, allure, charm. Cela m'a séduit du premier coup, it took my fancy at once.

séduisant [sedɥizɑ̃], *a.* **1.** Seductive, tempting. **2.** Fascinating, taking, engaging, attractive.

segment [sεgmɑ̃], *s.m.* **1.** (*a*) *Geom:* Segment. (*b*) Segment (of worm, insect, etc.). **2.** *I.C.E: Mch:* S. de piston, piston-ring, packing-ring.

segmentation [sεgmɑ̃tasjɔ̃], *s.f.* Segmentation.

segmenter [sεgmɑ̃te], *v.tr.* To segment; to divide into segments. se segmenter, to segment.

ségrégation [segregasjɔ̃], *s.f.* Segregation, setting apart; isolation.

séguedille [segədiːj], *s.f. Danc: Mus:* Seguidilla.

seiche[1] [sεʃ], *s.f.* Cuttle-fish. Os de seiche, cuttle-bone.

seiche[2], *s.f.* Seiche, tidal wave (on Swiss lakes).

séid [seid], *s.m. Moslem Civ:* Say(y)id; lord.

séide [seid], *s.m.* Devoted follower, blind supporter; henchman.

seigle [sεgl], *s.m.* **1.** Rye. Pain de s., rye bread. **2.** Faux seigle, rye-grass.

seigneur [sεɲœːr], *s.m.* **1.** (*a*) Lord. (*b*) Lord of the manor. (*c*) Nobleman, noble. Petit seigneur, lordling. Mener une vie de grand seigneur, to live like a lord. Faire le grand seigneur, trancher du grand seigneur, to lord it; to give oneself airs. **2.** Le Seigneur, God; the Lord. Notre-Seigneur, our Lord.

seigneurial, -aux [sεɲœrjal, -o], *a. A:* Seigniorial, manorial (rights, etc.).

seigneurie [sεɲœri], *s.f.* **1.** *A:* Seigniory. **2.** Lordship. (*a*) Domain, manor. (*b*) Votre Seigneurie, your Lordship.

seille [sεːj], *s.f.* (Wooden) pail; bucket.

sein [sε̃], *s.m.* Breast, bosom. *B:* Le sein d'Abraham, Abraham's bosom. Donner le sein à un enfant, to give the breast to a child. S.a. RÉCHAUFFER 1. Au sein de la famille, in the bosom of the family. Le sein de l'Église, the bosom of the Church.

seine [sεn], *s.f. Fish:* Seine, drag-seine; drawnet; tow-net.

seing [sε̃], *s.m. A:* Sign manual. *Jur:* Acte sous seing privé, simple contract. S.a. BLANC-SEING.

séisme [seism], *s.m.* Earthquake, seism.

séismique [seismik], *a.* = SISMIQUE.

seize [sεːz], *num.a.inv. & s.m.inv.* Sixteen. Louis Seize, Louis the Sixteenth. Le s. mai, (on) the sixteenth of May.

seizième [sεzjεm]. **1.** *num. a. & s.* Sixteenth. **2.** *s.m.* Sixteenth (part). *adv.* **-ment.**

séjour [seʒuːr], *s.m.* **1.** Stay, sojourn. *Rail:* Avec séjour facultatif, with liberty to break the journey. S.a. PERMIS 2. **2.** (Place of) abode; residence, resort. *Poet:* L'infernal séjour, the infernal regions.

séjourn|er [seʒurne], *v.i.* **1.** To stay, stop, sojourn, reside (in a place). **2.** Les eaux séjournent dans les fossés, the water lies stagnant in the ditches. *s.m.* **-ement.**

sel [sεl], *s.m.* **1.** Salt. (*a*) Sel blanc, table salt. S.a. GROS 1. Sel gemme, rock-salt. Vous êtes le sel de la terre, ye are the salt of the earth. (*b*) *Pharm:* Sel anglais, d'Angleterre, d'Epsom, Epsom salts. (*c*) *pl.* Sels (volatils) anglais, smelling-salts. Flacon de sels, (bottle of) smelling-salts. (*d*) *Ch:* Salt. Sel double, double salt. Sel ammoniac, sal-ammoniac. S.a. ESPRIT 2. **2.** *F:* Piquancy, wit. Conversation pleine de sel, witty conversation. Satire au gros sel, coarse satire. Sel attique, Attic salt, Attic wit.

sélecteur, -trice [selεktœːr, -tris]. **1.** *a. Phot:* Écran sélecteur, selective filter. **2.** *s.m. Tp:* Selector, selecting-switch.

sélectif, -ive [selεktif, -iːv], *a. W.Tel:* Selective.

sélection [selεksjɔ̃], *s.f.* **1.** Selection, choice. *Sp:* Match de sélection, trial game, selection match. *Biol:* Sélection naturelle, natural selection. **2.** *Mus:* Selection (sur, from).

sélectivité [selεktivite], *s.f. W.Tel:* Selectivity.

sélénite [selenit], *s.m.* Selenite; inhabitant of the moon.

sélénium [selenjɔm], *s.m. Ch:* Selenium.

sélénographie [selenɔgrafi], *s.f.* Selenography.

sélénographique [selenɔgrafik], *a.* Selenographic(al) (map, etc.).

self [self], *s.f. El:* (Bobine de) self(-induction), inductance-coil, self-induction coil, choking-coil.

selle [sɛl], *s.f.* **1.** (a) *A:* Seat, stool. (b) *Med:* Motion of the bowels; stool. **Aller à la selle,** to go to stool. **2.** (a) Saddle. **Cheval de selle,** saddle-horse. **Se mettre, sauter, en selle,** to mount, vault, into the saddle. **Se remettre en selle,** (i) to remount; (ii) *F:* to get into the saddle again (after a failure). **Être bien en selle,** (i) to have a good seat; (ii) *F:* to be firmly established. (b) (Bicycle) saddle. *S.* tandem, pillion seat (of motor cycle). **3.** *Cu:* Selle de mouton, saddle of mutton. **4.** *Ind:* Bench, support.

sell|er [sɛle], *v.tr.* To saddle (horse). *s.m.* **-age.**

sellerie [sɛlri], *s.f.* **1.** Saddlery. **2.** Harness-room, saddle-room.

sellette [sɛlɛt], *s.f.* **1.** (a) *A:* Stool of repentance. *F:* **Tenir, mettre, qn sur la sellette,** to call s.o. to account; *F:* to have s.o. on the mat. (b) (Small) seat, stool; esp. caulker's or painter's slung cradle; bosun's chair. **2.** Saddle (of draught-horse).

sellier [sɛlje], *s.m.* Saddler, harness-maker.

selon [s(ə)lɔ̃], *prep.* According to. **L'Évangile selon saint Luc,** the Gospel according to Saint Luke. *S. moi,* in my opinion. *S. les termes de cet article,* by the terms of this article. **C'est selon,** that is as may be; it all depends. **Selon que** + *ind.,* according as.

seltz [sɛls], *s.m.* **Eau de seltz,** seltzer-water, soda-water.

seltzogène [sɛlsɔʒɛn], *s.m.* Seltzogene, gazogene.

semailles [s(ə)maːj], *s.f.pl.* **1.** Sowing; seed-time. **2.** Sowings, seeds. [SEMER]

semaine [s(ə)mɛn], *s.f.* (a) Week. **Jour de semaine,** week-day. *Il est toujours à Paris en semaine,* he is always in Paris during the week. **Prêter à la petite semaine,** to lend at high interest. **La semaine sainte,** Holy Week. S.a. JEUDI. (b) Working week; week's work. **Semaine anglaise,** working week of five and a half days. **Faire la semaine anglaise,** to close at midday on Saturdays. (c) Week's pay, week's wages. (d) *Mil: etc:* Week's duty. **Être de semaine,** to be on duty for the week.

semainier, -ière [s(ə)mɛnje, -jɛːr]. **1.** *s.* Person on duty for a week. **2.** *s.m.* (a) Seven-day case of razors. (b) (Workman's) time-sheet.

semaison [s(ə)mɛzɔ̃], *s.f.* Seed-time. [SEMER]

sémantique [semãtik]. *Ling:* **1.** *a.* Semantic. **2.** *s.f.* Semantics, semasiology.

sémaphore [semafɔːr], *s.m.* Semaphore; signal-station. *Rail:* Semaphore signal.

semblable [sãblabl]. **1.** *a.* (a) Alike; similar (à, to); like. *Votre cas est s. au mien,* your case is similar to mine. *S. à son père,* like his father. *Alg:* Termes semblables, like terms. (b) Such. *En s. occasion,* on such an occasion. **Je n'ai rien dit de semblable,** I said nothing of the sort, no such thing. **2.** *s.* (a) *Vous ne trouverez pas son s.,* you will not find his like, his equal. (b) **Nos semblables,** our fellow-men, fellow-creatures.

semblablement [sãblabləmã], *adv.* Similarly, likewise.

semblant [sãblã], *s.m.* Semblance, appearance; (outward) show. **Faux semblant,** pretence, sham. *Faire un s. de résistance,* to make a show of resistance. **Faire semblant de faire qch.,** to

pretend to be doing sth.; to make a pretence of doing sth. **Faire s. d'être malade,** to sham illness. **Sans faire semblant de rien,** (i) surreptitiously; (ii) without seeming to take any notice.

sembler [sãble], *v.i.* (Aux. *avoir*) (a) To seem, to appear. *Voilà, ce me semble, un avis excellent,* that, to my mind, is excellent advice. (b) *Impers. Il me semblait rêver,* it seemed to me that I was dreaming. **A ce qu'il me semble,** as it strikes me; I fancy. *Ils pourront, quand bon leur semblera . . .,* they may, at any time. . . . **Faites comme bon vous semble(ra), ce que bon vous semble(ra),** ce qu'il vous semble bon, do as you think best, as you think fit, as you please. **Que vous en semble?** what do you think of it? *Il semble qu'il ne veut, ne veuille, pas y aller,* it looks as if he wouldn't go. *Il me semble que* + *ind.,* it seems to me that. . . . *Il ne me semble pas que* + *sub.,* it does not look to me as if. . . .

semelle [s(ə)mɛl], *s.f.* **1.** Sole (of shoe); foot (of stocking). *S. intérieure de liège,* cork insole. *Souliers à semelles épaisses,* thick-soled shoes. *F:* **Ne pas reculer d'une semelle,** not to give way an inch. **Battre la semelle,** (i) to be on the tramp; (ii) to warm one's feet (by beating them against those of another person). **2.** (a) *Const:* Ground-sill, sole-piece; footing (of an upright). (b) *S. de poutre,* girder-flange. (c) Bed-plate (of machine, lathe). (d) Shoe (of anchor, sledge). (e) Tread (of tyre, stirrup).

semence [s(ə)mãːs], *s.f.* **1.** Seed. *Blé de s.,* seed-corn. **2.** (a) **Semence de perles,** seed pearls. (b) (Tin)tacks, sprig nails. .

semer [s(ə)me], *v.tr.* (je **sème;** je **sèmerai**) **1.** To sow (seed). *S. un champ,* to sow a field. *S. à tout vent, à la volée,* to sow broadcast. *Prov:* **On recueille ce qu'on a semé,** we reap as we sow. S.a. VENT 1. **2.** To spread, strew, scatter (flowers, etc.); to disseminate, spread abroad (news). *S. des mines,* to lay mines. *Ciel semé d'étoiles,* star-spangled sky. *Herbe semée de pâquerettes,* grass dotted, starred, with daisies. **3.** *P:* To shake off, shed (an acquaintance). *S. un concurrent,* to leave a rival behind.

semestre [s(ə)mɛstr], *s.m.* **1.** Half-year. **2.** Six months' pay, duty, etc. **Être de semestre,** to be on duty (for six months). **Être en semestre,** to be on six months' leave or furlough. **3.** *Sch:* Semester; term (of six months).

semestriel, -elle [səmɛstriɛl], *a.* **1.** Half-yearly. **2.** Of six months' duration.

semeur, -euse [s(ə)mœːr, -øːz], *s.* (a) Sower. (b) Disseminator, spreader (of false news, etc,).

semi-circulaire, *a.* Semicircular.

semi-hebdomadaire, *a.* Half-weekly.

sémillance [semijãːs], *s.f.* Sprightliness.

sémillant [semijã], *a.* Sprightly, bright.

semi-mensuel, -elle, *a.* Half-monthly, fortnightly, bi-monthly.

séminaire [seminɛːr], *s.m.* Seminary. (a) **Grand séminaire,** training college (for the priesthood). **Petit séminaire,** secondary school (staffed by priests). (b) Training centre.

séminariste [seminarist], *s.m.* Seminarist.

semi-officiel, -elle, *a.* Semi-official.

semi-rigide, -elle, *a.* Semi-rigid (airship).

semis [s(ə)mi], *s.m.* **1.** Sowing. *S. à la volée,* broadcast sowing. *Fleurs qui proviennent de s.,* flowers raised from seed. **2.** Seed-plot. **3.** Seedlings. [SEMER]

Sémites [semit], *s.m.pl. Ethn:* Semites.

sémitique [semitik], *a.* Semitic.

sémitisme [semitism], *s.m.* Semitism.

semi-transparent, *a.* Semi-transparent.

semi-voyelle, *s.f. Ling:* Semivowel.
semoir [səmwaːr], *s.m.* Sowing-machine, seeder.
semonce [səmɔ̃ːs], *s.f.* **1.** (*a*) *A:* Summons. (*b*) *Navy:* Call (to a ship) to heave to. Coup de semonce, warning shot. **2.** Reprimand, scolding, *F:* lecture. *Verte s.,* good talking-to.
semoncer [səmɔ̃se], *v.tr.* (je semonçai(s); n. semonçons) To lecture, reprimand, sermonize.
semoule [s(ə)mul], *s.f.* Semolina.
sempiternel, -elle [sɛpitɛrnɛl], *a.* Sempiternal, never-ceasing. *adv.* **-ellement.**
sénat [sena], *s.m.* **1.** Senate. **2.** Senate-house.
sénateur [senatœːr], *s.m.* Senator.
sénatorial, -aux [senatɔrjal, -o], *a.* Senatorial.
senatus-consulte [senatyskɔ̃sylt], *s.m.* Senatus consult(um).
séné [sene], *s.m.* Senna.
sénéchal, -aux [seneʃal, -o], *s.m. A:* Seneschal.
sénéchaussée [seneʃose], *s.f. A:* (*a*) Seneschalsy, seneschal's jurisdiction. (*b*) Seneschal's court.
seneçon [sənsɔ̃], *s.m. Bot:* Groundsel.
Sénégal [senegal]. *Pr.n.m. Geog:* Senegal.
sénégalais, -aise [senegalɛ, -ɛːz], *a. & s.* Senegalese.
Sénèque [senɛk]. *Pr.n.m. Lt.Lit:* Seneca.
sénestre [senɛstr], *a. A:* Left. *Her:* Sinister.
senestrorsum [senɛstrɔrsɔm], *adv.* Counterclockwise.
sénevé [senve], *s.m.* **1.** *Bot:* Mustard. **2.** Mustard-seed.
sénile [senil], *a.* Senile.
sénilité [senilite], *s.f.* Senility.
senne [sɛn], *s.f. Fish:* = SEINE.
sens [sɑ̃ːs], *s.m.* **1.** Sense (of touch, etc.). *Les cinq sens,* the five senses. **Perdre, reprendre, ses sens,** to lose, regain, consciousness. **Il tombe sous le sens que . . .,** it is obvious, self-evident, that. . . . *Sens moral,* moral sense. **2.** Sense, judgment, intelligence, understanding. **Avoir le sens droit,** to have a clear judgment. **Sens commun** [sɑ̃kɔmœ̃], **bon sens** [bɔ̃sɑ̃(s)], common sense. *Agir en dépit du sens commun,* to act against all sense. *Tout homme jouissant de son bon sens,* any man in his senses. S.a. GROS 1. A **mon sens,** as I think, in my opinion. **J'abonde dans votre sens,** I am entirely of your opinion. S.a. NATIF 1, PRATIQUE¹ 1, RASSIS. **3.** Sense, meaning, import (of a word, etc.). *Mot à double sens,* word with a double meaning. *Faire un faux sens,* to misunderstand slightly (passage in a text). *Cf.* CONTRE-SENS 1. **S'exprimer, parler, dans le même sens,** to express oneself to the same effect. **4.** Direction, way. **Dans le (bon) sens,** in the right direction. **En sens inverse,** in a contrary direction, in the opposite direction. **Dans le sens des aiguilles d'une montre,** clockwise. **Retourner qch. dans tous les sens,** to turn sth. over and over. *Rue à deux sens,* street with two-way traffic. *Rue à sens unique,* one-way street. **"Sens interdit,"** 'no entry.' *Mth:* **Sens direct,** positive direction. **Sens rétrograde,** negative direction. **Nous avons pris des dispositions dans ce sens,** we have made provisions to this effect. **Sens dessus dessous** [sɑ̃tsysdəsu], upside down, topsy-turvy. **Sens** [sɑ̃] **devant derrière,** back to front.
sensation [sɑ̃sɑsjɔ̃], *s.f.* Sensation. **1.** Feeling. *Cela donne la sensation de . . .,* it feels like. . . . **2.** Excitement. **Roman à sensation,** thrilling, sensational, novel. **Faire sensation,** to create, make, a sensation.
sensationnel, -elle [sɑ̃sɑsjɔnɛl], *a.* Sensational, *F:* thrilling (news). *Roman s.,* *F:* thriller.
sensé [sɑ̃se], *a.* Sensible, judicious. *adv.* **-ment.**

sensibilisateur, -trice [sɑ̃sibilizatœːr, -tris]. *Phot: etc:* **1.** *a.* Sensitizing. **2.** *s.m.* Sensitizer.
sensibiliser [sɑ̃sibilize], *v.tr. Phot:* To sensitize (paper, collodion).
sensibilité [sɑ̃sibilite], *s.f.* Sensibility. **1.** Sensitiveness (of skin, of balance) (*à, pour,* to). **2.** Feeling, compassion, pity.
sensible [sɑ̃sibl], *a.* **1.** (*a*) Sensitive, susceptible, impressionable. **Avoir la peau sensible,** (i) to have a sensitive skin; (ii) *F:* to be thin-skinned. **Toucher, ouïe, peu sensible,** dull sense of touch, dull hearing. *Être s. au froid,* to feel the cold. *Être très s. à la douleur,* to be very susceptible to pain. *S. sur l'honneur,* sensitive about honour. *Être s. aux bontés de qn,* to appreciate s.o.'s kindness. *Mus:* **La note sensible,** the leading note. *F:* **Toucher la note, la corde, sensible,** to appeal to the emotions. (*b*) Sympathetic. *Se montrer s. aux malheurs de qn,* to sympathize with s.o. **Peu sensible,** callous. (*c*) Sensitive (thermometer, etc.). *Balance s. au milligramme,* balance sensitive to a milligramme. *Phot: Papier s.,* sensitized paper. (*d*) Painful when touched; sensitive, tender (tooth, etc.). **L'endroit sensible,** the tender spot, the sore point. **2.** Sensible; tangible, palpable, perceptible. **D'une manière sensible,** perceptibly, appreciably. *Faire des progrès sensibles,* to make perceptible progress.
sensiblement [sɑ̃sibləmɑ̃], *adv.* Appreciably, palpably, perceptibly. *S. plus âgé,* a good bit older.
sensiblerie [sɑ̃sibləri], *s.f.* Sentiment(ality), sentimentalism, mawkishness.
sensitif, -ive [sɑ̃sitif, -iːv]. **1.** *a.* (*a*) Sensitive; having feeling. (*b*) Sensory, sensorial (nerve). **2.** *s.f. Bot:* Sensitive, sensitive plant.
sensualisme [sɑ̃sɥalism], *s.m.* Sensualism.
sensualiste [sɑ̃sɥalist]. **1.** *s.m.* Sensualist. **2.** *a.* Sensual.
sensualité [sɑ̃sɥalite], *s.f.* Sensuality.
sensuel, -elle [sɑ̃sɥɛl]. **1.** *a.* Sensual, sensuous; carnal. **2.** *s.* Sensualist. *adv.* **-ellement.**
sentâ [sɑ̃tɑ̃], *a.* Sentient.
sent-bon [sɑ̃bɔ̃], *s.m.inv. Bot:* Tansy.
sente [sɑ̃ːt], *s.f.* Footpath; track.
sentence [sɑ̃tɑ̃ːs], *s.f.* **1.** Maxim. **2.** (*a*) Sentence, judgment. **Sentence de mort,** sentence of death. *Prononcer une s.,* to pass a sentence. (*b*) *Rendre une s. arbitrale,* to make an award.
sentencieu|x, -euse [sɑ̃tɑ̃sjø, -øːz], *a.* Sententious. *adv.* **-sement.**
senteur [sɑ̃tœːr], *s.f.* Scent, perfume. S.a. POIS 1.
sentier [sɑ̃tje], *s.m.* (Foot)path. *S. à mulets,* mule-track. *S. pour cavaliers,* bridle-path. **S'écarter du sentier battu,** to turn aside from the beaten track.
sentiment [sɑ̃timɑ̃], *s.m.* **1.** Feeling. (*a*) Sensation (of joy, hunger). (*b*) Sense, consciousness. **Privé de sentiment,** devoid of feeling; numb (limb). *Elle a le s. très vif du beau,* she is keenly alive to the beautiful. **Avoir le sentiment de l'heure,** to have a sense of time. **Juger par sentiment,** to judge by one's impressions. (*c*) *Faire appel aux bons sentiments de qn,* to appeal to s.o.'s better feelings. (*d*) *Le s. de la nature,* a feeling for nature. *Ses sentiments vis-à-vis de moi,* his feelings towards me. **Jouer avec sentiment,** to play (the piano, etc.) feelingly. **Faire du sentiment,** to sentimentalize. **2.** Opinion. *Au s. de mon père,* in my father's opinion. *Partager les sentiments de qn,* to share s.o.'s views. *Sentiments anglophiles,* Anglophile proclivities.

sentimental, -aux [sãtimãtal, -o], *a.* Sentimental. *adv.* **-ement.**
sentimentalisme [sãtimãtalism], *s.m.* Sentimentalism.
sentimentalité [sãtimãtalite], *s.f.* Sentimentality.
sentine [sãtin], *s.f. Nau :* Bilge, well (of ship). *F :* **Sentine de tous les vices,** sink of iniquity.
sentinelle [sãtinɛl], *s.f. Mil :* Sentry ; sentinel. *S.a.* PERDU 2. **Faire sentinelle,** to stand sentry. **En sentinelle,** on sentry-duty.
sentir [sãtiːr], *v.* (*pr.p.* **sentant**; *p.p.* **senti**; *pr.ind.* **je sens, il sent, n. sentons**; *pr.sub.* **je sente**; *p.h.* **je sentis**; *fu.* **je sentirai**) **1.** *v.tr.* (*a*) To feel. *Je sentis trembler le plancher,* I felt the floor tremble. *Je sens vivement qu'il ne m'écrive plus,* I feel it very much that he has stopped writing to me. **Sentir quelque chose pour qn,** to feel an inclination for s.o., to feel drawn to s.o. (*b*) To be conscious, sensible, of (sth.). *S.* **un danger,** to be conscious of danger. *Il ne sent pas les affronts,* he is thick-skinned. *Je sens que vous avez raison,* I have a feeling that you are right. **Faire sentir son autorité à qn,** to make s.o. feel one's authority. **L'effet se fera sentir,** the effect will be felt. **Se sentir dix ou de moins,** to feel ten years younger. (*c*) To smell (odour, flower). *F :* **Je ne peux pas le sentir,** I can't bear him, can't stand him. *F :* **Sentir qch. de loin,** to be aware of sth. a long way off. **Sentir qn de loin,** to see through s.o. **2.** *v.i.* (*a*) (With cogn. acc.) To taste of, smell of (sth.). *La pièce sent l'humidité,* the room smells, feels, damp. *La salle sentait le tabac à plein nez,* the room reeked of tobacco. *S. le cru,* to smack of, be redolent of, the soil. *S.a.* FAGOT 1, HUILE 1, SAPIN 2, TERROIR. (*b*) (With adv. **bon, mauvais**) **Sentir bon, mauvais,** to smell good, bad. *Fleurs qui sentent bon,* sweet-smelling flowers. *Affaire qui ne sent pas bon,* unsavoury business. (*c*) To smell, to stink. **se sentir. 1.** *Je me sens fatigué,* I feel tired. **2.** (*a*) *Elle se sentait mourir,* she felt she was dying. **Il ne se sent pas de joie,** he is beside himself for joy. (*b*) **Se sentir de qch.,** to be affected by sth. *Chacun se sent de ces améliorations,* everyone is the better for these improvements. **3.** (Of pers.) To be conscious of one's strength, of one's own importance.
senti, *a.* Strongly expressed ; true to life. *Paroles bien senties,* heartfelt words.
seoir [swaːr], *v.i.* **1.** (In *p.p.* **sis**) *Jur :* **Maison sise rue Saint-Honoré,** house situate(d) in the Rue Saint-Honoré. **2.** (Used only in *pr.p.* **seyant, séant** ; *pr.ind.* **il sied, ils siéent** ; *pr.sub.* **il siée** ; *p.d.* **il seyait, ils seyaient** ; *fu.* **il siéra**) To suit, become. *Cette robe vous sied,* that dress suits you (well). *Il lui sied mal de parler ainsi,* it ill becomes him to talk in that strain.
sépale [sepal], *s.m. Bot :* Sepal.
séparable [separabl], *a.* Separable, severable (*de,* from).
séparateur, -trice [separatœːr, -tris]. **1.** *a.* Separative. **2.** *s.m. Tchn :* Separator. *Aut : etc : S. d'huile,* oil-separator.
séparatif, -ive [separatif, -iːv], *a.* Separative, separating ; dividing (wall).
séparation [separasjɔ̃], *s.f.* **1.** Separation, severance, parting. *S. d'avec qn,* (i) separation from s.o. ; (ii) parting with s.o. *S. judiciaire,* judicial separation (of husband and wife). *Jur :* **Séparation de biens,** separate maintenance. *S.a.* CORPS 1. **Mur de séparation,** partition wall, dividing wall. **2.** Breaking up, dispersal (of meeting, of a family).

séparatisme [separatism], *s.m. Pol :* Separatism.
séparatiste [separatist], *s.m.* Separatist, secessionist.
séparément [separemã], *adv.* Separately. *Vivre s.,* to live apart.
séparer [separe], *v.tr.* To separate (*de,* from). **1.** To disunite, part. *S. les bons d'avec les mauvais,* to separate the good from the bad. *S. des chiffons,* to sort rags. *S. la tête du corps,* to sever the head from the body. *S. deux combattants,* to part, separate, two fighters. **2.** To divide, keep apart. *Mur qui sépare deux champs,* wall dividing two fields. *Une table le séparait de la porte,* a table was between him and the door. **se séparer. 1.** To separate, part (*de,* from) ; to part company. *Se s. de sa femme, d'avec sa femme,* to separate from one's wife. **Il n'y a si bonne compagnie qui ne se sépare,** the best of friends must part. **2.** (Of river, road, etc.) To divide, branch off. *Là où les routes se séparent,* at the parting of the ways. (Of salt) *Se s. à l'état cristallin,* to crystallize out. **3.** To break up, disperse. *L'assemblée s'est séparée dans le tumulte,* the meeting broke up in disorder.
séparé, *a.* **1.** Separate, different, distinct. **2.** Separated, apart.
sépia [sepja], *s.f.* **1.** *Moll :* Cuttle-fish. **2.** Sepia (colour).
sept [sɛ(t)], *num.a.inv. & s.m.inv.* Seven. (As *card. adj.* before a noun or adj. beginning with a consonant sound [sɛ] ; otherwise always [sɛt]) *Sept (petits) garçons* [sɛ(pti)garsɔ̃], seven, (little) boys. *Sept hommes* [sɛtɔm], seven men. *J'en ai sept* [sɛt], I have seven. *Le sept mai* [ləsɛtmɛ], the seventh of May. *Édouard Sept,* Edward the Seventh. **Bottes de sept lieues** [sɛljø], seven-league boots.
septante [sɛptãːt], *num.a.inv. & s.m.inv.* **1.** *A :* (Still used in S.-E. of Fr., in Belg. and Switz.) Seventy. **2.** **Les Septante,** the Seventy (translators of the Old Testament into Greek). **La version des Septante,** the Septuagint.
septembre [sɛptãːbr], *s.m.* September. **En septembre,** in September. **Au mois de septembre,** in the month of September. *Le premier, le sept, s.,* (on) the first, the seventh, of September.
septennal, -aux [sɛptɛnnal, -o], *a.* Septennial.
septentrion [sɛptãtriɔ̃], *s.m. Poet : Lit :* North. *Au s.,* in the north.
septentrional, -aux [sɛptãtriɔnal, -o]. **1.** *a.* Northern. **2.** *s.m.pl.* Northerners.
septicémie [sɛptisemi], *s.f. Med :* Septicaemia, sepsis ; blood-poisoning.
septicité [sɛptisite], *s.f. Med :* Septicity.
septième [sɛtjɛm]. **1.** *num. a. & s.* Seventh. **Demeurer au septième** (*étage*), to live on the seventh floor. **2.** *s.m.* Seventh (part). **3.** *s.f. Mus :* Seventh. *adv.* **-ment.**
septillion [sɛptiljɔ̃], *s.m.* Quadrillion (10^{24}) *U.S :* septillion.
septimo [sɛptimo], *adv.* In the seventh place.
septique [sɛptik], *a. Med :* Septic.
septuagénaire [sɛptɥaʒenɛːr], *a. & s.* Septuagenarian.
septuagésime [sɛptɥaʒezim], *s.f.* Septuagesima (Sunday).
septum [sɛptɔm], *s.m. Anat : Bot :* Septum, dissepiment.
septuor [sɛptɥɔːr], *s.m. Mus :* Septet(te).
septuple [sɛptypl], *a. & s.m.* Septuple, sevenfold. **Au septuple,** sevenfold.
sépulcral, -aux [sepylkral, -o], *a.* Sepulchral.
sépulcre [sepylkr], *s.m.* Sepulchre. **Le saint sépulcre,** the Holy-Sepulchre.

sépulture [sepylty:r], *s.f.* **1.** Burial, sepulture, interment. **Refuser la sépulture à qn,** to refuse Christian burial to s.o. **2.** Burial-place. *Violer une s.,* to despoil, rifle, a tomb. *Sépultures militaires,* war cemeteries.

séquanais, -aise [sekwanɛ, -ɛ:z]. **1.** *a.* Of the Seine. **2.** *s.m.pl. A.Hist:* **Séquanais,** Sequani.

séquelle [sekɛl], *s.f.* **1.** *Pej:* (*a*) Gang, set, crew. (*b*) String (of oaths). **2.** *pl. Med:* **Séquelles,** sequelae, after-effects (of measles, etc.).

séquence [sekã:s], *s.f.* Sequence. *Cards: S. de trois,* run of three.

séquestration [sekɛstrasjɔ̃], *s.f.* **1.** *Jur:* Sequestration (of goods). **2.** Isolation (of infected animals, etc.). **3.** Seclusion (of s.o.); esp. *Jur:* illegal restraint.

séquestre[1] [sekɛstr], *s.m.* **1.** *Jur:* Sequestration; embargo (on ship). **En, sous, séquestre,** sequestered. **Mettre sous séquestre les biens de qn,** to sequester, sequestrate, s.o.'s property. **2.** Property sequestrated. **3.** *Sch:* Room for disciplinary confinement.

séquestre[2], *s.m.* *Jur:* Depositary, trustee (of sequestrated property); sequestrator.

séquestrer [sekɛstre], *v.tr.* **1.** To sequester, sequestrate (property). *Nau:* To lay an embargo upon (ship). **2.** To isolate, seclude (lepers, etc.). *Jur:* To confine, shut up, (s.o.) illegally.

sequin [səkɛ̃], *s.m. Num: Cost:* Sequin.

ser-ai, -as, -ons, etc. See ÊTRE.

sérail [sera:j], *s.m.* Seraglio.

séraphin [serafɛ̃], *s.m.* Seraph. *Les séraphins,* the seraphs, the seraphim.

séraphique [serafik], *a.* Seraphic, angelic.

serbe [sɛrb], *a. & s. Geog:* Serb, Serbian.

Serbie [sɛrbi]. *Pr.n.f. Geog:* Serbia.

serbo-croate [sɛrbɔkrɔat], *a. & s. Geog:* Serbo-Croat(ian).

Sercq [sɛrk]. *Pr.n. Geog:* (The island of) Sark.

serein[1] [sərɛ̃], *a.* **1.** Serene, calm (sky). *Jours sereins,* halcyon days. **2.** (Of pers.) Serene; cheerful.

serein[2], *s.m.* Evening dew.

sérénade [serenad], *s.f.* Serenade.

sérénissime [serenisim], *a.* (Most) Serene.

sérénité [serenite], *s.f.* **1.** Serenity, calmness. **Avec sérénité,** serenely. **2.** Serenity (title of honour).

séreux, -euse [serø, -ø:z], *a.* Serous (fluid, etc.).

serf, serve [sɛrf, sɛrv]. **1.** *s.* Bond(s)man, bond(s)-woman; serf. **2.** *a.* (*a*) (Of pers.) In bondage. *Condition serve,* serfage, serfdom. (*b*) (Of land) In bondage, in villein tenure.

serfouette [sɛrfwɛt], *s.f. Hort:* Combined hoe and fork.

serfouir [sɛrfwi:r], *v.tr.* To hoe (vegetables); to loosen (the soil). *s.m.* **-issage.**

serge [sɛrʒ], *s.m. Tex:* (Woollen) serge.

sergent[1] [sɛrʒã], *s.m.* Sergeant. (*a*) **Sergent d'armes,** sergeant-at-arms. **Sergent de ville,** policeman; (*b*) *Mil:* Sergeant (of unmounted troops). *S. instructeur,* drill-sergeant. **Sergent major,** quartermaster-sergeant.

sergent[2], *s.m.* *Tls:* (= SERRE-JOINT) Cramp; holdfast; (carpenter's) clamp.

sergot [sɛrgo], *s.m. P:* Policeman.

sériciculteur [serisikyltœ:r], *s.m.* Seri(ci)culturist; breeder of silkworms.

séri(ci)culture [seri(si)kylty:r], *s.f.* Seri(ci)culture.

série [seri], *s.f.* **1.** (*a*) Series; succession (of accidents); range, line (of samples). *Mth: S. infinie,* infinite series. *Faire une s. de visites,* to go on a round of visits. *F:* **Série noire,** chapter of accidents; run of ill-luck. **En, par, série, in series,** serially. *El.E:* **Excité en série,** series-wound. *Ind:* **Fabrication en (grande) série,** mass production. **Voiture de série,** car of standard model. **Article hors série,** (i) specially manufactured article; (ii) *Cost:* outsize. **Fin de série,** *Com:* oddment, remnant; *Publ:* remainder. (*b*) Break (at billiards); run (of cannons). **2.** Set (of tools, flags).

sérier [serje], *v.tr.* (*a*) To arrange in series. (*b*) To standardize (production).

sérieux, -euse [serjø, -ø:z]. **1.** *a.* Serious. (*a*) Grave, sober. *F:* **Sérieux comme un évêque,** as solemn as a judge. (*b*) Serious-minded. (*c*) Earnest, genuine. *Êtes-vous s.?* are you in earnest? do you mean it? *Offre sérieuse,* bona-fide offer. *Acheteur s.,* genuine purchaser. **Peu sérieux,** irresponsible (person). (*d*) Grave, weighty, important (matter). *Maladie sérieuse,* serious illness. **2.** *s.m.* Seriousness, gravity. **Garder son sérieux,** to preserve one's gravity, to keep a straight face. **Prendre qch. trop au sérieux,** to take sth. too seriously. **Manque de sérieux,** (i) levity, (ii) irresponsibility. *adv.* **-sement.**

serin [s(ə)rɛ̃], *s.m.* (*a*) *Orn:* Canary. *a.inv.* **Des gants jaune serin,** canary-yellow gloves. (*b*) *F:* Silly, noodle, muff.

serine [s(ə)rin], *s.f.* Hen-canary.

seriner [s(ə)rine], *v.tr.* (*a*) *S. un serin; s. un air à une serin,* to teach a canary to sing by means of the bird-organ. (*b*) *F: S. un air,* to grind out a tune; to tootle a tune (on the flute, etc.). (*c*) *F: S. qn; s. qch. à qn,* to drum, din, sth. into s.o. (*d*) *P:* To bore (s.o.). *s.m.* **-age.**

serinette [s(ə)rinet], *s.f.* Bird-organ.

seringa(t) [s(ə)rɛ̃ga], *s.m. Bot:* Syringa, seringa.

seringue [s(ə)rɛ̃:g], *s.f.* Syringe, squirt. *Med: S. injectrice, s. de Pravaz,* hypodermic syringe. *Aut: S. à graisse,* grease-gun.

seringuer [s(ə)rɛ̃ge], *v.tr.* (*a*) To syringe (wound). (*b*) To squirt (liquid).

serment [sɛrmã], *s.m.* (Solemn) oath. **Prêter serment,** to take an oath, to be sworn; (of jury) to be sworn in. **Déférer le serment à qn,** (i) to swear s.o., (ii) to swear s.o. in. **Être sous la foi du serment,** to be on oath. **Faire serment de faire qch.,** to swear that one will do sth. **Certifier qch. sous serment,** to declare sth. on oath. *Déclaration sous s.,* sworn statement. **Faire un faux serment,** to commit perjury.

sermon [sɛrmɔ̃], *s.m.* (*a*) Sermon. S.a. MONTAGNE 1. (*b*) *F:* Talking-to, lecture.

sermonner [sɛrmɔne]. *F:* **1.** *v.i.* To sermonize; to preachify. **2.** *v.tr.* To sermonize, lecture, reprimand (s.o.); to give (s.o.) a talking-to; to read (s.o.) a lecture.

sermonneur, -euse [sɛrmɔnœ:r, -ø:z]. *F:* **1.** *a.* Sermonizing. **2.** *s.* Sermonizer.

sérosité [serozite], *s.f.* Serosity.

sérothérapie [serɔterapi], *s.f.* Serotherapy.

serpe [sɛrp], *s.f.* Bill-hook, hedging-bill. *Fait à coups de serpe,* roughly made, hacked out.

serpent [sɛrpã], *s.m.* **1.** *Rept:* Snake. *S. d'eau,* grass-snake. *S. de verre,* slow-worm, blind-worm. *S. à sonnettes,* rattlesnake. *S. à coiffe, à lunettes,* cobra. *Myth: S. de mer,* sea-serpent. **Langue de serpent,** (i) *F:* venomous tongue, (ii) *Bot:* adder's-tongue. S.a. RÉCHAUFFER 1. **2.** *Mus: A:* Serpent.

serpentaire[1] [sɛrpãtɛ:r], *s.f. Bot: Pharm:* Serpentaria. *S. de Virginie,* Virginia snake-root.

serpentaire[2], *s.m. Orn:* Serpent-eater, secretary-bird.

serpente [sɛrpãːt], *s.f.* Tissue paper.
serpenteau [sɛrpãto], *s.m.* **1.** Young snake. **2.** *Pyr:* Serpent, squib.
serpent|er [sɛrpãte], *v.i.* (Of river, etc.) To wind, curve, meander. *s.m.* **-ement.**
serpentin, -ine [sɛrpãtɛ̃, -in]. **1.** *a.* (*a*) Serpentine (dance, etc.). (*b*) **Marbre serpentin,** serpentine (marble); ophite. **2.** *s.m.* (*a*) Worm (of still); coil (of tubing). (*b*) Paper streamer. **3.** *s.f.* Serpentine. (*a*) *Miner:* Serpentine (marble, stone); ophite. (*b*) *Bot:* Snake-wood.
serpette [sɛrpɛt], *s.f.* (*a*) Pruning-knife. (*b*) Bill-hook.
serpillière [sɛrpijɛːr], *s.f.* **1.** Packing-cloth; sacking. **2.** (Tradesman's) apron.
serpolet [sɛrpɔlɛ], *s.m.* *Bot:* Wild thyme.
serrage [sɛraːʒ], *s.m.* Tightening (of knot, screw); screwing tight (of nut); clamping (of joint, etc.); grip, holding (of chuck). *S. des freins,* application of the brakes. *Typ:* *S. des formes,* locking up of the forms. **Clef de serrage,** wedge key. **Collier de serrage,** clamping-band; *Aut:* hose-clip. **Vis de serrage,** set-screw, locking-screw. **Écrou de serrage,** hold-down nut.
serre [sɛːr], *s.f.* **1.** Greenhouse, conservatory, glass-house. **Serre chaude,** hothouse. **2.** Pressing, squeezing (of grapes). **3.** (*a*) Grip. **Avoir la serre bonne,** (i) to have a strong grip; (ii) *F:* to be close-fisted. (*b*) Claw, talon (of bird of prey). (*c*) Clip; *Surg:* suture forceps.
serre-écrou, *s.m.inv.* *Tls:* Bolt-spanner.
serre-fil, *s.m.* *El:* Binding-screw (of terminal); binding-post. *pl. Des serre-fils.*
serre-file, *s.m.* **1.** *Mil:* File-closer. **Marcher en serre-file,** to march serrefile. **2.** *Navy:* Sternmost ship, rear ship (of a line ahead). *pl. Des serre-files.*
serre-frein(s), *s.m.* **1.** *Rail:* Brakesman. **2.** *Mec.E:* Brake adjuster. *pl. Des serre-freins.*
serre-joint, *s.m.* *Tls:* (Joiner's) cramp. *pl. Des serre-joints.*
serrement [sɛrmã], *s.m.* Squeezing, pressure. *S. de main,* hand-shake, grip of the hand. **Serrement de cœur,** pang.
serre-nez, *s.m.inv.* *Vet:* Twitch (for horse).
serre-papiers, *s.m.inv.* **1.** File (for papers). **2.** (Set of) pigeon-holes. **3.** Paper-clip. **4.** Paperweight.
serrer [sɛre], *v.tr.* **1.** To put away, stow away (in drawer, etc.). *S. qch. sous clef,* to lock sth. up. **2.** To press, squeeze, clasp. **Serrer la main à qn,** to clasp s.o.'s hand, to shake hands with s.o. *S. qn entre ses bras,* to clasp s.o. in one's arms; to hug s.o. **Serrer le cou à qn,** to strangle s.o. *S. qch. dans sa main,* to grip, grasp, sth. (Of dog) **Serrer la queue,** to hold its tail between its legs. *Cela me serre le cœur,* it wrings my heart. **3.** To tighten (knot, screw); to screw up, tighten (nut). *S. les freins,* to apply, put on, the brakes. *S. qch. dans un étau,* to grip sth. in a vice. **Serrer (les cordons de) sa bourse,** to tighten one's pursestrings. *S. les dents,* to clench, set, one's teeth. *S.a.* POING. *S. les côtes à son cheval,* to keep a tight grip on one's horse; to urge one's horse on. *F:* **Serrer les côtes à qn,** to prod, jog, s.o. on; to keep s.o. at it. **4.** To close, close up, press close together. *S. son style,* to condense one's style. *S. son jeu,* (i) (at draughts) to keep one's men in close formation; (ii) *F:* to play a close game, to take no risks. *Mil:* *S. les rangs,* to close the ranks. **5.** To keep close to (s.o., sth.). *S. la muraille,* to hug, skirt, the wall. **Serrer le vent,** to haul, hug, the wind. **Serrer qn de près,** to beset s.o.; to press s.o. hard. *S. le texte de*

près, to keep close to the text. *S. qn de questions,* to ply s.o. with searching questions. *Sp:* *Rac:* **Serrer un concurrent,** to jostle a competitor.
se serrer. 1. To stand, sit, close together; to crowd. **Serrez-vous!** close up! sit closer! **2.** To tighten, to become tighter. *Ses lèvres se serrèrent,* his lips tightened. **3.** To squeeze, pull in, one's figure; to tight-lace.
serré. 1. *a.* (*a*) Tight; close (texture); compact, serried, dense (ranks); closely-woven (fabric); close-grained (wood). **Oignons plantés en rangs serrés,** close-set onions. **Serrés comme des harengs en caque,** packed (in) like herrings (in a barrel). **Avoir le cœur serré,** to be sad at heart. *Surveillance serrée,* close supervision. *Logique, traduction, serrée,* close reasoning, close translation. (*b*) Close-fisted, avaricious. **2.** *adv.* (*a*) **Mordre serré,** to bite hard. (*b*) **Jouer serré,** to play a cautious game.
serre-tête, *s.m.inv.* **1.** (*a*) Headband. (*b*) Kerchief (tied over the hair). **2.** *Av:* Crash-helmet.
serrure [sɛryːr], *s.f.* Lock. *S. encastrée,* mortiselock. *S. à broche,* piped-key lock. **Brouiller la s.,** to tamper with the lock. **Trou de la serrure,** key-hole. **Faire jouer la serrure,** to unlock the door. *S.a.* BÉNARDE, PALASTRE. [SERRER]
serrurerie [sɛryr(ə)ri], *s.f.* **1.** (*a*) Locksmithing. (*b*) The locksmith's (shop). (*c*) Mechanism of a lock. **2.** Iron work, metal work. *S. d'art,* art metal-work. **Grosse serrurerie,** heavy iron-work; heavy smithing.
serrurier [sɛryrje], *s.m.* **1.** Locksmith. **2.** Ironworker, ironsmith.
sert|ir [sɛrtiːr], *v.tr.* (*a*) To set (precious stone) in a bezel. (*b*) *Vitres serties de plomb,* panes set in lead. *s.m.* **-issage.**
sertissure [sɛrtisyːr], *s.f.* Setting (of precious stone); bezel.
sérum [serɔm], *s.m.* Serum.
servage [sɛrvaːʒ], *s.m.* Serfdom; bondage, thraldom; bondservice.
serval [sɛrval], *s.m.* Serval, tiger-cat. *pl. Des servals.*
servant, -ante [sɛrvã, -ãːt]. **1.** *a.* Serving. *Frère s.,* lay brother. *Gentilhomme s.,* gentleman-in-waiting. **2.** *s.m.* (*a*) *Artil:* **Les servants,** the gun crew. (*b*) *Ten:* Server. **3.** *s.f.* **Servante.** (*a*) (Maid-)servant, servant-girl. (*b*) (i) Dinner-waggon. (ii) Butler's tray; dumb waiter.
serve [sɛrv], *s.f.* See SERF.
serveur, -euse [sɛrvœːr, -øːz], *s.* **1.** (*a*) Carver (at hotel, etc.). (*b*) Barman, barmaid. (*c*) (In restaurant) *La serveuse,* the waitress. **2.** *Cards:* Dealer. **3.** *Ten:* Server.
serviabilité [sɛrvjabilite], *s.f.* Obligingness.
serviable [sɛrvjabl], *a.* Obliging; willing to help.
service [sɛrvis], *s.m.* **1.** (*a*) Service. **Entrer en service,** to go into service. **Prendre qn à son service,** to take s.o. into one's service. **Être au service de qn,** to be in s.o.'s service, [in attendance on s.o. **Escalier de service,** backstairs. **Porte de service,** tradesmen's entrance. **Hors de service,** (i) (person) retired from service; (ii) (thing) out of service, unfit for service; (gun) out of action. *Mil:* *Navy:* **En activité de service,** on the active list. **Bon pour le service,** (of man) fit for (general) service; (of ship, etc.) serviceable. **Faire son (temps de) service,** to do one's military service. **Avoir du s.,** to have seen service. **Avoir vingt ans de service(s),** to have served twenty years. **Au service,** in the service. **Entrer au service,** to enter the service. (*b*) Department; administrative authority. *Entreprise de s. public, de s. de ville,* public utility undertaking. *S. des eaux,* water

supply. Com: *Services d'une maison*, departments of a firm. **Chef de service**, departmental head. (c) Service (of trains, liners, etc.). **Faire le service entre** . . . **et** . . ., to run, ply, between . . . and. . . . **Mettre un autobus en service**, to put a bus into service. **2.** (a) Duty. **Être de service**, to be on duty. **Officier de service**, orderly officer. (b) Attendance (in hotels, etc.). (c) Divine service. (d) Ten: Service. **3. Rendre (un) service à qn**, to do s.o. a service, a good turn. **A votre service**, at your service. *Ce livre m'a rendu grand s.*, this book was very useful to me. **Vêtements de bon service**, hard-wearing clothes. **4.** (a) Course (of a meal). (b) Rail: **Premier service**, first lunch or dinner. **5.** Set (of utensils, etc.). *S. de table*, dinner service, dinner set.

serviette [sɛrvjɛt], s.f. **1.** (a) (Table-)napkin. *S. de plateau*, tray-cloth. (b) *S. de toilette*, towel. *S. éponge*, Turkish towel. **2.** (Lawyer's, professor's) portfolio (carried under the arm).

servile [sɛrvil], a. Servile; slavish (imitation, imitator). *adv.* **-ment.**

servilité [sɛrvilite], s.f. Servility; cringing; slavishness (to fashion).

servir [sɛrviːr], v. (pr.p. **servant**; p.p. **servi**; pr.ind. **je sers, il sert**, n. **servons**; pr.sub. **je serve**; p.h. **je servis**; fu. **je servirai**) To serve. **I.** v.i. (a) To be useful (à qn, to s.o.); to be in use. *Ce livre lui a beaucoup servi*, the book has been of great use to him. (b) **Servir à qch., à faire qch.**, to be useful for sth., for doing sth. **Ne servir à rien**, to answer no purpose; to be useless. **A quoi cela sert-il?** what is the good, the use, of that? **Cela ne sert à rien de pleurer**, it's no good crying. (c) **Servir à qn à, pour, faire qch.** *Ce canif me sert à me faire les ongles*, I use this penknife to trim my nails. (d) **Servir de**, to serve as, be used as (s.o., sth.). *Les pupitres servent de tables*, the desks are used as tables. *S. de prétexte*, to serve as a pretext. *Sa fille lui sert de secrétaire*, his daughter acts as his amanuensis. (e) Impers. **Il ne sert à rien de pleurer**, rien ne sert de pleurer, it is no good crying. Prov: **Rien ne sert de courir, il faut partir à point**, it is no good hurrying, you must start punctually. **2.** v.tr. (a) To be a servant to (s.o.); to serve (s.o.). *S. sa patrie*, to serve one's country. *Je me sers moi-même*, I am my own servant. (b) Abs. To serve (in army, navy). **En âge de servir**, of military age. (c) To serve, wait on, attend to (customer, etc.). **Est-ce qu'on vous sert?** are you being attended to? *Madame est servie*, dinner is served, madam. Abs. *S. à table*, to wait at table. (d) *S. une livre de beurre à qn*, to serve s.o. with a pound of butter. **Servir une rente à qn**, to pay an annuity to s.o. (e) To serve up, dish up, bring in (dinner, etc.). (f) To serve out (the fish, etc.). *S. à boire à qn*, to fill s.o.'s glass. *Servez-vous*, help yourself. (g) To help, assist, be of service to (s.o.). **En quoi puis-je vous servir?** what can I do for you? (h) To serve (gun); to work, operate (gun, pump). (i) **Servir la messe**, to serve at mass. (j) Ten: To serve. **se servir. 1.** **Se s. chez qn**, to buy one's provisions, supply oneself with goods, at a shop. **2.** **Se s. de qch., de qn**, to use sth., s.o.; to make use of sth., of s.o. *Vous servez-vous de votre plume?* are you using your pen?

serviteur [sɛrvitœːr], s.m. Servant. *S. à gages*, hired servant. **"Votre serviteur,"** 'your obedient servant.'

servitude [sɛrvityd], s.f. **1.** (a) Servitude; (i) bondservice; (ii) slavery. **Réduire un peuple en servitude**, to reduce a people to bondage. (b) *La s. de la mode*, the tyranny of fashion. **2.** Jur: Easement, charge (on real estate).

servo-frein, s.m. Aut: etc: Servo-brake.

servo-moteur. I. s.m. Mch: Servo-motor, auxiliary motor. **2.** a. Aut: etc: Self-energized (brake, etc.).

ses [se, sɛ], poss.a. See SON[1].

sésame [sezam], s.m. Bot: Sesame, sesamum. (In the 'Arabian Nights') **Sésame, ouvre-toi!** open, sesame !

séséli [sezeli], s.m. Bot: Seseli; meadow saxifrage.

sesquibasique [sɛskɥibazik], a. Ch: Sesquibasic.

sesquioxyde [sɛskɥiɔksid], s.m. Ch: Sesquioxide.

sessile [sɛssil], a. Sessile (leaf, horn, tumour).

session [sɛsjɔ̃], s.f. **1.** Session, sitting. **2.** Jur: Sch: Session, term.

sétacé [setase], a. Setaceous, bristly.

setier [s(ə)tje], s.m. **1.** Ancient measure = approx. 8 pints. **2.** F: Demi-setier, half-pint.

sétifère [setifɛːr], a. Setiferous, bristly.

sétigère [setiʒɛːr], a. = SÉTIFÈRE.

séton [setɔ̃], s.m. Surg: Vet: *S. à mèche*, seton. *Vet: S. en rouelle, s. à rouelle*, rowel. **Blessure en séton**, flesh wound.

seuil [sœːj], s.m. **1.** Threshold (of door); doorsill, door-step. **Franchir le seuil**, to cross the threshold. *Être au s. de la célébrité*, to stand on the threshold of fame. **2.** Hyd.E: Ground-sill (of lock). **3.** Ocean shelf.

seul [sœl], a. **1.** (*Seul* preceding the noun) (a) Only, sole, single. **Un seul homme**, one man only; only one man. **Avancer comme un seul homme**, to advance as one man. *Son s. souci*, his one, only, care. **Mon seul et unique faux col**, my one and only collar. **Pas un seul**, not a single one. *s.f.* Com: **Seule de change**, sole of exchange. (b) *La seule pensée m'effraie*, the thought alone frightens me; the bare thought frightens me. **2.** (*Seul* following the noun or used predicatively) **Un homme seul**, a man alone, by himself. Rail: *Compartiment de dames seules*, carriage for ladies only. **Parler seul à seul**, to speak to s.o. alone. **Il était seul à seul avec soi-même**, he was alone with his thoughts. **Je l'ai fait tout seul, à moi seul**, I did it (by) myself, alone, single-handed. **Cela va tout seul**, it is plain sailing. **3.** *Seul un homme pourrait l'entreprendre*, only a man could undertake it.

seulement [sœlmã], adv. **1.** (a) Only. *Nous sommes s. deux*, there are only two of us. **Non seulement . . ., mais aussi . . ., mais encore . . .**, not only . . ., but also. . . . (b) Solely, merely. **2.** Even. **Sans seulement me regarder**, without even looking at me. **Si seulement il m'avait regardé!** if only, if even, he had looked at me ! *Je n'ai pas s. le prix de mon voyage*, I haven't so much as my fare.

seulet, -ette [sœlɛ, -ɛt], a. F: Alone, lonely.

sève [sɛːv], s.f. (a) Sap (of plant). **Plein de sève**, sappy. **Sans sève**, sapless. (b) F: Vigour, vim (of youth). **Plein de sève**, full of vitality.

sévère [sevɛːr], a. Severe. **1.** Stern, hard, harsh (judge, etc.). *Climat s.*, hard climate. *Être s. envers qn, pour qn*, to be hard on s.o. **2.** Strict, rigid (discipline). **Morale peu sévère**, lax morals. *adv.* **-ment.**

sévérité [severite], s.f. Severity (of sentence, taste, dress); sternness; strictness (of discipline).

sévices [sevis], s.m.pl. Jur: Maltreatment (envers, of); brutality, cruelty (envers, towards).

sévir [seviːr], v.i. **1.** *S. contre qn*, to deal severely with s.o. **2.** (Of pestilence, war) To rage; (of poverty) to be rife, rampant. *Le froid sévissait,* the cold was severe.

sevr|er [səvre], *v.tr.* (je **sèvre**; je **sèvrerai**) **1.** To wean (child, lamb): *F: S. qn de distractions,* to deprive s.o. of amusements. **2.** *Hort:* To separate (layer from a plant). *s.m.* **-age.**

Sèvres [sɛːvr]. **1.** *Pr.n. Geog:* Sèvres. **2.** *s.m. Service de sèvres,* set of Sèvres porcelain.

sexagénaire [sɛksaʒenɛːr], *a. & s.* Sexagenarian.

Sexagésime [sɛksaʒezim], *s.f. Ecc:* Sexagesima.

sexe [sɛks], *s.m.* Sex. *Enfant du s. masculin,* male child. *F:* **Le beau sexe,** the fair sex.

sexennal, -aux [sɛksɛnnal, -o], *a.* Sexennial.

sextant [sɛkstɑ̃], *s.m. Mth: Nau:* Sextant.

sextillion [sɛkstiljɔ̃], *s.m.* A thousand trillions (10^{21}); *U.S:* sex(t)illion.

sextuor [sɛkstyɔːr], *s.m. Mus:* Sextet(te).

sextuple [sɛkstypl], *a. & s.m.* Sextuple; sixfold.

sextupler [sɛkstyple]. **1.** *v.tr.* To sextuple (a number). **2.** *v.tr. & i.* To increase sixfold.

sexualisme [sɛksɥalism], *s.m.* Sexualism.

sexualité [sɛksɥalite], *s.f.* Sexuality.

sexué [sɛksɥe], *a.* Sexed (plant, statue, etc.).

sexuel, -elle [sɛksɥɛl], *a.* Sexual.

sey-ait, -ant¹ [sɛjɛ, -ɑ̃]. See SEOIR.

seyant² [sɛjɑ̃], *a.* Becoming (garment, colour).

sgraffite [sgrafit], *s.m. Art:* (S)graffito.

shak(e)spearien, -ienne [ʃɛkspirjɛ̃, -jɛn], *a.* Shakespearean.

shako [ʃako], *s.m. Mil:* Shako.

shant(o)ung [ʃɑ̃tuŋ], *s.m. Tex:* Shantung.

shunt [ʃœ̃t], *s.m. El:* Shunt.

shunter [ʃœ̃te], *v.tr. El:* To shunt (circuit, ammeter).

si¹ [si], *conj.* (By elision **s'** before *il, ils*) **1.** If. (*a*) *Je ne sortirai pas s'il pleut,* I shall not go out if it rains. *S'il avait vécu, Lit:* s'il eût vécu, if he had lived. *S'il vient, vous m'avertirez,* if he comes, you will let me know. *S'il venait, vous m'avertiriez,* if he should come, you would let me know. *Si j'avais su,* had I but known. **Si ce n'est toi,** *c'est donc ton frère,* if it is not you, then it is your brother. *Si ce n'était que je l'ai vu moi-même . . .,* but that I saw it myself. . . . **Si ce n'était mon rhumatisme,** were it not for my rheumatism. S.a. QUE³ 5. **Si je ne me trompe,** if I am not mistaken. **Si tant est que** + *sub.,* if so it be that. (*b*) (Concessive) *S'il fut sévère, il fut juste,* if severe, he was just. *Le père Martin, un brave homme s'il en fut,* old Martin, a worthy man if ever there was one. **2.** Whether. *Je me demande si c'est vrai, s'il viendra,* I wonder whether it is true, whether he will come. *F: Vous connaissez Paris?—Si je connais Paris!* you know Paris?—Of course, I know Paris! **3.** How; how much. *Vous savez si je vous aime,* you know how I love you. **4.** What if; suppose. *Et si elle l'apprend?* and what if she hears of it? *F: Si nous changions de sujet?* suppose we change the subject? *Si on faisait une partie de bridge?* what about a game of bridge? **5.** *s.m.* Tes si et tes mais, your ifs and buts.

si², *adv.* **1.** So; so much. (*a*) *Ne courez pas si fort,* don't run so fast. *Un si bon dîner,* such a good dinner, so good a dinner. *De si bons dîners,* such good dinners. (*b*) (= AUSSI in negative clause) *Il n'est pas si beau que vous,* he is not as handsome, not so handsome, as you. (*c*) (Still used = AUSSI in affirmative clause in the phrs.) **Donnez-m'en si peu que vous voudrez, si peu que rien,** give me the smallest little bit. (*d*) **Si bien que . . .,** with the result that. . . . **2.** (Concessive) **Si . . . que** + *sub.,* however. *Si jeune qu'il soit,* however young he may be.

Si peu que ce soit, (i) however little it may be; (ii) ever so little. *Si bien qu'il s'y prenne,* however skilfully he sets about it. **3.** (In answer to a neg. question) Yes. **Si fait,** yes indeed. *Ça ne fait rien.—Si, ça fait quelque chose,* it doesn't matter. *—It does matter! Il n'est pas parti?—Si,* he hasn't gone?—Yes (, he has). *Il ne s'en remettra pas.*—**Que si!** he will not get over it.—Of course, he will! Yes, he will!

si³, *s.m.inv. Mus:* (The note) B. *En si bémol,* in B flat.

siamois, -oise [sjamwa, -waːz], *a. & s.* Siamese. *Frères siamois, sœurs siamoises,* Siamese twins.

Sibérie [siberi]. *Pr.n.f. Geog:* Siberia. **Chien de Sibérie,** Siberian dog.

sibérien, -ienne [siberjɛ̃, -jɛn], *a. & s.* Siberian.

sibilant [sibilɑ̃], *a.* Sibilant, hissing.

sibylle [sibil], *s.f.* Sibyl. *F: Une vieille s.,* an old hag.

sibyllin [sibillɛ̃], *a.* Sibylline (books, etc.).

sicaire [sikɛːr], *s.m.* Bravo; hired assassin.

siccatif, -ive [sikatif, -iːv]. **1.** *a.* (Quick-)drying, siccative. **2.** *s.m.* (*a*) Siccative, dryer (as used by painters). (*b*) (Quick-drying) polish.

siccité [siksite], *s.f.* Dryness.

Sicile [sisil]. *Pr.n.f. Geog:* Sicily.

sicilien, -ienne [sisiljɛ̃, -jɛn], *a. & s.* Sicilian.

sicle [sikl], *s.m. B:* Shekel.

sidéral, -aux [sideral, -o], *a.* Sidereal (day, year).

sidération [siderasjɔ̃], *s.f.* **1.** *Astrol:* Sideration. **2.** Sudden stroke of apoplexy. **3.** Blasting (of tree by lightning).

sidéré [sidere], *a.* (*a*) Struck dead (by lightning or apoplexy). (*b*) *F:* Struck dumb, dazed (with astonishment); thunderstruck, *F:* flabbergasted.

sidérurgie [sideryrʒi], *s.f.* The metallurgy of iron; iron-smelting.

sidérurgique [sideryrʒik], *a.* Pertaining to the metallurgy of iron. *Usine s.,* ironworks.

sidi [sidi], *s.m.* **1.** Sayyid. **2.** *Mil: P:* African soldier. **3.** *P:* Man, fellow. *Drôle de s.,* funny sort of chap, queer card.

siècle [sjɛkl], *s.m.* **1.** Century. *Au vingtième s.,* in the twentieth century. **2.** Age, period (of time). *Fr.Hist:* **Le grand siècle,** the age of Louis XIV. *C'est un homme de son s.,* he is a man of the times. *F:* **Il y a un siècle que je ne vous ai vu,** I haven't seen you for ages. **3.** *Se séparer du s.,* to withdraw from the world, from worldly life.

sied [sje], **sié-e, -ent,** etc. See SEOIR.

siège [sjɛːʒ], *s.m.* **1.** (*a*) Seat, centre (of learning, disease, etc.). **Siège social,** registered offices (of company). *Le s. du gouvernement,* the seat of government. (*b*) *Ecc:* **Siège épiscopal,** see; diocesan centre. S.a. SAINT-SIÈGE. **2.** *Mil:* Siege. **Mettre le siège devant une ville,** to lay siege to a town. **Lever le siège,** to raise the siege. **Déclarer l'état de siège** (*dans une ville*), to declare martial law. **3.** Seat, chair; (coachman's) box. *Le s. du juge,* the judge's bench. *Prenez un s.,* take a seat. **4.** (*a*) Bottom (of chair, etc.). *Fauteuil à s. de cuir,* leather-bottomed easy-chair. (*b*) Sitting. **Bain de siège,** sitz-bath, hip-bath. (*c*) Seat(ing) (of valve, etc.).

siéger [sjeʒe], *v.i.* (je **siège,** n. **siégeons**; je **siégeai**(s); je **siégerai**) **1.** (Of company) To have its head office, (of malady) to be seated, (of bishop) to hold his see (in a place). **2.** (Of judge, assembly, etc.) To sit. **3.** (*a*) *S. à la Chambre,* to have a seat, to sit, in the Chamber (of Deputies). (*b*) *S. au tribunal,* to be on the bench.

sien, sienne¹ [sjɛ̃, sjɛn]. His, hers, its, one's. **1.** *poss.a. Un sien oncle,* an uncle of his, of hers. *Mes intérêts sont siens,* my interests are his. **2.** Le sien, la sienne, les siens, les siennes. (*a*) *poss.pron.* *Ma sœur est plus jolie que la sienne*, my sister is prettier than his, than hers. (*b*) *s.m.* (i) One's own, his own (property, etc.). *A chacun le sien*, to each one his own. **Y mettre du sien**, to contribute to an undertaking. **Ajouter du sien à un récit**, to improve upon a tale. (ii) *pl.* His own, her own, one's own (friends, etc.). (iii) *F:* *Il a encore fait des siennes*, he's been up to his old tricks. **Sienne²**. *Pr.n.f. Geog:* Sienna. *Com:* **Terre de Sienne naturelle, brûlée**, raw, burnt, sienna.

siér-a, -ont, etc. See SEOIR.

sieste [sjɛst], *s.f.* Siesta, *F:* nap. **Faire la sieste**, to take a nap (after dinner).

sieur [sjœːr], *s.m. Jur:* **Le sieur un tel**, Mr So-and-so. *Com:* **Notre sieur Martin**, our Mr Martin.

sifflant, -ante [siflɑ̃, -ɑ̃:t]. I. *a.* Hissing (sound); whistling (note); wheezing, wheezy (breath); sibilant (consonant). 2. *s.f. Ling:* **Sifflante**, sibilant.

siffl|er [sifle]. I. *v.i.* (*a*) To whistle; (of serpent, goose) to hiss; (of missile) to whirr, whizz; (of asthmatic pers.) to wheeze; (of food frying, of arc-lamp) to sizzle. (*b*) To blow a whistle; to blow the whistle. S.a. DISQUE 2. 2. *v.tr.* (*a*) To whistle (a tune). *Nau:* To pipe (a command). (*b*) To whistle for, whistle up (cab, etc.); to whistle to, after (dog, etc.). (*c*) *Th:* To hiss, boo, hoot (play, actor). *Être sifflé, F:* to get the bird. (*d*) *P:* To swig off, toss off (glass of beer). *s.m.* **-ement**.

sifflet [siflɛ], *s.m.* I. Whistle (instrument). *Navy:* (Boatswain's) pipe. **Coup de sifflet**, blast of the whistle; whistle. **Donner un coup de sifflet**, to whistle; to blow the whistle; *Navy:* to pipe. *P:* **Couper le sifflet à qn**, (i) to cut s.o.'s throat; (ii) to nonplus s.o., shut s.o. up. *Row:* **Attaquer en sifflet**, to catch a crab. *Carp:* **Assemblage en sifflet**, scarf joint. **Couper en sifflet**, to cut slantwise. 2. Whistle (sound). *Th:* Catcall, hiss.

siffleur, -euse [siflœːr, -øːz]. I. *s.* Whistler. *Th:* Hisser, booer. 2. *s.m. Orn:* Widgeon. 3. *a.* Whistling (bird, duck); hissing (serpent); wheezy (breath).

sifflot|er [siflɔte], *v.i.* I. To whistle to oneself, under one's breath. 2. To whistle by snatches. *s.m.* **-ement**.

sigillaire [siʒillɛːr], *a.* Sigillary. **Anneau sigillaire**, signet-ring.

sigisbée [siʒisbe], *s.m.* Cicisbeo.

signal, -aux [siɲal, -o], *s.m.* Signal. *Donner un s.*, to signal. *S. du départ*, signal for departure. *S. d'incendie*, fire-alarm. *Rail:* **Corde de signal d'alarme**, communication cord. *S. de détresse*, distress signal. *S. à éclats*, flashing signal. *Aut: Signaux de route*, road warnings. *Tp: S. d'appel*, calling signal. *S. horaire*, time signal; *F:* the pips.

signalement [siɲalmɑ̃], *s.m.* Description (of pers. on passport, of criminal); particulars (of a car).

signaler [siɲale], *v.tr.* I. (*a*) To signalize; to make (sth.) conspicuous. (*b*) *S. qch. à l'attention de qn*, to point out sth. to s.o.'s attention, to draw s.o.'s attention to sth. *S. l'influence de qn*, to point to, point out, s.o.'s influence. (*c*) To report (s.o., sth.) to the police, etc. 2. (*a*) To signal (train, ship). (*b*) *Abs.* To signal. 3. To give a description of (man wanted). **se signaler**, to signalize, distinguish, oneself (*par*, by).

signalé, *a.* I. Signal (service); conspicuous (bravery); well-known (author). 2. *Pej:* Notorious (criminal, etc.).

signalétique [siɲaletik], *a. Adm:* Descriptive.

signaleur [siɲalœːr], *s.m.* (*a*) *Mil: etc:* Signaller. (*b*) *Rail:* Signalman.

signalisateur [siɲalizatœːr], *s.m.* Signalling device. *Aut:* Traffic indicator. *S. anti-vol*, thief-alarm.

signalisation [siɲalizasjɔ̃], *s.f.* I. Signalling. *S. optique*, visual signalling. 2. Means of signalling; set of signals. **Poteau de signalisation**, traffic sign.

signataire [siɲatɛːr], *s. m. & f.* Signer, signatory, subscriber.

signature [siɲatyːr], *s.f.* I. Signing. 2. Signature. *Apposer sa s. à un acte*, to set one's hand to a deed. 3. *Typ:* Signature.

signe [siɲ], *s.m.* Sign. I. Indication (of rain, grief); symptom (of illness); mark, token (of friendship). *Ne donner aucun s. de vie*, **ne pas faire signe de vie**, to show no sign of life. 2. Symbol, mark. *S. algébrique*, algebraical sign. S.a. CROIX 1. 3. (Distinctive) mark (on the body). *Adm: Signes particuliers*, special peculiarities (of a person). 4. Gesture, motion. **Signe de tête**, nod. **Signe des yeux**, wink. **Faire signe à qn**, (i) to motion to s.o., make a sign to s.o.; (ii) to beckon to s.o. *Faire s. à qn de faire qch.*, to sign to s.o. to do sth. *Faire s. que oui*, to make an affirmative sign. **En signe de respect**, as a token of respect.

signer [siɲe], *v.tr.* I. To sign; to put or set one's name to (document). *Nau: S. l'engagement*, to sign on. 2. To stamp, mark (jewellery, etc.). **se signer**, to cross oneself.

signet [siɲɛ], *s.m. Bookb:* Book-mark(er), tassel.

significa|tif, -ive [siɲifikatif, -iːv], *a.* Significant. *adv.* **-ivement**.

signification [siɲifikasjɔ̃], *s.f.* I. Meaning, signification, sense, import. 2. *Jur:* Notification; service, serving (of writ).

signifier [siɲifje], *v.tr.* I. To mean, signify. *Cela ne signifie rien*, they don't mean anything by it. *F:* (Denoting indignation) **Qu'est-ce que cela signifie? que signifie?** what's the meaning of this? 2. To intimate clearly. *S. ses intentions à qn*, to notify s.o. of one's intentions. **Signifier son congé à qn**, (i) to give s.o. notice to quit; (ii) to give s.o. notice of dismissal. *Jur: S. un arrêt à qn*, to serve a notice on s.o.

silence [silɑ̃:s], *s.m.* I. Silence. *S. absolu*, dead silence. **Imposer silence à qn**, **réduire qn au silence**, to put, reduce, s.o. to silence; to silence s.o. **Rompre le silence**, to break (the) silence. **Garder, observer, le silence**, to keep silent (*sur*, about). **Faire silence**, to stop talking. **Silence!** silence! hush! **Passer qch. sous silence**, to pass over sth. in silence. 2. *Mus:* Rest.

silencieu|x, -euse [silɑ̃sjø, -øːz]. I. *a.* Silent. (*a*) Taciturn. (*b*) Noiseless (typewriter, etc.). (*c*) Still, peaceful. 2. *s.m. I.C.E:* Silencer. *adv.* **-sement**.

Silène [silɛn]. I. *Pr.n.m. Myth:* Silenus. 2. *s.m. Bot:* Silene, catch-fly. *S. enflé*, bladder campion.

silex [silɛks], *s.m.* Silex, flint. **Fusil à silex**, flint-lock (gun).

silhouette [silwɛt], *s.f.* (*a*) Silhouette. (*b*) Outline, form (of person, etc.); profile.

silhouett|er [silwɛte], *v.tr.* (*a*) To silhouette; to outline. (*b*) *Phot:* To block out. *s.m.* **-age**. **se silhouetter**, to stand out, show up (against the horizon, etc.).

silicate [silikat], *s.m. Ch:* Silicate. *S. de potasse,* water-glass.

silice [silis], *s.f. Ch:* Silica.

siliceux, -euse [siliso, -ø:z], *a.* Siliceous.

silicique [silisik], *a. Ch:* Silicic (acid).

silicium [silisjɔm], *s.m. Ch:* Silicon.

silique [silik], *s.f. Bot:* Siliqua, silique; pod.

sillage [sija:ʒ], *s.m.* **I.** (a) Wake, wash, track (of ship). *F:* **Marcher dans le sillage de qn,** to follow in s.o.'s wake. *F:* **Il fait plus de remous que de sillage,** it's a case of much cry and little wool. (b) *Av: etc:* Slip-stream. **2.** Sea-way, headway, speed (of ship).

sillet [sijɛ], *s.m.* Nut (of stringed instruments).

sillomètre [sijɔmɛtr], *s.m. Nau:* Patent log.

sillon [sijɔ̃], *s.m.* **I.** (a) Furrow. (b) Drill (= small furrow). *Semer la graine par sillons,* to sow the grain in drills. (c) *pl. Lit:* Fields. (d) Line (on the forehead, etc.); wrinkle. **2.** Track, trail (of wheel); wake (of ship); path (of projectile); trail, streak (of light). **Éclairs en sillons,** forked lightning. **3.** (a) *Anat:* Groove. (b) **Sillon sonore,** sound-groove (of gramophone).

sillonner [sijɔne], *v.tr.* (a) To furrow; to plough (the seas). (b) (Of lightning) To streak (the heavens). (c) To wrinkle, furrow (the brow).

silo [silo], *s.m. Husb:* Silo; store-pit; clamp (of potatoes). **Mettre en silo,** to silo, to clamp.

silure [sily:r], *s.m. Ich:* Silurus, sheat-fish.

silurien, -ienne [silyrjɛ̃, -jɛn], *a. Geol:* Silurian.

simagrée [simagre], *s.f.* (a) Pretence. (b) *pl.* Affected airs; grimaces; affectation. *Faire des simagrées,* to mince. *Ne faites pas tant de simagrées,* don't make so much fuss.

simarre [sima:r], *s.f.* (a) Magistrate's cassock (worn under gown). (b) (Bishop's) chimere.

simien, -ienne [simjɛ̃, -jɛn], *a. Z:* Simian.

simiesque [simjɛsk], *a.* Monkey-like, ape-like, apish (face, grimace).

similaire [similɛ:r], *a.* Similar (*à,* to); like. *Cannes et objets similaires,* walking-sticks and like objects. *adv.* **-ment.**

similarité [similarite], *s.f.* Similarity, likeness.

simili [simili]. **I.** *pref.* Imitation. *Similibronze,* imitation bronze. **2.** *s.m. F:* Imitation. *Bijoux en s.,* imitation jewellery. **3.** *F:* (a) *s.f.* = SIMILIGRAVURE. (b) *s.m.* Half-tone block.

similicuir [similikɥi:r], *s.m.* Imitation leather; leatherette.

similigraveur [similigravœ:r], *s.m.* Process-engraver, half-tone engraver.

similigravure [similigravy:r], *s.f.* Process-engraving, half-tone.

similiser [similize], *v.tr.* To silk-finish (cotton).

similitude [similityd], *s.f.* Similitude. **I.** Resemblance, likeness; similarity (of ideas, of triangles). **2.** *Rh:* Simile.

similor [similɔ:r], *s.m.* Imitation gold; pinchbeck.

simoniaque [simɔnjak]. *Ecc:* **I.** *a.* Simoniac(al). **2.** *s.m.* Simoniac, Simonist.

simonie [simɔni], *s.f. Ecc:* Simony.

simoun [simun], *s.m.* Simoon; sand-storm.

simple [sɛ̃:pl], *a.* Simple. **I.** (a) Single (flower, etc.). *s.m. Ten:* **Jouer un simple,** to play a single. *S. messieurs,* men's single. S.a. EFFET 2. (b) Not compound. *Avoir une chance s.,* to have even chances. *Ch:* **Corps simple,** element. **2.** (a) Ordinary, common. **Simple soldat,** private (soldier). **Simple matelot,** ordinary seaman. (b) *C'est une s. question de temps,* it is simply a matter of time. *La vérité pure et s.,* the plain truth. *Croire qn sur sa s. parole,* to believe s.o. on his word alone. *La s. prudence veut que . . .,* ordinary, elementary,

prudence demands that. . . . (c) Plain (fact, food, truth). *Gens simples,* plain, homely, unpretentious, people. (d) Easy, straightforward. *F:* **C'est simple comme bonjour,** it's as easy as ABC. **3.** (a) Simple-minded, unsophisticated. *Il est un peu s. d'esprit,* he's not all there. *Un cœur s.,* a simple heart. **Au cœur simple,** simple-hearted. (b) Half-witted. (c) Ingenuous, guileless, *F:* green. **4.** *s.m.pl.* **Simples,** simples, medicinal herbs. *adv.* **-ment.**

simplesse [sɛ̃plɛs], *s.f.* Simpleness, artlessness.

simplet, -ette [sɛ̃plɛ, -ɛt], *a. F:* Artless.

simplicité [sɛ̃plisite], *s.f.* **I.** (a) Simplicity; plainness (of dress, furniture). (b) Elementary nature (of atoms, etc.). **2.** Artlessness, simpleness, simple-mindedness.

simplificateur, -trice [sɛ̃plifikatœ:r, -tris]. **I.** *a.* Simplifying. **2.** *s.m.* Simplifier.

simplification [sɛ̃plifikasjɔ̃], *s.f.* Simplification.

simplifier [sɛ̃plifje], *v.tr.* To simplify; to reduce (a fraction) to its lowest terms.

simplisme [sɛ̃plism], *s.m.* Begging the question.

simpliste [sɛ̃plist], *a.* Simplistic, over-simple (explanation).

simulacre [simylakr], *s.m.* (a) Simulacrum, image. (b) Semblance. *S. de résistance,* show of resistance. **Faire le simulacre de faire qch.,** to make a show of doing sth. *S. de combat,* sham fight.

simulateur, -trice [simylatœ:r, -tris], *s.* Simulator, shammer. *Mil:* Malingerer.

simulation [simylasjɔ̃], *s.f.* Simulation, feint. *Mil:* Malingering.

simuler [simyle], *v.tr.* To simulate, feign, counterfeit, sham.

simulé, *a.* Feigned (illness); sham (fight); bogus (sale). S.a. FACTURE[2].

simultané [simyltane], *a.* Simultaneous. *adv.* **-ment.**

sinapiser [sinapize], *v.tr.* To add mustard to (bath, poultice). *Cataplasme sinapisé,* mustard poultice.

sinapisme [sinapism], *s.m. Med:* Mustard plaster; sinapism.

sincère [sɛ̃sɛ:r], *a.* Sincere. **I.** Frank, candid, open-hearted. **2.** (a) Genuine, true-hearted (person). (b) Genuine, unfeigned (joy, sorrow, etc.). *adv.* **-ment.**

sincérité [sɛ̃serite], *s.f.* (a) Sincerity, frankness, candour. (b) Genuineness (of regret).

sinécure [sinekyr], *s.f.* Sinecure.

sinécuriste [sinekyrist], *s. m. & f.* Sinecurist.

Singapour [sɛ̃gapu:r]. *Pr.n.m. Geog:* Singapore.

singe [sɛ̃:ʒ], *s.m.* **I.** (a) Monkey, ape. S.a. MONNAIE I. (b) *F:* Ape, imitator. **2.** *Mil: P:* Bully beef. **3.** *P:* Boss, guv'nor.

singer [sɛ̃ʒe], *v.tr.* (je singeai(s); n. singeons) To ape, mimic (s.o.); to take (s.o.) off.

singerie [sɛ̃ʒri], *s.f.* **I.** (a) Grimace, apish antic, monkey trick. (b) = SIMAGRÉE. (c) (Monkey-like) imitation. **2.** Monkey-house.

singeur, -euse, -eresse [sɛ̃ʒœ:r, -ø:z, sɛ̃ʒrɛs]. **I.** *a.* Aping, imitative. **2.** *s.* Imitator.

singleton [sɛ̃glətɔ̃], *s. m. Cards:* Singleton.

singulariser [sɛ̃gylarize], *v.tr.* To singularize (s.o.); to make (s.o.) conspicuous.

se singulariser, to make oneself conspicuous (by one's oddity).

singularité [sɛ̃gylarite], *s.f.* Singularity. **I.** (a) Peculiarity, special feature. (b) *La s. de ces faits,* the unusualness of these facts. **2.** Oddness, oddity, eccentricity.

singuli|er, -ère [sɛ̃gylje, -ɛ:r], *a.* Singular. **I.** (a) **Combat singulier,** single combat. *s. Gram:*

Au singulier, in the singular. (b) Peculiar (à, to). **2.** Peculiar, remarkable, uncommon. **3.** (a) Odd, curious, strange queer *Il est s. qu'il ne soit pas encore arrivé,* it is strange that he has not arrived yet. (b) Conspicuous: like nobody else. *adv.* **-èrement.**

sinistre [sinistr]. **1.** *a.* Sinister, fatal, ominous, baleful. *Événement s.,* fatal occurrence. *Sourire s., sinister* smile. **2.** *s.m.* Disaster, catastrophe, calamity (esp. fire, earthquake, or shipwreck).

sinistré, -ée [sinistre]. **1.** *a.* That has suffered a disaster. **2.** *s.* Victim of, sufferer from, a disaster.

sinistrorsum [sinistrɔrsɔm]. **1.** *a.inv.* Sinistrorsal (whorl, etc.). **2.** *adv.* Counter-clockwise: from right to left.

sinologie [sinɔlɔʒi], *s.f. Ling: etc:* Sinology.

sinologue [sinɔlɔg], *s. m. & f.* Sinologue, sinologist; Chinese scholar.

sinon [sinɔ̃], *con* **1.** Otherwise, (or) else, if not. *Il faut obéir,* **sinon gare!** you must obey, or else look out! **2.** Except. *Il ne fait rien s. manger et boire,* he does nothing except eat and drink. *Sinon que,* except that, save that. [SI NON]

sinople [sinɔpl], *s.m. Her:* Vert, sinople.

sinueux, -euse [sinɥø, -øːz], *a.* Sinuous; winding (path); meandering (stream).

sinuosité [sinɥozite], *s.f.* (a) Sinuosity, winding. (b) Bend (of river, etc.).

sinus¹ [sinyːs]. *s.m Anat:* Sinus, antrum. *Les sinus frontaux,* the frontal sinuses.

sinus², *s.m. Mth:* Sine.

sinusite [sinyzit], *s.f. Med:* Inflammation of a (facial) sinus; infected antrum.

sinusoïdal [sinyzɔidal], *a. Mth:* Sinusoidal; sine-(wave); *El:* sine-shaped (current).

sinusoïde [sinyzɔid], *s.f. Mth:* Sine curve.

sioniste [sjɔnist], *a. & s.* Zionist.

siphon [sifɔ̃], *s.m.* (a) *Ph:* Siphon. (b) Siphon à eau de seltz, (soda water) siphon (bottle). (c) Trap (of drain, etc.).

siphonner [sifɔne], *v.tr.* To siphon.

sire [siːr], *s.m.* **1.** (a) *A:* Lord, sir. **Beau sire,** fair sir. (b) *Pej:* Un triste sire, a sad specimen (of humanity). **2.** (Title of address) Sire.

sirène [siren], *s.f.* **1.** (a) Siren, mermaid. (b) *F:* Charmer, *P:* vamp. **2.** (a) Siren, hooter, buzzer. (b) Fog-horn. **Un coup de sirène,** a blast of the hooter.

siroc [sirɔk], *s.m.,* **siroco** [sirɔko], *s.m.* Sirocco.

sirop [siro], *s.m.* Syrup.

siroter [sirɔte], *v.tr. F:* (a) To sip (one's wine, etc.). (b) *Abs.* To tipple. [SIROP]

sis, sise [si, siːz]. See SEOIR.

sisal [sizal], *s.m. Bot:* Sisal. **(Fibre de) sisal,** sisal-hemp.

sismal, -aux [sismal, -o], *a. Meteor:* Seismal.

sismique [sismik], *a.* Seismic (movement).

sismographe [sismɔgraf], *s.m.* Seismograph.

sismographie [sismɔgrafi], *s.f.* Seismography.

sismologie [sismɔlɔʒi], *s.f.* Seismology.

sisymbre [sizɛ̃br], *s.m. Bot:* Sisymbrium.

Sisyphe [sizif]. *Pr.n.m. Myth:* Sisyphus. *F:* Un travail de Sisyphe, Sisyphean labour.

site [sit], *s.m.* **1.** (Picturesque) site. **2.** *Civ.E:* Mil: Lie of the ground. Mil: **Angle de site,** angle of sight.

sitôt [sito], *adv.* (a) = AUSSITÔT. **Sitôt que** + *ind.,* as soon as. (b) (With neg.) **Vous ne le reverrez pas de sitôt,** it will be long before you see him again.

sittelle [sitel], *s.f. Orn:* Sitta, nuthatch.

situation [sitɥasjɔ̃], *s.f.* Situation. **1.** (a) Position, site (of a town, etc.). (b) *Nau:* Bearing.

2. (a) State, condition. **Être en situation de faire qch.,** to be in a position to do sth *S. sociale,* station in life. *Ma s. de fortune,* my worldly circumstances. *S. difficile,* predicament. **L'homme de la situation,** the right man in the right place. (b) **Mot de situation,** appropriate word. **Peu en situation,** out of place, inappropriate. **3.** *Il a une belle s.,* he has a first-rate position, *F:* a fine billet, a fine job.

situer [sitɥe], *v.tr.* To place, situate, locate.

six, *num.a.inv. & s.m.* Six. **1.** *card. a.* (At the end of the word-group [sis]; before a noun or adj. beginning with a vowel sound [siz]; before a noun or adj. beginning with a consonant [si]) *Six hommes* [sizɔm], six men *Six petits enfants* [siptizɑ̃fɑ̃], six little children. *J'en ai six* [sis], I have six. **2.** (Always [sis]) *Six et demi* [sisɛdmi], six and a half. *Le six mai,* (on) the sixth of May.

six-huit [sisɥit], *s.m. Mus:* **1.** Six-eight time. **2.** Piece in six-eight time.

sixième [sizjɛm]. **1.** *num. a. & s.* Sixth. **2.** *s.m.* Sixth (part). **3.** *s.f. Sch:* First form (of upper school). *adv.* **-ment.**

six-quatre-deux (à la) [alasiskatdø], *adv.phr. F:* Faire qch. à la six-quatre-deux, to do sth. in a slap-dash manner.

sixte¹ [sikst], *s.f.* **1.** *Mus:* Sixth. **2.** *Fenc:* **Parer en sixte,** to parry in sixte.

Sixte². *Pr.n.m. Ecc.Hist:* **Sixte-Quint,** Sixtus the Fifth.

Sixtine [sikstin], *a.f.* **La chapelle Sixtine,** the Sistine Chapel.

sizain [sizɛ̃], *s.m.* Six-line stanza.

ski [ski], *s.m.* **1.** Ski. *Fixer les skis,* to bind on the skis. **2.** Skiing. **Faire du ski,** to ski; to go in for skiing.

skieur, -euse [skiœːr, -øːz], *s.* Ski-runner, skier.

skungs [skœ̃gz], **skunks** [skœ̃ks], *s.m. Com:* Skunk (fur).

slave [slaːv]. **1.** *a.* Slav, Slavonic. **2.** *s.* Slav. **3.** *s.m. Ling:* Le slave, Slavonic.

slavon, -onne [slavɔ̃, -ɔn], *a. & s.* Slavonian, Slavonic.

sleeping [slipiŋ], *s.m. Rail: F:* Sleeping-car.

Slesvig (le) [lɔslɛzvig]. *Pr.n.m. Geog:* Schleswig.

slip [slip], *s.m.* **1.** *Cost:* Slip. **2.** *Nau:* Slip-way. *Av:* Launching ways (for hydroplane).

sloop [slup], *s.m. Nau:* Sloop.

sloughi [slugi], *s.m.* Saluki; gazelle-hound.

slovaque [slɔvak], *a. & s. Geog: Ling:* Slovak.

smala(h) [smala], *s.f.* (a) (Arab chief's) retinue. (b) *F:* Large family or household.

smérinthe [smerɛ̃t], *s.m. Ent:* Hawk-moth.

smilax [smilaks], *s.m. Bot:* Smilax.

smoking [smɔkiŋ], *s.m.* Dinner-jacket.

snob [snɔb], *s.m.* Vulgar follower of fashion; pretentious fellow.

snobinette [snɔbinet], *s.f. F:* Vulgar follower of fashion; pretentious young woman.

snobisme [snɔbism], *s.m.* Vulgar infatuation for anything that is 'all the rage'; vulgar desire to be in the swim.

sobre [sɔbr], *a.* **1.** Temperate, abstemious (person); moderate (meal). **2.** *S. de paroles, de louanges,* sparing of words, chary of praise. *Dessin très s.,* restrained drawing. *adv.* **-ment.**

sobriété [sɔbriete], *s.f.* **1.** Temperateness, abstemiousness, sobriety (in food and drink); moderation (in speech, etc.). **2.** Quietness (in dress).

sobriquet [sɔbrike], *s.m.* Nickname.

soc [sɔk], *s.m.* Ploughshare.

sociabilité [sɔsjabilite], *s.f.* Sociability, sociableness, companionableness.

sociable [sɔsjabl], *a.* Sociable, companionable. **Peu sociable,** unsociable. *adv.* **-ment.**

social, -aux [sɔsjal, -o], *a.* Social. (*a*) **L'ordre social,** the social order. (*b*) *Com:* **Nom social, raison sociale,** name, style, of the firm or company. **Capital social,** registered capital. *adv.* **-ement.**

socialiser [sɔsjalize], *v.tr.* To socialize (property).

socialisme [sɔsjalism], *s.m.* Socialism.

socialiste [sɔsjalist]. **1.** *a.* Socialistic; socialist (doctrine, M.P.). **2.** *s.* Socialist.

sociétaire [sɔsjetɛːr], *s.m. & f.* (*a*) (Full) member (of corporate body). (*b*) *S. d'une société anonyme,* shareholder, stockholder.

sociétariat [sɔsjetarja], *s.m.* Full membership (esp. of the Comédie-Française).

société [sɔsjete], *s.f.* Society. **1.** (*a*) Community. (*b*) Company. *Une nouvelle venue dans notre s.,* a new-comer in our circle. **2.** (*a*) Association, fellowship. **La Société des Nations,** the League of Nations. *S. de gymnastique, de tir,* athletic club, rifle-club. (*b*) *Com:* *Ind:* Company. *S. par actions,* joint-stock company. *S. en nom collectif,* firm, (general) partnership, private company. **Acte de société,** (i) deed of partnership; (ii) memorandum of association. *S.a.* ANONYME 1, COMMANDITE, MUTUEL. *Cf.* COMPAGNIE 3. **3.** (*a*) Companionship (of one's fellows). (*b*) *Fréquenter la bonne s.,* to move in good society. *Talents de s.,* social gifts. *S.a.* JEU 2.

sociologie [sɔsjɔlɔʒi], *s.f.* Sociology.

sociologique [sɔsjɔlɔʒik], *a.* Sociological.

sociologue [sɔsjɔlɔg], *s.m.* Sociologist.

socle [sɔkl], *s.m.* Base, pedestal, plinth (of statue, column); stand (for apparatus); footing (of wall). *El:* *S. isolant,* insulating base.

socque [sɔk], *s.m.* **1.** Clog, patten. **2.** *Ancient Th:* (Comedian's) sock. *Lit:* *Le socque et le cothurne,* comedy and tragedy.

socquettes [sɔkɛt], *s.f.pl.* (Ladies' tennis or golf) ankle socks.

Socrate [sɔkrat]. *Pr.n.m.* Socrates.

socratique [sɔkratik], *a.* Socratic (method).

soda [sɔda], *s.m.* Soda water.

sodium [sɔdjɔm], *s.m.* *Ch:* Sodium.

sœur [sœːr], *s.f.* **1.** Sister. *Sœur de lait,* foster-sister. *Lit:* *Les neuf Sœurs,* the nine Muses. **2.** *Ecc:* Sister (of charity); nun. *La s. Ursule,* Sister Ursula.

sofa [sɔfa], *s.m.* Sofa, settee.

soffite [sɔfit], *s.m.* *Arch:* Soffit.

soi [swa], *pers.pron.* Oneself; himself, herself, itself, etc. **1.** (Reflexive or reciprocal) *Chacun pour soi,* everyone for himself. *Article en soi inoffensif,* article inoffensive in itself. *S.a.* ALLER I. 7. *Penser à soi(-même),* to think of oneself. *Petits services qu'on se rend entre soi,* small services that we do one another. **2.** *Faire qch. soi-même,* to do sth. oneself.

soi-disant [swadizɑ̃]. **1.** *a.inv.* (*a*) Self-styled, would-be (duke, etc.). (*b*) So-called. **2.** *adv.* Supposedly, ostensibly.

soie [swa], *s.f.* **1.** Bristle (of a hog). **2.** Silk. **Soie artificielle, végétale,** rayon, artificial silk. *Robe de s.,* silk dress. *Fr:* **Boucles de soie,** silken tresses. **Papier de soie,** tissue paper. **3.** (*a*) Tang, tongue (of tool, sword). (*b*) *Mch:* Pin (of crank).

soient [swa]. See ÊTRE.

soierie [swari], *s.f.* **1.** Silk fabric or fabrics; silk goods; silks. **Marchand de soieries,** silk mercer. **2.** Silk trade.

soif [swaf], *s.f.* Thirst. **Boire à sa soif, étancher sa soif,** to drink one's fill; to slake one's thirst.

Avoir soif, to be thirsty. **Avoir (la) soif de . . .,** to thirst, be eager, for (gold, fame, revenge, etc.). *S.a.* DONNER 2, POIRE 1.

soigner [swaɲe], *v.tr.* To look after, take care of, attend to (s.o., sth.). (*a*) *S. un malade,* to nurse, tend, a patient; (of doctor) to attend a patient. *Vous avez l'air d'être très bien soigné,* you seem to be very well looked after. (*b*) *S. le ménage,* to do the housekeeping; to look after the house. *S. sa toilette, sa mise,* to dress with care. **se soigner. 1.** To take care of oneself. **2.** *P:* To do oneself well.

soigné, *a.* (*a*) Well finished, carefully done. *Repas s.,* carefully cooked meal. *Chevaux bien soignés,* well-groomed horses. **Soigné de sa personne,** well-groomed, spruce. **Peu soigné dans sa mise,** slovenly in his attire; ill-groomed. *Moustache soignée,* trim, neat, moustache. (*b*) *P:* First-rate, first-class.

soigneur [swaɲœːr], *s.m.* **1.** (Boxer's) second. **2.** *Ind:* (Machine-)minder, tenter.

soigneu|x, -euse [swaɲø, -øːz], *a.* Careful (*de,* of); painsꜱaking; tidy. **Peu soigneux,** careless; untidy. *adv.* **-sement.**

soi-même. See SOI and MÊME.

soin [swɛ̃], *s.m.* Care. (*a*) Watching over (s.o., sth.). *Le s. des enfants,* the care of the children. **Avoir, prendre, soin de qn, de qch.,** to look after, take care of, s.o., sth. *Confier qn aux soins de qn,* to place s.o. under the care of s.o. (On letters, etc.) *"Aux (bons) soins de . . .,"* 'care of. . . .' **Par les soins de . . .,** through the good offices of. . . . (*b*) Attention, trouble. **Avoir soin, grand soin, bien soin, de faire qch.,** to take (good) care to do sth. **Avoir soin que** + *sub.,* to take care that (sth. shall be done); to be careful that (something is done). **Mettre un soin infini, tous ses soins, à faire qch.,** to do sth. with great care; to be at great pains, at great trouble, to do sth. *Je vous laisse le s. de décider,* I leave it to you to decide. *Je leur laissai le soin de la distraire,* I left them to entertain her. (*c*) **Avoir beaucoup de soin,** to be very orderly, very tidy. **Avec soin,** carefully; with care. **Sans soin,** (i) *adj.* careless, untidy, slipshod; (ii) *adv.* carelessly, untidily; in a slipshod manner. **Manque de soin,** carelessness. (*d*) *pl.* Attentions, solicitude. **Soins médicaux,** medical care, medical aid. **Premiers soins aux blessés,** first aid to the injured. **Être aux petits soins pour, avec, qn,** to be full of attentions for s.o.; to wait on s.o. hand and foot.

soir [swaːr], *s.m.* (*a*) Evening. **Ce soir,** this evening, to-night. **A ce soir!** I shall see you again in the evening. *Que faites-vous le s.?* what do you do of an evening, in the evening? *A dix heures du s.,* at ten o'clock p.m., at ten o'clock at night. **Demain (au) soir,** to-morrow evening. **Hier (au) soir,** last evening. **La veille au soir,** the evening before. **Par un beau soir d'été,** on a fine summer evening. **Robe du soir,** evening-dress. **Robe de grand soir,** low evening-dress. (*b*) Afternoon.

soirée [sware], *s.f.* **1.** (Duration of) evening. *Passer la s. chez un ami,* to spend the evening at a friend's house. **2.** (*a*) (Evening) party; at-home. **Soirée dansante,** dancing-party. *Donner une s. dansante,* to give a dance. **Nous allons en soirée,** we are going to a party, to a reception. **Complet de soirée,** dress-suit. *S.a.* TENUE 3. (*b*) *Th: etc:* **Représentation de soirée,** evening performance.

sois [swa]. See ÊTRE.

soit [swa], (before a vowel) swat]. (Third pers. of *pr.sub.* of *être*) **1.** (*a*) **Soit** [swat]**!** be it so!

agreed! all right! S.a. AINSI 1, ÊTRE I. 2.
(b) Suppose; if for instance. **Soit multiplié
par six,** suppose three multiplied by six. *Soit
A B C un angle quelconque,* let ABC be any angle.
2. (a) *conj.* **Soit** *l'un* **soit** *l'autre,* either one or the
other **Soit** *maintenant* ou *demain,* whether to-day
or to-morrow. (b) **Soit qu'il vienne, soit qu'il ne
vienne pas; soit qu'il vienne ou qu'il ne vienne
pas,** whether he comes or not.

soixantaine [swasɑ̃tɛn], *s.f.* (Approximately)
sixty, about sixty. *Une s. de francs,* some sixty
francs; sixty francs or so. **Avoir passé la
soixantaine.** to be in the sixties.

soixante [swasɑ̃:t], *num.a.inv. & s.m.inv.* Sixty.
S. et un, sixty-one. *S. et onze,* seventy-one.
S. et onzième, seventy-first.

soixante-dix, *num.a.inv. & s.m.inv.* **1.** Seventy.
2. *Hist:* 1870.

soixante-dixième, *num. a. & s.* Seventieth.

soixantième [swasɑ̃tjɛm], *num. a. & s.* Sixtieth.

sol¹ [sɔl], *s.m.* **1.** (a) Ground, earth. *El: Relier
un fil au sol,* to earth a wire. *F:* **Rester cloué au
sol,** to stand rooted to the spot. *Le sol natal,*
one's native soil. (b) *Agr:* Soil. **2.** *Her:* Field.

sol², *s.m.inv. Mus:* (a) (The note) G. *Clef de sol.*
treble clef, G clef. (b) The G string (of violin).

solaire [sɔlɛ:r], *a.* Solar (eclipse, etc.). **Cadran
solaire,** sun-dial. *Med:* **Traitement solaire,**
sunlight treatment.

solanées [sɔlane], *s.f.pl. Bot:* Solanaceae.

solariser [sɔlarize], *v.tr. Phot:* To solarize.

solbatu [sɔlbaty], *a. Vet:* Bruised in the hoof.

soldat [sɔlda] *s.m.* Soldier. *S. d'artillerie,*
artilleryman. *S. de cavalerie,* cavalryman,
trooper *S. de marine,* marine. **Simple soldat.**
private *Les simples soldats,* the rank and file.
S. de première classe, lance-corporal. **Le Soldat
inconnu,** the Unknown Warrior. **Se faire soldat,**
to go into the army. *Toys:* **Soldat de plomb,** tin
soldier.

soldatesque [sɔldatɛsk]. *Pej: A:* **1.** *a.* Of the
soldiery, of the barrack-room. **2.** *s.f.* (Licentious)
soldiery

solde¹ [sɔld], *s.f. Mil:* Navy: Pay. **Soldes et
indemnités,** ordinary pay and allowances. *S. de
non-activité,* demi-solde, unemployed pay, half-
pay *Officier en demi-s.,* officer on half-pay.
F: **Être à la solde de qn,** to be in s.o.'s pay

solde², *s.m. Com:* **1.** Balance *S. débiteur,* debit
balance. *Paiement pour s.,* payment of balance,
final instalment "Pour solde," 'in settlement.'
S. de dividende, final dividend. S.a. NOUVEAU 4.
2. (a) Surplus stock, job lot, remnant. (b) **Vente
de soldes,** clearance sale. *S. d'édition,* re-
mainder(s), remainder line (in books). **"(En)
solde,"** 'to clear.' *Prix de s.,* bargain prices.

solder¹ [sɔlde], *v.tr.* To pay (soldiers, spies).

solder², *v.tr. Com:* **1.** (a) To balance (an
account). (b) To settle, discharge, pay (off) (an
account). **2.** To sell off (surplus stock). *Publ:*
To remainder (book).

sole¹ [sɔl], *s.f.* Sole (of animal's hoof). *Vet:* **Sole
battue,** bruised hoof.

sole², *s.f.* (a) *Const:* Sleeper, sill. (b) *Mec.E:*
Sole(-plate), bed-plate, base-plate (of machine).

sole³, *s.f Ich:* Sole.

solécisme [sɔlesism], *s.m.* Solecism.

soleil [sɔlɛ:i], *s.m.* **1.** Sun (a) **Lever du soleil,**
sunrise **Coucher du soleil,** sunset, sundown.
Soleil levant, (i) rising sun, (ii) *F:* rising power.
Soleil couchant, (i) setting sun, (ii) *F:* declining
power. **Il n'y a rien de nouveau sous le soleil,**
there is nothing new under the sun. (b) **Faux
soleil,** parhelion, mock-sun. **2.** Sunshine. **Il fait

du soleil, the sun is shining; it is sunny. **Au
grand soleil,** in the bright sunshine, full in the
sun. **Avoir sa place au soleil,** to have one's place
in the sun. **Avoir du bien au soleil,** to have
landed property. **Prendre le soleil,** to bask in
the sun, to sun oneself. **Bains de soleil,** sun-
bathing. **Sans soleil,** sunless. **Coup de soleil,**
(i) *Med:* sunburn; (ii) *Med:* touch of sunstroke;
(iii) sunny interval; (iv) *F:* sudden blush or
flush (of confusion). *P:* **Piquer un soleil,** to
blush, to flush up. **3.** *Bot:* Sunflower. **4.** *Ecc:*
Monstrance. **5.** *Gym:* **Faire le grand soleil,** to
do the grand circle on the horizontal bar.
6. *Pyr:* Catherine-wheel.

solennel, -elle [sɔlanɛl], *a.* Solemn. **1.** (a) *Contrat s.,* solemn agreement. (b) Official. *Réception
solennelle,* state reception. **2.** *Parler d'un ton s.,*
to speak in a solemn, grave, tone.

solennellement [sɔlanɛlmɑ̃], *adv.* **1.** With
ceremony. **2.** Impressively, solemnly.

solennisation [sɔlanizasjɔ̃], *s.f.* Solemnization.

solenniser [sɔlanize], *v.tr.* To solemnize; to
celebrate.

solennité [sɔlanite], *s.f.* **1.** (a) Solemnity;
awfulness. (b) Solemn ceremony. **2.** *Parler avec
solennité,* to speak impressively, solemnly.

solénoïde [sɔlenɔid], *s.m. El:* Solenoid; coil-
winding.

solfatare [sɔlfata:r], *s.f.* Solfatara, sulphur-
spring.

solfège [sɔlfɛ:ʒ], *s.m. Mus:* Solfeggio; sol-fa.

solfier [sɔlfje], *v.tr. Mus:* To sol-fa, to solmizate.

solidage [sɔlida:ʒ], *s.f. Bot:* Solidago; golden-
rod.

solidaire [sɔlidɛ:r], *a.* **1.** *Jur:* Jointly responsible. **Responsabilité (conjointe et) solidaire,**
joint and several liability. *Être s. des actes de qn,*
to be responsible for s.o.'s acts. *Il n'est s. de
personne,* he is answerable to no one. **Obligation
solidaire,** obligation binding on all parties.
2. Interdependent, solidary. *Ses intérêts sont
solidaires des nôtres,* his interests are bound up with
ours. *Tchn:* **Roue s. d'une autre,** wheel rigidly
locked with another; wheel integral, solid, with
another.

solidairement [sɔlidɛrmɑ̃], *adv.* Jointly. *Jur:*
Conjointement et solidairement, jointly and
severally.

solidariser [sɔlidarize], *v.tr.* **1.** To render
jointly responsible. **2.** *Mécanisme à action
solidarisée,* interlocking gear.
　se solidariser. **1.** To join together in
liability. **2.** To make common cause (*avec,* with).

solidarité [sɔlidarite], *s.f.* **1.** Joint and several
liability; joint responsibility. **2.** (a) Inter-
dependence (of parts). (b) Fellowship, solidarity.
Grève de solidarité, sympathetic strike.

solide [sɔlid]. **1.** *a.* (a) Solid (body, food).
Geom: **Angle solide,** solid angle. (b) Solid,
strong; secure (foundation); sound (argument);
fast (colour). *Com:* Sound, solvent (person);
well-established (business). **Peu solide,** weak;
flimsy. *Un coup de poing s.,* a vigorous, hefty,
blow. **Garantie solide,** reliable, trustworthy,
guarantee. *Ami s.,* staunch, reliable, trusty,
friend. *Faire un repas s.,* to make a hearty meal.
Un gaillard s., un s. gaillard, a strapping, hefty,
fellow. **Être encore solide,** to be still hale and
hearty. **2.** *s.m.* (a) Solid (body). (b) **Bâtir sur le
solide,** to build on solid foundations. *adv.* **-ment.**

solidification [sɔlidifikasjɔ̃], *s.f.* Solidification.

solidifier [sɔlidifje], *v.tr.* To solidify.
　se solidifier, to solidify; to become solid.

solidité [sɔlidite], *s.f.* Solidity; strength (of

building, etc.); soundness (of a firm); strength, stability (of friendship).
soliloque [sɔlilɔk], *s.m.* Soliloquy.
soliste [sɔlist], *s.m. & f.* Soloist. *a. Violon s.*, solo violin.
solitaire [sɔlitɛːr]. **1.** *a.* Solitary, lonely, lonesome. S.a. VER I. **2.** *s.m.* (*a*) Hermit, recluse. (*b*) Solitaire (game). (*c*) Solitaire (diamond). *adv.* **-ment.**
solitude [sɔlityd], *s.f.* **1.** Solitude, loneliness. **2.** Lonely spot; wilderness; solitude.
solive [sɔliːv], *s.f. Const:* Joist, beam, balk, rafter. *F:* **Roi Solive** = *roi Soliveau.*
soliveau [sɔlivo], *s.m.* (*a*) Small joist; small girder. (*b*) *F:* **Un roi Soliveau,** a King Log; a nonentity.
sollicitation [sɔllisitasjɔ̃], *s.f.* **1.** Solicitation, entreaty, earnest request. **2.** Attraction, pull (of magnet).
solliciter [sɔllisite], *v.tr.* **1.** *A:* S. qn à faire qch., to incite s.o. to do sth. *S. son cheval,* to urge one's horse. **2.** To solicit (s.o., sth.); to request earnestly, beg for (favour, interview). *S. un emploi (de qn),* to apply (to s.o.) for a situation. *S. des voix,* to canvass for votes. **3.** (Of magnet) To attract; (of spring) to pull.
solliciteur, -euse [sɔllisitœːr, -øːz], *s.* Petitioner; solicitant; applicant (*de,* for). *S. de voix,* canvasser.
sollicitude [sɔllisityd], *s.f.* (*a*) Solicitude, (tender) care. (*b*) Anxiety, concern (*pour,* for).
solmisation [sɔlmizasjɔ̃], *s.f.* Solmization, sol-fa.
solo [sɔlo]. **1.** *s.m. Mus:* Solo. **Jouer en solo,** to play solo. *pl. Des solos, des soli.* **2.** *a.inv.* Violon solo, solo violin.
solstice [sɔlstis], *s.m.* Solstice.
solubiliser [sɔlybilize], *v.tr.* To render soluble.
solubilité [sɔlybilite], *s.f.* **1.** Solubility (of a body). **2.** Solvability (of a problem).
soluble [sɔlybl], *a.* **1.** Soluble (substance). **2.** Solvable (problem).
solution [sɔlysjɔ̃], *s.f.* **1.** Solution de continuité, gap; solution of continuity; break (in glacier). **2.** Solution (of solid in liquid). **3.** Solution; answer (to question, problem); settlement (of dispute). **4.** *Med:* Termination, solution (of disease). *S. fatale,* fatal termination.
solutionner [sɔlysjɔne], *v.tr.* To solve (difficulty).
solvabilité [sɔlvabilite], *s.f.* Solvency.
solvable [sɔlvabl], *a.* Solvent (financially).
Somalie [sɔmali]. *Pr.n.f. Geog:* Somaliland.
sombre [sɔ̃ːbr], *a.* Dark, sombre, gloomy. (*a*) *inv.* **Des robes bleu sombre,** dark blue dresses. (*b*) Dim (forest, room, etc.); dull, overcast (sky). S.a. COUPE² I. **Il fait sombre,** it is dark, dull, weather. (*c*) Dismal, melancholy; saturnine (temperament); black (despair). *s.* **Avoir du sombre dans l'âme,** (i) to feel gloomy; (ii) to be of a saturnine disposition. *adv.* **-ment.**
sombrer [sɔ̃bre], *v.i.* (Of ship) To founder (in bad weather); to go down; to sink. *Il vit s. sa fortune,* he saw his fortune engulfed. *Sa raison sombra complètement,* his mind entirely gave way.
sommaire [sɔmmɛːr]. **1.** *a.* (*a*) Summary, compendious, succinct, concise. *Tenue s.,* scant attire. (*b*) Summary, hasty, improvised. *Dîner s.,* scratch dinner. (*c*) *Jur:* **Affaire sommaire,** summary proceedings. **2.** *s.m.* Summary, abstract, synopsis. *adv.* **-ment.**
sommation¹ [sɔmasjɔ̃], *s.f. Jur:* Summons (*de faire qch.,* to do sth.); notice (to perform contract). **Faire les trois sommations légales,** to read the riot act.

sommation², *s.f. Mth:* Summation (of a series).
somme¹ [sɔm], *s.f.* (*a*) *A:* Pack-saddle. (*b*) **Bête de somme,** beast of burden. *Mulet de s.,* pack-mule.
somme², *s.f.* Sum, amount; sum of money. *Payer la forte s.,* to pay top price. **Faire la somme de dix nombres,** to add up, sum up, ten numbers. **Tout fait somme,** everything counts. **Somme toute . . .,** upon the whole . . ., when all is said and done. . . . **En somme . . .,** in short. . . .
somme³, *s.m.* Nap; short sleep; *F:* snooze. **Faire un somme,** to take a nap. **Ne faire qu'un somme, dormir d'un somme,** to sleep without a break; to sleep the night through.
sommeil [sɔmɛːj], *s.m.* **1.** Sleep, slumber. **Sommeil de mort, de plomb,** heavy sleep. *Dormir d'un s. de plomb,* to sleep like a log. **Avoir le sommeil léger, profond,** to be a light, a heavy, sleeper. **Avoir le sommeil dur,** to be hard to wake. **Nuit sans sommeil,** sleepless night. **Dormir du sommeil des justes,** to sleep the sleep of the just. **2.** Drowsiness, sleepiness. **Avoir sommeil,** to be sleepy, to feel drowsy. **Je tombe de sommeil,** I am dying with sleep; I am ready to drop with sleep. *Med:* **Maladie du sommeil,** sleeping sickness.
sommeiller [sɔmeje], *v.i.* **1.** To doze, nod; to sleep lightly; to slumber. **2.** (Of nature, etc.) To lie dormant.
sommelier [sɔmǝlje], *s.m.* **1.** (Wine-)butler. **2.** (*a*) Cellarman. (*b*) (In restaurant) Wine-waiter.
sommer¹ [sɔme], *v.tr. Mth:* To sum up; to find the sum of (terms of a series).
sommer², *v.tr.* To summon. *S. qn de faire qch.,* to call on s.o. to do sth.
sommes [sɔm]. See ÊTRE.
sommet [sɔme], *s.m.* Top, summit (of hill); vertex, apex (of angle, curve); crest (of wave); crown (of arch, of the head); *F:* zenith, pinnacle, acme (of power, fame).
sommier [sɔmje], *s.m.* **1.** Pack-animal; pack-horse. **2.** (*a*) *S. élastique* (i) spring-mattress, (ii) box-mattress. (*b*) Wind-chest (of organ). (*c*) Springer (of arch); transom, lintel, breast-summer (of door, etc.); stringer (of bridge); beam (of balance); stock (of heavy bell); bed (of machine). (*d*) *Rail: Veh:* Bolster.
sommier-divan, *s.m.* Divan-bed. *pl. Des sommiers-divans.*
sommité [sɔmmite], *s.f.* Summit, top (of mountain). *F:* **Sommités de l'art,** leading people, persons of influence, in the world of art.
somnambule [sɔmnãbyl]. **1.** *a.* (*a*) Somnambulistic. (*b*) Clairvoyant. **2.** *s.* (*a*) Somnambulist, sleep-walker. *Il est s.,* he walks in his sleep. (*b*) *s.f* Somnambule lucide, clairvoyante.
somnambulisme [sɔmnãbylism], *s.m.* **1.** Somnambulism, sleep-walking. **2.** Somnambulisme provoqué, hypnotic state.
somnifère [sɔmnifɛːr]. **1.** *a.* Sleep-inducing. **2.** *a. & s.m. Med:* Soporific, narcotic.
somnolence [sɔmnɔlãːs], *s.f.* Somnolence, sleepiness, drowsiness.
somnolent [sɔmnɔlã], *a.* Somnolent, sleepy, drowsy.
somnoler [sɔmnɔle], *v.i.* To drowse, doze.
somnose [sɔmnoːz], *s.f.* **1.** Hypnotic sleep. **2.** *Med:* Sleeping-sickness.
somptuaire [sɔ̃ptɥɛːr], *a.* Sumptuary (law).
somptueux, -euse [sɔ̃ptɥø -øːz], *a.* Sumptuous; *F:* gorgeous. *adv.* **-sement.**
somptuosité [sɔ̃ptɥozite], *s.f.* Sumptuousness.

son¹, **sa, ses** [sɔ̃ sa, sɛ], *poss.a* *Son* is used instead of *sa* before fem. nouns beginning with a vowe or h 'mute.') His, her, its, one's, *Son père*, *sa mere, et ses enfants.* (i) his father, mother, and children, (ii) her father, mother, and children. *Tirer son épée* to draw one's sword. *On ne connaît jamais son bonheur*, one never knows one's own happiness. *Un de ses amis*, a friend of his, of hers. *Ses père et mère*, his father and mother. *Son meilleur ami.* his best friend.

son², *s.m.* Sound. *Son d'une cloche*, sound, ringing, tinkle, of a bell; clang (of a big bell). *Annoncer une nouvelle à son de trompe*, de trompette, to blaɪe out a piece of news.

son³, *s.m.* Bran. *Eau de son*, bran-water. *F:* *Tache de son*, freckle. *Taché de son*, freckled.

sonate [sɔnat], *s.f. Mus:* Sonata.

sonatine [sɔnatin], *s.f. Mus:* Sonatina.

sondage [sɔ̃da:ʒ], *s.m.* **1.** (a) *Nau:* Sounding. *Min:* Boring. **Faire des sondages,** (i) to take soundings; (ii) to make borings. (b) *Med:* Probing (of wound). **2.** Bore-hole.

sonde [sɔ̃:d], *s.f.* **1.** *Nau:* (a) (Sounding-)lead, sounding-line, plummet. **Petite sonde,** hand-lead. **Grande sonde,** deep-sea lead. **Jeter la sonde,** to heave the lead. **Être sur la sonde** to be in soundings. (b) *Sondes d'une carte,* soundings marked on a chart. (c) (Of whale) **Faire la sonde,** to sound. **2.** (a) Sounding-rod. (b) *Surg:* Sound, probe (c) *Meteor.* *S. aérienne,* sounding-balloon. **3.** Taster (for cheese, etc.). **4.** *Min:* Borer, boring-machine. **Trou de sonde,** bore-hole.

sonder [sɔ̃de], *v.tr.* **1.** (a) *Nau:* To sound. *S. la côte,* to take soundings along the coast. *F:* On n'a jamais sondé ce mystère, this mystery has never been fathomed. (b) *v.i.* (Of whale) To sound. **2.** To sound, probe, examine, investigate. *S. un bois,* to explore a wood. *S. le passé,* to probe into the past. **Sonder le terrain,** (i) to make borings in the ground; (ii) *F:* to see how the land lies. *F:* Sonder qn, to sound s.o. (with regard to sth.). **3.** *Surg:* To probe (wound).

sondeur, -euse [sɔ̃dœ:r, -ø:z]. **1.** *s.m.* (a) *Nau:* Leadsman. (b) *Min:* Borer, driller (for wells, etc.). **2.** *s.* *F:* Sondeur de secrets, prober of secrets. **3.** *s.m.* *Nau:* Sounder, sounding-apparatus; depth-finder. **4.** *s.f.* *Min: etc:* Sondeuse, borer; drilling-machine.

songe [sɔ̃:ʒ], *s.m.* Dream. **Faire un songe,** to dream; to have a dream. **Clef des songes,** dream-book.

songe-creux, *s.m.inv.* Dreamer, visionary.

songer [sɔ̃ʒe], *v.i.* (je songeai(s); n. songeons) **1.** (a) To dream (de, of). (b) To muse (à, upon); to day-dream. *Je ne songeais guère que* . . ., little did I dream that. . . . *Je songeais en moi-même que* . . ., I thought to myself that. . . . *S.a.* CREUX I. **2.** (a) **Songer à qch.,** to think of sth.; to consider, think over, think of, sth. *Il ne faut pas y s.,* that's quite out of the question. **Sans songer à mal,** without evil intent. *S. à faire qch.,* to contemplate doing sth.; to think of doing sth. **Je n'étais pas sans songer à l'avenir,** I was not without thought of the future. (b) To imagine. *Songez donc!* just fancy! (c) To remember. *Songez à lui,* bear him in mind. *Je ne songeais pas que j'étais déjà pris.* I had forgotten that I already had an appointment.

songerie [sɔ̃ʒri], *s.f.* **1.** (Day-)dreaming, idle musing. **2.** Reverie; brown study. (b) *pl.* Day-dreams.

songeur, -euse [sɔ̃ʒœ:r, -ø:z]. **1.** *s.* *A.* & *B:* Dreamer. **2.** *a.* (a) Dreamy. (b) Pensive, thoughtful. **D'un air songeur,** musingly.

sonnaille [sɔna:j], *s.f.* Cattle-bell. [SONNER]

sonnailler [sɔnaje], *s.m.* Husb: Bell-wether.

sonnant [sɔnɑ̃], *a.* **1.** Horloge sonnante striking clock. **A dix heures sonnant(es),** on the stroke of ten. **2.** Sounding, resounding. **Monnaie sonnante,** hard cash.

sonner [sɔne]. **I.** *v.i.* To sound; (of clock) to strike; (of bell) to ring, to toll. *S. creux,* to sound hollow. *S. faux,* to ring false. *Cela sonne bien,* it sounds well. *Mot qui sonne mal,* word that offends the ear. **Faire s. une pièce d'argent,** to ring a coin (in order to test it). *Faire s. ses clefs,* to jingle one's keys. *Six heures sonnèrent,* the clock struck six. **2.** *v.tr.* (a) *S. la cloche,* to ring the bell. *Abs. On sonne,* the bell is ringing, there is a ring at the door. *Horloge qui sonne les heures,* clock that strikes the hours. *F:* **Ne pas sonner mot,** not to utter a word. *S. pour les morts,* to toll for the dead. *S. le dîner,* to ring the dinner-bell. *S. du clairon,* to sound the bugle. *Av: P:* **Être sonné,** to come under shell fire. (b) To ring for (s.o.). *S. qn au téléphone,* to ring s.o. up.

sonné, *a.* *Il est dix heures sonnées,* it is past ten. *F:* *Elle a quarante ans sonnés,* she is on the wrong side of forty.

sonnerie [sɔnri], *s.f.* **1.** (a) Ringing (of bells). (b) Set of bells; chimes. **2.** (a) Striking mechanism (of clock). **Pendule à sonnerie,** striking clock. **Montre à sonnerie,** repeater. (b) *S. électrique,* electric bell. *S. ronflante,* buzzer. **Bouton de sonnerie,** bell-push. **3.** *Mil:* (Trumpet-, bugle-) call. *S. aux morts,* last post.

sonnet [sɔnɛ], *s.m.* Sonnet.

sonnette [sɔnɛt], *s.f.* **1.** (a) Small bell. (b) Hand-bell. (c) House-bell. **Agiter la sonnette,** to ring the bell. **Cordon de sonnette,** bell-pull. **Coup de sonnette,** ring (at the door). **2.** Pile-driving apparatus; pile-driver. **3.** Serpent à sonnettes, rattlesnake. [SONNER]

sonnettiste [sɔnɛtist], *s. m. & f.* Sonnet-writer.

sonneur [sɔnœ:r], *s.m.* **1.** (a) Bell-ringer. (b) Sonneur de trompette, de clairon, trumpeter, bugler. **2.** *Tg:* Sounder (device).

sonore [sɔnɔ:r], *a.* Sonorous. **1.** Loud-sounding; resonant (metal); loud, resounding (laugh); echoing (vault). *Ph:* **Onde sonore,** sound-wave; acoustic wave. **Mettre une scène à l'écran sonore,** to turn a scene into a sound-film. *S.a.* PISTE I. **2.** (a) Deep-toned, ringing (voice). (b) *Ling:* Sonant, voiced (consonant).

sonoriser [sɔnɔrize], *v.tr.* *Cin:* **Sonoriser un film,** to add the sound effects to a film.

sonorité [sɔnɔrite], *s.f.* Sonorousness, sonority.

sont [sɔ̃]. See ÊTRE.

Sophie [sɔfi]. *Pr.n.f.* Sophia, Sophy. *F:* (Of girl) **Faire sa Sophie,** (i) to affect prudishness; (ii) to put on airs.

sophisme [sɔfism], *s.m.* Sophism. *Log:* Fallacy.

sophiste [sɔfist], *s.m.* Sophist.

sophisterie [sɔfistəri], *s.f.* Sophistry.

sophistication [sɔfistikasjɔ̃], *s.f.* Sophistication, adulteration (of wine, etc.).

sophistique [sɔfistik]. **1.** *a.* Sophistic(al). **2.** *s.f.* Sophistry. *adv.* **-ment,** -ally.

sophistiquer [sɔfistike]. **1.** *v.i.* To indulge in sophistry; to quibble. **2.** *v.tr.* To sophisticate, adulterate (wine, etc.).

soporatif, -ive [sɔpɔratif, -i:v]. **1.** *a.* Sleep-inducing, soporific. **2.** *s.m.* Soporific.

soporifique [sɔpɔrifik]. **1.** = SOPORATIF. **Potion soporifique,** sleeping-draught. **2.** *a.* *F:* Tedious (story).

sopraniste [sɔpranist], *s.m.* Sopranist; male soprano singer.

soprano [sɔprano], *s. m. & f.* Soprano.

sorbe [sɔrb], *s.f.* Sorb-apple, service-apple.

sorbet [sɔrbɛ], *s.m.* Sorbet; water-ice.

sorbétière [sɔrbetjɛːr], *s.f.* Ice-pail; freezer.

sorbier [sɔrbje], *s.m. Bot:* Sorb, service-tree. *S. des oiseaux,* rowan(-tree), mountain-ash.

Sorbonne [sɔrbɔn]. **1.** *Pr.n.f.* The Sorbonne (seat of the University in Paris). *Étudier à la S., en S.,* to study at the Sorbonne. **2.** *s.f. Ch:* Fume-cupboard.

sorcellerie [sɔrsɛlri], *s.f.* Witchcraft, sorcery.

sorcier, -ière [sɔrsje, -jɛːr], *s.* Sorcerer, *f.* sorceress; wizard, *f.* witch. *F:* **Vieille sorcière,** old hag; beldam(e). *a.* **Ce n'est pas bien sorcier,** there is no wizardry in that.

sordide [sɔrdid], *a.* Sordid, squalid. **1.** Filthy, dirty. **2.** Mean, base. *adv.* **-ment.**

sordidité [sɔrdidite], *s.f.* Sordidness.

sore [sɔːr], *s.m. Bot:* Sorus.

sorg(h)o [sɔrgo], *s.m. Bot:* Sorghum; Indian millet.

sorite [sɔrit], *s.m. Log:* Sorites.

Sorlingues (les) [lesɔrlɛ̃g]. *Pr.n.f.pl.* The Scilly Islands.

sornettes [sɔrnɛt], *s.f.pl.* Nonsense; idle talk. *Conter des sornettes à qn,* to humbug s.o.

sor-s, -t[1] [sɔːr]. See SORTIR.

sort[2] [sɔːr], *s.m.* **1.** Lot (in life). *Assurer le s. de ses enfants,* faire un sort à ses enfants, to provide for one's children. **2.** Destiny, fate. *Abandonner qn à son s.,* to leave s.o. to his fate. **Coup du sort,** stroke of fate. **3.** Chance, fortune, lot. **Tirer au sort,** to draw lots. **Tirage au sort,** drawing of lots; balloting; *Adm:* drawing (of lots) for conscription. **Le sort en est jeté,** the die is cast. **4.** Spell, charm. **Jeter un sort sur qn,** to cast a spell on, over, s.o.

sortable [sɔrtabl], *a.* Suitable (match, employment); eligible (young man).

sortant, -ante [sɔrtã, -ãːt], *a.* Coming out. *Numéro s.,* winning number (in lottery). *Membres (de comité) sortants,* retiring, outgoing, members. *Foule sortante,* outgoing crowd.

sorte [sɔrt], *s.f.* **1.** Manner, way. **Ne parlez pas de la sorte,** don't talk like that, in that strain. **En quelque sorte,** as it were, in a way, in a manner. *Conj.phr. Il est sorti sans pardessus,* de sorte qu'*il a attrapé un rhume,* he went out without his overcoat, so that he caught cold. *Parlez de (telle) sorte qu'on vous comprenne,* speak so as to be understood, so that you are understood. **En sorte que** + *sub.,* so that, in such a manner that. *Faites en s. que tout soit prêt à temps,* see to it that everything is ready in time. **2.** Sort, kind. *Toute(s) sorte(s) de choses,* des choses de toute(s) sorte(s), all sorts, kinds, of things. **Un homme de la sorte,** a man of that sort, of that kind. **Un homme de votre sorte,** a man like you, of your stamp. **Il n'est sorte de soins qu'il n'ait pris,** he spared no pains. **Je n'ai rien dit, rien fait, de la sorte,** I said, did, no such thing, nothing of the kind. *J'ai une s. d'impression qu'il viendra, F:* I sort of feel that he will come. **3.** *Typ:* Sort. *S. surabondante,* superfluous sort. *S. manquante,* missing sort, short sort.

sortilège [sɔrtilɛːʒ], *s.m.* Spell, charm.

sortir [sɔrtiːr], *v.* (*pr.p.* sortant; *p.p.* sorti; *pr.ind.* je sors, il sort, n. sortons; *pr.sub.* je sorte; *p.h.* je sortis; *fu.* je sortirai) I. *v.i.* **1.** (*a*) To go or come out; to leave the room or the house. *S. de la salle,* to go, walk, stalk, stride, out of the room. **Faire sortir qn,** (i) to take (child) out (for a walk); (ii) to order s.o. out of the room, out of the house. *Ne le laissez pas s.,* don't let him out. **Sortir de son lit,** (i) to leave one's bed; (ii) (of river) to overflow its banks. *Th:* Macbeth sort, exit Macbeth. *F:* **D'où sortez-vous?** where have you been all this time? (Of ship) *S. du port,* to leave harbour. *Source qui sort de la terre,* spring that gushes, issues, from the earth. *S. d'un emploi,* to leave a situation. *Cela m'est sorti de l'esprit,* it has dropped out of my mind. **Faire sortir la garde,** to turn out the guard. *Fin:* (Of bonds) **Sortir en tirage,** to be drawn. (*b*) (Of horseman) To ride out; (of driver or vehicle) to drive out; (of captain or ship) to sail out. (*c*) *S. en courant,* to run out. *S. précipitamment, se hâter de s.,* to hurry out. *S. furtivement,* to steal out. *Parvenir à s.,* to (manage to) get out. (*d*) (Of flowers, corn, etc.) To come up, spring up. *Il lui est sorti une dent,* he has cut a tooth. (*e*) To have just come out. *Je sors de table,* I have just risen from table. *S. du collège,* to have just left school. *Il sort d'ici,* he has just left. (*f*) *A. & F: Je sors de le voir,* I have just seen him. (*g*) *S. de son sujet,* to depart, wander, from one's subject. *S. de la question,* to wander from the point. (Of train) **Sortir des rails,** to jump the metals. *S.a.* GOND. **2.** To go out, go from home. *Madame est sortie; elle est sortie à trois heures,* Mrs X is out; she went out at three o'clock. *S. à cheval, à pied,* to go out riding, walking. *Elle sort beaucoup,* she is out a great deal. **3.** To get out; extricate oneself (from a difficulty, danger). *Aider qn à s. d'une difficulté,* to help s.o. out. *Il sortit vainqueur,* he came off victorious. **4.** To spring, issue, descend (from a good family, etc.). *Sorti du peuple,* sprung from the people. *Cheval sorti d'un bon haras,* horse that comes from a good stud. *Officier sorti des rangs,* officer who has risen from the ranks. **5.** (*a*) To stand out, stick out, protrude, project. *Yeux qui sortent de la tête,* protruding eyes. *Un navire sortit du brouillard,* a ship loomed out of the fog. (*b*) (Of figure in picture, of thought) To stand out, to be prominent.

II. sortir, *v.tr.* To take out, bring out, pull out. *Sortez-nous quelques chaises,* bring us out a few chairs. *S. les mains de ses poches,* to take one's hands out of one's pockets. *Il sortit son carnet de chèques,* he pulled out his cheque book. *S. un revolver,* to whip out a revolver. *S. la tête à la portière,* to put one's head out of the carriage window. *Typ:* **Sortir une ligne,** to run out a line (into the margin).

III. sortir, *s.m.* **Au sortir du théâtre, de l'école,** on coming out of the theatre, out of school. **Au s. de l'hiver,** at the end of winter. **Au s. de l'enfance,** on emerging from childhood.

sortie, *s.f.* **1.** (*a*) Going out, coming out, departure, exit. *A toutes mes sorties,* every time I go out. *A la s. des ateliers,* when the men leave work. **A ma sortie de classe,** on coming out of school. *F:* **Se ménager une porte de sortie,** to arrange a way out (of the difficulty) for oneself; to arrange a bolt-hole. *Th:* **Fausse sortie,** sham exit (from stage); 'offers to go.' *S.a.* BILLET 6. (*b*) Leaving (for good). **A ma sortie d'école,** on (my) leaving school. *A la s. de l'hiver,* when winter is over. (*c*) Flowing out (of liquid, etc.). *Com:* **Sorties de fonds,** expenses, outgoings. (*d*) *Com:* Exportation (of goods). **Droit de sortie,** export duty. **2.** Trip, excursion. **Jour de sortie,** day out; holiday. **3.** (*a*) *Mil:* Sally, sortie. *Fb:* Run out (by goal-keeper). (*b*) *F:* Outburst, tirade. **Faire une sortie à,** contre, to launch out at, pitch into, s.o.; to lash out at

s.o. 4. Exit; way out. *S. de secours*, emergency exit. **Par ici la sortie**, this way out. **5.** *Cost:* **Sortie de bal, de théâtre**, evening wrap, opera-cloak. **6.** *Ecc:* Concluding voluntary, outgoing voluntary.

sosie [sɔzi], *s.m.* *F:* (S.o.'s) double, counterpart.

so|t, sotte [so, sɔt]. **I.** *a.* (*a*) Silly, stupid, foolish. (*b*) Embarrassed, disconcerted. **Rester tout sot**, to look sheepish; to feel foolish. **2.** *s.* Fool, dolt, blockhead. **C'est un sot en trois lettres**, he's a downright fool. *Une petite sotte*, a little ninny, a little goose. *adv.* **-ttement.**

sottise [sɔtiːz], *s.f.* **I.** Stupidity, silliness, folly, foolishness. **2.** (*a*) Foolish act or word. *Faire, dire, des sottises*, to do, say, silly things. (*b*) Offensive remark; insult. *Dire des sottises à qn*, to abuse, slang, s.o.

sou [su], *s.m.* (In familiar, but no longer official use) Sou (= five centimes). *F:* **Pièce de cent sous**, five-franc piece. **Gros sou**, penny(-piece). *Une question de gros sous*, a question of £ s. d. **Le sou du franc**, the market penny. **Prendre garde à un sou**, to look twice at every penny. **N'avoir pas le sou, être sans le sou**, to be penniless, destitute. *Prov:* **Un sou amène l'autre**, money makes money. **Affaire de quatre sous**, twopenny-halfpenny business. **Je m'en moque comme de quatre sous**, I don't care a tuppenny damn. **Pas ambitieux pour deux sous, pour un sou**, not in the least ambitious. **Il n'a pas pour deux sous de courage**, he hasn't a ha'p'orth of pluck. **Journaliste à deux sous la ligne**, penny-a-liner.

soubassement [subɑsmɑ̃], *s.m.* **I.** (*a*) *Arch:* Sub-foundation, base; stylobate (of colonnade). *F:* **Le s. social**, the social substructure. (*b*) Base (-plate) (of machine-tool). (*c*) *Geol:* Bed-rock. **2.** (Bed-)valance.

soubresaut [subrəso], *s.m.* (*a*) Sudden start; bound, leap (of horse, etc.); jolt (of vehicle). (*b*) Sudden emotion, catch of the breath; gasp. (*c*) *pl.* Trembling, convulsive movements (of the limbs).

soubresauter [subrəsote], *v.i.* To leap, start, bound; (of vehicle) to jolt.

soubrette [subrɛt], *s.f.* *Th:* Soubrette, waiting-maid.

souche [suʃ], *s.f.* **I.** (*a*) Stump, stub, stock (of tree). *S. d'enclume*, anvil-block. *F:* **Rester (là) comme une souche**, to stand like a log. (*b*) *F:* Blockhead, dolt. **2.** Head, founder (of family). **Faire souche**, to found a family. **Chien de bonne souche**, pedigree dog. *Famille de vieille s.*, an old family. **3.** *Com:* Counterfoil, *U.S:* stub (of cheque, etc.). **Carnet, livret, à souche**, counterfoil book. **4.** Shaft, stack (of chimney).

souchet¹ [suʃɛ], *s.m.* **I.** *Bot:* (*a*) Cyperus, galingale. (*b*) *S. d'Amérique*, rattan(-cane). **2.** *Orn:* Spoonbill duck; shoveller.

souchet², s.m. Ragstone (of quarry).

souci¹ [susi], *s.m.* *Bot:* Marigold. *S. d'eau*, marsh-marigold.

souci², s.m. Care. **I.** Solicitude. *S. de la vérité*, regard for truth. **Prendre souci de qch.**, to have a care for sth. **2.** Anxiety, worry. **C'est le moindre de mes soucis**, that's the least of my worries. *Les noirs soucis*, black care. *Soucis d'argent*, money troubles, money worries. *Donner bien des soucis à qn*, to cause s.o. great anxiety. **Être en souci de qch.**, to worry about sth. **Sans souci, libre de soucis**, care-free.

soucier [susje], *v.tr. & i.* (Of thg) *S. qn, à qn*, to trouble, disturb, s.o.

se soucier, to trouble oneself, concern oneself

(*de*, about); to care (*de*, for); to mind. *Ne se s. de rien*, to care for nothing. *Il ne se souciait pas de cela*, he didn't bother his head about that. *F:* *Je m'en soucie comme de l'an quarante*, I don't care a hang, a button, a fig, a rap.

soucieu|x, -euse [susjø, -øːz], *a.* (*a*) Anxious, concerned (*de*, about). *Être s. de faire qch.*, to be anxious to do sth. *Être s. de ses propres intérêts*, to have a care for one's own interest. **Peu soucieux du lendemain**, careless of the morrow. (*b*) Full of care; worried. *adv.* **-sement.**

soucoupe [sukup], *s.f.* Saucer.

soudain [sudɛ̃]. **I.** *a.* Sudden, unexpected. **2.** *adv.* Suddenly; all of a sudden. *adv.* **-ement.**

soudaineté [sudɛnte], *s.f.* Suddenness.

soudant [sudɑ̃], *a.* *Metalw:* Welding, brazing. **Blanc soudant**, welding heat.

soudard [sudaːr], *s.m.* Usu. *Pej:* (Hardened) old soldier, old trooper.

soude [sud], *s.f.* **I.** *Bot:* Salt-wort; (prickly) glass-wort. **2.** Soda. **Carbonate de soude**, *F:* **cristaux de soude**, washing soda, common soda. **Bicarbonate de soude**, bicarbonate of soda, *F:* baking soda. *S. caustique*, caustic soda.

soud|er [sude], *v.tr.* (*a*) To solder. (*b*) To weld, braze. *S. à l'autogène*, to weld. *S. à l'étain*, to sweat, to soft-solder. **Lampe à souder**, blow-lamp. **Eau à-souder**, killed spirits. S.a. FER 3. *s.m.* **-age.** *s.m.* **-eur.**

se souder. **I.** To join together; to weld, to fuse together. **2.** (*a*) (Of bone) To knit. (*b*) (Of joints) To become anchylosed.

soudoir [sudwaːr], *s.m.* *Tls:* Soldering-iron; copper bit.

soudoyer [sudwaje], *v.tr.* (**je soudoie; je soudoierai**) (*a*) To hire (assassin, etc.). (*b*) *F:* To bribe.

soudure [sudyːr], *s.f.* **I.** (*a*) Soldering. (*b*) Welding, brazing. *S. autogène, à l'autogène*, oxy-acetylene welding. **2.** (*a*) Soldered joint. *S. à nœud*, wipe(d) joint. (*b*) (Welded, brazed) seam; weld. **Sans soudure(s)**, seamless. (*c*) Union, join (of bones, etc.). **3.** Solder.

soue [su], *s.f.* Pigsty.

soufflage [suflaːʒ], *s.m.* **I.** Glass-blowing. **2.** Blowing, blow, blast (of furnace). *El.E:* *S. d'étincelles*, blow-out.

souffle [sufl], *s.m.* Breath. **I.** (*a*) Puff, blast (of air, wind). (*b*) Blast (of exploding shell); muzzle-blast (of gun). (*c*) *Av:* Wash (of propeller). (*d*) **Le souffle poétique**, the divine afflatus. (Of poet) **Manquer de souffle**, to lack inspiration. **2.** Respiration, breathing. **Retenir son souffle**, to hold one's breath. **Couper le souffle à qn**, (i) to wind s.o.; (ii) to make s.o. gasp; to take s.o.'s breath away. **Dernier souffle**, last breath. **Exhaler son dernier souffle**, to breathe one's last. **N'avoir plus que le souffle**, to be at one s last gasp. **Être à bout de souffle**, to be winded, out of breath, short of wind.

souffl|er [sufle]. **I.** *v.i.* (*a*) To blow. *S. dans une trompette*, to blow a trumpet. (*b*) To recover one's breath. **Laisser souffler un cheval**, to let a horse get its wind; to give a horse a breather. (*c*) To pant; to puff. *F:* **Souffler comme un bœuf**, to blow like a grampus. (*d*) *Le vent souffle en tempête*, it is blowing a gale. **2.** *v.tr.* (*a*) To blow (glass); to blow up (toy balloon, etc.). (*b*) To blow (the organ); to blow up (the fire); to blow off (dust); to blow out (a candle). S.a. CHAUD 2. (*c*) To breathe, utter (a word, a sound). **Ne pas souffler mot de qch.**, not to breathe a word of sth. (*d*) **Souffler son rôle à un acteur**, to prompt an actor. (*e*) *Draughts:* To huff (a man). *F:* **Souffler** qch. à qn, to trick s.o. out of sth. *s.m.* **-ement.**

soufflé. 1. *a.* (*a*) *Ling:* Unvoiced (vowel). (*b*) Puffed up, puffy (face, etc.); soufflé (omelet). **2.** *s.m. Cu:* Soufflé.

soufflerie [suflǝri], *s.f.* **1.** Bellows (of organ, forge). **2.** *Ind:* Blast-engine; blower.

soufflet [suflɛ], *s.m.* **1.** (*a*) (Pair of) bellows. (*b*) Blowing-machine. (*c*) *Ind:* Fan, fanner. **2.** (*a*) Malle à soufflets, portmanteau with expanding sides. (*b*) *Rail:* 'Concertina' vestibule (joining coaches). (*c*) *Phot:* Bellows (of camera). (*d*) *Dressm:* Gusset, gore, inlay. **3.** (*a*) Box on the ear, slap in the face. (*b*) Affront, humiliation, snub.

souffleter [suflǝte], *v.tr.* (je soufflette; je souffletterai) (*a*) **Souffleter** qn, to box s.o.'s ears, to slap s.o.'s face. (*b*) *F:* To insult, affront (s.o.).

souffleur, -euse [suflœːr, -øːz], *s.* **1.** (*a*) *S. d'orgue,* organ-blower. *S. de verre,* glass-blower. (*b*) *F:* Puffer and blower. (*c*) *Th:* Prompter. **Trou du souffleur,** prompt-box (in front of stage). **2.** *s.m.* Blower (of locomotive, for ventilation, etc.). **3.** *s.m. Z:* Blower (dolphin).

soufflure [suflyːr], *s.f.* **1.** Blister (in paint, etc.). **2.** *Metall:* Blow(-hole), flaw.

souffrance [sufrɑ̃ːs], *s.f.* **1.** (*a*) *Jur:* Jour, vue, de souffrance, window or light on sufferance (overlooking neighbour's property). (*b*) Suspense. **En souffrance,** in suspense, in abeyance. *Colis en s.,* parcels hung up in transit or awaiting delivery. **2.** Suffering, pain.

souffrant [sufrɑ̃], *a.* **1.** *A:* Long-suffering. **2.** (*a*) Suffering; in pain. (*b*) Unwell, poorly, ailing.

souffre-douleur [sufrǝdulœːr], *s.m.,* occ. *f.,* inv. (*a*) Drudge. (*b*) Butt (of jokes, etc.).

souffreteux, -euse [sufrǝtø, -øːz], *a.* **1.** Destitute, needy. **2.** Sickly, peaky, half-starved (child).

souffrir [sufriːr], *v.* (*pr.p.* souffrant; *p.p.* souffert; *pr.ind.* je souffre, il souffre, n. souffrons; *p.h.* je souffris; *fu.* je souffrirai) To suffer. **1.** *v.tr.* (*a*) To endure, undergo, bear, put up with (pain, loss, insult, etc.). *Mil:* **S.** *une attaque,* (i) to be attacked; (ii) to sustain, withstand, an attack. *F:* **Je ne peux pas le souffrir,** I can't abide him. (*b*) To permit, allow. *Je ne saurais s. cela,* I cannot allow that. *Souffrez que je vous dise la vérité,* allow me to tell you the truth. *Situation qui ne souffre aucun retard,* situation that brooks no delay, that admits of no delay. **2.** *v.i.* (*a*) To feel pain. *Souffre-t-il?* is he in pain? *Mon bras me fait s.,* my arm pains me. *Je souffre de le voir si changé,* it pains, grieves, me to see him so changed. (*b*) To suffer injury; (of thg) to be injured, damaged (by frost, travel, etc.). *Les vignes ont souffert de la gelée,* the vines have suffered from the frost.

soufre [sufr], *s.m.* Sulphur, *F:* brimstone. **Fleur(s) de soufre, soufre en fleur(s),** flowers of sulphur.

soufr|er [sufre], *v.tr.* To sulphur; to treat (sth.) with sulphur; to sulphurate (wool); to stum (wine). *Allumette soufrée,* sulphur-match. *s.m.* **-age.**

soufrière [sufriɛːr], *s.f.* **1.** Sulphur-mine. **2.** *Geol:* Solfatara.

souhait [swɛ], *s.m.* Wish, desire, aspiration. *Présenter ses souhaits à qn,* to offer s.o. one's good wishes. **A souhait,** according to one's wishes; to one's liking. *Avoir tout à s.,* to have everything one can wish for.

souhaitable [swɛtabl], *a.* Desirable.

souhaiter [swɛte], *v.tr.* To wish. *S. les richesses,* to desire wealth; to wish for wealth. *Je*

souhaiterais (de) *pouvoir vous aider,* I should like to be able to help you. *Je vous souhaite une bonne année, P: je vous la souhaite bonne (et heureuse),* I wish you a Happy New Year. *F:* **Je vous en souhaite!** don't you wish you may get it! *S.a.* BIENVENUE².

souillard [sujaːr], *s.m.* (*a*) Sink-hole (in a stone flag). (*b*) Sink-stone.

souille [suːj], *s.f.* (Wild boar's) wallow. (Of boar) **Prendre souille,** to return to its wallow.

souiller [suje], *v.tr.* **1.** To soil, dirty (de, with); to foul. **2.** To pollute, defile; to taint. **3.** To tarnish, sully, besmirch (one's name, a memory).

souillon [sujɔ̃], *s.m.* & *f.* **1.** Sloven; esp. *f.* slut, draggle-tail, slattern. **2.** *s.f.* Scullery-wench.

souillure [sujyːr], *s.f.* **1.** Spot (of dirt); stain (on garment). **2.** Blot, blemish (on one's honour); defilement. **Sans souillure,** unsullied, undefiled.

soûl [su]. *F:* **1.** *a.* (*a*) Glutted, surfeited, gorged (with food, etc.). *Être s. de musique,* to be surfeited with music. (*b*) Drunk, tipsy. **Soûl comme une grive,** as drunk as a fiddler, as a lord. **2.** *s.m.* Manger, pleurer, tout son soûl, to eat, weep, one's fill. *Dormir tout son s.,* to have one's sleep out.

soulagement [sulaʒmɑ̃], *s.m.* Relief, alleviation, assuagement; solace, comfort. *Mch:* **Soupape de soulagement,** relief-valve.

soulager [sulaʒe], *v.tr.* (je soulageai(s); n. soulageons) To lighten the burden of (mule, etc.); to ease (pressure); to relieve, alleviate, assuage (pain, grief). *S. une poutre,* to relieve the strain on a beam.

se soulager. 1. *Se s. d'un fardeau,* to ease oneself of a burden. **2.** To relieve one's feelings, one's mind. **3.** *F:* To relieve nature.

soûlard [sulaːr], *s.m. P:* Drunkard, soaker.

soûler [sule], *v.tr. F:* **1.** To surfeit (s.o.). *Tout soûle à la fin,* one can have too much of a good thing. **2.** To intoxicate; to make (s.o.) drunk.

se soûler. 1. To gorge (de, on); to glut oneself (de, with). **2.** To get drunk.

soûlerie [sulri], *s.f.* **1.** Satiety. **2.** Drinking-bout.

soulèvement [sulɛvmɑ̃], *s.m.* (*a*) Rising, heaving; swell(ing) (of the waves). **Soulèvement de cœur,** nausea. (*b*) *Geol:* Upheaval, upthrust. (*c*) Revolt, rising (of a people). (*d*) Burst of indignation; general protest.

soulever [sulve], *v.tr.* (je soulève; je soulèverai) **1.** (*a*) To raise (usu. with effort); to lift (up) (a weight). *Poussière soulevée par le vent,* dust raised by the wind. *S.a.* CŒUR I. (*b*) To raise slightly. *S. le rideau,* to peep out under the curtain. (*c*) *S. une objection,* to raise an objection. *S. des doutes,* to raise doubts. **2.** (*a*) To rouse, stir up (people to revolt). (*b*) To excite, provoke, rouse (passion, indignation). [LEVER]

se soulever. 1. (*a*) To rise. *La mer se soulève,* the sea heaves, swells. *Tout mon être se soulève en colère contre lui,* my whole being rises in anger against him. (*b*) (Of the stomach) To heave, to turn. **2.** (*a*) To raise oneself (with one's hands, etc.). (*b*) To revolt; to rise (in rebellion).

soulier [sulje], *s.m.* Shoe. *F:* **Être dans ses petits souliers,** to be in an embarrassing, awkward, situation; to be ill at ease, on pins and needles. *Prov:* **Chacun sait où le soulier le blesse,** everyone knows best where his own shoe pinches. *Faute de souliers on va nu-pieds,* beggars cannot be choosers.

soulign|er [suliɲe], *v.tr.* (*a*) To underline, underscore (word). (*b*) To emphasize, lay stress on (word, fact). *s.m.* **-ement.**

soumettre [sumɛtr], *v.tr.* (Conj.) like METTRE **I.** To subdue, to bring into subjection. **2.** To submit, refer, put (question, etc.). *S. une demande à qn,* to lay a request before s.o. **3.** *S. qn à une operation,* to subject s.o. to an operation. *S. qch. à un examen,* to subject sth. to an examination.
se soumettre, to submit, give in, yield (*à,* to). *Se s. aux volontés de qn,* to comply with s.o.'s wishes. *Se s. à une operation chirurgicale,* to undergo an operation.
soumis, *a.* **I.** Submissive, obedient; biddable, dutiful (child). **2.** Subject amenable (to law, authority, etc.). *S. au timbre,* liable to stamp-duty
soumission [sumisjɔ̃], *s.f.* **I.** (*a*) Submission (of rebels, etc.) **Faire (sa) soumission,** to surrender, yield. (*b*) Profession of allegiance. (*c*) Obedience, submissiveness, amenableness (*à,* to). **2.** *Com:* Tender (for public works, etc.). **Faire une soumission pour un travail,** to send in tender, to tender, for a piece of work.
soumissionnaire [sumisjɔnɛːr], *s.m.* (*a*) Party tendering for contract; tenderer. (*b*) *Fin:* Underwriter.
soumissionner [sumisjɔne], *v.tr.* (*a*) To tender for, put in a tender for (public works, etc.). (*b*) *Fin:* To underwrite.
soupape [supap], *s.f.* Valve. (*a*) *S. à clapet, à charnière,* clack-valve, flap-valve. *S. en champignon,* poppet-valve, mushroom-valve. *S. à boulet,* ball-valve. *S. à pointeau,* needle-valve. *S. à cloche,* cup-valve. *S. à tiroir,* slide-valve. *S. de sûreté,* safety-valve. *S. de réglage, à papillon,* throttle-valve; damper (of stove-pipe). *S. d'admission, d'arrivée,* inlet valve, induction valve. *I.C.E: Soupapes en tête, en chandelle,* overhead valves. *Soupapes en chapelle,* side-valves. **Sans soupapes,** valveless. (*b*) *El.E: S. électrique,* current-rectifying valve; rectifier.
soupçon [supsɔ̃], *s.m.* Suspicion. **I.** *Devenir l'objet des soupçons,* to fall under suspicion. *J'en avais le s.!* I thought so! I suspected as much! *Endormir les soupçons,* to lull suspicion. *Faire naître les soupçons,* to arouse suspicion. **2.** Surmise, conjecture. **3.** *F:* Slight flavour, small quantity, dash, soupçon (of vinegar, garlic, etc.); touch (of fever, irony). *Pas un s. de chance,* not the ghost of a chance.
soupçonnable [supsɔnabl], *a.* Liable to suspicion; suspectable.
soupçonner [supsɔne], *v.tr.* **I.** To suspect. *S. qn de qch., d'avoir fait qch.,* to suspect s.o. of sth., of having done sth. **Soupçonner juste,** to be right in one's suspicions. *Je le soupçonne royaliste,* I suspect him of royalism. **2.** To surmise, conjecture.
soupçonneux, -euse [supsɔnø, -øːz], *a.* Suspicious, distrustful. **Peu soupçonneux,** unsuspicious. *adv.* **-sement.**
soupe [sup], *s.f* **I.** Sop; soaked slice of bread. *S au lait,* bread and milk. S.a. MONTER I. 2, TREMPER I. **2.** Soup. *S. grasse,* soup made with meat. *S. maigre,* vegetable soup. *S. à l'oignon,* onion soup. *F:* Venez manger la soupe avec nous, come and take pot-luck with us. Il était pensionnaire chez un marchand de soupe, he was a boarder at a Dotheboys Hall. **3.** Soup-kitchen.
soupente [supɑ̃ːt], *s.f.* (*a*) Loft, garret. (*b*) Closet. *S. d'escalier,* recess under the stair.
souper [supe] I. *v.i.* To have supper; to sup. *F:* J'en ai soupé, I have had enough of it.
II. **souper,** *s.m.* Supper.

soupeser [supəze], *v.tr.* (je soupèse; je soupèserai) To feel, try, the weight of (sth.); to weigh, poise, (sth.) in the hand. |PESER|
soupière [supjɛːr], *s.f.* Soup-tureen.
soupir [supiːr], *s.m.* **I.** Sigh. **Pousser un soupir,** to heave, fetch, a sigh. *S de soulagement,* sigh of relief. **Rendre le dernier soupir,** to breathe one's last. **Le Pont des Soupirs,** the Bridge of Sighs. *S. du vent,* sighing, sough, of the wind. **2.** *Mus:* Crotchet-rest. *Demi-s.,* quaver rest.
soupirail, -aux [supiraːj, -o], *s.m.* Air-hole; (cellar) ventilator; vent (in air-shaft).
soupirant [supirɑ̃], *s.m.* *F:* Suitor, wooer.
soupirer [supire], *v.i.* (*a*) To sigh. **En soupirant,** with a sigh. (*b*) *S. après, pour qch.,* to long, yearn, sigh, for sth.
souple [supl], *a.* Supple. (*a*) Pliant; flexible, pliable; lithe, lissom(e) (body, figure); flexible (voice); limp (binding). *Esprits.,* versatile mind. (*b*) Docile, pliant, tractable. S.a. ÉCHINE. *adv.* **-ment.**
souplesse [suplɛs], *s.f.* Suppleness. **I.** Flexibility, pliability pliancy; lissom(e)ness (of figure); litheness (of body); flexibility (of voice). *S. d'esprit,* versatility. **2.** Pliability (of character).
souquenille [sukniːj], *s.f.* A: Smock (as worn by man-servant).
souquer [suke], *v.tr.* **I.** *Nau:* To haul (rope) taut. **2.** *S. sur le avirons,* to pull away at the oars. *S. un coup,* to pull one stroke.
source [surs], *s.f.* Source. **I.** (*a*) Spring(-head), fountain(-head), well. **Eau de source,** spring water. *S. d'eau minérale,* mineral spring. *S. thermale,* hot spring. **Rivière qui prend sa source dans . . .,** river that takes its rise in . . ., that rises 'n. . . . *F:* Son récit coule de source, he tells a straightforward tale. (*b*) *S. de pétrole,* oil-spring. *S. boueuse,* mud-geyser. **2.** Origin. *Aller à la s. du mal,* to get to the root of the evil. *S. de la vie, s. de toute science* well-spring of life, fount of all knowledge. **Je le tiens de bonne source,** I have it on good authority.
sourcier, -ière [sursje, -jɛːr], *s.* Water-diviner; dowser.
sourcil [sursi], *s.m.* Eyebrow. *Sourcils épais,* shaggy eyebrows. **Froncer le(s) sourcil(s),** to knit one's brow; to frown, to scowl.
sourciller [sursije], *v.i.* **I.** To knit one's brows; to frown. **2.** To wince, flinch. **Sans sourciller,** without wincing, *F:* without turning a hair.
sourcilleux, -euse [sursijø, -øːz], *a.* (*a*) Supercilious, haughty. (*b*) Frowning (brow). *Il avait le front s.,* he looked worried.
sourd [suːr], *a.* **I.** (*a*) Deaf. *S. d'une oreille,* deaf in one ear. *F:* Sourd comme un pot, as deaf as a post. S.a. OREILLE 2. (*b*) *s.* Deaf person. *F:* Crier comme un sourd, to yell, to squeal. Taper comme un sourd, to lay about one. **2.** Dull (pain); dull, muffled (noise); muted (string); secret (rumour, desire). *Cela tomba avec un coup s.,* it fell with a thump, with a thud. **Lanterne sourde,** dark-lantern. *Hostilité sourde,* veiled hostility, hostile mutterings. *Ling:* **Consonne sourde,** voiceless consonant; surd. **3.** Sound-proof.
sourdement [surdəmɑ̃], *adv.* (*a*) With a dull, hollow, sound. *Le tonnerre grondait s.,* the thunder rumbled. (*b*) Secretly.
sourdine [surdin], *s.f.* **I.** (*a*) *Mus:* Mute. **Mettre une sourdine à un violon,** to mute a violin. **Violons en sourdine,** muted violins. (*b*) *W.Tel:* Damper. (*c*) *Aut:* Dimmer. **2.** Accompagnement (de voix) en sourdine,

hummed accompaniment. *F:* **Jurer en sourdine,** to swear under one's breath. **A la sourdine,** in secret on the sly

sourd-muet, sourde-muette [surmɥe, surdmɥet] **1.** *a.* Deaf-and-dumb. **2.** *s.* Deaf-mute. *pl Des sourds-muets.*

sourdre [surdr], *v.i.* (Used only in third pers. **il sourd, ils sourdent,** and in inf.) **1.** (Of water) To spring, to well (up). **2.** *F:* To result, arise, spring. *Que verra-t-on s. de ces événements?* what will spring from these events?

souriant [surjɑ̃], *a.* Smiling. *Elle était toute souriante,* she was all smiles.

souriceau [suriso], *s.m* Little mouse.

souricière [surisjɛːr], *s.f.* (a) Mouse-trap. (b) *F:* Trap, snare; *esp.* police-trap. **Tendre une souricière,** to set a trap (à, for).

sourire [suriːr]. **I.** *v.i.* (Conj. like RIRE) **1.** (a) To smile (à, to). **En souriant,** with a smile; smilingly. (b) *Pej:* To smirk, to simper. **2.** (Of thg) To prove attractive to (s.o.). *L'idée ne nous souriait pas,* we did not relish the idea.
II. sourire, *s.m.* Smile. *S. affecté,* smirk. *S. de mépris,* scornful smile; sneer. **Large sourire,** grin. **Garder le sourire,** to keep smiling.

souris[1] [suri], *s.f.* **1.** Mouse. *S. de terre,* field-mouse. *S. d'eau,* shrew-mouse. *F:* **On aurait entendu trotter une souris,** you could have heard a pin drop. *a.inv.* **(Couleur) gris (de) souris,** mouse-colour. **2.** Knuckle-end (of leg of mutton).

souris[2], *s.m.* A. & Poet: = SOURIRE II.

sournois, -oise [surnwa, -waːz]. **1.** *a.* Artful, sly, deep, crafty; cunning, shifty (look); underhand (dealings). **2.** *s.* Sneak, sly-boots. *adv.* **-ement.**

sournoiser'e [surnwazri], *s.f.* **1.** (Underhand) cunning; craftiness. **2.** Underhand trick.

sous [su], *prep.* **1.** Under(neath), beneath, below. *Tirer un tabouret de sous la table,* to draw a stool from under the table. *Sous terre,* underground, below ground. *Sous clef,* under lock and key. *Sous nos propres yeux,* under, before, our very eyes. *Connu sous le nom de . . .,* known by the name of. . . . *Travailler sous la pluie,* to work in the rain. *Sous les armes,* under arms; fighting. *Sous les drapeaux,* with the colours. *Sous le vent,* under the lee. *Sous les tropiques,* in the tropics. *Sous Louis XIV,* under Louis XIV. *Sous peine de mort,* on pain of death. *Écrire sous la dictée de qn,* to write at, from, s.o.'s dictation. **2.** Within the time of. *Je répondrai sous trois jours,* I shall reply within three days. S.a. PEU 2. **3. Sous-,** *pref.* Sub-, under-. *Sous-affréteur,* sub-charterer. *Sous-lacustre,* sub-lacustrine. *Sous-enveloppe,* under-covering.

NOTE. Compound nouns and adjectives of which the first element is *sous* vary in the plural.

sous-acétate, *s.m. Ch:* Subacetate.
sous-affermer, *v.tr.* **1.** To sub-let (land). **2.** To sub-lease (land).
sous-affréter, *v.tr.* (Conj. like FRÉTER) To sub-charter (ship).
sous-agence, *s.f.* Sub-agency.
sous-agent, *s.m.* Sub-agent.
sous-alimentation, *s.f.* Malnutrition.
sous-bail, *s.m.* Sub-lease, sub-let.
sous-barbe, *s.f. inv.* **1.** Under-jaw (of horse). **2.** Back-stay (of bridle). **3.** *Nau:* Bobstay.
sous-bibliothécaire, *s.* Sub-librarian.
sous-bois, *s.m.* Underwood, undergrowth.
sous-bras, *s.m. Cost:* Dress-shield.

sous-chef, *s.m.* **1.** Deputy chief clerk. **2.** Assistant manager. *S.-c. de gare,* deputy station-master.
sous-chlorure, *s.m. Ch:* Subchloride.
sous-classe, *s.f. Nat.Hist:* Subdivision; subtype, subclass.
sous-comité, *s.m.* Sub-committee.
sous-commission, *s.f.* Sub-committee; subcommission.
sous-couche, *s.f.* Substratum. *Phot: S.-c. antihalo,* non-halation undercoating.
souscripteur [suskriptœːr], *s.m.* Subscriber.
souscription [suskripsjɔ̃], *s.f.* **1.** (a) Execution, signing (of deed). (b) Subscription, signature. (c) Underline; bibliographical note (printed at end of book). **2.** (a) Subscription, application (à des actions, for shares). **Bulletin de souscription,** allotment letter. (b) **Bal par souscription,** subscription dance. **3.** Subscription, contribution (of sum of money). *Lancer une s.,* to start a fund. **4.** Entering (of horse for race).
souscrire [suskriːr], *v.tr.* (Conj. like ÉCRIRE) **1.** To sign, execute (deed); to subscribe, sign (bond); to draw (cheque, etc.). **2.** *S. un abonnement,* to take out a subscription (for library, etc.). *S. mille francs pour une œuvre de charité,* to subscribe a thousand francs to a charity. *S. des actions,* to apply for shares. **Capital souscrit,** subscribed capital. **3.** *Abs.* (a) *S. à une émission,* to apply for, subscribe to, an issue. (b) *S pour (la somme de) mille francs,* to subscribe a thousand francs. (c) *S. à une opinion,* to subscribe to an opinion.
souscrit, *a. Gr.Gram:* (Iota) subscript.
sous-cutané, *a.* Subcutaneous.
sous-diacre, *s.m.* Subdeacon.
sous-directeur, -trice, *s.* **1.** Sub-manager, sub-manageress. **2.** Vice-principal (of school).
sous-division, *s.f.* = SUBDIVISION.
sous-dominante, *s.f. Mus:* Subdominant.
sous-embranchement, *s.m. Biol:* Sub-genus, sub-family.
sous-entendre, *v.tr.* To understand; not to express; to imply.
sous-entendu, *s.m.* Thing understood; implication. *Suggérer qch. par sous-entendus,* to hint at sth.
sous-entente, *s.f.* Mental reservation.
sous-espèce, *s.f.* Subspecies.
sous-estimer, sous-évaluer, *v.tr.* To under-estimate, undervalue, underrate.
sous-exposer, *v.tr. Phot:* To under-expose.
sous-exposition, *s.f. Phot:* Under-exposure.
sous-ferme, *s.f.* Underlease (of land).
sous-fermier, -ière, *s.* Under-lessee, sub-lessee.
sous-fréter, *v.tr.* (je sous-frète; je sous-fréterai) To under-freight to underlet (a ship).
sous-garde, *s.f. Sm.a:* Trigger-guard.
sous-genre, *s.m. Z:* Sub-genus, sub-group.
sous-gérant, *s.m.* Assistant manager.
sous-gouverneur, *s.m.* Deputy governor, vice-governor.
sous-intendant, *s.m.* Under-steward.
sous-jacent, *a.* Subjacent, underlying.
sous-jupe, *s.f. Cost:* Underslip.
Sous-le-vent, *Pr.n. Geog:* **Les Iles Sous-le-vent,** the Leeward Islands.
sous-lieutenance, *s.f.* Second-lieutenancy, sub-lieutenancy.
sous-lieutenant, *s.m.* Second-lieutenant, sub-lieutenant. *Av: S.-l. aviateur,* pilot officer.
sous-locataire, *s. m. & f.* Subtenant, under-tenant, sub-lessee.

sous-location, *s.f.* **1.** *(a)* Sub-letting, under-letting. *(b)* Under-renting **2.** Under-tenancy, sub-lease. sub-let.

sous-louer, *v.tr.* **1.** To sub-let, underlet, sub-lease (house). **2.** To rent (house) from the tenant

sous-main, *\.m* Blotting-pad, writing-pad.

sous-maître, -maîtresse, *s.* *Sch:* Assistant master assistant mistress.

sous-marin. 1. *a.* Submarine (vessel, volcano); submerged (reef). *Courant s.-m.*, deep-sea current. **2.** *s.m.* Submarine (boat). *S.-m. de croisière.* ocean-going submarine.

sous-maxillaire, *a.* *Anat:* Submaxillary.

sous-médiante, *s.f.* *Mus:* Supertonic.

sous-mentionné, *a.* Undermentioned.

sous-multiple, *a. & \.m.* Submultiple (*de*, of).

sous-nappe, *s.f.* Under-tablecloth.

sous-œuvre, *s.m.* **1.** *Const:* *Civ.E:* Under-pinning **Reprendre un édifice en sous-œuvre,** (i) to underpin a building; (ii) to shore up a building **2.** Under-portion, under-side.

sous-off, *\.m* *F:* N.C.O. non-com.

sous-officier, *s.m.* **1.** Non-commissioned officer. **2.** *Navy:* Petty officer.

sous-ordre, *s.m.* **1.** *inv.* Subordinate, underling. **En sous-ordre,** subordinate(ly). **2.** *Nat.Hist:* Sub-order.

sous-pied, *s.m.* *(a)* Under-strap (of gaiters). *(b)* Trouser-strap.

sous-pose, *s.f.* *Phot:* Under-exposure.

sous-préfecture, *s.f* Sub-prefecture.

sous-préfet, *s.m.* *Adm:* Sub-prefect.

sous-preneur, *s.m.* *Jur:* Sub-lessee.

sous-principal, *s.m.* *Sch:* Vice-principal.

sous-production, *s.f.* Under-production.

sous-produit, *s.m.* *Ind:* By-product.

sous-secrétaire, *s. m. & f.* Under-secretary.

sous-secrétariat, *s.m.* **1.** Under-secretaryship. **2.** Under-secretary's office or department.

sous-seing, *s.m.* Private agreement, private contract

sous-sel, *s.m.* *Ch:* Subsalt; basic salt.

soussigner [susine], *v.tr.* To sign, undersign.

soussigné, -ée, *a. & s.* Undersigned. *Je s. déclare que . . .,* I the undersigned declare that.

sous-sol, *s.m.* **1.** *Geol:* Subsoil, substratum. **2.** *Const:* *(a)* Basement; basement-flat. *(b)* Cellar-kitchen

sous-station, *s.f.* *El.E:* Sub-station.

sous-tangente, *s.f.* *Geom:* Subtangent.

sous-tendre, *v.tr.* *Geom:* To subtend (an arc)

sous-titre, *s.m.* **1.** Sub-title. **2.** *Cin: etc:* Caption; *Cin:* cut-in.

soustractif, -ive [sustraktif, -i:v], *a.* Subtractive.

soustraction [sustraksjɔ̃], *s.f.* *(a)* Removal, taking away, withdrawal. abstraction. *(b)* *Mth:* Subtraction.

soustraire [sustre:r], *v.tr.* (Conj. like TRAIRE) **1.** To take away, withdraw, abstract, purloin (document, etc.). **2.** To screen, preserve, shield. *S. qn à la colère de qn,* to protect s.o. from s.o.'s wrath **3.** *Mth:* To subtract (*de*, from). **se soustraire** *à qch.,* to avoid, elude, escape, sth. *Se s. aux regards.* to retire from sight. *Je ne vois aucun moyen de m'y s.,* I see no means of getting out of it *Se s à la justice,* to abscond.

sous-traitant, *s.m.* Sub-contractor.

sous-traiter, *v.tr.* **1.** To sub-contract. **2.** To sub-let (a contract).

sous-traité, *s.m.* Sub-contract.

sous-variété, *s.f* Subvariety.

sous-ventrière, *s.f.* *Harn:* *(a)* Belly-band (attached to shafts). *(b)* Saddlegirth. *(c)* Surcingle (securing blanket).

sous-verge, *s.m.inv.* **1.** (Unridden) off-horse (of a pair). *S.-v. de devant,* off-leader. **2.** *F:* Underling, understrapper.

sous-verre, *s.m.* Passe-partout picture.

sous-vêtement, *s.m.* Undergarment.

sous-volteur, *s.m.* *El.E:* Negative booster.

soutache [sutaʃ], *s.f.* Braid.

soutacher [sutaʃe], *v.tr.* To braid.

soutane [sutan], *s.f.* Cassock, soutane. *F:* **Prendre la soutane,** to become a priest; to take (holy) orders. *Le respect dû à la s.,* the respect due to the cloth.

soutanelle [sutanel], *s.f.* **1.** Short cassock. **2.** Clerical frock-coat.

soute [sut], *s.f.* *Nau:* Store-room. *S. à charbon,* coal-bunker. **Mettre du charbon en soute,** to bunker coal. *S. aux câbles,* cable-locker. *S. à eau,* water-tank. *Soutes à mazout,* oil(-fuel) tanks. *S. à munitions,* magazine. *S. aux poudres,* powder-magazine. *S. aux bagages,* luggage-room.

soutenable [sutnabl], *a.* *(a)* Bearable, supportable (burden, existence). *(b)* Tenable (opinion); arguable (theory).

soutenance [sutnɑ̃:s], *s.f.* *Sch:* Maintaining (of a thesis).

soutenant, -ante [sutnɑ̃, -ɑ̃:t]. **1.** *a.* Sustaining (power). **2.** *s.* *Sch:* Maintainer (of a thesis).

soutènement [sutɛnmɑ̃], *s.m.* Supporting, support, propping, holding up. **Arche de soutènement,** relieving arch. **Mur de soutènement,** retaining wall.

souteneur [sutnœ:r], *s.m.* **1.** Upholder (of system, etc.). **2.** Bully; pimp.

soutenir [sutni:r], *v.tr.* (Conj. like TENIR) To sustain, support. **1.** *(a)* To hold up, prop up; to prevent (s.o.. sth.) from falling. *Aliments qui soutiennent,* sustaining food. *(b)* To keep, maintain (parents. family). *(c)* To back (up) (cause, person); to stand by, stand up for (s.o.); to back (s.o. financially); to be at the back of (s.o.). *(d)* To maintain, uphold (opinion); to affirm (fact). *Il soutient l'avoir vu,* he asserts, maintains, that he saw it. *Il soutient que . . .,* he will have it that. . . *e)* To keep up, sustain, maintain (conversation, speed, one's rank). **2.** To sustain, withstand, hold out against (attack).

se soutenir. 1. To support, maintain, oneself; to hold up, keep up. *Se s. sur ses pieds,* to stand (up) on one's feet. **2.** To last continue. *L'intérêt se soutient,* the interest is kept up, does not flag

soutenu, *a.* Sustained. **1.** Unremitting (attention); unceasing, earnest, constant (effort); unflagging, unfailing, continued (interest). *Effort s.* sustained effort. **2.** Lofty, stately (style).

souterrain [suterɛ̃]. **1.** *a.* Underground, subterranean. **Couloir, passage, souterrain,** subway. **2.** *s.m.* *(a)* (Large) cavern; caves. *(b* Underground passage; tunnel; subway *(c)* Vault.

soutien [sutjɛ̃], *s.m.* *(a)* Support, prop. *(b)* Supporter. upholder. **Soutien de famille,** bread-winner. [SOUTENIR]

soutien-gorge, *s.m.inv.* *Cost:* Bust-bodice, brassière.

soutien-vélo, *s.m.* Bicycle-stand. *pl. Des soutien-vélos.*

soutier [sutje], *s.m.* *Nau:* (Coal-)trimmer.

soutirer [sutire], *v.tr.* To draw off, rack (wine); to tap (electric supply). *F:* **S. de l'argent à qn,** to get, wheedle. squeeze. money out of s.o.

souvenance [suvnã:s], *s.f.* *A:* Remembrance, recollection (*de*, of).

souvenir [suvni:r]. I. *v.impers.* *Lit:* (Conj. like VENIR. Aux. *être*) To occur to the mind. *Il me souvient d'une histoire curieuse*, there comes to my mind a curious story. *Autant qu'il m'en souvient*, qu'il m'en souvienne, to the best of my recollection; as far, as near, as I can remember.
se souvenir *de qch.*, *de qn*, to remember, recall, sth., s.o. *Autant que je m'en souviens, que je m'en souvienne*, to the best of my recollection. *Faire souvenir qn de qch.*, to remind s.o. of sth. *Je tâcherai de m'en s.*, I shall try to bear it in mind. II. **souvenir**, *s.m.* 1. Remembrance, recollection, memory. *Je jouerais encore ce rôle de souvenir*, I could still act the part from memory. *Souvenirs de ma jeunesse*, memories of my youth. *Veuillez me rappeler à son bon souvenir*, please remember me kindly to him. *Faire qch. en souvenir de qn*, to do sth. in remembrance of s.o. 2. Memorial, memento. 3. Token of remembrance. (*a*) Keepsake, souvenir. (*b*) *S. offert à un fonctionnaire*, presentation.

souvent [suvã], *adv.* Often. **Peu souvent**, seldom, infrequently. **Assez souvent**, fairly often, not infrequently. *Plus s.*, oftener. **Le plus souvent**, as often as not; more often than not. *P:* **Plus souvent!** not if I know it! *Plus s. que j'irais!* no fear of my going!

souverain, -aine [suvrɛ̃, -ɛn]. 1. *a.* Sovereign (power, remedy). **Le souverain bien**, the sovereign good. *Jur:* **Cour souveraine**, final court of appeal; supreme court. **Jugement souverain**, final judgment. 2. (*a*) *s.* Sovereign (supreme ruler). (*b*) *s.m.* *Num:* Sovereign. *adv.* **-ement**.

souveraineté [suvrɛnte], *s.f.* Sovereignty. 1. (*a*) Supreme authority. **Droits de souveraineté**, sovereign rights. (*b*) Supremacy (of law, of right). 2. Territory, dominion(s) (of sovereign prince).

soviet [sɔvjɛt], *s.m.* Soviet.

soviétique [sɔvjetik], *a.* Soviet (organization).

soya [sɔja], *s.m.* *Bot:* Soya-bean, soy.

soyeux, -euse [swajø, -ø:z], *a.* Silky. [SOIE]

soy-ons, -ez. See ÊTRE.

spacieux, -euse [spasjø, -ø:z], *a.* Spacious, roomy, capacious. *adv.* **-sement**.

spadassin [spadasɛ̃], *s.m.* Bully, bravo. *S. à gages*, hired assassin, hired ruffian.

spaghetti [spagɛti], *s.m.pl.* Spaghetti.

spahi [spai], *s.m.* *Mil:* Spahi (Algerian trooper).

sparadrap [sparadra], *s.m.* *Med:* Adhesive plaster; sticking-plaster.

sparte[1] [spart], *s.m.* *Bot:* Esparto (grass).

Sparte[2]. *Pr.n.f.* *A.Geog:* Sparta.

sparterie [spartri], *s.f.* 1. Esparto factory. 2. Articles of esparto.

spartiate [sparsjat], *a. & s.* *A.Geog:* Spartan. *F:* **A la spartiate**, Spartanwise.

spasme [spasm], *s.m.* Spasm.

spasmodique [spasmɔdik], *a.* *Med:* Spasmodic, spastic. *adv.* **-ment**, -ally.

spath [spat], *s.m.* *Miner:* Spar. *S. d'Islande*, Iceland spar. *S. fluor*, *s. fusible*, fluor-spar, fluorite.

spathe [spat], *s.f.* *Bot:* (*a*) Spathe. (*b*) Shuck (of maize).

spatial, -aux [spasjal, -o], *a.* Spatial.

spatule [spatyl], *s.f.* 1. *Pharm:* etc: Spatula. **Doigts en spatule**, spatulate fingers. 2. *Orn:* Spoonbill.

spécial, -aux [spesjal, -o], *a.* Special, especial. *Je viens pour une affaire spéciale*, I have called on

particular business. *Privilège s. aux militaires*, privilege peculiar to military men. *adv.* **-ement**.

spécialisation [spesjalizasjɔ̃], *s.f.* Specialization.

spécialiser [spesjalize], *v.tr.* To specialize.
se spécialiser *dans qch.*, to specialize, be a specialist, in sth.

spécialiste [spesjalist], *s.m. & f.* Specialist, expert.

spécialité [spesjalite], *s.f.* Speciality, special feature, special function; specialty. **Faire sa spécialité des mathématiques**, to specialize in mathematics.

spécieux, -euse [spesjø, -ø:z], *a.* Specious; plausible. *adv.* **-sement**.

spécificatif, -ive [spesifikatif, -i:v], *a.* Specifying.

spécification [spesifikasjɔ̃], *s.f.* 1. Specification; determination of species. 2. *Tchn:* Working up (of material).

spécifier [spesifje], *v.tr.* 1. To specify; to mention specially, to state definitely. *S. des fonctions*, to lay down duties. *S. que . . .*, to lay down that. . . . 2. To determine (sth.) specifically.

spécifique [spesifik]. 1. *a.* Specific (function, remedy germ). *Ph:* **Poids spécifique**, specific gravity. 2. *s.m.* *Med:* Specific (remedy) (*contre*, for). *adv.* **-ment**, -ally

spécimen [spesimɛn], *s.m.* Specimen. *Publ:* Presentation copy. *a.inv.* **Page spécimen**, specimen page.

spéciosité [spesjozite], *s.f.* Speciousness.

spectacle [spɛktakl], *s.m.* 1. Spectacle, sight, scene. *F:* **Se donner en spectacle**, to make an exhibition of oneself. **Faire spectacle de qch.**, to show off, exhibit, advertise, sth. 2. (*a*) *Th:* Play, entertainment; *F:* show. *Aller au s.*, to go to the theatre. **Salle de spectacle**, theatre. **Taxe sur les spectacles**, entertainment tax. (*b*) **Spectacle payant**, side-show (at bazaar). 3. Show, display. *Th:* **Pièce à grand spectacle**, spectacular play.

spectaculaire [spɛktakylɛ:r], *a.* Spectacular.

spectateur, -trice [spɛktatœ:r, -tris], *s.* Spectator, onlooker, bystander; beholder; witness (of accident, etc.). *Acteurs et spectateurs*, actors and audience.

spectral, -aux [spɛktral, -o], *a.* Spectral. 1. Ghostly, ghostlike. 2. *Opt:* **Couleurs spectrales**, colours of the spectrum. **Analyse spectrale**, spectrum analysis.

spectre [spɛktr], *s.m.* 1. Spectre, ghost, apparition. 2. (*a*) *Opt:* (Solar) spectrum. *b*) *Phot:* *S. secondaire*, ghost; flare(-spot). 3. *Magn:* Magnetic tracing (in iron filings).

spectromètre [spɛktrɔmɛtr], *s.m.* *Opt:* Spectrometer.

spectrophotographie [spɛktrɔfɔtɔgrafi] *s.f.* Spectrophotography.

spectroscope [spɛktrɔskɔp], *s.m.* *Opt:* Spectroscope. *S. à réseau*, grating spectroscope.

spectroscopie [spɛktrɔskɔpi], *s.f.* Spectroscopy.

spéculaire [spekylɛ:r]. 1. *a.* (*a*) Specular (mineral). (*b*) **Écriture spéculaire**, mirror writing. 2. *s.f.* *Bot:* Specularia.

spéculateur, -trice [spekylatœ:r, -tris], *s.* 1. Speculator, theorizer. 2. *Fin:* Speculator.

spéculatif, -ive [spekylatif, -i:v], *a.* Speculative. *adv.* **-ivement**.

spéculation [spekylasjɔ̃], *s.f.* Speculation. 1. (*a*) Cogitation. (*b*) Theory, conjecture. 2. *S. à la baisse*, bear operations. *S. à la hausse*, bull operations. *Pure s.*, pure gamble.

spéculer [spekyle], *v.i.* 1. To speculate, cogitate (*sur*, upon). 2. *Fin:* To speculate (*sur*, in).

S. à la hausse, to speculate for a rise; to go a bull. *S. à la baisse*, to speculate for a fall; to go a bear.

spéléologie [speleɔlɔʒi], *s.f.* Spelaeology.

spergule [spɛrgyl], *s.f. Bot:* Spergula, spurrey.

spermaceti [spɛrmaseti] *s.m.* Spermaceti. Huile de spermaceti, sperm oil.

spermatozoïde [spɛrmatozoid], *s.m.*, **spermatozoaire** [spɛrmatozɔɛ:r], *s.m.* Spermatozoon.

sperme [spɛrm], *s.m* **1.** *Physiol:* Sperm. **2. Sperme de baleine**, spermaceti.

sphacèle [sfasɛl], *s.m.* Sphacelus, gangrene.

sphacéler [sfasele], *v.tr.* (il sphacèle: il sphacèlera) To sphacelate; to make gangrenous; to mortify.

se sphacéler, to become gangrenous.

sphagnacées [sfagnase], *s.f.pl. Bot:* Sphagnaceae, peat-mosses.

sphaigne [sfɛɲ], *s.f. Bot:* Sphagnum, peat-moss.

sphénoïdal, -aux [sfenɔidal. -o], *a. Anat:* Sphenoidal (fissure, sinus).

sphénoïde [sfenɔid], *a. & s.m. Anat:* Sphenoid.

sphère [sfɛ:r], *s.f.* Sphere. **1.** Globe, orb. *La s. céleste*, the celestial sphere. **2.** *F:* Circuit, orbit. *S. d'activité*, sphere, field, of activity. *F:* **Être hors de sa sphère**, to be out of one's sphere, out of one's element.

sphéricité [sferisite], *s.f.* Sphericity, curvature. S.a. ABERRATION 1.

sphérique [sferik], *a.* Spherical.

sphéroïde [sferɔid], *s.m.* Spheroid.

sphéromètre [sferɔmɛtr], *s.m.* Spherometer.

sphérule [sferyl], *s.f.* Spherule; small sphere.

sphincter [sfɛktɛ:r], *s.m. Anat:* Sphincter.

sphinx [sfɛ̃:ks], *s.m.* **1.** *Myth:* Sphinx. *F:* **Sourire de sphinx**, sphinx-like smile. **2.** *Ent:* Sphinx, hawk-moth.

sphygmographe [sfigmɔgraf], *s.m. Med:* Sphygmograph.

sphygmomètre [sfigmɔmɛtr], *s.m. Med:* Sphygmometer.

spic [spik], *s.m. Bot:* Spike-lavender, French lavender. **Essence de spic**, spike oil.

spica [spika], *s.m. Med:* Spica (bandage).

spicule [spikyl], *s.m.* Spicule, spikelet.

spiculé [spikyle], *a. Bot:* Spiculate(d).

spider [spidɛr], *s.m. Aut:* **1.** Dick(e)y(-seat). **2.** Two-seater with dickey.

spinal, -aux [spinal, -o], *a. Anat:* Spinal.

spinelle[1] [spinɛl], *a. & s.m. Miner:* Spinel.

spinelle[2], *s.f. Nat.Hist:* Spinule.

spinthariscope [spɛ̃tariskɔp], *s.m. Radiology:* Spinthariscope.

spinule [spinyl], *s.f. Bot: etc:* Spinule.

spiral, -aux [spiral, -o]. **1.** *a.* Spiral. **2.** *s.m.* Hair-spring (of watch). **3.** *s.f.* Spirale, spiral, helix. **En spirale**, (i) *adv.* in a spiral, spirally; (ii) *adj.* spiral, curly. *Escalier en spirale*, winding staircase. *Av:* **Descente en spirale**, spiral nose-dive.

spirante [spirɑ̃:t], *s.f. Ling:* Spirant.

spire [spi:r], *s.f.* Single turn, whorl (of spiral). *Conch:* Twirl.

spirée [spire], *s.f. Bot:* Spiraea. *S. ulmaire*, meadow-sweet.

spirite [spirit]. *Psychics:* **1.** *a.* Spiritualistic (séance). **2.** *s.* Spiritist, spiritualist.

spiritisme [spiritism], *s.m. Psychics:* Spiritism; spiritualism.

spiritualiser [spiritɥalize], *v.tr.* To spiritualize.

spiritualisme [spiritɥalism], *s.m. Phil:* Spiritualism; animism.

spiritualiste [spiritɥalist]. *Phil:* **1.** *a.* Spiritualistic (philosophy). **2.** *s.* Spiritualist.

spiritu|el, -elle [spiritɥɛl], *a.* **1.** Spiritual (being, etc.). *Exercices spirituels*, religious exercises. *Parents spirituels*, god-parents. **Concert spirituel**, sacred concert. **2.** Witty; humorous *adv.* **-ellement.**

spiritueux, -euse [spiritɥø, -ø:z]. **1.** *a.* Spirituous. **2.** *s.m.* Spirituous liquor. *Les spiritueux*, spirits.

spiroïdal, -aux [spirɔidal, -o], *a.* Spiral (motion).

spiromètre [spirɔmɛtr], *s.m.* Spirometer, pulmometer.

spleen [splin], *s.m.* Spleen; lowness of spirits. **Avoir le spleen**, to be in the dumps.

splendeur [splɑ̃dœ:r], *s.f.* Splendour. (a) Brilliance, radiance, brightness. (b) Magnificence, grandeur, display.

splendide [splɑ̃did], *a.* Splendid. **1.** Resplendent, brilliant. **2.** Magnificent (palace); sumptuous (meal); gorgeous (sunset); *F:* splendiferous (display). *adv.* **-ment.**

splénique [splenik], *a. Anat:* Splenic (artery).

spoliateur, -trice [spɔljatœ:r, -tris]. **1.** *s.* Despoiler. **2.** *a.* (a) Despoiling. (b) Spoliatory (law).

spoliation [spɔljasjɔ̃], *s.f.* Spoliation; despoiling; robbing (of s.o.); plundering, rifling (of tomb, etc.).

spolier [spɔlje], *v.tr.* To despoil, rob (s.o.) (*de*, of); to plunder, rifle (tomb, etc.). *On l'a spolié de son héritage*, he was robbed, deprived, of his inheritance.

spondaïque [spɔ̃daik], *a. Pros:* Spondaic.

spondée [spɔ̃de], *s.m. Pros:* Spondee.

spongiaires [spɔ̃ʒjɛ:r], *s.m.pl.* Spongiae.

spongieux, -euse [spɔ̃ʒjø, -ø:z], *a.* Spongy.

spongiosité [spɔ̃ʒjozite], *s.f.* Sponginess.

spontané [spɔ̃tane], *a.* Spontaneous. *I.C.E:* **Allumage spontané**, self-ignition. *adv.* **-ment.**

spontanéité [spɔ̃taneite], *s.f.* Spontaneity, spontaneousness.

sporadique [spɔradik], *a.* Sporadic (disease, plant). *adv.* **-ment, -ally.**

sporange [spɔrɑ̃:ʒ], *s.m. Bot:* Sporangium, spore-case.

spore [spɔ:r], *s.f. Bot: Bot:* Spore.

sporocarpe [spɔrɔkarp], *s.m. Bot:* Sporocarp.

sporozoaires [spɔrɔzɔɛ:r], *s.m.pl. Biol:* Sporozoa.

sport [spɔ:r], *s.m.* Sports (not including hunting, fishing, or horse-racing); games. *Sports athlétiques*, athletic sports. *S'adonner aux sports*, to go in for sports. *Aut:* **Machine grand sport, sports model.** S.a. NAUTIQUE.

sportif, -ive [spɔrtif, -i:v]. **1.** *a.* (a) Sporting; (of) sport. *Réunion sportive*, athletic meeting; athletic sports. *Ils n'ont pas l'esprit s.*, they are no sportsmen; they are bad losers. (b) *Biol:* **Variation sportive**, sport, *F:* freak (of nature). **2.** *s.* Devotee of outdoor games.

sport(s)man [spɔrt(s)man], *s.m.* **1.** = SPORTIF 2. **2.** Patron of the turf. *pl.* Des *sport(s)men* [spɔrt(s)mɛn].

sporule [spɔryl], *s.f. Bot:* Sporule, spore.

spot [spɔt], *s.m.* Spot lumineux, light-spot (of recording apparatus).

spumeux, -euse [spymø, -ø:z], *a.* Spumy, spumous, foamy, frothy (blood, saliva).

squale [skwal], *s.m. Ich:* Dog-fish (shark). *pl.* Squales, squali, sharks.

squame [skwam], *s.f.* Squama; scale (of skin).

squameux, -euse [skwamø, -ø:z], *a.* Squamous. scaly (skin, bone).

square [skwɛr, skwa:r], *s.m.* (Public) square (with garden).

squelette [skəlɛt], *s.m.* (*a*) Skeleton. *F:* C'est un vrai squelette, he is a living skeleton. (*b*) Carcass, skeleton, frame-work (of ship, etc.); outline (of play, novel).

squelettique [skəlɛtik], *a.* (*a*) Skeletal. (*b*) Skeleton-like.

squille [skiːj], *s.f.* 1. *Bot:* Squill. 2. *Crust:* Squill(-fish).

squirr(h)e [skiːr], *s.m. Med:* Scirrhus.

squirreux, -euse [skirrø, -øːz], *a. Med:* Scirrhous, scirrhoid (tumour).

st [st], *int.* Here! you there!

stabilisateur, -trice [stabilizatœːr, -tris]. 1. *a.* Stabilizing. 2. *s.m. Aer: etc:* Stabilizer.

stabilisation [stabilizasjɔ̃], *s.f.* 1. Stabilization; steadying. 2. *Mil:* Standstill (in trench warfare).

stabiliser [stabilize], *v.tr.* To stabilize; to steady.
se stabiliser, to become stable, steady.

stabilité [stabilite], *s.f.* 1. Stability, firmness (of building, etc.); steadiness; stiffness (of ship). 2. Permanence (of a conquest); durability. *S. d'emploi,* security of tenure.

stable [stabl], *a.* Stable. 1. Firm, steady; balanced; stiff (ship). *Ch: Corps s.,* stable substance. Équilibre stable, stable equilibrium. Peu stable, unstable. 2. Durable, permanent; lasting (peace).

stabulation [stabylasjɔ̃], *s.f.* Stalling (of cattle); stabling (of horses). Mettre les bêtes en stabulation, to bring in the cattle for the winter.

stade [stad], *s.m.* 1. *Gr.Ant:* Stadium. 2. (*a*) Stadium, sports ground. (*b*) Athletic club. 3. Stage, period (of disease, etc.).

staff [staf], *s.m. Const:* Staff (building material).

stage [staːʒ], *s.m.* Period of probation, of instruction. Faire son stage, (of law student) to keep one's terms; (of teacher, etc.) to go through one's probation.

stagiaire [staʒjɛːr]. 1. *a.* (Of student) Keeping terms, under instruction. *Période s.,* period of probation. 2. *s.* Person under instruction; probationer.

stagnant [stagnɑ̃], *a.* Stagnant (water, business); standing (water).

stagnation [stagnasjɔ̃], *s.f.* Stagnation; stagnancy (of water); dullness (of trade). En stagnation, at a standstill; stagnant.

stalactite [stalaktit], *s.f. Geol:* Stalactite.

stalagmite [stalagmit], *s.f. Geol:* Stalagmite.

stalle [stal], *s.f.* 1. Stall (in cathedral); (numbered) seat (in theatre). Stalles d'orchestre, orchestra stalls. 2. Stall, box (in stable). *S. mobile,* loose box.

staminé [stamine], *a. Bot:* Staminate, stamened.

staminifère [staminifɛːr], *a. Bot:* Staminiferous.

stance [stɑ̃ːs], *s.f.* Stanza.

stand [stɑ̃ːd], *s.m.* 1. Stand (on racecourse). 2. (*a*) Shooting-stand, shooting-gallery. (*b*) Rifle-range.

standard [stɑ̃daːr], *s.m. Tp:* House or office switchboard.

standardisation [stɑ̃dardizasjɔ̃], *s.f. Ind:* Standardization.

standardiser [stɑ̃dardize], *v.tr. Ind:* To standardize.

stannate [stannat], *s.m. Ch:* Stannate.

stanneux, -euse [stannø, -øːz], *a. Ch:* Stannous.

stannifère [stannifɛːr], *a.* Stanniferous, tin-bearing. *Gîte s.,* tin-deposit.

stannique [stannik], *a. Ch:* Stannic (acid).

staphylin¹ [stafilɛ̃], *s.m. Ent:* Cocktail (beetle), rove-beetle, *F:* devil's coach-horse.

staphylin², *a. Anat:* Staphyline.

staphylome [stafiloːm], *s.m. Med:* Staphyloma.

starter [startœːr], *s.m. Rac:* Starter (who gives the signal).

stase [staːz], *s.f. Med:* Stasis.

stater, statère [statɛːr], *s.m. Num:* Stater.

stathouder [statudɛːr], *s.m. Hist:* Stad(t)holder.

statice [statis], *s.m. Bot:* Statice, sea-lavender.

statif [statif], *s.m.* Stand (of microscope).

station [stasjɔ̃], *s.f.* Station. 1. (*a*) (Action of) standing. En station derrière un arbre, stationed, on the look-out, behind a tree. (*b*) Position. Mettre un théodolite en s., to set up a theodolite. (*c*) Attitude (of horse). 2. Break of journey; (short) halt, stay, stop. Faire une s. d . . ., to halt at . . . . 3. (*a*) (Railway) station (esp. underground); stage (on bus or tramway route); cab-rank, taxi-rank. (*b*) Station d'hiver, d'été, winter resort, summer resort. Station balnéaire, watering-place; spa or seaside resort. S.a. MONTAGNE 1, THERMAL. (*c*) (Wireless, etc.) station. (*d*) *El.E:* Station centrale, power-station, -house. (*e*) *Mil: etc:* Post, station. *Navy:* Cruising ground; (colonial) station. Navire en station, ship on station.

stationnaire [stasjɔnɛːr]. 1. *a.* Stationary. *Rester s.,* to stand still. *Chaudière s.,* fixed boiler. 2. *s.m.* Guardship.

stationnement [stasjɔnmɑ̃], *s.m.* 1. (*a*) Stopping, standing (of cabs, etc.). Auto en stationnement, stationary car, car drawn up at the kerb. "S. interdit," 'no parking. (*b*) *Mil:* Stationing, quartering; halt. (*c*) Congestion (in traffic). 2. (*a*) *Adm:* (i) Cab-rank, taxi-rank. (ii) (Parc, endroit, de) stationnement, parking place (in street); motor-car park. (*b*) *Mil:* Quarters.

stationner [stasjɔne], *v.i.* 1. To stop; to take up one's position; to halt. 2. (Of cabs, cars, etc.) To stand; to park (in street). "Défense de stationner," 'no parking here.' 3. (*a*) (Of troops) To be stationed. (*b*) (Of ships) To be on station.

statique [statik]. 1. *a.* Static (electricity). 2. *s.f.* Statics.

statisticien [statistisjɛ̃], *s.m.* Statistician.

statistique [statistik]. 1. *a.* Statistical. 2. *s.f.* Statistics.

stator [statɔːr], *s.m. Mch: El.E:* Stator (of turbine, of electric motor).

statuaire [statɥɛːr]. 1. *a.* Statuary (art, etc.). 2. *s.* Sculptor, sculptress. 3. *s.f.* (Art of) statuary.

statue [staty], *s.f.* Statue.

statuer [statɥe], *v.tr.* 1. To decree, enact, ordain, rule. *S. que + ind.,* to rule, ordain, that . . . . 2. *Abs. S. sur une affaire,* to pronounce judgment in a matter. *S. sur un litige,* to settle a dispute.

statuette [statɥɛt], *s.f.* Statuette.

statufier [statyfje], *v.tr. F:* To erect a statue to (s.o.).

statu quo [statyko], *s.m.* Status (in) quo. In statu quo, in statu quo.

stature [statyːr], *s.f.* Stature, height (esp. of person).

statut [staty], *s.m.* 1. Statute, ordinance, article (of society, company, etc.); rule, regulation. *S. local,* by(e)-law. 2. *Dipl: etc:* Status (of country, port). Le Statut de Tanger, the status of Tangiers. *S. personnel,* personal status.

statutaire [statytɛːr], *a.* Statutory, statutable.

stayer [stɛjœːr], *s.m. Sp:* Long-distance runner or cyclist; stayer.

stéarate [stearat], *s.m. Ch:* Stearate.

stéarine [stearin], *s.f. Ch:* Stearin.

stéarique [stearik], *a.* 1. *Ch:* Stearic (acid). 2. Bougie stéarique, stearin candle.

stéatite [steatit], *s.f.* *Miner*: Steatite, soapstone.
stéatose [steato:z], *s.f.* *Med*: Fatty degeneration.
steeple-chase [stiplət∫ɛs], *s.m.* *F*: steeple [stipl]. *s.m.* *Rac*: (Long-distance) hurdle-race (on track).
stèle ¡stɛl], *s.f.* Stele (bearing inscription).
stellaire [stɛllɛ:r]. **1.** *a.* Stellar (light, etc.). **2.** *s.f.* *Bot*: Stellaria; starwort.
stellionat ¡stɛlljɔna], *s.m.* *Jur*: Fraudulent misrepresentation as to mortgages on a property; stellionate.
stemmate [stɛmmat], *s.m.* Stemma; simple eye.
sténo [steno], *s.f.* *F:* = STÉNOGRAPHIE.
sténodactylographe [stenɔdaktilɔgraf], *F:* sténodactylo [stenɔdaktilo], *s.m.* & *f.* Short-hand-typist.
sténodactylographie [stenɔdaktilɔgrafi], *s.f.* Shorthand and typing.
sténogramme [stenɔgram], *s.m.* **1.** *Shorthand*: Outline; grammalogue, logogram. **2.** Verbatim report (of proceedings).
sténographe [stenɔgraf], *s.m.* & *f.* Steno-grapher; shorthand writer, shorthand reporter.
sténographie ¡stenɔgrafi], *s.f.* Stenography; shorthand.
sténographier [stenɔgrafje], *v.tr.* To take down (speech, etc.) in shorthand.
sténographique [stenɔgrafik], *a.* Stenographic, shorthand (writing, etc.).
sténopé [stenɔpe], *s.m.* *Phot*: Pin-hole.
Stentor [stãtɔ:r]. *Pr.n.m.* *Gr.Lit*: Stentor. Voix de Stentor, stentorian voice.
step-in [stepin], *s.m.* Cami-knickers. *pl.* Des step-ins.
steppe [stɛp], *s. m. or f.* Steppe.
stepper, steppeur [stɛpœ:r], *s.m.* (Of horse) High-stepper.
stercoraire [stɛrkɔrɛ:r]. **1.** *a.* Stercoraceous; stercoral (ulcer, fistula). **2.** *s.m.* (a) *Ent*: Dung-beetle. (b) *Orn*: Skua.
stercoral, -aux [stɛrkɔral, -o], *a.* Stercoral.
stère [stɛ:r], *s.m.* *Meas*: Stere, cubic metre (of firewood). Bois de stère, cord-wood.
stéréochimie [stereɔ∫imi], *s.f.* Stereochemistry.
stéréogramme [stereɔgram], *s.m.* *Opt*: *Phot*: Stereogram; stereoscopic image or slide.
stéréographe [stereɔgraf], *s.m.* *Opt*: *Phot*: Stereograph (instrument).
stéréographie [stereɔgrafi], *s.f.* *Geom*: Stereo-graphy.
stéréographique [stereɔgrafik], *a.* Stereo-graphic(al).
stéréoscope [stereɔskɔp], *s.m.* *Opt*: Stereoscope.
stéréoscopique [stereɔskɔpik], *a.* Stereoscopic.
stéréotélémètre [stereɔtelemɛtr], *s.m.* Stereo-scopic telemeter.
stéréotomie [stereɔtɔmi], *s.f.* *Geom*: Stereo-tomy
stéréotype [stereɔtip]. *Typ*: **1.** *a.* Stereotype (printing); stereotyped (edition). **2.** *s.m.* Stereo-type plate.
stéréotypler ¡stereɔtipe], *v.tr.* *Typ*: To stereo-type. *F*: Expression stéréotypée, stereotyped phrase, hackneyed phrase. *s.m.* -age.
stéréotypeur [stereɔtipœ:r], *s.m.* *Typ*: Stereo-typer.
stéréotypie [stereɔtipi], *s.f.* **1.** Stereotypy. **2.** Stereotype foundry.
stérler [stere], *v.tr.* (je stère; je stérerai) To measure (wood) by the stere. *s.m.* -age.
stérile [steril], *a.* Sterile, unfruitful; barren (female, land); childless (marriage); unpro-ductive (land); fruitless (efforts); unprofitable (work). *adv.* -ment.

stérilisant [sterilizã], *s.m.* Sterilizing agent.
stérilisateur [sterilizatœ:r], *s.m.* Sterilizer.
stérilisation [sterilizasjɔ̃], *s.f.* Sterilization.
stériliser [sterilize], *v.tr.* To sterilize.
stérilité [sterilite], *s.f.* Sterility, barrenness, unfruitfulness.
sterlet [stɛrlɛ], *s.m.* *Ich*: Sterlet.
sternal, -aux [stɛrnal, -o], *a.* *Anat*: Sternal.
sternum [stɛrnɔm], *s.m.* *Anat*: Sternum, breast-bone.
sternutatif, -ive [stɛrnytatif, -i:v], *a.* *Med*: Sternutatory; sneezing(-powder).
sternutation [stɛrnytasjɔ̃], *s.f.* Sternutation, sneezing.
sternutatoire [stɛrnytatwa:r], *a.* & *s.m.* *Med*: Sternutatory; sneezing(-powder).
stertoreux, -euse [stɛrtɔrø, -ø:z], *a.* *Med*: Stertorous (breathing).
stéthoscope [stetɔskɔp], *s.m.* *Med*: Stethoscope.
stibial, -aux [stibjal, -o], *a.* Stibial, antimonial.
stibié [stibje], *a.* *Pharm*: Impregnated with antimony; stibiated. Tartre stibié, tartar emetic.
stibieux, -euse [stibjø, -ø:z], *a.* *Ch*: Stibious, antimonious.
stibine [stibin], *s.f.*, stibnite [stibnit], *s.f.* *Miner*: Stibnite, stibine; gray antimony.
stick [stik], *s.m.* **1.** (Soldier's) swagger-stick. **2.** (Riding-)switch; riding-whip.
stigmate [stigmat], *s.m.* **1.** *A*: (a) Stigma, brand (on slave). (b) *F*: Stigma, brand of in-famy, stain (on character). **2.** (a) Mark, scar (of wound); pock-mark. (b) *Med*: Stigma (of hysteria). (c) *pl.* *Rel.H*: Stigmata. **3.** (a) *Bot*: Stigma. (b) *Ent*: Spiracle, stigma.
stigmatique [stigmatik], *a.* **1.** *Nat.Hist*: Stig-matic. **2.** *Opt*: (Ana)stigmatic.
stigmatiser [stigmatize], *v.tr.* **1.** (a) *A*: To brand (slave, animal). (b) *F*: To stigmatize (de, with); to brand (s.o.) with infamy; to set the stamp of shame on (sth.). **2.** To pock-mark (s.o.).
stigmatisé, -ée, *s.* *Rel.H*: Stigmatist.
stillation [stillasjɔ̃], *s.f.* Dripping; falling drop by drop; oozing (from rock).
stilligoutte [stilligut], *s.m.* Dropping-tube, dropper.
stimulant [stimylã]. **1.** *a.* Stimulating, stimula-tive. **2.** *s.m.* (a) *Med*: Stimulant; whet (to the appetite). (b) Stimulus, spur, incentive, induce-ment.
stimulateur, -trice [stimylatœ:r, -tris], *a.* Stimulative.
stimulation [stimylasjɔ̃], *s.f.* Stimulation.
stimuler [stimyle], *v.tr.* To stimulate. **1.** To in-cite; to spur (s.o.) on. *S. qn au travail*, to incite s.o. to work. **2.** To stimulate (the digestion); to whet (the appetite); to give a stimulus to (business).
stipe [stip], *s.m.* *Bot*: (a) Stipe(s) (of fern, of fungus); culm. (b) Stem (of palm-tree).
stipendiaire [stipãdjɛ:r], *a.* & *s.m.* Usu. *Pej*: (a) (Of soldier) Mercenary. (b) *F*: Hireling.
stipendier [stipãdje], *v.tr.* To keep (ruffians, etc.) in one's pay.
stipendié. **1.** *a.* Mercenary, hired (ruffian). **2.** *s.m.* = STIPENDIAIRE.
stipité [stipite], *a.* *Bot*: Stipitate, stalked.
stipulation [stipylasjɔ̃], *s.f.* Stipulation, provi-sion. *pl.* Conditions laid down (in an agreement).
stipule [stipyl], *s.f.* *Bot*: Stipule.
stipuler [stipyle], *v.tr.* To stipulate: to lay down (that . . .).
stock [stɔk], *s.m.* *Com*: Stock (of goods). *S. en magasin*, stock in hand.
stockler [stɔke], *v.tr* To stock (goods). *s.m.* -age.

stockiste [stɔkist], *s.m.* *Com:* Wholesale warehouseman; stockist, stocker. *Aut:* Agent. *a.* Agence stockiste, service-station.

stoïcien, -ienne [stɔisjɛ̃, -jɛn]. **1.** *a.* Stoical, stoic. **2.** *s.* Stoic.

stoïcisme [stɔisism], *s.m.* Stoicism, impassiveness.

stoïque [stɔik]. **1.** *a.* Stoic, stoical. **2.** *s.* = STOÏCIEN 2. *adv.* **-ment,** -ally.

stolon [stɔlɔ̃], *s.m.* *Bot:* Stolon, offset; runner, sucker.

stomacal, -aux [stɔmakal, -o], *a.* Stomachal, gastric.

stomachique [stɔmaʃik], *a. & s.m. Anat: Med:* Stomachic.

stop [stɔp]. **1.** *int.* Stop! **2.** *s.m. Aut:* Stop-light.

stoppage¹ [stɔpa:ʒ], *s.m.* **1.** Stoppage, stopping (of machine, etc.); countering (of motion). **2.** Obstruction, stoppage (in pipe). **3.** *Adm:* Deduction (of tax) at the source.

stoppage², *s.m.* Invisible mending; fine-darning.

stopper¹ [stɔpe]. **1.** *v.i.* (Of ship, train) To stop; to come to a stop. **2.** *v.tr.* (*a*) To stop (train, etc.); to check (chain or cable). (*b*) *Com:* To stop (payment of cheque). (*c*) *Adm:* To deduct (tax) at the source.

stopper², *v.tr.* To repair by invisible mending; to fine-darn.

stoppeur, -euse [stɔpœ:r, -ø:z], *s.* Fine-darner.

storax [stɔraks], *s.m. Pharm:* Storax.

store [stɔ:r], *s.m.* (Inside or outside window-) blind; carriage-blind. *S. à rouleaux,* roller-blind. *S. à l'italienne,* awning-blind.

strabique [strabik]. **1.** *a.* Squint-eyed, *F:* cross-eyed. **2.** *s.* Squinter.

strabisme [strabism], *s.m.* Strabism(us); squinting.

stramoine [stramwan], *s.f. Bot:* Stramonium, stramony, thorn-apple.

strangulation [strɑ̃gylasjɔ̃], *s.f.* Strangulation. **1.** *Jur:* Strangling, throttling. **2.** *Med:* Constriction.

strapontin [strapɔ̃tɛ̃], *s.m. Aut: Th: etc:* Flap-seat, folding seat, bracket-seat.

stras(s) [stras], *s.m.* Strass; paste (jewellery).

stratagème [strataʒɛm], *s.m.* Stratagem; artifice of war.

stratège [stratɛ:ʒ], *s.m.* **1.** *Gr.Ant:* Strategus. **2.** *F:* = STRATÉGISTE.

stratégie [strateʒi], *s.f.* Strategy; generalship.

stratégique [strateʒik], *a.* Strategic(al) (position, etc.). *adv.* **-ment,** -ally.

stratégiste [strateʒist], *s.m.* Strategist.

stratification [stratifikasjɔ̃], *s.f.* Stratification. *Geol:* Bedding.

stratifier [stratifje], *v.tr.* To stratify.

stratosphère [stratɔsfɛ:r], *s.f. Meteor:* Stratosphere; isothermal layer.

stratus [straty:s], *s.m. Meteor:* Stratus (cloud).

streptocoque [strɛptɔkɔk], *s.m. Bac:* Streptococcus.

strette [strɛt], *s.f. Mus:* Stretto (of fugue).

striation [striasjɔ̃], *s.f. Anat: etc:* Striation.

strict [strikt], *a.* Strict. (*a*) *Obligation stricte,* strict obligation. *Le s. nécessaire,* no more than is necessary. (*b*) Severe, exact (person). *adv.* **-ement.**

stridence [stridɑ̃:s], *s.f.* Harshness (of sound); stridency; shrillness.

strid|ent [stridɑ̃], *a.* Strident, shrill, harsh, grating (noise, voice). *adv.* **-emment.**

stridulant [stridylɑ̃], *a.* Chirring (insect).

stridulation [stridylasjɔ̃], *s.f.* Stridulation; chirring.

striduler [stridyle], *v.i.* To chirr, to stridulate.

striduleux, -euse [stridylø, -ø:z], *a. Med:* Stridulous. S.a. LARYNGITE.

strie [stri], *s.f.* **1.** Score, scratch. *Anat: etc:* Stria. *Geol: Stries glaciales,* glacial striae. **2.** (*a*) Rib, ridge. *Arch:* (= LISTEL) Fillet, stria. (*b*) Streak (of colour).

strier [strie], *v.tr.* **1.** To striate, score, scratch. **2.** (*a*) To flute, groove, rib, corrugate. (*b*) To streak.
    strié, *a.* **1.** Scored, scratched; striated. *Anat:* Striped, striated (muscle). **2.** (*a*) Fluted, grooved; ribbed (glass). (*b*) Streaked (marble).

strige [stri:ʒ], *s.f.* Vampire, ghoul.

strigile [striʒil], *s.m. Gr. & Rom.Ant:* Strigil.

striure [striy:r], *s.f.* Striation. **1.** (*a*) Score, scratch, groove. (*b*) Streak; stripe. **2.** Scoring, scratching.

strobile [strɔbil], *s.m. Bot:* Strobile, cone (of pine, hops).

stroboscope [strɔbɔskɔp], *s.m.* Stroboscope.

stroboscopique [strɔbɔskɔpik], *a.* Stroboscopic.

strontiane [strɔ̃sjan], *s.f. Ch:* Strontia.

strontium [strɔ̃sjɔm], *s.m. Ch:* Strontium.

strophe [strɔf], *s.f.* **1.** *Gr.Lit:* Strophe. **2.** *Pros:* Stanza, verse.

stropiat [strɔpja], *s.m. P:* Cripple (real or sham).

structural, -aux [stryktyral, -o], *a.* Structural. *adv.* **-ement.**

structure [strykty:r], *s.f.* Structure.

strumeux, -euse [strymø, -ø:z], *a. Med:* Strumous, scrofulous.

strychnine [striknin], *s.f.* Strychnin(e).

strychnisme [striknism], *s.m. Med:* Strychn(in)ism.

stuc [styk], *s.m. Const:* Stucco.

stucage [styka:ʒ], *s.m.* Stucco-work.

studieu|x, -euse [stydjø, -ø:z], *a.* Studious; bookish. *adv.* **-sement.**

studio [stydjo], *s.m.* **1.** *Cin:* Film-studio. *W.Tel: S. d'émission,* broadcasting studio. **2.** One-roomed flat with bathroom, etc.

studiosité [stydjozite], *s.f.* Studiousness.

stupéfaction [stypefaksjɔ̃], *s.f.* Stupefaction, amazement.

stupéfait [stypefɛ], *a.* Stupefied, amazed, aghast, astounded, dumbfounded.

stupéfiant [stypefjɑ̃]. **1.** *a.* (*a*) *Med:* Stupefying, stupefacient (drug). (*b*) Amazing, astounding (news). **2.** *s.m. Med:* Narcotic, stupefacient; *F:* drug. Faire usage de, s'adonner aux, stupéfiants, to take drugs, to drug oneself. Trafic des stupéfiants, drug-traffic.

stupéfier [stypefje], *v.tr.* (*a*) To bemuse. *Med:* To stupefy. (*b*) To astound, amaze, dumbfound.

stupeur [stypœ:r], *s.f.* Stupor. **1.** Dazed state. **2.** Amazement. Muet de stupeur, dumbfounded. Écouter avec stupeur, to listen in amazement.

stupide [stypid], *a.* Stupid. (*a*) Stunned with surprise; bemused. (*b*) Dull-witted, witless. (*c*) Silly (answer, etc.); foolish. *adv.* **-ment.**

stupidité [stypidite], *s.f.* **1.** Stupidity; foolishness. **2.** Piece of stupidity; stupid answer.

stupre [stypr], *s.m.* Debauchery.

stuquer [styke], *v.tr. Const:* To stucco.

stygien, -ienne [stiʒjɛ̃, -jɛn], *a.* Stygian (darkness).

style [stil], *s.m.* **1.** (*a*) *Ant:* Stylus, style (writing implement). (*b*) Graver, etching-needle. (*c*) Style, pin, gnomon (of sun-dial). (*d*) *Bot:* Style. **2.** *Lit: Arch: etc:* Style. *Écrivain qui n'a pas de s.,* writer who lacks style. Meubles style

Empire, furniture in the Empire style. **Robe de style,** period dress, picture frock.

styler [stile], *v.tr.* To train, form (s.o.). *S. qn aux usages du monde,* to school s.o. in society ways. *Domestique, cheval, bien stylé,* well-schooled servant, horse.

stylet [stilɛ], *s.m.* **1.** Stiletto, stylet. **2.** *Surg:* Stylet, probe.

styliser [stilize], *v.tr. Art:* To stylize, conventionalize (form, design).

styliste [stilist], *s. m. & f. Lit:* Stylist.

stylistique [stilistik], *s.f.* Stylistics.

stylite [stilit], *a. & s.m. Rel.H:* Stylite.

stylo [stilo], *s.m. F:* = STYLOGRAPHE.

stylobate [stilɔbat], *s.m. Arch:* Stylobate.

stylographe [stilɔgraf], *s.m.* (a) Stylograph (pen). (b) Fountain-pen.

stylomine [stilɔmin], *s.m.* Ever-sharp; propelling pencil.

styptique [stiptik], *a. & s.m.* Styptic, astringent.

styrax [stiraks], *s.m. Bot:* Styrax.

Styx [stiks]. *Pr.n.m. Myth:* The (river) Styx. *Visiter les bords du S.,* to visit the Stygian shores.

su [sy]. See SAVOIR.

suage[1] [sɥa:ʒ], *s.m.* Sweating, oozing (of wall).

suage[2], *s.m. Metalw:* **1.** *Tls:* (a) Swage. (b) Creasing-tool. **2.** Fillet(-border) (of silverplate).

suage[3], *s.m. Nau:* **1.** Paying, tallowing (of vessel). **2.** Paying stuff; tallow.

suager[1] [sɥaʒe], *v.tr.* (je suageai(s); n. suageons) *Metalw:* To swage, crease.

suager[2], *v.tr. Nau:* To pay, tallow (vessel).

suaire [sɥɛ:r], *s.m.* Winding-sheet; shroud. **Le saint Suaire,** the Sindon (of Christ).

suant [sɥɑ̃], *a.* **1.** Sweating; in a sweat; sweaty; (of walls, wood) oozing moisture. **2.** *Metalw:* **Chaleur suante, blanc suant,** welding heat, white heat.

suave [sɥa:v], *a.* (a) Sweet, pleasant (music, etc.); mild (cigar). (b) Suave, bland. *adv.* **-ment.**

suavité [sɥavite], *s.f.* (a) Sweetness (of perfume, etc.). (b) Suavity, blandness.

subaigu, -uë [sybɛgy], *a. Med:* Subacute.

subalpin [sybalpɛ̃], *a.* Subalpine.

subalterne [sybaltɛrn]. **1.** *a.* Subordinate, minor (official, part). *Employé s., F:* understrapper. **2.** *s.m.* (a) Underling, subaltern. (b) *Mil:* Officer of subaltern's rank or of captain's rank.

subdiviser [sybdivize], *v.tr.* To subdivide, to split up (en, into).

se subdiviser, to subdivide.

subdivision [sybdivizjɔ̃], *s.f.* Subdivision.

subéreux, -euse [sybero, -ø:z], *a. Bot:* Suberous, suberose; corky (layer).

subir [sybi:r], *v.tr.* To undergo, go through (operation, trial, etc.); to come under (an influence); to suffer, sustain (defeat); to submit to, suffer (punishment, one's fate). *S. sa peine,* to serve one's sentence. *S. une complète métamorphose,* to undergo a complete change. **Faire subir** *un examen à qn,* to put s.o. through an examination. *Faire s. une peine à qn,* to inflict a penalty on s.o.

subit [sybi], *a.* Sudden, unexpected (death, change). *adv.* **-ement.**

subito [sybito], *adv. F:* (a) All of a sudden. (b) At once.

subjacent [sybʒasɑ̃], *a.* Subjacent, underlying.

subject|if, -ive [sybʒɛktif, -i:v], *a. Phil: Gram:* Subjective. *adv.* **-ivement.**

subjonctif, -ive [sybʒɔ̃ktif, -i:v]. *Gram:* **1.** *a.* Subjunctive (mood). **2.** *s.m.* Subjunctive.

subjugation [sybʒygasjɔ̃], *s.f.* Subjugation.

subjuguer [sybʒyge], *v.tr.* To subjugate, subdue; to bring (people) into subjection. *F: S. tous les cœurs,* to captivate, conquer, all hearts.

sublimation [syblimasjɔ̃], *s.f. Ch:* Sublimation.

sublime [syblim], *a.* Sublime; lofty, exalted. *s.* **Le sublime,** the sublime. *adv.* **-ment.**

sublimer [syblime], *v.tr.* (a) *Ch:* To sublimate. (b) To purify, refine.

sublimé, *s.m. Ch:* Sublimate. *Pharm:* **Sublimé corrosif,** corrosive sublimate.

subliminal, -aux [sybliminal, -o], *a. Psy:* Below the threshold; subliminal (consciousness, memory).

sublimité [syblimite], *s.f.* Sublimity.

sublingual, -als, -aux [syblɛ̃gwal, -o], *a. Anat:* Sublingual.

submerger [sybmɛrʒe], *v.tr.* (je submergeai(s); n. submergeons) **1.** To submerge; to put under water. (a) To flood (meadow). (b) To swamp (boat). (c) To immerse. **2.** *F:* To overwhelm (with work, etc.).

submersible [sybmɛrsibl]. **1.** *a.* (a) Sinkable; submersible (boat). (b) Easily flooded. **2.** *s.m. Navy:* Submersible; high-reserve submarine.

submersion [sybmɛrsjɔ̃], *s.f.* Submersion. **1.** Immersion. **Mort par submersion,** death by drowning. **2.** Flooding.

subordination [sybɔrdinasjɔ̃], *s.f.* Subordination (à, to).

subordonner [sybɔrdɔne], *v.tr.* To subordinate (à, to).

subordonné, -ée. 1. *a. Gram:* Subordinate, dependent (clause). **2.** *s.s.* Subordinate, underling.

subornation [sybɔrnasjɔ̃], *s.f. Jur:* Intimidation or bribing (of witnesses); subornation.

suborn|er [sybɔrne], *v.tr.* **1.** To suborn, instigate (evil-doer). **2.** *Jur:* To suborn, to tamper with (witness). *s.* **-eur, -euse.**

subrécargue [sybrekarg], *s.m. Nau:* Supercargo.

subreptice [sybrɛptis], *a.* Surreptitious; clandestine. *adv.* **-ment.**

subrogation [sybrɔgasjɔ̃], *s.f. Jur:* **1.** Subrogation, substitution. **2.** Delegation (of powers, rights).

subroger [sybrɔʒe], *v.tr.* (je subrogeai(s); n. subrogeons) *Jur:* To subrogate; to appoint (s.o.) as deputy, as surrogate.

subrogé, *a.* Subrogated. **Subro e tuteur,** deputy guardian; surrogate guardian.

subséqu|ent [sypsɛkɑ̃], *a.* Subsequent. **1.** Ensuing. **2.** Later (testament, etc.). *adv.* **-emment.**

subside [sypsid], *s.m.* Subsidy.

subsidence [sypsidɑ̃:s], *s.f.* Subsidence.

subsidiaire [sypsidjɛ:r], *a.* Subsidiary, auxiliary, accessory (à, to). *adv.* **-ment.**

subsistance [sypsistɑ̃:s], *s.f.* **1.** Subsistence, sustenance, maintenance; (one's) keep. **2.** *pl.* Provisions.

subsistant [sypsistɑ̃], *a.* Subsisting, existing, still extant.

subsister [sypsiste], *v.i.* To subsist. **1.** To (continue to) exist; to be still extant, in existence. *Cette objection subsiste,* the objection stands, holds. **2.** To live (de, upon).

substance [sypstɑ̃:s], *s.f.* **1.** Substance. *Arguments sans substance,* insubstantial arguments. **En substance,** in substance, substantially. **2.** Matter, material, stuff. *El: S. isolante,* insulating material.

substanti|el, -elle [sypstɑ̃sjɛl], *a.* Substantial. *adv.* **-ellement.**

substantif, -ive [sypstătif, -i:v]. **1.** *a.* Substantive. **2.** *s.m. Gram:* Substantive, noun.

substituer [sybstitɥe], *v.tr.* **I.** To substitute (à, for). **2.** *Jur:* (*a*) Substituer un héritier, to appoint an heir in succession to another or failing another. (*b*) **Substituer un héritage**, to entail an estate. **se substituer** *à* qn, to serve as a substitute for s.o.; to take the place of s.o. **substitué**, *a. Jur:* Enfant substitué, suppositious child.

substitut [sybstity], *s.m.* Assistant or deputy (to official); locum tenens (of doctor); surrogate (of bishop). *Jur:* Deputy public prosecutor.

substitution [sybstitysjɔ̃], *s.f.* **I.** Substitution. **2.** *Jur:* Entail.

substrat [sybstra], *s.m.*, **substratum** [sybstratɔm], *s.m. Phil:* Substratum.

substruction [sybstryksjɔ̃], *s.f.* **I.** Substruction, substructure, foundation. **2.** Under-pinning.

subterfuge [sypterfy:ʒ], *s.m.* Subterfuge, shift. *User de s.*, to resort to subterfuge; to quibble.

subtil [syptil], *a.* Subtle. **I.** (*a*) Tenuous, thin (matter); rarefied (air). (*b*) Pervasive (scent). **2.** (*a*) Acute, keen (sense of smell, hearing); discerning, shrewd (mind). (*b*) Delicate, nice, fine (distinction). *adv.* **-ement.**

subtiliser [syptilize], *v.tr.* **I.** To subtilize. (*a*) To refine (a substance). (*b*) To make (an argument) too subtle. **2.** *P:* To sneak (s.o.'s watch, etc.); to nobble (s.o.'s money).

subtilité [syptilite], *s.f.* **I.** Subtlety (of poison, etc.); rarefied state (of air). **2.** (*a*) Acuteness, quickness (of hearing); shrewdness (of mind). (*b*) Subtlety (of argument). **3.** Subtle argument or distinction.

subulé [sybyle], *a. Nat.Hist:* Subulate(d), awl-shaped.

suburbain [sybyrbɛ̃], *a.* Suburban.

subvenir [sybvəni:r], *v.ind.tr.* (Conj. like VENIR. Aux. *avoir*) *S. aux besoins de* qn, to supply, provide for, the needs of s.o. *S. aux frais d'une maladie*, to meet, defray, the expenses of an illness. *Il a subvenu à tout*, he provided for everything.

subvention [sybvɑ̃sjɔ̃], *s.f.* Subsidy, subvention, grant (of money).

subventionner [sybvɑ̃sjɔne], *v.tr.* To subsidize. *Être subventionné par l'État*, to be subsidized by the State; to be State-aided.

subversif, -ive [sybversif, -i:v], *a.* Subversive (de, of).

subversion [sybversjɔ̃], *s.f.* Subversion (of morality); overthrow (of the State, etc.).

subvertir [sybverti:r], *v.tr.* To subvert.

suc [syk], *s.m.* (*a*) Juice. *Bot:* Sap. **Suc gastrique**, gastric juice. (*b*) *F:* Pith, essence, quintessence (of a book, etc.).

succédané [syksedane], *s.m.* Substitute, succedaneum (of, for).

succéder [syksede], *v.ind.tr.* (je succède; je succéderai) *S. à* qn, *à* qch., to succeed, follow after, s.o., sth. *S. au trône*, to succeed to the throne. *S. à une fortune*, to inherit, come into, a fortune. *Les années se succèdent*, the years follow one another.

succès [syksɛ], *s.m.* **I.** Result, issue (of an undertaking, etc.). *Bon, mauvais, s.*, favourable, unfavourable, issue. **2.** Success; favourable result. **Avoir du succès**, (of undertaking) to turn out a success; (of article of commerce) to take on. *Remporter un s. complet*, to be entirely successful. *Il s'en est tiré avec succès*, he got through successfully. *Tentative sans succès*, unsuccessful attempt. *Th:* **Pièce à succès**, hit. **Succès d'estime**, success due to the sympathy of friends.

successeur [syksɛsœ:r], *s.m.* Successor (de, to, of).

successif, -ive [syksɛsif, -i:v], *a.* Successive. *Trois jours successifs*, three days running.

succession [syksɛsjɔ̃], *s.f.* Succession. **I.** (*a*) Series, sequence (of ideas, etc.). (*b*) *S. à la couronne*, succession to the crown. **Prendre la succession** d'un ministre, to succeed a minister. *Prendre la s. d'une maison de commerce*, to take over a business. **2.** *Jur:* Inheritance. (*a*) Inheriting, coming into (property). **Droits de succession**, probate duty; death duties. (*b*) Estate.

successivement [syksɛsivmɑ̃], *adv.* Successively, in succession; one after another; seriatim.

succin [syksɛ̃], *s.m.* Succin; yellow amber.

succinct [syksɛ̃, syksɛ̃:(k)t], *a.* Succinct, brief, concise. *adv.* **-ement.**

succion [syksjɔ̃], *s.f.* **I.** Suction; sucking (of a wound). **2.** Down-draught (of sinking ship).

succomber [sykɔ̃be], *v.i.* To succumb. **I.** *S. sous le poids de* qch., to sink under the burden of sth. **2.** (*a*) To be worsted. *S. sous le nombre*, to succumb to odds, to force. (*b*) To yield (to grief, etc.). *S. à l'émotion*, to be overcome by emotion. (*c*) To die. *S. au poison*, to die poisoned.

succube [sykyb], *s.m.* Succubus, succuba.

succulence [sykylɑ̃:s], *s.f.* Succulence; juiciness.

succulent [sykylɑ̃], *a.* Succulent, juicy; tasty, toothsome (morsel).

succursale [sykyrsal], *s.f.* (*a*) Branch (establishment) (of stores, etc.); branch (of bank); suboffice. (*b*) *Ecc:* Chapel of ease.

sucer [syse], *v.tr.* (je suçai(s); n. suçons) To suck (milk, orange, etc.). *S e s. les doigts*, to suck one's fingers. *F:* Sucer qn jusqu'au dernier sou, jusqu'à la moelle des os, to suck s.o. dry.

sucette [sysɛt], *s.f.* (*a*) (Baby's) comforter, dummy. (*b*) Lollipop mounted on a stick.

suceur, -euse [sysœ:r, -ø:z]. **I.** *s.* Sucker. **2.** *s.m.* Nozzle (of vacuum cleaner). **3.** *a. Z:* Suctorial.

suçoir [syswa:r], *s.m. Ent: etc:* Sucker.

suçon [sysɔ̃], *s.m. F:* **I.** Mark made (on skin) by sucking, by a kiss. **2.** Stick of barley sugar.

suçoter [sysɔte], *v.tr. F:* To suck away at (a sweet).

sucre [sykr], *s.m.* Sugar. (*a*) *S. en pains*, loaf sugar. *S. en poudre* castor sugar. *S. cristallisé*, granulated sugar. *S. en morceaux, en tablettes*, lump sugar. **Sucre d'orge**, barley sugar. **Pince à sucre**, sugar-tongs. *F:* Casser du sucre sur le dos de qn, to run s.o. down; to make a scurrilous attack on s.o. (*b*) *Ch:* *S. de lait*, lactose. *S. de raisin*, grape sugar; glucose. *S. de saturne*, sugar of lead.

sucr|er [sykre], *v.tr.* To sugar; to sweeten. *s.m.* **-age.**

sucré, *a.* **I.** Sugared, sweetened (coffee, etc.); sweet (fruits, etc.). *Mon thé est trop s.*, my tea is too sweet. **Eau sucrée**, sugar and water. **2.** *F:* Sugary (words, smile).

sucrerie [sykrəri], *s.f.* **I.** Sugar-refinery. **2.** *pl.* Sweetmeats, sweets, confectionery.

sucrier [sykrie], *s.m.* **I.** Sugar-manufacturer. **2.** Sugar-basin.

sucrin [sykrɛ̃], *s.m.* Sugary melon.

sud [syd]. **I.** *s.m.* No *pl.* South. *Un vent du sud*, a southerly wind. *Le vent du sud*, the south wind. **Au sud**, in the south. *Astr:* **La Croix du Sud**, the Southern Cross. *Nau:* **Faire le sud**, to steer a southerly course. **Vers le sud**, southward. **2.** *a.inv.* South, southerly (wind); southern (part, latitude). *Le pôle sud*, the south pole.

sud-africain, -aine [sydafrikɛ̃, -ɛn], *a. & s.*
Geog: South-African. **L'Union Sud-africaine**,
the Union of South Africa.

sudation [sydasjɔ̃], *s.f. Med:* Sudation, sweating.

sud-est [sydɛst, *Nau:* sy(r)ɛ]. **1.** *s.m.* No *pl.*
South-east. **2.** *a.inv.* South-easterly (wind);
south-eastern (region).

sudoripare [sydɔripaːr], *a.* Sudoriferous, per-
spiratory; sweat(-gland).

sud-ouest [sydwɛst, *Nau:* syrwɛ, syrwa].
1. *s.m.* No *pl.* South-west. **2.** *a.inv.* South-
westerly (wind); south-western (region).

Suède [sɥɛd]. **1.** *Pr.n.f.* Sweden. **2.** *s.m.*
Leath: **Gants de suède**, suède gloves.

suédois, -oise [sɥedwa, -waːz]. **1.** *a.* Swedish.
2. *s.* Swede. **3.** *s.m. Ling:* Swedish.

suer [sɥe], *v.i.* To sweat. **1.** (a) To perspire.
S. à grosses gouttes, to sweat profusely. **Faire suer**
qn, (i) to make s.o. sweat; (ii) *P:* to annoy,
irritate, s.o. (b) (Of walls) To ooze, weep.
2. (With cogn. acc.) (a) To exude (poison, etc.).
(b) *S. du sang*, to sweat blood. S.a. SANG I.
S. l'égoïsme, to be steeped in selfishness. *Maison*
qui sue le crime, house that reeks of crime.
suée, *s.f. Med:* Sweating, sweat.

sueur [sɥœːr], *s.f.* Sweat, perspiration. **Être en**
sueur, to be sweating, in a perspiration. *Vivre*
à la sueur de son front, to live by the sweat of
one's brow.

suffire [syfiːr], *v.i.* (*pr.p.* **suffisant**; *p.p.* **suffi**;
pr.ind. **je suffis, n. suffisons, ils suffisent**; *p.h.* **je**
suffis; *fu.* **je suffirai**) (a) To suffice; to be
sufficient. *Cela ne me suffit pas*, that's not
enough, won't do, for me. *Prov:* **A chaque jour**
suffit sa peine, sufficient unto the day is the evil
thereof. *Impers:* **Il a suffi de quelques mots pour**
le persuader, a few words were enough to persuade him. *Il suffit qu'il le dise*, (it is) enough
that he should say so. *F:* (*Il*) **suffit!** enough!
that'll do! (b) *S. à qch., à faire qch.*, to be equal,
adequate, to sth., to doing sth. *Il ne peut pas s.*
à tout, he cannot cope with everything. *Il s'est*
toujours suffi, he has always supported himself.

suffisance [syfizãːs], *s.f.* **1.** Sufficiency, adequacy. *Avoir suffisance de qch.*, to have enough
of sth. *Avoir de qch. à suffisance, en suffisance*,
to have plenty of sth. **2.** Self-complacency;
self-conceit.

suffisant [syfizã], *a.* **1.** Sufficient, adequate,
enough. *C'est plus que s.*, that is more than
enough. *Quantité suffisante de vivres*, adequate
supply of food. **2.** Self-satisfied, self-mportant,
bumptious, conceited (air, tone). *s.* Conceited
person; prig. **Faire le suffisant**, to give oneself
airs. *adv.* **-amment**.

suffixe [syfiks], *s.m. Ling:* Suffix.

suffocant [syfɔkã], *a.* Suffocating, stifling.

suffocation [syfɔkasjɔ̃], *s.f.* Suffocation, choking.

suffoquer [syfɔke]. **1.** *v.tr.* (Of smell, etc.) To
suffocate, stifle. *Les sanglots la suffoquaient*, she
was choking with sobs. **2.** *v.i. S. de colère*, to
choke with anger.

suffragant [syfragã], *a. & s.m.* Suffragan
(bishop).

suffrage [syfraːʒ], *s.m.* Suffrage, vote. *S. univer-*
sel, universal franchise.

suffusion [syffyzjɔ̃], *s.f. Med:* Suffusion; flush.

suggérer [sygʒere], *v.tr.* (je suggère; je suggé-
rerai) To suggest (d, to). *S. une réponse à qn*, to
prompt s.o. with an answer.

suggestibilité [sygʒestibilite], *s.f.* Suggesti-
bility; susceptivity to impressions.

suggestif, -ive [sygʒestif, -iːv], *a.* Suggestive.

suggestion [sygʒestjɔ̃], *s.f.* Suggestion. *Sugges-*
tions en vue d'une amélioration, suggestions for
improvement. *Pas la moindre s. de . . .*, not the
slightest hint of. . . .

suicide¹ [sɥisid], *s.m.* Suicide, self-murder. **Faux**
suicide, attempted suicide.

suicide². **1.** *s.m.* = SUICIDÉ. **2.** *a.* Suicidal.

suicider (se) [səsɥiside], *v.pr.* To commit
suicide; to make away with oneself.

suicidé, -ée, *s.* Suicide, self-murderer.

suie [sɥi], *s.f.* **1.** Soot. **2.** *Agr:* = CHARBON 2 (a).

suif [sɥif], *s.m.* Tallow; *F:* candle-grease.
Chandelle de s., tallow candle. S.a. GOUTTE-DE-
SUIF. *P:* **Recevoir un suif**, to get a wigging, a
dressing-down.

suiffer [sɥife], *v.tr.* To tallow (leather, etc.); to
grease (a pole). *I.C.E:* **Bougie suiffée**, sooted
sparking-plug.

suin(t) [sɥɛ̃], *s.m.* Yolk, suint, (natural) grease
(of wool); wool fat, wool grease. **Laines en**
suint, wool in the yolk, in (the) grease.

suinter [sɥɛ̃te], *v.i.* (a) (Of water, rock) To ooze,
seep, sweat. (b) (Of vessel) To leak; (of wound)
to run. *s.m.* **-ement**.

suis¹, ² [sɥi]. See ÊTRE and SUIVRE.

Suisse¹ [sɥis]. *Pr.n.f.* Switzerland.

suisse². **1.** *a.* Swiss. S.a. AMIRAL I. **2.** *s.m.* (a) Un
Suisse, a Swiss. *Les Suisses*, the Swiss. (b) *Hist:*
Swiss mercenary. S.a. ARGENT 2. (c) *Ecc: etc:*
Church officer or hall porter (in full regalia).
(d) *Petit suisse*, small cream cheese.

Suissesse [sɥises], *s.f.* Swiss (woman).

suite [sɥit], *s.f.* **1.** (a) Continuation. **Faire suite**
à qch., to be a continuation of sth.; to follow
up sth. **"Comme suite à notre lettre d'hier,"** 'in
further reference to our letter of yesterday.'
Com: **Donner suite à une commande**, to carry
out an order. **Donner suite à une décision**, to
give effect to a decision. **A la suite les uns des**
autres, one after another. *Nous marchions à sa s.*,
we followed in his wake. *A la s. de la décision*
prise, following the decision arrived at. *Dix*
carrosses de suite, ten carriages in succession.
Dix heures de s., ten hours on end. *Dix jours de s.*,
ten days running. **Et ainsi de suite**, and so on.
Tout de suite, *F:* de suite, at once, immediately.
Dans la suite, subsequently, in process of time.
Par la suite, later on, afterwards. (b) Sequel (of
tale, etc.). **"Suite au prochain numéro,"** 'to be
continued in our next.' (c) Coherence, consistency (in reasoning). **Sans suite**, (i) incoherent;
(ii) disconnectedly, incoherently. **Manquer de**
suite, d'esprit de suite, to be lacking in sense
of sequence, in method. **2.** Suite, retinue, train,
attendants (of monarch, etc.). **Être à la suite de**
qn, to be in s.o.'s train. **3.** (a) Series, sequence,
succession (of events). *S. de malheurs*, chapter of
accidents. *Dans la s. des siècles*, in the course,
progress, of centuries. *S. de médailles*, set of
medals. (b) *Mus:* **Suite d'orchestre**, orchestral
suite. **4.** Consequence, result. *Mourir des suites*
d'une blessure, to die of a wound. **Par suite . . .**,
consequently. . . . **Par suite de**, in consequence
of. *Par s. d'une erreur*, by, through, an error.

suivant¹ [sɥivã], *prep.* **1.** In the direction of.
Coupe s. la ligne M N, section along the line M N.
2. According to, in accordance with (one's
means, etc.); pursuant to (instructions). *S. lui*,
in his opinion, according to him. **Suivant que**
+ *ind.*, according as. . . .

suivant², -ante [sɥivã, -ãːt]. **1.** *a.* Next,
following (page, etc.). *Au chapitre s.*, in the
following chapter. *Les trois jours suivants*, the
next three days. *Sch:* **Au suivant!** next boy !

2. *s.m.* Follower, attendant. **3.** *s.f. Th:* Suivante, waiting-maid.
suivre [sɥiːvr], *v.tr.* (*pr.p.* suivant; *p.p.* suivi; *pr.ind.* je suis, il suit, n. suivons, ils suivent; *p.h.* je suivis; *fu.* je suivrai) To follow. **I.** (*a*) To go behind (s.o.). *S. qn de près*, to follow close on s.o.'s heels. *S. qn des yeux*, to follow s.o.'s progress (with one's eyes); not to lose sight of s.o. **Faire suivre une lettre**, to forward a letter. (On letter) **"Prière de faire suivre,"** 'please forward.' *Typ:* **"(Faire) suivre,"** 'run on.' (In serial stories) **"A suivre,"** 'to be continued.' *Ten:* **Suivre la balle**, to follow through. *S.a.* AIMER 1. (*b*) To escort, attend, accompany (s.o.). (*c*) To pursue (animal, enemy). (*d*) To pay heed to, be attentive to (sth.). (*e*) To watch (over), observe (s.o.'s progress, etc.). (*f*) *S. une piste, une indication*, to follow up a clue. **2.** (*a*) To succeed; to come, happen, after (sth.). *Le printemps suit l'hiver*, spring follows winter. *Les événements se suivent de près*, the events tread on each other's heels. **Conditions ainsi qu'il suit**, terms as follows. (*b*) To result from, be the consequence of (sth.). *Impers.* **Il suit de là que** **. . .**, it follows (from this) that. **. . . Que s'en est-il suivi?** what came of it? what was the consequence? **3.** (*a*) To go, proceed, along (road, etc.). *S. son chemin*, to go on one's way; to pursue one's way. *La justice suivra son cours*, justice will take its course. (*b*) To obey, conform to (fashion, law); to follow, act upon (advice). *S. son penchant*, to follow one's bent. **4.** (*a*) *S. des conférences*, to attend, hear, lectures. (*b*) To practise, exercise (profession, calling).
suivi, *a.* **I.** Connected (speech); sustained, coherent (reasoning); close (business relations); steadfast, unwavering (policy); continuous (work). *Com:* Steady, persistent (demand). *Correspondance suivie*, close, uninterrupted, correspondence. **2. Prédicateur très suivi,** preacher who has a large following.
sujet¹, -ette [syʒɛ, -ɛt]. **I.** *a.* Subject. (*a*) Dependent. *Être s. aux lois*, to be subject, amenable, to law. *Je suis s. à l'heure*, my time is not my own. *Provinces sujettes*, subject provinces. **Tenir qn très sujet**, (i) to keep s.o. well under one's thumb; (ii) to keep s.o. very much tied. (*b*) Liable, prone, exposed (à, to). *S. à l'erreur*, liable to error. *Être s. à la goutte*, to be subject to gout. *S.a.* CAUTION 1. (*c*) *Contrat s. au droit du timbre*, agreement liable to stamp-duty. **2.** *s.* Subject (of a state).
sujet², *s.m.* **I.** Subject. (*a*) Cause, reason, object, ground (of complaint, etc.). *S. d'étonnement*, matter of wonder. *J'ai tout sujet d'espérer*, I have every reason to hope. *Si je me plains c'est que j'en ai s.*, if I complain I have good cause. **Au sujet de qch.**, relating to, concerning, about, sth. *Éprouver des craintes au s. de qch.*, to entertain fears as to sth. (*b*) Subject-matter (of speech, etc.); theme (of play, etc.); topic (of conversation). *Un beau s. de roman*, a fine subject for a novel. (*c*) *Gram:* **Sujet du verbe**, subject, nominative, of the verb. **2.** Individual, fellow. **Mauvais sujet**, (i) ne'er-do-well, bad lot; (ii) *Sch:* bad boy. **Bon sujet**, steady, well-behaved, fellow or boy.
sujétion [syʒesjɔ̃], *s.f.* **I.** Subjection (à, to); servitude. *Vivre dans la s.*, to live in subjection, in bondage. *S. aux lois*, subservience to the laws. **2.** Constraint, obligation.
sulfatation [sylfatasjɔ̃], *s.f. El:* Sulphating (of accumulator plates).
sulfate [sylfat], *s.m. Ch:* Sulphate. *S. de cuivre*,

copper sulphate. *El:* **Encrassé de sulfate**, sulphated (accumulator).
sulfat|er [sylfate], *v.tr. Ch: Ind:* To sulphate. *Vit:* To treat, dress, (vines) with copper sulphate. *s.m.* **-age**.
se sulfater, (of accumulator) to sulphate.
sulfhydrate [sylfidrat], *s.m. Ch:* Hydrosulphide.
sulfhydrique [sylfidrik], *a. Ch:* **Acide sulfhydrique**, hydrogen sulphide, sulphuretted hydrogen.
sulfite [sylfit], *s.m. Ch:* Sulphite.
sulfocarbonate [sylfɔkarbɔnat], *s.m. Ch:* Thiocarbonate.
sulfocyanure [sylfɔsjanyːr], *s.m. Phot:* Sulphocyanide.
sulfure [sylfyːr], *s.m. Ch:* Sulphide. *S. de fer*, iron pyrites. *S. de carbone*, carbon disulphide.
sulfuré [sylfyre], *a. Ch:* Sulphuretted.
sulfureux, -euse [sylfyrø, -øːz], *a.* (*a*) Sulphureous. (*b*) *Ch:* Sulphurous. *Anhydride s.*, sulphur dioxide.
sulfurique [sylfyrik], *a. Ch:* Sulphuric (acid).
sultan [syltã], *s.m.* Sultan.
sultane [syltan], *s.f.* **I.** Sultana, sultaness. **2. Poule sultane**, sultan hen; sultana.
sumac [symak], *s.m.* Sumac(h). *S. vénéneux*, poison-ivy.
summum [sɔmmɔm], *s.m.* Acme, height, summit (of civilization, etc.).
Sund (le) [ləsɔ̃ːd]. *Pr.n.m. Geog:* The Sound.
super [sype]. **I.** *v.tr.* (Of pump) *S. l'eau*, *Abs.* **super**, to suck. **2.** *v.i.* (*a*) (Of pipe) To get stopped (up), plugged up, juicy. (*b*) *Navire supé*, vessel stuck in the mud.
superbe [sypɛrb]. **I.** *a.* (*a*) *A. & Lit:* Proud, haughty, vainglorious, arrogant. (*b*) Superb; stately (building). (*c*) *F:* Magnificent (horse); splendid, first-rate. *S. de carbone*, a fine woman. *Il fait des affaires superbes*, his business is thriving; he is doing a roaring trade. **2.** *s.f. A. & Lit:* Pride, haughtiness. *adv.* **-ment**.
supercentrale [sypersãtral], *s.f. El.E:* Main generating station.
supercherie [sypɛrʃəri], *s.f.* (*a*) Deceit; fraud; swindle. (*b*) Hoax.
superfétation [syperfetasjɔ̃], *s.f.* Superfluity (of words, etc.); redundancy; supererogation.
superficie [syperfisi], *s.f.* (*a*) Superficies, surface. *La s. de la terre*, the earth's surface. (*b*) Area (of a field, of a triangle). (*c*) *F:* Mere surface (of things). **Son savoir est tout en superficie**, his knowledge is all on the surface, entirely superficial.
superfici|el, -elle [syperfisjɛl], *a.* Superficial; skin-deep (wound); shallow (mind). *Eau superficielle*, surface water. *adv.* **-ellement**.
superfin [syperfɛ̃], *a.* Superfine (cloth, etc.); of extra quality.
superflu [syperfly]. **I.** *a.* (*a*) Superfluous, unnecessary. (*b*) *Regrets superflus*, vain, useless, regrets. **2.** *s.m.* Donner de son s., to give of one's superfluity. *Avoir du s. en main-d'œuvre*, to be overstaffed.
superfluité [syperflyite], *s.f.* **I.** Superfluity, superabundance. **2.** *Se passer de superfluités*, to do without unnecessary things.
superhétérodyne [syperreterɔdin], *s.m. W.Tel:* Superheterodyne.
supérieur, -eure [syperjœːr]. **I.** *a.* (*a*) Upper (storey, limb). **Cours supérieur d'une rivière**, headwaters of a stream. *Le Rhin s.*, the Upper Rhine. *Typ:* **Chiffre supérieur**, superior number

(as a note reference). (*b*) Superior (*à*, to). *S. à la normale*, above normal. *Se montrer s. aux événements*, to rise above events. *Être s. à qn*, to rank above s.o. (*c*) Higher, upper. *Classes supérieures*, upper classes (of society); upper forms (in school). *Mathématiques supérieures*, higher mathematics. (*d*) *Com:* Of superior quality. **2.** *s.* Superior. (*a*) One's better. *Il est votre s.*, (i) he is your superior; (ii) he is a better man than you. (*b*) Head (of convent or monastery). **La Mère supérieure,** the Mother Superior.

supérieurement [syperjœrmã], *adv.* **I.** Superlatively well. **2.** *S. à* . . ., to a higher degree than . . ., better than. . . .

supériorité [syperjɔrite], *s.f.* **I.** (*a*) Superiority. *S. d'âge*, seniority. (*b*) *F:* *Toutes les supériorités étaient invitées*, all the people of rank and talent were invited. **2.** Superiorship (of convent).

superlat|if, -ive [syperlatif, -iːv]. **I.** *a.* Superlative (adjective, etc.). **2.** *s.m.* *Gram:* Superlative (degree). **Adjectif au superlatif,** adjective in the superlative. *adv.* **-ivement.**

superpos|er [syperpoze], *v.tr.* To superpose (*à*, (up)on); to superimpose. *a.* **-able.**

superposition [syperpozisjɔ̃], *s.f.* Superposition (of triangles, of strata); superimposition (of colours).

superstitieusement [syperstisjøzmã], *adv.* **I.** Superstitiously. **2.** *F:* Over-scrupulously.

superstitieux, -euse [syperstisjø, -øːz], *a.* Superstitious.

superstition [syperstisjɔ̃], *s.f.* **I.** Superstition. **2.** *F:* *Avoir la s. du passé*, to be foolishly attached to the past.

superstructure [syperstryktyːr], *s.f.* Superstructure; upper works (of ship); *Rail:* permanent way.

supin [sypɛ̃], *s.m.* *Gram:* Supine. **Au supin,** in the supine.

supination [sypinasjɔ̃], *s.f.* Supination. **En supination,** supine (patient).

supplantation [syplɑ̃tasjɔ̃], *s.f.*, **supplantement** [syplɑ̃tmã], *s.m.* Supplanting, supplantation; supersession.

supplanter [syplɑ̃te], *v.tr.* To supplant; to supersede.

suppléance [sypleɑ̃ːs], *s.f.* (*a*) Deputyship. **Obtenir la suppléance de qn,** to be appointed s.o.'s substitute. (*b*) Temporary post (during holder's absence); post ad interim; supply (post). **Remplir une suppléance,** to deputize, supply, for someone.

suppléant, -ante [sypleɑ̃, -ãːt]. **I.** *s.* (Of pers.) Substitute (*de*, for); deputy, locum tenens. *Th:* Understudy. **2.** *a.* Acting, temporary (official).

suppléer [syplee]. **I.** *v.tr.* (*a*) To supply, make up, make good (what is lacking). (*b*) To take the place of, act as deputy for, deputize for (s.o.). **Se faire suppléer,** to find a substitute; to arrange for a supply. **2.** *v.i.* *S. à qch.*, to make up for, supply the deficiency of, compensate for, sth. *S. à une vacance*, to fill a vacant post.

supplément [syplemã], *s.m.* (*a*) Supplement, addition. **En supplément,** additional. (*b*) Extra or additional payment; *Rail:* excess fare, extra fare. *S. de solde*, extra pay. (*c*) Supplement (to book, magazine). (*d*) (In restaurant) Extra (dish); extra charge (for special dish). (*e*) *Geom:* Supplement (of an angle).

supplémentaire [syplemɑ̃tɛːr], *a.* Supplementary, additional, extra, further. *Ind:* **Heures supplémentaires (de travail),** overtime. *Geom:*

Angles supplémentaires, supplemental angles. *Mus:* **Lignes supplémentaires,** leger lines.

supplétif, -ive [sypletif, -iːv], *a.* *Gram:* Suppletory (word).

suppliant, -ante [sypliã, -ãːt]. **I.** *a.* Suppliant, supplicating, imploring, pleading (look, etc.). **2.** *s.* Suppliant, supplicant.

supplication [syplikasjɔ̃], *s.f.* Supplication, beseeching, entreaty.

supplice [syplis], *s.m.* (*a*) (Severe corporal) punishment; torture. **Le dernier supplice,** capital punishment, the extreme penalty. (*b*) Torment, anguish, agony. **Mettre qn au supplice,** (i) to torture s.o., to agonize s.o.; (ii) *F:* to make s.o. squirm; (iii) *F:* to keep s.o. on tenterhooks. **Être au supplice,** to be on the rack, on thorns.

supplicier [syplisje], *v.tr.* (*a*) *A:* To execute (criminal). (*b*) *F:* = *Mettre au supplice.*

supplicié, -ée, *s.* Executed criminal, or criminal under torture and about to be executed.

supplier [syplie], *v.tr.* To beseech, implore. *S. qn de faire qch.*, to implore, entreat, beg, s.o. to do sth. *Taisez-vous, je vous en supplie*, be silent, I beg of you.

supplique [syplik], *s.f.* Petition.

support [sypɔːr], *s.m.* **I.** Support, prop, stay. **Il est sans support,** he has no one to back him up. **2.** Rest (for tools, etc.); stand (for lamp); bracket, bearer (of machine part, etc.); mount (of photograph); holder (for memo block). *Mec.E:* Pedestal, pillow(-block). *S. de bicyclette*, bicycle stand. *W.Tel:* *S. de lampe*, valve-holder. *Nau:* *S. de gui*, boom-crutch.

supportable [sypɔrtabl], *a.* **I.** Supportable, bearable, tolerable, endurable. **2.** *F:* Fairly good. *adv.* **-ment.**

supporter [sypɔrte], *v.tr.* To support. **I.** To prop, hold up, sustain (ceiling, arch); to support, back up (person). **2.** (*a*) To endure, suffer, bear (heat, misfortune). *Il n'a pas supporté l'épreuve*, he was not equal to the test. (*b*) To tolerate, put up with, stand (rudeness, etc.). *S. l'humeur de qn*, to bear with s.o.'s temper.

suppos|er[1] [sypoze], *v.tr.* **I.** To suppose, assume, imagine. *S. vrai ce qui est en question*, to beg the question. **En supposant que + *sub.*, à supposer que + *sub.*,** supposing that . . . *Supposons que + *sub.*,** let us take it that . . ., suppose that. . . . **On suppose que + *ind.*,** it is thought, inferred, that. . . . *On le suppose à Paris, on suppose qu'il est à Paris*, he is supposed to be in Paris. *On le supposait riche*, he was supposed, thought, to be wealthy. **2.** To presuppose, imply. *Cela lui suppose du courage*, it implies courage on his part. *a.* **-able.**

supposé[1]. **I.** *a.* Supposed, alleged (thief, etc.); assumed, false, fictitious (name, etc.). **2.** *prep.* Supposé même sa conversion, even if his conversion be assumed. *Conj.phr.* **Supposé que + *sub.*,** supposing that. . . .

supposer[2], *v.tr.* *Jur:* To put forward (sth.) as genuine. *S. un testament*, to present, produce, a forged will.

supposé[2], *a.* Supposititious (child); forged (will).

suppositif, -ive [sypozitif, -iːv], *a.* Suppositive, assumed.

supposition[1] [sypozisjɔ̃], *s.f.* Supposition. *S. gratuite*, gratuitous assumption. **Si par supposition il revenait,** supposing he came back.

supposition[2], *s.f.* *Jur:* Production of forged document(s); forging (of will); impersonation (of party to contract).

suppositoire [sypɔzitwa:r], *s.m. Pharm:* Suppository.

suppôt [sypo], *s.m.* (Of pers.) Tool, instrument (of another). *Les suppôts de la loi,* the myrmidons of the law. *F:* **Suppôt de Satan,** hell-hound, fiend.

suppression [sypresjɔ̃], *s.f.* (a) Suppression; discontinuance (of a service); cancelling (of a passage); quelling (of revolt). (b) Concealment (of a fact).

supprim|er [syprime], *v.tr.* **1.** (a) To suppress; to put down (abuse); to abolish, do away with (law, tax); to put an end to (competition); to withdraw (credit); to omit, leave out, cut out (word); to discontinue, cancel (train); to remove (difficulty); to quell (revolt). *F:* **Supprimer qn,** to kill s.o.; to make away, do away, with s.o. *Typ:* **"A supprimer,"** 'delete.' (b) *Jur:* To conceal (document); to suppress, withhold (fact). **2.** *S. qch. à qn,* to deprive s.o. of sth. *a.* **-able.**

suppuration [sypyrasjɔ̃], *s.f.* Suppuration, running (of sore, etc.).

suppurer [sypyre], *v.i.* (Of wound, sore) To suppurate, run.

supputation [sypytasjɔ̃], *s.f.* Computation, calculation.

supputer [sypyte], *v.tr.* To compute, calculate.

supraliminal, -aux [sypraliminal, -o], *a. Psy:* Supraliminal; above the threshold.

suprématie [sypremasi], *s.f.* Supremacy.

suprême [sypre:m], *a.* (a) Supreme; highest (degree); crowning (effort); paramount (importance). *Au suprême degré,* in the highest degree; eminently. (b) Last (honours). *L'heure,* **le moment, suprême,** the hour of death. *adv.* **-ment.**

sur[1] [syr], *prep.* **1.** (a) On, upon. *Assis sur une chaise,* sitting on a chair. *Sur toute la ligne,* all along the line. *Je n'ai pas d'argent sur moi,* I have no money on me, about me. *Sur ma parole,* upon my word. *Serrer qn sur son cœur,* to clasp s.o. to one's heart. *Page sur page,* page after page. *Faire sottise sur sottise,* to commit blunder upon blunder. *Chanter qch. sur un certain air,* to sing sth. to a certain tune. (b) Towards. *Avancer sur qn,* to advance on, against, s.o. *Tirer sur l'âge,* to be growing old. (c) Over, above. *Être toujours sur les livres,* to be for ever poring over books. *L'emporter sur qn,* to prevail over s.o. *Sur toute(s) chose(s),* above all (things). (d) About, concerning, respecting. *Interroger qn sur ses motifs,* to question s.o. as to his motives. **2.** (Of time) (a) About, towards. *Sur le soir, sur le tard,* towards evening. *Sur les trois heures,* about three o'clock. (b) *Sur ce,* sur quoi, *il nous quitta,* thereupon, whereupon, he left us. *Il est sur son départ,* he is on the point of departure. **3.** Out of. (a) *Un jour sur quatre,* one day out of four, every fourth day. *Une fois sur deux,* every other time. *Une fois sur mille,* once in a thousand times. (b) *Vous vous payerez sur le surplus,* you will pay yourself out of what remains over. **4.** *Huit pieds sur six,* eight foot by six.

sur[2] [sy:r], *a.* Sour (fruit, etc.); tart.

sûr [sy:r], *a.* Sure. **1.** (a) Safe, secure (locality, shelter). *Peu sûr,* insecure, unsafe. *Jouer au plus sûr,* to play for safety. *Pour le plus sûr,* to be on the safe side. S.a. LIEU 1. (b) Trustworthy, reliable; trusty, true, staunch (friend). *Coup d'œil sûr,* unerring glance. *Avoir la main sûre,* le *pied sûr,* to have a steady hand, to be sure-footed. *Com: Maison sûre,* house of established standing. **2.** Certain. *Remède sûr, poison sûr,* infallible

remedy; unfailing poison. *C'est une affaire sûre,* it's a certainty. *Être sûr de qch.,* to be sure, certain, of sth. *Je suis sûr de lui,* I can depend on him. **Sûr et certain,** absolutely certain. **A coup sûr,** assuredly, for certain; without fail. *F:* **Bien sûr! pour sûr!** to be sure! surely! **Bien sûr?** honour bright?

surabondance [syrabɔ̃dã:s], *s.f.* Superabundance.

surabond|ant [syrabɔ̃dã], *a.* Superabundant; superfluous. *adv.* **-amment.**

surabonder [syrabɔ̃de], *v.i.* To superabound; to be glutted (de, with).

surah [syra], *s.m. Tex:* Surah.

suraigu, -uë [syregy], *a.* **1.** Overshrill, high-pitched (voice, note). **2.** *Med:* Peracute (inflammation).

surajouter [syraʒute], *v.tr.* To superadd.

suralimentation [syralimɑ̃tasjɔ̃], *s.f.* **1.** *Med:* Feeding up. **2.** Overfeeding. **3.** *I.C.E:* Supercharging.

suralimenter [syralimɑ̃te], *v.tr.* **1.** *Med:* To feed up (person). **2.** *I.C.E:* To supercharge (engine).

suranné [syrane], *a.* Out of date; antiquated, old-fashioned.

sur-arbitre, *s.m.* Referee (deciding a tie between umpires). *pl. Des sur-arbitres.*

surate [syrat], *s.f.* Sura(h) (of the Koran).

surbaissement [syrbɛsmã], *s.m. Arch:* Surbasement.

surbaisser [syrbɛse], *v.tr.* **1.** *Arch:* To surbase, flatten (arch, vault). **2.** *Aut: etc:* To drop, undersling (frame, etc.).

surbaissé, *a.* **1.** *Arch:* Depressed, flattened (arch). **2.** *Aut: etc:* Dropped (axle, frame, etc.); extra-low, underslung (chassis).

surbau, -aux [syrbo], *s.m. Nau:* (Hatchway) coaming.

surcapitalisé [syrkapitalize], *a.* Over-capitalized.

surcharge [syrʃarʒ], *s.f.* **1.** Overloading, overstressing. **2.** (a) Overload; extra load; additional burden. *El:* Overcharge (of accumulator). (b) Excess weight (of luggage). (c) Weight-handicap (of racehorse). **3.** (a) Overtax, overcharge. (b) Additional charge (on account rendered). **4.** Surcharge (on postage stamp).

surcharger [syrʃarʒe], *v.tr.* (je surchargeai(s); n. surchargeons) **1.** (a) To overburden, overload; to overcharge (accumulator). (b) To overtax, overcharge. **2.** To surcharge (postage stamp).

surchauffe [syrʃo:f], *s.f.* **1.** = SURCHAUFFAGE. **2.** Superheat (in steam).

surchauff|er [syrʃofe], *v.tr.* **1.** To overheat (oven, etc.). *Metalw:* To burn (iron). **2.** To superheat (steam). *s.m.* **-age.**

surchauffeur [syrʃofœ:r], *s.m. Mch:* (Steam) superheater.

surchoix [syrʃwa], *s.m.* Finest quality. *Tabacs de s.,* choice tobaccos.

surclasser [syrklɑse], *v.tr. Sp:* To outclass (opponents).

surcomposé [syrkɔ̃poze], *a.* Double-compound (tense) (e.g. *Lorsque j'ai eu fini*).

surcompression [syrkɔ̃presjɔ̃], *s.f. I.C.E:* Supercharging.

surcomprimé [syrkɔ̃prime], *a. I.C.E:* Super-charged (engine).

surcontre [syrkɔ̃:tr], *s.m. Cards:* Redouble.

surcontrer [syrkɔ̃tre], *v.tr. Cards:* To redouble.

surcoupe [syrkup], *s.f. Cards:* Overtrumping.

surcouper [syrkupe], *v.tr. Cards:* To overtrump.

surcroissance [syrkrwasã:s], *s.f.* Overgrowth.

surcroît [syrkrwa], *s.m.* Addition, increase. *Il craint un s. de besogne*, he is afraid it means more work. **Par surcroît**, to boot, into the bargain, in addition, besides. **Pour surcroît de bonheur**, as a crowning happiness or piece of good luck. *Pour s. de malheur*, to make matters worse. S.a. SÛRETÉ I.

surdi-mutité, *s.f.* Deaf(-and)-dumbness, surdomutism.

surdité [syrdite], *s.f.* Deafness.

surdoré [syrdɔre], *a.* Double-gilt.

surdos [syrdo], *s.m.* **1.** *Harn:* Back-band, back-strap. **2.** (Porter's) carrying-pad.

sureau [syro], *s.m.* Elder(-tree). **Baie de sureau**, elder-berry.

suréchauffé [syreʃofe], *a.* Overheated.

surélévation [syrelεvasjɔ̃], *s.f.* **1.** *Const:* Heightening, raising. *Aut:* Upsweep(ing) (of frame). **2.** Additional storey.

surélever [syrelve], *v.tr.* (Conj. like ÉLEVER) **1.** (*a*) To heighten, to raise (the height of) (wall, building). (*b*) *Aut:* To upsweep (frame). **2.** To raise (prices, tariff) higher.

surelle [syrεl], *s.f.* Wood-sorrel.

sûrement [syrmɑ̃], *adv.* **1.** Steadily, confidently. **2.** Surely, certainly, assuredly; to be sure! *Il réussira s.*, he is sure to succeed. **3.** Surely, securely, safely, reliably.

suréminent [syreminɑ̃], *a.* Supereminent.

surenchère [syrɑ̃ʃεːr], *s.f.* Higher bid. *Faire une s. sur qn*, to outbid s.o.

surenchérir [syrɑ̃ʃeriːr], *v.i.* (*a*) To bid higher; to overbid. *S. sur qn*, to bid higher than s.o.; to outbid s.o. (*b*) To rise higher in price.

surenchérisseur, -euse [syrɑ̃ʃerisœːr, -øːz], *s.* Overbidder.

surérogation [syrerɔgasjɔ̃], *s.f.* Supererogation.

surestarie [syrεstari], *s.f.* *Nau:* Demurrage. **Jours de surestarie**, extra lay days.

surestimation [syrεstimasjɔ̃], *s.f.* Over-estimate, overvaluation.

surestimer [syrεstime], *v.tr.* To over-estimate, overvalue; to overrate (s.o.).

suret, -ette [syrε, -εt], *a.* Sourish, tart.

sûreté [syrte], *s.f.* **1.** Safety, security, safe-keeping. **Lieu de sûreté**, place of safety. **Être en sûreté**, to be safe, in a safe place, out of harm's way. **Être en sûreté de qch.**, to be safe from sth. **Pour plus de sûreté, pour surcroît de sûreté**, in order to make assurance double sure. **Agent de la sûreté**, detective. **La police de sûreté**, the detective force. **La Sûreté**, the Criminal Investigation Department, *F:* the C.I.D. **Rasoir de sûreté**, safety-razor. *Mécanisme de s.*, foolproof mechanism. **Mettre son fusil au cran de sûreté**, to put one's gun to safety, to half-cock. S.a. SOUPAPE. **2.** Sureness (of hand, foot); unerringness, soundness (of vision, judgment); unerringness (of blow). *S. de soi*, self-confidence, self-assurance. **3.** *Com:* Surety, security, guarantee. *Prendre toutes ses sûretés*, to secure all guarantees.

surexcitable [syrεksitabl], *a.* Easily excited; excitable.

surexcitant [syrεksitɑ̃]. **1.** *a.* Strongly exciting (drink, emotion). **2.** *s.m. Med:* (Strong) stimulant.

surexcitation [syrεksitasjɔ̃], *s.f.* Excitement.

surexciter [syrεksite], *v.tr.* (*a*) To over-stimulate. (*b*) To excite (s.o.).

surexposer [syrεkspoze], *v.tr. Phot:* To over-expose.

surexposition [syrεkspozisjɔ̃], *s.f. Phot:* Over-exposure.

surface [syrfas], *s.f.* Surface. (*a*) Outside. **Bruit de surface**, surface scratching (of gramophone record). (Of submarine) **Marcher en surface**, to progress on the surface. **Revenir en surface, faire surface**, to break surface; to surface. **Vitesse en surface**, surface speed. (*b*) *Geom:* *S. de révolution*, surface of revolution. (*c*) Area. *S. d'appui*, bearing surface. *Av:* *S. portante*, aerofoil.

surfaire [syrfεːr], *v.tr.* (Conj. like FAIRE) (*a*) To overcharge; to ask too much for (sth.). (*b*) To over-estimate, overrate (person, talent, etc.); to overpraise.

surfaix [syrfε], *s.m. Harn:* Surcingle.

surfin [syrfε̃], *a. Com:* Superfine.

surgeon [syrʒɔ̃], *s.m. Hort:* Sucker. (Of plant) *Pousser des surgeons*, to sucker.

surgeonner [syrʒone], *v.i.* (Of plant) To put forth suckers; to sucker.

surgir [syrʒiːr], *v.i.* (Aux. *avoir*, occ. *être*) To rise; to come into view; to loom (up). *S. brusquement*, to appear suddenly. *De nouvelles difficultés ont surgi*, fresh difficulties have arisen, have cropped up. **Faire surgir un souvenir**, to call forth a memory.

surhauss|er [syrose], *v.tr.* **1.** (*a*) To heighten, raise (wall, etc.). (*b*) *Rail:* To cant (outer rail). *Civ.E:* To bank (road at a corner). **2.** To increase, force up, the price of (sth.). *s.m.* **-ement.**

surhomme [syrɔm], *s.m.* Superman, overman.

surhumain [syrymε̃], *a.* Superhuman.

surimposer [syrε̃poze], *v.tr.* **1.** To superimpose. **2.** To increase the tax on (sth.). **3.** To overtax.

surimposition [syrε̃pozisjɔ̃], *s.f.* **1.** Superimposition. **2.** Increase of taxation. **3.** Overtaxation.

surin¹ [syrε̃], *s.m.* Young apple-tree stock.

surin², *s.m. P:* (Apache's) knife or dagger.

surin|er [syrine], *v.tr. P:* To knife (s.o.); to murder; *P:* to do (s.o.) in. *s.m.* **-eur.**

surintendance [syrε̃tɑ̃dɑ̃s], *s.f. Hist:* **1.** Superintendence, stewardship. **2.** Superintendent's offices.

surintendant [syrε̃tɑ̃dɑ̃], *s.m.* Superintendent, overseer, steward. *Hist: S. des finances*, financial secretary (under the old regime).

surintendante [syrε̃tɑ̃dɑ̃ːt], *s.f.* **1.** (Woman) superintendent. **2.** *Hist:* (*a*) Superintendent's wife. (*b*) Chief lady-in-waiting.

surir [syriːr], *v.i.* To turn sour.

surjaler [syrʒale]. *Nau:* **1.** *v.tr.* To foul (the anchor-stock). **2.** *v.i.* (Of anchor) To become unstocked.

surjet [syrʒε], *s.m.* (*a*) Overcasting, whipping (of seams). **Faire un surjet**, to overcast, whip, a seam. (*b*) Overcast seam.

surjeter [syrʒate], *v.tr.* (Conj. like JETER) To overcast, whip (seam).

sur-le-champ, *adv.* At once.

surlendemain [syrlɑ̃dmε̃], *s.m.* Next day but one. *Le s. de son arrivée*, two days, the second day, after his arrival. *Il arriva le s.*, he arrived two days later.

surmenage [syrmɔnaːʒ], *s.m.* Overworking; over-exertion. *S. intellectuel*, mental strain; brain-fag.

surmener [syrmɔne], *v.tr.* (Conj. like MENER) To overwork; to overtask (children); to override, overdrive (horse). *El:* To overrun (lamp).

se surmener, to overwork; to over-exert oneself; to work too hard; to overdo it.

surmené, *a.* Jaded (horse, mind); stale (team); *F:* fagged.

surmontable [syrmɔ̃tabl], *a.* Surmountable, superable.

surmonter [syrmɔ̃te], *v.tr.* **I.** To surmount; to (over-)top; to rise above, higher than (sth.). *Colonne surmontée d'une croix,* column topped by a cross. **2.** To overcome, surmount (obstacle, one's emotion); to get over (difficulty); to master (one's grief). **3.** (Of oil) To float to the top of (water).

se surmonter, to master, control, one's feelings or passions.

surmoulage [syrmula:ʒ], *s.m.* **I.** Retreading (of tyres). **2.** *Typ:* (a) Duplicating (of block). (b) Cast, mould, from existing plate.

surmouler [syrmule], *v.tr.* **I.** To retread (pneumatic tyre). **2.** *Typ:* (a) To duplicate (block). (b) To cast, mould, from existing plate.

surmulet [syrmylɛ], *s.m. Ich:* Surmullet.

surmulot [syrmylo], *s.m.* Brown rat, wharf-rat.

surnager [syrnaʒe], *v.* (je surnageai(s); n. surnageons) **I.** *v.tr.* To overfloat. **2.** *v.i.* (a) To float on the surface. (b) *Ce qui avait surnagé au naufrage,* what had remained afloat from the wreck. *F: Il a surnagé au crach,* he has survived the (financial) crash.

surnatur|el, -elle [syrnatyrɛl], *a.* (a) Supernatural, preternatural. *s.* **Le surnaturel,** the supernatural. (b) *F:* Extraordinary, out of the common; uncanny. *adv.* **-ellement.**

surnom [syrnɔ̃], *s.m.* (a) *Rom.Ant:* Agnomen. (b) Appellation. (c) Nickname.

surnombre [syrnɔ̃:br], *s.m.* Number over the regulation number. *S. des habitants,* overpopulation. **En surnombre,** supernumerary.

surnommer [syrnɔme], *v.tr.* Pred. *S. qn qch.,* (i) to name, call, s.o. sth.; (ii) to nickname s.o. sth.

surnuméraire [syrnymerɛ:r], *a. & s.m.* Supernumerary.

suroffre [syrɔfr], *s.f.* Better offer, better bid.

suroît [syrwa], *s.m. Nau:* **I.** South-west. **2.** Sou'wester (wind or hat).

suros [syro], *s.m. Farr:* Splint, fusee (on the cannon-bone); exostosis.

surpassable [syrpɑsabl], *a.* Surpassable.

surpasser [syrpɑse], *v.tr.* To surpass. **I.** To be higher than (s.o., sth.); to overtop (sth.). *S. qn de la tête,* to be a head taller than s.o. **2.** To go beyond, to exceed; to outdo. *S. qn par l'intelligence,* to surpass s.o. in intelligence. *S. qn en talent,* to transcend s.o. in talent. *S. qn en éclat,* to outshine s.o. *F:* **Cela me surpasse,** that beats me.

surpaye [syrpɛ:j], *s.f.* Extra pay; bonus.

surpayer [syrpeje], *v.tr.* (Conj. like PAYER) To overpay (s.o.); to pay too much for (sth.).

surpeuplé [syrpœple], *a.* Over-populated.

surpeuplement [syrpœpləmɑ̃], *s.m.* Overcrowding.

surplis [syrpli], *s.m. Ecc:* Surplice.

surplomb [syrplɔ̃], *s.m.* Overhang (of wall, rock). **Être en surplomb,** to overhang. *Rocher en s.,* overhanging rock.

surplomb|er [syrplɔ̃be]. **I.** *v.i.* (Of wall, rock) To overhang; to jut out. **2.** *v.tr.* To overhang, hang over (sth.). *a.* **-ant.** *s.m.* **-ement.**

surplus [syrply], *s.m.* Surplus, overplus, excess. **Au surplus,** besides, after all; moreover. *Vivres* **en surplus,** provisions in excess.

surpoids [syrpwa], *s.m.* Overweight, excessweight. **En surpoids,** in excess.

surprenant [syrprənɑ̃], *a.* Surprising, astonishing. **Chose surprenante . . .,** wonderful to relate . . ., strange to say . . ., for a wonder. . . . *Il est s. que vous le sachiez,* it is surprising that you should know of it.

surprendre [syrprɑ̃:dr], *v.tr.* (Conj. like PRENDRE) To surprise. **I.** (a) To come upon (s.o.) unexpectedly; to catch (s.o.) unawares. *La nuit nous surprit,* night overtook us. *Être surpris par la pluie,* to be caught in the rain. *S. qn en défaut* to catch s.o. napping. *S. qn à faire qch.,* to catch s.o. (in the act of) doing sth. *S. une ville,* to take a town by surprise. (b) To intercept (letter, glance); to overhear (conversation). (c) **Surprendre la bonne foi de qn,** to abuse s.o.'s good faith. **2.** To astonish. *Cela me surprendrait qu'il revienne, s'il revenait,* I should be surprised if he came back. *Cela ne me surprend pas,* I don't wonder at it; it is not to be wondered at; I am not surprised.

surpris, *a.* Surprised. *Il parut légèrement s.,* he seemed the least bit taken aback. *Être s. d'apprendre qch.,* to be surprised to hear of sth.

surpression [syrpresjɔ̃], *s.f.* **I.** Over-pressure. **2.** High pressure.

surprise [syrpri:z], *s.f.* **I.** Surprise. **A sa grande surprise,** to his great surprise, much to his surprise. *S'emparer d'une ville par surprise,* par un **coup de surprise,** to capture a town by surprise. *Quelle bonne s.!* what a pleasant surprise! **2.** Lucky dip; prize-packet.

surproduction [syrprɔdyksjɔ̃], *s.f.* Overproduction.

sursaturation [syrsatyrasjɔ̃], *s.f.* Supersaturation.

sursaturer [syrsatyre], *v.tr.* To supersaturate.

sursaut [syrso], *s.m.* (Involuntary) start, jump. **Faire, avoir, un sursaut,** to start, to give a jump. *Se réveiller en s.,* to wake up with a start.

sursauter [syrsote], *v.i.* To start (involuntarily); to give a jump. **Faire sursauter qn,** to startle s.o. *S. d'indignation,* to leap up with indignation.

surséance [syrseɑ̃:s], *s.f. Jur:* Suspension, delay (of judgment or trial); stay of proceedings.

sursel [syrsɛl], *s.m. Ch:* Supersalt; acid salt.

surseoir [syrswa:r], *v.ind.tr.* (*pr.p.* sursoyant; *p.p.* sursis; *pr.ind.* je sursois, n. sursoyons; *pr.sub.* je sursoie; *p.h.* je sursis; *fu.* je surseoirai) *Jur: S. à un jugement,* to suspend, delay, put off, stay, a judgment; to stay proceedings. *S. à une inhumation,* to postpone a burial.

sursis [syrsi], *s.m. Jur:* Delay; stay of proceedings; respite; reprieve (from execution). *Mil:* **Sursis d'appel,** postponement of joining (the service). **Mettre un homme en sursis,** to allow a man an extension of time before joining up.

surtaux [syrto], *s.m.* Over-assessment.

surtaxe [syrtaks], *s.f.* Supertax; surtax, extra tax. *S. d'une lettre,* extra postage, surcharge, on a letter.

surtension [syrtɑ̃sjɔ̃], *s.f.* **I.** Over-pressure, excess pressure. **2.** *El.E:* Over-voltage, voltrise. **Onde de surtension,** surge of current.

surtout[1] [syrtu], *adv.* Particularly, especially, principally, above all.

surtout[2], *s.m.* **I.** *Cost: A:* Overcoat, surtout. **2.** Centre-piece (on dinner table); epergne.

survanté [syrvɑ̃te], *a.* Overpraised.

survécu, -s, -t, etc. [syrveky]. See SURVIVRE.

surveillance [syrvɛjɑ̃:s], *s.f.* Supervision, watching, superintendence, surveillance. *Être sous la s. de la police,* to be under police supervision. **Comité de surveillance,** vigilance committee.

surveillant, -ante [syrvɛjɑ̃, -ɑ̃:t], *s.* **I.** Supervisor, superintendent, overseer; shop-walker. *Rail:* Inspector. *Freemasonry:* Warden. *Sch: S. général,* vice-principal. *S. des études,* master or mistress on duty; usher. **2.** Guardian, watchman. **3.** *s.f. Med:* Surveillante, (ward-) sister.

surveiller [syrvɛje], *v.tr.* **I.** To supervise, oversee, superintend; to tend (machine). **2.** To watch (over), observe, look after (s.o.). *S. la situation de près,* to keep a close eye on the situation. **se surveiller,** to keep a watch upon oneself; *F:* to mind one's p's and q's.

survenant, -ante [syrvɔnɑ̃, -ɑ̃:t]. **I.** *a.* Coming unexpectedly; supervening. **2.** *s.* Chance-comer.

survendre [syrvɑ̃:dr], *v.tr.* To overcharge for (sth.).

survenir [syrv(ə)niːr], *v.i.* (Conj. like VENIR. Aux. *être*) (Of events) To supervene, happen, occur; *F:* to crop up; (of difficulty) to arise; (of pers.) to arrive unexpectedly.

survenue, *s.f.* Unexpected arrival, chance coming; supervening.

survie [syrvi], *s.f. Jur:* **I.** Presumption of survival. **2.** Survivorship. **3.** Survival. *Ins:* Tables de survie, 'expectation of life' tables.

survivance [syrvivɑ̃:s], *s.f.* **I.** (*a*) Survival, outliving. *Biol:* Survivance du plus apte, des mieux adaptés, survival of the fittest. (*b*) Reversion (of estate, office). **2.** *Une s. des temps passés,* a survival, relic, of times past.

survivancier, -ière [syrvivɑ̃sje, -jɛːr], *s.* Reversioner (of estate, office).

survivant, -ante [syrvivɑ̃, -ɑ̃:t]. **I.** *a.* Surviving. **2.** *s.* Survivor.

survivre [syrviːvr], *v.ind.tr.* (Conj. like VIVRE. Aux. *avoir*) *S. à qn, à qch.,* to survive, outlive, s.o., sth.

survol [syrvɔl], *s.m. Av:* Flight over (a region).

survoler [syrvɔle], *v.tr. Av:* To fly over.

survolt|er [syrvɔlte], *v.tr. El.E:* **I.** To boost, step up (current). **2.** To overrun (lamp). *s.m.* **-age.**

survolteur [syrvɔltœːr], *s.m. El.E:* Booster, step-up transformer.

sus [sy(s)]. **I.** *adv. A:* (Up)on, against. (Still used in) Courir sus à son adversaire, to rush at one's opponent. **En sus,** in addition, extra, to boot. *En sus de ses gages,* over and above one's wages. **2.** *int.* Come on! now then! *Sus à l'ennemi!* at them!

susceptibilité [syseptibilite], *s.f.* **I.** Susceptibility, sensitiveness. **2.** Touchiness, irritability.

susceptible [syseptibl], *a.* Susceptible. **I.** *S. de qch.,* capable of, admitting of, liable to, sth. *S. d'amélioration,* open to improvement. *S. de se produire,* apt to occur. *Les documents susceptibles de vous intéresser,* the documents likely to interest you. **2.** (*a*) Sensitive, delicate. (*b*) Touchy, thin-skinned, easily offended.

susciter [syssite], *v.tr.* **I.** (*a*) To raise up. *Dieu suscita des libérateurs,* God raised up, set up, deliverers. (*b*) To create (enemies); to give rise to (difficulties). *S. des ennuis à qn,* to bring petty annoyances upon s.o. *Se s. des ennemis,* to incur enmity, hostility. **2.** To (a)rouse (envy); to instigate, stir up (revolt).

suscription [syskripsjɔ̃], *s.f.* Superscription, address (on letter).

sus-dénommé, -ée, *a. & s.* Above-named, afore-named.

susdit, -ite [sysdi, syzdi, -it], *a. & s.* Aforesaid, above-mentioned.

susmentionné, -ée [sysmɑ̃sjɔne], *a. & s.* Above-mentioned, aforesaid.

susnommé, -ée [sysnɔme], *a. & s.* Above-named.

suspect [syspɛ(kt)]. **I.** *a.* Suspicious, doubtful,

suspect. **Tenir qn pour suspect,** to hold s.o. in suspicion. *Devenir s.,* to arouse suspicion. *Être s. à qn de qch., de faire qch.,* to be suspected by s.o. of sth., of doing sth. **2.** *s.m.* Suspect. *La liste des suspects,* the black list.

suspecter [syspɛkte], *v.tr.* To suspect (s.o.) (*de,* of); to question, doubt (sth.).

suspendre [syspɑ̃:dr], *v.tr.* To suspend. **I.** To hang up. *S. un hamac,* to sling a hammock. **2.** (*a*) To defer, stay (judgment); to leave (decree) in abeyance; to stop (payment). *Aut: S. un permis de conduire,* to suspend a licence. (*b*) *S. un fonctionnaire,* to suspend an official. **se suspendre** *à une corde,* to hang by a rope, to hang on to a rope.

suspendu, *a.* **I.** Suspended, hanging. (*a*) **Pont suspendu,** suspension-bridge. *suspendue,* spring-cart, swing-cart. *Charrette non suspendue,* cart without springs. (*b*) *Lampe suspendue au plafond,* lamp hanging from the ceiling. *Il était s. à une corde,* he was hanging on to a rope. **2.** *Mus:* **Cadence suspendue,** suspended cadence.

suspens (en) [ɑ̃syspɑ̃], *adv.phr.* In suspense; (i) (of pers.) in doubt, in uncertainty; (ii) (of thg) in abeyance. *Questions en s.,* outstanding questions.

suspensif, -ive [syspɑ̃sif, -iːv], *a.* **I.** Suspensive (veto, etc.). **2.** *Gram:* Points suspensifs, points of suspension.

suspension [syspɑ̃sjɔ̃], *s.f.* Suspension. **I.** Hanging (up). **Mort par suspension,** death by hanging. **2.** (*a*) (Temporary) discontinuance, interruption (of work, etc.). *Gram:* **Points de suspension,** points of suspension. **Suspension d'armes,** truce, armistice. *S. de payements,* suspension of payment. *Jur:* **Arrêt de suspension,** injunction. (*b*) *S. d'un fonctionnaire,* suspension of an official. **3.** Hanging lamp. *S. électrique,* electrolier. **4.** *Veh:* Springing, springs (of a car, etc.).

suspensoir [syspɑ̃swaːr], *s.m.* **I.** *Surg:* Suspensory bandage. **2.** Suspending rod (of suspension-bridge).

suspente [syspɑ̃:t], *s.f. Nau:* Sling (of yard, etc.). *Aer:* Suspending ropes (of balloon car).

suspicion [syspisjɔ̃], *s.f. Esp. Jur:* Suspicion. *Être en suspicion,* to be suspected.

sustentateur, -trice [systɑ̃tatœːr, -tris], *a. Av:* Lifting (force, etc.). **Effort sustentateur,** lift. **Surface sustentatrice,** aerofoil.

sustentation [systɑ̃tasjɔ̃], *s.f.* (*a*) *Med:* Sustenance, sustentation. (*b*) Support. (*c*) *Aer:* **Force de sustentation,** lifting force.

sustenter [systɑ̃te], *v.tr.* To sustain, nourish, support.

susurration [sysyrasjɔ̃], *s.f.,* **susurrement** [sysyrmɑ̃], *s.m. Lit:* Susurration, whispering; murmuring (of sea); soughing (of wind); rustling (of trees).

susurrer [sysyre], *v.i. Lit:* To susurrate; to murmur, whisper.

sutural, -aux [sytyral, -o], *a. Anat:* Sutural.

suture [syty:r], *s.f. Anat:* Suture, join. *Surg:* Suture, stitching (of wound). **Point de suture,** stitch.

suturer [sytyre], *v.tr.* To stitch up (wound).

suzerain, -aine [syzrɛ̃, -ɛn]. **I.** *a.* Paramount, suzerain (lord, power). **2.** *s.* Suzerain, *f.* suzeraine.

suzeraineté [syzrɛnte], *s.f.* Suzerainty; lordship.

svastika [svastika], *s.m.* Swastika; fylfot.

svelte [svɛlt], *a.* Slender, slim, willowy (figure).

sveltesse [svɛltɛs], *s.f.* Slenderness, slimness.

sybarite [sibarit], *a. & s.* Sybarite; voluptuary.

sybaritique [sibaritik], *a.* Sybaritic.
sybaritisme [sibaritism], *s.m.* Sybaritism.
sycomore [sikɔmɔːr], *s.m. Bot:* **1.** (Érable) **sycomore**, sycamore (maple), great maple. **2.** Figuier **sycomore**, sycamore fig.
sycophante [sikɔfɑ̃ːt]. **1.** *s.m.* Sycophant, *F:* lickspittle, toady. **2.** *a.* Sycophantic.
sycophantisme [sikɔfɑ̃tism], *s.m.* Sycophancy.
syllabaire [sillabɛːr], *s.m.* Spelling-book.
syllabe [sillab], *s.f.* Syllable.
syllabique [sillabik], *a.* Syllabic.
syllepse [sillɛps], *s.f. Rh:* Syllepsis.
sylleptique [sillɛptik], *a.* Sylleptic.
syllogisme [sillɔʒism], *s.m.* Syllogism.
sylphe [silf], *s.m.*, **sylphide** [silfid], *s.f.* Sylph. *F:* Taille de sylphide, sylphlike waist.
sylvestre [silvɛstr], *a.* (*a*) Growing in the woods. (*b*) Woodland (tree).
sylvicole [silvikɔl], *a.* **1.** Sylvan; dwelling in woods. **2.** Relating to forestry.
sylviculteur [silvikyltœːr], *s.m.* Sylviculturist.
sylviculture [silvikylty:r], *s.f.* Forestry.
symbiose [sɛ̃bjoːz], *s.f. Biol:* Symbiosis.
symbole [sɛ̃bɔl], *s.m.* (*a*) Symbol. (*b*) Conventional sign. (*c*) *Ecc:* Creed. Le symbole des Apôtres, the Apostles' Creed. S.a. NICÉE.
symbolique [sɛ̃bɔlik], *a.* Symbolic(al). *adv.* -ment, -ally.
symboliser [sɛ̃bɔlize], *v.tr.* To symbolize.
symbolisme [sɛ̃bɔlism], *s.m.* Symbolism.
symétrie [simetri], *s.f.* Symmetry. Sans symétrie, unsymmetrical.
symétrique [simetrik], *a.* Symmetrical. *adv.* -ment.
sympathie [sɛ̃pati], *s.f.* Sympathy. (*a*) Instinctive attraction, fellow feeling. Avoir de la sympathie pour qn, to feel drawn to s.o.; to like s.o. Se prendre de sympathie pour qn, to take a liking to s.o.; to take to s.o. Sympathies et antipathies, likes and dislikes. (*b*) Idées qui ne sont pas en s., ideas that do not go together. (*c*) *Med: Physiol:* Sympathy (between organs).
sympathique [sɛ̃patik], *a.* **1.** Sympathetic. Être s. aux idées de qn, to be in sympathy with s.o.'s ideas. **2.** Likable, attractive. Personnalité peu sympathique, unattractive personality. Il me fut tout de suite s., I took to him at once. Il me devint s., I came to like him. Entourage s., congenial surroundings. **3.** Encre sympathique, sympathetic ink, invisible ink. **4.** *Anat: Physiol: etc:* Sympathetic (nerve, ophthalmia). *s.m.* Le grand sympathique, the sympathetic nerve. *adv.* -ment, -ally.
sympathiser [sɛ̃patize], *v.i.* To sympathize.
symphonie [sɛ̃fɔni], *s.f.* **1.** Symphony. *Cin: S.* folâtre, silly symphony. **2.** (*a*) Orchestra. (*b*) Strings of the orchestra.
symphonique [sɛ̃fɔnik], *a.* Symphonic.
symptomatique [sɛ̃ptɔmatik], *a.* Symptomatic.
symptôme [sɛ̃potːm], *s.m.* Symptom; *F:* sign, token, indication.
synagogue [sinagɔg], *s.f.* Synagogue.
synallagmatique [sinallagmatik], *a. Jur:* Synallagmatic. Contrat synallagmatique, bilateral contract; indenture.
synarthrose [sinartroːz], *s.f. Anat:* Synarthrosis.
synchrone [sɛ̃krɔn], *a.* Synchronous. *El.E:* In step.
synchronique [sɛ̃krɔnik], *a.* Synchronistic, synchronological (table of events).
synchronis|er [sɛ̃krɔnize], *v.tr.* To synchronize. *s.f.* -ation.
   synchronisé, *a.* Synchronized; *El.E:* in step.

synchroniseur [sɛ̃krɔnizœːr], *s.m.* **1.** *El.E:* Synchronizer. **2.** *Aut:* Synchromesh device.
synchronisme [sɛ̃krɔnism], *s.m.* Synchronism. En synchronisme, in synchronism, *El.E:* in step. Hors de synchronisme, out of synchronism; out of step.
synclinal, -aux [sɛ̃klinal, -o], *a. Geol:* Synclinal (valley).
syncope [sɛ̃kɔp], *s.f.* **1.** *Med:* Syncope; faint, fainting fit; swoon. *S. mortelle,* heart-failure. Tomber en syncope, to swoon; to faint. **2.** *Gram:* Syncope. **3.** *Mus:* (*a*) Syncopation. (*b*) Syncopated note.
syncoper [sɛ̃kɔpe], *v.tr.* To syncopate.
syncrétisme [sɛ̃kretism], *s.m. Phil:* Syncretism.
syndactyle [sɛ̃daktil], *a. Z:* Syndactyl(ous); web-fingered, -toed.
syndic [sɛ̃dik], *s.m.* Syndic. Syndic de faillite, assignee, official receiver (in bankruptcy).
syndical, -aux [sɛ̃dikal, -o], *a.* **1.** Syndical (chamber). Acte syndical, underwriting contract. **2.** Mouvement syndical, trade-union movement.
syndicalisme [sɛ̃dikalism], *s.m.* Syndicalism. Esp. Syndicalisme ouvrier, trade-unionism.
syndicaliste [sɛ̃dikalist], *s.m.* Trade-unionist.
syndicat [sɛ̃dika], *s.m.* **1.** Trusteeship (in bankruptcy). **2.** Syndicate. (*a*) *S. professionnel,* trade society, trade association. *S. patronal,* employers' federation. *S. industriel,* pool. *S. de garantie,* underwriting syndicate. S.a. INITIATIVE. (*b*) Syndicat ouvrier, trade union.
syndiquer [sɛ̃dike], *v.tr.* **1.** To syndicate (an industry). **2.** To form (workmen) into a trade union.
   se syndiquer. **1.** To combine; to syndicate. **2.** To form a trade union.
   syndiqué, *a.* Associated, combined. *Ouvriers syndiqués,* trade-unionists. *Ouvriers non syndiqués,* non-union men.
syndrome [sɛ̃drɔm, -oːm], *s.m. Med:* Syndrome.
synecdoche, synecdoque [sinɛkdɔk], *s.f. Rh:* Synecdoche.
synérèse [sinerɛːz], *s.f. Ling:* Synaeresis.
synergie [sinɛrʒi], *s.f.* Synergy.
synode [sinɔd], *s.m. Ecc:* Synod.
synonyme [sinɔnim], **1.** *a.* Synonymous (de, with). **2.** *s.m.* Synonym.
synonymie [sinɔnimi], *s.f.* Synonymy.
synoptique [sinɔptik], *a.* Synoptic(al). *Tableau s.,* conspectus (of a science, etc.).
synovial, -aux [sinɔvjal, -o], *a. Anat:* Synovial.
synovie [sinɔvi], *s.f. Anat: Physiol:* Synovia.
synovite [sinɔvit], *s.f. Med:* Synovitis.
syntactique [sɛ̃taktik], *a. Gram:* Syntactic(al).
syntaxe [sɛ̃taks], *s.f. Gram:* Syntax.
syntaxique [sɛ̃taksik], *a.* = SYNTACTIQUE.
synthèse [sɛ̃tɛːz], *s.f.* Synthesis.
synthétique [sɛ̃tetik], *a.* Synthetic(al). *adv.* -ment, -ally.
synthétiser [sɛ̃tetize], *v.tr.* To synthesize.
syntonie [sɛ̃tɔni], *s.f. W.Tel:* Syntonism, syntony.
syntonique [sɛ̃tɔnik], *a. W.Tel:* Syntonic, tuned.
syntonisateur, -trice [sɛ̃tɔnizatœːr, -tris]. *W.Tel:* **1.** *a.* Bobine syntonisatrice, tuning-coil. **2.** *s.m.* Tuning device; tuner.
syntonisation [sɛ̃tɔnizasjɔ̃], *s.f. W.Tel:* Tuning. Bobine de syntonisation, tuning-coil.
syntoniser [sɛ̃tɔnize], *v.tr. W.Tel:* To syntonize; to tune in (set).
syriaque [sirjak], *a. & s.m. Ling:* Syriac.
Syrie [siri]. *Pr.n.f. Geog:* Syria.
syrien, -ienne [sirjɛ̃, -jɛn], *a. & s.* Syrian.

systématique [sistɛmatik], *a.* (*a*) Systematic.
(*b*) *F:* Hide-bound (person). *adv.* **-ment,** -ally.
systématiser [sistɛmatize], *v.tr.* To systematize.
système [sistɛm], *s.m.* **1.** System. (*a*) *S. métrique*,
metric system. *Nouveau s. d'éclairage*, new
method of illumination. *Anat: Le s. nerveux*,
the nervous system. *F: Il me tape sur le système*,
he gets on my nerves. S.a. D. (*b*) **Agir par
système**, to act in a stereotyped manner. *Esprit*
de système, pigheadedness. (*c*) Set (of wheels,
of valves); network (of roads). **2.** (*a*) *Fusils de
divers systèmes*, rifles of various makes or types.
Bouton de col à système, patent collar-stud.
(*b*) Swivel rowlock.
systole [sistɔl], *s.f. Physiol:* Systole.
systolique [sistɔlik], *a.* Systolic.
syzygie [siziʒi], *s.f. Astr:* Syzygy. **Les marées
de syzygie**, the spring tides.

T

T, t [te], *s.m.* The Letter T, t. *Fer à, en,* T,
T-iron, tee. *Antenne en* T, T aerial. *Poutre en
double* T, H beam S.a. TÉ 1.
t'. See TE and TU¹.
ta [ta], *poss.a.f.* See TON¹.
tabac [taba], *s.m.* **1.** *Bot:* Tobacco(-plant).
2. (*a*) *T. haché*, cut tobacco. *T. en corde*, pigtail.
T. en carotte, twist. *T. à chiquer*, chewing
tobacco. **Blague à tabac, tabacco-pouch. Pot à
tabac**, tobacco-jar. **Débitant de tabac**, tobacconist. **Débit, bureau, de tabac**, tobacconist's
shop. *P:* (Esp. of the police) **Passer qn à tabac**,
to give s.o. a rough handling. (*b*) *T. à priser,
t. râpé*, snuff. **Prendre du tabac**, to take snuff.
S.a. PRISE 4. **3.** *a.inv.* Tobacco-coloured, snuff-
coloured.
tabagie [tabaʒi], *s.f.* Place reeking of stale
tobacco-smoke.
tabar(d) [tabaːr], *s.m.* (Herald's) tabard.
tabarin [tabarɛ̃], *s.m. A:* Buffoon. (From Jean
Salomon Tabarin, 1584-1633.)
tabarinade [tabarinad], *s.f. A.Th:* Broad farce.
tabatière [tabatjɛːr], *s.f.* (*a*) Snuff-box. (*b*) (**Fenêtre, lucarne, à) tabatière**, hinged skylight.
[TABAC]
tabellion [tabɛljɔ̃], *s.m.* (*a*) *Jur: A:* Scrivener.
(*b*) *Hum:* Limb of the law.
tabernacle [tabɛrnakl], *s.m.* Tabernacle.
tabes [tabɛs], *s.m. Med:* Tabes.
tabescence [tabɛssɑ̃ːs], *s.f. Med:* Tabescence.
tablature [tablatyːr], *s.f. Mus:* **1.** *A:* Tablature. *F: A:* **Donner de la tablature à qn**, to
cause s.o. trouble or embarrassment. **Savoir,
entendre, la tablature**, to know a thing or two.
2. Fingering chart (of wind instrument).
table [tabl], *s.f.* Table. **1.** (*a*) *T. de jeu*, card
table. *T. de billard*, billiard table. *T. de toilette*,
dressing table. *T. d'opération*, operating table.
(*b*) *La t. du festin*, the festive board. **Mettre,
dresser, la table**, to lay, set, the table. **Bière de
table**, table beer. **Se mettre à table**, to sit down
to table, to dinner. **Se lever, sortir, de table**, to
rise from the table, to leave the table. **Tenir
table ouverte**, to keep an open board. **Avoir
table et logement chez qn**, to board and lodge
with s.o. (*Service de*) *petites tables*, separate
tables (at restaurant). *Mil: T. d'officiers*, officers'
mess. *Ecc:* **La Sainte Table**, the Lord's Table,
the communion table. S.a. HÔTE 1. **2.** (*a*) Table
(of gem). *Mus:* **Table d'harmonie**, sound-board
(of piano); belly (of violin). (*b*) Face (of hammer); flange (of girder). *Mch: T. du tiroir*,
valve face. *T. de planeuse*, bed of a planing-
machine. **3.** (*a*) Slab (of stone, etc.); tablet.
B: **Les tables de la loi**, the Tables of the Law.
S.a. RAS¹ 1. (*b*) List, catalogue. *T. alphabétique*,
alphabetical list, table, or index. *T. de multiplication*, multiplication table. S.a. MATIÈRE 3.

tableau [tablo], *s.m.* **1.** (*a*) Board. *T. d'annonces*,
notice-board. *Sch:* **Tableau noir**, blackboard.
El.E: **Tableau de distribution**, switchboard.
Aut: **Tableau de bord** = *planche de bord, q.v.*
under PLANCHE 1. (*b*) *Bill:* Scoring-board.
(*c*) *Nau:* Name-board (of ship). (*d*) (In hotel)
Key-rack, -board. **2.** (*a*) Picture, painting.
T. d'autel, altar-piece. (*b*) *Th:* Tableau (at end
of act, etc.). (*c*) **Tableau vivant**, living picture,
tableau vivant. (*d*) *Th:* Scene or group of scenes
acted in one setting. **3.** (*a*) List, table. *Rail:*
Tableau de marche, time-table. **Tableau d'avancement**, promotion list, promotion roster. *T. de
service*, duty roster. *Aut:* **T. de graissage**,
lubrication chart. (*b*) Roll (of lawyers); panel
(of jurymen, doctors, etc.). **Former un tableau**,
to empanel a jury. *Être rayé du t.*, to be struck
off the rolls.
tableautin [tablotɛ̃], *s.m.* Small picture.
tabler [table], *v.i. F:* **Tabler sur qch.**, to count,
reckon, on sth.
tabletier [tablətje], *s.m.* Dealer in fancy articles
(of ebony, ivory, bone) and inlaid ware.
tablette [tablɛt], *s.f.* **1.** (*a*) Shelf (of bookcase,
etc.). *T. à coulisse*, pull-out slide (of table or
desk). (*b*) Flat slab; coping-stone. **Tablette de
cheminée**, mantelshelf, mantelpiece. **Tablette
de fenêtre**, window-sill. **2.** *pl. A:* Writing-
tablets. **Mettre qch. sur ses tablettes**, to make a
note of sth. **3.** Cake, slab (of chocolate).
Pharm: Tablet, lozenge.
tabletterie [tabletri], *s.f.* (*a*) Fancy-goods
industry. (*b*) Inlaid ware, knick-knacks, and
fancy goods.
tablier [tablie], *s.m.* **1.** Apron. *T. d'enfant*,
pinafore. **Tablier-blouse**, (lady's) overall. *F:*
Rendre son tablier, to give notice. **2.** *Veh:* Apron
(of carriage). *Artil:* Footboard (of limber).
Aut: Dashboard. **3.** (*a*) Register, blower (of
French fireplace). (*b*) *T. de tôle (d'un magasin)*,
sectional steel shutter. **4.** Superstructure,
flooring, deck, road(way) (of bridge); table (of
weigh-bridge); foot-plate (of locomotive).
tabou [tabu], **1.** *s.m.* Taboo. **2.** *a.* Taboo(ed).
F: Sujets tabous, forbidden subjects.
tabouret [taburɛ], *s.m.* **1.** (*a*) High stool. *T. de
piano*, piano stool. (*b*) Footstool. **2.** *Bot:*
Shepherd's-purse.
tabulateur [tabylatœːr], *s.m.* **1.** *Typewr:* Tabu-
lator. **2.** *Tp:* **Faire marcher le t.**, to work
the dial; to dial.
tac [tak], *s.m.* Click (of steel); clack (of mill);
tick-tack (of clock-work). **Riposter du tac au tac**
(i) *Fenc:* to parry with the riposte; (ii) *F:* to
make a lightning retort.
tacaud [tako], *s.m. Ich:* Whiting-pout.
tachant [taʃɑ̃], *a.* **1.** (Of material) Easily stained
or soiled. **2.** That stains, soils (other things).

tache [taʃ], *s.f.* (*a*) Stain, spot (of grease, mud); blob (of colour); flaw, blemish; bruise (on fruit); stigma, blot (on family record). *T. d'encre*, blot, blur. *T. de suie*, fleck of soot; smut. *T. solaire, t. du soleil*, sun-spot. *Enlever, effacer, faire disparaître, une t.*, to remove a stain. *Sans tache*, spotless; stainless; without blemish, without a blot; undefiled. **Faire tache, to stand out as a blemish.** S.a. HUILE I. (*b*) **Tache de rousseur**, freckle. **Tache de vin**, strawberry-mark (on skin).

tâche [tɑːʃ], *s.f.* Task. *Travail à la tâche*, piecework. *Ouvrier à la tâche*, (i) jobbing workman; (ii) *Ind:* piece-worker. **Prendre à tâche de faire qch.**, to make it one's duty to do sth.; to undertake to do sth.

tachéomètre [takeɔmɛtr], *s.m. Surv:* Tacheometer, tachymeter.

tachéométrie [takeɔmetri], *s.f. Surv:* Tacheometry, tachymetry.

tacher [taʃe], *v.tr.* To stain, spot (garment, etc.); to sully, tarnish, blemish (reputation).
se tacher. I. To soil one's clothes. **2.** (Of material) To stain, spot.

tâcher [tɑʃe], *v.i.* (*a*) To try, endeavour. *T. de faire qch.*, to strive to do sth. *J'y tâcherai*, I shall do my best. *Tâchez qu'on n'en sache rien*, try to keep it quiet. (*b*) To toil (and moil).

tâcheron [tɑʃrɔ̃], *s.m.* Jobbing workman; pieceworker.

tacheter [taʃte], *v.tr.* (je tachette; je tachetterai [taʃtre]) To mark with spots; to speckle, fleck, mottle. *Chat tacheté*, tabby cat, brindled cat.

tachycardie [takikardi], *s.f. Med:* Tachycardia.

tachygraphe [takigraf]. **I.** *s.m. & f.* Shorthand writer (esp. of ancient Greece and Rome). **2.** *s.m.* Recording tachometer.

tachymètre [takimɛtr], *s.m.* Tachometer, speedometer.

tacite[1] [tasit], *a.* Tacit (consent, etc.); implied, understood, implicit. *adv.* **-ment.**

Tacite[2]. *Pr.n.m. Lt.Lit:* Tacitus.

taciturne [tasityrn], *a.* Taciturn, uncommunicative, close-mouthed. **Guillaume le Taciturne,** William the Silent.

taciturnité [tasityrnite], *s.f.* Taciturnity.

tacot [tako], *s.m. Veh: F:* **I.** Shandrydan, rattletrap. **2.** (*a*) Engine of small local train; 'Puffing Billy.' (*b*) Small local train. **3.** (*a*) Old crock (of a motor car). (*b*) Motor car. [TAC]

tact [takt], *s.m.* **I.** (Sense of) touch. *Choisir une étoffe au t.*, to choose a cloth by feel. **2.** Tact. *Avoir du t., être plein de t.*, to be tactful. *Homme de tact*, tactful man. *Dépourvu de tact*, tactless. *Manque de tact*, tactlessness. *Agir avec tact, sans tact*, to act tactfully, tactlessly.

tacticien [taktisjɛ̃], *s.m.* Tactician.

tactile [taktil], *a.* Tactile.

tactique [taktik]. **I.** *a.* Tactical. **2.** *s.f.* Tactics.

tadorne [tadɔrn], *s.m. Orn:* Sheldrake.

taffetas [tafta], *s.m.* (*a*) *Tex:* Taffeta. (*b*) *Med:* **Taffetas d'Angleterre, taffetas gommé,** courtplaster, sticking-plaster. *T. imperméable*, oiled silk.

taïaut [tajo], *int. Ven:* Tally-ho!

taïcoun [taikun], *s.m.* Tycoon (of Japan).

taie [tɛ], *s.f.* **I.** **Taie d'oreiller,** pillow-case, -slip. **2.** *Med:* Albugo; white speck on the eye.

taillable [tajabl], *a. Hist:* Talliable; liable to tallage.

taillade [tajad], *s.f.* Cut, slash, gash.

taillader [tajade], *v.tr.* (*a*) To slash, gash. *Cost: Jupe tailladée*, slashed skirt. (*b*) *F:* *T. un article (de journal)*, to make cuts in an article.

tailladin [tajadɛ̃], *s.m.* (Thin) slice of lemon or orange.

taillanderie [tajɑ̃dri], *s.f.* **I.** Edge-tool industry. **2.** *Coll.* Edge-tools.

taillandier [tajɑ̃dje], *s.m.* Maker of edge-tools.

taillant [tajɑ̃], *s.m.* (Cutting) edge (of sword).

taille [tɑːj, tɑːj], *s.f.* **I.** (*a*) Cutting (of diamonds, garments); pruning, trimming (of shrubs); clipping (of hedge); (i) hewing, (ii) dressing (of stone). *T. de cheveux*, hair-cutting. **Une taille de cheveux,** a hair-cut. **Pierre de taille,** (i) freestone, (ii) ashlar. (*b*) *Surg:* Lithotomy, cutting for stone. **2.** Method of cutting; cut. *Je n'aime pas la t. de votre pantalon*, I don't like the cut of your trousers. *Tls: Lime à simple t.*, single-cut file. *T. douce*, smooth cut. **3.** (*a*) Edge (of sword, etc.). **Coup de taille,** cut, slash. S.a. ESTOC 2. (*b*) *For:* **Une jeune taille,** a coppice. (*c*) *Com:* Tally(-stick). **4.** (*a*) Stature, height (of pers.); dimensions (of monument, etc.). *Être de grande t., de t. moyenne*, to be very tall, of middle height. *F:* **Il est de taille à se défendre,** he is big enough, strong enough, to look after himself. (*b*) Figure, waist. **Tour de taille,** waist measurement. **Être bien pris de taille, dans sa taille,** to have an elegant figure. **Prendre qn par la taille,** (i) to seize, take, s.o. round the waist; (ii) to put an arm round s.o.'s waist. **Femme en taille,** woman wearing no jacket or wrap. **5.** *Hist:* Tall(i)age, tax, toll. *T. réelle*, property tax. **6.** *Mus: A:* Tenor.

taille-crayons, *s.m.inv.* Pencil-sharpener.

taille-douce, *s.f. Engr:* (Gravure en) tailledouce, copper-plate engraving. *pl. Des taillesdouces.*

taille-mer, *s.m.inv. N.Arch:* Cutwater (of bow).

taille-pain, *s.m.inv.* (*a*) Bread-knife. (*b*) Breadslicer.

tailler [taje, tɑje], *v.tr.* **I.** (*a*) To cut (diamond, grass); to hew (stone); to prune (tree); to trim, clip (hedge, beard). *T. un crayon*, to sharpen, point, a pencil. *T. le pain*, to cut the bread. *Tailler une armée en pièces*, to cut an army to pieces. *Se t. un chemin à travers la foule*, to carve one's way through the crowd. (*b*) **Tailler un vêtement,** to cut out a garment. *Complet bien taillé*, well-cut suit. *F:* **On m'a taillé de la besogne**, I have my work cut out for me. *Prov:* **Il faut tailler la robe selon le corps,** you must cut your coat according to your cloth. S.a. BAVETTE I, CROUPIÈRE. **2.** *Surg:* To operate on, cut, (s.o.) for stone. **3.** *Hist:* To tax (the people).

taillé, *a.* **I.** *Homme bien t.*, well set-up man. *Il est t. pour commander*, he is cut out for a leader. S.a. CÔTE I. **2.** Cristal taillé, cut glass.

taille-racines, *s.m.inv.* Vegetable-cutter.

tailleur, -euse [tajœːr, -øːz], *s.* **I.** (*a*) Cutter (of gems, etc.); hewer (of stone). (*b*) Tailor, tailoress. "Tailleur à façon," 'customers' own material made up.' *S'asseoir en tailleur*, to sit cross-legged. **2.** *Cost:* (Costume) tailleur, tailormade costume.

taille-vent, *s.m.inv. Nau:* Lug mainsail; lugsail.

taillis [taji], *s.m.* **I.** Copse, coppice, *Poet:* shaw. *a.* **Bois taillis**, copsewood, brushwood; bush. *Gagner le t.*, to take to the bush. **2.** *Mil:* Brushwood entanglement.

tailloir [tajwaːr], *s.m.* **I.** Trencher. **2.** *Arch:* Abacus.

taillole [tajɔl], *s.f. Cost:* (In Provence) Woollen trouser-belt or sash (worn by peasants).

tain [tɛ̃], *s.m.* Silvering (for mirrors); foil, tain. **Glace sans tain,** plate-glass.

taire [tɛːr], *v.tr.* (*pr.p.* taisant; *p.p.* tu; *pr.ind.* je tais, il tait, n. taisons, ils taisent; *p.h.* je tus; *fu.* je tairai) To say nothing about (sth.); to suppress, keep dark, hush up (sth.). *Une dame dont je tairai le nom*, a lady who shall be nameless. *T. qch. à qn*, to keep, hide, conceal, sth. from s.o. *F:* Taire sa langue = *se taire*.
se taire, to hold one's tongue, to hold one's peace, to be silent. *Toute la nature se tait*, all nature is hushed. *Se t. sur, de, qch.*, to pass sth. over in silence. **Tais-toi!** hold your tongue! be quiet! **Faire taire qn**, to silence s.o.; to reduce s.o. to silence; to keep (a child) quiet. *Prov:* **Mieux vaut se taire que mal parler**, least said soonest mended. **Qui se tait consent**, silence gives consent. *Iron:* **Taisez-vous donc!** nonsense! fiddlesticks!
Taïti [taiti]. *Pr.n. Geog:* Tahiti.
talc [talk], *s.m.* Talc; French chalk; soap-stone. *Toil:* (Poudre de) talc, talcum powder.
talent [talɑ̃], *s.m.* **1.** *Gr.Ant:* Talent (weight or coin). *F:* Enfouir son talent, to hide one's light under a bushel. **2.** Talent, faculty, gift. **Avoir du talent**, to be talented. **Homme de talent**, man of parts; talented man. **Avoir le talent des langues**, to have a talent for languages. **Faire appel à tous les talents**, to form an administration of all the talents.
talentueux, -euse [talɑ̃tɥø, -øːz], *a.* Talented.
talion [taljɔ̃], *s.m.* Talion, retaliation. **La loi du talion**, the lex talionis; the law of retaliation.
talisman [talismɑ̃], *s.m.* Talisman.
talle [tal], *s.f. Agr: Hort:* Sucker; tiller.
taller [tale], *v.i.* To throw out suckers; to sucker; to tiller; to stool.
taloche [talɔʃ], *s.f. F:* Cuff; clout on the head. **Flanquer une taloche à qn** = *talocher qn*.
talocher [talɔʃe], *v.tr.* To cuff; to clout (s.o.) on the head; to box (s.o.)'s ears.
talon [talɔ̃], *s.m.* **1.** Heel (of foot or shoe). **Marcher sur les talons de qn**, to follow close on s.o.'s heels. **Être toujours sur les talons de qn**, to dog s.o.'s footsteps. **Montrer les talons, jouer des talons**, to show a clean pair of heels. *S.a.* ESTOMAC. **Bas troués aux talons**, stockings out at heel. *Hist:* Talon rouge, aristocrat, courtier. **2.** *Tchn:* (a) Heel (of tool, mast); nut (of violin bow); butt (of billiard cue); flange, collar (on axle). (b) Catch, clip, hook, stud; beading. **Pneu à talons**, beaded tyre. *Nau:* **Donner un coup de talon**, to touch (the bottom); to bump. **3.** (a) (At cards, dominoes) Stock (not yet dealt out); talon. (b) Fag-end, remnant (of bread, cheese); heel (of loaf). (c) **Talon de souche**, counterfoil. **4.** *Arch:* Ogee-moulding; talon.
talonn|er [talɔne]. **1.** *v.tr.* (a) To follow (s.o.) closely; to follow on the heels of (s.o.); to dog (s.o.); to dun (s.o.). (b) To dig one's heels into (one's horse); to spur on, urge (horse). *F:* **T. un élève**, to spur on a pupil. (c) *Rugby Fb:* To heel out. **2.** *v.i. Nau:* (Of ship, boat) To touch, to bump; to strike. *s.m.* **-ement.**
talonnette [talɔnɛt], *s.f.* Heel-piece (of stocking, shoe).
talonnière [talɔnjɛːr], *s.f.* **1.** *Nau:* Heel, sole (of rudder). **2.** *pl. Myth:* (Mercury's) heel-wings.
talpack [talpak], *s.m. Mil: A:* Busby.
talus [taly], *s.m.* **1.** Slope, *Civ.E:* batter. **En talus**, sloping; battered. **2.** Bank, embankment, ramp.
tamanoir [tamanwaːr], *s.m. Z:* Great ant-eater.
tamarin[1] [tamarɛ̃], *s.m. Bot:* Tamarind.
tamarin[2], *s.m. Z:* Silky marmoset; tamarin.

tamarinier [tamarinje], *s.m.* Tamarind-tree.
tamaris(c) [tamaris(k)], *s.m. Bot:* Tamarisk.
tambour [tɑ̃buːr], *s.m.* **1.** Drum. **Battre du tambour**, to play the drum. **Battre le tambour**, (of town-crier) to beat the drum; to drum. **Peau de tambour**, drum-head. **Tambour de basque**, tambourine (with jingles). **Coup de tambour**, beat or roll on the drum. **Sans tambour ni trompette**, quietly, without fuss. *S.a.* BATTANT I. 1, BATTRE 2, DÉNICHER 2, FLÛTE I. **2.** Drummer. **Tambour de ville**, town-crier. **3.** (a) Drum (of oil, etc.). *Mec.E:* (Winding-) drum, barrel, roller (of winch); barrel (of capstan). *Fish:* Spool (of reel). *El.E:* (Cable-) drum. *Aut:* **Tambour de frein**, brake-drum. (b) Tambour; (embroidery) frame. **4.** (a) Tambour (of vestibule); revolving door. (b) *T. d'une roue à aubes*, paddle-box. **5.** Tambourine (pigeon).
tambourin [tɑ̃burɛ̃], *s.m.* (a) Long, narrow drum (of Provence); *A:* tabor. (b) Tambourine (without jingles).
tambourinaire [tɑ̃burinɛːr], *s.m.* (In S. of Fr.) (a) Pipe and tabor player. (b) Town-crier.
tambourin|er [tɑ̃burine]. **1.** *v.i.* (a) To beat a drum. (b) *F:* To drum, thrum (with the fingers); to beat the devil's tattoo (on table, etc.). (c) (Of machine part) To knock, hammer. **2.** *v.tr. T. une nouvelle, un objet perdu*, to cry a piece of news, a lost object; to make sth. known by beat of drum. *s.m.* **-age.**
tambourineur [tɑ̃burinœːr], *s.m.* Drummer; town-crier.
tambour-major, *s.m.* Drum-major. *pl.* **tambours-majors.**
taminier [taminje], *s.m. Bot:* Black bryony.
tamis [tami], *s.m.* Sieve, sifter; (for liquids) strainer; (for flour) bolter. *Ind:* Riddle, screen. **Toile à tamis**, bolting-cloth. **Passer qch. au tamis**, (i) to sift or strain sth.; to bolt (flour); (ii) *F:* to sift (evidence, etc.) thoroughly.
Tamise (la) [latamiːz]. *Pr.n.* The Thames.
tamis|er [tamize]. **1.** *v.tr.* To pass (sth.) through a sieve; to sift, screen (gravel); to bolt (flour); to strain, to tammy, to filter (liquids); to filter (air). *Rideaux qui tamisent la lumière*, curtains that soften, subdue, the light. **2.** *v.i.* (Of dust, light, etc.) To filter through. *s.m.* **-age.** *s.m.* **-eur.**
tampon [tɑ̃pɔ̃], *s.m.* **1.** (a) Plug, stopper; waste-plug. *T. de liège*, bung (of cask). (b) Wall-plug. (c) *T. d'égout*, manhole cover. **2.** *Mil:* (a) *Artil: T. de bouche*, (muzzle) tompion, tampion. (b) *P:* Orderly, batman. **3.** (a) *Surg:* Wad, plug, tampon; tent (of cotton-wool). (b) (Inking-)pad. *T. à timbrer*, stamp-pad. (c) Rubber stamp. **4.** **Tampon de choc**, buffer. *T. à ressort*, spring-buffer. **Coup de tampon**, collision. *El.E:* **Accumulateur en tampon**, balancing accumulator. *Dipl:* **État tampon**, buffer state. **5.** Bass-drumstick. *F:* **Coup de tampon**, thump, punch.
tamponnement [tɑ̃pɔnmɑ̃], *s.m.* **1.** Plugging (of wound). **2.** Dabbing (with pad). **3.** *Rail:* (End-on) collision.
tamponner [tɑ̃pɔne], *v.tr.* **1.** To plug, tent, tampon (wound); to plug (wall). **2.** To dab (with pad); to ink up (type). **Se t. les yeux**, to dab one's eyes. *Se t. le front*, to mop one's brow. **3.** (Of car, train) To run into, collide with, *F:* to bump into (another car or train).
tam-tam [tamtam], *s.m.* **1.** (Indian or African) tom-tom. *F:* **Faire du tam-tam autour de qch.**, to make a great to-do about sth. **2.** (Chinese) gong. *pl.* **Des tam-tams.**

tan [tɑ̃]. **I.** *s.m.* Tan; (tanner's) bark. **2.** *a.inv.* Tan(-coloured).

tanaisie [tanɛzi], *s.f.* Bot: Tansy.

tancer [tɑ̃se], *v.tr.* (je tançai(s); n. tançons) To rate, scold; F: to haul (s.o.) over the coals.

tanche [tɑ̃:ʃ], *s.f.* Ich: Tench.

tandem [tɑ̃dɛm], *s.m.* (*a*) Veh: Tandem. Conduire en tandem, to drive tandem. (*b*) Tandem bicycle.

tandis que [tɑ̃di(s)kə], *conj.phr.* (*a*) Whereas. *Lui s'amuse, t. que nous, nous travaillons,* he plays, whereas we have to work. (*b*) While, whilst. *Il s'amuse tandis que nous travaillons,* he plays while we work.

tangage [tɑ̃ga:ʒ], *s.m.* Pitching (of ship, aeroplane). Angle de tangage, angle of pitch.

tangence [tɑ̃ʒɑ̃:s], *s.f.* Geom: Tangency.

tangent, -ente [tɑ̃ʒɑ̃, -ɑ̃:t]. **I.** *a.* Tangential, tangent (*à,* to). **2.** *s.f.* Tangente, tangent. *F:* S'échapper par la tangente, prendre la tangente, (i) to fly off at a tangent, to dodge the question; (ii) to slip away.

tangentiel, -elle [tɑ̃ʒɑ̃sjɛl], *a.* Tangential.

Tanger [tɑ̃ʒe]. *Pr.n.* Geog: Tangier(s).

tangible [tɑ̃ʒibl], *a.* Tangible.

tango [tɑ̃go]. **I.** *s.m.* Danc: Tango. **2.** *a.inv.* Yellow-orange (colour); tango.

tangon [tɑ̃gɔ̃], *s.m.* **I.** Navy: (Swinging) boom. **2.** T. de spinnaker, spinnaker boom.

tanguer[1] [tɑ̃ge], *v.i.* (Of ship, aeroplane) To pitch. T. dur, to pitch heavily.

tanguer[2], *v.i.* To dance the tango; to tango.

tanière [tanjɛ:r], *s.f.* Den, lair (of badger, lion, etc.); hole, earth (of fox).

tanin [tanɛ̃], *s.m.* Ch: Ind: Tannin.

tannant [tanɑ̃], *a.* **I.** Jus tannant, tan liquor; pickle. **2.** P: Boring, tiresome (person).

tanne [tan], *s.f.* **I.** Spot (on leather). **2.** Blackhead (on face).

tann|er [tane], *v.tr.* **I.** To tan. **2.** P: (*a*) To tire, bore, pester (s.o.). (*b*) Tanner le cuir à qn, to thrash, leather, s.o.; to tan s.o.'s hide. *s.m.* -age.

   tanné. **I.** *a.* Tanned (face). **2.** *s.m.* Tan (colour).

   tannée, *s.f.* **I.** Spent tan. **2.** P: Thrashing, hiding, tanning.

tannerie [tanri], *s.f.* Tannery, tan-yard.

tanneur [tanœ:r], *s.m.* Tanner.

tannin [tanɛ̃], *s.m.* = TANIN.

tannique [tannik], *a.* Ch: Tannic (acid).

tant [tɑ̃], *adv.* **I.** (*a*) So much. Tant de bonté, so much, such, kindness. *Il a tant bu que . . .,* he has drunk so much that. . . . Si vous faites tant que de . . ., if you decide to. . . . Pour tant faire, *F:* tant qu'à faire, j'aimerais autant . . ., while I am at it, about it, if it comes to that, I would just as soon. . . . Tant pour cent, so much per cent. *s.* Le tant pour cent sur . . ., the percentage on. . . . Être tant à tant, to be even (at play). Il a tant et plus d'argent, he has any amount of money. Faire tant et si bien que . . ., to work to such good purpose that. . . . Tant s'en faut, far from it. Tant soit peu, ever so little; somewhat. Un tant soit peu vulgaire, just a little bit vulgar. Ils sont tant soit peu cousins, they are more or less cousins. Un tant soit peu trop long, a shade, a thought, too long. Tant (il) y a que + *ind.*, the fact remains that. . . . Si tant est qu'il le fasse, if indeed he does it at all. *F:* Vous m'en direz tant! (i) now I see! now I understand! (ii) you don't say so! (*b*) So many; as many. Tant de fois, so many times,

so often. Il a tant et plus d'amis, he has ever so many friends. Tous tant que vous êtes, every one of you. (*c*) (= *autant que*) Je ne mange pas tant que vous, I don't eat as much, so much, as you. Tant que vous voudrez, as much as you like. (*d*) So; to such a degree. Tant était grande sa discrétion que . . ., so great was his discretion that. . . . Tant il est vrai que . . ., so true is it that. . . . En tant que, in so far as. L'homme en tant qu'homme, man, qua man. (*e*) (Concessive, = QUELQUE) Tant aimable qu'il soit, however pleasant he may be. (*f*) Tant mieux, so much the better; I'm very glad! good! Tant pis! so much the worse; it can't be helped! what a pity! **2.** (*a*) As much, as well (as). J'ai couru tant que j'ai pu, I ran as hard as I could. S.a. BIEN I. 4. (*b*) As long, as far (as). Tant que je vivrai, as long as I live.

Tantale[1] [tɑ̃tal]. *Pr.n.m.* Myth: Tantalus. *Ph:* Vase de Tantale, Tantalus cup.

tantale[2], *s.m.* Ch: Tantalum.

tantaliser [tɑ̃talize], *v.tr.* To tantalize, tease.

tante [tɑ̃:t], *s.f.* Aunt. Tante à la mode de Bretagne, (i) first cousin once removed; (ii) *F:* very distant relative. T. par alliance, aunt-in-law. *P:* Chez ma tante, at the pawnbroker's; *P:* at my uncle's; up the spout.

tantième [tɑ̃tjɛm]. **I.** *a.* Soit à trouver la t. partie d'un tout, to find the required part of a whole. **2.** *s.m.* Percentage, share, quota (of profits, etc.). [TANT]

tantinet [tɑ̃tine], *s.m.* F: Tiny bit, least bit; wee drop (of wine); dash, touch, thought of irony). [TANT]

tantôt [tɑ̃to], *adv.* **I.** Soon, presently. Voici tantôt trois ans que . . ., it will soon be three years since. . . . Je reviens tantôt, I'll be back (i) presently, (ii) in the afternoon. A tantôt, good-bye for the present; *F:* so long! Sur le tantôt, towards evening. **2.** Just now; a little while ago. **3.** Tantôt . . ., tantôt . . ., at one time . . ., at another time . . .; sometimes . . ., sometimes. . . . T. triste, t. gai, now sad, now gay. [TANT TÔT]

taon [tɑ̃], *s.m.* Gad-fly, horse-fly, cleg.

tapage [tapa:ʒ], *s.m.* (Loud) noise; din, uproar; row. *Jur:* Tapage nocturne, disturbance of the peace at night. Faire du tapage, to kick up a row.

tapageu|r, -euse [tapaʒœ:r, -ø:z]. **I.** *a.* (*a*) Noisy (child, etc.); rowdy, uproarious, *F:* rackety (revellers, etc.). (*b*) Loud, flashy, showy (dress). **2.** *s.* (*a*) Roisterer, rowdy; brawler. (*b*) Petit t., noisy little beggar. *adv.* -sement.

tapant [tapɑ̃], *a.* F: (Of the hour) Striking. Arriver à l'heure tapante, to arrive on the stroke of the hour.

tape[1] [tap], *s.f.* **I.** (*a*) Tap, rap, pat, slap. T. sur l'épaule, slap on the shoulder. Il me donna une petite t. sur la joue, he patted my cheek. (*b*) *F:* Tape à la bourse, call on the purse. **2.** *P:* Quelle tape! what a sell! Ramasser une tape, to come a cropper; *Th:* to get the bird.

tape[2], *s.f.* Plug, stopper, bung. *Artil:* Tompion, tampion. *Nau:* T. d'écubier, hawse-plug; buckler.

tape-à-l'œil, *s.m.inv.* F: Flashy goods.

tapecu(l), tape-cul [tapky], *s.m.* **I.** See-saw. **2.** Counterpoise swing-gate. **3.** *Nau:* Jigger (sail). **4.** *Veh:* (*a*) Gig. (*b*) Hard-sprung carriage; rattletrap. *pl.* Des tape(-)culs.

tap|er [tape], *v.tr.* **I.** To tap, strike, hit. (*a*) T. du tambour, to beat the drum. Se t. les cheveux, to pat one's hair. Taper une lettre (à la machine), to type(write) a letter. (*b*) Abs. T. sur *qch.*, to tap, bang, on sth. **Se taper sur la cuisse,** to slap one's thigh. *T. sur le ventre à qn,* to give s.o. a dig in the waistcoat. *T. sur le piano,* to **strum. Commis qui sait taper,** clerk who can type. **Taper sur qn,** to abuse, slate, slang, s.o. **Tapez dessus,** pitch into him. (Of wine) **Taper à la tête,** to go to the head. (*c*) *F : T. qn de dix francs,* to tap, touch, s.o. for ten francs. *P :* **Tu peux te taper,** you may whistle for it ; nothing doing. **2.** To dab on (paint). **3.** *v.i. P :* To stink. *s.m.* **-ement.**

   tapé, *a.* **1.** Dried (fruit). **2.** *P :* First-rate, tip-top. **Réponse tapée,** smart answer ; crusher.

   tapée, *s.f. P :* Great quantity ; lots. *J'en ai une t.,* I've got heaps.

tapette [tapɛt], *s.f.* (*a*) Mallet. (*b*) Carpet-beater. (*c*) (Engraver's) pad, dabber. (*d*) Flapper ; fly-swatter. (*e*) *P :* **Elle a une fière tapette,** she is a great chatterbox ; she *can* talk !

tapin [tapɛ̃], *s.m. P :* Drummer. [TAPER]

tapinois, -oise [tapinwa, -wa:z]. **1.** *s. A :* Sly-boots. **2.** *Adv.phr.* **En tapinois,** stealthily, on the sly.

tapioca [tapjɔka], *s.m.* Tapioca.

tapir[1] [tapi:r], *s.m. Z :* Tapir.

tapir[2] **(se),** *v.pr.* To squat, cower ; to ensconce oneself ; (of game) to take cover. *Se t. derrière la porte,* to crouch behind the door.

tapis [tapi], *s.m.* **1.** Cloth, cover. *T. de table,* table cover. *T. de billard,* billiard-cloth. **Tapis vert,** gaming table. **Le tapis brûle !** put down your stakes ! **Mettre qch. sur le tapis,** to bring sth. up for consideration, for discussion. **Être sur le tapis,** to be on the tapis, on the carpet. **Amuser le tapis,** to keep the company amused (before main event). S.a. **NET 1. 2.** Carpet. *T. de haute laine, de laine rase,* long-pile carpet, short-pile carpet. **Tapis de gazon,** (green)sward. **3.** *Ind :* **Tapis roulant,** travelling band, endless belt (in mass production).

tapis-brosse, *s.m.* Coir mat, door-mat. *pl. Des tapis-brosses.*

tapisser [tapise], *v.tr.* **1.** To hang (wall) with tapestry. **2.** To paper (room). **3.** *Mur tapissé d'affiches,* wall plastered with advertisements. *Une membrane tapisse l'estomac,* a membrane lines the stomach. *Mur tapissé de lierre,* ivy-clad, ivy-mantled, wall.

tapisserie [tapisri], *s.f.* **1.** Tapestry-making. **2.** Tapestry, hangings. (At a ball) **Faire tapisserie,** to be a wall-flower. **3.** Tapestry-work ; crewel-work. **Pantoufles en tapisserie,** carpet-slippers. **4.** Wall-paper.

tapissier, -ière [tapisje, -jɛ:r], *s.* **1.** Tapestry-worker. **2. Tapissier garnisseur,** upholsterer. **3.** *s.f.* **Tapissière.** (*a*) Delivery-van. (*b*) Covered waggonette.

tapon [tapɔ̃], *s.m.* Plug, stopper ; screwed-up rag. **En tapon,** (of clothes) bundled up ; (of hair) screwed up into a knot.

taponner [tapone], *v.tr.* To screw up (handker-chief) ; to screw up (one's hair) into a knot.

tapoter [tapɔte], *v.tr. F :* To pat (child's cheek, etc.) ; to thrum (on the table). *T. un air (au piano),* to strum, thrum, a tune. [TAPER]

tapotis [tapɔti], *s.m.* Rattle (of typewriter).

tapure [tapy:r], *s.f. Metall :* Shrinkage crack.

taque [tak], *s.f. Ind :* Cast-iron plate.

taquet [takɛ], *s.m.* **1.** (*a*) Angle-block ; bracket. (*b*) Flange ; lug. **2.** *Mec.E :* etc : Stop(per), block. **Taquet d'arrêt,** (i) *Veh :* scotch ; (ii) *Rail :* stop-block. **3.** *Nau :* (*a*) **Taquet de tournage,** (belaying-)cleat. (*b*) *pl.* Ribs, whelps (of capstan or windlass). **4. Taquet de soupape,** valve-tappet.

taquin, -ine [takɛ̃, -in]. **1.** *a.* (Given to) teasing. **2.** *s.* Tease.

taquin|er [takine], *v.tr.* (*a*) To tease ; to plague, torment. (*b*) *Ça me taquine qu'il n'arrive pas,* I'm rather worried that he isn't here yet. *s.m.* **-age.**

taquinerie [takinri], *s.f.* **1.** Teasing disposition. **2.** Teasing. *Faire des taquineries à qn,* to tease s.o.

tarabiscot [tarabisko], *s.m.* **1.** Groove or channel (between mouldings). **2.** Moulding plane.

tarabiscoté [tarabiskɔte], *a.* **1.** Grooved. **2.** *F :* Over-elaborate, finicky (style, etc.).

tarabuster [tarabyste], *v.tr. F : A :* **1.** To worry, plague, pester. **2.** *Lit :* To upbraid (s.o.).

tarare[1] [tara:r], *int. A :* Fiddlesticks ! nonsense !

tarare[2], *s.m. Husb :* Winnowing machine.

tararer [tarare], *v.tr. Husb :* To winnow.

taratata [taratata], *int.* Fiddlesticks ! hoity-toity !

taraud [taro], *s.m. Tls :* (Screw-)tap.

taraudage [taroda:ʒ], *s.m.* Screw-cutting ; tapping, threading (of nut, rod).

tarauder [tarode], *v.tr.* To tap, thread (rod, nut, etc.). **Machine à tarauder,** tapping-machine.

taraudeuse [tarodø:z], *s.f. Tls :* Screw-cutter, thread-cutter.

tarbouch(e) [tarbuʃ], *s.m. Cost :* Tarboosh.

tard [ta:r], *adv.* Late. *Plus t.,* later on. **Au plus tard,** at the latest. **Tôt ou tard,** sooner or later. **Il est tard,** it is late. *Il se maria t.,* he married late in life. **Il se fait tard,** it is getting late. *Pas plus t. qu'hier,* only yesterday ; but yesterday. *s.m.* **Sur le tard,** (i) late in the day ; (ii) late in life. S.a. JAMAIS 2.

tarder [tarde], *v.i.* **1.** (*a*) To delay. *Pourquoi tarde-t-il?* why is he so long? *T. en chemin,* to loiter on the way. **Tarder à faire qch.,** (i) to put off, defer, doing sth. ; (ii) to be long in (starting, coming, etc.). **Sans tarder,** without delay. **Sans plus tarder,** without further delay ; without further loss of time. (*b*) *Nous ne tarderons pas à le voir venir,* it will not be long before he appears. **2.** *Impers. Il lui tarde de partir,* he is longing, anxious, to get away.

tard|if, -ive [tardif, -i:v], *a.* (*a*) Tardy, belated (regrets) ; late (hour, fruit) ; backward (fruit, intelligence). (*b*) *Cœurs tardifs à croire,* hearts slow to believe. *adv.* **-ivement.**

tardigrade [tardigrad], *a. & s.m. Z :* Tardigrade.

tardiveté [tardivte], *s.f.* Lateness, backwardness.

tare [ta:r], *s.f.* **1.** (*a*) *Com :* Depreciation, loss in value. (*b*) (Physical, moral) defect, blemish. *T. héréditaire,* taint (of insanity, etc.). **Cheval sans tare,** sound horse. (*c*) Stain of illegitimacy. **2.** (*a*) Tare ; allowance for weight. **Faire la tare,** to allow for the tare. (*b*) *Faire la t. d'un ressort,* to calibrate a spring.

tarentelle [tarɑ̃tɛl], *s.f. Danc : Mus :* Taran-tella.

tarentule [tarɑ̃tyl], *s.f. Arach :* Tarantula.

tarer [tare], *v.tr.* **1.** To spoil, damage (goods) ; to tarnish (reputation). **2.** (*a*) *Com :* To tare, to ascertain the weight of (packing-case, etc.). (*b*) To calibrate (spring, valve).

   taré, *a.* **1.** Spoilt, tainted ; damaged (goods). *Cheval t.,* unsound horse. **2.** (*a*) Of damaged reputation, of ill repute. (*b*) With a taint or a blot in the family history.

taret [tarɛ], *s.m. Moll :* Teredo ; ship-worm.

targette [tarʒɛt], *s.f.* Flat door-bolt ; sash-bolt.

targuer (se) [sətarge], *v.pr. Se t. de qch., de faire qch.,* to pride, plume, oneself on sth., on doing sth.

tarier [tarje], *s.m. Orn:* Whinchat. *T. saxicole,* stonechat.

tarière [tarjɛːr], *s.f.* **1.** *Tls:* (a) Auger. (b) Drill. **2.** *Ent:* Terebra.

tarif [tarif], *s.m.* (a) Tariff, price-list. (b) Scale or schedule of charges. *T. télégraphique,* telegraph rates. *Rail:* **Plein tarif,** (i) full tariff (for goods); (ii) adult fare, full fare. **Billet à demi-tarif,** half-fare ticket.

tarifer [tarife], *v.tr.* To tariff; to fix the rate of (duties), the price of (goods).

tar|ir [tariːr].' **1.** *v.tr.* (a) To dry up (spring, tears). (b) To exhaust (one's means). **2.** *v.i.* (a) (Of waters) To dry up, run dry. (b) (Of conversation, etc.) To cease, stop; *F:* to dry up. *Ne pas t. sur un sujet,* to be for ever expatiating on a subject. *s.m.* **-issement.**

tarlatane [tarlatan], *s.f. Tex:* Tarlatan (muslin).

tarmac [tarmak], *s.m. Civ.E:* Tarmac.

tarpon [tarpɔ̃], *s.m. Ich:* Tarpon.

tarse [tars], *s.m. Anat: Ent:* Tarsus; *F:* (of human foot) instep.

tarsien, -ienne [tarsjɛ̃, -jɛn], *a.* Tarsal (bone).

tartan [tartɑ̃], *s.m.* Tartan (cloth or plaid).

tartane [tartan], *s.f. Nau:* Tartan, tartane.

tartare[1] [tartaːr], *a. & s.* **1.** *Ethn:* Ta(r)tar. **2.** *Cu:* Sauce tartare, sharp mayonnaise sauce.

Tartare[2] **(le).** *Pr.n.m. Myth:* Tartarus.

tartaréen, -enne [tartareɛ̃, -ɛn], *a.* Tartarean (blackness).

tarte [tart], *s.f. Cu:* (Open) tart; flan.

tartelette [tart(ə)lɛt], *s.f. Cu:* Tartlet.

tartine [tartin], *s.f.* **1.** Slice of bread and butter, bread and jam, etc. **2.** *F:* Long-winded speech; screed, rigmarole, effusion.

tartiner [tartine], *v.tr.* (a) To spread (bread) with butter. (b) *El.E:* To paste (accumulator plates).

tartrate [tartrat], *s.m. Ch:* Tartrate.

tartre [tartr], *s.m.* **1.** *Ch:* Tartar. **Crème de tartre,** cream of tartar. **2.** (a) *Mch:* Scale, fur (of boiler). (b) *Dent:* Tartar (on teeth).

tartreux, -euse [tartrø, -øːz], *a.* **1.** Tartarous (sediment). **2.** Scaly, furry (boiler).

tartrique [tartrik], *a. Ch:* Tartaric (acid).

tartufe [tartyf], *s.m.* Tartuf(f)e; sanctimonious hypocrite. (From Molière's *Le Tartufe.*)

tartuferie [tartyfri], *s.f.* Hypocrisy, cant.

tas [tɑ], *s.m.* **1.** (a) Heap, pile (of stones, etc.). *Tas de foin,* hay-cock. **Prendre au tas, piquer dans le tas,** to help oneself. **Prendre qn sur le tas,** to catch s.o. in the act, red-handed. *Mettre des objets en tas,* to heap up, pile up, things. **Être sur le tas,** to be at work. (b) *F:* Lot, crew, gang, pack (of persons); heaps, lots (of things). *Tas de mensonges,* pack of lies. *Il y en a des tas,* there are heaps, bags, of it. **2.** *Metalw:* (a) Stake (-anvil). (b) *Tas à river,* dolly.

tasse[1] [tɑːs], *s.f.* Cup. *T. à café,* coffee-cup. *T. de café,* cup of coffee. *F:* **La grande tasse,** the sea, Davy Jones's locker. **Boire à la grande tasse,** to get drowned (at sea).

Tasse[2] **(le).** *Pr.n.m. Lit:* Tasso.

tasseau [tɑso], *s.m.* (a) Cleat, strip, batten (supporting shelf). (b) Bracket. (c) Lug (of casting). (d) Brick foundation (of shed).

tass|er [tɑse], *v.tr.* To compress, cram, squeeze, (objects) together; to ram, pack, tamp (earth, etc.). *s.m.* **-ement.** [TAS]
   se tasser. 1. (Of foundations) (a) To settle, set. (b) To sink, subside. *F:* **Ça se tassera,** things will settle down. **2.** To crowd (up) together; to huddle together; (of troops) to bunch. **Tassez-vous un peu,** squeeze up a bit; sit a little closer.

tassé, *a.* **1.** Squat, dumpy. **2.** *P:* Liberal (in quantity); full.

ta ta ta [tatata], *int.* Hoity-toity! fiddle-de-dee!

tât|er [tɑte]. **1.** *v.tr.* To feel, touch; to finger, handle (material). *T. qch. du bout du doigt,* to prod sth. **Tâter le pouls à qn,** (i) to feel s.o.'s pulse; (ii) *F:* to sound s.o. (on a matter). **Tâter le terrain,** to explore the ground; to throw out a feeler. *Avancer en tâtant,* to grope one's way forward. **2.** *v.ind.tr.* (a) *T. d'un mets,* to taste a dish. *F:* **Vous en tâterez,** it will come your way one of these days. (b) **Tâter d'un métier,** to try one's hand at a trade. *F:* **Il a tâté de la prison,** he has done time. *s.m.* **-age.** *s.m.* **-ement.**
   se tâter. 1. To feel one's muscle; to feel for a sore spot, etc. **2.** *F:* To think it over (before taking a step).

tatillon, -onne [tatijɔ̃, -ɔn]. **1.** *a.* (a) Meddlesome. (b) Niggling, finical. **2.** *s.* (a) Busybody. (b) Niggler.

tatillonn|er [tatijɔne], *v.i.* (a) To meddle. (b) To niggle; to be fussy over trifles. *s.m.* **-age.**

tâtonn|er [tɑtɔne], *v.i.* **1.** To grope (in the dark); to feel one's way; to grope about. **2.** To proceed cautiously, tentatively. *s.m.* **-ement.**

tâtons (à) [atɔ̃s], *adv.phr.* Gropingly. **Avancer à tâtons,** to go forward warily; to grope, feel, one's way (along).

tatou [tatu], *s.m. Z:* Armadillo, tatu.

tatou|er [tatwe], *v.tr.* To tattoo (the body). *s.m.* **-age.**

tatoueur [tatwœːr], *s.m.* Tattooer, tattooist.

taud [to]. *s.m.,* **taude** [toːd], *s.f. Nau:* Rainawning; tarpaulin.

taudis [todi], *s.m.* Miserable room; hovel. *Les t. de Paris,* the slums of Paris.

taule [toːl], *s.f. P:* (a) House. (b) Room. (c) *Mil:* Prison.

taulier [tolje], *s.m. Mil: P:* Prisoner.

taupe [toːp], *s.f.* **1.** *Z:* Mole. **2.** Moleskin. **3.** *Sch: P:* Class preparing for the *École polytechnique.* **4.** *P:* **Vieille taupe,** old crone, old hag.

taupé [tope], *a.* **Feutre taupé,** velours felt. *Chapeau t.,* velours hat.

taupe-grillon, *s.m. Ent:* Mole-cricket. *pl. Des taupes-grillons.*

taupier [topje], *s.m.* Mole-catcher.

taupière [topjɛːr], *s.f.* Mole-trap.

taupin [topɛ̃], *s.m.* **1.** *Sch: P:* Student reading for the *École polytechnique.* **2.** Spring-beetle, click-beetle, skipjack.

taupinière [topinjɛːr], *s.f.* Mole-hill, mole-cast.

taure [toːr], *s.f.* Heifer.

taureau [tɔro], *s.m.* **1.** Bull. *Pugiliste au cou de t.,* bull-necked pugilist. *Combat de taureaux,* bullfight. *F:* **Prendre le taureau par les cornes,** to take the bull by the horns. **2.** *Astr:* **Le Taureau,** Taurus, the Bull.

taurillon [tɔrijɔ̃], *s.m.* Bull-calf.

tautochrone [totokron], *a. Mth:* Tautochronous. **Courbe tautochrone,** tautochrone.

tautologie [totɔlɔʒi], *s.f.* Tautology, redundancy.

tautologique [totɔlɔʒik], *a.* Tautological.

taux [to], *s.m.* Rate (of wages, discount, etc.); established price of commodities). *T. de pension,* scale of pension. *T. du change,* rate of exchange. *T. d'intérêt,* rate of interest. S.a. ESCOMPTE **2.** *Mec:* *T. de charge,* load per unit area.

tavaïole [tavajɔl], *s.f. Ecc:* (a) Chrisom-cloth. (b) Napkin.

taveler (se) [sətavle], *v.pr.* **(il se tavelle)** (Of fruit) To become spotted, specked. **Panthère tavelée,** spotted panther.

taverne [tavɛrn], *s.f.* **I.** Tavern; public house. **2.** Café-restaurant.

tavernier [tavɛrnje], *s.m.* *A:* Tavern-keeper.

taxateur [taksatœːr], *s.m.* Taxer, assessor. *Jur:* Taxing master.

taxation [taksasjɔ̃], *s.f.* **I.** Fixing of prices, wages, etc. *Jur:* Taxing (of costs). **2.** *Adm:* (*a*) Taxation. (*b*) Assessment.

taxe [taks], *s.f.* **I.** (*a*) Fixed price, official price (of certain foodstuffs); fixed rate (of wages). (*b*) Charge (for service); rate. *T. postale*, postage. *T. supplémentaire*, (i) surcharge; (ii) late fee. **2.** Tax, duty. *T. sur les chiens*, dog-tax. *T. de séjour*, visitors' tax. *T. des pauvres*, poor rate. *T. sur les spectacles*, entertainment tax. **3.** *Jur:* Taxing, taxation (of costs).

taxer [takse], *v.tr.* **I.** (*a*) To regulate the price of (bread, etc.), the rate of (wages, postage). (*b*) To surcharge (letter). (*c*) *Tp:* To charge for (call). **2.** To tax, impose a tax on (s.o., luxuries, motor cars). **3.** *Jur:* **Mémoire taxé**, taxed bill of costs. **4.** To accuse. *T. qn de lâcheté*, to tax s.o. with cowardice. *Abs. Je ne taxe personne*, I am not accusing anybody.

taxi [taksi], *s.m.* *F:* Taxi(-cab). **Conducteur de taxi**, taxi-man, taxi-driver.

taxidermie [taksidɛrmi], *s.f.* Taxidermy.

taxidermique [taksidɛrmik], *a.* Taxidermal.

taxidermiste [taksidɛrmist], *s.m.* Taxidermist.

taxigaz [taksigɑːz], *s.m.* *F:* Slot (gas-)meter.

taximètre [taksimɛtr], *s.m.* Taximeter.

taxiphone [taksifɔn], *s.m.* *Tp:* Public call-box.

Tchad (le) [latʃad]. *Pr.n.m.* Lake Chad.

tchandals [tʃɑ̃dal], *s.m.pl.* *India:* Chandals; untouchables.

tchécoslovaque [tʃekɔslɔvak], *a. & s.* Czecho-Slovak.

Tchécoslovaquie [tʃekɔslɔvaki]. *Pr.n.f.* Czecho-Slovakia.

Tchéka (la) [latʃeka], *s.f.* *Russian Adm:* The Cheka.

tchèque [tʃɛk], *a. & s.* Czech.

te, before a vowel sound **t'** [t(ə)], *pers.pron. sg.*, unstressed. **I.** (*a*) (Acc.) You. *Il t'adore*, he adores you. (*b*) (Dat.) (To) you. *Il te l'a dit*, he told you so. (*c*) (With pr.vbs) *Tu te fatigues*, you are tiring yourself. *Va-t'en*, go away. **2.** Thee, thyself. (In addressing the Deity) *Nous te magnifions*, we magnify Thee.

té¹ [te], *s.m.* (The letter) T, tee. **En té**, T-shaped. *Fer à té*, T-iron. *Té à dessin*, *équerre en té*, tee-square, T-square.

té², *int.* *Dial:* (In S. of Fr.) Hullo! *Té, c'est Marius!* why, it's Marius!

técéfiste [tesefist], *s.m.* Member of the T.C.F. (Touring-Club de France).

technicien [tɛknisjɛ̃], *s.m.* Technician.

technique [tɛknik]. **I.** *a.* Technical. *Raisons d'ordre t.*, technical reasons. **2.** *s.f.* (*a*) Technique. (*b*) Technics. *T. électrique*, electrical engineering. *adv.* **-ment.**

technologie [tɛknɔlɔʒi], *s.f.* Technology.

technologique [tɛknɔlɔʒik], *a.* Technological.

te(c)k [tɛk], *s.m.* Teak(-tree or -wood).

tectonique [tɛktɔnik], *a.* Tectonic.

tectrice [tɛktris], *a.f. & s.f.* *Orn:* (**Plumes**) tectrices, tectrices, (wing-)coverts.

Te Deum [tedeɔm], *s.m.inv.* Te Deum.

tégument [tegymɑ̃], *s.m.* *Nat.Hist:* Tegument.

tégumentaire [tegymɑ̃tɛːr], *a.* Tegumentary.

teigne [tɛɲ], *s.f.* **I.** (*a*) Tinea, moth. *T. des draps*, clothes-moth. (*b*) *F:* Pest (of a child); shrew (of a woman). **2.** (*a*) *Med:* Tinea; scalp disease. *T. faveuse*, favus. *T. tonsurante*, *t. tondante*, ringworm. (*b*) Scurf, scale-(on old trees).

teign-e, -es, etc. See TEINDRE.

teigneux, -euse [tɛɲø, -øːz], *a. & s.* (Person) suffering from scalp-disease. *s.m.* *F:* Scurvy fellow.

teille [tɛːj], *s.f.* Harl (of hemp).

teill|er [tɛje], *v.tr.* To strip, scutch (hemp, flax). *s.m.* **-age.**

teindre [tɛ̃ːdr], *v.tr.* (*pr.p.* teignant; *p.p.* teint; *pr.ind.* je teins, il teint, n. teignons; *p.h.* je teignis; *fu.* je teindrai) **I.** To dye. *T. qch. en rouge*, to dye sth. red. **2.** To stain, tinge, colour. *F:* **Être teint de latin**, to have a smattering of Latin.

se teindre. I. To dye one's hair. **2.** To take on the tinge (*de*, of).

teint [tɛ̃], *s.m.* **I.** Dye, colour. **Bon teint, grand teint**, fast dye; 'dyed in the wool.' **2.** Complexion, colour. **Au teint frais**, fresh-complexioned. *Au t. jaune*, sallow.

teinte [tɛ̃ːt], *s.f.* (*a*) Tint, shade, hue. *Art:* **Teinte plate**, flat tint. **Demi-teinte**, half-tint. (*b*) **Légère teinte de . . .**, tinge of . . .; touch of (malice, irony). **Discours sans teinte de pédanterie**, speech untinged with pedantry.

teinter [tɛ̃te], *v.tr.* (*a*) To tint. **Papier teinté**, tinted or toned paper. (*b*) **Ciel teinté de rose**, sky tinged with pink.

teinture [tɛ̃tyːr], *s.f.* **I.** (*a*) Dyeing (of cloth, hair). (*b*) Tinting (of a drawing). **2.** (*a*) Dye. *Couvertures sans teinture*, undyed blankets. (*b*) Colour, hue, tinge. *F:* **Avoir une teinture de latin**, to have a tincture, a smattering, of Latin. (*c*) *Her:* Tincture. **3.** *Pharm:* *T. d'iode*, tincture of iodine.

teinturerie [tɛ̃tyrri], *s.f.* **I.** Dyeing. **2.** Dye-works.

teinturier, -ière [tɛ̃tyrje, -jɛːr], *s.* Dyer. **Teinturier dégraisseur**, dyer and cleaner.

tel, telle [tɛl], *a.* **I.** Such. (*a*) *Un tel homme*, such a man. *De telles choses*, such things. (*b*) *En tel lieu*, in such and such a place. *Je sais telle maison où . . .*, I could mention a house where. . . . *Prendre telles mesures qui paraîtront nécessaires*, to take such steps as shall be considered necessary. (*c*) *Sa bonté est telle que . . .*, such, so great, is her kindness that. . . . *A tel point*, to such an extent, to such a pitch. **De telle sorte que**, (i) + *ind.* (of event realized), (ii) + *sub.* (of event to be realized), in such a way that. **2.** (*a*) Like; as. **Tel père, tel fils**, like father like son. (*b*) **Tel que**, such as, like. *Un homme tel que lui*, a man like him. *La clause telle qu'elle est*, the clause as it stands. *Voir les hommes tels qu'ils sont*, to see men as they are. *Je vois les choses telles qu'elles sont*, I look the facts in the face. (*c*) *Il n'y a rien de tel, il n'est rien tel, que d'avoir . . .*, there is nothing like having. . . . (*d*) *Lit:* **Tel un éclair**, *il s'élance*, like (unto) lightning he dashes forward. (*e*) **Tel quel.** (i) Just as it is; just as he is. *Je vous achète la maison telle quelle*, I'll buy the house from you just as it stands. (ii) *C'est un homme tel quel*, he's just an ordinary person. *Une paix telle quelle*, a make-shift peace, a peace of sorts. (iii) *Tout laisser tel quel*, to leave everything unaltered, in statu quo. **3.** *pron.* (*a*) Such a one. *Tel l'en blâmait, tel l'en excusait*, one would blame him, another would excuse him. **Tel qui**, he who, many a one who. *Prov:* **Tel rit vendredi qui dimanche pleurera**, laugh on Friday, cry on Sunday. (*b*) *Pred. Tel fut son langage*, such were his words. *s.* **Un tel, une telle**, so-and-so. *Monsieur un tel, Un Tel, Mr So-and-so.*

S'adresser à tel et tel, to apply to this man and that. *Tel ou tel vous dira que . . .*, some people will tell you that. . . .

Télamon [telamɔ̃]. **I.** *Pr.n.m. Myth :* Telamon. **2.** *s.m. Arch :* Telamon, *pl.* telamones, atlantes.

télautographe [telotɔgraf], *s.m. Tg :* Telautograph, telewriter.

téléférique [teleferik], *a. & s.m.* = TÉLÉPHÉRIQUE.

télégonie [telegɔni], *s.f. Biol :* Telegony.

télégramme [telegram], *s.m.* Telegram. *T. sous-marin*, cable(-gram). *Envoyer un télégramme pour faire venir qn*, to wire for s.o.

télégraphe [telegraf], *s.m.* **I.** (*a*) *A :* Semaphore. *F :* **Faire le télégraphe**, to fling one's arms about; to gesticulate. (*b*) *Tls :* Bevel square. **2.** (Electric) telegraph. *T. enregistreur*, recording telegraph. *T. imprimeur*, ticker. *T. sous-marin*, cable. *Aviser qn par le t.*, (i) to wire, (ii) to cable, to s.o.

télégraphie [telegrafi], *s.f.* Telegraphy. *S.a.* FIL I.

télégraphier [telegrafje], *v.tr. & i.* To telegraph; (i) to wire, (ii) to cable.

télégraphique [telegrafik], *a.* Telegraphic. *Réponse t.*, reply (i) by wire, (ii) by cable. *Bureau t.*, telegraph office. *adv.* **-ment**, -ally.

télégraphiste [telegrafist], *s.m.* Telegraphist. *Facteur t.*, telegraph-messenger.

télémécanique [telemekanik]. **I.** *a.* Electrically controlled (at a distance). **2.** *s.f.* Telemechanics.

télémètre [telemɛtr], *s.m.* Telemeter. *Mil : etc :* Range-finder.

télémétrie [telemetri], *s.f.* Telemetry. *Mil : etc :* Range-finding.

télémétrique [telemetrik], *a.* Telemetric(al).

téléobjectif [teleɔbʒɛktif], *s.m. Phot :* Telephoto(graphic) lens; telelens.

téléologie [teleɔlɔʒi], *s.f. Phil :* Teleology.

téléologique [teleɔlɔʒik], *a. Phil :* Teleological.

télépathie [telepati], *s.f.* Telepathy, thought-transference.

télépathique [telepatik], *a.* Telepathic.

téléphérique [teleferik], *a. & s.m.* (Ligne) **téléphérique**, telpher railway; rope-way; teleferic.

téléphone [telefɔn], *s.m.* Telephone, *F :* phone. *T. automatique*, dial telephone. *Demoiselle du t.*, phone girl. *Coup de téléphone*, telephone call. *Armer le téléphone*, to lift the receiver. *Demander qch. par t.*, to phone for sth.

téléphoner [telefɔne], *v.tr. & i.* **I.** To telephone, *F :* to phone. **2.** *T. à qn*, to ring s.o. up; to phone to s.o. *Je vous téléphonerai*, I'll give you a ring.

téléphonie [telefɔni], *s.f.* Telephony. **Téléphonie sans fil**, wireless telephony, radio-telephony.

téléphonique [telefɔnik]. **I.** *a.* Telephonic. **Cabine, cabinet, téléphonique**, telephone booth, call-box. *Appel t.*, telephone call. **2.** *s.m.* **Téléphonique combiné**, instrument with combined mouth-piece and receiver; hand microphone.

téléphoniste [telefɔnist], *s.m. & f.* Telephonist; telephone operator.

téléphotographie [telefɔtɔgrafi], *s.f.* **I.** *Tg :* Photo-telegraphy. **2.** *Occ. Phot :* (*a*) Telephotography. (*b*) Telephotograph.

télépointage [telepwɛ̃taʒ], *s.m. Navy :* Directing of gun-fire by means of a director theodolite. **Hune de télépointage**, director top.

télescopage [teleskɔpaʒ], *s.m.* Telescoping (of parts, of trains, etc.).

télescope [teleskɔp], *s.m.* Reflecting telescope.

télescoper [teleskɔpe], *v.i., tr. & pr.* (Of railway coaches, etc.) To telescope; to crumple up.

télescopique [teleskɔpik], *a.* Telescopic.

télétype [teletip], *a. & s.m.* (Appareil) télétype, teleprinter.

téléviser [televize], *v.tr.* To televise.

téléviseur [televizœːr], *s.m.* Televisor.

télévision [televizjɔ̃], *s.f.* Television.

tellement [tɛlmã], *adv.* **I.** In such a manner; so. **2.** To such a degree; so. **Tellement que** + *ind.*, to such an extent that. *Il est t. sourd qu'il faut crier*, he is so deaf that one has to shout. *A :* **Tellement quellement**, after a fashion; tolerably well.

tellière [tɛljɛːr], *a.inv. & s.m.* Foolscap (paper). (From the Chancellor Le Tellier, 1603-85.)

tellure [tɛllyːr], *s.m. Ch :* Tellurium.

tellureux, -euse [tɛllyrø, -øːz], *a.* Tellurous.

tellurien, -ienne [tɛllyrjɛ̃, -jɛn], *a.* Tellurian; earth (current).

tellurique¹ [tɛllyrik], *a. Ch :* Telluric (acid).

tellurique², *a.* Telluric (fever); arising from the soil.

telphérage [tɛlfera:ʒ], *s.m. Ind :* Telpherage; overhead cable transport. **Ligne de telphérage**, telpher, telpher-way.

telphérer [tɛlfere], *v.tr.* (**je telphère**; **je telphérerai**) To telpher; to transport (goods) by telpherage.

telson [tɛlsɔ̃], *s.m. Crust :* Telson; terminal flap.

téméraire [temerɛːr], *a.* (*a*) Rash, reckless, foolhardy. (*b*) Rash (judgment, statement). *adv.* **-ment**.

témérité [temerite], *s.f.* **I.** Temerity, rashness, recklessness, foolhardiness. **2.** Rash deed; piece of daring.

témoignage [temwaɲa:ʒ], *s.m.* **I.** Testimony, evidence. (*a*) **Porter témoignage**, to bear witness, give evidence. **Rendre témoignage de qch.**, (i) to give evidence about sth.; (ii) to bear testimony to sth. *F :* **Je vous rends ce témoignage que . . .**, I will say this about you that. . . . **Appeler qn en témoignage**, to call s.o. as witness. **Faux témoignage**, false witness; perjury. (*b*) **Témoignage des sens**, evidence of the senses. **2.** *Jur :* Hearing (of witness). **3. En témoignage d'estime**, as a mark, as a token, of esteem.

témoigner [temwaɲe]. **I.** *v.i.* To testify; to bear witness; to give evidence. *T. en faveur de qn*, to give evidence in s.o.'s favour. *T. contre qn*, to bear witness against s.o. **2.** *v.tr. or ind.tr. T. (de) qch.*, to show, evince, prove, sth.; to bear testimony to, bear witness to, testify to, sth.; to give evidence of sth. *T. d'un goût pour . . .*, to show, display, evince, a taste for. . . . *T. sa reconnaissance à qn*, to give expression to one's gratitude to s.o. *Ses écrits témoignent de son industrie*, his writings attest, bear witness to, his industry. *Elle ne témoigna pas avoir rien remarqué*, she gave no indication of having noticed anything.

témoin [temwɛ̃], *s.m.* **I.** Witness. (*a*) *Être t. d'un accident*, to witness an accident. *T. à un acte*, witness to a signature. (*b*) *Jur : T. à charge*, à décharge, witness for the prosecution, for the defence. **Barre des témoins**, witness-box. *T. oculaire*, eye-witness. **Appeler, prendre, qn à témoin**, to call, take, s.o. as witness. *Dieu m'est témoin si je vous ai aimé!* God knows how much I loved you! **Témoin les coups que j'ai reçus**, witness the blows which I received. (*c*) Second (in duel). **2.** *A :* (= TÉMOIGNAGE) **En témoin de quoi . . .**, in witness whereof. **3.** (*a*) Boundary mark. *Aut : T. d'aile*, wing indicator; feeler. (*b*) *Ch :* Reference solution. **Échantillon témoin**, check sample. *Phot :* **Plaque témoin**, reference plate. *Épreuve t.*, pilot print. (*c*) *El.E : Ind :* **Lampe témoin**, telltale lamp, pilot lamp.

(d) *Sp:* Handkerchief, etc., passed from hand to hand in relay race.

tempe [tɑ̃:p], *s.f. Anat:* Temple.

tempérament [tɑ̃peramɑ̃], *s.m.* **1.** (a) (Physical) constitution, temperament. *Paresseux par tempérament*, constitutionally lazy. (b) *T. violent*, *placide*, violent, placid, temper. **2.** (a) *A:* Moderation; spirit of compromise. *Garder en tout un certain t.*, to observe a certain measure in all things. (b) *Mus:* Temperament (of the intervals of the scale). **3.** *Com:* A **tempérament**, by instalments, on the deferred payment system. *Vente à tempérament*, hire-purchase.

tempérance [tɑ̃perɑ̃:s], *s.f.* Temperance, moderation.

tempérant [tɑ̃perɑ̃], *a.* Temperate, moderate.

température [tɑ̃peraty:r], *s.f.* Temperature. *Med: F:* Avoir de la **température**, to have a (high) temperature.

tempérer [tɑ̃pere], *v.tr.* (je tempère; je tempérerai) To temper, moderate (sun's heat, etc.). se **tempérer**, (of the wind, etc.) to moderate.

tempéré, *a.* **1.** Temperate, moderate (climate, speech); restrained, sober (style). *Monarchie tempérée*, limited monarchy. **2.** *Mus:* *Gamme tempérée*, equally tempered scale.

tempête [tɑ̃pɛ:t], *s.f.* Storm (of wind); *Lit:* tempest *T. de neige*, blizzard, snow-storm. Le vent souffle en tempête, it is blowing a hurricane. *Battu par la t.*, storm-beaten (coast); storm-tossed (ship). *F:* Une **tempête dans un verre d'eau**, a storm in a tea-cup. *T. d'applaudissements*. storm of applause.

tempêter [tɑ̃pete], *v.i. F:* To storm; to rage.

tempétueu|x, -euse [tɑ̃petɥø, -ø:z], *a.* Tempestuous; stormy. *adv.* **-sement.**

temple [tɑ̃:pl], *s.m.* **1.** Temple. *Poet:* fane. **2.** Church. place of worship (of Protestants); 'chapel.' **3.** (Freemasons') lodge. **4.** *Hist:* Les chevaliers du Temple, the Knights Templars.

templier [tɑ̃plie], *s.m. Hist:* (Knight) Templar.

tempo [tɛpo, tempo], *s.m. Mus:* Tempo, time.

temporaire [tɑ̃pɔrɛ:r], *a.* **1.** Temporary; provisional. **2.** *Mus:* Valeur temporaire, time-value (of a note) *adv.* **-ment.**

temporal, -aux [tɑ̃pɔral, -o], *a. Anat:* Temporal (bone, artery).

temporel, -elle [tɑ̃pɔrɛl], *a.* (a) Temporal (as opposed to eternal). (b) Temporal (as opposed to spiritual). *Puissance temporelle*, temporal power.

temporisateur, -trice [tɑ̃pɔrizatœ:r, -tris]. **1.** *s.* Temporizer; procrastinator. **2.** *a.* Temporizing

temporisation [tɑ̃pɔrizasjɔ̃], *s.f.* Temporization, temporizing; calculated delay.

temporiser [tɑ̃pɔrize], *v.i.* To temporize.

temps [tɑ̃], *s.m.* **1.** Time. (a) *Mettre beaucoup de t. à faire qch.*, to take a long time over sth. *F:* Tuer le temps, to kill time. Vous avez bien le temps, vous avez (tout) le temps voulu, you have plenty of time. *Combien de t. faut-il pour . . .?* how long does it take to . . .? *Gagner du t.*, to gain time, to temporize, to play for time. Dans le cours du temps, avec le temps, in process of time, in course of time. *Usé par le t.*, time-worn. De temps en temps, de temps à autre, now and then, now and again; from time to time. *Une fois de t. à autre*, once in a while. En même temps, at the same time. *F:* Se donner du bon temps, to have a good time; to enjoy oneself. *Myth:* Le Temps, (Father) Time. (b) (i) While, period. *Chaque chose a son t.*, everything has its day. *En t. de*

guerre, in war-time. Il y a peu de temps, a little while ago. Peu de temps après, not long after. *Pendant quelque t.*, for a short while. *Au bout de quelque t.*, *d'un certain t.*, after a time. Entre temps, meanwhile. Il y a beau temps qu'il est parti, he went off a long time ago. *Faire un t. de galop*, to have a short gallop. Temps d'arrêt, pause, halt. Marquer un temps, to pause. (ii) Term (of service, etc.). Faire son temps, to serve one's time; (of convict) to do one's stretch. (c) Age, days, times. Le bon vieux temps, the good old days. Dans le temps, au temps jadis, in times past, in the old days; formerly. Dans la suite des temps, in the course of ages. Au temps de ma jeunesse, in the days of my youth. Dans le temps où j'étais jeune, (in the days) when I was young. *Les t. sont durs*, times are hard. *Il fut un t. où . . .*, time was when. . . . Par le temps qui court, as times go; in these days. Être de son temps, to move with the times; to be up to date. *Vous n'êtes pas de votre t.*, you are behind the times. Il n'en était pas ainsi de mon t., it was not so in my day. De tout temps, en tout temps, at all times. S.a. DERNIER 1, PREMIER 1. (d) Hour. Arriver à temps, to arrive in time. En temps voulu, utile, in due time. Il est grand temps de partir, it is high time to start. Il se fait temps de partir, it is nearly time to start. Il n'est plus temps, it is too late. Il y a temps pour tout, there is a time for everything. En temps et lieu, in proper time and place; in due course. **2.** Weather. Par tous les temps, in all weathers. Quel temps fait-il? how is the weather? Si le t. le permet, (wind and) weather permitting. Beau temps, fine weather. *Nau:* Gros temps, heavy weather. Coup de temps, sudden squall. Prévision du temps, weather forecast. Le t. est à la pluie, it looks like rain. **3.** *Gram:* Tense. Temps primitifs, principal parts (of the verb). **4.** (a) *Mus:* T. fort, strong beat, down-beat. T. faible, up-beat. Mesure à deux temps, common time, duple time. Mesure à trois temps, triple time. (b) *Gym: Mil:* Exercice en trois temps, exercise in three motions. Au temps! as you were! *F:* Je vais vous faire ça en deux temps, en trois temps, I'll have it done in less than no time. (c) *I.C.E:* Moteur à deux, à quatre, temps, two-, four-stroke engine; two-, four-cycle engine. S.a. MORT 1, MOTEUR 1.

tenable [tənabl], *a.* (Usu. with negation) **1.** Tenable, defensible (position). *La position n'était plus t.*, it was impossible to hold out any longer. **2.** Par cette chaleur, le bureau n'est pas tenable, in this heat the office is unbearable.

tenace¹ [tənas], *a.* Tenacious; adhesive (matter); clinging (plant, perfume); tough (metal); dogged, stubborn (will); retentive (memory). *adv.* **-ment.**

tenace², *s.f. Cards:* Tenace.

ténacité [tenasite], *s.f.* Tenacity; toughness (of iron); adhesiveness, stickiness (of glue); stiffness (of soil); retentiveness (of memory); stubbornness (of will). Avec ténacité, tenaciously.

tenaille [tənɑ:j], *s.f.* (a) T. de forge, blacksmith's tongs. *T. à vis*, hand-vice. (b) *pl.* Tenailles, pincers (for drawing nails).

tenailler [tənɑje], *v.tr. A:* To tear (criminal's flesh) with (red-hot) pincers. *F:* Tenaillé par le remords, racked, tortured, by remorse. *Tenaillé par la faim*, gnawed by hunger.

tenancier, -ière [tənɑ̃sje, -jɛ:r], *s.* **1.** Tenant-farmer. **2.** Keeper (of gambling-den); lessee (of bar, casino, etc.).

tenant, -ante [tənɑ̃, -ɑ̃:t]. **1.** *a.* (Used in) **Séance**

tenante, forthwith, then and there. **2.** *s.* (*a*) Champion, supporter (of an opinion); taker (of a bet). (*b*) *Sp:* Holder (of championship). **3.** *s.m.* (Of landed property) **Tout d'un tenant, d'un seul tenant,** continuous; all in one block. *pl.* **Tenants,** lands marching with an estate. **Tenants et aboutissants,** (i) adjacent parts (of estate); (ii) *F:* ins and outs, full details (of an affair).

tendage [tɑ̃daːʒ], *s.m.* Stretching (of rope, wire).

tendance [tɑ̃dɑ̃ːs], *s.f.* Tendency, propensity, trend. **La t. générale de son caractère,** the general bent of his character. **Avoir une t. à qch.,** to be inclined to sth. **T. à se griser,** propensity for getting drunk. **Livre à tendance,** tendentious book.

tendanciel, -elle [tɑ̃dɑ̃sjɛl], **tendancieux, -euse** [tɑ̃dɑ̃sjø, -øːz], *a.* Tendentious, tendential. *Jur:* **Question tendancieuse,** leading question.

tendelet [tɑ̃dlɛ], *s.m. Nau: Veh:* Awning.

tendeur, -euse [tɑ̃dœːr, -øːz]. **I.** *s.* (*a*) Layer (of carpets); hanger (of wall-paper). (*b*) Setter, layer (of traps). **2.** *s.m.* Stretcher, tightener; wire-strainer. *Cy:* **T. de chaîne,** chain-adjuster. *a. Fil t.,* bracing-wire.

tendineux, -euse [tɑ̃dinø, -øːz], *a.* Stringy, sinewy (meat).

tendoir [tɑ̃dwaːr], *s.m.* Clothes-line, drying-line.

tendon [tɑ̃dɔ̃], *s.m.* Tendon, sinew. **Le tendon d'Achille,** the Achilles tendon. **T. du jarret,** hamstring.

tendre[1] [tɑ̃ːdr]. **I.** *a.* Tender. (*a*) Soft; delicate (colour); new (bread); early (age). *Viande t.,* tender meat. (*b*) Fond, affectionate, loving. **2.** *s.m. F:* **Avoir un tendre pour qn,** to have a soft place in one's heart for s.o. *adv.* **-ment.**

tendre[2]. **I.** *v.tr.* (*a*) To stretch. **T. une courroie,** to tighten a belt. **T. la peau d'un tambour,** to brace a drum. **T. un ressort, un piège,** to set a spring, a trap. (*b*) To fix up (tent, etc.); to spread (sail); to lay (carpet); to hang (wall-paper, tapestry). **Église tendue de noir,** church hung, draped, with black. **Chambre tendue de (papier) bleu,** room papered in blue. (*c*) To stretch out, hold out. **Tendre la main,** (i) to hold out one's hand; (ii) to beg. **T. le cou,** to crane one's neck. S.a. BRAS 1. (*d*) To (over)strain. **II.** *v.i.* To tend, lead, conduce (*à,* to). *Où tendent ces questions?* what is the aim, the drift, of these questions?

se tendre, to become taut; (of relations) to become strained; (of prices) to harden.

tendu, *a.* Tense, taut, tight. *Rapports tendus,* strained relations. *Situation tendue,* tense situation. S.a. BRAS 1.

tendresse [tɑ̃drɛs], *s.f.* Tenderness; fondness, love. **Avec tendresse,** fondly, lovingly.

tendron [tɑ̃drɔ̃], *s.m.* **1.** *Bot:* Tender shoot. **2.** *Cu:* Gristle (of veal). **3.** *F:* Dainty maiden, young lass.

ténèbres [tenɛːbr], *s.f.pl.* Darkness, gloom. **Dans les ténèbres,** in the dark. **Œuvre de ténèbres,** deed of darkness.

ténébreux, -euse [tenebrø, -øːz], *a.* **1.** Gloomy, dark, sombre (wood, prison). **2.** Mysterious, sinister; deep (conspiracy). *adv.* **-sement.**

ténébrion [tenebriɔ̃], *s.m. Ent:* Tenebrio; meal-beetle, meal-worm.

teneur[1], **-euse** [tənœːr, -øːz], *s.* **1.** Holder; taker (of a bet). **2. Teneur de livres,** book-keeper.

teneur[2], *s.f.* **1.** Tenor, purport, terms (of document). **2.** Amount, percentage. **T. en eau,** degree of humidity. **Minerai de haute teneur,** high-grade ore.

ténia [tenja], *s.m.* Taenia, tapeworm.

tenir [təniːr], *v.* (*pr.p.* **tenant;** *p.p.* **tenu;** *pr.ind.* **je tiens, il tient, n. tenons, ils tiennent;** *p.d.* **je tenais;** *p.h.* **je tins, n. tînmes, ils tinrent;** *fu.* **je tiendrai**) **I.** *v.tr.* **1.** To hold. (*a*) **T. qch. à la main,** to hold sth. in one's hand, on one's lap. **La fièvre le tient,** the fever has him in its grip. **Je tiens mon homme,** I've got my man. **Tenir le mot de l'énigme,** to hold the key to the puzzle. **Tenir qn de près,** to hold, keep, s.o. under strict control. **Auto qui tient bien la route,** car that holds the road well. S.a. CORDE 1. *Prov:* **Un "tiens" vaut mieux que deux "tu l'auras,"** a bird in the hand is worth two in the bush. **Faire tenir qch. à qn,** (i) to make s.o. hold sth.; (ii) to put s.o. in possession of sth. *Abs. in the imp.* **Tiens!** **tenez!** look (you)! look here! hark! here! S.a. TIENS[2]. **Et tenez!** and behold (how things turn out)! S.a. CÔTE 1, DRAGÉE. (*b*) To contain, have capacity for (a certain quantity). **Auto qui tient six personnes,** motor car that holds six. *v.i.* **On tient douze à cette table,** this table seats twelve. *Tout ça tient en deux mots,* all that can be said in a couple of words. **Faire tenir beaucoup de faits en peu de lignes,** to crowd a great many facts into few lines. (*c*) *Baril qui tient l'eau,* barrel that holds water, that is watertight. (*d*) **Tenir de,** to have, get, derive, (sth.) from, to owe (sth.) to (some source). **T. qch. de mains sûres,** to have sth. on good authority. (*e*) To keep, stock (groceries, etc.). S.a. COMPTE. (*f*) **En tenir.** (Of partridge) **Elle en tient** (*i.e. du plomb*), she's winged. **2. T. un magasin, une école,** to keep, run, a shop, a school. **T. la caisse,** to have charge of the cash. **Mlle X tenait le piano,** Miss X was at the piano. **T. une séance,** to hold a sitting. **Le marché se tient le samedi,** the market is held on Saturdays. **3.** (*a*) To hold, maintain (opinion); to keep (one's word, promise). (*b*) **T. de grands discours,** to hold forth at great length. (*c*) **Tenir son rang,** to keep up, uphold, one's position. (*d*) **T. qn en grand respect,** to hold s.o. in great respect. **4.** To hold back, restrain (one's tongue). **Tenir un cheval,** to control a horse. **5.** (*a*) To hold, keep, preserve (in a certain position). *Il nous a tenus debout pendant deux heures,* he kept us standing for two hours. **T. qch. en état,** to keep sth. in good order. **T. qch. sous clef,** to keep sth. under lock and key. S.a. CHAUD 2. **Tenir votre gauche,** keep to the left. (*b*) **Tenir la chambre,** to be confined to one's room. (*c*) **Tenir la mer,** (of ship) to keep the sea. **Navire capable, incapable, de tenir la mer,** seaworthy ship, unseaworthy ship. **6.** To occupy, take up (space). **7.** *Pred.* **T. les yeux fermés,** to keep one's eyes shut. **T. qn captif,** to keep, hold, s.o. prisoner. *Je le tiens pour un honnête homme,* I consider him to be an honest man. **Tenez cela pour fait,** look upon that as done. **Tenez-vous-le pour dit,** I shall not tell, warn, you again. S.a. DÉSHONNEUR, HONNEUR 1.

II. tenir, *v.i.* **1.** (*a*) To hold; to adhere. *Clou qui tient bien,* nail that holds well. *Cela tient comme poix,* it sticks like pitch. S.a. CŒUR 3, FIL 1. (*b*) *Sa terre tient à la mienne,* his estate borders on mine. (*c*) To bide, remain. *Il ne tient plus sur ses jambes,* he is ready to drop (with fatigue). **Ne pas tenir en place,** to be restless. S.a. PEAU 1. **2.** (*a*) **Tenir (bon, ferme),** to hold out, to stand fast; to hold one's own; (of cable, etc.) to stand the strain, to hold. **T. jusqu'au bout,** to hold out to the end. **Tenez bon!** (i) hold tight! (ii) never say die! **Je n'y tiens plus,** I can't stand it any longer. (*b*) To last, endure. *Couleur qui tient bien,* fast colour. *Mon offre tient toujours,* my offer stands. Il n'est d'ordre qui tienne, *faites ce que je vous dis*, never mind orders, do as I tell you. **3.** Tenir pour, to hold for, be in favour of (s.o., sth.). En tenir pour qn, to be fond of s.o., in love with s.o. **4.** Tenir à qch. *(a)* To value, prize, sth. Tenir à faire qch., to be bent on doing sth. Je n'y tiens pas, (i) I don't care for it, (ii) I would rather not. *Tenez-vous beaucoup à y aller?* are you very keen on going? *Il tient à vous voir*, he is bent on seeing you. *Je tiens à savoir* . . ., I desire to know. . . . Tenir à ce qu'on fasse qch., to be anxious, insistent, that something shall be done. *(b)* To depend on, result from, sth.; to be due to sth. *Cela tient à son éducation*, that's the result, the fault, of his education. *A quoi cela tient-il?* what's the reason for it? what is it due to? *Impers. Il ne tient qu'à vous de le faire*, it rests, lies, entirely with you to do it. Qu'à cela ne tienne, never mind that, that need be no obstacle. S'il ne tient qu'à cela . . ., if that is all (the difficulty). **5.** Tenir de qn, to take after s.o. *T. de qch.*, to partake of the nature of sth. *Cela tient du miracle*, it sounds like a miracle. Cela tient de la famille, it runs in the family.

se tenir. 1. *(a)* To keep, be, remain, stand, sit. *Se t. chez soi*, to stay, remain, at home. S.a. DEBOUT 1. *Tenez-vous là!* stand there! stay where you are! *Tenez-vous droit*, (i) sit up, sit straight; (ii) stand upright. Se tenir tranquille, to keep quiet. *Se bien t. à cheval*, to sit a horse well. Tiens-toi, behave yourself. *(b) Se t. à qch.*, to hold on to sth. *Rail: Se t. aux courroies, F:* to strap-hang. *(c) La boisson, la misère, le crime, tout cela se tient*, drink, poverty, crime, all these hold together. **2.** To contain oneself. *Il ne se tient pas de joie*, he cannot contain himself for joy. *Je ne pus me t. de l'embrasser*, I couldn't resist giving her a kiss. *Je ne pus me t. d'admirer*, I could not help admiring. S.a. QUATRE. **3.** Se tenir à qch., to keep to sth.; to abide by sth. *Cards: Je m'y tiens*, content! S'en tenir à qch., to confine oneself to sth.; to be satisfied, contented, with sth. *Je m'en tiens à ce que j'ai dit*, I will not go beyond what I have said. *Nous nous en tenons à l'exécution du traité*, we abide by the treaty. Je ne sais pas à quoi m'en tenir, I don't know what to believe.

tenu. 1. *a. (a)* Bien tenu, well-kept (child); tidy (house); neat, trim (garden). Mal tenu, ill-kept, neglected, uncared-for; untidy. *(b)* Être tenu de, à, faire qch., to be bound, obliged, to do sth. *Jur:* Être tenu à restitution, to be bound to make restitution. S.a. IMPOSSIBLE. **2.** *s.m. Box:* Hold.

tenue, *s.f.* **1.** *(a)* (Manner of) holding (pen, etc.). *Selle qui n'a pas de t.*, badly shaped, ill-fitting, saddle. *Nau: T. de l'ancre*, hold of the anchor. Fond de bonne tenue, good holding ground. *(b)* Session, holding (of an assembly, of assizes). *(c)* Keeping, managing, running (of shop, etc.). Tenue des livres, book-keeping. *Mch: T. des chaudières*, care of the boilers. **2.** *(a)* Bearing, behaviour, carriage. Avoir de la tenue, (i) to behave oneself; to have good manners; (ii) to have dignified manners. *Arthur*, de la tenue! Arthur, behave yourself! *Equit: Avoir une bonne, mauvaise, t.*, to have a good, poor, seat. *(b) Aer:* Tenue en l'air, behaviour in the air; airworthiness. *Aut: T. en côte*, climbing ability. **3.** Dress, *F:* get-up. *T. de soirée*, evening dress. *T. de ville*, morning dress. *Il avait pris la t. d'un cheminot*, he had rigged himself out as a navvy. *Mil:* En tenue, in

uniform. *En grande t.*, in full dress (uniform) Petite tenue, undress. *T. de campagne*, (i) field-service uniform, (ii) heavy marching order. **4.** *Mus: (a)* Holding-note, sustained note. *(b)* Organ point.

tennis [tɛnis], *s.m.* **1.** Lawn tennis. **2.** (Lawn-) tennis court.

tenon [tənɔ̃], *s.m.* **1.** *Carp:* Tenon. **2.** *(a)* Shoulder, lug. *(b)* Stud.

tenonner [tənɔne], *v.tr. Carp:* To tenon.

ténor [tenɔːr], *s.m. Mus:* Tenor.

tenseur [tɑ̃sœːr], *a. & s.m.* **1.** *(a) Anat:* (Muscle) tenseur, tensor. *(b) s.m. Mth:* Tensor. **2.** *Tchn:* = TENDEUR 2.

tension [tɑ̃sjɔ̃], *s.f.* Tension. **1.** *(a)* Stretching (of muscles); tightening (of guy-rope). Écrou à tension, tightening nut. Tension d'esprit, close application. *(b) Mec: T. de rupture*, breaking strain or stress. **2.** *(a)* Tightness (of rope); tenseness (of relations); flatness (of trajectory). *Mec.E: T. de courroie*, belt tension. *T. des esprits*, tension in the public mind. Acier à haute tension, high-tensile steel. *(b) St.Exch:* Hardness, firmness (of prices). **3.** Pressure (of steam). *Med:* Tension artérielle, blood-pressure. *El.E: T. du courant*, tension, voltage, of the current. *Haute t.*, high voltage. Fil sous tension, live, charged, wire. (Of conductor) Sans tension, dead. Montage des piles en tension, connection of batteries in series. S.a. VENTRE 2.

tentaculaire [tɑ̃takylɛːr], *a. Z:* Tentacular.

tentacule [tɑ̃takyl], *s.m. Z:* Tentacle, feeler.

tentant [tɑ̃tɑ̃], *a.* Tempting, alluring, enticing.

tentateur, -trice [tɑ̃tatœːr, -tris]. **1.** *s.* Tempter, temptress. **2.** *a.* Tempting.

tentatif, -ive [tɑ̃tatif, -iːv]. **1.** *a.* Tentative. **2.** *s.f.* Tentative, attempt, endeavour. *T. d'évasion*, attempt to escape. *T. d'assassinat*, attempted murder.

tentation [tɑ̃tasjɔ̃], *s.f.* Temptation (*de faire qch.*, to do sth.). Succomber, céder, à la t., to succumb, yield, to temptation; to fall.

tente [tɑ̃ːt], *s.f. (a)* Tent. Dresser les tentes, to pitch (the) tents. Abattre, plier, les tentes, to strike tents. Coucher sous la tente, to sleep under canvas. *F:* Se retirer dans sa tente, to sulk in one's tent (like Achilles). *(b) Nau:* Awning.

tenter [tɑ̃te], *v.tr.* **1.** *(a) A. & B:* To tempt; to put (s.o.) to the test. *Dieu tenta Abraham*, God did tempt Abraham. *(b) F: T. la chance, la fortune*, to try one's luck. *T. Dieu*, to tempt Providence. **2.** To tempt (s.o.). Se laisser tenter, to allow oneself to be tempted. **3.** To attempt, try. *T. d'inutiles efforts pour* . . ., to make useless attempts to. . . . *T. de faire qch.*, to try, endeavour, to do sth.

tenture [tɑ̃tyːr], *s.f. (a)* Hangings, tapestry. *(b)* (Papier-)tenture, wall-paper.

ténu [teny], *a. (a)* Tenuous, thin; slender, fine (thread, etc.); subtle (distinction); thin, watery (fluid).

ténuité [tenɥite], *s.f.* Tenuity, tenuousness; slenderness; fineness (of sand, of distinction).

tenure [tənyːr], *s.f. Jur:* Tenure.

ter [tɛːr], *Lt. adv. (a)* Three times. *Mus:* Ter. *(b)* For the third time.

tératologie [teratɔlɔʒi], *s.f.* Teratology.

tératologique [teratɔlɔʒik], *a.* Teratological.

tercet [tɛrsɛ], *s.m. Pros:* Tercet. *Mus:* Triplet.

térébenthine [terebɑ̃tin], *s.f.* Turpentine. Essence de térébenthine, (oil of) turpentine. *F:* turps.

térébinthe [terebɛ̃ːt], *s.m. Bot:* Terebinth. turpentine-tree.

térébrant [terɛbrã], *a.* (*a*) Terebrant, boring (insect). (*b*) **Douleur térébrante,** terebrating pain.
térébration [terɛbrasjɔ̃], *s.f.* Terebration. **1.** Boring (of resinous tree, etc.). **2.** *Surg:* Trephining.
térèbre [terɛbr], *s.f. Moll:* Auger-shell.
tergal, -aux [tergal, -o], *a. Z:* Tergal.
tergiversation [tɛrʒiversasjɔ̃], *s.f.* Tergiversation; beating about the bush.
tergiverser [tɛrʒivɛrse], *v.i.* To tergiversate, equivocate; to beat about the bush.
terme[1] [tɛrm], *s.m.* **1.** Terminal (statue); term, terminus. *F:* Il ne bouge pas plus qu'un terme, he stands like a statue. **2.** Term, end, limit (of life, journey, etc.). *Toucher à son t.,* to be near one's end. **Mettre un terme à qch.,** to put an end, a stop, to sth. Il y a terme à tout, there is an end to everything. **Mener qch. à bon terme,** to bring sth. to a successful conclusion; to carry sth. through. **3.** (*a*) (Appointed) time. *Accouchement avant t.,* premature labour. *Mil: Navy:* Engagement à long terme, long service. *T. de rigueur,* latest time, latest date. **Marché à terme,** time-bargain. (Of bills) **A court terme, à long terme,** short-dated, long-dated. *St.Exch:* Le terme, the settlement. **Opérations à terme,** forward deals. (*b*) **Demander un terme de grâce,** to ask for time to pay. *Payable à deux termes,* payable in two instalments. **4.** (*a*) Quarter (of rent); term. (*b*) Quarter's rent. (*c*) Quarter day.
terme[2], *s.m.* **1.** Term, expression. *T. de métier,* technical term. *En termes de pratique,* in legal parlance. *Il m'a dit en termes propres, en termes exprès, que . . .,* he told me in so many words that. . . . *En d'autres termes,* in other words. *Peser, mesurer, ses termes,* to weigh one's words. *Il m'a parlé de vous en très bons termes,* he spoke very nicely about you. **Dans toute la force du terme,** in the full sense of the word. S.a. MOYEN[1] 1. **2.** *pl.* Wording (of clause, etc.); terms, conditions. **3.** *pl.* Terms, footing. **Être en bons termes avec qn,** to be on good terms, on friendly terms, with s.o.
terminaison [tɛrminɛzɔ̃], *s.f.* Termination, ending.
terminer [tɛrmine], *v.tr.* To terminate. **1.** To bound, limit (estate). **2.** (*a*) To end, finish; to bring to an end, to a close; to conclude (bargain, etc.); to complete (piece of work). (*b*) *v.i. Il faut en t.,* we must make an end. **Terminer court,** to come to an abrupt ending.
se terminer, to end; to come to an end.
terminologie [tɛrminɔlɔʒi], *s.f.* Terminology.
terminus [tɛrminyːs], *s.m.* (Railway) terminus; terminal point (of coach line, etc.).
termite [tɛrmit], *s.m. Ent:* Termite, white ant.
ternaire [tɛrnɛːr], *a.* Ternary (notation, compound). *Mus:* **Mesure ternaire,** triple time.
terne [tɛrn], *a.* Dull, lustreless, leaden (colouring, etc.). *Voix t.,* flat voice, colourless voice. *Style t.,* dull, lifeless, colourless, style.
tern|ir [tɛrniːr], *v.tr.* To tarnish, dull, dim, deaden. *T. une réputation,* to tarnish a reputation. *s.m.* **-issement.**
se ternir, to tarnish; to grow dull or dim.
ternissure [tɛrnisyːr], *s.f.* (*a*) Tarnished appearance; dull spot or patch. (*b*) Blemish, stain (on reputation).
terrain [tɛrɛ̃], *s.m.* Ground. (*a*) Piece of ground, plot of land. *T. à bâtir,* ground-plot, building-site. (*b*) Land. *T. accidenté,* hilly ground. *T. mou,* soft soil. (*c*) Duelling ground; football field; golf course. *T. de jeux,* (i) playground; (ii) playing-field. *T. de manœuvres,* drill-ground,

parade-ground. **Aller sur le terrain,** to fight a duel. *Mil:* **Gagner du terrain,** to gain ground. *F:* **Être sur son terrain,** to be on familiar ground. **Sonder, tâter, le terrain,** to see how the land lies.
terral [tɛral], *s.m. Nau:* Land-breeze, terral.
terrasse [tɛras], *s.f.* (*a*) Terrace; bank. **Jardin en terrasse,** terraced garden. (*b*) Pavement (in front of a café). (*c*) (**Toit en**) **terrasse,** flat roof.
terrassement [tɛrasmã], *s.m.* **1.** Banking, digging (of earth). **Travaux de terrassement,** navvying. **2.** Earthwork, embankment.
terrasser [tɛrase], *v.tr.* **1.** To bank up, embank. **2.** (*a*) To lay (s.o.) low; to throw, floor (wrestler). (*b*) *F:* To overwhelm, dismay, crush, nonplus.
se terrasser, *Mil:* to dig oneself in.
terrassier [tɛrasje], *s.m.* Navvy. **Travaux de terrassier,** navvying.
terre [tɛːr], *s.f.* **1.** Earth. (*a*) The world. **Être seul sur la terre,** to be alone in the world. **Être encore sur terre,** to be still in the land of the living. S.a. REMUER 1. (*b*) Ground, land. **Armée de terre,** land army. **Basses terres,** lowlands. **Hautes terres,** highlands. **Aller par terre,** to go by land, overland. **Tomber par terre,** to fall down (from standing position). **Tomber à terre,** to fall down (from height). *Être assis, couché, par t.,* to sit, lie, on the ground. **Mettre pied à terre,** to set foot to ground; to dismount (from horse). S.a. PIED-À-TERRE. *Attaquer une ville par t. et par mer,* to attack a town by land and sea. **Être sous terre, en terre,** to be in one's grave. **Porter qn en terre,** to bear s.o. to burial. *El.E:* **Mettre, relier, le courant à (la) terre,** to earth the current. *Mise à t.,* (i) earthing (of current); (ii) earth-connection, -lead. (Of ship) **Être à terre,** to be aground, ashore. **Mettre qn à terre,** to land s.o.; to put s.o. ashore. S.a. MISE 1. **Descendre à terre,** to land, disembark, go ashore. **Perdre terre,** (i) *Nau:* to lose sight of land; (ii) (in swimming) to get out of one's depth. *F:* **Être terre à terre,** to be matter-of-fact, earthbound. *s.* **Le terre à terre de sa pensée,** the lack of any elevation in his thought. **2.** Soil, land. *T. grasse,* rich soil. **3.** (*a*) Estate, property. *Il a une t. en Normandie,* he has an estate in Normandy. (*b*) *Terres étrangères,* foreign lands. **La Terre Sainte,** the Holy Land. *Geog:* **La Terre de Feu,** Tierra del Fuego. **4.** Loam, clay. *T. végétale,* mould, loam. *Parquet en t. battue,* mud floor. **Terre à potier,** potter's clay. **Terre de pipe,** pipe-clay. **Pipe en terre,** clay pipe. **Terre cuite,** (i) baked clay, (ii) terra cotta. **Terre pourrie,** rotten-stone, tripoli powder. S.a. FOULON, GLAISE, OMBRE[2].
terreau [tɛro], *s.m.* (Vegetable-)mould. *T. de feuilles,* leaf-mould.
Terre-Neuve. **1.** *Pr.n.f.* Newfoundland. **2.** *s.m.inv.* Newfoundland dog.
terre-neuvien, -ienne. **1.** (*a*) *a.* (Of) Newfoundland. (*b*) *s.* Newfoundlander. **2.** *s.m.* (*a*) Newfoundland fisherman. (*b*) Newfoundland fishing-vessel; banker.
terre-plein, *s.m.* **1.** *Fort:* Terreplein. **2.** (*a*) Earth platform; terrace. (*b*) Raised strip of ground (with trees, etc.) running along a street or boulevard. *pl. Des terre-pleins.*
terrer [tɛre], *v.tr.* **1.** To earth up (tree, plant). **2.** *Agr:* To warp (field). **3.** *Tex:* To full (cloth).
se terrer. **1.** (*a*) (Of rabbit) To burrow; (of fox) to go to ground. (*b*) (Of rabbit, partridge, etc.) To squat. **2.** *Mil:* To entrench oneself, *F:* to dig oneself in.
terrestre [tɛrɛstr], *a.* Terrestrial; ground-(plant); earthly, worldly (thoughts). **Paradis**

terrestre, earthly paradise. *Mil: Effectifs terrestres,* land forces.

terreur [tɛrœːr], *s.f.* Terror; (intense) fear; dread. *Fou de t.,* wild with fear; frightened out of one's wits. **Être dans la terreur,** to be in terror. *Fr.Hist:* **La Terreur,** the (Reign of) Terror (1793).

terreux, -euse [tɛrø, -øːz], *a.* (*a*) Earthy (taste, smell). (*b*) Grubby, dirty (hands). (*c*) Dull (colour); ashy, sickly (face).

terrible [tɛribl], *a.* Terrible, terrific, frightful, dreadful. *F: Un temps t.,* awful weather. **Enfant terrible,** 'enfant terrible'; *F:* a little terror. *adv.* **-ment.**

terrien, -ienne [tɛrjɛ̃, -jɛn]. **I.** *a.* Possessing land. *Propriétaire t.,* landed proprietor. **2.** *s.* (*a*) Landowner; landed proprietor. (*b*) *Nau:* Landsman.

terrier¹ [tɛrje], *s.m.* Burrow, hole (of rabbit); earth (of fox).

terrier², *a. & s.m.* Relating to lands. *Hist:* (*Papier*) **terrier,** terrier; register of landed property.

terrier³, *a.m. & s.m.* (Chien) **terrier,** terrier.

terrifiant [tɛr(r)ifjɑ̃], *a.* Terrifying, awe-inspiring.

terrifier [tɛr(r)ifje], *v.tr.* To terrify; *F:* to scare to death.

terrine [tɛrin], *s.f.* **I.** (*a*) Earthenware vessel, pan (for milk, etc.). (*b*) (Earthenware) pot (for *foie gras,* etc.). **2.** *pl.* Potted meats.

territoire [tɛritwaːr], *s.m.* Territory; area under jurisdiction. *T. maritime,* territorial waters.

territorial, -aux [tɛritɔrjal, -o]. **I.** *a.* Territorial. *Eaux territoriales,* territorial waters. **2.** *F:* (*a*) *s.m.* Territorial (soldier). (*b*) *s.f.* **La territoriale,** the territorial army.

terroir [tɛrwaːr], *s.m. Agr:* Soil. (Of wine) **Goût de terroir,** tang of the soil; native tang. **Sentir le terroir,** to smack of the soil; to be racy of the soil.

terroriser [tɛr(r)ɔrize], *v.tr.* To terrorize.

terrorisme [tɛr(r)ɔrism], *s.m.* Terrorism.

terroriste [tɛr(r)ɔrist], *s.m.* Terrorist.

tertiaire [tɛrsjɛːr], *a. Geol:* Tertiary (period).

tertre [tɛrtr], *s.m.* Hillock, mound, knoll. *Golf:* **Tertre de départ,** teeing ground.

tes [te], *a.poss.* See TON¹.

téséfiste [tesefist], *s. m. & f. F:* Wireless fan.

tesson [tɛsɔ̃], *s.m.* Potsherd. *T. de bouteille,* broken bottle end.

test¹ [tɛ(st)], *s.m.* = TÊT 2.

test² [tɛst], *s.m.* Test. *T. mental,* intelligence test.

testacé [tɛstase]. **I.** *a.* Testaceous, shelled. **2.** *s.m.* Shell-fish; testacean.

testament¹ [tɛstamɑ̃], *s.m.* Will, testament. *Mettre qn sur son t.,* to mention s.o. in one's will. **Mourir sans testament,** to die intestate.

testament², *s.m. B:* **L'ancien, le nouveau, Testament,** the Old, the New, Testament.

testamentaire [tɛstamɑ̃tɛːr], *a.* Testamentary. **Disposition testamentaire,** clause (of a will); devise. **Héritier testamentaire,** devisee. S.a. EXÉ-CUTEUR I.

testateur, -trice [tɛstatœːr, -tris], *s.* Testator, testatrix. *Jur:* Devisor.

tester [tɛste], *v.i.* To make one's will.

testicule [tɛstikyl], *s.m. Anat:* Testicle.

testif [tɛstif], *s.m. Com:* Camel's hair.

testimonial, -aux [tɛstimɔnjal, -o], *a.* (*a*) *Jur:* Deponed to by witness. *Preuve testimoniale,* proof by witnesses. (*b*) *Lettre testimoniale,* testimonial; certificate.

---

têt [te], *s.m.* **I.** *Ven: A:* Skull (of stag). **2.** (*a*) *Z:* Test, shell (of sea-urchin, etc.). (*b*) *Bot:* Testa, skin (of seed). **3.** *Ch:* Small fire-clay cup. (*a*) Cupel. (*b*) *Têt à gaz,* beehive shelf.

tétanie [tetani], *s.f. Med:* Tetany.

tétanique [tetanik], *a. Med:* Tetanic.

tétaniser [tetanize], *v.tr. Med:* To tetanize.

tétanisme [tetanism], *s.m. Med:* Tetanic state.

tétanos [tetanɔs], *s.m. Med:* Tetanus, lock-jaw.

têtard [tɛtaːr], *s.m.* **I.** Tadpole. **2.** *Arb:* Pollard. **3.** *Ich:* (*a*) Bull-head, miller's-thumb. (*b*) Chub.

tête [tɛːt], *s.f.* Head. **I.** (*a*) **De la tête aux pieds,** from head to foot. **Être tête nue,** to be bare-headed. **Monstre à deux têtes,** double-headed monster. **Corps sans tête,** headless body. **Tenir tête à qn,** to hold one's own against s.o.; to stand up to s.o. **Endetté par-dessus la tête,** over head and ears in debt. **J'en ai par-dessus la tête,** I can't stand it any longer; *F:* I'm fed up. **La tête en bas,** head downwards; (of thg) upside down. *La t. la première,* head foremost; head first. **Ne (pas) savoir où donner de la tête,** not to know which way to turn. **Dîner tête à tête,** to dine alone together. S.a. TÊTE-À-TÊTE. **Signe de tête,** nod. **Mal de tête,** headache. **Avoir mal à la tête,** to have a headache. *T. ronde,* bullet-head. *Hist: Tête ronde,* Roundhead. *Fb: Jouer le ballon de la t.,* to head the ball. *Swim:* **Piquer une tête,** to take a header. **Tête ou pile?** heads or tails? S.a. BAISSER I. 1, BONNET 1, COUP 1, HAUT I. 1, III. 2, LAVER, LEVER I. 1, MORT¹ 2. (*b*) Head of hair. (*c*) Face, appearance. *Th:* **Se faire la tête d'un rôle,** to make up for a part. *F:* **Faire une tête,** to pull a long face, to look glum. S.a. PAYER. **Il a une bonne tête,** (i) he looks a decent fellow; (ii) he looks a bit of a mug. (*d*) Head (of animal, fish); jowl (of fish). **2.** Head-piece, brains, mind. *Se creuser la t.,* to rack one's brains. **Avoir de la tête,** to have a good head on one's shoulders. **C'est une femme de tête,** she is a capable woman. *F:* **C'est une tête de bois,** he's a blockhead. **Se mettre en tête de faire qch.,** to take it into one's head to do sth. **Se mettre dans la tête que . . .,** to get it, take it, into one's head that. . . . *Il a quelque chose en t.,* he is planning something, *F:* he is up to something. **Forte tête,** strong-minded person. **Mauvaise tête,** unruly boy, workman, etc. **Tête chaude,** hot-head. **C'est une tête brûlée,** he has a bit of the devil in him. **Travail de tête,** brain-work. **Calculer de tête,** to reckon in one's head. **Calcul de tête,** mental arithmetic. **En faire à sa tête,** to have one's way. **Avoir sa petite tête à soi,** to have a will of one's own. *Où ai-je la t.!* what am I thinking about! *Conserver sa t.,* to keep cool; to remain calm and collected. **Perdre la tête,** to lose one's head, one's self-possession. *Est-ce que vous perdez la t.?* have you taken leave of your senses? **Avoir toute sa tête,** to be quite rational. *Il n'avait plus sa t. à lui,* he was off his head. **Il a la tête montée,** his blood is up. **La tête reposée,** at one's leisure. *Prov:* **Autant de têtes autant d'avis,** so many men so many minds. S.a. CASSER 1, COUP 4, SE PERDRE 2. **3.** (*a*) Leader (of undertaking). (*b*) Summit, crown, top (of volcano, etc.); head, top (of book). *I.C.E:* **Soupapes en tête,** overhead valves. *T. de chapitre,* chapter heading. (*c*) Head (of pin, nail, etc.); loaf, head (of cabbage). *Anat:* **Tête du fémur,** apophysis of the femur. S.a. BIELLE. (*d*) Front (place). **Colonne de tête,** leading column. *Rail:* **Voiture de tête,** front carriage. **Marcher en tête,** to lead the way, to lead the van. *Marcher à la t. du cortège,* to head the procession. *Être* *à la t. de la classe*, to be at the top of the form. *Rac*: **Prendre la tête**, to take the lead. *Rail*: etc: **Tête de ligne**, (i) starting point, terminus; (ii) rail-head.

tête-à-queue, *s.m.inv.* Slew round. **Faire (un) tête-à-queue**, (i) *Aut*: to slew round; (ii) (of horse) to whip round.

tête-à-tête, *s.m.inv.* Private interview, confidential conversation; tête-à-tête.

tête-bêche, *adv.* Head to foot (alongside of one another); head to tail.

tête-de-loup, *s.f.* Turk's-head brush; wall-broom. *pl. Des têtes-de-loup*.

tétée [tete], *s.f.* Suck. *L'heure de la t.*, (infant's) feeding-time.

teter [təte], *v.tr.* (il tette; il tettera) (Of infant or young) To suck. **Donner à teter à un enfant**, to give suck to a child. [TETTE]

téter [tete], *v.tr.* (il tète; il tétera) = TETER.

têtière [tetjɛːr], *s.f.* **1.** Infant's cap. **2.** *Harn*: Head-stall. **3.** Antimacassar. **4.** *Nau*: Head (of sail).

tétin [tetɛ̃], *s.m.*, **tetin** [tətɛ̃], *s.m.* Nipple, pap; teat (of woman); dug (of cow).

tétine [tetin], *s.f.*, **tetine** [tətin], *s.f.* **1.** Dug (of animal). (*a*) Udder. (*b*) Teat. **2.** (Rubber) teat (of feeding-bottle). *T. sur anneau*, baby's comforter.

téton [tetɔ̃], *s.m.*, **teton** [tətɔ̃], *s.m.* (Woman's) breast.

tétracorde [tetrakɔrd], *s.m. Mus*: A: Tetra-chord.

tétraèdre [tetraɛdr]. *Geom*: **1.** *a.* Tetrahedral. **2.** *s.m.* Tetrahedron.

tétragone [tetragɔn]. *Geom*: **1.** *a.* Tetragonal. **2.** *s.m.* Tetragon.

tétramètre [tetramɛtr], *s.m. Pros*: Tetrameter.

tétras [tetrɑ(s)], *s.m. Orn*: Grouse. *T. lyre*, black-cock; (*femelle*) grey hen. *Grand t.*, wood grouse, capercailzie.

tétrasyllabe [tetrasillab], **tétrasyllabique** [tetrasillabik], *a.* Tetrasyllabic.

tette [tet], *s.f. F*: Dug, teat (of animal).

tette-chèvre, *s.m. Orn*: Nightjar, goatsucker.

têtu [tety], *a.* Stubborn, obstinate; mulish. *F*: **Têtu comme un mulet, comme une mule**, as stubborn, as obstinate, as a mule. [TÊTE]

teuf-teuf [tœftœf], *s.m. F*: (Child's word) Puff-puff; train or motor car.

teuton, -onne [tøtɔ̃, -ɔn]. **1.** *a.* Teuton(ic). **2.** *s.* Teuton.

teutonique [tøtɔnik], *a.* Teutonic.

texte [tekst], *s.m.* (*a*) Text. **Erreur de texte**, textual error. **Revenons à notre texte**, let us return to our subject. *Bookb*: **Gravure hors texte**, plate; full-page engraving. S.a. CRITIQUE[2] I. (*b*) Letterpress (to illustration).

textile [tekstil], *a. & s.m.* Textile.

textu|el, -elle [tekstɥel], *a.* Textual. *adv.* **-ellement**.

texture [tekstyːr], *s.f.* Texture (of cloth, bone).

thalassique [talasik], *a.* Thalassic.

thalle [tal], *s.m. Bot*: Thallus.

thallium [talljɔm], *s.m. Ch*: Thallium.

thalweg [talveg], *s.m. Geol*: Thalweg.

thapsia [tapsja], *s.m. Pharm*: Thapsia plaster.

thaumaturge [tomatyrʒ], *s.m.* Thaumaturge, thaumaturgist; miracle-worker.

thaumaturgie [tomatyrʒi], *s.f.* Thaumaturgy.

thé [te], *s.m.* **1.** (*a*) Tea. *C'est l'heure du thé*, it is tea-time. **Boîte à thé**, (i) tea-caddy, (ii) tea-canister. (*b*) *Thé du Paraguay*, maté. **2.** Tea-party. *Thé musical*, musical afternoon.

théâtral, -aux [teatral, -o], *a.* Theatrical; *Pej*: stagy. *adv.* **-ement**.

théâtre [teɑːtr], *s.m.* **1.** Theatre, playhouse. *F*: *Le t. de la guerre*, the theatre, seat, of war. **2.** Stage, scene. *Paraître sur le t.*, to appear on the stage, on the boards. **Mettre une pièce au théâtre**, to stage, put on, a play. **3.** (*a*) Dramatic art. **Pièce de théâtre**, play. **Faire du théâtre**, to be an actor, to be on the stage. **Coup de théâtre**, dramatic, sensational, turn (to events). **En coup de théâtre**, with startling suddenness. (*b*) Plays, dramatic works (of s.o.). **Le théâtre anglais**, the English drama.

théière [tejɛːr], *s.f.* Teapot.

théisme[1] [teism], *s.m.* Theism; tea-poisoning.

théisme[2], *s.m. Theol*: Theism.

théiste [teist]. **1.** *a.* Theistic. **2.** *s.* Theist.

thème [tem], *s.m.* (*a*) Theme, topic; subject (of discourse, etc.). (*b*) *Sch*: Composition exercise. *T. latin*, Latin (prose) composition. *F*: **Fort en thème**, good at book-learning.

théocratie [teɔkrasi], *s.f.* Theocracy.

théocratique [teɔkratik], *a.* Theocratic.

théodicée [teɔdise], *s.f. Phil*: Theodicy.

théodolite [teɔdɔlit], *s.m. Surv*: Theodolite.

théogonie [teɔgɔni], *s.f.* Theogony.

théologal, -aux [teɔlɔgal, -o], *a.* Relating to theology. **Les trois vertus théologales**, the three theological virtues.

théologie [teɔlɔʒi], *s.f.* Theology. *Cours de t.*, divinity course. **Docteur en théologie**, doctor of divinity; D.D.

théologien [teɔlɔʒjɛ̃], *s.m.* Theologian; divine.

théologique [teɔlɔʒik], *a.* Theological.

théorème [teɔrem], *s.m. Mth*: Theorem. **Le théorème de Newton** [nøtɔ̃], the binomial theorem.

théoricien, -ienne [teɔrisjɛ̃, -jɛn], *s.* Theor(et)-ician, theorist.

théorie[1] [teɔri], *s.f.* **1.** Theory. **2.** *Mil*: (*a*) Theoretical instruction (as part of training). (*b*) Training-manual.

théorie[2], *s.f.* **1.** *Gr.Ant*: Theory, theoria. **2.** Procession, file (of persons).

théorique [teɔrik], *a.* Theoretic(al). *adv.* **-ment**, -ally.

théoriser [teɔrize], *v.tr. & i.* To theorize.

théoriste [teɔrist], *s.m. & f.* Theorist, theorizer.

théosophe [teɔzɔf], *s. m. & f.* Theosophist.

théosophie [teɔzɔfi], *s.f.* Theosophy.

thèque [tek], *s.f. Fung*: Theca, ascus.

thérapeute [terapøːt], *s.m.* Therapeutist.

thérapeutique [terapøtik]. **1.** *a.* Therapeutic. **2.** *s.f.* Therapeutics.

thermal, -aux [termal, -o], *a.* Thermal. *Eaux thermales*, hot springs, thermal springs. *Station thermale*, spa, watering-place.

thermes [term], *s.m.pl.* **1.** *Gr. & Rom. Ant*: Thermae, public baths. **2.** Thermal baths; hot springs.

thermidor [termidɔːr], *s.m. Fr.Hist*: Eleventh month (July-August) in the Fr. Republican calendar.

thermie [termi], *s.f. Ph*: Thermal unit = 1000 great calories; *U.S*: therm.

thermique [termik], *a., Ph*: Thermic, thermal. **Moteur thermique**, heat engine.

thermite [termit], *s.f. Metalw*: Thermit(e).

thermo-cautère, *s.m. Surg*: Thermo-cautery.

thermo-chimie, *s.f.* Thermochemistry.

thermo-dynamique, *s.f.* Thermodynamics.

thermo-électricité, *s.f.* Thermo-electricity.

thermo-électrique, *a. Ph*: Thermo-elec-tric(al). **Pince thermo-électrique**, thermo-couple.

thermogène [termɔʒɛn], *a. Physiol*: Thermo-genic, heat-producing. *Med*: **Ouate thermogène**, thermogene (wool).

thermoïonique [tɛrmɔjɔnik], *a.* *W.Tel:* Thermionic (valve, etc.).

thermomètre [tɛrmɔmɛtr], *s.m.* Thermometer. *T. à mercure*, mercury thermometer. *T. médical, de clinique*, clinical thermometer. *Le t. indiquait* 38° (*centigrades*), the thermometer stood at 100° (Fahrenheit).

thermométrie [tɛrmɔmetri], *s.f. Ph:* Thermometry.

thermométrique [tɛrmɔmetrik], *a.* Thermometric(al).

thermopile [tɛrmɔpil], *s.f. El:* Thermopile.

thermos [tɛrmɔs], *s.m.* **Bouteille thermos**, vacuum flask, thermos (flask).

thermostat [tɛrmɔsta], *s.m.* Thermostat.

thermothérapie [tɛrmɔterapi], *s.f. Med:* Heat treatment; thermotherapy.

thésauris|er [tezɔrize], *v.tr.* To hoard, pile up (money); *abs.* to hoard. *s.f.* **-ation**.

thésauriseur, -euse [tezɔrizœːr, -øːz]. **I.** *s.* Hoarder of treasure. **2.** *a.* Acquisitive.

thèse [tɛːz], *s.f.* **I.** Thesis, proposition, argument. *Soutenir une t.*, to uphold a thesis. **Pièce à thèse**, propaganda play; problem play. **En thèse générale . . .**, as a general principle . . ., generally speaking. . . . *F:* **Voilà qui change la thèse!** that alters the case! **Changer de thèse**, to change the subject (of conversation). **2.** *Sch:* Thesis (submitted for degree).

thibaude [tibo:d], *s.f.* Coarse haircloth.

Thibau(l)t [tibo]. *Pr.n.m.* Theobald.

thiosulfate [tjɔsylfat], *s.m. Ch:* Thiosulphate.

thlaspi [tlaspi], *s.m. Bot:* Thlaspi. *T. des champs*, pennycress.

thon [tɔ̃], *s.m. Ich:* Tunny(-fish).

thoracique [tɔrasik], *a. Anat:* Thoracic.

thorax [tɔraks], *s.m.* **I.** *Anat:* Thorax, chest. **2.** *Ent:* Thorax.

thorite [tɔrit], *s.f. Miner:* Thorite.

thorium [tɔrjɔm], *s.m. Ch:* Thorium.

thran [trã], *s.m.* Train-oil.

thrips [trips], *s.m. Ent:* Thrips, thysanopter.

thrombose [trɔ̃boːz], *s.f. Med:* Thrombosis.

thrombus [trɔ̃byːs], *s.m. Med:* Thrombus.

thune [tyn], *s.f. P:* Five-franc piece.

thuriféraire [tyriferɛːr], *s.m.* (*a*) *Ecc:* (i) Thurifer, incense-bearer; (ii) boat-bearer. (*b*) *F:* Flatterer, extoller; *P:* booster (of s.o.).

thurifère [tyrifɛːr], *a. Bot:* Thuriferous.

thuya [tyja], *s.m. Bot:* Thuja, thuya, arbor vitae.

thym [tɛ̃], *s.m. Bot:* Thyme.

thymique [timik], *a. Med:* Thymic.

thymol [timɔl], *s.m. Pharm:* Thymol.

thymus [timyːs], *s.m. Anat:* Thymus (gland).

thyroïde [tirɔid], *a. Anat:* Thyroid (gland).

thyroïdisme [tirɔidism], *s.m. Med:* Thyroidism.

thyrse [tirs], *s.m. Gr.Ant:* Bot: Thyrsus.

tiare [tjaːr], *s.f.* Tiara. *F:* Aspirer à la tiare, to aspire to the papacy.

Tibère [tibɛːr]. *Pr.n.m. Rom.Hist:* Tiberius.

tibétain, -aine [tibetɛ̃, -ɛn], *a. & s.* Tibetan.

tibia [tibja], *s.m. Anat:* Tibia, shin-bone. *S'érafler le t.*, to bark one's shin.

tibial, -aux [tibjal, -o], *a. Anat:* Tibial.

Tibre (le) [lɔtibr]. *Pr.n.m.* The (river) Tiber.

tic [tik], *s.m.* (*a*) *Med:* Tic; twitching. **Il a un tic**, his face twitches. **Tic douloureux**, facial neuralgia. (*b*) *Farr:* Vicious habit, stable vice (of horse). (*c*) *F:* (Unconscious) habit; mannerism; trick (of doing sth.).

ticket [tikɛ], *s.m.* Ticket (esp. on bus, at swimming-bath, etc.); numbered slip, check (at restaurant, cloak-room). *Rail: etc: T. de place,*

reserved-seat ticket. **Ticket d'appel**, (numbered) call-slip (at bus stages in Paris).

tic-tac [tiktak], *s.m.* Tick-tack, tick-tock; ticking (of clock); pit-a-pat (of heart). **Faire tic-tac**, to go tick-tack, pit-a-pat.

tiède [tjɛd], *a.* Tepid; lukewarm. *adv.* **-ment**.

tiédeur [tjedœːr], *s.f.* Tepidity, tepidness; lukewarmness (of water, friendship). **Agir avec tiédeur**, to act without zeal, half-heartedly.

tiédir [tjediːr]. **I.** *v.i.* To become tepid, lukewarm; (of friendship, etc.) to cool off. **2.** *v.tr.* To make tepid, lukewarm.

tien, tienne[1] [tjɛ̃, tjɛn]. Yours; thine. (For the use of *tien* as opp. to *votre, cf.* **TU**.) **I.** Occ. *poss. a. pred. Mes intérêts sont tiens*, my interests are yours, thine. **2. Le tien, la tienne, les tiens, les tiennes**. (*a*) *poss.pron. Ma sœur se promène avec la tienne*, my sister is out walking with yours. (*b*) *s.m.* (i) Your own (property, etc.); yours. **Il faut y mettre du tien**, you must contribute your share. (ii) *pl.* Your own (friends, etc.). (iii) *F:* **Tu as encore fait des tiennes**, you have been up to your old tricks.

tien-drai, -ne[2], **-s**[1], **-t**, etc. See **TENIR**.

tiens[2] .[tjɛ̃], *int.* **I.** Hullo! **2.** To be sure! **3. Tiens, tiens!** indeed! well, well! [**TENIR**]

tierce [tjɛrs]. **I.** See **TIERS**. *s.f.* (*a*) *Astr: Mth:* Third (= sixtieth part of a second). (*b*) *Cards: Fenc:* Tierce. (*c*) *Ecc:* Terce, tierce. (*d*) *Mus:* T. majeure, major third. (*e*) *Typ:* Final revise.

tiercelet [tjɛrs(ə)lɛ], *s.m.* Tercel; male falcon.

tiers, f. tierce [tjɛːr, tjɛrs]. **I.** *a. A:* Third. *Hist:* **Le tiers état**, the third estate, the commonalty. *Jur:* **En main tierce**, in the hands of a third party. *A.Med:* **Fièvre tierce**, tertian ague. *Mth:* n tierce, n triple dash (n‴). **2.** *s.m.* (*a*) Third (part). **Remise d'un t. (du prix)**, a third off. (*b*) Third person, third party. **Être en tiers**, to be present as a third party, to make a third. *F:* **Le tiers et le quart**, everybody, anybody. **Devoir au t. et au quart**, to owe money right and left. S.a. **SE MOQUER**.

tiers-arbitre [tjɛrarbitr], *s.m.* Referee (in case of tie between arbitrators).

tiers-point, *s.m.* **I.** *Arch:* Tierce-point. **2.** *Tls:* Triangular file; three-cornered file.

tige [tiːʒ], *s.f.* **I.** (*a*) Stem, stalk (of plant). (*b*) Trunk, bole (of tree). (**Arbres à hautes tiges**, tall standards.) (*c*) Stock (of family). **Faire tige**, to found a family, a house. **2.** (*a*) Shaft (of column); stem (of candlestick, etc.); shank (of rivet, key); stick (of violin bow). *T. de soupape*, valve-stem, -spindle. (*b*) Rod. *Mch: T. du piston*, piston-rod. *T. de tiroir*, slide-rod. *T. de paratonnerre*, lightning-rod. *Cy: T. de selle*, saddle-pillar. (*c*) Leg (of boot). **Bottes à tiges**, top-boots.

tignasse [tiɲas], *s.f.* Shock, mop (of hair).

tigre[1], **tigresse** [tigr, tigrɛs]. **I.** *s. Z:* Tiger, tigress. **2.** *s.m.* Small groom; tiger.

Tigre[2] **(le)**. *Pr.n.m.* The (river) Tigris.

tigré [tigre], *a.* Striped (fur); speckled, spotted (skin). **Chat t.**, tabby cat. **Lis tigré**, tiger-lily.

tillac [tijak], *s.m. Nau:* Deck. **Franc tillac**, flush deck, main deck.

tille[1] [tiːj], *s.f.* Bast, bass. **Paillasson de tille**, bass(-mat).

tille[2], *s.f. Nau:* Cuddy (of half-decked boat).

tille[3], *s.f. Tls:* (Cooper's) adze.

tilleul [tijœl], *s.m.* **I.** Lime-tree, linden-tree. **2.** (Infusion de) tilleul, lime-blossom tea.

timbale [tɛ̃bal], *s.f.* **I.** *Mus:* Kettledrum; *pl.* timpani. **2.** Metal drinking-cup or mug. *F:* **Dé-**

crocher la timbale, to win the prize (originally from the top of the greasy pole). **3.** *Cu:* Pie-dish.

timbalier [tɛ̃balje], *s.m.* Kettledrummer; (in orchestra) performer on the timpani.

timbre [tɛ̃:br], *s.m.* **1.** (a) (Fixed) bell (with striking hammer); gong (of clock). **Timbre électrique,** electric bell. **Coup de timbre,** stroke of the bell. *F:* **Avoir le timbre fêlé,** avoir un **coup de timbre,** to have a screw loose. (b) Shell (of helmet). (c) Snare (of drum). (d) Timbre, quality in tone (of voice, instrument). **2.** (a) Stamp (on document, etc.). **Timbre fixe, à empreinte,** impressed stamp, embossed stamp. **Timbre de la poste,** post-mark. (b) **Timbre mobile,** adhesive stamp. (c) Stamp(ing instrument). **Timbre sec,** embossing press. *T. humide,* rubber stamp. *T. à date, t. dateur,* date-stamp. (d) Stamp-duty. **3.** *Mch:* (a) Test-plate (of boiler). (b) Test pressure.

timbre-poste, *s.m.* Postage stamp. *pl. Des timbres-poste.*

timbre-quittance, *s.m.* Receipt stamp. *pl. Des timbres-quittance.*

timbr|er [tɛ̃bre], *v.tr.* **1.** To stamp (passport, etc.). *Lettre timbrée de Paris,* letter bearing the Paris post-mark. **2.** To put (boiler) through its test. *s.m.* **-age.**

timbré, *a.* **1.** Sonorous (voice). **2.** *F:* Cracked (brain); crack-brained (person). **3.** Stamped (paper, document).

timide [timid], *a.* Timid. (a) Timorous, apprehensive. (b) Shy, bashful; diffident (*envers,* with). **Peu timide,** not at all shy; bold. *adv.* **-ment.**

timidité [timidite], *s.f.* Timidity. (a) Timorousness. (b) Shyness, bashfulness, diffidence.

timon [timɔ̃], *s.m.* **1.** (a) Pole (of vehicle); beam (of plough). (b) *Occ. pl.* Shafts (of vehicle). **2.** *Nau: A:* Tiller. *F:* **Prendre le timon des affaires,** to take the helm.

timonerie [timɔnri], *s.f.* **1.** *Nau:* (a) Steering (of ship). **Kiosque de timonerie,** wheel-house. (b) (Naval) signalling. **Poste de timonerie,** signal station. **Maître de timonerie,** (in the navy) yeoman of signals; (in the merchant service) quartermaster. **2.** *Aut:* Steering-gear or brake-gear.

timonier [timɔnje], *s.m.* **1.** *Nau:* (a) *A:* Helmsman; man at the wheel. (b) Quartermaster. (c) *Navy:* Signalman. **2.** *Veh:* Wheel-horse; wheeler.

timoré [timɔre], *a.* Timorous, fearful. *Conscience timorée,* easily alarmed conscience.

tin [tɛ̃], *s.m.* **1.** Block; (boat-)chock. *pl. N.Arch:* Keel-blocks (in dry dock); stocks (on slip). **2.** Barrel-chock.

tinctorial, -aux [tɛ̃ktɔrjal, -o], *a.* Tinctorial. *Matières tinctoriales,* dye-stuffs.

tine [tin], *s.f.* Butt, water-cask.

tinette [tinɛt], *s.f.* **1.** Tub, firkin. **2.** *Hyg:* (Sanitary) soil-tub.

tin-s, -t, etc. See TENIR.

tintamarre [tɛ̃tamaːr], *s.m.* *F:* (a) Din, racket, noise. (b) Rough music. (c) **Faire du tintamarre autour d'un roman,** to give a novel wide publicity.

tint|er [tɛ̃te]. **1.** *v.tr.* To ring, toll (bell). **2.** *v.i.* (a) (Of bell) To ring, toll; (of small bells, etc.) to tinkle; (of coins) to chink; (of sleigh-bells) to jingle; (of glasses) to clink. **Faire tinter les verres,** to clink glasses. (b) (Of the ears) To buzz, tingle. **Les oreilles ont dû vous tinter hier soir,** your ears must have burned last night (*i.e.* you were talked about). *s.m.* **-ement.**

tintouin [tɛ̃twɛ̃], *s.m.* **1.** *A:* Buzzing (in the

ears). **2.** *F:* Trouble, worry. **Donner du tintouin,** to give trouble. [TINTER]

tipule [tipyl], *s.f. Ent:* Tipula; *F:* daddy-long-legs, crane-fly.

tique [tik], *s.f. Arach:* Tick, cattle-tick. *F:* **Être comme une tique après qn,** (i) to pester s.o.; (ii) to batten on s.o.

tiquer [tike], *v.i.* **1.** *F:* (a) To twitch (with the face, eyelid). (b) To wince; to show a slight sign of emotion or interest. *Il n'a pas tiqué,* he never turned a hair. **2.** (Of horse) To have a stable vice.

tiqueté [tikte], *a.* Speckled, mottled, variegated.

tiqueture [tiktyːr], *s.f.* Speckles.

tiqueur, -euse [tikœːr, -øːz], *s.* Horse, mare, with a stable vice; crib-biter.

tir [tiːr], *s.m.* **1.** (a) Shooting. *Mil:* Musketry. *Artil:* Gunnery. *Tir aux pigeons,* pigeon shooting. S.a. ARC 1. (b) Shooting-match. **2.** Fire, firing. *Tir à la cible,* target practice. *Tir à volonté,* individual fire. *Tir sur zone,* barrage. *Navy: Tir en chasse,* bow fire. **A tir rapide,** quick-firing. **3.** (a) Rifle-range. (b) Shooting-gallery. [TIRER]

tirade [tirad], *s.f.* (a) *Th:* Declamatory speech (of some length). (b) Tirade; vituperative speech. *Débiter des tirades contre qn,* to tirade against s.o.

tirage [tiraːʒ], *s.m.* **1.** (a) Pulling, hauling (of carts, etc.). **Cheval de tirage,** draught horse. *F:* **Il y a du tirage entre eux,** there is friction between them. (b) (i) Towing (of barges). (ii) Towing-path. (e) *Metalw:* Wire-drawing. (d) Quarrying, extraction (of stone). **2.** *Phot:* Extension, focal length (of camera). **3.** Draught (of flue). *T. forcé,* forced draught. **4.** Drawing (of lottery, of bonds). S.a. SORT[2] 3. **5.** *Typ: Phot:* (a) Printing (off). **Tirage à part,** off-print. (b) Number printed. *Journal à gros t.,* newspaper with a wide circulation.

tiraillement [tirajmɑ̃], *s.m.* **1.** Tugging; pulling about. **2. Tiraillements d'estomac,** gnawing of the stomach; pangs of hunger. **3.** *F:* Wrangling, friction.

tirailler [tiraje], *v.tr.* **1.** To pull (s.o., sth.) about. *F: Tiraillé entre deux émotions,* torn between two opposing feelings. **Se faire tirailler,** to need a lot of asking. **2.** *Abs.* (a) To shoot aimlessly, to blaze away. (b) *Mil: T. contre l'ennemi,* to pot, snipe, at the enemy. [TIRER]

tirailleur [tirajœːr], *s.m.* **1.** *Mil:* Skirmisher, sharp-shooter, tirailleur. **En tirailleurs,** in extended order. **2.** *F:* Free-lance journalist.

tirant [tirɑ̃], *s.m.* **1.** Purse-string. **2.** (a) Boot-tag. (b) *pl.* Braces (of drum). (c) *Aut: T. de portière,* check-strap. (d) Sinew (in meat). **3.** (a) Tie-beam (of roof); tie, tie-rod, truss-rod. (b) Stay, brace(-rod) (of boiler, machine). *T. de frein,* brake-rod. **4.** *Nau: Tirant d'eau,* (ship's) draught. *Avoir dix pieds de t. d'eau,* to draw ten feet of water.

tire [tiːr], *s.f.* Pull(ing). **Tout d'une tire,** at one go; with one jerk. **Voleur à la tire,** pickpocket. S.a. VOL[2] 1.

NOTE. In the following compounds TIRE is inv., the noun takes the plural.

tire-balle, *s.m.* Bullet-extractor.

tire-botte, *s.m.* (a) Boot-jack. (b) Boot-hook.

tire-bouchon, *s.m.* **1.** Corkscrew. **2.** *Hairdr:* Corkscrew curl.

tire-bouchonner. **1.** *v.i.* (Of smoke) To curl up; to rise in spirals. **2.** *v.tr. T. son mouchoir,* to screw up one's handkerchief.

tire-bourre, *s.m.inv. Sm.a : A :* Wad-extractor ; worm.

tire-bouton, *s.m.* Buttonhook.

tire-cartouche, *s.m.* Cartridge-extractor.

tire-clous, *s.m.* Nail-wrench.

tire-d'aile (à), *adv.phr.* S'envoler à tire-d'aile, to fly swiftly away.

tire-feu, *s.m.inv. Artil :* (Cordon) tire-feu, (firing) lanyard.

tire-fond, *s.m.inv.* **1.** Long bolt, screw-spike, foundation-bolt. *Carp :* Coach-screw. *Rail :* Sleeper-screw. **2.** Hook, ring (screwed into ceiling).

tire-goupille, *s.m. Tls :* Pin-extractor.

tire-laine, *s.m.inv. A :* Robber, cloak-snatcher.

tire-larigot (à) [atirlarigo], *adv.phr. F :* Boire à tire-larigot, (i) to drink wine from a height into the mouth ; (ii) to drink deep, *F :* like a fish.

tire-ligne, *s.m.* **1.** Drawing-pen. **2.** *Tls :* Scriber, scribing-awl.

tirelire[1] [tirliːr], *s.f.* **1.** Money-box. **2.** *P :* Face, mug.

tire-lire[2] **,** *s.m.* (Lark's) carol, tirra-lirra.

tire-lirer [tirlire], *v.i.* (a) (Of lark) To carol. (b) *F :* To sing like a lark.

tire-point, *s.m. Tls :* Pricker, stabbing-awl.

tirer [tire]. I. *v.tr.* **1.** (a) To pull out, lengthen (out), stretch. *T. des fils métalliques,* to draw wire. *T. ses chaussettes,* to pull up one's socks. *T. une affaire en longueur,* to spin out an affair. S.a. CAROTTE 3, ÉPINGLE 1, LANGUE 1. (b) *T. une vache,* to milk a cow. **2.** To pull, tug, draw, drag, haul. *T. qn par la manche,* to pluck s.o.'s sleeve. *Il s'est fait tirer pour consentir,* he consented very reluctantly. *T. les cheveux à qn,* to pull s.o.'s hair. *T. la jambe,* to limp. *Tirer les rideaux,* to draw the curtains (to or apart). *T. le verrou,* to draw the bolt (in or out). *Golf : etc :* *T. la balle, un coup,* to pull a stroke. *A :* Tirer un criminel à quatre (chevaux), to draw and quarter a criminal. *F :* Être tiré à quatre, to be worried on every side. **3.** (a) To pull off, draw off (shoes, stockings). (b) *Tirer son chapeau à qn,* to raise, lift, one's hat to s.o. S.a. RÉVÉRENCE 2. **4.** To pull out, draw out, take out, extract. *T. une dent à qn,* to pull out, draw, s.o.'s tooth. S.a. ÉPINE 2. Tirer son épée, tirer sabre au clair, to draw one's sword. S.a. COUTEAU. *T. de l'eau,* to draw water. Tirer les cartes, to tell fortunes by cards. *Cards :* *T. pour la donne,* to cut for deal. S.a. PAILLE 1, SORT[2] 3. *Tirer vanité de qch.,* to take pride in sth. Tirer plaisir de qch. to derive pleasure from sth. S.a. PARTI 4. *L'huile se tire des olives,* oil is extracted from olives. *T. la racine carrée d'un nombre,* to extract the square root of a number. *T. qn de son lit,* to drag s.o. out of bed. S.a. CLAIR 3, COUVERTURE 1, ÉCHELLE 1, ÉPINGLE 1, MARRON[1] 1, VER 2. **5.** (a) To draw (line). (b) To pull, print (off) (proof). Donner le bon à tirer d'un volume, to pass a book for press. *Épreuve* en bon à tirer, press-proof. *Auteur qui tire à vingt mille,* author whose first editions run to twenty thousand. (c) *Com :* To draw (bill of exchange). *T. à vue sur qn,* to draw on s.o. at sight. **6.** (a) To shoot, fire, let off (fire-arm, etc.). *On tirait le canon,* artillery was in action. *T. un coup de revolver à qn,* to fire, shoot, at s.o. with a revolver. *T. une flèche à qn,* to let fly an arrow at s.o. *T. un feu d'artifice,* to let off fireworks. S.a. BORDÉE 2. *T. un lièvre,* to shoot at a hare. *T. à blanc,* to fire (off) blank (cartridge). *T. sur qn,* to shoot, fire, at s.o. (b) *Fenc :* Tirer (des armes), to fence. (c) *Phot :* *T. le portrait de qn,*

to take s.o.'s photo(graph). *Se faire tirer,* to have one's portrait taken. **7.** *Nau : Vaisseau qui tire vingt pieds,* ship that draws twenty feet (of water). II. **tirer,** *v.i.* **1.** To pull. *T. sur sa barbiche,* to tug at one's beard. **2.** (a) To tend (to), incline (to) ; to verge (on). *Bleu tirant sur le vert,* blue tending to green. *Le jour tire à sa fin,* the day is drawing to its close. *Nos provisions tirent à leur fin,* our stores are running low, are giving out. Tirer sur l'âge, to be growing old. S.a. CONSÉ-QUENCE, LONGUEUR 1. (b) *T. sur la gauche,* to incline to the left. Tirer au large, (i) *Nau :* to stand out to sea ; (ii) *F :* to skedaddle. S.a. FLANC. **3.** (Of chimney) To draw.

se tirer. **1.** *Se t. d'un mauvais pas,* to extricate oneself from a fix. S'en tirer sans aucun mal, to escape uninjured. Se tirer d'affaire, (i) to tide over a difficulty ; to 'manage' ; (ii) to get out of trouble. **2.** *P :* (Of pers.) To be off, to make tracks ; *U.S :* to beat it.

tiré, -ée. **1.** *a.* (a) Drawn, worn-out, peaked, pinched, haggard (features). *Il avait les traits tirés,* his face was drawn. (b) Tiré par les cheveux, far-fetched. (c) *Golf :* Coup tiré, pulled drive ; pull. **2.** *s. Com :* Drawee.

tiret [tire], *s.m. Typ :* (a) Hyphen. (b) Dash.

tirette [tiret], *s.f.* **1.** Curtain cords. **2.** Writing-slide, tablet (of desk). **3.** Flue damper.

tireur, -euse [tirœːr, -øːz], *s.* **1.** One who draws ; drawer. (a) *T. de fils métalliques,* wire-drawer. (b) (Wine-, beer-)drawer. (c) *Com :* Drawer (of bill of exchange, of cheque). (d) Tireuse de cartes, fortune-teller. S.a. FLANC. **2.** (a) Shooter ; marksman. *Un bon t., un t. d'élite,* a good shot, a crack shot. S.a. FRANC-TIREUR. (b) Tireur d'armes, fencer.

tire-v(i)eille [tirv(j)ɛːj], *s.f. Nau :* **1.** Man-rope, ladder-rope. **2.** *pl.* Yoke-lines (of rudder).

tiroir [tirwaːr], *s.m.* **1.** Drawer (of table, etc.). *Lit :* Comédie à tiroir(s), episodic play. **2.** (a) Slide-valve (of steam-engine). Boîte à tiroir, steam-chest. (b) Slide (of slide-rule).

tisane [tizan], *s.f.* **1.** Infusion (of herbs, etc.). *T. de camomille,* camomile tea. **2.** Tisane de champagne, light champagne.

tison [tizɔ̃], *s.m.* **1.** (Fire-)brand ; half-burned log. *F :* Garder les tisons, to stick to one's chimney-corner. *F :* Un tison arraché du feu, a brand from the burning. Tison de discorde, fire-brand. **2.** Fusee (match).

tisonner [tizone], *v.tr.* To poke, stir (the fire). *F :* Tisonner une querelle, to fan a quarrel.

tisonnier [tizonje], *s.m.* Poker.

tiss|er [tise], *v.tr.* To weave. *s.m.* **-age.**

tisserand, -ande [tisrɑ̃, -ɑ̃d], *s.* Weaver.

tisseranderie [tisrɑ̃dri], *s.f.* Weaving(-trade).

tisserin [tisrɛ̃], *s.m. Orn :* Weaver-bird.

tisseur, -euse [tisœːr, -øːz], *s.* Weaver.

tissu [tisy], *s.m.* See TISTRE.

tissu-éponge, *s.m.* Sponge-cloth ; towelling. *pl. Des tissus-éponges.*

tissure [tisyːr], *s.f.* Texture.

tistre [tistr], *v.tr. A :* (Used only in *p.p.* tissu and compound tenses) To weave.

tissu. **1.** *a.* (a) *A :* Woven (material, etc.). (b) *F :* Systèmes fortement tissus l'un avec l'autre, closely interwoven systems. **2.** *s.m.* (a) Texture. (b) Fabric, tissue. *T. de crin,* hair-cloth. *T. métallique,* wire gauze. *F :* *T. de mensonges,* tissue of lies.

titan [titɑ̃], *s.m.* Titan. *F :* Travail de titan, titanic work. *Ind :* Grue titan, giant crane.

titanesque [titanɛsk], **titanique**[1] [titanik], *a.* Titanesque, titanic.

titanique², *a. Ch:* Titanic (acid, oxide).
Tite-Live [titli:v]. *Pr.n.m. Lt.Lit:* Livy.
titi [titi], *s.m. P:* Cheeky youth (of the boulevards); street arab.
titillation [titillasjɔ̃], *s.f.* Titillation, tickling.
titiller [titille], *v.tr.* To titillate; *to* tickle.
titrage [titra:ʒ], *s.m.* (*a*) *Ch: Ind:* Titration (of solution); assaying (of ore). (*b*) Sizing, numbering (of cotton, wire, etc.).
titre [ti:tr], *s.m.* **1.** (*a*) Title (of nobility, honour); official title. *Se donner le t. de . . .,* to style oneself. . . . (*b*) *Adj.phr.* **En titre,** titular; on the regular staff. *Professeur en t.,* titular professor. **Sans titre officiel,** without any official status. **2.** (*a*) Diploma, certificate. *Pourvu de tous ses titres,* fully certificated. (*b*) Voucher. (*c*) Titledeed. (*d*) **Titre de créance,** proof of debt. (*e*) *Fin: Com:* Warrant, bond, certificate; *pl.* stocks and shares, securities. **Titre de rente,** government bond. *T. au porteur,* bearer-bond. *Titres nominatifs,* registered securities. **3.** Title, claim, right. *Titres de gloire,* titles to fame. *Titres à un emploi,* qualifications for an appointment. **A titre de . . .,** by right of . . ., by virtue of. . . . *A t. d'office,* ex officio. *Montre envoyée à t. d'essai,* watch sent on approval. *A t. de faveur,* as a favour. **A bon titre, à juste titre,** fairly, rightly. **A quel titre?** by what right? upon what score? S.a. CONFIDENTIEL, GRACIEUX 2, GRATUIT, INDICATION 2, ONÉREUX. **4.** (*a*) Title (of book, song). (**Page du**) **titre,** title-page. **Faux titre,** half-title, bastard title. (*b*) Heading (of chapter). **5.** (*a*) Title, titre (of gold); grade, content (of ore); fineness (of coinage). *Ch:* Strength, titre (of solution). **Or au titre,** standard gold. (*b*) Size, number (of cotton, wire).
titrer [titre], *v.tr.* **1.** To give a title to (s.o., sth.). **2.** (*a*) To titrate (solution); to assay (ore); to determine the strength of (alcohol, etc.). (*b*) To size, number (cotton, wire).
titré, *a.* **1.** Titled (person). **2.** Certificated (teacher). **3.** Titrated, standard (solution).
titub|er [titybe], *v.i.* To reel (about); to lurch; to stagger. *s.f.* **-ation.**
titulaire [titylɛːr]. **1.** *a.* Titular (bishop, professor). **2.** *s.* Holder (of right, certificate, etc.); bearer (of passport); incumbent (of parish).
titulariser [titylarize], *v.tr. Adm: etc:* To put (s.o.) on the establishment; to confirm (s.o.) in his post or appointment.
tmèse [tmɛːz], *s.f. Gram:* Tmesis.
toast [tɔst], *s.m.* Toast. **1.** **Porter un toast,** to propose a toast. **2.** *T. beurré,* buttered toast.
toaster [tɔste], *v.tr.* To toast (s.o.); to drink (s.o.'s) health.
toboggan [tɔbɔgɑ̃], *s.m.* Toboggan. **Piste de toboggan,** toboggan run.
toc [tɔk]. **1.** (*a*) *int.* Tap, tap! (*b*) *s.m.* Tap, rap (on door, etc.). **2.** *s.m. F:* Sham gold; faked stuff. *Bijoux en toc,* imitation jewellery.
tocante [tɔkɑ̃ːt], *s.f. P:* Ticker, watch.
tocard, -arde [tɔkaːr, -ard], *a. & s. P:* Harebrained, feather-brained (person).
tocsin [tɔksɛ̃], *s.m.* Tocsin; (i) alarm-signal, (ii) alarm-bell.
toge [tɔːʒ], *s.f.* (*a*) *Rom.Ant:* Toga. (*b*) Gown, robe (of judge, etc.).
tohu-bohu [tɔyboy], *s.m. F:* Confusion, medley; hurly-burly; hubbub.
toi [twa], *stressed pers. pron.* (For the use of *toi,* *cf.* TU) (*a*) You (subject or object). *C'est toi,* it is you. *Tu as raison, toi,* you are right. *Ce livre est à toi,* this book is yours, belongs to you. *Tais-toi,* hold your tongue. (*b*) (To the Deity,

also in Quaker speech) Thou, thee. *Assieds-toi,* sit thee down.
toile [twal], *s.f.* **1.** (*a*) Linen, linen cloth. *T. bise,* écrue, unbleached linen; holland. *T. à chemises,* shirting. *T. à matelas,* tick, ticking. **Marchand de toile,** linen-draper. (*b*) Cloth. *T. de crin,* horsehair cloth. *T. de coton,* calico. **Toile cirée,** (i) American cloth, oilcloth; (ii) *Nau:* oilskin. *T. vernie,* oilskin. *T. à voiles,* canvas, sail-cloth. *T. d'emballage,* pack-cloth. *T. à sac,* sackcloth, sacking, bagging. *Reliure en 't.,* cloth binding. (*c*) Canvas. *Seau en t.,* canvas bucket. (*d*) *T. métallique,* wire gauze. (*e*) **Toile d'araignée,** cobweb; spider's web. **2.** (*a*) Oil painting (on canvas); canvas. (*b*) *Th:* Curtain. *T. de fond,* back-cloth, drop-scene. **3.** *Nau:* Sail. **Augmenter de toile,** to make more sail. **Forcer, diminuer, de toile,** to crowd, shorten, sail. **A sec de toile,** under bare poles.
toilette [twalɛt], *s.f.* **1.** (*a*) (Tailor's, dressmaker's) wrapper (for garments). (*b*) *Cu:* Caul (over mutton); crow (of pig). **2.** Toilet-cover, doily. **3.** (*a*) Wash-stand. (*b*) Toilet-table, dressing-table. (*c*) Toilet service. **4.** Toilet, washing, dressing. **Faire sa toilette,** to make one's toilet; to dress. **Cabinet de toilette,** (private) dressing-room. **Faire la toilette d'un mort,** to lay out a corpse. **5.** Lavatory. **6.** (Woman's) dress, costume. **Aimer la toilette,** to be fond of dress. **Être en toilette,** to be dressed up. **Faire toilette pour qn,** to dress up for s.o. *En grande t.,* in full dress. **Marchande à la toilette,** wardrobe dealer.
toi-même, *pers.pron.* See TOI and MÊME **1** (*c*).
toise [twaːz], *s.f.* **1.** *A:* Fathom. *F:* Mots longs d'une toise, words as long as one's arm. **2.** Measuring apparatus (for conscripts, etc.). **Passer à la toise,** to be measured (for height).
tois|er [twaze], *v.tr.* **1.** (*a*) To measure (conscript). (*b*) *Civ.E:* To survey for quantities, for work done. **2.** To take stock of (s.o.); to eye (s.o.) from head to foot. *s.m.* **-eur.**
toisé, *s.m.* Measuring (up); measurement; quantity surveying.
toison [twazɔ̃], *s.f.* **1.** Fleece. **La Toison d'or,** the Golden Fleece. **2.** *F:* Mop, shock (of hair).
toit [twa], *s.m.* **1.** Roof; house-top. *F:* **Habiter sous les toits,** to live in a garret. **Publier, crier, qch. sur les toits,** to proclaim sth. from the housetops. *Aut: T. découvrable,* sliding roof. **2.** (*a*) *F:* House, roof-tree. *Le t. paternel,* the home. (*b*) Lean-to roof; shed.
toiture [twaty:r], *s.f.* Roofing, roof.
tokai, tokay [tɔke], *s.m.* Tokay (wine).
tôle [toːl], *s.f.* **1.** Sheet-metal. (*a*) Sheet-iron. *T. ondulée,* corrugated iron. *T. vernie,* japanned iron. (*b*) *T. de cuivre,* copper sheets. **2.** (Steel-, iron-) plate (for boilers, etc.); boiler-plate. *Tôles de fond,* bottom-plates (of boiler). *T. de blindage,* armour-plate.
tolérable [tɔlerabl], *a.* Bearable, tolerable. *adv.* **-ment.**
tolérance [tɔlerɑ̃ːs], *s.f.* Tolerance. **1.** Toleration (in religious matters, etc.). **Par tolérance, on** sufferance. **2.** *Mec.E:* Margin, limits, tolerance. *T. sur l'épaisseur,* thickness-margin. *Cust: T. permise,* quantity permitted, allowance (of cigars, etc.). **3.** *Med:* (Of patient) Tolerance (of a drug).
tolérant [tɔlerɑ̃], *a.* Tolerant.
tolérantisme [tɔlerɑ̃tism], *s.m.* Religious toleration; latitudinarianism.
tolérer [tɔlere], *v.tr.* (**Je tolère; je tolérerai**) (*a*) To tolerate. (*b*) To allow tacitly, wink at (abuses, etc.). (*c*) *Med:* To tolerate (drug).

tôlerie [tolri], *s.f.* **1.** Sheet-iron and steel-plate trade. **2.** Rolling-mills; sheet-iron works. **3.** *Aut: etc:* Steel-work. [TÔLE]

tolet [tɔlɛ], *s.m. Nau:* Thole-pin. *T. à fourche,* swivel rowlock.

tollé [tɔlle], *s.m.inv.* Crier tollé contre qn, to raise a hue and cry against s.o.

Tolu [tɔly]. *Pr.n. Geog:* Tolu. Baume de Tolu, balsam of Tolu; *F:* tolu.

toluène [tɔlɥɛn], *s.m. Ch:* Toluene; methyl benzene.

tomahawk [tɔmaɔk], *s.m.* Tomahawk.

tomate [tɔmat], *s.f.* Tomato. Sauce tomate, tomato sauce. *F:* Être comme une tomate, to be as red as a tomato.

tombal, -aux [tɔbal, -o], *a.* Relating to tombs. Pierre tombale, tombstone.

tombant [tɔbɑ̃], *a.* (a) Falling. *A la nuit tombante,* at nightfall. (b) Flowing (hair); drooping (moustache, shoulders).

tombe [tɔ̃b], *s.f.* (a) Tomb, grave. Être dans la tombe, to be dead. Être au bord de la tombe, to be on the point of death; to have one foot in the grave. (b) Tombstone.

tombeau [tɔbo], *s.m.* Tomb; monument (over grave or vault). *T. de famille,* family vault. Fidèle jusqu'au tombeau, true till death. *F:* Être aux portes du tombeau, to be at death's door. Mettre un corps au tombeau, to entomb a body. Mise au tombeau, entombment.

tomber [tɔbe]. **I.** *v.i.* (Aux. is usu. *être*) **1.** To fall fall down, tumble down, drop down. *Tout tombe en pièces,* everything is falling to pieces. *Impers. Il tombe de la neige,* it is snowing. *Il a tombé de l'eau,* it has been raining. *Le sort tomba sur lui,* the lot fell on him. *T. à bas de l'échelle,* to fall off the ladder. *T. aux pieds de qn,* to fling oneself at s.o.'s feet. Tomber de fatigue, de sommeil, to be ready to drop (with fatigue, with sleep). S.a. MAL² 2. Faire tomber qn, qch., (i) to knock over, push over, s.o., sth.; (ii) to bring about the fall of (the Government, etc.). Laisser tomber qch., (i) to drop sth.; (ii) to allow sth. to fall. *Se laisser t. dans un fauteuil,* to drop, sink, into an arm-chair. *F:* (Of pers.) *T. comme une masse,* to fall all of a heap; to collapse. *F: Les bras m'en tombent,* I am dumbfounded. Fruits tombés, windfalls. S.a. HAUT III. 1, NUE. **2.** (Of wind, fever, etc.) To drop, abate, subside; (of conversation) to flag. Laisser tomber sa voix, to drop one's voice. *Le feu tombe,* the fire is dying down. *Le vent tomba,* the wind died away. **3.** *T. dans, entre, les mains de qn,* to fall into s.o.'s hands. *T. en disgrâce,* to fall into disgrace. *Nau:* Tomber sous le vent, to fall off; to fall to leeward. **4.** Tomber sur l'ennemi, to attack, fall on, the enemy. **5.** *T. sur qn, sur qch.,* to fall in with, light upon, come across, happen on, s.o., sth. *T. sur qn à l'improviste,* to drop in on s.o. unexpectedly. *Vous tombez bien,* you come opportunely. *Comme ça tombe!* what a coincidence! Tomber juste, (i) (of thg) to occur opportunely; (ii) (of pers.) to come at the right moment; (iii) to guess right. S.a. PARTAGE 2, PIC¹ 3. **6.** To fail. *La pièce est tombée (à plat),* the play was a failure. **7.** (Of hair, drapery, etc.) To fall, hang down. *Jupe qui tombe bien,* skirt that hangs, sits, well. **8.** Tomber amoureux de qn, to fall in love with s.o. *T. malade,* to fall ill. *T. mort,* to fall dead. **9.** *v.tr.* (a) Tomber un adversaire, (in wrestling) to throw, give a fall to, an opponent. (b) *Metalw:* *T. le bord d'une tôle,* to turn down the edge of a sheet. Tôle à bord tombé, flanged plate.

II. tomber, *s.m.* Au tomber du jour, at nightfall.

tombé, *a. Rugby Fb:* Coup de pied tombé, drop-kick.

tombée, *s.f.* Fall (of rain, night, etc. *Cf.* CHUTE). *Quelle t. de pluie!* what a downpour! A la tombée de la nuit, at nightfall.

tombereau [tɔbro], *s.m.* Tip-cart. *T. à ordures,* dust-cart. *Hist:* Tombereau des condamnés, tumbrel, tumbril (of Revolutionary period).

tombeur [tɔbœr], *s.m.* **1.** *Const:* Housebreaker. **2.** (Professional) wrestler. **3.** *A:* Tumbler, acrobat.

tombola [tɔbola], *s.f.* Tombola, charity lottery.

Tombouctou [tɔbuktu]. *Pr.n.m.* Timbuctoo.

tome [to:m, tɔm], *s.m.* (Heavy) volume; tome.

tom-pouce [tɔmpus], *s.m.* **1.** Tom Thumb dwarf, midget. **2.** Stumpy umbrella, Tom-Thumb umbrella. *pl. Des tom-pouces.*

ton¹, ta, tes [tɔ̃, ta, tɛ], *poss.a.* (*Ton* is used instead of *ta* before fem. words beginning with a vowel or h 'mute.' For the use of *ton* as opp. to *votre, cf.* TU) (a) Your. *Ton ami, ton amie,* your friend. *Un de tes amis,* a friend of yours. *Tes père et mère,* your father and mother. (b) (To the Deity, also in Quaker speech) Thy. *Que ta volonté soit faite,* Thy will be done.

ton², *s.m.* **1.** (a) Tone, intonation. *Parler d'un ton doux, sur un ton amical,* to speak gently, in a gentle tone, in a friendly tone. Hausser le ton, to raise one's voice. Faire baisser le ton à qn, to make s.o. sing small. *Elle le prend sur ce ton?* is that how she speaks to you? (b) Tone, manners, breeding. Le bon ton, good form. *C'est de mauvais ton,* it is bad form. **2.** *Mus:* (a) (Hauteur du) ton, pitch. Donner le ton, (i) to give (an orchestra) the tuning A; (ii) *F:* to set, lead, the fashion. (b) Key. *Le ton d'ut,* the key of C. (c) *Tons et demi-tons,* tones and semi-tones. (d) Ton de rechange, crook (of horn, trumpet). **3.** *Ling:* Pitch accent. **4.** Tone, tint, colour. *Tons chauds,* warm tints. **5.** *Med:* Tone.

tonal, -aux [tɔnal, -o], *a. Mus:* Tonal.

tonalité [tɔnalite], *s.f. Art: Mus:* Tonality.

tondeur, -euse [tɔdœːr, -øːz]. **1.** *s.* Shearer (of cloth, sheep); clipper (of horses, dogs, hedge). **2.** *s.f.* Tondeuse. (a) Shearing-machine; shears (for cloth, sheep); (hair) clippers. (b) Lawn-mower.

tond|re [tɔ:dr], *v.tr.* **1.** To shear (cloth, sheep); to clip (hair, hedge). *T. le gazon,* to mow the lawn. Tondre qn, (i) to clip, crop, s.o.'s hair; (ii) *F:* to fleece s.o. *F:* Il tondrait (sur) un œuf, he would skin a flint. S.a. MESURER 2, PELÉ. **2.** Les brebis tondaient l'herbe, the sheep were cropping the grass. *s.m.* -age.

tonifiant [tɔnifjɑ̃], *a.* Bracing, tonic.

tonifier [tɔnifje], *v.tr.* To brace, to tone up; to invigorate.

tonique [tɔnik], *a.* **1.** *Med:* (a) Convulsion tonique, tonic spasm; tonus. (b) *Médicament t., s.m.* tonique, tonic (medicine). **2.** *Ling:* Tonic (accent); accented, stressed (syllable). **3.** *Mus: Note t., s.f.* tonique, tonic, key-note.

tonitruant [tɔnitryɑ̃], *a.* Like thunder; stentorian (voice); violent, blustering (wind).

Tonkin (le) [lətɔ̃kɛ̃]. *Pr.n. Geog:* Ton(g)kin(g).

tonnage [tɔnaːʒ], *s.m. Nau:* **1.** Tonnage, burthen (of ship). *T. brut,* gross tonnage. *T. net,* register tonnage. **2.** Tonnage (of a port).

tonnant [tɔnɑ̃], *a.* **1.** Thundering. **2.** *I.C.E:* Mélange tonnant, explosive mixture.

tonne [tɔn], *s.f.* **1.** Tun (large) cask. **2.** (a) *Meas: Nau:* Metric to n(= 1000 kilograms).

(b) *Nau : T. d'encombrement*, measurement ton.
3. *Nau :* Nun-buoy.
tonneau [tɔno], *s.m.* **1.** (a) Cask, tun, barrel.
Bière au tonneau, draught beer. *F :* Du même
tonneau, of the same kind ; alike. *Petit t.,* keg.
(b) *T. mélangeur à béton,* concrete mixing-drum.
(c) *T. d'arrosage,* watering-cart. (d) (Jeu de)
tonneau, game of skill in which discs or *palets*
(*q.v.*) are aimed at various openings in the
tonneau. **2.** *Meas :* **Nau :** Ton. *Vaisseau de* 500
tonneaux, ship of 500 tons burden. **3.** *Veh :*
(a) Governess-cart. (b) Tonneau (of motor car).
4. *Av :* Horizontal spin ; roll.
tonnelet [tɔnlɛ], *s.m.* Small cask ; keg (of
brandy) ; drum (of oil).
tonnelier [tɔnəlje], *s.m.* Wet cooper.
tonnelle [tɔnɛl], *s.f.* (a) Arbour, bower.
Déjeuner sous la t., to lunch alfresco. (b) *Arch :*
Semi-circular arch ; barrel-vault.
tonnellerie [tɔnɛlri], *s.f.* **1.** Cooperage. **2.** Cooper's shop.
tonner [tɔne], *v.i.* **1.** To thunder. *Il tonne,* it is
thundering. **2.** (Of cannon, etc.) To thunder, to
boom. *F :* Tonner contre qn, to thunder,
inveigh, against s.o.
tonnerre [tɔnɛ:r], *s.m.* **1.** (a) Thunder. Coup de
tonnerre, clap, peal, of thunder ; thunder-clap.
F : T. d'applaudissements, thunder of applause.
(b) *F :* Thunderbolt, lightning. *Le t. est tombé
sur une maison,* a house was struck by lightning.
(c) *int.* Tonnerre de Dieu! mille tonnerres! by
thunder ! **2.** Breech (of fire-arm).
tonsillaire [tɔ̃sillɛ:r], *a. Anat :* Tonsillar.
Angine tonsillaire, tonsillitis.
tonsure [tɔ̃sy:r], *s.f.* Tonsure. Recevoir,
prendre, la tonsure, to enter the priesthood.
tonsurer [tɔ̃syre], *v.tr.* To tonsure (a cleric).
tonte [tɔ̃:t], *s.f.* **1.** (a) Sheep-shearing ; clipping.
(b) Clip. (c) Shearing-time. **2.** Shearing, cropping (of cloth). [TONDRE]
tontine [tɔ̃tin], *s.f. Ins :* Tontine.
tontisse [tɔ̃tis], *a. & s.f. Tex :* (Bourre) tontisse,
cropping flock. *Paperm :* Papier tontisse,
flock-paper.
tonton [tɔ̃tɔ̃], *s.m. F :* = TOTON.
tonture¹ [tɔ̃ty:r], *s.f.* **1.** (a) *Tex :* Shearing,
cropping (of cloth). (b) Mowing (of lawn) ;
clipping (of hedge). **2.** (a) *Tex :* Shearings,
croppings, flock. (b) Cut grass, hay (from the
lawn) ; clippings (of hedge).
tonture², *s.f. N.Arch :* Sheer, camber.
top [tɔp], *int.* (Voice signal in recording time
signals) *Un, deux, trois, top!* one, two, three,
now ! *s.m. W.Tel :* Les tops, the pips.
topaze [tɔpa:z], *s.f.* Topaz.
toper [tɔpe], *v.i. F :* To agree, consent ; to shake
hands on it. *Tope! tope là!* done ! agreed !
here's my hand on it !
topinambour [tɔpinãbu:r], *s.m. Bot :* Cu :
Jerusalem artichoke.
topique [tɔpik], *a.* (a) Local (divinity, etc.).
(b) *Med :* Remède t., *s.m.* topique, local remedy ;
topical remedy.
topo [tɔpo], *s.m. P :* **1.** (a) *Journ :* Popular
article. (b) *Sch :* Lecture, demonstration (by
master or pupil). **2.** *Mil :* Staff officer ; *F :* brass
hat.
topographe [tɔpɔgraf], *s.m.* Topographer.
topographie [tɔpɔgrafi], *s.f.* **1.** Topography,
surveying. **2.** Topographical map.
topographique [tɔpɔgrafik], *a.* Topographic(al).
Le service topographique, the Ordnance Survey.
Carte t., ordnance map.
toponymie [tɔpɔnimi], *s.f. Ling :* Toponymy.

toquade [tɔkad], *s.f. F :* (Passing) craze, fancy.
Avoir une toquade pour qn, to be infatuated
with s.o. ; *F :* to be gone on s.o.
toquante [tɔkã:t], *s.f. P :* = TOCANTE.
toque [tɔk], *s.f. Cost :* (a) Cap (of a chef, of
French magistrate). (b) Jockey's cap. (c) (Woman's) toque.
toquer [tɔke], *v.tr.* To send (s.o.) off his head ;
to turn (s.o.'s) head ; to infatuate (s.o.).
se toquer (*d'une actrice, etc.*), to become
infatuated with (an actress, etc.).
toqué, *a. F :* **1.** Crazy, cracked, dotty.
2. Être toqué de qn, to be infatuated, madly in
love, with s.o. ; *F :* to be gone on s.o.
toquet [tɔkɛ], *s.m.* (a) (Child's) brimless cap.
(b) Mob-cap, dust-cap.
torche [tɔrʃ], *s.f.* **1.** Torch, link. *F :* Torche de
discorde, fire-brand. (Of parachute) Se mettre
en torche, to fail to open. **2.** (a) Twist of straw.
(b) *T. d'osier,* rope-border (of basket). (c) Pad (on
head, for carrying loads). (d) Saddle-cushion.
torche-pot, *s.m. Orn :* Nuthatch. *pl. Des
torche-pots.*
torcher [tɔrʃe], *v.tr.* **1.** To wipe (sth.) clean (with
rag, etc.). Se torcher, (i) to wipe oneself ;
(ii) *P :* to fight, to have a set-to. **2.** *F :* To do
(sth.) in a hurry. *Ouvrage mal torché,* scamped,
botched, piece of work. **3.** *Const :* To daub (a
wall). **4.** To twist a rope-border on (basket).
torchère [tɔrʃɛ:r], *s.f.* (a) *A :* Cresset. (b) Stand-
ard-lamp. (c) Candelabrum, candelabra, torchère.
torchette [tɔrʃɛt], *s.f.* **1.** Wisp of straw (for
cleaning). **2.** Clout ; house flannel.
torchis [tɔrʃi], *s.m. Const :* Cob, daub. *Mur
en t.,* cob wall, mud wall. [TORCHER]
torchon [tɔrʃɔ̃]. **1.** *s.m.* (a) Twist of straw.
(b) (Kitchen) rubber ; floor-cloth ; dish-cloth,
-clout ; duster. *F :* Le torchon brûle chez eux,
they lead a cat and dog life. (c) *T. végétal,* loofah.
2. *a.inv.* (a) Dentelle torchon, torchon lace.
(b) Édition torchon, cheap edition (of book).
(c) *Art :* Papier torchon, torchon-paper.
torchonner [tɔrʃɔne], *v.tr. F :* **1.** To wipe,
rub clean (plates, etc.). **2.** *P :* To scamp, botch
(piece of work).
torcol [tɔrkɔl], *s.m. Orn :* Wryneck.
tordant [tɔrdã], *a. P :* Screamingly funny
(story, joke). *C'est t.,* it's a scream.
tord-boyaux, *s.m.inv. P :* **1.** Raw spirits ;
P : rot-gut. **2.** Rat-poison.
tordeur, -euse [tɔrdœ:r, -ø:z]. **1.** *s. Tex :*
Twister (of hemp, wool) ; throwster (of silk).
2. *s.f.* Tordeuse. (a) Cable-twisting machine.
(b) *Ent :* Tortrix ; leaf-roller moth.
tord-nez, *s.m.inv. Vet :* Twitch (for mastering
horse).
tordoir [tɔrdwa:r], *s.m.* Rack-stick.
tordre [tɔrdr], *v.tr.* To twist (hemp, etc.) ; to
wring (clothes). *T. le cou à qn,* to wring s.o.'s
neck. *T. la soie,* to throw silk. Tordre la bouche,
to make a wry mouth. *Traits tordus,* distorted
features. *T. le bras à qn,* to twist s.o.'s arm.
Se t. les mains, les bras, to wring one's hands.
se tordre, to writhe, twist. *F :* Se tordre (de
rire), rire à se tordre, to split one's sides with
laughter. La pièce fait tordre le public, the play
is screamingly funny.
tore [tɔ:r], *s.m. Arch : etc :* Torus.
toréador [tɔreadɔ:r], *s.m.* Toreador, bull-fighter.
torgn(i)ole [tɔrɲɔl], *s.f. P :* Cuff, slap.
tormentille [tɔrmãti:j], *s.f. Bot :* Tormentil.
tornade [tɔrnad], *s.f.* Tornado.
toron¹ [tɔrɔ̃], *s.m.* **1.** Strand (of rope). **2.** Wisp
(of straw).

toron², *s.m. Arch:* Lower torus.

torpédo [tɔrpedo], *s.m. or f. Aut:* Open touring-car, open tourer.

torpeur [tɔrpœːr], *s.f.* Torpor.

torpille [tɔrpiːj], *s.f.* **1.** *Ich:* Torpedo, numbfish. **2.** *Navy: Aer:* Torpedo.

torpiller [tɔrpije], *v.tr.* To torpedo (ship). *s.m.* **-age.**

torpilleur [tɔrpijœːr], *s.m. Navy:* **1.** Torpedo man. **2.** (Small) destroyer; *A:* torpedo-boat.

torque [tɔrk], *s.f.* **1.** *Archeol:* Torque (of ancient Gauls). **2.** Coil ((i) of wire, (ii) of tobacco). **3.** *Her:* Crest wreath.

torréfier [tɔrrefje], *v.tr.* To torrefy; to roast (coffee, maize, etc.); (of sun, etc.) to scorch.

torrent [tɔr(r)ɑ̃], *s.m.* Torrent. *F: Il pleut à torrents,* it is raining in torrents. *T. d'injures,* stream of abuse.

torrentiel, -elle [tɔr(r)ɑ̃sjɛl], *a.* Torrential. *adv.* **-ellement.**

torrentueux, -euse [tɔr(r)ɑ̃tɥø, -øːz], *a.* Torrent-like (river, etc.).

torride [tɔrrid], *a.* Torrid (zone, etc.). *F:* Scorching (heat, etc.); broiling (weather).

tors, *f.* **torse¹** [tɔːr, tɔrs]. **1.** *a.* (*a*) Twisted (thread, etc.); thrown (silk). (*b*) (*f.* occ. **torte**) *Jambes torses, tortes,* crooked, bandy, legs. *Cou tors,* wry neck. **2.** *s.m.* (*a*) Twist, lay (of rope). (*b*) *Furn:* Twisted cord.

torsade [tɔrsad], *s.f.* **1.** (*a*) Twisted fringe; torsade. *T. de cheveux,* twist, coil, of hair. (*b*) Thick bullion (of epaulet). **2.** *Arch:* Cable moulding. [TORS]

torsader [tɔrsade], *v.tr.* To twist.

torse² [tɔrs], *s.m.* Torso (of statue, *F:* of person).

torsion [tɔrsjɔ̃], *s.f.* Torsion; twisting. *Mec:* Effort de torsion, twist; torque reaction. Moment de torsion, torque.

tort [tɔːr], *s.m.* Wrong. **1.** Error, fault. *Avouer ses torts,* to confess one's faults. **Avoir tort, être dans son tort,** to be wrong, in the wrong. **Se mettre dans son tort,** to put oneself in the wrong. **Donner tort à qn,** to decide against s.o. **Avoir des torts envers qn,** to have behaved badly to(wards) s.o. **A tort,** wrongly. **A tort ou à raison,** rightly or wrongly. **A tort et à travers,** at random; without rhyme or reason. S.a. ABSENT 2. **2.** Injury, harm, detriment, hurt. (*a*) **Faire (du) tort à qn,** (i) to wrong s.o.; to do s.o. an injustice; (ii) to damage s.o.'s cause, business, or reputation. **Faire tort à la réputation de qn,** to injure s.o.'s reputation. (*b*) **Faire tort à qn de qch.,** to wrong s.o. of sth.; to defraud s.o. of sth.

torte [tɔrt]. See TORS 1.

torticolis [tɔrtikɔli], *s.m.* Crick, (w)rick, in the neck; stiff neck; wryneck; torticollis.

tortil [tɔrtil], *s.m. Her:* Baron's coronet.

tortillage [tɔrtijaːʒ], *s.m. F:* **1.** Quibbling, wriggling. **2.** Underhand intrigue. trickery.

tortillard [tɔrtijaːr]. **1.** *a.* (*a*) Cross-grained (wood). (*b*) *Bot:* Orme tortillard, dwarf elm. **2.** *s.m. P:* (*a*) Deformed cripple. (*b*) Meandering railway; small local railway.

tortiller [tɔrtije]. **1.** *v.tr.* (*a*) To twist (up) (paper, hair, etc.); to twirl, twiddle (one's moustache). (*b*) To kink (rope). **2.** *v.i.* (*a*) Tortiller des hanches, to swing the hips (in walking). (*b*) *F:* To shuffle, prevaricate, quibble, wriggle; to use subterfuges. *s.m.* **-ement.**
se tortiller. 1. (Of serpent) To wriggle, twist. **2.** To writhe, squirm.

tortillon [tɔrtijɔ̃], *s.m.* **1.** Twist (of paper); wisp (of straw). **2.** Pad on head, for carrying loads).

tortionnaire [tɔrsjɔnɛːr]. **1.** *a.* (*a*) (Instrument) of torture. (*b*) *Jur:* Cruelly excessive; iniquitous (law, etc.). **2.** *s.m.* Torturer, executioner.

tortu [tɔrty], *a.* Crooked. *Avoir l'esprit t.,* to have a crooked, tortuous, mind.

tortue [tɔrty], *s.f.* **1.** Tortoise. *T. de mer,* turtle. Aller à pas de tortue, to go at a snail's pace. **Soupe à la tortue,** turtle soup. **Tête de veau en tortue,** mock turtle. **Pont en carapace de t.,** turtle-back deck. **2.** *Ant:* Testudo, tortoise.

tortueux, -euse [tɔrtɥø, -øːz], *a.* Tortuous, winding, meandering; twisted (tree); crooked, underhand (conduct). *adv.* **-sement.**

torture [tɔrtyːr], *s.f.* Torture. **Mettre qn à la torture,** to put s.o. to the torture. *F:* **Être à la torture,** to be on the rack, on thorns.

torturer [tɔrtyre], *v.tr.* **1.** To torture. *Se t. l'esprit,* to rack, cudgel, one's brains. **2.** *F:* To strain, twist, pervert (meaning of words, etc.).

torve [tɔrv], *a.* **Regard torve,** grim look; menacing look.

toscan, -ane¹ [tɔskɑ̃, -an], *a. & s.* Tuscan.

**Toscane². ** *Pr.n.f. Geog:* Tuscany.

tôt [to], *adv.* (*a*) Soon. *Le plus tôt possible,* as soon as possible. *La semaine prochaine au plus tôt,* next week at the earliest. **Le plus tôt sera le mieux,** the sooner the better. **Tôt ou tard,** sooner or later. S.a. AUSSITÔT, BIENTÔT, SITÔT. (*b*) *Se lever tôt,* to rise early. *Venez tôt,* come early.

total, -aux [tɔtal, -o]. **1.** *a.* Total, complete, entire, whole. *Éclipse totale,* total eclipse. **2.** *s.m.* Whole, total. *T. global,* sum total, grand total. **Au total,** on the whole, all things considered. *adv.* **-ement.**

totalisateur, -trice [tɔtalizatœːr, -tris]. **1.** *a.* Adding (machine, etc.). **2.** *s.m.* Adding-machine. *Turf:* Totalizator, *P:* tote. **3.** *s.f.* Totalisatrice, cash-register.

totaliser [tɔtalize], *v.tr.* To totalize, total up.

totalité [tɔtalite], *s.f.* Totality, whole. **En totalité,** wholly, as a whole. **Pris dans sa totalité,** taken as a whole.

totem [tɔtɛm], *s.m.* Totem.

totémisme [tɔtemism], *s.m.* Totemism.

toto [tɔto], *s.m. P:* Louse, *P:* cootie.

toton [tɔtɔ̃], *s.m.* Teetotum.

touaille [twaːj], *s.f.* Roller-towel, jack-towel.

Touareg, *F:* **Touaregs** [twarɛg], *a.inv. & s.pl. Ethn:* Tuareg.

toubib [tubib], *s.m. P:* Army doctor; 'doc.'

toucan [tukɑ̃], *s.m. Orn:* Toucan.

touchant [tuʃɑ̃]. **1.** *a.* Touching, moving, affecting (speech). **2.** *prep.* Touching, concerning, about, with regard to.

touche [tuʃ], *s.f.* **1.** (*a*) Touch, touching. **Pierre de touche,** touchstone, test. (*b*) *Bill:* Hit. **Manque de touche,** miss. *Fenc:* Hit. (*c*) *Fish:* Bite, nibble. (*d*) *Typ:* Inking. (*e*) *Hockey:* Roll-in. *Fb:* Throw-in. **Ligne de touche,** touch-line. **Hors des touches,** out of touch. **Remise en touche,** throw-in. (*f*) Touch, manner (of painter). (*g*) *F:* (External) appearance, look. *Il a une drôle de t.,* he's a queer-looking fish. (*h*) *F:* **La Sainte-Touche,** pay-day. **2.** (*a*) Digital, (finger-)key (of piano); key (of typewriter). (*b*) Finger-board (of violin); *pl.* frets (of mandolin guitar). (*c*) Tab (of alphabetical register); *pl.* thumb-index (of dictionary, etc.). (*d*) Goad (for driving cattle). **3.** *El:* Contact. *Tg: T. d'interruption,* break-key.

touche-à-tout, *s. m. & f. inv.* Meddler, busybody.

toucher [tuʃe]. I. *v.* To touch. **1.** *v.tr.* (*a*) *T. qn à l'épaule,* to touch s.o. on the shoulder. *Bill: T. une bille,* to hit a ball. *Artil: etc: T. le but,* to hit the mark. *Fenc: T. son adversaire*, to score a hit. *F: Votre observation l'a touché au vif*, your remark has touched him on the raw. *T. les bœufs*, to goad the oxen. *T. un cheval (du fouet)*, to whip up, touch up, a horse. **Toucher le piano, l'orgue**, *v.ind.tr.* toucher du piano, de l'orgue, to play the piano, the organ. *A: Touchez là!* your hand on it! *F: put it there! T. ses appointements*, *Abs.* **toucher**, to draw, receive, one's salary; to be paid. *T. un chèque*, to cash a cheque. *Mil: T. des rations*, to draw rations. (*b*) To assay, test (precious metal with touchstone). (*c*) To move, affect (s.o.). *T. le cœur de qn*, to touch s.o.'s heart. *T. qn jusqu'aux larmes*, to move s.o. to tears. (*d*) To concern, affect. *En ce qui vous touche*, as far as concerns, regards, you. (*e*) *Nau:* **Toucher terre**, to touch land. *Abs. T. à un port*, to touch, call, at a port. (*f*) *Min:* **Toucher le pétrole, un filon**, to strike oil, a seam. (*g*) *Nau:* **Toucher (le fond)**, (i) to touch bottom, the rump; (ii) to be aground. *T. sur un écueil*, to strike a reef. 2. (*a*) *v.tr.* To touch on, dwell on, deal with (fact, subject); to touch (lightly) on, allude to (subject). *Je lui en toucherai un mot*, I shall mention it to him. (*b*) *v.ind.tr.* To meddle, interfere. *Ne touchez pas à ce qui est bien*, let well alone. *Ne touchez pas à mes outils*, don't meddle with my tools; leave my tools alone. **Ne pas toucher à un plat**, to leave a dish untasted. *F:* **Sans avoir l'air d'y toucher**, in a detached manner; as if quite unconsciously. *F:* **Avoir l'air de ne pas y toucher, n'avoir pas l'air d'y toucher**, to put on an innocent air. *Cf.* NITOUCHE. 3. *v.i.* (*a*) *T. à qch.*, to be in touch, in contact, with sth.; to be near, close, to sth.; to border on sth. *L'année touche à sa fin*, the year is drawing to a close. (*b*) *T. de naissance à qn*, to be related to s.o. *Cela touche de très près à mes intérêts*, it closely affects my interests. **En ce qui touche à cette question**, as far as this question is concerned. *a.* **-able**.

se toucher. 1. To touch, adjoin; to be contiguous. 2. (Of curves) To touch, osculate.

II. **toucher**, *s.m.* Touch. **Reconnaître qch. au toucher**, to know sth. by the touch, by the feel of it.

touchette [tuʃɛt], *s.f.* Fret (of mandolin, guitar).

toue [tu], *s.f. Nau:* 1. (*a*) Warping. (*b*) Kedging. 2. (*a*) (Flat-bottomed) barge. (*b*) Chain-ferry.

touer [twe], *v.tr. Nau:* 1. (*a*) To warp. (*b*) To kedge. 2. To chain-tow. 3. To tow. *s.m.* **-age**.

touée, *s.f. Nau:* 1. (*a*) Warping. (*b*) Kedging. **Ancre de touée**, kedge. 2. Warp; warping-rope, -cable. **Filer une touée**, to pay out a cable.

touffe [tuf], *s.f.* Tuft (of hair, etc.); wisp (of straw); clump, cluster (of trees).

touffeur [tufœ:r], *s.f.* Suffocating heat (of a room); *F:* fug. [ÉTOUFFER]

touffu [tufy], *a.* Bushy (beard); thick (wood, eyebrows); thickly wooded (hillside, etc.). *Style t.*, involved style. [TOUFFE]

toujours [tuʒu:r], *adv.* 1. Always, ever. **Pour toujours, à toujours**, for ever. 2. Still. *Demeure-t-il t. là?* is he still living there? *Cherchez t.*, go on looking. **Allez toujours!** proceed! go ahead! 3. Nevertheless, all the same. *Dites t. ce que vous essayer*, anyhow I can try. *Dites t. ce que vous savez*, anyhow tell us what you know. **Toujours est-il que . . .**, the fact remains that. . . . **C'est toujours ça**, that's something anyhow.

touline [tulin], *s.f.* (*a*) Boat-rope. (*b*) Heaving-line.

toundra [tundra], *s.f. Geog:* Tundra.

toupet [tupɛ], *s.m.* 1. (*a*) Tuft of hair. (*b*) Forelock. **Faux toupet**, transformation, toupet. (*c*) Forelock (of horse). 2. *F:* Cheek, impudence, effrontery. **Payer de toupet**, to brazen it out.

toupie [tupi], *s.f.* 1. Top; esp. peg-top, spinning-top. **Faire aller une toupie**, to spin a top. *F: Dormir comme une toupie*, to sleep like a top. 2. Vertical shaper, milled cutter (of moulding-machine). 3. *P: Vieille t.*, old frump.

toupiller [tupije]. 1. *v.i. F:* (*a*) To spin round (like a top); to twirl round. (*b*) To bustle about. 2. *v.tr. Tchn:* To shape (wood).

tour[1] [tu:r], *s.f.* 1. Tower. *Arch: T. à cheval*, ridge turret. 2. *Chess:* Castle, rook.

tour[2], *s.m.* 1. (*a*) (Turning-)lathe. **Fait au tour**, (i) machine-turned; (ii) *F:* shapely (leg, etc.). *T. à pédale*, foot-lathe. *T. revolver*, turret-lathe. *T. à fileter*, screw-cutting lathe. *T. à guillocher*, rose-engine. (*b*) *T. de potier*, potter's wheel. (*c*) Turn-box (of convent, foundling-hospital). 2. (*a*) Circumference, circuit. **Faire le tour du monde**, to journey, sail, round the world. *Faire le t. du parc*, to walk, drive, round the park. *Sp:* **Tour de piste, de circuit**, lap. *F:* **Faire le tour du cadran**, to sleep the clock round. **Faire le grand tour**, to take the longest way round. **Avoir quarante pouces de tour de taille**, to be forty inches round the waist. **Tour de poitrine**, chest or bust measurement. **Tour de tête**, size in hats. S.a. HANCHE 1. (*b*) **Tour de lit**, bed-valance. *Cost:* **Tour de cou**, necklet (of fur); neck-ribbon. (*c*) *Nau: T. de bitte*, turn round the bitt. *Prendre un t.*, to take a turn. (*d*) **Tours et retours d'un chemin**, twists and turns of a road. (*e*) **Turn** (of phrase); shape, contour (of face); course, direction (of business affair). **Donner un bon tour à qch.**, (i) to give sth. a favourable turn; (ii) to put sth. in a favourable light. *T. de pensée d'un écrivain*, cast of thought of a writer. (*f*) **Tour de reins**, twist, strain, in the back. 3. (*a*) Round, revolution, turn. 2000 *tours à la minute*, 2000 revolutions a minute. **Donner un tour de clef à la porte**, to lock the door. **Frapper à tour de bras**, to strike with all one's might. **Son sang n'a fait qu'un tour**, it gave him a dreadful shock. S.a. DEMI-TOUR. (*b*) Stroll. *(Aller) faire un t.*, to go for a stroll, to take a walk. (*c*) Trip, tour. *Faire un t. sur le continent*, to take a continental trip. 4. Rotation, turn. **A qui le tour?** whose turn is it? **Tour de service**, spell of duty. **Chacun à son tour**, each one in his turn. S.a. CHACUN 2. **Tour à tour**, by turns, in turn(s); turn and turn about. **A tour de rôle**, in turn, by roster. 5. Trick, feat. *Je fis exécuter quelques tours à mes animaux*, I put my animals through some tricks. **Faire, jouer, un mauvais tour à qn**, to play s.o. a nasty trick. **Le tour de main**, the knack (of doing sth.). **Tour d'adresse**, (i) piece of sleight of hand; (ii) feat of acrobatics. **Tour de force**, feat of strength. S.a. GOBELET, MAIN 1 (*c*), MÉTIER 1, PASSE-PASSE.

tourangeau, -elle [turãʒo, -ɛl], *a. & s.* (Native, inhabitant) (i) of Tours, (ii) of Touraine.

tourbe[1] [turb], *s.f.* Mob, rabble.

tourbe[2], *s.f.* Peat, turf. **Une motte de tourbe**, a peat. **Litière de tourbe**, peat litter.

tourbeux, -euse [turbø, -ø:z], *a.* 1. Peaty, boggy. 2. Growing in peat-bogs.

tourbier, -ière [turbje, -jɛ:r]. 1. *a.* Peaty (soil). 2. *s.m.* (*a*) Peat-worker. (*b*) Owner of peat-bogs. 3. *s.f.* Tourbière, peat-bog.

tourbillon [turbijõ], *s.m.* 1. Whirlwind; swirl (of dust). **Monter en tourbillons**, to swirl up. 2. (*a*) Whirlpool. (*b*) Eddy. (*c*) *F:* Whirl, bustle (of political life); vortex, **giddy round** (of pleasures, etc.).

tourbillonn|er [turbijɔne], *v.i.* To whirl (round); to eddy, swirl. *s.m.* **-ement.**

tour-du-cou, *s.m.* Neckband (of shirt).

tourelle [turɛl], *s.f.* (*a*) *Arch:* Turret. (*b*) *Navy:* (i) (Gun-)turret. (ii) *T. de contrôle, de veille,* conning-tower. (*c*) Turret, capstan (of lathe).

touret [turɛ], *s.m.* **1.** Small wheel (for spinning, etc.). **2.** (*a*) Reel. (*b*) Drum (of winch); *El.E:* cable-drum. **3.** *Tls:* Bow-drill. **4.** *Nau:* Thole-pin. [TOUR²]

tourie [turi], *s.f.* Carboy.

tourier, -ière [turje, -jɛːr], *s.* Monk, nun, in attendance at the turn-box of a convent.

tourillon [turijɔ̃], *s.m.* **1.** (*a*) Pivot(-pin), swivel-pin. (*b*) Gudgeon(-pin) (in piston or cross-head); link-pin (of roller-chain). **2.** (*a*) Journal (of shaft, of axle). (*b*) Trunnion (of gun, of oscillating cylinder). (*c*) Crank-pin.

tourisme [turism], *s.m.* Travel for pleasure; touring. **Bureau de tourisme,** travel agency, tourist agency. **Voiture de tourisme,** touring-car.

touriste [turist], *s. m. & f.* (*a*) Tourist. (*b*) Tripper.

touristique [turistik], *a.* Touristic.

tourlourou [turluru], *s.m.* **1.** *P: A:* Foot-soldier; 'soldier-boy.' **2.** *F:* Land-crab.

tourmaline [turmalin], *s.f. Miner:* Tour-malin(e).

tourment [turmɑ̃], *s.m.* (*a*) Torment, torture. *Il a fait le t. de ma vie,* he has been the bane of my life. (*b*) (Bodily, mental) anguish, pain. *Les tourments de la jalousie,* the pangs of jealousy.

tourmente [turmɑ̃t], *s.f.* Gale, storm, tempest. **Tourmente de neige,** blizzard. *F: La t. politique,* the turmoil of politics.

tourmenter [turmɑ̃te], *v.tr.* **1.** To torture, torment. **2.** (*a*) To harass, trouble, worry; *F:* to bother. (*b*) To plague, pester, tease, bait. *Ses créanciers le tourmentent,* his creditors are dunning him. *T. un bouton,* to fiddle with a button.

se tourmenter, to be uneasy; to fret, worry; *F:* to bother.

tourmenté, *a.* (*a*) Distorted, contorted. (*b*) Tormented, tortured. (*c*) Uneasy, agitated (mind); turbulent, seething (sea).

tournage [turnaːʒ], *s.m.* **1.** Turning (on the lathe); lathe-work. **2.** **Taquet de tournage,** belaying-cleat.

tournailler [turnaje]. *F:* **1.** *v.i.* (*a*) To keep wandering round and round. (*b*) To prowl (about). **2.** *v.tr.* To twiddle (sth.) round and round.

tournant [turnɑ̃]. **1.** *a.* (*a*) Turning; revolving (bookcase, etc.); slewing (crane, etc.); live (axle). **Pont tournant,** swing-bridge. **Plaque tournante,** turn-table. (*b*) Winding (road); spiral (staircase). **2.** *s.m.* (*a*) Turning, bend (of road, river); street corner. *Aut: T. brusque,* dangerous corner. *F:* **Les tournants de l'histoire,** the turning-points of history. (*b*) Whirlpool, eddy.

tourne-à-gauche, *s.m.inv. Tls:* **1.** (*a*) Wrench. (*b*) Stock (for dies). **2.** Saw-set.

tournebroche [turnəbrɔʃ], *s.m.* **1.** Roasting-jack. **2.** *A:* Turnspit (dog or boy).

tournedos [turnədo], *s.m. Cu:* Fillet steak.

tournelle [turnɛl], *s.f. A:* (*a*) Small tower. (*b*) Small castle.

tournemain [turnəmɛ̃], *s.m.* (= *tour de main*) **En un tournemain,** in a trice, in the twinkling of an eye.

tournement [turnəmɑ̃], *s.m.* **Tournement de tête,** vertigo, giddiness.

tourne-pierre, *s.m. Orn:* Turnstone.

tourner [turne], *v.* To turn. **I.** *v.tr.* (*a*) To fashion, shape, turn, (sth.) on a lathe. *F: Bien t. une phrase,* to give a neat turn to a phrase. *Cer: T. un pot,* to throw a pot. (*b*) To revolve, turn round, rotate (wheel, etc.). *T. qch. autour de qch.,* to wind sth. round sth. *T. la tête, les yeux, vers qn,* to turn one's head, one's eyes, towards s.o. **Tourner le dos à qn,** (i) to turn one's back on s.o.; (ii) to have one's back turned to s.o.; to face the other way. **Tourner le dos à ses assaillants,** to turn tail. *T. les pieds en dedans,* to turn in one's toes. S.a. POUCE 1. **Tourner bride,** to turn one's horse's head (and gallop away). *Cin:* **Tourner un film,** (i) to take, shoot, a film; (ii) to play, star, in a film. *T. une scène,* to film a scene. (*c*) To change, convert. *T. tout en mal,* to put a bad complexion upon everything. **Tourner qn en ridicule,** to hold s.o. up to ridicule. (*d*) To turn over (page, etc.). (*e*) *T. un pardessus,* to turn an overcoat. S.a. CASAQUE 1. (*f*) To get round (obstacle); to evade, dodge (difficulty, the law). (*g*) *Il lui a tourné la tête,* she has become infatuated with him. **Cela m'a tourné l'estomac,** it turned my stomach. **2.** *v.i.* (*a*) To revolve; to go round; (of top) to spin. *La terre tourne autour du soleil,* the earth revolves round the sun. *F:* **Allons, l'heure tourne!** come on, time is getting on! **Tourner autour du pot,** to beat about the bush. **Voilà huit jours qu'il tourne autour d'elle,** he's been dangling round her for a week. **Le pied lui a tourné,** he twisted his ankle. (*b*) To change in direction. *Tournez à gauche,* turn to the left. **Tourner court,** (i) to turn short, sharply; (ii) to make off. *F:* **Ne savoir de quel côté tourner,** not to know which way to turn. *Le temps tourne au froid,* it is turning cold. *Sa chance a tourné,* his luck has turned. (*c*) (Of fruit, etc.) To colour, ripen. (*d*) To turn out, result. (Of pers.) **Mal tourner,** to go to the bad. *Cela tournera mal,* evil will come of it. (*e*) *L'affaire tournait au tragique,* the affair was taking a tragic turn, was turning to tragedy. (Of wine) *T. au vinaigre,* to turn acid. *Abs. Lait qui tourne,* milk that is turning, curdling. **Faire t. qch.,** to curdle sth.; to turn sth. sour. (*f*) *Cin: T. dans un film,* to act for a film.

se tourner. I. (*a*) *Se t. vers qn, du côté de qn,* to turn towards s.o. (*b*) *Se t. contre qn,* to turn against s.o. (*c*) To turn round. *Tournez-vous un peu que je vous voie de côté,* turn round a little and let me see your side-face. **2.** *Le temps se tourne au beau,* the weather is turning fine.

tourné, *a.* **1.** Turned (on lathe). *Jeune fille bien tournée,* well set up, handsome, girl. *Phrase bien tournée,* neatly turned sentence. **Esprit mal tourné,** cross-grained mind. **2.** *Esprit t. aux plaisirs,* mind disposed to enjoyment. **3.** (*a*) Sour (milk, etc.). (*b*) **Avoir la tête tournée,** (i) to have one's head turned (by success, etc.); (ii) to be distracted (by fear, etc.).

tournée, *s.f.* **1.** Round, tour (of official); round of visits (of doctor); circuit (of judge). *La t. du facteur,* the postman's round. **Troupe en tournée,** theatrical company on tour. **Faire la tournée des musées,** to go round, *F:* to do, the picture galleries. *Faire une t. électorale,* to canvass a constituency. **2.** *F:* **Payer une tournée,** to stand a round (of drinks).

tournerie [turnəri], *s.f.* Turner's shop.

tournesol [turnəsɔl], *s.m.* **1.** *Bot:* Turnsole, sunflower. **2.** **Papier (de) tournesol,** litmus paper.

tournette [turnɛt], *s.f.* **1.** Reel; wool-winder. **2.** Washer cutter; circular glass-cutter. **3.** (*a*) Turn-table (for small objects). (*b*) (Drying) whirler. **4.** Squirrel's cage.

tourneur, -euse [turnœːr, -øːz]. **1.** *a.* Derviche tourneur, dancing dervish. **2.** *s.m.* Turner. *T. de vis*, screw-cutter. **3.** *s.f. Tex:* Tourneuse, (woman) reeler, winder (of silk).

tourne-vent, *s.m.inv.* Chimney-cowl.

tournevis [turnəvis], *s.m. Tls:* Screw-driver.

tourniole [turnjɔl], *s.f.* Whitlow, esp. felon.

tourniquet [turnikɛ], *s.m.* **1.** Tourniquet (-oompteur), turnstile. **2.** (*a*) Roller (for ropes, etc., to pass over). (*b*) Swivel. (*c*) Button, turnbuckle (on shutter, etc.). **3.** (*a*) Whirligig. (*b*) Catherine-wheel. (*c*) *Ph:* T. hydraulique, reaction wheel. **4.** *Surg:* Tourniquet. **5.** *Ent:* Whirligig-beetle.

tournis [turni], *s.m. Vet:* Staggers, sturdy.

tournoi [turnwa], *s.m.* Tournament, tourney; (whist) drive.

tournoiement [turnwamã], *s.m.* **1.** Whirling; swirling; wheeling (of birds). **2.** (*a*) Giddiness, dizziness. (*b*) = TOURNIS.

tournoy|er [turnwaje], *v.i.* (je tournoie; je tournoierai) To turn round and round; to whirl; (of water) to eddy, swirl. Faire tournoyer qch., to twirl, whirl, sth. *a.* **-ant.**

tournure [turnyːr], *s.f.* **1.** *Metalw:* Turnings (from a lathe). **2.** Turn, course (of events). *Les affaires prennent une vilaine t.*, things are shaping badly, are looking black. **3.** Shape, form, figure, appearance. *Quelqu'un avec votre 't.*, someone with your figure. **Tournure d'esprit,** cast, turn, of mind. *Donner une autre tournure à la chose,* to put a new face on the matter. **4.** *Cost: A:* Bustle; dress-improver.

tourte [turt], *s.f.* (*a*) Raised pie (of the *vol-au-vent* type); (covered) tart. (*b*) *P:* Duffer, muff.

tourteau [turto], *s.m.* **1.** Oil-cake (for cattle). **2.** Edible crab. **3.** Centre-boss (of wheel, crank). **4.** *Her:* Roundel.

tourtereau [turtəro], *s.m.* Young turtle-dove. *F:* **S'aimer comme deux tourtereaux,** to bill and coo.

tourterelle [turtərɛl], *s.f.* Turtle-dove.

tourtière [turtjɛːr], *s.f.* Pie-dish; baking-tin.

tous. See TOUT.

Toussaint (la) [latusɛ̃]. *Pr.n.f.* All Saints' day; All-Hallows. *La veille de la T.*, Hallowe'en.

touss|er [tuse], *v.i.* To cough. Tousser gras, to cough up phlegm. *s.* **-eur, -euse.**

tousserie [tusri], *s.f.* (Constant) coughing (esp. among audience).

toussoter [tusɔte], *v.i.* (*a*) To hem; to cough slightly. (*b*) To have a slight cough.

tout, toute, *pl.* **tous, toutes** [tu, tut, tu, tut]. (When *tous* is a pronoun it is pronounced [tuːs]) All. **I.** *a.* **1.** (Noun undetermined) Any, every, all. *Toute profession est honnête,* any, every, calling is honest. *Pour tout mobilier deux petits lits,* for sole furniture two small beds. **Tout autre que vous,** anybody but you. *J'ai toute raison de croire que . . .,* I have every reason to believe that. . . . **2.** (Intensive) *De toute force il nous faut . . .,* we absolutely must. . . . *Dans sa toute jeunesse,* when he was quite a child; in his early youth. *Des arbres de toute beauté,* most beautiful trees. **A toute vitesse, à toute allure, à toute bride, à toute vapeur,** at full speed. **Tout à vous,** entirely yours. *De toute importance,* of the first importance. **3.** The whole; all. *Toute la famille,* the whole family, all the family. *Pendant tout l'hiver,* throughout the winter; all

through the winter. *L'armée cédait sur toute la ligne,* the army was giving way all along the line. *Au milieu de tout ça . . .,* in the midst of it all. . . . S.a. MONDE 2. **4.** All, every. *Tous les invités,* all the guests. *Tous ces livres,* all these books. **Tous les jours,** every day. **Toutes les fois que . . .,** every time that . . .; whenever. . . . Au-dessus de toutes choses . . ., above all. . . . **5.** (With numerals) Tous (les) deux, both. *Tous (les) trois,* all three. Tous les deux jours, every other day. Tous les trois jours, every third day. **6.** (With *un*) *Tout un quartier de la ville a été incendié,* a whole quarter of the town was burnt. C'est toute une histoire, (i) it's a long story; (ii) *F:* it's no end of a job.

II. tout, *pron.* **1.** *sg.neut.* All, everything. *Il faut tout lui montrer, il faut lui tout montrer,* we must show him everything. **Tout** est bien qui finit bien, all's well that ends well. C'est tout ce qu'il y a de plus beau, de plus drôle, it is most beautiful; nothing could be funnier. *Il mange de tout,* he eats anything. *Vendre de tout,* to deal in all sorts of wares. Il est capable de tout, he is capable of anything. C'est tout dire, I needn't say more. C'est tout un, it's all one. En tout et pour tout . . ., first and last. . . . *P:* Drôle comme tout, ever so funny, awfully funny. *Rire comme tout,* to laugh like anything. **2.** *pl.* Une (bonne) fois pour toutes, once for all. *Venez tous* [tuːs]! come all of you! *Le meilleur de tous,* the best of them all. **Tous à la fois,** all together. Tous sans exception, all without exception; one and all.

III. tout, *s.m.* **1.** Le tout, the whole. *Le tout est de réussir,* the main thing is to succeed. *Il faut risquer le tout pour le tout,* we must stake everything; *F:* it's neck or nothing. Du tout au tout, entirely. *La situation a changé du tout au tout,* the situation has entirely changed. **En tout ou en partie,** wholly or partly. **Pas du tout,** *F:* du tout, not at all. S.a. METTRE I, RIEN I. 2. **2.** *Mth:* (*pl.* **touts**) Total. (In charades) Mon tout, all, my whole.

IV. tout, *adv.* (Intensive) (Before a fem.adj. beginning with a consonant or *h* 'aspirate' *tout* becomes *toute*) **1.** Quite, entirely, completely, very. *Tout nouveau(x), toute(s) nouvelle(s),* quite new. *Elle était encore toute petite,* she was still quite little. *Tout de noir vêtue, toute vêtue de noir,* dressed all in black. **Des lutteurs de tout premier ordre,** wrestlers of the very first order. *Une tout autre personne,* quite a different person. *Tout droit,* bolt upright. *Tout neuf,* brand new. *Tout nu,* stark naked. *Tout éveillé,* wide awake. **Vêtement tout fait,** ready-made garment. *Tout au bout,* right at the end. S.a. CONTRE I, 2. *Tout doux!* gently! **Tout à fait,** quite, entirely, altogether. **Tout au plus,** at the very most. **Tout au moins, tout le moins,** at the very least. (At end of letter) Tout à vous, yours very truly. S.a. AUTANT I, BON I. 12, COUP 4, COURT¹ 2, GO, HAUT II. I, HEURE 2, LONG 2, MÊME 3, SUITE I, UN I. **2.** (With gerund) Tout en parlant, while speaking. **3.** (Concessive) Tout ignorant qu'il est, qu'il soit, however ignorant he is; ignorant though he may be. **4.** (Invariable in) Être tout yeux, tout oreilles, to be all eyes, all ears. *Elle est tout le portrait de sa mère,* she is the living image of her mother.

tout-à-l'égout, *s.m.* Direct-to-sewer drainage; main-drainage.

toute-bonne, *s.f.* **1.** *Bot:* Clary. **2.** Variety of pear. *pl.* Des toutes-bonnes.

toutefois [tutfwa], *adv.* Yet, nevertheless, however.

toute-puissance, *s.f.* Omnipotence.

toutou [tutu], *s.m.* Doggie, bow-wow. *pl. Des toutous.*

Tout-Paris, *s.m.* F: The Paris-that-matters; fashionable Paris.

tout-puissant, *f.* **toute-puissante,** *a.* Almighty, omnipotent, all-powerful. *s.m.* Le Tout-Puissant, the Almighty. *pl. Tout-puissants, toutes-puissantes.*

toux, *s.f.* Cough. **Accès, quinte, de toux,** fit of coughing. *T. grasse,* loose cough.

toxémie [tɔksemi], *s.f.* Blood-poisoning.

toxicité [tɔksisite], *s.f.* Toxicity, poisonousness.

toxicologie [tɔksikɔlɔʒi], *s.f.* Toxicology.

toxicomane [tɔksikɔman], *s.m. & f.* Drug addict; F: dope-addict, dope-fiend.

toxicomanie [tɔksikɔmani], *s.f.* Drug-habit; toxicomania; F: dope-habit.

toxine [tɔksin], *s.f. Physiol:* Toxin.

toxique [tɔksik]. **I.** *a.* Toxic. **Gaz toxique,** poisonous gas; *Mil: F:* poison gas. **2.** *s.m.* Poison.

trac[1] [trak], *s.m. P:* Funk, fright; *Th:* stage-fright. **Avoir le trac,** to be in a funk, to get the wind up.

trac[2], *s.m.* **Tout à trac,** thoughtlessly; without reflection.

traçant [trasɑ̃], *a.* Running, creeping (root).

tracas [traka], *s.m.* Worry, trouble, bother. **Avoir du tracas,** to be worried.

tracasser [trakase], *v.tr.* To worry, bother, plague. *a.* **-ant.** *s.m.* **-ement.**
se tracasser, to worry.

tracasserie [trakasri], *s.f.* **I.** Worry, fuss (about nothing). **2.** Pestering, worrying (of s.o.). **3.** *pl.* Vexatious or ill-natured interference; pin-pricks.

tracassier, -ière [trakasje, -jɛːr]. **I.** *a.* (*a*) Vexatious. (*b*) Pestering, interfering (person). (*c*) Fussy (person). **Peu tracassier,** easy-going. **2.** *s.* Busybody; fussy person.

trace [tras], *s.f.* Trace. **I.** (*a*) Trail, track, spoor (of beast); foot-print(s), trail (of person); (wheel-)track (of vehicle). (Of hounds) **Perdre la trace,** to lose the trail. F: *Marcher sur les traces de qn,* to tread in s.o.'s footsteps. *Laisser une t. profonde,* to leave a deep impression behind. (*b*) Weal, scar, mark (of wound, etc.). (*c*) (Slight) trace. *Pas de traces de poison,* no traces of poison. **2.** *Geom: Traces d'une droite,* traces of a straight line.

tracelet [traslɛ], *s.m. Tls:* Scriber, tracing-awl.

tracer [trase], *v.* (je traçai(s); n. traçons) **I.** *v.tr.* To trace. (*a*) To lay out (road, railway); to mark out (tennis-court); to plot, set out (curve); to map out (route). *T. une ligne de conduite,* to lay down a line of conduct. (*b*) To draw (a line); to outline (plan, pattern). **Aiguille à tracer,** scriber. *T. quelques lignes,* to write, pen, a few lines. **2.** *v.i.* (*a*) (Of roots) To run out; to creep. (*b*) (Of moles) To burrow. *s.m.* **-çage.**
tracé, *s.m.* **I.** (*a*) Tracing, sketching; setting out, plotting (of curve, etc.); marking out (of tennis-court); laying out (of road). (*b*) Lay-out (of town, railway system, etc.); lie (of a road, etc.). **2.** (*a*) Outline, sketch, diagram, drawing. (*b*) Graph.

traceret [trasrɛ], *s.m.* = TRACELET.

traceur, -euse [trasœːr, -øːz], *a.* Tracer. **Projectile traceur,** balle traceuse, tracer-bullet.

trachéal, -aux [trakeal, -o], *a. Anat:* Tracheal.

trachée [traʃe], *s.f.* **I.** (*a*) *Ent:* Trachea. (*b*) *Bot:* Duct. **2.** = TRACHÉE-ARTÈRE.

trachée-artère, *s.f.* Trachea, windpipe.

trachéotomie [trakeotomi], *s.f.* Tracheotomy.

trachome [trakoːm], *s.m. Med:* Trachoma; granular conjunctivitis.

traçoir [traswaːr], *s.m.* = TRACELET.

tractation [traktasjɔ̃], *s.f. Pej:* (Underhand) deal or dealing; bargaining.

tracteur [traktœːr], *s.m.* Tractor, traction-engine.

tractif, -ive [traktif, -iːv], *a.* Tractive (effort, force). *Roues tractives,* traction-wheels (of locomotive). *Av:* **Hélice tractive,** tractor-propeller.

traction [traksjɔ̃], *s.f.* Traction. (*a*) Pulling. **Résistance à la traction,** tensile strength. **Effort de traction,** pull. *Gym:* **Faire une traction, des tractions,** to pull up to the bar. (*b*) Draught. *T. à bras,* man-haulage. *T. automobile,* motor traction. *Véhicule à t. mécanique,* mechanically propelled vehicle.

tradition [tradisjɔ̃], *s.f.* **I.** (*a*) Tradition. **Il est de tradition de . . ., que** + *sub.*, it is traditional to . . ., that. . . . (*b*) Folklore. **2.** *Jur:* Delivery, handing over (of property).

traditionnel, -elle [tradisjɔnɛl], *a.* Traditional; standing (custom). *adv.* **-ellement.**

traducteur, -trice [tradyktœːr, -tris]. **I.** *s.* Translator. **2.** *s.m. Cin:* **Traducteur phonique,** sound unit.

traduction [tradyksjɔ̃], *s.f.* **I.** Translating. **2.** Translation. **Traduction inexacte,** mistranslation.

traduire [tradɥiːr], *v.tr.* (*pr.p.* **traduisant;** *p.p.* **traduit;** *pr.ind.* **je traduis,** n. **traduisons;** *p.h.* **je traduisis;** *fu.* **je traduirai**) **I.** *Jur: T. qn en justice,* to sue, prosecute, indict, s.o. *T. qn en conseil de guerre,* to summon s.o. before a court martial. **2.** (*a*) To translate (*en,* into). (*b*) To decode (a cable). (*c*) To interpret, explain, express (sentiment, idea, etc.). *Vous traduisez mal ma pensée,* you misinterpret me. *Sa douleur se traduisit par des larmes,* his grief found expression in tears.

traduisible [tradɥizibl], *a.* **I.** *T. en justice,* liable to prosecution; liable to be sued. **2.** Translatable.

trafic [trafik], *s.m.* Traffic. **I.** (*a*) Trading, trade. (*b*) *Pej:* Illicit trading. *Le t. des stupéfiants,* the drug traffic. **Faire trafic de son influence,** to trade on one's influence. **2.** *T. de chemin de fer,* railway traffic. **Ligne à grand trafic,** busy line. **Heures de fort trafic,** busy hours; peak hours. **Heures de faible trafic,** slack hours.

trafiquant [trafikɑ̃], *s.m.* (*a*) Trader, trafficker. (*b*) *Pej:* Trafficker.

trafiquer [trafike]. **I.** *v.i.* To traffic, deal, trade (*en,* in). *Pej: T. de sa conscience,* to sell one's conscience. *T. de son honneur,* to make traffic of one's honour. **2.** *v.tr.* To negotiate (a bill, etc.).

trafiqueur, -euse [trafikœːr, -øːz], *s. Pej:* Trafficker (*de, en,* in).

tragédie [traʒedi], *s.f.* Tragedy. **I.** *Les tragédies de Racine,* the tragedies of Racine. **2.** The art of tragedy.

tragédien, -ienne [traʒedjɛ̃, -jɛn], *s.* Tragedian; *f.* tragedian, tragédienne.

tragi-comédie, *s.f.* Tragi-comedy.

tragi-comique, *a.* Tragi-comic(al).

tragique [traʒik]. **I.** (*a*) *a.* Tragic (writer, play); tragic(al) (event). (*b*) *s.m.* Tragicalness; tragic side (of an event). **Cela tourne au tragique,** the thing is becoming tragic. **Prendre qch. au tragique,** to make a tragedy of sth.; *F:* to get panicky. **2.** *s.m.* Tragic poet. **3.** *s.m.* **Le tragique,** the tragic art; tragedy. *adv.* **-ment,** -ally.

tragus [tragyːs], *s.m. Anat:* Tragus (of ear).

trahir [trair], *v.tr.* To betray. **1.** To reveal, disclose, *F:* give away (secret). **Trahir sa pensée, se trahir**, *F:* to give oneself away. **2.** *T. qn*, to play s.o. false. *Ne me trahissez pas*, do not betray me; *F:* don't give me away. *T. ses serments*, to be false to one's oaths.

trahison [traizɔ̃], *s.f.* **1.** (a) Treachery, perfidy. (b) *Jur:* Treason. **Haute trahison**, high treason. **2.** Betrayal, betraying.

traille [traːj], *s.f.* **1.** Trail-bridge or ferry. **2.** *Fish:* Trawl(-net). *Pêcher à la t.*, to trawl.

train [trɛ̃], *s.m.* **1.** (a) Train, string, line of vehicles, etc.). *T. de bois*, timber raft, float. **Train de roues**, (i) set of wheels; (ii) *Mec.E:* wheel train. *T. d'engrenages*, gear-train. **Train baladeur**, sliding gear. *W.Tel:* *T. d'ondes*, train of waves. (b) (Railway-)train. *T. de voyageurs*, passenger train. *T. de marchandises*, goods train. *T. omnibus*, stopping train. *T. direct*, through-train, non-stop train. **Monter dans le train**, to get in. **Descendre de train**, to get out. S.a. INTER-COMMUNICATION, MIXTE 2. (c) *Mil:* Train (of transport). **Le train des équipages**, *F:* le Train, approx. = the Army Service Corps. (d) Suite, attendants; train (of servants, etc.). (e) Quarters (of horse). *T. de derrière*, hind quarters. (f) *Av:* **Train d'atterrissage**, under-carriage. **2.** Movement. (a) Pace, rate. **Cheval au t. doux**, easy-paced horse. **Mener une auto bon train**, to drive a car at a good rate; to drive fast. **Aller bon train**, to go at a good round pace. **Aller son petit train**, to jog along. **A fond de train**, at full speed, at top speed. **Au train dont il va, à ce train-là**, at the rate he is going, at that rate. *Sp: Cy:* **Meneur de train**, pace-maker. (b) **Il y a quelque chose en train**, there is something afoot, something in the wind. **Mettre qch. en train**, to start sth.; to set sth. going. *Typ:* **Mettre en train**, to make ready. *C'est lui qui met tout en t.*, he is the life and soul of the whole thing. **L'affaire est mal en train**, the business is hanging fire. *Le malade est en bon t.*, the patient is doing well. **Être en train de faire qch.**, to be engaged in, busy, doing sth. *Il est en t. de travailler*, he is at work. **Le train ordinaire des jours**, the daily round. **Les choses vont leur train**, things are proceeding as usual; *F:* we are jogging along. *F:* **Être dans le train**, to be in the swim. (c) Mode of life. **Train de maison**, style of living. **Mener grand train**, to live on a grand scale. **Mener un train d'enfer**, to go the pace. **Faire du train, faire un train de tous les diables**, to kick up, raise, a dust, a shindy. **3.** Mood. **Être en train**, to be in good spirits, in good form. **Être mal en train**, to be out of sorts. *Je ne suis pas en t. de rire*, I am in no laughing mood.

traînage [trɛnaːʒ], *s.m.* Hauling, haulage; sledging, sleighing. **Câble de traînage**, haulage rope.

traînant [trɛnɑ̃], *a.* **1.** Dragging, trailing. **2.** Languid, listless (life); drawling (voice); shambling, shuffling (gait); drifting (clouds); lifeless (style).

traînard [trɛnaːr], *s.m.* (a) *Mil:* Straggler, laggard. (b) *F:* Slow-coach; dawdler.

traînasse [trɛnas], *s.f.* **1.** *Bot:* Knotgrass, hogweed. **2.** *Ven:* Drag-net.

traînasser [trɛnase], *v.i.* To loaf, loiter; to trail about.

traîne [trɛn], *s.f.* **1.** Being dragged. *Nau:* A la **traîne**, (i) in tow; (ii) astern. **2.** Object, rope, bundle, etc., dragged behind; esp. train (of lady's dress). **3.** Seine(-net), drag-net, trail-net.

traîneau [trɛno], *s.m.* Sledge, sleigh. **Chien de traîneau**, sledge-dog; husky.

traîn|er [trɛne]. **1.** *v.tr.* To drag, pull, trail, haul, draw, (sth.) along; to tow (barges); to drag on, drag out (one's existence); to spin out, drag out (speech); to drawl (one's words). *T. une vie de misère*, to drag out a wretched life. **Traîner la jambe**, to be lame, to have a limp. **Traîner le pied**, to lag behind. *S'avancer en traînant le pas*, to slouch, shamble, shuffle, along. *F:* **Traîner qn dans la boue**, to drag s.o., s.o.'s name, through the mud, through the mire. **2.** *v.i.* (a) To trail, draggle (in the dust, etc.). (b) To lag behind; to trail behind; to straggle. (c) To linger, loiter, dawdle. With cogn. acc. **Traîner la rue, traîner les rues**, to loaf. (d) **Laisser traîner son argent**, to leave one's money lying about. *Cela traîne partout*, it is found, met with, everywhere. (e) To flag, drag, languish. *L'affaire traîne*, the matter hangs fire. (Of lawsuit) **Traîner en longueur**, to go on very slowly, to drag (on). *Laisser t. un compte*, to leave an account unpaid. *s.m.* **-ement**.

se traîner. **1.** (a) To crawl (along). (b) **Se traîner aux genoux de qn**, to go on one's knees to s.o. **2.** To drag oneself along; to move with difficulty. *Des fumées se traînent dans le ciel*, trails of smoke drift across the sky.

traînée, *s.f.* **1.** (a) Trail (of smoke, etc.); train (of gunpowder). **Se répandre comme une traînée de poudre**, to spread like wildfire. (b) *Av:* **Effort de traînée**, drag. (c) Air lag (of bomb). **2.** *Fish:* Ground-line, bottom-line. **3.** *Bot:* Runner.

traîneur, -euse [trɛnœːr, -øːz], *s.* **1.** Dragger, trailer (of sth.); hauler. *F:* **Traîneur de sabre d'épée**, swaggerer, swashbuckler. **2.** Straggler, laggard. **3.** Sleigh-driver.

train-paquebot, *s.m.* Boat-train. *pl. Des trains-paquebots.*

train-poste, *s.m.* Mail-train, limited mail. *pl. Des trains-poste(s).*

train-train [trɛ̃trɛ̃], *s.m.* *F:* Round, routine. *Le t.-t. quotidien de la vie*, life's daily grind; the trivial round. *Les choses vont leur train-train*, we are jogging along.

traire [trɛːr], *v.pr.* (pr.p. trayant; p.p. trait; pr.ind. je trais, n. trayons, ils traient; fu. je trairai; no p.h.) **1.** *T. une vache*, to milk a cow. **2.** *T. le lait*, to draw the milk.

trait [trɛ], *s.m.* **1.** (a) Pulling. (At chess or draughts) **Avoir le trait**, to have first move. **Tout d'un trait**, at one stretch. **Cheval de trait**, draught-horse, cart-horse. (b) Trace (of harness); leash (of dog). **2.** (a) Projection, throwing, shooting (of missile). **Armes de trait**, missile weapons. (b) Arrow, dart, *Poet:* shaft. *F:* **Partir comme un trait**, to be off like an arrow, like a shot. *Les traits de Jupiter*, Jove's thunderbolts. *T. de satire*, gibe. **Envoyer, lancer, un trait à qn**, to have a dig, a fling, at s.o. (c) Beam (of light). *Le soleil darde ses traits*, the sun darts its beams. (d) Flash (of light). **Trait d'esprit**, flash of wit; witticism; sally. (e) *Mus:* (i) Brilliant passage; (ii) run; (iii) melodic passage. **3.** Draught, gulp. *D'un (seul) trait*, at one gulp, *F:* at one go. **4.** (a) Stroke, mark, line, streak, bar. *D'un t. de plume*, with a stroke of the pen. **Dessin au trait**, outline drawing. **Gravure au trait**, line engraving. **Décrire qch. à grands traits**, to give a bold outline of sth. *Tg:* **Points et traits**, dots and dashes. (b) **Trait d'union**, hyphen. (c) Kerf, saw-cut. **5.** (a) Feature, lineament (of face). (b) Trait (of character). **6.** Act, deed (of courage, kindness). **Trait de génie**, stroke of genius. *Ce sont là de ses traits*, those are some of his tricks. **7.** **Avoir trait à qch.**, to have reference to sth.; to refer to sth.

traitable [trɛtabl], *a.* Tractable, manageable, docile.

traitant [trɛtɑ̃]. **1.** *a.* **Médecin traitant**, practising doctor, medical practitioner. **2.** *s.m. Hist :* Farmer of revenue, of taxes.

traite [trɛt], *s.f.* **1.** Stretch (of road); stage (of journey). *J'ai fait une longue t.*, I have come a long way. **(Tout) d'une traite,** at a stretch. **2.** Transport (of goods); trading. *La t. des noirs, des nègres, Abs.* **la traite,** the slave-trade. **3.** *Com :* (*a*) Drawing (of a bill of exchange). (*b*) (Banker's) draft; bill (of exchange). **Faire traite sur qn,** to draw (a bill) on s.o. **4.** (*a*) Milking. (*b*) The milk (of one milking).

traitement [trɛtmɑ̃], *s.m.* **1.** Treatment. *Mauvais traitements,* ill-usage, maltreatment. *Med :* **Premier traitement,** first-aid. **2.** Salary ; (officers') pay. **Secrétaire sans traitement,** secretary unpaid.

traiter [trɛte], *v.tr.* To treat. **1.** (*a*) *T. qn avec civilité,* to deal civilly with, by, s.o. ; to treat s.o. civilly. *T. qn de haut en bas,* to show oneself patronizing to s.o. ; to put on airs with s.o. *T. qn comme un ami,* to treat s.o. like, as, a friend. *T. qn d'égal,* to treat s.o. as an equal. (*b*) *T. qn de lâche, d'enfant,* to call s.o. a coward, a child. (*c*) *T. un malade, une maladie,* to treat a patient, a disease. **Se faire traiter d'un cancer,** to undergo treatment for cancer. (*d*) To entertain. *Il nous a traités splendidement,* he treated us splendidly. **2.** (*a*) To negotiate (deal, marriage, etc.); to handle (business). (*b*) To discuss, handle, deal with (subject). **3.** *v.i.* (*a*) *T. de la paix,* to treat for peace. *T. avec ses créanciers,* to treat, negotiate, with one's creditors. (*b*) (Of book) *T. d'un sujet,* to treat of, deal with, a subject.

    traité, *s.m.* **1.** Treatise (*de, sur,* on). **2.** Treaty, compact, agreement. *Préparer, négocier, conclure, un t.,* to arrange, to negotiate, to conclude, a treaty (*avec,* with). **Être en traité avec qn pour . . .,** to be in treaty, to be negotiating, with s.o. for. . . .

traiteur [trɛtœːr], *s.m.* Keeper of an eating-house ; caterer.

traître, traîtresse [trɛːtr, trɛtrɛs]. **1.** *a.* Treacherous, traitorous ; vicious (animal) ; dangerous (stair, crevasse). *T. à l'honneur,* false to honour. *F :* Il n'en a pas dit un traître mot, he didn't breathe a word about it. **2.** *s.* (*a*) Traitor, traitress. **En traître,** treacherously. (*b*) *Th :* Le traître, the villain.

traîtreusement [trɛtrøzmɑ̃], *adv.* Treacherously.

traîtrise [trɛtriːz], *s.f.* Treachery.

trajectoire [traʒɛktwaːr], *s.f.* Trajectory.

trajet [traʒɛ], *s.m.* (*a*) Journey (by railway, etc.); (length of) ride, drive, flight, etc. ; passage (*e.g.* of food through the alimentary tract). *T. de mer, par mer,* passage, crossing. *J'ai fait une partie du t. en avion,* I flew part of the way. (*b*) Course (of artery, etc.); path (of projectile).

tralala [tralala], *s.m.* **1.** Tra la la, tol-de-rol. **2.** *F :* Fuss, ado (at social ceremony, etc.). **Faire du tralala,** to make a great display. **Être sur son tralala, en grand tralala,** to be in full fig, dressed up to the nines.

tramail [tramaːj], *s.m.* Trammel(-net), drag-net. *pl. Des tramails.*

trame [tram], *s.f.* **1.** *Tex :* Woof, weft. *F : La t. de la vie, d'un discours,* the web, thread, of life ; the texture of a speech. **2.** Plot, conspiracy. **Ourdir une trame,** to hatch, concoct, a plot. **3.** *Phot :* (Ruled half-tone) screen.

tramer [trame], *v.tr.* **1.** (*a*) *Tex :* To weave. (*b*) *T. une action,* to weave the plot (of novel,

play). (*c*) *T. un complot,* to hatch, weave, a plot. *Il se trame quelque chose,* there is something afoot. **2.** *Phot :* *T. un cliché,* to take a negative through a (ruled half-tone) screen.

tramontane [tramɔ̃tan], *s.f.* **1.** Tramontana, north wind (esp. in the Adriatic). **2.** (*a*) North. (*b*) North Star. *F :* **Perdre la tramontane,** to lose one's bearings ; *F :* to lose one's head.

tramway [tramwɛ], *s.m.* **1.** Tramway. **2.** Tram-car, *F :* tram.

tranchant [trɑ̃ʃɑ̃]. **1.** *a.* (*a*) Cutting, sharp (tool, sword); keen (edge). (*b*) Trenchant (words, opinion); sharp, peremptory (tone); self-assertive (person). (*c*) Sharply contrasted (colours); loud, glaring (colour). **2.** *s.m.* (Cutting) edge (of knife, etc.); thin edge (of wedge). **Mettre le tranchant à une lame,** to put an edge on a blade. **Épée, argument, à deux tranchants,** two-edged sword ; argument that cuts both ways.

tranche [trɑ̃ːʃ], *s.f.* **1.** (*a*) Slice (of bread, etc.), round (of beef); rasher (of bacon). **En tranches,** in slices, sliced. (*b*) Block, portion (of an issue of shares, etc.). *Ar :* **Tranche de trois chiffres,** group, period, of three figures. **2.** Slab (of marble, stone). **3.** (*a*) Face (of wheel, etc.). (*b*) Edge (of coin, plank). (*c*) (Cut) edge (of book). **Livre doré sur tranche,** gilt-edged book. (*d*) *Geom.* Drawing : *T. verticale,* vertical section. **4.** *Tls :* Set, chisel. **Tranche à froid,** cold set.

tranchefile [trɑ̃ʃfil], *s.f. Bookb :* Headband.

tranche-montagne, *s.m. F :* Braggart, blusterer, fire-eater, Captain Bobadil. *D'un air de t.-m.,* blusteringly.

tranche-papier, *s.m.inv.* Paper-knife.

tranch|er [trɑ̃ʃe]. **1.** *v.tr.* (*a*) To slice (bread, etc.); to cut. *T. la tête à qn,* to cut off s.o.'s head. **Trancher dans le vif,** (i) *Surg :* to use the knife ; (ii) *F :* to adopt drastic measures. (*b*) To cut short (discussion, s.o.'s career); to settle (question) out of hand, once and for all. **Trancher le mot,** to speak plainly ; to speak out. **S.a. MOT 1.** **Il tranche sur tout,** he is so positive, so cocksure ; he is Sir Oracle. (*c*) To decide, settle, solve (question). **2.** *v.i.* (*a*) (Of colours, etc.) To contrast strongly (*sur,* with); to stand out clearly. (*b*) **Trancher du bel esprit, du philosophe,** to set up for a wit, for a philosopher. **S.a. SEIGNEUR 1.** *s.m.* **-age.**

    tranchée, *s.f.* **1.** (*a*) Trench. *Agr :* Drain. *Rail :* Cutting. *Mil :* **Monter à la tranchée,** to go into the trenches. **Être de tranchée,** to be on trench duty. (*b*) Cutting (through forest). **2.** *pl.* Colic, gripes.

tranchet [trɑ̃ʃɛ], *s.m. Tls :* **1.** Anvil-cutter. **2.** (Shoemaker's) paring-knife.

tranchoir [trɑ̃ʃwaːr], *s.m.* **1.** *Cu :* Trencher, cutting-board. **2.** *Ich :* Zanclus.

tranquille [trɑ̃kil], *a.* Tranquil. (*a*) Calm, still, quiet (sea); steady (compass); placid (stream). *Il ne peut pas rester t.,* he can't keep still. **Se tenir tranquille,** to keep still ; to keep quiet. (*b*) Quiet, peaceful (town, people, etc.). (*c*) Undisturbed, untroubled, easy (mind). *Laissez-moi t.,* leave me alone ; let me be. **Soyez tranquille (là-dessus),** set your mind at rest, at ease (about that). *adv.* **-ment.**

tranquilliser [trɑ̃kilize], *v.tr.* To tranquillize ; to reassure (s.o.) (*sur,* on, about); to set at rest, to soothe (the mind).

    se tranquilliser. 1. (Of the sea, etc.) To calm down. **2.** *Tranquillisez-vous là-dessus,* set your mind at rest about that.

tranquillité [trɑ̃kilite], *s.f.* **1.** (*a*) Tranquillity, calm(ness), quiet, stillness. (*b*) Quietness (of horse). **2.** *T. d'esprit*, peace of mind.

transa(t) [trăza], *s.m. F:* = TRANSATLANTIQUE 2(*b*).

transaction [trăzaksjɔ̃], *s.f.* **1.** (*a*) *Com:* Transaction; *pl.* dealings, deals. (*b*) *pl. Transactions d'une société*, transactions, proceedings (of the Royal society, etc.). **2.** (*a*) *Jur:* Settlement arrived at by parties *inter se*; arrangement, compromise. (*b*) *Pej: T. avec sa conscience*, compromise with one's conscience.

transactionnel, -elle [trăzaksjɔnɛl], *a.* Of the nature of a compromise. *Arriver à une solution transactionnelle*, to effect a compromise.

transalpin [trăzalpɛ̃], *a.* Transalpine.

transatlantique [trăzatlătik]. **1.** *a.* Transatlantic. **2.** *s.m.* (*a*) (Atlantic) liner. (*b*) (Hammock) deck-chair. (*c*) *pl. F:* Transatlantic passengers, visitors, or tourists.

transbordement [trăsbɔrdmã], *s.m.* **1.** (*a*) Trans-shipment. (*b*) *Rail:* Transfer from one train to another. **2.** Ferrying across.

transborder [trăsbɔrde], *v.tr.* **1.** (*a*) To trans-ship (cargo, passengers). (*b*) *Rail:* To transfer (goods) from one train to another. **2.** To convey, ferry, (passengers, etc.) across river, etc.

transbordeur [trăsbɔrdœ:r], *s.m.* (Pont) transbordeur, transporter-bridge; aerial ferry.

transcendance [trăssădă:s], *s.f.* Transcendency, transcendence.

transcendant [trăssădă], *a.* **1.** Transcendent. **2.** *Mth:* Transcendental (quantity, geometry).

transcripteur [trăskriptœ:r], *s.m.* Transcriber.

transcription [trăskripsjɔ̃], *s.f.* **1.** Transcription, transcribing. *Book-k:* Posting (of journal). **2.** (*a*) Transcript, copy. (*b*) *Mus:* Transcription (of song for violin, etc.).

transcrire [trăskri:r], *v.tr.* (Conj. like ÉCRIRE) **1.** (*a*) To transcribe, write out (shorthand notes, etc.). (*b*) *Book-k: T. le journal au grand livre*, to post the journal into the ledger; to post up. **2.** *T. un morceau pour le piano*, to make a transcription of a piece for the piano.

transe [trã:s], *s.f.* **1.** Usu. *pl.* Fright, fear. Être dans des transes, to be shivering in one's shoes. **2.** (Hypnotic) trance.

transept [trăsɛpt], *s.m. Ecc.Arch:* Transept.

transférable [trăsferabl], *a.* Transferable.

transf|érer [trăsfere], *v.tr.* (je transfère; je transférerai) **1.** (*a*) To transfer; to convey, remove, from one place to another; to translate (bishop). (*b*) *T. ses biens à qn*, to make over, assign, one's goods to s.o. *T. une propriété*, to convey an estate. **2.** To shift, move, the date of (entertainment, etc.). *s.m.* **-èrement.**

transfert [trăsfɛ:r], *s.m.* **1.** Transference. *Phot:* **Papier de transfert**, transfer paper (in carbon process). **2.** Making over; transfer, assignment (of stock, rights, etc.); demise, conveyance (of estate). *Jur:* **Acte de transfert**, deed of assignment (in favour of creditors).

transfiguration [trăsfigyrasjɔ̃], *s.f.* Transfiguration.

transfigurer [trăsfigyre], *v.tr.* To transfigure. **se transfigurer**, to be, become, transfigured.

transfo [trăsfo], *s.m. W.Tel: F:* Transformer.

transformateur, -trice [trăsfɔrmatœ:r, -tris]. *El.E:* **1.** *a.* Transforming. **2.** *s.m.* Transformer. *T. rotatif*, rotary transformer; converter. *T. élévateur*, step-up transformer. **Poste, station, de transformateurs**, transformer station. *W.Tel: T. d'oscillations*, transformer, *F:* jigger.

transformation [trăsfɔrmasjɔ̃], *s.f.* **1.**(*a*) Transformation (*en*, into). **Acteur à transformations,**

quick-change artist(e). (*b*) *Log:* Conversion (of proposition). **2.** Transformation(-wig).

transform|er [trăsfɔrme], *v.tr.* (*a*) To transform, change (*en*, into). *Rugby Fb:* Transformer **un essai**, to convert a try. (*b*) *Log:* To convert (proposition). *a.* **-able.**

se transformer, to be transformed, to change, turn (*en*, into).

transfuge [trăsfy:ʒ], *s.m.* (*a*) *Mil:* Deserter to the other side. (*b*) *F:* Turncoat.

transfuser [trăsfyze], *v.tr.* To transfuse (blood).

transfusion [trăsfyzjɔ̃], *s.f.* Transfusion (of blood).

transgresser [trăsgrese], *v.tr.* To transgress, contravene, break, infringe (the law).

transgression [trăsgresjɔ̃], *s.f.* Transgression.

transhumance [trăzymã:s], *s.f.* Moving of flocks (to or from the Alpine pastures).

transhumer [trăzyme], *v.tr.* To move (flocks) to or from the Alpine pastures.

transiger [trăziʒe], *v.i.* (je **transigeai(s)**; n. **transigeons**) To compound, compromise; to effect a compromise. *T. sur, avec, l'honneur*, to palter with one's honour.

transir [trăsi:r], *v.tr.* (*a*) To chill, benumb (with cold). (*b*) To paralyse, overcome (with fear).

transi, *a.* Chilled; perished with cold. *F:* **Amoureux transi,** bashful lover.

transit [trăzit], *s.m.* **1.** *Cust:* Transit. **Maison de transit,** forwarding agency. **2.** *Rail:* Through traffic.

transitaire [trăzitɛ:r]. **1.** *a. Pays t.*, country through which goods are conveyed in transit. **2.** *s.m.* Forwarding agent, transport agent.

transit|if, -ive [trăzitif, -i:v], *a. Gram:* Transitive (verb). *adv.* **-ivement.**

transition [trăzizjɔ̃], *s.f.* Transition.

transitoire [trăzitwa:r], *a.* Transitory, transient; temporary (measure). *adv.* **-ment.**

translatif, -ive [trăslatif, -i:v], *a. Jur:* Translative. **Acte translatif** (*de propriété*), conveyance, transfer.

translation [trăslasjɔ̃], *s.f.* **1.** *Ecc:* Translation (of bishop, relics). *Jur:* Transferring, conveyance (of property). *Tg:* Retransmission (of message). **2.** *Mec:* Mouvement de translation, motion of translation.

translucide [trăslysid], *a.* Translucent.

translucidité [trăslysidite], *s.f.* Translucence.

transmetteur [trăsmɛtœ:r], *s.m.* (*a*) *Tg:* Transmitter. (*b*) *Nau: T. d'ordres*, (ship's) telegraph; transmitter.

transmettre [trăsmɛtr], *v.tr.* (Conj. like METTRE) **1.** To transmit (light, message); to pass on, convey (message, etc.); to hand (sth.) down (to posterity). **2.** *Jur:* To transfer, convey, make over (property); to assign (shares, patent).

transmigration [trăsmigrasjɔ̃], *s.f.* Transmigration (of peoples, of the soul).

transmigrer [trăsmigre], *v.i.* To transmigrate.

transmi-s, -t, etc. See TRANSMETTRE.

transmissible [trăsmisibl], *a.* (*a*) Transmissible, transmittable. (*b*) Transferable (right, etc.).

transmission [trăsmisjɔ̃], *s.f.* **1.** (*a*) Transmission, transmittal (of heat, message); passing on (of order); handing down (of tradition, etc.) *Tg:* sending (of message). *T. aux ondes dirigées*, beam transmission. *Mec.E:* **Arbre de transmission,** driving-shaft. *Navy:* Officier de transmissions, signal officer. (*b*) *Mec.E:* **La transmission,** the transmission gear; the shafting, belting, gearing, etc. *T. par courroie*, belt-transmission, belt-drive. **2.** *Jur:* Transfer(ence), making over, conveyance (of estate); assignment (of shares, patent). *Adm:* T. *des pouvoirs,* 'handing over.'

transmuable [trăsmɥabl], *a.* Transmutable.

transmuer [trăsmɥe], *v.tr.* To transmute.

transmutation [trăsmytasjɔ̃], *s.f.* Transmutation (*en,* into).

transparaître [trăspareːtr], *v.i.* (Conj. like PARAÎTRE) To show through.

transparence [trăsparɑ̃:s], *s.f.* Transparency.

transparent [trăsparɑ̃], **1.** *a.* Transparent. **2.** *s.m.* (*a*) Transparency (illuminated from behind). (*b*) Underlines, 'black lines' (supplied with writing-block). (*c*) *pl. Tail:* Vest slips. ·(*d*) *Cost:* Thin material worn over a foundation.

transperc|er [trăspɛrse], *v.tr.* (je transperçai(s); n. transperçons) To (trans)pierce; to transfix; to stab, pierce, (s.o., sth.) through. *T. qn du regard,* to look s.o. through and through. *s.m.* **-ement.**

transpiration [trăspirasjɔ̃], *s.f.* **1.** (*a*) Perspiring. (*b*) *Bot:* Transpiration. (*c*) Transpiring (of a secret, etc.). **2.** Sweat, perspiration.

transpirer [trăspire], *v.i.* **1.** (Aux. *avoir*) (*a*) To perspire. *Med:* Faire transpirer qn, to sweat s.o. (*b*) *Bot:* To transpire. **2.** (Aux. *avoir* or *être*) To transpire; (of news) to leak out, to get abroad. *Il n'en était rien transpiré,* nothing of it had transpired.

transplantation [trăsplătasjɔ̃], *s.f.,* **transplantement** [trăsplătmɑ̃], *s.m.* Transplantation, transplanting.

transplant|er [trăsplăte], *v.tr.* To transplant. *a.* **-able.** *s.m.* **-eur.**
se **transplanter,** to settle elsewhere.

transport [trăspɔːr], *s.m.* **1.** (*a*) Transport, conveyance, carriage (of goods, passengers). Frais de transport, freight charges; carriage. Compagnie de transport, carrying company, forwarding company. *Ind:* Courroie de transport, conveying belt. (*b*) *Jur:* Transport sur les lieux, visit (of experts, officials, etc.) to the scene of the occurrence. (*c*) *Geol:* Terrain de transport, alluvial deposit. **2.** *Navy:* Transport (-ship); troop-ship. **3.** (*a*) *Jur:* Transport (-cession), transfer, assignment, making over, conveyance (of property). (*b*) *Book-k:* (i) Transfer (from one account to another); (ii) balance brought forward. (*c*) *Lith:* Transfer (on to the stone). **Papier à transport,** transfer paper. **4.** Transport, rapture; outburst of feeling. *Dans un t. de joie,* in an ecstasy of joy. *Dans un t. de colère,* in a burst of passion. Accueillir une nouvelle avec transport, to receive news with transports of delight. **5.** *Med:* Transport au cerveau, rush of blood to the brain; 'brain-storm; stroke.

transportable [trăspɔrtabl], *a.* Transportable; (patient) fit to be (re)moved.

transportant [trăspɔrtɑ̃], *a.* Exciting, thrilling.

transportation [trăspɔrtasjɔ̃], *s.f.* **1.** Conveyance (of goods). **2.** (Penal) transportation (of convicts).

transporter [trăspɔrte], *v.tr.* **1.** (*a*) To transport, convey, remove, transfer, carry (goods, troops, etc., from one place to another). (*b*) *Jur:* To transport (convict). **2.** *Jur:* To transfer, make over, assign (rights). **3.** To transport, to carry away, to enrapture.
se **transporter,** to go, betake oneself, repair (to a place). *Jur:* (Of officials) Se t. sur les lieux, to visit the scene of the occurrence.

transporté, -ée, *s.* Transported convict.

transporteur [trăspɔrtœːr], *s.m.* **1.** Carrier; forwarding agent. **2.** *Ind:* (*a*) T. à vis, spiral

conveyor. *T. à bande,* belt-conveyor. (*b*) (Chariot) transporteur, travelling crane.

transposable [trăspozabl], *a.* Transposable.

transposer [trăspoze], *v.tr.* To transpose.

transpositeur [trăspozitœːr], *s.m. Mus:* Transposing instrument.

transposition [trăspozisjɔ̃], *s.f.* Transposition.

transrhénan [trăsrenă], *a.* Beyond the Rhine; transrhenane.

transsaharien, -ienne [trŏssaarjɛ̃, -jɛn], *a. Geog:* Trans-Saharan.

transsubstantiation [trăssypstăsjasjɔ̃], *s.f. Theol:* Transubstantiation.

transsudation [trăssydasjɔ̃], *s.f.* Transudation.

transsuder [trăssyde], *v.i.* (Of liquid) To transude; to ooze through.

transvas|er [trăsvaze, trăz-], *v.tr.* To decant (wine, etc.). *s.m.* **-ement.**
se **transvaser,** (of water) to siphon.

transversal, -aux [trăsversal, trăz-, -o], *a.* Transverse, transversal; cross-(section, gallery). *Mur t.,* partition(-wall). *Poutre transversale,* cross-girder. *Rue transversale,* cross-street, side-street. *N.Arch: Plan t.,* athwartship plane.

transversalement [trăsversalmă, trăz-], *adv.* Transversely, crosswise, athwart.

transverse [trăsvers, trăz-]. **1.** *a. Anat: Geom:* Transverse. **2.** *s.m. Anat:* Transverse (muscle).

tran-tran [trătrɑ̃], *s.m. A: =* TRAIN-TRAIN.

trapèze [trapɛːz], *s.m.* **1.** (*a*) *Geom:* Trapezium (with two sides parallel). (*b*) *Gym:* Trapeze. **2.** *a.* **Muscle trapèze,** trapezius (muscle).

trapéziste [trapezist], *s.m. & f. Gym:* Trapezist.

trapézoïde [trapezoid]. **1.** *a.* Trapezoid(al). *Anat:* Os trapézoïde, trapezium. **2.** *s.m. Geom:* Trapezoid; trapezium (with no sides parallel).

trapp [trap], *s.m. Geol:* Trap (rock).

trappe[1] [trap], *s.f.* **1.** *Ven:* Trap, pitfall. **2.** (*a*) Trap-door, flap-door. *Th:* Trap. (*b*) Register (of fireplace).

Trappe[2] (**la**). *Pr.n.f.* **1.** The convent of La Trappe (in Normandy). **2.** The Trappist order of monks.

trappeur [trapœːr], *s.m.* Trapper (of wild animals).

trappillon [trapijɔ̃], *s.m. Th:* Trap-door; slot.

trappiste [trapist], *a. & s.m.* Trappist (monk).

trapu [trapy], *a.* Thick-set, squat, dumpy, stocky (man, horse).

traquenard [traknaːr], *s.m.* (*a*) Trap, deadfall. *Pris au t.,* caught in a trap. *F: Pris dans son propre t.,* hoist with his own petard. *Les traquenards d'une langue,* the pitfalls of a language. (*b*) Ambush.

traquer [trake], *v.tr. Ven:* **1.** To beat (wood, etc.) for game; to beat up (game). **2.** (*a*) To enclose, surround, hem in (quarry, bandits). (*b*) To track down, hunt down, run to earth (criminal).

traquet [trakɛ], *s.m.* **1.** (Mill-)clapper, clack. **2.** *Orn: T.* motteux, wheatear, fallow-finch. *T. rubicole,* stonechat.

traqueur [trakœːr], *s.m. Ven:* Beater.

traulet [trolɛ], *s.m.* Dotting-pen.

traumatique [tromatik], *a. Med:* Traumatic (fever, shock).

traumatisme [tromatism], *s.m. Med:* Traumatism.

travail[1] [travaj], *s.m. Farr: Vet:* Sling or frame (in which a horse is placed to be shod or to be operated upon). *pl. Des travails.*

travail[2]**,-aux** [travaj, -o], *s.m.* Work. **1.** (*a*) Labour, toil. *T. de tête, t. intellectuel,* brain-work. *T. à la main, t. manuel,* manual labour. *Travaux*

des champs, agricultural labour. *T. à la pièce,*
aux pièces, piece-work. *T. à l'entreprise*, contract
work. *T. en série*, mass production. *T. à*
l'aiguille, needlework. *T. pour dames*, ladies'
fancy-work. *Costume, vêtements, de t.*, working
dress or clothes. Homme de (grand) travail,
hard-working man; hard worker. *Pol:* Le Parti
du travail, the Labour Party. Le Ministère
du Travail, the Ministry of Labour. Travaux
forcés, transportation with hard labour. *Myth:*
Les douze travaux d'Hercule, the twelve labours
of Hercules. Avoir le travail facile, lent, to
work easily, slowly. Se mettre au travail, to
get, set, to work. Cesser le travail, (i) to cease
work; (ii) (= *se mettre en grève*) to down tools.
(b) Working, operation. *T. du vin*, working,
fermenting, of wine. *Mec:* *T. à la tension,*
tension stress. Surface de travail, working face
(of valve, etc.). *Mch:* Pression de travail,
working pressure. S.a. PLEIN 1. *(c)* Travail
d'enfant, travail, labour, childbirth. Femme en
travail, woman in travail. *(d) Coup qui demande*
beaucoup de t., stroke that requires a lot of
practice. *(e)* Occupation, employment. *Donner*
du t. à qn, to give s.o. employment. Manque de
travail, lack of work; unemployment. Être sans
travail, to be out of work. Les sans-travail, the
unemployed. 2. *(a)* Piece of work. *(b)* (Literary,
etc.) work. *Auteur d'un t. sur les métaux*, author
of a work on metals. *(c) Travaux d'une société,*
proceedings, transactions, of a society. *(d) Adm:*
Travaux publics, public works. S.a. ART 2. 3. *Bijou*
d'un beau t., jewel of fine craftsmanship.
travailler [travaje]. 1. *v.tr.* *(a)* To torment.
Un désir le travaillait, he was tormented,
obsessed, with a desire. *Être travaillé de, par,*
la goutte, to be a prey, a martyr, to gout. Se
travailler l'esprit, to worry. *(b)* To work upon
(s.o., the feelings, etc.); to bring pressure to bear
upon (s.o.). *T. des témoins*, to tamper with
witnesses. *T. les ouvriers de qn*, to work up, stir
up, s.o.'s workmen. *(c)* To overwork, fatigue
(horse). *(d)* To work, fashion, shape (wood,
iron); to knead (dough); to elaborate (one's
style); to work up (a negative). *(e)* To work at,
study (one's part, music, etc.). 2.*v.i.* *(a)* To work,
labour, toil. *T. dur*, to work hard. *F:* Travailler
comme un nègre, comme quatre, to work like a
nigger. Se tuer à (force de) travailler, to kill
oneself with work; to work oneself to death.
Travailler pour le roi de Prusse, to get nothing
out of it. *T. contre qn*, to work, intrigue, against
s.o. *T. à la perte de qn*, to work for the undoing
of s.o. *(b)* (Of performing animals, etc.) To go
through their performance; to perform. *(c)* (Of
ship, cable) To strain; (of beam) to be in stress;
(of wine) to ferment, to work; (of wood) to
warp or shrink; (of walls) to crack.
    se travailler, to labour, to strain. *Se t. à*
produire l'effet, to strain after effect.
    travaillé, *a.* *(a)* Worked, wrought (iron). Non
travaillé, unworked; unwrought. *(b)* Laboured,
elaborate (style).
travailleur, -euse [travajœːr,-øːz]. 1.*(a) a.* Industrious, hard-working. *(b) s. C'est un rude t.,*
he's a hard worker. 2. *s.* *(a)* Worker, workman,
labourer. *T. en chambre*, home-worker. *(b) s.f.*
Ent: Travailleuse, worker (bee).
travailliste [travajist]. *Pol:* 1. *s.m.* Member of
the Labour party; *F:* labourite. 2. *a. Parti t.,*
député t., Labour party, Labour member.
travée [trave], *s.f.* 1. *Const:* *Arch:* Bay.
2. (i) Span, bay (of bridge); (ii) independent
girder (of bridge). 3. *Av:* Rib (of wing).

travers [travɛːr], *s.m.* 1. *(a)* Breadth. En
travers, across, transversely, crosswise. Profil
en travers, cross-section. En travers de, across,
athwart. A travers qch., au travers de qch.,
through sth. S.a. CHAMP¹ 1. *(b) Nau:* Beam,
broadside (of vessel). Vent de travers, wind on
the beam. Par le travers, abeam, on the beam,
on the broadside, athwartships. *Cabine par le t.,*
cabin amidships. *Collision par le t.*, collision
broadside-on. En travers, athwart. En travers
du vaisseau, athwartship(s). Venir en travers, to
broach to. 2. De travers, askew, awry, the wrong
way, amiss. *Tout alla de t.*, everything went
wrong. Regarder qn de travers, to look askance,
to scowl, at s.o. *Les tableaux pendaient de t.*, the
pictures were hung awry. *Il a des idées tout(es)*
de t., his ideas are all wrong. Entendre, prendre,
tout de travers, to put a wrong construction on
everything; to take up things wrong. 3. Failing,
bad habit, fault. *Malgré tous ses t.*, in spite of all
his faults.
traversable [traversabl], *a.* Traversable (desert,
etc.); fordable (river).
traversant [traversã], *a.* Traversing. Boulon
traversant, through-bolt.
traverse [travers], *s.f.* 1. (Chemin de) traverse,
cross-road, short cut. J'ai pris la traverse, I took
the short cut. 2. *(a)* (Barre de) traverse, cross-bar,
cross-piece; rail (of door); slat (of bed); rung
(of ladder). *Artil:* Cross-bar (of sight). *Rail:*
Sleeper. *Aut:* *etc:* Cross-member (of frame).
(b) Fort: Traverse. *(c) Mch:* Crosshead.
(d) Nau: Bar (at harbour mouth). 3. *(a)* Hitch,
set-back. *(b)* Se mettre à la traverse des projets
de qn, to oppose, thwart, cross, s.o.'s plans.
travers|er [traverse], *v.tr.* 1. To traverse
(region); to cross, go across, step across (street);
to go, pass, through (town, danger, crisis); to
make one's way through (crowd). *T. la rivière*
à la nage, en bateau, par le bac, to swim, row,
ferry, across the river. *Le pont qui traverse la*
rivière, the bridge that crosses, spans, the river.
T. la forêt à cheval, à bicyclette, en auto, to ride,
cycle, drive, through the forest. *Il eut la jambe*
traversée par une balle, he was shot through the
leg. *T. qch. de part en part*, to go clean through
sth. 2. To cross, thwart (s.o.'s plans).
s.m. **-ement.**
    traversée, *s.f.* 1. Passage, crossing (by sea).
Faire la t. de Douvres à Calais, to cross from
Dover to Calais 2. *Rail:* Traversée de voie,
railway crossing; cross-over.
traversier, -ière [traversje, -jɛːr]. 1. *a.* Cross,
crossing. *Rue traversière*, cross-street. *Nau:*
Vent t., leading wind. 2. *s.m.* Spreader (of fan
aerial).
traversin [traversɛ̃], *s.m.* 1. *(a)* Cross-bar,
cross-piece; thwart or stretcher (of rowing-boat).
(b) Nau: Cross-tree. *(c)* Beam (of balance).
2. Bolster (of bed).
traversine [traversin], *s.f.* 1. Cross-bar, cross-
beam. 2. (Crossing) plank (between two ships);
gang-plank.
travertin [travertɛ̃], *s.m. Geol:* Travertine
(stone); sinter.
travestir [travestiːr], *v.tr.* 1. To disguise (esp.
with ludicrous effect, or for fancy dress). *T. un*
homme en femme, to disguise a man as a woman.
Bal travesti, fancy-dress ball, costume ball.
2. *(a)* To travesty, parody, burlesque (play,
poem). *(b) F: T. la pensée de qn*, to misrepresent,
travesty, s.o.'s thought.
travestissement [travestismã], *s.m.* 1. *(a)* Disguising. *(b)* Disguise. *Th:* Rôle à **travestisse-**

ments, quick-change part. **2.** Travesty, misrepresentation (of facts).

tray-ant, -ais, etc. See TRAIRE.

trayon [trɛjɔ̃], *s.m.* Dug, teat (of cow, etc.).

trébucher [trebyʃe]. **I.** *v.i.* (a) To stumble, totter. *Marcher en trébuchant*, to stagger along. *Faire trébucher qn*, to trip s.o. up. (b) (Of coin) To turn the scale. **2.** *v.tr.* To test (coin) for weight.

trébuchet [trebyʃɛ], *s.m.* **I.** (a) Bird-trap. (b) Trap, deadfall. **2.** Precision balance; assay balance.

tréfil|er [trefile], *v.tr. Metalw:* To wire-draw. *Banc à t.*, drawing-frame. *s.m.* **-age.** *s.m.* **-eur.**

tréfilerie [ˌtrefilri], *s.f.* **I.** Wire-drawing. **2.** Wire-works, wire-mill, drawing-mill.

trèfle [trɛfl], *s.m.* **I.** *Bot:* (a) Trefoil, clover. *T. blanc*, wild white clover. *T. à quatre feuilles*, four-leaved clover. (b) **Trèfle d'eau**, marsh-trefoil; bog-myrtle. **2.** *Arch:* Trefoil. **3.** *Cards:* Clubs. *Jouer trèfle*, to play a club, to play clubs.

tréfoncier, -ière [trefɔ̃sje, -jɛːr]. **I.** *a.* Pertaining to the subsoil. **2.** *s.* Owner of the soil and subsoil.

tréfonds [trefɔ̃], *s.m.* Subsoil; minerals, etc., lying below the ground. *Vendre le fonds et le tréfonds*, to sell soil and subsoil. *F:* **Dans le tréfonds de mon cœur**, in my heart of hearts. *Savoir le fonds et le tréfonds d'une affaire*, to know all about a matter.

treillage [trɛjaːʒ], *s.m.* Trellis(-work); lattice-work. *T. en fil de fer*, wire netting.

treillager [trɛjaʒe], *v.tr.* (je treillageai(s); n. treillageons) To trellis, lattice (wall, etc.).

treille [trɛːj], *s.f.* (a) Vine-arbour. *T. à l'italienne*, pergola. (b) (Climbing) vine. *Le jus de la t.*, the juice of the grape; wine.

treillis [trɛji], *s.m.* **I.** Trellis(-work); lattice. *T. métallique*, wire netting. *N.Arch:* **Mât treillis**, trellis-mast. **2.** (a) Grating. (b) Grid (for maps, etc.). **3.** (Coarse) canvas (for working garments); sackcloth, sacking. *T. pour matelas*, ticking. *Mil:* **Jeu de treillis**, dungarees; fatigue dress.

treillisser [trɛjise], *v.tr.* (a) To trellis, lattice. (b) To enclose with wire netting.

treize [trɛːz], *num.a.inv. & s.m.inv.* Thirteen. *Le t. mai*, the thirteenth of May. **Louis Treize**, Louis the Thirteenth.

treizième [trɛzjɛm]. **I.** *num. a. & s.* Thirteenth. **2.** *s.m.* Thirteenth (part). *adv.* **-ment.**

trélingage [trelɛ̃gaːʒ], *s.m. Nau:* Cat-harpings.

trélinguer [trelɛ̃ge], *v.tr. Nau:* To swifter (the shrouds, etc.).

tréma [trema], *s.m.* Diaeresis.

tremblaie [trɑ̃blɛ], *s.f.* Aspen plantation.

tremblant [trɑ̃blɑ̃], *a.* **I.** Trembling; quivering (face); quaking (ground, voice); unsteady, flickering (light); tremulous, quavering (voice).

tremble [trɑ̃ːbl], *s.m.* **Peuplier tremble**, aspen; trembling poplar.

tremblement [trɑ̃bləmɑ̃], *s.m.* **I.** Trembling, quiver(ing), shaking; tremulousness, quavering (of voice). **2.** Tremor. **Tremblement de terre**, earth tremor; earthquake. *P:* **Et tout le tremblement**, and all the rest of it; and the whole boiling.

trembler [trɑ̃ble], *v.i.* (a) To tremble, shake; to quake; (of light) to quiver, flicker; (of voice) to quaver. *Le sol tremble*, the earth is shaking. *T. de colère, de froid*, to shake with anger; to shiver with cold. (b) To tremble, quake, with fear. *T. de tout son corps, de tous ses membres*, to shake all over; *F:* to be all of a tremble. *F:* **Trembler dans sa peau**, to quake, shake, in

one's shoes. **En tremblant**, tremblingly, tremulously. *Je tremble de le rencontrer*, I tremble at the thought of meeting him. *Elle tremblait qu'on (ne) la découvrît*, she was in deadly fear of being discovered. *Ça me fait trembler quand j'y pense*, it gives me the shivers to think of it.

tremblé, *a.* (a) Shaky (handwriting); wavy (line). (b) *Notes tremblées*, tremolo notes.

trembleur, -euse [trɑ̃blœːr, -øːz], *s.* **I.** *Rel.H:* (i) Quaker. (ii) Shaker. **2.** Timid, apprehensive, person. **3.** *El:* (a) *s.m.* Trembler; vibrator (of coil); hammer-break. *Tg: Tp:* Buzzer, ticker. (b) *a.* *Sonnerie trembleuse*, trembling electric bell.

tremblote [trɑ̃blɔt], *s.f. P:* **Avoir la tremblote**, to have the shivers, the shakes.

tremblot|er [trɑ̃blɔte], *v.i.* To tremble (slightly); to quiver; (of voice) to quaver, shake; (of light) to flicker; (of wings) to flutter. *T. de froid, de peur*, to shiver with cold, with fear. *a.* **-ant.** *s.m.* **-ement.**

trémie [tremi], *s.f.* (Mill-)hopper; loading funnel; cone (of blast-furnace).

trémière [tremjɛːr], *a.f.* **Rose trémière**, hollyhock.

trémouss|er [tremuse]. **I.** *v.tr.* To hustle (s.o.) up. **2.** *v.i.* (Of bird) *T. des ailes*, to flutter, flap, its wings. *s.m.* **-ement.**

se trémousser. I. (a) To have the fidgets; to fidget. (b) To jig up and down (in dancing, etc.). (c) (Of bird) To flutter about (in cage). **2.** To bestir oneself.

trempe [trɑ̃ːp], *s.f.* **I.** (a) Steeping, dipping, soaking. **Mettre qch. en trempe**, to steep sth.; to put sth. in soak. (b) *Metall:* Tempering, hardening. **Acier de trempe**, hardening steel. *T. à l'eau*, water-tempering. *T. par cémentation*, case-hardening. *T. glacée*, chilling. **2.** (a) Temper (of steel). **Donner la trempe à . . .**, to temper . . .; to harden. . . . (b) *F:* Quality. *Les hommes de sa t.*, men of his stamp, *F:* of his kidney.

tremp|er [trɑ̃pe]. **I.** *v.tr.* (a) To mix, dilute, with water. (b) To soak, steep; to drench. *T. qch. dans un liquide*, to dip or soak sth. in a liquid. *T. la soupe*, to pour the soup on the bread. *F:* **Être trempé comme une soupe**, to be wet to the skin. *T. sa plume dans l'encre*, to dip one's pen in the ink. *Tan: T. les peaux*, to steep, drench, the skins. (c) *Metall:* To harden (steel); to chill (cast iron). *F: T. les muscles*, to harden the muscles. **2.** *v.i.* (a) To soak, to steep, to lie in soak. (b) *F:* **Tremper dans un complot**, to have a hand in a plot. *s.m.* **-age.** *s.m.* **-age.**

trempé, *a.* (a) Wet, soaked. **Trempé jusqu'aux os**, wet through; soaked to the skin; drenched. (b) *F:* **Esprit bien trempé**, well-tempered mind.

trempette [trɑ̃pɛt], *s.f.* **I.** Sippet. **2.** *F:* **Faire la trempette**, to dip bread, biscuit, etc., in wine, in coffee, etc.

tremplin [trɑ̃plɛ̃], *s.m.* Spring-board; (spring) diving-board. **Faire le (saut du) tremplin**, to turn a somersault off the spring-board. *F:* **Être sur le tremplin**, to be about to take the plunge.

trentaine [trɑ̃tɛn], *s.f.* (About) thirty, some thirty. *Une t. de francs*, thirty francs or so. *Avoir passé la t.*, to be in the thirties.

trente¹ [trɑ̃ːt], *num.a.inv. & s.m.inv.* Thirty. *T. jours*, thirty days. *Le t. juin*, (on) the thirtieth of June. *F:* **Se mettre sur son trente et un**, to put on one's best Sunday-go-to-meeting clothes. *Ten:* **Trente à**, thirty all.

Trente². *Pr.n. Geog:* Trent (in Italy). **Le concile de Trente**, the Council of Trent.

trentenaire [trɑ̃tnɛːr], *a. Concession t.*, thirty years' lease (esp. of a grave).

trente-six [trɑ̃tsi, -sis, -siz; for rules of pronunciation see SIX], *num.a.inv. & s.m.inv.* Thirty-six. *F:* Voir trente-six chandelles, to see stars (after receiving a blow on the head). Il n'y va pas par trente-six chemins, he doesn't beat about the bush. Je le vois tous les trente-six [trɑ̃tsis] du mois, I see him once in a blue moon. Avoir trente-six raisons de faire qch., *F:* to have umpteen reasons for doing sth.

trentième [trɑ̃tjɛm]. **1.** *num. a. & s.* Thirtieth. **2.** *s.m.* Thirtieth (part).

trentin [trɑ̃tɛ̃]. *Geog:* **1.** *a.* Trentine, Tridentine. **2.** *Pr.n.m.* Le Trentin, the Trentino.

trépan [trepɑ̃], *s.m.* **1.** *Tls:* (a) Trepan; rock-drill. (b) *Surg:* Trepan, trephine. **2.** = TRÉPANATION.

trépanation [trepanasjɔ̃], *s.f. Surg:* Trepanning, trephining.

trépaner [trepane], *v.tr.* **1.** To bore, drill, into (rock, etc.). **2.** *Surg:* To trepan; to trephine.

trépas [trepɑ], *s.m.* Death, decease. Passer de vie à trépas, to pass away; to depart this life.

trépass|er [trepɑse], *v.i.* (Aux. *avoir*, occ. *être*) To die; to depart this life; to pass away. *s.m.* **-ement.**

trépassé, -ée, *a. & s.* Dead, deceased (person). Les trépassés, the dead, the departed. *Ecc:* Le Jour, la Fête, des Trépassés, All Souls' Day; All Souls.

tréphine [trefin], *s.f. Surg:* Trephine, perforator.

trépidant [trepidɑ̃], *a.* Agitated, vibrating.

trépidation [trepidasjɔ̃], *s.f.* **1.** Tremor (of the ground); trepidation, jarring (of machinery, etc.). **2.** Trepidation; agitation, flurry.

trépider [trepide], *v.i.* **1.** (Of machines, etc.) To vibrate, shake. **2.** *F:* To be in a nervous, trembling, state of apprehension.

trépied [trepje], *s.m.* Tripod. (a) Three-legged stool or stand. (b) Cu: Trivet. (c) (Three-legged) brazier. (d) Tripod mounting (of gun, rocket, theodolite).

trépign|er [trepiɲe]. **1.** *v.i.* T. de colère, de rage, to dance, prance, with rage. Il trépignait de partir, he was itching to start. **2.** *v.tr.* To trample down (earth). *s.m.* **-ement.**

trépointe [trepwɛ̃t], *s.f.* Welt (of shoe).

très [trɛ], *adv.* Very, most; (very) much. Très bon, (i) very good, (ii) most kind. Il n'est pas très lu aujourd'hui, he is not widely read to-day. Très estimé, much, highly, esteemed. Il est soldat et très soldat, he is a soldier and very much of a soldier. Prendre qch. très au sérieux, to take sth. very seriously. *F:* Avoir très faim, très soif, to be very hungry, very thirsty. Avoir très peur, to be very much afraid.

trésaillé [trezaje], *a.* Crackled (china).

trésaillure [trezajyːr], *s.f.* Crackle (in picture, porcelain).

Très-Haut (le) [lətreo]. *Pr.n.m.* The Almighty.

trésillon [trezijɔ̃], *s.m.* = ÉTRÉSILLON.

trésor [trezoːr], *s.m.* **1.** (a) Treasure. (b) *Jur:* Treasure-trove. (c) Treasure-house. **2.** *pl.* Entasser des trésors, to accumulate, hoard, riches. Les trésors de la terre, the treasures of the earth. **3.** Le Trésor (public), the (French) Treasury. **4.** *A:* Trésor de la langue grecque, thesaurus of the Greek language.

trésorerie [trezorri], *s.f.* **1.** Treasury. **2.** (a) Treasurership. (b) Treasurer's office.

trésorier, -ière [trezorje, -jɛːr], *s.* Treasurer; paymaster, paymistress. Oommis trésorier, treasury clerk. *Mil: Officier t.*, paymaster.

tressaillement [tresajmɑ̃], *s.m.* Start (of surprise); quiver; shudder (of fear); thrill (of joy); wince (from pain).

tressaillir [tresajiːr], *v.i.* (*pr.p.* tressaillant; *p.p.* tressailli; *pr.ind.* je tressaille, n. tressaillons; *p.h.* je tressaillis; *fu.* je tressaillirai) To start; to give a start, a jump (from surprise); to quiver; to shudder (from fear); to thrill (with joy); (of heart) to throb, bound. *T. de douleur*, to wince. Faire tressaillir qn, to startle s.o.

tressaut [treso], *s.m.* **1.** Start, jump (of surprise). **2.** Jolt.

tressaut|er [tresote], *v.i.* **1.** To start, jump (with fear, surprise). **2.** To jolt; to be jolted; to be tossed about. *s.m.* **-ement.**

tresse [tres], *s.f.* (a) Plait, tress (of hair). (b) Braid (of yarn, etc.); plait (of straw, etc.). *T. de coton*, cotton tape. *El.E:* Fil conducteur sous tresse, braided conductor wire.

tress|er [trese], *v.tr.* To plait (hair, straw); to braid (yarn); to weave (basket, garland). *s.m.* **-age.**

tresseur, -euse [tresœːr, -øːz], *s.* (a) Braider, plaiter. (b) Wig-maker.

tréteau [treto], *s.m.* **1.** Trestle, support, stand. **2.** *pl.* (Mountebank's) stage, boards (on trestles). Monter sur les tréteaux, (i) to take to barnstorming; (ii) *Iron:* to go on the stage.

treuil [trœːj], *s.m.* Winch, windlass, winding-drum.

trêve [trɛːv], *s.f.* (a) Truce. *Hist:* La trêve de Dieu, the truce of God. *Pol: F: T. des confiseurs*, political truce in the Chamber at New Year. (b) Respite, intermission. *F:* Trêve de plaisanteries, a truce to your nonsense; no more of your joking! Sans trêve, unceasing(ly); without intermission.

tri¹ [tri], *s.m.* Sorting (out); classifying. Faire le tri de ..., to sort out ...; to set aside.... *Rail: Bureau de tri*, sorting-office.

tri², *s.m.* (At bridge, whist) Odd trick.

triade [triad], *s.f.* Triad.

triage [triaʒ], *s.m.* Sorting (of coal, letters, etc.). *T. à la main*, hand-picking or -sorting. *Rail:* Manœuvres de triage, shunting operations. Gare de triage, marshalling yard. [TRIER]

triangle [triɑ̃ːgl], *s.m.* **1.** Triangle. **2.** (a) *Nau:* Triangular flag. (b) *Draw:* Set square. (c) *Mus:* Triangle.

triangulaire [triɑ̃gylɛːr], *a.* Triangular; three-square (file). *Nau:* Voile triangulaire, leg-of-mutton sail. *adv.* **-ment.**

triangulation [triɑ̃gylasjɔ̃], *s.f. Surv:* Triangulation.

trias [triɑs], *s.m. Geol:* Trias.

triasique [triazik], *a. Geol:* Triassic.

tribasique [tribazik, -bɑ-], *a. Ch:* Tribasic.

tribord [triboːr], *s.m. Nau:* Starboard. A tribord, on the starboard side; to starboard. La barre toute à tribord! hard-a-starboard! Venez sur tribord! port (the helm)! *Row:* Aviron de tribord, bow-side oar.

tribordais [triborde], *s.m.* Man of the starboard watch.

Triboulet [tribulɛ], *s.m.* (a) (Type of) tragic buffoon. (From V. Hugo's Le Roi s'amuse.)

tribraque [tribrak], *s.m. Pros:* Tribrach.

tribu [triby], *s.f.* Tribe. Membre d'une t., tribesman.

tribulation [tribylasjɔ̃], *s.f.* Tribulation; trouble, trial.

tribun [tribœ̃], *s.m.* (a) *Rom.Hist:* Tribune. (b) *F:* Democratic leader.

tribunal, -aux [tribynal, -o], *s.m.* Tribunal. (a) Judge's seat, bench. (b) Court of justice, law-court; (the) magistrates. **En plein tribunal,** in open court. *T. de simple police,* police-court. *T. militaire,* military tribunal. *F: Le t. de l'opinion publique,* the tribunal, the bar, of public opinion. **Gazette des tribunaux,** law reports. S.a. INSTANCE I. *(c) Navy : T. de prise,* prize court.

tribune [tribyn], *s.f.* **I.** Tribune, rostrum, (speaker's) platform. **Monter à la tribune,** to go up to the tribune (in Fr. Parliament); to address the House. **Éloquence de la tribune,** parliamentary eloquence. **2.** *(a)* Gallery (in church, etc.). *Parl: La t. publique,* the strangers' gallery. *(b)* (At races) Grand stand. **Les tribunes,** the stands. *(c) T. de l'orgue,* organ-loft.

tribut [triby], *s.m.* Tribute. **Payer tribut,** to pay tribute. *F:* **Payer le tribut à la nature,** to pay the debt of nature; to die. *Apporter son t. d'éloges,* to bring, offer, one's tribute of praise, one's meed of praise.

tributaire [tribytɛːr], *a. & s.m.* **I.** Tributary. *Être t. de l'étranger,* to be dependent upon foreign supplies. **2.** Tributary (river).

tri-car, *s.m.* Tricar. **I.** Motor-tricycle. **2.** Cycle-car, *F:* three-wheeler.

tricentenaire [trisɑ̃tnɛːr], *a. & s.m.* Tercentenary.

tricher [triʃe], *v.i. & tr.* To cheat; to trick (s.o.).

tricherie [triʃri], *s.f.* Cheating (at cards, etc.); trickery.

tricheur, -euse [triʃœːr, -øːz]. **I.** *a.* Given to cheating. **2.** *s.* Cheat; trickster.

trichine [triʃin, trikin], *s.f. Med:* Trichina, thread-worm.

trichiné [triʃine, trikine], *a.* Trichinous, trichinosed.

trichinose [triʃinoːz, trikinoːz], *s.f. Med:* Trichinosis.

trichrome [trikroːm], *a.* Three-colour(ed); trichromatic (photography).

trick [trik], *s.m. Cards:* Odd trick.

tricoises [trikwaːz], *s.f.pl.* (Farrier's) pincers.

tricolore [trikɔlɔːr], *a.* Tricolour(ed). **Le drapeau tricolore,** the French flag, the Tricolour.

tricorne [trikɔrn]. **I.** *a.* Three-horned; three-cornered. **2.** *s.m.* Three-cornered hat.

tricot [triko], *s.m.* **I.** *(a)* Knitting; knitted wear. **Faire du tricot,** to knit. *(b) Tex:* Stockinet. **2.** *(a)* (Knitted) jersey, jumper; *F:* woolly. *(b)* (Under)vest.

tricot|er [trikote], *v.tr.* **I.** To knit. **Aiguilles à tricoter,** knitting-needles. **Machine à tricoter,** knitting-machine. **2.** *F:* To run fast, to leg it; (on bicycle) to scorch along. *s.m.* **-age.**

tricoteuse, -euse [trikotœːr, -øːz]. **I.** *s.* Knitter. **2.** *s.f.* **Tricoteuse,** knitting-machine.

trictrac [triktrak], *s.m.* **I.** Click, rattle (of dice, etc.). **2.** *Games:* *(a)* Backgammon. *(b)* Backgammon-board.

tricuspide [trikyspid], *a.* Tricuspid, three-pointed.

tricycle [trisikl], *s.m.* Tricycle.

tridactyle [tridaktil]. **I.** *a. Z:* Tridactyl(ous). **2.** *s.m. (a) Ent:* Mole-cricket. *(b) Orn:* Button-quail.

trident [tridɑ̃], *s.m.* **I.** Trident (of Neptune). **2.** *(a)* Fish-spear. *(b)* Three-pronged (pitch-)fork.

tridenté [tridɑ̃te], *a.* Tridentate.

trièdre [triɛdr], *a. & s.m.* Trihedral (angle).

triennal, -aux [triɛnnal, -o], *a.* Triennial. **I.** Lasting three years. **2.** Recurring every third year. *Agr: Assolement t.,* three-course rotation.

triennat [triɛnna], *s.m. (a)* Triennium. *(b)* Three-years' spell of office.

trier [trie], *v.tr. (a)* To sort (letters); *Rail:* to marshal (trucks). *(b)* To pick out, sort out (the best). *T. à la main,* to hand-pick. S.a. VOLET I.

triérarchie [trierarʃi], *s.f. Gr.Ant:* Trierarchy.

triérarque [trierark], *s.m.* Trierarch.

trieur, -euse [triœːr, -øːz]. **I.** *s.* Sorter (of letters, etc.). **2.** *s.m. Ind:* Screening-machine. **3.** *s.f.* **Trieuse,** wool-picking machine.

trifouill|er [trifuje], *v.tr. & i. F: T. dans un tiroir,* to rummage in a drawer. *Ne trifouillez pas le mécanisme,* don't fiddle about with the mechanism. *s.m.* **-age.** *s.* **-eur, -euse.**

trigame [trigam], **I.** *a. Jur: Bot:* Trigamous. **2.** *s. Jur:* Trigamist.

trigle [trigl], *s.m. Ich:* Trigla, gurnard.

triglyphe [triglif], *s.m. Arch:* Triglyph.

trigone [trigɔn], *a.* Trigonal, three-cornered.

trigonométrie [trigɔnɔmetri], *s.f.* Trigonometry. *T. rectiligne,* plane trigonometry.

trigonométrique [trigɔnɔmetrik], *a.* Trigonometric(al). *adv.* **-ment,** -ally.

trigyne [triʒin], *a. Bot:* Trigynous. **Plante trigyne,** trigyn.

trihebdomadaire [triɛbdɔmadɛːr], *a.* Tri-weekly; appearing, occurring, thrice weekly.

trijumeau, -elle [triʒymo, -ɛl]. **I.** *s.* Triplet, trilling. **2.** *a. & s.m.* **(Nerfs) trijumeaux,** trigeminal nerves.

trille [triːj], *s.m. Mus:* Trill, shake.

triller [trije], *v.tr. Mus:* To trill, shake (a note).

trillion [triljɔ̃], *s.m.* Billion (10^{12}); *U.S:* trillion.

trilobé [trilobe], *a.* **I.** *Arch:* Three-cusped, trefoiled (arch). **2.** *Bot:* Trilobate.

trilogie [trilɔʒi], *s.f. Lit:* Trilogy.

trimard [trimaːr], *s.m. P:* High road. **Battre le trimard, être sur le trimard,** to be on the tramp, on the pad.

trimarder [trimarde], *v.i. P:* To be on the tramp; to pad the hoof.

trimardeur [trimardœːr], *s.m. P:* Tramp, *U.S:* hobo.

trimbal|er [trɛ̃bale], *v.tr. F:* To carry about; to drag, lug, about (parcels, etc.); to trail (children, etc.) about. *s.m.* **-age.** *s.m.* **-ement.** **se trimbaler,** to wander along (heavily and slowly).

trimer [trime], *v.i. P:* To drudge; to fag; to toil (and moil). **Faire trimer qn,** to keep s.o. at it.

trimestre [trimɛstr], *s.m.* **I.** Quarter; three months; trimester. *Sch:* Term. **Par trimestre,** quarterly. **2.** Quarter's salary, quarter's rent. *Sch:* Term's fees.

trimestriel, -elle [trimɛstriɛl], *a.* Quarterly (magazine, payment). *Sch:* **Bulletin trimestriel,** end-of-term school report.

trimètre [trimɛtr], *s.m. Pros:* Trimeter.

trimoteur [trimɔtœːr], *a. & s.m.* Three-engined (aeroplane).

tringa [trɛga], *s.m. Orn:* Tringa, sandpiper.

tringlage [trɛglaːʒ], *s.m. Mec.E:* (System of) rods.

tringle [trɛːgl], *s.f.* **I.** *(a)* Rod. *T. de rideau,* curtain-rod. *T. d'un pneu,* wire of a tyre. *(b)* Bar. *Rail: T. de manœuvre,* switch-bar (of points). **2.** Line, mark (made by chalked string). **3.** *Arch:* Tringle; square moulding.

tringler [trɛgle], *v.tr. Const: etc:* To line out (piece of timber); to chalk (a line).

tringlerie [trɛglari], *s.f.* = TRINGLAGE.

tringlette [trɛglɛt], *s.f.* Small rod.

tringlot [trɛglo], *s.m. Mil: P:* Soldier of the French Army Service Corps.

trinitaire [trinitɛːr], *s.m. or f. (a) Ecc:* Trinitarian, Redemptionist (monk or nun). *(b) Theol:* Trinitarian.

trinité [trinite], *s.f.* **1.** *Theol:* Trinity. (Fête de) la Trinité, Trinity Sunday. **2.** *Geog:* (Ile de) la Trinité, Trinidad.

trinitrotoluène [trinitrɔtɔlɥɛn], *s.m.*, **trinol** [trinɔl], *s.m. Exp:* Trinitrotoluene, trinitrotoluol, trotyl, *F:* T.N.T.

trinôme [trino:m], *a. & s.m. Mth:* Trinomial.

trinquart [trɛ̃ka:r], *s.m. Fish:* Herring-boat.

trinquer [trɛ̃ke], *v.i.* **1.** (*a*) To clink glasses (before drinking). *T. avec qn*, to take wine with s.o. (*b*) *F:* To hobnob (*avec*, with). **2.** *P:* To suffer a loss; to get the worst of it; to 'catch it.'

trinquet [trɛ̃kɛ], *s.m. Nau:* Foremast (in lateen-rigged vessel).

trinquette [trɛ̃kɛt], *s.f. Nau:* **1.** Storm-jib. **2.** Fore-topmast staysail.

trinqueur [trɛ̃kœ:r], *s.m. F:* Drinker, tippler.

trio [trio], *s.m. Mus: etc:* Trio.

triode [triɔd], *a. & s.f. W.Tel:* (Lampe) triode, three-electrode lamp.

triolet [triɔlɛ], *s.m.* **1.** *Pros:* Triolet. **2.** *Mus:* Triplet. **3.** (*a*) Dutch clover. (*b*) Black medick.

triomphal, -aux [triɔ̃fal, -o], *a.* Triumphal.

triomphalement [triɔ̃falmɑ̃], *adv.* Triumphantly; in triumph.

triomphant [triɔ̃fɑ̃], *a.* Triumphant.

triomphateur, -trice [triɔ̃fatœ:r, -tris]. **1.** *a.* Triumphing. **2.** *s.m.* Triumpher.

triomphe [triɔ̃:f], *s.m.* Triumph. Porter qn en triomphe, to carry s.o. shoulder high; to chair s.o. Arc de triomphe, triumphal arch.

triompher [triɔ̃fe], *v.i.* **1.** (*a*) *Rom.Ant:* To triumph. (*b*) To triumph (*de, sur*, over); to get the better (of s.o.). *T. d'une difficulté*, to overcome a difficulty. **2.** To exult, glory; to gloat (*de*, over).

tripaille [tripɑ:j], *s.f. F:* Garbage; offal.

tripang [tripɑ̃], *f. Echin:* Trepang, sea-slug.

triparti, -ite [triparti, -it], *a.* Tripartite.

tripartition [tripartisjɔ̃], *s.f.* Tripartition.

tripatouill|er [tripatuje], *v.tr.* **1.** *F:* To tamper, tinker, with (literary work); to garble (news, etc.); to cook (accounts); to gerrymander (an election). **2.** *P:* To paw, cuddle (s.o.). *s.m.* **-age.**

tripe¹ [trip], *s.f.* Usu. *pl.* (*a*) *F:* Intestines, guts. (*b*) *Cu:* Tripe. Tripes à la mode de Caen, braised tripe and onions.

tripe², *s.f. Tex:* Tripe de velours, mock velvet; velveteen.

tripenné [tripɛnne], *a. Bot:* Tripinnate.

triperie [tripri], *s.f.* Tripe-shop or -trade.

tripette [tripɛt], *s.f. A:* Small tripe. *F:* Ne pas valoir tripette, to be utterly worthless.

triphasé [trifaze], *a. El.E:* Triphase, three-phase (current).

triphtongue [triftɔ̃:g], *s.f. Ling:* Triphthong.

tripier, -ière [tripje, -jɛ:r], *s.* Tripe-dealer.

triplace [triplas], *a. & s.m.* Three-seater (car, plane).

triplan [triplɑ̃], *a. & s.m. Av:* Triplane.

triple [tripl], *a. & s.m.* Treble, threefold, triple. Des forces triples des nôtres, forces three times as great as ours. *F:* Menton à t. étage, triple chin. Facture en triple exemplaire, en triple expédition, invoice in triplicate. *Mth:* Raison triple, triple ratio. *F:* Aller au triple galop, to ride hell for leather. Un t. coquin, a villain of the deepest dye. S.a. ALLIANCE 1.

triplement¹ [tripləmɑ̃], *adv.* Trebly; threefold.

tripl|er [triple], *v.tr. & i.* To treble, triple; to increase threefold. *s.m.* **-ement².**

triplet [triplɛ], *s.m. Opt:* Triplet lens.

triplicata [triplikata], *s.m.inv.* Triplicate; third copy.

Triplice [triplis], *s.f. Hist:* La Triplice, the Triple Alliance.

Tripoli [tripɔli]. **1.** *Pr.n. Geog:* Tripoli. **2.** *s.m.* Tripoli (stone). *T. anglais*, rottenstone.

triporteur [tripɔrtœ:r], *s.m.* **1.** Carrier-tricycle. **2.** (Commercial) tricar.

tripot [tripo], *s.m.* Gambling-den.

tripotage [tripota:ʒ], *s.m.* **1.** (*a*) Messing round; fiddling about. (*b*) Odd jobs. Les tripotages du ménage, the daily chores. **2.** Underhand work; intrigue; jobbery.

tripoter [tripɔte]. **1.** *v.i.* (*a*) To fiddle about; to do odd jobs. *T. dans l'eau*, to dabble, mess about, in the water. (*b*) To engage in underhand dealings, in shady business. *T. dans la caisse*, to tamper with the cash. **2.** *v.tr.* (*a*) To finger, handle (sth.); to paw (s.o.); to meddle with (sth.). *T. sa chaîne de montre*, to fiddle with one's watch-chain. Qu'est-ce que vous tripotez là? what are you up to? (*b*) To deal shadily, dishonestly, with (money). Il se tripote quelque chose, there is something afoot.

tripotée, *s.f. P:* **1.** Dressing down, drubbing, licking. **2.** Large quantity; lots.

tripoteur, -euse [tripotœ:r, -ø:z], *s.* Schemer; esp. shady speculator.

tripotier, -ière [tripɔtje, -jɛ:r]. **1.** *s.* Keeper of a gambling-den. **2.** *a.* Scheming (person).

triptyque [triptik], *s.m.* **1.** *Art:* Triptych. **2.** *Aut:* Triptyque (for international travel).

trique [trik], *s.f. F:* Cudgel; heavy stick.

triqueballe [trikbal], *s.m. or f.* **1.** Sling-cart, devil-carriage. **2.** Timber-cart. **3.** Logging-wheels.

trique-madame, *s.f. Bot:* White stonecrop.

trirème [trirɛm], *s.f. Gr.Ant:* Trireme.

trisaïeul, -e [trizajœl], *s.* Great-great-grandfather; great-great-grandmother. *pl. Des tri-saïeul(e)s.*

trisannuel, -elle [trizan(n)ɥɛl], *a.* Triennial.

trisecteur, -trice [trisɛktœ:r, -tris]. *Geom:* **1.** *a.* Trisecting. **2.** *s.m.* Trisector.

trisser [trise], *v.i.* (Of swallow) To twitter.

tris(s)yllabe [trisillab]. **1.** *s.m.* Trisyllable. **2.** *a.* Trisyllabic.

tris(s)yllabique [trisillabik], *a.* Trisyllabic.

Tristan [tristɑ̃]. *Pr.n.m. Mediev.Lit:* Tristram.

triste [trist], *a.* Sad. **1.** (*a*) Sorrowful, doleful, woeful; melancholy (news). Sourire t., sad, wan, smile. (*b*) Dreary, dismal, cheerless. Campagne t., bleak, depressing, countryside. Faire triste mine à qn, to give s.o. a poor reception. Faire triste figure, to pull a long face. *F:* Triste comme un jour de pluie, comme un bonnet de nuit, dull as ditchwater. **2.** Unfortunate, painful (news, duty). En cette triste occasion, on this sad occasion. C'est une triste affaire, it's a bad business, a bad job. **3.** *F:* Poor, sorry, wretched (meal, excuse). Faire triste figure, to look sadly out of place. *adv.* **-ment.**

tristesse [tristɛs], *s.f.* (*a*) Sadness; melancholy, gloom. Avec tristesse, sadly. (*b*) Dullness, dreariness, dismalness, cheerlessness; bleakness (of landscape).

Triton¹ [tritɔ̃]. **1.** *Pr.n.m. Myth:* Triton. **2.** *s.m. Amph:* Triton, water-salamander, *F:* newt, eft.

triton², *s.m. Mus:* Tritone; augmented fourth.

trituration [trityrasjɔ̃], *s.f.* Trituration, grinding.

triturer [trityre], *v.tr.* (*a*) To triturate, grind, reduce to powder. (*b*) To masticate.

triumvir [triɔmvi:r], *s.m. Rom.Hist:* Triumvir.

triumvirat [triɔmvira], *s.m.* Triumvirate.
trivalent [trivalã], *a. Ch:* Trivalent, tervalent.
trivelin [trivlɛ̃], *s.m. A.Th:* Buffoon.
trivial, -als [trivjal]. **1.** *a.* (*a*) *A:* Trite, hackneyed, commonplace. (*b*) Vulgar, low, coarse (expression, etc.). **2.** *s.m. Tomber dans le t.,* to lapse into vulgarity. *adv.* **-ement.**
trivialiser [trivjalize], *v.tr.* To vulgarize (one's style, etc.).
trivialité [trivjalite], *s.f.* **1.** (*a*) *A:* Triteness. (*b*) Vulgarity, coarseness. **2.** Vulgarism; coarse expression.
troc [trɔk], *s.m.* Truck; exchange (in kind); barter; *F:* swopping. **Faire un troc,** *F:* to do a swop. *Donner qch. en t. pour qch.,* to barter sth. for sth. **Troc pour troc,** even-handed exchange.
trocart [trɔka:r], *s.m. Surg:* Trocar.
trochaïque [trɔkaik], *a. & s.m. Pros:* Trochaic.
trochanter [trɔkãte:r], *s.m. Anat:* Trochanter.
trochée¹ [trɔʃe], *s.m. Pros:* Trochee.
trochée², *s.f.* Tuft of twigs (on tree-stump).
trochet¹ [trɔʃe], *s.m. Bot:* Cluster.
trochet², *s.m.* Cooper's block.
trochile [trɔkil], *s.m.* Humming-bird.
trochisque [trɔʃisk], *s.m. Pharm:* Troche; lozenge.
trochlée [trɔkle], *s.f. Anat:* Trochlea.
trochoïde [trɔkɔid]. **1.** *a.* (*a*) *Anat:* Trochoid. (*b*) *Geom:* Trochoidal. **2.** *s.m. Geom:* Spherical lune. **3.** *s.f.* (*Courbe*) **trochoïde,** cycloid, trochoid, roulette.
troène [trɔɛn], *s.m. Bot:* Privet.
troglodyte [trɔglɔdit], *s.m.* **1.** Troglodyte; cave-dweller. **2.** *Orn:* Wren.
trogne [trɔɲ], *s.f.* Bloated face. *Il a une t. d'ivrogne,* he has a beery face.
trognon [trɔɲɔ̃], *s.m.* **1.** Core (of apple); stump (of cabbage); cabbage runt. **2.** *P:* = TÊTE.
Troie [trwa]. *Pr.n.f. A.Geog:* Troy. **La guerre de Troie,** the Trojan War.
trois [trwa], before a vowel sound [trwaz], *num.a.inv. & s.m.* Three. *F: Les trois quarts du temps,* most of the time. *Entrer par trois,* to come in in threes, three by three. *Le trois août* [lətrwa(z)u], the third of August. *Henri Trois,* Henry the Third. *Th: Le décor du trois,* the scenery of the third act.
trois-étoiles, *s.m. F: Cognac t.-é.,* three-star brandy. **Madame Trois-Étoiles,** (*Mme ****), Mrs X.
troisième [trwazjɛm]. **1.** *num.a. & s.* Third. **Demeurer au troisième (étage),** to live on the third floor. *F: De troisième ordre,* third-rate, third-class. **2.** *s.f.* (*a*) *Sch:* (Classe de) **troisième,** approx. = fourth form (of upper school). (*b*) *Rail:* **Voyager en troisième,** to travel third (-class). *adv.* **-ment.**
trois-mâts, *s.m.inv.* Three-masted ship. *T.-m. carré,* square-rigged three-master.
trois-pièces, *s.m.inv.* (Lady's) three-piece suit.
trois-quarts, *s.m.inv.* **1.** Three-quarter violin. **2.** *Fb:* **Les trois-quarts,** the three-quarters.
trois-quatre, *s.m.inv. Mus:* **1.** Three-four (time). **2.** Piece in three-four time.
trois-six, *s.m. Dist:* Proof spirit.
trôle¹ [tro:l], *s.f.* **Ouvrier à la trôle,** cabinet-maker who hawks his own wares from house to house.
trôle², *s.f. Fish:* Dragging, trawling. **Filet à la trôle,** drag-net; trawl(-net).
trôler [trole]. **1.** *v.tr. F:* (*a*) To take, drag, (s.o.) about; to have (s.o.) in tow. (*b*) To hawk (furniture). **2.** *v.i. F:* To wander about; to loaf.
trôleur [trolœ:r], *s.m.* (*a*) Hawker. (*b*) Vagrant, vagabond, tramp; loafer.

troll [trɔl], *s.m. Norse Myth:* Troll.
trolley [trɔlɛ], *s.m.* **1.** *Ind:* Troll(e)y, truck (of aerial ropeway). **Transport par trolley,** overhead transport. **2.** *El. Tramways:* Troll(e)y-pole and wheel. **Autobus à trolley,** trolley-bus.
trombe [trɔ̃:b], *s.f.* **1.** Waterspout. **2.** *T. de vent,* whirlwind. *F:* **Entrer, sortir, en trombe,** to burst in, out.
trombine [trɔ̃bin], *s.f. P:* Face, head; *P:* mug.
tromblon [trɔ̃blɔ̃], *s.m.* **1.** Blunderbuss. **2.** Grenade-sleeve (fitted to rifle).
trombone [trɔ̃bɔn], *s.m.* Trombone (instrument or performer). *T. à coulisse,* slide-trombone.
tromboniste [trɔ̃bɔnist], *s.m.* Trombone-player.
trompe [trɔ̃:p], *s.f.* **1.** (*a*) Trump, horn. *T. de chasse,* hunting-horn. *F: Publier qch. à son de trompe,* to trumpet sth. abroad. (*b*) Hooter, steam-whistle. (*c*) *Aut:* (Reed) horn. **2.** Proboscis; trunk (of elephant). **3.** *Anat:* **Trompe d'Eustache,** Eustachian tube. **4.** *Ind:* Aspirator.
trompe-l'œil, *s.m.inv.* **1.** *a. Art:* Still-life deception. (*b*) Dummy window, etc. **2.** *Pej:* Deceptive appearance; illusion; eye-wash; piece of bluff, of camouflage.
tromper [trɔ̃pe], *v.tr.* To deceive. **1.** (*a*) To cheat; to impose upon, take in (s.o.). **Se laisser tromper aux apparences,** to be taken in by appearances. (*b*) To betray; be unfaithful to (wife, husband). **2.** (*a*) *T. qn sur ses intentions,* to mislead s.o. as to one's intentions. *T. les espérances de qn,* to disappoint s.o.'s hopes. *C'est justement ce qui vous trompe,* that is just where you are mistaken. (*b*) To outwit, baffle. (*c*) To beguile (grief, tedium); to while away (the time).

se tromper, to be mistaken; to be wrong; to make a mistake. *Se t. dans son calcul,* to be out in one's reckoning. *Je me suis trompé de maison, de route,* I went to the wrong house, took the wrong road. *Se t. d'heure,* to mistake the time. **Elle ressemble à sa sœur à s'y tromper,** she is remarkably like her sister. **Il n'y a pas à s'y tromper,** there is no doubt about it. **Vous m'avez fait tromper,** you made me commit a mistake; you put me off.
tromperie [trɔ̃pri], *s.f.* **1.** (*a*) Deceit, deception, fraud. (*b*) Illusion. **2.** Piece of deceit; fraud.
trompeter [trɔ̃pɛte], *v.* (**je trompette;** **je trompetterai**) **1.** *v.tr.* To trumpet (news) abroad. **2.** *v.i.* (Of the eagle) To scream.
trompette [trɔ̃pɛt]. **1.** *s.f.* (*a*) Trumpet ((i) instrument, (ii) trumpeter or orchestral performer). *Sonnerie de t.,* trumpet-call. *F:* **Emboucher, entonner, la trompette,** to adopt a high-flown style, an epic style. S.a. TAMBOUR 1. **La trompette du jugement dernier,** the last trump. (*b*) **Trompette électrique, d'appel,** buzzer. (*c*) *Aut:* Horn. **2.** *s.m. Mil:* Trumpeter.
trompeu|r, -euse [trɔ̃pœːr, -øːz]. **1.** *a.* (*a*) Deceitful. (*b*) Deceptive, delusive, misleading. *Prov: Les apparences sont trompeuses,* appearances are deceptive. **2.** *s.* Deceiver, cheat. **Le trompeur trompé,** the biter bit. *adv.* **-sement.**
tronc [trɔ̃], *s.m.* **1.** (*a*) Trunk (of tree, of body); bole, body, stem (of tree); barrel (of ox). (*b*) *Arch:* Trunk, drum (of column). (*c*) Parent stock (of family). **2.** Collecting-box (in church). **3.** *Geom:* Frustum (of a cone, of a pyramid).
tronche [trɔ̃:ʃ], *s.f.* **1.** (*a*) Log, esp. yule-log. (*b*) *P:* Head, pate. **2.** *For:* Stem-pruned tree.
tronçon [trɔ̃sɔ̃], *s.m.* **1.** (Broken) piece, end, stub, stump (of sword, mast); frustum (of column). *T. de bois,* log.
tronçonn|er [trɔ̃sɔne], *v.tr.* To cut (anything of

cylindrical shape) into pieces, into sections, into lengths; to cut up. *s.m.* **-ement.**

trône [tro:n], *s.m.* Throne. **Monter au trône, sur le trône,** to mount, ascend, the throne. *Mettre qn sur le t.,* to seat, instal, s.o. upon the throne. **Discours du trône,** King's speech.

trôner [trone], *v.i.* (a) To sit enthroned. (b) *F:* To occupy a place of honour; to sit in state; *F:* to throne it, to lord it.

tronquer [trɔ̃ke], *v.tr.* (a) To truncate (tree); to mutilate (statue). (b) *F:* To curtail, cut down (novel).

tronqué, *a.* (a) Truncated. **Mât tronqué,** stub mast. (b) *F: Édition tronquée,* abbreviated edition.

trop [tro]. **1.** *adv.* Too. (a) (With adj.) Too, over-. *C'est trop difficile,* it is too difficult. *Trop fatigué,* over-tired. *Trop fatigué pour courir,* too tired to run. (b) (With vb) Too much, overmuch, unduly, over-. *Trop travailler,* to over-work, to work too hard. *Boire trop, trop boire,* to drink to excess. *Je l'ai trop aimé* [tropeme], I loved him too well. *Ne vous y fiez pas trop,* don't count on it too much. *Il parle trop,* he is too talkative. *On ne saurait trop le répéter, le trop répéter,* it cannot be too often repeated. **Je ne sais trop que dire,** I hardly know what to say. **2.** *s.m.* Too much, too many. **Le trop ne vaut rien,** enough is as good as a feast. *Trop de bruit,* too much noise. *Trop d'amis,* too many friends. **De trop,** too much, too many. **Être de trop,** to be in the way, unwelcome. *Ils sont trop!* they are too many! *Ils sont de trop,* they are not wanted. **Par trop,** (altogether) too (much). *Être par trop généreux,* to be far too generous.

trope [trɔp], *s.m. Rh:* Trope.

trophée [trɔfe], *s.m.* Trophy (of war, etc.).

tropical, -aux [trɔpikal, -o], *a.* Tropical.

tropique [trɔpik]. **1.** *a.* Tropical (year). **2.** *s.m.* (a) *Astr: Geog:* Tropic. (b) *pl.* The tropics. *F:* **Maladie des tropiques,** yellow fever.

trop-plein [troplɛ̃], *s.m.* Overflow (of bath, etc.). **(Tuyau de) trop-plein,** waste-pipe, overflow-pipe.

troqu er [trɔke], *v.tr.* To exchange, barter, truck, *P:* swop (sth.). *T. qch. contre qch.,* to exchange, barter, sth. for sth. *F:* **Troquer son cheval borgne contre un aveugle,** to swop bad for worse. *s.* **-eur, -euse.**

trot [tro], *s.m.* Trot. **Aller le trot, au trot,** to trot. *Au petit t.,* at a gentle, easy, trot. **Partir au trot,** to trot off. (Of horse) **Prendre le trot,** to break into a trot.

trotte [trɔt], *s.f. F:* Distance, stretch, run. *Il y a une bonne t. d'ici là,* it is a good step from here. *Tout d'une trotte,* without stopping, at a stretch.

trotte-menu, *a.inv. F:* Pitter-patter, scampering (steps of mice).

trotter [trɔte]. **1.** *v.i.* To trot; (of mice) to scamper. *F:* **Elle est toujours à trotter,** she is always on the trot, on the go. **2.** *v.tr.* To put (horse) to the trot; to trot (horse).

se trotter, *F:* = S'EN ALLER.

trotterie [trɔtri], *s.f. F:* Toddling steps (as of child or old person); toddle.

trotteur, -euse [trɔtœ:r, -ø:z]. **1.** *s.* (a) Trotter; trotting horse or mare. (b) *F:* Quick walker. **2.** *s.f.* Trotteuse. (a) Centre-seconds hand (of watch). (b) Go-cart (for teaching infant to walk).

trottin [trɔtɛ̃], *s.m.* (Dressmaker's) errand-girl.

trottiner [trɔtine], *v.i.* **1.** *a) Equit:* To trot short. (b) *F:* To jog along (on one's horse). **2.** *F:* To trot about (from one room to another); to pit-pat (about or along); (of child) to toddle.

trottinette [trɔtinɛt], *s.f.* Scooter.

trottoir [trɔtwa:r], *s.m.* **1.** (a) Footway, footpath, pavement. **Bordure du trottoir,** kerb. *Aut:* **Heurter le t.,** to strike the kerb. **Artiste de trottoir,** pavement artist. (b) *Rail:* (Station) platform. **2. Trottoir roulant,** escalator; moving stairway.

trou [tru], *s.m.* Hole. **1.** (a) *T. dans un bas,* hole in a stocking. **Percer un trou,** to cut, bore, or prick, a hole (*dans,* in). *F:* **Faire son trou,** to come to the fore; to work oneself into a good position. S.a. LUNE 1. (b) *T. dans une haie,* gap in a hedge. **2.** *T. dans une route,* pot-hole in a road. *T. d'obus,* shell-hole. *Av:* **Trou d'air,** air-pocket, *F:* bump. *T. de souris,* mouse-hole. *F:* **Habiter un petit trou mort,** to live in a dead-and-alive little hole. *Golf:* **Partie par trous,** match-play. *Th:* **Trou du souffleur,** prompter's box. **3.** *Mch: etc:* **Trou d'homme,** manhole.

troubade [trubad], *s.m. Mil: F:* Foot-slogger.

troubadour [trubadu:r], *s.m. Lit.Hist:* Troubadour; minstrel (of Provence).

troublant [trublɑ̃], *a.* Disturbing. **1.** Disquieting, disconcerting. **2.** Perturbing. *Parfum t.,* heady perfume.

trouble¹ [trubl], *a.* **1.** Turbid, cloudy, muddy (liquid); dim (glasses, eyes); murky, overcast (sky). **Avoir la vue trouble,** to be dim-sighted. *Situation t.,* situation that is far from clear. *F:* **Pêcher en eau trouble,** to fish in troubled waters. *Adv.* **Voir trouble,** to be dim-sighted. **2.** Confused (mind); turbid (conscience). *Joie t. et presque douloureuse,* uneasy and almost painful joy.

trouble², *s.m.* **1.** (a) Confusion, disorder (in the ranks, in s.o.'s ideas, etc.). **Porter le trouble dans une cérémonie,** to disturb a ceremony. *Troubles de digestion,* derangement of the digestion. *Troubles de vision,* eyesight trouble. (b) Agitation, perturbation, uneasiness. **Jeter le trouble dans l'esprit de qn,** to disturb s.o.'s mind; to perturb s.o. (c) *pl.* Public disturbances. *Troubles ouvriers,* disturbances due to labour. **2.** *Jur:* **Trouble de jouissance,** disturbance of possession.

trouble-fête, *s.m.inv.* Spoil-sport, wet blanket, kill-joy.

troubler [truble], *v.tr.* **1.** To make (liquid, etc.) cloudy, thick, muddy; to muddy (water). *Yeux troublés de larmes,* eyes blurred with tears. **2.** To disturb; to interfere with (activities). *T. le silence,* to break (in upon) the silence. **Troubler le repos, l'ordre public,** to make, create, a disturbance; *Jur:* to break the peace. *T. la digestion de qn,* to upset s.o.'s digestion. *Imagination troublée,* disordered imagination. **3.** To perturb. (a) To confuse, upset, discompose (s.o.); to disquiet (s.o.); to make (s.o.) uneasy; to put (s.o.) out. *Elle était toute troublée,* she was all in a flutter. (b) To agitate, excite, upset, stir. *Parfums qui troublent les sens,* scents that stir, thrill, the senses.

se troubler. 1. To become turbid; (of wine, etc.) to get cloudy; (of sky) to become overcast, to cloud over; (of vision) to become blurred, hazy; to grow dim; (of voice) to waver, to break (with emotion). **2.** To show perturbation; to falter; to get confused. **Sans se troubler,** unconcerned, unruffled.

trouer [true], *v.tr.* To hole; to make a hole or holes in (wall, etc.); to perforate. **Avoir les bas troués,** to have holes in one's stockings. **Troué aux coudes,** out at elbows. **Artiste qui a bien de la peine à trouer,** artist who has much difficulty in coming to the front.

se trouer. I. To wear into holes. **2.** To open up; to show an opening.

trouée, s.f. Gap, opening, breach. **F: Faire sa trouée,** to come to the fore.

troupe [trup], s.f. **I.** (a) Troop, band, company, throng (of people); gang, set (of thieves). (b) *Th:* Troupe; (theatrical) company. (c) Herd, drove (of cattle, deer); flock (of sheep, geese). **Ces animaux vivent en troupe,** these animals herd together, are gregarious. **2.** *Mil:* (a) Troop; body of soldiers. (b) (i) N.C.O.'s and men; (ii) men (as opp. to officers). **Officiers et troupe,** officers and other ranks. **Enfant de troupe,** soldier's son or orphan (brought up and schooled in the barracks). **Chevaux de troupe,** army remounts. (c) *pl.* Troops, forces.

troupeau [trupo], s.m. Herd, drove (of cattle); flock (of sheep, geese, etc.).

troupier [trupje], s.m. *Mil:* Soldier, private. *F:* **Vieux troupier,** old campaigner.

trousse [trus], s.f. **I.** Bundle, package; truss (of hay). **2.** *pl.* *A.Cost:* Trunk-hose. *F:* **Être aux trousses de qn,** to be after s.o., on s.o.'s heels. **3.** Case, kit (of instruments, tools). *T. de toilette,* dressing-case. *T. à réparations,* (cyclist's, etc.) repair outfit.

trousseau [truso], s.m. **I.** Bunch. Esp. **Trousseau de clefs,** bunch of keys. **2.** (a) Outfit (of clothing), esp. school outfit. (b) (Bride's) trousseau.

trousse-queue, s.m.inv. *Harn:* Dock-piece.

troussequin [truskɛ̃], s.m. **I.** Cantle (of saddle). **2.** = TRUSQUIN.

trouss|er [truse], v.tr. **I.** (a) To tuck up, pin up (skirt, etc.); to turn up (one's trousers). (b) *Cu:* To truss (fowl). **2.** *F:* To dispatch, get through, (work, business) promptly; to polish off (meal). s.m. **-age.** **se trousser,** to tuck up one's clothes.

troussé, a. **I.** Bundled up; tucked-up (skirt, etc.); trussed (fowl, etc.). **2.** *F:* **Bien troussé,** well-arranged, neat (object); dapper (individual); well-prepared (meal); neatly turned (compliment).

troussis [trusi], s.m. Tuck (in garment).

trouvaille [truva:j], s.f. Find, lucky find, godsend, windfall.

trouv|er [truve], v.tr. To find. **I.** (a) *Je ne peux pas t. mes clefs,* I cannot find my keys. *Je lui trouve d'excellentes qualités,* I find in him excellent qualities. *Ces plantes se trouvent partout,* these plants are met with everywhere. **Aller trouver qn,** to go to s.o.; to go and see s.o. (b) To discover, invent (process). **2.** *T.* (qch.) *par hasard,* to discover, hit upon, come upon, come across (sth.). *T. qn en faute,* to catch s.o. napping. **Bureau des objets trouvés,** lost-property office. *T. un filon,* une idée, to strike upon a vein, an idea. **C'est bien trouvé!** happy thought! **Trouver à qui parler,** to meet one's match. **Il trouva la mort à . . .,** he met his death at. . . . *S.a.* ENFANT, REDIRE 2. **3.** To think, deem. *Je la trouve jolie,* I consider her pretty. **Vous trouvez?** you think so? *S.a.* BON I.7, MAUVAIS. a. **-able.** s. **-eur, -euse.** **se trouver. I.** (a) To be. *Je me trouvais alors à Paris,* I was then in Paris. *Se t. pris,* to be caught. *Trouvez-vous ici à quatre heures,* be here at four o'clock. (b) To feel. *Je me trouve très bien ici,* I feel very comfortable here. **Se trouver bien de qch.,** to feel all the better for sth. *Se t. bien d'avoir fait qch.,* to find it an advantage to have done sth. *Je me trouve mieux,* I feel better. *Je m'en trouve mieux,* I feel better for it. *S.a.* MAL³ 2. **2.** To happen; to turn out.

Cela se trouve bien, this is most opportune. *Je me trouve avoir du temps devant moi,* I happen to have some spare time. *Impers.* **Il se trouve que** + *ind.,* it happens that. . . .

trouvère [truvɛ:r], s.m. *Lit.Hist:* Trouvere; minstrel (of N. of Fr., 11th cent.).

troyen, -enne [trwajɛ̃, -ɛn], a. & s. Trojan.

truand, -ande [tryɑ̃, -ɑ̃:d], s. *A. & Hum:* Sturdy beggar; vagrant.

truble [trybl], s.f. *Fish:* Hoop-net; shove-net.

trublion [trybliɔ̃], s.m. Trouble-maker.

truc [tryk], s.m. *F:* **I.** (a) Knack. **Avoir le truc pour faire qch.,** to have the knack of doing sth. (b) Trick, dodge. *Th:* **Pièce à trucs,** play with elaborate stage effects. *T. d'optique,* optical illusion. **2.** *P:* (a) Thingumbob, thingummy. (b) Thing, contraption, gadget.

trucage [tryka:ʒ], s.m. **I.** Faking; *F:* cooking (of accounts). **2.** Fake. *Cin:* Trick picture.

truchement [tryʃmɑ̃], s.m. *A:* **I.** Dragoman. **2.** Go-between; spokesman (for s.o.).

truck [tryk], s.m. *Rail:* Truck.

truculence [trykylɑ̃:s], s.f. Truculence.

truculent [trykylɑ̃], a. Truculent.

trudgeon [trydʒɔ̃], s.m. *Swim:* Trudgen stroke.

truelle [tryɛl], s.f. **I.** Trowel. **2.** *T. à poisson,* fish-slice.

truellée [tryɛle], s.f. Trowelful.

truffe [tryf], s.f. (a) Truffle. (b) *F:* Bulbous nose.

truff|er [tryfe], v.tr. **I.** To stuff with truffles. **Dinde truffée,** truffled turkey. **2.** To grangerize (book). s.m. **-age.**

trufficulteur [tryfikyltœ:r], s.m. Truffle-grower.

truie [trɥi], s.f. Sow. **Peau de truie,** pigskin.

truisme [tryism], s.m. Truism.

truite [trɥit], s.f. *Ich:* Trout. **Truite saumonée,** salmon trout.

truité [trɥite], a. Red-spotted; speckled; spotted (dog); flea-bitten (horse); crackled (china). [TRUITE]

trumeau [trymo], s.m. **I.** (a) *Arch:* Pier. (b) *Furn:* Pier-glass. **2.** *Cu:* Leg of beef; gravy beef.

truquage [tryka:ʒ], s.m. = TRUCAGE.

truqu|er [tryke]. **I.** v.tr. To fake; *F:* to cook (accounts). *T. une élection,* to gerrymander an election. **Article truqué,** fake. **2.** *Abs.* To sham. [TRUC] s. **-eur, -euse.**

trusquin [tryskɛ̃], s.m. *Tls:* Marking-gauge, mortise gauge. **Compas à trusquin,** beam-compass.

tsar [tsa:r], s.m. Czar, tsar.

tsarévitch [tsarevitʃ], s.m. Czarevitch, tsarevitch.

tsarine [tsarin], s.f. Czarina, tsarina.

tsé-tsé, tsétsé [tsetse], s.f. *Ent:* Tsetse(-fly).

tu¹ [ty], pers.pron.nom. (Familiar form of address to relations, intimate friends, children, animals) (a) You. *Qui es-tu, toi?* who are you? *F:* **Être à tu et à toi avec qn,** to be on familiar terms with s.o. *P:* (Abbreviated to t') *T'entends bien!* you understand! (b) (In Biblical style; also in Quaker speech) Thou.

tu². See TAIRE.

tuant [tɥɑ̃], a. *F:* **I.** Killing, laborious (work). **2.** Boring; exasperating.

tub [tœb], s.m. *Toil:* Tub, (sponge-)bath.

tuba [tyba], s.m. *Mus:* (Sax-)tuba; bass-tuba.

tube [tyb], s.m. **I.** (a) Tube, pipe. **Tube acoustique,** speaking-tube. *W.Tel:* **T. redresseur,** rectifying valve. *T. de pâte de couleur,* tube of colour. *Mch:* *T. de niveau,* glass gauge, gauge-glass. **Chaudière à tubes,** tubular boiler. (b) *Anat:* Tube, duct. **2.** *Artil:* (i) Inner tube (of gun). (ii) *F:* Gun. **3.** *pl.* *Dressm:* Bugles. **4.** *P:* Top hat, *F:* topper.

tub|er [tybe], *v.tr.* To tube. *s.m.* **-age.**

tubercule [tybɛrkyl], *s.m.* **I.** *Bot:* Tuber. **2.** *Med:* Tubercle.

tuberculeux, -euse [tybɛrkylø, -øːz]. **I.** *a.* (*a*) *Bot:* Tubercular (root). (*b*) *Med:* Tuberculous (lung). **2.** *s.* Tubercular patient; consumptive.

tuberculose [tybɛrkyloːz], *s.f.* Tuberculosis.

tubéreux, -euse [tyberø, -øːz]. *Bot:* **I.** *a.* Tuberous. **2.** *s.f.* **Tubéreuse,** tuberose.

tubulaire [tybylɛːr], *a.* Tubular. *Voie souterraine t.,* tube railway.

tubulure [tybylyːr], *s.f. Hyd.E:* etc: Tubulure, tubulature; pipe; nozzle. *Flacon à trois tubulures,* three-neck bottle. *I.C.E:* T. *d'échappement,* exhaust manifold.

tudesque [tydɛsk], *a.* Teutonic, Germanic.

tudieu [tydjø], *int. A:* Zounds! 'sdeath!

tue-mouches, *s.m.inv.* **I.** *Bot:* Fly agaric. **2.** (*a*) Fly-swatter. (*b*) **Papier tue-mouches,** fly-paper.

tuer [tɥe], *v.tr.* To kill. **I.** To slaughter, butcher (animal). **2.** To slay, make away with (s.o.). *T. qn d'un coup de couteau,* to stab s.o. dead. *Il fut tué d'une balle au cœur,* he was shot through the heart. **Tuer qn raide,** (i) to kill s.o. on the spot; (ii) to shoot s.o. dead. **Se faire tuer,** (i) to seek death; (ii) to get killed. **Tué à l'ennemi,** killed in action. *F:* **Tuer le temps,** to kill time.

se tuer. I. (*a*) To kill oneself; to commit suicide. (*b*) To get killed. **2.** *Se t. à force de boire,* to drink oneself to death. *Je me tue à vous le dire,* I am sick and tired of telling you.

tuerie [tyri], *s.f.* Slaughter, butchery, carnage.

tue-tête (à), *adv.phr.* At the top of one's voice. *Crier à t.-t.,* to bawl, yell.

tueur [tɥœːr], *s.m.* (*a*) Butcher, slaughterman. (*b*) Killer, slayer. *T. de lions,* lion-killer.

tuf [tyf], *s.m.* **I.** *Geol:* (*a*) **Tuf volcanique,** tuff. (*b*) **Tuf calcaire,** calcareous tufa; chalky subsoil. **2.** *F:* Bottom, bed-rock, foundation (of one's mind, being). *Descendre jusqu'au tuf,* to get down to bed-rock. *Com:* (Of prices) **Toucher le tuf,** to touch bottom.

tuile [tɥil], *s.f.* **I.** (Roofing) tile. *T. flamande, en S,* pantile. *T. faîtière,* ridge tile. **Couvrir un comble en tuiles,** to tile a roof. **2.** *P:* Unlucky event; crusher.

tuilerie [tɥilri], *s.f.* (*a*) Tile-works. (*b*) **Les Tuileries,** the Tuileries ((i) *Hist:* Palace, (ii) Gardens, in Paris).

tulipe [tylip], *s.f.* **I.** Tulip. **2.** (Tulip- or bell-shaped) shade (for electric light).

tulle [tyl], *s.m. Tex:* Tulle; net (fabric).

tullerie [tylri], *s.f.* **I.** Tulle-making. **2.** Tulle-factory.

tuméfaction [tymefaksjɔ̃], *s.f.* Tumefaction, swelling.

tuméfier [tymefje], *v.tr.* To tumefy; to cause (joint, etc.) to swell.

se tuméfier, to tumefy; to swell.

tumeur [tymœːr], *s.f. Med:* **I.** Tumour; *F:* growth. **2.** Swelling.

tumulaire [tymylɛːr], *a.* Tumulary; sepulchral. **Pierre tumulaire,** tombstone, gravestone.

tumulte [tymylt], *s.m.* Tumult, hubbub, turmoil, uproar. **Tumulte,** in an uproar, in confusion.

tumultueu|x, -euse [tymyltɥø, -øːz], *a.* Tumultuous, noisy, riotous. *adv.* **-sement.**

tumulus [tymylyːs], *s.m.* Tumulus, barrow; sepulchral mound. *pl. Des tumulus, des tumuli.*

tungstate [tœ̃kstat], *s.m. Ch:* Tungstate.

tungstène [tœ̃kstɛn], *s.m. Ch:* Tungsten. **Acier au tungstène,** tungsten steel.

tunique [tynik], *s.f.* **I.** *Cost:* Tunic. *Ecc:* Tunicle. **2.** *Biol: Bot:* Tunic; coat, envelope (of an organ).

Tunisie [tynizi]. *Pr.n.f. Geog:* Tunis (the Protectorate, with cap. Tunis).

tunnel [tynɛl], *s.m.* (*a*) Tunnel. *Aer:* **Tunnel aérodynamique,** wind tunnel. (*b*) *El.E:* T. *de câbles,* cable subway.

turban [tyrbã], *s.m.* Turban. *F:* **Prendre le turban,** to go over to Islam.

turbidité [tyrbidite], *s.f.* Turbidity, cloudiness, muddiness (of liquid).

turbin [tyrbɛ̃], *s.m. P:* Work, grind. *Maison où il y a beaucoup de t.,* house where there is a lot to do. [TURBINER]

turbine [tyrbin], *s.f.* **I.** Turbine. *T. à choc,* impulse turbine. *T. à réaction,* reaction turbine. *T. hydraulique,* water turbine, water-wheel. *T. à vapeur,* steam turbine. **2.** (Rotary) fan (of vacuum-cleaner, etc.).

turbiné [tyrbine], *a.* Turbinate(d); whorled.

turbiner [tyrbine], *v.i. P:* To work, toil.

turbo-alternateur, *s.m. El.E:* Turbo-alternator.

turbo-électrique, *a. Mch:* Turbo-electric.

turbo-moteur, *s.m.* Turbo-motor; turbine.

turbot [tyrbo], *s.m. Ich:* Turbot.

turbotière [tyrbotjɛːr], *s.f. Cu:* Turbot-kettle.

turbotin [tyrbotɛ̃], *s.m. Ich:* Young turbot.

turbulence [tyrbylãːs], *s.f.* Turbulence. (*a*) Unruliness, insubordination. (*b*) Boisterousness.

turbulent [tyrbylã], *a.* Turbulent. (*a*) Restless, unruly (crowd). (*b*) Boisterous, stirring (child).

turc, *f.* **turque** [tyrk]. **I.** *a.* Turkish. **Être assis à la turque,** to sit cross-legged. **2.** (*a*) *s.* Turk. **Tête de Turc,** (i) try-your-strength machine (at fairs); hence (ii) butt, scapegoat. (*b*) *s.m. Ling:* Turkish.

turco [tyrko], *s.m. Mil: F:* Turco; Algerian rifleman.

turcoman [tyrkomã], *s.m. Ethn: Ling:* Turcoman, Turkoman.

turelure [tyrlyːr], *s.f. F:* Refrain (of song); fol-de-rol. *F:* **C'est toujours la même turelure,** it's the old story.

turf [tyrf], *s.m.* **I.** Race-course. **2.** Le turf, racing; the turf.

turfiste [tyrfist], *s.m.* Race-goer.

turgescence [tyrʒɛssãːs], *s.f.* Turgescence, turgidity.

turgescent [tyrʒɛssã], *a.* Turgescent.

turlupin [tyrlypɛ̃], *s.m.* (*a*) Clown, buffoon, merry-andrew. (*b*) Scamp.

turlupinade [tyrlypinad], *s.f. A:* Piece of clownery, of low buffoonery.

turlurette [tyrlyrɛt], *int.* Fiddle-de-dee!

turlutaine [tyrlyten], *s.f.* **I.** *A:* Bird-organ. **2. C'est sa turlutaine,** he is always harping on that.

turlututu [tyrlytyty], *int. F:* Fiddlesticks! fiddle-de-dee! hoity-toity!

turne [tyrn], *s.f. P:* (*a*) Diggings, digs. (*b*) Sanctum, den.

turnep(s) [tyrnɛp(s)] *s.m.* Turnip-cabbage, kohl-rabi.

turpitude [tyrpityd], *s.f.* Turpitude. **I.** Depravity, baseness. **2.** (*a*) Scurvy trick, base deed. (*b*) *Débiter des turpitudes,* to talk smut.

turque [tyrk], *a. & s.f.* See TURC.

turquet [tyrkɛ], *s.m.* **I.** Maize; Indian corn. **2.** Pug(-dog).

turquette [tyrkɛt], *s.f. Bot:* Rupture-wort.

Turquie [tyrki]. *Pr.n.f. Geog:* Turkey. *F:* **Blé de Turquie,** Turkish wheat; maize.

turquin [tyrkɛ̃], *a.* **Bleu turquin,** slate-blue, bluish-grey (marble, etc.).

turquoise [tyrkwaːz], **I.** *s.f.* Turquoise. **2.** *a.inv. & s.m.inv.* Turquoise (blue).

tu-s, -t, etc. See TAIRE.

tussilage [tysilaːʒ], *s.m. Bot:* Coltsfoot.

tussor [tysɔːr], *s.m. Tex:* Tussore silk.

tutélaire [tytelɛːr], *a.* Tutelary (divinity); guardian (angel). *Jur:* **Gestion tutélaire,** guardianship.

tutelle [tytɛl], *s.f.* **I.** *Jur:* Tutelage, guardianship. **Enfant en tutelle,** child under guardianship. **2.** *F:* Protection. **Prendre qn sous sa tutelle,** *F:* to take s.o. under one's wing. **Tenir qn en tutelle,** to keep s.o. under one's thumb.

tuteur, -trice [tytœːr, -tris]. **I.** *s.* (*a*) *Jur:* Guardian; tutor (of a minor). (*b*) *F:* Protector. **2.** *s.m. Hort:* Prop, support, stake.

tut|oyer [tytwaje], *v.tr.* (**je tutoie; je tutoierai**) To address (s.o.) as *tu* and *toi* (instead of *vous*); to be on familiar terms with (s.o.). *s.m.* **-oiement.**

tutu [tyty], *s.m.* **I.** (Child's word) Bottom, behind. **2.** (Ballet dancer's) 'sticking-out' skirt.

tuyau, -aux [tɥijo, tɥijo], *s.m.* **I.** (*a*) Pipe, tube. *T. de descente* (*d'une maison*), rain-water pipe, down pipe. *T. d'évent,* blow-off pipe (of cesspool). *T. flexible, t. en caoutchouc,* (i) rubber tubing; (ii) hose(-pipe). **Tuyau d'incendie,** fire-hose. *T. d'arrosage,* garden-hose. **Tuyau de cheminée,** chimney-flue. **Tuyau de poêle,** (i) stove-pipe; (ii) *P:* top hat, topper. **Tuyau acoustique,** speaking-tube. **Tuyau d'orgue,** organ-pipe. *F:* **Dire qch. à qn dans le tuyau de l'oreille,** to whisper sth. in s.o.'s ear (whence the meaning 2 below). (*b*) Stem (of tobacco-pipe); nozzle (of bellows). (*c*) Barrel (of quill). (*d*) Stalk (of corn). (*e*) *Laund:* Flute, goffer, quill. **2.** *F:* (at horse-racing); wrinkle, hint. **Avoir des tuyaux,** to be in the know.

tuyauter [tɥijote, tɥijote], *v.tr.* **I.** *Laund:* To flute, goffer, quill (linen). **Fer à tuyauter,** goffering tongs. **2.** *Rac: etc: F:* To give a tip, a wrinkle, to (s.o.); to put (s.o.) up to all the tips.

tuyauterie [tɥijotri, tɥijotri], *s.f.* Pipe and tube works, factory or trade.

tuyauteur [tɥijotœːr, tɥijotœːr], *s.m. F:* Tipster.

tuyère [tɥjɛːr], *s.f.* (*a*) *Metall:* Tuyere, twyer,

blast-pipe, nozzle. (*b*) *T. d'injecteur.* injector nozzle.

tympan [tɛ̃pɑ̃], *s.m.* **I.** *Anat:* Drum (of ear). **Membrane du tympan,** tympanic membrane; ear-drum. *Bruit à briser le t.,* ear-splitting noise. **2.** *Typ:* Tympan. **3.** *Arch:* Tympanum.

type [tip], *s.m.* **I.** Type. *Com:* Sample piece; pattern. **Motocyclette type,** motor bicycle of standard design. **2.** (*a*) *F:* Personality. **Drôle de type,** queer chap, rum stick. (*b*) *P:* Fellow, chap, bloke. *T'es un chic type,* you're a brick, a trump. **3.** *Typ:* Type.

typesse [tipɛs], *s.f. P:* Woman, girl.

typha [tifa], *s.m. Bot:* Typha, (cat's)-tail.

typhlite [tiflit], *s.f. Med:* Typhlitis.

typhoïde [tifoid], *a.* **Fièvre typhoïde,** typhoid (fever); enteric fever.

typhoïque [tifoik]. **I.** *a.* Typhoidal. **2.** *s.* Patient suffering from typhoid.

typhon [tifɔ̃], *s.m. Meteor:* Typhoon.

typhus [tifyːs], *s.m. Med:* Typhus (fever).

typifié [tipifje], *a.* Typical; standardized.

typique [tipik], *a.* Typical. **I.** Symbolical. **2.** True to type.

typographe [tipɔgraf], *s.m., F:* **typo** [tipo], *s.m.* Typographer, printer.

typographie [tipɔgrafi], *s.f.* **I.** Typography. **2.** Printing-works.

typographique [tipɔgrafik], *a.* Typographic(al). **Erreur typographique,** misprint. *adv.* **-ment,** -ally.

typolithographie [tipɔlitɔgrafi], *s.f.* Typolithography.

typotélégraphe [tipɔtelegraf], *s.m.* Printing telegraph.

tyran [tirɑ̃], *s.m.* Tyrant. *Femme qui est un tyran domestique,* woman who is a domestic tyrant. *Il est le t. de sa famille,* he tyrannizes his family.

tyranneau [tirano], *s.m.* Petty tyrant.

tyrannie [tirani], *s.f.* Tyranny.

tyrannique [tiranik], *a.* Tyrannical, tyrannous. *adv.* **-ment.**

tyranniser [tiranize], *v.tr.* To tyrannize over (s.o.); to tyrannize (s.o.).

tyrolien, -ienne [tirɔljɛ̃, -jɛn]. **I.** *a. & s.* Tyrolese. **2.** *s.f.* **Tyrolienne,** Tyrolienne; yodelled song or melody.

tzigane [tsigan], *s.m. & f.* Tzigane; Hungarian gipsy.

U

U, u [y], *s.m.* (The letter) U, u. **Fer en U,** channel iron. *Porte-objectif en U,* stirrup lens-front.

ubiquiste [ybikɥist], *a. & s. F:* Ubiquitous (person).

ubiquité [ybikɥite], *s.f.* Ubiquity.

udomètre [ydɔmɛtr], *s.m.* Udometer, pluviometer, rain-gauge.

uhlan [ylɑ̃], *s.m.* (Pronounced as with h 'aspirate') Uhlan. **Les uhlans** [leylɑ̃], the uhlans.

ukase [ykɑːz], *s.m.* Ukase. *F: U. paternel,* paternal fiat.

ulcération [ylsɛrasjɔ̃], *s.f.* Ulceration.

ulcère [ylsɛːr], *s.m.* Ulcer; sore. *U. rongeant,* rodent ulcer.

ulcérer [ylsere], *v.tr.* (**il ulcère; il ulcérera**) (*a*) *Med:* To ulcerate. (*b*) *F:* To wound, embitter (s.o.). **s'ulcérer,** to ulcerate; to fester.

ulcéré, *a.* Ulcerated. *F:* **Avoir une conscience ulcérée,** to suffer pangs of conscience. *Cœur u.,* cankered heart.

ulcéreux, -euse [ylserø, -øːz], *a. Med:* Ulcerous; ulcerated.

ulex [ylɛks], *s.m. Bot:* Ulex, furze, gorse, whin.

uliginaire [yliʒinɛːr], **uligineux, -euse** [yliʒinø, -øːz], *a.* Uliginous; uliginal (plant). **Terrain uliginaire,** swampy ground; swamp, marshland.

ulmaire [ylmɛːr], *s.f. Bot:* Meadow-sweet.

ulnaire [ylnɛːr], *a. Anat:* Ulnar.

ultérieur, -eure [ylterjœːr], *a.* Ulterior. **I.** *Geog:* Further, thither. **2.** Subsequent (*d, to*); later (news, date). *Com: Ordres ultérieurs,* further orders.

ultérieurement [ylterjœrmɑ̃], *adv.* Ulteriorly, later on, subsequently, hereafter.

ultimatum [yltimatɔm], *s.m.* Ultimatum.

ultime [yltim], *a.* Ultimate, final, last.
ultimo [yltimo], *adv.* Lastly, finally.
ultra [yltra], *s.m. Pol:* Ultra(ist), extremist.
ultramarine [yltramarin], *s.f.* Lapis lazuli.
ultramontain [yltramɔ̃tɛ̃]. **1.** *a.* Ultramontane; beyond the Alps (as from France). **2.** *s.m. Theol: Pol:* Ultramontanist, Vaticanist.
ultra-royaliste, *a. & s.* Ultra-royalist.
ultra-sonore, *a. Ph:* Above the audible range; supersonic.
ultra-violet, -ette, *a. Opt:* Ultra-violet.
ululation [ylylasjɔ̃], *s.f.,* **ululement** [ylylmɑ̃], *s.m.* Ululation (of owls); hoot(ing).
ululer [ylyle], *v.i.* (Of owl) To ululate; to hoot.
Ulysse [ylis]. *Pr.n.m.* Ulysses.
un, une [œ̃, yn]. **1.** *num. a & s.* (a) One. *Il n'en reste qu'un,* there is only one left. **Les Mille et Une Nuits,** the Thousand and One Nights. **Un à un** [œ̃naœ̃], **un par un,** one by one. **En colonne par un,** in single file. **Une heure,** one o'clock. **Sur les une** [leyn] **heure,** about one (o'clock). *Page un,* page one. *Un et un* [œ̃ e œ̃] *font deux,* one and one are two. *Th:* **Le un** [ləœ̃], the first act. *F:* **En savoir plus d'une,** to know a thing or two. *Il vient un jour sur deux, de deux jours l'un,* he comes one day out of two, every other day. *De trois l'un,* one out of every three. **Une, deux, trois, partez!** one, two, three, go! (b) One (and indivisible). **Dieu est un,** God is one. **C'est tout un** [tutœ̃], it's all one, all the same. *F:* **Ils ne font qu'un,** they are hand in glove together. **2.** *Indef. pron.* One. **(L')un de nous, (l')un d'entre nous,** one of us. **Les uns disent que . . .,** some say that. . . . **L'un et l'autre, l'un ou l'autre, l'un l'autre,** see AUTRE I. **Pas un,** see PAS² 2. **3.** *Indef.art. (pl. des, q.v.* under DE III.) A, an (*pl.* some). (a) *Un jour, une pomme, une heure,* a day, an apple, an hour. *Un père et une mère,* a father and mother. *Venez me voir un lundi,* come and see me on a Monday, some Monday. *Pour une raison ou pour une autre,* for some reason or other. (b) Such a one as. *Sans doute un Worth vous aurait-il mieux habillée,* no doubt a (firm like) Worth would have dressed you better. (c) (Intensive) **J'ai eu un monde aujourd'hui!** I've had such a lot of people to-day! *Tu m'as fait une peur!* you gave me such a fright!
unanime [ynanim], *a.* Unanimous (*dans,* in); of one mind. *Ils sont unanimes à vous accuser,* they are unanimous in accusing you.
unanimement [ynanimmɑ̃], *adv.* Unanimously; with one accord.
unanimité [ynanimite], *s.f.* Unanimity. *A l'unanimité,* unanimously. *A l'u. des voix,* without one dissentient voice.
uncial, -aux [ɔ̃sjal, -o], *a.* = ONCIAL.
unguéal, -aux [ɔ̃gɥeal, -o], *a. Anat:* Ungual.
unguifère [ɔ̃gɥifɛːr], *a. Z:* Unguiferous; clawed.
uniate [ynjat], *s.m. & a. Rel.H:* Uniat(e).
unicellulaire [yniselylɛːr], *a. Biol:* Unicellular.
unicité [ynisite], *s.f.* **1.** *Phil:* Oneness, uniquity. **2.** Uniqueness, singleness.
unicolore [ynikɔlɔːr], *a.* Unicolour; one-coloured, whole-coloured (stuff, etc.).
unicorne [ynikɔrn]. **1.** *a.* Single-horned. **2.** *s.m.* = LICORNE.
unième [ynjɛm], *num.a.* (Used only in compounds) First. *Trente et unième,* thirty-first.
unification [ynifikasjɔ̃], *s.f.* Unification; consolidation (of loans, etc.); standardization (of weights and measures); amalgamation (of industries).

unifier [ynifje], *v.tr.* To unify (ideas); to consolidate (loans); to standardize; to amalgamate (industries).
uniform|e [ynifɔrm]. **1.** *a.* Uniform, unvarying. *Taux u.,* flat rate (of interest, etc.). **2.** *s.m.* Uniform. **Grand uniforme,** full uniform. *F:* **Endosser l'uniforme,** to become a soldier. **Quitter l'uniforme,** to leave the service. *adv.* **-ément.**
uniformiser [ynifɔrmize], *v.tr.* To make uniform; to standardize.
uniformité [ynifɔrmite], *s.f.* Uniformity.
unilatéral, -aux [ynilateral, -o], *a.* Unilateral; one-sided (contract, etc.). *adv.* **-ement.**
unilingue [ynilɛ̃ːg], *a.* Unilingual (dictionary).
uniloculaire [ynilɔkylɛːr], *a. Bot:* Unilocular; one-celled (ovary).
uniment [ynimɑ̃], *adv.* Smoothly, evenly.
uninominal, -aux [yninɔminal, -o], *a.* Uninominal. **Scrutin uninominal,** voting for a single member, for one member only.
union [ynjɔ̃], *s.f.* Union. **1.** Coming together. S.a. TRAIT 4. **2.** Society, association. **L'Union Sud-africaine,** the South African Union. **Union ouvrière,** trade union. **Union chrétienne de jeunes gens,** Young Men's Christian Association. **3.** Marriage. **4.** *F:* Unity, concord, agreement. **L'union fait la force,** unity is strength. **5.** *Tchn:* Union(-joint); coupling.
unipare [ynipaːr], *a. Biol:* Uniparous.
unipersonnel, -elle [ynipɛrsɔnɛl], *a. Gram:* **1.** Unipersonal (verb). **2.** Imper.onal (verb).
uniphasé [ynifɑze], *a. El.E:* Single-phase.
unipolaire [ynipɔlɛːr], *a. El.E:* Unipolar; single-pole (dynamo, switch).
uniprix [ynipri], *a.inv.* **Magasin uniprix,** one-price store.
unique [ynik], *a.* **1.** Sole, only, single; that stands alone. **Fils unique,** only son. **Rue à sens unique,** one-way road, street. **2.** Unique, unrivalled, unparalleled. *F:* **Vous êtes unique!** you're the limit! *adv.* **-ment.**
unir [yniːr], *v.tr.* **1.** To unite, join. *Faits étroitement unis,* facts closely linked together. *Être uni par le mariage à . . .,* to be joined in wedlock to. . . . **Unir à nouveau,** to reunite. **2.** To smooth, level, make plane.
s'unir. 1. To unite, join. *S'u. à qn,* (i) to join forces with s.o.; (ii) to marry s.o. **2.** To become smooth, even.
uni, *a.* **1.** (a) United, harmonious (family). (b) **Le Royaume-Uni,** the United Kingdom. **Les États-Unis,** the United States. **2.** Smooth, level, even (ground). **3.** Plain (material, colour); self-colour(ed) (material). *Tulle uni,* plain net.
uniréfringent [ynirefrɛ̃ʒɑ̃], *a. Ph:* Monorefringent (crystal).
unisexué [yniseksɥe], **unisexuel, -elle** [yniseksɥɛl], *a. Biol:* Unisexual, unisexed.
unisson [ynisɔ̃], *s.m. Mus:* Unison. **A l'unisson,** (i) in unison (*de,* with); (ii) in keeping (with).
unitaire [ynitɛːr], *a.* **1.** = UNITA(I)RIEN. **2.** Unitary (system, etc.). *Com:* **Prix unitaire,** unit-price. *Mec.E:* **Allongement unitaire,** elongation per unit-length.
unitairien [yniterjɛ̃], **unitarien, -ienne** [ynitarjɛ̃, -jɛn], *a. & s. Rel.H:* Unitarian.
unité [ynite], *s.f.* **1.** (a) Unit (of measure, etc.). (b) *Mth:* Unity, one. *Com:* **Prix de l'unité,** price of one (article). **2.** Unity. (a) Oneness (of God). (b) Uniformity (of plan, action). *Il n'y a pas d'u. dans sa conduite,* there is no unity, no consistency, in his conduct. *Lit:* **Les unités dramatiques,** the dramatic unities.

univalent [ynivalɑ̃], *a. Ch*: Univalent, monovalent.

univalve [ynivalv], *a.* (a) *Bot*: Univalvular. (b) *Moll*: Univalve.

univers [yniveːr], *s.m.* Universe. **Par tout l'univers,** all over the world.

universaliser [yniversalize], *v.tr.* To universalize ; to make (sth.) universal.

universalité [yniversalite], *s.f.* **1.** Universality, universalness. **2.** Sum total.

univers|el, -elle [yniversel], *a.* Universal. *Réputation universelle,* world-wide reputation. *F:* H̶o̶m̶m̶e̶s̶ u̶n̶i̶v̶e̶r̶s̶e̶l̶s̶, all-rounders. **Légataire universel,** residuary legatee. *adv.* **-ellement.**

universitaire [yniversiteːr]. **1.** *a.* University (studies, town). **2.** *s.* Member of the *Université de France* (*q.v.* below) ; member of the teaching profession.

université [yniversite], *s.f.* **1.** University. *Il avait étudié à l'u.,* he had been through the university ; *F:* he had been to college. **2. L'Université de France,** the whole body of university and school teachers, professors, inspectors, etc.

univoque [ynivɔk], *a.* Univocal.

Untel [œ̃tɛl], *s.m. Hum*: M. Untel, Mr So-and-so. Cf. TEL 3.

upas [ypɑs], *s.m.* **1.** Upas(-tree). **2.** Upas (juice).

upsilon [ypsilɔn], *s.m. Gr.Alph*: Upsilon.

urane [yran], *s.m. Ch*: Uranium oxide.

uranium [yranjɔm], *s.m. Ch*: Uranium.

uranographie [yranɔgrafi], *s.f.* Uranography.

urate [yrat], *s.m.* **1.** *Ch*: Urate. **2.** *Agr*: Urate fertilizer.

urbain [yrbɛ̃]. **1.** *a.* Urban (population); town (house). *Architecture urbaine,* town planning. **2.** *s.m.* Town-dweller ; city-dweller.

urbaniser [yrbanize], *v.tr.* To urbanize (rural district, etc.).

urbanisme [yrbanism], *s.m.* Town-planning.

urbaniste [yrbanist], *s.m.* Town-planner.

urbanité [yrbanite], *s.f.* Urbanity. **Avec urbanité,** urbanely.

urée [yre], *s.f. Ch*: Urea.

urémie [yremi], *s.f. Med*: Uraemia.

urémique [yremik], *a. Med*: Uraemic.

urètre [yrɛtr], *s.m. Anat*: Urethra.

urgence [yrʒɑ̃s], *s.f.* Urgency. **En cas d'urgence,** in case of emergency. **Il y a urgence,** the case is pressing. **A adresser d'urgence,** to be sent immediately. **Convoquer d'urgence les sociétaires,** to call an extraordinary meeting of the shareholders. *Parl*: **Demander l'urgence,** to call for a vote of urgency.

urg|ent [yrʒɑ̃], *a.* Urgent, pressing ; instant (need). *Cas u.,* urgent case ; emergency. *Post*: "Urgent," 'urgent' ; 'for immediate delivery.' *adv.* **-emment.**

urinaire [yrineːr], *a. Anat*: Urinary.

urinal, -aux [yrinal, -o], *s.m.* Urinal (vessel).

urine [yrin], *s.f.* Urine. **Évacuer l'urine,** to pass water.

uriner [yrine], *v.i.* To urinate ; to make water.

urinoir [yrinwaːr], *s.m.* (Public) urinal.

urique [yrik], *a.* Uric (acid, concretion).

urne [yrn], *s.f.* (a) Urn. (b) **Urne de scrutin,** ballot-box.

ursuline [yrsylin], *s.f. Ecc*: Ursuline (nun). *F: Les Ursulines,* Ursuline convent-school.

urticacées [yrtikase], *s.f.pl Bot*: Urticaceae.

urticaire [yrtikeːr], *s.f. Med*: Nettle-rash.

urticant [yrtikɑ̃], *a.* Urticating, stinging.

urtication [yrtikasjɔ̃], *s.f. Med*: Urtication.

urus [yryːs], *s.m. Z*: Urus. aurochs.

us¹ [y], *s.m.pl. A*: Usages. (Still used in) **Les us et coutumes** [yzekutym] *d'un pays,* the ways and customs of a country.

us² [yːs]. (The Lt. ending) us. *F*: **Mots en us,** learned words.

usable [yzabl], *a.* Liable to deteriorate through wear ; liable to wear out.

usage [yzaːʒ], *s.m.* **1.** (a) Use, using, employment. **Mettre un article en usage,** to put an article into use. **Faire usage de qch.,** to use, make use of, sth. **Faire bon usage de qch.,** to make good use of sth. ; to put sth. to good use. **Faire mauvais usage de qch.,** to make bad use of sth. ; to put sth. to (a) bad use ; to misuse sth. *Pharm*: "Pour l'usage externe," 'for external application.' **Article à mon usage,** article for my personal use. **Article d'usage,** article for everyday use. **Hors d'usage,** (i) out of use ; (ii) obsolete. (b) Wear, service (of garments, etc.). **Faire un bon usage,** faire de l'usage, to wear well, do good service. **Garanti à l'usage,** warranted to wear well. **2.** *Jur*: **Droit d'usage continu,** (right of) user. **3.** (a) Usage ; use (and wont) ; custom, practice. *Usages locaux,* local customs. **Phrases d'usage,** conversational commonplaces. **Comme d'usage,** as usual. *Selon l'u., suivant l'u.,* according to custom. **Il est d'usage de** + *inf.,* it is customary to. . . . (b) Practice, experience. *Prov*: **Usage rend maître,** practice makes perfect. **Avoir l'usage de qch.,** to be used to sth. **L'usage du monde,** good breeding. **Avoir l'usage du monde,** to have a knowledge of the ways of society. **Manquer d'usage,** to lack breeding.

usagé [yzaʒe], *a.* (Article) that has been used or worn ; second-hand (car, etc.). **Non usagé,** new.

usager, -ère [yzaʒe, -ɛːr]. **1.** *s.* User (of sth.). *Les usagers de la route,* those who use the road ; road-users. **2.** *a.* (Of articles) Of everyday use. *Cust*: **Effets usagers,** articles for personal use.

usance [yzɑ̃s], *s.f. Com*: Usance (of 30 days).

usant [yzɑ̃], *a.* Wearing (life, work) ; abrading (powder).

user [yze]. I. **1.** *v.ind.tr.* **User de qch,** to use sth., make use of sth. *U. bien, mal, de qch.,* to make good use, bad use, of sth. *U. de force, de violence,* to resort to force, to violence. **En bien user avec qn,** to treat s.o. well. **En mal user avec qn,** to treat s.o. badly ; to use s.o. ill. *Est-ce ainsi que vous en usez avec lui?* is that how you deal with him, how you treat him? **2.** *v.tr.* (a) To use (up), consume (sth.). *U. toutes ses provisions,* to use up all one's provisions. (b) To wear (sth.) (out, away, down) ; to abrade. *U. ses vêtements,* to wear out one's clothes. **Meule à user,** abrading wheel.
s'user, to wear (away). *Sa résistance s'usera à la fin,* his resistance will wear down, break down, in due course.
II. **user,** *s.m.* **Étoffe d'un bon user,** material that wears well.

usé, *a.* (Of metal, stone) Worn ; (of garment) shabby, threadbare ; (of rope) frayed. **Sujet usé,** hackneyed, stale, threadbare, trite, trivial, subject. *Cheval usé,* worn-out horse. *Terre usée,* exhausted land.

usine [yzin], *s.f.* Works, (manu)factory, mill. *U. à gaz,* gas-works. *El.E*: **U. centrale,** power-station, power-house. **Ouvrier d'usine,** factory-hand, mill-hand.

usin|er [yzine], *v.tr.* **1.** *Metalw*: To machine, to tool (castings, etc.) ; to machine-finish (parts). **Parties usinées,** bright parts. **2.** *P*: To sweat (labour, artists, etc.). *s.m.* **-age.**

usinier [yzinje], *s.m.* Manufacturer; mill-owner.

usité [yzite], *a.* Used; in use; current. *Le mot n'est plus u.*, the word is obsolete.

ustensile [ystãsil], *s.m.* Utensil, implement, tool. *U. de ménage*, household utensil. *Ustensiles de toilette*, toilet requisites.

usu|el, -elle [yzµel], *a.* Usual, customary, habitual, common. *Les arts usuels*, arts and crafts. *Connaissances usuelles*, knowledge of everyday things. *adv.* **-ellement.**

usufruit [yzyfrµi], *s.m. Jur:* Usufruct; life interest.

usufruitier, -ière [yzyfrµitje, -jɛːr], *a. & s. Jur:* Usufructuary. *s.* Tenant for life.

usuraire [yzyrɛːr], *a.* Usurious (interest).

usure[1] [yzyːr], *s.f.* Usury. *Pratiquer l'u.*, to practise usury. *F:* **Rendre un bienfait avec usure,** to repay a service with interest.

usure[2], *s.f.* (*a*) Wear (and tear). *U. par frottement*, attrition. *Mil:* **Guerre d'usure,** war of attrition. (*b*) *Geol:* Wearing away; erosion.

usurier, -ière [yzyrje, -jɛːr]. **1.** *s.* Usurer. **2.** *a.* Usurious.

usurpateur, -trice [yzyrpatœːr, -tris]. **1.** *s.* Usurper. **2.** *a.* (*a*) Usurping. (*b*) Encroaching.

usurpation [yzyrpasjɔ̃], *s.f.* (*a*) Usurpation. (*b*) Encroaching, encroachment (*de*, upon).

usurpatoire [yzyrpatwaːr], *a.* Usurpatory.

usurper [yzyrpe]. **1.** *v.tr.* (*a*) To usurp (*sur*, from). (*b*) To encroach upon, usurp (s.o.'s rights, etc.). **2.** *v.i. U. sur les droits de qn*, to encroach, usurp, (up)on s.o.'s rights.

ut [yt], *s.m.inv. Mus:* (The note) C. *Ut dièse*, C sharp. *Clef d'ut*, C clef. *Clef d'ut quatrième ligne*, tenor clef.

utérin [yterɛ̃], *a.* Uterine. **Frère utérin,** half-brother on the mother's side.

utile [ytil], *a.* Useful, serviceable. *Si je puis vous être u. à quelque chose*, if I can be of any use, of any assistance, to you. *Puis-je être u. en rien?* can I do anything? can I be of any use? *Cela m'a été bien u.*, it came in very handy, stood me in good stead. **En temps utile,** in (good) time; duly. *Prendre toutes dispositions utiles*, to make all necessary arrangements. *Dictionnaire u. à consulter*, dictionary that may be usefully consulted. *Mec:* **Effet utile,** useful effect; effective power. *s.m.* **Joindre l'utile à l'agréable,** to join pleasure and profit. *adv.* **-ment.**

utilisable [ytilizabl], *a.* Utilizable; capable of being turned to account.

utilisation [ytilizasjɔ̃], *s.f.* Utilization (of sth.); turning (of sth.) to account.

utiliser [ytilize], *v.tr.* To utilize; to make use of (sth.); to turn (sth.) to account.

utilitarisme [ytilitarism], *s.m.* Utilitarianism.

utilité [ytilite], *s.f.* **1.** Utility, use(fulness); useful purpose; service, avail. *Être d'une grande u.*, to be of great use. *Outil de première u.*, essential tool. **Sans utilité,** useless(ly). *S'entremettre sans grande u.*, to intervene to little purpose. **2.** *Th:* Utility actor or actress. **Les utilités, the small** parts.

utopie [ytɔpi], *s.f.* Utopia.

utopique [ytɔpik], *a.* Utopian.

utopiste [ytɔpist]. **1.** *s.* Utopian, utopist. **2.** *a.* Utopian.

utriculaire [ytrikylɛːr], *s.f. Bot:* Utricularia, bladder-wort.

utricule [ytrikyl], *s.m. Nat.Hist:* Utricle.

uval, -aux [yval, -o], *a.* Pertaining to grapes. *Med:* **Cure uvale,** grape-cure.

uviforme [yvifɔrm], *a. Bot:* Grape-shaped.

uvulaire [yvylɛːr]. **1.** *a. Anat:* Uvular. **2.** *s.f. Bot:* Uvularia.

uvule [yvyl], *s.f. Anat:* Uvula.

V

V, v [ve], *s.m.* (The letter) V, v. **Double v(é),** W, w. *I.C.E:* **Moteur à cylindres en V,** V-type engine.

va [va]. See ALLER.

vacance [vakãːs], *s.f.* **1.** Vacancy; vacant office or post. **2.** *pl.* Vacation, holidays; (of parliament) recess. *Sch:* **Les grandes vacances,** the summer holidays; (of university) the long vacation. **En vacance(s),** on holiday. **Un jour de vacance,** a (day's) holiday.

vacant [vakã], *a.* Vacant, unoccupied, tenantless (house, etc.). **Place vacante,** (i) vacant seat, (ii) vacancy (of office).

vacarme [vakarm], *s.m. F:* Uproar, din, racket, hubbub. **Faire du vacarme,** to kick up a row.

vacation [vakasjɔ̃], *s.f.* **1.** (*a*) Attendance, sitting (of officials); day's scale (at an auction). (*b*) *pl.* Fees (of lawyer). **2.** *pl. Jur:* Vacation, recess (of law-courts). **3.** Abeyance (of succession, etc.).

vaccin [vaksɛ̃], *s.m. Med:* Vaccine, lymph.

vaccinateur [vaksinatœːr], *s.m.* Vaccinator.

vaccination [vaksinasjɔ̃], *s.f. Med:* (*a*) Vaccination. (*b*) Inoculation.

vaccine [vaksin], *s.f.* **1.** (*a*) *Vet:* Vaccinia, cow-pox. (*b*) *Med:* Inoculated cow-pox. **2.** = VACCINATION.

vacciner [vaksine], *v.tr. Med:* (*a*) To vaccinate. (*b*) To inoculate.

vache [vaʃ], *s.f.* **1.** (*a*) Cow. *V. laitière, v. à lait,* milch-cow. *F:* **Le plancher des vaches,** terra firma. **Parler français comme une vache espagnole,** to murder the French language. **Manger de la vache enragée,** to have a rough time of it. *Nau:* **Nœud de vache,** granny's knot. (*b*) **Vache de Tartarie,** yak. **Vache marine,** sea-cow. (*c*) *P:* (i) Fat woman. (ii) Policeman. (iii) Disagreeable fellow; swine. **2.** Cow-hide. *Valise en v.*, leather suit-case.

vacher, -ère [vaʃe, -ɛːr], *s.* Cowherd, neat-herd.

vacherie [vaʃri], *s.f.* **1.** Cow-byre, cow-house. **2.** *P:* Dirty trick.

vacillant [vasillã, -ijã], *a.* **1.** Unsteady (table); unsteady, flickering (flame); uncertain, staggering (gait). **2.** Vacillating; wavering, undecided (mind); uncertain (health).

vacillation [vasillasjɔ̃, -ija-], *s.f.* **1.** Unsteadiness; wobbling; flickering (of flame). **2.** Vacillation, shilly-shallying; wavering (of opinion).

vacillement [vasijmã], *s.m.* = VACILLATION **1.**

vaciller [vasille, -ije], *v.i.* **1.** (*a*) To be unsteady. *Entrer, sortir, en vacillant*, to stagger in, out; to lurch in, out. (*b*) (Of light) To flicker. **2.** To vacillate, waver.

va-comme-je-te-pousse, *s. m. & f. inv. F:* Easy-going man or woman.

vacuité [vakµite], *s.f.* Vacuity, emptiness.

vacuole [vakµɔl], *s.f. Biol:* Vacuole.

vacuum [vakµɔm], *s.m.* Vacuum.

vade-mecum ʃvademekɔm], *s.m.inv.* Vade-mecum.

vadrouille [vadru:j], *s.f.* **1.** *Nau:* (*a*) Pitch-mop. (*b*) (Deck-)swab. **2.** *P:* (*a*) Faire la vadrouille, aller en vadrouille, to go on the spree; to gallivant. (*b*) Roving fellow or woman on the spree; runagate, rollicker, gadabout. (*c*) Party out on the spree, on the loose.

vadrouill|er [vadruje], *v.i.* *P:* (*a*) To gallivant; to go on the loose. (*b*) *V. par le monde*, to roam; to knock about the world. *s.* **-eur, -euse.**

va-et-vient, *s.m.inv.* **1.** (*a*) Movement to and fro; (i) backward and forward motion; (ii) seesaw motion. (Of ferry-boat) Faire le va-et-vient *entre . . . et . . .,* to ply between . . . and. . . . *a.inv.* **Porte va-et-vient,** swing door. (*b*) Coming and going (of persons). **2.** (*a*) Ferry-boat. (*b*) *El:* Two-way wiring (system). *a.inv.* Commutateur va-et-v ent, two-way switch. (*c*) *Mec.E:* Reciprocating gear.

vagabond, -onde [vagabɔ̃, -ɔ̃:d]. **1.** *a.* Vagabond; wandering, roving (life); *El:* stray (current). **2.** *s.* Vagabond; vagrant, tramp.

vagabondage [vagabɔ̃da:ʒ], *s.m.* Vagrancy, vagabondage.

vagabonder [vagabɔ̃de], *v.i.* **1.** To be a vagabond. *V. par le monde,* to rove about the world; to roam. **2.** (Of the mind) To wander.

vagir [vaʒi:r], *v.i.* (Of new-born infant) To cry, wail; (of hare) to squeak.

vagissement [vaʒismɑ̃], *s.m.* Vagitus, cry, wail(ing) (of new-born infant); squeak(ing) (of hare).

vague[1] [vag], *s.f.* Wave. **Grosse vague,** billow, sea. *Une v. balaya le pont,* the deck was swept by a sea. *V. de fond,* tidal wave. *F:* **Vague de chaleur,** heat wave. *El:* Vague de courant, surge of current.

vague[2]. **1.** (*a*) *a.* Vague, indefinite; dim (recollection); hazy (knowledge). *Quelque v. écrivain,* (i) a writer of some sort; (ii) some writer or other. (*b*) *a. & s.m. Anat:* (**Nerf**) vague, vagus (nerve). **2.** *s.m.* Vagueness, indefiniteness. *adv.* **-ment.**

vague[3]. **1.** *a.* Empty, vacant. (Still so used in) Regard vague, vacant stare. **Terrains vagues,** waste ground, *F:* no man's land. **2.** *s.m.* Empty space. **Fixer les yeux dans le vague,** to gaze into vacancy.

vaguemestre [vagmɛstr], *s.m.* **1.** *Mil:* *A:* Baggage-master. **2.** (*a*) *Mil:* Post orderly. (*b*) *Navy:* Postman.

vaguer [vage], *v.i.* To wander, roam, ramble (about). **Laisser vaguer ses pensées,** to let one's thoughts wander.

vaigrage [vɛgra:ʒ], *s.m. N.Arch:* Ceiling, inner planking, inner plating.

vaigre [vɛ:gr], *s.f. N.Arch:* (*a*) Ceiling-plate, inner plank. (*b*) Bottom-board (of small boat).

vaillance [vajɑ̃:s], *s.f.* Valour, bravery, courage, gallantry.

vaill|ant [vajɑ̃]. **1.** *a.* (*a*) Valiant, brave, courageous, spirited; stout (heart); *Mil:* gallant. (*b*) *F:* Être vaillant, to be in good health. **2.** *adv.* Elle a cent mille francs vaillant, she has a hundred thousand francs of her own, at her own disposal. *N'avoir pas un sou v.,* to be penniless. **3.** *s.m. Perdre, dépenser, tout son v.,* to lose, spend, one's all. *adv.* **-amment.**

vaillantise [vajɑ̃ti:z], *s.f. A. & Iron:* Valiant deed; deed of derring-do.

vaill-e, -es, etc. See VALOIR.

vain [vɛ̃], *a.* **1.** Vain. (*a*) Sham, unreal, empty (title, etc.). *Vaine gloire,* vainglory. *De vains*

amusements, futile amusements. *Vaines promesses,* hollow promises. (*b*) Ineffectual, useless, fruitless (efforts). *Adv.phr.* **En vain,** in vain; ₰vainly. (*c*) **Terres vaines et vagues,** waste land. **2.** Vain, conceited.

vaincre [vɛ̃:kr], *v.tr.* (*pr.p.* vainquant; *p.p.* vaincu; *pr.ind.* je vaincs, il vainc, n. vainquons; *p.h.* je vainquis; *fu.* je vaincrai) **1.** (*a*) To vanquish, conquer, defeat (adversary). *Malheur aux vaincus!* woe to the vanquished! (*b*) *Sp:* etc: To beat (rival). *V. qn en générosité,* to outdo s.o. in generosity. **2.** To overcome, master, conquer (disease, difficulties). **Se laisser vaincre à la tentation,** to give way to temptation.

vainement [vɛnmɑ̃], *adv.* Vainly, in vain; to no purpose.

vainqu-e, etc. See VAINCRE.

vainqueur [vɛ̃kœ:r]. **1.** *s.m.* (*a*) Vanquisher (*de qn,* of s.o.); victor, conqueror. (*b*) *Sp:* etc: Winner. **2.** *a.m.* Vanquishing, conquering, victorious.

vair [vɛ:r], *s.m.* **1.** *Her:* Vair. **2.** *Com:* (Whole-) squirrel fur.

vairon [vɛrɔ̃]. **1.** *a.* (*a*) *Aux yeux vairons,* with eyes of different colours. (*b*) Wall-eyed (horse). **2.** *s.m.* Minnow.

vais [vɛ]. See ALLER.

vaisseau [vɛso], *s.m.* **1.** Vessel, receptacle. *V. de terre,* earthenware pan. **2.** Ship, vessel. *V. à voiles,* sailing vessel. *V. à vapeur,* steamship. *V. de mer,* sea-going ship. *V. de guerre,* warship. *V. amiral,* flagship. *V. marchand,* merchantman; merchant ship. *F:* **Brûler ses vaisseaux,** to burn one's boats. S.a. FANTÔME. **3.** Nave (of church); body, hall (of building). **4.** *Anat:* *Bot:* Vessel, canal, duct. *V. sanguin,* blood-vessel.

vaisseau-école, *s.m.* Training-ship.

vaisselier [vɛsəlje], *s.m. Furn:* Dresser.

vaisselle [vɛsɛl], *s.f.* Table-service; plates and dishes. *V. de terre,* crockery, earthenware. **Vaisselle plate,** silver plate. **Laver, faire, la vaisselle,** to wash up. **Eau de vaisselle,** dishwater. **Marchand de vaisselle,** china merchant.

vaissellerie [vɛsɛlri], *s.f.* Household cooperage.

val [val], *s.m.* (Narrow) valley, vale. The *pl.* is usu. **vals,** except in the phr. **Par monts et par vaux,** *q.v.* under MONT.

valable [valabl], *a.* Valid, good (title, excuse). *Billet v. pour deux mois,* ticket available, good, for two months.

valablement [valabləmɑ̃], *adv.* Validly.

Val-de-Grâce (le), *s.m.* The Military Hospital (in Paris).

Valence[1] [valɑ̃:s]. **1.** *Pr.n.f.* (*a*) Valencia (in Spain). (*b*) Valence (in France). **2.** *s.f.* Valencia orange.

valence[2], *s.f. Ch:* Valence, valency.

valenciennes [valɑ̃sjɛn], *s.f.* Valenciennes lace.

valériane [valerjan], *s.f. Bot:* Valerian, all-heal.

valet [valɛ], *s.m.* **1.** (*a*) *A:* = VARLET. (*b*) *Cards:* Knave, jack. **2.** *V. de chambre,* valet, man-servant. *V. de pied,* footman, *F:* flunkey. *V. d'écurie,* groom, stable-boy. *V. de ferme,* farm-hand. *Prov:* **Tel maître, tel valet,** like master, like man. *A:* Ame de valet, servile nature. **Faire le plat valet,** to toady, to fawn. **3.** (*a*) Door counterweight. (*b*) Clamp, holdfast. (*c*) Support, rest, stand (of mirror, etc.).

valetaille [val(a)ta:j], *s.f. A:* Flunkeys, menials.

valet/er [valte], *v.tr.* (je valette; je valetterai) (*a*) To valet (s.o.). (*b*) *F:* To fetch and carry. *s.m.* **-age.**

valétudinaire [valetydinɛ:r]. **1.** *a.* Valetudinary. **2.** *s.* Valetudinarian.

valeur [valœːr], *s.f.* **1.** (a) Value, worth. *Augmenter en v.*, to advance, rise, increase, in value. *Bijou de valeur*, valuable jewel. *Artiste de v.*, talented artist. *Homme de v.*, man (i) of real ability, (ii) of merit. **De première valeur**, (article) of the best quality; (man) of outstanding merit. **De nulle valeur**, worthless. **Valeur en fabrique**, cost price. *Com:* **Valeur reçue**, for value received. *Papier de v. douteuse*, dubious bills. *Cust:* **Droit sur la valeur**, ad valorem duty. *Colis avec valeur déclarée*, (i) registered parcel; (ii) insured parcel. **Mettre une terre en valeur**, to develop land. (b) *Mus:* (Time-)value, length (of a note). (c) Import, weight, value. *Votre argument n'est pas sans v.*, there is force in what you say. *Renseignements sans valeur*, valueless information. **Valeur des mots**, import, full meaning, of words. **Mettre un mot en valeur**, to emphasize, give importance to, a word. **2.** *Fin:* (a) Asset. *F:* (Of pers.) **C'est une de nos valeurs**, he is one of our assets. (b) *pl.* Bills, shares, securities. *Valeurs mobilières*, transferable securities; stocks and shares. *Valeurs actives*, assets. *Valeurs passives*, liabilities. **3.** Valour, gallantry. **Se battre avec valeur**, to fight gallantly.

valeureu|x, -euse [valœrø, -øːz], *a.* Valorous, brave, gallant (in battle). *adv.* **-sement**.

validation [validasjɔ̃], *s.f.* Validation (of election, marriage); ratifying (of law).

valide [valid], *a.* **1.** Valid (contract, marriage). **2.** *Mil:* etc: Fit for service; able-bodied. *adv.* **-ment**.

valider [valide], *v.tr.* To validate (election, marriage); to ratify (contract, etc.); to authenticate (document).

validité [validite], *s.f.* Validity (of contract, election, passport, etc.). **Durée de validité d'un billet**, availability of a ticket. **Établir la validité d'un testament**, to prove a will.

valise [valiːz], *s.f.* (a) Valise; (small) portmanteau. (b) Suit-case. (c) *V. diplomatique*, embassy dispatch-bag.

vallée [vale], *s.f.* Valley.

vallon [valɔ̃], *s.m.* Small valley; dale, dell, vale; *Scot:* glen.

vallonné [valɔne], *a.* Cut up by dells; undulating (country).

vallum [vallɔm], *s.m. Rom.Ant:* Vallum.

valoir [valwaːr], *v.tr. & i.* (*pr.p.* valant; *p.p.* valu; *pr.ind.* je vaux, il vaut, n. valons, ils valent; *pr.sub.* je vaille, n. valions, ils vaillent; *p.h.* je valus; *fu.* je vaudrai) **1.** (a) To be worth. *Maison valant cent mille francs*, house worth one hundred thousand francs. *Combien vaut le beurre aujourd'hui?* what is butter selling at to-day? **A valoir sur** (*une somme*), on account of (a sum). *Payer dix francs à v.*, to pay ten francs on account. **A valoir sur qn**, on account of s.o.; for account of s.o. **Ne pas valoir grand'chose**, not to be worth much. *Comme acteur il ne vaut pas cher*, as an actor he is not up to much. *S'il n'est pas mort, il n'en vaut guère mieux*, if he is not dead, he is not far from it. **Ne valoir rien pour la santé**, to be bad for the health. **Ce n'est rien qui vaille**, it is not worth having, it is nothing of any value. **Un, une, rien qui vaille** = *un vaurien, une vaurienne*. (b) To be equivalent to. *Le premier coup en vaut deux*, the first blow is half the battle. *C'est une façon qui en vaut une autre*, it is as good a way as any other. **L'un vaut l'autre**, one is as good, as bad, as the other. *Il ne vaut pas mieux que son frère*, he is no better than his brother. **Cela vaut fait**, it is as good as done. (c) *Impers.* **Il vaut mieux, i! vaudrait mieux**,

rester à la maison, it is, would be, better to stay at home. **Il vaut mieux qu'il en soit ainsi**, (it is) better that it should be so. **Il vaut mieux + *inf.* que (de) + *inf.***, it is better to + *inf.* than to + *inf.* **Mieux vaut tard que jamais**, better late than never. *Autant vaut rester ici*, we may as well stay here. *C'est une affaire faite ou autant vaut*, it is as good as done. (d) **Faire valoir qch.**, to make the most of sth.; to set sth. off to advantage. *Monture qui fait v. la pierre*, setting that shows off the stone. **Faire v. ses opinions**, to command respect for one's opinions. **Faire v. ses droits à . . .**, to assert, enforce, one's claims to. . . . *Faire v. son bon droit*, to vindicate one's rights. *J'ai fait v. que . . .*, I pointed out, urged, that. . . . **Se faire valoir**, to push oneself forward. *Faire v. son argent*, to invest one's money to good account. **Faire v. une terre**, to develop an estate. S.a. MARCHANDISE. **2.** To be worth, to deserve, merit (sth.). **Un service en vaut un autre**, one good turn deserves another. *Le livre vaut d'être lu*, the book is worth reading. **Cela vaut la peine de faire le voyage**, it is worth taking the journey. *F:* **Cela vaut le coup**, it's worth trying. **3.** **Valoir qch. à qn.** (a) To bring in, yield, fetch (so much). *Cette terre lui vaut dix mille francs de rente*, this land brings him in an income of ten thousand francs. **Vaille que vaille**, (i) whatever it may be worth; (ii) at all costs, come what may. (b) To obtain, win, gain. *Cette action lui a valu la croix*, this act won him the cross. **Qu'est-ce qui me vaut cet honneur?** to what do I owe this honour?

valorisation [valɔrizasjɔ̃], *s.f. Com: Fin:* Valorization (of product, etc.); stabilization (of price of commodity).

valoriser [valɔrize], *v.tr. Com: Fin:* To valorize; to stabilize (price of commodity).

Vals [vals], *Pr.n. Eau de Vals*, table-water from Vals-les-Bains.

valse [vals], *s.f.* Waltz. **Faire un tour de valse**, to waltz round the room.

vals|er [valse], *v.i.* **1.** To waltz. **J'ai fait valser Mlle X**, I waltzed with Miss X. **2.** *F:* (a) *J'ai valsé de dix mille francs*, I lost a clear ten thousand francs. (b) **Faire valser qn**, (i) to lead s.o. a dance; (ii) to show s.o. the door. **Faire valser l'argent**, to make the money fly. *s.* **-eur, -euse**.

valve [valv], *s.f.* **1.** *Nat.Hist:* Valve. **2.** *Mec.E:* Valve (esp. of clack-valve or ball-valve type). *V. de retenue*, non-return valve. *V. de pneumatique*, tyre-valve. **3.** *W.Tel:* (a) *V. redresseuse*, rectifying valve. (b) = *Lampe valve, q.v.* under LAMPE 2. S.a. CUPROXYDE. **4.** *Cin:* *V. de lumière*, light-valve.

valvule [valvyl], *s.f.* Valvule.

vampire [vɑ̃piːr], *s.m.* **1.** (a) *Myth:* Vampire. (b) *F:* Vampire, extortioner, blood-sucker. **2.** *Z:* Vampire(-bat).

vampirisme [vɑ̃pirism], *s.m.* Vampirism. **1.** Belief in vampires. **2.** *F:* Blood-sucking; extortion.

van [vɑ̃], *s.m. Husb:* (a) Winnowing-basket; sieve. (b) Winnowing-machine; fan.

vanadium [vanadjɔm], *s.m. Ch:* Vanadium. **Acier au vanadium**, vanadium steel.

Vandale [vɑ̃dal], *s.m. & a.* **1.** *Hist:* Vandal. **2.** *F:* Vandal, destroyer of works of art, etc.

vandalisme [vɑ̃dalism], *s.m.* Vandalism.

vandoise [vɑ̃dwaːz], *s.f. Ich:* Dace.

vanesse [vanɛs], *s.f. Ent:* Vanessa (butterfly).

vanille [vaniːj], *s.f.* Vanilla. **Gousse de vanille**, vanilla bean.

vanillé [vanije], *a.* Flavoured with vanilla.

vanillier [vanije], *s.m. Bot:* Vanilla plant.

vanité¹ [vanite], *s.f.* Vanity. **1.** Futility (of worldly pleasures). La foire aux vanités, vanity fair. **2.** Conceit, vainglory. Faire vanité, tirer vanité, de qch., to take an empty pride in sth. Faire qch. par vanité, to do sth. out of vanity.

vaniteu|x, -euse [vanitø, -ø:z], *a.* Vain, conceited, vainglorious. *adv.* **-sement.**

vannage¹ [vana:ʒ], *s.m. Hyd.E :* **1.** Sluicing (of water-gate). **2.** (System of) sluice-gates.

vanne [van]. **1.** *s.f.* (a) Sluice(-gate), water-gate. Lever les vannes, to open the flood-gates. Mettre les vannes, to close the flood-gates. (b) *Mch :* Butterfly valve. *V. d'eau,* water valve. (c) *Husb :* Shutter (of fan). (d) Blade (of blower). (e) *Nau :* Cock. S.a. NOYAGE. **2.** *a.* Eaux vannes, waste-water (from factories); cess-water (from houses).

vanneau [vano], *s.m. Orn :* Lapwing, peewit. *Cu : Œufs de v.,* plovers' eggs.

vann|er [vane], *v.tr.* **1.** To winnow, fan, sift (grain). **2.** *P :* To tire out, exhaust. *Être vanné,* to be dead beat, done up. [VAN] *s.m.* **-age².**

vannerie [vanri], *s.f.* **1.** Basket-making, basket-trade. **2.** Basket-work, wicker-work. [VAN]

vanneur, -euse [vanœ:r, -ø:z]. **1.** *s.* Winnower. **2.** *s.f.* Vanneuse, winnowing-machine.

vannier [vanje], *s.m.* Basket-worker, -maker.

vanmure [vany:r], *s.f. Husb :* Husks, chaff.

vantail, -aux [vãta:j, -o], *s.m.* Leaf (of door, shutter, sluice-gate). Porte à deux vantaux, folding door.

vantard, -arde [vãta:r, -ard]. **1.** *a.* Boasting, boastful, bragging. **2.** *s.* Braggart, boaster; *F :* bragger.

vantardise [vãtardi:z], *s.f.* **1.** Bragging, boastfulness; braggadocio. **2.** Boast; piece of bounce.

vanter [vãte], *v.tr.* To praise up (s.o., sth.); to speak highly of (sth.); *F :* to cry up, crack up (s.o., sth.). S.a. MARCHANDISE.

se vanter, to boast, brag. *Se v. d'être . . .,* to pride oneself on being. . . .

vanterie [vãtri], *s.f.* **1.** Bragging, boasting. **2.** Boast.

va-nu-pieds [vanypje], *s. m. & f. inv.* Tatterdemalion; barefoot tramp.

vapeur¹ [vapœ:r], *s.f.* **1.** Vapour; haze; fumes. **2.** (a) *V. d'éther, d'alcool,* ether vapour, alcoholic vapour. (b) Vapeur d'eau, steam. Machine à vapeur, steam-engine. Bateau à vapeur, steamer, steamship. Mettre la vapeur, to put steam on. Navire sous vapeur, ship under steam. A toute vapeur, (at) full steam, at full speed, full steam ahead. **3.** *pl. A.Med :* Vapours. Il lui prit une vapeur, she had a fit of dizziness.

vapeur², *s.m.* Steamer, steamship.

vaporeu|x, -euse [vaporø, -ø:z], *a.* (a) Vaporous, vapoury; steamy (atmosphere). (b) *F :* Filmy, hazy (ideas). *adv.* **-sement.**

vaporisateur [vaporizatœ:r], *s.m.* **1.** (a) Vaporizer, atomizer. *Hort :* Sprayer. (b) Scent-spray. **2.** *Ind :* Evaporator.

vaporisation [vaporizasjɔ̃], *s.f.* (a) Vaporization; evaporation. (b) Atomization.

vaporis|er [vaporize], *v.tr.* **1.** (a) To vaporize, volatilize (liquid). (b) To atomize, spray (liquid). **2.** To spray (sth.) with scent. *a.* **-able.**

se vaporiser, to become vaporized; to vaporize.

vaquer [vake], *v.i.* **1.** (a) (Of situation) To be vacant. (b) (Of Parliament, law-courts) To be in vacation, not to be sitting. **2.** Vaquer à qch., to attend to sth.; to be occupied with, concern oneself with, sth. *V. aux soins du ménage,* to see to the household duties.

varangue [varã:g], *s.f. N.Arch :* Floor-timber, floor-frame.

varappe [varap], *s.f.* Rock-face (to be climbed).

varappeur [varapœ:r], *s.m.* Rock-climber.

varec(h) [varɛk], *s.m.* Wrack, seaweed, varec(h); kelp. Ramasseur de varech, kelp-gatherer.

vareuse [varø:z], *s.f.* **1.** *Nau :* (a) (Sailor's) jersey, jumper. (b) Pilot-coat, pea-jacket. **2.** *Mil :* Field-service tunic, fatigue jacket. **3.** Dark-blue close-fitting jacket buttoning to the neck (worn by artists, students).

variabilité [varjabilite], *s.f.* (a) *Biol : Gram : etc :* Variability. (b) Changeableness (of mood, weather).

variable [varjabl]. **1.** *a.* (a) *Biol : Gram : Mth :* Variable. (b) Changeable, altering (mood, etc.); unsteady (barometer). *Temps v.,* changeable, unsettled, weather. *Astr : Étoile v.,* variable star. **2.** *s.f. Mth :* Variable.

variant, -ante [varjã, -ã:t]. **1.** *a.* Variable, fickle (character). **2.** *s.f.* Variante, variant (reading of text, spelling of word); various reading.

variation [varjasjɔ̃], *s.f.* **1.** Variation. *V. du temps* change in the weather. *Nau : V. du compas,* compass error. **2.** *Mus :* Air avec variations, theme with variations.

varice [varis], *s.f. Med :* Varix, varicosity. varicose vein.

varicelle [varisɛl], *s.f. Med :* Varicella, chicken-pox.

varier [varje]. **1.** *v.tr.* To vary; to diversify (occupations, etc.); to variegate (colours). **2.** *v.i.* To vary, change; (of markets) to fluctuate. *Les auteurs varient souvent,* authors often differ, are often at variance. *V. de méthode,* to vary one's methods. *Mth : Lorsque y varie dans le même sens que et proportionnellement à x,* when y varies as x.

varié, *a.* Varied; varying (types, etc.); miscellaneous (news); variegated (plumage); chequered (existence). *Mus :* Air varié, air with variations. *Mec :* Mouvement varié, variable motion.

variété [varjete], *s.f.* **1.** Variety (de, of); diversity (of opinions); variedness (of landscape). Donner de la variété au menu, (i) to vary the menu; (ii) to lend variety to the menu. **2.** *Nat.Hist :* Variety (of flower, etc.).

variole [varjɔl], *s.f.* **1.** *Med :* Variola, smallpox. **2.** *V. des vaches,* cow-pox.

varioleux, -euse [varjolø, -ø:z]. **1.** *a. Med :* Variolous (pustules, patient). **2.** *s.* Smallpox patient.

variqueux, -euse [varikø, -ø:z], *a.* **1.** *Med :* Varicose. **2.** Varicated (shell).

varlet [varlɛ], *s.m. Hist :* Varlet; page.

varlope [varlɔp], *s.f. Tls :* Trying-plane, jointer.

Varsovie [varsɔvi]. *Pr.n.f. Geog :* Warsaw.

vas [va]. See ALLER.

vasculaire [vaskylɛ:r], **vasculeux, -euse** [vaskylø, -ø:z], *a.* Vascular (tissue, etc.). Pression vasculaire, blood-pressure.

vase¹ [va:z], *s.m.* **1.** Vase, vessel, receptacle. *V. à fleurs,* flower vase. *V. de nuit,* chamber(-pot). *El : V. d'un élément de pile,* battery-jar. *V. poreux,* porous cell. **2.** *Bot :* Calyx, vase (of tulip).

vase², *s.f.* Mud, silt, slime, ooze, sludge. Banc de vase, mud-bank.

vaseline [vazlin], *s.f.* Vaseline. Enduire de vaseline, to smear with vaseline. *Pharm :* Huile de vaseline, vaseline liquide, liquid paraffin.

vaseux, -euse [vazø, -ø:z], *a.* **1.** Muddy, slimy. **2.** *P :* (a) Knocked-up; seedy. (b) Without any guts.

vasistas [vazistɑːs], *s.m.* Fanlight (over door); ventilator (in window, over door).

vaso-constricteur, -trice. *Anat:* **1.** *a.* Vaso-constrictive. **2.** *s.m.* Vaso-constrictor.

vaso-moteur, -trice, *a. & s.m. Anat:* Vaso-motor (nerve-centre).

vasque [vask], *s.f.* **1.** Basin (of fountain). **2.** *V. (lumineuse) en albâtre,* alabaster bowl (for electric light).

vassal, -ale, -aux [vasal, -o], *s. & a.* Vassal.

vassalité [vasalite], *s.f.*, **vasselage** [vaslaːʒ], *s.m.* **1.** Vassalage. **2.** *F:* Bondage.

vaste [vast], *a.* Vast, immense, spacious; of wide extent. *adv.* **-ment.**

vastitude [vastityd], *s.f.* Vastitude. **1.** Vastity, vastness. **2.** Vast expanse.

vastringue [vastrɛ̃ːg], *s.f. Carp:* Spoke-shave.

Vatican (le) [lɔvatikɑ̃]. *Pr.n.m.* The Vatican.

vaticination [vatisinasjɔ̃], *s.f.* Vaticination.

vaticiner [vatisine], *v.i.* To vaticinate.

va-tout [vatu], *s.m.inv.* The whole of one's stakes. *Jouer son va-tout,* to stake one's all.

vau (à) [avo], *adv.phr.* A vau-l'eau, down-stream, with the stream. *F:* Tout va à vau-l'eau, everything is going to rack and ruin. **A vau-de-route,** in utter confusion, helter-skelter. [VAL]

vaudeville [vodvil], *s.m.* **1.** *Lit.Hist:* Topical or satirical song (with refrain). **2.** *Th:* Vaudeville, light comedy (with occasional song).

vaudevilliste [vodvilist], *s.m.* Vaudevillist; writer of vaudevilles.

vaudois, -oise [vodwa, -waːz], *a. & s.* **1.** (Native, inhabitant) of Vaud (Swiss canton); Vaudois. **2.** *Rel.H:* Waldensian.

vaudr-ai, -as, etc. See VALOIR.

vaurien, -ienne [vorjɛ̃, -jɛn], *s.* (a) Waster, rotter, bad lot. (b) *F: Petit v.!* you little scamp! you little rascal! [VAUT RIEN]

vaut [vo]. See VALOIR.

vautour [votuːr], *s.m. Orn:* Vulture.

vautrait [votrɛ], *s.m. Ven:* Boar-hunting pack.

vautre [voːtr], *s.m.* Boar-hound.

vautr|er (se) [səvotre], *v.pr.* (a) (Of pig) To wallow (in mud). *F: Se v. dans le vice,* to wallow in vice. (b) *F:* To sprawl on one's stomach (on grass, on a sofa). *s.m.* **-ement.**

vauvert [vovɛːr]. See DIABLE 1.

vaux [vo]. See VALOIR.

vavassal, -aux [vavasal, -o], *s.m.*, **vavasseur** [vavasœːr], *s.m. Hist:* Vavasour.

va-vite (à la) [alavavit], *adv.phr.* Travail fait à la va-vite, scamped work, rushed work.

vé [ve], *s.m.* (The letter) vee, v.

veau [vo], *s.m.* **1.** (a) Calf. *Le veau gras,* the fatted calf. *F:* Pleurer comme un veau, to weep copiously; to blubber. (b) **Veau marin,** sea-calf, seal. (c) *F:* Lumpish fellow, lump, clod. **2.** *Cu:* Veal. *Côtelette de v.,* veal cutlet. But **Gelée de pied de veau,** calves-foot jelly. **Tête de veau,** calf's-head. **3.** Calf(-leather), calfskin. *V. chromé,* box-calf.

vecteur [vɛktœːr], *s.m. Mth:* Vector. **Rayon vecteur,** radius vector.

vectoriel, -elle [vɛktɔrjɛl], *a. Mth:* Vectorial.

vécu [veky]. See VIVRE.

vedette [vɔdɛt], *s.f.* **1.** *Mil:* Vedette; mounted sentry. **Être en vedette,** to be on vedette duty. **2.** (a) *Navy:* Vedette-boat; scout; picket-boat. (b) Small steamer, motor boat (on cross-harbour service, etc.). **3.** (a) Écrire, imprimer, qch. en vedette, to write, print, sth. in a line by itself. **Mots en vedette,** words displayed in bold type. (Of actor) **Se trouver, être mis, en vedette sur l'affiche,** to head, top, the bill. *F:* Être en

vedette, to be in the limelight. (b) *Th:* Star *V. de l'écran,* film star.

védique [vedik], *a. Rel.H:* Vedic.

védovelli [vedɔvelli], *s.m. W.Tel:* Shell insulator.

végétal, -aux [veʒetal, -o]. **1.** *a.* Plant-(life, etc.); vegetable (kingdom). **2.** *s.m.* Plant.

végétarien, -ienne [veʒetarjɛ̃, -jɛn], *a. & s.* Vegetarian.

végétarisme [veʒetarism], *s.m.* Vegetarianism.

végétatif, -ive [veʒetatif, -iːv], *a.* Vegetative.

végétation [veʒetasjɔ̃], *s.f.* **1.** Vegetation. **2.** *pl. Med:* Vegetations. **Végétations adénoïdes,** adenoid growths; *F:* adenoids.

végéter [veʒete], *v.i.* (je végète; je végéterai) **1.** (Of plant) To vegetate, grow. **2.** *F:* To vegetate; to lead an aimless or uneventful life.

véhémence [veemɑ̃ːs], *s.f.* Vehemence. **Avec véhémence,** vehemently.

véhément [veemɑ̃], *a.* Vehement, violent. *adv.* **-ement.**

véhiculaire [veikylɛːr], *a.* Vehicular.

véhicule [veikyl], *s.m.* Vehicle.

véhiculer [veikyle], *v.tr.* To convey, carry (sth.) (by vehicle); to cart (sth.).

Vehme [vem]. *Pr.n.f. Hist:* La sainte Vehme, the Vehmgericht.

veille [vɛːj], *s.f.* **1.** (a) Sitting up, staying up (at night); watching (by night). *Être accoutumé aux veilles,* to be accustomed to late nights. (b) Vigil (of nun, etc.). (c) *Mil:* (Night) watch. *Nau:* Look-out. *Nau:* **Homme de veille,** look-out (man). **Ancre de veille,** sheet-anchor. (d) Wakefulness. **Entre la veille et le sommeil,** between waking and sleeping. *Causer à qn bien des veilles,* to cause s.o. many a sleepless night. **2.** (a) Eve; preceding day. **La veille de Noël,** Christmas Eve. *Je l'avais vu la v.,* I had seen him the day before. **La veille au soir,** the night before. (b) **Être à la veille de la ruine, d'une guerre,** to be on the brink, on the verge, of ruin, of a war. *A la v. de la réunion,* just before the meeting.

veiller [veje]. **1.** *v.i.* (a) To sit up, stay up, keep awake. (b) To watch, be on the look-out; to keep a good look-out; to stand by. (c) *V. sur qn,* to look after s.o.; to take care of s.o. (d) *V. à qch.,* to watch over, see to, sth. *V. aux intérêts de qn,* to attend to, look after, s.o.'s interests. *V. à la besogne,* to keep an eye on the work. *V. à ce que qch. se fasse,* to see to it that sth. is done. *F:* **Veiller au grain,** to look out for squalls; to keep one's weather eye open. **2.** *v.tr.* To sit up with, look after, watch over, attend to (sick person, etc.). *V. un mort,* to sit up with the corpse.

veillée, *s.f.* **1.** Night-nursing (of the sick); watching, vigil (by dead body). **Veillée de corps irlandaise,** Irish wake. **2.** Evening (spent in company). **Faire la veillée chez des voisins,** to spend the evening socially with neighbours (esp. among the peasantry during the winter months).

veilleur, -euse [vejœːr, -øːz]. **1.** *a.* **(a)** *s.m.* Watcher (by night); keeper of a vigil. **Veilleur de nuit,** night-watchman. **(b)** *s.f.* Nun keeping vigil (beside the dead). **2.** *s.f.* **Veilleuse.** (a) Night-light. **Lumière en veilleuse** light turned low. *Mettre l'électricité en v.,* to dim the lights. *Aut:* **Mettre les phares en v.,** to dim the head-lights. (b) By-pass (of gas-burner); pilot-light.

veinard, -arde [vɛnaːr, -ard], *a. & s. F:* Lucky (person, player). *C'est un v.,* he has all the luck. **Veinard!** you lucky devil!

veine [vɛn], *s.f.* **1.** (a) *Anat:* Vein. *Anat:* **Veine cave,** vena cava. (b) (Underground)

stream, rivulet. (c) Vein (in wood, marble).
2. (a) Geol : Vein ; lode (of ore) ; seam (of coal).
(b) Vein, inspiration, humour. *F :* **Être en veine
de faire qch.**, to be in the mood, in the humour,
to do sth. *Être en v. de générosité,* to be in a
generous mood. (c) *F :* Luck. **Être en veine,**
avoir de la veine, to be in luck('s way). **Porter
veine à qn,** to bring s.o. good luck. **Coup de
veine,** (i) stroke of luck ; (ii) fluke.

ein|er [vene], *v.tr.* To vein, grain (door, etc.).
s.m. **-age.**

veineux, -euse [vɛnø, -øːz], *a.* **1.** Venous
(system, blood). **2.** Veiny (wood, etc.).

einule [venyl], *s.f.* Veinlet.

élaire [velɛːr], *a. & s.f. Ling :* Velar (guttural) ;
back (consonant).

élarium [velarjɔm], *s.m. Rom.Ant :* Velarium.

vêl|er [vele], *v.i.* (Of cow) To calve. [VEAU]
s.m. **-age.** *s.m.* **-ement.**

vélin [velɛ̃], *s.m.* **1.** Vellum (parchment).
2. (Papier) **vélin,** wove paper.

vélite [velit], *s.m. Rom.Ant :* Velite ; light-armed
soldier.

velléitaire [vɛlleitɛːr], *a.* Impulsive, erratic.

velléité [vɛlleite], *s.f.* Slight desire or inclination ;
stray impulse.

vélo [velo], *s.m. F :* (= VÉLOCIPÈDE) Bike, push-
bike ; *U.S :* wheel. **Aller à vélo,** to cycle ;
F : to bike. **Faire du vélo,** to go in for cycling.

vélocipède [velɔsipɛd], *s.m.* **1.** *A :* Velocipede.
2. *Adm :* Cycle (of any type).

vélocité [velɔsite], *s.f.* Speed, velocity, swiftness.

vélodrome [velɔdroːm], *s.m.* Cycle-racing track.

vélomoteur [velɔmɔtœːr], *s.m.* Motorized bicycle.

velours [v(ə)luːr], *s.m.* Velvet. **1.** *Tex :* *V. uni,
v. plain,* plain velvet. *V. façonné,* figured velvet.
V. bouclé, frisé, épinglé, uncut velvet ; terry.
V. à côtes, cannelé, ribbed velvet, corduroy velvet.
V. de coton, velveteen. S.a. PATTE 1. **2.** *F :* **Le
chemin de velours,** the primrose path. **Être
sur le velours,** to be on velvet ; *Golf :* to be
dormy (2, 3, etc.). **3.** *F :* Incorrect 'liaison'
consisting of an epenthetic [z], as : *J'ai été*
[ʒezete], *il leur a dit* [ilœrzadi].

velouter [v(ə)lute], *v.tr.* To give a velvety
appearance to (sth.) ; (of haze, etc.) to soften
(contour).

velouté. 1. *a.* Velvety ; velvet-like ; soft as
velvet ; downy (peach, cheeks). **2.** *s.m.* (a) Vel-
vetiness, softness (of material, voice) ; bloom
(of peach). (b) **Velouté de laine,** velour(s) (cloth).

velouteux, -euse [v(ə)lutø, -øːz], *a.* Velvety,
soft.

velpeau [velpo], *s.m. Surg : Sp : Box :* **Bande
Velpeau, un velpeau,** crape bandage.

velu [vəly], *a.* Hairy ; villous (leaf, etc.).

vélum [velɔm], *s.m.* Awning.

velvantine, velventine [velvɑ̃tin], *s.f. Tex :*
Velveteen.

velvote [velvɔt], *s.f. Bot : F :* Toad-flax.

venaison [vənɛzɔ̃], *s.f. Cu :* Venison.

venaissin [vənɛsɛ̃], *a.* Pertaining to Vaucluse.

vénal, -als, -aux [venal, -o], *a.* **1.** Venal,
purchasable (privilege, etc.). *Com :* **Valeur
vénale,** market value. **2.** *Pej :* Venal, mercenary,
corruptible ; corrupt (press). *adv.* **-ement.**

vénalité [venalite], *s.f.* Venality.

venant [vənɑ̃]. **1.** *a.* Thriving. **2.** *s.m.* **A tout
venant, à tous venants,** to all comers, to all and
sundry. S.a. ALLANT 2.

vendable [vɑ̃dabl], *a.* Saleable, vendible,
marketable.

vendange [vɑ̃dãːʒ], *s.f.* **1.** (Often in *pl.*) Vintage

(season). **2.** (a) Vintaging ; grape-gathering ;
vine-harvest, wine-harvest. *F :* **Adieu, paniers,
vendanges sont faites,** the business is over (and
done with). (b) The grapes.

vendang|er [vɑ̃dãʒe], *v.tr. & i.* **(je vendangeai(s) ;
n. vendangeons)** To vintage ; to gather (the
grapes). *s.* **-eur, -euse.**

vendéen, -enne [vɑ̃deɛ̃, -ɛn], *a. & s. Geog :*
Vendean ; of Vendée.

vendémiaire [vɑ̃demjɛːr], *s.m. Fr.Hist :* First
month of the Fr. Republican calendar (Sep.-Oct.).

vendetta [vɛdɛtta, vǎ-], *s.f.* Vendetta.

vendeur, -euse [vɑ̃dœːr, -øːz], *s.* **1.** *Com :*
Seller (of goods) ; (in shop) salesman, saleswoman ; assistant ; shopman, shop-girl. **2.** *Jur :*
(f. venderesse) Vendor.

vendre [vɑ̃ːdr], *v.tr.* **1.** To sell. *V. qch. à qn,* to
sell s.o. sth. ; to sell sth. to s.o. *V. à terme,* to
sell on credit. *V. comptant,* to sell for cash. *V.
cher, chèrement, sa vie,* to sell one's life dearly.
V. un objet trois francs, occ. pour trois francs, to
sell an object for three francs. *Ces cuillers se
vendent à dix francs pièce,* these spoons sell at
ten francs each. **Maison à vendre,** house for
sale. **L'art de vendre,** salesmanship. *V. ses droits,
sa liberté,* to barter away one's rights, one's
liberty. **Vendre qn comme esclave,** to sell s.o.
for a slave, into slavery. **2.** *F :* **Vendre qn,** to
sell s.o. up (for debt). **3. Vendre qn,** to betray
s.o. *V. un secret,* to betray a secret.

vendu, *s.m.* Traitor.

vendredi [vɑ̃dradi], *s.m.* Friday. **Le vendredi
saint,** Good Friday.

venelle [vənɛl], *s.f. A :* Alley, *Scot :* vennel.
(Still used in) *F :* **Enfiler la venelle,** to slip away ;
to take to one's heels.

vénéneux, -euse [venenø, -øːz], *a.* Poisonous
(plant, food). *Cf.* VENIMEUX.

vener [vəne], *v.i.* (je **vène ; je venerai) Faire
vener la viande,** to hang meat (till it is high).

vené, *a.* High (meat).

vénérabilité [venerabilite], *s.f.* Venerability.

vénérable [venerabl]. **1.** *a.* Venerable. **2.** *s.m.*
Worshipful master (of masonic lodge). *adv.*
-ment.

vénérateur, -trice [veneratœːr, -tris], *s.* Vener-
ator, reverencer.

vénération [venerasjɔ̃], *s.f.* Veneration, reverence. **Avoir de la vénération pour qn,** to hold
s.o. in veneration.

vénérer [venere], *v.tr.* (je **vénère ; je vénérerai)**
(a) To venerate, reverence, revere. (b) To
worship (saint, relics).

vénérie [venri], *s.f.* Venery ; (science of)
hunting. *Termes de v.,* hunting terms.

venette [vənɛt], *s.f. P :* **Avoir la venette,** to be
in a blue funk ; to have, get, the jitters. **Donner
la venette à qn,** to put s.o. in a funk.

veneur [vənœːr], *s.m. Ven : A :* Huntsman.

vengeance [vɑ̃ʒãːs], *s.f.* **1.** Revenge. **Par vengeance,** in revenge. **Tirer vengeance d'une injure,**
to be revenged for an insult. **Tirer, prendre,
vengeance de qn, exercer sa vengeance sur qn,**
to be avenged on s.o. **2.** Vengeance, retribution, requital. **Crime qui crie vengeance,** crime
that cries for vengeance (contre, against).

venger [vɑ̃ʒe], *v.tr.* (je **vengeai(s) ; nous vengeons)**
To avenge. *V. qn d'une injure,* to avenge s.o. for
the insult offered.

se venger, to be revenged ; to have one's
revenge. *Se v. d'une injure,* to take vengeance for
an insult ; to requite an insult. *Se v. sur qn (de
qch.),* to revenge oneself on s.o. (for sth.) ; to
pay s.o. out.

vengeur', -eresse [vãʒœːr, -ərɛs]. **1.** *s.* Avenger, revenger. **2.** *a.* Avenging, vengeful.
véni|el, -elle [venjɛl], *a.* Venial (sin). *adv.* **-ellement.**
venimeux, -euse [vənimø, -øːz], *a.* Venomous. (*a*) Poisonous (bite, serpent). *Glandes venimeuses,* poison-glands. (*b*) *F:* Spiteful.
venin [vənɛ̃], *s.m.* Venom. (*a*) Poison (of adder). (*b*) *F:* Spite, malice. *Jeter tout son venin,* to vent all one's spleen. S.a. MORT[1] 1.
venir [v(ə)niːr]. **I.** *v.i.* (*pr.p.* venant; *p.p.* venu; *pr.ind.* je viens, il vient, n. venons, ils viennent; *pr.sub.* je vienne; *p.h.* je vins, n. vinmes, v. vîntes, ils vinrent; *p.sub.* je vinsse; *fu.* je viendrai. Aux. *être*) To come. **1.** (*a*) *Je viens!* I'm coming! *Ne faire qu'aller et venir,* (i) to be always on the move, on the go. (ii) *Je ne ferai qu'aller et venir,* I shall come straight back. *Venez par ici,* step this way. *D'où venez-vous?* where have you come from? *Il vint à moi, vers moi,* he came up to me. *Il vint sur moi,* he advanced on me (threateningly). *Venir au monde,* to be born. *Ses succès à venir,* his future successes. *Vienne un peu de soleil et tout le monde est gai,* the minute the sun comes out everyone is cheerful. *Il aura dix ans vienne (la) Noël,* he will be ten come Christmas. *Faire venir qn,* to send for, call in, summon, fetch, s.o. *Voir venir qn,* to see s.o. coming. *F: Je vous vois venir!* I see what you are getting at. *Le voici venir, le voici qui vient,* here he comes. *Se faire bien venir de qn,* to ingratiate oneself with s.o. *Être bien, mal, venu,* to be welcome, unwelcome. *Je serais mal venu à . . .,* it would ill beseem me to. . . . *Impers. Est-il venu quelqu'un?* has anyone called? *F:* has anybody been? *Il est venu deux lettres pour vous,* two letters have come for you. *Nau: Venir dans le vent,* to come round. *Venir sur bâbord, sur tribord,* to alter course to port, to starboard. (*b*) **Venir + inf.** (i) *Il vint tomber à mes pieds,* he fell at my feet. (ii) *Venez me trouver à quatre heures,* come to me, come and see me, at four o'clock. *Je viens vous voir,* I have come to see you. *V. chercher qch., qn, v. prendre qch.,* to come and fetch sth.; to call for s.o. (*c*) *Venir de faire qch.* (*pr. & p.d.* only), to have (only) just done sth. *Il vient, venait, de sortir,* he has just, had just, gone out. **2.** (Denoting origin) (*a*) *Il vient d'Amérique,* he hails from America. *Mot qui vient du latin,* word derived from Latin. *Ce bien lui est venu de famille,* this property was a family inheritance. *Tout cela vient de ce que . . .,* all this is the result of. . . . (*b*) *Impers.* D'où vient(-il) que . . .? how is it that . . .? how comes it that . . .? **3.** (*a*) To occur, to come. *Le premier exemple venu,* the first instance that comes to hand. *L'idée me vient que . . .,* il me vient à l'esprit que . . ., il me vient l'idée que . . ., the thought strikes me, it comes to my mind, that . . .; it occurs to me that. . . . (*b*) *Venir à faire qch.,* to happen to do sth., to chance to do sth. **4.** (*a*) To attain, reach. *L'eau leur venait aux genoux,* the water was up to their knees. (*b*) *Venir à rien,* to come to nothing. *Venir à bien,* to succeed, prosper. S.a. BOUT 1. (*c*) *En venir à qch., à faire qch.,* to come to sth., to the point of doing sth. *En v. aux coups, aux mains,* to come to blows. *Il en était venu à mendier,* he had come down to begging. *Les choses en sont-elles venues là?* have things come to such a pass? *Je comprends où vous voulez en v.,* I see what you are driving at. **5.** (Of plants, teeth, children, etc.) To come up, grow, grow up. *Bien venir,* to thrive. *Sujet mal venu,* stunted offspring. *Faire*

venir du blé, to grow corn. (Of photograph, etc. *Être bien venu,* to be successful. *Metall:* Ven de forge, de fonte, avec . . ., forged, cast, in on piece with . . .
     s'en venir, *F:* to come along.
II. venir, *s.m.* (Used in) *J'ai eu l'aller pour l venir,* I had my journey for my trouble.
venu, -ue[1], *s.* (With *premier, dernier, nouveau* Comer. *Les nouveaux venus,* the new-comers S.a. PREMIER 1.
venue[2], *s.f.* **1.** Coming, arrival; advent approach (of spring); rush, irruption (of water) S.a. ALLÉE 1. *Lors de ma venue au monde . . .,* when I was born. . . . **2.** Growth (of tree, etc.) *D'une belle venue,* well-grown. *Tout d'un venue,* (of legs, etc.) straight up and down shapeless.
Venise [v(ə)niːz]. *Pr.n.f.* Venice. **Point d** Venise, Venetian lace.
vénitien, -ienne [venisjɛ̃, -jɛn], *a. & s.* Vene tian. S.a. LANTERNE 1.
vent [vã], *s.m.* **1.** (*a*) Wind. *Nau: V. frais* strong breeze. *Grand v., v. fort,* high wind; gale *Coup de vent,* gust of wind; squall. *F: Entrer sortir, en coup de vent,* to dash in, out. *F: Jete la plume, la paille, au vent,* to trust to chance *A l'abri du vent,* (i) sheltered from the wind (ii) *Nau:* under the lee. *Mus: Instrument à vent,* wind instrument. S.a. FUSIL 3, MOULIN *Il fait du vent,* it is windy (weather). *Pression d vent,* wind pressure; *Metall:* blast pressure *Aller comme le vent,* to go like the wind. *F: l a le vent en poupe,* he is on the high road t success. *Aller vent arrière,* to sail, run, before the wind. *Contre le vent,* against the wind, i the teeth of the wind. *Sous le vent, alee;* t leeward. *Au vent,* (i) a-weather; (ii) to wind ward. *Au v. de . . .,* to windward of. . . S.a. BOUÉE 1. *Mettre la barre au vent,* to pu the helm up, alee. *Côté du vent,* weather-side *Côté sous le vent,* lee-side. *Avoir l'avantage d vent,* to have the weather-gauge. *F: Regarde de quel côté vient le vent,* to watch which wa the wind is blowing. *F: Tourner, virer, à tou les vents,* to be a weathercock. *Prov: Qui sèm le vent récolte la tempête,* he who sows the winc shall reap the whirlwind. S.a. ABATTRE 5, ALIZÉ AUTANT 1, BREBIS 2, COULIS[1], DEBOUT 2, ÉCORNER 1 MARÉE 1. (*b*) *Aire de vent,* point of the compass *F: Logé aux quatre vents,* exposed to the fou winds of heaven. (*c*) *Air. Marché, assemblée en plein vent,* open-air market, meeting S.a. MARCHAND 1. *Mettre qch. au vent,* to hang sth. out to air. S.a. FLAMBERGE. *Donner vent à un tonneau,* to make a vent in a barrel. *F: Don ner vent à sa colère,* to give vent to one's anger (*d*) Blast (of bellows, gun). (*e*) Wind, breath breathing. *Prendre vent,* to recover one's wind one's breath. (*f*) *Med:* Flatulence, wind **2. Ven:** Scent. *Avoir le vent de son gibier, to* have the wind of one's game. *F: Avoir vent de qch.,* to get wind of sth.
vente [vãːt], *s.f.* **1.** Sale. *V. aux enchères,* sale by auction. *V. judiciaire,* sale by order of the court *V. de charité,* (charity) bazaar. **Marchandise de bonne vente,** goods that sell well. **Salle des ventes,** auction-mart. **Salle de vente,** sale-room. **Vente publique,** public sale; auction(-sale). *En vente chez . . .,* on sale at . . ., to be had from. . . . **Offrir qch. en vente,** to offer sth. for sale. (Of book) **Avoir rencontré la forte vente,** to be a best seller. S.a. ACTE 2, AMIABLE. **2.** Timber felled. **Jeune(s) vente(s),** new undergrowth.

venter [vɑ̆te], *v.impers.* To blow, to be windy. *Il vente fort*, it is blowing fresh; it is very windy.

venteux, -euse [vɑ̃tø, -øːz], *a.* (*a*) Windy (weather); windswept (country). (*b*) Causing flatulence; *F:* windy (food).

ventilateur [vɑ̃tilatœːr], *s.m.* Ventilator. **1.** Ventilating aperture or pipe. **2.** *V. rotatif*, fan; blower. *V. électrique*, electric fan.

ventilation [vɑ̃tilasjɔ̃], *s.f.* Ventilation.

ventiler [vɑ̃tile], *v.tr.* To ventilate, air (room).

ventôse [vɑ̃toːz], *s.m. Hist:* Sixth month of the Fr. Republican calendar (Feb.-March).

ventouse [vɑ̃tuːz], *s.f.* **1.** (*a*) *Med:* Cupping-glass. *V. scarifiée*, wet-cup. *V. sèche*, dry-cup. *Appliquer des ventouses à qn*, to cup s.o. *F:* Faire ventouse, to adhere by suction. (*b*) Sucker (of leech). (*c*) Nozzle (of vacuum-cleaner). (*d*) Sucking-disk. *Cendrier à ventouse*, suction-grip ash-tray (for motor car). **2.** Air-hole, ventilator, vent(-hole).

ventouser [vɑ̃tuze], *v.tr. Med:* To cup.

ventral, -aux [vɑ̃tral, -o], *a.* Ventral.

ventre [vɑ̃ːtr], *s.m.* **1.** (*a*) Abdomen, belly. *Se coucher à plat ventre*, to lie flat on one's belly, on one's stomach. *F:* Se mettre à plat ventre devant qn, to grovel before s.o. (Of horse) *Ventre à terre*, at full speed. *Avoir mal au ventre*, to have the belly-ache. *Avoir du ventre*, to be stout. *Prendre du ventre*, to grow stout; to develop a corporation. *Se serrer le ventre*, to tighten, pull in, one's belt; to be on short commons. S.a. CŒUR 3, DÉBOUTONNER, TAPER 1. (*b*) Stomach, paunch. *Être porté sur son ventre, faire un dieu de son ventre*, to make a god of one's belly. *N'avoir rien dans le ventre*, (i) to be starving; (ii) *F:* to have no guts. **2.** *Tchn:* (*a*) Bulge, paunch, swell (of bottle, girder); belly, sag (of sail); belly (of ship). *Faire ventre*, (i) to bulge out, to belly out; (ii) to sag. (*b*) *Ph:* Antinode; ventral segment. *Ventre de potentiel, de tension*, antinode, loop, of potential (in circuit or aerial).

ventrebleu [vɑ̃trəblø], *int. A:* Gadzooks!

ventrée [vɑ̃tre], *s.f. F:* Bellyful.

ventricule [vɑ̃trikyl], *s.m. Anat:* Ventricle.

ventriloque [vɑ̃trilɔk]. **1.** *a.* Ventriloquous. **2.** *s.* Ventriloquist.

ventriloquie [vɑ̃trilɔki], *s.f.* Ventriloquy, ventriloquism.

ventripotent [vɑ̃tripotɑ̃], *a. F:* = VENTRU 1.

ventru [vɑ̃try], *a.* **1.** Corpulent, portly, *F:* pot-bellied. **2.** (Of cover, diaphragm, etc.) Dished.

vénusté [venyste], *s.f. A:* Charm, grace.

vêpres [veːpr], *s.f.pl. Ecc:* Vespers; evensong.

ver [veːr], *s.m.* **1.** Worm. (*a*) *Ver de terre*, earth-worm. *Ver des pêcheurs, ver rouge*, lobworm. (*b*) *Med:* Ver solitaire, tapeworm. *F:* Tuer le ver, to drink a glass of neat spirits before breaking one's fast. **2.** (*a*) Grub, larva, maggot. *Ver blanc*, grub (of cockchafer). *Ver de viande*, maggot. *Ver de farine*, meal-worm. *Rongé, piqué, des vers*, worm-eaten, moth-eaten. *Ver rongeur*, (i) cankerworm, canker; (ii) the worm that gnaws; remorse; (iii) constant drain on the resources. *Rose rongée de vers*, cankered rose. *F:* Tirer les vers du nez de qn, to worm secrets out of s.o. (*b*) *Ver luisant*, glow-worm. (*c*) *Ver à soie*, silk-worm.

véracité [verasite], *s.f.* Veracity. **1.** Truthfulness. **2.** Truth (of a statement).

véranda [verɑ̃da], *s.f.* Veranda(h).

verbal, -aux [verbal, -o], *a.* **1.** (Of promise, order) Verbal; by word of mouth. S.a. PROCÈS-

VERBAL. **2.** *Gram:* Verbal (adjective, etc.). *adv.* **-ement.**

verbalisation [verbalizasjɔ̃], *s.f. Jur:* Official entry (by policeman, etc.) of (motoring, etc.) offence. *Cf.* PROCÈS-VERBAL.

verbaliser [verbalize], *v.i. Jur:* (*a*) (Of policeman) *V. contre un conducteur d'auto*, to take a motorist's name, and full particulars of the offence. (*b*) To draw up an official report (of an offence, etc.); to minute (a meeting).

verbe [verb], *s.m.* **1.** *A. & Lit:* Tone of voice; speech. *Avoir le verbe haut*, to be loud of speech. **2.** *Theol:* Le Verbe, the Word. **3.** *Gram:* Verb.

verbeux, -euse [verbø, -øːz], *a.* Verbose, long-winded; prosy (orator).

verbiage [verbjaːʒ], *s.m.* Verbiage.

verbosité [verbozite], *s.f.* Verbosity, wordiness.

ver-coquin [verkɔkɛ̃], *s.m.* **1.** Vine-grub. **2.** *Vet:* (*a*) Stagger-worm. (*b*) (Blind) staggers. *pl. Des vers-coquins.*

verdal [verdal], *s.m. Const:* Pavement-glass; basement-light. *pl. Des verdals.*

verdâtre [verdɑːtr], *a.* Greenish.

verdelet, -ette [verdəlɛ, -ɛt], *a.* **1.** (Of wine) Tart; slightly acid. **2.** (Of old people) Hale and hearty; enjoying a green old age.

verdeur [verdœːr], *s.f.* **1.** (*a*) Greenness (of immaturity). (*b*) Sap (in wood); greenness (of wood). **2.** Tartness, acidity (of fruit, wine, *F:* of speech). **3.** *F:* Vigour, vitality (of old people); greenness (of old age).

verdict [verdikt], *s.m. Jur:* Finding of the jury; verdict. *Prononcer, rendre, un verdict*, to return a verdict; to find (for or against s.o.).

verdier [verdje], *s.m.* **1.** Greenfinch, green linnet. **2.** *Hist:* Verderer. [VERT]

verdir [verdiːr]. **1.** *v.tr.* To make or paint (sth.) green. **2.** *v.i.* (*a*) (Of vegetation) To grow, become, turn, green. (*b*) (Of copper) To become covered with verdigris.

verdoyant [verdwajɑ̃], *a.* Verdant, green.

verdoyer [verdwaje], *v.i.* (il verdoie; il verdoiera) (Of field, etc.) To take on a green colour.

verdunis|er [verdynize], *v.tr.* To chlorinate (water). [VERDUN] *s.f.* **-ation.**

verdure [verdyːr], *s.f.* **1.** (*a*) Greenness. (*b*) Verdure, greenery. *Cabinet de verdure*, green arbour. *Tapis de v.*, greensward; green. **2.** *Cu:* Green-stuff, greens.

véreux, -euse [verø, -øːz], *a.* **1.** Wormy, maggoty (fruit). **2.** *F:* Of dubious character; *F:* fishy. *Financier v.*, shady financier. *Affaire véreuse*, bubble scheme; fishy business. *Dettes véreuses*, bad debts. [VER]

verge [verʒ], *s.f.* (*a*) Rod, wand, switch. *F:* Gouverner avec une verge de fer*, to rule with a rod of iron. *Être sous la verge de qn*, to be ruled by s.o. *V. d'huissier*, usher's wand. *A:* Huissier à verge*, tipstaff. (*b*) (*Poignée de) verges*, birch-rod, birch. *Battre de verges un enfant*, to birch a child. (*c*) Shank (of anchor); rod (of pendulum); beam (of balance); stick (of rocket). *V. de piston*, piston-rod. (*d*) *Bot:* Verge d'or*, golden-rod, Aaron's rod.

vergé [verʒe], *a.* **1.** *Tex:* (*a*) Badly dyed; streaky. (*b*) Corded. **2.** Laid (paper). *s.m. V. blanc*, cream-laid paper.

verger [verʒe], *s.m.* Orchard.

vergette [verʒɛt], *s.f.* **1.** Small cane, switch. **2.** *pl.* Clothes-whisk. [VERGE]

vergeture [verʒətyːr], *s.f.* Weal, red mark (caused by lash of whip, etc.).

vergeure [verʒyːr], *s.f.* Wire-mark (on laid paper). [VERGE]

verglas [vɛrglɑ], *s.m.* Glazed frost, silver thaw.
vergogne [vɛrgɔɲ], *s.f. A:* Shame. (Still used in) **Sans vergogne,** shameless(ly).
vergue [vɛrg], *s.f. Nau:* Yard. **Grande vergue,** main-yard. **Bout de vergue,** yard-arm. **Avoir (le) vent sous vergue, être vent sous vergue,** to scud before the wind.
véridicité [veridisite], *s.f.* = VÉRACITÉ.
véridique [veridik], *a.* Veracious (person, account). *adv.* **-ment.**
vérificateur [verifikatœːr], *s.m.* **1.** Verifier, inspector, examiner. **Vérificateur de comptes,** auditor. **2.** Testing device; gauge, calipers. *V. de pression (des pneus),* tyre pressure-gauge.
vérification [verifikasjɔ̃], *s.f.* Verification (of statement); inspection, examination, checking (of work, etc.); scrutiny (of votes). **Vérification de comptes,** audit(ing) of accounts.
vérifi|er [verifje], *v.tr.* **1.** To verify; to inspect, examine, check (work, etc.); to overhaul (machinery); to audit (accounts); to scrutinize (votes). *V. des références,* to take up references. **2.** To verify, prove, confirm (statement, etc.). *a.* **-able.**
vérin [verɛ̃], *s.m. Tchn:* Jack. *V. à vis,* screw-jack. *V. hydraulique,* hydraulic jack.
véritable [veritabl], *a.* **1.** True (story, etc.). **2.** Real, genuine, veritable. *Le v. prix des choses,* the real, true, value of things. *Des larmes véritables,* genuine tears. *Un v. artiste,* a real, true, artist. *C'est un v. coquin,* he's a regular rogue. *adv.* **-ment.**
Véritas [veritɑːs], *s.m. Nau:* **1.** Le (Bureau) **Véritas** = Lloyd's. **2.** Le **Véritas** = Lloyd's List.
vérité [verite], *s.f.* **1.** Truth, verity (of statement). **Dire la vérité,** to speak the truth. **La vérité se découvre toujours,** truth will out. **A la vérité,** as a matter of fact. **En vérité,** really, actually; *B:* verily. **2.** Fact, truth. *F:* **C'est la vérité vraie,** it's an actual fact; it's the honest truth. **Dire à qn (toutes) ses vérités, ses quatre vérités,** to tell s.o. a few home truths. S.a. LA PALICE. **3.** Sincerity, truthfulness.
verjus [vɛrʒy], *s.m.* **1.** Verjuice. **2.** Verjuice grape.
verjuté [vɛrʒyte], *a.* Verjuiced; acid, sour.
vermeil, -eille [vɛrmɛːj]. **1.** *a.* Vermilion, bright red; ruby (lips); rosy (cheeks). **2.** *s.m.* Silver-gilt, vermeil.
vermicel(le) [vɛrmisɛl], *s.m. Cu:* Vermicelli.
vermicide [vɛrmisid]. *Pharm:* **1.** *a.* Vermicidal (drug). **2.** *s.m.* Vermicide.
vermiculaire [vɛrmikylɛːr], *a.* Vermicular, worm-shaped. *Anat:* **Appendice vermiculaire,** vermiform appendix.
vermiculé [vɛrmikyle], *a.* **1.** *Arch:* Vermiculated (stone-work). **2.** Engine-turned (watch-case, etc.). **3.** *Nat.Hist:* Vermiculate (markings).
vermiforme [vɛrmiform], *a.* Vermiform, vermicular. *Anat:* **Appendice vermiforme,** vermiform appendix.
vermifuge [vɛrmify:ʒ], *a. & s.m.* Vermifuge, anthelmintic. **Poudre vermifuge,** worm-powder.
vermillon [vɛrmijɔ̃], *s.m.* **1.** Vermilion; cinnabar. **2.** Vermilion (colour); bright red.
vermine [vɛrmin], *s.f.* Vermin. **Couvert de vermine,** *F:* **grouillant de vermine,** verminous.
vermisseau [vɛrmiso], *s.m.* Small earthworm.
vermouler (se) [səvɛrmule], *v.pr.* (Of wood) To become worm-eaten.
vermoulu [vɛrmuly], *a.* (*a*) Worm-eaten (wood, etc.). (*b*) *F:* Out-of-date; tottering to a fall; decrepit. [MOUDRE]

vermoulure [vɛrmuly:r], *s.f.* **1.** Worm-hole (in wood). **2.** Wood dust (from worm-hole). **3.** Worm-eaten state (of wood); decrepitud (of an empire).
vermout(h) [vɛrmut], *s.m.* Vermouth.
vernal, -aux [vɛrnal, -o], *a.* Vernal.
vernier [vɛrnje], *s.m.* Vernier; sliding-gauge.
vernir [vɛrniːr], *v.tr.* **1.** To varnish (picture); t polish (mahogany); to japan (iron, leather) *V. au tampon,* to french-polish. **2.** *Cer:* (= VER NISSER) To glaze.
verni, *a.* (*a*) Varnished. **Cuir verni,** paten leather. *F:* **Être verni,** (i) to bear a charme life; (ii) to be drunk, to be well oiled. (*b*) *Tuil en grès v.,* vitrified drain tile.
vernis [vɛrni], *s.m.* **1.** Varnish, polish, glaze gloss. *V. à l'alcool,* spirit varnish. *V. à l'essence* turpentine varnish. *V. cellulosique,* cellulos varnish. *V. japonais,* japan. *V. au tampon,* french polish. *Cer:* *V. luisant,* glaze. *V. de plomb,* lea glaze. **2.** *Bot:* **Vernis du Japon,** varnish-tree lacquer-tree, tree of heaven.
vernissage [vɛrnisaːʒ], *s.m.* (*a*) Varnishing glazing, cr japanning. (*b*) Varnishing-day (at th Salon).
vernisser [vɛrnise], *v.tr.* To glaze (pottery).
vernissé, *a.* (*a*) Glazed. (*b*) *F:* Glossy S.a. BRIQUE 1.
vernisseur, -euse [vɛrnisœːr, -øːz], *s.* **1.** Varnisher or japanner. **2.** *Cer:* Glazer.
vernissure [vɛrnisy:r], *s.f.* **1.** (*a*) Varnishing (*b*) *Cer:* Glazing. **2.** (*a*) Varnish. (*b*) Glaze.
vérole [verɔl], *s.f. Med:* **Petite vérole,** smallpox *Marques de la petite v.,* pock-marks. **Petit vérole volante,** chicken-pox.
véronal [veronal], *s.m. Pharm:* Veronal.
Véronique [veronik]. **1.** *Pr.n.f.* (St) Veronica **2.** *s.f.* (*a*) *Ecc:* Veronica. (*b*) *Bot:* Speedwell
verr-ai, -as, etc. [vɛre, -a]. See VOIR.
verrat [vɛra], *s.m. Breed:* Boar.
verre [vɛːr], *s.m.* **1.** Glass. *V. moulé,* pressed glass. *V. laminé, à glaces,* plate-glass. *Verre: dalles,* pavement lights. *V. armé, v. grillagé* wired glass. *V. de couleur,* stained glass. **Article de verre,** glass-ware. **Un œil en verre,** a glass eye **Peintre sur verre,** artist in stained glass. **Sous verre,** under glass, in a glass case. **Coton de verre, fil de verre,** spun glass. **Papier de verre,** glass-paper or sand-paper. S.a. MOUSSELINE 2. **2.** (Object made of glass) *V. de lunettes,* lens. *V. grossis-sant,* magnifying glass. *V. ardent,* burning glass *V. de montre,* watch-glass. *V. de lampe,* lamp-glass, -chimney. *Nau: V. de hublot,* bull's-eye. **3.** (*a*) **Verre à boire,** (drinking-)glass. *V. gobelet* tumbler. *V. à liqueur,* liqueur glass. *V. gradué* graduated measure. (*b*) Glass(ful). *V. de vin* glass of wine. **Plein verre,** bumper. **Boire un petit verre,** to have a drop of spirits. *F:* a dram. *F:* **Tempête dans un verre d'eau,** storm in a tea-cup. **4.** **Verre soluble,** water-glass.
verré [vɛre], *a.* **1.** **Papier verré,** glass-paper or sand-paper. **2.** **Cuve verrée,** glass-lined tank.
verrerie [vɛr(ə)ri], *s.f.* **1.** Glass-works. **2.** Glass-ware.
verrier [vɛrje], *s.m.* **1.** Glassmaker, glass-blower. *a.* **Peintre verrier,** artist in stained glass. **2.** Glass-rack.
verrière [vɛrjɛːr], *s.f.* **1.** Glass casing (to protect shrine, etc.). **2.** Stained glass window.
verrine [vɛrin], *s.f.* **1.** = VERRIÈRE 1. **2.** *Hort:* Bell-glass. **3.** *Nau:* Glazed-in light; lantern.
verroterie [vɛrɔtri], *s.f.* Small glass-ware; esp glass beads (for trading with natives).

verrou [vɛru], *s.m.* **1.** Bolt, bar. **Fermer une porte au verrou**, to bolt a door. **S'enfermer au verrou**, to bolt oneself in; to deny one's door to visitors. *Pousser le v.*, to bolt the door. **Tirer le(s) verrou(s)**, to unbolt the door. **Sous les verrous**, under lock and key in safe custody. **2.** *Sm.a:* Breech-bolt (of shot-gun).

verrouill|er [vɛruje], *v.tr.* To bolt (door). *V. qn*, to bolt s.o. in; to lock s.o. up. *Sm.a:* *V. la culasse*, to lock the breech. *s.m.* **-age**.

verrue [vɛry], *s.f.* Wart.

verruqueux, -euse [vɛrrykø, -øːz], *a.* Warty (hand). *Bot:* Verrucose, warted (branch, etc.).

vers¹ [vɛːr], *s.m. Pros:* Verse, line (of poetry). **Faire des vers**, to write poetry. **Vers de société**, society verse. *Méchants vers*, doggerel. *Vers blancs*, unrhymed verse.

vers², *prep.* **1.** (Of place) Toward(s), to. (At marine station) *"Vers le bateau,"* 'to the boat.' **2.** (Of time) (a) Toward(s). *Vers la fin du siècle*, towards the end of the century. (b) About. *Venez vers (les) trois heures*, come about three.

versant [vɛrsɑ̃], *s.m.* Slope, side, versant (of mountain); bank (of canal, etc.). *V. de colline*, hillside.

versatile [vɛrsatil], *a.* **1.** Changeable, fickle, inconstant, unstable (disposition). **2.** *Bot:* Versatile (anther).

versatilité [vɛrsatilite], *s.f.* Inconstancy, fickleness.

verse¹ [vɛrs], *s.f.* **1.** Lodging, laying (of corn by wind, etc.). **2. A verse**, in torrents. *Il pleut à v.*, it is pouring. [VERSER]

verse², *a.* *Geom:* Sinus verse. versed sine; versine.

versé [vɛrse], *a.* Versed, experienced, practised, well up (*dans, en,* in); conversant (with).

Verseau (le) [ləvɛrso]. *Pr.n. Astr:* Aquarius, the Water-bearer.

versement [vɛrs(ə)mɑ̃], *s.m.* **1.** Pouring (out) (of liquid, etc.). **2.** *Fin:* Payment. *V. partiel*, instalment. *En plusieurs versements*, by instalments. *Bank:* **Bulletin de versement**, pay-in slip.

verser [vɛrse]. **1.** *v.tr.* (a) To overturn, upset (vehicle); (of wind, etc.) to lodge, lay (crops). (b) To pour (out) (liquid, etc.). *V. à boire à qn*, to pour out a drink for s.o. *V. des décombres*, to shoot rubbish. (c) To shed (tears, blood, light). (d) To pay (in), to deposit (money). **Capitaux versés**, paid-up capital. (e) *V. des hommes à un régiment, dans une arme*, to assign or transfer men to a regiment, to an arm. **2.** *v.i.* (Of vehicle) To turn over (on its side); to upset; (of crops) to be lodged, beaten down, laid flat. **se verser**, (of river) to flow, pour (*dans*, into).

verset [vɛrsɛ], *s.m.* **1.** Verse (of Bible). **2.** *Typ:* Versicle.

verseur, -euse [vɛrsœːr, -øːz]. **1.** *s.* Pourer (of liquids). **La verseuse**, (i) the barmaid, (ii) the coffee-maid. **2.** *s.f.* **Verseuse**, coffee-pot.

versicolore [vɛrsikɔlɔːr], *a.* Versicolour(ed), particoloured, variegated.

versicule [vɛrsikyl], *s.m.* Versicle; little verse.

versificateur, -trice [vɛrsifikatœːr, -tris], *s.* Versifier.

versification [vɛrsifikasjɔ̃], *s.f.* Versification.

versifier [vɛrsifje]. **1.** *v.i.* To versify; to write poetry. **2.** *v.tr.* To versify; to write (sth.) in verse.

version [vɛrsjɔ̃], *s.f.* **1.** *Sch:* Translation (from foreign into mother tongue). **2.** Version, account (of event).

verso [vɛrso], *s.m.* Verso, back, reverse (of sheet of paper); left-hand page (in book). **"Voir au verso,"** 'see overleaf.'

versoir [vɛrswaːr], *s.m. Agr:* Mould-board (of plough). [VERSER]

vert [vɛːr]. **1.** *a.* (a) Green; *Poet:* verdant. *F:* **Vert comme pré**, as green as grass. **Légumes verts**, greens. (b) *Bois v.*, green wood. **Pois verts**, green peas. **Fruits verts**, unripe fruit. *Prov:* Ils sont trop verts, the grapes are sour. **Cuir vert**, raw hide, green hide. *La verte jeunesse*, callow youth. S.a. ARBRE 1. (c) *Verte vieillesse*, green old age. (d) Sharp (reprimand); severe (punishment). (e) *F:* Spicy (story). (f) Langue verte, slang. **2.** *s.m.* (a) (The colour) green. *Her:* Vert. **Des rubans vert bouteille**, vert chou, bottlegreen, cabbage-green, ribbons. *V. pomme*, apple-green. (b) Green grass; fresh vegetation. **Mettre un cheval au vert**, to turn a horse out to grass. *F:* **Prendre qn sans vert**, to catch s.o. napping. S.a. DIABLE 1. **3.** *s.f. F:* **Une verte**, an absinthe.

vert-de-gris, *s.m.* Verdigris.

vert-de-grisé, *a.* Verdigrised; coated with verdigris.

vertébral, -aux [vɛrtebral, -o], *a.* Vertebral. *Colonne vertébrale*, spine; backbone.

vertèbre [vɛrtɛːbr], *s.f. Anat:* Vertebra.

vertébré [vɛrtebre], *a. & s.m. Z:* Vertebrate.

vertement [vɛrtəmɑ̃], *adv. F:* **Tancer qn vertement**, to reprimand s.o. sharply; to give s.o. a sharp scolding. [VERT]

vertical, -aux [vɛrtikal, -o]. **1.** *a.* Vertical; perpendicular, plumb; upright. **2.** *s.f.* **Verticale**, vertical. *adv.* **-ement**.

verticalité [vɛrtikalite], *s.f.* Verticality.

verticille [vɛrtisil], *s.m. Bot:* Verticil, whorl.

verticillé [vɛrtisille], *a.* Verticillate, whorled.

vertige [vɛrtiːʒ], *s.m.* **1.** Dizziness, swimming of the head, giddiness. **Être pris de vertige**, to become dizzy. *Avoir le v.*, to feel dizzy. **2.** Height fear.

vertigineux, -euse [vɛrtiʒinø, -øːz], *a.* Vertiginous; dizzy, giddy (height). *F: Allure vertigineuse*, giddying speed.

vertu [vɛrty], *s.f.* **1.** *A:* Courage, valour. **2.** Virtue. **Faire de nécessité vertu**, to make a virtue of necessity. **3.** Chastity. **4.** Quality, property (of remedy, etc.). *Plantes qui ont la v. de guérir*, plants that have healing virtues. **En vertu de**, in pursuance of, by virtue of.

vertueu|x, -euse [vɛrtɥø, -øːz], *a.* **1.** Virtuous. **2.** *f.* Chaste. *adv.* **-sement**.

vertugadin [vɛrtygadɛ̃], *s.m. A:* Farthingale.

verve [vɛrv], *s.f.* Animation, zest, verve; *F:* go. **Être en verve**, to be in capital form. *Plein de v.*, full of life; lively, spirited.

verveine [vɛrvɛn], *s.f. Bot:* Vervain, verbena.

verveu|x¹, -euse [vɛrvø, -øːz], *a.* Animated, lively, spirited. *adv.* **-sement**.

verveux², *s.m. Fish:* Hoop-net.

vesce [vɛs], *s.f. Bot:* Vetch, tare.

vésicatoire [vezikatwaːr], *a. & s.m. Med:* Vesicatory. **Appliquer un vésicatoire à qn**, to blister s.o.

vésicule [vezikyl], *s.f.* **1.** Vesicle. *Bot:* Air-cell. *V. biliaire*, gall-bladder. *Ich: V. aérienne*, air-bladder. **2.** Blister (on the skin, in a casting).

vespasienne [vɛspazjɛn], *s.f.* Street urinal.

vessie [vesi], *s.f.* **1.** Bladder. *F:* **Prendre des vessies pour des lanternes**, to believe that the moon is made of green cheese. S.a. NATATQIRE. **2.** *F:* Blister (filled with serum).

vestale [vastal], *s.f. Rom.Ant:* Vestal (virgin).

veste [vɛst], s.f. Cost: (Short) jacket (as worn by waiters, page-boys, etc.). F: Retourner sa veste, to turn one's coat. Remporter une veste, to fail; to meet with a rebuff. S.a. MANCHE¹ 1.

vestiaire [vɛstjɛːr], s.m. 1. (a) Cloakroom (of theatre, etc.). (b) Wardrobe room (of boarding-school). (c) Changing-room (of sports pavilion); robing-room (of judges). 2. Hat-and-coat rack.

vestibule [vɛstibyl], s.m. Vestibule, (entrance-) hall, lobby.

vestige [vɛstiː3], s.m. 1. Mark, trace, footprint. 2. F: Vestige, remains, trace (of former habitations, etc.).

veston [vɛstɔ̃], s.m. (Man's) jacket; lounge-coat. Nau: Monkey-jacket. Complet veston, lounge suit. [VESTE]

Vésuve [vezyːv]. Pr.n.m. Geog: Vesuvius.

vêtement [vɛtmɑ̃], s.m. Garment. pl. Clothes, clothing, apparel; F: things. Étoffes pour vêtements, dress materials. Vêtements sacerdotaux, canonicals. Enlever ses vêtements de dehors, to take off one's outdoor things. Vêtements de dessous, underwear, underclothing. La nourriture et le v., food and raiment.

vétéran [vetɛrɑ̃], s.m. 1. Veteran; old campaigner. 2. Student, pupil, who repeats a course.

vétérinaire [veterinɛːr]. 1. a. Veterinary. 2. s.m. Veterinary surgeon; F: vet.

vétille [vetiːj], s.f. Bagatelle, trifle; peccadillo; mere nothing.

vétiller [vetije], v.i. 1. To trifle. 2. To stick at trifles; to split hairs.

vétilleur, -euse¹ [vetijœːr, -øːz], s. Quibbler, caviller.

vétilleux, -euse² [vetijø, -øːz], a. 1. Delicate, ticklish, finicky (business). 2. Captious, finicky (person).

vêtir [vetiːr], v.tr. (pr.p. vêtant; p.p. vêtu; pr.ind. je vêts, n. vêtons; p.h. je vêtis; fu. je vêtirai. The forms vêtissant, vêtissons, vêtissais, etc., are also met with more and more.) 1. To clothe; to dress, attire (s.o.) (de, in). Chaudement vêtu, warmly clad. Collines vêtues de vignes, vine-clad hills. 2. A: (= REVÊTIR) To put on, don (garment).

se vêtir, to dress (oneself) (de, in); to clothe oneself.

veto [veto], s.m. Veto. Mettre son veto à qch., to veto sth.

vétusté [vetyste], s.f. Decay, decrepitude.

veuf, veuve [vœf, vœːv]. 1. a. Widowed (man, woman). 2. s. Widower, f. widow. P: La Veuve, the guillotine.

veuil-e, -es, etc. [vœːj]. See VOULOIR.

veule [vœːl], a. Weak, feeble, flabby (person, etc.); toneless (voice); drab, flat (existence). adv. -ment.

veulent [vœl]. See VOULOIR.

veulerie [vœlri], s.f. Inertia, flabbiness, listlessness; tonelessness (of voice); dullness, emptiness (of existence).

veut [vø]. See VOULOIR.

veuvage [vœvaːʒ], s.m. Widowhood or widowerhood.

veuve. See VEUF.

veux [vø]. See VOULOIR.

vexant [vɛksɑ̃], a. Vexing, provoking, annoying.

vexateur, -trice [vɛksatœːr, -tris], a. Vexatious.

vexation [vɛksasjɔ̃], s.f. Vexation. (Restricted in meaning to) 1. Harassing, F: plaguing. 2. Vexatious measure.

vexatoire [vɛksatwaːr], a. Vexatious.

vexer [vɛkse], v.tr. To vex. 1. To plague, harass.

2. To annoy, provoke. Être vexé de, par, qch., to be vexed, chagrined, at sth.

se vexer de qch. to get vexed, annoyed chagrined, at sth.

vexillaire [vɛksillɛːr], s.m. Rom.Ant: Vexillary; standard-bearer.

viabilité¹ [viabilite, vja-], s.f. Viability (of newborn child, etc.).

viabilité², s.f. Traffic condition (of road). Mettre une route en état de v., to fit a road for traffic; to recondition a road.

viable¹ [viabl, vjabl], a. Viable (infant); capable of living.

viable², a. (Road) fit for traffic.

viaduc [vjadyk], s.m. Viaduct.

viager, -ère [vjaʒe, -ɛːr]. 1. a. (a) For life. Rente viagère, life annuity. (b) F: Transitory (glory, fame). 2. s.m. Life interest. Placer son argent en viager, to invest one's money in a life annuity; to buy an annuity.

viagèrement [vjaʒɛrmɑ̃], adv. For life; during one's lifetime.

viande [vjɑ̃ːd], s.f. Meat. 1. A: Food, viands Prov: Il n'est viande que d'appétit, hunger is the best sauce. 2. Flesh. Grosse viande, v. de boucherie, butcher's meat. V. fraîche, fresh meat V. de cheval, horse-flesh. (On menu) Viande froides, cold buffet. S.a. MOUCHE 1.

viatique [vjatik], s.m. Viaticum. 1. Ecc: & F. Money, provisions, for a journey. 2. Ecc: Last sacrament.

vibrant [vibrɑ̃], a. 1. Vibrating, vibrant. L public se montra v. et réceptif, the public was eage and receptive. 2. (a) Resonant, ringing (voice) (b) Rousing, stirring (speech).

vibrateur [vibratœːr], s.m. El.E: Buzzer.

vibration [vibrasjɔ̃], s.f. 1. Vibration. 2. Reson ance (of voice).

vibratoire [vibratwaːr], a. Vibratory. W.Tel Circuit vibratoire, oscillatory circuit. Med Massage vibratoire, vibro-massage.

vibrer [vibre], v.i. To vibrate. Faire v. le cœu de qn, to thrill s.o., s.o.'s heart.

vibreur [vibrœːr], s.m. El.E: Trembler, vibra tor, buzzer.

vibrion [vibriɔ̃], s.m. Biol: Vibrio. V. septique gas bacillus.

vibrionner [vibriɔne], v.i. F: (Of opinions To breed, propagate; (of sedition) to ferment.

vicaire [vikɛːr], s.m. Ecc: (a) V. apostolique apostolic vicar. Grand vicaire, vicaire général vicar-general. (b) Curate (of parish). Cf. CURÉ (c) (Erroneous translation) Le Vicaire de Wake field, the Vicar of Wakefield.

vice [vis], s.m. 1. (a) Vice, depravity, corruption Bourbier du vice, sink of iniquity. (b) Vice moral failing. 2. Fault, defect, blemish, flaw imperfection. V. de prononciation, faulty utter ance. Jur: Vice de forme, flaw (in a deed, etc.) faulty drafting. Vice propre, inherent defec S.a. RÉDHIBITOIRE.

NOTE. In the following compounds VICE is inv.; the noun takes the plural.

vice-amiral, -aux, s.m. Vice-admiral.

vice-chancelier, s.m. Vice-chancellor.

vice-consul, s.m. Vice-consul.

vice-consulat, s.m. 1. Vice-consulship. 2. Vice consulate.

vice-gérant, s.m. Deputy-manager, actin manager.

vicennal, -aux [visɛnnal, -o], a. Vicennial.

vice-présidence, s.f. (a) Vice-presidency (b) Vice-chairmanship.

vice-président, *s.m.* (a) Vice-president. (b) Vice-chairman.

vice-roi, *s.m.* Viceroy.

vice versa [visevɛrsa], *Lt.adv.phr.* Vice versa; conversely.

Vichy [viʃi]. *Pr.n. Geog:* Vichy. **Eau de Vichy,** Vichy (water). **Pastille de Vichy,** Vichy tablet, digestive tablet.

viciateur, -trice [visjatœːr, -tris], *a.* Vitiating, contaminating.

viciation [visjasjɔ̃], *s.f.* Vitiation; corruption (of morals); contamination (of the air); poverty (of blood).

vicier [visje], *v.tr.* **1.** To vitiate, corrupt, spoil. *V. l'air,* to taint the air. **2.** *Jur:* To vitiate, invalidate (deed). **se vicier,** to become tainted.

vicié, *a.* Vitiated, corrupt; tainted (food); poor, thin (blood). *Air v.,* stale, foul, air.

vicieux, -euse [visjø, -øːz], *a.* Vicious. **1.** Depraved. **2.** Defective, fau'ty. **Cercle vicieux,** vicious circle. **3.** Tricky, restive, bad-tempered (horse).

vicinal, -aux [visinal, -o], *a.* **Chemin vicinal,** by-road, local road, parish road.

vicissitude [visissityd], *s.f.* Vicissitude, mutability (of fortune, etc.).

vicomte [vikɔ̃ːt], *s.m.* Viscount.

vicomté [vikɔ̃te], *s.f.* **1.** Viscountcy, viscountship. **2.** Viscounty.

vicomtesse [vikɔ̃tɛs], *s.f.* Viscountess.

victime [viktim], *s.f.* **1.** Victim (of sacrifice). **2.** Victim, sufferer. *Être la v. d'une illusion,* to labour under a delusion. S.a. ACCIDENT 1.

victoire [viktwaːr]. **1.** *s.f.* Victory. **Remporter la victoire,** to gain a, the, victory (*sur,* over); to carry, win, the day. *F:* **Chanter victoire,** to crow, to triumph. **2.** *Pr.n.f.* Victoria.

victorien, -ienne [viktɔrjɛ̃, -jɛn], *a.* Victorian.

victorieu|x, -euse [viktɔrjø, -øːz], *a.* Victorious. *Être v.,* to win the day; to gain the victory. *Être v. de qn,* to be victorious over s.o. *adv.* **-sement.**

victuailles [viktɥaːj], *s.f.pl.* Victuals, eatables.

vidange [vidãːʒ], *s.f.* **1.** (a) Voidance, emptying (of cesspools, etc.). **Matières de vidange,** night-soil. (b) Draining, emptying (of sump); blowing off (of boiler). **Bouchon de vidange,** drain-cock; blow-off cock; sump-plug; draining-plug. **Robinet de vidange,** drain-cock. **Tonneau en vidange,** broached cask. **2.** Usu. *pl.* (a) Night-soil. (b) Sediment, sludge.

vidanger [vidãʒe], *v.tr.* (je vidangeai(s); n. vidangeons) To empty (cesspool, radiator); to drain (engine sump); to blow off (boiler).

vidangeur [vidãʒœːr], *s.m.* Nightman; scavenger (of cesspools).

vide [vid]. **1.** *a.* Empty; blank (space in document); unoccupied (seat). *Revenir les mains vides,* to return empty-handed. *F: Avoir la tête v.,* to be empty-headed. **Vide de sens,** void, devoid, of meaning. *Phrases vides,* empty words; claptrap. **2.** *s.m.* (a) Empty space; gap; cavity; void; blank (in document). **Combler les vides,** to fill up the gaps. (b) *Ph:* Vacuum. **Pompe à vide,** vacuum pump. **Nettoyage par le vide,** vacuum cleaning. *El:* **Lampe à vide,** vacuum-lamp. *V. très poussé,* very high vacuum. (c) Emptiness. *Taper dans le v.,* to (hit out and) miss the mark. *Regarder dans le v.,* to stare into vacancy. *Voiture revenant à vide,* carriage returning empty. (Of machine) **Marcher à vide,** to run on no load, to run light. *F:* **Usine qui mâche à vide,** factory eating its head off. *Mus:* **Corde à vide,** open string.

vide-citron, *s.m.* Lemon-squeezer.

vide-poche(s), *s.m.inv. Furn:* (a) (Dressing-table) tidy; pin-tray. (b) Pouch-table.

vide-pomme, *s.m.* Apple-corer.

vid|er [vide], *v.tr.* **1.** To empty; to clear out (room, drawer); to drain (cask, one's glass); to drain off (pond); to exhaust (mind, brain); to blow off (boilers); to blow (an egg). **Vider les lieux,** to vacate the premises; *F:* to clear out, to quit. **Le juge ordonna de faire vider la salle,** the judge ordered the court to be cleared. S.a. ARÇON 1. **2.** To eviscerate (carcass); to gut, clean (fish); to draw (fowl); to core (apple); to stone (fruit). **3.** To settle (question). *V. une querelle,* (i) to adjust, settle, a difference; (ii) to fight it out; to have it out. *s.m.* **-age.** *s.m.* **-ement.**

se vider, to empty; to become empty.

vidé, *a.* Emptied, exhausted. *F:* **C'est un homme vidé,** he is played out.

viduité [vidɥite], *s.f.* Widowhood.

vie [vi], *s.f.* Life. **1.** **Être en vie,** to be alive. **Donner là vie à un enfant,** to give birth to a child. **Avoir la vie dure,** to be hard to kill; to die hard. *Question de vie et de mort,* life-and-death question. **Il y va de la vie,** it's a case of life and death. *Sauver la vie à qn,* to save s.o.'s life. *F:* **Sur ma vie!** as I live! **Sans vie,** lifeless. *Elle déborde de vie,* she is bubbling over with vitality. *Musique pleine de vie,* music full of go. **2.** Lifetime. *De toute ma vie je n'ai entendu chose pareille!* in all my born days I never heard the like! **Pour la vie,** for life; till death. **Entre eux c'est à la vie à la mort,** they are sworn friends. *Une fois dans la vie,* once in a lifetime. **Pension à vie,** life pension. **Nommé à vie,** appointed for life. **3.** Existence, mode of life, way of living. *Ainsi va la vie! c'est la vie!* such is life! **Changer de vie,** to mend one's ways. **Rendre la vie dure à qn,** to make life a burden for s.o. *F:* **Faire la vie,** (i) to live fast, riotously; (ii) to kick up a row. **Mauvaise vie,** loose living. **4.** Living, livelihood. *Niveau de vie,* standard of living. *Prix de la vie,* cost of living. *Gagner sa vie,* to earn, get, one's living, one's livelihood.

vieil, vieille. See VIEUX.

vieillard [vjɛjaːr], *s.m.* (f. usu. **vieille,** q.v. under VIEUX) Old man, greybeard. *Les vieillards,* the aged; old people.

vieilleries [vjɛjri], *s.f.pl.* Old stuff, old thing; outworn ideas.

vieillesse [vjɛjɛs], *s.f.* (Old) age; oldness (of custom, etc.). *Dans leur v.,* in their old age. **Pension de vieillesse,** old age pension. S.a. BÂTON 1.

vieill|ir [vjɛjiːr]. **1.** *v.i.* (a) To grow old. (b) To age (in appearance). (c) (Of custom, word) To become obsolete, antiquated. **2.** *v.tr.* To age (s.o.); to make (s.o.) look older. *s.m.* **-issement.**

vieillot, -otte [vjɛjo, -ɔt], *a.* **1.** Oldish. *s. Petite vieillotte,* little old woman. **2.** Antiquated, old-fashioned. **3.** Wizened (face).

vielle [vjɛl], *s.f.* Hurdy-gurdy. (*N.B.* Not barrel-organ.)

viendr-ai, -as, etc. [vjɛ̃dre, -a]. See VENIR.

vienn-e, -es, etc. [vjɛn]. See VENIR.

vien-s, -t [vjɛ̃]. See VENIR.

vierge [vjɛrʒ]. **1.** *s.f.* (a) Virgin, maid(en). **La (Sainte) Vierge,** the Blessed Virgin (Mary). **Chapelle de la Vierge,** Lady-chapel. S.a. FIL 1. (b) *Astr:* **La Vierge,** Virgo. **2.** *a.* Virgin, virginal; pure, intact, spotless. **Terre, forêt, vierge,** virgin soil, forest. *Page v.,* blank page.

vieux, vieil, f. **vieille** [vjø, vjɛ(ː)j], *a.* (The form *vieil* is used before masc. nouns beginning with a vowel or *h* 'mute,' but *vieux* also occurs in this position) **1.** (Of pers.) Old. (*a*) (In years) **Se faire vieux,** to be getting old, to be getting on in years. **Vivre vieux, vieille,** to live to an old age. *s.* **Un vieux, une vieille,** an old man, an old woman. *F:* **Eh bien, mon vieux!** well, old man, old chap! **Mes vieux,** my old people, my parents. (*b*) Of long standing. **Un vieil ami,** an old friend, a friend of long standing. **Une vieille fille,** an old maid. *s. F:* **Un vieux de la vieille** (*i.e. de la vieille garde de Napoléon*), one of the old guard; a veteran. **2.** (Of thgs) (*a*) Old, ancient (building, etc.); stale (bread, news); worn, shabby (hat). *V. papiers,* waste paper. **Vieux comme le Pont-Neuf, comme les rues, comme Hérode,** as old as Adam, as the hills. **Le bon vieux temps,** the good old times. **C'est une vieille histoire,** it is an old story. *Adj.phr.inv.* **Vieux jeu,** old-fashioned. *Doctrines v. jeu,* antiquated doctrines, outworn shibboleths. (*b*) *inv.* **Des rubans vieil or,** old-gold ribbons. **3.** *s.f.* *Ich:* **Vieille,** wrasse, sea-wife.

vif, vive [vif, viːv]. **1.** *a.* (*a*) Alive, living. *Être brûlé vif,* to be burnt alive. **De vive force,** by main force. **De vive voix,** by word of mouth; viva voce. *Haie vive,* quickset hedge. **Eau vive,** running water, spring water. **Vives eaux** [vivzo], spring-tide. *Le plus vif de nos intérêts,* our most vital interests. *S.a.* CHAUX, FORCE 2, ŒUVRE 4. (*b*) Lively, animated; fast, brisk (action, discussion); brisk, hot (fire). *Enfant vif,* lively child. *Vive allure, allure vive,* rapid gait, brisk pace. *Vif à répliquer,* quick to retort. *Il y eut un échange de paroles vives,* words ran high. *Cheval vif,* high-spirited horse. (*c*) Sharp (wind, reprimand). *L'air est vif,* there is a tang in the air. *Vive arête,* sharp edge. *adv.* **Il gèle vif,** it is freezing hard. (*d*) Keen, quick (wit, etc.); vivid (imagination). *Vif plaisir,* keen pleasure. *Vive satisfaction,* lively satisfaction. (*e*) *Couleurs vives,* bright, vivid, colours. **2.** *s.m. Jur:* Living person. **3.** *s.m.* (*a*) **Peindre au vif, sur le vif,** to paint from life. (*b*) Heart (of tree); shaft (of column). (*c*) Living flesh; quick. *F:* **Blessé, piqué, au vif,** stung to the quick. **Entrer dans le vif de la question,** to come to the heart of the matter.

vif-argent [vifarʒɑ̃], *s.m.* Quicksilver, mercury.

vigie [viʒi], *s.f. Nau:* (*a*) Look-out. **Être de vigie, en vigie,** to be on the look-out. (*b*) Look-out (man). (*c*) Watch-tower. *V. de signaux,* signal-cabin.

vigilance [viʒilɑ̃:s], *s.f.* (*a*) Vigilance. (*b*) *V. méfiante,* watchfulness. **Surprendre la vigilance de qn,** to catch s.o. napping.

vigil|ant [viʒilɑ̃], *a.* Vigilant, watchful, alert. *adv.* **-amment.**

vigile [viʒil], *s.f. Ecc:* Vigil(s).

vigne [viɲ], *s.f.* **1.** *Vit:* (*a*) Vine. **Feuille de vigne,** vine-leaf. (*b*) Vineyard. *F:* **Être dans les vignes du Seigneur,** to be in one's cups. **2.** *Bot:* **Vigne vierge,** Virginia creeper.

vigneron, -onne [viɲrɔ̃, -ɔn], *s.* (*a*) Vine-grower, vineyardist. (*b*) Vine-dresser.

vignette [viɲɛt], *s.f.* **1.** Vignette. *Typ:* Text illustration; head- or tail-piece; ornamental border. **2.** *Bot: F:* (*a*) Meadow-sweet. (*b*) Clematis.

vignettiste [viɲɛtist], *s.m.* Vignettist.

vignoble [viɲɔbl]. **1.** *s.m.* Vineyard. **2.** *a. Région v.,* wine region.

vigogne [vigɔɲ], *s.f.* (*a*) *Z:* Vicuña, vicuna. (*b*) *Tex:* Vicuña (wool or cloth).

vigoureu|x, -euse [vigurø, -øːz], *a.* Vigorous, strong, sturdy. *Faire une opposition vigoureuse à*

un projet, to offer strenuous opposition to a plan. *adv.* **-sement.**

vigueur [vigœːr], *s.f.* **1.** Vigour, strength. **Donner de la vigueur à qn,** to invigorate s.o.; **to brace s.o. (up).** *Dans la vigueur de l'âge,* in the prime of life. **2.** (Of decree, etc.) **En vigueur,** in force. **Entrer en vigueur,** to come into force, into effect, into operation. **Mettre une loi en vigueur,** to enforce a law. **Cesser d'être en vigueur,** to lapse.

vil [vil], *a.* **1.** Cheap, low-priced. **Vendre qch. à vil prix,** to sell sth. at a low price, *F:* dirt cheap. **2.** Low(ly) (origin, condition, etc.); base (metal). **3.** Vile, base (person, soul, motive). *Une vile calomnie,* a foul calumny. *adv.* **-ement.**

vilain, -aine [vilɛ̃, -ɛn]. **1.** *s.* (*a*) *Hist:* Villein. (*b*) Scurvy fellow. *Prov:* **A vilain vilain et demi,** set a thief to catch a thief. (*c*) *F:* **Oh, la vilaine!** for shame, you naughty girl! (*d*) *A:* Miser. **2.** *a.* (*a*) Nasty, bad, unpleasant. *Un v. tour,* a mean, scurvy, dirty, trick. *C'est une vilaine histoire,* it is not a nice story. (*b*) Ugly; shabby (hat, etc.); sordid, wretched (street, etc.) (*c*) Mean; *F:* stingy. *adv.* **-ement.**

vilainage [vilɛnaːʒ], *s.m. Hist:* Villeinage.

vilebrequin [vilbrəkɛ̃], *s.m.* **1.** *Tls:* (i) (Bit-)brace; (ii) brace and bit. *V. à conscience,* breast-drill. **2.** (*Arbre à*) **vilebrequin,** crank-shaft.

vilenie [vilɔni], *s.f.* **1.** Meanness, stinginess. **2.** (*a*) Mean, vile, low, action; foul deed. (*b*) *Dire des vilenies à qn,* to hurl foul abuse at s.o.

vileté [vilte], *s.f.* **1.** (*a*) **Vileté de prix,** cheapness; low price. (*b*) Worthlessness. **2.** (*a*) Vileness (of character). (*b*) Low action.

vilipender [vilipɑ̃de], *v.tr.* To vilipend, vilify, abuse; to run (s.o.) down.

villa [vil(l)a], *s.f.* Villa; suburban residence.

village [vilaːʒ], *s.m.* Village. **Gens de village,** country-folk. *F:* **Il est bien de son village,** (i) he is still awkward (in manner); (ii) he is still very green. *S.a.* COQ¹ 1.

villageois, -oise [vilaʒwa, -waːz]. **1.** *s.* Villager; countryman, countrywoman. **2.** *a.* (*a*) Rustic country (customs, etc.). (*b*) Boorish, clownish.

villanelle [villanɛl], *s.f. A:* Villanelle; pastoral poem.

ville [vil], *s.f.* Town. *Grande v.,* city. **Ville d'eaux,** watering-place, spa. **Demeurer dans la ville,** to live in the heart of the town. **Demeurer à la ville,** to live in town. **Être en ville,** to be in town, not at home. **"En ville,"** (on letters) 'local.' **Toilette de ville,** out-door dress, street dress. **Costume de ville,** (i) (of uniformed officials) plain clothes, *F:* 'mufti'; (ii) (at a reception) morning dress. **Hôtel, maison, de ville,** town-hall. *Tp:* **"La ville, s'il vous plaît!"** 'Exchange, please!'

villégiateur [vil(l)eʒjatœːr], *s.m.* Person on holiday; visitor (at a resort).

villégiature [vil(l)eʒjaty:r], *s.f.* (*a*) Stay in the country. (*b*) Holiday (out of town). **En villégiature,** on holiday.

villeux, -euse [villø, -øːz], *a.* Villous, villose, hairy.

villosité [villozite], *s.f. Anat: etc:* Villosity.

vin [vɛ̃], *s.m.* Wine. *Les grands vins,* the wine from the famous vineyards. *Vin ordinaire, vin de table,* dinner wine, beverage wine. *Vin gris (de Bourgogne), vin rosé (d'Anjou),* light-bodied pink table wine; rosé wine. *Vin mousseux,* sparkling wine. *Vin chaud,* mulled wine. *S.a.* CRU² ENSEIGNE 1, LIE². *Vin en cercles,* wine in the wood, in the cask. **Marchand de vin,** wine-shop, keeper; publican. **Négociant en vins,** wine merchant. Offrir un vin d'honneur à qn, to hold an official reception in honour of s.o. and drink his health (c.s.p. as a leave-taking). Être pris de vin, to be intoxicated. Avoir le vin gai, triste, to be merry, maudlin, in one's cups. Entre deux vins, F: half-seas over. *Prov:* Le vin est tiré, il faut le boire, it is too late to draw back now. Mettre de l'eau dans son vin, (i) to water one's wine ; (ii) F: to moderate one's pretensions.

vinaigre [vinɛːgr], *s.m.* Vinegar. (a) V. à l'estragon, tarragon vinegar. (b) V. de toilette, toilet-vinegar. V. rosat, rose-vinegar. Sel de vinaigre, smelling-salts.

vinaigrer [vinɛgre], *v.tr.* To season with vinegar. F: V. sa louange, to give an acid flavour to one's praise.

vinaigrerie [vinɛgrəri], *s.f.* **1.** Vinegar factory. **2.** Vinegar-making ; vinegar trade.

vinaigrette [vinɛgrɛt], *s.f.* **1.** Cu: Vinegar sauce ; oil and vinegar dressing. **2.** A: Two-wheeled sedan.

vinaigrier [vinɛgrie], *s.m.* **1.** Vinegar-maker. **2.** Vinegar-cruet.

vinasse [vinas], *s.f.* F: Washy wine ; F: hogwash, swipes.

vindas [vɛ̃dɑ(ː)s], *s.m.*, **vindau, -aux** [vɛ̃do], *s.m.* **1.** Windlass, winch. **2.** *Gym:* Giant-stride.

vindicat|if, -ive [vɛ̃dikatif, -iːv], *a.* Vindictive, spiteful, revengeful. *adv.* **-ivement.**

vindicte [vɛ̃dikt], *s.f. Jur:* Prosecution (of crime). V. publique, vindication of society. F: Exposé à la v. publique, held up to public obloquy.

vineux, -euse [vinø, -øːz], *a.* **1.** (Of wine) Full-bodied. **2.** (a) Vinous (flavour) ; wine-flavoured (peach). (b) Wine-stained (napkin). F: Nez v., ruby, winy, bibulous, nose. **3.** (Of region) Rich in vintage.

vingt [vɛ̃], *num.a.inv. & s.m.inv.* Twenty ; a score. V. mille francs, twenty thousand francs. Vingt et un [vɛ̃teœ̃], twenty-one. Vingt-deux [vɛ̃tdø], twenty-two. Numéro v., number twenty. Avoir plus de vingt ans [vɛ̃tɑ̃], to be out of one's teens. Aut: F: Une v. chevaux, a 'twenty.' (As a card. adj. takes an s when multiplied ; see QUATRE-VINGTS, QUINZE-VINGTS.)

vingtaine [vɛ̃tɛn], *s.f.* (About) twenty ; a score.

vingtième [vɛ̃tjɛm]. **1.** *num. a. & s.* Twentieth. **2.** *s.m.* Twentieth (part).

vinicole [vinikɔl], *a.* Wine-growing (district).

vin-s, -t [vɛ̃], **vinss-e,** etc. [vɛ̃s]. See VENIR.

Vintimille [vɛ̃timiːj]. *Pr.n. Geog:* Ventimiglia.

viol [vjɔl], *s.m. Jur:* Rape. [VIOLER]

violacé [vjɔlase], *a.* Purplish-blue. (Of pers.) Prendre une teinte violacée, to go blue.

violateur, -trice [vjɔlatœːr, -tris], *s.* Violator ; transgressor (of laws, etc.).

violation [vjɔlasjɔ̃], *s.f.* Violation, infringement, breach (of law, etc.). V. des règles, breaking of the rules. Agir en v. d'une règle, to act in contravention of a rule. V. de foi, breach of faith. V. de promesse de mariage, breach of promise. V. de frontière, trespass of frontier.

violâtre [vjɔlɑːtr], *a.* Purplish. [VIOLET]

viole [vjɔl], *s.f. Mus:* Viol.

violence [vjɔlɑ̃ːs], *s.f.* Violence, force. Faire violence à qn, to do violence to s.o. Se faire violence, to do violence to one's feelings.

viol|ent [vjɔlɑ̃], *a.* Violent ; high, buffeting (wind) ; fierce (encounter). Mourir de mort violente, to die a violent death. F: C'est par trop violent! it is really too bad ! *adv.* **-emment.**

violenter [vjɔlɑ̃te], *v.tr.* To do violence to (s.o.).

violer [vjɔle], *v.tr.* To violate ; to transgress (law) ; to break (law, treaty, faith). V. le repos dominical, to break the Sabbath. V. une sépulture, to desecrate a grave.

violet, -ette[1] [vjɔlɛ, -ɛt], *a.* Violet, purple (-coloured). *s.m.* (The colour) violet.

violette[2] [vjɔlɛt], *s.f. Bot:* Violet. P: Faire sa violette, to affect excessive modesty.

violier [vjɔlje], *s.m. Bot:* F: **1.** Stock. **2.** V. jaune, wallflower.

violon [vjɔlɔ̃], *s.m.* **1.** (a) Violin, F: fiddle. F: C'est son violon d'Ingres, it is a hobby in which he takes more pride than in his art (or regular vocation). (b) Violin (player). F: Payer les violons, to pay the piper. **2.** P: Le violon, the cells, the lock-up. **3.** (Poulie à) violon, fiddle-block. **4.** Nau: Violons de mer, fiddles (for the tables).

violoncelle [vjɔlɔ̃sɛl], *s.m.* (a) Violoncello, 'cello. (b) 'Cello (player).

violoncelliste [vjɔlɔ̃selist], *s.m. & f.* Violoncellist, 'cellist.

violoner [vjɔlɔne], *v.i.* F: To fiddle.

violoneur [vjɔlɔnœːr], *s.m.*, **violoneux** [vjɔlɔnø], *s.m.* F: Fiddler.

violoniste [vjɔlɔnist], *s.m. & f.* Violinist.

viorne [vjɔrn], *s.f. Bot:* Viburnum.

vipère [vipɛːr], *s.f.* Viper, adder. F: Langue de vipère, viperish, venomous, tongue.

vipereau [vipro], *s.m.* Young viper.

vipérin, -ine [viperɛ̃, -in]. **1.** *a.* Viperine. **2.** *s.f.* Vipérine. (a) Bot: Viper's bugloss. (b) Rept: Viperine snake.

virage [viraːʒ], *s.m.* **1.** Turning, sweeping round, cornering (of car, cycle, etc.) ; turning (round) ; slewing round, swinging round (of crane, etc.). Nau: Tacking, going about. Av: V. incliné, bank(ing). **2.** Aut: (a) (Sharp) turn, corner, bend (in road or track). (b) Banked corner, bank (of racing-track). Prendre un virage, to corner. **3.** (a) (Of coloured material) Changing of colour. V. au rouge, turning red. (b) Phot: Toning (of proofs). [VIRER]

virago [virago], *s.f.* Virago, termagant.

vire [viːr], *s.f.* Winding mountain track ; traverse.

virelai [virlɛ], *s.m. Lit: A:* Virelay.

virement [virmɑ̃], *s.m.* **1.** = VIRAGE 1, 3. **2.** V. d'eau, turn of the tide. **3.** Bank: Transfer. Banque de virement, clearing-bank.

virer [vire]. **1.** *v.i.* To turn ; to sweep round. (a) Aut: etc: To take a bend or a corner ; to corner. V. sur place, to turn in one's own length. (b) Av: To bank. (c) (Of crane, etc.) To slew round, swing round. (d) Nau: Virer de bord, (i) to tack, go about ; (ii) (of steamship) to turn. V. de bord cap pour cap, to turn 16 points. V. vent arrière, to wear (ship). S.a. LOF 1. V. vent devant, to go about in stays. Bateau lent à virer, ship slack in stays. Pare à virer! ready about! (e) V. au cabestan, to heave at the capstan. V. à pic, to heave short. (f) (Of coloured material) To change colour. Encre qui vire au noir en séchant, ink that turns black on drying. (g) Phot: (Of print) To tone. **2.** *v.tr.* (a) To turn (ship.) over. Virer une crêpe, to toss a pancake. (b) Bank: (i) To transfer (a sum). (ii) To clear (cheques). (c) Phot: To tone (print).

vireux, -euse [virø, -øːz], *a.* Poisonous, noxious (plant) ; malodorous.

virevolte [virvɔlt], *s.f. Equit:* Quick circling (of horse). F: V. de la fortune, sudden change of fortune.

virevolter [virvɔlte], *v.i.* (a) (Of horse) To circle. (b) F: (Of pers.) To spin round.

43

virginal, -aux [virʒinal, -o], *a.* Virginal; maiden(ly) (modesty). *Bot:* Lis **virginal,** pure white lily. **Lait virginal,** benzoin skin lotion.

virginité [virʒinite], *s.f.* Virginity; maidenhood.

virgule [virgyl], *s.f.* (a) *Gram:* Comma. **Point et virgule,** semicolon. *Med:* **Bacille virgule,** comma bacillus. (b) *Mth:* = Decimal point. **Trois virgule cinq** (3,5) = three point five (3.5).

viril [viril], *a.* **1.** Virile. (a) Male. **Toge virile,** toga virilis. (b) Manly (action, soul). **L'âge viril,** man's estate; manhood. **2.** *Jur:* Portion virile, lawful share (of succession).

virilement [virilmã], *adv.* Like a man; in a manly fashion.

virilité [virilite], *s.f.* Virility, manliness.

virole [virɔl], *s.f.* Ferrule, thimble (of walking-stick, etc.). *Mec.E:* Collar, hoop, sleeve. **Virole à air** (*d'un brûleur à gaz*), air-clip (of gas-burner).

viroller [virɔle], *v.tr.* To ferrule (tool-handle, tubes of boiler, etc.). *s.m.* **-age.**

virtuel, -elle [virtɥɛl], *a.* Virtual (intention; image, focus).

virtuellement [virtɥɛlmã], *adv.* Virtually; to all intents and purposes.

virtuose [virtɥoːz], *s.m. & f.* Virtuoso.

virtuosité [virtɥozite], *s.f.* Virtuosity.

virulence [virylãːs], *s.f.* Virulence.

virulent [virylã], *a.* Virulent.

virure [viryːr], *s.f. N.Arch:* Strake.

virus [viryːs], *s.m. Med:* Virus. **V. filtrant,** filterable virus.

vis [vis], *s.f.* Screw. **1.** (a) *Vis sans fin,* endless screw, worm(-screw). *Vis* (*sans fin*) *et secteur,* worm and segment. *Hyd.E: Vis d'Archimède,* Archimedean screw. *Ind: Vis de transport,* spiral conveyor. (b) Thread. *Vis à droite, à gauche,* right-, left-handed screw or thread. **Tige à vis,** screwed, threaded, rod. *F:* **Serrer la vis à qn,** to put the screw on s.o. (c) **Escalier à vis,** spiral staircase. **2.** *Vis à bois,* wood screw. *Vis à oreilles, à ailettes,* thumb-screw, wing-screw. *Vis à tête cylindrique,* cheese-head screw. *Vis d'arrêt,* stop-screw. **Fermer une boîte à vis,** to screw down (the lid of) a box.

vi-s, -t, etc. [vi]. See VOIR and VIVRE.

visa [viza], *s.m.* (a) Visa, visé (on passport). **Apposer un visa à un passeport,** to stamp, visé, a passport. (b) Signature (on document, etc.); initials (of supervisor).

visage [vizaːʒ], *s.m.* Face, countenance, visage. *Homme au v. agréable,* pleasant-faced man. **Changer de visage,** to change countenance. **Faire son visage,** to make one's face up; *F:* to make up. **A deux visages,** double-faced. **Avoir bon visage,** to look well. **Faire bon, mauvais, visage à qn,** to smile, frown, on s.o. *F:* **Trouver visage de bois,** to find nobody at home.

vis-à-vis [vizavi]. **1.** *Adv.phr.* Opposite. *La maison* (*qui est*) *v.-à-v.,* the house over the way. *Assis v.-à-v.,* sitting face to face. **2.** *Prep.phr.* **Vis-à-vis de** (qn, qch.). (a) Opposite, facing (s.o., sth.). (b) Towards, with respect to, with regard to, in relation to (s.o., sth.). *Ses sentiments v.-à-v. de moi,* his feelings towards me. **3.** *s.m.* Person opposite (at table, etc.). *Cards:* Partner. *Danc:* Vis-à-vis. **Faire vis-à-vis à qn,** to be, stand, sit, opposite s.o.

viscéral, -aux [visseral, -o], *a. Anat:* Visceral.

viscère [visseːr], *s.m. Anat:* Viscus; internal organ. *Les viscères,* the viscera.

viscose [viskoːz], *s.f. Ch: Ind:* Viscose; cellulose thiocarbonate.

viscosité [viskozite], *s.f.* Viscosity, viscidity; stickiness.

viser[1] [vize]. **1.** *v.i.* To aim (*à*, at). *V. à l'effet,* to aim at effect. *V. à faire qch.,* to aim at doing sth.; to aspire to do sth. **2.** *v.tr.* (a) To aim, take aim, at (s.o., sth.). *V. haut,* to aim high ((i) with gun, (ii) = to be ambitious). *Golf: V. la balle,* to address the ball. (b) *Surv:* To sight; to take a sight on (sth.). (c) To have (sth.) in view; to relate to (sth.). *Accusation visant qn,* accusation directed against s.o. (d) To allude to (s.o.). *Je ne vise personne,* I am not alluding to anybody in particular.

visée, *s.f.* **1.** Aim. *Mil: Surv:* Aiming, sighting. **Prendre sa visée,** to take aim. **Ligne de visée,** line of sight. **Point de visée,** point aimed at. **2.** *pl.* Aims, designs. *Avoir de hautes visées,* to have high aims, great ambitions; to aim high.

viser[2], *v.tr. Adm: Com: etc:* To visé (passport); to countersign, initial (document).

viseur, -euse [vizœːr, -øːz]. **1.** *s.* Aimer. **2.** *s.m.* (a) *Phot:* View-finder. (b) (Of surveying instrument, etc.) Sighting-tube, eye-piece. *Av: V. de lancement,* bomb-sights (of bombing-plane).

visibilité [vizibilite], *s.f.* Visibility.

visible [vizibl], *a.* **1.** (a) Visible, perceptible. **Il n'y avait personne de visible,** there was nobody about. (b) *F:* Obvious, manifest, evident (falsehood, etc.). **Très visible,** conspicuous. **2.** (a) Ready to receive company. *Je ne suis pas v.,* I am not at home. (b) Disengaged. *Je ne serai pas v. avant trois heures,* I can't see anybody before three o'clock. (c) (Collection) accessible, open, to the public. *adv.* **-ment.**

visière [vizjɛːr], *s.f.* **1.** (a) *Archeol:* Visor, vizor (of helmet). *F:* **Rompre en visière à, avec, qn,** (i) to quarrel openly with s.o.; (ii) to take up a diametrically opposite view to that of s.o. (b) Peak (of cap). (c) Eye-shade. **2.** Inspection hole (of kiln, etc.).

vision [vizjɔ̃], *s.f.* Vision. **1.** (a) Eyesight. (b) Sight (of sth.). *V. momentanée,* glimpse (of sth.). **2.** *Les visions d'un poète,* a poet's visions. **3.** Fantasy; phantom.

visionnaire [vizjɔnɛːr], *a. & s.* Visionary; dreamer.

visitandine [vizitãdin], *s.f.* Nun of the Order of the Visitation.

visite [vizit], *s.f.* Visit. **1.** (a) (Social) call. **Faire des visites,** to pay calls. *Faire une petite v. à qn,* to drop in on s.o. **Faire, rendre, visite à qn;** **faire une visite à qn,** to visit s.o.; to call on s.o. **Rendre une visite, rendre sa visite à qn,** to return s.o.'s call. **En visite chez qn,** on a visit to s.o. *V. de digestion,* party call; formal call (after dinner-party). **Carte de visite,** visiting-card. **Carnet de visites,** visiting-book. **Heures de visite,** (i) calling hours; (ii) visiting hours (at hospital, etc.). (b) Caller, visitor. **2.** Attendance (of doctor). **3.** (a) Inspection; overhauling (of machinery); survey (of ship). **Faire la visite,** to go on one's round of inspection. *V. médicale,* medical examination. *V. des malles, de la douane,* customs examination. **Trou de visite,** man-hole (of sewer, etc.). (b) Search (of house, ship, etc.). *Nau:* **Droit de visite,** right of search.

visiter [vizite], *v.tr.* **1.** (a) (Of doctor) To visit, attend (patient). (b) *Ne pas v. ses voisins,* not to be on visiting terms with one's neighbours. **2.** (a) To examine, inspect, view, go over (premises, etc.); to overhaul (engine); to examine (ship for contraband); to survey (ship). *J'ai visité toutes les pièces,* I have been into every room. **Permis de visiter,** order to view (house). (b) (Of police) To visit, search (house).

visiteur, -euse [vizitœːr, -øːz]. **1.** s. (a) Caller, visitor. (b) Les visiteurs du musée, visitors to the museum. (c) Inspector. Cust: Searcher. **2.** a. Visiting.

vison [vizõ], s.m. Z: Vison; American mink.

visqueux, -euse [viskø, -øːz], a. Viscous, gluey, sticky; tacky (rubber solution); thick (oil); slimy (secretion).

viss|er [vise], v.tr. To screw, screw on, screw in, screw down, screw up (sth.). F: Se visser sur sa chaise, to sit tight on one's chair. s.m. **-age.**

visu|el, -elle [vizɥɛl], a. Visual. Champ visuel, field of vision. adv. **-ellement.**

vit [vi]. See VIVRE and VOIR.

vital, -aux [vital, -o], a. Vital. Parties vitales, vitals. F: Question vitale, vital question.

vitalisme [vitalism], s.m. Biol: Vitalism.

vitaliste [vitalist]. **1.** a. Vitalistic (doctrine, etc.). **2.** s. Vitalist.

vitalité [vitalite], s.f. Vitality.

vitamine [vitamin], s.f. Bio-Ch: Vitamin(e).

vite [vit]. **1.** a. Swift, rapid, speedy. Voitures légères et vites, light speedy cars. Cheval v., fleet horse. Fb: Avants vites, speedy forwards. **2.** adv. Quickly, fast, swiftly. Nau: "Plus vite!" 'increase speed!' Vous allez v. en besogne, you aren't long about it. Ça ne va pas v., it is slow work. Vous serez v. guéri, you'll soon be better. Faites vite! make haste! look sharp! look alive! Allons, et plus v. que cela! now then, be quick about it! Au plus vite, as quickly as possible. Avoir vite fait de faire qch., to be quick about doing sth.

vitellin [vitɛllɛ̃], a. Biol: Vitelline. Membrane vitelline, vitelline membrane, yolk-sac.

vitellus [vitɛllyːs], s.m. Biol: Vitellus, yolk.

vitelotte [vitlɔt], s.f. Kidney potato.

vitement [vitmã], adv. A: Quickly, speedily.

vitesse [vites], s.f. Speed, swiftness, rapidity, fleetness; velocity (of light, projectile); rate (of going). A la vitesse de . . ., avec une vitesse de . . ., at the rate of. . . . F: En vitesse, with all speed. De toute sa vitesse, at the top of one's speed. Aller à toute vitesse, to go (at) full speed; to tear along. Vitesse folle, breakneck speed. Nau: En avant à toute v., full speed ahead. Il lutta de vitesse avec le renard, he ran a race with the fox. Gagner qn de vitesse, (i) to outstrip s.o.; (ii) to overtake, pass, s.o.; (ii) to steal a march on s.o. (Of train, etc.) Prendre de la vitesse, to pick up speed, to gather pace. Aut: etc: Faire de la vitesse, to speed. Indicateur de vitesse, speedometer. Av: V. aérodynamique, air speed. Perdre de la vitesse, to stall. Perte de vitesse, stalling. Rail: Train de grande vitesse, express passenger train. Colis en grande vitesse, parcel by fast goods service. En petite vitesse, by slow goods service. Mec: V. uniformément accélérée, uniform acceleration. V. acquise, impetus. Aut: Changement de vitesse, (i) change of gear, (ii) change-speed gear. Boîte de vitesses, gear-box. Passer les vitesses, to go through the gears. Première vitesse, first gear, bottom gear. Filer en quatrième v., to drive in top (gear).

viticole [vitikɔl], a. Viticultural; wine (industry).

viticulteur [vitikyltœːr], s.m. Vine-grower.

viticulture [vitikyltyːr], s.f. Vine-growing, viticulture.

vitrage [vitraːʒ], s.m. **1.** Glazing. **2.** (a) Windows, glass-work (of church, etc.). (b) Glass partition or door.

vitrail, -aux [vitraːj, -o], s.m. Leaded glass window; esp. stained glass (church) window.

vitre [vitr], s.f. Pane (of glass); window-pane. F: Casser les vitres, (i) to kick up a shindy; (ii) to blurt out everything.

vitrer [vitre], v.tr. To glaze (window, etc.). **vitré,** a. **1.** Glazed. **2.** Vitreous, glassy. Esp. Humeur vitrée, corps vitré, vitreous humour, vitreous body (of the eye).

vitrerie [vitrəri], s.f. Glaziery.

vitreux, -euse [vitrø, -øːz], a. Vitreous (mass); glassy (appearance). Yeux vitreux, glassy, glazed, eyes (of corpse).

vitrier [vitrie], s.m. **1.** Maker of glass (for windows). **2.** Glazier. **3.** pl. P: Les vitriers, the chasseurs à pied, the light infantry.

vitrification [vitrifikasjõ], s.f. Vitrification.

vitrifi|er [vitrifje], v.tr. To vitrify (sand, etc.). Brique vitrifiée, glazed brick. a. **-able.**

vitrine [vitrin], s.f. **1.** Shop-window. **2.** Glass case, glass cabinet. Com: Show-case.

vitriol [vitriɔl], s.m. Vitriol. (a) V. bleu, blue vitriol, copper sulphate. V. vert, green vitriol, ferrous sulphate. (b) (Huile de) vitriol, oil of vitriol, concentrated sulphuric acid. F: Plume trempée dans du v., pen dipped in vitriol; vitriolic pen.

vitriol|er [vitriɔle], v.tr. **1.** Tex: To sour (material). **2.** To throw vitriol at (s.o.). s.m. **-age.**

vitrioleur, -euse [vitriɔlœːr, -øːz], s. Vitriol-thrower.

vitupération [vityperasjõ], s.f. Vituperation.

vitupérer [vitypere], v.tr. (je vitupère; je vitupérerai) A: To vituperate, blame (s.o.).

vivace [vivas], a. (a) Long-lived. (b) Bot: Hardy. (c) Bot: Perennial. Pois vivace, ever-lasting pea. (d) F: Haine v., undying, inveterate, hatred. Souvenirs encore vivaces, memories still green.

vivacité [vivasite], s.f. **1.** V. à agir, promptness to act. **2.** (a) Hastiness (of temper); petulance. Avec vivacité, hastily. (b) Hasty utterance; outburst of temper. **3.** (a) Acuteness (of feeling); heat (of a discussion); fire, intensity (of a passion). (b) Vividness, brilliancy (of colour, light). V. du teint, high colour. **4.** Vivacity, vivaciousness, sprightliness, liveliness. V. d'esprit, readiness of mind. Avoir de la vivacité, to be vivacious, full of life. Avec vivacité, vivaciously.

vivandier, -ière [vivɑ̃dje, -jɛːr], s. Sutler, canteen-keeper; f. vivandière.

vivant [vivɑ̃]. **1.** a. (a) Alive, living. Pas une âme vivante, not a living soul. Portrait vivant, lifelike portrait. Être le portrait vivant de qn, to be the very image of s.o. Langue vivante, modern language. S.a. TABLEAU 2. (b) Lively, animated (street, scene). (c) Vivid, live (narrative). **2.** s.m. (a) Living being. Les vivants et les morts, the quick and the dead. (b) Bon vivant, (i) jolly good fellow, boon companion; (ii) man who enjoys life. **3.** s.m. En, de, son vivant, during his lifetime; in his day.

vivat [vivat], int. & s.m. Hurrah, vivat.

vive¹ [viːv], s.f. Ich: Weever, sting-fish.

vive². See VIF.

vive³, int. See VIVRE I. 1 (a).

vive-eau [vivo], s.f., **vives-eaux** [vivzo], s.f.pl. Nau: Spring-tide.

vive-la-joie, s.m.inv. F: Jolly fellow; jovial soul.

vivement [vivmã], adv. **1.** (a) Briskly, sharply, smartly. (b) Réprimander v. qn, to give s.o. a sharp reprimand. Répondre v., to answer sharply. **2.** (Of feelings) (a) Keenly, deeply, acutely. (b) Remercier v. qn, to thank s.o. warmly.

viveur, -euse [vivœːr, -øːz], s. Man, woman, who goes the pace; rake; gay dog.

vivier [vivje], *s.m.* **1.** (*a*) Fish-pond; fish-preserve. (*b*) Breeding-ground (*de*, for). **2.** (In boat) Fish-well.

vivifiant [vivifjɑ̃], **vivificateur, -trice** [vivifikatœːr, -tris], *a.* Vivifying, quickening; (of air, etc.) invigorating, bracing.

vivifier [vivifje], *v.tr.* To vivify, quicken; to endue (sth.) with life; (of air, etc.) to invigorate.

vivipare [vivipaːr]. **1.** *a.* Viviparous. **2.** *s.m.pl.* Vivipares, vivipara.

vivisection [vivisɛksjɔ̃], *s.f.* Vivisection.

vivoter [vivɔte], *v.i.* F: To live sparely; to keep body and soul together. [VIVRE]

vivre [viːvr]. I. *v.i.* (*pr.p.* vivant; *p.p.* vécu; *pr.ind.* je vis, il vit, n. vivons, ils vivent; *p.h.* je vécus; *fu.* je vivrai) To live. **1.** (*a*) To be alive. *V. longtemps*, to live long. **Cesser de vivre**, to die. *Être las de v.*, to be tired of life. **Vive le roi!** long live the King! *Vive(nt) les vacances!* hurray for the holidays! *Vive la joie!* let us be merry! *Mil:* **Qui vive?** who goes there? S.a. QUI-VIVE. **Ne rencontrer âme qui vive**, to meet no one, not a living soul. *Prov:* **Qui vivra verra**, time will show. (*b*) *Ouvrage qui vivra*, work that will endure. *Traditions qui vivent encore*, traditions that are still alive. **2.** To spend one's life. *V. à Paris*, to live in Paris. **Être aisé à vivre**, commode à vivre, to be easy to get on with. **Savoir vivre**, to know how to behave; to be well-bred. S.a. SAVOIR-VIVRE. **Apprendre à vivre à qn**, to teach s.o. manners. **Se laisser vivre**, to take life easily. *Il fait bon v. ici*, life is pleasant here. **3.** To subsist. *On vivait bien juste*, we could just manage, just rub along. *V. bien*, to live well; to keep a good table. *Travailler pour v.*, to work for one's living. **Il fait cher vivre ici**, living is dear here. **Faire vivre sa famille**, to support, keep, one's family. **Vivre au jour le jour**, to live from hand to mouth. *V. de sa plume*, to live by one's pen. *De quoi vit-il?* what does he live on? **Avoir de quoi vivre**, to have enough to live on. II. **vivre**, *s.m.* (*a*) Living. (*b*) Food. **Le vivre et le couvert**, board and lodging. (*c*) *pl.* Provisions, supplies, victuals. *Mil:* Rations. **Couper les vivres à qn**, (i) to cut off s.o.'s supplies; (ii) to stop s.o.'s allowance.

vécu, *a.* **1.** Choses vécues, actual experiences. **2.** (Play, novel) true to life.

vizir [viziːr], *s.m.* Vizier.

v'là [vla], *prep.* P: = VOILÀ.

vlan, v'lan [vlɑ̃], *int.* Slap(-bang)! whack!

vocable [vɔkabl], *s.m.* **1.** Vocable, word. **2.** *Ecc:* Name-patronage (of saint). *Église sous le v. de saint Pierre*, church under the invocation of Saint Peter.

vocabulaire [vɔkabylɛːr], *s.m.* Vocabulary.

vocal, -aux [vɔkal, -o], *a.* Vocal. *adv.* **-ement.**

vocalique [vɔkalik], *a.* Vocalic; vowel (change, sound).

vocalisation [vɔkalizasjɔ̃], *s.f.* Vocalization.

vocalise [vɔkaliːz], *s.f. Mus:* Exercise in vocalization.

vocaliser [vɔkalize], *v.tr.* To vocalize (a melody, a consonant).

vocatif [vɔkatif], *s.m. Gram:* Vocative case. **Au vocatif**, in the vocative (case).

vocation [vɔkasjɔ̃], *s.f.* Vocation. **1.** (Divine) call. *Je ne me sens pas la v. de la prêtrise*, I feel no call to the Church. **2.** Calling, bent, inclination. *Avoir de la v. pour le commerce*, to have a turn for business. *Manquer sa v.*, to mistake, miss, one's vocation.

vocero [vɔtʃero], *s.m.* (Corsican) funeral chant.

vociférant [vɔsiferɑ̃], *a.* Vociferous, clamorous.

vociférateur, -trice [vɔsiferatœːr, -tris], *s.* Vociferator; noisy clamourer.

vociférations [vɔsiferasjɔ̃], *s.f.pl.* Vociferation(s).

vociférer [vɔsifere], *v.i.* (je vocifère; je vociférerai) To vociferate (*contre*, against); to shout, bawl, yell.

vœu, -x [vø], *s.m.* **1.** Vow. **Faire vœu de faire qch.**, to make, take, a vow to do sth. *Ecc:* Prononcer ses vœux, to take one's vows. *Les vœux de baptême*, the baptismal vows. **2.** Wish. **Émettre un v.**, to express a wish; (at meeting) to pass a resolution. **Appeler qch. de tous ses vœux**, to pray for the coming of sth. **Tous mes vœux!** all good wishes!

vogue [vɔg], *s.f.* Fashion, vogue. **Mettre qch. en vogue**, to bring sth. into vogue. **Avoir de la vogue**, être en vogue, to be popular, in favour, in request. **Entrer en vogue**, to come into vogue. *C'est la grande v.*, it's all the rage.

voguer [vɔge], *v.i. Nau:* To sail. F: *Les nuages voguant dans le ciel*, the clouds sailing by. **Voguer à pleines voiles**, to forge ahead; to advance from success to success. S.a. GALÈRE.

voici [vwasi], *prep.* **1.** Here is, are. **Me voici, les voici**, here I am, here they are. *Du pain?* En voici, bread? Here is some, F: here you are. **En voici bien d'une autre!** here's something new! **La voici qui vient**, here she comes. **Voici venir Jeanne**, here comes Jeanne. **Mon ami que voici vous le dira**, my friend here will tell you. *V. ce qu'il m'a dit*, this is what he told me. **La petite histoire que voici**, the following little story. *V. Noël!* Christmas is here! **2.** (= *il y a*) *Je l'ai vu v. trois ans*, I saw him three years ago.

voie[1] [vwa], *s.f.* **1.** (*a*) Way, road, route, track. *V. publique*, public thoroughfare; public highway. S.a. LACTÉ 1. **Être toujours par voie et par chemin**, to be always on the move. *V. fluviale*, voie d'eau, water-way. (Cf. 1 (*f*).) **Par voie de terre**, by land; overland. **Par voie de mer**, by sea. *Mec.E:* **Voie de roulement pour billes**, ball-race. *Min:* **Voie d'aérage**, air-way, windgate. *Av:* **Voie de départ**, runway. (*b*) *Ven:* (Often *pl.*) Tracks (of game); slot (of deer). **Mettre les chiens sur la voie**, to put the dogs on the scent. F: *Mettre qn sur la v.*, to put s.o. on the right track. (*c*) *Rail:* **Voie ferrée**, railway track; railway line. *V. de service, de garage*, siding. **Changement de voie**, points. **Largeur de voie**, gauge. (*d*) (i) Gauge (of wheels of vehicle). *V. charretière*, cart-gauge. (ii) Tracks (of vehicle). (*e*) (i) Kerf, clearance (of a tool); (ii) set (of a saw). **Donner de la voie à une scie**, to set (of a saw). (*f*) *Nau:* **Voie d'eau**, leak. (Cf. 1 (*a*).) **Faire une voie d'eau**, to spring a leak. (*g*) *Anat:* Passage, duct. *Les voies urinaires*, the urinary passages. **2.** (*a*) Way. *La v. étroite*, the narrow way; the strait way. **Voies et moyens**, ways and means. *La v. des armes*, recourse to arms. **Par voie diplomatique**, through the channels of diplomacy. S.a. HIÉRARCHIQUE. *Une v. dangereuse*, a dangerous course. **Affaire en bonne voie**, affair going well. **En voie de formation**, in process of formation. *Être en v. de faire qch.*, to be in a fair way to do sth. *Être en (bonne) v. de réussir*, to be on the (high) road to success. *Jur:* **Voies de droit**, recourse to legal proceedings. **Voies de fait**, acts of violence; assault and battery. *En venir aux voies de fait*, to come to blows. (*b*) *Ch: etc:* **Voie sèche, humide**, dry, wet process. *Essai par la v. sèche*, dry test.

voie[2]. See VOIR.

voilà [vwala], *prep.* **1.** (*a*) There is, are. **Le voilà, les voilà**, there he is, there they are. *V. où il* *demeure*, that is where he lives. **En voilà assez!** that's enough (of it)! that will do! **En voilà une idée!** what an idea! **Voilà tout**, that's all. **Le voilà qui entre, voilà qu'il entre,** there he is coming in. **Voilà qui s'appelle danser!** that's something like dancing! **Voilà comme elle est; la voilà bien!** that's just· like her! *F:* (Ne) **voilà-t-il pas qu'il pleut!** there now! if it isn't raining! **En voilà-t-il!** what a lot! (In restaurants) **Voilà, monsieur!** coming, sir! (*b*) *F:* Often = VOICI. **Me voilà!** here I am! **Le voilà,** here he comes. **2.** (= *il y a*) *En juin* **voilà** *trois ans,* June three years ago. *V. dix ans que je le connais,* I've known him these ten years.

voile [vwal]. **I.** *s.f.* Sail. **Grande voile,** mainsail. *V. carrée,* square sail. *Déployer, établir, une v.,* to set a sail. **Bateau à voiles,** sailing-boat. **Aller à la voile,** to sail. **Vaisseau sous voile(s),** ship under sail. **A toutes voiles,** at full sail. **Faire voile, mettre à la voile,** to set sail (*pour,* for). **Faire force de voiles,** to crowd on all sail. **Toutes voiles dehors,** in full sail, all sails set. S.a. PLEIN I. **II. voile,** *s.m.* **1.** (*a*) Veil. *Ecc:* **Prendre le voile,** to take the veil. *F:* **Sous le voile de la religion,** under the cloak of religion. (*b*) *Tex:* Voile. (*c*) *Anat:* **Voile du palais,** soft palate; velum. (*d*) *Phot:* Fog (on the negative). **2.** *Mec.E:* Buckle (of wheel, etc.); warping.

voiler[1] [vwale], *v.tr.* **1.** (*a*) To veil. *Se v. la face,* (i) to veil one's face; (ii) to hide one's face in horror. (*b*) To veil, obscure, dim, cloud (light, etc.); to muffle (sound, drum, etc.); to shade (light). (*c*) *Phot:* To fog (plate, print). **2.** (*a*) To buckle, warp (wheel, etc.). (*b*) *v.i.* (Of wheel, rod) To buckle, to bend; (of wood) to warp.
  se voiler. 1. (Of sky, etc.) To become overcast, to cloud over. **2.** = *voiler* 2 (*b*).
  voilé, *a.* **1.** (*a*) Veiled, dim (light); dim (eyes); veiled, obscure (meaning); muffled (drum). (*b*) Fogged (plate, print). **2.** (Of wheel, etc.) Buckled; out of true.
voiler[2], *v.tr. Nau:* To rig (ship) with sails.
voilerie, [vwalri], *s.f.* **1.** Sail-loft. **2.** Sail-making.
voilette [vwalɛt], *s.f.* **1.** (Hat-)veil. **2.** *V. de chaise,* antimacassar.
voilier, -ière [vwalje, -jɛːr]. **1.** *a.* **Bâtiment bon voilier, mauvais voilier,** good, bad, sailer. **2.** *s.m.* Sailing-ship, sailing-boat; *F:* windjammer. **3.** *s.m.* Sail-maker.
voilure[1] [vwalyːr], *s.f.* (*a*) Sails (of ship). *Réduire la v.,* to shorten sail. (*b*) *Av:* Wings, flying surface, aerofoil.
voilure[2], *s.f.* Buckling, bending (of wheel, etc.); warping (of board).
voir [vwaːr], *v.tr.* (*pr.p.* **voyant;** *p.p.* **vu;** *pr.ind.* je **vois,** il **voit,** n. **voyons,** ils **voient;** *pr.sub.* je **voie;** *p.h.* je **vis;** *fu.* je **verrai**) To see. **1.** (*a*) To set eyes upon (s.o., sth.); to sight (ship). *F:* Il ne voit pas plus loin que son nez, he can't see further than the end of his nose. *Il faut le v. pour le croire,* it must be seen to be believed. **Voir c'est croire,** seeing is believing. *Je le vois qui arrive,* I see him coming. *On lui voit beaucoup d'amis,* he appears to have a lot of friends. **A le voir on dirait . . .,** by the look of him, to judge by his looks, one would say. . . . *Monument qui se voit de loin,* monument that can be seen from afar. *Son jupon se voit,* her petticoat is showing. *Abs.* **Je n'y vois pas,** I can't see (for want of light). **Je n'y vois plus,** I can't see any more. **Voir rouge,** to see red. **Voir trouble,** to see things through a mist. **Voyez vous-même!** see for yourself! *Lit:* **Que vois-je?** what is this

(that I see)? *Iron:* **Voyez un peu!** behold him! S.a. CLAIR 2, COULEUR I, FEU[1] I. 4, GOUTTE 4. **Il faut y aller voir,** we must go and see. **Faire voir, laisser voir, qch. à qn,** to show sth. to s.o.; to let s.o. see sth. *Laisser v. son ignorance,* to reveal, betray, one's ignorance. **Faites voir!** let me see it! *F:* **Voyons voir,** (i) let us see, let me see; (ii) show it to me. **Montrez voir,** just let me see it. **Dites voir,** let us hear it. S.a. ATTENDRE I. (*b*) *Com:* To sight (a bill of exchange). (*c*) (Of building) **Voir sur . . .,** to look out on. . . . **2. Voir** + *inf.* (*a*) *V. venir qn,* to see s.o. coming. *Quels acteurs avez-vous vus jouer ce rôle?* what actors have you seen in this part? (*b*) **Voir faire qch.,** to see sth. done. *V. faire qch. à qn,* to see s.o. do sth. *Quelles pièces avez-vous vu jouer?* what plays have you seen acted? **3.** (*a*) (As aux. of the passive voice) *Je me vis forcé de partir,* I was compelled to depart. (*b*) (In quasi passive constructions) *Il se voyait refuser les fournitures les plus urgentes,* he was refused the most urgent supplies. *Je me vois reprocher les bévues de mes collègues,* I am taken to task for my colleagues' mistakes. **4.** (*a*) To visit (s.o., sth.). **Aller voir qn,** to go to see s.o.; to go and see s.o. *Nous avons vu les musées,* we visited the museums. **Voir du pays,** to travel. (*b*) **Voir qn,** to receive s.o.'s visit. *Il ne voit personne,* he receives no one; he is not at home to anyone. *Nous nous voyons souvent,* we often meet. **5.** (*a*) To understand. *Je vois où vous voulez en venir,* I see, understand, what you are driving at. **Voir de loin; voir bien loin,** to have foresight and perspicacity. *F:* **Ni vu ni connu,** nobody is, was, any the wiser for it. (*b*) To perceive, observe (sth.). *Il la voyait moins attentive,* he noticed she was less attentive. **On verra de quel bois je me chauffe,** I'll show them what stuff I am made of. **A ce que je vois,** from what I can see. *Cela se voit,* that is obvious. *Vous voyez ça d'ici,* you can imagine what it was like. **6.** (*a*) *V. une affaire à fond,* to look into a matter thoroughly. **Faire qch. seulement pour voir,** to do sth. just as an experiment. *Eh bien, je verrai,* well, I'll see about it. *C'est ce que nous verrons!* that remains to be seen. *P:* **Va-t'en voir s'ils viennent!** tell me another! **Il n'a rien à voir là-dedans,** it is nothing to do with him; it is no business of his. *Vous n'avez rien à y v.,* it is no concern of yours. **Cela n'a rien à voir à l'affaire,** that has nothing to do with the matter. (*b*) **Voir à** + *inf. Voyez à nous loger,* see that we are housed. **Voir que** + *sub. C'est à vous à v. que rien ne nous fasse défaut,* it is for you to see that we lack nothing. (*c*) *int.* **Voyons!** (i) let us see; (ii) come! come! **7. Se faire bien voir de qn,** to gain s.o.'s favour, s.o.'s goodwill; *F:* to get into s.o.'s good books. **Se faire mal voir de qn,** to get into s.o.'s bad books. **Être bien vu de tous,** to be highly esteemed, well thought of, by all. **Mal vu,** held in suspicion; disliked. S.a. NOIR 3. *F:* **Je ne peux pas le voir,** I can't bear the sight of him.
vu [vy]. **I.** *s.m.* (*a*) **Au vu de tous,** openly, publicly. **Au vu et au su de tous,** to everybody's knowledge, as everyone knows. **Sur le vu de la facture,** upon presentation of the invoice. (*b*) *Jur:* **Le vu d'un arrêt,** the preamble of a decree. **2.** *prep.* Considering, seeing. *Vu la chaleur je voyagerai de nuit,* in view of the heat, owing to the heat, I shall travel by night. **Vu que** + *ind.,* seeing that . . .; (in legal preambles) whereas . . .
vue, *s.f.* **1.** (*a*) Sight. **Perdre la vue,** to lose one's (eye)sight. **Avoir la vue courte, basse,** to

be short-sighted. *F: Toilette qui donne dans la vue*, conspicuous dress. **Connaître qn de vue**, to know s.o. by sight. **Garder qn à vue**, to keep a close watch on s.o. **Perdre qn de vue**, (i) to lose sight of s.o.; (ii) to lose touch with s.o. **A perte de vue**, as far as the eye can reach. **Personnes les plus en vue**, people most in the public eye. *Faire qch.* **à la vue de tous**, to do sth. in sight of everybody. *Se tenir hors de vue*, to keep out of sight. **A vue d'œil**, (i) at a rough estimate; (ii) visibly. **Visible à la vue simple**, visible to the naked eye. (b) *Psychics:* **Seconde vue**, second sight. **2.** (a) View. *Vues saines*, sound views. (b) View, survey. *La vue n'en coûte rien*, it costs nothing to look at it. **Dessin à vue**, free-hand drawing. **3. A la vue de qn**, at the sight of s.o. **A première vue**, at first sight, off-hand. *Mus:* Lecture à vue, reading at sight. **A vue, en vue, de terre**, (with)in sight of land; in view of land. S.a. NEZ I. *Com:* **Payable à vue**, payable at sight. **A sept jours de vue**, seven days after sight. **4.** View. (a) Prospect, outlook. **Chambre qui a vue, qui prend vue, sur le jardin**, room that looks out on the garden. *Vue en coupe*, sectional drawing, cross-section. *Vues de Paris*, views of Paris. *Voir 'qch. sous un autre point de vue*, to see sth. in another light. **Échappée de vue**, vista. S.a. OISEAU I, POINT[1] 3. (b) Window, light (of house). *Jur:* **Droit de vues**, ancient lights. *Condamner les vues*, to block up the windows. (c) Intention, purpose, design. *Entrer dans les vues de qn*, to agree with s.o.'s views. **Avoir qch. en vue**, to have sth. in view. *Avoir des vues pour qn*, to have plans for s.o.'s future. **Avoir des vues sur qn**, to have designs on s.o. *Prep.phr.* **En vue de**, with a view to. **Travailler en vue de l'avenir**, to work with an eye to the future. *En vue de plaire*, with a view to pleasing, in order to please. **5.** (a) Vue (*pour projections*), (lantern-)slide. **Vues fondantes**, dissolving views. (b) *Cin:* **Prendre les vues**, to shoot the film. *Appareil de prise de vues*, motion-picture camera. (c) *Vues stéréoscopiques*, stereoscopic slides.

voire [vwaːr], *adv.* **1.** *A:* In truth. **2.** Nay. **Voire même**, and even, or even, (and) indeed. *J'en suis ahuri, v. révolté*, I am astounded, nay, disgusted.

voirie [vwari], *s.f.* **1. La grande voirie**, the high roads. **Le Service de voirie**, the Highways Department. *Travaux de v.*, road labour. *Travailleur de la v.*, scavenger. **2.** (a) Refuse-dump; garbage-heap. *Jeter les ordures à la voirie*, to dump the refuse. (b) Refuse, garbage.

voisin, -ine [vwazẽ, -in]. **1.** *a.* Neighbouring, adjoining. *La chambre voisine*, the next room. *Être v. de qch.*, to be next to, near, sth. *Émotion voisine de la terreur*, emotion bordering on terror. **2.** *s.* Neighbour. *V. d'à côté*, next-door neighbour. **Agir en bon voisin**, to act in a neighbourly way.

voisinage [vwazina:ʒ], *s.m.* **1.** Proximity, vicinity, nearness. *Le v. de la gare est un avantage*, proximity to the station is an advantage. **2.** Neighbourhood, vicinage, surrounding district. **3.** Neighbourly intercourse. **Relations de bon voisinage**, neighbourliness.

voisiner [vwazine], *v.i.* **1.** To visit one's neighbours. *Nous voisinons avec les nouveaux locataires*, we are on friendly terms with the new tenants. **2.** (Of thgs) To be placed side by side; to adjoin.

voiturage [vwatyra:ʒ], *s.m.* Cartage, carriage, conveyance (of goods, etc.).

voiture [vwaty:r], *s.f.* *A:* Conveyance, transportation. (Still so used in) *Com:* **Lettre de voiture**, way-bill, consignment note. **2.** (a) Conveyance, vehicle, carriage, motor car. *V. publique*, public conveyance. *V. de place*, hackney-carriage; cab; taxi. *V. de maître*, private carriage. *V. à deux chevaux*, carriage and pair. *V. automobile*, motor car. **Avoir voiture, avoir sa voiture à soi**, to keep a carriage or a car. **Aller en voiture**, to drive. *Partir en v.*, to drive away. *F:* **Nous avons pris la voiture dès cordeliers, des capucins**, we came on Shanks's mare. (b) Cart, van. *V. de roulier*, waggon. *V. de livraison*, delivery van. *V. de laitier*, milk-cart. *V. à bras*, barrow, hand-cart. **Petites voitures**, (in Paris) costers' barrows. *V. d'enfant, de bébé*, baby-carriage, perambulator. *V. cellulaire*, prison-van. *V. de malade*, invalid chair, Bath-chair. *V. de saltimbanques*, caravan. **Voiture de chemin de fer**, railway coach, carriage; *U.S:* car. **Voiture-restaurant**, dining-car. **"En voiture!"** 'take your seats!'

voiturée [vwatyre], *s.f.* Carriageful (of people); cart-load (of goods).

voiturer [vwatyre], *v.tr.* To convey, transport (goods, etc.).

voiturette [vwatyret], *s.f.* Trap; small spring-cart. *Aut:* Light car; 'baby car.'

voiturier, -ière [vwatyrje, -jɛːr]. **1.** *a.* (a) Carriageable. **Avenue voiturière**, carriage-drive. (b) *L'industrie voiturière*, the carrying trade. **2.** *s.m.* Carter, carrier.

voix [vwa], *s.f.* **1.** Voice. **Parler à haute voix**, to speak aloud. S.a. HAUT I. 1. **Parler à voix basse, à mi-voix**, to speak in a low voice, under one's breath. *Élever la v.*, to speak out; to raise one's voice. **A portée de (la) voix**, within earshot, within call. **Hors de portée de la voix**, out of hearing, out of earshot. (Of dogs) **Donner de la voix**, to bark, to give tongue, to bay. *Mus: V. de poitrine*, chest-voice. *V. de tête*, head-voice. **Chanter à plusieurs voix**, to sing in parts. **2. Demeurer sans voix**, to remain speechless. **De vive voix**, by word of mouth; viva voce. *La v. de la nature*, the call of nature. *La v. du peuple*, public opinion. **D'une commune voix**, by common consent. **Donner sa voix à qn**, to vote for s.o. **Mettre une question aux voix**, to put a question to the vote. *La Chambre alla aux v.*, the House divided. *F:* **Avoir voix au chapitre**, to be entitled to give one's opinion; to have a say in the matter. **3.** *Gram:* A la voix active, passive, in the active voice, in the passive (voice).

vol[1] [vɔl], *s.m.* **1.** (a) Flying, flight. **Prendre son vol**, (i) (of bird) to take wing; (ii) *Av:* to fly off. **Au vol**, on the wing. *F:* **Saisir l'occasion au vol**, to grasp the opportunity. **A vol d'oiseau**, as the crow flies. **Vue à vol d'oiseau**, bird's-eye view. **Oiseau de haut vol**, high-flying bird. *F: Ame de haut vol*, lofty soul. (b) *Av:* **Vol à voile**, gliding; sail-planing. *Vol piqué*, dive. *Vols de virtuosité*, trick flying. S.a. PLANÉ[2]. **2.** Flock, flight (of birds flying together); covey (of game birds); swarm (of locusts). **3.** *Chasse* au vol, hawking.

vol[2], *s.m.* **1.** Theft; stealing, robbery. *Jur:* **Vol qualifié**, aggravated theft; robbery. **Vol de nuit avec effraction**, burglary. **Vol à la tire**, pocket-picking. **Vol à l'étalage**, shop-lifting. **Vol à l'américaine**, confidence trick. **Vol de grand chemin**, highway robbery. *Commettre plusieurs vols*, to commit several thefts. **2.** Stolen goods or object.

volable [vɔlabl], *a.* **1.** Worth stealing. **2.** (Man) easy to rob.

volage [vɔlaːʒ], a. Fickle, inconstant, flighty. adv. -ment.

volaille [vɔlaːj], s.f. 1. Poultry, fowls. Marchand de volaille, poulterer. 2. Cu: Fowl.

volailler [vɔlaje], s.m. 1. Poulterer. 2. Poultry-yard.

volant [vɔlɑ̃]. I. a. 1. Flying; fluttering (ribbons, tresses). Ich: Poisson volant, flying fish. Navy: Escadre volante, flying squadron. 2. Loose; movable. Feuille volante, loose leaf, detachable slip. Table volante, occasional table. El: Fiche volante, wander-plug. Nau: Cabestan volant, portable winch. Pont volant, flying bridge. II. volant, s.m. 1. Games: Shuttlecock. Jeu de volant, (game of) battledore and shuttlecock. Volant au filet, badminton. 2. Sail (of windmill). 3. (a) Fly-wheel (of engine); fly (in clockwork). Former volant, to act as a fly-wheel. (b) (i) Head of steam. (ii) Steadying force or factor; reserve supply; store of energy (for smooth working). 4. Hand-wheel. Aut: Volant de direction, steering-wheel. Tenir le volant, to drive. Se mettre au volant, to take the wheel. 5. Talon et volant, counterfoil and leaf. 6. Dressm: (i) Flounce. (ii) Shaped panel.

volatil [vɔlatil], a. Volatile.

volatile [vɔlatil], s.m. or f. Winged creature; bird.

volatilisation [vɔlatilizazjɔ̃], s.f. Volatilization.

volatiliser [vɔlatilize], v.tr. Ch: To volatilize. se volatiliser, to volatilize.

volatilité [vɔlatilite], s.f. Volatility.

vol-au-vent [vɔlovɑ̃], s.m.inv. Cu: Puff-pie (filled with goose-liver, kidneys, truffles, mushrooms, sweetbreads, etc.); vol-au-vent.

volcan [vɔlkɑ̃], s.m. Volcano.

volcanique [vɔlkanik], a. Volcanic (rock, etc.).

vole [vɔl], s.f. Cards: Vole; all the tricks.

voler¹ [vɔle], v.i. To fly. (a) F: Voler de ses propres ailes, to fend for oneself. On aurait entendu voler une mouche, you could have heard a pin drop. Voler en éclats, to fly into pieces. Faire voler un cerf-volant, to fly a kite. Av: V. la tête en bas, to fly upside down. Voler à voile, to glide. (b) (Of the mind) To soar. (c) F: To travel fast; to move with speed. Le temps vole, time flies. Faire voler une nouvelle, to spread a piece of news.

volée, s.f. 1. Flight (of bird, projectile, etc.). Prendre sa volée, to take wing. Tirer à toute volée, to fire (a gun) (i) at maximum elevation, (ii) at random. Rugby Fb: Coup de volée, punt. Signifier un arrêt de volée, to make one's mark. Ten: V. haute, smash. V. basse, low volley. F: Entre bond et volée, at a lucky moment. Tirer un oiseau à la volée, to shoot a bird on the wing. Agr: Semer à la v., to broadcast. 2. Flock, flight (of crows, etc.); covey (of partridges). Une danseuse de la première volée, a dancer of the first rank. Joueur de la première v., crack player, first-class player. 3. (a) Volley (of missiles). (b) V. de coups de bâton, shower of blows. Recevoir une bonne volée, to get a sound thrashing. (c) V. de cloches, full peal of bells. Sonner à toute volée, (i) to set all the bells a-ringing; (ii) (of bells) to ring a full peal. 4. Volée d'escalier, flight of stairs, pair of stairs. 5. Jib (of crane). 6. Chase (of gun).

voler², v.tr. 1. To steal. V. qch. à qn, to steal sth. from s.o.; to rob s.o. of sth. F: Il ne l'a pas volé, he richly deserves it. 2. (a) To rob (s.o.). (b) F: To swindle, cheat, do (s.o.).

volerie [vɔlri], s.f. Thieving, robbery.

volet [vɔlɛ], s.m. 1. (a) Sorting-board (for seeds,

etc.). F: Trié sur le volet, very select (company, etc.). (b) Float-board, paddle (of water-wheel). 2. (a) (i) Inside shutter (of window); (ii) (= CONTREVENT) outside shutter; (iii) shop shutter. Mettre les volets, to put up the shutters. Enlever les volets, to take down the shutters. (b) Phot: Shutter (of plate-holder). (c) I.C.E: Butterfly valve (of carburetter). (d) El.E: Indicateur à volets, drop indicator (of annunciator board, etc.). (e) Av: Flap. V. d'intrados, split flap.

voleter [vɔlte], v.i. (il volette; il volettera) (Of bird) To flutter. V. d'arbre en arbre, to flit from tree to tree. [VOLER¹]

volettement [vɔletmɑ̃], s.m. (a) Fluttering, flutter (of wings, of flag). (b) Flitting (hither and thither).

voleur¹ [vɔlœːr], a. Faucon haut, bas, voleur, high-, low-flying hawk.

voleur², -euse [vɔlœːr, -øːz]. 1. s. (a) Thief, robber, burglar. Voleur de grand chemin, footpad, highwayman. Voleur à la tire, pickpocket. Voleuse à l'étalage, shop-lifter. Au voleur! stop thief! (b) V. d'idées, stealer of ideas. V. de moutons, sheep-stealer. 2. a. Thieving, thievish; fleecing, rapacious (tradesman).

volière [vɔljɛːr], s.f. (a) Aviary. (b) Pigeon-run.

volige [vɔliːʒ], s.f. Const: (a) Scantling, batten. Caisse en voliges, crate. (b) Slate-lath.

voliger [vɔliʒe], v.tr. (je voligeai(s); n. voligeons) Const: (a) To batten. (b) To lath. s.m. -eage.

volitif, -ive [vɔlitif, -iːv], a. Volitional, volitive.

volition [vɔlisjɔ̃], s.f. Volition.

volontaire [vɔlɔ̃tɛːr], a. 1. Voluntary; spontaneous (act). Homicide v., voluntary homicide. Mil: Engagé v., s.m. volontaire, voluntarily enlisted man; volunteer. 2. Self-willed, wilful, headstrong. Menton v., firm, determined, chin. adv. -ment.

volontariat [vɔlɔ̃tarja], s.m. Mil: A: Period of service shortened to one year in consideration of payment.

volonté [vɔlɔ̃te], s.f. 1. Will. (a) V. de fer, will of iron, iron will. Manque de volonté, lack of will, infirmity of purpose. Ne pas avoir de v., to have no will of one's own. (b) Bonne volonté, mauvaise volonté, goodwill, ill-will. Travailler de bonne volonté, to work with a will. Faire qch. de bonne v., to do sth. of one's own free will, with a good grace. Homme de bonne volonté, volunteer (for dangerous enterprise, etc.). S.a. ACTE 1. (c) Suivre sa volonté; en faire à sa volonté, to have one's own way. A volonté, at will, at pleasure, ad lib. Mil: Feu à volonté, independent firing. De sa propre volonté, of one's own accord; spontaneously. S.a. ACTE 2. 2. pl. (a) Les dernières volontés de . . ., the last will and testament of. . . . (b) Whims, caprices. Elle fait ses quatre volontés, she does just what she pleases.

volontiers [vɔlɔ̃tje], adv. (a) Willingly, gladly, with pleasure. Il cause v., he is fond of talking. (b) Readily. On croit v. que . . ., we are apt to think that. . . .

volt [vɔlt], s.m. El.Meas: Volt.

voltage [vɔltaːʒ], s.m. El: Voltage.

voltaïque [vɔltaik], a. El: Voltaic (cell, pile).

voltampère [vɔltɑ̃pɛːr], s.m. El.Meas: Volt-ampere; watt.

volte [vɔlt], s.f. 1. Equit: Fenc: Volt. 2. Gym: (Exercices de) volte, exercises on the vaulting-horse; vaulting.

volte-face, s.f.inv. Turning round; volte-face; wheel round; face-about. Faire volte-face, to face about.

voltige [vɔltiːʒ], *s.f.* **1.** *Equit:* Mounted gymnastics. *Haute v.*, trick-riding. *Saut en v.*, flying leap into the saddle. **2.** (*a*) Slack rope. (*b*) Slackrope gymnastics. (*c*) Flying-trapeze exercises.

voltigement [vɔltiʒmã], *s.m.* Fluttering, flitting.

voltiger [vɔltiʒe], *v.i.* (je voltigeai(s); n. voltigeons) **1.** *Gym: Equit: etc:* To perform on horseback, on the slack rope, on the flying trapeze. **2.** (Of bird, insect) To fly about; to flit; (of curtain, flag, etc.) to flutter, flap.

voltigeur, -euse [vɔltiʒœːr, -øːz], *s.* **1.** Performer on horseback, on the slack rope, on the flying trapeze. **2.** *s.m. A:* Light infantryman.

voltmètre [vɔltmetr], *s.m. El:* Voltmeter.

volubilis [vɔlybilis], *s.m. Bot:* Convolvulus.

volubilité [vɔlybilite], *s.f.* Volubility; glibness of tongue.

volume [vɔlym], *s.m.* **1.** Volume, tome. *Il faudrait des volumes pour raconter . . .*, it would take volumes to relate. . . . **2.** (*a*) Volume, bulk, mass (of solid or fluid). *Nau:* **Chargé en volume**, laden in bulk. (*b*) Volume (of sound, of the voice). (*c*) Capacity (of bunkers, etc.).

volume-contrôle, *s.m.* Volume-control (of gramophone, of wireless set).

volumétrique [vɔlymetrik], *a.* Volumetric(al). *adv.* **-ment**, -ally.

volumineux, -euse [vɔlyminø, -øːz], *a.* **1.** Voluminous, bulky, large. **2.** Voluminous (writer).

volupté [vɔlypte], *s.f.* (Sensual) pleasure or delight. *Toutes les voluptés*, every pleasurable sensation.

voluptuaire [vɔlyptɥɛːr], *a. Jur:* (Of expenses) For embellishment.

voluptueu|x, -euse [vɔlyptɥø, -øːz]. **1.** *a.* Voluptuous. **2.** *s.* Voluptuary, sensualist. *adv.* **-sement.**

volute [vɔlyt], *s.f.* (*a*) Volute, helix; scroll (of violin). *Ressort en volute*, helical spring. *V. de fumée*, twirl, wreath, of smoke. (*b*) *Conch:* Whorl.

volvox [vɔlvɔks], *s.m. Prot:* Volvox.

vomer [vɔmeːr], *s.m.* **1.** *Anat:* Vomer; ploughshare bone. **2.** *Ich:* Moon-fish.

vomique [vɔmik]. **1.** *a.* **Noix vomique**, nux vomica. **2.** *s.f. Med:* Vomica((i) cavity; (ii) pus).

vomiquier [vɔmikje], *s.m.* Nux vomica (tree).

vomir [vɔmiːr], *v.tr.* (*a*) To vomit; to bring up (food). *Envie de vomir*, squeamish feeling; nausea. *Avoir envie de v.*, to feel squeamish, sick. **Faire des efforts pour vomir**, to retch, to heave. (*b*) (Of chimney, volcano, etc.) To vomit, belch forth (smoke, flames).

vomissement [vɔmismã], *s.m.* **1.** Vomiting. **2.** Vomit.

vomitif, -ive [vɔmitif, -iːv], *a. & s.m. Med:* Emetic; vomitory.

vomitoire [vɔmitwaːr], *s.m. Rom.Ant:* Vomitorium; vomitory (of amphitheatre).

vont [vɔ̃]. See ALLER.

vorace [vɔras], *a.* Voracious. *adv.* **-ment.**

voracité [vɔrasite], *s.f.* Voracity, voraciousness.

vortex [vɔrtɛks], *s.m.* (*a*) Whorl. (*b*) Vortex-ring.

vos [vo]. See VOTRE.

votant, -ante [vɔtã, -ãːt]. **1.** *a.* Having a vote; voting (assembly, member). **2.** *s.* Voter.

votation [vɔtasjɔ̃], *s.f.* Voting.

vote [vɔt], *s.m.* **1.** (*a*) Vote. (*b*) Voting, ballot(ing), poll. **Droit de vote**, franchise. **Prendre part au vote**, to go to the poll; to vote. **Bulletin de vote**, voting-paper, ballot-paper. **Section de vote**, polling district or station. **2. Vote d'une loi**, passing of a bill. **Vote de confiance**, vote of confidence. **Le vote est pour, contre, the ayes, the noes, have it.**

voter [vɔte]. **1.** *v.i.* To vote. *V. à main levée*, to vote by (*a*) show of hands. **2.** *v.tr.* (*a*) To pass, carry (a bill). (*b*) To vote (money, etc.). *V. des remercîments à qn*, to pass a vote of thanks to s.o.

votif, -ive [vɔtif, -iːv], *a.* Votive (offering, mass).

votre, *pl.* **vos** [vɔtr, vo], *poss.a.* Your. *Votre fils et votre fille*, your son and (your) daughter. *Vos père et mère*, your father and mother.

vôtre [voːtr]. **1.** Occ. *poss.a.* Yours. *Je suis tout vôtre*, I am entirely at your service. **2. Le vôtre, la vôtre, les vôtres.** (*a*) *poss.pron.* Yours; your own. *Com: J'ai reçu la vôtre du 6 mai*, I am in receipt of yours of May the 6th. *F:* **A la vôtre!** here's to you! (*b*) *s.m.* (i) Your own (property, etc.). **Il faut y mettre du vôtre**, you must do your share. (ii) *pl.* Your own (friends, etc.); your own folk. (iii) *F:* **Vous avez encore fait des vôtres**, you've been up to some of your tricks again.

voudr-ai, etc. [vudre]. See VOULOIR.

vouer [vwe], *v.tr.* To vow, dedicate, consecrate. *Vouer obéissance au roi*, to pledge one's allegiance to the king. *Se v. au service de Dieu*, to dedicate one's life to the service of God. *V. sa vie, se vouer, à l'étude*, to devote, give up, one's life to study. *F:* **Il ne sait (pas) à quel saint se vouer**, he is at his wits' end.

vouloir [vulwaːr]. **1.** *v.tr.* (*pr.p.* voulant; *p.p.* voulu; *pr.ind.* je veux, il veut, n. voulons, ils veulent; *pr.sub.* je veuille, n. voulions, ils veuillent; *imp.* in **1.** voulez, otherwise veuille, veuillez; *p.h.* je voulus; *fu.* je voudrai) **1.** To will (sth.); to be determined on (sth.). *Ce que Dieu veut*, the will of God. **Dieu le veuille!** please God! *Prov:* **Vouloir, c'est pouvoir**, where there's a will there's a way. *Voulez et vous pourrez*, if you put forth your will you will manage it. **Vous l'avez voulu!** you have only yourself to blame! **2.** (*a*) To want, to wish (for), to desire (sth.). *Il sait ce qu'il veut*, he knows what he wants, he knows his own mind. **Faites comme vous voudrez**, do as you please. *Je ne veux pas de cela*, I'll have none of that. *Ils ne veulent pas de moi*, they won't have me. *En voulez-vous?* do you want any? will you have some? *Adv.phr.* **En veux-tu, en voilà**, as much as ever you like. *Il y en avait à bouche que veux-tu*, there was any amount. (*b*) *Pred.* **Vouloir qn pour roi**, to want s.o. for a king, as a king. *Je te veux heureuse*, I want you to be happy. (*c*) *V. du bien, du mal, à qn*, to wish s.o. well, harm. **En vouloir à qn**, to bear s.o. ill-will, a grudge. *Ne m'en veuillez pas*, don't be vexed with me. *En v. à qn de qch.*, to owe s.o. a grudge for sth. **A qui en voulez-vous?** what ails you? *S'en vouloir*, to be angry, vexed, with oneself. **3. Vouloir + inf.** (expressed or understood); **vouloir que + sub.** (*a*) To will, to require, to demand. *Le mauvais sort voulut qu'il arrivât trop tard*, ill-luck would have it that he should get there too late. *Je veux être obéi*, I intend, mean, to be obeyed. **Vouloir absolument, à toute force, faire qch.**, to insist upon doing sth., to be determined to do sth. *Le moteur ne veut pas démarrer*, the engine won't start. (*b*) To want, wish. *Il voulait me frapper*, he wanted to hit me. *Il ne voulait pas s'en aller*, he was loath to go. *J'aurais voulu y* *rester toujours*, I would, could, have stayed there for ever. *Il aurait voulu être mort*, he wished himself dead. *Je voudrais bien être à votre place*, I wish I were in your place. *Je veux que vous sachiez que* . . ., I will, would, have you know that. . . . *Que voulez-vous que je fasse?* what would you have me do? *Rentrons, voulez-vous?* let us go in, shall we? (*c*) To try to (do sth.). *Il voulut arrêter le coup*, he made an endeavour to stop the blow. *Il voulut me frapper*, he tried, offered, to strike me. (*d*) To mean, intend. *Il voulait me rendre service*, he meant to do me a service. **Faire qch. sans le vouloir**, to do sth. unintentionally, without meaning it. S.a. DIRE I. 5. (*e*) **Vouloir bien** taire qch., to consent, be willing, to do sth. *Je veux bien que vous veniez*, I am willing that you should come. *Voulez-vous bien attendre un instant*, will you kindly wait a moment. *Veuillez* (*bien*) *vous asseoir*, (i) kindly sit down; (ii) do please sit down; pray be seated. *Venez-vous avec nous?*—Je veux bien, are you coming with us?—I don't mind; by all means. S[i] **vous voulez**, if you like. *Je viens quand je veux*, I come when I choose, when I like, when I please. **Dieu veuille que** . . ., God send, grant, that. . . . (*f*) (*Bien* used as an intensive) **Voulez-vous bien vous taire!** *will* you be silent! do shut up! **4.** To be convinced, to insist. *Il veut absolument que je me sois trompé*, he will have it that I was mistaken. **5.** (Of thg) To require, need, demand (sth.). *La vigne veut un terrain crayeux*, vines require a chalky soil. *Ce verbe veut l'accusatif*, this verb takes the accusative. **II. vouloir**, *s.m.* Will. (*a*) *Le v. de Dieu*, the will of God. (*b*) **Bon, mauvais, vouloir**, goodwill, ill-will (*pour, envers*, towards).

voulu, *a.* **1.** Required, requisite (formalities, etc.). *Cela se fera à l'heure voulue*, it will be done in due time. **2.** Deliberate, intentional. *Impertinence voulue*, studied impertinence.

vous [vu], *pers. pron. sg. & pl.* **1.** (*a*) (Subject) You; *A. & Lit:* pl. ye. (*b*) (Object) You, to you. *Il vous en parlera*, he will speak to you about it. *F:* (Ethic dative) *La mule vous lui détacha un coup de sabot*, the mule let fly a kick at him. (*c*) (Refl.) *Vous vous êtes donné bien de la peine*, you have given yourself, yourselves, much trouble. *Taisez-vous*, be silent. (*d*) (Reciprocal) *Vous vous connaissez*, you know one another. **2.** (Stressed) (*a*) (Subject) You. *Vous et votre femme*, you and your wife. *Vous autres Anglais*, you English. *Faites-le vous-même*, do it yourself. (*b*) (Object) *Ces gants sont à vous*, these gloves are yours, belong to you. *C'est à vous de jouer*, it is your turn to play.

vous-même(s) [vumɛːm], *pers.pron.* See MÊME.

vousseau [vuso], *s.m.*, **voussoir** [vuswaːr], *s.m.* Voussoir, arch-stone.

voussure [vusyːr], *s.f.* Curve, bend (of arch); arching.

voûte [vut], *s.f.* Vault, arch. (*a*) *Arch: V. d'arête*, groined arch. *V. en ogive*, ogival vault. *V. à plein cintre*, semi-circular vault. S.a. CLEF 3. (*b*) *La* **voûte** *céleste*, the vault, canopy, of heaven. *Anat: V. du crâne*, dome of the skull. *V. du palais*, roof of the mouth.

voûter [vute], *v.tr.* (*a*) To arch, vault (roof). (*b*) *L'âge voûte la taille*, age bows the back. **se voûter**, to become bent, bowed.

voûté, *a.* (*a*) Vaulted, arched. (*b*) Stooping, bent. *Dos voûté*, bent back.

vouv|oyer [vuvwaje], *v.tr.* (je vouvoie; je **vouvoierai**) To address (s.o.) as *vous* (instead of *tu*). *s.m.* **-oiement.**

voyable [vwajabl], *a. F: Je ne suis pas v.*, I am not fit to be seen. [VOIR]

voyage [vwajaːʒ], *s.m.* Journey, trip, tour, run. *Aimer les voyages*, to be fond of travel. *Les voyages de Gulliver*, Gulliver's travels. *V. en chemin de fer*, railway journey. *V. sur mer*, voyage. **Faire un voyage**, to go on a journey or on a voyage. **Petit voyage d'agrément**, pleasure trip. **Voyage de noces**, honeymoon trip. **Vaisseau engagé au voyage**, ship engaged by the run. **Se mettre en voyage** *pour l'Australie*, to set forth for Australia. *Il est en voyage*, he is travelling. **Costume de voyage**, travelling costume, travelling dress. **Compagnon de voyage** (i) travelling companion, (ii) fellow-traveller or -passenger. **Bon voyage!** pleasant journey!

voyager [vwajaʒe], *v.i.* (je voyageai(s); n. voyageons) **1.** (*a*) To travel; to make a journey, a trip. *Il a beaucoup voyagé*, he has been a great traveller. *Personne qui a beaucoup voyagé*, much-travelled person. (*b*) *Com:* To travel; *F:* to be on the road. *V. pour les vins*, to travel in wine. (*c*) (Of birds) To migrate. **2.** (Of goods, etc.) To be transported.

voyageur, -euse [vwajaʒœːr, -øːz]. **I.** *s.* (*a*) Traveller; (in train, etc.) passenger; (in cab) fare. (*b*) *Esp. Hist:* Voyager, explorer. (*c*) *Voyageur de commerce*, commercial traveller. **2.** *a.* (*a*) Travelling. **Commis voyageur**, commercial traveller. (*b*) **Oiseau voyageur**, migratory bird. **Pigeon voyageur**, carrier pigeon.

voyant, -ante [vwajã, -ãːt]. **I.** *a. & s.* (*a*) Seeing (person); seer (as opposed to blind). (*b*) Clairvoyant. **2.** *a.* Gaudy, loud, garish (colour); showy, conspicuous (monument, etc.). **3.** *s.m.* (*a*) Mark, signal; *Surv:* slide-vane, sight (of levelling-rod); *Nau:* sphere (of light-ship). (*b*) Sighting-slit of scientific instrument).

voyelle [vwajɛl], *s.f.* Vowel.

voyer [vwaje], *s.m. & a.m.* (Agent) voyer, road surveyor.

voy-ez, -ons, etc. [vwaje, -ɔ̃]. See VOIR.

voyou, -oute [vwaju, -ut]. **I.** *s. F:* (*a*) Cheeky street-arab; gutter-snipe. (*b*) (Young) loafer, hooligan, corner-boy. **2.** *a. Verve voyoute*, gutter wit.

voyoucratie [vwajukrasi], *s.f. F:* The mob, the riff-raff.

vrac [vrak], *s.m.* (Used in) **En vrac**, loose, in bulk. **Charger en v.**, to lade in bulk. *Marchandises en v.*, loose goods (not packed).

vrai [vrɛ]. **1.** *a.* (*a*) True, truthful. **C'est vrai comme l'Évangile**, it's (the) gospel truth. **C'est** (**bien**) **vrai!** true! *F:* (Pour) de vrai, really, in earnest. *C'est pour de v.*, I am in earnest. (*b*) True, real, genuine. *Le v. Dieu*, the true God. *Un v. ami*, a real friend. *F: Un vrai des vrais*, a true blue; one of the lads. (*c*) Downright, arrant, regular (swindler, etc.). **2.** *adv.* Truly, really, indeed. **Dire vrai**, to tell the truth. **A vrai dire**, *à dire vrai*, if the truth must be told; as a matter of fact. *F: Tu m'aimes, vrai?* you *do* love me? **Vrai de vrai!** as true as true! honest Injun! *Vous m'écrirez*, vrai? you *will* write to me, won't you? **3.** *s.m. Distinguer le v. du faux*, to distinguish truth from falsehood. **Être dans le vrai**, to be right. *Il y a du v. dans ce bruit*, there is some truth in the rumour.

vraiment [vrɛmã], *adv.* Really, truly, in truth. *Vous êtes v. trop bon*, you are really too kind. **Vraiment?** indeed? is that so? **Oui vraiment**, yes indeed.

vraisemblable [vrɛsɑ̃blabl]. **I.** *a.* Probable, likely. *Il n'est pas v. que + sub.*, it is (i) hardly

credible, (ii) hardly to be expected, that. . . .
Excuse peu vraisemblable, unconvincing excuse.
2. *s.m.* What is probable, likely. **Au delà du**
vraisemblable, beyond the bounds of probability.
adv. **-ment.**

vraisemblance [vrɛsɑ̃blɑ̃:s], *s.f.* Probability,
likelihood, verisimilitude. **Selon toute vraisem-**
blance, in all probability.

vrille [vri:j], *s.f.* **1.** *Bot:* Tendril. **2.** *Tls:*
Gimlet, borer, piercer. *F:* **Yeux percés en**
vrille, yeux en trou de vrille, gimlet eyes.
3. *Av:* Tail spin. **Descente en vrille,** spinning
dive.

vrill|er [vrije]. **1.** *v.tr.* To bore (with a gimlet).
2. *v.i.* (*a*) (Of rocket, etc.) To ascend in a spiral.
(*b*) (Of thread, rope) To twist, kink ; to corkscrew.
s.m. **-age.**
   vrillé, *a.* (*a*) Spiral ; twisted, kinked (thread).
(*b*) *Bot:* With tendrils ; tendrilled.
   vrillée, *s.f. Bot: F:* Bindweed.

vrillette [vrijɛt], *s.f. Ent:* Death-watch
(beetle).

vromb|ir [vrɔ̃bi:r], *v.i.* (Of flies) To buzz ; (of
top, aeroplane) to hum ; (of engine) to throb,
to hum. *s.m.* **-issement.**

vu, vue [vy]. See VOIR.

vulcanisation [vylkanizasjɔ̃], *s.f. Ind:* Vulcanization (of rubber).

vulcaniser [vylkanize], *v.tr. Ind:* To vulcanize
(rubber).

vulcanite [vylkanit], *s.f.* Vulcanite, ebonite.

vulgaire [vylgɛ:r]. **1.** *a.* Vulgar. (*a*) Common,
everyday (custom). **Langue vulgaire,** vernacular.
(*b*) Low, unrefined, coarse. **2.** *s.m.* (*a*) **Le vul-**
gaire, the common people, the vulgar herd.
(*b*) **Donner dans le vulgaire,** to lapse into vulgarity. *adv.* **-ment.**

vulgarisateur, -trice [vylgarizatœːr, -tris], *s.*
Popularizer (of knowledge).

vulgarisation [vylgarizasjɔ̃], *s.f.* Popularization
(of knowledge). **Ouvrage de vulgarisation,**
popular work, popular treatise.

vulgariser [vylgarize], *v.tr.* **1.** To popularize
(knowledge). **2.** To coarsen, vulgarize.
   se vulgariser, to grow vulgar.

vulgarisme [vylgarism], *s.m.* Vulgarism.

vulgarité [vylgarite], *s.f.* Vulgarity.

vulnérabilité [vylnɛrabilite], *s.f.* Vulnerability.

vulnérable [vylnɛrabl], *a.* Vulnerable.

vulnéraire [vylnerɛːr]. **1.** *Pharm:* (*a*) *a.* Vulnerary, healing. **Eau vulnéraire,** lotion for
wounds. (*b*) *s.m.* Vulnerary. **2.** *s.f. Bot:* Kidney
vetch, wound-wort.

vulpin [vylpɛ̃], *s.m. Bot:* Foxtail (grass).

vultueux, -euse [vyltɥø, -øːz], *a.* (Of the face)
Red and puffy ; bloated ; purply.

W

W, w (double v) [dublǝve], *s.m.* (The letter) W, w.

wagnérien, -ienne [vagnerjɛ̃, -jɛn], *a. & s.*
Mus: Wagnerian.

wagon [vagɔ̃], *s.m. Rail:* Carriage, coach, car
(for passengers) ; waggon, truck (for goods).
W. à bagages, luggage-van. *W. à bestiaux,* cattle-
truck. *W. à chevaux,* horse-box. **Monter en**
wagon, to get into the train.

   NOTE. In the following compounds both
nouns vary in the plural.

wagon-bar, *s.m.* Refreshment-car.

wagon-citerne, *s.m.* Tank-car, tank-waggon.

wagon-couloir, *s.m.* Corridor carriage.

wagon-écurie, *s.m.* Horse-box.

wagon-frein, *s.m.* Brake-van.

wagon-lit, *s.m.* Sleeping-car ; *F:* sleeper.

wagon(n)et [vagɔnɛ], *s.m. Min:* Tip-truck,
tip-waggon.

wagon-poste, *s.m.* Mail-van. *pl. Des wagons-poste.*

wagon-restaurant, *s.m.* Restaurant-car ;
dining-car.

wagon-salon, *s.m.* Saloon(-car, -carriage).

Walkyrie [valkiri], *s.f. Myth:* Valkyrie.

wallace [valas], *s.f. F:* (Also **Fontaine Wallace**)
Drinking-fountain (of which a number were
presented to Paris by Sir Richard Wallace).

wallon, -onne [valɔ̃, -ɔn]. **1.** *a. & s. Ethn:*
Walloon. **2.** *s.m. Ling:* Walloon.

wapiti [wapiti], *s.m. Z:* Wapiti.

warrant [varɑ̃:t, varɑ̃:t], *s.m. Com: Jur:* (Warehouse or dock) warrant. *W. en marchandises,*
produce warrant.

warrant|er [varɑ̃te], *v.tr. Com:* To issue a
warehouse warrant for (goods). *Marchandises*
warrantées, goods covered by a warehouse
warrant. *s.m.* **-age.**

water-closet [watɛrklɔzɛt], *s.m.* Water-closet,
w.-c. *pl. Des water-closets.*

wateringue [vatǝrɛ̃ːg], *s.f.* (In the N. of Fr. and
in Flanders) **1.** Drainage-works. **2.** Draining
syndicate.

waterproof [watɛrpruf], *s.m.* Waterproof (coat) ;
mackintosh.

watt [wat], *s.m. El.Meas:* Watt, ampere-
volt.

wattage [wata:ʒ], *s.m. El.E:* Wattage.

watt-heure [watœːr], *s.m. El. Meas:* Watt-hour.
pl. Des watt-heures.

wattman [watman], *s.m.* Driver (of electric
tramway or train). *pl. Des wattmen* [watmɛn].

wattmètre [watmɛtr], *s.m. El.E:* Watt-hour
meter ; wattmeter.

wesleyen, -enne [wɛslejɛ̃, -ɛn], *a. & s.* Wesleyan.

whisky [wiski], *s.m.* Whisky. *pl. Des whiskys.*

whist [wist], *s.m.* Whist. *W. à trois avec un mort,*
dummy whist.

wiesnérie [visneri], *s.f. Bot:* Alisma, water-
plantain.

wisigoth, -othe [vizigo, -ɔt]. *Hist:* **1.** *a.* Visi-
gothic. **2.** *s.* Visigoth.

wolfram [vɔlfram], *s.m. Miner:* Wolfram ;
tungsten ore.

wootz [vuts], *s.m. Metall:* Wootz (steel) ; India
steel.

X, x [iks], *s.m.* (The letter) X, x. *Ph :* Rayons X, X rays. *P :* L'X, the *École polytechnique. F :* Fort en x, strong in mathematics.
xanthéine [gzātein], *s.f. Ch :* Xanthein.
xanthine [gzātin], *s.f. Ch :* Xanthin(e).
xanthophylle [gzātɔfil], *s.f. Ch : Bot :* Xanthophyll.
xénon [ksenɔ̃], *s.m. Ch :* Xenon.
xénophobe [ksenɔfɔb], *a. & s.* Xenophobe.
xénophobie [ksenɔfɔbi], *s.f.* Xenophobia.
xéranthème [kserātɛm], *s.m. Bot :* Xeranthemum.
xérasie [kserazi], *s.f. Med :* Xerasia.
Xérès [kerɛs, gzerɛs]. **1.** *Pr.n. Geog :* Jerez. **2.** *s.m.* (Also vin de **Xérès**) Sherry.

xérodermie [kserɔdermi], *s.f. Med :* Xeroderm(i)a.
xi [ksi], *s.m. Gr.Alph :* Xi.
xiphias [ksifjaːs], *s.m. Ich :* Xiphias, swordfish.
xiphoïde [ksifɔid], *a. Anat :* Xiphoid, ensiform. L'appendice **xiphoïde,** the xiphoid appendage, cartilage, or process ; the xiphoid.
xylographe [ksilɔgraf], *s.m.* Wood-engraver.
xylographie [ksilɔgrafi], *s.f.* **1.** Xylography, wood-engraving. **2.** Xylograph, wood-cut.
xylonite [ksilɔnit], *s.f.* Xylonite, celluloid.
xylophone [ksilɔfɔn], *s.m. Mus :* Xylophone.
xystre [ksistr], *s.m. Surg : Dent :* Xyster.

Y

Y, y[1] (i grec) [igrɛk], *s.m.* (The letter) Y, y.
y[2] [i], *adv. & pron.* **1.** *adv.* There ; here ; thither. *Est-il à Paris?—Oui, il y est,* is he in Paris?—Yes, he is (there). *F : J'y suis, j'y reste !* here I am and here I stay ! *Madame y est-elle?* is Mrs X at home? *En quittant la table j'y laissai ma lettre,* on rising from the table I left my letter on it. *F :* Ah, **j'y suis !** ah, now I understand ! *Y* **êtes-vous?** *F :* do you tumble to it? *Vous n'y êtes pas du tout,* you are all at sea. *Pendant que vous y êtes,* while you are about it. **2.** *pron.inv.* (a) *J'y pense sans cesse,* I am always thinking of it. *J'y gagnerai,* I shall gain by it. *Je m'y attendais,* I expected as much. (b) (Standing for clause governed by d) *Venez nous voir.—Je n'y manquerai pas,* come and see us.—I shall not fail to do so. (c) (Standing for person just mentioned) *Pensez-vous à lui?—Oui, j'y pense,* do you think of him?—Yes, I do. **3.** (Indeterminate uses) **Je vous y prends !** I have caught you (in the act) ! **Ça y est** [sajɛ] ! (i) it's done ! that's it ! (ii) all right ! done ! (iii) there now, I was sure it would happen ! **Il y est pour quelque chose,** he has a hand in it. **Je n'y suis pour rien,** I had no art or part in it. S.a. ALLER 6, 7, AVOIR 8, FAIRE IV. 2. **4.** *Vas-y* [vazi], go there. *Penses-y* [pɑ̃szi], think of it.

yachmak [jaʃmak], *s.m.* (Moslem woman's) veil ; yashmak.
yacht [jak(t), jat, jɔt], *s.m. Nau :* Yacht. *Y. de plaisance,* pleasure yacht. **Croisière en yacht,** yachting cruise.
yachteur [jatœːr, jɔtœːr], *s.m.* Yachtsman.
ya(c)k [jak], *s.m. Z :* Yak.
yahourt [jaurt], *s.m. Cu :* Yaourt, yogurt.
yatagan [jatagɑ̃], *s.m.* Yataghan.
yèble [jɛbl], *s.f. Bot :* = HIÈBLE.
yeuse [jøːz], *s.f. Bot :* Ilex, holm-oak, holly-oak.
yeux. See ŒIL.
yod [jɔd], *s.m. Ling :* Yod.
yog(h)ourt(h) [jɔgurt], *s.m.* = YAHOURT.
yole [jɔl], *s.f. Nau :* Gig, skiff, yawl. *Y. d'amiral,* galley.
yoleur [jɔlœːr], *s.m. Nau :* Gigsman.
yougoslave [jugɔslaːv], *a. & s. Geog :* Yugo-Slav, Jugo-Slav.
Yougoslavie (la) [lajugɔslavi]. *Pr.n.f. Geog :* Yugo-Slavia, Jugo-Slavia.
youyou [juju], *s.m. Nau :* Dinghy. *pl. Des youyous.*
ypérite [iperit], *s.f. Ch :* Yperite ; mustard-gas.
ypréau, -aux [ipreo], *s.m. Bot :* **1.** Broad-leaved elm, wych-elm. **2.** White poplar.
yttrium [itriɔm], *s.m. Ch :* Yttrium.
yucca [juka], *s.m. Bot :* Yucca.

Z, z [zɛd], *s.m.* (The letter) Z, z.
zabre [zɑːbr], *s.m. Ent:* Zabrus; caraboid beetle.
zagaie [zagɛ], *s.f.* Assegai.
zain [zɛ̃], *a.m.* Whole-coloured (horse, with no white hairs).
Zambèze (le) [lɑzɑ̃bɛːz]. *Pr.n.* The Zambezi (river).
zan(n)i [zani], *s.m.inv. A.Th:* Zany; buffoon, merry-andrew.
zébie [zebi], *s.f.* (Meaningless term used in) *P:* Peau de zébie, (i) trash, rubbish, take-in; (ii) nothing, nix.
zèbre [zɛbr], *s.m.* Zebra.
zébrer [zebre], *v.tr.* (je zèbre; je zébrerai) To mark (sth.) with stripes; to streak.
    zébré, *a.* Striped (*de*, with); stripy.
zébrure [zebryːr], *s.f.* **1.** Stripe. **2.** (Series of) stripes; zebra markings.
zébu [zeby], *s.m. Z:* Zebu; humped ox.
zédoaire [zedɔɛːr], *s.f. Bot:* Zedoary.
zée [ze], *s.m. Ich:* Zeus. *Zée forgeron,* (John) Dory.
Zélande [zelɑ̃ːd]. *Pr.n.f.* **1.** Zealand (Holland). **2.** La Nouvelle Zélande, New Zealand.
zélateur, -trice [zelatœːr, -tris]. **1.** *s.* Zealot. *Z. d'une cause,* enthusiastic worker for a cause. **2.** *a.* Zealous.
zèle [zɛːl], *s.m.* Zeal, ardour (*pour,* for). Avec zèle, zealously. Brûler de zèle pour qch., to be fired with enthusiasm for sth. Faux zèle, misguided zeal. *F:* Faire du zèle, (i) to make a show of zeal; (ii) to go beyond one's orders.
zélé, -ée [zele], *a. & s.* Zealous. Trop zélé, over-zealous. Peu zélé, *F:* slack, remiss.
zélote [zelɔt], *s.m. B.Hist:* Zealot.
zémindar [zemɛ̃daːr], *s.m.* (In India) Zemindar.
zénana [zenana], *s.m.* **1.** (In India) Zenana. **2.** *Tex:* Zenana(-cloth).
zénith [zenit], *s.m.* Zenith. *F: Parvenu au z. de sa gloire,* having reached the zenith of his fame.
zénithal, -aux [zenital, -o], *a.* Zenithal.
zéolit(h)e [zeolit], *s.f. Miner:* Zeolite.
zéphire, zéphyr(e) [zefiːr], *s.m.* **1.** (*a*) *Myth:* Zephyr, the West Wind. (*b*) Balmy breeze; zephyr. (*c*) *P:* Soldier of the African Disciplinary Companies. **2.** *Tex:* Laine zéphire, zephyr.
zeppelin [zeplɛ̃], *s.m. Aer:* Zeppelin.
zéro [zero], *s.m.* **1.** Cipher, nought. *F:* C'est un zéro, he is a mere cipher, a nonentity, a nobody. *Ten:* Trois à zéro, three love. **2.** Starting point, zero (of various scales). Point zéro, zero point. S.a. ABSOLU. Correction du zéro, mise au point zéro, index correction, initial adjustment (of surveying instrument, etc.). *El.E:* "Zéro," 'off' (on electric stove, etc.). Interrupteur à zéro, no-load release.
zérotage [zerɔtaːʒ], *s.m.* Calibration of thermometers, etc.); determination of the zero point.
zest [zɛst]. **1.** *int. A:* Pish! tush! **2.** *s.m.* Être entre le zist et le zest, to be neither one thing nor the other; to be betwixt and between; (of health) to be middling, not up to much.
zeste [zɛst], *s.m.* (*a*) *Cu:* Peel (of orange, lemon). *Z. confit,* candied peel. (*b*) Partition quartering the kernel (of walnut). *F: Cela ne vaut pas un zeste,* it is not worth a straw.
zester [zɛste], *v.tr.* To peel the outer skin off (lemon, orange).

zesteuse [zɛstøːz], *s.f.* Orange-peeler; lemon-peeler.
zêta [zeta], *s.m. Gr.Alph:* Zeta.
zeugme [zøːgm], **zeugma** [zøgma], *s.m. Gram: Rh:* Zeugma.
Zeus [zøːs]. *Pr.n.m. Myth:* Zeus.
zézaiement [zezɛmɑ̃], **zézayement** [zezɛjmɑ̃], *s.m.* Lisping, lisp.
zézayer [zezeje], *v.i. & tr.* (je zézaie, je zézaye; je zézaierai, je zézayerai) To lisp.
zibeline [ziblin], *s.f.* **1.** *Z:* (Martre) zibeline, sable. **2.** *Cost:* Sable (fur).
zig [zig], *s.m. P:* Fellow, chap. Esp. Un bon zig, a decent chap.
zigouiller [ziguje], *v.tr. P:* To kill, murder, knife (s.o.); to bayonet (s.o.).
zigue [zig], *s.m. P:* = ZIG.
zigzag [zigzag], *s.m.* **1.** Zigzag. Éclair en zigzag, forked lightning. *Tranchées en z.,* zigzag trenches. Faire des zigzags, to stagger along (when tipsy); to zigzag along. *Nau:* Faire route en zigzag, to steer a zigzag course. La route fait des zigzags, the road runs zigzag. *Mec.E: Disposés en z.,* staggered (rivets, etc.). **2.** Lazy-tongs.
zigzaguer [zigzage], *v.i.* To zigzag. *s.m.* **-ement.**
    zigzagué, *a. Éclair z.,* forked lightning.
zinc [zɛ̃g], *s.m.* **1.** Zinc. *Com:* Spelter. *Poussière de z.,* zinc powder. *Z. à souder,* spelter solder. *Pharm:* Pommade à l'oxyde de zinc, zinc-ointment. S.a. BLANC II. 4. **2.** *P:* (Zinc) counter (of public-house); bar. **3.** Gravure sur zinc, zincograph. **4.** *Av: P:* Aeroplane.
zincographie [zɛ̃kɔgrafi], *s.f.* Zincography.
zincographier [zɛ̃kɔgrafje], *v.tr.* To zincograph; to reproduce (design) by zincography.
zincogravure [zɛ̃kɔgravyːr], *s.f. Phot.Engr:* **1.** Zincography. **2.** (*a*) Zincograph, zincotype. (*b*) Zinc block; *F:* zinco.
zingage [zɛ̃gaːʒ], *s.m.* **1.** Covering (of roof, etc.) with zinc. **2.** *Metall:* Coating with zinc; zincing. *Z. au trempé, F:* galvanizing (of iron).
zingaro [zɛ̃garo], *s.m.* Gipsy, zingaro. *pl. Des zingari.*
zinguer [zɛ̃ge], *v.tr.* **1.** To cover (roof, etc.) with zinc. **2.** *Metall:* To coat with zinc; to zinc; *F:* to galvanize (iron). Fer zingué, *F:* galvanized iron.
zinguerie [zɛ̃gri], *s.f.* **1.** Zinc-works. **2.** Zinc-trade. **3.** Zinc-ware.
zingueur [zɛ̃gœːr], *s.m.* (*a*) Zinc-worker. (*b*) Zinc-roofer.
zinzolin, -ine [zɛ̃zɔlɛ̃, -in], *a. & s.m.* Reddish purple.
zinzoliner [zɛ̃zɔline], *v.tr.* To dye (sth.) a reddish purple.
zircon [zirkɔ̃], *s.m. Miner:* Zircon.
zirconium [zirkɔnjɔm], *s.m. Ch:* Zirconium.
zist [zist], *s.m.* See ZEST.
zizanie [zizani], *s.f.* (*a*) *A:* Tare, darnel. (*b*) *F:* Semer la zizanie entre les familles, to sow discord between families. Perpétuellement en zizanie, perpetually quarrelling, at loggerheads.
zoanthaire [zɔɑ̃tɛːr], *a. & s.m. Coel:* Zoantharian. *s.m.pl.* Zoanthaires, zoantharia.
zodiacal, -aux [zɔdjakal, -o], *a. Astr:* Zodiacal (star, light).
zodiaque [zɔdjak], *s.m.* Le zodiaque, the zodiac.

Zoïle [zɔil]. *Pr.n.m. Lit:* (*a*) Zoilus (severe critic of Homeric poems). (*b*) *s.m. F:* Ill-natured critic, criticaster.

zona [zona], *s.m. Med:* Shingles, zona.

zonaire [zɔnɛːr]. **1.** *a.* Zoned (alabaster, etc.). **2.** *s.f. Algae:* Zonaria.

zonal, -aux [zɔnal, -o], *a.* Zonal.

zone [zoːn], *s.f.* **1.** *A.Cost: Lit:* Zone, girdle. **2.** Zone. (*a*) *Geom: Geog:* Z. *sphérique,* spherical zone. Z. *torride,* torrid zone. Z. *des alizés,* trade-wind belt. Z. *houillère,* coal-belt. (*b*) *Adm:* Z. *postale,* postal area. *Tp: etc:* Z. *suburbaine,* suburban area. *Mil:* Z. *militaire,* military area. (In war) La z. *des armées,* the war zone, the army zone. *W.Tel:* Z. *de silence,* silent zone.

zonier [zonje], *s.m.* (*a*) Dweller in the military zone round Paris. (*b*) *pl. F:* Dregs of the population about Paris.

zoobiologie [zɔɔbjɔlɔʒi], *s.f.* Zoobiology.

zoochimie [zɔɔʃimi], *s.f.* Zoochemistry.

zooglée [zɔɔgle], *s.f. Biol:* Zooglœa.

zoolithe [zɔɔlit], *s.m.* Zoolite.

zoologie [zɔɔlɔʒi], *s.f.* Zoology.

zoologique [zɔɔlɔʒik], *a.* Zoological. Jardin zoologique, zoological garden(s) ; *F:* Zoo.

zoologiste [zɔɔlɔʒist], *s.m.* Zoologist.

zoophage [zɔɔfaːʒ]. **1.** *a.* Zoophagous, carnivorous. **2.** *s.m.* Zoophagan. *pl.* Les zoophages, the zoophaga.

zoophytes [zɔɔfit], *s.m.pl. Biol:* Zoophytes, zoophyta ; phytozoa.

zoospore [zɔɔspɔːr], *s.f. Biol:* Zoospore, swarm-spore.

zootrope [zɔɔtrɔp], *s.m. Toys:* Zootrope, zoetrope ; wheel of life.

zostère [zɔstɛːr], *s.f. Bot:* Grass-wrack, sea-wrack, sea-grass ; zostera.

zouave [zwaːv], *s.m. Mil:* Zouave. *F:* Faire le zouave, to play the giddy goat.

zoulou [zulu], *a. & s. Usu. inv. in f.* Zulu. *pl. Des zoulous.*

Zoulouland [zululã(ːd)]. *Pr.n. Geog:* Zululand.

zozoter [zɔzɔte], *v.i. F:* = ZÉZAYER.

zut [zyt], *int. P:* (*a*) (Of disappointment, anger) Botheration ! hang it all ! dash (it) ! (*b*) (Of contempt) Rats ! shut up ! (*c*) I can't be bothered !

Zuyderzée (le) [lɔzɥidɛrze]. *Pr.n. Geog:* The Zuyder Zee.

zyeuter [zjøte], *v.tr. P:* To have a look, a squint, at (sth.). *Zyeute-moi ça !* just look at that !

zygoma [zigɔma], *s.m. Anat:* Zygoma ; cheek-bone.

zygomatique [zigɔmatik], *a. Anat:* L'arcade zygomatique, the zygomatic arch.

zygote [zigɔt], *s.m. Biol:* Zygote.

zymase [zimɑːz], *s.f. Ch:* Zymase.

zymologie [zimɔlɔʒi], *s.f.* Zymology.

zymotique [zimɔtik], *a. Med:* Zymotic.

SUPPLEMENT

PART ONE
FRENCH—ENGLISH

PART ONE
FRENCH—ENGLISH

abri] **A** [axe

abri, *s.m.* A. *de sous-marins,* submarine pen.
accaparant [akaparɑ̃], *a.* Engrossing.
accaparer, *v.tr.* To seize upon.
accident, *s.m.* **1.** (*b*) A. *d'avion, d'aviation,* plane crash, air crash.
accord, *s.m.* **1.** (*b*) F: **D'accord,** yes, I agree.
accrochage, *s.m.* **1.** (*d*) *Sp:* Recovery (from a losing position).
accueil, *s.m.* **Centre d'accueil,** rest-centre.
acquis, **2.** *s.m. Il a de l'a.,* he's been through the mill (of an artist, writer, etc.).
ad hoc [adɔk]. *Lt.adv.phr:* Ad hoc, for the purpose, special.
aéronautique. **2.** *s.f.* (*b*) **L'Aéronautique navale** = the Fleet Air Arm.
aéroporté [aerɔpɔrte], *a.* Airborne. *Troupes aéroportées,* airborne forces.
affectation, *s.f.* **2.** (*b*) *Mil:* Avoir une, être en, *a. spéciale* = to be in a reserved occupation.
ahurissant, *a. F:* Breath-taking.
aigrement, *adv.* Acidly.
ailleurs. **2.** *Adv.phrs.* (*a*) **D'ailleurs,** (iii) however. (*b*) **Par ailleurs,** (iv) incidentally.
air, *s.m.* l. **1.** (*a*) *École de l'Air,* Air College. **2.** *Coup d'air dans l'œil,* cold in the eye.
ajournement, *s.m. Mil:* Deferment.
ajourner, *v.tr.* (*b*) *Mil:* To grant deferment to (s.o.).
alerte. **2.** *s.f.* Air-raid warning.
allergie [alɛrʒi], *s.f. Med:* Allergy.
allergique [alɛrʒik], *a. Med:* Allergic.
allocation, *s.f.* **2.** *Les allocations familiales* = family allowances.
allongé, *a.* **3.** *Sp:* Coup a., follow-through.
alvéole, *s.m. or f.* **4.** *Artil:* Gun-pit.
amphibie. **1.** *a. Mil: Nav: Av: Opération a.,* combined operation.
ancien. **5.** *s.m.* (*c*) *F: Mil:* Veteran.
angle, *s.m.* **3.** Angle, point of view.
annonce, *s.f.* **2.** *Petites annonces,* classified advertisements.
annonceur, -euse [anɔ̃sœːr, -øːz], *s. W.Tel:* Announcer.
antiaérien, -ienne, *a.* **Défense antiaérienne,** ack-ack.
antiblindé, [ɑ̃tiblɛ̃de], *a. Mil:* Anti-tank.
antigel [ɑ̃tiʒɛl], *s.m.inv.* Anti-freeze.
anti-personnel [ɑ̃tipɛrsɔnɛl], *a.inv.* **Bombe anti-personnel,** anti-personnel bomb.
appeler, *v.tr.* **1.** (*c*) *Tp:* Appeler qn., to ring someone up. **Appeler à l'automatique,** to dial.
apponter [apɔ̃te], *v.i. Av:* To land (on deck of aircraft carrier).
Arabie [arabi]. *Pr.n.f. Geog:* Arabia. **L'Arabie séoudite,** Saudi Arabia.
arbitraire, *a.* **2.** High-handed. **3.** *s.m.* Arbitrariness, high-handedness.
armée, *s.f.* (*a*) *A. aérienne,* air task force. *A. de métier,* professional army. *A. de terre,* land forces.
aromatiser, *v.tr. Cu:* To flavour.

arrière. **1.** *adv.* (*c*) *La casquette en a.,* with his cap tilted back. **3.** *s.m.* (*a*) *Aut:* Tout à l'arrière, rear-engined type.
arrière-pays, *s.m.inv.* Hinterland.
art, *s.m.* **2.** (*b*) Method. (*c*) Talent.
artisanat, *s.m.* **2.** Cottage industry.
asdic [asdik], *s.m. Nav:* Asdic.
aspirant, -ante. **2.** (*b*) *Mil.Av:* Acting pilot officer.
assistance, *s.f.* **3.** **Assistance sociale,** welfare work.
assistant, -ante, *s.* **2.** (*c*) **Assistant(e) social(e),** welfare worker.
assurance, *s.f.* **2.** (*b*) *A. chômage,* unemployment insurance. *Assurances sociales,* social insurance. *A. contre les accidents du travail,* workmen's compensation insurance.
atomique, *a. Ch: Ph:* Bombe a., atom, atomic, bomb. *Guerre a.,* atomic warfare. *Énergie a.,* atomic energy. *F:* Microscopic, very small.
attaque, *s.f.* **1.** (*a*) Hold-up (of a car, a train).
attendre, *v.tr.* **1.** Attendez! Just a moment!
attention, *s.f.* (*a*) *Com:* A l'a. de M. —, attention of Mr —.
atténuant, *a. Jur:* Mitigating.
atterrissage, *s.m.* **2.** *Av:* A. forcé, forced landing. *A. sur le ventre,* pancake landing.
attribution, *s.f.* **1.** Awarding. *L'a. de bourses de voyage,* the awarding of travel grants.
auditeur, -trice, *s. W.Tel: Programme des auditeurs,* request programme.
autant, *adv.* **1.** (*a*) Autant ça qu'autre chose, I don't really care which, it is six of one and half-a-dozen of the other.
auto-école [otoekɔl], *s.f.* School of motoring. *pl. Des auto-écoles.*
autogare [otogaːr], *s.f.* Coach station; bus station.
autogire [otoʒiːr], *s.m. Av:* Autogiro.
automatique. **2.** *s.m.* Automatic telephone, dial-telephone.
avance, *s.f.* **4.** (*a*) **Compte d'avances,** working capital fund. **5.** (*a*) *Retenir ses places trois mois d'a.,* to book seats three months ahead. (*d*) *Tout est en a. cette année,* everything is forward this year.
avantage, *s.m.* **1.** *J'ai l'a. de vous informer que . . .,* I am pleased to inform you that. . . .
avant-première [avɑ̃prəmjɛːr], *s.f. Cin:* Preview. *pl. Des avant-premières.*
avenir, *s.m. C'est un homme d'a.,* he is a coming man.
aviation, *s.f.* **1.** *Av: Nav:* **L'aviation embarquée,** carrier-borne aircraft. **2.** *Notre a. de chasse a abattu* 20 *appareils ennemis,* our fighters shot down 20 enemy aircraft.
avion, *s.m. A. torpilleur,* torpedo-carrying aircraft. *A. de transport,* transport aircraft.
axe, *s.m.* **1.** *Conduire sur l'axe de la chaussée,* to drive on the crown of the road. **3.** *Pol:* Axis.

689

bac, *s.m.* **1.** (*c*) Pontoon.

balai, *s.m.* **1.** (*a*) *F*: Balai électrique, vacuum-cleaner.

balance, *s.f.* **3.** (*b*) B. des pouvoirs, balance of power. *B. politique,* (i) balance of parties, (ii) balance of power.

balayage [balɛjaːʒ], *s.m.* Sweeping.

balle¹, *s.f.* **1.** *Ten:* "*Balle!*", "Service !"

bar², *s.m.* Bar tabacs, bar and tobacconist.

base, *s.f.* **3.** *Traitement de b.,* basic salary.

basket(-ball) [baskɛt(bal)], *s.m. Games:* Basketball.

bâtiment, *s.m.* **3.** *Nav:* Bâtiment de débarquement, landing-craft.

bâton, *s.m.* **1.** (*a*) B. d'agent de police, truncheon.

beaucoup. 1. *s.m.inv.* (*a*) Il y est pour b., he has had a great deal to do with it.

beauté, *s.f.* **1.** *Crème de b.,* face, beauty, cream. *Soins de b.,* beauty treatment.

bellicisme [bɛllisism], *s.m.* War-mongering.

belliciste [bɛllisist], *s.m. & f.* War-monger.

bénef [benɛf], *s.m. P:* Petits bénefs, perks.

Bénélux [benelyks]. *Pr.n.m.* Benelux.

biscuiterie [biskɥitri], *s.f.* (*a*) Biscuit factory. (*b*) Biscuit trade.

black-out [blakut], *s.m.* Black-out. *Faire le b.-o.,* to black-out.

blague, *s.f.* **2.** (*a*) B. à part, joking apart.

blanc. 1. *a.* **1.** *Parl:* Livre blanc, white paper.

blanchisserie, *s.f.* **1.** (*b*) B. automatique, launderette.

blédard [bledaːr], *s.m. F:* Colonist, settler (in the interior).

blindé, *a.* **4.** *s.m.pl.* Les blindés, the armour.

blocage, *s.m.* **4.** *Pol.Ec:* Pegging, freezing. *B. des prix et des salaires,* price and wage freeze.

blondin², *s.m.* Cableway.

blouson [bluzɔ̃], *s.m.* (Lumber-)jacket. Blouson de golf, wind-cheater, golfing-jacket.

bombardier, *s.m.* **3.** *Av:* (*a*) (*Pers.*) Bomb-aimer. (*b*) Bombardier en piqué, dive-bomber.

bonimenter [bɔnimɑ̃te], *v.i. P:* To kid.

se borner. 2. To amount, *F:* boil down (à, to).

boulanger¹, -ère. 2. (*b*) *Danc:* Boulangère, Paul Jones.

bouquet, *s.m.* **3.** *F:* Ça, c'est le bouquet! That takes the biscuit !

bourratif [buratif], *a. P:* Stodgy, filling.

box, *s.m.* **4.** *Jur:* Être dans le box des accusés, to be in the dock.

boy-scout [bɔjskaut, -skut], *s.m.* Boy-scout. *pl. Des boy-scouts.*

bravoure, *s.f. Lit: Morceau de b.,* purple passage.

bricolage [brikɔlaːʒ], *s.m. F:* Pottering about.

brin, *s.m.* **2.** *F:* Un b. de toilette, a lick and a promise.

brouillard, *s.m.* **1.** *Televis:* B. de fond, background mush.

brûler. 1. *v tr.* **2.** (*b*) *Aut:* B. les signaux to shoot the traffic lights.

brûlot, *s.m.* **2.** *Av:* Flare.

bull-dozer [byldozɛːr], *s.m.* Bulldozer.

busc, *s.m. Dressm:* Whalebone.

but¹, *s.m.* **1.** Un coup au but, a direct hit.

C

cabine, *s.f.* (*b*) C. (téléphonique), phone box, (telephone) call-box.

cachette, *s.f. Adv.phr. Vendre, donner, en c.,* to sell, give, under the counter.

café, *s.m.* **1.** (*b*) Café crème, (white) coffee.

café-crème [kafekrɛm], *s.m.* (White) coffee. *pl. Des cafés-crème.*

cafeteria, caféterie [kafə)tɛrja, kafet(ə)ri], *s. f.* Cafeteria. (*b*) Cafeteria.

cafetier, -ière. 2. *s.f.* Cafetière. C. automatique, c. russe, percolator.

camion-atelier [kamjɔ̃atəlje], *s.m.* Mobile workshop. *pl. Des camions-ateliers.*

canadien, -ienne, *a. & s.* **1.** *Aut:* (Carrosserie) canadienne, shooting-brake, station-waggon (body). **2.** *s.f.* Canadienne. (*a*) Sheepskin jacket, waist-coat. (*b*) Canadian canoe.

canarder. 2. *v.tr.C. qn,* to take pot-shots at s.o.

cancer, *s.m.* **2.** *Med:* Malignant growth.

canoë [kanu], *s.m.* (Canadian) canoe.

canoéisme [kanuism], *s.m.* Canoeing.

canoéiste [kanuist], *s.m. & f.* Canoeist.

capitaine, *s.m.* (*a*) *Mil.Av:* C. aviateur, flight lieutenant.

caporal, -aux, *s.m.* **1.** *Av:* Leading aircraft-man.

caporal-chef, *s.m. Mil:* Lance-sergeant. *pl. Des caporaux-chefs.*

carnet, *s.m.* C. de timbres(-poste), book of stamps.

carotte, *s.f.* **1.** *F:* Ses carottes sont cuites, he's done for. *F:* Les carottes sont cuites, it's as good as settled. **2.** Tobacconist's sign (in France).

casser, *v.tr.* **1.** *F:* Une attaque à tout c.,* an all-out attack. *F:* C. les oreilles à qn, to bother, importune, s.o.

catapultage [katapyltaːʒ], *s.m. Av:* Catapult-launching, catapulting.

catapulter [katapylte], *v.tr. Av:* To catapult.

catch [katʃ], *s.m.* Le catch, catch as catch can.

ceinture, *s.f.* **2.** C. de verdure, green belt.

cellulite [sɛlylit], *s.f. Med:* Fibrositis.

centre, *s.m. Fb:* Les centres, the insides. *Ph:* Centre d'attraction, de gravitation, centre of attraction.

certificat, *s.m. Sch:* Certificat de Licence, d'Études supérieures, (i) each of the four examinations for the degree of *Licencié,* (ii) Certificate obtained on passing an examination for the degree of *Licencié.*

cesse, *s.f.* Elle parle sans c., she never stops talking.

chaîne, *s.f.* **1.** (*a*) Chaîne de montage, assembly conveyor. **2.** Travail à la chaîne, chain work.

chaise, *s.f.* **1.** (*a*) Le jeu, la polka, des chaises, musical chairs. (*c*) C. électrique, (electric) chair.

chambre, *s.f.* **1.** (*a*) Faire c. à part, to sleep in separate rooms (of married couple). *C. à grand lit, c. à deux (personnes)*, double room. (*c*) *C. à gaz*, gas-chamber.

chance, *s.f.* **I.** *Chance aléatoire, douteuse*, off chance. *Ne pas avoir chance de . . .*, to be unlikely to. . . .

changement, *s.m.* "*Changement de propriétaire*," "under new ownership."

chanter. 2. *v.i.* (*b*) *F:* *Est-ce que cela vous chante?* Do you like the idea of it?

chanteur, -euse, *s.* **Chanteur de charme,** crooner.

chantier, *s.m.* **2.** Site, depot. *C.* (*de construction*), building yard. *Rail: C. de voies de garage et de triage*, shunting yard.

chapeau, *s.m.* **I.** *C. de chasse*, deer-stalker (hat). *Faire passer le c.*, to send round the hat.

chapeauté [ʃapote], *a.* Capped, covered.

chapelet, *s.m.* **I.** *C. de bombes*, stick of bombs.

char, *s.m.* **2.** *C. à bœufs*, ox-cart, bullock-cart.

charge, *s.f.* **5.** **Deux enfants à charge,** two dependent children.

charger, *v.tr.* **I.** (*c*) *El: Accumulateur chargé à fond, à refus*, fully charged battery.

charitable, *a.* **Oeuvres charitables,** charities.

charme¹, *s.m.* **2.** *F:* *Faire du c.*, to make oneself pleasant, charming.

charnière, *s.f.* **I.** Stamp-hinge. **2.** *Mil:* Bridge, point of contact.

chasse, *s.f.* **I.** (*a*) **La chasse,** the hunt. **2.** *F:* *Tirer la c.* (*d'eau*), to pull the (lavatory) chain.

chasseur, -euse. 4. *s.m.* *Av:* Fighter.

chausson, *s.m.* **I.** (*d*) *C.* (*tricoté*) *de bébé*, bootee.

chef, *s.m.* **2.** *Av:* **Chef de bord,** captain.

chemise, *s.f.* **2.** (*b*) *C. couvre-livre*, book-cover.

chemisier, -ière [ʃmizje, -jɛːr]. **I.** *s.* (*a*) Shirtmaker. (*b*) Haberdasher. **2.** *s.m.* Shirt (blouse), sports blouse.

chercher, *v.tr.* **I.** *F:* *Je l'ai cherché*, I asked for it.

cheveu, -eux, *s.m.* **2.** *P:* *Avoir mal aux cheveux*, to have a hang-over.

chevroter, *v.i.* To bleat (of goat).

chic. 3. *int.* *F:* *Chic* (*alors*)! Fine!

chiendent, *s.m.* **2.** *Brosse en, de, c.*, scrubbing-brush.

chiffrer. 2. *v.tr.* (*c*) To code (a message).

chinois. 2. (*b*) *s.m.* *Ling:* Chinese.

chiqué, *s.m.* *P:* Eye-wash. *Faiseur de c.*, swank. *Tout ça c'est du c.*, that's all eye-wash.

chocolat. I. *s.m.* *C. à croquer*, eating chocolate.

chômeur, -euse [ʃomœːr, ʃomoːz], *s.* Out-of-work.

chute, *s.f.* **I.** (*a*) *C. de montagne*, landslide.

ciné-journal [sineʒurnal], *s.m.* Not used in *pl.* News-reel.

cinglé [sɛ̃gle], *a.* *P:* Cracked, daft.

citoyen, -enne, *s.* *C. d'honneur* = Freeman of a city.

civique, *a.* *Centre c.*, civic centre.

clandestin, -ine, *a.* Underground.

classe, *s.f.* **I.** *Nau: Voyager en dernière c.*, to go steerage. **3.** *Mil:* Age-group.

client, -ente, *s.* *C.* (*d'un portraitiste*), sitter.

climatisation [klimatizasjɔ̃], *s.f.* (*Registered Trade Name*) = Air-conditioning.

clip [klip], *s.m.* (*Jewel*) clip.

clouer, *v.tr.* **I.** *Mil: C. au sol*, to pin down.

clouté [klute], *a.* Studded, bradded (shoes).

clown [klun], *s.m.* Clown; buffoon; funny-man.

cocktail [kɔktɛl], *s.m.* (*a*) Cocktail. (*b*) Cocktail-party.

cœur, *s.m.* **I.** (*a*) *F:* *Joli c.*, sissy.

coin-coin [kwɛ̃kwɛ̃], *s.m.* & *int.* (*Of ducks*) Quacking. Quack! quack! *F:* *Aut:* Honk! honk!

collaborateur, -trice, *s.* *Pol:* Collaborationist.

collège, *s.m.* **2.** School. (Revised article.) Secondary grammar school. *C. moderne* = Secondary Modern School. *C. libre*, private (secondary) school.

colonel, *s.m.* *Mil. Av:* Group captain.

colonne, *s.f.* **2.** (*c*) *Pol:* **Cinquième colonne,** fifth column.

combine [kɔ̃bin], *s.f.* Scheme, trick.

commandant. 2. *s.m.* *Mil. Av: C. de groupe*, squadron leader.

commando [kɔmãdo], *s.m.* *Mil:* Commando.

communication, *s.f.* **I.** (*a*) *Faire une c.* (*à une société savante*), to read a paper (to a learned society). *Livre envoyé en c.*, book sent on approval. (In a public library) *C. de livres*, issue. (*b*) *Tp:* Communication urbaine, local call. *W.Tel: Nous vous mettons en c. avec Rome*, we take you over to Rome.

communisant, -e [kɔmynizã, -ãt]. *F:* (*a*) *a.* Communistic. (*b*) *s.* Fellow-traveller.

compagnon, *s.m.* **I.** (*a*) *Pol:* *C. de route*, fellow-traveller.

complet, -ète. I. *a.* (*b*) *excl.* Complet! full up!

concentré, *a.* **3.** *s.m.* Extract. **Concentré de viande,** meat extract. **Concentré de tomate,** tomato sauce.

conduite, *s.f.* **I.** (*b*) *Aut: C. à gauche*, left-hand drive. *Av:* **Conduite intérieure,** enclosed cockpit, closed cabin.

conférence, *s.f.* **I.** *C. de presse*, press conference.

congé, *s.m.* **I.** (*c*) *Ind:* **Congé payé,** holidays with pay.

conseiller², -ère, *s.* **I.** *C. fiscal* = chartered accountant. **2.** *C. général* = county councillor.

consultation, *s.f.* (*b*) "**Consultation externe**" "out-patients' department."

contact, *s.m.* **I.** *Prendre contact avec qn*, to get into touch with s.o., to contact s.o. *Prise de c.*, preliminary conversation.

contacter [kɔ̃takte], *v.tr.* To contact (s.o.).

contingent, *s.m.* **2.** (*b*) Ration, allocation.

contrôle, *s.m.* **3.** (*b*) *Fin:* **Contrôle des changes,** exchange control.

convention, *s.f.* **I.** (*a*) **Convention collective** = collective bargaining.

cordée [kɔrde], *s.f.* *Mountaineering:* Roped (climbing) party. *Premier de cordée*, leader, first on the rope.

cornet, *s.m.* **2.** (*a*) *C. de crème glacée*, ice(-cream) cone.

corps, *s.* *Le c. médical*, the medical profession.

correspondant, -ante. 2. *s.* (*c*) Pen-friend.

coupure, *s.f.* **2.** (*c*) *Coupure* (*de courant*), (electricity) cut.

crawl [krol], *s.m.* *Swim:* Crawl(-stroke).

crayon, *s.m.* **I.** (*a*) *C. à copier, c. à encre* (*indélébile*), indelible pencil. **2.** *C. à lèvres*, lipstick.

crayon-lèvres, *s.m.* Lipstick. *pl. Des crayons-lèvres.*

criminalité [kriminalite], *s.f.* **Criminalité juvénile,** juvenile delinquency.

crise, *s.f.* **I.** *Pol: La c. du logement*, the housing shortage.

croquette [krɔkɛt], *s.f.* *Cu:* Rissole, croquette.

cure, *s.f.* **2.** (*c*) *R.C.Ch:* Presbytery.

cyclomoteur [siklɔmotœːr], *s.m.* Auto-cycle.

débarquement, *s.m. Nav:* Péniche de débarquement, landing-barge.

débrayer, *v.tr.* **3.** *F:* (a) To go on strike. (b) (Of workman) To knock off.

se débrouiller. 2. *Débrouillez-vous!* that's your look-out l *F: Se d. sur le voisin,* to pass the buck.

décade, *s.f.* **1.** Period of ten years.

déchoir, *v.i. Ce serait d.,* it would mean loss of prestige.

découvert, *a. Manège d.,* open-air riding-school.

défense, *s.f.* **1. Défense passive,** Civil Defence, Air Raid Precautions (A.R.P.). *Poste de d. passive,* warden's post. *D. contre avions,* anti-aircraft defence.

déficience [defisjɑ̃:s], *s.f.* Deficiency.

défilé, *s.m.* **2.** *Av: D. (d'avions),* fly-past.

défrichage [defriʃa:ʒ], *s.m.* = défrichement.

dégager, *v.tr.* **2.** (b) *Abs: F: Dégagez, s'il vous plait,* gangway, please ; *Rail:* mind your backs, please. (e) *Arch: D. les vues,* to open vistas.

dégivrage [deʒivra:ʒ], *s.m. Av:* De-icing.

degré, *s.m.* **2.** *Sch:* **Enseignement du second degré,** secondary education.

déjà, *adv.* **3.** *F: Comment s'appelle-t-il déjà?* what's his name again?

délégué, -ée, *a. & s.* (c) *Ind: D. d'usine, du personnel,* shop steward.

délestage [delɛsta:ʒ], *s.m. El:* Load-shedding.

délester, *v.tr.* (c) *El:* To shed the load.

délinquant, -ante, *s. Jur: Un d. primaire,* a first offender.

démaquillage [demakija:ʒ], *s.m. Toil:* **Crème de démaquillage,** cleansing cream.

démarquer, *v.tr.* **1.** (b) *Com:* To mark down (goods).

déminer [demine], *v.tr.* To clear (a field) of mines.

dépistage [depista:ʒ], *s.m.* Tracking-down.

déplacé, *a.* **3.** *Pol.Ec:* **Personnes déplacées,** displaced persons.

derm(at)ite [dɛrm(at)it], *s.f. Med:* Dermatitis.

dérogeant [derɔʒɑ̃], *a.* Derogatory.

diététicien, -enne [djetetisjɛ̃, -jɛn], *s. Diet* etician, nutritionist.

dire. 1. *v.tr.* **4.** (a) *Qu'est-ce que dit le temps* what's the weather like?

dirigé, *a.* Controlled. *Sch: Jeux dirigés,* organised games. **Économie dirigée,** planned economy

dirigisme [diriʒism], *s.m.* (a) *Pol.Ec:* Planning Dirigisme économique, planned economy, planning. (b) Controlled finance.

discutable, *a. Un bienfait d.,* a doubtful blessing

disponibilité, *s.f.* **1.** *Mil: Mettre qn en d.,* tc release s.o.

dissolvant², *s.m.* **Dissolvant (pour ongles),** (nail-varnish) remover.

distance, *s.f. Mil: Gym:* **Prendre ses distances** to dress.

distributeur, -trice. **2.** *s.m. I.C.E: Pièce mobile du d.,* distributor arm ; rotor.

distribution, *s.f. Th: W.Tel:* Characters.

docker [dɔkɛr], *s.m.* Docker.

doigt, *s.m.* **1.** (b) **Doigt de chocolat,** bar o chocolate.

dommage, *s.m.* **2.** *pl.* **Dommages de guerre,** war damage compensation.

donner, *v.tr.* **1.** *Med: D. du sang,* to donate blood. *D. de la vitesse,* to get up speed.

doryphore [dɔrifɔ:r], *s.m. Ent:* Colorado beetle.

double. **1.** *a. Maisons doubles,* semi-detached houses. **2.** *s.m.* (b) *Typewr:* Carbon copy.

drapeau, -eaux, *s.m. Mil:* **Présentation du drapeau** = trooping the colour(s).

dribbler [drible], *s.m. Fb:* To dribble.

dur, *a.* **1.** *F: Const:* **En dur,** in concrete in stone. **5.** *s.m.* *P:* Tough.

E

eau, eaux, *s.f.* **2.** (d) 'Eau de a ville,' 'main water.'

éberluer, *v.tr.* To flabbergast.

échantillon, *s.m. Post:* **Echantillons sans valeur,** sample post, samples of no value.

échelle, *s.f.* **1.** (a) *É. à crochet,* (fireman's) hook-ladder.

échelon, *s.m.* **1.** *A l'é. ministériel,* at ministerial level.

éclaircie, *s.f.* **1.** Fair period.

éclaireur, *s.m.* **1.** (c) *Av: Avion é.,* reconnaissance aircraft.

écoute¹, *s.f. W.Tel:* **Ne quittez pas l'écoute,** don't switch off.

effarant [ɛfarɑ̃], *a.* *F:* Bewildering.

élection, *s.f.* **1.** *Pol:* **É. partielle,** by-election.

électoral, -aux, *a. Agent é.,* electioneering agent.

élevage, *s.m.* **1.** Animal husbandry.

embobiner [ɑ̃bɔbine], *v.tr.* *F:* To coax, wheedle, get round (s.o.) ; to hoodwink (s.o.).

emboîter, *v.tr.* **2.** (c) *F:* **Emboîter le pas à qn,** to follow suit.

embouteillage, *s.m.* **3.** *F:* Traffic-jam.

émetteur-récepteur [emɛtœ:r-resɛptœir], *s.m. W.Tel:* Transmitter-receiver ; *F:* walkie-talkie.

empoussiéré [ɑ̃pusjere], *a.* Covered with dust ; dusty.

encorder [ɑ̃kɔrde], *v.tr.* *Mountaineering:* To rope (climbers) together.

endurance, *s.f.* **2.** Staying-power.

énergie, *s.f.* **2.** (a) **Énergie atomique,** atomic energy. (b) *Ind:* Fuel and power.

enfant, *s.m. & f.* **Enfant difficile,** problem child.

engagement, *s.m.* **2.** (a) Commitment.

s'engager. 2. (c) *Sp:* S'e. pour une course, to enter for a race.

ennuyé [ɑ̃nɥije], *a.* **1.** Annoyed. **2.** Bored. **3.** Worried.

enquêtrice [ɑ̃kɛtris], *s.f. Journ:* Woman interviewer.

entêté, *a.* Wilful, perverse.

entraînant, *a.* Catchy (music).

entrepreneur, -euse, *s.* **Entrepreneur de chargement et de déchargement,** stevedore.

envergure, *s.f. Une offensive d'e.,* a large-scale offensive.

épargne, *s.f.* **I.** *Pol.Ec:* Dépôts d'épargne, savings. Bon d'épargne = national savings certificate.

épilé [epile], *a.* *Sourcils épilés,* plucked eyebrows.

épuisé, *a.* **I.** *El:* Pile épuisée, dead cell.

équipe, *s.* **I 2.** *É. de secours,* rescue squad.

éreinté [erɛ̃te], *a.* *F:* All in.

erreur, *s.f.* *F:* Faire erreur, to be mistaken.

espionnage, *s.m.* *E. et contre-espionnage* = the Secret Service.

esprit, *s.m.* **5.** *Avoir bon e.,* to be well-meaning. *Les esprits sont très montés,* feeling is running very high.

esquimau, -aux, *s.m.* **2.** *F:* Choc-ice. **3.** *Cost:* Child's woolly suit.

établir, *v.tr.* **2.** *Établi d'après,* compiled from.

étatique [etatik], *a.* Under State control.

étatisme, *s.m.* Etatism.

étonnant, *a.* *Vous êtes é.!* You surprise me! **étudier,** *v.tr.* (*a*) *É.* (*son piano*), to practise (on the piano).

évacué, -ée [evakye], *s.* Evacuee.

évasion, *s.f.* **3.** Escapism. *Littérature d'é.,* escapist literature.

exclure, *v.tr.* (*a*) To preclude.

extravagant. **2.** *s.m.* Eccentric, crank.

F

faire, *v.tr.* **I. 3.** (*c*) *P: Tu es fait, mon vieux!* You've had it, chum !

familial, -e, -aux. **2.** *s.f.* Familiale, *Aut:* seven-seater saloon.

fantôme, *s.m.* *Pol: Gouvernement f.,* shadow government.

fauteuil, *s.m.* **I.** *Jur:* *U.S.:* F. électrique, electric chair.

fécondateur, -trice [fekɔ̃datœːr, -tris], *a. & s.* (*a*) *a.* Fertilizing. (*b*) *s.* Fertilizer, fertilizing agent.

femme-agent [famaʒɑ̃], *s.f.* Police woman. *pl. Des femmes-agents.*

fer, *s.m.* **3.** *Tls:* Fer électrique, electric iron.

ferme², *s.f.* **I.** (*b*) Ferme laitière, dairy farm.

ferry(-boat) [feri(bot)], *s.m.* Train-ferry. *pl. Des ferry(-boats).*

fête, *s.f.* **2.** *F. d'aviation,* f. aéronautique, air display, pageant.

feuille, *s.f.* **3.** *F.* de paye, pay-roll.

fil, *s.m.* **I.** (*a*) *Laine trois fils,* three-ply wool. (*b*) *El.E:* Les fils de ligne, the mains.

fichu¹, *a.* **4.** (*b*) *F: Être mal f.,* to be out of sorts, off colour.

fièvre, *s.f.* **2.** Excitement, restlessness.

figue, *s.f.* **I.** *F:* Mi-figue, mi-raisin, wavering.

file, *s.f.* Fumeur de cigarettes à la file, chain-smoker.

filtrant, *a.* **2.** (*a*) Bout f. (*cigarette*), filter-tip.

fin¹, *s.f.* **I.** Fin de semaine, week-end. **2.** (*a*) *À toutes fins utiles,* to all intents and purposes.

fission [fisjɔ̃], *s.f.* Fission. *F. de l'atome,* splitting of the atom, nuclear fission.

flancher, *v.i.* *F:* **2.** (*b*) *J'ai flanché en histoire,* I came a cropper in history.

flèche, *s.f.* **I.** (*b*) *Aut:* F. de direction, trafficator.

fleur, *s.f.* **2.** Avoir les nerfs à fleur de peau, to be on edge.

folie, *s.f.* **I.** La folie des grandeurs, megalomania.

forain, -aine. **2.** *a.* Fête foraine, fun fair.

force, *s.f.* **2.** (*c*) *Mil:* F. d'intervention, task force.

format, *s.m.* (*a*) *F.* standard, standard gauge. (*b*) Appareil de petit f., miniature camera.

fourrure, *s.f.* **2.** *Aut:* F. de frein, brake lining.

fric [frik], *s.m.* *P:* Dough, money.

Frigidaire [friʒidɛːr]. *Pr.n.m.* Refrigerator, Frigidaire (registered trade mark).

fromage, *s.m.* **I.** F. fondu, industriel, processed cheese.

front, *s.m.* **2.** *Mil:* Le front, the front, the front line. Front de mer, water-front. *Pol:* F. populaire, Popular Front.

fumé, *a.* Smoked, smoke-cured. Verres fumés, sun-glasses.

fusil, *s.m.* **3.** (*a*) F. de chasse, shot-gun.

G

galerie, *s.f.* **5.** *Aut:* Roof rack.

garde-bébé, *s.m.* Baby-sitter. *pl. Des garde-bébés.*

gardien, -ienne, *s.* Watchman.

gauche, *a.* **3.** (*d*) *s.f.Pol:* De gauche, left-wing.

gaulois, -oise. **3.** *s.f.* Gauloise, a popular brand of cigarette.

général, -ale, -aux. *Replace present entry by:* **2.** *s.m.* (i) *Mil:* General. G. de brigade, brigadier. G. de division, major-general. G. de corps d'armée, lieutenant-general. (ii) *Av:* G. d'armée aérienne, air chief marshal. G. de brigade aérienne, air commodore. G. de division aérienne, air vice-marshal. G. de corps aérien, air marshal.

génération, *s.f.* **2.** La g. qui monte, the rising generation.

gin [ʒin], *s.m.* Gin.

giration, *s.f.* Carrefour à giration, roundabout.

goûter. **II.** *s.m.* (Afternoon) tea.

gras, grasse, *a.* **I.** (*a*) *Cu:* Matières grasses, fats.

grattement [grat(ə)mɑ̃], *s.m.* Scratching.

grève, *s.f.* **2.** G. perlée, go-slow policy. G. d'avertissement, symbolique, token strike.

guerre, *s.f.* **I.** Guerre totale, total war(fare). *F:* Guerre éclair, blitzkrieg. Guerre froide, cold war. Usine de g., munition factory.

guide¹, *s.m. & f.* **I.** (*c*) *s.f.* Girl guide.

haleine, *s.f.* *Politique de longue h.,* long-term policy.
*haut-de-forme [odfɔrm], *s.m.* Top hat. *pl. Des hauts-de-forme.*
*haut-parleur, *s.m.* Amplifier (in stations, etc.).
herbicide [ɛrbisid], *s.m.* Weed-killer.
heureux, -euse, *a.* I. *H. comme un poisson dans l'eau,* as happy as a sand-boy.

*holà, *int.* 2. Whoa (back) !
homme-grenouille [ɔmgrənu:j], *s.m.* *Nau:* Frogman. *pl. Des hommes-grenouilles.*
*hors-bord, *s.m. inv. in pl. F:* Speedboat. *Moteur h.-b.,* outboard motor.
hôte, hôtesse, *s.* I. *Av:* Hôtesse de l'air, air-hostess.
*housse, *s.f.* I. *(a)* Loose cover.

I

ignorer, *v.tr. Nul n'est censé i. la loi,* ignorance of the law is no excuse.
illusion, *s.f.* I. *Se bercer d'illusions,* to live in a fool's paradise.
îlot, *s.m.* 2. *Chef d'i.,* air-raid warden.
impôt, *s.m. Retenue de l'i. à la base,* pay as you earn.
imprimé, *s.m.* 2. *Tex:* Print.
inadaptation [inadaptasjɔ̃], *s.f.* Maladjustment.
inadapté [inadapte], *a. & s.* Maladjusted. *Les inadaptés,* the social misfits.
inconfort [ɛ̃kɔ̃fɔr], *s.m.* Discomfort.
indemnisation, *s.f.* Compensation.
indétraquable [ɛ̃detrakabl], *a.* Fool-proof (mechanism).
indicatif. 3. *s.m. W.Tel: I. (musical),* signature-tune.
indisponible, *a.* 2. *(b)* (Car, etc.) Out of commission.
industrie-clef, *s.f.* Key-industry. *pl. Des industries-clefs.*

inexploité, *a. Ressources inexploitées,* untapped resources.
infanterie, *s.f.* Infanterie portée, lorry-borne infantry.
infantile, *a. Paralysie i.,* infantile paralysis.
infroissable [ɛ̃frwasabl], *a. Tex:* Creaseless ; uncreasable.
ingénieur, *s.m. Cin: I. du son,* sound engineer. *I. radio,* radio-engineer.
inquisiteur. I. *s.m. (b)* Snooper.
inscrire, *v.tr.* I. *(b) Ind: I. (un employé) à l'arrivée,* to book in (an employee).
intellectuel, -elle, 2. *s.* Professional man, woman.
intendant, *s.m.* I. *(c) Sch:* Bursar.
intime, *a.* 2. Cosy.
inviolable, *a.* Burglar-proof (lock).
Israël. *Pr.n.m. Geog:* Israel.
issue, *s.f.* I. Outcome.

J

jaquette, *s.f. (c)* (Book) jacket.
jardin, *s.m. Jardins ouvriers,* allotments.
jardinier, -ière. 2. *s. Sch:* Jardinière d'enfants, kindergarten mistress. 3. *s.f.* Jardinière, *(d)* Window-box.
jeep [(d)ʒip], *s.f. Aut:* Jeep.
joindre, *v.tr.* I. *(d) Je vous joindrai à . . .,* I shall meet, join, you at. . . .
judiciaire. I. *a. Erreur judiciaire,* miscarriage of justice.

jumeau, -elle. I. *a. & s. (b)* Maisons, villas, jumelles, semi-detached houses.
jumelé, *a.* Maison jumelée, semi-detached house.
jusque, *prep.* 2. *(a) Venez jusqu'ici,* come over here.
justice, *s.f.* I. *Ce n'est que justice,* it is only just. (Of murderer) *Se faire j.,* to commit suicide.

K

kidnapper [kidnape], *v.tr.* To kidnap.
kidnappeur, -euse [kidnapœ:r, -ø:z]. Kidnapper.

klaxonner [klaksɔne], *v.i. Aut:* To hoot.

lampe, *s.f.* **2.** (*a*) *Aut:* L. *de bord, de tablier,* dash-board light. *Lampes-satellites,* side lights.

lance-flammes, *s.m. inv. Mil:* Flame-thrower.

langue, *s.f.* **1.** *Prendre l.,* (i) to establish contact, to start preliminary conversations, (ii) to open up a conversation ; *F:* to break the ice.

leader [lidœr], *s.m.* (*a*) *Pol:* Leader. (*b*) *Journ:* Leader.

liaison, *s.f.* **1.** (*d*) *Mil:* *Faire, effectuer, la l.,* to liaise.

libre, *a.* **2.** (*a*) Libre possession, vacant possession.

licence, *s.f.* **1.** (*a*) *Adm:* L. *d'importation,* import licence.

lieutenant, *s.m. Mil.Av:* Flying officer.

lieutenant-colonel, *s.m. Mil.Av:* Wing commander.

ligne, *s.f.* **1.** (*c*) Garder la ligne, soigner la ligne, to keep one's figure. *F: C'est dans ma l.,* it's in my line, that's right up my street.

linotypiste [linɔtipist], *s.* Linotype operator.

livre², *s.m.* (*a*) L. *à succès, à fort tirage, à forte vente,* best-seller.

local, -aux. 2. *s.m.* (*c*) *Fb:* Les locaux, the home side.

location, *s.f.* (*a*) L. *de voitures sans chauffeur,* self-drive cars for hire.

loisir, *s.m.* Les loisirs, spare-time activities.

lune, *s.f.* **1.** *L'homme de la l.,* the man in the moon.

M

machine, *s.f.* **1.** (*a*) *F: Trois pages de m.,* three typewritten pages.

magasin, *s.m.* **1.** (*a*) Magasin à succursales multiples, chain-stores.

   se maintenir. 2. *St.Exch: Ces actions se maintiennent à . . .,* these shares remain firm at. . . . **3.** *Le temps se maintient au beau,* the weather remains fine.

maison, *s.f.* **3.** *a.* Pâté maison (*on menu*), special pâté of the establishment.

Malaisie. *Pr.n.f.* **2.** *Geog:* La Malaisie (britannique), Malaya.

malle, *s.f.* **1.** (*a*) M. *de tôle,* tin trunk.

malpoli [malpoli], *a. F:* Impolite.

manche¹, *s.f.* **1.** (*b*) *Av:* Manche à air, windsock.

manège, *s.m.* **1.** (*a*) *Maître de manège,* ringmaster (of circus).

maniabilité, *s.f. Av:* Manœuvrability.

manquant. 3. *s.m. Com:* Les manquants, (the) shortages.

manquement, *s.m.* M. *aux devoirs de la profession,* unprofessional conduct.

maquette, *s.f.* (*e*) Scale model.

maquis, *s.m.* Maquis, underground forces.

maquisard [makiza:r], *s.m.* Member of the maquis.

maraîcher, -ère. 1. *a.* (*b*) *Produits maraîchers,* market-garden produce.

marche², *s.f.* **3.** (*b*) Motion. *M. avant,* forward motion.

marché, *s.m.* **1.** (*a*) M. *noir,* black market.

marge, *s.f.* **1.** (*b*) *Typ: Illustrations à marges perdues,* bled-off illustrations.

marine, *s.f.* **5.** *a. F:* Navy-blue, navy. *Un costume m.,* a navy-blue suit.

marmite, *s.f.* **1.** (*a*) M. *sous-pression,* pressure-cooker.

marque¹, *s.f.* **3.** (*e*) *Sp: A vos marques!* (to runners) on the mark, on your marks !

marquer. 1. *v.tr.* (*b*) *Games:* M. *trente points,* to score thirty. *Ne m. aucun point,* to fail to score.

marrant, *a.* **3.** *P:* Odd, strange, queer.

masochisme [mazɔʃism], *s.m. Psy:* Masochism.

match, *s.m. Sp: Row:* M. *d'aviron,* boat-race. *Games:* M. *prévu,* fixture. M. *de championnat* (*professionnel*), league match.

matériel, -elle. 2. *s.m.* Equipment. *Mil: Le service du m.,* ordnance.

matraque, *s.f.* Matraque en caoutchouc, rubber truncheon.

matraquer [matrake], *v.tr.* To bludgeon.

mec [mɛk], *s.m. P:* Fellow, bloke.

médaillon, *s.m.* **1.** (*c*) Pat (of butter).

même. 3. *Adv.phr. Mais tout de m.!* Hang it all !

mer, *s.f.* (*a*) M. *fermée,* inland sea. *M. libre* open sea.

mère-patrie, *s.f.* Mother country.

météo [meteo]. **1.** *s.f. F:* (*a*) Weather report. (*b*) = *Bureau central de météorologie.* **2.** *s.m. F:* Meteorologist (in aircraft, etc.).

météorologie, *s.f. Bureau de m.,* weather bureau.

météorologique, *a. Station m.,* weather-station.

Micheline [miʃlin], *s.f.* = Autorail.

microfilm [mikrɔfilm], *s.m. Phot:* Microfilm.

microfilmer [mikrɔfilme], *v.tr. Phot:* To microfilm.

mille¹. 1. *num. a.inv. & s.m.inv. C'est m. fois dommage,* it's a thousand pities.

mine-piège [minpjɛ:ʒ], *s.f.* Booby-trap.

minimum. 1. *s.m. Pol.Ec:* Minimum vital, minimum living wage.

   se miter [samite]. To become moth-eaten.

mitraillage [mitrɑja:ʒ], *s.m.* Machine-gunning.

mitrailler, *v.tr.* To machine-gun.

mitraillette [mitrɑjɛt], *s.f.* Sub-machine-gun.

mitrailleur, *a. Fusil m.,* Bren-gun.

mobiliser, *v.tr.* Un mobilisé, a serviceman.

modeste, *a. Gens modestes,* people with modest incomes.

moins. 1. *adv.* (*b*) Pour le moins, at (the very) least ; to say the least of it. *F:* Au moins, *Tu as fait ton travail, au m.?* I can take it you have done your work?

monde, *s.m.* **1.** (*b*) Il faut de tout pour faire un monde, it takes all sorts to make a world.

monnaie, *s.f.* **1.** *Pol.Ec:* Monnaie forte, hard currency.

mordu, -e [mɔrdy], *a. F:* Mad. M. *du cinéma,* mad on the cinema.

motoriser [mɔtɔrize], *v.tr.* To motorize.

   se mourir, to die away, die out.

nègre. 1. *s.* (*b*) F: Stooge.
nid, *s.m.* **1.** *Navy:* N. *de sous-marins*, submarine pen.
nippon, -one [nipɔ̃, -ɔn], *a. & s.* Nipponese, Japanese.
noir, -e. 3. *s.m.* (*f*) *Typ:* En noir, Clarendon.
nom, *s.m.* **1.** *Com:* N. *déposé*, registered (trade) name, trade name.

nouilles. 2. (In sg.) *a. & s.f.* P: *C'est une nouille*, he, she, is a drip, has no guts.
numéro, *s.m.* (*a*) *Dernier n., n. du jour, de la semaine*, current issue, number.
nurse [nœrs], *s.f.* Nannie, nanny, (children's) nurse.
nylon [nilɔ̃], *s.m.* *Tex:* Nylon.

O

objecteur [ɔbʒɛktœːr], *s.m.* Objecteur de conscience, conscientious objector.
objet, *s.m.* **1.** (*a*) *Objets trouvés*, lost property
œil, *pl.* **yeux,** *s.m.* **1.** P: Mon œil! My foot!
œuf, *s.m.* **1.** (*a*) O. *en poudre*, dried egg. *Œufs du jour*, new-laid eggs.
office. 1. *s.m.* (*a*) *Gagner d'o.*, to have a walk-over. (*d*) O. *de la main-d'œuvre*, Labour Exchange.
ogive, *s.f.* *Arch:* Voûte d'ogives, ribbed vault.
onde, *s.f.* **3.** *Mettre en ondes*, to produce, put on the air.
ordre, *s.m.* **4.** (*b*) O. *des avocats* = the Bar.
oreille, *s.f.* **1.** *Il commence à m'échauffer les oreilles*, he is beginning to annoy me.
    s'organiser, *v.pr.* To get settled ; to settle down.

orgue, *s.m.* **1.** (*c*) Orgue de cinéma, theatre organ.
orient, *s.m.* **1.** (*b*) Le moyen Orient, the Middle East.
original, -aux, *a. & s.* **1.** *Typewr:* Top copy.
osciller, *v.i.* **1.** To flicker (of speedometer needle).
ouïe, *s.f.* **1.** (*a*) *Être tout o.*, to be all ears, all attention.
ouverture, *s.f.* **2.** (*c*) *Phot:* Aperture. **3.** *Av:* Drop (of parachute). O. *retardée*, delayed drop.
ouvreur, -euse, *s.* *Cin:* Ouvreuse, usherette.
ouvrier, -ère. 2. *a.* (*a*) *Logements ouvriers*, tenement house(s), tenement(s).
oxygéner, *v.tr.* *Haird:* F: To wash in peroxide, to bleach (hair).

P

paillette, *s.f.* **2.** (*b*) *Savon en paillettes*, soap flakes.
Pakistan [pakistɑ̃]. *Pr.n.m. Geog:* Pakistan.
panaché. 3. *s.m.* Shandy(-gaff).
panda [pɑ̃da], *s.m.* Z: Panda.
panne², *s.f.* **2.** P. *d'essence*, failure of engine through shortage of petrol.
papier, *s.m.* **1.** (*a*) P. *beurre, p. parcheminé*, grease-proof paper. (*b*) P. *à calquer*, tracing-paper.
papillotement, *s.m.* **2.** *Televis:* Flicker.
parachutage [paraʃytaːʒ], *s.m.* Parachute landing (of men, supplies) ; parachuting, drop.
parachute, *s.m.* **1.** *Aer:* *Sauter en p.*, to bale out.
parachuter [paraʃyte], *v.tr. & i.* To parachute, to drop by parachute.
parachutiste. 1. *s.m. & f.* Parachutistes, para-troops. **2.** *a.* Parachute.
parc, *s.m.* **2.** P. *d'attractions*, fun fair. P. *pour enfants*, play-pen, nursery pen.
parfum, *s.m.* Flavour (of ice-cream).
parpaing, *s.m.* *Const:* Breeze-block.
partir. 2. *v.i.* (*a*) *Le lait part*, the milk is boiling over. (*b*) *Ces allumettes partent mal*, these matches strike badly.
partout, *adv.* (*a*) *Un peu p.*, all over the place.
passionner, *v.tr.* To interest greatly.

pastis [pastis], *s.m.* Aniseed aperitif.
pâte, *s.f.* **1.** (*a*) *Cu:* P. *lisse, à frire*, batter.
patin, *s.m.* **3.** (*b*) Brake-block.
pause, *s.f.* **1.** *Fb:* Half-time.
peinture, *s.f.* **1.** (*a*) P. *au pistolet*, spray-painting.
pékiné [pekine], *a.* Candy-striped.
péniche, *s.f.* **2.** *Mil:* P. *de débarquement*, landing-craft, -barge.
pénicilline [penisilin], *s.f.* Penicillin.
pépin¹, *s.m.* F: *Avoir un p.*, to strike a snag.
percuter, *v.tr.* (*a*) *L'avion percuta une colline*, the plane crashed into a hill-side. *Abs: L'avion percuta au sol*, the plane crashed into the ground.
périphraser [perifraze], *v.i.* To be long-winded, prolix.
perle, *s.f.* **1.** *Sch:* Gem, howler.
perméable, *a.* **2.** *Mil:* Vulnerable.
petit, -ite, *a.* **2.** (*b*) Feeble, poor, delicate. *Il a une petite santé*, he is always ailing.
peuplier, *s.m.* P. d'Italie, Lombardy poplar.
photostat [fɔtɔstɑ̃], *s.m.* Photostat.
piaule [pjol], *s.f.* P: Digs.
pic¹, *s.m.* **1.** (*a*) P. *pneumatique*, pneumatic drill, pick.
pickpocket [pikpɔkɛ(t)], *s.m.* Pickpocket.
pied, *s.m.* **1.** (*a*) F: *Ça lui fera les pieds*, that will serve him right.
pierre¹, *s.f.* (*a*) *Pierres de gué*, stepping-stones.

pile³, *s.f.* *F:* 'Ça tombe pile, that falls just right.
pilote, *s.m.* **1.** *Av:* Pilote convoyeur, pilote de convoyage, ferry pilot. Pilote automatique, automatic pilot, *F:* George. *P. d'essais,* test pilot.
pipeline [piplin], *s.m.* Pipe-line.
piqué, *a.* **6.** *s.m. Av:* Attaque en p., dive-bombing attack. *Attaquer en p.,* to dive-bomb.
piquet¹, *s.m.* **1.** *(a) Fb: P. de coin,* corner-flag.
piste, *s.f.* **1.** *(a) Aut: P. de vitesse,* racing-track. *(c) Av: P. d'envol,* runway.
plain-pied. **2.** *Adv.phr.* **De plain-pied avec,** flush with ; *F:* on an equal footing with.
plaisantin [plɛzɑ̃tɛ̃], *s.m.* Practical, malicious joker.
planifier [planifje], *v.i.* *Pol.Ec:* To plan.
planque [plɑ̃:k], *s.f.* *P:* *(a)* Hiding-place, hideout. *(b)* Soft job.
plastique. **3.** *s.m. Generally in pl. Ind:* Plastics.
pliable, *a.* Foldable.
pliant. **1.** *a.* *(b) Aut: Capote pliante,* collapsible hood.
plonger. **1.** *v.i.* *(b) Nau: P. raide,* to crash-dive.
poil, *s.m.* **4.** *(c) F:* Mood, temper.
police¹, *s.f.* **2. Appeler Police Secours = to dial 999.** *P. judiciaire =* Criminal Investigation Department, *F:* C.I.D.
pomme, *s.f.* **1.** *(b) Cu: Pommes de terre à l'anglaise* boiled potatoes. *Pommes chips,* potato crisps.
pompiste [pɔ̃pist], *s.m. Aut:* Pump assistant.
pompon, *s.m.* **1.** *F:* Ça, c'est le p.! that's the limit !
pont¹, *s.m.* **2.** *Navy: Tout le monde sur le p.!* clear lower deck !
port¹, *s.m.* **2.** *(a)* "*P. de la libération,*" "Mulberry."

porte-chars [pɔrtəʃa:r], *s.m. inv.in pl. Mil:* Tank transporter.
poser. **2.** *v.tr.* *(b) P. une vitre,* to put in a pane of glass.
possession, *s.f.* **4. Possession de soi-même,** self-control.
poste², *s.m.* **1.** *(c) Rail: P. de signaux, d'aiguillage,* signal-box.
poumon, *s.m.* *P. d'acier,* iron lung.
poutre, *s.f.* **1. Aux poutres apparentes,** half-timbered.
précédent. **2.** *s.m. Jur: Les précédents,* = case-law.
préfabriqué [prefabrike], *a.* Prefabricated.
première, *s.f.* **1.** Head saleswoman.
près. **2.** *Adv.phr.* *(a) Je ne suis pas à cela près,* I haven't come down to that.
presse, *s.f.* **2.** *Publ:* **Service de presse,** publicity (department).
pression, *s.f.* *(a) Graissage sous p.,* pressure greasing.
prêt¹, *a.* **Fin prêt,** absolutely ship-shape.
prêt-bail [prɛbɑ:j], *s.m. no pl. Pol. Ec:* Lease-lend.
se prêter. **1.** *Si le temps s'y prête,* weather permitting.
printing [prɛ̃tɛ̃], *s.m.* *F:* Teleprinter.
prise, *s.f.* **3.** *(a) Mil: P. d'armes,* parade under arms. *(c) Televis: P. de vue directe,* live broadcast.
prolonge, *s.f.* **2. Prolonge d'artillerie,** gun-carriage (at military funeral).
providence, *s.f.* *F:* L'Etat providence, the Welfare State.
psychiatre, *s.m.* Psychiatrist.
punch² [pœnʃ], *s.m. Box:* Punch.
puzzle [pyzl], *s.m.* Jig-saw puzzle.

Q

quadruplé [kwadryple], *s.m.* Quadruplet, *F:* quad. | **quintuplé** [k(y)ɛ̃typle], *s.m.* Quintuplet, *F:* quin.

R

radar [radar], *s.m.* Radar. *R. d'avion,* airborne radar.
radiographier, *v.tr.* To X-ray.
radio-phono [radjofono], *s.m.* Radiogram.
radio-reporter [radjorɔpɔrtɛ:r], *s.m.* *W.Tel:* Commentator. *pl. Des radio-reporters.*
ralenti. **2.** *s.m. Travail au r.,* go-slow policy.
randonneur, -euse [rɑ̃dɔnœ:r, -ø:z], *s.* Excursionist.
rappel, *s.m.* **7.** Suspicion, touch, faint smell.
rapporter, *v.tr.* **3.** *(a) Vous n'auriez pas dû le r.,* you should not have repeated it.
rasoir, *s.m.* *R. électrique,* electric razor, shaver.
rassemblement, *s.m.* **1.** *Mil:* Parade. *Retard au r.,* late on parade.
rayon¹, *s.m.* **2.** *Avion à grand r. d'action,* long-range aircraft.
réacteur [reaktœ:r], *s.m.* **1.** *El.E:* Reactor, choking-coil, *F:* choke. **2.** *Av:* Jet engine.
réaménager [reamenaʒe], *v.tr.* To refit.
recensement, *s.m.* *(a) Mil:* Registration.

recenser, *v.tr.* *(a) Mil:* To register.
reclassement [rəklasmɑ̃], *s.m.* **1.** Fresh classifying ; regrouping. **2.** Rehabilitation ; re-housing. **3.** Regrading (of civil servants, etc.).
récupération, *s.f.* **1.** *(b)* Salvage.
récupérer, *v.tr.* **1.** *(b)* To salve. **2.** To make up.
rééducatif, -ive [reedykatif, -i:v], *a. Thérapie rééducative,* occupational therapy.
rééducation, *s.f. Med:* Rehabilitation.
refonte, *s.f.* **2.** Reconstruction.
réfrigérateur [refriʒeratœ:r], *s.m.* Refrigerator.
régisseur, *s.m. Cin:* Assistant director.
régénérescence [reʒenerɛsɑ̃:s], *s.f. Med: etc:* Rejuvenation.
régulier, -ière, *a.* **1.** *(a)* Valid (passport).
remaniement, remaniment, *s.m.* **2.** *R. ministériel,* Cabinet reshuffle.
rembobiner [rɑ̃bɔbine], *v.tr. Cin: Typewr:* To re-wind (film, ribbon).
rembrayer [rɑ̃breje], *v.tr.* **1.** *Aut:* To let the clutch in again. **2.** *F:* To start work again.

remettre, *v.tr.* **2.** (*a*) To send in.
remonte-pentes [rəmɔ̃:tpɑ̃:t], *s.m.inv. in pl.*
Sp: Ski-lift; ski-train.
rentable [rɑ̃tabl], *a.* Profit-earning.
rentrant, -ante. I. *a.* (*b*) *Av:* Retractable.
II. **rentrer,** *v.tr.* **I.** *Av:* To retract.
repiquer, *v.tr.* **I.** (*d*) *Plant à r.*, bedding plant.
reprendre, *v.tr.* **I.** (*d*) *Reprenons les faits,* let
us recapitulate the facts.
reprise, *s.f.* **2.** (*b*) *Mouvement de r.*, upward
movement. (*d*) *A trois reprises,* three times
running.
reproduction, *s.f.* **I.** (*b*) *Journ:* Droits de r. en
feuilleton, serial rights.
résidentiel, -elle [rezidɑ̃sjɛl], *a.* Residential.
resquillage [rɛskija:ʒ], *s.m.,* **resquille** [rɛski:j],
s.f. F: Wangling.
resquiller [rɛskije], *v.tr. F:* To wangle
resquilleur, -euse, *s.* (*b*) *F:* Wangler.
retardement [rətardmɑ̃], *s.m. Mil:* Action de

r., delaying action. *Bombe à r.*, delayed action
bomb; time bomb.
retour, *s.m.* **2.** *Med:* R. d'âge, change of life
I.C.E: Avoir des retours, to back-fire.
revers, *s.m.* **I.** (*a*) *R. de pantalon,* trouser turn-up
rien. I. *pron. indef. m.* **2.** (*b*) *Pour trois fois rien*
for next to nothing.
rimaye [rimɑ:j], *s.f. Mountaineering:* Berg-
schrund.
ring [ring], *s.m. Box:* Ring.
robe, *s.f.* **I.** (*a*) *R. d'intérieur,* house coat.
II. **ronde,** *s.f.* **I.** (*b*) *Fort: Chemin de r.*,
wall-walk, parapet walk.
rond-point, *s.m.* Roundabout.
roue, *s.f.* (*d*) *N.Arch: Bateau à roue(s),* paddleboat.
roulant. 4. *s.f.* Roulante. *F: Mil:* Field kitchen.
routier^d, -ière, *a. & s.* (*f*) *Gare routière,* bus,
coach station.

S

sabordage [sabɔrda:ʒ], **sabordement,** *s.m.*
Nau: Scuttling.
sac¹, *s.m.* **I.** (*a*) *Sac en bandoulière,* shoulder-bag.
saharien, -ienne [saarjɛ̃, -jɛn]. **I.** *a.* Saharic,
Saharian. **2.** .*f.* Saharienne, bush-shirt.
salle, *s.f.* **I.** *S. de séjour,* living-room.
sanguin, -ine. I. *a.* **I.** Groupe sanguin, blood-
group.
sans-abri [sɑ̃zabri], *s.m.inv.* Homeless (person).
sauvette [sovɛt], *s.f. F:* A la sauvette, on the
run; ready to beat it quick.
scénariste [senarist], *s.m. Cin:* Script-writer.
scout [skut]. (*a*) *s.m.* Boy-scout. (*b*) *a.* Scout, -e,
scout.
secours, *s.m.* Poste de s., first-aid post.
sergent-chef, *s.m. Mil.Av:* Flight sergeant.
serre-livres [sɛrli:vr], *s.m.inv.* Book-ends.
service, *s.m.* **2.** (*b*) Libre service, self-service (at
shop, etc.).
servir. 2. *v.tr.* (*c*) *Tout le monde est servi?* Any
more fares, please?
servitude, *s.f.* **2.** *Jur:* Servitude de passage,
right of way.
short [ʃɔrt], *s.m. Cost:* Shorts.
signal, *s.m. Adm:* Signaux lumineux, traffic lights.

ski, *s.m.* **I.** *Saut à ski,* ski-jump. **3.** *Ski nautique,*
water-skiing.
skier [skie], *v.i.* To ski.
soldat, *s.m.* Serviceman, *Av:* aircraftman. *S. de*
première classe, aircraftman first-class.
sonorisation [sɔnɔrizasjɔ̃], *s.f. Cin:* Scoring.
spécialiste, *s.m. Mil:* etc.: Tradesman.
standard, *s.m.* **2.** Le standard de l'existence, de
vie, the standard of living.
standardiste [stɑ̃dardist], *s.m. & f. Tp:*
Switchboard operator.
star [sta:r], *s.f. Cin:* Star.
station-service [stasjɔ̃sɛrvis], *s.f. Aut:* Service
station; repair station.
stylo, *s.m.* Stylo à bille, ball-point pen.
succès, *s.m.* **2.** Livre à succès, best-seller.
supercarburant [sypɛrkarbyrɑ̃], *s.m.* High-grade
petrol.
super-impôt [sypɛrɛpo], *s.m.* Surtax.
sûreté, *s.f.* **I.** La Sûreté = Scotland Yard.
surréalisme [syrrealism], *s.m.* Surrealism.
sursis, *s.m. Mil:* S. d'appel, deferment (of
call-up). *Mettre en s.,* to defer.
sympathisant, -e [sɛpatizɑ̃, -ɑ̃:t], *s.* Sympathiser.

T

tabac, *s.m.* **2.** (*a*) *F: C'est un pot à t.,* he is a
tubby little man.
table, *s.f.* **I.** (*a*) *T. de malade,* bed-table.
taille, *s.f.* **7.** *Min:* Coal face.
tank [tɑ̃:k], *s.m.* Tank.
tankiste [tɑ̃kist], *s.m.* Member of a tank crew.
taxe, *s.f.* **2.** *T. de luxe* = purchase tax.
télécinéma [telesinema], *s.m.* Telecine.
téléguidage [telegida:ʒ], *s.m.* Radio-control.
téléguider [telegide], *v.tr.* To radio-control.
téléimprimeur [teleɛ̃primœ:r], *s.m.* Teleprinter.

télérécepteur [teleresɛptœ:r], *s.m.* Television
set.
téléscripteur [teleskriptœ:r], *s.m.* Teleprinter.
téléspectateur, -trice [telespɛktatœ:r, -tris],
s. Televiewer, viewer.
téléviseur [televizœ:r], *s.m.* = TÉLÉRÉCEPTEUR.
tenaille, *s.f.* (*b*) *Mil: Manœuvre en tenailles,*
pincer movement.
tenu. I. *a.* (*b*) *Tenu! (d'un pari),* done! (of a
bet).
terre, *s.f.* **I.** (*b*) *Mil: Tactique de la t. brûlée,*
scorched earth policy.

errifiant, *a. Roman t.,* thriller.
tête, *s.f.* **3.** (d) *Mil:* **Tête de pont,** (i) bridge-head, (ii) beach-head.
thé, *s.m.* **I.** (a) *Thé de Ceylan,* Indian tea.
théâtre, *s.m.* **I.** *T. de verdure,* open-air theatre.
thérapie [terapi], *s.f. Med:* Therapy.
toit, *s.m.* **I.** *Aut: T. ouvrant,* sunshine roof.
tomber. **I.** *v.i.* **5.** *Ce livre m'est tombé sous la main,* I came across this book.
tondeur, -euse. **2.** *s.f.* (b) *Tondeuse (de gazon) automobile, à moteur,* motor mower, automower.
topo, *s.m. F:* **I.** (c) Plan.
totalitaire [tɔtalitɛːr], *a.* Totalitarian.
tourelle, *s.f.* (b) *Av: T. de mitrailleuse,* gun-ring; gun-turret.
tournage, *s.m.* **3.** *Cin:* Shooting.
traçant. (b) *Ball: s.m.* **Un traçant,** a tracer-shell. *s.f.* **Une traçante,** a tracer-bullet.
tract [trakt], *s.m.* **I.** Tract. **2.** Leaflet.
traction, *s.f.* (b) *Aut: F:* **Une traction avant,** a car with front-wheel drive.

Trafalgar [trafalgaːr]. *Pr.n.* **I.** *Geog:* Trafalgar. **2.** *F:* **Un coup de Trafalgar,** an unexpected disaster.
train, *s.m.* **I.** (b) *T. supplémentaire,* relief train. **2.** (a) *Sp:* **Mener le train,** to set the pace.
tranche, *s.f.* **I.** *T. napolitaine,* Neapolitan (ice-cream).
transat [trɑ̃zat]. **I.** *s.m.* = TRANSATLANTIQUE. **2.** (a), (b). **2.** *s.f. F:* **La Transat** = La Compagnie Générale Transatlantique.
transmission, *s.f.* **I.** (a) *W.Tel: Antenne de t.,* sending aerial, transmitting aerial. *Mil: Trans-missions* = signals.
transposition, *s.f. Cin:* Dubbing.
travailler. **2.** *v.i.* (a) *P: T. du chapeau,* to have a screw loose.
tribune, *s.f.* **2.** (b) *Sp: T. d'honneur,* grand stand.
trombone, *s.m.* **2.** *F:* Wire paper-clip.
truffer, *v.tr.* **3.** *F: Truffé de balles,* riddled with bullets.

U

un, une. **I.** (a) *F: Il était moins une,* that, it, was as near as dammit.
urbanification [yrbanifikasjɔ̃], *s.f.* Town-planning.
Ursse [yrs]. *Geog: Pr.n.: F:* U.S.S.R.

usuel, -elle, *a.* Everyday. *L'anglais usuel,* everyday English.
utilitaire [ytilitɛːr], *a. & s.m. & f.* Utilitarian. *Aut:* **Véhicules utilitaires,** commercial vehicles.

V

varappe, *s.f. Mountaineering:* **2.** Rock-climbing.
varapper [varape], *s.f. Mountaineering:* To climb a rock face.
vaser [vɑze], *v.i. P:* To do badly (at an examination, etc.).
vaseux, -euse. *a.* **2.** (c) *F: Des idées vaseuses,* woolly ideas.
vedette, *s.f.* **2.** (a) *Navy: V. lance-torpilles,* motor torpedo boat, M.T.B.
vente, *s.f.* **I.** *En v. libre,* for sale unrationed, off the ration. *Mise en v. libre,* derationing.
verglacé [vɛrglase], *a.* **Route verglacée,** icy road.
verrière, *s.f.* **3.** Glass-roof (of a railway station).

verser. **I.** *v.tr.* (e) *Mil:* To draft (dans, into).
Viet-Nam [vjɛtnam]. *Pr.n.m. Geog:* Viet-Nam.
vietnamien, -ienne [vjɛtnamjɛ̃, -jɛn], *a. & s.* Native inhabitant of Viet-Nam.
vilain. **I.** *s.* (e) Trouble. *Il y aura du v.,* there is going to be trouble.
visibilité, *s.f. Av: Vol sans v., vol en P.S.V.* (*pilotage sans v.*), blind flying.
voie¹, *s.f.* **I.** (a) *Grande v. de communication,* main artery, arterial road.
volet, *s.m.* **I.** (a) *F:* **Trié sur le volet,** hand-picked.
vrille, *s.f.* **3.** *Av:* Spin. *V. à plat,* flat spin. *V. serrée,* steep spin.

Y

yodler [jɔdle], *v.i. Mus:* To yodel

Z

zéro, *s.m.* **2. Partir de zéro,** to start from scratch.
zigoto [zigoto], *s.m. P: C'est un drôle de z.,* he is a queer customer. *Faire le z.,* to play the fool.
zone, *s.f.* **I. Zone verte,** green belt.

AR., *Aut : Arrière,* rear.
AV., *Aut : Avant,* front.
C.F.T.C., *Confédération française des travailleurs chrétiens.*
c.u., *Charge utile,* useful load.
D.A.T., *Défense antiaérienne du territoire.*
D.D.T., *Ch : Dichloro-diphenyl-trichloroethane,* D.D.T.
D.P., 1. *Défense passive,* Civil Defence, C.D. **2.** *Personne déplacée,* displaced person.
E.O.R., *Élève officier de Réserve,* cadet.
F.M., 1. *Fusil mitrailleur.* **2.** *Post : Franchise militaire.*
J.E.C., *Jeunesse étudiante catholique.*
J.O.C., *Jeunesse ouvrière catholique.*
O.N.M., *Office national météorologique* = Central Forecasting Office.
O.N.U., *Organisation des nations unies,* United Nations Organisation, U.N.O.

P.C., 3. *Parti communiste français.*
p.m., *Poids mort,* dead weight.
P.M.E., *Préparation Militaire Élémentaire.*
P.M.S., *Préparation Militaire Supérieure* = Senior Training Corps.
P.S.V., *Pilotage sans visibilité.*
R.I., *Mil : Régiment d'Infanterie,* Infantry Regi ment.
R.T.F., *Radiodiffusion et Télévision Françaises.*
S.A.R.L., *Société à responsabilité limitée.*
S.F.F., *Services féminins de la Flotte* = W.R.N.S
S.I., *Syndicat d'initiative.*
S.N.C.F., *Société Nationale des Chemins de fe Français.*
U.N.E.S.C.O., *Organisation des Nations Unie pour l'Éducation, la Science et la Culture,* th United Nations Educational, Scientific and Cul tural Organisation.

MANSION'S SHORTER

FRENCH AND ENGLISH
DICTIONARY

Part Two

PREFACE

THE publication of this volume completes the Shorter French and English Dictionary, and in presenting it to the public the publishers wish to pay a tribute to its late Editor, Mr J. E. Mansion, who, for nearly twenty-five years, devoted his unremitting labour and great intellectual gifts to the compilation first of the Standard French and English Dictionary and later of this Shorter French and English Dictionary—an abridged edition of the parent work. Although he was denied the satisfaction of seeing this last volume in book form, the publishers wish to put on record here that the work is his, the whole of the manuscript having been reviewed and passed by him before his death. The subsequent routine operation of seeing it through to press has been carried out by the staff who worked under him for many years, and whose one consideration has been to produce the volume exactly as he would have had it.

The plan and general arrangement of this Shorter Dictionary remain substantially the same as in the Standard Dictionary, but for the benefit of those who have not access to the larger work the following explanations are given:

(1) Adverbs ending in -ly are entered at the end of the adjectives from which they are formed, and hence are not always in their strict alphabetical position.
E.g., *tardily* is under *tardy*, and not before *tardiness*.

(2) TREATMENT OF VERBS. First the simple verb is dealt with, and then follow in the same paragraph the various compound forms (*give in*, *give up*, etc.), each with its past participle, present participle and gerund (if these require treatment). Then come the past participle and -ing forms of the simple verb, and lastly any hyphenated compounds of the simple verb.
E.g., to **break;** . . . to **break down, break-down,** *s.,* **broken down,** *adj.;* . . . to **break up, break-up,** *s.,* **breaking up; broken,** *adj.,* **-ly,** *adv.,* **broken-backed,** etc.; **breaking,** *s.,* **breaking-point; break-neck.**

Each of these sub-entries is printed in heavy black type to enable the reader's eye to catch the required word with the minimum of difficulty.

(3) Hyphenated words of types other than those illustrated under (2) are entered at the end of the paragraph dealing with the first element, while those compounds written in one word without the hyphen have a separate entry in their correct alphabetical place.
E.g., *duck-pond, duck-shooting*, etc., appear at the end of *duck*, while *duckweed* is entered after *duckling*.

Frequently, the question of hyphen or no hyphen is a moot point, and in these cases the form used in the Shorter Oxford Dictionary has been adopted.

REPRESENTATION OF THE PRONUNCIATION

THE notation adopted in this second part of the Shorter Dictionary is that of th
International Phonetic Association, with the following modifications: the symbol [æ]
replaced by [a]; [o] appears only in the group [ou] or in foreign words; 'obscur
a and o are represented by [*a*], [*o*]; 'mute' r is represented by [r].

The stress is indicated by an accent preceding the stressed syllable: *abbey* ['abi
aberration [abə'reiʃ(ə)n].

TABLE OF PHONETIC SYMBOLS

VOWELS

[iː]	bee, fever, sea, police	[ɔːə]	boar, four
[iːə]	beer, appear, real	[ɔi]	boil, toy, oyster, loyal
[i]	bit, belated, physic	[ou]	low, soap, rope
[e]	bet, menace, leopard, said, bury	[oːu]	chose, clove, hose
[ei]	date, day, nail	[*o*]	obey, indigo, plutocrat
[eːi]	gaze, rave	[u]	put, into, full, frugality
[ɛə]	bear, bare, there, heir, airy	[uː]	shoe, prove, too, frugal
[a]	bat, add	[uə]	poor, sure, tour, boorish
[ai]	aisle, height, life, fly, type	[ʌ]	cut, sun, son, some, cover, rough
[aːi]	exercise, chives	[ər]	supper, martyrdom, sugar
[ɑː]	art, car, ask	[əːr]	burn, learn, herb, whirl, myrrh
[au]	fowl, house, bough	[ə]	rodent, guttural, treacherous
[*a*]	abet, sofa, Sophia	[y]	
[o]	lot, was, what	[ø]	In foreign words as in Part I
[ɔː]	all, haul, short, saw	[œ]	

CONSONANTS

[p]	pat, tap	[ʃ]	sham, dish, issue, ocean, natio
[b]	bat, tab		machine
[m]	mat, ram, prism	[tʃ]	chat, search, chisel, thatch, rich
[f]	fat, laugh, ruff, rough, elephant	[ʒ]	pleasure, azure, vision
[v]	vat, avail, rave	[dʒ]	rage, edge, verger, pigeon, jet, digi
[t]	tap, pat, patter, trap		spinach
[d]	dab, bad, build	[k]	cat, ache, pique, kitten
[n]	nab, ban, banner, pancake	[ks]	except, exercise, expect
[nj]	pinion, onion	[kʃ]	action, eviction
[s]	sat, scene, mouse, psychology	[g]	go, ghost, guard, again, egg
[θ]	thatch, ether, faith, breath	[gz]	exist, exact
[z]	zinc, buzz, houses	[h]	hat, cohere
[dz]	adze, adds	[χ]	loch, pibroch
[ð]	that, the, mother, breathe	[ŋ]	bang, sing, link, anchor
[l]	lad, all, table, chisel	[ŋg]	anger, finger, English
[lj]	bullion, pillion	[r]	rat, arise, barring
		[r]	(Not sounded in southern Englis
			furnish, varnish, born, finge
			(sounded when final and carri
			on to the next word, as in) fing
			in the pie.

SEMI-CONSONANTS

[j]	yam, yet, beauty, pure, duration, picture	[w]	wall, well, await
[hj]	hew, hue, huge	[hw]	what, awhile

iv

ABBREVIATIONS

a. — Adjective
A: — Archaism; ancient; in former use
Abs. — Absolutely
Ac: — Acoustics
acc. — Accusative
adj. — Adjective; adjectival
Adm: — Administration
adv. — Adverb; adverbial
Aer: — Aeronautics
Agr: — Agriculture
Alg: — Algebra
Amph: — Amphibia
Anat: — Anatomy
Ann: — Annelida
Ant: — Antiquity, -ies
Anthr: — Anthropology
Ap: — Apiculture
Ar: — Arithmetic
Arach: — Arachnida
Arb: — Arboriculture
Arch: — Architecture
Archeol: — Archeology
Artil: — Artillery
Astr: — Astronomy
Astrol: — Astrology
attrib. — Attributive
Aut: — Automobilism
aux. — Auxiliary
Av: — Aviation

B: — Biblical; Bible
Bac: — Bacteriology
Ball: — Ballistics
Bank: — Banking
Bill: — Billiards
Bio-Ch: — Bio-Chemistry
Biol: — Biology
Bookb: — Bookbinding
Book-k: — Book-keeping
Bootm: — Bootmaking
Bot: — Botany
Box: — Boxing
Breed: — Breeding
Brew: — Brewing
Brickm: — Brickmaking

Carp: — Carpentry
Cer: — Ceramics
Ch: — Chemistry
Chr: — Chronology
Cin: — Cinematography
Civ: — Civilization
Civ.E: — Civil Engineering
Cl: — Classical
Clockm: — Clock and watch making
Coel: — Coelenterata
cogn.acc. — Cognate accusative
Coll. — Collective
Com: — Commerce
comb.fm — Combining form
comp. — Comparative
Conch: — Conchology
condit. — Conditional
conj. — Conjunction
Conj. like — Conjugated like
Const: — Construction

Coop: — Cooperage
Corr: — Correspondence
Cost: — Costume
Cr: — Cricket
Crust: — Crustacea
Cryst: — Crystallography
Cu: — Culinary; cuisine
Cust: — Customs
Cy: — Cycles; cycling

Danc: — Dancing
dat. — Dative
def. — (i) Definite; (ii) defective
dem. — Demonstrative
Dent: — Dentistry
Dial: — Dialectal
Dipl: — Diplomacy
Dist: — Distilling
Dom.Ec: — Domestic Economy
Draw: — Drawing
Dressm: — Dressmaking
Dy: — Dyeing

Ecc: — Ecclesiastical
Echin: — Echinodermata
El: — Electricity
El.-Ch: — Electro-Chemistry
El.E: — Electrical Engineering
Eng. — English; England
Engr: — Engraving
Ent: — Entomology
Equit: — Equitation
esp. — Especially
Ethn: — Ethnology
excl. — Exclamation; exclamative
Exp: — Explosives

f. — Feminine
F: — Familiar
Farr: — Farriery
Fb: — Football
Fenc: — Fencing
Fin: — Finance
Fish: — Fishing
For: — Forestry
Fort: — Fortification
Fr. — French; France
fu. — Future
Fung: — Fungi
Furn: — Furniture

Gasm: — Gasmaking
Geog: — Geography
Geol: — Geology
Geom: — Geometry
Glassm: — Glassmaking
Gr. — Greek
Gr.Alph: — Greek Alphabet
Gram: — Grammar
Gym: — Gymnastics

Hairdr: — Hairdressing
Harn: — Harness
Hatm: — Hatmaking
Her: — Heraldry

Hist: — History; historical
Hort: — Horticulture
Hum: — Humorous
Husb: — Husbandry
Hyd: — Hydraulics; hydrostatics
Hyg: — Hygiene

i. — Intransitive
I.C.E: — Internal Combustion Engines
Ich: — Ichthyology
imp. — Imperative
impers. — Impersonal
ind. — Indicative
Ind: — Industry
indef. — Indefinite
ind.tr. — Indirectly transitive
inf. — Infinitive
Ins: — Insurance
int. — Interjection
interr. — Interrogative
inv. — Invariable
Iron: — Ironical(ly)

Jew. — Jewish
Join: — Joinery
Journ: — Journalism
Jur: — Jurisprudence; law

Lap: — Lapidary Arts
Laund: — Laundering
Leath: — Leatherwork
Ling: — Linguistics
Lit: — Literary use; literature; literary
Lith: — Lithography
Locksm: — Locksmithery
Log: — Logic
Lt. — Latin

m. — Masculine
Magn: — Magnetism
Mapm: — Mapmaking
Mch: — Machines; steam engines
Meas: — Weights and measures
Mec: — Mechanics
Mec.E: — Mechanical Engineering
Med: — Medicine; medical
Mediev: — Medieval
Metall: — Metallurgy
Metalw: — Metalworking
Meteor: — Meteorology
Mil: — Military
Mill: — Milling
Min: — Mining and quarrying
Miner: — Mineralogy
M.Ins: — Maritime Insurance
Moll: — Molluscs
Mth: — Mathematics
Mus: — Music
Myr: — Myriapoda
Myth: — Myth and legend, mythology

N.Arch:	Naval Architecture	pref.	Prefix	sub.	Subjunctive
Nat.Hist:	Natural History	prep.	Preposition; prepo-	suff.	Suffix
Nau:	Nautical		sitional	Sug.-R:	Sugar-Refining
Needlew:	Needlewor	Pr.n.	Proper name	sup.	Superlative
neg.	Negative	pron.	Pronoun	Surg:	Surgery
neut.	Neuter	Pros:	Prosody	Surv:	Surveying
nom.	Nominative	Prot:	Protozoa	Swim:	Swimming
Num:	Numismatics	Prov:	Proverb		
num.a.	Numeral adjective	pr.p.	Present participle	Tail:	Tailoring
		Psy:	Psychology	Tan:	Tanning
Obst:	Obstetrics	p.t.	Past tense	Tchn:	Technical
Oc:	Oceanography	Publ:	Publishing	Televis:	Television
occ.	Occasionally	Pyr:	Pyrotechnics	Ten:	(i) Tennis; (ii) lawn
Opt:	Optics				tennis
Orn:	Ornithology	qch.	Quelque chose	Tex:	Textile.
Ost:	Ostreiculture	qn	Quelqu'un	Tg:	Telegraphy
				Th:	Theatre
P:	Popular; slang	Rac:	Racing	Theol:	Theology
Paint:	Painting trade	Rad.-A:	Radio-Activity	thg	Thing
Pal:	Paleography	Rail:	Railways	Tls:	Tools
Paleont:	Paleontology	R.C.Ch:	Roman Catholic	Toil:	Toilet
Paperm:	Papermaking		Church	Tp:	Telephony
Parl:	Parliament	rel.	Relative	tr.	Transitive
Pej:	Pejorative	Rel:	Religion(s)	Trig:	Trigonometry
perf.	Perfect	Rel.H:	Religious History	Typ:	Typography
pers.	Person; personal	Rept:	Reptilia	Typewr:	Typewriting
Ph:	Physics	Rh:	Rhetoric		
Pharm:	Pharmacy	Rom.	Roman	U.S:	United States
Phil:	Philosophy	Ropem:	Ropemaking	usu.	Usually
Phot:	Photography	Row:	Rowing		
Phot.Engr:	Photo-Engraving;			v.	Verb
	process work	s., sb.	Substantive	V:	Vulgar
phr.	Phrase	S.a.	See also	Veh:	Vehicles
Physiol:	Physiology	Sch:	Schools and univer-	Ven:	Venery
Pisc:	Pisciculture		sities	Vet:	Veterinary science
pl.	Plural	Scot:	Scottish	Vit:	Viticulture
Plumb:	Plumbing	Sculp:	Sculpture		
P.N:	Public notices	Ser:	Sericulture	Wine-m:	Wine-making
Poet:	Poetical	sg.	Singular	Wr:	Wrestling
Pol:	Politics	Sm.a:	Small arms	W.Tel:	Wireless Telephony
Pol.Ec:	Political Economy	s.o.	Someone		and Telegraphy
poss.	Possessive	Soapm:	Soapmaking	W.Tg:	Wireless Telegraph
Post:	Postal Service	Sp:	Sport	W.Tp:	Wireless Telephony
p.p.	Past participle	Spong:	Sponges		
pr.	(i) Present; (ii) pro-	St.Exch:	Stock Exchange	Y:	Yachting
	nominal	sth.	Something		
pred.	Predicate; predica-	Stonew:	Stoneworking	Z:	Zoology
	tive				

The symbol = is used to indicate a correspondence between French and English institutions, when the terms thus brought together cannot be considered strictly as translations one of the other. Thus *Regimental sergeant-major* = adjudant chef.

SHORTER
FRENCH AND ENGLISH DICTIONARY

PART TWO
ENGLISH—FRENCH

A

A, a¹ [ei]. **1.** (La lettre) A, a *m*. *It is spelt with two a's*, cela s'écrit avec deux a. *F:* Not to know A from B, être absolument nul. **A1** [ei'wʌn], (i) *Nau:* A1 (*at Lloyd's*), de première cote (au Lloyd); (ii) *F:* de première qualité; de premier ordre. **2.** *Mus:* La *m*. *In A flat*, en la bémol. **a²**, *before a word beginning with a vowel* an [*stressed* ei,'an; *unstressed* ə, ən], *indef. art.* **1.** Un, une. *A man*, un homme. *A history*, une histoire. *A unit*, une unité. *A man and* (*a*) *woman*, un homme et une femme. *A wife and mother*, une épouse et mère. **2.** (*Def. art. in Fr.*) (*a*) *To have a big mouth*, avoir la bouche grande. (*b*) *To have a taste, a contempt, for sth.*, avoir le goût, le dédain, de qch. *A fine excuse indeed!* la belle excuse! (*c*) (*Generalizing use*) *A woman takes life too seriously*, les femmes prennent la vie trop au sérieux. **3.** (*Distributive use*) (*a*) *Apples at fivepence a pound*, pommes à cinq pence la livre. *Five francs a head*, cinq francs par tête. (*b*) (*Time*) *Three times a week, a month, a year*, trois fois par semaine, par mois, par an, *occ.* trois fois l'an. **4.** (*a*) (= *A certain, a particular*) *I know a Doctor Smith*, je connais un certain docteur Smith. (*b*) (= *The same; with 'at', 'of'*) *To eat two at a time*, en manger deux à la fois. *To come in two at a time*, entrer deux par deux. **To be of a size,** être de la même grandeur, de (la) même taille. (*c*) (= *A single*) *I haven't understood a word*, je n'ai pas compris un seul mot. **5.** (*Omitted in Fr.*) (*a*) (*Before unqualified pred. nouns*) *He is an Englishman*, *a father*, il est Anglais; il est père. *He was a barrister*, il était avocat. (*But* C'est un Anglais de passage.) (*b*) (*Before nouns in apposition*) *Caen, a large town in Normandy*, Caen, grande ville de Normandie. (*c*) (*In many verb-phrases*) *To put an end to sth.*, mettre fin à qch. *To make a fortune*, faire fortune. (*d*) *What a man!* quel homme! *What a pity!* quel dommage! (*e*) *In a cab*, en fiacre. *To live like a prince*, vivre en prince. *To sell sth. at a loss*, vendre qch. à perte. *Within a short time*, à bref délai.

aback [a'bak], *adv.* (*a*) *Nau:* (Voile) masquée, coiffée. (*Of ship*) **To be aback,** avoir le vent dessus. **To be caught aback, taken aback,** être pris devant, vent dessus; être masqué; faire chapelle. (*b*) *F:* **To be taken aback,** être, rester, déconcerté, interdit; se déconcerter.

abacus, *pl.* **-ci** ['abakəs, -sai], *s.* **1.** *Mth:* Boulier compteur *m*, abaque *m*. **2.** *Arch:* Abaque, tailloir *m*.

abaft [a'bɑːft]. *Nau:* **1.** *adv.* Sur l'arrière; vers l'arrière. **2.** *prep.* **Abaft the mast,** sur l'arrière du mât.

abandon¹ [a'bandən, abã'dɔ̃], *s.* (*a*) Abandon *m*; laisser-aller *m*. (*b*) Entrain *m*.

abandon² [a'bandən], *v.tr.* Abandonner; délaisser (sa famille, etc.); renoncer à (un plan, des poursuites). *Nau:* **To abandon ship,** abandonner, évacuer, le bâtiment. *To a. oneself to despair*, s'abandonner, se livrer, se laisser aller, au désespoir. **abandoned,** *a.* Dévergondé; dépravé.

abandonment [a'bandənmənt], *s.* Abandon *m*, abandonnement *m* (de qn, de qch.).

abase [a'beis], *v.tr.* Abaisser, *F:* ravaler (qn). *To a. oneself*, s'abaisser, s'humilier.

abasement [a'beismənt], *s.* Abaissement *m*. **1.** *F:* Ravalement *m*; humiliation *f*. **2.** Humilité *f*.

abash [a'baʃ], *v.tr.* Confondre, interloquer, décontenancer, déconcerter, interdire. *To be abashed at sth.*, être confus de qch. *Nothing can a. him*, *F:* rien ne le démonte.

abashment [a'baʃmənt], *s.* Confusion *f*, embarras *m* (de qn).

abate [a'beit]. **1.** *v.tr.* Diminuer (l'orgueil, le zèle); affaiblir (le courage); relâcher, ralentir (son activité); diminuer, faire cesser (la douleur, le bruit, etc.). **2.** *v.i.* (*Of storm, courage*) Diminuer, faiblir, s'affaiblir; (*of storm, fear, pain*) se calmer, s'apaiser; se modérer; (*of flood*) baisser, diminuer. *The wind abated*, le vent tomba.

abatement [a'beitmənt], *s.* **1.** Diminution *f*, affaiblissement *m*; apaisement *m* (de la tempête); relâchement *m* (du temps); baisse *f* (des eaux). **2.** *Com:* Rabais *m*, remise *f* (sur le prix).

abbacy ['abəsi], *s.* **1.** Dignité *f* d'abbé. **2.** Abbaye *f*, bénéfice *m*.

abbess ['abes], *s.f.* Abbesse; supérieure (de couvent); mère abbesse.

abbey ['abi], *s.* **1.** Abbaye *f*. **2.** Église abbatiale.

abbot ['abət], *s.m.* Abbé (d'un monastère); (père) supérieur.

abbreviate [a'briːvieit], *v.tr.* Abréger.

abbreviation [abriːvi'eiʃ(ə)n], *s.* Abréviation *f*.

ABC, abc [eibiː'siː]. **1.** ABC, abc *m*. *F:* **To be only at the ABC,** en être encore aux rudiments. *Rail:* **The ABC (guide),** l'indicateur alphabétique. *S.a.* SIMPLE **1**. **2.** *s. Sch:* Abécédaire *m*.

abdicate ['abdikeit], *v.tr.* **1.** Abdiquer (un trône); se démettre d'(une charge); renoncer à (un droit). **2.** *Abs.* Abdiquer; résigner le pouvoir.

abdication [abdi'keiʃ(ə)n], *s.* Abdication *f*; renonciation *f*; démission *f*.

abdomen [ab'doumen, 'abdomen], *s.* Abdomen *m*.

abdominal [ab'dɔminəl], *a.* Abdominal, -aux.

abduct [ab'dʌkt], *v.tr. Jur:* Enlever (qn).

abduction [ab'dʌkʃ(ə)n], *s. Jur:* Enlèvement *m* (de qn). *A. by force*, rapt *m*.

abductor [ab'dʌktər], s. Jur: Ravisseur m; auteur m de l'enlèvement.

abeam [a'bi:m], adv. Nau: Par le travers; en belle.

abed [a'bed], adv. Au lit; couché. To lie (late) a., faire la grasse matinée.

aberration [abə'reiʃ(ə)n], s. **1.** Aberration f, déviation f. **2.** (a) Égarement m (des passions, etc.). Mental aberration, égarement d'esprit; aberration; Jur: démence f. (b) Écart m (de conduite). **3.** Astr: Mth: Opt: Aberration. **4.** Biol: Structure anormale; anomalie f.

abet [a'bet], v.tr. (abetted) **1.** To abet s.o. in a crime, encourager qn à un crime. Jur: To aid and abet s.o., être le complice, le fauteur, de qn. **2.** Encourager (un vice, le crime). **abetting,** s. (Aiding and) abetting, complicité f.

abettor [a'betər], s. A. of a crime, complice mf, fauteur, -trice, d'un crime.

abeyance [a'be(i)əns], s. Suspension f (d'une loi); vacance f (de droits); vacance f (d'un poste). The matter is still in a., la question est toujours pendante, en suspens. Law in a., loi inappliquée.

abhor [ab'hɔːr], v.tr. (abhorred) Abhorrer; avoir horreur de; avoir (qn, qch.) en horreur.

abhorrence [ab'hɔrəns], s. Horreur f (of, de); extrême aversion f (of, poːr, de).

abhorrent [ab'hɔrənt], a. **1.** (Of pers., thg) To be abhorrent to s.o., être répugnant, en horreur, à qn. **2.** (Of thg) Abhorrent to, from, sth., contraire à qch.; incompatible avec qch.

abide [a'baid], v. (p.t. abided, abode [a'boud]; p.p. abided, abode) **1.** v.i. (a) A. & Lit: Rester, demeurer. To a. at, in, a place, séjourner dans un lieu; habiter un lieu. (b) To abide by a promise, rester fidèle à, tenir, une promesse. To a. by a resolve, maintenir une résolution. I a. by what I said, je maintiens mon dire. (c) (Of thg) Durer, subsister, demeurer. **2.** v.tr. (a) To abide the test, subir l'épreuve. (b) Attendre. I a. my time, j'attends l'occasion. (c) (Neg. and interr.) I can't a. him, je ne peux pas le sentir. **abiding,** a. Permanent, durable.

abigail ['abigeil], s.f. Suivante, soubrette.

ability [a'biliti], s. **1.** (a) Capacité f, pouvoir m (to do sth., de faire qch.). (b) Jur: Habilité f (à succéder, etc.); capacité légale. **2.** Habileté, capacité, intelligence f. To do sth. to the best of one's ability, faire qch. dans la mesure de ses moyens; faire qch. de son mieux.

abject ['abdʒekt], a. **1.** Abject, misérable. To live in a. poverty, F: ramper dans la misère. **2.** (a) Bas, vil. (b) Servile. **-ly,** adv. Abjectement. **1.** Misérablement. **2.** Bassement.

abjection [ab'dʒekʃ(ə)n], s. Abjection f, misère f.

abjuration [abdʒu'reiʃ(ə)n], s. Abjuration f.

abjure [ab'dʒuər], v.tr. Abjurer (sa foi, ses erreurs); renier (sa religion); renoncer (sous serment) à (ses droits).

ablative ['ablətiv], a. & s. Gram: Ablatif (m). In the a., à l'ablatif. A. absolute, ablatif absolu.

ablaut ['aplaut], s. Ling: Apophonie f.

ablaze [a'bleːiz], adv. & pred.a. En feu; en flammes; enflammé, embrasé. To be a., flamber. A. with light, resplendissant de lumière. A. with anger, enflammé de colère.

able ['eibl], a. **1.** (a) Capable, compétent, habile. A very a. man, un homme de haute capacité. Jur: Able in body and mind, sain de corps et d'esprit. S.a. SEAMAN **1.** (b) To be able to do sth., (i) savoir, être capable de, faire qch.; (ii) (as infinitive to the vb. CAN) pouvoir, être à même de, être en état de, faire qch. I shall not be a. to come,

je ne pourrai pas venir. Better a. to do sth., plus capable, mieux à même, de faire qch. A. to pay, en mesure de payer. (c) Jur: Able to devise property, to inherit, apte, habile, à léguer, à succéder. **2.** A. piece of work, œuvre de talent; travail bien fait. **ably,** adv. Habilement; avec maîtrise. **able-'bodied,** a. Fort, robuste, vigoureux. Mil: (i) Valide; (ii) bon pour le service. S.a. SEAMAN.

abloom [a'blu:m], adv. & pred.a. En fleur(s).

ablution [ab'luːʃ(ə)n], s. Ablution f.

abnegation [abne'geiʃ(ə)n], s. **1.** Abnégation f; renoncement m, renonciation f. **2.** Désaveu m, reniement m (d'une doctrine, etc.).

abnormal [ab'nɔːrməl], a. Anormal, -aux. **-ally,** adv. Anormalement.

abnormalism [ab'nɔːrməlizm], **abnormality** [abnɔːr'maliti], s. **1.** Caractère anormal (de qch.); anomalie f. **2.** (a) Difformité f. (b) Bizarrerie f.

abnormity [ab'nɔːrmiti], s. **1.** = ABNORMALITY. **2.** (a) Monstruosité f. (b) Monstre m.

aboard [a'bɔːrd]. **1.** adv. A bord. To go aboard, aller, monter, à bord; s'embarquer. All aboard! embarquez! **2.** prep. Aboard (a) ship, à bord d'un navire.

abode¹ [a'boud], s. **1.** Demeure f, habitation f, résidence f. **2.** (Lieu m de) séjour m. To take up one's abode in the country, s'installer à la campagne. Jur: Place of abode, domicile m. Of, with, no fixed abode, sans domicile fixe.

abode². See ABIDE.

abolish [a'bɔliʃ], v.tr. Abolir, supprimer.

abolishment [a'bɔliʃmənt], **abolition** [abo'liʃ(ə)n], s. Abolissement m, abolition f; suppression f.

abolitionist [abo'liʃənist], s. & a. Hist: Abolition(n)iste mf, antiesclavagiste mf.

abominable [a'bɔminəbl], a. Abominable; odieux. **-ably,** adv. Abominablement.

abominate [a'bɔmineit], v.tr. Abominer; avoir (qch.) en abomination, en horreur. To a. doing sth., détester faire qch.

abomination [abɔmi'neiʃ(ə)n], s. Abomination f.

aboriginal [abo'ridʒinəl]. **1.** a. (a) Primitif. (b) Indigène, aborigène. **2.** s. Aborigène m, indigène m.

aborigines [abo'ridʒiniːz], s.pl. Aborigènes m, indigènes m.

abortion [a'bɔːrʃ(ə)n], s. **1.** (Miscarriage) Avortement m, esp. avortement provoqué. **2.** F: (a) (Dwarfed creature) Avorton m. (b) Œuvre mal venue.

abortive [a'bɔːrtiv]. **1.** a. & s. Abortif (m). **2.** a. (Of plan, etc.) Avorté, mort-né, manqué. (Of plan) To prove abortive, ne pas aboutir; n'aboutir à rien; échouer, avorter.

abound [a'baund], v.i. Abonder (in, with, en); foisonner. **abounding,** a. Abondant.

about [a'baut], adv. & prep. **1.** (a) Autour (de). The hills (round) a. the town, les collines autour de la ville. About us, les gens autour de nous, qui nous entourent. He went a long way a., il fit un long détour. (b) De côté et d'autre. To stroll a., se promener de ci, de là. Don't leave those papers lying a., ne laissez pas traîner ces papiers. About here, par ici, dans ces parages. To walk a. the streets, marcher dans, par, les rues. He is about again, il est de nouveau sur pied. (c) There was a look of kindness a. his face, il y avait sur sa figure un air de bonté. There is something uncommon a. him, il y a dans sa personne quelque chose de pas ordinaire. There's something about a horse that . . ., il y a chez

le cheval un je ne sais quoi qui. . . . *(d) To do sth.* turn (and turn) about, faire qch. à tour de rôle, tour à tour. *S.a.* DAY I, TURN[1] 4. **2. To turn sth.** about, retourner qch. **To turn about,** faire demi-tour; se retourner qch. *Mil:* **About turn!** about face! demi-tour! *S.a.* RIGHT-ABOUT. *Nau:* **Ready about!** paré à virer! *S.a.* GO ABOUT I, PUT ABOUT 3, TACK[2] 2. **3.** Environ, presque. *There are a.* thirty, il y en a environ trente; il y en a une trentaine. *A. as big, a.* peu près aussi grand. *That's about right,* c'est à peu près cela. *It is about time,* (i) il est presque temps; (ii) *Iron:* il est grand temps! *He came a.* three o'clock, il est venu vers trois heures, sur les trois heures. *A. midday, a.* one o'clock, sur les midi, sur les une heure. **4.** Au sujet de. *To quarrel a.* nothing, se quereller à propos de rien. *Much ado about nothing,* beaucoup de bruit pour rien. *About that,* là-dessus, à ce sujet, à cet égard. *About what? what about?* à quel sujet? à quel propos? *What is it all about?* de quoi s'agit-il? *To speak a. sth.,* parler de qch. *To be uneasy a. s.o.,* être inquiet à l'égard, sur le compte, de qn. *F: What a. my bath?* et mon bain? *How about a game of bridge?* si on faisait un bridge? **5.** (a) **To be about to do sth.,** être sur le point de, près de, faire qch. *What were you a. to say?* qu'est-ce que vous alliez dire? *(b)* **To go about one's task,** faire sa besogne. *This is how I go a. it,* voici comment je m'y prends. *To know what one is a.,* savoir, connaître, son affaire. *What are you a.?* qu'est-ce que vous faites là? *Mind what you are a.!* faites attention! *You haven't been long a. it,* il ne vous a pas fallu longtemps (pour le faire). *While you are a. it,* pendant que vous y êtes. *To send s.o. a. his business,* envoyer promener qn.
above [a'bʌv], *adv. & prep.* **I.** Au-dessus (de). *(a) The water reached a. their knees,* l'eau leur montait jusqu'au-dessus des genoux. *(b) To hover a. the town,* planer au-dessus de la ville. *The tenants of the flat a.,* les locataires du dessus. **A voice from above,** une voix d'en haut. **The Powers above,** les puissances célestes. *(c) A mountain rises a. the lake,* une montagne s'élève au-dessus du lac, domine le lac. *His voice was heard a. the din,* on entendait sa voix par-dessus le tumulte. *The Seine basin a. Paris,* le bassin de la Seine à l'amont de Paris. *(d) He is a. me in rank,* il est mon supérieur hiérarchique. *Brought up a. his station,* élevé au-dessus de sa condition. *You must show yourself a. prejudice,* il faut vous montrer supérieur aux préjugés. **To live above one's means,** vivre au delà de ses moyens. *A. criticism,* hors de l'atteinte de la critique. *S.a.* LAW 2. **Above all** . ., surtout . . ., sur toutes choses . . ., (surtout et) avant tout . . ., par-dessus tout. . . . **2.** *(In book)* Ci-dessus. *See the paragraph a.,* voir le paragraphe ci-dessus. **As above,** comme ci-dessus. **3.** *(Of pers.)* To be a. *(all)* suspicion, être au-dessus de tout soupçon. *I am a. doing that,* je me respecte trop pour faire cela; je dédaigne de faire cela. *He is a. telling a lie,* il ne saurait s'abaisser jusqu'à mentir. **4.** *(a) A. twenty,* plus de vingt. *(b) He can trace his descent a. four hundred years,* il fait remonter sa descendance au delà de quatre cents ans. **a′bove-board. I.** *adv. To play fair and a.-b.,* jouer cartes sur table; agir ouvertement, loyalement. **2.** *Pred.a.* Loyal; franc, franche. *His conduct was a.-b.,* sa conduite a été franche et ouverte. **a′bove-ground,** *a.* Au-dessus de terre; superficiel. **a′bove-′mentioned, a′bove-′named,** *a.* Sus-mentionné, susnommé, susdit; mentionné ci-dessus.

abrade [a'breid], *v.tr.* User (qch.) par le frottement, par abrasion; écorcher (la peau, etc.).
abrasion [a'breiʒ(ə)n], *s.* **I.** (Usure par le) frottement *m.* **2.** *Med:* Écorchure *f,* éraflure *f.*
abrasive [a'breisiv], *a. & s.* Abrasif *(m).*
abreast [a'brest], *adv.* De front; sur la même ligne. *Navy:* **Line abreast,** en ligne de front. **To come abreast of a car,** arriver à la hauteur d'une voiture. *(b) (Of pers.) To walk a.,* marcher côte à côte. **To march two abreast,** marcher par deux. **To be abreast with, of, the times,** être de son temps; être à la hauteur des idées actuelles; *F:* être à la page.
abridge [a'bridʒ], *v.tr.* **I.** Abréger. **Abridged edition,** édition réduite. **2.** Diminuer, restreindre, retrancher (l'autorité, les droits, de qn).
abridg(e)ment [a'bridʒmənt], *s.* **I.** *(a)* Raccourcissement *m. (b)* Diminution *f;* restriction *f.* **2.** Abrégé *m,* précis *m,* résumé *m.*
abroad [a'brɔːd], *adv.* **I.** *(a)* A l'étranger; en voyage. *To live a.,* vivre hors de l'Angleterre. *He is just back from a.,* il revient de l'étranger. *Troops serving a.,* troupes en service actif hors de la Grande-Bretagne. *S.a.* HOME I. 2. *(b) (Of pers.)* Sorti; (au) dehors. **2.** Au loin. *Scattered a.,* éparpillé de tous côtés. *The news got a.,* la nouvelle se répandit. *There is a rumour a. that . . .,* le bruit court que. . . . *S.a.* NOISE[2], TRUMPET[2] 2. **3. He is all abroad,** il est tout désorienté. *I am all a.,* j'y perds mon latin.
abrogate ['abrogeit], *v.tr.* Abroger (une loi).
abrogation [abro'geiʃ(ə)n], *s.* Abrogation *f.*
abrupt [a'brʌpt], *a.* **I.** (Départ, personne) brusque; (départ) brusqué, précipité; (ton) cassant; (style) heurté, saccadé, abrupt. **2.** *A. mountain,* montagne abrupte, escarpée, à pic. **-ly,** *adv.* **I.** Brusquement. **2.** Abruptement; à pic.
abruptness [a'brʌptnəs], *s.* **I.** *(a)* Brusquerie *f. (b)* Précipitation *f. (c)* Saccadé *m* (du style). **2.** Escarpement *m;* raideur *f* (d'un sentier).
abscess ['abses], *s.* Abcès *m;* foyer purulent. *To lance, drain, an a.,* ouvrir, percer, vider, un abcès.
abscissa, *pl.* **-ae, -as** [ab'sisa, -iː, -əz], *s. Mth:* Abscisse *f.*
abscond [ab'skɔnd], *v.i. (a)* Se soustraire à la justice; s'enfuir, s'évader *(from,* de). *(b) F:* Décamper, filer. **absconding[1],** *a.* En fuite. **absconding[2],** *s.* Fuite *f,* évasion *f.*
absconder [ab'skɔndər], *s.* **I.** Fugitif *m.* **2.** *Jur:* Contumace *m.*
absence ['abs(ə)ns], *s.* **I.** Absence *f,* éloignement *m (from,* de). **To be conspicuous by one's absence,** briller par son absence. *Jur:* **Sentenced in his, her, absence,** condamné(e) par contumace. **2. In the absence of definite information,** faute de, à défaut de, renseignements précis. **3. Absence of mind,** distraction *f,* préoccupation *f.*
absent[1] ['abs(ə)nt], *a.* **I.** Absent *(from,* de). *Why were you a. from church?* pourquoi avez-vous manqué l'office? *Prov:* **Long absent, soon forgotten,** les absents ont tort; loin des yeux, loin du cœur. *(b)* Manquant. **2.** *Occ. = absent-minded.* **absent-′minded,** *a.* Distrait. **-ly,** *adv.* Distraitement; d'un air distrait. **absent-′mindedness,** *s.* Distraction *f.*
absent[2] [ab'sent], *v.pr. To a. oneself,* s'absenter *(from* de).
absentee [absən'tiː], *s.* **I.** .. *(a)* Absent *m. (b)* Manquant *m* (à l'appel). **2.** *a. & s. Hist:* **Absentee (landlord),** absentéiste *m.*

absinth(e) ['absinθ], s. Absinthe f.
absolute ['absəl(j)u:t]. **1.** a. (a) Absolu. A. power, pouvoir absolu, illimité. A. alcohol, alcool absolu. Jur : **Decree absolute**, décret irrévocable. (b) Autoritaire ; (ton) absolu. (c) F : An a. knave, un coquin achevé. It's an a. scandal, c'est un véritable scandale. **2.** s. Phil : **The absolute**, l'absolu m. **-ly**, adv. Absolument. It is a. forbidden to . . ., il est formellement interdit de. . . .
absolution [absə'l(j)u:ʃ(ə)n], s. Ecc : Absolution f.
absolve [ab'zɔlv], v.tr. **1.** (a) Absoudre (s.o. from a sin, qn d'un péché). (b) Remettre (un péché). **2.** To a. s.o. from a vow, affranchir, délier, dispenser, qn d'un vœu.
absorb [ab'sɔ:rb], v.tr. **1.** (a) Absorber (un liquide, la chaleur). (b) To a. a shock, a sound, amortir un choc, un son. **2.** (a) His business absorbs him, ses affaires l'absorbent. (b) To become absorbed in sth., s'absorber dans qch. **absorbing**, a. Absorbant.
absorbedly [ab'sɔ:rbidli], adv. D'un air absorbé.
absorbent [ab'sɔ:rbənt], a. & s. Absorbant (m). Med : **Absorbent cotton-wool**, coton hydrophile.
absorber [ab'sɔ:rbər], s. **1.** Ch : Ph : Absorbeur m. **2.** Amortisseur m (de son, d'oscillations).
absorption [ab'sɔ:rpʃ(ə)n], s. **1.** Absorption f (de chaleur, etc.). **2.** Absorbement m (de l'esprit). **3.** A. of sounds, of a shock, amortissement m de sons, d'un coup.
abstain [abs'tein], v.i. **1.** S'abstenir (from sth., from doing sth., de qch., de faire qch.). R.C.Ch : To a. from meat, faire maigre. **2.** Abs. S'abstenir de spiritueux.
abstainer [abs'teinər], s. Abstème mf ; buveur d'eau. **To be a total abstainer** (from alcohol), ne pas boire d'alcool ; ne boire que de l'eau.
abstemious [abs'ti:miəs], a. (a) Sobre, tempérant, abstinent. (b) An a. meal, un repas frugal. **-ly**, adv. Sobrement ; frugalement.
abstemiousness [abs'ti:miəsnəs], . Sobriété f, tempérance f ; abstinence f.
abstention [abs'tenʃ(ə)n], s. **1.** Abstention f, abstinence f (from, de). **2.** Pol : Abstention.
abstinence ['abstinəns], s. (a) Abstinence f (from, de). (b) **Total abstinence**, abstinence complète de boissons alcooliques.
abstract[1] ['abstrakt]. **1.** a. Abstrait. (a) A. number, nombre abstrait. Gram : **Abstract noun**, nom abstrait. (b) F : Abstrus. **2.** s. **The abstract**, l'abstrait m. To know sth. in the a., avoir une connaissance abstraite, théorique, de qch.
abstract[2] ['abstrakt], s. Résumé m, abrégé m.
abstract[3] [abs'trakt], v.tr. **1.** (a) Soustraire, dérober, voler (sth. from s.o., qch. à qn). (b) Détourner (l'attention de qn). **2.** (a) To a. a quality, a conception, faire abstraction d'une qualité, d'une conception. (b) Ch : Ind : Extraire (par distillation). **3.** Résumer, abréger (un livre) ; relever (un compte). **abstracted**, a. Distrait ; rêveur. **-ly**, adv. = ABSENT-MINDEDLY.
abstraction [abs'trakʃ(ə)n], s. **1.** Soustraction f (d'argent, de papiers, etc.) ; détournement m, vol m. **2.** (a) Phil : Abstraction f. (b) Idée abstraite. **3.** A. of mind, distraction f, préoccupation f.
abstruse [abs'tru:s], a. Abstrus.
abstruseness [abs'tru:snəs], s. Caractère abstrus (de qch.) ; complexité f.
absurd [ab'sɔ:rd], a. Absurde ; déraisonnable. It's absurd! F : c'est idiot! **-ly**, adv. Absurdement

absurdity [ab'sɔ:rditi], **absurdness** [ab'sɔ:rdnəs], s. Absurdité f.
abundance [a'bʌndəns], s. **1.** Abondance f, affluence f. He has got a. of friends, il a des amis en abondance. **In abundance**, en abondance, F : à foison. A. of heart, l'abondance du cœur. **To live in abundance**, vivre dans l'abondance. **2.** (At solo whist) Demande f de neuf levées.
abundant [a'bʌndənt], a. Abondant (in, en) ; fertile (en blé, etc.) ; copieux. **-ly**, adv. Abondamment ; copieusement.
abuse[1] [a'bju:s], s. **1.** (a) Abus m (of, de). A. of administrative authority, abus d'autorité, de pouvoir. A. of trust, prévarication f. (b) To remedy an a., redresser un abus. (c) Emploi abusif (d'un terme). (d) Dommage (infligé). A. of the highway, dommage, dégradations fpl, à la route. **2.** Insultes fpl, injures fpl.
abuse[2] [a'bju:z], v.tr. **1.** Abuser (de son autorité, etc.) ; mésuser (de son pouvoir) ; faire abus de (qch.). **2.** Maltraiter, houspiller (qn). **3.** (a) Médire, dire du mal, de (qn) ; dénigrer (qn). (b) Injurier ; dire des injures, des sottises, à (qn).
abuser [a'bju:zər], s. Détracteur, -trice.
abusive [a'bju:siv], a. **1.** (Emploi) abusif (d'un mot). **2.** (Propos) injurieux ; (homme) grossier. **-ly**, adv. **1.** (Employer un mot) abusivement. **2.** (Parler) injurieusement.
abusiveness [a'bju:sivnəs], s. Grossièreté f.
abut [a'bʌt], v.i. & tr. (abutted) **1.** To a. sth. ; to a. on, against, sth., aboutir, confiner, à un endroit. Our fields a., nos champs se touchent, sont attenants. **2.** Const : To a. on, against (a wall, etc.), s'appuyer, buter, contre (une paroi). **3.** Carp : v.i. (S')abouter. (b) v.tr. Abouter (deux pièces). **abutting**, a. **1.** Aboutissant, attenant (on, à). **2.** A. joint, assemblage en about. A. surface, surface de contact.
abutment [a'bʌtmənt], s. **1.** Carp : Aboutement m. **2.** (a) Arc-boutant m (d'une muraille) ; contrefort m. (b) Butée f, culée f (d'un pont) ; pied-droit m (d'une voûte).
abysmal [a'bizməl], a. Sans fond ; insondable ; (ignorance) profonde.
abyss [a'bis], s. Abîme m, gouffre m.
abyssal [a'bisəl], a. Oc : Geol : Abyssal, -aux.
Abyssinia [abi'sinjə]. Pr.n. Geog : L'Éthiopie f ; l'Abyssinie f.
Abyssinian [abi'sinjən], a. & s. Éthiopien, abyssinien.
acacia [a'keiʃa], s. Bot : Acacia m.
academic [aka'demik], a. Académique. (a) Phil : Qui se rapporte à l'école platonicienne. (b) A. discussion, débat académique ; discussion abstraite. (c) Pej : (Style) compassé, guindé. (d) (Carrière, etc.) universitaire. (e) Art : (Peinture, etc.) académique.
academical [aka'demik(ə)l]. **1.** a. Universitaire. **2.** s.pl. **Academicals**, costume m académique.
academician [akadə'miʃ(ə)n], s. Académicien m. Esp. **Royal Academician, R.A.**, membre de la 'Royal Academy' (des Beaux-Arts).
academy [a'kadəmi], s. **1.** Gr.Phil : L'Académie f (de Platon). **2.** (a) Académie. **The Royal Academy (of Arts)**, (i) l'Académie royale des Beaux-Arts ; (ii) le Salon (de Londres). Fencing a., salle f d'escrime. (b) Military Academy, École f militaire. **3.** (a) A : École (privée) ; pension f, pensionnat m. (b) (In Scot.) École secondaire ; collège m. **4.** Art : Academy(-figure), académie (d'après le modèle nu).
acanthus [a'kanθəs], s. **1.** Bot : Acanthe f. **2.** Arch : (Feuille f d')acanthe.

accede [ak′si:d], *v.i.* **1.** To … to an office, entrer en possession d'une charge. *To a. to the throne,* monter sur le trône. **2.** (*a*) *To a. to a treaty,* accéder à un traité. *To a. to a reques.,* accueillir une demande. (*b*) *To a. to a party,* adhérer, se ioindre, à un parti.

accelerate [ak′seləreit]. **1.** *v.tr.* (*a*) Accélérer (la marche, un travail) ; précipiter (les événements) ; activer (un travail). *Abs. Aut :* Accélérer. (*b*) Hâter, précipiter (le depart, la mort, de qn). **2.** *v.i.* (*Of motion, etc.*) S'accélérer. **accelerated,** *a.* (Mouvement) accéléré. **accelerating,** *a.* Accélérateur, -trice.

acceleration [akselə′reiʃ(ə)n], *s.* Accélération *f.* *Negative a.,* accélération retardatrice. négative ; retardation *f.* *Constant a.,* accélération uniforme. *Uniform a.,* vitesse uniformément accélérée.

accelerator [ak′seləreitər]. **1.** *a. & s.* Accélérateur, -trice. **2.** *s. Aut :* *Clockm : Phot :* Accélérateur *m.* *Aut :* **Accelerator pedal,** pédale d'accélération, de gaz.

accent[1] [′aks(ə)nt], *s.* Accent *m.* **1.** (*a*) *To have a German a.,* avoir l'accent allemand. (*b*) In **broken accents,** d'une voix brisée, entrecoupée. **2.** (*a*) *Pros :* Temps marqué. (*b*) *Mus :* (i) Temps fort ; (ii) accent (mélodique). **3.** *Grammatical accents,* accents grammaticaux. *Acute a., grave a.,* accent aigu, accent grave.

accent[2] [ak′sent], *v.tr.* Accentuer (une syllabe, une voyelle, etc.) ; appuyer sur (une syllabe).

accentuate [ak′sentjueit], *v.tr.* Accentuer, souligner, appuyer sur, faire ressortir, rehausser (un détail, etc.). **accentuated,** *a.* Fortement marqué ; accentué.

accentuation [aksentju′eiʃ(ə)n], *s.* Accentuation *f.*

accept [ak′sept], *v.tr. & ind.tr.* **1.** Accepter (un cadeau, une offre) ; agréer (les prières de qn) ; admettre (les raisons, les excuses, de qn) ; agréer (un prétendant) ; donner son adhésion à (un traité). *To be accepted,* être accepté ; passer. *The accepted custom,* l'usage admis. *Com :* *To a. a bill,* accepter un effet. **2.** *To a. of a gift,* daigner accepter un cadeau.

acceptable [ak′septəbl], *a.* Acceptable, agréable (*to,* à). *Your cheque was most a.,* votre chèque est arrivé fort à propos. **-ably,** *adv.* Acceptablement ; assez bien.

acceptance [ak′septəns], *s.* (*a*) Acceptation *f* ; consentement *m* à recevoir (qch.) ; accueil *m* favorable (de qch.). *A. of a proposal,* agrément donné à une proposition. *To beg s.o.'s a. of sth.,* prier qn d'accepter qch. **To secure acceptance of sth.,** faire accepter qch. **This proposal met with general acceptance,** cette proposition a rallié tous les suffrages. *Com :* **To present a bill for acceptance,** présenter une traite à l'acceptation. (*b*) *Th :* Réception *f* (d'une pièce par le comité de lecture). (*c*) *Com : Ind :* Réception (d'un article commandé). **Acceptance test or trial,** essai de réception, de recette. (*d*) **Acceptance of persons,** partialité *f.* **Without acceptance of persons,** sans faire acception de personne.

acceptation [aksep′teiʃ(ə)n], *s.* Acception *f,* signification *f* (d'un mot).

acceptor [ak′septər], *s. Com :* Tiré *m* ; accepteur *m* (d'une lettre de change).

access [′akses], *s.* **1.** Accès *m,* abord *m.* **Difficult of access,** d'un accès difficile, d'un abord difficile ; difficile à approcher. **Easy of access,** abordable, accostable. **Door that gives access to a room,** porte qui donne accès à, qui commande, une pièce. *A. to the door is by a flight of steps,* on accède à la porte par un escalier. **To find, obtain,**

access to s.o., trouver accès auprès de qn. **To have access to s.o.,** avoir accès chez, auprès de qn ; avoir son entrée, ses entrées, chez qn. **2.** *A. of fever, of rage,* accès de fièvre, de rage. *A. of joy,* saisissement *m* de joie.

accessibility [aksesi′biliti], *s.* Accessibilité *f* ; commodité *f* d'accès.

accessible [ak′sesibl], *a.* **1.** (Endroit) accessible, approchable. *Knowledge a. to everyone,* connaissances à la portée de tout le monde, accessibles à tous. **2.** (*Of pers.*) (*a*) Accueillant. (*b*) *A. to pity,* accessible à la pitié.

accession [ak′seʃ(ə)n], *s.* **1.** *A. of light, of air,* admission *f* de lumière, d'air. *A. of funds from abroad,* arrivage *m* de fonds de l'étranger. **2.** (*a*) Accroissement *m* (par addition). *A. to one's income,* augmentation *f* de revenus. (*b*) Adhésion *f* (à un parti). **3.** (*a*) *A. to manhood,* arrivée *f* à l'âge d'homme. (*b*) *A. to power,* accession *f* au pouvoir. *A. to the throne,* avènement *m* au trône. *A. to an estate,* entrée en possession, en jouissance, d'un patrimoine.

accessory [ak′sesəri]. **1.** *a.* Accessoire, subsidiaire (*to,* à). **2.** *s.* (*a*) Accessoire *m* (d'une machine, etc.) ; article *m* d'équipement. *Toilet accessories,* objets *m,* ustensiles *m,* de toilette. (*b*) *pl. Th :* Accessoires *mpl* (d'une pièce). **3.** *s. & pred. a. A. to a crime,* complice *m,* fauteur *m,* d'un crime. *Jur :* **Accessory before the fact,** complice par instigation. **Accessory after the fact,** complice après coup.

accidence [′aksidəns], *s. Gram :* Morphologie *f.*

accident [′aksidənt], *s.* **1.** (*a*) Accident *m.* **By accident,** accidentellement. **By a mere accident,** par pur hasard. (*b*) *Serious a.,* accident grave. *Fatal a.,* accident mortel. *A. to the engines,* avarie *f* de machines. **To meet with, to have, an accident,** être, se trouver, victime d'un accident. *Prov :* **Accidents will happen,** on ne peut pas parer à tout ; on ne saurait tout prévenir. *S.a.* CHAPTER I. **2.** Accident, inégalité *f* (du terrain).

accidental [aksi′dent(ə)l]. **1.** *a.* (*a*) Accidentel, fortuit ; de hasard. (*b*) Accessoire, subsidiaire. **2.** *s. Mus :* Accident *m* ; signe accidentel. **-ally,** *adv.* Accidentellement. (*a*) Par hasard, fortuitement. (*b*) Par mégarde.

acclaim [ə′kleim], *v.tr.* Acclamer ; accueillir (qn) par des acclamations. *Charlemagne was acclaimed emperor,* Charlemagne fut acclamé, proclamé, empereur.

acclamation [aklə′meiʃ(ə)n], *s.* Acclamation *f.* **Carried by acclamation,** adopté par acclamation.

acclimatization [əklaimətai′zeiʃ(ə)n], *s.* Acclimatation *f,* accoutumance *f* (*to,* à).

acclimatize [ə′klaimətaiz], *v.tr.* Acclimater. **To get, become, acclimatized,** s'acclimater.

acclivity [ə′kliviti], *s.* Montée *f,* côte *f* ; rampe *f.*

accolade [ako′leid], *s.* Accolade *f* ((i) coup du plat de l'épée ; (ii) trait de plume).

accommodate [ə′kɔmodeit], *v.tr.* **1.** (*a*) Accommoder, approprier, conformer (ses goûts à ceux d'un autre). *To a. oneself to circumstances,* s'accommoder, s'adapter, aux circonstances. (*b*) Ajuster, adapter (qch. à qch.). (*c*) Arranger (une querelle) ; concilier (des opinions). **2.** **To accommodate s.o.** (i) Accommoder, servir, obliger, qn. (ii) *To a. s.o. with sth.,* donner, fou~nir, qch. à qn ; fournir qn de qch. *To a. s.o. with a loan,* mettre un prêt à qn. **3.** Loger, recevoir (tant de personnes). **accommodating,** *a.* (*a*) Complaisant, obligeant, serviable, accommodant ; peu difficile (*with regard to,* sur). (*b*) *Pej :* (*Of morals, religion, etc.*) Accommodant, commode. **-ly,** *adv.* Complaisamment.

accommodation [akɔmo'deiʃ(ə)n], *s.* **1.** (*a*) Ajustement *m*, adaptation *f* (*to*, à). (*b*) Accommodement *m*, arrangement *m*, ajustement (d'une dispute). *To come to an a.*, arriver à un compromis; s'arranger (à l'amiable). **2.** (*a*) Commodité *f*, facilités *fpl*. *It would be a great a. to me*, cela me serait bien commode, cela m'arrangerait. *For your accommodation*, pour votre commodité. *Com:* **Accommodation bill**, billet de complaisance. *Nau:* **Accommodation ladder**, échelle de poupe, de coupée; échelle de commandement. (*b*) Logement *m*; installation matérielle. **Accommodation for man and beast**, (ici) on loge à pied et à cheval. (*c*) Avance *f*, prêt *m* (d'argent).

accompaniment [ə'kʌmpənimənt], *s.* (*a*) Accompagnement *m*; accessoires *mpl*. (*b*) *Mus:* Accompagnement (*on the piano*, au piano).

accompanist [ə'kʌmpənist], *s. Mus:* Accompagnateur, -trice.

accompany [ə'kʌmpəni], *v.tr.* Accompagner. **1.** *To be accompanied by s.o.*, être accompagné de (*occ.* par) qn. **2.** (*a*) *He accompanied these words with a cuff*, il accompagna ces mots d'une taloche. (*b*) *Fever accompanied by, with, delirium*, fièvre accompagnée de délire. **3.** *Mus: To a. s.o. on the piano*, accompagner qn au piano. **accompanying**, *a.* (Symptôme, etc.) concomitant.

accomplice [ə'kɔmplis], *s.* Complice *mf*. *To be an a. in a crime*, tremper dans un crime, être complice d'un crime.

accomplish [ə'kɔmpliʃ], *v.tr.* Accomplir, exécuter, achever, venir à bout de (qch.); mener à bonne fin (une tâche); réaliser (une prédiction). *To a. one's object*, atteindre son but. **accomplished**, *a.* (*a*) (Musicien, etc.) accompli, achevé. (*b*) Qui possède de nombreux talents.

accomplishment [ə'kɔmpliʃmənt], *s.* **1.** (*a*) Accomplissement *m*, achèvement *m*, exécution *f*, consommation *f* (d'une tâche); réalisation *f* (d'un projet). **Difficult of accomplishment**, difficile à réaliser. (*b*) Chose accomplie, réalisée. **2.** *Usu.pl.* Art(s) *m* d'agrément, talent(s) *m* (d'agrément).

accord[1] [ə'kɔːrd], *s.* **1.** Accord *m*, consentement *m*. **With one accord**, d'un commun accord. **To be in accord, out of accord, with sth.**, être d'accord, en désaccord, avec qch. **2.** *To do sth. of one's own accord*, faire qch. de son plein gré, de son propre gré, de sa propre volonté.

accord[2], *v.i.* S'accorder, être d'accord, concorder (*with*, avec). **2.** *v.tr.* Accorder, concéder, octroyer (*to*, à). **according**, *adv. Used only in :* **1.** *Conj.phr.* According as, selon que, suivant que, + *ind. We see things differently a. as we are rich or poor*, on voit les choses différemment selon qu'on est riche ou pauvre. **2.** *Prep.phr.* According to the orders, selon, suivant, d'après, les ordres; conformément aux ordres. *A. to age, to height*, par rang d'âge, de taille. (*b*) **According to him**, d'après lui; à l'en croire; à ce qu'il dit. **According to that**, d'après cela. The Gospel **according to St Luke**, l'Évangile selon saint Luc. **-ly**, *adv.* **1.** (*a*) To act accordingly, agir en conséquence, à l'avenant. (*b*) **Accordingly as** = *according as*. **2.** (*Therefore*) *A. I wrote to him*, je lui ai donc écrit; en conséquence je lui ai écrit.

accordance [ə'kɔːrdəns], *s.* Accord *m*, conformité *f*. **In accordance with your instructions**, en conformité avec, conformément à, vos ordres; suivant vos ordres. *Statement in a. with truth*, affirmation conforme à, d'accord avec, la vérité.

accordion [ə'kɔːrdiən], *s.* Accordéon *m*. *Dressm:*

A.-pleated, (plié) en accordéon; en plis d'accordéon.

accost [ə'kɔst], *v.tr.* Accoster, aborder.

account[1] [ə'kaunt], *s.* **1.** (*Calculation*) To cast an account, faire un calcul. **2.** (*a*) *Com: Fin:* Compte *m*, note *f*. **Detailed account**, compte spécifié. *Book-k:* **Accounts payable**, dettes passives. **Accounts receivable**, dettes actives. **Account current, current account**, compte courant. *My bank a.*, mon compte en banque. **To settle an account**, régler une note, un compte. **The accounts** (*of a firm*), la comptabilité. **To keep the accounts**, tenir les livres, les écritures, les comptes. **In account with s.o.**, en compte avec qn. *To pay a sum on account*, payer une somme en acompte, à compte, à valoir; payer un acompte. *To give ten pounds on a.*, donner un acompte de dix livres. **On, for, account of s.o.**, pour le compte de qn, à valoir sur qn. (*b*) Exposé *m*, état *m*, note. *A. of expenses*, état, note, de dépenses. (*c*) To find one's account in . . ., trouver son compte à. . . . **To turn, put, sth. to account**, tirer parti, avantage, de qch.; faire valoir qch.; utiliser qch. *To turn sth. to the best a.*, tirer tout le profit, parti, possible de qch. *He can turn everything to a.*, il fait profit de tout; il fait flèche de tout bois. (*d*) **To call s.o. to account** (*for sth., for doing sth.*), demander une explication à qn; demander compte à qn (de qch.); prendre qn à partie (d'avoir fait qch.). **To bring s.o. to account**, faire payer ses méfaits à qn. **He has gone to his account**, il est mort; il a payé sa dette à la nature. **To give account of sth.**, rendre raison de qch. *F: He gave quite a good a. of himself*, il s'est bien acquitté; il s'en est bien tiré. **3.** (*a*) (*Person, thing*) **of some account, of high account, of small account**, (personne, chose) qui compte, qui compte pour beaucoup, qui ne compte guère. *Competitors of little a.*, des concurrents peu dangereux, peu sérieux. *To make much, little, account of sth.*, faire grand cas, peu de cas, de qch. **To be held in account**, *to be of some a.*, être (tenu) en grande estime. **To take sth. into account**, *to take a. of sth.*, tenir compte de qch. **To leave sth. out of account**, *to take no a. of sth.*, ne pas tenir compte de qch.; négliger (une circonstance). (*b*) On **account of s.o.**, à cause de, par égard pour, qn. *I was nervous on his a.*, j'avais peur pour lui. **On account of sth.**, à cause de, en considération de, qch. **On every account**, sous tous les rapports. **On no account, not on any account**, dans aucun cas, pour rien au monde. (*c*) To act on one's own account, agir à sa propre initiative, de soi-même. **4.** Récit *m*, relation (d'un fait). **To give an account of sth.**, faire le récit, la relation, de qch. *To give an a. of the position of affairs*, faire un exposé de la situation. *To give an a. of oneself*, (i) rendre compte de ses faits et gestes; (ii) décliner ses titres et qualités. **By his own account . . .**, (i) d'après son propre dire . . . , selon son dire . . ., à ce qu'il dit . . .; (ii) à l'en croire. . . . **By all accounts**, au dire de tout le monde. **ac'count-day**, *s. St.Exch:* (Jour de) règlement *m*.

account[2], *v.tr. & ind.tr.* **1.** *Pred. To a. s.o. (to be) wise, guilty*, tenir qn pour sage, coupable; regarder, considérer, qn comme sage, coupable. **To account oneself lucky**, s'estimer heureux. **2.** (*a*) **To account for** (sth.), rendre raison de, justifier (de) (sa conduite); expliquer (une circonstance). *To a. for a sum of money, for an expenditure*, rendre compte d'une somme; justifier une dépense. (*b*) *I can't a. for it*, je n'y comprends rien, je ne me l'explique pas. **There is no accounting for tastes**, des goûts et des couleurs, on ne discute pas ; chacun son goût. *(c)* F: To account for (= *kill*) **s.o.**, faire son affaire à qn. **accounting,** *s.* = ACCOUNTANCY. **The accounting department**, la comptabilité. **accountable** [a'kauntəbl], *a. To be a. to s.o. for sth.*, être responsàble de qch. envers qn. *To be a. for a sum of money*, être redevable d'une somme d'argent. *He is not a. for his actions*, il est irresponsable.

accountancy [a'kauntənsi], *s.* **I.** Comptabilité *f;* profession *f* de comptable. **2.** Tenue *f* des livres. **accountant** [a'kauntənt], *s.* *(a)* Agent *m* comptable ; comptable *m;* teneur *m* de livres. *Chief a.,* chef *m* de (la) comptabilité ; chef comptable. **The accountant's department**, la comptabilité. *(b)* **Chartered accountant, C.A.,** = expert *m* comptable.

accoutre [a'ku:tər], *v.tr. (Used chiefly in p.p.) (a)* Accoutrer (un chevalier, etc.). *(b) Accoutred with pistols*, équipé de pistolets.

accoutrement(s) [a'ku:tərmənt(s)], *s.(pl.) (a)* Harnachement *m;* caparaçon *m* (d'un destrier). *(b)* Équipement *m,* fourniment *m* (du soldat).

accredit [a'kredit], *v.tr.* **I.** Accréditer (qn, qch.) ; mettre (qn, qch.) en crédit, en réputation. **2.** *To a. an ambassador to a government*, accréditer un ambassadeur auprès d'un gouvernement. **accredited,** *a.* **I.** *(Of pers.)* Accrédité, autorisé. **2.** *A.* opinions, opinions reçues, orthodoxes. **accretion** [a'kri:∫(ə)n], *s. (a)* Accroissement *m* organique. *(b)* Accroissement par alluvion, par addition ; addition *f (to,* à).

accrue [a'kru:], *v.i.* **I.** *(a)* Provenir, dériver *(from,* de). *(b) (Of moneys, land, etc.) To a. to s.o.,* revenir à qn. **2.** *(Of interest)* Courir, s'accumuler.

accumulate [a'kjumjuleit], **I.** *v.tr.* Accumuler, amasser (une fortune, etc.) ; amonceler. **2.** *v.i.* S'accumuler, s'amonceler.

accumulation [əkjumju'lei∫(ə)n], *s.* **I.** Accumulation *f,* amoncellement *m. A. of capital*, accroissement *m* du capital (auquel viennent s'ajouter les intérêts). **2.** Amas *m,* monceau *m,* accumulation. **accumulative** [a'kjumjuleitiv], *a.* Qui s'accumule.

accumulator [a'kjumjuleitər], *s.* **I.** *(Pers.)* Accumulateur, -trice. **2.** *(a) Mec.E : Civ.E :* Accumulateur *m* (d'énergie). *(b) El : (Storage battery)* Accumulateur, F: accu *m.*

accuracy ['akjurəsi], *s. (a)* Exactitude *f;* (degré *m* de) justesse *f;* précision *f. (b)* Fidélité *f* (de mémoire), d'une citation).

accurate ['akjurət], *a. (a)* Exact, juste, précis. **To be (strictly) accurate** . . ., pour être tout à fait exact. . . . *To take a.* aim, viser juste. *(b)* (Mémoire, citation) fidèle ; (dessin) correct, fidèle. **-ly,** *adv.* Exactement, avec précision.

accursed [a'kə:rsid], *a. Lit :* **I.** Maudit. **2.** *F:* Maudit, exécrable, détestable.

accusation [akju'zei∫(ə)n], *s.* Accusation *f; Jur :* incrimination *f.*

accusative [a'kju:zətiv], *a.* & *s. Gram :* (Cas) accusatif *m;* régime direct.

accuse [a'kju:z], *v.tr.* Accuser *(s.o. of sth., of doing sth.*, qn de qch., de faire qch.) ; *Jur :* incriminer (qn). **accused,** *s. Jur :* **The accused,** le, la, prévenu(e). **accusing,** *a.* Accusateur, -trice. **-ly,** *adv.* D'une manière accusatrice.

accuser [a'kju:zər], *s.* Accusateur, -trice.

accustom [a'kʌstəm], *v.tr.* Accoutumer, habituer *(s.o. to sth., to do sth.*, qn à qch., à faire qch.) ;

aguerrir (qn à, contre, la fatigue, etc.). *To a. oneself to discipline*, se faire à la discipline. **accustomed,** *a.* **I.** Accoutumé, habitué *(to,* à). **To be accustomed to . . .,** *(i)* avoir coutume de . . ., *(ii)* être accoutumé à. . . . **To get accustomed to sth.**, s'accoutumer à qch. ; se faire à qch. *That is not what I am a.* to, *(i)* ce n'est pas dans mes habitudes ; *(ii)* ce n'est pas à quoi je suis accoutumé. **2.** Habituel, coutumier, familier, ordinaire ; d'usage.

ace [eis], *s.* **I.** *(Of dice, dominoes, cards)* As *m.* **2.** *Av: (Of pers.)* As. **3.** *F:* Within an ace of sth., à deux doigts de qch. *I was within an ace of* + *ger.,* j'ai bien failli, bien manqué + *inf.*

acerbity [a'sə:rbiti], *s.* Acerbité *f;* aigreur *f,* âpreté *f* (de ton).

acetate ['aseteit], *s. Ch:* Acétate *m.*

acetic [a'setik, a'si:tik], *a. Ch:* Acétique. *Glacial a. acid*, acide acétique concentré.

acetify [a'setifai]. **I.** *v.tr.* Acétifier. **2.** *v.i.* S'acétifier ; tourner au vinaigre.

acetone ['asetoun], *s. Ch:* Acétone *f.*

acetylene [a'setili:n], *s. Ch:* Acétylène *m. A. lamp,* lanterne à acétylène.

ache[1] [eik], *s.* Mal *m,* douleur *f. Headache,* toothache, mal de tête, mal de dents. *Heartache,* chagrin *m;* peine *f* de cœur. *I have a headache,* j'ai mal à la tête. *F:* **All aches and pains**, tout courbaturé, tout moulu.

ache[2], *v.i.* My head aches, la tête me fait mal ; j'ai mal à la tête. *It makes my head a.,* cela me donne le, un, mal de tête. *The exercise has made my legs a.,* l'exercice m'a fatigué, courbaturé, les jambes. **It makes my heart ache,** cela me serre le cœur. **aching,** *a.* Douloureux, endolori. *An a. tooth,* une dent malade. **Aching heart,** cœur dolent. *S.a.* VOID II.

achene [a'ki:n], *s. Bot:* Akène *m.*

achieve [a't∫i:v], *v.tr.* **I.** Accomplir (une tâche) ; exécuter, réaliser (une entreprise). **2.** Acquérir (de l'honneur) ; parvenir (aux honneurs) ; se faire (une réputation). **3.** Atteindre (à), arriver à (un but). **To achieve one's purpose, one's end,** parvenir à ses fins. *To a. victory*, remporter la victoire. *He has achieved the impossible*, il est venu à bout d'une tâche qui semblait impossible. *He will never a. anything*, il n'arrivera jamais à rien. **achieving,** *s.* **I.** Accomplissement *m,* exécution *f.* **2.** Obtention *f* (d'un résultat).

achievement [a't∫i:vmənt], *s.* **I.** Accomplissement *m,* réalisation *f,* exécution *f* (d'un projet, etc.). **2.** *(a)* Exploit *m,* (haut) fait. *(b) When we consider his a.,* lorsque nous considérons l'effort qu'il a accompli.

Achilles [a'kili:z]. *Pr.n.m.* Achille. **Achilles tendon,** tendon d'Achille.

acid ['asid]. **I.** *a. (a)* Acide. **Acid drops,** bonbons acidulés. *(b)* Revêche, aigre. *S.a.* TEST[1] I *(b).* **2.** *s.* Acide *m.* **'acid-proof, 'acid-resisting,** *a.* Qui résiste aux acides.

acidity [a'siditi], *s.* **I.** Acidité *f;* verdeur *f* (des fruits, du vin). **2.** *F:* Aigreur *f* (d'une réponse).

acierate ['asiəreit], *v.tr. Metall:* Aciérer (par cémentation).

acknowledge [ak'nɔledʒ], *v.tr.* **I.** *(a)* Reconnaître, avouer (qch.) ; reconnaître (qn). *He acknowledged having organized the plot*, il reconnut avoir organisé le complot. *He was acknowledged as king*, il fu. reconnu pour roi. *To a. oneself beaten*, s'avouer, se reconnaître, vaincu. *Fenc:* **To acknowledge a hit,** accuser un coup. *(b)* Reconnaître (un service). **2.** Répondre à (une courtoisie, un salut, etc.). **To acknowledge (receipt of) a letter,** accuser réception d'une lettre. **acknowledged,** *a.* **1.** (Fait) reconnu, avéré, notoire. **2.** Qui fait autorité.

acknowledg(e)ment [ak'nɔledʒmənt], *s.* **1.** (*a*) Constatation *f*; reconnaissance *f* (d'un bienfait). *Com:* Reçu *m*, quittance *f* (d'un payement). **Acknowledgement of receipt,** accusé *m* de réception (d'une lettre, d'un colis). **To make an acknowledgement of sth.,** reconnaître qch. (*b*) Aveu *m* (d'une faute). **2. Acknowledgements,** remerciements *mpl.*

acme ['akmi], *s.* Plus haut point; comble *m* (de la perfection, du bonheur); sommet *m*, faîte *m* (de la gloire, des honneurs); apogée *m* (de la puissance); plus haut période (de la gloire, de l'éloquence).

acne ['akni], *s. Med:* Acné *f.* **Acne rosacea,** couperose *f.*

acolyte ['akolait], *s. Ecc. & F:* Acolyte *m.*

aconite ['akonait], *s. Bot:* Aconit *m.*

acorn ['eikɔːrn], *s. Bot:* Gland *m* (du chêne). **To gather, get in, the acorns,** faire la glandée. '**acorn-cup,** *s. Bot:* Cupule *f.*

acotyledon [akɔti'liːdən], *s. Bot:* Acotylédone *f,* acotylédonée *f.*

acoustic(al) [ə'kaustik(əl), -'ku-], *a.* Acoustique.

acoustics [ə'kaustiks, -'ku-], *s.pl.* (*With sg. or pl. const.*) Acoustique *f. A. is the science of sound,* l'acoustique est la science des sons. *The a. of this hall are excellent,* cette salle a une bonne acoustique.

acquaint [ə'kweint], *v.tr.* **1. To acquaint s.o. with sth., of a fact,** informer, avertir, qn de qch. ; faire savoir qch. à qn. *To a. s.o. with the facts* (*of the case*), mettre qn au courant (des faits); mettre qn au fait (de la situation). **2.** (*a*) **To be acquainted with s.o., sth.,** connaître qn; connaître, savoir, qch. (*b*) **To become, make oneself, acquainted with s.o.,** faire, lier, connaissance avec qn. *To become, make oneself, acquainted with sth.,* prendre connaissance (des faits); apprendre, s'initier à, étudier (une langue, une science).

acquaintance [ə'kweintəns], *s.* **1.** Connaissance *f* (*with,* de). (*a*) *His a. with the classical tongues,* sa connaissance des langues classiques. (*b*) *Long a. with s.o.,* relations *f* de longue date avec qn. **To make s.o.'s acquaintance,** faire la connaissance de qn. **To make a. with s.o.,** faire connaissance avec qn. *I have not the honour of his a.,* je n'ai pas l'honneur de le connaître. **He improves upon acquaintance,** il gagne à être connu. **2.** (*Pers.*) Personne *f* de connaissance ; connaissance. **To have a wide circle of acquaintances, a wide acquaintance,** avoir des relations très étendues.

acquaintanceship [ə'kweintənsʃip], *s.* **1.** Relations *fpl,* rapports *mpl.* **2.** *Coll.* Cercle *m* de connaissances, relations. **Wide acquaintanceship,** relations étendues.

acquiesce [akwi'es], *v.i.* Acquiescer (*in a request,* à une demande); donner son assentiment (*in,* à).

acquiescence [akwi'esns], *s.* **1.** Acquiescement *m* (*in,* à); assentiment *m.* **2.** Soumission *f* (*in,* à).

acquiescent [akwi'esnt], *a.* Disposé à acquiescer; consentant.

acquire [ə'kwaiər], *v.tr.* Acquérir (qch.); se rendre propriétaire de (qch.). *To a. a habit,* prendre, contracter, une habitude. *To a. a taste for sth.,* prendre goût à qch. *To a. a language,* apprendre une langue.

acquirement [ə'kwaiərmənt], *s.* **1.** Acquisition *f* (*of,* de). **2.** (*a*) Talent (acquis). (*b*) *pl.* Connaissances *fpl.*

acquirer [ə'kwaiərər], *s.* Acquéreur *m.*

acquisition [akwi'ziʃ(ə)n], *s.* Acquisition *f.*

acquisitive [ə'kwizitiv], *a.* **1.** Thésauriseur. **2.** Apre au gain.

acquit [ə'kwit], *v.tr.* (**acquitted**) **1.** *To a. a debt,* s'acquitter d'une dette, acquitter une dette. **2.** Acquitter (un accusé). **To acquit s.o. of sth.,** absoudre qn de qch. **3.** (*a*) *To a. oneself of a duty, of a task,* s'acquitter d'un devoir, d'une tâche. (*b*) *To a. oneself well, ill,* se bien, mal, acquitter.

acquittal [ə'kwit(ə)l], *s.* **1.** *Jur:* Acquittement *m* (d'un accusé, d'un débiteur). **2.** Exécution *f,* accomplissement *m* (d'un devoir).

acre ['eikər], *s.* **1.** (*a*) *A:* Champ *m,* pré *m.* (*Still so used in*) *God's acre,* le champ de repos, le cimetière. (*b*) *pl.* Proud *of his broad acres,* fier de ses terres, de ses arpents. **2.** *Meas:* Acre *f* (0.4 hectare); (*approx.* =) arpent *m,* demi-hectare *m.*

acreage ['eikəredʒ], *s.* Superficie *f* (en mesures agraires).

acrid ['akrid], *a.* **1.** (Goût, fumée) âcre. **2.** (Style) mordant; (critique) acerbe. **-ly,** *adv.* Avec âcreté ; avec acerbité.

acridity [a'kriditi], *s.* Acreté *f.*

acrimonious [akri'mounjəs], *a.* Acrimonieux, atrabilaire ; (*of woman*) acariâtre. **-ly,** *adv.* Avec acrimonie ; acrimonieusement.

acrimony ['akriməni], **acrimoniousness** [akri'mounjəsnəs], *s.* Acrimonie *f* ; aigreur *f.*

acrobat ['akrobat], *s.* Acrobate *mf.*

acrobatic [akro'batik], *a.* **1.** *a.* Acrobatique. *A. feat,* tour d'acrobatie. **2.** *s.pl.* **Acrobatics,** acrobatie *f.*

acropolis [ə'krɔpolis], *s.* Acropole *f.*

across [ə'krɔs], *adv. & prep.* En croix; en travers (de). **1. With arms,** *Nau:* **with yards, across,** les bras, les vergues, en croix. *With arms folded a. his breast,* les bras croisés sur la poitrine. **2.** (*a*) **To walk across (a street),** traverser (une rue). *To go a. a bridge,* passer (sur) un pont; franchir un pont. *We shall soon be a.,* (i) nous serons bientôt de l'autre côté ; (ii) la traversée sera bientôt faite. (*b*) **To lay sth. across (sth.),** mettre qch. en travers (de qch.). *To throw a bridge a. a river,* jeter un pont sur une rivière. (*c*) **To come, drop, across a person,** rencontrer (par hasard) une personne. **3.** (*a*) **The distance across,** (i) la distance en largeur ; (ii) la longueur de la traversée. *The river is a mile a.,* le fleuve a un mille de large. (*b*) **He lives across the street,** il demeure de l'autre côté de la rue.

acrostic [ə'krɔstik], *a. & s.* Acrostiche (*m*).

act¹ [akt], *s.* **1.** Acte *m.* (*a*) **Act of justice, of kindness,** acte de justice, de bonté. (*b*) **Act of Parliament,** loi *f,* décret *m.* (*c*) (*Instrument in writing*) **The Acts of the Apostles,** les Actes des Apôtres. *I deliver this as my act and deed,* signé de ma main ; fait de ma main. **2.** Action *f.* **The act of walking,** l'action de marcher. *An act of folly,* une folie. **To catch s.o. in the (very) act,** prendre qn sur le fait, en flagrant délit. *Jur:* **M.Ins: Act of God,** (i) (cas *m* de) force majeure ; (ii) cas fortuit ; cause naturelle. **3.** *Th:* Acte (d'une pièce).

act². **1.** *v.tr.* (*a*) **To act a play, a character,** jouer, représenter, une pièce, un personnage. *To act a part,* remplir un rôle. *To act Hamlet,* jouer, faire, Hamlet. *To act the ass,* faire l'imbécile. (*b*) **To act a part,** feindre ; faire, jouer, la comédie. *To act fear,* simuler la crainte. **He was only acting,** il faisait semblant. (*c*) **To act the part of an honest man,** se conduire, agir, en honnête homme. **2.** *v.i.* Agir ; prendre des mesures. (*a*) *It is time to act,* il est temps d'agir. **He did not know how to act,** il ne savait quel parti prendre. *To act like a friend*, agir en ami, se conduire en ami. *I acted for the best*, j'ai fait pour le mieux. *To act for s.o.*, agir au nom de qn; représenter qn. *To act as secretary*, faire office, exercer les fonctions, de secrétaire. *His daughter acts as his secretary*, sa fille lui sert de secrétaire. *To act upon advice*, suivre un avis. *To act up to one's principles*, agir conformément à ses principes ; mettre ses principes en pratique. (*b*) *The pump is not acting well*, la pompe ne fonctionne, ne marche, pas bien. *The engine acts as a brake*, le moteur fait fonction de frein. (*c*) *To act (up)on the brain, the bowels*, agir, exercer une action, sur le cerveau, sur l'intestin. (*d*) *Th: Cin:* Jouer (bien, mal). *To act for the films*, faire du cinéma. *To act in a film*, tourner dans un film. **acting**[1], *a.* **1.** Remplissant les fonctions de . . .; (i) suppléant; (ii) intérimaire. **Acting manager,** (i) directeur gérant ; (ii) directeur intérimaire ; gérant provisoire. *Lieutenant a. captain*, lieutenant faisant fonction de capitaine. **2.** *Th:* **Acting company,** troupe de comédiens. **acting**[2], *s.* **1.** Action *f.* **2.** (*a*) *Th:* Jeu *m* (d'un acteur); exécution *f*, production *f* (d'une pièce de théâtre). **Acting over** (*of a play*), répétition *f* (d'une pièce). **Acting play,** pièce destinée à la scène, qui peut se jouer. (*b*) *To go in for a.*, faire du théâtre. (*c*) *F:* **It is mere acting,** c'est une comédie. **actinic** [ak'tinik], *a.* *Ph:* Actinique. **Actinic spectrum,** spectre chimique.

actinometer [akti'nɔmetər], *s.* *Ph: Phot:* Actinomètre *m* ; photomètre *m* de tirage, de pose.

action ['akʃ(ə)n], *s.* **1.** Action *f* (d'une personne, d'un remède, etc.). *To take action*, agir ; prendre des mesures. *Man of action*, homme de main, d'action. *To suit the action to the word*, joindre le geste à la parole. *To put, set, sth. in action; to bring, call, sth. into action*, mettre qch. en action, en œuvre, en jeu, en train, en mouvement ; faire agir, faire marcher, faire jouer, faire fonctionner, qch. *To come into action*, entrer en action, en jeu. *To bring the law into a.*, faire intervenir la loi. *Out of action*, hors de service. *To put* (sth.) *out of action*, (i) débrayer, dégager (une machine, etc.); (ii) *I.C.E:* arrêter, couper (l'allumage, etc.); (iii) détraquer, mettre en panne (une machine, etc.). **2.** (*Deed*) Action, acte *m*, fait *m*. *Splendid a.*, action d'éclat ; haut fait. **3.** *Th:* Action (d'une pièce). **The scene of action is . . .**, la scène se passe à. . . . **4.** (*a*) Action, gestes *mpl* (d'un joueur) ; train *m*, allure *f*, action (d'un cheval). (*b*) Mécanisme *m* (d'une montre, etc.) ; jeu *m* (d'une pompe, d'une serrure) ; mécanique *f* (d'un piano, d'un orgue). **5.** *Jur:* **Action at law,** action en justice ; procès *m* (civil ou criminel). *To bring an action against s.o.*, intenter une action, un procès, à, contre, qn ; exercer des poursuites contre qn. **6.** *Mil: Navy:* Action, combat *m*, engagement *m*. *Naval a.*, combat naval. *To go into action*, engager le combat ; donner. *Killed in action*, tué au feu, à l'ennemi. *Out of action*, hors de combat.

actionable ['akʃənəbl], *a.* *Jur:* (Mot, action) qui expose à des poursuites judiciaires.

activate ['aktiveit], *v.tr.* Activer.

active ['aktiv], *a.* **1.** Actif ; agile, alerte. *To be still a.*, être encore allant, alerte, ingambe. *A. volcano*, volcan en activité. *There is an active demand for wool*, les laines sont très recherchées. *A. brain*, cerveau éveillé. *A. imagination*, imagination vive. **2.** *Gram:* **Verb in the active voice,** verbe à l'actif, à la voix active. **3.** *To be an active party to sth., to take an active part in sth.*, prendre une part active, effective, à qch. **4.** **Active list,** *Mil: Navy:* cadre d'activité, *Mil:* rôles de 'armée active. (*Of official*) *To be in active employment, Mil:* to be on the active list, être en activité (de service). *Mil:* **Active service,** (i) service actif ; (ii) *F:* (= *field service*) service en campagne. *On a. service*, en campagne.

activity [ak'tiviti], *s.* **1.** Activité *f.* **Man of activity,** homme actif. *The a. of a large town*, le mouvement d'une grande ville. **2.** *That does not come within my activities*, cela ne rentre pas dans mes fonctions ; c'est en dehors de ma sphère d'action.

actor ['aktər], *s.* (*a*) Acteur *m* ; comédien *m*. *Tragic a.*, tragédien *m*. **Film actor,** acteur de cinéma. (*b*) *The chief a. in this event*, le principal acteur dans cet événement.

actress ['aktres], *s.f.* Actrice ; comédienne.

actual ['aktjuəl], *a.* **1.** Réel, véritable. *It's an a. fact*, c'est un fait positif. *To take an a. case*, pour prendre un cas concret. *To give the a. figures*, donner les chiffres mêmes. *A. possession*, possession de fait. *In actual fact . . .*, en fait. . . . **2.** (*Present*) Actuel, présent. *The a. position of affairs*, l'état de choses actuel. **-ally,** *adv.* **1.** (*a*) Réellement, véritablement, effectivement, positivement ; de fait. (*b*) *I a. found the door open*, à mon grand étonnement je trouvai la porte ouverte. *He a. swore*, il alla (même) jusqu'à lâcher un juron. **2.** Actuellement ; à présent ; à l'heure actuelle.

actuality [aktju'aliti], *s.* (*a*) Réalité *f.* (*b*) Actualité *f* ; le temps présent.

actualize ['aktjuəlaiz], *v.tr.* **1.** Réaliser (une conception). **2.** Faire revivre (une époque).

actuary ['aktjuəri], *s.* *Ins:* Actuaire *m.* **Actuaries' tables,** tables *f* de mortalité.

actuate ['aktjueit], *v.tr.* **1.** Mettre en action, mettre en mouvement, mener, actionner (une machine). **2.** Animer, pousser, faire agir (qn). *Actuated by jealousy*, poussé, mû, inspiré, par la jalousie. **actuating,** *a.* **1.** (Mécanisme) de commande, de manœuvre. **2.** (Motif) qui fait agir.

acuity [a'kjuiti], *s.* Acuité *f* ; acutesse *f.*

acumen [a'kju:men], *s.* Pénétration *f*, finesse *f* (d'esprit) ; clairvoyance *f*, perspicacité *f.*

acute [a'kjut], *a.* **1.** (*a*) (Angle) aigu ; (pointe) aiguë. (*b*) *Gram:* **Acute accent,** accent aigu. **2.** (*a*) (Son) aigu ; (douleur) aiguë, intense ; vif. *A. remorse*, remords cruels, poignants. (*b*) *A. stage of disease*, période aiguë d'une maladie. **3.** (*a*) **Acute ear,** oreille fine, ouïe fine. *A. sight*, vue perçante. (*b*) (Esprit) fin, pénétrant. **-ly,** *adv.* **1.** Vivement ; intensément. **2.** Avec finesse ; finement.

acuteness [a'kjutnəs], *s.* **1.** Aiguité *f* (d'un angle). **2.** (*a*) Acuité *f* (d'une douleur, d'un son) ; intensité *f* (d'une douleur, d'un remords). (*b*) Caractère aigu (d'une maladie). **3.** (*a*) Finesse *f* (d'ouïe) ; acuité *f* (de la vision) ; vivacité *f* (d'un sentiment). (*b*) Pénétration *f*, perspicacité *f* (de l'esprit).

adage ['adedʒ], *s.* Adage *m* ; maxime *f.*

adagio [a'dɑːdʒjo], *adv. & s.* Adagio (*m*).

Adam ['adəm], *Pr.n.m.* Adam. **Adam's apple,** pomme d'Adam ; nœud *m* de la gorge. *F:* **Not to know s.o. from Adam,** ne connaître qn ni d'Ève ni d'Adam. *To cast off the old A.,* dépouiller le vieil homme. *S.a.* OLD 3.

adamant ['adəmənt], *s.* **1.** *A:* (*a*) Diamant *m.*

(*b*) Aimant *m.* **2.** *F:* **Heart of adamant,** cœur de bronze, de pierre. **Frame of adamant,** corps d'acier. *On this point he is a.,* sur ce point il ne transige pas.

adamantine [adə'mantain], *a.* *Miner:* Adamantine spar, spath adamantin. *F: A. fortitude,* courage indomptable.

adapt [a'dapt], *v.tr.* Adapter, ajuster, approprier (*sth. to sth.,* qch. à qch.). **To adapt oneself to circumstances,** s'adapter, s'ajuster, s'accommoder, aux circonstances. *To a. one's language to the circumstances,* approprier son langage aux circonstances. **adapted,** *a.* **1.** *A.* **to sth.,** approprié à, fait pour, qch. *Well a. for a purpose,* bien adapté à un but; qui se prête à un but. **2.** Play adapted from the French, pièce adaptée du français.

adaptability [adaptə'biliti], *s.* Faculté *f* d'adaptation; souplesse *f.*

adaptable [a'daptəbl], *a.* **1.** (*a*) Adaptable, ajustable, qui peut s'adapter (*to,* à). (*b*) Susceptible d'être utilisé (*for,* pour; *to an end,* dans un but). **2.** *A. person,* personne qui s'accommode à toutes les circonstances. *A. mind,* esprit souple.

adaptation [adap'teiʃ(ə)n], *s.* **1.** Adaptation *f,* appropriation *f* (*of sth. to sth.,* de qch. à qch.). **2.** Adaptation (littéraire).

adapter [a'daptər], *s.* **1.** Auteur *m* d'une adaptation; remanieur *m.* **2.** Intermédiaire *m* de raccord. *El:* Raccord *m* (de lampe). *Phot:* **Plate adapter,** cadre *m* intermédiaire. **Lens adapter,** bague *f* porte-objectif.

add [ad], *v.tr.* **1.** (*a*) Ajouter, joindre (*to,* à). *To add s.o. to a committee,* adjoindre qn à un comité. *To add the interest to the capital,* ajouter l'intérêt au capital. *This news adds to our joy,* cette nouvelle augmente, accroît, notre joie. **Added to which . . .,** en outre de quoi. . . . **To add to my work . . .,** par surcroît de besogne. . . . *To add to my distress . . .,* pour mettre le comble à mon chagrin. . . . **To add sth. in,** ajouter, inclure, qch.; faire entrer qch. en ligne de compte. (*b*) (*Say besides*) Ajouter. *He added that . . .,* il ajouta que. . . . **2.** *Ar:* *To add (up, together) ten numbers,* additionner dix nombres. **To add up a column of figures,** totaliser une colonne de chiffres. (*Passive use*) *The assets add up to two millions,* l'actif se totalise par deux millions. **'adding-machine,** *s.* Additionneuse *f;* totalisateur *m.*

addendum, *pl.* **-a** [a'dendəm, -a], *s.* (*a*) Addenda *m inv.* (*b*) Addition *f* (à un livre, etc.); supplément *m.*

adder ['adər], *s.* Vipère *f* (fer-de-lance). *Young a.,* vipereau *m.*

addict[1] ['adikt], *s.* Personne adonnée à (l'opium, etc.); **-mane** *mf.* **Morphia addict,** morphinomane.

addict[2] [a'dikt], *v.tr.* To addict oneself to study, drink, s'adonner, se livrer, à l'étude, à la boisson.

addiction [a'dikʃ(ə)n], *s.* (*a*) *A. to study, science, good, evil,* attachement *m* à l'étude, inclination *f* pour les sciences, penchant *m* au bien, au mal. (*b*) *A. to morphia,* morphinomanie *f.*

addition [a'diʃ(ə)n], *s.* **1.** Addition *f.* *A welcome a. to my salary,* un heureux surcroît d'appointements. *Additions to the staff,* adjonction *f* de personnel. **In addition,** en outre, en sus, de plus, par surcroît. *In a. to sth.,* en plus, en sus, de qch. **2.** *Mth:* Addition. **additional** [a'diʃənəl], *a.* Additionnel, supplémentaire. *A. postage,* surtaxe *f.* *Com:* *A. payment,* supplément *m.* *A. reason,* nouvelle raison, raison de plus. **-ally,** *adv.* En outre (*to,* de); en sus.

addle[1] [adl], *a.* **1.** (Œuf) pourri, gâté, couvi. **2.** *F:* (Cerveau) (i) vide, creux, (ii) trouble, brouillé. **Addle-headed,** *s.* **addle-brain, -pate,** (homme) écervelé.

addle[2]. **1.** *v.tr.* (*a*) Pourrir, gâter (un œuf). (*b*) *F:* Troubler, brouiller (le cerveau, la tête). **2.** *v.i.* (*Of egg*) Se pourrir, se gâter.

address[1] [a'dres], *s.* **1.** Adresse *f,* habileté *f.* **2.** Adresse (d'une personne, d'une lettre). **What is your address?** où demeurez-vous? **3.** (*a*) Abord *m.* *To be of pleasing a.,* avoir l'abord aimable. *Young man of good a.,* jeune homme qui se présente bien. (*b*) **To pay one's addresses to a lady,** faire la cour à une femme. **4.** Discours *m,* allocution *f.* **5.** **Form of address,** titre *m* (à donner en s'adressant à qn). **ad'dress-book,** *s.* Carnet *m* d'adresses.

address[2], *v.tr.* **1.** (*a*) *To a. a letter to s.o.,* adresser une lettre à qn. (*b*) **To address a letter,** mettre, écrire, l'adresse sur une lettre. **2.** (*a*) *To a. one's prayers to God,* adresser ses prières à Dieu. (*b*) **To address s.o.,** (i) aborder, accoster, qn; (ii) adresser la parole à qn. **To address oneself to s.o.,** s'adresser à qn. (*c*) **To address the crowd,** haranguer la foule. *When he addresses the House,* quand il parle à la Chambre; (*in Fr.*) quand il monte à la tribune. **3.** *Golf:* Viser (la balle). **4. To address oneself to a task,** se mettre à une tâche.

addressee [adre'si:], *s.* Destinataire *mf.*

adduce [a'dju:s], *v.tr.* Alléguer, apporter (des raisons, des preuves); produire (un témoin); invoquer, citer (une autorité).

adenoids ['adenɔidz], *s.pl.* *Med:* Végétations *f* adénoïdes.

adenoma [ade'nouma], *s.* *Med:* Adénome *m.*

adept. **1.** *a.* [a'dept]. *To be a. in sth., at doing sth.,* être expert, habile, à qch., à faire qch. **2.** *s.* ['adept]. Adepte *mf;* initié(e); expert *m* (*in,* en).

adequacy ['adikwəsi], *s.* Suffisance *f* (d'une récompense, etc.); justesse *f.*

adequate ['adikwet], *a.* **1.** (*a*) Suffisant (*to,* à). *A. reward,* juste récompense; récompense adéquate, suffisante. *A. help,* aide efficace. (*b*) Proportionné (*to,* à). **2.** *I can find no one a. to the task,* je ne trouve personne qui soit à la hauteur de la tâche. **-ly,** *adv.* Suffisamment, congrûment, convenablement, en juste proportion.

adhere [ad'hi:ər], *v.i.* **1.** (*Of thg*) Adhérer, se coller. (*Of clay, cigarette*) *To a. to the tongue, to the lips,* happer à la langue, aux lèvres. **2.** (*Of pers.*) (*a*) **To adhere to a proposal, to a party,** adhérer, donner son adhésion, à une proposition, à un parti. (*b*) **To adhere to one's decision,** persister dans sa décision. *I a. to my statement,* je maintiens mon dire.

adherence [ad'hi:ərəns], *s.* **1.** (*Of thg*) Adhérence *f,* adhésion *f* (*to,* à). **2.** (*Of pers.*) (*a*) Attachement *m* (à un parti). (*b*) Accession *f,* adhésion (à un parti).

adherent [ad'hi:ərənt]. **1.** *a.* Adhérent (*to,* à); collé, attaché (*to,* à). **2.** *s.* Adhérent *m;* partisan *m.*

adhesion [ad'hi:ʒ(ə)n], *s.* **1.** Adhésion *f* (*to,* à); accession *f* (à un parti); approbation *f* (d'un projet). **2.** *Mec:* *Med:* *Surg:* Adhérence *f.*

adhesive [ad'hi:siv], *a.* **1.** Adhésif, collant; agglutinant. **2.** *Mec:* *A. capacity,* pouvoir adhérent. *S.a.* PLASTER[1] 1.

adieu [a'dju:]. **1.** *int.* Adieu! **2.** *s.* **To bid s.o. adieu,** dire adieu, faire ses adieux, à qn.

ad infinitum [adinfi'naitəm], *Lt.adv.phr.* A l'infini; *F:* à n'en plus finir.

ad interim [ad'intərim], *Lt.adv.phr.* *Jur :* Par intérim ; provisoire.

adipose ['adipous], *a.* Adipeux.

adit ['adit], *s.* **1.** *Min :* Galerie *f* (d'accès) à flanc de coteau. **2.** Accès *m* d'un lieu.

adjacency [a'dʒeis(ə)nsi], *s.* Contiguïté *f* (*to a place*, à un lieu) ; proximité *f*.

adjacent [a'dʒeis(ə)nt], *a.* (Angle, terrain) adjacent ; (terrain) contigu, attenant (*to*, à) ; (pays) limitrophe (*to*, de).

adjectival [adʒek'taiv(ə)l], *a.* *Gram :* Adjectif. **-ally,** *adv.* Adjectivement.

adjective ['adʒektiv], *s.* Adjectif *m*.

adjoin [a'dʒoin]. **1.** *v.tr.* Avoisiner (un lieu) ; être contigu à (qch.) ; toucher à, attenir à (qch.). **2.** *v.i.* The two houses adjoin, les deux maisons sont contiguës, se touchent. **adjoining,** *a.* (*a*) Contigu, -uë ; avoisinant. *Garden a. mine,* jardin attenant au mien. (*b*) *The a. room,* la pièce voisine.

adjourn [a'dʒə:rn]. **1.** *v.tr.* To a. sth. to, till, the next day, for a week, ajourner, différer, remettre, renvoyer, qch. au lendemain, à huitaine. **2.** *v.i.* (*a*) (*Of meeting, etc.*) (i) S'ajourner (*until*, à) ; (ii) lever la séance ; clore les débats. (*b*) *F :* (*Of persons*) To adjourn to a place, se transporter dans un endroit. *To a. to the drawing-room,* passer au salon.

adjournment [a'dʒə:rnmənt], *s.* (*a*) Ajournement *m*, suspension *f* (d'une séance, etc.). (*b*) Renvoi *m*, remise *f* (d'une affaire, etc.).

adjudge [a'dʒʌdʒ], *v.tr.* **1.** Prononcer sur, juger, décider judiciairement (une querelle, etc.). **2.** *Pred.* To adjudge s.o. (to be) guilty, déclarer qn coupable. **3.** To adjudge a prize to s.o., adjuger, décerner, une récompense à qn.

adjudicate [a'dʒu:dikeit], *v.tr.* & *i.* Juger, décider (une affaire) ; prononcer sur (une affaire). *To a. a claim,* juger une réclamation.

adjudication [adʒu:di'keiʃ(ə)n], *s.* Jugement *m*, décision *f*, arrêt *m*. *A. of bankruptcy,* jugement déclaratif de faillite.

adjudicator [a'dʒu:dikeitər], *s.* (*a*) Arbitre *m* ; juge *m*. (*b*) (*In musical competitions, etc.*) Membre *m* du jury.

adjunct ['adʒʌŋkt], *s.* **1.** (*a*) (*Pers.*) Adjoint (*to*, de) ; auxiliaire *mf*. (*b*) (*Thg*) Accessoire *m* (*of*, de). **2.** *Gram :* Complément *m*, adjoint *m* (du verbe, etc.).

adjuration [adʒuə'reiʃ(ə)n], *s.* Adjuration *f*.

adjure [a'dʒuər], *v.tr.* To a. s.o. to do sth., adjurer, conjurer, supplier, qn de faire qch.

adjust [a'dʒʌst], *v.tr.* **1.** Arranger (une affaire, une querelle) ; concilier, régler (un différend). **2.** (*a*) Ajuster (qch. à qch.). *To a. oneself to new conditions,* s'adapter aux conditions nouvelles. (*b*) Régler, ajuster (une balance, une montre, etc.) ; monter (un appareil) ; étalonner (un instrument) ; mettre un microscope, un moteur) au point ; égaliser (la pression, etc.). *Nau :* To a. the compasses, compenser, corriger, les compas. (*c*) Ajuster, arranger (son chapeau, ses vêtements).

adjusting, *s.* Mise *f* au point ; réglage *m*. *Adjusting screw,* vis de réglage.

adjustable [a'dʒʌstəbl], *a.* (*a*) (Différend) susceptible d'accommodement. (*b*) *Mec.E :* etc : Ajustable, réglable.

adjustment [a'dʒʌstmənt], *s.* **1.** Ajustement *m* (d'un différend, etc.) ; arrangement *m* (d'une affaire). **2.** Ajustement (d'une balance) ; rectification *f* (d'un outil, d'un instrument) ; réglage *m* (d'un mécanisme). *Nau :* Compensation *f*, correction *f* (des compas). *Final a.,* mise *f* au point.

adjutancy ['adʒutənsi], *s.* *Mil :* Fonctions *fpl* de capitaine adjudant major.

adjutant ['adʒutənt], *s.* *Mil :* Battalion, regimental, a., capitaine *m* adjudant major ; *F :* le major. Adjutant general, *approx.* = chef *m* d'état-major. **'adjutant(-bird, -crane, -stork),** *s.* *Orn :* Adjudant *m*, marabout *m* (des Indes).

ad libitum, ad lib. [ad'libitəm, ad'lib], *Lt.adv.phr.* A volonté ; (*of food*) à discrétion.

administer [ad'ministər], *v.tr.* (*a*) Administrer, régir (un pays) ; gérer (des affaires, des biens) ; appliquer (les lois). To administer justice, dispenser, rendre, la justice. (*b*) *To a. the last sacraments, a remedy, to s.o.,* administrer les derniers sacrements, un médicament, à qn. To administer an oath, the oath, to s.o., faire prêter serment à qn ; assermenter qn.

administration [adminis'treiʃ(ə)n], *s.* **1.** (*a*) Administration *f*, gestion *f* (d'une fortune, etc.) ; régie *f* (d'une succession, etc.). (*b*) *Jur :* Curatelle *f* (des biens d'un mineur). (*c*) Administration (de la justice, des sacrements, d'un remède). **2.** *Coll.* L'Administration, le Gouvernement.

administrative [ad'ministreitiv], *a.* Administratif. *A. details,* détails d'ordre administratif.

administrator [ad'ministreitər], *s.* **1.** Administrateur *m* ; gestionnaire *m*. **2.** *Jur :* Curateur *m*.

administratorship [ad'ministreitərʃip], *s.* Gestion *f*, gérance *f*. *Jur :* Curatelle *f*.

admirable ['admirəbl], *a.* Admirable. **-ably,** *adv.* Admirablement. *He succeeded a.,* il a réussi à merveille.

admiral ['admirəl], *s.* **1.** (*a*) Amiral *m*, *pl.* -aux. *A. Nelson,* l'amiral Nelson. (*b*) Commandant *m* en chef d'une flotte marchande). **2.** *Ent :* Red Admiral, vulcain *m*. White Admiral, petit sylvain.

admiralty ['admirəlti], *s.* The Admiralty, l'Amirauté *f* ; (*in France*) le Ministère de la Marine, *F :* la Marine. First Lord of the Admiralty, = Ministre de la Marine. Court of Admiralty, Tribunal maritime.

admiration [admi'reiʃ(ə)n], *s.* (*a*) Admiration *f* (*of, for,* pour). To be struck with admiration, être saisi d'admiration. To cry out in admiration, *F :* crier merveille. (*b*) *To be the a. of everyone,* faire l'admiration de tous.

admire [ad'maiər], *v.tr.* **1.** Admirer. *To a. oneself in a glass,* se mirer dans une glace. **2.** *F :* Exprimer son admiration de (qch.). **admiring,** *a.* (Regard, ton, etc.) admiratif. **-ly,** *adv.* Avec admiration.

admirer [ad'maiərər], *s.* (*a*) Admirateur, -trice. (*b*) Adorateur *m*, soupirant *m* (d'une femme).

admissibility [admisi'biliti], *s.* Admissibilité *f*.

admissible [ad'misibl], *a.* (Idée, projet) admissible. *Jur :* (Pourvoi) recevable.

admission [ad'miʃ(ə)n], *s.* **1.** Admission *f*, accès *m* (à une école, à un emploi). Admission free, entrée libre. **2.** (*a*) Admission, acceptation *f* (d'un argument, d'une preuve). (*b*) *Jur :* Reconnaissance *f* (d'un fait allégué) ; confession *f* (d'un crime, etc.) ; aveu *m*. To make full admissions (of guilt), faire des aveux complets. **3.** *Mch :* I.C.E : Admission, aspiration *f* (de la vapeur, des gaz, etc.) ; injection *f* (de l'eau). Admission pipe, tuyau, conduite, d'amenée.

admit [ad'mit], *v.* (admitted) **1.** *v.tr.* (*a*) Admettre (qn à qch., dans un endroit) ; laisser entrer (qn) ; livrer passage à (qn). 'Admit bearer,' "laissez passer." *The key admits to the garden,* la clé donne entrée au jardin. *To a. s.o. to one's friendship,* admettre qn dans son intimité. (*b*) *The windows do not a. enough air,* les fenêtres ne laissent pas entrer assez d'air. (c) *Harbour that admits large ships*, port qui reçoit de grands bâtiments. (d) Admettre (une vérité, des excuses) ; reconnaître (un principe, sa faute) ; concéder (qu'on a tort). **It must be admitted that . . .,** il faut reconnaître que + *ind. To a. one's guilt*, s'avouer coupable ; faire des aveux ; avouer. *I was wrong, I admit*, j'ai eu tort, j'en conviens. **Let it be admitted!** avouons-le ! (e) *To a. a claim*, faire droit à, accueillir, une réclamation. **2.** *v.ind.tr. It admits of no doubt*, cela ne permet, ne souffre, aucun doute. **admitted,** *a.* **1.** *A. custom*, usage admis. **2.** *A. truth*, vérité reconnue, avouée. *An a. thief*, un voleur avéré. **-ly,** *adv. A. incorrect*, reconnu (pour, comme) incorrect. *The country is a. ill-governed*, le pays de l'aveu général est mal gouverné.

admittance [ad'mitəns], *s.* Permission *f* d'entrer ; entrée *f* (*to*, dans) ; accès *m* (à un endroit, auprès de qn). **To give s.o. admittance,** laisser entrer qn ; admettre qn. *He was denied, refused, a.*, on ne voulut pas le laisser entrer. **No admittance,** entrée interdite.

admixture [ad'mikstjər], *s.* **1.** Mélange *m.* **2.** *Pharm:* (Ad)mixtion *f. Water with an a. of alcohol*, eau additionnée d'alcool.

admonish [ad'mɔniʃ], *v.tr.* **1.** (a) Admonester, reprendre (qn). (b) **To admonish s.o. to do sth.,** exhorter qn à faire qch. **2.** *A : To a. s.o. of a danger*, avertir, prévenir, qn d'un danger.

admonishment [ad'mɔniʃmənt], **admonition** [admo'niʃ(ə)n], *s.* Remontrance *f*, admonestation *f. Ecc :* Admonition *f*, exhortation *f.*

admonitory [ad'mɔnitəri], *a.* (Lettre, etc.) de remontrances.

ado [a'du:], *s.* **1.** Agitation *f*, activité *f* ; bruit *m*, affairement *m. Without (any) more ado, without further ado*, sans plus de façons, de cérémonie, d'embarras. **To make much ado about nothing,** faire beaucoup de bruit pour rien. **2.** Difficulté *f*, peine *f.*

adobe [a'doubi, a'doub], *s.* Adobe *m* (brique ou maison).

adolescence [ado'les(ə)ns], *s.* Adolescence *f.*

adolescent [ado'les(ə)nt], *a. & s.* Adolescent.

adopt [a'dɔpt], *v.tr.* **1.** Adopter (un enfant). *Pred. To a. s.o. as son*, adopter qn pour fils. **2.** Adopter (une ligne de conduite) ; choisir, embrasser (une carrière). *The course to a.*, la marche à suivre. **adopted,** *a.* (Enfant, mot) adopté. *A. son*, fils adoptif. **My adopted country,** mon pays d'adoption.

adoption [a'dɔpʃ(ə)n], *s.* Adoption *f* (d'un enfant, d'une coutume, d'un pays) ; choix *m* (d'une carrière).

adoptive [a'dɔptiv], *a.* (Enfant, père) adoptif.

adorable [a'dɔ:rəbl], *a.* Adorable. **-ably,** *adv.* Adorablement ; à ravir.

adoration [ado'reiʃ(ə)n], *s.* Adoration *f. F : His a. for my cousin*, l'amour, le culte, qu'il portait à ma cousine.

adore [a'dɔ:ər], *v.tr.* Adorer (qn, qch) ; aimer (qn) à l'adoration.

adorer [a'dɔ:rər], *s.* Adorateur, -trice. *Her adorers*, ses adorateurs ; ses soupirants.

adorn [a'dɔ:rn], *v.tr.* Orner, parer, embellir (*with*, de). *Writer who adorns his age*, écrivain qui est l'ornement de son siècle. *To a. oneself*, se parer (*with*, de) ; se faire beau, belle.

adornment [a'dɔ:rnmənt], *s.* **1.** Ornementation *f.* **2.** Ornement *m*, parure *f. In all her adornments*, dans tous ses atours.

Adrian ['eidriən]. *Pr.n.m.* Adrien.

Adrianople [eidria'noupl]. *Pr.n.* Andrinople.

Adriatic [eidri'atik], *a. & s. Geog :* (La mer) Adriatique.

adrift [a'drift], *adv. Nau :* A la dérive. (*Of ship*) **To run, go, adrift,** aller à la dérive ; dériver. **To break adrift,** partir en dérive. **To be adrift,** être en dérive, à l'abandon. *F : You are all adrift*, vous divaguez ! *F :* **To turn s.o. adrift,** abandonner qn ; mettre qn sur le pavé. *He was turned a. in the world*, il fut abandonné à ses propres ressources. **To cut a boat adrift,** couper l'amarre. *F : To cut (oneself) a. from s.o.*, rompre avec qn.

adroit [a'drɔit], *a.* Adroit ; habile. **-ly,** *adv.* Adroitement.

adroitness [a'drɔitnəs], *s.* Adresse *f*, dextérité *f.*

adulate ['adjuleit], *v.tr.* Aduler, flatter, flagorner.

adulation [adju'leiʃ(ə)n], *s.* Adulation *f*, flatterie *f.*

adulator ['adjuleitər], *s.* Adulateur, -trice.

adulatory ['adjulətəri], *a.* Adulateur, -trice.

adult [a'dʌlt], *a. & s.* Adulte (*mf*).

adulterate [a'dʌltəreit], *v.tr.* Adultérer (une substance) ; altérer, falsifier (les monnaies) ; frelater (du vin, du lait).

adulteration [a'dʌltə'reiʃ(ə)n], *s.* Adultération *f* ; altération *f*, falsification *f* (des monnaies) ; frelatage *m* (des boissons).

adulterer, f. -eress [a'dʌltərər, -əres], *s.* Adultère *mf* (violateur, -trice, de la foi conjugale).

adulterine [a'dʌltərain], *a.* (Enfant) adultérin.

adulterous [a'dʌltərəs], *a.* Adultère.

adultery [a'dʌltəri], *s.* Adultère *m* (violation de la foi conjugale).

adumbrate [a'dʌmbreit], *v.tr.* **1.** Ébaucher, esquisser (un plan). **2.** Faire pressentir, laisser pressentir (de nouvelles démarches).

adumbration [adʌm'breiʃ(ə)n], *s.* **1.** Ébauche *f*, esquisse *f.* **2.** (a) Signes précurseurs. (b) Pressentiment *m.*

ad valorem [adva'lɔ:rem], *Lt.phr. Com : Ind :* **Ad valorem duty,** droit sur la valeur ; droit proportionnel.

advance[1] [ad'va:ns], *s.* **1.** (a) Marche *f* en avant ; mouvement *m* en avant. **To make an advance,** avancer. *A. towards sth.*, acheminement à, vers, qch. *Adm :* **Advance in seniority,** majoration *f* d'ancienneté. *Mil :* **Advance guard,** avant-garde *f.* **Advance party,** pointe *f* d'avant-garde. (b) **In advance,** (i) en avant ; (ii) en avance. *To arrive in a.*, arriver en avance. *To arrive in a. of others*, arriver avant les autres. *To pay in a.*, payer d'avance, par avance. *'All my thanks in a.*,' "tous mes remercîments par avance." *Th :* **To book in a.,** louer à l'avance. **Advance payment,** paiement par anticipation. (c) *I.C.E :* **A. of the ignition, of the spark,** avance *f* à l'allumage. **2.** Avancement *m*, progrès *m*, développement *m* (des sciences, etc.). *The a. of thought*, le cheminement, le progrès, de la pensée. **3. To make an advance, advances, to s.o.,** faire une avance, des avances, à, auprès de, qn ; faire les premières démarches. **To respond to s.o.'s advances,** répondre aux invites de qn. (*Of woman*) *To make advances to a man*, provoquer, *F :* aguicher, un homme. **4.** *Com : Fin :* (a) Avance (de fonds). *Advances on securities*, prêts *m* sur titres. (b) Augmentation *f* (de prix) ; renchérissement *m* ; hausse *f.*

advance[2]. I. *v.tr.* **1.** (a) Avancer (le pied, *Chess :* un pion). (b) Avancer (l'heure d'un payement). *I.C.E :* **To advance the spark,** mettre de l'avance à l'allumage. (c) Avancer, présenter, mettre en avant (une opinion). **2.** (a) Faire progresser, faire avancer (les sciences, etc.) ; faire avancer (des troupes) ; reculer (une frontière). (*b*) Élever, faire avancer (qn à un grade supérieur). **3.** Augmenter, hausser (le prix de qch.). **4.** *To a. s.o. money*, avancer de l'argent à qn. II. **advance,** *v.i.* **1.** S'avancer (*towards*, vers) ; (*of troops*) se porter en avant. *He advanced on me (threateningly*), il vint sur moi. **2.** (*a*) Avancer (en âge, dans ses études). *The work is advancing*, l'ouvrage avance, fait des progrès. *S.a.* YEAR. (*b*) (*Of officers, etc.*) Recevoir de l'avancement ; monter (en grade). **3.** Augmenter de prix ; hausser. **advanced,** *a.* **1.** (*a*) (Poste) avancé ; (études, opinions) avancées. *More a.* natives, indigènes plus évolués. *To be very advanced,* to hold very advanced ideas, avoir des idées très avancées. (*b*) *A.* mathematics, mathématiques supérieures. *A.* students, étudiants déjà avancés. **2.** *The night is a.,* il est tard dans la nuit. *The season is a.,* c'est la fin de saison. **3.** *The a.* cost of living, l'augmentation du coût de la vie.

advancement [ad′vɑːnsmənt], *s.* Avancement *m* (d'une personne, des sciences) ; progrès *m.*

advantage¹ [ad′vɑːntedʒ], *s.* **1.** Avantage *m.* To have the advantage of, over, s.o. : to gain the advantage over s.o., avoir, remporter, l'avantage sur qn ; l'emporter sur qn ; avoir le dessus. To take s.o. at advantage, prendre qn au dépourvu. To have the advantage of, in, numbers, avoir l'avantage du nombre. *I gained little a. from it*, j'en ai eu, j'en ai remporté, peu de profit. *You might with a. apply to . . .,* vous pourriez utilement vous adresser à. . . . To take advantage of sth., profiter de qch. ; tirer avantage, profit, de qch. To take a. of s.o., abuser de la crédulité, de la bonne volonté, de qn ; exploiter qn. To turn sth. to advantage, tirer parti de qch. ; mettre qch. à profit ; faire tourner qch. à son avantage. (*Of event*) To turn out to s.o.'s advantage, tourner à l'avantage de qn ; profiter à qn. To show off sth. to advantage, faire valoir qch. To show to (great) advantage, faire (très) bonne figure. *To execute an order to the best a.,* exécuter un ordre au mieux. *Ten:* Advantage in, advantage server, avantage dedans, au servant. Advantage out, advantage striker, avantage dehors, au relanceur. **2.** *Mec:* Multiplication *f* (d'un levier).

advantage², *v.tr.* Avantager, favoriser (qn, qch.).

advantageous [advan′teidʒəs], *a.* Avantageux (*to*, pour) ; profitable, utile. **-ly,** *adv.* Avantageusement ; utilement.

advent [′advent], *s.* **1.** *Ecc:* (*a*) Avent *m.* Advent Sunday, le premier dimanche de l'Avent. (*b*) The second Advent, le second Avènement. **2.** Arrivée *f* ; venue *f. The a.* of the motor car, l'avènement *m* de l'automobile.

adventitious [adven′tiʃəs], *a.* Adventice. (*a*) (Fait) accessoire. (*b*) Accidentel, fortuit.

adventure¹ [ad′ventʃər], *s.* **1.** Aventure *f.* (*a*) Entreprise hasardeuse. *Life of a.,* vie d'aventure, vie aventureuse. (*b*) Événement *m* (qui arrive à qn). *He told us all his adventures*, il nous a raconté toutes ses aventures. **2.** Spéculation hasardée.

adventure², **1.** *v.tr.* Aventurer, hasarder, risquer (sa fortune, sa vie, etc.). **2.** *v.i.* & *pr. To a.* (*oneself*) (*up*)on an undertaking, s'aventurer, se hasarder, dans une entreprise.

adventurer [ad′ventʃərər], *s.* (*In all senses*) Aventurier *m* ; homme *m* d'aventures. *Pej:* Chevalier *m* d'industrie ; rastaquouère *m*, *F:* rasta *m.*

adventuress [ad′ventʃəres], *s.f. Pej:* Aventurière ; intrigante.

adventurous [ad′ventʃərəs], *a.* Aventureux.

adverb [′advəːrb], *s. Gram:* Adverbe *m.*

adverbial [ad′vəːrbiəl], *a. Gram:* Adverbial, -aux. **Adverbial phrase**, locution adverbiale. **-ally,** *adv.* Adverbialement.

adversary [′advərsəri], *s.* Adversaire *m.*

adverse [′advəːrs], *a.* **1.** Adverse. (*a*) Contraire, opposé (*to,* à). *A. wind,* vent contraire. (*b*) Ennemi (*to, de*) ; hostile (*to,* à, envers). *A. fortune,* fortune adverse. (*c*) Défavorable. **2.** Opposé ; en face. *The a.* page, la page ci-contre. **-ly,** *adv.* (*a*) *To act a. to s.o.,* agir (tout) au contraire de qn ; prendre le contre-pied de ce que fait qn. (*b*) *To influence s.o. a.,* exercer une influence défavorable sur qn.

adversity [ad′vəːrsiti], *s.* Adversité *f*, infortune *f.*

advert [ad′vəːrt], *v.i. To a. to sth.,* faire allusion à qch. ; parler de qch. ; citer qch.

advertise [′advərtaiz], *v.tr.* & *i.* **1.** *A :* Avertir (*s.o. of sth.,* qn de qch.). **2.** (*a*) (i) (Faire) annoncer, faire savoir, faire connaître (un événement dans les journaux) ; (ii) afficher (une vente, etc.). *To a. in a paper,* (faire) insérer une annonce dans un journal. (*b*) Faire de la réclame, de la publicité, de la propagande, pour (un produit). *Abs.* Faire de la réclame, de la publicité. *F : You needn't a.* the fact, vous n'avez pas besoin de le crier sur les toits. **advertising,** *s.* Publicité *f*, réclame *f* ; annonces *fpl.* Advertising medium, agency, agent, organe, bureau, entrepreneur, de publicité. Advertising manager, chef de la publicité.

advertisement [ad′vəːrtizmənt], *s.* **1.** Publicité *f.* **2.** (*a*) (*In newspaper*) Annonce *f.* Advertisement manager, annoncier *m.* (*b*) (*On a wall*) Affiche *f.* (*c*) (Puffing) advertisement, réclame *f.*

advertiser [′advərtaizər], *s.* (*a*) Auteur *m* de l'annonce. (*b*) Faiseur *m* de réclame.

advice [ad′vais], *s.* (*The pl. is rare, except in* 3) **1.** Conseil(s) *m(pl)*, avis *m.* Piece of advice, conseil. To ask for advice, demander des conseils. To ask, seek, s.o.'s advice, prendre conseil de qn ; prendre l'avis de qn. *To take s.o.'s a.,* suivre le conseil de qn ; se conformer à l'avis de qn. To act on s.o.'s advice, agir selon, sur, le conseil de qn. To take medical advice, consulter un médecin. *At, by, on, under, s.o.'s a.,* sur l'avis de qn ; suivant les conseils de qn. **2.** Avis. *Com:* Advice-note, letter of advice, lettre, note, d'avis. **3.** *pl.* Nouvelles *f*, avis. *We have advices from abroad,* nous avons reçu des informations, des avis, de l'étranger. **ad′vice-boat,** *s. Navy:* Aviso *m*, mouche *f* (d'escadre).

advisability [advaizə′biliti], *s.* = ADVISABLENESS.

advisable [ad′vaizəbl], *a.* **1.** (Démarche) recommandable, conseillable, judicieuse. *It would be a.* to lock up these papers, il serait prudent d'enfermer ces papiers. **2.** Opportun, à propos ; convenable (*for,* pour). *It might be a. to . . .,* peut-être conviendrait-il de. . . . As shall be deemed advisable, ainsi qu'on le jugera utile ; ainsi qu'il appartiendra. *If you deem it a.,* si bon vous semble.

advisableness [ad′vaizəblnəs], *s.* Opportunité *f*, convenance *f.*

advise [ad′vaiz]. I. *v.tr.* **1.** (*a*) *To a. s.o.,* conseiller qn. *To a. s.o. to do sth.,* conseiller à qn de faire qch. *I strongly a. you to . . .,* je vous recommande (instamment) de. . . . *What do you a. me to do?* que me conseillez-vous ? (*b*) *To a. sth.,* recommander qch. (à qn). (*c*) To advise s.o. against sth., against doing sth., déconseiller qch. à qn ; déconseiller à qn de faire qch. **2.** To advise s.o. on a question, renseigner qn sur une question. *To a. on a question,* servir de conseil pour une question. **3.** To advise s.o. of sth., avertir, prévenir, instruire, qn de qch. *To a. s.o. that . . .,* avertir, prévenir, qn que. . . . II. **advise,** *v.i.* To advise with s.o., (i) consulter qn; (ii) se consulter avec qn. **advised,** *a.* **1.** (Acte) réfléchi, délibéré. **2.** *See* ILL-ADVISED, WELL-ADVISED.

advisedly [ad'vaizidli], *adv.* **1.** De propos délibéré; à dessein. **2.** En connaissance de cause; après mûre considération.

adviser [ad'vaizər], *s.* Conseiller *m.* **Legal adviser,** conseiller juridique. **Spiritual adviser,** directeur *m* de conscience.

advisory [ad'vaizəri], *a.* Consultatif.

advocacy ['advokəsi], *s.* **1.** Profession *f* ou fonction *f* d'avocat. **2.** *A. of a cause,* plaidoyer *m* en faveur d'une cause; appui donné à une cause.

advocate[1] ['advoket], *s.* **1.** *Jur:* (*In Scot.*) Avocat *m.* **The Lord Advocate** = le Procureur général (en Écosse). **2.** Avocat; défenseur *m* (d'une doctrine, etc.). *The advocates of free trade,* les partisans du libre-échange.

advocate[2] ['advokeit], *v.tr.* Plaider en faveur de (qch.); préconiser (un remède).

advowson [ad'vausən], *s.* *Ecc:* Droit *m* de présentation (à un bénéfice).

adze [adz], *s.* *Tls:* (H)erminette *f*; doloire *f.*

aedile ['iːdail], *s.* *Rom.Ant:* Édile *m.*

Aegean [iː'dʒiːən], *a. & s.* *Geog:* (La mer) Égée.

aegis ['iːdʒis], *s.* *Gr.Myth:* Égide *f.* *F:* **Under the aegis of . . .,** sous l'égide de. . . .

Aeneas [iː'niːəs]. *Pr.n.m.* *Lt.Lit:* Énée.

Aeneid ['iːniid], *s.* **The Aeneid,** l'Énéide *f.*

Aeolian [iː'oulian], *a.* *A.Geog:* Éolien. **Aeolian harp,** harpe éolienne.

aeon ['iːən], *s.* Durée *f* (de l'univers); éon *m.* *F:* **During aeons upon aeons,** pendant des siècles; pendant des éternités.

aerate ['ɛəreit], *v.tr.* **1.** (a) Aérer. (b) *Physiol:* Artérialiser (le sang). **2.** Gazéifier (l'eau); champagniser (le vin). **aerated,** *a.* (a) (Pain) aéré. (b) (Eau) gazeuse; (vin) gazéifié, champagnisé.

aeration [ɛə'rei∫(ə)n], *s.* Aération *f.*

aerial ['ɛəriəl]. **1.** *a.* Aérien. *A. railway,* voie ferrée aérienne. **2.** *s.* *W.Tel:* Antenne *f.* **Aerial wire,** brin, fil, d'antenne. *Frame a., loop a.,* antenne en cadre; cadre *m* de réception. *Av:* *Trailing a.,* antenne pendante.

aerie, aery ['ɛəri, 'iːəri], *s.* = EYRIE, EYRY.

aerobatics [ɛərə'batiks], *s.pl.* *Av:* *F:* Acrobaties (aériennes).

aerodrome ['ɛərədroum], *s.* Aérodrome *m.*

aerodynamic [ɛərədai'namik, -di-], *a.* *Aut: etc:* (= STREAMLINED) Aérodynamique.

aerodynamics [ɛərədai'namiks, -di-], *s.pl.* (*Usu. with sg. const.*) Aérodynamique *f.*

aero-engine ['ɛəroendʒin], *s.* Aéromoteur *m.*

aerofoil ['ɛərofoil], *s.* *Av:* Plan *m* à profil d'aile; voilure *f*; surface portante.

aerograph ['ɛərograf], *s.* **1.** *Meteor:* (*Instrument*) Aérographe *m.* **2.** = AIR-BRUSH.

aerolite ['ɛərolait], **aerolith** ['ɛəroliθ], *s.* Aérolithe *m.*

aeronaut ['ɛərono:t], *s.* Aéronaute *m.*

aeronautic(al) [ɛəro'no:tik(l)], *a.* Aéronautique.

aeronautics [ɛəro'no:tiks], *s.pl.* (*Usu. with sg. const.*) Aéronautique *f*, aérostation *f.*

aerophotography [ɛərofo'tografi], *s.* Photographie aérienne.

aeroplane ['ɛəroplein], *s.* Aéroplane *m*; avion *m.* *Commercial a.,* avion de transport.

aerostatics [ɛəro'statiks], *s.pl.* (*Usu. with sg. const.*) Aérostatique *f.*

Aeschylus ['iːskiləs]. *Pr.n.m.* Eschyle.

Aesculapius [iːskju'leipiəs]. *Pr.n.m.* *Myth:* Esculape. **Aesculapius's staff,** caducée *m.*

Aesop ['iːsop]. *Pr.n.m.* *Gr.Lit:* Ésope.

aesthete ['iːsθiːt], *s.* Esthète *mf.*

aesthetic(al) [iːs'θetik(l)], *a.* **1.** Esthétique. **2.** *F:* De bon goût. **-ally,** *adv.* Esthétiquement.

aesthetics [iːs'θetiks], *s.pl.* (*Usu. with sg. const.*) Esthétique *f.*

aestival [iːs'taivəl], *a.* Estival, -aux.

afar [a'fɑːr], *adv.* From afar, de loin. **Afar off,** au loin; éloigné.

affability [afə'biliti], *s.* Affabilité *f* (*towards,* envers, avec); aménité *f*, courtoisie *f.*

affable ['afəbl], *a.* Affable, courtois (to, with, envers, avec). **-ably,** *adv.* Avec courtoisie, avec affabilité.

affair [a'fɛər], *s.* Affaire *f.* **That is my affair,** ça, c'est mon affaire. (Love-)affair, affaire de cœur. *A. of honour,* affaire d'honneur; duel *m.* *The affairs of this world,* les choses *f* de ce monde. *F:* *The building is a poor a.,* le bâtiment n'est pas grand'chose, n'est rien.

affect[1] [a'fekt], *v.tr.* **1.** (a) Affecter (une forme). (b) Affecter (une manière, une vertu, etc.). *To a. to do sth., to be sth.,* affecter de faire qch., d'être qch. *To a. big words,* affecter les grands mots. *He affects the high-brow,* il se donne des airs d'intellectuel. (c) Simuler (la piété, etc.). *To a. stupidity,* faire la bête. **2.** (*Of animals*) Fréquenter, hanter (une région). **affected**[1], *a.* (*Of pers., manners*) (a) Affecté, maniéré, mignard, affété (*of pers.*) minauder, grimacier. (b) Simulé. **-ly,** *adv.* Avec affectation.

affect[2], *v.tr.* **1.** (a) Atteindre, attaquer, toucher (qn); affecter (un organe, etc.); influer sur (qch.). *To be affected by a fall in prices,* être atteint par une baisse de prix. *The climate has affected his health,* le climat a altéré sa santé. **It affects me personally,** cela me touche, m'intéresse, personnellement. (b) *Med:* Intéresser. *Bowel complaint that also affects the liver,* maladie intestinale qui intéresse le foie. **2.** Affecter, affliger, toucher (qn). *To be affected at the sight of sth.,* se laisser attendrir au spectacle de qch. **3.** Toucher, concerner (qn, qch.). *That does not a. the matter,* cela ne fait rien à l'affaire. *To a. events,* influer sur les événements. **affected**[2], *a.* (a) *To be well, ill, a. towards s.o.,* être bien, mal, disposé pour qn. (b) *To be a. with a disease,* être atteint d'une maladie. *The lung is a.,* le poumon est atteint, attaqué, touché. (c) Ému, touché. *To be much a. by sth.,* ressentir vivement qch.

affecting, *a.* Touchant, attendrissant.

affectation [afek'tei∫(ə)n], *s.* **1.** *A. of interest,* affectation *f*, simulation *f*, d'intérêt. **2.** Affectation; afféterie *f*, apprêt *m* (de langage); mignardise *f*, mièvrerie *f*; simagrées *fpl.*

affectedness [a'fektidnəs], *s.* Affectation *f.*

affection [a'fek∫(ə)n], *s.* **1.** Impression (ressentie). **2.** Affection *f*, tendresse *f*; amitié *f*, attachement *m.* **To have an affection for s.o., to feel affection towards s.o.,** avoir, ressentir, de l'affection pour qn; affectionner qn. **To gain, win, s.o.'s affection,** se faire aimer de qn. **3.** *Med:* Affection (de poitrine, etc.).

affectionate [a'fek∫ənet], *a.* Affectueux, aimant. *Your a. son,* votre fils affectionné. **-ly,** *adv.* Affectueusement, affectionnément. **Yours affectionately,** à vous de (tout) cœur; bien affectueusement le vôtre.

affiance [a'faiəns], *v.tr.* *Lit:* Fiancer (s.o. to s.o., qn avec qn). **affianced,** *a.* To be affianced to s.o., être fiancé(e) à qn. *She became a. to him,* elle devint sa fiancée ; elle se fiança avec lui. The affianced couple, les deux fiancés. *A.* bride, fiancée *f.*

affidavit [afi'deivit], *s. Jur:* Déclaration par écrit et sous serment, enregistrée sur acte timbré ; affirmation. *Evidence taken on a.,* dépositions recueillies sous serment.

affiliate [a'filieit], *v.tr.* **1.** (*Of a society*) To a. members, s'affilier des membres. **2.** *To a. a member to, with, a society,* affilier un membre à une société. *To a.* (*oneself*) *to, with, a society,* s'affilier à une société. Affiliated firm, filiale *f.*

affiliation [afili'eiʃ(ə)n], *s.* (*a*) Affiliation *f* (à une société). (*b*) *U.S: Political affiliations,* attaches *f* politiques.

affinity [a'finiti], *s.* (*a*) Affinité *f* (*with, to,* avec ; *between,* entre). *Spiritual a.,* affinité spirituelle. (*b*) Conformité *f* de caractère. (*c*) *Ch:* Affinity for a body, affinité pour un corps. (*d*) Parenté *f* par alliance ; affinité.

affirm [a'fəːrm], *v.tr.* **1.** Affirmer, soutenir (*that,* que). *To a. sth. to s.o.,* affirmer, assurer, qch. à qn. **2.** *Jur:* Confirmer, homologuer (un jugement).

affirmation [afər'meiʃ(ə)n], *s.* **1.** (*a*) Affirmation *f,* assertion *f.* (*b*) *Jur:* Déclaration solennelle (tenant lieu de serment) (p. ex. lorsque le témoin n'a pas de foi religieuse). **2.** *Jur:* Confirmation *f,* homologation *f* (d'un jugement).

affirmative [a'fəːrmətiv]. **1.** *a.* Affirmatif. *To make an a. sign,* faire signe que oui. **2.** *s. If he replies* in the affirmative, s'il répond affirmativement. *The answer is in the a.,* la réponse est oui. **-ly,** *adv.* Affirmativement.

affirmatory [a'fəːrmətəri], *a.* Affirmatif.

affix [a'fiks], *v.tr.* Attacher (*sth. to sth.,* qch. à qch.). *To a. a seal, a stamp, to a document,* apposer un sceau, un timbre, à, sur, un document.

afflatus [a'fleitəs], *s.* Souffle *m* (divin, du génie).

afflict [a'flikt], *v.tr.* Affliger, tourmenter ; désoler. *s.* The afflicted, les affligés. **afflicting,** *a.* Affligeant.

affliction [a'flikʃ(ə)n], *s.* **1.** Affliction *f. These forms are my a.,* ces formules font mon désespoir. **2.** Calamité *f,* revers *m.* **3.** The afflictions of old age, les infirmités *f* de la vieillesse.

afflictive [a'fliktiv], *a.* Pénible.

affluence ['afluəns], *s.* **1.** Affluence *f* ; grand concours (de gens, etc.). **2.** Abondance *f,* richesse *f.*

affluent[1] ['afluənt], *a.* **1.** Abondant, riche (*in,* en). **2.** Opulent, riche. *In a. circumstances,* dans l'aisance.

affluent[2], *s. Geog:* Affluent *m* (d'une rivière).

afflux ['aflʌks], *s.* **1.** Afflux *m,* affluence *f* (du sang, etc.). **2.** Concours *m* (de gens). *A sudden a. of strangers,* une affluence inopinée d'étrangers.

afford [a'fɔːrd], *v.tr.* **1.** (*Usu. with 'can'*) (*a*) Avoir les moyens (pécuniaires) (de faire qch.) ; être en mesure (de faire qch.). *I cannot a. to be idle,* je ne suis pas à même de ne rien faire. **I can't afford it,** mes moyens ne le permettent pas ; c'est trop cher pour moi. *He can well a. to build,* il a largement les moyens de bâtir. *I* **can afford to wait,** je peux attendre. *Can you a. the time?* disposez-vous du temps (nécessaire) ? **2.** (*Give, provide*) Fournir, offrir. *These trees afforded us but little shelter,* ces arbres ne nous fournissaient qu'un piètre abri.

afforest [a'fɔrest], *v.tr.* (*a*) Boiser (une terre, une région) ; soumettre (une région) au régime forestier. (*b*) Reboiser.

afforestation [afɔres'teiʃ(ə)n], *s.* (*a*) Boisement *m,* afforestation *f.* (*b*) Reboisement *m.*

affranchise [a'frantʃaiz], *v.tr.* Affranchir.

affranchisement [a'frantʃizmənt], *s.* Affranchissement *m* (d'un serf, d'un esclave).

affray [a'frei], *s.* **1.** Bagarre *f,* échauffourée *f.* **2.** (*Between two men*) Rixe *f.*

affright [a'frait], *v.tr. A:* = FRIGHTEN.

affront[1] [a'frʌnt], *s.* Affront *m,* offense *f. To put an a. upon s.o., to offer an a. to s.o.,* faire (un) affront, faire une avanie, à qn. **To suffer an affront** (*at the hands of s.o.*), essuyer une avanie (de la part de qn). *To pocket an a.,* avaler un affront.

affront[2], *v.tr.* (*a*) Insulter, offenser ; faire (un) affront à (qn). (*b*) Faire rougir, faire honte à (qn).

afield [a'fiːld], *adv. Lit: To be a.,* (*of labourer*) être aux champs ; (*of warrior*) être en campagne. (*b*) *F:* **To go far afield, farther afield,** aller très loin, plus loin.

afire [a'faiər], *adv. & pred.a. A. & Lit:* En feu ; embrasé. **To be** (*all*) **afire with the desire to . . .,** brûler du désir de. . . .

aflame [a'fleim], *adv. & pred. a. Lit:* En flammes ; embrasé. **To be aflame with colour,** briller de vives couleurs ; rutiler. *To be a. with curiosity,* brûler de curiosité. *This rumour had set Vendée a.,* cette rumeur avait mis le feu à la Vendée.

afloat [a'flout], *adv. & pred. a.* **1.** (*a*) A flot ; sur l'eau ; à la mer. (*Of ship, F: of pers.*) **To be afloat,** être à flot. **To set a ship afloat,** lancer, mettre à la mer, mettre à l'eau, un navire. *To keep a ship a.,* maintenir un navire à flot. *What had remained a. from the wreck,* ce qui avait surnagé au naufrage. *F:* (*Of pers.*) **To keep afloat,** se maintenir à flot ; surnager. (*b*) **Service afloat,** service à bord. *To serve a.,* servir sur mer. **2.** (*Of rumour, etc.*) To be a., courir, circuler. *This notion is a. again,* cette idée revient sur l'eau.

afoot [a'fut], *adv.* **1.** To be, to go, to come, a., être, aller, venir, à pied. **2.** To be afoot, être sur pied, en mouvement. *She is early a.,* elle est levée, debout, sur pied, de bonne heure. **3.** *F: A plan is a. to . . .,* on envisage, on a formé, un projet pour . . . ; on a formé le projet de. . . . **There's something afoot,** il se prépare, il se trame, quelque chose. *There is mischief a.,* il se prépare un mauvais coup.

afore [a'fɔːər], *adv. & prep.* **1.** *Nau:* Afore the mast, sur l'avant (du mât). **2.** *A. & Dial:* = BEFORE. **3.** Afore-cited, -mentioned, -named, aforesaid, précité, susmentionné, susdit.

aforethought [a'fɔːərθɔːt], *a. Jur:* **With, of,** malice aforethought, avec préméditation.

afraid [a'freid], *pred. a.* Pris de peur. **To be afraid** (**of s.o., of sth.**), avoir peur (de qn, de qch.) ; craindre (qn, qch.). *Don't be a.,* n'ayez pas peur ; ne craignez rien. *To make s.o. a.,* faire peur à qn ; effrayer qn. **To be afraid to do, of doing, sth.,** ne pas oser faire qch. ; avoir peur, craindre, de faire qch. *I am a. he will die,* je crains qu'il ne meure. *I am not a. of his dying,* je ne crains pas qu'il meure. *I am a. that he will not come, of his not coming,* j'ai peur qu'il ne vienne pas. **I'm afraid it is so!** j'en ai (bien) peur ! *F: I'm a. I can't tell you,* je ne saurais guère vous le dire. *I am a. he is out,* je crois bien qu'il est sorti. *I'm a. that it is too true,* je crains bien que ce ne soit que trop vrai.

afresh [a'freʃ], *adv.* De nouveau, à nouveau. **To start sth. afresh,** recommencer qch.

Africa ['afrika]. *Pr.n. Geog:* L'Afrique *f.*

African ['afrikən], *a. & s. Geog:* Africain.

aft [ɑːft], *adv. Nau:* Sur, à, vers, l'arrière. *To berth aft*, coucher à l'arrière. **Aft of the mast**, sur l'arrière du mât. *S.a.* FORE-AND-AFT. **'aft-gate,** *s.* Porte *f* d'aval (d'une écluse).

after ['ɑːftər]. I. *adv.* Après. **1.** (*Place, order*) **To come after**, venir après, venir à la suite. *You speak first, I shall speak a.*, parlez d'abord, je parlerai ensuite. **2.** (*Time*) *I never spoke to him a.*, je ne lui ai jamais parlé après. *I heard of it a.*, je l'ai appris plus tard. *He was ill for months after*, il en est resté malade pendant des mois. **Soon, long, after**, bientôt, longtemps, après. *The night, the week, a.*, la nuit, la semaine, d'après. *S.a.* DAY I, EVER I, MORNING I. II. **after**, *prep.* Après. **1.** (*Place*) (*a*) **To walk a.** *s.o.*, marcher après qn. *He closed the door a. him*, il referma la porte sur lui. (*b*) *To run, shout, a. s.o.*, courir, crier, après qn. *F:* **To be after s.o.**, sth, être après qn, qch.; être en quête de qn, de qch. *The police are a. you*, la police est à vos trousses. *The boys are a. your fruit*, les gamins en veulent à vos fruits. **What is he after?** (i) qu'est-ce qu'il a en tête? (ii) qu'est-ce qu'il cherche? *I see what you're a.*, je vois où vous voulez en venir. **2.** (*Time*) **To reign a.** *s.o.*, régner après qn. **After this date . . .**, passé cette date. **. . . On and after the 15th**, à partir du quinze. **After all** (*said and done*), au bout du compte; à la fin des fins; après tout; enfin. *The day a. the battle*, le lendemain de la bataille. **The day after to-morrow**, après-demain. *It is a. five* (*o'clock*), il est plus de cinq heures; il est cinq heures passées. *They entered one after the other*, ils entrèrent à la file, les uns après les autres. *He read page a. page*, il lut page sur page. **Time after time**, maintes (et maintes) fois. *S.a.* DAY I. **3.** (*Order*) (*a*) **'After you, sir,'** "après vous, monsieur." (*b*) *I put Milton a. Dante*, je mets Milton au-dessous de Dante. **4.** (*Manner*) **After a pattern**, d'après, suivant, selon, un modèle. *Landscape a. Turner*, paysage d'après Turner à la manière de Turner. III. **after**, *conj.* Après que + *ind.* *I come a. he goes*, je viens après qu'il est parti. IV. **after-**, *a.* **1.** Après. **2.** A venir. **3.** Arrière. *S.a.* GUN¹ 1. **'after-ages,** *s.pl.* **1.** Les siècles futurs; la postérité. **2.** Les époques postérieures. **'after-cabin,** *s. Nau:* Chambre *f* de l'arrière. **'after-care,** *s.* Surveillance *f* (de convalescents, de jeunes criminels). **'after-damp,** *s. Min:* Gaz *m* délétères (provenant d'une explosion de grisou); mofette *f*. **'after-days,** *s.pl.* La suite des temps. **In after-days**, (i) dans les jours à venir; (ii) dans les jours qui suivirent; dans la suite. **'after-deck,** *s. Nau:* Arrière-pont *m*, pont arrière. **'after-effect(s),** *s.*(*pl.*) Suites *fpl*, contre-coup *m*, répercussion *f* (d'un événement); séquelles *fpl* (d'une maladie). **'after-growth,** *s.* = AFTERCROP. **'after-life,** *s.* **1.** La vie future. **2.** Suite *f* de la vie. **In after-life**, plus tard dans la vie. **'after-mentioned,** *a.* Mentionné ci-après. **'after-taste,** *s.* Arrière-goût *m*; (*of wine*) déboire *m*.

aftercrop ['ɑːftərkrɔp], *s.* Regain *m* (de foin); seconde récolte.

afterglow ['ɑːftərglou], *s.* Dernières lueurs, derniers reflets, du soleil couchant.

aftermath ['ɑːftərmaθ], *s.* **1.** *Agr:* Regain *m*. **2.** Suites *fpl* (d'un événement).

aftermost ['ɑːftərmoust], *a. Nau:* **The a. part**, la partie la plus en arrière, la plus à l'arrière.

afternoon [ɑːftər'nuːn], *s.* Après-midi *m or f*, après-dîner *m*. *I shall see him this a.*, je le verrai cet(te) après-midi. *At half past two in the a.*, à deux heures et demie de l'après-midi; *Jur: etc:* à deux heures et demie du soir. *Every a.*, tous les après-midi. *I saw him on Tuesday a.*, je l'ai vu mardi après-midi. **Good afternoon!** bonjour! *S.a.* TEA I.

afterthought ['ɑːftərθɔːt], *s.* Réflexion *f* après coup.

afterwards ['ɑːftərwərdz], *adv.* Après, plus tard, ensuite; dans la suite, par la suite. *I only heard of it a.*, je ne l'ai su qu'après coup.

again [ə'gein], *adv.* With a *vb. often rendered by the pref.* re-: *to begin a.*, recommencer; *to bring a.*, ramener, rapporter; *to do a.*, refaire; *to come down, up, a.*, redescendre, remonter. **1.** (*a*) De nouveau, encore; *Lit:* derechef. **Once again**, encore une fois, une fois de plus. **Here we are again!** *F:* nous revoilà! *Don't do it a.!* ne recommencez pas! **Never again**, (ne . . .) jamais plus; plus jamais (. . . ne). **Again and again**, time and again, maintes et maintes fois; à plusieurs reprises. **Now and again**, ever and again, de temps en temps; de temps à autre. **As much again**, deux fois autant. *As large a.*, deux fois aussi grand. **Half as much again**, moitié plus. (*b*) (*Back*) **To send, give, sth. back a.**, renvoyer, rendre, qch. **To come a.**, revenir. (*c*) *F:* **What's his name again?** comment s'appelle-t-il déjà? (*d*) (*Intensive*) *The blow made his ears ring again*, ce fut un coup à lui faire tinter les oreilles. *The loaded table groaned a.*, la table chargée gémissait sous le poids. **2.** (*a*) De plus, d'ailleurs, en outre. (*b*) (**Then**) **again**; (**and**) **again**, d'autre part; d'un autre côté.

against [ə'geinst], *prep.* Contre. **1.** (*a*) **To fight a. s.o.**, se battre contre qn. **To march a. the enemy**, marcher à l'ennemi. *I have nothing to say a. it*, je n'ai rien à dire là-contre. **To be a. sth. being done**, être opposé à ce que quelque chose se fasse. *They fought man a. man*, ils se battirent homme à homme. *I did it a. my will*, je l'ai fait malgré moi, à contre-cœur. *Action that is a. the rules*, action contraire aux règlements. *Conditions are a. us*, les conditions (nous) sont défavorables. *There is no law a. it*, il n'y a pas de loi qui s'y oppose. **To brush a hat against the nap**, brosser un chapeau à contre-poil, à rebours. (*b*) *Warned a. s.o.*, sth., mis en garde contre qn, qch. (*c*) *To run, dash, a. the wall*, courir, donner, contre le mur. *F:* **To run up a. s.o.**, rencontrer qn par hasard. *S.a.* COME UP, UP¹ 1. 5. (*d*) *Leaning a. the wall*, appuyé contre le mur. (*e*) A l'encontre de. *Never go a. Nature*, il ne faut jamais aller à l'encontre de la Nature. **2.** (*a*) *My rights* (*as*) *a. the Government*, mes droits vis-à-vis du Gouvernement. (*b*) *Over against the school*, en face de l'école, vis-à-vis de l'école. **3.** *To show up a. a background*, se détacher sur un fond. **4.** *To make preparation a. his return*, faire des préparatifs pour son retour. *To buy preserves a. the winter*, acheter des conserves en prévision de l'hiver. **5.** *Three deaths this year as against thirty in 1934*, trois morts cette année contre trente, comparées à trente, en 1934.

agape [ə'geip], *adv. & pred. a.* Bouche bée.

agaric ['agarik, ə'garik], *s. Fung:* Agaric *m*. **Fly-agaric**, (amanite *f*) tue-mouches *m*.

agate ['aget], *s.* Agate *f*.

agave [ə'geivi], *s. Bot:* Agave *m*.

age¹ [eidʒ], *s.* **1.** Age *m*. (*a*) Middle age, âge mûr. **To be past middle age**, être sur le retour; être sur le déclin de la vie. **Of uncertain age**, entre deux âges. **To be twenty years of age**, être âgé de vingt ans. **What age are you?** quel âge avez-vous? *He has a daughter your age*, il a une fille de votre âge. *At his age*, à son âge, à l'âge qu'il a. **To be under age**, être mineur. **Full age**, âge légal ; (état *m* de) majorité *f*. **To be of (full) age**, être majeur. **To come of age**, atteindre sa majorité. **Coming of age**, entrée *f* en majorité. *On, at, his coming of age*, à sa majorité. **To be over age to do sth.**, être trop âgé pour faire qch. **To be of an age to marry**, être en âge de se marier. **He does not look his age**, il ne porte pas son âge. *She might be any age*, elle n'a pas d'âge. **They are of an age**, ils sont du même âge. (*b*) (Old) age, vieillesse *f*. *S.a.* OLD I. **2.** (*a*) Age, époque *f*, siècle *m*. **From age to age**, d'âge en âge. *The age we live in*, le siècle où nous vivons ; notre siècle. **In our age**, à notre époque. *The present age*, la génération actuelle. *Archeol :* **The stone age**, l'âge de pierre. **The iron age**, l'âge du fer. *Hist :* **The Middle Ages**, le moyen âge. *Myth :* **The golden age**, l'âge d'or. **The iron age**, l'âge de fer. (*b*) *F :* It is an age, it is ages, since I saw him, *I haven't seen him for ages*, il y a une éternité que je ne l'ai vu.

age², *v.* (aged [eidʒd], ag(e)ing ['eidʒiŋ]) I. *v.i.* Vieillir ; prendre de l'âge. **2.** *v.tr.* Vieillir ; rendre (qn) vieux. **aged**, *a.* I. ['eidʒid] Âgé, vieux. *An a. man*, un vieillard. *s. The a.*, les vieillards ; *F :* les vieux. **2.** [eidʒd] (*a*) *A. twenty years*, âgé de vingt ans. (*b*) *I found him greatly a.*, je le trouvai bien vieilli. **ageing¹**, *a.* Vieillissant. **ageing²**, *s.* Vieillissement *m*.

agency ['eidʒənsi], *s.* I. (*a*) Action *f*, opération *f*. *Through the a. of water*, par l'action de l'eau. (*b*) Agent *m. Natural agencies*, agents naturels. (*c*) Entremise *f. Through s.o.'s a.*, par l'entremise, par l'intermédiaire *m*, de qn. **2.** *Com :* Agence *f*, bureau *m*. **Agency office**, bureau d'affaires.

agenda [a'dʒendə], *s.pl.* (*Usu. with sing. concord*) Ordre *m* du jour (d'une réunion).

agent ['eidʒənt], *s.* I. (*a*) Agent *m*. **To be a free agent**, avoir son libre arbitre. (*b*) Homme *m* d'affaires ; régisseur *m* (d'une propriété). *Com :* Agent, représentant *m*. *On the spot*, agent à demeure. *To be sole a. for* . . ., avoir la représentation exclusive de. . . . *Mercantile a.*, commissionnaire *m*. **Bank agent**, directeur *m* d'une succursale de banque. (*c*) Mandataire *m*f ; fondé(e) de pouvoir. *S.a.* PRINCIPAL II. I. **2.** *Chemical a.*, agent chimique.

agglomerate, [a'glɔməreit]. I. *v.tr.* Agglomérer. **2.** *v.i.* S'agglomérer.

agglomeration [aglɔmə'reiʃ(ə)n], *s.* Agglomération *f*.

agglutinate [a'glu:tineit]. I. *v.tr.* Agglutiner. **2.** *v.i.* S'agglutiner.

aggrandize ['agranda:iz], *v.tr.* Agrandir ; exagérer (un incident).

aggrandizement [a'grandizmənt], *s.* Agrandissement *m*.

aggravate ['agrəveit], *v.tr.* I. (*a*) Aggraver (une faute, une difficulté) ; empirer (un mal) ; envenimer (une querelle). *Jur :* **Aggravated larceny**, vol qualifié. (*b*) Augmenter (l'indignation, la douleur). **2.** *F :* Agacer, exaspérer (qn). **aggravating**, *a.* I. *A. circumstance*, circonstance aggravante. **2.** Exaspérant, assommant.

aggravation [agrə'veiʃ(ə)n], *s.* I. (*a*) Aggravation *f* (d'un crime, d'une maladie) ; envenimement *m* (d'une querelle). (*b*) *F :* Agacement *m*, exaspération *f*. **2.** Circonstance aggravante.

aggregate¹ ['agregeit]. I. *a.* (*a*) Collectif. *Ind :* *A. output*, rendement global, total, d'ensemble. (*b*) *Bot : Geol : Z :* Agrégé. **2.** *s.* (*a*) Ensemble *m*, total *m*. (*b*) Masse *f*, assemblage *m*, agrégation *f*.

Miner : Agrégat *m*. **In the aggregate**, en somme, dans l'ensemble.

aggregate² ['agregeit]. I. *v.tr.* (*a*) *Ph :* Agréger. (*b*) *To a. s.o. to a society*, agréger qn à une compagnie. **2.** *v.i.* (*a*) *These armies aggregated 300,000 men*, ces armées s'élevaient à un total de 300,000 hommes. (*b*) *Ph :* S'agréger.

aggregation [agre'geiʃ(ə)n], *s.* I. (*a*) *Ph :* Agrégation *f* agglomération *f*.. (*b*) *A. of people*, assemblage *m* de personnes. **2.** Agrégat *m*.

aggression [a'greʃ(ə)n], *s.* Agression *f*.

aggressive [a'gresiv], *a.* Agressif. *A. policy*, politique militante. **-ly**, *adv.* D'une manière agressive ; d'un ton agressif.

aggressor [a'gresər], *s.* Agresseur *m*.

aggrieve [a'gri:v], *v.tr.* (*Usu. passive*) Chagriner, blesser.

aghast [a'gɑ:st], *pred. a.* Consterné. *To stand a. (at sth.)*, être stupéfait, consterné (de qch.).

agile ['adʒail], *a.* Agile, leste. **-ly**, *adv.* Agilement.

agility [a'dʒiliti], *s.* Agilité *f*.

agitate ['adʒiteit], *v.tr.* I. Agiter, remuer (qch.). **2.** Agiter, émouvoir, troubler (qn, l'esprit de qn). **3.** (*a*) Agiter (une question). (*b*) *Abs. To a. for sth., against sth.*, faire de l'agitation en faveur de qch., contre qch. **agitated**, *a.* Agité ; ému ; troublé. **agitating**, *a.* Émotionnant ; troublant.

agitation [adʒi'teiʃ(ə)n], *s.* I. Agitation *f* (de la mer) ; mouvement *m*. **2.** (*a*) Agitation, émotion *f*, trouble *m*. (*b*) Agitation (ouvrière, etc.) ; troubles. **3.** Discussion *f* (d'une question).

agitator ['adʒiteitər], *s.* Agitateur *m. Political a.*, fauteur *m* de troubles ; meneur *m*.

agleam [a'gli:m], *pred. a.* *Lit :* = GLEAMING¹.

aglow [a'glou], *adv. & pred. a.* I. (*Of thg*) Enflammé, embrasé. *To be a. with colour*, briller de vives couleurs. **2.** (*Of pers.*) *I was all a.*, (l'exercice, etc.) m'avait fouetté le sang. *Face a. with health*, visage resplendissant de santé.

agnail [a'gneil], *s.* Envie *f* (filet de peau qui s'est détaché de l'ongle).

agnostic [ag'nɔstik], *a. & s.* Agnosticiste (*m*f) ; agnostique (*m*f) ; libre penseur *m*.

ago [a'gou]. I. *a.* *Ten years ago*, il y a dix ans ; cela date de dix ans. *He arrived an hour ago*, il est arrivé il y a déjà une heure ; il est là depuis une heure. *A little while ago*, tout à l'heure ; tantôt. **2.** *adv.* **Long ago**, il y a longtemps. *Not long ago*, il n'y a pas longtemps ; naguère. *How long ago is it since* . . . ? combien de temps y a-t-il que. . . . ? *So long ago, as long ago*, as 1840, déjà en 1840 ; dès 1840. *No longer ago than last week*, pas plus tard que la semaine dernière.

agog [a'gɔg], *adv. & pred. a.* **To be agog for sth.**, être dans l'attente, dans l'expectative, de qch. *To be (all) a. (with excitement) about sth.*, être en l'air, en émoi, à cause de qch. **To be (all) agog to do sth.**, être impatient de faire qch. ; griller d'envie de faire qch. *The whole town was a.*, toute la ville était en émoi. **To set s.o. (all) agog**, mettre qn en train, en émoi ; *F :* aguicher qn. *To set the town a.*, mettre la ville en rumeur.

agoing [a'gouiŋ], *adv.* **To set sth., s.o., agoing**, mettre qch., qn, en marche, en train, en branle ; faire aller qch. *F :* **Just agoing to begin**, sur le point de commencer.

agonize [a'gona:iz]. I. *v.tr.* Torturer ; mettre (qn) au supplice, au martyre, à la torture. **2.** *v.i.* *Lit :* Être au supplice, au martyre. **agonized**, *a.* I. (Cri) d'agonie, d'angoisse. **2.** *I was a. at the thought that* . . ., j'étais au supplice, angoissé, à l'idée que. . . . **agonizing**, *a.* (*Of pain*) Atroce ; (*of spectacle*) navrant, poignant, angoissant. *A. cry*, cri déchirant.

agony ['agoni], *s.* **1.** Angoisse *f.* To suffer agonies, to be in agonies, être au supplice, au martyre. *Journ:* Agony column, annonces personnelles. **2.** To be in the death agony, être à l'agonie.

agouti, agouty [a'gu:ti], *s.* Z: Agouti *m.*

agrarian [a'grɛəriən]. **1.** *a.* (Loi, mesure) agraire. **2.** *a. & s. Pol:* Agrarien (*m*).

agree [a'gri:]. **I.** *v.i. & tr.* **1.** Consentir, donner son adhésion (*to*, à) ; faire droit (à une requête). *To a. formally to sth.*, approuver qch. officiellement. *To a. to do sth.*, accepter, convenir, de faire qch. ; consentir à faire qch. *I a. that he was mistaken*, je vous accorde, j'admets, qu'il s'est trompé. *To a. upon, as to, certain conditions*, convenir de, accepter, tomber d'accord sur, certaines conditions. *They have agreed about the prices*, ils sont convenus des prix. *To a. to sth. being done*, accepter que qch. se fasse. *Unless otherwise agreed*, sauf arrangement contraire. **2.** (*Of pers.*) (*a*) S'accorder ; être d'accord ; tomber d'accord. (*b*) *To a. with s.o.*, entrer dans les idées de qn ; donner raison à qn ; penser comme qn. *To a. with s.o. on, in, a matter*, être du même avis que qn sur une question ; s'accorder, être d'accord, avec qn sur une question. *I quite a. with you on that point*, je suis tout à fait de votre avis là-dessus. (*c*) "*That is so*," he agreed, "c'est vrai," acquiesça-t-il. **3.** (*Of thgs*) (*a*) S'accorder, concorder (ensemble) ; (*of ideas, opinions*) se rencontrer. (*b*) *Gram:* S'accorder. (*c*) Convenir (*with*, à). *The climate, wine, does not a. with him*, le climat ne lui convient pas ; le vin lui est contraire. **II. agree**, *v.tr. Book-k:* *To a. the books*, faire accorder les livres. **agreed**, *a.* **1.** (*Of pers.*) *To be a.* (*with s.o.*), être, demeurer, d'accord (avec qn) (*on, about, sth.*, sur qch.). *We are a. about the prices*, nous sommes convenus des prix. **2.** (*Of thgs*) Agreed upon, convenu. (That is) agreed! c'est convenu ! c'est entendu ! soit ! d'accord ! **Agreed unanimously**, adopté à l'unanimité.

agreeable [a'gri:əbl], *a.* **1.** Agréable (*to*, à) ; (*of pers.*) aimable (*to*, envers). *If that is a. to you*, si cela vous convient. **2.** *Pred. F:* (*Of pers.*) Consentant. *To be a. to sth., to do sth.*, consentir à qch., à faire qch. ; accepter de faire qch. *I am* (*quite*) *a.*, je veux bien. **-ably**, *adv.* **1.** Agréablement. **2.** Conformément (*to, with*, à).

agreeableness [a'gri:əblnəs], *s.* (*a*) (*Of pers.*) Amabilité *f.* (*b*) (*Of place, etc.*) Agrément *m.*

agreement [a'gri:mənt], *s.* **1.** Convention *f,* acte *m,* contrat *m,* traité *m,* arrangement *m.* *Jur:* Real agreement, bail *m. Written a.*, convention par écrit. To enter into, conclude, an agreement with s.o., passer un traité, un contrat, avec qn. **2.** (*a*) Accord *m.* **To be in agreement with s.o.**, être d'accord avec qn. *To be in a. with a decision*, se rallier à, approuver, une décision. **To come to an agreement**, tomber d'accord. **By mutual agreement**, de gré à gré ; à l'amiable. (*b*) *A. between powers*, concert *m* des puissances. *Ind:* *A. between producers*, entente *f* entre producteurs. **3.** (*a*) Conformité *f,* concordance *f.* (*b*) *Gram:* Accord (*with*, avec) ; concordance.

agricultural [agri'kʌltjurəl], *a.* (Nation, produit) agricole ; (peuple) agriculteur. *A. engineer*, ingénieur agronome. **Agricultural college**, ferme école.

agriculture ['agrikʌltjər], *s.* Agriculture *f.*

agriculturist [agri'kʌltjurist], *s.* Agriculteur *m,* agronome *m.*

agrimony ['agrimoni], *s. Bot:* **1.** Common agrimony, aigremoine *f.* **2.** Hemp agrimony, chanvre *m* d'eau.

agronomic(al) [agro'nomik(əl)], *a.* Agronomique.

agronomist [a'gronomist], *s.* Agronome *m.*

agronomy [a'gronomi], *s.* Agronomie *f.*

aground [a'graund], *adv. Nau:* Échoué ; au sec ; amorti. **To run a ship aground**, (faire) échouer un navire ; mettre un navire à la côte. (*Of ship*) To run aground, échouer (à la côte).

ague ['eigju:], *s. Med:* Fièvre (paludéenne) intermittente. **Fit of ague**, accès *m* de fièvre.

ah! [a:], *int.* Ah ! ha ! heu !

aha [a'ha:], *int.* Haha !

ahead [a'hed], *adv.* **1.** *Nau:* (*a*) To be ahead, être sur l'avant, en avant (du navire). *The ship was right a.*, le navire était droit devant. **To draw ahead** of s.o., a ship, dépasser qn, un navire ; gagner l'avant d'un navire. **To go ahead**, aller de l'avant ; avancer ; faire route. **Full speed ahead!** en avant à toute vitesse ! en avant toute ! (*b*) **Wind ahead**, vent debout. **2.** *F:* (*Of pers., car, etc.*) (*a*) To get ahead, prendre de l'avance. **To go on ahead**, prendre les devants. *Go on a.!* filez devant ! **Ahead of s.o.**, en avant de qn. **To be two hours ahead of s.o.**, avoir deux heures d'avance sur qn. *He is going a.*, il fait des progrès, il va de l'avant. **To look ahead**, penser à l'avenir. (*b*) **Go ahead!** (i) allez ! marchez ! (ii) continuez !

ahem [(h)mm], *int.* Hum !

ahoy [a'hɔi], *int. Nau:* **1.** Boat ahoy! ohé, du canot ! **2.** All hands ahoy! tout le monde sur le pont !

aid¹ [eid], *s.* **1.** Aide *f,* assistance *f,* secours *m,* appui *m.* **·With, by, the aid of s.o., sth.**, avec l'aide de qn ; à l'aide de qch. **To go to s.o.'s aid**, aller, se porter, au secours de qn. *To lend one's aid to an undertaking*, prêter son concours à une entreprise. **In aid of**, au profit de. *Mutual aid*, entr'aide *f* ; secours mutuels. *Medical aid*, soins médicaux. *S.a.* FIRST-AID. **2.** *Usu.pl.* Aids to health, conseils *m* pour se bien porter. **3.** (*Pers.*) Aide *mf* ; auxiliaire *mf.* **'aid-post**, *s. Mil:* Poste *m* de secours.

aid², *v.tr.* **1.** Aider, assister, secourir (qn) ; venir en aide à, venir à l'aide de (qn). *To aid s.o. to do sth.*, aider (à) qn à faire qch. *To aid one another*, s'aider les uns les autres ; s'entr'aider. *S.a.* ABET 1. **2.** Soutenir, venir en aide à (une entreprise). **aiding**, *s.* Aide *f. S.a.* ABETTING.

aide-de-camp ['eid(ə)kɔŋ], *s.* (*pl.* aides-de-camp ['eid(d)əkɔŋz]) *Mil:* Officier *m* d'ordonnance.

aigrette ['eigret], *s.* Aigrette *f.*

ail [eil], *v.tr.* (*With indef. subject, esp. in interrog.*) Faire souffrir (qn). **What ails you?** de quoi souffrez-vous ? qu'est-ce que vous avez ? **ailing**, *a.* Souffrant, malade, mal portant. *She has been a. for a long time*, elle souffre depuis longtemps.

aileron ['eilərɔn], *s. Av:* Aileron *m.*

ailment ['eilmənt], *s.* Mal *m* ; maladie (légère).

aim¹ [eim], *s.* **1.** (*a*) Action *f* de viser. **To miss one's aim**, (i) (*with fire-arm*) manquer le but, manquer son coup ; (ii) frapper à faux. **To take aim at s.o.**, viser, ajuster, qn ; coucher qn en joue. *Abs. To take aim*, mettre en joue. (*b*) But *m. Missiles that fall short of their aim*, projectiles qui n'atteignent pas le but. **2.** But, objet *m,* dessein *m* ; visées *fpl. He has one aim and object in life*, sa vie n'a qu'un (seul) but. **With the aim of doing sth.**, dans le dessein de faire qch.

aim². **I.** *v.tr.* (a) To aim a stone, a blow, at s.o., lancer une pierre, porter, allonger, un coup, à qn. (b) Viser. *Artil*: Pointer. **To aim a gun, a pistol, at s.o.**, ajuster, viser, qn. *Well-aimed fire*, feu bien ajusté. (c) **To aim one's remarks at s.o.**, parler à l'adresse de qn. *Measures aimed against our trade*, mesures dirigées contre notre commerce. **2.** *v.ind.tr.* (a) **To aim at s.o.** (with a gun), ajuster, viser, qn; mettre, coucher, qn en joue. (b) **To aim at becoming sth.**, aspirer, viser, à devenir qch. **What are you aiming at?** quel but poursuivez-vous? *Decree that aims at altering . . .*, arrêt qui vise à changer. . . . **aiming,** *s.* Visée *f*. *Artil*: Pointage *m*.

aimless ['eimləs], *a.* Sans but, sans objet. *An a. sort of life*, une vie désœuvrée, qui ne mène à rien. **-ly,** *adv.* Sans but.

ain't [eint]. *A. & P.* := am not, is not, are not.

air¹ ['ɛər], *s.* **I.** Air *m*. (a) *Breath of air*, souffle *m* (d'air). *Fresh air*, air frais. *Foul air*, air vicié. *S.a.* OPEN¹ 2, OPEN-AIR. *The fowls of the air*, les oiseaux des cieux. *To expose water to the air*, aérer de l'eau. *F*: **I can't live on air**, je ne peux pas vivre de l'air du temps. *To carry goods by air*, transporter des marchandises par la voie des airs. *Journey by air*, voyage aérien, en avion. *To throw sth. into the air*, jeter qch. en l'air. *F*: **To walk on air**, ne pas se sentir de joie. **There is something in the air**, il se prépare, il se trame, quelque chose. **It's all in the air as yet**, ce ne sont encore que de vagues projets. *Mil*: *Their left flank was in the air*, le flanc gauche était en l'air, exposé. *All that money has vanished into thin air*, tout cet argent a passé au bleu. (b) *Attrib.* **Air raid**, raid aérien. *Adm*: *Air representative*, représentant aérien. (c) *W.Tel*: *F*: **To be on the air**, parler à la radio. *His speech will be put on the air*, son discours sera radiodiffusé. **II. air.** *Mus*: Air. **III. air.** Air, mine *f*, apparence *f*. *There is an air of comfort everywhere*, il y a partout une apparence, un air, de confort. *F*: **He has an air about him**, il a beaucoup de cachet, de chic; il a du panache. *To carry it off with an air*, y mettre du panache. **To give oneself airs, to put on airs**, se donner des airs; prendre de grands airs; faire des embarras. *To put on airs with s.o.*, traiter qn de haut. **'air-base,** *s.* Base *f* d'aviation. **'air-bed,** *s.* Matelas *m* pneumatique, à air. **'air-bladder,** *s.* **I.** *Ich*: Vésicule aérienne; vessie *f* natatoire. **2.** *Algae*: Vésicule, aérocyste *f*. **'air-brake,** *s.* Frein *m* à air comprimé. **'air-brush,** *s.* *Paint*: Aérographe *m*; pinceau *m* à air; pistolet *m* vaporisateur. **'air-bump,** *s.* *Av*: Trou *m* d'air. **'air-cell,** *s.* Vésicule (aérienne, pulmonaire). **'air-chamber,** *s.* **I.** Chambre *f* a air; (*of torpedo, etc.*) réservoir *m* d'air comprimé. **2.** Cloche *f* d'air (d'une pompe). **'air-channel,** *s.* Conduit *m* d'air; conduit à vent; *Min*: buse *f* d'aérage. **'air-cooled,** *a.* Refroidi par l'air; (moteur) à refroidissement par air. **'air-cushion,** *s.* Coussin *m* à air, pneumatique. **'air-drill,** *s.* *Tls*: Perforatrice *f* à air comprimé. **'air-duct,** *s.* **I.** Canal aérien (des poissons, etc.). **2.** *Ind*: *etc*: Porte-vent *m inv*. **'air-engine,** *s.* Moteur *m* à air; aéromoteur *m*, éolienne *f*. **'air-fleet,** *s.* Flotte aérienne; aéroflotte *f*. **'air-force,** *s.* Aviation *f* (de guerre); armée *f* de l'air. *Our air-f.*, nos forces aériennes, notre aviation. **'air-gun,** *s.* Carabine *f* à air comprimé; fusil *m* à vent. **'air-hole,** *s.* **I.** (*Ventilator*) Aspirail *m*, soupirail *m*; trou *m* d'évent; prise *f* d'air. *Air-holes of bellows*, venteaux *m* d'un soufflet. **2.** (*In metal*) Soufflure *f*;

bulle *f* d'air; globule *m*. **'air-inlet, -intake,** *s.* Prise *f* d'air. **'air-line,** *s.* Service *m* de transports aériens, de transport par avion. **'air-liner,** *s.* Grand avion de transport. **'air-lock,** *s.* **I.** (a) *Civ.E*: Écluse *f*, sas *m* pneumatique, à air, clapet *m* à air (d'un caisson). (b) *Nau*: Sas (de la chaufferie). **2.** *Mch*: *etc*: Poche *f* d'air, retenue *f* d'air. **'air-mail,** *s.* Poste aérienne; service postal aérien. **By airmail,** par avion, par poste aérienne. **'airmattress,** *s.* = AIR-BED. **'air-mechanic,** *s.m.* Mécanicien d'avion. **'air-minded,** *a.* Qui a le plein sentiment de l'importance de l'aviation; conscient du progrès, des avantages, de l'aviation. **'air-passages,** *s.pl.* *Anat*: Voies *f* aérifères. **'air-pilot,** *s.m.* Pilote aviateur. **'air-pocket,** *s.* **I.** *Av*: Trou *m* d'air. **2.** *Hyd.E*: Poche *f* d'air (dans une canalisation). **'air-port¹,** *s.* *Av*: Aéroport *m*. **'air-port²,** *s.* *Nau*: Sabord *m* d'aérage; hublot *m*. **'air-pressure,** *s.* Pression *f* atmosphérique. **'air-pump,** *s.* Pompe *f* à air. *Ph*: Machine *f* pneumatique. **'air-screw,** *s.* *Av*: Hélice *f*. **'air-shaft,** *s.* *Min*: Puits *m*, buse *f*, d'aérage. *Nau*: Manche *f* (à vent, à air). **'air-station,** *s.* Aéroport *m*; centre *m* d'aviation. **'air-tight,** *a.* (Clôture) hermétique; (récipient) à clôture hermétique, étanche (à l'air); (vêtement) imperméable à l'air. **'air-tightness,** *s.* Hermétícité *f*; étanchéité *f*, imperméabilité *f*, à l'air. **'air-tube,** *s.* **I.** Tuyau *m* à air. **2.** Chambre *f* à air (d'un pneu). **'air-valve,** *s.* Soupape *f* à air; reniflard *m*.

air², *v.tr.* **I.** (a) **To air a room,** aérer, rafraîchir, une chambre; renouveler l'air d'une chambre. *To air clothes* (*out of doors*), mettre des effets à l'air, au vent. *To air linen, a bed*, chauffer, aérer, le linge; bassiner un lit; (*before the fire*) donner un coup de feu au linge. (b) **The question needs to be aired,** la question demande à être ventilée. *To air personal grievances*, exposer des griefs personnels. **2. To air one's opinions, one's knowledge,** faire parade de ses opinions, de son savoir. **airing,** *s.* **I.** (a) Ventilation *f*, renouvellement *m* de l'air (d'une salle, etc.); aérage *m*, aération *f*. (b) Éventage *m* (de vêtements); exposition *f* à l'air. *Airing-cupboard*, chauffe-linge *m*. **2.** (Petite) promenade. **To take an airing,** prendre l'air; faire un petit tour.

aircraft ['ɛərkrɑːft], *s.* **I.** Navigation aérienne (en tant que science). **2.** *Coll.* Aéronefs *mpl* or *fpl* et avions *mpl*. *S.a.* CARRIER 3.

airiness ['ɛərinəs], *s.* **I.** (a) Situation aérée. (b) Bonne ventilation. **2.** Légèreté *f* (d'esprit); désinvolture *f*.

airless ['ɛərləs], *a.* **I.** Privé d'air; renfermé. **2.** (Temps) calme, tranquille, sans vent.

airman, -men ['ɛərmən, -men], *s.m.* Aviateur.

airplane ['ɛərplein], *s.* *U.S*: = AEROPLANE.

airship ['ɛərʃip], *s.* (Ballon) dirigeable *m*.

airwoman, -women ['ɛərwumən, -wimen], *s.f.* Aviatrice.

airworthiness ['ɛərwəːrðinəs], *s.* Tenue *f* en l'air, navigabilité *f* (d'un dirigeable, etc.).

airworthy ['ɛərwəːrði], *a.* *Aer*: Navigable.

airy ['ɛəri], *a.* **I.** Bien aéré; ouvert à l'air. **2.** *Poet*: Élevé, aérien. **3.** (*Of material, etc.*) Léger, ténu. **4.** (a) (*Of conduct, etc.*) Léger, insouciant, désinvolte, dégagé. (b) *A.* promises, promesses vaines; promesses en l'air. **-ily,** *adv.* Légèrement; avec désinvolture.

aisle [ail], *s.* **I.** *Ecc.Arch*: Nef latérale; bas-côté *m*. **2.** *U.S*: Passage *m* (entre bancs).

aitch [eitʃ], *s.* (La lettre) h *m*. **To drop one's**

aitches, ne pas aspirer les h, ou les aspirer mal à propos (indice d'un niveau social peu élevé).

aitch-bone ['eitʃboun], s. Culotte f (de bœuf).

ajar [a'dʒɑːr], adv. & pred. a. (Of door) Entrebâillé, entr'ouvert.

a-kimbo [a'kimbo], adv. With arms a-kimbo, les (deux) poings sur les hanches.

akin [a'kin], adv. & pred. a. **1.** A. to s.o., parent de qn; apparenté à, avec, qn. **2.** To be akin to sth., ressembler à qch.; avoir des rapports avec qch. Passion a. to love, passion qui tient de l'amour. Trades closely a., métiers connexes.

alabaster [ala'bɑːstər], s. Albâtre m.

alack [a'lak], int. A. & Poet: Hélas!

alacrity [a'lakriti], s. Empressement m, alacrité f.

alarm¹ [a'lɑːrm], s. **1.** Alarme f, alerte f. **To raise the alarm,** donner l'éveil. To give the a. to s.o., donner l'alarme, l'alerte, à qn; alerter qn. To sound the alarm, sonner le tocsin, l'alarme, l'appel aux armes. **Alarms and excursions,** (i) Th: A: alertes et échauffourées fpl; (ii) F: alertes, remue-ménage m. **To take (the) alarm,** prendre l'alarme; s'alarmer. False alarm, fausse alerte. **2.** (a) Avertisseur m, signal m. Mch: **Low-water alarm,** sifflet-avertisseur m de bas niveau. (b) = ALARM-CLOCK. **a'larm-bell,** s. (a) Tocsin m; cloche f d'alarme. (b) Timbre avertisseur; sonnerie f d'alarme. **a'larm (-clock),** s. Réveille-matin m; réveil m. **a'larm-gun,** s. Canon m d'alarme. **a'larm-signal,** s. Signal m d'alarme.

alarm², v.tr. **1.** (a) Alarmer, donner l'alarme à (qn). (b) Alerter (des troupes). **2.** (Frighten) Alarmer, effrayer. **To be alarmed at sth.,** s'alarmer, s'émouvoir, de qch. **alarming,** a. Alarmant; angoissant. **-ly,** adv. D'une manière alarmante.

alarmist [a'lɑːrmist], s. Alarmiste mf.

alarum [a'lɛərəm, a'lærəm], s. **1.** A: = ALARM¹ **1.** Esp. Th: A: Alerte f. **2.** Réveille-matin m inv.

alas [a'lɑːs], int. Hélas!

alb [alb], s. Ecc.Cost: Aube f.

Albania [al'beinja]. Pr.n. Geog: L'Albanie f.

albatross ['albatrɔs], s. Albatros m.

albeit [ɔː'biːit], conj. Quoique, bien que, + sub.

Albert ['albərt]. **1.** Pr.n.m. Albert. **2.** s. Albert (chain), chaîne (de montre) giletière à gros maillons.

Albigenses [albi'dʒensiːz], s.pl. Albigeois m.

albino, pl. **-os** [al'biːno, -ouz], s. **1.** (Of pers.) Albinos mf. **2.** (Of animals) A. rabbit, lapin blanc.

album ['albəm], s. Album m. Loose-leaf a., album à feuilles mobiles.

albumen [al'bjuːmen], s. **1.** Albumen m; blanc d'œuf. **2.** Albumine f (du sang). **3.** Bot: Albumen (de l'embryon).

alchemist ['alkemist], s.m. Alchimiste.

alchemy ['alkemi], s. Alchimie f.

alcohol ['alkohɔl], s. Alcool m. Pure a., alcool absolu. Denatured a., alcool dénaturé.

alcoholic [alko'hɔlik]. **1.** a. Alcoolique. **2.** s. (Pers.) Alcoolique mf.

alcoholism ['alkohɔlizm], s. Med: Alcoolisme m.

alcoholize ['alkohɔlaiz], v.tr. Alcooliser.

Alcoran [alko'rɑːn], s. = KORAN.

alcove ['alkouv, al'kouv], s. **1.** Alcôve f (de chambre). **2.** Niche f, enfoncement m (dans un mur).

alder ['ɔldər], s. Bot: **1.** Aune m. **2.** Black alder, alder buckthorn, bourdaine f, frangule f.

alderman, -men ['ɔldərmən, -men], s.m. Alderman, magistrat (municipal).

Alderney ['ɔldərni]. Pr.n. Geog: Aurigny m.

ale [eil], s. **1.** Bière anglaise (légère); ale f. **Pale ale,** bière blanche, blonde; pale-ale m. **2.** See GINGER-ALE. **'ale-house,** s. Cabaret m.

aleatory ['eiliətɔri], a. (Contrat, etc.) aléatoire.

Alec(k) ['alek]. Pr.n.m. Alexandre. F: A smart Aleck, un finaud; un monsieur je-sais-tout.

alee [a'liː], adv. Nau: Sous le vent. To put the helm a., mettre la barre dessous.

alembic [a'lembik], s. Alambic m.

alert [a'ləːrt]. **1.** a. (a) Alerte, vigilant, éveillé. (b) Actif, vif, preste. **2.** s. Alerte f. **To be on the alert,** être sur le qui-vive. To keep s.o. on the a., tenir qn en éveil. **-ly,** adv. D'une manière alerte; prestement.

alertness [a'ləːrtnəs], s. **1.** (a) Vigilance f. (b) Promptitude f. **2.** Vivacité f, prestesse f.

Alexander [aleg'zɑːndər]. Pr.n.m. Alexandre.

Alexandrian [aleg'zɑːndriən], a. & s. Alexandrin.

Alexandrine [aleg'zɑːndrain], a. & s. Pros: Alexandrin (m).

alfa(-grass) ['alfa(grɑːs)], s. Bot: Alfa m.

alfalfa [al'falfa], s. Bot: U.S: Luzerne f.

alfresco [al'fresko], a. & adv. En plein air.

alga, pl. **-ae** ['alga, 'aldʒi:], s. Bot: Algue f.

algebra ['aldʒebra], s. Algèbre f.

algebraic(al) [aldʒe'breiik(l)], a. Algébrique. **-ally,** adv. Algébriquement.

Algeria [al'dʒiːəriə]. Pr.n. Geog: L'Algérie f.

Algerian [al'dʒiːəriən], a. & s. **1.** (Of Algeria) Algérien, -ienne. **2.** (Of Algiers) Algérois.

Algiers [al'dʒiːərz]. Pr.n. Geog: Alger m.

alias ['eilias]. **1.** adv. Autrement dit, autrement nommé, alias. **2.** s. (pl. **aliases** ['eiliasiz]) Nom d'emprunt, faux nom.

alibi ['alibai], s. Alibi m. **To plead an alibi,** plaider l'alibi. **To produce an alibi,** fournir un alibi. **To establish an alibi,** prouver son alibi.

alien ['eiljən]. **1.** a. & s. Étranger (non naturalisé). **2.** a. A. from sth., étranger à qch., éloigné de qch. A. to sth., contraire, opposé, à qch.; qui répugne à qch.

alienable ['eiljənəbl], a. Jur: (Bien) aliénable, mutable.

alienate ['eiljəneit], v.tr. **1.** Jur: Aliéner (des biens, etc.). **2.** Détacher, éloigner, (s')aliéner (qn).

alienation [eiljə'neiʃ(ə)n], s. **1.** Jur: Aliénation f (de biens). **2.** Aliénation (de cœurs); désaffection f. **3.** Mental alienation, aliénation (mentale); égarement m d'esprit.

alienist ['eiljənist], s. (Médecin) aliéniste m.

alight¹ [a'lait], v.i. Descendre. **1.** To a. from horseback, from a carriage, descendre de cheval, de voiture; mettre pied à terre. **2.** (a) (Of birds) S'abattre, se poser. (b) (Of pers.) To a. (safely) on one's feet, tomber debout, retomber sur ses pieds. (c) Av: Atterrir; (on sea) amerrir. **alighting,** s. Av: Atterrissage m; amérissage m.

alight², pred. a. Allumé; en feu. **To catch alight,** s'allumer; prendre feu. **To set sth. alight,** mettre le feu à qch.

align [a'lain]. **1.** v.tr. Aligner (des soldats, etc.); mettre (des objets) en ligne. **2.** v.i. S'aligner; se mettre en ligne.

alignment [a'lainmənt], s. Alignement m. **Out of alignment,** désaligné; Typ: (ligne) sortante.

alike [a'laik]. **1.** pred. a. Semblable, pareil, ressemblant. **You are all alike!** vous vous ressemblez tous! vous êtes tous pareils! All things are a. to him, tout lui est égal, indifférent. **2.** adv. Pareillement; de même; de la même manière; également. Dressed a., habillés de même. Winter and summer a., été comme hiver.

aliment ['alimənt], *s.* Aliment *m.*
alimentary [ali'mentəri], *a.* Alimentaire.
alimentation [alimen'teiʃ(ə)n], *s.* Alimentation *f.*
alimony ['aliməni], *s. Jur:* Pension *f* alimentaire.
aliquot 'alikwɔt], *a. & s. Mth:* A. (*part*), (parti *f*) aliquote (*f*).
alive [ə'laːiv], *a.* (*Always pred. unless modified by an adv.* Cf. DEAD-ALIVE) **1.** (*a*) (*Of pers.*) To be (*still*) a., être (encore) vivant, en vie; vivre (encore). *If he is still a.,* s'il est encore au monde. To keep s.o. alive, maintenir qn en vie. To be burnt, buried, alive, être brûlé, enterré, vif. It's good to be alive! il fait bon vivre! Dead or alive, mort ou vif. *Misjudged while a.,* méconnu de son vivant. The best man alive, le meilleur homme du monde. *He will do it better than any man a.,* il le fera mieux que personne. *F:* Man alive! par exemple. *Man a.! is it you?* c'est vous? pas possible! (*b*) (*Of thg*) To keep the fire, a memory, a., entretenir le feu; garder, entretenir, un souvenir. *To keep courage a.,* soutenir, maintenir, le courage. **2.** To be alive to an impression, ressentir une impression. *I am fully a. to the honour they have done me,* je suis très sensible à cet honneur. *To be fully a. to the danger,* avoir pleinement conscience du danger. *To be a. to the importance of . . .,* se rendre compte de l'importance de. . . . *I am a. to the fact that . . .,* je n'ignore pas que. . . . **3.** He is very much alive, (i) il est très remuant; (ii) il a l'esprit très éveillé. Look alive! remuez-vous (donc)! dépêchez-vous! **4.** *The cheese was a. with worms,* le fromage grouillait de vers. *The heath is a. with game,* la lande foisonne de gibier. *The street was a. with people,* la rue fourmillait de monde. **5.** *El.E:* (Fil, etc.) sous tension.
alkali ['alkəlai], *s. Ch:* Alcali *m.*
alkaline ['alkəlain], *a. Ch:* Alcalin.
alkaloid ['alkəlɔid], *a. & s.* Alcaloïde (*m*).
all [ɔːl]. I. *a., pron., & adv.* **1.** Tout, tous. (*a*) (*With noun or pronoun expressed*) *All France,* toute la France. All day, (pendant) toute la journée. All men, tous les hommes. All the others, tous les autres. *Try to be all things to all men,* tâchez d'être tout à tous. *All his life,* toute sa vie. All the way, tout le long du chemin. *Is that all the luggage you are taking?* c'est tout ce que vous emportez de bagages? For all his wealth . . ., en dépit de, malgré, sa fortune. . . . With all speed, au plus vite, à toute vitesse. At all hours, à toute heure. You are not as ill as all that, vous n'êtes pas malade à ce point-là; vous n'êtes pas (aus)si malade que ça. (*b*) *Almost all,* presque tous. All of us, nous tous; tous tant que nous sommes. All together, tous, toutes, à la fois, ensemble. All whom I saw, tous ceux, toutes celles, que j'ai vu(e)s. (*c*) *We all love him,* nous l'aimons tous. I know it all, (i) je sais tout cela; (ii) (*of poem, etc.*) je le sais en entier. *Take it all,* prenez le tout. *Games:* We are five all, nous sommes cinq à cinq. *Ten:* Four all, quatre jeux partout. *Fifteen all,* quinze à, quinze A. (*d*) *neut. Almost all,* presque tout. All is lost, tout est perdu. *All (that) I did,* tout ce que j'ai fait. For all he may say, en dépit de ses dires; quoi qu'il en dise. That's all, c'est tout, voilà tout. *Is that all?* (i) est-ce tout? (ii) *Iron:* n'est-ce que cela? la belle affaire! *If that is all (the difficulty),* s'il ne tient qu'à cela. All's well, tout va bien. *S.a.* WELL[3] II. **2.** When all is said and done, somme toute; quand tout est dit. **2.** (*a*) Once for all, une fois pour toutes. For all I know, autant que je sache. For all I care, pour (tout) ce que cela me fait. *S.a.* FOR[1] I. 9.

Thirty men in all, trente hommes en tout. (*b*) Most of all, surtout; le plus. (*The*) best of all would be to . ., le mieux serait de. . . . *S.a.* FIRST III. 1. (*c*) At all. (i) *Did you speak at all?* avez-vous dit quoi que ce soit? *Do you know him at all?* le connaissez-vous aucunement? Not at all, pas du tout; *F:* du tout! Nothing at all, rien du tout. *I don't know at all,* je n'en sais rien (du tout). (ii) *If he comes at all,* si tant est qu'il venne. *If you hesitate at all . . .,* pour peu que vous hésitiez. . . . *If you are at all anxious,* si vous êtes tant soit peu inquiet. *If there is any wind at all,* s'il y a le moindre vent. (*d*) All but. *All but impossible,* presque impossible. *I all but fell,* j'ai failli tomber. *He all but embraced me,* c'est tout juste s'il ne m'embrassa pas. (*e*) All in all. *Taking it, take it, all in all,* à tout prendre. *They were all in all to each other,* ils étaient dévoués l'un à l'autre. *He imagines that he is all in all to the business,* il s'imagine qu'il est indispensable. (*f*) *F:* And all, et (tout, le reste. **3.** *adv.* Tout. He is, she is, all alone, il est tout seul, elle est toute seule. *To be (dressed) all in black,* être habillé tout en noir, tout de noir. *His hands were all tar,* ses mains étaient couvertes de goudron. She is all ears, all impatience, elle est tout oreilles, tout impatience. *He is not all bad,* il n'est pas entièrement mauvais. All the better, all the worse (*for me*), tant mieux, tant pis (pour moi). *You will be all the better for it,* vous vous en trouverez (d'autant) mieux. *The hour came all too soon,* l'heure n'arriva que trop tôt. All at once, (i) (*suddenly*) tout à coup, subitement; (ii) (*at one time*) tout d'un coup, tous à la fois. II. all, *s.* Tout *m,* totalité *f.* My all, mon tout; tout mon avoir. *We must stake our all,* il faut risquer le tout pour le tout. To lose one's little all, perdre son pécule, tout son petit avoir. **'All 'Fools' Day,** *s.* Le premier avril. **'All 'Hallows' (Day),** *s.* (Le jour de) la Toussaint. **all-im'portant,** *a.* De la plus haute importance; de toute importance. **'all-in,** *a.* **1.** *El:* All-in agreement, police mixte (force et lumière). *Ins:* All-in policy, police tous risques. **2.** *Sp:* All-in wrestling, pancrace *m.* **'all-night** *a.* (Veillée, etc.) de la nuit entière. *Adm:* All-night service, permanence de nuit. *Mil: etc:* All-night pass, permission de la nuit. **all-'powerful,** *a.* Tout-puissant, toute-puissante. **'all-'purpose,** *a.* Répondant à tous les besoins; universel; "à tout faire." **'all-'round,** *a. F:* (Athlète, etc.) complet. *An a.-r. man,* un homme universel. *A.-r. improvement,* amélioration totale, sur toute la ligne. **all-'rounder,** *s. F:* Homme universel. **'All 'Saints' Day,** *s.* (Le jour de) la Toussaint. **'All 'Souls' Day,** *s.* Le jour, la fête, des Morts. **'all-weather,** *a.* De toute saison. *Aut: A.-w.-body,* carrosserie "tous temps."
allay [ə'lei], *v.tr.* (*a*) Apaiser, calmer (une tempête, une colère); tempérer, modérer (l'ardeur). (*b*) Apaiser (une querelle); calmer (la frayeur); endormir, dissiper (les soupçons). (*c*) Alléger, calmer, amortir, assoupir (la douleur); apaiser (la soif, la faim). **allaying,** *s.* Apaisement *m,* soulagement *m.*
allegation [ale'geiʃ(ə)n], *s.* Allégation *f.*
allege [ə'ledʒ], *v.tr.* **1.** Alléguer, prétendre (*that,* que + *ind.*). *To a. an urgent appointment,* prétexter un rendez-vous urgent. *He was alleged to be dead,* on le prétendait mort, on le disait mort. **2.** Plaider, citer (un exemple). **alleged,** *a. A. reason,* raison alléguée. *The a. thief,* le voleur présumé.
allegiance [ə'liːdʒ(ə)ns], *s.* **1.** Fidélité *f,* obéis-

sance f (to, à). **Profession of allegiance,** soumission f. *To own a. to a party,* être inféodé à un parti. *To cast off one's a. to a party,* se détacher d'un parti. **2.** (*Engl.*) **To take the oath of allegiance,** prêter serment d'allégeance.

allegoric(al) [ale'gɔrik(l)], a. Allégorique. **-ally,** adv. Allégoriquement; par allégorie.

allegory ['alegɔri], s. Allégorie f.

alleviate [a'li:vieit], v.tr. Alléger, soulager (la douleur); adoucir (le chagrin); apaiser (la soif).

alleviation [ali:vi'eiʃ(ə)n], s. Allègement m (de la douleur); soulagement m, adoucissement m.

alley ['ali], s. (a) (*In garden*) Allée f; (*in town*) ruelle f, passage m. *S.a.* BLIND¹ 3. (b) See BOWLING-ALLEY, SKITTLE 2. **'alley-way,** s. **1.** *U.S:* Ruelle f. **2.** *N.Arch:* Coursive f.

alliance [a'laiəns], s. **1.** Alliance f. **To enter into an alliance,** s'allier (*with*, avec). **2.** *A. by marriage,* alliance; apparentage m.

alligator ['aligeitər], s. **1.** *Rept:* Alligator m. **2.** *Bot:* Alligator pear, (poire f d') avocat m.

alliteration [alitə'reiʃ(ə)n], s. Allitération f.

alliterative [a'litəreitiv], a. Allitératif.

allocate ['alokeit], v.tr. (a) Allouer, assigner (qch. à qn, à qch.). (b) *To a. a sum amongst several people,* répartir une somme entre plusieurs personnes. *To a. duties,* attribuer, distribuer, des fonctions (*to*, à).

allocation [alo'keiʃ(ə)n], s. **1.** (a) Allocation f, affectation f (d'une somme). (b) Répartition f (de dépenses); attribution f (de fonctions). (c) *A. of contract,* adjudication f. **2.** Part ou somme assignée.

allocution [alo'kju:ʃ(ə)n], s. Allocution f.

allot [a'lɔt], v.tr. (**allotted**) **1.** *To a. sth. to s.o.,* attribuer, assigner, qch. à qn. *To a. sth. to, for, an object,* affecter, destiner, qch. à un but. *Mil:* *To a. a portion of one's pay to a relative,* déléguer une portion de solde à un parent. **2.** Répartir, distribuer (des fonctions, des sièges, *Fin:* des actions).

allotment [a'lɔtmənt], s. **1.** (a) Attribution f (de qch. à qn); affectation f (d'une somme à un but). *Mil: Navy:* *A. of pay (to wife, etc.),* délégation f de solde (à une épouse, etc.). (b) Partage m, répartition f; distribution f; lotissement m. *A. of time,* emploi m du temps. **2.** (a) Portion f, part f, lot m. (b) Lopin m de terre. **Allotments,** lotissements; jardins ouvriers.

allow [a'lau], v.tr. **1.** (a) Admettre. **To allow sth. to be true,** admettre, reconnaître, qch. pour vrai. *He allows it to be true,* il admet, il convient, que c'est vrai. (b) *To a. a request, a claim,* faire droit à une demande, à une réclamation; admettre une requête. **2.** (a) (*Permit*) Permettre, souffrir, tolérer, admettre (qch.). **To allow s.o. sth.,** permettre qch. à qn. **To allow s.o. to do sth.,** permettre à qn de faire qch. *A. me to tell you the truth,* souffrez que je vous dise la vérité. *Circumstances will not a. it,* les circonstances s'y opposent. **Allow me!** permettez(-moi)! *The law allows you twenty days' grace,* la loi vous impartit, vous accorde, un délai de vingt jours. *To allow an item of expenditure,* allouer une dépense. (b) *To a. sth. to be lost,* laisser perdre qch. *To a. oneself to be led, to be deceived,* se laisser mener, se laisser tromper. (c) *ind.tr.* (*Of thg*) *Tone which allowed of no reply,* ton qui n'admettait pas de réplique. *The matter allows of no delay,* l'affaire ne souffre pas de retard. *His condition would not a. of his going out,* son état ne lui permettait pas de sortir. **3.** (a) *To a. s.o. £100 a year,* faire, accorder, allouer, à qn une rente de £100. **To allow a debtor time to pay,** accorder un délai à

un débiteur. (b) *Com: Fin:* **To allow s.o. a discount,** consentir, accorder, faire, une remise à qn. (c) *ind.tr.* **To allow for sth.,** tenir compte de qch. ; faire la part de qch. ; avoir égard à qch. *After allowing for . . . ,* déduction faite de. . . . *To a. for readjustments,* prévoir des rectifications. *To a. so much for carriage,* (i) ajouter tant pour le port; (ii) déduire tant pour le port. *Allowing for the circumstances . . . ,* eu égard aux circonstances. . . .

allowable [a'lauəbl], a. Admissible, admis, légitime.

allowance [a'lauəns], s. **1.** (a) Tolérance f (d'un abus, etc.). (b) *Jur:* **Allowance of items in an account,** allocation f des articles dans un compte. **2.** (a) Pension f alimentaire; rente f. (b) *Adm:* *Jur:* Allocation; dégrèvement m (pour charges de famille, etc.). (c) *Mil: Navy: etc:* Field-allowance, indemnité f de campagne. Mess a., indemnité de table. *Adm: Office a.,* frais mpl de bureau. *Travelling a.,* frais de route, de voyage; indemnité de déplacement. (d) (*Of food, etc.*) Ration f. **To put s.o. on (short) allowance,** mettre qn à la ration; rationner qn. **3.** *Com:* Remise f, rabais m, déduction f, concession f. **4.** (a) *Mec.E: etc:* Tolérance f. *Mint:* Tolérance; faiblage m. (b) **To make allowance(s) for sth.,** tenir compte de, faire la part de, avoir égard à, qch.

allowedly [a'lauidli], adv. De l'aveu de tous; de l'aveu général.

alloy¹ [a'lɔi], s. Alliage m. *F:* **Happiness without alloy,** bonheur sans mélange.

alloy², v.tr. Allier (l'or avec l'argent, etc.). *F: Nothing happened to a. our happiness,* rien ne vint altérer, diminuer, notre bonheur.

allude [a'l(j)u:d], v.ind.tr. *To a. to sth., to s.o.,* (*of pers.*) faire allusion à qch., à qn; (*of phrase*) avoir trait à, se rapporter à, qch., qn.

allure [a'l(j)uər], v.tr. **1.** *To a. s.o.(wards) oneself, (in)to a party,* attirer qn à, vers, soi; à, dans, un parti. **2.** Attirer, allécher, séduire.

alluring, a. Attrayant, alléchant, séduisant.

allurement [a'l(j)uərmənt], s. Attrait m; appât m, amorce f; allèchement m, séduction f.

allusion [a'l(j)u:ʒ(ə)n], s. Allusion f.

allusive [a'l(j)u:siv], a. (Style, etc.) allusif, plein d'allusions. **-ly,** adv. Par (voie d')allusion(s).

alluvial [a'l(j)u:viəl], a. *Geol:* (Terrain) alluvial, d'alluvion; (gîte) alluvien, alluvionnaire.

alluvion [a'l(j)u:viən], s. Alluvion f.

alluvium, pl. **-ia** [a'l(j)u:viəm, -ia], s. *Geol:* (a) Alluvion f; atterrissement m; lais m. (b) pl. Terrains alluviaux, terres f d'alluvion.

ally¹ ['alai], s. Allié m, coalisé m. *To become allies,* s'allier (ensemble); se coaliser.

ally² [a'lai]. **1.** v.tr. Allier (qn, qch.) (*to, with,* à, avec). *To a. by marriage,* apparenter (deux familles, etc.). **2.** v.i. S'allier (*to, with,* à, avec).

allied, a. **1.** Allié (*to, with,* à, avec). **The allied Powers,** les Puissances alliées. *The a. nations,* les nations coalisées. **2.** *Biol: Med:* De la même famille, du même ordre, de la même nature. *Nearly a. species,* espèces voisines. *Closely a. industries,* industries connexes.

Alma Mater ['alma'meitər], s. L'université f où l'on a fait ses études; alma mater f.

almanac ['ɔ:lmənak], s. **1.** Almanach m. **2.** Annuaire m.

almighty [ɔ:l'maiti], a. & s. **1.** Tout-puissant, omnipotent. **The Almighty,** le Tout-Puissant, le Très-Haut. **2.** *F:* = MIGHTY II.

almond ['a:mənd], s. **1.** Amande f. *Sweet a.,* amande douce. **Burnt almonds,** amandes grillées; pralines f. *Shelled almonds,* amandes décorti-

quées. **Ground almonds,** amandes pilées.
Almond(-shaped) eyes, yeux (taillés) en
amande. *S.a.* SUGAR-ALMOND. **2. Almond(-tree),**
amandier *m.* **'almond-'oil,** *s.* Huile *f*
d'amande. *Sweet-a. oil,* huile d'amandes douces.
'almond-'willow, *s. Bot:* Osier brun ; osier-
amandier *m.*
almoner [ˈɑːmənər, ˈalmənər], *s.* Aumônier *m.*
Lady almoner, aumônière *f* (d'un hôpital).
almost [ˈɔːlmoust], *adv.* Presque ; à peu près ;
quasi. **Almost always,** presque toujours. *It is a.
noon,* il est près de midi, bientôt midi. *He a. fell,*
peu s'en fallut qu'il ne tombât ; il faillit tomber.
He is a. the master here, il est quasi, quasiment,
le maître ici.
alms [ɑːmz], *s.sg. or pl.* Aumône *f. To give a. to
s.o.,* donner, faire, l'aumône à qn ; faire la
charité à qn. **'alms-giving,** *s.* L'aumône *f.*
'alms-house, *s.* **I.** Asile *m* d'indigents, de
vieillards ; maison *f* de retraite pour les vieillards.
2. *U.S:* (*Workhouse*) Hospice *m.*
almsman, *pl.* **-men** [ˈɑːmzmən, -men], *s.m.*
(Vieillard) hospitalisé.
almswoman, *pl.* **-women** [ˈɑːmzwumən,
-wimen], *s.f.* (Vieille femme) hospitalisée.
aloe [ˈalou], *s.* **I.** *Bot:* Aloès *m.* **2.** *pl.* (*Usu. with
sg. constr.*) *Pharm:* **Aloes** [ˈalouz], aloès. **Bitter
aloes,** amer *m* d'aloès.
aloft [əˈlɔft], *adv.* (*a*) *Nau:* En haut (dans la
mâture). **Aloft there!** ohé de la hune ! *Away a.!*
en haut les gabiers ! (*b*) *Av:* (Appareil) en vol.
(*c*) *F: Caps were thrown a.,* on jetait les cas-
quettes en l'air.
alone [əˈloun], *pred. a.* **I.** Seul. *He lives (all) a.,*
il demeure (tout) seul. *An expert a. could advise
us,* seul un expert pourrait nous conseiller. **I did
it alone,** je l'ai fait à moi seul. *London a. has a
population equal to . . .,* Londres à lui seul a une
population égale à. . . . *To believe s.o. on his
word a.,* croire qn sur (sa) simple parole. *I want
to speak to you a.,* je voudrais vous parler seul à
seul. *His silence a. is sufficient proof against him,*
rien que son silence le condamne. **With that
charm which is his alone,** avec ce charme qui lui
est propre, qui n'appartient qu'à lui. **2.** (*a*) **To
let, leave s.o., sth., alone,** (i) laisser qn tranquille,
en paix ; (ii) laisser qn faire ; (iii) ne pas se mêler
de qch. *Your work is all right, leave it a.,* votre
travail est bien, n'y retouchez pas. *Prov:* **Let
well alone,** le mieux est (souvent) l'ennemi du
bien. (*b*) *F:* **Let alone . . .,** sans parler de . . .,
sans compter. . . . **3.** *adv.* **Not alone in London
was it rife,** ce n'est pas qu'à Londres que cet
abus sévissait.
along [əˈlɔŋ]. **I.** *prep.* Le long de. (*a*) *To walk
a. the shore,* longer la plage, se promener (tout)
le long de la plage. *To go a. a street,* suivre une
rue ; passer par une rue. **To sail along the land,
the coast,** serrer la terre ; longer, suivre, la côte.
To creep up the wall, se faufiler le long du mur.
(*b*) *Trees a. the river,* arbres qui bordent la
rivière, sur le bord de la rivière. **2.** *adv.* (*Often
expletive, with a general implication of progress*)
(*a*) **To move along,** avancer. *To walk, stride, a.,*
avancer à grandes enjambées ; *F:* arpenter le
terrain. *Come a. with me,* venez-vous-en avec
moi. **Come along !** arrivez donc ! venez donc !
(*b*) *I knew that all along,* je le savais dès, depuis,
le commencement. (*c*) *F:* Along with, avec.
alongshore [əˈlɔŋˈʃɔːr], *adv.* Le long de la
côte. *To sail a.,* longer la terre.
alongside [əˈlɔŋˈsaid], *adv. & prep. Nau:* Ac-
costé (le long de . . .). *To make a boat fast
(close) a. a ship,* amarrer (un canot) le long du

bord. *To come a.* (*a ship*), *a. of a ship,* accoster,
aborder (un navire). **Come alongside ! accostez !**
A. the quay, le long du quai, bord à quai. *To come
a.* (*the quay*), aborder à quai.
aloof [əˈluːf], *adv. & pred. a.* **I.** *Nau:* Au large
et au vent. **Keep aloof !** passez au large ! **2.** To
keep, hold, aloof (from sth.), se tenir (visiblement)
à l'écart, à distance, éloigné (de qch.) ; s'abstraire
(de qch.). *To stand a. from a cause,* se tenir en
dehors d'une cause. **To hold, stand, aloof,**
s'abstenir (lorsqu'il s'agit de faire qch.). *He kept
very much a.,* il s'est montré très distant.
aloofness [əˈluːfnəs], *s.* Attitude distante ;
désintéressement *m,* réserve *f* (*from,* à l'égard de).
aloud [əˈlaud], *adv.* A haute voix ; (tout) haut.
alp [alp], *s.* Alpe *f* ; pâturage *m* de montagne.
Geog: **The Alps,** les Alpes.
alpaca [alˈpaka], *s.* **I.** *Z:* Alpaca *m.* **2.** *Tex:*
Alpaga *m.*
alpenstock [ˈalpənstɔk], *s.* Alpenstock *m* ; bâton
ferré.
alpha [ˈalfa], *s. Gr.Alph:* Alpha *m.* **'alpha
rays,** *s.pl. Ph:* Rayons *m* alpha.
alphabet [ˈalfəbet], *s.* Alphabet *m.*
alphabetical [alfəˈbetik(ə)l], *a.* Alphabétique.
-ally, *adv.* Alphabétiquement.
alpine [ˈalpain], *a.* (Club, chasseur) alpin ; (site,
paysage, climat) alpestre. *Geog:* **A.** *range,*
chaîne de montagnes alpique. *A. climbing,* alpinisme *m. Bot: A. plants,* *s.* alpines, plantes
alpines, alpicoles.
alpinist [ˈalpinist], *s.* Alpiniste *mf.*
already [ɔːlˈredi], *adv.* Déjà ; dès à présent. *Ten
o'clock a.!* déjà dix heures !
Alsatian [alˈseiʃən], *a. & s. Geog:* Alsacien.
Alsatian wolf-hound, chien de berger alsacien ;
chien-loup *m.*
also [ˈɔːlso], *adv.* Aussi. *I a. discovered that . . .,*
(i) moi aussi j'ai trouvé que . . ., (ii) j'ai encore
trouvé que. . . . *He saw it a.,* il l'a vu également.
Not only . . . but also . . ., non seulement . . . ;
mais encore . . ., mais aussi. . .
altar [ˈɔːltər], *s.* Autel *m.* **High altar,** maître(-)
autel *m. To set up an a.,* dresser un autel. *F:* **To
lay one's ambitions on the altar,** sacrifier ses
ambitions ; faire le sacrifice de ses ambitions.
'altar-cloth, *s.* Nappe *f* d'autel. **'altar-
piece,** *s.* Tableau *m* d'autel ; retable *m.*
'altar-rail, *s.* Balustrade *f* ou grille *f* (du
sanctuaire) de l'autel. *To kneel at the a.-r. (for
communion),* s'approcher de la table sainte.
'altar-screen, *s.* Retable *m.* **'altar-stone,
-table,** *s.* Pierre *f* d'autel.
alter [ˈɔːltər]. **I.** *v.tr.* (*a*) Remanier (une comédie) ; retoucher (un dessin) ; modifier (ses
plans) ; changer de (plans). *To a. the place of
sth.,* changer de place. *To a. one's mind,*
changer d'avis. *That alters matters,* **alters the
case,** voilà qui change les choses ; *F:* ça, c'est
une autre paire de manches. *To a. sth. for the
better,* améliorer qch. *To a. sth. for the worse,*
altérer qch. **To alter one's course,** changer de
route. *Nau:* **To alter (the) course,** changer,
modifier, la route. (*b*) Fausser (les faits) ; altérer
(un texte). **2.** *v.i.* **He was greatly altered,** il a
bien changé. *To a. for the better,* s'améliorer ;
s'amender. (*of pers.*) changer en mieux. *To a.
for the worse,* s'altérer, perdre.
alteration [ɔːltəˈreiʃ(ə)n], *s.* (*a*) Remaniement *m,*
retouche *f,* modification *f* ; changement *m. To
make an a. to a dress,* faire une modification, une
retouche, à une robe. (*b*) **Marginal alteration,**
renvoi *m* en marge.

altercation [ɔltər'keiʃ(ə)n], s. Altercation f, dispute f, querelle f.
alternate¹ [ɔl'təːrnet], a. **I.** Alternatif, alterné, alternant. *The a. action of sun and rain,* l'action alternative, alternée, du soleil et de la pluie. *To come on a. days,* venir de deux jours l'un, tous les deux jours. *Trees planted in a. rows,* arbres en quinconce. *Professors lecturing on a. days,* professeurs alternants. **2.** Geom: Bot: (Angles, feuilles) alternes. **3.** Pros: (Rimes) croisées. **-ly,** adv. Alternativement; tour à tour.
alternate² [ɔ'ltərneit]. **I.** v.tr. Faire alterner; employer tour à tour, alternativement. **2.** v.i. Alterner (with, avec); se succéder (tour à tour). **alternating,** a. **I.** Alternant, alterné. **2.** (a) El.E: (Courant) alternatif. (b) Mec.E: (Mouvement) alternatif, de va-et-vient.
alternation [ɔltər'neiʃ(ə)n], s. **I.** Alternation f (d'un mouvement). **2.** Alternance f (du jour et de la nuit, etc.). **3.** Alternations of rain and sun, alternatives f de pluie et de soleil.
alternative [ɔl'təːrnətiv]. **I.** a. (a) Alternatif. *An a. proposal,* une contre-proposition. (b) An a. route, un second, un autre, itinéraire. **2.** s. Alternative f. *The a. of death or the Koran,* l'alternative de la mort ou du Coran. *To have no alternative,* n'avoir pas le choix. **-ly,** adv. **I.** Alternativement; tour à tour. **2.** Avec l'alternative de. . . .
alternator ['ɔltərneitər], s. El.E: Alternateur m.
although [ɔl'ðou], conj. = THOUGH I. I.
altimeter [al'timetər], s. Av: etc: Altimètre m.
altitude ['altitjuːd], s. **I.** (a) Altitude f, élévation f (au-dessus du niveau de la mer). (b) Hauteur f (d'un astre, d'un triangle). **2.** Usu.pl. Hauteur(s).
alto ['alto], s. Mus: **I.** Alto m. **2.** (a) (Male) Haute-contre f. (b) (Female) Contralto m.
altogether [ɔːltu'geðər], adv. (a) (Wholly) Entièrement, tout à fait. *You are a. right,* vous avez entièrement, grandement, raison. (b) (On the whole) Somme toute. . . . *Taking things a.; taken a.,* à tout prendre. (c) How much a.? combien en tout? combien tout compris?
alto-relievo ['ɑltɔri'liːvo], s. Haut-relief m.
altruism ['altruizm], s. Altruisme m.
altruist ['altruist], s. Altruiste mf.
altruistic [altru'istik], a. Altruiste.
alum¹ ['aləm], s. Alun m., Alum works, mine, aluminière f, alunière f. Alum manufacturer, alunier m. Phot: Alum bath, bain aluné.
alum², v.tr. Aluminer, aluner.
alumina [a'ljuːmina], s. Miner: Alumine f.
aluminium [alju'miniəm], s. Aluminium m. Aluminium works, aluminerie f.
aluminum [a'luːminəm], s. U.S: = ALUMINIUM.
alumnus, pl. **-i** [a'lʌmnəs, -ai], s.m. Esp.U.S: (a) Élève (d'un collège). (b) Étudiant (à une université); gradué (d'une université).
alveole ['alvioul], s. Alvéole m or f.
always ['ɔːlwəz, -weiz], adv. Toujours. (a) He is nearly a. here, il est presque toujours ici. Office always open, permanence f. (b) F: There is a. the workhouse, il y a toujours l'hospice.
alyssum [a'lisəm], s. Bot: Alysson m, alysse m.
am [am]. See BE.
amain [a'mein], adv. A. & Poet: To smite sth. amain, frapper qch. de toutes ses forces.
amalgam [a'malgəm], s. Amalgame m.
amalgamate [a'malgəmeit]. **I.** v.tr. (a) Amalgamer (l'or, etc.). (b) Amalgamer (des idées); fusionner (des sociétés); unifier (les industries). **2.** v.i. (a) (Of metals) S'amalgamer. (b) (Of ideas)

S'amalgamer; (of companies) fusionner; (of races) se mélanger.
amalgamation [amalgə'meiʃ(ə)n], s. **I.** Amalgamation f (des métaux). **2.** Fusion f, fusionnement m (de deux sociétés); mélange m (de races, etc.).
amanuensis, pl. **-es** [amanju'ensis, -iːz], s. Secrétaire mf.
amarant(h) ['amarant, -anθ], s. Bot: Amarante f. A. (-coloured) ribbons, des rubans amarante.
amarant(h)ine [ama'rantain, -θain], a. **I.** (D')amarante. **2.** Lit: Impérissable, immortel.
amass [a'mas], v.tr. Amasser, accumuler.
amateur [amə'təːr, 'amətjuər], s. Amateur m. He is an a. of painting, il est amateur en peinture. Pej: He is an a. at painting, il peint en amateur.
amateurish [amə'təːriʃ, amə'tjuəriʃ], a. Pej: (Travail, etc.) d'amateur. **-ly,** adv. En amateur.
amateurishness [amə'təːriʃnəs, -'tjuər-], s. **I.** Inexpérience f. **2.** Dilettantisme m.
amative ['amətiv], a. Porté à l'amour.
amatory ['amətəri], a. (Sentiment) amoureux; (lettre) d'amour; (poète, poème) érotique.
amaze [a'meːiz], v.tr. Confondre, stupéfier, frapper de stupeur; F: ébahir, ébaubir.
amazed, a. Confondu, stupéfait; F: ébahi.
amazing, a. Stupéfiant; F: renversant; P: épatant. **-ly,** adv. Étonnamment.
amazedly [a'meːizidli], adv. Avec stupéfaction.
amazement [a'meizmənt], s. Stupéfaction f; stupeur f; F: ébahissement m.
Amazon ['amazən]. **I.** s.f. Myth. & F: Amazone. **2.** Pr.n. Geog: The river Amazon, le fleuve des Amazones; l'Amazone f.
ambassador [am'basədər], s. Ambassadeur m.
ambassadorship [am'basədərʃip], s. Ambassade f.
ambassadress [am'basədres], s.f. Ambassadrice.
amber ['ambər], s. **I.** Ambre m. Yellow a., ambre jaune; succin m. A. colour, nuance ambrée. Adm: Amber light, feu jaune. **'amber-coloured,** a. Ambré.
ambergris ['ambərgriːs], s. Ambre gris.
ambidext(e)rous [ambi'dekst(ə)rəs], a. Ambidextre.
ambient ['ambiənt], a. Ambiant.
ambiguity [ambi'gjuiti], s. **I.** Ambiguïté f. **2.** Équivoque f.
ambiguous [am'bigjuəs], a. **I.** Ambigu, f. -uë; équivoque. **2.** Incertain. **3.** Obscur; (style) confus. **-ly,** adv. Avec ambiguïté; d'une manière équivoque.
ambit ['ambit], s. **I.** Circuit m, tour m (d'une ville, etc.). **2.** Bornes fpl, limites fpl (d'un terrain, etc.). **3.** Étendue f, portée f (d'une action).
ambition [am'biʃ(ə)n], s. Ambition f. The a. to shine, l'ambition de briller. To make it one's a. to do sth., mettre son ambition à faire qch.
ambitious [am'biʃəs], a. Ambitieux. To be a. of power, ambitionner le pouvoir. To be a. to do sth., ambitionner de faire qch. **-ly,** adv. Ambitieusement.
ambitiousness [am'biʃəsnəs], s. **I.** Ambition f. **2.** Caractère ambitieux.
amble¹ [ambl], s. **I.** Equit: (a) Amble m, entrepas m. (b) (Of horse) Traquenard m. **2.** (Of pers.) Pas m tranquille; allure f tranquille.
amble², v.i. **I.** Equit: (a) Aller (à) l'amble. (b) (Of horse) Aller le traquenard. **2.** (Of pers.) To a. along, aller, marcher, d'un pas tranquille.
ambler ['amblər], s. Promeneur m sans but; flâneur m.
Ambrose ['ambrouz]. Pr.n.m. Ambroise.
ambrosia [am'brouzia], s. Ambroisie f.

ambrosial [am'brouziǝl], *a.* Ambrosiaque ; au parfum d'ambroisie.

ambulance ['ambjulǝns], *s.* Ambulance *f.* **1.** Hôpital ambulant. *Attrib.* **Ambulance man,** ambulancier(-brancardier) *m* ; infirmier *m. A. nurse,* ambulancière *f* ; infirmière *f.* **2.** Ambulance (waggon), (voiture *f* d')ambulance. *A. train, plane,* train, avion, sanitaire.

ambulatory[1] ['ambjulǝtǝri], *a.* Ambulant, mobile.

ambulatory[2], *s.* Promenoir *m*, préau *m. Ecc. Arch :* (Dé)ambulatoire *m.*

ambuscade[1] [ambʌs'keid], *s.* = AMBUSH[1].

ambuscade[2], *v.tr. & i.* = AMBUSH[2].

ambush[1] ['ambuʃ], *s.* Embuscade *f* ; guet-apens *m, pl.* guets-apens. *To lay an a.,* dresser une embuscade. *To fall into an a.,* donner, tomber, dans une embuscade. **To be, lie, in ambush,** être, se tenir, en embuscade ; être à l'affût. **Troops in ambush,** troupes embusquées.

ambush[2]. **1.** *v.tr. To a. the enemy,* attirer l'ennemi dans un piège. **To be ambushed,** tomber dans une embuscade. **2.** *v.i.* S'embusquer.

ameer [a'miːǝr], *s.m.* Émir.

ameliorate [a'miːljǝreit], **1.** *v.tr.* Améliorer. **2.** *v.i.* S'améliorer, s'amender.

amelioration [ami:lio'reiʃ(ǝ)n], *s.* Amélioration *f.*

amen [ɑːˈmen, eiˈmen], *int.* Amen ; ainsi soit-il.

amenable [a'miːnǝbl], *a.* **1.** *Jur :* Justiciable, ressortissant, relevant (*to a court,* d'un tribunal) ; responsable (*to s.o.,* envers qn). *A. to a fine,* passible d'une amende. **2.** (*a*) Soumis (à la loi, à la discipline) ; docile (aux conseils) ; sensible (à la bonté). **Amenable to reason,** raisonnable. (*b*) (Enfant) soumis, docile.

amenableness [a'miːnǝblnǝs], *s.* **1.** *Jur :* Justiciabilité *f* (*to, de*) ; responsabilité *f* (*to, envers*). **2.** Soumission *f*, docilité *f.*

amend [a'mend]. **1.** *v.tr.* (*a*) Amender, modifier (un projet de loi) ; rectifier (un compte) ; corriger (un texte). (*b*) Réformer (sa vie). *To a. one's ways,* s'amender. **2.** *v.i.* S'amender, se corriger.

amending, *a.* Correctif.

amendment [a'mendmǝnt], *s.* (*a*) Modification *f* ; rectification *f* ; redressement *m* (d'une erreur). (*b*) *Parl : etc :* Amendement *m.*

amends [a'mendz], *s.pl.* Réparation *f*, dédommagement *m*, compensation *f. Used esp. in* **To make amends for an injury,** réparer un tort.

amenity [a'miːniti], *s.* **1.** Aménité *f*, agrément *m*, charme *m* (d'un lieu). **2.** Aménité, amabilité *f*, affabilité *f.* **3.** *pl.* **Amenities.** (*a*) Aménités, civilités *fpl.* (*b*) *The amenities of life,* les commodités *f* de l'existence.

America [a'merikǝ]. *Pr.n.* L'Amérique *f. North, South, A.,* l'Amérique du Nord, du Sud.

American [a'merikǝn], *a. & s.* **1.** Américain, -aine. **2.** Des États-Unis. *S.a.* CLOTH I.

amethyst ['ameθist], *s.* Améthyste *f.*

amiability [eimjǝ'biliti], *s.* Amabilité *f* (*to, envers*).

amiable ['eimjǝbl], *a.* Aimable (*to, envers*). *To make oneself a. to s.o.,* faire l'aimable auprès de qn. **-ably,** *adv.* Aimablement.

amicable ['amikǝbl], *a.* **1.** (*Of manner, etc.*) Amical ; (*of pers.*) bien disposé. **2.** *Jur :* Amicable settlement, arrangement à l'amiable. **-ably,** *adv.* (i) Amicalement ; (ii) à l'amiable.

amice[1] ['amis], *s.* Amict *m* (de prêtre).

amice[2], *s.* Aumusse *f* (de chanoine).

amid(st) [a'mid(st)], *prep.* Au milieu de ; parmi.

amidships [a'midʃips], *adv. Nau :* **1.** Au milieu du navire ; par le travers. *The boat parted*

a., le navire s'ouvrit par le milieu. **2.** *To put the helm a.,* mettre la barre droite.

amiss [a'mis], *adv. & pred. a.* **1.** (*Wrongly*) Mal ; de travers. *To judge a.,* mal juger. **To take sth. amiss,** prendre qch. de travers, en mal, en mauvaise part. **2.** (*Out of order*) Mal à propos. *That would not come a.,* cela n'arriverait pas mal (à propos). *Something is a.,* il y a quelque chose qui cloche.

amity ['amiti], *s.* Amitié *f*, concorde *f*, bonne intelligence. *A. between two countries,* bons rapports, bonnes relations, entre deux pays.

ammeter ['ametǝr], *s. El :* Ampèremètre *m.*

ammonia [a'mounjǝ], *s. Ch :* Ammoniaque *f* ; gaz ammoniac. *A. hydrate, a. solution, F :* **ammonia,** (solution aqueuse d')ammoniaque.

ammoniac [a'mounjak], *a.* Ammoniac, -aque. *Esp.* Sal ammoniac, sel ammoniac.

ammoniated [a'mounjeitid], *a. Pharm : etc :* Ammoniacé, ammoniaqué.

ammonium [a'mounjǝm], *s. Ch :* Ammonium *m.* **Ammonium carbonate,** carbonate d'ammoniaque.

ammunition [amju'niʃ(ǝ)n], *s. Mil :* **1.** Munitions *fpl* de guerre. *S.a.* ROUND[1] II. 6. **2.** *Attrib.* D'ordonnance. **ammu'nition-wagon,** *s. Artil :* Caisson *m.*

amnesia [am'niːzia], *s. Med :* Amnésie *f.*

amnesty[1] ['amnesti], *s.* Amnistie *f.*

amnesty[2], *v.tr.* Amnistier.

amoeba, *pl.* **-as, -ae** [a'miːba, -ǝz, -iː], *s.* Amibe *f.*

amok [a'mʌk], *adv.* = AMUCK.

among(st) [a'mʌŋ(st)], *prep.* Parmi, entre. (*a*) *Sitting a. her children,* assise au milieu de ses enfants. *To wander a. the ruins,* errer dans les ruines. (*b*) *We are a. friends,* nous sommes entre amis. (*c*) *To count s.o. a. one's friends,* compter qn au nombre de ses amis. *He is a. those who . . .,* il est du nombre de ceux qui. . . . *A. them are several . . .,* parmi eux il y en a plusieurs. . . . *Not one a. them,* pas un d'entre eux. **He is one among a thousand,** il est un entre mille. (*d*) *Nations divided a. themselves,* nations divisées entre elles. *Do it a. you,* faites-le entre vous.

amoral [ei'mɔrǝl], *a.* Amoral, -aux.

amorous ['amǝrǝs], *a.* Amoureux (*of s.o.,* de qn) ; porté vers l'amour. **Amorous verse,** poésie érotique. **-ly,** *adv.* Amoureusement.

amorousness ['amǝrǝsnǝs], *s.* Tempérament amoureux ; amativité *f.*

amorphous [a'mɔːrfǝs], *a.* **1.** *Biol : etc :* Amorphe. **2.** *F :* (Opinions) sans forme ; (projet) vague, amorphe.

amortization [amɔːrti'zeiʃ(ǝ)n], *s.* Amortissement *m* (d'une dette, etc.).

amortize [a'mɔːrtiz], *v.tr.* **1.** Amortir (une dette). **2.** *Jur :* Aliéner (une terre) en mainmorte.

amount[1] [a'maunt], *s.* **1.** *Com :* Somme *f*, montant *m*, total *m* (d'une facture, etc.). *Have you the right a.?* avez-vous votre compte? *What is the a. of their business?* quel est leur chiffre d'affaires? (*Up*) *to the amount of . . .,* jusqu'à concurrence de. . . . **2.** (*a*) Quantité *f.* **In small amounts,** par petites quantités. *F :* **To spend any amount of money,** dépenser énormément d'argent. *He has any a. of money,* il a de l'argent tant et plus. *Any a. of people saw it,* nombre de gens l'ont vu. (*b*) (*Percentage*) Teneur *f. A. of grease in a leather,* teneur en graisse d'un cuir. **3.** Valeur *f*, importance *f* (d'une affirmation, etc.). *These facts are of little a.,* ces faits ne signifient pas grand'chose.

amount², *v.i.* **1.** (*Of money, etc.*) S'élever, (se) monter (*to*, à). *Com: The stocks a. to so much*, les stocks s'élèvent à tant, atteignent tant. *I don't know what my debts a. to*, j'ignore le montant de mes dettes. **2.** (*Be equivalent*) Équivaloir, revenir (*to*, à). *It amounts to the same thing*, cela revient au même; *F:* c'est tout comme. **3.** *F:* He will never amount to muoh, il ne sera, ne fera, jamais grand'chose.

amour [a'muər], *s.* Intrigue galante.

amp [amp], *s.* *F:* = AMPERE.

amperage ['ampəredʒ], *s.* *El:* Ampérage *m.*

ampere ['ampeər], *s.* *El.Meas:* Ampère *m.*

amphibia [am'fibia], *s.pl.* *Z:* Amphibiens *mpl.*

amphibian [am'fibiən], *a. & s.* Amphibie (*m*).

amphibious [am'fibiəs], *a.* *Z. & F:* Amphibie.

amphitheatre ['amfiθiːətər], *s.* Amphithéâtre *m.* *A. of mountains*, cirque *m* de montagnes.

amphora, *pl.* **-ae** ['amfora, -iː], *s.* Amphore *f.*

ample [ampl], *a.* Ample. **1.** *An a. garment*, un ample, large, vêtement. *A. resources*, d'abondantes ressources. **2.** (*Enough*) *You have a. time*, vous avez amplement, grandement, largement, le temps. *To make a. apologies*, faire d'amples excuses. **-ply**, *adv.* Amplement, grandement.

ampleness ['amplnəs], *s.* Ampleur *f*; abondance *f* (de ressources).

amplification [amplifi'keiʃ(ə)n], *s.* Amplification *f.*

amplifier ['amplifaiər], *s.* **1.** *Phot:* (Lentille) amplificatrice. **2.** *W.Tel:* Amplificateur *m.*

amplify ['amplifai], *v.tr.* **1.** Amplifier (une idée, *El:* le courant). *To a. a story*, développer une histoire. **2.** Exagérer, amplifier (une nouvelle). **amplifying**, *a.* Amplificateur, -trice.

amplitude ['amplitjuːd], *s.* **1.** Amplitude *f.* *Ph:* *A. of swing*, amplitude des oscillations (d'un pendule). **2.** Abondance *f*, ampleur *f* (de style).

ampulla, *pl.* **-ae** [am'pʌla, -iː], *s.* Ampoule *f.*

amputate ['ampjuteit], *v.tr.* Amputer, faire l'amputation de (la jambe, etc.). *His right leg was amputated*, il fut amputé de la jambe droite.

amputation [ampju'teiʃ(ə)n], *s.* Amputation *f.*

amuck [a'mʌk], *adv.* **To run amuck. 1.** Tomber dans la folie furieuse de l'amok, des Malais. **2.** *F:* (*a*) Perdre tout son sang-froid. (*b*) Faire les cent coups.

amulet ['amjulet], *s.* Amulette *f.*

amuse [a'mjuːz], *v.tr.* Amuser, divertir, égayer, faire rire (qn). *To a. oneself by, with, doing sth.*, s'amuser, se récréer, à faire qch., en faisant qch. *To a. oneself with sth.*, s'amuser avec qch. *To be amused at, by, sth.*, être amusé de qch.; s'amuser de qch. **amusing**, *a.* Amusant, divertissant. *Highly a.*, désopilant. *The a. thing about it is that . . .*, le plaisant de l'affaire c'est que. . . . **-ly**, *adv.* D'une manière amusante.

amusement [a'mjuːzmənt], *s.* **1.** Amusement *m*; divertissement *m.* *Place of a.*, lieu de plaisir. *We have few amusements here*, nous avons ici peu de distractions. **2.** *Money for one's amusements*, argent pour menus plaisirs.

Amy ['eimi]. *Pr.n.f.* Aimée.

an [an]. *See* A².

anachronism [a'nakronizm], *s.* Anachronisme *m.*

anachronistic [anakro'nistik], *a.* Anachronique. *A. errors*, fautes d'anachronisme.

anacoluthon, *pl.* **-a** [anako'ljuːθɔn, -a], *s.* Anacoluthe *f.*

anaconda [ana'kɔnda], *s.* Anaconda *m*, eunecte *m.*

anaemia [a'niːmia], *s.* Anémie *f.* **Pernioious anaemia**, anémie pernicieuse progressive.

anaemic [a'niːmik], *a.* Anémique. *To become a.*, s'anémier.

anaesthesia [anes'θiːzia], *s.* Anesthésie *f.*

anaesthetic [anes'θetik], *a. & s.* Anesthésique (*m*).

anaesthetist [a'niːsθetist], *s.* Anesthésiste *m.*

anaesthetization [aniːsθeti'zeiʃ(ə)n], *s.* Administration *f* d'un anesthésique; insensibilisation *f.*

anaesthetize [a'niːsθetaːiz], *v.tr.* *Med:* Anesthésier; *F:* endormir.

anaglyph ['anaglif], *s.* Opt: Anaglyphe *m or f.*

anagram ['anagram], *s.* Anagramme *f.*

anal ['einəl], *a.* *Anat:* Anal, -aux.

analgesic [anal'dʒiːsik], **analgetic** [anal'dʒetik], *a. & s.* *Med:* Analgésique (*m*); anodin (*m*).

analogical [ana'lɔdʒ(ə)l], *a.* Analogique. **-ally**, *adv.* Analogiquement; par analogie.

analogous [a'nalogəs], *a.* Analogue (*to, with*, à).

analogue ['analɔg], *s.* Analogue *m.*

analogy [a'nalodʒi], *s.* Analogie *f* (*to, with*, avec; *between*, entre). **To argue from analogy**, raisonner par analogie. **On the analogy of . . .**, par analogie avec. . . .

analyse ['analaːiz], *v.tr.* Analyser; faire l'analyse de (qch.). *Gram: To a. a sentence*, faire l'analyse logique d'une phrase.

analysis, *pl.* **-es** [a'nalisis, -iːz], *s.* Analyse *f.* *Ch:* *Quantitative a.*, dosage *m.* *Wet a.*, analyse par voie humide. *Dry a.*, analyse par voie sèche. *Gram:* *A. of a sentence*, analyse logique d'une phrase.

analyst ['analist], *s.* *Ch:* Analyste *m.*

analytic(al) [ana'litik(əl)], *a.* Analytique.

anapaest ['anapiːst, -pest], *s.* *Pros:* Anapeste *m.*

anarchic(al) [a'nɔːrkik(əl)], *a.* Anarchique. **-ally**, *adv.* Anarchiquement.

anarchism ['anarkizm], *s.* Anarchisme *m.*

anarchist ['anarkist], *s.* Anarchiste *mf.*

anarchy ['anarki], *s.* Anarchie *f.*

anastigmat [ana'stigmat], *s.* *Opt:* *Phot:* Objectif *m* anastigmatique; anastigmat *m.*

anastigmatic [anastig'matik], *a.* *Opt:* Anastigmate, anastigmatique.

anathema [a'naθəma], *s.* Anathème *m* ((i) malédiction; (ii) personne frappée de malédiction).

anathematize [a'naθəmataːiz], *v.tr.* (*a*) Anathématiser (qn); frapper (qn) d'anathème. (*b*) *F:* Maudire (qn).

anatomical [ana'tɔmik(ə)l], *a.* Anatomique. *A. specimen*, pièce d'anatomie. **-ally**, *adv.* Anatomiquement.

anatomist [a'natomist], *s.* Anatomiste *m.*

anatomy [a'natomi], *s.* Anatomie *f.*

ancestor ['ansəstər], *s.* Ancêtre *m*; aïeul *m*, *pl.* aïeux.

ancestral [an'sestrəl], *a.* (*a*) Héréditaire; de famille. *His a. castle*, le château de ses ancêtres. (*b*) *Biol:* Ancestral, -aux.

ancestress ['ansəstres], *s.f.* Ancêtre, aïeule.

ancestry ['ansəstri], *s.* **1.** Race *f*; lignée *f*, lignage *m*; longue suite d'ancêtres; ascendance *f.* **2.** *Coll.* Ancêtres *mpl*; ascendants *mpl*; aïeux *mpl.*

anchor¹ ['aŋkər], *s.* **1.** *Nau:* Grappling *m*, grappin *m.* *S.a.* BOWER², KEDGE¹, SHEET-ANCHOR. **Stand by the anchor!** paré à mouiller! **To let go, drop, the anchor**, jeter, mouiller, l'ancre. **Let go the anchor!** mouillez! **To come to anchor**, s'ancrer, mouiller. *F:* (*Of pers.*) **To cast anchor, to come to anchor**, s'ancrer (quelque part). **To lie, ride, at anchor**, être à l'ancre; être mouillé, au mouillage. **Foul anchor**, ancre surjalée, engagée. **'anchor-plate**, *s.* *Civ.E:* Plaque *f* d'ancrage; contre-plaque *f.* **'anchor-tie**, *s.* *Const: etc:* Tige *f* d'ancrage. **'anchor-watch**, *s.* *Nau:* Quart *m* au mouillage; quart de rade.

anchor². **1.** *v.tr.* (*a*) Ancrer (un navire); mettre

(un navire) à l'ancre, au mouillage. (*b*) *Const :* Affermir (qch.) par des ancres. **2.** *v.i.* (*a*) Jeter l'ancre ; mouiller. *To a. by the stern,* mouiller par l'arrière. (*b*) *F :* S'ancrer (dans un lieu). **anchored,** *a.* (*a*) Ancré, mouillé ; à l'ancre. *Fish : A. net,* rets sédentaire. (*b*) *F : Firmly a. faith,* foi solidement ancrée. **anchoring,** *s.* Ancrage *m,* mouillage *m.* **Anchoring-gear,** appareaux *mpl* de mouillage. **Anchoring-ground, -place, -berth,** ancrage, mouillage.
anchorage¹ ['aŋkəredʒ], *s. Nau :* (*a*) Ancrage *m,* mouillage *m. To leave the a.,* dérader. (*b*) Droits *mpl* d'ancrage, de stationnement.
anchorage², *s.* Retraite *f* d'anachorète.
anchorite ['aŋkɔrait], *s.* Anachorète *m.*
anchovy ['antʃovi, an'tʃouvi], *s.* Anchois *m.* Anchovy paste, beurre *m,* pâte *f,* d'anchois.
anchylose ['aŋkilo:uz]. **1.** *v.tr.* Ankyloser. **2.** *v.i.* S'ankyloser. (*Of bones*) *To become anchylosed,* s'ankyloser, se souder.
anchylosis [aŋki'lousis], *s. Med :* Ankylose *f.*
ancient ['einʃənt], *a.* Ancien. (*a*) De vieille date. *Family of a. descent,* famille ancienne, de longue lignée. *A. oak,* chêne centenaire. *Poet. & Hum : An a. man,* un vieillard, un ancien. *s. B :* **The Ancient of Days,** l'Ancien des jours ; l'Éternel. *S.a.* LIGHT¹ 4. (*b*) **Ancient Rome,** la Rome antique. *The a. world,* le monde antique. *s.* **The ancients,** les anciens. *S.a.* HISTORY 1.
ancillary [an'siləri], *a.* Subordonné, ancillaire.
and [and, ənd], *conj.* Et. **1.** (*a*) *A knife and fork,* un couteau et une fourchette. (*b*) (*With numerals*) (i) *A. & Lit :* Five and twenty (= *twenty-five*), vingt-cinq. (ii) *Two hundred and two,* deux cent deux. *Four and a half,* quatre et demi. *Four and three quarters,* quatre trois quarts. *An hour and twenty minutes,* une heure vingt minutes. (*c*) *Coffee and milk,* café au lait. *Carriage and pair,* voiture à deux chevaux. **To walk two and two,** marcher deux à deux, deux par deux. (*d*) (*After 'without'*) Ni. *He had come without pencils and pens,* il était venu sans plumes ni crayons. (*e*) (*Intensive repetition*) *For miles and miles,* pendant des milles et des milles. **Better and better,** de mieux en mieux. **Worse and worse,** de pis en pis. *Smaller and smaller,* de plus en plus petit. *I knocked and knocked, but . . .,* je frappai tant et plus, mais. . . . **2.** (*Connecting clauses*) (*a*) *He sang and danced,* il chantait et dansait. (*b*) *Go and look for it,* allez le chercher. *Come and see me,* venez me voir. *F :* Wait and see, attendez voir. *Try and help me,* tâchez de m'aider.
Andalusia [anda'lu:zia]. *Pr.n.* L'Andalousie *f.*
Andalusian [anda'lu:ziən], *a. & s.* Andalou, -ouse.
Andes ['andi:z]. *Pr.n.* The Andes, les Andes *f.*
andiron ['andaiərn], *s.* (*a*) Landier *m.* (*b*) Chenet *m.*
Andrew ['andru:]. *Pr.n.m.* André.
anecdotage ['anekdoutedʒ], *s.* **1.** Recueil *m* d'anecdotes. **2.** *F :* In his anecdotage, dans sa conteuse vieillesse.
anecdotal ['anekdoutəl], *a.* Anecdotique.
anecdote ['anekdout], *s.* Anecdote *f.*
anecdotist ['anekdoutist], *s.* Anecdotier, -ière.
anemometer [ane'mɔmitər], *s.* Anémomètre *m.*
anemone [a'neməni], *s. Bot :* Anémone *f.*
anent [a'nent], *prep. A : & Scot :* A propos de.
aneroid ['anərɔid], *a. & s.* **Aneroid (barometer),** (baromètre *m*) anéroïde (*m*).
aneurism, aneurysm ['anjurizm], *s. Med :* Anévrisme *m.*
anew [a'nju:], *adv.* **1.** (*Once more*) De nouveau.

To begin a., recommencer. **2.** (*In a new way*) A nouveau. *To create sth. a.,* créer qch. à nouveau.
anfractuosity [anfraktju'ɔsiti], *s.* (*a*) *Lit.* Anfractuosité *f.* (*b*) *pl.* Sinuosités *f ;* détours *m.*
angel ['eindʒəl], *s. Ange m. Little a.,* angelet *m. F : An a. of a woman,* une femme angélique. *She is my guardian angel,* c'est mon ange gardien. Angels' visits, visites très espacées. *Prov :* **Talk of angels and you will hear the flutter of their wings,** quand on parle du loup on en voit la queue. **'angel-fish,** *s. Ich :* Ange *m* de mer.
angelic [an'dʒelik], *a.* Angélique. *An a. smile,* un sourire d'ange.
angelica [an'dʒelika], *s. Bot : Cu :* Angélique *f.*
angelus ['andʒeləs], *s. Ecc :* Angélus *m.* **The angelus-bell,** l'angélus.
anger¹ ['aŋgər], *s.* Colère *f ;* emportement *m ; Lit :* courroux *m. Fit of a.,* accès *m* de colère. *To act in a.,* agir sous le coup de la colère. *In great a.,* courroucé.
anger², *v.tr.* Irriter, *Lit :* courroucer (qn) ; mettre (qn) en colère. *He is easily angered,* il se met facilement en colère ; il est irascible.
angered, *a.* Irrité, furieux.
Angevin(e) ['andʒivin], *a.* Angevin ; d'Anjou.
angina [an'dʒaina], *s. Med :* **1.** Angine *f.* **2.** Angina pectoris ['pektoris], angine de poitrine, crampe *f* de poitrine.
angle¹ [angl], *s.* (*a*) Angle *m. Acute a.,* angle aigu. *Obtuse a.,* angle obtus. *Sharp a.,* angle vif. **At an angle of . . .,** sous un angle de. . . . **At an angle,** en biais. *The house stands at an a. to the street,* la maison fait angle sur la rue. *S.a.* RIGHT¹ I. 1. (*b*) (*Corner, nook*) Coin *m.* **'angle-bar,** *s.* Cornière *f* (en fer). **'angle-brace,** *s. Tls :* Foret *m* à angle. **'angle-iron,** *s.* Cornière *f ;* fer *m* d'angle.
angle², *v.i.* Pêcher à la ligne. *To a. for trout,* pêcher la truite. *F : To a. for compliments,* quêter des compliments. *To a. for a husband,* essayer de pêcher un mari. **angling,** *s.* Pêche *f* à la ligne. *A. for trout,* la pêche de la truite. *F : A. for husbands,* la pêche aux maris.
angler ['anglər], *s.* Pêcheur *m* à la ligne.
Anglican ['aŋlikən], *a. & s. Ecc :* Anglican, -ane. **The Anglican Church,** l'Église anglicane.
Anglice ['anglisi], *Lt.adv.* En anglais.
Anglicism ['anglisizm], *s.* (*In speaking or writing French*) Anglicisme *m.*
Anglo-Catholic ['aŋlo'kaθolik], *a. & s. Rel.H :* Anglo-catholique (*mf*).
Anglo-Indian ['aŋlo'indjən], *a. & s.* Anglo-Indien, -ienne. **1.** *Adm :* (Métis) issu du croisement entre Anglais(e) et Hindou(e). **2.** *F :* (Anglais) (i) né dans l'Inde, aux Indes, (ii) servant ou ayant servi dans l'Inde.
Anglomaniac [aŋlo'meiniak], *s.* Anglomane *mf.*
Anglo-Norman ['aŋlo'nɔ:rmən], *a. & s.* Anglo-Normand, -ande.
Anglophil(e) ['anglofil], *s.* Anglophile *mf.*
Anglo-Saxon ['aŋlo'saksən]. **1.** *a. & s.* Anglo-Saxon, -onne. **2.** *s. Ling :* L'anglo-saxon *m.*
angry ['aŋgri], *a.* Fâché, irrité, courroucé (*with s.o. about sth.,* contre qn de qch.). *He was a. at being kept waiting,* il était irrité qu'on le fît attendre. *To get angry,* se mettre en colère ; se fâcher, s'irriter. *To get a. with s.o.,* se fâcher contre qn. *To make s.o. a.,* fâcher, exaspérer, qn ; mettre qn en colère. *A. voices,* voix irritées, colères. *The a. sea, Lit :* la mer courroucée, en courroux. *A. sky,* ciel à l'orage. *Med : A. sore,* plaie irritée, enflammée. **-ily,** *adv.* En colère, avec colère.

anguish ['aŋgwiʃ], s. Angoisse f; douleur f. *To be in a.*, être au supplice.
angular ['aŋgjulər], a. **I.** (Vitesse, etc.) angulaire. **2.** (Rocher, visage) anguleux. *F:* (*Of pers.*) Maigre, décharné.
angularity [aŋgju'lariti], s. Angularité f.
anhydride [an'haidraid], s. *Ch:* Anhydride m.
anhydrous [an'haidrəs], a. *Ch:* Anhydre.
anil ['anil], s. **I.** (a) *Bot:* Anil m, indigotier m. (b) *Dy:* Indigo m. **2.** *Ch:* Anil.
aniline ['anilain], s. *Ch:* *Dy:* Aniline f. **Aniline dyes,** colorants azoïques.
animadversion [animad'vəːrʃ(ə)n], s. Animadversion f, censure f, blâme m.
animadvert [animad'vəːrt], v.i. *To a. on s.o.'s action,* critiquer, blâmer, censurer, l'action de qn.
animal ['anim(ə)l]. **I.** s. Animal m. *A. painter,* animalier m. **2.** a. *A. life,* vie animale. *The a. kingdom,* le règne animal. *A. nature,* animalité f.
animate[1] ['animet], a. Animé; doué de vie.
animate[2] ['animeit], v.tr. (a) Animer. *To be animated by the best intentions,* être animé des meilleures intentions. (b) Encourager, stimuler.
animated, a. Animé. *To become a.,* s'animer.
animation [ani'meiʃ(ə)n], s. **I.** Animation f; vivacité f; chaleur f (du style); feu m, entrain m, verve f (d'un orateur). **2.** Stimulation f, encouragement m.
animosity [ani'mɔsiti], s. Animosité f.
anise ['anis], s. *Bot:* Anis m.
aniseed ['anisiːd], s. (Graine f d')anis m.
anisette [ani'zet], s. Anisette f (liqueur).
ankle [aŋkl], s. Cheville f (du pied). **Ankle-deep,** jusqu'à la cheville. **Ankle-ring,** anneau de cheville. **'ankle-bone,** s. Astragale m. **'ankle-joint,** s. Cheville f; attache f du pied. **'ankle-strap,** s. Barrette f (de soulier).
anklet ['aŋklet], s. **I.** Anneau attaché autour de la cheville. (a) Manille f (de forçat). (b) Bracelet m de jambe, de cheville. **2.** (a) Guêtron m (de chasseur). (b) Molletière f cycliste.
anna ['ana], s. *Num:* (¹⁄₁₆ *rupee*) Anna m.
annalist ['anəlist], s. Annaliste m.
annals ['anəlz], s.pl. Annales f.
Anne [an]. *Pr.n.f.* Anne. *F:* **Queen Anne's dead,** c'est de l'histoire ancienne.
anneal [a'niːl], v.tr. *Metall:* Recuire, adoucir (un métal, le verre). **annealing,** s. Recuit m, recuite f.
annelid, pl. **-ida** ['anelid, a'nelida], s. Annélide m.
annex[1] [a'neks], v.tr. **I.** Annexer (*sth. to sth.*, qch à qch.); ajouter, joindre (une pièce à un mémoire). **2.** *To a. a province,* annexer une province.
annex(e)[2] ['aneks, a'neks], s. Annexe f (d'un hôtel, etc.).
annexation [anek'seiʃ(ə)n], s. Annexion f (*of,* de); mainmise f (*of,* sur).
annihilate [a'naihileit], v.tr. Anéantir (une flotte, etc.); annihiler, supprimer (le temps, etc.).
annihilation [anaihi'leiʃ(ə)n], s. Anéantissement m; annihilation f.
annihilator [a'naihileitər], s. (*Pers.*) Annihilateur, -trice; destructeur m.
anniversary [ani'vəːrsəri], s. Anniversaire m.
annotate ['anoteit], v.tr. Annoter (un livre, etc.); commenter (un texte).
announce [a'nauns], v.tr. Annoncer (qn, qch.). *He announced his intentions to me,* il me fit part de ses intentions.
announcement [a'naunsmənt], s. Annonce f, avis m; (*of birth, marriage, etc.*) faire-part m.

announcer [a'naunsər], s. **I.** Annonceur m. **2.** *W.Tel:* Micrphoniste mf.
annoy [a'nɔi], v.tr. **I.** (*Vex*) Contrarier, tracasser. **2.** (a) (*Inconvenience*) Gêner, incommoder, ennuyer, importuner. (b) (*Molest*) Molester (qn); harceler (l'ennemi). **annoyed,** a. Contrarié, ennuyé. **To get annoyed at sth.,** se vexer de qch. **annoying,** a. Contrariant, ennuyeux, ennuyant.
annoyance [a'nɔiəns], s. **I.** Contrariété f, chagrin m. *Look of a.,* air contrarié, fâché. **2.** Désagrément m, ennui m.
annual ['anjuəl]. **I.** a. Annuel. **2.** s. (a) *Bot:* Plante annuelle. *S.a.* HARDY **2.** (b) (*Book, etc.*) Annuaire m; publication annuelle. **-ally,** *adv.* Annuellement; tous les ans.
annuitant [a'njuitənt], s. **I.** Pensionnaire mf. **2.** Rentier, -ière (en viager).
annuity [a'njuiti], s. **I.** *A. in redemption of debt,* annuité f. **2.** Rente (annuelle). **Government annuity,** rente sur l'État. **Life annuity,** rente viagère, pension viagère. **To pay s.o. an annuity,** servir, faire, une rente à qn.
annul [a'nʌl], v.tr. (annulled) Annuler, résilier (un acte); dissoudre (un mariage); abroger (une loi).
annular ['anjulər], a. (Éclipse, doigt, espace) annulaire.
annulment [a'nʌlmənt], s. Annulation f, résiliation f; dissolution f (d'un mariage); abrogation f (d'une loi).
annunciate [a'nʌnʃieit], v.tr. Annoncer, proclamer (une nouvelle, la venue du Messie).
annunciation [anʌnsi'eiʃ(ə)n], s. *Ecc:* **The Annunciation,** l'Annonciation f.
annunciator [a'nʌnʃieitər], s. **I.** Annonciateur, -trice (du Messie, etc.). **2.** *Tp:* (*Device*) Avertisseur m, annonciateur. **Annunciator-board,** tableau indicateur.
anode ['anoud], s. *El:* Anode f. **Anode voltage,** tension f de plaque.
anodyne ['anodain], a. & s. *Med:* Anodin (m); calmant (m); antalgique (m).
anoint [a'nɔint], v.tr. Oindre. *To a. s.o. with oil,* oindre qn d'huile. *Pred.* *To a. s.o. king,* sacrer qn roi. **The Lord's Anointed,** l'Oint du Seigneur.
anointing, s. **I.** Onction f. **2.** Sacre m (d'un roi, d'un évêque).
anomalous [a'nɔmələs], a. **I.** Anomal, -aux. **2.** *F:* Anormal, -aux. **-ly,** *adv.* Irrégulièrement.
anomaly [a'nɔməli], s. Anomalie f.
anon[1] [a'nɔn], *adv.* *A.* & *Hum:* Tout à l'heure, bientôt; à l'instant. *S.a.* EVER **I.**
anon[2], a. = ANONYMOUS.
anonymity [ano'nimiti], s. Anonyme m, anonymat m.
anonymous [a'nɔniməs], a. Anonyme. *A. writer,* anonyme m. **To remain anonymous,** garder l'anonyme, l'anonymat. **-ly,** *adv.* Anonymement.
anopheles [a'nɔfiliːz], s. *Ent:* Anophèle m.
another [a'nʌðər], a. & pron. **I.** (*An additional*) Encore (un). *A. cup of tea,* encore une tasse de thé. *In a. ten years,* dans dix ans d'ici. *I have received a. three hundred francs,* j'ai reçu trois cents autres francs. *Without a. word. . . .,* sans plus . . .; sans un mot de plus. . . . **2.** (*A similar*) Un(e) autre, un(e) second(e). **Such another,** un autre du même genre, du même modèle. *There is not such a. man,* il n'a pas son pareil. **3.** (a) (*A different*) Un(e) autre. *A. was there before me,* un autre m'avait devancé. **That is (quite) another matter,** c'est tout autre chose; *F:* c'est une autre paire de manches. **Another**

time, une autre fois. (b) *She now has a. husband,* elle a maintenant un nouvel époux. **4. One** . . **another.** (a) *Science is one thing, art is a.,* la science est une chose, l'art en est une autre. (b) **(Taking) one year with another,** bon an mal an. *Taking one (thing) with a.,* l'un dans l'autre; l'un portant l'autre. *S.a.* THING 3. (c) *(Reciprocal pron.)* **One another,** l'un l'autre, les uns les autres. *Love one a.,* aimez-vous les uns les autres. *Near one a.,* l'un près de l'autre; près l'un de l'autre. *To help one a.,* s'entr'aider.

answer¹ [ˈɑːnsər], *s.* **I.** Réponse *f* (à une question, à une lettre); réplique *f* (à une observation, à une critique). *To give an a. to s.o. about sth.,* répondre, faire une réponse, à qn sur qch., au sujet de qch. *He has an a. to everything,* il a réponse à tout. *I could find no a.,* je n'ai rien trouvé à répondre. **Answer to a charge,** réponse à une accusation. *Her only a. was to break into sobs,* pour toute réponse, elle éclata en sanglots. **'An answer will oblige,'** "réponse, s'il vous plaît." *Com:* **In answer to your favour** . . ., en réponse à votre honorée. . . . **2.** Solution *f* (d'un problème).

answer², *v.tr. & i.* **I.** Répondre. (a) *To a. s.o.,* répondre à qn. *Not to a. a syllable,* ne pas répondre un mot. *He answered that he knew nothing about it,* il répondit qu'il n'en savait rien; il répondit n'en rien savoir. (b) *To a. a question,* *a letter,* répondre, faire réponse, à une question, à une lettre. *The question was not answered,* il ne fut pas répondu à la question. **To answer for** (= *instead of*) s.o., répondre pour qn. (*Cp.* 3.) (c) **To answer the roll, to answer one's name,** répondre à l'appel. **To answer the bell,** répondre à un coup de sonnette. **To answer the door,** aller ouvrir; venir ouvrir. (d) *(Of ship)* **To answer the helm,** obéir à la barre. (e) *To a. a charge,* répondre à, réfuter, une accusation. (*f*) *To a. a description,* répondre à un signalement. (*g*) *To a. a prayer,* exaucer une prière. **2.** *To a. the requirements of* . . ., répondre aux besoins de. . . . **To answer the purpose,** remplir le but. *That will a. my purpose,* cela fera mon affaire. *His scheme didn't a.,* son projet n'a pas réussi, n'a pas abouti. **3. To answer** (= *vouch*) **for** s.o., for s.o.'s honesty, répondre de qn; se porter, se rendre, garant de qn, de l'intégrité de qn. (*Cp.* 1 (b).) *I will a. for it that* . . ., je vous suis caution que. . . . **He has a lot to answer for,** il est responsable de bien des choses. **answering,** *a.* **I.** *An a. cry,* un cri jeté en réponse. **2.** Qui répond, correspond, est équivalent (to, à).

answerable [ˈɑːnsərəbl], *a.* **I.** (a) Garant, responsable, comptable (*to s.o. for sth.,* envers qn de qch.). (b) *To be a. to an authority,* relever d'une autorité. **2.** *The question is not a.,* c'est une question (i) à laquelle on ne peut pas répondre, (ii) que l'on ne peut pas résoudre. **-ably,** *adv.* Conformément (to, à).

ant [ant], *s.* Fourmi *f. Wood ant, red ant,* fourmi rouge, fauve. **White ant,** fourmi blanche; termite *m.* **'ant-bear,** *s.* Z: Tamanoir *m.* **'ant-eater,** *s.* Z: Fourmilier *m.* **'ant-hill,** *s.* Fourmilière *f.*

Antaeus [anˈtiːəs]. *Pr.n.m. Myth:* Antée.

antagonism [arˈtagonizm], *s.* Antagonisme *m,* opposition *f.*

antagonist [anˈtagonist], *s.* Antagoniste *mf,* adversaire *m.*

antagonistic [antagoˈnistik], *a.* Opposé, contraire (to, à). *A. environment,* milieu antagonique.

antagonize [anˈtagonaiz], *v.tr.* **I.** *(Of a force)* S'opposer à (une autre force); contrarier (une

force). **2.** Éveiller l'antagonisme, l'hostilité, de (qn).

antarctic [anˈtɑːrktik]. **I.** *a.* Antarctique. **2.** *s.* **The Antarctic,** l'Antarctique *m.*

antecedence [antiˈsiːdəns], *s.* **I.** (a) Antériorité *f.* (b) Priorité *f.* **2.** *Astr:* Antécédence *f.*

antecedent [antiˈsiːdənt]. **I.** *a.* Antécédent; antérieur (*to,* à). **2.** *s.* (a) *Gram: etc :* Antécédent *m.* (b) *Mus:* Thème *m* (d'une fugue). (c) *pl. His antecedents,* ses antécédents.

antechamber [ˈantitʃeimbər], *s.* Antichambre *f.*

antedate [ˈantideit], *v.tr.* **I.** Antidater (un document). **2.** Précéder; venir avant (un événement).

antediluvian [antidiˈljuːviən], *a. & s.* Antédiluvien, -ienne.

antelope [ˈantiloup], *s.* Z: Antilope *f.*

ante meridiem [antimeˈridiem], *Lt.phr.* (*Abbr.* a.m. [ˈeiˈem]) Avant midi. *Five a.m.,* cinq heures du matin.

ante-natal [antiˈneit(ə)l], *a.* Prénatal, -als.

antenna, *pl.* **-ae** [anˈtena, -iː], *s.* **I.** *Ent:* Crust: Antenne *f. Moll:* Tentacule *m;* corne *f* de limaçon. **2.** *W.Tel:* Antenne.

antepenult [antipeˈnʌlt], **antepenultimate** [antipeˈnʌltimet], *a. & s.* Antépénultième (*f*).

anterior [anˈtiːəriər], *a.* Antérieur (to, à).

ante-room [ˈantirum], *s.* Antichambre *f.*

anthem [ˈanθem], *s.* **I.** *Ecc.Mus:* Motet *m.* **2. National anthem,** hymne national.

anther [ˈanθər], *s. Bot:* Anthère *f.*

anthology [anˈθɔlodʒi], *s.* Anthologie *f,* florilège *m.*

Anthony [ˈantoni]. *Pr.n.m.* Antoine.

anthracite [ˈanθrasait], *s. Min:* Anthracite *m.*

anthrax [ˈanθraks], *s.* (a) *Vet: Med :* Charbon *m.* (b) *Med:* Pustule charbonneuse.

anthropoid [ˈanθropoid], *a. & s.* (a) Anthropoïde (*m*). (b) Z: (Singe *m*) anthropomorphe; anthropoïde (*m*).

anthropological [anθropoˈlodʒik(ə)l], *a.* Anthropologique.

anthropologist [anθroˈpolodʒist], *s.* Anthropologiste *m,* anthropologue *m.*

anthropology [anθroˈpolodʒi], *s.* Anthropologie *f.*

anthropometry [anθroˈpometri], *s.* Anthropométrie *f.* **Criminal anthropometry department,** service anthropométrique.

anthropomorphism [anθropoˈmɔːrfizm], *s. Rel.H:* Anthropomorphisme *m.*

anthropophagi [anθroˈpofadʒai], *s.pl.* Anthropophages *m.*

anthropophagy [anθroˈpofadʒi], *s.* Anthropophagie *f.*

anti-aircraft [antiˈɛərkrɑːft], *a.* **Anti-aircraft gun,** canon anti-aérien, contre-avion(s).

anti-body [ˈantibodi], *s. Physiol:* Anticorps *m.*

antic [ˈantik], *s.* (*Usu. pl.*) (a) Bouffonnerie *f,* singerie *f,* cocasserie *f.* **To play, perform, one's antics,** faire le bouffon, faire des singeries, des farces. (b) *pl.* Gambades *f,* cabrioles *f.*

anticathode [antiˈkaθoud], *s. El:* Anticathode *f.*

antichrist [ˈantikraist], *s.* Antéchrist *m.*

anticipate [anˈtisipeit], *v.tr.* **I.** (a) *To a. events, one's income,* anticiper sur les événements, sur son revenu. *To a. a pleasure,* savourer un plaisir d'avance. (b) Escompter (un résultat, un vote). **2.** *To a. s.o.,* prévenir, devancer, qn. *To a. s.o.'s orders, s.o.'s desires,* prévenir les ordres de qn; aller au-devant des désirs de qn. **3.** Anticiper, avancer (un payement, l'heure de son arrivée). **4.** Prévoir, envisager, s'attendre à (une difficulté, etc.); se promettre (un plaisir).

anticipation [antisi'peiʃ(ə)n], *s.* Anticipation *f.* **1.** Action *f* d'escompter (un résultat, etc.). *Com*: 'Thanking you in anticipation,' "avec mes remercîments anticipés." **2.** Prévision *f.* **3.** Attente *f*, expectative *f.*

anticipatory [an'tisipeitəri], *a.* Anticipé, anticipatif; par anticipation.

anticlerical [anti'klerik(ə)l], *a. & s.* Anticlérical, -aux.

anticlimax [anti'klaimaks], *s.* **1.** *Rh:* Anticlimax *m*; gradation *f* inverse. **2.** *F:* The *fifth act forms an a.*, avec le cinquième acte nous retombons dans l'ordinaire, dans le trivial.

anti-clockwise [anti'klɔkwa:iz], *adv. & pred. a.* = COUNTER-CLOCKWISE.

anticyclone [anti'saikloun], *s.* Anticyclone *m.*

anti-dazzle ['antidazl], *a.* Anti-aveuglant. *Aut:* Anti-dazzle shield, pare-lumière *m.* Anti-dazzle head-lights, phares-code *m.*

antidote ['antidout], *s.* Antidote *m*, contre-poison *m.*

anti-freeze [anti'fri:z], *s. Aut:* Solution *f* incongelable.

anti-freezing [anti'fri:ziŋ], *a. Aut: etc:* Anti-congélateur, -trice; anti-gel *inv. A.-f. solution*, solution incongelable.

anti-French [anti'frenʃ], *a.* (Démonstration, etc.) gallophobe.

anti-friction [anti'frikʃ(ə)n], *a. Mec.E:* (Garniture, etc.) anti-friction.

anti-knock [anti'nɔk], *a. I.C.E:* (Produit) antidétonant.

Antilles (the) [ðian'tili:z]. *Pr.n.pl. Geog:* Les Antilles *f.*

antilogarithm [anti'lɔgəriθm], *s. Mth:* Cologarithme *m.*

antimacassar [antima'kasər], *s.* Têtière *f*, voile *m* (de fauteuil, de chaise).

antimony ['antimoni], *s.* Antimoine *m.* Grey antimony, stibine *f*, stibnite *f.*

antinode ['antinoud], *s. Ph:* Antinœud *m*, ventre *m* (d'onde).

antinomy [an'tinomi], *s.* Antinomie *f.*

Antioch ['antiɔk]. *Pr.n. A.Geog:* Antioche *f.*

antipathetic(al) [antipa'θetik(ə)l], *a.* Antipathique (*to*, à).

antipathy [an'tipaθi], *s.* Antipathie *f* (*to*, *against*, pour, contre).

antiphon ['antifɔn], *s. Ecc.Mus:* Antienne *f.*

antiphonal [an'tifɔnəl]. **1.** *a.* (*a*) (En forme) d'antienne. (*b*) En contre-chant. **2.** *s.* = ANTI-PHONARY.

antiphonary [an'tifɔnəri], *s.* Antiphonaire *m.*

antipodes [an'tipodi:z], *s.pl. Geog:* The **antipodes**, les antipodes *m.*

antipoison ['antipɔizn], *s.* Contre-poison *m.*

antipope ['antipoup], *s. Ecc.Hist:* Antipape *m.*

antipyretic [antipai'retik], *a. & s. Med:* Fébrifuge (*m*).

antipyrin(e) [anti'pairi:n], *s. Pharm:* Anti-pyrine *f.*

antiquarian [anti'kwɛəriən]. **1.** *a.* Archéologique. *A. taste*, goût de l'antique. *A. collection*, collection d'antiquités. **2.** *s.* (*a*) = ANTIQUARY. (*b*) *Com:* Antiquaire *m.*

antiquarianism [anti'kwɛəriənizm], *s.* Goût *m* des antiquités.

antiquary ['antikwəri], *s.* Archéologue *m*; amateur *m* d'antiquités.

antiquated ['antikweitid], *a.* Vieilli; désuet, -ète. *A. dress*, habit démodé, suranné. *A. person*, personne vieux jeu.

antique [an'ti:k]. **1.** *a.* Antique. (*a*) *A:* Des anciens. (*b*) *Lit: & Hum:* Ancien, vénérable. (*c*) Suranné. (*d*) *A. books*, *prints*, livres anciens, gravures anciennes. **2.** *s.* (*a*) *Art:* The antique, l'antique *m.* (*b*) Objet *m* antique. Antique shop, magasin d'antiquités. Antique dealer, antiquaire *m.*

antiquity [an'tikwiti], *s.* **1.** (*a*) Ancienneté *f* (d'un usage, etc.). (*b*) L'antiquité (grecque, romaine). **2.** *pl.* Antiquités.

antirrhinum [anti'rainəm], *s. Bot:* Muflier *m*, gueule-de-loup *f.*

anti-Semite [anti'si:mait], *s.* Antisémite.

anti-Semitism [anti'semitizm], *s.* Antisémitisme *m.*

antiseptic [anti'septik], *a. & s. Med:* Antiseptique (*m*).

antisepticize [anti'septisa:iz], *v.tr.* Antiseptiser.

anti-skidding [anti'skidiŋ], *a. Aut: etc: A.-s. device*, antipatinant *m*, antidérapant *m.*

antisocial [anti'souʃ(ə)l], *a.* Antisocial, -aux.

antistrophe [an'tistrofi], *s.* Antistrophe *f.*

anti-tank [anti'taŋk], *attrib. a. Mil:* (Canon) antichars.

antithesis, *pl.* **-es** [an'tiθesis, -i:z], *s.* **1.** Antithèse *f* (*between*, entre; *to*, *of*, de). **2.** Opposé *m*, contraire *m* (de).

antithetic(al) [anti'θetik(ə)l], *a.* Antithétique. **-ally,** *adv.* Par antithèse.

antitoxin [anti'tɔksin], *s. Med:* Antitoxine *f.*

anti-trade ['anti'treid], *a. & s. Nau:* (Vent) contre-alizé (*m*).

antivivisectionist ['antivivi'sekʃənist], *s.* Antivivisection(n)iste *mf.*

antler ['antlər], *s.* Andouiller *m* (d'un cerf, etc.). The antlers, le bois, les bois.

Antony ['antoni]. *Pr.n.m.* Antoine. Mark Antony, Marc Antoine.

antonym ['antonim], *s.* Antonyme *m.*

antonymous [an'tɔniməs], *a.* Antonyme.

antrum ['antrʌm], *s. Anat:* Antre *m*, sinus *m.*

Antwerp ['antwə:rp]. *Pr.n. Geog:* Anvers *m.*

anvil ['anvil], *s.* **1.** *Metalw:* Enclume *f.* Two-horned *a.*, bigorne *f. F:* To have a new book on the anvil,ₜ avoir un nouveau .ivre sur le métier, sur le chantier. **2.** *Anat:* Enclume (de l'oreille).

anxiety [aŋ'zaiəti], *s.* (*a*) Inquiétude *f.* Deep *a.*, anxiété *f*, angoisse *f.* (*b*) *A. for s.o.'s safety*, sollicitude *f* pour la sûreté de qn. (*c*) *A. for knowledge*, désir *m* de savoir.

anxious ['aŋ(k)ʃəs], *a.* **1.** (*a*) Inquiet, soucieux (*about*, sur, de, au sujet de). Very *a.*, extremely *a.*, tourmenté, angoissé. *To be a. for s.o.'s safety*, (i) être plein de sollicitude pour la sûreté de qn; (ii) craindre pour qn. (*b*) Inquiétant. An *a. moment*, un moment d'anxiété. **2.** Désireux. *To be a. for sth.*, désirer vivement qch. *To be a. to do sth.*, désirer faire qch.; tenir à faire qch.; être désireux, soucieux, impatient, de faire qch. *Not very a. to meet her*, peu soucieux de se rencontrer avec elle. *I am very a. that he should come*, je tiens beaucoup à ce qu'il vienne. **-ly,** *adv.* **1.** (*a*) Avec inquiétude; soucieusement. (*b*) Anxieusement. **2.** Avec sollicitude. **3.** Avec impatience.

any ['eni]. I. *a. & pron.* **1.** (*Some(one)*; *in interr. and hypothetical sentences*) Is there any Englishman who . . .? y a-t-il un Anglais qui. . . .? Have you any milk? avez-vous du lait? Have you any? en avez-vous? If any of them should see him, si aucun d'entre eux le voyait. In any hamlet of any importance, dans tout hameau tant soit peu considérable. *There is little, are few, if any,* il y en a peu, si tant est qu'il y en ait du tout. *He knows English if any man does,* il sait l'anglais comme pas un. **2.** (*a*) **Not any,** ne . . . aucun, nul. *He hasn't any reason to complain,* il n'a aucune raison de se plaindre. *I don't owe any man a penny,* je ne dois un centime à qui que ce soit. *I can't find any,* je n'en trouve pas. *I don't think any of them have arrived,* je ne pense pas qu'aucun d'eux soit arrivé. (*b*) (*With implied negation*) *The impossibility of giving him any education,* l'impossibilité de lui donner aucune éducation. **3.** (*a*) (*No matter which*) N'importe (le)quel. *Come any day* (*you like*), venez n'importe quel jour. *Not under any pretext,* pas sous aucun prétexte. *You may bring along any person you like,* vous amènerez qui vous voudrez. **Any but he would have refused,** tout autre que lui aurait refusé. **That may happen any day,** cela peut arriver d'un jour à l'autre. *Draw any two cards,* tirez deux cartes quelconques. (*b*) (*Any and every*) *Any pupil who forgets his books* . . ., tout élève qui oubliera ses livres. . . . **At any hour of the day,** à toute heure de la journée. **II. any,** *adv.* (*Not translated*) *I cannot go any further,* je ne peux aller plus loin. *Will you have any more tea?* voulez-vous encore du thé?

anybody ['enibɔdi], **anyone** ['eniwʌn], *s. & pron.* **I.** (= '*Someone*' *in hypothetical and interr. sentences*) Quelqu'un ; (*with implied negation*) personne. *Do you see a. over there?* voyez-vous quelqu'un là-bas? *Does a. dare to say so?* y a-t-il personne qui ose le dire? *F:* **Is he anybody?** est-il quelqu'un? **2.** (*In neg. sentences*) **Not any-body,** not anyone, ne . . . personne. *There was hardly a.,* il n'y avait presque personne. **3.** (*No matter who*) N'importe qui ; tout le monde. *A. will tell you so,* le premier venu vous le dira. *A. would think him mad,* on le croirait fou. *A. who had seen him at that time* . . ., quiconque l'aurait vu alors. . . . *Anyone but he,* tout autre que lui. *S.a.* ELSE 2.

anyhow ['enihau]. **I.** *adv.* **To do sth. anyhow,** faire qch. (i) d'une manière quelconque, (ii) n'importe comment, tant bien que mal. **Things are (going) all anyhow,** tout est en désordre, en pagaille. **2.** *conj.* (*At any rate*) En tout cas, de toute façon. *A. you can try,* vous pouvez toujours essayer.

anything ['eniθiŋ], *pron. & s.* **I.** (= *Something, in interr. and hypothetical sentences*) Quelque chose ; (*with implied negation*) rien. **Can I do anything for you?** puis-je vous être utile à quelque chose? *Is there a. more pleasant than* . . .? est-il rien de plus agréable que . . .? **If anything should happen to him** . . ., s'il lui arrivait quelque malheur. . . . **2.** (*In neg. sentences*) **Not anything,** ne . . . rien. *He doesn't do a.,* il ne fait rien. **Without doing anything,** sans rien faire. *Hardly a.,* presque rien. **3.** (*No matter what*) N'importe quoi ; tout. **He eats anything,** il mange de tout. **Anything you like,** tout ce que vous voudrez. **He is anything but mad,** il n'est rien moins que fou. *S.a.* BUT 3, ELSE, IF 1. **4.** *Adv.phr.* (*Intensive*) *F:* **Like anything.** *To work like a.,* travailler avec acharnement. *To run like a.,* courir à toutes jambes. *It is raining like a.,* il pleut tant qu'il peut.

anyway ['eniwei], *adv. & conj.* = ANYHOW.

anywhere ['enihwɛər], *adv.* **I.** N'importe où ; dans quelque endroit que ce soit. *Can you see it a.?* pourra-t-il le voir quelque part? **Anywhere else,** partout ailleurs. **2.** **Not** . . . **anywhere,** nulle part ; en aucun endroit, en aucun lieu.

anywise ['eniwaːiz], *adv.* (*also* **in anywise**) **I.** D'une manière quelconque. **2.** En aucune façon ; d'aucune façon. *If he has* **in anywise** *offended you,* s'il vous a offensé en aucune façon.

Anzac ['anzak], *s.m. Hist:* Membre de l'*Australian and New Zealand Army Corps* (1914-1918).

aorist ['ɛərist], *a. & s. Gram:* Aoriste (*m*).

aorta [ei'ɔːrta], *s. Anat:* Aorte *f.*

apace [ə'peis], *adv. Lit:* A grands pas ; vite, rapidement. *Winter is coming on a.,* voici déjà l'hiver.

Apache [ə'patʃe], *s.* **I.** *Ethn:* Apache *m.* **2.** *F:* [ə'paʃ] (*Hooligan*) Apache.

apanage ['apaned3], *s.* Apanage *m.*

apart [ə'pɑːrt], *adv.* A part. **I.** (*Aside*) De côté. **To take s.o. apart,** prendre qn à part. **To hold oneself apart,** se tenir à part, à l'écart. **A class apart,** un genre à part. **2.** (*Asunder, separate*) **To get two things apart,** séparer deux choses, *The boys and girls were kept a.,* on tenait séparés les garçons et les filles. **To move apart,** se séparer. **To come apart,** se détacher, se défaire, se désunir. **To take a machine apart,** démonter, désassembler, une machine. **It is difficult to tell them apart,** il est difficile de les distinguer l'un de l'autre. **To stand with one's feet wide apart,** se tenir les jambes écartées. **3.** (*a*) (*Distant*) *They are a mile a.,* ils sont à un mille l'un de l'autre. *Lines ten centimetres a.,* lignes espacées de dix centimètres. (*b*) **Apart from the fact that** . . ., hormis que . . ., outre que . . . *A. from these reasons* . . ., en dehors de ces raisons . . ., ces raisons mises à part. . . . **Jesting, joking, apart,** plaisanterie à part ; *P:* sans blague.

apartment [ə'pɑːrtmənt], *s.* (*a*) Salle *f*, chambre *f* ; pièce *f.* (*b*) (*Usu. pl.*) Logement *m* ; appartement *m.* **To take apartments,** retenir, prendre, un appartement. **To let furnished apartments,** louer en meublé, *Pej:* en garni.

apathetic [apə'θetik], *a.* Apathique, indifférent. **-ally,** *adv.* Apathiquement ; nonchalamment.

apathy ['apəθi], *s.* Apathie *f*, nonchalance *f.*

ape[1] [eip], *s.* (*a*) *Z:* (*Grand*) singe (sans queue). (*b*) *F:* Singe. **To play the ape,** faire le singe.

ape[2], *v.tr.* Singer ; imiter ; mimer ; contrefaire.

apeak [ə'piːk], *adv.* **I.** (*Ancre*) à pic, dérapée. **2.** *Yard-arms apeak,* vergues en pantenne, apiquées. **Oars apeak,** avirons mâtés.

aperient [ə'piːəriənt], *a. & s. Med:* Laxatif (*m*).

aperiodic [apiːəri'odik], *a. Mec:* Apériodique.

aperture ['apərtjuər], *s.* (*a*) Ouverture *f*, orifice *m.* (*b*) *Phot:* Ouverture (d'un objectif, du diaphragme).

apex, *pl.* **apexes, apices** ['eipeks, -iz, 'eipisiːz], *s.* Sommet *m* (d'un triangle, d'une montagne). *F:* Point culminant, apogée *m* (d'une carrière).

aphasia [ə'feiziə], *s. Med:* Aphasie *f.*

aphelion [ə'fiːliən], *s. Astr:* Aphélie *f.*

aphis, *pl.* **-ides** ['afis, -idiːz], *s. Ent:* Aphidé *m* ; puceron *m.*

aphorism ['aforizm], *s.* Aphorisme *m.*

aphrodisiac [afro'diziak], *a. & s.* Aphrodisiaque (*m*).

Aphrodite [afro'daiti]. *Pr.n.f. Gr.Myth:* Aphrodite.

aphtha, *pl.* **-ae** ['afθa, -iː], *s.* (*a*) Pustule aphteuse. (*b*) *pl.* Aphte *m.*

apiarist ['eipiərist], *s.* Apiculteur *m.*

apiary ['eipiəri], *s.* Rucher *m.*

apices. *See* APEX.

apiculture ['eipikʌltjər], *s.* Apiculture *f.*

apiece [ə'piːs], *adv.* Chacun. *To cost a penny a.,* coûter un penny (la) pièce. *He gave them five francs a.,* il leur donna cinq francs chacun.

apish ['eipiʃ], *a.* **1.** Simiesque. *A. trick*, singerie *f.* **2.** Imitateur, -trice. **-ly,** *adv.* En singe.
apishness ['eipiʃnəs], *s.* Singeries *fpl*; sotte imitation.
apocalypse [a'pɔkalips], *s.* Apocalypse *f.*
apocalyptic [apɔka'liptik], *a.* Apocalyptique.
apocope [a'pɔkopi], *s.* Ling: Apocope *f.*
Apocrypha (the) [ðia'pɔkrifa], *s.pl. B.Lit:* Les Apocryphes *m.*
apocryphal [a'pɔkrifəl], *a.* Apocryphe.
apodosis, *pl.* **-es** [a'pɔdosis, -iːz], *s.* Apodose *f.*
apogee ['apɔdʒiː], *s.* Apogée *m.* **The moon is at apogee,** la lune est à son apogée.
Apollo [a'pɔlo]. *Pr.n.m. Myth:* Apollon.
Apollyon [a'pɔljən]. *Pr.n.m.* L'Ange de l'abîme; Satan (dans le 'Voyage du Pèlerin' de John Bunyan).
apologetic [apɔlo'dʒetik], *a.* **1.** (Ton, etc.) d'excuse. *He was quite a. about it,* il s'en excusa vivement. **2.** (Livre, etc.) apologétique. **-ally,** *adv.* **1.** En manière d'excuse; pour s'excuser; en s'excusant. **2.** Sous forme d'apologie.
apologist [a'pɔlodʒist], *s.* Apologiste *m.*
apologize [a'pɔlodʒaːiz], *v.i.* To apologize to s.o. for sth., s'excuser de qch. auprès de qn. *To a. for doing sth.*, s'excuser de faire qch. *To a. for one's attire,* s'excuser sur sa tenue.
apologue ['apɔlɔg], *s.* Apologue *m.*
apology [a'pɔlodʒi], *s.* **1.** (*a*) Excuses *fpl.* *Letter of apology,* lettre d'excuses. **To make, offer, an apology,** faire, présenter, des excuses. *To demand an a.,* exiger des excuses. *To be profuse in one's apologies,* se répandre, se confondre, en excuses. (*b*) *F:* An a. for a dinner, un semblant de dîner, un piètre dîner. **2.** Apologie *f* (*for,* de); justification *f.*
apophony [a'pɔfoni], *s. Ling:* Alternance *f* (de voyelles); ablaut *m*; apophonie *f.*
apophthegm ['apɔθem], *s.* Apophtegme *m.*
apophysis [a'pɔfisis], *s.* Apophyse *f.*
apoplectic [apo'plektik], *a.* (Personne) apoplectique; (attaque) d'apoplexie.
apoplexy ['apopleksi], *s. Med:* Apoplexie *f*; congestion (cérébrale). *Heat apoplexy,* coup *m* de chaleur; coup de soleil.
apostasy, apostacy [a'pɔstəsi], *s.* Apostasie *f.*
apostate [a'pɔstet], *a. & s.* Apostat (*m*).
apostle [a'pɔsl], *s.* Apôtre *m.* **The Apostles' Creed,** le Symbole des Apôtres.
apostleship [a'pɔslʃip], *s.*, **apostolate** [a'pɔstolet], *s.* Apostolat *m.*
apostolic(al) [apo'stɔlik(əl)], *a.* Apostolique.
apostrophe [a'pɔstrofi], *s.* Apostrophe *f.*
apostrophize [a'pɔstrofaːiz], *v.tr.* Apostropher.
apothecary [a'pɔθikəri], *s.* Apothicaire *m*, pharmacien *m.* *Apothecary's shop,* pharmacie *f.*
apotheosis, *pl.* **-oses** [apɔθi'ousis, -'ousiːz], *s.* Apothéose *f.*
appal [a'pɔːl], *v.tr.* (**appalled**) Consterner; épouvanter. **appalling,** *a.* Épouvantable, effroyable. **-ly,** *adv.* Épouvantablement, effroyablement.
apparatus, *pl.* **-us, -uses** [apa'reitəs, -əsiz], *s.* (*Pl. more usu.* **pieces of apparatus**) (*a*) Appareil *m*, dispositif *m.* (*b*) *Fishing a.,* attirail *m* de pêche.
apparel[1] [a'parəl], *s.* (*No pl.*) Vêtement(s) *m*, habillement *m*, habits *mpl.*
apparel[2], *v.tr.* (**apparelled**) (*a*) Vêtir, revêtir (qn). (*b*) Parer (qn).
apparent [a'parənt, a'pɛərənt], *a.* (Qui est ou qui semble être) apparent, manifeste, évident. *The truth became a. to him,* la vérité lui apparut. *In spite of his a. indifference,* malgré son air

d'indifférence. *S.a.* HEIR. **-ly,** *adv.* **1.** Évidemment, manifestement. **2.** Apparemment. *This is a. true,* il paraît que c'est vrai.
apparition [apa'riʃ(ə)n], *s.* **1.** Apparition *f.* **2.** Fantôme *m*, revenant *m.*
apparitor [a'paritər], *s.m.* Appariteur.
appeal[1] [a'piːl], *s.* **1.** Appel *m*, recours *m.* *A. to arms,* recours aux armes. *Jur:* Appeal at law, appel. *A. from a sentence,* appel d'une condamnation. *Court of Appeal,* cour d'appel. *To hear an a. from a decision,* juger en appel d'une décision. *Without appeal,* sans appel; en dernier ressort. *Notice of appeal,* intimation *f.* *To lodge an appeal,* interjeter appel. *To lodge an a. with the Supreme Court,* se pourvoir en cassation. **2.** (*a*) *To make an a. to s.o.'s generosity,* faire appel à la générosité de qn. (*b*) *The a. of the sea,* l'attrait *m* de la mer. **3.** Prière *f*, supplication *f.*
appeal[2], *v.i.* **1.** *Jur: etc:* (*a*) To appeal to the law, invoquer l'aide de la justice, de la loi. *To a. from a judgment,* appeler d'un jugement. *To a. to the Supreme Court,* se pourvoir en cassation. *To a. to the sword, to the country,* en appeler à l'épée, au pays. *To a. to s.o.'s indulgence,* faire appel à l'indulgence de qn. (*b*) *Abs.* Interjeter appel. **2.** *To a. to s.o. for help,* demander des secours à qn; avoir recours à qn; faire appel à qn. **3.** *To a. to s.o.'s imagination,* s'adresser à l'imagination de qn; (*of thg*) attirer, séduire, charmer, l'imagination. *The plan appeals to me,* le projet me sourit. *That doesn't appeal to me,* cela ne me dit rien. **appealing,** *a.* **1.** (Regard, etc.) suppliant. **2.** (Ton) émouvant. **3.** (Personnalité) sympathique. **-ly,** *adv.* D'un ton, d'un regard, suppliant.
appear [a'piːər], *v.i.* **1.** (*Become visible*) Paraître; apparaître; devenir visible; se montrer. *When Christ shall a.,* quand le Christ paraîtra. *A ghost appeared to him,* un spectre lui apparut. **2.** (*Present oneself publicly*) (*a*) Se présenter. *Jur: To a. before a court,* comparaître devant un tribunal. *To appear for s.o.,* représenter qn; (*of counsel*) plaider pour qn. (*b*) (*Of actor*) To appear on the stage, entrer en scène; paraître sur la scène. (*c*) (*Of book*) Paraître. **3.** (*a*) (*Seem*) *To a. sad,* paraître, sembler, triste. *He appeared to hesitate,* il paraissait hésiter. *So it appears, so it would appear,* il paraît que oui. *It appears not,* il paraît que non. *The boat, it appears, did not call at . . .*, le navire, à ce qu'il paraît, n'a pas fait escale à. . . . (*b*) (*Be manifest*) *As will presently a.,* comme on le verra bientôt.
appearance [a'piːərəns], *s.* **1.** (*a*) Apparition *f*; entrée *f.* *To make an appearance, one's appearance,* paraître, faire son apparition, se montrer, se présenter, arriver. **To put in an appearance,** faire acte de présence. *Th:* First appearance of Miss X, début *m* de Mlle X. **To make one's first appearance,** débuter; faire ses débuts. (*b*) *Jur:* Comparution *f* (devant un tribunal). (*c*) *Publ:* Parution *f* (d'un livre). **2.** (*a*) (*Look, aspect*) Apparence *f*, aspect *m*, air *m*, figure *f*, mine *f*, dehors *m.* *A pleasing a.,* un extérieur aimable; des dehors agréables. *To have a good a.,* avoir une bonne présentation; faire bonne figure. *He makes a good a.,* il (se) présente bien. *The a. of the streets,* l'aspect des rues. *At first appearance,* à première vue; au premier abord. *One should not judge by appearances,* il ne faut pas juger sur l'apparence, sur les dehors. (*b*) (*Semblance*) Apparence. *To, by, all appearance(s),* selon toute apparence; apparemment. **For the sake of appearances,** pour sauver les apparences; pour la forme.

ppease [ə'piːz], *v.tr.* (*a*) Apaiser, tranquilliser (qn). (*b*) Apaiser, assouvir (la faim).
ppeasement [ə'piːzmənt], *s.* (*a*) Apaisement *m.* (*b*) Assouvissement *m.*
ppellant [ə'pelənt], *a. & s. Jur:* Appelant *m.*
ppellation [ape'leiʃ(ə)n], *s.* Appellation *f*, nom *m*, titre *m*, désignation *f.*
ppend [ə'pend], *v.tr.* (*a*) Attacher, joindre (qch. à qch.). *Esp.* (*b*) **To append a signature to a document**, apposer une signature sur un document. *To a. a document to a dossier*, annexer un document à un dossier. *To a. notes*, ajouter des notes.
ppendage [ə'pendedʒ], *s.* **1.** Accessoire *m*, apanage *m* (*to*, de). *The house and its appendages*, la maison et ses dépendances *f*, et ses annexes *f*. **2.** *Anat: Nat.Hist:* Appendice *m.*
ppendicitis [apendi'saitis], *s.* Appendicite *f.*
ppendix, *pl.* **-ixes, -ices** [ə'pendiks, -iksiz, -isiːz], *s.* Appendice *m.* **1.** *Anat:* Vermiform appendix, appendice vermⅰrorme. **2.** Annexe *f* (d'un rapport, etc.); appendice (d'un livre).
ppertain [apər'tein], *v.i. Adm. & Lit:* **1.** Appartenir (*to*, à). **2.** *As appertains to my office*, comme il appartient à mes fonctions. **3.** Se rapporter (*to*, à).
ppetite ['apetait], *s.* (*a*) Appétit *m. To have a good a.*, avoir bon appétit. **To spoil, take away, s.o.'s appetite**, gâter, couper, l'appétit à qn. **To eat with (an) appetite**, manger de bon appétit. (*b*) **Appetite for revenge**, soif *f* de vengeance.
ppetizer ['apetaizər], *s.* Apéritif *m.*
ppetizing ['apetaiziŋ], *a.* Appétissant, alléchant
pplaud [ə'plɔːd], *v.tr.* **1.** Applaudir (qn). **2.** *To a. s.o.'s efforts*, applaudir aux efforts de qn.
pplause [ə'plɔːz], *s.* **1.** Applaudissements *mpl. To meet, be greeted, with a.*, être applaudi. **To win applause**, se faire applaudir (*from*, par, de). **2.** Approbation *f.*
pple [apl], *s.* **1.** Pomme *f. Eating a., dessert a.*, pomme au couteau. *Stewed apples*, compote *f* de pommes; pommes en compote. *Baked a.*, pomme cuite. *S.a.* ADAM. **2.** Apple of the eye, prunelle *f* de l'œil. **apple-'brandy**, *s.* Calvados *m.* **'apple-cart**, *s.* Voiture *f* à bras (de marchand des quatre saisons). *F:* **To upset s.o.'s apple-cart**, bouleverser, chambarder, les plans de qn. **'apple-cheeked**, *a.* Aux joues pleines et vermeilles; à figure de pomme d'api. **'apple-core**, *s.* Trognon *m* de pomme. **apple-'green**, *a. & s.* Vert pomme *m inv.* **'apple-orchard**, *s.* Pommeraie *f.* **apple-'pie**, *s.* Tourte *f* aux pommes. *F:* In 'apple-pie order, en ordre parfait. 'Apple-pie bed, lit *m* en portefeuille. **apple-'sauce**, *s.* Compote *f* de pommes. **apple-'tart**, *s.* Tourte *f*, tarte *f*, aux pommes. **'apple-tree**, *s.* Pommier *m.*
ppliance [ə'plaiəns], *s.* (*a*) Appareil *m*, instrument *m*, dispositif *m.* (*b*) *pl.* Accessoires *m* (d'une machine, etc.); attirail *m.*
pplicable ['aplikəbl], *a.* **1.** Applicable (*to*, à). **2.** Approprié (*to*, à).
pplicant ['aplikənt], *s.* **1.** *A. for a place*, candidat *m* à une place; postulant, -ante, solliciteur *m*, d'une place. **2.** *Jur:* Demandeur, -deresse; requérant, -ante.
pplication [apli'keiʃ(ə)n], *s.* **1.** (*a*) Application *f*, applicage *m* (*of sth. to sth.*, de qch. à, sur, qch.). *Pharm:* **"For external application,"** "pour l'usage externe." (*b*) (*Thing applied*) Application; enduit *m.* (*c*) *Industrial applications of a discovery*, applications industrielles d'une découverte. *Practical applications of a process*, réalisations *f* d'un

procédé. **2.** Assiduité *f*, application (à l'étude, etc.). **3.** Demande *f*, sollicitation *f*, requête *f. A. for a job, for help, for a patent*, demande d'emploi, de secours, de brevet. *To make a. to s.o. for sth.*, s'adresser à qn pour avoir qch. *Samples are sent* **on application**, on envoie des échantillons sur demande.
apply [ə'plai], *v.tr. & i.* **1.** (*a*) Appliquer (*sth. to sth.*, qch. sur qch.); faire l'application de (qch. à qch.). *To a. a poultice*, appliquer un cataplasme. (*b*) *To a. a system*, appliquer un système; mettre un système en pratique. *This applies to my case*, ceci s'applique à mon propre cas. (*c*) *To a. one's mind to sth.*, appliquer son esprit à qch.; s'appliquer à qch. *To a. oneself to one's work*, travailler avec application; s'attacher à son travail. **2.** *To a. to s.o. for sth.*, s'adresser, recourir, avoir recours, à qn pour obtenir qch. *To a. for a post*, poser sa candidature à un emploi; solliciter un emploi. **applied**, *a.* **The applied sciences**, les sciences appliquées. **Applied art**, arts industriels.
appoggiatura [apɔdʒja'tuːra], *s. Mus:* Appog(g)iature *f.*
appoint [ə'pɔint], *v.tr.* **1.** Nommer. (*a*) *Pred: To a. s.o. (to be) mayor*, nommer qn maire. (*b*) *To a. s.o. to sth., to do sth.*, nommer qn à qch.; désigner qn pour faire qch. *To a. s.o. to a post, to a hip*, désigner qn à, pour, un poste, un vaisseau. **2.** (*a*) Fixer, désigner, assigner (l'heure, l'endroit); arrêter (un jour). (*b*) *To a. that sth. shall be done*, décider que qch. se fera; prescrire que qch. se fasse. **appointed**, *a.* **1.** Désigné. (*a*) *At the a. time*, à l'heure dite, convenue, indiquée. (*b*) *A. agent*, agent attitré. **2.** Équipé, monté. **Well-appointed house**, maison bien installée.
appointment [ə'pɔintmənt], *s.* **1.** Rendez-vous *m*; (*for business*) entrevue *f*; *Adm:* convocation *f. To make, accept, an a. for three o'clock*, prendre rendez-vous pour trois heures. **To break an appointment**, manquer au rendez-vous. **2.** (*a*) *A. of s.o. to a post, to a ship*, nomination *f* de qn à un emploi; *Adm:* désignation *f* de qn pour un emploi, un navire. **Purveyor by special appointment to His Majesty**, fournisseur breveté, attitré, de sa Majesté. (*b*) Place *f*, charge *f*, emploi *m.* **3.** *pl.* Aménagement *m*, installation *f* (d'une maison); équipement *m* (d'une auto, etc.).
apportion [ə'pɔːrʃ(ə)n], *v.tr. Fin:* Répartir (les frais); lotir (une propriété). *To a. sth. to s.o.*, assigner qch. à qn.
apportionment [ə'pɔːrʃənmənt], *s.* Partage *m*, répartition *f*; allocation *f*; lotissement *m.*
apposite ['apozit], *a.* Juste; approprié (*to*, à); (fait) à propos. **-ly**, *adv.* A propos; convenablement.
appositeness ['apozitnəs], *s.* Justesse *f*, à-propos *m*; opportunité *f* (d'une action).
apposition [apo'ziʃ(ə)n], *s. Gram: etc:* Apposition *f.* **Words in apposition**, mots appositifs.
appraisal [ə'preiz(ə)l], **appraisement** [ə'preizmənt], *s.* Évaluation *f*, estimation *f*, appréciation *f.* **Official appraisement**, expertise *f.*
appraise [ə'preiz], *v.tr.* Priser, estimer, évaluer (qch.) (*at so much*, à tant); faire l'expertise (des dégâts).
appraiser [ə'preizər], *s.* Estimateur *m*, priseur *m*, évaluateur *m.* **Official appraiser** (*of property, etc.*), commissaire-priseur *m*; expert *m.*
appreciable [ə'priːʃjəbl], *a.* Appréciable; sensible. **-ably**, *adv.* Sensiblement.
appreciate [ə'priːʃieit]. **1.** *v.tr.* (*a*) Évaluer (des

marchandises); estimer la valeur de (qch.).
(b) Apprécier; faire cas de (qch.). *Songs greatly
appreciated*, chansons très goûtées. **I fully appreciate the fact that** . . ., je me rends clairement
compte que. . . . *I fully a. all you have done*,
je ne méconnais pas vos services. **2.** *Fin:*
(a) *v.tr.* Hausser la valeur de (qch.). *To a. the
coinage*, rehausser les monnaies. (b) *v.i.* (*Of goods*)
Augmenter de valeur; hausser de prix; monter.
appreciation [ə'priːʃiˈeiʃ(ə)n], s. **I.** (a) Appréciation *f* ((i) du prix, de la valeur, de qch.; (ii) d'un
service, de la situation, etc.); estimation *f* (de la
valeur de qch.); évaluation *f*. (b) *To give, write,
an a. of a new play*, faire la critique d'une nouvelle
pièce. **2.** Accroissement *m*, hausse *f*, de valeur.
appreciative [ə'priːʃjətiv], **appreciatory**
[ə'priːʃjətəri], a. **I.** (Jugement, etc.) élogieux.
2. *To be appreciative of music*, être sensible à la
musique; apprécier la musique. **-ively**, *adv.*
(a) Favorablement. (b) Avec satisfaction.
appreciator [ə'priːʃieitər], s. Appréciateur,
-trice.
apprehend [apri'hend], *v.tr.* **I.** *Jur:* Arrêter
(qn); appréhender (qn) (au corps); saisir (qn)
au corps. **2.** *Lit:* (a) Percevoir. (b) Comprendre,
saisir (le sens d'une phrase). **3.** *Lit:* Appréhender, redouter.
apprehensible [apri'hensibl], a. Appréhensible
(*to, by, the senses*, par les sens); perceptible.
apprehension [apri'henʃ(ə)n], s. **I.** Arrestation *f*; prise *f* de corps. **2.** (a) Perception *f*;
compréhension *f*. (b) *Psy:* Entendement *m*.
3. Appréhension *f*, crainte *f*.
apprehensive [apri'hensiv], a. **I.** *The a. faculty*,
la faculté de comprendre, de percevoir. *The a.
faculties*, les facultés perceptives. **2.** Timide,
craintif. *To be apprehensive of danger*, redouter
le danger. *To be a. of failure*, craindre d'échouer.
-ly, *adv.* Avec appréhension, avec crainte.
apprentice[1] [ə'prentis], s. (a) Apprenti, -ie.
(b) *Nau:* Apprenti marin; novice *m*. (c) Élève
(d'un architecte).
apprentice[2], *v.tr.* *To apprentice s.o. to s.o.*,
placer, mettre, qn (i) en apprentissage chez qn,
(ii) comme élève chez un architecte. **appren-
ticed,** a. En apprentissage (*to*, chez).
apprenticeship [ə'prentisʃip], s. Apprentissage *m*.
apprise [ə'praiz], *v.tr.* *Lit:* *To apprise s.o. of
sth.*, apprendre qch. à qn; prévenir qn de qch.
To be apprised of a fact, avoir connaissance
d'un fait.
approach[1] [ə'proutʃ], s. Approche *f*. **I.** (a) *The
a. of death*, l'approche, les approches, de la mort.
(b) Abord *m*. *Man easy of approach*, homme
qui est d'un abord facile. (c) *To make approaches
to s.o.*, faire des avances à qn. **2.** Voie *f* d'accès.
The a. to a town, les abords, les approches, d'une
ville. **3.** Rapprochement *m*. *It is an a. to perfection*, cela approche de la perfection. **4.** *Golf:*
Approach shot, coup *m* d'approche.
approach[2]. **I.** *v.i.* Approcher, s'approcher.
Golf: Jouer le coup d'approche. *To a. to perfection*, approcher de la perfection. **2.** *v.tr.* (a) *We
are approaching London*, nous approchons de
Londres. (b) S'approcher de (qn); aborder,
approcher (qn); entrer en communication avec
(qn). *To a. s.o. on the subject of* . . ., faire une
démarche auprès de qn au sujet de. . . . **To be
easy, difficult, to approach**, avoir l'abord facile,
difficile. (c) *To a. a question*, aborder, s'attaquer
à, une question. **approaching,** a. Approchant.
(a) *His a. death*, sa mort prochaine. (b) *The a.
car*, la voiture qui venait en sens inverse.

approachable [ə'proutʃəbl], a. Accessibl[e]
approchable; (personne, côte) abordable.
approbation [apro'beiʃ(ə)n], s. Approbation[.]
I. Agrément *m*, consentement *m*. **2.** Jugement
favorable. *To show one's a.*, manifester so[n]
approbation. *Smile of a.*, sourire approbateu[r.]
3. *Com:* Goods on approbation, *F:* on appro[,]
marchandises à condition, à l'examen, à l'essai.
appropriate[1] [ə'proupriet], a. **I.** Appropri[é.]
Style a. to the subject, style qui convient au sujet[.]
style approprié au sujet. **2.** Propre, convenabl[e]
(*to, for*, à). *The remark is a.*, l'observation es[t]
juste, à propos. **-ly**, *adv.* Convenablemen[t]
proprement; à propos; comme il convient.
appropriate[2] [ə'prouprieit], *v.tr.* **I.** S'appro[-]
prier (qch.); s'emparer de (qch.). **2.** Appropri[er,]
affecter, consacrer (*sth. to, for, a purpose*, qch. [à]
une destination).
appropriateness [ə'prouprietnəs], s. Conven[-]
ance *f*, justesse *f*, à-propos *m*, applicabilité *f*.
appropriation [ə'proupri'eiʃ(ə)n], s. **I.** Appro[-]
priation *f*, prise *f* de possession (*of*, de). **2.** (a) Ap[-]
propriation, affectation *f* (de qch. à un usage)[.]
(b) Affectation de fonds. **3.** Crédit *m* (budgé[t]
aire); budget *m*.
approval [ə'pruːv(ə)l], s. **I.** Approbation [*f,*]
agrément *m*. *I hope it will meet with your a.[,]*
j'espère que vous en serez satisfait. *Gesture, sign*
of approval, geste, signe, approbateur. *To no[d]*
approval, approuver de la tête. **2.** *Adm:* Ratifica[-]
tion *f*, homologation *f*. **3.** *Com:* = APPROBA[-]
TION 3.
approve [ə'pruːv]. **I.** *v.tr.* (a) *A:* *To a. oneself[,]*
faire ses preuves. *The old approved methods*, le[s]
méthodes classiques. (b) Approuver, sanctionne[r]
(une action); ratifier, homologuer (une décision)[.]
Read and approved, lu et approuvé. *Adm:* Ap[-]
proved society, compagnie d'assurances agréé[e]
par l'État. **2.** *v.ind.tr.* **To approve of sth.**,
approuver qch. *To a. of a suitor*, agréer un
prétendant. *I don't a. of your friends*, vos amis
ne me plaisent pas. *To a. of s.o.'s doing sth.*,
approuver, trouver bon, que qn fasse qch.
approving, a. Approbateur, -trice; approbatif.
-ly, *adv.* D'un air, d'un ton, approbateur.
approver [ə'pruːvər], s. Approbateur, -trice.
approximate[1] [ə'proksimet], a. **I.** *Biol:* *Ph:*
Rapproché, proche, voisin. **2.** (Calcul, etc.)
approximatif, approché. **-ly**, *adv.* Approximativement.
approximate[2] [ə'proksimeit]. **I.** *v.tr.* Rapprocher (deux cas, etc.). **2.** *v.i.* *To a. to the truth*,
approcher, se rapprocher, de la vérité.
approximation [ə'proksi'meiʃ(ə)n], s. **I.** Rapprochement *m*. **2.** Approximation *f*. *A. to reality*,
approximation de la réalité. *To be satisfied with
an a.*, se contenter d'un à peu près.
appurtenance [ə'pəːtinəns], s. **I.** *Jur:* (a) Ap-
partenance *f*. (b) Droit *m* accessoire, servitude *f*
(d'un immeuble). **2.** *pl.* Accessoires *m*, attirail *m*.
appurtenant [ə'pəːtinənt], a. *Jur:* (a) *A. to
sth.*, appartenant à qch.; dépendant de qch.
(b) Propre, particulier (*to*, à).
apricot ['eiprikɔt], s. **I.** Abricot *m*. **2.** Apri-
cot(-tree), abricotier *m*.
April ['eipril], s. Avril *m*. *In A.*, au mois d'avril,
en avril. (*On*) *the first, the seventh, of A.*, le
premier, le sept, avril. **April-fool-day**, le premier
avril. **To make an April-fool of s.o.**, donner,
faire, un poisson d'avril à qn.
apron ['eiprən], s. **I.** *Cost:* Tablier *m*.
2. (a) *Veh:* *Aut:* Tablier. (b) *Th:* Apron
(-stage), avant-scène *f*. **'apron-strings**, *s.pl.*
Cordons *m* de tablier. *F:* **To be tied to one's**

mother's apron-strings, être pendu aux jupes, aux jupons, de sa mère.

apse [aps], *s. Ecc.Arch:* Abside *f*, apside *f*.

apt [apt], *a.* **1.** (Mot) juste, fin; (expression) heureuse, qui convient. **2. Apt to do sth.** (*a*) (*Of pers.*) Enclin, porté, à faire qch. *He is apt to forget*, il oublie facilement. *We are apt to believe that . . .*, on croit volontiers que. . . . (*b*) (*Of thg*) Sujet à, susceptible de, faire qch. *Toys apt to go wrong*, jouets sujets à se détraquer. *Iron is apt to rust*, le fer se rouille facilement. **3.** (Élève, etc.) intelligent. *To be apt at sth., at doing sth.*, être habile à qch., à faire qch. **-ly**, *adv.* **1.** Avec justesse; convenablement; avec à-propos. **2.** Adroitement, habilement.

aptera ['aptərə], *s.pl. Z:* Aptères *m*.

apterous ['aptərəs], *a. Bot: Z:* Aptère.

aptitude ['aptitjuːd], *s.* **Aptitude for sth.**, aptitude *f* à, pour, qch.; disposition(s) *f* pour qch.

aptness ['aptnəs], *s.* **1.** Justesse *f*, à-propos *m*. **2.** Penchant *m*, tendance *f* (*to do sth.*, à faire qch.). **3.** = APTITUDE.

aqua ['akwa], *s.* (*Used to form compounds in*) *Ch: Pharm:* **Aqua fortis**, eau-forte *f*. **Aqua regia** ['riːdʒia], eau régale. **Aqua vitae** ['vaitiː], eau-de-vie *f*.

aquafortist [akwa'fɔːrtist], *s. Engr:* Aquafortiste *mf*.

aquamarine [akwama'riːn], *s.* Aigue-marine *f*.

aquarium [a'kwɛəriəm], *s.* Aquarium *m*.

aquatic [a'kwatik], *a.* **1.** (Plante, etc.) aquatique. **2. Aquatic sports**, sports nautiques.

aquatint ['akwatint], *s. Engr:* Aquatinte *f*.

aqueduct ['akwidʌkt], *s.* Aqueduc *m*.

aqueous ['eikwiəs], *a.* **1.** Aqueux. **2.** *Geol:* (Roche) sédimentaire.

aquiline ['akwilain], *a.* Aquilin. **Aquiline nose**, nez aquilin, busqué, en bec d'aigle.

Arab ['arəb], *a. & s.* **1.** *Ethn:* Arabe (*mf*). *S.a.* STREET-ARAB. **2.** (Cheval) arabe (*m*).

Arabia [a'reibia]. *Pr.n.* L'Arabie *f*.

Arabian [a'reibiən]. **1.** *a.* Arabe, d'Arabie. **The Arabian Gulf**, le golfe Arabique. **2.** *s.* Arabe *mf*.

Arabic ['arəbik]. **1.** *a.* (Gomme) arabique; (langue) arabe. **2.** *s. Ling:* L'arabe *m*.

arable ['arəbl], *a.* (Terre) arable, labourable.

arachnid, *pl.* **-ida** [a'raknid, -ida], *s. Z:* Arachnide *m*; acarien *m*.

arbiter ['aːrbitər], *s.* Arbitre *m*.

arbitral ['aːrbitrəl], *a.* Arbitral, -aux.

arbitrament [aːr'bitrəmənt], *s.* Arbitrage *m*; décision arbitrale. **The arbitrament of war**, l'arbitrage de la guerre.

arbitrary ['aːrbitrəri], *a.* Arbitraire. **-ily**, *adv.* Arbitrairement.

arbitrate ['aːrbitreit]. **1.** *v.tr.* Arbitrer, juger, trancher (un différend). **2.** *v.i.* Décider en qualité d'arbitre; arbitrer.

arbitration [aːrbi'treiʃ(ə)n], *s.* Arbitrage *m*. **Procedure by arbitration**, procédure arbitrale. **Arbitration court**, tribunal arbitral.

arbitrator ['aːrbitreitər], *s. Jur:* Arbitre *m*; arbitre-juge *m*.

arboreal [aːr'bɔːriəl], *a.* **1.** D'arbre(s). **2.** (Animal) arboricole; (existence) sur les arbres.

arborescence [aːrbo'res(ə)ns], *s.* Arborescence *f*.

arborescent [aːrbo'res(ə)nt], *a.* Arborescent. *A. shrub*, arbuste *m*.

arboriculture ['aːrborikʌltjər], *s.* Arboriculture *f*.

arboriculturist [aːrbori'kʌltjərist], *s.* Arboriculteur *m*, pépiniériste *m*.

arbour ['aːrbər], *s.* Berceau *m* de verdure; tonnelle *f*, charmille *f*. **Vine arbour**, treille *f*.

arbutus ['aːrbjutəs], *s. Bot:* Arbousier *m*. **Arbutus berry**, arbouse *f*.

arc [aːrk], *s.* **1.** Arc *m*. *Arc of a circle*, arc de cercle. **2. Electric arc, voltaic arc**, arc électrique, voltaïque. **'arc-lamp**, *s.* Lampe *f* à arc.

arcade [aːr'keid], *s.* (*a*) Arcade(s) *f* (en bord de rue); galeries *fpl*. (*b*) Passage *m* (à boutiques).

arch[1] [aːrtʃ], *s.* **1.** Voûte *f*, arc *m*; cintre *m*. *Row of arches*, arcade *f*. **Centre arch**, voûte maîtresse. *A. of a vault*, arceau *m*. *Semicircular a., round a.*, arc (en) plein cintre, arc roman. *Pointed, segmental, a.*, ogive *f*. **2.** (*a*) *Civ.E:* Arche *f* (d'un pont, d'un viaduc). **Railway arch**, pont *m* de chemin de fer (franchissant une rue). (*b*) *A. of a furnace*, voûte d'un fourneau. **3.** *A. of a saddle*, arcade *f* d'une selle. *Anat: A. of the eyebrows*, arc des sourcils. **The orbital arches**, les arcades orbitaires. *A. of the instep*, cambrure *f* du pied. **'arch-stone**, *s. Arch:* Voussoir *m*, claveau *m*.

arch[2]. **1.** *v.tr.* (*a*) Voûter (une porte, un passage). (*b*) Arquer, cintrer; cambrer. *The cat arches its back*, le chat bombe, arque, le dos, fait le gros dos. **2.** *v.i.* Se voûter, former voûte, bomber. **arched**, *a.* (*a*) A arc, en voûte; voûté; voussé. *A. window*, fenêtre (i) cintrée, (ii) en ogive. (*b*) Arqué, cintré; cambré. *A. nose*, nez busqué.

arch[3], *a.* (*Usu. attrib. and only of women and children*) Espiègle; malin, *f.* -igne; malicieux. *An a. glance*, un coup d'œil espiègle et moqueur. **-ly**, *adv.* D'un air espiègle, malin; malicieusement.

arch-, *a. & pref.* Archi-, grand, insigne. *A.-traitor*, traître insigne; architraître. *A.-deceiver*, maître en fourberie.

archaeologic(al) [aːrkio'lɔdʒik(əl)], *a.* Archéologique.

archaeologist [aːrki'ɔlodʒist], *s.* Archéologue *m*.

archaeology [aːrki'ɔlodʒi], *s.* Archéologie *f*.

archaic [aːr'keik], *a.* Archaïque.

archaism ['aːrkeizm], *s.* Archaïsme *m*.

archangel ['aːrkeindʒəl], *s.* Archange *m*.

archbishop [aːrtʃ'biʃəp], *s.m.* Archevêque.

archbishopric [aːrtʃ'biʃəprik], *s.* **1.** Archevêché *m*. **2.** Archiépiscopat *m*.

archdeacon [aːrtʃ'diːkən], *s.m.* Archidiacre.

archduchess [aːrtʃ'dʌtʃes], *s.f.* Archiduchesse.

archduke [aːrtʃ'djuːk], *s.m.* Archiduc.

archer ['aːrtʃər], *s.* **1.** Archer *m*. **2.** *Astr:* **The Archer**, le Sagittaire.

archery ['aːrtʃəri], *s.* Tir *m* à l'arc.

archetype ['aːrkitaip], *s.* Archétype *m*.

archfiend [aːrtʃ'fiːnd], *s.* **The a.**, Satan *m*.

Archimedean [aːrki'miːdiən], *a.* D'Archimède.

archipelago, *pl.* **-oes** [aːrki'peləgou(z)], *s.* Archipel *m*. **The Indian Archipelago**, l'Insulinde *f*.

architect ['aːrkitekt], *s.* **1.** Architecte *m*. **2. Naval architect**, ingénieur *m* des constructions navales, du génie maritime.

architecture ['aːrkitektjər], *s.* Architecture *f*.

architrave ['aːrkitreːiv], *s.* **1.** *Arch:* Architrave *f*. **2.** *Const:* Encadrement *m* (de porte, de fenêtre).

archives ['aːrkaːivz], *s.pl.* Archives *f*.

archivist ['aːrkivist], *s.* Archiviste *mf*.

archness ['aːrtʃnəs], *s.* (*Of women and children*) Malice *f*, espièglerie *f* (du regard, du sourire).

archpriest [aːrtʃ'priːst], *s.m.* Archiprêtre.

archway ['aːrtʃwei], *s.* Passage voûté; porte cintrée, voûte *f* d'entrée; arcade *f*, portail *m*.

arctic ['aːrktik], *a.* Arctique.

ardent ['aːrdənt], *a.* Ardent. **1.** *A. heat*, chaleur ardente. **2.** *A. in pursuit of the enemy*, ardent à poursuivre l'ennemi. **-ly**, *adv.* Ardemment; avec ardeur.

ardour ['ɑ:rdər], s. Ardeur f.
arduous ['ɑ:rdjuəs], a. (Sentier, travail) ardu; (chemin) escarpé; (travail) rude. **-ly**, adv. Péniblement, malaisément.
arduousness ['ɑ:rdjuəsnəs], s. Arduité f, difficulté f.
are [ɑːr, ər]. See BE.
area ['ɛəriə], s. **1.** (a) Terrain vide, inoccupé. (b) Parterre m (de salle de concert, de cinéma). **2.** Cour f d'entrée en sous-sol (sur la rue). **3.** (a) Aire f, superficie f, contenance f (d'un cercle, d'un champ, etc.). (b) Surface f. Wall a., surface de paroi. **4.** Étendue f (de pays); territoire m, région f. Disturbed a., zone troublée. Postal area, zone postale. The whole London a., l'agglomération londonienne.
areca ['arika], s. Bot: Arec m. **Areca palm(-tree),** aréquier m. **Areca-nut,** (noix d')arec.
arena, pl. **-as** [a'ri:na, -əz], s. (a) Arène f. (b) Champ m (d'une activité, etc.). The a. of the war, le théâtre de la guerre.
aren't [ɑːrnt]. (a) = Are not. (b) P: = Am not.
areola, pl. **-ae** [a'ri:ola, -i:], s. Aréole f.
areometer [ɛəri'ɔmetər], s. Ph: Aréomètre m.
Areopagus [ari'ɔpagəs]. Pr.n. & s. Aréopage m.
argent ['ɑːrdʒənt]. Her: & Poet: **1.** s. Argent m. **2.** a. Argenté; Her: d'argent, argent inv.
Argentina [ɑːrdʒen'tainə]. Pr.n. Geog: L'Argentine f; la République Argentine.
argentine[1] ['ɑːrdʒəntain], a. Argentin.
Argentine[2], a. Geog: **The Argentine Republic,** F: the Argentine, la République Argentine.
argillaceous [ɑːrdʒi'leiʃəs], a. Argileux.
argle-bargle ['ɑːrgl'bɑːrgl], v.i. F: Argumenter, raisonner.
argon ['ɑːrgon], s. Ch: Argon m.
Argonaut ['ɑːrgonɔːt], s. **1.** Gr.Myth: Argonaute m. **2.** Moll: Voilier m, argonaute.
argosy ['ɑːrgosi], s. A: & Poet: Caraque f.
arguable ['ɑːrgjuəbl], a. Discutable, soutenable.
argue ['ɑːrgjuː]. (arguing; argued) **1.** v.tr. (a) (Indicate) Prouver, indiquer, démontrer. His action argues him (to be) a coward, son action prouve, accuse, décèle, sa lâcheté. (b) Discuter, débattre; raisonner sur (une question, une affaire, etc.). To a. that sth. is impossible, soutenir, prétendre, que qch. est impossible. **2.** v.i. (a) Argumenter (against s.o., contre qn; about sth., sur qch.). To argue from sth., tirer argument de qch. (b) Discuter, (se) disputer, raisonner (with s.o. about sth., avec qn sur qch.); plaider (for, against, sth., pour, contre, qch.). **argue down,** v.tr. Réduire (qn) au silence (à force d'arguments).
arguer ['ɑːrgjuər], s. Argumentateur, -trice.
argufy ['ɑːrgjufai], v.i. (a) Argumenter, raisonner; faire le raisonneur. (b) Disputailler.
argument ['ɑːrgjumənt], s. **1.** Argument m (for, against, en faveur de, contre). To follow s.o.'s (line of) a., suivre le raisonnement de qn. His a. is that gold should be done away with, sa thèse est qu'il faudrait abolir l'or. For the sake of a., (i) pour le plaisir de discuter; (ii) à titre d'exemple. **2.** Discussion f, dispute f, débat m. **3.** (a) A: Argument, thèse f (d'un discours, d'une pièce de théâtre). (b) (Synopsis) Argument, sommaire m.
argumentation [ɑːrgjumen'teiʃ(ə)n], s. Argumentation f.
argumentative [ɑːrgju'mentətiv], a. **1.** (Ouvrage) raisonné, critique. **2.** (Of pers.) Raisonneur; disposé à argumenter, à disputailler.
argumentativeness [ɑːrgju'mentətivnəs], s. Disposition f à argumenter; esprit raisonneur.

Argus ['ɑːrgəs]. Pr.n.m. Myth: Argus. **Argus-eyed,** aux yeux d'Argus.
aria ['ɑːria], s. Mus: Aria f.
Ariadne [ari'adni]. Pr.n.f. Gr.Myth: Ariane.
Arian ['ɛəriən], a. & s. Rel.H: Arien, -ienne.
arid ['arid], a. (Terre, sujet) aride.
aridity [a'riditi], **aridness** ['aridnəs], s. Aridité f.
aright [a'rait], adv. Bien, juste, correctement.
Ariosto [ari'ɔsto]. Pr.n.m. Lit.Hist: L'Arioste.
arise [a'raiz], v.i. (arose [a'rouz]; arisen [a'rizn]) **1.** S'élever. (a) (Of pers.) A prophet arose, un prophète surgit, se révéla. (b) (Of thg) Along the road buildings soon arose, le long de la route s'élevèrent bientôt des bâtiments. (c) A. & B: To a. from the dead, ressusciter (des morts). **2.** (Of thg) (a) S'élever, surgir, survenir, s'offrir, se présenter, se produire. A storm arose, il survint une tempête. Another difficulty then arose, alors survint, surgit, se présenta, une nouvelle difficulté. Should the occasion arise . . ., le cas échéant. . . . (b) Émaner, provenir, résulter (from, de). Obligations that a. from a clause, obligations qui émanent d'une clause. **Arising from** (this proposal, etc.), comme suite à (cette proposition, etc.).
aristocracy [aris'tɔkrəsi], s. Aristocratie f.
aristocrat ['aristokrat, a'ris-], s. Aristocrate mf.
aristocratic [aristo'kratik], a. Aristocratique.
Aristophanes [aris'tɔfaniːz]. Pr.n.m. Aristophane.
Aristotelian [aristo'tiːljən], a. & s. Aristotélicien; (doctrine) aristotélique.
Aristotle ['aristɔtl]. Pr.n.m. Aristote.
arithmetic [a'riθmetik], s. Arithmétique f, calcul m.
arithmetical [ariθ'metik(ə)l], a. Arithmétique. **-ally,** adv. Arithmétiquement.
ark [ɑːrk], s. Arche f. **1.** Noah's ark, l'arche de Noé. **2.** The Ark of the Covenant, l'Arche d'alliance, l'Arche sainte.
arm[1] [ɑːrm], s. **1.** Bras m (de personne; Farr: de cheval). **Upper arm,** haut m du bras, arrière-bras m. S.a. FOREARM. **To carry a child in one's arms,** porter un enfant au bras, dans ses bras. **To have s.o. on one's arm,** avoir qn à son bras. **To give one's arm to s.o.,** donner le bras à qn. **Arm-in-arm,** bras dessus bras dessous. She took my arm, elle me prit le bras; elle passa sa main dans mon bras. **To put one's arm round s.o.,** prendre qn par la taille. **To carry sth. at arm's length,** porter qch à bras tendu, à bout de bras. F: **To keep s.o. at arm's length,** tenir qn à distance. **2.** Bras (de mer, d'un fleuve, de fauteuil, de levier, de manivelle); fléau m (de balance); accoudoir m (de fauteuil). **'arm-badge,** s. **1.** Mil: Brassard m. **2.** Plaque f (de commissionnaire, etc., portée au bras). **'arm-band,** s. Brassard m; esp. brassard de deuil. **'arm-chair,** s. Fauteuil m. **'arm-hole,** s. Emmanchure f, entournure f. **'arm-rest,** s. Veh: Accoudoir m, accotoir m.
arm[2], s. Usu. pl. **1.** Arme f. (a) **Fire-arm(s),** arme(s) à feu. **Small-arms,** armes portatives. **Side-arms,** armes blanches. **To take up arms, to rise up in arms,** prendre les armes (against, contre). **To arms!** aux armes! **To bear, carry, arms,** porter les armes. **To lay down one's arms,** mettre bas les armes; rendre les armes. **Nation in arms, under arms,** nation sous les armes. **Arms factory,** fabrique d'armes. (b) Mil: (Branch of service) Arme. F: **The fourth arm,** l'aviation f. **2.** pl. Her: Armoiries f, armes. S.a. COAT[1] 1.

arm³. I. *v.tr.* (*a*) Armer. *F: To arm oneself with an umbrella,* s'armer, se nantir, d'un parapluie. (*b*) *Tchn:* Armer (une poutre, un aimant, etc.); renforcer (une poutre, etc.). **2.** *v.i.* S'armer; prendre les armes. **armed¹,** *a.* Armé (*with,* de). *A. ship,* (i) navire armé en guerre; (ii) vaisseau cuirassé. *Armed to the teeth,* armé jusqu'aux dents. *Armed at all points,* armé de toutes pièces, de pied en cap. **arming,** *s.* **I.** Arming of a fuse, armement *m* d'une amorce. **2.** *Nau:* Suif *m* (de la grande sonde).

armada [ɑːrˈmeidə], *s.* (*a*) *Hist:* The Invincible Armada, l'Invincible Armada *f.* (*b*) *F:* Grande flotte de guerre.

armadillo [ɑːrməˈdilo], *s.* **I.** *Z:* Tatou *m.* **2.** *Crust:* (*Wood-louse*) Armadille *m* or *f.*

Armageddon [ɑːrməˈgedən], *s.* (*a*) *B.Lit:* Armageddon *m.* (*b*) La lutte suprême.

armament [ˈɑːrməmənt], *s.* **I.** Armement *m.* *Naval armaments,* armements navals. *Armament maker,* fabricant de matériel de guerre. **2.** Forces *fpl*; armée *f,* flotte navale.

armature [ˈɑːrmatjuər], *s.* **I.** *Biol: etc:* Armure *f.* **2.** *El:* Induit *m* (de condensateur, dynamo); armature *f* (de magnéto). *A. winding,* enroulement *m* d'induit.

-armed² [ɑːrmd], *a.* Long-armed, au(x) bras long(s).

Armenia [ɑːrˈmiːnjə]. *Pr.n.* L'Arménie *f.*

Armenian [ɑːrˈmiːnjən], *a. & s.* Arménien.

armful [ˈɑːrmful], *s.* Brassée *f.* *In armfuls, by the a.,* à pleins bras, plein les bras.

armistice [ˈɑːrmistis], *s.* Armistice *m.* *Armistice day,* l'anniversaire de l'Armistice (de 1918).

armlet [ˈɑːrmlet], *s.* **I.** Bracelet (porté au-dessus du coude). **2.** Brassard *m.* **3.** Petit bras de mer.

armorial [ɑːrˈmɔːriəl], *a.* Armorial, -aux; héraldique. *A. bearings,* armoiries *fpl.*

armour¹ [ˈɑːrmər], *s.* **I.** Armure *f* (de chevalier, etc.). *Suit of armour,* armure complète. *In full armour,* armé de pied en cap. **2.** (*a*) Blindage *m* (de train blindé). (*b*) *N.Arch:* Cuirasse *f,* blindage. **'armour-bearer,** *s. A:* Écuyer *m.* **'armour-belt,** *s. N.Arch:* Cuirasse *f* de ceinture; ceinture blindée, cuirassée. **'armour-clad,** *a.* Blindé, cuirassé. **'armour-plate,** *s. N.Arch: etc:* Plaque *f* de cuirasse, de blindage. **'armour-plated,** *a.* Cuirassé; blindé.

armour², *v.tr.* Cuirasser (un navire); blinder (un train, etc.); *El.E:* armer (un câble).

armourer [ˈɑːrmərər], *s.* Armurier *m.*

armoury [ˈɑːrməri], *s.* **I.** Magasin *m* d'armes. **2.** (*In barracks*) Armurerie *f.*

armpit [ˈɑːrmpit], *s.* Aisselle *f.*

army [ˈɑːrmi], *s.* **I.** (*a*) Armée *f.* *To be in the army,* être dans l'armée; être soldat, militaire. *To go into the army, to join the army,* s'engager, s'enrôler; se faire soldat; entrer au service. *Standing army, regular army,* armée permanente, active. (*b*) The Salvation Army, l'Armée du Salut. **2.** *F:* Foule *f,* multitude *f* (d'hommes, etc.). **'army-corps,** *s.inv.* Corps *m* d'armée. **'Army-list,** *s.* L'Annuaire *m* militaire.

arnica [ˈɑːrnikə], *s.* Arnica *f.*

aroma [əˈroumə], *s.* Arome *m*; bouquet *m* (d'un vin, d'un cigare).

aromatic [aroˈmatik]. **I.** *a.* Aromatique; (*parfum*) balsamique. **2.** *s.* Aromate *m.*

aromatize [əˈroumataːiz], *v.tr.* Aromatiser.

around [əˈraund]. **I.** *adv.* Autour, à l'entour. *All around,* tout autour. *The woods (all) a.,* les bois d'alentour. **2.** *prep.* Autour de. *The country a. the town,* les environs de la ville.

arouse [əˈrauːz], *v.tr.* **I.** (*a*) Réveiller, éveiller (qn). *To a. s.o. from his sleep,* tirer qn de son sommeil. (*b*) Secouer (qn) (de sa paresse); stimuler (qn). **2.** Exciter, éveiller, susciter (un sentiment); soulever (des passions).

arpeggio [ɑːrˈpedʒjo], *s. Mus:* Arpège *m.*

arraign [əˈreːin], *v.tr.* (*a*) Mettre (qn) en accusation; accuser, inculper (qn) (*for,* de); traduire (qn) devant un tribunal. (*b*) Attaquer (qn, une opinion); s'en prendre à (qn).

arraignment [əˈreinmənt], *s.* **I.** *Jur:* (*a*) Mise *f* en accusation. (*b*) Acte *m* d'accusation. **2.** Censure *f*; critique *f* hostile.

arrange [əˈreindʒ], *v.tr.* Arranger, aménager. **I.** (*a*) (*Set in order*) Disposer, ranger (les meubles, etc.); ordonner (un cortège). *To a. one's affairs,* régler ses affaires. (*b*) *Piece arranged for the piano,* morceau adapté, arrangé, pour piano. **2.** (*Plan beforehand*) *To a. a marriage,* arranger un mariage. *To a. to do sth.,* (i) s'arranger, prendre ses dispositions, pour faire qch; (ii) s'arranger avec qn pour faire qch.; convenir de faire qch. *To a. a time for sth.,* fixer une heure pour qch. *It was arranged that . . .,* il fut convenu que. . . . **3.** (*Settle*) Accommoder, ajuster, arranger (un différend). **arranging,** *s.* Arrangement *m,* aménagement *m,* ajustement *m,* règlement *m.*

arrangement [əˈreindʒmənt], *s.* **I.** Arrangement *m,* disposition *f,* aménagement *m,* mise *f* en ordre. *To make arrangements to do sth., for sth. to be done,* prendre des dispositions, des mesures, faire des préparatifs, pour faire qch., pour que qch. se fasse. *Mus: A. for piano,* arrangement, adaptation *f,* réduction *f,* pour piano. **2.** Accommodement *m* (d'un différend); accord *m,* entente *f.* *Jur:* Transaction *f.* *Com:* To come to an arrangement with s.o., entrer en arrangement, passer un compromis, avec qn. *Price by arrangement,* prix à débattre. **3.** Dispositif *m* (de mise en marche, etc.).

arrant [ˈarənt], *a.* Insigne, achevé. *A. rogue,* coquin fieffé; franc coquin.

arras [ˈarəs], *s. A:* Tenture(s) *f*; tapisserie(s) *f.*

array¹ [əˈrei], *s.* **I.** (*a*) Rangs *mpl.* *In close array,* en rangs serrés. *In battle array,* en ordre de bataille. (*b*) Étalage *m.* *An a. of figures,* une rangée de chiffres. **2.** *Poet:* Parure *f,* atours *mpl.*

array², *v.tr.* **I.** Ranger, mettre en ordre; disposer, déployer (des troupes) (en ordre de bataille). *They arrayed themselves against the King,* ils se rangèrent du parti hostile au roi. **2.** *Poet:* Revêtir, orner, parer (*s.o. in sth.,* qn de qch.).

arrear(s) [əˈriːər(z)], *s.* Arriéré *m,* arrérages *mpl.* *Arrears of rent,* arriéré de loyer. *Arrears of wages,* arrérages de salaires. *Rent in arrear,* loyer arriéré, en retard. *To get, fall, into arrears,* (*of pers.*) se mettre en retard; s'arriérer. *Arrears of interest,* intérêts arriérés; arrérages.

arrest¹ [əˈrest], *s.* **I.** (*a*) Arrestation *f.* *Jur:* Prise *f* de corps. *Under arrest,* en état d'arrestation. *S.a.* WARRANT¹ 3. (*b*) *Mil:* Arrêts *mpl.* *Under arrest,* aux arrêts. **2.** Arrêt *m,* suspension *f* (d'un mouvement, du progrès).

arrest², *v.tr.* **I.** Arrêter (un mouvement, le progrès). **2.** Arrêter (un malfaiteur); appréhender (qn) au corps. **3.** Arrêter, fixer, retenir (l'attention, les regards). **4.** *Jur:* To arrest judgment, suspendre l'exécution d'un jugement.

arresting, *a.* Attachant, frappant; qui arrête l'attention.

arris [ˈaris], *s.* Arête vive (d'un prisme, d'une cannelure).

arrival [əˈraivəl], *s.* **I.** (*a*) Arrivée *f.* On arrival, à l'arrivée. (*b*) *Com:* Arrivage *m* (de marchandises). (*c*) *Nau:* Entrée *f* (d'un vaisseau).

S.a. PLATFORM 2, **2.** (*Of pers.*) A new arrival, un nouveau venu, un nouvel arrivant.
arrive [a'ra:iv], *v.i.* **1.** (*a*) Arriver (*at, in,* à, dans). *We arrived at three o'clock,* nous sommes arrivés à trois heures. *As soon as he arrived in London,* dès son arrivée à Londres. *To a. upon the scene, to a. unexpectedly,* survenir. (*b*) *To a. at the age of sixty,* atteindre, parvenir à, l'âge de soixante ans. **2.** *To a. at a conclusion,* arriver, aboutir, à une conclusion. *To a. at a price,* fixer un prix.
arrogance ['arogəns], **arrogancy** ['arogənsi], *s.* Arrogance *f*; morgue *f.*
arrogant ['arogənt], *a.* Arrogant. *A. tone,* ton rogue. **-ly,** *adv.* Avec arrogance.
arrogate ['arogeit], *v.tr.* **1.** To arrogate sth. to oneself, s'arroger qch., s'attribuer qch. **2.** To arrogate sth. to s.o., attribuer injustement qch. à qn.
arrow ['aro], *s.* Flèche *f.* *To shoot, let fly, an a.,* lancer, décocher, une flèche. *F: The arrows of calumny,* les traits *m* de la calomnie. *Adm:* Broad **arrow** = marque *f* de l'État. **'arrow-head,** *s.* **1.** *Bot:* Marante *f.* **2.** *Cu:* Arrow-root *m.* **'arrow-root,** *s.* Tête *f,* fer *m,* pointe *f,* de flèche.
arsenal ['ɑːrsənəl], *s.* Arsenal *m,* -aux.
arsenic¹ ['ɑːrsnik], *s.* Arsenic *m.*
arsenic² [ɑːr'senik], *a. Ch:* (Acide) arsénique.
arsenical [ɑːr'senik(ə)l], *a.* Arsenical, -aux.
arson ['ɑːrsn], *s.* Incendie *m* volontaire, par malveillance. *Jur:* Crime *m* d'incendie.
art¹ [ɑːrt], *s. See* BE. ·
art², *s.* **1.** Art *m.* (*a*) The (fine) arts, les beaux-arts. *Work of art,* œuvre d'art. *S.a.* GALLERY 2. (*b*) The liberal arts, les arts libéraux. *S.a.* BACHELOR 3, MASTER¹ 2. **The useful arts,** les arts mécaniques. **Arts and crafts,** arts et métiers. (*c*) *The art of war,* l'art militaire. **The black art,** la magie noire. **The noble art,** la boxe. **2.** (*a*) (*Dexterity, cunning*) Adresse *f,* habileté *f,* artifice *m,* art. *To use every art in order to . . .,* user de tous les artifices pour. . . . (*b*) **To have art and part in sth.,** être fauteur et complice de qch. *I had no art or part in it,* je n'y suis pour rien. **'art-critic,** *s.* Critique *m* d'art. **'art-exhibition,** *s.* Exposition *f* des beaux-arts. **'art-school,** *s.* École *f* des beaux-arts; *esp.* école, académie *f,* de dessin.
arterial [ɑːr'tiːəriəl], *a.* **1.** *Anat:* Artériel. **2. Arterial road,** grande voie de communication. *Rail: A. line,* grande ligne.
artery ['ɑːrtəri], *s.* **1.** *Anat:* Artère *f.* **2.** *F: Traffic a.,* artère de circulation.
artesian [ɑːr'tiːzjən, -'tiːʒən], *a.* Artésien; de l'Artois. *Esp.* Artesian well, puits artésien.
artful ['ɑːrtful], *a.* (*a*) Adroit, habile, ingénieux. (*b*) Rusé, artificieux, astucieux; *F:* malin, *f.* -igne. **-fully,** *adv.* **1.** Adroitement. **2.** Artificieusement.
artfulness ['ɑːrtfulnəs], *s.* **1.** Art *m,* adresse *f,* habileté *f,* ingéniosité *f.* **2.** Astuce *f.*
arthritic [ɑːr'θritik], *a. Med:* Arthritique.
arthritis [ɑːr'θraitis], *s. Med:* Arthrite *f.* **Rheumatoid arthritis,** rhumatisme *m* articulaire.
arthropod, *pl.* **-s, -oda** ['ɑːrθropɔd, -z, ɑːr'θropoda], *s. Z:* Arthropode *m.*
Arthurian [ɑːr'θjuəriən], *a. Lit.Hist:* (Cycle *m,* etc.) d'Arthur; (roman) arthurien.
artichoke ['ɑːrtitʃouk], *s.* **1.** Artichaut *m.* **2. Jerusalem artichoke,** topinambour *m.*
article¹ ['ɑːrtikl], *s.* **1.** *Bot: Ent:* Article *m;* point *m* d'articulation. **2.** (*a*) *Com: Jur:* Article, clause *f* (d'un contrat, d'un traité). **Articles of apprenticeship, of a partnership,** contrat *m* d'apprentissage, de société; acte *m* de société.

Articles of war, *Mil:* code *m* (de justice) militaire; *Navy:* code de justice maritime. (*b*) **Article of faith,** article de foi. *Theol:* **The Articles of Religion, the Thirty-nine Articles,** les Articles de religion (de l'Église anglicane). (*c*) *Jur:* Chef *m* d'accusation. **3.** Article (de journal, de revue). *S.a.* LEADING² 2. **4.** (*a*) Article, objet *m.* **Toilet articles,** objets de toilette. (*b*) *A. of luggage,* pièce *f* de bagage; colis *m.* *A. of clothing,* pièce d'habillement. **5.** *Gram:* **Definite, indefinite, article,** article défini, indéfini.
article², *v.tr.* *To a. s.o. to an architect, etc.,* placer qn (comme élève) chez un architecte, etc. **Articled clerk,** clerc d'avoué, de *solicitor,* lié par un contrat d'apprentissage.
articulate¹ [ɑːr'tikjulet], **1.** *a. & s.* Z: Articulé (*m*). **2.** *a.* (*a*) *A. speech,* langage articulé. (*b*) (*Of utterance*) Net, distinct.
articulate² [ɑːr'tikjuleit], *v.tr. & i.* **1.** *Anat:* Articuler (un squelette, etc.). **2.** Articuler, énoncer (un mot, etc.). *He doesn't a. his words,* son énonciation est mauvaise.
articulation [ɑːrtikju'leiʃ(ə)n], *s.* Articulation *f.*
artifice ['ɑːrtifis], *s.* **1.** Artifice *m,* ruse *f;* combinaison *f.* **2.** Art *m,* habileté *f,* adresse *f.*
artificer [ɑːr'tifisər], *s.* Artisan *m,* ouvrier *m.* *Mil:* Artificier *m.* *Navy:* **Engine-room artificer,** mécanicien *m.*
artificial [ɑːrti'fiʃ(ə)l], *a.* **1.** Artificiel; simili-. *A. stone,* similipierre *f.* *A. leg,* jambe artificielle. *A. hair, teeth,* cheveux postiches, fausses dents. *Agr:* **Artificial manure,** engrais chimiques. *S.a.* SILK 1. **2.** Factice, simulé. *A. tears,* larmes factices, feintes. **-ally,** *adv.* Artificiellement.
artillery [ɑːr'tiləri], *s.* (*Ordnance, gunnery,* or *one of the arms of the service*) Artillerie *f.* **Heavy a.,** artillerie lourde. **Naval a.,** artillerie de bord. *S.a.* FIELD-ARTILLERY, HORSE-ARTILLERY.
artillery-waggon, *s. Mil:* Caisson *m.*
artilleryman, *pl.* **-men** [ɑːr'tilərimən, -men], *s.m.* Artilleur.
artisan [ɑːrti'zan], *s.* Artisan *m,* ouvrier *m.* **The artisan class,** la classe ouvrière; l'artisanat *m.*
artist ['ɑːrtist], *s.* (*a*) Artiste *mf.* *Esp.* (*b*) Artiste-peintre *m.* *He is an a.,* il est peintre.
artiste [ɑːr'tiːst], *s.* *Th:* Artiste *mf.*
artistic(al) [ɑːr'tistik(əl)], *a.* (*Arrangement*) artistique; (style, tempérament) artiste. **-ally,** *adv.* Artistement, avec art, artistiquement.
artistry ['ɑːrtistri], *s.* Art *m* (avec lequel qch. a été ordonné, truqué, etc.).
artless ['ɑːrtləs], *a.* **1.** Sans art. **2.** Naturel; sans artifice. **3.** Naïf, ingénu, candide. **-ly,** *adv.* **1.** Sans art. **2.** Naturellement, simplement. **3.** Naïvement, ingénument.
artlessness ['ɑːrtləsnəs], *s.* **1.** Naturel *m,* simplicité *f.* **2.** Naïveté *f,* ingénuité *f,* candeur *f.*
arum ['εərəm], *s. Bot:* Arum *m;* *F:* gouet *m.* **Arum lily,** arum; richardie *f.*
Aryan ['εəriən], *a. & s. Ethn: Ling:* Aryen.
as [az, əz]. I. *adv.* **1.** (*In principal clause*) Aussi, si. *I am as tall as you,* je suis aussi grand que vous. *Is it as high as that?* est-ce si haut que ça? **2.** *I shall help you as far as I can,* je vous aiderai autant que je pourrai. *I worked as hard as I could,* j'ai travaillé tant que j'ai pu. *S.a.* SOON 1. **3. As regards that, as for that, as to that,** quant à cela. *S.a.* FOR¹ I. 9. *To question s.o. as to his motives,* interroger qn sur ses motifs. *To entertain fears as to sth.,* éprouver des craintes au sujet de qch. **As to you,** quant à vous; pour ce qui est de vous. II. *as, conj. & rel. adv.* (*In subordinate clause*) **1.** (*Degree*) (*a*) Que. *You are as tall as he,* vous êtes aussi grand que lui. *You*

are not so tall as he, vous n'êtes pas si, aussi, grand que lui. *He is as generous as he is wealthy*, il est libéral autant que riche. *By day as well as by night*, le jour comme la nuit ; de jour comme de nuit. *S.a.* WELL[3] I. 4. (*b*) (*In intensifying similes*) Comme. *As pale as death*, pâle comme un mort. *As white as a sheet*, blanc comme un linge. **2.** (*Concessive*) *Delightful as London is* . . ., si agréable que soit Londres. . . . *Ignorant as he is* . . ., tout ignorant qu'il est. . . . *S.a.* MUCH 4. **Be that as it may**, quoi qu'il en soit. **3.** (*Manner*) (*a*) Comme. **Do as you like**, faites comme vous voudrez. *Pronounce the a as in father*, prononcez l'*a* comme dans *father*. *As often happens* . . ., comme il arrive souvent . . . ; ainsi qu'il arrive souvent. . . . A is to B as C is to D, A est à B comme C est à D. *Leave it as it is*, laissez-le tel quel, tel qu'il est. **As it is, we must** . . ., les choses étant ainsi, il nous faut. . . . *S.a.* BE 6 (*c*), GO[2] 2, 3, IF 1 (*e*), SO I. 1, THOUGH I. 3. (*b*) **As** . . ., **so.** . . . (*Just*) *as we must know how to command, so must we know how to obey*, de même qu'il faut savoir commander, (de même) il faut savoir obéir. *As the parents do so will the children*, tel font les parents, tel feront les enfants. **As of you, so of me**, il en est de moi comme de vous. (*c*) *He will keep silent*, as I am an honest man, il se taira, (sur ma) foi d'honnête homme. *As I live, I saw him strike the blow!* aussi vrai que je suis en vie, je l'ai vu frapper le coup ! (*d*) *To consider s.o. as a friend*, considérer qn comme un ami. *To treat s.o. as a stranger*, traiter qn en étranger. *I had him as a master*, je l'ai eu pour maître. *He was often ill as a child*, enfant il fut souvent malade ; il fut souvent malade dans son enfance. **To act as secretary**, (i) servir de secrétaire ; (ii) agir en qualité de secrétaire. *A study of Dumas as writer and as man*, une étude de Dumas en tant qu'écrivain et en tant qu'homme. **To act as a father**, agir en père. **To be dressed as a page**, être habillé en page. **4.** (*Time*) (*a*) *He went out* (*just*) *as I came in*, il sortit comme, au moment (même) où, j'entrais. *One day as I was sitting* . . ., un jour que j'étais assis. . . . *They were murdered as they lay asleep*, ils furent assassinés pendant qu'ils dormaient, pendant leur sommeil. *S.a.* JUST II. 1. (*b*) *He grew more charitable as he grew older*, il devenait plus charitable à mesure qu'il vieillissait, en vieillissant. **5.** (*Reason*) *As you are not ready, we cannot go*, comme, puisque, vous n'êtes pas prêt, nous ne pouvons pas partir. **6.** (*Result*) *He so arranged matters as to please everyone*, il arrangea les choses de manière, de façon, à contenter tout le monde. *Be so good as to come*, soyez assez bon pour venir. *He is not so foolish as to believe it*, il n'est pas assez stupide pour le croire. *S.a.* SO I. 4. III. **as**, *rel.pron.* *I had the same trouble as you*, j'ai eu les mêmes difficultés que vous. *Beasts of prey*, (such) *as the lion or tiger*, les bêtes fauves, telles que, comme, le lion ou le tigre.

asbestos [az'bestəs], *s.* Asbeste *m*, amiante *m*. **Asbestos-board, -sheet**, carton *m* d'amiante.

ascaris, *pl.* **-ides** ['askaris, as'karidi:z], *s.* Ascaride *m*, ascaris *m*, lombric (intestinal).

ascend [a'send]. **I.** *v.i.* (*a*) Monter, s'élever. (*b*) (*Of genealogical line*) Remonter. **2.** *v.tr.* (*a*) *To ascend the throne*, monter sur le trône. (*b*) *To a. a mountain, a hill*, faire l'ascension d'une montagne ; gravir une colline. (*c*) *To a. a river*, remonter un fleuve. **ascending**, *a.* **I.** *Astr: Mth: etc:* Ascendant. *Mus:* *A. scale*, gamme ascendante. **2.** (*Sentier*) montant, remontant.

ascendancy, -ency [a'sendənsi], *s.* **I.** Ascendant *m*, pouvoir *m*, influence *f* (*over s.o.*, sur qn). **2.** (*Of nation, etc.*) *To rise to ascendancy*, arriver à la suprématie.

ascendant, -ent [a'sendənt]. **I.** *a.* Ascendant. **2.** *s.* (*a*) *Astrol:* Ascendant *m*. *To be in the ascendant*, (i) (*of point of the ecliptic*) être à l'ascendant ; (ii) *F:* avoir le dessus ; s'affirmer ; prédominer. (*b*) *Jur:* (*Father, grandfather, etc.*) Ascendant.

ascension [a'senʃ(ə)n], *s.* Ascension *f*. *Esp: Ecc:* **Ascension-day**, jour, fête, de l'Ascension.

ascent [a'sent], *s.* **I.** Ascension *f* (d'une montagne) ; montée *f* (d'une tour, etc.). *Balloon a.*, ascension en ballon. **2.** Montée, pente *f*, rampe *f*. **3.** *Jur:* Line of ascent, ascendance *f*.

ascertain [asər'tein], *v.tr.* Constater (un fait) ; s'assurer, s'informer, de (la vérité de qch.). *It is difficult to a. whether* . . ., il est difficile de savoir si. . . .

ascertainment [asər'teinmənt], *s.* Constatation *f* (d'un fait).

ascetic [a'setik]. **I.** *a.* Ascétique. **2.** *s.* Ascète *mf*, ascétique *mf*.

asceticism [a'setisizm], *s.* Ascétisme *m*.

ascidium, *pl.* **-a** [a'sidiəm, -a], *s.* **I.** *Bot:* Ascidie *f*. **2.** *Moll:* Ascidie ; *F:* outre *f* de mer.

ascribable [a'skra:ibəbl], *a.* Attribuable, imputable (*to*, à).

ascribe [a'skra:ib], *v.tr.* Attribuer, imputer (*to*, à).

ascription [a'skripʃ(ə)n], *s.* Attribution *f*, imputation *f* (*of sth. to sth.*, de qch. à qch.).

asepsis [a'sepsis], *s. Med:* Asepsie *f*.

aseptic [a'septik], *a. & s. Med:* Aseptique (*m*).

ash[1] [aʃ], *s. Bot:* Frêne *m*. *S.a.* MOUNTAIN ASH. **'ash-key**, *s. Bot:* Samare *f* de frêne.

ash[2], *s.* (*Usu. in pl.*) **I.** (*a*) Cendre(s) *f*(*pl*). *Cigar ash*, cendre de cigare. **To reduce, burn, sth. to ashes**, réduire (le bois, une ville) en cendres. *S.a.* SACKCLOTH 2. (*b*) *pl. Mch:* Escarbilles *f*. **2.** Cendres (des morts) ; dépouille mortelle. *Peace* (be) *to his ashes!* paix à ses cendres ! *S.a.* DUST 2. **'ash-bin**, *s.* Cendrier *m* ; boîte *f* à ordures. **'ash-blond**, *a.* Blond cendré *inv.* **'ash-box**, *s.* Cendrier *m* (de locomotive). **'ash-bucket**, *s.* (*a*) Cendrier *m*. (*b*) *Nau:* Seau *m* à escarbilles. **'ash-coloured, ash-'grey**, *a.* Cendré ; gris cendré *inv.* **'ash-heap**, *s. Metall:* Cr ssier *m*. **'ash-hole, -pit**, *s.* **I.** Trou *m* à cendres ; fosse *f* aux cendres. **2.** Cendrier *m*, fosse à escarbilles (de foyer de machine). **'ash-pan**, *s.* Cendrier *m* (de poêle) ; garde-cendres *m inv.* **'ash-tray**, *s.* Cendrier *m* (de fumeur). **Ash 'Wednesday**, *s.* Le mercredi des Cendres.

ashamed [a'ʃeimd], *a.* **I.** Honteux, confus. **To be ashamed of s.o.**, **of sth.**, avoir honte de qn, de qch. *I am a. of you*, vous me faites honte. *To be, feel, a. to do sth., of doing sth.*, avoir honte, être honteux, de faire qch. ; avoir honte à faire qch. *You make me feel a.*, (i) vous me rendez confus ; (ii) vous me faites honte. **You ought to be ashamed of yourself**, vous devriez avoir honte. **2.** *Unable to work, and a. to beg*, incapable de travailler, et trop fier pour mendier.

ashen[1] [aʃn], *a.* De frêne, en frêne.

ashen[2], *a.* Cendré ; couleur de cendres ; (*of face*) pâle comme la mort.

ashlar [aʃlər], *s.* (*a*) Pierre *f* de taille ; moellon *m* d'appareil. **Ashlar work**, appareil en moellons. (*b*) Parements *mpl*, revêtement *m* (des murs d'un édifice).

ashore [a'ʃɔːr], *adv. Nau:* **I.** A terre. *To go a.*, aller, descendre, à terre ; débarquer. *To set, put,* (*passengers*) *a.,* débarquer (des passagers). **2.** Échoué. (*Of ship*) *To run ashore,* s'échouer ; faire côte.

ashy [´aʃi], *a.* **1.** Cendreux ; couvert de cendres. **2.** = ASHEN². *He went ashy pale,* il devint blême.

Asia [´eiʃa]. *Pr.n. Geog:* L'Asie *f. Asia Minor,* l'Asie Mineure.

Asiatic [eiʃi´atik], *a. & s.* Asiatique (*mf*) ; d'Asie.

aside [a´said]. **1.** *adv.* De côté ; à l'écart ; à part. *To draw* (*a curtain*) *a.,* écarter (un rideau). *To lay, put, sth. a.,* mettre qch. de côté. *S.a.* LAY ASIDE. *To stand aside,* (i) se tenir à l'écart, à part ; (ii) se ranger. *To step a.,* s'écarter, se ranger. *To turn aside,* se détourner (*from,* de). *Putting that a. . . .,* laissant cela de côté. . . . *I took, drew, him a.,* je le pris à part, à l'écart. *Th: Words spoken a.,* paroles dites en aparté. *S.a.* SET ASIDE. **2. Aside from,** a part. *A. from my own interest, I think . . .,* mon propre intérêt à part, je pense que. . . . **3.** *s.* Remarque faite à l'écart ; à-côté *m. Th:* Aparté *m. In an aside,* en aparté.

asinine [´asinain], *a.* (*a*) (Race) asine. (*b*) **F:** Stupide, sot ; digne d'un âne.

ask [ɑːsk], *v.tr. & i.* (asked [ɑːs(k)t]) Demander. **1.** (*Inquire*) *To ask s.o. sth.,* demander qch. à qn. *Ask* (*him*)·*his name,* demandez(-lui) son nom. *To ask the time,* demander l'heure. *To ask s.o. a question,* poser, faire, adresser, une question à qn. *Ask the constable,* adressez-vous à l'agent de police. **2.** (*Beg for, request to be given*) (*a*) *To ask a favour of s.o., to ask s.o. a favour,* demander une faveur à qn ; solliciter une grâce de qn. (*b*) (*Of price*) *How much are you asking for it?* combien en voulez-vous ? *To ask six francs for sth.,* demander six francs pour qch., de qch. **3.** (*Request*) (*a*) *To ask to do sth.,* demander à faire qch. ; demander la permission, l'autorisation, de faire qch. *He asked to be admitted,* il demanda qu'on le laissât entrer. (*b*) *To ask s.o. to do sth.,* demander à qn, prier qn, de faire qch. **4.** (*a*) *To ask about sth.,* se renseigner sur qch. *To ask s.o. about·sth.,* interroger qn sur qch. ; se renseigner sur qch. auprès de qn. (*b*) *To ask after s.o., after s.o.'s health,* demander des nouvelles de (la santé de) qn ; s'informer de la santé de qn. **5.** (*a*) *To ask for s.o.,* demander à voir qn. *I asked for the manager,* je demandai à parler au gérant. (*b*) *To ask for sth.,* demander qch. ; solliciter qch. *To ask s.o. for sth.,* demander qch. à qn. *To ask for something to eat,* demander à manger. *To ask for something to read,* demander qch. à lire. **6.** *To ask s.o. to lunch,* inviter qn à déjeuner. *To ask s.o. in, out,* demander à qn, prier qn, d'entrer, de sortir, de monter. **ask back,** *v.tr.* **1.** *To ask for sth. back,* redemander (un objet prêté, son argent, etc.). **2.** *To ask s.o. back,* (i) réinviter qn ; (ii) inviter qn pour lui rendre la politesse. **asking,** *s.* **You may have it for the asking,** il est à vous pour la peine de le demander ; il n'y a qu'à (le) demander.

askance [a´skans], *adv.* De côté, du coin de l'œil, obliquement. *Esp. To look askance at s.o., at sth.,* regarder qn, qch., de travers, avec méfiance, d'un œil malveillant.

askew [a´skjuː], *adv.* De biais, de côté. *His nose is a.,* il a le nez de travers.

aslant [a´slɑːnt], *adv.* Obliquement, de travers, de biais.

asleep [a´sliːp], *adv. & pred. a.* Endormi. **1.** *To be a.,* dormir, sommeiller. **To be fast, sound, asleep,** être profondément endormi, plongé dans

le sommeil ; dormir profondément. **He lay asleep,** il dormait. **To fall, drop, asleep,** s'endormir. **2.** *My foot is asleep,* j'ai le pied engourdi, endormi.

asp [asp], *s.* (Vipère *f*) aspic *m.*

asparagus [as´paragəs], *s. Coll.* Asperges *fpl. A stick of asparagus,* une asperge. *A. tips,* pointes d'asperges. *Bundle of a.,* botte d'asperges.

aspect [´aspekt], *s.* **1.** Exposition *f,* vue *f* ; orientation *f. To have a northern a.,* être exposé au nord ; avoir une exposition nord. **2.** Aspect *m,* air *m. All the aspects of a subject,* tous les aspects d'un sujet. *To see sth. in its true aspect,* voir qch sous son vrai jour.

aspen [´aspən], *s. Bot:* (Peuplier *m*) tremble *m. Aspen leaf,* feuille de tremble.

aspergillum [aspər´dʒiləm], *s. Ecc:* Goupillon *m.*

asperity [as´periti], *s.* **1.** (*a*) Âpreté *f.* (*b*) Rigueur *f,* sévérité *f* (du climat). (*c*) Rudesse *f* (de caractère) ; aspérité *f* (de style). **2.** (*Rough excrescence*) Aspérité.

asperse [a´spəːrs], *v.tr.* (*a*) Calomnier, diffamer, dénigrer (qn). (*b*) *To a. s.o.'s good name,* salir, éclabousser, la réputation de qn.

aspersion [a´spəːrʃ(ə)n], *s.* **1.** (*Sprinkling*) Aspersion *f.* **2.** Calomnie *f.* **To cast aspersions upon s.o.,** répandre des calomnies sur qn ; dénigrer qn.

asphalt¹ [´asfalt], *s.* Asphalte *m* ; (*often loosely*) bitume *m* ; goudron minéral.

asphalt², *v.tr.* Asphalter, bitumer.

asphodel [´asfodel], *s. Bot:* Asphodèle *m.*

asphyxia [as´fiksia], *s.* Asphyxie *f.*

asphyxiate [as´fiksiet], *v.tr.* Asphyxier.

aspic¹ [´aspik], *s.* = ASP.

aspic², *s. Cu:* Aspic *m.*

aspirant [a´spairənt], *s.* Aspirant, -ante (*to, after,* à) ; candidat *m.*

aspirate¹ [´aspiret]. *Ling:* **1.** *a.* Aspiré. **2.** *s.* (*a*) (Lettre) aspirée *f.* (*b*) (La lettre) h.

aspirate² [´aspireit], *v.tr.* Aspirer (une voyelle, un liquide). **Aspirating filter,** filtre à vide.

aspiration [aspi´reiʃ(ə)n], *s.* **1.** Aspiration *f* ((i) de l'air, d'un fluide ; (ii) de l'h). **2.** *A. for, after, renown,* aspiration à la gloire.

aspirator [´aspireitər], *s.* **1.** *Ph: Med:* Aspirateur *m.* **2.** *Husb:* Tarare *m.* **3.** (*Filter-pump*) Trompe *f.*

aspiratory [a´spairətəri], *a.* Aspirateur, -trice.

aspire [a´spaiər], *v.i.* Aspirer. *To a. to, after, sth.,* aspirer, prétendre, viser, à qch. ; ambitionner qch. *To a. to do sth.,* aspirer à faire qch.

aspiring [a´spaiəriŋ], *a.* Ambitieux.

aspirin [´aspirin], *s. Pharm:* Aspirine *f. F:* Take an a., prenez un comprimé d'aspirine.

ass [as, ɑːs], *s.* **1.** Âne, *f.* ânesse. *Ass's foal, ass's colt,* ânon *m. Ass's milk,* lait d'ânesse. **2.** *F:* Sot, *f.* sotte ; âne. *He is a perfect ass,* c'est un âne bâté ; il est bête à manger du foin. *S.a.* SILLY 1. *F: To behave like an ass,* to play the ass, faire l'imbécile, le sot, l'âne, l'idiot. *To make an ass of oneself,* (i) agir d'une manière stupide, idiote ; faire des âneries ; (ii) se donner en spectacle ; se faire moquer de soi. **´ass-driver,** *s.* Ânier *m.*

assail [a´seil], *v.tr.* **1.** (*a*) Assaillir, attaquer (l'ennemi, une place forte). (*b*) *To a. an author,* s'attaquer à un auteur. **2.** (*Of noise*) *To a. the ear,* frapper l'oreille.

assailant [a´seilənt], *s.* Assaillant *m.*

assassin [a´sasin], *s.* Assassin *m.*

assassinate [a´sasineit], *v.tr.* Assassiner.

assassination [asasi´neiʃ(ə)n], *s.* Assassinat *m.*

assault¹ [a'sɔlt], *s.* **1.** (*a*) Assaut *m.* **To take, carry, a town by assault,** prendre une ville d'assaut. *Fenc:* **Assault of, at, arms,** assaut d'armes. (*b*) Attaque (brusquée). **2.** *Jur:* Tentative *f* de voie de fait. **Unprovoked assault,** agression *f.* **Assault and battery,** (menaces *fpl* et) voies de fait ; coups *mpl* et blessures *fpl.* **To commit an assault,** se porter, se livrer, à des voies de fait (*on*, sur).

assault², *v.tr.* **1.** Attaquer, assaillir (une position); donner l'assaut à (une ville, etc.). **2.** Attaquer (qn). **To be assaulted,** être victime d'une agression.

assaulter [a'sɔltər], *s.* Assaillant *m*, agresseur *m.*

assay¹ [a'sei], *s.* Essai *m* (d'un métal précieux, d'un minerai).

assay², *v.tr.* Essayer, titrer (un métal précieux, un minerai). **assaying,** *s.* Essai *m*, titrage *m.*

assegai ['asigai], *s.* Zagaie *f*, sagaie *f.*

assemblage [a'sembledʒ], *s.* **1.** Assemblage *m* (de pièces de menuiserie, etc.). **2.** (*a*) Réunion *f*, concours *m* (de personnes). (*b*) Collection *f* (d'objets).

assemble [a'sembl]. **1.** *v.tr.* (*a*) Assembler (des personnes); convoquer (un parlement). *Mil:* Rassembler (des troupes). (*b*) Assembler (des pièces de menuiserie, etc.); ajuster, monter (une machine). **2.** *v.i.* S'assembler ; se rassembler. **assembling,** *s.* Assemblage *m* ; rassemblement *m* ; convocation *f.*

assembler [a'semblər], *s. Ind:* Monteur, -euse ; ajusteur, -euse.

assembly [a'sembli], *s.* **1.** (*a*) Assemblée *f.* **In open assembly,** en séance publique. (*b*) *Mil:* (Sonnerie *f* du) rassemblement *m.* (*c*) *Jur:* Unlawful assembly, attroupement *m.* **2.** Assemblement *m*, réunion *f. Place of a.,* lieu de réunion. **3.** Assemblage *m*, montage *m* (d'une machine).

assent¹ [a'sent], *s.* Assentiment *m*, consentement *m*, acquiescement *m. Jur:* Agrément *m.* **The royal assent,** le consentement, la sanction, du Roi. *S.a.* NOD².

assent², *v.i.* **1.** (*a*) Accéder, acquiescer, donner son assentiment (*to*, à). (*b*) (*Of sovereign, etc.*) Sanctionner (une loi, etc.). **2.** *To a. to the truth of sth.,* reconnaître la vérité de qch. *To a. to a theory,* admettre une théorie.

assert [a'sə:rt], *v.tr.* **1.** (*a*) **To assert one's rights,** revendiquer, faire valoir, ses droits. (*b*) **To assert oneself,** soutenir ses droits ; s'affirmer ; s'imposer. **2.** Affirmer. *To a. that . . .,* affirmer, prétendre, soutenir, que. . . . **To assert one's innocence,** protester de son innocence.

assertion [a'sə:r∫(ə)n], *s.* **1.** *A. of one's rights,* revendication *f* de ses droits. **2.** Affirmation *f. S.a.* SELF-ASSERTION.

assertive [a'sə:rtiv], *a.* (*a*) = SELF-ASSERTIVE. (*b*) (Ton, etc.) péremptoire, cassant. **-ly,** *adv.* Avec assurance ; d'un ton cassant.

assertiveness [a'sə:rtivnəs], *s.* Assurance *f* ; ton *m* ou manière *f* autoritaire.

assess [a'ses], *v.tr.* **1.** (*a*) Répartir, établir (un impôt). (*b*) Estimer, inventorier, évaluer. *Jur:* **To assess the damages,** fixer les dommages-intérêts. **2.** *To a. a loan, etc., upon s.o.,* imposer un prêt, etc., à qn. **3.** *Adm:* *To a. s.o. in, at, so much,* coter, imposer, taxer, qn à tant. **4.** *To a. a property (for taxation),* évaluer une propriété. **Assessed taxes,** impôts directs.

assessable [a'sesəbl], *a.* **1.** (Dommage) évaluable. **2.** (Propriété) imposable.

assessment [a'sesmənt], *s.* **1.** (*a*) Répartition *f*, assiette *f* (d'un impôt). (*b*) Évaluation *f* (de dégâts, *Nau:* d'avarie). *Jur:* *A. of damages,*

fixation *f* de dommages-intérêts. (*c*) Imposition *f* (d'une commune, d'un immeuble). (*d*) Cotisation *f* (du contribuable). **2.** (*Amount*) Cote *f* ; taxe officielle. *A. on landed property,* cote foncière. *A. on income,* impôt *m* sur le revenu.

assessor [a'sesər], *s.* **1.** *Jur:* Assesseur (adjoint à un juge). **2.** **Assessor of taxes,** contrôleur *m* des contributions (directes).

asset ['aset], *s.* **1.** Chose *f* dont on peut tirer avantage ; possession *f* ; avoir *m. He is one of our assets,* c'est une de nos valeurs. **II.** **assets,** *s.pl.* **1.** *Jur:* Masse *f* d'une succession, d'une société. **Personal assets,** biens *m* meubles. **Real assets,** biens immobiliers. **2.** *Com:* Actif *m* ; avoir *m.*

asseverate [a'sevəreit], *v.tr.* Affirmer (solennellement) (*that*, que + *ind.*).

asseveration [asevə'rei∫(ə)n], *s.* Affirmation (solennelle) ; protestation *f* (d'innocence).

assiduity [asi'djuiti], *s.* Assiduité *f*, diligence *f* (*in doing sth.,* à faire qch.).

assiduous [a'sidjuəs], *a.* **1.** (*Of pers.*) Assidu ; diligent. **2.** (Travail) assidu. **-ly,** *adv.* Assidûment.

assign¹ [a'sain], *s. Jur:* Ayant cause *m*, ayant droit *m* (*pl.* ayants cause, ayants droit) ; délégué ; mandataire *mf.*

assign², *v.tr.* **1.** Assigner (*to*, à). (*a*) Donner (qch.) en partage à (qn). (*b*) **To assign a reason for sth.,** donner la raison de qch. *Object assigned to a certain use,* objet affecté, consacré, à un certain usage. *To a. a salary to an office,* attribuer un traitement à un emploi. (*c*) *To a. an hour, a place,* fixer une heure, un lieu. (*d*) *To a. a task to s.o.,* assigner, attribuer, une tâche à qn. **2.** *Jur:* *To a. a property to s.o.,* céder, transférer, une propriété à qn.

assignable [a'sainəbl], *a.* **1.** (*a*) Assignable, attribuable (*to*, à). (*b*) (Date, etc.) que l'on peut fixer, que l'on peut déterminer. **2.** *Jur:* (Bien) cessible, transférable.

assignation [asig'nei∫(ə)n], *s.* **1.** Distribution *f*, répartition *f*, attribution *f* (de biens). **2.** *Jur:* Cession *f*, transfert *m* (de biens, de dettes). (*In bankruptcy*) **Deed of assignation,** acte de transfert ; acte attributif. **3.** (*a*) Fixation *f* (d'une heure, etc.). (*b*) Rendez-vous *m.*

assignee [asi'ni:], *s. Jur:* **1.** (*a*) = ASSIGN¹. (*b*) (Administrator-)séquestre *m* ; syndic *m.* **2.** Cessionnaire *mf* (d'une créance, etc.).

assignment [a'sainmənt], *s.* **1.** (*a*) = ASSIGNATION I, 2. (*b*) (*Allocation*) Affectation *f*, allocation *f*, attribution *f* (de qch. à qch., à qn). (*c*) Citation *f*, production *f* (de raisons) ; attribution (de cause) (*to*, à). **2.** *Sch:* *U.S:* Tâche assignée.

assimilable [a'siməbl], *a.* **1.** (Aliment) assimilable. **2.** Comparable, assimilable (*to*, à).

assimilate [a'simileit], *v.tr.* **1.** (*a*) Assimiler, comparer (*to*, à). (*b*) *v.i.* (*Of consonants*) S'assimiler. **2.** *To a. food,* assimiler des aliments.

assimilation [asimi'lei∫(ə)n], *s.* **1.** (*a*) Assimilation *f* (*to, with,* à). (*b*) (*Comparison*) Assimilation (*to*, à) ; comparaison *f* (*to*, avec). **2.** Assimilation (des aliments).

assist [a'sist]. **1.** *v.tr.* (*a*) Aider (qn) ; prêter son concours, prêter assistance, à (qn). *To a. one another,* s'entr'aider. *To a. s.o. in doing sth.,* aider qn à faire qch. *To a. s.o. to the door,* aider qn à gagner la porte. (*b*) *To a. s.o. in misfortune,* secourir, assister, qn dans le malheur. **2.** *v.i.* *To a. at a ceremony,* (i) prendre part à une cérémonie ; (ii) (*be present*) assister à une cérémonie.

assistance [a'sistəns], *s.* Aide *f*, secours *m*, assistance *f.* **To come to s.o.'s assistance,** venir à l'aide de, en aide à, au secours de, qn. **With the assistance of sth., of s.o.**, à l'aide de qch., avec l'aide de qn. **To be of assistance to s.o.**, aider qn, être utile à qn.

assistant [ə'sistənt]. **I.** *a.* Qui aide ; auxiliaire ; adjoint ; sous-. **Assistant-professor**, professeur adjoint. **Assistant-master**, sous-maître *m*. **A.-stoker**, aide-chauffeur *m*. **2.** *s.* Aide *mf* ; adjoint, -ointe ; auxiliaire *mf*. *Com:* Commis *m* (de magasin) ; demoiselle *f* de magasin ; employé, -ée. *S.a.* SHOP-ASSISTANT.

assize [ə'saiz], *s.* (*Usu. in pl.*) *Jur:* (**Court of**) assizes, assize-court, (cour *f* d')assises *fpl*.

associate[1] [ə'souʃiet]. **I.** *a.* Associé. **Associate judge**, juge-assesseur *m*. **2.** *s.* (*a*) Associé *m*, adjoint *m* ; membre correspondant (d'une académie). *Associates in crime, in intrigue*, consorts *m*. (*b*) Compagnon *m*, camarade *mf*.

associate[2] [ə'souʃieit]. **I.** *v.tr.* Associer (*with*, avec qn, à qch.). *To a. oneself with s.o. in an undertaking*, s'associer avec qn pour une entreprise. *To be associated with a plot*, tremper dans un complot. *Phil:* **To a. ideas**, associer des idées. **2.** *v.i.* (*a*) *To a. with s.o. in doing sth.*, s'associer avec qn pour faire qch. (*b*) *To a. with s.o.*, fréquenter qn ; frayer avec qn.

association [əsousi'eiʃ(ə)n], *s.* **I.** (*a*) Association *f* (d'idées, etc.). *Land full of historic associations*, pays fertile en souvenirs historiques. (*b*) Fréquentation *f* (*with s.o.*, de qn). *To form associations*, se faire des relations. (*c*) **Association football**, football *m* association. **2.** Association, société *f* ; amicale *f* (de professeurs, etc.). **Young Men's Christian Association**, Union chrétienne de jeunes gens. *To form an a.*, constituer une société.

assonance ['asonəns], *s. Pros:* Assonance *f*.

assort [ə'sɔːrt]. **I.** *v.tr.* (*a*) Assortir (*with*, à). *To a. colours*, assortir des couleurs ; marier des couleurs. (*b*) Classer, ranger (*with*, parmi). **2.** *v.i.* *To a. well, ill, with sth.*, (s')assortir bien, mal, avec qch. *To a. well, ill*, aller ensemble, ne pas aller ensemble.

assortment [ə'sɔːrtmənt], *s.* **I.** Assortiment *m* ; jeu *m* (d'outils). **2.** Classement *m*, classification *f* (par sortes).

assuage [ə'sweidʒ], *v.tr.* Apaiser, adoucir ; soulager (les souffrances) ; apaiser, satisfaire (un appétit. (*Of pain*) *To be assuaged*, se calmer.

assuagement [ə'sweidʒmənt], *s.* Apaisement *m*, adoucissement *m*, soulagement *m* (de la douleur).

assumable [ə'sjuːməbl], *a.* **I.** (*a*) (Titre, etc.) appropriable. (*b*) (Responsabilité) dont on peut se charger. **2.** Supposable, présumable. *It is a. that . . .*, il est à présumer que. . . . **-ably**, *adv.* A ce qu'on peut supposer.

assume [ə'sjuːm], *v.tr.* **I.** Prendre, se donner (un air, une mine) ; affecter, revêtir (une forme, un caractère). *The judges a. their robes*, les juges revêtent leur toge. **2.** (*a*) Prendre sur soi, prendre à son compte, assumer (une charge, une responsabilité) ; se charger (d'un devoir). *Com:* *To a. all risks*, assumer tous les risques. (*b*) *To a. power, authority*, prendre possession du pouvoir. **3.** S'attribuer, s'arroger, s'approprier (un droit, un titre). *To a. a name*, adopter un nom. *Jur:* **To assume ownership**, faire acte de propriétaire. **4.** Simuler, affecter (une vertu). **5.** Présumer, supposer (qch.) ; tenir (qch.) comme établi. *Geom:* Admettre (qch.) en postulat. *I a. that he will come*, je présume qu'il viendra. *He was assumed to be wealthy*, on le supposait riche. *Let us a. that such is the case*, mettons qu'il en soit ainsi. *Assuming the truth of*

the story . . .*, en supposant que l'histoire soit vraie. . . .* **assumed**, *a.* Supposé, feint, faux. *With a. nonchalance*, avec une affectation d'indifférence. *A. piety*, fausse dévotion. **Assumed name**, pseudonyme *m* ; nom de guerre.

assuming, *a.* Présomptueux, prétentieux.

assumption [ə'sʌm(p)ʃ(ə)n], *s.* **I.** *Ecc:* Assomption *f* (de la Vierge). **2.** (*a*) Action *f* de prendre (une forme, un caractère). (*b*) *A. of office*, entrée *f* en fonctions. **3.** (*a*) Affectation *f* (de vertu, etc.). (*b*) Arrogance *f*, prétention(s) *f*, présomption *f*. **4.** Supposition *f*, hypothèse *f*. *Phil:* Postulat *m*.

assurable [ə'ʃuərəbl], *a.* Assurable.

assurance [ə'ʃuərəns], *s.* **I.** (*a*) (*Certainty*) Assurance *f*. **To make assurance double sure**, pour plus de sûreté ; pour surcroît de sûreté. (*b*) Promesse (formelle). (*c*) Affirmation *f*. **2.** *Ins:* Life-assurance, assurance sur la vie. *Cf.* INSURANCE. **3.** (*a*) Assurance, fermeté *f* ; *F:* aplomb *m*. *S.a.* SELF-ASSURANCE. (*b*) Hardiesse *f*, présomption *f* ; *F:* toupet *m*.

assure [ə'ʃuər], *v.tr.* (*a*) (*Make safe*) *To a. s.o. against sth.*, assurer qn contre qch. *To a. s.o.'s life*, assurer la vie de qn. *To a. one's life*, s'assurer (sur la vie). (*b*) (*Make certain*) *To a. the peace, the happiness, of s.o.*, assurer la paix, le bonheur, de qn. (*c*) (*Affirm*) *To a. s.o. of sth.*, assurer qn de qch. ; assurer qch. à qn. *He will do it*, **I can assure you!** il le fera, je vous en réponds! **You may rest assured that . . .**, vous pouvez tenir pour certain que. . . . **Be well assured that . . .**, soyez certain que. . . .

assuredly [ə'ʃuəridli], *adv.* Assurément ; à coup sûr. **Assuredly not**, non certes.

Assyria [ə'siria]. *Pr.n.* *A.Geog:* L'Assyrie *f*.

astatic [ə'statik], *a.* *El:* Astatique.

aster ['astər], *s. Bot:* Aster *m*. **China aster**, aster de Chine ; reine-marguerite *f*.

asterisk ['astərisk], *s.* Astérisque *m*.

astern [ə'stəːrn]. **I.** *adv.* (*a*) (*Position on ship*) A l'arrière, sur l'arrière. (*b*) (*Backwards*) **To go, come, astern**, culer ; aller de l'arrière ; marcher en arrière. **Full speed astern!** en arrière à toute vitesse! (*c*) (*Behind*) **To make a boat fast a.**, amarrer un canot derrière. **To have the wind a.**, avoir le vent en arrière. **2. Astern of a ship**, derrière un vaisseau ; sur l'arrière d'un vaisseau.

asteroid ['astərɔid]. **I.** *a.* En forme d'étoile. **2.** *s.* Astéroïde *m*.

asthenia [as'θiːnia], *s.* *Med:* Asthénie *f*.

asthma [as(θ)ma], *s.* Asthme *m*. **To suffer from a.**, être asthmatique.

asthmatic [as(θ)'matik], *a.& s.* Asthmatique (*mf*).

astigmatic [astig'matik], *a.* Astigmate.

astigmatism [a'stigmatizm], *s.* Astigmatisme *m*.

astir [ə'stəːr], *adv. & pred. a.* **I.** Actif ; en mouvement ; animé. **To set sth. astir**, mettre qch. en mouvement, en branle. **2.** Debout, levé. **3.** En émoi ; agité.

astonish [ə'stɔniʃ], *v.tr.* Étonner, surprendre. *You a. me*, vous m'étonnez. *To be astonished at seeing sth., to see sth.*, être étonné, s'étonner, de voir qch. *I am astonished that . . .*, cela m'étonne que + *sub.* **astonishing,** *a.* Étonnant, surprenant. **-ly**, *adv.* Étonnamment.

astonishment [ə'stɔniʃmənt], *s.* Étonnement *m*, surprise *f*. *My a. at seeing him*, mon étonnement, l'étonnement où j'étais, de le voir. *A look of blank a.*, un air ébahi.

astound [ə'staund], *v.tr.* Confondre, abasourdir ; stupéfier ; *F:* ébahir. **astounding,** *a.* (*a*) Abasourdissant ; *F:* mirobolant. (*b*) (*Désastre*) épouvantable ; (nouvelle) atterrante.

astraddle [a'stradl], adv. & pred. a. A califour-chon, à cheval (sur qch.).
astragal ['astragəl], s. Astragale m, chapelet m (d'une colonne).
Astrak(h)an [astra'kan]. **1.** Pr.n. Geog: Astrak(h)an. **2.** s. (Fur) Astrakan m.
astral ['astrəl], a. Astral, -aux.
astray [a'strei], adv. & pred. a. (i) Égaré; (ii) Pej: dévoyé. **To go astray,** (i) s'égarer; s'écarter de la route, faire fausse route; (ii) Pej: se dévoyer. **To lead s.o. astray,** (i) égarer qn; induire qn en erreur; (ii) débaucher, dévoyer, qn.
astride [a'straid], adv., pred.a., & prep. A califourchon; jambe deçà, jambe delà (sur qch.). **To sit a. sth.,** être à cheval, chevaucher, être à califourchon, sur qch.
astringent [a'strindʒənt], a. & s. Astringent (m); styptique (m), constipant (m).
astrologer [a'strɔlodʒər], s. Astrologue m.
astrological [astro'lɔdʒik(ə)l], a. Astrologique.
astrology [a'strɔlodʒi], s. Astrologie f.
astronomer [a'strɔnomər], s. Astronome m.
astronomic(al) [astro'nɔmik(əl)], a. Astronomique.
astronomy [a'strɔnomi], s. Astronomie f.
astute [as'tjuːt], a. **1.** Fin, avisé, pénétrant. **2.** Pej: Astucieux, matois, rusé. **-ly,** adv. **1.** Avec finesse. **2.** Astucieusement.
astuteness [as'tjuːtnəs], s. **1.** Finesse f, sagacité f; pénétration f. **2.** Pej: Astuce f.
asunder [a'sandər], adv. **1.** Éloignés, écartés (l'un de l'autre). **2.** To tear sth. a., déchirer qch. en deux. (Of parts) **To come asunder,** se désunir, se disjoindre.
asylum [a'sailəm], s. **1.** (a) Hist: Asile m (inviolable). (b) Asile, (lieu m de) refuge m. **To afford asylum to s.o.,** donner asile, offrir un asile, à qn. **2.** (a) Hospice m. (b) F: (Lunatic) asylum, maison f, hospice, asile, d'aliénés; F: maison de fous. Private a., maison de santé.
asymmetry [a'simetri], s. Asymétrie f.
asymptote ['asim(p)tout], s. Asymptote f.
at [at], prep. A. **1.** (Position) (a) At the centre, at the top, au centre, au sommet. At table, at church, at school, à table, à l'église, à l'école. **The dog was at his heels,** le chien marchait sur ses talons. At hand, sous la main. At sea, at war, en mer, en guerre. (b) At home, à la maison, chez soi. At the tailor's, chez le tailleur. (c) To sit at the window, se tenir (au)près de la fenêtre. He came in at the window, il entra par la fenêtre. **2.** (Time) At six o'clock, à six heures. At present, à présent. Two at a time, deux par deux; deux à la fois. S.a. TIME¹ 5. At night, la nuit, le soir. **3.** (Price) At two francs a pound, à deux francs la livre. **4.** At my request, sur ma demande. **At all events,** en tout cas. **5.** Swift at repartee, prompt à la repartie. Good at games, habile aux jeux. **6.** (a) To look at sth., regarder qch. To be surprised at sth., être étonné de qch. To catch at sth., s'accrocher à qch. (b) To laugh at s.o., se moquer de qn. To swear at s.o., jurer contre qn. (c) To be at work, être au travail, être à travailler. To be at sth., être occupé à faire qch. She's at it again (i.e. crying, etc.), voilà qu'elle recommence! **While we are at it,** why not . . ., pendant que nous y sommes, pourquoi ne pas. . . . (d) To be at s.o., être acharné contre qn; rudoyer qn. They are at me again, voilà encore qu'on s'en prend à moi. Mil: At them! chargez! en avant! (To dog) At him! pille! pille!
atavism ['atavizm], s. Atavisme m.

atavistic [ata'vistik], a. Atavique.
ataxy [a'taksi, 'ataksi], s. Med: Ataxie f. Locomotor ataxy, ataxie locomotrice progressive.
ate [eit]. See EAT.
atheism ['eiθiizm], s. Athéisme m.
atheist ['eiθiist], s. Athée mf.
athenaeum [aθe'niːəm], s. Athénée m.
Athenian [a'θiːnjən], a. & s. Athénien, -ienne; d'Athènes; attique.
Athens ['aθenz]. Pr.n. Athènes f.
athirst [a'θəːrst], pred. a. Lit: Altéré, assoiffé (for, de).
athlete ['aθliːt], s. **1.** Athlète m. **2.** Fervent m du sport.
athletic [aθ'letik], a. **1.** Athlétique. A. exercises, exercices gymnastiques. A. club, société de gymnastique. A. meeting, réunion sportive. **2.** An a. young fellow, un gaillard vigoureux, solide, bien taillé, sportif. **-ically,** adv. Athlétiquement.
athleticism [aθ'letisizm], s. Athlétisme m.
athletics [aθ'letiks], s.pl. (Usu. with sg. const.) Sports m (athlétiques); culture f physique.
at-home [at'houm], s. Réception f; soirée f. Our a.-h. day is Thursday, nous recevons le jeudi. What is your a.-h. day? quel est votre jour?
athwart [a'θwɔːrt]. **1.** adv. En travers; Nau: par le travers. **2.** prep. En travers de.
a-tilt [a'tilt], adv. Incliné, penché; soulevé (d'un côté). With hat a-tilt, le chapeau sur l'oreille.
Atlantic [at'lantik], a. & s. The Atlantic (Ocean), l'océan Atlantique.
Atlas ['atləs]. **1.** Pr.n.m. Gr.Myth: Atlas. **2.** s. (pl. atlases ['atləsiz]) Atlas m. **3.** s. Arch: (pl. atlantes [at'lantiːz]) Atlante m, télamon m.
atmosphere ['atmosfiːər], s. **1.** Atmosphère f. F: A. of vice, ambiance f de vice. **2.** Ph: (Pressure of 15 lb. per sq. inch) Atmosphère.
atmospheric(al) [atmos'ferik(əl)]. **1.** a. Atmosphérique. **2.** s.pl. W.Tel: Atmospherics, perturbations f, parasites m, atmosphériques.
atoll [a'tɔl, 'atɔl], s. Atoll m; île f de corail.
atom ['atəm], s. Atome m. Not an a. of common sense, pas un grain de bon sens. Smashed to atoms, réduit en miettes.
atomic(al) [a'tɔmik(əl)], a. Atomique.
atomize ['atəmaiz], v.tr. Pulvériser (un liquide); vaporiser.
atomizer ['atəmaizər], s. **1.** Pulvérisateur m, atomiseur m. **2.** I.C.E: Gicleur-pulvérisateur m.
atone [a'toun], v.tr. or ind.tr. To atone (for) a fault by doing sth., expier, racheter, réparer, une faute en faisant qch.
atonement [a'tounmənt], s. Expiation f, réparation f (for, de). Theol: Rachat m. To make atonement for a fault, réparer une faute. Jew.Rel: Day of Atonement, jour des propitiations.
atonic [a'tɔnik]. **1.** a. Med: (Of muscle, etc.) Atonique. **2.** a. & s. (Syllabe) atone (f).
atony ['atoni], s. Med: Atonie f; F: aveulissement m.
atop [a'tɔp], adv. En haut, au sommet.
atrabilious [atra'biljəs], a. Atrabilaire.
atrip a'trip], adv. Nau: With anchor atrip, l'ancre dérapée, guindée.
atrocious [a'trouʃəs], a. **1.** (Crime) atroce. **2.** F: (Jeu de mots) exécrable (chapeau) affreux. **-ly,** adv. **1.** Atrocement. **2.** F: Exécrablement.
atrociousness [a'trouʃəsnəs], **atrocity** a'trɔsiti], s. Atrocité f.
atrophy¹ ['atrofi], s. Atrophie f.

atrophy². **1.** *v.tr.* Atrophier. **2.** *v.i.* S'atrophier.
attach [a'tat]. **1.** *v.tr.* (*a*) Attacher, lier, fixer (*sth. to sth.*, qch. à qch.); annexer (un document). (*b*) *Jur:* Arrêter (qn); contraindre (qn) par corps; saisir, mettre une saisie-arrêt sur (des biens mobiliers). (*c*) *To attach credence to sth.*, ajouter foi à qch. *S.a.* IMPORTANCE. **2.** *v.i.* S'attacher. *The blame which attaches to a crime*, la honte qui s'attache à un crime. **attached,** *a.* (*a*) Attaché (*to*, à); adjoint (à un personnel). *Official temporarily a. to another department*, fonctionnaire détaché à un autre service. (*Of ship*) *To be a. to a squadron*, faire partie d'une escadre. *Salary a. to a post*, traitement afférent à un emploi. (*b*) *To be deeply a. to s.o.*, être fortement attaché à qn.
attachable [a'tatʃəbl], *a.* **1.** Qui peut être attaché (*to*, à); facile à attacher, à fixer. **2.** *Jur:* (*Of property*) Saisissable.
attaché [a'taʃe], *s.* *Dipl:* *etc:* Attaché *m.*
at'taché-case, *s.* Mallette *f* (pour documents).
attachment [a'tatʃmənt], *s.* **1.** (*a*) Action *f* d'attacher (qch. à qch.); attachement *m.* (*b*) Attache *f*, lien *m.* **2.** Accessoire *m* (d'une machine à coudre, etc.). **3.** (*Affection*) Attachement *m* (*of s.o. for s.o.*, de qn pour qn); affection *f* (*for*, pour). *To entertain an attachment for s.o.*, être épris de qn. **4.** *Jur:* (*a*) Saisie-arrêt *f*, opposition *f.* (*b*) Contrainte *f* par corps.
attack¹ [a'tak], *s.* **1.** Attaque *f*, assaut *m.* *To make an attack upon s.o.*, sth., attaquer qn, qch.; s'attaquer à (un problème, un travail). *Mil:* Surprise attack, coup *m* de main. *To rush to the a.*, se précipiter à l'assaut. *To return to the attack*, revenir à la charge. **2.** (*a*) Attaque, crise *f* (de goutte, etc.). *A. of fever, of giddiness*, accès *m* de fièvre, de vertige. *A. of nerves*, crise de nerfs. (*b*) *A. on s.o.'s life*, attentat *m* à la vie de qn.
attack², *v.tr.* (*a*) *Mil:* Attaquer (l'ennemi). *The attacking forces*, les troupes engagées dans l'attaque. *To be attacked*, subir une attaque; être attaqué. (*b*) *To a. s.o., s.o.'s rights*, attaquer qn, les droits de qn; s'en prendre à qn; s'attaquer à qn. (*c*) *To a. a task*, s'attaquer à un travail.
attacker [a'takər], *s.* Attaquant *m*; agresseur *m.*
attain [a'tein]. **1.** *v.tr.* Atteindre, arriver à (un endroit); atteindre, parvenir à, arriver à (un grand âge). *To attain knowledge*, acquérir des connaissances. **2.** *v.ind.tr.* *To a. to perfection*, atteindre à la perfection.
attainable [a'teinəbl], *a.* Accessible; que l'on peut atteindre; à la portée (*by*, de).
attainder [a'teindər], *s.* *Jur:* *A:* Act, Bill, of attainder, décret *m* de confiscation de biens et de mort civile.
attainment [a'teinmənt], *s.* **1.** (*No pl.*) Arrivée *f* (à ses fins); obtention *f*, réalisation *f.* *For the attainment of his purpose*, pour atteindre, arriver, à ses fins. *End easy, difficult, of attainment*, but facile, difficile, à atteindre. **2.** (*Often in pl.*) Connaissance(s) *f*; savoir *m.*
attar [a'tər], *s.* Attar of roses, essence *f* de roses.
attempt¹ [a'tem(p)t], *s.* **1.** Tentative *f*, essai *m*, effort *m.* *A. at theft*, tentative de vol. *To make an a. at sth., at doing sth., to do sth.*, essayer, tâcher, de faire qch.; s'essayer à faire qch. *You made a good a. at it*, (i) vous vous êtes acquitté de façon très méritoire; (ii) vous êtes arrivé fort près du but. *No attempt will be made to . . .*, on n'essaiera pas de. . . *First attempt*, coup *m* d'essai; première tentative. *To be successful at the first a.*, réussir du premier coup; emporter une affaire d'emblée. *F:* **I will do it or perish in**

the attempt, je le ferai ou j'y perdrai la vie. *To give up the attempt*, y renoncer. **2.** *Attempt on s.o.'s life*, attentat *m* contre la vie de qn.
attempt², *v.tr.* **1.** (*a*) *To a. to do sth.*, essayer, tenter, s'efforcer, tâcher, de faire qch. *He attempted to rise*, il voulut se lever. (*b*) *To a. resistance*, essayer de résister. *He attempted a smile*, il s'efforça de sourire. *To attempt impossibilities*, tenter l'impossible. Attempted murder, theft, tentative *f* d'assassinat, de vol. **2.** *To attempt s.o.'s life*, attenter à la vie de qn.
attend [a'tend]. **1.** *v.ind.tr.* (*Give heed*) (*a*) *To a. to sth.*, faire, prêter, attention à qch. (*b*) *To a. to s.o.*, écouter qn. *I shall a. to you in a minute*, je serai à vous dans une minute. (*c*) *To a. to sth.*, s'occuper, se charger, se préoccuper, de qch. *To a. to one's studies*, s'appliquer à ses études. (*d*) *To a. to a customer*, servir un client. **2.** *v.tr.* (*Of doctor*) Soigner, donner des soins à (un malade). *To a. the poor*, visiter les pauvres. **3.** *v.tr.* & *ind.tr.* (*a*) *To a. s.o.; to a. on, upon, s.o.*, (i) servir qn, être au service de qn, être de service auprès de qn; (ii) se rendre auprès de qn, se rendre aux ordres de qn. *To a. (upon) a prince*, suivre, accompagner, un prince. (*b*) *Measure attended by unexpected consequences*, mesure suivie, accompagnée, de conséquences inattendues. *Method attended by great difficulties*, méthode qui comporte de grandes difficultés. **4.** *v.tr.* *To attend church, school*, aller à l'église, à l'école. *To attend a lecture, a meeting*, assister à une conférence, à une réunion. *To a. (a course of) lectures*, suivre un cours.
attendance [a'tendəns], *s.* **1.** (*a*) (*In hotel, shop*) Service *m.* *A. included*, service compris. (*b*) (*Of doctor*) *A. on s.o.*, soins *mpl* pour qn; visites *fpl* à qn. (*c*) *To be in attendance* (up)on the king, être de service auprès du roi. **2.** *A. at a meeting*, présence *f* à une réunion. Regular attendance, assiduité *f*; régularité *f* de présence. **3.** *There was a good a. at the meeting*, il y avait une nombreuse assistance à la réunion.
attendant [a'tendənt]. **1.** *a.* (*a*) *A. on s.o.*, qui escorte, qui suit, qui accompagne, qui sert, qn. (*b*) *The a. crowd*, la foule qui y assistait. **2.** *s.* (*a*) Serviteur *m*, domestique *mf*; surveillant, -ante; *Adm:* préposé, -ée; (*in museum, etc.*) gardien, -ienne; (*in theatre*) ouvreuse *f*; (*in laboratory*) appariteur *m.* (*b*) (*Usu.pl.*) Suivants *m*, gens *m* (d'un roi, etc.); personnel *m* (d'un magasin, etc.); personnel de service. *The prince and his attendants*, le prince et sa suite, et son cortège.
attention [a'tenʃ(ə)n], *s.* **1.** (*a*) Attention *f* (*to*, à) *To give one's a. to sth.*, se préoccuper de qch. *To turn one's attention to sth.*, diriger son attention vers qch.; porter son attention sur qch. *We will now turn our a. to . . .*, nous allons maintenant nous occuper de. . . *To pay attention to sth.*, faire attention à qch.; tenir compte de qch. *To pay particular a. to sth.*, s'attacher (surtout) à qch. *To pay a. to s.o.*, *to give one's a. to s.o.*, prêter (son) attention à qn. **Pay attention!** faites attention! *To call, attract, draw,* (*s.o.'s*) *a. to sth.*, appeler, attirer, porter, l'attention (de qn) sur qch. *To catch s.o.'s a.*, attirer, fixer, l'attention de qn. *To attract s.o.*, se faire remarquer. (*b*) Soins *mpi*, entretien *m.* *The batteries require daily a.*, les accus exigent un entretien journalier. **2.** (*Often in pl.*) Attention(s), soins, prévenance(s) *f.* *F:* **To pay one's attentions to a lady**, faire la cour à une dame; être attentif auprès d'une dame. **3.** *Mil:* **Attention!** *F:* **'shun!** garde à vous! **To come**

to attention, se mettre au garde-à-vous. **To stand at attention,** prendre l'attitude militaire ; être, se tenir, au garde-à-vous.
attentive [a'tentiv], a. **1.** Attentif (to, à) ; soigneux, soucieux (to, de). **2.** A. to s.o., assidu, empressé, auprès de qn ; prévenant pour qn ; plein d'égards d'attentions, pour qn. To be very a. to s.o., être aux petits soins pour qn ; être très attentionné pour qn. **-ly,** adv. Attentivement ; avec attention.
attentiveness [a'tentivnəs], s. **1.** Attention f. **2.** Prévenances fpl (to s.o., pour qn).
attenuate [a'tenjueit]. **1.** v.tr. Atténuer. (a) Amincir. (b) Raréfier (un gaz, etc.). (c) To a. a statement, atténuer une affirmation. **2.** v.i. S'atténuer ; (of gas) se raréfier.
attest [a'test]. **1.** v.tr. (a) Attester, certifier (un fait). Facts that a. his industry, faits qui témoignent de son activité. To a. that . . ., attester, certifier, que + ind. (b) Affirmer sous serment. Attested copy, copie certifiée. To a. a signature, légaliser une signature. (c) v.ind.tr. To a. to sth., (i) témoigner de qch. ; (ii) attester qch. ; se porter garant, témoin, de qch. **2.** (a) Jur : Assermenter (qn). (b) Mil : Faire prêter serment à (des volontaires). (c) v.i. Mil : Prêter serment.
attestation [ates'teiʃ(ə)n], s. **1.** Jur : (a) Déposition f ; témoignage m. (b) Attestation f ; légalisation f. **2.** (a) Assermentation f (d'une recrue). (b) Prestation f de serment.
Attic[1] ['atik], a. Attique.
attic[2], s. (a) Mansarde f. To live in the attics, F : loger sous les toits. (b) F : Grenier m.
Attica ['atika]. Pr.n. A.Geog : L'Attique f.
atticism ['atisizm], s. Atticisme m.
attire[1] [a'taiər], s. (a) Vêtement(s) m ; costume m. (b) Poet : Parure f, atours mpl (de femme).
attire[2], v.tr. Lit : (Usu. passive or reflexive) Vêtir ; parer. With her head neatly attired, coiffée avec soin.
attitude ['atitjud], s. (a) Attitude f, pose f ; port m (de la tête). (b) A. of mind, manière f de penser, de voir ; disposition f d'esprit. To maintain a firm a., (i) rester ferme ; (ii) garder bonne contenance. S.a. STRIKE[2] I. 10.
attitudinize [ati'tjudina:iz], v.i. Poser ; faire des grâces ; F : la faire à la pose.
attitudinizer [ati'tjudina:izər], s. Poseur, -euse.
attorney[1] [a'tə:rni], s. Jur : **1.** A : Attorney-at-law = SOLICITOR. S.a. PETTIFOG. **2.** U.S : Avoué m. **3.** Attorney-general, Avocat m du Gouvernement (avec fonctions ministérielles, et toujours membre du Parlement) et Chef du Barreau. **4.** Mandataire m ; fondé m de pouvoir(s).
attorney[2], s. Letter, power, warrant, of attorney, procuration f, mandat m, pouvoirs mpl.
attract [a'trakt], v.tr. **1.** Attirer (to, à, ~ers). A magnet attracts iron, l'aimant attire le fer. S.a. ATTENTION I. **2.** Séduire, attirer ; exercer une attraction sur (qn) ; avoir de l'attrait pour (qn).
attraction [a'trakʃ(ə)n], s. **1.** Attraction f (to, towards, vers). The attraction of gravity, l'attraction. S.a. CENTRE[1] I. **2.** (Usu. in pl.) Séduction f ; attractions, attraits mpl. **3.** The chief attraction (at a party, etc.), le clou (de la fête, etc.).
attractive [a'traktiv], a. **1.** (Of magnet, etc.) Attractif, attirant. **2.** (Of pers., offer, manner) Attrayant, attirant, séduisant ; alléchant. **-ly,** adv. D'une manière attrayante.
attractiveness [a'traktivnəs], s. Attrait m, charme m, agrément m, attraction f.

attributable [a'tribjutəbl], a. Attribuable, imputable (to, à).
attribute[1] ['atribjut], s. **1.** Attribut m, qualité f, apanage m. Speech is an a. of man, la parole est un attribut de l'homme. **2.** Symbole m, attribut. The sword, as an a. of justice, le glaive, en tant qu'attribut de la justice. **3.** Gram : Épithète f.
attribute[2] [a'tribjut], v.tr. Attribuer, imputer (to, à). You a. to him qualities that he does not possess, vous lui prêtez des qualités qu'il n'a pas.
attribution [atri'bju:ʃ(ə)n], s. **1.** Attribution f, imputation f (to, à). **2.** That lies outside of my attributions, cela sort de mes attributions.
attributive [a'tribjutiv], a. Gram : **Attributive** adjective, épithète f ; adjectif qualificatif.
attrition [a'triʃ(ə)n], s. Attrition f ; usure f par le frottement. War of attrition, guerre d'usure.
attune [a'tju:n], v.tr. Lit : Accorder, harmoniser (to, avec). Tastes attuned to mine, goûts à l'unisson des miens.
auburn ['ɔ:bərn], a. A. hair, cheveux blond ardent, clair-bruns, châtain roux.
auction[1] ['ɔ:kʃ(ə)n], s. (Sale by) auction, auction-sale, vente f à l'enchère, aux enchères ; vente à l'encan ; (vente à la) criée f. To put sth. up to, for, auction, mettre qch. aux enchères. S.a. BRIDGE[3]. **auction-room,** s. Salle f des ventes.
auction[2], v.tr. Vendre (qch.) aux enchères, à l'encan ; mettre (qch.) aux enchères ; vendre (des denrées) à la criée.
auctioneer [ɔ:kʃə'ni:ər], s. **1.** (Auctioneer and valuer) Commissaire-priseur m. **2.** Directeur m de la vente ; crieur m.
audacious [ɔ:'deiʃəs], a. **1.** Audacieux, hardi, intrépide. **2.** Pej : Effronté, hardi, cynique.
audaciousness [ɔ:'deiʃəsnəs], **audacity** [ɔ:'dasiti], s. Audace f. **1.** Intrépidité f, hardiesse f. **2.** Pej : Effronterie f, hardiesse, cynisme m.
audibility [ɔ:di'biliti], **audibleness** ['ɔ:dibl-nəs], s. Perceptibilité f (d'un son).
audible ['ɔ:dibl], a. Perceptible (à l'oreille) ; (of speech, voice) distinct, intelligible ; qu'on peut entendre. He was scarcely a., on l'entendait à peine. **-ibly,** adv. Distinctement, intelligiblement.
audience ['ɔ:djəns], s. **1.** Audience f. To grant s.o. an a., accorder audience à qn. **2.** (At meeting, etc.) Assistance f, assistants mpl ; (at theatre) spectateurs mpl, auditoire m, public m ; (at concert) auditeurs mpl.
audit[1] ['ɔ:dit], s. Vérification f, apurement m (de comptes) ; vérification(s) comptable(s). Adm : Audit Office, Cour des comptes.
audit[2], v.tr. Vérifier, apurer (des comptes).
audition [ɔ'diʃ(ə)n], s. **1.** Ouïe f. **2.** Séance f d'essai (d'un chanteur, etc.) ; audition f.
auditive ['ɔ:ditiv], a. = AUDITORY.
auditor ['ɔ:ditər], s. **1.** Auditeur m (d'une conférence, etc.). **2.** (a) Adm : Commissaire m aux comptes ; vérificateur m des comptes. (b) Expert m comptable ; vérificateur comptable.
auditorium [ɔ:di'tɔ:riəm], s. **1.** Th : Salle f. **2.** Ecc : Parloir m (d'un couvent).
auditory ['ɔ:ditəri], a. Auditif.
Augean [ɔ'dʒiːən], a. F : The Augean stables, les écuries d'Augias.
Augeas [ɔ'dʒiːas]. Pr.n.m. Gr.Myth : Augias.
auger ['ɔ:gər], s. Tls : **1.** Perçoir m, foret m ; tarière f. **2.** Min : Sonde ; tarière (de sondage). **'auger-shell,** s. Conch : Térèbre f.
aught [ɔ:t], s. Lit : B : Quelque chose m ; quoi que ce soit. If you have a. to say, si vous avez quelque chose à dire. For aught I know, (pour) autant que je sache.

augment¹ ['ɔːgmənt], *s. Gram:* Augment *m.*
augment² [ɔg ment]. **1.** *v.tr.* Augmenter, accroître *(with, by,* de). **2.** *v.i.* Augmenter, s'accroître.
augmentation [ɔːgmen'teiʃ(ə)n], *s.* Augmentation *f,* accroissement *m* (de fortune, etc.).
augur¹ ['ɔːgər], *s. Rom.Ant:* (*Pers.*) Augure *m.*
augur², *v.tr. & i.* Augurer, présager, prédire. It augurs no good, cela ne présage, n'annonce, rien de bon. It augurs well, ill, cela est de bon, de mauvais, augure.
augury ['ɔːgjuri], *s.* **1.** Augure *m*; *F:* présage *m. The priests took the auguries,* les prêtres prirent les augures. **2.** Science *f* des augures.
august¹ [ɔ'gʌst], *a.* Auguste; imposant, majestueux. **-ly,** *adv.* Majestueusement, augustement.
August² ['ɔːgəst], *s.* Août *m. In A.,* au mois d'août. *On the fifth of A.,* le cinq août.
Augustan [ɔ'gʌstən], *a.* The Augustan age, (i) *Lt.Lit:* le siècle d'Auguste; (ii) *Engl.Lit:* l'époque de la reine Anne.
Augustus [ɔ'gʌstəs]. *Pr.n.m.* Auguste.
auk [ɔːk], *s. Orn:* **1.** Pingouin *m. Great auk,* grand pingouin. **2. Little auk** = RAZOR-BILL.
auld [ɔːld], *a. Scot:* = OLD. Auld lang syne, le temps jadis; le bon vieux temps. 'Auld Reekie,' la vieille Enfumée (Édimbourg).
aunt [ɑːnt], *s.f.* **1.** Tante. *A.-in-law,* tante par alliance. **2.** *F:* **Aunt Sally** = jeu *m* de massacre.
auntie, aunty ['ɑːnti], *s.f. F:* Ma tante.
aural ['ɔːrəl], *a.* De l'oreille. *A. surgeon,* auriste *m.* **-ally,** *adv.* Avec l'oreille; (perçu) par l'oreille.
Aurelius [ɔ'riːljəs]. *Pr.n.m. Hist:* Marcus Aurelius, Marc Aurèle.
aureola [ɔ'riːola], **aureole** ['ɔːrioul], *s. Art:* Auréole *f,* gloire *f* (d'un saint).
auricle ['ɔːrikl], *s.* (a) Auricule *f*; pavillon *m* (de l'oreille). (b) Oreillette *f* (du cœur).
auricular [ɔ'rikjulər]. **1.** *a.* Auriculaire. (a) De l'oreille, des oreillettes du cœur. (b) **Auricular confession,** confession auriculaire. **Auricular witness,** témoin auriculaire. **2.** *s.* (*Little finger*) Auriculaire *m.*
auriferous [ɔ'rifərəs], *a.* Aurifère.
aurist ['ɔːrist], *s. Med:* (*Ear specialist*) Auriste *m,* auriculiste *m.*
aurochs ['ɔːrɔks], *s.* Aurochs *m*; bœuf *m* urus.
Aurora [ɔ'rɔːra]. **1.** *Pr.n.f. Myth:* Aurore. **2.** *s.* Aurore *f.* **Aurora borealis,** aurore boréale.
auscultation [ɔskəl'teiʃ(ə)n], *s.* Auscultation *f.*
auspices ['ɔːspisiz], *s.pl.* Auspices *m. Under favourable a.,* sous d'heureux auspices.
auspicious [ɔs'piʃəs], *a.* **1.** (a) (Vent, etc.) propice, favorable. (b) (Signe) de bon augure. **2.** (Age) heureux, prospère, de prospérité. **-ly,** *adv.* (a) Sous d'heureux auspices. (b) Favorablement.
auspiciousness [ɔs'piʃəsnəs], *s.* Aspect *m* favorable, propice (d'une entreprise, etc.).
Aussie ['ɔsi], *s.m. F:* = AUSTRALIAN.
austere [ɔs'tiːər], *a.* Austère; (appartement) sans luxe, d'un goût sévère. **-ly,** *adv.* Austèrement; avec austérité.
austereness [ɔs'tiːərnəs], **austerity** [ɔs'teriti], *s.* Austérité *f*; absence *f* de luxe; sévérité *f* de goût.
austral ['ɔːstrəl], *a.* Austral, -als, -aux.
Australia [ɔs'treiljə]. *Pr.n.* L'Australie *f.* South Australia, l'Australie méridionale.
Australian [ɔs'treiljən], *a. & s.* Australien, -ienne.
Austria ['ɔːstriə]. *Pr.n.* L'Autriche *f.*
Austrian ['ɔːstriən], *a. & s.* Autrichien, -ienne.
authentic [ɔ'θentik], *a.* Authentique; digne de foi. **-ally,** *adv.* Authentiquement.

authenticate [ɔ'θentikeit], *v.tr.* **1.** Certifier, homologuer, légaliser, valider, viser (un acte, etc.). **2.** Établir l'authenticité de (qch.); vérifier.
authenticated, *a.* **1.** Authentique. **2.** D'une authenticité établie.
authentication [ɔθenti'keiʃ(ə)n], *s.* Certification *f* (d'une signature, etc.); homologation *f,* légalisation *f,* validation *f.*
authenticity [ɔθen'tisiti], *s.* Authenticité *f.*
author ['ɔːθər], *s.* Auteur *m.*
authoress ['ɔːθəres], *s.f.* Femme auteur; femme écrivain.
authoritarian [ɔθɔri'teəriən], *a. & s.* Autoritaire (*m*); partisan *m* de l'autorité.
authoritative [ɔ'θɔritətiv], *a.* **1.** (Caractère) autoritaire; (ton) péremptoire, d'autorité. **2.** Revêtu d'autorité. (a) (Document) qui fait foi, qui fait autorité. (b) (Renseignement) de bonne source. **-ly,** *adv.* **1.** Autoritairement; péremptoirement. **2.** Avec autorité.
authority [ɔ'θɔriti], *s.* Autorité *f.* **1. To have, exercise, authority over s.o.,** (i) avoir, exercer, une autorité sur qn; (ii) avoir de l'ascendant sur qn. **Who is in authority here?** qui est-ce qui commande ici? *To be under s.o.'s a.,* être sous les ordres de qn. **2.** Autorisation *f,* mandat *m.* **To have authority to act,** avoir qualité *f* pour agir. *To give s.o. a. to do sth.,* autoriser qn à faire qch. **To act on s.o.'s authority,** agir sur l'autorité de qn *To do sth. without a.,* faire qch. sans autorisation, sans mandat. **3.** (a) **To be an authority on sth.,** faire autorité en matière de qch. (b) **To have sth. on good authority,** tenir, savoir, qch. de bonne part, de source autorisée. **4.** *Adm:* **Public authority, administrative authority,** corps constitué; service administratif. **The authorities,** l'administration; les autorités.
authorization [ɔθərai'zeiʃ(ə)n], *s.* Autorisation *f (to do sth.,* de faire qch.); pouvoir *m*; mandat *m.*
authorize ['ɔːθəraːiz], *v.tr.* Autoriser (qch.). *To a. s.o. to do sth.,* autoriser qn à faire qch. **Authorized by custom,** sanctionné par l'usage. **authorized,** *a.* Autorisé. *To apply to an a. person,* s'adresser à qui de droit. **The Authorized Version** (*of the Bible*), la traduction de là Bible de 1611 (dénommée la "Traduction autorisée").
authorship ['ɔːθərʃip], *s.* **1.** Profession *f* ou qualité *f* d'auteur. **2.** *To establish the a. of a book,* identifier l'auteur d'un livre.
autobiographer [ɔːtɔbai'ɔgrəfər], *s.* Autobiographe *m.*
autobiographic(al) [ɔːtɔbaiɔ'grafik(əl)], *a.* Autobiographique.
autobiography [ɔːtɔbai'ɔgrəfi], *s.* Autobiographie *f.*
autocracy [ɔː'tɔkrəsi], *s.* Autocratie *f.*
autocrat ['ɔːtɔkrat], *s.* Autocrate *m.*
autocratic(al) [ɔːtɔ'kratik(əl)], *a.* Autocratique; (*of pers.*) autocrate; (caractère) absolu. **-ally,** *adv.* Autocratiquement.
autograph¹ ['ɔːtɔgraf, -grɑːf]. **1.** *s.* (a) Autographe *m.* **Autograph album,** keepsake *m.* (b) Reproduction autographiée. **2.** *a. A. letter of Byron,* lettre autographe de Byron.
autograph², *v.tr.* **1.** Écrire (une lettre, etc.) de sa propre main. **2.** Écrire son autographe dans (un livre); signer, dédicacer (un exemplaire). **3.** *Lith:* Autographier.
autographic(al) [ɔːtɔ'grafik(əl)], *a.* **1.** (Lettre) autographe. **2.** *Lith:* (Encre, papier) autographique.
autogyro [ɔːtɔ'dʒairo], *s. Av:* Autogyre *m.*
auto-ignition [ɔːtoig'niʃ(ə)n], *s. I.C.E:* Auto-allumage *m.*

automatic [ɔːtoˈmatik], a. (a) Automatique. **Automatic machine** (*delivering sweets, etc.*), distributeur m. *Sm.a:* Automatic pistol, automatique m. (b) Automatic motion, mouvement inconscient, machinal. **-ally,** adv. **1.** Automatiquement. **2.** Machinalement.

automaton, pl. **-ons, -a** [ɔːˈtɔmatən, -ənz, -a], s. Automate m.

automobile [ˈɔːtomobiːl], s. U.S: Automobile f; F: auto f, voiture f.

autonomous [ɔːˈtɔnoməs], a. Autonome.

autonomy [ɔːˈtɔnomi], s. Autonomie f.

autopsy [ɔːˈtɔpsi, ˈɔːtopsi], s. Autopsie f.

autumn [ˈɔːtəm], s. L'automne m; l'arrière-saison f. *In a.*, en automne. *Late a.*, l'arrière-automne m.

autumnal [ɔːˈtʌmnəl], a. Automnal; d'automne.

auxiliary [ɔɡˈziliəri], a. & s. Auxiliaire (mf); subsidiaire (*to*, à). *Gram:* Auxiliary verb, verbe auxiliaire.

avail¹ [əˈveil], s. Avantage m, utilité f. Of no avail, sans effet. To be of little avail to s.o., être peu utile à qn. *To work to no a.*, travailler sans résultat. *It is of no a.*, cela ne sert à rien. Without avail, sans effet; inutile(ment).

avail², v.tr. & i. **1.** Servir, être utile, à (qn); être efficace. *Nought availed*, rien n'y faisait; rien n'y fit. **2.** To avail oneself of sth., se servir, s'aider, de qch.; user de qch.; profiter de qch. To a. oneself of a right, user d'un droit; se prévaloir d'un droit. To a. oneself of the opportunity to do sth., saisir l'occasion de faire qch.

availability [əveiləˈbiliti], s. **1.** Disponibilité f (de matériaux, d'hommes). **2.** *Rail: etc:* (Durée et rayon de) validité f (d'un billet).

available [əˈveiləbl], a. **1.** (a) Disponible. To try every a. means, essayer de tous les moyens dont on dispose. *A. funds*, fonds liquides, disponibles. *Capital that can be made a.*, capitaux mobilisables. (b) Accessible. Train a. for passengers covering a distance of . . ., train accessible aux voyageurs effectuant un parcours de. . . . **2.** (*Of ticket, etc.*) Valable, bon, valide (pour deux mois, etc.).

avalanche [ˈavalɑːnʃ], s. Avalanche f.

avarice [ˈavəris], s. Avarice f.

avaricious [avəˈriʃəs], a. Avare, avaricieux. **-ly,** adv. Avaricieusement.

avariciousness [avəˈriʃəsnəs], s. Avarice f.

avast ˌ[əˈvɑːst], int. *Nau:* Tiens bon! tenez bon! baste! *A. heaving!* tenez bon virer!

avaunt [əˈvɔːnt], int. *A:* Arrière! retire-toi! loin de moi!

ave [ˈeivi, ˈɑːvi]. **1.** Lt.int. Ecc. & Lit: (a) Salut! (b) Adieu! **2.** s. Avé (Maria) m. **ˈave-bell,** s. Angélus m.

avenge [əˈvendʒ], v.tr. Venger (qn, une injure). To avenge oneself, be avenged, on one's enemies, se venger de, sur, ses ennemis; prendre, tirer, vengeance de ses ennemis. *To a. s.o. for the insult offered*, venger qn d'une injure. **avenging,** a. Vengeur, f. -eresse.

avenger [əˈvendʒər], s. Vengeur, -eresse.

avens [ˈavənz], s. *Bot:* Wood avens, benoîte f. Water avens, benoîte des ruisseaux.

avenue [ˈavənjuː], s. (a) Avenue f. (b) Esp. U.S: (Belle) rue; boulevard m. (c) Chemin m d'accès. (d) Promenade plantée d'arbres.

aver [əˈvəːr], v.tr. (averred) **1.** Avérer, déclarer, affirmer (que). **2.** *Jur:* Prouver (son dire).

average¹ [ˈavəred3], s. **1.** Moyenne f. On an average, en moyenne; F: l'un portant l'autre. To take an a. of results, faire la moyenne des résultats. **2.** *M.Ins:* Avarie(s) f. Particular average, avarie particulière. General average, avaries communes. Average adjustment, dispache f.

average², a. Moyen. The a. Englishman, l'Anglais moyen, l'Anglais en général. Man of a. abilities, homme ordinaire. A. specimen, échantillon normal.

average³, v.tr. & i. **1.** Prendre, établir, faire, la moyenne (des résultats, etc.). **2.** (a) To average (up to) so much, donner, atteindre, rendre, une moyenne de tant. (b) He averages eight hours' work a day, il travaille en moyenne huit heures par jour.

averment [əˈvəːrmənt], s. **1.** Affirmation f. *Jur:* Allégation f. **2.** *Jur:* Preuve f (d'une allégation).

averse [əˈvəːrs], a. Opposé. To be a. to, from, sth., répugner à qch.; être opposé à qch. *I am a. to acknowledge that* . . ., il me répugne d'admettre que. . . . He is not averse to a glass of beer, il prend volontiers un verre de bière.

averseness [əˈvəːrsnəs], s. Aversion f (to, from, pour); répugnance f (to, from, à).

aversion [əˈvəːrʃ(ə)n], s. **1.** Aversion f, répugnance f. *To feel an a. to, for, s.o.*, se sentir de l'aversion pour, envers, qn. *To feel a. to doing sth.*, répugner à faire qch. To have an a. to s.o., avoir qn en aversion. To take, conceive, an a. to s.o., prendre qn en aversion, en grippe. **2.** F: Objet m d'aversion. *F: My pet aversion*, ma bête noire.

avert [əˈvəːrt], v.tr. **1.** Détourner (les yeux, etc.) (from, de). **2.** Écarter, éloigner, prévenir (des soupçons, un danger); détourner (un coup).

aviary [ˈeiviəri], s. Volière f.

aviation [eiviˈeiʃ(ə)n], s. Aviation f.

aviator [ˈeivieitər], s. Aviateur, -trice.

avid [ˈavid], a. Avide (of, for, de). **-ly,** adv. Avidement; avec avidité.

avidity [əˈviditi], s. Avidité f (for, de, pour).

avocation [avoˈkeiʃ(ə)n], s. (a) Occupation f. (b) Vocation f, métier m, état m, profession f.

avoid [əˈvoid], v.tr. **1.** Éviter. To a. doing sth., éviter de faire qch. *To a. s.o., the world*, se cacher à qn, au monde. **2.** (Evade) Se soustraire (au châtiment); esquiver (un coup, une difficulté). To avoid notice, se dérober aux regards. **3.** *Jur:* Résoudre, résilier, annuler (un contrat, etc.).

avoidable [əˈvoidəbl], a. Évitable.

avoidance [əˈvoidəns], s. **1.** Action f d'éviter. *For the a. of ill*, pour éviter le malheur. **2.** *Jur:* A. of an agreement (owing to breach, etc.), résolution f, annulation f, résiliation f, d'un contrat.

avoirdupois [avərdəˈpɔiz], s. Poids m du commerce. *Ounce a.*, once f avoirdupois, du commerce.

avow [əˈvau], v.tr. **1.** *Pred.* (a) Reconnaître His father avowed him for his son, son père le reconnut pour fils. (b) To a. oneself a free-trader, se déclarer, s'avérer, partisan du libre-échange. **2.** A. & Lit: Déclarer, affirmer (que). **3.** Avouer, admettre (une faute). **avowed,** a. (Ennemi, etc.) avéré.

avowable [əˈvauəbl], a. Avouable.

avowal [əˈvauəl], s. Aveu m. To make an a., faire un aveu.

avowedly [əˈvauidli], adv. Ouvertement, franchement.

await [əˈweit], v.tr. **1.** (a) (Of pers.) Attendre (qch., occ. qn). *Com:* Awaiting your orders, dans l'attente de vos ordres. (b) Work awaiting performance, travail en souffrance. **2.** The fate that awaits him, le sort qui l'attend, qui lui est réservé.

awake¹ [a'weik], v. (p.t. awoke [a'wouk] ; p.p. awoke, awaked [a'weikt]) **1.** v.i. (a) S'éveiller, se réveiller. (b) **To awake to the danger,** se rendre compte, prendre conscience, du danger. **2.** v.tr. (a) Éveiller, réveiller (qn, les remords) ; éveiller (la curiosité, les soupçons). (b) = AWAKEN 1. **awake²,** pred.a. **1.** Éveillé. To lie a., to keep a., rester éveillé. I was a., je ne dormais pas. To keep s.o. a., tenir qn éveillé. **Wide awake,** (i) bien éveillé, tout éveillé ; (ii) F: averti, malin, avisé. He's wide a.! il a l'œil ouvert ! **2. To be awake to a danger,** avoir conscience d'un danger, se rendre compte d'un danger.

awaken [a'weik(ə)n], v.tr. & i. **1.** To a. s.o. to a sense of his position, ouvrir les yeux à qn sur sa position. **2.** = AWAKE¹. **awakening¹,** a. (Passion, etc.) qui s'éveille. **awakening²,** s. (a) Réveil m. (b) F: A rude a., un amer désillusionnement.

award¹ [a'wɔːrd], s. **1.** Jur: Arbitrage m; sentence arbitrale ; décision (arbitrale) ; adjudication f. To make an a., rendre un jugement (arbitral). **2.** (a) Jur: Dommages-intérêts mpl. (b) Sch: etc: Récompense f. To make an a., décerner un prix, une récompense.

award², v.tr. Adjuger, décerner (sth. to s.o., qch. à qn) ; adjuger (un contrat) ; conférer (un bénéfice, une dignité). **awarding,** s. Décernement m (d'un prix, etc.) ; adjudication f (d'un contrat).

aware [a'wɛər], a. Avisé, informé, instruit (of sth., de qch.). **To be aware of sth.,** avoir connaissance, avoir conscience, de qch. ; savoir, ne pas ignorer, qch. Fully a. of the gravity of . . ., conscient de la gravité de. . . . Not that I am aware of, pas que je sache. **To become aware of sth.,** apprendre qch. ; prendre connaissance (d'un fait). I became a. of a smell of burning, j'ai perçu une odeur de brûlé.

awash [a'wɔʃ], adv. **1.** (Of submarine, etc.) A fleur d'eau. Reef awash, écueil ras. **2.** Flottant sur l'eau ; surnageant. **3.** The street was a., la rue était inondée.

away [a'wei], adv. Loin ; au loin. **1.** (With verbs expressing sense of removal) (a) To go a., partir, s'en aller. To walk, drive, ride, a., partir à pied, en voiture, à cheval. To gallop a., partir, s'éloigner, au galop. The ball rolled a., la balle roula plus loin. **To drive dull care away,** chasser les noirs soucis. S.a. MAKE AWAY. (b) (Sense shown by a prefix en-, em-) To run, fly, a., s'enfuir, s'envoler. To take s.o., sth., a., emmener qn, emporter qch. **To carry away,** emporter. (Uses (a) and (b) above are dealt with under the respective verbs ; see GET, GIVE, PUT, SEND, THROW, etc.). **2.** (Elliptical uses) Away with you! allez-vous-en ! F: fichez le camp ! A. with it! emportez-le ! A. with him! qu'on l'emmène ! **Away with fear!** bannissons la crainte ! One, two, three, and away! un, deux, trois, partez ! I must a.! il me faut partir ! **3.** (Continuousness) (a) To work a., travailler toujours ; continuer à travailler. Sing a.! continuez à chanter ! (b) To do sth. right away, faire qch. tout de suite, sur-le-champ. S.a. FIRE², RIGHT¹ III. 1. **4.** (Distant) Loin. (a) **Far away,** dans le lointain ; au loin. **Away back in the distance,** tout au loin. **We are five miles away from the station,** nous sommes à huit kilomètres de la gare. Five paces a. stood . . ., à cinq pas de là se tenait. . . . **This is far and away the best,** c'est de beaucoup le meilleur. That is far and a. better, cela vaut infiniment mieux. (b) **To hold sth. away from sth.,** tenir qch. éloigné, loin, de qch. **To turn (one's face) a. from sth.,** détourner la tête de qch.

S.a. LOOK AWAY. (c) **Away from home,** absent (de chez lui, de chez moi). When he is a., lorsqu'il n'est pas là. When I have to be a., lorsque je dois m'absenter. My occupation keeps me a. from town, mon occupation me tient éloigné de la ville. **To stay away,** rester absent, ne pas venir. **To keep away,** se tenir à l'écart. **5.** (Time) I knew him away back in 1900, je l'ai connu dès 1900.

awe¹ [ɔː], s. Crainte f, terreur f; occ. respect m. To strike s.o. with awe, (i) (of pers.) imposer à qn un respect mêlé de crainte ; (ii) (of phenomenon) frapper qn d'une terreur mystérieuse. **To hold, keep, s.o. in awe,** (en) imposer à qn ; tenir qn en respect. **To stand in awe of s.o.,** (i) craindre, redouter, qn ; (ii) avoir une crainte respectueuse de qn. **'awe-inspiring,** a. Terrifiant, imposant, impressionnant. Awe-i. sight, spectacle grandiose. **'awe-stricken, 'awe-struck,** a. **1.** Frappé d'une terreur profonde, mystérieuse, etc. **2.** Intimidé.

awe², v.tr. = To strike with awe, q.v. above.

awesome ['ɔːsəm], a. = AWE-INSPIRING.

awful ['ɔːful], a. **1.** Terrible, redoutable, effroyable. To die an a. death, mourir d'une mort terrible. **2.** (a) Terrifiant. (b) Imposant, solennel. **3.** (Intensive) F: What an a. scoundrel! c'est un fameux coquin ! An a. hat, un chapeau affreux. You were an a. fool! vous avez été rudement bête ! What a. weather! quel chien de temps ! **-fully,** adv. **1.** Terriblement, effroyablement. **2.** Solennellement. **3.** F: (Intensive) I am a. sorry, je regrette infiniment. A. funny, drôle comme tout. A. ugly, affreusement laid. **Thanks awfully !** merci mille fois !

awfulness ['ɔːfulnəs], s. Caractère imposant ; solennité f ; caractère terrible (de la situation).

awhile [a'hwail], adv. Pendant quelque temps ; un moment. Wait a., attendez un peu.

awkward ['ɔːkwərd], a. **1.** (Clumsy) Gauche, maladroit, disgracieux. To be a., avoir l'air emprunté. **The awkward age,** l'âge ingrat. A. fellow, F: empoté m. Mil: F: **The awkward squad,** le peloton des arriérés ; les bleus. To be a. with one's hands, avoir la main maladroite. A. sentence, phrase gauche. **2.** (Ill at ease) Embarrassé, gêné. **3.** Fâcheux, malencontreux, embarrassant, gênant. An a. situation, un mauvais pas. **4.** Incommode, peu commode. A. tool, outil peu maniable. A. corner, virage difficile, assez dangereux. F: He's an awkward customer, c'est un homme difficile ; il n'est pas commode. **-ly,** adv. **1.** (a) Gauchement, maladroitement. (b) Mal à propos. **2.** D'une manière embarrassée ; d'un ton embarrassé, gêné. **3.** D'une façon gênante, embarrassante. To be a. situated, se trouver dans une situation embarrassante.

awkwardness ['ɔːkwərdnəs], s. **1.** (a) Gaucherie f ; maladresse f. (b) Manque m de grâce ; balourdise f. **2.** Embarras m, gêne f. **3.** (Of situation) Inconvénient m, incommodité f.

awl [ɔːl], s. Tls: Alène f, poinçon m, perçoir m.

awn [ɔːn], s. Bot: Barbe f, barbelure f (d'avoine, etc.) ; arête f.

awning ['ɔːniŋ], s. **1.** (a) Tente f, vélum m. banne f (de boutique) ; bâche f (de charrette) ; tendelet m (de voiture). (b) Nau: Tente, tendelet m. **2.** (a) Rail: Portique m (de quai). (b) Marquise f (de théâtre, d'hôtel, etc.).

awoke [a'wouk]. See AWAKE¹.

awry [a'rai], adv. & pred.a. De travers, de guingois. (Of plans, etc.) **To go all awry,** aller tout de travers ; avorter.

ax, axe, pl. **axes** [aks, 'aksiz], s. **1.** Hache f. Woodman's axe, felling axe, hache d'abattage ;

cognée *f* de bûcheron. *Broad axe*, doloire *f*. *F:* To have an axe to grind, avoir un intérêt personnel à servır ; agir dans un but intéressé. *S.a.* BATTLE-AXE, ICE-AXE, POLE-AXE¹. **2.** *F:* The axe, coup. *f* sombre dans les prévisions budgétaires ; réductions *fpl* sur les traitements ; diminutions *fpl* de personnel. **axe′head,** *s.* Fer *m* de hache.

ıxial [′aksiəl], *a.* Axial, -aux.

ıxil [′aksil], **axilla** [ak′silə], *s. Bot:* Aisselle *f* (d'une feuille).

ıxiom [′aksiəm], *s.* Axiome *m*.

ıxiomatic(al) [aksio′matik(əl)], *a.* (*a*) Axiomatique. (*b*) *F:* Évident.

ıxis, *pl.* **-es** [′aksis, ′aksi:z], *s.* Axe *m*. Major axis of an ellipse, grand axe d'une ellipse. *Opt: A. of vision*, axe visuel.

ıxle [aksl], *s.* **I.** Axle(-tree), essieu *m*. Live axle, essieu tournant. Dead axle, essieu fixe. Driving-axle, essieu moteur ; (*of electric locomotive*) pont *m*. *Aut:* Rear axle, pont (arrière) ; essieu arrière. **2.** Tourillon *m*, arbre *m*, axe *m* (d'une roue, etc.).

′axle-box, *s.* Boîte *f* de l'essieu ; boîte à graisse. **′axle-cap,** *s. Veh:* Chapeau *m*, capot *m*, de moyeu. **′axle-shaft,** *s. Aut:* Demi-essieu *m* (du pont arrière).

ay(e)¹ [ai]. **I.** *adv. & int.* (*a*) (*Esp. in Scot.*) Oui ; mais oui. (*b*) *Nau:* Ay(e), ay(e), sir! (i) oui commandant! bien, capitaine! (ii) paré! **2.** *s.* (*In voting*) Ayes and noes, voix *f* pour et contre. The ayes have it, le vote est pour. *Thirty ayes and twenty noes*, trente oui et vingt non.

ay(e)² [ei], *adv. Lit:* Toujours. For (ever and) aye, pour toujours ; à tout jamais.

ayah [′aia], *s.f.* Ayah ; bonne d'enfant (hindoue).

azalea [a′zeiljə], *s. Bot:* Azalée *f*.

azimuth [′aziməθ], *s.* Azimut *m*. Azimuth compass, compas de relèvement.

Azores (the) [ðia′zɔ:ərz]. *Pr.n.pl.* Les Açores *f*.

Aztec [′aztek], *a. & s. Ethn: Hist:* Aztèque (*mf*).

azure [′aʒər, ′eiʒər], *s.* Azur *m*. **2.** *Attrib. An a. sky*, un ciel d'azur. **′azure-spar, -stone,** *s.* Lapis-lazuli *m inv*.

B

B, b [bi:]. **I.** (La lettre) B, b *m*. *F:* Not to know B from a bull's foot, ne savoir ni A ni B ; ne savoir rien de rien. **2.** *Mus:* Si *m*. B flat, si bémol.

baa¹ [bɑ:], *s.* Bêlement *m*. *Baa!* bê! Baa-lamb, petit agneau.

baa², *v.i.* (baaed, baa'd [bɑ:d]) Bêler.

Baal, *pl.* **Baalim** [′beiəl, ′beiəlim], *s. Rel.H:* (*a*) Baal *m*. (*b*) *F:* Faux dieu.

Babbit-metal, *F:* **babbit** [′babit(met(ə)l)], *s.* Métal *m* antifriction ; régule *m*.

babble¹ [babl], *s.* **I.** Babil *m*, babillage *m*, babillement *m*. **2.** Jaserie *f*, bavardage *m*. **3.** Murmure *m* (d'un ruisseau).

babble². **I.** *v.i.* (*a*) Babiller. (*b*) Bavarder, jaser. (*c*) (*Of stream*) Murmurer, babiller. **2.** *v.tr.* To b. (*out*) a secret, laisser échapper un secret. **babbling,** *a.* Babillard, bavard, jaseur ; (*of stream*) murmurant.

babbler [′bablər], *s.* **I.** Babillard, -arde ; bavard, -arde. **2.** Jaseur, -euse (qui laisse échapper des secrets).

babe [beib], *s.* Enfant *m* (en bas âge) ; petit enfant. *F: Story that is no food for babes*, histoire qui n'est p..s pour les jeunes filles.

Babel [′beibəl]. **I.** *Pr.n.* The Tower of Babel, la Tour de Babel. **2.** *s. F:* Babel of talk, brouhaha *m* de conversation. *It was an absolute B.*, c'était un vacarme à ne pas s'entendre.

baboo, babu [′bɑ:bu:], *s.* Babou *m*.

baboon [ba′bu:n], *s. Z:* Babouin *m*. Dog-faced baboon, cynocéphale *m*.

baby [′beibi], *s.* **I.** (*m., f., or neut.*) Bébé *m* ; poupon *m*, poupard *m*. I have known him from a baby, je l'ai vu naître. The baby of the family, le benjamin. *S.a.* CRY-BABY. *F:* To hold, carry, the baby, avoir l'entreprise sur les bras. **2.** *Attrib.* (*a*) D'enfant, de bébé. Baby talk, babil enfantin. *F:* Baby face, visage poupin, poupard. (*b*) *F:* De petites dimensions. *Esp.* Baby grand, piano *m* (à) demi-queue ; crapaud *m*. *Aut:* Baby car, voiturette *f*. **′baby-farm,** *s.* Pouponnière *f*,

nourricerie *f* ; garderie *f* d'enfants. **′baby-farmer,** *s.* Gardeuse *f* d'enfants. **′baby-linen,** *s.* Layette *f*. **′baby-ribbon,** *s.* Ruban *m* comète.

babyhood [′beibihud], *s.* Première enfance : bas âge.

babyish [′beibiiʃ], *a. F:* De bébé ; puéril.

Babylon [′babilən]. *Pr.n.* Babylone *f*. *F:* The modern Babylon, la Babylone moderne (Londres).

Bacchanal [′bakənəl], *s.* (*a*) = BACCHANT. (*b*) (*Reveller*) Tapageur, -euse ; noceur, -euse. (*c*) (*Revelry*) Bacchanal *m*. (*d*) (*Dance*) Bacchanale *f*.

Bacchanalia [bakə′neiljə], *s.pl.* Bacchanales *f*.

Bacchanalian [bakə′neiljən], *a.* Bachique.

Bacchant [′bakənt], *s.* Prêtre ou prêtresse de Bacchus ; (*when f.*) bacchante.

bacchante [ba′kanti], *s.f.* Bacchante, ménade.

Bacchic [′bakik], *a.* Bachique.

baccy [′baki], *s. P:* = TOBACCO.

bachelor [′batʃələr], *s.m.* **I.** *Hist:* Bachelier (aspirant à la chevalerie). **2.** Célibataire, garçon. Old bachelor, vieux garçon. Bachelor uncle, oncle non marié. *F:* Bachelor girl, jeune fille indépendante. **3.** *Sch:* Bachelier, -ière (en tant que détenteur, -trice, d'un diplôme de fin d'études universitaires). Bachelor of Arts, of Science, approx. = licencié ès lettres, ès sciences. *B. of Medicine, of Laws, of Divinity*, bachelier en médecine, en droit, en théologie.

bachelorhood [′batʃələrhud], *s.* Célibat *m*.

bacillary [ba′siləri], *a. Biol:* Bacillaire.

bacillus, *pl.* **-i** [ba′siləs, -ai], *s. Biol:* Bacille *m*.

back¹ [bak]. **I.** *s.* **I.** (*a*) Dos *m*. To fall on one's b., tomber à la renverse. *F:* I have no clothes, I haven't a rag, to my back, je n'ai rien à me mettre sur le dos. She wears her hair down her b., elle porte les cheveux dans le dos. To carry, sling, sth. across one's b., porter, mettre, qch. en bandoulière. To be at the back of s.o., (i) être derrière qn ; (ii) soutenir qn. The Government has a broad back, le gouvernement a bon dos.

To do sth. behind s.o.'s back, faire qch. à l'insu de qn. To turn one's back on s.o., (i) tourner le dos à qn ; (ii) abandonner qn. To stand, sit, with one's back to s.o., tourner le dos à qn. To be glad to see the back of s.o., être content de voir partir qn, d'être débarrassé de qn. To be on one's back, (i) être étendu sur le dos ; (ii) (to be ill) être alité. The cat sets up its b., le chat fait le gros dos, arque le dos. F: To put, set, get, s.o.'s back up, mettre qn en colère ; fâcher qn ; faire rebiffer qn. To make a back (at leap-frog), faire le mouton. To make a back for s.o., to lend a back to s.o., faire la courte échelle à qn. Back to back, dos à dos ; adossés. Back to front, sens devant derrière. With one's back to the wall, (i) adossé au mur ; (ii) poussé au pied du mur ; acculé ; aux abois. F: To put one's back into sth., s'appliquer à qch. ; s'y mettre énergiquement. S.a. PAT², SCRATCH² I. (b) Les reins m ; F: l'échine f. S.a. SMALL II. To break one's back, se casser les reins, l'échine. To break the back of the work, faire le plus dur, le plus fort, du travail. (c) (Of ship) To break her back, se briser en deux ; se casser. 2. (a) Dos (d'un couteau, d'un livre) ; envers m (d'une étoffe) ; verso m (d'une page, d'une carte postale) ; dos, verso (d'un chèque). Fin: Bills as per back, effets comme au verso. (b) Dossier m (d'une chaise). (c) Revers m (d'une colline, d'une médaille). The back of the hand, le revers de la main. (d) Derrière m (de la tête, d'une maison) ; arrière m (d'une maison, d'une voiture). Phot: Back of a camera, corps m arrière, arrière-cadre m. The frock fastens at the b., la robe s'agrafe dans le dos. F: The third floor back, le troisième sur la cour, sur le derrière. Idea at the back of one's mind, idée de derrière la tête ; arrière-pensée f. There is something at the back of it, il y a une raison secrète derrière tout cela. To get to the back of a policy, voir le dessous des cartes. 3. Arch: Extrados m (d'une voûte). 4. (a) Fond m (d'une armoire, d'une salle). Th: The back of the stage, le fond de la scène ; l'arrière-scène. At the very back of . . ., au fin fond de. . . . S.a. BEYOND 3. (b) Derrières (de la ville, de l'armée). 5. Fb: Arrière. The backs, l'arrière-défense f. S.a. HALF-BACK. II. back, a. (Place, etc.) arrière, de derrière. Back apartment, pièce sur le derrière. The back streets of a town, les derrières m d'une ville. Mil: The back area, l'arrière m. Back wheel, roue arrière. III. back, adv. 1. (Of place) (a) En arrière. Stand back! arrière ! rangez-vous ! To step b. a pace, faire un pas en arrière. Far back, loin derrière (les autres, etc.). House standing b. from the road, maison écartée du chemin ; maison en retrait. (b) Dans le sens contraire. To hit, strike, back, rendre coup pour coup. If anyone hits me, I'll hit back, si on me frappe, je rends la pareille. It was a bit of his own back, c'était une revanche. (With a v. often rendered by the pref. re-) To call s.o. back, rappeler qn. To come back, revenir. To go, drive, ride, sail, walk, back, (i) retourner (to,à) ; (ii) rebrousser chemin. To drive, chase, s.o. back, faire rebrousser chemin à qn. To make one's way back, s'en retourner. Ship chartered to Lisbon and b. to London, navire affrété pour voyage à Lisbonne avec retour sur Londres. To hasten back, retourner en toute hâte. (c) When will he be b.? quand sera-t-il de retour ? As soon as I get b., dès mon retour. S.a. THERE I. 1. Attrib. Back-action, mouvement inverse. Back current, contre-courant m. 2. (Of time) Some few years back, il y a (déjà) quelques années. Far back in

the Middle Ages, à une période reculée du moyen âge. As far b. as 1914, déjà en 1914 ; dès 1914. **back-'answer,** s. F: Réplique impertinente. **'back-band,** s. Harn: Surdos m. **back-'bencher,** s. Parl: Membre m sans portefeuille. **'back-breaking,** a. (Travail, etc.) éreintant. **'back-chat,** s. P: Impertinence f. **'back-cloth, -curtain,** s. Th: Toile f de fond ; arrière-scène f. **back-'door,** s. Porte f de derrière, de service. F: To get into a profession through the b.-d., entrer dans une profession par la petite porte. **back-'fire¹,** s. I.C.E: (a) Allumage prématuré ; contre-allumage m. Back-fire kick, retour m de manivelle. (b) Retour de flamme (au carburateur). **back-'fire²,** v.i. I.C.E: 1. S'allumer prématurément ; pétarder. 2. Donner des retours de flamme. **back-'garden,** s. Jardin m de derrière. **back-'hair,** s. Chignon m. **'back-hand,** s. 1. Back-hand blow, coup m de revers. 2. Écriture renversée, penchée à gauche. **'back-handed,** a. 1. Back-handed blow, coup inattendu, déloyal. B.-h. compliment, compliment équivoque, à rebours. 2. Back-handed writing, écriture renversée, penchée à gauche. **'back-hander,** s. F: 1. Coup m du revers de la main. 2. Riposte inattendue ; attaque indirecte, déloyale. **'back-iron,** s. Tls: Contre-fer m (de rabot). **back-'kitchen,** s. Arrière-cuisine f. **'back-lash,** s. 1. Mec.E: Jeu m (nuisible) ; secousse f, battement m, saccade f. 2. Contre-coup m, répercussion f (d'une explosion). **back-'number,** s. (a) Vieux numéro (d'un journal). (b) F: Objet démodé. (Of pers.) To be a b.-n., être vieux jeu. **back-'pay,** s. Mil: Navy: Arriéré m de solde ; rappel m de solde. **back-'pedal,** v.i. Contre-pédaler. **'back-pressure,** s. 1. Contre-pression f. Back-pressure valve, clapet de retenue. 2. El: Contre-tension f. **'back-scratching,** s. P: 1. Flagornerie f. 2. = LOG-ROLLING. **back-'seat,** s. Siège m de derrière ; siège arrière. To take a back-seat, (i) s'asseoir sur un banc de derrière ; (ii) F: passer au second plan ; se trouver relégué au deuxième rang ; céder le pas à d'autres. **'back-set,** s. 1. Contre-courant m. 2. Revers m (de fortune) ; échec m. **back-'shop,** s. Arrière-boutique f, pl. -boutiques. **back-'sight,** s. Sm.a: Hausse f. (Sighting notch of) back-sight, cran m de mire. **'back-stitch,** s. Needlew: Point m arrière, arrière-point m, point de piqûre. **'back-strap,** s. Harn: Dossière f ; surdos m. **'back-street,** s. 1. Petite rue écartée. 2. Pej: Rue pauvre, mal fréquentée. **'back-stroke,** s. 1. (a) Coup m de revers. (b) Contre-coup m. 2. Course f de retour (d'un piston, etc.). 3. Swim: Nage f, brasse f, sur le dos. **back-'tooth,** s. Dent f du fond ; molaire f. **back-'yard,** s. Arrière-cour f.

back², I. v.tr. 1. (a) Renforcer (un mur, une carte) ; endosser (un livre) ; maroufler (une toile). (b) To back (up) s.o., sth., soutenir, appuyer, qn, qch. ; prêter son appui à qn. Sp: To back a horse, parier, miser, sur un cheval ; jouer un cheval. Well-backed horse, cheval très coté. Com: etc: To back s.o., financer qn. To back a bill, endosser un effet. (c) Phot: Ocrer (une plaque). 2. (a) Reculer (une charrette) ; faire (re)culer (un cheval). Mch: Mettre (une machine) en arrière ; refouler (un train). (b) Nau: To back the oars, to back water, (i) ramer à rebours, nager à culer ; (ii) (to stop way) scier, dénager. (c) Nau: Masquer, coiffer (une voile). 3. Servir de fond (à qch.). The hills that b. the *town*, les collines auxquelles la ville est adossée. **II. back,** *v.i.* **1.** (*a*) Aller en arrière; marcher à reculons; (*of horse*) reculer; *Aut: etc:* faire marche arrière. *Aut: To b. into the garage*, entrer dans le garage en marche arrière. (*b*) *Nau:* (*Of wind*) (Re)descendre, ravaler. **2.** *The house backs on the high road*, la maison donne par derrière sur le grand chemin. **back down,** *v.i.* **1.** (*a*) Descendre (une échelle, etc.) à reculons. (*b*) *The engine is backing down*, la machine revient sur le train. **2.** (*a*) Avouer qu'on est dans son tort; rabattre de ses prétentions; en rabattre. (*b*) *P:* Caner; caler; filer doux. **back out,** *v.i.* **1.** (*Of pers., etc.*) Sortir à reculons; (*of car*) sortir en marche arrière. **2.** *F:* Retirer sa promesse; se dédire, se dérober. *To b. out of an argument*, se soustraire à une discussion. **back up,** *v.tr. See* BACK² I. 1 (*b*). **backed,** *a.* **1.** *B. on to sth.*, adossé à qch. **2.** (*a*) A dos, à dossier. *Backed saw*, scie à dosseret. (*b*) *Broad-backed*, à large dos, qui ‹ le dos large. *S.a.* HUMPBACKED. **3.** *Phot:* **Backed plate**, plaque à enduit antihalo; plaque ocrée. **backing,** *s.* **1.** (*a*) Renforcement *m* (d'un mur, d'une carte). *Bookb:* Endossage *m* (d'un livre). (*b*) *Sp:* B. of a horse, paris *mpl* sur un cheval. **2.** (*a*) Renfort *m*, support *m*, soutien *m* (d'un mur). (*b*) *Phot:* (Enduit *m*) anti-halo *m*. **3.** (*a*) Recul *m*, reculement *m* (d'un cheval, d'une charrette); acculement *m* (d'un cheval); refoulement *m* (d'un train). (*b*) Nage *f* à culer (d'un canot). (*c*) Renversement *m* (du vent).

backache ['bakeik], *s.* (*a*) Douleurs *fpl* de reins. (*b*) Courbature *f*.

backbite ['bakbait], *v.tr.* Médire de (qn). **backbiting,** *s.* Médisance *f*.

backbiter ['bakbaitər], *s.* Médisant, -ante; mauvaise langue.

backbone ['bakboun], *s.* (i) Épine dorsale, colonne vertébrale; échine *f*; (ii) grande arête (de poisson). *F:* English to the backbone, anglais jusqu'à la moelle des os. *He has got backbone*, il a du caractère. *He has no backbone*, il manque de fermeté, d'énergie, de caractère. *He is the b. of the movement*, c'est lui qui mène le mouvement.

backer ['bakər], *s.* **1.** *Sp:* esp. *Rac:* Parieur, -euse. **2.** *Com:* (*a*) B. of a bill, donneur *m* d'aval. (*b*) Commanditaire *m*. **3.** Partisan *m*.

backgammon [bak'gamən], *s.* (Jeu *m* de) trictrac *m*; (jeu de) jacquet *m*.

background ['bakgraund], *s.* Fond *m*, arrière-plan *m*. *In the b.*, dans le fond, à l'arrière-plan. *Against a dark b.*, sur (un) fond sombre. *F:* To keep (oneself) in the background, s'effacer; se tenir dans l'ombre.

backless ['bakləs], *a.* (Robe, etc.) sans dos; (banc, etc.) sans dossier.

backmost ['bakmoust], *a.* Dernier; le plus éloigné, le plus reculé.

backsheesh ['bakʃiːʃ], *s.* = BAKSHEESH.

backslide ['bakslaid], *v.i.* (backslid) Retomber dans l'erreur, dans le vice; rechuter. **backsliding,** *s.* Rechute *f* dans le péché, dans le vice; récidive *f*.

backslider ['bakslaidər], *s.* Relaps, *f.* relapse.

backstair(s) [bak'stɛər(z)], *s.* (i) Escalier *m* de service; (ii) escalier dérobé. *F:* 'Backstair influence, (i) protections en haut lieu; (ii) menées sourdes, secrètes. 'Bac stair ossip, propos d'antichambre.

backward ['bakwərd]. **1.** *a.* (*a*) B. motion, mouvement rétrograde, en arrière. *B. glance*, regard en arrière. (*b*) B. harvest, moisson en retard. *B. child*, enfant attardé, arriéré. (*c*) **To be backward in doing sth.**, être lent, peu empressé, à faire qch. **2.** *adv.* = BACKWARDS.

backwardness ['bakwərdnəs], *s.* **1.** Retard *m* (d'un enfant, de la moisson); lenteur *f* d'intelligence. **2.** B. in doing sth., hésitation *f*, lenteur, à faire qch.

backwards ['bakwərdz], *adv.* En arrière. *To jump, lean, b.*, sauter, se pencher, en arrière. *To go, walk, b.*, aller, marcher, à reculons. *To fall b.*, tomber à la renverse. (*Of water*) *To flow b.*, couler à contre-courant; refouler. *To reckon b. to a date*, remonter jusqu'à une date. *To stroke the cat b.*, caresser le chat à contre-poil, à rebrousse-poil. **Backwards and forwards**, d'avant en arrière et d'arrière en avant. *To walk b. and forwards*, aller et venir; se promener de long en large; faire les cent pas.

backwash ['bakwəʃ], *s.* Remous *m*.

backwater¹ ['bakwɔːtər], *s.* **1.** Eau arrêtée (par un bief, etc.). **2.** Bras *m* de décharge (d'une rivière). **3.** Remous *m* (d'une roue à aubes).

backwater², *v.i.* = *back water, q.v. under* BACK² I. 2.

backwoodsman, *pl.* **-men** [bak'wudzmən, -men], *s.m.* Colon des forêts (de l'Amérique du Nord).

bacon ['beik(ə)n], *s.* Lard *m*; porc salé et fumé; bacon *m.* *F:* To save one's bacon, sauver sa peau. *P:* To pull bacon at s.o., faire un pied de nez à qn.

bacterial [bak'tiːəriəl], *a.* Bactérien.

bacteriologist [baktiːəri'ɔlɔdʒist], *s.* Bactériologiste *m*.

bacteriology [baktiːəri'ɔlɔdʒi], *s.* Bactériologie *f*.

bacterium, *pl.* **-ia** [bak'tiːəriəm, -ia], *s.* Bactérie *f*.

bad [bad]. **I.** *a.* (worse [wəːrs], worst [wəːrst]) Mauvais. **1.** (*a*) (*Inferior*) *Bad food*, mauvaise nourriture; nourriture de mauvaise qualité. *Bad air*, air vicié. *Bad meat*, viande gâtée, avariée. *Bad coin*, pièce fausse. **Bad debt**, mauvaise créance; créance douteuse, véreuse, irrécouvrable. *Very bad work*, travail détestable. *Nau: Bad holding-ground*, fond sans tenue. (*Of food, etc.*) **To go bad**, se gâter, s'avarier. (*b*) (*Incorrect*) *Bad translation*, mauvaise traduction, traduction incorrecte. *He speaks bad French*, il parle mal le français; son français est mauvais. *Bad shot*, coup mal visé; coup qui manque le but. **To be bad at** (*lying, etc.*), s'entendre mal à (mentir, etc.). *F:* It's not bad, not so bad: it isn't half bad, ce n'est pas mal du tout; c'est très passable. (*c*) (*Unfortunate*) It's a bad business! *F:* it's a bad job! c'est une mauvaise affaire! c'est une triste affaire! **To be in a bad plight**, *F:* in a bad way, être en mauvais, piteux, état; être dans de beaux draps; (*health*) filer un mauvais coton. *He will come to a bad end*, il finira mal. *He has a bad name*, il a une mauvaise réputation. *It would not be a bad thing, a bad plan, to . . .*, on ne ferait pas mal de. . . . *Things are going from bad to worse*, les choses vont de mal en pis. (*d*) *Jur:* Bad claim, réclamation mal fondée. *Bad voting paper*, bulletin de vote nul. *This is bad law, bad history*, c'est fausser la loi, l'histoire. (*e*) *Word taken* in a bad sense, mot avec un sens péjoratif. **2.** (*a*) (*Wicked*) *Bad man*, méchant homme. *Bad book*, mauvais livre. *Bad life*, mauvaise vie; vie déréglée. **Don't call people bad names**, n'injuriez pas les gens. **He's a bad lot,** *P:* a bad egg, c'est un vilain personnage, un vilain coco, une gouape, une fripouille. **He isn't as bad as he looks**, il n'est pas si diable qu'il est noir. (b) (*Unpleasant*) *Bad news*, mauvaise nouvelle. *Bad smell*, mauvaise odeur. *To have a bad cold, a bad headache*, avoir un gros rhume, un violent mal de tête. **To be on bad terms with s.o.**, être mal, en mauvais termes, avec qn. *It is very bad of you to . . .*, c'est très mal à vous, de votre part, de. . . . **It is (really) too bad! that's too bad!** c'est (par) trop fort! par trop violent! ça c'est raide! *It's too bad of him!* ce n'est vraiment pas bien de sa part! (c) *Bad accident*, grave accident. *Bad mistake*, lourde méprise. **To be bad for s.o., for sth.**, ne rien valoir à qn, pour qch. *It is bad for the health*, cela ne vaut rien pour la santé. (d) *F:* (*Ill, diseased*) *She is very bad to-day*, elle est très mal aujourd'hui. **I feel bad**, je ne me sens pas bien. *She has a bad finger*, elle a mal au doigt. *My bad leg*, ma jambe malade. *F:* **I'm not so bad**, je ne vais pas trop mal. *How's business?—Not so bad*, comment vont les affaires?—*As I said. P:* **She took bad, was taken bad**, elle s'est sentie indisposée, a été prise d'un malaise. **-ly**, *adv.* (worse, worst) **1.** Mal. *B. dressed*, mal habillé. **To do, come off, badly**, mal réussir. *I came off .b. in that affair*, cette affaire a tourné à mon désavantage. **To be doing badly**, faire de mauvaises affaires. *Things are going, turning out, b.*, les choses vont mal, tournent mal. *He took it very badly*, il a très mal pris la chose. (*Of machine, etc.*) **To work b.**, mal fonctionner. **2. Badly wounded**, gravement, grièvement, blessé. *B. beaten*, battu à plate couture. **3.** **To want sth. badly**, avoir grand besoin de qch. **II. bad**, *s.* Ce qui est mal ou mauvais. (a) **To take the bad with the good**, accepter la mauvaise fortune aussi bien que la bonne. (b) (*Of pers.*) **To go to the bad**, mal tourner. (c) *I am 500 francs to the bad*, je suis en perte de 500 francs. **bad-'looking**, *a. F: He is not b.-l.*, il n'est pas mal (de sa personne). **bad-'tempered**, *a.* Grincheux; acariâtre.

bade [bad, beid]. *See* BID².

badge [badʒ], *s.* **1.** (a) Insigne *m* (d'un membre d'une société); insigne de casquette; plaque *f* (de cocher); médaille *f* (de porteur, etc.); *Mil:* attribut *m* (d'un régiment, etc.). *Sporting b.*, insigne sportif. (b) = ARM-BADGE. (c) (*Of boy-scout*) Brevet *m*. **2.** Symbole *m*, marque *f*; signe distinctif.

badger¹ ['badʒər], *s.* **1.** *Z:* Blaireau *m*. **2.** (*Brush*) Blaireau.

badger², *v.tr.* Harceler, tourmenter, tracasser, importuner (qn). *To b. s.o. for sth.*, harceler qn pour obtenir qch.

badminton ['badmintən], *s. Games:* Volant *m* au filet.

badness ['badnəs], *s.* **1.** (a) Mauvaise qualité; mauvais état. (b) *The b. of the weather*, le mauvais temps. **2.** (*Of pers.*) Méchanceté *f.*

baffle¹ [bafl], *s.* Déflecteur *m*; chicane *f*; contre-porte *f.*

baffle², *v.tr.* **1.** (a) Confondre, déconcerter, dérouter (qn); dépister (la police); dérouter (les soupçons). (b) Déjouer, faire échouer (un projet); frustrer, décevoir (un espoir); tromper, éluder (la vigilance). *To b. definition*, échapper à toute définition. **2.** Établir des chicanes dans (un conduit, etc.).

bag¹ [bag], *s.* **1.** Sac *m*. *Money-bag*, (i) bourse *f*; (ii) (*of tramway conductors, etc.*) sacoche *f*. *Travelling bag*, sac de voyage. *Paper bag*, sac de, en, papier. *S.a.* BRIEF-BAG, CARPET-BAG, GAME-BAG, GAS-BAG, HAND-BAG, ICE-BAG, KIT-BAG, MAIL-BAG, NOSE-BAG, POST-BAG, SLEEPING-BAG, TOOL-BAG, WORK-BAG. *F:* **To pack up bag and**

baggage, plier bagage; prendre ses cliques et ses claques; faire son baluchon. *P:* **There are bags of it**, il y en a des tas. **2.** (a) *Nat.Hist:* Sac, poche *f*. **Tear bag**, sac lacrymal. **Poison bag**, glande *f*, vésicule *f*, à venin. (b) *F: Bags under the eyes*, poches sous les yeux. *Bags at the knees*, poches aux genoux (d'un pantalon). **3.** *Ven:* The bag, le tableau. *To secure a good bag*, faire bonne chasse. **4.** *pl. F:* Pantalon *m.*

bag², *v.* (bagged) **1.** *v.tr.* (a) *To bag (up) sth.*, mettre qch. en sac; ensacher (du minerai, etc.). (b) *Ven:* Abattre, tuer (du gibier). (c) *F:* Empocher; s'emparer de (qch.); mettre la main sur (qch.). (d) *P:* Voler, chiper. **2.** *v.i.* (Se) gonfler, s'enfler; (*of garment, etc.*) bouffer, avoir trop d'ampleur; (*of sail, etc.*) faire sac.

bagging, *s.* **1.** Mise *f* en sac. **2.** Toile *f* à sac.

bagatelle [baga'tel], *s.* **1.** Bagatelle *f.* **2.** Billard anglais; *A:* trou-madame *m.*

bagful ['bagful], *s.* Sac plein; plein sac; sachée *f.*

baggage ['bagedʒ], *s.* **1.** (a) *Mil:* Bagage *m.* (b) *F:* A saucy baggage, une jeune effrontée. **2.** *U.S:* = LUGGAGE.

baggy ['bagi], *a.* (Vêtement) trop ample, trop lâche, mal coupé; (pantalon) flottant, bouffant. *B. cheeks*, joues pendantes; bajoues *f.*

bagpipe(s) ['bagpaip(s)], *s.* Cornemuse *f.*

Bahama [bə'hɑːma]. *Pr.n. The Bahama Islands, F: the Bahamas*, les Lucayes *f.*

bail¹ [beil], *s. Jur:* (a) Cautionnement *m.* (b) (*Pers.*) Caution *f*, garant *m*, répondant *m.* (c) Somme fournie à titre de cautionnement. **To go bail for s.o.**, se porter, se rendre, garant de qn; fournir caution pour qn (pour sa libération provisoire). **To find bail**, fournir caution.

bail², *v.tr. To bail s.o. (out)*, se porter caution pour obtenir l'élargissement provisoire de qn.

bail³, *s.* **1.** (*Swinging*) bail (*in stable*), bat-flanc(s) *m inv.* **2.** *pl. Cr:* Barrettes *f*, bâtonnets *m* (qui couronnent le guichet).

bail⁴, *v.tr. To bail a boat (out)*, to bail (out) the water, écoper, vider, un canot; vider, écoper, l'eau d'une embarcation.

bailer ['beilər], *s.* Écope *f*; épuisette *f.*

bailey ['beili], *s. F: The Old Bailey* (= *the Central Criminal Court*), le tribunal principal de Londres en matière criminelle.

bailiff ['beilif], *s.* **1.** *Sheriff's bailiff*, agent *m* de poursuites; huissier *m*; porteur *m* de contraintes. **2.** Régisseur *m*, intendant *m* (d'un domaine). *S.a.* WATER-BAILIFF. **3.** *Hist:* Bailli *m.*

bairn [bɛərn], *s. Dial:* (*In Scot.*) Enfant *mf.*

bait¹ [beit], *s.* (a) *Fish:* Amorce *f*, appât *m*, achée *f.* (b) *F:* Appât; leurre *m.* **To take, nibble at, rise to, swallow, the bait**, mordre à l'hameçon, à l'appât; gober l'appât; *F:* gober le morceau.

bait². **1.** *v.tr.* Harceler (un animal). *To b. a bull with dogs*, lancer, faire combattre, des chiens contre un taureau. *F: To bait s.o.*, harceler, tourmenter, qn. **2.** *v.tr.* Faire manger (un cheval pendant une halte). (b) *v.i.* S'arrêter pour se rafraîchir; se restaurer. **3.** *v.tr* Amorcer, appâter, garnir (un hameçon, etc.). **baiting**, *s.* **1.** Harcelage *m*, harcèlement *m.* **2.** Amorçage *m*, amorcement *m* (d'un hameçon, d'un piège).

baize [beiz], *s.* (a) Serge *f*, reps *m*, grosse étoffe (d'ameublement). **Green baize**, tapis vert. **(Green-) baize door**, porte rembourrée, matelassée. (b) *Oil baize*, toile cirée.

bake [beik]. **1.** *v.tr.* (a) Cuire, faire cuire (qch.) (au four). *To b. bread*, cuire le pain. *Abs. Do you know how to b.?* savez-vous boulanger? *S.a.* HALF-BAKED. (b) Cuire (des briques).

F: Earth baked by the sun, soi durci, desséché, par le soleil. **2.** *v.i.* (*Of bread, etc.*) Cuire (au four). *F: We are baking in the heat,* nous brûlons par cette chaleur. **baking,** *s.* **1.** (*a*) Cuisson (du pain etc.). *Mil:* The baking section, la boulangerie. (*b*) Cuisson, cuite (des briques, de la porcelaine). **2.** (*Batch*) (*a*) Fournee (de pain). (*b*) Cuite (de briques, etc.). **'baking-powder,** *s. Cu:* Poudre *f* à lever; levure artificielle.

bakehouse ['beikhaus], *s.* Fournil *m*, boulangerie *f*.

bakelite ['beikəlait], *s.* Bakélite *f*.

baker ['beikər], *s.* Boulanger *m.* The baker's wife, la boulangère. Baker's man, garçon boulanger. Baker's shop, boulangerie *f. S.a.* DOZEN 2.

bakery ['beikəri], *s.* (*a*) Boulangerie *f.* (*b*) *Mil: etc:* Manutention *f.*

baksheesh ['bakʃi:ʃ], *s.* Bakhchich *m*; pot-de-vin *m.*

Balaclava [balə'klɑ:və]. *Pr.n. Geog:* Balaklava Balaclava helmet, passe-montagne *m.*

balance[1] ['baləns], **1.** Balance *f.* Roman balance, balance romaine. Spring balance, peson *m. Analytical, chemical, precision, b.,* balance de précision; (*if small*) trébuchet *m.* To turn the balance, faire pencher la balance. *F:* To be, hang, in the balance, être, rester, en balance. **2.** Équilibre *m*, aplomb *m.* To keep, lose, recover, one's balance, se tenir en équilibre; perdre l'équilibre; retrouver, reprendre, son équilibre. To throw s.o. off his balance, (i) faire perdre l'équilibre à qn; (ii) *F:* interloquer qn. Mind off its balance, esprit désaxé, déséquilibré. *Hist:* The balance of power, l'équilibre des puissances; la balance politique. **3.** *Com:* Fin (*a*) Solde *m*, reliquat *m* (d'un compte). Balance in hand, solde créditeur. Balance carried forward, report *m* à nouveau, solde à nouveau. Balance due, (i) solde débiteur; (ii) solde de compte. (*b*) Bilan *m.* To strike a balance, dresser, établir, le bilan. On balance . . ., à tout prendre. . . . *S.a.* CREDIT[1]4, DEBIT[1]. **'balance-beam,** *s.* Fléau *m.* verge *f*, de balance. **'balance-sheet,** *s. Com:* Bilan *m* (d'inventaire); tableau *m* par doit et avoir. **'balance-weight,** *s.* Contrepoids *m.* **'balance-wheel,** *s. Clockm: etc:* Balancier *m* (de montre); roue *f* de rencontre (d'une horloge).

balance[2]. **1.** *v.tr.* (*a*) Balancer, peser (les conséquences, etc.). (*b*) Mettre, maintenir, (un objet) en équilibre; équilibrer, stabiliser, compenser (des forces); faire contrepoids à (qch.). *To b. oneself on one foot,* s'équilibrer sur un seul pied. (*c*) *One thing balances another,* une chose balance, compense, l'autre. (*d*) *Com: Fin:* Balancer, solder (un compte). *Book-k:* To b. the books, régler les livres. To balance the budget, équilibrer le budget. **2.** *v.i.* (*a*) Se faire contrepoids. (*Of scales*) Se faire équilibre. (*Of accounts*) Se balancer, s'équilibrer, se solder. (*b*) Osciller, balancer. (*Of pers.*) Hésiter; balancer (entre deux partis). **balanced,** *a.* **1.** Équilibré, compensé. *F:* To have a well-, ill-balanced mind, avoir l'esprit bien, mal, équilibré. **2.** En nombre égal; de force ou de valeur égale. **balancing**[1], *a.* **1.** (*a*) (Mouvement) basculaire. (*b*) (Caractère) hésitant. **2.** (*a*) (*Of power*) Pondérateur, -trice. (*b*) (*Of spring, etc.*) Compensateur, -trice. **balancing**[2], *s.* **1.** Balancement *m*, hésitation *f* (entre deux choses). **2.** (*a*) Mise *f* en équilibre; équilibrage *m*; stabilisation *f.* (*b*) *B. of accounts,* règlement *m*, solde *m*, alignement *m*, des comptes. **3.** Ajustement *m* (de deux choses);

compensation *W.Tel:* **Balancing aerial,** antenne de compensation. **'balancing-pole,** *s.* Contrepoids *m* de danseur de corde).

balancer ['balənsər], *s.* **1.** Balancier *m.* **2.** *Ent:* Balancier, aileron *m* (des diptères).

balcony ['balkəni], *s.* **1.** Balcon *m.* **2.** *Th. Esp. U.S:* Fauteuils *mpl* stalles *fpl,* de deuxième galerie.

bald [bɔ:ld], *a.* **1.** Chauve. *B. patch,* région chauve; (*on head*) petite tonsure. *To be b. at the temples,* avoir les tempes dégarnies. **2.** (*Of style, etc.*) Décharné; plat; sec, *f.* sèche. **3.** (*Marked with white*) Bald horse, cheval belle-face. **-ly,** *adv.* Nûment, platement, sèchement. **'bald-head,** *s.* Tête *f* chauve; *F:* caillou déplumé. *F: An old b.-h.,* un vieux déplumé. **bald-headed,** *a.* (A la tête) chauve. *F:* To go at it bald-'headed, y aller tête baissée. **'bald-pate,** *s.* = BALD-HEAD.

baldachin ['baldəkin], *s.* Baldaquin *m.*

balderdash ['bɔ:ldərdaʃ], *s.* Bêtises *fpl,* balivernes *fpl,* fadaises *fpl.*

baldness ['bɔ:ldnəs], *s.* **1.** (*a*) Calvitie *f*, alopécie *f.* (*b*) Nudité (d'une montagne, etc.). **2.** Platitude *f,* pauvreté *f,* sécheresse *f* (du style, etc.).

baldric ['bɔldrik], *s. A:* Baudrier *m.*

bale[1] [beil], *s. A. & Poet:* **1.** Malheur *m.* The Day of Bale, le jugement dernier. **2.** Tourment *m. Souls in b.,* âmes en peine.

bale[2], *s. Com:* Balle *f*, ballot *m* (de marchandises).

bale[3], *v.tr.* Emballotter, paqueter, empaqueter.

baling, *s.* Mise *f* en balles; paquetage *m.*

bale[4], *v.i. Av:* To bale out, avoir recours au parachute.

Balearic [bali'arik], *a. Geog:* The Balearic islands, les îles Baléares.

baleful ['beilful], *a. Lit:* Sinistre, funeste. **-fully,** *adv.* Sinistrement.

balk[1] [bɔ:k], *s.* **1.** *Agr:* (*a*) Bande *f* de délimitation entre deux champs. (*b*) Billon *m.* **2.** (*a*) (i) Pierre *f* d'achoppement; obstacle *m*; contretemps *m*; (ii) déception *f.* (*b*) *Bill:* Espace *m* derrière la ligne de départ. **3.** *Const:* (Grosse) poutre, solive *f*, billon.

balk[2]. **1.** *v.tr.* Contrarier. (*a*) *To b. s.o.'s plans,* déjouer, contrecarrer, les desseins de qn. *To b. s.o. of his prey,* frustrer qn de sa proie. (*b*) *To* mettre en travers de (qn qui va sauter, etc.); entraver (qn). (*c*) Éviter (un sujet); se soustraire à (une obligation); laisser passer (une occasion). **2.** *v.i.* (*Of horse*) Refuser; se dérober. *F:* To balk at sth., s'arrêter, reculer, hésiter, devant qch.; regimber contre qch.

Balkan ['bɔ:lkən], *a. Geog:* The Balkan mountains, the Balkans, les (monts) Balkans *m.* The Balkan States, les États balkaniques. The Balkan Peninsula, la péninsule des Balkans.

ball[1] [bɔ:l], *s.* **1.** (*a*) Boule *f* (de croquet, de neige); balle *f* (de cricket, de tennis, de hockey, etc.); ballon *m* (d'enfant, de football); bille *f* (de billard); balle (de fusil); boulet *m* (de canon); pelote *f*, peloton *m* (de laine, de ficelle). *To wind wool into a b.,* (em)peloter, pelotonner, de la laine; mettre (de la laine) en pelote. The three (golden) balls, *P:* the three brass balls, les trois boules (enseigne du prêteur sur gages). *Meteor:* Ball of fire, ball lightning, globe *m* de feu; éclair *m* en boule. *S.a.* FIRE-BALL. *Sm.a:* To load with ball, charger à balle. *Ten: etc:* To knock the balls about, peloter; *Bill:* caramboler les billes. *F:* To keep the ball rolling, continuer, soutenir, la conversation; ne pas laisser languir la conversation, le jeu. To start the ball rolling,

to set the ball a-rolling, déclencher la conversation; mener le branle. **To have the ball at one's feet** avoir la balle belle, avoir la partie belle; n'avoir qu'à saisir l'occasion. (b) *Mec.E:* Bille (de roulement). *S.a.* RACE¹ 4. (c) **Ball-(and-socket) joint**, (i) *Anat:* emboîtement *m* réciproque; énarthrose *f*; (ii) *Mec.E:* joint *m* à rotule, à boulet, à genou; joint sphérique. **2.** (a) Lentille *f* (de pendule). (b) Éminence métatarsienne (du pied); éminence thénar (du pouce). **To walk on the b. of the foot**, marcher sur la demi-pointe des pieds. (c) Globe *m* (de l'œil). **3.** *Cu:* Meat-ball, boulette *f*. **4.** *U.S:* **Ball (game)** = BASEBALL. **'ball-bearing(s)**, *s.(pl.) Mec.E:* Roulement *m* à billes. **'ball-cartridge**, *s.* Cartouche *f* à balle. **'ball-cock**, *s.* Robinet *m*, soupape *f*, à flotteur. **'ball-shaped**, *a.* Sphérique. **'ball-valve**, *s.* **1.** Soupape *f* à boulet; clapet *m* sphérique. **2.** = BALL-COCK.

ball². **1.** *v.tr.* (a) Agglomérer. *Metall:* Baller (le fer). (b) *Tex:* Mettre (la laine) en pelote. **2.** *v.i.* S'agglomérer. (*of snow*) so botter.

ball³, *s. Danc:* Bal *m, pl.* bals. *S.a.* FANCY¹ II, MASK² I. **To open the ball,** (i) ouvrir le bal; mettre le bal en train; (ii) *F:* mettre les choses en branle; *F:* ouvrir le bal. **'ball-room**, *s.* Salle *f* de bal.

ballad ['baləd], *s.* **1.** *Mus:* Romance *f*. **2.** *Lit:* Récit en vers disposé par strophes régulières; ballade *f*. **'ballad-singer**, *s.* (a) Chanteur, -euse, de romances. (b) *A:* Chanteur, -euse, des rues.

ballade [ba'lɑ:d], *s. Lit:* Ballade *f*.

ballast¹ ['baləst], *s.* **1.** *Nau: Aer:* Lest *m*. **Ship in ballast(-trim)**, navire sur lest. **To take in b.**, faire son lest. **To discharge, throw out, b.**, se délester; jeter du lest. *F:* (Of pers.) **To have ballast**, avoir l'esprit rassis. **To lack ballast**, ne pas avoir de plomb dans la cervelle. **2.** (a) *Civ.E:* Pierraille *f*, cailloutage *m*. (b) *Rail:* Ballast *m*, empierrement *m*.

ballast², *v.tr.* **1.** *Nau: Aer:* Lester. **2.** *Civ.E:* (a) Empierrer, caillouter. (b) *Rail:* Ballaster.

ballerina [balə'ri:na], *s.f.* Ballerine.

ballet ['bale], *s.* **1.** Ballet *m*. **2.** Corps *m* de ballet. **'ballet-dancer**, *s.* Danseur, -euse, d'opéra; *f* ballerine. **'ballet-girl**, *s.f.* Figurante.

ballistics [ba'listiks], *s.pl.* Balistique *f*.

ballon(n)et ['balonet], *s. Aer:* **1.** Ballonnet compensateur. **2.** = GAS-BAG 2 (b).

balloon¹ [ba'lu:n], *s.* **1.** (a) *Aer:* Ballon *m*, aérostat *m*. **To go up in a b.**, monter en ballon. **The Balloon Service**, l'Aérostation *f*. **Balloon corps**, corps d'aérostiers militaires. *S.a.* DIRIGIBLE, KITE-BALLOON. (b) *Air-balloon*, toy-balloon, ballon à air. **2.** *Ch:* Balloon-(flask), ballon. **bal'loon-tyre**, *s.* Pneu *m* ballon.

balloon², *v.i.* Bouffer; se ballonner.

balloonist [ba'lu:nist], *s.* Aéronaute *m*, aérostier *m*.

ballot¹ ['balət], *s.* **1.** Ballot-(ball), boule *f* de scrutin. **2.** (a) Tour *m* de scrutin. **To vote by ballot**, voter au scrutin. (b) Scrutin *m*, vote *m*. **To take a ballot**, procéder à un vote, à un vote. **3.** *Parl:* Tirage *m* au sort (pour la priorité du droit de soumettre des résolutions, etc.). **'ballot-box**, *s.* Urne *f* de scrutin. **'ballot-paper**, *s.* Bulletin *m* de vote.

ballot², *v.i.* (a) Voter au scrutin (secret). **To b. against s.o.**, voter contre qn; *F:* blackbouler qn. (b) Tirer au sort. **To b. for a place**, tirer une place au sort. **balloting**, *s.* **1.** Élection *f* au scrutin. **2.** Tirage *m* au sort.

balm [bɑ:m], *s.* **1.** Baume *m*. *F: A b. to a wounded soul*, un baume pour une âme meurtrie. **2.** *Bot:* Mélisse officinale; citronnelle *f*.

balmy ['bɑ:mi], *a.* **1.** Balsamique. **2.** (a) (Air, temps) embaumé, parfumé; d'une douceur délicieuse. (b) *Lit:* Calmant, adoucissant. **3.** *P:* Toqué, loufoque.

balsam ['bɔlsəm], *s.* **1.** Baume *m*. **Copaiba balsam**, baume de Copahu. **Balsam of Peru**, baume du Pérou. **2.** *Bot:* Garden, yellow, balsam, balsamine *f*. **3.** Balsam fir, sapin baumier.

balsamic [bɔl'samik], *a.* Balsamique.

Baltic ['bɔ:ltik], *a. & s.* **1.** The Baltic (Sea), la (mer) Baltique. **2.** Baltic port, port balte.

baluster ['baləstər], *s.* **1.** Balustre *m*. **2.** *pl.* = BANISTERS.

balustrade [baləs'treid], *s.* (a) Balustrade *f*. (b) Accoudoir *m*, allège *f*, appui *m* (de fenêtre, etc.).

bamboo [bam'bu:], *s.* Bambou *m*.

bamboozle [bam'bu:zl], *v.tr. F:* Mystifier, enjôler, emboeliner (qn). **To b. s.o. out of sth.**, (i) frauder qn de qch.; (ii) soutirer qch. à qn.

ban¹ [ban], *s.* (a) (*Sentence of banishment, of outlawry*) Ban *m*, bannissement *m*, proscription *f*. (b) *Ecc:* Interdit *m*. **To place s.o. under the ban of public opinion**, mettre qn au ban de l'opinion.

ban², *v.tr.* (banned) Interdire (qn, qch.); mettre (un livre) à l'index. **To be banned by public opinion**, être au ban de l'opinion (publique).

banality [ba'naliti], *s.* Banalité *f*.

banana [ba'nɑ:na], *s.* Banane *f*. **Banana-tree**, bananier *m*.

band¹ [band], *s.* **1.** (a) Lien *m* (de fer); frette *f*; cercle *m* (d'un tonneau); bandage *m* (d'une roue); ruban *m* (d'un chapeau). *Bookb:* Nerf *m*, nervure *f*. *Narrow b.*, bandelette *f*. **Crape band** (round arm), brassard *m* de deuil. **Elastic b.**, anneau *m* en caoutchouc; *F:* élastique *m*. *S.a.* NECK-BAND, WAISTBAND. *Aut: etc:* **Brake band**, ruban de frein. *Mil:* **Cap-band**, bandeau *m*. *Nau:* (*In Merchant Service*) **Bands**, galons *mpl*. (b) Bande *f* (de gazon, de toile). **Paper band**, bande de papier; (*round cigar*) bague *f*. (c) *Opt:* **Bands of the spectrum**, bandes du spectre. (d) *W.Tel:* **Frequency band**, bande de fréquence. **2.** *Mec.E:* Bande, courroie *f* (de transmission). *Ind:* **Endless band** (*in mass production*), band-conveyor, tapis roulant; transporteur *m* à toile sans fin. **Moving-band production**, travail à la chaîne. **3.** *pl. Ecc.Cost: etc:* **Bands**, rabat *m*. **'band-brake**, *s.* Frein *m* à collier, à bande. **'band-clutch**, *s.* Embrayage *m* à ruban. **'band-pulley**, *s.* Poulie *f* à courroie. **'band-saw**, *s.* Scie *f* à ruban; scie sans fin.

band², *v.tr.* Bander (un ballot); fretter (un four, etc.); mettre (un journal) sous bande.

band³, *s.* **1.** (a) Bande *f*, troupe *f*. (b) Compagnie *f*; *Pej:* clique *f*. **2.** *Mus:* (a) Orchestre *m*. (b) *Mil: etc:* Musique *f*. **The regimental b.**, la musique du régiment. **Brass band**, fanfare *f*. **Brass and reed band**, harmonie *f*. *Mil:* **The drum and bugle band**, la batterie. **The members of the b.**, les musiciens.

band⁴, *v.i.* **To band (together)**, (i) se bander; se réunir en bande; (ii) s'ameuter.

bandage¹ ['bandedʒ], *s.* (a) *Esp. Med:* Bandage *m*, bande *f*; (*for blindfolding*) bandeau *m*. **Crêpe b.**, bande Velpeau. (b) *Surg:* Bande de pansement; pansement *m*. *Head swathed in bandages*, tête enveloppée de linges. **To remove a b. from a wound**, débander une plaie.

bandage², *v.tr.* Bander (un bras cassé); poser un appareil, mettre un pansement, sur (une plaie).

bandbox ['bandbɔks], s. Carton m à chapeau(x) ; carton de modiste. **To look as if one had just stepped out of a bandbox,** être tiré à quatre épingles.

banderol(e) ['bandərɔl], s. Banderole f.

bandit ['bandit], s. Bandit m, brigand m.

bandmaster ['bandmɑːstər], s. (a) Chef m d'orchestre. (b) Mil: etc: Chef de musique, de fanfare.

bandoleer, bandolier [bando'liːər], s. 1. Bandoulière f. 2. Cartouchière (portée en écharpe).

bandsman, pl. **-men** ['bandzmən, -men], s.m. Musicien (d'un orchestre, d'une fanfare).

bandstand ['bandstand], s. Kiosque m à musique.

bandy[1] ['bandi], v.tr. (Se) renvoyer (une balle, des paroles) ; échanger (des plaisanteries, des coups). **To bandy words,** se chamailler.

bandy[2], a. 1. **Bandy legs,** jambes arquées, bancales. 2. (Of pers.) = BANDY-LEGGED. **'bandy-legged,** a. (Of pers.) Bancal, -als.

bane [bein], s. 1. Fléau m, peste f. 2. A : Poison m.

baneful ['beinful], a. Funeste, fatal, -als ; pernicieux. **-fully,** adv. Pernicieusement.

bang[1] [baŋ], s. Coup (violent) ; détonation f ; fracas m ; claquement m (de porte). (Of firework, etc.) **To go off with a b.,** détoner.

bang[2]. 1. v.i. (a) **To b. at, on, the door,** frapper à la porte avec bruit ; heurter à la porte. **To b. on the table with one's fist,** frapper à la table du poing. (b) (Of door) **To bang,** claquer, battre. 2. v.tr. (a) Frapper (violemment). I banged his head on a stone, je lui ai cogné la tête sur une pierre. (b) **To bang the door,** (faire) claquer la porte, fermer la porte avec fracas, frapper la porte. **To bang down the lid,** abattre violemment le couvercle. **banging,** s. (a) Coups violents ; claquement m. (b) Détonations fpl.

bang[3]. 1. int. Pan ! v'lan ! boum ! F: **Bang went saxpence !** j'ai dépensé six pence d'un seul coup ! 2. adv. F: **To go bang,** éclater. **Bang off,** sur-le-champ.

bang[4], s. Coiffure f à la chien.

bangle [baŋgl], s. Bracelet m. **Slave-bangle,** bracelet esclave.

banian ['banjən], s. 1. (a) (Trader) Banian m. (b) Robe f de chambre (portée aux Indes). 2. Bot: Banian(-tree), arbre m des banians ; banian ; figuier m de l'Inde.

banish ['baniʃ], v.tr. 1. Bannir, exiler ; proscrire (qn). 2. **To b. fear, care,** bannir, chasser, la crainte, les soucis.

banishment ['baniʃmənt], s. Bannissement m, proscription f, exil m.

banister ['banistər], s. (Usu. in pl.) 1. Balustres m (d'escalier). 2. Rampe f (d'escalier).

banjo, pl. **-os, -oes** ['bandʒou(z)], s. 1. Mus: Banjo m. 2. Aut: Carter m du différentiel.

bank[1] [baŋk], s. 1. (a) Talus m ; terrasse f. Civ.E: Banquette f, remblai m. Rail: Rampe f. B. of flowers, tertre m de fleurs. (b) (In river, sea) Banc m (de sable, de roches). S.a. ICE-BANK, SAND-BANK. Geog: **The Banks of Newfoundland,** le Banc de Terre-Neuve. (c) Digue f. 2. (a) (Steep side) Berge f (d'une rivière, etc.). (b) (Side) Bord m, rive f (d'une rivière, d'un lac). 3. Av : Virage incliné.

bank[2]. 1. v.tr. (a) **To b. a river,** endiguer une rivière. (b) **To bank up,** remblayer, terrasser, amonceler (de la terre, de la neige). Civ.E: **To bank a road** (at a corner), surhausser, relever, un virage. Banked edge (of road, etc.), berge f. (c) Mch: **To bank (up) fires,** couvrir, coucher, les feux. 2. v.i. (Of snow, clouds, etc.) S'entasser,

s'accumuler, s'amonceler. 3. v.i. Av : Pencher l'avion ; vire.' (sur l'aile). **banking**[1], s. 1. (a) Remblayage m ; surhaussement m (d'un virage). (b) Banking up of a river, haussement m du niveau d'une rivière. 2. Remblai m. 3. Av : Virage incliné.

bank[3], s. 1. (a) Banque f. **The Bank of England,** la Banque d'Angleterre. **Bank account,** compte en banque. **Bank clerk,** commis, employé, de banque. (b) Bureau m de banque. **Branch bank,** succursale f. 2. Gaming : Banque (de celui qui tient le jeu). **To break the bank,** faire sauter la banque. **'bank-bill,** s. Effet (tiré par une banque sur une autre). **'bank-book,** s. Livret m de banque. **bank-'holiday,** s. (Jour m de) fête légale (où les banques n'ouvrent pas). **bank-'messenger,** s. Garçon m de recette. **'bank-note,** s. Billet m de banque.

bank[4], v.tr. & i. 1. Mettre, déposer, (de l'argent) en banque. 2. Gaming : Tenir la banque. 3. F: **To bank on sth.,** compter sur qch. ; caver, miser, sur (un événement). **banking**[2], s. 1. (Affaires fpl, opérations fpl, de) banque f. **Banking house,** maison de banque. **Banking account,** compte en banque. 2. Profession f de banquier ; la banque.

bank[5], s. 1. Nau: A: (a) Banc m (de rameurs). (b) Rang m (de rames, d'avirons). 2. Mus: Clavier m (d'un orgue). Organ with three banks, orgue à trois claviers. 3. Ind: Groupe f, batterie f (de chaudières, de cornues, de lampes électriques, etc.).

banker[1] ['baŋkər], s. 1. Banquier m. 2. Gaming : Banquier, tailleur m.

banker[2], s. Banquier m, banquais m (qui pêche la morue) ; morutier m ; terre-neuvien m.

bankrupt[1] ['baŋkrʌpt], a. & s. 1. (a) (Commerçant) failli (m). **To go bankrupt,** (i) faire faillite ; (ii) (of business) F: sauter. **To be b.,** être en faillite. S.a. UNDISCHARGED 1. (b) Fraudulent or negligent b., banqueroutier m. (c) F: **B. of intelligence,** dépourvu d'intelligence. B. of honour, perdu d'honneur. 2. F: (Homme) criblé de dettes, sans ressources.

bankrupt[2], v.tr. Mettre (qn) en faillite.

bankruptcy ['baŋkrʌptsi], s. 1. (a) Faillite f. (b) Fraudulent bankruptcy, banqueroute f. 2. F: Ruine f.

banner ['banər], s. (a) Bannière f, étendard m. (b) Ecc : Bannière.

bannock ['banək], s. (In Scot.) Pain plat et rond cuit sans levain.

banns [banz], s.pl. Bans m (de mariage). **To put up, publish, the banns,** (faire) publier les bans. **To forbid the banns,** faire, mettre, opposition à un mariage.

banquet[1] ['baŋkwet], s. Banquet m ; dîner m de gala, d'apparat. Wedding b., repas m de noces.

banquet[2]. 1. v.tr. Offrir un banquet, un dîner de gala, à (qn). 2. v.i. F: Banqueter ; faire festin.

banqueter ['baŋkwetər], s. Banqueteur m.

banshee ['banʃiː], s. (In Ireland and Scot.) Fée f (dont les cris présagent la mort).

bantam ['bantəm], s. 1. Coq m, poule f, (de) Bantam ; coq nain. 2. Mil: F: **Bantams,** (bataillon composé d')hommes au-dessous de la taille réglementaire. **'bantam-weight,** s. Box: Poids m bantam ; poids coq.

banter[1] ['bantər], s. (a) Badinage m. (b) Ironie f, raillerie f ; persiflage m.

banter[2], v.tr. & i. (a) Badiner. (b) Gouailler, railler ; (ill-naturedly) persifler. **bantering,** a. Railleur, -euse ; goguenard.

Bantu ['ban'tu], *a. & s. Ethn:* Bantou, -oue.
baptism ['baptizm], *s.* Baptême *m.* **To receive baptism,** recevoir le baptême. **Certificate of baptism,** extrait de baptême ; extrait baptistaire.
baptismal [bap'tizm(ə)l], *a.* (Registre) baptistaire ; (nom) de baptême.
baptist ['baptist], *s.* **1.** John the Baptist, saint Jean-Baptiste. **2.** *Ecc:* Anabaptiste *mf.*
baptist(e)ry ['baptist(ə)ri], *s.* Baptistère *m.*
baptize [bap'ta:iz], *v.tr.* **1.** Baptiser. **To be baptized,** recevoir le baptême. **2.** Baptiser, bénir (une cloche, un navire).
bar¹ [ba:r], *s.* **1.** (a) Barre *f* (de fer, de bois, de chocolat) ; barre, brique *f* (de savon) ; lingot *m* (d'or). *Bar of a medal,* barrette *f* d'une médaille. *Bar of a door,* bâcle *f* d'une porte ; barre de porte. *Gym:* **Parallel bars,** barres parallèles. **Horizontal bar,** barre fixe. (b) *pl.* Barreaux *m* (d'une fenêtre, d'une grille, d'une cage). *The bars of the grate,* la grille du foyer. *To be behind prison bars,* être sous les grilles (d'une prison) ; être sous les verrous. (c) *pl.* Barrettes (de souliers de dames). (d) *pl.* Barres (de la bouche d'un cheval). (e) *(In river, harbour)* I ar-e (de sable) ; traverse *f. To cross the bar,* passer, franchir, la barre. *S.a.* SAND-BAR. **2.** (a) Empêchement *m,* obstacle *m. To be a bar to sth.,* être un empêchement, faire obstacle, à qch. (b) *Jur:* Exception *f* ; fin *f* de non-recevoir. *S.a.* PLEA I. **3.** *Jur:* (a) Barre (des accusés). **The prisoner at the bar,** l'accusé. **To appear at the bar,** paraître à la barre. (b) Barreau (des avocats). **To be called, to come, go, to the bar,** être reçu, se faire inscrire, au barreau ; être reçu avocat. **4.** (a) Bar *m* ; (in N. of Fr.) estaminet *m. Rail: Th:* Buvette *f. S.a.* QUICK-LUNCH. (b) *(In public house)* Comptoir *m,* bar. **5.** (a) Barre *f,* ligne *f,* trait *m.* (b) *Mus:* **Bar(-line),** barre. **Double bar,** double barre ; division *f.* (c) *Mus:* Mesure *f.* 'bar-iron, *s. Com:* Fer *m* en barres ; fer carillon.
bar², *v.tr.* (barred) **1.** Barrer (une porte) ; griller (une fenêtre). **To bar oneself in,** se barricader. **2.** (a) *(Obstruct)* Barrer (un chemin). **To bar s.o.'s way,** barrer la route à qn. (b) = DEBAR. **3.** (a) Défendre, prohiber, interdire (une action) ; exclure (un sujet de conversation). (b) *F:* Ne pas supporter, ne pas approuver (une personne, une habitude). (c) *Jur:* Opposer une fin de non-recevoir à (une action). **4.** Rayer (de lignes) ; barrer. **barred,** *a.* **1.** (a) Barré ; muni d'une grille, de barreaux. *B. window,* fenêtre grillée. (b) *Mus:* **Barred C,** C barré. **2.** (Drap, etc.) rayé. **3.** (Port) obstrué par une barre de sable.
bar³, barring, *prep. F:* Excepté, sauf ; à l'exception de. **Barring accidents,** sauf accident, à moins d'accident(s). **Bar none,** sans exception.
bar⁴, *s. Ich:* Maigre *m.*
barb¹ [ba:rb], *s.* **1.** (a) Barbillon *m* (d'un hameçon) ; barbelure *f* (d'une flèche). (b) *Engr: Metalw:* Barbe *f,* bavure *f* (de métal). **2.** *pl.* (a) *Ich: Vet:* Barbillons. *Bot:* Arêtes *f.* (b) Barbes (d'une plume).
barb², *v.tr.* Garnir de barbelures, de barbillons.
barbed, *a.* **1.** *Bot:* Aristé ; hameçonné. **2.** Barbelé. **Barbed wire,** fil de fer barbelé. *Mil:* **Barbed-wire entanglements,** les barbelés *m.*
barb³, *s.* Cheval *m* barbe ; barbe *m.*
Barbado(e)s [ba:r'beidouz], *Pr.n.* La Barbade.
Barbaresque [ba:rba'resk], *a.* Barbaresque.
barbarian [ba:r'beəriən], *a. & s.* Barbare (*mf*).
barbaric [ba:r'barik], *a.* Barbare.
barbarism ['ba:rbərizm], *s.* **1.** *Gram: Ling:* Barbarisme *m.* **2.** Barbarie *f.*
barbarity [ba:r'bariti], *s.* Barbarie *f,* cruauté *f.*

barbarous ['ba:rbərəs], *a.* **1.** Barbare. **2.** Cruel, barbare, inhumain. **-ly,** *adv.* Cruellement.
Barbary ['ba:rbəri]. *Pr.n. Geog:* La Barbarie ; les États *m* barbaresques.
barbecue ['ba:rbikju:], *s. U.S:* Grande fête en plein air (où l'on rôtit des animaux tout entiers).
barbel ['ba:rbəl], *s. Ich:* Barbeau *m.* **2.** *pl.* Barbillons *m,* palpes *f,* barbes *f* (d'un poisson).
barber ['ba:rbər], *s.* Barbier *m,* coiffeur *m.* **Barber's pole,** enseigne de barbier.
barberry ['ba:rberi], *s. Bot:* Épine-vinette *f.*
barbican ['ba:rbikən], *s. Archeol:* Barbacane *f.*
barcarol(l)e ['ba:rkaroul], *s. Mus:* Barcarolle *f.*
bard¹ [ba:rd], *s.* **1.** (a) *(Celtic, esp. of Wales)* Barde *m.* (b) *(Of ancient Greece)* Aède *m.* **2.** *F:* Poète *m.*
bard², *s.* **1.** *Archeol:* Barde *f* (de cheval d'armes). **2.** *Cu:* Barde (de lard).
bare¹ ['beər], *a.* **1.** Nu ; dénudé. *B. legs,* jambes nues. *F:* **Bare as the back of my hand,** nu comme la main. *B. country-side,* pays nu, dénudé, pelé. *The trees are already b.,* les arbres sont déjà dépouillés. *B. cupboard,* cupboard b. of food, placard vide ; buffet dégarni. **To lie, sleep, on the bare ground, on the bare boards,** coucher sur la dure. **To lay bare,** mettre à nu, exposer (une surface, son cœur) ; dévoiler (un secret, une fraude). *B. chest,* poitrine découverte. *El:* **Bare wire,** fil dénudé. *Nau:* **To run, scud, under bare poles,** filer, courir, fuir, à sec (de toiles). *Cards:* **Ace bare, king bare,** as sec, roi sec. **2. To earn a bare living,** gagner tout juste, à peine, de quoi vivre ; gagner sa vie et rien de plus. *S.a.* NECESSARY 2. *B. majority,* faible majorité. *The b. thought frightens me,* cette seule pensée m'effraie. *A b. thank you,* un merci tout sec. **-ly,** *adv.* **1. Room b. furnished,** (i) pièce dont le mobilier se réduit à l'essentiel ; (ii) pièce pauvrement meublée. **2.** A peine, tout juste. *I b. know him,* c'est à peine si je le connais. *He is b. thirty,* c'est tout juste s'il a trente ans. 'bare-backed, *a.* A dos nu, le dos nu. *B.-b. horse,* cheval nu, à poil. **2.** *adv.* = BAREBACK. 'bareheaded, *a. & adv.* Nu-tête, (la) tête nue ; découvert. 'bare-legged, *a. & adv.* Nu-jambes ; (les) jambes nues ; aux jambes nues.
bare², *v.tr.* Mettre (qch.) à nu ; découvrir (une plaie, etc.) ; se découvrir (la tête) ; déchausser (une dent, des racines, etc.).
bare³. See BEAR².
bareback ['beərbak], *adv.* **To ride bareback,** monter (un cheval) à nu, à cru, à poil.
barefaced ['beərfeist], *a.* **1.** A visage imberbe. **2.** (a) Sans masque. (b) *F:* (Mensonge, etc.) éhonté, cynique.
barefacedly ['beər'feisidli], *adv.* Effrontément.
barefoot ['beərfut]. **1.** *adv.* Nu-pieds ; (à) pieds nus. **2.** *a.* = BAREFOOTED.
barefooted ['beər'futid], *a.* Aux pieds nus ; à pieds nus. *Ecc:* **Barefooted Carmelites,** carmes déchaussés.
bareness ['beərnəs], *s.* **1.** Nudité *f,* dénuement *m.* **2.** Pauvreté *f,* sécheresse *f* (de style).
bargain¹ ['ba:rgən], *s.* **1.** Marché *m,* affaire *f.* **To make a good bargain,** faire une bonne affaire, un bon marché. **To get the best of the bargain,** avoir l'avantage dans un marché. **To strike, drive, a bargain with s.o.,** conclure un marché avec qn. *S.a.* BEST¹ 1. *A real b.,* une véritable occasion. **Into the bargain,** par-dessus le marché ; par surcroît ; en plus. **It's a bargain!** c'est entendu ! c'est convenu ! **2.** (a) **Bargain sale,** vente de soldes. *B. prices,* prix de solde. (b) *(Of article) To be a b.,* être en vente emplette.

'bargain-counter, s. *Com:* Rayon m des soldes.
bargain², v.i. (a) Entrer en négociations, négocier (with s.o., avec qn). To b. with s.o. for sth., traiter, faire marché, de qch. avec qn. F: I didn't bargain for that, je ne m'attendais pas à cela. F: He got more than he bargained for, il a eu du fil à retordre. (b) (Haggle) To b. with s.o., marchander qn. To b. over an article, marchander un article.
barge¹ [bɑːrdʒ], s. (a) Chaland m, péniche f. Canal barge, balandre f. Motor barge, chaland à moteur. (b) (With sails) Gabare f. (c) Bateau-maison m, pl. bateaux-maisons (appartenant à un club de l'aviron). (d) Navy: Deuxième canot m. Admiral's barge, canot de l'amiral. (e) State barge, barque f de cérémonie. **'barge-pole,** s. Gaffe f. F: I wouldn't touch it with a barge-pole, je n'en veux à aucun prix. I wouldn't touch him with a b.-p., il me dégoûte.
barge², v.i. F: To barge into, against, s.o., veni˙ se heurter contre qn; bousculer qn. To barge in, intervenir mal à propos.
bargee [bɑːrˈdʒiː], s. (a) Chalandier m. (b) Gabarier m. (c) F: Batelier m, marinier m.
bargemaster [ˈbɑːrdʒmɑːstər], s. Patron m de chaland ou de gabare.
barium [ˈbɛəriəm], s. Ch: Baryum m.
bark¹ [bɑːrk], s. I. Écorce f (d'arbre). Inner bark, liber m. To strip the b. off a tree, écorcer un arbre. Peruvian bark, quinquina m. 2. Tanner's bark, tan m.
bark², v.tr. (a) Écorcer, décortiquer (un arbre). (b) F: To bark one's shins, s'érafler les tibias.
bark³, s. (a) Aboiement m, aboi m. To give a bark, pousser un aboiement. F: His bark is worse than his bite, il aboie plus qu'il ne mord; il fait plus de bruit que de̱ mal. (b) (Of fox) Glapissement m.
bark⁴, v.i. I. (a) Aboyer (at, après, contre). To bark up the wrong tree, suivre une fausse piste; accuser qn à tort. (b) (Of fox) Glapir. 2. Dire (qch.) d'un ton sec, cassant. 3. F: Tousser.
barking¹, a. (Chien) aboyeur. B: criticism, critique aboyeuse. **barking²,** s. (a) Aboiement m. (b) (Of fox) Glapissement m.
bark⁵, s. I. Nau: Trois-mâts barque m. 2. Poet: Barque f.
barker [ˈbɑːrkər], s. I. Aboyeur, -euse. 2. P: Pistolet m ou revolver m.
barley [ˈbɑːrli], s. Orge f; but m. in: hulled barley, orge mondé, and pearl barley, orge perlé. **'barley-sugar,** s. Sucre m d'orge. **'barley-water,** s. Tisane f d'orge.
barleycorn [ˈbɑːrlikɔːrn], s. Grain m d'orge. F: John Barleycorn, le whisky.
barm [bɑːrm], s. Levure f (de bière).
barmaid [ˈbɑːrmeid], s.f. Demoiselle de comptoir, fille de comptoir (d'un débit de boisson).
barman, -men [ˈbɑːrmən, -men], s.m. Garçon de comptoir (d'un débit de boisson); serveur.
barn [bɑːrn], s. I. Grange f. (b) U.S: Étable f ou écurie f. **barn-'door,** s. Porte f de grange. **'Barn-door fowls,** volaille de basse-cour. **barn-'floor,** s. Aire f (de grange). **'barn-owl,** s. Orn: Effraie f. **'barn-stormer,** s. F: Cabotin m. **'barn-yard,** s. Basse-cour f.
barnacle¹ [ˈbɑːrnəkl], s. I. Orn: Barnacle (goose), bernacle f, bernache f; oie marine. 2. (a) Crust: Stalked or ship barnacle, bernache, bernacle; anatif(e) m. (b) F: Individu cramponnant.
barograph [ˈbɑːrograf], s. Baro(métro)graphe m.

barometer [baˈrɔmetər], s. Baromètre m. Recording b., baromètre enregistreur. The b. points to rain, to set fair, le baromètre est à la pluie, au beau fixe. S.a. ANEROID
barometric(al) [baroˈmetrik(əl)], a. Barométrique.
baron [ˈbarən], s. I. (a) Baron m. (b) U.S: F: Grand manitou (industriel). 2. Baron of beef, double aloyau m; selle f de bœuf.
baronage [ˈbarənedʒ], s. I. Baronnage m. 2. Annuaire m de la noblesse.
baroness [ˈbarənes], s.f. Baronne.
baronet [ˈbarənet], s.m. Baronnet.
baronetage [ˈbarəɪnetedʒ],s. I. Les baronnets m. 2. Annuaire m des baronnets.
baronetcy [ˈbarənetsi], s. Dignité f de baronnet. To be given a b., être élevé au rang de baronnet.
baronial [baˈrounjəl], a. Baronnial. F: B. hall, demeure seigneuriale.
barrack(s)¹ [ˈbarək(s)], s. I. (a) Mil: (Usu. in pl.) Caserne f; (of cavalry) quartier m. To live in barracks, (i) (of officers) loger, vivre, à la caserne au quartier; (ii) (of soldiers) être casernés. Life in barracks, la vie de caserne. Confinement to barracks, F: C.B., consigne au quartier. To be confined to barracks, être consigné. (b) Naval barracks, dépôt m des équipages de la flotte. 2. Pej: F: Grand bâtiment qui ressemble à une caserne; F: caserne. **barrack room,** s. Chambrée f. **Barrack-room language,** expressions de caserne, de chambrée. **barrack 'square,** s. Cour f du quartier.
barrack², v.tr. P: Conspuer, huer (une équipe de joueurs). Abs. Faire du chahut; chahuter.
barrage [ˈbaredʒ], s. I. Hyd.E: Barrage m (d'un fleuve). 2. Mil: (also [baˈrɑːʒ]) Tir m de barrage; tir sur zone.
barratry [ˈbarətri], s. Nau: Baraterie f.
barrel¹ [ˈbarəl], s. I. (a) Tonneau m, barrique f, futaille f, fût m (de vin, etc.); caque f, baril m (de harengs). (b) Biscuit barrel, seau m à biscuits. 2. (a) Cylindre m; partie f cylindrique, fût, caisse f (d'un tambour); tuyau m (de plume d'oiseau); canon m ((i) de fusil, (ii) de seringue, (iii) de serrure, de clef); corps m, barillet m (de pompe); cylindre, barillet (de serrure); fusée f, mèche f, tambour m, cloche f (de cabestan, de treuil). Clockm: Barillet, boîte à ressort (de montre). Mus: Cylindre noté (d'un orgue mécanique). S.a. LOCK² 3. (b) Anat: Barrel of the ear, caisse du tympan. **barrel-'head,** s. Fond m de tonneau. **'barrel-organ,** s. Mus: (a) Orgue m mécanique. (b) (Of street-player) (i) Orgue de Barbarie; (ii) piano m mécanique (à cylindre). **'barrel-roof,** s. Toit cintré. **'barrel-stand,** s. Porte-fût(s) m inv; chantier m. **'barrel-vault,** s. (Voûte f en) tonnelle f.
barrel², v.tr. (barrelled) Mettre (qch.) en fût; entonner, enfutailler (du vin); (en)caquer, embariller (des harengs).
barren [ˈbarən], a. I. a. (a) Stérile, improductif; (terrain) aride. (b) B: subject, sujet maigre, ingrat, aride. Life b. of good works, vie stérile en bonnes œuvres. Mind b. of ideas, esprit peu fertile en idées. 2. s. Lande f; pays nus. **-ly,** adv. Stérilement; sans résultats.
barrenness [ˈbarənnes], s. Stérilité f.
barricade¹ [bariˈkeid], s. Barricade f.
barricade², v.tr. Barricader.
barrier [ˈbariər], s. Barrière f. Rail: Ticket barrier, portillon m d'accès. B. to progress, obstacle m au progrès. The Great Barrier Reef, la Grande Barrière f.
barrister [ˈbaristər], s. Jur: Barrister-at-law,

avocat m. Consulting b., avocat consultant, avocat conseil.
barrow¹ ['baro], s. **1.** (Wheel-)barrow, brouette f. **2.** = HAND-BARROW. **3.** (a) (With two wheels) Hawker's b., baladeuse f; voiture f à bras. (b) Rail: Luggage-barrow, diable m.
barrow², s. Archeol: Tumulus m; tertre m (funéraire); tombeau m.
barrowful ['barəful], s. Brouettée f.
barter¹ ['bɑːtər], s. Échange m; troc m.
barter², v.tr. To b. sth. for sth., échanger, troquer, qch. contre qch. **barter away**, v.tr. Pej: Vendre, faire trafic de (son honneur, etc.).
barterer ['bɑːtərər], s. Troqueur, -euse.
Bartholomew [bɑːr'θɔlɔmjuː]. Pr.n.m. Barthélemy. Hist: The Massacre of St Bartholomew, le Massacre de la Saint-Barthélemy.
barytes [bə'raitiːz], s. Miner: Barytine f.
barytone ['baritoun]. Mus: (a) s. Baryton m. (b) a. Barytone voice, voix de baryton.
basal ['beisəl], a. Fondamental, -aux. Cryst: (Clivage) basique.
basalt [ba'sɔːlt, 'basɔːlt], s. Basalte m.
base¹ [beis], s. **1.** (a) Base f (de triangle, etc.). Aviation base, base d'aviation. S.a. NAVAL, PRISONER 3. (b) Mth: Base (loga.ˈthmique, d'un système de numération). (c) Ch: Base (d'un sel). **2.** (a) Partie inférieure; fondement m; base; Arch: Const: soubassement m; (of apparatus) socle m, pied m, embase f. El: Insulating base, socle isolant. Phot: Cin: B. of the film, support m du film, de l'émulsion. (b) Her: Pied (de l'écu). **3.** (Metal) base (of sporting cartridge, electric lamp), culot m. S.a. WHEEL-BASE. **'base-ball,** s. U.S: Sp: Base-ball m. **'base-line,** s. **1.** (a) Surv: Base f. (b) Mch: Ligne f zéro (du diagramme). (c) Ten: Ligne de fond. **2.** Art: Ligne de fuite.
base², v.tr. Baser, fonder (on, sur). To b. oneself on sth., se fonder, se baser, sur qch.
base³, a. (a) Bas, vil. B. motive, motif bas, indigne. B. action, action ignoble, lâche. (b) (Of little value) Base metals, métaux vils. (c) Base coin(age), (i) monnaie de mauvais aloi; (ii) fausse monnaie. **-ly,** adv. Bassement, vilement. **'base-born,** a. De basse extraction, de basse naissance.
Basel ['bɑːz(ə)l]. Pr.n. Geog: Bâle.
baseless ['beisləs], a. Sans base, sans fondement; (critique) qui manque de fondement.
basement ['beismənt], s. **1.** Soubassement m (d'une construction); allège f (d'une fenêtre). **2.** Sous-sol m. Basement flat, sous-sol.
baseness ['beisnəs], s. Bassesse f. B. of birth, (i) bassesse de naissance; (ii) illégitimité f.
bash¹ [baʃ], s. F: (a) Coup m, enfoncement m. The tea-pot has had a b., la théière est bosselée. (b) Esp. Scot.) Coup (sur la figure); coup de poing violent.
bash², v.tr. F: To bash one's head, se cogner la tête. To bash (in) a hat, aplatir, cabosser, un chapeau (d'un coup de poing). To b. in a box, défoncer une boîte. To bash s.o. about, houspiller, maltraiter, qn. He bashed him on the head, il l'assomma.
basher ['baʃər], s. F: Cogneur m, pugiliste m.
bashful ['baʃful], a. (a) Timide. B. lover, amoureux transi. (b) Modeste, pudique. **-fully,** adv. (a) Timidement. (b) Pudiquement.
bashfulness ['baʃfulnəs], s. Timidité f; fausse honte.
basic ['beisik], a. **1.** (Principe, etc.) fondamental. Ling: Basic vocabulary, vocabulaire de base. **2.** (a) Ch: Geol: Basique. Basic slag, scorie

basique. (b) Ch: Sous-. Basic salt, sous-sel m. B. nitrate, sous-nitrate m. **-ally,** adv. Fondamentalement; à la base.
basil¹ ['bazil], s. Bot: Basilic m.
basil², s. Leath: Basane f.
basilica [ba'silika], s. Basilique f.
basilisk ['bazilisk], s. Myth: Rept: Basilic m.
basin ['beis(i)n], s. **1.** (a) Bassin m; (for soup, etc.) écuelle f, bol m; (for milk) jatte f. B. of a fountain, vasque f, coupe f, d'une fontaine. S.a. SUGAR-BASIN. (b) (Wash-hand-)basin, (i) cuvette f; (ii) (lavatory-basin) lavabo m. **2.** Geog: Bassin (d'un fleuve). **3.** (a) Geog: Port naturel; rade fermée. (b) Nau: Bassin. (c) (In canal, river) Garage m.
basinful ['beis(i)nful], s. **1.** Plein bol, écuellée f (de soupe, etc.). **2.** Pleine cuvette (d'eau).
basis ['beisis], pl. **bases** [-iːz], s. Base f (de négociations, etc.); fondement m (d'une opinion, etc.). B. of a tax, assiette f d'un impôt.
bask [bɑːsk], v.i. To b. in the sun, se chauffer (au soleil); prendre le soleil.
basket ['bɑːsket], s. **1.** (Without a handle) Corbeille f; (with a handle) panier m; (carried in front) éventaire m; (carried on the back) hotte f; (for coal, etc.) banne f, manne f; (small) banneau m, bannette f. Laundry basket, corbeille à linge. Linen-basket, panier à linge. S.a. WORK-BASKET. Basket handle, anse de panier. Arch: Basket-handle arch, arc en anse de panier. **2.** Ent: Pollen basket (of bee), corbeille. **'basket-hilt,** s. (Of sword) (Garde f en) coquille f; pas-d'âne m **'basket-maker,** s. Vannier m. **'basket-work,** s. Vannerie f.
basketful ['bɑːsketful], s. Plein panier; panerée f.
Basle [bɑːl]. Pr.n. Geog: Bâle.
Basque [bask], a. & s. Ethn: etc: Basque (mf).
bas-relief ['bɑːriliːf], s. Bas-relief m.
bass¹ [bas], s. Ich: **1.** Perche commune. **2.** Bar(s) m.
bass² [bas], s. **1.** (a) Bot: Liber m. (b) Tille f, filasse f. **2.** (a) Bass(-mat), paillasson m en fibre, en tille, etc. (b) (Basket) (Workman's) bass, cabas m. **'bass-wood,** s. Bot: Com: Tilleul m d'Amérique.
bass³ [beis], a. & s. Mus: Basse f. **1.** (a) Bass voice, voix de basse. Deep bass, basse profonde. S.a. CLEF. (b) (In brass bands) E-flat bass, B-flat bass, contrebasse f en mi bémol, en si bémol. S.a. DOUBLE-BASS, DRUM¹ **1.** **2.** Figured bass, basse chiffrée.
basset ['baset], s. (Chien) basset m.
bassinet(te) [basi'net], s. **1.** Berceau m; bercelonnette f ou moïse m. **2.** Voiture f d'enfant.
bassoon [ba'suːn], s. Basson m. Double bassoon, contrebasson m.
bast [bast], s. = BASS² **1.**
bastard ['bastərd], a. & s. **1.** Bâtard m. Jur: Enfant naturel. **2.** Faux, f. fausse; bâtard. (Of paper, book, etc.) Bastard size, format bâtard. Bookb: Bastard leather backing, reliure à dos brisé.
bastardy ['bastərdi], s. Bâtardise f. Jur: Bastardy case, action en désaveu de paternité.
baste¹ [beist], v.tr. Needlew: Bâtir, faufiler, baguer (un corsage, etc.). **basting¹,** s. Bâti m, faufilure f.
baste², v.tr. **1.** Cu: Arroser (de sa graisse) (un rôti, une volaille). **2.** F: Bâtonner (qn). **basting²,** s. **1.** Arrosement m, arrosage m (d'un rôti). **2.** F: Bastonnade f; rossée f.
bastinado¹ [basti'neido], s. Bastonnade f.
bastinado², v.tr. Donner la bastonnade à (qn).
bastion ['bastiən], s. Fort: Bastion m.

bat¹ [bat], s. Z: Chauve-souris f, pl. chauves-souris. S.a. BLIND¹ 1. F: To have bats in the belfry, avoir une araignée au plafond ; être toqué.
bat², s. 1. Batte f (de cricket, de base-ball). Cr: To carry (out) one's bat, rester au guichet jusqu'à la fin de la partie. F: To do sth. off one's own bat, faire qch. de sa propre initiative, de son (propre) chef. 2. Palette f, raquette f (de ping-pong) ; battoir m (de blanchisseuse). 3. (Harlequin's) bat, batte.
bat³, v.i. (batted) Manier la batte (au cricket, au base-ball). Cr: Être au guichet.
bat⁴, s. F: Pas m, allure f. He went off at a rare bat, il est parti à toute allure.
batch [batʃ], s. 1. Fournée f (de pain). F: B. of prisoners, fournée de prisonniers. A whole b. of letters, tout un paquet de lettres. 2. Lot m (de marchandises).
bate [beit], v.tr. A: Réduire, diminuer, retrancher. To speak with bated breath, parler en baissant la voix, dans un souffle.
bath¹, pl. **baths** [bɑːθ, bɑːðz], s. 1. Bain m. To take, have, a b., prendre un bain. To give a child a b., baigner un enfant. Public baths, (i) établissement m de bains ; (ii) (swimming) piscine f. Turkish baths, hammam m. The Order of the Bath, l'Ordre du Bain. S.a. FOOT-BATH, SHOWER-BATH, SWIMMING-BATH. 2. (a) Baignoire f. (b) Phot: etc: Cuvette f. 3. (Liquid) Acid, alkaline, bath, bain acide, alcalin. Phot: Alum bath, hardening bath, bain aluné. **'bath-heater,** s. Chauffe-bain m. **'bath-mat,** s. Descente f de bain. **'bath-room,** s. Salle f de bain(s). **'bath-tub,** s. Baignoire f ; tub m. **'bath-wrap,** s. Peignoir m de bain.
bath². 1. v.tr. Baigner, donner un bain à (qn). 2. v.i. Prendre un bain.
Bath³. Pr.n. Geog: Bath (ville d'eaux thermales). F: Go to Bath! va-t'en au diable ! **'Bath brick,** s. Brique anglaise (à nettoyer). **'Bath 'bun,** s. 'Bun' (q.v.) saupoudré de sucre. **'Bath-'chair,** s. Voiture de promenade (tirée ou poussée à bras) ; voiture de malade.
bathe¹ [beiːð], s. Bain m (de rivière, en mer) ; baignade f.
bathe². 1. v.tr. (a) Baigner. To b. one's face, se baigner la figure. Face bathed in tears, visage baigné, arrosé, de larmes. (b) Laver, lotionner (une plaie). (c) The seas that b. England, les mers qui baignent l'Angleterre. 2. v.i. Se baigner.
bathing ['beiːðiŋ], s. 1. Bains mpl (de mer, de rivière) ; baignades fpl. Sea bathing, bains de mer. S.a. SUN-BATHING. 2. Bassinage m, lotion f (d'une plaie, etc.). **'bathing-cap,** s. Bonnet m de bain. **'bathing-costume,** s. Costume m de bain(s). Skin-tight b.-c., maillot m (de bain). **'bathing-drawers,** s.pl. Caleçon m de bain. **'bathing-gown,** s. = BATHING-WRAP. **'bathing-hut,** s. Cabine f de bains (de plage). **'bathing-resort,** s. Station f balnéaire ; F: plage f. **'bathing-wrap,** s. Peignoir m de bain ; baigneuse f.
bather ['beiðər], s. Baigneur, -euse.
bat-horse ['batɔːrs], s. Mil: Cheval m de bât.
bathos ['beiθɔs], s. 1. L'ampoulé m (du style) ; enflure f ; affectation f ridicule du sublime.
batiste [ba'tiːst], s. Tex: Batiste f.
batman, pl. **-men** ['batmən, -men], s. Mil: Brosseur m ; ordonnance m or f ; P: tampon m.
baton ['bat(ə)n], s. 1. Bâton m. Conductor's b., bâton de chef d'orchestre. Field-marshal's b., bâton de maréchal. 2. = TRUNCHEON.
batrachian [ba'treikiən], a. & s. Batracien (m).

batsman, pl. **-men** ['batsmən, -men], s.m. Cr: Batteur f.
battalion [ba'taljən], s. Mil: Bataillon m.
batten¹ ['bat(ə)n], s. 1. (a) (i) (Bead or moulding) Couvre-joint m ; baguette f ; (ii) latte f. (b) Nau: Barre f, latte, tringle f. 2. Th: The battens, les herses f (d'éclairage). 3. Planche f (de parquet).
batten², v.tr. (a) Carp: Latter, voliger. (b) Nau: To batten down the hatches, (i) mettre les panneaux en place ; (ii) condamner les panneaux, les descentes ; assujettir, coincer, les panneaux.
batten³, v.i. Lit: S'engraisser, se bourrer, se repaître (on, de). To b. on others, s'enrichir aux dépens des autres.
batter¹ ['batər], s. 1. Cu: Pâte f lisse ; pâte à frire. 2. Typ: (a) Écrasement m (des caractères). (b) Caractère écrasé.
batter². 1. v.tr. (a) Battre. Artil: Battre en brèche, canonner (une ville). (b) Bossuer (de la vaisselle d'argent, etc.). 2. v.i. To batter at the door, frapper avec violence à la porte. **battered,** a. Délabré, bossué. Old b. hat, vieux chapeau cabossé. B. face, visage meurtri. **'battering-ram,** s. Mil: A: Bélier m.
batter³, s. Civ.E: (a) Fruit m (d'un mur, etc.). (b) Batter of an embankment, talus m d'un remblai.
battery ['batəri], s. 1. Jur: (a) Rixe f. (b) Voie f de fait. S.a. ASSAULT¹ 2. 2. Artil: Batterie f. Horse battery, batterie à cheval, batterie volante. Battery fire, tir par salves. 3. (a) Batterie (de fours à coke, de chaudières, etc.). (b) Phot: B. of lenses, trousse f d'objectifs. (c) El: Pile f ou batterie. (d) El: (Storage-)battery, accumulateur m, F: accu m.
battle¹ ['batl], s. Bataille f, combat m. Pitched battle, bataille rangée. Army drawn up in battle array, in battle order, armée rangée en bataille. S.a. ORDER¹ 3. To fight a battle, livrer une bataille, un combat. To give, offer, battle, donner, livrer, bataille ; engager le combat. To win a battle, gagner une bataille ; remporter une victoire. Lit: To do battle for, against, s.o., livrer bataille pour qn ; livrer bataille à, contre, qn. To join battle with s.o., entrer en lutte avec qn. That's half the battle, c'est bataille à moitié gagnée. F: To fight s.o.'s battles, prendre le parti de qn ; livrer bataille pour qn. Battle royal, bataille en règle ; mêlée générale. **'battle-axe,** s. Hache f d'armes. **'battle-cruiser,** s. Nau: Croiseur m de combat, de bataille. **'battle-cry,** s. Cri m de guerre. **'battle-field,** s. Champ m de bataille.
battle², v.i. Se battre, lutter, rivaliser (with s.o. for sth., avec qn pour qch.). To battle with, against, public opinion, combattre l'opinion. To b. against the wind, lutter contre le vent.
battledore ['batldɔːr], s. 1. (a) Laund: Battoir m. (b) Bak: Pelle f à enfourner. 2. Sp: Raquette f (de jeu de volant). To play at battledore and shuttlecock, jouer au volant.
battlements ['batlmənts], s.pl. (a) Créneaux m. (b) Parapet m, rempart m.
battleship ['batlʃip], s. Cuirassé m (de ligne).
bauble [bɔːbl], s. 1. Jester's bauble, marotte f. 2. (Worthless thing) Babiole f.
baulk¹,² [bɔːk], s. & v. = BALK¹,².
bauxite ['bɔːksait], s. Miner: Bauxite f.
Bavaria [ba'veəria]. Pr.n. La Bavière.
Bavarian [ba'veəriən], a. & s. Bavarois, -oise.
bawdy ['bɔːdi], a. Obscène, impudique. B. talk, propos orduriers.
bawl [bɔːl], v.tr. & i. (a) Brailler ; crier à tue-tête ; F: beugler ; P: gueuler (at s.o., contre qn).

To bawl out abuse, brailler, hurler, des injures. (b) **To b. for help,** crier au secours.

bay¹ [bei], s. *Bot:* **Sweet bay,** bay laurel, laurier commun. **Bay-tree,** laurier. **Bay wreath, bays,** couronne f de laurier(s). *F:* **To carry off the bays,** remporter les lauriers.

bay², s. *Geog:* Baie f; (if small) anse f. **Hudson Bay,** la Baie d'Hudson. **The Bay of Biscay,** le Golfe de Gascogne.

bay³, s. **1.** (Of bridge, roof, etc.) Travée f. **2.** (a) Enfoncement m. (Space for door, etc.) Baie f. S.a. SICK-BAY. (b) Ind: Hall m (d'usine). **bay-'window,** s. Fenêtre f en baie, en saillie; baie f.

bay⁴, s. Aboi m, aboiement m (d'un chien de chasse). **To bring a stag to bay,** mettre un cerf aux abois; acculer un cerf. **To be at bay,** être aux abois.

bay⁵, v.i. (a) (Of hound) Aboyer; donner de la voix. (b) **To bay (at) the moon,** hurler, aboyer, à la lune. **baying,** s. Aboiement m.

bay⁶, a. & s. (Cheval) bai (m). **Light bay,** bai châtain; (cheval) isabelle (m).

bayonet¹ ['beiənet], s. *Mil:* Baïonnette f. **To fix bayonets,** mettre (la) baïonnette au canon. **Bayonet charge,** charge à la baïonnette. **'bayonet-joint,** s. Joint m en baïonnette. **Bayonet-joint base, socket,** culot, douille, à baïonnette (de lampe électrique).

bayonet², v.tr. (bayoneted) Percer (qn) d'un coup de baïonnette.

bay-salt ['beisɔlt], s. Sel gris, sel marin; gros sel.

bazaar [ba'zaːr], s. **1.** (a) Bazar m (oriental). (b) Bazar; magasin m à bon marché. **2.** Vente f de charité.

be [bi(ː)], v.i. (pr. ind. am, art, is, pl. are; past ind. was, wast, was, pl. were; pr. sub. be; past sub. were, wert, were; pr. p. being, p.p. been; imp. be) Être. **1.** (a) *Mary is pretty,* Marie est jolie. *The weather was fine,* le temps était beau. *Seeing is believing,* voir c'est croire. *Yours, his, is a fine house,* c'est une belle maison que la vôtre, que la sienne. *Isn't he lucky?* n'est-ce pas qu'il a de la chance? (b) *His father is a doctor,* son père est médecin. *He is an Englishman,* il est Anglais, c'est un Anglais. *If I were you,* à votre place; si j'étais (que) de vous. (c) *Unity is strength,* l'union fait la force. *Three and two are five,* trois et deux font cinq. *You would be as well to . . .,* vous feriez (aussi) bien de. . . . **2.** (a) *The books are on the table,* les livres sont, se trouvent, sur la table. *He was a long time reaching the shore,* il mit longtemps à gagner le rivage. *Don't be long,* ne tardez pas (à revenir). *To be in danger,* se trouver en danger. *I was at the meeting,* j'ai été, j'ai assisté, à la réunion. **I don't know where I am,** (i) je ne sais pas où je suis; (ii) F: je suis tout désorienté; je ne sais pas où j'en suis. **Here I am,** me voici. *So you are back again,* vous voilà donc de retour. (b) (Of health) **How are you?** comment allez-vous? comment vous portez-vous? *I am better,* je vais mieux, je me trouve mieux; je me sens mieux. (c) **How much is that?** combien cela coûte-t-il? *How much is that in all?* combien cela fait-il? **How far is it to London?** combien y a-t-il d'ici à Londres? *It is a mile from here,* c'est à un mille (d'ici). (d) (Time) *When is the concert?* quand le concert aura-t-il lieu? *Christmas is on a Sunday this year,* Noël tombe un dimanche cette année. *To-morrow is Friday,* c'est demain vendredi. **3.** (a) **To be** (= feel) **cold, afraid,** etc., avoir froid, peur, etc. S.a. AFRAID, ASHAMED, COLD, etc. *My hands are cold,*

j'ai froid aux mains. *How cold your hands are!* comme vous avez les mains froides! (b) **To be twenty (years old),** avoir vingt ans, être âgé de vingt ans. *The wall is six foot high,* le mur a six pieds de haut, est haut de six pieds. **4.** (Exist. occur, remain) (a) **To be or not to be,** être, ou ne pas être. *The time of steel ships was not yet,* on n'en était pas encore au temps des navires d'acier. *The greatest genius that ever was,* le plus grand génie qui ait jamais existé, qui fut jamais. *That may be,* cela se peut. *So be it!* ainsi soit-il! *Well, be it so!* eh bien, soit! *Everything must remain just as it is,* tout doit rester tel quel. *However that may be,* quoi qu'il en soit. *How is it that . . .?* comment se fait-il que + sub., d'où vient(-il) que . . .? (b) Impers. **There is, there are.** (i) Il y a. *There is a man in the garden,* il y a un homme dans le jardin. *What is there to see?* qu'est-ce qu'il y a à voir? *There will be dancing* on dansera. *There were a dozen of us,* nous étions une douzaine. (ii) (In a wide, permanent sense) est. *There are men on whom Fortune always smiles* il est des hommes à qui tout sourit. (iii) *There was once a princess,* il était une fois une princesse **5.** (Go or come) *Are you for Bristol?* allez-vous à Bristol? *I have been to see Jones,* j'ai été voir Jones. *He had been and inspected the land,* il était allé inspecter le terrain. *I have been into every room,* j'ai visité toutes les pièces. *He was into the room like a flash,* il entra dans la pièce en coup de foudre. *Where have you been?* d'où venez-vous? *Has anyone been?* est-il venu quelqu'un? **6.** Impers. (a) *It is six o'clock,* il est six heures *It is late,* il est tard. *It is a fortnight since I saw him,* il y a quinze jours, voilà quinze jours, que je ne l'ai vu. (b) *It is fine, cold,* etc., il fait beau (temps), il fait froid, etc. (c) *It is easy to do so,* il est facile de + inf. (d) *It is right that . . .,* il est juste que + sub. *It is said that . . .,* on dit que. . . . *It is you I am speaking to,* c'est à vous que je parle. *It is for you to decide,* c'est à vous à décider. **What is it?** (i) que voulez-vous? (ii) de quoi s'agit-il? qu'est-ce qu'il y a? *As it were,* pour ainsi dire; en quelque sorte. *Were it only to please me,* ne fût-ce que pour me plaire. *Were it not for my rheumatism,* si ce n'était mon rhumatisme. *Had it not been for the rain . . .,* n'eût été la pluie. . . . *Had it not been for him . . .,* sans lui . . ., n'eût été lui. **7.** (Auxiliary uses) (a) *I am, was, doing sth.,* je fais, je faisais, qch.; je suis, j'étais, en train de faire qch. *They are always laughing,* ils sont toujours à rire. *The house is building, is being built,* on est en train de bâtir la maison. *I have (just) been writing,* je viens d'écrire. *I have been waiting for a long time,* il y a longtemps que j'attends; j'attends depuis longtemps. (Emphatic) *Why are you not working?—I am working!* pourquoi ne travaillez-vous pas?—Mais si je travaille! mais je travaille, voyons! (b) *The sun is set,* le soleil est couché. *The guests were all gone,* les invités étaient tous partis. (c) (Forming passive voice) (i) *He was killed,* il fut tué. *He is respected by all,* il est respecté de tous. *The loft was reached by means of a ladder,* on accédait au grenier au moyen d'une échelle. *He is allowed to smoke,* on lui permet de fumer. *He was laughed at,* on s'est moqué de lui. (ii) *He is to be pitied,* il est à plaindre, on doit le plaindre. *The house is to be let,* la maison est à louer. *How is it to be done?* comment le faire? *What is to be done?* que faire? (d) (Denoting futurity) *I am to see him to-morrow,* je dois le voir demain. *He was never to see them again,* il ne devait plus les revoir. *I was to have*

come, but . . ., je devais venir, mais. . . .
(e) (*Necessity, duty*) *Am I to do it or not?* faut-il
que je le fasse ou non? *You are to be at school
to-morrow*, il faut que vous soyez à l'école
demain. **8.** (a) **The bride to-be,** la future, la
fiancée. *s.* **The to-be,** l'avenir. *S.a.* HAS-BEEN.
(b) **To be for s.o.,** sth., tenir pour qn, qch. *I am
for reform*, je suis pour, je suis partisan de, la
réforme. (c) (*Belong*) **The battle is to the strong,**
la victoire est aux forts. **9.** (*Elliptical*) *Is your
book published?*—*It is*, est-ce que votre livre est
imprimé?—Oui, il l'est. *Are you happy?*—*I am*,
êtes-vous heureux?—Oui, or je le suis, or oui, je
le suis, or mais oui! *You are angry.*—*No, I'm
not.*—*Oh, but you are!* vous voilà fâché.—Pas
du tout.—Oh, mais si! *He is back.*—*Is he?* il
est de retour.—Vraiment? *So you are back, are
you?* alors vous voilà de retour? **being¹,** *a.*
For the time being, pour le moment, pour le
quart d'heure, pour l'heure. **being²,** *s.* **I.** Existence *f*, être *m.* (a) **Those to whom you owe your
being,** ceux qui vous ont donné l'être. (b) **To come
into being,** prendre forme, prendre naissance.
The coming into b. of a new industry, la naissance
d'une nouvelle industrie. *To bring a plan into b.*,
réaliser un projet. **2.** Être. (a) **All my being
revolts at the idea,** tout mon être se révolte à
cette idée. (b) **A human being,** un être humain.
Human beings, le genre humain, les humains.
The Supreme Being, l'Être Suprême.
beach¹ [biːtʃ], *s.* Plage *f*, grève *f*, rivage *m.*
S.a. PEBBLE I. **'beach-comber,** *s.* **I.** Vague
déferlante. **2.** *F:* (*Of pers.*) Batteur *m* de grève.
beach², *v.tr.* **I.** Échouer, mettre à l'échouage (un
navire). **2.** Tirer (une embarcation) à sec.
beacon ['biːkən], *s.* **I.** (a) *A:* Feu m d'alarme.
(b) Tour *f* ou colline *f* du feu d'alarme. **2.** Feu
de joie. **3.** *Nau: Av:* Beacon(-light), fanal *m*,
phare *m.* Airway b., phare de ligne. **4.** *Nau:*
Balise *f.*
bead¹ [biːd], *s.* **I.** (*For prayers*) Grain *m.* (String
of) beads, chapelet *m.* **To tell one's beads,**
égrener, dire, son chapelet; dire le rosaire.
2. (a) (*For ornament*) Perle *f* (de verroterie,
d'émail). (String of) beads, collier *m.* To thread
beads, enfiler des perles. (b) (*Drop*) Goutte *f*,
perle. Beads of dew, perles de rosée. (c) Bulle *f*
(sur le vin, l'eau-de-vie). (d) *Arch:* Joint: Perle,
baguette *f*, arête *f* (de moulure). **3.** (*Of tyre*)
Talon *m*, bourrelet *m.* Clincher bead, talon à
crochet. **4.** *Sm.a:* Guidon *m*, mire *f* (de fusil);
grain-d'orge *m.* *F:* **To draw a bead on s.o.**,
ajuster, viser, qn.
bead², **I.** *v.tr.* (a) Couvrir, orner, (qch.) de perles.
(b) Joint: Appliquer une baguette sur (qch.).
2. *v.i.* (*Of liquids*) Perler, faire la perle.
beaded, *a.* **I.** *Tex:* (*Of material*) Perlé.
2. Beaded edge, talon *m* (de pneu). Beaded tyre,
pneu à talons, à bourrelets. Beaded rim, jante
à rebord. **3.** Brow b. with perspiration, front
emperlé de sueur. **beading,** *s.* **I.** Garniture *f*
de perles. **2.** (a) Joint: Baguette *f.* (b) (*Of tyre*)
Talon *m*, bourrelet *m.*
beadle [biːdl], *s.m.* **I.** Bedeau. **2.** (*In university*)
Appariteur, massier.
beagle [biːgl], *s.* (Chien *m*) bigle *m*; briquet *m.*
beak¹ [biːk], *s.* Bec *m* (d'oiseau, de tortue,
d'enclume); *F:* nez crochu.
beak², *s.m.* *P:* Magistrat (du commissariat de
police).
beaked [biːkt], *a.* **I.** (Animal) à bec. **2.** (Nez)
crochu.
beaker ['biːkər], *s.* Gobelet *m*; coupe *f.*

beam¹ [biːm], *s.* **I.** (a) Poutre *f* (en bois); solive *f*,
madrier *m*; (*small*) poutrelle *f.* **Main beam,**
maîtresse poutre. **Longitudinal beam,** longeron
m, longrine *f.* *S.a.* CROSS-BEAM I, TIE-BEAM.
(b) Fléau *m*, verge *f* (d'une balance). (c) Age *m*,
timon *m*, flèche *f* (d'une charrue). (d) Balancier *m*
(d'une machine à vapeur). **2.** *N.Arch:* Bau *m.*
Deck-beam, barrot *m* de pont. **The beams,** les
barrots. **On the starboard beam,** par le travers
tribord. **On the weather b.,** par le travers au vent.
(**Breadth of) beam** (*of a ship*), largeur *f* (d'un
navire). **Broad in the beam,** (i) (vaisseau) à larges
baux; (ii) *F:* (personne) aux larges hanches.
3. (a) Rayon *m* (de lumière, de soleil). *Stray b. of
sunshine*, coulée *f* de soleil. *The sun darts its beams*,
le soleil darde ses traits. *F:* **B. of delight,** large
sourire *m.* (b) **B. of rays,** faisceau lumineux.
Beam of a lighthouse or head-light, faisceau d'un
phare. *W.Tg:* **Beam system,** émission aux ondes
dirigées. **'beam-compass,** *s.* Compas *m* à
trusquin, à verge (de dessinateur). **beam-
'ends,** *s.pl.* (*Of ship*) **To be on her beam-ends,**
être engagé. *To throw a ship on her b.-ends,*
coucher un navire. *F:* (*Of pers.*) **To be on one's
beam-ends,** être, se trouver, à bout de ressources.
beam². **I.** *v.tr.* (*Of the sun*) **To beam** (forth)
rays, envoyer, lancer, darder, des rayons.
2. *v.i.* (a) (*Of the sun*) Rayonner. (b) (*Of pers.*)
To beam (**with satisfaction**), rayonner (de satisfaction). **beaming,** *a.* Rayonnant; (soleil,
visage) radieux.
bean [biːn], *s.* **I.** Fève *f*; (*small variety*) gourgane *f.* **Broad bean,** grosse fève; fève des marais.
Kidney bean, haricot bean, haricot *m*, soissons *m*;
flageolet *m.* **French beans,** haricots verts. **Dried
beans,** haricots secs. *S.a.* BUTTER-BEAN, RUNNER
3, SOYA-BEAN. *F:* **To be full of beans,** (i) être
gaillard; se porter à merveille; (ii) être plein
d'entrain. **To give s.o. beans,** (i) attraper qn;
donner un savon, laver la tête, à qn; (ii) battre
qn à plate couture. *He knows how many beans
make five*, c'est un malin. *He hasn't a bean*, il
n'a pas le sou, *P:* pas un radis. **2.** Grain *m* (de
café). **'bean-feast,** *s.* *F:* **I.** Petite fête
(annuelle) offerte aux ouvriers par le patron.
2. Partie *f* de plaisir; noce *f*, régal *m.* **'bean-
stalk,** *s.* Tige *f* de fève ou de haricot.
bear¹ ['bɛər], *s.* **I.** (a) Ours *m.* **She-bear,** ourse *f.*
Young bear, bear's cub, ourson *m.* **Polar bear,**
ours blanc. *S. a.* GRIZZLY 2. *F:* **What a bear!**
quel maussade! quel ours! (b) *Astr:* **The Great,
Little, Bear,** la Grande, la Petite, Ourse.
2. *St.Exch:* Baissier *m*; joueur *m* à la baisse.
'bear-fight, *s.* *F:* Scène *f* de désordre; bousculade *f.* **'bear-garden,** *s.* **I.** Fosse *f* aux ours.
2. *F:* Pétaudière *f.* **To turn the place into a
bear-garden,** mettre le désordre partout. **'bear-
leader,** *s.* (a) Montreur *m* d'ours; meneur *m*
d'ours. (b) *F:* Précepteur *m* qui accompagne son
élève en voyage. *F:* cornac *m.*
bear², *v.tr. & i.* (*p.t.* bore ['bɔːr], *A. & B:*
bare ['bɛər]; *p.p.* borne [bɔːrn]) (a) Porter (un
fardeau, des armes, un nom, une date). *The
document bears your signature*, le document est
revêtu de votre signature. **To bear a good character,** jouir d'une bonne réputation. **To bear
oneself well,** se bien comporter. *The love she bore
him*, l'affection qu'elle lui portait. (b) Supporter,
soutenir (un poids); supporter, endurer (la
souffrance); supporter (les frais, les conséquences); souffrir (la douleur, la fatigue, une
perte). *To b. the penalty of one's misdeeds*, porter
la peine de ses méfaits. **To bear a part in sth.**,
jouer un rôle dans qch. **The charge will not bear

examination, cette accusation ne supporte pas l'examen. He could bear it no longer, il ne pouvait plus y tenir. *S.a.* GRIN². I cannot bear him, bear the sight of him, je ne peux pas le souffrir, le sentir. I cannot bear to see it, je ne peux pas en supporter la vue. To bear with s.o., être, se montrer, indulgent pour qn. (*c*) (*Press*) We were borne backwards (*by the crowd, etc.*), nous fûmes refoulés (par la foule, etc.). It was gradually borne in upon him that . . ., peu à peu il se laissa persuader que. . . . To bear to the right, prendre à droite; appuyer à droite. To bear hard, heavily, on s.o., (i) (*of pers.*) être dur pour qn; (ii) (*of thg*) peser lourdement sur qn. Law that bears unjustly on s.o., loi qui défavorise injustement qn. Question that bears on the welfare of the country, question qui intéresse le bien-être du pays. That does not b. on the question, cela n'a aucun trait à la question. (*Of pers.*) To bear on a lever, peser sur un levier. (*d*) Bring to bear. To bring all one's strength to b. on a lever, peser (de toutes ses forces) sur un levier. To bring one's mind to bear on sth., porter son attention sur qch. *S.a.* PRESSURE 2. To bring a telescope to bear on sth., braquer une lunette sur qch. To bring a gun to bear on a mark, pointer un canon sur un but. (*e*) *Nau:* The cape bears north-north-west, on relève le cap au nord-nord-ouest. How does the land bear? comment relève-t-on la terre? (*f*) (*Produce*) To bear a child, donner naissance à un enfant, mettre au jour un enfant. She has borne him three sons, elle lui a donné trois fils. *S.a.* BORN. Capital that bears interest, capital qui porte intérêt. *S.a.* FRUIT 1. **bear away,** *v.tr.* Emporter, enlever (qch.). To b. away the prize, remporter le prix. **bear down.** 1. *v.tr.* To bear down the enemy, accabler l'ennemi. To bear down all resistance, briser, vaincre, venir à bout de, toute résistance. 2. *v.i. Nau:* To bear down (up)on sth., courir sur qch. To b. down on the enemy, foncer, laisser porter, arriver, sur l'ennemi. **bear off.** 1. *v.tr.* = BEAR AWAY. 2. *v.i. Nau:* To bear off from the land, s'éloigner, s'écarter de la terre. **bear out,** *v.tr.* 1. To bear out a body, etc., emporter un cadavre, etc. 2. To bear out a statement, confirmer, justifier, une assertion. To bear s.o. out, corroborer le dire de qn. **bear up.** 1. *v.tr.* Soutenir (qn, qch.). 2. *v.i.* To bear up against pain, résister à la douleur. To bear up against, under, misfortune, faire face, tenir tête, au malheur. Bear up! tenez bon! du courage! **bearing**¹, *a.* 1. Porteur, -euse. Bearing axle, essieu porteur. Bearing surface, surface d'appui; surface portante. 2. (*a*) (Sol) productif. (*b*) Interest-bearing capital, capital producteur d'intérêts; capital qui rapporte. (*c*) (*In scientific compounds often*) -fère. Lead-bearing, plombifère. Silver-bearing, argentifère. **'bearing-rein,** *s.* Harn. Fausse rêne. **bearing**², *s.* 1. (*a*) Port *m* (d'armes, de nouvelles). (*b*) (*Of pers.*) Port, maintien *m*, conduite *f*. Majestic b., port majestueux. Modest b., maintien modeste. Soldierly b., allure martiale. (*c*) *pl. Her:* (Armorial) **bearings,** armoiries *f*, blason *m*. 2. (*a*) Capacité *f* de supporter (des maux, des souffrances). Beyond (all) bearing, insupportable. (*b*) (Appareil *m* d')appui *m* (d'un pont métallique); surface *f* d'appui (d'une poutre); portée *f* (de poutres); chape *f* (d'une balance). (*Of beam, etc.*) To take its bearing on sth., prendre appui sur qch. (*c*) *Mec.E:* (i) Palier *m*; roulement *m*; (ii) coussinet *m*. Thrust bearing, coussinet de butée. Big end bearing, coussinet de tête de bielle. **Bearing-brasses,** coussinet antifriction. *F:* (*To pers.*)

Bearings hot? ça vous a échauffé la bile? *S.a.* BALL-BEARING(S). (*d*) *Nau:* Relèvement *m*. To take the bearings of a coast, relever une côte. To take the ship's bearings, faire le point. Radio bearing station, poste radiogoniométrique. *F:* To take one's bearings, s'orienter, se repérer. To lose one's bearings, perdre le nord; se trouver désorienté. To find, get, one's bearings, se retrouver, se reconnaître. (*e*) Portée *f* (d'une question, d'un argument). Bearing on a question, rapport *m* avec une question. I had not understood the b. of his words, je n'avais pas saisi la portée de ses paroles. To examine a question in all its bearings, examiner une question sous tous ses aspects. 3. (*a*) (*Of tree, etc.*) To be in full bearing, être en plein rapport. (*b*) Bearing of a child, mise *f* au monde d'un enfant. **bearable** ['bɛərəbl], *a.* Supportable. **beard**¹ ['biərd], *s.* (*a*) Barbe *f*. To have a b., avoir de la barbe; porter la barbe. Man with a b., homme barbu. (*b*) *Bot:* Arête *f* (d'épi). (*c*) Barbelure *f* (d'une flèche, d'un hameçon). **beard**², *v.tr.* Braver, défier, narguer (qn). *F:* To beard the lion in his den, aller défier qn chez lui. **bearded** ['biərdid], *a.* (Homme, blé, poisson) barbu; (blé) aristé. Black-bearded man, homme à barbe noire. **beardless** ['biərdləs], *a.* Imberbe; sans barbe. **bearer** ['bɛərər], *s.* 1. (*Pers.*) (*a*) Porteur, -euse. B. of good news, (ap)porteur de bonnes nouvelles. B. of evil tidings, messager *m* de malheur. *S.a.* STANDARD-BEARER, STRETCHER-BEARER. (*b*) Bearer of a cheque, of a passport, porteur d'un chèque, titulaire *mf* d'un passeport. Fin: Bearer-bond, titre au porteur. (*c*) (*At funeral*) The bearers, les porteurs. 2. (*Of tree*) To be a good bearer, être de bon rapport. 3. Support *m*. Bearers of a rolling-mill, colonnes *f* du laminoir. **bearish** ['bɛəriʃ], *a.* (*a*) (Manières) d'ours. (*b*) (*Of pers.*) Bourru. **bearskin** ['bɛərskin], *s.* 1. Peau *f* d'ours. 2. *Mil.Cost:* Bonnet *m* à poil; bonnet d'oursin. **beast** [bi:st], *s.* 1. Bête *f*; *esp.* quadrupède *m*. Wild b., (i) bête sauvage; (ii) bête féroce. The brute beasts, les brutes *f*. The king of the beasts, le roi des animaux. 2. (*a*) Bête de somme ou de trait. (*b*) *pl. Husb:* Bétail *m*, bestiaux *mpl*; cheptel *m*. Herd of forty beast(s), troupeau de quarante têtes de bétail. 3. *F:* To make a beast of oneself, s'abrutir. What a b.! quel animal! **beastliness** ['bi:stlinəs], *s.* 1. Bestialité *f*, brutalité *f*. 2. *F:* Saleté *f* (d'esprit). **beastly** ['bi:stli]. 1. *a.* (*a*) Bestial, brutal, -aux. (*b*) *F:* Sale, dégoûtant, infect. What beastly weather! quel sale temps! 2. *adv. F:* (*Intensive*) Terriblement, bigrement. **beat**¹ [bi:t], *s.* 1. (*a*) Battement *m* (du cœur, etc.); pulsation *f* (du cœur); batterie *f* (de tambour); son *m* (du tambour). (*b*) *Mus:* Mesure *f*, temps *m*. Strong b., temps fort. 2. *Ph:* Battement (d'ondes sonores). 3. Secteur *m* de surveillance (d'une sentinelle, etc.); ronde *f* (d'un agent de police). *F:* It's off my beat altogether, ça n'est pas de ma compétence. 4. *Ven:* (Terrain de) battue *f*. **beat**², *v. (beat; beaten)* Battre (qn, qch.). 1. (*a*) To b. s.o. with a stick, donner des coups de bâton à qn. To beat s.o. black and blue, meurtrir, rouer, qn de coups; mettre qn en capilotade. To b. one's breast, se frapper la poitrine. To b. on the door, frapper, cogner, à la porte. To b. a drum, battre du tambour. To beat to arms, battre le rappel. To b the retreat (on drum), battre la retraite. To beat a retreat,

(i) *Mil:* battre en retraite ; (ii) *F:* se retirer, se dérober. **To beat time** (*to music*), battre la mesure. *His heart beats with joy,* son cœur bat de joie. **To beat a wood** (*for game*), battre un bois. *F:* **To beat about the bush,** tourner autour du pot. *Not to b. about the bush,* (i) aller droit au but, droit au fait ; (ii) répondre sans ambages, carrément. *Nau:* **To beat to windward,** against the wind, louvoyer ; tirer des bordées ; gagner au vent. *U.S: P:* **To beat it,** tirer au large. **Now then, beat it!** allons, file ! décampe ! (*b*) (*Of bird*) **To b.** *its wings,* battre de l'aile. **2.** (*Conquer, surpass*) (*a*) **To b.** *the enemy,* battre l'ennemi. *To b. s.o. at chess,* battre qn aux échecs. *S.a.* HOLLOW[1] II. *F:* **That beats me!** cela me passe ! ça me dépasse ! **That beats everything!** ça c'est fort ! ça c'est le comble ! (*b*) **To beat the record,** battre le record. **beat back,** *v.tr.* Repousser, refouler (qn). *To b. back the flames,* rabattre les flammes. **beat down.** **1.** *v.tr.* (*a*) *To b. sth. down,* (r)abattre qch. *The rain has beaten down the corn,* la pluie a couché les blés. (*b*) **To beat down the price of sth.,** marchander sur le prix de qch. **To beat s.o. down,** marchander (avec) qn. **2.** *v.i. The sun beats down upon our heads,* le soleil donne (à plomb) sur nos têtes. **beat in,** *v.tr.* Enfoncer, défoncer (une porte). **beat off,** *v.tr. To b. off an attack,* repousser un assaut. **beat out,** *v.tr.* **1.** (*a*) *To b. out a path,* frayer un chemin. (*b*) *To b. out iron,* battre, aplatir, le fer. **2. To beat s.o.'s brains out,** assommer qn. **beat up.** **1.** *v.tr.* (*a*) *To b. up eggs, cream,* battre, fouetter, les œufs, la crème. (*b*) **To beat up game,** *F:* customers, rabattre, traquer, le gibier, des clients. (*c*) **To beat up s.o.,** relancer qn. **2.** *v.i. Nau:* **To beat up,** louvoyer vers la terre ; gagner vers la terre. *To b. up to windward,* remonter le vent. **beaten,** *a.* **1. The beaten track,** le chemin battu ; les vieux sentiers rebattus. *House off the b. track,* maison écartée. **2.** (Or, fer) battu, martelé. *S.a.* WEATHER-BEATEN. **beating,** *s.* **1.** (*a*) Battement *m* (d'ailes, du cœur, etc.). (*b*) *Tchn:* Battage *m.* **2.** (*a*) Coups *mpl* ; raclée *f,* rossée *f.* (*b*) Défaite *f.*

beater ['bi:tər], *s.* **1.** (*Pers.*) (*a*) Batteur, -euse. (*b*) *Ven:* Rabatteur *m,* traqueur *m.* **2.** Batte *f* ; battoir *m* (de laveuse) ; fouloir *m* (de foulon).

beatific [bia'tifik], *a.* Béatifique.

beatify [bi'atifai], *v.tr. Ecc:* Béatifier.

beatitude [bi'atitju:d], *s.* Béatitude *f.*

beau, *pl.* **beaus, beaux** [bou, bouz], *s.m.* **1.** Élégant, dandy ; petit-maître, *pl.* petits-maîtres. *An old b.,* un vieux beau. **2.** Prétendant (d'une jeune fille) ; galant.

beauteous ['bju:tjəs], *a. Poet:* = BEAUTIFUL.

beautiful ['bju:tiful], *a.* **1.** (Très) beau, (très) belle. *A b. face,* un très beau visage. *At twenty she was b.,* à vingt ans c'était une beauté. **2.** *F:* Magnifique ; admirable. **3.** *s.* The beautiful, le beau. **-fully,** *adv.* Admirablement ; on ne peut mieux ; parfaitement.

beautify ['bju:tifai], *v.tr.* Embellir, enjoliver.

beauty ['bju:ti], *s.* Beauté *f.* **1.** *To be in the flower of one's b.,* être dans toute sa beauté. *Prov:* Beauty is in the eye of the beholder, il n'y a point de laides amours. *F:* **The beauty of it is that . . .,** le beau côté, le joli, de l'affaire, c'est que. . . . **That's the beauty of it!** (i) voilà ce qui en fait le charme ! (ii) c'est là le plus beau de l'affaire ! **2.** *She was a b. in her day,* elle a été une beauté dans le temps. *F:* **Well, you're a beauty!** eh bien, tu es encore un drôle de type,

toi ! **The Sleeping Beauty,** la Belle au bois dormant. **'beauty-sleep,** *s.* Sommeil *m* avant minuit. **'beauty-spot,** *s.* **1.** (*Applied on face*) Mouche *f.* **2.** Site *m,* coin *m,* pittoresque.

beaver ['bi:vər], *s.* Castor *m.* ‹

becalm [bi'ka:m], *v.tr.* Abriter, déventer (un navire). (*Of ship*) **To be becalmed,** être accalminé.

became [bi'keim]. *See* BECOME.

because [bi'kɔ(:)z]. **1.** *conj.* Parce que. *I eat b. I'm hungry,* je mange parce que j'ai faim. *If I said so it was b. it had to be said,* si je l'ai dit c'est qu'il fallait le dire. *B. he dashed off a sonnet he thinks himself a poet,* pour avoir bâclé un sonnet il se croit poète. **2.** *Prep.phr.* **Because of sth.,** à cause de, en raison de, qch.

beck[1] [bek], *s.* Ruisseau *m* (de montagne).

beck[2], *s.* Signe *m* (de tête, de la main). **To have s.o. at one's beck and call,** avoir qn à ses ordres. **To be at s.o.'s beck and call,** obéir à qn au doigt et à l'œil.

becket ['beket], *s. Nau:* Garcette *f.*

beckon ['bek(ə)n], *v.tr. & i.* Faire signe (*to s.o.,* à qn) ; appeler (qn) de la main, d'un geste. **To beckon s.o. in,** faire signe à qn d'entrer.

become [bi'kʌm], *v.* (**became** [bi'keim] ; **become**) **1.** *v.i.* Devenir ; se faire. (*a*) *To b. great, king, etc.,* devenir grand, roi, etc. *To b. old, thin, etc.,* vieillir, maigrir. *They have b. more amiable,* ils se sont faits plus aimables. *To b. a priest, a doctor,* se faire prêtre, médecin. *To b. accustomed, interested,* s'accoutumer, s'intéresser. (*Of pers.*) *To b. known,* commencer à être connu ; se faire connaître. (*b*) **What has become of X?** qu'est devenu X? qu'est-il advenu de X? **2.** *v.tr.* Convenir à, aller (bien) à. *Hat that does not b. him,* chapeau qui ne lui sied pas, qui ne lui va pas. *S.a.* ILL III. **2. becoming,** *a.* **1.** (*a*) Convenable, bienséant. (*b*) *B. to the occasion,* digne de l'occasion. **2.** (*Of dress, etc.*) Seyant (*to,* à) ; qui sied (à) ; qui va bien (à). *B. dress,* robe avantageuse. **-ly,** *adv.* Convenablement ; comme il convient.

bed[1] [bed], *s.* Lit *m* ; *Lit:* couche *f.* **1.** (*a*) **Single bed,** lit en une place, pour une personne. **Double bed,** lit à deux places, pour deux personnes. **Spare bed,** lit d'ami. *S.a.* AIR-BED, CAMP-BED, FEATHER-BED, TRUCKLE-BED, WATER-BED. **To give bed and board to s.o.,** donner à qn le logement et la nourriture, le vivre et le couvert. **The marriage bed,** le lit conjugal. *Jur:* **Separation from bed and board,** séparation de corps (et de biens). *To sleep in separate beds,* faire lit à part. **To be brought to bed of a boy,** accoucher d'un petit garçon. **To be in bed,** (i) être couché ; (ii) (*through illness*) être alité, garder le lit. **To go to bed,** se coucher. **To take to one's bed,** s'aliter. **To keep to one's bed,** garder le lit. *Bed of sickness,* lit de douleur. *S.a.* SICK-BED. *Three days in bed,* trois jours d'alitement. **To get into bed,** se mettre au lit. **To get out of bed,** se lever. *To put a child to bed,* coucher un enfant. *To make the beds,* faire les lits. *Prov:* **As you make your bed so you must lie on it,** comme on fait son lit on se couche. *S.a.* DEATH-BED, ROSE[1] I. (*b*) = BEDSTEAD. (*c*) Spring-bed, sommier *m* élastique. **2.** (*a*) (Lit (d'une rivière) ; banc *m* (d'huîtres). *Hort:* (Rectangular) bed, planche *f,* carré *m* (de légumes, etc.). (Flower-)bed, parterre *m,* plate-bande *f, pl.* plates-bandes. *S.a.* OYSTER-BED, SEED-BED. (*b*) *Geol:* Assise *f* ; couche *f.* *Miner:* Gisement *m.* *S.a.* COAL-BED. *Const:* Bed of concrete, assise de béton. (*c*) (Engine-)bed, support *m,* bâti *m,* de moteur. **'bed-bug,** ‹. Punaise *f* des lits. **'bed-**

clothes, s.pl. Couvertures f et draps m de lit. 'bed-cover, s. Dessus m de lit. 'bed-head, s. Chevet m; tête f (du lit). 'bed-linen, s. Draps mpl de lit et taies fpl d'oreillers. 'bed-post, s. Colonne f de lit; quenouille f (de lit à colonnes). 'bed-rest, s. Dossier m de malade. 'bed-ridden, a. Cloué au lit. 'bed-rock, s. (a) Geol: Roche f de fond; tuf m. (b) F: Fondement m (de sa croyance, etc.). To get down to bed-rock, descendre jusqu'au tuf, au fond des choses. Bed-rock price, dernier prix; prix le plus bas.

bed². 1. v.tr. (bedded) (a) To bed (up, down) the horses, faire la litière aux chevaux. (b) To bed (out) plants, dépoter des plantes. To bed (in) seedlings, repiquer des plants. (c) Const: Sceller (une poutre dans un mur, etc.); asseoir (une pierre, les fondations). 2. v.i. (a) (Of animal) Se gîter. (b) (Of foundations, etc.) To bed (down), prendre son assiette; se tasser. bedding, s. 1. (a) Parcage m (des huîtres). (b) Civ.E: Enrochement m (d'un bâtardeau, etc.). (c) Scellement m (d'une poutre dans un mur, etc.); assiette f (d'une pierre). (d) Hort: Bedding-out, dépotage m, dépotement m (de plantes). 2. (a) Literie f; fournitures fpl (d'un lit). (b) Mil: Navy: (Matériel m de) couchage m. 3. (a) Husb: Litière f. (b) Civ.E: Matériau m d'enrochement, d'assise. 4. Lit (d'une chaudière).

bedabble [bi'dabl], v.tr. Éclabousser, souiller.

bedaub [bi'dɔ:b], v.tr. Barbouiller (de peinture).

bedchamber ['bedtʃeimbər], s. A: Chambre f à coucher. (At court) The Gentlemen of the Bedchamber, les gentilshommes de la chambre.

bedeck [bi'dek], v.tr. Lit: Parer, orner (s.o. with sth., qn de qch.). To b. oneself, s'attifer.

bedew [bi'dju:], v.tr. Lit: Humecter de rosée. Cheeks bedewed with tears, joues baignées de larmes.

bedfellow ['bedfelo], s. Camarade mf de lit.

bedim [bi'dim], v.tr. (bedimmed) Lit: Obscurcir (l'esprit, les yeux). Eyes bedimmed with tears, yeux voilés de larmes.

bedizen [bi'daizn], v.tr. Attifer, chamarrer.

Bedlam ['bedlam]. 1. Pr.n. (Corrupt. of Beth-lehem) Hôpital m (d'aliénés) de Ste-Marie-Bethléem. 2. s. F: (a) Maison f de fous, d'aliénés. (b) Charivari m, tohu-bohu m.

bedlamite ['bedləmait], s. F: Fou, f. folle; échappé de Charenton.

Bedouin ['beduin, -i:n], a. & s. inv. Bédouin, -ine.

bedrabbled [bi'drabld], bedraggled [bi-'dragld], a. (a) Crotté. (b) Dépenaillé.

bedroom ['bedrum], s. Chambre f à coucher. Spare bedroom, chambre d'ami.

bedside ['bedsaid], s. Chevet m; bord m du lit. At s.o.'s b., au chevet de qn. Bedside carpet, rug, descente f de lit, saut-de-lit m. Bedside lamp, lampe de chevet. Bedside table, table de nuit, de chevet. Bedside books, livres de chevet.

bedspread ['bedspred], s. Courtepointe f; dessus m de lit.

bedstead ['bedsted], s. Châlit m; bois m de lit. Iron, mahogany, b., lit de fer, lit en acajou.

bedtime ['bedtaim], s. Heure f du coucher. It is b., il est l'heure d'aller se coucher.

bee [bi:], s. 1. Abeille f. Hive-bee, abeille domestique. Working bee, abeille neutre, abeille ouvrière. To keep bees, élever des abeilles. F: To have a bee in one's bonnet, (i) être timbré; avoir une araignée au plafond; (ii) avoir une idée fixe. S.a. BUMBLE-BEE, HONEY-BEE, QUEEN-BEE. 2. U.S: (a) Réunion f (pour

travaux en commun). (b) Concours m. S.a. SPELLING-BEE. 'bee-keeper, s. Apiculteur m. 'bee-line, s. Ligne f à vol d'abeille, à vol d'oiseau. In a bee-line, à vol d'abeille, d'oiseau. F: To make a bee-line for sth., aller droit vers qch. 'bee-master, s. Apiculteur m.

beech [bi:tʃ], s. Hêtre m; fayard m. Copper beech, hêtre rouge. Beech furniture, meubles en hêtre. 'beech-grove, s. Foutelaie f, hêtraie f. 'beech-mast, s. Faînes fpl. 'beech-nut, s. Faîne f.

beef [bi:f], s. (No pl.) Cu: Bœuf m. Roast beef, rôti m de bœuf; rosbif m. Chilled beef, bœuf frigorifié. Salt beef, corned beef, bœuf de conserve. F: To have plenty of beef, avoir du muscle; P: être costaud. 'beef-'steak, s. Cu: Bifteck m, tournedos m. 'beef-'tea, s. Bouillon m.

beefeater ['bi:fi:tər], s. Hallebardier m ((i) de la garde du corps, (ii) à la Tour de Londres).

beefy ['bi:fi], a. F: Musculeux, musclé; P: costaud.

beehive ['bi:haiv], s. Ap: Ruche f.

Beelzebub [bi'elzibʌb]. Pr.n.m. 1. B.Lit: Belzébuth. 2. F: Le Diable.

been [bi:n]. See BE.

beer [bi'ər], s. Bière f. Bottled b., bière en can(n)ette. Small beer, petite bière. F: To think no small beer of oneself, ne pas se prendre pour de la petite bière; P: se gober. To chronicle small beer, enregistrer des détails insignifiants. Fortune made in b., fortune faite dans la brasserie. 'beer-house, s. Cabaret m; brasserie f.

beery ['bi:əri], a. 1. (Atmosphère) qui sent la bière. 2. Un peu gris. Beery voice = voix avinée.

beeswax ['bi:zwaks], s. (a) Cire f d'abeilles. (b) Cire à parquet.

beeswing ['bi:zwiŋ], s. 1. Pellicules fpl (du vin de Porto). 2. Vieux porto.

beet [bi:t], s. Betterave f. White beet, (i) (bette) poirée f; (ii) betterave à sucre. Beet sugar, sucre de betterave.

beetle¹ ['bi:tl], s. Mailloche f, masse f (en bois); maillet m; (for paving) hie f, demoiselle f; dame f. Laund: Battoir m.

beetle², s. Ent: Coléoptère m; hister m, escarbot m, scarabée m. S.a. BLACK-BEETLE, POTATO-BEETLE, STAG-BEETLE, etc.

beetle³, a. Beetle brows, (i) front bombé; sourcils touffus; (ii) front sourcilleux.

beetle⁴, v.i. Surplomber. beetling, a. 1. (Of rock) Surplombant, menaçant. B. height, précipice m. 2. = BEETLE³.

beetroot ['bi:tru:t], s. Betterave potagère.

befall [bi'fɔ:l], v.tr. & i. (Conj. like FALL; used only in 3rd pers.) Arriver, survenir (à qn). It so befell that ..., il arriva que. ...

befit [bi'fit], v.tr. (befitted) (Used only in 3rd pers.) Convenir, seoir (à qn). befitting, a. Convenable, seyant.

befog [bi'fɔg], v.tr. 1. Envelopper de brouillard. 2. Obscurcir (la pensée, etc.).

before [bi'fɔ:ər]. 1. adv. (a) (In space) En avant; devant. To go on before, marcher en avant, prendre les devants; (take precedence) passer le premier. There were trees both b. and behind, il y avait des arbres devant et derrière. This page and the one before, cette page et la précédente. (b) (In time) Auparavant, avant. Two days b., deux jours auparavant; l'avant-veille f. The day before, le jour précédent; la veille. The evening before, la veille au soir. The year before, l'année d'auparavant. A moment before, un moment auparavant, le moment d'auparavant. *I have seen him b.*, je l'ai déjà vu. *I have never seen him before*, je le vois pour la première fois. **2.** *prep.* *(a)* *(Place)* Devant. **To stand before s.o.**, se tenir devant qn. **Before my (very) eyes**, sous mes (propres) yeux. *He said so b. me*, il l'a dit en ma présence. *S.a.* WIND¹ I. *(b)* *(Time)* Avant. **Before Christ**, B.C., avant Jésus-Christ, av. J.-C. **Before long**, avant (qu'il soit) longtemps. **It ought to have been done before now**, ce devrait être déjà fait. **To arrive an hour before the time**, arriver (avec) une heure d'avance. *We are b. our time*, nous sommes en avance. *The day b. the battle*, la veille de la bataille. *Two days b. Christmas*, l'avant-veille de Noël. *B. answering*, avant de répondre. *Fin:* Redemption before due date, remboursement anticipé. *(c)* *(Preference, order)* **Before everything else . .**, avant tout. . . . *Ladies b. gentlemen*, les dames avant les messieurs. **3.** *conj.* Avant que (ne) + *sub.* *(a)* *Come and see me b. you leave*, venez me voir avant que vous (ne) partiez, avant de partir, avant votre départ. *It will be long b. we see him again*, on ne le reverra pas d'ici longtemps. *It was long b. he came*, il fut longtemps a venir. *(b)* **I will die before I yield**, je préfère mourir plutôt que de céder.

beforehand [bi'fɔ:rhand], *adv.* Préalablement, au préalable ; d'avance ; auparavant. *You ought to have told me b.*, vous auriez dû me prévenir. *To pay b.*, payer d'avance. *To rejoice b.*, se réjouir par avance. *To be b. with the rent*, (i) payer son loyer avant le terme ; (ii) avoir en main l'argent du terme.

befriend [bi'frend], *v.tr.* Venir en aide à, à l'aide de (qn) ; secourir (qn) ; se montrer l'ami de (qn).

beg [beg], *v.tr. & i.* (begged) **1.** Mendier ; tendre la main. **To beg (for) one's bread**, mendier son pain. *(To dog)* Beg! fais le beau! **These jobs go (a-)begging**, ce sont des emplois qui trouvent peu d'amateurs. **2.** **To beg a favour of s.o.**, solliciter une faveur de qn. *To beg (of) s.o. to do sth.*, prier, supplier, qn de faire qch. **I beg (of) you!** de grâce! je vous en prie! **To beg the question**, supposer vrai ce qui est en question ; faire une pétition de principe. *S.a.* PARDON¹ I. **begging¹**, *a.* (Frère, ordre) mendiant. **begging²**, *s.* **1.** Mendicité *f.* **2.** Begging the question, pétition *f* de principe.

began [bi'gan]. *See* BEGIN.

beget [bi'get], *v.tr.* (begot [bi'gɔt], B: begat, [bi'gat] ; begotten [bi'gɔtn]) **1.** Engendrer, procréer. *Abraham begat Isaac*, Abraham engendra Isaac. **2.** Causer, susciter ; faire naître (des difficultés, etc.).

beggar¹ ['begər], *s.* **1.** Beggar(-man, -woman), mendiant, -e, gueux, -euse, pauvre, -esse. **Sturdy beggar**, truand *m.* *Prov:* Beggars cannot be choosers, ne choisit pas qui emprunte. *S.a.* HORSEBACK. **2.** *F:* Individu *m.* *Funny little b.*, drôle *m* de petit bonhomme. **Poor beggar!** pauvre diable! **Lucky beggar!** veinard!

beggar², *v.tr.* (beggared ['begərd]) **1.** To beggar s.o., réduire qn à la mendicité ; mettre qn sur la paille. **2.** *F:* To beggar description, défier toute description.

beggarly ['begərli], *a.* Chétif, minable, misérable, mesquin. *B. wage*, salaire dérisoire.

beggary ['begəri], *s.* Mendicité *f*, misère *f.* **To be reduced to beggary**, être réduit à la mendicité ; être dans la misère.

begin [bi'gin], *v.tr. & i.* (began [bi'gan] ; begun [bi'gʌn]) Commencer (un discours, une tâche) ; entamer, amorcer (une conversation). *To b. at the beginning*, commencer par le commencement. *He began life as a ploughboy*, il débuta dans la vie comme valet de charrue. *Before winter begins*, avant le début de l'hiver. *The day began well, badly*, la journée s'annonça bien, mal. **To begin to do sth.**, to begin doing sth., commencer à, de, faire qch. *To b. to laugh, to cry; to b. laughing, crying*, se mettre à rire, à pleurer ; se prendre à pleurer. **To begin by doing sth.**, débuter, commencer, par faire qch. **To begin with**, tout d'abord ; pour commencer. **To begin again**, recommencer. *Prov:* Well begun is half done, a moitié fait qui commence bien. **beginning**, *s.* Commencement *m*; début *m* (d'une carrière, etc.); origine *f*, naissance *f* (du monde, etc.). **In the beginning**, au commencement, au début. **From the beginning**, dès le commencement. **From beginning to end**, depuis le commencement jusqu'à la fin ; de bout en bout. **To make a beginning**, commencer, débuter. *To start again from the very b.*, reprendre le travail à pied d'œuvre. *Aut:* B. of a skid, amorce *f* de dérapage. *Prov:* A good beginning is half the battle, a moitié fait qui commence bien.

beginner [bi'ginər], *s.* **1.** Premier *m* à agir ; auteur *m* (d'une querelle, etc.). **2.** Commençant, -ante, débutant, -ante ; novice *mf.*

begone [bi'gɔn], *p.p.* *(Used as imp.)* Va-t'en! allez-vous-en! partez! hors d'ici!

begot(ten) [bi'gɔt(n)]. *See* BEGET.

begrime [bi'graim], *v.tr.* Noircir, salir, barbouiller. *Begrimed with smoke*, noirci de fumée.

begrudge [bi'grʌdʒ], *v.tr.* Donner (qch.) à contre-cœur. *To b. s.o. sth.*, (i) mesurer, (ii) envier, qch. à qn.

begrudgingly [bi'grʌdʒiŋli], *adv.* **1.** A contre-cœur. **2.** Envieusement. **3.** Chichement.

beguile [bi'gail], *v.tr. Lit:* **1.** Enjôler, séduire, tromper (qn). *B:* The serpent beguiled me, le serpent m'a séduite. *To b. s.o. with promises*, bercer qn de promesses. *To b. s.o. out of sth.*, soutirer qch. à qn. **2.** Distraire, charmer, amuser. *To b. the time doing sth.*, tromper son ennui en faisant qch. *To b. s.o.'s leisure*, charmer les loisirs de qn.

begun [bi'gʌn]. *See* BEGIN.

behalf [bi'hɑ:f], *s.* **1.** On behalf of s.o., au nom de qn ; *Com:* au compte, au profit, de qn. *I come on b. of Mr X*, je viens de la part de M. X. **2.** *To plead in, on, s.o.'s b.*, plaider en faveur de qn. **3.** *Don't be uneasy on my b.*, ne vous inquiétez pas à mon sujet.

behave [bi'heiv], *v.i.* *(Usu. with adv.)* **To b. well, badly, prudently, like a man of honour**, se conduire, se comporter, bien, mal, prudemment, en homme d'honneur. *To b. well to, towards, s.o.*, bien agir envers qn ; se bien conduire à l'égard de, envers, qn. **To know how to behave**, savoir vivre. *(To child)* Behave yourself! sois sage! **behaved**, *a.* *(With adv. prefixed, e.g.)* Well-behaved, sage ; poli ; qui se conduit bien. **Ill-behaved, badly behaved**, qui se conduit mal ; sans tenue.

behaviour [bi'heivjər], *s.* **1.** Façon *f* de se comporter, d'agir ; tenue *f*, maintien *m* ; conduite *f* (to, towards, s.o., avec, envers, qn). *Good b.*, bonne conduite. **To be on one's best b.**, se surveiller ; se conduire de son mieux. **2.** Allure *f*, fonctionnement *m* (d'une machine) ; tenue (d'une auto).

behead [bi'hed], *v.tr.* Décapiter ; faire tomber la tête de (qn). *He was beheaded*, on lui coupa le cou. **beheading**, *s.* Décapitation *f.*

beheld [bi'held]. *See* BEHOLD.

5

behest [bi'hest], *s. Lit:* Commandement *m*, ordre *m.* **At s.o.'s behest,** sur l'ordre de qn.

behind [bi'haind]. **1.** *adv.* Derrière ; par derrière. (*a*) *Hair cropped close b.*, cheveux coupés ras par derrière. *To attack s.o. from b.*, attaquer qn par derrière. *To come b.*, venir derrière ; suivre. *To ride b.*, (i) suivre à cheval ; (ii) monter en croupe. **To fall, lag, behind, s'attarder** ; traîner en arrière ; se laisser distancer. **To stay, remain, behind,** rester, demeurer, en arrière. (*b*) **To be behind with one's studies, with one's work,** être en retard pour ses études, dans son travail. **2.** *prep.* (*a*) Derrière. *He hid b. it,* il se cacha derrière. **Look behind you,** regardez derrière vous. **To walk, follow, close behind s.o.,** marcher sur les talons de qn. **What is behind all this?** qu'y a-t-il derrière tout cela ? **To be behind** (= *to support*) s.o., soutenir qn. **To put a thought behind one,** rejeter une pensée. (*b*) En arrière de, en retard sur (qn, qch.). *Country (far) b. its neighbours,* pays (très) en arrière de ses voisins. *Here we are far b. Paris,* ici nous sommes très en retard sur Paris (en matière de modes, etc.). *S.a.* TIME¹ 4, 6. **3.** *s. F:* **To kick s.o.'s behind,** botter le derrière de, à, qn.

behindhand [bi'haindhand], *adv. & pred. a.* En arrière ; en retard ; attardé. *To be b. with the rent,* être en retard pour, avec, le loyer. *He is not b. in generosity,* il n'est pas en reste de générosité.

behold [bi'hould], *v.tr.* (beheld [bi'held] ; beheld) *Lit:* **1.** Voir ; apercevoir. **2.** *imp.* Behold! voyez ! *B., he cometh!* voici qu'il vient !

beholden [bi'houldn], *a.* **To be beholden to s.o.,** être redevable à qn (*for,* de).

beholder [bi'houldər], *s.* Spectateur, -trice ; assistant, -ante ; témoin *m.*

behoof [bi'hu:f], *s.* To, for, on, s.o.'s behoof, à l'avantage, au profit, de qn. *For one's own b.,* dans son propre intérêt.

behove [bi'ho:uv], *v.tr. impers.* **1.** Incomber (à). *It behoves him to . . .,* il lui appartient de. . . . **2.** *It does not behove him to boast,* mal lui sied de se vanter.

being [bi:iŋ], *s. See* BE.

belabour [bi'leibər], *v.tr. To b. s.o.* (soundly), battre qn à coups redoublés ; rouer qn de coups.

belated [bi'leitid], *a.* **1.** (Voyageur, etc.) attardé ; surpris par la nuit. **2.** (Repentir, renseignement) tardif ; (invité) en retard.

belaud [bi'lɔ:d], *v.tr.* Combler (qn) de louanges.

belay [bi'lei], *v.tr. Nau:* Tourner, amarrer (une manœuvre). **Belay!** (i) amarrez ! (ii) *F:* en voilà assez. **be'laying-pin,** *s.* Cabillot *m,* taquet *m.*

belch¹ [bel(t)ʃ], *s.* **1.** Éructation *f* ; (*not in polite use*) rot *m.* **2.** Vomissement *m* (de flammes, etc.).

belch². **1.** *v.i.* Éructer ; (*not in polite use*) roter. **2.** *v.tr.* **To belch (forth, out) flames, smoke,** vomir des flammes, de la fumée.

beldam(e) ['beldəm], *s.f.* Vieille sorcière ; mégère.

beleaguer [bi'li:gər], *v.tr.* Assiéger.

belemnite ['belemnait], *s.* Bélemnite *f.*

belfry ['belfri], *s.* Beffroi *m,* clocher *m. S.a.* BAT¹.

Belgian ['beldʒjən], *a. & s.* Belge (*mf*) ; de Belgique.

Belgium ['beldʒjəm]. *Pr.n.* La Belgique.

belie [bi'lai], *v.tr.* (*pr.p.* belying [bi'laiiŋ]) Donner un démenti à (des paroles) ; démentir (une promesse, des espérances) ; faire mentir (un proverbe).

belief [bi'li:f], *s.* **1.** Croyance *f,* conviction *f.*

B. in ghosts, croyance aux revenants. *B. in God,* croyance en Dieu. **To the best of my belief,** à ce que je crois ; autant que je sache. **2.** *B. in s.o.,* in sth., foi *f,* confiance *f,* en qn, en qch.

believable [bi'li:vəbl], *a.* Croyable.

believe [bi'li:v]. **1.** *v.tr.* (*a*) Croire (une nouvelle, etc.) ; ajouter foi à (une rumeur) ; accorder créance à (une affirmation). *I b.* (*that*) *I am right,* je crois avoir raison. *The house was believed to be haunted,* la maison passait pour être hantée. *He is believed to have a chance,* on lui croit des chances (de réussir). **I believe not,** je crois que non ; je ne le crois pas. **I believe so,** je crois que oui ; je le crois. **Seeing is believing,** voir c'est croire. *To make s.o. b. that . . .,* faire accroire à qn que. . . . (*b*) **To believe s.o.,** croire qn ; accorder créance au dire de qn. *If he is to be believed . . .,* à l'en croire . . . ; s'il faut l'en croire. . . . **2.** *v.i.* (*a*) **To believe in God,** croire en Dieu. *To b. in one God,* croire à un seul Dieu. (*b*) **To believe in s.o.'s word,** croire à la parole de qn. *I don't b. in doctors,* je n'ai pas confiance dans les médecins. **3.** **To make believe to do** sth., feindre, faire semblant, de faire qch. *S.a.* MAKE-BELIEVE.

believer [bi'li:vər], *s.* **1.** Croyant, -ante. **2.** **To be a believer in sth.,** (i) croire à qch. ; (ii) être partisan de qch.

belittle [bi'litl], *v.tr.* Rabaisser, déprécier, amoindrir (le mérite de qn) ; décrier (qch).

bell¹ [bel], *s.* **1.** (*a*) (Clapper-)bell (*in church, etc.*), cloche *f* ; (*smaller*) clochette *f* ; (*in house*) sonnette *f* ; (*fixed bell*) timbre *m* ; (*for cattle, sheep*) clochette, clarine *f,* sonnaille *f.* **Globular bell, sleigh-bell,** grelot *m.* **Electric bell,** sonnerie *f* (électrique). *Med: etc:* **Hand-bell,** sonnette de nuit. **Set of bells** (*of church, etc.*), sonnerie. **Great bell** (*of church*), bourdon *m.* **Chime of bells,** carillon *m.* **There's a ring at the bell, there's the bell,** on sonne. **To ring the bell,** (i) sonner ; (ii) (*handbell*) agiter la sonnette ; (iii) (*at a fair*) faire sonner le timbre de la tête de Turc. *Hence: F:* **To ring, bear (away), the bell,** décrocher la timbale ; l'emporter sur les autres. *S.a.* CANTERBURY, SOUND⁶ I. 1. (*b*) **The dinner-bell,** la cloche du dîner. *S.a.* PASSING-BELL. (*c*) *Nau:* **To strike the bells,** piquer l'heure. **Six bells,** six coups (de cloche). **To strike eight bells,** piquer midi. **2.** Calice *m,* clochette (d'une fleur) ; pavillon *m* (d'une trompette, etc.). **3.** *Hort:* Cloche. **'bell-buoy,** *s.* Bouée *f* à cloche. **'bell-crank,** *attrib.* Bell-crank lever, levier coudé, à renvoi. **'bell-flower,** *s.* Campanule *f.* **'bell-founder,** *s.* Fondeur *m* de cloches. **'bell-handle,** *s.* **1.** Tirant *m* (de cloche, de sonnette). **2.** Poignée *f* (de sonnette à main). **'bell-hanger,** *s.* Poseur *m* de sonnettes. **'bell-metal,** *s.* Métal *m,* bronze *m,* de cloche(s). **'bell-mouth,** *s.* Évasement *m,* égueulement *m.* **'bell-pull,** *s.* Cordon *m* de sonnette. **'bell-push,** *s.* Bouton *m* de sonnerie (électrique) ; bouton poussoir. **'bell-ringer,** *s.* (*a*) Sonneur *m.* (*b*) Carillonneur *m.* **'bell-tower,** *s.* Clocher *m* ; campanile *m.* **'bell-wether,** *s.m.* **1.** *Husb:* Sonnailler, bélier meneur du troupeau. **2.** *Pej:* Chef de bande ; meneur.

bell². **1.** *v.tr. F:* **To bell the cat,** attacher le grelot. **2.** *v.i.* (*Of skirt, etc.*) Faire cloche ; ballonner.

bell³, *s.* Bramement *m* (du cerf).

bell⁴, *v.i.* (*Of deer*) Bramer, raire.

belladonna [belə'dɔnə], *s.* Belladone *f.*

belle [bel], *s.f.* (*Pers.*) Beauté. **The belle of the ball,** la reine, la beauté, du bal.

bellicose ['belikous], a. Belliqueux.
belligerent [be'lidʒərənt], a. & s. Belligérant (m).
bellow[1] ['belo], s. (a) Beuglement m, mugissement m. (b) F: Hurlement m (de douleur, etc.).
bellow[2]. **1.** v.i. (Of bull) Beugler, mugir; F: (of pers., ocean) mugir, hurler. **2.** v.tr. To bellow (out) a song, vociférer, F: beugler, une chanson.
bellows ['beloz], s.pl. **1.** Soufflet m (pour le feu). A pair of bellows, un soufflet. **2.** Soufflerie f (d'un orgue, d'une forge).
belly[1] ['beli], s. **1.** Ventre m; P: panse f, bedaine f. **2.** (a) Ventre, panse (d'une cruche). (b) Mus: Table f d'harmonie (d'un violon, d'un piano). **3.** Nau: Creux m, fond m (d'une voile).
'belly-ache, s. F: Mal m de ventre; colique f.
belly[2]. Nau: **1.** v.tr. (Of wind) To belly (out) the sails, enfler, gonfler, les voiles. **2.** v.i. (Of sail) Faire (le) sac.
bellyful ['beliful], s. Plein ventre; F: ventrée f. F: To have had a bellyful, en avoir une gavée; en avoir tout son soûl.
belong [bi'lɔŋ], v.i. **1.** Appartenir, être (to, à). That book belongs to me, ce livre m'appartient, est à moi. It belongs to me to decide, il m'appartient de décider. That belongs to my duties, cela relève de mes attributions. (Of land) To b. to the Crown, dépendre de la Couronne. **2.** (Be appropriate) Être propre (à qch.). Such amusements do not b. to his age, ces amusements ne sont pas de son âge. **3.** (Be connected) To belong to a society, faire partie, être membre, d'une société. To belong to a place, (i) être (natif, originaire) d'un endroit; (ii) résider à un endroit. I belong here, je suis d'ici.
belongings [bi'lɔŋiŋz], s.pl. Affaires f, effets m (appartenant à qn). Personal belongings, objets personnels. With all one's belongings, F: avec armes et bagages.
beloved. 1. p.p. & pred. a. [bi'lʌvd] Aimé. B. by all, aimé de tous. Beloved of the gods, aimé, chéri, des dieux. **2.** a. ' & s. [bi'lʌvid] Bien-aimé(e), chéri(e). My beloved, mon, ma, bien-aimé(e).
below [bi'lou]. **1.** adv. (a) En bas, (au-)dessous. The tenants (of the flat) below, les locataires du dessous. Here below (on earth), ici-bas. Nau: All hands below! tout le monde en bas! S.a. DOWN[3] I. 2. (b) Jur: The court below, le tribunal inférieur. (c) The passage quoted below, le passage cité (i) ci-dessous, (ii) plus loin, ci-après. **2.** prep. Au-dessous de. (a) B. the knee, au-dessous du genou. On the table and b. it, sur la table et (au-)dessous. S.a. BELT[1] I. (b) Below the average, au-dessous de la moyenne. Temperature below normal, température inférieure à la normale. (c) Below the surface, sous la surface. (d) Below the bridge, en aval du pont. (e) To be below s.o. in station, occuper un rang inférieur à qn.
belt[1] [belt], s. **1.** (a) (Waist-)belt, ceinture f, Mil: ceinturon m. (Shoulder-)belt, baudrier m, banderole f. (Ladies') suspender belt, gaine f de hanches. S.a. HALF-BELT, LIFE-BELT. Box: Blow below the belt, coup bas, coup déloyal. F: To hit s.o. below the belt, donner à qn un coup en traître; frapper qn déloyalement. (b) N.Arch: Armour belt, ceinture cuirassée. **2.** Mec.E: Courroie f (de transmission). **3.** Belt of hills, ceinture de collines. B. of land, bande f de terre. Coal belt, zone houillère. The belts of Jupiter, les zones, les bandes, de Jupiter. Trade-wind belt, zone des (vents) alizés. Standard-time belt, fuseau m horaire.

belt[2], v.tr. **1.** Ceinturer, ceindre (qn, qch.). **2.** (Surround) Entourer (qch.) d'une ceinture.
belted, a. Ceinturé; à ceinture; (croiseur) cuirassé. F: Belted earl, seigneur haut et puissant. **belting,** s. **1.** (a) Ceinture(s) f(pl). (b) Matière f à courroies. **2.** Mec.E: Transmission f. **3.** F: To give a child a good belting, administrer une correction à un enfant (avec une courroie).
belvedere ['belvedi:ər], s. Arch: Belvédère m.
bemired [bi'maiərd], a. Embourbé.
bemoan [bi'moun], v.tr. Pleurer, déplorer (qch.).
bemuse [bi'mju:z], v.tr. Stupéfier.
Ben[1] [ben]. Pr.n.m. Benjamin. S.a. BIG BEN.
ben[2], s. Geog: (Scot.) Sommet m, pic m. Ben Nevis, le mont Nevis.
bench [benʃ], s. **1.** (a) Banc m; banquette f; gradin m (d'amphithéâtre). Parl: The Treasury Bench, le banc ministériel. The episcopal bench, le banc des évêques (à la Chambre des Lords). Jur: The judge's bench, le siège du juge. (b) Jur: The Bench, la magistrature. (c). (The judges) La Cour. **2.** (a) Établi m (de menuisier). (b) Mec.E: Testing bench, banc d'essai. **3.** Civ.E: Accotement m, berme f (d'un chemin). **'bench-mark,** s. Surv: Repère m. **'bench-test,** s. Mec.E: Essai m au banc.
bencher ['benʃər], s. Avocat appartenant au corps des doyens des 'Inns of Court', q.v. under INN 2.
bend[1] [bend], s. Nau: Nœud m, ajut m. Fisherman's bend, nœud de pêcheur; nœud anglais.
bend[2], s. Her: Bande f, lanière f. Bend sinister, barre f de bâtardise.
bend[3], s. **1.** Courbure f; courbe f; (of road, pipe) coude m; (of road) tournant m, angle m, Aut: virage m; (of river) méandre m, sinuosité f. Aut: To take a bend, prendre un virage; virer. **2.** mec: U.S: The bends, mal m des caissons.
bend[4], v.tr. & i. (bent; p.p. bent, Lit: occ. bended) **1.** Courber (un osier, le corps); plier (le coude, etc.); ployer, fléchir (le genou); baisser (la tête); arquer (le dos); cambrer, cintrer (un tuyau, un rail). To b. one's head over a book, pencher la tête sur le livre. To b. to s.o.'s will, se plier à, fléchir devant, la volonté de qn. Better bend than break, mieux vaut plier que rompre. The road, river, bends to the right, la route, la rivière, tourne, s'infléchit, fait un coude, vers la droite. To b. beneath a burden, plier, fléchir, se courber, sous un fardeau. S.a. KNEE I. **2.** (a) v.tr. To b. a rod, a key, out of shape, forcer, fausser, une barre de fer, une clef. (b) v.i. To bend under a strain, (of wood, iron) arquer; (of rod, wheel) (se) voiler. **3.** (Make tense) Tendre, bander (un arc, un ressort). **4.** (Direct) (a) To bend one's steps towards a place, diriger, porter, ses pas, se diriger, vers un endroit. (b) Lit: To bend one's gaze on sth., fixer ses regards sur qch. **5.** Nau: (a) Étalinguer (un câble); frapper (une manœuvre); enverguer (une voile). (b) Abouter (deux cordages). **bend back. 1.** v.tr. Reployer en arrière; replier; recourber (une ame, etc.). **2.** v.i. Se recourber; se réfléchir. (b) (Of pers.) Se pencher en arrière. **bend down. 1.** v.tr. Courber, ployer (une branche). **2.** v.i. Se courber, se baisser. **bend forward,** v.i Se pencher en avant. **bent. 1.** (a) Courbé, plié, arqué. B. back, dos vouté. (b) Faussé, fléchi, gauchi. To become bent, se s'arquer, se courber; (with age) se voûter; (ii) (of rod, spring, etc.) fléchir, gauchir. **2.** (Determined) Déterminé, résolu, décidé (on doing sth., à faire qch.). He is b. on

ruining you, il est acharné à votre perte. *He is b. on seeing me*, il veut absolument me voir. *To be b. on gain*, être âpre au gain. **3. To be homeward bent**, diriger ses pas, s'acheminer, vers la maison. **bending,** *s.* (*a*) Ployage *m*, cintrage *m.* (*b*) *Mec.E:* etc: Arcure *f*, arqûre *f.* (*c*) *Mec:* Bending strength, résistance à la flexion. **Bending moment**, moment de flexion.

beneath [bi'ni:θ]. **1.** *adv.* Dessous, au-dessous, en bas. **From beneath**, de dessous. **2.** *prep.* (*a*) (*Lower than*) Au-aessous de; sous. *F:* **It is beneath him to complain**, il est indigne de lui de se plaindre; il dédaigne de se plaindre. *S.a.* MARRY¹ 2. (*b*) (*Under*) **Habitations b. the ground**, habitations sous terre. **To bend beneath a burden**, plier sous un fardeau.

benedick ['benedik], *s.m. F:* Vieux garçon nouveau marié.

Benedict ['benedikt]. *Pr.n.m.* Benoît, Benoist.

benedictine [bene'diktin]. **1.** *Ecc:* a. & s. Bénédictin, -ine. **2.** *s.* (*also* [-ti:n]) (*Liqueur*) Bénédictine *f.*

benediction [bene'dikʃ(ə)n], *s.* **1.** Bénédiction *f.* **2.** (*At meals*) Bénédicité *m.*

benefaction [bene'fakʃ(ə)n], *s.* **1.** Bienfait *m.* **2.** (*a*) Œuvre *f* de bienfaisance. (*b*) Donation *f.*

benefactor, -tress ['benefaktər, -tres], *s.* **1.** Bienfaiteur, -trice. **2.** Donateur, -trice.

benefice ['benefis], *s. Ecc:* Bénéfice *m.*

beneficence [be'nefis(ə)ns], *s.* **1.** Bienfaisance *f.* **2.** Œuvre *f* de bienfaisance.

beneficent [be'nefis(ə)nt], *a.* **1.** Bienfaisant. **2.** Salutaire. **-ly,** *adv.* **1.** Avec bienfaisance. **2.** Salutairement.

beneficial [bene'fiʃ(ə)l], *a.* Salutaire, profitable, utile, avantageux. **-ally,** *adv.* Avantageusement.

beneficiary [bene'fiʃəri], *a.* & *s. Ecc: Jur:* Bénéficier, -ière; bénéficiaire (*m*); ayant-droit *m.*

benefit¹ ['benefit], *s.* **1.** Avantage *m*, profit *m. To derive, reap, b. from sth.*, profiter de qch. *Performance for the b. of the poor*, représentation au profit des pauvres. *Jur:* **Benefit of the doubt**, bénéfice *m* du doute. **Benefit club, benefit society**, société de secours mutuels. *Th: Sp:* **Benefit (performance, match)**, représentation, match, au bénéfice de qn. **2.** *Adm:* Indemnité *f*, allocation *f.* **Unemployment benefit**, indemnité de chômage; prestation *f.* **Medical benefit**, secours médical.

benefit². **1.** *v.tr.* Faire du bien, être avantageux, profiter, à (qn, qch.). **2.** *v.i.* **To benefit by sth.**, profiter de qch.; gagner à qch.; se trouver bien de qch.

benevolence [be'nevoləns], *s.* **1.** Bienveillance *f*, bonté *f.* **2.** Bienfait *m*; don *m* charitable.

benevolent [be'nevolənt], *a.* **1.** Bienveillant (*to, envers*). **2.** Bienfaisant, charitable (*to, envers*). **Benevolent society**, association de bienfaisance; société de secours mutuels. **-ly,** *adv.* Avec bienveillance.

Bengal [ben'gɔ:l]. *Pr.n. Geog:* Le Bengale. **Bengal light**, feu *m* de Bengale.

benighted [bi'naitid], *a.* **1.** Anuité; surpris par la nuit. **2.** Plongé dans les ténèbres de l'ignorance.

benign [bi'nain], *a.* (*a*) Bénin, *f.* bénigne; doux, *f.* douce; favorable. (*b*) *Med:* Bénin.

benignant [be'nignənt], *a.* Bénin, *f.* bénigne; bon, bienveillant. **-ly,** *adv.* Avec bienveillance.

benignity [be'nigniti], *s.* **1.** Bienveillance *f*, bonté *f.* **2.** Bénignité *f* (du climat, d'une fièvre).

Benjamin¹ ['bendʒamin]. *Pr.n.m.* Benjamin. *F:* **The Benjamin**, le Benjamin (de la famille); le favori, le gâté.

benjamin², *s. Bot:* Benjoin *m.*

bent¹ [bent], *s.* **1.** *Bot:* **Bent(-grass)**, (i) jonc *m*; (ii) agrostide *f.* **2.** Lande *f*, prairie *f.*

bent², *s.* Penchant *m*, inclination *f*, disposition *f* (*for*, pour). **To have a bent towards sth.**, avoir du goût pour qch., un penchant à qch., des dispositions naturelles pour qch. *S.a.* TOP¹ I. 6.

bent³. *See* BEND⁴.

benumb [bi'nʌm], *v.tr.* (*a*) Engourdir, transir. (*b*) *F:* Paralyser, engourdir (l'esprit).

benzene, benzine ['benzi:n], *s.* Benzine *f.*

benzoin ['benzoin], *s.* (*Gum*) **benzoin**, benjoin *m.*

benzol ['benzol], *s. Ch: Com:* Benzol *m.*

bequeath [bi'kwi:ð], *v.tr.* Léguer (*to, à*).

bequest [bi'kwest], *s.* Legs *m.*

bereave [bi'ri:v], *v.tr.* (*p.t. & p.p.* **bereft** [bi'reft], **bereaved**; *usu.* **bereft** *in* 1 *and* **bereaved** *in* 2) Priver, déposséder (*s.o. of sth.*, qn de qch.). **1.** *Indignation had bereft him of speech*, l'indignation l'avait privé de la parole. **2.** *An accident bereaved him of his father, of his parents*, un accident lui a ravi son père, l'a rendu orphelin. *s.pl.* **The bereaved**, la famille du mort; les affligés.

bereavement [bi'ri:vmənt], *s.* Perte *f* (d'un parent); deuil *m.*

bereft. *See* BEREAVE.

beret ['bere, 'beret], *s. Cost:* Béret *m.*

bergamot¹ ['bə:rgamot], *s.* (*Orange or lemon*) Bergamote *f.* **Bergamot tree**, bergamotier *m.*

bergamot², *s.* (*Pear*) Bergamote *f*, crassane *f.*

berm [bə:rm], *s. Civ.E:* Berme *f*, banquette *f.*

Bermudas (the) [ðəbə(:)r'mju:dəz]. *Pr.n. Geog:* Les Bermudes *f.*

berry¹ ['beri], *s.* **1.** *Bot:* Baie *f.* **2.** (*a*) Frai *m* (de poisson). (*b*) Œufs *mpl* (de crustacé).

berry², *v.i.* **1.** (*Of shrub*) Se garnir de baies. **2.** **To go berrying**, aller à la cueillette des mûres.

berth¹ [bə:rθ], *s.* **1.** *Nau:* (*a*) Évitée *f*, évitage *m.* **To give a ship a wide berth**, éviter, parer, un navire; passer au large d'un navire. *F:* **To give s.o. a wide berth**, éviter qn. (*b*) (*Anchoring*) **berth**, poste *m* de mouillage, d'amarrage. (*c*) Poste à quai; emplacement *m.* **2.** (*a*) *Nau: Rail:* Couchette *f* (de voyageur). (*b*) *Nau:* Cadre *m* (d'officier, d'homme d'équipage). **3.** (*a*) Emplacement (de qch.); place *f* (dans une diligence, etc.). (*b*) *F:* Place, emploi *m.*

berth². **1.** *v.tr.* (*a*) Donner, assigner, un poste à (un navire). (*b*) Accoster (un navire) le long du quai. **2.** *v.i.* (*a*) (*Of ship*) (i) Mouiller. (ii) Aborder à quai. (*b*) **To berth forward, aft**, coucher à l'avant, à l'arrière.

beryl ['beril], *s. Miner:* Béryl *m.*

beseech [bi'si:tʃ], *v.tr.* (*besought* [bi'sɔ:t]) *Lit:* **1.** Supplier, adjurer, conjurer (*s.o. to do sth.*, qn de faire qch.). **2.** **To b. s.o.'s pardon**, implorer le pardon de qn. **beseeching,** *a.* (Air, ton) suppliant.

beseem [bi'si:m], *v.tr.* (*Only in 3rd pers.*) *Lit: To b. s.o.* (*well, ill*), convenir, seoir, (bien, mal) à qn. **beseeming,** *a.* Convenable, seyant.

beset [bi'set], *v.tr.* (*p.t.* beset; *p.p.* beset; besetting) *Lit:* **1.** Cerner (des troupes); assaillir, obséder (qn); serrer (qn) de près. **Beset with dangers, with difficulties**, environné, entouré, de dangers, de difficultés. **2.** Assiéger (un endroit). **3.** (*Of misfortunes, etc.*) Assaillir (qn). **besetting,** *a.* **Besetting sin**, péché d'habitude.

beside [bi'said], *prep.* **1.** A côté, auprès, de (qn, qch.). *Seated b. me*, assis à côté de moi. *There is no one to set b. him*, il n'y a personne qui lui soit comparable. **2.** (*a*) **Beside the question**,

beside the point, à côté de la question ; en dehors du sujet. (b) **To be beside oneself,** être hors de soi ; (with joy) être transporté de joie.
besides [bi'saidz]. I. adv. (a) En outre, en plus. **Many more besides,** encore bien d'autres. **Nothing besides,** rien de plus. (b) It is too late ; b., I am tired, il est trop tard ; d'ailleurs, du reste, je suis fatigué. 2. prep. Others b. him, d'autres que lui. We were four b. John, nous étions quatre sans compter Jean.
besiege [bi'si:dʒ], v.tr. Assiéger ; mettre le siège devant (une ville) ; faire le siège (d'une ville).
besieger [bi'si:dʒər], s. Assiégeant m.
beslaver [bi'slavər], v.tr. Couvrir (qch.) de bave ; baver sur (qch.). F : To b. s.o., flagorner qn.
besmear [bi'smiːər], v.tr. Barbouiller, souiller.
besmirch [bi'sməːrtʃ], v.tr. Salir, tacher, souiller (qch.) ; salir, ternir (la mémoire de qn, etc.).
besom ['bi:zəm], s. Balai m (de jonc, de bruyère).
besot [bi'sɔt], v.tr. (besotted) Abrutir (with, de).
besotted, a. Abruti (par la boisson, etc.).
besought [bi'sɔːt]. See BESEECH.
bespangle [bi'spaŋgl], v.tr. Lit : = SPANGLE².
bespatter [bi'spatər], v.tr. Éclabousser. Be-spattered with mud, tout couvert de boue.
bespeak [bi'spi:k], v.tr. (Conj. like SPEAK) I. Commander (des souliers, etc.) ; retenir, arrêter (une place, une chambre à l'hôtel). 2. Accuser, annoncer. His conversation bespeaks a man of wit, sa conversation annonce un homme d'esprit. **bespoke,** a. (a) Bespoke garment, vêtement (fait) sur commande, sur mesure. (b) Bespoke shoemaker, cordonnier à façon.
besprinkle [bi'spriŋkl], v.tr. Lit : (a) Arroser, asperger (with, de). (b) Saupoudrer (with, de). (c) Parsemer (with, de).
Bess [bes]. Pr.n.f. F : A : Brown Bess, fusil m à pierre ; mousquet m, flingot m. Hist : F : Good Queen Bess, la bonne reine Élisabeth (1533-1603).
best¹ [best]. I. a. & s. (a) (Le) meilleur, (la) meilleure ; (neuter) le meilleur. Best man (at a wedding), garçon d'honneur. We drank of the best, of his best, nous avons bu du meilleur, de son meilleur. (Dressed) in one's best (clothes), endimanché ; · (of woman) dans ses plus beaux atours ; F : sur son trente et un. He can sing with the best, il chante comme pas un. The best of the matter, the best of it, is that . . ., le plus beau de l'affaire c'est que . . . The best part of the way, of the year, la plus grande partie du chemin, de l'année. To know what is best for s.o., savoir ce qui convient le mieux à qn. It would be b. to . . ., the best plan would be to . . ., le mieux serait de. . . . To do one's best, the best one can, faire de son mieux, faire tout son possible. I did my b. to comfort her, je la consolai de mon mieux. He did his b. to smile, il s'efforça de sourire. To look one's best, être, paraître, à son avantage ; (of woman) être en beauté. To be at one's best, être en train, en forme. She was at her b. at thirty, c'est à trente ans qu'elle a été le plus belle. To get, have, the best of it, of the bargain ; to come off best, l'emporter ; avoir l'avantage ; avoir le dessus. To make the best of sth., s'accommoder de qch. To make the best of a bad job, of a bad bargain, faire bonne mine à mauvais jeu ; faire contre mauvaise fortune bon cœur. S.a. FOOT¹ I, NEXT I. 2, SECOND-BEST. (b) Adv.phr. At (the) best. To sell at b., vendre au mieux. At (the) b. it is a poor piece of work, pour dire le mieux c'est un piètre travail. To act for the best, agir pour le mieux. To do sth. to the best of one's

ability, faire qch. de son mieux. To the best of my belief, knowledge, recollection, à ce que je crois ; autant que je sache ; (pour) autant que je puisse m'en souvenir. 2. adv. (a) He does it (the) best, c'est lui qui le fait le mieux. I comforted her as best I could, je la consolai de mon mieux. You know best, c'est vous (qui êtes) le mieux placé pour en juger. Do as you think b., faites comme bon vous semble(ra). (b) The b. dressed man, l'homme le mieux habillé. The b. known book, le livre le mieux, le plus, connu. **best-'seller,** s. F : I. Livre m à succès, à fort tirage. 2. Auteur m à gros tirages.
best², v.tr. F : L'emporter sur (qn).
bestial ['bestjəl], a. Bestial, -aux.
bestiality [besti'aliti], s. Bestialité f.
bestir [bi'stəːr], v.pr. (Conj. like STIR) To b. oneself, se remuer, s'actionner, s'activer.
bestow [bi'stou], v.tr. I. Accorder, octroyer, donner (sth. upon s.o., qch. à qn). To b. a title on s.o., conférer un titre à qn. To b. one's affection on s.o., placer son affection sur qn. To bestow one's hand on s.o., faire don de sa main à qn. To bestow the hand of one's daughter upon s.o., accorder à qn la main de sa fille. 2. A : To b. sth. somewhere, déposer qch. quelque part.
bestowal [bi'stouəl], s Don m, octroi m (de qch.).
bestrew [bi'stru:], v.tr. (p.t. bestrewed) ; p.p. be-strewed or bestrewn [bi'stru:n]) Lit : Parsemer, joncher (with, de).
bestride [bi'straid], v.tr. (bestrode [bi'stroud], bestridden [bi'stridn]) I. (a) Être à cheval, à califourchon, sur (qch.). (b) Se tenir les jambes écartées au-dessus de (qch.). 2. (a) Enjamber (un fossé). (b) Enfourcher (un cheval).
bet¹ [bet], s. Pari m, gageure f. To make, lay, a bet, parier ; faire un pari. To take (up) a bet, tenir, accepter un pari. S.a. EVEN² 3.
bet², v.tr. (p.t. & p.p. bet ; betting) Parier (une somme). To bet ten to one that . . ., parier à dix contre un que. . . . To bet two to one, parier le double contre le simple. To bet against s.o., parier contre qn. To bet on sth., parier sur qch. I'll bet you anything you like, j'en gagerai ma tête à couper. **betting,** s. Les paris m. The b. ran high, on a parié gros.
betake [bi'teik], v.pr. (Conj. like TAKE). To b. oneself to a place, (s'en) aller, se rendre, dans, à, un endroit.
betel [bi:tl], s. Bétel m. Betel-nut, (noix f d')arec m.
bethink [bi'θiŋk], v.pr. (Conj. like THINK) I. To b. oneself, réfléchir, considérer. To b. oneself of sth., to do sth., s'aviser de qch., de faire qch. 2. Se rappeler (that, que).
bethought [bi'θɔːt]. See BETHINK.
betide [bi'taid], v. (Used only in 3rd sing. pres. sub.) A. & Lit : I. v.i. Whate'er betide, quoi qu'il arrive ; advienne que pourra. 2. v.tr. Woe betide him if ever . . ., malheur à lui si jamais. . . .
betimes [bi'taimz], adv. Lit : De bonne heure.
betoken [bi'toukə n], v.tr. I. Être signe de (qch.) ; accuser, dénoter, révéler. Here everything betokens peace, ici tout respire la paix. 2. Présager, annoncer (le beau temps, etc.).
betony ['betəni], s. Bot : Bétoine f.
betook [bi'tuk]. See BETAKE.
betray [bi'trei], v.tr. I. Trahir (qn, sa patrie, sa foi) ; vendre (qn). To b. s.o. into s.o.'s hands, livrer qn aux mains de qn (par trahison). 2. To b. s.o. into error, entraîner qn dans l'erreur 3. Révéler, montrer, laisser voir, laisser deviner, trahir (son ignorance, son émotion) ; livrer, révéler (un secret).

betrayal [bi'treiəl], *s.* **1.** Action *f* de trahir ; trahison *f.* **2.** Révélation *f* (de son ignorance, etc.).
betrayer [bi'treiər], *s.* (*a*) Traître, -esse. *B. of his country*, traître envers sa patrie. (*b*) Révélateur, -trice (d'un secret).
betroth |bi'tro:uð], *v.tr. Lit:* Promettre (sa fille) en mariage (*to*, à) ; fiancer (*to*, à, avec).
betrothed, *a. & s. Lit :* Fiancé(e).
betrothal [bi'trouðəl], *s.* Fiançailles *fpl* (*to*, avec).
better[1] ['betər]. **1.** *a. & s.* Meilleur. *B. days*, des jours meilleurs. *F :* **They have seen better days,** ils ont eu des malheurs. *S.a.* DAY 3. *You will find no b.* hotel, vous ne trouverez pas mieux comme hôtel. *He's a b.* man *than you,* il est votre supérieur ; il vaut plus que vous. (*At games, etc.*) *You are b.* than *I,* vous êtes plus fort que moi. *He is no b.* than his brother, il ne vaut pas mieux que son frère. **The respect due to your betters,** le respect dû à vos supérieurs. **A street of better-class houses,** une rue de maisons de bonne apparence, de maisons cossues. *I had hoped for b. things,* j'avais espéré mieux. *For the b. part of the day,* pendant la plus grande partie du jour. *S.a.* HALF 1, WORLD 1. **2.** (*Neuter*) Mieux. (*a*) **That's better,** voilà qui est mieux. *Nothing could be b.,* it couldn't be b., c'est on ne peut mieux. **So much the better,** tant mieux. **To do** sth. for better or worse, faire qch. vaille que vaille. *To take s.o. for b. or worse,* prendre qn pour les bons comme pour les mauvais jours. **To get better,** (i) (*of thgs*) s'améliorer, s'amender ; (ii) (*of pers.*) guérir, se remettre, se rétablir. **The weather is better,** il fait meilleur. **To be better** (*in health*), aller, se porter, mieux. **Change for the better,** amélioration. *There is a change for the b.,* il y a un mieux. **To get the better of s.o.,** (i) l'emporter sur qn ; (ii) (*cheat*) refaire qn ; mettre qn dedans ; rouler qn. **To be (all) the better for doing sth.,** se trouver bien d'avoir fait qch. *S.a.* ALL I. 3. **To go one better than s.o.,** (r)enchérir, surenchérir, sur qn ; *F :* damer le pion à qn. (*b*) *It is b. that it should be so ;* better so, il vaut mieux qu'il en soit ainsi. *It is b. to go away than stay,* il vaut mieux, mieux vaut, partir que de rester. *It is b. to suffer than to lie,* plutôt souffrir que mentir. *It would be b. to see him again,* il serait préférable de le revoir. **3.** *adv.* (*a*) Mieux. **Better and better,** de mieux en mieux. *I know that b. than you,* je sais cela mieux que vous. *I can understand it all the* **better because . . .,** je le conçois d'autant mieux que. . . . **You had better stay,** il vaut mieux que vous restiez ; vous ferez, feriez, bien de rester. **To think better of it,** changer d'opinion ; se raviser. **Better still . . .,** (i) mieux encore . . ., (ii) qui mieux est. . . . *S.a.* LATE II. 1. (*b*) **Better dressed,** mieux habillé. *B. known,* plus connu.
better[2]. **1.** *v.tr.* (*a*) Améliorer ; rendre meilleur. **To better oneself,** améliorer sa position, sa condition. (*b*) Surpasser (un exploit). **2.** *v.i.* (*Of thg*) S'améliorer.
better[3], **bettor** ['betər], *s.* Parieur *m.*
betterment ['betərmənt], *s.* Amélioration *f.*
between [bi'twi:n]. **1.** *prep.* Entre. (*a*) *B. the two hedges,* entre les deux haies. **No one can come between us,** personne ne peut nous séparer. *S.a.* DEVIL[1] 1, FIRE[1] 4, STOOL[1] 1. (*b*) *B. eight and nine o'clock,* entre huit et neuf heures. *B. now and Monday,* d'ici (à) lundi. *B. twenty and thirty,* de vingt à trente. (*c*) **You must choose between them,** il faut choisir entre les deux. (*d*) **We bought it between us,** nous l'avons acheté à nous deux, à nous trois, etc. (*e*) *They shared the loot b. them,* ils se sont partagé le butin. **Between ourselves,**

entre nous ; de vous à moi. **2.** *adv. He separated them by rushing b.,* il les a séparés en se jetant entre eux. *S.a.* FAR-BETWEEN, GO-BETWEEN.
be'tween-decks. *Nau :* **1.** *adv.* Dans l'entrepont ; sous barrots. **2.** *s.* L'entrepont *m.*
be'tween-time(s), -while(s), *adv.* **1.** Dans l'intervalle ; entre-temps. **2.** De temps en temps.
betwixt [bi'twikst]. **1.** *prep.* = BETWEEN. **2.** *adv. F :* **Betwixt and between,** entre les deux.
bevel[1] ['bev(ə)l], *s.* **1.** Angle *m* oblique. (*a*) Biseau *m,* biais *m.* **Bevel-edge,** bord biseauté, en chanfrein. (*b*) Conicité *f* (d'un engrenage, etc.). **Bevel-gear,** engrenage à biseau ; engrenage conique, d'angle. **Bevel-wheel,** roue dentée conique ; pignon conique. **2.** *Tls :* **Bevel-rule, -square,** fausse équerre.
bevel[2], *v.* (bevelled) **1.** *v.tr.* Biseauter, chanfreiner ; tailler (qch.) en biseau, en sifflet. **2.** *v.i.* (*Of thg*) Biaiser ; aller de biais ; aller en biseau. **bevelled,** *a.* (Bord) biseauté, en biseau.
bevelling, *s.* Biseautage *m,* équerrage *m,* chanfreinage *m.*
beverage ['bevəredʒ], *s.* Breuvage *m,* boisson *f.*
bevy ['bevi], *s.* **1.** Bande *f,* troupe *f. Esp.* Bevy of maidens, bande, essaim *m,* de jeunes filles. **2.** *Ven :* (*Of larks, quails*) Volée *f ;* (*of roes*) harde *f,* troupe.
bewail [bi'weil], *v.tr.* Pleurer (qch.). *To b. one's lot,* se lamenter sur son sort.
beware [bi'weər], *v.ind.tr., & Poet : v.tr.* (*Only in inf. and imp.*) *To b. of s.o.,* se méfier, se défier, de qn. *To b. of sth.,* se garder de qch. ; prendre garde à qch. Beware! prenez garde ! 'Beware of pickpockets,' "se méfier des pickpockets." *To b. of doing sth.,* se garder de faire qch.
bewilder [bi'wildər], *v.tr.* Désorienter, égarer (qn) ; *F :* ahurir (qn). **bewildered,** *a.* (*a*) Désorienté ; *F :* ahuri. *B. air,* air hébété. **I am bewildered,** j'y perds la tête. (*b*) Abasourdi, confondu. **bewildering,** *a.* Déroutant ; *F :* ahurissant.
bewilderment [bi'wildərmənt], *s.* (*a*) Désorientation *f ;* trouble *m ; F :* ahurissement *m.* (*b*) Abasourdissement *m.*
bewitch [bi'witʃ], *v.tr.* Ensorceler. (*a*) Jeter un sort sur (qn). (*b*) *F :* Charmer, enchanter (qn). **bewitching,** *a.* Ensorcelant, ravissant ; enchanteur, -eresse.
beyond [bi'jɔnd]. **1.** *adv.* Au delà, par delà, plus loin. **2.** *prep.* Au delà de, par delà. (*a*) *The house is b.* the church, la maison est au delà de, plus loin que, l'église. *The countries b. the Rhine, b. the seas,* les pays d'outre-Rhin, d'outre-mer. **To be beyond the pale,** être au ban de la société. *S.a.* REACH[1] 2. (*b*) **To stay beyond one's time,** rester trop longtemps. *B. a certain date,* passé une certaine date. (*c*) (*Surpassing*) Beyond all praise, au-dessus de tout éloge. **To succeed beyond one's hopes,** réussir au delà de ses espérances. *To go b. one's authority,* outrepasser ses pouvoirs. *This work is beyond me,* ce travail dépasse mes forces, mes moyens. **It is beyond me,** cela me dépasse ; je n'y comprends rien. *S.a.* CONTROL[1] 1, POWER 1. **Beyond doubt,** hors de doute. **Beyond belief,** incroyable(ment). *S.a.* MEASURE[1] 3, QUESTION[1] 2. **That is (going) beyond a joke,** cela dépasse les bornes de la plaisanterie. (*d*) (*Except*) *He has nothing b. his wages,* il n'a rien que ses gages. **3.** *s.* The beyond, l'au-delà. *F :* At the back of beyond, tout au bout du monde.
bezel ['bez(ə)l], *s.* **1.** *Lap :* Biseau *m* (d'une pierre taillée). **2.** Chaton *m,* portée *f* (de bague). **3.** Drageoir *m,* biseau (de boîtier de montre).
bezique [be'zi:k], *s. Cards :* Bésigue *m.*

bias[1] ['baiəs], s. **1.** *Needlew:* Biais *m.* **Material cut on the bias,** étoffe coupée en biais, de biais. **2.** *Bowls:* (*a*) Décentrement *m,* fort *m* (de la boule). (*b*) Déviation *f.* **3.** (*a*) Prévention *f* (*towards,* en faveur de; *against,* contre); parti pris. (*b*) Penchant *m* (pour qch.). **4.** *W.Tel:* Grid bias, polarisation *f* de la grille.

bias[2], *v.tr.* (bias(s)ed) **1.** *Bowls:* Décentrer (la boule). **2.** Rendre (qn) partial; prédisposer, prévenir (qn) (*towards,* en faveur de; *against,* contre). **biased,** *a.* Partial, -aux. **To be b. against s.o.,** avoir une prévention contre qn.

bib ⌊bib⌋, *s.* **1.** Bavette *f* (d'enfant). **2.** Baverette *f* (de tablier). *F:* (*Of woman*) **To put on one's best bib and tucker,** se mettre sur son trente et un.

bibber ['bibər], *s.* Buveur *m.* *See* WINE-BIBBER.

Bible [baibl], *s.* Bible *f.* **Bible-oath,** serment prêté sur la Bible. **Bible class,** (i) classe d'histoire sainte; (ii) (classe du) catéchisme.

biblical ['biblik(ə)l], *a.* Biblique.

bibliographer [bibli'əgrəfər], *s.* Bibliographe *m.*

bibliographic(al) [biblio'grafik(əl)], *a.* Bibliographique.

bibliography [bibli'əgrəfi], *s.* Bibliographie *f.*

bibliomaniac [biblio'meiniak], *s.* Bibliomane *m.*

bibliophile ['bibliofil], *s.* Bibliophile *m.*

bibulous ['bibjuləs], *a.* Adonné à la boisson; buveur. *F:* **Bibulous nose,** nez d'ivrogne.

bicarbonate [bai'kɑːrbonet], *s.* Bicarbonate *m.*

biceps ['baiseps], *s.* *Anat:* Biceps *m.*

bichromate [bai'kroumet], *s.* Bichromate *m.* *Phot:* **Gum bichromate,** gomme bichromatée.

bicker ['bikər], *v.i.* **1.** Se quereller, se chamailler. **2.** (*Of stream*) Murmurer. **bickering**[1], *a.* **1.** Querelleur. **2.** (*Of stream*) Murmurant. **bickering**[2], *s.* Querelles *fpl;* chamailleries *fpl.*

biconcave [bai'kɔnkeiv], *a.* Biconcave.

biconvex [bai'kɔnveks], *a.* Biconvexe.

bicycle[1] ['baisikl], *s.* Bicyclette *f.* *A:* '*Ordinary*' *b.,* vélocipède *m.* **Bicycle track,** piste cyclable. **bicycle**[2], *v.i.* **1.** Faire de la bicyclette. **2.** *To b.* **to Bristol,** aller à bicyclette à Bristol. **bicycling,** *s.* Cyclisme *m.*

bicyclist ['baisiklist], *s.* (Bi)cycliste *mf.*

bid[1] [bid], *s.* (*a*) Enchère *f,* offre *f,* mise *f.* **To make a bid for a property,** (i) faire une offre pour, (ii) mettre (une) enchère sur, un immeuble. **Further bid, higher bid,** surenchère *f;* offre supérieure. **The last bid,** la dernière mise. *F:* **To make a bid for power,** (i) viser au pouvoir; (ii) tenter un coup d'État. (*b*) *Cards:* Appel *m;* demande *f.* (*At bridge*) **To raise the bid,** relancer.

bid[2], *v.tr. & i.* (*p.t.* **bade** [bad, beid], **bid;** *p.p.* **bidden** [bidn], **bid;** **bidding**) **1.** Commander, ordonner (*s.o.* (*to*) *to do sth.,* à qn de faire qch.). **Bid him come in,** dites-lui d'entrer. **Do as you are bid,** faites ce que vous vous dit. **2.** (*a*) *To bid s.o. to dinner,* inviter qn à dîner. (*b*) *To bid* **s.o. welcome, good-day,** souhaiter la bienvenue, donner le bonjour, à qn. *S.a.* DEFIANCE, FAREWELL. (*c*) **The weather bids fair to be fine,** le temps s'annonce beau. **3.** (*p.t. & p.p.* bid) (*a*) (*At auction sale*) *To bid* for sth., (i) faire une offre pour qch.; (ii) mettre une enchère sur qch. *To bid ten pounds,* faire une offre de dix livres. (*b*) *Cards:* **To bid three diamonds,** demander, appeler, trois carreaux. **bidding,** *s.* **1.** (*a*) Commandement *m,* ordre *m.* **To be at s.o.'s b.,** être aux ordres de qn. (*b*) Invitation *f.* **2.** (*a*) Enchères *fpl,* mises *fpl.* (*b*) *Cards: etc:* **The b. is closed,** l'enchère est faite.

biddable ['bidəbl], *a.* Obéissant, docile.

bidder ['bidər], *s.* (*At sale*) Enchérisseur *m.*

The highest bidder, le plus offrant; le dernier enchérisseur.

bide [baid], *v.tr. & i.* (bided) *A: =* ABIDE. (*Still used in*) **To bide one's time,** attendre l'heure, attendre le bon moment; se réserver.

biennial [bai'enjəl]. **1.** *a.* Biennal, -aux. **2.** *a. & s.* *Bot:* Biennial (plant), plante bisannuelle. **-ally,** *adv.* Tous les deux ans.

bier ['biːər], *s.* (*a*) Civière *f* (pour porter un mort). (*b*) (*Hearse*) Corbillard *m.*

bif(f) [bif], *s.* *P:* Gnon *m,* beigne *f,* torgnole *f.*

bifocal [bai'fouk(ə)l], *a.* *Opt:* Bifocal, -aux.

bifurcate ['baifəːrkeit]. **1.** *v.tr.* Bifurquer. **2.** *v.i.* (Se) bifurquer.

bifurcation [baifəːr'keiʃ(ə)n], *s.* Bifurcation *f,* embranchement *m.*

big [big]. (**bigger** ['bigər]; **biggest**) **1.** *a.* (*a*) (*Large*) Grand; (*bulky*) gros. **Big hotel,** grand hôtel. *Big man,* (i) homme de grande taille, (ii) gros homme, (iii) homme marquant. **Big girl,** grande jeune fille. **Big enough to defend oneself,** de taille à se défendre. **Big fortune,** grosse fortune. **Big drop in prices,** forte baisse de prix. **The big scene** (*of the play*), la grande scène. **To grow big(ger),** (i) grandir; (ii) grossir. **Big drum,** grosse caisse. *Ven:* **Big game,** (i) gros gibier; (ii) les grands fauves. *S.a.* END[1] I, STICK[1] I. (*b*) **Big with child,** grosse, enceinte. **Big with consequences,** gros, lourd, de conséquences. **2.** *adv.* **To talk big,** faire l'important; fanfaronner. **'big-bellied,** *a.* Ventru, pansu. **'Big Ben,** *s.* La grosse cloche du Palais du Parlement. (Ainsi nommée en l'honneur de Sir Benjamin Hall.) **'big-boned,** *a.* Ossu; fortement charpenté.

bigamist ['bigəmist], *s.* Bigame *mf.*

bigamous ['bigəməs], *a.* Bigame.

bigamy ['bigəmi], *s.* Bigamie *f.*

bigaroon [bigə'ruːn], *s.* *Hort:* Bigarreau *m.*

bigger ['bigər], **biggest** ['bigəst]. *See* BIG.

bigness ['bignəs], *s.* **1.** Grandeur *f.* **2.** Grosseur *f.*

bigot ['bigət], *s.* Fanatique *mf* (en politique, etc.); sectaire *mf.*

bigoted ['bigətid], *a.* Fanatique; au zèle ou à l'esprit étroit.

bigotry ['bigətri], *s.* Fanatisme *m;* étroitesse *f* d'esprit.

bigwig ['bigwig], *s.* *F:* Personnage important; gros bonnet.

bike[1] [baik], *s.* *F:* (= BICYCLE) Vélo *m,* bécane *f.*

bike[2], *v.i.* *F:* = BICYCLE[2].

bilateral [bai'latərəl], *a.* Bilatéral, -aux.

bilberry ['bilbəri], *s.* *Bot:* = WHORTLEBERRY.

bile ⌊bail⌋, *s.* *Physiol:* Bile *f.* *F:* **To stir s.o.'s bile,** échauffer la bile à qn. **'bile-stones,** *s.pl.* *Med:* Calculs *m* biliaires.

bilge ⌈bildʒ⌉, *s.* *Nau:* (*a*) Fond *m* de cale. **The bilges,** les mailles *f.* (*b*) Bilge(-water), eau *f* de cale. *F:* **Get rid of all that b.,** débarrassez-vous de tout ce fatras. **'bilge-keel,** *s.* Quille *f* de bouchain; quille de roulis. **'bilge-pump,** *s.* Pompe *f* de cale.

biliary ['biljəri], *a.* *Physiol:* Biliaire.

bilinear [bai'liniər], *a.* *Mth:* Bilinéaire.

bilingual [bai'liŋgwəl], *a.* Bilingue.

bilious ['biljəs], *a.* Bilieux; (*tempérament*) bilieux. **Bilious attack,** accès *m* de bile.

biliousness ['biljəsnəs], *s.* Attaque *f* de bile; crise *f* hépatique; bile *f.*

bilk [bilk], *v.tr.* *F:* **1.** Tromper, escroquer (qn); payer (qn) en monnaie de singe. **2.** Fausser compagnie à (qn); filouter (un conducteur de taxi).

bill¹ [bil], *s. Archeol:* Hallebarde *f.* **'bill-hook,** *s. Tls:* Vouge *m*; serpe *f.*
bill², *s.* **1.** Bec *m* (d'oiseau, d'ancre). *S.a.* CRANE'S-BILL, RAZOR-BILL, SCISSOR-BILL. **2.** *Geog:* Bec, promontoire *m.* **Portland Bill,** le Bec de Portland.
bill³, *v.i.* (*Of birds*) Se becqueter. *F:* (*Of pers.*) **To bill and coo,** faire les tourtereaux.
bill⁴, *s.* **1.** *Com:* Note *f*, facture *f*, mémoire *m*; (*in restaurant*) addition *f.* **To make out a bill,** faire, rédiger, une facture. *Jur:* **Bill of costs,** état *m* de frais. **2.** (*a*) Effet *m* (de commerce); billet *m.* **Long(-dated) bills,** papier, effets, à longue échéance. **Bill of exchange,** lettre *f* de change; traite *f.* (*b*) *U.S:* Billet de banque. **3.** Affiche *f*, placard *m*, écriteau *m.* **To stick bills on a wall,** placarder un mur. **Stick no bills!** défense d'afficher. *Th:* (Play-)bill, affiche; programme *m* du spectacle. *S.a.* FLY-BILL, HANDBILL. **4.** (*a*) **Bill of fare,** carte *f* du jour; menu *m.* (*b*) *Nau:* **Bill of lading,** connaissement *m*; police *f* de chargement. (*c*) **Bill of sale,** acte *m*, contrat *m*, de vente; facture. *S.a.* ATTAINDER. **6.** *Jur:* Résumé des chefs d'accusation (présenté au jury). (*Of Grand Jury*) **To find a true bill against s.o.,** déclarer fondés les chefs d'accusation. **'bill-board,** *s.* Panneau *m* (d'affichage). **'bill-poster, -sticker,** *s.* Afficheur *m.* **'bill-posting, -sticking,** *s.* Affichage *m.*
bill⁵, *v.tr.* **1.** Facturer (des marchandises). **2.** Afficher; *Th:* mettre (une pièce) à l'affiche.
Bill⁶. *Pr.n.m.* (*Dim. of William*) Guillaume.
billet¹ ['bilet], *s. Mil:* **1.** (*a*) Billet *m* de logement. (*b*) Logement *m* (chez l'habitant). **Every bullet has its billet,** toute balle a sa destination; on ne lutte pas contre le sort. **2.** *F:* Place *f*, emploi *m.*
billet², *v.* (billeted) **1.** *v.tr. Mil:* **To billet troops on s.o., on, in, a town,** loger des troupes chez qn; cantonner des troupes dans une ville. **2.** *v.i. Mil:* Loger (avec, chez).
billet³, *s.* **1.** Bûche *f*; rondin *m*; bille *f*, billette *f* (de bois de chauffage, etc.). **2.** *Metall:* Billette (d'acier); lopin *m.*
billiards ['biljədz], *s.pl.* (Jeu *m* de) billard *m.* **To play billiards,** jouer au billard. **To have a game of b.,** faire une partie de billard. **Billiard-ball,** bille *f* de billard. **Billiard cloth,** tapis *m* de billard. **Billiard cue,** queue *f* de billard. **'billiard-room,** *s.* (Salle *f* de) billard *m.* **'billiard-table,** *s.* Billard *m.*
Billingsgate ['biliŋzgeit]. **1.** *Pr.n.* Marché *m* au poisson (à Londres). **2.** *s. F:* Langage *m* des halles, des poissardes.
billion ['biljən], *s.* **1.** Trillion *m* (10^{12}). **2.** *U.S:* Billion *m*, milliard *m.*
billow¹ ['bilou], *s.* Grande vague; lame *f* (de mer).
billow², *v.i.* (*Of the sea*) Se soulever en vagues; (*of crowds, flames*) ondoyer.
Billy ['bili]. **1.** *Pr.n.m.* Guillaume. **2.** *s.* (*In Austr.*) Billy(-can), gamelle *f*; bouilloire *f* (à thé).
billycock ['bilikɔk], *s. F:* (Chapeau *m*) melon *m.*
billygoat ['biligout], *s.* Bouc *m.*
bimanous ['baimanəs], *a. Z:* Bimane.
bimetallism bai'metəlizm], *s. Pol.Ec:* Bimétallisme *m.*
bi-monthly [bai'mʌnθli]. **1.** *a.* (*a*) Bimensuel, semi-mensuel. (*b*) Bimestriel. **2.** *adv.* (*a*) Bimensuellement. (*b*) Tous les deux mois.
bin [bin], *s.* (*a*) Coffre *m*, huche *f*, boîte *f.* **Corn-bin** (*in stable*), coffre à avoine. *S.a.* DUST-BIN. (*b*) **Wine-bin,** casier à bouteilles.
binary ['bainəri], *a. Mth: etc:* Binaire.

bind¹ [baind], *s.* **1.** *Mus:* Ligature *f*, liaison *f.* **2.** (*a*) Coincement *m*, grippage *m.* (*b*) Gommage *m.*
bind², *v.tr.* (bound [baund]; bound) Attacher, lier. **1.** (*Tie fast*) (*a*) **To b. a prisoner,** *s.o.'s hands,* lier, attacher, ligoter, un prisonnier; lier les mains à qn. **Bound hand and foot,** pieds et poings liés. **Bound by a spell,** retenu par un charme. *S.a.* SPELL-BOUND. **To be bound to s.o. by gratitude,** être attaché à qn par la reconnaissance. (*b*) **To bind sth. (down) to, on, sth.,** attacher, fixer, qch. à qch.; serrer (une pièce sur l'établi). (*c*) **To bind a bargain,** ratifier, confirmer, un marché. (*d*) **Food that binds the bowels,** nourriture constipante. **2.** (*a*) **To bind (up) a wound,** bander, panser, une blessure. **To b. an artery,** ligaturer une artère. (*b*) **To b. a wreath about s.o.'s head,** ceindre d'une couronne la tête de qn. (*c*) **Border** (un manteau, un chapeau); border (une étoffe). **3.** (*Tie together*) (*a*) **To bind (up) a sheaf,** lier une gerbe. (*b*) **Relier** (un livre). **Bound in paper, paper-bound,** broché. **Bound in boards,** cartonné. **Full-bound in morocco,** relié en plein maroquin. (*c*) (i) **Lier,** agglutiner (du sable, etc.). (ii) *v.i.* (*Of gravel, etc.*) Se lier, s'agglomérer; s'agréger; (*of cement*) durcir, prendre. (*d*) *v.i.* (*Of machine parts, etc.*) (Se) coincer; (*of bearings*) gripper; (*of cylinders, etc.*) coller, gommer. **4.** Lier, engager (qn). **To b. s.o. to obedience,** s'engager à l'obéissance. **To b. oneself to do sth.,** s'engager à faire qch. **bind down,** *v.tr.* **To bind s.o. down to do sth.** **bind over,** *v.tr. Jur:* **To bind s.o. over to keep the peace,** exiger de qn sous caution qu'il ne procédera à aucune voie de fait. **bound,** *a.* **1.** (*a*) Lié. **They are very much bound up in each other,** ils sont très attachés l'un à l'autre. **The present is b. up with the past,** le présent se relie au passé, est lié au passé. (*b*) (*With s. prefixed, e.g.*) **Tide-bound,** retenu par la marée. *S.a.* HIDE-BOUND, ICE-BOUND, SNOW-BOUND, WEATHER-BOUND, WIND-BOUND. **2.** (*a*) **To be bound to do sth.,** être obligé, tenu, de faire qch. **You are in duty bound to do it,** votre devoir vous y oblige. **To be in honour bound to do sth.,** être engagé d'honneur à faire qch.; mettre son honneur à faire qch. **To be b. by strict rules,** être soumis à des règles strictes. (*b*) **He's bound to come,** il ne peut pas manquer de venir. **It's b. to happen,** c'est fatal. **We are b. to be successful,** nous réussirons à coup sûr. (*c*) *F:* **He'll come, I'll be bound,** il viendra, j'en suis sûr! je veux le promets! **binding¹,** *a.* **1.** (*Agent*) agglomératif, agglutinateur. **2.** Obligatoire (*upon s.o.,* pour qn). **Agreement binding (up)on s.o.,** contrat qui lie qn. **3.** *Med:* Astringent, constipant, échauffant.
binding², *s.* **1.** (*a*) Agglutination *f*, agrégation *f.* (*b*) Fixation *f*; serrage *m*; cerclage *m* (d'une roue). **Binding screw,** (i) vis de pression; (ii) *El:* serre-fil *m.* (*c*) = BIND¹ 2. **2.** (*a*) Lien *m*, ligature *f*; bandage *m* (d'une poutre, etc.); frette *f. El.E:* Armature binding, frette d'induit. (*b*) Reliure *f* (d'un livre). **Quarter-binding,** demi-reliure *f.* **Library binding,** reliure amateur. **Spring binding** (*for holding papers*), reliure électrique; auto-relieur *m. S.a.* LIMP³. (*c*) Bordure *f*, liséré *m* (d'une robe, etc.).
binder ['baindər], *s.* **1.** (*Pers.*) (*a*) Husb: etc: Lieur, -euse. (*b*) = BOOKBINDER. **2.** (*Thg*) (*a*) Husb: Lieuse *f* (de gerbes); lien *m*, hart *f* (de fagot, etc.). (*b*) Bande *f*, ceinture *f* (de flanelle); bandage *m* de corps. (*c*) (**Spring-back**) **binder,** auto-relieur *m.* (*f*) *Civ.E:* Liant *m*,

agglomératif *m* ; matière d'agrégation (d'une route).

bindery ['baɪndəri], *s.* Atelier *m* de reliure.

bindweed ['baindwi:d], *s. Bot:* Liseron *m.*

bine [bain], *s. Bot:* Sarment *m* ; tige *f* (de houblon, etc.). *S.a.* WOODBINE.

binge [bindʒ], *s. P:* Ribote , , bombe *f.*

binnacle ['binəkl], *.. Nau:* Habitacle *m.*

binocular [bai'nɔkjulər, bi-]. *Opt:* **1.** *a.* Binoculaire. **2.** *s.pl.* **Binoculars,** jumelle(s) *f.*

binomial [bai'noumiəl]. *Mth:* **1.** *a.* Binôme. **The binomial theorem,** le théorème de Newton. **2.** *s.* Binôme *m.*

biochemistry [baɪo'kemɪstrɪ], *s.* Biochimie *f.*

biographer [bai'ɔgrəfər], *s.* Biographe *m*

biographic(al) [baio'grafik(əl)], *a.* Biographique.

biography [bai'ɔgrəfi], *s.* Biographie *f.*

biologis [bai'ɔlodʒist], *s* Biologiste *m*, biologue *m.*

biology [bai'ɔlodʒi], *s.* Biologie *f.*

bipartite [bai'pɑ:rtait], *a.* **1.** *Nat.Hisi:* Biparti, -ite. **2.** (Document) rédigé en double.

biped ['baiped], *a. & s,* Bipède (*m*).

biphase ['baife:iz], *a. El.E:* Biphasé, diphasé.

biplane ['baiplein], *s.* Avion biplan ; biplan *m.*

bipolar [bai'poulər], *a. El:* Bipolaire.

biquadratic [baikwɔ'dratik], *a. Mth:* Bicarré.

birch[1] [bə:rtʃ], *s.* **1.** *Bot:* Bouleau *m.* **Lady birch, silver birch white birch,** bouleau blanc. **2. Birch(-rod),** verge *f*, poignée *f* de verges (pour fouetter).

birch[2], *.tr.* Donner les verges, e fouet, à (qn).

bird [bə:rd], *s.* **1.** (*a*) Oiseau *m.* **Hen bird,** oiseau femelle. **Song-bird,** oiseau chanteur. **Little bird,** oiselet *m*, oisillon *m. F: A little bird told me so,** mon petit doigt me l'a dit. **To give s.o. the bird,** (i) envoyer promener qn ; (ii) *Th: etc:* huer, siffler, qn. *Prov:* **The early bird catches the worm,** à qui se lève matin Dieu aide et prête la main. **A bird in the hand is worth two in the bush,** un tiens vaut mieux que deux 'tu l'auras.' *S.a.* CHAFF[1] I, KILL[2] I. (*b*) *Cu:* Volaille *f.* (*c*) *The birds are shy this year,* le gibier est timide cette année. **2.** *P:* Type *m*, individu *m.* **Who's that old bird?** qu'est-ce que c'est que ce vieux type-là? **'bird-cage,** *s.* Cage *f* d'oiseau ; (*if large*) volière *f.* **'bird-call,** *s.* Appeau *m*, pipeau *m.* **'bird-catcher,** *s.* Oiseleur *m.* **'birdfancier,** *s.* (*a*) Oiselier *m* ; aviculteur *m.* (*b*) Connaisseur *m* en oiseaux. **'bird-lime,** *s.* Glu *f.* **'bird's-eye,** *s.* **1.** *Bot:* Véronique *f.* **2. Bird's-eye view,** perspective, vue, perspective, à vol d'oiseau. **3.** Bird's-eye mahogany, acajou moucheté. **Bird's-eye maple,** érablé à broussin, érablé madre. **4.** Tabac cordé et haché. **'bird's-nest**[1], *s.* **1.** Nid *m* d'oiseau. **2.** *Cu:* Nid de salangane **bird's-'nest**[2], *v.i.* Denicher des oiseaux.

biretta [bi'reta], *s. Ecc.Cost:* Barrette *f.*

birth [bə:rθ], *s.* **1.** Naissance *f.* **Premature birth,** accouchement *m* avant terme. **To give birth to** a child, donner naissance, donner le jour, à un enfant. *F: To give b. to a poem,* enfanter un poème. **Irish by birth,** Irlandais de naissance. **Of high birth,** de haute naissance. **By right of birth,** par droit de naissance. **The birth of an idea,** la genèse d'une idée. **2.** Mise *f* bas (d'un animal). (*Of animal*) **To give birth to . . .,** mettre bas. . . **'birth-cer'tificate,** *s.* Acte *m* ou extrait *m* de naissance. **'birth-control,** *s.* Restriction *f* de la natalité. **'birth-mark,** *s.* Envie *f* ; tache *f* de naissance. **'birth-place,** *s.* (*a*) Lieu *m* de naissance ; (i) pays natal ;

(ii) maison natale. (*b*) *F:* Berceau *m* (d'une religion, etc.). **'birth-rate,** *s.* Natalité *f.*

birthday ['bə:rθdei], *s.* Anniversaire *m* de naissance ; jour natal ; *F:* jour de naissance. **Birthday present** = cadeau de fête.

birthright ['bə:rθrait], *s.* **1.** Droit *m* d'aînesse. **2.** Droit de naissance, droit du sang.

Biscay ['biskei]. *Pr.n. Geog:* La Biscaye (en Espagne). **The Bay of Biscay,** le golfe de Gascogne.

biscuit ['biskit], *s.* **1.** (*a*) Biscuit *m.* **Fancy biscuits,** gâteaux secs ; petits fours. *P: He takes the biscuit!* à lui le pompon ! *That takes the biscuit!* ça, c'est fort ! (*b*) *a. & s.* (*Colour*) Biscuit *inv*, isabelle *inv.* **2.** *Cer:* **Biscuit ware,** biscuit.

bisect [bai'sekt], *v.tr.* Couper, diviser, (une ligne, un angle) en deux parties égales.

bisection [bai'sekʃ(ə)n], *s.* Bissection *f.*

bisector [bai'sektər], *s.* Bissectrice *f.*

bishop[1] ['biʃəp], *s.* **1.** *Ecc:* Évêque *m.* **Bishop's palace,** palais épiscopal ; évêché *m.* **2.** *Chess:* Fou *m.*

bishop[2], *v.tr. Farr:* Maquignonner (un cheval).

bishopric ['biʃəprik], *s.* Évêché *m.*

bismuth ['bizməθ], *s. Miner:* Bismuth *m.*

bison ['baisən, 'baizən], *s.* Bison *m* ; taureau *m* à bosse.

bisque[1] [bisk], *s. Ten:* Bisque *f.*

bisque[2], *s. Cer:* a) Biscuit *m.* (*b*) Porcelaine blanche sans couverte.

bissextile [bi'sekstail, -til]. **1.** *a.* Bissextil. **2.** *s.* Année bissextile.

bistoury ['bisturi], *s. Surg:* Bistouri *m.*

bistre ['bistər], *s. & a.* Bistre (*m*).

bisulphite [bai'sʌlfait], *s. Ch:* Bisulfite *m.*

bit[1] [bit], *s.* **1.** *Harn:* Mors *m* (d'une bride). **To champ the bit,** (*of horse*) mâcher son mors ; *F:* (*of pers.*) ronger son frein. (*Of horse, F: of pers.*) **To take the bit between its, one's, teeth,** prendre le mors aux dents ; s'emballer. *S.a.* BRIDLE-BIT, CURB-BIT. **2.** *Tls:* (*a*) Mèche *f* de vilebrequin ; mèche. *S.a.* CENTRE-BIT, SPOONBIT, TWIST-BIT. (*b*) **Copper-bit, soldering-bit,** fer *m* à souder.

bit[2], *s. F:* **1.** (*a*) Morceau *m* (de pain, de fromage, etc.). *F:* **To have a bit of something,** manger un morceau. (*b*) Bout *m*, brin *m. Bit of paper, of string,* bout *m* de papier, de ficelle. *Bit of straw,* brin *m* de paille. *A (little) bit of hope,* un peu, un petit brin, d'espoir. *I did my bit,* j'ai servi pendant la guerre. (*c*) *F:* (*Coin*) Pièce *f.* **Threepenny bit,** pièce de trois pence. **2.** (*a*) **A bit (of),** un peu (de). *A tiny little bit,* un tout petit peu. *He is a bit jealous,* il est quelque peu jaloux. *He is a bit of a liar,* il est tant soit peu menteur. **Wait a bit!** attendez un peu, un instant ! **A good bit older,** sensiblement plus âgé. **Bit by bit,** peu à peu ; petit à petit ; brin à brin. **Not a bit (of it)!** pas le moins du monde ! n'en croyez rien ! **It's not a bit of use,** cela ne sert absolument à rien. *S.a.* EVERY. (*b*) *F: A bit of news,* une nouvelle. *A bit of advice,* un conseil. *A bit of luck,* une chance : une aubaine.

bit[3]. See BITE[2].

bitch [bitʃ], *s.* **1.** (*a*) Chienne *f.* (*b*) **Terrier bitch,** terrier *m* femelle. (*c*) Femelle *f* (du renard, du loup). **2.** *P:* (*Of wom. n*) Garce *f.*

bite[1] [bait], *s.* **1.** (*a*) Coup *m* de dent. *S.a.* BARK[3], CHERRY I. (*b*) *Fish:* Touche *f.* *P:* **Got a bite?** ça mord? **2.** (*a*) (*Wound*) Morsure *f.* *S.a.* FROSTBITE. (*b*) Piqûre *f*, morsure (d'un insecte). *S.a.* FLEA-BITE. **3.** *F:* Bouchée *f*, morceau *m.*

I haven't had a bite all day, je n'ai rien mangé de la journée. **Without bite or sup,** sans boire ni manger. **4.** (*a*) *Tchn:* Mordant *m* (d'une lime, etc.). (*b*) Piquant *m* (d'une sauce). **bite²,** *v.tr.* (*p.t.* bit; *p.p.* bitten, *A:* bit, *see* BITER) Mordre. **I.** Donner un coup de dent à (qn, qch.); (*of insect*) piquer. *To b.* one's lips, one's nails, se mordre les lèvres, se ronger les ongles. **To bite the dust,** mordre la poussière. *The fish bites,* le poisson mord (à l'hameçon). *Prov:* **Once bitten, twice shy,** chat échaudé craint l'eau froide. *S.a.* THUMB¹. **To get bitten,** se faire mordre; se faire piquer. **To be bitten with a desire to do sth.,** brûler de faire qch. *I've been badly bitten,* on m'a mis dedans. **2.** *The wind bites the face,* le vent coupe le visage. *Frost bites the leaves,* la gelée brûle les feuilles. *Pepper bites the tongue,* le poivre pique la langue. **bite off,** *v.tr.* Enlever, détacher, (qch.) avec les dents, d'un coup de dent(s). *F:* **To bite** s.o.'s **head off,** rembarrer qn. **To bite off more than one can chew,** entreprendre une trop forte tâche; tenter qch. au-dessus de ses forces. **biting,** *a.* Mordant; (*of cold*) cuisant, âpre, perçant; (*of wind*) cinglant, piquant; (*of style, wit, epigram*) mordant, caustique. **-¹y,** *adv.* D'un ton mordant.

biter ['baitər], *s.* (*a*) Animal *m* qui mord. (*b*) *F:* **The biter bit,** le trompeur trompé.

bitter ['bitər]. **I.** *a.* (Goût) amer; (vin) acerbe; (vent) aigre, piquant; (ennemi) implacable; (conflit) aigu; (temps) rigoureux; (ton) aigre, âpre. *B.* cold, wind, froid, vent, glacial, cinglant. **Bitter beer,** bière fortement houblonnée. *B. enemies,* ennemis à mort. *B. hatred,* haine acharnée. *B. remorse,* remords cuisants. *B. experience,* amère déception; expérience cruelle. *S.a.* PILL. **To be bitter against a project,** critiquer un projet avec âpreté. **2.** *s.* (*a*) = *bitter beer.* (*b*) *pl.* **Bitters,** bitter(s) *m,* amer(s) *m.* **To have a bitters,** prendre l'apéritif. **-ly,** *adv.* Amèrement, avec amertume, avec aigreur. *It was b. cold,* il faisait un froid de loup. *To feel sth. b.,* ressentir beaucoup d'amertume de qch. **'bitter-'sweet. I.** *a.* Aigre-doux, -douce. **2.** *s. Bot:* Douce-amère *f.*

bitter-end [bitər'end], *s. Nau:* Étalingure *f* du puits. **To the bitter-end,** à outrance; jusqu'au bout.

bittern ['bitərn], *s. Orn:* Butor *m.*

bitterness ['bitərnəs], *s.* **I.** (*a*) Amertume *f.* (*b*) Rigueur *f,* âpreté *f* (du temps); aigreur *f,* acrimonie *f* (de paroles, d'une querelle). **2.** Rancune *f,* rancœur *f.*

bitts [bits], *s.pl. Nau:* Bittes *f* (d'amarrage).

bitumen ['bitjumən, bi'tju:men], *s.* Bitume *m*; goudron minéral; asphalte minéral.

bituminize [bi'tju:mina:iz], *v.tr.* Bituminer, bitumer.

bituminous [bi'tju:minəs], *a.* Bitumineux. **Bituminous coal,** houille grasse, collante.

bivalent ['baivələn . *Ch:* Bivalent, divalent.

bivalve ['baivalv], *a. & s. Moll:* Bivalve (*m*).

bivouac¹ ['bivuak], *s. Mil:* Bivouac *m.*

bivouac², *v.i.* (bivouacked) Bivouaquer.

bizarre [bi'za:r], *a.* Bizarre.

blab¹ [blab], **blabber** ['blabər], *s. F:* Jaseur, -euse; indiscret, -ète; bavard, -arde.

blab², *v.* (blabbed) **I.** *v.i.* Jaser, bavarder; causer (indiscrètement). **2.** *v.tr.* **To blab out a secret,** laisser échapper un secret.

black¹ [blak]. **I.** *a.* Noir. **I.** (*a*) *B. coat,* habit noir. *B. spot* (*on furniture, etc.*), noircissure *f.* **The night was as black as pitch,** il faisait noir comme dans un four. **As black as ebony,** d'un

noir d'ébène. *S.a.* PITCH-BLACK. **To be black in the face,** avoir le visage tout congestionné. **To look black,** faire une vilaine figure, une vilaine moue. *To look as b. as thunder,* avoir l'air furieux. **To beat** s.o. **black and blue,** meurtrir, rosser, qn de coups. *To be b. and blue (all over),* être tout meurtri (de coups); être couvert de bleus. **Black eye,** œil poché; *F:* œil au beurre noir. *S.a.* EYE¹ I. *Hist:* **The Black Death,** la Peste Noire. *S.a.* LIST². *Geog:* **The Black Sea,** la Mer Noire. *S.a.* COAL-BLACK, CURRANT I, JACK III. 3, JET-BLACK, MARIA, RUST¹ 2, SHEEP. (*b*) **The black races,** les races noires. **Black troops,** troupes indigènes. **Black woman,** négresse *f. B. servant,* domestique nègre. (*c*) *His hands were b.,* il avait les mains sales, les mains toutes noires. *F:* **The Black Country,** la région sidérurgique (du Staffordshire et du Warwickshire); le "Pays Noir" de l'Angleterre. **2.** *B. despair,* sombre désespoir. *B. tidings,* triste(s) nouvelle(s). *B. ingratitude,* noire ingratitude. *S.a.* ART². **II. black,** *s.* Noir *m.* **I.** Ivory black, noir d'ivoire. **Bone black,** noir animal. **Lamp black,** noir de fumée. **Brunswick black,** laque *f* à l'asphalte. **2.** (*a*) *She always wears b.,* elle est toujours en noir. (*b*) **To work in black and white,** faire du dessin à l'encre, au crayon noir. **Black-and-white artist,** dessinateur à l'encre. **To set sth. down in black and white,** coucher qch. par écrit. **'black-beetle,** *s.* (i) Blatte *f,* cafard *m*; (ii) escarbot *m.* **'black-coated,** *a.* Vêtu de noir; à jaquette noire. **The black-coated workers,** les employés de bureau (par opposition à l'artisanat). **'black-cock,** *s. Orn:* Tétras *m* lyre; petit coq de bruyère. **black(-)'hole,** *s.* Cachot *m.* **black-'lead,** *s.* **I.** Mine *f* de plomb; plombagine *f.* **2.** Crayon de mine de plomb. **'black letter,** *s. Typ:* Caractères *m* gothiques. **'black-list,** *v.tr.* **I.** Inscrire, mettre, (qn) sur la liste des punitions, des suspects. *Cf. black list, under* LIST². **2.** Mettre (un livre, un atelier) à l'index. **Black-listed,** à l'index. **black-'pudding,** *s. Cu:* Boudin *m.*

black², *v.tr.* **I.** Noircir (qch.). **To b. boots,** cirer des bottes, des bottines. *F:* **To black** s.o.'s **eye,** pocher l'œil à qn. **2. To black sth. out,** effacer, rayer, qch. (d'un gros trait noir). **To black out,** (i) couper la lumière; (ii) obscurcir (une ville, etc.). **blacking,** *s.* Cirage *m* (de ou pour chaussures). **'blacking-brush,** *s.* Brosse *f* à cirer. **black-'out,** *s.* **I.** Panne *f* d'éclairage, d'électricité. **2.** Obscurcissement *m* (d'une ville).

blackamoor ['blakamuər], *s.* Noir; nègre, *f.* négresse; moricaud.

blackball ['blakbɔːl], *v.tr.* Blackbouler (qn).

blackberry ['blakbəri], *s.* Mûre *f* (de ronce). **Blackberry bush,** ronce *f,* mûrier *m,* des haies.

blackbird ['blakbəːrd], *s. Orn:* Merle *m.*

blackboard ['blakbɔːrd], *s.* Tableau noir.

blackcap ['blakkap], *s.* Fauvette *f* à tête noire.

blacken ['blakn]. **I.** *v.tr.* Noircir (un mur, la réputation de qn); obscurcir (le ciel); (*with smoke*) enfumer. **To blacken** s.o.'s **character,** calomnier (qn). **2.** *v.i.* (Se) noircir; devenir noir; s'assombrir. **blackening,** *s.* Noircissement *m.*

blackguard¹ ['blaga:rd], *s.* Ignoble personnage *m*; canaille *f,* gouape *f,* vaurien *m.*

blackguard², *v.tr.* Lancer des injures à (qn); agonir (qn) de sottises.

blackguardism ['blaga:rdizm], *s.* Canaillerie *f.*

blackguardly ['blaga:rdli], *a.* Ignoble, canaille.

blackhead ['blakhed], *s.* Comédon *m*; tanne *f*; point noir (sur le visage).

blackish [′blakiʃ], *a.* Noirâtre; tirant sur le noir.

blackleg¹ [′blakleg], *s.* *Ind:* *F:* Renard *m*; jaune *m*; traître *m*.

blackleg², *v.tr.* (blacklegged) *Ind:* Prendre la place (des grévistes, etc.).

blackmail¹ [′blakmeil], *s.* *F:* Chantage *m*; extorsion *f* (sous menace de scandale).

blackmail², *v.tr.* Soumettre (qn) à un chantage; *F:* faire chanter (qn).

blackmailer [′blakmeilər], *s.* Maître-chanteur *m*.

blackness [′blaknəs], *s.* Noirceur *f*; (*of the night*) obscurité *f*.

Blackshirt [′blakʃəːrt], *s.* Fasciste *m*; chemise noire.

blacksmith [′blaksmiθ], *s.* Forgeron *m*; maréchal ferrant.

blackthorn [′blakθɔːrn], *s.* **1.** *Bot:* Épine noire. **2.** Gourdin *m* (d'épine).

bladder [′bladər], *s.* (*a*) *Anat:* Vessie *f.* (*b*) *Anat:* *Bot:* Vésicule *f.* *S.a.* AIR-BLADDER, GALL-BLADDER. (*c*) Outre remplie d'air. *Fb:* Vessie (de ballon). ′**bladder-wort**, *s.* *Bot:* Utriculaire *f.* ′**bladder-wrack**, *s.* *Algae:* Raisin *m* de mer.

blade [bleid], *s.* **1.** Brin *m* (d'herbe); pampe *f* (de blé). **Corn in the blade**, blé en herbe. **2.** (*a*) Lame *f* (de couteau, d'épée, de rasoir, *Bot:* de feuille); feuille , lame (d'une scie). (*b*) *F:* Sabre *m* ou épée *f.* *F:* He's a (regular, jolly) **blade**, c'est un gaillard, un luron. **3.** Pelle *f*, plat *m*, pale *f* (d'aviron); aile *f*, pale, branche *f* (d'hélice); ailette *f*, vanne *f* (de ventilateur); ailette, aube *f* (de turbine); fer *m* (de bêche). **4.** Blade of the tongue, plat de la langue. *S.a.* SHOULDER-BLADE. ′**blade-bone**, *s.* **1.** *Anat:* Omoplate *f.* **2.** *Cu:* Paleron *m*.

bladed [′bleidid], *a.* A lame(s), à aile(s), à pales, à ailettes. **Three-bladed propeller**, hélice à trois ailes, à trois pales.

blame¹ [bleim], *s.* **1.** Reproches *mpl*; condamnation *f.* **To deserve b.**, mériter des reproches. **2.** Responsabilité *f*; faute *f.* **The b. is mine**, la faute en est à moi. **To lay, put, cast, the blame (for sth.) upon s.o.**, rejeter, faire retomber, le blâme ou la faute (de qch.) sur qn; incriminer qn. **To bear the blame**, supporter le blâme; endosser la faute.

blame², *v.tr.* **1.** Blâmer, condamner (qn). **To b. s.o. for sth.**, blâmer qn de qch.; reprocher qch. à qn; attribuer (un malheur, etc.) à qn. **To b. s.o. for doing sth.**, reprocher à qn de faire, d'avoir fait, qch. **They each other**, ils s'en prennent l'un à l'autre. **I am not blaming you**, ce n'est pas à vous que j'en ai. **To have only oneself to blame**, n'avoir à s'en prendre qu'à soi-même. **He is to blame**, il y a de sa faute. **2. To b. sth. for an accident**, *etc.*, attribuer un accident, etc., à qch.

blameless [′bleimləs], *a.* Innocent, irréprochable; sans tache. **-ly**, *adv.* Irréprochablement.

blameworthy [′bleimwəːrði], *a.* **1.** Blâmable; digne de reproches. **2.** (*Of conduct*) Répréhensible.

blanch [blɑːnʃ], **1.** *v.tr.* (*a*) Blanchir (des légumes, un métal). **To blanch almonds**, monder, dérober, des amandes. (*b*) *Poet:* (*Of illness, etc.*) Pâlir, rendre pâle (qn, le teint de qn); (*of fear, etc.*) blêmir (le visage). **2.** *v.i.* (*Of hair, etc.*) Blanchir. (*b*) (*Of pers.*) Blêmir, pâlir.

blancmange [blɑ′mɔnʒ], *s.* Blanc-manger *m*.

bland [bland], *a.* **1.** (*Of pers., speech*) (*a*) Doux, *f.* douce; aimable; affable; débonnaire. *Iron:* Doucereux. (*b*) (*Sourire*) narquois. **2.** (*Of air,* *food, drink*) Doux, suave. **-ly**, *adv.* (*a*) Avec affabilité; *Iron:* mielleusement. (*b*) D'un air un peu narquois.

blandish [′blandiʃ], *v.tr.* Cajoler, flatter.

blandishment [′blandiʃmənt], *s.* Flatterie *f.* *Usu. pl.* Cajoleries *fpl*, câlineries *fpl*.

blandness [′blandnəs], *s.* **1.** (*a*) Douceur *f*, suavité *f*, affabilité *f.* (*b*) Affabilité un peu narquoise. **2.** Douceur (du climat, etc.).

blank [blaŋk]. I. *a.* **1.** (*a*) B. paper, papier blanc. *B.* page, page vierge, blanche. (*b*) **Blank cheque**, credit, chèque, crédit, en blanc. (*c*) *B. space*, espace en blanc; blanc *m.* **Blank map**, carte muette. (*d*) **Blank verse**, vers blancs, non rimés. *S.a.* CARTRIDGE I. **2.** (*a*) *B. existence*, existence vide. *B. look*, regard sans expression. (*b*) **To look blank**, avoir l'air confondu, déconcerté. *S.a.* ASTONISHMENT. (*c*) *B. despair*, profond découragement. *B. impossibility*, impossibilité absolue. **-ly**, *adv.* **1.** **To look b. at s.o.**, regarder qn (i) d'un air confondu, déconcerté, (ii) sans expression. **2.** **To deny sth. b.**, nier qch. absolument, carrément. II. **blank**, *s.* **1.** (*a*) (*In document, etc.*) Blanc *m*, vide *m*; (*in one's memory*) trou *m*, lacune *f*, vide. **Paper signed in blank**, blanc-seing *m*, *pl.* blancseings. *To leave blanks*, laisser des blancs. *F:* His death leaves a blank, sa mort laisse un vide. **His mind is a blank**, (i) sa mémoire est une table rase; (ii) il a, il se sent, la tête vide. (*b*) **To fire off blank (shot)**, tirer à blanc. (*c*) Blanc (d'une cible). *S.a.* POINT-BLANK. (*d*) *Dominoes:* Double blank, double blanc *m.* **2.** (*In lottery*) Billet blanc, billet perdant. *S.a.* DRAW² 3. **3.** (*a*) *Mint:* Flan *m* (de métal). (*b*) *Metalw:* Flan; masselotte *f.*

blanket¹ [′blaŋket], *s.* **1.** Couverture *f* (de lit, de cheval). **To toss s.o. in a blanket**, berner qn. *S.a.* WET BLANKET. (*b*) Couverture ou pagne *m* (d'indigène). **2.** *Typ:* (Press-)blanket, blanchet *m.* **3.** *Attrib.* *U.S:* Général; applicable à tous les cas. **Blanket order**, ordre d'une portée générale.

blanket², *v.tr.* **1.** Mettre une couverture à (qch.). **2.** (*a*) *Nau:* Déventer, abriter (un navire, un yacht); manger le vent à (un autre navire). (*b*) *Navy:* Se mettre en travers du feu de ses propres vaisseaux).

blankness [′blaŋknəs], *s.* **1.** Air confus, décontenancé. **2.** Vide *m*, néant *m* (de la pensée, etc.).

blare¹ [′blɛər], *s.* Sonnerie *f*, accents cuivrés (de la trompette).

blare². **1.** *v.i.* (*Of trumpet*) Sonner. *Mus:* Cuivrer le son. **2.** *v.tr.* **The band blared (out)** a quickstep, la fanfare fit retentir une marche.

blarney¹ [′blɑːrni], *s.* *F:* Eau bénite de cour; patelinage *m*; boniments *mpl* à la graisse d'oie.

blarney², *v.tr.* Cajoler, enjôler (qn).

blaspheme [blas′fiːm], *v.i. & tr.* Blasphémer.

blasphemer [blas′fiːmər], *s.* Blasphémateur, -trice.

blasphemous [′blasfiməs], *a.* (*Of pers.*) Blasphémateur, -trice; (*of words*) blasphématoire, impie.

blasphemy [′blasfəmi], *s.* Blasphème *m*.

blast¹ [blɑːst], *s.* **1.** (*a*) Bouffée *f* de vent, coup *m* de vent; rafale *f.* **Blast of steam**, jet *m* de vapeur. (*b*) Souffle *m* (du vent). **2.** *B. on the whistle*, on the siren, coup de sifflet, de sirène. *B. on the trumpet*, sonnerie *f* de trompette. *Nau:* **To sound a blast**, faire entendre un coup de sirène. **3.** *Metall:* Air *m*, vent *m* (de la soufflerie); soufflerie *f*, soufflage *m* (d'un haut-fourneau). (*Of furnace*) **To be in blast**, être allumé, en marche. **To be in full blast**, être en pleine activité. *S.a.* SAND-BLAST¹. **4.** (*a*) *Ball:* Souffle. (*b*) *Min:* (i) Coup de mine. (ii) Charge *f* d'explosif.

'**blast-furnace**, s. Haut-fourneau. '**blast-pipe**, s. Metall: Tuyère f.

blast². **1.** v.tr. (a) Min: Faire sauter (à la dynamite, etc.); pétarder (des roches). (b) Brûler, flétrir (une plante); ruiner, briser (l'avenir de qn); détruire, anéantir (des espérances). Blasted heath, lande désolée. (c) (Of lightning) Foudroyer (un arbre, etc.). **2.** v.i. (Of brass instrument) Cuivrer. **blasting**, s. **1.** (a) Travail m aux explosifs; exploitation f à la mine; abattage m à la poudre. S.a. GELATINE. (b) Anéantissement m (d'un espoir, etc.); ruine f (d'une carrière). (c) Foudroiement m (d'un arbre). **2.** W.Tel: Poussées fpl d'intensité (dans le haut-parleur); réception hurlante. '**blasting-powder**, s. Poudre f de mine, de démolition.

blatancy ['bleitənsi], s. Vulgarité criarde.

blatant ['bleitənt], a. **1.** (Of pers., manners) D'une vulgarité criarde. **2.** (Injustice) criante. **-ly**, adv. Avec une vulgarité criarde.

blather ['blaðər], v. & s. = BLETHER ¹, ².

blaze¹ [bleiz], s. **1.** (a) Flamme(s) f, feu m, conflagration f, flambée f. In a blaze, en feu, en flammes. To set sth. in a b., enflammer, embraser, qch. F: The whole of Europe was in a b., toute l'Europe était en feu. To burst (out) into a b., se mettre à flamber; s'enflammer. In the blaze of day, en plein midi. (b) Blaze of anger, éclat m de colère. **2.** Flamboiement m (du soleil); éclat (des couleurs, des diamants, etc.). **3.** pl. F: (= HELL) (a) Go to blazes! allez au diable! (b) (Intensive) What the blazes . . ., que diable (me veut-il, etc.). To work like blazes, travailler furieusement. To run like blazes, courir à toute vitesse.

blaze², v.i. (a) (Of fire, etc.) Flamber; (of sun, colours) flamboyer; (of jewels, metals) étinceler. Uniforms blazing with gold lace, uniformes resplendissants de galons d'or. (b) F: (Of pers.) To blaze with anger, être enflammé de colère; être furieux. **blaze away**, v.i. **1.** (Of fire) Continuer à flamber. **2.** To b. away at the enemy, maintenir un feu nourri contre l'ennemi. To b. away at the pheasants, tirer sans désemparer sur les faisans. **blaze down**, v.i. (Of sun) Darder, déverser, ses rayons (on, sur). **blaze out**, v.i. **1.** (a) (Of fire) Se mettre à flamber. (b) (Of the sun) Apparaître tout à coup (parmi les nuages). **2.** Éclater en reproches, en injures, etc. To b. out at s.o., s'en prendre violemment à qn. **blaze up**, v.i. **1.** S'embraser, s'enflammer. **2.** (Of pers.) S'emporter; se fâcher tout rouge. To b. up at a proposal, s'insurger contre une proposition. **blazing**, a. **1.** (a) En feu; enflammé; embrasé. (b) (Feu, soleil) flambant, ardent. (c) Ven: Blazing scent, fumet tout récent; piste toute fraîche. **2.** F: To commit a blazing indiscretion, commettre une indiscrétion formidable.

blaze³, s. **1.** (On face of horse, ox) Étoile f. **2.** (On tree) Blaze(-mark), blanchis m, griffe f.

blaze⁴, v.tr. Griffer, blanchir, marquer (un arbre). To blaze a trail, tracer un chemin, frayer le chemin; poser des jalons (dans une science, etc.).

blaze⁵, v.tr. To blaze a rumour abroad, répandre un bruit partout. To b. the news, proclamer partout la nouvelle.

blazer ['bleizər], s. **1.** Cost: Sp: Blazer m. **2.** F: Mensonge m énorme.

blazon¹ [bleizn], s. Her: (a) Blason m. (b) Armoiries fpl. (c) Étendard armorié.

blazon², v.tr. **1.** Her: Blasonner; marquer (qch.) aux armoiries de qn. **2.** Embellir, orner

(de dessins héraldiques). **3.** Célébrer, exalter (les vertus de qn). **4.** To blazon forth, out, sth., publier, proclamer, qch.

bleach¹ [bli:tʃ], s. Agent m de blanchiment; -décolorant m.

bleach², v.tr. & i. Blanchir; Ch: etc: (se) décolorer. To b. the hair, décolorer, blondir, les cheveux. Tex: Half-bleached, demi-blanc, mibis. **bleaching**, s. Blanchiment m; Ch: décoloration f. '**bleaching-field**, s. Tex: Pré m de blanchiment. '**bleaching-powder**, s. Poudre f à blanchir; chlorure m de chaux. '**bleaching-water**, s. Eau f de Javel.

bleak¹ [bli:k], s. Ich: Ablette f, alburne f.

bleak², a. **1.** (Terrain) désert, sans abri, exposé au vent. **2.** (Temps) triste; (vent) froid. **3.** B. prospects, avenir morne. B. smile, sourire pâle. **-ly**, adv. Froidement, tristement; d'un air morne.

blear¹ ['bliːər], a. **1.** (Of eyes) Troubles, larmoyants. **2.** (Of outline) Vague, indécis, imprécis. '**blear-eyed**, a. Aux yeux troubles, larmoyants.

blear², v.tr. **1.** Rendre (les yeux) troubles. **2.** Obscurcir, embrumer, estomper (des contours).

bleat¹ [bli:t], s. Bêlement m.

bleat². **1.** v.i. Bêler. **2.** v.tr. F: (Of pers.) (a) To bleat out a protest, protester d'une voix chevrotante. (b) He went and bleated it all over the place, il est allé chanter ça partout. **bleating¹**, a. Bêlant. **bleating²**, s. Bêlement m.

bleb [bleb], s. **1.** Bouillon m, bulle f, cloche f (dans le verre, etc.). **2.** Bouton m, petite ampoule (sur la peau).

bleed [bli:d], v. (bled; bled) **1.** v.tr. Saigner. To b. s.o. in the arm, saigner qn au bras. F: To b. s.o. (for money), saigner, gruger, qn; extorquer de l'argent à qn; P: faire casquer, faire cracher, qn. To b. oneself white to pay, se saigner aux quatre veines pour payer. **2.** v.i. (a) Saigner; perdre du sang. He is bleeding at the nose, his nose is bleeding, il saigne du nez, le nez lui saigne. To b. for one's country, verser son sang pour sa patrie. (b) (Of tree, etc.) Pleurer, perdre sa sève. (c) Civ.E: etc: (Of riveted joints; of water, gas, etc.) Fuir. **bleeding¹**, a. Saignant; (i) en train de saigner; (ii) ensanglanté. With a b. heart, le cœur navré de douleur. **bleeding²**, s. **1.** (a) Écoulement m de sang, de sève; (of vine, etc.) pleurs mpl. B. at the nose, saignement m de nez. (b) Surg: Saignée f. **2.** Fuite f (de gaz, etc.).

blemish¹ ['blemiʃ], s. **1.** Défaut m; défectuosité f, imperfection f. **2.** Souillure f, tache f, tare f.

blemish², v.tr. **1.** Tacher, entacher, souiller (une réputation, etc.). **2.** Abîmer, gâter (un travail).

blench¹ [blenʃ], v.i. Sourciller, broncher.

blench², v.i. Pâlir, blêmir.

blend¹ [blend], s. Mélange m (de thés, etc.).

blend², v. (p.t. & p.p. blended, Lit: blent) **1.** v.tr. (a) To b. sth. with sth., mêler qch. à, avec, qch.; joindre, unir, qch. à qch. To b. one colour with another, (i) mélanger une couleur avec une autre; (ii) fondre deux couleurs; (iii) allier, marier, deux couleurs. (b) Mélanger (des thés, des cafés; F: des races). **2.** v.i. Se mêler, se mélanger, se confondre (into, en); (of voices, etc.) se marier harmonieusement; (of colours) s'allier, se marier; (of parties, etc.) fusionner. **blending**, s. Mélange m (de thés, de tabacs, etc.); alliance (de deux qualités)

bless [bles], v.tr. (p.t. & p.p. blessed [blest], A. & Poet: blest) Bénir. **1.** To b. God, bénir, adorer, Dieu. **2.** (Of God, of the priest) To b. the *people*, bénir le peuple. *To b. a bell*, consacrer, baptiser, une cloche. **God bless you!** que (le bon) Dieu vous bénisse! **3.** *F:* *God blessed them with children*, Dieu leur ac orda le bonheur d'avoir des enfants. *F:* **To be blessed, blest, with sth.**, jouir de qch. ; avoir le bonheur de posséder qch. *I blessed my star. that .*, je me félicitai de ce que . . . ; je bénis mon étoile de ce que. **God bless me!** miséricorde! mon Dieu! **Bless my soul!** tiens, tiens, tiens! Well, I'm blest! par exemple! (*I'll be) blest if I know*, que le diable m'emporte si je le sais. **blessed** ['blesid], *a.* (*a*) **The Blessed Virgin**, la Sainte Vierge. **Blessed be Thy name**, que votre nom soit sanctifié. (*b*) *R.C.Ch:* **The B. Thomas More**, le bienheureux Thomas More. **Blessed are the poor in spirit**, bienheureux sont les pauvres en esprit. (*c*) *P:* (*Intensive*) *What a b. nuisance! quel fichu contretemps!* *The whole b. day*, toute la sainte journée. **blessing**, ʿ Bénédiction *f.* **To give, pronounce, the blessing**, donner la bénédiction. **To ask ₋ blessing** (*at a meal*), dire le bénédicité. **With the b. of God**, par la grâce de Dieu. *The blessings of civilization, etc.*, les avantages *m*, bienfaits *m*, de la civilisation, etc. *Blessings upon you!* Dieu vous bénisse!

blest [blest], *a.* (*Cf.* BLESS) Bienheureux.

blether[1] ['bleðər], *s. Scot:* Paroles *fpl* en l'air ; sottises *fpl*, bêtises*fpl.*

blether[2], *v.i. Scot:* Parler à tort et à travers ; dire des inepties, des bêtises.

blew [blu:]. *See* BLOW [2,4]

blight[1] [bla.t], *s.* **1.** (*a*) Rouille *f*, brûlure *f* ; charbon *m*, nielle *f* (des céréales) ; brunissure *f* (des pommes de terre) ; cloque *f* (des pêches, etc.). (*b*) (*By the sun*) Brouissure *f.* **2.** *Ent:* (*Plant-louse*) Puceron *m.* **3.** *F:* Influence *f* néfaste ; fléau *m.*

blight[2], *v.tr.* Rouiller, nieller (le blé) ; (*of the sun*) brouir ; (*of the wind*) flétrir. **To blight s.o.'s hopes**, flétrir les espérances de qn.

blighter ['blaitər], *s. P:* **1.** Bon à rien You **blighter!** espèce d'animal! **2.** Individu *m* **A poor blighter**, un pauvre hère. **You lucky blighter!** veinard!

blighty ['blaiti], *s. Mil: P:* **1.** L'Angleterre *f* ; (le) retour dans les foyers. **2. A blighty**, la bonne blessure.

blimp [blimp], *s. Aer:* Dirigeable *m* de reconnaissance.

blind[1] [blaind], *a.* **1.** Aveugle. (*a*) **Blind in one eye**, borgne. **A blind man, woman**, un, une, aveugle. **The blind**, les aveugles. **It is a case of the blind leading the blind**, c'est un aveugle qui en conduit un autre. **He is as blind as a bat**, a mole, il n'y voit pas plus clair qu'une taupe. *F:* **To turn a blind eye to sth.**, refuser de voir qch. (comme l'amiral Nelson à la bataille de Copenhague). **In blind man's holiday**, entre chien et loup. *S.a.* COLOUR-BLIND, DAY-BLIND, STONE-BLIND, *etc.* (*b*) **To be blind to one's interests, to s.o.'s faults**, ne pas voir ses propres intérêts, les défauts de qn. (*c*) *adv. P:* **To go at a thing blind**, se lancer à l'aveugle dans une entreprise. *Av:* **To fly blind**, voler à l'aveuglette. *S.a.* DRUNK 1. **2.** (*Hidden*) **Blind ditch**, saut *m* de loup. *Needlew:* **Blind hemming**, point d'ourlet invisible. *S.a.* CORNER[1] 3. **3. Blind path**, chemin sans issue. **Blind alley**, cul-de-sac *m*, impasse *f.* **Blind-alley occupation**, occupation sans avenir. *Arch:* **B. door, window**, fausse porte ; fenêtre feinte, aveugle. **-ly**, *adv.* Aveuglément ; en aveugle ; à l'aveuglette. **'blind-man's-'buff**, *s.* Colin-maillard *m.* **'blind-**

stor(e)y, s. *Arch:* Triforium *m.* **'blind-worm**, *s. Rept:* Orvet *m.*

blind[2], *v.tr.* **1.** Aveugler. (*a*) Rendre (qn) aveugle ; frapper (qn) de cécité ; crever les yeux à (qn). **Blinded ex-service men**, aveugles de guerre. (*b*) Éblouir. **2.** (*a*) Ensabler (une chaussée, une voie .errée). (*b*) *Min:* Blinder (une galerie).

blind[3], *s.* **1.** (Awning-)blind, (outside sun-)blind, store *m* (à l'italienne) ; abat-jour *m inv.* **Roller blind**, store sur rouleau. **Venetian blind**, jalousie *f* (à lames mobiles). **2.** *His piety is only a b.*, sa piété n'est qu'un masque, qu'une feinte.

blindfold[1] ['blaindfould], *a. & adv.* **1.** Les yeux bandés. **2.** (*Recklessly*) Aveuglément.

blindfold[2], *v.tr.* Bander les yeux à, de (qn).

blindness ['blaindnəs], *s.* **1.** Cécité *f. S.a.* COLOUR-BLINDNESS, DAY-BLINDNESS, *etc.* **2.** (*Ignorance, folly*) Aveuglement *m. B. to the facts*, refus *m* d'envisager les faits.

blink[1] [bliŋk], *s.* **1.** Battement *m*, clignotement *m*, de paupières. **2.** (*Gleam*) Lueur (momentanée) ; (*glimpse*) vision momentanée.

blink[2]. **1.** *v.i.* (*a*) Battre des paupières ; cligner des paupières ; clignoter. (*b*) (*Of light*) Papilloter. **2.** Fermer les yeux à demi. (*a*) *v.tr.* **To blink the facts**, fermer les yeux sur la vérité. **To blink the question**, esquiver la question. *There is no blinking the fact that . . .* il n'y a pas à dissimuler que. . . (*b*) *v.i.* **To blink at a fault**, fermer les yeux sur un défaut. **blinking**[1], *a. F:* (*a*) Clignotant. (*b*) (*Feu*) papillotant. **2.** *P: Euphemism for* BLOODY 2. **blinking**[2], *s.* **1.** (*a*) Clignotement *m.* (*b*) Papillotage *m.* **2. Blinking of a fact**, refus *m* d'envisager un fait.

blinkers ['bliŋkərz], *s.pl. Harn:* Œillères *f.*

bliss [blis], *s.* Béatitude *f*, félicité *f.*

blissful ['blisful], *a.* (Bien)heureux. **B. days**, jours sereins. **-fully**, *adv.* Heureusement.

blister[1] ['blistər], *s.* (*a*) (*On skin*) Ampoule *f*, bulle *f.* **Water blister**, cloque *f.* (*b*) Cloque, boursouflure *f* (de la peinture). *Glassm:* Bulle, cloche *f. Metall:* Soufflure *f*, paille *f.* (*c*) *Med:* Vésicatoire *m.*

blister[2]. **1.** *v.tr.* (*a*) Couvrir d'ampoules ; faire venir des ampoules à (la main, etc.). (*b*) *Med:* Appliquer un vésicatoire. **2.** *v.i.* Se couvrir d'ampoules ; (*of paint*) (se) cloquer ; gondoler. **blistering**, *s.* **1.** *Med:* Vésication *f.* **2.** Formation *f* d'ampoules. **3.** Cloquage *m*, gondolage *m.*

blithe(some) ['blaːið(səm)], *a.* Joyeux, folâtre. **blithely** ['blaiðli], *adv.* Joyeusement.

blithering ['bliðəriŋ], *a. F:* = BLETHERING. **Blithering idiot**, (type absolument) idiot.

blizzard ['blizərd], *s.* Tempête *f*, rafale *f*, de neige.

bloat [blout], *v.tr.* Boursoufler ; gonfler ; bouffir. **bloated**, *a.* (*a*) Boursouflé, gonflé, bouffi. (*b*) **B. face**, visage congestionné.

bloater ['bloutər], *s.* Hareng bouffi ; craquelot *m.*

blob [blɔb], *s.* (*a*) Tache *f* (de couleur) ; pâté *m* (d'encre). (*b*) Goutte *f* d'eau (sur la table, etc.).

block[1] [blɔk], *s.* **1.** (*a*) Bloc *m* (de marbre, de fer) ; bille *f*, tronçon *m* (de bois) ; quartier *m* (de roche) ; tête *f* à perruque (de perruquier) ; poupée *f* (de modiste). *I.C.E:* Four-cylinder *b.*, bloc de quatre cylindres. *Toys:* **Building blocks**, cubes *mpl* ; jeu *m* de constructions. *S.a.* CALENDAR, CHIP[1], HAT-BLOCK, *etc.* (*b*) (Chopping-, anvil-)block, billot *m. Hist:* **To perish on the block**, périr sur le billot. (*c*) (Mounting-)block, horse-block, montoir *m.* (*d*) (*Chock*) Tin *m*, hausse *f*, cale *f.* (*e*) Sabot *m* (de frein). (*f*) *P:* Tête *f* ; *P:* caboche *f.* **2.** (*a*) Pâté *m*, îlot *m*, de maisons (entre quatre rues) ; ensemble *m* de bâtiments. (*b*) Lot *m* (de terrains). (*c*) *Fin:*

Block of shares, tranche *f* d'actions. 3. (*a*) Traffic block, encombrement *m*, embarras *m* (de voitures); embouteillage *m*. (*b*) *Cr:* Point en avant du guiche où le batteur appuie sa batte. 4. *Rail:* Tronçon *m* (de ligne`; canton *m*. Block system, cantonnement *m*; block-système *m*. 5. *Engr:* Planche *f*; bois *m*; (*metal*) cliché *m*. 6. Poulie *f*; moufle *m*. *Differential b.*, mouflette *f*. block-'capitals, *s.pl.* Majuscules *f* imitant l'imprimerie. 'block-'letter, *s.* (*a*) *Typ:* Lettre moulée; caractère gras. (*b*) *pl.* = BLOCK-CAPITALS. 'block-maker, *s.* (*a*) Photo-graveur *m.* (*b*) *Typ:* Clicheur *m*.

block², *v.tr.* I. Bloquer, obstruer. *To b. the traffic*, entraver, gêner, la circul.tion. *To b. s.o.'s way*, barrer le passage à qn. 'Road blocked,' "rue barrée." *To b. progress*, arrêter le progrès. *To b. a wheel*, bloquer, enrayer, une roue. *Rail:* To block the line, fermer la voie. 2. *Games:* (*a*) *Cr:* To block the ball, arrêter la balle sans la relancer; bloquer la balle. (*b*) *Dominoes:* To block the game, fermer le jeu. (*c*) *Fb:* Gêner (un adversaire). 3. *Bookb:* Gaufrer, frapper (la couverture d'un livre). block out, *v.tr.* I. (*Of censor*) Caviarder (un passage d'un journal). 2. Ébaucher (une statue, etc.). block up, *v.tr.* (*a*) Boucher, bloquer (un trou); condamner, murer (une porte, une fenêtre); *Nau:* bâcler (un port). (*b*) Obstruer (un tuyau, etc.). block-ing, *s.* I. Encombrement *m*. 2. *Bookb:* Gau-frage *m*, frappe *f*.

blockade¹ [blo'ke:id], *s.* Blocus *m*. To run the blockade, forcer le blocus. To raise the blockade, lever le blocus. bloc'kade-runner, *s.* For-ceur *m* de blocus. bloc'kade-running, *s.* Forcement *m* de blocus.

blockade², *v.tr.* Bloquer (une ville, un port); faire le blocus (d'une place forte).

blockhead ['blokhed], *s.* *F:* Lourdaud *m*; sot *m*. *He's a b.*, c'est une tête de bois.

blockhouse ['blokhaus], *s.* *Mil:* Blockhaus *m*.

bloke [blouk], *s.* *P:* Individu *m*, type *m*.

blond, *f.* blonde [blond], *a.* & *s.* I. Blond, -e. 2. *F:* Blondin, -ine. 3. Blonde (lace), blonde *f*.

blood¹ [blʌd], *s.* I. Sang *m*. (*a*) To shed, spill, blood, répandre, verser, le sang. *Without shedding of b.*, sans effusion de sang. To draw blood, faire saigner qn. *To flog s.o. till one draws b.*, fouetter qn jusqu'au sang. *To fight until b. is drawn* (*and no longer*), se battre au premier sang. *To spit b.*, cracher du sang; cracher rouge. *F:* He's out for blood, il va se montrer intraitable, féroce. *Prov:* One can't get blood out of a stone, on ne saurait tirer de l'huile d'un mur. The blood stream, le cours du sang. It makes my blood boil, cela me fait bouillir le sang; cela m'indigne. *His b. boiled*, his blood was up, le sang lui bouillait dans les veines; il était monté. His blood ran cold, son sang se glaça, se figea (dans ses veines). To commit a crime in cold blood, commettre un crime de sang-froid. His blood is on his own head, son sang est sur lui. There is bad blood, ill blood, between them, il y a de vieilles rancunes entre eux. To infuse new blood into an under-taking, vivifier une entreprise. The committee needs new b., le comité a besoin d'être rajeuni. *S.a.* FLESH 2, PRESSURE I. (*b*) (*Kindred*) They are near in b., ils sont proches parents. It runs in the blood, cela tient de famille; c'est dans le sang. The call of the blood, la voix du sang. (*c*) (*Birth, race*) Prince of the blood, prince du sang. Blue blood, sang royal, aristocratique. *Prov:* Blood will tell, bon sang ne peut mentir. Blood horse, cheval de sang, de race; (cheval)

pur-sang *m*. 2. (*a*) *A:* Petit-maître *m*, dandy *m*. (*b*) *F:* Young blood, un des jeunes du parti (politique, etc.). 'blood-curdling, *a.* A vous tourner les sangs; qui (vous) fige le sang. 'blood-giver, *s.* *Surg:* Donneur *m* de sang. 'blood-letting, *s.* *Med:* *A:* Saignée *f*. 'blood-orange, *s.* (Orange) sanguine *f*. 'blood-poisoning, *s.* *Med:* Empoisonne-ment *m* du sang; septicémie *f*, toxémie *f*. 'blood-red, *a.* Rouge sang. blood-re'la-tion, *s.* Parent(e) par le sang. 'blood-stain, *s.* Tache *f* de sang. 'blood-stained, *a* Taché de sang, souillé de sang. 'blood-stone, *s.* *Lap:* Sanguine *f*. 'blood-sucker, *s.* I. *Ann:* Sangsue *f*. 2. *F:* Sangsue, vampire *m*. 'blood-tax, *s.* L'impôt *m* du sang. 'blood-vessel, *s.* Vaisseau sanguin.

blood², *v.tr* (*a*) *Ven:* Acharner (les chiens), leur donner le goût du sang. (*b*) *Mil:* To b. the troops, donner aux troupes le baptême du feu.

-blooded ['blʌdid], *a.* Warm-, cold-blooded animals, animaux à sang chaud, à sang froid. *S.a.* COLD-BLOODED, etc.

bloodhound ['blʌdhaund], *s.* I. Chien *m* de Saint-Hubert; limier *m*. 2. *F:* (*Of pers.*) Limier.

bloodless ['blʌdləs], *a.* I. Exsangue, anémié. 2. Bloodless victory, victoire sans effusion de sang.

bloodshed ['blʌdʃed], *s.* I. Effusion *f* de sang. 2. Carnage *m*.

bloodshot ['blʌdʃot], *a.* Bloodshot eye, œil injecté de sang. (*Of eye*) To become b., s'injecter.

bloodthirstiness ['blʌdθə:rstinəs], *s.* Soif *f* de sang.

bloodthirsty ['blʌdθə:rsti], *a.* Sanguinaire; altéré de sang, assoiffé de sang.

bloody ['blʌdi], *a.* I. Sanglant, ensanglanté, taché de sang; (*combat*) sanglant, sanguinaire; (*tyran*) sanguinaire, cruel. 2. *P:* (*Not in decent use; usu. spelt b. . . .*) *a.* Sacré. A b. . . . liar, un sacré menteur. (*b*) *adv.* It is b. . . . hot! quelle sacrée chaleur!

bloom¹ [blu:m], *s.* I. (i) Fleur *f*; (ii) floraison *f*, épanouissement *m*. To burst into bloom, fleurir. *Flower in b.*, fleur éclose. In full bloom, épanoui; en pleine fleur. *F:* In the b. of youth, à, dans, la fleur de l'âge; en pleine jeunesse. Beauty that has lost its bloom, beauté défraîchie. 2. Velouté *m*, duvet *m* (du raisin, d'une pêche).

bloom², *v.i.* Fleurir; être en fleur. To bloom into sth., devenir qch. (de beau). blooming¹, *a.* I. (*a*) Fleurissant; en fleur. (*b*) (*Flourishing*) Florissant. 2. *P:* Ain't he a b. toff! ce qu'il est rupin! You b. idiot! sacré imbécile! bloom-ing², *s* Floraison *f*, fleuraison *f*.

bloom³, *s.* *Metall:* Masse *f* de fer cinglé; loupe *f*, bloom *m*, lopin *m*, masseau *m*.

bloomer ['blu:mər], *s.* *P:* Bévue *f*, gaffe *f*.

bloomers ['blu:mərz], *s.pl.* *Cost:* Culotte bouf-fante (de femme), pour cyclisme, etc., ou jupe courte comme costume de gymnas-tique).

Bloomsbury ['blu:mzbəri]. *Pr.n.* I. *A:* Quar-tier *m* (de Londres) de bonne bourgeoisie. 2. Quartier d'hôtels et de pensions de famille. 3. (En voie de devenir) le "quartier latin."

blossom¹ ['blosəm], *s.* Fleur *f* (des arbres). Tree in blossom, arbre en fleur(s). Orange blossom, fleur d'oranger.

blossom², *v.i.* (*Of tree*) Fleurir. To blossom (out) into sth., devenir qch. (de beau). blossom out, *v.i.* S'épanouir. blossoming, *s* Fleu-raison *f*, floraison *f*.

blot¹ [blot], *s.* (*a*) Tache *f*; (*of ink*) pâté *m*.

(b) A b. on s.o.'s honour, une tache, une souillure, à l'honneur de qn.

blot², *v.tr.* (blotted) **1.** *(a)* Tacher, souiller. *(b) (Of ink)* Faire des pâtés sur (qch.). *(c)* **To blot (up) the ink,** l'encre (d'une lettre, etc.). **To blot (up) the ink,** passer le buvard sur l'encre. **3.** *Abs. (Of blotting-paper)* Boire l'encre. **blot out,** *v.tr.* **1.** Effacer. **2.** *(Of fog, etc.)* Cacher, masquer (l'horizon, etc.). **3.** *Lit:* Exterminer (une race). **blotting,** *s.* **1.** Séchage *m* (au papier buvard). **2.** Maculage *m* (du papier). **'blotting-pad,** *s.* (Bloc) buvard *m*; sous-main *m*. **'blotting-paper,** *s.* Papier buvard, papier brouillard.

blotch¹ [blɔtʃ], *s.* **1.** Tache *f*, éclaboussure *f* (d'encre, de couleur). **2.** *(a)* Tache rouge (sur la peau). *(b)* Pustule *f*.

blotch², *v.tr.* Couvrir (la peau) de taches, de rougeurs. *The cold blotches the skin,* le froid marbre la peau.

blotchiness ['blɔtʃinəs], *s.* Couperose *f*.

blotchy ['blɔtʃi], *a.* **1.** (Teint) brouillé, couperosé; peau couverte de rougeurs. **2.** Tacheté.

blotter ['blɔtər], *s.* Buvard *m*; bloc buvard. **Hand-blotter,** tampon *m* buvard.

blouse [blɑːuz], *s.* **1.** Blouse *f.* **2.** *Mil: U.S:* Vareuse *f.*

blow¹ [blou], *s.* **1.** Coup *m* de vent. *To go for a b.,* sortir prendre l'air. **2.** Souffle *m. Every morning he has a b. at his trombone,* tous les matins il souffle dans son trombone. **3.** = FLY-BLOW.

blow², *v.* (blew [bluː]; blown [bloun], *P:* blowed [blo:ud]) I. *v.i.* Souffler. **1.** *(a) (Of wind) It is blowing,* il fait du vent, il vente. *It is blowing hard,* le vent souffle fort; il fait grand vent. *It is blowing a gale,* le vent souffle en tempête, le vent fait rage. *It was blowing great guns,* il faisait un vent à (d)écorner les bœufs. *It is blowing up for rain,* le vent annonce de la pluie. *S.a.* WIND¹ 1. *F:* Blow high, blow low . . ., quoi qu'il advienne. . . . *S.a.* FRESH 1. 5, HOT 1. *(b) Pred.* The door blew open, la porte s'ouvrit sous la poussée du vent. **2.** *(a) (Of pers.)* To b. on one's fingers, souffler dans ses doigts. *(b)* To let the horses blow, laisser souffler les chevaux. *(c) (Of whale)* Rejeter l'eau par les évents. *F: (Of pers.)* To blow like a grampus, souffler comme une baleine, comme un phoque, comme un bœuf. **3.** To blow upon s.o.'s reputation, ternir une réputation. **4.** *(Of electric lamp)* Claquer, griller; *(of fuse)* fondre, sauter. II. **blow,** *v.tr.* **1.** The wind blows the rain against the windows, le vent chasse la pluie contre les vitres. *(Of wind)* To b. a ship ashore, pousser un navire à la côte. **2.** *(a) (Of pers.)* To b. the dust off a book, souffler sur un livre (pour enlever la poussière). *F:* To blow s.o. a kiss, envoyer un baiser à qn. *(b)* To blow (up) the fire, ranimer le feu. To b. the organ, souffler l'orgue. *(c)* To blow one's nose, se moucher. To blow a trumpet, souffler dans une trompette. To b. the horn, sonner du cor. *F:* To blow one's own trumpet, chanter ses propres louanges. *(d)* To b. air into sth., insuffler de l'air dans qch. *Mch:* To blow a boiler, évacuer une chaudière. *Nau:* To blow the tanks (of a submarine), chasser aux ballasts. To blow bubbles, faire des bulles de savon. To blow glass, souffler le verre. **3.** Essouffler (un cheval, etc.). **4.** *El:* To blow a fuse, faire fondre un fusible; faire sauter les plombs. **5.** *(Of fly)* Gâter la viande (en y pondant des œufs). *(Cf.* FLY-BLOWN.) **6.** *P:* Blow the expense! expense be blowed! je me moque de la dépense! You be blowed! zut pour vous! I'll be blowed if . . ., que le diable m'emporte si. . . . **blow about. 1.** *v.i. (Of leaves, etc.)* Voler çà et là. **2.** *v.tr.* Ballotter; faire voler (qch.) çà et là; disperser (des feuilles, etc.). **blow away,** *v.tr.* Emporter. **1.** To b. away the dust, souffler sur la poussière (pour l'enlever). **2.** The sails were blown away, les voiles furent emportées par le vent. **blow down,** *v.tr. (Of wind)* Abattre, renverser (un arbre); verser (les blés). **blow in. 1.** *v.tr. (Of wind, etc.)* Enfoncer (une vitre, une porte). **2.** *v.i. (a) The wind blows in at the window,* le vent entre par la fenêtre. *(b) F: (Of pers.)* Entrer en passant; s'amener. **blow off. 1.** *v.tr. (a) The wind has blown his hat off,* le vent a emporté son chapeau. To b. the dust off, souffler la poussière. *(b) Mch:* To blow off steam, purger, souffler sur la poussière (pour l'enlever), lâcher, de la vapeur. *S.a.* STEAM¹. **2.** *v.i. (Of hat)* S'envoler. **blow out. 1.** *v.tr. (a)* Souffler, éteindre (une bougie). *(b)* To b. out one's cheeks, gonfler, enfler, les joues. *(c)* To b. the air out (from gas-pipes, etc.), chasser, expulser, l'air. To b. out a boiler, évacuer l'eau d'une chaudière. *S.a.* BRAIN¹ 2. **2.** *v.i. (a) (Of candle, etc.)* S'éteindre. *(b) Aut: (Of tyre)* Éclater; faire hernie. *(c) El: (Of fuse)* Sauter. **blow-'out,** *s. P:* Gueuleton *m.* **blow over. 1.** *v.tr.* = BLOW DOWN. **2.** *v.i. (a) The storm has blown over,* la tempête s'est calmée, est passée. *The scandal soon blew over,* le scandale fut bientôt oublié. *(b) (Of crops)* Verser. **blow up. 1.** *v.i. (a) (Of mine, etc.)* Éclater, sauter; *(of boiler)* crever, exploser. *(b) Nau:* It is blowing up for a gale, il vente grand frais. **2.** *v.tr. (a)* Faire sauter (une mine, un pont, etc.); (faire) exploser (une mine). *(b)* Gonfler (un pneu). *F:* Blown up with pride, bouffi d'orgueil. *(c) F:* Semoncer, tancer. **blowing up,** *s.* **1.** Explosion *f.* **2.** Gonflement *m* (d'un pneu). **3.** Semonce *f.*; à bout de souffle. **2.** *(Of food)* Gâté. **blowing,** *s.* **1.** Soufflement *m* (du vent). **2.** Soufflage *m* (d'un fourneau, etc.). **'blow-ball,** *s. Bot:* Chandelle *f* (de pissenlit); voyageur *m.* **'blow-cock,** *s. Mch:* Robinet *m* de vidange. **'blow-fly,** *pl.* **-flies,** *s.* Mouche *f* à viande. **'blow-hole,** *s.* **1.** Évent *m* (d'une baleine). **2.** Ventilateur *m* (d'un tunnel). **'blow-lamp, -torch,** *s.* **1.** Lampe *f* à souder, à braser. **2.** Brûloir *m* (de peintre en bâtiments). **'blow-pipe,** *s.* **1.** Sarbacane *f.* **2.** *(a) Ch: Metall:* Chalumeau *m. (b) Glassm:* Canne *f* (de souffleur).

blow³, *s. (In the phr.)* In full blow, en pleine fleuraison, en plein épanouissement.

blow⁴, *v.i.* (blew; blown) *(Of flower)* S'épanouir, fleurir.

blow⁵, *s.* **1.** Coup *m*; *(with fist)* coup de poing; *(with stick)* coup de bâton. *At the first b.,* du premier coup. *At a (single) b.,* d'un (seul) coup. To strike a blow, porter, asséner, donner, un coup. Without striking a blow, sans coup férir. To deal s.o. a blow, porter un coup à qn. *S.a.* FETCH² 5. To come to blows, en venir aux coups, aux mains; *Jur:* en arriver aux voies de fait. *Blows fell thick and fast,* il pleuvait des coups. Knock-out blow, (i) coup d'assommoir; (ii) *Box:* knock-out *m. Prov:* The first blow is half the battle, le premier coup en vaut deux. *B.* to s.o.'s credit, atteinte *f* au crédit de qn. To aim a blow at s.o.'s authority, porter atteinte à l'autorité de qn. **2.** Coup (du sort). *It came as a crushing b. to us,* ce fut un coup d'assommoir pour nous.

blower ['blouər], *s.* **1.** *(a)* Souffleur, -euse (de verre, etc.). *b)* **Horn-blower,** sonneur *m* de cor. **2.** *(a)* Tablier *m*, rideau *m* (de cheminée). *(b) Ind: etc:* Ventilateur soufflant; machine *f* à vent souffleur *m.* (*c*) Insufflateur *m*, soufflet *m* (à poudre insecticide).

blowy ['bloui], *a.* Venteux ; tempétueux.

blowzy ['blauzi], *a.* (*Of woman*) (*a*) Rougeaude. (*b*) Ébouriffée ; mal peignée.

blubber¹ ['blʌbər], *s.* **I.** Graisse *f*, lard *m*, de baleine. **2.** *F:* (*Jelly-fish*) Méduse *f*.

blubber², *attrib. a.* **Blubber lip**, lippe *f*. **Blubber-lipped**, lippu.

blubber³. *F:* **I.** *v.i.* (*a*) Pleurer bruyamment, *F:* pleurer comme un veau (*over*, sur). (*b*) Pleur-nicner. **2.** *v.tr.* (*a*) To blubber out sth., dire qch. en pleurant. (*b*) *Cheeks blubbered with tears*, joues barbouillées de larmes, bouffies par les larmes.

blubberer ['blʌbərər], *s.*, **blubbering**, *a.* Pleurard, -arde ; pleurnicheur, -euse.

bluchers ['bluːkərz], *s.pl.* Demi-bottes *f*.

bludgeon¹ ['blʌdʒən], *s.* Gourdin *m*, matraque *f*.

bludgeon², *v.tr.* Asséner un coup de gourdin, de matraque, à (qn).

blue¹ [bluː]. I. *a.* (*a*) Bleu, azuré. *B.* spectacles, lunettes bleutées. **Blue ribbon**, (i) ruban bleu (des buveurs d'eau) ; (ii) prix principal (d'une réunion de courses, etc.). *F:* **Blue water**, the **blue sea**, la haute mer ; le large **The blue-water school**, les partisans d'une marine puissante. *S.a.* **BLOOD¹** I, **BOOK¹** I, **DEVIL¹** 2, **PETER¹** 2, *etc.* (*b*) (*Of pers.*) To go blue, prendre une teinte violacée. *You may talk till you are b. in the face*, dites à all's blue, vous aurez beau parler. *S.a.* **BLACK¹** I. I. {*c*) *F:* To look blue, avoir l'air (i) triste, sombre, (ii) déconcerté. **To feel blue**, avoir le cafard. (*d*) To tell blue stories, raconter des grivoiseries. II. **blue**, *s.* **I.** Bleu *m*, azur *m*. **A light blue dress**, une robe bleu clair. **Dark blue socks**, des chaussettes bleu foncé. **Sky-blue**, bleu céleste ; azur *m inv.* **Cambridge blue**, bleu clair. **Oxford blue**, bleu foncé. **Steely blue**, bleuté. **Navy blue**, **sea blue**, bleu marine *inv.* **The blue (sky)**, la voûte azurée. **Out of the blue**, soudainement. *S.a.* **BOLT¹** 2. **2.** *Pol:* A true blue, un patriote ; *F:* un vrai de vrai. To win, get, one's blue, être choisi pour repré-senter son université dans un match universitaire. **3.** (Washing-)blue, indigo *m* ; bleu (d'empois). **4.** *s.pl.* The blues, humeur noire, papillons noirs. To have (a fit of) the blues, avoir des idées noires ; avoir le cafard. '**blue bag**, *s. Laund:* Sachet *m* à bleu. '**blue-bell**, *s.* **I.** Jacinthe *f* des prés, des bois. **2.** *Scot:* Campanule *f*. '**blue-'black**, *a.* Noir tirant sur le bleu. **blue-'eyed**, *a.* **I.** Aux yeux bleus. **2.** *F:* Innocent, candide. **blue-'grass**, *s. Bot:* Pâturin *m* des prés. '**blue-grey**, *a. & s.* Gris bleuté. '**blue jacket**, *s.* Marin *m*, matelot *m*, de l'État ; col-bleu *m*. **blue-'pencil**, *v.tr.* Marquer au crayon bleu. '**blue-stocking**, *s.* (*Of woman*) Bas-bleu *m*.

blue², *v.tr.* **I.** (*a*) Bleuir ; teindre (qch.) en bleu. *Laund:* Azurer (le linge) ; mettre, passer, (le linge) au bleu. (*b*) **Blued spectacles**, lunettes bleu-tées **2.** *F:* To blue one's money, gaspiller, manger, son argent.

Bluebeard ['bluːbiəd]. *Pr.n.m.* Barbe-bleue *m*.

bluebottle ['bluːbɔtl], *s.* **I.** Bluet *m*, bleuet *m*. **2.** Mouche *f* à viande.

bluff¹ [blʌf]. I. *a.* (*a*) (*Of cliff, coast*) Accore, escarpé ; à pic. *Nau:* **Bluff(-bowed)**, (navire) renflé de l'avant. (*b*) (*Of pers.*) Brusque ; un peu bourru. *A straightforward, bluff, man*, un homme tout rond. II. **bluff**, *s. Geog:* Cap *m* à pic ; à-pic *m* ; falaise *f*.

bluff², *s.* (*a*) *Cards:* (*At poker*) Bluff *m*. (*b*) *F:* Bluff, battage *m*. (*c*) Menaces exagérées. **To call**

s.o.'s bluff, (i) (*at poker*) inviter l'adversaire à mettre cartes sur table ; (ii) *F:* relever un défi.

bluff³, *v.tr.* *Cards & F:* Bluffer (qn). *Abs.* Faire du bluff, de l'épate.

bluffness ['blʌfnəs], *s.* Brusquerie (amicale) ; franc-parler *m*.

bluish ['bluːiʃ], *a.* Bleuâtre ; bleuté.

blunder¹ ['blʌndər], *s.* Bévue *f*, maladresse *f*, erreur *f*. *B. in behaviour*, *social b.*, solécisme *m* de conduite ; *F:* gaffe *f*, impair *m.* **Egregious b.**, grosse maladresse.

blunder², *v.i. & tr.* **I.** Faire une bévue, une gaffe, une maladresse, un faux pas ; *F:* gaffer. **2.** To blunder against, into, s.o., se heurter contre qn ; heurter qn. *To b. one's way along*, avancer à l'aveuglette. *To b. upon the truth*, découvrir la vérité par hasard. **He managed to blunder through**, il s'en est tiré tant bien que mal. **blundering**, *a.* Brouillon, maladroit. **-ly**, *adv.* A l'aveuglette ; au petit bonheur.

blunderbuss ['blʌndərbʌs], *s.* Tromblon *m*, espingole *f*.

blunderer ['blʌndərər], *s.* Brouillon, -onne ; maladroit, -e ; gaffeur, -euse.

blunderhead ['blʌndərhed], *s.* = **DUNDERHEAD**.

blunt¹ [blʌnt], *a.* **I.** (*Not sharpened*) Mousse ; (*having lost its edge*) émoussé ; (*having lost its point*) épointé ; (instrument) contondant ; (angle) obtus. **2.** (*Of pers.*) Brusque, carré. **The blunt fact**, le fait brutal. **-ly**, *adv.* Brusquement, carrément. *To announce news b.*, annoncer une nouvelle sans ménagements. '**blunt-witted**, *a.* A l'esprit épais, obtus.

blunt², *v.tr.* Émousser (un couteau) ; épointer (un crayon). *F:* To b. the feelings, émousser les sentiments. *To b. the palate*, blaser le palais.

bluntness ['blʌntnəs], *s.* **I.** État émoussé, épointé ; manque *m* de tranchant. **2.** Brusquerie *f*, franchise *f*. *B. of speech*, franc-parler *m*.

blur¹ [bləːr], *s.* **I.** Tache *f*, macule *f*, barbouillage *m* (d'encre, etc.). **2.** (*a*) Apparence confuse ; brouillard *m*. (*b*) Buée *f* (sur un miroir, etc.). **3.** Ternissure *f*.

blur², *v.tr.* (blurred) **I.** Barbouiller (d'encre, etc.). *Typ:* Maculer. **2.** Brouiller, troubler. *Eyes blurred with tears*, yeux voilés de larmes. **blur out**, *v.tr.* Effacer, cacher (l'horizon).

blurt [bləːrt], *v.tr.* To blurt out a secret, laisser échapper, trahir maladroitement, un secret.

blush¹ [blʌʃ], *s.* **I.** Aspect *m.* **At the first blush**, au premier abord, au premier aspect. **In the first blush of youth**, aux prémices de la jeunesse. **2.** (*a*) Rougeur *f* (de modestie, de honte). **To put s.o. to the blush**, (i) faire rougir qn ; (ii faire honte à qn. (*b*) Incarnat *m* (des roses). *The first b. of dawn*, les premières rougeurs de l'aube.

blush², *v.i.* (*Of pers.*) Rougir. *To b. for shame*, rougir de honte. **I blush for you**, vous me faites rougir. **To blush to the roots of one's hair**, rougir jusqu'au blanc des yeux, jusqu'aux oreilles. **2.** (*Of flower, dawn*) Rougir. **blushing**, *a.* **I.** Rougissant ; timide. **2.** (*Of flower, etc.*) Rouge, rougissant.

bluster¹ ['blʌstər], *s.* (*a*) Fureur *f*, fracas *m* (de l'orage). (*b*) Bravacherie *f*, rodomontades *fpl*.

bluster², *v.i.* (*a*) (*Of wind*) Souffler en rafales. (*b*) (*Of pers.*) Faire du fracas ; parler haut ; faire le rodomont. *v.tr.* **To bluster out threats**, se répandre en menaces ; déblatérer des menaces. **blustering**, *a.* (*a*) (Vent) violent. (*b*) Bravache, tonitruant. **-ly**, *adv.* D'un air bravache.

blusterer ['blʌstərər], *s.* Bravache *m*, rodomont *m*.

boa ['boua], *s.* **I.** *Z:* Boa *m.* **Boa constrictor**, boa constricteur. **2.** *Cost:* **Feather boa**, boa.

boar ['bɔːr], s. Verrat m. **Wild boar**, sanglier m. **'boar-hound**, s. Vautre m. **'boar-hunting**, s. Chasse f au sanglier. **'boar-spear**, s. Épieu m. **board**[1] [bɔːrd], s. **I.** (a) Planche f, ais m; (thick) madrier m. **Bread board**, planche à couper le pain. **Ironing board**, planche à repasser. S.a. DIVING-BOARD, KNIFE-BOARD, etc. (b) **(Notice-) board**, tableau m de publicité, d'annonces, d'affichage. Sp: **Telegraph board**, tableau d'affichage. Aut: Av: **(Fascia-)board**, (instrument-)board, tableau de bord, de manœuvre; planche de bord; Aut: planche tablier. S.a. DASH-BOARD, SIGN-BOARD, etc. (c) pl. Th: **The boards**, la scène, le théâtre, F: les planches. **To go on the boards**, aborder la scène; monter sur les planches, sur les tréteaux. (d) **(Cardboard)** Carton m. Bookb: (i) **(Binding in) paper boards**, cartonnage m, emboîtage m. **In paper boards**, cartonné. **(Binding in) cloth boards**, emboîtage pleine toile. (ii) pl. **The boards**, les plats m (d'un livre). **2.** (a) Table f. **The festive board**, la table du festin. (b) Table, nourriture f, pension f. **Board and lodging**, b. (and) residence, pension et chambre(s). Partial b., demi-pension f. With b. and lodging, nourri et logé. (c) **(Gaming) board**, table de jeu. **To clean the b.**, faire tapis net. (d) Chess: Tablier m (de l'échiquier). **3.** (a) **Board of enquiry**, commission f d'enquête. **Board of examiners**, jury m, commission, d'examen. (b) **The Board of Trade** = le Ministère du Commerce. **The Board of Education** = le Ministère de l'Éducation nationale. **The Board of Works** = le Ministère des Travaux publics. (c) Com: **Board of Directors, of Managers**, (conseil m d')administration f; bureau m (d'une société). **Boar meeting**, réunion du conseil. **4.** Nau: (a) Bord m. **On board (ship)**, à bord d'un navire. **On b. my ship**, à mon bord. **To take goods on b.**, embarquer des marchandises. **To go on board**, monter à bord; s'embarquer. **To go by the board**, s'en aller par-dessus bord; tomber à la mer. (b) Bordée f, bord. **To make a board**, courir une bordée; courir un bord. **'board-room**, s. Salle f de réunion, du conseil. **'board-school**, s. A: = École primaire communale. **board-'wages**, s.pl. Indemnité f de logement, de nourriture. **To be on b.-w.**, toucher pour sa nourriture.

board[2]. **I.** v.tr. (a) Planchéier (le sol d'un appartement). (b) Bookb: Cartonner (un livre). **2.** (a) v.i. Être en pension. **To b. with the family**, prendre pension dans la famille. **To b. at the school**, être pensionnaire à l'école. (b) v.tr. Nourrir (des élèves, etc.). **3.** v.tr. Nau: (a) Aborder, accoster, Adm: arraisonner (un navire). (b) Aller, monter, à bord d'un navire. U.S: **To b. a train**, monter dans un train. (c) Navy: Aborder (un navire). **board out**, v.tr. Mettre (des enfants) en pension; placer (des enfants) dans une famille. **board up**, v.tr. Boucher (une fenêtre); condamner (une porte). **boarding**, s. **I.** (a) Const: Planchéiage m. (b) Cartonnage m (d'un livre). **2.** (a) Nau: Accostage m; Arraisonnement m. (b) Navy: Abordage m. **3.** Coll. Planches fpl. **'boarding-house**, s. **I.** Pension f de famille. **2.** Sch: Maison f où logent les internes. **'boarding-school**, s. Pension f, pensionnat m, internat m. **To send a child to a b.-s.**, mettre un enfant en pension.

boarder ['bɔːrdər], s. Pensionnaire mf; (in schools) interne mf.

boast[1] [boust], s. Vanterie f. **To make a b. of sth.**, se faire gloire, se glorifier, de qch. **boast**[2]. **I.** v.i. Se vanter; F: hâbler. **To b. that**

one can do, has done, sth., se vanter de pouvoir faire, d'avoir fait, qch. **To b. of, about, sth.**, se vanter, se faire gloire, de qch. **That's nothing to boast of**, il n'y a pas là de quoi être fier. **Without wishing to· boast . .**, sans vanité . . .; sans forfanterie. . . . **2.** v.tr. (Se glorifier de) posséder (qch.). **The school boasts a fine library**, l'école possède une belle bibliothèque. **boasting**, s. Vantardise f; gloriole f; jactance f.

boaster ['boustər], s. Vantard m, fanfaron m.

boastful ['boustful], a. Vantard. **-fully**, adv. Avec vanterie, avec jactance.

boastfulness ['boustfulnəs], s. Vantardise f, jactance f.

boat[1] [bout], s. Bateau m; (i) canot m; barque f (de pêcheur); embarcation f; (ii) navire (marchand). Ship's b., embarcation de bord. **Canal-boat**, péniche f. S.a. FERRY-BOAT, FISHING-BOAT, MAIL-BOAT, etc. **We took (the) boat at . . .**, nous nous sommes embarqués à . . ., nous avons pris le bateau à. . . . **To go by boat**, prendre le bateau. **To lower the boats**, mettre les embarcations à la mer. F: **To be all in the same boat**, être tous logés à la même enseigne; être tous dans le même cas. **To burn one's boats**, brûler ses vaisseaux. **'boat-builder**, s. Constructeur m de canots, de bateaux. **'boat-deck**, s. Nau: Pont m des embarcations. **'boat-hook**, s. Nau: Gaffe f; croc m de marinier. **'boat-house, -shed**, s. Hangar m à bateaux, pour canots; garage m (pour canots). **'boat-keeper**, s. Loueur m d'embarcations. **'boat-race**, s. Course f de bateaux; esp. match m d'aviron; régate(s) f(pl). **'boat-train**, s. Rail: Train m du bateau; train-paquebot m.

boat[2], v.i. Aller, se promener, en bateau; canoter; faire du canotage. **boating**, s. Canotage m. **Boating-club**, cercle de canotage, d'aviron.

boater ['boutər], s. (Hat) Canotier m.

boatman, pl. **-men** ['boutmən, -men], s.m. **I.** Batelier m. **2.** Loueur m de canots. **3.** Good b., bon canotier.

boatswain [bousn, 'boutswein], s. Nau: (F: bos'n, bosun) Maître m d'équipage **Boatswain's mate**, quartier-maître. **Bosun's chair, cradle**, chaise de riveur, de calfat.

bob[1] [bɔb], s. **I.** (a) Lentille f (d'un pendule); plomb m (d'un fil à plomb); queue f (d'un cerf-volant). (b) Fish: Bouchon m (de ligne). **2.** (a) Bob of hair, chignon m. (b) Coiffure f à la Ninon, à la Jeanne d'Arc. (c) Queue écourtée (d'un cheval). **3.** U.S: (a) Patin m (de traîneau). (b) = BOB-SLEIGH. **'bob-sled, -sleigh**, s. Bob-sleigh m; bob m. **'bob-tail**, a. & s., **'bob-tailed**, a. (Cheval, chien) à queue écourtée.

bob[2], v.tr. (bobbed) **I.** (Of woman) **To bob one's hair**, se faire couper les cheveux à la nuque; porter les cheveux à la Ninon. **2. To bob a horse's tail**, écourter la queue d'un cheval. **bob**[3], v.i. Se mouvoir de haut en bas et de bas en haut; s'agiter. **I.** Something was bobbing on the water, quelque chose s'agitait sur l'eau. **To bob up and down in the water**, danser sur l'eau. **2. To bob to s.o., to bob a curtsey**, faire une petite révérence (à qn). **3. To bob for apples**, chercher à saisir avec les dents des pommes flottant dans un baquet. **bob down**, v.i. Baisser brusquement la tête. **bob under**, v.i. (Of fisherman's float) Plonger. **bob up**, v.i. Surgir brusquement. **To bob up again**, revenir à la surface; revenir sur l'eau.

bob[4], s. **I.** Petite secousse f; petit coup m. **2.** (Curtsy) Petite révérence. **3.** Bellringing:

(a) Carillon m. (b) Chacune des variations du carillon. **Bob⁵.** **1.** Pr.n.m. Robert. **2.** s.m. F: (At Eton College) Dry bob, joueur m de cricket. Wet bob, canotier m.

bob⁶, s.inv. P: Shilling m. Five bob, cinq balles.

bobbin ['bɔbin], s. **1.** (a) Bobine f. (b) Lace bobbin, bloquet m, fuseau m, pour dentelles. **2.** El: Corps m de bobine. **'bobbin-frame,** s. Tex: Bobinoir m.

Bobby ['bɔbi]. **1.** Pr.n.m. Dim. of ROBERT. **2.** s. F: = POLICEMAN.

bobstay ['bɔbstei], s. Nau: Sous-barbe f inv.

Boccaccio [bɔk'katʃjo]. Pr.n.m. Boccace.

bode [boud], v.tr. & i. Présager. It bodes no good, cela ne présage, n'annonce, rien de bon. To bode well, ill, être de bon, de mauvais, augure. **boding,** s. (a) Présage m, augure m. (b) Pressentiment m.

bodice ['bɔdis], s. Corsage m. Under-bodice, cache-corset m inv.

-bodied ['bɔdid], a. Strong-bodied, fort, robuste. Able-bodied, valide. Full-bodied wine, tobacco, vin, tabac, qui a du corps.

bodiless ['bɔdiləs], a. Sans corps.

bodily ['bɔdili]. **1.** a. Corporel, physique. To supply one's b. wants, pourvoir à ses besoins matériels. B. pain, douleur physique. To go about in bodily fear, craindre pour sa sûreté personnelle. **2.** adv. (a) Corporellement. (b) They resigned b., ils ont donné leur démission en corps.

bodkin ['bɔdkin], s. **1.** (a) Passe-lacet m, passe-cordon m. (b) Needlew: Poinçon m. (c) (Grande) épingle. **2.** F: To ride, sit, bodkin (in carriage), être en lapin.

body ['bɔdi], s. Corps m. **1.** (a) Human b., corps humain. To belong to s.o. body and soul, appartenir, être, à qn corps et âme. To keep body and soul together, vivre tout juste; vivoter. Body linen, linge de corps. S.a. SOUND⁵ I. 1. (b) (Dead) body, corps (mort); cadavre m. The resurrection of the body, la résurrection de la chair. (c) Sève f, générosité f (d'un vin). To give b. to wine, corser le vin. (d) Consistance f. Paper without enough b., papier qui manque de consistance, de corps. **2.** (a) Legislative body, corps législatif. Public b., corporation f. Examining b., jury m d'examen. Electoral b., collège électoral. (b) Large body of people, nombreuse société; foule nombreuse. Little b. of disciples, petite bande de disciples. To come in a body, venir en masse, en corps. (c) Jur: Strong b. of evidence, forte accumulation de preuves. B. of laws, recueil m de lois. **3.** F: (Person) (a) A very decent old body, une vieille personne très respectable. (b) A queer body, un drôle de corps; un drôle de type. **4.** (Main part) (a) Corps (de document, de bâtiment); vaisseau m (d'église); fuselage m (d'avion). The b. of a speech, le fond, la substance, d'un discours. (b) Veh: Bâti m, corps, caisse f; carrosserie f. **5.** Astr: Ch: Corps. Heavenly body, astre m; corps céleste. **'body-colour,** s. Couleur f opaque. Art: Gouache f. To paint in b.-c., peindre à la gouache. **'body-guard,** s. **1.** (a) Garde f du corps; sauvegarde f. (b) Cortège m (à la suite de qn). **2.** Garde m du corps. **'body-snatcher,** s. Déterreur m de cadavres; résurrectionniste m.

Bœotian [bi'ouʃjən], a. & s. Béotien, -ienne.

bog¹ [bɔg], s. Fondrière f; marécage m. **'bog bean,** s. = BUCK-BEAN. **'bog berry,** s. Bot: Baie f des marais. **'bog-trotter,** s. Hist: F: Irlandais m.

bog², v. (bogged) **1.** v.tr. Embourber, enliser.

To get bogged, s'embourber, s'enliser. **2.** v.i. (Of horse, etc.) To bog down, s'enfoncer dans une fondrière.

bogey ['bougi], s. **1.** (a) Épouvantail m. (b) Griche-dents f inv. **2.** Golf: (Colonel) Bogey, la normale du parcours. **'bogey-man,** s. The b.-m., croque-mitaine m; le Père Fouettard (des enfants).

boggle [bɔgl], v.i. (a) Rechigner (at, over, sth. devant qch.; at, about, doing sth., à faire qch.). (b) (Bungle) To b. over an exercise, over the adverbs, ►patauger dans un devoir, parmi les adverbes.

boggy ['bɔgi], a. Marécageux, tourbeux.

bogie ['bougi], s. Rail: Bog(g)ie m. Bogie carriage, voiture à bog(g)ie.

bogle [bougl], s. Scot: **1.** = BOGEY 1. **2.** Spectre m, revenant m.

bogus ['bougəs], a. Faux, f. fausse; feint, simulé. Com: Bogus company, (i) société qui n'existe pas; (ii) société fantôme; (ii) sòciété véreuse.

bogy ['bougi], s. = BOGEY 1.

Bohemia [bo'hi:mjə]. Pr.n. **1.** Geog: La Bohême. **2.** (Unconventional life) Bohème f.

Bohemian [bo'hi:mjən]. **1.** a. & s. Geog: Bohémien, -ienne. **2.** s. (a) (Gipsy) Bohémien, -ienne. (b) Bohème m. a. B. life, vie de bohème. B. habits, mœurs débraillées.

boil¹ [bɔil], s. Med: Furoncle m, F: clou m.

boil², s. **1.** (Of water, etc.) To come to the boil, commencer à bouillir. The kettle is on the boil, l'eau bout. To go off the boil, cesser de bouillir. **2.** Tourbillon m (dans un cours d'eau); remous m.

boil³. **1.** v.i. Bouillir; (violently) bouillonner. To begin to b., entrer en ébullition. To b. fast, gently, bouillir à gros, à petits, bouillons. Cu: Allow to b. gently, slowly, faites mijoter. To keep the pot boiling, (i) faire bouillir la marmite; (ii) F: pourvoir aux besoins du ménage; (iii) F: maintenir l'entrain (dans une réunion). S.a. BLOOD¹ 1. **2.** v.tr. (a) Faire bouillir (de l'eau, etc.); cuire (du sucre). Cu: Cuire, faire cuire, (des pois, etc.) à l'eau. Boiled egg, œuf à la coque. (b) Laund: Lessiver (le linge). **boil away,** v.i. (Of sauce, etc.) Se réduire. **boil down.** **1.** v.tr. Réduire (une solution); (apr) réduire un sirop, etc.). F: To b. down a newspaper article, résumer, condenser, un article de journal. **2.** v.i. Se réduire. **boil over,** v.i. (Of liquid in pan) S'en aller, se sauver. F: To boil over with rage, bouillir de colère. **boil up,** v.i. (Of milk, etc.) Monter, partir. **boiling¹,** a. Bouillant, bouillonnant. adv. Boiling hot, tout ébullition f. **2.** P: The whole boiling, toute la bande; tout le bazar; toute la boutique. **'boiling-point,** s. Point m d'ébullition.

boiler ['bɔilər], s. **1.** Fabricant m, raffineur m (de sucre, etc.). **2.** Chaudière f. Direct-tube b., chaudière à flamme directe. French .oiler, chaudière à bouilleurs. Oil-fuel b., chaudière au mazout. Dom.Ec: Range boiler, chaudière de cuisine; bain-marie m. **'boiler-deck,** s. Nau: Pont inférieur (d'un vapeur). **'boiler-house,** s. Ind: Salle f, bâtiment m, des chaudières. **'boiler-maker,** s. Chaudronnier m. **'boiler-plate,** s. Tôle f à chaudières. **'boiler-room,** s. **1.** = BOILER-HOUSE. **2.** Nau: Chambre f de chauffe. The boiler-rooms, la chaufferie. **'boiler-suit,** s. Ind: Bleus mpl; combinaison f. **'boiler-tube,** s. **1.** (Fire-tube) Tube m de chaudière, de fumée. **2.** (Water-tube) Bouilleur m; tube d'eau.

boisterous ['boistərəs], *a.* (*Of pers.*) Bruyant, turbulent ; tapageur ; (*of wind*) violent ; (*of sea*) tumultueux, (*of weather*) tempétueux. *B. spirits*, gaieté débordante, bruyante. **-ly,** *adv.* (*a*) Bruyamment ; avec une gaieté bruyante. (*b*) Tempétueusement.

boisterousness ['boistərəsnəs], *s.* Turbulence*f* ; violence *f* (du vent) ; agitation *f* (de la mer).

bold [bould], *a.* **1.** Hardi ; (i) peu timide ; (ii) audacieux, téméraire ; (ton, regard) assuré, confiant. *Bold stroke,* (i) coup hardi ; (ii) coup d'audace. *B. to act,* hardi à agir. **To make bold with s.o.,** prendre des libertés avec qn. **To make (so) bold (as) to do sth.,** s'enhardir jusqu'à faire qch. ; oser faire qch. ; se permettre de faire qch. **To put a bold face on the matter,** payer d'audace. **2.** Impudent, effronté. *A b. hussy,* une effrontée. **As bold as brass,** effronté comme un page. *To answer as b. as brass,* répondre sans sourciller. **3.** (*Prominent*) (*a*) *B. headland,* promontoire à pic, accore. *B. cliff,* falaise escarpée. *S.a.* TYPE¹ 2. (*b*) *Art:* *B. style,* style hardi. *In b. relief,* en puissant relief. **-ly,** *adv.* **1.** Hardiment ; audacieusement ; avec audace. *To assert sth. b.,* affirmer qch. carrément, avec confiance. **2.** Effrontément. **3.** *The coast rises b.,* la côte s'élève à pic. **'bold-faced,** *a.* **1.** Effronté. **2.** Bold-faced type, caractères gras.

boldness ['bouldnəs], *s.* **1.** Hardiesse *f* (de conduite, etc.) ; audace *f*, intrépidité *f*. **2.** Effronterie *f*. **3.** Escarpement *m* (d'une falaise).

bole [boul], *s.* Fût *m,* tronc *m,* tige *f* (d'un arbre).

boll [boul], *s.* Capsule *f* (du cotonnier, du lin). **'boll-weevil,** *s.* *Ent:* Anthonome *m* des cultures de cotonnier.

bollard ['bolərd], *s.* *Nau:* (*a*) (*On wharf*) Pieu *m,* canon *m,* borne *f,* d'amarrage. (*b*) (*On ship*) Bitte *f* (de tournage).

Bologna [bo'lounjə]. *Pr.n.* *Geog:* Bologne *f.* *Bologna sausage,* mortadelle *f.*

Bolshevik ['bolʃevik], **Bolshevist** ['bolʃevist], *a. & s.* Bolchevik (*mf*), bolcheviste (*mf*).

Bolshevism ['bolʃevizm], *s.* Bolchevisme *m.*

bolster¹ ['boulstər], *s.* **1.** Traversin *m* ; coussin *m* (de canapé). **2.** Épaulement *m* (de couteau, etc.). **3.** (*a*) *Mec.E:* Coussinet *m.* (*b*) *Metalw:* Matrice *f* ; étampe inférieure. **4.** *Const:* Racinal, -aux *m* ; sous-poutre *f.*

bolster², *v.tr.* **To bolster s.o. up,** (i) soutenir, relever, la tête de qn avec des oreillers ; (ii) *F:* appuyer, soutenir, qn (qui a tort).

bolt¹ [boult], *s.* **1.** Carreau *m* (d'arbalète). *F:* **He has shot his last bolt,** il a vidé son carquois. **2.** Éclair *m* ; coup *m* de foudre. *F:* *Bolt from the blue,* événement imprévu. **3.** (*a*) (*Sliding*) *bolt,* verrou *m* (de porte) ; pêne *m* (de serrure). **To shoot the bolts,** pousser, mettre, les verrous. (*b*) *Sm.a:* Rifle-bolt, culasse .*f* mobile ; fermeture *f* de culasse. *S.a.* SAFETY. **4.** *Mec.E:* Boulon *m* ; cheville *f.* *Main bolt,* cheville ouvrière. *S.a.* EYE-BOLT, KING-BOLT, RING-BOLT, SCREW-BOLT, *etc.* **5.** (*a*) Pièce *f* (de toile). (*b*) Botte *f* (d'osier). **'bolt-head,** *s.* **1.** Tête *f* de boulon. **2.** Tête mobile (de fusil). **'bolt-lever,** *s.* Levier *m* (de fusil). **'bolt-rope,** *s.* *Nau:* Ralingue *f.*

bolt². **1.** *v.i.* (*a*) (*Of pers.*) *F:* (i) Décamper, déguerpir. (*Of game*) *To b. from cover,* débouler. (ii) *To b. out of the room,* sortir précipitamment, brusquement, de la salle. (*Of horse*) S'emballer, s'emporter. **2.** *v.tr.* Gober ; avaler à grosses bouchées, sans mâcher. **To bolt one's dinner,** expédier, *F:* bouffer, son dîner. **3.** *v.tr.* (*a*) Verrouiller ; fermer (une porte) au verrou ; bâcler

(une porte). **To bolt the door,** mettre les verrous. (*b*) Boulonner, cheviller. **bolt in,** *v.tr.* Enfermer (qn) au verrou. **bolt out,** *v.tr.* Mettre les verrous contre (qn).

bolt³, *adv.* Bolt upright, tout droit ; droit comme un piquet.

bolt⁴, *s.* *F:* Élan soudain ; fuite *f.* **To make a bolt for sth.,** s'élancer sur, vers, qch. **To make a bolt for it,** décamper, déguerpir, filer.

bolt⁵, *v.tr.* *Mill:* Bluter, tamiser, sasser (la farine). **bolting,** *s.* Blutage *m,* tamisage *m.*

bolter ['boultər], *s.* Cheval porté à s'emballer.

bolus ['bouləs], *s.* *Vet:* Bol *m* ; grosse pilule.

bomb¹ [bom], *s.* (*a*) Bombe (explosive). *Aerial b.,* bombe aérienne, d'avion. *To release a b.,* lâcher, larguer, une bombe. (*b*) *Dynamite bomb,* machine infernale. (*c*) Mills bomb, grenade *f* de Mills. **'bomb-carrier,** *s.* Avion *m* de bombardement. **'bomb-crater,** *s.* *Mil:* Entonnoir *m.* **'bomb-proof,** *a.* A l'épreuve des bombes. *B.-p. dug-out,* abri blindé. **'bomb-shell,** *s.* (= SHELL) Obus *m.* *Esp. F:* *This was a b.-s. to us all,* cette nouvelle nous consterna. *This letter came like a b.-s.,* cette lettre nous tomba des nues. **'bomb-sight,** *s.* *Av:* Viseur *m.*

bomb², *v.tr.* *Esp. Av:* Lancer des bombes sur (une ville). **bombing,** *s.* **1.** Bombardement *m.* Bombing plane, avion de bombardement ; bombardement *m.* **2.** Attaque *f* à la grenade.

bombard [bom'bɑːrd], *v.tr.* *Mil:* *Navy:* Bombarder (une ville, un port).

bombardier [bombər'diːər], *s.* **1.** *A:* Bombardier *m.* **2.** *Artil:* (*In Brit. army*) Brigadier *m.*

bombardment [bom'bɑːrdmənt], *s.* Bombardement *m.*

bombasine [bombə'ziːn], *s.* *Tex:* Bombasin *m.*

bombast ['bombast], *s.* Emphase *f,* enflure *f,* boursouflure *f* (de style) ; grandiloquence *f.*

bombastic [bom'bastik], *a.* (Style) ampoulé, enflé, emphatique.

bomber ['bomər], *s.* **1.** (*Pers.*) (*a*) Grenadier *m.* (*b*) *Av:* Bombardier *m.* **2.** (*Machine*) Avion *m* de bombardement.

bona fide ['bounə'faidi], *a. & adv.* De bonne foi. *B. f. offer,* offre sérieuse.

bona fides [bounə'faidiːz], *Lt.s.* Bonne foi.

bonanza [bou'nanzə], *s.* *U.S:* Bonanza *f* ; filon riche. *To strike a b.,* rencontrer un filon riche. *F:* *The enterprise proved a b.,* l'entreprise est devenue une vraie mine d'or.

bond¹ [bond], *s.* Lien *m* ; attache *f.* **1.** *pl.* Fers *m,* liens, chaînes *f.* *To burst one's bonds, to break from one's bonds,* rompre, briser, ses liens. **2.** (*a*) Lien (d'osier, pour fagots, etc.). *F:* *Bonds of friendship,* liens d'amitié. (*b*) *Const:* (System of) bond, appareil *m* (en liaison). *Old English bond,* appareil anglais. (*c*) Assemblage *m* ou joint *m.* *Thermit(e) bond,* joint à la thermite. **3.** (*a*) Engagement *m,* contrat *m* ; obligation *f.* *Mortgage bond,* titre *m* hypothécaire. (*b*) *Fin:* Bon *m.* *Treasury bonds,* bons du Trésor. *Bearer b.,* bon au porteur. *Registered b.,* bon nominatif. *Government bonds,* (i) rentes *f* sur l'État ; (ii) titres de rente. *National war bonds,* bons de la défense nationale. (*c*) *Jur:* Caution *f.* **4.** *Com:* Dépôt *m,* entreposage *m.* (*Of goods*) *To be in bond,* être à l'entrepôt, être entreposé. *To take goods out of b.,* dédouaner des marchandises. **'bond-stone,** *s.* *Const:* Parpaing *m,* boutisse *f.*

bond², *v.tr.* *Const:* **1.** Liaisonner (des pierres). (*b*) Appareiller (un mur). **2.** *Com:* Entreposer, mettre en dépôt, à l'entrepôt (des marchandises). *S.a.* WAREHOUSE¹ 1.

bondage ['bondedʒ], *s.* **1.** Esclavage *m,* servitude *f,* asservissement *m.* To be in bondage to s.o., être sous la coupe, sous la férule, de qn. **2.** *Hist:* Servage *m.* **3.** *Poet:* Captivité *f.*

bondholder ['bɔndhouldər], *s. Fin:* Obligataire *m* ; porteur *m* de bons, d'obligations.

bondmaid(en) ['bɔndmeid(n)], *s.f. A:* Jeune esclave.

bondman, *pl.* **-men** ['bɔndmən, -men], *s.m.* (*a*) *Hist:* Serf. (*b*) *F:* Esclave.

bondsman, *pl.* **-men** ['bɔndzmən, -men], *s.m.* **1.** = BONDMAN. **2.** To be bondsman for s.o., être le garant de qn ; s'être porté caution pour qn.

bone[1] [boun], *s.* **1.** Os *m.* Fish-bone, arête *f. S.a.* ANKLE-BONE, BACKBONE, CHEEK-BONE, WHALE-BONE, *etc.* Horse with plenty of bone, cheval fortement membré. *F:* Hard words break no bones, une parole rude ne casse rien. He is (nothing but) a bag of bones, il n'a que la peau et les os. He won't make old bones, il ne fera pas de vieux os. I feel it in my bones, j'en ai le pressentiment. To make no bones about doing sth., ne pas se gêner, ne pas faire de manières, pour faire qch. ; ne pas hésiter à faire qch. *S.a.* BREED[2] I., CHILL[3] 1, CONTENTION 1, PICK[3] 3. **2.** *pl.* (*a*) (*Of the dead*) Ossements *m.* (*b*) *F:* (i) Dés *m* à jouer. (ii) Dominos *m.* (*c*) (i) *Mus:* Cliquettes *f.* (ii) Le joueur de cliquettes (dans une troupe nègre). **'bone-black,** *s.* Noir *m* animal. **'bone-dry,** *a.* Sec à l'absolu. **'bone-lace,** *s.* Dentelle *f* au fuseau. **'bone-setter,** *s.* Rebouteur *m.* **'bone-shaker,** *s.* **1.** *A: F:* Vélocipède *m* à bandages de fer. **2.** (*Of car, bicycle*) *F:* Vieux clou ; vieille guimbarde. **'bone-spavin,** *s. Vet:* Éparvin calleux.

bone[2], *v.tr.* **1.** Désosser (la viande) ; ôter les arêtes (du poisson). **2.** Garnir (un corset) de baleines. **3.** *P:* Chiper, escamoter, voler (qch).

boneless ['bounləs], *a.* **1.** Désossé ; sans os ; sans arêtes. **2.** *F:* Mou ; sans énergie.

bonfire ['bɔnfaiər], *s.* Feu *m* de joie.

bonnet ['bɔnet], *s.* **1.** *Cost:* (*a*) (*Men*) Bonnet (écossais) ; béret (écossais). *S.a.* BEE 1. (*b*) (*Women*) Chapeau *m* à brides ; capote *f,* bonnet ; béguin *m* (d'enfant). **2.** *Aut: Av:* Capot *m.* **3.** *Nau:* Bonnette maillée (de voile).

bonny ['bɔni], *a. Scot:* Joli ; gentil, *f.* gentille.

bonus, *pl.* **-uses** ['bounəs, -əsiz], *s.* Surpaye *f,* boni *m* ; prime *f* ; part *f* de bénéfice ; gratification *f.* Cost-of-living bonus, indemnité *f* de cherté de vie. B. on shares, bonification *f* sur les actions.

bony ['bouni], *a.* **1.** Osseux. **2.** (*a*) (*Personne*) à gros os ; (corps) anguleux. (*b*) (Doigt, visage) décharné. **3.** (*Of meat*) Plein d'os ; (*of fish*) plein d'arêtes.

boo[1] [bu:]. **1.** *int.* Hou ! (d'aversion ou de mépris). **2.** *s.* Huée *f.*

boo[2], *v.tr. & i.* To boo (at) s.o., huer, conspuer, qn. To be booed off the stare, quitter la scène au milieu des huées. **booing,** *s.* Huées *f.pl.*

booby ['bu:bi], *s.* **1.** (*a*) Nigaud, benêt *m,* grand dadais. (*b*) Le dernier (dans un concours, etc.). **2.** *Orn: F:* Fou *m.* **'booby-trap,** *s.* Attrape-nigaud *m.*

boodle [bu:dl], *s. P:* Argent *m, P:* pèze *m.*

boohoo[1] [bu'hu:]. **1.** *int.* Heu, heu, heu ! **2.** *s. F:* Pleurnichement *m.*

boohoo[2], *v.i. F:* Pleurer bruyamment ; pleurnicher.

book[1] [buk], *s.* **1.** (*a*) Livre *m.* Old books, vieux bouquins. *F:* To talk like a book, parler comme un livre. To speak by the book, citer ses autorités. Book knowledge, connaissances livresques. Class book, livre classique, de classe. *Reward*

books, livres de prix. (*b*) Livret *m* (d'un opéra). (*c*) (*Bible*) To swear on the Book, prêter serment sur la Bible. (*d*) Blue book, (i) *Adm:* = livre jaune ; (ii) *U.S:* registre *m* des employés de l'État. **2.** Registre. (*a*) Account book, livre de comptes. Bank-book, livret, carnet *m,* de banque. *S.a.* DAY-BOOK, NOTE-BOOK, PASS-BOOK, *etc.* To keep the books of a firm, tenir les livres d'une maison. *F:* To be in s.o.'s good books, être en faveur auprès de qn. To be in s.o.'s bad books, être mal dans les papiers de qn. To bring s.o. to book for sth., forcer qn à rendre compte de qch. (*b*) *Nau:* Ship's books, livres de bord. (*c*) Exercise-book, cahier *m* (de devoirs, d'écolier). (*d*) *Turf:* Betting-book, livre de paris. To make a book, faire un livre. *F:* That just suits my book, ça fait mon beurre. (*e*) Savings-bank book, livret de caisse d'épargne. B. of tickets, carnet de billets. *Mil:* (Soldiers') 'small book,' livret individuel. (*f*) The telephone book, l'annuaire *m* du téléphone. **3.** Book of needles, sachet *m* d'aiguilles. **'book-ends,** *s.pl.* Serre-livres *m inv.* **'book-hunter,** *s.* Bibliophile *m,* bouquineur *m.* **'book-hunting,** *s.* Bouquinerie *f.* **'book-keeper,** *s.* Teneur *m* de livres ; comptable *m.* **'book-keeping,** *s.* Tenue *f* des livres ; comptabilité *f.* **'book-learning,** *s.* Savoir acquis dans les livres ; connaissances *f* livresques. **'book-maker,** *s.* **1.** Faiseur *m* de livres. **2.** *Turf:* Book-maker *m, F:* book *m.* **'book-mark(er),** *s.* Signet *m.* **'book-muslin,** *s. Tex:* Organdi *m.* **'book-plate,** *s.* Ex-libris *m.* **'book-post,** *s.* Service postal des imprimés (journaux exceptés). **'book-rest,** *s.* Appui-livre(s) *m inv* ; liseuse *f.* **'book-shelf,** *s.* -ves, *s.* Rayon *m* ; planche réservée aux livres. **'book-trade,** *s.* Industrie *f* du livre ; (commerce *m* de) librairie *f.* **'book-worm,** *s.* **1.** *Ent:* Anobion *m,* ptine *m.* **2.** *F:* (*Of pers.*) Dévoreur de livres ; bouquineur *m.*

book[2], *v.tr.* **1.** Inscrire, enregistrer (une commande, etc.). **2.** Retenir, réserver (une chambre, une place) ; louer (une place) d'avance. **3.** *Rail:* Délivrer un billet à (un voyageur). *Abs.* (*Of passenger*) To book, prendre son billet. **booking,** *s.* Enregistrement *m,* inscription *f. Th:* B. of tickets, location *f* de billets. *Rail:* B. of seats, réservation *f* des places. **'booking-clerk,** *s. Rail:* Préposé *m* à la distribution des billets. **'booking-office,** *s. Rail:* (*a*) Guichet *m.* (*b*) Parcel booking-office, bureau *m* de messagerie.

bookbinder ['bukbaindər], *s.* Relieur *m.*

bookbindery ['bukbaindri], *s.* Atelier *m* de reliure ; maison *f* de reliure.

bookbinding ['bukbaindin], *s.* Reliure *f.*

bookcase ['bukkeis], *s.* Bibliothèque *f.*

bookish ['bukiʃ], *a.* **1.** Adonné à la lecture ; studieux. **2.** Pédantesque, livresque.

booklet ['buklet], *s.* Livret *m* ; opuscule *m.*

booklover ['buklʌvər], *s.* Bibliophile *m.*

bookseller ['bukselər], *s.* Libraire *m.* Second-hand bookseller, bouquiniste *m.* Bookseller's shop, librairie *f.*

bookshop ['bukʃɔp], *s.* Librairie *f.*

bookstall ['bukstɔ:l], *s.* **1.** Étalage *m* de livres. Second-hand b.-s., étalage de bouquiniste. **2.** *Rail:* Bibliothèque *f* (de gare).

boom[1] [bu:m], *s.* **1.** (*At harbour mouth*) (Pannes *f.pl* de) barrage *m* ; chaîne *f* (de fermeture) ; barre *f.* **2.** *Nau:* (*a*) Bout-dehors *m* (de foc) ; gui *m.* Spinnaker boom, tangon *m,* bout-dehors, de spinnaker. *S.a.* JIB-BOOM. (*b*) Swinging boom, tangon. (*c*) Derrick-boom, mât *m* de charge. **3.** *Av:* Longeron *m.*

boom², s. Grondement m, retentissement m, bruit m (du canon, du tonnerre); mugissement m (du vent); tons m sonores (de la voix); ronflement m (de l'orgue); bourdonnement m.

boom³, v.i. (Of wind, etc.) Retentir, gronder, mugir (sourdement); (of organ) gronder, tonner; (of organ) ronfler; (of insects) bourdonner.

boom⁴, s. Com: 1. Hausse f rapide; boom m. 2. (a) Vague f de prospérité. (b) (Période de) vogue f.

boom⁵. 1. v.tr. Faire une grosse publicité en faveur de (qch.); faire du battage autour de (qn, qch.). 2. v.i. Être en hausse. Trade is booming, le commerce va très fort.

boomerang ['bu:mərəŋ], s. Boumerang m.

boon¹ [bu:n], s. 1. Don m, faveur f. To grant a b., accorder une faveur. 2. Bienfait m, avantage m.

boon², a. Boon companion, gai compagnon; bon vivant; vive-la-joie m inv.

boor ['buər], s. Rustre m, rustaud m; goujat m.

boorish ['buəriʃ], a. Rustre, rustaud, grossier; malappris. **-ly,** adv. Grossièrement; en rustre.

boorishness ['buəriʃnəs], s. Grossièreté f; manque m de savoir-vivre.

boost [bu:st], v.tr. 1. U.S: F: Faire de la réclame, du battage, pour, en faveur de (qn, qch.). 2. El.E: Survolter. **boosting,** s. 1. F: Battage m, réclame f; puffisme m. 2. El.E: Survoltage m.

booster ['bu:stər], s. 1. Prôneur m, réclamiste m; puffiste m. 2. El.E: Survolteur m.

boot¹ [bu:t], s. 1. Chaussure f, bottine f; (high b.) botte f; (strong, laced b.) brodequin m. Lace boots, button(ed) boots, elastic-sided boots, bottines à lacets, à boutons, à élastiques. Riding-boots, bottes à l'écuyère. Boot and shoe manu-facturer, fabricant de chaussures. To put on one's boots, (i) se chausser; (ii) (top-boots) se botter. To take off one's boots, se déchausser. S.a. JACK-BOOTS, TOP-BOOTS, etc. Mil: To sound the boot and saddle, sonner le boute-selle. F: The boot is on the other leg, (i) c'est tout (juste) le contraire; (ii) les rôles sont renversés. P: To give s.o. the (order of the) boot, mettre, flanquer, qn à la porte. To get the boot, être saqué. S.a. HEART I, PUSS I. 2. Veh: Coffre m, caisson m. **'boot-black,** s. Décrotteur m, cireur m (de chaussures). **'boot-jack,** s. Arrache-chaussures m inv, tire-botte m (pour se débotter). **'boot-maker,** s. Bottier m, cordonnier m. **'boot-polish,** s. Crème f à chaussures. **'boot-tree,** s. 1. Embauchoir m (pour botte). 2. Tendeur m (pour chaussures).

boot², s. (In the phrase) To boot, par surcroît, en sus, de plus.

boot³, v.tr.impers. A. & Lit: What boots it to . . .? à quoi sert-il de . . .? It boots not to . . ., rien ne sert de . . .

booted ['bu:tid], a. Booted and spurred, chaussé de ses bottes et de ses éperons.

bootee [bu'ti:], s. 1. (a) Bottine f d'intérieur (pour dame). (b) Bottine d'enfant; chausson tricoté (de bébé).

booth [bu:ð], s. Baraque f, tente f (de marché, de forains); loge f (de foire).

bootlace ['bu:tleis], s. Lacet m (de chaussure).

bootleg ['bu:tleg], v.i. U.S: F: Faire la contre-bande des boissons alcooliques. **bootlegging,** s. Contrebande f de l'alcool.

bootlegger ['bu:tlegər], s. U.S: F: Contre-bandier m de boissons alcooliques.

bootless¹ ['bu:tləs], a. Sans chaussures.

bootless², a. A. & Lit: Inutile, vain.

boots [bu:ts], s. Garçon m d'étage (dans un hôtel); cireur m de chaussures (dans un pen-sionnat, etc.).

booty ['bu:ti], s. 1. Butin m. 2. (a) To play booty, faire exprès de perdre au début de la partie pour allécher la victime. (b) To play b. with s.o., être de mèche avec qn.

booze¹ [bu:z], v.i. P: Boire (la) ribote.

booze², s. P: 1. Boisson f (alcoolique). 2. To be on the booze, être en ribote.

boozer ['bu:zər], s. P: Ivrogne m, poivrot m.

bo-peep [bou'pi:p], s. To play (at) bo-peep, jouer à cache-cache (avec un enfant); faire coucou.

boracic [bo'rasik], a. Ch: Borique. Boracic ointment, pommade à l'acide borique. Boracic powder, poudre boriquée. S.a. LINT.

borage ['borədʒ], s. Bot: Pharm: Bourrache f.

borax ['bo:raks], s. Borax m.

border¹ ['bo:rdər], s. 1. Bord m (d'un lac); lisière f, bordure f (d'un bois); marge f (d'un chemin); frontière f, confins mpl (d'un pays). The Border, la frontière écossaise (et les comtés limitrophes). Border town, ville frontière. 2. (a) (Edging) Galon m, bordé m (d'un habit); bordure (d'un tableau, d'un tapis, etc.); encadre-ment m (d'un panneau). Black border (on letter paper), baguette f. (b) Grass border, turf border, plate-bande f, pl. plates-bandes; cordon m de gazon. **'border-land,** s. (a) Pays m frontière, limitrophe; marche f. (b) Les confins m de l'au-delà. **'border-line,** s. 1. Ligne f de séparation (entre deux catégories, etc.); pl. limites fpl, bornes fpl (d'une catégorie, etc.); frontière f (entre deux états). 2. Border-line case, (i) cas limite; (ii) cas indéterminé.

border². 1. v.tr. (a) Border (un habit, un chemin); lisérer (un mouchoir); encadrer. (b) Border; confiner à (un pays, etc.). 2. v.i. To border on (sth.). (a) (Of territory) Toucher, confiner, à (un autre pays); être limitrophe (d'un autre pays). (b) To border on insanity, approcher, être voisin, de la folie; friser la folie. **bordering,** a. (a) Contigu, -uë, touchant, aboutissant (on, à); voisin (on, de); limitrophe (on, de). (b) Colour bordering on red, couleur qui tire sur le rouge. Statement b. on truth, on untruth, déclaration qui côtoie la vérité, qui frise le mensonge.

borderer ['bo:rdərər], s. Habitant, -ante, (i) de la frontière, esp. (ii) de la frontière d'Écosse; frontalier m.

bore¹ ['bo:ər], s. 1. (a) Calibre m, alésage m (d'un tuyau, etc.); calibre (d'une arme à feu). (b) Ame f (d'une arme à feu). 2. Min: Trou m de sonde. **'bore-hole,** s. Min: 1. Trou m de sonde. 2. Trou de mine.

bore², v.tr. & i. 1. To bore (out), creuser; (i) forer, (ii) foncer (un puits); forer, percer (un trou); aléser (un cylindre). To bore through sth., percer, perforer, qch. Min: To bore for water, minerals, faire un sondage, sonder, pour trouver de l'eau, des minéraux. 2. (Of horse) Bourrer, encenser. 3. (a) Turf: Abs. Couper un con-current, couper la ligne. (b) (Of pers.) To b. (one's way) through the crowd, se frayer (brutale-ment) un chemin à travers la foule. **boring¹,** s. 1. Percement m. Mec.E: Forage m, perçage m; (of cylinder) alésage m. Min: Sondage m. **'boring-machine,** s. Foreuse f, perceuse f; (for cylinders) aléseuse f, alésoir m, aléseuse f.

bore³, s. (a) (Of pers.) Fâcheux, -euse; importun m; raseur, -euse. (b) (Of thg) Ennui m, scie f, corvée f.

bore⁴, v.tr. F: Ennuyer; F: raser, assommer

(qn) ; *P:* scier le dos à (qn). **To bore s.o. to death ;** *P:* **to bore** s.o. **stiff,** ennuyer qn à mourir. *To be bored to death, bored stiff,* s'ennuyer à mourir ; se morfondre ; *F:* avoir le cafard. *To be bored with doing sth.,* s'ennuyer à faire qch. **boring²,** *a.* Ennuyeux, ennuyant, *F:* assommant, rasant, sciant.

bore⁵, *s.* (*In tidal wave*) Mascaret *m* ; raz *m* de marée ; barre *f* d'eau.

bore⁶. *See* BEAR².

boreal ['bɔriəl], *a.* Boréal, -aux.

boredom ['bɔːrdəm], *s.* Ennui *m.*

borer ['bɔːrər], *s.* 1. Foreur *m,* perceur *m* ; sondeur *m* (de puits). 2. Appareil *m* ou outil *m* de perforation. (*a*) Foret *m,* tarière *f* ; perçoir *m,* vrille *f.* (*b*) Alésoir *m.* (*c*) *Civ.E:* Perforatrice *f.* 3. Cheval *m* qui se braque.

boric ['bɔrik], *a. Ch:* Borique.

born [bɔːrn]. 1. *p.p.* **To be born,** naître ; venir au monde. **To be born again,** renaître. *To have been b.,* être né. *London born,* natif de Londres. *French b.,* Français de naissance. *He was b. in* 1870, il naquit, il est né, en 1870. *In this town a hundred children are b. every month,* il naît dans cette ville cent enfants par mois. *S.a.* CAUL 1, PURPLE II. **High-born,** de haute naissance. *S.a.* BASE-BORN, HIGH-BORN, NEW-BORN, *etc. Confidence is b. of knowledge,* la confiance vient du savoir. 2. *a.* **He is a born poet, a poet born,** il est né poète. *A gentleman b.,* un gentilhomme de naissance. **A Londoner born and bred,** un vrai Londonien de Londres. *F:* **Born fool,** parfait idiot. 3. *s.* *Her latest born,* son dernier né, sa dernière née.

borne [bɔːrn]. *See* BEAR².

boron ['bɔːrɔn], *s. Ch:* Bore *m.*

borough ['bʌrə], *s.* (*a*) Ville *f* (avec municipalité). **County borough,** commune *f* de plus de 50,000 habitants. (*b*) Circonscription électorale (urbaine). *Hist:* **Rotten borough,** bourg pourri.

borrow ['bɔrou], *v.tr.* Emprunter (*from, of,* à). *To b. at interest,* emprunter à intérêt. *Borrowed feathers, plumes,* plumes d'emprunt. *To live by borrowing,* vivre d'emprunts.

borrower ['bɔrouər], *s.* Emprunteur, -euse.

bort [bɔːrt], *s. Lap:* Égrisée *f* ; boort *m.*

borzoi ['bɔːrzɔi], *s.* Lévrier *m* russe ; borzoï *m.*

bosh [bɔʃ], *s. & int. F:* Bêtises *fpl,* blague *f* ; propos idiots. *That's all b.,* tout ça c'est de la blague.

bosk(et) ['bɔsk(et)], *s.* Bosquet *m* ; fourré *m.*

bos'n [bousn]. *See* BOATSWAIN.

bosom ['buːzəm], *s.* 1. (*a*) Giron *m,* sein *m. To hide a letter in one's b.,* cacher une lettre dans son sein. **The wife of his bosom,** sa femme bienaimée. (*b*) **In the bosom of one's family,** au sein de sa famille ; dans le giron de l'Église. (*c*) **Bosom of a dress,** devant *m* d'un corsage. 2. Poitrine *f.* 3. *a. See* FRIEND 1. **-bosomed** [buːzəmd], *a.* **Broad-bosomed,** à large poitrine.

Bosphorus ['bɔsfərəs], **Bosporus** ['bɔspɔrəs]. *Pr.n. Geog:* **The Bosphorus,** le Bosphore.

boss¹ [bɔs], *s.* Protubérance *f,* renflement *m. Arch: etc:* Bosse *f. Archeol:* Ombon *m* (de bouclier). *Mec.E:* Mamelon *m,* portée *f. Av: Nau:* **Boss of the propeller,** moyeu *m* de l'hélice.

boss², *s. F:* (*a*) **The boss,** le patron, le chef. *She's the b.,* c'est elle qui porte la culotte. (*b*) *Ind:* Contremaître *m.*

boss³, *v.tr. F:* Mener, diriger (qn, qch.). **To boss the show,** contrôler, conduire, toute l'affaire. *He bosses everybody,* il régente tout le monde.

bossy ['bɔsi], *a. F:* Autoritaire. *A b. fellow,* un monsieur Jordonne.

bosun [bousn], *s. See* BOATSWAIN.

bot(t) [bɔt], *s. Ann:* Larve *f* d'œstre. **'bot-fly,** *s* Œstre *m* ; mouche *f* des chevaux.

botanic(al) [bo'tanik(əl)], *a.* Botanique.

botanist ['bɔtənist], *s.* Botaniste *mf.*

botanize ['bɔtənaːiz], *v.i.* Herboriser, botaniser. **botanizing,** *s.* Herborisation *f.*

botany ['bɔtəni], *s.* Botanique *f.*

botch¹ [bɔtʃ], *s. F:* Travail mal fait ; *F:* travail bousillé. *To make a b. of sth.,* saboter un travail.

botch², *v.tr. F:* 1. Bousiller, saboter (un travail, etc.). 2. **To botch up,** réparer grossièrement, rafistoler (des souliers, un appareil, etc.).

both [bouθ]. 1. *a. & pron.* Tous (les) deux, toutes (les) deux ; l'un(e) et l'autre. *B.* (*of them*) *are dead,* ils sont morts tous (les) deux. **Both of these possibilities** *must be taken into account,* il faut tenir compte de l'une et de l'autre de ces possibilités. **To hold sth. in both hands,** tenir qch. à deux mains. *On b. sides,* des deux côtés. *S.a.* SIDE¹ 3, 4. **Both alike,** l'un comme l'autre. **Both of us saw it,** nous l'avons vu tous (les) deux. 2. *adv.* **Both you and I,** (et) vous et moi. *B. John and I came, John and I b. came,* Jean et moi sommes venus tous les deux. *She b. attracts and repels me,* elle m'attire et me repousse à la fois. *I am fond of music b. ancient and modern,* j'aime la musique tant ancienne que moderne.

bother¹ ['bɔðər], *s.* Ennui *m, F:* embêtement *m,* tracas *m,* aria *m.* **Bother!** zut !

bother². 1. *v.tr.* Gêner, ennuyer, tracasser, tourmenter (qn) ; *F:* embêter (qn). *To b. s.o. about sth.,* importuner qn au sujet de qch. *Don't b. me!* laissez-moi tranquille ! *Don't b.* (*your head*) *about me!* ne vous inquiétez pas de moi ! *F:* **I can't be bothered,** ça m'embête. **Bother it!** **bother the thing!** zut ! *B. the man!* qu'il aille au diable ! 2. *v.i.* *He doesn't bother about anything,* il ne s'inquiète de rien. **bothered,** *a.* Inquiet ; embarrassé.

botheration [bɔðə'reiʃ(ə)n]. *F:* 1. *s.* Ennui *m.* 2. *int.* Zut !

bothersome ['bɔðərsəm], *a.* Importun, gênant.

bottle¹ [bɔtl], *s.* 1. Bouteille *f* ; (*small*) flacon *m* ; fiole *f* ; (*wide-mouthed*) bocal *m.* **Wicker-bottle,** bouteille clissée. **Wine bottle,** bouteille à vin. *B. of wine,* bouteille de vin. **Half-bottle** (*of wine*), demi-bouteille. *Cider in a stone bottle,* du cidre dans un cruchon. **Cider in bottle,** cidre bouché. 2. **Feeding bottle, child's bottle,** biberon *m.* *Child brought up on the bottle,* enfant élevé au biberon. 3. **Hot-water bottle,** boule *f* à eau chaude ; bouillotte *f* (de lit) à eau chaude ; (*of stone*) cruchon *m. F:* moine *m.* **'bottle-brush,** *s.* Goupillon *m* ; hérisson *m.* **'bottle-drainer,** *s.* Égouttoir *m* à bouteilles ; hérisson *m.* **'bottle-green,** *s. & a.* Vert bouteille (*m*) *inv.* **'bottle-holder,** *s.* *Box:* Soigneur *m,* second *m.* **'bottle-imp,** *s.* 1. *Ph:* Ludion *m.* 2. Génie enfermé dans une bouteille. **'bottle-neck,** *s.* 1. Goulot *m* (de bouteille). 2. Étranglement *m,* embouteillage *m* (dans une rue) ; goulet *m* (d'un port). **'bottle-nosed,** *a.* A gros nez. **'bottle-rack,** *s.* Porte-bouteilles *m inv.* **'bottle-washer,** *s.* Laveur, -euse, de bouteilles ; plongeur *m. F:* **Head cook and bottlewasher,** (i) factotum *m* ; (ii) homme qui mène toute l'affaire.

bottle², *v.tr.* Mettre (du vin) en bouteilles ; mettre (des fruits) en bocal. **Bottled wine,** vin en bouteilles. *S.a.* BEER. **bottle up,** *v.tr.* 1. Embouteiller (une flotte, la circulation). 2. *F:* To *b. up one's feelings, one's anger*, étouffer ses sentiments; comprimer, ravaler, sa colère.

bottling, s. Mise f en bouteille(s), en bocal.

ottle³, s. Botte f (de foin, etc.). *S.a.* NEEDLE I.

ottler ['bɔtlər], s. Metteur m en bouteilles.

ottom¹ ['bɔtəm], s. **1.** (*a*) Bas m (d'une colline, d'un escalier, d'une robe, d'une page). *S.a.* TOP¹ I. 1. (*b*) Fond m (d'un puits, d'une boîte, de la mer); ballast m, assiette f (d'une chaussée, etc.). *At the b. of the garden*, au fond du jardin. *At the b. of the table, of the class*, au (bas) bout de la table, à la queue de la classe. *To send a ship to the bottom*, envoyer un bâtiment au fond, par le fond. (*Of ship*) *To go to the bottom*, couler à fond. *Prices have touched b.*, les prix sont au plus bas. (*Of swimmer*) *To find bottom again*, reprendre fond; reprendre pied. *To sift sth. to the bottom*, examiner qch. à fond. *At bottom he's not a bad fellow*, au fond ce n'est pas un mauvais garçon. *From the very bottom of the heart*, du fond du cœur. *To be at the bottom of sth.*, (*of pers.*) être l'instigateur de qch. *Nau: Gravel b.*, fond de gravier. *Rocky b.*, fond de roche. (*c*) Résistance f, fond. *Horse with bottom*, cheval qui a du fond. **2.** Basfond m (de terrain); creux m; vallée f. *U.S: Bottom lands*, terres d'alluvion; bonnes terres. **3.** (*a*) (i) Fond m, (ii) dessous m (d'assiette, de verre, etc.); siège m (d'une chaise). *To set sth. bottom up(wards)*, mettre qch. sens dessus dessous. *F: To knock the bottom out of an argument*, démolir un argument. *The bottom has fallen out of the market*, le marché s'est effondré. *F: Every tub must stand on its own bottom*, il faut se montrer indépendant d'autrui. (*b*) *Bill: To put bottom on a ball*, faire de l'effet rétrograde; faire un rétro. **4.** *F: Derrière m*, postérieur m, fondement m (d'une personne). *To kick s.o.'s bottom*, *F:* enlever le ballon à qn. **5.** *Nau:* (*a*) Carène f, fond (d'un navire). *Double b.*, double fond. (*b*) Navire m. *In British bottoms*, sous pavillon anglais. **6.** *Bottom half (of a box, etc.)*, partie inférieure. *B. boy of the class*, dernier élève de la classe. *U.S: F: My bottom dollar*, mon dernier sou. *S.a.* GEAR¹ 3.

bottom². **1.** *v.tr.* (*a*) Mettre ou remettre un fond à (une boîte), un siège à (une chaise). (*b*) *To b. an argument upon sth.*, baser, fonder, asseoir, un argument sur qch. **2.** *v.i.* (*Of ship*) Toucher le fond. **-bottomed**, *a.* *Leather-bottomed easy chair*, fauteuil à siège de cuir. *Flat-bottomed boat*, bateau à fond plat.

bottomless ['bɔtəmləs], *a.* Sans fond. **1.** (Chaise) sans siège. **2.** Insondable. *B: The bottomless pit*, l'abîme m.

bottomry ['bɔtəmri], s. *Nau:* Emprunt m à la grosse aventure.

bough [bau], s. Branche f, rameau m (d'arbre).

bought [bɔːt]. *See* BUY.

bougie ['buːʒiː], s. *Surg:* Bougie f.

boulder ['bouldər], s. (Gros) bloc de pierre roulé; gros galet. *Geol:* Bloc erratique.

boulevard ['bulvɑːr], s. **1.** Boulevard m. **2.** *U.S:* Grande voie de communication.

bounce¹ [bauns], s. **1.** (*Of ball*) Rebond m, rebondissement m; bond m. *To take, catch, the ball on the bounce*, prendre la balle au bond. **2.** *F:* (*Of pers.*) Jactance f, vantardise f, épate f.

bounce². **1.** *v.i.* (*a*) (*Of ball*) Rebondir. (*b*) (*Of pers.*) *To bounce in, out*, entrer, sortir, en coup de vent, à l'improviste. (*c*) *F:* (*Of pers.*) Faire l'important; faire de l'esbrouffe, de l'épate. **2.** *v.tr.* (*a*) Faire rebondir (une balle). (*b*) *F:* Ne

pas laisser à (qn) le temps de réfléchir. *To bounce s.o. into doing sth.*, arriver à force d'esbrouffe à faire faire qch. à qn. (*c*) *U.S: F:* Donner son congé à (qn); flanquer (qn) à la porte (du cabaret, etc.). **bouncing**, *a.* **1.** Rebondissant. **2.** *F:* *Bouncing lass*, jeune fille pleine de vie et de santé.

bound¹ [baund], s. (*Usu. pl.*) Limite(s) f, bornes fpl. *Sch: The village is out of bounds*, l'accès du village est défendu aux élèves. *Golf: Fb: etc:* Out of bounds, hors des limites, hors du jeu. *F: To set bounds to one's ambition*, mettre des bornes, fixer une limite, à son ambition; borner son ambition. *To go beyond all bounds, to pass all bounds, to know no bounds*, dépasser toutes les bornes, n'avoir pas de bornes. *To keep within bounds*, rester dans la juste mesure; user de modération. *Within the bounds of probability*, dans les limites du probable. *S.a.* BREAK² I. 4.

bound², *v.tr.* Borner, limiter.

bound³, s. Bond m, saut m. *At a bound*, d'un (seul) bond, d'un saut.

bound⁴, *v.i.* Bondir, sauter; (*of ball, etc.*) rebondir; (*of horse*) soubresauter. *To bound away*, (*of pers.*) s'en aller en bondissant; (*of ball*) (re)bondir au loin. *His heart bounded with joy*, son cœur tressaillit, sursauta, de joie.

bound⁵, *a.* *Nau:* Ship bound for a country, navire en partance pour, en route pour, allant à, un pays. *The ship was b. for India*, le navire (i) partait pour, (ii) faisait route vers, les Indes.

bound⁶. *See* BIND².

boundary ['baundəri], s. Limite f, bornes fpl, frontière f; bornage m (d'une concession, etc.). *Boundary (line)*, ligne frontière, ligne de démarcation; *Sp:* limites du jeu. **Boundary post, stone**, poteau m, pierre f, de bornage; borne.

bounden ['baundən], *a.* (Devoir) impérieux.

bounder ['baundər], s. *F:* Épateur m, plastronneur m; homme prétentieux et mal élevé.

boundless ['baundləs], *a.* Sans bornes; illimité, infini. **-ly**, *adv.* Infiniment.

boundlessness ['baundləsnəs], s. Infinité f.

bounteous ['bauntiəs], *a.* **1.** (*Of pers.*) Libéral, -aux; généreux. **2.** *B. harvest*, moisson abondante. **-ly**, *adv.* Libéralement, généreusement.

bounteousness ['bauntiəsnəs], s. **1.** Libéralité f, générosité f. **2.** (*Of crops, etc.*) Abondance f.

bountiful ['bauntiful], *a.* **1.** Bienfaisant. *B. rains*, pluies fécondes. **2.** Généreux; libéral, -aux.

bounty ['baunti], s. **1.** *Lit:* Générosité f, munificence f. **2.** (*a*) Don m, gratification f (à un employé, etc.). (*b*) *Adm: Ind:* Indemnité f; prime f (d'exportation, etc.); subvention f. (*c*) *Mil: Nau:* Prime d'engagement.

bouquet [bu'kei, 'buke], s. **1.** Bouquet m (de fleurs, de feu d'artifice). **2.** ['buke] Bouquet (du vin).

bourn(e) ['buərn], s. *Poet:* **1.** terme m, but m. **2.** Frontière f. *The b. from which no traveller returns*, l'au-delà m dont on ne revient pas.

bout¹ [baut], s. **1.** (*At games*) Tour m, reprise f. *Fencing b.*, passe f d'armes. *Wrestling b.*, assaut m de lutte. **2.** Accès m (de fièvre); attaque f (de fièvre, d'influenza); crise f (de rhumatisme).

'bout², *adv.* (= ABOUT) *Nau:* 'Bout ship! envoyez!

bovine ['bouvain]. **1.** *a.* (*a*) Bovin. (*b*) *F:* (Esprit) lourd. **2.** *s.pl.* Bovines, bovidés m.

bow¹ [bou], s. **1.** Arc m. *To draw a bow*, bander, tendre, un arc. *To draw the bow*, tirer de l'arc.

To have two strings to one's bow, avoir deux cordes à son arc. I have still one string to my bow, il me reste encore une ressource. **2.** *Mus:* (a) Archet *m* (de violon, etc.). (b) Coup *m* d'archet. **3.** Nœud *m* (de ruban). Butterfly bow, nœud (de) papillon. **4.** *Harn:* (Saddle-)bow, arçon *m*, pontet *m*. 'bow-compass, *s.* (*Also* pair of bow-compasses) Compas *m* à balustre. 'bow-drill, *s.* *Tls:* Foret *m* à arçon; touret *m*. 'bow-legged, *a.* Bancal, -als. 'bow-legs, *s.pl.* Jambes bancales, arquées. 'bow-saw, *s.* *Tls:* Scie *f* à chantourner. 'bow-tie, *s.* *Cost:* Nœud carré. bow-'window, *s.* Fenêtre *f* en saillie (courbe); bow-window *m inv.*

bow² [bou], *v.tr.* **I.** Courber (qch.). *Nau:* To bow a mast, arquer un mât. **2.** *Mus:* To bow a passage, gouverner l'archet dans un passage. **bowing**, *s.* **I.** Courbage *m.* **2.** *Mus:* Manière *f* de gouverner l'archet.

bow³ [bau], *s.* Salut *m*; (i) révérence *f*; (ii) inclination *f* de tête. To make one's bow to the company, se présenter; débuter. To make one's bow to the company (and depart), tirer sa révérence à la compagnie. With a bow, en saluant, en s'inclinant. To make a deep, low, bow to s.o., saluer qn profondément.

bow⁴ [bau]. **I.** *v.i.* (a) (i) S'incliner; baisser la tête; (ii) faire une génuflexion. To bow to s.o., adresser un salut à qn; saluer qn. To bow low to s.o., faire un grand salut à qn. To bow and scrape to s.o., faire force révérences à qn. To bow (down) to, before, s.o., (i) se prosterner devant qn; (ii) faire des courbettes devant qn. (b) *With cogn. acc.* To bow one's assent, signifier son consentement d'une inclination de tête. To bow one's thanks to s.o., remercier qn d'un salut. (c) To bow to s.o., s'incliner devant qn. To bow to the inevitable, s'incliner devant les faits. **2.** *v.tr.* (a) Incliner, baisser (la tête); fléchir (le genou). (b) Courber, voûter (le dos, les épaules, de qn). *To become bowed*, se voûter. **bow down**, *v.i.* Se baisser. **bow in**, *v.tr.* To bow s.o. in, faire entrer qn (avec force saluts). **bow out**, *v.tr.* To bow s.o. out, (i) prendre conge de qn (a la porte) avec force saluts; (ii) congédier qn avec un salut.

bow⁵ [bau], *s.* **I.** *Nau:* (*Often in pl.*) Avant *m*, étrave *f*; *A. & Lit:* proue *f.* On the bow, par l'avant, par le bossoir. On the port bow, par bâbord devant. To cross the bows of a ship, couper la route d'un navire. **2.** *Aer:* Nez *m* (d'un dirigeable). **3.** *Row:* Nageur *m* de tête; le brigadier. 'bow-chaser, *s.* *Navy:* Canon *m* de chasse. 'bow-side, *s.* *Row:* Tribord *m.*

Bowden ['boud(ə)n], *s.* *Mec.E:* Bowden wire, commande *f* Bowden; *F:* bowden *m.*

bowdlerize ['baudləraiz], *v.tr.* Expurger (une œuvre littéraire).

bowel ['bauəl], *s.* *Anat: etc:* (a) Intestin *m.* (b) *pl.* Intestins, entrailles *f*, *F:* boyaux *m.* Bowel complaint, affection intestinale. To have one's bowels open, free, avoir le ventre libre. *F:* The bowels of the earth, les entrailles, le sein, de la terre. (c) Bowels of compassion, sentiment *m* de compassion; *F:* entrailles.

bower¹ ['bauər], *s.* **I.** Berceau *m* de verdure; charmille *f*, tonnelle *f.* **2.** *Poet: A:* (a) Demeure *f.* (b) Appartement *m* (d'une dame); boudoir *m.*

bower², *s.* *Nau:* Bower(-anchor), ancre *f* de bossoir.

bowie(-knife, *pl.* -ves ['boui(naif, -naivz)], *s.*, *U.S:* Couteau-poignard *m*; couteau *m* de chasse.

bowl¹ [boul], *s.* **I.** Bol *m*, jatte *f*; (*small wooden*)

sébile *f* (de mendiant); coupe *f* (de cristal, etc.) *Mil:* Gamelle *f.* **2.** Fourneau *m* (de pipe à tabac); cuilleron *m* (de cuiller); culot *m* (de lampe). *Nau:* Cuvette *f* (du compas).

bowl², *s.* Boule *f.* **(Game of) bowls**, (i) (jeu *m* de boules; (ii) *U.S:* (jeu de) quilles *f.*

bowl³, *v.tr.* (a) Rouler, faire courir (un cerceau). (b) *Bowls:* Lancer, rouler (la boule). (c) *Cr:* Bôler, servir (la balle). **bowl along**, *v.i.* (*O carriage*) Rouler rapidement; (*of ship*) vogue rapidement. **bowl (out)**, *v.tr.* To bowl s.o out, (i) *Cr:* renverser le guichet de qn; mettr qn hors jeu; (ii) *F:* renverser (un ministère etc.); (iii) *F:* réduire (qn) à quia. **bowl over** *v.tr.* (a) Renverser (les quilles avec la boule (b) *F:* Déconcerter, renverser (qn). You can' bowl him over, il ne se laisse pas démonter; rien ne l'épate. **bowling**, *s.* **I.** (a) Jeu *m* de boules Bowling match, match de boules. (b) *U.S:* Jeu de quilles. **2.** *Cr:* Lancement *m* de la balle 'bowling-alley, *s.* Jeu *m* de boules. 'bowling-green, *s.* (Terrain *m* pour) jeu *m* de boules; *A:* boulingrin *m.*

bowler¹ ['boulər], *s.* **I.** Joueur *m* de boules boulomane *m.* **2.** *Cr:* Bôleur *m*, serveur *m.*

bowler², *s.* Bowler (hat), chapeau rond, (chapeau melon *m.*

bowful ['boulful], *s.* Plein bol (de qch.).

bowline ['boulain], *s.* *Nau:* Bouline *f.* Bowline-knot, -hitch, nœud *m* de chaise, nœud de bouline. To sail on a bowline, courir près du vent.

bowman¹, *pl.* -men ['boumən, -men], *s.m.* Archer.

bowman², *pl.* -men ['baumən, -men], *s.m.* *Row:* Brigadier (d'un canot).

bowshot ['bouʃɔt], *s.* Portée *f* de trait. Within b., à portée d'arc, de trait.

bowsprit ['bousprit], *s.* *Nau:* Beaupré *m.*

bowstring ['boustriŋ], *s.* **I.** Corde *f* d'arc. **2.** (*As mode of execution*) Lacet *m*, cordon *m.*

bow-wow ['bau'wau]. **I.** *int.* Ouâ-ouâ! **2.** *s.* *F:* Toutou *m.*

box¹ [bɔks], *s.* Bot: Buis *m.*

box², *s.* **I.** (a) Boîte *f*; (*small*) coffret *m*; (*large wooden*) caisse *f*, coffre *m*; (*for packing*) caisse, layette *f*; (*for shrubs*) bac *m*; (*for travelling*) malle *f*; (*of cardboard*) carton *m* (à chapeaux, etc.); (*for dicing*) cornet *m.* **Tool-box**, coffre à outils. Jewel-box, coffret à bijoux. Bathing-box, cabine *f.* *F:* To be, find oneself, in the wrong box, s'être trompé (d'endroit, dans ses calculs, etc.); s'être fourvoyé. To be in the same box, se trouver dans le même cas. *S.a.* CHRISTMAS-BOX, LETTER-BOX, SNUFF-BOX, etc. (b) *Ecc:* (For alms) Tronc *m.* **2.** *Veh:* Siège *m* (du cocher). **3.** (a) *Th:* Loge *f.* (b) (*In stable*) Stalle *f.* (c) *Jur:* Witness-box = barre *f* des témoins. To be in the box, paraître à la barre. (d) *Mil:* Sentry-box, guérite *f.* *Rail:* Signal-box, cabine *f* (de signaleur); poste *m* d'aiguillage. (e) (**Fishing-, shooting-)box**, pavillon *m* (de pêche, de chasse). (f) *Rail:* (**Horse-)box**, wagon *m* à chevaux; wagon-box(e) *m.* **4.** *Tchn:* Boîte (d'essieu, de frein); moyeu *m* (de roue); palastre *m* (d'une serrure). *Aut:* (*Of gear*) Carter *m.* *Mec.E:* Coupling box, manchon *m* d'accouplement, d'assemblage. *S.a.* FIRE-BOX, SOUND-BOX, etc. 'box-attendant, *s.* *Th:* Ouvreuse *f.* 'box-bed, *s.* Lit clos; lit en armoire. 'box-camera, *s.* *Phot:* Détective *m.* 'box-keeper, *s.* *Th:* Ouvreuse *f* de loges. 'box-kite, *s.* Cerf-volant *m* cellulaire. 'box-office, *s.* *Th:* Bureau *m* de location. 'box-pleat, *s.* *Dressm:* Pli creux. 'box-room, *s.* Chambre *f* de débarras. 'box-

seat, *s.* Place *f* à côté du siège du cocher.
'box-spanner, *s.* *Tls:* Clef *f* à douille.
ox³, *v.tr.* (*a*) Emboîter, encaisser, encartonner (qch.); mettre (qch.) en boîte. *To box a horse,* mettre un cheval dans une stalle à part, dans un box. (*b*) **To box the compass,** (i) *Nau:* réciter, dire, la rose des vents; répéter le compas; (ii) *F:* revenir à son point de départ (dans ses opinions). **boxed,** *a.* *Com: Ind:* En boîte ou en étui. **Boxed in,** encaissé; sans issue. *To feel boxed up,* se sentir à l'étroit. **boxing¹,** *s.* Emboîtage *m*; encaissement *m* (d'un oranger).
ox⁴, *s.* Box on the ear, gifle *f*, claque *f*.
ox⁵. **1.** *v.tr.* To box s.o.'s ears, gifler qn; flanquer une claque à qn. **2.** *v.i. Sp:* Boxer; faire de la boxe. **boxing²,** *s.* La boxe, le pugilat.
'boxing-gloves, *s.pl.* Gants bourrés; gants de boxe. **'boxing-match,** *s.* Match *m* de boxe.
ox-calf ['bɔks'kɑːf], *s* *Leath:* Veau chromé.
boxer ['bɔksər], *s.* Boxeur *m*, pugiliste *m*.
oxful ['bɔksful], *s.* Pleine boîte, pleine caisse.
oxing-day ['bɔksiŋdei], *s.* Le lendemain de Noël (jour d'étrennes aux fournisseurs, etc.).
oxwood ['bɔkswud], *s.* Buis *m.*
oy [bɔi], *s.m.* **1.** (*a*) Garçon; (*on the street*) gamin. *Little boy,* garçonnet. *An English boy,* un jeune Anglais. *Blind boy,* jeune aveugle. *S.a.* SCOUT¹ **1** When I was a boy, quand j'étais petit; quand j'étais enfant. I have known him from a boy, je le connais (i) depuis ma jeunesse, (ii) depuis sa jeunesse. Boys will be boys, il faut que jeunesse se passe. *F:* My dear boy! mon cher (ami)! mon bon! Old boy! mon vieux! The old boy, (i) le paternel; (ii) le patron. (*b*) *Sch:* Élève *m.* An old boy, un ancien élève. (*c*) *F:* One of the boys, un joyeux vivant, un gai luron, un vive-la-joie *inv.* (*d*) *P:* Her boy (friend), son petit jeune homme. (*e*) *F:* This is my boy, voici mon fils, mon garçon. **2.** (*a*) (*In the Colonies, etc.*) Domestique *m* ou ouvrier indigène; boy (*b*) *Nau:* = SHIP('S) BOY. (*c*) *The grocer's boy,* le garçon épicier. *S.a.* STABLE-BOY, TELEGRAPH BOY.
boycott¹ ['bɔikɔt], *s.* Mise *f* en interdit; boycottage *m.*
boycott², *v.tr.* Boycotter (qn).
boycotter ['bɔikɔtər], *s.* Boycotteur *m.*
boyhood ['bɔihud], *s.* Enfance *f*, première jeunesse, ou adolescence *f* (d'un garçon).
boyish ['bɔiiʃ], *a.* **1.** Puéril, enfantin, d'enfant. **2.** (Nature) jeune. **3.** (Manières) de garçon.
Boyle [bɔil]. *Pr.n.* *Ph:* Boyle's law, la loi de Mariotte.
boylike ['bɔilaik]. **1.** *a.* De gamin. **2.** *adv.* En vrai enfant; en vrai(s) garçon(s).
brace¹ [breis], *s.* **1.** *Const: etc:* (*In tension*) Attache *f*, lien *m*, entretoise *f*, étrésillon *m*; croisillon *m*; (*in compression*) contrefiche *f*, moise *f*; jambe *f* de force. (Anchor-)brace, ancre *f*, ancrure *f*. Cross-brace, diagonal brace, écharpe *f*; moise en écharpe. **2.** (*a*) *pl. Cost:* Bretelles *f* pl. (*b*) Tirant *m*, corde *f* (de tambour). **3.** *inv.* Couple *f* (de perdrix); paire *f* (de pistolets, etc.). *S.a.* SHAKE¹ **1.** **4.** *Tls:* Brace (and bit), vilebrequin *m* (à main). Brace-chuck, porte-outil(s) *m inv.* **5.** *Nau:* Bras *m* (de vergue). **6.** *Mus: Typ:* Accolade *f.*
brace², *v.tr.* **1.** *Const: etc:* Ancrer, amarrer (une construction); armer (une poutre); entretoiser, étrésillonner (une charpente); moiser (des étais); hauban(n)er (un mât). **2.** Fortifier (le corps); tonifier (les nerfs). To brace s.o. up, retremper qn; (re)donner de la vigueur à qn; *F:* remonter, ravigoter, qn. *To b. oneself* (*up*) *to*

---

do sth., raidir ses forces, se raidir, pour faire qch. **3.** Bander (un tambour). *To b. the knees,* tendre les jarrets. **4.** *Typ:* Accolader, accoler (des mots). *Mus:* Accolader (les portées). **5.** *Nau:* Brasser (les vergues). **bracing¹,** *a.* (Air, etc.) fortifiant, tonifiant. **bracing²,** *s.* **1.** Ancrage *m*, entretoisement *m*; armement *m* (d'une poutre); consolidation *f*, renforcement *m* (d'un mur). **2.** Retrempe *f* (du corps); tonification *f* (des nerfs). **3.** *Nau:* Brassage *m* (des vergues).
bracelet ['breislet], *s.* **1.** Bracelet *m.* Curb-bracelet, gourmette *f.* **2.** *pl. P:* = HANDCUFFS.
brachycephalic [brakise'falik], *a.* Brachycéphale.
bracken ['brak(ə)n], *s.* Fougère arborescente.
bracket¹ ['braket], *s.* **1.** Support *m.* (*a*) Console *f*; potence *f.* *Arch:* Corbeau *m.* (*b*) Tasseau *m*; taquet *m* de soutien. (*c*) (Gas-)bracket, applique *f* (à gaz). *Cy:* Lamp-bracket, porte-lanterne *m inv.* **2.** (*a*) *Typ: etc:* Square bracket, crochet *m.* Round bracket, parenthèse *f.* (*b*) (Brace) Accolade *f.* (*c*) *Artil:* (*In ranging*) Fourchette *f.* **'bracket-seat,** *s.* Strapontin *m.*
bracket², *v tr* (bracketed) **1.** Mettre (des mots) entre crochets. **2.** Réunir (des mots) par une accolade; accolader, accoler (deux mots, etc.); placer (deux candidats) ex æquo. **3.** *Artil:* Encadrer (le but); prendre (le but) en fourchette.
brackish ['brakiʃ], *a.* Saumâtre.
brackishness ['brakiʃnəs], *s.* Caractère *m* saumâtre (d'une eau stagnante).
bract [brakt], *s.* *Bot:* Bractée *f.*
brad [brad], *s.* Pointe *f*; clou *m* à tête perdue.
bradawl ['bradɔːl], *s.* *Tls:* Alêne plate; poinçon *m.*
Bradshaw ['bradʃɔː], *s.* Indicateur *m* des chemins de fer britanniques.
brae [breː], *s.* *Scot:* Pente *f*, côte *f*, colline *f.*
brag¹ [brag], *s.* **1.** (Piece of) brag, vanterie *f*, vantardise *f*, hâblerie *f*, fanfaronnade *f.* **2.** (Pers.) Fanfaron *m*; vantard *m.*
brag², *v.i.* (bragged [bragd]) Hâbler, se vanter; fanfaronner. *To b. of, about, sth.,* se vanter de qch. **bragging¹,** *a.* Vantard. **bragging²,** *s.* Vantardise *f.*
braggadocio [braga'doutʃiou], *s.* **1.** (Pers.) Bravache *m*, fanfaron *m.* **2.** Fanfaronnade *f.*
braggart ['bragərt], *a.* & *s.* Fanfaron (*m*), vantard (*m*); *F:* avaleur *m* de gens.
brahman, brahmin ['brɑːmən, -min], *s.m.* Brahmane, brame.
brahma(pootra) ['brɑːma('puːtra)], *s.* *Husb:* Coq *m* brahma, poule *f* brahma.
braid¹ [breid], *s.* **1.** (*a*) Tresse *f* (de cheveux). (*b*) *Poet:* Bandeau *m* (pour les cheveux). **2.** (*a*) Galon *m*, ganse *f*, tresse. Gold braid (of officers), galon. (*b*) *El.E:* Guipage *m* (de fils conducteurs).
braid², *v.tr.* **1.** (*a*) Tresser, natter (ses cheveux, de la paille). (*b*) *Poet:* Mettre un bandeau sur (ses cheveux). **2.** Galonner, soutacher; passementer. **3.** *El.E:* Tresser, guiper (un câble).
braiding, *s.* **1.** Tressage *m.* **2.** (Garniture *f* de) galon *m*; soutache *f.*
brail¹ [breil], *s.* *Nau:* Cargue *f.*
brail², *v.tr.* *Nau:* To brail (up), carguer (une voile).
braille [breil], *s.* Système *m* d'écriture de Braille. Braille type, caractères *mpl* Braille.
brain¹ [brein], *s.* **1.** Cerveau *m.* *B: diseases,* maladies cérébrales. *F:* To turn s.o.'s brain, tourner la tête à qn. To have an idea on the brain, être monomane; avoir l'obsession d'une idée. *To get sth. on the b.,* être hanté par l'image,

par la pensée, de qch. **2.** *pl.* **Brains,** cervelle *f.*
(a) Matière cérébrale. *Cu:* **Calves' brains,** cervelle de veau. **To blow s.o.'s brains out,** brûler,
faire sauter, la cervelle à qn. (b) **To rack, cudgel,
one's brains,** se creuser la cervelle, le cerveau,
l'esprit. **Man of brains,** homme de tête. **He has
brains,** il est intelligent. **'brain-fag,** *s.*
Épuisement cérébral. **'brain-fever,** *s. Med:*
(a) Fièvre cérébrale. (b) Fièvre chaude. **'brain-
pan,** *s.* Crâne *m*; boîte cranienne. **'brain-
storm,** *s.* Transport *m* au cerveau. **'brain-
wave,** *s.* **1.** *Psychics:* Onde *f* télépathique.
2. *F:* Inspiration *f*, bonne idée; trouvaille *f.*
'brain-work, *s.* Travail cérébral; travail de
tête.
brain³, *v.tr.* Défoncer le crâne à (qn); casser la
tête à (qn); assommer (qn).
braininess ['breininəs], *s. F:* Intelligence *f.*
brainless ['breinləs], *a. F:* Sans cervelle;
stupide.
brainy ['breini], *a. F:* Intelligent, débrouillard.
braise [bre:z], *v.tr. Cu:* Braiser; cuire (qch.)
à l'étouffée. *Braised beef,* bœuf en daube.
brake¹ [breik], *s.* Fourré *m*, hallier *m.*
brake², *s. Veh: etc:* Frein *m. Aut:* **Four-wheel
brakes,** freins sur quatre roues; freinage intégral.
Band-brake, frein à ruban, à bande. **Hand-brake,**
frein à main; frein de stationnement. **Brake
gear,** timonerie *f. Cy:* Rim brake, frein sur
jante. **To put on, apply, the brake,** serrer le
frein. *S.a.* RELEASE² 2. **'brake-block,** *s.*
Sabot *m* de frein; patin *m.* **'brake-drum,** *s.
Aut:* Tambour *m* de frein. **'brake-van,** *s.
Rail:* Wagon-frein; fourgon *m.*
brake³, *v.tr.* Appliquer le frein sur (les roues).
Abs. Serrer le frein; freiner; enrayer. **braking,** *s.* Freinage *m*; serrage *m* des freins.
brakesman, *pl.* **-men,** *U.S:* **brakeman,**
pl. **-men** ['breik(s)mən, -men], *s.m. Rail:*
Serre-frein(s).
bramble [brambl], *s.* **1.** Ronce sauvage, commune; mûrier m des haies. **2. Brambles,** ronces.
'bramble-berry,'s. Mûre *f* sauvage.
bran [bran], *s. Mill:* Son *m*; remoulage *m.*
'bran-mash, *s. Husb:* Son mouillé; eau
blanche; mash *m.* **bran-'pie, 'bran-tub,** *s.*
Baquet rempli de son où l'on plonge la main
pour en retirer une surprise (à une vente de
charité, à une soirée enfantine).
branch¹ [brɑ:n(t)ʃ], *s.* **1.** Branche *f*, rameau *m*
(d'un arbre). **2.** (a) Ramification *f*; rameau
(d'une chaîne de montagnes); branche, bras *m*
(d'un fleuve); embranchement *m* (d'une route,
d'un chemin de fer). (b) Branche (d'une famille,
etc.). (c) Succursale *f*, filiale *f* (d'une société,
d'une maison de commerce). **'branch-line,** *s.
Rail:* Embranchement *m*; ligne *f* d'intérêt local.
branch². **1.** *v.i. (Of plants)* To branch (forth),
pousser des branches. **To branch (out),** se
ramifier; *(of an organization, etc.)* étendre au
loin ses ramifications. **2.** *v.i. (Of road(s), etc.)*
To branch (off, away), (se) bifurquer, s'embrancher *(from,* sur). **3.** *v.tr. El:* Brancher (un
circuit); dériver (le courant). **branching¹,** *a.*
1. *(Of tree)* Branchu, rameux. **2.** *(Of road, etc,)*
D'embranchement. **branching²(off),** *s.* Bifurcation *f*, branchement *m*, dérivation *f.*
branchia ['braŋkiə], *s.pl.,* **branchiae** ['braŋ-
kii:], *s.pl.* Branchies *f*; ouïes *f.*
brand¹ [brand], *s.* **1.** Brandon *m*, tison *m.*
F: **A brand from the burning,** un tison arraché
au feu; un nouveau converti. **2.** *Poet:* Flambeau *m.* **3.** (a) Fer chaud. (b) Marque (faite
avec un fer chaud); flétrissure *f.* **4.** *Com:*

(a) Marque (de fabrique). (b) *F:* Sorte *f*,
qualité *f* (d'une marchandise). **5.** *Poet:* Glaive *m*,
épée *f.* **'brand-'new,** *a.* Tout (battant) neuf,
tout flambant neuf.
brand², *v.tr.* **1.** **To b. with a hot iron,** marque
au fer chaud; flétrir (qn). **2.** *F: To b. sth. o*
s.o.'s memory, graver qch. dans la mémoire d
qn. **3.** *To b. s.o. with infamy,* flétrir, stigmatiser
qn; noter qn d'infamie. **branding,** *s.* Impression *f* au fer chaud. **'branding-iron,** *s.* Fer *m*
à marquer.
Brandenburg ['brandənbə:rg]. **1.** *Pr.n. Geog*
Le Brandebourg. **2.** *s.pl. Cost:* Brandebourgs *m.*
brandish ['brandiʃ], *v.tr.* Brandir (une arme
etc.). **brandishing,** *s.* Brandissement *m.*
brandling ['brandliŋ], *s. Fish:* Ver *m* rouge.
brandy ['brandi], *s.* Eau-de-vie *f*, cognac *m*
Liqueur brandy, fine champagne. **Brandy an**
soda, fine *f* à l'eau.
bran-new ['bran'nju:], *a.* = BRAND-NEW.
brass [brɑ:s], *s.* **1.** Cuivre *m* jaune; laiton *m*
Lit: airain *m. B.* foundry, fonderie *f* de cuivre
robinetterie *f.* **Brass plate,** plaque de cuivre
F: **Brass-hat,** officier d'état-major. **2.** (a) Le
cuivres, robinets, etc. (du ménage, à bord). **T**
do the brass(es), faire les cuivres. (b) *Usu. pl*
Mec.E: Coussinet *m* de bielle, de palier
coquille *f* (de coussinets). (c) *Mus:* **The bras**
(in band, orchestra), les cuivres. **3.** *P:* Argent *m*
pépète *f*, galette *f.* **4.** *P: (Cheek)* Toupet *m*
culot *m.* **'brass-ware,** *s.* Dinanderie *f*
'brass-work, *s.* **1.** Les cuivres *m.* **2.** *Ind*
Cuivrerie *f.*
brassière [bra'sjɛ:ər], *s.* Soutien-gorge *m inv.*
brassy¹ ['brɑ:si], *s. Golf:* Brassie *m.*
brassy², *a.* **1.** (a) *(Of colour, etc.)* Qui ressembl
au cuivre; cuivré. (b) (Son) cuivré, clairon
nant. **2.** *P: (Of pers.)* Effronté.
brat [brat], *s. Usu. Pej:* Marmot *m*, mioche *m*
moutard *m.*
bravado [bra'vɑ:dou], *s.* Bravade *f.* **Out o**
bravado, par bravade.
brave¹ [bre:iv]. **1.** *a.* (a) Courageux, brave
(b) *A. & F:* (i) Beau, élégant. (ii) Excellent
fameux. **2.** *s.* Brave *m* (guerrier Peau-rouge
-ly, *adv.* Courageusement.
brave², *v.tr.* Braver, défier (qn); affronter (u
danger, etc.). **To brave it out,** ne pas se laisse
démonter.
bravery ['breivəri], *s.* **1.** Bravoure *f*, vaillance *f*
2. *A. & F:* Beaux habits.
bravo¹, *pl.* **-os, -oes** ['brɑ:vou, -ouz], *s.* Brav
m, *pl.* bravi; spadassin *m.*
bravo², *int.* Bravo!
brawl¹ [brɔ:l], *s.* **1.** Rixe *f*, bagarre *f. Drunken b*
querelle *f* d'ivrognes. **2.** = BRAWLING² 2.
brawl², *v.i.* **1.** *(Of pers.)* Brailler; se chamaille
2. *(Of streams)* Murmurer, bruire. **brawling**
a. **1.** *(Of pers.)* Braillard, tapageur. **2.** *(O*
stream) Murmurant, bruissant. **brawling²,**
1. Braillement *m*, clabauderie *f.* **2.** Murmure *m*
bruissement *m* (d'un ruisseau, etc.).
brawler ['brɔ:lər], *s.* **1.** Braillard, -arde; tapageur
-euse; querelleur, -euse.
brawn [brɔ:n], *s.* **1.** Muscles *mpl*; partie charnu
(des membres). **2.** *Cu:* Fromage *m* de cochon
de hure.
brawny ['brɔ:ni], *a. (Of pers.)* Musclé; *F:* bie
bâti.
bray¹ [brei], *s.* **1.** Braiment *m* (d'un âne
2. Son éclatant (d'une trompette).
bray², *v.i.* **1.** *(Of ass)* Braire. **2.** *(Of trumpe*
etc.) Émettre un son strident, éclatant.

bray³, *v.tr.* Broyer, piler, concasser.

braze [breːiz], *v.tr.* Braser; souder (qch.) au laiton. **brazing,** *s.* Brasage *m*; soudure *f* (au laiton); soudure forte.

brazen¹ [breizn], *a.* **1.** D'airain. **2.** *F:* Brazen (-faced), au front d'airain; effronté, impudent, cynique. *To tell a b. lie,* mentir impudemment, cyniquement. **-ly,** *adv.* Effrontément, cyniquement.

brazen², *v.tr.* To brazen it out, payer d'effronterie, de toupet; crâner.

brazenness ['breiznnəs], *s.* Cynisme *m.*

brazier¹ ['breiziər, -ʒjər], *s.* Chaudronnier *m*, dinandier *m.*

brazier², *s.* Brasero *m* (à charbon de bois).

Brazil [brə'zil]. *Pr.n. Geog:* Le Brésil. **Bra'zil-'nut,** *s.* Noix *f* du Brésil.

Brazilian [brə'ziljən], *a. & s.* Brésilien, -ienne.

breach¹ [briːtʃ], *s.* **1.** Infraction *f. B. of rules,* infraction aux règles. *B. of the law,* violation *f* de la loi. *B. of duty,* manquement *m* au devoir. *B. of faith,* violation de foi; manque *m* de parole. Breach of trust, abus *m* de confiance. Breach of privilege, atteinte portée aux privilèges. *B. of police regulations,* contravention *f.* Breach of the peace, attentat *m*, délit *m*, contre l'ordre public. Breach of promise, (i) manque de parole; (ii) violation de promesse de mariage. *S.a.* CONTRACT¹ 2. **2.** Brouille *f*, rupture *f* (entre deux amis, etc.). **3.** Brèche *f* (dans un mur, etc.). *Mil:* To make a b. in the enemy's lines, trouer, percer, les lignes de l'ennemi.

breach². **1.** *v.tr.* Ouvrir une brèche dans (une digue, un mur). **2.** *v.i.* (a) (Of embankment, etc.) Se rompre. (b) (Of whale) Sauter, émerger.

bread [bred], *s.* Pain *m. Brown b.,* pain bis, pain de son. *New b.,* pain frais. Ship's bread, biscuit *m* (de mer). A loaf of bread, un pain, une miche. Bread and butter, (i) pain beurré; (ii) *F:* moyens de subsistance. *Slice of b. and butter,* tartine de beurre, tartine beurrée. *F:* To quarrel with one's bread and butter, casser la marmite. He knows on which side his bread is buttered, il sait où est son avantage, son intérêt. To live on bread and cheese, vivre chichement, frugalement. Bread and milk, panade *f* au lait; soupe *f* au lait. To be on bread and water, être au pain (sec) et à l'eau. *Ecc:* The bread and wine, les espèces *f.* To take the bread out of s.o.'s mouth, ôter le pain à qn. **'bread-basket,** *s.* **1.** Corbeille *f* à pain. **2.** *P:* Estomac *m*, bedaine *f.* **'bread-bin,** *s.* Huche *f* au pain; maie *f.* **'bread-crumb¹,** *s.* (a) Mie *f* (du pain); mie de pain. (b) Miette *f* (de pain). *Cu:* Bread-crumbs, chapelure *f*; (when cooked) gratin *m.* **'bread-crumb²,** *v.tr. Cu:* Paner (des côtelettes); gratiner (une sole). **'bread-fruit,** *s. Bot:* Fruit *m* à pain. Bread-fruit tree, arbre *m* à pain; jaquier *m.* **'bread-'poultice,** *s.* Cataplasme *m* à la mie de pain. **'bread-'sauce,** *s.* Sauce *f* à la mie de pain. **'bread-stuffs,** *s.pl.* **1.** Farines *f.* **2.** Céréales *f* panifiables. **'bread-winner,** *s.* Gagne-pain *m inv*; (i) soutien *m* de famille, chef *m* de famille; (ii) instrument *m* de travail.

breadth [bredθ], *s.* **1.** Largeur *f.* Finger's breadth, travers *m* de doigt. Breadth of wings (of bird, aeroplane), envergure *f.* The table is three feet in breadth, la table a trois pieds de large. **2.** Largeur (de pensée, de vues); facture *f* large (d'un tableau); ampleur *f* (de style). *S.a.* LENGTH 1.

break¹ [breik], *s.* **1.** Rupture *f.* (a) Brisure *f*, cassure *f*, fracture *f*; trouée *f*, percée *f*, brèche *f*, ouverture *f* (dans une haie); éclaircie *f* (à travers les nuages); lacune *f* (dans une succession). Break in the voice, (i) altération *f* de la voix (par l'émotion); (ii) mue *f* (à la puberté). Break of continuity, solution *f* de continuité. *B. in a journey,* arrêt *m.* To work without a break, travailler sans interruption, sans désemparer. *El.E:* Break in the circuit, rupture *f* du circuit. (b) Break in the weather, changement *m* de temps. (c) B. between two friends, rupture, brouille *f*, entre deux amis. (d) Brisure (d'une ligne). (e) Déviation *f.* *Games:* Effet *m* (de la balle). **2.** (a) (Moment *m* de) repos *m*, répit *m.* With an hour's b. for lunch, avec une heure de battement pour déjeuner. (b) *Sch:* Intervalle *m* entre les classes; récréation *f.* **3.** Break of day, point *m* du jour; aube *f*, aurore *f.* **4.** *Bill:* Série *f*, suite *f* (de carambolages, etc.).

break², *v.* (broke [brouk], *A:* brake [breik]; *p.p.* broken [broukn], *F:* broke) I. *v.tr.* **1.** (a) Casser, briser (un verre); casser, rompre (un bâton); briser, rompre (ses chaînes); rompre (les rangs). To b. one's arm, one's neck, se casser le bras, se rompre le cou. To break sth. in(to) pieces, mettre, briser, qch. en morceaux. To break bread with s.o., rompre le pain avec qn. To b. the enemy's lines, enfoncer, rompre, les lignes ennemies. To b. the skin, entamer la peau. To break (new) ground, (i) défricher une terre; donner les premiers coups de pioche; (ii) *F:* faire œuvre de pionnier. (b) Décompléter, dépareiller (un service d'argenterie). (c) *El:* Interrompre (le courant); rompre, couper, ouvrir (le circuit). (d) To break step, rompre le pas. To break a charm, (the) silence, one's fast, rompre un charme, le silence, le jeûne. To break one's journey à . . ., interrompre son voyage à . . .; faire étape à . . .; *Nau:* faire escale à . . . . **2.** To b. a branch from a tree, détacher une branche d'un arbre. **3.** To break s.o. of a bad habit, faire perdre à qn une mauvaise habitude. **4.** (a) To break a way, se frayer, s'ouvrir, un chemin. (b) To break gaol, forcer sa prison; s'évader de prison. *Mil: etc:* To break bounds, violer la consigne. **5.** To break s.o.'s heart, briser, crever, le cœur à qn. *S.a.* HEART¹ 1. *To b. s.o.'s spirit,* briser le courage de qn. To break (down) s.o.'s resistance, briser la résistance de qn. To b. s.o. into a kind of work, rompre qn à un travail. *Equit:* To break a horse, rompre un cheval. *S.a.* BREAK IN 1. **6.** (a) To break a fall, a blow, amortir une chute, un coup. (b) To break the news gently to s.o., apprendre une (mauvaise) nouvelle doucement à qn. **7.** (a) To break s.o., (i) (of losses, etc.) ruiner qn; (ii) (of grief) briser qn; (iii) (of age, illness) casser qn. To break the bank, faire sauter la banque. (b) *Mil:* Casser (un officier). **8.** (a) Violer, enfreindre, ne pas observer (la loi); rompre, enfreindre, violer (une trêve). To break the peace, troubler, violer, l'ordre public. To break one's word, one's promise, manquer de parole (à qn); fausser parole (à qn); violer sa promesse. *To b. an appointment,* manquer à un rendez-vous. (b) Résilier (un contrat). **9.** *Nau:* To break a flag, déferler un signal. II. **break,** *v.i.* I. (a) (Se) casser, se rompre, se briser; (of limb, etc.) se fracturer; (of wave) déferler; (of bubble, abscess) crever. The clouds are breaking, les nuages se dissipent, se dispersent. (b) (Of troops) Se débander. **2.** (a) (Of heart) Se briser; se fendre, crever; (of health) s'altérer, se détraquer; (of weather) changer, (i) s'améliorer, (ii) se gâter; (of heat-wave) passer. The frost has *broken*, le temps est, se met, au dégel. (*b*) *Their spirit did not b.*, ils ne se laissèrent pas abattre. *His voice is beginning to b.*, sa voix commence à muer. *His voice broke (with emotion*), sa voix s'altéra, se troubla. **3.** (*Of merchant*) Faire faillite ; (*of bank*) sauter. **4.** To break with s.o., with the traditional ways of living, rompre, briser, avec qn, avec la vie traditionnelle. **5.** (*a*) To break into a house, entrer de force, pénétrer, dans une maison ; (*of burglar*) cambrioler une maison. *To b. into a cake*, entamer un gâteau. (*b*) To break (out) into a laugh, into sobs, éclater de rire, en sanglots. To break into praise of s.o., entonner les louanges de qn. To break into a trot, prendre le trot. **6.** (*a*) To break out of prison, s'échapper, s'évader, de prison. (*b*) *A cry broke from his lips*, un cri s'échappa de ses lèvres. (*c*) (*Of ideas, etc.*) To break in upon s.o., se présenter, s'offrir, à (l'esprit de) qn. (*d*) Day was beginning to break, le jour commençait à poindre, à luire. **7.** *Sp :* The ball breaks, la balle fait faux bond. **break away. 1.** *v.tr.* Détacher (qch.) (*from*, de). **2.** *v.i.* (*a*) (*Of thg*) Se détacher (*from*, de) ; (*of pers.*) se dégager, se détacher (*from*, de) ; (*of prisoner*) s'échapper, s'évader. *Box :* To make fighters b. away, briser un corps-à-corps. Break (away)! séparez ! (*b*) *Mil :* (*Of troops*) Rompre les rangs. '**break-away,** *s.* **1.** Sécession *f*, désertion *f* (*from*, de). **2.** *Box :* Séparation *f*. **3.** *Rail :* Dérive *f* (de wagons). **break down. 1.** *v.tr.* (*a*) Abattre, démolir, renverser (un mur, etc.) ; rompre (un pont). *To b. down all opposition*, vaincre, avoir raison de, toute opposition. (*b*) *To b. down a substance*, (i) concasser, broyer, (ii) *Ch :* décomposer, une substance. **2.** *v.i.* (*a*) (*Of health*) S'altérer, se détraquer ; (*of the mind*) s'ébranler, sombrer ; (*of plan*) échouer, s'effondrer ; (*of bridge*) s'effondrer. (*b*) (*Of pers.*) (i) S'arrêter tout court, demeurer court (dans un discours) ; (ii) éclater en sanglots, fondre en larmes ; (iii) tomber malade (de fatigue). (*c*) (*Of motor car, train*) Rester en panne, avoir une panne. '**break-down,** *s.* **1.** Insuccès *m* (d'une tentative) ; rupture *f* (de négociations) ; écroulement *m* (d'un système) ; arrêt complet (dans un service). **2.** *B.-d. in health*, débâcle *f*, écroulement, de la santé. **Nervous break-down**, épuisement nerveux. **3.** (*a*) *Aut :* *Nau :* *etc :* Avarie *f* de route ; panne *f* ; *Mch :* arrêt inopiné. **Break-down gang,** (i) *Aut :* équipe de dépannage ; (ii) *Rail :* corvée de secours. **Break-down lorry,** dépanneuse *f*. To have a break-down, rester en panne. (*b*) *Ind :* *Rail :* *etc :* Perturbation *f* dans le service. **broken down,** *a.* (*Of pers.*) Cassé ; brisé (par la douleur) ; (*of horse*) usé, fourbu ; (*of health, furniture*) délabré ; (*of motor car, etc.*) (i) en panne ; (ii) en mauvais état ; (*of any mechanism*) détraqué. **break forth,** *v.i.* *Lit :* (*Of light, water*) Jaillir ; (*of rage, storm*) éclater, se déchaîner. *To b. forth into explanations*, se répandre en explications. **break in. 1.** *v.tr.* (*a*) Enfoncer (une porte, etc.) ; défoncer (un tonneau). (*b*) Rompre, mater, dresser (un cheval). *To b. oneself in to sth.*, se rompre à qch. **2.** *v.i.* (*Of roof, etc.*) Se défoncer, s'effondrer. **3.** *v.i.* (*a*) To break in (up)on s.o., (up)on a conversation, interrompre une conversation. *To b. in upon a company*, faire irruption dans une compagnie. *Abs.* To break in, intervenir, s'interposer. (*b*) (*Of burglars, etc.*) S'introduire par effraction. **breaking in,** *s.* **1.** (*a*) Enfoncement *m* (d'une porte) ; défonçage *m*, défoncement *m* (d'un tonneau). (*b*) Effraction *f*. **2.** Dressage *m*

(d'un cheval). **3.** Irruption *f* (dans une compagnie) ; interruption *f* (d'une conversation). **break loose,** *v.i* **1.** Se dégager de ses liens ; s'évader, s'échapper, s'affranchir (*from*, de). (*Of dog*) Casser sa chaîne. **2.** *His fury broke loose*, sa fureur se déchaîna. **3.** (*Of ship*) Partir à la dérive. **break off. 1.** *v.tr.* (*a*) Casser, rompre (qch.) ; détacher (qch.) (*from*, de). (*b*) Interrompre, abandonner (son travail, une discussion) ; cesser (des relations d'affaires, etc.) ; rompre (des négociations). The engagement is broken off, le mariage est rompu. **2.** *v.i.* (*a*) Se détacher se dégager (*from sth.*, de qch.) ; se détacher (net) ; se casser (net). (*b*) Discontinuer. To b. off talking, s'interrompre de parler. (*c*) To break off with s.o., rompre avec qn. **breaking off,** *s.* Rupture *f* (d'un mariage, des négociations) interruption *f* (d'un travail). **break open,** *v.tr.* To b. open a door, a safe, a case, enfoncer, forcer une porte ; forcer une serrure, un coffre-fort enfoncer une caisse. **break out,** *v.i.* **1.** (*a*) (*Of war, fire, disease*) Éclater ; se déclarer. (*b*) (*Of the face, etc.*) To break out into pimples, se couvrir de boutons. To b. out into a sweat, se mettre à transpirer ; entrer en moiteur. **2.** (*a*) S'échapper s'évader (de prison, etc.). (*b*) Faire une fugue *To b. out into excesses*, se livrer à des excès **3.** S'écrier. **break through,** *v.tr.* To b. through a barrier, abs. to break through, enfoncer une barrière ; se frayer un passage. *To b. through a wall*, faire une brèche dans, à, un mur. *The sun breaks through (the clouds*), le soleil perce les nuages. *Mil :* To b. through (*the enemy lines*) faire une percée. **break up. 1.** *v.tr.* Mettre (qch.) en morceaux ; démolir (un bâtiment, etc.) défoncer, ameublir (un terrain) ; *Ch :* résoudre (un composé) ; morceler (une propriété) ; démembrer, fragmenter (un empire) ; disperser (la foule) ; dissoudre (une assemblée) ; rompre interrompre (une conférence) ; rompre (une coalition). *The country was broken up into factions* le pays était divisé en factions. **2.** *v.i.* (*a*) (*Of empire, ship, etc.*) Se démembrer ; (*of crowd, etc.* se disperser ; (*of road surface, etc.*) se désagréger (*of ice*) débâcler. *Ship breaking up*, navire en perdition. *F : He is beginning to b. up*, il commence à se casser, à décliner. (*b*) (*Of company meeting*) Se séparer ; (*of groups*) se disjoindre (*c*) *Sch :* Entrer en vacances. *We b. up on the fourth*, nos vacances commencent le quatre (*d*) (*Of weather*) Se gâter, se brouiller '**break-up,** *s.* **1.** Dissolution *f*, fin *f* (d'un empire, d'une assemblée) ; affaissement *m* (de forces physiques) ; bris *m* (d'un navire). **2.** *Sch* Entrée *f* en vacances. **3.** Changement *m* (d temps) ; débâcle *f* (des glaces). **breaking up,** *s* **1.** Démolition *f* ; défoncement *m* (d'un terrain) décomposition *f* (d'une substance) ; dissolution *f* (d'une assemblée) ; dispersion *f* (d'une foule) morcellement *m* (d'une propriété) ; démembrement *m* (d'une empire). **2.** (*a*) Séparation *f*. O the b. up of the meeting, au sortir, à l'issue, de la réunion. (*b*) *Sch :* Entrée *f* en vacances (*c*) Débâcle *f* (des glaces). **broken,** *a.* (*a*) Cassé brisé, rompu. Broken meat, rogatons *mpl*. *B ribs*, côtes enfoncées. He is broken in health, sa santé est délabrée, détraquée. *His spirit is b.*, i est abattu, découragé. A broken man, (i) u homme ruiné ; (ii) un homme au cœur brisé (*b*) (*Terrain*) accidenté ; (chemin) raboteux défoncé ; (sommeil) interrompu ; (temps) incertain, variable. *B. outline*, contour anfractueux *B. sea*, mer battue. *B. water*, brisants *mpl*. In a **broken voice**, d'une voix entrecoupée, altérée, e broken French, en mauvais français. **-ly,** adv. Sans suite ; par à-coups ; (parler) à mots entre-coupés. **broken-'backed,** a. (a) Aux reins cassés, brisés. (b) Nau : (Navire) arqué, cassé. **broken-'hearted,** a. Au cœur brisé. To die b.-h., mourir de chagrin. **broken-'kneed,** a. (Cheval) couronné. **broken-'winded,** a. (Cheval) poussif. **breaking,** s. **1.** (a) Rupture f ; brisement m (d'une statue) ; concassage m (du minerai) Jur : (i) Bris m (d'une vitre, de scellés) ; (ii) levée f (de scellés). El.E : B. of the circuit, rupture du circuit. (b) **Breaking into a house,** entrée f par effraction dans une maison. (c) **Break-ing of the law,** violation f de la loi, infraction f à la loi. B. of one's word, manque m de parole. (d) Amortissement m (d'une chute). **2. Breaking of the voice,** (i) (at manhood) mue f ; (ii) (with emotion) altération f de la voix. **'breaking(-'down) point,** s. Mec.E : Limite f critique (de résistance) ; point m de rupture. **'break-neck,** a. It was a b.-n. path, le sentier était un véritable casse-cou. To go at a b.-n. pace, filer à une allure folle ; galoper à tombeau ouvert.

•**reak³,** s. **1.** Veh : Break m. **2.** Voiture f de dressage (des chevaux).

•**reakable** ['breikəbl]. **1.** a. Cassant, fragile. **2.** s.pl. Breakables, objets m fragiles.

•**reakage** ['breikedʒ], s. **1.** Rupture f ; bris m, fracture f (du verre, etc.). **2.** Casse f.

•**reaker** ['breikər], s. **1.** (Pers.) (a) Casseur, briseur. (b) Dresseur, entraîneur (de chevaux). (c) Violateur, -trice (d'une loi). **2.** Brisoir m, concasseur m. **3.** Nau : Brisant m ; vague déferlante. Breakers ahead ! des brisants devant !

•**reakfast¹** ['brekfəst], s. (Petit) déjeuner. To have breakfast, to eat one's breakfast, déjeuner.

•**reakfast²,** v.i. Déjeuner (le matin).

•**reakwater** ['breikwɔ:tər], s. **1.** Brise-lames m ; môle m ; jetée f. **2.** Éperon m (d'un pont).

•**ream** [bri:m], s. Ich : Brème f.

•**reast¹** [brest], s. **1.** Sein m, mamelle f. To give a child the b., donner le sein à un enfant. Child at the b., enfant à la mamelle. **2.** Poitrine f ; poitrail m (de cheval). Cu : Blanc m (de volaille) ; avant-cœur m (du bœuf). B. of a coat, of a shirt, devant m d'un habit, d'une chemise. To press s.o. to one's b., serrer qn sur son cœur. Shot under the left b., atteint d'une balle au-dessous du sein gauche. F : To make a clean breast of it, tout avouer ; faire des aveux complets. **3.** Min : Front m de taille, d'abattage. **'breast-band,** s. Harn : Tablier m. **'breast-'deep,** adv. Jusqu'à la poitrine. **'breast-drill,** s. Tls : Vilebrequin m à engrenages ; porte-foret m à conscience. **'breast-harness,** s. Bricole f. **'breast-'high,** adv. **1.** A hauteur de poitrine. F : Angine f de poitrine. **'breast-plate,** s. **1.** (a) Plastron m ; cuirasse f. (b) Ecc : Pectoral m. **2.** Tls : Conscience f (de vilebrequin). **breast-'pocket,** s. Poche f de poitrine. Inside b.-p., poche intérieure. **'breast-strap,** s. Harn : Poitrail m. **'breast-stroke,** s. Swim : Brasse f sur le ventre ; nage f en grenouille. **'breast-wall,** s. Mur m de soutènement.

•**reast²,** v.tr. Affronter, faire front à, lutter contre (une tempête, un danger). To b. a hill, affronter, gravir, une colline.

•**reastbone** ['brestboun], s. Anat : Sternum m ; bréchet m (d'un oiseau).

•**reastwork** ['brestwə:rk], s. Parapet m, garde-corps m inv. Nau : Rambarde f.

•**reath** [breθ], s. Haleine f, souffle m, respiration f. To draw breath, respirer. To draw a deep,

long, b., respirer profondément. To draw one's last breath, exhaler son dernier souffle ; rendre le dernier soupir. To have a sweet b., avoir l'haleine douce. To have a bad b., avoir mauvaise haleine. F : It is the very b. of life to me, cela m'est aussi précieux que la vie même. All in the same breath, tout d'une haleine. To hold one's breath, retenir son souffle. To gasp for breath, haleter. He caught his breath, il eut un sursaut ; la respiration lui manqua. To lose one's breath, perdre haleine. To waste one's breath, perdre son temps en discours inutiles ; perdre ses paroles. To be short of breath, (i) avoir l'haleine courte ; (ii) être essoufflé. Out of breath, hors d'haleine ; à bout de souffle ; essoufflé. To get out of b., perdre haleine. To take s.o.'s breath away, couper la respiration, le souffle, à qn ; suffoquer, interloquer, qn. To take breath ; to get, recover, one's breath, souffler ; reprendre haleine. To speak below, under, one's breath, parler à (de)mi-voix, à voix basse. To swear under one's b., jurer en sourdine. The first breath of spring, les premiers effluves du printemps. There is not a breath of wind, il n'y a pas un souffle de vent. B. of stale tobacco, relent m de tabac. S.a. AIR¹ I. 1, BATE.

breathable ['bri:ðəbl], a. Respirable.

breathe [bri:ð]. I. v.i. Respirer, souffler. To b. hard, (i) haleter ; respirer avec peine ; (ii) souffler fort, à pleins poumons. To b. heavily, (i) respirer bruyamment ; (ii) respirer péniblement. To b. on one's fingers, souffler dans ses doigts. The spirit that breathes through his work, l'esprit qui anime ses œuvres. II. **breathe,** v.tr. **1.** Respirer (l'air). To breathe in, breathe out, the air, aspirer, exhaler, l'air. To b. air into sth., insuffler de l'air dans qch. **2.** To breathe courage into s.o., inspirer du courage à qn. **3.** (a) To breathe a sigh, exhaler, laisser échapper, un soupir. To b. a prayer, murmurer une prière. To breathe one's last, rendre le dernier soupir. Don't breathe a word of it ! n'en soufflez pas un mot ! (b) To breathe forth, breathe out, threats, s'exhaler en menaces ; proférer des menaces. (Of a flower) To b. forth perfume, exhaler un parfum. (c) To b. simplicity, health, respirer la simplicité, la santé. (d) Ling : Aspirer (un son). **4.** Laisser souffler (un cheval). **breathing¹,** a. (Of picture, statue) Vivant ; qui respire. **breathing²,** s. **1.** Respira-tion f ; souffle m. Heavy b., (i) respiration bruyante ; (ii) respiration pénible ; oppression f. B. apparatus, appareil respiratoire. **2.** Ling : (a) Aspiration f (d'un son). (b) Gr.Gram : Rough, smooth, breathing, esprit rude, doux. **'breathing-space,** s. Le temps de souffler, de respirer ; répit m.

breather ['bri:ðər], s. F : Moment m de repos. To give a horse a b., laisser souffler un cheval.

breathless ['breθləs], a. **1.** Hors d'haleine ; essoufflé, haletant. B. with running, essoufflé d'avoir couru. **2. Breathless suspense,** attente fiévreuse. **-ly,** adv. **1.** En haletant. **2.** (Attendre, écouter) en retenant son haleine.

breathlessness ['breθləsnəs], s. Essoufflement m ; (of patient) manque m de souffle ; oppression f.

bred [bred]. See BREED².

breech¹ [bri:tʃ], s. **1.** A : Le derrière ; le cul. **2.** (a) (Pair of) breeches ['britʃiz], culotte f. To put a child into breeches, mettre un enfant en culotte. (b) F : Pantalon m, f : culotte. **3.** Artil : Sm.a : Culasse f. **Breech action,** mécanisme m de culasse. **'breech-block,** s. Artil : Bloc m de culasse. **'breeches-buoy,** s. Nau : Bouée f culotte. **'breech-loader,** s.

Fusil *m*, pièce *f*, se chargeant par la culasse.
'breech-loading, *s.* Chargement *m* par la culasse. *B.-l. rifle,* fusil se chargeant par la culasse.
breech², *v.tr.* *F: A:* Mettre (un enfant) en culotte. **breeching,** *s.* *Harn:* Avaloire *f*; (courroie *f* de) reculement *m.*
breed¹ [bri:d], *s.* Race *f* (d'hommes, d'animaux); lignée *f.* *S.a.* CROSS-BREED¹. HALF-BREED. *Prov:* Breed will tell, bon sang ne peut mentir.
breed², *v.* (bred; bred) I. *v.tr.* 1. Produire, engendrer; faire naître, donner naissance à (des vices, etc.). *S.a.* FAMILIARITY 1. 2. (*a*) Élever (du bétail, etc.). *Abs.* Faire de l'élevage. *Prov:* What's bred in the bone will come out in the flesh, (i) bon chien chasse de race; (ii) chassez le naturel, il revient au galop. (*b*) He was bred (up) to the law, il fut destiné au barreau. *He had been bred a sailor,* il avait été élevé pour faire un marin. *Country-bred,* élevé à la campagne. *S.a.* BORN 2, HALF-BRED, ILL-BRED, PURE-BRED. II. **breed,** *v.i.* (*a*) (*Of animals, people*) Multiplier; se reproduire. (*b*) *F:* (*Of opinions, etc.*) Se propager. **breeding,** *s.* 1. (*a*) Reproduction *f.* (*b*) Élevage *m* (d'animaux domestiques, etc.). *He goes in for b.,* il fait de l'élevage. **Silkworm breeding,** éducation *f* des vers à soie. 2. (*a*) Éducation (d'un enfant, etc.). (*b*) (**Good) breeding,** bonnes manières; savoir-vivre *m.* *S.a.* ILL-BREEDING. **'breeding-season,** *s.* (*Of birds*) Couvaison *f*; (*of domestic animals*) monte *f.*
breeder ['bri:dər], *s.* 1. Reproducteur, -trice. *Good b.,* (jument) bonne poulinière. 2. Éleveur *m* (d'animaux). *S.a.* SILKWORM.
breeks [bri:ks], *s.pl.* *F:* (*In Scot.*) = breeches, *q.v. under* BREECH¹ 2.
breeze¹ [bri:z], *s.* 1. Vent assez fort; brise *f.* Land breeze, brise de terre. Sea breeze, brise de mer, du large. *Nau: Strong b., stiff b.,* vent frais, grosse brise. 2. *F:* Scène *f*, querelle *f.*
breeze², *s.* (*Cinders*) Braise *f* de houille; fraisil *m.*
breeziness ['bri:zinəs], *s.* *F:* Cordialité bruyante; jovialité *f*; verve *f* (d'un discours).
breezy ['bri:zi], *a.* 1. Venteux. 2. *F:* (*Of pers., manners*) Jovial; désinvolte; (*of speech*) plein de verve. *B. welcome,* accueil cordial (et bruyant). **-ily,** *adv.* *F:* Avec jovialité.
Bremen ['bremən]. *Pr.n.* *Geog:* Brême.
brent-goose ['brentgu:s], *s.* *Orn:* Bernache *f*, barnache *f*; oie marine.
brethren ['breðrən], *s.pl.* *See* BROTHER.
Breton ['bretən]. 1. *a. & s.* Breton, -onne. 2. *s. Ling:* Le breton.
breve [bri:v], *s.* 1. *Hist:* Bref *m* (du pape). 2. *Pros:* Brève *f.*
brevet ['brevet], *s.* *Mil:* Brevet *m.* *B. officer,* officier breveté. **Brevet rank,** grade honoraire.
breviary ['bri:viəri], *s.* *Ecc:* Bréviaire *m.*
brevity ['breviti], *s.* Brièveté *f.* 1. Concision *f.* 2. Courte durée (de la vie, etc.).
brew¹ [bru:], *s.* 1. (*a*) Brassage *m* (de la bière). (*b*) Brassin *m*, cuvée *f.* 2. Infusion *f* (de thé); tisane *f* (de plantes).
brew². 1. *v.tr.* (*a*) Brasser (la bière). (*b*) *Abs.* Brasser; faire de la bière. (*c*) To brew tea, faire infuser le thé. 2. *v.i.* (*a*) (*Of tea, etc.*) S'infuser. (*b*) *F:* There is a storm brewing, un orage couve, se prépare. There is something brewing, il se trame quelque chose.
brewer ['bruər], *s.* Brasseur *m.*
brewery ['bruəri], *s.* Brasserie *f.*
briar ['braiər], *s.* (*a*) Wild briar, églantier commun; rosier *m* sauvage. Sweet briar, églantier odorant. (*b*) *F:* Briars, ronces *f.* **'briar-rose,** *s.* Églantine *f.*

bribe¹ [braib], *s.* Payement *m* illicite; *F:* pot-de-vin *m.* *To take a b., bribes,* se laisser corrompre.
bribe², *v.tr.* Corrompre, acheter, soudoyer; *F:* graisser la patte à (qn). *To b. a witness,* suborner un témoin. **bribing,** *s.* Corruption *f*; subornation *f* (de témoins).
briber ['braibər], *s.* Corrupteur, -trice; suborneur *m.*
bribery ['braibəri], *s.* Corruption *f.* **Open to bribery,** corruptible.
bric-à-brac ['brikəbrak], *s.* Bric-à-brac *m.*
brick¹ [brik], *s.* 1. (*a*) Brique *f.* *Glazed b.,* brique vernissée. **Brick house,** maison en briques. *F:* To drop a brick, faire une boulette, une bourde, une gaffe. *S.a.* WALL¹. (*b*) (*Toy*) Box of bricks, boîte de constructions. 2. *F:* He's a brick! c'est un chic type. *Be a b.!* soyez chic! 3. Bloc *m* (de thé); pain *m* (de savon). **'brick-clay,** *s.* Argile *f*, terre *f*, à briques. **'brick-field,** *s.* Briqueterie *f.* **'brick-kiln,** *s.* Four *m* à briques.
brick², *v.tr.* Briqueter; garnir (qch.) en briques. To brick up a window, murer une fenêtre.
brickbat ['brikbat], *s.* Fragment *m* de brique; briquaillon *m.*
bricklayer ['brikleiər], *s.* Maçon *m.*
brickmaker ['brikmeikər], *s.* Briquetier *m.*
brickwork ['brikwə:rk], *s.* Briquetage *m*; maçonnerie *f* de brique.
bridal ['braid(ə)l]. 1. *s.* *Poet:* Noce(s) *f.* 2. *a.* Nuptial, -aux, de noce(s). **Bridal wreath,** couronne de mariée.
bride [bra:id], *s.f.* 1. Future, fiancée (sur le point de se marier). 2. Épousée; (nouvelle) mariée. The bride and bridegroom, (i) les futurs conjoints; (ii) les nouveaux mariés. **'bride('s)-cake,** *s.* = WEDDING-CAKE.
bridegroom ['braidgrum], *s.m.* 1. Futur, prétendu (sur le point de se marier). 2. (Nouveau) marié. *S.a.* BRIDE.
bridesmaid ['braidzmeid], *s.f.* Demoiselle *d'honneur* (de la mariée).
bridge¹ [bridʒ], *s.* 1. Pont *m.* *To throw a b. across a river,* jeter un pont sur un fleuve. Swing-bridge, pont tournant. 2. *Nau:* (*a*) Passerelle *f* (de commandement). (*b*) (*From ship to shore*) Ladder bridge, passerelle à taquets. 3. *El:* (*a*) Measuring-bridge, pont de mesure. Induction bridge, balance *f* d'induction. (*b*) Bridge-piece, pont polaire (d'accus). 4. Dos *m*, arête *f* (du nez); chevalet *m* (d'un violon). **'bridge-head,** *s.* *Mil:* Tête *f* de pont. **'bridge-house,** *s.* *Nau:* Roufle central. **'bridge-train,** *s.* *Mil:* (i) Train *m* de pontons; (ii) corps *m* des pontonniers.
bridge², *v.tr.* To bridge (over) a river, jeter, construire, un pont sur un fleuve; (*with pontoons*) ponter un fleuve. *To bridge a gap,* relier les bords d'une brèche; combler une lacune.
bridge³, *s.* *Cards:* Bridge *m.* **Auction bridge,** bridge aux enchères. **Contract bridge,** bridge contrat. **Bridge player,** bridgeur, -euse. **Bridge-marker,** carnet-bloc *m* (de bridge). **Bridge-party,** (i) soirée, (ii) réunion de bridge.
bridle¹ [braidl], *s.* 1. (*a*) *Harn:* Bride *f.* To give a horse the bridle, lâcher, rendre, la bride à un cheval. (*b*) *F:* Frein *m.* *To put a b. on one's passions,* mettre un frein à ses passions. 2. *Nau:* Branche *f.* 3. Frein, filet *m* (de la langue). **'bridle-bit,** *s.* *Harn:* Mors *m* de bride. **'bridle-path,** *s.* Sentier *m* pour cavaliers; piste cavalière.
bridle². 1. *v.tr.* (*a*) Brider, rêner (un cheval).

(b) Maîtriser, brider, mettre un frein à, refréner (ses passions). *S.a.* TONGUE[1] **1**. **2.** *v.i.* **To bridle (up),** (i) redresser la tête ; se rengorger ; (ii) se rebiffer ; prendre la mouche.

bridoon [bri'du:n], *s. Harn :* Bridon *m.*

brief[1] [bri:f], *a.* Bref, *f.* brève ; court. *B. sojourn,* séjour passager, de peu de durée. **In brief, en** raccourci, en résumé. **To be brief . . .,** bref. . . . **-ly,** *adv.* Brièvement ; en peu de mots.

brief[2], *s.* **1.** *Ecc :* Bref *m.* **Apostolic brief, bref** apostolique, bref du pape. **2.** Abrégé *m,* résumé *m,* exposé *m. Jur :* Dossier *m* (d'une procédure). **To hold a brief,** être chargé d'une cause. *To hold a b. for s.o.,* représenter qn en justice. **'brief-bag,** *s.* Sac rond (en cuir).

brief,[3] *v.tr.* **1. To brief a case,** rédiger, établir, le dossier d'une affaire. **2. To brief a barrister,** confier une cause à un avocat ; constituer un avoué.

briefless ['bri:fləs], *a.* (Avocat) sans cause.

briefness ['bri:fnəs], *s.* Brièveté *f* ; concision *f.*

brier ['braiər], *s.* **1.** Bruyère (arborescente). **2.** Brier (pipe), pipe *f* en bruyère. **'brier-root,** *s.* Racine *f* de bruyère.

brig [brig], *s. Nau :* Brick *m.*

brigade[1] [bri'geid], *s.* **1.** Brigade *f* (de cavalerie, d'artillerie). *F :* **One of the old brigade,** un vieux de la vieille ; (*of woman*) une vieille garde. **2.** Corps organisé (pour un service public, etc.). *See esp.* FIRE-BRIGADE.

brigade[2], *v.tr. Mil :* Embrigader.

brigadier [briga'di:ər], *s. Mil :* Général *m* de brigade.

brigand ['brigənd], *s.* Brigand *m,* bandit *m.*

brigandage ['brigəndedʒ], *s.* Brigandage *m.*

bright [brait], *a.* **1.** Lumineux. (*a*) (*Of star, gem, etc.*) Brillant ; (*of sun*) éclatant. *B. fire,* feu clair, vif. *B. light,* lumière vive. *B. eyes,* yeux brillants, lumineux. *B. steel,* acier poli. *F :* **As bright as a button, as a sixpence,** brillant comme un sou neuf. (*b*) (*Of day, weather*) Clair. **To become brighter,** s'éclaircir. (*c*) (*Of colour*) Vif, éclatant. **Bright red,** rouge vif. (*d*) *Brighter days,* des jours plus heureux. **To see the bright side of things,** prendre les choses par le bon côté. **2.** (*a*) (*Vivacious*) Vif, animé, sémillant. (*b*) *F :* **Bright lad,** garçon éveillé, intelligent. *A b idea,* une idée lumineuse. (*c*) **To keep a bright look-out,** avoir l'œil au guet. **-ly,** *adv.* **1.** Brillamment ; avec éclat. **2.** *To reply b.,* répondre (i) gaiement, (ii) avec intelligence.

brighten ['brait(ə)n]. **1.** *v.tr.* **To brighten sth. (up),** faire briller, faire reluire, qch. ; fourbir (le métal) ; aviver (une couleur) ; égayer (la conversation). (*Of joy, etc.*) *To b. s.o.'s face,* dérider, faire épanouir, le visage de qn. **2.** *v.i.* **To brighten (up),** (*of face*) s'épanouir, s'éclaircir, se dérider ; (*of weather*) s'éclaircir. *His eyes brightened,* ses yeux s'allumèrent.

brightness ['braitnəs], *s.* Éclat *m* (du soleil, du teint) ; intensité *f* d'éclairage ; brillant *m* (de l'acier) ; clarté *f* (du jour) ; vivacité *f* (de l'intelligence, d'une couleur) ; intelligence *f* (d'un enfant).

brill [bril], *s. Ich :* Barbue *f.*

brilliance ['briljəns], **brilliancy** ['briljənsi], *s.* Éclat *m,* brillant *m,* lustre *m.*

brilliant[1] ['briljənt], *a.* (*a*) (*Fait d'armes,* éclairage) brillant, éclatant. (*b*) *B. idea,* idée lumineuse. **-ly,** *adv.* Brillamment ; avec éclat. *B. intelligent,* d'une intelligence brillante.

brilliant[2], *s. Lap :* Brillant *m.*

brim[1] [brim], *s.* Bord *m* (de verre, de chapeau, etc.). **To fill s.o.'s glass to the brim,** verser du vin à qn à ras bord. **'brim-'full,** *a.* Plein jusqu'au bord ; débordant.

brim[2], *v.* (brimmed) **1.** *v.tr.* **To brim the bowl,** remplir la coupe jusqu'au bord. **2.** *v.i.* **To brim over (with sth.),** déborder, regorger (de qch.). **Brimming (over),** débordant (*with,* de). *Eyes b. (over) with tears,* yeux noyés de larmes.

brimful ['brimful], *a. F :* **Brimful of health, of life,** débordant de santé, de vie.

brimstone ['brimstən], *s.* Soufre (brut).

brindle(d) [brindl(d)'], *a.* (Chat) tacheté, tavelé.

brine [brain], *s.* Eau salée ; saumure *f.*

bring [brin], *v.tr.* (*p.t.* brought [brɔ:t] ; *p.p.* brought) (*a*) Amener (qn, un animal, une voiture) ; apporter (qch., une réponse, des nouvelles). *To b. s.o. on his way,* accompagner qn un bout de chemin. *He was brought before the judge,* on l'amena, on le fit comparaître, devant le juge. *To be brought before the assizes,* être traduit en cour d'assises. *S.a.* WORD[1] 3. (*b*) **To bring tears (in)to. s.o.'s eyes,** faire venir, faire monter, les larmes aux yeux de qn. *To b. s.o. luck, ill luck,* porter bonheur, malheur, à qn. *S.a.* LUCK I. *To b. misfortune on s.o.,* attirer un malheur sur qn. **You have brought it on yourself,** vous vous l'êtes attiré vous-même. (*c*) **To bring an action against s.o.,** intenter un procès à qn. *S.a.* CHARGE[1] 6. (*d*) *To b. s.o. into difficulties, into danger,* mettre qn dans l'embarras, dans le danger. **To bring sth. into question,** mettre qch. en question. **To bring sth. into action, into play,** mettre qch. en œuvre. *S.a.* FASHION[1] 3. (*e*) **To bring s.o. to beggary,** réduire qn à la mendicité. **To bring sth. to perfection,** porter qch. à la perfection. *To b. sth. to a successful issue,* faire aboutir qch. *S.a.* END[1] 3, HOME II. 2, JUSTICE I, LIGHT[1] I, LOW[1] I. 2, MIND[1] I, NOTICE[1] 3, TRIAL I. (*f*) **To bring sth. to pass,** amener, faire arriver, qch. *S.a.* BEAR[2] (*d*). (*g*) *To b. s.o. to do sth.,* amener qn à faire qch. **To bring oneself to do sth.,** se résoudre, se décider, à faire qch. **bring about,** *v.tr.* **1.** (*a*) (*Cause*) Amener, causer, déterminer, occasionner (qch.). *To b. about s.o.'s ruin,* entraîner la ruine de qn. *To b. about an accident, a reform,* provoquer un accident, une réforme. (*b*) Effectuer, accomplir, opérer (qch.). *To b. about a change,* opérer un changement. **2.** *Nau :* Retourner, faire virer (un navire). **bring along,** *v.tr.* Amener (qn) ; apporter (qch.). **bring away,** *v.tr.* Emmener (qn) ; emporter (qch.). **bring back,** *v.tr.* Rapporter (qch.) ; ramener (qn). **This brings back to me my childhood,** cela me rappelle mon enfance. **bring down,** *v.tr.* **1.** (*a*) Abattre (un arbre, du gibier) ; faire tomber (le fruit d'un arbre) ; faire crouler, faire effondrer (une maison) ; terrasser (un adversaire). *Th : F :* **To bring down the house,** faire crouler la salle (sous les applaudissements). (*b*) *Ar :* To *b. down a figure,* abaisser un chiffre. **2.** (*a*) Faire descendre (qn). (*b*) Descendre (un objet du grenier, etc.). **3.** (*a*) Abaisser (l'orgueil de qn). (*b*) *Drink has brought him down,* c'est l'ivrognerie qui a été sa ruine, sa perte. (*c*) Abaisser, faire baisser (le prix). **4.** (*a*) *To b. down a sword on s.o.'s head,* abattre un sabre sur la tête de qn. (*b*) *To b. down s.o.'s wrath on s.o.,* attirer la colère de qn sur qn. **5.** *To b. down a swelling,* réduire une enflure. **6.** *To b. down a history to modern times,* amener une histoire jusqu'aux temps modernes. **bring forth,** *v.tr.* **1.** Mettre au monde (des enfants) ; (*of animal*) mettre bas (des petits) ; (*of plant*) produire (des fruits). *What the future will b. forth,* ce que l'avenir produira, apportera. **2.** *To b.*

forth protests, provoquer des protestations. **bring forward,** *v.tr.* (*a*) Avancer (une chaise, etc.); faire avancer, faire approcher (qn); produire (un témoin); avancer (un argument). (*b*) Avancer (une réunion, etc.). (*c*) *Com:* Reporter (une somme). **Brought forward,** à reporter; report *m.* **bring in,** *v.tr.* **1.** (*a*) Introduire, faire entrer (qn); apporter, rentrer (qch.). (*b*) Introduire (une coutume); lancer (une mode). (*c*) Faire intervenir (qn). **2.** (*Of capital, investment*) To bring in interest, rapporter; porter intérêt. **3.** (*a*) Déposer, présenter (un projet de loi). (*b*) (*Of jury*) To bring in a verdict, rendre un verdict. To bring s.o. in guilty, déclarer qn coupable. **bring off,** *v.tr.* **1.** (*a*) Ramener (qn) à bord ou à terre. (*b*) Renflouer (un navire). **2.** Réussir, boucler, conduire à bien (une affaire). *F:* To bring it off, réussir le coup. **bring on,** *v.tr.* **1.** Produire, occasionner (une maladie, etc.). **2.** *The sun is bringing on the plants,* le soleil fait pousser les plantes. **3.** *Th:* Amener ou apporter sur la scène. **4.** *To b. on a subject for discussion,* introduire un sujet de discussion. **bring out,** *v.tr.* **1.** Apporter (qch.) dehors; faire sortir (qn); conduire (qn) dehors. *To b. sth. out (of a box, etc.),* sortir qch. **2.** Faire ressortir, mettre en relief, mettre en évidence (le sens de qch.); faire valoir (une couleur); mettre en lumière (un défaut, etc.). **3.** (*a*) Introduire, faire débuter, (une jeune fille) dans le monde; lancer (une actrice). (*b*) *The sun brings out the roses,* le soleil fait épanouir les roses. (*c*) Publier, faire paraître (un livre). **bringing out,** *s.* Publication *f* (d'un livre); lancement *m* (d'une actrice); présentation *f* (d'une jeune fille) dans le monde. **bring over,** *v.tr.* **1.** Transporter, amener (*from,* de). **2.** To bring s.o. over to a cause, convertir, gagner, qn à une cause. **bring round,** *v.tr.* **1.** Apporter (qch.); amener, faire venir (qn). **2.** (*a*) Rappeler, ramener, (qn) à la vie; faire reprendre connaissance à (qn). (*b*) Remettre (qn) de bonne humeur. **3.** (*a*) Rallier (qn à un parti). (*b*) *To b. the conversation round to a subject,* (r)amener la conversation sur un sujet. **bring through,** *v.tr.* **1.** Faire passer, faire traverser (qn, qch.). **2.** *To b. a patient through,* sauver un malade. **bring to,** *v.tr.* **1.** *Nau:* Mettre (un navire) en panne; couper l'erre à (un navire). *v.i.* (*Of ship*) Mettre en panne, prendre la panne. **2.** To bring s.o. to, faire reprendre connaissance à qn. **bring together,** *v.tr.* Réunir; mettre (des personnes) en contact; affronter (des plaques de métal). *To b. persons together again,* réconcilier des personnes. *I brought them together,* je leur fis faire connaissance. *Chance brought us together,* le hasard m'a fait la rencontrer. **bring under,** *v.tr.* **1.** Soumettre, subjuguer, assujettir (qn). **2.** (*Prep. use*) *To b. s.o. under discipline,* plier qn à la discipline. **bring up,** *v.tr.* **1.** (*a*) Monter (du vin de la cave); faire monter (qn). (*b*) *To bring up one's food,* vomir; rendre ce qu'on a mangé. **2.** Apporter, approcher, avancer (qch.); amener, faire approcher (qn). *B. up your chair to the fire,* approchez votre chaise du feu. **3.** Élever (des enfants). **4.** *To b. s.o. up before the court,* citer qn en justice. **5.** (*Bring to a standstill*) (*a*) Arrêter (une voiture, etc.). *To be brought up short by sth.,* buter contre qch.; s'aheurter à qch. (*b*) *Nau:* Mouiller ou arrêter (un navire). *v.i.* (*Of ship*) Mouiller; casser son erre; accoster (*along,* le long de). *S.a.* STANDING¹ 4. **6.** *To bring up a subject,* mettre une question sur le tapis, en avant. *To b. up a subject again,* revenir

sur un sujet. *To b. sth. up against s.o.,* objecter qch. à qn. **bringing up,** *s.* **1.** Apport *m* (de munitions, etc.). **2.** Éducation *f* (des enfants). *He had a hard b. up,* il fut élevé à la dure. *S.a.* UPBRINGING.

brink [briŋk], *s.* Bord *m* (d'un précipice, d'un fleuve). *To be on the b. of ruin,* être à deux doigts, à la veille, de la ruine; être sur le bord de l'abîme. *To be on the b. of tears* avoir peine à retenir ses larmes; être près d'éclater en sanglots.

briny ['braini]. **1.** *a.* Saumâtre, salé. **2.** *s. F:* The briny, la mer, la grande tasse.

briony ['braioni], *s.* = BRYONY.

brisk¹ [brisk], *a.* **1.** Vif, actif, alerte, animé; plein d'entrain. *B. old man,* vieillard ingambe, guilleret. **Brisk-looking children,** enfants à l'air éveillé. **At a brisk pace,** à vive allure. **Brisk trade,** commerce actif. *B. market,* marché animé. *B. fire,* (i) feu vif; (ii) *Mil:* feu nourri. **2.** (*a*) (Air) vivifiant. (*b*) (Champagne) pétillant; (bière) qui mousse bien; (eau de Seltz) bien gazeuse. **-ly,** *adv.* Vivement, activement; avec entrain.

brisk². **1.** *v.tr.* To brisk s.o. up, animer, activer, émoustiller, qn. **2.** *v.i.* To brisk up, s'animer.

brisket ['brisket], *s. Cu:* Poitrine *f* (de bœuf).

briskness ['brisknəs], *s.* **1.** (*a*) Vivacité *f,* animation *f,* entrain *m.* (*b*) Activité *f* (des affaires). **2.** Fraîcheur *f* (de l'air).

bristle¹ [brisl], *s.* **1.** Soie *f* (de porc, de brosse); poil *m* raide (de la barbe). *F:* To set up one's bristles, se hérisser. **2.** *Bot:* Soie, poil.

bristle². **1.** *v.tr.* (*Of animal*) Hérisser (ses poils, ses soies). **2.** *v.i.* (*a*) (*Of animal, hair, etc.*) To bristle (up), se hérisser; *F:* (*of pers.*) se rebiffer, se hérisser. (*b*) *F:* To bristle with bayonets, with difficulties, être hérissé de baïonnettes, de difficultés. **bristling,** *a.* Hérissé (*with,* de).

bristly ['brisli], *a.* Couvert ou garni de soies, de poils raides; poilu. **Bristly moustache,** moustache hérissée, raide.

Britain ['britən]. *Pr.n.* **1.** *Hist:* La Bretagne (plus tard l'Angleterre). **2.** *Geog:* **Great Britain,** la Grande-Bretagne.

Britannia [bri'tanjə]. *Pr.n.* (Nom symbolique de) la Grande-Bretagne. *Com:* **Britannia metal,** *F:* britannia, métal (blanc) anglais.

Britannic [bri'tanik], *a.* **His Britannic Majesty,** Sa Majesté Britannique.

British ['britiʃ], *a.* **1.** Britannique; de la Grande-Bretagne; (*in Fr. usu.*) anglais, d'Angleterre. **The British Isles,** les Iles Britanniques. *B. India,* l'Inde anglaise. *s.pl.* **The British,** les Anglais. **2.** *Hist:* Breton (de la Grande-Bretagne).

Briton ['britən], *s.* **1.** *Hist:* Breton, -onne (de la Grande-Bretagne). **2.** *F:* Anglais, -aise.

Brittany ['britəni]. *Pr.n.* La Bretagne.

brittle [britl], *a.* Fragile, cassant. *Metalw:* Aigre.

brittleness ['britlnəs], *s.* Fragilité *f. Metalw:* Aigreur *f.*

broach¹ ['broutʃ], *s.* **1.** *Cu:* Broche *f* (à rôtir). **2.** *Arch:* Flèche *f,* aiguille *f* (d'église). **3.** *Tls:* (*a*) Équarrissoir *m;* alésoir *m.* (*b*) *Coop:* Perçoir *m.*

broach², *v.tr.* **1.** *Cu:* Embrocher. **2.** (*a*) *Metalw:* Aléser (un trou, un tube); équarrir. (*b*) *Coop:* Percer, entamer (un fût); mettre (un fût, du vin) en perce. **3.** *F:* Entamer, aborder (une question, etc.). **broaching,** *s.* **1.** Alésage *m;* mandrinage *m.* **2.** Mise *f* en perce (d'un fût).

broach³, *v. Nau:* **1.** *v.i.* (*Of ship*) **To broach (to),** venir en travers; faire chapelle. **2.** *v.tr. To b. a ship to,* lancer un vaisseau dans le vent.

broad [brɔːd]. **I.** *a.* (*a*) Large. *The road is forty foot b.*, la route est large de quarante pieds, a quarante pieds de arge, de largeur. *The b. sea*(*s*), le vaste océan. **To have a broad back,** (i) avoir une forte carrure; (ii) *F:* avoir bon dos. *B. grin,* sourire épanoui. **In broad daylight,** en plein jour; au grand jour. *F:* **It is as broad as it is long,** cela revient au même; c'est bonnet blanc et blanc bonnet. *S.a.* ARROW, OUTLINE¹ 2. (*b*) **The broad facts,** les faits tout simples. *B. rule,* règle de principe. (*c*) **Broad accent, speech,** accent, langage, rustique. **To speak b.** Scotch, parler l'écossais avec un accent prononcé. *S.a.* HINT¹. (*d*) **Broad story,** histoire hardie, risquée, *F:* salée, corsée. *B. humour,* grosse gaieté. *To be b. in one's conversation,* être libre, leste, dans ses discours. (*e*) **Broad Church,** Église libérale *B. views,* idées larges. **2.** *s.* (*a*) **The broad of the back,** toute la largeur du dos; le milieu du dos. (*b*) *pl. Geog:* **The (Norfolk) Broads,** la région de lacs et de mar..c..ges du Norfolk. **3.** *adv.* **Broad awake,** tout éveillé. **-ly,** *adv.* Largement. **Broadly speaking,** généralement parlant. **'broad-'brimmed,** *a.* A larges bords. **broad-'minded,** *a. To be b.-m.,* avoir l'esprit large, les idées larges; être tolérant. **broad-'mindedness,** *s.* Largeur *f* d'esprit; tolérance *f.* **broad-'shouldered,** *a.* Large d'épaules, trapu.

broadcast¹ ['brɔːdkɑːst]. **I.** *adv. Agr:* **To sow broadcast,** semer à tout vent, à la volée. **2.** *a.* (*a*) *Agr:* Semé à la volée. (*b*) *W.Tel:* (Omni)diffusé. **Broadcast announcement,** radio-émission *f;* annonce *f* par radio.

broadcast². **I.** *v.tr.* (broadcast; broadcast) **I.** (*a*) *Agr:* Semer (le grain) à la volée. (*b*) *F:* Faire savoir (qch.) partout, de tous côtés; répandre (une nouvelle). **2.** *W.Tel:* (broadcasted; broadcast(ed)) Radiodiffuser. **broadcasting,** *s.* **I.** *Agr:* Semaille à la volée. **2.** *W.Tel:* Radio-émission *f,* radio-diffusion *f,* radiophonie *f.* **Broadcasting station,** station de radio-diffusion; poste émetteur. **II. broadcast,** *s.* *W.Tel:* Émission *f* (de nouvelles); radio-émission; audition (musicale, etc.).

broadcaster ['brɔːdkɑːstər], *s.* *W.Tel:* **I.** (Appareil) émetteur *m,* diffuseur *m.* **2.** (*Pers.*) Microphoniste *mf.*

broadcloth ['brɔːdklɔθ], *s.* *Tex:* Drap noir fin, de première qualité.

broaden ['brɔːd(ə)n]. **I.** *v.tr.* Élargir. **2.** *v.i.* S'élargir; s'évaser.

broadness ['brɔːdnəs], *s.* **I.** Largeur *f.* **2.** Grossièreté *f,* vulgarité *f* (d'une plaisanterie, etc.).

broadsheet ['brɔːdʃiːt], *s.* **I.** *Typ:* In-plano *m inv.* **2.** *Lit.Hist:* Canard *m;* feuille imprimée (relatant ou satirisant un fait du jour).

broadside ['brɔːdsaid], *s.* **I.** *Nau:* (*a*) Flanc *m,* travers *m* (du navire). **On the broadside,** par le travers. (*Of ship*) **To be broadside on to sth.,** présenter le côté, le travers, à qch. **Collision broadside on,** abordage par le travers. (*b*) **To fire a broadside,** tirer une bordée. **2.** = BROADSHEET.

broadsword ['brɔːdsɔːrd], *s.* Sabre *m;* latte *f.*

brocade¹ ['bro'keid], *s.* *Tex:* Brocart *m.* **Gold b.,** brocart, drap *m,* d'or.

brocade², *v.tr. Tex:* Brocher.

brocket ['brɔket], *s.* *Ven:* Daguet *m.*

brogue¹ [broug], *s.* **I.** *A:* Chaussure *f* en cuir cru. **2.** Soulier *m* de golf. **3.** *Fishing brogues,* brodequins *m* de pêche.

brogue², *s.* (*a*) Accent *m* de terroir. (*b*) Accent irlandais.

broil¹ [broil], *s.* Querelle *f;* bagarre *f;* rixe *f.*

broil², *s.* Viande grillée; grillade *f.*

broil³, *v.tr. & i.* Griller; (faire) cuire sur le gril. **broiling,** *a.* *F:* (*Of the sun*) Ardent, brûlant. *B. weather,* chaleur torride.

broke [brouk]. **I.** *See* BREAK². **2.** *a. P:* (= broken) **To be (stony) broke, dead broke,** être sans le sou, dans la purée; être décavé, à sec.

broken, -ly. *See* BREAK².

broker ['broukər], *s.* **I.** (*a*) Courtier *m* (de commerce). **Bill-broker,** courtier de change. *Cotton-b.,* courtier en coton. *S.a.* PAWNBROKER, SHIP-BROKER. (*b*) **Stock-broker,** agent *m* de change. *S.a.* EXCHANGE¹ 2. **2.** (*Second-hand*) Brocanteur.

brokerage ['broukəredʒ], *s.* **I.** (*Profession*) Courtage *m.* **2.** (*Commission*) (Frais *mpl* de) courtage.

bromide ['broumaid], *s.* *Ch:* Bromure *m.* *Phot:* **Bromide paper,** papier au gélatinobromure; papier au bromure (d'argent).

bromine ['broumi(ː)n, -ain], *s.* *Ch:* Brome *m.*

bronchia ['brɔŋkiə], *s.pl.* *Anat:* Bronches *f.*

bronchial ['brɔŋkiəl], *a.* *Anat:* Bronchial, -aux; des bronches.

bronchitis [brɔŋ'kaitis], *s.* *Med:* Bronchite *f.*

bronco ['brɔŋko], *s.* Cheval non dressé.

bronze¹ [brɔnz]. **I.** *s.* (*a*) Bronze *m.* (*b*) *Art:* (Objet *m* en) bronze. **2.** *Attrib.* (*a*) *B. statue,* statue de, en, bronze. (*b*) (Cuir) bronzé, mordoré.

bronze². **I.** *v.tr.* (*a*) Bronzer (le fer, etc.). *F:* **Bronzed skin,** peau bronzée, basanée. (*b*) Mordorer (le cuir). **2.** *v.i.* Se bronzer. **bronzing,** *s.* Bronzage *m.*

brooch [broutʃ], *s.* *Cost:* Broche *f,* épingle *f.* **Brooch pin,** queue de broche.

brood¹ [bruːd], *s.* **I.** Couvée *f* (de poussins); volée *f* (de pigeons); naissain *m* (d'huîtres). **2.** *F:* (*a*) Enfants *mpl* *F:* marmaille *f.* (*b*) *Pej: B. of scoundrels,* engeance *f* de scélérats. **'brood-hen,** *s.f.* Couveuse. **'brood-mare,** *s.f.* (Jument) poulinière.

brood², *v.i.* (*Of hen*) Couver. **2.** *F:* (*a*) Broyer du noir; rêver noir. **To brood on, over, sth.,** rêver à qch.; songer sombrement à qch.; ruminer (une idée); couver (un projet). *To b. over the fire,* couver le feu. (*b*) *Night, silence,* broods over the scene, la nuit, le silence, plane sur la scène.

brooder ['bruːdər], *s.* (Poule) couveuse *f.*

broody ['bruːdi], *a.* (*a*) *B. hen,* poule couveuse, qui demande à couver. (*b*) *F:* (*Of pers.*) Distrait, rêveur.

brook¹ [bruk], *s.* Ruisseau *m.*

brook², *v.tr.* (*In neg. sentences*) (Ne pas) souffrir; (ne pas) endurer. **The matter brooks no delay,** l'affaire ne souffre pas de retard.

brooklet ['bruklet], *s.* Ruisselet *m;* petit ruisseau.

brookweed ['brukwiːd], *s.* Pimprenelle *f* aquatique; mouron *m* d'eau.

broom [bruːm], *s.* **I.** *Bot:* Genêt *m* (à balai). **2.** Balai *m.* *Small b.,* balayette *f.* **Wall-broom,** tête-de-loup *f.* *Prov:* **A new broom sweeps clean,** il n'est ferveur que de novice.

broomstick ['bruːmstik], *s.* **I.** Manche *m* à balai. **2.** *pl. F:* Jambes *f* comme des allumettes.

broth [brɔθ], *s.* (*a*) Bouillon *m,* potage *m.* (*b*) **Scotch broth,** soupe *f* (de tête de mouton) avec orge et légumes.

brother, *pl.* **-ers;** (*in sense* 2) *pl.* **brethren** ['brʌðər, -ərz, 'breðrən]. **I.** Frère *m.* *Younger b.,* (frère) cadet *m.* **2.** (*a*) (*Fellow-member of a society, pl. usu.* brethren) Frère. *Ecc:* **Dearly beloved brethren,** mes très chers frères. (*b*) (*pl.* Brethren) Confrère *m* (d'un

corps de métier). **3.** *Ecc.* (*pl. Brothers*) Frère (d'une communauté). **4.** *Attrib.* Brother-'writer, -'teacher, -'doctor, -'officer, *etc.*, confrère *m*, collègue *m*. **'brother-in-'arms,** *s.m.* (*pl.* brothers-in-arms) Compagnon d'armes; frère d'armes. **'brother-in-law,** *s.m.* Beau-frère, *pl.* beaux-frères.
brotherhood ['brʌðərhud], *s.* **1.** Fraternité *f*. **2.** Confraternité *f*, société *f*; (*religious*) confrérie *f*.
brotherlike ['brʌðərlaik], **brotherly** ['brʌðərli]. **1.** *a.* De frère; fraternel. **2.** *adv.* En frère; fraternellement.
brotherliness ['brʌðərlinəs], *s.* **1.** Amour fraternel. **2.** Confraternité *f*.
brougham ['bru:əm, bru:m],*s. Veh :* Brougham *m*. *Aut :* Coupé *m* (de ville).
brought [brɔ:t]. *See* BRING.
brow [brau], *s.* **1.** (*Usu. pl.*) (*a*) Arcades sourcilières. (*b*) Sourcil(s) *m*. **To pucker one's brows,** froncer les sourcils. *S.a.* KNIT² 2. **2.** (*Forehead*) Front *m*. **3.** *F:* Front, croupe *f* (de colline); bord *m* (de précipice).
browbeat ['braubi:t], *v.tr.* Intimider, brusquer, rudoyer (qn).
-browed [braud], *a.* High-browed, au front haut. **Brazen-browed,** au front d'airain. **Heavy-browed,** aux sourcils épais.
brown¹ [braun]. **1.** *a.* (*a*) Brun, marron. *B. hair,* cheveux bruns, cheveux châtains. **Light-brown hair,** cheveux châtain clair. **Brown boots,** chaussures jaunes. *Tex :* **Brown holland,** toile écrue. *Cu :* **Brown butter,** beurre roux, beurre noisette. (*b*) Bruni par le soleil; bronzé. **2.** *s.* Brun *m*; marron *m*.
brown². **1.** *v.tr.* (*a*) Brunir. *Face browned by the sun,* teint bruni au soleil. (*b*) *Cu :* Rissoler (la viande); faire dorer (le poisson); faire roussir (une sauce). *Metall :* Bronzer, brunir. **2.** *v.i.* (*a*) (Se, brunir. (*b*) *Cu :* Prendre couleur; roussir.
browning¹, *s.* **1.** Brunissement *m*; bronzage *m*. **2.** *Cu :* Caramel *m*.
brownie ['brauni], *s.* **1.** *Scot :* Farfadet *m*. **2.** Membre *m* de la section des "petites" des *"Girl Guides."*
Browning² ['brauniŋ], *s. Sm.a :* Browning *m*; pistolet *m* automatique.
brownish ['brauniʃ], *a.* Brunâtre.
browse¹ [brauz], *s.* Brout *m*; jeunes pousses *f*.
browse², *v.tr. & i.* (*a*) *To b.* (*on*) *leaves,* brouter des feuilles. (*b*) *F:* (= GRAZE) Brouter (l'herbe); paître. *F: To b. among books,* butiner dans les livres.
Bruin ['bruin]. *Pr.n. Lit :* Brun *m*; l'Ours *m*.
bruise¹ [bru:z], *s.* Meurtrissure *f*; contusion *f*; bleu *m*; (*on fruit*) talure *f*; (*on metal*) bosse *f*. *Surg :* Coup *m* orbe.
bruise², *v.tr.* **1.** (*a*) Meurtrir, contusionner, froisser (une partie du corps); écraser (un fruit, un doigt). *To b. one's arm,* se meurtrir le bras. (*b*) (*With passive force*) (*Of fruit*) Se meurtrir, se tacher. **2.** Bosseler, bossuer. **3.** Broyer.
bruising, *s.* **1.** Écrasement *m* (des chairs); contusion *f*, froissement *m*. **2.** Broyage *m*.
bruiser ['bru:zər], *s. Box: F:* Boxeur (brutal); cogneur *m*.
bruit [bru:t], *v.tr.* To bruit sth. abroad, about, faire courir le bruit de qch.; ébruiter qch.
Brummagem ['brʌmədʒəm], *s. F:* (= *Birmingham*) Brummagem ware, joaillerie *f*, *etc.*, de camelote, en toc.
brunch [brʌnʃ],*s. F:* Déjeuner *m* à la fourchette (tenant lieu de "*breakfast*" et de "*lunch*").
brunette [bru'net], *a. & s.* (*Of woman*) Brune. A small brunette, une brunette.

brunt [brʌnt], *s.* Choc *m*. **To bear the brunt of the attack,** soutenir le plus fort, le choc, de l'attaque. *The b. of the battle,* le plus fort de la bataille. *To bear the b.* (*of work or fight*), payer de sa personne.
brush¹ [brʌʃ], *s.* **1.** (*a*) = BRUSHWOOD. (*b*) *U.S: etc:* Brousse *f*. **2.** (*a*) Brosse *f*; (*for bottles*) goupillon *m*. **Sweeping brush,** balai *m*. **Long-handled (Turk's head) brush,** tête-de-loup *f*. **Hearth-, banister-brush,** balayette *f*, époussette *f*. (*b*) **(Paint-)brush,** pinceau *m*. **Flat brush,** queue-de-morue *f*. **Paste-brush,** pinceau à colle **Whitewash brush,** badigeon *m*. **Air-brush,** pinceau vaporisateur. (*c*) *Ven:* Queue *f* (de renard). (*d*) *El.E:* Balai (de commutateur) **3.** Faisceau *m* de rayons électriques. **4.** Coup *m* de brosse (à des vêtements, etc.). **5.** Rencontre *f*, échauffourée *f* (avec l'ennemi). *F:* **At the first brush,** au premier abord. **'brush-holder,** *s.* Porte-balais *m inv* (de dynamo). **'brush-maker,** *s.* Brossier *m*; fabricant *m* de brosses. **'brush-work,** *s.* **1.** Travail *m* au pinceau. **2.** *Art:* Touche *f* (du peintre); facture *f*.
brush². **1.** *v.tr.* (*a*) Brosser (un habit, les cheveux); balayer (un tapis). *To b. one's hair,* se brosser les cheveux. (*b*) Effleurer, raser, frôler (une surface). (*c*) Gratter (la laine). (*d*) *To b. the dust off sth.,* enlever la poussière de qch. (à la brosse). *To b. sth. clean,* nettoyer qch. avec une brosse, à la brosse. **2.** *v.i.* **To brush against, by,** past, s.o., froisser, frôler, qn en passant. **brush aside,** *v.tr.* Écarter (une pensée, une difficulté). **brush away,** *v.tr.* Enlever (la boue, etc.) d'un coup de brosse ou du balai. **brush down,** *v.tr.* Donner un coup de brosse à (qn); brosser, panser (un cheval). **brush out,** *v.tr.* **1.** *To b. out one's hair,* se démêler les cheveux (à la brosse). **2.** *To b. out a room,* nettoyer une pièce (avec un balai). **brush over,** *v.tr.* Enduire (une surface) à la brosse; badigeonner (une surface) (*with*, de). **brush up,** *v.tr.* (*a*) Donner un coup de brosse à (un chapeau, etc.). *F:* **To brush up a subject,** se remettre à un sujet; repasser, rafraîchir, un sujet. *To b. up one's French,* dérouiller son français. (*b*) *To b. up wool,* gratter la laine. (*c*) *To b. up the crumbs,* ramasser les miettes (avec la brosse). **brush-'up,** *s.* **1.** Coup *m* de brosse. **2.** *To give one's French a b.-up,* dérouiller son français.
brushwood ['brʌʃwud], *s.* (*a*) Broussailles *f pl*; bois taillis; fourré *m*. (*b*) Mort-boi: *m*; menu bois.
brushy ['brʌʃi], *a.* **1.** En brosse; hérissé. **2.** *B. tail,* queue bien fournie.
brusque [brusk], *a.* Brusque; (ton) rude, bourru. **-ly,** *adv.* Avec rudesse, avec brusquerie.
brusqueness ['brusknəs], *s.* Brusquerie *f*, rudesse *f*.
Brussels [braslz]. *Pr.n. Geog:* Bruxelles.
brutal ['brut(ə)l], *a.* Brutal, -aux; (instinct) animal, de brute. **-ally,** *adv.* Brutalement.
brutality [bru'taliti], *s.* **1.** Brutalité *f* (*to*, envers). **2.** *Jur:* Sévices *m pl* (envers).
brutalization [brutəlai'zeiʃ(ə)n], *s.* Abrutissement *m*.
brutalize ['brutəlaiz], *v.tr.* Abrutir.
brute [bru:t]. **1.** *s.* (*a*) Brute *f*; bête *f* brute. *Alcohol turns men into brutes,* l'alcool abrutit les hommes. (*b*) *F:* (*Of pers.*) Brute; brutal, -aux *m*. (*c*) *F:* **It was a brute of a job,** c'était un métier, un travail, de chien. **2.** *a.* (*a*) **Brute beast,** bête brute. (*b*) **Brute force,** la force brutale. **By brute force,** de vive force. (*c*) **Brute matter,** matière brute.

brutish ['brutiʃ], *a.* **1.** De brute ; bestial, -aux. **2.** Abruti.

brutishness ['brutiʃnəs], *s.* **1.** Bestialité *f.* **2.** Abrutissement *m.*

bryony ['braiɔni], *s. Bot:* **1.** White bryony, bryone *f*, couleuvrée *f.* **2.** Black bryony, taminier *m.*

bubble[1] [bʌbl], *s.* **1.** (*a*) Bulle *f* (d'air, de savon) ; (*in boiling liquid*) bouillon *m.* (*b*) *Glassm:* Metall: Soufflure *f* ; *Cer:* cloche *f.* **2.** Projet *m* chimérique ; chimère *f*, illusion *f* ; tromperie *f.* The bubble **Reputation,** cette chose vaine qu'on appelle Renommée. **Bubble scheme,** entreprise véreuse ; duperie *f.* **3.** Bouillonnement *m.* '**bubble-and-'squeak,** *s. Cu:* Réchauffé *m* en friture de pommes de terre et de choux.

bubble[2], *v.i.* (*a*) Bouillonner ; dégager des bulles ; (*of wine*) pétiller ; (*of gas through liquid*) barboter. (*b*) (*Of liquid poured*) Faire glouglou ; glouglouter. **bubble over,** *v.i.* Déborder. *F:* To b. over *with vitality, with high spirits,* déborder de vie, de gaîté. **bubble up,** *v.i.* (*Of spring*) Sortir à gros bouillons. **bubbling,** *a.* Bouillonnant ; (*of wine*) pétillant.

bubbly-jock ['bʌblidʒɔk], *s. Scot:* Dindon *m.*

bubo, *pl.* **-oes** ['bjuːbou, -ouz], *s. Med:* Bubon *m.*

bubonic [bjuˈbɔnik], *a. Med:* Bubonique.

buccaneer [bʌkəˈniːər], *s.* (*a*) *Hist:* Flibustier *m.* (*b*) *F:* Boucanier *m*, flibustier ; pirate *m.*

buck[1] [bʌk], *s.* **1.** (*a*) Daim *m* ou chevreuil *m* (mâle). (*b*) Mâle *m* (du renne, du chamois, du lapin, du lièvre). (*c*) *U.S:* Indien mâle. **2.** *F:* (*a*) *A:* & *Hist:* Dandy *m*, élégant *m.* Old buck, vieux marcheur. (*b*) Old buck! mon vieux ! **3.** *Equit:* = BUCK-JUMP[1]. **4.** *U.S:* *P:* = DOLLAR 1. '**buck-jump**[1], *s.* (*Of horse*) Saut *m* de mouton. '**buck-jump**[2], *v.i.* (*Of horse*) Faire le saut de mouton ; faire un haut-le-corps. '**buck-shot,** *s. Ven:* Chevrotine *f* ; gros plomb. '**buck-teeth,** *s.pl.* Dents saillantes.

buck[2]. **1.** *v.i.* = BUCK-JUMP[2]. **2.** *v.tr.* (*Of horse*) To buck s.o. off, désarçonner qn.

buck[2]. **1.** *v.tr* To buck s.o. up, remonter le courage de qn ; stimuler, ragaillardir, qn. *I was tremendously bucked to hear the news,* j'ai été enchanté d'apprendre la nouvelle. **2.** *v.i.* To buck up, (i) reprendre courage ; se ressaisir ; (ii) se hâter ; se remuer.

buck-bean ['bʌkbiːn], *s. Bot:* Trèfle *m* d'eau.

bucket ['bʌkit], *s.* **1.** (*a*) Seau *m. Canvas b., wooden b.,* seau en toile, en bois. *S.a.* DROP[1] 1, KICK[2] 2. (*b*) *Ind:* Baquet *m. Nau:* Tar b., baille *f* à goudron. **2.** Piston *m* (à clapet) (d'une pompe) ; heuse *f.* **3.** *Hyd.E:* (*a*) Auget *m* (d'une roue hydraulique). (*b*) Chain of buckets, (pompe à) chapelet *m.* **4.** Godet *m*, benne *f* (d'une drague). **5.** *Mil:* Botte *f* (pour carabine) ; godet (pour hampe de lance, etc.). '**bucket-seat,** *s. Aut:* (Siège *m* en) baquet *m.* '**bucket-shop,** *s. Fin:* Bureau *m* d'un courtier marron.

bucketful ['bʌkitful], *s.* Plein seau. *F: It is raining (in) bucketfuls,* il pleut à seaux.

buckle[1] [bʌkl], *s.* **1.** Boucle *f*, agrafe *f.* **2.** *Tchn:* Flambement *m*, gauchissement *m* (d'une tige, d'une surface) ; voile *m* (d'une roue) ; flambage *m.*

buckle[2]. **1.** *v.tr.* (*a*) Boucler (une valise, un soulier, etc.) ; agrafer, serrer, attacher (une ceinture, etc.). To buckle on *one's sword,* ceindre son épée. (*b*) *Tchn:* Déjeter ; gauchir ; voiler (une roue) ; faire flamber (une tige de métal, etc.). **2.** *v.i.* (*a*) (*Of shoe, belt*) Se boucler. (*b*) *F:* (*Of pers.*) To buckle to a task, s'appliquer, s'atteler, à un travail. To buckle to, s'y atteler ; s'y mettre. **3.** *v.i.* To buckle (up), (*of metal, etc.*)

se déformer, se déjeter, (se) gondoler, gauchir, flamber, arquer ; (*of wheel*) se voiler. **buckling,** *s.* **1.** Agrafage *m.* **2.** (*Of metal*) Déformation *f*, flambage *m*, gauchissement *m*, déjettement *m*, voilure *f* ; gondolage *m* (d'une tôle, de plaques d'accu). **3.** *F:* Buckling to, (i) application assidue au travail ; (ii) commencement *m* du travail.

buckler ['bʌklər], *s.* **1.** *Archeol:* Écu *m*, bouclier *m.* **2.** *Nau:* Tampon *m*, tape *f* (d'écubier).

buckram ['bʌkrəm], *s.* **1.** *Tex:* Bougran *m.* **2.** *F:* Raideur *f*, empesé *m* (du style, etc.).

buckshee ['bʌkʃiː], *adv. P:* Gratis ; à l'œil.

buckskin ['bʌkskin], *s.* Peau *f* de daim. *B. breeches, s.pl.* buckskins, culotte *f* de peau.

buckthorn ['bʌkθɔːrn], *s. Bot:* Nerprun *m.*

buckwheat ['bʌkhwiːt], *s.* Sarrasin *m* ; blé noir.

bucolic [bjuˈkɔlik], *a.* & *s.* Bucolique (*f*).

bud[1] [bʌd], *s.* **1.** Bourgeon *m* ; œil *m* (d'une plante). (*Of tree*) To be in bud, bourgeonner. *F:* Sedition in the bud, sédition en germe. *S.a.* NIP[2] 2. **2.** *Bot:* Bouton *m* (de fleur).

bud[2], *v.* (budded) **1.** *v.i.* (*a*) (*Of tree, plant*) Bourgeonner ; se couvrir de bourgeons. (*b*) (*Of flower*) Boutonner ; commencer à éclore. (*c*) *F:* (*Of talent, etc.*) Commencer à éclore, à se révéler. **2.** *v.tr.* Greffer (un arbre fruitier) par œil détaché ; écussonner (un arbre). **budding**[1], *a.* (*a*) Qui bourgeonne ou qui boutonne. *A b. rose,* un bouton de rose ; une rose en bouton. (*b*) *F:* Budding artist, artiste en herbe. **budding**[2], *s.* **1.** (*a*) Bourgeonnement *m.* (*b*) Poussée *f* des boutons. **2.** Greffe *f* par œil détaché.

Buddha ['budə], *s.* (Le) Bouddha.

Buddhist ['budist]. **1.** *s.* Bouddhiste *mf.* **2.** *a.* Bouddhique.

budge [bʌdʒ]. **1.** *v.i.* (*a*) Bouger, céder ; reculer. *I won't b. an inch,* je ne reculerai pas d'un centimètre. (*b*) Bouger, remuer. **2.** *v.tr. I couldn't b. him,* il est resté inébranlable.

budgerigar [bʌdʒeriˈgɑːr], *s.* Perruche *f* inséparable.

budget[1] ['bʌdʒet], *s.* **1.** Tas *m*, collection *f* (de papiers, etc.) ; recueil *m* (d'anecdotes, etc.) ; paquet *m* (de lettres). **2.** Budget *m.* To introduce, open, the budget, présenter le budget. To pass the b., voter le budget. *S.a.* BALANCE[2] 1.

budget[2], *v.i.* To budget for *a certain expenditure,* porter, inscrire, certaines dépenses au budget.

budgetary ['bʌdʒetəri], *a.* Budgétaire.

buff[1] [bʌf], *s.* **1.** Peau *f* de buffle ; cuir épais. Buff-leather, buffle *m. A:* Buff-coat, -jerkin, pourpoint de buffle. **2.** Couleur *f* chamois ; jaune clair *inv.* **3.** *F:* In buff tout nu. To strip to the buff, se mettre dans le costume d'Adam ; *P:* se mettre à poil. '**buff-stick,** *s.* Buffle *m*, polissoir *m.*

buff[2], *v.tr.* Polir, émeuler (un métal, etc.) (au buffle). **buffing,** *s.* Polissage *m*, émeulage *m*, '**buffing-wheel,** *s.* Meule *f* à polir.

buffalo ['bʌfəlo], *s. Z:* (*a*) Buffle *m. Young b.,* bufflon *m.* (*b*) *U.S: F:* Bison *m.*

buffer[1] ['bʌfər], *s.* Appareil *m* de choc ; amortisseur *m.* **1.** (*a*) *Rail:* Tampon *m* (de choc). *El.E:* Accumulator forming buffer, accumulateur en tampon. (*b*) = BUFFER-STOP. **2.** *Artil:* Recoil-buffer, frein *m* (de tir) ; accul *m.* '**buffer-stop,** *s. Rail:* Butoir *m*, heurtoir *m* ; tampon *m* d'arrêt.

buffer[2], *s.* *F:* Old buffer ; vieux copain ; (ii) vieux bonze.

buffet[1] ['bʌfet], *s.* Coup *m* (de poing).

buffet[2], *v.tr.* & *i.* (*a*) Flanquer une torgn(i)ole à (qn) ; bourrer (qn) de coups. (*b*) To buffet (with) **the waves**, lutter contre les vagues. (*Of ship*) *Buffeted by the waves, by the wind*, battu, ballotté, par les vagues ; secoué par le vent. **buffeting**, *s.* Succession *f* de coups, de chocs. *We got a b. in the Bay of Biscay*, nous avons été fortement secoués dans le golfe de Gascogne.

buffet³, *s.* **1.** ['bʌfet] (*Sideboard*) Buffet *m.* **2.** ['bufe] (*On menu*) **Cold buffet**, viandes froides ; assiette anglaise.

buffoon [bʌ'fuːn], *s.* Bouffon *m*, paillasse *m.*

buffoonery [bʌ'fuːnəri], *s.* Bouffonneries *fpl.*

bug [bʌg], *s.* **1.** (*a*) Punaise *f.* (*b*) *U.S:* *F:* Insecte *m.* **2.** *F:* (*Of pers.*) **Big bug**, gros bonnet. **The big bugs**, les huiles *f.* 'bug-hunter, *s.* *P:* Entomologiste *m* ; naturaliste *m.*

bugaboo ['bʌgəbuː], *s.* (*a*) Objet *m* d'épouvante (pour les enfants) ; *F:* croquemitaine *m*, loupgarou *m.* (*b*) *F:* Sujet *m* de grosse inquiétude ; cauchemar *m.*

bugbear ['bʌgbɛər], *s.* (*a*) = BUGABOO. (*b*) *F:* *That man's my b.*, cet homme-là, je ne peux pas le sentir.

buggy ['bʌgi], *s.* *Veh:* Boghei *m*, buggy *m.*

bugle¹ [bjugl], *s.* Clairon *m.* **Key(ed) b.**, bugle *m.* **Bugle band**, fanfare *f.* *S.a.* CALL¹ 2.

bugle², *v.i.* Sonner du clairon.

bugle³, *s.* *Bot:* Bugle *f.*

bugler ['bjuglər], *s.* Clairon *m* ; sonneur *m* de clairon.

bugles [bjuglz], *s.pl.* *Dressm:* Tubes *m* (de verre) ; verroterie noire.

bugloss ['bjuglɔs], *s.* *Bot:* **1.** **Corn, field, bugloss**, buglosse *f.* **2.** **Viper's bugloss**, vipérine *f* ; herbe *f* aux vipères. **3.** **Dyer's bugloss**, orcanette *f.*

buhl [buːl], *s.* (Marqueterie *f* de) Boul(l)e *m.* **Buhl cabinet**, cabinet de boulle.

build¹ [bild], *s.* **1.** Construction *f* ; façons *fpl* (d'un navire, etc.) ; style *m* (d'un édifice). **2.** Carrure *f*, taille *f*, conformation *f* (d'une personne). *Man of powerful b.*, homme à forte membrure. *Man of slight b.*, homme fluet.

build², *v.tr.* (built [bilt] ; built) **1.** Bâtir (une maison, etc.) ; construire (un vaisseau, un pont, une route, une machine) ; édifier (un temple). *To b. over, upon, a piece of land*, bâtir un terrain. *The stables are built on to the house*, les écuries tiennent à la maison. *F:* *To b. upon sand*, bâtir sur le sable. *F:* *I'm built that way*, je suis comme ça. *I'm not built that way*, cela ne s'accorde pas avec mes principes ; cela ne rentre pas dans mes goûts. **2.** **To build vain hopes on sth.**, fonder de vaines espérances sur qch. **build in**, *v.tr.* **1.** Murer, boucher, bloquer (une fenêtre, etc.). **2.** **Built-in beam**, poutre encastrée. **build up**, *v.tr.* (*a*) Affermir (la santé). (*b*) Bâtir, échafauder (une théorie, etc.). *To b. up a connection*, se créer une clientèle. (*c*) (*Of magnetic field*) **To build up**, s'amorcer. (*d*) **Built-up area**, agglomération (urbaine). **building up**, *s.* **1.** Affermissement *m* (de la santé, etc.). **2.** *El.E:* Amorçage *m* (du champ, d'une dynamo).

built, *a.* British built, de construction anglaise. *F:* **Well-built man**, homme bien bâti, solidement charpenté. **building**, *s.* **1.** Construction *f.* **Building ground, building land**, terrain à bâtir. **Building contractor**, entrepreneur de bâtiment. **The building-trade**, le bâtiment. **2.** Bâtiment *m* ; maison *f* ; local *m*, -aux ; (*large b.*) édifice *m.* **Public building**, édifice public ; monument *m.* 'building-slip, *s.* *N.Arch:* Cale *f* de construction.

builder ['bildər], *s.* Entrepreneur *m* (en bâtiments) ; constructeur *m* (de navires) ; *F:* créa-

teur, -trice, fondateur, -trice (d'un empire, etc.).

built [bilt]. *See* BUILD².

bulb [bʌlb], *s.* **1.** *Bot:* Bulbe *m*, oignon *m* (de tulipe, etc.). **2.** *Anat:* **Hair-bulb**, bulbe pileux. **3.** *El:* Ampoule (incandescente) ; lampe *f.* *Vacuum b.*, lampe dans le vide. **4.** *Ph:* Boule *f*, ampoule (de thermomètre). **5.** *Phot:* Poire *f* (de déclencheur). 'bulb-holder, *s.* *El:* Porteampoule *m inv.*

bulbous ['bʌlbəs], *a.* Bulbeux. **Bulbous nose**, nez en pied de marmite ; truffe *f.*

Bulgaria [bʌl'gɛəria]. *Pr.n.* La Bulgarie.

Bulgarian [bʌl'gɛəriən], *a. & s.* Bulgare (*mf*).

bulge¹ [bʌldʒ], *s.* Bombement *m*, ventre *m*, renflement *m* ; (*of vase, etc.*) panse *f.*

bulge², *v.tr. & i.* To bulge (out), bomber, ballonner ; faire ventre ; faire saillie. *Sack bulging with potatoes*, sac bourré de pommes de terre. **bulging**, *a.* (*Front*, etc.) bombé ; (*ventre*) ballonnant. *B. eyes*, yeux protubérants ; *F:* yeux en boules de loto.

bulk¹ [bʌlk], *s.* **1.** *Nau:* Charge *f* ; chargement arrimé. **To break bulk**, désarrimer ; rompre charge ; entrer en déchargement. *To load (a ship) in b.*, charger un navire en volume, en vrac. *Com:* **In bulk**, en bloc, globalement ; en gros, en quantité. **2.** Grandeur *f*, grosseur *f*, masse *f*, volume *m* (d'un colis). **3.** *The (great) b. of mankind*, la masse, la plupart, des hommes. *To lose the b. of one's goods*, perdre le plus gros de ses biens.

bulk², *v.i.* To bulk large, occuper une place importante, faire figure importante (*in s.o.'s eyes*, aux yeux de qn).

bulkhead [bʌlkhed], *s.* *N.Arch:* Cloison *f.*

bulky ['bʌlki], *a.* **1.** Volumineux, encombrant, peu portatif. **2.** Gros, *f.* grosse.

bull¹ [bul], *s.* **1.** (*a*) Taureau *m.* *F:* **To take the bull by the horns**, prendre le taureau par les cornes. *He is like a bull in a china shop*, il est comme un taureau en rupture d'étable. (*b*) **Bull elephant, whale**, éléphant *m* mâle, baleine *f* mâle. (*c*) *Astr:* **The Bull**, le Taureau. **2.** *St.Exch:* Spéculateur *m* à la hausse ; haussier *m.* **3.** *F:* = BULL'S-EYE 4. 'bull-baiting, *s.* Combat *m* de chiens contre un taureau. 'bull-calf, *s.* **1.** Jeune taureau *m* ; taurillon *m.* **2.** *F:* Niais *m*, innocent *m.* 'bull-dog, *s.* **1.** Bouledogue *m.* **2.** *F:* (i) Personne d'un courage obstiné ; (ii) appariteur *m* du censeur (aux universités d'Oxford et de Cambridge). *F:* **One of the bull-dog breed**, un homme qui a du cran. 'bull-fight, *s.* Course *f*, combat *m*, de taureaux. 'bull-fighter, *s.* Toréador *m.* 'bull-fighting, *s.* Combats *mpl*, courses *fpl*, de taureaux. 'bull-frog, *s.* Grenouille mugissante. 'bull-pup, *s.* Petit chien bouledogue. 'bull-ring, *s.* Arène *f* (pour les courses de taureaux). 'bull's-eye, *s.* **1.** *Glassm:* Boudine *f.* **2.** *Nau:* (Verre *m* de) hublot *m* ; lentille *f.* **3.** **Bull's-eye window**, œil-de-bœuf *m*, *pl.* œils-de-bœuf. **Bull's-eye lantern**, lanterne sourde. **4.** Noir *m*, blanc *m*, mouche *f* (d'une cible). **To make a bull's-eye**, mettre, donner, dans le noir. **5.** *F:* Gros bonbon (en boule) à la menthe. **bull-'terrier**, *s.* (Chien) bull-terrier *m.*

bull², *v.tr.* (*a*) **To bull the market**, chercher à faire hausser les cours. (*b*) *Abs.* Spéculer à la hausse.

bull³, *s.* *Ecc:* Bulle *f.*

bull⁴, *s.* **Irish bull**, inconséquence *f* ; coq-à-l'âne *m.*

bullet ['bulet], s. Balle f (de fusil, de revolver). **'bullet-headed**, a. **1.** À tête ronde **2.** U.S: F: Entêté. **'bullet-proof**, a A l'épreuve des balles.

bulletin ['buletin], s. Bulletin m, communiqué m. News bulletin, bulletin d'actualités; W.Tel: journal parlé.

bullfinch ['bulfinʃ], s. **1.** Orn: Bouvreuil m. **2.** Equit: Haie f avec fossé.

bullion¹ ['buljən], s. Or m en barres; or, argent m, en lingot(s); valeurs fpl en espèces. Bullion reserve, réserve métallique.

bullion², s. Tex: (a) Cannetille f. (b) Mil: Torsades fpl; franges fpl.

bullock ['bulə/k], s. Husb: Bœuf m. Young b., bouvillon m. **'bullock-cart**, s. Char m à bœufs.

bully¹ ['buli], s. **1.** (a) A: Bravache m. To play the bully, faire le fendant. (b) F: Brute f, tyran m. Sch: Brimeur m. (c) Homme m de main (d'un aventurier politique, etc.). **2.** (Pimp) Souteneur m.

bully², v.tr. Intimider, malmener, brutaliser. To b. s.o. into doing sth., faire faire qch. à qn à force de menaces. **bullying¹**, a. Brutal, -aux; bravache. **bullying²**, s. **1.** Intimidation f, brutalité f. **2.** Sch: Brimades fpl.

bully³, a. & int. U.S: P: Fameux, épatant, bœuf.

bully⁴, s. Hockey: Engagement m (du jeu).

bully⁵, v.i. Hockey: To bully (off), engager (le jeu); mettre la balle en jeu.

bully⁶, s. F: Bully (beef), bœuf m de conserve.

bulrush ['bulrʌʃ], s. Bot: **1.** Jonc m des marais. **2.** Massette f, quenouille f.

bulwark ['bulwə/k], s. **1.** A.Fort: Rempart m, boulevard m. **2.** pl. Nau: Pavois m, bastingage m.

bum¹ [bʌm], s. F: Derrière m; P: cul m.

bum². U.S: P: **1.** a. Sans valeur; misérable, P: moche. **2.** s. Fainéant m.

bum³, v.i. (bummed) U.S: P: Flâner, fainéanter.

bumble-bee ['bʌmblbiː], s. Ent: Bourdon m.

bumboat ['bʌmbout], s. Bateau m à provisions.

bumkin ['bʌmkin], s. Nau: Minot m; boutdehors m (de tapecul).

bump¹ [bʌmp], s. **1.** Choc (sourd); secousse f, heurt m, coup m; cahot m (d'une voiture). **2.** Bosse f; (in phrenology) protubérance f, bosse. Bumps in a road, inégalités f, cahots, d'un chemin. To have the bump of invention, avoir la bosse de l'invention. **3.** Av: Trou m d'air.

bump². **1.** v.tr. Cogner, frapper. To b. one's head on, against, sth., se cogner la tête contre qch. **2.** v.i. (a) Se cogner, se heurter, buter (into, against, sth., contre qch.); entrer en collision (avec qch.). To bump along (in cart, etc.), avancer avec force cahots. (b) Nau: (Of ship) Talonner; toucher (le fond). **bump off**, v.tr. U.S: P: Assassiner, supprimer (qn). **bumping**, s. Heurtement m, cahotement m.

bump³, adv. & int. Pan! boum!

bumper¹ ['bʌmpə/r], s. **1.** Rasade f (de champagne, etc.). F: Bumper crop, récolte magnifique. Th: Bumper house, salle comble. **2.** (a) Rail: U.S: Tampon m. (b) Aut: Pare-choc(s) m inv.

bumpkin ['bʌm(p)kin], s. **1.** Rustre m, lourdaud. **2.** Nau: = BUMKIN.

bumptious ['bʌm(p)ʃəs], a. Présomptueux, suffisant, outrecuidant. **-ly**, adv. D'un air suffisant; avec suffisance.

bumptiousness ['bʌm(p)ʃəsnəs], s. Suffisance f, outrecuidance f.

bumpy ['bʌmpi], a. **1.** (Chemin, etc.) cahoteux, défoncé. **2.** Couvert de bosses.

bun [bʌn], s. **1.** Cu: Petit pain au lait (avec ou sans raisins). **2.** (Cheveux enroulés en) chignon m.

bunch¹ [bʌnʃ], s. (a) Botte f (de radis); bouquet m (de fleurs); grappe f (de raisin); houppe f (de plumes); trousseau m (de clefs); flot m (de rubans); régime m (de bananes); poignée f (de brindilles, etc.). (b) F: Groupe m (de personnes). F: He's the best of the bunch, c'est lui le meilleur (de la bande).

bunch². **1.** v.tr. Grouper; botteler (des radis, etc.); lier (des fleurs) en bouquet. **2.** v.i. To bunch (together), se presser en foule; se serrer; se pelotonner.

bundle¹ ['bʌndl], s. Paquet m (de linge, etc.); ballot m (de marchandises); botte f (d'asperges, etc.); faisceau m (de cannes, de fils); liasse f (de papiers); fagot m (de bois).

bundle², v.tr. (a) To bundle (up), empaqueter; mettre, lier, (qch.) en paquet; mettre (des documents) en liasse. F: To b. everything up, tout ramasser en pagaïe. (b) F: To bundle s.o. out of the house, jeter, flanquer, qn à la porte. To b. sth. into a corner, fourrer qch. dans un coin. To bundle s.o. off, se débarrasser de qn (sans cérémonie).

bung¹ [bʌŋ], s. Bondon m (de fût); tampon m de liège. **'bung-hole**, s. Bonde f.

bung², v.tr. To bung (up), bondonner (un fût); boucher (un orifice). F: Eyes bunged up, yeux pochés.

bung³, v.tr. P: Lancer, jeter (des pierres, etc.).

bungalow ['bʌŋgalo, -ou), s. **1.** (In India) Bungalow m; villa f à véranda. **2.** F: Maison f sans étage.

bungle¹ ['bʌŋgl], s. Gâchis m, maladresse f, bousillage m. To make a bungle of sth., bousiller, gâcher, qch.

bungle², v.tr. Bousiller, gâcher, saboter, P: louper (un travail); rater (une affaire). **bungling¹**, a. Maladroit. B: attempt, tentative gauche. **bungling²**, s. **1.** Bousillage m, gâchis m. **2.** Maladresse f.

bungler ['bʌŋglə/r], s. (a) Bousilleur, -euse (de travail); gâcheur, -euse. (b) Maladroit, -e.

bunion ['bʌnjən], s. Med: F: Oignon m.

bunk¹ [bʌŋk], s. (a) Lit-placard m. (b) Nau: Rail: Couchette f.

bunk², v.i. & s. F: To bunk (off), to do a bunk, déguerpir, filer, décamper.

bunk³, s. U.S: P: = BUNKUM.

bunker¹ ['bʌŋkə/r], s. **1.** Nau: Soute f (à charbon, etc.). **2.** Golf: Banquette f.

bunker², v.tr. **1.** Nau: Mettre (du charbon) en soute. **2.** To be bunkered, (i) Golf: se trouver derrière une banquette; (ii) F: se trouver dans une impasse.

bunkum ['bʌŋkəm], s. F: Blague f, bêtises fpl. That's all bunkum! tout ça c'est des histoires, des balivernes!

bunny ['bʌni], s. F: Jeannot lapin m.

bunting¹ ['bʌntiŋ], s. Orn: Bruant m. Corn bunting, common bunting, bruant proyer.

bunting², s. **1.** Tex: Étamine f (à pavillon). **2.** Coll: Drapeaux m, pavillons m. To put out bunting, pavoiser.

buoy¹ [bɔi], s. Nau: Bouée f; balise flottante. Mooring-buoy, (bouée de) corps-mort m. To put down a buoy, mouiller une bouée. S.a. BELL-BUOY, BREECHES-BUOY, LIFE-BUOY. **'buoy-rope**, s. Orin m.

buoy², v.tr. Nau: **1.** To buoy up an object, faire flotter un objet; soutenir un objet sur l'eau.

F: To buoy s.o. up, soutenir, appuyer, qn. **2.** Baliser (un chenal).

buoyancy ['bɔiənsi], s. **1.** (a) Flottabilité f (d'un objet); légèreté f sur l'eau. (b) Poussée f (d'un liquide). Centre of buoyancy, centre de poussée. **2.** F: Entrain m; élasticité f de caractère.

buoyant ['bɔiənt], a. **1.** (a) Flottable; léger. (b) *Salt water is more b. than fresh,* l'eau salée porte mieux que l'eau douce. **2.** F: (Of pers.) Plein d'entrain; qui a du ressort. B. step, pas élastique. Com: B. market, marché soutenu.

bur [bə:r], s. Bot: (a) Capsule épineuse. (Of burdock) Bouton m de pompier; teigne f (de bardane). Chestnut-bur, bogue f. Teasel-bur, carde f. (b) = BURDOCK. (c) F: (Of pers.) Crampon m. 'bur-walnut, s. (Plaqué m en) ronce de noyer.

Burberry ['bə:rberi], s. Imperméable m (de la marque Burberry).

burble¹ [bə:rbl], s. Murmure m (de paroles); sons inarticulés.

burble², v.i. (a) Murmurer (des sons inarticulés). (b) F: Débiter des inepties.

burbot ['bə:rbət], s. Ich: Lotte f, barbot m.

burden¹ [bə:rdn], s. **1.** (a) Fardeau m, charge f. The burden of years, of taxation, le poids des années, des impôts. Jur: Burden of proof, charge de la preuve. To be a b. to s.o., être à charge à qn. To become a b. on s.o., tomber à la charge de qn. To make s.o.'s life a b., rendre la vie dure à qn. Beast of burden, bête de somme, de charge. (b) Nau: Charge, contenance f, d'un navire. Ship of five thousand tons burden, navire qui jauge cinq mille tonneaux. **2.** (a) Refrain m (d'une chanson). (b) Substance f, fond m (d'un discours, d'une plainte).

burden², v.tr. Charger, alourdir (s.o. with sth., qn de qch.). Burdened estate, domaine grevé d'hypothèques.

burdensome ['bə:rdnsəm], a. Onéreux (to, à); fâcheux, ennuyeux.

burdock ['bə:rdɔk], s. Bardane f, glouteron m.

bureau, pl. -eaux ['bjuərou, -ouz], s. **1.** Furn: Bureau m; secrétaire m. **2.** (a) (Office) Bureau. *Information b.,* office m de renseignements. (b) U.S: Bureau; service m (du gouvernement).

bureaucracy [bjuə'roukrəsi], s. Bureaucratie f.

bureaucrat ['bjuərokrat], s. Bureaucrate m; F: rond-de-cuir m.

burette [bjuə'ret], s. **1.** Ecc: Burette f. **2.** Ch: Éprouvette graduée.

burgee [bə:r'dʒi:], s. Nau: Guidon m, cornette f (d'un yacht).

burgeon¹,² ['bə:rdʒ(ə)n], s. & v.i. Lit: = BUD¹,².

burgess ['bə:rdʒes], s.n. Bourgeois m, citoyen m.

burgh ['bʌrə], s. Scot: Bourg m.

burgher ['bə:rgər], s. Hist: Bourgeois m, citoyen m.

burglar ['bə:rglər], s. Cambrioleur m; dévaliseur m de maisons. S.a. CAT-BURGLAR. 'burglar-proof, a. (Coffre-fort) incrochetable, inviolable.

burglarious [bə:r'glɛəriəs], a. (Tentative) de cambriolage. -ly, adv. Avec effraction.

burglary ['bə:rgləri], s. (a) Jur: Vol m de nuit avec effraction. (b) F: Vol avec effraction; cambriolage m.

burgle [bə:rgl], v.tr. F: Cambrioler, dévaliser (une maison).

burgomaster ['bə:rgomɑːstər], s. Bourgmestre m.

Burgundian [bə:r'gʌndiən], a. & s. Geog: Bourguignon, -onne.

Burgundy ['bə:rgəndi]. **1.** Pr.n. La Bourgogne. **2.** s. (Vin m de) bourgogne m.

burial ['beriəl], s. Enterrement m, inhumation f. Christian burial, sépulture f en terre sainte. 'burial-ground, s. Cimetière m. 'burial-service, s. Office m des morts.

burke [bə:rk], v.tr. Étouffer, étrangler (un scandale). To burke the question, escamoter la vraie question.

burlap ['bə:rlap], s. Toile f d'emballage.

burlesque¹ [bə:r'lesk]. **1.** a. Burlesque. **2.** s. (a) Burlesque m. (b) Parodie f.

burlesque², v.tr. Travestir, parodier.

burly ['bə:rli], a. Solidement bâti. A big burly fellow, un grand gaillard de forte carrure.

Burma(h) ['bə:rma]. Pr.n. La Birmanie.

Burman ['bə:rmən], **Burmese** [bə:r'mi:z], a. & s. Birman, -ane.

burn¹ [bə:rn], s. Brûlure f.

burn², v. (burnt; burnt; occ. burned; burned) **1.** v.tr. (a) Brûler. To b. sth. to ashes, réduire qch. en cendres. To b. one's fingers, se brûler les doigts. F: He burnt his fingers over it, il lui en a cuit. To be burnt alive, être brûlé vif. To be burnt to death, être brûlé vif; (in house fire, etc.) être carbonisé. F: Money burns his fingers, burns a hole in his pocket, l'argent lui fond dans les mains. To have money to burn, avoir de l'argent à n'en savoir que faire. S.a. BOAT¹, CANDLE I. (b) Ind: Cuire (des briques). (c) Surg: Cautériser (une plaie). F: This memory has burnt (itself) into my mind, ce souvenir s'est gravé, reste gravé, dans ma mémoire. **2.** v.i. (a) Brûler. To burn like matchwood, flamber comme une allumette. To burn like tinder, brûler comme de l'amadou; brûler sec. My head burns, la tête me brûle. My wound was burning, ma blessure cuisait. To burn with desire, brûler de désir. To b. to do sth., brûler de faire qch. To b. with impatience, griller d'impatience. (b) I.C.E: (Of mixture) Exploser. **burn away. 1.** v.tr. Brûler, consumer (qch.). **2.** v.i. Se consumer. **burn down,** v.tr. Brûler, incendier (une ville, etc.). **burn in,** v.tr. Graver (qch.) par le feu. **burn off,** v.tr. Brûler, décaper (la peinture). **burn out. 1.** v.tr. (a) To burn s.o.'s eyes out, brûler les yeux à qn. (b) To burn s.o. out, chasser qn par le feu. (c) The candle has burnt itself out, la chandelle s'est brûlée jusqu'au bout. (d) El: Brûler, court-circuiter (une bobine); griller (une lampe). **2.** v.i. Se consumer; brûler; (of electric lamp) griller. **burn up. 1.** v.tr. Brûler (entièrement); consumer. **2.** v.i. (Of fire) Se ranimer, flamber.

burnt, a. **1.** (a) Brûlé, carbonisé. A burnt child dreads the fire, expérience passe science. (b) Face b. by the sun, figure bronzée par le soleil. **2.** Burnt taste, goût de brûlé. **burning¹,** a. **1.** Brûlant, ardent. Burning question, question brûlante. **2.** B. coals, du charbon embrasé, allumé. B. town, ville incendiée, en feu. burning-'hot, a. Brûlant. **burning²,** s. **1.** Brûlage m; incendie m (d'une maison). B. sensation, (i) sensation de chaleur; (ii) douleur cuisante. There is a smell of burning, ça sent le brûlé. **2.** (a) Cuite f, cuisson f (de briques, de tuiles). (b) Fournée f.

burn³, s. Scot: Ruisseau m.

burner ['bə:rnər], s. **1.** (Pers.) Brûleur, -euse. **2.** (a) (Of gas-cooker, etc.) Brûleur. (b) Bec m (de gaz). Incandescent burner, bec Auer.

burnet ['bə:rnet], s. Bot: Grande pimprenelle.

burnish¹ ['bə:rniʃ], s. Bruni m, brunissure f.

burnish². 1. v.tr. (a) Brunir; polir, lisser (un métal). (b) Phot: Satiner (une épreuve). **2.** v.i. Se polir; prendre de l'éclat. burnish-

ing, s. (a) Brunissage m, polissage m, lissage m. (b) Satinage m.

urnisher ['bə:rniʃər], s. **1.** (Pers.) (a) Brunisseur m. (b) Satineur m. **2.** Tls: Brunissoir m.

urr¹ [bə:r], s. = BURR.

urr², s. **1.** Engr: Metalw: Barbe f, bavure f. **2.** Ling: 'R' de la gorge (fricative postpalatale). To speak with a burr, prononcer l'r de la gorge.

urr³, v.tr. **1.** To burr one's r's, prononcer l'r de la gorge. **2.** Mater (l'extrémité d'un boulon, etc.); rabattre (un clou).

urrow¹ ['bʌro], s. Terrier m (de renard, de lapin). F: Never to leave one's b., ne jamais sortir de sa coquille.

urrow². **1.** v.i. (Of rabbits, etc.) (i) Fouir la terre; (ii) (se) terrer. F: To b. into the archives, fouiller dans les archives. **2.** v.tr. To b. one's way underground, creuser un chemin sous terre.

urrower ['bʌroər, -rouər], s. (Animal) fouisseur m.

oursar ['bə:rsər], s. **1.** (At Engl. universities) Économe m. **2.** (In Scot.) Boursier, -ière.

bursary ['bə:rsəri], s. **1.** Économat m. **2.** (In Scot.) Bourse f (d'études).

burst¹ [bə:rst], s. **1.** Éclatement m, explosion f (d'une bombe, etc.). **2.** Jaillissement m, jet m (de flamme); coup m (de tonnerre); éclat m (de rire); salve f (d'applaudissements). B. of activity, emballement m; poussée f d'activité. B. of gun-fire, rafale f. Sp: B. of speed, emballage m.

burst², v. (burst; burst) **1.** v.i. (a) (Of boiler, bomb, etc.) Éclater, exploser, faire explosion; (of boiler) sauter; (of abscess) crever, percer; (of bubble, tyre) crever; (of bud) éclore. To burst in pieces, voler en éclats. (b) The sacks were bursting, les sacs étaient pleins à crever; les sacs regorgeaient. To be bursting with laughter, crever de rire. To be bursting with health, déborder, regorger, de santé. Bursting with impatience, bouillant d'impatience. I was bursting to tell him so, je mourais d'envie de le lui dire. (c) A cry burst from his lips, un cri s'échappa de ses lèvres. (d) (Of flower) To burst into bloom, fleurir, s'épanouir. The horses burst into a gallop, les chevaux prirent le galop. To burst into tears, se mettre à pleurer; avoir une crise de larmes. S.a. FLAME¹ 1, SONG 1. (e) To burst into a room, entrer dans une chambre en coup de vent. (Of sun) To b. through a cloud, percer un nuage. (f) To burst upon s.o.'s sight, se présenter, se découvrir, aux yeux de qn. The truth burst (in) upon me, soudain la vérité m'apparut. **2.** v.tr. Faire éclater (qch.); crever, éclater (un ballon); faire sauter (une chaudière); rompre (ses liens). To burst a door open, enfoncer, briser, une porte. **burst asunder. 1.** v.tr. Rompre (ses liens). **2.** v.i. Se rompre. **burst forth,** v.i. (Of sun) Se montrer tout à coup; (of blood) jaillir. To b. forth into explanations, se répandre en explications. **burst in. 1.** v.tr. Enfoncer (une porte). **2.** v.i. Faire irruption; (of pers.) entrer en coup de vent. **burst open. 1.** v.tr. Enfoncer (une porte); faire sauter (le couvercle). **2.** v.i. (Of door) S'ouvrir tout d'un coup. **burst out,** v.i. (Of pers.) S'écrier, s'exclamer; (of liquid) jaillir. To burst out laughing, éclater, pouffer, de rire. **'burst-up,** F: **'bust-up,** s. **1.** Débâcle f (d'un système); faillite f (d'une maison de commerce). **2.** To have a b.-up with s.o., avoir une prise de bec avec qn; rompre avec qn. **bursting,** s. Éclatement m, explosion f (d'une chaudière); crevaison f (de pneu); rupture f (de liens).

burthen ['bə:rðən], s. & v.tr. Lit:= BURDEN¹, ².

bury ['beri], v.tr. (p.p. & p.t. buried) Enterrer, inhumer, ensevelir (un mort); enfouir (une bête). Buried in the ruins, enseveli sous les décombres. To b. a dagger in s.o.'s breast, enfoncer, plonger, un poignard dans la poitrine de qn. To bury one's face in one's hands, se couvrir la figure de ses mains. To b. oneself in one's studies, s'enfermer dans ses études. I found it buried under my papers, je l'ai trouvé enfoui sous mes papiers. **burying¹,** a. (Insecte) enfouisseur. **'burying beetle,** s. Ent: Nécrophore m. **burying²,** s. **1.** Enterrement m; ensevelissement m. **2.** Enfouissement m.

bus¹, pl. **buses** [bʌs, 'bʌsiz], s. Omnibus m. (Motor-)bus, autobus m. We went there by bus, nous y sommes allés en autobus. To miss the bus, (i) manquer, rater, l'autobus; (ii) F: laisser échapper l'occasion.

bus², v.i. F: Aller (i) en omnibus, (ii) en autobus.

busby ['bʌzbi], s. Bonnet m de hussard; colback m.

bush¹ [buʃ], s. **1.** (a) Buisson m; (of lilac, etc.) arbrisseau m. Rose-bush, rosier m. **Raspberry-bush,** framboisier m. (b) Fourré m, taillis m. S.a. BEAT² 1. **2.** (Vintner's) Bouchon m. S.a. WINE¹. **3.** (In Brit. Colonies) The bush, la brousse. **'bush-fighter,** s. Guérillero m. **'bush-fighting,** s. Guerre f de buissons, d'embuscades. **'bush-ranger,** s. Coureur m des bois, de la brousse.

bush², s. Mec.E: Fourrure f métallique; bague f; coussinet m (de palier).

bush³, v.tr. Mec.E: Baguer, manchonner; mettre un coussinet à (un palier). **bushing,** s. **1.** Manchonnage m. **2.** Manchon m; coussinet m métallique; douille f, bague f.

bushel [buʃl], s. Boisseau m (= approx. 36 litres).

bushman, pl. **-men** ['buʃmən, -men], s. **1.** Ethn: (In S. Africa) Boschiman m. **2.** Colon m (de la brousse australienne).

bushy ['buʃi], a. Touffu; épais, -aisse; buissonneux, broussailleux.

business ['biznəs], s. **1.** (a) Affaire f, besogne f, occupation f, devoir m. To make it one's business to do sth., se faire un devoir, se mettre en devoir, de faire qch. To have business with s.o., avoir affaire avec qn. That's the manager's b., ça c'est l'affaire du gérant. It is my business to . . ., c'est à moi de. . . . It's none of your business, ce n'est pas votre affaire; cela ne vous regarde pas. What b. had you to tell him so? était-ce à vous de le lui dire? F: To send s.o. about his business, envoyer promener qn. S.a. MIND² 2. It's a bad, a sorry, business, c'est une malheureuse affaire. F: Good business! à la bonne heure! (b) Business meeting, séance de travail (d'une société). The business before the meeting, l'agenda m; l'ordre m du jour. **2.** (a) Les affaires f. Business is business, les affaires sont les affaires. To set up in business as a grocer, s'établir épicier. To go into business, entrer dans les affaires. To follow a business, exercer un métier. To do business with s.o., faire des affaires avec qn. To give up business, se retirer des affaires. He is in b. for himself, il travaille à son compte. To be out of business, être retiré des affaires. Piece of business, affaire f; opération f (commerciale). To mean business, avoir des intentions sérieuses; ne pas plaisanter. Attrib. Business hours, heures d'ouverture, d'affaires, des affaires. Business house, maison de commerce. Business man, homme d'affaires. Big-

business man, brasseur *m* d'affaires. (*b*) Fonds *m* de commerce. *Manager of two different businesses,* directeur de deux établissements différents. **3.** *Th:* Jeux *mpl* de scène. **4.** *F:* Métier *m.* *To make a b. of one's religion,* faire métier de sa religion. **'business-like,** *a.* **1.** (*Of pers.*) Capable ; pratique ; (*of transaction*) régulier, sérieux. **2.** (*Of style*) Net, précis ; (*of manner*) sérieux, carré.

busk¹ [bʌsk]. *s.* Busc *m* (de corset).

busk², *v.i.* *Th:* *P:* (*Of actor*) Faire les plages en été ; cabotiner.

busker ['bʌskər], *s.* *Th:* *P:* Cabotin *m.*

buskin ['bʌskin], *s.* *Ant:* Cothurne *m.*

busman, *pl.* **-men** ['bʌsmən, -men], *s.m.* (i) Conducteur (d'autobus) ; (ii) receveur. *F:* *To take a busman's holiday,* faire du métier en guise de congé ou de loisirs.

bust [bʌst], *s.* **1.** *Sculp:* Buste *m.* **2.** Buste, gorge *f,* poitrine *f* (de femme). **'bust-bodice,** *s.* *Cost:* Soutien-gorge *m inv.*

bustard ['bʌstərd], *s.* *Orn:* Outarde *f.*

bustle¹ [bʌsl], *s.* Remue-ménage *m.*

bustle². **1.** *v.i.* To bustle (about), se remuer, s'activer, s'affairer ; faire l'empressé. *They bustle in and out,* ils entrent et sortent d'un air affairé. **2.** *v.tr.* Faire dépêcher (qn). *To bustle s.o. out of the house,* pousser qn dehors.

bustling, *a.* Affairé ; agissant, allant ; empressé.

bustle³, *s.* *Cost:* A: Tournure *f* (de derrière de jupe).

bust-up ['bʌstʌp], *s.* *P:* See BURST-UP.

busy¹ ['bizi], *a.* (busier) Affairé, occupé ; actif, allant. *B. day,* jour chargé. **The busy hours,** les heures de fort trafic ; (*in shops, etc.*) les heures d'affluence. *B. street,* rue mouvementée, passante. *To be busy at, with, over, sth.,* être occupé à, de, qch. *To be busy doing sth.,* être occupé à faire qch. ; être en train de faire qch. *To keep oneself busy,* s'activer. *F:* *To get busy,* se mettre à la tâche ; s'y mettre. **-ily,** *adv.* **1.** Activement ; avec empressement ; d'un air affairé. **2.** Avec trop de zèle.

busy², *v.tr. & pr.* *To b. oneself, one's hands, with sth.,* s'occuper à, se mêler de, qch. *To b. oneself* (*with*) *doing sth.,* s'occuper à, de, faire qch.

busybody ['bizibodi], *s.* Officieux, -euse ; tatillon, -onne ; important *m* ; la mouche du coche.

but [bʌt]. **1.** *conj.* (*a*) Mais. *A poor but honest family,* une famille pauvre mais honnête. *F:* *But I tell you I saw it !* (mais) puisque je vous dis que je l'ai vu ! *But yet . . .,* néanmoins ., toutefois. . . . (*b*) (*Subordinating*) *I never pass there but I think of you,* je ne passe jamais par là sans penser à vous. *Never a year passes but he writes to us,* il ne se passe jamais une année qu'il ne nous écrive. *Who knows but that he may come?* qui sait s'il ne viendra pas ? **I cannot but believe that . . .,** il m'est impossible de ne pas croire que. . . . *I do not doubt but that he will consent,* je ne doute pas qu'il (ne) consente. **Not but that I pity you,** non que je ne vous plaigne. **2.** *adv.* Ne . . . que ; seulement. *She is but a child,* ce n'est qu'une enfant. *He talks but little,* il parle assez peu. **But a moment ago,** il n'y a qu'un instant. **But yesterday,** pas plus tard qu'hier. *Had I but known!* si j'avais su ! *If I could but see him!* si je pouvais seulement le voir ! *S.a.* ALL I. 2. **3.** *conj. or prep.* (*Except*) (*a*) *Who will do it but me?* qui le fera si ce n'est moi, sinon moi? *All but he, but him,* tous excepté lui ; tous sauf lui. **None but he,** personne d'autre que lui. *Anyone but me,* tout autre que moi. *Anything but that,* tout plutôt que cela. *He is anything but a hero,*

il n'est rien moins qu'un héros. **There is nothing for it but to obey,** il n'y a qu'à obéir. *What could I do but invite him?* que pouvais-je faire d'autre que de l'inviter? *How could I but laugh?* comment pouvais-je faire autrement que de rire? (*b*) **But for, sans.** *But for you I was done for,* sans vous j'étais perdu. **But for that,** à part cela ; excepté cela.

butcher¹ ['butʃər], *s.* (*a*) Boucher *m.* **Butcher's shop, trade,** boucherie *f.* (*b*) *F:* Boucher, massacreur *m.* (*c*) *F:* Chirurgien incompétent ; *P:* charcutier *m.* **'butcher's 'broom,** *s. Bot:* Faux buis.

butcher², *v.tr.* **1.** Égorger, massacrer. **2.** *F:* Massacrer, saboter (un travail, une symphonie). (*Of surgeon*) *To b. a patient,* charcuter un patient.

butchering, *s.* **1.** Tuerie *f,* massacre *m* (*of,* de). **2.** *F:* The *b. trade,* la boucherie.

butchery ['butʃəri], *s.* **1.** (*Trade*) Boucherie *f.* **2.** *F:* Tuerie *f,* boucherie, massacre *m.*

butler ['bʌtlər], *s.* Maître *m* d'hôtel (d'une maison privée).

butt¹ [bʌt], *s.* (*a*) Barrique *f,* futaille *f* ; gros tonneau. (*b*) Tonneau *m* (pour l'eau de pluie).

butt², *s.* **1.** Bout *m* ; souche *f* (d'arbre, de chèque). *Join: etc:* Butt and butt, bout à bout. **2.** Gros bout, talon *m* (d'une canne à pêche). **3.** *Bill:* Masse *f,* talon (de la queue). **4.** *Sm.a:* Crosse *f* (de fusil). **5.** Poisson plat. **butt-'end,** *s.* **1.** Extrémité inférieure ; bout *m* ; gros bout. **2.** Couche *f* (d'un fusil). **'butt-joint,** *s.* *Carp: Mec.E: etc:* Assemblage *m* bout à bout ; joint *m* en about.

butt³, *s.* **1.** *Mil:* (*Stop-butt*) Butte *f.* **The butts,** le champ de tir. **2.** (*Thing aimed at*) But *m.* *Esp.* (*Of pers.*) Souffre-douleur *m inv.* **To be a butt for s.o.'s jokes,** servir de plastron à qn.

butt⁴, *s.* Coup *m* de (la) tête ; coup de corne (d'un bélier, etc.).

butt⁵, *v.i. & tr.* To butt (into, against) sth., donner du front, buter, contre qch. (*Of ram, etc.*) *To b.* (*at*) *s.o.,* donner un coup de corne à qn. *F:* *To b. into the conversation,* to butt in, intervenir sans façon dans la conversation).

butter¹ ['bʌtər], *s.* **1.** Beurre *m.* *Whiting with melted b.,* merlan sauce au beurre. *With brown butter sauce,* au beurre noir, au roux. *F:* Butter wouldn't melt in her mouth, elle a l'air de ne pas y toucher. **2.** *P:* Flatterie *f,* flagornerie *f.* **'butter-bean,** *s.* *Hort:* Haricot *m* beurre. **'butter-cloth, -muslin,** *s.* Gaze *f* à envelopper le beurre ; étamine *f.* **'butter-dish,** *s.* Beurrier *m.* **'butter-fingered,** *a.* Maladroit, empoté. **'butter-fingers,** *s.* Maladroit, -e ; empoté, -ée. **'butter-scotch,** *s.* Caramel *m* au beurre.

butter², *v.tr.* Beurrer (du pain). *S.a.* BREAD. *F:* *To butter s.o. up,* flatter, pateliner, qn.

buttercup ['bʌtərkʌp], *s.* *Bot:* Renoncule *f* des champs ; *F:* bouton *m* d'or.

butterfly ['bʌtərflai], *s.* **1.** *Ent:* Papillon *m.* *S.a.* BOW¹ 3. **2.** *F:* Personne *f* frivole ; papillon.

buttermilk ['bʌtərmilk], *s.* Babeurre *m.*

buttery ['bʌtəri], *s.* *Sch:* Dépense *f,* office *f.*

buttock ['bʌtək], *s.* **1.** (*a*) Fesse *f.* (*b*) *pl.* The buttocks, le derrière, le postérieur, les fesses. (*c*) *Cu:* Culotte *f* (de bœuf). **2.** *pl.* Croupe *f* (de cheval, de bœuf).

button¹ [bʌtn], *s.* **1.** Bouton *m* (pour attacher). *Bachelor's buttons,* boutons mobiles (pour vêtements). **Button boots,** bottines à boutons. **Boy in buttons,** *F:* buttons, chasseur *m* (d'hôtel, de club) ; groom *m.* **2.** (*a*) Bouton(-pressoir) *m* (de sonnerie électrique, d'appareil photographique). *F:* **You've only to press the button,** ça se fait tout seul ; c'est automatique. (*b*) Bouton, mouche *f* (de fleuret). (*c*) Bouton (pour tourner). *Knurled b.*, bouton moleté. (*d*) *Bot:* Bouton (de rose, de champignon). **'button-hole¹,** *s.* **1.** Boutonnière *f.* *F:* **To wear a button-hole,** porter une fleur à sa boutonnière. **Button-hole stitch,** point de feston, de boutonnière. **2.** *Surg:* Boutonnière ; petite incision. **'button-hole²,** *v.tr.* *F:* *To b.-h. s.o.*, retenir, cramponner, accrocher, qn (au passage). **'button-hook,** *s.* Tire-bouton *m.* **'button-stick,** *s.* *Mil: etc:* Patience *f.*

button², *v.tr.* **1.** (*a*) **To button (up) sth.,** boutonner qch. (*b*) (*With passive force*) *Dress that buttons behind*, robe qui se boutonne par derrière. **2.** *Fenc:* Moucheter (une épée).

buttress¹ ['bʌtres], *s.* *Const:* Contrefort *m,* contre-boutant *m.* *F:* **The buttresses of society,** les piliers *m* de la société. *S.a.* FLYING-BUTTRESS.

buttress², *v.tr.* *Const:* Arc-bouter, étayer.

buxom ['bʌksəm], *a.* (Femme) aux formes plastiques ; (femme) fraîche et rondelette

buy [bai], *v.tr.* (**bought; bought**) (*a*) Acheter (*sth. from, of, s.o.*, qch. à qn) ; prendre (un billet de chemin de fer, etc.). *I bought this horse cheap*, j'ai eu ce cheval à bon marché. **To buy and sell,** brocanter ; faire le brocantage. *Money cannot buy it*, cela ne se paie pas. **A dear-bought advantage,** un avantage chèrement payé. (*b*) **To buy s.o. sth.,** acheter qch. à, pour, qn. **buy back,** *v.tr.* Racheter. **buying back,** *s.* Rachat *m.* **buy in,** *v.tr.* **1.** (*At auction sales*) Racheter (pour le compte du vendeur). **2.** S'approvisionner de (denrées, etc.). **buy off,** *v.tr.* Se débarrasser de (qn) en lui payant une somme d'argent ; *F:* acheter (qn). **buy out,** *v.tr.* Désintéresser (un associé). **buy over,** *v.tr.* Corrompre, acheter (qn). **buy up,** *v.tr.* Rafler, accaparer (des denrées, etc.). **buying up,** *s.* Accaparement *m.*

buyer ['baiər], *s.* **1.** Acheteur, -euse ; acquéreur *m.* **2.** *Com:* Chef *m* de rayon.

buzz¹ [bʌz], *s.* Bourdonnement *m,* vrombissement *m* (d'un insecte) ; brouhaha *m* (de conversations). *W.Tel:* Ronflement *m* ; (bruits *mpl* de) friture *f.*

buzz². **1.** *v.i.* Bourdonner, vrombir. **My ears were buzzing,** les oreilles me tintaient. **2.** *v.tr.* *P:* Lancer (une pierre, etc.). **buzz about, around,** *v.i.* *F:* S'activer ; faire l'empressé ; faire la mouche du coche. **buzz off,** *v.i.* *P:* Décamper, filer. **buzzing,** *s.* = BUZZ¹. **Buzzing in the ears,** tintement *m* des oreilles ; *Med:* bourdonnement *m.*

buzzard ['bʌzərd], *s.* *Orn:* Buse *f,* busard *m.*

buzzer ['bʌzər], *s.* (*a*) *Nau:* *Ind:* Sirène *f.* (*b*) *Aut:* Klaxon *m.* (*c*) *El:* *Tp:* Appel *m* phonique ; vibreur *m,* vibrateur *m.*

by [bai]. I. *prep.* **1.** (*Near*) (*a*) (Au)près de, à côté de. *Sitting by the fire*, assis près du feu. *By the sea*, au bord de la mer. **By oneself,** seul ; à l'écart. *He kept by himself*, il se tenait à l'écart. **I have no money by me,** (i) je n'ai pas d'argent sous la main ; (ii) je n'ai pas d'argent disponible. (*b*) *North by East*, Nord quart nord-est. **2.** (*Along, via*) Par. **By land and sea,** par terre et par mer. **3.** (*Agency, means*) (*a*) Par, de. *To be punished by s.o.*, être puni par qn. *To die by one's own hand*, mourir de ses propres mains. **Made by hand, by machinery,** fait à la main, à la machine. **Known by the name of X,** connu sous le nom d'X. **By force,** de force. **By (an) error,** par suite d'une erreur. **By chance,** par hasard. **To do sth. (all) by oneself,** faire qch. (tout) seul. **Three feet by two,** trois pieds sur deux. **To travel by rail,** voyager par le, *F:* en, chemin de fer. **By tram, by car, by motor cycle, by mule,** en tramway, en auto, à motocyclette, à dos de mulet. (*b*) (*With gerund*) *By doing that you will offend him*, en faisant cela vous l'offenserez. *What do you gain by doing that?* que gagnez-vous à faire cela ? *We shall lose nothing by waiting*, nous ne perdrons rien pour attendre. **4. By rote,** par routine. **By right,** de droit. **By rights,** à la rigueur. *By the clock it is three*, d'après l'horloge il est trois heures. *To judge by appearances*, juger sur l'apparence. **By (the terms of) article 5 . . .,** aux termes, selon les termes, de l'article 5. . . . **To sell sth. by the pound,** vendre qch. à la livre. **5. By degrees,** par degrés. **By turn(s),** tour à tour. **One by one,** un à un. *By twos and threes*, par deux ou trois. **6. By day,** de jour, le jour. **7.** (*Of point in time*) *He will be here by three o'clock*, il sera ici avant, pour, trois heures. *By Monday*, d'ici lundi. *He ought to be here* **by now, by this time,** il devrait être déjà ici. **8.** *Longer by two feet*, plus long de deux pieds. **By far,** de beaucoup. **9. I know him by name, by sight,** je le connais de nom, de vue. *He is a grocer by trade*, il est épicier de son métier. **To do one's duty by s.o.,** faire son devoir envers qn. **10.** (*In oaths*) **By God,** au nom de Dieu. *To swear by all one holds sacred*, jurer par tout ce qu'on a de plus sacré. II **by,** *adv.* **1.** Près. **Close by, hard by,** tout près, ici près, tout à côté. *Nau:* **By and large!** près et plein ! *F:* **Taking it by and large . . .,** à tout prendre. . . . **2.** (*Aside*) **To lay, set, put, sth. by,** mettre qch. de côté. **3.** (*Past*) **To go, pass, by,** passer. *The time is gone by when . . .*, le temps est passé où. . . . **4.** *Adv.phr.* **By and by,** tout à l'heure, bientôt, tantôt. **By the by(e) . . .,** à propos. . . . III. **by(e¹),** *a.* **By(e) effect,** effet secondaire, indirect ; contre-coup *m.* **'by-election,** *s.* *Parl:* Élection *f* de remplacement. **'by-issue,** *s.* Question *f* d'intérêt secondaire. **'by-motive,** *s.* Mobile *m* secondaire. **'by-name,** *s.* = NICKNAME¹. **'by-pass¹,** *s.* **1.** *Mch: etc:* Conduit *m* de dérivation. **2.** (*Of gas burner*) Veilleuse *f.* **3.** *Aut: etc:* **By-pass (road),** route *f* d'évitement, de contournement. **4.** *W.Tel:* Filtre *m.* **By-pass condenser,** condensateur shunté. **'by-pass²,** *v.tr.* **1.** (*a*) *Mch:* Amener (la vapeur, etc.) en dérivation. (*b*) *W.Tel:* Filtrer (un poste émetteur). **2.** (*a*) (*Of road or pers.*) Contourner, éviter (une ville, etc.). (*b*) *To by-p. the traffic*, dévier la circulation. **'by-path,** *s.* Sentier écarté, détourné. **'by-play,** *s.* *Th:* Jeu *m* accessoire ; aparté mimé. **'by-plot,** *s.* *Th:* Intrigue *f* secondaire. **'by-product,** *s.* *Ind:* Sous-produit *m* ; produit secondaire ; dérivé *m.* **'by-road,** *s.* (*a*) Chemin détourné. (*b*) Chemin vicinal. **'by-street,** *s.* Rue écartée ; ruelle *f.* **'by-way,** *s.* Chemin détourné, voie indirecte. **By-ways of history,** à-côtés *m* de l'histoire. **'by-word,** *s.* **1.** Proverbe *m,* dicton *m.* **2. To be the by-word of the village,** être la fable, la risée, du village.

bye² [bai], *s.* **1.** *Cr:* Balle passée. **2.** *Sp:* (*Of player*) **To have a bye,** être exempt (d'une épreuve dans un tournoi).

bye-bye ['bai 'bai]. **1.** *int.* *F:* Adieu ! au revoir ! **2.** *s.* *F:* **To go to bye-bye,** aller faire dodo.

by(e)-law ['bailɔː], *s.* Statut *m* émanant d'une autorité locale ; arrêté municipal.

bygone ['baigɔn]. **1.** *a.* Passé, écoulé, ancien, d'autrefois. *In b. days*, dans l'ancien temps.

2. *s.pl.* **Let bygones be bygones,** oublions le passé; passons 'éponge (là-dessus).
byre ['baiər], *s.* Vacherie *f*; étable *f* à vaches.
Byronic [bai'rɔnik], *a.* Byronien.

bystander ['baistandər], *s.* Assistant *m*; spectateur, -trice.
Byzantine [bi'zantain], *a. & s.* Byzantin, -ine.
Byzantium [bi'zan∫jəm]. *Pr.n. Geog:* Byzance *f*

C

C, c [siː]. **1.** (La lettre) C, c *m.* **2.** *Mus:* Ut *m*, do *m. In C sharp,* en ut dièse. **3.** *Mil: F:* C.B., *see* BARRACK[1] **1. 4. A C3 man,** homme classé dans la dernière catégorie par le conseil de révision. *F:* C3 *nation,* nation aveulie.
cab [kab], *s.* **1.** Voiture *f* de place. (*a*) Fiacre *m.* (*b*) *A:* (*Hansom cab*) Cab *m.* (*c*) Taxi *m* (automobile). *To call a cab,* héler un taxi; faire avancer un taxi. **2.** Guérite *f*, cabine *f* (de conducteur de camion, etc.); abri *m*, poste *m* de conduite (de locomotive). **'cab-driver,** *s.* = CABMAN. **'cab-horse,** *s.* Cheval *m* de fiacre. **'cab-rank, -stand,** *s.* Station *f* de fiacres; stationnement *m.* **'cab-spectacles, -windows,** *s. pl. Rail:* Lunettes *f* (de la locomotive).
cabal[1] [ka'bal], *s.* **1.** Cabale *f*, brigue *f*. **2.** Coterie *f*.
cabal[2], *v.i.* (caballed) Cabaler, comploter.
cabaret ['kabərei], *s.* **1.** Cabaret *m* (genre montmartrois). **2. Cabaret (show),** concert *m* genre music-hall (donné dans un restaurant, etc.).
cabbage ['kabedʒ], *s.* Chou *m, pl.* choux. **Garden cabbage,** chou pommé, chou cabus. **'cabbage-lettuce,** *s.* Laitue pommée. **'cabbage-patch,** *s.* Carré *m*, plant *m*, de choux. **'cabbage-stump,** *s.* Trognon *m* de chou.
cab(b)ala ['kabala], *s. Jew.Rel.H:* Cabale *f*.
cab(b)alistic [kaba'listik], *a.* Cabalistique.
cabby ['kabi], *s. F:* Cocher *m* (de fiacre).
caber ['keibər], *s. Sp:* Tronc *m* de mélèze, de pin, ou de sapin. **Tossing the caber,** sport écossais qui consiste à lancer le tronc (tenu verticalement par le petit bout) de manière à le faire retomber aussi loin que possible sur le gros bout.
cabin[1] ['kabin], *s.* **1.** (*a*) Cabane *f*, case *f*. (*b*) *Rail:* Guérite *f*, cabine *f*, vigie *f* (de signaux). (*c*) *El.Rail:* Driver's cabin, loge *f*; poste *m* de conduite. **2.** *Nau:* Cabine. (*b*) *Av:* Carlingue *f.* **'cabin-boy,** *s.m. Nau:* Mousse. **'cabin-trunk,** *s.* Malle *f* (de) cabine; malle (de) paquebot.
cabin[2], *v.tr.* Enfermer (qn à l'étroit).
cabinet ['kabinet], *s.* **1.** (*a*) Meuble *m* à tiroirs. Music-cabinet, casier *m* à musique. (*b*) Wireless cabinet, coffret *m*, ébénisterie *f*, de poste de radio. (*c*) Glass cabinet, vitrine *f*. **2.** (*a*) *A:* Petite chambre; cabinet *m.* (*b*) *Pol:* Cabinet, ministère *m.* Cabinet minister, ministre d'État. *C. crisis,* crise ministérielle. **3.** *Phot:* Cabinet size, format album. **'cabinet-maker,** *s.* Ébéniste *m.* **'cabinet-work,** *s.* Ébénisterie *f*.
cable[1] ['keibl], *s.* **1.** *Nau: etc:* Câble *m.* Cable('s)-length (*one-tenth of a nautical mile,* = 185.2 *m.*), encâblure *f*. **2.** *Nau:* Chaîne *f* (d'ancre). **3.** *El.E:* Câble. **To lay a cable,** poser un câble. **4.** = CABLEGRAM. **'cable-address,** *s.* Câble-adresse *f*. **'cable-laid,** *a.* (Cordage) commis en grelin. **'cable-laying,** *s.* Pose *f* de câbles sous-marins. **'cable-'rail-**

way, *s.* Funiculaire *m.* **'cable-re'lease,** *s.* *Phot:* Déclencheur *m.* **'cable-ship,** *s.* Câblier *m* **'cable-stitch,** *s. Knitting:* Point natté.
cable[2], *v.tr.* Câbler (un message). *Abs.* **To cable (to) s.o.,** câbler à qn; aviser qn par câble.
cablegram ['keiblgram], *s.* Câblogramme *m.*
cabman, *pl.* **-men** ['kabmən, -men], *s.m.* Cocher de fiacre.
caboodle [ka'buːdl], *s. P:* **The whole caboodle,** tout le bazar; tout le tremblement.
caboose [ka'buːs], *s. Nau:* Cuisine *f*.
ca'canny ['kɑː'kani]. **1.** *int. Scot:* Allez-y doucement! **2.** *v.i. F:* **To ca'canny,** travailler sans se (la) fouler; *Ind:* faire la grève perlée.
cacao [ka'kɑːo, ka'keio], *s.* **1.** Cacao(-bean), cacao *m.* **2.** Cacaotier *m.*
cachalot ['ka∫alɔt], *s. Z:* Cachalot *m.*
cache[1] [ka∫], *s.* Cache *f*, cachette *f* (d'explorateur).
cache[2], *v.tr.* Mettre (des provisions, etc.) dans une cache.
cachet ['ka∫e], *s.* **1.** (*Of a work, etc.*) *To have a certain c.,* avoir un certain cachet. **2.** (i) Cachet (d'aspirine), (ii) capsule *f* (d'huile de foie de morue).
cachou ['ka∫uː], *s.* Cachou *m.*
cackle[1] [kakl], *s.* **1.** (*Of hen, F: of pers.*) Caquet *m. F:* **Cut your cackle!** en voilà assez! **2.** Ricanement *m*; rire saccadé.
cackle[2], *v.i.* **1.** (*Of hen*) Caqueter. **2.** Ricaner; faire entendre un petit rire sec.
cacophony [ka'kɔfoni], *s.* Cacophonie *f*.
cactus ['kaktəs], *s. Bot:* Cactus *m*, cactier *m.*
cad [kad], *s.m.* **1.** Goujat, pleutre, cuistre *m.* **2.** Canaille *m; P:* fripouille *f*, arsouille *m.*
cadastral [ka'dastr(ə)l], *a.* Cadastral, -aux. *C. survey,* cadastre *m.*
cadaveric [kada'verik], *a.* (Rigidité) cadavérique
cadaverous [ka'davərəs], *a.* Cadavéreux.
caddie[1] ['kadi], *s. Golf:* Cadet *m*, caddie *m*
caddie[2], *v.i. Golf:* Servir de cadet (*for s.o.,* à qn).
caddis ['kadis], *s.* Caddis(-fly), phrygane *f.* Caddis(-worm), *Fish:* caddis-bait, larve *f* de phrygane.
caddish ['kadi∫], *a. F:* Voyou, arsouille.
caddishness ['kadi∫nəs], *s.* Goujaterie *f*.
caddy ['kadi], *s.* (Tea-)caddy, boîte *f* à thé.
cadence ['keidəns], *s.* **1.** Cadence *f*, rythme *m*, battement *m.* **2.** *Mus:* Cadence. **3. Cadence o!** the voice, (i) chute *f* de la voix; (ii) intonation *f*
cadet [ka'det], *s.m.* **1.** *A:* (*Younger son*) Cadet. **2.** (*a*) Élève d'une école militaire; cadet. (*b*) *Sch:* Membre d'un bataillon scolaire. **Cadet corps,** bataillon scolaire.
cadge [kadʒ], *v.tr. & i.* **1.** Colporter. **2.** (*a*) Mendier. (*b*) Écornifler, chiner (qch.).
cadger ['kadʒər], *s.m.* **1.** Marchand ambulant; colporteur *m.* **2.** (*a*) Mendiant. (*b*) Écornifleur ; chineur.
Cadiz ['keidiz]. *Pr.n. Geog:* Cadix.
cadmium ['kadmiəm], *s. Ch:* Cadmium *m.*

Caesar ['si:zər]. *Pr.n.m.* **Julius Caesar,** Jules César.

caesium ['si:ziəm], *s. Ch:* Césium *m.*

caesura [si'zjuərə], *s. Pros:* Césure *f.*

café ['kafe], *s.* Café(-restaurant) *m.*

cafeteria [kafə'ti:əriə], *s.* Restaurant *m* où les clients se servent eux-mêmes ; caféterie *f.*

cage¹ [ke:idʒ], *s.* **I.** Cage *f.* **2.** (*a*) Cabine *f* (d'ascenseur). (*b*) *Min:* **Shaft-cage,** cage de puits. **'cage-bird,** *s.* Oiseau *m* de volière.

cage², *v.tr.* Encager ; mettre (un oiseau) en cage.

cahoot [kə'hu:t], *s. U.S: F:* **To be in cahoot(s) with s.o.,** être d'intelligence avec qn ; *F:* être de mèche avec qn.

caiman ['keimən], *s. Rept:* = CAYMAN.

Cain [kein]. *Pr.n.m. B:* Caïn. *F:* **To raise Cain,** (i) faire un bruit infernal ; (ii) faire une scène (à propos de qch.).

cairn ['kɛərn], *s.* Cairn (commémoratif) ; mont-joie *m, pl.* monts-joie.

Cairo ['kairo]. *Pr.n. Geog:* Le Caire.

caisson ['keis(ə)n], *s. Hyd.E:* Caisson *m,* bâtardeau *m.*

caitiff ['keitif], *s. A:* Misérable *m* ; lâche *m.*

cajole [kə'dʒoul], *v.tr.* Cajoler ; enjôler. **To c. s.o. into doing sth.,** persuader à qn de faire qch. **To c. sth. out of s.o.,** obtenir qch. de qn à force de cajoleries ; soutirer (de l'argent) à qn.

cajoling, *a.* Cajoleur, -euse.

cajolery [kə'dʒouləri], *s.* Cajolerie(s) *f(pl)* ; enjôlement *m.*

cake¹ [keik], *s.* **I.** (*a*) Gâteau *m. S.a.* CHEESE-CAKE, FRUIT-CAKE, SPONGE-CAKE. *F:* **To take the cake,** remporter la palme. *He takes the c.!* à lui le pompon ! **They're going, selling, like hot cakes,** ça se vend comme des petits pains. (*b*) (Small) cakes, pâtisserie légère ; gâteaux, pâtisseries. (*c*) *Scot:* (Oat-)cake ; galette *f* d'avoine. (*d*) Rissole *f. S.a.* FISH-CAKE. **2.** (*a*) Pain *m* (de savon, etc.) ; tablette *f* (de chocolat). (*b*) Oil-, linseed-cake, tourteau *m* de lin. **3.** Masse *f,* croûte *f* (de sang coagulé) ; motte *f* (de terre, etc.) ; agglutination *f* (de houille, etc.). **'cake-shop,** *s.* Pâtisserie *f.*

cake², *v.i.* (*a*) Former une croûte ; faire croûte. (*b*) (*Of coal, etc.*) (Se) coller ; se prendre ; s'agglutiner ; (*of blood, etc.*) se cailler. **Caked with mud, with blood,** plaqué de boue, de sang.

caking, *s.* Agglomération *f,* agglutination *f* (de la houille) ; coagulation *f* (du sang).

calabash ['kaləbaʃ], *s.* Calebasse *f,* gourde *f.*

Calabria [kə'leibriə]. *Pr.n. Geog:* La Calabre.

calamary ['kaləmɛəri], *s. Moll:* Calmar *m.*

calamine ['kalamin], *s. Miner:* Calamine *f.*

calamitous [kə'lamitəs], *a.* Calamiteux, désastreux. **-ly,** *adv.* Calamiteusement, désastreusement.

calamity [kə'lamiti], *s.* **I.** Calamité *f,* infortune *f,* malheur *m.* **2.** Désastre *m* ; sinistre *m.*

calamus ['kaləməs], *s. Bot:* **I.** Calamus *m,* rotin *m.* **2.** Sweet calamus, jonc odorant.

calcareous [kal'kɛəriəs], *a. Miner:* Calcaire.

calceolaria [kalsio'lɛəriə], *s. Bot:* Calcéolaire *f.*

calcify ['kalsifai]. **I.** *v.tr.* Calcifier. (*a*) Convertir en carbonate de chaux. (*b*) Pétrifier (le bois). **2.** *v.i.* Se calcifier.

calcination [kalsi'neiʃ(ə)n], *s. Ch: Ind:* Calcination *f* ; cuisson *f* ; grillage *m.*

calcine ['kalsain]. **I.** *v.tr.* Calciner ; cuire (le gypse, etc.). *Metall:* Griller (le minerai). **2.** *v.i.* Se calciner

calcium ['kalsiəm], *s. Ch:* Calcium *m.* **Calcium carbide,** carbure *m* de calcium.

calculate ['kalkjuleit], *v.tr. & i.* **I.** (*a*) Calculer,

évaluer ; estimer (une distance) ; calculer, mesurer (ses paroles) ; faire le compte de (sa fortune). *Abs.* Faire un calcul ; compter. (*b*) *To c. upon sth., on doing sth.,* compter sur qch. ; compter faire qch. **2.** *U.S:* Croire, supposer (*that,* que). **calculated,** *a.* (*a*) *C.* insolence, insolence délibérée, calculée. (*b*) *News c. to astonish him,* nouvelle faite pour l'étonner. *Words c. to reassure us,* paroles propres à nous rassurer. (*Of pers.*) Calculateur, -trice ; réfléchi. **calculating²,** *s.* Calcul *m,* estimation *f.* **Calculating machine,** machine à calculer.

calculation [kalkju'leiʃ(ə)n], *s.* Calcul *m.* *To be out in one's calculations,* être loin de son compte.

calculator ['kalkjuleitər], *s.* **I.** (*Pers.*) Calculateur, -trice. **2.** Machine *f* à calculer.

calculus ['kalkjuləs], *s.* **I.** *Med:* (*pl.* **calculi** ['kalkjulai]) Calcul (vésical, etc.). **2.** *Mth:* Calcul infinitésimal.

Caledonia [kale'dounjə]. *Pr.n. A:* La Calédonie, l'Écosse *f.*

Caledonian [kale'dounjən], *a. & s.* (*a*) Calédonien, -ienne. (*b*) *Hum:* Écossais, -aise.

calendar ['kaləndər], *s.* **I.** Calendrier *m.* **Tear-off calendar, block-calendar,** calendrier bloc ; calendrier éphéméride, à effeuiller. **2.** *Jur:* Liste *f* des accusés, des causes au criminel ; rôle *m* des assises.

calender¹ ['kaləndər], *s.* Calandre *f.*

calender², *v.tr.* Calandrer, cylindrer (des étoffes, etc.). **calendering,** *s.* Calandrage *m.*

calends ['kaləndz], *s.pl. Rom.Ant:* Calendes *f.* *F:* **On the Greek calends,** aux calendes grecques.

calf¹, *pl.* **calves** [kɑ:f, kɑ:vz], *s.* **I.** (*a*) Veau *m.* **Cow in, with, calf,** vache pleine. *Attrib.* Calf love, amours enfantines ; les premières amours. (*b*) *Leath:* Veau ; vachette *f. C. boots,* souliers en veau mégis. *S.a.* BOX-CALF. **2.** (*a*) Petit *m* de certains animaux. **Whale-calf,** baleineau *m.* **Elephant-calf,** éléphanteau *m.* (*b*) Glaçon (détaché d'un iceberg) ; veau. **'calf's-foot jelly, 'calves-foot jelly,** *s. Cu:* Gelée *f* de pied de veau.

calf², *pl.* **calves,** *s.* Mollet *m* (de la jambe).

calfskin ['kɑ:fskin], *s.* (Cuir *m* de) veau *m.*

calibrate ['kalibreit], *v.tr.* Étalonner (un compteur) ; calibrer (un tube) ; graduer (un thermomètre) ; tarer (un ressort).

calibration [kali'breiʃ(ə)n], *s.* Étalonnage *m* ; calibrage *m* (d'un tube) ; tarage *m* (d'un ressort).

calibre ['kalibər], *s.* (*a*) Calibre *m,* alésage *m* (d'un canon, d'un tube). (*b*) *F: A man of his c.,* un homme de son calibre, de son envergure.

-calibred ['kalibərd], *a.* **Small-, large-calibred,** de petit, gros, calibre.

calico ['kaliko], *s. Tex:* (*a*) Calicot *m.* **Printed calico,** indienne *f.* (*b*) *Dressm:* Percaline *f* (pour doublures).

California [kali'fɔ:rnjə]. *Pr.n.* La Californie.

Californian [kali'fɔ:rnjən], *a. & s.* Californien, -ienne.

caliper ['kalipər], *s.* = CALLIPER.

caliph ['keilif, 'kalif], *s.* Calife *m.*

calk¹ [kɔ:k], *s.* Crampon *m* (de fer à cheval).

calk², *v.tr.* Ferrer (un cheval) à glace.

calkin ['kɔ:kin, 'kalkin], *s. Farr:* **I.** Crampon *m* (de fer à cheval). **2.** Clou *m* à glace.

call¹ [kɔ:l], *s.* **I.** (*a*) (*Shout*) Appel *m,* cri *m* ; cri d'appel. (*b*) Cri (d'un oiseau). *S.a.* BIRD-CALL. **2.** (*Summons*) (*a*) Appel. **To come at, to answer s.o.'s call,** venir, répondre, à l'appel de qn. **To be within call,** être à portée de voix. **To give s.o. a call,** appeler qn. *To answer the c. of duty,* se rendre à son devoir. **You have no call to do so,** vous n'avez aucune raison de le faire. *U.S: F:* **To have a close call,** l'échapper belle. *S.a.* BECK², BLOOD¹ I. (*b*) *Mil:* Bugle-call, trumpet-call, sonnerie *f*, coup *m*, appel, de clairon, de trompette. (*c*) (Roll-)call, appel nominal. (*d*) He felt **a call** (*to the ministry*), il se sentait la vocation. (*e*) *Tp:* Telephone call, appel téléphonique; coup de téléphone. *Local c.,* communication locale, urbaine. **I'll give you a call,** je vous téléphonerai *To put a c. through,* donner la communication. *To pay for twenty calls,* payer vingt conversations *f*. *S.a.* TRUNK-CALL. (*f*) *Cards:* (*At bridge*) Appel; (*at solo whist*) demande *f*. **Call for trumps,** invite *f* d'atout. *A c.* of three diamonds, une annonce de trois carreaux. (*g*) *Th:* Rappel *m* (d'un acteur). *When she took her call,* lorsqu'elle parut devant le rideau. **3.** Visite *f*. **To pay, make, a call on s.o.,** faire (une) visite à qn. *To pay calls,* faire des visites. **'Party' call** (*after a dinner*), visite de digestion. *Nau:* Port of call, port d'escale, de relâche. **4.** Demande (d'argent). *Fin:* Appel de fonds, de versement. **Payable at call,** remboursable sur demande, à présentation, à vue. **'call-box,** *s. Tp:* Cabine *f*, guérite *f* (téléphonique). **'call-boy,** *s. Th:* Avertisseur *m*.

call². I. *v.tr.* **I.** (*a*) Appeler (qn); crier (qch.). *Abs. Who is calling?* qui est-ce qui appelle? **To call** (out) 'fire,' crier au feu. **To call the banns,** publier les bans. **To call a halt,** (i) crier halte; (ii) faire halte. **To call the roll,** faire l'appel. *W.Tel:* London calling! ici (poste de) Londres! *Nau:* To call the soundings, chanter le fond. (*b*) To call to s.o. to do sth., crier à qn de faire qch. **2.** (*a*) (*Summon*) Appeler (qn); héler (un taxi); convoquer (une assemblée). *Th:* Rappeler (un acteur). *To c. a cab* (*off the rank*), faire avancer un taxi. **To call** (in) **the doctor,** faire venir, appeler, le médecin. *Mil:* **To call to arms,** battre la générale. **To call into play** all one's powers, faire appel à toutes ses facultés. *S.a.* ACCOUNT¹ 2, BAR¹ 3, MIND¹ I. (*b*) Call me at six o'clock, réveillez-moi à six heures. **3.** *He is called John,* il s'appelle Jean. **To call s.o. after** s.o., donner le nom de qn à qn. *To c. oneself a colonel,* se qualifier de colonel. **To call s.o. names,** injurier, invectiver, qn. *To c. s.o. a liar,* traiter qn de menteur. *F:* **We'll call it three francs,** (i) mettons trois francs; (ii) va pour trois francs. **4.** *Cards:* Appeler, déclarer (des carreaux, etc.). **5.** To call a strike, décréter, ordonner, une grève. II. **call,** *v.i.* (*a*) *To c. at s.o.'s house,* (i) faire une visite chez qn; (ii) passer, se rendre, se présenter, chez qn. *Has anyone called?* est-il venu quelqu'un? *I must c. at the grocer's,* il faut que je passe chez l'épicier. **To call again,** repasser (*on, chez*). (*b*) *The train calls at every station,* le train s'arrête à toutes les gares. *Nau:* (*Of ship*) To call at a port, faire escale, relâcher, toucher, à un port. **call aside,** *v.tr.* Prendre, tirer, (qn) à part. **call away,** *v.tr.* *I am called away on business,* je suis obligé de m'absenter pour affaires. **call back. I.** *v.tr.* Rappeler (qn). **2.** *v.tr.* I called back "don't forget," je me suis retourné pour crier "n'oubliez pas." **3.** *v.i.* I shall call back for it, je repasserai le prendre. **call down,** *v.tr.* (*a*) Faire descendre (qn). (*b*) To call down curses on s.o.'s head, appeler des malédictions sur la tête de qn. **call for,** *v.ind.tr.* (*a*) Appeler, faire venir (qn); faire apporter (qch.); commander (une consommation, etc.). *To c. for help,* appeler, crier, au secours. (*b*) Venir prendre, venir chercher (qn, qch.).

'To be (left till) called for,' 'à laisser jusqu'à ce qu'on vienne le chercher'; *Post:* 'poste restante'; *Rail:* 'en gare.' (*c*) **To call for** an explanation, for an apology, demander, exiger, une explication, des excuses. (*d*) Demander, comporter, réclamer, exiger (l'attention, des réformes). **call forth,** *v.tr.* (*a*) Produire, faire naître (des protestations); évoquer (un souvenir); exciter (l'admiration). (*b*) Faire appel à (tout son courage). (*c*) Évoquer (un esprit). **call in,** *v.tr.* **I.** Faire entrer (qn); faire rentrer (les enfants). **2.** Retirer (une monnaie) de la circulation. **3.** *To c. in a specialist,* faire appel, avoir recours, à un spécialiste. **call off. I.** *v.tr.* (*a*) Rappeler (un chien). (*b*) **To call off a strike,** décommander une grève. *To c. off a deal,* rompre, annuler, un marché. **2.** *v.i.* Se dédire; revenir sur sa parole. **call on,** *v.i.* **I.** Faire visite chez (qn); passer chez (qn); aller voir (qn). *To c. on s.o. again,* repasser chez qn. **2.** = CALL UPON. **call out. I.** *v.tr.* (*a*) Faire sortir (qn); appeler (les pompiers). *To c. out the military,* faire intervenir la force armée. (*b*) Provoquer (qn) en duel. **2.** *v.i.* (*a*) Appeler; appeler au secours. (*b*) *To c. out for sth.,* demander qch. à grands cris. **call over,** *v.tr.* (*a*) *To c. over* (*the names*), faire l'appel. (*b*) I called him over, je lui fis signe de venir nous retrouver. **'call-over,** *s. Sch: etc:* L'appel *m*. **call together,** *v.tr.* Convoquer, réunir (une assemblée); assembler (des gens). **call up,** *v.tr.* **I.** Faire monter (qn). **2.** Évoquer (un esprit, un souvenir). **3.** Appeler (qn) au téléphone. **4.** *Mil: Navy:* Mobiliser (un réserviste); appeler (qn) sous les armes. **call upon,** *v.i.* (*a*) Invoquer (le nom de Dieu). (*b*) *To c. upon s.o. for sth.,* demander qch. à qn; réclamer qch. à qn. (*c*) *To c. upon s.o. to do sth.,* sommer qn de faire qch. *To c. upon s.o.'s help,* faire appel à qn, à l'aide de qn. *To c. upon s.o. to apologize,* exiger de qn qu'il fasse des excuses. **I feel called upon** *to warn you that . . .,* je me sens dans l'obligation de vous avertir que. . . . I now call upon Mr S., la parole est à M. S. **calling,** *s.* **I.** (*a*) Appel *m*, cri *m*. (*b*) Convocation *f* (d'une assemblée, etc.). **2.** Visite *f* (*on,* à). Calling hours, heures de visite. **3.** Vocation *f*, état *m*, métier *m*.

caller [ˈkɔːlər], *s.* **I.** Personne *f* qui appelle. **2.** Visiteur, -euse. **3.** Caller(-up), éveilleur, -euse.

calligraphy [kəˈligrəfi], *s.* Calligraphie *f*.

cal(l)iper [ˈkalipər], *s.* (*Sg. only in compounds*) Calliper compasses, (pair of) callipers, compas *m* à calibrer. *In and out callipers,* maître *m* de danse. *Figure-of-eight c.,* huit-de-chiffre(s) *m*. **Calliper square,** pied *m* à coulisse.

callosity [kæˈlɔsiti], *s.* Callosité *f*, durillon *m*.

callous [ˈkaləs], *a.* **I.** (*Of skin*) Calleux. **2.** (Homme, cœur) insensible, endurci; (homme) dur, sans cœur. **-ly,** *adv.* Sans pitié, sans cœur.

callousness [ˈkaləsnəs], *s.* Insensibilité *f* (*to,* à); dureté *f*; manque *m* de cœur, de pitié.

callow [ˈkalo], *a.* (*Of fledgling*) Sans plumes. *F:* Callow youth, la verte jeunesse. *F: A c. youth,* un blanc-bec.

callus [ˈkaləs], *s.* **I.** Callosité *f*. **2.** *Surg:* Cal *m*, *pl.* cals.

calm¹ [kɑːm], *s.* Calme *m*, tranquillité *f*, sérénité *f* (d'esprit). Dead calm, calme plat.

calm², *a.* Calme, tranquille. *F:* **The sea was** as calm as a mill-pond, nous avions une mer d'huile. **To remain calm and collected,** rester serein; ne pas perdre la tête. **To keep calm,** rester calme; se modérer. **-ly,** *adv.* Avec calme; tranquillement; sans s'émouvoir.

calm³. I. *v.tr.* Calmer, apaiser (la tempête); tranquilliser (l'esprit); atténuer, adoucir (la douleur). **Calm yourself,** remettez-vous! To **calm s.o.** down, pacifier qn. **2.** *v.i.* (*Of storm, grief*) To calm down, se calmer, s'apaiser. **calming (down),** s. Apaisement m; adoucissement m.
calmness ['kɑːmnəs], s. Tranquillité f, calme m.
caloric [kə'lɔrik], s. *Ph:* Calorique m. **Caloric energy,** énergie thermique.
calorie ['kalɔri], s. *Ph:* Calorie f.
calorimeter [kalɔ'rimetər], s. Calorimètre m.
calorimetric(al) [kalɔri'metrik(əl)], a. *Ph:* Calorimétrique.
calorimetry [kalɔ'rimetri], s. *Ph:* Calorimétrie f.
calory ['kalɔri], s. = CALORIE.
calotte [kə'lɔt], s. *R.C.Ch:* *Geol:* Calotte f.
caltrop ['kaltrɔp], s. **I.** *Mil:* A: Chausse-trape f, pl. chausse-trapes. **2.** pl. *Bot:* Chardon étoilé; chausse-trape (étoilée). **Water caltrops,** macre f, cornue f; châtaigne f d'eau.
calumniate [kə'lʌmnieit], v.tr. Calomnier.
calumniation [kalʌmni'eiʃ(ə)n], s. Calomnie f.
calumniator [kə'lʌmnieitər], s. Calomniateur, -trice.
calumny ['kaləmni], s. Calomnie f.
Calvary ['kalvəri]. **I.** *Pr.n.* (Mount) Calvary, le Calvaire. **2.** s. Calvaire m.
calve [kɑːv], v.i. (*Of cow, iceberg*) Vêler. **calving,** s. Vêlage m, vêlement m.
calves¹,². See CALF¹,².
Calvinist ['kalvinist], s. *Rel.H:* Calviniste mf.
calyx, pl. **-yxes, -yces** ['keiliks, 'kaliks, -iksiːz, -isiːz], s. *Bot:* Calice m; vase m (de tulipe).
cam [kam], s. *Mec.E:* Came f; excentrique m.
'cam-shaft, s. *Mec.E:* Arbre m à cames. *I.C.E:* Arbre de distribution.
camber¹ ['kambər], s. Cambrure f (d'une poutre); courbure f; bombement m (d'une chaussée). **Rise of camber,** flèche f (d'une poutre).
camber², v.tr. Bomber (une chaussée); cambrer (une poutre). **cambered,** a. Arqué, courbé, cambré. **cambering,** s. Bombement m, cambrage m; cintrement m.
Cambodia [kam'boudiə]. *Pr.n.* *Geog:* Le Cambodge.
Cambrian ['kambriən], a. & s. **I.** *Geog:* Gallois, -oise. **2.** *Geol:* Cambrien, -ienne.
cambric ['keimbrik], s. *Tex:* Batiste f (de lin).
came¹ [keim], s. Plombure f (d'un vitrail). The cames, la résille.
came². See COME.
camel ['kaməl], s. **I.** Chameau m. **She-camel,** chamelle f. **Racing camel,** méhari m. **Camel's hair,** poil de chameau. **Camel('s)-hair brush,** pinceau en petit-gris (pour l'aquarelle). **2.** *Nau:* Chameau m (de renflouage). **'camel-driver,** s. Chamelier m.
camellia [kə'miːlja], s. *Bot:* Camélia m.
cameo ['kamio], s. Camée m.
camera ['kamərə], s. **I.** (a) *Phot:* Appareil m. **Plate camera,** appareil à plaques. **Film camera,** appareil à pellicules. **Hand camera,** appareil à main. **Folding camera,** appareil pliant; folding m. *Cin:* Motion-picture camera, caméra f. (b) *Opt:* Camera obscura, chambre noire. **2.** *Jur:* Cabinet m du Président; chambre du Conseil. In camera, à huis clos. **'camera-man,** pl. **-men,** s. **I.** Photographe m de presse. **2.** *Cin:* Opérateur m.
Cameroons (the) [ðəkamə'ruːnz]. *Pr.n.pl.* *Geog:* Le Cameroun.

cami-knickers [kami'nikərz], s.pl. *Cost:* Chemise-culotte f.
camisole ['kamisoul], s. Cache-corset m inv.
camlet ['kamlet], s. *Tex:* Camelot m.
camomile ['kamomail], s. *Bot:* **I.** Camomille f. **2.** **Stinking camomile,** camomille puante; maroute f. **'camomile-'tea,** s. (Tisane f de) camomille f.
camouflage¹ ['kamuflɑːʒ], s. Camouflage m.
camouflage², v.tr. Camoufler. To c. the truth, farder la vérité.
camp¹ [kamp]. s. Camp m; campement m. **To pitch a camp,** asseoir, établir, un camp. **To strike, break (up), camp,** lever le camp. **'camp-bed,** s. Lit m de sangle. **'camp-chair,** s. Chaise pliante. **camp-'followers,** s.pl. A: Non-combattants à la suite de l'armée **'camp-stool,** s. Pliant m.
camp². **I.** *v.i.* To camp (out), camper. **2.** v.tr. Camper (une armée). **camping,** s. **I.** *Mil:* etc: Campement m. **2.** To go camping, faire du camping. **'camping-ground,** s. (a) Campement m (de bohémiens, etc.). (b) Terrain m de camping.
campaign¹ [kam'pein], s. Campagne f (militaire). *F:* Electoral campaign, campagne électorale. *F:* To lead, conduct, a campaign against s.o., mener (une) campagne contre qn.
campaign², v.i. Faire (une) campagne; faire des campagnes. **campaigning,** s. Vie f de soldat; campagnes fpl.
campaigner [kam'peinər], s. **I.** Soldat m en campagne. **2.** Old campaigner, vieux soldat; vieux routier; vétéran m.
campanile [kampa'niːle], s. *Arch:* Campanile m.
campanula [kam'panjula], s. *Bot:* Campanule f.
Campeachy [kam'piːtʃi]. *Pr.n.* *Geog:* Campêche m. Campeachy wood, bois de Campêche.
camper ['kampər], s. **I.** Homme m sous la tente. **2.** Camper (out), amateur, -trice, de camping.
camphor ['kamfər], s. Camphre m.
camphorated ['kamforeitid], a. **Camphorated oil,** huile camphrée.
campion ['kampiən], s. *Bot:* Lychnis m. **White campion,** compagnon blanc. **Bladder campion,** silène enflé.
can¹ [kan], s. **I.** (a) Bidon m, broc m, pot m (pour liquides). *S.a.* WATER-CAN. (b) Milk-can, boîte f à lait. (c) *Ind:* Burette f (à huile, etc.). **2.** *U.S:* Cannette m métal; boîte (de viande conservée) **'can-opener,** s. *U.S:* Ouvre-boîte(s) m.
can², v.tr. *U.S:* Mettre, conserver, (de la viande, etc.) en boîte. **canned,** a. (*Of meat*) Conservé en boîtes (de fer blanc). *U.S:* *P:* Canned music, musique enregistrée; *F:* musique de conserve. **canning,** s. Canning-industry, industrie des conserves alimentaires. **Canning factory,** conserverie f.
can³, modal aux. v. (pr. can, canst, can, pl. can; neg. cannot ['kanɔt], canst not; p.t. could [kud], could(e)st; inf., pr.p. & p.p. wanting; defective parts are supplied from 'to be able to.' 'Cannot' and 'could not' are often contracted into can't [kɑːnt], couldn't ['kudnt]) **I.** Pouvoir. *I can do it,* je peux, je puis, le faire. *I cannot allow that,* je ne saurais permettre cela. *As soon as I can,* aussitôt que je pourrai. *As often as I possibly can,* aussi souvent que faire se peut. *I took every step that I possibly could,* j'ai fait toutes les démarches possibles. *He will do what he can,* il fera ce qu'il pourra; il fera son possible. *F:* I will help you all I can, je vous aiderai de mon mieux. *Make all haste you can,* faites toute la diligence

possible. *It cannot be done,* cela ne peut pas se faire; c'est impossible (à faire). *That cannot be,* cela ne se peut pas. *What can it be?* qu'est-ce que cela peut bien être? *Can it be that . . .?* se peut-il, est-il possible, que + *sub.? (c) (Emphatic) I never could understand music,* je n'ai jamais été capable de comprendre la musique. *Mr X? what 'can he want?* M. X? qu'est-ce qu'il peut bien me vouloir? *How 'could you?* vous! faire ça! à quoi pensez-vous? *She is as pleased as can 'be,* elle est on ne peut plus contente. *As soon as can 'be,* aussi tôt que possible. **2.** *Savoir. I can swim,* je sais nager. **3.** (a) *You don't know how silly a girl can be,* vous ne savez pas à quel point les jeunes filles sont parfois sottes. *(b) (Permission, = 'may') When can I move in?* quand pourrai-je emménager? *(To inferior) You can go,* vous pouvez vous retirer. **4.** (*Not translated*) *I can understand your doing it,* je comprends que vous le fassiez. *I can see nothing,* je ne vois rien. *Hoẃ can you tell?* comment le savez-vous? **5.** *(a) He could have done it if he had wanted to,* il aurait pu le faire s'il avait voulu. *(b) I could have wished it otherwise,* j'aurais préféré qu'il en fût autrement. *(c) I could have wept,* je me sentais près de pleurer; j'en aurais pleuré! **6.** *You cannot but succeed,* vous ne pouvez pas ne pas réussir. *You can but try,* vous pouvez toujours essayer.

Canada ['kanədə]. *Pr.n. Geog:* Le Canada. *In Canada,* au Canada.

Canadian [kə'neidiən], *a. & s.* Canadien, -ienne.

canal [kə'nal], *s.* **I.** Canal *m,* -aux. *Branch c.,* canal de dérivation. **2.** *Anat:* The alimentary canal, le canal alimentaire.

canalization [kanəlai'zeiʃ(ə)n], *s.* Canalisation *f.*

canalize ['kanəla:iz]. **I.** *v.tr.* Canaliser. **2.** *v.i.* (*Of opinion, etc.*) Se canaliser.

Canary [kə'nɛəri]. **I.** *Pr.n. Geog:* The Canary Islands, the Canaries, les îles Canaries. **2.** *s. Orn:* Serin *m.* *Canary yellow,* jaune serin *inv.* **ca'nary-seed,** *s.* (*Grains mpl de*) millet *m.*

cancel[1] ['kans(ə)l], *s.* **I.** *Typ:* Cancel(-page), onglet *m.* **2.** Oblitérateur *m,* poinçon *m.*

cancel[2], *v.tr.* (**cancelled**) **I.** Annuler (une commande); résilier, résoudre, *Jur:* rescinder (un contrat); révoquer (un acte); rappeler (un message); contremander (un ordre); rapporter (une décision); supprimer (un train); décommander (une réunion); infirmer (une lettre); oblitérer (un timbre); biffer (un mot). *Mil:* Lever (une consigne). *To c. one's booking,* décommander sa place. **2.** *Mth:* To cancel x, y, éliminer x, y. **cancel out,** *v.i. Mth:* (*Of terms*) S'annuler, s'éliminer.

cancellation [kansə'leiʃ(ə)n], *s.* Annulation *f;* résiliation *f* (d'une commande); résolution *f* (d'une vente). *C. of an order,* contre-ordre *m.*

cancer ['kansər], *s.* **I.** Cancer *m.* *C. serum,* sérum anticancéreux. *Cancer patient,* cancéreux, -euse. **2.** *Astr:* Le Cancer.

cancerous ['kansərəs], *a. Med:* Cancéreux.

candelabra, *pl.* **-as** [kandi'leibrə, -əz], **candelabrum,** *pl.* **-a** [kandi'leibrʌm, -a], *s.* Candélabre *m.*

candescent [kan'des(ə)nt], *a.* D'une blancheur éblouissante.

candid ['kandid], *a.* **I.** Franc, *f.* franche; sincère. **2.** Impartial, -aux. **-ly,** *adv.* **I.** Franchement, sincèrement, de bonne foi. **2.** Impartialement.

candidate ['kandidet], *s.* Candidat *m,* aspirant *m,* prétendant *m* (*for sth.,* à qch.). *To be a c.,* être sur les rangs.

candidature ['kandidetjər], *s.* Candidature *f.*

candidness ['kandidnəs], *s.* = CANDOUR.

candle [kandl], *s.* **I.** *Wax candle,* bougie *f.* *Tallow candle,* chandelle *f.* *Church candle,* cierge *f.* *F:* To burn the candle at both ends, brûler la chandelle par les deux bouts. *The game is not worth the candle,* le jeu ne vaut pas la chandelle. *He cannot hold a candle to you,* il vous est très inférieur. **2.** *Pyr:* Roman candle, chandelle romaine. **candle-'end,** *s.* Bout *m* de chandelle; lumignon *m.* **'candle-grease,** *s.* Suif *m.* **'candle-power,** *s. Ph.Meas:* Bougie *f.* *Sixty c.-p. lamp,* lampe de soixante bougies.

candlelight ['kandllait], *s.* Lumière *f* de chandelle, de bougie. *By candlelight,* à la chandelle, à la bougie.

Candlemas ['kandlmas], *s. Ecc:* La Chandeleur.

candlestick ['kandlstik], *s.* Chandelier *m.* *Flat candlestick,* bougeoir *m.*

candour ['kandər], *s.* **I.** Franchise *f,* bonne foi, sincérité *f.* **2.** Impartialité *f.*

candy ['kandi], *v.tr.* (a) Faire candir (le sucre). *(b)* Glacer (des fruits). **candied,** *a.* (a) Candi; confit (au sucre). *S.a.* PEEL[1]. *(b) A. & Lit:* (Discours) mielleux.

candytuft ['kanditʌft], *s. Bot:* Ibéride *f.*

cane[1] [kein], *s.* (a) Canne *f,* jonc *m;* rotin *m.* *Raspberry cane,* tige *f* de framboisier. *(b) (Walking-stick)* Canne. *Malacca cane,* (canne de) jonc. *(c) (Switch)* Badine *f.* *(d) (For chastisement)* Canne. *To get the cane,* être fouetté. **'cane(-bottomed) chair,** *s.* Chaise cannée. **'cane-juice,** *s. Sug.-R:* Vesou *m.* **'cane-plantation,** *s.* Cannaie *f.* **'cane-sugar,** *s.* Sucre *m* de canne.

cane[2], *v.tr.* **I.** Battre, frapper, (qn) à coups de canne. **2.** Canner (une chaise). **caning,** *s.* **I.** *Sch:* Correction *f.* **2.** Cannage *m* (de chaises).

canful ['kanful], *s.* Plein bidon, plein broc.

canicular [kə'nikjulər], *a.* Caniculaire.

canine ['kanain], *a.* **I.** *a.* Canin; de chien. **2.** *s.* Canine (tooth), canine *f;* (dent) œillère *f.*

canister ['kanistər], *s.* **I.** Boîte *f* (en fer blanc). **2.** *Mil:* Mitraille *f.*

canker[1] ['kaŋkər], *s.* . **I.** *Hort: Med:* Chancre *m.* **2.** *F:* Influence corruptrice; plaie *f,* fléau *m.* **3.** *Vet:* Crapaud *m* (au sabot).

canker[2], *v.tr.* (a) Ronger (un arbre); nécroser (le bois). *(b)* Corrompre (une âme). **cankered,** *a.* Atteint par le chancre; rongé.

cankerworm ['kaŋkərwəːrm], *s.* Ver rongeur.

cannel [kanl], *s.* Houille grasse.

cannery ['kanəri], *s.* Conserverie *f.*

cannibal ['kanibəl], *s. & a.* Cannibale (*mf*); anthropophage (*mf*).

cannibalism ['kanibəlizm], *s.* Cannibalisme *m,* anthropophagie *f.*

cannibalistic [kanibə'listik], *a.* Cannibale.

cannon[1] ['kanən], *s.* **I.** *Artil:* (*pl. usu.* cannon) Canon *m;* pièce *f* d'artillerie. **2.** *Harn:* Cannon (-bit), canon (du mors). **3.** *Bill:* Carambolage *m.* **4.** Canon (de clef). **'cannon-ball,** *s.* Boulet *m* (de canon). **'cannon-bone,** *s.* Canon *m* (de la jambe du cheval). **'cannon-fodder,** *s. F:* Chair *f* à canon. **'cannon-shot,** *s.* (a) Coup *m* de canon. *(b) Within cannon-shot,* à portée de canon.

cannon[2], *v.i.* (**cannoned**) **I.** *Bill:* Caramboler. *To cannon off the red,* caramboler par la rouge. **2.** *To cannon into s.o.,* heurter violemment qn.

cannonade [kanə'neid], *s.* Canonnade *f.*

cannot ['kanɔt]. See CAN[3].

canny ['kani], *a.* Prudent, finaud. *C. answer,* réponse de Normand. *S.a.* CA'CANNY. **-ily,** *adv.* Prudemment.

canoe [ka'nu:], s. **1.** Sp : Canadian canoe, canoë m. Rob-Roy canoe, périssoire f. **2.** (Of savages) Pirogue f. S.a. PADDLE³.
canoeing [ka'nuiŋ], s. To go in for c., faire de la périssoire, du canoë.
canoeist [ka'nuist], s. Canotier m.
canon¹ ['kanən], s. **1.** (a) Canon m (de la messe). Canon law, droit canon. (b) Règle f, critère m. **2.** Mus : Canon.
canon², s. Ecc : Chanoine m.
canoness ['kanənes], s.f. Ecc : Chanoinesse.
canonical [ka'nɔnik(ə)l], a. **1.** (Devoir) canonial, -aux ; (droit) canonique. **2.** Canonical dress, s.pl. canonicals, vêtements sacerdotaux.
canonization [kanənai'zeiʃ(ə)n], s. Canonisation f.
canonize ['kanənaiz], v.tr. Ecc : **1.** Canoniser (qn). **2.** Sanctionner (un usage).
canonry ['kanənri], s. Canonicat m.
canopy¹ ['kanəpi], s. **1.** Dais m (d'un trône) ; baldaquin m (de lit) ; ciel m (d'autel) ; (over doorway) auvent m, marquise f. F : The canopy of heaven, la voûte du ciel. **2.** Arch : Gable m (de fenêtre).
canopy², v.tr. Couvrir d'un dais, d'un dôme de verdure. **canopied,** a. Recouvert d'un dais.
cant¹ [kant], s. **1.** Arch : Carp : Pan coupé. Mec.E : Arête f (de boulon). **2.** (a) (Slope) Inclinaison f, dévers m. (b) To have a c., pencher. **'cant-hook,** s. Croc m à levier.
cant². **1.** v.tr. (a) Carp : To cant off an angle, délarder une arête. (b) To cant a beam, incliner une poutre. Rail : To c. the outer rail, surhausser le rail extérieur. (c) Renverser. Nau : To cant a boat for repairs, cabaner un canot pour le réparer. **2.** v.i. (a) S'incliner. (b) Pencher. (c) (Of ship) Éviter.
cant³. **1.** s. (a) Jargon m, argot m. (b) Langage m hypocrite ; tartuferie f. **2.** a. Cant phrase, cliché m.
can't [kɑ:nt]. F : = cannot, q.v. under CAN³.
cantaloup ['kantəlup], s. Hort : Cantaloup m.
cantankerous [kan'taŋkərəs], a. Revêche, acariâtre ; d'humeur hargneuse ; tracassier. To be c., avoir mauvais caractère. **-ly,** adv. D'une manière acariâtre.
cantankerousness [kan'taŋkərəsnəs], s. Humeur f revêche, acariâtre.
cantata [kan'tɑːtə], s. Mus : Cantate f.
canteen [kan'tiːn], s. **1.** Cantine f. **2.** Mil : (a) Bidon m. (b) Gamelle f. **3.** Canteen of cutlery, service m de table en coffret.
canter¹ ['kantər], s. Equit : Petit galop. Rac : To win in a canter, arriver bon premier ; F : arriver dans un fauteuil.
canter². **1.** v.i. Aller au petit galop. **2.** v.tr. Faire aller (un cheval) au petit galop.
Canterbury ['kantərbəri]. Pr.n. Cantorbéry m. **Canterbury bell,** campanule f à grosses fleurs.
cantharis, pl. **cantharides** ['kanθaris, kan-'θaridiːz], s. Cantharide f.
canticle ['kantikl], s. Cantique m.
cantilever ['kantili:vər], s. (a) Arch : Encorbellement m. (b) Civ.E : Cantilever m.
canting ['kantiŋ], a. **1.** Hypocrite. A c. hypocrite, un tartufe. **2.** Her : Canting arms, armes parlantes.
canto ['kanto], s. Chant m (d'un poème).
canton [kan'tɔn], s. Canton m.
cantonment [kan'tuːnmənt], s. Cantonnement m.
canvas ['kanvəs], s. **1.** Tex : (a) (Grosse) toile ; toile à voiles, toile de tente. Aut : C. of a tyre, toiles d'un pneu. **Under canvas,** (i) Mil : sous

la tente ; (ii) Nau : sous voile. S.a. STRETCHER 1. (b) Needlew : Canvas work, tapisserie au, sur, canevas. **2.** Art : A fine c., une belle toile.
'canvas-back, s. Canard m d'Amérique.
canvass¹ ['kanvəs], s. Sollicitation f de suffrages ; tournée électorale.
canvass², v.tr. **1.** Discuter (une affaire) ; éplucher (une réputation). **2.** Solliciter (des suffrages, des commandes). Abs. To canvass, faire une tournée électorale. Com : To canvass from door to door, faire la place. **canvassing,** s. **1.** Discussion f ; épluchage m (de réputations). **2.** Sollicitation f (de suffrages).
canvasser ['kanvəsər], s. Solliciteur, -euse. Com : Placier m (de marchandises). Pol : Courtier électoral.
canyon ['kanjən], s. Cañon m ; gorge profonde.
caoutchouc ['kautʃuːk], s. Caoutchouc m.
cap¹ [kap], s. **1.** (a) (Brimless) Bonnet m; (with peak) casquette f ; toque f (de jockey, universitaire) ; képi m (de militaire) ; béret m (de marin) ; barrette f (de cardinal). Skull cap, calotte f. Cap of liberty, bonnet phrygien. Scotch cap, béret. Sp : To win one's cap, être choisi comme membre de la première équipe. Cap and bells, marotte f (de bouffon). Sch : In cap and gown, en toque et en toge ; en costume académique. To come cap in hand, se présenter le bonnet à la main. F : (Of woman) To set one's cap at a man, entreprendre la conquête d'un homme. If the cap fits, wear it! qui se sent morveux se mouche ! à bon entendeur salut ! S.a. THINKING². (b) Orn : Capuchon m, chapeau m (d'un oiseau). **2.** (a) Chapeau m (de colonne) ; chapeau (de champignon). Arch : Comble m en dôme. (b) Tchn : Chapeau (de protection) ; capuchon (de porte-plume à réservoir). Mec.E : Lubricator cap, chapeau graisseur. **3.** Exp : Amorce f, capsule f. **'cap-screw,** s. Vis f à tête cubique. **'cap-stone,** s. Const : Chaperon m (d'un toit).
cap², v.tr. (capped [kapt]) **1.** (a) Coiffer (qn). (b) Sch : (In Scot.) To cap a candidate, conférer un grade à un candidat. (c) Sp : Choisir (qn) comme membre de la première équipe. **2.** Coiffer, couronner (sth. with sth., qch. de qch.) ; capsuler (une bouteille) ; armer (un aimant) ; amorcer (un obus). **3.** F : Donner un coup de chapeau à (qn). **4.** F : (Outdo) Surpasser. To cap it all . . ., pour comble. . . . **capping,** s. **1.** (a) Capsulage m (d'un flacon). (b) Amorçage m (d'un obus). (c) Nau : Capelage m (de câbles). **2.** Chapeau m, chape f (d'une charpente).
cap³, s. Typ : F : = CAPITAL² II. 2.
capability [keipə'biliti], s. **1.** Capacité f (of doing sth., pour faire qch.) ; faculté f (to do sth., de faire qch.). **2.** The boy has capabilities, c'est un enfant bien doué.
capable ['keipəbl], a. **1.** (a) Capable (of sth., de qch.). (b) Very c. doctor, médecin très compétent. C. woman, maîtresse femme. **2.** Susceptible (d'amélioration). **-ably,** adv. Avec compétence.
capacious [ka'peiʃəs], a. Vaste, spacieux ; ample.
capaciousness [ka'peiʃəsnəs], s. Amples proportions fpl (d'une salle, etc.).
capacitance [ka'pasitəns], s. El : Résistance f de capacité.
capacitate [ka'pasiteit], v.tr. **1.** Rendre (qn) capable (for sth., de qch.). **2.** Jur : Donner qualité à (qn) (to act, pour agir).
capacity [ka'pasiti], s. **1.** (a) Capacité f (d'un cylindre, El : d'un accumulateur) ; contenance f (d'un tonneau). Nau : C. of the bunkers, volume m

des soutes. (*b*) Rendement *m* (d'une loco-motive); débit *m* (d'un cours d'eau). **Carrying capacity,** charge *f* utile. *S.a.* LIFTING. **Seating capacity,** nombre *m* de places (dans une voiture, etc.). **House filled to capacity,** salle comble. **2.** Capacité (*for,* pour). *C. for doing sth.,* aptitude *f* à faire qch. **To show one's c.,** donner sa mesure. **3. To have capacity to act,** avoir qualité pour agir.

cap-à-pie ['kapa'pi:], *adv.* (Armé) de pied en cap.

caparison [ka'parizn], *s. A:* Caparaçon *m.*

cape[1] [keip], *s.* **I.** *Cost:* (*a*) Pèlerine *f,* cape *f*; (*small*) collet *m.* (*b*) *Ecc:* Camail *m, pl.* -ails. **2.** *Orn:* Collier *m.*

cape[2], *s.* Cap *m,* promontoire *m. Geog:* **The Cape (of Good Hope),** le Cap (de Bonne Espé-rance). **Cape Colony,** la colonie du Cap. **Cape pigeon,** pétrel du Cap.

caper[1] ['keipər], *s. Bot:* **I.** Câpre *f.* **2. Caper (-bush, -plant),** câprier *m.*

caper[2], *s.* Entrechat *m,* cabriole *f,* gambade *f.* **To cut capers,** (i) faire des entrechats; (ii) *F:* faire des siennes.

caper[3], *v.i.* **To caper (about),** faire des entrechats, des cabrioles; gambader.

capercailzie, capercailye [kapər'keili], *s.* Coq *m* de bruyère (d'Écosse); grand tétras.

capful ['kapful], *s.* Pleine casquette. *Nau:* **A capful of wind,** une bouffée de vent.

capillarity [kapi'lariti], *s. Ph:* Capillarité *f.*

capillary [ka'piləri], *a.* Capillaire.

capital[1] ['kapit(ə)l], *s. Arch:* Chapiteau *m.*

capital[2]. **I.** *a.* **I.** Capital, -aux. **Capital letter,** *s.* **capital,** (lettre) capitale, (lettre) majuscule (*f*). **Capital town,** *s.* **capital,** (ville) capitale (*f*). **2.** *Jur: C. punishment,* peine capitale. **3.** **It is of capital importance,** c'est de la plus haute importance. *S.a.* SHIP[1]. **4.** *A c. fellow,* un excellent garçon. **Capital!** fameux! **-ally,** *adv.* Admirablement (bien). **II. capital,** *s.* **I.** *Fin:* Capital *m,* capitaux *mpl,* fonds *mpl.* **Paid-up capital,** capital versé. **Working c.,** fonds de roulement. *F:* **To make capital out of sth.,** profiter de qch.; exploiter qch. **Capital levy,** prélèvement *m* sur le capital. **2.** *Typ: Large capitals, F: large caps,* grandes capitales; majuscules *f.*

capitalism ['kapitəlizm], *s.* Capitalisme *m.*

capitalist ['kapitəlist], *s.* Capitaliste *mf.*

capitalistic [kapitə'listik], *a.* Capitaliste.

capitalization [kapitəlai'zeiʃ(ə)n], *s.* Capitalisa-tion *f* (des intérêts).

capitalize ['kapitəlaiz], *v.tr.* **I.** Capitaliser. **2.** Écrire (un mot) avec une majuscule.

capitate ['kapitet], **capitated** ['kapiteitid], *a. Bot:* En capitule; capité.

capitation [kapi'teiʃ(ə)n], *s. Adm:* **Capitation grant,** allocation *f* (de tant) par tête.

capitular [ka'pitjulər], *a.* **I.** *Jur:* Capitulaire. **2.** *Bot:* Capité.

capitulary [ka'pitjuləri], *s. Hist:* Capitulaire *m.*

capitulate [ka'pitjuleit], *v.i.* Capituler.

capitulation [kapitju'leiʃ(ə)n], *s.* **I.** Énuméra-tion *f* des chapitres, des articles (d'un traité). **2.** Capitulation *f,* reddition *f* (d'une place forte).

capon ['keipən], *s. Cu:* Chapon *m,* poulet *m.*

caprice [ka'pri:s], *s.* **I.** Caprice *m,* lubie *f.* **2.** *Mus:* Caprice.

capricious [ka'priʃəs], *a.* Capricieux. **-ly,** *adv.* Capricieusement.

capriciousness [ka'priʃəsnəs], *s.* Humeur capri-cieuse, inégale. *C. of temper,* inégalité *f* d'humeur.

Capricorn ['kaprikɔ:rn], *s. Astr:* Le Capricorne.

caprine ['kaprain], *a. Z:* Caprin.

capriole[1] ['kaprioul], *s. Equit:* Cabriole *f.*

capriole[2], *v.i.* (*Of horse*) Cabrioler.

capsicum ['kapsikəm], *s.* **I.** *Bot:* Piment *m.* **2.** *Cu:* Piment, poivron *m.*

capsize [kap'saiz]. **I.** *v.i.* (*Of boat*) Chavirer. (*Of motor car*) Capoter; faire panache. **2.** *v.tr.* Faire chavirer. **capsizing,** *s.* Chavirement *m;* capotage *m.*

capstan ['kapstən], *s.* **I.** Cabestan *m. To man the c.,* armer le cabestan. **2.** *Mec.E:* Revolver *m* (de tour). *S.a.* LATHE 1.

capstone ['kapstəun].

capsular ['kapsjulər], *a.* (Fruit) capsulaire.

capsule ['kapsju:l], *s.* Capsule *f* (de fleur, de bouteille, pharmaceutique).

captain[1] ['kaptən], *s.* **I.** (*a*) Chef *m,* capitaine *m.* (*b*) *Sp:* Chef d'équipe. *Artil: C. of the gun,* chef de pièce. **2.** *Mil: Nau:* (*Rank*) Capitaine. *Mil.Av:* Group captain, colonel *m.* **3.** *Ich:* Grondin gris.

captain[2], *v.tr.* **I.** Commander (une compagnie). **2.** *F:* Conduire (une expédition). *Sp: To c. a team,* mener, diriger, une équipe.

captaincy ['kaptənsi], *s.* **I.** Grade *m* de capi-taine. **To obtain one's captaincy,** passer capi-taine. **2.** Conduite *f,* commandement *m.*

captainship ['kaptənʃip], *s.* **I.** = CAPTAINCY. **2.** *To handle one's troops with consummate c.,* diriger ses troupes avec l'art d'un grand capitaine.

caption ['kapʃ(ə)n], *s.* **I.** (*In book*) En-tête *m. Cin:* Sous-titre *m. Journ:* Rubrique *f.* **2.** *Jur:* Arrestation *f.* **3.** *Jur:* Indication *f* d'origine.

captious ['kapʃəs], *a.* **I.** (Raisonnement) cap-tieux, insidieux. **2.** (*Of pers.*) Pointilleux, chica-neur, vétilleux. **-ly,** *adv.* Pointilleusement.

captiousness ['kapʃəsnəs], *s.* **I.** Caractère *m* sophistique (d'un argument). **2.** Pointillerie *f.*

captivate ['kaptiveit], *v.tr.* Charmer, captiver. **captivating,** *a.* Séduisant; captivant.

captivation [kapti'veiʃ(ə)n], *s.* Séduction *f.*

captive ['kaptiv]. **I.** *a.* (*a*) Captif. (*b*) *C. state,* état *m* de captivité. **2.** *s.* Captif, prisonnier.

captivity [kap'tiviti], *s.* Captivité *f.*

captor ['kaptər], *s.* **I.** Celui qui s'est emparé de qn; ravisseur *m.* **2.** *Navy:* Capteur *m.*

capture[1] ['kaptʃər], *s.* **I.** (*Action*) Capture *f,* prise *f.* **2.** (*Thg or pers. taken*) Prise.

capture[2], *v.tr.* **I.** Capturer (un vaisseau); prendre (une ville) (*from,* sur). **2.** *W.Tel: To c. Hertzian waves,* capter des ondes hertziennes.

capturing, *s.* **I.** Capture *f* (d'un navire); prise *f* (d'une ville). **2.** *W.Tel:* Captage *m.*

Capuchin ['kapjutʃin], *s.* **I.** *Ecc:* Capucin. **2.** *Cost:* Capeline *f.* **3.** (*Monkey*) Saï *m.*

capybara [kapi'bɑ:ra], *s. Z:* Cabiai *m.*

car [kɑ:r], *s.* **I.** *Lit:* (*Chariot*) Char *m.* **2.** (**Motor**) **car,** automobile *f; F:* auto *f,* voiture *f. Light car,* voiturette *f.* **3.** *Rail:* Dining-car, wagon-restaurant *m. S.a.* SLEEPING-CAR. **4.** Nacelle *f* (d'un pont transbordeur, d'un ballon). **'car-licence,** *s.* Permis *m* de circulation.

carabineer [karabi'niər], *s. Mil:* Carabinier *m.*

caracal ['karakal], *s. Z:* Caracal *m, pl.* -als.

caracole[1] ['karakoul], *s. Equit:* Caracole *f.* **2.** *Arch:* Escalier en spirale, en colimaçon.

caracole[2], *v.i. Equit:* Caracoler.

carafe [ka'raf], *s.* Carafe *f.*

caramel [ka'ramel], *s.* **I.** Caramel *m.* **2.** Bon-bon *m* au caramel.

carapace ['karapeis], *s. Crust:* Carapace *f;* bouclier *m.*

carat ['karət], *s. Meas:* Carat *m.* **Eighteen-carat gold,** or au titre 750.

caravan ['karavan], s. **1.** Caravane f. **2.** Veh:
(a) Roulotte f. (b) Aut: Caravane.
caravanserai [kara'vansərai], s. Caravansérail m.
caravel ['karavel], s. Nau.: A: Caravelle f.
caraway ['karawei], s. Bot: Carvi m. **'caraway-
seeds,** s.pl. Graines f de carvi.
carbide ['kɑːrbaid], s. Ch: Ind: Carbure m.
carbine ['kɑːrbain], s. Carabine f.
carbo-hydrate ['kɑːrbo'haidret], s. Ch: Hydrate m de carbone.
carbolated ['kɑːrbɔleitid], a. Phéniqué.
carbolic [kɑːr'bɔlik], a. Ch: Phénique. Com:
Carbolic acid, phénol m.
carbolize ['kɑːrbɔlaiz], v.tr. Med: Phéniquer.
carbon ['kɑːrbən], s. **1.** Ch: Carbone m.
Carbon dioxide, anhydride m carbonique.
2. (a) Gas carbon, charbon m de cornue. (b) Phot:
Carbon print, épreuve au charbon. (c) I.C.E:
etc: Carbon deposit, calamine f. **3.** Typewr:
(a) Papier m carbone. (b) = CARBON-COPY.
4. Lap: Carbonado m. **'carbon-copy,** s.
Typewr: Copie f, double m, au (papier) carbone.
'carbon paper, s. **1.** Phot: Papier m au
charbon. **2.** Typewr: Papier carbone.
carbonaceous [kɑːrbə'neiʃəs], a. **1.** Ch: Car-
boné. **2.** Geol: Charbonneux.
carbonate ['kɑːrbənet], s. Ch: Carbonate m.
carbonic [kɑːr'bɔnik], a. Ch: Carbonique.
Carbonic acid gas, anhydride m carbonique.
carboniferous [kɑːrbə'nifərəs], a. Carbonifère ;
(bassin) houiller.
carbonization [kɑːrbənai'zeiʃ(ə)n], s. **1.** Carbonisation f. **2.** I.C.E: Calaminage m.
carbonize ['kɑːrbənaiz], v.tr. Carboniser ;
I.C.E: carburer. **carbonizing,** s. = CAR-
BONIZATION.
carborundum [kɑːrbo'rʌndəm], s. Carborundum m. C. wheel, meule en carborundum.
carboy ['kɑːrbɔi], s. Tourie f ; bonbonne f.
carbuncle ['kɑːrbʌŋkl], s. **1.** Lap: Escarboucle f.
2. Med: Anthrax m ; bourgeon m (sur le nez).
carburant ['kɑːrbjuːr t], s. I.C.E: Carbur-
an. m.
carburate ['kɑːrbjureit], v.tr. Carburer.
carburation [kɑːrbju'reiʃ(ə)n], s. Carburation f.
carburetted ['kɑːrbjuretid], a. Carburé. Carburetted hydrogen, méthane m ; Min: grispu m.
carburetter, -or [kɑːrbju'retər], s. I.C.E:
Carburateur m.
carburetting ['kɑːrbjuretiŋ], s. Carburation f.
carburize ['kɑːrbjuraiz], v.tr. **1.** Carburer (un
gaz). **2.** Metall: Carburer (l'acier).
carcase, carcass ['kɑːrkəs], s. **1.** F: (i) Cadavre
(humain) ; (ii) corps m. F: To save one's
carcase, sauver sa peau. **2.** Cadavre, carcasse f
(d'un animal). **3.** Carcasse (d'une maison).
card¹ [kɑːrd], s. **1.** (Playing-)card, carte f (à
jouer). Game of cards, partie de cartes. Pack of
cards, jeu de cartes. F: To play one's cards well,
bien jouer son jeu. To lay one's cards on the table,
mettre cartes sur table. To have a card up one's
sleeve, avoir encore une ressource. It is (quite)
on the cards that . . ., il est bien possible
que. . . . S.a. THROW IN 4. He's a queer card,
c'est un drôle de type. He's a knowing card,
c'est une fine mouche. He's a card, c'est un
original. **2.** (a) (Visiting-)card, carte (de visite).
Business card, carte d'adresse, d'affaires. (b) Admission card, carte, billet m, d'entrée. (c) Correspondence card, carte correspondance. (d) Com:
(Index-)card, (carte-)fiche f. (e) Golf: Carte du
parcours. Rac: Programme m des courses.
(f) Mec.E: (Indicator) card, diagramme m
d'indicateur. (g) Dance card, carnet m de bal.

3. Dominoes: Dé m. **'card-case,** s. Porte-
cartes m inv. **'card index¹,** s. Fichier m ;
classeur m. **card-'index²,** v.tr. Mettre sur
fiches. **'card-playing,** s. Jeu m. **'card-
sharper,** s. Tricheur m ; bonneteur m, escroc m.
'card-table, s. Table f de jeu.
card², v.tr. Mettre (des notes) sur fiche.
card³, s. Tex: Carde f, peigne m. **'card-
thistle,** s. Chardon m à foulon.
card⁴, v.tr. Tex: Carder, peigner (la laine, etc.).
cardamine ['kɑːdamain], s. Bot: Cardamine f.
cardamom ['kɑːrdaməm], s. Bot: Cardamome m.
cardan ['kɑːrdən], s. Mec.E: Cardan joint, joint
m de Cardan, joint universel.
cardboard ['kɑːrdbɔːrd], s. Carton m.
carder ['kɑːrdər], s. Tex: (a) (Pers.) Cardeur.
(b) (Machine) Cardeuse f.
cardiac ['kɑːrdiak]. **1.** a. Med: Cardiaque,
cardiaire. **2.** s. Pharm: Cordial m, pl. -aux.
cardigan ['kɑːrdigən], s. Gilet m de tricot.
cardinal ['kɑːrdinəl]. I. a. **1.** Cardinal, -aux.
The cardinal numbers, points, les nombres,
points, cardinaux. The c. virtues, les vertus
cardinales. **2.** (Colour) Pourpre ; cardinal inv.
-ally, adv. Fondamentalement. II. **cardinal,**
s. **1.** Cardinal m. **2.** Orn: Cardinal(-bird),
cardinal. **'cardinal-flower,** s. Bot: Car-
dinale f.
cardoon [kɑːr'duːn], s. Hort: Cardon m.
care¹ ['keər], s. **1.** Souci m, inquiétude f. My
greatest c., ma plus grande préoccupation.
Gnawing care, soucis rongeurs. Prov: Care
killed the cat, il ne faut pas se faire de bile.
2. Soin(s) m(pl), attention f, ménagement m.
Constant c., soins assidus. Tender c., sollicitude f.
C. for details, attention aux détails. To take care
in doing sth., apporter du soin à faire qch. To
take care not to do sth., se garder, prendre garde,
de faire qch. Take care! have a care! (i) faites
attention ! prenez garde ! (ii) ne vous y frottez
pas ! To take c. of one's health, ménager sa santé.
To take c. that sth. shall be done, veiller à ce que
qch. se fasse. That matter will take care of itself,
cela s'arrangera tout seul. 'Glass with care,'
"fragile." **3.** Soin(s), charge f, tenue f. C. and
treatment of animals, soins et traitement des
animaux. Write to me care of Mrs X, c/o Mrs X,
écrivez-moi aux bons soins de Mme X, chez
Mme X. C. of a car, entretien m d'une voiture.
Want of care, incurie f, négligence f. **4.** Cares of
State, responsabilités f d'État. That shall be my c.,
je m'en charge. **'care-free,** a. Libre de soucis ;
insouciant ; sans souci. **'care-taker,** s. Concierge mf (de maison) ; gardien m (d'un immeuble, d'un musée). **'care-worn,** a. Rongé
par le chagrin.
care², v.i. **1.** Se soucier, s'inquiéter, se préoccuper (for, about, de). That's all he cares about,
il n'y a que cela qui l'intéresse. I don't c. what
he says, peu m'importe ce qu'il dit. What do I
care? qu'est-ce que cela me fait? I don't c.
much for it, je n'y tiens pas. To care for nothing,
se désintéresser de tout ; ne se soucier de rien.
Not that I care, non pas que ça me fasse quelque
chose. For all I care, pour (tout) ce que ça me
fait. I don't care! as if I cared! ça m'est égal !
I don't c. either way, cela m'est indifférent.
F: I don't care a red cent, je m'en moque pas
mal ; ça m'est absolument égal ; F: je m'en
fiche. He doesn't c. for anybody or anything, il se
moque du tiers comme du quart. **2.** To care for
invalids, soigner les malades. Well cared-for
appearance, apparence soignée. **3.** To care for
s.o., aimer qn. He doesn't c. for her, elle ne lui

8

plaît pas. *I don't c. for this music,* cette musique ne me dit rien. *F:* I don't care if I do, je veux bien ; je ne dis pas non. *If you c. to join us,* si vous voulez vous joindre à nous. If you care to, si le cœur vous en dit.

careen [ka'ri:n]. **1.** *v.tr.* (a) Abattre, mettre, (un navire) en carène. (b) Caréner (un navire) ; nettoyer la carène (d'un navire). **2.** *v.i.* (*Of ship*) Donner de la bande. **careening,** *s.* **1.** Carénage *m* ; abattage *m* en carène. Careening basin, bassin de carénage. **2.** *Nau :* Bande dangereuse.

career[1] [ka'ri:ər], *s.* **1.** Course (précipitée). To stop in mid career, rester, demeurer, en (beau) chemin. **2.** Carrière *f.* To take up a c., embrasser une carrière.

career[2], *v.i.* Courir rapidement, follement. To career along, être en pleine course.

careful ['keərful], *a.* **1.** Soigneux (*of,* de) ; attentif (*of,* à). Be c. of it! ayez-en soin ! Be c. what you are doing, faites attention à ce que vous faites. Be careful! prenez garde! faites attention! **2.** Prudent, circonspect. *C. housewife,* ménagère très regardante. *A c. answer,* une réponse bien pesée. **-fully,** *adv.* **1.** Soigneusement, avec soin ; attentivement. **2.** Prudemment ; avec circonspection. To live c., (i) soigner sa santé ; (ii) vivre avec économie.

carefulness ['keərfulnəs], *s.* **1.** Soin *m,* attention *f.* **2.** Prudence *f.*

careless ['keərləs], *a.* **1.**(a) Insouciant (*of, about,* de) ; nonchalant. (b) *A c. remark,* une observation à la légère. *C. mistake,* faute d'inattention. **2.** Négligent ; sans soin. **-ly,** *adv.* Avec insouciance ; négligemment ; sans soin.

carelessness ['keərləsnəs], *s.* **1.**(a) Insouciance*f.* (b) Inattention *f.* Piece of carelessness, étourderie *f.* **2.** Manque *m* de soin ; négligence *f.*

caress[1] [ka'res], *s.* Caresse *f.*

caress[2], *v.tr.* (a) Caresser. (b) *F:* Mignoter (qn). **caressing,** *a.* Caressant. *C. tones,* tons câlins. **-ly,** *adv.* D'une manière caressante.

caret ['karet], *s. Typ :* Signe *m* d'omission.

cargo, *pl.* **-oes** ['ka:rgo, -ouz], *s. Nau :* Cargaison*f,* chargement *m.* To take in c., charger des marchandises. '**cargo-boat,** *s.* Cargo *m.*

Carib ['karib], *a. & s. Ethn :* Caraïbe (*mf*).

Caribbean [kari'bi:ən], *a.* Caribbean Sea, Islands, mer des Caraïbes ; îles Caraïbes.

caribou [kari'bu:], *s. Z :* Caribou *m, pl.* -ous.

caricature[1] ['karikatjuər], *s.* Caricature *f,* charge*f.*

caricature[2] [karika'tjuər], *v.tr.* Caricaturer. *Th :* To caricature a part, charger un rôle.

caricaturist [karika'tjuərist], *s.* Caricaturiste *m.*

caries ['keərii:z], *s. Med :* Carie *f.*

carillon [ka'riljən], *s. Mus :* Carillon *m.*

carinate ['karinet], *a. Nat.Hist :* Caréné

carious ['keəriəs], *a. Med :* (Os) carié.

carking ['ka:rkiŋ], *a.* Carking care, soucis rongeurs.

carline ['ka:rlin], *s.* Carline thistle, carline *f* vulgaire.

carman, *pl.* **-men** ['ka:rmən, -men], *s.m.* (a) Camionneur, charretier. (b) *Com :* Livreur. Carman and contractor, entrepreneur de camionnage.

Carmelite ['ka:rmelait], *s. Rel.H :* Carme *m.* Carmelite nun, carmélite *f.* The Carmelite order, l'ordre du Carmel.

carmine ['ka:rmain, -min], **1.** *s.* Carmin *m.* **2.** *a.* Carminé ; carmin *inv.*

carnage ['ka:rned3], *s.* Carnage *m.*

carnal ['ka:rn(ə)l], *a.* **1.** Charnel ; (i) sensuel ;

(ii) sexuel. Carnal sins, péchés de la chair. **2.** Mondain. **-ally,** *adv.* Charnellement, sensuellement.

carnation[1] [ka:r'neiʃ(ə)n]. (a) *s.* Incarnat *m.* (b) *a.* (Teint) incarnat, incarnadin.

carnation[2], *s. Bot :* Œillet *m.*

carnival ['ka:rnivəl], *s.* **1.** Carnaval *m, pl.* -als. **2.** *C. of bloodshed,* orgie *f* de sang.

carnivora [ka:r'nivora], *s.pl. Z :* Carnassiers *m.*

carnivore ['ka:rnivo:ər], *s.* **1.** *Z :* Carnassier *m.* **2.** *Bot :* Plante *f* carnivore.

carnivorous [ka:r'nivorəs], *a.* **1.** (*Of animal*) Carnassier. **2.** (*Of pers., plant*) Carnivore.

carob ['karəb], *s.* **1.** Carob(-bean), caroube *f,* carouge *f.* **2.** Carob(-tree), caroubier *m.*

carol[1] ['karəl], *s.* (a) Chant *m,* chanson *f.* Christmas carol, noël *m.* (b) Tire-lire *m* (de l'alouette).

carol[2], *v.i. & tr.* (**carolled**) (a) Chanter (joyeusement). (b) (*Of lark*) Tire-lirer.

carom[1] ['karəm], *s. Bill : U.S :* Carambolage *m.*

carom[2], *v.i. Bill : U.S :* Caramboler ; faire un carambolage.

carotid [ka'rɔtid], *a. & s. Anat :* Carotide (*f*).

carousal [ka'rauzəl], **carouse**[1] [ka'ra:uz], *s.* B(e)uverie *f ; F :* bombe *f ;* bamboche *f.*

carouse[2], *v.i.* Faire la fête, *F :* la bombe.

carouser [ka'rauzər], *s.* Fêtard *m,* noceur *m.*

carp[1] [ka:rp], *s.* (*Usu. inv. in pl.*) *Ich :* Carpe *f.*

carp[2], *v.i.* Épiloguer, gloser (*at,* sur). *To c. at sth.,* trouver à redire à qch. **carping**[1], *a.* Chicanier. *C. criticism,* critique pointilleuse. **-ly,** *adv.* Pointilleusement. **carping**[2], *s.* Critique (malveillante).

carpal ['ka:rp(ə)l]. *Anat :* **1.** *a.* Carpien ; du carpe. **2.** *s.* Os carpien.

carpel ['ka:rpəl], *s. Bot :* Carpelle *m,* carpophylle *m.*

carpellary ['ka:rpeləri], *a. Bot :* Carpellaire.

carpenter ['ka:rpəntər], *s.* Charpentier *m ;* menuisier *m* en bâtiments. *Nau :* Ship's carpenter, matelot *m* charpentier. Carpenter's shop, atelier de menuiserie.

carpentry [ka:rpəntri], *s.* **1.** Charpenterie *f.* **2.** Charpente *f.*

carper ['ka:rpər], *s.* (a) Critique malveillant. (b) *F :* Ronchonneur.

carpet[1] ['ka:rpet], *s.* Tapis *m.* (a) Brussels carpet, moquette *f* de Bruxelles. To lay a c., poser un tapis. *F :* To be on the carpet, être sur la sellette. (b) Tapis (de verdure, etc.). **carpet-** '**bag,** *s. A :* Sac *m* de voyage, de nuit. **carpet-** '**bagger,** *s. F :* Candidat (au Parlement) étranger à la circonscription. '**carpet-broom,** *s.* Balai *m* de jonc. '**carpet-knight,** *s.m.* Héros de salon. '**carpet-'slippers,** *s.pl.* Pantoufles *f* en tapisserie. '**carpet-sweeper,** *s.* Balai *m* mécanique.

carpet[2], *v.tr.* **1.** Recouvrir d'un tapis. **2.** *F : A :* Mettre (qn) sur la sellette. **carpeted,** *a.* Couvert d'un tapis. Slope c. with flowers, pente tapissée de fleurs. **carpeting,** *s.* **1.** (a) Pose *f* de tapis. (b) *Coll.* Tapis *mpl* en pièce. **2.** *F : A :* Semonce *f.*

carpus ['ka:rpəs], *s. Anat : Z :* Carpe *m.*

carriage ['kared3], *s.* **1.** Port *m,* transport *m. Com :* Carriage free, franc de port ; franco. Carriage paid, port payé ; franc de port. Carriage forward, (en) port dû. **2.** Port, maintien *m. Free, easy, c.,* allure dégagée. **3.** (a) *Veh :* Voiture *f ;* équipage *m,* attelage *m.* Carriage and pair, voiture à deux chevaux. Baby carriage, voiture d'enfant. (b) *Rail :* Voiture, wagon *m. You change carriages at . . .,* on change de voiture à. . . . **4.** (a) *Artil :* (Gun-)carriage, affût *m.*

(b) *Veh:* Train *m* (de la voiture). (c) *Mec.E:* Chariot *m* (d'un tour, d'une machine à écrire). **'carriage-builder,** *s.* Carrossier *m.* **'carriage-building,** *s.* Carrosserie *f.* **'carriage-drive,** *s.* Avenue *f* pour voitures; grande avenue. **'carriage-entrance,** *s.* Porte cochère. **'carriage-window,** *s.* Glace *f* (de voiture). **carrick bend** ['karik'bend], *s. Nau:* Nœud *m* de vache, d'aju(s)t.

carrier ['kariər], *s.* **1.** (*Pers.*) (a) Porteur. (b) *Com:* Camionneur *m,* messagiste *m,* roulier *m. Jur:* Common **carrier,** voiturier public. (c) *Mil:* (*Of ammunition*) Ravitailleur *m.* **2.** (a) Shade **carrier** (*of lamp*), support *m* d'abat-jour. (b) (Luggage-)**carrier,** porte-bagages *m inv.* (c) *Mec.E:* Toc *m,* doguin *m* (de tour); (*heart-shaped*) cœur *m* de tour. *Sm.a:* Cartridge **carrier,** chargeur *m.* (d) *Ind:* Overhead **carrier,** transporteur aérien. **3.** *Navy:* Aircraft **carrier,** (navire *m*) porte-avions *m inv.* **4.** Carrier-pigeon, pigeon voyageur. **5.** *Art:* Véhicule *m* (pour couleurs). **6.** *W.Tel:* Carrier wave, onde porteuse.

carrion ['kariən], *s.* Charogne *f. S.a.* CROW[1] 1.

carron-oil [karən'ɔil], *s. Pharm:* Liniment *m* oléo-calcaire (pour brûlures).

carrot ['karət], *s. Hort:* Carotte *f. F:* Carrots, (i) cheveux *m* rouges; (ii) (*pers.*) rouquin, -ine.

carroty ['karəti], *a. F:* Roux, *f.* rousse.

carry[1] ['kari], *s.* **1.** *Mil:* Sword at the **carry,** sabre en main. **2.** (a) Portée *f* (d'un fusil). (b) *Golf:* Trajet *m* (d'une balle). **3.** Portage *m* (entre cours d'eau).

carry[2], *v.tr.* (carried) **1.** Porter (un fardeau); transporter, camionner (des marchandises); rentrer (la moisson). *To c. one's life in one's hands,* risquer sa vie. *S.a.* FETCH[2] 1, LEG[1] 1. **2.** (*Of wires*) Conduire (le son); (*of ropes*) amener (l'eau). **3.** *To c. pipes under a street,* faire passer des tuyaux par-dessous une rue. *To c. sth. in one's head,* retenir qch. dans sa tête. *Liberty carried to the point of effrontery,* licence poussée jusqu'au cynisme. **To carry sth. into effect,** mettre qch. à exécution. **4.** Enlever (une forteresse); emporter (une position) d'assaut. **To carry all before one,** (i) remporter tous les prix; (ii) vaincre toutes les résistances. **To carry one's hearers with one,** entraîner son auditoire. **To carry one's point,** imposer sa manière de voir. *S.a.* DAY 1 (b), FOOT[1] 1. **5.** (i) Adopter, (ii) faire adopter (une proposition). (*Of a bill*) **To be carried,** être voté. **6.** (a) Porter (une montre) sur soi. **To carry authority,** avoir du poids, de l'autorité. (*Of money*) To carry interest, porter intérêt. (b) (*Of shop*) Avoir (des marchandises) en magasin, en dépôt. **7.** *Mil:* **To carry swords,** mettre le sabre en main. **8.** **To carry one's head high,** porter la tête haute. **To carry one's liquor well,** bien supporter la boisson. **9.** Porter, supporter (une poutre, une voûte). **10.** *Ar:* **To carry a figure,** retenir un chiffre. Carry two and seven are nine, deux de retenue et sept font neuf. **11.** *Abs.* (*Of gun*) Porter. *His voice carries well,* il a une voix qui porte bien. **12.** *St.Exch:* Accorder un crédit à (un client). **carry across,** *v.tr.* Transporter (qch.) de l'autre côté. **carry along,** *v.tr.* Emporter, entraîner (qn, qch.). *The mud carried along by the stream,* la vase charriée par le ruisseau. **carry away,** *v.tr.* **1.** = CARRY OFF 1. **2.** Transporter (qn de joie). *Carried away by his feelings,* entraîné par ses émotions. **carry back,** *v.tr.* **1.** Rapporter (qch.); ramener (qn). **2.** Reporter (qch.); remmener (qn). **carry down,** *v.tr.* Descendre (qch.). **carry forward,** *v.tr.*

1. Avancer (qch.). **2.** *Book-k:* To c. an item **forward,** reporter un article. **Carried forward,** report *m*; à reporter. **carry-'forward,** *s. Book-k:* Report *m.* **carry off,** *v.tr.* **1.** Emporter (qch.); emmener, enlever (qn). **2.** *To c. off,* (i) faire passer la chose; (ii) réussir le coup. *S.a.* AIR[1] III. **carrying off,** *s.* Enlèvement *m* (de qn). **carry on.** **1.** *v.tr.* Poursuivre; continuer (une tradition); exercer (un commerce); entretenir (une correspondance); soutenir (une conversation). **2.** *v.i.* (a) *To c. on during s.o.'s absence,* (i) continuer le travail, (ii) diriger les affaires, pendant l'absence de qn; *Adm:* assurer l'intérim. *Mil:* Carry on! continuez! (b) Persévérer, persister. *I shall c. on to the end,* j'irai jusqu'au bout. (c) *F:* Se comporter. *I don't like the way she carries on,* je n'aime pas ses façons. (d) *F: She carried on dreadfully,* elle nous a fait une scène terrible. *Don't c. on like that!* ne vous emballez pas comme ça! (e) *F:* To carry on with s.o., faire des coquetteries à qn. **carrying on,** *s.* **1.** Continuation *f* (d'un travail, de la guerre). **2.** *F:* Such carryings on! quelle manière de se conduire! **carry out,** *v.tr.* **1.** Porter (qch.) dehors. **2.** Mettre à exécution, effectuer (un projet); remplir (les instructions de qn); exécuter (un programme); exercer (un mandat); se décharger (d'une commission); s'acquitter (d'une fonction). *To c. out the law,* appliquer la loi. *Mil: Movement smartly carried out,* mouvement bien enlevé. **carry over,** *v.tr.* **1.** Transporter (une somme) de l'autre côté. **2.** *Book-k:* Reporter (une somme). *To c. over a balance,* transporter un solde. **3.** *St.Exch:* To c. over stock, reporter des titres. **'carry-over,** *s. St.Exch:* Report *m.* **carrying over,** *s.* **1.** Transport *m.* **2.** *St.Exch:* Report *m.* **carry through,** *v.tr.* **1.** Transporter (qch.). **2.** Mener (une entreprise) à bonne fin. **3.** *His strong constitution carried him through (his illness),* sa forte santé l'aida à surmonter cette maladie. **carry up,** *v.tr.* Monter (qch.). **carrying,** *s.* **1.** (a) Port *m,* transport *m.* Carrying business, entreprise de transports. Carrying capacity, (capacité de) charge *f* utile. (b) Carrying of arms, port d'armes. **2.** Enlèvement *m* (d'une forteresse). **3.** Adoption *f,* vote *m* (d'un projet de loi).

cart[1] [kɑːrt], *s.* Charrette *f. Mil:* Fourgon *m.* Tip-cart, tombereau *m. F:* **To put the cart before the horse,** mettre la charrue devant les bœufs. *P:* **To be in the cart,** être dans le pétrin, dans de beaux draps. **'cart-grease,** *s.* Vieux oing. **'cart-horse,** *s.* Cheval *m* de (gros) trait. **'cart-house,** *s.* Hangar *m,* remise *f,* chartil *m.* **'cart-load,** *s.* Charretée *f,* voiturée *f* (of, de). *C.-l. of coal* tombereau *m* de charbon. *F:* A cart-load of trouble, toute une accumulation de malheurs. **'cart-road, -track, -way,** *s.* Chemin *m* de charroi; route charretière, chemin charretier. **'cart-shed,** *s.* = CART-HOUSE. **'cart-wheel,** *s.* **1.** (a) Roue *f* de charrette. (b) *P:* Thune *f.* **2.** *Gym:* To turn cart-wheels, faire la roue (sur les pieds et les mains).

cart[2], *v.tr.* Charrier, charroyer. **cart about,** *v.tr. F:* Trimbaler (qn, qch.). **carting,** *s.* = CARTAGE.

cartage ['kɑːrtedʒ], *s.* ●Charroi *m,* charriage *m.*

carte (à la) [alɑ'kɑːrt]. *Fr.a.phr. & adv.phr.* A la carte dinner, dîner à la carte.

cartel ['kɑːrtel], *s.* (a) Cartel *m.* (b) Cartel(-ship), navire *m* parlementaire.

carter ['kɑːrtər], *s.* Charretier *m,* roulier *m,* camionneur *m.*

Cartesian [kɑːrˈtiːziən], *a. & s. Phil: Mth:* Cartésien. *Ph:* Cartesian diver, imp, ludion *m.*

cartful [ˈkɑːrtful], *s.* Charretée *f.*

Carthusian [kɑːrˈθjuziən], *a. & s.* Chartreux ; des chartreux. *The C. friars,* les chartreux.

cartilage [ˈkɑːrtiledʒ], *s.* Cartilage *m.*

cartilaginous [kɑːrtiˈladʒinəs], *a.* Cartilagineux.

cartographer [kɑːrˈtɔgrəfər], *s.* Cartographe *m.*

cartographical [kɑːrtoˈgrafik(ə)l], *a.* Cartographique.

cartography [kɑːrˈtɔgrəfi], *s.* Cartographie *f.*

cartomancy [ˈkɑːrtomansi], *s.* Cartomancie *f.*

carton [ˈkɑːrtən], *s.* (*a*) Carton *m.* (*b*) Petite boîte en carton.

cartoon[1] [kɑːrˈtuːn], *s.* **1.** *Art:* Carton *m* (dessin ou peinture sur carton). **2.** *Journ:* (*a*) Dessin *m* (humoristique ou satirique) sur les événements du jour. (*b*) Portrait caricaturé.

cartoon[2], *v.tr.* Faire la caricature de (qn).

cartouche [kɑːrˈtuːʃ], *s.* *Arch: etc:* Cartouche *m.*

cartridge [ˈkɑːrtridʒ], *s.* **1.** (*a*) Cartouche *f.* To fire blank cartridge, tirer à blanc. (*b*) Gargousse *f* (de grosse pièce). **2.** *Ind:* Filter cartridge, cartouche filtrante ; cartouche à filtre. **3.** *Phot: U.S:* (Pellicule *f* en) bobine *f.* 'cartridge-belt, *s.* **1.** Ceinture-cartouchière *f.* **2.** Bande-chargeur *f* (de mitrailleuse). 'cartridge-case, *s.* **1.** Étui *m,* douille *f.* **2.** *Artil:* Gargoussier *m.* 'cartridge-paper, *s.* Papier fort. 'cartridge-pouch, *s.* Cartouchière *f.*

cartulary [ˈkɑːrtjuləri], *s.* Cartulaire *m.*

cartwright [ˈkɑːrtrait], *s.* Charron *m.*

caruncle [ˈkarəŋkl, kaˈrʌŋkl], *s.* Caroncule *f.*

carve [kɑːrv], *v.tr.* **1.** Sculpter, graver, ciseler. To carve one's way, se tailler un chemin. **2.** Découper (la viande) ; dépecer (un poulet). *F:* To carve up a country, démembrer un pays.

carving, *s.* **1.** *Art:* Sculpture *f,* gravure *f,* ciselure *f.* **2.** Découpage *m* de la viande.

carvel [ˈkɑːrvel], *s.* *A :* = CARAVEL. 'carvel-built, *a.* Bordé à franc-bord.

carver [ˈkɑːrvər], *s.* **1.** (*a*) Ciseleur *m.* (*b*) (*At table*) Découpeur ; (*hotel*) serveur. **2.** Couteau *m* à découper. *pl.* Service *m* à découper.

caryatid [kariˈatid], *s.* Caryatide *f.*

caryopsis [kariˈɔpsis], *s.* *Bot:* Caryopse *m.*

cascade[1] [kasˈkeid], *s.* Chute *f* d'eau ; cascade *f.*

cascade[2], *v.i.* Tomber en cascade ; cascader.

case[1] [keis], *s.* **1.** Cas *m.* The case in point, le cas dont il s'agit. *Jur:* A case in point, un cas d'espèce. *F:* To quote a case in point, citer un exemple topique. Should the case occur, le cas échéant. This is not the case, ce n'est pas le cas ; il n'en est rien. *If that is the c.,* s'il en est ainsi. That is often the c., cela arrive souvent. That alters the case, c'est une autre affaire ; *F:* c'est une autre paire de manches ! It is a hard case, c'est dur pour lui. It is a case for the doctor, c'est affaire au médecin. *F:* It's a case, les voilà épris l'un de l'autre. In any case, en tout cas ; dans tous les cas ; de toute façon. As in the case of . . ., comme pour. . . . Do it, just in case, faites-le à tout hasard. *Such being the c. . . .,* cela étant. *. . . In most cases,* en général. **2.** *Med:* (*a*) Cas (de choléra). (*b*) *F:* Malade *mf* ; blessé. *Mil:* The serious cases, les grands blessés. **3.** *Jur:* (*a*) Cause *f,* affaire. Famous cases, causes célèbres. To state the case, faire l'exposé des faits. (*b*) The case for the Crown, l'accusation *f.* There is no case against you, vous êtes hors de cause. You have no case, vous serez débouté (de votre demande). To make out a case, établir une

réclamation. **4.** *Gram:* Cas. The case-endings, les flexions casuelles. 'case-book, *s.* Recueil *m* de jurisprudence.

case[2], *s.* **1.** Case of goods, caisse *f* de marchandises ; colis *m.* *Mil:* Uniform case, cantine *f* (d'officier). **2.** (*a*) Étui *m* ; écrin *m* (pour bijoux) ; trousse *f* (d'instruments) ; boîte *f* (de violon). (*b*) (**Display**) case, vitrine *f.* **3.** (*a*) Coffre *m,* caisse (de piano) ; buffet *m* (d'orgue). (*b*) Boîtier *m* (de montre). **4.** = CASING 2. **5.** (*a*) *Bookb:* Couverture *f.* (*b*) Filing-case, carton *m.* **6.** *Dom.Ec:* Pillow-case, taie *f* d'oreiller. **7.** *Typ:* Casse *f.* Upper case, haut *m* de casse. Lower-case letters, lettres (de) bas de casse ; minuscules *f.* 'case-binding, *s.* *Bookb:* Emboîtage *m* ; reliure *f* Bradel. 'case-bottle, *s.* Bouteille carrée ; flacon *m.* 'case-harden, *v.tr.* Cémenter, aciérer (le fer). 'case-hardened, *a.* **1.** Cémenté, aciéré. **2.** *F:* (*Of pers.*) Endurci. 'case-opener, *s.* Ciseau *m* à déballer.

case[3], *v.tr.* **1.** To case goods (up), encaisser des marchandises. **2.** (*a*) Envelopper (*with,* de). To c. a boiler, chemiser une chaudière. To c. a turbine, bâcher une turbine. (*b*) *Bookb:* Cartonner (un livre). **3.** To case a well, tuber, cuveler, un puits. **casing,** *s.* **1.** (*a*) Encaissement *m* (de marchandises) ; clissage *m* (d'une bouteille). *Bookb:* Casing (in), cartonnage *m.* (*b*) Coffrage *m* (d'un puits de mine). **2.** Enveloppe *f* (d'une pompe) ; chemise *f* (d'un cylindre) ; bâche *f* (d'une turbine) ; revêtement *m* (d'une maçonnerie) ; chambranle *m* (d'une porte). *Min:* Boisage *m* (d'une galerie). *N.Arch:* Cadre *m* (d'une hélice). *El.E:* Armature casing, enveloppe d'induit. *Aut:* Differential casing, carter *m* du différentiel. Tyre casing, enveloppe (extérieure), carcasse *f,* de pneu.

casein [ˈkeisiin], *s.* *Ch: Ind:* Caséine *f.*

casemate [ˈkeismeit], *s.* *Fort:* Casemate *f,* coffre *m.* *N.Arch:* Gun *c.,* réduit *m.*

casement [ˈkeismənt], *s.* Châssis *m* de fenêtre à deux battants. 'casement-cloth, *s.* Toile *f* pour rideaux. 'casement-window, *s.* Croisée *f.*

cash[1] [kaʃ], *s.* *No pl.* Espèces *fpl* ; argent comptant ; valeurs *fpl* en espèces. To be out of cash, n'être pas en fonds ; *F:* être à sec. Hard cash, espèces sonnantes. Cash down, argent (au) comptant. 'Terms cash,' "payable au comptant." 'Cash less discount,' "comptant avec escompte." Cash price, prix au comptant. 'C. on delivery' parcel, colis grevé de remboursement. Cash with order, payable à la commande. *Book-k:* Cash in hand, espèces en caisse. To balance the cash, faire la caisse. 'cash-account, *s.* Compte *m* de caisse. 'cash-book, *s.* Livre *m* de caisse ; sommier *m.* 'cash-box, *s.* Caisse *f* ; cassette *f.* 'cash-clerk, -keeper, *s.* Caissier *m.* 'cash-desk, *s.* Caisse *f.* 'cash-register, *s.* Caisse enregistreuse. 'cash-sale, *s.* Transaction *f* au comptant.

cash[2], *v.tr.* Toucher (un chèque) ; encaisser (un coupon).

cash[3], *s.* *Num:* Sapèque *f.*

cashew [kaˈʃuː], *s.* *Bot:* Acajou *m* à pommes ; anacardier *m.* Cashew nut, noix *f* d'acajou.

cashier[1] [kaˈʃiːər], *s.* Caissier. Cashier's desk, office, caisse *f* ; comptoir *m* de recette.

cashier[2], *v.tr.* Casser (un officier).

Cashmere [ˈkaʃmiːər]. **1.** *Pr.n.* Le Cachemire. **2.** *s.* *Tex:* Cachemire *m.* Cashmere shawl, cachemire de l'Inde.

casino [kaˈsiːno], *s.* Casino *m.*

cask [kɑːsk], s. (a) Barrique f, fût m, tonneau m. (b) (For dry goods) Boucaut m.
casket ['kɑːsket], s. Coffret m, cassette f.
Caspian [ˌkaspiən], a. The Caspian Sea, la mer Caspienne m.
cassava [kaˈsɑːva], s. Cassave f, manioc m.
casserole ['kasəroul], s. Cu: 1. Cocotte f (en terre). 2. Ragoût m en cocotte.
cassia ['kasia], s. 1. Bot: (a) Casse f, canéfice f. (b) Cassia(-tree), cassier m. 2. Pharm: Casse.
cassock ['kasək], s. Ecc: Soutane f.
cassowary ['kasoweəri], s. Orn: Casoar m.
cast[1] [kɑːst], s. 1. (a) Jet m (d'une pierre); coup m (de dés); lancer m (du filet). Nau: Cast oı the lead, coup de sonde. (b) Fish: Bas m de ligne. 2. (a) Earth-worm casts, déjections t de lombric. (b) Husb: Agneaux pl mis bas. 3. Ap: Jet (d'abeilles); rejet m (d'essaim). 4. (a) Metall: Coulée f. (b) Pièce moulee. Plaster cast, moulage m au plâtre. To take a c. of sth., mouler qch. 5. (a) A man of his cast, un homme de sa trempe. Cast of mind, tournure f d'esprit. Cast of features, physionomie f. (b) (Arrangement) Cast of a sentence, ordonnance f, allure f, d'une phrase. 6. To have a cast in one's eye, avoir une tendance à loucher. 7. Addition f (de chiffres). 8. Th: Distribution f (des rôles); la troupe.
cast[2], v.tr. (p.t. cast; p.p. cast) 1. (a) Jeter, lancer (une pierre); projeter (une ombre). The die is cast, le dé, le sort, en est jeté. You needn't c. it in his teeth, ce n'est pas la peine de revenir là-dessus. Nau: To cast the lead, donner un coup de sonde. S.a. ASPERSION 2. (b) (Of reptile) To cast its slough, jeter sa dépouille. (Of bird) To c. its feathers, muer. (Of pers.) To c. a garment, se dévêtir de qch.; ôter un vêtement. S.a. SHOE[1] 2. (c) Husb: (Of dam) To c. her young, mettre bas (un petit) avant terme. 2. Fish: To c. the line, lancer la ligne. 3. Donner (un suffrage). Number of votes cast, nombre de voix, de suffrages. 4. Astrol: To cast a horoscope, dresser un horoscope. S.a. LOT 1. 5. To cast (up) figures, additionner des chiffres. S.a. ACCOUNT[1] 1. 6. To c. a horse, jeter un cheval par terre. 7. (a) Jur: To be cast in damages, être condamné à des dommages-intérêts. (b) Mil: Réformer (un cheval). 8. Metall: Fondre (du métal); mouler (un cylindre). To c. a statue, couler une statue. Cast in one piece, coulé en bloc. Typ: To c. a page, clicher une page. S.a. MOULD[2] 2. 9. Th: To cast a play, distribuer les rôles d'une pièce. To c. s.o. for a part, assigner un rôle à qn. **cast about.** 1. v.tr. To c. one's eyes about, promener ses regards de tous côtés. 2. v.i. (a) To cast about for an excuse, chercher une excuse. (b) Nau: Virer. **cast aside**, v.tr. Se défaire de (qch.); mettre (qch.) de côté, F: au rancart. **cast away**, v.tr. (a) Jeter au loin; rejeter. (b) Nau: To be cast away, faire naufrage. **cast back.** 1. v.tr. (a) Renvoyer (une pierre, etc.). (b) Ramener, reporter, (ses pensées) en arrière. 2. v.i. Revenir sur ses pas. **cast down**, v.tr. (a) Jeter bas. (b) Baisser (les yeux). (c) To be cast down, être abattu, déprimé. **cast in**, v.tr. To cast in one's lot with s.o., épouser le parti de qn; partager le sort de qn. **cast loose**, v.tr. Nau: Larguer (une amarre). Abs. To cast loose, larguer. **cast off.** 1. v.tr. (a) Rejeter. He was cast off by his family, il a été renié par sa famille. (b) Se dévêtir de (ses vêtements). Cast-off clothing, cast-offs, vêtements mpl de rebut; défroque f. (c) To c. off all sense of shame, abjurer toute pudeur. (d) To c. off the hawsers, larguer les

amarres. (e) Knitting: To c. off five stitches, fermer cinq mailles. Abs. To cast off, rabattre les mailles. (f) Typ: To cast off a manuscript, évaluer le nombre de pages imprimées auquel se montera un manuscrit. 2. v.i. (Of ship) Abattre sous le vent. **cast out**, v.tr. Mettre (qn) dehors; exorciser (des démons). **cast up**, v.tr. 1. Lever (les yeux) au ciel. 2. To cast sth. up to s.o., reprocher qch. à qn. 3. Flotsam cast up on the shore, épaves rejetées sur le rivage. **cast**[3], a. 1. Art: Cast shadow, ombre portée. 2. Cast horses, chevaux de réforme. 3. Metall: Coulé. Cast 'iron, fonte de fer; (fer de) fonte. 'Cast-iron discipline, discipline de fer. **casting**[1], a. The chairman has the c. vote, la voix du président est prépondérante. To give the c. vote, départager les voix. **casting**[2], s. 1. (a) Jet m (d'une pierre). (b) Metall: Moulage m, fonte f. (c) Mil: Réforme f (de chevaux). (d) Th: Distribution f des rôles. (e) Casting (up) of figures, addition f de chiffres. 2. Metall: Pièce coulée, pièce de fonte. Heavy castings, grosses pièces. 'cast(ing)-net, s. Fish: Épervier m.
castanets [kasta'nets], s.pl. Castagnettes f.
castaway ['kɑːstəwei], s. (a) Naufragé. (b) = OUTCAST.
caste [kɑːst], s. Caste f. F: To lose caste, déroger (à son rang).
castellan ['kastelən], s. A: Gouverneur m (du château).
castellated ['kasteleitid], a. 1. Crénelé. 2. (Immeuble) bâti dans le style féodal.
castigate ['kastigeit], v.tr. Châtier, corriger (qn).
castigation [kasti'geiʃ(ə)n], s. Châtiment m, correction f.
castigator ['kastigeitər], s. Châtieur m.
Castile [kas'tiːl]. Pr.n. Geog: La Castille. Com: Castile soap, savon blanc.
Castilian [kas'tilian], a. & s. Castillan.
castle[1] ['kɑːsl], s. 1. Château (fort). F: To build castles in the air, bâtir des châteaux en Espagne. Prov: An Englishman's home is his castle, charbonnier est maître chez lui. 2. Chess: Tour f. 'castle-nut, s. Écrou crénelé, à entailles.
castle[2], v.tr. Chess: To castle the king, abs. to castle, roquer. **castling**, s. Chess: Roque m.
castor[1] ['kɑːstər], s. 1. Saupoudroir m. S.a. SUGAR[1] 1. 2. Roulette f (de fauteuil).
castor[2], s. Châtaigne f (de jambe de cheval).
castor oil ['kɑːstər'ɔil], s. Huile f de ricin.
castrate [kas'treit], v.tr. 1. Châtrer. 2. F: Expurger, émasculer (un livre).
castration [kas'treiʃ(ə)n], s. Castration f.
casual ['kaʒjuəl]. 1. a. (a) Fortuit, accidentel. To engage in c. conversation, parler de choses et d'autres. Casual labour, main-d'œuvre d'emploi intermittent. Casual labourer, homme à l'heure. Casual profit, produit casuel. (b) F: Insouciant. To give a c. answer, répondre d'un air désinvolte. 2. s. Indigent de passage. Casual ward, asile m de nuit (d'un hospice). -ally, adv. (a) Fortuitement, par hasard, en passant. (b) Négligemment; avec désinvolture.
casualty ['kaʒjuəlti], s. 1. Accident m (de personne). Casualty ward, salle des accidentés. (b) pl. Mil: Pertes f. 2. Mort m; blessé m.
casuist ['kazjuist], s. Casuiste m.
casuistic(al) [kazju'istik(ə)l], a. De casuiste.
casuistry ['kazjuistri], s. Casuistique f.
cat [kat], s. 1. (a) Chat, f. chatte. Tom cat, matou m. F: To be like a cat on hot bricks, être sur des épines. To see which way the cat jumps, prendre l'air du vent. There's not room to swing a cat in his study, son cabinet est grand

comme un mouchoir de poche. **To let the cat out of the bag**, éventer la mèche. *The cat is out of the bag*, le grand mot est lâché. *They quarrel like cat and dog*, ils s'accordent comme chien et chat. *S.a.* RAIN². It would make a cat laugh, c'est à mourir de rire. *Prov:* **A cat may look at a king**, un chien regarde bien un évêque. **When the cat's away the mice will play**, le chat parti les souris dansent. *S.a.* CARE¹ I, GRIN². (b) *F:* (*Of pers.*) **An old cat**, une vieille chipie. **2.** *Z:* **Wild cat**, chat sauvage. *The (great) cats*, les grands félins. **3.** = CAT-O'-NINE-TAILS. **'cat-'burglar**, *s.* *F:* Monte-en-l'air *m inv.* **'cat-fish**, *s.* Loup marin; chat marin. **'cat-footed**, *a.* Qui marche à pas feutrés. **'cat-ice**, *s.* *Nau:* Glace pourrie. **'cat-lap**, *s.* *F:* Lavasse *f*; thé *m* trop faible. **cat-o'-'nine-tails**, *s.* *Nau:* Chat *m* à neuf queues. **'cat's-'cradle**, *s.* (Jeu *m* de la) scie; (jeu du) berceau. **'cat's-eye**, *s.* *Lap:* Œil-de-chat *m*. **'cat's-meat**, *s.* Mou *m*, tripes *fpl*, abats *mpl*. **'cat's-paw**, *s.* **I.** Petite bouffée de vent. **2.** *F:* To be made a c.-p. of, tirer les marrons du feu (pour qn). **'cat's-tail**, *s.* *Bot:* Massette *f*. **'cat-walk**, *s.* *Aer:* Coursive *f* (de dirigeable).

cataclysm ['katəklizm], *s.* Cataclysme *m*.
catacombs ['katəkoumz], *s.pl.* Catacombes *f*.
catafalque ['katəfalk], *s.* Catafalque *m*.
catalepsy ['katəlepsi], *s.* **I.** *Med:* Catalepsie *f*. **2.** *Phil:* Compréhension *f*.
cataleptic [katə'leptik], *a. & s.* *Med:* Cataleptique (*mf*).
catalogue¹ ['katələg], *s.* **I.** Catalogue *m*, liste *f*. **Subject catalogue**, catalogue raisonné. **2.** *Com:* Catalogue, prix-courant *m*.
catalogue², *v.tr.* Cataloguer.
catalysis [kə'talisis], *s.* *Ch:* Catalyse *f*.
catalytic [katə'litik], *a.* *Ch:* Catalytique.
cataplasm ['katəplazm], *s.* *Med:* Cataplasme *m*.
catapult¹ ['katəpʌlt], *s.* **I.** Lance-pierre *m*. **2.** *Av:* Catapulte *f* (de lancement). **Catapult-launched**, (avion) catapultable.
catapult², *v.tr.* *Av:* Lancer (un avion). **catapulting**, *s.* Lancement *m*.
cataract ['katərakt], *s.* Cataracte *f* (d'un fleuve, de l'œil).
catarrh [kə'tɑːr], *s.* *Med:* Catarrhe *m*.
catastrophe [kə'tastrofi], *s.* **I.** Catastrophe *f*; désastre *m*. *The victims of the c.*, les sinistrés. **2.** *Gr.Drama:* Catastrophe, dénouement *m*.
catastrophic [katə'strɔfik], *a.* Désastreux; *F:* catastrophique.
catcall ['katkɔːl], *s.* *Th:* (Coup *m* de) sifflet *m*.
catch¹ [katʃ], *s.* **I.** Prise *f*. (a) *Cr:* Prise au vol de la balle. (b) **Catch of the breath**, soubresaut *m*. **2.** (a) *Fish:* Prise, pêche *f*. *To have a good c.*, faire (une) bonne pêche. (b) *F:* Bon parti (à épouser). (c) *F:* **It's no great catch**, ce n'est pas le Pérou. **3.** Fragment *m*, bribe *f* (de conversation). **4.** (*On door*) Loquet *m*, loqueteau *m*; (*of buckle*) ardillon *m*; (*on garment*) agrafe *f*. *Mec.E:* Déclic *m*; cliquet *m*. *Phot:* **Infinity catch**, accrochage *m* à l'infini. **5.** (*Deception*) Attrape *f*. **There's a catch in it**, c'est une attrape. *Sch:* **Catch question**, colle *f*. **6.** *Mus:* Chant *m* à reprises; canon *m*.
catch², *v.* (*p.t.* **caught** [kɔːt]; *p.p.* **caught**) **I.** *v.tr.* **I.** (a) Attraper, prendre (un poisson); attraper, saisir (une balle); ne pas manquer (le train); *Fish: Ven:* **To catch nothing**, revenir bredouille. *Nau:* (*Of sail, etc.*) **To catch the wind**, prendre le vent. *S.a.* BREATH, HARE¹. (b) = CATCH UP 3. (c) **To catch s.o. doing sth.**, surprendre qn à

faire qch. *If I c. them at it!* si je les y prends! *F:* **Catch me (doing such a thing)!** il n'y a pas de danger! *You won't catch me doing that again!* on ne m'y reprendra plus! (d) *We were caught in the storm*, l'orage nous a surpris. *Cart caught in a bog*, charrette enlisée dans un marais. **2.** (a) Saisir (des sons); rencontrer (le regard de qn). *A sound caught my ear*, un son me frappa l'oreille. *The artist has caught the likeness*, l'artiste a bien saisi la ressemblance. (b) **I did not catch what you said**, je n'ai pas bien entendu ce que vous disiez. *I didn't quite c. that*, pardon? plaît-il? (c) Accrocher, happer. *A nail caught my frock*, un clou a accroché ma robe. *The car caught two passers-by*, l'auto happa deux passants. **3.** Attraper (une maladie); contracter (une habitude). **4.** (a) **To catch s.o. a blow**, flanquer un coup à qn. (b) **You'll catch it!** vous allez être grondé! votre affaire est bonne! **5.** *F:* (*Entrap*) Attraper. **You don't catch me!** ça ne prend pas (avec moi)! **II. catch**, *v.i.* **I. To catch at sth.**, s'accrocher à qch. **2.** (a) (*Of cog-wheel*) Mordre; (*of door-bolt*) s'engager. (b) (*Of fi: 2*) Prendre. **3.** *Cu:* **To catch in the pan**, attacher. **catch on**, *v.i.* *F:* (*Of play*) Prendre, réussir. **catch out**, *v.tr.* *F:* Prendre (qn) sur le fait. *To c. s.o. out in a lie*, surprendre qn à mentir. **catch up**, *v.tr.* **I.** Saisir (qch.). *We were caught up in this wave of enthusiasm*, nous fûmes gagnés par cette vague d'enthousiasme. **2.** *To c. s.o. up* (*in a speech*), relever les paroles de qn. **3.** (*Overtake*) **To catch s.o. up**, *v.i.* **to catch up with s.o.**, rattraper qn. *He caught us up at the village*, il nous a rejoints au village. **catching¹**, *a.* (*Of disease*) Contagieux, infectieux; (*of laughter*) communicatif; (*of melody*) (i) entraînant, (ii) facile à retenir. **catching²**, *s.* Prise *f*. (a) Capture *f*. (b) Accrochage *m*. **'catch-as-catch-'can**, *s.* *Wr:* Lutte *f* libre. **'catch-basin**, *s.* *Geol:* Bassin *m* de captation. **'catch-points**, *s.pl.* *Rail:* Aiguille prise en pointe.
catcher ['katʃər], *s.* Attrapeur; preneur.
catchment ['katʃmənt], *s.* *Hyd.E:* (a) (**Water-**) **catchment**, captage *m* (d'eaux). (b) **Catchment (basin)**, bassin *m* de réception.
catchpenny ['katʃpeni], *s.* (*Of thg*) Attrape-sou *m*; camelote *f* de réclame.
catchword ['katʃwəːd], *s.* **I.** (a) *Pol:* Mot *m* de ralliement. (b) *F:* Scie *f*, rengaine *f*. **2.** *Typ:* Mot-souche *m*. **3.** *Th:* Réplique *f*.
catchy ['katʃi], *a.* **I.** (i) Entraînant; (ii) facile à retenir. **2.** *C. question*, question insidieuse.
catechism ['katekizm], *s.* Catéchisme *m*.
catechist ['katekist], *s.* Catéchiste *m*.
catechize ['katekaːiz], *v.tr.* **I.** Catéchiser. **2.** *F:* Poser une série de questions à (qn).
catechizer ['katekaːizər], *s.* **I.** Catéchiste *m*. **2.** Interrogateur, -trice.
catechu ['katiʃuː], *s.* Cachou *m*. *Pale c.*, gambir *m*.
categoric(al) [kate'gɔrik(əl)], *a.* Catégorique; **-ally**, *adv.* Catégoriquement.
category ['kategəri], *s.* Catégorie *f*.
catenary [kə'tiːnəri], **catenarian** [kati'nɛəriən], *a. & s.* Caténaire (*f*); (ligne *f* de) chaînette *f*. *C. curve*, funiculaire *f*.
cater ['keitər], *v.i.* *To c. for s.o.*, (i) approvisionner qn; (ii) pourvoir aux plaisirs de qn. **cater for all tastes**, pourvoir à tous les goûts.
catering, *s.* Approvisionnement *m*. **Catering department**, rayon d'alimentation.
caterer ['keitərər], *s.* **I.** Approvisionneur; pourvoyeur. **2.** (*Supplying banquet*) Traiteur *m*.
caterpillar ['katərpilər], *s.* **I.** Chenille *f*.

2. (a) Caterpillar(-tractor), auto-chenille f. (b) Caterpillar wheel, roue à chenille.

caterwaul ['katərwɔ:l], v.i. **1.** Miauler. **2.** F: Crier (comme les chats la nuit); faire un vrai sabbat. **caterwauling**, s. **1.** Miaulements mpl. **2.** F: Sabbat m de chats; charivari m.

catgut ['katgʌt], s. Corde f de boyau.

cathedral [ka'θi:drəl]. **1.** a. Cathédral, -aux. Cathedral church, église cathédrale. **2.** s. Cathédrale f. Cathedral town, ville épiscopale.

Catherine ['kaθərin]. Pr.n.f. Catherine. Pyr: Catherine wheel, soleil m; roue f à feu. F: To turn Catherine wheels, faire la roue.

cathode ['kaθoud], s. El: Cathode f. Cathode rays, rayons cathodiques.

cathodic [ka'θɔdik], a. El: Cathodique.

catholic ['kaθolik]. **1.** a. (a) Universel. (b) Tolérant. C. mind, esprit large. C. taste, goûts éclectiques. **2.** a. & s. Ecc: (a) Orthodoxe (mf), catholique (mf). The Catholic Church, toute la chrétienté. (b) (Roman Catholic) Catholique (romain).

catholicism [ka'θɔlisizm], s. Catholicisme m.

catholicity [kaθo'lisiti], s. **1.** (a) Universalité f. (b) Largeur f (d'esprit); tolérance f; éclectisme m. **2.** Theol: Orthodoxie f.

cation ['kataiən], s. El: Cation m.

catkin ['katkin], s. Bot: Chaton m, iule m.

catmint ['katmint], s. Cataire f; herbe f aux chats.

catsup ['katsʌp], s. = KETCHUP.

cattiness ['katinəs], s. = CATTISHNESS.

cattish ['katiʃ], a. F: (Esp. of woman) Méchant(e), rosse. C. answer, réponse aigre-douce. **-ly**, adv. Méchamment.

cattishness ['katiʃnəs], s. F: Méchanceté f, rosserie f.

cattle [katl], s. Coll. inv. **1.** Bétail m; bestiaux mpl. Horned cattle, bêtes fpl à cornes. **2.** F: Chevaux mpl. **'cattle-drover**, s. Bouvier m; meneur m de bœufs. **'cattle-lifter**, s. Voleur m de bétail. **'cattle-shed**, s. Bouverie f; étable f. **'cattle-show**, s. Comice m agricole. **'cattle-truck**, s. Fourgon m à bestiaux.

catty ['kati], a. F: = CATTISH. C. remark, rosserie f.

caucus ['kɔ:kəs], s. Comité électoral; clique f politique.

caudal ['kɔ:d(ə)l], a. Z: Caudal, -aux.

caught. See CATCH².

caul [kɔ:l], s. **1.** Coiffe f (de nouveau-né). Born with a caul, né coiffé. **2.** Cu: Crépine f.

cauldron ['kɔ:ldrən], s. **1.** (a) Chaudron m. (b) Ind: Chaudière f. **2.** Oc: Gouffre m.

cauliflower ['kɔliflauər], s. Chou-fleur m.

caulk [kɔ:k], v.tr. **1.** (a) Calfater (un navire). (b) Calfeutrer (une fenêtre). **2.** Mater (un rivet). **caulking**, s **1.** (a) Calfatage m (d'un navire). (b) Calfeutrage m, calfeutrement m. **2.** Matage m (de tôles). **'caulking-iron**, s. **1.** Calfait m; ciseau m de calfat. **2.** Metalw: Matoir m.

caulker ['kɔ:kər], s. Calfat m.

causal ['kɔ:z(ə)l], a. Causal (no mpl). Gram: Causal conjunction, conjonction causative.

cause¹ [kɔ:z], s. **1.** Cause f. Prime c., cause première. To be the c. of an accident, être (la) cause d'un accident. **2.** Raison f, motif m, sujet m. C. for litigation, matière f à procès. I have c. to be thankful, j'ai lieu d'être reconnaissant. To have good cause for doing sth., faire qch. à bon droit. To show cause, exposer ses raisons. To give serious cause for complaint, donner de grands sujets de plainte. **3.** (a) Jur: Cause;

procès m. To plead s.o.'s cause, plaider la cause de qn. (b) F: To take up s.o.'s c., épouser la querelle de qn. To work in a good cause, travailler pour une bonne cause. **'cause-list**, s. Jur: Rôle m d'audience.

cause², v.tr. **1.** Causer, occasionner (un malheur). To c. a fire, déterminer un incendie. **2.** To cause s.o. to do sth., faire faire qch. à qn. To c. s.o. to be punished, faire punir qn.

causeway ['kɔ:zwei], s. (a) Chaussée f. (b) Levée f, digue f.

caustic ['kɔ:stik]. **1.** a. Caustique. C. wit, esprit mordant. **2.** s. Pharm: Caustique m. **-ally**, adv. D'un ton mordant.

cauterization [kɔ:tərai'zeiʃ(ə)n], s. Cautérisation f.

cauterize ['kɔ:təraiz], v.tr. Cautériser.

cautery ['kɔ:təri], s. Cautère m.

caution¹ ['kɔ:ʃ(ə)n], s. **1.** Précaution f, prévoyance f, prudence f, circonspection f. To do sth. with great c., faire qch. avec de grands ménagements. **2.** (a) Avis m, avertissement m. Caution! steep incline, attention! descente rapide. (b) Mil: Commandement m préparatoire. (c) Réprimande f. He was let off with a caution, il s'en est tiré avec une réprimande. To inflict a punishment as a c. to others, infliger une punition pour l'exemple. **3.** F: A caution, un drôle de numéro; une drôle de femme; un vrai type.

caution², v.tr. **1.** Avertir (qn); mettre (qn) sur ses gardes. To c. s.o. against sth., mettre qn en garde contre qch. **2.** Menacer (qn) de poursuites à la prochaine occasion.

cautionary ['kɔ:ʃənəri], a. D'avertissement.

cautious ['kɔ:ʃəs], a. Circonspect, prudent. C. judgment, jugement retenu. To be c. in doing sth., faire qch. avec circonspection. To play a c. game, jouer serré. **-ly**, adv. Avec circonspection; prudemment; avec ménagement(s).

cautiousness ['kɔ:ʃəsnəs], s. Prudence f.

cavalcade [kaval'keid], s. Cavalcade f.

cavalier [kavə'li:ər]. **1.** s.m. (a) Cavalier; gentilhomme. (b) F: Galant; chevalier servant (d'une dame). **2.** a. Cavalier, désinvolte. **-ly**, adv. Cavalièrement.

cavalry ['kavəlri], s. Cavalerie f.

cavalryman, pl. **-men** ['kavəlrimən, -men], s.m. Mil: Cavalier; soldat de cavalerie.

cave¹ [keiv], s. **1.** Caverne f, antre m, souterrain m, grotte f. **2.** Pol: (a) Scission f. (b) Dissidents mpl. **'cave-man**, pl. **-men**, s.m. **1.** Anthr: Troglodyte. **2.** F: Homme à la manière forte (avec les femmes).

cave², v.i. To cave in. **1.** S'effondrer, s'ébouler. **2.** (Of pers.) Céder, se rendre.

cave³ ['keivi], int. P: Pet! vingt-deux! To keep cave, faire le guet; P: faire le pet.

caveat ['keiviat], s. Jur: (a) Opposition f (to, à). To enter a caveat, mettre opposition (against, à). (b) Avis m d'opposition.

cavendish ['kavəndiʃ]. s. Tabac foncé édulcoré.

cavern ['kavərn], s. Caverne f; souterrain m.

cavernous ['kavərnəs], a. Caverneux.

caviar(e) ['kavi'a:r], s. Caviar m.

cavil ['kavil], v.i. (cavilled) Chicaner, ergoter. He is always cavilling, il trouve à redire sur tout. To c. at sth., pointiller sur qch. **cavilling**, a. Argutieux; chicaneur.

cavity ['kaviti], s. Cavité f; creux m; alvéole m or f; trou m, pl. trous. The nasal cavity, les fosses nasales.

cavy ['keivi], s. **1.** Cobaye m; cochon m d'Inde. **2.** Water cavy, cabiai m.

caw¹ [kɔ:], s. Croassement m.

caw², v.i. (Of crow) Croasser. **cawing,** s. Croassement m.

Cayenne [kei'en]. **1.** Pr.n. Geog: Cayenne f. **2.** s. **Cayenne (pepper),** poivre m de Cayenne.

cayman ['keimən], s. Rept: Caïman m.

cease¹ [si:s], s. **Without cease,** sans cesse.

cease², v.tr. & i. **1.** Cesser ((from) doing sth., de faire qch.). He has ceased to see anybody, il ne voit plus personne. **2.** Cesser (ses efforts, etc.). **To cease from work,** cesser son travail. **To cease work,** cesser le travail; arrêter les travaux. The noise ceased, le bruit cessa. **ceasing,** s. Cessation f. Without ceasing, sans arrêt.

ceaseless ['si:sləs], a. Incessant; sans arrêt; sans fin. **-ly,** adv. Sans cesse, sans arrêt.

cedar ['si:dər], s. Bot: **Cedar(-tree, -wood),** cèdre m.

cede [si:d], v.tr. Céder (un bien immobilier).

cedilla [se'dilə], s. Cédille f.

ceiling ['si:liŋ], s. **1.** Plafond m. **Ceiling light, lamp,** plafonnier m. **2.** Av: (Valeur f de) plafond (d'un avion). **3.** Nau: Vaigres fpl, vaigrage m.

-ceilinged ['si:liŋd], a. **High-, low-ceilinged,** haut, bas, de plafond.

celandine ['selandain], s. Bot: Éclaire f.

celebrant ['selebrənt], s. Ecc: Célébrant m.

celebrate ['selebreit], v.tr. **1.** Ecc: Célébrer (la messe). **2.** Célébrer, glorifier (la mémoire de qn); commémorer (un événement). **celebrated,** a. Célèbre for, par); renommé (for, pour).

celebration [sele'breiʃ(ə)n], s. **1.** Ecc: Célébration f (de la messe). **2.** Célébration, commémoration f (d'un événement, etc.).

celebrator ['selebreitər], s. Célébrateur m.

celebrity [se'lebriti], s. **1.** Célébrité f, renommée f. **2.** (Pers.) Célébrité.

celerity [se'leriti], s. Célérité f.

celery ['seləri], s. Hort: Céleri m. **Head of celery,** pied m de céleri.

celestial [se'lestjəl], **1.** a. Céleste. **2.** s. Chinois.

celibacy ['selibəsi], s. Célibat m.

celibate ['selibet]. **1.** a. (Personne) célibataire; (vie) de célibataire. **2.** s. Célibataire mf.

cell [sel], s. **1.** Compartiment m. (a) (In monastery) Cellule f; (in prison) cellule, cachot m. Mil: **The cells,** la prison, P: le bloc. (b) Ap: Cellule, alvéole m or f. (c) El: **The brain cells,** les territoires cérébraux. **2.** El: Élément m (de pile); couple m. **Dry cell,** pile sèche. **3.** Biol: Cellule. **Cell-wall,** paroi f cellulaire. **4.** (a) Mil: Groupe m de combat. (b) **Communist cell,** cellule communiste; noyau m communiste.

cellar ['selər], s. Cave f; (small) caveau m. F: **To keep a good cellar,** avoir une bonne cave. **'cellar-kitchen,** s. Cuisine f en sous-sol.

cellarage ['selərdʒ], s. **1.** Emmagasinage m (en cave). **2.** Coll. Caves fpl.

cellarman, pl. **-men** ['selərmən, -men], s.m. Caviste; sommelier.

celled [seld], a. **1.** Biol: Cellulé. **2.** Biol: etc: **-celled.** One-c., two-c., à une cellule, à deux cellules.

'cellist ['tʃelist], s. = VIOLONCELLIST.

'cello ['tʃelo], s. = VIOLONCELLO.

cellophane ['seləfein], s. Cellophane f.

cellular ['seljulər], a. **1.** Biol: Cellulaire, celluleux. **2.** Cellulaire, alvéolaire. C. girder, poutre cellulaire. I.C.E: **Cellular radiator,** radiateur cellulaire, à nid d'abeilles.

cellule ['selju:l], s. Nat.Hist: Cellule f.

celluloid ['seljulɔid], s. Celluloïd(e) m.

cellulose ['seljulous]. **1.** a. Celluleux. **2.** s. Cellulose f. **Cellulose varnish,** vernis cellulosique.

Celt [selt], s. Ethn: Celte mf.

Celtic ['seltik, (of Wales) 'keltik]. **1.** a. Celtique; celte. **2.** s. Ling: Le celtique.

cement¹ [si'ment], s. **1.** Const: Ciment m. **Hydraulic cement,** mortier m hydraulique. **2.** Cer: Dent: etc: Mastic m, lut m. **3.** Anat: Cément m (d'une dent). **4.** Metall: Cément.

cement², v.tr. **1.** Cimenter (des pierres); F: cimenter, consolider (une amitié). **2.** Lier au ciment; coller. **Cemented lens,** objectif à lentilles collées. **3.** Metall: Cémenter (le fer).

cementation [si:men'teiʃ(ə)n], s. **1.** Cimentage m, cimentation f; collage m. **2.** Metall: Cémentation f.

cemetery ['semetəri], s. Cimetière m.

cenotaph ['senotaf], s. Cénotaphe m.

cense [sens], v.tr. Ecc: Encenser.

censer ['sensər], s. Ecc: Encensoir m.

censor¹ ['sensər], s. Adm: Censeur m. **The Board of Censors,** la censure. Banned by the C., interdit par la censure.

censor², v.tr. **1.** Interdire (une pièce de théâtre). **2. To be censored,** (i) (of play, etc.) passer par la censure; (of letter) passer par le contrôle; (ii) être interdit, supprimé, par la censure; (iii) être expurgé. **censoring,** s. Censure f (des journaux, etc.).

censorial [sen'sɔ:riəl], a. Censorial, -aux.

censorious [sen'sɔ:riəs], a. Porté à censurer; sévère (of, upon, pour).

censorship ['sensərʃip], s. Adm: (a) **The Censorship,** la censure. (b) **Postal censorship,** contrôle postal.

censurable ['sensərəbl], a. Censurable, blâmable.

censure¹ ['sensər], s. Censure f, blâme m. Deserving of c., réprimandable. **To pass censure on the Government,** blâmer le Gouvernement. **Vote of censure,** vote de blâme.

censure², v.tr. Censurer; (i) blâmer, condamner; (ii) critiquer.

census ['sensəs], s. Recensement m. Adm: **To take a census of the population,** faire le recensement de la population; dénombrer la population.

cent [sent], s. **1.** Num: (a) U.S: Cent m. (b) F: (Small coin) Sou m, liard m. I haven't got a red cent, je n'ai pas le sou. S.a. CARE² 1. **2.** Com: Per cent, pour cent.

cental ['sent(ə)l], s. Meas: Quintal m, -aux.

centaur ['sentɔ:r], s.m. Myth: Centaure.

centaury ['sentɔ:ri], s. Bot: Centaurée f.

centenarian [senti'nɛəriən], a. & s. Centenaire (mf).

centenary [sen'ti:nəri, -'ten-], a. & s. (Anniversaire) centenaire (m).

centennial [sen'tenjəl], a. Centennal, -aux; séculaire.

center ['sentər], s. & v. U.S: = CENTRE¹,².

centesimal [sen'tesim(ə)l], a. Centésimal, -aux.

centigrade ['sentigreid], a. Centigrade.

centigramme ['sentigram], s. Centigramme m.

centilitre ['sentili:tər], s. Centilitre m.

centimeter, centimetre ['sentimi:tər], s. Centimètre m.

centipede ['sentipi:d], s. Myr: Centipède m; F: mille-pattes m inv.

central ['sentr(ə)l], a. Central, -aux. S.a. SCHOOL¹ 1 (a). **-ally,** adv. Centralement.

centralization [sentrəlai'zeiʃ(ə)n], s. Centralisation f.

centralize ['sentrəlaiz]. **1.** v.tr. Centraliser. **2.** v.i. Se centraliser.

centre¹ ['sentər], s. **I.** Centre m (d'un cercle, etc.); milieu m (d'une table); foyer m (d'érudition, d'infection). **In the centre,** au centre. **Centre of attraction,** F: clou m (d'une fête, etc.). S.a. DEAD-CENTRE. **2.** Mec.E: Pointe f (d'un tour). **3.** Attrib. Central, -aux. **The centre arch,** l'arche centrale, du centre. Fr.Pol: **The Centre party,** les membres du Centre; les centristes. **'centre-bit,** s. Tls: Mèche anglaise. **'centreboard,** s. Nau: (Quille f de) dérive f. **centre-'forward,** s. Fb: (Pers.) Avantcentre m. **centre-'half,** s. Fb: (Pers.) Demicentre m. **'centre-line,** s. Ligne médiane. **'centre-piece,** s. Pièce f de milieu, surtout m. **'centre-pin,** s. Cheville ouvrière. **'centrepunch,** s. Tls: Pointeau m. **'centresecond(s),** s. Clockm: Grande aiguille trotteuse. **centre²**. **I.** v.tr. (a) Placer (qch.) au centre. **To centre one's affections on s.o.,** concentrer, rassembler, toute son affection sur qn. (b) Centrer (une pièce sur le tour). (c) Fb: Centrer (le ballon); abs. centrer. **2.** v.i. **To centre in, on, round, s.o., sth.,** se concentrer dans, sur, autour de, qn, qch. **-centred,** a. **Two-centred arch,** arc à deux centres. S.a. SELF-CENTRED. **centring,** s. **I.** Centrage m (d'une pièce sur le tour, etc.). **2.** Const: (a) Cintrage m (d'une voûte). (b) Cintre m.
centric(al) ['sentrik(əl)], a. Du centre; central, -aux.
centrifugal [sen'trifjug(ə)l], a. Centrifuge.
centripetal [sen'tripet(ə)l], a. Centripète.
centuple¹ ['sentjupl], a. & s. Centuple (m).
centuple², v.tr. Centupler.
century ['sentjuri], s. **I.** Siècle m. **In the nineteenth century,** au dix-neuvième siècle. **2.** Cr: Centaine f.
cephalic [se'falik], a. Céphalique.
cephalopod ['sefalopɔd], s. Moll: Céphalopode m.
ceramics [se'ramiks], s.pl. (Usu. with sg. const.) La céramique.
ceramist ['seramist], s. Céramiste m.
Cerberus ['sə:rbərəs]. Pr.n.m. Myth: Cerbère. S.a. SOP¹ I.
cere ['siːər], s. Orn: Cire f (du bec d'un oiseau).
cereal [si:riəl], a. & s. Céréale (f).
cerebellum [sere'beləm], s. Anat: Cervelet m.
cerebral ['serebr(ə)l], a. Cérébral, -aux.
cerebrum ['serebrəm], s. Anat: Cerveau m.
cerement(s) ['si:ərmənt(s)], s. (Usu. pl.) **I.** Toile(s) f d'embaumement. **2.** Lit: Linceul m, suaire m.
ceremonial [sere'mounjəl]. **I.** a. De cérémonie. **2.** s. Cérémonial m. **-ally,** adv. En grande cérémonie.
ceremonious [sere'mounjəs], a. Cérémonieux. **-ly,** adv. Cérémonieusement.
ceremony ['sereməni], s. Cérémonie f. **With ceremony,** solennellement. **Without ceremony,** sans cérémonie, sans façon. **To stand (up)on ceremony,** faire des façons. **To attend a c.,** assister à une cérémonie.
cerise [sə'riːz], a. & s. (Colour) Cerise (m) inv.
cert [sə:rt], s. P: = CERTAINTY. **A dead cert,** une certitude (absolue); une affaire sûre. **It's a cert,** c'est couru.
certain ['sə:rt(ə)n], a. Certain. **I.** (Assured) (a) **This much is certain, that . . .,** ce qu'il y a de sûr, de certain, c'est que. . . . **He is certain to come,** il viendra sûrement; il est certain qu'il viendra. (b) (Of pers.) **To be certain of sth.,** être certain, sûr, de qch. **I am almost c. of it,** j'en ai la presque certitude. **I am not c. that he**

will come, je ne suis pas certain qu'il vienne. (c) **To know sth. for certain,** être bien sûr de qch.; savoir qch. à n'en pouvoir douter. (d) **To make certain of sth.,** (i) s'assurer de qch.; (ii) s'assurer qch. **To make c. of a seat,** s'assurer une place. **2.** (a) (Undetermined) **There are c. things that . . .,** il y a certaines choses que. . . . Pej: **A c. person,** (une) certaine personne. **C. people,** (de) certaines gens; certains mpl. **A certain Mr Smith,** un certain M. Smith. (b) **He used to write on a c. day,** il m'écrivait à jour fixe. **-ly,** adv. (a) Certainement; certes; assurément; à coup sûr. (b) (Assent) Assurément; parfaitement. **You allow me?—Certainly!** vous permettez?—Comment donc! **Certainly not!** non certes! non, par exemple!
certainty ['sə:rtnti], s. (a) Certitude f; chose certaine, fait certain. **For a certainty, of a c.,** à coup sûr; certainement. **It's a dead certainty,** c'est une certitude absolue. **To bet on a certainty,** parier à coup sûr. (Cf. CERT.) (b) Certitude (morale); conviction f.
certifiable [sə:rti'faiəbl], a. Que l'on peut certifier. **C. lunatic,** personne dont un médecin se jugera autorisé à attester l'aliénation mentale. F: **He's certifiable,** il est fou à lier.
certificate¹ [sə:r'tifiket], s. **I.** (a) Certificat m, attestation f. Fin: Titre m (d'actions). (b) Jur: (Acte m de) concordat m (entre un failli et ses créanciers). **2. Certificate (of competency),** certificat (d'aptitude); diplôme m, brevet m. Nau: **Master's certificate,** brevet de capitaine. **3.** Acte. **Birth certificate,** acte de naissance. **Death certificate,** (i) acte de décès; (ii) extrait m mortuaire. S.a. REGISTRY I.
certificate² [sə:r'tifikeit], v.tr. Diplômer, breveter (qn). **certificated,** a. **I.** Diplômé, titré. **2.** Jur: **Certificated bankrupt,** concordataire mf.
certifier ['sə:rtifaiər], s. Certificateur m.
certify ['sə:rtifai], v.tr. **I.** (a) Certifier, déclarer, attester. **To c. a death,** constater un décès. Jur: **Certified lunatic,** aliéné interdit. (b) Authentiquer, homologuer, légaliser (un document). S.a. COPY¹ I. (c) Diplômer, breveter (qn). **Certified broker,** courtier attitré. **2.** v.ind.tr. **To certify to sth.,** attester qch. **certifying¹,** a. (Document) certificatif. **certifying²,** s. **I.** Attestation f. **2.** Approbation f (d'un document); homologation f.
certitude ['sə:rtitjud], s. Certitude f.
cerulean [se'ru:liən], a. Bleu céleste inv; cérulé, céruléen, azuré.
cervical ['sə:rvik(ə)l, sər'vaik(ə)l], a. Anat: Cervical, -aux.
cessation [se'sei∫(ə)n], s. Cessation f, arrêt m.
cession ['se∫(ə)n], s. Cession f; abandon m (de marchandises, de droits, etc.).
cessionary ['se∫ənəri]. **I.** a. Cessionnaire. **2.** Jur: Ayant cause m, pl. ayants cause.
cesspit ['sespit], s. **I.** Fosse f à fumier et à purin. **2.** = CESSPOOL.
cesspool ['sespu:l], s. Fosse f d'aisance. F: **A cesspool of iniquity,** un cloaque de vice.
cetacea [si:'teisia, -∫ia], s.pl. Z: Les cétacés m.
cetacean [si:'teisian, -∫ian], a. & s. Les Cétacé (m).
Ceylon [si'lɔn]. Pr.n. Geog: Ceylan m.
chad [t∫ad], s. Ich: **I.** Dorade (bilunée). **2.** = SHAD.
chafe¹ [t∫eif], s. **I.** = CHAFING. **2.** Écorchure f.
chafe². **I.** v.tr. (a) Frictionner, dégourdir (les membres). (b) User, échauffer, (qch.) par le frottement; écorcher (la peau); érailler (un cordage). (c) Irriter, énerver (qn). **2.** v.i. (a) S'user par le frottement; (of rope) s'érailler,

raguer. (b) (Of caged animal) To chafe against the bars, s'user en vains efforts contre les barreaux. F: (Of pers.) To chafe at, under, sth., s'énerver de qch. To c. under restraint, ronger son frein. **chafing,** s. **1.** Friction f. **2.** (a) Écorchement m (de la peau). (b) Usure f, frottement m, échauffement m (d'une corde). **3.** (Of pers.) Irritation f, énervement m. **'chafing-dish,** s. Cu: Réchaud m (de table).

chafer ['tʃeifər], s. Ent: = COCKCHAFER.

chaff¹ [tʃɑːf], s. **1.** (a) Balle(s) f (du grain). Prov: **Old birds are not to be caught with chaff,** on ne prend pas les vieux merles à la pipée. (b) Husb: (i) Menue paille, paille d'avoine; (ii) paille hachée. (c) F: Choses fpl sans importance; vétilles fpl. **2.** F: Raillerie f; persiflage m.

chaff², v.tr. Railler, taquiner (qn); persifler (qn).

chaffer¹ ['tʃæfər], s. F: Railleur m; persifleur m.

chaffer² ['tʃæfər], v.i. Marchander, barguigner. To chaffer with s.o., marchander qn. To chaffor over the price, débattre le prix.

chaffinch ['tʃæfin(t)ʃ], s. Orn: Pinson m.

chagrin¹ [ʃa'griːn], s. Chagrin m, dépit m; vive contrariété; déplaisir m.

chagrin², v.tr. Chagriner, dépiter (qn). To be chagrined at sth., être mortifié de qch.

chain¹ [tʃein], s. **1.** (a) Chaîne f; (small) chaînette f. To put a dog on the chain, mettre un chien à l'attache, à la chaîne. **Prisoner in chains,** prisonnier enchaîné. F: To burst one's chains, rompre ses chaînes; briser ses fers. **Watch-chain,** chaîne de montre. Mec.E: **Driving chain,** chaîne de transmission. (b) Chaîne (de montagnes); enchaînement m (d'idées); suite f, série f (d'événements); cordon m (de sentinelles). **2.** Surv.Meas: Longueur f de 20 m, 116; double décamètre. **'chain-adjuster,** s. Tendeur m de chaîne; patte f de tension. **'chain-'armour,** s. Archeol: (a) Mailles fpl. (b) Cotte f de mailles. **'chain-case,** s. Cy: Carter m. **'chain-gang,** s. A. & U.S: Chaîne f, cadène f (de forçats). **'chain-stitch,** s. Needlew: Point m de chaînette. **'chain-store,** s. Succursale f de grand magasin. **'chain-stores,** s. Grand magasin à succursales.

chain², v.tr. **1.** To chain sth. to sth., attacher qch. à qch. par une chaîne, par des chaînes. **2.** To chain sth. down, retenir qch. par une chaîne, par des chaînes. To chain s.o. (down), enchaîner qn. To chain up a dog, mettre un chien à la chaîne, à l'attache. Chained up, chained together, à la chaîne. **3.** Fermer (un port, etc.) avec des chaînes. **4.** Surv: Chaîner (un champ).

chainman, pl. -men ['tʃeinmən, -men], s.m. Surv: Chaîneur; aide (d'arpenteur).

chair¹ [tʃɛər], s. **1.** (a) Chaise f, siège m. **Folding chair,** chaise pliante; pliant m. **Grandfather chair,** bergère f à oreilles. To take a chair, s'asseoir. S.a. ARM-CHAIR, BATH-CHAIR, BOAT-SWAIN, DECK-CHAIR, EASY-CHAIR, INVALID², LADY-CHAIR, ROCKING-CHAIR. (b) Sch: Chaire f (de professeur de faculté). (c) Siège (de juge); fauteuil m (de président). To be in the chair; to occupy, fill, the chair, occuper le fauteuil présidentiel; présider. To take the chair, prendre la présidence. To leave, vacate, the chair, lever la séance. **Chair! Chair!** à l'ordre! à l'ordre! **2.** Rail: Coussinet m, chaise (de rail). **'chair-back,** s. Dossier m de chaise. **'chair-maker,** s. Chaisier; fabricant m de chaises. **'chair-mender,** s. Rempailleur de chaises. **'chair-rail,** s. **1.** Barreau m, bâton m (de chaise). **2.** Antebois m (d'une salle).

chair², v.tr. Porter (qn) en triomphe.

chairman, pl. -men ['tʃɛərmən, -men], s. **1.** Président, -ente. **Mr Chairman, Madam Chairman,** Monsieur le Président, Madame la Présidente. **2.** Chaisier m; loueur m de chaises. **3.** A: Porteur m (de chaise à porteurs).

chairmanship ['tʃɛərmənʃip], s. Présidence f.

chaise [ʃeiz], s. Veh: A: Chaise f, cabriolet m.

chalcedony [kal'sedəni], s. Lap: Calcédoine f.

Chaldea [kal'diːa]. Pr.n. A.Geog: La Chaldée.

Chaldean [kal'diːən], **Chaldee** [kal'diː], a. & s. A.Geog: Chaldéen.

chalice ['tʃalis], s. Ecc: Calice m.

chalk¹ [tʃɔːk], s. **1.** (a) Craie f; (coloured c. for drawing) pastel m. Bill: Blanc m. **French chalk,** talc m, stéatite f. S.a. RED 1. F: **He doesn't know chalk from cheese,** il ne sait rien de rien. (b) Geol: Calcaire m. (c) Pharm: **Precipitated chalk,** carbonate m de chaux précipité. **2.** Compte m des consommations (à l'ardoise). F: **Not by a long chalk,** tant s'en faut. **'chalk-pit,** s. (i) Carrière f de craie; crayère f; (ii) plâtrière f. **'chalk-stone,** s. Med: Concrétion f calcaire.

chalk², v.tr. **1.** (a) Marquer (qch.) à la craie. (b) Blanchir (sa figure, etc.) avec de la craie. (c) Talquer; saupoudrer de talc. **2.** To chalk (up) sth. on sth., écrire qch. à la craie sur qch. F: To chalk up the drinks, inscrire les consommations à l'ardoise. **3.** F: To chalk out a plan, tracer un plan (de conduite).

chalkiness ['tʃɔːkinəs], s. **1.** Nature crayeuse (du sol). **2.** F: Extrême pâleur (du teint).

chalky ['tʃɔːki], a. **1.** Crayeux, crétacé. S.a. DEPOSIT¹ 3. **2.** (Teint) pâle, terreux.

challenge¹ ['tʃalendʒ], s. **1.** (a) Défi m; provocation f (en duel, etc.). Sp: **To issue a challenge,** lancer un challenge. (b) Mil: Interpellation f, sommation f (par une sentinelle); qui-vive m inv. **2.** Jur: Récusation f (du jury). **'challenge-cup,** s. Sp: Coupe f que se disputent annuellement toutes les équipes, certains yachts d'un club, etc.; coupe-challenge f.

challenge², v.tr. **1.** (a) (i) To c. s.o. to fight, défier qn au combat; provoquer qn en duel; demander à qn satisfaction (d'une offense). (ii) Porter un défi à (un champion). To c. s.o. to do sth., défier qn de faire qch. (b) Mil: (Of sentry) To challenge s.o., interpeller qn. **2.** (a) Disputer, relever (une affirmation); mettre en question, en doute (la parole de qn). (b) Récuser (un juré). **3.** Provoquer (l'admiration, etc.). **challenging,** a. (Of look, remark) Provocateur, -trice; (air) de défi.

challengeable ['tʃalendʒəbl], a. **1.** Qu'on peut disputer, critiquer. **2.** (Juré) récusable.

challenger ['tʃalendʒər], s. **1.** (a) Provocateur, -trice. (b) Sp: Lanceur m d'un challenge. **2.** Jur: Récusant.

chalybeate [ka'libiet], a. Ch: Ferrugineux.

chamber ['tʃeimbər], s. **1.** (a) A. & Lit: (Room) Chambre f, pièce f, salle f. (Still so used in) **Audience chamber,** salle d'audience. S.a. COUNCIL-CHAMBER, LETHAL. (b) Lit: (Bed)chamber, chambre (à coucher). **Gentleman of the Privy Chamber,** gentilhomme de la Chambre du Roi. (c) **Chamber(-pot),** pot m de chambre. **2. Chamber of Commerce, of Trade,** chambre de commerce, de métiers. Pol: **The double chamber system,** le système bicaméral. **3.** pl. **Chambers.** (a) Appartement m de garçon. (b) Cabinet m de consultation (d'un avocat); étude f (d'un avoué). (c) Jur: **To hear a case in chambers,** juger une cause en référé. S.a. COUNSEL¹ 4. **4.** Tchn: (a) Cavité f alvéolaire; alvéole m or f. (b) Chambre, tonnerre m (d'une arme à feu). I.C.E:

Chambre d'explosion ; culasse *f.* **'chamber-music,** *s.* Musique *f* de chambre.
chambered ['tʃeimbərd], *a.* Évidé, chambré.
Six-chambered revolver, revolver à six coups.
chamberlain ['tʃeimbərlen], *s.* Chambellan *m.*
chambermaid ['tʃeimbərmeid], *s.f.* Fille, femme, de chambre (d'hôtel).
chameleon [kə'miːliən], *s.* *Rept:* Caméléon *m.*
chamfer[1] ['tʃamfər], *s.* Biseau *m,* chanfrein *m.*
chamfer[2], *v.tr.* **1.** *Carp: etc:* Biseauter, chanfreiner ; abattre (une arête). **2.** Canneler (une colonne, etc.).
chamois ['ʃamwɑː], *s.* Chamois *m.* **chamois-leather** ['ʃamiˈleðər], *s.* (Peau *f* de) chamois *m.*
champ [tʃamp], *v.tr.* (*Of horse, etc.*) Mâcher bruyamment (le fourrage) ; ronger, mâcher, mâchonner (le mors). **champing,** *s.* Mâchonnement *m.*
Champagne [ʃamˈpein]. **1.** *Pr.n.* *Geog:* La Champagne. **2.** *s.* Vin *m* de Champagne ; champagne *m.* **Light champagne,** tisane *f* de Champagne.
champaign ['tʃampein, tʃamˈpein], *s.* *A. & Lit:* Plaine *f* ; campagne ouverte.
champion[1] ['tʃampjən], *s.* **1.** (*a*) Champion *m.* (*b*) *Sp:* Recordman *m* ; champion, -ionne. **2.** *Attrib.* *C. driver,* champion de vitesse. *F: C. cabbage,* maître chou.
champion[2], *v.tr.* Soutenir, défendre (une cause) ; prendre fait et cause pour (qn).
championship ['tʃampjənʃip], *s.* **1.** *Sp:* etc. Championnat *m.* **2.** Défense *f* (d'une cause).
chance[1] [tʃɑːns], *s.* **1.** (*a*) Chance *f,* hasard *m,* sort *m.* *Game of chance,* jeu de hasard. **By (mere) chance,** par hasard. *Shall we see you there by any chance?* est-ce qu'on vous y verra par extraordinaire ? **Chance so ordained it that . . .,** le hasard voulut, le hasard fit, que + *ind.* or *sub.* *To leave everything to c.,* s'en remettre au hasard. **The chances are against me,** les chances sont contre moi. **The chances are that . . .,** il y a fort à parier que. . . . **Off chance,** chance moyenne. **To do sth. on the off chance,** faire qch. à tout hasard. (*b*) *To submit to the c. of war,* se soumettre au sort, à la fortune, de la guerre. **To look, have an eye, to the main chance,** ne pas perdre de vue son propre intérêt ; s'attacher au solide. **2.** Occasion *f.* **Now's your chance!** vous avez beau jeu ! *To have a good c. of doing sth.,* avoir beau jeu, une belle occasion, de faire qch. **To stand a chance,** avoir des chances de succès. **He hasn't the ghost of a chance of succeeding,** il n'a pas la moindre chance, l'ombre d'une chance, de réussir. **To have even chances,** avoir des chances égales. **To give s.o. a chance,** (i) mettre qn à l'essai ; (ii) *F:* entendre qn jusqu'au bout ; agir loyalement avec qn. **To take one's chance,** risquer les chances. **3.** *Esp. U.S:* Risque *m.* **To take a chance,** encourir un risque. **To take a long chance,** risquer beaucoup. **4.** *Attrib.* Fortuit, accidentel. **A chance acquaintance,** une connaissance fortuite, de rencontre. **Chance comer,** survenant *m.*
chance[2]. **1.** *v.i.* (*a*) *To c. to do sth.,* faire qch. par hasard. *If I c. to find it,* si je viens à le trouver. (*b*) *To chance upon s.o.,* upon sth.,* trouver, rencontrer, qn, qch., par hasard. **2.** *v.tr.* Risquer. **To chance it,** risquer le coup.
chancel ['tʃɑːnsəl], *s.* *Ecc.Arch:* **1.** Sanctuaire *m.* **2.** Chœur *m.*
chancellery, -ory ['tʃɑːnsələri], *s.* Chancellerie *f.*
chancellor ['tʃɑːnsələr], *s.* Chancelier *m.* **Chan-**

cellor of the Exchequer = Ministre *m* des Finances.
chancellorship ['tʃɑːnsələrʃip], *s.* Cancellariat *m.*
chancery ['tʃɑːnsəri], *s.* **1.** *Jur:* (Court of) Chancery, cour *f* de la chancellerie. *S.a.* WARD[1] 1. **2.** *Wr:* Hold in chancery, cravate *f.* *F:* To put one's head in chancery, se mettre à la merci de ses adversaires.
chancy ['tʃɑːnsi], *a.* *F:* Chanceux, incertain ; risqué.
chandelier [ʃandəˈliːər], *s.* Lustre *m* (d'éclairage).
chandler ['tʃɑːndlər], *s.* (*a*) Épicier-droguiste *m.* (*b*) Fournisseur *m.* *S.a.* CORN-CHANDLER, SHIP-CHANDLER.
chandlery ['tʃɑːndləri], *s.* **1.** Épicerie-droguerie *f.* **2.** Ship's chandlery, fournitures *fpl* pour la marine.
change[1] [tʃeindʒ], *s.* **1.** Changement *m* ; retour *m* (de la marée) ; revirement *m* (d'opinion, de fortune). **Change of abode,** changement de domicile ; déplacement *m.* **Change for the better, worse,** changement en mieux, en mal. **Barometer at 'change,'** baromètre à "variable." **To make a change,** effectuer un changement (*in,* à). *This journey will be* (*a bit of*) *a c. for you,* ce voyage vous changera un peu. **For a change,** comme distraction ; pour changer. *Physiol:* **Change of life,** retour *m* d'âge. *El:* **Change of connection,** commutation *f.* **Change of front,** (i) *Mil:* mouvement *m* de conversion ; (ii) *F:* volte-face *f* *inv* (politique). **2.** (*a*) **Change of clothes,** vêtements de rechange. (*b*) **Change of horses,** relais *m.* **3.** (*Exchange*) Change *m.* **4.** (*a*) Monnaie *f.* **Small change,** petite monnaie. *To give c. for £5,* donner, rendre, la monnaie de cinq livres. **'No change given,'** "on ne rend pas de monnaie" ; "le public est tenu de faire l'appoint." *P:* He won't get much change out of me, il perdra ses peines avec moi. (*b*) = EXCHANGE[1] 3 (*a*). **5.** *F:* To ring the changes on a subject, ressasser, rabâcher, un sujet.
change[2]. **1.** *v.tr.* Changer. (*a*) Modifier (ses plans). *To c. one thing* (*in*)*to another,* changer, transformer, une chose en une autre. *F:* **To change one's note, one's tune,** changer de ton. **To change the subject,** changer de sujet ; passer à autre chose. *S.a.* MIND[1] 2. (*b*) **To change one's clothes,** *abs.* to change, changer de vêtements ; se changer. *S.a.* GEAR[1] 3, HORSE 1. (*c*) *To c. one's seat,* changer de place. *Rail: To c. trains, abs.* to change, changer de train. **All change!** tout le monde descend ! **To change colour,** changer de couleur, de visage. **To change front,** (i) *Mil:* changer de front ; (ii) *F:* faire volte-face. **To change the guard,** relever la garde. *S.a.* HAND[1] 5, PLACE[1] 2, SIDE[1] 5. (*d*) *To c. one thing for another,* échanger, troquer, une chose contre une autre. (*e*) **To change a banknote,** (i) changer un billet de banque ; (ii) donner la monnaie d'un billet de banque. **2.** *v.i.* (*a*) Changer (*into,* en) ; se modifier ; varier. *To c. for the better,* changer en mieux ; (*of weather*) tourner au beau. *I could not wish it changed,* je ne voudrais pas qu'il en fût autrement. *S.a.* CHOP[5] 1, MANNER 3.
change about, *v.i.* Faire volte-face. **change down,** *v.i.* *Aut:* Passer à une vitesse inférieure.
change over, *v.i.* **1.** Passer (d'un système à un autre). **2.** (*Of sentries*) Se relever. **3.** *El:* Permuter, commuter. **change-'over,** *s.* **1.** Changement *m* (d'un système à un autre). **2.** Renversement *m* (politique, etc.). **3.** Relève *f* (de factionnaires). **4.** *El:* Commutation *f.*
change up, *v.i.* *Aut:* Passer à une vitesse supérieure ; monter les vitesses. **changing**[1], *a.* Changeant ; (expression) mobile. **changing**[2], *s.*

Changement *m*; relève *f* (de la garde). **'chang-ing-room,** *s.* Vestiaire *m*.
changeability [tʃeindʒəˈbiliti], **changeable-ness** ['tʃeindʒəblnəs], *s.* Variabilité *f* (du temps); mobilité *f* (de caractère); versatilité *f*.
changeable ['tʃeindʒəbl], *a.* **1.** (*Of pers., colour, etc.*) Changeant; (*of weather*) variable, inconstant; (*of character*) mobile. **2.** *C. at will,* modifiable à discrétion.
changeless ['tʃeindʒləs], *a.* Immuable.
changeling ['tʃeindʒliŋ], *s.* Enfant changé en nourrice, ou par les fées.
changer ['tʃeindʒər], *s.* **1.** *See* MONEY-CHANGER. **2.** *W.Tel:* Frequency changer, changeur *m* de fréquence.
channel[1] [tʃanl], *s.* **1.** Lit *m* (d'une rivière). **2.** (*a*) Passe *f*, chenal *m* (d'un port). (*b*) *Geog:* Détroit *m*, canal *m*. The (English) Channel, la Manche. The Channel Islands, les îles Anglo-normandes. **3.** Canal, conduit *m*. Oil-channel, rainure *f* de graissage; *pl.* pattes *f* d'araignée. **4.** Cannelure *f*, rainure (d'une colonne); gorge *f*, goujure *f* (d'une poulie). **5.** Rigole *f* (d'irrigation, de rue). **6.** Voie *f*. *Adm:* To go through official channels, suivre la filière, suivre la voie hiérarchique. *Through the ordinary channels of diplomacy,* par voie diplomatique. Channels of communication (*of a country*), artères *f* (d'un pays). **7.** New channels for trade, nouveaux débouchés pour le commerce.
channel[2], *v.tr.* (channelled) **1.** Creuser des rigoles dans (un terrain). **2.** (*a*) Canneler, rainurer. To channel out a groove, tailler une rainure. (*b*) Évider (une lame de sabre, etc.).
chant[1] [tʃɑːnt], *s.* *Mus:* Chant *m* (monotone); (*in church*) (i) plain-chant *m*, (ii) psalmodie *f*.
chant[2], *v.tr.* (*a*) *A:* Chanter. (*Still in*) To chant s.o.'s praises, chanter les louanges de qn. (*b*) *Ecc:* Psalmodier.
chanter ['tʃɑːntər], *s.* **1.** *Ecc:* Chantre *m.* **2.** *Mus:* Chalumeau *m*, "musette" *f* (de la cornemuse).
chanticleer [tʃanti'kliːər], *s.* *Lit. & Hum:* Chantecler *m* (le coq).
chantry ['tʃɑːntri], *s.* *Ecc:* **1.** Fondation *f* de messes (pour le repos de l'âme du fondateur). **2.** Chantrerie *f*.
chanty ['ʃɑːnti, 'ʃanti], *s.* (Sea-)chanty, chanson *f* de bord.
chaos ['keiɔs], *s.* Chaos *m*.
chaotic [kei'ɔtik], *a.* Chaotique, désorganisé. **-ally,** *adv.* Sans ordre.
chap[1] [tʃap], *s.* Gerçure *f*, crevasse *f*.
chap[2], *v.tr.* (chapped) Gercer, crevasser (la peau).
chap[3], *s.* (*Usu. pl.*) Bajoue(s) *f* (d'un cochon). *Cu:* Bath chap, béquet *m*. **'chap-fallen,** *a.* Penaud, décontenancé.
chap[4], *s.* **1.** *A:* = CHAPMAN. **2.** *F:* Garçon *m*, type *m*, individu *m*. Old chap, mon vieux. *A queer c.,* un drôle de corps, de bonhomme. **'chap-book,** *s.* Livre *m* de colportage.
chapel [tʃapl], *s.* **1.** (*a*) Chapelle *f*; oratoire (particulier). *Sch:* To keep a chapel, faire acte de présence à un office. Chapel of ease, (chapelle de) secours *m*. (*b*) Temple *m* (dissident).
chaperon[1] ['ʃapəroun], *s.* Chaperon *m*. *To act as c.,* jouer le rôle de chaperon.
chaperon[2], *v.tr.* (chaperoned) Chaperonner (une jeune fille).
chaplain ['tʃaplən], *s.* *Ecc:* Aumônier *m*.
chaplet ['tʃaplet], *s.* **1.** *Ecc:* Chapelet *m* (d'un tiers du rosaire). **2.** *Arch:* Moulure *f* en perles.
chapman, *pl.* **-men** ['tʃapmən, -men], *s.m.* Colporteur.

chapter ['tʃaptər], *s.* **1.** Chapitre *m*. *F:* To give chapter and verse, citer ses autorités, fournir des documents. *F:* A chapter of accidents, une suite de malheurs. **2.** *Ecc:* Chapitre (de chanoines).
'chapter-house, *s.* *Ecc:* Salle *f* du chapitre.
char[1] [tʃɑːr], *s.* *Ich:* Ombre *m* chevalier.
char[2], *s.f.* *P:* = CHARWOMAN.
char[3], *v.i.* *F:* To go out charring, travailler à la journée; aller en journée; faire des ménages.
char[4]. **1.** *v.tr.* (charred) Carboniser. **2.** *v.i.* Se carboniser. **charring,** *s.* Carbonisation *f*.
char-à-banc ['ʃarəbaŋ, -bɑ̃], *s.* Autocar *m*.
character ['karəktər], *s.* **1.** *Typ:* Caractère *m*, lettre *f*. **2.** (*a*) Caractère; marque distinctive. *Books of that c.,* les livres de ce genre. To be in character with sth., être à l'unisson de qch.; s'harmoniser avec qch. It is out of character with . . ., cela ne s'accorde guère avec. . . . In his character of . . ., en (sa) qualité de. . . . (*b*) *Work that lacks c.,* œuvre qui manque de caractère, de cachet. To assume, take on, character, se caractériser. **3.** Man of (strong) character, homme de caractère, de volonté. *He lacks (strength of) c.,* il n'a pas de (force de) caractère. **4.** (*a*) *Of bad c.,* de mauvaise réputation; mal famé. (*b*) *F:* Certificat *m* (de moralité). *F:* To give s.o. a good character, dire du bien de qn. **5.** (*Of acting*) Personnage *m* (de roman, etc.). (*Of acting*) In character, dans le ton, la note. Out of character, hors de propos. *Th:* A rôle. Character actor, acteur de genre. (*b*) A public character, une personnalité. A bad character, un mauvais sujet. *F:* He's a character, c'est un type, un original.
characteristic [karəktə'ristik]. **1.** *a.* Caractéristique. *Adm:* Characteristic signs, signalement *m*. **2.** *s.* (*a*) Trait *m*, signe *m*, de caractère, particularité *f*. (*b*) *Mth:* Caractéristique *f* (d'un logarithme). **-ally,** *adv.* D'une manière caractéristique.
characterization [karəktərai'zeiʃ(ə)n], *s.* Caractérisation *f*.
characterize ['karəktəraiz], *v.tr.* Caractériser; être caractéristique de (qn).
characterless ['karəktərləs], *a.* **1.** Dépourvu de caractère. **2.** Dépourvu de certificat (de bonne conduite).
charade [ʃəˈrɑːd], *s.* Charade *f*. Dumb charade, charade mimée.
charcoal ['tʃɑːrkoul], *s.* **1.** (*a*) Charbon *m* (de bois). (*b*) Animal charcoal, noir animal, charbon animal. **2.** *Art:* Fusain *m*. Charcoal drawing, (dessin *m* au) fusain. **'charcoal-burner,** *s.* Charbonnier *m*.
chard [tʃɑːrd], *s.* *Cu:* Carde *f*. Swiss chard, bette poirée.
charge[1] [tʃɑːrdʒ], *s.* **1.** (*a*) Charge *f* (de salut). cartouche). Blank charge, charge de salut. *S.a.* DEPTH-CHARGE. (*b*) (*Of kiln, etc.*) Fournée *f*. (*c*) *El:* Charge. **2.** (*a*) Frais *mpl*, prix *m*; *Adm:* droits *mpl*. List of charges, tarif *m*. Charge for admittance, prix des places. No c. for admission, entrée gratuite. To make a charge for sth., compter qch. Free of charge, (i) exempt de frais, sans frais; (ii) gratis, franco; (iii) à titre gratuit; à titre gracieux. At a charge of . . ., moyennant. . . . *S.a.* EXTRA 1. (*b*) Charges on an estate, charges d'une succession. To be a charge on s.o., être à la charge de qn. **3.** (*a*) Commission *f*, devoir *m*. (*b*) Charge; emploi *m*; fonction *f*; (*of clergy*) cure *f*. **4.** (*a*) Garde *f*, soin *m*. To take charge of s.o., (i) se charger, avoir soin, de qn; (ii) (*provide for*) prendre qn à sa charge. Nurse in charge of a child, bonne commise à la garde d'un enfant. Child in charge of a nurse, enfant

sous la garde d'une bonne. **To give s.o. charge of, over, sth.**, confier qch. à (la garde de) qn. *(Of official)* **To have charge, be in charge, of sth.**, être préposé à la garde de qch. **Person in charge,** préposé *(of,* à). *Jur:* **To take s.o. in charge,** arrêter qn. **To give s.o. in charge,** faire arrêter qn. *Mil:* **To take sth. on charge,** porter qch. sur les contrôles. *(b)* Personne, chose, confiée à la garde de qn. **5.** Recommandation *f,* exhortation *f*; résumé *m* (du juge après cause entendue). **6.** *Jur:* Charge; chef *m* d'accusation. **To bring, lay, a charge against s.o.**, porter une accusation, porter plainte, contre qn. **To lay sth. to s.o.'s charge,** charger, accuser, qn de qch. **On a charge of . . .**, sous l'inculpation de. . . . **7.** *(a) Mil:* Charge, attaque *f.* *F:* **To return to the charge,** revenir à la charge. *(b) Fb:* Choc *m,* charge.

charge², *v.tr.* **1.** Charger (un fusil, un accumulateur) *(with,* de). *El:* **Charged conductor,** conducteur chargé, sous tension. **2.** *(a)* **To charge s.o. with a commission,** charger qn d'une commission. *(b) Jur: (Of judge)* **To charge the jury,** faire le résumé des débats. **3.** **To charge s.o. with a crime,** imputer un crime à qn. **To c. s.o. with having done sth.**, accuser qn, reprocher à qn, d'avoir fait qch. **4.** *(a) Com:* Charger, imputer. **To c. the postage to the customer,** débiter les frais de poste au client. **To c. an expense on, to, an account,** imputer, passer, mettre, une dépense à un compte. **C. it on the bill,** portez-le sur la note. *(b)* **To c. s.o. a price for sth.**, prendre, compter, demander, un prix à qn pour qch. **To c. five francs a yard** *(for sth.),* demander cinq francs du mètre. *How much will you c. for the lot?* combien me faites-vous le tout? **5.** *v.tr. & i.* Charger (l'ennemi). *F:* **To charge into sth.**, donner (de la tête) contre qch. **To charge down upon s.o.**, foncer sur qn. **charging,** *s.* Chargement *m*; remplissage *m.* *El.E:* **Battery charging, (re)-charge** *f* des accus.

chargeable ['tʃɑːrdʒəbl], *a.* **1.** *(Of pers.)* Accusable, inculpable *(with,* de). **2.** *(Of pers., thg)* A la charge *(to,* de). **3.** Imputable *(to a cause,* à une cause). **4.** *(Of land)* Affectable; grevé (d'un impôt).

charger ['tʃɑːrdʒər], *s.* **1.** Cheval *m* de bataille. **2.** Chargeur *m* (d'accumulateur); chargeuse *f* mécanique. *S.a.* TRICKLE-CHARGER.

chariness ['tʃɛərinəs], *s.* **1.** Circonspection *f,* prudence *f (of doing sth.,* à faire qch). **2.** Parcimonie *f* (de paroles, de louanges).

chariot ['tʃɑriət], *s.* Char *m.*

charioteer [tʃɑrio'tiːər], *s.* Conducteur *m* de char.

charitable ['tʃɑritəbl], *a.* **1.** (Personne) charitable. **2.** (Œuvre) de bienfaisance, de charité. **-ably,** *adv.* Charitablement.

charity ['tʃɑriti], *s.* **1.** Charité *f.* **Out of charity, for charity's sake,** par charité. **To be in charity with one's neighbour,** vouloir du bien à son prochain. *Prov:* **Charity begins at home,** charité bien ordonnée commence par soi(-même). **2.** *(a)* Acte *m* de charité. *(b)* Charité, aumônes *fpl,* bienfaisance *f.* **To live on charity,** vivre d'aumônes, être à la charité. **Charity ball,** bal de bienfaisance. **3.** Œuvre *f* de bienfaisance, de charité; fondation pieuse. **'charity-boy, -girl,** *s.* Enfant élevé(e) dans un orphelinat. **'charity-school,** *s.* Orphelina *m.*

charlady ['tʃɑːleidi], *s.f. Hum:* = CHARWOMAN.

charlatan ['ʃɑːrlətan], *s.* Charlatan *m.*

charlatanry ['ʃɑːrlətənri], *s.* Charlatanerie *f.*

Charley, Charlie ['tʃɑːrli]. *Pr.n.m.* Charlot.

charlock ['tʃɑːrlɔk], *s. Bot:* Sanve *f.*

Charlotte ['ʃɑːrlɔt]. **1.** *Pr.n.f.* Charlotte. **2.** *s. Cu:* **Apple charlotte,** charlotte *f* aux pommes.

charm¹ [tʃɑːrm], *s.* **1.** Charme *m (against,* contre); sortilège *m,* sort *m.* **To be under the charm,** se trouver sous le charme. **2.** *(a)* Amulette *f,* fétiche *m.* *(b)* Breloque *f*; porte-bonheur *m inv.* **3.** Charme, agrément *m.* **To be devoid of c.**, manquer de charme.

charm², *v.tr.* **1.** Charmer, enchanter. **To charm away s.o.'s cares,** charmer les ennuis de qn. **He bears a charmed life,** sa vie est sous un charme; *F:* il est verni. **2.** *Charmed to see you!* charmé, enchanté, de vous voir! **charming,** *a.* Charmant, ravissant.

charmer ['tʃɑːrmər], *s.* Charmeur, -euse.

charmless ['tʃɑːrmləs], *a.* Sans charme.

charnel-house ['tʃɑːrnəlhaus], *s.* Charnier *m,* ossuaire *m.*

chart¹ ['tʃɑːrt], *s.* **1.** *Nau:* Carte *f* (marine). **Mercator's chart,** projection *f* de Mercator. **Wind chart,** carte des vents. **2.** *(a) (Of statistics, etc.)* Graphique *m,* diagramme *m.* *(b)* Tableau *m* (de graissage, etc.). **'chart-house, -room,** *s.* *Nau:* Cabine *f,* chambre *f,* des cartes; kiosque *m* de navigation.

chart², *v.tr.* **1.** *Nau:* *(a)* Porter (un rocher, etc.) sur une carte. *(b)* Dresser la carte (d'une côte, etc.); faire l'hydrographie (d'une mer, etc.). **2.** Établir le graphique (d'une série de relèvements). **charting,** *s.* Reconnaissance *f* (du littoral); relèvement *m* (d'un récif, etc.).

charter¹ ['tʃɑːrtər], *s.* **1.** Charte *f* (d'une ville). **Bank charter,** privilège *m* de la Banque. **2.** *Nau:* Affrètement *m.* **Trip charter, time charter,** affrètement au voyage, à temps. **'charter-party,** *s.* *Nau:* Charte-partie *f, pl.* chartes-parties.

charter², *v.tr.* **1.** Instituer (une compagnie) par charte. **2.** *Nau:* Affréter, fréter. **chartered,** *a.* (Compagnie) à charte. **Chartered bank,** banque privilégiée. *F:* **Chartered libertine,** fantasque à qui l'on permet tout. *S.a.* ACCOUNTANT. **chartering,** *s.* (Af)frètement *m,* nolisement *m.*

charterer ['tʃɑːrtərər], *s.* *Nau:* (Af)fréteur *m,* nolis(at)eur *m.*

Charterhouse ['tʃɑːrtərhaus], *s.* *A:* Couvent *m* de chartreux.

chartless ['tʃɑːrtləs], *a.* *(a)* (Littoral, etc.) non hydrographié. *(b)* (Navire) sans cartes marines.

charwoman, *pl.* **-women** ['tʃɑːrwumən, -wimen], *s.f.* Femme de journée, femme de ménage.

chary ['tʃɛəri], *a.* **1.** Prudent, circonspect. **To be c. of, in, doing sth.**, hésiter à faire qch. **2.** Chary of praise, avare de louanges. **C. of one's words,** économe, chiche, de paroles. **-ily,** *adv.* **1.** Avec circonspection. **2.** Parcimonieusement.

chase¹ [tʃeis], *s.* **1.** *(a)* Chasse *f,* poursuite *f.* **To give chase to s.o.**, donner la chasse à qn. *F:* **Wild goose chase,** poursuite vaine. **To go on a wild goose c.**, courir après la lune. **2.** *Ven:* Chasse (à courre). **2.** (Terrain non enclos réservé à la) chasse.

chase², *v.tr.* **1.** Chasser, pourchasser (le cerf). **2.** Poursuivre; donner la chasse à (un voleur, etc.). **To chase away a dog,** chasser un chien. **3.** *v.i.* *F:* **To chase off after sth.**, partir à la poursuite de qch.

chase³, *v.tr.* **1.** *(a)* Ciseler, bretteler (l'or). *(b)* Relever (le métal) en bosse; repousser (le métal). **2.** Enchâsser, sertir (un diamant). **chasing,** *s.* *(a)* Ciselage *m,* ciselure *f,* brettelure *f.* *(b)* Repoussage *m.*

chase⁴, s. *Typ:* Châssis *m* (de mise en pages).
chaser ['tʃeisər], s. **1.** Chasseur *m* (du cerf).
2. *Navy:* (*a*) (Navire) chasseur. **Submarine-chaser**, chasseur de sous-marins. (*b*) Pièce *f* de canon. *S.a.* BOW-CHASER, STERN-CHASER. **3.** *F:* Pousse-café *m inv.*
chasm [kazm], s. **1.** Gouffre béant; chasme *m.* **2.** Abîme *m* (entre deux personnes). **3.** Vide *m* (norme.
chassis ['ʃasi:], s. *inv. Aut: etc:* Châssis *m.*
chaste [tʃeist], a. **1.** (*Of pers.*) Chaste, pudique. **2.** (*Of style*) Pur, châtié. **-ly,** adv. Chastement, pudiquement; purement.
chasten [tʃeisn], v.tr. (*a*) Châtier, éprouver (qn). (*b*) Châtier (ses passions, son style). (*c*) Rabattre l'orgueil de (qn); assagir (qn). **chastened,** a. Assagi (par un déboire); désillusionné; radouci.
chasteness ['tʃeistnəs], s. = CHASTITY, *esp.* 2.
chastise [tʃas'taiz], v.tr. Châtier; infliger une correction à (qn); corriger (un enfant).
chastisement ['tʃastizmənt], s. Châtiment *m.*
chastiser [tʃas'taizər], s. Châtieur *m.*
chastity ['tʃastiti], s. **1.** Chasteté *f.* **2.** *Art: etc:* Pureté *f,* simplicité *f* (de style).
chasuble ['tʃazjubl], s. *Ecc:* Chasuble *f.*
chat¹ [tʃat], s. Causerie *f,* causette *f. To have a c. with s.o.,* tailler une bavette avec qn.
chat², v.i. (**chatted**) Causer, bavarder.
chat³, s. *Orn:* Tarier *m.*
chattel [tʃatl], s. *Jur:* (*a*) Bien *m* meuble, bien mobilier. (*b*) *pl.* Objets mobiliers; meubles *m. F: Goods and chattels,* biens et effets *m.*
chatter¹ ['tʃatər], s. **1.** Caquet(age) *m,* jacasserie *f* (d'oiseaux, de commères); bavardage *m.* **2.** Claquement *m* (d'une machine).
chatter², v.i. **1.** (*Of birds*) Caqueter, jacasser, jaser; (*of pers.*) bavarder, caqueter. *To chatter like a magpie,* jaser comme une pie (borgne). **2.** (*a*) (*Of teeth*) Claquer. (*b*) (*Of machinery, etc.*) Faire du bruit; cogner. **chattering,** s. **1.** = CHATTER¹. **2.** Claquement *m* (des dents).
chatterer ['tʃatərər], *F:* **chatterbox** ['tʃatərbɔks], s. Babillard, -arde; grand(e) bavard(e).
chatty ['tʃati], a. (*Of pers.*) Causeur; (dîner) très causant. *C. article on . . .,* article sur le ton de la conversation sur. . . .
chauffeur [ʃou'fə:r], s. Chauffeur *m*; conducteur *m* (d'une auto).
chaw¹ [tʃɔ:], s. Chique *f* (de tabac).
chaw², v.tr. *F:* (*a*) Mâcher. (*b*) Chiquer (du tabac). **'chaw-bacon,** s. *F:* Rustre *m,* croquant *m.*
cheap [tʃi:p], **1.** a. (*a*) (A) bon marché. *To buy sth. cheap,* acheter qch. (à) bon marché, à bon compte, pour pas cher. **Cheaper,** (à) meilleur marché, moins cher. *It comes cheaper to take a whole bottle,* on a avantage à prendre la bouteille entière. *Dirt cheap,* à vil prix; pour rien. *C. seats* (*in theatre, etc.*), places populaires, petites places. *To do sth. on the cheap,* faire qch. (i) à peu de frais, (ii) chichement. (*b*) De peu de valeur. *C. music,* musiquette *f. F: To feel cheap,* (i) être honteux; (ii) ne pas être dans son assiette. *To make oneself cheap,* déroger; se déprécier. *To hold sth. cheap,* faire bon marché, peu de cas, de qch. *S.a.* JACK¹ II 1. **2.** adv. *F:* = CHEAPLY. **-ly,** adv. (A) bon marché; à bas prix; à peu de frais. *F: He got off cheap(ly),* il en est quitte à bon compte.
cheapen [tʃi:pn], **1.** v.tr. (Ra)baisser le prix de (qch.); diminuer la valeur de (qch.). **2.** v.i. Diminuer de prix.

cheapness ['tʃi:pnəs], s. **1.** Bon marché; bas prix (de qch.). **2.** Médiocrité *f* (de qch.).
cheat¹ [tʃi:t], s. **1.** (*a*) Trompeur *m*; escroc *m.* (*b*) (*At games*) Tricheur *m.* **2.** *A:* Tromperie *f,* fourberie *f,* escroquerie *f.*
cheat², v.tr. **1.** Tromper; frauder (qn); voler (qn). *To cheat the gallows,* échapper à la potence. *To cheat s.o. out of sth.,* frustrer qn de qch. **2.** (*At games*) Tricher (qn); *abs.* tricher.
cheating¹, a. **1.** Trompeur. **2.** Tricheur.
cheating², s. **1.** Tromperie *f*; fourberie *f.* **2.** *Cards:* Tricherie *f.*
check¹ [tʃek], s. **1.** (*a*) *Chess:* Échec *m. To give check to the king,* faire échec au roi. **'Check!'** "échec au roi!" (*b*) Revers *m,* échec. (*c*) *Ven:* (*Of pack*) *To come to a check,* venir à bout de la voie; perdre la voie. **2.** Arrêt *m,* pause *f,* anicroche *f,* à-coup *m.* **3.** (*a*) (*Restraint*) Frein *m. To keep, to hold, the enemy in check,* tenir l'ennemi en échec; faire échec à l'ennemi. (*b*) *Geol:* Accident *m* de terrain. **4.** Butée *f,* arrêt. *Aut: etc:* **Door-check,** arrêt de porte. **5.** Contrôle *m.* (*a*) *Com:* Vérification *f* (d'un compte, etc.). **Check sample,** échantillon témoin. (**Cross-)checks** (**on information**), (moyens *m* de) recoupement *m. To keep a check on sth.,* contrôler qch. (*b*) Billet *m*; (*at cloakroom, etc.*) ticket *m.* **Luggage check,** bulletin *m* de bagages. (*c*) *U.S:* Jeton *m* de présence (à une séance). **6.** *U.S:* = CHEQUE. **'check-nut,** s. Contre-écrou *m.* **'check-screw,** s. Contre-vis *f inv.* **'check-valve,** s. *Mch: Hyd.E:* Soupape *f* de retenue.
check². **1.** v.tr. (*a*) *Chess:* Mettre (le roi) en échec; faire échec (au roi). (*b*) Faire échec à (qn, qch.); contenir (l'ennemi); enrayer (une crise); arrêter (une attaque). *Nau:* Stopper (un câble). (*c*) Refouler, comprimer, retenir (ses larmes, sa colère); modérer (sa violence); réprimer, refréner (une passion); freiner (la production). (*d*) Réprimander, reprendre (un enfant, etc.). (*e*) Vérifier, apurer (un compte); collationner, compulser (un document). *Typ:* (i) Réviser, (ii) conférer (des épreuves). *To check (off),* pointer (des noms sur une liste). *To check (up) information,* contrôler des renseignements. (*f*) Contrôler (une expérience, etc.); *Rail:* les billets. (*g*) (Faire) enregistrer (ses bagages). **2.** v.i. Hésiter, s'arrêter (*at,* devant); (*of horse*) refuser. **checking,** s. **1.** Répression *f*; enrayage *m.* **2.** (*a*) Contrôle *m*; vérification *f*; apurement *m*; pointage *m.* (*b*) Enregistrement *m* (de bagages).
check³, s. *Tex:* Carreau *m*; (étoffe) à carreaux, en damier.
checked [tʃekt], a. A carreaux; quadrillé.
checker¹ ['tʃekər], s. Contrôleur *m,* pointeur *m.*
checker², s. & v.tr. = CHEQUER¹, ².
checkers ['tʃekərz], s.pl. *U.S:* Jeu *m* de dames. **'checker-board,** s. Damier *m.*
checkmate¹ ['tʃekmeit], s. *Chess:* Échec et mat *m.*
checkmate², v.tr. **1.** *Chess: A:* = MATE². **2.** *F:* Faire échec et mat à (qn). **3.** *F:* Contrecarrer, déjouer (les projets de qn).
cheddar ['tʃedər], s. (Fromage de) Cheddar *m.*
cheek¹ [tʃi:k], s. **1.** Joue *f.* **Cheek by jowl with s.o.,** côte à côte avec qn. *S.a.* TONGUE¹ 1. **2.** *F:* (*a*) Toupet *m,* effronterie *f,* impudence *f. To have the cheek to do, say, sth.,* avoir l'aplomb de faire, de dire, qch. *What cheek!* quel toupet! (*b*) Impertinences *fpl.* **3.** Joue (de poulie, de coussinet); flasque *m,* bras *m* (de manivelle);

mâchoire *f* (d'étau). **'cheek-bone,** *s.* Pommette *f*; os *m* malaire.

cheek², *v.tr.* F: Faire l'insolent avec (qn). **-cheeked** [tʃi:kt], *a.* Rosy-cheeked, aux joues vermeilles. *S.a.* APPLE-CHEEKED.

cheekiness ['tʃi:kinəs], *s.* F: Effronterie *f*.

cheeky ['tʃi:ki], *a.* F: Effronté. **-ily,** *adv.* F: D'un air ou d'un ton effronté.

cheep¹ [tʃi:p], *s.* Piaulement *m*.

cheep², *v.i.* (Of young birds) Piauler.

cheer¹ ['tʃiər], *s.* **1.** Bonne disposition (d'esprit). (So used esp. in) Words of cheer, paroles consolatrices, d'encouragement. F: What cheer? comment ça va? **2.** (Fare) Bonne chère. **3.** Hourra *m*; *pl.* acclamations *f*, bravos *m*, vivats *m*. 'Loud cheers,' "vifs applaudissements." To give three cheers = accorder un ban à qn. Three cheers for X! vive X!

cheer². **1.** *v.tr.* (a) To cheer s.o. (up), égayer, ragaillardir, dérider, qn; relever le moral de qn. To cheer s.o. on (to do sth.), encourager qn (à faire qch.). (b) Acclamer, applaudir (qn). **2.** *v.i.* (a) To cheer up, reprendre sa gaieté; se ragaillardir. Cheer up! courage! (b) Pousser des hourras, des vivats; applaudir. **cheering¹,** *a.* Encourageant, réjouissant. **cheering²,** *s.* Acclamation *f*; applaudissements *mpl.*

cheerful ['tʃiərful], *a.* (Of pers.) Gai; de bonne humeur; allègre; (of room) d'aspect agréable, riant; (of fire, news) réconfortant; (of conversation, music) égayant. **-fully,** *adv.* **1.** Gaiement, allégrement. **2.** De bon cœur; volontiers.

cheerfulness ['tʃiərfulnəs], *s.* (a) (Of pers.) Gaieté, gaîté *f*, belle humeur; contentement *m*. His c. in misfortune, sa sérénité dans le malheur. (b) Aspect riant (du paysage); air *m* agréable (d'un intérieur).

cheerio ['tʃiəri'ou], *int.* P: **1.** A bientôt! bon courage! adieu! **2.** A la vôtre! à la tienne!

cheerless ['tʃiərləs], *a.* Morne, triste, sombre.

cheery ['tʃiəri], *a.* **1.** (Of pers.) Joyeux, gai, guilleret. **2.** = CHEERING¹. **-ily,** *adv.* Gaiement.

cheese¹ [tʃi:z], *s.* **1.** Fromage *m*. F: To believe the moon is made of green cheese, prendre des vessies pour des lanternes. *S.a.* CHALK¹. **2.** (With *pl.* cheeses) A cheese, un fromage (entier). **3.** Gelée *f* (de prunes de Damas, etc.). *S.a.* LEMON-CHEESE. **'cheese-biscuit,** *s.* Biscuit non sucré. **'cheese-cake,** *s.* Cu: Tartelette *f* à la frangipane au citron. **'cheese-cloth,** *s.* Gaze *f*; étamine *f*. **'cheese-cover,** *s.* Cloche *f* à fromage. **'cheese-maker,** *s.* Fromager, -ère. **'cheese-paring,** *s.* **1.** Pelure *f* de fromage. **2.** Parcimonie *f*, lésine *f* *a.* Cheese-paring economy, économies de bouts de chandelle.

cheese², *s.* P: That's the cheese! ça c'est à la hauteur! à la bonne heure! Hard cheese! ça, c'est de la déveine!

cheesemonger ['tʃi:zmʌŋgər], *s.* Marchand de fromage.

cheesy ['tʃi:zi], *a.* **1.** Caséeux, caséiforme. **2.** (Odeur) de fromage.

cheetah 'tʃi:ta], *s.* Z: Guépard *m*.

chef [ʃef], *s.m.* Chef de cuisine.

chemical ['kemik(ə)l], **1.** *a.* Chimique. C. balance, balance de laboratoire. **2.** *s.pl.* Chemicals, produits *m* chimiques. Com: Ind: Drogues *f*. **-ally,** *adv.* Chimiquement.

chemise [ʃə'mi:z], *s.* Chemise *f* (de femme).

chemisette [ʃemi'zet], *s.* Cost: Guimpe *f*.

chemist ['kemist], *s.* **1.** Pharmacien *m*. Chemist's shop, pharmacie *f*. **2.** Chimiste *m*. Analytical chemist, chimiste (analyste).

chemistry ['kemistri], *s.* Chimie *f*. Inorganic c., chimie minérale. Organic c., chimie organique.

chenopodium [keno'pɔdiəm], *s.* Bot: Chénopode *m*; patte-d'oie *f*.

cheque [tʃek], *s.* Com: Chèque *m*. Crossed c., chèque barré. Open, uncrossed, c., chèque ouvert, non barré. *S.a.* BLANK I. **1.** **'cheque-book,** *s.* Carnet *m* de chèques.

chequer¹ ['tʃekər], *s.* Usu. pl. Quadrillage *m*. **'chequer-wise,** *adv.* En échiquier.

chequer², *v.tr.* **1.** Quadriller (une étoffe, etc.). **2.** Diaprer, bigarrer. **3.** F: Diversifier, varier.

chequered, *a.* **1.** Quadrillé, à carreaux, en damier, en échiquier. **2.** Diapré, bigarré. **3.** Chequered career, vie accidentée, mouvementée. **chequering,** *s.* Quadrillage *m* (d'une étoffe); guillochage *m* (d'une montre).

cherish ['tʃeriʃ], *v.tr.* **1.** Chérir; soigner tendrement (un enfant). **2.** Bercer, caresser (un espoir); nourrir, entretenir (une idée).

cheroot [ʃə'ru:t], *s.* Manille *m* (à bouts coupés).

cherry ['tʃeri]. **1.** *s.* Cerise *f*. Black-heart cherry, guigne noire. White-heart cherry, bigarreau *m*. Wild cherry, merise *f*. F: Not to make two bites at a cherry, ne pas s'y prendre à deux fois; y aller sans hésiter. **2.** *s.* Cherry(-tree, -wood), cerisier *m*. Wild cherry(-tree), merisier *m*. Heart-cherry(-tree), guignier *m*. **3.** *a.* Cherry (-red), cerise *inv*; (of lips) vermeil. **cherry-'bay,** -'laurel, *s.* Bot: Laurier-cerise *m*. **'cherry-orchard,** *s.* Cerisaie *f*. **cherry-'pie,** *s.* Tourte *f* aux cerises. **cherry-'ripe.** **1.** *int.* Aux cerises mûres! **2.** *a.* F: (Mûr) à point. **'cherry-stone,** *s.* Noyau *m* de cerise. **'cherry-wood,** *s.* (Bois *m* de) cerisier *m*. C.-w. pipe, pipe en merisier.

cherub, *pl.* B: **cherubim,** F: **cherubs** ['tʃerəb, -(j)ubim, -z], *s.* Chérubin *m*.

cherubic [ʃe'r(j)u:bik], *a.* Chérubique; chérubin.

chervil ['tʃə:rvil], *s.* Bot: Cerfeuil *m*.

chess [tʃes], *s.* Jeu *m* d'échecs. **'chess-board,** *s.* Échiquier *m*. **'chess-men,** *s.pl.* Pièces *f* (du jeu d'échecs).

chest [tʃest], *s.* **1.** Coffre *m*, caisse *f*, boîte *f*. Furn: Chest of drawers, commode *f*. Sea chest, coffre de marin. *S.a.* ICE-CHEST, MEDICINE-CHEST, STEAM-CHEST, TEA-CHEST, TOOL-CHEST. **2.** Anat: Poitrine *f*. Cold on the chest, chest cold, rhume de poitrine. To have a weak c., avoir les bronches délicates. To throw out one's chest, bomber la poitrine, le torse. F: To get it off one's chest, dire ce qu'on a sur le cœur. **'chest-voice,** *s.* Voix *f* de poitrine.

-chested ['tʃestid], *a.* Broad-chested, à large poitrine.

chesterfield ['tʃestərfi:ld], *s.* Furn: Canapé rembourré et capitonné (à deux accoudoirs).

chestnut ['tʃes(t)nʌt]. **1.** *s.* (a) (Sweet, Spanish) chestnut, (i) châtaigne *f* (comestible); (ii) (if very large) marron *m*. *S.a.* FIRE¹ **1**, HORSE-CHESTNUT. (b) (Sweet) chestnut(-tree), châtaignier commun; marronnier *m*. (c) F: Plaisanterie usée; vieille histoire. **2.** Attrib. (a) (Wood) De châtaignier. (b) (Colour) Châtain; (cheval) alezan. **'chestnut-grove,** *s.* Châtaigneraie *f*. **'chestnut-man,** *s.m.* -men, *s.m.* Marchand de marrons.

chesty ['tʃesti], *a.* **1.** U.S: P: Vaniteux. **2.** P: Délicat des bronches.

cheval-glass [ʃə'valglɑ:s], *s.* Furn: Psyché *f*.

chevron ['ʃevrən], *s.* Her: Mil: Chevron *m*.

chew¹ [tʃu:], *s.* **1.** To have a chew at sth., mâchonner qch. **2.** Chique *f* (de tabac).

chew², *v.tr.* Mâcher, mastiquer (des aliments, etc.); chiquer (du tabac); mâchonner (un cigare). *F:* **To chew over sth.**, méditer sur qch.; ruminer (une idée). **To chew sth. up**, abîmer qch.; mettre qch. en morceaux. *S.a.* CUD.
chewing, *s.* Mastication *f*, mâchonnement *m*. **'chewing-gum,** *s.* Gomme *f* à mâcher. *Pharm:* ■Masticatoire *m*. **'chewing tobacco,** *s.* Tabac *m* à chiquer.
chewer ['tʃuːər], *s.* Chiqueur *m* (de tabac).
chicane¹ [ʃi'keːin], *s.* Chicane *f*; avocasserie *f*.
chicane². **1.** *v.i.* Chicaner. **2.** *v.tr.* Chicaner (qn).
chicanery [ʃi'keinəri], *s.* **1.** Chicanerie *f*, chicane *f*, tracasserie *f*. **2.** Arguties *fpl*; subtilités *fpl*.
chick [tʃik], *s.* (i) (*Unfledged*) Poussin *m*; (ii) poulet *m*. *F:* **To have neither chick nor child,** être sans enfant.
chickabiddy ['tʃikəbidi], *s.* *F:* Cocot(t)e *f* (poule ou enfant).
chicken ['tʃikən], *s.* **1.** (*a*) (*Recently hatched*) Poussin *m*. (*b*) (*Fledged*) Poulet *m*. *F:* **Don't count your chickens before they are hatched,** il ne faut pas vendre la peau de l'ours avant de l'avoir tué. **She is no chicken,** elle n'est plus dans sa première jeunesse. *Orn:* *F:* **Mother Car(e)y's chicken,** pétrel *m* de tempête. **2.** *Cu:* Poulet. **Spring chicken,** poussin. **'chicken-hearted,** *a.* Poltron; *F:* capon. **'chicken-pox,** *s.* *Med:* Varicelle *f*. **'chicken-run,** *s.* Enclos grillagé d'un poulailler.
chickling ['tʃiklin], *s.* *Bot:* Gesse *f*.
chick-pea [tʃik'piː], *s.* *Bot:* Pois *m* chiche.
chickweed ['tʃikwiːd], *s.* *Bot:* Mouron *m* des oiseaux. '
chicory ['tʃikəri], *s.* *Bot:* Chicorée *f*. **Broad-leaved chicory,** endive *f*. **Wild chicory,** (i) *Bot:* chicorée sauvage; (ii) *Hort:* barbe-de-capucin *f*.
chide [tʃaid], *v.tr. & i.* (*p.t.* chid, *occ.* chided; *p.p.* chidden *or* chid, *occ.* chided) *A. & Lit:* Réprimander, gronder (qn). *To c. s.o. for sth., for doing sth.*, reprocher à qn d'avoir fait qch.
chief [tʃiːf]. **I.** *s.* (*a*) (*Pers.*) Chef *m* (de tribu). *F:* **The c.**, le patron. (*b*) **In chief,** en chef. **Commander-in-chief,** commandant en chef. **II. chief,** *a.* Principal, -aux; premier; (*en*) chef. *C. engineer*, ingénieur en chef. *C. stoker*, chef de chauffe. *C. object*, but principal. *To play a c. part in . . .*, jouer un rôle capital dans. . . . **-ly,** *adv.* **1.** Surtout, avant tout. **2.** Principalement.
chieftain ['tʃiːftən], *s.m.* Chef (de clan).
chiffon ['ʃifən], *s.* **1.** *Tex:* Chiffon *m*, gaze *f*. **2.** *pl.* Chiffons, atours *m* (de toilette).
chiffonier [ʃifo'niːər], *s.* *Furn:* Chiffonnier *m* (à tiroirs).
chilblain ['tʃilblein], *s.* Engelure *f*.
child, *pl.* **children** [tʃaild, 'tʃildrən], *s. m, f, or neut.* (*a*) Enfant *mf*. **Be a good child!** sois sage! *I'm taking the c. with me,* *F:* j'emmène le petit, la petite. **From a child . . .**, dès son enfance, depuis son plus jeune âge. . . . **To be with child,** être enceinte. (*b*) *Lit:* *B:* Descendant; enfant. **Our children's children,** nos arrière-neveux *m*. **'child-bearing,** *s.* **1.** = CHILD-BIRTH. **2.** Gestation *f*, grossesse *f*. **'child-bed,** *s.* Couches *fpl*. **'child-birth,** *s.* Enfantement *m*; couches *fpl*; accouchement *m*. **'child-mur-der,** *s.* Infanticide *m*. **'child's-play,** *s.* Jeu *m* d'enfant. **To make child's-play of sth.**, faire qch. en se jouant.
child(e) [tʃaild], *s.m.* *Lit:* *A:* Titre donné dans les anciennes *ballads* aux fils de famille noble.

childhood ['tʃaildhud], *s.* (*a*) Enfance *f*. (*b*) **one's second childhood,** retombé en enfance.
childish ['tʃaildiʃ], *a.* **1.** Enfantin, d'enfant, d'enfance. **2.** *Pej:* (*Of grown-up pers.*) Enfant, puéril, *F:* bébête. **Don't be so childish,** ne faites pas l'enfant. **3.** (*Of aged pers.*) **To grow childish,** retomber en enfance. **-ly,** *adv.* Comme un enfant; puérilement.
childishness ['tʃaildiʃnəs], *s.* *Pej:* Enfantillage *m*, puérilité *f*.
childless ['tʃaildləs], *a.* Sans enfant(s).
childlike ['tʃaildlaik], *a.* Enfantin; naïf.
chill¹ [tʃil], *s.* **1.** (*a*) *Med:* Coup *m* de froid. **To catch a chill,** prendre froid; attraper un chaud et froid. (*b*) **Chill of fear,** frisson *m* de crainte. **2.** (*a*) Froideur *f* (de l'eau, etc.). **To take the chill off (sth.),** (faire) dégourdir, (faire) tiédir (l'eau); chambrer (le vin). (*b*) **To cast a chill over the company,** jeter un froid sur l'assemblée. **3.** *Metall:* **Chill(-mould),** moule *m* en fonte; coquille *f*.
chill², *a.* Froid, glacé. **The wind blows chill,** il souffle un vent glacial. (*Of blood*) **To run chill,** se glacer.
chill³. **1.** *v.tr.* (*a*) Refroidir, glacer; faire frissonner (qn); donner le frisson à (qn). *F:* **Chilled to the bone,** morfondu; transi de froid. (*b*) Réfrigérer (la viande, etc.). **Chilled meat,** viande frigorifiée. (*c*) *Metall:* **To chill(-harden),** tremper, couler, (le fer) en coquille. **2.** *v.i.* refroidir, se glacer. **chilling**¹, *a.* (*Vent, accueil*) glacial, -als. **chilling**², *s.* **1.** Réfrigération *f* (des aliments). **2.** *Metall:* Trempe *f* en coquille.
chilli ['tʃili], *s.* *Cu:* Piment *m*. **Red chilli,** piment rouge.
chilliness ['tʃilinəs], *s.* (*a*) Froid *m*, froideur *f*, fraîcheur *f*. (*b*) Froideur (d'un accueil).
chilly ['tʃili], *a.* **1.** (*Of pers.*) (*a*) Frileux. (*b*) **To feel c.**, avoir froid. **2.** (*Of weather, etc.*) Frais, *f.* fraîche; (un peu) froid. *It is getting c.*, il commence à faire frisquet. **3.** (*Of pers., manner*) Froid. **Chilly politeness,** politesse glaciale.
chime¹ [tʃaim], *s.* **1.** Chime, chimes (*of bells*), carillon *m*. **The full chimes,** la grosse sonnerie. **2.** **To keep chime with sth.**, s'accorder, s'harmoniser, avec qch.
chime². **1.** *v.i.* Carillonner. *F:* **To chime together,** s'accorder, être d'accord. **To chime in with s.o.'s ideas,** s'harmoniser, tomber d'accord, avec les idées de qn. *F:* **To chime in,** placer son mot, intervenir (dans la conversation). *To c. in with the laughter*, s'associer aux rires. **2.** *v.tr.* (*Of clock*) *To c. the hour*, carillonner l'heure. **chiming**¹, *a.* Carillonnant. **Chiming clock,** pendule à carillon. **chiming**², *s.* Carillonnement *m*, carillon *m*, sonnerie *f*.
chime³, *s.* Jable *m* (d'un tonneau).
chimera [ki'miːərə, kai-], *s.* Chimère *f*.
chimerical [ki'merik(ə)l, kai-], *a.* Chimérique. **-ally,** *adv.* Chimériquement.
chimney ['tʃimni], *s.* **1.** Cheminée *f* (de maison). *C. on fire*, feu *m* de cheminée. *A:* **Chimney boy,** petit ramoneur. **2.** (*Funnel*) Cheminée (de bateau à vapeur). **Lamp chimney,** verre *m* de lampe. **3.** *Mountaineering:* Cheminée, varappe *f*. **'chimney-corner,** *s.* Coin *m* de cheminée; coin du feu. **'chimney-jack,** *s.* Mitre *f* (de cheminée) à tête mobile; gueule-de-loup *j*. **'chimney-piece,** *s.* Chambranle *m* de cheminée; *F:* dessus *m* de cheminée. **'chimney-pot,** *s.* **1.** Mitre *f*; pot *m* de cheminée. **2.** *F:* **Chimney-pot (hat),** *F:* tube *m*; tuyau *m* de poêle; huit-reflets *m*. **'chimney-stack, -stalk,**

1. (Corps de) cheminée *f*; souche *f*. 2. Cheminée d'usine. '**chimney-sweep**, *s.* (*Pers.*) Ramoneur *m*. '**chimney-sweeping**, *s.* Ramonage *m*.
himpanzee [tʃimpan'ziː], *s.* Chimpanzé *m*.
hin [tʃin], *s.* Menton *m*. *F:* **To wag one's chin**, faire aller sa langue. '**chin-rest**, *s.* Mentonnière *⸔* (de violon). '**chin-strap**, *s. Mil:* Jugulaire *f*, (sous-)mentonnière *f* (de casque, etc.). '**chin-wag**, *s. F:* Conversation *f*, causette *f*.
China ['tʃainə]. 1. *Pr.n. Geog:* La Chine. 2. *s.* (*No pl.*) (i) Porcelaine *f*; faïence fine; (ii) vaisselle *f* de porcelaine. '**china-clay**, *s.* Terre *f* à porcelaine; kaolin *m*. '**China-paper**, *s. Paperm:* Papier *m* de Chine.
Chinaman, *pl.* -**men** ['tʃainəmən, -men], *s.m.* Chinois.
Chinatown ['tʃainətaun]. *Pr.n.* Quartier chinois (d'une ville).
chinchilla [tʃin'tʃilə], *s.* (*Rat, rabbit*) Chinchilla *m*.
hin-chin ['tʃin'tʃin], *int. & s. F:* 1. (*a*) Salut *m*, bonjour *m*. (*b*) Adieu *m*; au revoir *m*. 2. A la vôtre!
hine[1] [tʃain], *s. Geol:* Ravinée *f*, ravin *m*.
hine[2], *s.* 1. *Anat:* Échine *f*. 2. Arête *f*, crête *f* (d'une montagne).
Chinee [tʃai'niː], *s. P:* Chinois *m*.
Chinese [tʃai'niːz]. 1. *a. & s. inv.* Chinois, -oise. Chinese white, blanc de Chine. 2. *s. Ling:* Le chinois.
hink[1] [tʃiŋk], *s.* Fente *f*, crevasse *f*, lézarde *f* (dans un mur); entre-bâillement *m* (de la porte).
hink[2], *s.* 1. Tintement *m* (du métal, du verre). *I heard a c. of money*, j'entendis sonner des pièces d'argent. 2. *P:* Argent *m*, galette *f*.
hink[3]. 1. *v.tr.* Faire sonner (son argent); faire tinter (des verres, etc.). 2. *v.i.* Sonner (sec).
Chink[4], *s. P:* Chinois *m*.
'**hinless** ['tʃinləs], *a.* Au menton fuyant.
chinned [tʃind], *a.* **Double-chinned**, à double menton.
hintz [tʃints], *s. Tex:* Perse *f*, indienne *f*.
hip[1] [tʃip], *s.* 1. Éclat *m*, copeau *m* (de bois); écaille *f*, éclat (de marbre). *F:* **He is a chip of the old block**, c'est bien le fils de son père. 2. (*Fracture*) Brisure *f*, écornure *f* (d'assiette). 3. *Cu:* Chip potatoes, chips, pommes de terre frites. Game chips, croustilles *f*. 4. *Cards: etc:* Jeton *m*. '**chip-carving**, *s.* Sculpture *f* sur bois.
hip[2], *v.tr.* (**chipped**) 1. Tailler par éclats; hacher ou doler (le bois). 2. (*a*) Ébrécher (un couteau); écorner (un meuble). *To c. a piece off sth.*, enlever un morceau à qch. (*b*) Piquer (les incrustations d'une chaudière). (*c*) *F:* **To chip in** (at) s.o., persifler qn; se moquer de qn. **chip in**, *v.i.* 1. *Cards:* Miser. 2. *F:* Intervenir; placer son mot. **chip off**. 1. *v.i.* (*Of paint, etc.*) S'écailler. 2. *v.tr. To c. off the scale of a boiler*, piquer une chaudière. **chipped**, *a.* 1. Ébréché, écaillé. 2. Chipped potatoes, pommes de terre frites. **chipping**, *s.* 1. (*a*) Taille *f* par éclats; écaillement *m*; clivage *m* (de pierre); burinage *m* (de métal); piquage *m* au marteau (d'une chaudière). (*b*) *F:* Persiflage *m*, taquinerie *f*. 2. *pl.* Chippings, éclats *m*, copeaux *m*.
hip[3], *s. Wr:* Croc *m* en jambe.
hippy ['tʃipi], *a.* 1. *F:* (*Esp. of food*) Sec, *f.* sèche; sans saveur. 2. *P:* **To feel chippy**, avoir la gueule de bois.
chiromancer ['kairomansər], *s.* Chiromancien.
chiromancy ['kairomansi], *s.* Chiromancie *f*.
chiropodist [kai'rɔpodist], *s.* Pédicure *m*.

chiropody [kai'rɔpodi], *s.* Chirurgie *f* pédicure, *m*.
chirp[1] [tʃəːrp], *s.* Pépiement *m*, gazouillement *m*. gazouillis *m* (d'oiseaux); grésillement *m* (du grillon).
chirp[2], *v.i.* (*Of bird*) Pépier, gazouiller, ramager; (*of grasshopper*) grésiller. **chirp up**, *v.i. F:* (*a*) Faire entendre sa petite voix. (*b*) Se ragaillardir.
chirpiness ['tʃəːrpinəs], *s. F:* Humeur gaie, gaillarde.
chirpy ['tʃəːrpi], *a. F:* D'humeur gaie; bien en train.
chirr[1] [tʃəːr], *s.* Grésillement *m* (du grillon).
chirr[2], *v.i.* (*Of cricket*) Grésiller, chanter.
chirrup ['tʃirəp], *s. & v.i.* = CHIRP[1,2].
chisel[1] [tʃizl], *s.* 1. Ciseau *m*. **Mortise chisel**, bédane *m*. *S.a.* COLD-CHISEL. 2. *Engr:* Burin *m*. 3. Anvil chisel, tranche *f*.
chisel[2], *v.tr.* Ciseler; buriner (le métal). **To chisel sth. off**, enlever, détacher, qch. au ciseau, au burin. *F:* **Chiselled features**, traits finement ciselés. **chiselling**, *s.* Ciselure *f*; burinage *m*.
chit[1] [tʃit], *s. F: Usu. Pej:* Mioche *mf*, gosse *mf*; bambin *m*.
chit[2], *s. F:* = CHITTY.
chit-chat ['tʃittʃat], *s. F:* Bavardages *mpl*, commérages *mpl*.
chitterlings ['tʃitərliŋz], *s.pl. Cu:* Andouille *f*.
chitty ['tʃiti], *s. F:* (*In India*) 1. Lettre *f*, billet *m*. 2. Autorisation *f* par écrit; permis *m*; laissez-passer *m inv*.
chivalrous ['ʃivəlrəs, 'tʃ-], *a.* Chevaleresque; courtois. -**ly**, *adv.* Chevaleresquement.
chivalrousness ['ʃivəlrəsnəs, 'tʃ-], *s.* = CHIVALRY 2.
chivalry ['ʃivəlri, 'tʃ-], *s.* 1. Chevalerie *f*. 2. Conduite *f* chevaleresque; courtoisie *f*.
chives [tʃaivz], *s.pl.* Ciboulette *f*, civette *f*.
chivy, **chivvy** ['tʃivi], *v.tr.* Poursuivre, chasser. **To chivvy s.o. about**, ne laisser aucun repos à qn.
chloral ['klɔːr(ə)l], *s. Ch:* Chloral *m*.
chlorate ['klɔːret], *s. Ch:* Chlorate *m*.
chloric ['klɔːrik], *a. Ch:* Chlorique.
chloride ['klɔːraid], *s. Ch:* Chlorure *m*.
chlorinate ['klɔrineit], *v.tr.* 1. Chlorurer. 2. *Hyg:* Javelliser (l'eau).
chlorination [klɔri'neiʃ(ə)n], *s.* 1. Chloruration *f*. 2. *Hyg:* Javellisation *f*.
chlorine ['klɔːriːn], *s. Ch:* Chlore *m*.
chloroform[1] ['klɔrofɔːrm], *s. Med:* Chloroforme *m*. *To give c. to s.o.*, chloroformer, chloroformiser, qn.
chloroform[2], *v.tr.* Chloroformer, chloroformiser.
chlorophyl(l) ['klɔːrofil], *s.* Chlorophylle *f*.
chlorosis [klɔ'rousis], *s. Med: Bot:* Chlorose *f*.
chock[1] [tʃɔk], *s.* Cale *f*; tin *m*, coin *m*. *Av: etc:* *To withdraw the chocks*, enlever les cales.
chock[2], *v.tr.* **To chock (up)**, caler (un meuble); coincer (des rails). **chocking**, *s.* 1. Calage *m*. 2. Coinçage *m*.
chock-a-block ['tʃɔkə'blɔk], *a.* 1. (Poulie) à bloc. 2. *F:* = CHOCK-FULL.
chock-full ['tʃɔk'ful], *a. F:* Plein comme un œuf. *Th: The house was c.-f.*, la salle était comble.
chocolate ['tʃɔkolet]. 1. *s.* Chocolat *m*. Cake of *c.*, tablette *f* de chocolat. *F:* **A chocolate**, une crotte de chocolat. 2. *a.* (De couleur) chocolat *inv*. '**chocolate-maker**, *s.* Chocolatier, -ière.
choice[1] [tʃɔis], *s.* 1. Choix *m*. (*a*) Préférence *f*. **For choice**, de préférence. **The country of my choice**, mon pays d'élection. (*b*) Alternative *f*.

9

You have no *c.* in the matter, vous n'avez pas le choix. **2.** (*Variety*) Assortiment *m*, choix. *To have a wide c.*, trouver grandement de quoi choisir.
choice², *a.* **1.** Bien choisi. **2.** *Com:* C. *article*, article de choix ; article surfin.
choiceness ['tʃɔisnəs], *s.* Excellence *f.*
choir ['kwaiər], *s.* **1.** *Arch:* Chœur *m* (d'église). **2.** Chœur (de chanteurs). **Male-voice choir,** orphéon *m.* **'choir-boy,** *s. Ecc:* Enfant *m* de chœur. **'choir-master,** *s.* Maître *m* de chapelle.
choirman, *pl.* **-men** ['kwaiərmən, -men], *s. Ecc:* Chantre *m.*
choke¹ [tʃouk], *s.* **1.** (*a*) Étranglement *m* (de canon de fusil). (*b*) *I.C.E:* Étrangleur *m.* *To pull out the c.*, fermer l'étrangleur. **2.** *El:* = CHOKING-COIL. **3.** Étranglement (de la voix).
choke². I. *v.* **1.** *v.tr.* (*a*) Étouffer, suffoquer, étrangler (qn). *Voice choked with sobs*, voix suffoquée par les sanglots. (*b*) Étrangler (une cartouche). (*c*) *To choke* (*up*) *a pipe*, obstruer, engorger, boucher, un tuyau (*with*, de). *I.C.E:* *Choked jet* (*of carburettor*), gicleur bouché. *Harbour choked* (*up*) *with sand*, port ensablé. **2.** *v.i.* (*a*) Étouffer, étrangler (*with*, de). *To c. with laughter*, suffoquer de rire. (*b*) S'engorger, s'obstruer, se boucher (*with*, de) ; (*of filter, etc.*) se colmater. **choke back**, *v.tr.* Refouler (ses larmes). **choke off,** *v.tr.* *F:* (*a*) *To c. s.o. off from doing sth.*, dissuader qn de faire qch. (*b*) Se débarrasser de (qn) ; écarter (un importun).
choking, *s.* **1.** Étouffement *m*, suffocation *f*, étranglement *m.* **2.** Engorgement *m*, obstruction *f* ; ensablement *m.* **'choking-coil,** *s. El:* Bobine *f* d'impédance, de réactance ; self *f.* II. **choke-,** *comb.fm.* **'choke-bore,** *s. Sm.a:* **1.** Étranglement *m* (du canon). *Fusil m de chasse à choke-bore.* **'choke-coil,** *s.* = CHOKING-COIL. **'choke-damp,** *s. Min:* Mofette *f.* **'choke-pear,** *s.* Poire *f* d'angoisse. **'choke-tube,** *s.* Buse *f* (du carburateur). **'choke-weed,** *s. Bot:* Orobanche *f.*
choker ['tʃoukər], *s. F:* **1.** Foulard *m* (d'ouvrier). **2.** = CHOKE¹ I (*b*).
choky ['tʃouki], *a. F: To feel c.*, étouffer d'émotion. *C. atmosphere*, atmosphère suffocante.
choler ['kɔlər], *s. Med: Poet:* Bile *f.*
cholera ['kɔlərə], *s.* Choléra *m.* *A c. patient*, un, une, cholérique. *Summer c.*, cholérine *f.* **'cholera-belt,** *s.* Ceinture *f* de flanelle.
choleric ['kɔlərik], *a.* Colérique, irascible.
cholerine ['kɔlərain, -iːn], *s. Med:* Cholérine *f.*
choose [tʃuːz], *v.tr.* (chose [tʃouz] ; chosen [tʃouzn]) **1.** (*a*) Choisir ; faire choix de (qch.). *To c. a method*, adopter une méthode. *Pred. To choose s.o.* (*for a*) *king*, choisir qn comme roi. (*b*) *He cannot choose but obey*, il ne peut faire autrement qu'obéir. (*c*) *To choose from, between, several persons*, choisir, opter, entre plusieurs personnes. *To c. an apple from the basket*, choisir une pomme dans le panier. *War or peace: they chose war*, la guerre ou la paix : ils optèrent pour la guerre. *There is nothing to choose between them*, l'un vaut l'autre ; ils se valent. **2.** *I do not choose to do so*, il ne me plaît pas de le faire. *When I choose*, quand je voudrai. *To do sth. when one chooses*, faire qch. à son bon plaisir.
chosen, *a.* Choisi. *To address a c. few*, s'adresser à quelques auditeurs choisis. *s. The chosen*, les élus. **choosing,** *s.* Choix *m.* *The difficulty of choosing*, l'embarras du choix.
chop¹ [tʃɔp], *s.* **1.** Coup *m* de hache, de couperet. **2.** *Cu:* Côtelette *f* (de mouton, de porc).

3. Clapotage *m*, clapotis *m* (de la mer). **4.** *Ten:* Chop(-stroke), volée coupée-arrêtée. **'chop house,** *s.* Restaurant *m* populaire.
chop², *v.* (chopped) **1.** *v.tr.* (*a*) Couper, fendre (du bois), hacher (des légumes). **Chopped wood**, menu bois. *To c. sth. to pieces*, hacher qch. en morceaux. (*b*) *To c. one's speech*, hacher se paroles. (*c*) *Ten: To c. the ball*, couper la balle **2.** *v.i.* (*Of sea*) Clapoter. **chop away,** *v.tr* Détacher (qch. à coups de cognée) ; tranche (qch.). **chop down,** *v.tr.* Abattre (un arbre) **chop off,** *v.tr.* Trancher, couper, abattre **chop up,** *v.tr.* Couper (qch.) en morceaux **'chopping-block,** *s.* Hachoir *m*, billot *m.*
chop³, *s.* = CHAP³. *To lick one's chops*, se (pour) lécher les babines. **The chops of the Channel** l'entrée *f* de la Manche.
chop⁴, *s.* Chop of the wind, saute *f* de vent *F:* Chops and changes, girouetteries *f.*
chop⁵. **1.** *v.i.* (*a*) *To chop and change*, manque de suite ; girouetter. (*b*) *Nau: The wind keep chopping about*, le vent varie à chaque instant **2.** *v.tr.* *F: To chop logic*, ergoter.
chop⁶, *s. Com:* (*In Far East*) Marque *f* (d qualité) ; étiquette *f.* *F:* First chop, de première qualité.
chopper ['tʃɔpər], *s.* Couperet *m*, hachoir *m.*
choppiness ['tʃɔpinəs], *s.* Agitation *f* (de la mer)
choppy¹ ['tʃɔpi], *a. Nau:* Clapoteux. *C. sea* mer hachée ; lame courte.
choppy², *a.* (Vent) changeant, variable.
chop-sticks ['tʃɔpstiks], *s.pl.* (*Chinese Civ.* Bâtonnets *m*, baguettes *f.*
choral ['kɔːrəl], *a. Mus:* **1.** Choral (*no m.pl.* **2.** Chanté en chœur.
choral(e) [kɔ'rɑːl], *s. Mus:* Choral *m*, -als.
chord¹ [kɔːrd], *s.* **1.** *Poet:* Corde *f* (d'une harpe) *F: To touch the right chord*, faire vibrer la corde sensible. **2.** = CORD¹ (*d*). **3.** *Geom:* Corde (d'un arc).
chord², *s. Mus:* Accord *m.* **Common chord** accord parfait.
chorea [kɔ'riːa], *s.* Chorée *f* ; danse *f* de Saint-Guy.
choreography [kɔre'ɔgrəfi], *s.* Chorégraphie *f*
chorister ['kɔristər], *s.m.* Choriste ; *esp. Ecc:* chantre ou enfant de chœur.
chortle¹ [tʃɔːrtl], *s. F:* Gloussement *m* (de gaieté).
chortle², *v.i. F:* Glousser de joie.
chorus¹, *pl.* **-uses** ['kɔːrəs, -əsiz], *s.* **1.** Chœur *m.* (*a*) Chorus of praise, concert *m* de louanges. (*b*) *She belongs to the c.*, elle fait partie du chœur. **2.** Refrain *m* (d'une chanson). **To join in the** chorus, faire chœur. **'chorus-girl,** *s.f.* Gir (de music-hall). **'chorus-singer,** *s.* (*In opera*) Choriste *mf.*
chorus², *v.* (chorused) *v.i.* Faire chorus ; reprendre en chœur. **2.** *v.tr. To chorus sth.*, répéter qch. en chœur.
chose [tʃouz], **chosen** [tʃouzn]. *See* CHOOSE.
chough [tʃʌf], *s. Orn:* Crave *m*
chouse [tʃaus], *v.tr. F:* Filouter, duper (qn). *To chouse s.o.* (*out*) *of sth.*, soutirer, souffler, qch. à qn.
chow [tʃau], *s.* (*a*) (Chien) chow-chow (*m*).
chowder ['tʃaudər], *s. Cu:* Bouillabaisse *f.*
chrestomathy [kres'tɔmaθi], *s.* Chrestomathie *f.*
chrism [krizm], *s. Ecc:* (Saint) chrême.
Christ [kraist]. *Pr.n.m.* Le Christ ; Jésus-Christ.
christen [krisn]. *v.tr.* Baptiser (qn, un navire). *To c. a child after s.o.*, donner à un enfant le nom de qn. **christening,** *s.* Baptême *m.*
Christendom ['krisndəm], *s.* La chrétienté.

Christian ['krɪstjən], *a & s.* Chrétien, -ienne. The Christian era, l'ère chrétienne. *S.a.* BURIAL, NAME¹ 1 *F:* To behave like a decent C., se conduire en homme civilisé.

Christianity [kristi'aniti], *s.* Christianisme *m.*

Christmas ['krɪsməs], *s.* Noël *m. At C.*, à Noël, à la Noël. A merry Christmas! joyeux Noël! Father Christmas, le Bonhomme Noël. Christmas comes but once a year, ce n'est pas tous les jours fête. Christmas gift, étrennes *fpl.* '**Christmas-box**, *s.* = Étrennes *fpl*; gratification *f.* '**Christmas-card**, *s.* Carte *f* de Noël. **Christmas-'carol**, *s.* Chant *m* de Noël; noël *m.* **Christmas-'day**, *s.* Le jour de Noël. **Christmas-'eve**, *s.* La veille de Noël. '**Christmas-tide**, *s.* Le moment de Noël.

chromate ['kroumeit], *s. Ch:* Chromate *m.*

chromatic [kro'matik], *a.* Chromatique. 1. (Impression) polychrome. 2. *Mus:* Chromatic scale, gamme chromatique.

chrome [kroum], *s.* (a) Chrome leather, cuir chromé Chrome-tanning, tannage aux sels de chrome (b) Chrome steel, acier chromé. (c) Chrome yellow, jaune de chrome.

chromic ['kroumik], *a. Ch:* Chromique.

chromium ['kroumiəm], *s. Ch:* Chrome *m.* Chromium steel, acier chromé, au chrome. '**chromium-plated**, *a.* Chromé. '**chromium-plating**, *s.* Chromage *m.*

chromolithograph [kroumo'liθogra:f, -graf], *F:* **chromo** ['kroumo], *s.* (Colour-print) Chromolithographie *f*; *F:* chromo *m.*

chromolithography [kroumoli'θogrəfi], *s.* (Process) Chromolithographie *f.*

chronic ['krɔnik], *a.* 1. (a) *Med:* Chronique. *C. ill-health*, invalidité *f.* (b) *F:* Constant, continuel. 2. *P:* Insupportable. A c. headache, un mal de tête fou. **-ally**, *adv.* Chroniquement

chronicle¹ ['krɔnikl], *s.* Chronique *f.*

chronicle², *v.tr.* To c. events, faire la chronique des événements ; enregistrer, raconter, les faits.

chronicler ['krɔniklər], *s.* Chroniqueur *m.*

chronologer [krɔ'nɔlodʒər], *s.* Chronologiste *m.*

chronological [krɔno'lɔdʒik(ə)l], *a.* Chronologique. In chronological order, par ordre de dates. **-ally**, *adv.* Chronologiquement.

chronologist [krɔ'nɔlodʒist], *s.* = CHRONOLOGER.

chronology [krɔ nɔlodʒi], *s.* Chronologie *f.*

chronometer [krɔ'nɔmetər], *s.* Chronomètre *m.*

chrysalis ['krisəlis], pl. **chrysalides, chrysalises** ['krisəliz, kri'salidi:z, 'krisəlisiz], *s.* Chrysalide *f.*

chrysanthemum [kri'sanθiməm], *s.* Chrysanthème *m.*

chub [tʃʌb], *s.* Chabot *m* de rivière ; chevesne *m.*

chubby ['tʃʌbi], *a.* Boulot, -otte ; (of face) joufflu, '**chubby-cheeked**, *a.* Joufflu.

chuck¹ [tʃʌk]. 1. *s.* Gloussement *m* (de la volaille). 2. (Call to fowls) Chuck! chuck! petit! petit!

chuck², *v.i.* (a) (Of fowls) Glousser (b) *F:* (Of pers.) Clapper (de la langue).

chuck³, *s.* 1. Petite tape (sous le menton). 2. Action de lancer qch. *F:* To give s.o. the chuck, (i) *P:* plaquer qn ; (ii) congédier (un employé) To get the chuck, recevoir son congé.

chuck, *v.tr.* 1. To chuck s.o. under the chin, relever le menton à qn. 2. *F:* (a) Jeter, lancer (une pierre). (b) Lâcher, plaquer (qn). (c) *P:* Chuck it en voilà assez! **chuck about**, *v.tr. F:* Gaspiller (son argent), faire l'important. **chuck out**, *v.tr. F:* Flanquer (qn) à la porte **chuck up**, *v.tr. F:* (a) Abandonner (un travail). To chuck it up, y renoncer ; quitter la partie. (b) To c. up one's job, lâcher son emploi ; démissionner.

chuck⁵, *s.* Mandrin *m*, plateau *m* (d'un tour).

chuckle¹ [tʃʌkl], *s.* Rire étouffé ; petit rire.

chuckle², *v.i.* Rire tout bas, en soi-même, sous cape (at, over, sth., de qch.).

chuckle-head ['tʃʌklhed], *s. F:* Nigaud *m*, benêt *m.*

chuckle-headed ['tʃʌklhedid], *a. F:* Sans cervelle.

chum¹ [tʃʌm], *s. F:* Camarade *mf*; copain *m*, copine *f.*

chum², *v.i.* (chummed) To chum (up) with s.o., se lier d'amitié avec qn.

chummy ['tʃʌmi], *a. F:* Familier, intime. To be c. with s.o., être copain avec qn.

chump [tʃʌmp], *s.* 1. (a) Tronçon *m* (de bois). (b) Chump-chop, côtelette *f* de gigot. 2. *P:* (a) (Head) Tête *f*, caboche *f.* Off one's chump, timbré, loufoque. (b) A (silly) chump, un nigaud, une cruche.

chunk [tʃʌŋk], *s.* Gros morceau (de bois, etc.); quignon *m* (de pain).

church [tʃə:rtʃ], *s.* 1. Église *f*; (protestant) temple *m.* 2. (a) The Established Church, l'Église établie. The Church of England, l'Église anglicane. To go into the Church, entrer dans les ordres. To be received into the Church, (i) prendre le voile ; (ii) faire sa première communion ; (iii) devenir chrétien par le baptême. (b) Church service, office *m* ; service (divin). To go to church, aller à l'office, (in Fr.) à la messe. It is church time, il est l'heure de l'office. *I shall see you after c.*, je vous verrai après l'office. To be a church-goer, être assidu(e) aux offices divins. '**church-worker**, *s.* Personne *f* qui prend une part active aux œuvres de l'église.

churchman, pl. **-men** ['tʃə:rtʃmən, -men], *s.* 1. Homme *m* d'église ; ecclésiastique *m.* 2. *He's a good c.*, c'est un bon anglican.

churchwarden ['tʃə:rtʃwɔ:rdən], *s.* 1. Marguillier *m.* 2. Longue pipe (en terre) ; pipe hollandaise.

churchyard ['tʃə:rtʃ'ja:rd], *s.* Cimetière *m.* *F:* Churchyard cough, toux qui sent le sapin.

churl [tʃə:rl], *s.* (a) *Hist:* Manant *m.* (b) *F:* Rustre *m.* (c) *F:* Grincheux *m.*

churlish ['tʃə:rliʃ], *a.* (a) Mal élevé ; grossier. (b) Hargneux, grincheux. **-ly**, *adv.* Avec mauvaise grâce.

churlishness ['tʃə:rliʃnəs], *s.* (a) Grossièreté *f.* (b) Temperament hargneux.

churn¹ [tʃə:rn], *s.* 1. Baratte *f.* 2. *Rail:* Bidon *m* à lait.

churn², *v.tr.* (a) Baratter (la crème) ; battre (le beurre). (b) *F:* To churn up the foam, brasser l'écume.

chute [ʃu:t], *s.* (a) Chute *f* d'eau. (b) *Geol:* Couloir *m.* (c) *Sp:* Piste *f*, glissière *f* (pour toboggans).

chutney ['tʃʌtni], *s. Cu:* Chutney *m* (condiment épicé).

chyle [kail], *s. Physiol:* Chyle *m.*

chyme [kaim], *s. Physiol:* Chyme *m.*

ciborium [si'bɔ:riəm], *s. Ecc:* Ciboire *m.*

cicada [si'ka:də], *s. Ent:* Cigale *f.*

cicatrice, cicatrix, pl. **-ices** ['sikatris, -triks, sika'traisi:z], *s.* Cicatrice *f.*

cicatrization [sikatrai'zeiʃ(ə)n], *s.* Cicatrisation *f.*

cicatrize ['sikatra:iz]. 1. *v.tr.* Cicatriser. 2. *v.i.* Se cicatriser.

Cicero ['sisəro]. *Pr.n.m.* Cicéron.

cicerone [tʃitʃe'roune], *s.* Cicerone *m.*

cicisbeo [tʃitʃiz'beio], *s.* Sigisbée *m.*

cider ['saidər], *s.* Cidre *m.* '**cider-cup**, *s.*

Boisson glacée au cidre. **'cider-press,** *s.*
Pressoir *m* (à pommes).
cigar [si'gɑːr], *s.* Cigare *m.* **ci'gar-case,** *s.*
Étui *m* à cigares. **ci'gar-cutter,** *s.* Coupe-
cigares *m inv.* **ci'gar-holder,** *s.* Fume-cigare *m,*
porte-cigare *m.*
cigarette [sigə'ret], *s.* Cigarette *f. Packet of*
c. paper, cahier *m* de papier à cigarettes.
ciga'rette-case, *s.* Étui *m* à cigarettes.
ciga'rette-holder, *s.* Porte-cigarette *m.*
cilia ['silia], *s.pl. Biol :* Cils *m* vibratiles.
cilice ['silis], *s. Ecc :* Cilice *m.*
cinch [sinʃ], *s. U.S :* **1.** *Harn :* Sangle *f ;* sous-
ventrière *f.* **2.** *P :* Certitude *f.* **It's a cinch,**
c'est certain.
cinchona [siŋ'kouna], *s.* Quinquina *m.*
cincture ['siŋktjər], *s.* **1.** *Poet :* Ceinture *f.*
Ecc : Alb and c., l'aube et la ceinture. **2.** Enceinte *f ;* ceinture *f* (de murailles).
cinder ['sindər], *s.* **1.** Cendre *f. To cook a joint*
to a c., calciner un rôti. **To rake out the cinders,**
racler les cendres (du foyer). **2.** *pl.* (*a*) (*Partly*
burnt coal) Escarbilles *fpl.* (*b*) *Metall :* Scorie(s)
f(pl). **'cinder-path, -track,** *s.* Piste (en)
cendrée. **Cinder-track race,** course sur cendrée.
'cinder-sifter, *s.* Crible *m* à escarbilles.
Cinderella [sində'rela], *Pr.n.f.* Cendrillon.
Cinderella dance, sauterie *f* (qui se termine à
minuit).
cine-camera [sini'kaməra], *s. Cin :* Camera *f.*
cinema ['sinima], *s. F :* (*a*) Le cinéma, le ciné.
He is a c. actor, il fait du ciné(ma). (*b*) (Salle *f* de)
cinéma. **'cinema-star,** *s.* Vedette *f* de l'écran.
cinematograph[1] [sini'matogrɑːf, -graf], *s.* Cinématographe *m, F :* cinéma *m.*
cinematograph[2], *v.tr.* Cinématographier ;
filmer.
cine-projector ['siniprodʒektər], *s.* Cinéprojecteur *m.*
cineraria [sinə'rɛəria], *s. Bot :* Cinéraire *f.*
cinerary ['sinərəri], *a.* Cinéraire.
cinnabar ['sinabɑːr], *s.* (*a*) *Miner :* Cinabre *m ;*
vermillon naturel. (*b*) *Ind :* Vermillon.
cinnamon ['sinamən], *s.* **1.** Cinnamon(-bark),
cannelle *f.* **2.** Cinnamon(-tree), cannelier *m.*
cinquecento [tʃiŋkwe'tʃento], *s.* La Renaissance
.talienne : l'art italien du XVIᵉ siècle.
cinq(ue)foil ['siŋkfoil], *s.* Potentille rampante.
cipher[1] ['saifər], *s.* **1.** *Mth :* Zéro *m. F :* **He's a**
mere cipher, c'est une nullité, un homme qui ne
compte pas. **2.** (*a*) (*Secret writing*) Chiffre *m.*
To send a message in c., transmettre une dépêche
en chiffre. (*b*) Message chiffré. (*c*) Clef *f* (d'un
chiffre). **3.** (*Monogram*) Chiffre. **4.** *Mus :* Cornement *m* (d'un tuyau d'orgue).
cipher[2]. **1.** *v.tr.* Chiffrer (une dépêche).
2. *v.i.* (*a*) Chiffrer, calculer. (*b*) *Mus :* (*Of organ*
pipe) Corner.
circle[1] ['səːkl], *s.* **1.** (*a*) Cercle *m. To stand in*
a c., faire cercle. **To have circles round the eyes,**
avoir les yeux cernés. *Aut :* Turning circle,
rayon *m* de braquage. (*b*) *Gym :* **To do the**
grand circle, faire le grand soleil. (*c*) *Log :* Vicious
circle, cercle vicieux. **2.** Révolution *f,* orbite *m or f*
(d'une planète). **To come full circle,** compléter
son orbite. **3.** Inner circle, (chemin *m* de fer de)
petite ceinture. **4.** *Th :* Upper circle, seconde
galerie. **5.** Milieu *m,* coterie *f. The family c.,*
le sein de la famille. *In certain circles,* dans
certains milieux. *In theatrical circles,* dans le
monde des théâtres. *To move in fashionable*
circles, fréquenter les salons.
circle[2]. **1.** *v.tr.* (*a*) Ceindre, entourer (*with,* de).
(*b*) (*Go round*) Faire le tour de (qch.). **2.** *v.i.* (*a*) To

c. round, about, sth., tournoyer autour de qch.
(*b*) *The bottle circled round,* la bouteille circulait.
circled, *a.* Encerclé, cerclé.
circuit ['səːkit], *s.* **1.** (*a*) Pourtour *m* (d'une
ville) ; enceinte *f* (de murailles). (*b*) *Sp :* Circuit *m,*
parcours *m* (d'une course d'avions, etc.).
2. (*a*) Révolution *f* (du soleil). (*b*) **To make the c.**
of the town, faire le tour de la ville. (*c*) Tournée *f,*
circuit. (*Of judge*) **To go on circuit,** aller en
tournée. (*d*) Circonscription *f* (de tournée).
3. Détour *m. To make a wide c.,* faire un grand
détour. **4.** *El :* Circuit. *Branch c.,* branchement *m.*
To close, make, the circuit, fermer le circuit.
To break the circuit, rompre le circuit. **Short**
circuit, court-circuit *m.* **'circuit-breaker,** *s.*
El.E : Coupe-circuit *m inv,* interrupteur *m.*
'circuit-closer, *s. El.E :* Conjoncteur *m.*
circuitous [sər'kjuitəs], *a.* (Chemin) détourné.
To take a c. road, faire un détour. *By c. means,*
par des moyens détournés.
circular ['səːkjulər]. **1.** *a.* Circulaire. (*a*) *C. arc,*
arc de cercle. (*b*) **Circular letter,** lettre circulaire ;
circulaire *f.* **Circular tour,** tour circulaire.
2. *s.* (*a*) = circular letter. (*b*) **The Court circular,**
la chronique mondaine. **-ly,** *adv.* Circulaire-
ment ; en rond.
circularize ['səːkjulərɑːiz], *v.tr.* Envoyer des
circulaires à (ses clients, etc.). **circularizing,** *s.*
Envoi *m* de circulaires.
circulate ['səːkjuleit]. **1.** *v.i.* Circuler. **2.** *v.tr.*
(*a*) Faire circuler (l'air, le vin, etc.). (*b*) Mettre en
circulation (de l'argent, des nouvelles) ; faire
circuler (un bruit). **circulating,** *s.* Circulation *f.*
circulation [səːkju'leiʃ(ə)n], *s.* Circulation *f* (du
sang, de l'argent) ; tirage *m* (d'un journal). *C. of*
capital, roulement *m* de fonds. *Newspaper with*
a wide c., journal à grand tirage. *To restore the c.*
in one's legs, se dégourdir les jambes. *To put forged*
notes into c., écouler de faux billets. *I.C.E :*
Gravity circulation , circulation (de l'eau) par
gravité. *Forced-feed c.,* circulation sous pression
(de l'eau, de l'huile).
circumcise ['səːkəmsaːiz], *v.tr.* Circoncire.
circumcised, *a.* Circoncis.
circumcision [səːrkəm'siʒ(ə)n], *s.* Circoncision *f.*
circumference [sər'kʌmfərəns], *s.* Circonférence *f ;* périphérie *f ;* pourtour *m* (d'un
piston). **On the circumference,** à la circonférence.
circumflex ['səːrkəmfleks], *a. & s.* **Circumflex**
(accent), accent *m* circonflexe.
circumlocution [səːrkəmlo'kju:ʃ(ə)n], *s.* Circonlocution *f,* ambages *fpl.*
circumscribe ['səːrkəmskraib], *v.tr.* **1.** Circonscrire. **2.** Limiter (des pouvoirs). **circum-**
scribed, *a.* **1.** *Geom :* Circonscrit. **2.** Restreint,
limité. *C. intellect,* esprit borné.
circumscription [səːrkəm skripʃ(ə)n], *s.*
1. *Geom :* Circonscription *f.* **2.** Restriction *f.*
3. Région *f,* circonscription (administrative).
circumspect ['səːrkəmspekt], *a.* Circonspect ;
avisé. **-ly,** *adv.* Prudemment ; avec circonspection.
circumspection [səːrkəm spekʃ(ə)n], *s.* Circonspection *f.*
circumstance ['səːrkəmstəns], *s.* **1.** *pl.* (*a*) Circonstances *f.* **In, under, the circumstances,** dans
ces circonstances ; puisqu'il en est ainsi. **Under**
any circumstances, en tout état de cause. **In no**
circumstances, en aucun cas ; sous aucun prétexte. *Under similar circumstances,* en pareille

occasion. **That depends on circumstances**, c'est selon. *We must take the circumstances into account,* il faut tenir la part des circonstances. *Circumstances alter cases,* les cas changent avec les circonstances. (*b*) *If his circumstances allow,* sı ses moyens le permettent. *In easy circumstances* dans l'aisance. **My worldly circumstances,** ma situation de fortune. **2.** sing. Circonstance, détail, fait. *Without omitting a single c.,* sans omettre aucun détail. *Were it not for the c. that . . .,* n'était le fait que. . . **3.** sing. Pompe *f. To receive s.o with pomp and circumstance,* recevoir qn en grande cérémonie.

circumstanced ['sɜ:rkəmstənst], *a.* **Well circumstanced,** dans l'aisance. **Poorly c.** *people,* gens peu fortunés. **As I was circumstanced,** dans la situation où je me trouvais.

circumstantial [sɜ:rkəm'stanʃ(ə)l], *a.* **1.** Circonstanciel. *C. evidence,* preuves indirectes. **2.** Accessoire, accidentel. **3.** (Récit) circonstancié, détaillé. **-ally,** *adv.* **1.** Accessoirement. **2.** En détail.

circumvallation ['sɜ:rkəmva'leiʃ(ə)n], *s.* Circonvallation *f;* retranchements *mpl.*

circumvent [sɜ:rkəm'vent], *v.tr.* Circonvenir.

circus, *pl.* **-uses** ['sɜ:rkəs, -əsiz], *s.* **1.** (*a*) *Rom. Ant:* Cirque *m.* (*b*) *Ph.Geog:* Cirque. (*c*) (*Of roads*) Rond-point *m.* **2.** (*a*) **Travelling circus,** cirque forain. (*b*) *Mil.Av: F:* Escadrille *f.*

cirrhosis [si'rousis], *s. Med:* Cirrhose *f.*

cirrus, *pl.* **-ri** ['sirəs, -rai], *s. Meteor:* Cirrus *m;* nuage *m* en queue de vache.

cisalpine [sis'alpain], *a. A.Hist:* Cisalpin.

cist [sist], *s.* Sépulture *f* préhistorique en dalles de pierre.

Cistercian [sis'tɜ:rʃ(ə)n], *a. & s.* Cistercien, -ienne. **The Cistercian Order,** l'ordre de Cîteaux.

cistern ['sistərn], *s.* (*a*) Réservoir *m* à eau (sous les combles). (*b*) (*Underground*) Citerne *f.*

citadel ['sitadel], *s.* (*a*) Citadelle *f.* (*b*) *F:* Lieu *m* de refuge.

citation [sai'teiʃ(ə)n], *s* **1.** *Jur:* = SUMMONS. **2.** Citation *f* d'un auteur, d'une autorité.

cite [sait], *v.tr.* **1.** (*a*) Citer (qn devant un tribunal). (*b*) Assigner (un témoin). **2.** (*a*) Citer (un auteur). (*b*) Alléguer (un auteur).

citizen ['sitiz(ə)n], *s.* Citoyen, -enne; bourgeois, -oise; citadin *m.* **My fellow-citizens,** mes concitoyens.

citizenship ['sitizənʃip], *s.* **1.** Droit *m* de cité, de bourgeoisie. **2. Good citizenship,** civisme *m.*

citrate ['sitreit], *s. Ch:* Citrate *m.*

citric ['sitrik], *a. Ch:* Citrique.

citron ['sitrən], *s.* Cédrat *m.*

citrus ['sitrəs], *s. Bot:* Citron *m.*

city ['siti], *s.* **1.** (*a*) Grande ville; *Poet:* cité *f.* **The city dwellers,** la population urbaine. (*b*) Cité, agglomération *f.* **Garden-city,** (i) cité-jardin *f;* (ii) (*for workmen*) cité ouvrière. **2. The City,** la Cité de Londres. *F:* **He's in the City,** il est dans les affaires.

civet ['sivet], *s.* Civet(-cat), civette *f.*

civic ['sivik], *a.* Civique. **The c.** *authorities,* les autorités municipales.

civics ['siviks], *s.pl.* (*Usu. with sg. const.*) *Sch:* Instruction *f* civique.

civil ['sivil], *a.* **1.** Civil. **Civil rights,** droits civiques. **In civil life,** dans le civil. *Adm:* **The Civil List,** la liste civile. **Civil List pension,** pension sur les fonds de la Couronne. **2.** Poli, honnête, courtois. **-illy,** *adv.* Civilement, poliment. **'civil-spoken,** *a.* Courtois.

civilian [si'viljən]. **1.** *s.* Bourgeois *m;* civil *m;*

Mil: P: pékin *m.* **2.** *a.* Civil. **In civilian life,** dans le civil.

civility [si'viliti], *s.* Civilité *f;* politesse *f.*

civilization [sivilai'zeiʃ(ə)n], *s.* Civilisation *f.*

civilize ['sivilaːiz], *v.tr.* Civiliser. **To become civilized,** se civiliser.

civilizer ['sivilaizər], *s.* Civilisateur, -trice.

clack[1] [klak], *s.* **1.** Bruit sec; claquement *m.* **Clack-clack,** clic-clac *m.* **2.** (*a*) **Clack(-valve),** (soupape *f* à) clapet *m.* (*b*) (**Mill-**)**clack,** traquet *m.* **3.** *F:* = CHATTER[1] I.

clack[2], *v.i.* **1.** (*Of thg*) Claquer. **2.** *F:* (*Of pers.*) Caqueter, bavarder, jacasser.

clad [klad]. *See* CLOTHE.

claim[1] [kleim], *s.* **1.** Demande *f* (de secours, etc.); revendication *f,* réclamation *f.* **2.** Droit *m,* titre *m,* prétention *f* (*to sth.,* à qch.). **To lay claim to** sth., (i) prétendre à qch.; (ii) s'attribuer qch. *Legal c.* **to sth.,** titre juridique à qch. **To put in a claim,** faire valoir ses droits. *To set up a c.,* émettre une revendication. **3.** (*Debt*) Créance *f.* **4.** (*a*) *Jur:* Réclamation. **To set up a claim,** faire une réclamation. *To make, put in, a c. for damages,* réclamer des dommages-intérêts. *Adm:* **Disputed claims office,** le contentieux. (*b*) *I have some claims on his friendship,* j'ai des titres à son amitié. *I have many claims on my time,* mon temps est entièrement pris. **5.** (*In U.S. and Austr.*) Concession (minière).

claim[2], *v.tr.* (*a*) Réclamer (un droit); revendiquer (un honneur); demander (de l'attention). *To c. sth. from s.o.,* réclamer qch. à qn. *To c. a privilege,* prétendre à un privilège. *To c. the right to do sth.,* revendiquer le droit de faire qch. **To claim one's due,** faire valoir ses droits. (*b*) *To c. that . . .,* prétendre, avancer, affirmer, soutenir, que. . . . *To c. a virtue,* s'attribuer une vertu. *To c. kinship with s.o.,* se prétendre parent de qn. *Family that claims descent from . . .,* famille qui rapporte son origine à. . . .

claimant ['kleimənt], **claimer** ['kleimər], *s.* Prétendant, -ante; revendicateur *m;* *Jur:* réclamant, -ante; demandeur, -eresse. **Rightful claimant,** ayant droit *m. Estate without a c.,* succession vacante.

clairvoyance [klɛər'vɔiəns], *s.* **1.** Lucidité *f* (somnambulique). **2.** (*Penetration of mind*) Clairvoyance *f.*

clairvoyant [klɛər'vɔiənt]. **1.** *a.* (*a*) Doué de seconde vue. (*b*) (*Shrewd*) Clairvoyant. **2.** *s.* (*f. occ.* **clairvoyante**) Voyant, -ante; somnambule *mf* lucide.

clam [klam], *s. Moll:* Palourde *f.*

clamant ['klamənt, 'klei-], *a.* (*a*) *C. injustice,* injustice criante. (*b*) *C. need for sth.,* besoin urgent de qch.

clamber[1] ['klambər], *s.* Ascension *f* raide; escalade *f.*

clamber[2], *v.i.* Grimper (des pieds et des mains). *To c. over a wall,* escalader un mur.

clamminess ['klaminəs], *s.* Moiteur froide.

clammy ['klami], *a.* **1.** (*Of skin*) (Froid et) moite; (*of atmosphere*) (froid et) humide. **2.** Gluant, collant.

clamorous ['klamərəs], *a.* Bruyant, braillard. *A c. crowd,* une foule vociférante. **-ly,** *adv.* Bruyamment; à grands cris.

clamour[1] ['klamər], *s.* Clameur *f;* cris *mpl.*

clamour[2], *v.i.* Vociférer; pousser des clameurs. *To c. for sth.,* réclamer qch. à grands cris.

clamp[1] [klamp], *s.* (*a*) Crampon *m,* presse *f;* main *f* de fer. (*b*) *Const:* Agrafe *f,* happe *f.* (*c*) Bride *f* de serrage; patte *f* d'attache. (*d*) *Carp:*

Serre-joint *m*, valet *m*. (*e*) Mordache *f* (d'étau).
(*f*) El.E: Attache-fil(s) *m inv* ; borne *f*.
clamp² [klamp], *v.tr* (*a*) Agrafer (deux pierres) ; brider
(un tuyau). (*b*) Bloquer ; caler (un télescope).
clan¹ [klan], *s*. **1**. Clan *m*. **The head of the clan,**
le chef de clan. **2**. (*a*) Tribu *f*. (*b*) *F* : Coterie *f*.
clan², *v.i.* (clanned) *F* : **To clan together,** se
soutenir mutuellement.
clandestine [klan'destin], *a*. Clandestin, subreptice. **-ly,** *adv*. Clandestinement ; à la dérobée.
clang¹ [klan], *s*. Son *m* métallique ; bruit strident,
retentissant ; résonnement *m* (de cloches).
clang², *v.i.* Retentir, résonner. **clanging,** *s.* =
CLANG¹.
clangorous ['klaŋgərəs], *a*. Retentissant, strident.
clangour ['klaŋgər], *s.* = CLANG¹.
clank¹ [klaŋk], *s*. Bruit sec (de fers) ; cliquetis *m*.
clank². **1**. *v.i.* Rendre un bruit métallique (sans
résonance). **2**. *v.tr*. *The prisoners c. their chains,*
les prisonniers font sonner leurs fers. **clanking,** *s.* = CLANK¹.
clannish ['klaniʃ], *a*. Dévoué aux intérêts de sa
coterie.
clannishness ['klaniʃnəs], *s.* Esprit *m* de corps
(des membres d'une coterie).
clansman, *pl.* **-men** ['klanzmən, -men], *s.*
Membre *m* d'un clan, d'une tribu.
clap¹ [klap], *s*. **1**. (*a*) Battement *m* (de mains) ;
applaudissements *mpl*. **To give s.o. a clap,**
applaudir qn. (*b*) Coup *m*, tape *f* (de la main).
2. (Thunder-)clap, coup de tonnerre.
clap². **1**. *v.tr*. (clapped) (*a*) **To clap one's hands,**
battre, claquer, des mains. **To clap s.o. on the
back,** donner à qn une tape dans le dos. *To c. a
performer,* applaudir un artiste. (*b*) (*Of bird*) *To
c. its wings,* battre des ailes. (*c*) *To c. s.o. in prison,*
fourrer qn en prison. *To c. a pistol to s.o.'s head,*
appuyer brusquement un pistolet sur la tempe de
qn. **To clap on one's hat,** camper son chapeau
sur sa tête. **To clap on more sail,** augmenter de
toile. *F:* **To clap eyes on s.o.,** voir qn (tout à
coup). **2**. *v.i.* Applaudir. **clap to,** *v.i.* Se
refermer (avec un bruit sec). **clapping,** *s.*
Battement *m* des mains ; applaudissements *mpl*.
clapper ['klapər], *s*. **1**. Battant *m* (de cloche) ;
claquet *m*, traquet *m* (de moulin). **2**. *Ecc :* Claquette *f*. **3**. (*Pers.*) Applaudisseur *m* ; (*hired*)
claqueur *m*. *The* (*hired*) *clappers,* la claque.
claptrap ['klaptrap], *s*. Boniment *m* ; phrases *f*
vides. **To talk claptrap,** parler pour la galerie ;
parler pour ne rien dire.
clarendon ['klarəndən], *s*. *Typ :* Caractère gras.
claret ['klaret], *s*. (*a*) Vin *m* de Bordeaux (rouge) ;
bordeaux *m*. (*b*) *P:* **To tap s.o.'s claret,** faire
saigner du nez. **'claret-cup,** *s*. Boisson
sucrée au vin rouge.
clarify ['klarifai], *v.tr*. Clarifier (le beurre, le
sirop) ; éclaircir (l'esprit).
clarinet [klari'net], *s*. Clarinette *f*. •
clarion ['klariən], *s*. *Poet:* Clairon *m*.
clarity ['klariti], *s*. Clarté *f*.
clash¹ [klaʃ], *s*. Choc violent et sonore. **1**. Fracas
m ; résonnement *m* (de cloches) ; choc (de verres) ;
cliquetis *m* (d'épées). **2**. (*a*) Conflit *m*, choc
(d'opinions) ; (*between mobs*) échauffourée *f*.
(*b*) Disparate *f* (de couleurs).
clash². **1**. *v.i.* (*a*) (*Of bells*) Résonner (bruyamment) ; (*of arms*) s'entre-choquer. (*b*) (*Of colours*)
Jurer ; faire disparate ; (*of opinions, etc.*)
s'opposer ; (*of interests*) se heurter. *The two
dates c.,* les deux réunions, etc., tombent le même
jour. **2**. *v.tr*. Faire résonner (des cymbales).
clasp¹ [klɑːsp], *s*. **1**. Agrafe *f* (de broche) ; fermeture *f* (de collier) ; fermoir *m* (de livre, de

porte-monnaie). **Staple-clasp** (*for padlocking*),
moraillon *m*. **2**. Étreinte *f*. **Hand-clasp,** serrement *m* de mains. **'clasp-knife,** *s*. Couteau
pliant ; *F:* eustache *m* ; (*with lock-back*) couteau
à cran d'arrêt.
clasp², *v.tr*. **1**. Agrafer (un bracelet). **2**. (*a*) Serrer, étreindre (qn). *To c. s.o. to one's breast,* serrer
qn contre sa poitrine. *To be clasped in each other's
arms,* se tenir étroitement embrassés. (*b*) *To c.
s.o.'s hand,* serrer la main à qn.
class¹ [klɑːs], *s*. Classe *f*. **1**. **The upper class,** les
gens du monde. **Class consciousness,** (i) esprit
de caste ; (ii) conscience de classe. **Class war,**
lutte des classes. **The lower classes,** le prolétariat. **The middle class,** la bourgeoisie. *P:* **She
is no class,** elle n'est pas de notre monde. (*Of
sportsman*) *He is not c. enough,* il n'est pas à la
hauteur. **2**. *Sch:* **The French class,** la classe de
français. **Evening classes,** cours *m* du soir.
Dancing c., cours de danse. **3**. (*a*) Catégorie *f*,
sorte *f*, genre *m*. *Arrangement in classes,* classification *f*. *This article stands in a c. by itself,* cet
article est unique. *C. of ships,* type *m* de vaisseaux. (*b*) *Ins:* **Class of a ship,** cote *f* d'un
navire (au Lloyd). **'class-book,** *s*. *Sch:* Livre
m de classe. **'class-room,** *s*. *Sch:* (Salle *f* de)
classe *f*.
class², *v.tr*. (*a*) Classer ; ranger (des candidats)
par classes. (*b*) *Ins:* Coter (un navire).
classic ['klasik]. **I**. *a*. Classique. **2**. *s*. (*a*) Classique *m* (grec, etc.). (*b*) *Sch:* Humaniste *m*.
(*c*) *pl.* (*Usu. with sg. const.*) Études *f* classiques ;
humanités *f*. **To study classics,** faire ses
humanités.
classical ['klasik(ə)l], *a*. Classique. **Classical
scholar,** humaniste *m*.
classification [klasifi'keiʃ(ə)n], *s*. Classification *f*
(des plantes) ; classement *m* (de papiers) ; cote *f*
(d'un navire) ; codification *f* (des lois).
classify ['klasifai], *v.tr*. Classifier, classer.
classy ['klɑːsi], *a*. *F:* Bon genre ; chic.
clatter¹ ['klatər], *s*. **1**. Bruit *m*, vacarme *m* ;
ferraillement *m*. **2**. *F:* Brouhaha *m* (de conversation).
clatter², *v.i.* Faire du bruit ; se choquer avec
fracas. **To clatter downstairs,** descendre bruyamment l'escalier. **To come clattering down,** dégringoler.
clause [klɔːz], *s*. **1**. Clause *f*, article *m* (d'un
traité). *C. of a will,* disposition *f* testamentaire.
Customary c., clause d'usage. **2**. *Gram:* Membre
m de phrase. **Head c., main c.,** proposition
principale.
claustral ['klɔːstr(ə)l], *a*. Claustral, -aux.
clavicle ['klavikl], *s*. *Anat:* Clavicule *f*.
claw¹ [klɔː], *s*. **1**. Griffe *f* (de félin) ; serre *f*
(d'oiseau de proie) ; pince *f* (d'une écrevisse).
(*Of cat*) *To sharpen its claws,* faire ses griffes.
To draw in its claws, faire patte de velours.
F: **To cut s.o.'s claws,** rogner les ongles à qn.
2. Coup *m* de griffe, d'ongle, de patte. **3**. (*a*) (*Of
bench*) Valet *m* ; (*of vice*) mordache *f*. (*b*) **Claw
of a grapnel,** patte *f* d'un grappin. (*c*) (*Of hammer*)
Panne fendue. **'claw-hammer,** *s*. Marteau *m*
à panne fendue.
claw². **1**. *v.tr*. Griffer, égratigner ; déchirer
(qch.) avec ses griffes. **2**. *v.i.* **To claw at sth.,**
s'accrocher à qch. ; agripper qch.
clay [klei], *s*. **1**. Argile *f* ; (terre-)glaise *f*. **Pottery
clay,** argile figuline. *C. soil,* sol argileux, glaiseux.
2. Clay(-pipe), pipe *f* en terre. **'clay-pit,** *s*.
Argilière *f*, glaisière *f*.
clayey ['kleii], *a*. Argileux, glaiseux.
clean¹ [kliːn]. **I**. *a*. **1**. Propre, net. *F:* **As clean**

as a new pin, propre comme un sou neuf. *To make sth. c.*, nettoyer qch. *To keep sth. c.*, tenir qch. propre. *C. plate*, assiette nette. **Clean land**, terrain sans herbes. *Nau:* **Clean anchorage**, mouillage sain. **Clean jump**, saut franc. **Clean break**, cassure nette, franche. *Nau:* **Clean bill of health**, patente nette. **Clean hands**, (i) mains propres; (ii) (*clean from crime*) mains nettes. **2.** **Clean** (out)lines, contours nets. *Car with c. lines*, auto qui a de la ligne. *Nau:* **Clean ship**, navire fin. *Farr: C. hocks (of horse)*, jarrets vidés. **II. clean**, *adv.* **1.** *F:* Tout à fait. **I clean forgot**, j'ai absolument oublié. *They got c. away*, ils ont décampé sans laisser de traces. **2. To cut clean through** sth., couper, trancher, qch. de part en part. *To break off c.*, casser net. **clean-'handed**, *a.* Aux mains nettes. **clean-'shaven**, *a.* Sans barbe ni moustache; (visage) glabre.

clean², *s.* Nettoyage *m.* **To give sth. a clean** (up), nettoyer qch.

clean³, *v.tr.* Nettoyer (qch.); récurer (les casseroles); balayer (les rues); faire (une chambre); vider (le poisson); sarcler (un champ); défricher (un terrain). *Nau: To c. the brasswork*, faire le fourbissage. *To c. one's teeth, one's nails*, se nettoyer les dents; se curer les ongles. *F:* **To clean oneself** (up), se débarbouiller. **clean out**, *v.tr.* **1.** Ranger (une armoire); curer, décrasser (un fourneau); vidanger (une fosse). *I.C.E: To c. out the jet*, déboucher le gicleur. **2.** *F:* **To clean s.o.** out, mettre qn à sec. **Cleaned out**, décavé. **clean up**, *v.tr.* **1.** Nettoyer (un champ). **2.** *Abs.* Faire le nettoyage. **clean-'up**, *s.* Nettoyage *m.* **cleaning**, *s.* Nettoyage *m.* **'cleaning-rod**, *s.* Baguette *f* (de fusil).

cleaner ['kli:nər], *s.* **1.** (*Pers.*) Nettoyeur, -euse; décrotteur *m.* French, dry, cleaner, nettoyeur à sec. **2.** (*Device*) Nettoyeuse *f.* *S.a.* VACUUM-CLEANER.

cleanliness ['klenlinəs], *s.* Propreté *f*; netteté *f.*

cleanly¹ ['klenli], *a.* Propre (par habitude).

cleanly² ['kli:nli], *adv.* Proprement, nettement.

cleanness ['kli:nnəs], *s.* **1.** Propreté *f.* **2.** Netteté *f* (de contours).

cleanse [klenz], *v.tr.* **1.** Assainir, curer (un égout). **2.** Purifier, dépurer (le sang). **cleansing¹**, *a.* Assainissant, purifiant. **cleansing²**, *s.* **1.** Assainissement *m*, curage *m* (d'un égout). **2.** Purification *f* (du sang, de l'âme).

clear¹ [kli:ər]. **I.** *a.* **1.** (*a*) Clair, limpide; net. *On a c. day*, par temps clair. *F:* As clear as day, **as crystal**, clair comme le jour, comme de l'eau de roche. **As clear as mud**, pas clair du tout. (*b*) *C. conscience*, conscience nette. (*c*) *C. voice*, voix claire, nette. **2.** (*Manifest*) *C. indication*, signe certain, évident *C. case of bribery*, cas de corruption manifeste. **3.** *To make one's meaning*, *oneself*, *c.*, se faire comprendre. *I wish to make it c. that . . .*, je tiens à préciser que. . . . *C. thinker*, esprit lucide. *To send a message in clear*, transmettre une dépêche en clair. **4. To be clear about sth.**, être convaincu, certain, de qch. **5.** (*a*) *C. profit*, bénéfice clair et net. **Clear loss**, perte sèche. **Clear majority**, majorité absolue. (*b*) *Jur:* **Three clear days**, trois jours francs. **6.** Libre, dégagé (of, de). *C. estate*, bien franc d'hypothèque. *C. space*, espace libre. *C. road*, chemin libre; route bien dégagée. (*Of pers.*) *To be c. of sth.*, être débarrassé de qch *The train was c. of the station*, le train était sorti de la gare. *Horizon c. of haze*, horizon dégagé de brume. *The town was c. of the enemy*, la ville avait été

évacuée par l'ennemi. *The roads are c.*, les routes sont débloquées. *Rail:* **Clear road**, 'road clear,' "voie libre." *'All clear!*" *Mil:* "fin d'alerte"; *Nau:* "paré!" **Clear coast**, côte saine. *F:* **The coast is clear**, le champ est libre. **II. clear**, *a. or adv.* *To steer c. of a rock*, passer au large d'un écueil. **To stand clear**, s'écarter, se garer (pour éviter un danger). *F:* **To keep, steer, clear of sth.**, éviter qch.; se garer de qch. **Stand clear of the doorway!** dégagez la porte! *I keep c. of him as far as possible*, je l'évite le plus possible. *To get c. of debt*, se débarrasser de ses dettes. **To get clear**, se tirer d'affaire. **-ly**, *adv.* **1.** Clairement, nettement. *To see, speak, c.*, voir, parler, clair. *It was too dark to see c.*, il faisait trop noir pour bien distinguer. **You must clearly understand that . . .**, il vous faut bien comprendre que. . . . **2.** Évidemment. (*a*) *He is c. wrong*, il est clair qu'il a tort. (*b*) *I was wrong?*—Clearly, j'ai eu tort?—Évidemment. **'clear-cut**, *a.* *C.-c. features*, traits nettement dessinés. *C.-c. division*, division nette. **'clear-headed**, *a.* **1.** Perspicace. **2. I was quite clear-headed**, j'avais toute ma tête, toute ma lucidité d'esprit. **clear-'headedness**, *s.* Perspicacité *f.* **'clear-sighted**, *a.* Clairvoyant; qui voit juste.

clear², *v.* **I.** *v.tr.* **1.** (*a*) Éclaircir. **To clear the air**, (i) (*of thunderstorm*) rafraîchir l'air; (ii) (*of discussion*) mettre les choses au point. (*b*) Clarifier (un liquide); dépurer (le sang). **2. To clear s.o. of a charge**, innocenter qn d'une accusation. *To c. oneself*, se disculper. **3.** Dégager (une route); désencombrer (une salle); défricher (un terrain); (*from rubbish*) déblayer (un terrain); *Jur:* To clear the court, faire évacuer la salle. **To clear one's conscience**, décharger sa conscience. **Clear the way!** faites place! *To c. a way for oneself*, se frayer un passage. *F:* **To clear the ground for negotiations**, déblayer le terrain. **To clear the table**, enlever le couvert. *Navy:* **To clear (the decks) for action**, faire le branle-bas de combat. **A cup of coffee clears the head**, une tasse de café dégage le cerveau. *Com:* **To clear goods**, solder des marchandises. **To clear," "to sell," "solde."** 'Must be cleared,' "vente à tout prix." *Nau:* **To clear a cable, an anchor**, parer un câble, une ancre. *Rail:* **To clear the line**, dégager la voie; (*after an accident*) déblayer la voie. *To c. a choked pipe*, désobstruer un tuyau. *To c. a filter*, décolmater un filtre. **4.** *To c. one's plate*, faire assiette nette. *To c. the letter-box*, lever les lettres. *To c. the bowels*, purger, dégager, les intestins. **5.** (*a*) *To c. a barrier (by three inches)*, franchir une barrière (avec trois pouces de reste). *To jack up a wheel till it clears the ground*, soulever une roue jusqu'à ce qu'elle ne touche plus le sol. (*b*) *Nau:* **To clear the harbour**, sortir du port; quitter le port. **To clear the land**, prendre la terre. **6.** (*a*) Acquitter (une dette); affranchir (une propriété); solder, liquider (un compte). (*b*) *Nau:* (*Of ship*) **To clear its quarantine**, purger la quarantaine. *To c. goods*, dédouaner des marchandises. **7. To clear ten per cent**, faire un bénéfice net de dix pour cent. *Not to c. one's expenses*, ne pas faire ses frais. **8.** *Fin:* Compenser, virer (un chèque). **II. clear**, *v.i.* **1.** (*a*) (*Of the weather*) **To clear** (up), s'éclaircir; se mettre au beau. (*Of mist*) **To clear** (away), se dissiper. *The sky is clearing*, le ciel se dégage. *His brow clears*, son front se rasséréna. (*b*) (*Of liquid*) Se clarifier. **2.** (*Of ship*) Prendre la mer. **clear away**, *v.tr.* Enlever, ôter (qch.); écarter (un obstacle). **clear off.** **1.** *v.tr.* S'acquitter de (ses dettes). *Com:* Solder (des marchandises).

To c. off arrears of work, rattraper l'arriéré de besogne. **2.** *v.i. (Of intruders)* S'enfuir, filer, décamper. **clear out. 1.** *v.tr.* Nettoyer (une chambre); vider (une armoire); balayer (tout le personnel). **2.** *v.i.* Filer, déguerpir. **Clear out!** filez! hors d'ici! **clear-'out,** *v.tr.* Nettoyage *m.* **clear up,** *v.tr.* Éclaircir, élucider (un mystère). *To c. up a matter,* tirer une affaire au clair. **clearing,** *s.* **1. Clearing of s.o.** *(from a charge),* désinculpation *f* de qn. **2.** Dégagement *m,* déblaiement *m* (d'une voie); enlèvement *m* (de débris); défrichement *m* (d'un terrain). **3.** Franchissement *m* (d'une barrière). **4.** *(a) Cust:* Dédouanement *m. (b)* Acquittement *m* (de dettes). *(c) Fin:* Compensation *f* (de chèques). **Country clearing,** virement *m.* **5.** *(In forest)* Éclaircie *f,* clairière *f.* **'clearing-bank,** *s. Bank:* Banque *f* de virement. **'clearing-house,** *s.* **1.** *Fin:* Comptoir *m* de règlement. **2.** *Rail:* Bureau central.

clearance ['kliːərəns], *s.* **1. Clearance sale,** vente *f* de soldes. **2.** *(a) Cust:* Dédouanage *m,* dédouanement *m.* **Clearance certificate,** lettre *f* de mer. **Clearance inwards,** permis *m* d'entrée. *(b) Nau:* Départ *m* (du port). **3.** Compensation *f* (de chèques). **4.** *Tchn:* Espace *m* libre; jeu *m;* voie *f* (d'une scie). **Permissible c.,** jeu tolérable. *There is not enough c. for the barges under the bridge,* le pont manque de hauteur pour laisser passer les péniches.

clearness ['kliːərnəs], *s.* **1.** Clarté *f* (de l'atmosphère). **2.** Netteté *f* (d'une image, des idées).

cleat [kliːt], *s.* Tasseau *m,* taquet *m.*

cleavable ['kliːvəbl], *a.* Fissile; *Miner:* clivable.

cleavage ['kliːvedʒ], *s.* **1.** Fendage *m. Miner:* Clivage *m.* **2.** Scission *f* (dans un parti).

cleave[1] [kliːv], *v. (p.t. cleaved,* **cleft** [kleft], *Lit:* **clove** [kloːv]; *p.p.* **cleaved, cleft,** *Lit:* **cloven** [klouvn])** **1.** *v.tr. (a)* Fendre (le bois, le fer). **Cleft stick,** piquet fourchu. *F:* **To be in a cleft stick,** se trouver dans une impasse. **Cleft palate,** palais fendu. **Cloven hoof,** pied fourchu. *F:* **To show, display, the cloven hoof,** montrer le pied fourchu; laisser passer le bout de l'oreille. *(b) Miner:* Cliver (un cristal). *(c) (Of bird, ship)* Fendre (l'air, les eaux). **2.** *v.i. (a)* **To cleave (asunder),** se fendre. *(b) (Of crystals)* Se cliver.

cleave[2], *v.i. (p.t.* **cleaved** [kliːvd], *Lit:* **clave** [kleːiv]; *p.p.* **cleaved** [kliːvd]) Adhérer, s'attacher, être fidèle (à un parti).

cleaver ['kliːvər], *s.* Fendoir *m;* *(for meat)* couperet *m.*

cleavers ['kliːvərz], *s. Bot:* Grateron *m.*

clef [klef], *s. Mus:* Clef *f.* **The bass clef,** la clef de fa. **The treble clef,** la clef de sol. **The C clef,** la clef d'ut.

cleft[1] [kleft], *s.* Fente *f,* fissure *f,* crevasse *f.*

cleft[2]. *See* CLEAVE[1].

clematis ['klematis], *s. Bot:* Clématite *f.*

clemency ['klemənsi], *s.* **1.** Clémence *f* (*to,* envers, pour). **2.** Douceur *f* (du temps).

clement ['klemənt], *a.* **1.** Clément, indulgent (*to,* envers, pour). **2.** *(Of weather)* Doux, douce. **-ly,** *adv.* Avec clémence, avec indulgence.

clench [klenʃ], *v.tr.* **1.** = CLINCH[2] **1. 2.** Serrer (les dents, le poing). **With clenched hands,** les mains crispées. **3.** *v.i.* Se serrer; se crisper.

clerestory ['kliːərstoːri], *s. Ecc.Arch:* Claire-voie *f.*

clergy ['kləːrdʒi], *s. (No pl.)* **1.** *Coll.* Clergé *m.* **2.** *(With pl. const.)* Membres *m* du clergé.

clergyman, *pl.* **-men** ['kləːrdʒimən, -men], *s.m.* Ecclésiastique; ministre (du culte); pasteur (protestant).

---

cleric ['klerik], *s.* = CLERGYMAN.

clerical ['klerik(ə)l], *a.* **1.** Clérical, -aux; du clergé. **2.** *(a)* **Clerical error,** faute de copiste; *Book-k:* erreur d'écritures. *(b)* **Clerical work,** travail d'écritures.

clerk [klaːrk], *s.* **1.** *(a)* Employé, -ée, de bureau; commis *m;* buraliste *mf;* clerc *m* (d'avoué). **Chief c.,** chef m de bureau. *Junior c.,* petit employé. *(b) Jur:* Clerk of the court, greffier *m. C. of the court's office,* greffe *m.* **2.** *Ecc:* **Clerk (in holy orders),** clerc; ecclésiastique *m.* **3.** *(a)* **Clerk of the works,** conducteur *m* des travaux. *(b) F:* **The Clerk of the weather,** la providence qui régit la pluie et le beau temps. *(c) Rac:* **Clerk of the course,** commissaire *m* de la piste.

clerkly ['klaːrkli], *a.* **1.** De bureau. *C. hand,* écriture moulée. **2.** *A:* Docte, savant, lettré.

clerkship ['klaːrkʃip], *s.* Emploi *m* ou place *f* de commis, d'employé, *Jur:* de clerc.

clever ['klevər], *a.* **1.** Habile, adroit. *He is c. with his hands,* il est adroit de ses mains. *C. at doing sth.,* habile, ingénieux, à faire qch. *To be c. with one's pencil,* se servir adroitement de son crayon. **2.** *(a)* **To be clever,** être intelligent. *A c. child,* un enfant à l'intelligence éveillée. *Sch:* **Clever at mathematics,** fort en mathématiques. *(b) F: (Smart) He was too c. for us,* il nous a roulés. *(c) A c. parody,* une parodie pleine de finesse. *(d) C. device,* dispositif ingénieux. **-ly,** *adv.* Habilement, adroitement; avec intelligence.

cleverness ['klevərnəs], *s.* **1.** Habileté *f,* adresse *f,* dextérité *f. C. at doing sth.,* habileté à faire qch. **2.** Intelligence *f.* **3.** Ingéniosité *f.*

clew[1] [kluː], *s.* **1.** Pelote *f* (de fil). **2.** *Nau: (a)* Araignée *f* (de hamac). *(b)* Point *m* d'écoute (de voile). **3.** = CLUE 2. **'clew-garnet, -line,** *s.* *Nau:* Cargue-point *m.*

clew[2], *v.tr.* **To clew (up)** *the sails,* carguer les voiles.

cliché ['kliːʃe], *s.* Cliché *m.*

click[1] [klik], *s.* **1.** Bruit sec; clic *m;* cliquetis *m* (d'épées). **2. Click (of the tongue),** claquement *m* (de la langue). **3.** *Tchn:* Cliquet *m;* déclic *m.* **'click-beetle,** *s.* Élatère *m;* *F:* taupin *m.* **'click-clack,** *s.* Tic-tac *m* (d'un moulin). **'click-wheel,** *s.* Roue *f* à cliquet, à rochet.

click[2], *v.tr. & i.* Cliqueter; faire tic-tac. **To click one's heels,** (faire) claquer les talons (en saluant). **clicking,** *s.* = CLICK[1] 1, 2.

click[3], *v.i.* **1.** *P: (a) (Of two pers.)* Se plaire du premier coup. *(b) (Of things)* Aller ensemble. *(c)* Avoir de la veine. **2.** *Mil:* *To c. for a fatigue,* écoper d'une corvée.

client ['klaiənt], *s.* **1.** *Rom.Ant:* Client *m.* **2.** *(a)* Client, -ente (dans les professions libérales). *(b) Com:* = CUSTOMER 1.

clientele [klaiən'tiːl, kliãtel], *s.* Clientèle *f.*

cliff [klif], *s. (On sea-shore)* Falaise *f; (inland)* escarpement *m,* varappe *f.*

cliffsman, *pl.* **-men** ['klifsmən, -men], *s.* Escaladeur *m* de falaises; varappeur *m.*

climacteric [klaimak'terik], *a.* Climatérique *f.*

climate ['klaimet], *s.* Climat *m.*

climatic [klai'matik], *a.* **1.** Climat(ér)ique. *(b) Biol: C. variation,* variation climatologique *f.*

climax ['klaimaks], *s.* **1.** *Rh:* Gradation (ascendante). **2.** *F:* Comble *m,* apogée *m;* plus haut point. *This brought matters to a c.,* ce fut le comble. *Th: etc:* **To work up to a climax,** corser l'action; amener la grande scène.

climb[1] [klaim], *s.* **1.** Ascension *f. Aut: Sp:* **Hill climb,** course *f* de côte. **2.** Côte *f,* montée *f.*

climb[2], *v.tr. & i.* **1.** *(a)* Monter, gravir (l'escalier); grimper à (un arbre); monter à (l'échelle); escalader (une falaise) **To c.** *a mountain*, faire l'ascension d'une montagne. **To climb over** *the wall*, franchir le mur. **To climb down** *the cliff*, descendre la falaise. **To climb out** *of a hole*, grimper en dehors d'un trou; se tirer d'un trou. (b) *The road climbs*, la route va en montant. **2. To climb to power**, s'élever au pouvoir. **3.** *Av:* Prendre de l'altitude. **climb down,** *v.i.* **1.** Descendre. **2.** *F:* En rabattre; baisser pavillon; *P:* se dégonfler. **'climb-down,** *s.* **1.** Descente *f.* **2.** *F:* Défaite *f. A miserable c.-d.*, une honteuse reculade. **climbing',** *a* Climbing plant, plante grimpante. *Av:* Climbing flight, vol ascendant. **climbing²,** *s.* Escalade *f*; montée *f.* Alpine climbing, alpinisme *m. Aut:* Climbing ability, tenue en côte. Climbing speed, vitesse en montée. **'climbing-irons,** *s.pl.* Crampons *m.*

climber ['klaimər], *s.* **1.** (a) Ascension(n)iste *m* (de montagne); grimpeur *m* (à une paroi). *S.a.* ROCK-CLIMBER. (b) *These planes are good climbers*, ces avions montent vite. **2.** *F:* Arriviste *mf.* **3.** (a) *Bot:* Plante grimpante. (b) *Orn:* Grimpeur.

clime [klaim], *s. Poet:* Climat *m*; pays *m.*

clinch ['klinʃ], *s.* **1.** (a) Rivet *m*, crampon *m.* (b) *Nau:* Étalingure *f.* **2.** *Box:* Corps-à-corps *m.* **clinch².** **1.** *v.tr.* (a) River. (b) *Nau:* Étalinguer (une chaîne). (c) Conclure (un marché). *That clinches it, F:* voilà qui vous rive votre clou. **2.** *v.i. Box:* Se prendre corps-à-corps. **'clinch-nail,** *s.* Clou rivé, à river.

clincher ['klinʃər], *s.* **1.** *F:* Argument *m* sans réplique. *That was a c. for him!* ça lui a rivé son clou! **2.** *Aut: Cy:* (Of wheel-rim) Gouttière *f.* **Clincher tyre,** pneu à talon.

cling [kliŋ], *v.i.* (clung [klʌŋ]; clung) (a) (Of pers.) S'attacher, s'accrocher, se cramponner (to, à); (of burr) s'attraper (to, à) *She clung to me*, elle se prit à moi. **To cling close to s.o.,** se serrer, se coller, contre qn. **To cling together, to one another,** (i) rester attachés l'un à l'autre; rester étroitement unis; (ii) se tenir étroitement enlacés. (b) **To cling to an opinion**, rester attaché à une opinion. (c) Adhérer (to, à). (Of garment) *To c. to the figure*, coller au corps. *Clinging material*, étoffe qui moule le corps. (d) *Clinging nature*, naturel affectueux.

clingstone ['kliŋstoun], *s.* **Clingstone (peach),** pavie *f*, alberge *f.*

clinic ['klinik], *s. Med:* Clinique *f.*

clinical ['klinik(ə)l], *a.* (Leçon, etc.) clinique. **Clinical thermometer,** thermomètre médical.

clink¹ [kliŋk], *s.* Tintement *m*, choc *m* (de verres); cliquetis *m* (d'épées).

clink². **1.** *v.i.* (Of glasses) Tinter. **2.** *v.tr.* Faire tinter, faire résonner. **To clink glasses,** trinquer.

clink³, *s. P:* Prison *f*; *Mil: P:* bloc *m*, taule *f.* **To go to clink,** être fourré au bloc.

clinker¹ ['kliŋkər], *s.* **1.** Brique vitrifiée. **2.** Mâchefer *m*; scories vitreuses; escarbilles *fpl.*

clinker². *s.* **1.** (a) = CLINCHER 1. (b) *F:* Personne ou chose épatante. **2.** = CLINCH-NAIL. **'clinker-built,** *a. N.Arch:* Bordé à clin(s).

clinkstone ['kliŋkstoun], *s.* Phonolite *f.*

clinometer [klai'nɔmetər], *s. Surv: Nau:* Clinomètre *m. Aut: Av:* Indicateur *m* de pente.

clip¹ [klip], *s.* **1.** Pince *f*, attache *f*; griffe *f*, collier *m*, ou étrier *m* de serrage. **Paper-clip,** agrafe *f* (pour papiers); attache-papiers *m inv*; (wire) attache trombone. **Fountain-pen clip,** bague-agrafe *f. Surg:* **Artery-clip,** pince hémo-

statique **2.** *El:* Cosse *f* (de fil). **3.** *Mil:* (Loading-)clip, chargeur *m* (pour cartouches).

clip², *v.tr.* (clipped [klipt]) Pincer, serrer. *To c. papers together*, agrafer des papiers.

clip³, *s.* **1.** (a) Tonte *f* (de moutons). (b) Tonte de la saison. **2.** *P:* Taloche *f. Box:* Cli on the jaw, coup sec à la mâchoire.

clip⁴, *v.tr.* **1.** Tondre (un mouton); tailler (une haie); rogner, cisailler (la monnaie). *To c. the wings of a bird*, rogner les ailes à une volaille. *F.* **To clip s.o.'s claws,** rogner les ongles à qn. *F:* **To clip one's words,** écourter ses mots. **2.** Poinçonner (un billet) **clipping,** *s.* **1.** (a) Tondage *m* (de chevaux); tonte *f* (de moutons). (b) Poinçonnage *m* (de billets). **2.** (a) *U.S:* Coupure (prise dans un journal). (b) *pl.* Rognures *f.*

clipper ['klipər], *s.* **1.** (*Pers.*) Tondeur, -euse. **2.** *pl Tls:* Tondeuse *f.* **3.** *Nau:* Fin voilier. **Clipper-built,** à formes élancées.

clique [kli:k], *s.* Coterie *f*; petite chapelle.

cliquishness ['kli:kiʃnəs], *s* Esprit *m* de coterie.

cloak¹ [klouk], *s.* Manteau *m. Evening c.*, sortie *f* de bal, de théâtre **Under the cloak of night,** sous le voile de la nuit. *Under the of religion*, sous le manteau de la religion. **Cloak-and-dagger story,** roman de cape et d'épée **'cloak-room,** *s.* **1.** *Th:* Vestiaire *m.* **'Ladies' cloak-room,'** "Dames." **2.** *Rail:* Consigne *f.*

cloak², *v.tr.* (a) Couvrir revêtir, (qn) d'un manteau. (b) Masquer (ses projets).

clock¹ [klɔk], *s.* (a) (*Large*) Horloge *f*; (*smaller*) pendule *f. Nau:* Montre *f. Aut: Dashboard c.*, montre de bord. **Town clock,** horloge de ville. **Grandfather clock,** horloge de parquet. **Wall clock,** cartel *m.* **What o'clock is it?** quelle heure est-il? **It is one, two, o'clock,** il est une heure, deux heures. *It took him ten minutes by the c.*, cela lui a pris dix minutes montre en main. *F:* **To sleep the clock round,** faire le tour du cadran. *F:* (*Intensive*) **Like one o'clock,** fameusement, rondement. *You get on together like one o'clock*, vous vous entendez à merveille. *Everything went like one o'clock*, tout a marché comme sur des roulettes. (b) **Clock of taxi-cab,** appareil *m* horo-kilométrique.

clock². **1.** *v.tr. F:* Chronométrer. **2.** *v.i.* (a) *Av:* (Of engine) **To clock over,** tourner au (grand) ralenti. (b) *Ind:* **To clock on, off,** pointer à l'arrivée, au départ.

clock³, *s.* (On sock) Baguette *f.*

clockwise ['klɔkwaiz], *a.* Dans le sens des aiguilles d'une montre; à droite; dextrorsum.

clockwork ['klɔkwə:rk], *s.* Rouage *m* d'horloge; mouvement d'un horlogerie. *C. train*, chemin de fer mécanique. *F:* **Everything is going like clockwork,** tout va comme sur des roulettes.

clod [klɔd], *s.* **1.** (a) Motte *f* (de terre). *Agr:* **To break (up) the clods,** émotter la terre. (b) *F:* **The clod,** la terre (des champs). (c) *Lit:* Le corps (opposé à l'âme); la matière. **2.** = CLOD-HOPPER. **'clod-hopper,** *s.* Rustre *m*, lourdaud *m.*

clog¹ [klɔg], *s.* **1.** (a) Entrave *f*; billot *m* (pour vache). (b) *F:* Empêchement *m.* **2.** (a) (*Over-shoe*) Socque *f*, galoche *f.* (b) Gros brodequin à semelle de bois et à bout ferré. **'clog-dance,** Danse *f* à claquettes.

clog², *v.* (clogged) **1.** *v.tr.* (a) Entraver (une bête). (b) Boucher, obstruer (un tuyau); colmater (un filtre); empâter (une lime). *To c. the wheels of the administration*, entraver la marche des services. **2.** *v.i.* Se boucher, s'obstruer.

cloister[1] ['klɔistər], s. **1.** Cloître m. **2.** pl. **Cloisters**, péristyle m, ambulatoire m.

cloister[2], v.tr. Cloîtrer. To lead a cloistered life, mener une vie monacale.

cloistral ['klɔistrəl], a. Claustral, -aux.

close[1] [klous]. I. a. **1.** (a) Bien fermé; clos. To draw a fastening c., serrer un lien. Ling: Close vowel, voyelle fermée, entravée. (b) C. air, air renfermé. The room smells close, ça sent le renfermé ici. Close weather, temps lourd. (c) C. secret, secret impénétrable. (d) C. corporation, société exclusive. (e) Ven: Close time, season, chasse fermée. **2.** Typ: C. matter, composition compacte. C. grain, grain fin, dense. In close order, Navy: à distance serrée; Mil: en rangs serrés. **3.** When I saw him at c. quarters, quand je le vis de près. C. connexion between two facts, rapport étroit entre deux faits. Close friend, ami(e) intime. C. resemblance, ressemblance exacte. C. translation, traduction fidèle. C. attention, attention soutenue. To keep c. watch on s.o., surveiller qn de près. C. prisoner, prisonnier étroitement gardé. To cut hair c., couper les cheveux ras. Rac: C. finish, arrivée serrée. C. election, élection vivement contestée. **4.** Peu communicatif. To be close about sth., être réservé à l'égard de qch. To play a close game, jouer serré. **5.** Avare, regardant. **-ly,** adv. **1.** = CLOSE[1] II. 1. **2.** (a) C. guarded, étroitement gardé. (b) C. cut, tondu ras. C. contested, vivement contesté. (c) (Surveiller qn) de près; (interroger qn) à fond; (écouter) attentivement. **3.** C. packed in a box, serrés dans une boîte. II. **close,** adv. **1.** C. shut, étroitement, hermétiquement, fermé ou bouché. **2.** Près, de près, auprès. To follow c. behind s.o., suivre qn de près. To keep c. to the door, se tenir tout près de la porte. (Of garment) To fit close, bien prendre la taille. To stand c. together, se tenir serrés. **3.** To lie close, se tenir tapi. **4.** (a) Close at hand, close by, tout près, tout proche; à peu de distance. (b) Nau: To stand close in (to the land), serrer la terre. (c) Close (up)on nine o'clock, tout près de neuf heures. To be c. on fifty, friser la cinquantaine. (d) Close to, close by (sth.), tout près, à proximité, de (qch.). C. to the door, tout contre la porte. C. to the ground, à fleur de terre. **close-'cropped, -'cut,** a. (Of hair) Coupé ras; (of grass) tondu de près. **close-'fisted,** a. Ladre; F: pingre. **'close-fitting,** a. (Vêtement) ajusté, collant. **close-'grained,** a. (Of wood) Serré; à grain(s) fin(s). **close-'hauled,** a. Nau: Au plus près serré. **close-'meshed,** a. A petites mailles. **close-'mouthed,** a. Économe de paroles; peu communicatif. **close-'ranked,** a. En rangs serrés. **close-'reefed,** a. Nau: Au bas ris. **close-'set,** a. (Of eyes, etc.) Rapprochés. **close-'shaven,** a. Rasé de près. **close-'up,** s. Cin: (Vue f de) premier plan.

close[2] [klous], s. **1.** Jur: Clôture f. **2.** (a) Clos m, enclos m. (b) Enceinte f (de cathédrale). **3.** (In Scot.) Passage m.

close[3] [klo:uz], s. **1.** Fin f, conclusion f; bout m (de l'année); clôture f (d'une séance). The evening drew to a c., la soirée prit fin. Close of the season, fermeture f de la pêche, de la chasse. **2.** (Of wrestlers) To come to a close, en venir au corps-à-corps.

close[4] [klo:uz]. I. v.tr. **1.** Fermer; replier (un parapluie); barrer (une rue); Nau: bâcler (un port). Road closed to motor traffic, route interdite à la circulation automobile. Cold closes the pores, le froid resserre les pores. Book-k: To close

the books, régler les livres; balancer les comptes. **2.** Conclure, terminer; clore, fermer (un débat); arrêter (un compte). To declare the discussion closed, prononcer la clôture des débats. **3.** To close the ranks, serrer les rangs. Navy: To close the columns, resserrer les colonnes. II. **close,** v.i. **1.** (Se) fermer; se refermer. The theatres c. on Good Friday, les théâtres font relâche le vendredi saint. El.E: The cut-out has closed, le conjoncteur est collé. **2.** Finir; se terminer. The day is closing, le jour tire à sa fin. **3.** To close about, round (s.o.), cerner, encercler (qn). **4.** To close with s.o., (i) conclure le marché avec qn; toper; (ii) se prendre corps à corps avec qn. **close down.** **1.** v.tr. Fermer (une usine). **2.** v.i. (a) (Of factory) Fermer; chômer. (b) W.Tel: Terminer l'émission. **close in,** v.i. (a) The night closes in, la nuit tombe. The days are closing in, les jours (se) raccourcissent. (b) To close in on s.o., cerner qn de près. **close up.** **1.** v.tr. (a) Boucher; barrer. (b) Typ: Rapprocher (les caractères). **2.** v.i. (a) (Of aperture) S'obturer. (b) Se serrer, se tasser. Mil: Close up! serrez les rangs! **closed,** a. Fermé; (of pipe) obturé, bouché. With c. eyes, les yeux clos. 'Road closed,' "rue barrée." Th: 'Closed,' "relâche." 'Closed for the season," "clôture." **closing**[1], a. (a) Qui (se) ferme. (b) Dernier; final, -als. The c. bid, la dernière enchère. C. session, séance de clôture. Closing prices, derniers cours. **closing**[2], s. **1.** Fermeture f. Closing (-down) of a factory, fermeture d'une usine. Com: Sunday closing, repos m hebdomadaire. 'Closing time!' "on ferme!" **2.** Clôture f (d'un compte, d'une séance). **closeness** ['klousnəs], s. **1.** (a) Rapprochement m, proximité f. The c. of their friendship, leur grande intimité. (b) Contexture serrée (d'une étoffe, etc.). **2.** Exactitude f. The c. of the resemblance, la ressemblance frappante. **3.** (a) Manque m d'air. (b) Lourdeur f (du temps). **4.** Réserve f, caractère peu communicatif (de qn). **5.** Ladrerie f. **closet**[1] ['klɔzet], s. **1.** (a) Cabinet m. (b) A: Boudoir m; cabinet de travail. (c) = WATER-CLOSET. **2.** Armoire f, placard m; (under staircase) soupente f. **closet**[2], v.tr. (closeted) To be closeted with s.o., être enfermé avec qn (pour conférer). **closure**[1] ['klouʒər], s. **1.** (a) Clôture f, fermeture f (d'une séance). (b) Parl: To move the closure, voter la clôture. **2.** Fermeture, occlusion f (d'une soupape, etc.). **closure**[2], v.tr. Clôturer (un débat). **clot**[1] [klɔt], s. Caillot m (de sang); bourbillon m (d'encre). Clot on the brain, embolie cérébrale. **clot**[2], v. (clotted) **1.** v.i. (Of milk) Se cailler; (of blood) se figer, se coaguler. **2.** v.tr. Caillebotter, cailler (le lait); figer (le sang). Clotted cream, crème caillebottée (par échaudage). F: Clotted nonsense, absurdités fpl. **clotting,** s. Caillement m, figement m. **cloth,** pl. **cloths** [klɔθ, klɔ:θs], s. **1.** Tex: (a) Étoffe f de laine; drap m. F: Story invented out of whole cloth, histoire inventée de toutes pièces. (b) (Linen, cotton) Toile f. Map mounted on c., carte entoilée. (c) American cloth, (i) (also oil-cloth) toile cirée; (ii) (also Lancaster cloth) molesquine f. **2.** (a) Linge m; (for cleaning) torchon m. (b) (Table-)cloth, tapis m (de table); (of linen) nappe f. To lay the cloth, (i) mettre la nappe; (ii) mettre, dresser, le couvert. (c) Tapis (de billard). (d) Th: Toile f (de décor). (e) Nau: F: Ship that spreads much cloth, navire qui porte une forte voilure. S.a. FLOOR-CLOTH,

HORSE-CLOTH, TEA-CLOTH, TRAY-CLOTH. **3.** *F:* The cloth, (i) l'habit *m* ecclésiastique; (ii) le clergé. **'cloth-hall,** *s. A:* Halle *f* aux draps. **clothe** [klo:uð], *v.tr.* (*p.t. & p.p.* **clad** [klad] *or* **clothed** [klo:uðd]) Vêtir, revêtir, habiller (*in, with,* de). *Warmly clad,* chaudement vêtu. *F:* **Wall clad with ivy,** mur revêtu, tapissé, de lierre. *S.a.* IRON-CLAD. **clothing,** *s.* **I.** Action *f* de vêtir ou de se vêtir. *The c. trades,* les industries du vêtement. **2.** *Coll.* Habillement *m*; vêtements *mpl.* **clothes** [klo:uðz], *s.pl.* **I.** Vêtements *m*, habits *m*, effets *m.* **Suit of clothes,** complet *m. In one's best c.,* dans ses habits de cérémonie; *F:* endimanché. **To put on, take off, one's clothes,** s'habiller, se vêtir; se déshabiller, se dévêtir. *S.a.* LONG-CLOTHES, MOTH I, READY-MADE, SUNDAY, SWADDLING-CLOTHES. **2.** Linge *m. Soiled c.,* linge sale. **3.** = BED-CLOTHES. **'clothes-basket,** *s.* Panier *m* au linge sale. **'clothes-horse,** *s.* Chevalet *m* pour linge; séchoir *m.* **'clothes-line,** *s.* Corde *f* à (étendre le) linge; étendoir *m.* **'clothes-peg,** *s.* Pince *f*; fichoir *m.* **'clothes-prop,** *s.* Perche *f* d'étendoir. **clothier** ['klouðiər], *s.* (*a*) Drapier *m.* (*b*) Marchand *m* de confections. **cloud¹** [klaud], *s.* **I.** Nuage *m*; *Poet:* nuée *f*, nue *f. F:* **To be in the clouds,** être dans les nuages. (*Of stranger, etc.*) **To drop from the clouds,** tomber des nues. *Prov:* **Every cloud has a silver lining,** après la pluie le beau temps. **To be under a cloud,** (i) avoir eu un revers de fortune; (ii) être l'objet de soupçons. **2.** Nuage, voile *m* (de fumée, de poussière). *F:* **Under the cloud of night,** sous le voile de la nuit. **3.** (*In liquid*) Nuage, turbidité *f*; (*on glass*) buée *f.* **4.** Nuée (de sauterelles, de flèches). **'cloud-burst,** *s.* Trombe *f*; rafale *f* de pluie. **cloud².** **I.** *v.tr.* Couvrir, voiler, obscurcir (le ciel): troubler (un liquide); couvrir (une vitre) de buée; ternir (un miroir). *To c. s.o.'s mind,* troubler, obscurcir, la raison de qn. *To c. the issue,* embrouiller la question. **2.** *v.i.* (*Of sky*) **To cloud (up, over),** se couvrir, se voiler, de nuages. *His brow clouded (over),* son front s'assombrit. **clouded,** *a.* (Ciel) couvert (de nuages); (verre) embué, couvert de buée; (liquide) trouble. **cloudiness** ['klaudinəs], *s.* **I.** Aspect nuageux (du ciel). **2.** Turbidité *f* (d'un liquide). **cloudless** ['klaudləs], *a.* (Ciel) sans nuages. **cloudy** ['klaudi], *a.* **I.** (Temps) couvert; (ciel) nuageux, assombri. **2.** (Liqu·ide) trouble. *C. ideas,* idées fumeuses, nébuleuses. **clout¹** [klaut], *s.* **I.** Chiffon *m*, linge *m*, torchon *m.* **2.** *pl. F:* Frusques *f*, nippes *f. Prov:* **Ne'er cast a clout till May be out** = en avril ne quitte pas un fil. **3.** *F:* Beigne *f*, claque *f*, taloche *f* (sur la tête). **clout²,** *v.tr.* **I.** *A. & Dial:* Rapiécer, rapetasser (un vieil habit). **2.** *F:* **To clout s.o. on the head,** flanquer une taloche, *P:* une beigne, à qn. **clove¹** [klo:uv]. See CLEAVE¹. **clove²,** *s.* Clove of garlic, gousse *f* d'ail. **clove³,** *s.* **I.** Clou *m* de girofle. **Clove-tree,** giroflier *m.* **2.** *Bot:* **Clove-pink,** œillet *m* des fleuristes. **clove-hitch** ['klo:uvhitʃ], *s. Nau:* Demi-clefs *fpl* à capeler. **cloven** [klouvn]. See CLEAVE¹. **cloven-'footed, -'hoofed,** *a. Z:* Fissipède; au pied fourchu. **clover** ['klouvər], *s. Bot:* Trèfle *m*; *F:* lupinelle *f. F:* **To be,** to live, (like dogs) in clover, être, vivre, comme un coq en pâte. **'clover-leaf,** *s.* Feuille *f* de trèfle.

clown¹ [klaun], *s.* **I.** *A:* Paysan *m.* **2.** Rustre *m.* manant *m.* **3.** *Th:* (*a*) Bouffon *m* paillasse *m* pitre *m.* (*b*) Clown *m* (de cirque). **clown²,** *v.i.* Faire le clown, le pitre. **clownery** ['klaunəri], *s.* Bouffonnerie *f.* **clownish** ['klauniʃ], *a.* **I.** *A:* Campagnard, agreste. **2.** (*a*) Gauche, empoté. (*b*) Grossier; mal élevé. **3.** (Tour) de paillasse. **cloy** [klɔi], *v.tr.* (*Of food*) Rassasier; écœurer. **cloying,** *a.* Rassasiant, affadissant. **club¹** [klʌb], *s.* **I.** (*a*) Massue *f*, gourdin *m*, assommoir *m. Gym:* Indian club, mil *m.* (*b*) *Golf:* Crosse *f*, club *m.* **2.** *Cards:* Trèfle *m.* **3.** (*a*) Club *m* (politique, littéraire, etc.). (*b*) *Literary c.,* cercle *m*, cénacle *m*, littéraire. (*c*) Association *f*, société *f*, club. *C for young people,* patronage *m.* Tennis club, club de tennis. **'club-foot,** *s.* Pied bot *m.* **'club-footed,** *a.* (Qui a le) pied bot. **'club-house,** *s. Sp:* Pavillon *m.* **'club-land,** *s.* Quartier *m* des clubs à Londres (St James' et Piccadilly). **'club-law,** *s.* La loi du plus fort. **club²,** *v.* (clubbed) **I.** *v.tr.* Frapper (qn) avec une massue, avec un gourdin. *To c. s.o. to death,* assommer qn à coups de gourdin. **2.** *v.tr. To c. one's resources (together),* mettre ses ressources en commun; faire bourse commune. **3.** *v.i.* (*a*) Se réunir, s'associer (avec d'autres pour faire qch.). (*b*) **To club together,** se cotiser; mettre son argent en commun. **cluck¹** [klʌk], *s.* (*Of hen*) Gloussement *m.* **cluck²,** *v.i.* (*Of hen*) Glousser. **clucking,** *s.* Gloussement *m.* **clue** [klu:], *s.* **I.** = CLEW¹ I, 2. **2.** Indication *f*, indice *m.* **To get, find, the clue to sth.,** trouver, découvrir, la clef de qch., le fin mot. **To give s.o. a clue,** mettre qn sur la voie, sur la piste. **The clues of a cross-word puzzle,** les définitions *f.* **clump¹** [klʌmp], *s.* **I.** (*a*) Bloc *m*, masse *f* (de bois, d'argile). (*b*) Groupe *m*, bouquet *m* (d'arbres); massif *m* (de fleurs). **2.** Pas lourd. **3.** *P:* **To give s.o. a clump on the head,** flanquer une taloche à qn. **clump².** **I.** *v.i.* Se grouper en masse compacte. **2.** (*a*) *v.i.* **To clump (about),** marcher lourdement. (*b*) *v.tr.* **To clump s.o.'s head,** flanquer une taloche à qn. **clumsiness** ['klʌmzinəs], *s.* Maladresse *f*, gaucherie *f.* **clumsy** ['klʌmzi], *a.* **I.** Maladroit, malhabile, gauche. **2.** (*Of shape*) Lourd, informe. **-ily,** *adv.* Maladroitement, gauchement. **clung** [klʌŋ]. See CLING. **cluster¹** ['klʌstər], *s.* Bouquet *m* (de fleurs); massif *m*, groupe *m* (d'arbres); grappe *f* (de raisins); nœud *m* (de diamants); amas *m* (d'étoiles); agglomération *f* (d'îles). **cluster².** **I.** *v.tr.* Grouper; rassembler en groupes. **2.** *v.i.* **To cluster round s.o., sth.,** se grouper, se rassembler, autour de qn, de qch. (*Of particles, etc.*) **To cluster together,** s'agglomérer. **clustered,** *a. Arch:* Clustered columns, colonnes en faisceau. **clutch¹** [klʌtʃ], *s.* **I.** (*a*) Griffe *f* (d'un animal); serre *f* (d'un oiseau de proie). *F:* **To be in s.o.'s clutches,** être dans les griffes de qn. **To fall into s.o.'s clutches,** tomber sous la patte de qn. **To escape from s.o.'s clutches,** se tirer des pattes de qn. (*b*) **To make a clutch at sth.,** tâcher de saisir qch. **2.** *Mec.E:* (Manchon *m* d')embrayage *m. Aut:* Single-plate c., embrayage à plateau, par disque unique. *Multiple-disc c.,* embrayage à disques. **To let in the clutch,** embrayer. *To disengage, put out, the c.,* débrayer. **'clutch-**

stop, s. *Aut:* Frein *m* de débrayage, d'embrayage. **clutch²,** *v.tr.* & *ind.tr.* Saisir, empoigner, étreindre. *To c. sth. with both hands,* saisir qch. à deux mains. **To clutch at sth.,** to clutch hold of sth., se raccrocher, s'agripper, à qch. *F:* To clutch at every straw, se raccrocher à tout. *To c. at shadows,* essayer de saisir des ombres. **clutch³,** s. Couvée *f* (d'œufs). **clutter¹** ['klʌtər], s. Encombrement *m*, mélimélo *m*, confusion *f*. **clutter².** **1.** *v.i.* = CLATTER². **2.** *v.tr.* To clutter up a room, encombrer une chambre (*with,* de). **coach¹** [koutʃ], s. **1.** *A:* Carrosse *m* ou coche *m*. Coach and six, carrosse à six chevaux. *F:* To drive a coach and four through an Act of Parliament, passer outre à la loi. *You could drive a c. and four through his story,* son histoire ne tient pas debout. **2.** *Rail:* Voiture *f*, wagon *m*. **3.** (*a*) *Sch:* Professeur *m* qui donne des leçons particulières (pour préparer à un examen); répétiteur *m*. *My mathematical c.,* mon répétiteur de mathématiques. (*b*) *Sp:* Entraîneur *m*. **'coach-builder,** s. Carrossier *m*. **'coach-building,** s. Carrosserie *f*. **'coach-built,** *a. Aut:* (Voiture) carrossée. **'coach-horse,** s. **1.** Cheval *m* de carrosse. **2.** *Ent:* Devil's coach-horse, staphylin *m*. **'coach-house,** s. Remise *f*. **'coach-screw,** s. Tire-fond *m inv* (de carrosserie). **'coach-work,** s. Carrosserie *f*. **coach²,** *v.tr.* (*a*) *Sch:* Donner des leçons particulières à (qn); *F:* chauffer (qn). *F:* To coach s.o. up, faire la leçon à qn. *Th:* To c. s.o. in a part, faire répéter son rôle à qn. (*b*) *Sp:* Entraîner (une équipe) **coaching,** s. **1.** The old coaching days, le temps où l'on voyageait en diligence. **2.** (*a*) *Sch:* Répétitions *fpl.* To give private coaching, donner des répétitions. (*b*) *Sp:* Entraînement *m* (de l'équipe). **coachman,** *pl.* -men ['koutʃmən, -men], s.m. Cocher. **coagulable** [ko'agjuləbl], *a.* Coagulable. **coagulant** [ko'agjulənt], s. Coagulant *m*. **coagulate** [ko'agjuleit]. **1.** *v.tr.* Coaguler, figer; cailler (le lait). **2.** *v.i.* Se coaguler se figer: (*of milk*) se cailler. **coagulation** [koagju'leiʃ(ə)n], s. Coagulation *f*, figement *m*. **coal¹** [koul], s. (*a*) Charbon *m* (de terre); houille *f*. *C. industry,* industrie houillère. (*b*) Morceau *m* de charbon. Live coals, braise *f*; charbons ardents. *F:* To carry coals to Newcastle, porter de l'eau à la rivière, à la mer. To heap coals of fire on s.o.'s head, amasser des charbons ardents sur la tête de qn. To haul s.o. over the coals, réprimander, semoncer, qn. **'coal-barge,** s. Chaland *m* à charbon. **'coal-bearing,** *a* Carbonifère; houiller,-ère. **'coal-bed,** s Couche *f*. banc *m*, de houille. **'coal-black,** *a.* Noir comme du charbon. **'coal-cellar,** s. Cave *f* au charbon. **'coal-field,** s. *Min:* Bassin houiller. **'coal-gas,** s. Gaz *m* de houille; gaz d'éclairage. **'coal-heaver,** s. Porteur *m*, coltineur *m*, de charbon; (*from ship*) déchargeur *m*. **'coal-hole,** s Cave *f* ou réduit *m* à charbon **'coal-merchant,** s. **1.** Négociant *m* en charbon. **2.** Marchand *m* de charbon; charbonnier *m*. **'coal-mine,** s. Mine *f* de houille; houillère *f*. **'coal-miner,** s. (Ouvrier) mineur *m*, houilleur *m*. **'coal-mining,** s. Exploitation *f* de la houille; charbonnage *m*. **'coal-owner,** s. Propriétaire *m* de mines de charbon. **'coal-pit,** s. = COAL-MINE. **'coal-scuttle,** s. Seau *m* à charbon. **'coal-seam,** s. = COAL-BED. **'coal-shovel,**

'coal-scoop, s. Pelle *f* à charbon. **'coal-tar,** s. Goudron *m* de houille. **coal²,** *v.tr.* Approvisionner (un navire) de charbon. To coal ship, abs. to coal, faire le charbon. **coaling,** s. *Nau:* Charbonnage *m*. **coalesce** [koə'les], *v.i.* **1.** (*a*) S'unir; se fondre (ensemble). (*b*) *Ch:* Se combiner. **2.** (*Of parties,* etc.) Fusionner. **coalescing,** s. **1.** Union *f*, coalescence *f*. **2.** Fusion *f*, fusionnement *m* (de partis). **coalescence** [koə'lesəns], s. (*a*) Coalescence *f*, fusion *f*. (*b*) *Ch:* Combinaison *f*. **coalite** ['koulait], s. Semi-coke *m*; coalite *f*. **coalition** [koə'liʃ(ə)n], s. Coalition *f*. *Pol:* The left wing coalition, le cartel, le bloc, des Gauches. **coalman,** *pl.* -men ['koulmən, -men], s.m. Charbonnier. **coaming** ['koumiŋ], s. *Nau:* Hiloire *f*. **coarse** [kɔːrs], *a.* **1.** Grossier, vulgaire. *C. laugh,* rire brutal; gros rire. *C. voice,* voix commune. *C. words,* mots grossiers; grossièretés *f*. **2.** (*a*) (*Of material*) Gros, grossier, rude. *To have a c. skin,* avoir la peau rude. (*b*) (*Of food*) Grossier. **-ly,** *adv.* Grossièrement. **'coarse-'cut,** *a.* (Tabac) haché gros. **'coarse-fibred, -grained,** *a.* A gros grain(s); à grain grossier; (*of wood*) à gros fil. **coarsen** ['kɔːrsən]. **1.** *v.tr.* Rendre plus grossier, plus rude. **2.** *v.i.* Devenir plus grossier; (*of features*) s'épaissir. **coarseness** ['kɔːrsnəs], s. **1.** Grossièreté *f*, brutalité *f* (des manières, etc.). **2.** Rudesse *f* (de la peau); grosseur *f* de fil (d'une étoffe); gros grain (de la pierre, du bois). **coast¹** [koust], s. **1.** (*Of pers. or ship*) Côte *f*, rivage *m*; (*flat*) plage *f*; (*extensive*) littoral *m*. **2.** Descente *f* (en toboggan); *Cy:* descente en roue libre. **'coast-guard,** s. Garde-côte *m*, *pl.* gardes-côte. **coast²,** *v.i.* & *tr.* **1.** *Nau:* (*a*) To coast (along), suivre la côte; côtoyer le rivage. (*b*) *Com:* Caboter. **2.** To coast (down a hill), descendre en toboggan; *Cy:* descendre en roue libre; *Aut:* descendre (une côte) le moteur débrayé. **coasting,** s. **1.** (*a*) Navigation côtière. (*b*) Cabotage *m*. Coasting vessel, caboteur *m*. **2.** (*a*) *Cy:* *Aut:* Descente *f* de côte en roue libre. (*b*) *Aut:* Marche *f* au débrayé. **coaster** ['koustər], s. **1.** (*Of pers. or ship*) Caboteur *m*. **2.** Dessous *m* de bouteille, de carafe **coastline** ['koustlain], s. Littoral *m*. **coastwise** ['koustwaiz]. **1.** *adv.* Le long de la côte. **2.** *a.* Côtier. Coastwise trade, commerce caboteur. **coat¹** [kout], s. **1.** (*a*) (*For men*) Habit *m*. Dress coat, habit (à queue); frac *m*. Morning-coat, jaquette *f*. (Over)coat, (top-)coat, pardessus *m*. *Archeol:* Coat of mail, cotte *f* de mailles. *Prov:* It is not the coat that makes the man, l'habit ne fait pas le moine. *F:* To cut one's coat according to one's cloth, subordonner ses dépenses à son revenu. (*b*) (*For women*) (*short*) Jaquette *f*; (*long*) manteau *m*. Coat and skirt, costume *m* tailleur; *F:* tailleur *m*. (*c*) *A:* Casaque *f* (de livrée). *F:* To turn one's coat, tourner casaque. (*d*) *Her:* Coat armour, cotte d'armes, armes *fpl*, armoiries *fpl*, écusson *m*. **2.** (*a*) Robe *f* (d'un chien, d'un cheval). (*b*) *C. of snow,* manteau *m* de neige. **3.** (*a*) Couche *f*, application *f* (de peinture); enduit *m* (de goudron). Ground coat, première couche; couche d'impression Final coat, couche de teinte, de finition. (*b*) *Anat:* Paroi *f* (de l'estomac, du crane). **'coathanger,** s. Cintre *m*; porte-vêtements *m inv*. **'coat-hook, -peg,** s. Patère *f*.

coat², *v.tr.* Enduire (*sth. with paint, tar, etc.*, qch. de peinture, de goudron, etc.). *El.E:* To c. *a cable*, revêtir, couvrir, armer, un câble (*with,* de). **coated**, *a.* Enduit, couvert, recouvert, enrobé (*with,* de). Coated tongue, langue chargée, pâteuse. Coated paper, papier couché. **coating**, *s.* **1.** Enduisage *m.* **2.** Enduit *m,* revêtement *m,* couche *f* (de peinture, etc.). *Anat:* Paroi *f* (de l'estomac). *Const:* Rough coating (*of plaster*), crépi *m.* **3.** *Com:* Étoffe *f* pour habits.

coax [kouks], *v.tr.* Cajoler, enjôler, câliner. To coax s.o. into a cooked hat, (i) battre qn à plates coatures; (ii) abasourdir qn. **3.** To cook a gun, armer le chien.

cock⁴, *s. Agr:* Meulon *m,* meule *f* (de foin).

cockade [kɔ'keid], *s.* Cocarde *f.*

cockatoo [kɔka'tu:], *s. Orn:* Cacatoès *m,* cacatois *m.*

cockatrice ['kɔkatrais], *s. Myth:* Basilic *m.*

cockchafer ['kɔkt∫eifər], *s. Ent:* Hanneton *m.*

Cocker ['kɔkər]. *Pr.n. F:* According to Cocker, conforme à la règle; réglementaire.

cockerel ['kɔkərəl], *s.* Jeune coq.

cock-eyed ['kɔkaid], *a. F:* **1.** Qui louche. **2.** De biais, de travers.

cockiness ['kɔkinəs], *s.* Toupet *m,* suffisance *f.*

cockle¹ [kɔkl], *s.* **1.** *Bot:* (Corn-)cockle, nielle *f* des champs, des blés. **2.** *Agr:* (*Disease*) Nielle.

cockle², *s* (*a*) *Moll:* Bucarde *f,* clovisse *f.* (*b*) *Hist:* Coquille *f* de pèlerin. (*c*) *A:* Cockles of the heart, le cœur. *S.a.* WARM³ **1.** 'cockle-shell, *s.* **1.** Bucarde *f,* coque *f.* **2.** *F:* (*Boat*) Coquille *f* de noix.

cockle³. **1.** *v.tr.* (Re)coquiller (une feuille de papier); faire goder (une étoffe). **2.** *v.i.* Se recroqueviller; (*of paper*) (se) gondoler; se crisper; (*of tissue*) goder, coquiller. **cockling,** *s.* Gondolement *m,* gondolage *m.*

cockney ['kɔkni], *a. & s.* Londonien, -ienne. *C. accent,* accent faubourien (de Londres).

cockpit ['kɔkpit], *s.* **1.** Arène *f,* parc *m,* de combats de coqs. **2.** *Navy: A:* Poste *m* des blessés. **3.** *Av:* Carlingue *f;* poste *m* du pilote; cockpit *m.*

cockroach ['kɔkrout∫], *s. Ent:* Blatte *f; F:* cafard *m.*

cockscomb ['kɔkskoum], *s.* **1.** Crête *f* de coq. **2.** *Bot:* Célosie *f* à crête(s); crête-de-coq *f.*

cockspur ['kɔkspəːr], *s.* Ergot *m* de coq.

cocktail ['kɔkteil], *s.* (*Drink*) Cocktail *m.*

cocky ['kɔki], *a. F:* Suffisant, outrecuidant. **-ily,** *adv.* Effrontément; avec suffisance.

coco(a¹) ['koukou], *s.* **1.** Coco(a)-nut, (i) (noix *f* de) coco *m;* (ii) *P:* tête *f,* caboche *f.* Coco(a)-nut milk, eau *f,* lait *m,* de coco. Coco(a)-nut fibre, fibre *f* de coco; coir *m.* Coco(a)-nut shy, jeu *m* de massacre. **2.** Coco(a)-nut palm, cocotier *m.*

cocoa², *s.* **1.** Cacao *m.* **2.** Cocoa-tree, cacaotier *m,* cacaoyer *m.* 'cocoa-bean, *s.* Graine *f,* fève *f,* de cacao. 'cocoa-nib, *s.* Graine *f* de cacao décortiquée.

cocoon [kɔ'ku:n], *s.* Cocon *m* (de ver à soie, etc.).

cocoonery [kɔ'ku:nəri], *s.* Magnanerie *f.*

cod¹ [kɔd], *s.* (*Cod-fish*), morue *f.* Dried cod, morue sèche; merluche *f.* 'cod-bank, *s. Fish:* Banc *m* de morues. 'cod-fisher, *s.* Morutier *m,* moruyer *m.* 'cod-fishing, *s.* Pêche *f* de la morue. 'cod-liver-'oil, *s. Pharm:* Huile *f* de foie de morue.

cod², *v.tr. & i.* (codded) *P:* Tromper; mettre (qn) dedans.

coddle [kɔdl], *v.tr.* Gâter, choyer; élever (qn) dans le coton, dans la ouate. To coddle oneself, s'écouter; se dorloter.

code¹ [koud], *s.* **1.** Code *m. The highway c.,* le code de la route. **2.** (*a*) *Tg: etc:* Telegraphic code, code télégraphique. Code word, mot convenu. Code letter, indicatif littéral. (*b*) (*Secret*) Chiffre *m.* To write a dispatch in code, chiffrer une dépêche.

code², *v.tr.* **1.** Codifier (une dépêche). **2.** Mettre en chiffre, chiffrer (une dépêche).

---

coat², *v.tr.* Enduire (*sth. with paint, tar, etc.*, qch. de peinture, de goudron, etc.). *El.E:* To c. *a cable*, revêtir, couvrir, armer, un câble (*with,* de). **coated**, *a.* Enduit, couvert, recouvert...

l'oreille: (ii) relever, retrousser, son chapeau. **Cooked hat,** (i) chapeau à cornes; (*two-pointed*) bicorne *m;* (*three-pointed*) tricorne *m. F:* To knock s.o. into a cooked hat...

coax s.o. into sth., faire faire qch. à qn à force de cajoleries. To coax sth. out of s.o., obtenir qch. de qn en le cajolant. **coaxing¹,** *a.* Câlin, cajoleur. **-ly,** *adv.* D'un ton cajoleur. **coaxing²,** *s.* Cajolerie *f,* enjôlement *m.*

coaxer ['kouksər], *s.* Cajoleur, -euse; enjôleur, -euse; câlin, -e.

cob¹ [kɔb], *s.* **1.** (*Horse*) Cob *m,* bidet *m.* **2.** Cob (-swan), cygne *m* mâle. **3.** Cob(-nut), grosse noisette. **4.** (Corn-)cob, épi *m* de maïs. **5.** Cob(-coal), cobs, gaillette *f,* gailletin *m.*

cob², *s. Const:* Pisé *m,* torchis *m.*

cobalt ['koubɔlt], *s. Ch:* Cobalt *m.* Cobalt blue, cobalt d'outremer; bleu de cobalt.

cobble¹ [kɔbl], *s.* **1.** Cobble(-stone), galet *m,* caillou *m* (de chaussée). **2.** *pl.* (Charbon *m* en) gaillette(s) *f(pl).*

cobble², *v.tr.* Paver en cailloutis.

cobble³, *v.tr.* Carreler (des souliers).

cobbler ['kɔblər], *s.* Cordonnier *m* (qui fait les raccommodages); savetier *m.* 'cobbler's 'wax, *s.* Poix *f* de cordonnier.

coble [koubl], *s.* Barque *f* de pêche à fond plat.

cobra ['koubrə], *s. Rept:* Cobra *m;* serpent *m* à lunettes.

cobweb ['kɔbweb], *s.* **1.** Toile *f* d'araignée. *F:* To blow away the cobwebs, prendre l'air; se rafraîchir les idées. **2.** Fil *m* d'araignée.

cocaine [ko'kein], *s. Pharm:* Cocaïne *f.* Cocaine-addict, cocaïnomane *mf.*

Cochin-China [kɔt∫in't∫ainə]. *Pr.n. Geog:* La Cochinchine.

cochineal ['kɔt∫ini:l], *s. Dy: Ent:* Cochenille *f. Bot:* Cochineal-fig, -cactus, cochenillier *m,* nopal *m.*

cock¹ [kɔk], *s.* **1.** (*a*) Coq *m. F:* As bold as a cock on his own dunghill, hardi comme un coq sur son fumier. The cock of the walk, of the roost, le coq du village, de la paroisse. Old cock! mon vieux! ma vieille branche! Cock-and-bull story, histoire de pure invention. (*b*) Cock-bird, oiseau *m* mâle. Cock lobster, homard *m* mâle. **2.** (*a*) Robinet *m.* 'Nau: Sea-cock, robinet de prise d'eau à la mer. (*b*) *Sm.a:* Chien *m* (de fusil). At full cock, au cran d'armé. *S.a.* HALF-COCK. 'cock-a-doodle-'doo! Cocorico! 'cock-a-'hoop, *a. & adv.* (En) jubilant; triomphant, exultant. 'cock-crow, *s.* At cock-crow, au (premier) chant du coq; à l'aube. 'cock-fight, *s.* Combat *m* de coqs. **cock-'sure,** *a.* Sûr de soi; outrecuidant. To be c.-s. of, about, sth., n'avoir aucun doute sur qch. **cock-'sureness,** *s.* Outrecuidance *f.*

cock², *s.* **1.** Cock of the eye, œillade *f;* clignement *m* d'œil. **2.** Retroussis *m. To give one's hat a saucy c.,* retrousser crânement son chapeau.

cock³, *v.tr* **1.** (*a*) To cock one's eye at s.o., lancer une œillade à qn; regarder qn de côté. (*b*) (*Of horse*) To cock its ears, dresser les oreilles. To cock one's little finger, (i) dresser le petit doigt; (ii) *F:* lever le coude. **2.** To cock one's hat, (i) mettre son chapeau de travers, sur

codex, *pl.* **-ices** ['koudeks, -isi:z], *s.* **1.** Manuscrit (ancien). **2.** *Pharm:* Codex *m.*
codger ['kɔdʒər], *s.* *F:* Old codger, vieux bonhomme. *Funny old c.*, drôle de type.
codicil ['kɔdisil], *s.* Codicille *m* (d'un testament).
codification [koudifi'keiʃ(ə)n], *s.* Codification *f.*
codify ['koudifai], *v.tr.* Codifier.
co-director [koudi'rektər, -dai'rektər], *s.* Codirecteur *m*; co-administrateur *m.*
codlin(g) ['kɔdlin, -iŋ], *s.* Pomme *f* à cuire.
co-education [koedju'keiʃ(ə)n], *s.* Coéducation *f.*
coefficient [koe'fiʃənt], *s.* Coefficient *m.* *Mec.E:* Coefficient of safety, facteur *m* de sûreté, de sécurité.
cœlenterata [si:lentə'reita], *s.pl.* *Z:* Cœlentérés *m.*
coequal [ko'i:kwəl], *a. & s.* Égal, -aux.
coerce [ko'ə:rs], *v.tr.* Fcrcer, contraindre (*s.o. into doing sth.*, qn à faire qch.).
coercible [ko'ə:rsibl], *a.* **1.** (*Of pers.*) Contraignable. **2.** (*Of gas*) Coercible.
coercion [ko'ə:rʃ(ə)n], *s.* Coercition *f*, contrainte *f.* To act under coercion, agir par contrainte ; agir à son corps défendant.
coercive [ko'ə:rsiv], *a.* Coercitif ; *Jur:* coactif. **-ly**, *adv.* Par la force, par contrainte.
coeval [ko'i:v(ə)l], *a. C. with sth.*, contemporain de qch. ; de l'âge de qch.
coexist [koueg'zist], *v.i.* Coexister (*with*, avec).
coexistence [koueg'zistəns], *s.* Coexistence *f.*
coexistent [koueg'zistənt], *a.* Coexistant (avec).
coffee ['kɔfi], *s.* Café *m.* Black coffee, café noir ; café nature. *F:* White coffee, café au lait ou café crème. **'coffee-bean**, *s.* Grain *m* de café. **'coffee-coloured**, *a.* (Couleur) café au lait *inv.* **'coffee-cup**, *s.* Tasse *f* à café. **'coffee-grounds**, *s.pl.* Marc *m* de café. **'coffee-house**, *s. A:* Café *m.* **'coffee-mill**, *s.* Moulin *m* à café. **'coffee-pot**, *s.* Cafetière *f.* **'coffee-room**, *s.* Salle *f* des voyageurs, salle à manger (d'hôtel). **'coffee-stall**, *s.* Bar *m*, cantine *f*, de coin de rue (sur roulettes).
coffer ['kɔfər], *s.* **1.** Coffre *m.* *The coffers of State*, les fonds publics. **2.** *Arch:* Caisson *m* (de plafond).
cofferdam ['kɔfərdam], *s.* *Hyd.E:* Bâtardeau *m*; caisson *m* hydraulique.
coffin ['kɔfin], *s.* **1.** Cercueil *m*, bière *f.* **2.** *Farr:* Cavité *f* du sabot (d'un cheval). **'coffin-bone**, *s.* *Farr:* Phalangette *f.*
coffin², *v.tr.* Mettre (qn) en bière.
cog¹ [kɔg], *s.* *Mec.E:* Dent *f* (d'une roue dentée). *F:* I am only a cog in the machinery, je ne suis qu'un rouage de la machine. *To slip a cog*, (i) (*of pawl*) glisser sur une dent ; (ii) *F:* (*of the mind*) avoir un moment d'absence. **'cog-rail**, *s.* *Rail:* Crémaillère *f.* **'cog-wheel**, *s.* *Mec.E:* Roue dentée.
cog², *v.* (cogged) **1.** *v.tr.* Denter, endenter (une roue). **2.** *v.i.* (*Of wheels*) S'engrener.
cog³, *v.tr.* Piper (des dés). Cogged dice, dés pipés.
cogency ['koudʒənsi], *s.* Force *f*, puissance *f* (d'un argument).
cogent ['koudʒənt], *a.* (Argument) irrésistible ; (motif) puissant ; (raison) valable. **-ly**, *adv.* Avec force ; fortement.
cogitate ['kɔdʒiteit], **1.** *v.i.* Méditer, réfléchir (*upon, over*, sur). **2.** *v.tr.* To c. mischief, méditer un mauvais coup.
cogitation [kɔdʒi'teiʃ(ə)n], *s.* Réflexion *f*, délibération *f* (*upon, over*, sur).
cognate ['kɔgneit], **1.** *s.* *Jur:* Cognat *m* ; parent *m.* **2.** *a. C.* (*with sth.*), qui a du rapport (avec

qch.) ; analogue (à qch.). *C. words*, mots congénères, apparentés.
cognizance ['kɔgnizəns, *Jur:* 'kɔnizəns], *s.* **1.** Connaissance *f.* *Jur:* To take cognizance of sth.*, prendre connaissance de qch. **2.** *Jur:* Compétence *f.* Within the cognizance of a court, du ressort d'une cour.
cognizant ['kɔgnizənt, *Jur:* 'kɔnizənt], *a.* To be c. of a fact, être instruit d'un fait.
cognomen [kɔg'noumen], *s.* **1.** *Rom.Hist:* Cognomen *m.* **2.** (*a*) Surnom *m*, sobriquet *m.* (*b*) Nom *m* de famille.
cohabit [ko'habit], *v.i.* (cohabited) Cohabiter.
cohabitation [kohabi'teiʃ(ə)n], *s.* Cohabitation *f.*
coheir, *f.* **-ess** [ko'ɛər, -es], *s.* Cohéritier, -ière.
cohere [ko'hiːər], *v.i.* (*a*) (*Of whole, of parts*) Se tenir ensemble ; adhérer. (*b*) S'agglomérer. (*c*) (*Of argument*) Être conséquent ; se tenir.
coherence, -ency [ko'hiːərəns, -ənsi], *s.* **1.** = COHESION. **2.** (*Of argument, style*) Suite *f* (logique) ; cohérence *f.*
coherent [ko'hiːərənt], *a.* **1.** Cohérent(s) ; lié(s) ensemble. **2.** (*Of argument, etc.*) Conséquent, cohérent ; (*of thinker*) qui a de la suite dans ses idées. **-ly**, *adv.* (Parler) avec cohérence.
cohesion [ko'hiːʒ(ə)n], *s.* (*a*) Cohésion *f* ; adhérence *f.* (*b*) *Attack that lacks c.*, attaque qui manque d'ensemble.
cohesive [ko'hiːsiv], *a.* Cohésif.
cohort ['kouhɔːrt], *s.* Cohorte *f.*
coif [kɔif], *s.* (*a*) *A:* Coiffe *f*, béguin *m.* (*b*) Cornette *f* (de nonne).
coign [kɔin], *s.* Coign of vantage, position avantageuse.
coil¹ [kɔil], *s.* **1.** (*a*) Rouleau *m* (de corde) ; *Nau:* glène *f* (de câble). *Coils of hair*, torsades *f* de cheveux. (*b*) (Coiled tube) Serpentin *m.* **2.** (*a*) Pli *m*, repli *m* (d'un cordage) ; repli, anneau *m* (d'un serpent). (*b*) *Coils of smoke*, tourbillons *m* de fumée. **3.** *El:* Enroulement *m*, bobine *f.* Coil winding, solénoïde *m.*
coil². **1.** *v.tr.* (En)rouler, gléner (un cordage). *El:* Bobiner (des fils). To coil (itself) up, (*of snake*) s'enrouler, se lover ; (*of cat*) se mettre en rond. Coiled spring, ressort en spirale ; ressort à boudin. **2.** *v.i.* Serpenter. **coiling**, *s.* Enroulement *m* ; bobinage *m.*
coil³, *s. A:* Tumulte *m.* *F:* To shuffle off this mortal coil, s'échapper du tumulte de ce monde.
coin¹ [kɔin], *s.* **1.** Pièce *f* de monnaie. **2.** *Coll:* Monnaie(s) *f*, numéraire *m*, espèces *fpl.* Small c., monnaie divisionnaire. *F:* To pay in coin of the realm, payer en espèces. *S.a.* PAY BACK 2.
coin², *v.tr.* **1.** *To c. money*, (i) frapper de la monnaie, battre monnaie ; (ii) faire des affaires d'or. **2.** Inventer (un mot nouveau).
coinage ['kɔinedʒ], *s.* **1.** (*a*) Monnayage *m* ; frappe *f* (de la monnaie). (*b*) Invention *f* (d'un mot). **2.** (*a*) Système *m* monétaire (d'un pays). (*b*) Monnaie(s) *f* ; numéraire *m.*
coincide [kouin'said], *v.i.* **1.** Coïncider (*with*, avec). **2.** S'accorder, être d'accord (with, avec).
coincidence [kou'insidəns], *s.* **1.** (*In space, time*) Coïncidence *f.* **2.** Coïncidence, rencontre *f*, concours *m* (d'événements).
coincident [kou'insidənt], *a.* Coïncident ; d'accord (with, avec).
coiner ['kɔinər], *s.* **1.** Monnayeur *m.* **2.** Faux monnayeur *m.* **3.** *F:* Fabricateur *m*, inventeur *m* (d'un mensonge, etc.).
coir [kɔiər], *s.* Coir *m* ; fibre *f* de coco ; bastin *m.* *C. mat*, paillasson *m* ; tapis-brosse *m.*
coke [kouk], *s.* Coke *m.*
cokernut ['koukərnʌt], *s.* *P:* = cocoa-nut.

col [kɔl], s. *Geog:* Col *m*, ensellement *m*.

colander ['kʌləndər], s. *Cu:* Passoire *f*.

colchicum ['kɔlkikəm], s. *Bot:* Colchique *m*.

cold[1] [kould], a. Froid. **I.** (a) **It is cold**, il fait froid. **To get, grow, cold**, se refroidir. **Cold steel**, l'arme blanche. *Soluble when c.*, soluble à froid. *Com:* **Cold storage**, conservation par le froid. **Cold room** (*for storage*), chambre frigorifique. **Cold store**, entrepôt frigorifique. **Cold meat**, (i) viande froide; (ii) viande frigorifiée. *F:* **Cold pig**, douche d'eau froide (jetée sur qn qui dort, pour l'éveiller). **To be cold**, to feel cold, avoir froid. *My feet are as cold as ice*, j'ai les pieds glacés. **2.** A **cold reception**, un accueil froid. *To be c. with s.o.*, se montrer froid avec qn. *F: That leaves me cold*, cela ne me fait ni chaud ni froid. **3.** Cold-pressed, pressé à froid. **Cold rivetting**, rivure à froid. **-ly**, *adv.* Froidement. **'cold-blooded**, a. **I.** (Animal) à sang froid. **2.** (*Of pers.*) Froid, insensible; (*of action*) prémédité, délibéré. **cold-'chisel**, s. Ciseau *m* à froid. **'cold-'cream**, s. *Pharm:* Cold-cream *m*. **'cold-drawn**, a. *Metalw:* Étiré à froid. **'cold-hammer**, *v.tr.* Écrouir (le fer); battre, marteler, (le fer) à froid. **cold-'hearted**, a. Au cœur froid, sec. **cold-'shoulder**, *v.tr.* Battre froid à (qn); tourner le dos à (qn).

cold[2], s. **I.** Froid *m*. **'Cold wave**, vague de froid. *F:* **To leave s.o. out in the cold**, laisser qn à l'écart. **2.** *Med:* Rhume *m*. **To have a cold**, être enrhumé; avoir un rhume. **Cold in the head**, rhume de cerveau. **Cold on the chest**, chest cold, rhume de poitrine. **To catch** (a) **cold**, attraper un rhume; s'enrhumer; prendre froid. *F: You will catch your death of cold*, vous allez attraper la mort par ce froid.

coldness ['kouldnəs], s. **I.** Froideur *f*; froidure *f* (du climat). **2.** *There is a c. between them*, il y a de la froideur, du froid, entre eux.

coleopter [kɔli'ɔptər], s. *Ent:* Coléoptère *m*.

colic ['kɔlik], s. *Med:* Colique *f*, épreintes *fpl*. **Colic belt**, ceinture *f* de flanelle

Coliseum (the) [ðɔkɔli'si:əm], s. Le Colisée.

collaborate [kɔ'læboreit], *v.i.* Collaborer (*with*, avec).

collaboration [kɔlabo'reiʃ(ə)n], s. Collaboration *f*.

collaborator [kɔ'læboreitər], s. Collaborateur, -trice.

collapse[1] [kɔ'laps], s. **I.** (a) Écroulement *m*; effondrement *m*; dégonflement *m* (d'un ballon); débâcle *f* (d'un pays). (b) *Mec.E: etc:* Gauchissement *m*, flexion *f* (d'une plaque, etc.). (c) *Com:* Chute *f* (de prix); effondrement (du marché); dégringolade *f* (du franc). **2.** *Med:* Affaissement subit; prostration *f*.

collapse[2], *v.i.* **I.** (a) S'affaisser, s'écrouler, s'effondrer; (*of balloon*) se dégonfler; (*of pers.*) s'effondrer; tomber comme une masse. (b) *Mec.E: etc:* (*Of support, etc.*) Gauchir, fléchir. (c) (*Of car hood*) Se rabattre. (d) (*Of prices*) S'effondrer. **2.** *Med:* (*Of pers.*) S'affaisser (subitement).

collapsible [kɔ'lapsibl], a. (*Of chair, etc.*) Pliant, repliable, démontable; (*of handle, etc.*) rabattable.

collar[1] ['kɔlər], s. **I.** (a) Col *m* (de robe); collet *m* (de manteau); tour *m* de cou (en fourrure, etc.); collier *m* (d'un ordre, etc.). **Lace collar**, collerette *f*. (*Non-detachable*) *shirt c.*, col de chemise. **To seize s.o. by the collar**, prendre, saisir, qn au collet. (b) (**Detachable**) **collar**, faux

col. **Soft c.**, col mou, souple. **Stiff c.**, col raide, empesé. **Size in collars**, encolure *f*. **2.** Collier (de chien, de cheval). *F:* **I am once more in collar**, j'ai repris le collier. **3.** *Mec.E:* Anneau *m*; collier, collet. **Set collar**, bague *f* d'arrêt, de butée. **'collar-bone**, s. Clavicule *f*.

collar[2], *v.tr.* **I.** (a) Colleter (qn); saisir, prendre, (qn) au collet. (b) *Fb:* Arrêter (l'adversaire). **To collar s.o. low**, ceinturer qn. (c) *F:* Saisir, pincer, mettre la main sur (qn, qch.). **2.** *Cu:* Mettre (du poisson) en roulades.

collate [kɔ'leit], *v.tr.* Collationner, conférer (un texte) (*with*, avec).

collateral [kɔ'latərəl], a. **I.** Collatéral, -aux. **2.** (*Of knowledge*) Concomitant, additionnel. *Com:* **Collateral security**, garantie additionnelle, accessoire. **-ally**, *adv.* **I.** Parallèlement (*with*, à). **2.** Indirectement, subsidiairement.

collation [kɔ'leiʃ(ə)n], s. **I.** Collation *f*, confrontation *f* (de textes). **2.** *F:* Collation, goûter *m*. *Cold c.*, repas froid.

colleague ['kɔli:g], s. Collègue *mf*; confrère *m*.

collect[1] ['kɔlekt], s. *Ecc:* (*Prayer*) Collecte *f*.

collect[2] [kɔ'lekt]. **I.** *v.tr.* (a) Rassembler (la foule); assembler (des matériaux); relever (les blessés); amasser (une fortune); recueillir (des données). *To c. the letters*, lever les lettres; faire la levée des lettres. *Rail: To c. the luggage*, prendre les bagages à domicile. *Civ.E: To c. the water*, capter, réunir, les eaux. (b) Collectionner (des timbres, etc.). (c) Percevoir, lever (les impôts); toucher (une traite). **To collect a debt**, faire rentrer une créance; faire un recouvrement. *Abs.* **To collect for the poor**, quêter, faire la quête, pour les pauvres. **Collecting-box**, tronc *m* (d'église, de quêteur). (d) *F:* Aller chercher (sa valise, etc.). (e) *F:* Recueillir, rassembler (ses idées); ramasser (ses forces). *To c. oneself*, se reprendre. *To c. one's thoughts*, se recueillir. **2.** *v.i.* (*Of pers.*) S'assembler, se rassembler; (*of things*) s'amasser. **collected**, a. (a) Recueilli. (b) (Plein) de sang-froid. **-ly**, *adv.* (a) Avec recueillement. (b) Avec calme; avec sang-froid.

collection [kɔ'lekʃ(ə)n], s. **I.** Rassemblement *m*; relèvement *m* (des blessés); recouvrement *m* (d'une somme); perception *f* (des impôts); encaissement *m* (d'un billet); levée (des lettres); enlèvement *m*, prise *f* à domicile (de colis); captage *m* (d'eau, de courant électrique, etc.); collectionnement *m* (de tableaux, de livres). **2.** *Ecc: etc:* Quête *f*, collecte *f*. **To take up a collection**, faire la quête. **3.** Amas *m*, assemblage *m*. **4.** Collection *f* (de papillons, de timbres); recueil *m* (de proverbes).

collective [kɔ'lektiv], a. Collectif. **-ly**, *adv.* Collectivement; en commun.

collectivity [kɔlek'tiviti], s. Collectivité *f*.

collector [kɔ'lektər], s. **I.** (a) Encaisseur *m* (d'un chèque, d'un billet); quêteur, -euse (d'aumônes); collecteur, -trice (de cotisations). *Rail:* **Ticket-collector**, contrôleur *m*. (b) Encaisseur (de la Compagnie du gaz, etc.). *Adm:* Percepteur *m* (des contributions directes); receveur *m* (des contributions indirectes). (c) Collectionneur, -euse. *S.a.* STAMP-COLLECTOR. **2.** (*Device*) Collecteur (d'huile, etc.). *El.E:* **Current collector**, prise *f* de courant.

college ['kɔledʒ], s. **I.** Collège *m*. **2.** École *f* (militaire, navale). **3.** (*School*) Collège; école secondaire.

collegiate [kɔ'li:dʒiet], a. Collégial, -aux.

collet ['kɔlet], s. **I.** Douille *f* (de serrage). **2.** Chaton *m* (de bague); sertissure *f*.

collide ['kɔ'laid], *v.i.* (*Of vehicles, etc.*) Se rencontrer, se heurter; entrer en collision. *To c. with sth.*, heurter qch.; *Nau:* aborder (un navire).

collie ['kɔli], *s.* Chien de berger écossais.

collier ['kɔljər], *s.* **1.** (*Pers.*) Houilleur *m*; mineur *m* (de charbon). **2.** *Nau:* (Navire *m*) charbonnier *m*.

colliery ['kɔljəri], *s.* Houillère *f*; mine *f* de houille.

collimator ['kɔlimeitər], *s. Opt:* Collimateur *m*.

collision [kɔ'liʒ(ə)n], *s.* Collision *f*, rencontre *f*; tamponnement *m* (de trains); abordage *m* (de navires). **To come into collision with . . .,** entrer en collision avec (un train, etc.); se heurter à, contre (qn).

collocate ['kɔlokeit], *v.tr.* Arranger, disposer (des troupes, des faits).

collodion [kɔ'loudiən], *s.* Collodion *m*.

colloid ['kɔloid], *a. & s. Ch:* Colloïde (*m*).

colloidal [kɔ'loid(ə)l], *a. Ch:* Colloïdal, -aux.

collop ['kɔləp], *s.* Tranche *f* de viande. Minced collops, hachis *m*.

colloquial [kɔ'loukwiəl], *a.* Familier; de (la) conversation. **-ally,** *adv.* Familièrement.

colloquialism [kɔ'loukwiəlizm], *s.* Expression familière.

colloquy ['kɔlokwi], *s.* Colloque *m*, entretien *m*.

collotype ['kɔlotaip], *s.* **1.** Phototype *m*. **2.** (*Process*) Phototypie *f*; collotypie *f*.

collusion [kɔ'lju:ʒ(ə)n], *s.* Collusion *f*. *To act in c. with s.o.*, agir de complicité, de connivence, avec qn.

colon[1] ['koulən], *s. Anat:* Côlon *m*.

colon[2], *s.* Deux-points *m*.

colonel ['kə:n(ə)l], *s.* Colonel *m*.

colonelcy ['kə:nəlsi], **colonelship** ['kə:nəlʃip], *s.* Grade *m* de colonel.

colonial [kɔ'lounjəl], *a. & s.* Colonial, -aux.

colonist ['kɔlənist], *s.* Colon *m*.

colonization [kɔlənai'zei∫(ə)n], *s.* Colonisation *f*.

colonize ['kɔlənaːiz], *v.tr.* Coloniser.

colonizer ['kɔlənaizər], *s.* Colonisateur *m*.

colonnade [kɔlo'neid], *s.* Colonnade *f*.

colony ['kɔləni], *s.* Colonie *f*. *To live in the* **colonies,** vivre aux colonies.

colophon ['kɔlofən], *s. Typ:* Chiffre *m* (de l'éditeur); marque *f* typographique.

coloration [kʌlə'rei∫(ə)n], *s.* Coloration *f*; coloris *m*.

colossal [kɔ'lɔs(ə)l], *a.* Colossal, -aux; démesuré.

colossus, *pl.* **-i, -uses** [kɔ'lɔsəs, -ai, -əsiz], *s.* Colosse *m*.

colour[1] ['kʌlər], *s.* **1.** (*a*) Couleur *f*. *What c. is it?* de quelle couleur est-ce? *To take the c. out of sth.*, décolorer qch. **The colour problem,** le problème des races de couleur. **To see an affair in its true colours,** voir une affaire sous son vrai jour. *F:* Not to have seen the colour of s.o.'s money, ne pas avoir encore vu la couleur de l'argent de qn. (*b*) *Art: etc:* Coloris *m*. **2.** (*Material*) Matière colorante; pigment *m*. **Water colour,** couleur à l'eau, à l'aquarelle. **Oil colour,** couleur à l'huile. **3.** Teint *m*, couleurs. **To lose colour,** perdre ses couleurs; devenir pâle. **To change colour,** changer de visage. **High colour,** vivacité *f* de teint. *F:* **To be off colour,** être pâle; n'être pas dans son assiette. **4.** *Usu. pl.* Couleurs (d'un parti). *Nau:* Pavillon *m*. **To show, display, one's colours,** montrer son pavillon; montrer les couleurs. (**Regimental) colours,** drapeau *m*. **Colour party,** garde *f* du drapeau. *S.a.* TROOP[2] 2. **To call s.o. to the colours,** appeler qn sous les drapeaux. **To be with the colours,** être

sous les drapeaux. **With colours flying,** (à) enseignes déployées. *F:* **To pass (an examination) with flying colours,** passer haut la main. **To sail under false colours,** (i) naviguer sous un faux pavillon; (ii) *F:* se faire passer pour quelqu'un d'autre. *F:* **To stick to one's colours,** rester fidèle à ses principes. **To show oneself in one's true colours,** jeter le masque. **To nail one's colours to the mast,** clouer son pavillon. **5.** (*a*) To give, lend, colour to a story, rendre une histoire vraisemblable; *F:* colorer un récit. **To put a false colour on things,** mal voir les choses. *Jur:* To have colour of title to sth., avoir un titre coloré à qch. (*b*) Fausse apparence. **Under colour of law, of reason,** sous l'apparence de la légalité, du bon sens. **'colour-bearer,** *s. Mil:* Porte-drapeau *m inv.* **'colour-blind,** *a.* Daltonien. **'colour-blindness,** *s.* Daltonisme *m*. **'colour-box,** *s.* Boîte *f* de couleurs. **'colour-man,** *pl.* **-men,** *s.m.* Marchand de couleurs; droguiste. **'colour-print,** *s. F:* Chromo *m*. **'colour-sergeant,** *s. Mil:* = Sergent *m* fourrier, sergent chef.

colour[2]. **1.** *v.tr.* (*a*) Colorer; colorier (une carte); enluminer (une gravure). *To c. sth. blue,* colorer qch. en bleu. (*b*) Donner de l'éclat à (une description); imager (son style). (*c*) Présenter (un fait) sous un faux jour; déguiser (un mensonge). **2.** *v.i.* (*a*) (*Of thg*) Se colorer. (*b*) (*Of pers.*) Rougir. **coloured,** *a.* **1.** Coloré; (*of drawing*) colorié. *C. shirt,* chemise de couleur. *C. person,* personne de couleur. *C. sketch,* croquis en couleurs. **2.** *Highly c. narrative,* récit coloré.

colouring, *s.* **1.** Coloration *f*, coloriage *m* (de cartes, etc.). **2.** (*a*) *Art:* Coloris *m*. (*b*) Teint *m*. *People with high c.,* gens hauts en couleur. **3.** Apparence *f*. *To give a false c. to the facts,* dénaturer, travestir, les faits.

colourable ['kʌlərəbl], *a.* **1.** Plausible; (argument) spécieux. **2.** Trompeur. **Colourable imitation,** contrefaçon *f*.

colourful ['kʌlərful], *a.* (Ciel, style) coloré; (style) pittoresque.

colourless ['kʌlərləs], *a.* **1.** Sans couleur; incolore. **2.** (*a*) Terne; (visage) décoloré; (lumière) pâle, falote. (*b*) *C. style,* style incolore.

colporteur [kɔlpɔ:r'tə:r], *s.* Distributeur *m* de Bibles.

colt[1] [koult], *s.* **1.** Poulain *m*, pouliche *f*. **2.** *F:* Débutant *m*, novice *m*.

Colt[2]. *Pr.n. Sm.a: U.S:* **Colt revolver,** revolver Colt. **Colt pistol,** pistolet automatique.

coltish ['koultiʃ], *a.* **1.** Sans expérience. **2.** Folâtre.

coltsfoot ['koultsfut], *s. Bot:* Tussilage *m*.

columbine[1] ['kɔləmbain], *s. Bot:* Ancolie *f*.

Columbine[2]. *Pr.n.f. Th:* Colombine.

Columbus [kɔ'lʌmbəs]. *Pr.n.m.* **Christopher Columbus,** Christophe Colomb.

column ['kɔləm], *s.* **1.** Colonne *f*. *Anat:* **Spinal column,** colonne vertébrale. **2.** *Av:* **Control column,** levier de commande. *Aut:* **Steering column,** tube *m*, colonne, de direction. **3.** *Mil:* *C. of fours,* colonne par quatre. **4.** *Page of two columns,* page de deux colonnes. *Journ:* **The theatrical column,** le courrier, la rubrique, des théâtres.

colza ['kɔlza], *s. Bot:* Colza *m*.

coma[1] ['kouma], *s. Med:* Coma *m*.

coma[2], *pl.* **-ae** ['kouma, -iː], *s.* **1.** *Bot:* Barbe *f*, chevelure *f*. *Astr:* Chevelure (d'une comète). **3.** *Opt:* Aigrette *f*.

comatose ['koumatous], *a. Med:* (État) comateux; (sommeil) soporeux.

comb¹ [koum], *s.* **I.** Peigne *m.* *Large-tooth c.,* démêloir *m.* **Tooth-comb,** peigne fin. **2.** (*a*) *Tex:* Peigne, carde *f.* (*b*) *El:* Collecteur *m.* **3.** (*a*) Crête *f* (de coq). *F:* To cut s.o.'s comb, rabaisser la crête à qn ; rabattre le caquet à qn. (*b*) Crête (de colline, de vague). **4.** = HONEYCOMB¹.

comb², *s.* *F:* To give one's hair a comb, donner un coup de peigne à ses cheveux

comb³. **I.** *v.tr.* (*a*) Peigner (les cheveux). To comb down a horse, étriller un cheval. (*b*) *Tex:* Peigner, carder (la laine). **2.** *v.t.* (*Of wave*) Se briser en écumant ; déferler. **comb out,** *v.tr.* **I.** Démêler (les cheveux). **2.** *F:* (*a*) "Ratisser," "éplucher" (les services administratifs, etc.) pour appeler sous les drapeaux les embusqués. (*b*) (*Of police*) To c. out a district, faire une rafle (de suspects). (*c*) To c. out a department, éliminer les incapables, les non-valeurs, d'un service.

combing, *s.* **I.** (*a*) Coup *m* de peigne. (*b*) *Tex:* Peignage *m*, cardage *m.* **2.** *pl.* **Combings,** peignures *f*, démêlures *f.*

combat¹ ['kɔmbat, 'kʌm-], *s.* Combat *m.*

combat². **I.** *v.i.* (combated) Combattre (*with,* *against,* contre). **2.** *v.tr.* Lutter contre, combattre (une maladie).

combatant ['kɔmbatənt, 'kʌm-], *a. & s.* Combattant (*m*).

combative ['kɔmbativ, 'kʌm-], *a.* Combatif ; batailleur.

comber ['koumər], *s.* **I.** Peigneur, -euse ; cardeur, -euse (de laine). **2.** Longue lame déferlante.

combination [kɔmbi'neiʃ(ə)n], *s.* **I.** Combinaison *f.* (*a*) To enter into c. with . . ., se combiner avec. . . . (*b*) *Ch:* Combiné *m*, mélange *m.* **2.** Association *f* (de personnes) ; *Pej:* coalition *f.* **3.** *pl.* *Cost:* (A pair of) combinations, une combinaison-culotte (en laine).

combine¹ ['kɔmbain], *s.* Combinaison financière ; entente industrielle ; cartel *m.*

combine² [kɔm'bain]. **I.** *v.tr.* Combiner ; allier (des qualités, des mots, etc.) (*with,* à). To combine forces, one's efforts, joindre ses forces, ses efforts. To combine business with pleasure, joindre l'utile à l'agréable. **2.** *v.i.* (*a*) (*Of pers.*) S'unir, s'associer (*against,* contre) ; (*of workers*) se syndiquer. (*b*) (*Of parties*) Fusionner. (*c*) *Ch:* (*Of elements*) Se combiner. **combined,** *a.* C. efforts, efforts réunis, conjugués. C. work, travail fait en collaboration. *Mec.E:* Combined strength, résistance composée.

combustible [kɔm'bʌstibl]. **I.** *a.* (*a*) Combustible, comburable. (*b*) *F:* (*Of a crowd, etc.*) Inflammable. **2.** *s.* (*a*) Matière *f* inflammable. (*b*) (*Fuel*) Combustible *m.*

combustion [kɔm'bʌstʃ(ə)n], *s.* Combustion *f.* Spontaneous c., inflammation spontanée ; auto-allumage *m.* Internal combustion engine, moteur à explosion, à combustion interne. Slow-combustion stove, poêle à combustion continue.

come [kʌm], *v.i.* (*p.t.* came [keim] ; *p.p.* come) **I.** Venir, arriver. (*a*) To c. to a place, venir, arriver, à un endroit. He has just come from Paris, il arrive de Paris. *F:* Let 'em all come! qu'ils viennent tous ! ils seront tous les bienvenus. He comes this way every week, il passe par ici tous les huit jours. Here he comes! le voilà qui arrive ! Coming ! voilà ! on y va ! j'y vais ! Come to see me, *F:* come and see me, to-morrow, venez me voir, me trouver, demain. To come for s.o., for sth., venir chercher qn, qch. To come to s.o., venir trouver qn. *F:* You have come to the wrong person, vous vous adressez mal. To come to the throne, monter sur le trône. To come to years of discretion, arriver à l'âge de raison. *F:* What are things coming to? où allons-nous ? To come and go, aller et venir. To c. to the surface again, remonter sur l'eau. *int.* Come now! allons ! voyons ! Come, come! *a little silence!* allons, allons ! un peu de silence ! *Prov:* Easy come easy go; light come light go, ce qui vient par la flûte s'en va par le tambour (*b*) To come to oneself, (i) reprendre connaissance ; (ii) recouvrer sa raison ; (iii) revenir de ses erreurs ; se ressaisir. (*c*) *F:* A week come Tuesday, il y aura mardi huit jours. He will be ten come January, il aura dix ans au mois de janvier. **2.** (*Occur, happen*) (*a*) That comes on the next page, cela se trouve à la page suivante. Come what may, advienne que pourra. (*b*) How does the door come to be open? comment se fait-il que la porte soit ouverte ? Now that I come to think of it, maintenant que j'y songe. **3.** (*a*) What will come of it? qu'en adviendra-t-il? qu'en résultera-t-il? *That's what comes of doing* . . ., voilà ce qu'il en est de faire. . . . (*b*) To come of a good family, être, sortir, d'une bonne famille. **4.** (*a*) *The total comes to ten shillings,* la somme s'élève à dix shillings. How much does it come to? combien cela fait-il? *It comes to this, that* . . ., cela revient à ceci, que. . . . *S.a.* NOTHING II. **2.** (*b*) If it comes to that . . ., à ce compte-là. . . . It must come to that, il faudra bien en arriver là. What he knows does not come to much, ce qu'il sait ce n'est pas grand'chose. He will never c. to much, il ne sera, ne fera, jamais grand'chose. (*c*) That doesn't come within my duties, cela ne rentre pas dans mes fonctions. **5.** (*a*) That comes easy, natural, to him, cela lui est facile, naturel. To come expensive, cheap, coûter cher, revenir cher ; coûter peu. (*Of seam, etc.*) To come unstitched, se découdre. (*b*) You come first, vous venez en premier ; c'est vous le premier. You c. third, vous êtes le troisième. **6.** I have come to believe that . . ., j'en suis venu, j'en suis arrivé, à croire que. . . . *This plan came to be realized,* ce projet finit par se réaliser. I came to like him, il me devint sympathique. *When she came to know him,* quand elle vint à le connaître. **7.** The time to come, le temps à venir ; l'avenir *m.* The life to come, la vie future. *For three months to c.,* pendant trois mois encore. **8.** *F:* To come it strong, exagérer ; y aller fort. To come it over s.o., faire la loi à qn. To come the old soldier over s.o., la faire au vieux sergent ; chercher à en imposer à qn ; rudoyer qn. **come about,** *v.i.* **I.** Arriver, se passer, se produire, avoir lieu. **2.** (*a*) *Nau:* Virer de bord. (*b*) (*Of the wind*) Tourner. **come across,** *v.i.* (*a*) Traverser (la mer, les champs). (*b*) Trouver, rencontrer, (qn, qch.) sur son chemin ; tomber sur (qn). **come after,** *v.i.* **I.** (*Prep. use*) (*a*) Suivre (qn, qch.). (*b*) Succéder à (qn). **2.** (*Adv. use*) Suivre ; venir plus tard. **come again,** *v.i.* Revenir. *S.a.* CUT² **I.** **come against,** *v.i.* (*Prep. use*) Heurter, frapper (qch.). **come along,** *v.i.* **I.** Arriver, venir ; *P:* s'abouler. Come along! (i) amène-toi ! arrive ! (ii) allons-y ! allons-nous-en ! **2.** *F:* Survenir. **come apart, asunder,** *v.i.* (*a*) Se séparer, se défaire. (*b*) Se décoller. **come away,** *v.i.* **I.** Partir, s'en aller (d'un lieu) ; quitter (un lieu). **2.** Se détacher ; se décoller. **come back,** *v.i.* **I.** Revenir. *It's all coming back to me,* cela me revient à la mémoire. To come back to what I was saying . . ., pour en revenir à ce que je disais. . . . **2.** (*Of fashion etc.*) Revenir en vogue. **come before,** *v.i.*

1. *These cases c. before a conciliation court*, ces affaires ressortissent à la justice de paix. **2.** Précéder (qn, qch.). **3.** (*Of thg*) Primer (qch. en importance) ; (*of pers.*) prendre le pas sur (qn). **come between,** *v.i.* Intervenir, s'entremettre, s'interposer, entre (deux personnes). **come by,** *v.i.* **1.** (*a*) To come by the house, passer par la maison. (*b*) To come by money, obtenir de l'argent. *Honestly come by*, honnêtement acquis. **2.** *I heard him come by*, je l'ai entendu passer. **come down,** *v.i.* **1.** Descendre (l'échelle, l'escalier) ; faire la descente de (la montagne, etc.). **2.** (*a*) *To c. down to breakfast*, descendre déjeuner. *To c. down to s.o.'s level*, s'abaisser jusqu'au niveau (d'esprit) de qn. *F:* To come down (in the world), déchoir. *Prices are coming down*, les prix baissent, sont en baisse. *F:* To come down a peg, (i) en rabattre ; déchanter ; (ii) descendre d'un cran. (*b*) *F:* To come down upon s.o., (i) semoncer vertement qn ; (ii) blâmer sévèrement qn. (*c*) *F:* To come down handsomely, se montrer généreux ; *F:* se fendre. (*d*) (*Of rain, etc.*) Tomber. (*e*) *Her hair came down to her knees*, ses cheveux lui descendaient jusqu'aux genoux. (*f*) Venir (de nos aïeux). *All the tales that have come down to us*, tous les contes qui nous ont été transmis par la tradition. (*g*) (*Of pers., horse*) S'abattre ; (*of structure*) s'écrouler. (*h*) (*Of problem, etc.*) Se résumer. *The expenses c. down to board and lodging*, les dépenses se réduisent aux frais de pension. **come-'down,** *s. F:* Humiliation *f* ; déchéance *f*. **come forth,** *v.i.* Sortir, s'avancer. **come forward,** *v.i.* **1.** S'avancer. **2.** *To c. forward as a candidate*, se présenter comme candidat ; se porter candidat. **come in,** *v.i.* **1.** Entrer. *F:* That's just where the mistake comes in, voilà justement où est l'erreur. **2.** (*Of tide*) Monter ; (*of ship*) arriver ; (*of year*) commencer ; (*of fashion*) entrer en vogue. *As soon as oysters come in*, dès que les huîtres sont de saison. **3.** (*Of funds*) Rentrer. **4.** (*a*) To come in useful to s.o., for sth., servir à qn, à qch. (*b*) *Sp:* To come in first, second, arriver premier, second. **5.** To come in for sth., recevoir (une part des bénéfices, une semonce, etc.). *To c. in for a fortune*, succéder à une fortune. *F:* And where do I come in? et moi, qu'est-ce que j'y gagne ? **come into,** *v.i.* **1.** Entrer dans (une chambre). (*Of idea*) *To c. into s.o.'s mind*, se présenter à l'esprit de qn. **2.** To come into a property, entrer en possession d'un domaine. **come off,** *v.i.* **1.** (*Prep. use*) (*a*) Descendre de (la table, etc.). *To c. off one's horse*, tomber de (son) cheval. (*b*) To come off the gold standard, abandonner l'étalon or. **2.** (*Adv. use*) (*a*) (*Of button, etc.*) Se détacher, sauter ; (*of smell, etc.*) se dégager ; (*of stain, etc.*) s'enlever, s'en aller. *The colour came off on my dress*, la couleur a déteint sur ma robe. (*b*) (*Of ship aground*) Se déséchouer ; partir. (*c*) (*Of event*) Avoir lieu ; (*of attempt, etc.*) réussir, aboutir. *The marriage didn't c. off*, le mariage a manqué. (*d*) (*Of pers.*) To come off badly, s'en mal tirer. *He came off victorious*, il en sortit vainqueur. **come on,** *v.i.* (*a*) S'avancer. *Come on, boys!* (i) allons-y, les gars ! (ii) arrivez, mes enfants ! *Come on, let's have a game!* allons ! faisons une partie ! *Come on!* (i) en avant ! (ii) arrivez ! (iii) *P:* (*as a challenge*) viens-y donc ! (*b*) (*Of plants, children, etc.*) (Bien) venir ; se développer ; faire des progrès. (*c*) (*Of illness, etc.*) Survenir ; (*of winter, etc.*) venir, arriver ; (*of night*) tomber. *When the wind comes on to blow*, quand le vent se met à souffler. (*d*) (*Of question*) To come on

(*for discussion*), venir en discussion. (*Of lawsuit*) To come on for trial, venir devant la cour. *The case comes on to-morrow*, la cause sera entendue demain. (*e*) *Th:* (*Of actor*) Entrer en scène. **come out,** *v.i.* **1.** (*Prep. use*) To come out of a place, of a room, sortir d'un lieu, quitter une salle. **2.** (*Adv. use*) (*a*) Sortir. *Ind:* To come out (on strike), se mettre en grève. (*b*) Do come out to India, venez donc nous retrouver aux Indes ! (*c*) *Sch:* To c. out first, second, être reçu premier, second. (*d*) (*Of stars*) Paraître ; (*of buds*) éclore ; *Phot:* (*of image*) se développer, se révéler ; (*of rash, pimples*) sortir, se montrer ; (*of the truth*) se découvrir (*Of pers.*) To come out in a rash, (i) avoir une poussée de boutons ; (ii) avoir une poussée d'urticaire. (*e*) (i) *Art: etc:* (*Of details*) Ressortir ; se détacher (sur le fond). (ii) *Phot:* (*Of detail in negative*) Apparaître. (iii) *Phot: You have come out well (in the group)*, vous êtes très réussi. (*f*) (*Of stain*) S'enlever, s'effacer. (*g*) (*Of book*) Paraître. (*h*) (*Of problem*) Se résoudre. (*Of average, etc.*) To come out at . . ., être de . . ., être de l'ordre de . . ., se monter à. . . . . (*i*) (*Of pers.*) Débuter (au théâtre) ; débuter, faire son entrée dans le monde. (*j*) *F:* To come out with a remark, lâcher, laisser échapper, une observation. **coming out,** *s.* (*a*) Sortie *f* (du public) ; chute *f* (des cheveux). (*b*) Apparition *f* (du soleil, etc.) ; éclosion *f* (des fleurs). (*c*) Apparition, parution *f* (d'un livre). (*d*) Début *m* (au théâtre, dans le monde). **come over,** *v.i.* **1.** (*Prep. use*) (*a*) Traverser (la mer). (*b*) Envahir, gagner, saisir (qn). *What has come over you?* qu'est-ce qui vous prend ? **2.** (*Adv. use*) (*a*) *To c. over from a place*, arriver, venir, d'un lieu. (*b*) *To c. over to s.o.'s side*, passer du côté de qn. (*c*) *F:* To come over funny, queer, se sentir mal ; *F:* se sentir tout chose. **come round,** *v.i.* **1.** (*Prep. use*) (*a*) Entourer (qn). (*b*) Faire le tour de (qch.) ; contourner (qch.). **2.** (*Adv. use*) (*a*) Faire le tour, un détour. *Conversation that comes round to the same subjects again*, conversation qui retombe sur les mêmes sujets. (*b*) *F:* Come round and see me one day, venez me voir un de ces jours. (*c*) The time has come round, les temps sont révolus. (*d*) Reprendre connaissance ; revenir à soi. (*e*) *To c. round to s.o.'s way of thinking*, se ranger à l'avis de qn. **come through,** *v.i.* **1.** (*Prep. use*) (*a*) Passer par, à travers (le bois). *The rain has c. through his clothes*, la pluie a traversé, percé, ses vêtements. (*b*) *To c. through trials*, passer par des épreuves. *To c. through an illness*, surmonter une maladie. **2.** (*Adv. use*) (*a*) *The water, the rain, is coming through*, l'eau, la pluie, pénètre. (*b*) *He came through without a scratch*, il s'en est tiré indemne. **come to,** *v.i.* = COME ROUND 2 (*d*). **come together,** *v.i.* S'assembler, se réunir. **come under,** *v.i.* **1.** *To c. under s.o.'s influence*, être soumis à, tomber sous, subir, l'influence de qn. **2.** *To c. under a heading*, être compris sous un article. **come up,** *v.i.* **1.** (*Prep. use*) Monter (l'échelle, etc.). **2.** (*Adv. use*) (*a*) *Come up to my rooms*, montez chez moi. *To c. up out of the abyss*, surgir de l'abîme. *To c. up to the surface again*, remonter sur l'eau. (*b*) To come up to town, venir en ville. *To c. up (to the university)*, commencer ses études. (*c*) *To c. up to s.o.*, s'approcher de qn. *Ten: To c. up to the net*, monter au filet. *Jur:* To come up before the Court, comparaître (devant le tribunal). (*d*) (*Of plants*) Sortir de terre ; pousser. (*e*) To come up (for discussion), venir en discussion ; venir sur le tapis. *The case comes up for hearing to-*

morrow, l'affaire passera demain. (*f*) **To come up to sth.**, atteindre, s'élever, jusqu'à qch. *He does not c. up to my waist*, il ne me vient pas à la ceinture. **To come up to s.o's expectations,** répondre à l'attente de qn. (*g*) *As a violinist he doesn't c. up to X*, comme violoniste il n'égale pas X, il ne vaut pas X. (*h*) **To come up against sth.,** se heurter, se cogner, à, contre, qch. *To c. up against s.o.*, entrer en conflit avec qn. (*i*) **To come up with s.o.,** rattraper, rejoindre, qn. **come upon,** *v.i.* (*a*) Tomber, fondre, sur (qn). (*b*) **To come upon s.o. for a sum,** réclamer une somme à qn. (*c*) **To come upon the parish,** tomber à la charge de la paroisse. (*d*) **To come upon s.o.,** rencontrer qn par hasard. (*e*) (*Of idea*) **To come upon s.o.,** venir à l'esprit, à la mémoire, de qn. **come within,** *v.i.* Rentrer dans (les fonctions de qn); être couvert par (une définition). **coming**[1], *a.* **I.** *The c. year*, l'année qui vient, l'année prochaine. *The c. storm*, l'orage qui approche. *The c. generations*, les générations futures. **A coming man,** un homme d'avenir. **2.** *A. & Lit:* Accueillant. **coming**[2], *s.* Venue *f*, arrivée *f*; approche *f* (de la nuit, etc.); avènement *m* (du Messie). **Comings and goings,** allées et venues. **'come-and-go,** *s.* Va-et-vient *m*.

comedian [kɔ'mi:djən], *s.* (*a*) Comédien, -ienne. (*b*) Comique *m* (de music hall, etc.).

comedy ['kɔmedi], *s.* **I.** La comédie; le genre comique. **2.** (*Play*) Comédie.

comely ['kʌmli], *a.* (*Of pers.*) Avenant; (femme) fraîche et accorte.

comer ['kʌmər], *s.* **I.** Arrivant, -ante; venant, -ante. **Comers and goers,** allants *m* et venants *m*; entrants *m* et sortants *m*. **All comers,** tout le monde. **2. First comer,** premier venu.

comet ['kɔmet], *s.* Comète *f*.

comfit ['kʌmfit], *s.* Bonbon *m*.

comfort[1] ['kʌmfərt], *s.* **I.** Consolation *f*; motif *m* de consolation; soulagement *m*. **Be of good comfort!** prenez courage! *To take c.*, se consoler. *That is cold comfort*, c'est là une piètre consolation. *To be a great c. to s.o.*, être un grand sujet de consolation à qn. *F:* **A little drop of comfort,** une petite goutte de réconfort. **2.** Bien-être *m*. *I like c.*, j'aime mes aises. **3.** Confort *m*; confortable *m*; aisance *f*. (*At hotel, etc.*) **Every modern comfort,** tout le confort moderne. **To live in comfort,** vivre dans l'aisance, à l'aise. **4.** *pl. The comforts of life,* les commodités *f*, les agréments *m*, les douceurs *f*, de la vie.

comfort[2], *v.tr.* **I.** Consoler, soulager. **2.** (*a*) (*Of beverage*) Réconforter. (*b*) Redonner du courage à (qn). **comforting,** *a.* Réconfortant. *C. words,* paroles de consolation, de réconfort.

comfortable ['kʌmfərtəbl], *a.* **I.** (*a*) (*Of bed, etc.*) Confortable; (*of dress*) commode, aisé; (*of warmth*) agréable. *These shoes are c.*, on est à l'aise dans ces chaussures. **To make oneself comfortable,** se mettre à son aise. *To feel c.*, se trouver bien; se sentir à l'aise **It is so comfortable here,** on est si bien ici; il fait si bon ici. (*b*) (*Of patient*) **To be comfortable,** ne pas souffrir **2. Comfortable income,** revenu suffisant. *To make s.o. c. for the rest of his days,* assurer la vie de qn pour le restant de ses jours. **3.** Sans inquiétude; tranquille. *Make yourself c. about that,* tranquillisez-vous, rassurez-vous, là-dessus. **-ably,** *adv.* Confortablement, commodément, agréablement. **To be comfortably off,** avoir de quoi (vivre); être à l'aise. *To live c.,* vivre à l'aise, à son aise.

comforter ['kʌmfərtər], *s.* **I.** Consolateur, -trice.

2. Cache-nez *m inv* (de laine). **3.** (*Baby's*) Tétine *f* (sur anneau).

comfortless ['kʌmfərtləs], *a.* Incommode; sans commodité.

comfrey ['kʌmfri], *s. Bot:* Consoude *f*.

comic ['kɔmik]. **I.** *a.* Comique. **Comic opera,** opéra bouffe. **2.** *s.* Comédien, -ienne (de music hall); comique *m*.

comical ['kɔmik(ə)l], *a.* Comique, risible; qui prête à rire. **What a comical idea!** quelle drôle d'idée! **-ally,** *adv.* Comiquement; drôlement.

comicality [kɔmi'kaliti], *s.* **I.** Comique *m* (d'une situation). **2.** Drôlerie *f*.

comity ['kɔmiti], *s.* Courtoisie *f*, politesse *f*. **The comity of nations,** le bon accord entre les nations.

comma ['kɔma], *s.* (*a*) Virgule *f*. (*b*) **Inverted commas,** guillemets *m*. *Between inverted commas,* entre guillemets.

command[1] [kɔ'mɑ:nd], *s.* **I.** Ordre *m*, commandement *m*. **Done at, by, s.o.'s command,** fait d'après les ordres de qn. **To be at s.o.'s command,** être aux ordres de qn. **Word of command,** commandement. **By royal command,** sur l'invitation du Roi. **2.** Commandement (*of, de; over, sur*); gouvernement *m* (d'une place forte). **Second in command,** commandant *m* en second. **Under (the) command of . . .,** sous le commandement de. . . . *Mil:* **The Higher Command,** le commandement supérieur. **3.** (*a*) **To be in command of a pass,** commander, dominer, un défilé. (*b*) Connaissance *f*, maîtrise *f* (d'une langue). **To have several languages at one's command; to have a command of several languages,** posséder plusieurs langues. (*c*) **Command over oneself,** maîtrise *f* de soi. (*d*) **Command of the seas,** maîtrise des mers. (*e*) **The money at my command,** les fonds à ma disposition.

command[2], *v.tr.* **I.** Ordonner, commander (*s.o. to do sth.*, à qn de faire qch.). **2.** (*a*) Commander (un régiment). *Abs.* **To command in chief,** commander en chef. (*b*) **To command oneself,** rester maître de soi. **With money one commands the world,** avec de l'argent on est maître du monde. **3.** Avoir (qch.) à sa disposition. *You may c. me,* vous pouvez disposer de moi. **4.** (*a*) **To command respect, admiration,** commander, inspirer, le respect, l'admiration. (*b*) *To c. a high price,* se vendre à un haut prix. **5.** (*Of fort, etc.*) Commander, dominer (une ville, etc.). **commanding,** *a.* **I.** Commanding officer, officier commandant; *Mil:* chef *m* de corps. **2.** (Ton) d'autorité, de commandement. **3.** *C. presence,* air, port, imposant **4.** (Lieu) éminent.

commandant [kɔman'dant], *s.* Commandant *m*.

commandeer [kɔman'di:ər], *v.tr.* Réquisitionner.

commander [kɔ'mɑ:ndər], *s.* **I.** (*a*) *Mil:* Commandant *m*. **Commander-in-chief,** commandant en chef; généralissime *m*. (*b*) *Navy:* Capitaine *m* de frégate. **2.** (*Of knights*) Commandeur *m*.

commandment [kɔ'mɑ:ndmənt], *s.* Commandement (divin).

commemorate [kɔ'memoreit], *v.tr.* Commémorer (qn, le souvenir de qn); solenniser, célébrer, le souvenir de (qn, qch.).

commemoration [kɔmemo'reiʃ(ə)n], *s.* Commémoration *f*. *In c. of,* en mémoire de qn.

commence [kɔ'mens], *v.tr. & i.* Commencer (*sth., qch.*). *To c. to do sth., to c. doing sth.,* commencer à, de, faire qch. **C. work!** au travail! *Mil:* **To c. operations,** entamer les opérations.

commencement [kɔ'mensmənt], *s.* Commencement *m*, début *m*.

commend [kɔ'mend], *v.tr.* **1.** Recommander, confier (qch. à qn, aux soins de qn). **2.** (*a*) Louer. *To c. s.o. for his bravery*, louer qn de sa bravoure. *To c. s.o. for doing sth.*, approuver qn d'avoir fait qch. (*b*) *A course of action that did not c. itself to me*, une ligne de conduite qui n'était pas à mon goût.

commendable [kɔ'mendəbl], *a.* Louable.

commendation [kɔmen'deiʃ(ə)n], *s.* Éloge *m*, louange *f*, approbation *f*.

commendatory [kɔ'mendətəri], *a.* **1.** Élogieux. **2.** *Ecc:* (Abbé, abbaye) commendataire.

commensurable [kɔ'menʃərəbl], *a.* **1.** Commensurable (*with, to,* avec). **2.** = COMMENSURATE 2.

commensurate [kɔ'menʃəret], *a.* **1.** Coétendu (*with,* à). **2.** Proportionné (*to, with,* à). **-ly,** *adv.* Proportionnellement (*to, with,* à).

comment[1] ['kɔment], *s.* Commentaire *m*. *No comments, please!* point d'observations, s'il vous plaît.! *To call for comment,* provoquer des critiques.

comment[2] ['kɔment, kɔ'ment], *v.i.* **1.** *To c. on a text,* commenter un texte. **2.** *F: To c. on s.o.'s behaviour,* critiquer la conduite de qn. *Several people commented on his absence,* plusieurs firent des observations sur son absence.

commentary ['kɔmentəri], *s.* **1.** Commentaire *m*, glose *f*. **2.** **Running commentary,** (i) lecture expliquée ; (ii) radio-reportage *m*.

commentator ['kɔmenteitər], *s.* **1.** Commentateur, -trice. **2.** Radio-reporter *m*.

commerce ['kɔmərs], *s.* Le commerce ; les affaires *f*. **'commerce-destroyer,** *s.* Bâtiment armé en course. **'commerce-destroying,** *s.* Guerre *f* de course.

commercial [kɔ'mə:rʃ(ə)l], **1.** *a.* (*a*) Commercial, -aux. *C. bank,* banque commerciale, de commerce. *C. car,* automobile industrielle. *C. efficiency (of machine),* rendement économique. **The commercial world,** le commerce. (*b*) (Esprit) mercantile. **2.** *s.m. F:* Commis voyageur. **Commercial room,** salle réservée aux voyageurs de commerce. **-ally,** *adv.* Commercialement.

comminatory ['kɔminətəri], *a.* Comminatoire.

commingle [kɔ'mingl]. **1.** *v.tr.* Mêler ensemble ; mélanger. **2.** *v.i.* Se mêler (*with,* avec).

comminute ['kɔminjut], *v.tr.* **1.** Pulvériser ; réduire en fragments. *Surg:* **Comminuted fracture,** fracture esquilleuse. **2.** Morceler (une propriété).

comminution [kɔmi'nju:ʃ(ə)n], *s.* **1.** Comminution *f* ; pulvérisation *f*. **2.** Morcellement *m*.

commiserate [kɔ'mizəreit], *v.tr. & i. To commiserate (with)* s.o., s'apitoyer sur le sort de qn.

commiseration [kɔmizə'reiʃ(ə)n], *s.* Commisération *f*, compassion *f* (*with,* pour).

commiserative [kɔ'mizərətiv], *a.* Compatissant.

commissariat [kɔmi'sɛəriət], *s. Mil:* Intendance *f*.

commissary ['kɔmisəri], *s.* **1.** Commissaire · *m*, délégué *m*. **2.** *Mil:* **Commissary general,** intendant général d'armée. **3.** *Ecc:* Grand vicaire (délégué par l'évêque).

commission[1] [kɔ'miʃ(ə)n], *s.* Commission *f*. **1.** Délégation *f* (d'autorité). **2.** Brevet *m*. **Commission of the peace,** charge *f* de juge de paix. *Mil:* **To get a, one's, commission,** être nommé officier. *To resign one's c.,* démissionner. **3.** Ordre *m*, mandat *m*. *To carry out a c.,* s'acquitter d'une commission. **4.** **Royal Commission,** commission d'enquête ordonnée par décret parlementaire.

5. *Nau:* Armement *m* (d'un navire). **To put a ship into commission,** armer un vaisseau. *Aeroplane in c.,* avion en service. **6.** *Com:* Commission ; pourcentage *m*. *Illicit c.,* remise *f* illicite ; *F:* pot *m* de vin. **7.** Perpétration *f* (d'un crime). **com'mission-agency,** *s.* Maison *f* de commission. **com'mission-agent,** *s.* Commissionnaire *m* en marchandises.

commission[2], *v.tr.* **1.** (*a*) Commissionner (qn). (*b*) Préposer, déléguer, (qn) à une fonction ; nommer (un officier) à un commandement. (*c*) Commander (un livre, un tableau). **2.** *Nau:* (*a*) Armer (un navire). (*b*) *v.i.* (*Of ship*) Armer.

commissioned, *a.* **1.** Muni de pouvoirs ; commissionné. **2.** **Commissioned officer,** officier *m*.

commissionaire [kɔmiʃə'nɛər], *s.* Commissionnaire *m*. **1.** Chasseur *m* (d'hôtel). **2.** Messager patenté.

commissioner [kɔ'miʃənər], *s.* Commissaire *m*. (*a*) Membre *m* d'une commission. (*b*) Délégué *m* d'une commission. **Commissioner of police** = préfet *m* de police. **Commissioner for oaths,** officier ministériel ayant qualité pour recevoir les déclarations sous serment.

commissure ['kɔmiʃjuər], *s.* Commissure *f*.

commit [kɔ'mit], *v.tr.* (**committed**) **1.** Commettre, confier (*sth. to s.o.'s care,* qch. aux soins, à la garde, de qn). **To commit sth. to writing,** coucher qch. par écrit. **2.** **To commit s.o. to prison,** *abs.* **to commit s.o.,** envoyer qn en prison. **To commit s.o. for trial,** renvoyer (un prévenu) aux assises. **3.** (*a*) Engager (sa parole, etc.). (*b*) **To commit oneself,** se compromettre. *I am too deeply committed to draw back,* je suis trop engagé pour reculer. *Without committing myself,* sous toutes réserves. **4.** Commettre (un crime, une erreur). *S.a.* SUICIDE[2].

commitment [kɔ'mitmənt], *s.* **1.** = COMMITTAL. **2.** Engagement financier.

committal [kɔ'mit(ə)l], *s.* **1.** Délégation *f* (d'une tâche, etc.) (*to,* à). **2.** (*a*) *C. of a body to the earth,* mise *f* en terre d'un cadavre. (*b*) *Jur:* Mise en prison. **Committal order,** mandat de dépôt. **3.** Perpétration *f* (d'un délit). **4.** Engagement *m* (de sa parole).

committee [kɔ'miti], *s.* **1.** Comité *m*, commission *f*, conseil *m*. *To be on a c.,* faire partie d'un comité. *C. of management,* conseil d'administration. *Organizing c.,* comité d'organisation. *To send a bill to a c.,* renvoyer un projet de loi à une commission. **Committee rooms** (*of parliamentary candidate*), permanence électorale. **2.** *Jur:* [kɔmi'ti:] Tuteur, -trice, curateur, -trice (d'un faible d'esprit).

commode [kɔ'moud], *s. Furn:* **1.** Commode *f*. **2.** Night commode, chaise percée.

commodious [kɔ'moudjəs], *a.* Spacieux.

commodiousness [kɔ'moudjəsnəs], *s.* Amples dimensions *f* (d'une maison, d'une pièce).

commodity [kɔ'mɔditi], *s.* Marchandise *f*, denrée *f*, article *m*. *Primary c.,* produit *m* de base.

commodore ['kɔmodɔ:r], *s.* (*a*) *Navy:* Chef *m* de division (par intérim) ; commodore *m*. (*b*) Le capitaine (d'un corps de pilotes, d'un yacht-club).

common[1] ['kɔmən], *a.* **1.** Commun (*to,* à). *C. wall,* mur mitoyen. *C. report,* rumeur publique. *Jur:* commune renommée. *C. property,* choses communes. *The c. opinion,* l'opinion courante. *Gram:* **Common noun,** nom commun. *Mth:* **Common divisor,** diviseur commun. *Common crier,* crieur public. **2.** (*a*) Ordinaire. *C. occurrence,* chose fréquente. *C. honesty,* la probité la plus élémentaire. **In common use,** d'usage courant. **In common parlance,** en langage ordinaire. (*Of news, etc.*) To be common talk, courir les rues. They are as common as blackberries, les rues en sont pavées. (*b*) De peu de valeur. *C. material,* étoffe ordinaire. *The c. people,* les gens du peuple; le menu peuple. **3.** Vulgaire; trivial, -als. *C. manners,* manières vulgaires, communes. **-ly,** *adv.* **I.** Communément, ordinairement. **2.** Vulgairement. **'common-room,** *s. Sch:* **I.** Salle commune. **2.** Salle des professeurs.

common², *s.* **I.** (*a*) Pâtis *m*, friche *f*. (*b*) Terrain, pré, communal. **2.** To have sth. in common with s.o., avoir qch. en commun avec qn. *They have nothing in c.,* ils n'ont rien de commun. *It is out of the c.,* cela sort de l'ordinaire. **Nothing out of the common,** rien d'extraordinaire.

commonalty ['kɔmənəlti], *s.* **I.** Le commun des hommes. **2.** La bourgeoisie.

commoner ['kɔmənər], *s.* **I.** Homme *m* du peuple; bourgeois *m*. **2.** *Sch:* Étudiant *m* ordinaire.

commonness ['kɔmənnəs], *s.* **I.** Fréquence *f* (d'un événement). **2.** Banalité *f*; vulgarité *f*.

commonplace ['kɔmənpleis]. **I.** *s.* (*a*) Lieu commun. (*b*) Banalité *f*. **Commonplace-book,** recueil *m* de faits notables. **2.** *a.* Banal, -aux.

commons ['kɔmənz], *s.* **I.** Le peuple; les tiers état. **The House of Commons,** la Chambre des Communes. **2.** *Sch:* Ordinaire *m* (de la table). *F:* To be on short commons, faire maigre chère.

commonweal (the) [ðə'kɔmənwiːl], *s.* Le bien public; la chose publique.

commonwealth ['kɔmənwelθ], *s.* (*a*) État *m*; république *f*. (*b*) **The Commonwealth,** la chose publique.

commotion [kɔ'mouʃ(ə)n], *s.* **I.** Confusion *f*, agitation *f*, commotion *f*, ébranlement *m*. *In a state of c.,* en émoi. *The c. in the streets,* le brouhaha de la rue. **2.** Troubles *mpl*. *Popular c.,* mouvement *m* populaire.

communal ['kɔmjun(ə)l], *a.* Communal, -aux. *Jur:* Communal estate, communauté (conjugale).

commune¹ ['kɔmjuːn], *s. Adm:* Commune *f*.

commune² [kɔ'mjuːn], *v.i. Lit:* Converser, s'entretenir (*with s.o.,* avec qn). **To commune with oneself,** se recueillir.

communicable [kɔ'mjuːnikəbl], *a.* Communicable. *Med:* Contagieux.

communicant [kɔ'mjuːnikənt], *s.* **I.** Informateur, -trice. **2.** *Ecc:* Communiant, -ante.

communicate [kɔ'mjuːnikeit]. **I.** *v.tr.* To c. (sth.) to sth., to s.o., communiquer (la chaleur, etc.) à qch.; communiquer, faire connaître (une nouvelle) à qn. **2.** *v.i.* (*a*) To c. with s.o., communiquer avec qn. *To c. by letter,* communiquer par lettre. (*b*) *Rooms that c. with one another,* chambres qui communiquent entre elles. **3.** *Ecc:* (*a*) *v.tr.* Communier (qn). (*b*) *v.i.* Communier; recevoir la communion.

communication [kɔmjuːni'keiʃ(ə)n], *s.* **I.** (*a*) *C. of a piece of news to s.o.,* communication *f* d'une nouvelle à qn. (*b*) *To read a c.,* lire une communication. **2.** To get into communication with s.o., communiquer avec qn. *To be in close c. with one another,* être en relations suivies. **3.** Line of communication, voie d'intercommunication. **Means of communication,** moyens (i) de communication, (ii) de transport.

communicative [kɔ'mjuːnikətiv], *a.* Communicatif; expansif.

communicativeness [kɔ'mjuːnikətivnəs], *s.* Caractère expansif; humeur bavarde.

communicator [kɔ'mjuːnikeitər], *s.* Communicateur *m* (de mouvement, etc.).

communion [kɔ'mjuːnjən], *s.* **I.** Relations *fpl*, rapports *mpl* (*with s.o.,* avec qn). **Self-communion,** recueillement *m*. **2.** **The communion of saints,** la communion des saints. **3.** *Ecc:* **The (Holy) Communion,** la communion, la (Sainte) Cène. **The Communion table,** la Sainte Table.

communism ['kɔmjunizm], *s.* Communisme *m*.

communist ['kɔmjunist], *s.* **I.** Communiste *mf*. **2.** *Fr.Hist:* Communard *m*.

community [kɔ'mjuːniti], *s.* **I.** Communauté *f* (de biens); solidarité *f* (d'intérêts). **2.** *Ecc:* Communauté (religieuse). **3.** (*a*) **The community,** l'État *m*; le public. *All classes of the c.,* toutes les classes de la société. (*b*) **Community singing,** chant en commun.

commutability [kɔmjutə'biliti], *s.* **I.** Permutabilité *f*. **2.** *Jur:* Commuabilité *f* (d'une peine).

commutable [kɔ'mjuːtəbl], *a.* **I.** Permutable; interchangeable. **2.** (Peine) commuable.

commutate ['kɔmjuteit], *v.tr. El.E:* Commuter, permuter.

commutation [kɔmju'teiʃ(ə)n], *s.* (*a*) *C. of sentence,* commutation *f* de peine. (*b*) *C. of an easement,* rachat *m* d'une servitude.

commutative [kɔ'mjuːtətiv], *a.* Commutatif.

commutator ['kɔmjuteitər], *s. El:* Commutateur *m*. *C. ring,* bague de collecteur.

commute [kɔ'mjuːt], *v.tr.* **I.** Interchanger. **2.** Échanger (*for,* pour, contre); racheter (une servitude). **3.** *El.E:* = COMMUTATE.

compact¹ ['kɔmpakt], *s.* Convention *f*, accord *m*, pacte *m*.

compact² [kom'pakt], *a.* **I.** Compact; serré; tassé; (style) concis. **2.** Formé, composé (*of,* de).

compact³ ['kɔmpakt], *s. Toil:* **I.** Poudre compacte. **2.** Poudrier *m* (de sac à main).

compactness [kom'paktnəs], *s.* Compacité *f*; concision *f* (de style).

companion¹ [kom'panjən], *s.* **I.** (*a*) Compagnon, *f.* compagne. *Companions in distress,* compagnons d'infortune. (*b*) **(Lady-)companion,** dame *f* de compagnie. (*c*) Compagnon (d'un ordre). **2.** (*a*) Manuel *m*. (*b*) **Lady's companion,** nécessaire *m* à ouvrage. **3.** Pendant *m* (à un tableau).

companion², *s. Nau:* **I.** Companion(-hatch), capot *m* (de descente). **2.** Companion(-ladder), échelle *f* d'honneur, de commandement. **Companion(-way),** escalier *m* des cabines.

companionable [kom'panjənəbl], *a.* D'une société agréable. **-ably,** *adv.* Sociablement.

companionship [kom'panjənʃip], *s.* (*a*) Compagnie *f*. (*b*) Camaraderie *f*.

company¹ ['kʌmpəni], *s.* **I.** Compagnie *f*. **To keep s.o. company,** tenir compagnie à qn. **To part company (with s.o.),** (i) se séparer (de qn); (ii) n'être plus d'accord (avec qn). *Prov:* Two's company, three's none, deux s'amusent, trois s'embêtent. **2.** (*a*) Assemblée *f*, compagnie; bande *f*. **Select company,** assemblée choisie. **Present company excepted,** les présents exceptés. (*b*) (*Guests*) Monde *m*. *We are expecting c.,* nous attendons des visites. *We see very little c.,* nous voyons très peu de monde. **To put on one's company manners,** soigner sa tenue, son langage. **3.** (*Associates*) Compagnie, société *f*. **To keep good company,** fréquenter la bonne compagnie. *Avoid bad c.,* prenez garde aux mauvaises fréquentations. **A man is known by his company,** dis-moi qui tu hantes, je te dirai qui tu es. *F:* He is very good company, il est fort amusant. **4.** *Com: Ind:* (*a*) (i) Compagnie; (ii) société (commerciale). *The Railway companies,* les compagnies de chemins de fer. *Gas c.,* compagnie du gaz. **Joint stock company,** société par actions.

Limited (liability) company, société (anglaise) à responsabilité limitée. **Smith and Company** (*usu.* **and Co.**), Smith et Compagnie ; Smith et Cie. (*b*) Corporation *f* de marchands. **5.** (*a*) *Th:* Troupe *f*. *The Odéon c.*, la troupe de l'Odéon. *Touring c.*, troupe ambulante. (*b*) *Nau:* **The ship's company**, l'équipage *m*. **6.** *Mil:* Compagnie. **Half-company**, peloton *m*. *F:* **To get one's company**, être promu capitaine.

company², *v.i.* **To c. with s.o.**, (i) fréquenter qn ; (ii) vivre, voyager, en compagnie de qn.

comparable ['kɔmpərəbl], *a.* Comparable (*with, to, avec, à*). **-ably,** *adv.* Comparablement.

comparative [kɔm'parətiv], *a.* **1.** (*a*) Comparatif. *Gram:* **C. adverb**, adverbe comparatif. *C. degree*, le comparatif. (*b*) **Comparative philology**, philologie comparée. **2.** Relatif. *This would be c. wealth*, ce serait l'aisance relative. **-ly,** *adv.* **1.** Comparativement, par comparaison (*to*, à). **2.** Relativement.

compare¹ [kɔm'pɛər], *s. Poet. & Hum:* Beyond compare, hors de comparaison ; (beauté) sans pareille.

compare². **1.** *v.tr.* (*a*) Comparer (*to, with*, à, avec). *C. the two things!* faites la comparaison ! *They are not to be compared*, on ne saurait les comparer. (**As**) compared **with**, **to . . .**, en comparaison de . . .,auprès de. . . . *To c. a copy with the original*, confronter une copie avec l'original. *F:* **To compare notes**, échanger ses impressions avec qn. (*b*) *To c. an adjective*, former les degrés de comparaison d'un adjectif. **2.** *v.i. He can't c. with you*, il ne vous est pas comparable. **To compare favourably with sth.**, ne le céder en rien à qch. **comparing,** *s.* Comparaison *f*.

comparison [kɔm'parisən], *s.* Comparaison *f*. *In c. with . . .*, en comparaison de . . . ; auprès de . . . *Gram:* **Degrees of comparison**, degrés de comparaison.

compartment [kɔm'pɑːtmənt], *s.* **1.** Compartiment *m*. *N.Arch:* **Watertight compartment**, compartiment étanche. *Rail:* **Smoking c.**, compartiment fumeurs. **2.** Case *f* (d'un tiroir).

compass¹ ['kʌmpəs], *s.* **1.** (**A pair of) compasses**, un compas. *Proportional compasses*, compas à, de, réduction. **2.** (*a*) Limite(s) *f(pl)* (d'un endroit). (*b*) Pourtour *m* (d'un bâtiment). **To fetch a compass**, faire un détour. **3.** (*a*) Étendue *f*. *Knowledge within my compass*, connaissances à la portée de mon esprit. **In small compass**, sous un volume restreint. (*b*) *Mus:* Étendue, registre *m* (de la voix) ; clavier *m* (de la clarinette). **4.** (*With moving needle*) Boussole *f* ; (*with moving card*) compas. **Pocket compass**, boussole de poche. **Mariner's compass**, compas (de mer). **The points of the compass**, les aires *f* de vent. *Nau:* **To take a compass bearing**, prendre un relèvement au compas. **'compass-card,** *s. Nau:* Rose *f* des vents. **'compass-saw,** *s.* Scie *f* à chantourner.

compass², *v.tr.* **1.** Faire le tour de (qch.). **2.** *Compassed about by, with, enemies*, entouré d'ennemis. **3.** Comprendre ; saisir. **4.** *Jur:* Comploter (la mort, la ruine, de qn). **5.** Atteindre (son but).

compassion [kɔm'paʃ(ə)n], *s.* Compassion *f*. **To have compassion on s.o.**, avoir compassion de qn. **To arouse c.**, faire pitié.

compassionate [kɔm'paʃənet], *a.* Compatissant (*to, towards*, à, pour). **-ly,** *adv.* Avec compassion.

compatibility [kɔmpati'biliti], *s.* Compatibilité *f*.

compatible [kɔm'patibl], *a.* Compatible (*with*, avec).

compatriot [kɔm'patriət]; *s.* Compatriote *mf*.

compeer [kɔm'piːər], *s.* **1.** Égal *m*, pair *m*. **2.** Compère *m*, compagnon *m*.

compel [kɔm'pel], *v.tr.* (**compelled**) **To compel s.o. to do sth.**, contraindre, forcer, obliger, qn à, *occ.* de, faire qch. **To be compelled to do sth.**, se voir forcé de faire qch. *He compels respect*, il impose le respect. **compelling,** *a.* *C.* force, force compulsive. *C. curiosity*, curiosité irrésistible.

compendious [kɔm'pendiəs], *a.* Abrégé, succinct. **-ly,** *adv.* En abrégé ; succinctement.

compendium, *pl.* **-ums** [kɔm'pendiəm(z)], *s.* **1.** Abrégé *m*, compendium *m inv* (d'une science, etc.). *C. of laws*, recueil *m* des lois. **2.** (*a*) Pochette *f* (de papeterie). (*b*) **Compendium of games**, malle *f* de jeux.

compensate ['kɔmpənseit]. **1.** *v.tr.* (*a*) **To compensate s.o. for sth.**, dédommager qn de qch. (*b*) Rémunérer (qn). (*c*) *Mec:* Compenser (un pendule, etc.). *These errors c. one another*, ces erreurs se compensent. **2.** *v.i.* **To compensate for sth.**, (i) remplacer, racheter, qch. ; (ii) compenser qch. *Mec.E:* **To c. for wear**, compenser l'usure. **compensating,** *a.* **1.** Compensating errors, erreurs qui se compensent. **2.** Compensateur, -trice. **Compensating magnet**, aimant correcteur.

compensation [kɔmpən'seiʃ(ə)n], *s.* Compensation *f* ; dédommagement *m* ; indemnité *f*. *F:* **In compensation**, en revanche. *Ph:* **C. for temperature**, compensation en température.

compensator ['kɔmpənseitər], *s. El: Ph:* Compensateur *m*. *Aut:* Palonnier *m* (du frein).

compete [kɔm'piːt], *v.i.* **1.** **To compete with s.o.**, faire concurrence à qn. **2.** **To c. for a prize**, concourir pour un prix. **To c. with s.o. for a prize**, disputer un prix à qn. **3.** **To compete with s.o. in talent**, ardeur, le disputer en talent avec qn ; rivaliser d'ardeur avec qn.

competence ['kɔmpetəns], **competency** ['kɔmpetənsi], *s.* **1.** Suffisance *f* de moyens d'existence. **To enjoy a competency**, avoir de quoi vivre. *He has a small c.*, c'est un petit rentier. **To have a bare competency**, avoir tout juste de quoi vivre. **2.** **Competence in a subject**, compétence *f* en un sujet. **3.** Attributions *fpl* (d'un fonctionnaire) ; *Jur:* compétence. *It lies beyond my c.*, cela dépasse ma compétence.

competent ['kɔmpetənt], *a.* **1.** Capable. **2.** Compétent (*in a matter*, en une matière). **3.** (Tribunal) compétent. **4.** **Competent knowledge of English**, connaissance suffisante de l'anglais. **-ly,** *adv.* **1.** Avec compétence. **2.** D'une manière suffisante.

competition [kɔmpe'tiʃ(ə)n], *s.* **1.** Rivalité *f*, concurrence *f*. *There was keen c. for it*, il y avait un grand nombre de concurrents. **2.** Concours *m*. *Chess c.*, tournoi *m* d'échecs. *The place will be filled by open c.*, le poste sera mis au concours. **Not for competition**, hors concours. **3.** *Com:* Concurrence. **Unfair competition**, concurrence déloyale.

competitive [kɔm'petitiv], *a.* *C.* spirit, esprit de concurrence. *C. design*, dessin de concours.

competitor, -tress [kɔm'petitər, -tres], *s.* Concurrent, -ente. **To be a c.**, être sur les rangs.

compilation [kɔmpi'leiʃ(ə)n], *s.* Compilation *f*.

compile [kɔm'pail], *v.tr.* Compiler. **To c. a catalogue**, dresser un catalogue.

compiler [kɔm'pailər], *s.* Compilateur, -trice.

complacence [kɔm'pleisəns], **complacency**

[kɔm'pleisənsi], *s.* **I.** Satisfaction *f.* **2.** Contentement *m* de soi-même ; suffisance *f.*
complacent [kɔm'pleisənt], *a.* Content de soi-même. *C. air*, air suffisant. *C. optimism*, optimisme béat. **-ly,** *adv.* Avec satisfaction ; avec suffisance.
complain [kɔm'plein], *v.i.* **I.** Se plaindre (*of* de). *To c. that* . . ., se plaindre que + *sub. or ind.*, de ce que + *ind. He complains of the heat*, il se plaint de la chaleur. *I have nothing to c. of*, je n'ai pas à me plaindre ; je n'ai à me plaindre de rien. **2.** Porter plainte (*against s.o.*, contre qn). *What do you complain of?* sur quoi porte votre plainte ? **3.** *Poet :* Se lamenter.
complainant [kɔm'pleinənt], *s. Jur :* Plaignant *m.*
complainer [kɔm'pleinər], *s.* Réclamant, -ante ; mécontent, -ente.
complaint [kɔm'pleint], *s.* **I.** *Lit :* (*a*) Plainte *f*, doléances *fpl.* (*b*) *Lit.Hist :* Complainte *f.* **2.** (*a*) Grief *m.* *I have no cause of complaint*, je n'ai aucun sujet de plainte. *Let us hear your complaints*, exposez vos griefs. (*b*) **To lodge a complaint against** s.o., porter plainte contre qn. **3.** Maladie *f*, mal *m.* *What is your complaint?* de quoi souffrez-vous ?
complaisance [kɔm'pleizəns], *s.* Complaisance *f.* obligeance *f.*
complaisant [kɔm'pleizənt], *a.* Complaisant, obligeant. **-ly,** *adv.* Avec complaisance.
complement¹ ['kɔmplimənt], *s.* **I.** (*a*) Plein *m* (de combustibles, etc.). (*b*) *Navy :* etc. Effectif *m.* *Full c.*, effectif complet. **2.** Complément *m* (d'un verbe, d'un angle, d'un logarithme).
complement² [kɔmpli'ment], *v.tr.* Compléter.
complementary [kɔmpli'mentəri], *a.* (Angle, etc.) complémentaire.
complete¹ [kɔm'pli:t], *a.* **I.** (*a*) Complet, -ète ; entier, total. *My happiness is c.*, rien ne manque à mon bonheur. *The staff is c.*, le personnel est au complet. (*b*) Terminé. *My report is not yet c.*, mon rapport n'est pas encore achevé. **2.** Parfait, achevé, accompli. *The complete angler*, le pêcheur accompli. **-ly,** *adv.* Complètement, totalement.
complete², *v.tr.* **I.** Compléter, achever, accomplir. *He has completed his twentieth year*, il a vingt ans révolus. *To complete the misfortune* . . ., pour comble de malheur. . . . **2.** *To c. a form*, remplir une formule.
completeness [kɔm'pli:tnəs], *s.* État complet ; plénitude *f* (d'une victoire).
completion [kɔm'pli:ʃ(ə)n], *s.* **I.** Achèvement *m*, complètement *m.* **In process of completion**, en (cours d')achèvement. *Near c.*, près d'être achevé. **2.** Accomplissement *m* (d'un vœu) ; pleine réalisation.
complex ['kɔmpleks]. **I.** *a.* Complexe. **2.** *s.* (*a*) Tout (formé de parties). (*b*) *Psy :* Complexe *m.* Inferiority complex, complexe d'infériorité.
complexion [kɔm'plekʃ(ə)n], *s.* **I.** Teint *m.* *To have a fine c.*, avoir un joli teint. **Complexion cream**, crème de beauté. **2.** Aspect *m.* *The affair has assumed a serious complexion*, l'affaire a revêtu un caractère grave.
-complexioned [kɔm'plekʃ(ə)nd], *a.* To be fair-, dark-complexioned, être blond, brun. **Fresh-complexioned**, teint frais.
complexity [kɔm'pleks ti], *s.* Complexité *f.*
compliance [kɔm'plaiəns], *s.* **I.** Acquiescement *m* (*with*, à). **In compliance with your wishes**, en conformité de vos désirs. **To refuse compliance with an order**, refuser d'obéir à un ordre. **2.** *Pej :* (Base) compliance, soumission (abjecte). *To show c.*, *F :* courber l'échine

compliant [kɔm'plaiənt], *a.* Obligeant, accommodant. **-ly,** *adv.* Complaisamment, servilement.
complicate ['kɔmplikeit], *v.tr.* Compliquer (*with*, de). **complicated,** *a.* Compliqué ; (affaire) embrouillée.
complication [kɔmpli'keiʃ(ə)n], *s.* Complication *f.*
complicity [kɔm'plisiti], *s.* Complicité *f* (*in*, à).
compliment¹ ['kɔmplimənt], *s.* Compliment *m.* **To pay a compliment to** s.o., faire, adresser, un compliment à qn. *Mil : Navy :* **To pay compliments**, rendre les honneurs *m.* (*At end of letter*) **To send one's compliments to** s.o., se rappeler au bon souvenir de qn. **Compliments of the season**, meilleurs souhaits de nouvel an. **With the publisher's compliments**, hommage de l'éditeur.
compliment² ['kɔmpliment, kɔmpli'ment], *v.tr.* Complimenter, féliciter (qn) (*on*, de).
complimentary [kɔmpli'mentəri], *a.* Flatteur, -euse. **Complimentary copy**, exemplaire 'en hommage.
complin(e) ['kɔmplin], *s. Ecc :* Complies *fpl.*
comply [kɔm'plai], *v.i. To c. with* (*sth.*), se conformer à (une formalité) ; se soumettre à (la loi) ; observer (une règle) ; accéder à (une demande) ; obéir à (un ordre). *He complied gracefully*, il s'exécuta avec grâce. *Your wishes have been complied with*, vos désirs ont reçu satisfaction.
component [kɔm'pounənt]. **I.** *a.* **Component parts**, parties constituantes. *Mec :* **Component forces**, forces composantes. **2.** *s.* (*a*) Composant *m* ; partie composante. (*b*) Organe *m* (d'une machine). (*c*) *Opt :* **Four-component lens**, objectif à quatre lentilles.
comport [kɔm'pɔ:rt]. **I.** *v.i.* S'accorder, convenir (*with*, à). **2.** *v.pr.* **To comport oneself**, se comporter.
comportment [kɔm'pɔ:rtmənt], *s.* Conduite *f*, maintien *m.*
compose [kɔm'pouz], *v.tr.* **I.** Composer. *Typ : To c. a line*, composer une ligne. *An engine is composed of many parts*, un moteur se compose, est composé de nombreux organes. **2.** *Art : To c. the figures in a picture*, arranger les personnages d'un tableau. **3.** Arranger, accommoder (un différend). **4.** (*a*) *To c. one's features*, se composer le visage. *To c. oneself to sleep*, se disposer au sommeil. (*b*) **Compose yourself!** calmez-vous ! **composed,** *a.* Calme, tranquille. **composing,** *s*, Composition *f.* *Typ :* **Composing-stick**, composeur *m.*
composedly [kɔm'pouzidli], *adv.* Tranquillement ; avec calme.
composer [kɔm'pouzər], *s.* Compositeur, -trice (de musique).
composite ['kɔmpozit]. **I.** *a.* (*a*) (Fleur) composée. *Arch :* (Chapiteau) composite. (*b*) (Train) mixte. (*c*) *Cin :* **Composite shot**, impression combinée. **2.** *s.* Composé *m.*
composition [kɔmpo'ziʃ(ə)n], *s.* **I.** (*a*) Action *f* de composer ; composition *f* (de qch.). *Mec : C. of forces*, la composition des forces. (*b*) Composition, constitution *f* (de l'air, etc.). (*c*) *Art :* Composition. **2.** Mélange *m*, composé *m.* **Non-conducting composition**, enduit *m* calorifuge. **3.** (*a*) A musical composition, une composition musicale. (*b*) *Sch :* Dissertation *f*, rédaction *f.* (*c*) *Sch :* Thème *m.* *To do a paper in French c.*, composer en thème français. **4.** (*a*) Accommodement *m*, entente *f.* **To enter into a composition with** s.o. over sth., composer avec qn sur qch. (*b*) Transaction *f.* **Composition for stamp duty,**

(taxe *f* d')abonnement *m* au timbre. (*c*) Accommodement (avec des créanciers) ; concordat *m*.
compositor [kɔm'pɔzitər], *s.* *Typ:* Compositeur *m*, typographe *m*.
compos mentis ['kɔmpɔs 'mentis], *a.* *Jur:* Sain d'esprit. **Non compos (mentis)**, aliéné.
compost ['kɔmpɔst], *s.* *Hort:* Compost *m*.
composure [kɔm'pouʒər], *s.* Calme *m*, sang-froid *m*. *To retain one's c.*, garder son sang-froid.
compound[1] ['kɔmpaund]. I. *a.* (*a*) Composé. *Gram:* **C. word**, mot composé. **Compound interest**, intérêts composés. *S.a.* FRACTURE[1] I. (*b*) Complexe. *C. addition*, addition des nombres complexes. (*c*) **Compound steel**, acier compound *inv.* *El.E:* **C. wound**, à enroulement compoundé. II. **compound**, *s.* I. (Corps *m*) composé *m*. 2. *Tchn:* Composition *f*, mastic *m*.
compound[2] [kɔm'paund]. I. *v.tr.* (*a*) Composer, mélanger (une boisson, etc.) ; combiner (des éléments). (*b*) Accommoder, arranger (un différend) ; régler (un différend) à l'amiable. (*c*) **To compound a felony**, pactiser avec un crime. (*d*) *El.E:* Compounder (une dynamo). 2. *v.i.* S'arranger, composer (*with s.o.*, avec qn) ; transiger (avec sa conscience). **compounding**, *s.* I. Composition *f* ; confection *f* (de drogues). 2. *El.E:* Compoundage *m*.
compound[3] ['kɔmpaund], *s.* (*In India, China*) Enceinte fortifiée (affectée aux Européens) ; compound *m*.
comprehend [kɔmpri'hend], *v.tr.* Comprendre. I. Se rendre compte de (qch.). 2. Englober.
comprehensible [kɔmpri'hensibl], *a.* Compréhensible, intelligible.
comprehension [kɔmpri'henʃ(ə)n], *s.* Compréhension *f*. I. Entendement *m*. 2. Portée *f*, étendue *f*.
comprehensive [kɔmpri'hensiv], *a.* Compréhensif. I. *Phil:* **The comprehensive faculty**, l'entendement *m*. 2. **Comprehensive study**, étude d'ensemble. *C. knowledge*, connaissances étendues. **-ly**, *adv.* Dans un sens très étendu.
comprehensiveness [kɔmpri'hensivnəs], *s.* Étendue *f*, portée *f* (d'un mot, d'une offre).
compress[1] ['kɔmpres], *s.* *Surg:* Compresse *f*.
compress[2] [kɔm'pres], *v.tr.* I. Comprimer (un gaz) ; bander (un ressort) ; (*of compressor*) refouler (l'air). 2. Condenser (un discours) ; concentrer (son style).
compressible [kɔm'presibl], *a.* Compressible, comprimable.
compression [kɔm'preʃ(ə)n], *s.* I. Compression *f*. *I.C.E:* **Compression tap**, robinet de décompression. 2. Concentration *f* (du style).
compressive [kɔm'presiv], *a.* Compressif. **Compressive stress**, effort de compression.
comprise [kɔm'praiz], *v.tr.* Comprendre, comporter, renfermer.
compromise[1] ['kɔmprɔmaiz], *s.* Compromis *m*. *To agree to a c.*, accepter une transaction ; transiger. **Policy of compromise**, politique d'accommodements. *Policy of no c.*, politique intransigeante.
compromise[2]. I. *v.tr.* (*a*) Compromettre (son honneur, etc.). *To c. oneself with s.o.*, se compromettre avec qn. (*b*) Arranger (un différend). 2. *v.i.* Compromettre, transiger. *If he agrees to c.*, s'il accepte un compromis. **compromising**[1], *a.* Compromettant. **compromising**[2], *s.* I. Compromission *f* (de son honneur). 2. Composition *f* (d'un différend).
comptroller [kɔn'troulər], *s.* I. Administrateur *m* (d'une maison royale, etc.). 2. Contrôleur *m* ; vérificateur *m* (de comptes).

compulsion [kɔm'pʌlʃ(ə)n], *s.* Contrainte *f*. **Under compulsion**, par contrainte. *To obey only under c.*, n'obéir qu'à son corps défendant.
compulsory [kɔm'pʌlsəri], *a.* I. Obligatoire. *C. loan*, emprunt forcé. 2. *C. powers*, pouvoirs coercitifs. **-ily**, *adv.* Obligatoirement.
compunction [kɔm'pʌŋ(k)ʃ(ə)n], *s.* Componction *f* ; remords *m*. *F:* **Without compunction**, sans scrupule.
computable [kɔm'pju:təbl], *a.* Calculable.
computation [kɔmpju'teiʃ(ə)n], *s.* Calcul *m*, estimation *f*. *To make a c. of sth.*, calculer qch. **Beyond computation**, incalculable.
compute [kɔm'pju:t], *v.tr.* Computer, calculer, estimer. *Computed horse-power*, chevaux-vapeur estimés.
comrade ['kɔmred], *s.* Camarade *m*, compagnon *m*. **Comrades in arms**, compagnons d'armes.
comradeship ['kɔmredʃip], *s.* Camaraderie *f*.
con[1] [kɔn], *v.tr.* (**conned**) Étudier (un rôle).
con[2], *v.tr.* *Nau:* Gouverner (un navire). *To con the ship*, diriger, commander, la manœuvre. **'conning-tower,** *s.* *Navy:* Blockhaus *m* ; kiosque *m* (de sous-marin).
concatenation [kɔnkati'neiʃ(ə)n], *s.* Enchaînement *m* (d'idées) ; concours *m* (de circonstances).
concave ['kɔnkeiv], *a.* Concave, incurvé.
concavity [kɔn'kaviti], *s.* Concavité *f*.
conceal [kɔn'si:l], *v.tr.* (*a*) Cacher ; celer, dissimuler (la vérité, son chagrin, etc.) ; masquer (ses projets, une fenêtre) ; voiler (ses pensées). **I do not conceal the fact that it is so**, je ne dissimule pas qu'il en est ainsi, qu'il n'en soit ainsi. *To c. sth. from s.o.*, cacher qch. à qn ; taire qch. à qn. *To c. one's movements from the enemy*, dérober sa marche à l'ennemi. (*b*) *Jur:* Recéler (un malfaiteur, un objet volé).
concealed, *a.* Caché, dissimulé, invisible. **Concealed turning**, virage masqué.
concealment [kɔn'si:lmənt], *s.* I. Dissimulation *f*. 2. *Jur:* (*a*) Cel *m*, recel *m*. (*b*) Réticence *f*. 3. Action *f* de cacher ou de se cacher. *To find a place of concealment*, trouver une cachette, une retraite.
concede [kɔn'si:d], *v.tr.* I. Concéder. *I will c. nothing*, je ne ferai aucune concession. 2. *To c. that one is wrong*, concéder, admettre, qu'on a tort.
conceit [kɔn'si:t], *s.* I. Vanité *f*, suffisance *f*. **Eaten up with conceit**, pétri d'amour-propre. 2. **He has got a very good c. of himself**, il est très satisfait de sa petite personne. 3. *A:* Trait *m* d'esprit. *pl.* Conceits, concetti *m*.
conceited [kɔn'si:tid], *a.* Suffisant, vaniteux. *A c. puppy*, un jeune prétentieux. *A c. little hussy*, une petite mijaurée. **-ly**, *adv.* Avec suffisance.
conceivable [kɔn'si:vəbl], *a.* Concevable, imaginable. **-ably**, *adv.* *He may c. have reached the summit*, il est concevable qu'il ait pu atteindre jusqu'au sommet.
conceive [kɔn'si:v], *v.tr.* I. Concevoir (un enfant). *Who was conceived by the Holy Ghost*, qui a été conçu du Saint-Esprit. 2. (*a*) Concevoir (un projet). *To conceive a dislike for s.o.*, prendre qn en aversion. (*b*) *I cannot c. why you should allow it*, je ne conçois pas pourquoi vous le permettriez. 3. (*Of document*) Conceived as follows, ainsi conçu. 4. *v.i.* **To conceive of sth.**, (s')imaginer, comprendre, qch. *That is not the case, as you may well c.*, vous pouvez bien vous imaginer qu'il n'en est pas ainsi.
concentrate ['kɔnsentreit]. I. *v.tr.* Concentrer (des troupes, son attention). *Mil:* **To c. the fire of a battery**, faire converger les feux d'une bat-

terie. **2.** *v.i.* (*a*) Se concentrer. (*b*) To concentrate on sth., concentrer son attention sur qch.
concentration [kɔnsen'treiʃ(ə)n], *s.* **I.** (*a*) Concentration *f* (d'une solution, etc.); *Mil:* convergence *f* (des feux). **Concentration camp,** camp de concentration. (*b*) *Ch:* **(Degree of) concentration,** titre *m* ,d'un acide). **2. Power of concentration,** faculté *f* de concentration, d'application **3.** **Hostile concentration,** rassemblement ennemi.
concentric [kɔn'sentrik], *a.* Concentrique.
-ally, *adv.* Concentriquement.
concept ['kɔnsept], *s.* Concept *m*; idée générale.
conception [kɔn'sepʃ(ə)n], *s.* Conception *f* (d'un enfant, d'une idée) *To have a clear c. of sth.*, se représenter clairement qch. par la pensée. *F:* I **haven't the remotest conception,** je n'en ai pas la moindre idée.
concern[1] [kɔn'sə:rn], *s.* **I.** (*a*) Rapport *m*. (*b*) Intérêt *m* (in, dans). **It's no concern of mine,** cela ne me regarde pas; ce n'est pas mon affaire. **2.** Souci *m*, anxiété *f*, inquiétude *t* (*about*, à l'égard de). **He enquired with concern** . ., il demanda avec sollicitude *f.* . . . *He showed deep c. at the news,* il s'est montré très affecté de cette nouvelle. **3.** (*a*) *Com: Ind:* Entreprise *f*; maison *f* de commerce, fonds *m* de commerce. *The whole c. is for sale,* toute l'entreprise est mise en vente. (*b*) *F:* Appareil *m*, machin *m*.
concern[2], *v.tr.* **I.** (*a*) Concerner, regarder, intéresser (qn, qch.); se rapporter à (qn, qch.). *That does not concern me,* cela ne me regarde pas. *You are the most closely concerned,* c'est vous le premier intéressé. *It concerns him to know* . . ., il lui importe de savoir. . . . *Treaty concerning a country,* traité relatif à un pays. *As concerns* . . ., quant à . . ., pour ce qui est de. . . . (*b*) **To concern oneself with, about, in, sth.,** s'intéresser à, s'occuper de, se mêler de, qch. **2.** (*a*) **To be concerned in, with, sth.,** s'intéresser à, s'occuper de, qch.; être en cause. *His honour is concerned,* il s'agit de son honneur. **The parties, persons, concerned,** les intéressés **As far as I am concerned,** en ce qui me concerne; quant à moi. (*b*) **To be concerned about sth.,** s'inquiéter, être inquiet, de qch. *I am concerned for his health,* sa santé me donne des inquiétudes. *He looked very much concerned,* il avait l'air très soucieux.
concerning, *prep.* Concernant, touchant, en ce qui concerne, au sujet de (qn, qch.).
concernedly [kɔn'sə:rnidli], *adv.* Avec inquiétude; d'un air soucieux.
concert[1] ['kɔnsərt], *s.* **I.** Concert *m*, accord *m*. **To sing in concert,** chanter à l'unisson. **To act in concert (with s.o.),** agir de concert, d'accord (avec qn). **2.** *Mus:* Concert; séance musicale. **Wireless concerts,** auditions musicales. '**concert-'grand,** *s. Mus:* Piano *m* à grande queue. '**concert-hall,** *s.* Salle *f* de concert. '**concert-pitch,** *s.* Diapason *m* de concert (anglais). *F:* **To keep up to concert-pitch,** se maintenir en forme.
concert[2] [kɔn'sə:rt]. **I.** *v.tr.* Concerter (des mesures). **2.** *v.i.* Se concerter, tenir conseil (*with*, avec).
concertina [kɔnsər'ti:na], *s.* **I.** *Mus:* Accordéon hexagonal **2.** *Rail:* **Concertina vestibule** (*joining coaches*), soufflet *m*.
concession [kɔn'seʃ(ə)n], *s.* Concession *f* (de terrain, d'opinion). *Mining c.,* concession minière.
concessive [kɔn'sesiv], *a.* Concessif.
conch [kɔŋk], *s.* Conque *f*.
concha ['kɔŋka], *s.* **I.** Conque *f* (de l'oreille); oreille *f* externe. **2.** Voûte *f* d'abside.

conchoidal [kɔŋ'kɔid(ə)l], *a.* Conchoïdal, -aux.
conciliate [kɔn'silieit], *v.tr.* **I.** Concilier, réconcilier (des intérêts opposés). **2.** *To c. s.o.'s favour,* se concilier la faveur de qn.
conciliation [kɔnsili'eiʃ(ə)n], *s.* Conciliation *f.* *Ind:* **Conciliation board,** conseil *m* d'arbitrage.
conciliatory [kɔn'siliətəri], *a.* Conciliant.
concise [kɔn'sais], *a.* Concis. **-ly,** *adv.* Avec concision.
conciseness [kɔn'saisnəs], *s.* Concision *f*
concision [kɔn'siʒ(ə)n], *s.* Concision *f*.
conclave ['kɔnkleiv], *s.* **I.** *R.C.Ch:* Conclave *m*. **2.** *F:* (*a*) Assemblée *f*, réunion *f*. (*b*) Conseil (tenu à huis clos).
conclude [kɔn'klu:d], *v.tr. & i.* **I.** Conclure (un traité, etc.); arranger, régler (une affaire). **2.** (*a*) Terminer, conclure, achever. **To conclude by saying** . . ., dire en terminant. . . **To be concluded in our next,** la fin au prochain numéro. (*b*) *v.i. The report concludes as follows,* le rapport se termine comme il suit. **3.** *From this I conclude that* . ., de ceci je conclus, j'estime, que. . . **4. To conclude in favour of a course of action,** conclure à une ligne de conduite. **concluding,** *a.* Final, -als.
conclusion [kɔn'klu:ʒ(ə)n], *s.* **I.** Conclusion *f* (d'un traité). **2.** Fin *f*, conclusion (d'une lettre); clôture *f* (d'une session). **In conclusion,** pour conclure. **3.** (*a' Log:* Conclusion (d'un syllogisme). (*b*) **Conclusions arrived at,** décisions prises. **To come to the conclusion that** . . ., conclure que. . . . *It was a foregone c.,* c'était prévu. *F:* **To try conclusions with s.o.,** se mesurer avec, contre, qn.
conclusive [kɔn'klu:siv], *a.* Concluant, décisif. **-ly,** *adv.* D'une manière concluante.
concoct [kɔn'kɔkt], *v.tr.* **I.** Composer (un cocktail); confectionner (un plat). **2.** Imaginer, combiner (un plan); tramer (un complot).
concoction [kɔn'kɔkʃ(ə)n], *s.* **I.** (*a*) Confectionnement *m* (d'un plat, etc.). (*b*) Boisson *f*, potion *f*. **2.** (*a*) Conception *f*; machination *f* (d'un complot). (*b*) *C. of lies,* tissu *m* de mensonges.
concomitant [kɔn'kɔmitənt]. **I.** *a.* Concomitant (*with*, de). **2.** *s.* Accessoire *m*, accompagnement *m*.
concord ['kɔnkɔ:rd], *s.* **I.** Concorde *f*, harmonie *f*. **To live in concord,** vivre en bon accord (*with*, avec). **2.** *Gram:* Concordance *f.* **The concords,** les règles *f* d'accord.
concordance [kɔn'kɔ:rdəns], *s.* Concordance *f*, accord *m* (*with*, avec); harmonie *f*.
concordant [kɔn'kɔ:rdənt], *a.* **I.** Qui s'accorde, concordant (*with*, avec). **2.** *Mus:* Consonant.
concordat [kɔn'kɔ:rdat], *s.* Concordat *m*.
concourse ['kɔnkɔ:rs], *s.* **I.** (*a*) Foule *f*, rassemblement *m*, concours *m* (de personnes). (*b*) Convergence *f* d'allées; carrefour *m*. **2.** *Unforeseen c. of circumstances,* concours inattendu de circonstances.
concrescence [kɔn'kres(ə)ns], *s.* *Biol:* Concrétion *f*.
concrete[1] ['kɔnkri:t]. **I.** *a.* Concret, -ète. *Jur:* **Concrete case,** cas d'espèce. **2.** *s.* Béton *m* (de ciment). **Reinforced concrete,** béton armé; ciment armé. **-ly,** *adv.* D'une manière concrète.
concrete[2] [kɔn'kri:t]. **I.** *v.tr. Const:* Bétonner. **2.** *v.i.* Se solidifier; se prendre en masse.
concretion [kɔn'kri:ʃ(ə)n], *s.* Concrétion *f*.
concubine ['kɔŋkjubain], *s.f.* Concubine.
concupiscence [kɔn'kju:pisəns], *s.* Concupiscence *f*.
concur [kɔn'kə:r], *v.i.* (**concurred**) **I.** (*a*) (*Of events*) Concourir, coïncider. (*b*) *To c. to produce a result,* contribuer à produire un résultat.

2. (*Of pers.*) Être d'accord (*with s.o.*, avec qn); partager l'opinion (de qn). *All c. in the belief that* . . ., tous s'accordent à croire que. . . .

concurrence [kon'kʌrəns], *s.* **1.** (*a*) Concours *m* (de circonstances); coopération *f* (de personnes). *Geom:* Point of concurrence, point de concours. (*b*) Simultanéité *f.* **2.** (*Of pers.*) (*a*) Accord *m.* (*b*) Assentiment *m*, approbation *f.*

concurrent [kon'kʌrənt], *a.* **1.** (*a*) *Geom:* Concurrent lines, lignes concourantes. (*b*) Simultané; coexistant. (*c*) Concurrent cause, cause contribuante. **2.** Unanime, concordant. **-ly,** *adv.* Concurrement (*with*, avec). *Jur:* The two sentences to run c., avec confusion des deux peines.

concussion [kon'kʌʃ(ə)n], *s.* Secousse *f*, ébranlement *m.* *Med:* Commotion (cérébrale). *Artil:* Concussion fuse, fusée percutante.

condemn [kon'dem], *v.tr.* Condamner. **1.** *To c. s.o. to death*, condamner qn à (la) mort. **Condemned cell**, cellule des condamnés. *The condemned man (on the scaffold)*, le patient. *F:* Condemned to lead a hopeless existence, condamné à vivre sans espoir. **2.** *To c. stores*, condamner, réformer, du matériel. **3.** Déclarer coupable. *F: His looks condemn him*, sa mine le condamne. **4.** Censurer, blâmer.

condemnation [kondem'neiʃ(ə)n], *s.* **1.** (*a*) Condamnation *f.* (*b*) Censure *f*, blâme *m.* **2.** *Mil:* Réforme *f* (du matériel).

condensable [kon'densəbl], *a.* Condensable.

condensation [konden'seiʃ(ə)n], *s.* **1.** Condensation *f* (de la vapeur, d'un gaz). **2.** Liquide condensé.

condense [kon'dens]. **1.** *v.tr.* Condenser (un gaz, une pensée); serrer (son style); concentrer (un produit). **2.** *v.i.* Se condenser.

condenser [kon'densər], *s.* **1.** (*a*) *Mch: Gasm:* Condenseur *m.* (*b*) *Nau:* Fresh-water condenser, distillateur *m.* **2.** *El: Opt:* Condensateur *m.*

condescend [kondi'send], *v.i.* **1.** Condescendre (*to do sth.*, à faire qch.); s'abaisser (à, jusqu'à, faire qch.). **2.** Se montrer condescendant (*to s.o.*, envers qn). **condescending,** *a.* Condescendant (*to*, envers). **-ly,** *adv.* Avec condescendance. *To treat s.o. c.*, traiter qn de haut en bas.

condescension [kondi'senʃ(ə)n], *s.* **1.** Condescendance *f* (*to*, envers, pour). **2.** Complaisance *f.* Out of condescension to s.o., par déférence *f* pour qn.

condign [kon'dain], *a.* (Châtiment) mérité, exemplaire; juste (punition).

condiment ['kondimənt], *s.* Condiment *m*; assaisonnement *m.*

condition[1] [kon'diʃ(ə)n], *s.* Condition *f.* **1.** To impose conditions on s.o., poser des conditions à qn. *Conditions laid down in an agreement*, stipulations *f* d'un contrat. On condition that . . ., à (la) condition que. . . . **2.** (*a*) État, situation *f.* In (*a*) good, bad, c., en bon, mauvais, état. To be in a (fit) c. to do sth., être à même, en état, de faire qch. Not in a c. to do sth., hors d'état de faire qch. To keep oneself in condition, se maintenir en forme. (*b*) État civil. **To change one's condition**, changer d'état; se marier. (*c*) People of humble condition, gens de simple condition. **3.** *pl.* Weather conditions, conditions atmosphériques.

condition[2], *v.tr.* **1.** *To c. that sth. be done*, stipuler qu'on fasse qch. **2.** Soumettre (qch.) à une condition. *The receipts are conditioned by the capacity of the hall*, les recettes dépendent de la capacité de la salle. **3.** *Ind:* Conditionner (la soie, l'air d'un cinéma, etc.). **conditioned,** *a.* **1.** If I were so conditioned, si j'étais dans une

position semblable. **2.** (*Of proposition*) Conditionné.

conditional [kon'diʃənəl]. **1.** *a.* Conditionnel. (*a*) *My promise was c.*, ma promesse était soumise à certaines réserves. (*b*) **Conditional on sth.**, dépendant de qch. *Cheapness is c. upon abundance*, le bon marché est fonction de l'abondance. (*c*) *Gram:* Conditional mood, mode conditionnel. **2.** *s. Gram:* Verb in the conditional, verbe au conditionnel. **-ally,** *adv.* Conditionnellement; sous certaines conditions. **Conditionally on** . . ., à la condition que. . . .

condolatory [kon'doulətəri], *a.* (Lettre, etc.) de condoléance.

condole [kon'doul], *v.i.* **To condole with s.o.**, exprimer ses condoléances à qn.

condolence [kon'doulans], *s.* Condoléance *f.*

condonation [kondou'neiʃ(ə)n], *s.* Pardon *m*; indulgence *f* (*of*, pour).

condone [kon'doun], *v.tr.* **1.** Pardonner. **2.** (*Of action*) Racheter (une offense).

condor ['kondɔ:r], *s. Orn:* Condor *m.*

conduce [kon'dju:s], *v.i.* Contribuer, tendre (*to*, à). *Virtues that c. to success*, vertus qui favorisent le succès.

conducive [kon'dju:siv], *a.* Qui contribue (à qch.); favorable (à qch.).

conduct[1] ['kondʌkt], *s.* Conduite *f.* **1.** *C. of affairs*, conduite, gestion *f*, maniement *m*, des affaires. *S.a.* SAFE-CONDUCT. **2.** Allure *f*; manière *f* de se conduire. *C. towards s.o.*, conduite à l'égard de, envers, qn.

conduct[2] [kon'dʌkt], *v.tr.* **1.** Conduire, (a)mener (qn). **Conducted tours**, excursions accompagnées. **2.** (*a*) Mener, gérer (des affaires); diriger (des opérations). *Who will c. the negotiations?* qui va mener les négociations? *Jur: To c. one's own case*, plaider soi-même sa cause. (*b*) *Mus:* Diriger (un orchestre). **3.** To conduct oneself, se comporter, se conduire (bien, mal). **4.** *Ph:* Être conducteur de. . . . *Substance that conducts heat*, substance conductrice de la chaleur. **conducting,** *a.* Conducteur, -trice.

conductance [kon'dʌktəns], *s. El:* Conductance *f.*

conductible [kon'dʌktibl], *a. Ph:* Conductible.

conduction [kon'dʌkʃ(ə)n], *s. Ph:* Conduction *f*, transmission *f* (de la chaleur).

conductive [kon'dʌktiv], *a.* Conducteur, -trice.

conductivity [kondʌk'tiviti], *s. Ph:* Conductivité *f*, conductibilité *f.*

conductor [kon'dʌktər], *s.* **1.** (*a*) Conducteur *m* (de personnes); accompagnateur *m* (de touristes). (*b*) Receveur *m* (d'un tramway). *Rail: U.S:* Chef *m* de train. (*c*) *Mus:* Chef d'orchestre. **2.** Conducteur (de la chaleur, de l'électricité). *S.a.* LIGHTNING-CONDUCTOR.

conductress [kon'dʌktres], *s.f.* Conductrice; receveuse (d'un tramway).

conduit ['kʌndit, 'kond(w)it], *s.* (*a*) *Hyd.E:* Conduit(-pipe), conduit *m*; tuyau conducteur. (*b*) *El.E:* Cable-conduit, tube *m* guide-fils; manchon *m* pour câbles.

Condy ['kondi]. *Pr.n.m.* **Condy's fluid**, solution aqueuse de permanganate de soude ou de potasse.

cone [koun], *s.* **1.** Cône *m.* **Truncated cone**, tronc *m* de cône. *Ball:* Cone of fire, gerbe *f* (de dispersion). **2.** *Blast-furnace c.*, cloche *f*, trémie *f*, de haut-fourneau. *S.a.* STORM-CONE. **3.** *Bot:* Pomme *f*, cône (de pin, de houblon). **4.** Cône (d'un volcan). **'cone-bearing,** *a. Bot:* Conifère. **'cone-pulley,** *s.* Poulie étagée. **'cone-wheel,** *s. Mec.E:* Roue *f* conique (à friction).

coney ['kouni], *s.* = CONY.

confabulation [kɔnfabju'leiʃ(ə)n], *s.* Causerie *f* intime ; entretien familier ; colloque *m*.

confection [kon'fekʃ(ə)n], *s.* Confection *f*.

confectioner [kon'fekʃənər], *s.* Confiseur *m*.

confectionery [kon'fekʃənəri], *s.* Confiserie *f*.

confederacy [kon'fedərəsi], *s.* **1.** Confédération *f* (d'États). **2.** Conspiration *f*.

confederate[1] [kon'fedərət]. **1.** *a.* Confédéré (*with*, avec). **2.** *s.* (*a*) Confédéré *m*. (*b*) *Jur:* Complice *m* (*with*, de). (*c*) *F:* Conjuror's c., comparse *m*.

confederate[2] [kon'fedəreit]. **1.** *v.tr.* Confédérer (des États). **2.** *v.i.* (*a*) Se confédérer (*with*, avec). (*b*) Conspirer (*against*, contre).

confederation [konfedə'reiʃ(ə)n], *s.* Confédération *f*.

confer [kon'fəːr], *v.* (**conferred**) **1.** *v.tr.* Conférer (*a title on s.o.*, un titre à qn). To c. a favour on s.o., accorder une faveur à qn. **2.** *v.i.* Conférer, entrer en consultation (*with s.o. on sth., about sth.*, avec qn sur qch.). **conferring**, *s.* **1.** = CON-FERMENT **2.** Consultation *f*.

conference ['kɔnfərəns], *s.* **1.** Conférence *f*, entretien *m*, consultation *f*. **2.** Educational conference, congrès *m* de l'enseignement. Industrial conference, comice industriel.

conferment [kon'fəːrmənt], *s.* **1.** Collation *f* (d'un titre). **2.** Octroi *m* (d'une faveur).

confess [kon'fes], *v.tr.* (*a*) Confesser, avouer (une faute). To c. oneself (to be) guilty, s'avouer coupable. I was wrong, I confess, j'ai eu tort, je l'avoue, j'en conviens. (*b*) *Abs.* (*Of criminal*) Faire des aveux. (*c*) *v.ind.tr.* To confess to a crime, avouer un crime. To c. to a liking for . . ., avouer avoir un penchant, un faible, pour. . . . **2.** *Ecc:* (*a*) To c. one's sins, confesser ses péchés. To confess (oneself), se confesser (*to s.o.*, à qn, auprès de qn). (*b*) (*Of priest*) Confesser (un pénitent). **3.** To confess the faith, confesser sa foi. **confessed,** *a.* Confessé, avoué. The c. murderer a . . ., le meurtrier avoué de. . .

confessedly [kon'fesidli], *adv.* **1.** De l'aveu général. **2.** Ouvertement.

confession [kon'feʃ(ə)n], *s.* **1.** Confession *f*, aveu (de qch.). To make a full confession, faire des aveux complets. By general confession, de l'aveu de tout le monde. **2.** *Ecc:* Auricular confession, confession auriculaire, privée. The seal of confession, le secret du confessionnal. To go to confession, aller à confesse. To hear s.o.'s confession, confesser qn. **3.** Confession of faith, confession de foi.

confessional [kon'feʃən(ə)l]. **1.** *a.* Confessionnel. **2.** *s. Ecc:* Confessionnal *m*.

confessor [kon'fesor], *s.* **1.** Personne *f* qui avoue (un crime). **2.** (*Priest*) Confesseur *m*. **3.** Confesseur (de sa foi).

confetti [kon'feti], *s.pl.* Confetti *m*.

confidant, *f.* **confidante** [kɔnfi'dant], *s.* Confident, -ente.

confide [kon'faid]. **1.** *v.tr.* Confier. (*a*) He confided to me that . . ., il m'avoua en confidence que. . . . (*b*) To c. sth. to s.o.'s care, confier qch. à la garde de qn. **2.** *v.i.* To confide in s.o., (i) se fier à qn ; (ii) se confier à qn. **confiding,** *a.* Confiant ; sans soupçons. To be of a c. nature, être peu soupçonneux. **-ly,** *adv.* Avec confiance ; d'un air confiant.

confidence ['kɔnfidəns], *s.* **1.** (*a*) Confiance *f* (*in*, en). To put one's c. in s.o., mettre sa confiance en qn. To have every confidence in s.o., faire toute confiance à qn. To lose the c. of the public, perdre toute créance. *Parl:* To ask for a vote of

c., poser la question de confiance. (*b*) Assurance *f*, confiance, hardiesse *f*. I have every confidence that he will succeed, j'ai l'assurance qu'il réussira. **2.** Confidence *f*. To tell s.o. sth. in c., dire qch. à qn en confidence. In strict confidence, à titre essentiellement confidentiel. **3.** To make a confidence to s.o., faire une confidence à qn. **4.** Confidence-trick, vol *m* à l'américaine. Confidence man, chevalier *m* d'industrie.

confident ['kɔnfidənt]. **1.** *a.* (*a*) Assuré, sûr (*of*, de) ; confiant. C. of success, sûr de réussir. (*b*) *Pej:* Plein de hardiesse ; effronté. **2.** *s.* Confident, -ente. **-ly,** *adv.* **1.** Avec confiance. **2.** Avec assurance.

confidential [kɔnfi'denʃ(ə)l], *a.* **1.** (*Avis*, etc.) confidentiel. **2.** To be c. with s.o., faire des confidences à qn. **3.** Confidential clerk, homme de confiance. C. secretary, secrétaire particulier. **-ally,** *adv.* Confidentiellement ; à titre confidentiel.

configuration [kɔnfigju'reiʃ(ə)n], *s.* Configuration *f*.

confine [kon'fain]. **1.** *v.tr.* (*a*) (R)enfermer (qn dans une prison, etc.). To be confined to bed, être obligé de garder le lit ; être alité. (*b*) To confine oneself to doing sth., se borner, se limiter, à faire qch. To c. oneself to facts, s'en tenir aux faits. (*c*) Resserrer (une rivière dans son lit). To be confined (for space), être à l'étroit. Confined space, espace resserré, restreint. (*d*) (*Of woman*) To be confined, faire ses couches. **2.** *v.i.* To c. with a country, confiner à un pays.

confinement [kon'fainmənt], *s.* **1.** Emprisonnement *m*, réclusion *f*. In close confinement, in solitary confinement, au secret ; dans une réclusion rigoureuse. **2.** (*a*) C. to one's bed, alitement *m*. (*b*) Couches *fpl*, accouchement *m*. **3.** Limitation *f*, restriction *f* (*to*, à).

confines ['kɔnfainz], *s.pl.* (*a*) *Lit:* Confins *m* (d'un lieu, etc.). (*b*) Eaux *f* (d'un port).

confirm [kon'fəːrm], *v.tr.* **1.** (R)affermir (son pouvoir) ; fortifier (une résolution) ; confirmer (qn dans une opinion). **2.** Confirmer (un traité) ; *Jur:* entériner (une décision) ; homologuer (un arrêt). **3.** Confirmer, corroborer (une nouvelle). Confirming my letter, en confirmation de ma lettre. **4.** *Ecc:* Confirmer To be confirmed, recevoir la confirmation. **confirmed,** *a.* (Habitude) invétérée ; (ivrogne) incorrigible ; (célibataire) endurci.

confirmation [kɔnfər'meiʃ(ə)n], *s.* **1.** (R)affermissement *m* (de l'autorité de qn) ; confirmation *f* (d'un traité, d'une nouvelle). In confirmation of . . ., pour confirmer. . . . **2.** *Ecc:* Confirmation *f*.

confirmative [kon'fəːrmətiv], *a.* Confirmatif (*of*, de).

confiscate ['kɔnfiskeit], *v.tr.* Confisquer.

confiscation [kɔnfis'keiʃ(ə)n], *s.* Confiscation *f*.

conflagration [kɔnfla'greiʃ(ə)n], *s.* (*a*) Conflagration *f*, embrasement *m*. (*b*) Incendie *m*.

conflict[1] ['kɔnflikt], *s.* Conflit *m*, lutte *f* ; antagonisme *m* (d'intérêts). To come into conflict with s.o., entrer en conflit avec qn.

conflict[2] [kon'flikt], *v.i.* **1.** *A:* Lutter (*with*, contre). **2.** Être en conflit, en contradiction, en désaccord (*with*, avec). When interests c., lorsque les intérêts se heurtent. **conflicting,** *a.* Opposé (*with*, à) ; incompatible (*with*, avec). C. evidence, témoignages discordants.

confluence ['kɔnfluəns], *s.* **1.** Confluent *m* (de voies). **2.** *A:* Affluence *f*, concours *m* (de monde).

confluent ['kɔnfluənt]. **1.** *a.* (*Of streams*) Qui

confluent ; (of marks, spots) qui se confondent. **2.** s. Affluent m (d'un fleuve).

conform [kɔn'fɔ:rm]. **I.** v.tr. Conformer (sth. to sth., qch. à qch.). **2.** v.i. Se conformer (to, with, à). (a) To c. to fashion, suivre la mode. To c. to the law, obéir aux lois. (b) (Of a part) To c. (in shape) to another part, s'adapter à une autre pièce. (c) Rel.H : Faire acte de conformité.

conformable [kɔn'fɔ:rməbl], a. **I.** Conforme (to, à). **2.** (Of pers.) (a) Accommodant. (b) Docile, soumis (to, à). -**ably**, adv. Conformably to . . ., conformément à (vos désirs, etc.).

conformation [kɔnfɔr'meiʃ(ə)n], s. Conformation f, structure f.

conformity [kɔn'fɔ:rmiti], s. Conformité f (to, with, à). In c. with your instructions, conformément à vos ordres.

confound [kɔn'faund], v.tr. **I.** Confondre, déconcerter (les plans de qn). **2.** Bouleverser, confondre (qn). **3.** Lit : (a) Mêler, brouiller. (b) To c. sth. with sth., confondre qch. avec qch. **4.** Confound him! que le diable l'emporte! C. it! zut! **confounded**, a. F : Maudit, satané, sacré. -**ly**, adv. F : It was c. cold, il faisait bigrement froid.

confraternity [kɔnfra'tə:rniti], s. **I.** Confrérie f. **2.** Treaty of c., traité de confraternité.

confront [kɔn'frʌnt], v.tr. **I.** To c. s.o., être en face, se trouver en présence, de qn. **2.** To c. the enemy, a danger, affronter, faire face à, l'ennemi, un danger. **3.** To c. s.o. with witnesses, confronter qn avec des témoins.

confrontation [kɔnfrʌn'teiʃ(ə)n], s. Confrontation f (de témoins, etc.).

confuse [kɔn'fju:z], v.tr. **I.** Mêler, brouiller. To c. accounts, embrouiller des comptes. **2.** To c. sth. with sth., confondre qch. avec qch. **3.** (a) Embrouiller (qn). To get confused, s'embrouiller. (b) Bouleverser, troubler (qn). To get confused, se troubler. **confused**, a. **I.** (a) Embrouillé. C. mind, esprit trouble. (b) Bouleversé, F : ahuri. (c) Confus, interdit. **2.** C. speech, discours confus. **confusing**, a. Embrouillant. It is very confusing, on s'y perd.

confusedly [kɔn'fju:zidli], adv. Confusément.

confusion [kɔn'fju:ʒ(ə)n], s. **I.** (Of pers.) Confusion f. To put s.o. to confusion, couvrir qn de confusion, de honte. **2.** Désordre m, remueménage m. Everything was in confusion, tout était sens dessus dessous. To retire in c., se retirer à la débandade. To fall into confusion, se désorganiser. Confusion worse confounded, le comble de la confusion. **3.** Confusion of sth. with sth., confusion de qch. avec qch.

confutation [kɔnfju'teiʃ(ə)n], s. Réfutation f.

confute [kɔn'fju:t], v.tr. **I.** Convaincre (qn) d'erreur **2.** Réfuter (un argument).

congeal [kɔn'dʒi:l]. **I.** v.tr. (a) Congeler, geler. (b) Coaguler ; . cailler (le sang) ; figer (l'huile, le sang). **2.** v.i. (a) Se congeler ; geler. (b) (Of oil, blood) Se figer ; (of jelly) se prendre.

congealable [kɔn'dʒi:ləbl], a. Congelable ; concrescible.

congealment [kɔn'dʒi:lmənt], **congelation** [kɔndʒe'leiʃ(ə)n], s Congélation f.

congener [ˈkɔndʒenər]. **I.** s. Congénère m (of, de). **2.** a. Congénère (to, de).

congeneric [kɔndʒe'nerik], a. Congénère.

congenial [kɔn'dʒi:njəl], a. (a) C. with sth., du même caractère, de la même nature, que qch. We have c. tastes, nous avons des goûts en commun. (b) Congenial spirit, esprit sympathique, aimable. C. employment, travail agréable. **2.** Propre, convenable, qui convient (to, à). If I could

find some c. employment, si je pouvais trouver un emploi qui me convienne. -**ally**, adv. Agréablement ; d'un ton aimable.

congeniality [kɔndʒi:ni'aliti], s. Accord m de sentiments, d'humeur ; communauté f (de goûts).

congenital [kɔn'dʒenit(ə)l], a. Congénital, -aux. Congenital idiot, (i) idiot de naissance ; (ii) F : parfait idiot. -**ally**, adv. De naissance.

conger [ˈkɔŋgər], s. Ich : Conger(-eel), congre m ; anguille f de mer.

congeries [kɔn'dʒeriiz, -'dʒi:əriiz], s. Entassement m, amas m, accumulation f, masse f (d'objets disparates, etc.).

congest [kɔn'dʒest]. **I.** v.tr. (a) Med : Congestionner ; engorger. (b) Encombrer, embouteiller (la circulation, les rues, etc.). **2.** v.i. (a) Med : Se congestionner. (b) (Of traffic, etc.) S'embouteiller. **congested**, a. **I.** Med : Congestionné. **2.** (Of traffic) Encombré, embouteillé. Congested area, région surpeuplée.

congestion [kɔn'dʒestʃ(ə)n], s. **I.** Med : Congestion f ; engorgement m. Congestion of the brain, of the lungs, congestion cérébrale, pulmonaire. **2.** (a) Encombrement m de rue, de circulation ; presse f. (b) Surpeuplement m.

conglomerate[1] [kɔn'glɔmərət]. **I.** a. Congloméré. **2.** s. Geol : Conglomérat m, aggloméré m.

conglomerate[2] [kɔn'glɔməreit]. **I.** v.tr. Conglomérer. **2.** v.i. Se conglomérer. Geol : S'agglomérer.

conglomeration [kɔnglɔmə'reiʃ(ə)n], s. Conglomération f ; agrégation f (de roches, etc.).

congratulate [kɔn'gratjuleit], v.tr. To c. s.o. on sth., féliciter qn de qch. I congratulate you, (je vous en fais) mes compliments.

congratulation [kɔngratju'leiʃ(ə)n], s. Félicitation f. Congratulations! je vous en félicite !

congratulatory [kɔn'gratjulətəri], a. (Lettre) de félicitations.

congregate [ˈkɔŋgregeit]. **I.** v.tr. Rassembler, réunir. **2.** v.i. Se rassembler, s'assembler.

congregation [kɔŋgre'geiʃ(ə)n], s. **I.** Rassemblement m. **2.** (a) A : Assemblée f. (b) (In church) L'assistance f, les paroissiens m. To preach to a large c., prêcher devant une nombreuse assistance.

congregational [kɔŋgre'geiʃən(ə)l], a. Rel.H : The Congregational Church, l'Église congrégationaliste.

congress [ˈkɔŋgres], s. **I.** Réunion f (d'atomes, de personnes). **2.** Congrès m.

congressman, pl. -**men** [ˈkɔŋgresmən, -men], s.m. U.S : Membre du Congrès.

congruence [ˈkɔŋgruəns], **congruency** [ˈkɔŋgruənsi], s. Conformité f (with, avec).

congruent [ˈkɔŋgruənt], a. **I.** Conforme (with, à). **2.** Mth : Congruent (with, à).

congruity [kɔŋ'gruiti], s. = CONGRUENCE.

congruous [ˈkɔŋgruəs], a. = CONGRUENT **I.** -**ly**, adv. Congrûment, convenablement (to, with, à).

conic(al) [ˈkɔnik(əl)], a. Geom : Conique. Conic sections, sections coniques.

conicity [ko'nisiti], s. Conicité f.

conics [ˈkɔniks], s.pl. Mth : Sections f coniques.

conifer [ˈkounifər], s. Bot : Conifère m.

coniferous [ko'nifərəs], a. Bot : Conifère.

conjectural [kɔn'dʒektjur(ə)l], a. Conjectural, -aux.

conjecture[1] [kɔn'dʒektjər], s. Conjecture f.

conjecture[2], v.tr. Conjecturer.

conjoin [kɔn'dʒɔin]. **I.** v.tr. Conjoindre. **2.** v.i. S'unir ; se joindre ensemble ; s'associer.

conjoined, a. Conjoint ; (planètes) en conjonction.

conjoint [kon'dʒɔint], *a.* Conjoint, associé. **-ly,** *adv* Conjointement, ensemble.

conjugal ['kɔndʒug(ə)l], *a.* Conjugal, -aux. **-ally,** *adv.* Conjugalement.

conjugate[1] ['kɔndʒuget], *a.* Conjugué.

conjugate[2] ['kɔndʒugeit], **1.** *v.tr.* Conjuguer (un verbe). **2.** *v.i.* *Biol:* (*Of cells*) Se conjuguer

conjugation [kɔndʒu'gei∫(ə)n], *s.* Conjugaison *f.*

conjunct [kon'dʒʌŋkt], *a.* Conjoint, associé. **-ly,** *adv.* Conjointement.

conjunction [kon'dʒʌŋ(k)∫(ə)n], *s.* Conjonction *f.* In conjunction with s.o., de concert avec qn.

conjunctiva [kɔndʒʌŋk'taivə], *s.* Conjonctive *f* (de l'œil).

conjunctive [kon'dʒʌŋ(k)tiv]. **1.** *a.* (Tissu) conjonctif. **2.** *a.* & *s.* *Gram:* (Mode) conjonctif (*m*).

conjuncture [kon'dʒʌŋ(k)tʃər], *s.* Conjoncture *f,* circonstance *f,* occasion *f.*

conjuration [kɔndʒu'rei∫(ə)n], *s.* Conjuration *f.* **1.** Évocation *f* (des démons). **2.** Incantation *f.*

conjure, *v.* **1.** [kon'dʒuər], *v.tr.* Conjurer (*s.o. to do sth.,* qn de faire qch.). **2.** ['kʌndʒər] (*a*) *v.tr.* Conjurer (un démon). **To conjure up,** évoquer (un esprit). *F:* *To c. up memories,* évoquer des souvenirs. *F:* **A name to conjure with,** un nom tout-puissant. (*b*) *v.i.* Faire des tours de passe-passe. **conjuring,** *s.* **1.** Conjuration *f* (des esprits). Conjuring up, évocation *f.* **2.** Presti-digitation *f;* tours *mpl* de passe-passe.

conjurer, conjuror ['kʌndʒərər], *s.* Presti-digitateur *m.*

conk [kɔŋk], *v.i.* *Aut:* *P:* (*Of engine*) Flancher; avoir des ratés. **To conk out,** (se) caler.

conker ['kɔŋkər], *s.* *F:* Marron *m* d'Inde.

connate ['kɔneit], *a.* (*a*) **Connate ideas,** idées innées. (*b*) **Connate with . . .,** né en même temps que. . .

connect [kɔ'nekt]. **1.** *v.tr.* (*a*) (Re)lier, (ré)unir; rattacher, joindre (*with, to,* à). **Connected by telephone,** relié par téléphone. *Tp:* *To c. two subscribers,* mettre deux abonnés en communica-tion. *El:* *To c. to earth,* relier à la terre. *Con-nected to the mains,* branché sur le secteur. (*Of power stations*) **Connected up,** interconnectés. (*b*) Associer (*with,* avec, à); relier (des idées). (*c*) (*Of pers.*) **To be connected with a family,** être allié à, avec, une famille. **2.** *v.i.* Se lier, se relier, se joindre, se réunir. *Rail:* *etc:* **To connect with a train,** faire correspondance avec un train. **connected,** *a.* **1.** (*a*) *C. speech,* discours suivi. (*b*) *Two closely c. trades,* deux métiers affins, connexes. **2.** (*Of pers.*) **To be well connected,** être bien apparenté. **3.** *Bot:* *Jur:* Connexe. **-ly,** *adv.* *To think c.,* avoir de la suite dans les idées. **connecting,** *a.* **Connecting wire,** fil de connexion. *C. gear,* embrayage *m.* Connecting-rod, bielle motrice.

connection [kɔ'nek∫(ə)n], *s.* **1.** Rapport *m,* liaison *f* (des choses); connexion *f,* suite *f* (des idées). *This question has no c. with . . .,* cette question n'a rien à voir avec. . . . In connection with . . ., à propos de . . ., relatif à. . . . In this connection, à ce propos; à cet égard. In another connection, d'autre part. **2.** **To form a connection with s.o.,** établir des rapports, des relations, avec qn. **To break off a connection,** rompre des relations. **3.** (*a*) Parenté *f;* liens *mpl* de famille. (*b*) *He, she, is a c. of mine,* c'est un(e) de mes parent(e)s. **4.** *Com:* **Wide connection,** belle clientèle; achalandage *m* considérable. *Commercial traveller with a wide c.,* commis voyageur bien relationné. **5.** *Rail:* Corres-pondance *f;* train correspondant. **6.** *Mec.E:*

Connexion; assemblage *m;* embrayage *m.* *Tp:* **Wrong connection,** fausse communication. **7.** (*a*) Raccord *m* (entre deux tuyaux). (*b*) *El.E:* Contact *m;* prise *f* de courant.

connective [kɔ'nektiv], *a.* Connectif. *Anat:* Connective tissue, tissu cellulaire connectif, conjonctif.

connexion [kɔ'nek∫(ə)n], *s.* = CONNECTION.

connivance [kɔ'naivəns], *s.* Connivence *f;* complicité *f* (*at, in,* dans). *This was done with his c.,* cela s'est fait d'intelligence avec lui.

connive [kɔ'naiv], *v.i.* **To connive at an abuse,** fermer les yeux sur un abus.

connoisseur [kɔnə'sɔːr], *s.* Connaisseur *m.*

connotation [kɔno'tei∫(ə)n], *s.* **1.** Signification *f* (d'un mot). **2.** *Phil:* Compréhension *f* (d'un nom générique).

connote [kɔ'nout], *v.tr.* **1.** *Log:* Connoter. **2.** Comporter (une signification secondaire, etc.). **3.** *F:* Signifier; impliquer.

connubial [kɔ'njuːbiəl], *a.* Conjugal, -aux.

conquer ['kɔŋkər], *v.tr.* **1.** Conquérir. *To c. all hearts,* subjuguer tous les cœurs. **2.** Vaincre.
conquering, *a.* **1.** Conquérant. **2.** Victorieux. *The c. hero,* le héros triomphant.

conqueror ['kɔŋkərər], *s.* **1.** Conquérant *m* (d'un pays). *Eng.Hist:* **The Conqueror,** Guillaume le Conquérant. **2.** Vainqueur *m.*

conquest ['kɔŋkwest], *s.* Conquête *f.* *F:* **To make a conquest of s.o., of s.o.'s heart,** faire la conquête de qn.

consanguinity [kɔnsaŋ'gwiniti], *s.* **1.** Consan-guinité *f;* parenté *f* du côté du père. **2.** *F:* Pa-renté.

conscience ['kɔn∫əns], *s.* Conscience *f.* **With a clear conscience,** en (toute) sûreté de conscience. **To have no conscience,** être sans conscience. *I did it for c. sake,* je l'ai fait par acquit de conscience. In (all) conscience, en vérité, assuré-ment, certes. I would not have the conscience to do it, cela irait contre ma conscience de le faire. **'conscience-money,** *s.* Somme resti-tuée au fisc par remords de conscience. **'con-science-stricken,** *a.* Pris de remords.

conscientious [kɔn∫i'en∫əs], *a.* **1.** Conscien-cieux. **2.** **Conscientious scruple,** scrupule de conscience. **Conscientious objector,** réfractaire *m;* objecteur *m* de conscience. **-ly,** *adv.* Con-sciencieusement.

conscientiousness [kɔn∫i'en∫əsnəs], *s.* Con-science *f;* droiture *f.*

conscious ['kɔn∫əs], *a.* **1.** (*a*) **To be conscious of sth.,** avoir conscience de qch.; sentir qch. *I was not c. of having moved,* je n'avais pas conscience d'avoir bougé. **To become conscious of sth.,** s'apercevoir de qch. *I was c. that he was looking at me,* je sentais qu'il me regardait. (*b*) **Conscious movement,** mouvement conscient. (*c*) *Phil:* **Man as a c. being,** l'homme en tant qu'être conscient. **2.** **To be conscious,** avoir sa connaissance. *To become c.,* reprendre connais-sance; revenir de son évanouissement. **-ly,** *adv.* Consciemment.

consciousness ['kɔn∫əsnəs], *s.* **1.** (*a*) Con-science *f,* sentiment *m* (*of,* de). *The c. of being watched,* le sentiment qu'on vous regarde. (*b*) Sentiment intime, persuasion *f* intime. *C. that all is not well,* pressentiment *m* de malheur. **2.** *Phil:* (*a*) Conscience (de l'être conscient). (*b*) Moral consciousness, conscience morale. **3.** **To lose consciousness,** perdre connaissance; s'évanouir. **To regain consciousness,** revenir à soi.

conscript[1] ['kɔnskript], *a.* & *s.* Conscrit (*m*).

conscript² [kon'skript], *v.tr.* Enrôler, engager (des troupes).

conscription [kon'skripʃ(ə)n], *s.* Conscription *f.*

consecrate¹ ['kɔnsekret], *a.* Consacré (*to*, à).

consecrate² ['kɔnsekreit], *v.tr.* **1.** (*a*) *Ecc:* Consacrer (une église); bénir (le pain); sacrer (un évêque). (*b*) *Custom consecrated by time*, coutume consacrée par le temps. **2.** *To c. one's life to a work*, consacrer sa vie à un travail. **consecrated,** *a.* (*Of church, phrase*) Consacré; (*of bread*) bénit. **In consecrated ground**, en terre sainte, en terre bénite.

consecration [kɔnse'kreiʃ(ə)n], *s.* **1.** Consécration *f*; sacre *m* (d'un roi). **2.** *The c. of a whole life to a single object*, le dévouement d'une vie entière à un seul but.

consecutive [kon'sekjutiv], *a.* Consécutif. **1.** *On three c. days*, trois jours de suite. *Mus:* *C. fifths*, quintes consécutives. **2.** *Gram:* **Consecutive clause**, proposition consécutive. **-ly,** *adv.* Consécutivement; de suite.

consensus [kon'sensəs], *s.* Consensus *m*, unanimité *f* (d'opinions, de témoignages).

consent¹ [kon'sent], *s.* Consentement *m*, assentiment *m.* *C. to a request*, agrément donné à une requête. **By common consent**, d'une commune voix; de l'aveu de tout le monde. **With one consent**, d'un commun accord. **By mutual consent**, de gré à gré.

consent², *v.i.* **To consent to sth.**, consentir à qch. *I consent*, j'y consens; je veux bien.

consequence ['kɔnsekwəns], *s.* **1.** Conséquence *f*; suites *fpl.* **In consequence**, par conséquent. **In consequence of** ..., par suite de .... **To take the consequences**, **to put up with the consequences**, subir, accepter, les conséquences. **2.** Importance *f*; *F:* conséquence. **It is of no consequence**, cela ne tire pas à conséquence; cela ne fait rien. **He is of no consequence**, il ne compte pas. **To set up for a man of consequence**, faire l'important.

consequent¹ ['kɔnsekwənt], *s.* **1.** *Mth:* Conséquent *m.* **2.** *Log:* Conclusion *f.*

consequent², *a.* **1.** Résultant. *Infirmity c. on a wound*, infirmité consécutive à une blessure. **2.** *Log:* Conséquent (*from*, de). **3.** (*Consistent*) Conséquent, logique. **-ly.** **1.** *adv. & conj.* Par conséquent; conséquemment. **2.** *adv.* Logiquement.

consequential [kɔnse'kwenʃ(ə)l], *a.* **1.** Conséquent, consécutif (*to*, à). **2.** (*Of pers.*) Suffisant; plein d'importance. **-ally,** *adv.* **1.** Indirectement, secondairement. **2.** D'un air important.

conservancy [kon'sə:rvənsi], *s.* **1.** Commission *f* de conservation. **The Thames Conservancy**, la Commission fluviale (de la Tamise). **2.** Conservation *f*, protection *f* (des forêts, etc.).

conservation [kɔnsər'veiʃ(ə)n], *s.* Conservation *f*, protection *f.* *C. of forests*, conservation forestière.

conservative [kon'sə:rvətiv]. **1.** *a.* (*a*) Préservateur, -trice; conservateur, -trice. (*b*) *At a c. estimate*, au bas mot. *On c. lines*, selon la méthode consacrée par l'usage. **2.** *a. & s. Pol:* Conservateur.

conservator ['kɔnsərveitər], *s.* Conservateur, -trice (d'une forêt, d'un musée).

conservatory [kon'sə:rvətəri], *s. Hort:* Serre *f.*

conserve [kon'sə:rv], *v.tr.* Conserver, préserver.

conserves [kon'sə:rvz], *s.pl. Cu:* Confiture(s) *f*, conserves *f* (de fruits).

consider [kon'sidər], *v.tr.* **1.** (*a*) Considérer (une question); envisager (une possibilité). *I will c. it*, j'y réfléchirai; j'y songerai. **Considered opinion**, opinion motivée, réfléchie. **All things considered**,

tout bien considéré; (toute) réflexion faite. (*b*) Prendre (une offre) en considération: étudier, examiner (une proposition). **2.** (*a*) **To consider s.o., s.o.'s feelings**, avoir égard à la sensibilité de qn; ménager qn. *To c. the expense*, regarder à la dépense. (*b*) *When one considers that* ..., quand on pense que. ... **3.** (*a*) *Pred. I c. him (to be) crazy*, je le considère, regarde, comme fou; je le tiens pour fou. **Consider it as done**, tenez cela pour fait. *He is considered rich*, on le dit riche. *To c. oneself happy*, s'estimer heureux. (*b*) *We c. that he ought to do it*, à notre avis il doit le faire.

considering, *prep.* Eu égard à (qch.). *C. his age*, étant donné son âge. *C. the circumstances*, vu les circonstances. **Considering that** ..., vu, attendu, que. ... *F: It is not so bad considering*, somme toute, ce n'est pas si mal.

considerable [kon'sidərəbl], *a.* Considérable. *A c. number of* ..., un nombre considérable de, pas mal de. ... *To a c. extent*, dans une forte mesure. **-ably,** *adv.* Considérablement.

considerate [kon'sidəret], *a.* Prévenant, plein d'égards (*towards*, pour, envers). *If you had been more c.*, si vous aviez tenu compte de son état, etc. ... **-ly,** *adv.* Avec égards, avec prévenance.

considerateness [kon'sidəretnəs], *s.* Attentions *fpl*, égards *mpl* (*to, for*, envers, pour).

consideration [kɔnsidə'reiʃ(ə)n], *s.* **1.** Considération *f.* (*a*) **To take sth. into consideration**, prendre qch. en considération; tenir compte de qch. **Taking all things into c.**, tout bien considéré. *Fact that has been left out of c.*, fait auquel on n'a pas pris garde. **In consideration of** ..., en considération de ..., eu égard à. ... **Question under consideration**, question en délibération, à l'examen, à l'étude. **After due consideration**, après mûre réflexion; tout bien considéré. *A list for your kind c.*, une liste que nous vous prions de bien vouloir examiner. (*b*) *Money is always the first c.*, la question d'argent vient toujours en premier. *Material considerations*, préoccupations matérielles. **On no consideration** ..., à aucun prix ..., pour rien au monde. ... **2.** Compensation *f*, rémunération *f.* **For a consideration**, contre espèces; *F:* moyennant finance. **3.** *Out of consideration for s.o.*, par égard, par considération, pour qn. *To treat s.o. with c.*, to show s.o. c., ménager qn. **4.** *Of great, of no, consideration*, de grande importance; d'aucune importance. *Money is no c.*, l'argent n'entre pas en ligne de compte.

consign [kon'sain], *v.tr.* **1.** Consigner, expédier (des marchandises) (*to s.o.*, à qn, à l'adresse de qn); envoyer (des marchandises) en consignation (à qn). **2.** Confier, livrer (*sth. to s.o.'s care*, qch. à qn, entre les mains de qn). **To consign sth. to oblivion**, ensevelir qch. dans l'oubli.

consignee [kɔnsai'ni:], *s.* Consignataire *m.*

consignment [kon'sainmənt], *s.* **1.** (*a*) Envoi *m*, expédition *f* (de marchandises). *For c. abroad*, à destination de l'étranger. **Consignment note**, (i) lettre *f* de voiture; (ii) *Rail:* récépissé *m.* (*b*) *Com:* **On consignment**, en consignation, en dépôt (permanent). **2.** Envoi, arrivage *m* (de marchandises).

consignor [kon'sainər], *s. Com:* Consignateur *m*, expéditeur *m.*

consist [kon'sist], *v.i.* (*a*) **To consist of sth.**, consister en, dans, se composer de, qch. (*b*) *True happiness consists in desiring little*, le vrai bonheur consiste à modérer ses désirs.

consistence [kon'sistəns], *s.* Consistance *f* (d'un sirop, etc.); compacité *f* (du sol, etc.).

consistency [kɔn'sistənsi], s. **1.** = CONSISTENCE.
2. Uniformité f (de conduite). *Your actions
lack c.*, vos actions manquent de suite f, de
logique f.
consistent [kɔn'sistənt], a. **1.** (*Of pers.*) Conséquent; logique. *Ideas that are not c.*, idées qui
ne se tiennent pas. **2.** Compatible, d'accord (*with*,
avec). **-ly,** adv. **1.** Conséquemment; avec
conséquence, avec logique. **2.** Conformément
(*with*, à).
consistory [kɔn'sistəri], s. *Ecc:* Consistoire m.
consolable [kɔn'souləbl], a. Consolable.
consolation [kɔnso'leiʃ(ə)n], s. Consolation f.
Consolation prize, prix de consolation.
console[1] ['kɔnsoul], s. **1.** *Arch:* Console f.
2. Console (d'orgue). *Wireless c.*, meuble m pour
T.S.F.
console[2] [kɔn'soul], v.tr. Consoler (*s.o. for a loss*,
qn d'une perte). **consoling,** a. Consolant;
consolateur, -trice.
consoler [kɔn'soulər], s. Consolateur, -trice.
consolidate [kɔn'sɔlideit]. **1.** v.tr. (a) Consolider, (r)affermir. (b) Consolider, (ré)unir (deux
propriétés); unifier (une dette). **The consolidated annuities,** les fonds consolidés. **2.** v.i. Se
consolider; (*of road*) se tasser.
consolidation [kɔnsɔli'deiʃ(ə)n], s. **1.** Consolidation f, (r)affermissement m; tassement m
(de terres). **2.** Unification f (des lois, etc.).
consols [kɔn'sɔlz], s.pl. *Fin:* Fonds consolidés.
consonance ['kɔnsonəns], s. **1.** Consonance f;
Mus: accord m. **2.** Accord, communion f
(d'idées).
consonant[1] ['kɔnsonənt], a. **1.** Consonant.
2. Consonant with duty, qui s'accorde avec le
devoir.
consonant[2], s. *Ling:* Consonne f.
consort[1] ['kɔnsɔːrt], s. **1.** Époux, -ouse. **Queen
consort,** reine consort(e). **2. To act in consort
with s.o.,** agir de concert avec qn. *Nau:* **To sail
in consort,** naviguer de conserve.
consort[2] [kɔn'sɔːrt], v.i. **To consort with s.o.,**
frayer avec qn; fréquenter qn.
conspectus [kɔn'spektəs], s. Aperçu général.
conspicuous [kɔn'spikjuəs], a. **1.** Qui donne
dans la vue; (repère) voyant. *In a c. position*, bien
en évidence. *To be c.*, attirer les regards. *F:* **To
be conspicuous by one's absence,** briller par son
absence. **2.** Frappant, marquant. **To make
oneself conspicuous,** se faire remarquer; se
singulariser; se signaler (*by*, through, par). *C.
gallantry*, bravoure insigne. **-ly,** adv. Manifestement; bien en évidence.
conspiracy [kɔn'spirəsi], s. **1.** Conspiration f,
conjuration f. **2.** *Jur:* Entente délictueuse.
conspirator [kɔn'spirətər], s. Conspirateur,
-trice; conjuré m.
conspire [kɔn'spaiər], v.i. (a) Conspirer (*against*,
contre); agir de concert (avec qn). **To conspire
to do sth.,** comploter de faire qch.; s'entendre
pour faire qch. (b) (*Of events*) Concourir,
conspirer (*to*, à).
constable ['kʌnstəbl], s. **1.** (a) *Hist:* Connétable
m. (b) Gouverneur m (d'un château). **2.** (Police)
constable, gardien m de la paix. **Chief constable**
= commissaire m de police. **Special constable,**
citoyen assermenté faisant fonction d'agent de
police.
constabulary [kɔn'stabjuləri], s. La police.
constancy ['kɔnstənsi], s. **1.** Constance f, fermeté f (de caractère); fidélité f (d'un ami).
2. Constance (de la température); régularité f
(du vent).
constant ['kɔnstənt]. **1.** a. (a) Constant; (équi-

libre) stable; (pression) invariable; *El:* (courant) continu. (b) Incessant, continuel; (travail)
assidu, soutenu. (c) (Ami) loyal, -aux; (au cœur)
fidèle. **2.** s. *Mth: Ph:* Constante f. **-ly,** adv.
Constamment, continuellement.
constellation [kɔnste'leiʃ(ə)n], s. Constellation f.
consternation [kɔnstər'neiʃ(ə)n], s. Consternation f; atterrement m. *They looked at each other
in c.*, ils se regardaient atterrés, consternés.
constipate ['kɔnstipeit], v.tr. *Med:* Constiper.
constipating, a. Constipant; échauffant.
constipation [kɔnsti'peiʃ(ə)n], s. Constipation f.
constituency [kɔn'stitjuənsi], s. **1.** Collège
(électoral); électeurs mpl. **2.** Circonscription
électorale.
constituent [kɔn'stitjuənt]. **1.** a. Constituant,
constitutif. **2.** s. Élément constitutif; composant m. **3.** s.pl. Mandants m (d'un député); électeurs m.
constitute ['kɔnstitjuːt], v.tr. Constituer. **1. Constituted authority,** les autorités constituées. *To
c. s.o. arbitrator*, constituer, nommer, qn arbitre.
2. Constituer, faire (le bonheur de qn). **3.** *So
constituted that . . .*, ainsi fait que. . . .
constitution [kɔnsti'tjuːʃ(ə)n], s. **1.** Constitution f, composition f (de qch.). **2.** Complexion f,
constitution (du corps). *Iron c.*, santé f de fer.
3. *Pol:* Constitution (d'un État). **4.** pl. *Hist:*
Constitutions, arrêts m.
constitutional [kɔnsti'tjuːʃ(ə)nl]. **1.** a. (a) (Monarque) constitutionnel. (b) *Med:* (Affection)
diathésique. **2.** s. **To take, go for, one's constitutional,** faire sa promenade quotidienne.
-ally, adv. **1.** Constitutionnellement. **2.** Par
tempérament.
constitutive ['kɔnstitjutiv], a. Constitutif.
constrain [kɔn'strein], v.tr. **1. To constrain s.o.
to do sth.,** contraindre, forcer, qn à, de, faire qch.
To feel constrained to do sth., se voir dans la
nécessité de faire qch. **2.** (a) (*Of clothing*) Contraindre (le corps). (b) Retenir (qn) de force;
tenir (qn) en contrainte. **constrained,** a.
(Sourire) forcé; (air) gêné.
constraint [kɔn'streint], s. **1.** Contrainte f.
To put s.o. under constraint, retenir qn de force;
enfermer, interner (un aliéné). **2.** (a) (*Of manner*)
Gêne f, contrainte. (b) Retenue f. *To speak without constraint,* parler à cœur ouvert.
constrict [kɔn'strikt], v.tr. **1.** Resserrer, étrangler, rétrécir (une ouverture). **2.** Brider, serrer,
gêner. *Constricted figure*, taille étranglée par le
corset.
constriction [kɔn'strikʃ(ə)n], s. Resserrement m,
étranglement m; *Med:* strangulation f (des
artères).
constrictor [kɔn'striktər], s. **1.** (Muscle) constricteur (m). **2.** = boa-constrictor, q.v. under BOA.
construct [kɔn'strʌkt], v.tr. Construire; bâtir
(un édifice); établir (un chemin de fer); *F:* confectionner, charpenter (un drame).
construction [kɔn'strʌkʃ(ə)n], s. **1.** (a) Construction f, établissement m (d'une machine, d'un
édifice. **Under construction, in course of
construction,** en construction. (b) Construction,
édifice m, bâtiment m. **2.** (a) *Gram:* Construction (de la phrase). (b) **To put a good, bad,
construction on s.o.'s words,** interpréter en bien,
en mal, les paroles de qn. *To put a wrong c. on
sth.,* mésinterpréter qch.; entendre qch. de
travers; prendre le contre-sens des paroles de qn.
constructional [kɔn'strʌkʃənl], a. De construction. **Constructional engineering,** construction f mécanique. *S.a.* IRONWORK.
constructive [kɔn'strʌktiv], a. **1.** Constructif;

(esprit) créateur. **2.** *Jur:* Par déduction. *S.a.* LOSS 2.

constructor [kən'strʌktər], *s.* Constructeur *m*; ingénieur *m* (des constructions navales).

construe ['kɔnstruː, kən'struː], *v.tr.* **I.** (*a*) *Sch:* Faire le mot à mot (d'un passage); analyser, décomposer (une phrase). *To c.* Homer, expliquer Homère. *Sentence that does not c.*, phrase qui manque de construction. (*b*) *Gram: Preposition construed with the dative*, préposition qui gouverne le datif. **2.** Interpréter (les paroles de qn); expliquer (la conduite de qn).

consul ['kɔnsəl], *s.* Consul *m*.

consular ['kɔnsjulər], *a.* Consulaire.

consulate ['kɔnsjulet], *s.* Consulat *m*.

consult [kən'sʌlt]. **I.** *v.tr.* (*a*) Consulter (*s.o. on, about, sth.*, qn sur qch.). (*b*) *To c. one's own interests, one's own safety*, consulter ses intérêts; pourvoir à sa propre salut. *To c. s.o.'s feelings*, avoir égard à la sensibilité de qn. **2.** *v.i.* Consulter (avec qn). *To c. together*, délibérer; se consulter. **consulting,** *a.* Consulting physician, médecin consultant. Consulting engineer, ingénieur conseil. **con'sulting-hours,** *s. pl.* Heures *f* de consultation. **con'sulting-room,** *s.* Cabinet *m* de consultation.

consultant [kən'sʌltənt], *s.* (*a*) Médecin ou chirurgien consultant. (*b*) *Ind:* Expert *m* conseil.

consultation [kɔnsəl'teiʃ(ə)n], *s.* **I.** Consultation *f* (d'un dictionnaire, etc.). **2.** Consultation, délibération *f* (entre médecins, etc.). *To hold a consultation*, consulter, délibérer, conférer.

consultative [kən'sʌltətiv], *a.* Consultatif.

consume [kən'sjuːm], *v.tr.* (*a*) (*Of fire*) Consumer, dévorer. *The town was consumed by fire*, la ville fut la proie des flammes. (*b*) Consommer (des vivres). (*c*) *Engine that consumes a ton of coal per hour*, machine qui consomme, qui brûle, une tonne de charbon par heure. (*d*) *To be consumed with thirst*, être consumé par la soif. *To be consumed with desire, jealousy*, brûler de désir; être dévoré, rongé, de jalousie. *To be consumed with boredom*, sécher d'ennui. (*e*) Épuiser (ses vivres, etc.).

consumer [kən'sjuːmər], *s.* Consommateur, -trice (d'une denrée). *Consumers of gas*, abonnés au gaz.

consummate[1] [kən'sʌmet], *a.* (*a*) (Art, artiste) consommé, achevé. *To be a c. master of one's craft*, être passé maître dans son métier. (*b*) *F: C. liar*, menteur achevé; fieffé menteur.

consummate[2] ['kɔnsəmeit], *v.tr.* Consommer (un mariage, un sacrifice).

consummation [kɔnsə'meiʃ(ə)n], *s.* **I.** Consommation *f* (d'un mariage, d'un crime). **2.** Perfection *f* (d'un art, etc.). **3.** Fin *f*; but *m*; comble *m* (des désirs). *The c. of a splendid life*, le couronnement d'une belle vie.

consumption [kən'sʌm(p)ʃ(ə)n], *s.* **I.** (*a*) Consommation *f* (de denrées). (*b*) Consommation, dépense *f* (de chaleur, de charbon). **2.** *Med:* Phtisie *f*; consomption *f* pulmonaire. *To go into consumption*, devenir phtisique, poitrinaire.

consumptive [kən'sʌm(p)tiv], *a. & s. Med:* Poitrinaire (*mf*), phtisique (*mf*), tuberculeux, -euse. *C. cough*, toux de poitrinaire. **-ly,** *adv. C. inclined*, prédisposé à la phtisie. *To cough c.*, tousser en poitrinaire.

contact ['kɔntakt], *s.* Contact *m*. **I.** (*a*) Point of contact, point de contact, de tangence, d'attouchement (de deux courbes, etc.). (*b*) **To be in contact with s.o.**, être en contact, en rapport, avec qn. **2.** *El:* (*a*) *C. to earth*, contact avec la terre;

mise *f* à terre. **To make contact**, établir le contact. **To break contact**, rompre le contact; couper le circuit. (*b*) **Contact(-piece)**, contact, touche *f*; (*button*) goutte-de-suif *f*; (*stud*) plot *m*. **Floor contact**, pédale *f* de parquet. *S.a.* SLIDE-CONTACT. **3.** *Med:* **Immediate contact** (*without vehicle*), contage immédiat. **'contact-breaker,** *s. El.E:* Dispositif *m* de rupture; (inter)rupteur *m*; trembleur *m*. **'contact-pin,** *s. El.E:* Cheville *f* de contact.

contagion [kən'teidʒ(ə)n], *s.* Contagion *f*.

contagious [kən'teidʒəs], *a.* (*Of disease, laughter*) Contagieux; (*of laughter*) communicatif.

contagiousness [kən'teidʒəsnəs], *s.* Contagiosité *f*.

contain [kən'tein], *v.tr.* **I.** (*a*) Contenir. (*b*) (*Comprise, include*) Contenir, renfermer; comprendre, comporter. *Machine that contains all the latest improvements*, machine qui comporte tous les derniers perfectionnements. *Substance that contains arsenic*, substance où il entre de l'arsenic. **2.** (*Restrain*) Contenir, maîtriser (son indignation); retenir, refouler (ses sentiments). *He cannot c. himself for joy*, il ne se sent pas de joie. **3.** *Mil:* Contenir, maintenir (l'ennemi).

container [kən'teinər], *s.* (*a*) Récipient *m*; réservoir *m*. *El:* Bac *m* (d'accumulateur); vase *m*. (*b*) *Com:* Boîte *f*.

contaminate [kən'tamineit], *v.tr.* Contaminer; corrompre; souiller. *Contaminated air*, air vicié.

contaminating, *a.* Viciateur, -trice.

contamination [kɔntami'neiʃ(ə)n], *s.* Contamination *f*, souillure *f*.

contango, *pl.* -oes [kən'taŋgo(z)], *s. St.Exch:* (Intérêt *m* de) report *m*. **Payer of contango,** reporté *m*.

contemn [kən'tem], *v.tr. A. & Lit:* Mépriser.

contemplate ['kɔntempleit], *v.tr.* **I.** (*a*) Contempler, considérer. (*b*) *v.i.* Se recueillir; méditer. **2.** (*a*) Prévoir, envisager (qch.). (*b*) *To contemplate sth., doing sth.*, projeter, se proposer, qch., de faire qch. *To c. suicide*, songer au suicide.

contemplation [kɔntem'pleiʃ(ə)n], *s.* **I.** (*a*) Contemplation *f*. (*b*) Recueillement *m*, méditation *f*. **2.** (*a*) **To have sth. in contemplation**, projeter qch. *It is as yet only in c.*, ce n'est encore qu'à l'état de projet. (*b*) **In contemplation of an attack**, en prévision d'une attaque.

contemplative ['kɔntempleitiv], *a.* Contemplatif, recueilli.

contemplator ['kɔntempleitər], *s.* Contemplateur, -trice.

contemporaneous [kɔntempo'reinjəs], *a.* Contemporain (*with*, de). **-ly,** *adv.* Contemporaneously with . . ., à la même époque que. . . .

contemporary [kən'tempərəri]. **I.** *a.* Contemporain (*with*, de). **Contemporary events**, événements actuels. **2.** *s.* Our contemporaries, nos contemporains *m*; *Journ:* nos confrères *m*.

contempt [kən'tem(p)t], *s.* **I.** Mépris *m*; dédain *m*. **To hold s.o. in contempt**, mépriser qn; tenir qn en mépris. **To bring s.o. into contempt**, faire tomber qn dans le mépris; faire mépriser qn. **In contempt of . . .**, au, en, mépris de. . . . **Beneath contempt**, tout ce qu'il y a de plus méprisable. **2.** *Jur:* Contempt of court, (i) outrage *m* ou offense *f* à la Cour; désobéissance *f*; (ii) refus *m* de comparaître; contumace *f*.

contemptible [kən'tem(p)tibl], *a.* Méprisable; (conduite) indigne. *Hist:* **The Old Contemptibles,** les survivants *m* de "la misérable petite armée britannique" de 1914. **-ibly,** *adv.* D'une manière méprisable.

contemptuous [kɔn'tem(p)tjuəs], *a.* **1.** Dédaigneux (*of*, de). **2.** (Air) méprisant; (geste)
de mépris. **-ly,** *adv.* Avec mépris; d'un air,
d'un ton, méprisant.
contend [kɔn'tend]. **1.** *v.i.* Combattre, lutter
(*with, against*, contre); disputer, discuter (avec
qn sur qch.). *To have a powerful enemy to c.
with*, avoir affaire à forte partie. **To contend with
s.o. for sth.**, disputer, contester, qch. à qn.
2. *v.tr.* **To contend that . . .** , prétendre, soutenir, que + *ind.* **contending,** *a.* C. *parties,*
contestants *m*; partis *m* en lutte. *C. armies,*
armées opposées.
content[1] ['kɔntent, kɔn'tent], *s.* **1.** (*a*) Contenance *f* (d'un vase). (*b*) *pl.* **Contents,** contenu *m*
(d'une bouteille, d'une lettre, etc.). (*Of book*)
(Table of) contents, table des matières. **2.** *Ch:
Miner:* Teneur *f*, titre *m*. **Gold-content,** teneur
en or.
content[2] [kɔn'tent], *s.* **1.** Contentement *m*,
satisfaction *f. S.a.* HEART[1] 2. **2.** (*In House of
Lords*) (*a*) Vote affirmatif. (*b*) Membre *m* qui a
voté pour la motion.
content[3] [kɔn'tent], *a.* **1.** Satisfait (*with*, de).
To be content to do sth., s'accommoder de qch.
I am c. to live at home, je n'en demande pas
davantage que de vivre à la maison. *To be c. with
sth.*, se contenter de qch. *Cards:* **Content!** je
m'y tiens! **2.** (*In House of Lords*) **Content,** not
content, pour, contre.
content[4] [kɔn'tent], *v.tr.* **1.** Contenter, satisfaire
(qn). **2. To content oneself with (doing) sth.**, se
contenter de (faire) qch.; se borner à faire qch.
contented, *a.* Satisfait, content (*with*, de).
-ly, *adv.* Sans se plaindre; (vivre) content.
contention [kɔn'tenʃ(ə)n], *s.* **1.** Dispute *f*,
démêlé *m*, débat *m. To be a bone of contention,*
être un sujet de dispute, une pomme de discorde;
donner lieu à des contestations. **2.** Affirmation *f*,
prétention *f*. **My contention is that . . .** , je
soutiens que + *ind.*
contentious [kɔn'tenʃəs], *a.* **1.** Disputeur, -euse;
disputailleur, -euse. **2.** (*Of issue*) Contentieux.
contentment [kɔn'tentmənt], *s.* Contentement
m de son sort.
contest[1] ['kɔntest], *s.* (*a*) Combat *m*, lutte *f* (*with*,
avec, contre; *between*, entre). (*b*) Concours *m*
(de musique), etc.). *F:* **C. of eloquence,** joute *f*
oratoire.
contest[2] [kɔn'test]. **1.** *v.tr.* (*a*) Contester,
débattre (une question). (*b*) *To c. s.o.'s right to do
sth.*, contester à qn le droit de faire qch. *Sp:* To
c. a race, se mettre sur les rangs. *It was a well-
contested match*, la lutte a été chaude. **To contest
a seat in Parliament,** disputer un siège au Parlement. (*c*) *Jur:* Attaquer (un testament); contester (une dette). **2.** *v.i.* (*a*) Se disputer (*with,
against*, avec). (*b*) *To c. for a prize*, disputer
un prix.
contestable [kɔn'testəbl], *a.* Contestable;
(question) débattable; (testament) attaquable.
contestant [kɔn'testənt], *s.* **1.** Contestant, -ante.
2. Compétiteur, -trice; concurrent *m*.
contestation [kɔntes'teiʃ(ə)n], *s.* Contestation *f*
(d'un droit). *Matters in contestation,* matières
en contestation, en litige.
context ['kɔntekst], *s.* Contexte *m*.
contiguity [kɔnti'gjuːiti], *s.* Contiguïté *f*. In
contiguity, contigu, -uë (*with*, à).
contiguous [kɔn'tigjuəs], *a.* Contiguous to sth.,
contigu, -uë, à qch., avec qch.; attenant à qch.
To be c., se toucher.
continence ['kɔntinəns], *s.* Continence *f*,
chasteté *f*.

continent[1] ['kɔntinənt], *a.* Continent, chaste.
continent[2] **,** *s. Geog:* (*a*) Continent *m*. (*b*) *F:* The
Continent, l'Europe (continentale).
continental [kɔnti'nent(ə)l], *a.* Continental, -aux.
contingency [kɔn'tindʒənsi], *s.* (*a*) Éventualité *f*;
cas imprévu. **Should a contingency arise, in case
of a contingency,** en cas d'imprévu. (*b*) *Com:*
Contingencies, faux frais divers. *To provide for
contingencies,* parer à l'imprévu.
contingent [kɔn'tindʒənt]. **1.** *a.* (*a*) *Phil:* Contingent. (*b*) Éventuel, fortuit, accidentel; (profit)
aléatoire. *C. expenses,* dépenses imprévues. (*c*) *C.
on sth.*, sous (la) réserve de qch. (*Of event*) *To be
c. upon sth.*, dépendre de qch. **2.** *s. Mil:* Contingent *m*.
continual [kɔn'tinjuəl], *a.* Continuel. **-ally,**
adv. Continuellement; sans cesse, sans arrêt.
continuance [kɔn'tinjuəns], *s.* Continuation *f*.
1. Perpétuation *f* (de l'espèce). **2.** Persistance *f*,
durée *f*. **Of long continuance,** prolongé; de
longue durée.
continuation [kɔntinju'eiʃ(ə)n], *s.* **1.** Continuation *f. Sch:* **Continuation course,** cours
postscolaire. **2.** Prolongement *m* (d'un mur);
suite *f* (d'un roman).
continue [kɔn'tinjuː]. **1.** *v.tr.* (*a*) Continuer;
prolonger (une droite); poursuivre (un travail);
reprendre (une conversation). *Journ:* '**To be
continued,**' ''à suivre.'' (*b*) Perpétuer (la race,
une tradition); maintenir (qn dans un emploi).
(*c*) **To continue (on) one's way,** continuer son
chemin; se remettre en marche. (*d*) **To continue to do sth.**, continuer à, de, faire qch.
2. *v.i.* (*a*) (Se) continuer, se soutenir; (*of line*)
prolonger. (*b*) *To c. impenitent,* rester impénitent.
To c. in office, garder sa charge.
continuity [kɔnti'njuːiti], *s.* **1.** Continuité *f*.
El: Uniformité *f* (du courant). **To break the
continuity of s.o.'s ideas,** couper le fil des idées
de qn. **2.** *Cin:* Scénario *m*.
continuous [kɔn'tinjuəs], *a.* Continu. *C. studies,*
études suivies. *El:* **Continuous waves,** ondes
entretenues. *Cin:* **Continuous performance,**
spectacle permanent. **-ly,** *adv.* Continûment;
sans interruption.
contort [kɔn'tɔːrt], *v.tr.* Tordre, contourner (les
traits, etc.); dévier (un organe). *Face contorted
by pain,* visage tordu par la douleur. **contorted,**
a. Contorsionné, contourné.
contortion [kɔn'tɔːrʃ(ə)n], *s.* Contorsion *f*.
contortionist [kɔn'tɔːrʃənist], *s.* Contorsion-
niste *m*; *F:* homme-serpent *m*.
contour[1] ['kɔntuər], *s.* Contour *m*; profil *m* (du
terrain); tracé *m* (d'un plan). '**contour-line,** *s.
Surv:* Courbe *f* de niveau. '**contour-map,** *s.*
1. Carte *f* en courbes de niveau. **2.** *Aut:* Carte
des profils de la route.
contour[2] **,** *v.tr. Surv:* Lever les courbes de
niveau de (la région).
contra ['kɔntra], *s. Book-k:* **Per contra,** par
contre. **As per contra,** en contre-partie, porté
ci-contre. **Contra entry,** écriture *f* inverse;
contre-écriture *f*.
contraband ['kɔntraband], *s.* Contrebande *f*.
Contraband goods, marchandises de contrebande.
contract[1] ['kɔntrakt], *s.* **1.** (*a*) Pacte *m*; contrat
m (de mariage). (*b*) Acte *m* de vente; contrat
translatif de propriété. **By private contract,** à
l'amiable; de gré à gré. *S.a.* SIMPLE 1. **2.** Entreprise *f*; soumission *f* ou adjudication *f*. *To make
a c. for a supply of coal*, passer marché pour une
fourniture de charbon. *C. for a bridge,* entreprise
d'un pont. **Contract work,** travail à l'entreprise,
à forfait. **To enter into a contract,** passer (un)

contrat (*with*, avec). **To put work up to contract,** mettre un travail en adjudication. **To put work out to contract,** mettre un travail à l'entreprise. *To place the* c. *for an undertaking,* concéder, adjuger, l'exécution d'une entreprise. **To get, secure, a contract for sth.,** être déclaré adjudicataire de qch. **Breach of contract,** rupture de contrat. **3.** *Rail:* U.S: (Carte *f* d')abonnement *m*. **4.** *Cards:* (*Bridge*) Déclaration *f*; contrat. **To make one's contract,** réaliser son contrat. *S.a.* BRIDGE².

contract² [kon'trakt], *v*. I. **1.** *v.tr.* (*a*) Contracter; crisper (les traits); rétrécir, resserrer (les tissus). (*b*) *Ling:* *To* c. *'shall not' into 'shan't,'* contracter "shall not" en "shan't." **2.** *v.i.* Se contracter, se resserrer, se rétrécir. II. **contract.** **1.** *v.tr.* (*a*) Contracter (une obligation, une dette, une maladie); prendre, contracter (une habitude). *To* c. *a liking for sth.,* prendre goût à qch. (*b*) *Com:* **To contract to do sth.,** s'engager par traité à faire qch. **2.** *v.i. Com: To* c. *for a supply of sth.,* entreprendre une fourniture. **To contract for work,** entreprendre des travaux à forfait.

contracting, *a.* (*a*) **High contracting parties,** hautes parties contractantes. (*b*) *Com:* **Contracting party,** contractant *m*; *esp.* partie *f* adjudicataire.

contractible [kon'traktibl], *a.* Contractile.

contraction [kon'trak'ʃ(ə)n], *s.* **1.** (*a*) Contraction *f*; rétrécissement *m*; retrait *m* (des métaux). (*b*) *Com:* Amoindrissement *m* (de crédit). **2.** (*a*) Contraction (de deux mots en un seul). (*b*) Mot contracté; contraction. **3.** Prise *f* (d'une habitude). *C. of debts* endettement *m*.

contractor [kon'traktər], *s.* Entrepreneur *m*, pourvoyeur *m*; (*of public works*) adjudicataire *m*. *Army* c., fournisseur *m* de l'armée.

contractual [kon'traktjuəl], *a.* Contractuel.

contradict [kontra'dikt], *v.tr.* Contredire (qn); démentir (qn, un bruit). *To* c. *a statement,* opposer un démenti à une déclaration.

contradiction [kontra'dik'ʃ(ə)n], *s.* Contradiction *f.* **1.** Démenti *m. To give a flat* c. *to a statement,* démentir formellement une assertion. **2.** **In contradiction with . . .,** en contradiction avec. . . . **Contradiction in terms,** contradiction dans les termes.

contradictory [kontra'diktəri], *a.* Contradictoire; opposé (*to*, à).

contradistinction [kontradis'tiŋ(k)ʃ(ə)n], *s.* **In contradistinction to . . .,** par opposition à. . . .

contra-indicate [kontra'indikeit], *v.tr. Med:* Contre-indiquer (un régime, etc.).

contralto [kon'tralto], *s. Mus:* Contralte *m.*

contraption [kon'trapʃ(ə)n], *s.* F: Dispositif *m*, machin *m*; truc *m.*

contrapuntal [kontra'pʌnt(ə)l], *a. Mus:* (Morceau, accompagnement) en contrepoint.

contrariety [kontra'raiəti], *s.* Contrariété *f* (d'intérêts, d'opinions).

contrariness [kon'treərinəs], *s.* F: Esprit de contradiction, de contrariété.

contrariwise ['kontrəriwaiz], *adv.* **1.** Au contraire; d'autre part. **2.** En sens opposé. **3.** F: [kon'treəriwaiz] Par esprit de contrariété.

contrary ['kontrəri]. **I.** *a.* (*a*) Contraire (*to*, à); (*of interests, etc.*) opposé (à), en opposition (avec). **In a contrary direction,** en sens opposé, inverse. **Contrary to nature,** contre nature. **Contrary winds,** vents contraires. (*b*) F: [kon'treəri] Indocile; qui prend plaisir à contrarier. **2.** *s.* Contraire *m. Quite the contrary,* tout au contraire; c'est tout l'opposé. **On the contrary,** au contraire. **Unless you hear to the contrary,** à moins d'avis contraire; sauf contre-avis. **I have nothing to say to the contrary,** je n'ai rien à objecter; je n'ai rien à dire contre. **3.** *adv* Contrairement (*to*, à); en opposition (*to* à, avec); à, au, rebours (*to*, de). **Contrary to accepted opinions,** à l'encontre des idées reçues. *C. to his usual custom,* contrairement à son habitude.

contrast¹ ['kontra:st], *s.* Contraste *m* (*between*, entre). **In contrast with sth.,** par contraste avec qch. **Colours in contrast,** couleurs en opposition. **To form a contrast to . . .,** faire contraste avec. . **To stand out in sharp contrast to** sth., se détacher nettement sur, contre, qch.

contrast² [kon'tra:st]. **1.** *v.tr* Faire contraster, mettre en contraste (*with*, avec); opposer (le vice à la vertu). **2.** *v.i.* Contraster, faire contraste (*with*, avec). **To contrast strongly,** trancher (*with*, sur). **Contrasting colours,** tons opposés.

contravene [kontra'vi:n], *v.tr.* **1.** Transgresser, enfreindre (la loi, etc.). **To contravene the regulations,** contrevenir aux règlements. **2.** Aller à l'encontre de (qch.); opposer un démenti à (une affirmation).

contravention [kontra'venʃ(ə)n], *s. C. of a law,* contravention *f*, infraction *f*, à la loi. *To act in* c. *of a rule,* agir en violation d'une règle.

contribute [kon'tribjut], *v.tr. & i.* **To contribute one's share,** payer sa (quote-)part. *To* c. *a sum of money,* contribuer pour une somme. **To contribute to a charity,** contribuer à, souscrire pour, une bonne œuvre. *To* c. *to a newspaper,* collaborer à un journal. **To contribute to the success,** aider au succès.

contribution [kontri'bju:ʃ(ə)n], *s.* **1.** (*a*) Contribution *f* (à une œuvre de bienfaisance, etc.); cotisation *f. Fin:* Contribution of capital, apport *m* de capitaux. (*b*) *Mil: etc:* Contribution; réquisition *f. The whole country has been laid under* c., on a fait contribuer tout le pays. *F:* To lay one's friends under contribution, mettre ses amis à contribution. **2.** **Contribution to a** newspaper, article écrit pour un journal.

contributive [kon'tribjutiv], *a.* Contributif.

contributor [kon'tribjutər], *s.* **1.** *Fin:* Apporteur *m* (de capitaux). **2.** Collaborateur, -trice (*to a paper,* d'un journal).

contributory [kon'tribjutəri], *a.* Contribuant, contributif. *Jur: Ins:* Contributory negligence, manque *m* de précautions, imprudence *f*, de la part de l'accidenté.

contrite ['kontrait], *a.* Contrit, pénitent, repentant.

contrition [kon'triʃ(ə)n], *s.* Contrition *f*, pénitence *f.*

contrivance [kon'traivəns], *s.* **1.** Invention *f* (d'un appareil); combinaison *f*, adaptation *f* (d'un moyen). **2.** Invention; artifice *m.* **3.** Appareil *m*, dispositif *m*; *F:* truc *m.*

contrive [kon'traiv], *v.tr.* (*a*) Inventer, imaginer, combiner. (*b*) Pratiquer, ménager. **To contrive to do sth.,** trouver moyen de, venir à bout de, faire qch. (*c*) *Abs.* Se débrouiller; se tirer d'affaire; s'arranger.

control¹ [kon'troul], *s.* **1.** (*a*) Autorité *f. To have* c. *of an undertaking,* être à la tête d'une entreprise. *She has no* c. *over the children,* elle ne sait pas tenir ses élèves. (*b*) Maîtrise *f*, contrainte *f. Circumstances beyond our control,* circonstances en dehors de notre action. (*Of pers.*) **To get out of control,** s'affranchir de toute autorité; *F:* s'émanciper. **To have one's horse under control,** avoir son cheval bien en main. **To have absolute control over s.o.,** avoir un empire absolu sur qn. **To lose control of oneself,** ne plus se maîtriser. *Adm: Aut:* **Control signals,** signalisation routière. (*c*) Gouverne *f*, manœuvre *f* (d'un train, d'un navire). *The driver had lost c. of the train,* le mécanicien n'était plus maître du train. **Ship out of control,** navire qui n'est plus maître de sa manœuvre. **Control lever,** levier *m* de commande, d'asservissement ; *Aut :* manette *f* de commande. *Av :* **Control column,** levier de commande. (*d*) Surveillance *f.* **Under government control,** assujetti au contrôle du gouvernement. **2.** *Tchn :* (Organe *m* de) commande *f. I.C.E :* Ignition control, commande d'allumage. *W.Tel :* Volume control, contrôle *m* de volume ; modérateur *m* de son. **Remote control,** commande à distance. **3.** *Sp :* (*In reliability run, etc.*) **Control point,** contrôle *m. Med :* **Control case,** cas témoin.

control², *v.tr.* (controlled) **1.** Diriger (des affaires, la production) ; régler (la dépense). **To control men, one's fate,** commander aux hommes, au destin. *He cannot c. his boys,* il ne sait pas tenir ses élèves. *Adm :* **To c. the traffic,** réglementer la circulation. **2.** Maîtriser, gouverner (un cheval) ; réprimer (un soulèvement) ; gouverner, dompter (ses passions). **To control oneself,** se maîtriser, se dominer. **Control yourself!** modérez-vous ! retenez-vous !

controllable [kon'trouləbl], *a.* **1.** Qui peut être gouverné ; (machine, vaisseau) maniable, manœuvrable. **2.** (Passion, cheval) maîtrisable.

controller [kon'troulər], *s.* **1.** *Pers.*) (*a*) Contrôleur, -euse. (*b*) = COMPTROLLER. **2.** (Appareil) contrôleur *m* ; commande *f.*

controversial [kɔntro'vəːrʃ(ə)l], *a.* **1.** Controversable. **2.** (*Of pers.*) Enclin à la controverse ; disputailleur, -euse.

controversialist [kɔntro'vəːrʃəlist], *s.* Controversiste *m,* polémiste *m.*

controversy ['kɔntrovəːrsi], *s.* Polémique *f* ; controverse *f.* **To hold, carry on, a controversy (with, against, s.o.) on sth.,** soutenir une polémique, une controverse, (contre qn) au sujet de qch. **Beyond controversy,** hors de controverse.

controvert ['kɔntrovəːrt], *v.tr.* **1.** Controverser (une question). **2.** Disputer ; mettre en doute (la vérité de qch.).

controvertible [kɔntro'vəːrtibl], *a.* Controversable.

contumacious [kɔntju'meiʃəs], *a.* Rebelle, récalcitrant. *Jur :* Contumace.

contumacy ['kɔntjuməsi], *s.* Entêtement *m,* obstination *f. Jur :* Contumace *f.*

contumely ['kɔntjumili], *s. Lit :* **1.** Insolence *f* ; souverain mépris. **2.** Honte *f.*

contuse [kon'tjuːz], *v.tr.* Contusionner. **Contused wound,** plaie contuse.

contusion [kon'tjuːʒ(ə)n], *s.* Contusion *f.*

contusive [kon'tjuːziv], *a.* Contondant.

conundrum [ko'nʌndrəm], *s.* **1.** Devinette *f.* **2.** Énigme *f.*

convalesce [kɔnvə'les], *v.i.* Relever de maladie. *He is convalescing at Brighton,* il est en convalescence à Brighton.

convalescence [kɔnvə'les(ə)ns], *s.* Convalescence *f.*

convalescent [kɔnvə'les(ə)nt], *a. & s.* **1.** Convalescent, -ente. **2.** **Convalescent home,** maison de convalescence.

convection [kon'vek∫(ə)n], *s. Ph :* Convection *f.*

convene [kon'viːn]. **1.** *v.tr.* Convoquer, réunir (une assemblée). **2.** *v.i.* S'assembler, se réunir.

convenience [kon'viːnjəns], *s.* **1.** Commodité *f,* convenance *f.* **Marriage of convenience,** mariage de convenance, de raison. **At your convenience,**

à votre convenance, à votre bon plaisir. **At your earliest convenience,** le plus tôt (qu'il vous sera) possible. **It is a great convenience to be able to . . .,** c'est bien commode, pratique, de pouvoir. . . . **2.** (Public) **convenience,** cabinets *m* d'aisances ; chalet *m* de nécessité **3.** *pl.* Commodités, agréments *m.* **All modern conveniences,** tout le confort moderne.

convenient [kon'viːnjənt], *a.* Commode. *If it is c. to you,* si cela ne vous dérange pas ; si vous n'y voyez pas d'inconvénient. **To make it convenient to do sth.,** s'arranger de manière à faire qch. **-ly,** *adv.* Commodément ; sans inconvénient.

convent ['kɔnvənt], *s.* Couvent *m* (de femmes). **To enter a convent,** entrer au couvent.

convention [kon'venʃ(ə)n], *s.* **1.** (*a*) Convention *f.* **The Hague Conventions,** les conventions, les actes *m,* de la Haye. (*b*) Accord *m,* contrat *m.* **2.** *Usu. pl.* Convenances *fpl,* bienséances *fpl.* **Social conventions,** les conventions sociales. **3.** *Hist :* Assemblée *f,* convention.

conventional [kon'venʃən(ə)l], *a.* **1.** Conventionnel ; de convention. *Art :* **C. design,** dessin stylisé. **2.** Courant ; normal, -aux. *The c. type of car,* la voiture ordinaire, classique.

converge [kon'vəːrdʒ]. **1.** *v.i.* Converger (*on,* sur). **2.** *v.tr.* Faire converger (des rayons lumineux, etc.). **converging,** *a.* Convergent, concourant. **Converging point,** point de concours.

convergence [kon'vəːrdʒəns], *s.* Convergence *f.*

convergent [kon'vəːrdʒənt], *a.* Convergent.

conversant ['kɔnvərsənt], *a.* Familier, intime (avec qn). **Conversant with sth.,** versé dans, au courant de, qch. ; compétent en matière de (finance).

conversation [kɔnvər'seiʃ(ə)n], *s.* Conversation *f,* entretien *m.* **To hold a conversation with s.o.,** s'entretenir avec qn. **To enter, fall, into conversation (with s.o.),** entrer en conversation, entrer en propos (avec qn). **To be the subject of conversation,** défrayer la conversation ; faire les frais de la conversation. *Art :* **Conversation piece,** scène *f* d'intérieur ; tableau *m* de genre.

conversational [kɔnvər'seiʃən(ə)l], *a.* **1.** De (la) conversation. **In a conversational tone,** sur le ton de la conversation. **2.** (*Of pers.*) Qui aime à causer.

conversazione, *pl.* **-es, -i** [kɔnvərsatsi'ouni, -iz, -iː], *s.* Réunion *f* (littéraire, artistique).

converse¹ [kon'vəːrs], *v.i.* Causer. **To converse with s.o., on, about, sth.,** converser avec qn sur qch. ; s'entretenir avec qn de qch.

converse² [ˈkɔnvəːrs], *a. & s.* **1.** *Log :* (Proposition) converse (*f*). **2.** *Mth :* (Proposition) réciproque (*f*).

conversely [kon'vəːrsli], *adv.* Réciproquement.

conversion [kon'vəːrʃ(ə)n], *s.* **1.** Conversion *f* (de qn). **2.** (*a*) **C. of water into steam,** conversion de l'eau en vapeur. *Improper c. of funds,* détournement *m* de fonds. (*b*) **Conversion of a room to office use,** accommodation *f* d'une salle aux usages d'un bureau.

convert¹ ['kɔnvərt], *s.* Converti, -ie. **To become a convert to sth.,** se convertir à qch.

convert² [kon'vəːrt], *v.tr.* **1.** Convertir (qn) (à une religion). **2.** Transformer, changer, convertir (*sth. into sth.,* qch. en qch.). (*a*) **To c. a tourer into a closed car,** transformer une torpédo en conduite intérieure. *Rugby Fb :* **Converted goal,** but de transformation. *S.a.* TRY 2. (*b*) **To convert a room to office use,** accommoder une salle aux usages d'un bureau. **3.** **To c. funds to one's own use,** détourner des fonds.

converter [kon'vəːrtər], s. (Appareil) convertisseur m. *El.E:* Static **converter,** convertisseur, transformateur m. **Rotary converter,** commutatrice f.

convertible [kon'vəːrtibl], a. Convertible, convertissable *(into,* en). *Phot:* (Objectif) dédoublable. **Convertible car,** voiture décapotable, transformable.

convex ['kɔnveks], a. **I.** Convexe. **Double convex,** biconvexe. **2.** *C. road,* chaussée bombée.

convey [kon'vei], v.tr. **I.** Transporter, porter, conduire; (a)mener (qn); voiturer (des marchandises). **2.** *(Of air, etc.)* Transmettre (le son, une odeur). **3.** Transmettre (un ordre, des remerciements); communiquer (une nouvelle) *(to,* à). **To convey one's meaning,** communiquer, rendre, sa pensée. **To convey to s.o. that . . .,** faire comprendre à qn que. . . . *The name conveys nothing to me,* ce nom ne me dit rien. **4.** *Jur:* Faire cession (d'un bien); transmettre, céder (un bien) *(to,* à).

conveyance [kon'veiəns], s. **I.** Transport m; moyens m de transport; transmission f. **Public means of conveyance,** les transports en commun. **2.** *Jur:* Transmission, translation f, transfert m (de biens). **3.** *Jur:* Acte translatif de propriété. **4.** Véhicule m (de transport); voiture f. *Jur:* **Public conveyance,** véhicule de transport(s) en commun; voiture publique.

conveyor, -er [kon'veiər], s. *Ind:* (Appareil) transporteur m; transporteuse f. **Conveyer-belt, belt-conveyer,** bande transporteuse; courroie f de transport. **Spiral conveyer,** vis transporteuse; transporteur à vis (sans fin). *Mec.E:* **Assembly conveyor,** chaîne f de montage; tapis roulant.

convict [ˈkɔnvikt], s. Forçat m. **Convict prison** = maison centrale.

convict² [kon'vikt], v.tr. *(a) To c. s.o. of a crime,* convaincre qn d'un crime. *He was convicted,* il fut déclaré, reconnu, coupable. *(b) To c. s.o. of error,* convaincre qn d'erreur. *(c) You stand convicted by your own words,* vos propres paroles vous condamnent.

conviction [kon'vikʃ(ə)n], s. **I.** Condamnation f. *Jur: Previous convictions,* dossier m du prévenu. **2. To be open to conviction,** être accessible à la persuasion; ne demander qu'à être convaincu. **3.** *(Belief)* Conviction. *(Of evidence, etc.)* To **carry conviction,** emporter conviction. *It is my c. that* je suis persuadé que. . . *S.a.* COURAGE.

convince [kon'vins], v.tr Convaincre, persuader *(s.o. of sth.,* qn de qch.). *I am convinced that he is still alive,* j'ai la conviction, je suis persuadé, qu'il est encore vivant. **convincing,** a. (Argument) convaincant; (langage) persuasif. **-ly,** adv. D'un ton, d'un air, qui emporte conviction.

convivial [kon'viviəl], a. **I. Convivial evening,** dîner entre camarades; soirée passée à table ou à boire. *C. songs,* chansons à boire. **2.** *(Of pers.)* Jovial (à table); bon convive.

convocation [kɔnvo'keiʃ(ə)n], s. **I.** Convocation f (d'une assemblée). **2.** *Ecc:* Assemblée f, synode m

convoke [kon'vouk], v.tr Convoquer (une assemblée)

convolution [kɔnvo'ljuːʃ(ə)n], s. Circonvolution f (du cerveau, etc.).

convolvulus [kon'vɔlvjuləs], s. *Bot:* Volubilis m.

convoy¹ ['kɔnvɔi], s. *Mil: Nau:* Convoi m. **Convoy-ship,** convoyeur m; (bâtiment d')escorte f. **To sail under convoy,** naviguer de conserve, en convoi.

convoy² [kon'vɔi], v.tr. *Mil: Nau:* Convoyer, escorter.

convulse [kon'vʌls], v.tr. **I.** Bouleverser (qn, la vie de qn); ébranler (la terre). **2.** *Med:* Convulsionner; convulser (un muscle); donner des convulsions à (qn). *F:* **To be convulsed with laughter,** se tordre de rire. *Face convulsed with terror,* visage décomposé par la terreur.

convulsion [kon'vʌlʃ(ə)n], s. **I.** *Med:* (Usu. pl.) **To throw s.o. into convulsions,** donner des convulsions f à qn. **2. To be seized with convulsions of laughter,** se tordre de rire. **3.** Bouleversement m, commotion f.

convulsive [kon'vʌlsiv], a. Convulsif. *C. movements (of the limbs),* soubresauts m.

cony ['kouni], s. **I.** *A. & U.S:* Lapin m. **2.** *Com:* Cony(-skin), peau f de lapin. *S a.* SEAL¹ 2.

coo¹ [kuː], s. Roucoulement m.

coo², v.i. Roucouler; *(of baby)* gazouiller. *S.a.* BILL³. **cooing,** s. Roucoulement m.

cook¹ [kuk], s. *(a)* Cuisinier, -ière. **Plain cook,** cuisinière bourgeoise. **Cook-general,** cuisinière et bonne à tout faire. *(b) Nau:* Cuisinier; maître-coq m. **'cook-house,** s. *Mil: Nau:* Cuisine f. **'cook-shop,** s. Gargote f.

cook². **I.** v.tr. *(a)* (Faire) cuire (de la viande, etc.). *Abs.* Faire la cuisine; cuisiner *S.a.* READY-COOKED. *F:* **To cook s.o.'s goose,** (i) contrecarrer qn; (ii) faire son affaire à qn. *His goose is cooked,* il a son compte; il est flambé. *P:* **He is cooked,** (i) *(drunk)* il a sa cuite; (ii) *(of athlete, etc.)* il est à bout de forces, à plat. *(b) F:* **To cook accounts,** cuisiner, fricoter, truquer, les comptes. **2.** v.i. *(Of food)* Cuire. **cooking,** s. **I.** Cuisson f (de la viande, etc.). **2.** Cuisine f. **Plain cooking,** cuisine bourgeoise. **Cooking utensils,** articles de cuisine. **3.** Cooking of accounts, trucage m des comptes; tripotages mpl de caisse. **'cooking-range, -stove,** s. Fourneau m de cuisine; cuisinière f.

cooker ['kukər], s. *(Kitchen stove)* Cuisinière f. **Electric cooker,** cuisinière, fourneau m, électrique. **Gas-cooker,** cuisinière à gaz; réchaud-four m. *S.a.* PRESSURE-COOKER.

cookery ['kukəri], s. (L'art de la) cuisine. **Cookery-book,** livre de cuisine.

cool¹ [kuːl]. **I.** a. (a) Frais, *f.* fraîche. *C. drink,* boisson rafraîchissante. **It is cool,** il fait frais. **It is turning cool,** le temps se rafraîchit. 'To be **kept in a cool place,'** "craint la chaleur"; "tenir au frais." *(b)* **To keep cool (and collected),** garder son sang-froid. *F:* **As cool as a cucumber,** avec un sang-froid imperturbable. **Keep cool!** du calme! *F:* ne vous emballez pas! *(c)* **To be cool towards s.o.,** être froid, tiède, envers qn. **To give s.o. a cool reception,** faire un accueil froid à qn. *(d) F:* **He is a cool customer,** il ne se laisse pas démonter; il en prend à son aise. **He answered as cool as you please,** il répondit sans se laisser démonter **2.** s. **In the cool,** au frais, **In the cool of the evening,** dans la fraîcheur du soir; à la fraîche. **To enjoy the c. of the evening,** prendre le frais. **-lly,** adv **I.** Fraîchement. **2.** (Agir) de sang-froid, de sens rassis. **3.** (Recevoir qn) avec froideur, froidement. **4.** Effrontément; sans gêne. **cool-'headed,** a. A l'esprit calme; que rien ne démonte.

cool². **I.** v.tr. Rafraîchir, refroidir (l'eau, l'air); rafraîchir (le sang). *S.a.* AIR-COOLED. **2.** v.i. *(Of liquid)* Se rafraîchir, (se) refroidir; *(of anger, etc.)* se refroidir. **cool down.** **I.** v.i. *(After exertion)* Se rafraîchir; *(after anger)* s'apaiser, se calmer.

cool off, v.i. *F: (Of affection, enthusiasm)* Se

refroidir, tiédir. **cooling**[1], *a.* Rafraîchissant.
cooling[2], *s.* Rafraîchissement *m*, refroidissement *m*. *I.C.E : etc :* Air cooling, refroidissement par courant d'air. *Ind :* Cooling tower, tour *f* de réfrigération ; refroidisseur *m*.
cooler ['ku:lər], *s.* (*a*) (Appareil) rafraîchisseur *m*. Butter-cooler, beurrier *m*. *S.a.* WINE-COOLER. (*b*) *Ind :* Réfrigérant *m*, refroidisseur *m*.
coolie ['ku:li], *s.m.* Homme de peine ou portefaix (aux Indes et en Chine) ; cooli(e).
coolness ['ku:lnəs], *s.* **I.** Fraîcheur *f* (de l'air, du soir). **2.** (*a*) Sang-froid *m*, flegme *m*. (*b*) *F :* Aplomb *m* ; toupet *m*. **3.** Froideur *f* (de qn, d'un accueil).
coon [ku:n], *s.* *U.S : F :* **I.** He's a gone coon, il est fichu. **2.** Nègre *m*. Coon songs, chansons nègres.
coop[1] [ku:p], *s.* (*a*) Cage *f* à poules ; mue *f*. (*b*) Poussinière *f*.
coop[2], *v.tr* Enfermer (des poules) dans une mue. *F :* To coop s.o. up, tenir qn enfermé ; claquemurer, cloîtrer, qn.
cooper ['ku:pər], *s.* **I.** (Wet) cooper, tonnelier *m*. Dry cooper, boisselier *m*. **2.** = WINE-COOPER.
cooperage ['ku:pəredʒ], *s.* Tonnellerie *f*. White cooperage, boissellerie *f*.
co-operate [ko'ɔpəreit], *v.t.* **I.** Coopérer (*with s.o. in sth.*, avec qn à qch.) ; agir en commun. **2.** (*Of thgs*) Concourir, contribuer (*in*, à)
co-operation [koɔpə'reiʃ(ə)n], *s.* Coopération *f*, concours *m* (*in*, à).
co-operative [ko'ɔpərətiv], *a.* Coopératif. Co-operative (supply) stores, société coopérative de consommation ; *F :* coopérative *f*.
co-operator [ko'ɔpəreitər], *s.* Coopérateur, -trice.
co-opt [ko'ɔpt], *v.tr.* Coopter.
co-optation [koɔp'teiʃ(ə)n], **co-option** [ko-'ɔpʃ(ə)n], *s.* Cooptation *f*.
co-ordinate[1] [ko'ɔ:rdinet], **I.** *a. Gram :* (*Of clause*) Coordonné. **2.** *s. Mth :* Coordonnée *f*.
co-ordinate[2] [ko'ɔ:rdineit], *v.tr.* Coordonner (*with*, à).
co-ordination [koɔrdi'neiʃ(ə)n], *s.* Coordination *f*.
coot [ku:t], *s. Orn :* (Bald-)coot, foulque noire.
cop[1] [kɔp], *s. Tex :* Cannette *f* de fil.
cop[2], *s. P :* = COPPER[2]. *S.a.* SPEED[1] I.
cop[3], *v.tr. P :* Attraper, pincer (qn). To get copped, se faire pincer. To cop it, (i) écoper ; (ii) recevoir un savon.
copaiba [ko'paiba], *s.* Copahu *m*.
copal ['koupəl], *s.* (Gum) copal, copal *m*.
copartner [kou'pɑ:rtnər], *s. Com :* Coassocié *m*.
copartnership [kou'pɑ:rtnərʃip], *s.* Coassociation *f* ; société *f* en nom collectif.
cope[1] [koup], *s. Ecc :* Chape *f* ; pluvial *m*, -aux. *F :* The cope of heaven, la voûte céleste ; la calotte des cieux. Under the cope of night, sous le manteau de la nuit **'cope-stone, 'coping-stone,** *s.* Couronnement *f* (d'un mur, *F :* d'une carrière).
cope[2], *v.i.* (*a*) To c. with s.o., with the enemy, tenir tête à qn, à l'ennemi. (*b*) To c. with a situation, faire face à une situation. To c. with a difficulty, venir à bout d'une difficulté.
Copenhagen [koupən'heigən], *Pr.n.* Copenhague *f*.
copier ['kɔpiər], *s.* **I.** Copiste *mf*. **2.** Imitateur, -trice.
copious ['koupjəs], *a.* (*a*) Copieux, abondant, ample. (*b*) (Style) riche. **-ly,** *adv.* Copieusement.
copper[1] ['kɔpər], *s.* **I.** Cuivre *m* (rouge).

2. (*a*) Cuve *f* à lessive ; lessiveuse *f*. (*b*) *F :* (*Coin*) Pièce *f* de deux sous ; penny *m* *pl* Petite monnaie. (*c*) *P :* To have hot coppers, avoir la gueule de bois. **3.** *Attrib.* (*a*) De cuivre, en cuivre. Copper wire, fil de cuivre. (*b*) *C.* complexion, teint cuivré, bronzé. *S.a.* BEECH.
'copper-smith, *s.* Chaudronnier *m* en cuivre.
'copper-ware, *s.* Dinanderie *f*.
copper[2], *s. P :* (*Policeman*) Sergot *m*, flic *m*.
copperplate[1] ['kɔpərpleit], *s.* **I.** Plaque *f* de cuivre. **2.** Copperplate engraving, (gravure *f* en) taille-douce *f* ; gravure sur cuivre. *F :* Copperplate writing, écriture moulée, calligraphiée.
copperplate[2], *v.tr.* Cuivrer (un métal).
coppice ['kɔpis], *s.* Taillis *m*, hallier *m*.
copra ['kɔpra], *s. Com :* Copra *m*.
co-property [kou'prɔpərti], *s. Jur :* Copropriété *f*
co-proprietor [koupro'praiətər], *s. Jur :* Copropriétaire *m*.
copse [kɔps], *s.* = COPPICE.
copy[1] ['kɔpi], *s.* **I.** Copie *f*, reproduction *f*. **2.** (*a*) Copie, transcription *f* (d'une lettre. etc.). Rough copy, brouillon *m*. Fair copy, copie (au net). To take a copy of a letter, prendre copie d'une lettre (*b*) *Jur :* Expédition *f* (d'un acte). Certified copy, copie authentique ; ampliation *f*. **3.** Modèle *m*, exemple *m* (d'écriture). **4.** Exemplaire *m* (d'un livre) ; numéro *m* (d'un journal) **5.** (*a*) Manuscrit (destiné à l'impression) ; copie. (*b*) *Journ :* Matière *f* à reportage ; sujet *m* d'article. **'copy-book,** *s.* Cahier *m* d'écriture.
copy[2], *v.tr.* Copier. **I.** (*a*) Imiter, reproduire (une œuvre d'art, etc.). Copied from the original, copié sur l'original. (*b*) To c. s.o., se modeler sur qn. *Art : Lit :* To c. s.o.'s style, copier, pasticher, le style de qn. (*c*) *Journ :* 'Australian papers please copy,' "prière d'insérer dans les journaux australiens." **2.** To copy (out) a letter, copier, transcrire, une lettre. Copying clerk, expéditionnaire *m*. **copying,** *s.* Transcription *f*, imitation *f*. *S.a.* INK[1].
copyist ['kɔpiist], *s.* Copiste *mf* ; scribe *m*.
copyright[1] ['kɔpirait], *s* Droit *m* d'auteur ; propriété *f* littéraire. Out of copyright, (tombé) dans le domaine public. **'Copyright reserved,'** "tous droits réservés."
copyright[2], *v.tr. Publ :* Déposer (un livre).
copyright[3], *a.* (Livre) qui est protégé par des droits d'auteur ; (article) dont le droit de reproduction est réservé.
coquetry ['koukətri], *s.* Coquetterie *f*, chatteries *fpl*.
coquette [ko'ket], *s.* Coquette *f*.
coquet(te)[2], *v.i.* Faire la coquette ; flirter.
coquettish [ko'ketiʃ], *a.* (*a*) (Petit chapeau, etc.) coquet. (*b*) (Sourire) provocant, *F :* aguichant. **-ly,** *adv.* D'un air provocant.
coral ['kɔrəl], *s.* **I.** Corail *m*, -aux. Coral fisher, corailleur *m*. Coral fishery, la pêche du corail. Coral island, île corallienne, de corail. Coral necklace, collier de corail. **2.** Hochet *m* ou anneau *m* de corail (pour bébés qui font leurs dents).
coralline ['kɔralain], *a.* (*a*) Corallien. (*b*) (Pinkish-red) Corailline *f*.
corbel[1] ['kɔrbəl], *s. Arch :* Corbeau *m*, console *f*.
corbel[2], *v.tr.* Encorbeller. To be corbelled out, porter en saillie. **corbelled,** *a. Arch :* En encorbellement. **corbelling,** *s.* Encorbellement *m*.
cord[1] [kɔ:rd], *s.* (*a*) Corde *f* (mince) ; cordon *m* ; ficelle *f*. Stranded, twisted, cord, cordon câblé. (*b*) *El.E :* Conducteur *m* souple ; cordon.

(c) Bandereau *m* (de trompette). *Dressm: Tail:* Ganse *f. Bookb:* Nerf *m* (de dos de livre). *(d) Anat:* **The vocal cords,** les cordes voćlaes. **The spinal cord,** le cordon médullaire. **The umbilical cord,** le cordon ombilical.

cord², *v.tr.* Corder; attacher, lier, avec une corde; ligoter (un fagot, etc.). **corded,** *a.* **1.** *(a) Tex:* Côtelé; à côtes. *(b) Needlew:* Corded cotton, coton perlé. **2.** *Aut:* Corded tyre, pneu à cordes.

cordage ['kɔːrdedʒ], *s. Coll.* Cordages *m pl,* filin *m.*

cordate ['kɔːrdet], *a.* Cordé, cordiforme; en forme de cœur.

cordial ['kɔːrdjəl]. **1.** *a.* Cordial, -aux; chaleureux. **2.** *s.* Cordial *m.* **-ally,** *adv.* Cordialement, chaleureusement.

cordiality [kɔːrdiˈaliti], *s.* Cordialité *f.*

cordon ['kɔːrdən], *s.* **1.** *(a)* Cordon *m,* tresse *f.* *(b)* [kɔr'dɔ̃] Cordon (d'un ordre de chevalerie). **2.** Cordon (de police, de troupes).

Cordova ['kɔːrdova]. *Pr.n. Geog:* Cordoue *f.*

corduroy ['kɔːrdjurɔi], *s. & a. Tex:* Velours (de coton) côtelé, à côtes. *F:* **Corduroy road,** chemin de rondins; route fascinée.

core¹ ['kɔːr], *s.* **1.** Cœur *m* (du bois, etc.); trognon *m* (d'une pomme, etc.). **Selfish to the core,** d'un égoïsme foncier. *S.a.* ROTTEN 1. **In my heart's core,** au plus profond de mon cœur. **2.** Bourbillon *m* (d'un abcès); cornillon *m* (d'un cor). **3.** *(a) Geol: Metall:* Noyau *m.* *(b) El:* Noyau (d'un aimant). *(c)* Mèche *f,* âme *f* (d'un câble).

core², *v.tr.* **1.** To core an apple, enlever le cœur d'une pomme; vider une pomme. **2. To core (out) a mould,** noyauter, évider, un moule.

co-religionist [kouriˈlidʒənist], *s.* Coreligionnaire *m.*

co-respondent [koureˈspɔndənt], *s. Jur:* Codéfendeur *m* (en adultère).

Corfu [kɔːrˈfuː, -ˈfjuː]. *Pr.n. Geog:* Corfou *m.*

Corinth ['kɔrinθ]. *Pr.n. A.Geog:* Corinthe *f.*

Corinthian [koˈrinθiən], *a. & s.* Corinthien, -ienne.

cork¹ [kɔːrk], *s.* **1.** Liège *m.* **Cork sole,** semelle de, en, liège. **2.** Bouchon *m* (de liège). **To draw the cork of a bottle,** déboucher une bouteille. **'cork-oak,** *s. Bot:* Chêne-liège *m, pl.* chênes-lièges.

cork², *v.tr.* **1.** *(a)* To cork (up) a bottle, boucher une bouteille. *(b)* Garnir (un filet, etc.) de bouchons. **2.** Se noircir (le visage) au bouchon. **corked,** *a.* *(Of wine)* Qui sent le bouchon.

corker ['kɔːrkər], *s. P:* **1.** *(a)* Mensonge un peu fort. *(b)* Réponse *f* qui vous en bouche un coin. **2. He's a corker,** c'est un type épatant.

corkscrew¹ ['kɔːrkskruː], *s.* Tire-bouchon *m.* **Hairdr:** Corkscrew curl, tire-bouchon; boudin *m.* *S.a.* STAIRCASE.

corkscrew², *v.i. (Of wire, etc.)* Vriller.

cormorant ['kɔːrmorənt], *s.* **1.** *Orn:* Cormoran *m.* **2.** *F:* Homme *m* d'une rapacité de cormoran.

corn¹ [kɔːrn], *s.* **1.** Grain *m* (de blé, de poivre, etc.). **2.** *(Coll. sg.)* Grains, blé(s) *m(pl).* **Winter corn,** semis *m* d'hiver. **Corn crops,** céréales *f.* *F:* **There's corn in Egypt,** les provisions ne manquent pas. **3.** Indian corn, *U.S:* corn, maïs *m.* **4.** *Esp. Scot:* Avoine *f.* **'cornchandler,** *s. Com:* Marchand *m* de grains. **'corn-cob,** *s.* Épi *m* de maïs. **'corn-field,** *s.* Champ *m* de blé, *U.S:* de maïs. **'corn-salad,** *s. Bot:* Mâche *f.*

corn², *s.* **1.** Cor *m* (à l'orteil); oignon *m* (au pied); durillon *m* (sous le pied). **Soft corn,** œil-de-perdrix, *pl.* œils-de-perdrix. *F:* **To tread**

on s.o.'s **corns,** toucher qn à l'endroit sensible; froisser qn. **2.** *Vet:* Bleime *f.*

corncrake ['kɔːrnkreik], *s. Orn:* Râle *m* des genêts.

cornea ['kɔːrnia], *s. Anat:* Cornée *f* (de l'œil).

corned [kɔːrnd], *a.* **Corned beef,** bœuf salé; bœuf de conserve.

cornel(-berry) ['kɔːrnəl(bəri)], *s. Bot:* Cornouille *f.* **Cornel(-tree),** cornouiller *m.*

cornelian [kɔːrˈniːljən], *s. Lap:* Cornaline *f.*

corner¹ ['kɔːrnər], *s.* **1.** Coin *m,* angle *m.* *F:* **To rub the corners off** s.o., dégourdir, dégrossir, qn. **2.** Coin; encoignure *f* (d'une salle, etc.); commissure *f* (des lèvres). **To put a child in the corner,** mettre un enfant en pénitence. **To drive** s.o. **into a corner,** (i) acculer qn; (ii) *F:* mettre qn au pied du mur. **Corner seat,** place de coin. **Chimney corner,** coin du feu. **Nooks and corners,** coins et recoins. *S.a.* FOUR. *Fb:* **Corner(-kick),** coup de pied de coin. **3.** *(a)* Coin, angle (de rue). **Corner house,** maison qui fait le coin, l'angle, de la rue. **C. shop,** boutique d'angle. **You will find the grocer's round the c.,** vous trouverez l'épicerie en tournant le coin. *F:* **To turn the corner,** passer le moment critique. *(b)* Tournant *m;* *Aut: Sp:* virage *m.* **He disappeared round the c.,** il a disparu au tournant. *Aut:* **Blind corner,** virage masqué. **To take a corner,** virer; prendre un virage. **4.** *Com:* Monopole *m.* **To make a corner in wheat,** accaparer le blé. **'corner-cupboard,** *s.* Encoignure *f.* **'corner-plate,** *s.* Équerre *f* en fer, en tôle. **'corner-stone,** *s. Const:* Pierre *f* angulaire; pierre de refend.

corner², *v.tr.* **1.** *(a)* Acculer (qn); mettre (un animal) à l'accul. *(b) F:* Mettre (qn) au pied du mur, à quia. **2.** Accaparer (une denrée, le marché). **3.** *Abs. Aut:* Prendre un virage; virer. **To corner sharply,** virer court. **-cornered,** *a.* **Sharp-cornered,** à angles saillants. **Three-cornered,** à trois coins.

cornet¹ ['kɔːrnet], *s.* **1.** *Mus:* Cornet *m* à pistons; piston *m.* **2.** Cornet (en papier). **Ice-cream cornet,** oublie *f,* plaisir *m.*

cornet², *s.* **1.** Cornette *f* (de religieuse). **2.** *Mil: A:* *(a)* Étendard *m* (de cavalerie). *(b)* *(Pers.)* Cornette *m.*

cornflour ['kɔːrnflauər], *s.* Farine *f* de maïs.

cornflower ['kɔːrnflauər], *s. Bot:* Bleuet *m,* bluet *m,* barbeau *m.* **Cornflower blue,** bleu barbeau *inv.*

cornice ['kɔːrnis], *s.* Corniche *f.*

Cornish ['kɔːrniʃ], *a.* Cornouaillais.

cornucopia, *pl.* **-as** [kɔːrnjuˈkoupia, -əz], *s.* Corne *f* d'abondance.

Cornwall ['kɔːrnwəl]. *Pr.n.* (Le comté de) Cornouailles.

corolla [koˈrɔla], *s. Bot:* Corolle *f.*

corollary [koˈrɔləri], *s. Log: Mth:* Corollaire *m.*

corona, *pl.* **-ae** [koˈrouna, -iː], *s.* Couronne *f* (solaire, d'une dent, etc.).

coronation [korəˈnei(ʃ)ən], *s.* Couronnement *m,* sacre *m.*

coroner ['korənər], *s. Jur:* Coroner *m* (officier civil chargé d'instruire en cas de mort suspecte). *S.a.* INQUEST.

coronet ['koronet], *s.* *(a)* (Petite) couronne (ducale, etc.); cercle *m;* tortil *m* (de baron). *(b) (Lady's)* Diadème *m* ou bandeau *m.*

corporal¹ ['kɔːrpor(ə)l], *a.* Corporel. *S.a.* PUNISHMENT.

corporal², *s. Mil:* *(Of infantry)* Caporal *m,* -aux; *(of cavalry, artillery)* brigadier *m.*

corporate ['kɔːrporet], *a.* **1.** *Jur:* Body corporate, **corporate body**, corps constitué ; personne morale, civile, juridique. **2. Corporate feeling**, esprit *m* de corps.

corporation [kɔːrpoˈreiʃ(ə)n], *s.* **1.** (*a*) Corporation *f*; corps constitué. (*b*) *Hist:* Corps de métier. **2.** *Com:* Société enregistrée. **3.** *Jur:* Personne morale, civile. **4.** **Municipal corporation**, conseil municipal. **5.** *F:* Bedaine *f*, bedon *m.* **To develop a c.**, prendre du ventre.

corporeal [kɔːrˈpoːriəl], *a.* Corporel, matériel.

corps [kɔːr, *pl.* kɔːrz], *s. inv.* Corps *m.* **Army corps**, corps d'armée. **The diplomatic c.**, le corps diplomatique.

corpse [kɔːrps], *s.* (*a*) Cadavre *m*; corps (mort). (*b*) (*At a burial*) Dépouille mortelle.

corpulence [ˈkɔːrpjuləns], *s.* Corpulence *f.*

corpulent [ˈkɔːrpjulənt], *a.* Corpulent.

corpus [ˈkɔːrpəs], *s.* **1.** (*a*) Corpus *m*, recueil *m* (d'inscriptions, etc.). (*b*) *Jur:* **Corpus delicti** [diˈliktai], le corps du délit. **2. Corpus Christi** [ˈkristi], la Fête-Dieu.

corpuscle [ˈkɔːrpʌsl], *s.* **1.** Corpuscule *m.* **Blood corpuscles**, globules sanguins. **2.** *F:* = Atome *m*, molécule *f.*

corral [koˈral], *s.* Corral *m, pl.* -als.

correct[1] [koˈrekt], *v.tr.* **1.** Relever les fautes (d'un thème, etc.); corriger (une épreuve, une mauvaise habitude). **2.** Rectifier (une erreur). **3.** Reprendre, faire la leçon à (un enfant). **To stand corrected**, reconnaître son erreur. **To correct oneself**, se reprendre. **4.** Neutraliser, contrebalancer (une influence).

correct[2], *a.* **1.** Correct, exact; (réponse) juste. *His prediction proved c.*, sa prédiction s'est vérifiée. **2.** Bienséant; conforme à l'usage. **It's the correct thing**, c'est l'usage. **-ly**, *adv.* Correctement, exactement, justement.

correction [koˈrekʃ(ə)n], *s.* **1.** Correction *f* (d'une épreuve, d'un devoir, etc.); rectification *f* (d'une erreur). **Under correction**, sauf erreur, sauf correction. **2.** Correction, châtiment *m*, punition *f.*

correctness [koˈrektnəs], *s.* Correction *f*, convenance *f* (de tenue, etc.); exactitude *f*, justesse *f*; pureté *f* (de style).

corrector [koˈrektər], *s.* Correcteur, -trice.

correlate [ˈkoreleit], *v.i.* Correspondre, être corrélatif (*with, to*, à). **2.** *v.tr.* Mettre (qch.) en corrélation (*with*, avec).

correlation [koreˈleiʃ(ə)n], *s.* Corrélation *f.*

correlative [koˈrelətiv], *a. & s.* Corrélatif (*m*). **-ly**, *adv.* Corrélativement.

correspond [koresˈpond], *v.i.* **1.** (*a*) Correspondre, être conforme (*with, to*, à). (*b*) Correspondre (*to*, avec). *The two windows do not c.*, les deux fenêtres ne correspondent pas, ne se répondent pas. **2.** (*Communicate*) Correspondre (*with s.o.*, avec qn). *They correspond*, ils s'écrivent.

corresponding, *a.* Correspondant. *C. to the original*, conforme à l'original. *Book-k:* **Corresponding entry**, écriture conforme. **-ly**, *adv.* Également; à l'avenant.

correspondence [koresˈpondəns], *s.* **1.** Correspondance *f* (*with, to*, avec). **2.** (*a*) **To be in correspondence with s.o.**, être en relations, en correspondance, avec qn. (*b*) Correspondance, courrier *m.* *Sch:* **Correspondence course**, cours *m* par correspondance.

correspondent [koresˈpondənt], *s.* Correspondant *m.* *Journ:* **Answers to correspondents**, la petite poste. **From our special correspondent**, de notre envoyé spécial.

corridor [ˈkoridoːr], *s.* Couloir *m*, corridor *m.* *Rail:* **Corridor carriage**, wagon *m* à couloir.

wagon-couloir *m.* *Geog:* **The Polish Corridor**, le Couloir de Dantzig.

corroborate [koˈrɔboreit], *v.tr.* Corroborer, confirmer (une déclaration). *The facts c. his statements*, les faits viennent à l'appui de ce qu'il dit.

corroboration [korɔboˈreiʃ(ə)n], *s.* Corroboration *f*, confirmation *f.* **In corroboration of . . .**, à l'appui de. . . .

corroborator [koˈrɔboreitər], *s.* Témoin *m* à l'appui.

corrode [koˈroud]. **1.** *v.tr.* Corroder, attaquer (le métal); ronger (le métal, le cœur). **2.** *v.i.* Se corroder.

corrodent [koˈroudənt], *s.* Corrodant *m.*

corrosion [koˈrouʒ(ə)n], *s.* Corrosion *f.*

corrosive [koˈrousiv], *a. & s.* Corrosif (*m*), corrodant (*m*). **Non-corrosive**, inoxydable.

corrugate [ˈkorjugeit], *v.tr.* Strier de nervures; strier (le verre); onduler (la tôl); gaufrer (le papier). **corrugated**, *a.* Ridé, plissé, rugueux; (verre) strié, cannelé; (papier) gaufré; (carton) ondulé. **Corrugated iron**, tôle ondulée.

corrugation [korjuˈgeiʃ(ə)n], *s.* Plissement *m*, ondulation *f*, cannelure *f.*

corrupt[1] [koˈrʌpt], *a.* Corrompu. (*a*) **Corrupt practices**, (i) tractations malhonnêtes; (ii) trafic *m* d'influence. *C. press*, presse vénale. (*b*) (Texte) corrompu, altéré.

corrupt[2]. **1.** *v.tr.* Corrompre, altérer (la viande, un texte, le caractère); suborner (un témoin); dépraver, dévoyer (la jeunesse). **2.** *v.i.* Se corrompre.

corrupter [koˈrʌptər], *s.* Corrupteur, -trice, démoralisateur, -trice.

corruption [koˈrʌpʃ(ə)n], *s.* **1.** (*a*) Corruption *f*, putréfaction *f.* (*b*) Dépravation *f.* **2.** *Jur:* Subornation *f* (de témoins). **Bribery and corruption**, corruption, subornation.

corsair [ˈkɔːrseər], *s.* **1.** Corsaire *m* (vaisseau ou marin). **2.** Flibustier *m*, pirate *m.*

corset [ˈkɔːrsət], *s.* (*Often pl.*) *Cost:* Corset *m.* **Corset-belt**, corset ceinture. **'corset-maker**, *s.* Corsetier, -ière.

Corsica [ˈkɔːrsika]. *Pr.n. Geog:* La Corse.

Corsican [ˈkɔːrsikən], *a. & s.* Corse (*mf*).

cortex, *pl.* **-ices** [ˈkɔːrteks, -isiːz], *s.* **1.** *Bot:* Enveloppe subéreuse. **2.** *Anat:* Substance corticale.

corundum [koˈrʌndəm], *s.* *Miner:* Corindon *m.* *Ind:* **Corundum wheel**, meule en corindon.

coryphaeus [kɔriˈfiːəs], *s.* Coryphée *m.*

cos [kos], *s.* *Hort:* **Cos** (lettuce) (laitue) romaine *f.*

cosine [ˈkousain], *s.* *Trig:* Cosinus *m.* **Cosine curve**, cosinusoïde *f.*

cosiness [ˈkouzinəs], *s.* Confortable *m* (d'un fauteuil); chaleur *f* agréable (du coin du feu, etc.).

cosmetic [kozˈmetik], *a. & s.* Cosmétique (*m*).

cosmic(al) [ˈkozmik(əl)], *a.* Cosmique.

cosmogony [kozˈmogoni], *s.* Cosmogonie *f.*

cosmography [kozˈmografi], *s.* Cosmographie *f.*

cosmopolitan [kozmoˈpolitən], *a. & s.* Cosmopolite (*mf*).

cosmopolis [kozˈmopolis], *s.* Cité *f* cosmopolite

cosmos [ˈkozmos], *s.* Cosmos *m.* **The cosmos**, l'univers *m.*

Cossack [ˈkosak], *a. & s.* Cosaque (*mf*).

cost[1] [kost], *s.* **1.** Coût *m*, frais *mpl.* **Cost of living**, coût de la vie. **To bear the cost of an undertaking**, faire les frais d'une entreprise; défrayer une entreprise. **To live at s.o.'s cost**, vivre aux dépens, aux crochets, de qn. **At the cost of one's life**, au prix de sa vie. **At little cost.**

à peu de frais. **At great cost,** à grands frais. **At any cost, at all costs,** à tout prix ; à toute force ; coûte que coûte. *I learnt it* to my cost, je l'ai appris à mes dépens. *Com :* **Prime cost, net cost,** prix de revient, prix coûtant. *S.a.* PRICE¹. **2.** *pl. Jur :* Frais d'instance ; dépens *mpl.* **To allow costs,** accorder les frais et dépens. *They were ordered to pay costs,* ils furent condamnés aux frais.

cost². **1.** *v.i.* (cost ; cost) Coûter. *His house has cost him* 50,000 *francs,* sa maison lui revient à 50,000 francs. *That will c. him a lot of trouble,* cela lui coûtera beaucoup de peine. *The attempt cost him his life,* cette tentative lui coûta la vie. **Cost what it may,** coûte que coûte. *It costs me a little civility,* j'en suis quitte pour une petite politesse. **2.** *v.tr.* (costed ; costed) *Com : Ind :* **To cost an article,** établir le prix de revient d'un article. *To c. a job,* évaluer le coût d'un travail.

costing, *s.* Établissement *m* du prix de revient.

coster(monger) ['kɔstər(mʌŋgər)], *s.* Marchand ambulant ; marchand des quatre saisons. **Coster's cart,** baladeuse *f* ; voiture *f* à bras.

costive ['kɔstiv], *a.* Constipé.

costliness ['kɔstlinəs], *s.* **1.** Somptuosité *f* (de l'ameublement, etc.). **2.** Haut prix ; prix élevé.

costly ['kɔstli], *a.* **1.** (*a*) Précieux ; de grand prix. (*b*) (Ameublement, etc.) riche, somptueux ; de luxe. **2.** Coûteux, dispendieux.

costmary ['kɔstmɛəri], *s. Bot :* Balsamite *f.*

costume ['kɔstjum], *s.* Costume *m.* **1.** *Th :* **Costume play,** pièce historique. **2.** (*With pl.* **costumes**) **(Lady's) tailor-made)** costume, costume tailleur.

costum(i)er [kɔs'tju:m(i)ər], *s.* Costumier *m.*

cosy ['kouzi]. **1.** *a.* Chaud, confortable ; (*of pers.*) bien au chaud. *It is c. here,* il fait bon ici. **2.** *s.* = EGG-COSY, TEA-COSY. **-ily,** *adv.* Confortablement ; douillettement.

cot¹ [kɔt], *s.* **1.** *Poet :* (Cottage) Chaumière *f,* chaumine *f.* **2.** Abri *m.*

cot², *s.* (*a*) Lit *m* d'enfant ; couchette *f.* (*b*) **Basket cot,** moïse *m.*

cotangent [kou'tandʒənt], *s. Trig :* Cotangente *f.*

cote [kout], *s.* **Dove-cote,** colombier *m,* pigeonnier *m.* **Hen-cote,** poulailler *m.*

coterie ['koutəri], *s.* Coterie *f* ; cénacle *m* (littéraire, etc.).

cotill(i)on [ko'tiljən], *s. Danc :* Cotillon *m.*

cottage ['kɔtedʒ], *s.* **1.** Chaumière *f.* **2.** Villa *f* ; petite maison de campagne. **Cottage hospital,** (i) hôpital de petite ville ; (ii) hôpital réparti en villas ou chalets. *S.a.* LOAF¹.

cottager ['kɔtedʒər], *s.* **1.** Paysan, -anne ; villageois, -oise.

cottar¹, cotter¹ ['kɔtər], *s. Scot :* = COTTAGER.

cottar², cotter², *s. Mec.E :* etc : (*Also* **cotter-pin**) Clavette *f,* goupille *f.*

cotter², *v.tr. Mec.E :* Claveter ; goupiller ; caler (une pièce).

cotton¹ [kɔt(ə)n], *s.* **1.** (*a*) *Bot :* Cotonnier *m.* (*b*) Coton *m.* **Raw c.,** coton en laine. **Cotton industry,** industrie cotonnière. *Pharm :* **Absorbent cotton,** coton hydrophile. **2.** *Tex :* (*a*) **Cotton yarn,** coton filé ; fil *m* de coton. (*b*) **Cotton goods, stuffs,** cotonnades *f.* **Cotton(-cloth),** (toile ᶠ de) coton ; cotonnade, percale *f.* **Printed cotton,** indienne *f.* **3.** **Sewing-cotton,** fil à coudre ; fil d'Écosse ; fil de coton. '**cotton-cake,** *s. Husb :* Tourteau *m.* '**cotton-mill,** *s.* Filature ᶠ de coton ; cotonnerie *f.* '**cotton-plantation,** *s.* Cotônnerie *f.* '**cotton-spinner,** *s.* **1.** (*Owner*) Filateur *m* de coton. **2.** (*Worker*) Fileur, -euse,

de coton. **cotton-'wool,** *s.* Ouate *f.* *F :* **To bring up a child in cotton-wool,** élever un enfant dans du coton.

cotton², *v.i.* **1.** (*Of material*) (Se) cotonner. **2.** *F :* **To cotton (with s.o.),** s'accorder, faire bon ménage (avec qn). **3.** **To cotton up to s.o.,** faire des avances à qn. **4.** (*a*) **To cotton (on) to s.o.,** se sentir attiré par qn ; prendre qn en amitié. (*b*) **To c.** (*on*) *to* (*sth.*), mordre à (l'algèbre, etc.).

cottonwood ['kɔtnwud], *s.* *U.S :* (Variété *f* de) peuplier *m.*

cottony ['kɔtəni], *a.* Cotonneux.

cotyledon [kɔti'li:dən], *s. Bot :* Cotylédon *m.*

cotyledonous [kɔti'li:dənəs], *a.* Cotylédoné.

couch¹ [kautʃ], *s.* **1.** *Lit :* Lit *m,* couche *f.* **2.** *Furn :* Canapé *m,* divan *m* ; chaise-longue *f.*

couch². **1.** *v.tr.* (*a*) *Lit :* **To be couched on the ground,** être couché par terre. (*b*) Mettre (sa lance) en arrêt. (*c*) *A. & Adm :* **To couch a request in writing,** coucher une demande par écrit. *Letter couched in these terms,* lettre ainsi conçue. **2.** *v.i.* (*a*) (*Of animal*) Se coucher, être couché (dans sa tanière) ; se terrer ; gîter. (*b*) (*Of dog, pers.*) Se tapir (devant qn) ; s'aplatir. (*c*) Se tenir embusqué.

couch³(-grass) ['kautʃ(grɑːs), 'kuːtʃ-], *s. Bot :* Chiendent *m.*

cougar ['kuːgər], *s. Z :* Couguar *m,* puma *m.*

cough¹ [kɔf], *s.* Toux *f.* **To have a cough,** tousser. *He gave a cough to warn .me,* il toussa pour m'avertir. '**cough-drop, -lozenge,** *s.* Pastille pectorale.

cough². **1.** *v.i.* Tousser. **2.** *v.tr.* **To cough out** sth., cracher qch. (en toussant). *P : To c. up money,* abs. **to cough up,** payer, *P :* cracher.

coughing, *s.* Toux *f.*

could [kud]. *See* CAN³.

coulter ['koultər], *s.* Coutre *m* (de charrue).

council ['kaunsil], *s.* **1.** Conseil *m.* **Town-council, city-council,** conseil municipal. **County council** = conseil général ou conseil départemental. **To hold council** ; **to be, meet, in council,** tenir conseil. *S.a.* ORDER¹ 11, PRIVY I. 2. **2.** *Ecc :* Concile *m.* '**council-chamber,** *s.* Salle *f* du conseil. '**council-school,** *s.* = École municipale.

councillor ['kaunsilər], *s.* Conseiller *m* ; membre *m* du conseil.

counsel¹ ['kauns(ə)l], *s.* **1.** Délibération *f* ; consultation *f.* **To take counsel with s.o.,** (i) prendre conseil de qn ; (ii) délibérer, consulter, avec qn. *To take c. together,* se consulter, se concerter. **2.** Conseil *m,* avis *m.* *F :* **Counsel of perfection,** idéal *m* difficile à atteindre. *S.a.* PILLOW¹ 1. **3.** Dessein *m,* intention *f.* **To keep one's (own) counsel,** garder ses projets pour soi ; observer le silence. **4.** *Jur :* (*a*) Avocat *m* ; conseil *m.* **To be represented by counsel,** comparaître par avoué. **Counsel in chambers,** avocat consultant. (*b*) **King's counsel,** conseiller du Roi (titre conféré à des membres éminents du barreau de Londres).

counsel², *v.tr.* (counselled) *Lit :* Recommander (une ligne de conduite) *To c. s.o. to do sth.,* conseiller, recommander, à qn de faire qch.

counsellor ['kaunsələr], *s.* Conseiller *m.*

count¹ [kaunt], *s.* **1.** (*a*) Compte *m,* calcul *m* ; (*of votes*) dépouillement *m* ; (*of people*) dénombrement *m.* **To keep count of . . . ,** compter . . . ; tenir le compte de. . . . **To lose count,** perdre le compte. **To ask for a count,** demander le scrutin. (*b*) Total *m.* **2.** *Jur :* Chef *m* (d'accusation). **3.** *Tex :* Numéro *m* (du fil). **4.** *Box :* Compte (de dix secondes). **To take the count**

(out), rester sur le plancher pour le compte; être mis knock-out.

count². **I.** *v.tr.* (*a*) Compter; dénombrer (ses troupeaux, etc.). **To count the cost,** compter, calculer, la dépense. **To count up sth.,** compter, faire le compte de, qch. *S.a.* CHICKEN I. **To count the votes** (*at election*), dépouiller le scrutin. **Counting from to-morrow . . .,** à compter de demain. (*b*) **To count s.o. among one's friends,** compter qn parmi ses amis. (*c*) *Pred.* **To c. s.o. as dead,** tenir, compter, qn pour mort. **2.** *v.i.* (*a*) *A:* Faire des projets. (*b*) **To count on, upon, s.o.,** compter sur qch. **To count on doing sth.,** compter faire qch. **3.** *v.i.* (*a*) *He counts among my best friends,* il compte parmi, au nombre de, mes meilleurs amis. *Cards: Card that counts,* (carte) marquante. *This person counts as two,* cette personne compte pour deux. *He doesn't c. for much,* il ne compte guère. (*b*) Avoir de l'importance. *Every minute counts,* il n'y a pas une minute à perdre. *Every penny counts,* il faut regarder à chaque sou. **count in,** *v.tr.* Faire entrer en ligne de compte. **count out,** *v.tr.* **I.** Compter (de l'argent, etc.) pièce par pièce. **2.** *Box:* **To be counted out,** rester sur le plancher pour le compte. **3.** *F:* **You can count me out of that show,** ne comptez pas sur moi dans cette affaire. **counting,** *s.* Compte *m*, calcul *m*; dépouillement *m* (du scrutin); dénombrement *m* (de personnes). **'counting-frame,** *s.* Boulier compteur. **'counting-house,** *s.* (Bureau *m* de) la comptabilité.

count³, *s.m.* Comte (français, italien, etc. *Cp.* EARL).

countenance¹ ['kauntinəns], *s.* **I.** Expression *f* du visage; visage, figure *f*, mine *f*. **To keep one's countenance,** (i) ne pas se laisser décontenancer; (ii) se donner, se faire, une contenance. **To put s.o. out of countenance,** décontenancer qn. **To lose countenance,** se décontenancer; perdre contenance. **To stare s.o. out of countenance,** dévisager qn. **2.** **To give, lend, countenance to s.o., to sth.,** appuyer, favoriser, encourager, qn, qch.; accréditer (une nouvelle, etc.).

countenance², *v.tr.* **I.** Autoriser, approuver, sanctionner (une action). **2.** Encourager, appuyer, soutenir (qn) (*in*, dans).

counter¹ ['kauntər], *s.* **I.** (*Pers.*) Compteur, -euse. **2.** *Mec.E:* Compteur *m.* **3.** *Games:* (i) (*Square*) Fiche *f* (en os, etc.). (ii) (*Round*) Jeton *m.* **4.** (*a*) (*In bank, etc.*) Guichets *mpl* (*d'une banque*). (*b*) (*In shop*) Comptoir *m.* **'counter-jumper,** *s.* *F:* Commis *m* (de magasin).

counter², *s.* **I.** *N.Arch:* Voûte *f* d'arcasse. **2.** Creux *m* (d'un poinçon, etc.).

counter³, *s.* *Bootm:* Contrefort *m.*

counter⁴. **I.** *s.* (*a*) *Fenc:* Contre *m.* (*b*) *Box:* Coup *m* d'arrêt; contre. **2.** *a.* (*a*) Contraire, opposé (*to*, à). (*b*) *In compounds often translated by* contre-. **3.** *adv.* En sens inverse; à contresens **To run counter to one's orders,** agir contrairement à ses instructions; aller à l'encontre de ses instructions. **'counter-ad'vice,** *s.* Contre-avis *m.* **'counter-at'tack¹,** *s.* Contre-attaque *f.* **'counter-at'tack²,** *v.tr. & i.* Contre-attaquer. **'counter-at'traction,** *s.* **I.** Attraction opposée. **2.** Attraction destinée à faire concurrence au clou de la fête. **'counter-brace¹,** *s.* *Civ.E:* Entretoise *f.* **'counter-brace²,** *v.tr.* Entretoiser. **'counter-charge,** *s.* Contre-accusation *f.* **'counter-charm,** *s.* Contre-charme *m.* **'counter-check,** *s.* *Mec:* Force opposée; force antagoniste. **'counter-claim¹,** *s.* *Jur:* Demande reconventionnelle;

défense *f* au contraire. **'counter-claim²,** *v.tr.* *Jur:* Faire, opposer, une demande reconventionnelle (en dommages-intérêts, etc.) **'counter-'clockwise,** *adv.* En sens inverse des aiguilles d'une montre; sinistrorsum. **'counter-'current,** *s.* Contre-courant *m.* **'counter-decla'ration,** *s.* Contre-déclaration *f.* **'counter-'effort,** *s.* Contre-effort *m.* **'counter-en'quiry,** *s.* *Jur:* Contre-enquête *f.* **'counter-'irritant,** *a. & s.* *Med:* (Médicament) révulsif (*m*), dérivatif (*m*). **'counter-'melody,** *s.* *Mus:* Contre-chant *m.* **'counter-o'ffensive,** *s.* *Mil:* Contre-offensive *f.* **'counter-propo'sition,** *s.* Contre-proposition *f.* **'counter-punch,** *s.* *Tls:* Contre-poinçon *m.* **'counter-revo'lution,** *s.* Contre-révolution *f.* **'counter-seal,** *s.* Contre-sceau *m.* **'counter-'signature,** *s.* **I.** Contreseing *m.* **2.** Approuvé *m.* **'counter-stroke,** *s.* *Mil:* Retour offensif.

counter⁵, *v.tr.* Aller à l'encontre de, contrarier (qn, qch.); contrecarrer (les desseins de qn). *Box:* **To counter** (*a blow*), parer, bloquer (un coup) et riposter en même temps.

counteract [kauntə'rakt], *v.tr.* Neutraliser (une influence); parer à (un résultat).

counteraction [kauntə'rak∫(ə)n], *s.* **I.** Action *f* contraire; mouvement opposé; opposition *f.* **2.** Neutralisation *f* (d'une influence, etc.).

counterbalance¹ ['kauntərbaləns], *s.* Contrepoids *m.*

counterbalance² [kauntər'baləns], *v.tr.* Contrebalancer; faire contrepoids à (qch.); compenser (une force, etc.).

countercharge ['kauntərt∫ɑ:rdʒ], *s.* *Jur:* Contre-accusation *f.*

counterfeit¹ ['kauntərfi:t]. **I.** *a.* Contrefait; faux. **Counterfeit coin,** fausse monnaie. **2.** *s.* Contrefaçon *f.*

counterfeit², *v.tr.* **I.** Contrefaire (la monnaie, etc.). **2.** Simuler, feindre (une passion, etc.). **To counterfeit poverty,** faire le pauvre. **counterfeiting,** *s.* **I.** (*a*) Contrefaction *f.* (*b*) Contrefaçon *f.* **2.** Simulation *f.*

counterfeiter ['kauntərfi:tər], *s.* **I.** Contrefacteur *m*; faux monnayeur. **2.** Simulateur, -trice.

counterfoil ['kauntərfoil], *s.* Souche *f*, talon *m* (de chèque).

counterfort ['kauntərfo:rt], *s.* *Arch:* Éperon *m* (d'un mur). *Ph.Geog:* Contrefort *m.*

countermand [kauntər'mɑ:nd], *v.tr.* Contremander; décommander (une grève); révoquer, rappeler (un ordre). **Unless countermanded,** sauf contre-ordre, sauf contre-avis.

countermarch ['kauntərmɑ:rt∫], *s.* Contremarche *f.*

countermine [kauntər'main], *v.tr. & i.* Contreminer.

counterpane ['kauntərpein], *s.* Courtepointe *f*; couvre-lit *m*, couvre-pied(s) *m.*

counterpart ['kauntərpɑ:rt], *s.* Contre-partie *f*; pendant *m* (d'un tableau, etc.); duplicata *m*, double *m* (d'un document).

counterplot ['kauntərplɔt], *s.* Contre-ruse *f*, contre-trame *f.*

counterpoint ['kauntərpoint], *s.* *Mus:* Contrepoint *m.*

counterpoise¹ ['kauntərpɔiz], *s.* **I.** Contrepoids *m.* **2.** Équilibre *m.* **In counterpoise,** en équilibre.

counterpoise², *v.tr.* Contre-balancer; faire contrepoids à (qch.).

counterscarp ['kauntərskɑ:rp], *s.* *Fort:* Contrescarpe *f.*

countershaft ['kauntərˌʃɑ:ft], s. *Mec.E*: Arbre *m* intermédiaire, de renvoi *Aut*: Contre-arbre *m*.

countersign¹ ['kauntərsain], s. **1.** Contreseing *m*. **2.** Mot *m* d'ordre; mot de ralliement.

countersign² [kauntərˈsain], *v.tr.* Contresigner, signer en second, viser.

countersink¹ ['kauntərsiŋk], s. **1.** *Tls*: Fraise *f*. **2.** Countersink (hole), fraisure *f* (d'un trou); noyure *f* (pour tête de vis).

countersink², *v.tr.* (*Conj. like* SINK) **1.** Fraiser (un trou). **2.** Encastrer (la tête d'un rivet); noyer (la tête d'une vis).

countervail [kauntərˈveil]. **1.** *v.tr.* Contrebalancer, compenser. **2.** *v.i.* Prévaloir (*against*, contre).

counterweight ['kauntərweit], s. Contrepoids *m*.

countess ['kauntes], *s.f.* Comtesse.

countless ['kauntləs], *a.* Innombrable.

countrified, countryfied ['kʌntrifaid], *a.* Aux allures campagnardes; agreste.

country ['kʌntri], s. **1.** (*a*) Pays *m*, contrée *f*, région *f*. To go up country, remonter vers l'intérieur du pays. Open country, rase campagne. (*b*) (*Native country*) Patrie *f*. To die for King and country, mourir pour la patrie. **2.** (*a*) (*Opposed to capital*) Province *f*. In the country, en province. Country cousin, cousin de province. (*b*) (*Opposed to town*) Campagne *f*. In the country, à la campagne. Surrounding country, pays d'alentour; (*of large town*) banlieue *f*. Country life, vie de, à la, campagne; vie champêtre. Country girl, (jeune) paysanne *f*. **country 'dance,** s. Danse *f* rustique. **country-'house, -'seat,** s. **1.** Maison *f* de campagne. **2.** Château *m*. **country-'side,** s. **1.** La région. **2.** La population de la région.

countryman, *pl.* **-men** ['kʌntrimən, -men], *s.m.* **1.** Compatriote, concitoyen. **2.** Paysan, campagnard.

countrywoman, *pl.* **-women** ['kʌntriwumən, -wimen], *s.f.* **1.** Compatriote, concitoyenne. **2.** Paysanne, campagnarde.

county ['kaunti], *s.* Comté *m*. County town, chef-lieu *m* de comté, *pl.* chefs-lieux. County court = tribunal *m* d'arrondissement. A county family, une des familles terriennes du comté. County society, the county set, l'aristocratie et la haute bourgeoisie du comté. *S.a.* COUNCIL I.

coupé ['ku:pe], *s. Veh*: Coupé *m*.

couple¹ [kʌpl], s. **1.** Couple *f* (d'attache, pour chiens de chasse). **2.** Couple *f* (de pigeons, d'œufs, etc.). To work in couples, se mettre à deux pour travailler. **3.** (*a*) Couple *m* (de chiens de chasse). *F*: To go, hunt, run, in couples, être toujours ensemble (*b*) Couple *m* (d'époux, de danseurs). The newly married couple, les nouveaux mariés; le nouveau ménage. *The young c.*, les deux jeunes époux. 'Respectable c. wanted,' "on demande un ménage recommandable." **4.** *Mec*: Couple *m* (de torsion); couple moteur.

couple², *v.tr.* (*a*) Coupler, accoupler (des bœufs, deux idées); associer, accoler (des noms, etc.). *Organ*: To c. two manuals, accoupler deux claviers. (*b*) *Mec.E*: *etc*: Engrener, embrayer (une machine); raccorder (des tuyaux). Coupled direct to the motor, en prise directe avec le moteur. (*c*) *El*: Associer, grouper, accoupler (des piles); faire communiquer (des organes). (*d*) *Rail*: To couple up, couple on, a carriage, atteler, accrocher, un wagon. **coupling,** s. **1.** Accouplement *m* (de deux choses); appariement *m* (des animaux); association *f* (d'idées, etc.); accolement *m* (de deux noms). **2.** *Tchn*: (*a*) Accouplement,

assemblage *m*, couplage *m* (de deux roues, etc.); emmanchement *m* (de deux tuyaux). **Coupling-box, coupling-sleeve,** manchon *m* d'accouplement. (*b*) *Rail*: Attelage *m*, accrochage *m* (des wagons). (*c*) *El*: Couplage, association *f*, groupement *m* (d'éléments de pile, etc.). **3.** (*Coupling device*) Accouplement, raccord *m*; (*for transmitting motion*) embrayage *m*. *Rail*: Attelage *m*.

coupler ['kʌplər], *s. Organ*: (i) Tirant *m* à accoupler; (ii) pédale *f* d'accouplement.

couplet ['kʌplət], s. *Pros*: Distique *m*.

coupon ['ku:pɔn], s. **1.** Coupon *m*. *Com*: Freegift coupon, bon-prime *m*, *pl.* bons-primes. **2.** *Pol*: Recommandation officielle donnée à un candidat par le chef d'un parti.

courage ['kʌredʒ], s. **1.** Courage *m*. To have courage, avoir du cœur. To have the courage of one's convictions, avoir le courage de ses opinions. To take, pluck up, muster up, courage, prendre son courage à deux mains; faire appel à tout son courage. *S.a.* DUTCH.

courageous [kəˈreidʒəs], *a.* Courageux. **-ly,** *adv.* Courageusement.

courier ['kuriər], *s.* **1.** Courrier *m*, messager *m*. **2.** *Journ*: The Northern C., le Courrier du Nord.

course¹ [kɔːrs], s. **1.** (*a*) Cours *m* (d'un fleuve, du temps); courant *m* (des affaires, etc.); cours, marche *f* (des événements); cours, trajet *m* (d'une balle, etc.). *Geol*: Direction *f* (d'un filon). In the course of the sitting, au cours de la séance. In (the) course of time, avec le temps; à la longue. In the course of nature, in the ordinary course of things, normalement. To do sth. in due course, faire qch. en temps voulu, en temps utile. In due course . . ., quand les temps furent révolus. . . . In course of construction, en cours de construction. The fever must run its course, il faut que la fièvre suive son cours. To let nature take her course, donner libre cours à la nature. Let things take their course, *F*: laissez faire. (*b*) Of course, bien entendu; naturellement. (*c*) That is a matter of course, cela va sans dire; cela va de soi. As a matter of course, comme de juste, comme de raison. **2.** (*a*) *Sch*: Cours. To give a course of lectures, professer un cours. To go through a course, suivre un cours (de physique, etc.). *To publish a c. in French*, publier une méthode de français. (*b*) *Med*: Traitement *m*, régime *m*. (*c*) *Agr*: Four-course rotation, assolement quadriennal. **3.** (*a*) Route *f*, direction *f*. To hold (on) one's course, suivre tout droit son chemin; *Nau*: maintenir son cap. To change one's course, changer de direction; *Nau*: changer le cap. *Nau*: To set the course (on the chart), tracer la route (sur la carte). To steer a course, suivre une route. (*b*) To take a course of action, adopter une ligne de conduite. To take one's own course, agir à sa guise. There was no c. open to me but flight, je n'avais d'autre ressource que la fuite. To hesitate between two courses, hésiter entre deux partis. The best course, the right course, le parti le plus sûr; la bonne voie. To be given over to evil courses, avoir une mauvaise conduite. *S.a.* MIDDLE I. (*c*) *Mch*: Upward course *of a piston*, course ascendante, ascensionnelle, d'un piston. **4.** (*Of meal*) Service *m*, plat *m*. **5.** *Sp*: (*a*) Champ *m*, terrain *m* (de courses). (*b*) Piste *f*. Closed course, circuit *m* (sur piste). **6.** Lit *m* (d'un cours d'eau). *S.a.* MILL-COURSE, WATER-COURSE. **7.** *Const*: Assise *f* (de briques, de charpente). *S.a.* DAMP-COURSE. **8.** *Fin*: Course of exchange, cote *f* des changes. **9.** *Nau*: Basse voile.

course². **I.** *v.tr.* (*a*) *Ven:* Courir (un lièvre). (*b*) Faire courir (un chien, un cheval). **2.** *v.i.* (*Of liquids*) Courir, couler. *The blood courses through the veins*, le sang circule dans les veines. **coursing,** *s.* Chasse *f* à courre au lièvre. **courser** ['kɔːrsər], *s. Poet:* Coursier *m.*

court¹ [kɔːrt], *s.* **I.** (*a*) = COURTYARD. *Poet:* The courts of heaven, les célestes parvis. (*b*) *A:* Château *m*, manoir *m.* (*c*) (*Off street*) Ruelle *f*; cul-de-sac *m*, *pl.* culs-de-sac; impasse *f.* **2.** (*a*) Cour (royale). **The Court of St James's,** la cour du Roi d'Angleterre. *Lit:* **Court epic,** épopée courtoise. (*b*) **To make, pay, court to s.o.,** faire la cour à qn. **3.** *Jur:* (*a*) Cour, tribunal *m.* **Court-room,** salle *f* d'audience. **The Law Courts,** le palais de justice. **Police court,** tribunal de simple police. **In open court,** en plein tribunal, en pleine audience; à huis ouvert. **To arrange, settle, a case out of court,** arranger une affaire à l'amiable. **To be ruled, put, out of court,** être mis hors de cour; être débouté de sa demande. (*b*) *Mil: Navy:* **Court of inquiry,** commission *f* d'enquête. **4.** (*a*) (i) Jeu *m* de paume. (ii) Terrain *m* (de jeu de paume). (*b*) (i) Tennis *m.* (ii) **Court** *m* (de tennis). (iii) **Service-court,** rectangle *m* de service. **'court-card,** *s. Cards:* Figure *f*; carte peinte. **'court-dress,** *s.* (*a*) Habit *m* de cour. (*b*) (*Of lady*) Robe *f* de cour. **'court-house,** *s.* Palais *m* de justice; tribunal *m.* **court-'martial¹,** *s.* (*pl.* courts-martial) *Mil:* Conseil *m* de guerre. **To be tried by court-martial,** passer en conseil de guerre. **court-martial²,** *v.tr.* (court-martialled) Faire passer (qn) en conseil de guerre.

court², *v.tr.* **I.** Courtiser; faire la cour à (une femme). **2.** Briguer, rechercher (une alliance, etc.); chercher, solliciter (les applaudissements, etc.). **To court danger,** aller au-devant du danger. **courting,** *s.* **To go a-courting,** aller faire sa cour.

courteous ['kɔːrtjəs, 'kɔːrt-], *a.* Courtois, poli, gracieux (*to, towards,* envers). **-ly,** *adv.* Courtoisement.

courteousness ['kɔːrtjəsnəs, 'kɔːrt-], *s.* Courtoisie *f*, politesse *f.*

courtesan ['kɔːrtizan], *s.* Courtisane *f.*

courtesy ['kɔːrtəsi, 'kɔːrtəsi], *s.* Courtoisie *f*, politesse *f.* **By courtesy, as a matter of courtesy,** à titre gracieux. *C. of the road,* chevalerie *f* de la route (entre automobilistes, etc.). **Exchange of courtesies,** échange de bons procédés. **Courtesy title,** titre de courtoisie.

courtier ['kɔːrtiər], *s.* Courtisan *m.*

courtliness ['kɔːrtlinəs], *s.* **I.** Courtoisie *f.* **2.** Élégance *f*; grand air.

courtly ['kɔːrtli], *a.* **I.** Courtois. **2.** Élégant; à l'air digne et aristocratique.

courtship ['kɔːrtʃip], *s.* Cour (faite à une femme).

courtyard [kɔːrt'jɑːrd], *s.* Cour *f* (de maison).

cousin [kʌzn], *s.* Cousin, -ine. **First cousin,** cousin(e) germain(e). **Second cousin,** cousin(e) issu(e) de germain.

cove¹ [kouv], *s. Ph.Geog:* Anse *f*; petite baie.

cove², *s.* *P:* Type *m*, individu *m.*

covenant¹ ['kʌvənənt], *s.* **I.** *Jur:* Convention *f*, contrat *m.* **2.** *Pol:* Pacte *m*, traité *m.* **3.** *B:* Alliance *f* (entre Dieu et les Israélites).

covenant². **I.** *v.tr.* (*a*) Promettre, accorder, (qch.) par contrat. (*b*) Stipuler (une somme). (*c*) *To c. to do sth.,* convenir de, s'engager à, faire qch. **2.** *v.i. To c. with s.o. for sth.,* convenir (par contrat) de qch. avec qn.

covenanter ['kʌvənəntər], *s.* **I.** Partie contrac-

tante. **2.** *Eng.Rel.Hist:* [kʌvə'nantər] Covenantaire *m.*

Coventry ['kʌvəntri]. *Pr.n. Geog:* Ville industrielle du comté de Warwick. *F:* **To send s.o. to Coventry,** mettre qn en quarantaine; frapper qn d'ostracisme.

cover¹ ['kʌvər], *s.* **I.** Couverture *f*; tapis *m* (de table); dessus *m* (de buffet); fourreau *m* (de parapluie); bâche *f* (d'automobile). **Loose cover** (*of chair*), housse *f.* **Outer cover** *of tyre,* enveloppe *f* de pneu. **2.** Couvercle *m* (de marmite, etc.); cloche *f* (pour plat). **Chain cover,** carter *m* de chaîne. *I.C.E:* **Timing-case cover,** couvercle de distribution. *Nau:* **White cap-c.,** coiffe blanche. *S.a.* DISH-COVER. **3.** Couverture (d'un livre); *Bookb:* les plats *m.* **To read a book from cover to cover,** lire un livre d'un bout à l'autre. **4.** *Post:* Enveloppe *f.* **Under separate cover,** sous pli séparé. **5.** (*a*) Abri *m.* **To give s.o. cover,** abriter qn. **To seek, take, cover, se mettre à l'abri; s'abriter. **To be under cover,** être à couvert, à l'abri. (*b*) *Ven:* (i) Abri, couvert *m*, fourré *m*; (ii) gîte *m*, retraite *f.* **To break cover,** sortir de son terrier, d'un fourré; débucher. *Mil: To take c. from the enemy's fire,* se défiler du feu de l'ennemi. (*c*) *To place troops under c.,* embusquer des troupes. *To take c.,* s'embusquer. **6.** Voile *m*, masque *m.* **Under the cover of darkness,** of night, sous le couvert de la nuit. *Under (the) c. of friendship,* sous le masque de l'amitié. **7.** *Com: Ins:* Couverture, provision *f*, marge *f.* *To operate without cover,* opérer à découvert. *Fin: Call for additional c.,* appel *m* de marge. *Ins:* **Full cover,** garantie totale. **8.** *Covers were laid for four,* la table était de quatre couverts. **'cover-glass, -slip,** *s.* (Lamelle *f*) couvre-objet *m* (d'une préparation microscopique).

cover², *v.tr.* **I.** (*a*) Couvrir (qn, qch.) (*with,* de). *To c. one's head,* se couvrir (la tête); se coiffer. **To stand covered,** rester couvert. (*b*) **To cover s.o. with ridicule,** couvrir qn de ridicule. **2.** *The cavalry covered the retreat,* la cavalerie couvrait la retraite. **3.** Couvrir, recouvrir, gainer, envelopper, revêtir. *To c. a book,* recouvrir un livre (de papier gris). *El.E: etc: To cover a wire,* guiper un fil conducteur. **4. To cover a distance,** couvrir, franchir, parcourir, une distance. **5.** Couvrir, dissimuler (son inquiétude, etc.). **6. To cover s.o. with a revolver,** braquer un revolver sur qn. **7.** Comprendre, englober. *This explanation does not c. all the facts,* cette explication n'embrasse pas tous les faits. *In order to c. all eventualities . . .,* pour parer à toute éventualité. . . . **8.** (*a*) Couvrir (un risque, son banquier). *To c. a bill,* faire la provision d'une lettre de change. (*b*) *To cover (one's) expenses,* faire ses frais; couvrir ses dépenses. *To c. a deficit,* combler un déficit. **cover in, cover over,** *v.tr.* Recouvrir (une canalisation sous terre, etc.); remplir (la tranchée). **cover up,** *v.tr.* Couvrir entièrement; recouvrir; dissimuler (la vérité). **covering¹,** *a.* **Covering letter,** lettre confirmative (d'une autre); lettre d'introduction. *Com:* **Covering note,** garantie *f* (de qch.). **covering²,** *s.* **I.** Couverture *f* (de qch.). **2.** Couverture *f*, enveloppe *f*, revêtement *m*, recouvrement, gainage *m.* *El.E:* Guipage *m* (d'un câble, etc.).

coverlet ['kʌvərlet], *s.* Couvre-lit *m*; dessus *m* de lit; couvre-pied(s) *m inv.*

covert¹ ['kʌvərt], *a.* (*Of threat, etc.*) Caché, voilé; (*of attack*) indirect; (*of enemy*) couvert, secret. **-ly,** *adv.* Secrètement; en secret.

covert², *s.* **I.** *Ven:* = COVER¹ 5 (*b*). **2.** *Orn:* Tail-

coverts, wing-coverts, plumes tectrices de la queue, des ailes.
covet ['kʌvet], *v.tr.* (coveted) (*a*) Convoiter. (*b*) Ambitionner (qch.); aspirer à (qch.).
coveter ['kʌvetər], *s.* Convoiteur, -euse.
covetous ['kʌvetəs], *a.* **1.** Avide (*of gain*, de gain). **2.** *To be c. of sth.*, convoiter qch. *To cast c. eyes on sth.*, convoiter qch. des yeux ; regarder qch. d'un œil de convoitise. **-ly,** *adv.* Avec convoitise ; avidement.
covetousness ['kʌvetəsnəs], *s.* **1.** Cupidité *f*, avidité *f*. **2.** Convoitise *f*.
covey ['kʌvi], *s.* **1.** Compagnie *f*, vol *m* (de perdrix). **2.** *F:* Troupe *f*, bande *f* (de personnes).
cow¹ [kau], *s.* (*pl.* cows, *A:* kine [kain]) **1.** Vache *f*. *The time of the lean kine,* l'ère des vaches maigres. *F:* Wait till the cows come home, attendez jusqu'à la semaine des quatre jeudis. **2.** (*Of elephant, seal, etc.*) Femelle *f.* **'cow-bell,** *s.* Clochette *f*, sonnette *f* (pour bétail). **'cow-boy,** *s.m.* **1.** Jeune vacher. **2.** *U.S:* Cowboy. **'cow-catcher,** *s. U.S:* Chasse-bestiaux *m inv*, chasse-corps *m inv* (de locomotive). **'cow-'heel,** *s. Cu:* Pied *m* de vache en gelée. **'cow-hide,** *s. Leath:* (Peau *f* de) vache *f.* **'cow-house,** *s.* Vacherie *f*, étable *f.* **'cow-keeper,** *s.* Nourrisseur *m.* **'cow-lick,** *s.* Épi *m* (de cheveux). **'cow-man,** *pl.* **-men,** *s.m.* Vacher. **'cow-parsley,** *s.* Cerfeuil *m* sauvage.
cow², *v.tr* **1.** Intimider, dompter (qn). *Cowed look,* air de chien battu. **2.** Accouardir (un chien).
coward ['kauərd], *s. & a.* **1.** Lâche (*mf*). **2.** *F: I'm a terrible c. in the dark,* je suis très poltron quand il fait nuit.
cowardice ['kauərdis], **cowardliness** ['kauərdlinəs], *s.* Lâcheté *f.*
cowardly ['kauərdli]. **1.** *a.* Lâche. **2.** *adv.* Lâchement ; en lâche.
cower ['kauər], *v.i.* Se blottir, se tapir (à terre). *To cower before s.o.,* trembler, se faire tout petit, devant qn.
cowherd ['kauhə:rd], *s.* Vacher *m* ; bouvier *m.*
cowl [kaul], *s.* **1.** (*a*) Capuchon *m* (de moine). *Penitent's cowl,* cagoule *f. Prov:* The cowl does not make the monk, l'habit ne fait pas le moine. *To take the cowl,* prendre le capuchon. (*b*) Têtière *f* (d'un capuchon). **2.** (*a*) Capuchon, mitre *f*, abat-vent *m inv* (de cheminée). (*b*) *Av: Nau:* Capot *m* (de moteur, de cheminée).
cowled [kauld], *a.* Capuchonné ; encapuchonné.
cowling ['kaulin], *s.* **1.** Capuchonnement *m* (de cheminée). **2.** Capot *m*, capotage *m* (de moteur).
cowrie ['kauri], *s.* **1.** *Conch: Moll:* Porcelaine *f.* **2.** (*Money*) Cauri(s) *m.*
cowslip ['kauslip], *s. Bot:* (Fleur *f* de) coucou *m.*
cox¹ [kɔks], *s. F:* = COXSWAIN.
cox², *v.tr.* Diriger, gouverner (un canot).
coxal ['kɔksəl], *a. Anat:* Coxal, -aux.
coxalgia [kɔks'aldʒiə], *s. Mea:* Coxalgie *f.*
coxcomb ['kɔkskoum], *s.* Petit-maître *m*, *pl.* petits-maîtres ; fat *m.*
coxswain ['kɔkswein, kɔksn], *s.* **1.** *Nau:* Patron *m* (d'une chaloupe). **2.** *Row:* Barreur *m.*
coy [kɔi], *a.* **1.** (*Of girl*) Timide, modeste, farouche. **2.** *Coy of speech,* réservé en paroles. **-ly,** *adv.* Modestement, timidement.
coyness ['kɔinəs], *s.* Timidité *f*, réserve *f.*
coyote [kɔi'jout], *s. Z:* Coyote *m.*
coyp(o)u ['kɔipu], *s. Z:* Coypou *m*
coz [kʌz], *s. A: F:* = COUSIN.
cozen [kʌzn], *v.tr.* **1.** Tromper, duper (qn). *To cozen s.o. out of sth.,* filouter qch. à qn.
crab¹ [krab], *s.* **1.** *Crust:* Crabe *m*, cancre *m.*

Shore crab, green crab, crabe commun. *F:* (*Rowing*) To catch a crab, (i) engager un aviron ; (ii) attaquer en sifflet ou faire fausse rame. **2.** *Astr:* = CANCER 2. **3.** *Ind: etc:* Treuil (roulant, portatif) ; chèvre *f.* Ceiling crab, chariot (transporteur) à poutre de plafond. **'crab-pot,** *s.* Nasse *f*, casier *m* (à crabes).
crab², *s.* Crab(-apple), pomme *f* sauvage. Crab-tree, pommier *m* sauvage.
crab³, *v.tr.* (crabbed) **1.** (*Of hawks*) To crab each other, se griffer. **2.** *F:* (*a*) Décrier, dénigrer (qn, qch.); *P:* débiner (qn). (*b*) Mettre des bâtons dans les roues à (qn).
crabbed ['krabid], *a.* **1.** (*Of pers.*) Maussade, grognon, grincheux, revêche. **2.** Crabbed style, style pénible, rébarbatif. *C. writing,* écriture illisible, en pattes de mouche.
crabwise ['krabwa:iz], *adv.* Comme un crabe ; (marcher) de biais.
crack¹ [krak]. I. *s.* **1.** (*a*) Craquement *m* (de branches, etc.) ; claquement *m*, clic-clac *m* (de fouet) ; détonation *f*, coup sec (de fusil). (*b*) *F:* Crack on the head, coup violent sur la tête. **2.** (*a*) Fente *f*, fissure *f*; (*in skin*) gerçure *f*, crevasse *f*; (*in wall, ground*) crevasse, lézarde *f*; (*in pottery, bell, etc.*) fêlure *f*. (*b*) Entre-bâillement *m* (d'une porte). *F:* Open the window a crack, ouvrez la fenêtre un petit peu. **3.** *Scot:* Causerie *f*, causette *f*. II. **crack,** *a. F:* Fameux ; d'élite ; de première force. Crack player, etc., as *m*, crack *m.* **'crack-'brained,** *a.* Au cerveau timbré, fêlé.
crack², *int.* Clac ! crac ! pan !
crack³. I. *v.tr.* **1.** Faire claquer (un fouet) ; faire craquer (ses doigts, etc.). **2.** (*a*) Fêler (une cloche, un verre) ; gercer, crevasser (la peau) ; lézarder, crevasser (un mur) ; fendre, fendiller (une pierre, etc.) ; fracturer (un os). (*b*) Casser (une noisette). To crack one's skull, se casser la tête. *F:* To crack a bottle (with s.o.), vider, boire, une bouteille (avec qn). (*c*) *Ind:* Fractionner, "craquer" (une huile lourde). **3.** To crack a joke, faire, lâcher, lancer, une plaisanterie. II. **crack,** *v.i.* **1.** Craquer ; (*of whip*) claquer. *A rifle cracked,* un coup de fusil partit. **2.** Se fêler ; se fissurer ; se crevasser ; (*of wall*) se lézarder ; (*of skin*) se gercer ; se fendre, se tendiller. **3.** (*Of voice*) Se casser, se fausser ; (*at puberty*) muer. **4.** *Scot:* Causer, faire la causette (avec qn). **crack on,** *v.tr.* To crack on sail, faire force de voiles. **crack up.** **1.** *v.tr. F:* Vanter, prôner (qn, qch.). **2.** *v.i.* (*Of empire*) Se démembrer. **cracked,** *a.* **1.** Fêlé, fendu (*of wall*) lézardé ; (*of tree, timber*) gerçuré. Cracked voice, voix cassée. *To sound c.,* sonner le fêlé. **2.** *F:* Timbré toqué ; *P:* loufoque. **cracking,** *s.* **1.** Claquement *m*, craquement *m.* **2.** Fendillement *m* ; craquelure *f* (de la peinture). **3.** Fractionnement *m*, craquage *m* (d'une huile lourde) **'crack-jaw,** *a.* (Nom, etc.) impossible à prononcer.
cracker ['krakər], *s.* **1.** (*Pers.*) (*a*) Cracker of jokes, faiseur, -euse, de plaisanteries. (*b*) Cracker-up, prôneur, -euse. **2.** *F:* Mensonge *m*, craque *f.* **3.** (*a*) Pétard *m* Jumping cracker, crapaud *m.* (*b*) (Christmas-)cracker, diablotin *m* ; papillote *f* à pétard. **4.** (Nut-)crackers, casse-noisette(s) *m inv*, casse-noix *m inv.* **5.** *U.S:* Biscuit (dur) ; craquelin *m.* **6.** *pl. P:* (Hair-curlers) Papillotes.
crackle¹ ['krakl], *s.* **1.** Craquemen *m* crépitement *m. W. Tel:* Crachements *mpl.* **2.** Fendillement *m.*
crackle². **1.** *v.i.* (*a*) Craqueter ; (*of salt on fire*,

etc.) crépiter ; (*of sth. frying*) grésiller ; (*of fire*) pétiller. *W.Tel:* **Crackling** noise, friture *f*. (*b*) Se fendiller. **2.** *v.tr.* Fendiller. **crackling,** *s.* **1.** = CRACKLE[1]. **2.** (*a*) Peau croquante (du porc rôti) ; couenne *f*. (*b*) *pl. Dial:* **Cracklings,** cretons *m*.

cracknel ['kraknəl], *s.* (*Biscuit*) Craquelin *m*.

cracksman, *pl.* **-men** ['kraksmən, -men], *s.m. F:* Cambrioleur.

Cracow ['krakou]. *Pr.n. Geog:* Cracovie *f*.

cradle[1] [kreidl], *s.* **1.** Berceau *m*. **Wicker cradle,** moïse *m*. **Child in the cradle,** enfant au berceau. **2.** *Ind:* Berceau (d'une machine) ; cadre *m*. *N.Arch:* Ber *m* (de lancement). **3.** *Const:* Échafaud(age) volant ; pont volant. **'cradle-song,** *s.* Berceuse *f*.

cradle[2], *v.tr.* Mettre, coucher, dans un berceau. *F:* **Cradled in luxury,** bercé dans le luxe.

craft [krɑːft], *s.* **1.** (*a*) *A:* Habileté *f*, adresse *f*. (*b*) Ruse *f*, artifice *m* ; fourberie *f*. **2.** (i) Métier manuel ; (ii) profession *f*. *Prov:* **Every man to his craft,** chacun son métier. **3.** Corps *m* de métier **4.** *Coll.* (*With pl. construction*) *Nau:* Embarcations *f* ; petits navires.

craftiness ['krɑːftinəs], *s.* Ruse *f*, astuce *f*.

craftsman, *pl.* **-men** ['krɑːftsmən, -men], *s.m.* **1.** Artisan, ouvrier ; homme de métier. **2.** Artiste dans son métier.

craftsmanship ['krɑːftsmənʃip], *s.* **1.** Dextérité manuelle. **2.** (*In writer, etc.*) Connaissance *f* du métier ; "métier."

crafty ['krɑːfti], *a.* Artificieux, astucieux, rusé, cauteleux. **-ily,** *adv.* Artificieusement, astucieusement, cauteleusement.

crag [krag], *s.* (*a*) Rocher ou flanc de montagne escarpé ; rocher à pic. (*b*) (*From the climber's point of view*) Varappe *f*.

cragged ['kragid], *a.* Rocailleux, anfractueux.

craggedness ['kragidnəs], **cragginess** ['kraginəs], *s.* Aspect anfractueux, rocailleux (d'une montagne, etc.).

craggy ['kragi], *a.* = CRAGGED.

cragsman, *pl.* **-men** ['kragzmən, -men], *s.m.* Varappeur.

cram[1] [kram], *s. F:* **1.** Chauffage *m* (pour un examen). **2.** Presse *f* à étouffer, foule serrée (à une réunion mondaine, etc.). **3.** Mensonge *m*, craque *f* blague *f*. **'cram-'full,** *a.* Tout plein, regorgeant (*of*, de) ; bondé.

cram[2], *v.* (**crammed**) **1.** *v.tr.* (*a*) Fourrer (*sth. into sth.*, qch. dans qch.). **To c. one's hat over one ear,** enfoncer son chapeau sur l'oreille. **Book crammed with quotations,** livre qui regorge de citations. *Th:* **The house was crammed,** la salle était bondée. **Cupboards crammed with linen,** armoires bourrées de linge. (*b*) **To c. s.o. with sth.,** bourrer qn de qch. (*c*) *Husb:* Empâter, gaver, gorger (une volaille). (*d*) *Sch:* Chauffer (un candidat pour un examen). **To c. a pupil with Greek,** bourrer, gaver, un élève de grec. **2.** *v.i. F:* (*a*) S'entasser (*into*, dans). (*b*) Se gorger de nourriture ; s'empiffrer, se gaver (*with*, de). (*c*) *To c. for an examination,* préparer un examen. **cramming,** *s.* **1.** Entassement *m*. **2.** Gavage *m*. **3.** *Sch:* Chauffage *m* (pour un examen).

crammer ['kramər], *s. Sch:* Chauffeur *m*, préparateur *m*.

cramp[1] [kramp], *s. Med:* Crampe *f*.

cramp[2], *s.* **1.** (*a*) *Const:* Happe *f*, agrafe *f*, crampon *m*. (*b*) *Tls:* Serre-joint *m*. (*c*) *Typ:* Cornière *f*. **2.** *F:* Entrave *f* ; contrainte *f*. **'cramp-iron,** *s.* = CRAMP[2] I (*a*).

cramp[3], *v.tr.* **1.** Donner des crampes à (qn). **Limbs cramped by the cold,** membres engourdis

par le froid. **2.** Gêner (les mouvements, etc.). *F:* **To cramp s.o.'s style,** priver qn de ses moyens. **3.** (*a*) *Const:* Cramponner, agrafer (des pierres, etc.). (*b*) Presser, serrer (à l'étau, au serre-joint). **cramped,** *a.* A l'étroit ; gêné. **To be, feel, cramped for room,** être, se sentir, à l'étroit. **Cramped handwriting,** écriture gênée. *C. style,* style contraint.

cranberry ['kranbəri], *s. Bot:* Airelle *f* coussinette.

crane[1] [krein], *s.* **1.** *Orn:* Grue *f*. **2.** *Mec.E:* Grue. **Overhead travelling crane,** pont-grue *m* ; pont roulant ; (chariot *m*) transporteur *m*. **'crane-fly,** *s. Ent:* Tipule *f*. **'crane's-bill,** *s. Bot:* Bec-de-grue *m* ; géranium *m*.

crane[2]. **1.** *v.tr.* **To crane one's neck,** tendre, allonger, le cou. **2.** *v.i.* **To crane forward,** allonger le cou, la tête, en avant.

cranial ['kreiniəl], *a.* Cranien.

craniometry [kreini'ɔmetri], *s.* Craniométrie *f*.

cranium, *pl.* **-ia** ['kreiniəm, -ia], *s.* Crâne *m*.

crank[1] [kraŋk], *s. Mec.E:* Manivelle *f*. *S.a.* BELL-CRANK. **'crank-arm,** *s.* Bras *m*, corps *m*, de manivelle. **'crank-axle,** *s.* **1.** Essieu coudé. **2.** *Cy:* Axe pédalier. **'crank-case,** *s. I.C.E:* Carter *m* (du moteur). **'crank-pin,** *s.* Tourillon *m*, maneton *m*, de manivelle. **'crank-shaft,** *s.* Vilebrequin *m* ; arbre-manivelle *m*, arbre coudé.

crank[2], *v.tr.* **1.** Couder (un essieu). **2.** **To crank up a car,** lancer une auto à la main à la manivelle.

crank[3], *s. F:* **1.** (*a*) Marotte *f*, manie *f*. (*b*) Mot plaisant ; paradoxe *m*. **2.** (*Pers.*) Maniaque *mf*, excentrique *mf*, original *m*.

crank[4], *a.* (*Of machinery*) Détraqué ; délabré.

crank[5], *a.* (*Navire*) instable, mal équilibré.

crankiness ['kraŋkinəs], *s.* **1.** Humeur *f* difficile. **2.** (*a*) État délabré. (*b*) Chavirabilité *f*, instabilité *f* (d'un navire).

cranky ['kraŋki], *a.* **1.** D'humeur difficile ; capricieux. **2.** (*a*) = CRANK[4]. (*b*) = CRANK[5].

cranny ['krani], *s.* (*a*) Fente *f*, crevasse *f*. (*b*) Enfoncement *m*, niche *f*.

crape[1] [kreip], *s. Tex:* Crêpe noir. *Cp.* CRÊPE.

crape[2], *v.tr.* Draper de crêpe (en signe de deuil).

crape[3], *v.tr.* Crêper (les cheveux).

crapulous ['krapjuləs], *a.* Crapuleux.

crash[1] [kraʃ], *s.* **1.** Fracas *m. A c. of thunder,* un coup de tonnerre. **2.** Catastrophe *f*, débâcle *f*. *Fin:* Krach *m*. **3.** Écrasement *m* ; chute *f*. *Av:* Atterrissage brutal. *Aut:* Collision *f*, accident *m*. **4.** *int.* Patatras ! *He went, drove,* **crash into the wall,** il alla s'emboutir contre le mur. **'crash-dive,** *v.i.* Plongée *f* raide (d'un sous-marin). **'crash-helmet,** *s. Av: etc:* Serre-tête *m inv* ;. casque protecteur.

crash[2]. **1.** *v.i.* (*a*) Retentir ; éclater avec fracas. (*b*) **To crash** (down), tomber avec fracas ; s'abattre. **The roof crashed in,** le toit s'effondra. **To crash into a shop-window,** enfoncer une vitrine. *Aut:* **To c. into a tree,** s'emboutir sur, tamponner, un arbre. (*c*) *Av:* (i) (*Of plane*) S'écraser sur le sol. (ii) (*Of pilot*) Atterrir brutalement ; *F:* casser du bois. **2.** *v.tr.* Briser, fracasser. *Av:* Écraser (son appareil) sur le sol.

crash[3], *s. Tex:* Toile *f* à serviettes (de toilette).

crass [kras], *a.* Crass stupidity, stupidité grossière. **Crass ignorance,** ignorance crasse.

crate[1] [kreit], *s.* Caisse *f* à claire-voie.

crate[2], *v.tr.* Emballer (des marchandises) dans une caisse à claire-voie.

crater [kreitər], *s.* **1.** Cratère *m* (de volcan). **2.** (*Shell-hole*) Entonnoir *m*. **3.** Cratère (de l'arc électrique).

cravat [kra'vat], *s.* **1.** *A:* Cravate *f.* **2.** Foulard *m.*

crave [kreːiv], *v.tr. & i.* **1.** To c. sth. *from s.o.,* of s.o., implorer avec instance qch. de qn. To crave s.o.'s pardon, demander pardon à qn. To c. the attention of the audience, solliciter l'attention du public. **2.** To crave for, after, sth., désirer ardemment qch. **craving,** *s.* Désir ardent, obsédant ; appétit *m* insatiable (*for,* de). To have a c. for praise, être assoiffé de louanges ; avoir soif de louanges.

craven [kreivn], *a. & s.* Poltron (*m*), lâche (*m*). **-ly,** *adv.* Lâchement.

cravenness ['kreivnnəs], *s.* Lâcheté *f,* couardise *f.*

crawfish ['krɔːfiʃ], *s.* = CRAYFISH.

crawl[1] [krɔːl], *s.* (a) *Pisc:* Vivier *m.* (b) Parc *m* à tortues, à homards.

crawl[2], *s.* **1.** Rampement *m* (d'un serpent). **2.** Mouvement traînant (d'une personne). *F:* Cab on the crawl, taxi en maraude. *S.a.* PUBCRAWL. **3.** *Swim:* Crawl *m.*

crawl[3], *v.i.* **1.** Ramper. To crawl in, out, entrer, sortir, en rampant. *F:* To crawl before s.o., ramper, s'aplatir, devant qn. **2.** (a) (*Of pers.*) To crawl (along), se traîner. To c. on one's hands and knees, aller à quatre pattes. (b) Avancer lentement. (*Of taxi*) Marauder. **3.** To be crawling with vermin, grouiller de vermine. **crawling,** *a.* **1.** Rampant. **2.** Crawling cab, taxi en maraude. **3.** Grouillant (*with,* de).

crawler ['krɔːlər], *s.* **1.** *Rept:* Reptile *m.* **2.** *Swim:* Crawleur *m.* **2.** Taxi *m* en maraude ; maraudeur. **3.** *pl. Cost:* Crawlers, tablier-combinaison *m* ; barboteuse *f* (pour enfants).

crawly ['krɔːli], *a.* Crawly feeling, (i) fourmillement *m* ; (ii) chair *f* de poule.

crayfish ['kreifiʃ], *s. Crust:* **1.** (Fresh-water) crayfish, écrevisse *f.* **2.** *F:* (= *spiny lobster*) Langouste *f.*

crayon[1] ['kreiən], *s.* **1.** (i) Craie *f* à dessiner ; crayon *m* de pastel ; (ii) fusain *m.* **2.** Dessin *m* au pastel ou au crayon conté. **3.** *El:* Crayon (d'une lampe à arc). **'crayon-holder,** *s.* Porte-fusain *m inv.*

crayon[2], *v.tr.* **1.** Dessiner (qch.) au pastel, au crayon conté. **2.** Crayonner (une esquisse) ; esquisser (un portrait, etc.).

craze[1] [kreiz], *s.* Manie *f,* toquade *f* (*for sth.,* de qch.).

craze[2], *v.tr.* Rendre (qn) fou ; déranger (l'esprit).

craziness ['kreizinəs], *s.* **1.** (*Of pers.*) Folie *f,* démence *f.* **2.** (*Of building, etc.*) Délabrement *m,* décrépitude *f.*

crazy ['kreizi], *a.* **1.** (*Of pers.*) Fou, *f.* folle (à lier) ; toqué. C. with fear, affolé (de terreur). To drive, send, s.o. crazy, rendre qn fou ; affoler qn. To be crazy over, about, s.o., être fou de qn. To be crazy to do sth., brûler de faire qch. **2.** (*Of building*) Délabré ; qui menace ruine. C. furniture, meubles branlants. Crazy ship, navire hors d'état de tenir la mer. **3.** Composé de morceaux rapportés ; irrégulier. Crazy paving, dallage irrégulier. **-ily,** *adv.* Follement.

creak[1] [kriːk], *s.* Cri *m,* grincement *m* (de gonds, etc.) ; craquement *m.*

creak[2], *v.i.* (*Of hinge, etc.*) Crier, grincer ; (*of timber, shoes*) craquer. *Prov:* A creaking gate hangs long, pot fêlé dure longtemps.

cream[1] [kriːm], *s.* **1.** (a) Crème *f* (du lait). Clotted cream, Devonshire cream, crème caillée (par échaudage). Cream bun, chou *m* à la crème. To take the c. off the milk, écrémer le lait. (b) *F:* (Le) meilleur ; (le) dessus du panier. The

cream of society, la crème de la société. The cream of the joke, le plus beau, le plus drôle, le piquant, de l'histoire. **2.** (a) Coffee cream, crème au café. (b) Cream of tartar, crème de tartre. (c) Crème (à chaussures, de beauté, etc.). **3.** *Attrib.* Cream(-coloured), crème *inv* ; (cheval) isabelle *inv.* **'cream-jug,** *s.* Pot *m* à crème.

cream[2]. **1.** *v.tr.* Écrémer. **2.** *v.i.* (*Of milk*) Se couvrir de crème ; crémer ; (*of ale, etc.*) mousser.

creamery ['kriːməri], *s.* **1.** Crémerie *f.* **2.** Consortium laitier. Creamery butter, beurre fabriqué industriellement.

creamy ['kriːmi], *a.* **1.** Crémeux. **2.** Rich c. voice, voix veloutée.

crease[1] [kriːs], *s.* (Faux) pli *m* ; (*in paper*) fronce *f.*

crease[2]. **1.** *v.tr.* (a) Plisser, faire des (faux) plis à (qch.). Well-creased trousers, pantalon avec un pli impeccable. (b) Chiffonner, froisser (une robe, etc.). **2.** *v.i.* Se plisser ; prendre un faux pli. **creasing,** *s.* **1.** Plissement *m* ; froncement *m.* **2.** Pli *m.*

create [kriˈeit], *v.tr. & i.* Créer. To create s.o. a knight, créer qn chevalier. **2.** (a) Créer, faire naître, susciter (une difficulté) ; faire, produire (une impression). To create a scandal, (i) causer un scandale ; (ii) faire de l'esclandre. (b) *Abs. P:* To create, faire une scène (*about,* à propos de). (c) *Com:* To c. a fashion, créer, lancer, une mode.

creation [kriˈeiʃ(ə)n], *s.* Création *f.* The brute creation, l'espèce animale ; les bêtes *fpl. F:* That beats creation! ça dépasse tout au monde ! *F:* The latest creations, les dernières modes, créations.

creative [kriˈeitiv], *a.* Créateur, -trice ; créatif.

creator [kriˈeitər], *s.* Créateur, -trice.

creature ['kriːtjər], *s.* **1.** Créature *f,* être *m* ; *esp.* être vivant. **2.** Animal *m,* bête *f.* Dumb creatures, les bêtes, les animaux. **3.** Poor creature! le pauvre homme ! la pauvre femme ! le, la, pauvre enfant ! Not a c. was to be seen, on ne voyait âme qui vive. **4.** The c. of some great man, la créature, l'âme damnée, d'un homme puissant. **5.** Man is the creature of circumstances, l'homme dépend des circonstances. **6.** *Attrib.* Creature comforts. l'aisance matérielle.

crèche [kreːʃ], *s.* Asile *m* de jour pour bébés ; crèche *f* ; pouponnière *f.*

credence ['kriːdəns], *s.* **1.** Créance *f,* croyance *f,* foi *f.* To give, attach, credence to sth., ajouter foi à qch. **2.** *Ecc:* Credence(-table), crédence *f.*

credentials [kreˈdenʃəlz], *s.pl.* **1.** (a) Lettres *fpl* de créance. (b) Certificat *m* (d'un domestique, etc.). To show one's credentials, (i) montrer ses pouvoirs ; (ii) exhiber son certificat. **2.** Pièces justificatives d'identité.

credibility [krediˈbiliti], *s.* Crédibilité *f.*

credible ['kredibl], *a.* Croyable ; digne de foi. **-ibly,** *adv.* D'une façon qui inspire la confiance. To be credibly informed of sth., tenir qch. de bonne source.

credit[1] ['kredit], *s.* **1.** Croyance *f,* créance *f,* foi *f.* To give credit to a report, ajouter foi à un bruit. (*Of report*) To gain credit, s'accréditer. Facts that lend credit to a rumour, faits qui accréditent un bruit. **2.** Crédit *m,* influence *f,* réputation *f* (*with,* auprès de). He has credit at court, il est bien en cour. **3.** Mérite *m,* honneur *m.* To take credit for an action, s'attribuer le mérite d'une action. He came out of it with c., il en est sorti à son honneur. *Sch:* To pass an examination with credit, être reçu avec mention assez bien. I gave him c. for more sense, je lui croyais, lui supposais, plus de jugement. **It must be said to his credit that . . .,** on doit dire à son honneur que. . . **It does him credit, it reflects great credit on him,** cela lui fait (grand) honneur. **4.** (a) *Com:* Crédit. **To give s.o. credit,** faire crédit à qn. **To sell on credit,** vendre à crédit, à terme. **Credit slip,** bulletin de versement. *Bank:* **Letter of credit,** lettre de crédit; lettre accréditive. **To enter, put, a sum to s.o.'s credit,** porter une somme au crédit, à l'actif, de qn. **Credit balance,** solde créditeur. (b) *Book-k:* **Credit side,** avoir *m.* **5.** *Com:* Réputation de solvabilité; crédit. **6.** *Parl:* = Douzième *m* provisoire.

credit², *v.tr.* **I.** Ajouter foi à, donner, accorder, créance à (un bruit); croire (qn). **2.** (a) Attribuer, prêter (*s.o. with a quality,* une qualité à qn). *I credited you with more sense,* je vous croyais plus de jugement. **To be credited with having done sth.,** passer pour avoir fait qch *He hasn't as much money as people c. him with,* il n'a pas la grosse fortune qu'on lui prête. (b) *To c. s.o. with a quality,* reconnaître une qualité à qn. **3.** *Com:* **To credit a sum to s.o., to credit s.o. with a sum,** créditer qn d'une somme; porter une somme au crédit de qn.

creditable ['kreditəbl], *a.* (Action) estimable, honorable. **-ably,** *adv.* Honorablement; avec honneur.

creditor ['kreditər], *s.* **I.** Créancier, -ière. **2.** *Book-k:* **Creditor side** (*of balance*), compte créditeur; compte avoir.

credulity [kre'dju:liti], *s.* Crédulité *f.*

credulous ['kredjuləs], *a.* Crédule **-ly,** *adv.* Crédulement; avec crédulité.

credulousness ['kredjuləsnəs], *s.* Crédulité *f.*

creed [kri:d], *s.* **I.** *Theol:* Credo *m,* symbole *m.* **2.** Croyance *f;* foi (confessionnelle). **3.** *F:* Profession *f* de foi; credo (politique).

creek [kri:k], *s.* **I.** Crique *f,* anse *f.* **2.** *U.S:* (a) Ruisseau *m,* affluent *m.* (b) Petite vallée; cluse *f.*

creel [kri:l], *s.* (a) Panier *m* de pêche. (b) Casier *m* à homards.

creep¹ [kri:p], *s.* **I.** *pl.* *F:* **To give s.o. the creeps,** donner la chair de poule à qn. **2.** Glissement *m,* cheminement *m* (d'un pneu sur la jante, etc.).

creep², *v.i.* (**crept** [krept]; **crept**) **I.** Ramper; (*of pers.*) se traîner, se glisser; *F:* ramper (devant les grands). *To c. into bed,* se glisser dans son lit. *To c. into the room,* entrer tout doucement, à pas de loup, dans la chambre. *To c. into a hole,* se couler dans un trou. *A feeling of uneasiness creeps over me,* une inquiétude commence à me gagner. *S.a.* FLESH I. **2.** (*Of rails, etc.*) Cheminer; (*of transmission belt*) glisser, ramper; (*of tyre*) glisser, cheminer, sur la jante. **3.** (*Of plant, accumulator acid, etc.*) Grimper. **creep along,** *v.i.* S'avancer en rampant, furtivement. *To c. along the wall,* se faufiler le long du mur. **creep away,** *v.i.* S'éloigner (i) en rampant, (ii) à pas de loup. **creep on,** *v.i.* Avancer lentement. *Old age is creeping on,* la vieillesse s'approche à pas lents. **creeping,** *s.* **I.** Rampement *m.* **2.** Grimpement *m,* ascension *f* capillaire (de l'acide d'un accu). **3.** (*Of skin*) Chair *f* de poule.

creeper ['kri:pər], *s.* **I.** *Bot:* Plante rampante ou grimpante. *S.a.* VIRGINIA I. **2.** Vis *f* de transport.

creepy ['kri:pi], *a.* *F:* **I.** Rampant. **2. To feel creepy,** avoir la chair de poule. *C. story,* récit qui donne la chair de poule. **'creepy-'crawly,**

a. *F:* **I.** Creepy-crawly **feeling,** (i) fourmillement *m;* (ii) chair *f* de poule. **2.** (*Of pers.*) Rampant, servile.

creese [kri:s], *s.* Criss (malais).

cremate [kre'meit], *v.tr.* Incinérer (un mort).

cremation [kre'mei∫(ə)n], *s.* Incinération *f;* crémation *f.*

crematorium [kremə'tɔ:riəm], *s.* Crématorium *m;* (four *m*) crématoire *m.*

crenate ['kri:neit], **crenated** ['kri:neitid], *a.* *Bot:* *Z:* Crénelé, créné.

crenel(l)ate ['kreneleit], *v.tr.* Créneler.

crenel(l)ation [krene'lei∫(ə)n], *s.* Crénelure *f,* crénelage *m.*

creole ['kri:oul], *a.* & *s.* Créole (*mf*).

creosote¹ ['kri:osout], *s.* *Ch:* Créosote *f.*

creosote², *v.tr.* Créosoter; injecter (le bois) à la créosote.

crepe [kre:p], *s.* **I.** *Tex:* Crêpe (blanc ou de couleur, mais non noir). *Cp.* CRAPE. **2. Crêpe (-rubber) soles,** semelles *f* (de) crêpe.

crepitate ['krepiteit], *v.i.* Crépiter.

crepitation [krepi'tei∫(ə)n], *s.* Crépitation *f.*

crept [krept]. *See* CREEP².

crepuscular [kre'pʌskjulər], *a.* Crépusculaire.

crescent ['kres(ə)nt]. **I.** *s.* (a) Le premier quartier de la lune. (b) Croissant *m* (de la lune qui croît ou décroît). (c) *Her:* etc: Croissant. (d) Rue *f* ou côté *m* de rue en arc de cercle. **2.** *a.* **The crescent moon,** le croissant de la lune.

cress [kres], *s.* *Bot:* Cresson *m.*

cresset ['kreset], *s.* **I.** Torchère *f* (d'une tour). **2.** *Ch:* Creusote *f.*

Cressy ['kresi]. *Pr.n.* *Geog:* *Hist:* Crécy *m.*

crest¹ [krest], *s.* **I.** Crête *f* (de coq); huppe *f* (d'alouette); aigrette *f* (de paon). **2.** Cimier *m,* crête (de casque). **3.** Crête, sommet *m,* arête *f* (de colline); crête (d'une vague). **4.** *Arch:* Crête, faîte *m,* faîtage *m.* **5.** *Her:* (On helmet) Cimier; (*on escutcheon*) timbre *m.* **6.** (*On seal*) Armoiries *fpl;* écusson *m.* **'crest-fallen,** *a.* (*Of pers.*) Abattu, découragé; (*of look*) déconfit, penaud.

crest², *v.tr.* (a) Gravir (une colline) jusqu'à la crête. (b) Franchir la crête (d'une vague).

crested, *a.* **I.** *Orn:* etc: Huppé; houppé. **2.** (a) (*Of helmet*) Orné d'un cimier. (b) *F:* Armorié.

cretaceous [kre'tei∫əs], *a.* Crétacé, crayeux.

Cretan ['kri:tən], *a.* & *s.* Crétois, -oise.

Crete [kri:t]. *Pr.n.* *Geog:* L'île de Candie.

cretin ['kri:tin, 'kre-], *s.* Crétin *m.*

cretinism ['kri:tinizm, 'kre-], *s.* Crétinisme *m.*

cretinous ['kri:tinəs, 'kre-], *a.* Crétineux.

cretonne [krə'tɔn], *s.* *Tex:* Cretonne *f.*

crevasse¹ [krə'vas], *s.* Crevasse *f* (glaciaire).

crevasse², *v.i.* (*Of ice*) Se crevasser, se fissurer.

crevice ['krevis], *s.* Fente *f;* crevasse *f,* lézarde *f,* (de mur); fissure *f* (de rocher).

crew¹ [kru:], *s.* **I.** *Nau:* Équipage *m;* (*of rowing boat*) équipe *f.* **2.** (*Gang*) Équipe. *Artil:* Gun **crew,** servants *mpl* d'une pièce. **3.** *Pej:* Bande *f,* troupe *f.* *Sorry crew!* triste engeance *f!*

crew². *See* CROW⁴.

crewel ['kru:əl], *s.* Laine *f* à broder ou à tapisserie. **'crewel-work,** *s.* Tapisserie *f* (sur canevas).

crib¹ [krib], *s.* **I.** Mangeoire *f,* râtelier *m.* **2.** Lit *m* d'enfant; couchette *f.* *Ecc:* Crèche *f.* **3.** *F:* (a) Plagiat *m.* (b) *Sch:* Traduction *f* (d'auteur), corrigé *m* (de thèmes, etc.) (employés subrepticement). **4.** *F:* Emploi *m* place *f.*

crib², *v.tr.* (**cribbed**) **I.** *A:* Claquemurer, enfermer. **2.** *F:* (a) *To c. from an author,* plagier un auteur. (b) *Sch:* *To c. an exercise from another*

boy, copier un devoir sur un camarade. **crib-bing,** *s. Sch :* Emploi déloyal de traductions.
crick¹ [krik], *s.* **I.** Crampe *f.* **Crick in the neck,** torticolis *m.* **2.** Effort *m*, foulure *f.* **Crick in the back,** tour *m* de reins.
crick², *v.tr.* **To c.** *one's neck,* se donner le torticolis. **To c.** *one's back,* se donner un tour de reins.
cricket¹ ['kriket], *s. Ent :* Grillon *m* ; cricri *m.*
cricket², *s. Games :* Cricket *m.* **F :** **That's not cricket,** cela n'est pas loyal ; cela ne se fait pas. **'cricket-shirt,** *s.* Chemise blanche à col ouvert.
cricketer ['kriketər], *s.* Joueur *m* de cricket.
crier ['kraiər], *s.* **I.** (*a*) Crieur *m* (à une vente, etc.). (*b*) **Public crier, town-crier,** crieur public. (*c*) **Court crier,** audiencier *m* (du tribunal). **2.** **Crier up,** prôneur, -euse.
crikey ['kraiki], *int. P :* Mazette !
crime [kraim], *s.* (*a*) Crime *m.* (*b*) Délit *m.* (*c*) *Mil :* Manquement *m* à la discipline ; infraction *f*, faute *f.* **Crime sheet,** feuille *f* de punitions.
Crimea [krai'miːa]. *Pr.n. Geog :* La Crimée.
Crimean [krai'miːən], *a.* **The Crimean War,** la guerre de Crimée.
criminal ['krimin(ə)l]. **I.** *a.* Criminel. **To take criminal proceedings against s.o.,** poursuivre qn criminellement, au criminel. **The Criminal Investigation Department,** *F :* **the C.I.D.** [siːaiˈdiː], la Sûreté ; la police secrète. **2.** *s.* (*a*) Criminel *m.* **Habitual criminal,** repris *m* de justice ; récidiviste *mf.* (*b*) *F :* Le coupable. **-ally,** *adv.* Criminellement.
criminalist ['kriminəlist], *s.* Criminaliste *m.*
criminate ['krimineit], *v.tr.* **I.** Incriminer, accuser (qn). **2.** Convaincre (qn) d'un crime.
crimination [krimi'neiʃ(ə)n], *s.* Incrimination *f.*
criminologist [krimi'nɔlɔdʒist], *s.* Criminaliste *m.*
criminology [krimi'nɔlɔdʒi], *s.* Criminologie *f.*
crimp¹ [krimp], *s.* Racoleur *m* (de marins, etc.).
crimp², *v.tr.* Racoler (des marins, etc.). **crimping¹,** *s.* Racolage *m.*
crimp³, *s.* Gaufrage *m* ; pli *m* (d'un drap) ; frisure *f* (des cheveux).
crimp⁴, *v.tr.* (*a*) Gaufrer (à la paille), plisser, crêper, friser (l'étoffe, etc.). (*b*) Friser, frisotter, crêper (les cheveux). (*c*) Onduler (la tôle). **crimping²,** *s.* Plissement *m*, gaufrage *m*, crêpage *m.*
crimson [krimz(ə)n], *a. & s.* Cramoisi (*m*) ; pourpre (*m*).
cringe¹ [krindʒ], *s.* **I.** Mouvement craintif. **2.** Courbette *f* servile.
cringe², *v.i.* **I.** Se faire tout petit ; se dérober (par crainte d'un coup). **2.** S'humilier, ramper, se mettre à plat ventre (*to, before, s.o.,* devant qn). **cringing,** *a.* **I.** (Geste) craintif. **2.** Servile, obséquieux. **-ly,** *adv.* **I.** Craintivement. **2.** Servilement, obséquieusement.
crinkle¹ [kriŋkl], *s.* Pli *m*, ride *f* ; tronce *f* (dans le papier).
crinkle². **I.** *v.tr.* Froisser, chiffonner (le papier). **Crinkled paper,** papier ondulé, gaufré ; papier crêpe. **2.** *v.i.* Se froisser et ratatiner.
crinkly [kriŋkli], *a.* Ratatiné ; plein de rides.
cripple¹ [kripl], *s.* Estropié, -ée ; boiteux, -euse ; infirme *mf.*
cripple², *v.tr.* (*a*) Estropier (qn). (*b*) Disloquer (une machine) ; paralyser (l'industrie, la volonté) ; désemparer (un navire).
crisis, *pl.* **crises** ['kraisis, -iːz], *s.* Crise *f.*
crisp [krisp]. **I.** *a.* (*a*) (Cheveux) crêpés, crépus, frisés. (*b*) (Biscuit) croquant, croustillant, cassant. (*c*) (Style) nerveux ; (ton) tranchant (*d*) *The c.*

air of an autumn morning, l'air vif d'une matinée d'automne. **2.** *s.* **Potato-crisps,** croustilles *f* ; pommes *f* chip.
crispness ['krispnəs], *s.* **I.** Qualité croustillante (d'un gâteau, etc.). **2.** Netteté *f* (de style, *Mus :* d'exécution). **3.** Froid vif (de l'air).
criss-cross¹ ['kriskrɔs]. **I.** *a.* (*a*) Entre-croisé, treillissé. (*b*) (Humeur, personne) revêche. **2.** *s.* Entre-croisement *m.* *C.-c. of wires,* enchevêtrement *m* de fils de fer.
criss-cross². **I.** *v.tr.* Entre-croiser. **2.** *v.i.* S'entre-croiser.
criterion, *pl.* **-ia** [krai'tiəriən, -ia], *s.* Critérium *m*, critère *m* ; *F :* pierre *f* de touche.
critic ['kritik], *s.* (*a*) Critique *m* (littéraire, etc.). *F :* **Armchair critic,** critique en chambre. (*b*) Censeur *m* (de la conduite d'autrui, etc.) ; critiqueur *m.*
critical ['kritik(ə)l], *a.* Critique. **I.** **To look on sth. with a critical eye,** regarder qch. d'un œil (de) connaisseur. **2.** *Textual and critical notes,* remarques littérales et critiques. **3.** *Critical situation,* situation critique, dangereuse. *Med :* *In a c. state,* dans un état dangereux. **4.** *Ph :* **Critical temperature,** température critique ; point de transformation. *Opt :* **Critical angle,** angle limite. **-ally,** *adv.* **I.** **To look at sth. c.,** considérer qch. en critique. **2.** **Critically ill,** dangereusement malade.
criticaster ['kritikastər], *s.* Un Zoïle.
criticism ['kritisizm], *s.* Critique *f.*
criticize ['kritisaiz], *v.tr.* **I.** Critiquer, faire la critique de (qch.). **2.** Censurer, blâmer.
criticizer ['kritisaizər], *s.* Critiqueur, -euse ; censeur *m.*
croak¹ [krouk], *s.* Coassement *m* (de grenouille) ; croassement *m* (de corbeau).
croak², *v.i.* **I.** (*Of frog*) Coasser ; (*of raven*) croasser. **2.** (*Of pers.*) Grogner, ronchonner. **3.** *P :* Mourir. **croaking,** *s.* Coassement *m* ; croassement *m.*
croaker ['kroukər], *s.* **I.** Ronchonneur *m* ; grognon *mf.* **2.** Prophète *m* de malheur ; prêche-malheur *mf inv.*
croaky ['krouki], *a.* (Voix) enrouée, rauque.
crochet¹ ['krouʃei, -ʃi], *s.* (*Also* **crochet-work**) (Travail *m* au) crochet *m.* **'crochet-hook,** *s.* Crochet *m.*
crochet², *v.tr.* (*p.p. & p.t.* **crocheted** ['krouʃeid, -ʃid]) Faire (qch.) au crochet. *Abs.* Faire du crochet.
crock¹ [krɔk], *s.* (*a*) Cruche *f.* (*b*) Pot *m* de terre.
crock², *s. P :* **I.** Cheval claqué ; vieille rosse. **2.** (*Of motor car, etc.*) Vieux clou ; (*of pers.*) bonhomme fini, claqué.
crock³. *s. v.i. P :* **To crock (up),** tomber malade ; flancher. **2.** *v.tr.* Mettre (un athlète) hors de combat ; claquer, abîmer (un cheval).
crockery ['krɔkəri], *s.* Faïence *f*, poterie *f.*
crocodile ['krɔkədail], *s.* (*a*) Crocodile *m.* **Crocodile tears,** larmes de crocodile. (*b*) *Hum :* (i) Jeunes filles d'un pensionnat marchant deux à deux, en rang(s) d'oignons. (ii) Procession *f*, défilé *m* (d'automobiles).
crocus, *pl.* **-uses** ['kroukəs, -əsiz], *s.* **I.** *Bot :* Crocus *m.* **2.** Rouge *m* à polir.
croft [krɔft], *s.* **I.** Petit clos. **2.** Petite ferme.
crofter ['krɔftər], *s.* (*a*) Petit fermier. (*b*) (*In N. of Scot.*) Fermier d'une terre divisée entre affermataires.
cromlech ['krɔmlek], *s. Archeol :* Dolmen *m.*
crone [kroun], *s.* Vieille (femme) ; commère *f.*
crony ['krouni], *s.* Compère *m*, commère *f.* **An old crony,** *F :* un vieux copain.

crook¹ [kruk], *s.* **1.** (*a*) Croc *m*, crochet *m*. (*b*) Houlette *f* (de berger); crosse *f* (d'évêque). (*c*) *Mus:* Ton *m* de rechange (d'un cor d'harmonie). **2.** (*a*) Angle *m* ou courbure *f*; détour *m*, coude *m*. (*b*) *F:* **To get sth. on the crook,** obtenir qch. par fraude. **3.** *U.S:* *F:* Escroc *m*; chevalier *m* d'industrie. **'crook-back,** *s.* Bossu, -ue. **'crook-backed,** *a.* Bossu.

crook², *v.tr.* Courber, recourber. **crooked** ['krukid], *a.* **1.** (*a*) Courbé (en crosse); crochu; tordu, recourbé; (*of path*) tortueux; (*of limb, tree*) contourné, déjeté. (*b*) Malhonnête, déshonnête. *C. means,* moyens obliques. **2.** [krukt] (Canne, etc.) à béquille. **-ly** ['krukidli], *adv.* **1.** Tortueusement. **2.** De travers.

crookedness ['krukidnəs], *s.* **1.** Sinuosité *f* (d'un sentier etc.). **2.** (*a*) Perversité *f*. (*b*) Manque *m* de franchise, de droiture.

Crookes [kru:ks]. *Pr.n. Ph:* **Crookes tube,** tube *m* de Crookes.

croon¹ [kru:n], *s.* (*a*) Chanson *f* à demi-voix; fredonnement *m*. (*b*) Plainte *f*; gémissement plaintif.

croon², *v.tr.* Chantonner; fredonner (une chanson).

crooner ['kru:nər], *s.* Fredonneur, -euse.

crop¹ [krɔp], *s.* **1.** Jabot *m* (d'un oiseau). **2.** Manche *m* (d'un fouet). **Hunting-crop,** stick *m* de chasse. **3.** Récolte *f*, moisson *f*; (*of apples, etc.*) cueillette *f*. **Second crop,** regain *m*. **The crops,** la récolte. **4.** Coupe *f* (des cheveux). **To give s.o. a close crop,** tondre les cheveux de qn. **Eton crop,** cheveux *mpl* à la garçonne. **'crop-eared,** *a.* **1.** (Chien) courtaud, essorillé. **2.** *Hist:* (Têtes-rondes) aux cheveux coupés ras.

crop², *v.* (cropped) **1.** *v.tr.* (*a*) Tondre, tailler, couper (une haie, etc.); écourter, couper (les oreilles, la queue); essoriller (un chien). *Tex:* Tondre, raser (une étoffe). *Hair cropped close,* cheveux coupés ras. (*b*) (*Of cattle*) Brouter, paître (l'herbe). **2.** *v.i.* (*Of land*) Donner une récolte. **crop out,** *v.i.* **1.** *Geol:* (*Of seam*) Affleurer. **2.** *F:* (*Of taint, etc.*) Réapparaître, pointer. **crop up,** *v.i.* **1.** *Geol:* Affleurer. **2.** *F:* Surgir.

cropper ['krɔpər], *s.* **1.** (*Pers.*) Tondeur *m* (de drap). **2.** (Pigeon *m*) boulant *m*. **3.** *F:* **To come a cropper,** (i) faire une chute (de cheval, de bicyclette); faire la culbute; (ii) faire faillite; (iii) se heurter à un obstacle imprévu. *I came a c. in history,* j'ai été collé en histoire.

croquet¹ ['kroukei, -ki], *s.* (Jeu *m* de) croquet *m*. **croquet²,** *v.tr.* (croqueted ['kroukeid, -kid]) To (tight-)croquet, croquer (la boule). To (loose-)croquet, roquer (la boule).

croquette [kro'ket], *s. Cu:* Croquette *f*.

crosier ['krouʒər], *s.* Crosse *f* (d'évêque).

cross¹ [krɔs], *s.* **1.** Croix *f*. **To make the sign of the cross,** tracer, faire, le signe de la croix; se signer. **Fiery cross,** croix de feu. **Market cross,** croix de la place du marché. (*Of crusader*) To take the cross, prendre la croix; se croiser. **Maltese cross,** croix de Malte. **The Red Cross,** la Croix rouge (de Genève). **To sign with a cross,** signer d'une croix. **2.** Contrariété *f*, ennui *m*. **3.** *Husb:* (*a*) Croisement *m* (de races). (*b*) Métis, -isse. *F:* **To be a c. between sth. and sth.,** être un mélange de qch. et de qch. **4.** Carrefour *m*. **5.** (*a*) (*Of stuff*) Biais *m*. **On the cross,** en biais. (*b*) *F:* **He has been on the cross all his life,** il a toujours vécu d'escroquerie. **'cross-bearer,** *s.* Porte-croix *m inv.* **'cross-stitch,** *s. Needlew:* Point croisé.

cross², **1.** *v.tr.* (*a*) Croiser (deux bâtons, etc.).

(*b*) *Ecc:* **To cross oneself,** faire le signe de la croix; se signer. (*c*) Barrer (un chèque); mettre les barres à (ses t). (*d*) Passer (la mer); traverser (la rue, la mer); franchir (le seuil). *To c. a bridge,* passer (sur) un pont. (*Of thought*) To cross s.o.'s mind, passer par, traverser, l'esprit de qn. (*e*) Croiser (qn dans la rue). *F:* **To cross s.o.'s path,** se mettre en travers de la volonté, des visées, de qn. *F:* **To cross s.o., s.o.'s plans,** contrecarrer qn, les desseins de qn. *Crossed in love,* contrarié dans ses amours. (*f*) **To cross breeds,** croiser, métisser, des races. **2.** *v.i.* (*a*) (*Of roads, breeds*) Se croiser. (*b*) Passer (d'un lieu à un autre). **To cross (over)** *from Dover to Calais,* faire la traversée de Douvres à Calais.

cross out, *v.tr.* Biffer, barrer, rayer (un mot). **cross over,** *v.i.* Passer de l'autre côté (de la rue, etc.). **'cross-over,** *s.* Croisement *m*. *Rail:* Voie *f* de croisement, de passage. **crossing,** *s.* **1.** Barrement *m* (d'un chèque). **2.** (*a*) Traversée *f* (de la mer); passage *m* (d'un fleuve, des Alpes). (*b*) (**Street-**)**crossing,** passage (d'un trottoir à l'autre). *Pedestrian c.,* passage pour piétons. **3.** Croisement *m* (de lignes, de fils, etc.); intersection *f* (de voies). *Rail:* **Level crossing,** passage à niveau. **4.** *Breed:* Croisement, mélange *m* (de deux espèces). **'crossing-place,** *s.* Passage *m*. **'crossing-sweeper,** *s.* A: Balayeur *m* (entre trottoirs).

cross³. **1.** *a. & comb.form.* (*a*) Transversal, -aux; oblique; mis en travers. (*b*) (*Intersecting*) (Entre-)croisé. (*c*) (*Opposed*) Contraire, opposé (*to, à*). **2.** *a. F:* (*Of pers.*) Maussade, de mauvaise humeur, fâché. **To be as cross as two sticks, as a bear,** être d'une humeur massacrante; être comme un crin. **Don't be cross with me,** il ne faut pas m'en vouloir. **-ly,** *adv.* Avec (mauvaise) humeur. **'cross-bar,** *s.* (*a*) (Barre *f* de) traverse *f*; entretoise *f*; (*of window*) croisillon *m*. (*b*) *Fb:* Barre (de but). **'cross-beam,** *s. Const:* Sommier *m*, traverse *f*. **'cross-'bearings,** *s.pl. Nau:* Relèvements croisés, simultanés. **'cross-belt,** *s. Mil: etc:* Bandoulière *f*. **'cross-bench,** *s.* Banquette transversale. *Parl:* **To sit on the cross-benches,** être (un député) du Centre. **'cross-bencher,** *s. Parl:* Membre *m* du Centre. **'cross-bones,** *s.pl.* Os *m* en croix. *S.a.* SKULL. **'cross-bow,** *s.* Arbalète *f*. **'cross-brace¹,** *s.* Entretoise *f*; croisillon *m*. **'cross-brace²,** *v.tr.* Entretoiser; croisillonner. **'cross-'bred,** *a.* Métis, -isse. **'cross-'breed,** *s.* **1.** *Husb:* Race croisée. **2.** *F:* Métis, -isse. **'cross-'breed²,** *v.tr.* (*p.t. & p.p.* cross-bred) Croiser, métisser (des races). **'cross-'breeding,** *s.* Croisement *m* de races; métissage *m*. **'cross-'check,** *s. Surv: etc:* Recoupement *m*. **'cross-'country,** *attrib. a.* (Chemin, promenade, etc.) à travers champs. **'cross-cut,** *s.* **1.** (*a*) Coupe *f* en travers. (*b*) Contre-taille *f*. **2.** Accourcie *f*; (chemin *m* de) traverse *f*. **cross-exami'nation,** *s. Jur:* Interrogatoire *m* contradictoire. **cross-ex'amine,** *v.tr. Jur:* Interroger (qn) contradictoirement; *F:* mettre (qn) sur la sellette. **cross-ex'aminer,** *s.* Interrogateur, -trice. **'cross-eye,** *s. Med:* Strabisme *m*. **'cross-eyed,** *a.* Louche; qui louche; strabique. **'cross-fire,** *s.* Feu croisé. **Exposed to cross-fire,** pris entre deux feux. **'cross-grained,** *a.* **1.** (*Of wood*) Aux fibres irrégulières. **2.** *F:* (*Of pers.*) Revêche, grincheux. (*b*) Bourru, ronchonneur. **'cross-hairs,** *s.pl. Opt:* Fils *m* en croix, fils d'araignée; réticule *m*. **'cross-hatch,** *v.tr. Engr:* Contre-hacher, contre-tailler. **'cross-hatching,** *s.*

Contre-hachure *f.* **'cross-'head,** *s.* **1.** *Mch:* Pied *m* de bielle; crosse *f,* tête *f* (de piston). **2.** (Barre *f* de) traverse *f.* **'cross-'keys,** *s.pl.* *Her: etc:* Clefs *f* en sautoir. **'cross-'legged,** *a.* Les jambes croisées. **'cross-'lines,** *s.pl.* = CROSS-HAIRS. **'cross-'patch,** *s.* *F:* Grincheux, -euse; grognon *mf.* **'cross-'piece,** *s.* (Barre *f* de) traverse *f;* entretoise *f;* moise *f.* **'cross-'purposes,** *s.pl.* Malentendu *m,* quiproquo *m.* **We are at cross-purposes,** (i) il y a malentendu; (ii) nous nous contrecarrons. **cross-'question,** *v.tr.* = CROSS-EXAMINE. **cross-'reference,** *s.* Renvoi *m* (dans un livre). **'cross-road,** *s.* **1.** Chemin *m* de traverse. **Main cross-road** (*between highways*), chemin de grande communication. **2. Cross-roads,** carrefour *m;* croisée *f* de chemins. *F:* **We are now at the cross-roads,** c'est l'heure des décisions irrévocables. **'cross-'section,** *s.* Coupe *f* en travers; section transversale. **'cross-'street,** *s.* (*a*) Rue latérale. (*b*) Rue transversale; rue de traverse. **'cross-'talk,** *s.* Répliques *fpl.* **'cross-'threads,** *s.pl.* = CROSS-HAIRS. **cross-wind** ['krɔs'wind], *s.* Vent *m* contraire. **'cross-'wires,** *s.pl.* = CROSS-HAIRS. **cross-word,** *s.* **'Cross-word puzzle, 'cross-'words,** mots croisés. **crossbill** ['krɔsbil], *s.* *Orn:* Bec-croisé *m.* **crossbowman,** *pl.* -**men** ['krɔsboumən, -men], *s.m.* *A:* Arbalétrier. **crosswise** ['krɔswaːiz], *adv.* En croix, en travers; en sautoir. *Bus with seats arranged c.,* *adj.* **with crosswise seats,** autobus avec places disposées en travers. **crotch** [krɔtʃ], *s.* Fourche *f,* enfourchure *f* (d'un arbre). **crotchet** ['krɔtʃet], *s.* **1.** *Mus:* Noire *f.* **2.** *F:* (*a*) Lubie *f,* caprice *m,* toquade *f.* (*b*) Idée *f* fixe; manie *f.* (*c*) *pl.* Préjugés *m.* **crotchetiness** ['krɔtʃətinəs], *s.* Caractère capricieux; inégalité *f* d'humeur. **crotchety** ['krɔtʃəti], *a.* Sujet à des lubies; capricieux, fantasque; à l'humeur difficile. **crouch¹** [krautʃ], *s.* Accroupissement *m.* **crouch²,** *v.i.* Se blottir, se tapir, s'accroupir. **croup¹** [kruːp], *s.* Croupe *f* (de cheval). **croup²,** *s.* *Med:* Croup *m;* angine striduleuse. **croupier** ['kruːpiər, kruːˈpiːər], *s.* Croupier *m.* **crow¹** [krou], *s.* **1.** *Orn:* Corneille *f.* **The crows** (*as a class*), les corbeaux *m.* **Carrion crow,** corneille noire. *F:* **As the crow flies,** à vol d'oiseau. **To have a crow to pluck with s.o.,** avoir maille à partir avec qn. **2.** *Tls:* Crow(-bar), pince *f* (à levier); aspect *m.* **'crow's-foot,** *pl.* -**feet,** *s.* Patte *f* d'oie (au coin de l'œil). **'crow's-nest,** *s.* *Nau:* Nid *m* de pie. **crow²,** *s.* *Cu:* Fraise *f,* toilette *f* (de porc). **crow³,** *s.* Chant *m* du coq; *F:* coquerico *m,* cocorico *m.* **crow⁴,** *v.i.* (*p.t.* crowed [kroud], *Lit:* crew [kruː]; *p.p.* crowed) **1.** (*Of cock*) Chanter. *F:* **To crow over s.o.,** chanter victoire sur qn. **2.** (*Of infant*) Gazouiller; pousser de petits cris de joie. **crowing,** *s.* **1.** Chant *m* (du coq). **2.** Gazouillement *m* (de bébé). **crowd¹** [kraud], *s.* **1.** (*a*) Foule *f,* affluence *f,* rassemblement *m.* **To force one's way through the c.,** fendre la presse. **It might pass in a crowd,** ce n'est pas bon mais cela passerait. (*b*) **To rise above the crowd,** s'élever au-dessus de la foule, du vulgaire. **2.** *F:* Grande quantité, tas *m* (de choses). **Come along to help to make up a c.,** venez pour faire nombre. **3.** *F:* (*a*) Bande *f* (de personnes). *Pej:* **I don't belong to that c.,** je ne suis pas de ce monde-là. (*b*) *Th: Cin:* The

crowd, les figurants *m.* **4.** *Nau:* **Under a crowd of sail,** toutes voiles dehors. **crowd².** **1.** *v.tr.* (*a*) Serrer, (en)tasser. *We are too crowded here,* on est gêné ici. (*b*) Remplir, bourrer. *Room crowded with furniture,* pièce encombrée de meubles. *The hall was crowded with people,* la salle était bondée. *The streets were crowded,* il y avait foule dans les rues. **Crowded cities,** cités surpeuplées. *Th:* **Crowded house,** salle comble. **Crowded profession,** profession encombrée. *Streets crowded with traffic,* rues à circulation intense. (*c*) *Sp:* **To crowd a competitor,** entraver la marche d'un concurrent. *To be crowded off the pavement,* être forcé de quitter le trottoir. (*d*) *Nau:* **To crowd (on) sail,** faire force de voiles. **2.** *v.i.* (*a*) **To crowd (together),** se presser en foule; s'attrouper. *Here memories c. on me,* ici des souvenirs se pressent dans ma mémoire. (*b*) *Nau:* Se hâter, se presser; (*of sailing ship*) courir à toutes voiles. **crowd in,** *v.i.* Entrer en foule. **crowd out.** **1.** *v.i.* Sortir en foule. **2.** *v.tr.* (*a*) Ne pas laisser de place à (qn, qch.). *Journ:* **Matter crowded out,** matière restée sur le marbre. (*b*) *U.S:* Évincer (qn). **crowfoot** ['kroufut], *s.* *Bot:* Renoncule *f.* **crown¹** [kraun], *s.* **1.** (*a*) Couronne *f* (de fleurs, d'or). (*b*) **To come to the crown,** monter sur le trône. (*c*) **Crown lands,** terres relevantes de la Couronne. **Crown lawyer,** avocat du Gouvernement. **Crown prince,** prince héritier. **2.** Couronne (de cinq shillings). **Half a crown,** une demi-couronne. **3.** Sommet *m,* haut *m* (de la tête). **4. Crown of a hat,** calotte *f,* forme *f,* d'un chapeau. **5.** Couronne (de dent); sommet, clef *f* (de voûte); bombement (d'un pont); cime *f* (d'un arbre). *Aut:* **To drive on the c. of the road,** conduire sur l'axe *m* de la chaussée. **'crown-'colony,** *s.* Colonie *f* de la Couronne. **'crown-'jewels,** *s.pl.* Joyaux *m* de la Couronne. **'crown-wheel,** *s.* *Mec.E:* Roue dentée sur une surface latérale; roue de champ. **crown²,** *v.tr.* **1.** Couronner. **To crown s.o. king,** couronner, sacrer, qn roi. **Crowned with roses,** couronné de roses. **2.** (*a*) Couronner, récompenser (les efforts de qn). (*b*) *F:* **To crown all,** pour y mettre le comble. **That crowns all!** ne manquait plus que cela! **3.** (*At draughts*) Damer (un pion). **4.** Couronner (une dent). **crowning¹,** *a.* Final, -als; suprême. *That would be the c. mistake,* il ne manquerait plus que cela! **crowning²,** *s.* **1.** Couronnement *m* (d'un prince, etc.). **2.** Bombement *m* (d'une route). -**crowned** [kraund], *a.* **High-, low-crowned hat,** chapeau haut, bas, de forme. **crozier** ['krouʒjər], *s.* = CROSIER. **crucial** ['kruːʃəl, 'kruːʃ(ə)l], *a.* (Point) décisif, critique. *The c. test,* l'épreuve décisive. **crucible** ['kruːsibl], *s.* *Ind:* Creuset *m.* **crucifer** ['kruːsifər], *s.* *Bot:* Crucifère *f.* **cruciferous** [kruːˈsifərəs], *a.* *Bot:* Crucifère. **crucifix** ['kruːsifiks], *s.* Crucifix *m,* christ *m.* **Roadside crucifix,** calvaire *m.* **crucifixion** [kruːsiˈfik∫(ə)n], *s.* Crucifixion *f,* crucifiement *m;* mise *f* en croix. **cruciform** ['kruːsifɔːrm], *a.* Cruciforme. **crucify** ['kruːsifai], *v.tr.* Crucifier (qn, la chair, etc.); mettre (qn) en croix. **crude** [kruːd], *a.* **1.** (*a*) (A l'état) brut. (*b*) (*Of fruit*) Vert; (*of colour*) cru. *C. expression,* expression crue. (*c*) (*Of method, style*) Informe, grossier. *C. manners,* manières frustes. *C. statement of the facts,* exposition brutale des faits. (*d*) (*Of literary work*) Indigeste. **2.** *Physiol:*

(Aliment) non assimilé. **-ly,** *adv.* **1.** Crûment, grossièrement. **2.** D'une manière fruste.
crudeness ['kru:dnəs], **crudity** ['kru:diti], *s.* Crudité *f* (de l'eau, d'expression, *Art :* de tons).
cruel ['kruəl], *a* Cruel. *(a) C. disposition,* naturel brutal. *(b) A c. death,* une mort cruelle. **-lly,** *adv.* Cruellement.
cruelty ['kruəlti], *s. (a)* Cruauté *f (to, towards,* envers). **Society for the prevention of cruelty to animals,** société protectrice des animaux. *(b) Jur :* Sévices *mpl (to one's wife,* envers sa femme).
cruet ['kruet], *s.* Burette *f* (à huile). **Cruet-stand,** ménagère *f,* huilier *m.*
cruise[1] ['kru:z], *s.* Croisière *f. Pleasure c.,* voyage *m* d'agrément (en mer).
cruise[2], *v.i.* **1.** *Nau :* Croiser. *Navy : To be cruising,* tenir croisière. **2.** *F : (Of taxi)* Faire la maraude. **cruising,** *a.* **1.** En croisière. **Cruising fleet,** croisière *f.* **2.** *F : (Of taxi)* En maraude.
cruiser ['kru:zər], *s. Navy :* Croiseur *m.* **Armed merchant cruiser,** croiseur auxiliaire.
'cruiser-weight, *s. Box :* Poids mi-lourd.
crumb[1] [krʌm], *s. (a)* Miette *f* (de pain). *He didn't leave a c.,* il n'en a pas laissé une miette. *F :* **Crumb of comfort,** brin *m* de consolation. *(b) Cu :* **Bread crumbs,** chapelure *f. Fried in bread crumbs,** pané. **2.** *(Opposed to crust)* Mie *f.*
'crumb-scoop, *s.* Ramasse-miettes *m inv.*
crumb[2], *v.tr. Cu :* Paner (des côtelettes, etc.).
crumble [krʌmbl]. **1.** *v.tr.* Émietter (du pain) ; effriter (les pierres). *To c. glass,* gruger le verre. **To crumble sth. up,** réduire qch. en miettes. **2.** *v.i. (Of bread)* S'émietter ; *(of stone)* s'effriter ; *(of masonry)* s'écrouler ; *(of earth)* s'ébouler ; *(of empire)* crouler. **crumbling,** *s.* **1.** Émiettement *m,* effritement *m,* désagrégation *f.* **2.** Éboulement *m ;* écroulement *m.*
crumbly ['krʌmbli], *a.* Friable, ébouleux.
crumpet ['krʌmpet], *s.* **1.** Sorte de crêpe peu sucrée (pour le thé). **2.** *P :* Tête *f,* caboche *f.* **Off one's crumpet,** maboul, loufoque.
crumple [krʌmpl]. **1.** *v.tr.* Friper, froisser. *Aut : Crumpled (up)* mudguard, aile en accordéon. **2.** *v.i.* **To crumple (up).** *(a)* Se friper, se froisser ; *(of leaves, parchment)* se recroqueviller. *(b) (Of opposition ; Sp : of pers., horse)* S'effondrer. *(c) (Of mudguard, car)* Se mettre en accordéon.
crunch[1] [krʌnʃ], *s.* **1.** Coup *m* de dents. **2.** Bruit *m* de broiement.
crunch[2]. **1.** *v.tr.* Croquer, broyer (qch. avec les dents). **2.** *v.i. (Of snow, etc.)* Crier, craquer ; s'écraser.
crupper ['krʌpər], *s.* **1.** *Harn :* Croupière *f,* culière *f.* **2.** Croupe *f* (de cheval).
crusade [kru'seid], *s.* Croisade *f.*
crusader [kru'seidər], *s.* Croisé *m.*
cruse [kru:z], *s. B :* Pot *m,* jarre *f. F : It's like the widow's cruse,* c est une source intarissable.
crush[1] [krʌʃ], *s.* **1.** Écrasement *m.* **2.** Presse *f,* foule *f ;* bousculade *f. F : An awful c.,* un monde fou. **3.** *U.S : P :* **To have a crush on s.o.,** avoir un béguin pour qn. **'crush-'hat,** *s.* (Chapeau) claque *m ;* gibus *m.*
crush[2]. **1.** *v.tr. (a)* Écraser ; aplatir (un chapeau) ; pressurer (des fruits). *To c. one's leg in falling,* se froisser la jambe en tombant. *To c. sth. into a box,* fourrer qch. dans une boîte. *We were nearly crushed to death,* la presse était à mourir. *(b) F :* **Crushed with grief,** accablé de douleur. *(c)* Froisser (une robe). *(d) Min : etc :* Broyer, concasser. **2.** *v.i.* Se presser en foule. **To crush one's way through the crowd,** se frayer un chemin à travers la foule. *F :* **Please crush up a little,** voudriez-vous vous serrer un peu ?

crushing[1], *a.* **1.** *(Of roller)* Concasseur. **2.** *(Of news, defeat)* Écrasant. **crushing**[2], *s.* Aplatissage *m,* écrasement *m ;* broyage *m* (du minerai).
crusher ['krʌʃər], *s.* **1.** *Min : etc :* Broyeur *m,* écraseur *m ;* concasseur *m. Ore-c.,* pileur *m* de minerai. **2.** *F :* Malheur accablant. **What a crusher!** quelle tuile !
crust[1] [krʌst], *s.* **1.** *(a)* Croûte *f* (de pain, de pâté). *Not a c. to eat,* pas une croûte à manger. *(b)* **Piece of crust,** croûton *m.* **2.** Écorce *f,* croûte (terrestre) ; carapace *f* (de homard) ; paroi *f* (de sabot de cheval) ; couche *f* (de rouille). *F :* **The upper crust,** la fine fleur de la société. **3.** Dépôt *m* (de vin en bouteille). **4.** Croûte (d'une plaie).
crust[2]. **1.** *v.tr.* Encroûter ; couvrir d'une croûte (de rouille). **2.** *v.i.* Se couvrir d'une croûte.
crusted, *a.* **1.** Crusted over, couvert d'une croûte. *F :* **Crusted ignorance,** croûte d'ignorance. **2.** (Vin) qui a du dépôt. *Old c. port,* vieux porto de derrière les fagots.
crustacea [krʌs'teiʃiə], *s.pl. Z :* Crustacés *m.*
crustacean [krʌs'teiʃən], *s.* Crustacé *m.*
crustiness ['krʌstinəs], *s.* **1.** Dureté *f* de croûte (du pain). **2.** Humeur bourrue.
crusty ['krʌsti], *a.* **1.** *Cu :* (Pain) qui a une forte croûte. *(b)* (Pâté, biscuit) croustillant. **2.** *F : (Of pers.) (a)* Bourru. *(b)* Hargneux, irritable. *He's a c. fellow,* c'est un ours. **-ily,** *adv. (a)* D'un ton bourru. *(b)* Avec humeur.
crutch [krʌtʃ], *s.* **1.** Béquille *f.* **2.** *(a) Ind : Const :* Support *m ;* béquille ; étançon *m. (b) Row :* Tolet *m* à fourche. *(c)* Support arrière (de motocyclette).
crux [krʌks], *s.* Nœud *m* (d'une difficulté, de la question).
cry[1] [krai], *s.* **1.** Cri *m. Within cry,* à portée de voix. *To be a far cry from here to . .,* il y a loin d'ici à. . . *War-cry,* cri de guerre. *The pack is in full cry,* toute la meute aboie. *F : The thief fled with the street in full cry after him,* le voleur détala, avec toute la rue à ses trousses. *Much cry and little wool,* grand bruit et petite besogne. **2.** Cri (de douleur) ; plainte *f.* **3.** Action *f* de pleurer ; pleurs *mpl.* **To have a good cry,** donner libre cours à ses larmes. **To have one's cry out,** pleurer tout son content.
cry[2], *v.tr. & i.* (cried [kraid] ; cried) **1.** *(a)* Crier ; pousser un cri, des cris. *To cry aloud,* pousser de grands cris. **To cry for help,** crier au secours. *Evil that cries for a remedy,* mal qui réclame un remède. *(b)* **To cry fish** (for sale), crier son poisson (dans la rue) *F :* **To cry stinking fish,** dénigrer sa propre marchandise. *(c) Ven : (Of hounds)* Donner de la voix ; aboyer. **2.** S'écrier. *"That is false!" he cried,* "c'est faux !" s'écria-t-il. **3.** Pleurer ; verser des larmes. **To cry for sth.,** demander qch. en pleurant. **To cry one's eyes out,** pleurer toutes les larmes de ses yeux. **cry down,** *v.tr.* Décrier, déprécier (qn, qch.).
cry off. **1.** *v.i.* Se dédire, se récuser. **2.** *v.tr.* **To cry off a deal,** annuler une affaire. **cry out.** **1.** *v.tr. To cry out a name,* crier un nom. **2.** *v.i. (a)* Pousser des cris ; s'écrier. *(b) To cry out against s.o.,* se récrier contre qn. **crying**[1], *a.* **1.** Crying injustice, injustice criante. *C. evil,* abus scandaleux. **2.** Pleurant ; qui pleure. **crying**[2], *s.* Cri(s) *m(pl) ;* clameur *f.* **2.** Pleurs *mpl,* larmes *fpl* Fit of crying, crise *f* de larmes.
'cry-baby, *s.* Pleurard, -arde.
crypt [kript], *s.* Crypte *f.*
cryptic ['kriptik], *a.* Secret, occulte. *To maintain a c. silence,* se renfermer dans un silence énigmatique. **-ally,** *adv.* (Parler) à mots couverts.
cryptogam ['kriptəgam], *s. Bot :* Cryptogame *f.*

cryptogamic [kripto'gamik], **cryptogamous** [krip'tɔgaməs], a. Bot: Cryptogamique.
cryptogram ['kriptogram], s. Cryptogramme m.
crystal ['krist(ə)l], s. **1.** Cristal m, -aux. F: Crystal clear, clair comme le jour. **2.** (a) Crystal (-glass), cristal. (b) a. The c. waters of the fountain, les eaux cristallines, limpides, de la source. **3.** Psychics: Boule f de cristal. **'crystal-gazer,** s. Voyant, -ante, qui pratique la divination par la boule de cristal.
crystalline ['kristalain], a. Cristallin.
crystallizable [krista'laizəbl], a. Cristallisable.
crystallization [kristalai'zeiʃ(ə)n], s. Cristallisation f.
crystallize ['kristala:iz]. **1.** v.tr. (a) Cristalliser. (b) Crystallized fruits, fruits candis. **2.** v.i. (Se) cristalliser.
ctenoid ['ti:nɔid], a. Z: Cténoïde, pectiné.
cub [kʌb], s. Petit m (d'un animal); (of fox) renardeau m; (of bear) ourson m; (of lion) lionceau m; (of wolf) louveteau m. F: Unlicked cub, ours mal léché. **'cub-hunting,** s. Chasse f au renardeau.
cubage ['kjubedʒ], **cubature** ['kjubatʃər], s. Cubage m.
cubby-hole ['kʌbihoul], s. **1.** Retraite f. **2.** Placard m.
cube¹ [kju:b], s. **1.** Cube m. Cube root, racine cubique. **2.** Tablette f (de soupe); dé m (de pain).
cube², v.tr. Mth: Cuber.
cubic ['kjubik], a. **1.** (Cube-shaped) Cubique. **2.** Meas: Cubic foot, pied cube. C. capacity, volume m; Mch: cylindrée f. **3.** Cubic equation, équation du troisième degré.
cubical ['kjubik(ə)l], a. Cubique; en (forme de) cube.
cubicle ['kjubikl], s. **1.** Alcôve f (d'un dortoir). **2.** Cabine f (d'une piscine, etc.).
cubism ['kjubizm], s. Art: Cubisme m.
cubit ['kjubit], s. A.Meas: Coudée f.
cubitus ['kjubitəs], s. Anat: Cubitus m.
cuckoo ['kuku:], s. **1.** (a) Orn: Coucou m. (b) int. Coucou! **2.** F: Niais m, benêt m. **'cuckoo-clock,** s. (Pendule f à) coucou m. **'cuckoo-pint,** s. Bot: Arum maculé; gouet m.
cucumber ['kju:kʌmbər], s. Concombre m.
cud [kʌd], s. Bol m alimentaire (d'un ruminant). To chew the cud, ruminer.
cudbear ['kʌdbeər], s. Bot: Dy: Orseille f.
cuddle¹ [kʌdl], s. F: Étreinte f, embrassade f.
cuddle². F: **1.** v.tr. Serrer (qn) doucement dans ses bras. **2.** v.i. (a) Se peloter (l'un l'autre). (b) To cuddle up to s.o., se pelotonner contre qn.
cuddy ['kʌdi], s. Nau: Tille f; (of barge) rouf(le) m.
cudgel¹ ['kʌdʒəl], s. Gourdin m, trique f. F: To take up the cudgels for s.o., prendre fait et cause pour qn.
cudgel², v.tr. (cudgelled) Bâtonner. To c. s.o. to death, assommer qn à coups de gourdin.
cudgelling, s. (Volée f de) coups mpl de bâton.
cue¹ [kju:], s. (a) Th: Fin f de tirade; réplique f. To take (up) one's cue, donner la réplique. (b) Avis m, mot m, indication f. To give s.o. the cue, (i) donner le mot à qn; (ii) faire la leçon à qn. (c) Mus: Indication f de rentrée (d'un instrument).
cue², s. Queue f (de billard). **'cue-rack,** s. Bill: Porte-queues m inv. **'cue-tip,** s. Bill: Procédé m.
cuff¹ [kʌf], s. **1.** Poignet m (de chemise); (starched) manchette f. **2.** (Of coat sleeve) Parement m.
cuff², s. Taloche f, calotte f.

cuff³, v.tr. Talocher, calotter (qn); flanquer une taloche à (qn).
cuirass [kwi'ras], s. Cuirasse f.
cuirassier [kwira'siːər], s. Mil: Cuirassier m.
cuisse [kwis], s. Archeol: Cuissard m.
culinary ['kju:linəri], a. Culinaire.
cull [kʌl], v.tr. Lit: **1.** Choisir, recueillir (from, dans). **2.** Cueillir (des fleurs, des fruits).
culm [kʌlm], s. Bot: Chaume m, stipe m, tige f.
culminant ['kʌlminənt], a. **1.** (Astre) culminant, au méridien. **2.** F: (Point) culminant.
culminate ['kʌlmineit], v.i. **1.** (Of star) Culminer; passer au méridien. **2.** To culminate in sth., se terminer en qch. Culminating point, point culminant.
culmination [kʌlmi'neiʃ(ə)n], s. **1.** Astr: Culmination f. **2.** F: Point culminant.
culpability [kʌlpə'biliti], s. Culpabilité f.
culpable ['kʌlpəbl], a. Coupable. To hold s.o. culpable, tenir qn pour coupable. **-ably,** adv. Coupablement.
culprit ['kʌlprit], s. **1.** Jur: Accusé, -ée; prévenu, -ue. **2.** Coupable mf.
cult [kʌlt], s. Culte m (of, de).
cultivate ['kʌltiveit], v.tr. **1.** (a) Cultiver, exploiter (la terre, un champ). (b) Cultiver (des légumes). **2.** To c. s.o.'s friendship, cultiver l'amitié de qn. To c. the Muses, se vouer au culte des Muses. **cultivated,** a. (Voix) qui accuse une bonne éducation; (esprit) cultivé.
cultivation [kʌlti'veiʃ(ə)n], s. Culture f. Fields under c., cultures fpl. To bring land into cultivation, mettre des terres en valeur.
cultivator ['kʌltiveitər], s. Agr: Cultivateur m. Power-driven cultivator, motoculteur m.
culture ['kʌltʃər], s. **1.** Culture f (des champs). **2.** Bac: Culture. Culture tube, tube à culture. **3.** He lacks c., il n'a aucune culture.
cultured ['kʌltʃərd], a. Cultivé, lettré. The cultured, les gens cultivés.
culvert ['kʌlvərt], s. Civ.E: (a) Ponceau m. (b) Open culvert, rigole f, cassis m. Closed culvert, canal couvert. **2.** El.E: Conduit souterrain.
cumber ['kʌmbər], v.tr. Embarrasser, encombrer (with, de). To c. s.o. with parcels, charger qn de paquets.
cumbersome ['kʌmbərsəm], **cumbrous** ['kʌmbrəs], a. Encombrant, gênant, incommode.
cumulative ['kjumjulətiv], a. Cumulatif. **-ly,** adv. Cumulativement.
cumulus, pl. **-li** ['kjumjuləs, -lai], s. Cumulus m.
cuneiform ['kju:niifɔːrm], a. Cunéiforme.
cunning¹ ['kʌniŋ], s. **1.** (a) Ruse f, finesse f. (b) Pej: Fourberie f, astuce f. Man of low c., homme plein d'astuce. **2.** Adresse f, habileté f.
cunning², a. **1.** Rusé; malin, f. maligne; madré, astucieux. **2.** (a) A: Adroit. (b) C. device, dispositif ingénieux. **-ly,** adv. **1.** Avec ruse; astucieusement. **2.** A: Habilement.
cup¹ [kʌp], s. **1.** Tasse f. Tea-cup, tasse à thé. Cup of tea, tasse de thé. **2.** (Metal) Gobelet m, timbale f. **3.** (a) Lit: Coupe f. Ecc: Calice m (du saint Sacrement). To drink a parting cup, boire le coup de l'étrier. To drain the cup (of sorrow) to the dregs, boire le calice jusqu'à la lie. Prov: There's many a slip 'twixt the cup and the lip, il y a loin de la coupe aux lèvres. F: To be in one's cups, être pris de boisson. To be quarrelsome in one's cups, avoir le vin mauvais. (b) Sp: To win a cup, remporter une coupe. **4.** (a) Bot: (i) Calice (d'une fleur); (ii) = CUPULE. (b) Anat: Emboîture f (de l'os). (c) Cup-and-ball, (jeu m de) bilboquet m. Mec.E: Cup-and-ball joint, joint à rotule. (d) Mec.E: Lubricating cup, godet

graisseur. (e) *Med:* Dry cup, ventouse sèche. **Wet cup,** ventouse scarifiée. **'cup-bearer,** s. Échanson m. **'cup-final,** s. *Fb:* Finale f du championnat. **'cup-tie,** s. *Fb:* Match m éliminatoire. **'cup-valve,** s. Soupape f à cloche.

cup², *v.tr.* (cupped) *Surg:* Ventouser (qn).

cupping, s. Application f de ventouses. **Cupping glass,** ventouse f.

cupboard ['kʌbərd], s. **1.** Armoire f; (in wall) placard m. *F:* **Cupboard love,** amour intéressé. **2.** *A:* Buffet m.

cupel¹ ['kju:pəl], s. *Metall:* Coupelle f.

cupel², *v.tr.* (cupelled ['kju:pəld]) Coupeller (l'or, l'argent).

cupful ['kʌpful], s. Pleine tasse. *Add two cupfuls of milk,* ajoutez deux tasses de lait.

Cupid ['kju:pid]. **1.** *Pr.n.m.* Cupidon. **2.** s. *Chubby little Cupids,* Amours joufflus.

cupidity [kju'piditi], s. Cupidité f.

cupola ['kju:pola], s. *Arch:* Coupole f.

cupreous ['kju:priəs], a. Cuivreux.

cupric ['kju:prik], a. *Ch:* (Acide) cuprique.

cuprous ['kju:prəs], a. *Ch:* (Sel) cuivreux.

cuproxide [kju'prɔksaid], s. Cuproxyde m.

cupule ['kjupjul], s. *Bot: Z:* Cupule f.

cur-[kə:r], s. **1.** Roquet m; chien m sans race. **2.** *F:* Homme m méprisable; cuistre m.

curable ['kjuərəbl], a. Guérissable; curable.

curacy ['kjuərəsi], s. *Ecc:* Vicariat m, vicairie f.

curate ['kjuəret], s. Vicaire m. **Curate in charge,** desservant m.

curative ['kjuərətiv], a. & s. Curatif (m).

curator [kjuə'reitər], s. **1.** Conservateur m (de musée). **2.** (*Scot.*) Tuteur, -trice, curateur m (d'un dément).

curb¹ [kə:rb], s. **1.** *Harn:* Gourmette f. *F:* **To put a curb on one's passions,** mettre un frein à ses passions. **2.** Curb(-stone), bordure f (de trottoir); margelle f (de puits). *Aut:* **To strike the c.,** heurter le trottoir. **'curb-bit,** s. *Harn:* Mors m de bride. **'curb-roof,** s. *Arch:* Comble brisé; toit m en mansarde.

curb², *v.tr.* **1.** Gourmer (un cheval). **2.** Réprimer, refréner, contenir (sa colère); brider (ses passions).

curd [kə:rd], s. **1.** (Lait) caillé m; caillebotte f. **Curds and whey,** lait caillé sucré. **2.** **Soap curds,** grumeaux m de savon.

curdle [kə:rdl]. **1.** *v.tr.* Cailler (le lait); *F:* glacer, figer (le sang). **2.** *v.i.* (Of milk) Se cailler; (of blood) se figer.

cure¹ ['kjuər], s. **1.** Guérison f. **To effect cures,** opérer des guérisons. **2.** (a) Cure f. **Milk cure,** cure de lait. **To take a cure,** suivre un traitement. (b) Remède m. **There is a c. for everything but death,** il y a remède à tout fors à la mort. **3.** *Ecc:* **Cure of souls,** cure, charge f, d'âmes.

cure², *v.tr.* **1.** **To c. s.o. of an illness,** guérir qn d'une maladie. *Prov:* **What can't be cured must be endured,** où il n'y a pas de remède il faut se résigner. **2.** (a) Saler, fumer (la viande); saurer (des harengs). (b) *Leath:* Saler (les peaux). (c) Vulcaniser (le caoutchouc). **curing,** s. **1.** Guérison f. **2.** (a) Salaison f. (b) Vulcanisation f (du caoutchouc). **'cure-all,** s. Panacée f.

cure³, s. *P:* Drôle de garçon; original m. **He's a cure!** c'est un numéro!

curfew ['kə:rfju:], s. Couvre-feu m inv.

curio ['kjuərio], s. **1.** Curiosité f; bibelot m. **Curio hunter,** bibeloteur m. **'curio-dealer,** s. Marchand m de curiosités.

curiosity [kjuəri'ɔsiti], s. **1.** Curiosité f. **I was burning with curiosity,** je brûlais d'en savoir plus long; j'étais fort intrigué. **2.** *I referred to it as a* matter of curiosity, j'en ai fait mention pour la curiosité du fait. **3.** (a) Old curiosities, curiosités; bibelots m antiques. **Old curiosity shop,** boutique de bric-à-brac. (b) (Of pers.) Original m, -aux; excentrique m.

curious ['kjuəriəs], a. **1.** (a) Curieux. *I felt c. to know,* la curiosité me prit de savoir. (b) *Pej:* Curieux; indiscret, -ète. **2.** Curieux, singulier. **The c. part about it,** le curieux de l'affaire. **-ly,** adv. **1.** Curieusement. **2.** Singulièrement. **Curiously enough . . .,** chose assez singulière. . . .

curl¹ [kə:rl], s. **1.** (a) Boucle f (de cheveux); frisure f. **Loose curls,** boucles éparses. **False curls,** *F:* chichis m. (b) Spirale f (de fumée); volute f. **2.** (a) Action f de se recourber. **Curl of the lips,** moue f de dédain. (b) (Of hair) **In curl,** bouclé, frisé. **My hair is out of c.,** je suis toute défrisée. **'curl-paper,** s. Papillote f.

curl². **1.** *v.tr.* (a) Boucler, friser (les cheveux). (b) **To curl one's lip,** faire la moue. (c) **To c. sth. round sth.,** enrouler qch. autour de qch. **2.** *v.i.* (a) (Of hair) Boucler, friser; (of paper) se recroqueviller. (b) (Of smoke) S'élever en spirales; tire-bouchonner; (of waves) onduler ou déferler; (of lip) s'abaisser avec dédain. **curl up. 1.** *v.tr.* (a) **To curl up one's lip,** retrousser la lèvre. (b) **To c.** (oneself) **up,** se rouler en boule. **2.** *v.i.* (a) (Of paper) S'enrouler; (of nail, point) se rebrousser. (b) (Of hedgehog) Se mettre en boule.

curling, s. Frisure f (des cheveux); ondulation f (des vagues). *S.a.* PIN¹ 1. **'curling-irons,** **-tongs,** s.pl. Fer m à friser; frisoir m.

curlew ['kə:rlju:], s. *Orn:* Courlis m, courlieu m.

curly ['kə:rli], a. Bouclé, frisé; en spirale. **'curly-headed,** a. A la tête bouclée; (of negro) crépu.

curmudgeon [kə:r'mʌdʒən], s. **1.** Bourru m. **2.** Grippe-sou m; pingre m.

currant ['kʌrənt], s. **1.** Groseille f (à grappes). **Red currant,** groseille rouge. **Black currant,** cassis m. **2.** Raisin m de Corinthe. **'currant-bush,** s. Groseillier m.

currency ['kʌrənsi], s. **1.** Circulation f, cours m. **To give currency to a rumour,** mettre un bruit en circulation. **2.** Terme m d'échéance, échéance f (d'une lettre de change). **3.** Unité f monétaire (d'un pays); monnaie f. **Payable in currency,** payable en espèces de cours.

current¹ ['kʌrənt], a. Courant; en cours. **Current number** (of a periodical), dernier numéro (d'une publication); numéro du jour. *C. reports,* bruits qui courent. **To be current,** être accepté; avoir cours. **In current use,** d'usage courant; très usité. **Current events,** actualités f. **-ly,** adv. Couramment. **It is currently reported that . . .,** le bruit court que. . . .

current², s. **1.** (a) Courant m; fil m de l'eau. *Nau:* **Back current,** revolin m. **To drift with the current,** se laisser aller au fil de l'eau. (b) **The current of events,** le cours des événements. **2.** **Electric current,** courant électrique. **Direct current,** courant continu. **Alternating current,** courant alternatif.

curriculum [kʌ'rikjuləm], s. *Sch:* Programme m d'études; plan m d'études.

currier ['kʌriər], s. Corroyeur m.

curry¹ ['kʌri], s. *Cu:* Cari m.

curry², *v.tr. Cu:* Apprêter (des œufs, etc.) au cari.

curry³, *v.tr.* **1.** Étriller (un cheval). **2.** Corroyer (le cuir). **3.** **To curry favour with s.o.,** chercher à plaire à qn. **'curry-comb,** s. Étrille f.

curse[1] [kəːrs], s. **1.** (a) Malédiction f, anathème m. *A c. on the day when . . .!* maudit soit le jour où . . .! *To lie under a curse,* être sous le coup d'une malédiction. (b) Imprécation f; juron m; gros mot. **2.** Fléau m, calamité f. *Here the rabbits are a c.,* ici les lapins sont un fléau.

curse[2]. **1.** v.tr. Maudire, anathématiser. *He is cursed with a violent temper,* il est affligé d'un mauvais caractère. **Curse it!** malédiction! **2.** v.i. Blasphémer; sacrer, jurer. **cursed** [ˈkəːrsid, kəːrst], a. **1.** Maudit. **2.** F: *What c. weather!* quel fichu temps! **cursing,** s. **1.** Malédiction(s) f(pl). **2.** F: Jurons mpl; gros mots pl.

cursive [ˈkəːrsiv], a. Cursif. *C. handwriting,* s. cursive, cursive f.

cursory [ˈkəːrsəri], a. (Coup d'œil) rapide, superficiel. **-ily,** adv. Rapidement; à la hâte.

curt [kəːrt], a. Brusque; sec, f. sèche. *C. answer,* réponse sèche, brève. *He might have been a little less c.,* il aurait pu le prendre sur un ton moins cassant. **-ly,** adv. Brusquement, sèchement.

curtail [kərˈteil], v.tr. **1.** Raccourcir; écourter; tronquer (un ouvrage). **2.** Diminuer (l'autorité de qn); restreindre (ses dépenses). **3.** *To curtail s.o. of his privileges,* enlever ses privilèges à qn.

curtailment [kərˈteilmənt], s. Raccourcissement m; restriction f, diminution f (d'autorité).

curtain[1] [ˈkəːrt(ə)n], s. **1.** (a) Rideau m. Door-curtain, portière f. (b) Blind curtain, store m. **2.** Th: Rideau. *To ring down the curtain,* sonner pour le baisser du rideau. *The curtain rises at eight sharp,* rideau à huit heures précises. Fire-proof curtain, safety curtain, rideau métallique. F: (*In narrative*) Curtain! tableau! **3.** Fort: Courtine f. 'curtain-lecture, s. Semonce conjugale; sermon d'alcôve. 'curtain-raiser, s. (*Short play*) Lever m de rideau. 'curtain-rod, s. Tringle f de rideau.

curtain[2], v.tr. Garnir de rideaux.

curtness [ˈkəːrtnəs], s. Brusquerie f.

curts(e)y[1] [ˈkəːrtsi], s. Révérence f (que fait une femme en pliant le genou).

curts(e)y[2], v.i. (*Of woman*) Faire une révérence (*to s.o.,* à qn); F: tirer sa révérence (à qn).

curvature [ˈkəːrvətʃər], s. **1.** (a) Courbe f. Flat c., courbe ouverte. *Taking of curves* (*by train*), inscription f des courbes. *C. of an arch,* voussure f d'une voûte. (b) C. in the road, tournant m.; Aut: virage m. **2.** Draw: French curve, pistolet m.

curve[1] [kəːrv], s. **1.** (a) Courbe f. Flat c., courbe ouverte. *Taking of curves* (*by train*), inscription f des courbes. *C. of an arch,* voussure f d'une voûte. (b) C. in the road, tournant m.; Aut: virage m. **2.** Draw: French curve, pistolet m.

curve[2]. **1.** v.tr. Courber, cintrer. **2.** v.i. Se courber; décrire une courbe. **curved,** a. Courbé, courbe.

curvet[1] [kərˈvet], s. Equit: Courbette f.

curvet[2], v.i. (curvet(t)ed) Equit: Faire des courbettes.

curvilinear [kəːrviˈliniər], a. Curviligne.

curvometer [kəːrˈvɔmetər], s. Curvimètre m, cartomètre m.

cushion[1] [ˈkuʃ(ə)n], s. **1.** Coussin m. **2.** Bill: Bande f. Off the cushion, par la bande. *To play off the c.,* bricoler. **3.** Mch: Steam cushion, matelas m de vapeur. **4.** (Pad) Bourrelet m. **5.** Fourchette f (de sabot de cheval). 'cushion-tyre, s. Cy: Bandage plein avec canal à air.

cushion[2], v.tr. **1.** (a) Garnir (un siège) de coussins. (b) Rembourrer (un siège). **2.** Amortir (un coup). Mch: Matelasser (le piston).

cushy [ˈkuʃi], a. P: (Emploi) facile et grassement rétribué; P: pépère.

cusp [kʌsp], s. **1.** Pointe f. Cusp of the moon, corne f de la lune. **2.** Geom: Point m de re-

broussement (d'une courbe). **3.** Bot: Cuspide f.

cuspidate [ˈkʌspidet], a. Bot: Cuspidé.

cuss [kʌs], s. U.S: F: (= curse) **1.** Juron m. **2.** (*Of pers.*) Individu m, type m.

cussedness [ˈkʌsidnəs], s. U.S: F: (= cussedness) Perversité f. Out of pure, sheer, cussedness, rien que pour embêter le monde.

custard [ˈkʌstərd], s. Cu: Crème f (au lait); œuf(s) m au lait. Baked custard, flan m. Caramel custard, crème brûlée, renversée, au caramel. 'custard-apple, s. Bot: Corossol m.

custodian [kʌsˈtoudiən], s. Gardien, -ienne f; (*of museum*) conservateur m.

custody [ˈkʌstədi], s. **1.** Garde f (d'enfants, etc.). In safe custody, sous bonne garde, en lieu sûr. **2.** Emprisonnement m; détention f. *To take s.o. into custody,* arrêter qn; constituer qn prisonnier. *To be in c.,* être en détention préventive.

custom [ˈkʌstəm], s. **1.** Coutume f, usage m, habitude f. The manners and customs (*of a country*), les us m et coutumes. **2.** Jur: Droit coutumier, coutume (d'un pays). **3.** pl. Adm: Douane f. Customs officer, douanier m. Customs station, poste de douane. Custom(s) duties, droits de douane. The customs examination, la visite douanière. **4.** Com: (a) (*Of shop*) Achalandage m; (*of business*) clientèle f. *The shop draws plenty of c.,* la boutique est bien achalandée. *S.a.* LOSS I. (b) Patronage m (du client). 'custom-house, s. (Bureau m de la) douane.

customary [ˈkʌstəməri], a. (a) Accoutumé, habituel, d'usage. It is customary to . . ., il est de coutume, d'usage, de. . . (b) Jur: Customary clause, clause d'usage. **-ily,** adv. Ordinairement, habituellement.

customer [ˈkʌstəmər], s. **1.** (*Of shop*) Chaland, -ande f; pratique f; (*of business*) client, -ente. *He is a c. of ours,* il se fournit chez nous. **2.** F: A queer customer, un drôle de type. Rough, ugly, customer, vilain bonhomme; sale type. Sly, shifty, customer, faux bonhomme.

cut[1] [kʌt], s. **1.** (a) Coupe f. *To make a clean cut,* trancher nettement. (b) Coupure f (dans une pièce de théâtre). (c) Wage cuts, réductions f de salaires, sur le traitement. (d) Cards: Coupe. Cut for partners, tirage m pour les places. (e) Cr: Ten: Coup tranchant. (f) F: *To give s.o. the cut direct,* passer près de qn sans le saluer. **2.** (a) Coup m (d'épée); taillade f. (b) Cut with a whip, coup de fouet; cinglon m. The unkindest cut of all, le coup de pied de l'âne. **3.** Metalw: etc: (a) Taille f, entaille f (d'une lime). (b) Passe f (de machine-outil). (c) Saw cut, trait m de scie. **4.** (a) (*Wound, gash*) Coupure; balafre f; entaille. (b) Hort: Enture f. (c) Civ.E: Tranchée f. Mec.E: Saignée f (pour graissage). **5.** (a) Illustration f, gravure f; (*woodcut*) gravure sur bois. (b) Diagramme m. **6.** Coupe (d'un vêtement); taille (d'une pierre précieuse). **7.** F: *To be a cut above s.o.,* être supérieur à qn. *That's a cut above me,* ça me dépasse. **8.** Cu: Cut off the joint, tranche f, morceau m, de rôti. Prime cut, morceau de (premier) choix. **9.** Short cut, raccourci m; chemin m de traverse.

cut[2], v.tr. & i. (*p.t. cut; p.p. cut; pr.p. cutting*) **1.** Couper, tailler; (*in slices*) trancher; hacher (le tabac). *To cut one's finger,* se couper au doigt. *To have one's hair cut,* se faire tailler les cheveux. *This remark cut him to the quick,* cette parole le piqua au vif. F: *That cuts both ways,* c'est un argument à deux tranchants. To cut and come again, revenir au plat. To cut into a loaf, entamer un pain. Bill: *To cut the cloth,* faire un accroc au tapis. *Com:* To cut prices, faire des prix de concurrence. *Aut: etc:* To cut a corner (close), prendre un virage à la corde. *Nau:* To cut one's moorings, couper ses amarres. To cut and run, (i) *Nau:* filer le câble ; (ii) *F:* filer (en vitesse) ; prendre ses jambes à son cou. **2.** (a) To cut sth. to ribbons, déchiqueter qch. (b) To cut an actor's lines, faire des coupures dans le rôle d'un acteur. To cut sth. short, couper court à qch. *To cut a speech short,* raccourcir un discours. *To cut s.o. short,* couper la parole à qn. *To cut a long story short she left him,* tant (il) y a qu'elle l'a quitté. *F:* Cut it short! abrégez! **3.** *To cut an opening in a wall,* pratiquer une ouverture dans un mur. **4.** (a) To cut one's way through the wood, se frayer un chemin à travers le bois. To cut across country, couper à travers champs. (b) To cut into the conversation, intervenir dans la conversation. **5.** *Cards:* Couper (les cartes). To cut for deal, tirer pour la donne. **6.** *Cr: Ten:* Trancher, couper (la balle). **7.** To cut s.o. (dead), faire semblant de ne pas voir qn. *He cut me dead,* il m'a passé raide (sans me saluer). **8.** *F:* (a) Manquer exprès à (un rendez-vous). *Sch:* Sécher (un cours, une classe). (b) To cut the whole concern, abandonner l'affaire ; renoncer à l'affaire. **cut away,** v.tr. (a) Retrancher, élaguer. (b) Évider. **cut back.** **1.** v.tr. Élaguer. **2.** v.i. *F:* Rebrousser chemin. **cut down,** v.tr. **1.** (a) Couper (un arbre). (b) Sabrer (un adversaire) ; faucher (les troupes ennemies). **2.** Rogner (des dépenses). *Ind:* Restreindre (la production). **cut in,** v.i. **1.** *Cards:* (R)entrer dans le jeu. (*Cf.* CUT OUT 4.) **2.** Se mêler à la conversation. **3.** *Rac:* Couper un concurrent. *Aut:* Couper la route à qn (après avoir doublé). **4.** v.tr. *El:* To cut in a resistance, intercaler une résistance. **cut off.** **1.** v.tr. (a) Couper, détacher. To cut off s.o.'s head, trancher, abattre, la tête à qn. To be cut off in one's prime, être fauché à la fleur de l'âge. (b) To cut off s.o.'s retreat, couper la retraite à qn. (c) *Tp:* Don't cut me off, ne coupez pas. (d) *El:* To cut off the current, interrompre le courant. *To cut off s.o.'s supplies,* couper les vivres à qn. (e) To cut s.o. off with a shilling, déshériter qn. **2.** v.i. *F:* Décamper. *I told him to cut off,* je lui ai dit de filer. **cut out,** v.tr. **1.** (a) Couper, enlever ; exciser. (b) *F:* To cut s.o. out, supplanter qn. **2.** Découper (des images). *To cut out a garment,* tailler un vêtement. *F:* To be cut out for sth., être fait, taillé, pour qch. ; avoir des dispositions pour qch. **3.** Supprimer, retrancher (un organe). To cut out superfluous details, élaguer des détails superflus. **4.** v.i. *Cards:* Couper à qui se retirera du jeu. **cut-'out,** s. *El.E:* Coupe-circuit m inv. **cut up,** v.tr. **1.** Couper, débiter (le bois) ; découper, dépecer (une volaille) ; *F:* critiquer sévèrement (un livre). *To cut up the bread,* tailler le pain par morceaux. *A battalion has been cut up,* un bataillon a été taillé en pièces. *Road cut up by the rains,* route ravinée par les pluies. **2.** *F:* (a) Don't be so cut up about it, ne vous affligez pas ainsi. (b) v.i. To cut up rough, se fâcher ; se mettre en colère. *He cut up very rough (about it),* il a très mal pris la chose. **cut³,** a. **1.** Cut glass, cristal taillé. Well-cut suit, complet de bonne coupe. Low-cut dress, robe décolletée. Cut and dried opinions, opinions toutes faites. **2.** Cut prices, prix réduits. **cutting¹,** a. **1.** Cutting edge, tranchant m (d'un outil). **2.** Cutting wind, vent cinglant. **3.** Cutting remark, réponse mordante. **cutting²,** s. **1.** (a) Coupe f, coupage m. (b) Taille f (d'un diamant). (c) Découpage m (de

la tôle, d'un film). (d) Cutting of prices, réduction f des prix. **2.** (*Piece cut off*) (a) Coupon m, bout m (d'étoffe, etc.). C. from a newspaper, coupure prise dans un journal. (b) *Hort:* Bouture f. **3.** *Civ.E: etc:* Tranchée f ; voie f en tranchée. *Road running through a c.,* route encaissée.

cutaneous [kju'teiniəs], a. Cutané.

cute [kjuːt], a. *F:* **1.** (a) (*Of pers.*) Malin, -igne ; rusé. (b) Cute idea, idée originale. **2.** *U.S:* Gentil, -ille ; coquet, -ette. **-ly,** adv. *F:* Avec ruse ; ingénieusement.

cuteness ['kjuːtnəs], s. *F:* Intelligence f, finesse f.

cuticle ['kjuːtikl], s. **1.** Épiderme m. **2.** *Bot: Biol:* Cuticule f.

cutis ['kjuːtis], s. *Anat:* Derme m.

cutlass ['kʌtləs], s. **1.** *Nau:* Sabre m d'abordage. **2.** *U.S:* Couteau m de chasse.

cutler ['kʌtlər], s. Coutelier m.

cutlery ['kʌtləri], s. Coutellerie f.

cutlet ['kʌtlet], s. Côtelette f (de mouton) ; escalope f (de veau).

cutter ['kʌtər], s. **1.** (*Pers.*) Coupeur m ; tailleur m (de pierre). **2.** *Tls:* Coupoir m, lame f. Rotary cutter, roue f à couteaux. **3.** *Nau:* (a) Canot m (d'un bâtiment de guerre). (b) Revenue cutter, patache f de la douane.

cutthroat ['kʌtθrout], s. **1.** Coupe-jarret m ; escarpe m. Cutthroat den, coupe-gorge m inv. **2.** Cutthroat competition, concurrence acharnée.

cuttle [kʌtl], s. *Moll:* Cuttle(-fish), seiche f.

cutwater ['kʌtwɔːtər], s. **1.** *N.Arch:* (Taquet m de) taille-mer m ; éperon m ; guibre f. **2.** *Civ.E:* Bec m (d'une pile de pont).

cyanide ['saianaid], s. *Ch:* Cyanure m. Cyanide process, procédé de cyanuration.

cyanogen [sai'anodʒen], s. *Ch:* Cyanogène m.

cyanosis [saia'nousis], s. *Med:* Cyanose f.

cyclamen ['siklamen], s. *Bot:* Cyclamen m.

cycle¹ [saikl], s. **1.** Cycle m (de mouvements, de poèmes) ; *Geol:* période f. *Ph:* Carnot's cycle, le cycle de Carnot. *I.C.E:* Four-stroke cycle, cycle à quatre temps. **2.** = BICYCLE¹. Cycle path, piste f cyclable. Cycle-racing track, vélodrome m.

cycle², v.i. Faire de la bicyclette ; aller à bicyclette ; *F:* pédaler. **cycling,** s. Cyclisme m.

cyclic(al) ['siklik(əl)], a. Cyclique.

cyclist ['saiklist], s. Cycliste mf.

cycloid ['saikloid], s. *Geom:* Cycloïde f.

cycloidal [sai'kloid(ə)l], a. Cycloïdal, -aux.

cyclometer [sai'klɔmetər], s. Compteur m kilométrique (pour bicyclettes).

cyclone ['saikloun], s. *Meteor:* Cyclone m.

cyclopaedia [saiklo'piːdia], s. = ENCYCLOPAEDIA.

Cyclopean [saiklo'piːən], a. Cyclopéen ; gigantesque.

Cyclops ['saiklɔps], s. *Myth:* Cyclope m.

cyclostyle ['saiklostail], s. Appareil m à polycopier par stencils.

cygnet ['signet], s. *Orn:* Jeune cygne m.

cylinder ['silindər], s. **1.** *Geom:* Cylindre m. **2.** Cylindre (de machine à vapeur) ; barillet m (de revolver). *Typewr:* Rouleau m porte-papier. C. of compressed gas, bouteille f cylindre, de gaz comprimé. A six-cylinder car, *F:* une six-cylindres.

cylindrical [si'lindrik(ə)l], a. Cylindrique.

cyma, pl. -mas ['saima(z)], s. **1.** *Arch:* Cimaise f (de corniche). **2.** *Bot:* = CYME.

cymbal ['simb(ə)l], s. Cymbale f.

cyme [saim], s. *Bot:* Cyme f.

Cymric ['kimrik], *a.* Kymrique ; gallois.
cynegetic [saini'dʒetik], *a.* Cynégétique.
cynegetics [saini'dʒetiks], *s.pl.* (*With sg. const.*) Cynégétique *f.*
cynic ['sinik]. **1.** *a. & s. Hist. of Phil :* Cynique (*m*). **2.** *s.* Censeur *m* caustique ; railleur *m* ; sceptique *m.*
cynical ['sinik(ə)l], *a.* **1.** *Hist. of Phil :* Cynique. **2.** Sarcastique ; sceptique. **-ally,** *adv.* D'un ton sceptique ; caustiquement.
cynicism ['sinisizm], *s.* **1.** *Hist. of Phil :* Cynisme *m.* **2.** Scepticisme railleur. **3.** Mot *m* caustique.
cynocephalus [saino'sefələs], *s.* *Z :* Cynocéphale *m.*
cynosure ['sainɔsjuər], *s.* *F :* The cynosure of every eye, le point de mire de tous les yeux.
cypher ['saifər], *s.* = CIPHER.

cypress ['saipres], *s.* *Bot :* Cyprès *m.*
Cyprian ['siprian]. **1.** *a. & s. Geog :* Cypriot (*mf*). **2.** *A. & Lit :* (*a*) *a.* Débauché, dévergonde (*b*) *s.f.* Courtisane.
Cypriote ['sipriət], *a. & s. Geog :* Cypriote (*mf*
Cyprus ['saiprəs]. *Pr.n.* L'île de Chypre.
cyst [sist], *s.* **1.** (*a*) *Biol :* *Anat :* Sac *m* ; vésicule *f* (*b*) *Bot :* Kyste *m.* **2.** *Med :* Kyste.
cytisus ['sitisəs], *s.* *Bot :* Cytise *m.*
cytoblast ['saitoblɑːst], *s.* *Biol :* Cytoblaste *m*
czar [tsɑːr, zɑːr], *s.* Tsar *m.*
czarevitch ['tsɑːrevitʃ], *s.* Tsarévitch *m.*
czarina [tsɑ'riːna, zɑ-], *s.f.* Tsarine.
Czech [tʃek], *a. & s.* Tchèque (*mf*).
Czecho-Slovak [tʃeko'slouvak], *s.* Tchéco slovaque *mf.*
Czecho-Slovakia [tʃekoslo'vakia]. *Pr.n.* L Tchécoslovaquie.

D

D, d [diː], *s.* **1.** (La lettre) D, d *m.* **D joint,** chape *f.* **2.** *Mus :* Ré *m.* **3.** (*Abbr. for Lt. 'denarius'*) Penny *m,* pence *mpl.*
dab[1][dab], *s.* **1.** Coup léger ; tape *f.* **2.** (*a*) Tache *f* (d'encre, de peinture). A dab of butter, un petit morceau de beurre. (*b*) Petit coup de tampon.
dab[2], *v.tr.* (**dabbed**) **1.** Lancer une tape à (qn). **2.** Tapoter ; (*with pad*) tamponner. To dab one's eyes with a handkerchief, se tamponner les yeux.
dab[3], *s.* *Ich :* Limande *f,* carrelet *m.*
dab[4], *s.* *F :* To be a dab (hand) at sth., s'entendre à qch. He's a dab at algebra, il est à cheval sur l'algèbre ; *P :* il est calé en algèbre.
dabble [dabl]. **1.** *v.tr.* Humecter, mouiller. **2.** *v.i.* (*a*) Barboter (dans l'eau). (*b*) *F :* To dabble in, at, law, s'occuper un peu de droit.
dace [deis], *s.* *Ich :* Vandoise *f* ; dard *m.*
dacoit [da'kɔit], *s.* Dacoït *m* (brigand de l'Inde).
dactyl ['daktil], *s.* *Pros :* Dactyle *m.*
dactyloscopy [dakti'lɔskɔpi], *s.* Dactyloscopie *f* ; étude *f* des empreintes digitales.
dad [dad], *s.* *F :* Papa *m* ; petit père.
daddy ['dadi], *s.* = DAD. **daddy-'long-legs,** *s. Ent : F :* Tipule *f.*
dado ['deido], *s.* **1.** *Arch :* (*a*) Dé *m* (de piédestal). (*b*) Cimaise *f.* **2.** *Typ :* Croix *f.*
dago [deigo], *s.* *P :* Sud-américain *m* (de race latine) ; métèque *m.*
dahlia ['deiljə], *s.* *Bot :* Dahlia *m.*
daily ['deili]. **1.** *a.* Journalier, quotidien. D. servant domestique à la journée. **2.** *adv.* Journellement quotidiennement, tous les jours. **3.** *s. Journ :* Quotidien *m.* **Our leading dailies,** nos grands quotidiens.
daintiness ['deintinəs], *s.* Délicatesse *f,* raffinement *m* (de goût) ; mignonnesse *f* (de taille).
dainty[1] ['deinti], *s.* Friandise *f.*
dainty[2], *a.* **1.** (*Of food*) Friand, délicat. **2.** (*Of*

pers.) Délicat, exquis. She's a d. little thing *F :* elle est mignonne. **3.** To be d., être délica sur la nourriture. **-ily,** *adv.* Délicatement d'une manière raffinée.
dairy ['dɛəri], *s.* **1.** Laiterie *f.* **2.** (*Shop*) Laiterie (*small restaurant*) crémerie *f.* **'dairy-farm,** (Ferme *f*) vacherie *f.* **'dairy-farming,** L'industrie laitière. **'dairy-produce,** *s.* Produits laitiers ; laitages *mpl.*
dairymaid ['dɛərimeid], *s.f.* Fille de laiterie.
dairyman, *pl.* **-men** ['dɛərimən, -men], *s.m* **1.** *Husb :* Nourrisseur. **2.** *Com :* Laitier crémier.
dais [deis], *s.* (*a*) Estrade *f* (d'honneur) ; dais *m* (*b*) Dais (recouvrant l'estrade).
daisy ['deizi], *s.* **1.** *Bot :* Marguerite *f.* Common daisy, pâquerette *f.* **Daisy-chain** guirlande *f* de pâquerettes. **2.** *P :* She's a daisy, c'est une perle
dale [deil], *s.* Vallée *f,* vallon *m*
dalesman, *pl.* **-men** ['deilzmən, -men], *s.m* Habitant des vallées (du nord de l'Angleterre).
dalliance ['daliəns], *s. Lit :* Flirtage *m* ; échange *m* de tendresses ; badinage *m.*
dally ['dali], *v.i. Lit :* **1.** (*a*) To dally with a idea, caresser une idée. (*b*) Badiner, flirter (*with* avec). **2.** Tarder, baguenauder.
dalmatic [dal'matik], *s. Ecc.Cost :* Dalmatique *f*
daltonism ['dɔltənizm], *s. Med :* Daltonisme *m.*
dam[1] [dam], *s. Hyd.E :* (*a*) Barrage *m* de retenu (d'un grand réservoir). (*b*) *F :* Eau retenue (pa un barrage) : retenue *f.*
dam[2], *v.tr.* (**dammed**) To dam (up), contenir endiguer (un cours d'eau, un lac).
dam[3], *s.* Mère *f* (en parlant des animaux).
damage[1] ['damedʒ], *s.* **1.** Dommage(s) *m(pl)* dégâts *mpl* ; (*to engine, ship, etc.*) avarie(s) *f(pl)* D. in transit, avarie(s) en cours de route *F :* There's no end of d. done, il n'y a pas grand mal. **2.** Préjudice *m,* tort *m.* To cause s.o damage, porter préjudice à qn. **3.** *pl. Jur :* Dommages-intérêts *m,* indemnité *f.* To sue s.o. for damages, poursuivre qn en dommages-intérêts **4.** *F :* What's the damage? à combien se monte la note ? c'est combien ?
damage[2], *v.tr.* **1.** Endommager ; avarier (une marchandise, une machine) ; abîmer (qch.). **2.** Faire tort, nuire, à (qn). **damaged,** *a*

Avarié, endommagé. **damaging,** a. Préjudiciable, nuisible.

damascene [dama'si:n], v.tr. Metalw: Damasquiner.

Damascus [da'maskəs]. Pr.n. Geog: Damas m.

damask ['daməsk], a. & s. **I.** Tex: Damask (silk, linen), damas m; soie damassée, linge damassé **2.** Damask steel, acier damassé. **3.** (a) Damask rose, rose de Damas. (b) Damask (colour), incarnat m. Her d. cheeks, ses joues vermeilles.

dame [deim], s. A: = lady. F: An old d., une vieille dame. **'dame-school,** s. École enfantine (tenue par une femme).

damn¹ [dam], s. (Often written d——) Juron m; gros mot. Not to be worth a (tuppenny) damn, ne pas valoir chipette.

damn², v.tr. **I.** (a) Condamner, critiquer défavorablement (un livre). (b) Perdre, ruiner (qn, un projet). **2.** (a) Theol: Damner; (of God) réprouver. (b) F: Well, I'm damned [damd]! ça c'est fort! I'll see him damned first! qu'il aille au diable! **3.** (a) Damn your impudence! que le diable vous emporte! (b) int. Sacristi! sacrebleu! Damn it! zut! **damned,** a. **I.** Damné, réprouvé. The damned, les damnés. **2.** F: (Often written d——d) (a) Sacré, satané. (b) adv. Diablement, bigrement. (c) s. To do one's damnedest ['damdəst], faire tout son possible. **damning¹** ['damniŋ, 'damiŋ], a. Portant condamnation. Damning evidence, preuves accablantes. **damning²** ['damiŋ], s. **I.** Condamnation f. **2.** Damnation f.

damnable ['damnəbl], a. **I.** Damnable. **2.** F: Maudit, odieux. **-ably,** adv. Odieusement; diablement (mauvais, etc.).

damnation [dam'neiʃ(ə)n], s. **I.** Damnation f. **2.** Éreintement m (d'une pièce de théâtre, etc.). **3.** int. F: Sacrebleu!

Damocles ['daməkli:z]. Pr.n.m. The sword of Damocles, l'épée de Damoclès.

damp¹ [damp], s. **I.** (a) Humidité f. (b) To cast a damp over the company, jeter un froid sur la compagnie. **2.** Min: (Black) damp = CHOKE-DAMP. S.a. FIRE-DAMP. **'damp-course,** s. Const: Couche isolante, hydrofuge. **'damp-proof,** a. Hydrofuge; imperméable.

damp², v.tr. **I.** Mouiller; humecter (le linge); amoitir (la peau). **2.** Étouffer (le feu); assourdir (un son). To damp down a furnace, boucher un haut fourneau. **3.** Ph: (a) Damped waves, ondes amorties. (b) v.i. The oscillations d. down, les vibrations s'amortissent. **4.** Refroidir (l'ardeur, le courage). To damp s.o.'s spirits, décourager qn. **damping,** s. **I.** (a) Humectation f. (b) A general d. of spirits, un froid général jeté sur la compagnie. **2.** Amortissement m.

damp³, a. Humide, (of skin) moite. D. heat, chaleur humide, moite.

dampen ['dampən]. **I.** v.tr. U.S: = DAMP² I, 4. **2.** v.i. (a) Devenir humide. (b) (Of ardour) Se refroidir.

damper ['dampər], s. **I.** F: (a) (Pers.) Rabat-joie m inv. (b) Événement déprimant. To put a damper on the company, jeter un froid sur la compagnie. **2.** (In Austr.) Pain m en galette, sans levain. **3.** (Of piano, sound) Étouffoir m. **4.** Registre m (de foyer). **5.** Mec.E: El.E: Aut: Amortisseur m.

dampness ['dampnəs], s. Humidité f; moiteur f (de la peau).

damsel ['damzəl], s.f. A. & Lit: Demoiselle f, jeune fille.

damson ['damzən], s. (a) Prune f de Damas. (b) Prunier m de Damas.

dance¹ [dɑ:ns], s. **I.** (a) Danse f. F: To lead s.o. a dance, (i) donner du fil à retordre à qn; (ii) faire voir bien du chemin à qn. The Dance of Death, la danse macabre. (b) (Air m de) danse. **2.** Bal m, pl. bals; soirée dansante. **'dance-hall,** s. Bal public; dancing m.

dance². **I.** v.i. (a) Danser. To d. with s.o., faire danser qn. F: I'll make him dance to a different tune! je vais le faire chanter sur un autre ton. (b) To dance for joy, danser de joie. To d. with rage, trépigner de colère. **2.** v.tr. (a) Danser (une valse, etc.). (b) To dance attendance on s.o., faire l'empressé auprès de qn; faire les trente-six volontés de qn. **dancing¹,** a. Dansant. Dancing dervish, derviche tourneur. **'dancing-girl,** s.f. Bayadère. **dancing²,** s. Danse f. **'dancing-hall,** s. Salle f de danse; dancing m. **'dancing-master,** s. Maître m de danse.

dancer ['dɑ:nsər], s. Danseur, -euse.

dandelion ['dandilaiən], s. Bot: Pissenlit m.

dander ['dandər], s. F: To get s.o.'s dander up, mettre qn en colère. He got his d. up, la moutarde lui a monté au nez.

dandified ['dandifaid], a. Vêtu en dandy. D. young man, (i) jeune gommeux; (ii) jeune fat.

dandle [dandl], v.tr. **I.** (a) Faire sauter (un enfant, sur ses genoux). (b) Dodeliner (un enfant). **2.** Câliner, dorloter (qn).

dandruff ['dandrəf], s. Pellicules fpl (du cuir chevelu).

dandy ['dandi]. **I.** s. Dandy m, gommeux m. **2.** a. U.S: Épatant.

Dane [dein], s. **I.** Danois, -oise. **2.** (Dog) (Great) Dane, (grand) danois.

danger ['deindʒər], s. Danger m, péril m. To be in danger, courir un danger. Out of danger, hors de danger; F: hors d'affaire. To run into d., s'exposer au danger. To be in d. of falling, courir le risque de tomber. To ward off a d., écarter un danger. Rock that is a d. to navigation, écueil dangereux pour la navigation. 'Danger, road up,' "attention aux travaux." Rail: Signal at danger, signal à l'arrêt. **'danger-signal,** s. Rail: Arrêt m.

dangerous ['deindʒərəs], a. (a) Dangereux, périlleux. D. illness, maladie grave. F: You are on dangerous ground, vous êtes sur un terrain brûlant. D. situation, mauvais pas. (b) D. example, exemple pernicieux. **-ly,** adv. Dangereusement.

dangle [dangl]. **I.** v.i. Pendiller, pendre. With one's legs dangling, les jambes ballantes. F: To dangle after a woman, être pendu aux jupes d'une femme. **2.** v.tr. Faire pendiller. F: To dangle a prospect before s.o.'s eyes, faire miroiter une perspective aux yeux de qn.

Danish ['deiniʃ]. **I.** a. Danois. **2.** s. Ling: Le danois.

dank [daŋk], a. (Cachot) humide (et froid).

Daphne ['dafni]. **I.** Pr.n.f. Myth: Daphné. **2.** s. Bot: Daphné m, lauréole f.

dapper ['dapər], a. **I.** Pimpant. A d. little man, un petit homme tiré à quatre épingles. **2.** Sémillant.

dapple [dapl], v.tr. Tacheter. **dappled,** a. Tacheté; (of horse, sky) pommelé. **dapple-grey,** a. & s. (Cheval) gris pommelé.

darbies ['dɑ:rbiz], s.pl. P: Menottes f.

Darby ['dɑ:rbi]. Pr.n.m. F: Darby and Joan, Philémon et Baucis.

dare ['deər], v. **I.** Modal aux. (3rd sg.pr. he dare; p.t. durst [də:rst], occ. dared, dare; no p.p.) Oser.

He dared not contradict me, il n'osa (pas) me contredire. *Don't you d. touch him!* n'ayez pas l'audace de le toucher! *How dare you!* vous avez cette audace! *I dare say,* sans doute; peut-être bien; je (le) crois bien. **2.** *v.tr.* (*3rd sg.pr.* he dares; *p.t.* dared; *p.p.* dared) (*a*) *To d. to do sth.,* oser faire qch. *To d. all things,* tout oser. (*b*) Braver, affronter (la mort). *To d. the perils of a journey,* affronter, risquer, les périls d'un voyage. (*c*) *To dare s.o. to do sth.,* défier qn de faire qch. **daring**[1], *a.* (i) Audacieux, hardi; (ii) téméraire. *Greatly daring,* fort osé. **-ly,** *adv.* Audacieusement, témérairement. **daring**[2], *s.* (i) Audace *f,* hardiesse *f;* (ii) témérité *f.* **'dare-devil.** **1.** *s.* Casse-cou *m inv;* cervelle brûlée. **2.** *a.* Qui ne craint ni Dieu ni diable.

dark[1] [dɑːk], *a.* **1.** Sombre, obscur, noir. *It is dark,* il fait nuit, il fait noir. *It is getting d.,* il commence à faire sombre. *The sky grew d.,* le ciel s'assombrit. **2.** (*Of colour*) Foncé, sombre. *Dark blue* (*dresses*), (des robes *f*) bleu foncé. **3.** (*Of pers.*) Brun; basané. **4.** *The dark race,* la race nègre. **5.** (*a*) Sombre, triste. *D. future,* sombre avenir. *To look on the dark side of things,* voir tout en noir. (*b*) Ténébreux, mauvais. *To utter d. threats,* proférer de sourdes menaces. **6.** *D. saying,* mot mystérieux. *To keep sth. dark,* tenir qch. secret. *Keep it d.!* gardez le secret! *Dark horse,* (i) *Turf:* cheval dont on ne sait rien; (ii) *F:* concurrent que l'on ne croyait pas dangereux. **7.** *The Dark Ages,* l'âge des ténèbres. **-ly,** *adv.* (*a*) Obscurément. (*b*) *To look darkly at s.o.,* regarder qn d'un air sombre. **'dark-'eyed,** *a.* Aux yeux noirs. **'dark-'lantern,** *s.* Lanterne sourde. **'dark-room,** *s.* *Phot:* Cabinet noir. **'dark-'skinned,** *a.* **1.** A peau brune. **2.** (*Race*) nègre. **'dark-slide,** *s.* *Phot:* Châssis négatif.

dark[2], *s.* **1.** Ténèbres *fpl,* obscurité *f.* *After dark,* à (la) nuit close. *The dark of the moon,* la nouvelle lune. **2.** *To be* (*kept*) *in the dark,* être (laissé) dans l'ignorance. *We are in the d. as to his plans,* nous ignorons ses projets.

darken ['dɑːk(ə)n]. **1.** *v.tr.* Obscurcir; assombrir (le ciel); brunir (le teint); foncer (une couleur); attrister (la vie de qn). *A cloud darkened the sun,* un nuage voila la face du soleil. *Never darken my doors again!* ne remettez plus les pieds chez moi! **2.** *v.i.* S'obscurcir; (*of sky, brow*) s'assombrir. **darkening,** *s.* Assombrissement *m.*

darkness ['dɑːknəs], *s.* **1.** Obscurité *f,* ténèbres *fpl.* *The room was in complete d.,* il faisait tout à fait noir dans la salle. **2.** Teinte foncée. *D. of complexion,* teint bronzé. **3.** Ignorance *f* (*as to,* de).

darky ['dɑːki], *s.* *F:* Moricaud, -aude.

darling ['dɑːliŋ], *s. & a.* Favori, -ite; bien-aimé, -ée. *My darling!* ma chérie! *She's a little d.,* c'est un petit amour. *A mother's d.,* un enfant gâté. *The d. of the people,* l'idole *f* du peuple.

darn[1] [dɑːn], *s.* Reprise *f,* passefilure *f.*

darn[2], *v.tr.* Raccommoder, ravauder; repriser (des bas). **darning,** *s.* Reprise *f,* ravaudage *m.* **'darning-egg,** *s.* Œuf *m* à repriser. **'darning-needle,** *s.* Aiguille *f* à repriser.

darnel ['dɑːnəl], *s.* *Bot:* Ivraie (enivrante).

dart[1] [dɑːt], *s.* **1.** (*a*) Dard *m,* trait *m,* javelot *m.* (*b*) *Games:* Fléchette *f.* (*c*) *Dressm:* Pince *f,* suçon *m.* **2.** Mouvement soudain en avant. *To make a sudden dart on sth.,* foncer, se précipiter, sur qch.

dart[2]. **1.** *v.tr.* Darder (des rayons); lancer (un harpon, un regard). **2.** *v.i.* Se précipiter, s'élancer, foncer (*at, upon,* sur). *To dart in, out, entrer,* sortir, comme un trait.

Dartmoor ['dɑːtmɔːr]. *Pr.n.* Prison *f* pour forçats.

dartre ['dɑːrtər], *s.* *Med:* Dartre *f.*

dartrous ['dɑːrtrəs], *a.* Dartreux; herpétique.

dash[1] [daʃ], *s.* **1.** Coup *m,* heurt *m,* choc *m.* **2.** Soupçon *m,* goutte *f* (de cognac, etc.); pointe *f* (de vanille, etc.); filet *m* (de vinaigre). **3.** *Dash of colour,* tache *f* de couleur (dans le paysage, etc.); touche *f* de couleur (dans un tableau). **4.** Trait *m* (de plume, de l'alphabet Morse). *Typ:* (i) Tiret *m;* (ii) moins *m.* *Mth:* *A dash* (*A′*), a prime. **5.** (i) Attaque soudaine; (ii) course *f* à toute vitesse; élan *m;* ruée *f.* *To make a dash forward,* s'élancer en avant. *To make a d. at sth.,* se précipiter, se ruer, sur qch. *D. across the desert,* raid *m* à travers le désert. **6.** Élan, impétuosité *f,* fougue *f,* entrain *m,* allant *m.* *Mus:* *To play with d.,* jouer avec brio. **7.** *F:* *To cut a dash,* faire (brillante) figure; faire de l'effet; faire de l'épate. **8.** (*a*) = DASH-BOARD 2. (*b*) *Aut:* Auvent *m.* **'dash-board,** *s.* **1.** *Veh:* Garde-boue *m inv,* pare-boue *m inv.* **2.** *Aut:* Tablier *m;* planche *f* de bord.

dash[2]. **1.** *v.tr.* (*a*) Lancer violemment (qch. contre qch.); jeter, *F:* flanquer (qch. par terre). *To dash sth. to pieces,* fracasser qch.; briser qch. en morceaux. *To d. one's head against sth.,* se casser la tête contre qch. (*b*) *To d. water over sth.,* jeter, flaquer, de l'eau sur qch. (*c*) *To d. sth. with mud,* éclabousser qch. de boue. *Dashed with colour,* rehaussé de touches de couleur. (*d*) Déconcerter, confondre (qn); anéantir, détruire (les espérances). *To dash s.o.'s spirits,* abattre le courage, l'entrain, de qn. (*e*) *int.* *P:* *Euphemism for DAMN*[2] 3 (*b*). **2.** *v.i.* (*a*) *To dash against sth.,* se heurter, se jeter, contre qch. (*b*) *To dash at s.o., at sth.,* se précipiter, s'élancer, sur qn, qch. *To d. down the street,* descendre la rue à toute vitesse. **dash along,** *v.i.* Avancer, filer, à fond de train. **dash away.** **1.** *v.tr.* Écarter violemment (qch.). **2.** *v.i.* S'éloigner en coup de vent. **dash in,** *v.i.* Entrer en trombe, précipitamment. **dash off.** **1.** *v.tr.* Dessiner (un croquis) en un tour de main; bâcler, enlever (une lettre, etc.). **2.** *v.i.* = DASH AWAY 2. **dash out.** **1.** *v.tr.* *To dash out one's brains,* se fracasser la cervelle. **2.** *v.i.* S'élancer dehors. **dashed,** *a.* *Euphemism for DAMNED 2.* **dashing,** *a.* (*Of pers.*) Impétueux; plein d'élan; (*of horse*) fougueux. *D. young man,* beau cavalier. **-ly,** *adv.* (S'habiller) avec une élégance tapageuse.

dastard ['dastərd], *s.* *Lit:* Lâche *m.*

dastardliness ['dastədlinəs], *s.* **1.** Lâcheté *f.* **2.** Infamie *f* (d'une action).

dastardly ['dastərdli], *a.* **1.** Lâche. **2.** (Crime, etc.) infâme.

data ['deita], *s.pl.* See DATUM.

date[1] [deit], *s.* *Bot:* **1.** Datte *f.* **2.** Date(-palm), dattier *m.*

date[2], *s.* Date *f;* (*on coins, books*) millésime *m;* (*of month*) quantième *m.* *Under the date of June 4th,* en date du 4 juin. *To be up to date,* être au niveau des derniers progrès; être dans le train; *F:* être à la page. *To be up to d. with one's work,* être à jour dans son travail. *To bring up to date,* remettre au point (une question, etc.). *To bring, keep, one's diary up to d.,* mettre, tenir, son journal à jour. *Out of date,* (i) (*of pers.*) de la vieille école; (ii) (*of thg*) démodé. *Com:* *Interest to date,* intérêts à ce jour. *Date of a bill,* terme *m,* échéance *f,* d'un billet. **Three months**

after date, at three months' date, à trois mois de date. *F:* To have a date with s.o., avoir rendez-vous avec qn. **'date-marker, -stamp,** *s.* Dateur *m*; timbre *m* à date.

date³. **1.** *v.tr.* (*a*) Dater (une lettre, etc.); composter (un billet de chemin de fer, etc.). *S.a.* LONG-DATED, SHORT-DATED. (*b*) Assigner une date à (une œuvre). **2.** *v.i.* (*a*) Church dating from, dating back to, the XIIIth century, église qui remonte au XIIIᵉ siècle, qui date du XIIIᵉ siècle. (*b*) His style is beginning to d., son style commence à dater.

dateless ['deitləs], *a.* Sans date.

dative ['deitiv], *a. & s. Gram:* Datif (*m*). In the dative, au datif.

datum, *pl.* **data** ['deitəm, 'deitə], *s.* **1.** Donnée *f.* **2.** (*a*) *Surv:* Datum-line, ligne *f* de repère; ligne de niveau. (*b*) *Mec.E:* etc: (Point *m* de) repère *m*.

daub¹ [dɔːb], *s.* **1.** (*a*) Enduit *m*, barbouillage *m*. (*b*) *Const:* Torchis *m*, gobetage *m*. **2.** (*Picture*) Croûte *f*.

daub², *v.tr.* **1.** Barbouiller, enduire (*with*, de). *Wall daubed with clay*, mur enduit de torchis. **2.** *Art:* *F:* Peintur(lur)er, barbouiller (une toile).

dauby ['dɔːbi], *a.* **1.** Gluant, visqueux, poisseux. **2.** (*Of picture, etc.*) Barbouillé.

daughter ['dɔːtər], *s.f.* Fille (par rapport au père et à la mère). **'daughter-in-law,** *s.f.* Belle-fille, *pl.* belles-filles; bru.

daughterly ['dɔːtərli], *a.* Filial, -als, -aux.

daunt [dɔːnt], *v.tr.* Intimider, décourager. *Nothing daunted*, aucunement intimidé; sans se laisser abattre.

dauntless ['dɔːntləs], *a.* Intrépide. **-ly,** *adv.* Intrépidement.

Dauphin, Dauphiness ['dɔːfin, -ines], *s. Fr.Hist:* Dauphin, -ine.

davenport ['davənpɔːrt], *s.* Petit bureau-pupitre.

davit ['davit], *s. Nau:* Bossoir *m*, davier *m* (d'embarcation).

davy ['deivi], *s. F:* (*Affidavit*) To take one's davy that . . ., donner sa parole que. . . .

dawdle [dɔːdl]. **1.** *v.i.* Flâner, musarder, lambiner. **2.** *v.tr.* To dawdle away one's time, passer son temps à flâner; gaspiller le temps.

dawdling¹, *a.* Flâneur, musard, lambin.

dawdling², *s.* Flânerie *f*, musarderie *f*.

dawdler ['dɔːdlər], *s.* Flâneur, -euse; lambin, -ine; traînard *m*.

dawn¹ [dɔːn], *s.* **1.** Aube *f*, aurore *f*. At dawn, au point du jour. **2.** *F:* Aube (de la vie, de l'histoire); commencement *m* (de la civilisation); naissance *f* (d'une idée).

dawn², *v.i.* (*Of day*) Poindre; (commencer à) paraître; naître. *Day is dawning*, le jour se lève. *At length it dawned on me that* . . ., enfin il me vint à l'esprit que. . . . *The truth dawned on him*, la vérité se fit jour dans son esprit. **dawning,** *a.* (Jour, espoir) naissant.

day [dei], *s.* **1.** (*a*) Jour *m*; (*whole day in regard to work, etc.*) journée *f*. *It's a fine day*, il fait beau aujourd'hui. To work day and night, travailler nuit et jour. All day (long), all the day, toute la journée. To work by the day, travailler à la journée. *F:* It's all in the day's work, ça fait partie de ma routine; j'en vois bien d'autres! Twice a day, deux fois par jour. This day, ce jour-ci, aujourd'hui. This day week, (d')aujourd'hui en huit. The day before sth., la veille de qch. Two days before sth., l'avant-veille *f* de qch. The day after (sth.), le lendemain (de qch.). *Two days after, later*, deux jours après; le

surlendemain. Every other day, day about, tous les deux jours. Day after day, tous les jours. Day in day out, du matin au soir; sans trêve. Day by day, jour par jour; de jour en jour. From day to day, de jour en jour. (*b*) To carry, win, the day, gagner la journée; remporter la victoire. **2.** (*a*) Before day, avant le jour. At break of day, au point du jour. (*b*) (*Daylight*) To travel by day, *in the day*, voyager le jour, de jour. It was broad day, il faisait grand jour. **3.** (*a*) Day of the month, quantième *m* du mois. *What is the day of the month?* c'est le combien aujourd'hui? One summer day, par un jour d'été. One day, some day, one of these (fine) days, un de ces (beaux) jours. *I saw him the other day*, je l'ai vu l'autre jour. *He may arrive any day*, il peut arriver d'un jour à l'autre. It will be a long day before I go there again, il fera beau quand j'y retournerai. *It is many a long day since you did that*, il y a beau jour que vous n'avez (pas) fait cela. *Thursday is my (at-home) day*, mon jour (de réception) est le jeudi. Day off, jour de congé (d'un employé). *F:* To name the day, fixer le jour du mariage. *Prov:* The better the day the better the deed, bon jour bonne œuvre. *S.a.* TIME¹ 6. (*b*) Fête *f*. All Saints' Day, la fête de la Toussaint. Easter Day, le jour de Pâques. **4.** The good old days, le bon vieux temps. *In the days of* . . ., au temps de . . ., du temps de. . . . In the days of old, autrefois; au temps jadis. In these days, in our days, de nos jours; de notre temps. *I was a student in those days*, j'étais étudiant à ce moment-là, à cette époque. At, to, this (very) day, encore aujourd'hui. In days to come, dans un temps futur. *Of other, former, days*, d'autrefois. *The man of the day*, l'homme du jour. (*Of theory, etc.*) To have had its day, avoir fait son temps. **'day-blind,** *a.* Nyctalope. **'day-blindness,** *s.* Nyctalopie *f*. **'day-boarder,** *s. Sch:* Demi-pensionnaire *mf*. **'day-book,** *s. Com:* Journal *m*, -aux; main courante; brouillard *m*. **'day-boy,** *s.m. Sch:* Externe. **'day-break,** *s.* Point *m* du jour; lever *m* du jour; aube *f*. At day-break, au jour levant. **'day-dream¹,** *s.* Rêverie *f*, rêvasserie *f*. **'day-dream²,** *v.i.* Rêver creux; rêvasser. **day-dreaming,** *s.* Rêverie *f*, songerie *f*. **'day-dreamer,** *s.* Rêveur, -euse; songe-creux *m inv.* **'day-'labourer,** *s.* Journalier *m*; ouvrier *m* à la journée. **'day-nursery,** *s.* **1.** Salle *f* des enfants. **2.** *Adm:* Pouponnière *f*; garderie *f* (d'enfants). **'day-scholar,** *s.* Externe *mf*. **'day-school,** *s.* Externat *m*. **'day-time,** *s.* Le jour, la journée. In the day-time, pendant la journée.

daylight ['deilait], *s.* **1.** Jour *m*; lumière *f* du jour. By daylight, de jour, le jour. In broad daylight, en plein jour; au grand jour. *It is broad d.*, il fait grand jour. Before daylight, avant le jour. **2.** Espace *m* libre; ouverture *f*; jour, intervalle *m*. *F:* To (begin to) see daylight through a piece of work, (i) apercevoir la fin du travail; approcher du but; (ii) voir jour dans une affaire.

daze [deːz], *s.* Étourdissement *m*, stupéfaction *f*. To be in a daze, être hébété, stupéfait.

daze², *v.tr.* **1.** (*a*) (*Of drug, etc.*) Stupéfier, hébéter. (*b*) (*Of blow*) Étourdir. (*c*) *F:* Abasourdir, ahurir (qn). **2.** = DAZZLE². **dazed,** *a.* (*a*) Stupéfié (par un narcotique); hébété. (*b*) Tout étourdi (par un coup). (*c*) *F:* Abasourdi, ahuri, sidéré.

dazzle¹ [dazl], *s.* **1.** Éblouissement *m*; aveuglement *m*. **2.** *Navy:* Camouflage *m*.

dazzle², *v.tr.* Éblouir, aveugler. **dazzling**, *a.* Éblouissant, aveuglant.

deacon ['di:kən], *s.* *Ecc:* **1.** Diacre *m.* **2.** (*Presbyterian Ch.*) Membre *m* du Conseil de fabrique.

deaconess ['di:kənes], *s.f.* Diaconesse.

dead [ded]. I. *a.* **1.** Mort. (*a*) *He is d.*, il est mort, décédé. **The dead man, woman,** le mort, la morte. *S.a.* SHOE¹ 1. *Prov:* **Dead men tell no tales,** morte la bête mort le venin. *S.a.* FLOG. **To strike, kill, s.o.** (stone) **dead,** tuer qn raide. **To drop down dead,** tomber mort. *F:* **Dead as a door-nail, as mutton,** mort et bien mort. **Dead and gone, dead and buried,** mort et enterré. **Dead to the world,** mort pour le monde. *F:* **Dead and done for,** flambé, fichu, fini. (*Of regulation*) **To become a dead letter,** tomber en désuétude. *Post:* **Dead letters,** lettres tombées au rebut. (*b*) (Doigt) mort, engourdi par le froid. (*Of limb*) **To go dead,** s'engourdir. **2. Dead to honour,** mort à tout sentiment d'honneur. *D. to reason,* sourd à la raison. **3.** *D. coal,* charbon éteint. **Dead colour,** couleur terne. **Dead white,** blanc mat. *D. sound,* son sourd, mat. **Dead well,** puits perdu. *El.E:* **Dead wire,** fil (i) hors courant, (ii) sans tension, sans courant. *El:* **Dead cell,** pile épuisée, à plat. *Typ:* **Dead matter,** matière à distribuer. **4. Dead season,** morte-saison. **The dead hours,** (i) la nuit; (ii) *Ind: etc:* les heures creuses. *D. spring,* ressort qui a perdu son élasticité. **Dead axle,** essieu fixe. *Fb:* **Dead ball,** ballon mort. *Ph:* **Dead beat,** oscillation amortie. **5. Dead stop,** arrêt brusque, halte subite. *To come to a d. stop,* s'arrêter net. *Nau:* **Dead calm,** calme plat. **Dead silence,** silence de mort. **Dead secret,** profond secret. *D. level,* niveau parfait. **To be dead on time,** être à la minute. **Dead loss,** perte sèche. **To be in dead earnest,** être tout à fait sérieux. **He's a dead shot,** il ne manque, ne rate, jamais son coup. *Golf:* (*Of ball*) **To lie dead,** être au bord du trou. II. **dead,** *s.* **1.** *pl.* **The dead,** les morts *m*; les trépassés *m.* **To rise from the dead,** ressusciter des morts. **2. At dead of night,** au milieu de la nuit. **In the dead of winter,** au (plus) fort de l'hiver. III. **dead,** *adv.* (*a*) Absolument. **Dead drunk,** ivre mort. *D. tired,* mort de fatigue; éreinté. *D. sure,* absolument certain. **To go dead slow,** aller au grand ralenti. (*b*) **To stop dead,** s'arrêter net. (*c*) (*Of pers.*) **To be dead against sth.,** être absolument opposé à qch. *D. smooth surface,* surface parfaitement plane. **'dead(-and)- a'live,** *a.* (Endroit) mort, triste, sans animation. **'dead-'beat¹,** *attrib. a. El:* (Instrument) apériodique. **'dead-'beat²,** *a.* F: Épuisé, éreinté, fourbu. **'dead-'centre,** *s.* **1.** *Mch:* Point mort (du piston). **2.** (*Of lathe*) Pointe *f* de la poupée mobile. **dead-'end,** *s.* **1.** Cul-de-sac *m.* **2.** *El:* Spires mortes (d'un enroulement). **'dead-eye,** *s. Nau:* Cap *m* de mouton. **'dead-fall,** *s.* (Piège *m*) assommoir *m*; traquenard *m.* **'dead-head,** *s.* F: *Th: etc:* Personne *f* en possession d'un billet de faveur, *P:* qui entre à l'œil. **'dead-light,** *s.* **1.** *Nau: F:* (*a*) Mantelet *m* de sabord. (*b*) Couvercle *m* de panneau. **2.** *Const:* Fausse fenêtre. **'dead-lock,** *s.* **1.** Serrure *f* à pêne dormant. **2.** Impasse *f*; situation *f* inextricable. **'dead-march,** *s. Mus:* Marche *f* funèbre. **'dead-'weight,** *s.* **1.** Poids mort; *F:* poids accablant (de dettes, etc.). *To be a d.-w.,* faire poids (inutile). **2.** *Nau:* Portée *f* en poids. **'dead-wood,** *s.* Bois mort.

deaden [dedn], *v.tr.* Amortir (un coup);

assourdir, étouffer (un son); émousser, assoupir, aveulir (les sens). *To d. one's footsteps,* ouater, feutrer, ses pas. **deadening,** *s.* Amortissement *m*; assourdissement *m* (du bruit, d'un son).

deadliness ['dedlinəs], *s.* Nature mortelle (d'un poison, etc.).

deadly ['dedli]. **1.** *a.* (*a*) (*Of poison, blow, etc.*) Mortel. **Deadly hatred,** haine mortelle, implacable. **Deadly insult,** insulte mortelle. **The seven deadly sins,** les sept péchés capitaux. (*b*) = DEATH-LIKE. **2.** *adv.* Mortellement. **Deadly pale,** d'une pâleur mortelle. *It was d. cold,* il faisait un froid de loup. *S.a.* DULL¹ 5.

deadness ['dednəs], *s.* Torpeur *f*; engourdissement *m* (des membres); stagnation *f* (des affaires).

deaf [def], *a.* Sourd. **Deaf and dumb,** sourd-muet. **Deaf as a door-post,** sourd comme un pot. **To turn a deaf ear to s.o.,** faire la sourde oreille à ce que dit qn; refuser d'écouter qn. **'deaf-'mute,** *s.* Sourd-muet, *f.* sourde-muette.

deafen [defn], *v.tr.* Assourdir (qn); rendre (qn) sourd. **deafening,** *a.* Assourdissant.

deafness ['defnəs], *s.* Surdité *f.*

deal¹ [di:l], *s.* (*Usu.* a great deal, a good deal) (Grande) quantité; beaucoup. **A good deal to do,** bien des choses à faire. **That's saying a good deal,** ce n'est pas peu dire. *adv.* **He is a good deal better,** il va beaucoup mieux. *He is a great d. wiser than you,* il est de beaucoup plus sage que vous.

deal², *s.* **1.** *Cards:* La donne; la main. **Whose deal is it?** à qui de faire, de donner? **2.** *Com:* *F:* Affaire *f*, marché *m.* **To do a deal with s.o.,** conclure un marché avec qn. *F:* **To give s.o. a square deal,** agir loyalement envers qn. *Pej:* Deal between parties, tractation *f* entre partis.

deal³, *v.* (dealt [delt]; dealt) I. *v.tr.* **1.** To deal out gifts, distribuer, répartir, partager, des dons (*to, among,* entre). **2. To deal a blow,** donner, porter, allonger, asséner, un coup (*at,* à). **3.** Donner, distribuer (les cartes). II. **deal,** *v.i.* **1.** (*a*) **To have to deal with s.o.,** avoir affaire à, avec, qn. *Man easy to d. with,* homme commode, accommodant. (*b*) **To deal with a subject,** traiter, s'occuper, d'un sujet. **2.** (*a*) **To deal with a piece of business,** conclure, terminer, une affaire. *To d. with a difficulty,* venir à bout d'une difficulté. (*b*) **To deal with a culprit,** disposer d'un coupable; faire justice à un coupable. *I know how to d. with him,* je sais comment il faut le traiter. **To deal well, badly, by s.o.,** en user bien, mal, avec qn. **3.** *Com:* **To deal with s.o.,** traiter, négocier, avec qn. **To deal in leather,** faire le commerce des cuirs. *F:* *To d. in politics,* se mêler de politique. **4.** *Cards:* Faire la donne; donner; *F:* faire. **dealing,** *s.* **1. Dealing (out),** distribution *f* (de dons, etc.); distribution, donne *f* (de cartes). **2.** *pl.* (*a*) **To have dealings with s.o.,** avoir des relations, des rapports, entretenir des relations, avec qn. (*b*) *Pej:* Accointances *f*, tractations *f* (*with,* avec); tripotage *m.* Underhand dealings, menées sourdes, sournoises. **3.** (*a*) Conduite *f*, procédé *m.* **Fair, square, dealing(s),** loyauté *f*, honnêteté *f* (en affaires). *S.a.* DOUBLE-DEALING. (*b*) **One's dealings with the world,** le commerce de la vie.

deal⁴, *s.* **1.** (*a*) Madrier *m.* (*b*) Planche *f* (à planchéier). **2.** Bois *m* de pin ou de sapin; *esp.* white deal, sapin blanc, bois blanc.

dealer ['di:lər], *s.* **1.** *Cards:* Donneur *m.* **2.** *Com:* (*a*) Négociant *m* (in, en); distributeur *m* (in, de). (*b*) Marchand *m*, -ande, fournisseur *m* (in, de). (*c*) *St.Exch:* = JOBBER 3.

dean [di:n], *s. Ecc: Sch:* Doyen *m.*
deanery ['di:nəri], *s. Ecc:* 1. Doyenné *m.*
2. Résidence *f* du doyen.
dear ['di:ər]. I. *a.* (*a*) Cher (*to*, à). To hold s.o.
dear, chérir, aimer, qn. *F:* My dear fellow,
mon cher ; mon ami. Dear Madam, Madame,
Mademoiselle. Dear Sir, *D. Mr Smith,* Cher
Monsieur. To run for dear life, courir de toutes
ses forces. (*b*) Cher, coûteux. (*Of food, etc.*) To
get dear, dearer, enchérir, renchérir. **-ly,** *adv.*
1. Cher, chèrement. *You shall pay d. for this,*
cela vous coûtera cher. 2. Dearly loved, tendrement aimé(e), bien aimé(e). *He d. loves his house,*
il est fort attaché à sa maison. II. **dear,** *s.*
Cher, *f.* chère. My dear, cher ami, mon ami(e).
III. **dear,** *adv.* 1. (Vendre, payer) cher. 2. He
sold his life dear, il vendit chèrement sa vie.
IV. **dear,** *int.* Dear dear! dear me! mon Dieu,
mon Dieu ! Oh dear! (i) oh là là ! (ii) hélas !
dearness ['di:ərnəs], *s.* 1. Cherté *f* (des vivres,
etc.). 2. (*a*) Tendresse *f.* (*b*) Degré *m* d'affection.
dearth [də:rθ], *s.* Disette *f,* pénurie *f* (de vivres,
de livres, etc.) ; dénuement *m,* stérilité *f* (d'idées).
death [deθ], *s.* 1. Mort *f*; *Lit:* trépas *m.* To
die a violent death, mourir de mort violente.
Till death, pour la vie. Faithful unto death,
fidèle jusqu'au tombeau. You will catch your
death *if you go out in this weather,* vous allez
attraper la mort si vous sortez par ce temps.
F: He'll be the death of me, (i) il me fera mourir ;
(ii) il me fait mourir de rire. *F:* To be death on
sth., ne pas souffrir qch. To put s.o. to death,
mettre qn à mort ; exécuter qn. To do s.o. to
death, faire souffrir une mort cruelle à qn ;
F: égorger qn. *F:* Meat done to death, viande
carbonisée. Fashion that has been done to death,
mode qui a été copiée jusqu'à la nausée. *Wounded
to the death,* blessé à mort. To be sick (un)to
death, être malade à mourir. To drink oneself
to death, se tuer à force de boire. To be in at
the death, (i) *Ven:* être à la curée, à l'hallali ;
(ii) *F:* être présent au bon moment, pour le
bouquet. 2. *Jur:* Décès *m.* To notify a death,
notifier un décès. Death notices (*in newspaper*),
avis *m* mortuaires. *Journ:* Deaths, Nécrologie *f.*
3. La mort. To be at death's door, être à toute
extrémité ; être à l'article de la mort. **'death-
bed,** *s.* Lit *m* de mort. Death-bed confession,
aveu fait au lit de mort. **'death-bell,** *s.* Glas *m.*
'death-blow, *s.* Coup mortel, fatal. **'death-
chamber,** *s.* Chambre *f* mortuaire. **'death-
duty,** *s. Adm:* Droit *m* de mutation par décès ;
droit de succession. **'death-mask,** *s.* Masque *m*
mortuaire. **'death-rate,** *s.* (Taux *m* de la)
mortalité. **'death-rattle,** *s.* Râle *m* (de la
mort). **'death-roll,** *s.* Liste *f* des morts ;
nécrologe *m.* **'death's-head,** *s.* Tête *f* de mort.
'death-trap, *s.* Endroit dangereux pour la vie ;
coupe-gorge *m inv,* casse-cou *m inv.* **'death-
warrant,** *s. Jur:* Ordre *m* d'exécution ; arrêt *m*
de mort. **'death-watch(-beetle),** *s. Ent:*
Horloge *f* de la mort ; vrillette *f.* **'death-
wound,** *s.* Blessure mortelle.
deathless ['deθləs], *a.* Impérissable, immortel.
deathlike ['deθlaik], *a.* De mort ; (teint)
cadavéreux.
deathly ['deθli]. *Lit:* 1. *a.* (*a*) = DEADLY 1 (*a*).
(*b*) = DEATHLIKE. 2. *adv.* D. pale, d'une pâleur
mortelle.
debar [di'bɑ:r], *v.tr.* (debarred) 1. To debar s.o.
from sth., exclure, priver, qn de qch. To debar
s.o. from doing sth., défendre, interdire, à qn de
faire qch. 2. To debar s.o. a right, refuser un
droit à qn ; priver qn d'un droit.

debase [di'beis], *v.tr.* 1. Avilir, ravaler, dégrader
(qn) ; rabaisser, trivialiser (son style). 2. (*a*) Altérer (la monnaie). (*b*) Déprécier (la monnaie).
debasing, *a.* Avilissant.
debasement [di'beismənt], *s.* 1. Avilissement *m,*
dégradation *f.* 2. Altération *f* (des monnaies).
debatable [di'beitəbl], *a.* Contestable, discutable.
debate[1] [di'beit], *s.* Débat *m,* discussion *f*;
conférence *f* contradictoire. The question in
debate, under debate, la question en discussion.
debate[2]. 1. *v.tr.* Débattre contradictoirement,
discuter, agiter (une question, etc.). *A much
debated question,* une question fort controversée.
I was debating in my mind whether . . ., je
délibérais si. . . . 2. *v.i.* Discuter, disputer (*with
s.o. on sth.,* avec qn sur qch.). Debating society,
parlot(t)e *f.*
debauch[1] [di'bɔ:tʃ], *s.* 1. La débauche. 2. *To
have a d.,* faire une débauche ; faire la noce.
debauch[2], *v.tr.* Débaucher, corrompre (qn) ;
vicier (le goût). **debauched,** *a.* Débauché,
corrompu.
debauchee [debɔ:'(t)ʃi:], *s.* Débauché *m.*
debauchery [di'bɔ:ʃəri], *s.* Débauche *f*; dérèglement *m* de mœurs.
debenture [di'bentjər], *s. Fin:* Obligation *f.*
Mortgage debenture, obligation hypothécaire.
de'benture-'holder, *s. Fin:* Porteur, -euse,
d'obligations ; obligataire *m.*
debilitate [di'biliteit], *v.tr.* Débiliter.
debility [di'biliti], *s. Med:* Débilité *f.*
debit[1] ['debit], *s. Book-k:* Débit *m,* doit *m.* To
enter sth. to the debit(-side) of an account, porter
qch. au débit, au doit, d'un compte. Debit
balance, solde débiteur. *Account showing a d.
balance,* compte déficitaire.
debit[2], *v.tr. Book-k:* 1. Débiter (un compte).
2. To d. s.o. with a sum, inscrire, porter, une
somme au débit de qn.
debonair [debɔ'nɛər], *a. Lit:* Jovial, -aux.
debouch [di'bu:ʃ], *v.i.* Déboucher (*into,* dans).
debouchment [di'bu:ʃmənt], *s.* 1. Débouchement *m* (de troupes, d'un fleuve). 2. Débouché *m,*
sortie *f* (d'un défilé, etc.).
Debrett [di'bret]. *Pr.n.* Debrett's Peerage, almanach *m* nobiliaire.
debris ['debri:], *s.* Débris *mpl* ; détritus *mpl*
(géologiques).
debt [det], *s.* Dette *f* ; créance *f.* Bad debts,
mauvaises créances, créances véreuses. To be in
debt, être endetté ; avoir des dettes. *F:* To be
head over ears, up to the eyes, in debt, être
criblé de dettes ; avoir des dettes par-dessus la
tête. *I shall always be in your d.,* je serai toujours
votre obligé ; je vous serai toujours redevable.
To be twenty francs in d., avoir vingt francs de
dettes. To be out of debt, être quitte de dettes ;
n'avoir plus de dettes. Funded debt, consolidated debt, fonds consolidés. *F:* To pay the
debt of, to, nature, payer sa dette, le tribut,
à l'humanité, à la nature. **'debt-collector,** *s.
Com:* Agent *m* de recouvrements.
debtor ['detər], *s.* 1. Débiteur, -trice. *I am your
d. for £100,* je vous suis redevable de £100.
2. *Book-k:* Debtor side, débit *m,* doit *m.* Debtor
account, compte débiteur. Debtor and creditor
account, compte par doit et avoir.
debunk [di'bʌŋk], *v.tr. P:* Débronzer (un grand
nom). 'Napoleon debunked,' "Napoléon dégonflé."
début ['debu:, de'by:], *s.* Début *m* ; (*in society*)
entrée *f* dans le monde.
débutante [deby'tɑ̃t], *s.f.* Débutante.

decade [′dekəd, di′keid], *s.* **1.** Période *f* de dix ans. **2.** *Ecc:* Dizain *m* de chapelet.

decadence [′dekadəns, di′keidəns], *s.* Décadence *f*.

decadent [′dekadənt, di′keidənt], *a.* En décadence; décadent.

decagon [′dekagən], *s. Geom:* Décagone *m.*

decamp [di′kamp], *v.i.* **1.** *Mil:* Lever le camp. **2.** *F:* Décamper, filer.

decant [di′kant], *v.tr.* Décanter, transvaser (un liquide); tirer (un liquide) au clair.

decantation [di:kan′teiʃ(ə)n], *s.* Décantation *f*, décantage *m*; transvasement *m.*

decanter [di′kantər], *s.* Carafe *f* (à liqueur, à vin).

decapitate [di′kapiteit], *v.tr.* Décapiter; couper la tête à (qn).

decapitation [dikapi′teiʃ(ə)n], *s.* Décapitation *f.*

decarbonization [di:kɑ:rbənai′zeiʃ(ə)n], *I.C.E:* Décarbonisation *f*, décalaminage *m*, décrassage *m* (du moteur)

decarbonize [di:′kɑ:rbənaiz], *v.tr.* **1.** *Metall: Ind:* Décarburer (la fonte, etc.). **2.** *I.C.E:* Décarboniser, décalaminer (un cylindre).

decarburize [di:′kɑ:rbjuraiz], *v.tr. Ind:* = DE-CARBONIZE I.

decasyllable [deka′siləbl], *a. & s. Pros:* Décasyllabe ‚*m*).

decay[1] [′di′kei], *s.* **1.** Décadence *f* (d'une famille, d'un pays); déclin *m* (de la beauté, d'une fortune); délabrement *m* (d'un bâtiment). Senile decay, affaiblissement *m* sénile. To fall into decay, (*of house*) tomber en ruine, se délabrer; (*of state*) tomber en décadence; (*of custom*) tomber en désuétude. To be in a state of d., être en ruine, en décadence. **2.** (*a*) Pourriture *f*, corruption *f*; putréfaction *f*; altération *f* (du caoutchouc, etc.). (*b*) Carie *f* (des dents).

decay[2]. **1.** *v.i.* (*a*) Tomber en décadence; (*of building*) tomber en ruine; se délabrer; (*of race, plant*) dépérir; (*of empire*) décliner; (*of custom*) se perdre. (*b*) (*Of meat, fruit*) Se gâter, s'altérer, s'avarier, pourrir; (*of teeth*) se carier. **2.** *v.tr.* Pourrir (le bois, etc.); carier (les dents).

decayed, *a.* **1.** (Famille) déchue, ruinée; (fleur, beauté) passée, flétrie; (maison, fortune) délabrée. Decayed gentlewoman, dame (bien née) tombée dans la gêne. **2.** (Bois) pourri; (fruit) gâté. Decayed tooth, dent gâtée.

decease[1] [di′si:s], *s. Jur: Adm:* Décès *m.*

decease[2], *v.i. Jur: Adm:* Décéder. **deceased. 1.** *a.* (*a*) Décédé. Mary Smith, deceased, feue Mary Smith. (*b*) D'un décédé. Deceased estate, succession *f.* **2.** *s.* Le défunt, la défunte. The house of the d., la maison mortuaire.

deceit [di′si:t], *s.* Tromperie *f*, duperie *f*, fourberie *f.* A piece of deceit, une supercherie.

deceitful [di′si:tful], *a.* Trompeur, -euse; fourbe; faux, *f.* fausse; (regard) mensonger. **-fully,** *adv.* **1.** Frauduleusement; par supercherie. **2.** Faussement; avec duplicité.

deceitfulness [di′si:tfulnəs], *s.* Nature trompeuse; fausseté *f.*

deceive [di′si:v], *v.tr.* Tromper, abuser (qn); en imposer à (qn). To d. oneself, se tromper, s'abuser. To d. oneself with a fond hope, se leurrer d'un espoir. I thought my eyes were deceiving me, *F:* j'ai cru avoir la berlue. **deceiving,** *a.* Trompeur, -euse; décevant. **-ly,** *adv.* Trompeusement.

deceiver [di′si:vər], *s.* Trompeur, -euse; fourbe *m.*

December [di′sembər], *s.* Décembre *m.* In December, au mois de décembre, en décembre.

(*On*) the first, the seventh, of D., le premier, le sept, décembre.

decency [′di:sənsi], *s.* **1.** Décence *f*, bienséance *f* (de costume, etc.). **2.** Bienséance, convenance(s) *f(pl)*, décence, honnêteté *f.* The decencies, common decency, les convenances (sociales); le respect humain. **3.** (Sense of) decency, pudeur *f.*

decennial [di′senjəl], *a.* Décennal, -aux. **-ally,** *adv.* Tous les dix ans.

decent [′di:sənt], *a.* **1.** (*a*) Bienséant, convenable. (*b*) Décent, honnête, modeste. **2.** *F:* Passable; assez bon. To have a d. competence, avoir une honnête aisance. **3.** *F:* A very decent (sort of) fellow, un très bon garçon; un brave garçon. Quite d. people, des gens très comme il faut. **4.** *adv. F:* Decent-sized house, maison d'une grandeur raisonnable. **-ly,** *adv.* **1.** Décemment, convenablement. **2.** Passablement; assez bien.

decentralization [di:sentrəlai′zeiʃ(ə)n], *s.* Décentralisation (administrative, etc.).

decentralize [di:′sentrəlaiz], *v.tr.* Décentraliser.

deception [di′sepʃ(ə)n], *s.* **1.** Tromperie *f*, duperie *f*; fraude *f.* **2.** (Piece of) deception, supercherie *f.*

deceptive [di′septiv], *a.* (Of thg, appearance) Trompeur, -euse; décevant, mensonger. **-ly,** *adv.* Trompeusement, mensongèrement.

decide [di′said]. **1.** *v.tr.* (*a*) Décider (une question, une querelle); trancher (une question); juger (un différend); statuer sur (une affaire). (*b*) Décider de (qch.). To d. s.o.'s fate, décider du sort de qn. Nothing has been decided yet, il n'y a encore rien de décidé. (*c*) To decide s.o. to do sth., décider qn à faire qch. (*d*) To decide to do sth., se décider, se résoudre, à faire qch.; décider, résoudre, de faire qch. It was decided to await his reply, on décida d'attendre sa réponse. I have decided what I shall do, mon parti est pris. **2.** *v.i.* To decide (up)on sth., se décider à qch. To d. on doing sth., se décider à, décider de, faire qch. To d. upon a day, fixer un jour. To decide for, in favour of, s.o., se décider pour, en faveur de, qn. **decided,** *a.* **1.** (*a*) They are quite d. about it, ils sont tout à fait décidés (là-dessus). (*b*) (Of opinion) Arrêté; (of manner) décidé. In a d. tone, d'un ton net, résolu, tranchant. A d. refusal, un refus catégorique. **2.** (Of improvement, etc.) Incontestable. A decided difference, une différence marquée. **-ly,** *adv.* **1.** (Agir, répondre) résolument, avec décision. **2.** Incontestablement, décidément. **deciding,** *a.* Décisif. The deciding game, la belle.

deciduous [di′sidjuəs], *a.* Caduc, *f.* caduque.

decigram [′desigram], *s. Meas:* Décigramme *m.*

decimal [′desim(ə)l]. **1.** *a.* Décimal, -aux. *Mth:* Decimal point = virgule *f.* **2.** *s.* Décimale *f.* Recurring decimal, fraction *f* périodique. Correct to five places of decimals, exact jusqu'à la cinquième décimale.

decimate [′desimeit], *v.tr.* Décimer (des mutinés, etc.).

decimation [desi′meiʃ(ə)n], *s.* Décimation *f.*

decimetre [′desimi:tər], *s. Meas:* Décimètre *m.*

decipher [di′saifər], *v.tr.* Déchiffrer; transcrire en clair (une dépêche chiffrée). **deciphering,** *s.* Déchiffrement *m*; transcription *f* en clair.

decipherable [di′saifərəbl], *a.* Déchiffrable.

decision [di′siʒ(ə)n], *s.* **1.** (*a*) Décision *f* (d'une question), délibération *f* (d'une assemblée). (*b*) Décision, jugement *m*, arrêt *m.* **2.** Décision, résolution *f.* To come to, reach, a decision, arriver à, prendre, une décision; prendre un

parti. *To abide by one's d.*, s'en tenir à sa décision.
3. Résolution (de caractère) ; fermeté *f*, décision.
decisive [di'saisiv], *a.* **1.** Décisif ; *(of experiment)* concluant. **2.** *(a)* (Ton) tranchant, net. *(b)* = DE-
CIDED **2.** **-ly,** *adv.* Décisivement.
deck[1] [dek], *s.* **1.** *(a) Nau :* Pont *m.* Aft(er)-deck, pont arrière. Lower deck, pont inférieur ; premier pont. Upper deck, pont supérieur ; pont des gaillards. To come, go, on deck, monter sur le pont. *Navy :* The lower-deck ratings, *F :* the lower deck, le personnel non officier. Upper-deck ratings, hommes du pont. *(b)* Top deck *(of bus, etc.),* impériale *f.* **2.** *Civ.E :* Tablier *m* ; plancher *m* (d'un pont). **'deck-chair,** *s.* Transatlantique *m* ; *F :* transa(t) *m.* **'deck-hand,** *s.* Homme *m* de pont, matelot *m* de pont. **'deck-house,** *s. Nau :* Rouf *m*, roufle *m.* **'deck-light,** *s. Nau :* Claire-voie *f* (dans le pont).
deck[2], *v.tr.* **1.** Parer, orner, agrémenter *(with,* de). To deck oneself out, s'endimancher ; se mettre sur son trente et un. *S.a.* FLAG[4] 1. **2.** *N.Arch :* To deck a ship, ponter un navire. **-decked,** *a. Nau :* Two-, three-decked, à deux, à trois, ponts.
decking, *s.* **1.** Decking (out), décoration *f.* **2.** Pontage *m* (d'un navire). **3.** *Coll.* (Les) ponts *m* (d'un navire).
-decker ['dekər], *s. Nau :* A three-decker, un vaisseau à trois ponts ; un trois-ponts.
deckle-edged ['dekl'edʒd], *a.* (Papier) à bords non ébarbés, à bords déchiquetés.
declaim [di'kleim]. **1.** *v.i.* Déclamer *(against,* contre). **2.** *v.tr.* Déclamer.
declamation [deklə'mei§(ə)n], *s.* Déclamation *f.*
declamatory [di'klamətəri], *a.* (Style) déclamatoire, déclamateur.
declaration [deklə'rei§(ə)n], *s.* *(a)* Déclaration *f.* Customs declaration, déclaration de, en, douane. *(b) Cards :* Annonce *f.*
declare [di'klɛər]. **1.** *v.tr. (a)* Déclarer *(sth. to s.o.,* qch. à qn). He declared he had seen nothing, il déclara, affirma, n'avoir rien vu. To declare war, déclarer la guerre *(on, against,* à). *(At the customs)* Have you anything to declare ? avez-vous quelque chose à déclarer ? *F :* Well, I declare! par exemple ! *S.a.* POLL[1] 2. *(b) Pred.* To d. *s.o.* guilty, déclarer qn coupable. To d. *s.o.* King, déclarer qn roi. *F :* To declare the bargain off, rompre le marché. *(c) Cards :* To declare trumps, appeler l'atout. *Abs.* To declare, annoncer son jeu. *F :* To declare one's hand, avouer ses intentions. *(d)* To declare oneself, (i) prendre parti ; (ii) *(of lover)* faire sa déclaration. *(Of disease)* To d. *itself,* se déclarer, éclater. **2.** *v.i.* To declare for, against, sth., se déclarer, se prononcer, pour, contre, qch. **declared,** *a.* Ouvert, avoué, déclaré.
declaredly [di'klɛəridli], *adv.* Ouvertement.
declension [di'klen§(ə)n], *s. Gram :* Déclinaison *f.*
declinable [di'klainəbl], *a. Gram :* Déclinable.
declination [dekli'nei§(ə)n], *s. Astr :* Déclinaison *f.*
decline[1] [di'klain], *s.* **1.** Déclin *m* (du jour, d'un empire) ; baisse *f* (de prix). To be on the decline, être sur le déclin ; décliner ; *(of pers.)* être sur le retour (d'âge) ; *(of prices)* être en baisse. **2.** Maladie *f* de langueur ; consumption *f*, étisie *f.* To go into a decline, entrer en consomption.
decline[2]. **1.** *v.tr.* **1.** *(a)* Refuser courtoisement (une invitation): décliner (un honneur). *Abs.* S'excuser. *(b)* Refuser ; repousser (l'intervention de qn). To d. to do sth., refuser de faire qch.

2. *Gram :* Décliner (un nom, etc.). **II. decline,** *v.i.* **1.** *(Of ground, etc.)* S'incliner ; être en pente. **2.** *(a) (Of sun, etc.)* Décliner ; *(of day)* tirer à sa fin. *(b) (Of health, etc.)* Décliner, baisser ; *(of empire)* tomber en décadence ; *(of prices)* baisser ; être en baisse. **declining,** *a.* Sur son déclin. *D. sun,* soleil couchant. In one's declining years, au déclin de la vie.
declivitous [di'klivitəs], *a.* Déclive ; escarpé.
declivity [di'kliviti], *s.* Déclivité *f*, pente *f.*
declutch [di:'klʌt§], *v.i. Aut :* Débrayer, désembrayer.
decode [di:'koud], *v.tr.* Déchiffrer, transcrire en clair (une dépêche). **decoding,** *s.* Déchiffrement *m* ; transcription *f* en clair.
decoke [di:'kouk], *v.tr. F :* = DECARBONIZE 2.
decompose [di:kom'pouz]. **1.** *v.tr. (a)* Décomposer, analyser (la lumière, etc.). *(b)* Décomposer, corrompre (la matière). **2.** *v.i. (a)* Se décomposer. *(b)* Entrer en décomposition ; pourrir.
decomposition [di:kompo'zi§(ə)n], *s.* Décomposition *f.* **1.** Résolution *f* en parties simples. **2.** Désintégration *f* ; putréfaction *f.*
decompression [di:kom'pre§(ə)n], *s. Mch : etc :* Décompression *f.*
decompressor [di:kom'presər], *s. I.C.E :* Décompresseur *m.*
deconsecrate [di:'konsekreit], *v.tr.* Séculariser, désaffecter (une église).
deconsecration [di:konse'krei§(ə)n], *s.* Sécularisation *f*, désaffectation *f.*
decorate ['dekoreit], *v.tr.* **1.** *(a)* Décorer, orner, agrémenter *(with,* de) ; pavoiser (une rue). *(b)* Peindre et tapisser, décorer (un appartement). **2.** Médailler, décorer (un soldat, etc.).
decoration [deko'rei§(ə)n], *s.* **1.** *(a)* Décoration *f* ; parement *m* (d'une façade) ; pavoisement *m* (des rues). *(b)* Remise *f* d'une décoration (à qn). **2.** *(a) Usu. pl.* (Les) décorations (d'une ville en fête, etc.) ; décor *m* (d'un appartement, etc.). *(b)* Décoration, médaille *f.*
decorative ['dekorətiv], *a.* Décoratif.
decorator ['dekoreitər], *s.* Décorateur *m.* (House) decorator, peintre décorateur (d'appartements) ; tapissier *m.*
decorous [de'kɔ:rəs, 'dekərəs], *a.* Bienséant, convenable ; comme il faut.
decorticate [di'kɔ:rtikeit], *v.tr.* Décortiquer.
decorum [de'kɔ:rəm], *s.* Décorum *m*, bienséance *f.*
decoy[1] [di'kɔi], *s.* Appât *m*, piège *m*, leurre *m*, amorce *f.* **Decoy-bird,** oiseau *m* de leurre ; moquette *f* ; *F :* chanterelle *f.* **Decoy-duck,** (i) canard privé ; (ii) compère *m* (d'un escroc).
decoy[2], *v.tr.* **1.** Piper, leurrer (des oiseaux). **2.** Leurrer, amorcer (qn). To d. *s.o. into a trap,* entraîner, attirer, qn dans un piège. To d. *s.o. into doing sth.,* entraîner qn à faire qch.
decrease[1] ['di:kri:s], *s.* Diminution *f*, décroissance *f*, amoindrissement *m.* D. in speed, ralentissement *m.* Imports are on the decrease, les importations sont en décroissance.
decrease[2] [di'kri:s]. **1.** *v.tr.* Diminuer, faire décroître, amoindrir. **2.** *v.i.* Diminuer ; décroître ; s'amoindrir. **decreasing,** *a.* Décroissant, diminuant. **-ly,** *adv.* De moins en moins.
decree[1] [di'kri:], *s.* **1.** *Adm :* Décret *m*, édit *m*, arrêté *m* ; ordonnance (royale). To issue a decree, promulguer un décret. **2.** *Jur :* Décision *f*, arrêt *m*, jugement *m.* Decree nisi ['naisai], jugement provisoire (en matière de divorce).
decree[2], *v.tr.* Décréter, ordonner.

decrement ['dekrimənt], s. **1.** Décroissement m, décroissance f. **2.** Perte f, diminution f.

decrepit [di'krepit], a. **1.** (Of pers.) Décrépit; caduc, -uque. **2.** (Of thg) Vermoulu; qui tombe en ruine.

decrepitude [di'krepitjud], s. **1.** Décrépitude f; caducité f. **2.** Vermoulure f.

decrescent [di'kres(ə)nt], a. Décroissant; en décroissance.

decry [di'krai], v.tr. Décrier, dénigrer.

decuple[1] ['dekjupl], a. & s. Décuple (m).

decuple[2]. **1.** v.tr. Décupler. **2.** v.i. Se décupler.

dedicate ['dedikeit], v.tr. **1.** Dédier, consacrer (une église). To d. oneself, one's life, to sth., se vouer à qch. **2.** Dédier (un livre, etc.) (to, à).

dedication [dedi'keiʃ(ə)n], s. **1.** Dédicace f, consécration f (d'une église). **2.** Dédicace (d'un livre).

dedicatory [dedi'keitəri], a. Dédicatoire.

deduce [di'dju:s], v.tr. Déduire, inférer, conclure (from, de).

deduct [di'dʌkt], v.tr. Déduire, retrancher (from, de). To d. sth. from the price, rabattre qch. sur le prix.

deduction [di'dʌkʃ(ə)n], s. **1.** Déduction f (from a quantity, sur une quantité); (of pay) retenue f. **2.** (a) Raisonnement déductif; déduction. (b) Déduction, conclusion f (from, tirée de).

deductive [di'dʌktiv], a. Déductif.

deed [di:d], s. **1.** (a) Action f, acte m. **Man of deeds**, homme d'action, d'exécution. (b) Deed of valour, haut fait; exploit m. (c) Foul deed, forfait m. S.a. ILL I. **1.** (d) Fait. He was ruler in deed, though not in name, c'était lui, dans le fait, qui était le chef, bien qu'il n'en portât pas le titre. Cf. INDEED. **2.** Jur: Acte notarié, sur papier timbré, et signé par les parties. To draw up a d., rédiger un acte. **'deed-box**, s. Coffret m à documents. **'deed-'poll**, s. Jur: Acte unilatéral.

deem [di:m], v.tr. Juger, estimer, croire. I do not d. it necessary to . . ., je ne juge pas, ne crois pas, nécessaire de. . . . To deem highly of s.o., avoir une haute opinion de qn. S.a. ADVISABLE 2.

deemster ['di:mstər], s. Juge m (dans l'île de Man).

deep [di:p]. I. a. **1.** (a) Profond. To be ten feet deep, avoir dix pieds de profondeur; être profond de dix pieds. **Deep end**, bout le plus profond (de la piscine). P: To go (in) off the deep end, (i) se mettre en colère; (ii) prendre les choses au tragique. Deep in debt, in study, criblé de dettes; absorbé, plongé, dans l'étude. S.a. ANKLE, KNEE-DEEP, WAIST-DEEP. (b) D. shelves, rayons larges. Man d. in the chest, homme à forte poitrine. Mil: Two, four, deep, sur deux, quatre, rangs. The crowd on the pavement was twelve deep, sur le trottoir la foule formait une haie d'une douzaine de rangs. (c) D. sigh, profond soupir. D. thinker, penseur profond. **2.** (a) (Of colour) Foncé, sombre. (b) (Of sound) Profond, grave. In a deep voice, d'une voix profonde. **3.** D. sorrow, despair, chagrin profond, profond désespoir. D. concern, vive préoccupation. S.a. MOURNING 2. **4.** (Of conduct) Difficile à pénétrer; (of pers.) rusé, malin, astucieux. D. scheme, projet ténébreux. **-ly**, adv. Profondément. To go d. into sth., pénétrer, entrer, fort avant dans qch. II. deep, adv. **1.** Profondément. **Deep-lying causes**, causes profondes. Prov: Still waters run deep, il n'y a pire eau que l'eau qui dort. **2.** The harpoon sank d. into the flesh, le harpon pénétra très avant dans les chairs.

D. into the night, très avant dans la nuit. III. **deep**, s. **1.** The deep. (a) Les profondeurs f, l'abîme m, le gouffre. (b) L'océan m. To commit a body to the deep, immerger un mort. **2.** In the deep of winter, au plus profond de l'hiver. **'deep-'chested**, a. (Homme) à forte poitrine. **'deep-'drawn**, a. (Soupir) profond. **'deep-'laid**, a. (Complot) ténébreux. **'deep-'rooted**, a. Profondément enraciné. **'deep-'sea**, attrib. a. **Deep-sea fishery**, (i) pêche hauturière; (ii) grande pêche (de Terre-Neuve, etc.). S.a. PILOT[1] 1. **'deep-'seated**, a. Profond, enraciné. **'deep-'set**, a. (Yeux) enfoncés, creux.

deepen [di:pn]. **1.** v.tr. (a) Approfondir, creuser (un puits, etc.). (b) Rendre (un sentiment) plus intense. (c) Foncer (une couleur); rendre (un son) plus grave, plus sonore. **2.** v.i. (a) Devenir plus profond; s'approfondir. The river deepens below London, le fleuve prend de la profondeur en aval de Londres. (b) (Of colour) Devenir plus foncé; (of sound) devenir plus grave. **deepening**, s. **1.** Approfondissement m. **2.** Augmentation f de profondeur, d'intensité.

deepness ['di:pnəs], s. **1.** Profondeur f (de la voix, etc.). Mus: Gravité f (d'un son). **2.** Astuce f (d'une personne).

deer [di:ər], s. inv. (Red) deer, (i) cerf commun; (ii) Coll. cervidés mpl. **Fallow deer**, daim m. **'deer-hound**, s. Limier m; lévrier m d'Écosse. **'deer-stalker**, s. **1.** Chasseur m (de cerf) à l'affût. **2.** Chapeau m de chasse. **'deer-stalking**, s. Chasse f (du cerf) à l'affût.

deerskin ['di:ərskin], s. Peau f de daim.

deface [di'feis], v.tr. Défigurer; mutiler (une statue); dégrader (une porte); lacérer (une affiche); oblitérer (un timbre).

defacement [di'feismənt], s. Défiguration f, mutilation f (d'une statue, etc.); lacération f (d'une affiche); oblitération f.

defalcate [di'falkeit], v.i. Détourner des fonds.

defalcation [di:fal'keiʃ(ə)n], s. **1.** Détournement m de fonds. **2.** Fonds manquants: déficit m (de caisse).

defamation [di:fa'meiʃ(ə)n], s. Diffamation f.

defamatory [di'famətəri], a. Diffamatoire, diffamant.

defame [di'feim], v.tr. Diffamer (qn); salir le nom de (qn).

defamer [di'feimər], s. Diffamateur, -trice.

default[1] [di'fɔ:lt], s. **1.** (a) Manquement m (à un engagement). (b) St.Exch: Déconfiture f. **2.** Jur: Défaut m; non-comparution f; (criminal law) contumace f. Judgment by default, jugement par défaut, par contumace. Sp: Match won by default, match gagné par forfait. **3.** Carence f. (a) Com: Default in paying, défaut de paiement. (b) Jur: Default of heirs, déshérence f. (c) Prep.phr. In default of . . ., à, au, défaut de . . .; faute de. . . .

default[2], v.i. (a) Jur: Faire défaut; être en état de contumace. (b) St.Exch: Manquer à ses engagements; tomber en déconfiture.

defaulter [di'fɔ:ltər], s. **1.** (a) Délinquant -ante. (b) Jur: Contumace mf. Mil: Navy: (a) Retardataire m, réfractaire m (Undergoing punishment) Consigne m. **2.** Auteur m de détournements de fonds; (of public money) concussionnaire m. St.Exch: Défaillant m.

defeat[1] [di'fi:t], s. **1.** Défaite f. To suffer, sustain a defeat, essuyer une défaite. **2.** Renversement m (d'un projet); insuccès m (d'une entreprise).

defeat[2], v.tr. **1.** Battre, défaire, vaincre (une armée). **2.** Renverser, faire échouer (un projet)

To d. the ends of justice, contrarier la justice. *To d. one's own object,* aller à l'encontre de ses propres intentions.

defeatism [di'fi:tizm], *s.* Défaitisme *m.*

defeatist [di'fi:tist], *s.* Défaitiste *mf.*

defect [di'fekt], *s.* **1.** Défaut *m,* insuffisance *f,* manque *m* (*of,* de). **2.** Défaut, imperfection *f*; (*in horse*) tare *f.* **Defect of eyesight,** trouble visuel. **Physical defect,** défaut; vice *m* de conformation.

defection [di'fekʃ(ə)n], *s.* Défection *f.*

defective [di'fektiv]. **1.** *a.* (*a*) Défectueux, imparfait; (*of formation*) vicieux. *D. child,* enfant anormal. *S.a.* MENTALLY. **Defective brakes,** freins mauvais. (*b*) *Gram:* (Verbe, etc.) défectif. **2.** *s.* **Mental defective,** *see* MENTAL. **-ly,** *adv.* Défectueusement.

defence [di'fens], *s.* **1.** Défense *f,* protection *f.* *S.a.* SELF-DEFENCE. **2.** *Mil:* Défences, défenses. **3.** (*a*) Défense, justification *f,* apologie *f.* (*b*) *Jur:* Défense. **Counsel for the defence,** défenseur *m*; (*in civil law*) avocat *m* de la défense. **Witness for the defence,** témoin *m* à décharge. **To set up a defence,** établir, présenter, une défense. **In his defence** *it may be said that* . . ., l'on pourrait dire, à sa décharge, que. . . .

defenceless [di'fensləs], *a.* Sans défense. **1.** (*a*) Sans protection. (*b*) Incapable de se défendre. **2.** Désarmé; sans moyen de défense.

defend [di'fend], *v.tr.* **1.** Défendre, protéger (*from, against,* contre). **2.** (*a*) Faire l'apologie de (qn). (*b*) Défendre, justifier (une opinion). **3.** *Jur:* Défendre (un accusé).

defendant [di'fendənt], *a. & s. Jur:* (*a*) Défendeur, -eresse. (*b*) (*In criminal case*) Accusé, -ée.

defender [di'fendər], *s.* Défenseur *m.*

defensible [di'fensibl], *a.* **1.** (Frontière, cause) défendable. **2.** (Opinion) soutenable. **-ibly,** *adv.* D'une manière justifiable.

defensive [di'fensiv]. **1.** *a.* Défensif. **2.** *s.* Défensive *f.* **To be, stand, on the defensive,** se tenir, rester, sur la défensive. **-ly,** *adv.* Défensivement.

defer[1] [di'fə:r], *v.tr.* (deferred) Différer, ajourner, renvoyer, retarder (une affaire); reculer (un payement); suspendre (un jugement). *To d. doing sth.,* différer à, de, faire qch. **deferred,** *a.* (*Of share, telegram, etc.*) Différé. **Deferred payment,** paiement par versements échelonnés.

defer[2], *v.i.* Déférer. *To defer to s.o.'s opinion,* déférer, se rendre, à l'avis de qn.

deference ['defərəns], *s.* Déférence *f.* **To pay, show, deference to s.o.,** témoigner de la déférence à, envers, qn. **In, out of, deference to** . . ., par déférence pour. . . . *With all due deference to you,* sauf votre respect. *With all due d. to your father,* n'en déplaise à monsieur votre père.

deferential [defə'renʃ(ə)l], *a.* (Air, ton) de déférence.

deferment [di'fə:rmənt], *s.* Ajournement *m,* remise *f* (d'une affaire).

defiance [di'faiəns], *s.* Défi *m.* **To bid defiance to** s.o., narguer, porter, jeter, un défi à qn. **To set s.o. at defiance,** défier qn. **In defiance of the law,** au mépris de la loi.

defiant [di'faiənt], *a.* (*a*) Provocant; (regard, parole) de défi. (*b*) Qui repousse les avances; ntraitable. **-ly,** *adv.* D'un air de défi.

deficiency [di'fiʃənsi], *s.* **1.** Manque *m,* insuffisance *f,* défaut *m* (*of,* de) *S.a.* MENTAL. **2.** Défaut, faiblesse *f,* imperfection *f.* **3.** Déficit *m.* **4.** *Med:* Carence *f* (*in, of,* de); déficience *f.*

deficient [di'fiʃənt], *a.* (*a*) Défectueux, insuffisant, incomplet. *To be d. in sth.,* manquer, être dépourvu, de qch. (*b*) (Personne) à petite mentalité. *S.a.* MENTAL, MENTALLY.

deficit ['defisit, 'di:fisit], *s. Fin: Com:* Déficit *m.* *Budget that shows a d.,* budget en déficit, déficitaire.

defilade ['defileid], *v.tr. Fort:* Défiler (un ouvrage).

defile[1] ['di:fail], *s.* Défilé *m* (entre montagnes).

defile[2] [di'fail], *v.i.* (*Of troops*) Défiler. **defiling,** *s.* Défilé *m.*

defile[3] [di'fail], *v.tr.* Souiller, salir (ses mains); polluer (un lieu saint).

defilement [di'failmənt], *s.* Souillure *f*; pollution *f.* **Free from defilement,** sans tache, sans souillure.

definable [di'fainəbl], *a.* Définissable.

define [di'fain], *v.tr.* **1.** Définir. **To define one's position,** préciser son attitude (politique, etc.). **2.** Déterminer (l'étendue de qch.); délimiter (un territoire). **3.** **Well-defined outlines,** contours nettement dessinés.

definite ['definit], *a.* **1.** Défini; bien déterminé. *D. answer,* réponse catégorique. *D. intentions,* intentions bien arrêtées. *Com:* **Definite order,** commande ferme. **2.** *Gram:* **Definite article,** article défini. **Past definite,** passé défini. **-ly,** *adv.* D'une manière précise, bien déterminée. *He is d. better,* il va décidément mieux. *D. superior,* nettement supérieur.

definiteness ['definitnəs], *s.* Précision *f,* exactitude *f,* netteté *f.*

definition [defi'niʃ(ə)n], *s.* **1.** Définition *f.* **2.** *Opt:* Netteté *f* (de l'image).

definitive [de'finitiv], *a.* (Jugement, résultat) définitif. **-ly,** *adv.* Définitivement; en définitive.

deflagrate ['deflagreit]. *Ch:* **1.** *v.tr.* Faire déflagrer (du salpêtre, etc.). **2.** *v.i.* Déflagrer, fuser.

deflagration [deflə'greiʃ(ə)n], *s. Ch:* Déflagration *f.*

deflate [di'fleit], *v.tr.* (*a*) Dégonfler. **Deflated tyre,** pneu aplati, à plat. (*b*) *To d. the currency, abs.* **to deflate,** amener la déflation de la monnaie.

deflation [di'fleiʃ(ə)n], *s.* **1.** Dégonflement *m* (d'un ballon). **2.** *Fin:* Déflation *f.*

deflect [di'flekt]. **1.** *v.tr.* (Faire) dévier; détourner, défléchir. **2.** *v.i.* (*a*) (Se) dévier, se détourner, défléchir. (*b*) S'incurver; faire flèche.

deflection, deflexion [di'flekʃ(ə)n], *s.* **1.** Déflexion *f* (de la lumière); déviation *f* (de l'aiguille du compas). **2.** Déjettement *m,* déformation *f.* (*Sag*) Flèche *f,* flexion *f.*

deflower [di'flauər], *v.tr.* Déflorer.

defoliate [di:'foulieit], *v.tr.* Défeuiller (un arbuste, etc.).

deforest [di:'forest], *v.tr.* **1.** Déboiser. **2.** Défricher.

deforestation [di:fores'teiʃ(ə)n], *s.* **1.** Déboisement *m.* **2.** Défrichement *m.*

deform [di'fɔ:rm], *v.tr.* Déformer. **deformed,** *a.* **1.** (*Of pers.*) Contrefait, difforme. **2.** *Ph:* Deformed wave, onde faussée, déformée.

deformation [di:fɔ:r'meiʃ(ə)n], *s.* Déformation *f.*

deformity [di'fɔ:rmiti], *s.* Difformité *f.*

defraud [di'frɔ:d], *v.tr.* **1.** Frauder (le fisc, etc.). **2. To defraud s.o. of sth.,** frustrer qn de qch.; escroquer qch. à qn. **defrauding,** *s.* **1.** Fraude *f.* **2.** Frustration *f* (de ses créanciers, etc.).

defrauder [di'frɔ:dər], *s.* Fraudeur *m* (du fisc).

defray [di'frei], *v.tr.* **To defray s.o.'s expenses,**

défrayer qn. **To defray the cost of sth.**, couvrir les frais de qch.

defrayable [di'freiəbl], *a.* A la charge (*by*, de).

defrost [di:'frɔst], *v.tr.* **1.** Déglacer (un réfrigérateur). **2.** Décongeler (la viande frigorifiée).

deft [deft], *a.* Adroit, habile. *D. hand*, main exercée; main preste. **-ly,** *adv.* Adroitement, prestement.

deftness ['deftnəs], *s.* Adresse *f*, habileté *f*, dextérité *f*, prestesse *f*.

defunct [di'fʌŋkt], *a.* Défunt, -e; décédé, -ée.

defy [di'fai], *v.tr.* Défier (qn); mettre (qn) au défi. **I defy you to do so**, je vous mets au défi, je vous défie, de le faire. **To defy description,** défier toute description.

degeneracy [di'dʒenərəsi], *s.* Dégénération *f*.

degenerate[1] [di'dʒenəret], *a. & s.* Dégénéré, -ée.

degenerate[2] [di'dʒenəreit], *v.i.* Dégénérer (*from*, de; *into*, en); s'abâtardir.

degeneration [didʒenə'reiʃ(ə)n], *s.* Dégénérescence *f*, dégénération *f*; abâtardissement *m*.

degradation [degrə'deiʃ(ə)n], *s.* **1.** Dégradation *f*; cassation *f* (d'un officier, etc.). **2.** Avilissement *m*, dégradation, abrutissement *m*. **3.** *Geol:* Dégradation, effritement *m* (des roches).

degrade [di'greid], *v.tr.* (*a*) Dégrader, casser (un officier, etc.). (*b*) Avilir, dégrader (qn). (*c*) *Geol:* Effriter, dégrader (des roches). **degrading,** *a.* Avilissant, dégradant.

degree [di'gri:], *s.* **1.** *A:* Degré *m*, marche *f* (d'autel). **2.** (*a*) **To some degree,** à un certain degré; (jusqu')à un certain point. **In the highest degree,** au plus haut degré, au suprême degré. **In some degree,** dans une certaine mesure. *F:* **To a degree,** au plus haut degré; éminemment. **By degrees,** par degrés; petit à petit. **By slow degrees,** graduellement, lentement. *Gram:* **Degree of comparison,** degré de comparaison. **Degree of humidity,** titre *m* d'eau; teneur *f* en eau. *U.S: F:* **Third degree,** passage *m* à tabac; cuisinage *m*. **To put a prisoner through the third d.,** cuisiner un prisonnier. (*b*) *Mth: Ph: etc:* Degré (d'un cercle, de température). **Angle of 30 degrees,** angle de 30 degrés. **Twenty degrees west of Greenwich,** sous le méridien de vingt degrés à l'ouest de Greenwich. **3.** *Mus:* Échelon *m* (de la gamme); degré (de la portée). **4.** *A. & Lit:* Rang *m*, condition *f*. **Of high degree,** de haut rang, de haut lignage. **Of low degree,** *F:* de bas étage. **5.** *Sch:* Grade *m* (universitaire). **To take one's degree,** prendre ses grades.

dehydrate [di:'haidreit], *v.tr.* Déshydrater.

deification [di:ifi'keiʃ(ə)n], *s.* Déification *f*.

deify ['di:ifai], *v.tr.* Déifier.

deign [dein], *v.tr.* **1. To deign to do sth.**, daigner faire qch.; condescendre à faire qch. **2.** *Usu. neg.* **He did not deign me an answer,** il ne daigna pas me répondre.

deism ['di:izm], *s.* Déisme *m*.

deity ['di:iti], *s.* **1.** Divinité *f* (de Jésus-Christ, etc.). **2.** Dieu *m*, déesse *f*; déité *f*, divinité.

deject [di'dʒekt], *v.tr.* Abattre, décourager, déprimer (qn). **dejected,** *a.* Triste, abattu, déprimé. **-ly,** *adv.* D'un air découragé; tristement.

dejection [di'dʒekʃ(ə)n], *s.* **1.** Découragement *m*, tristesse *f*, abattement *m*. **2.** *Med:* Déjection *f*.

delaine [di'lein], *s.* *Tex:* Mousseline *f* de laine.

delation [di'leiʃ(ə)n], *s.* Délation *f*; dénonciation *f*.

delay[1] [di'lei], *s.* **1.** Sursis *m*, remise *f*; délai *m*, retard *m*. *Without d.,* sans délai; tout de suite.

Without further delay, sans plus tarder. **To make no delay,** ne pas traîner, ne pas tarder (*in doing sth.,* à faire qch.). *The law's delays,* les lenteurs *f* de la loi. **2.** Retardement *m*, arrêt *m*, entrave *f* (du progrès).

delay[2]. **1.** *v.tr.* (*a*) Différer, retarder, remettre (une affaire); arriérer (un payement). **Delayed-action fuse,** fusée à retard. (*b*) Retenir, arrêter, retarder (qn); entraver, retarder (le progrès). **2.** *v.i.* (*a*) Tarder, différer (*in doing sth.,* à faire qch.). (*b*) S'attarder.

delectable [di'lektəbl], *a.* *Lit. & Hum:* Délectable, délicieux. **-ably,** *adv.* Délectablement.

delectation [di:lek'teiʃ(ə)n], *s.* Délectation *f*.

delegate[1] ['deliget], *s.* Délégué *m*.

delegate[2] ['deligeit], *v.tr.* Déléguer.

delegation [deli'geiʃ(ə)n], *s.* (*a*) Délégation *f*, subrogation *f* (de droits, etc.). (*b*) Délégation (de qn). (*c*) *A delegation*, une délégation.

delete [di'li:t], *v.tr.* Effacer, rayer (un mot, etc.). *Typ:* '**Delete,**' "à supprimer."

deleterious [dele'ti:əriəs], *a.* **1.** Nuisible à la santé. **2.** (Gaz, etc.) délétère.

deletion [di'li:ʃ(ə)n], *s.* **1.** Rature *f*, suppression *f* (d'un passage). **2.** Passage supprimé.

delf(t) [delf(t)], *s.* *Cer:* Faïence *f* de Delft. **Delft blue,** bleu *m* de faïence.

deliberate[1] [di'libəret], *a.* **1.** Délibéré, prémédité, intentionnel, voulu. *D. insolence,* insolence calculée. **2.** (*Of pers.*) (*a*) Réfléchi, circonspect, avisé. (*b*) Lent; sans hâte. *His d. tread,* son pas mesuré. **-ly,** *adv.* **1.** De propos délibéré; à dessein; exprès; à bon escient. **2.** (Agir) posément, sans hâte, délibérément.

deliberate[2] [di'libəreit], *v.tr. & i.* Délibérer (*on, de,* sur). **To deliberate over, on, a question,** délibérer une question, d'une question.

deliberateness [di'libəretnəs], *s.* **1.** Intention marquée, bon escient (d'une insulte). **2.** Sage lenteur *f*, mesure *f* (dans les actions).

deliberation [dilibə'reiʃ(ə)n], *s.* **1.** (*a*) Délibération *f*. *After due d.,* après mûre délibération; après mûre réflexion. (*b*) *The deliberations of an assembly,* les débats *m* d'une assemblée. **2.** (*a*) **To act with d.,** agir avec circonspection, après réflexion. (*b*) Sage lenteur *f*. *With d.,* posément; sans hâte.

deliberative [di'libərətiv], *a.* (*a*) *A:* **Deliberative voice,** voix délibérative. (*b*) **Deliberative assembly,** assemblée délibérante.

delicacy ['delikəsi], *s.* Délicatesse *f*. **1.** (*a*) Finesse *f* (d'un dessin); sensibilité *f* (d'un instrument de précision). (*b*) Délicatesse, faiblesse *f* (de santé). (*c*) **To outrage s.o.'s delicacy,** faire outrage à la délicatesse, à la pudeur, de qn. **To feel a delicacy about doing sth.,** se faire scrupule de faire qch. **2.** **Table delicacies,** délicatesses, friandises *f*, de table.

delicate ['deliket], *a.* Délicat. **1.** (*a*) **To have a delicate touch,** avoir de la légèreté de touche, de doigté. **To have a delicate wit,** avoir l'esprit fin. (*b*) *D. feelings,* sentiments délicats, raffinés. **2.** *D. situation,* situation délicate, difficile. *D. question,* question épineuse. *F:* **To tread on delicate ground,** toucher à des questions délicates. **3.** *D. health,* santé délicate, faible. **-ly,** *adv.* Délicatement; avec délicatesse.

delicious [di'liʃəs], *a.* **1.** (Paysage) ravissant. **2.** (Mets) délicieux, exquis. **-ly,** *adv.* Délicieusement.

delight[1] [di'lait], *s.* **1.** Délices *fpl*, délice *m*, délectation *f*. *It is such a d. to* . . ., c'est si bon de. . . . *S.a.* TURKISH DELIGHT. **2.** Joie *f*. **Much to the delight of** . . ., to the great delight of . . ., à la grande joie de. . . . **3.** To take delight in sth. = to delight in sth.

delight². **1.** v.tr. Enchanter, ravir, réjouir (qn); faire les délices de (qn). **2.** v.i. To delight in sth., se délecter à (l'étude), dans (le péché); faire ses délices de qch. To d. in doing sth., se complaire à faire qch. **delighted,** a. Enchanté, ravi (with, at, de). To be delighted to do sth., être enchanté de faire qch. I shall be delighted, je ne demande pas mieux. **-ly,** adv. Avec joie.

delightful [di'laitful], a. Délicieux, ravissant; enchanteur, -eresse; charmant. **-fully,** adv. Délicieusement; (chanter, etc.) à ravir.

Delilah [di'lailə]. Pr.n.f. Dalila.

delimit [di'limit], v.tr. Délimiter (un terrain, des pouvoirs).

delimitation [dilimi'teiʃ(ə)n], s. Délimitation f.

delineate [di'linieit], v.tr. **1.** Tracer, décrire (un triangle, etc.). **2.** Dessiner (un paysage); délinéer (un profil).

delineation [dilini'eiʃ(ə)n], s. **1.** Délinéation f. **2.** Tracé m, dessin m.

delinquency [di'linkwənsi], s. **1.** Culpabilité f. **2.** Délit m, faute f; écart m de conduite.

delinquent [di'linkwənt], a. & s. Délinquant, -ante; coupable (mf).

delirious [di'liriəs], a. (Malade) en délire, délirant; (divagations) du délire. To be delirious, avoir le délire; délirer. F: D. with joy, fou, délirant, de joie.

delirium [di'liriəm], s. Délire m.

deliver [di'livər], v.tr. **1.** Délivrer (s.o. from sth., qn de qch.). To deliver s.o. from death, sauver qn de la mort. To deliver s.o. from, out of, captivity, (re)tirer qn de (la) captivité. **2.** (a) To deliver a woman (of a child), (faire) accoucher une femme. (b) To be delivered of a child, accoucher d'un enfant. (c) To deliver oneself of an opinion, émettre, exprimer, une opinion. **3.** To deliver s.o., sth., (up, over) to s.o., livrer, délivrer, qn, qch., à qn. S.a. STAND² I. 3. To deliver up, restituer, rendre (to, à). To deliver over, céder, transférer, transmettre (un bien, etc.) (to, à). **4.** (a) Remettre, délivrer (un paquet, etc.); distribuer (des lettres); livrer (des marchandises). To d. sth. into s.o.'s charge, confier qch. à qn, à la garde de qn. To deliver a message, faire une commission. Com: Delivered free, rendu à domicile; livraison franco. (b) (Of dynamo, etc.) Débiter, fournir (du courant); (of pump) refouler (l'eau). **5.** Porter, donner (un coup); faire, lancer (une attaque); livrer (bataille). **6.** Faire, prononcer (un discours); faire (une conférence). Jur: Prononcer, rendre (un jugement).

deliverance [di'livərəns], s. **1.** Délivrance f, libération f (from, de). **2.** Déclaration f, expression f (d'opinion).

deliverer [di'livərər], s. **1.** Libérateur, -trice; sauveur m. **2.** Distributeur, -trice (de prospectus, etc.); livreur, -euse (de marchandises).

delivery [di'livəri], s. **1.** Mil: Reddition f (d'une ville, d'un prisonnier). S.a. GAOL-DELIVERY. **2.** (a) D. of a message, exécution f d'une commission. (b) Livraison f, délivrance f, remise f (d'un paquet, etc.); remise (d'une lettre); distribution f (des lettres). Jur: D. of a writ, signification f d'un acte. Delivery note, bulletin m de livraison. Free delivery, livraison franco. Delivery-man, livreur m. To pay on delivery, payer sur livraison. Payment on delivery, livraison contre remboursement. Ind: To accept delivery of sth., prendre qch. en recette. **3.** (a) Delivery of a speech, prononciation f d'un

discours. (b) Débit m, diction f (d'un orateur). **4.** (a) Distribution (de courant électrique, etc.). (b) Débit (de courant, etc.); refoulement m (d'une pompe). Delivery pipe, tuyau m, conduite f, d'amenée.

dell [del], s. Vallon m, combe f.

Delphi ['delfai]. Pr.n. A.Geog: Delphes f.

Delphic ['delfik], a. The Delphic Oracle, l'Oracle m de Delphes.

delphinium [del'finiəm], s. Bot: Delphinium m; F: pied-d'alouette m.

delta ['delta], s. Gr.Alph: Geog: Delta m.

deltoid ['deltoid], a. & s. Anat: (Muscle m) deltoïde m.

delude [di'lju:d], v.tr. **1.** Abuser, tromper (qn); induire (qn) en erreur. To d. oneself, s'abuser; se faire illusion. To delude oneself with false hopes, se bercer, se leurrer, de vaines espérances. **2.** Duper (qn); en faire accroire à (qn).

deluge¹ ['deljudʒ], s. Déluge m.

deluge², v.tr. Inonder (with, de). F: To be deluged with letters, être inondé de lettres.

delusion [di'lju:ʒ(ə)n], s. Illusion f, hallucination f, erreur f. To be under a delusion, se faire illusion; s'abuser; s'illusionner.

delusive [di'lju:siv], a. Illusoire; trompeur, -euse. **-ly,** adv. Illusoirement; trompeusement.

delve [delv], v.i. (a) A. & Lit: Fouiller le sol. (b) (Of path, etc.) S'abaisser. (c) F: To delve into one's pocket, fouiller dans sa poche.

demagnetization [di:mægnətai'zeiʃ(ə)n], s. Désaimantation f.

demagnetize [di:'mægnətaiz], v.tr. Démagnétiser; désaimanter.

demagogue ['deməgɔg], s. Démagogue m.

demagogy ['deməgɔgi, -dʒi], s. Démagogie f.

demand¹ [di'mɑ:nd], s. **1.** Demande f, réclamation f, revendication f. Payable on demand, payable sur demande, à vue. **2.** Pol.Ec: Supply and demand, l'offre et la demande. To be in (great, little) demand, être (très, peu) demandé, recherché. **3.** pl. The demands of the case, les nécessités f du cas. To make great demands upon s.o.'s energy, exiger de qn beaucoup d'énergie. I have many demands upon my time, je suis très pris.

demand², v.tr. **1.** To demand sth. of, from, s.o., demander (formellement), réclamer, qch. à qn; exiger qch. de qn. To d. to know whether . . ., insister pour savoir si. . . . To d. that . . ., demander, exiger, que + sub. **2.** The matter demands great care, l'affaire demande, exige, réclame, beaucoup de soin.

demarcate ['di:mɑ:rkeit], v.tr. Délimiter (un terrain).

demarcation [di:mɑ:r'keiʃ(ə)n], s. Démarcation f; délimitation f.

demean¹ [di'mi:n], v.pr. To demean oneself honourably, se comporter en homme d'honneur.

demean², v.pr. To demean oneself, s'abaisser, se dégrader.

demeanour [di'mi:nər], s. Air m, tenue f, maintien m.

demented [di'mentid], a. Fou, f. folle; en démence. F: He was running like one demented, il courait comme un fou.

dementia [di'menʃia], s. Med: Démence f.

demesne [di'mein, -'mi:n], s. **1.** Jur: Possession f. **2.** Domaine m.

demi-circle ['demisə:rkl], s. Surv: Demi-cercle m.

demigod ['demigɔd], s. Demi-dieu m

demijohn ['demidʒɔn], s. Ind: etc: Dame-jeanne f, bombonne f, tourie f.

demilitarization [di:militərai'zeiʃ(ə)n], s. Démilitarisation f.

demilitarize [di:'militəraiz], v.tr. Démilitariser.

demilune ['demilu:n], s. Fort: Demi-lune f.

demise[1] [di'ma:iz], s. **1.** Jur: Cession f, transmission f (par testament, etc.); transfert m (d'un titre, etc.). **2.** F: Décès m, mort f (de qn).

demise[2], v.tr. Jur: Céder, transmettre (un bien).

demit [di'mit], v.tr. (demitted) To demit office, se démettre de ses fonctions; démissionner.

demobilization [di:moubilai'zeiʃ(ə)n], s. Démobilisation f.

demobilize [di:'moubila:iz], v.tr. Mil: Démobiliser.

democracy [de'mokrəsi], s. Démocratie f.

democrat ['demokrat], s. Démocrate mf.

democratic [demo'kratik], a. Démocratique. **-ally**, adv. Démocratiquement.

demolish [di'moliʃ], v.tr. **1.** Démolir. **2.** F: Avaler, dévorer (un pâté, etc.).

demolisher [di'moliʃər], s. Démolisseur, -euse (of, de).

demolition [demo'liʃ(ə)n, di:-], s. Démolition f.

demon ['di:mən], s. **1.** (a) Gr.Myth: Démon m, esprit m. (b) Myth: Démon, génie m. **2.** Démon, diable m. F: He's a demon for work, c'est un travailleur acharné.

demonetize [di:'monita:iz], v.tr. Démonétiser (une monnaie).

demoniac [di'mounjak], a. & s. Démoniaque (mf).

demoniacal [di:mo'naiək(ə)l], a. Démoniaque, diabolique.

demonstrability [dimonstrə'biliti], s. Démontrabilité f.

demonstrable [di'monstrəbl], a. Démontrable. **-ably**, adv. Statement d. false, affirmation dont la fausseté peut être prouvée.

demonstrate [di'monstreit, 'demonstreit]. **1.** v.tr. (a) Démontrer (une vérité). (b) Décrire, expliquer (un système). **2.** v.i. Pol: Manifester; prendre part à une manifestation.

demonstration [demon'streiʃ(ə)n], s. **1.** (a) Démonstration f (d'une vérité). Proved to demonstration, prouvé sans contredit. (b) Practical demonstration, démonstration pratique (d'un appareil). **2.** F: Demonstrations of love, témoignages m, démonstrations, de tendresse. **3.** Manifestation f (politique). To make a d., manifester.

demonstrative [di'monstrətiv], a. Démonstratif. **-ly**, adv. (Accueillir qn) avec effusion.

demonstrator ['demonstreitər], s. **1.** (a) Démonstrateur m. (b) Sch: Préparateur m (d'un professeur de sciences, etc.); démonstrateur (en anatomie). **2.** Manifestant m (politique).

demoralization [dimorəlai'zeiʃ(ə)n], s. Démoralisation f.

demoralize [di'morəla:iz], v.tr. **1.** Dépraver, corrompre. **2.** Démoraliser (les troupes, etc.).

demote [di'mout], v.tr. Mil: etc: U.S: Réduire à un grade inférieur, à une classe inférieure.

demur[1] [di'mə:r], s. Hésitation f. To make no demur, ne faire aucune difficulté, aucune objection.

demur[2], v.i. (demurred) Faire des difficultés; soulever des objections (at, to, contre).

demure [di'mjuər], a. (Used chiefly of young women) **1.** Posé(e), grave; réservé(e). **2.** D'une modestie affectée. D. look, petit air de Sainte-Nitouche. **-ly**, adv. **1.** D'un air posé, modeste. **2.** Avec une modestie affectée; d'un air de Sainte-Nitouche.

demureness [di'mjuərnəs], s. **1.** Gravité f de maintien. **2.** Modestie affectée; air m de Sainte-Nitouche.

demurrage [di'mʌredʒ], s. **1.** Nau: Surestarie(s) f(pl). **2.** Rail: Magasinage m.

den [den], s. **1.** Tanière f, antre m, repaire m (de bêtes féroces). B: Den of lions, fosse f aux lions. S.a. BEARD[2]. Den of thieves, retraite f de voleurs. **2.** F: Cabinet m de travail ou fumoir m; P: turne f. **3.** F: Bouge m. S.a. GAMBLING.

denationalize [di:'naʃənəla:iz], v.tr. Dénationaliser (qn).

denaturalize [di:'natʃərəla:iz], v.tr. **1.** Dénaturer (qch.). **2.** To denaturalize oneself, se dénaturaliser, se dénationaliser.

denaturation [di:neitjə'reiʃ(ə)n], s. Dénaturation f (de l'alcool, etc.).

denature [di:'neitjər], **denaturize** [di:'neitjəra:iz], v.tr. Dénaturer (un produit).

dendrite ['dendrait], s. Miner: Cryst: Arborisation f, dendrite f.

dene-hole ['di:nhoul], s. Puits artificiel dans le calcaire.

deniable [di'naiəbl], a. Niable.

denial [di'naiəl], s. **1.** (Refusal) Déni m, refus m. I will take no d., il faut absolument que vous veniez, que vous le fassiez, etc. **2.** Dénégation f, démenti m (de la vérité de qch.). **3.** B: (Le) reniement (de saint Pierre).

denigrate ['denigreit], v.tr. Lit: (a) Noircir (la réputation de qn); diffamer (qn). (b) Dénigrer (qn, un projet).

denigration [deni'greiʃ(ə)n], s. Lit: (a) Diffamation f. (b) Dénigrement m.

denigrator ['denigreitər], s. Lit: (a) Diffamateur m. (b) Dénigreur m.

denizen ['deniz(ə)n], s. Poet: Habitant, -ante. Denizens of the forest, hôtes m, habitants, des bois.

Denmark ['denma:rk]. Pr.n. Le Danemark.

denominate [di'nomineit], v.tr. Dénommer.

denomination [dinomi'neiʃ(ə)n], s. **1.** Dénomination f. **2.** Ecc: Culte m, secte f, confession f. **3.** Catégorie f. Coins of all denominations, pièces de toutes valeurs.

denominational [dinomi'neiʃən(ə)l], a. Confessionnel, sectaire. D. school, école confessionnelle.

denominator [di'nomineitər], s. Mth: Dénominateur m. Common denominator, dénominateur commun.

denotation [di:no'teiʃ(ə)n], s. **1.** Désignation f (of sth. by sth., de qch. par qch.). **2.** Denotations of an uneasy conscience, indications f d'une conscience troublée. **3.** Signification f (d'un mot).

denote [di'nout], v.tr. **1.** Dénoter. Face that denotes energy, visage qui dénote l'énergie. Here everything denotes peace, ici tout respire la paix. **2.** Signifier.

dénouement [de'nu:mã], s. Dénouement m.

denounce [di'nauns], v.tr. **1.** (a) Dénoncer. To d. s.o. to the authorities, déférer qn à la justice. (b) Démasquer (un imposteur). (c) Pred. To d. s.o. as an impostor, taxer qn d'imposture. **2.** S'élever contre (un abus). **3.** To denounce a treaty, dénoncer un traité.

de novo [di:'nouvou], Lt.adv.phr. A nouveau.

dense [dens], a. **1.** Ph: Dense. **2.** (Of smoke) Épais, -aisse. D. darkness, obscurité profonde. D. crowd, foule compacte. **3.** Stupide, bête. D. mind, esprit lourd, obtus. **4.** Phot: D. negative, cliché opaque. **-ly**, adv. D. wooded country, pays couvert de forêts épaisses. D. crowded streets, rues où se presse une foule compacte.

denseness ['densnəs], s. = DENSITY 2, 3.

density ['densiti], s. I. *Ph:* Densité f.
2. Épaisseur f (du brouillard); compacité f (du
sol); densité (de la population). **3.** Stupidité f.
4. *Phot:* Opacité f (d'un cliché).
dent¹ [dent], s. (a) Marque f de coup ; bosselure f ;
renfoncement m. (b) Brèche f (dans une lame).
dent², v.tr. (a) Bosseler, bossuer. (b) Ébrécher
(une lame).
dental ['dent(ə)l], a. I. Dentaire. **Dental surgeon,** chirurgien dentiste. **2.** *Ling:* Dental,
-aux. s. (Consonne) dentale f.
dentate ['denteit], a. Denté.
dentation [den'teiʃ(ə)n], s. I. Dentelure f.
denticulation [dentikju'leiʃ(ə)n], s. Dentelure f.
dentifrice ['dentifris], s. Dentifrice m.
dentist ['dentist], s. Dentiste m.
dentistry ['dentistri], s. Art m dentaire.
dentition [den'tiʃ(ə)n], s. Dentition f.
denture ['dentʃər], s. I. Z: Denture f. **2.** (Of
artificial teeth) Dentier m ; F: râtelier m.
denudation [denju'deiʃ(ə)n], s. Dénudation f.
denude [di'nju:d], v.tr. Dénuder (qch.). *Tree
denuded of leaves,* arbre dégarni de feuilles.
denunciation [dinʌnsi'eiʃ(ə)n], s. I. Dénonciation f. **2.** (a) Condamnation f (d'un abus).
(b) Accusation publique (de qn). **3.** Dénonciation
(d'un traité).
denunciative [di'nʌnsieitiv], **denunciatory**
[di'nʌnsiətəri], a. Dénonciateur, -trice.
denunciator [di'nʌnsieitər], s. Dénonciateur,
-trice.
deny [di'nai], v.tr. I. Nier (un fait); démentir
(une nouvelle). *Jur:* Dénier (un crime); repousser (une accusation). **I don't deny it,** je
n'en disconviens pas. *I cannot d. (but) that you
are right,* je ne saurais nier que vous n'ayez
raison. **There is no denying the fact,** c'est un
fait indéniable. **I do not deny the fact that . . .,**
j'apprécie le fait que. . . . **There's no denying
that . . .,** on ne saurait nier que. . . . **2.** (a) Renier (qn, sa foi). **To d. God,** nier Dieu. (b) *To d.
one's signature,* désavouer sa signature. **3.** *To
deny s.o. sth.,* refuser qch. à qn. *To d. the door
to s.o.,* fermer sa porte à qn. *To be denied a right,*
se voir frustré d'un droit. **He is not to be denied,**
il n'acceptera pas de refus. **4.** (a) *To deny oneself sth.,* se refuser qch. ; se priver de qch. (b) *To
deny oneself,* faire abnégation de soi-même.
deodar ['di:odɑ:r], s. Cèdre m de l'Himalaya.
deodorize [di'oudəraiz], v.tr. Dé(s)odoriser.
deodorizer [di'oudəraizər], s. Dé(s)odorisa-
teur m.
deoxidize [di:'ɔksidaiz], v.tr. *Ch:* Désoxyder.
depart [di'pɑ:rt], v.i. I. (a) S'en aller, partir ;
(*of train*) partir. *To d. from a place,* quitter un
lieu. (b) *To depart (from) this life,* mourir ;
quitter ce monde. **2.** *To d. from a rule,* sortir
d'une règle. **departed,** a. I. (*Of glory, etc.*)
Passé, évanoui. **2.** Mort, défunt. **The departed,**
(i) le défunt ; (ii) *pl.* les morts.
department [di'pɑ:rtmənt], s. I. (a) *Adm:* Département m, service m. *The different departments,*
les différents bureaux. *Heads of departments,*
chefs de service. (b) (*In shop*) Rayon m, comptoir m. *U.S:* **Department store,** grand magasin.
2. *Fr.Geog:* Département.
departmental [di:pɑ:rt'ment(ə)l], a. Départemental, -aux ; qui se rapporte à un service.
departure [di'pɑ:rtʃər], s. I. Départ m. *To take
one's departure,* s'en aller ; partir. **2.** *D. from a
principle,* déviation f d'un principe. *A d. from his
usual habits,* procédé m contraire à ses habitudes.
3. **A new departure,** (i) une nouvelle tendance ;
(ii) *F:* un nouvel usage.

depend [di'pend], v.i I. *A:* Pendre (*from,* à).
2. Dépendre (*on,* de). **That depends entirely on
you,** cela ne tient qu'à vous. **That depends, it
all depends,** cela dépend ; *F:* c'est selon.
3. (a) *To depend on s.o.,* se trouver à la charge
de qn ; recevoir une pension de qn. (b) *To d.
on foreign supplies,* être tributaire de l'étranger.
To d. on oneself, F: voler de ses propres ailes.
4. (*Rely*) *To depend upon s.o.,* compter sur,
faire fond sur, qn. *I can d. on him,* je suis sûr
de lui. *You may d. upon it that what I say is true,*
vous pouvez vous fier à la vérité de mes paroles.
(**You may) depend upon it,** comptez là-dessus.
dependable [di'pendəbl], a. (*Of pers.*) Digne de
confiance ; (*of information*) sûr, bien fondé.
dependant [di'pendənt], s. Protégé, -ée. *pl.* **Dependants,** (i) domesticité f ; (ii) charges f de
famille.
dependence [di'pendəns], s. I. (a) *D. on s.o.,*
dépendance f de qn. (b) *D. on s.o.,* le fait d'être
à la charge de qn. **2.** Confiance f (*on,* en). **To
place dependence on s.o.,** se fier à qn.
dependency [di'pendənsi], s. Dépendance f.
Esp. pl. **Dependencies of an estate,** dépendances
d'une terre.
dependent [di'pendənt]. I. a. (a) Dépendant
(*on,* de). *To be d. on alms,* subsister d'aumônes.
(b) *Gram:* Dependent clause, proposition
subordonnée. (c) *To be d. on s.o.,* être à la charge
de qn. **2.** s. = DEPENDANT.
depict [di'pikt], v.tr. Peindre, dépeindre.
depilate ['depileit], v.tr. Épiler ; peler (des
peaux).
depilation [depi'leiʃ(ə)n], s. Épilation f.
deplenish [di'pleniʃ], v.tr. Dégarnir (une
maison) ; démunir (*of,* de) ; vider (ses poches).
deplete [di'pli:t], v.tr. Épuiser (des provisions,
etc.).
depletion [di'pli:ʃ(ə)n], s. Épuisement m (des
ressources).
deplorable [di'plɔ:rəbl], a. Déplorable, lamentable. **-ably,** adv. Lamentablement.
deplore [di'plɔ:r], v.i. Déplorer ; regretter
vivement. *To d. one's fate,* se lamenter sur son
sort.
deploy [di'plɔi]. *Mil: Navy:* I. v.tr. Déployer
(une armée). **2.** v.i. Se déployer.
deployment [di'plɔimənt], s. *Mil: Navy:* Déploiement m.
depolarize [di:'pouləraiz], v.tr. Dépolariser.
deponent [di'pounənt], a. & s. I. *Gram:*
(Verbe) déponent (m). **2.** *Jur:* (Témoin)
déposant m.
depopulate [di:'pɔpjuleit], v.tr. Dépeupler.
depopulation [di:pɔpju'leiʃ(ə)n], s. Dépopulation f (d'un pays); dépeuplement m (d'une
forêt).
deport [di'pɔ:rt]. I. v.tr. Expulser (un étranger).
2. v.pr. *To deport oneself,* se comporter (bien,
mal).
deportation [di:pɔ:r'teiʃ(ə)n], s. Expulsion f
(d'un étranger). *D. order,* arrêté m d'expulsion.
deportment [di'pɔ:rtmənt], s. (a) Tenue f,
maintien m. (b) Conduite f ; manière f d'agir.
depose [di'pouz], v.tr. I. (a) *A:* Poser (qch.).
(b) Déposer (un roi). **2.** *Jur:* (a) Témoigner ;
témoigner (*that,* que + *ind.*). (b) v.i. *To depose
to a fact,* témoigner d'un fait.
deposit¹ [di'pɔzit], s. I. *Bank d.,* dépôt m en
banque. **Deposit account,** compte m de dépôts.
2. To pay a deposit, verser une somme par
provision. **3.** Dépôt(s) m(pl); sédiment m,
Geol: Gisement m, couche f. **River deposits,**
alluvions f. *To form a d.,* se déposer. *Med.*

Chalky d., encroûtement *m* calcique. *I.C.E:*
Carbon d., encrassement charbonneux ; *F :* cala-
mine *f*. **deposit²**, *v.tr.* **I.** Déposer (*sth. on sth.*, qch. sur
qch.). **2.** (*a*) To deposit money with s.o., con-
signer de l'argent chez qn. (*b*) *Cust :* To *d. the
duty (repayable)*, cautionner les droits. **3.** (*Of
liquid*) Déposer.
depositary [di'pɔzitəri], *s.* Dépositaire *m.*
deposition [di:po'ziʃ(ə)n], *s.* **I.** Déposition *f*
(d'un roi). `2.` Déposition, témoignage *m.*
3. Dépôt *m* (d'un sédiment).
depositor [di'pɔzitər], *s. Bank :* Déposant *m.*
depository [di'pɔzitəri], *s.* Dépôt *m*, entrepôt *m.*
Furniture depository, garde-meubles *m inv.*
depot ['depou], *s.* **I.** *Mil :* Navy : Dépôt *m.*
Navy: Depot ship, (transport) ravitailleur *m.*
2. (*a*) *Com :* Dépôt, entrepôt *m.* (*b*) *Tramway d.*,
garage *m* de(s) tramways.
depravation [di:pra'veiʃ(ə)n], *s.* Dépravation *f.*
deprave [di'preiv], *v.tr.* Dépraver.
depravity [di'praviti], *s.* Dépravation *f* ; perversité *f.*
deprecate ['deprekeit], *v.tr.* Désapprouver,
déconseiller (une action). **deprecating**, *a.*
Désapprobateur, -trice.
deprecation [depre'keiʃ(ə)n], *s.* Désapprobation *f.*
deprecatory ['deprekeitəri], *a.* (Rire) qui va
au-devant des reproches, de la critique.
depreciate [di'pri:ʃieit]. **I.** *v.tr.* (*a*) Déprécier ;
avilir (les marchandises). (*b*) Déprécier, dénigrer
(qn). **2.** *v.i.* Se déprécier ; diminuer de valeur.
depreciation [dipri:ʃi'eiʃ(ə)n], *s.* **I.** (*a*) Dépréciation *f* (de l'argent) ; moins-value *f.*
(*b*) *Ind :* *Annual d.*, amortissement annuel.
2. Dépréciation, dénigrement *m.*
depreciative [di'pri:ʃiətiv], **depreciatory**
[di'pri:ʃiətəri], *a.* Dépréciateur, -trice.
depreciator [di'pri:ʃieitər], *s.* Dépréciateur,
-trice ; dénigreur, -euse.
depredation [depre'deiʃ(ə)n], *s.* Déprédation *f.*
depredator ['depredeitər], *s.* Déprédateur,
-trice.
depress [di'pres], *v.tr.* **I.** Abaisser ; baisser
(qch.) ; appuyer sur (la pédale). **2.** (*a*) Abattre
(les forces) ; faire languir (le commerce). (*b*) Attrister, décourager. **depressed**, *a.* **I.** *Arch :*
(Arc) surbaissé. **2.** *Com :* (Marché) languissant.
3. Triste, abattu. *He is easily d.*, un rien l'abat.
To feel d., *F :* avoir le cafard. **depressing**, *a.*
Attristant. *D. landscape*, paysage triste, maussade.
depression [di'preʃ(ə)n], *s.* **I.** (*a*) Abaissement *m*
(de qch.). (*b*) *Astr :* Dépression *f* (d'un astre).
2. *Meteor :* Dépression, baisse *f.* **3.** Dépression,
creux *m* (de terrain). **4.** *Com :* Affaissement *m*,
marasme *m* (des affaires). **5.** Découragement *m*,
abattement *m.*
deprival [di'praivəl], *s.* Privation *f* (*of*, de).
deprivation [depri'veiʃ(ə)n], *s.* **I.** Privation *f*,
perte *f* (de droits). **2.** Dépossession *f.*
deprive [di'praiv], *v.tr.* **I.** *To d. s.o. of sth.*,
priver qn de qch. *To deprive oneself*, s'infliger
des privations. **2.** Déposséder (qn) d'une charge ;
destituer (un prêtre).
depth [depθ], *s.* **I.** Profondeur *f.* *At a d. of*
50 *fathoms*, par 50 brasses de fond. **2.** Fond *m*,
hauteur *f* (de l'eau). **To get out of one's depth**,
(i) perdre fond ; (ii) *F :* sortir de sa compétence.
3. Hauteur (d'un faux col) ; épaisseur *f* (d'une
couche). **4.** (*a*) Gravité *f* (d'un son). (*b*) Portée *f*
(de l'intelligence). (*c*) Intensité *f* (de coloris).
5. Fond (d'une forêt, d'une caverne) ; milieu *m*
(de la nuit). **In the depth of winter**, au plus fort

de l'hiver. **6.** *pl.* The depths. (*a*) *Lit :* L'abîme *m*,
le gouffre. (*b*) Profondeurs (de l'océan) ; ténèbres *f* (de l'ignorance). **In the depths of despair**, dans le plus profond désespoir. **'depth-
charge**, *s. Navy :* Grenade sous-marine.
depurate ['depjureit], *v.tr. Med :* Dépurer.
depurative [de'pjuərətiv, 'depjureitiv], *a. & s.
Med :* Dépuratif (*m*).
deputation [depju'teiʃ(ə)n], *s.* Députation *f*,
délégation *f.*
depute [di'pju:t], *v.tr.* **I.** Déléguer (*powers to
s.o.*, des pouvoirs à qn). **2.** *To d. s.o. to do sth.*,
députer, déléguer, qn pour faire qch.
deputize ['depjuta:iz], *v.i. To d. for s.o.*, faire
l'intérim de qn ; remplacer qn.
deputy ['depjuti], *s.* Fondé *m* de pouvoir.
I. Substitut *m* (d'un juge) ; délégué *m* (d'un
fonctionnaire). *To act as d. for s.o.*, suppléer qn.
Deputy-chairman, vice-président *m.* **Deputy-
governor**, sous-gouverneur *m.* **Deputy-judge**,
juge *m* suppléant. **2.** (*a*) Délégué. (*b*) *Fr.Pol :*
Député *m.*
deracinate [di'rasineit], *v.tr.* Déraciner.
deracination [dirasi'neiʃ(ə)n], *s.* Déracinement *m.*
derail [di'reil], *v.tr.* Faire dérailler (un train).
derailment [di'reilmənt], *s.* Déraillement *m.*
derange [di'reindʒ], *v.tr.* Déranger.
derangement [di'reindʒmənt], *s.* Dérèglement *m.*
Derangement of mind, dérangement *m* d'esprit.
derate [di:'reit], *v.tr.* Dégrever (une industrie).
derating, *s.* Dégrèvement *m.*
Derby ['dɑ:rbi]. *Pr.n. Sp :* **The Derby**, la course
classique du Derby ; le Derby. *F :* Derby dog,
(i) le chien fatal qui traverse la piste ; (ii) incident
fâcheux et imprévu.
derelict ['derelikt]. **I.** *a.* Abandonné, délaissé,
à l'abandon. **2.** *s.* (*a*) Objet abandonné. *Esp.
Nau :* Navire abandonné (en mer) ; épave *f.*
(*b*) Épave humaine.
dereliction [dere'likʃ(ə)n], *s.* **I.** Abandon *m*,
délaissement *m.* **2. Dereliction of duty**, manquement *m* au devoir.
derestrict [di:re'strikt], *v.tr.* **To derestrict a road**,
libérer une route de toute restriction de vitesse.
deride [di'raid], *v.tr.* Tourner en dérision ;
bafouer, railler, se moquer de (qn).
derision [di'riʒ(ə)n], *s.* **I.** Dérision *f.* Object of
derision, objet de risée. **To hold s.o. in derision**,
se moquer de qn. **2.** Objet *m* de dérision.
derisive [di'raisiv], *a.* **I.** Moqueur, -euse.
2. *D. offer*, offre dérisoire. **-ly**, *adv.* D'un air
moqueur.
derivation [deri'veiʃ(ə)n], *s.* Dérivation *f.*
derivative [di'rivətiv]. **I.** *a. & s. Gram :* (Mot)
dérivé (*m*). **2.** *s.* (*a*) *Ch :* *Ind :* Dérivé *m.*
(*b*) *Mth :* Dérivée *f.* (*c*) *Mus :* Accord dérivé.
derive [di'ra:iv], *v.tr. & i.* **I.** (*a*) *To d. sth. from
sth.*, tirer (son origine) de qch. ; devoir (son bonheur) à qch. ; trouver (du plaisir) à qch. *Income
derived from an investment*, revenu provenant
d'un placement. *To d. an idea from an author*,
puiser une idée chez un auteur. (*b*) *Ling :* *Word
derived from Latin*, mot qui vient du latin.
2. To be derived, *v.i.* to derive, dériver, (pro)-
venir (*from*, de).
derm [də:rm], *s. Anat :* Derme *m.*
dermal ['də:rm(ə)l], *a.* Cutané.
dermatitis [də:rmə'taitis], *s. Med :* Dermite *f.*
dermatology [də:rmə'tɔlodʒi], *s.* Dermatologie *f.*
derogate ['derogeit], *v.i.* **I.** *A :* To *d. from a
right*, porter atteinte à un droit. *To d. from s.o.'s
authority*, diminuer l'autorité de qn. **2.** *.To d.
(from one's dignity)*, déroger (à sa dignité).

derogation [dero'geiʃ(ə)n], s. **1.** D. of a law, dérogation f à une loi. **2.** D. from a right, atteinte portée à un droit. **3.** Without derogation, sans déroger (from dignity, à la dignité).

derogatory [di'rɔgətəri], a. **1.** (a) Dérogatoire (from, à). (b) D. to a right, attentatoire à un droit. **2.** Dérogeant, qui déroge (to, à). To do sth. d. to one's position, se manquer à soi-même.

derrick ['derik], s. (a) Chevalement m; potence f, chèvre f. (b) Nau: Mât m de charge.

derring-do ['deriŋ'du:], s. Bravoure f. Deeds of derring-do, hauts faits.

dervish ['də:viʃ], s. Derviche m.

descant [des'kant], v.i. Discourir, s'étendre (on, sur).

descend [di'send]. **1.** v.i. (a) Descendre; (of rain) tomber. (b) To descend on s.o., s'abattre, tomber, sur qn. (c) To descend to s.o.'s level, s'abaisser au niveau de qn. To d. to lying, descendre jusqu'au mensonge. (d) To descend, be descended, from s.o., descendre de qn ; tirer son origine (d'une maison royale, etc.). Well descended, de bonne famille. (e) (Of property) To d. from s.o. to s.o., passer de qn à qn. **2.** v.tr. Descendre, dévaler (une colline, un escalier).

descendant, -ent [di'sendənt], s. Descendant, -ante. pl. Descendants, descendance f, postérité f.

descent [di'sent], s. **1.** Descente f. **2.** (Lineage) Descendance f. Person of noble d., personne de haut parage. **3.** Jur: Transmission f (d'un bien) par héritage.

describable [dis'kraibəbl], a. Descriptible.

describe [dis'kraib], v.tr. **1.** (a) Décrire, dépeindre. (b) Pred. To d. s.o. as . . ., qualifier qn de . . ., représenter qn comme. . . . (c) Signaler (un homme recherché par la police). **2.** Décrire (une courbe).

description [dis'kripʃ(ə)n], s. **1.** (a) Description f. Beyond description, indescriptible. (b) (For police purposes) Signalement m. To answer to the description, répondre au signalement. (c) Com: Désignation f (de marchandises). **2.** F: Sorte f, espèce f, genre m. People of this description, les gens de cette espèce, de cette sorte.

descriptive [dis'kriptiv], a. Descriptif. D. catalogue, catalogue raisonné.

descry [dis'krai], v.tr. Apercevoir, aviser (dans le lointain).

desecrate ['desekreit], v.tr. Profaner (un lieu saint).

desecration [dese'kreiʃ(ə)n], s. Profanation f.

desecrator ['desekreitər], s. Profanateur, -trice.

desensitize [di:'sensitaiz], v.tr. Phot: Désensibiliser (une plaque).

desensitizer [di:'sensitaizər], s. Phot: Désensibilisateur m.

desert[1] [di'zə:rt], s. Mérite m. Usu. pl. Mérites ; ce qu'on mérite ; dû m. To everyone according to his deserts, à chacun son dû. To get one's deserts, avoir ce que l'on mérite.

desert[2] ['dezərt]. **1.** a. (Of region, etc.) Désert. **2.** s. Désert m.

desert[3] [di'zə:rt], v.tr. (a) Déserter. (b) Abandonner, délaisser (qn). Pol: To d. one's party, faire défection. deserted, a. (Of pers.) Abandonné ; (of place) désert.

deserter [di'zə:rtər], s. Déserteur m.

desertion [di'zə:rʃ(ə)n], s. **1.** Abandon m, délaissement m (de qn). **2.** Mil: Désertion f. Pol: D. of one's party, défection f.

deserve [di'zə:rv], v.tr. Mériter (qch.). To d. praise, être digne d'éloges. He richly deserves it!

F: il ne l'a pas volé ! **deserving**, a. (Of pers.) Méritant ; (of action) méritoire. Deserving case, cas digne d'intérêt.

deservedly [di'zə:rvidli], adv. A juste titre ; à bon droit.

desiccate ['desikeit], v.tr. Dessécher.

desiccation [desi'keiʃ(ə)n], s. Dessiccation f; dessèchement m.

desideratum, pl. **-a** [disidə'reitəm, -a], s. Desideratum m, pl. desiderata.

design[1] [di'zain], s. **1.** (a) Dessein m, intention f, projet m. By design, à dessein. (b) With this design . . ., dans ce but. . . . **2.** (Decorative) design, dessin m d'ornement. **3.** Ind: Étude f, avant-projet m (d'une machine, etc.). **4.** Dessin, modèle m (d'une machine, etc.). Machine of faulty design, machine mal étudiée, de construction fautive. Battleships of different designs, cuirassés de types différents. Car of the latest d., voiture dernier modèle.

design[2], v.tr. **1.** Destiner (for, à). **2.** Machine designed for a special purpose, machine construite, étudiée, dans un but spécial. **3.** Projeter, se proposer (de faire qch.). **4.** (a) Préparer (un projet) ; combiner (un coup). (b) Créer (une robe) ; établir (un avion). Well designed premises, local bien agencé. **designing**[1], a. Artificieux, intrigant. **designing**[2], s. Dessin m, création f (d'une machine).

designate ['dezigneit], v.tr. **1.** (a) Désigner, nommer (s.o. to an office, qn à une fonction). (b) To d. s.o. as, for, one's successor, désigner qn pour, comme, son successeur. **2.** Designated by the name of . . ., désigné sous le nom de. . . . Rulings designated as arbitrary, décisions qualifiées d'arbitraires. **3.** (Of things) Indiquer (qch.).

designation [dezig'neiʃ(ə)n], s. **1.** Désignation f (d'une personne). **2.** D. to a post, nomination f à un emploi. **3.** Désignation, nom m. Known under several designations, connu sous plusieurs noms.

designedly [di'zainidli], adv. A dessein.

designer [di'zainər], s. **1.** Ind: Com: Dessinateur, -trice. Th: Stage designer, décorateur m de théâtre. **2.** Intrigant, -ante.

desilverize [di:'silvəraiz], v.tr. Désargenter.

desirability [dizaiərə'biliti], **desirableness** [di'zaiərəblnəs], s. Caractère m désirable ; avantage m ; attrait m (d'une femme).

desirable [di'zaiərəbl], a. Désirable. (a) A désirer ; souhaitable ; avantageux. (b) (Of pers., esp. of woman) Attrayant. **-ably**, adv. Avantageusement.

desire[1] [di'zaiər], s. **1.** Désir m, souhait m. I feel no d. to . . ., je n'éprouve aucune envie de. . . . Consumed with d., consumé par le désir. **2.** At, by, s.o.'s desire, à, sur la demande de qn.

desire[2], v.tr. **1.** Désirer (qch.) ; avoir envie de (qch.). To d. to do sth., désirer faire qch. Since you desire it, puisque vous y tenez. It leaves much to be desired, cela laisse beaucoup à désirer. **2.** (a) To d. sth. of s.o., demander qch. à qn. (b) To d. s.o. to do sth., prier qn de faire qch.

desirous [di'zaiərəs], a. Désireux (of, de).

desist [di'zist], v.i. Lit: **1.** Cesser (from doing sth., de faire qch.). **2.** To d. from sth., renoncer à qch. ; se désister de qch.

desk [desk], s. **1.** Pupitre m; (in office) bureau m; (schoolmaster's) chaire f. Pedestal desk, bureau à deux corps de tiroirs. **2.** = PAY-DESK. Pay at the desk! payez à la caisse !

desolate[1] ['desolet], a. **1.** (Lieu) désert. **2.** Affligé.

desolate² ['desəleit], *v.tr.* Désoler. **1.** Ravager (un pays). **2.** Affliger (qn).

desolation [desə'leiʃ(ə)n], *s.* Désolation *f.*

despair¹ [dis'peər], *s.* Désespoir *m.* **To be in despair,** être au désespoir. *A dumb d.,* un accablement muet. *To give up (the attempt) in d.,* y renoncer en désespoir de cause. **To drive s.o. to despair,** désespérer qn. **To give way to despair,** se livrer au désespoir.

despair², *v.i.* (*a*) Désespérer (*of,* de). *To d. of doing sth.,* désespérer de faire qch. (*b*) *Abs.* Perdre espoir ; (se) désespérer. **despairing,** *a.* Désespéré. *In a d. tone,* d'un ton de désespoir. **-ly,** *adv.* En désespéré.

despatch [dis'patʃ], *s. & v.* = DISPATCH¹, ².

desperado [despə'reido], *s.m.* Homme capable de tout ; cerveau brûlé ; risque-tout *inv.*

desperate ['despərət], *a.* **1.** (*a*) (*Of condition, malady*) Désespéré. (*b*) **Desperate remedy,** remède héroïque. **Desperate cases require desperate remedies,** aux grands maux les grands remèdes. (*c*) *He's a d. fellow,* c'est un homme capable de tout. **2.** (*a*) *A d. man,* un désespéré. (*b*) *D. energy,* l'énergie du désespoir. *D. conflict,* combat acharné. **To do something desperate,** *F:* faire un malheur. **3.** *A d. earthquake,* un tremblement de terre affreux, épouvantable. **-ly,** *adv.* **1.** (Lutter) désespérément, avec acharnement. **2. Desperately wounded,** atteint de blessures terribles. **3.** *F: D. in love,* éperdument amoureux (*with,* de).

desperation [despə'reiʃ(ə)n], *s.* (Outrance *f* du) désespoir *m.* **To drive s.o. to desperation,** pousser qn à bout. **In desperation,** en désespoir de cause. *I was in desperation,* j'étais aux cent coups.

despicable ['despikəbl], *a.* Méprisable. *D. apology,* excuses plates, basses. **-ably,** *adv.* Bassement.

despise [dis'paiz], *v.tr.* (*a*) Mépriser (qn) ; faire mépris de (qch.). (*b*) Dédaigner (qch.).

despite [dis'pait]. **I.** *s. Lit:* Dépit *m.* **2.** *prep. & prep.phr.* **Despite, in despite of** (sth.), en dépit de (qch.).

despoil [dis'pɔil], *v.tr.* Dépouiller (qn) (*of,* de).

despoiler [dis'pɔilər], *s.* Spoliateur, -trice.

despond¹ [dis'pɔnd], *s.* **The slough of despond,** le bourbier du découragement.

despond², *v.i.* Perdre courage. *To d. of the future,* voir l'avenir en noir.

despondency [dis'pɔndənsi], *s.* Découragement *m,* abattement *m.*

despondent [dis'pɔndənt], *a.* Découragé, abattu. *To feel d.,* se sentir déprimé. **-ly,** *adv.* D'un air découragé.

despot ['despɔt], *s.* Despote *m* ; tyran *m.*

despotic [des'pɔtik], *a.* **1.** (Pouvoir) despotique. **2.** (*Of pers.*) Arbitraire, despote. **-ally,** *adv.* Despotiquement, arbitrairement.

despotism ['despotizm], *s.* Despotisme *m.*

desquamate ['deskwəmeit], *v.i.* Se desquamer.

dessert [de'zə:rt], *s.* Dessert *m.* **des'sert-spoon,** *s.* Cuiller *f* à dessert.

destination [desti'neiʃ(ə)n], *s.* Destination *f.*

destine ['destin], *v.tr.* Destiner. *He was destined for the church,* il fut destiné à l'église. *I was destined to be unhappy,* j'étais destiné à être malheureux. *He was destined never to see her again,* il ne devait plus la revoir. **2.** *Lit: The ship was destined for the Cape,* le vaisseau était en partance pour le Cap.

destiny ['destini], *s.* Destin *m,* destinée *f* ; le sort.

destitute ['destitjut], *a.* **1.** Dépourvu, dénué (*of,* de). **2.** Indigent ; sans ressources ; *F:* sans le sou. *The d. indigents, s.* the destitute, les pauvres. *To be utterly d.,* manquer de tout.

destitution [desti'tju:ʃ(ə)n], *s.* Dénuement *m,* indigence *f* ; la misère. *Reduced to d. in food and clothing,* réduit au manque de nourriture et de vêtements.

destroy [dis'trɔi], *v.tr.* **1.** Détruire ; anéantir (des espérances). *To d. one's eyes by reading,* user ses yeux à (force de) lire. **2.** Tuer, abattre (une bête). **To destroy oneself,** se suicider. **destroying,** *a.* Destructeur, -trice.

destroyer [dis'trɔiər], *s.* **1.** Destructeur, -trice. **2.** *Navy:* (Torpedo-boat) destroyer, (contre-) torpilleur *m,* destroyer *m.*

destructible [dis'trʌktibl], *a.* Destructible.

destruction [dis'trʌkʃ(ə)n], *s.* Destruction *f.* *He is rushing to his own d.,* il court à sa perte. *The d. caused by the fire,* les ravages *m* du feu. **Gambling was his destruction,** le jeu causa sa perte.

destructive [dis'trʌktiv], *a.* Destructeur, -trice ; destructif. *A d. child, F:* un brise-tout *inv.* **-ly,** *adv.* D'une façon funeste.

destructiveness [dis'trʌktivnəs], *s.* **1.** Effet destructeur, pouvoir destructeur (d'un explosif). **2.** (*Of child*) Penchant *m* à détruire.

destructor [dis'trʌktər], *s.* **1.** Destructeur, -trice. **2.** Refuse destructor, incinérateur *m.*

desuetude ['deswitju:d], *s.* Désuétude *f.* *Law fallen into d.,* loi caduque, désuète.

desultory ['desəltəri], *a.* Décousu ; sans suite. *D. conversation,* conversation à bâtons rompus. *D. reading,* lectures décousues. **-ily,** *adv.* D'une manière décousue ; sans suite, sans méthode, à bâtons rompus.

detach [di'tatʃ], *v.tr.* **1.** Détacher, séparer (*from,* de) ; dételer (des wagons). **2.** *Mil:* Détacher (des troupes). **detached,** *a.* Détaché. **1.** Séparé (*from,* de) ; à part. **2.** *D. house,* maison détachée. *Mil:* **Detached post,** poste isolé. **2.** (*a*) (*Of pers.*) Désintéressé. (*b*) *D. manner,* manière désinvolte.

detachable [di'tatʃəbl], *a.* Détachable ; amovible. *Engine with d. head,* moteur à culasse rapportée.

detachment [di'tatʃmənt], *s.* **1.** (*a*) Séparation *f* (*from,* de). (*b*) Action de se détacher ; décollement *m.* **2.** (*a*) Détachement *m* (de l'esprit) (*from,* de). (*b*) Indifférence *f* (*from,* envers). **3.** *Mil:* Détachement. **On detachment,** en détaché.

detail¹ ['di:teil, di'teil], *s.* **1.** Détail *m,* particularité *f.* **To go, enter, into all the details,** donner, entrer dans, tous les détails. **In every detail,** de point en point. **2.** Organe *m,* pièce composante (d'une machine). **3.** *Mil:* Détachement *m* (de corvée).

detail², *v.tr.* **1.** Détailler ; raconter (des faits). **To d. the facts,** énumérer les faits. **2.** *Mil: To d. s.o. for a duty,* désigner qn à un service.

detain [di'tein], *v.tr.* **1.** Détenir (qn en prison). **2.** (*a*) Retenir (qn) ; empêcher (qn) de partir. (*b*) Consigner (un élève).

detect [di'tekt], *v.tr.* **1.** Découvrir (le coupable). **To detect s.o. in the act,** prendre qn en flagrant délit. **2.** Apercevoir. *Object easy to d.,* but facile à discerner. **3.** *W.Tel:* Détecter.

detection [di'tekʃ(ə)n], *s.* **1.** Découverte *f.* **To escape detection,** (i) se dérober aux recherches ; (ii) (*of mistake*) passer inaperçu. **2.** *W.Tel:* Détection *f.*

detective [di'tektiv]. **1.** *a.* Révélateur, -trice. **2.** *s.* Agent *m* de la police secrète. **Private detective,** détective *m.* **Detective novel,** roman policier.

detector [di'tektər], *s.* **1.** (*Pers.*) Découvreur, -euse (d'erreurs, etc.). **2.** *Tchn:* (*a*) Détecteur *m* (de grisou). (b) Signal m d'alarme (d'incendie); avertisseur m.

détente [de'tɑ:nt], s. Détente f (diplomatique).

detention [di'tenʃ(ə)n], s. **1.** (a) Détention f (en prison). **House of detention,** maison f d'arrêt. (b) Sch: Consigne f, retenue f. **2.** (a) Retard m (inévitable); arrêt m. (b) Nau: Arrêt (d'un vaisseau).

deter [di'tə:r], v.tr. (**deterred**) Détourner, décourager (s.o. from doing sth., qn de faire qch.). **Nothing will deter him,** rien ne le fera hésiter.

detergent [di'tə:rdʒənt], a. & s. Détersif (m).

deteriorate [di'ti:rioreit]. **1.** v.tr. Détériorer. **2.** v.t. (a) (Se) détériorer. (b) Diminuer de valeur (c) (Of race) Dégénérer.

deterioration [diti:ərio'reiʃ(ə)n], s. (a) Détérioration f (b) Diminution f de valeur. (c) Dégénération f (d'une race).

determinable [di'tə:rminəbl], a. **1.** (Quantité) déterminable. **2.** Jur: (Contrat) résoluble.

determinate [di'tə:rminet], a. (a) Déterminé; précis; bien défini. (b) Définitif.

determination [ditə:rmi'neiʃ(ə)n], s. **1.** (a) Détermination f (d'une date). (b) Délimitation f (d'une frontière). **2.** (Of pers.) Détermination, résolution f. **To come to a determination,** se décider. **Air of determination,** air résolu. **3.** Jur: (a) Décision f (d'une affaire). (b) Arrêt m, décision. **4.** (a) Jur: Résolution (d'un contrat, etc.). (b) Expiration f (d'un contrat).

determinative [di'tə:rminətiv]. **1.** a. Déterminant. **2.** a. & s. Gram: Déterminatif (m).

determine [di'tə:rmin], v.tr. & i. **1.** (a) Déterminer (une date). Conditions to be determined, conditions à fixer. (b) Délimiter (une frontière). (c) Constater (la nature de qch.). **2.** Décider (une question). **3.** To d. to do sth., décider de faire qch. To d. that . . ., décider, résoudre, que. . . **4.** Jur: (a) v.tr. Résoudre (un contrat). (b) v.i. (Of lease) Prendre fin. **determined,** a. **1.** (Prix) déterminé. **2.** (Of pers.) Déterminé, résolu. D. chin, menton volontaire. **3. To be determined to do sth.,** être résolu de, vouloir absolument, faire qch. **-ly,** adv. Résolument.

deterrent [di'terənt], s. **To act as a d.,** exercer un effet préventif.

detest [di'test], v.tr. Détester.

detestable [di'testəbl], a. Détestable. **-ably,** adv. Détestablement.

detestation [di:tes'teiʃ(ə)n], s. **1.** Détestation f (of, de). **To hold sth. in detestation,** détester qch. **2.** Chose f détestable.

dethrone [di'θroun], v.tr. Détrôner.

dethronement [di'θrounmənt], s. Détrônement m.

detonate ['di:toneit, 'detoneit]. **1.** v.tr. Faire détoner (un explosif). **2.** v.i. Détoner. **detonating,** a. Détonant, explosif.

detonation [di:to'neiʃ(ə)n, de-], s. Détonation f, explosion f.

detonator ['di:toneitər, 'de-], s. **1.** Détonateur m; amorce f. **2.** Rail: Pétard m.

detour [di'tuər], s. Détour m.

detract [di'trakt]. **1.** v.i. To detract from s.o.'s merit, rabaisser le mérite de qn. **2.** v.tr. To d. something from s.o.'s pleasure, diminuer un peu le plaisir de qn.

detractor [di'traktər], s. Détracteur, -trice.

detrain [di'trein], v.i. (Of troops) Débarquer (du train). **detraining,** s. Débarquement m (d'un train).

detriment ['detrimənt], s. Détriment m, dommage m. **To the detriment of . . .,** au détriment, au préjudice, de. . . .

detrimental [detri'ment(ə)l], a. Nuisible (to, à). It would be d. to my interests, cela desservirait mes intérêts. **-ally,** adv. Nuisiblement.

detritus [di'traitəs], s. Geol: Détritus m(pl).

deuce[1] [dju:s], s. **1.** (Of dice, dominoes, cards) Deux m. **2.** Ten: A deux; égalité f (à quarante).

deuce[2], s. F: Diantre m, diable m. **Go to the deuce!** allez vous promener! va-t-en au diable! **To play the deuce with sth.,** ruiner, gâcher, qch. **He's the deuce of a liar,** c'est un satané menteur. **A deuce of a mess,** un joli gâchis.

deuced ['dju:sid]. **1.** a. F: A d. lot of trouble, une peine du diable. **2.** adv. What d. bad luck! quelle fichue guigne! **-ly,** adv. Diablement, diantrement.

devaluate [di:'valjueit], v.tr. Pol.Ec: Dévaluer (le dollar, etc.).

devaluation [di:valju'eiʃ(ə)n], s. Pol.Ec: Dévaluation f.

devastate ['devəsteit], v.tr. Dévaster, ravager. **devastating,** a. **1.** (Of storm) Dévastateur, -trice. **2.** F: (Argument) accablant; (charme) fatal. **-ly,** adv. F: **Devastatingly funny,** d'un comique à se tordre.

devastation [devə'steiʃ(ə)n], s. Dévastation f.

devastator ['devəsteitər], s. Dévastateur, -trice.

develop [di'veləp], v. (**developed** [di'veləpt]) I. v.tr. **1.** Geom: Mth: Développer (une surface, une fonction). **2.** (a) Développer (les facultés). (b) Développer, amplifier (une pensée). (c) Mil: To d. an attack, développer une attaque. **3.** To d. a district, exploiter, mettre en valeur, une région. **4.** To d. heat, engendrer de la chaleur. **5.** Contracter (une maladie, une mauvaise habitude); manifester (une tendance à . . .). **6.** Phot: Révéler, développer (une plaque). II. **develop,** v.i. **1.** (a) (Of the body) Se développer. We must let things d., il faut laisser dérouler les choses. Bot: (Of plant) To d. imperfectly, avorter. (b) London developed into the general mart of Europe, Londres devint peu à peu le grand marché de l'Europe. **2.** Se manifester.

developing, s. **1.** Développement m; mise f en valeur (d'une région). **2.** Phot: Développement. D. of prints, tirage m par développement. **Developing bath,** (bain) révélateur m. **Developing dish,** cuvette f.

developer [di'veləpər], s. Phot: Révélateur m.

development [di'veləpmənt], s. **1.** Geom: Mth: Développement m (d'une surface, d'une fonction). **2.** (a) Développement (des facultés). (b) Développement, amplification f (d'un sujet). **3.** Exploitation f, mise f en valeur (d'une région). **4.** Phot: Développement. **5.** Développement; déroulement m (des événements). **6.** Fait nouveau. **To await further developments,** attendre les événements.

deviate ['di:vieit], v.i. Dévier, s'écarter (from, de). Ph: (Of beam) S'infléchir. (Of projectile) Dériver.

deviation [di:vi'eiʃ(ə)n], s. Déviation f (from, de); écart m. D. from one's instructions, dérogation f à ses instructions.

device [di'vais], s. **1.** (a) Expédient m, moyen m. **To leave s.o. to his own devices,** abandonner qn à ses propres moyens; livrer qn à lui-même. (b) Stratagème m, ruse f. **2.** Dispositif m, appareil m; F: truc m. **3.** Emblème m, devise f.

devil[1] ['dev(i)l], s. **1.** (a) Diable m. **To be between the devil and the deep sea,** être entre l'enclume et le marteau; être entre Charybde et Scylla. **Talk of the devil and he's sure to appear,** quand on parle du loup, on en voit la queue. **To paint the devil blacker than he is**, faire le diable plus noir qu'il n'est. **The devil rebuking sin**, le diable qui s'est fait ermite. **Devil take it!** que le diable l'emporte! **To go to the devil**, se ruiner. **Go to the devil!** allez au diable! **To play the devil with sth.**, mettre la confusion dans qch. **The devil's in it!** le diable s'en mêle! (b) F: **What the devil are you doing?** que diable faites-vous là? **How the devil . . .?** comment diable . . .? **To work like the devil**, travailler avec acharnement. **There'll be the devil to pay**, les conséquences seront sérieuses. (Of a task, etc.) **It's the devil**, c'est le diable. **A d.** of a business, une diable d'affaire. **Devil a one!** pas un! personne! **Devil a bit!** pas du tout! **2.** Démon m. F: **To raise the devil in s.o.**, évoquer les pires passions chez qn. F: **Blue devils**, diables bleus; humeur noire; le cafard. **3.** F: (a) Nègre m (d'un avocat). (b) Typ: **Printer's devil**, apprenti imprimeur. **'devil-fish**, s. Pieuvre f, poulpe m. **'devil-may-'care**, a. & s. Cerveau brûlé; tête brûlée. D.-m.-c. **spirit**, esprit (i) téméraire, (ii) insouciant.

devil², v. (devilled) **1.** v.i. F: **To devil for s.o.**, servir de nègre à (un avocat). **2.** v.tr. Faire griller et poivrer fortement (de la viande).

devilish ['devliʃ]. **1.** a. (a) Diabolique. (b) F: Maudit, satané. **2.** adv. F: **It's d. hot!** il fait diablement chaud! **-ly**, adv. Diaboliquement.

devilment ['devlmənt], **devilry** ['devlri], s. **1.** Méchanceté f. There's some d. afoot, il se trame quelque chose. **2.** To be full of d., avoir le diable au corps.

devious ['di:viəs], a. Détourné, tortueux. **-ly**, adv. D'une façon détournée.

deviousness ['di:viəsnəs], s. Détours mpl, tortuosité f.

devise¹ [di'vaiz], s. **1.** Dispositions f testamentaires de biens immobiliers. **2.** Legs (immobilier).

devise², v.tr. **1.** Combiner (un projet); inventer, imaginer (un appareil); tramer (un complot). To d. some good plan, s'aviser d'un bon expédient. **2.** Jur: Disposer par testament de (biens immobiliers).

devoid [di'void], a. **1.** Dénué, dépourvu (of, de). **2.** D. of cares, exempt de soucis.

devolution [devo'lju:ʃ(ə)n], s. **1.** Biol: Dégénération f (d'une espèce). **2.** Jur: Dévolution f; transmission f. **3.** Pol: (a) Délégation f (de pouvoir). (b) Décentralisation administrative.

devolve [di'volv]. **1.** v.tr. Déléguer, transmettre (des fonctions). **2.** v.i. (a) Incomber (on, upon, à). The duty devolved upon me to . . ., le devoir m'échut de. . . . (b) Jur: (Of property) To d. to, upon, s.o., être dévolu à qn. The estate devolved upon him, c'est lui qui a hérité.

devote [di'vout], v.tr. Vouer, consacrer; accorder (du temps à qch.). To d. oneself to sth., se vouer à (une occupation); s'adonner à (l'étude). **devoted**, a. **1.** Dévoué, attaché (to, à). D. to work, assidu au travail. **2.** A. & Lit: Voué au malheur. Blows fell thick and fast upon his devoted head, il courbait la tête sous les coups du malheur. **-ly**, adv. Avec dévouement.

devotee [devo'ti:], s. Fervent m (of sport, du sport). Surrounded by his devotees, entouré de thuriféraires m.

devotion [di'vouʃ(ə)n], s. **1.** Dévotion f (à Dieu). **2.** To be at one's devotions, faire ses dévotions, ses prières. **3.** Dévouement m (to s.o., à, pour, qn). D. to work, assiduité f au travail.

devotional [di'vouʃən(ə)l], a. (Livre) de dévo-

tion. D. attitude, attitude de prière. **-ally**, adv. Avec dévotion.

devour [di'vauər], v.tr. Dévorer. **devouring**, a. Dévorateur, -trice.

devourer [di'vauərər], s. Dévorateur, -trice.

devout [di'vaut], a. **1.** Dévot, pieux. **2.** (Of wish) Fervent, sincère. **-ly**, adv. **1.** Dévotement. **2.** Sincèrement. F: It is d. to be hoped that . . ., on ne saurait trop espérer que. . . .

devoutness [di'vautnəs], s. Dévotion f, piété f.

dew¹ [dju:], s. Rosée f. Evening dew, serein m; rosée du soir. Dew is falling, il tombe de la rosée. **'dew-berry**, s. Bot: (a) Mûre f des haies. (b) (The shrub) Ronce bleue. **'dew-claw**, s. Z: Ergot m (des chiens, etc.). **'dew-fall**, s. Serein m. **'dew-point**, s. Ph: Meteor: Point m de rosée.

dew², v.tr. Humecter (l'herbe) de rosée. Eyes dewed with tears, yeux mouillés de larmes.

dewdrop ['dju:drop], s. (a) Goutte f de rosée. (b) F: Goutte au bout du nez; roupie f.

dewlap ['dju:lap], s. Fanon m (de la vache).

dewy ['dju:i], a. Humecté de rosée.

dexterity [deks'teriti], s. Dextérité f; habileté f.

dext(e)rous ['dekst(ə)rəs], a. Adroit, habile (in doing sth., à faire qch.). **-ly**, adv. Avec dextérité; habilement.

diabetes [daia'bi:ti:z], s. Med: Diabète m.

diabetic [daia'bi:tik], a. & s. Diabétique (mf).

diabolical [daia'bolik(ə)l], a. (Cruauté) diabolique; (complot) infernal, -aux. D. grin, ricanement satanique. **-ally**, adv. Diaboliquement.

diacritical [daia'kritik(ə)l], a. Gram: (Signe) diacritique.

diadem ['daiədem], s. Diadème m, bandeau m.

diaeresis, pl. **-eses** [dai'i:rəsis, -esi:z], s. Gram: Tréma m.

diagnose [daiag'no:uz], v.tr. Diagnostiquer.

diagnosis, pl. **-oses** [daiag'nousis, -ousi:z], s. Med: Diagnostic m (d'une maladie).

diagnostic [daiag'nostik], a. Diagnostique.

diagonal [dai'agon(ə)l]. **1.** a. Diagonal, -aux. **2.** s. Diagonale f. **-ally**, adv. Diagonalement; en diagonale.

diagram ['daiagram], s. **1.** Diagramme m, tracé m, schéma m. **2.** Graphique m (de température, de pression, etc.). Mch: **Indicator diagram**, diagramme d'indicateur

diagrammatic [daiagra'matik], a. Schématique. **-ally**, adv. Schématiquement.

dial¹ ['daial], s. **1.** (a) Cadran m. S.a. SUN-DIAL. (b) Nau: Compass dial, rose f des vents. (c) Tp: To work the d., faire aller le tabulateur. **2.** P: Visage m. **'dial-'telephone**, s. Téléphone m automatique.

dial², v.tr. (dialled) Tp: To dial a number, composer un numéro. **dialling**, s. Tp: Composition f du numéro. **Dialling tone**, signal m de numérotage.

dialect ['daialekt], s. Dialecte m. Provincial d., patois m.

dialectal [daia'lekt(ə)l], a. Dialectal, -aux.

dialectic(s) [daia'lektik(s)], s. (pl.) Dialectique f.

dialectician [daialek'tiʃ(ə)n], s. Dialecticien, -ienne.

dialogue ['daialog], s. Dialogue m.

diameter [dai'ametər], s. Diamètre m. Wheel 60 inches in diameter, roue qui a 60 pouces de diamètre. Opt: Magnification of eight diameters, grossissement m de huit fois.

diametrical [daia'metrik(ə)l], a. Diamétral, -aux. **-ally**, adv. Diamétralement. That is d. opposed to the truth, c'est le rebours de la vérité.

diamond ['dai(ə)mənd], s. **1.** Diamant m. *D. of the first water*, diamant de première eau. *Rough d.*, diamant brut. *F: He's a rough diamond*, c'est un homme très capable sous des dehors frustes. *F: Diamond cut diamond*, à malin malin et demi. *Tls:* Cutting diamond, diamant de vitrier. **2.** (a) Losange m. Diamond panes, vitres en forme de losange. (b) *Cards:* Carreau m. (c) *Sp:* U.S: Terrain m de baseball. **3.** *Typ:* Corps m quatre. **diamond-shaped,** a. En losange. **'diamond-'wedding,** s. Noces fpl de diamant.

Diana [dai'anə]. *Pr.n.f.* Diane.

diapason [daia'peizən], s. **1.** (a) A. & *Lit:* Crescendo harmonieux. (b) Diapason m, étendue f (d'un instrument). **2.** Diapason, (hauteur f du) ton m (d'un instrument). **3.** Principaux jeux de fond (d'un orgue).

diaper ['daiəpər], s. **1.** *Tex:* Linge ouvré; toile gaufrée. **2.** (a) Serviette (ouvrée). (b) (*For babies*) Couche f.

diaphanous [dai'afənəs], a. Diaphane.

diaphragm ['daiafram], s. **1.** *Anat:* Diaphragme m. **2.** (a) Diaphragme, membrane f. *Porous d.*, membrane poreuse. *Gramophones:* D. of the sound-box, membrane du diaphragme. (b) *Phot:* Iris diaphragm, diaphragme iris.

diarist ['daiarist], s. Auteur m d'un journal (particulier).

diarrhoea [daia'ri:a], s. *Med:* Diarrhée f; dérangement m de corps.

diary ['daiari], s. **1.** Journal (particulier). **2.** (*Memorandum book*) Agenda m.

diathermy ['daiaθə:rmi], s. *Med:* Diathermie f.

diathesis, pl. **-eses** [dai'aθesis, -esi:z], s. *Med:* Diathèse f; prédisposition f (à l'arthrite, etc.).

diatom ['daiatom], s. *Algae:* Diatomée f.

diatomic [daia'tomik], a. *Ch:* Diatomique, biatomique.

diatonic [daia'tonik], a. (Gamme) diatonique.

diatribe ['daiatraib], s. Diatribe f.

dibasic [dai'beisik], a. *Ch:* Bibasique, dibasique.

dibber ['dibər], **dibble** [dibl], s. *Tls:* Plantoir m.

dibbling ['dibliŋ], s. Semis m en poquets.

dibs [dibz], s.pl. **1.** (*Game*) Osselets mpl. **2.** *F:* Argent m; *P:* pognon m, pépette f. He's got the dibs, c'est un richard.

dice¹ [dais], s.pl. See DIE¹ I. **'dice-box,** s. Cornet m à dés.

dice². **1.** v.i. Jouer aux dés. **2.** v.tr. (a) To dice away a fortune, perdre une fortune au jeu. (b) *Cu:* Couper (des légumes) en cubes.

dichotomy [dai'kotomi], s. Dichotomie f.

dickens ['dikənz], s. *F:* Euphemism for DEVIL, DEUCE, (*q.v.*) *in such phrases as* What the dickens . . .?

dicky¹, dickey ['diki], s. *F:* **1.** Bourricot m, âne m. **2.** Dicky(-bird), petit oiseau. **3.** Faux plastron (de chemise). **4.** *Aut:* Spider m. Two-seater with a d., spider.

dicky², a. *F:* (a) Défectueux; peu solide. (b) Malade, indisposé.

dicotyledon [daikoti'li:dən], s. *Bot:* Dicotylédone f, dicotylédonée f.

dicotyledonous [daikoti'li:dənəs], a. *Bot:* Dicotylédone, dicotylédonée.

dictate¹ ['dikteit], s. Commandement m. The dictates of conscience, la voix de la conscience.

dictate² [dik'teit]. **1.** v.tr. Dicter (une lettre, des conditions de paix). *Abs. F:* Faire la loi. *His words are dictated by wisdom*, c'est la sagesse qui dicte ses paroles. **2.** v.i. *F: I won't be*

dictated to, je n'ai pas d'ordres à recevoir; on ne me régente pas.

dictation [dik'tei∫(ə)n], s. **1.** Dictée f. *To write to s.o.'s d.*, écrire sous la dictée de qn. *Passage taken down from d.*, passage dicté. *Sch:* To do dictation, faire la dictée. **2.** Étalage m d'autorité.

dictator [dik'teitər], s. , **1.** Personne qui dicte. **2.** *Pol:* Dictateur m.

dictatorial [diktə'tɔ:riəl], a. **1.** (Pouvoir) dictatorial, -aux. **2.** (Ton) impérieux.

dictatorship [dik'teitər∫ip], s. Dictature f.

diction ['dik∫(ə)n], s. Style m (d'un orateur).

dictionary ['dik∫ənəri], s. Dictionnaire m; glossaire m.

dictum, pl. **-ums, -a** ['diktəm, -əmz, -a], s. **1.** Affirmation f. **2.** Maxime f, dicton m. **3.** Opinion prononcée par un juge.

did [did]. See DO¹.

didactic [di'daktik, dai-], a. Didactique. **-ally,** adv. Didactiquement.

didactics [di'daktiks], s.pl. La didactique.

diddle [didl], v.tr. *P:* Duper, rouler, carotter (qn).

die¹ [dai], s. I. pl. dice [dais]. **1.** Dé m (à jouer); (*with twelve faces*) cochonnet m. *The cast of the die*, le coup de dés. *The die is cast*, le sort en est jeté. **2.** pl. To play dice, jouer aux dés. To cast the dice, jeter les dés. II. die, pl. dies [dai:z]. **1.** *Arch:* Dé. **2.** *Minting:* Coin m. **3.** *Metalw:* Matrice f. Stamping die, étampe f.

die², v.i. (died [daid]; dying ['daiiŋ]) **1.** Mourir; (*prematurely*) périr; (*of animals*) crever. *To be dying*, être à l'agonie. *He died yesterday*, il est mort hier. *It is five years since he died*, il y a cinq ans qu'il est mort. *To die a natural death*, mourir de sa belle mort. *To die before one's time*, mourir avant l'âge. *To die a martyr to the cause*, mourir martyr pour une cause. *They died like heroes*, ils se firent tuer en braves. *To die by one's own hand*, périr de sa propre main. *To die by inches*, mourir à petit feu. *To die hard*, (*of pers.*) vendre chèrement sa vie; (*of an abuse, etc.*) être dur à tuer. *This superstition will die hard*, cette superstition aura la vie dure. *Never say die!* il ne faut pas jeter le manche après la cognée. **2.** To die of laughing, mourir de rire. *I am dying with sleep*, je tombe de sommeil. *To be dying to do sth.*, brûler, mourir d'envie, de faire qch. **3.** *His fortune dies with him*, sa fortune s'éteindra avec lui. *His secret died with him*, il emporta son secret dans le tombeau. *My heart dies within me*, le cœur me manque. **die away,** v.i. (*Of sound*) S'affaiblir; (*of voice*) s'éteindre; *Mth:* (*of curve, etc.*) décroître. *The sound died away in the distance*, le son alla se perdre au loin. **die down,** v.i. (*Of fire*) Baisser; (*of wind*) s'apaiser; (*of sound*) s'éteindre; (*of excitement*) se calmer. **die off,** v.i. Mourir les uns après les autres. **die out,** v.i. (*Of fire*) S'éteindre; (*of custom*) disparaître; (*of race*) s'éteindre. **dying¹,** a. Mourant, agonisant. *In a d. voice*, d'une voix éteinte. The dead and the dying, les morts m et les moribonds m. Prayers for the dying, prières des agonisants. **dying²,** s. Agonie f, mort f. To one's dying day, jusqu'au dernier soupir. Dying words, dernières paroles. **'diehard,** s. Conservateur m à outrance; misoné iste endurci; jusqu'auboutiste m. The die-hards, les irréductibles m.

dielectric [daii'lektrik], a. & s. Diélectrique (m).

dies non ['daii:z'nɔn], s. *Jur:* **1.** Jour férié. **2.** Jour dont il n'est pas tenu compte.

diet¹ ['daiet], s. **1.** Nourriture f. *He needs an abundant d.*, il lui faut une nourriture abondante.

2. To be on a diet, être au régime. *Milk d.,* régime lacté, diète lactée. *Starvation d.,* diète absolue.

diet², *v.tr.* Mettre (qn) au régime.

diet³, *s. Pol:* Diète *f.*

dietary ['daiətəri], *s.* Régime *m* (alimentaire) (d'un malade, d'une prison).

dietetic [daiə'tetik], *a.* Diététique.

differ ['difər], *v.i.* **1.** Différer (*from,* de); être différent (de). **2. To differ in opinion,** différer d'opinion. **To differ about sth.,** ne pas s'accorder sur qch. **I beg to differ,** permettez-moi d'être d'un autre avis. **To agree to differ,** garder chacun son opinion.

difference ['difərəns], *s.* **1.** Différence *f,* écart *m* (*between,* entre). *I don't quite see the d.,* je ne saisis pas la nuance. *What a difference from . . .,* quelle différence avec. . . . *Difference in age,* différence d'âge. *D. in temperature,* écart de température. *With a slight difference,* à peu de chose près. *With this difference that . . .,* à la différence que. . . . *It makes no d.* (*to me*), cela ne (me) fait rien; cela m'est parfaitement égal. *It will make no d., F:* cela ne fera ni chaud ni froid. *That makes all the difference,* voilà qui change les choses du tout au tout. **2.** Différence (entre deux nombres). *Com:* **To split the difference,** partager le différend. *Rail:* **To pay the difference,** payer le supplément. **3.** *Dispute f,* différend *m. Differences arose,* des démêlés *m* survinrent. *Settle your differences,* mettez-vous d'accord.

different ['difərənt], *a.* **1.** Différent (*from, to,* de). *I feel a d. man,* je me sens tout autre. *To do sth. quite a d.,* faire tout autre chose. *To do sth. out of a desire to be d. from other people,* faire qch. par esprit de singularité. *That's quite a different matter,* ça, c'est une autre affaire. *He wears a d. suit every day,* il met tous les jours un nouveau costume. **2.** Divers, différent. *D. people saw him,* différentes personnes l'ont vu. *At different times,* à diverses reprises. **-ly,** *adv.* **1.** Différemment. *He speaks d. from you,* il parle autrement que vous. **2.** Diversement.

differential [difə'renʃ(ə)l]. **1.** *a.* (*a*) Différentiel. *Mth:* **Differential calculus,** calcul différentiel. (*b*) Distinctif. **2.** *s.* (*a*) *Mth:* Différentielle *f.* (*b*) *Aut:* Différentiel *m.*

differentiate [difə'renʃieit], *v.tr.* (*a*) Différencier (*sth. from sth.,* qch. de qch.). *Abs. To d. between two things,* faire la différence entre deux choses. (*b*) *Mth:* Différentier (une fonction).

differentiation [difərenʃi'eiʃ(ə)n], *s.* Différenciation *f.*

difficult ['difikəlt], *a.* (*a*) Difficile, malaisé. *There's nothing d. in that,* cela ne présente aucune difficulté. *Only the beginning is d.,* il n'y a que le premier pas qui coûte. *Person d. of approach,* personne d'accès difficile. *It is difficult to deny that . . .,* on ne saurait nier que. . . . *It is d. to believe that . . .,* on a peine à croire que + *sub.* (*b*) (*Of pers., character*) Difficile; peu commode. **Person difficult to get on with,** personne difficile à vivre.

difficulty ['difikəlti], *s.* Difficulté *f.* **1.** *Work of some d.,* travail assez difficile. *There will be no d. about that,* cela ne fera pas de difficulté. **The difficulty is to . . .,** le difficile, c'est de. . . . *The d. of choice,* l'embarras *m* du choix. *With great d.,* à grand'peine. **2.** Obstacle *m. I see no d. about it,* je n'y vois pas d'inconvénient. **To raise, make, difficulties,** soulever des objections *f;* faire des difficultés. *To look for difficulties where there are none, F:* chercher midi à quatorze

heures. **3.** Embarras *m,* ennui *m.* **To be in a difficulty,** être dans l'embarras. **Ship in difficulties,** navire en détresse. *Pecuniary difficulties,* soucis *mpl* d'argent; la gêne. **To get out of one's difficulties,** se tirer d'affaire. *He knows how to get out of a d.,* il sait se débrouiller.

diffidence ['difidəns], *s.* Manque *m* d'assurance; modestie excessive.

diffident ['difidənt], *a.* Qui manque d'assurance. *To be d.,* se défier de soi-même. *I was d. about speaking to him,* j'hésitais à lui parler. **-ly,** *adv.* Timidement; en hésitant.

diffract [di'frakt], *v.tr. Opt:* Diffracter.

diffraction [di'frakʃ(ə)n], *s. Opt:* Diffraction *f.*

diffractive [di'fraktiv], *a. Opt:* Diffractif, diffringent.

diffuse¹ [di'fju:s], *a.* (*Of light*) Diffus; (*of style*) diffus, prolixe. **-ly,** *adv.* Avec prolixité.

diffuse² [di'fju:z], *v.tr.* Répandre; diffuser. **Diffused lighting,** éclairage diffusé.

diffusion [di'fju:ʒ(ə)n], *s.* Diffusion *f. Ph:* Dispersion *f* (des rayons).

dig¹ [dig], *s. F:* **1.** *I've been having a dig in, at, the garden,* je viens de donner un coup de bêche au jardin. **2.** (*a*) **To give s.o. a dig in the ribs,** enfoncer son doigt dans les côtes de qn; cogner qn du coude. (*b*) **To have a dig at s.o.,** donner un coup de patte, de bec, à qn; lancer un sarcasme à qn. *That's a dig at you,* c'est une pierre dans votre jardin. (*c*) *P:* **To have a dig at sth.,** essayer qch.

dig², *v.* (dug [dʌg]; dug; digging) **1.** *v.tr.* (*a*) Bêcher, retourner (la terre). (*b*) **To dig (up) potatoes,** arracher des pommes de terre. (*c*) Creuser (un trou). *To dig a grave,* creuser une fosse. (*d*) *Abs.* Travailler la terre; fouir. *To dig into, through, sth.,* creuser, percer, qch. **2.** *v.tr.* Enfoncer (*sth. into sth.,* qch. dans qch.). *To dig one's spurs into one's horse,* piquer des deux. **To dig s.o. in the ribs =** *to give s.o. a dig in the ribs.* **3.** *v.i. F:* Loger en garni. **dig in,** *v.tr.* (*a*) Enterrer (du fumier). *Mil:* **To dig oneself in,** se terrer. (*b*) **To dig one's toes in,** s'assurer; se tenir de pied ferme. **dig out,** *v.tr.* (*a*) Extraire, déterrer (qch.). (*b*) *F:* Déterrer (un secret). *Documents dug out of the archives,* documents exhumés des archives. **dig up,** *v.tr.* Déraciner (une plante); mettre à jour (un trésor); piocher (la rue). **digging,** *s.* **1.** (*a*) Bêchage *m* (de la terre); excavation *f.* (*b*) Fouilles *fpl.* **2.** *pl.* **Diggings.** (*a*) *Min:* Placer *m.* (*b*) (*Often abbr. to digs*) *F:* Logement *m,* garni *m.* **To live in digs, in diggings,** loger en garni.

digest¹ ['daidʒest], *s.* Sommaire *m,* abrégé *m,* résumé *m* (d'une science).

digest² [di'dʒest, dai-], *v.tr.* **1.** (*a*) Mettre en ordre (des faits). (*b*) Résumer (un compte rendu). **2.** Digérer, élaborer (un projet). **3.** (*a*) Digérer (les aliments). (*b*) *F:* To digest an insult, avaler une insulte. (*c*) *To d. what one reads,* digérer, s'assimiler, ce qu'on lit.

digestible [di'dʒestibl, dai-], *a.* Digestible.

digestion [di'dʒestʃ(ə)n, dai-], *s.* (*a*) Digestion *f.* (*Of food*) **To be hard of digestion,** être difficile à digérer. (*b*) Sluggish digestion, digestion laborieuse. **To spoil one's digestion,** s'abîmer l'estomac.

digestive [di'dʒestiv, dai-], *a.* Digestif.

digger ['digər], *s.* Bêcheur *m;* piqueur *m* (de la houille); terrassier *m* (de fossés).

digit ['didʒit], *s.* **1.** (*a*) Doigt *m.* (*b*) Doigt de pied; orteil *m.* **2.** *Meas: A:* (Grandeur *f* d'un travers de) doigt. **3.** *Mth:* Chiffre *m* (arabe). *The ten digits,* les neuf chiffres et le zéro.

digital ['didʒit(ə)l]. **1.** a. Digital, -aux. **2.** s. Mus : Touche f (du piano).

digitalis [didʒi'teilis], s. **1.** Bot: Digitale f. **2.** Pharm: Digitaline f.

dignify ['dignifai], v.tr. Donner de la dignité à (qch.); revêtir (qch.) d'un air de majesté.

dignified, a. Plein de dignité; (air) digne. **To assume a dignified air**, se draper dans sa dignité.

dignitary ['dignitəri], s. Dignitaire m.

dignity ['digniti], s. **1.** Dignité f. To preserve one's dignity, soutenir sa dignité. **To be, stand, on one's dignity (with s.o.),** se tenir sur son quant-à-soi; le prendre de haut (avec qn). It is beneath your dignity to accept, vous ne pouvez pas vous abaisser (jusqu')à accepter. **2.** Dignité; haut rang. To maintain the d. of one's (official) position, représenter.

digress [dai'gres, di-], v.i. Faire une digression (from, de); s'écarter (du sujet).

digression [dai'greʃ(ə)n, di-], s. Digression f, écart m. This by way of digression, ceci soit dit en passant.

digs [digz], s.pl. See DIGGING 2 (b).

dihedral [dai'hi:drəl, -'hedrəl]. **1.** a. Dièdre. **2.** s. Angle m dièdre.

dihedron [dai'hi:drən, -'hedrən], s. Dièdre m.

dike¹ [daik], s. **1.** (a) Digue f, levée f. (b) Chaussée surélevée. **2.** A: Fossé m. **3.** Scot: Mur m de clôture en pierres sèches.

dike², v.tr. Protéger (un terrain) par des digues.

dilapidate [di'læpideit], v.tr. Délabrer, dégrader (un édifice). **dilapidated**, a. Délabré, décrépit; F: calamiteux. **Dilapidated-looking car,** auto décrépite. D. hat, chapeau dépenaillé.

dilapidation [dilæpi'deiʃ(ə)n], s. (a) Délabrement m, dégradation f (d'un mur). (b) pl. Jur: Dilapidations, détériorations f, dégradations.

dilatable [dai'leitəbl, di-], a. Dilatable.

dilatation [dailə'teiʃ(ə)n, di-], **dilation** [dai-'leiʃ(ə)n, di-], s. Dilatation f.

dilate [dai'leit, di-]. **1.** v.tr. Dilater. **2.** v.i. (a) (Of eyes) Se dilater. (b) To dilate (up)on a topic, s'étendre sur un sujet.

dilatoriness ['dilətərinəs], s. Lenteur f (à agir).

dilatory ['dilətəri], a. (Of pers.) Lent (à agir); (of action) tardif.

dilemma [dai'lema, di-], s. **1.** Log: Dilemme m. **2.** F: To be in a dilemma, être fort embarrassé.

dilettante, pl. **-ti** [dile'tante, -ti], s. Dilettante m.

dilettantism [dile'tantizm], s. Dilettantisme m.

diligence ['dilidʒəns], s. Assiduité f, application f, diligence f.

diligent ['dilidʒənt], a. Assidu, appliqué, diligent. **-ly**, adv. Avec assiduité, avec application; diligemment.

dill [dil], s. Bot: Aneth odorant.

dilly-dally ['dilidali], v.i. F: Lanterner, traînasser; P: pivoter.

dilute¹ [dai'lju:t, di-], a. **1.** (Of acid) Dilué. **2.** Atténué; (socialisme) à l'eau de rose.

dilute², v.tr. **1.** Diluer; mouiller, arroser (le vin, le lait). **2.** Atténuer, édulcorer (une doctrine).

dilution [dai'lju:ʃ(ə)n, di-], s. **1.** Dilution f; arrosement m (du vin). **2.** Dilution of labour, adjonction f de main-d'œuvre non professionnelle.

diluvial [di'lju:viəl]; **diluvian** [di'lju:viən], a. Geol: Diluvien; diluvial, -aux.

dim¹ [dim], a. (dimmer) (Of light) Faible, pâle; (of colour) effacé; (of sight) faible; (of memory) incertain, vague. **Eyes dim with tears,** yeux voilés de larmes. Dim forebodings, d'obscurs pressentiments. The fire was dim, le feu brûlait faiblement. **To grow dim,** (of light) baisser; (of recollection) s'effacer; (of understanding) s'affaiblir; (of sight) se troubler; (of colour) pâlir. **-ly**, adv. Faiblement, sans éclat; vaguement.

dim², v. (dimmed) **1.** v.tr. (a) Obscurcir; ternir (un miroir). **Eyes dimmed with weeping,** yeux ternis de pleurs. (b) Réduire (la lumière); mettre (l'électricité) en veilleuse. Aut: To dim the head-lights, baisser les phares. (c) Rejeter dans l'ombre (la gloire de qn). **2.** v.i. (Of light) Baisser; (of eyes) s'obscurcir; (of outlines) s'effacer.

dimension¹ [dai'menʃ(ə)n, di-], s. Dimension f; Ind: cote f. **Dimension figures of a machine,** cotes d'une machine.

dimension², v.tr. Coter (un dessin).

dimensional [dai'menʃənəl, di-], a. Two-, three-dimensional space, espace à deux, à trois, dimensions.

diminish [di'miniʃ]. **1.** v.tr. Diminuer, réduire, amoindrir. **2.** v.i. Diminuer, décroître; aller en diminuant. **diminished**, a. Diminué, amoindri. F: To hide one's diminished head, baisser la tête (honteusement).

diminution [dimi'nju:ʃ(ə)n], s. Diminution f; réduction f; amoindrissement m.

diminutive [di'minjutiv]. **1.** a. & s. Gram: Diminutif (m). **2.** a. F: Tout petit; minuscule.

dimity ['dimiti], s. Tex: Basin m, brillanté m.

dimmer ['dimər], s. Réducteur m d'éclairage. Aut: Réducteur "code."

dimness ['dimnəs], s. **1.** Faiblesse f (d'éclairage, de la vue); obscurité f (d'une salle). **2.** Imprécision f (d'un contour).

dimple [dimpl], s. (On cheek, chin) Fossette f.

dimpled [dimpld], a. A fossette(s).

din¹ [din], s. Tapage m, fracas m, vacarme m. F: To kick up a din, faire un charivari de tous les diables. What a din! quel vacarme!

din², v. (dinned) **1.** v.tr. To din sth. into s.o.'s ears, corner qch. aux oreilles à qn. **2.** v.i. (Of voice) To din in s.o.'s ears, retentir dans l'oreille de qn.

dine [dain]. **1.** v.i. Dîner. To dine on, off, sth., dîner de qch. To dine out, dîner en ville. **2.** v.tr. All these people will have to be dined, il faudra donner à dîner à tout ce monde.

dining, s. Dîner m. **dining-car,** s. Wagon-restaurant m. **dining-room,** s. Salle f à manger.

diner ['dainər], s. **1.** Dîneur, -euse. **2.** Rail: = DINING-CAR.

ding-dong ['diŋ'dɔŋ]. **1.** adv. Digue-din-don. **2.** s. Tintement m (des cloches). **3.** a. D.-d. match, partie durement disputée.

dinghy ['diŋgi], s. Nau: Canot m, youyou m. **Collapsible dinghy,** berthon m.

dinginess ['dindʒinəs], s. Aspect enfumé, manque m de fraîcheur (du mobilier); propreté douteuse (d'une maison, du mobilier).

dingle [diŋgl], s. Vallon (boisé).

dingo ['diŋgo], s. Dingo m; chien m sauvage.

dingy ['dindʒi], a. Qui manque d'éclat, de fraîcheur; (of furniture) défraîchi; (of colour) terne; (of linen) crasseux. D. white, d'un blanc sale.

dinky ['diŋki], a. F: Coquet, mignon.

dinner ['dinər], s. Dîner m. I have s.o. in to d., j'ai quelqu'un à dîner. To be at dinner, être à table. We were having d., nous étions en train de dîner. To go out to dinner, dîner (i) en ville, (ii) chez des amis. Public dinner, banquet m. Rail: Second dinner, deuxième service m. **'dinner-can,** s. Potager m (d'ouvrier).

'dinner-dance, .. Dîner suivi de bal.
'dinner-hour, s. L'heure *f* du dîner.
'dinner-jacket, s. (Veston *m*) smoking *m*.
'dinner-lift, s. Monte-plats *m inv.* **'dinner-**
.mat, s. Dessous *m* de plat ; garde-nappe *m*.
'dinner-party, s. Dîner prié. **To have a**
dinner-party, avoir du monde à dîner. **'dinner-**
service, -set, s. Service *m* de table. **'dinner-**
time, s. L'heure *f* du dîner. **'dinner-wagon,** s.
Furn: Servante *f*.
dinosaur ['dainosɔ:r], s. Dinosaurien *m*.
dint[1] [dint], s. **1.** = DENT[1]. **2.** By dint of . . .,
à force de. . . .
dint[2], *v.tr.* = DENT[2].
diocesan [dai'ɔsisən], a. & s. *Ecc:* Diocésain (*m*).
diocese ['daiosi(:)s], s. Diocèse *m*.
Diogenes [dai'ɔdʒeni:z]. *Pr.n.m.* Diogène.
diopter [dai'ɔptər], s. *Opt.Meas:* Dioptrie *f*.
dioxide [dai'ɔksaid], s. *Ch:* Bioxyde *m*.
dip[1] [dip], s. **1.** Plongement *m*, immersion *f* (de
qch. dans un liquide). *F:* To have a dip into a
book, jeter un coup d'œil dans un livre.
2. (a) Inclinaison *f* (de l'aiguille aimantée).
(b) Plongée *f* (du terrain) ; déclivité *f*. **3.** *Nau:*
Salut *m* (avec le pavillon). **Flag at the dip,**
pavillon à mi-drisse. **4.** Baignade *f*. *I'm going*
for a dip, je vais me baigner. **5.** **Sheep-dip,** bain
parasiticide (pour moutons). **'dip-needle,** s.
Boussole *f* d'inclinaison. **'dip-rod, -stick,** s.
Aut: Réglette-jauge *f*; pige *f* de niveau d'huile.
dip[2], *v.* (dipped) **I.** *v.tr.* **1.** Plonger, tremper (les
mains dans l'eau). *F:* I am always dipping my
hand into my pocket, je suis toujours à débourser.
2. Immerger, décaper, dérocher (un métal).
Husb: To dip the sheep, baigner les moutons
(dans un bain parasiticide). **3.** Baisser (qch.)
subitement. *Aut:* To dip the head-lights, faire
basculer les phares ; baisser les phares. **To 'dip**
and switch,' se mettre en code. *Nau:* To dip
one's flag, *abs.* to dip, to a ship, saluer un vaisseau
avec son pavillon ; *abs.* saluer. **4.** He dipped his
spoon into the pot, il puisa dans la marmite avec
sa cuiller. II. dip, *v.i.* **1.** Plonger (dans l'eau).
2. (Of sun) Baisser. The sun dipped below the sea,
le soleil s'enfonça dans la mer. **3.** (Of compass-
needle) Incliner ; (of scale) pencher. The road dips
sharply, la route plonge brusquement. **4.** To dip
into a book, feuilleter un livre. To dip into one's
purse, puiser dans sa bourse. **To dip deep into**
the past, sonder le passé. **dipping,** s. Plongée *f*,
immersion *f*; *Metalw:* dérochage *m*, décapage *m*.
'dipping-needle, s. = DIP-NEEDLE.
diphtheria [dif'θiːəria], s. *Med:* Diphtérie *f*.
diphthong ['difθɔŋ], s. *Ling:* Diphtongue *f*.
diplogen ['diplɔdʒən], s. *Ch:* Hydrogène lourd ;
deutérium *m*.
diploma [di'ploumа], s. Diplôme *m*.
diplomacy [di'ploumɔsi], s. Diplomatie *f*.
diplomat ['diplomɑt], s. Diplomate *m*.
diplomatic [diplo'matik], a. **1.** Diplomatique.
To enter the diplomatic service, entrer dans la
diplomatie. **2.** Adroit, prudent. **-ally,** adv.
1. Diplomatiquement. **2.** Avec tact.
diplomatist [di'ploumatist], s. Diplomate *m*.
dipper ['dipər], s. **1.** *Ind:* (Pers.) Plongeur,
-euse. **2.** *Orn:* Merle m d'eau. **3.** (a) *U.S:*
Cuiller *f* à pot. (b) *Astr:* *U.S:* The (Great)
Dipper, la Grande Ourse. **4.** (a) *I.C.E:* Oil
dipper, plongeur *m* (de tête de bielle). (b) *Aut:*
= DIP-ROD. **5.** *Aut:* Basculeur *m* (pour phares).
dipsomania [dipso'meinia], s. Dipsomanie *f*.
dipsomaniac [dipso'meiniak], a. & s. Dipsomane (*mf*).
dipter ['diptər], s. *Ent:* Diptère *m*.

diptera ['diptəra], *s.pl.* *Ent:* Diptères *m*. ·
dipterous ['diptərəs], a. *Ent:* Diptère.
diptych ['diptik], s. Diptyque *m*.
dire ['daiər], a. Désastreux, néfaste, affreux.
Dire necessity, nécessité implacable. *D. poverty*,
misère noire. *D. forebodings*, pressentiments
lugubres. **To be in dire distress,** se trouver dans
la dernière misère.
direct[1] [dai'rekt, di-], *v.tr.* **1.** Adresser (une
lettre) (to s.o., à qn). Letter directed to s.o., lettre
à l'adresse de qn. **2.** Gouverner (sa conduite) ;
gérer, régir (une entreprise). **3.** (a) To d. s.o.'s
attention to sth., attirer l'attention de qn sur qch.
(b) To direct one's steps towards . . ., diriger
ses pas, se diriger, vers. . . . To d. one's efforts
to(wards) an end, orienter ses efforts vers un but.
4. To direct s.o. to the station, indiquer la gare
à qn. **5.** (a) To direct s.o. to do sth., ordonner
à qn, charger qn, de faire qch. **As directed,**
selon les instructions. I was directed to . . ., je
reçus l'ordre de. . . . Do as duty directs, faites
ce que le devoir vous ordonne. (b) (Of judge) To
direct the jury, instruire le jury.
direct[2]. **1.** a. (a) Direct. **Direct cause,** cause
immédiate. **Direct taxation,** contributions directes. **To be a direct descendant of s.o.,**
descendre de qn en ligne directe. **The direct**
opposite of sth., juste l'opposé de qch. *Gram:*
Direct object, complément direct. (b) (Of pers.)
Franc, *f.* franche. (c) Absolu, formel. *D. answer*,
réponse catégorique. (d) *El:* **Direct current,**
courant continu. **2.** adv. (Aller) directement, tout
droit. **-ly.** **1.** adv. (a) (Aller) directement, tout
droit. To go d. to the point, aller droit au fait.
I am not d. concerned, cela ne m'intéresse pas
personnellement. **2.** Absolument. *D. contrary*,
diamétralement opposé (to, à). He lives d.
opposite the church, il demeure juste en face de
l'église. (c) Tout de suite, tout à l'heure. The
doctor came d., le médecin vint aussitôt. **2.** conj.
F: Aussitôt que, dès que. I will come d. I've
finished, je viendrai dès que j'aurai fini.
direction [dai'rekʃ(ə)n, di-], s. **1.** Direction *f*,
administration *f* (d'une société). **Under the**
direction of . . ., sous la conduite de. . . .
2. Adresse *f* (d'une lettre). **3.** (a) Direction,
sens *m*. In every direction, en tous sens. In the
opposite direction, en sens inverse. To lose one's
sense of direction, perdre le sens de l'orientation *f*.
Mth: **Positive direction,** sens direct. **Negative**
direction, sens rétrograde. (b) Improvements in
many directions, améliorations sous bien des rapports *m*. **4.** (Usu. pl.) Instruction(s) *f(pl)*. *Sailing*
directions, instructions nautiques. **Stage direction,**
indication *f* scénique. **di'rection-finder,** s.
W.Tel: Radiogoniomètre *m*. **di'rection-**
finding, s. Radiogoniométrie *f*. **di'rection-**
post, s. Poteau indicateur.
directional [dai'rekʃən(ə)l, di-], a. **Directional**
wireless, radiogoniométrie *f*. **Directional-finding**
station, station radiogoniométrique.
directive [dai'rektiv, di-], a. Directif.
directness [dai'rektnəs, di-], s. Franchise *f*
(d'une réponse).
director [dai'rektər, di-], s. **1.** (Pers.) (a) Administrateur *m*, directeur *m* (d'une société) ;
gérant *m* (d'une entreprise). (b) *R.C.Ch:* Directeur de conscience. **2.** (a) *Navy:* **Director top,**
hune *f* de télépointage. (b) Appareil *m* de visée
(de torpille). (c) *Mec.E:* etc: Guide *m* (d'un
mouvement).
directorate [dai'rektərət, di-], s. (Conseil *m*
d')administration *f*; direction *f* (des chemins
de fer).

directorship [dai'rektərʃip, di-], *s.* Directorat *m*.
directory [dai'rektəri, di-], *s.* **I.** Répertoire *m* d'adresses ; *(in France)* le Bottin ; annuaire *m* (des téléphones). **2.** *Fr.Hist:* The Directory, le Directoire.
directress [dai'rektres, di-], *s.f.* Directrice.
direful ['daiərful], *a.* *Poet:* = DIRE. **-fully, adv.** Désastreusement, affreusement.
dirge [də:rdʒ], *s.* Hymne *m* ou chant *m* funèbre.
dirigible ['diridʒibl], *a. & s.* Dirigible balloon, *F:* dirigible, (ballon) dirigeable (*m*).
dirk [də:rk], *s.* Poignard *m*.
dirt [də:rt], *s.* Saleté *f.* **I.** (*a*) Boue *f*, crotte *f*, ordure *f*; (*body dirt*) crasse *f.* Hands ingrained with dirt, mains encrassées. *F:* To throw dirt at s.o., éclabousser la réputation de qn. To treat s.o. like dirt, traiter qn comme le dernier des derniers. *P:* To eat dirt, être forcé de faire des excuses. (*b*) *I.C.E:* D. in the carburettor, encrassement *m* du carburateur. (*c*) *Min:* Terre *f* aurifère. **2.** Malpropreté *f.* **'dirt-proof,** *a.* Insalissable. **'dirt-track,** *s.* *Sp:* Piste *f* en cendrée.
dirtiness ['də:rtinəs], *s.* Saleté *f*, malpropreté *f.*
dirty[1] ['də:rti], *a.* **I.** Sale, malpropre, crasseux ; crotté ; encrassé. *D. hands*, mains sales. *D. face*, visage barbouillé. *D. shoes*, souliers crottés. *D. streets*, rues fangeuses. *Don't get your gloves d.*, ne salissez pas vos gants. **2.** Dirty weather, mauvais temps ; *Nau:* gros temps. **3.** *D. mind*, esprit tourné vers la saleté, vers l'obscénité. **4.** To play s.o. a dirty trick, jouer un vilain tour à qn. *It's a dirty business*, c'est une sale affaire. *P:* To do, play, the dirty on s.o., faire une crasse à qn ; jouer un sale coup à qn. **-ily, adv.** Salement. **1.** Malproprement. **2.** Bassement.
dirty[2]. **I.** *v.tr.* Salir, crotter, encrasser. *To d. one's hands*, se salir les mains. **2.** *v.i.* (*Of stuff*) *To d. easily*, se salir facilement.
disability [disə'biliti], *s.* **I.** (*a*) Incapacité *f.* (*b*) Physical disability, infirmité *f.* (*c*) *Adm:* Invalidité *f.* **2.** *Jur:* Inhabilité *f* (à faire qch).
disable [dis'eibl], *v.tr.* Mettre (qn) hors de combat ; estropier (qn) ; désemparer (un navire). Disabled soldier, invalide *m*. Disabled ex-service-men, mutilés *m* de guerre. (*Of ship*) To be disabled, avoir des avaries ; être en panne.
disablement [dis'eiblmənt], *s.* **I.** Mise *f* hors de combat. **2.** Invalidité *f*; incapacité *f* de travail.
disabuse [disə'bju:z], *v.tr.* Désabuser (*of*, de) ; désaveugler (qn).
disaccustom [disə'kʌstəm], *v.tr.* Désaccoutumer, déshabituer (*s.o. to sth.*, qn de qch.).
disadvantage [disad'va:ntedʒ], *s.* Désavantage *m*, inconvénient *m*. *To take s.o. at a disadvantage*, prendre qn au dépourvu. *To show oneself to disadvantage*, se montrer sous un jour désavantageux.
disadvantageous [disadvan'teidʒəs], *a.* Désavantageux, défavorable (*to*, à).
disaffected [disə'fektid], *a.* Désaffectionné.
disaffection [disə'fekʃ(ə)n], *s.* Désaffection *f.*
disagree [disə'gri:], *v.i.* **I.** (*a*) Être en désaccord, n'être pas d'accord (*with*, avec). (*b*) To d. with s.o., donner tort à qn. *I disagree*, je ne suis pas de cet avis. **2.** (*a*) (*Quarrel*) Se brouiller (*with*, avec). (*b*) *They had always disagreed*, ils avaient toujours vécu en mésintelligence. **3.** *The climate disagrees with him*, le climat ne lui convient pas. *Wine disagrees with him*, le vin lui est contraire.
disagreeable [disə'gri:əbl], *a.* (*a*) Désagréable (*to*, à) ; déplaisant (*to*, à). (*b*) *A d. incident*, un incident fâcheux. (*c*) (*Of pers.*) Désagréable,

maussade. **-ably, adv.** Désagréablement ; fâcheusement.
disagreeableness [disə'gri:əblnəs], *s.* **I.** Désagrément *m.* **2.** (*a*) Mauvaise humeur. (*b*) Désobligeance *f* (*to*, envers).
disagreement [disə'gri:mənt], *s.* **I.** Différence *f* (*between*, entre) ; discordance *f.* **2.** Désaccord *m* (*with s.o. on, about, sth.*, avec qn sur qch.). **3.** (*a*) Différend *m*, querelle *f.* (*b*) Mésintelligence *f*, mésentente *f* (*between*, entre).
disallow [disə'lau], *v.tr.* **I.** Ne pas admettre (une réclamation). *Jur:* Rebuter, rejeter (un témoignage). **2.** Ne pas permettre ; interdire.
disappear [disə'pi:ər], *v.i.* Disparaître (*from a place*, d'un endroit) ; (*of difficulties*) s'aplanir. *He disappeared from our sight*, il disparut à nos yeux. *Since he disappeared*, depuis sa disparition.
disappearing, *a.* (*Cible*) à éclipse.
disappearance [disə'pi:ərəns], *s.* Disparition *f.*
disappoint [disə'pɔint], *v.tr.* (*a*) Désappointer (qn) ; (*after promising*) manquer de parole à (qn). (*b*) Décevoir, chagriner (qn). *Are you disappointed?* c'est une déception? *He was sorely disappointed*, il a eu un grave mécompte. *To be disappointed in love*, avoir des chagrins d'amour. (*c*) Décevoir (les espérances de qn) ; tromper (l'attente de qn). *I was much disappointed with it*, cela ne répondait aucunement à mon attente.
disappointing, *a.* **I.** Décevant. **2.** *How d.!* quel contretemps !
disappointment [disə'pɔintmənt], *s.* Déception *f*, désappointement *m* ; mécompte *m*. *Keen d.*, crève-cœur *m inv*. *To suffer many disappointments*, essuyer bien des déboires *m*.
disapprobation [disapro'beiʃ(ə)n], *s.* Désapprobation *f* (*of*, de).
disapproval [disə'pru:vəl], *s.* Désapprobation *f* (*of*, de). *Look of d.*, regard désapprobateur.
disapprove [disə'pru:v]. **I.** *v.tr.* Désapprouver (qn) ; réprouver. **2.** *v.i.* To disapprove of sth., désapprouver qch. *To d. of sth. being done*, désapprouver, trouver mauvais, que l'on fasse qch.
disapprovingly [disə'pru:viŋli], *adv.* D'un air ou d'un ton désapprobateur.
disarm [dis'a:rm]. **I.** *v.tr.* Désarmer (un prisonnier, etc.). **2.** *v.i.* Désarmer. **disarming**[1], *a.* (Franchise, etc.) qui vous désarme. **disarming**[2], *s.* Désarmement *m*.
disarmament [dis'a:rməmənt], *s.* Désarmement *m*.
disarrange [disə'reindʒ], *v.tr.* Déranger ; mettre (qch.) en désordre. *Disarranged hair*, cheveux défaits.
disarrangement [disə'reindʒmənt], *s.* Dérangement *m*, désajustement *m*, désordre *m*.
disarray[1] [disə'rei], *s.* Désarroi *m* ; désordre *m*.
disarray[2], *v.tr.* (*a*) Mettre (des troupes) en désarroi, en déroute. (*b*) Mettre en désordre.
disarticulate [disa:r'tikjuleit], *v.tr.* Désarticuler.
disaster [di'za:stər], *s.* Désastre *m* ; (*by shipwreck, fire, flood*) sinistre *m*. *Public d.*, calamité publique. *Railway d.*, catastrophe *f* de chemin de fer. *He is heading for d.*, il court à sa perte.
disastrous [di'za:strəs], *a.* Désastreux ; funeste. **-ly, adv.** Désastreusement.
disavow [disə'vau], *v.tr.* Désavouer ; renier (sa foi, une action).
disavowal [disə'vauəl], *s.* Désaveu *m* ; reniement *m* (de sa foi).
disband [dis'band]. **I.** *v.tr.* Licencier, congédier (des troupes). **2.** *v.i.* (*Of troops*) (*a*) Se débander.

(b) Être licencié. **disbanding,** s. Licenciement m.

disbar [dis'bɑːr], v.tr. (disbarred) Rayer (un avocat) du tableau de l'ordre.

disbelief [disbi'liːf], s. **1.** Disbelief in sth., incrédulité f à l'égard de qch.; refus m de croire à qch. **2.** Theol: Incrédulité.

disbelieve [disbi'liːv]. **1.** v.tr. Ne pas croire (qch.); refuser créance à (qn). **2.** v.i. To d. in sth., ne pas croire à qch.

disbeliever [disbi'liːvər], s. Incrédule mf.

disbud [dis'bʌd], v.tr. (disbudded) Ébourgeonner, épincer (un arbre fruitier).

disburden [dis'bəːrdn], v.tr. **1.** Décharger. To d. one's mind of a secret, décharger sa conscience d'un secret. **2.** Déposer (un fardeau).

disburse [dis'bəːrs], v.tr. Débourser (de l'argent).

disbursement [dis'bəːrsmənt], s. **1.** Déboursement m. **2.** pl. Disbursements, débours mpl.

disc [disk], s. = DISK.

discard¹ [dis'kɑːrd], s. (a) (At cribbage) Écart m (action ou carte). (b) (At bridge) Défausse f.

discard², v.tr. (a) (At cribbage) Écarter (une carte). (b) (At bridge) To d. a suit, se défausser d'une couleur. Abs. To discard, se défausser. **2.** Mettre (qch.) de côté; se défaire de (qch.). To d. one's winter clothing, laisser de côté ses vêtements d'hiver. **discarding,** s. **1.** Cards: (a) Défausse f. (b) (At bridge) Défausse f. **2.** Mise f de côté (de qch.); mise au rancart (d'une théorie).

discern [di'zəːrn, di'səːrn], v.tr. (a) Distinguer, discerner, apercevoir. To d. no difference, ne percevoir aucune différence. (b) To d. good from bad, discerner le bien d'avec le mal. **discerning,** a. (Of pers.) Judicieux; (of intelligence) pénétrant; (of taste) sûr.

discernible [di'zəːrnibl, di'səːrnibl], a. Perceptible.

discernment [di'zəːrnmənt, di'səːrn-], s. Discernement m.

discharge¹ [dis't͡ʃɑːrdʒ], s. **1.** Déchargement m (d'un navire). **2.** Décharge f (d'artillerie). **3.** (a) Décharge, déversement m; dégagement m (de gaz); débit m (d'une pompe). (b) El: Décharge. (c) Med: Écoulement m. **4.** (a) Renvoi m (d'un employé). (b) Libération f (d'un militaire); (after active service) démobilisation f. To take one's discharge, prendre son congé. **5.** Jur: (a) Mise f en liberté, élargissement m (d'un prisonnier). (b) Acquittement m (d'un accusé). (c) Discharge in bankruptcy, réhabilitation f (d'un failli). **6.** Accomplissement m (d'un devoir). In the discharge of his duties, dans l'exercice m de ses fonctions. **7.** (a) Payement m (d'une dette). (b) Quittance f. In full discharge, pour acquit.

discharge². I. v.tr. **1.** Décharger (un navire). **2.** (a) Décharger (une arme à feu). (b) El: Décharger (une pile, etc.). **3.** (a) Décharger, débarder (une cargaison). (b) (Of vehicle) To d. passengers, déposer des voyageurs. **4.** (a) Congédier (un employé); débaucher (un ouvrier); destituer (un fonctionnaire). (b) Libérer (un homme) du service militaire. Navy: Débarquer (un équipage). (c) To discharge a patient (from hospital), renvoyer un malade guéri. **5.** Jur: (a) Libérer (un prisonnier). (b) Acquitter (un accusé). **6.** Discharged bankrupt, failli réhabilité. **7.** (a) Lancer (un projectile). (b) (Of abscess) To d. pus, jeter du pus. Abs. To discharge, (of abscess) se dégorger; (of wound) suppurer. (c) (Of chemical reaction) Dégager, émettre (un gaz). (d) River that discharges into a lake, rivière

qui se déverse dans un lac. **8.** (a) S'acquitter de (son devoir). (b) Acquitter (une dette). II. **discharge,** v.i. **1.** (Of ship) Être en déchargement. **2.** (Of gun) Partir. **discharging,** s. Décharge f, déchargement m.

disciple [di'saipl], s. Disciple m.

disciplinarian [disipli'nɛəriən], s. Disciplinaire m. He is a good d., il a de la discipline.

disciplinary ['disiplinəri], a. (Punition) disciplinaire; (établissement) de discipline.

discipline¹ ['disiplin], s. Discipline f. Iron d., discipline de fer, à la prussienne. To enforce d., maintenir la discipline.

discipline², v.tr. (a) Discipliner (des élèves). (b) Disciplined in the school of adversity, formé, élevé, à l'école de l'adversité.

disclaim [dis'kleim], v.tr. **1.** Renoncer à (un droit). **2.** Désavouer (qch.). To d. all responsibility, dénier toute responsabilité. **3.** Renier (l'autorité de qn).

disclaimer [dis'kleimər], s. (a) Jur: D. of a right, renonciation f à un droit. (b) D. of responsibility, déni m de responsabilité.

disclose [dis'klo:uz], v.tr. Découvrir, révéler (qch.); divulguer (un secret).

disclosure [dis'klou:ʒər], s. Mise f à découvert (d'un trésor); révélation f (de sa pensée); divulgation f (d'un secret).

discolour [dis'kʌlər], v.tr. (a) Décolorer. (b) Ternir, délaver (un tissu).

discolo(u)ration [diskʌlə'reiʃ(ə)n], s. Décoloration f.

discomfit [dis'kʌmfit], v.tr. **1.** Lit: Déconfire (une armée). **2.** F: Décontenancer, déconcerter (qn).

discomfiture [dis'kʌmfitjər], s. **1.** Lit: Déconfiture f (d'une armée). **2.** Déconvenue f (de qn).

discomfort [dis'kʌmfərt], s. (a) Manque m de confort. (b) Malaise m, gêne f.

discommode [disko'moud], v.tr. Incommoder (qn).

discompose [diskom'po:uz], v.tr. Troubler, agiter (qn). Discomposed countenance, visage défait.

discomposure [diskom'pou:ʒər], s. Trouble m, agitation f; perturbation f (d'esprit).

disconcert [diskon'sə:rt], v.tr. Déconcerter, interloquer (qn). **disconcerting,** a. Déconcertant, troublant.

disconnect [disko'nekt], v.tr. **1.** Désunir, disjoindre (sth. with, from, sth., qch. de qch.); décrocher (des wagons); débrayer (une machine). **2.** El: Déconnecter (un secteur). To d. a telephone line, couper la communication. **disconnected,** a. **1.** (a) Détaché, isolé. (b) Tchn: Débrayé; déconnecté. **2.** (Of speech) Décousu. **-ly,** adv. (Parler, penser) sans suite, à bâtons rompus.

disconnectedness [disko'nektidnəs], s. Incohérence f, manque m de suite (des idées).

disconsolate [dis'kɔnsolet], a. Tout triste; inconsolable; désolé.

discontent [diskon'tent], s. (a) Mécontentement m. (b) Sujet m de mécontentement; grief m.

discontented [diskon'tentid], a. (a) Mécontent (with, de); peu satisfait (de son sort). (b) D. spirits, esprits factieux.

discontentedness [diskon'tentidnəs], s. Mécontentement m (de son sort).

discontinuance [diskon'tinjuəns], s. Discontinuation f, cessation f (de fabrication).

discontinue [diskon'tinju:]. **1.** v.tr. Discontinuer (qch.). To d. one's visits, cesser ses visites. To d. a *newspaper*, se désabonner à un journal. **2.** *v.i.* Cesser.

discontinuity [diskɔntiˈnjuiti], *s.* **1.** Discontinuité *f.* **2.** Solution *f* de continuité; intervalle *m.*

discontinuous [diskɔnˈtinjuəs], *a.* Discontinu. *Mth:* **Discontinuous quantity**, quantité discrète.

discord [ˈdiskɔːrd], *s.* **1.** Dıscorde *f*, désunion *f*. *Civil d.*, dissensions civiles. **2.** *Mus:* (i) Dissonance *f*; (ii) accord dissonant.

discordance [disˈkɔːrdəns], *s.* **1.** Discordance *f* (des sons). **2.** *D. of opinions*, désaccord *m* d'opinions.

discordant [disˈkɔːrdənt], *a.* **1.** (*a*) (*Of sound*) Discordant; peu harmonieux. (*b*) *Mus:* Dissonant. **2.** *D. opinions*, opinions opposées.

discount[1] [ˈdiskaunt], *s.* **1.** *Com:* Remise *f*, rabais *m.* **To sell sth. at a discount**, vendre qch. au rabais. *D. for quantities*, réductions *fpl* sur la quantité. *D. for cash*, escompte *m* au comptant. **2.** *Fin:* Escompte. (*Of shares*) **To stand at a discount**, accuser une perte. *F: Politeness is at a d.*, on fait peu de cas de la politesse. ˈ**discount bank**, *s.* Comptoir *m* d'escompte. ˈ**discount price**, *s. Com:* Prix *m* faible.

discount[2] [disˈkaunt, ˈdiskaunt], *v.tr.* **1.** *Fin:* Escompter; faire l'escompte (d'un effet). **2.** (*a*) Ne pas tenir compte de (qn, qch.). (*b*) *F:* Faire peu de cas de (l'avis de qn). *To d. news*, faire la part de l'exagération dans une nouvelle.

discountenance [disˈkauntinəns], *v.tr.* **1.** Décontenancer, déconcerter (qn). **2.** Décourager (un projet); désapprouver.

discourage [disˈkʌredʒ], *v.tr.* Décourager, abattre (qn). **To become discouraged**, se décourager. **discouraging**, *a.* Décourageant. **-ly**, *adv.* D'une manière décourageante.

discouragement [disˈkʌredʒmənt], *s.* **1.** Découragement *m.* **2.** Désapprobation *f* (d'un projet).

discourse[1] [ˈdiskɔːrs], *s.* **1.** *Lit:* Discours *m*; dissertation *f* (*on*, sur). **2.** *Lit. & Hum:* **To hold discourse with s.o.**, s'entretenir avec qn (*on*, de).

discourse[2] [disˈkɔːrs], *v.i. Lit:* (*a*) Discourir (*on*, *of*, de). (*b*) Causer, s'entretenir (de).

discourteous [disˈkəːrtiəs, -ˈkɔːr-], *a.* Discourtois, impoli. **-ly**, *adv. To behave d. to s.o.*, faire une impolitesse à qn.

discourtesy [disˈkəːrtəsi, -ˈkɔːr-], *s.* Impolitesse *f*.

discover [disˈkʌvər], *v.tr.* **1.** Découvrir, trouver. (*a*) *To d. a new gas*, découvrir un gaz nouveau. (*b*) *I discovered too late that . . .*, je m'aperçus trop tard que. . . . **2.** (*a*) *A. & Lit:* Révéler, laisser voir (qch.); divulguer (un secret). (*b*) *Th:* **To be discovered at the rise of the curtain**, être en scène au lever du rideau.

discoverer [disˈkʌvərər], *s.* Découvreur, -euse.

discovery [disˈkʌvəri], *s.* **1.** Découverte *f. A great d.*, (i) une grande découverte; (ii) *F:* (*of a find*) une trouvaille. **2.** *A. & Lit:* Révélation *f* (d'un secret); divulgation *f*.

discredit[1] [disˈkredit], *s.* **1.** Doute *m.* **To throw discredit upon a statement**, mettre en doute une affirmation. **2.** Discrédit *m* (de qn, de qch.); déconsidération *f* (de qn). *To reflect d. on . . .*, jeter du discrédit sur. . . .

discredit[2], *v.tr.* **1.** Ne pas croire (un bruit); mettre en doute (un bruit). **2.** Discréditer (une opinion); déconsidérer (qn).

discreditable [disˈkreditəbl], *a.* **1.** Peu digne. *Conduct d. to a barrister*, conduite indigne d'un avocat. *D. acquaintances*, connaissances interlopes. **2.** *D. examination-paper*, composition qui

ne fait pas honneur au candidat. **-ably**, *adv.* De façon indigne, déshonorante.

discreet [disˈkriːt], *a.* **1.** Avisé, sage. *A d. smile*, un petit sourire contenu. **2.** Discret, -ète. **-ly**, *adv.* **1.** Avec réserve. **2.** Discrètement.

discrepancy [disˈkrepənsi], *s.* Désaccord *m*; divergence *f* (de témoignages). *There is a d. between the two stories*, les deux récits ne cadrent pas.

discrepant [ˈdiskripənt, disˈkrepənt], *a.* Différent (*from*, de). *D. accounts*, récits contradictoires.

discrete [disˈkriːt], *a. Mth:* Discret, -ète; discontinu.

discretion [disˈkreʃ(ə)n], *s.* **1.** Discrétion *f.* **I shall use my own discretion**, je ferai comme bon me semblera. **To leave sth. to s.o.'s discretion**, laisser qch. à la discrétion de qn. **2.** Sagesse *f*, jugement *m*, prudence *f.* **To use discretion**, agir avec discrétion. *To come to years of d.*, atteindre l'âge de raison. *F: He thought discretion the better part of valour*, il abandonne le champ à de plus dignes. **3.** Discrétion; silence judicieux.

discretionary [disˈkreʃənəri], *a.* (Pouvoir) discrétionnaire.

discriminate [disˈkrimineit]. **1.** *v.tr.* Distinguer (*from*, de, d'avec). **2.** *v.i.* (*a*) Distinguer, établir une distinction (*between*, entre). (*b*) **To discriminate in favour of s.o.**, faire des distinctions en faveur de qn. **discriminating**, *a.* **1.** (*Of pers.*) Plein de discernement. *D. purchaser*, acheteur avisé. *D. ear*, oreille fine. **2.** *Adm:* **Discriminating tariff**, tarif différentiel. **-ly**, *adv.* Avec discernement.

discrimination [diskrimiˈneiʃ(ə)n], *s.* **1.** Discernement *m.* **2.** Jugement *m. Man of d.*, homme judicieux. **3.** Distinction *f*, préférence *f.*

discursive [disˈkəːrsiv], *a.* **1.** (Style) décousu, sans suite. *He is too d.*, il ne s'attache pas assez à son sujet. **2.** *Log:* Discursif, déductif. **-ly**, *adv.* **1.** D'une manière décousue. **2.** *Log:* Par déduction.

discuss [disˈkʌs], *v.tr.* **1.** Discuter, débattre (un problème); délibérer (d'une question); agiter (une question). *D. the matter with him*, concertez-vous avec lui là-dessus. **2.** *F:* **To discuss a bottle**, déguster, vider, une bouteille.

discussion [disˈkʌʃ(ə)n], *s.* Discussion *f*; agitation *f* (d'une question). *Oral d.*, débat *m. Question under discussion*, question en discussion. *To start a d.*, entamer une discussion.

disdain[1] [disˈdein], *s.* Dédain *m* (*of*, de).

disdain[2], *v.tr.* Dédaigner.

disdainful [disˈdeinful], *a.* Dédaigneux (*of*, de). **-fully**, *adv.* Dédaigneusement.

disease [diˈziːz], *s.* Maladie *f*; mal *m*, affection *f.*

diseased [diˈziːzd], *a.* **1.** Malade. **2.** *D. meat*, viande contaminée. **3.** Morbide.

disembark [disemˈbaːrk], *v.tr. & i.* Débarquer.

disembarkation [disembaːrˈkeiʃ(ə)n], *s.* Débarquement *m.*

disembarrass [disemˈbarəs], *v.tr.* Débarrasser (*of*, de); dégager (*from*, de).

disembody [disemˈbɔdi], *v.tr.* **1.** Désincorporer. **Disembodied spirit**, esprit désincarné. **2.** Licencier (des troupes).

disembowel [disemˈbauəl], *v.tr.* Éventrer; éviscérer.

disenchanted [disenˈtʃaːntid], *a.* Désenchanté, désabusé.

disencumber [disenˈkʌmbər], *v.tr.* (*a*) Débarrasser (*of*, de); désencombrer (qn). (*b*) Purger l'hypothèque sur (une terre).

14

disendow [disen'dau], *v.tr.* Priver (une Église) de ses dotations.

disendowment [disen'daumənt], *s.* Sécularisation *f* des biens et dotations (d'une Église).

disengage [disen'geidʒ]. **I.** *v.tr.* (*a*) Dégager (*sth. from sth.*, qch. de qch.). (*b*) *Mec.E:* Déclencher; désengrener; débrayer. (*c*) *Ch:* To **disengage oxygen**, dégager de l'oxygène. (*d*) *Abs. Fenc:* Dégager (le fer). **2.** *v.i.* (*a*) Se dégager. (*b*) Se déclencher. **disengaged,** *a.* **I.** (*Of pers.*) Libre, inoccupé, visible. **2.** (*Of seat*) Libre; pas occupé.

disentail [disen'teil], *v.tr. Jur:* Libérer (une propriété substituée).

disentangle [disen'taŋgl], *v.tr.* (*a*) Dégager, *F:* dépêtrer (*from*, de). (*b*) Démêler, désentortiller (une ficelle); débrouiller (une situation).

disentanglement [disen'taŋglmənt], *s.* Débrouillement *m*, dégagement *m*; démêlage *m* (d'un écheveau).

disestablish [dises'tabliʃ], *v.tr.* Séparer (l'Église) de l'État.

disestablishment [dises'tabliʃmənt], *s.* Séparation *f* de l'Église et de l'État.

disfavour [dis'feivər], *s.* Défaveur *f*. **To fall into disfavour,** tomber en disgrâce. **At the risk of incurring s.o.'s disfavour,** au risque de déplaire à qn.

disfiguration [disfigju'reiʃ(ə)n], *s.* = DISFIGUREMENT.

disfigure [dis'figər]; *v.tr.* Défigurer; enlaidir. *Factory chimneys that d. the view,* cheminées d'usine qui gâtent le paysage.

disfigurement [dis'figərmənt], *s.* Défiguration *f*; enlaidissement *m*.

disfranchise [dis'franʃaːiz], *v.tr.* Priver (qn) du droit électoral; priver (un bourg pourri, etc.) de ses droits de représentation.

disfranchisement [dis'franʃizmənt], *s.* Privation *f* du droit de vote, des droits civiques.

disfrock [dis'frɔk], *v.tr. Ecc:* Défroquer.

disgorge [dis'gɔːrdʒ], *v.tr.* (*a*) Dégorger, rendre (la nourriture). (*b*) *River that disgorges its waters into . . .,* rivière qui décharge ses eaux dans. . . . (*c*) *F:* Dégorger (ce qu'on a volé, etc.).

disgrace[1] [dis'greis], *s.* **I.** Disgrâce *f*. **To be in disgrace,** être dans la disgrâce; (*of child*) être en pénitence *f*. **2.** Honte *f*, déshonneur *m*. **To bring d. on one's name,** déshonorer sa famille. **To be a disgrace to one's family,** être la honte de sa famille.

disgrace[2], *v.tr.* **I.** Disgracier (un courtisan, etc.). **2.** Déshonorer.

disgraceful [dis'greisful], *a.* Honteux, déshonorant, scandaleux. **-fully,** *adv.* Honteusement; d'une manière scandaleuse. *He acted d.,* sa conduite a été indigne.

disgruntled [dis'grʌntld], *a. F:* Contrarié, mécontent (*at*, de); maussade.

disguise[1] [dis'gaːiz], *s.* **I.** Déguisement *m*; travestissement *m*. **In disguise,** déguisé. **2.** Feinte *f*; fausse apparence. **To throw off all disguise,** laisser tomber le masque.

disguise[2], *v.tr.* **I.** Déguiser, travestir (qn). **2.** (*a*) Déguiser (sa pensée); masquer (une odeur). (*b*) **There is no disguising the fact that . . .,** il faut avouer que. . . . (*c*) *To d. one's feelings,* dissimuler ses sentiments.

disguisement [dis'gaizmənt], *s.* = DISGUISE[1].

disgust[1] [dis'gʌst], *s.* **I.** Dégoût (profond) (*at, for, towards,* pour). **2.** Profond mécontentement. **He resigned in disgust,** écœuré, il donna sa démission.

disgust[2], *v.tr.* Dégoûter; écœurer. **To be disgusted at, with, by, sth.,** être profondément mécontent de qch. **disgusting,** *a.* Dégoûtant. **I.** Qui répugne au goût, à l'odorat, à la vue. **2.** Écœurant. **-ly,** *adv. He is d. mean,* il est d'une ladrerie dégoûtante.

dish[1] [diʃ], *s.* **I.** Plat *m*. **Vegetable dish,** légumier *m*. **To wash (up) the dishes,** laver la vaisselle. **2.** *Cu:* Plat (de viande); mets *m*. **Dainty dish,** mets délicat. **3.** Récipient *m*. *Ch:* Capsule *f*. *Phot:* Cuvette *f*. **'dish-cloth,** *s.* **I.** Torchon *m*. **2.** Lavette *f*. **'dish-cover,** *s.* **I.** Couvercle *m* (de plat). **2.** Cloche *f*. **'dish-water,** *s.* Eau *f* de vaisselle.

dish[2], *v.tr.* **I.** **To dish (up) meat,** servir, dresser, la viande. *F:* **To dish up well-known facts in a new form,** donner un réchauffé de faits bien connus. **2.** *F: To d. one's opponents,* rouler, enfoncer, ses adversaires. **To dish oneself,** s'enferrer. **3.** Donner une forme concave ou convexe à (une surface). *Veh:* **Dished wheel,** roue désaxée. *Metalw:* **Dished plate,** tôle emboutie; tôle bombée.

dishabille [disa'biːl], *s.* **I. In dishabille,** er déshabillé. **2.** *Cost:* Négligé *m*.

dishearten [dis'hɑːrt(ə)n], *v.tr.* Décourager abattre, démoraliser, rebuter. *Don't get disheartened,* ne perdez pas courage. **disheartening,** *a.* Décourageant; (travail) ingrat.

dishevel [di'ʃev(ə)l], *v.tr.* Ébouriffer (qn, les cheveux). **dishevelled,** *a.* **I.** Échevelé, dépeigné; ébouriffé. **2.** Aux vêtements chiffonnés.

dishonest [dis'ɔnest], *a.* Malhonnête; déloyal, -aux. **-ly,** *adv.* Malhonnêtement.

dishonesty [dis'ɔnesti], *s.* Improbité *f*, malhonnêteté *f*. **Piece of dishonesty,** malhonnêteté.

dishonour[1] [dis'ɔnər], *s.* **I.** Déshonneur *m*. **To bring dishonour on one's family,** déshonorer sa famille. **2.** Chose déshonorante.

dishonour[2], *v.tr.* **I.** Déshonorer. **2.** (*a*) *To d. one's word,* manquer à sa parole. (*b*) *Com:* **To dishonour a bill,** ne pas honorer un effet. **Dishonoured cheque,** chèque impayé.

dishonourable [dis'ɔnərəbl], *a.* **I.** (*Of pers.*) Sans honneur. **2.** (*Of action*) Déshonorant, honteux, indigne. **-ably,** *adv.* D'une façon peu honorable.

disillusion[1] [disi'ljuːʒ(ə)n], *s.* Désillusion *f*, désabusement *m*, désenchantement *m*.

disillusion[2], **disillusionize** [disi'ljuːʒənaːiz], *v.tr.* Désillusionner, désabuser, désenchanter.

disillusionment [disi'ljuːʒənmənt], *s.* Désillusionnement *m*, désenchantement *m*.

disinclination [disinkli'neiʃ(ə)n], *s.* Répugnance *f*, aversion *f* (*for, to,* pour). **To show a disinclination to do sth.,** montrer peu d'empressement à faire qch.

disincline [disin'klain], *v.tr. To d. s.o. to, for, sth.,* éloigner, détourner, qn de qch. **disinclined,** *a.* Peu disposé (*for, to, sth.,* à qch.).

disinfect [disin'fekt], *v.tr.* Désinfecter.

disinfectant [disin'fektənt], *a. & s.* Désinfectant (*m*).

disinfection [disin fekʃ(ə)n], *s.* Désinfection *f*.

disingenuous [disin'dʒenjuəs], *a.* Sans franchise; faux, *f.* fausse. **-ly,** *adv.* Sans franchise.

disingenuousness [disin'dʒenjuəsnəs], *s.* Manque *m* de franchise; mauvaise foi.

disinherit [disin'herit], *v.tr.* Déshériter.

disintegrate [dis'integreit], *v.tr.* **I.** Désagréger; effriter (la pierre). **2.** *v.i.* Se désagréger.

disintegration [disinte'greiʃ(ə)n], *s.* Désagrégation *f*, effritement *m*.

disinter [disin'tə:r], *v.tr.* (**disinterred**) Déterrer, exhumer.

disinterested [dis'intərestid], *a.* Désintéressé. *His action is not entirely d.*, *F*: ce qu'il en fait ce n'est pas pour vos beaux yeux. **-ly,** *adv.* Avec désintéressement.

disinterestedness [dis'int(ə)restidnəs],*s.* Désintéressement *m.*

disinterment [disin'tə:rmənt], *s.* Déterrement *m* ; exhumation *f.*

disjoin [dis'dʒɔin], *v.tr.* Disjoindre, désunir.

disjoint [dis'dʒɔint],*v.tr.* Disjoindre, démembrer (une volaille). *Surgⁱ*: Désarticuler (l'épaule).

disjointed, *a.* Disjoint, disloqué ; (discours) sans suite ; (style) décousu.

disjunctive [dis'dʒʌŋ(k)tiv], *a.* Disjonctif.

disk [disk], *s.* (*a*) Disque *m* (de la lune). (*b*) Disque, rondelle *f. Mil:* **Identity disk,** plaque *f* d'identité. **Gramophone disk,** disque de phonographe. *Rail:* **Disk signal,** disque. *Aut:* **Wheel-disk,** flasque *m.*

dislike¹ [dis'laik], *s.* Aversion *f*, répugnance *f* (*to, of, for,* pour). **To take a dislike to s.o.,** prendre qn en grippe.

dislike², *v.tr.* Ne pas aimer ; détester. *He dislikes you,* vous lui êtes antipathique. *I don't d. him,* il ne me déplaît pas. *I d. his coming so often,* je n'aime pas qu'il vienne si souvent. *To be disliked by all,* être mal vu de tous.

dislocate ['dislokeit], *v.tr.* (*a*) Disloquer (une machine) ; désorganiser (les affaires). (*b*) Luxer, déboîter (un membre). (*Of horse*) *To d. its hip,* se déhancher.

dislocation [dislo'keiʃ(ə)n], *s.* (*a*) Dislocation *f* (d'une machine) ; désorganisation *f* (des affaires). (*b*) Luxation *f*, déboîtement *m* (d'un membre). *Vet:* *D. of the hip,* déhanchement *m.*

dislodge [dis'lɔdʒ], *v.tr.* **I.** Déloger. *The enemy were easily dislodged from the hill,* on parvint sans peine à déloger l'ennemi de la colline. **2.** Détacher. *Several bricks had become dislodged,* plusieurs briques s'étaient détachées.

disloyal [dis'lɔiəl], *a.* Infidèle (à l'amitié) ; déloyal, -aux. *A d. act,* une déloyauté. **-ally,** *adv.* Infidèlement, déloyalement.

disloyalty [dis'lɔiəlti], *s.* Infidélité *f*, déloyauté *f.*

dismal ['dizməl], *a.* Sombre, triste ; lugubre ; (paysage) morne. **-ally,** *adv.* Lugubrement, tristement.

dismantle [dis'mantl], *v.tr.* **I.** Dégarnir (*of,* de). **2.** (*a*) Démanteler (une forteresse). (*b*) Démonter (une machine).

dismast [dis'mɑ:st], *v.tr.* Démâter.

dismay¹ [dis'mei], *s.* Consternation *f* ; épouvante *f.* **In (blank) dismay,** consterné.

dismay², *v.tr.* Consterner, épouvanter. *Be not dismayed,* n'ayez point de crainte.

dismember [dis'membər], *v.tr.* Démembrer (un poulet). *His body was dismembered,* son corps fut écartelé.

dismemberment [dis'membərmənt], *s.* Démembrement *m.*

dismiss [dis'mis], *v.tr.* **I.** Congédier (qn) ; donner congé à (qn) ; chasser (un domestique) ; révoquer, destituer (un fonctionnaire). **2.** (*a*) Congédier (aimablement) (qn). (*b*) Congédier, éconduire (un importun, etc.). (*c*) Dissoudre (une assemblée). (*d*) *To d.* **troops** (*after service*), renvoyer des troupes dans leurs foyers. **3. To dismiss sth. from one's thoughts,** bannir, chasser, qch. de ses pensées. **4. Let us dismiss the subject,** n'en parlons plus ; brisons là. *The subject is not lightly to be dismissed,* l'on ne saurait écarter cette question aussi légèrement. **5.** (*a*) Écarter

(une proposition). *Jur:* Rejeter (une demande). **To dismiss a charge,** rendre une ordonnance de non-lieu. (*b*) **To dismiss the accused,** acquitter l'inculpé. **6.** *Mil:* **Dismiss!** rompez (les rangs) !

dismissal [dis'misəl], *s.* **I.** Congédiement *m*, renvoi *m* (d'un employé) ; révocation *f*, destitution *f* (d'un fonctionnaire). *He threatened him with d.,* il menaça de le renvoyer. **2.** *Jur:* (*a*) Fin *f* de non-recevoir ; rejet *m* (d'un appel). (*b*) Acquittement *m* (de l'inculpé).

dismount [dis'maunt]. **I.** *v.i.* To dismount (*from a horse*), descendre (de cheval) ; mettre pied à terre. **2.** *v.tr.* (*a*) Démonter (un cavalier). (*b*) *Mil:* Mettre à pied (des troupes montées). **3.** *v.tr.* Démonter (un canon, une machine).

disobedience [diso'bi:djəns], *s.* Désobéissance *f* (*to s.o.,* à qn ; *of a rule,* à une règle).

disobedient [diso'bi:djənt],*a.* Désobéissant. **To be disobedient to s.o.,** désobéir à qn.

disobey [diso'bei], *v.tr.* Désobéir à (qn). *My orders were disobeyed,* mes ordres ont été désobéis.

disoblige [diso'blaidʒ], *v.tr.* Désobliger (qn).

disobliging, *a.* Désobligeant.

disoblingness [diso'blaidʒiŋnəs], *s.* Désobligeance *f* ; manque *m* de complaisance (*to, envers*).

disorder¹ [dis'ɔ:rdər], *s.* **I.** Désordre *m*, confusion *f.* **In disorder,** en désordre. **To throw the ranks into disorder,** mettre le désordre dans les rangs. *They fled in d.,* ils s'enfuirent à la débandade. **2.** Désordre, tumulte *m.* **3.** *Med:* Désordre ; affection *f. Disorders of the mind,* dérangement *m* d'esprit.

disorder²,*v.tr.* **I.** Déranger ; mettre le désordre, la confusion, dans (les rangs, etc.). **2.** Déranger (l'estomac) ; *F:* détraquer (la santé). **disordered,** *a.* **I.** Désordonné ; en désordre. **2.** (Estomac) dérangé.

disorderliness [dis'ɔ:rdərlinəs],*s.* **I.** Désordre *m.* **2.** Conduite *f* contraire aux bonnes mœurs. **3.** Turbulence *f.*

disorderly [dis'ɔ:rdərli], *a.* **I.** Qui manque d'ordre ; désordonné ; en désordre. **2.** (*Of mob*) Turbulent. **3.** (*Of pers.*) Désordonné, déréglé. *To lead a d. life,* vivre dans le dérèglement.

disorganization [disɔ:rgənai'zeiʃ(ə)n], *s.* Désorganisation *f.*

disorganize [dis'ɔ:rgəna:iz], *v.tr.* Désorganiser.

disorientate [dis'ɔ:rienteit], *v.tr.* Désorienter.

disown [dis'oun], *v.tr.* Désavouer (une œuvre) ; renier (l'autorité de qn, sa signature).

disparage [dis'paredʒ], *v.tr.* **I.** Déprécier, dénigrer ; battre (qn) en brèche. **2.** Déshonorer, discréditer. **disparaging,** *a.* **I.** (Terme) de dénigrement ; dépréciateur, -trice. **2.** Peu flatteur ; déshonorant. **-ly,** *adv.* **To speak disparagingly of s.o.,** parler de qn en termes peu flatteurs.

disparagement [dis'paredʒmənt],*s.* **I.** Dénigrement *m*, dépréciation *f.* **2.** *To his everlasting d.* *he signed the decree,* à son déshonneur éternel, il signa le décret.

disparager [dis'paredʒər], *s.* Dénigreur, -euse ; détracteur, -trice.

disparity [dis'pariti], *s.* Inégalité *f*, disconvenance *f* (*of, de*). **Disparity of age,** différence *f* d'âge.

dispassionate [dis'paʃənet], *a.* **I.** Sans passion ; calme. **2.** Impartial, -aux. **-ly,** *adv.* **I.** Sans passion ; avec calme. **2.** Sans parti pris.

dispatch¹ [dis'patʃ], *s.* **I.** Expédition *f* ; envoi *m* (de qn, de qch.). **2.** Mise *f* à mort (d'un condamné). **3.** (*a*) Expédition (d'une affaire.)

(b) Promptitude f, diligence f. **With dispatch,** promptement. **With all possible dispatch, with the utmost dispatch,** en toute diligence ; au plus vite. **4.** Dépêche f. *Mil :* **To be mentioned in dispatches,** être cité à l'ordre (du jour) ; *F :* être cité. **5.** *Nau :* Dispatch(-boat, -vessel), aviso *m.*

dis'patch-box, *s.* Valise f diplomatique.

dis'patch-case, *s.* Serviette f (de voyageur).

dis'patch-rider, *s. Mil :* Estafette f.

dispatch², *v.tr.* **1.** Dépêcher (un courrier) ; expédier (des marchandises) ; envoyer (qn) ; faire partir (des troupes). **2.** (a) To dispatch a wounded animal, achever un animal. (b) *The executioner soon dispatched the prisoners,* le bourreau eut vite fait d'expédier les prisonniers. **3.** *To d. current business,* expédier les affaires courantes. **4.** *F :* Expédier (un repas).

dispel [dis'pel], *v.tr.* (dispelled) Chasser, dissiper (les illusions, les craintes).

dispensary [dis'pensəri], *s.* **1.** (a) Dispensaire *m,* policlinique f. (b) (*In a hospital*) Dépense f. **2.** (a) Officine f (d'une pharmacie). (b) Pharmacie f.

dispensation [dispen'sei∫(ə)n], *s.* **1.** Dispensation f, distribution f (des aumônes). **2.** Décret *m,* arrêt *m* (de la Providence). **3.** *Ecc :* Dispensation from fasting, dispense f du jeûne. **4.** Dispensation from sth., fait *m* d'être dispensé de qch.

dispense [dis'pens]. **1.** *v.tr.* (a) Dispenser, distribuer (des aumônes). (b) Administrer (la justice). (c) *Pharm :* Préparer (des médicaments). **To dispense a prescription,** exécuter une ordonnance. **2.** *v.tr.* **To dispense s.o. from sth.,** dispenser qn de qch. **3.** *v.i.* **To dispense with sth.,** se passer de qch. **dispensing,** *s.* **1.** Dispensation f, distribution f (des aumônes). **2.** *Pharm :* Préparation f (des ordonnances). (*In large stores*) Dispensing department, rayon *m* d'ordonnances médicales.

dispenser [dis'pensər], *s.* **1.** (a) Dispensateur, -trice (d'aumônes). (b) (*In hospital*) Dépensier, -ière. (c) Pharmacien *m.* **2.** Administrateur *m* (des lois).

dispersal [dis'pə:rsəl], *s.* = DISPERSION.

disperse [dis'pə:rs]. **1.** *v.tr.* (a) Disperser ; dissiper (les nuages). (b) Répandre, disséminer (des nouvelles). (c) *Med :* Résoudre (une tumeur). (d) *Opt :* (*Of prism, etc.*) Disperser (la lumière). **2.** *v.i.* Se disperser.

dispersion [dis'pə:r∫(ə)n], *s.* Dispersion f.

dispirit [dis'pirit], *v.tr.* Décourager, abattre (qn).

displace [dis'pleis], *v.tr.* **1.** Déplacer (qch.). *El.E :* **To displace the brushes,** décaler les balais. **2.** (a) Déplacer, destituer (un fonctionnaire). (b) Remplacer (by, par). (c) Évincer (qn). **To displace s.o. in s.o.'s affections,** supplanter qn.

displacement [dis'pleismənt], *s.* (a) Déplacement *m* (de qch.) ; changement *m* de place. *El.E :* Décalage *m* (des balais). (b) *N.Arch :* Déplacement (d'un navire). **Light displacement,** déplacement lège. **Load displacement,** déplacement en charge.

display¹ [dis'plei], *s.* **1.** Étalage *m,* déploiement *m* (de marchandises) ; manifestation f (de colère). **Air display,** fête f aéronautique. *Com :* **Display case,** coffret *m* d'étalage. **D. of courage,** déploiement de courage. **2.** Étalage (de luxe) ; parade f, apparat *m* ; *F :* affichage *m* (d'opinions). *To make a great d. of sorrow,* faire montre de douleur, afficher sa douleur. **3.** *Typ :* Lignes fpl, matières fpl, en vedette.

display², *v.tr.* **1.** Exhiber, étaler, exposer (des marchandises). **To display a notice,** afficher un avis. **2.** Montrer, manifester (du courage) ; faire preuve de (courage). **To display a taste for . . .,** témoigner d'un goût pour. . . . **3.** Étaler, afficher (son luxe). **4.** Découvrir, révéler (son ignorance). **5.** *Typ :* Mettre (une ligne, etc.) en vedette.

displease [dis'pli:z], *v.tr.* Déplaire à (qn) ; contrarier, mécontenter (qn). **To be displeased at sth., with s.o.,** être mécontent de qch., de qn.

displeasing, *a.* Déplaisant, désagréable (to, à).

displeasure [dis'pleʒər], *s.* Déplaisir *m,* mécontentement *m.* **To incur s.o.'s displeasure,** s'attirer le courroux de qn.

disport [dis'pɔ:rt], *v. pr. & i.* **To disport (oneself),** (i) se divertir, s'amuser ; (ii) s'ébattre ; folâtrer.

disposal [dis'pouzəl], *s.* **1.** (a) Action f de disposer (de qch.). *The d. of one's money,* ce qu'il faut faire de son argent. *D. of a piece of business,* expédition f d'une affaire. **Disposal of a question,** résolution f d'une question. (b) **At s.o.'s disposal,** à la disposition de qn. *It is quite at your d.,* c'est tout à votre service. **The means at my disposal,** les moyens dont je dispose. **2.** Disposition f, cession f (de biens). **For disposal,** à vendre. **3.** *Com :* Délivrance f (de marchandises). **4.** Disposition (des troupes sur le terrain).

dispose [dis'pouz], *v.tr. & i.* **1.** (a) Disposer, arranger (des objets) ; ordonner (une maison). **Man proposes, God disposes,** l'homme propose et Dieu dispose. (b) *To d. of s.o.'s fate,* décider du sort de qn. **2.** **To dispose of sth.,** se défaire de qch. **To dispose of an opponent,** vaincre un adversaire. *To d. of a matter,* régler une affaire. *F :* **To dispose of a meal,** expédier un repas. **3.** *Com :* (*Sell*) **To dispose of goods, of an article,** écouler des marchandises ; vendre, placer, un article. *To d. of one's business,* céder son fonds. **To be disposed of,** à vendre, à céder. **Goods easily disposed of,** marchandises d'un écoulement facile. **4.** Disposer, incliner, porter (*s.o. to do sth.,* qn à faire qch.). **5.** **To dispose oneself to sleep,** se disposer à dormir. **disposed,** *a.* **1.** Intentionné, disposé. **To be friendly disposed,** être d'humeur affable. **If you feel so disposed,** si le cœur vous en dit. **2.** (a) Disposed to sth., enclin, porté, à qch. *To be d. to pity,* incliner à la pitié. (b) *I am d. to help you,* je suis (tout) disposé à vous aider.

disposition [dispo'zi∫(ə)n], *s.* **1.** (a) Disposition f, agencement *m.* (b) *Jur :* Disposition (testamentaire). **2.** = DISPOSAL 1 (b). **3.** Caractère *m,* naturel *m,* humeur f. *He is of a kindly d.,* c'est une bonne nature. **4.** (a) Disposition to do sth., désir *m* de faire qch. *There was a general d. to remain,* tous étaient disposés à rester. (b) Penchant *m,* tendance f (to, à).

dispossess [dispo'zes], *v.tr.* Déposséder (of, de).

disproof [dis'pru:f], *s.* Réfutation f.

disproportion [dispro'pɔ:r∫(ə)n], *s.* Disproportion f ; défaut *m* de proportion. **D. in age,** disconvenance f d'âge.

disproportionate [dispro'pɔ:r∫ənet], *a.* Disproportionné (to, à). **-ly,** *adv.* D'une façon disproportionnée.

disprove [dis'pru:v], *v.tr.* Réfuter (un dire) ; démontrer la fausseté d'un dire).

disputable ['dispjutəbl], *a.* Contestable.

disputation [dispju'tei∫(ə)n], *s.* Débat *m.*

dispute¹ [dis'pju:t], *s.* **1.** Contestation f, débat *m.* **The matter in dispute,** l'affaire dont il s'agit. **Beyond dispute,** incontestable. **Without dispute,**

sans contredit. *Jur:* **Case under dispute,** cas en litige. **2.** Querelle *f,* dispute *f (as to,* relative à).

dispute². I. *v.i. (a)* To dispute with s.o. about sth., débattre qch. avec qn. *(b)* Se disputer. **2.** *v.tr. (a)* Débattre (une question); contester (une affirmation). *(b)* To dispute (the possession of) sth. with s.o., disputer qch. à qn.

disqualification [diskwɔlifi'keiʃ(ə)n], *s.* **I.** Incapacité *f; Jur:* inhabilité *f (to act,* à agir). **2.** Cause *f* d'incapacité *(for,* à). **3.** *(a)* Mise *f* en état d'incapacité. *(b) Sp:* Disqualification *f.*

disqualify [dis'kwɔlifai], *v.tr.* **I.** Rendre incapable *(for sth.,* de faire qch.). **2.** *Jur:* Disqualified *from making a will,* inhabile à tester. **3.** *Sp:* Disqualifier (un joueur).

disquiet¹ [dis'kwaiet], *s.* Inquiétude *f;* agitation *f.*

disquiet², **disquieten** [dis'kwaietən], *v.tr.* Inquiéter; troubler. **disquieting,** *a.* Inquiétant; peu rassurant.

disquietude [dis'kwaietju:d], *s.* **I.** Inquiétude *f,* anxiété *f.* **2.** Manque *m* de calme; agitation *f.*

disquisition [diskwi'ziʃ(ə)n], *s.* Dissertation *f (on,* sur).

disrate [dis'reit], *v.tr. Navy:* Déclasser (un homme).

disregard¹ [disri'gɑ:rd], *s.* Indifférence *f,* insouciance *f (of, for,* à l'égard de). *D. of the law,* inobservation *f* de la loi.

disregard², *v.tr.* Ne tenir aucun compte de (qn, qch.); méconnaître (un devoir).

disregardful [disri'gɑ:rdful], *a.* Insouciant, dédaigneux, négligent *(of,* de); indifférent *(of,* à).

disrepair [disri'pɛər], *s.* Délabrement *m* (d'une maison). **To fall into disrepair,** tomber en ruines; se délabrer, se dégrader.

disreputable [dis'repjutəbl], *a.* **I.** *(Of action)* Déshonorant; honteux. **2.** *(Of pers.)* De mauvaise réputation; taré. **3.** *(Of garments)* Minable. *D. old hat,* vieux chapeau digne d'un chiffonnier.

dis'reputable-looking, *a.* De mauvaise mine; d'aspect louche.

disrepute [disri'pju:t], *s.* **To bring sth. into disrepute,** discréditer qch.; faire tomber qch. dans le discrédit. **To fall into disrepute,** tomber dans le mépris.

disrespect [disris'pekt], *s.* Manque *m* d'égards, de respect *(for,* envers). **To treat s.o. with disrespect,** manquer de respect à qn.

disrespectful [disris'pektful], *a.* Irrespectueux, irrévérencieux. **To be disrespectful to s.o.,** manquer de respect à qn. **-fully,** *adv.* **To speak disrespectfully of s.o.,** parler de qn avec irrévérence.

disrobe [dis'roub]. **I.** *v.tr.* Aider (un magistrat) à se dévêtir de sa robe. **2.** *v.i. (Of judge)* Se dévêtir de sa robe.

disrupt [dis'rʌpt], *v.tr.* **I.** Rompre, briser, disloquer. *Disrupted ground,* terrain bouleversé. **2.** Démembrer (un empire).

disruption [dis'rʌpʃ(ə)n], *s.* **I.** Dislocation (violente). **2.** Démembrement *m* (d'un empire).

dissatisfaction [dissatis'fakʃ(ə)n], *s.* Mécontentement *m (with, at,* de).

dissatisfy [dis'satisfai], *v.tr.* Mécontenter; ne pas satisfaire. **dissatisfied,** *a.* Mécontent *(with, at,* de).

dissect [di'sekt], *v.tr.* Disséquer.

dissection [di'sekʃ(ə)n], *s.* Dissection *f.*

dissemble [di'sembl], *v.tr.* Dissimuler (ses sentiments); passer (un fait) sous silence. *Abs.* User de dissimulation; déguiser sa pensée. **dissembling,** *s.* Dissimulation *f.*

dissembler [di'semblər], *s.* Dissimulateur, -trice.

disseminate [di'semineit], *v.tr.* Disséminer.

dissemination [disemi'neiʃ(ə)n], *s.* Dissémination *f.*

dissension [di'senʃ(ə)n], *s.* Dissension *f.*

dissent¹ [di'sent], *s.* **I.** Dissentiment *m;* avis *m* contraire. **2.** *Ecc:* Dissidence *f.*

dissent², *v.i.* **I.** Différer *(from s.o. about sth.,* de qn sur qch.). **2.** *Ecc:* Être dissident.

dissenting, *a.* Dissident.

dissenter [di'sentər], *s.* Dissident *m.*

dissentient [di'senʃənt], *a. & s.* Dissident *m. With one d. vote,* à l'unanimité moins une voix.

dissepiment [di'sepimənt], *s. Anat: Bot:* Cloison *f,* septum *m.*

dissert [di'sə:rt], *v.i.* Disserter *(on,* sur).

dissertation [disər'teiʃ(ə)n], *s.* Dissertation *f.*

disservice [dis'sə:rvis], *s.* Mauvais service rendu. *To do s.o. a d.,* desservir qn.

dissidence ['disidəns], *s.* Dissidence *f.*

dissident ['disidənt], *a. & s. (a)* Dissident *(m). (b)* Membre dissident (d'un parti).

dissimilar [di'similər], *a.* Dissemblable *(to,* à, de); différent *(to,* de).

dissimilarity [disimi'lariti], *s.* Dissemblance *f,* dissimilitude *f (to,* de).

dissimulate [di'simjuleit], *v.tr. (a)* Dissimuler; cacher (un fait). *(b) Abs.* Feindre.

dissimulation [disimju'leiʃ(ə)n], *s.* Dissimulation *f.*

dissimulator [di'simjuleitər], *s.* Dissimulateur, -trice.

dissipate ['disipeit]. **I.** *v.tr.* Dissiper (une fortune). *To d. one's efforts,* disperser ses efforts. **2.** *v.i.* Se dissiper. **dissipated,** *a.* Dissipé. *D. man, woman,* noceur, noceuse.

dissipation [disi'peiʃ(ə)n], *s.* **I.** Dissipation *f* (du brouillard); gaspillage *m* (d'une fortune). **2.** Divertissement *m.* **3.** Dissipation; vie désordonnée; le plaisir.

dissociate [di'souʃieit], *v.tr. (a)* Désassocier (des personnes) *(from,* de). *(b) Ch:* Dissocier (un composé).

dissociation [disouʃi'eiʃ(ə)n, -si'eiʃ(ə)n], *s. Ch:* Dissociation *f.*

dissolute ['disɔljut], *a.* Dissolu, débauché. *To lead a d. life,* vivre dans la débauche. **-ly,** *adv.* Dissolument.

dissoluteness ['disɔljutnəs], *s.* Dérèglement *m.*

dissolution [disɔ'lju:ʃ(ə)n], *s.* **I.** Dissolution *f,* fonte *f,* liquéfaction *f.* **2.** Dissolution (d'une assemblée, d'un mariage).

dissolve [di'zɔlv]. **I.** *v.tr. (a)* Dissoudre, faire dissoudre (un sel, etc.). *(b)* Dissoudre (une assemblée, un mariage). **2.** *v.i. (a)* Se dissoudre; fondre. *(b) (Of Parliament)* Se dissoudre. *(c) Cin:* **Dissolving views,** fondus *m.*

dissonance ['disonəns], *s.* Dissonance *f.*

dissonant ['disonənt], *a.* Dissonant.

dissuade [di'sweid], *v.tr.* **To dissuade s.o. from doing sth.,** dissuader, détourner, qn de faire qch.

dissuasion [di'sweiʒ(ə)n], *s.* Dissuasion *f.*

dissuasive [di'sweisiv], *a.* Dissuasif.

distaff ['distɑ:f], *s.* Quenouille *f.* **The distaff** side *(of a family),* le côté maternel.

distance ['distəns], *s.* **I.** *(a)* Distance *f,* éloignement *m.* **Within speaking distance,** à portée de voix. **It is no distance (away),** *F:* ce n'est qu'une promenade. *Seen from a d.,* vu de loin. **Distance** lends enchantment to the view, tout paraît beau vu de loin. *Customers who come from a d.,* clients venus du dehors. *(b)* Lointain *m.* **Away in the distance,** dans le lointain. *Art:* **Middle-distance,**

second plan. 2. *To go part of the d. on foot,* faire une partie du trajet à pied. 3. *Distance, intervalle* m. **To keep s.o. at a distance,** tenir qn à distance. *Rail:* D. *between rails,* écartement m de voie. 4. **Distance of manner,** air distant; réserve f.
distant ['distənt], a. 1. **Three miles distant,** à trois milles de distance. **Not far distant from . . .,** à peu de distance de. . . . 2. *(a)* (Endroit) éloigné; (pays) lointain. **To have a distant view of sth.,** voir qch. de loin. *Rail:* **Distant signal,** signal à distance; signal avancé. **Distant look,** regard perdu dans le vague. **Distant likeness,** faible, vague, ressemblance. *(b)* (*In time*) Éloigné, reculé. D. *recollection,* souvenir lointain. **In the distant future,** dans un avenir lointain. 3. *(Of pers.)* Réservé, froid, distant. **-ly,** *adv.* 1. De loin. **Distantly related,** d'une parenté éloignée. 2. Avec réserve; froidement.
distaste [dis'teist], s. Dégoût m (*for,* de); aversion f, répugnance f (*for,* pour).
distasteful [dis'teistful], a. 1. Désagréable au goût. 2. Désagréable, déplaisant, antipathique (*to,* à). *To be d. to s.o.,* répugner à qn.
distemper[1] [dis'tempər], s. *(a)* A: Maladie f. *(b) Vet:* Maladie des chiens.
distemper[2], *v.tr.* A: Rendre (qn) malade. **Distempered mind,** esprit dérangé, troublé.
distemper[3], s. 1. *Art:* Détrempe f. 2. (*For house-decoration*) Détrempe, badigeon m.
distend [dis'tend]. 1. *v.tr. (a)* Dilater, gonfler (un ballon). *(b)* Distendre, dilater, ballonner (l'estomac); *Vet:* météoriser (l'estomac). 2. *v.i. (a)* Se dilater, enfler. *(b)* Se distendre.
distension [dis'ten∫(ə)n], s. Dilatation f, distension f, gonflement m.
distich ['distik], s. *Pros:* Distique m.
distil [dis'til], v. (distilled) 1. *v.tr. (a)* Distiller. *(b)* Laisser tomber goutte à goutte. F: **To distil poison into s.o.'s mind,** faire couler du poison dans l'âme de qn. 2. *v.i. (a)* To distil (over), se distiller. *(b)* Distiller, couler doucement.
distillation [disti'lei∫(ə)n], s. Distillation f.
distiller [dis'tilər], s. Distillateur m.
distillery [dis'tiləri], s. Distillerie f.
distinct [dis'tiŋ(k)t], a. 1. Distinct, différent (*from,* de). **To keep two things d.,** distinguer entre deux choses. 2. (*Clear*) Distinct, net. D. *memory,* souvenir clair. D. *promise,* promesse formelle. 3. Caractérisé, marqué. D. *preference,* préférence marquée. **-ly,** *adv.* 1. *(a)* (Parler) distinctement, clairement. *(b) I told him d.,* je le lui ai dit expressément. 2. Indéniablement, décidément. *He is d. better,* il y a un mieux sensible.
distinction [dis'tiŋ(k)∫(ə)n], s. 1. Distinction f (*between,* entre). 2. *Academic distinctions,* distinctions académiques. 3. (*Excellence*) Distinction. **To gain distinction,** se distinguer. *Man of d.,* homme distingué.
distinctive [dis'tiŋ(k)tiv], a. Distinctif.
distinctness [dis'tiŋ(k)tnəs], s. 1. Clarté f, netteté f. 2. D. *of sth. from sth.,* caractère nettement différent de deux choses.
distinguish [dis'tiŋgwi∫]. 1. *v.tr. (a)* Distinguer, discerner. *(b)* Distinguer, différencier (*from,* de). **Distinguishing mark,** signe distinctif. *(c)* **To distinguish oneself by . . .,** se signaler, se faire remarquer, par. . . . 2. *v.i.* Faire une distinction (*between,* entre). **distinguished,** a. 1. Distingué. D. *writer,* écrivain de distinction. D. *people,* personnages de marque. *He is d. for his strength,* il est remarquable par sa force. 2. **To look distinguished,** avoir l'air distingué.
distinguishable [dis'tiŋgwi∫əbl], a. 1. Que l'on

peut distinguer (*from,* de). 2. Perceptible, reconnaissable.
distort [dis'to:rt], *v.tr. (a)* Tordre, contourner (qch.); décomposer, déformer. *(b)* Défigurer (la vérité); fausser, dénaturer (les faits). **distorted,** a. Tordu, contourné, tourmenté. *Face d. by rage,* visage convulsé par la fureur. D. *ideas,* idées biscornues. *Phot:* **Distorted image,** image déformée.
distortion [dis'to:r∫(ə)n], s. 1. *(a)* Distorsion f; décomposition f (des traits). *(b)* Déformation f (des faits). 2. *(a) Opt:* Déformation, distorsion. *(b) W. Tel:* Déformation (de la réception).
distract [dis'trakt], *v.tr.* 1. *(a)* Distraire, détourner (*the attention from,* l'attention de). *(b)* Brouiller (l'esprit). 2. Affoler (qn). **distracted,** a. Affolé, éperdu. *I shall go d.,* je deviendrai fou. *Like one d.,* comme un affolé. **-ly,** *adv.* 1. Comme un affolé. 2. (Aimer qn) éperdument. **distracting,** a. Affolant.
distraction [dis'trak∫(ə)n], s. 1. Distraction f. *(a)* Divertissement m. *(b)* Interruption f. 2. Confusion f, désordre m. 3. Affolement m. **To drive s.o. to distraction,** mettre qn hors de soi. **To love s.o. to distraction,** aimer qn éperdument.
distrain [dis'trein], *v.i. Jur:* **To distrain upon s.o.'s belongings,** saisir les meubles de qn. *To d. upon a debtor,* exécuter un débiteur.
distrainable [dis'treinəbl], a. *Jur:* Saisissable.
distraint [dis'treint], s. *Jur:* Saisie f.
distraught [dis'tro:t], a. *Lit:* = DISTRACTED.
distress[1] [dis'tres], s. 1. Détresse f, angoisse f. 2. Misère (profonde); gêne f. 3. Détresse, embarras m. **Companions in distress,** compagnons d'infortune. *Nau:* **Distress signal,** signal de détresse. 4. *Jur:* = DISTRAINT.
dis'tress-warrant, s. *Jur:* Mandat m de saisie.
distress[2], *v.tr.* 1. Affliger, angoisser, chagriner. 2. Épuiser, excéder. **distressed** [dis'trest], a. 1. Affligé, désolé. 2. **Distressed gentlewomen,** dames réduites à la misère. **Distressed areas,** régions ruinées par la crise économique. 3. Épuisé, essoufflé. **distressing,** a. Affligeant, angoissant.
distressful [dis'tresful], a. = DISTRESSING.
distribute [dis'tribjut], *v.tr.* Distribuer, répartir. *To d. a dividend,* répartir un dividende. *Load evenly distributed,* charge uniformément répartie. *Typ:* **To distribute the type,** distribuer la composition.
distribution [distri'bju:∫(ə)n], s. 1. (Mise f en) distribution f; répartition f. *Pol.Ec:* **Distribution of wealth,** répartition des richesses. 2. *Typ:* Mise en casse.
distributor [dis'tribjutər], s. 1. Distributeur, -trice. 2. *El.E:* Distributeur de courant.
district ['distrikt], s. 1. Région f, contrée f, territoire m, district m. *Mining d.,* région minière; bassin houiller. 2. *Adm: (a)* District, secteur m. *Electoral d.,* circonscription électorale. *(b)* Quartier m (d'une ville). **district-'nurse,** s.f. Infirmière d'hygiène sociale; infirmière visiteuse. **district-'visitor,** s.f. Dame de charité.
distrust[1] [dis'trʌst], s. Méfiance f, défiance f.
distrust[2], *v.tr.* Se méfier, se défier, de (qn). *To d. one's own eyes,* n'en pas croire ses propres yeux.
distrustful [dis'trʌstful], a. 1. Défiant, méfiant (*of,* de); soupçonneux. 2. Timide. *He was d. of his own capabilities,* il manquait de foi en ses propres capacités. **-fully,** *adv.* Avec méfiance, avec défiance.
disturb [dis'tə:rb], *v.tr.* 1. Déranger; troubler (le repos); agiter, remuer (une surface). **Please**

don't disturb yourself, ne vous dérangez pas. **2.** *Ph:* Ébranler (l'éther) ; amener de la perturbation dans (le champ magnétique). **3.** Inquiéter, troubler (qn). *To d. s.o.'s mind,* jeter le trouble dans l'esprit de qn. **disturbing,** *a.* Perturbateur, -trice.

disturbance [dis'tə:rbəns], *s.* **1.** Trouble *m* ; dérangement *m.* *Atmospheric d.,* perturbation *f* atmosphérique. **2.** Bruit *m,* tapage *m* ; émeute *f.* **To make a disturbance,** troubler l'ordre public. **3.** Agitation *f,* trouble (d'esprit).

disturber [dis'tə:rbər], *s.* **1.** Dérangeur, -euse. **2.** Perturbateur, -trice (de l'ordre).

disulphide [dai'sʌlfaid], *s.* *Ch:* Bisulfure *m.*

disunion [dis'ju:njən], *s.* Désunion *f.*

disunite [disju'nait], *v.tr.* Désunir.

disuse [dis'ju:s], *s.* Désuétude *f.* **To fall into disuse,** (i) tomber en désuétude ; (ii) être mis au rancart.

disused [dis'ju:zd], *a.* Hors d'usage.

disyllabic [disi'labik], *a.* (Mot) dissyllabe ; (vers) dissyllabique.

disyllable [di'siləbl], *s.* Dissyllabe *m.*

ditch¹ [ditʃ], *s.* Fossé *m* ; *(between fields)* douve *f.* *F:* **To die in a ditch,** mourir sur le bord de la route. **'ditch-water,** *s.* Eaux stagnantes (d'un fossé). *F:* **It's as clear as ditch-water,** c'est la bouteille à l'encre.

ditch², *v.tr.* (a) Entourer (un champ) de fossés ; creuser des fossés. (b) *Aut:* **To d.** *one's car,* verser son auto dans le fossé. *U.S: P:* **To be ditched,** (i) échouer ; (ii) être dans le pétrin.

dither ['diðər], *v.i.* *F:* Trembloter.

dittany ['ditəni], *s.* *Bot:* Dictame *m.*

ditto ['dito], *a. & s.* *(Abbr.* do) Idem ; de même. **To say ditto,** opiner du bonnet.

ditty ['diti], *s.* Chanson *f.* **Old ditties,** vieux refrains, vieilles chansons.

ditty-bag, -box ['ditibag, -boks], *s.* *Nau:* Nécessaire *m* de marin.

diuretic [daiju'retik], *a.* Diurétique.

diurnal [dai'ə:rn(ə)l], *a.* Diurne.

diva [di'va], *s.f.* *Th:* Diva, cantatrice.

divagate ['daivageit], *v.i.* Divaguer. **1.** Errer çà et là. **2.** S'écarter de son sujet.

divagation [daivə'geiʃ(ə)n], *s.* Divagation *f.*

divalent ['daivələnt], *a.* *Ch:* Divalent; bivalent.

divan [di'van], *s.* Divan *m.*

dive¹ [da:iv], *s.* **1.** (a) Plongeon *m.* **High dive,** plongeon de haut vol. (b) Plongée *f* (d'un sous-marin). (c) *Av:* Vol piqué ; piqué *m.* **Spinning d.,** descente *f* en vrille. **Dive-bombing,** attaque *f* en piqué. **2.** *U.S: P:* (a) Cabaret *m* borgne (en sous-sol). (b) Gargote *f* (en sous-sol).

dive², *v.i.* **1.** (a) Plonger *(into,* dans) ; *(head first)* piquer une tête. *To d. for pearls,* pêcher des perles. *Nau: F:* *(Of ship)* **To d.** *into it,* piquer du nez. (b) *Av:* **To** *(nose-)dive,* piquer (du nez). **To dive down on an enemy,** piquer de haut sur un ennemi. (c) *(Of submarine)* Plonger ; effectuer une plongée. **2.** *F:* **To d.** *into the street,* s'enfoncer dans la rue. **'diving-bell,** *s.* Cloche *f* à, de, plongeur(s). **'diving-board,** *s.* Plongeoir *m,* tremplin *m.* **'diving-dress, -suit,** *s.* Scaphandre *m.*

diver ['daivər], *s.* **1.** (a) Plongeur *m.* (b) *(In diver's dress)* Scaphandrier *m.* **2.** *Orn:* Plongeon *m.*

diverge [dai'və:rdʒ], *v.i.* *(Of roads, lines)* Diverger, s'écarter. *To d. from the beaten track,* s'écarter du chemin battu. **diverging,** *a.* Divergent.

divergence [dai'və:rdʒəns], *s.* Divergence *f.*

divergent [dai'və:rdʒənt], *a.* Divergent.

divers ['daivərz], *a.pl.* **On divers occasions,** en diverses occasions ; à diverses reprises.

diverse [dai'və:rs, di-], *a.* **1.** Divers, différent. **2.** Divers, varié. **-ly,** *adv.* Diversement.

diversify [dai'və:rsifai, di-], *v.tr.* Diversifier.

diversion [dai'və:rʃ(ə)n, di-], *s.* **1.** Détournement *m* (de la circulation) ; dérivation *f* (d'un cours d'eau). **2.** *Mil:* Diversion *f.* **3.** (a) Diversion (de l'esprit). **To create a diversion,** faire diversion. (b) Divertissement *m,* distraction *f,* jeu *m.*

diversity [dai'və:rsiti, di-], *s.* Diversité *f.*

divert [dai'və:rt, di-], *v.tr.* **1.** Détourner, dériver (un cours d'eau) ; écarter (un coup) ; détourner (la circulation) *(from,* de). *To d. s.o.'s attention,* distraire l'attention de qn. **2.** Divertir, amuser. **diverting,** *a.* Divertissant, amusant.

Dives ['daivi:z], *s.* *B:* Le mauvais riche.

divest [dai'vest], *v.tr.* **1.** **To divest s.o.** *of his clothes,* dévêtir qn. **2.** Dépouiller, priver (qn de qch.). *To d. oneself of a right,* renoncer à un droit.

divide¹ [di'vaid], *s.* *Geol:* *U.S:* Ligne *f* de partage des eaux.

divide². **1.** *v.tr.* (a) Diviser (un héritage). *To d. into parts,* diviser en parties ; sectionner, fractionner. *Divided between hatred and pity,* partagé entre la haine et la pitié. *Parl:* **To divide the House,** aller aux voix. (b) *(Share out)* Partager, répartir *(among,* entre). *We d. the work among us,* nous nous partageons le travail. (c) *Mth:* Diviser. **Twelve divides by three,** douze est divisible par trois. (d) Séparer *(from,* de). (e) Désunir (une famille). *House divided against itself,* maison désunie. (f) **Opinions are divided,** les avis sont partagés. *A divided mind,* un esprit indécis. **2.** *v.i.* (a) Se diviser, se partager *(into,* en) ; *(of road)* fourcher. (b) *Parl:* Aller aux voix. **divide up,** *v.tr.* Démembrer (un royaume) ; détailler (la viande, etc.). **dividing,** *a.* (Ligne) de démarcation. **Dividing wall,** mur mitoyen.

dividend ['dividend], *s.* *Mth: Fin:* Dividende *m.* *D. on shares,* dividende d'actions. **Interim dividend,** dividende provisoire. **Final dividend,** solde *m* de dividende.

dividers [di'vaidərz], *s.pl.* Compas *m* à pointes sèches.

divination [divi'neiʃ(ə)n], *s.* Divination *f.*

divine¹ [di'vain]. **1.** *a.* (a) Divin. **The divine afflatus,** le souffle poétique. (b) *F:* Divin, admirable. **2.** *s.* (a) *Theol:* Théologien *m.* (b) *A:* Ecclésiastique *m.* **-ly,** *adv.* Divinement.

divine², *v.tr.* Deviner (l'avenir). **di'vining-rod,** *s.* Baguette *f* divinatoire ; baguette de sourcier.

diviner [di'vainər], *s.* Devin *m,* devineresse *f.*

divinity [di'viniti], *s.* **1.** (a) *(Divine nature)* Divinité *f.* (b) Divinité, dieu *m.* **2.** (a) Théologie *f.* **Doctor of Divinity,** docteur en théologie. (b) *Sch:* Enseignement religieux.

divisible [di'vizibl], *a.* Divisible *(by,* par). *Fin:* **D. profits,** profits répartissables.

division [di'viʒ(ə)n], *s.* **1.** Division *f,* partage *m (into,* en) ; scission *f* (d'un parti). **2.** Répartition *f,* partage (des bénéfices). **3.** Division, désunion *f.* **4.** *Mth:* Division. **5.** *Parl:* Vote *m.* *There will be a d.,* on ira aux voix. **To challenge a division,** provoquer un vote. **6.** (a) Division (d'un livre). (b) *Biol:* ' Groupe *m,* classe *f.* (c) *Mil:* Division. (d) **Parliamentary division,** circonscription électorale. **7.** Cloison *f.*

divisor [di'vaizər], *s.* *Mth:* Diviseur *m.*

divorce¹ [di'vɔːrs], *s.* Divorce *m.*
divorce², *v.tr. Jur:* (a) (*Of judge*) Divorcer (deux époux). (b) (*Of husband or wife*) To divorce s.o., divorcer d'avec qn. (c) *F:* Séparer (*from,* de). *To d. Church from State,* séparer l'Église et l'État.
divot ['divət], *s. Golf:* Motte *f* (de gazon).
divulgation [divʌl'geiʃ(ə)n, dai-], **divulgement** [di'vʌldʒmənt, dai-], *s.* Divulgation *f.*
divulge [di'vʌldʒ, dai-], *v.tr.* Divulguer.
dixie, dixy ['diksi], *s. Mil: F:* Gamelle *f;* marmite *f* (de campement).
dizziness ['dizinəs], *s.* Étourdissement *m,* vertige(s) *m(pl).* Fit of dizziness, éblouissement *m.*
dizzy ['dizi], *a.* **1.** Pris d'étourdissement; pris de vertige. To feel dizzy, avoir le vertige. *To make s.o. d.,* étourdir qn. *My head is d.,* la tête me tourne. **2.** *F:* (*Of height, speed*) Vertigineux.
do¹ [duː]. I. *v.tr. (pr. ind. sg. 1st pers.* do; *2nd pers.* doest ['duest], *as aux.* dost [dʌst]; *3rd pers.* does [dʌz], *A:* doth [dʌθ], doeth ['dueθ]; *pl.* do; *past ind.* did, didst; *pr. sub. sg. & pl.* do; *p.p.* done [dʌn]) **1.** (a) (*Perform*) Faire (une bonne action, son devoir). *What do you do?* qu'est-ce que vous faites? quel est votre état? *What are you doing?* qu'est-ce que vous êtes en train de faire? To do good, faire le bien. *To do right,* bien faire. He did brilliantly at his examination, il s'est acquitté brillamment à son examen. *You would do well to . . .,* vous feriez bien de. . . . He is doing medicine, il fait sa médecine. To do three miles on foot, faire trois milles à pied. *The car was doing sixty,* l'auto faisait du soixante, filait à soixante. *To do ten years (in prison),* faire dix ans de prison. *Are you doing anything to-morrow?* avez-vous quelque chose en vue pour demain? Those things are not done; *F:* it isn't done, cela ne se fait pas. *It is as good as done,* c'est une affaire faite ou autant vaut. *Prov:* What is done cannot be undone, à chose faite point de remède. *I shall do nothing of the sort, no such thing,* je n'en ferai rien. *What is to be done?* que faire? *It cannot be done,* c'est (chose) impossible. *She did nothing but cry,* elle ne faisait que pleurer. *What can I do for you?* en quoi puis-je vous servir? What do you do for water? comment faites-vous pour vous procurer de l'eau? *I had much to do in getting him to come,* j'ai eu bien de la peine à le faire venir. *Do what we would . . .,* malgré tous nos efforts. . . . Well done! très bien! bravo! à la bonne heure! (b) *He came to see what was doing,* il est venu voir ce qui se faisait. *Com:* There is nothing doing, le marché est mort, est nul. *F:* Nothing doing! rien à faire! ça ne prend pas! **2.** (a) Faire (la correspondance, une chambre, les cheveux à qn). He does repairs, il se charge des réparations. (b) Cuire, faire cuire (la viande). Done to a turn, cuit à point. (c) *To do a sum, a problem,* faire un calcul; résoudre un problème. (d) Book done into English, livre traduit, rendu, en anglais. (e) (*Act a part*) Faire (Hamlet, etc.). *F:* To do the polite, faire l'aimable. (f) *F:* To 'do' a town, a picture-gallery, visiter une ville, un musée. (g) *F:* (*Cheat*) Refaire, faire, enfoncer (qn); mettre (qn) dedans. To do s.o. out of sth., soutirer, filouter, qch. à qn. *To do s.o. out of a job,* supplanter qn. (h) They do you very well at this hotel, on mange très bien à cet hôtel. *P:* To do oneself well, faire bonne chère. (i) *Com: F:* We can do you this article at . . .., nous pouvons vous faire cet article à. ... . **3.** (*Past participle*) (a) To have done, avoir fini. *The day is done,* le jour est à son déclin; la journée tire à sa fin. *Have done*

(*with*) *crying!* finissez de pleurer! assez de larmes! Be done! have done! finissez donc! (b) *P:* (*Of pers.*) To be done (to the world), être éreinté, exténué. (c) (*After a bargain made*) Done! tope là! c'est marché fait! **4.** How do you do? comment vous portez-vous? comment allez-vous? To be doing well, être en bonne voie, faire de bonnes affaires; (*of invalid*) être en voie de guérison; (*of business*) bien aller, réussir. *He is a lad who will do well,* c'est un garçon qui réussira. **5.** (*To serve, suffice*) That will do, (i) c'est bien (comme cela); cela va; (ii) cela suffira; en voilà assez! *This room will do for the office,* cette pièce ira bien pour le bureau. *That will not do,* cela ne fera pas l'affaire. That won't do here, cela ne passe pas ici. *It would hardly have done to . . .,* il n'aurait pas été convenable de. . . . I will make it do, je m'en arrangerai. *You must make do with what you have,* il faut vous arranger avec ce que vous avez. To have just enough to do on, avoir tout juste de quoi vivre. That will do me, cela fera mon affaire. *Nothing would do but I must go home with him,* il a fallu absolument que je rentre avec lui. II. do, *verb substitute.* **1.** *I replied as the others had done,* j'ai répondu comme avaient fait les autres. Why act as you do? pourquoi agir comme vous le faites? *He writes better than I do,* il écrit mieux que moi. He envies me as much as I do him, il me porte autant d'envie que je lui en porte. **2.** (*Elliptical auxiliary*) May I open these letters?—Please do, puis-je ouvrir ces lettres?—Faites donc! Je vous en prie! *Did you see him?—I did,* l'avez-vous vu?—Oui (, je l'ai vu). *Do you like her?—I do not,* l'aimez-vous? —Non (, je ne l'aime pas). *I like coffee; do you?* j'aime le café; et vous? *You like him, don't you?* vous l'aimez, n'est-ce pas? *You like him, do you?* vous l'aimez, alors? *He said so, did he?* il a dit cela, ah vraiment? Don't! ne faites pas cela! finissez! **3.** I wanted to see him and I did so, j'ai voulu le voir, et je l'ai vu. *You like Paris?* so do I, vous aimez Paris? moi aussi. III. **do,** *v.aux.* **1.** (*For emphasis*) He 'did go, il y est bien allé. *He threatened to go, and he 'did go, and go he 'did,* il menaça de partir, et il partit en effet. *Why don't you work?—I 'do work!* pourquoi ne travaillez-vous pas?—Mais si, je travaille! *'Did he indeed?* non vraiment? Do sit down, veuillez (donc) vous asseoir; asseyez-vous donc! *Do shut up!* voulez-vous bien vous taire! **2.** (*Inversion*) Never did I spend such a night, jamais je n'ai passé une nuit pareille. **3.** (*Usual form in questions and negative statements*) Do you see him? le voyez-vous? We do not know, nous ne le savons pas. Don't do it! n'en faites rien! *F:* D'you mind? ça ne vous fait rien? IV. **do** with certain prepositions. **1.** To do well, badly, by s.o., bien, mal, agir envers qn. He has been hard done by, il a été traité durement. *Do as you would be done by,* ne faites pas à autrui ce que vous ne voudriez pas qu'on vous fît. **2.** *F:* To do for. (a) To do for s.o., faire, tenir, le ménage de qn. *He can do for himself,* il peut se subvenir à lui-même. (b) Tuer (qn); faire son affaire à (qn). I'm done for, j'ai mon compte; je suis perdu. (c) Détruire, ruiner, couler (qn). **3.** (a) To have to do with s.o., avoir affaire à qn. To have to do with sth., (*of pers.*) être mêlé à qch.; avoir à voir à qch. (*of thg*) avoir rapport à qch. To have nothing to do with a matter, (*of pers.*) n'être pour rien dans une affaire. *Jealousy has a lot to do with it,* la jalousie y est pour beaucoup. (b) I cannot do with any noise, je ne peux pas sup-

porter le bruit. **He does with very little food,** il s'accommode de très peu de nourriture. (c) **How many can you do with?** combien en désirez-vous? combien vous en faut-il? *I could do with a cup of tea,* je prendrais une bonne tasse de thé. **4. Do without,** se passer de (qch.). V. **do,** *s.* F: **1.** Attrape *f,* fourberie *f,* escroquerie *f.* **2.** Soirée *f* (de réception); réception *f.* **do again,** *v.tr.* **1.** Refaire (qch.). **2.** *I won't do it again,* je ne le ferai plus, je ne recommencerai plus. **do away,** *v.* **To do away with,** abolir (un usage); supprimer (des frais, etc.); détruire, faire disparaître (un édifice); tuer, F: supprimer (qn); se défaire de (qn). **do in,** *v.tr.* P: (a) Tuer, assassiner (qn). (b) *I'm feeling absolutely done in,* je me sens absolument fourbu, éreinté. **do out,** *v.tr.* Faire, nettoyer (une chambre, une salle). **do up,** *v.tr.* **1.** (a) Réparer (qch.); remettre (qch.) à neuf; décorer (une maison, etc.). F: *To do oneself up,* faire toilette. **Done up to kill,** sur son grand tralala. (b) Blanchir (le linge). **2.** *Cu:* Accommoder (un plat, des restes). **3.** Faire, envelopper, ficeler (un paquet); emballer, empaqueter (des marchandises); mettre (un journal) sous bande; boutonner, agrafer (un vêtement). **4.** F: **To be done up,** être éreinté, fourbu. **doing,** *s.* **1.** (a) Action *f* de faire. **There is a great difference between doing and saying,** il y a loin du faire au dire. **That requires some doing,** ce n'est pas facile. (b) **This is so-and-so's doing,** cela est du fait d'un tel. **2.** (*Usu. in pl.*) Ce qu'on fait. (a) *Pej:* Agissements *mpl. Fine doings these!* une jolie conduite! *That's some of Tom's doings!* c'est encore Tom qui a fait des siennes! (b) *Doings and sayings,* faits *m* et dits *m.* **Great doings in the Balkans,** grands événements, grande activité, dans les Balkans.
do² [dou], *s. Mus:* **1.** (*Fixed do*) Do *m,* ut *m.* **2.** (*Movable do*) La tonique.
do³ ['dito] = DITTO.
docile ['dousail], *a.* Docile. **-ely,** *adv.* Docilement.
docility [do'siliti], *s.* Docilité *f.*
dock¹ [dɔk], *s. Bot:* Patience *f.* **Sour dock,** oseille *f.*
dock², *v.tr.* **1.** *To d. a horse, a horse's tail,* couper la queue à, écourter, un cheval. **2.** (a) Diminuer, rogner, ou supprimer (le traitement de qn). (b) **To dock s.o. of his ration,** retrancher sa ration à qn. **'dock-tailed,** *a.* **Dock-tailed horse,** (cheval) courtaud *m.*
dock³, *s. Nau:* (a) Bassin *m* (d'un port). **Outer dock,** avant-bassin *m.* **Inner dock,** arrière-bassin *m.* **Flooding dock,** bassin à flot. **To go into dock,** entrer au bassin. **The docks,** les docks *m.* (b) **Dry dock,** graving dock, cale sèche; bassin de radoub. *Ship in dry d.,* navire en radoub. (c) **Floating dock,** dock flottant. (d) *pl.* **Naval docks** = DOCKYARD.
dock⁴. **1.** *v.tr.* Faire entrer (un navire) au bassin. **2.** *v.i.* (*Of ship*) Entrer au bassin. **docking,** *s.* Entrée *f* au bassin.
dock⁵, *s. Jur:* Banc *m,* box *m,* des accusés, des prévenus. **To be in the dock,** être au banc des prévenus.
dockage ['dɔkedʒ], *s. Nau:* Droits *mpl* de bassin.
docker ['dɔkər], *s.* Déchargeur *m,* débardeur *m.*
docket¹ ['dɔket], *s.* Étiquette *f,* fiche *f* (d'un document). **Wages docket,** bordereau *m* de paye.
docket², *v.tr.* Étiqueter, classer (des papiers).
dockyard ['dɔkjɑːrd], *s.* Chantier *m* de construction de navires. *Esp.* **Naval dockyard,** arsenal *m* maritime.

doctor¹ ['dɔktər], *s.* **1.** A: (*Learned man*) Docteur *m.* **2.** *Sch:* **Doctor of Divinity,** docteur en théologie. **Doctor of Science,** docteur ès sciences. **3.** Docteur, médecin *m.* **Woman doctor,** docteur femme. **Doctor** (*abbr.* Dr) **Smith,** (Monsieur) le docteur Smith. **To call in a doctor,** appeler un médecin. **Come in, Doctor,** entrez, docteur.
doctor², *v.tr.* **1.** (a) Soigner, F: droguer (un malade). (b) *Turf:* Droguer, doper (un cheval). **2.** F: Réparer, raccommoder (un objet). **3.** F: Falsifier, fausser, truquer (des comptes); frelater (du vin, etc.). **doctoring,** *s.* **1.** Soins (donnés à qn). **2.** F: Profession *f* de médecin.
doctoral ['dɔktər(ə)l], *a.* Doctoral, -aux.
doctorate ['dɔktoret], *s. Sch:* Doctorat *m.*
doctrinarian [dɔktri'nɛəriən], *s.* Pédant *m;* théoricien *m,* idéologue *m.*
doctrine ['dɔktrin], *s.* Doctrine *f.*
document¹ ['dɔkjumənt], *s.* Document *m,* pièce *f,* titre *m;* F: papier *m. Legal d.,* acte *m* authentique. *Jur:* **Documents pertaining to the case,** dossier *m* (de l'affaire); pièces en instance.
document² ['dɔkjument], *v.tr.* Documenter.
documentary [dɔkju'mentəri], *a.* Documentaire. *S.a.* EVIDENCE¹ 3.
documentation [dɔkjumen'teiʃ(ə)n], *s.* Documentation *f.*
dodder¹ ['dɔdər], *s. Bot:* Cuscute *f.*
dodder², *v.i.* (*Of aged pers.*) Trembloter. **To dodder along,** (i) marcher en branlant bras et jambes; (ii) *Aut:* F: rouler à la papa. **doddering,** *a.* **1.** *D. gait, head,* démarche, tête, branlante. **2.** (*Of pers.*) Gaga *inv.*
dodderer ['dɔdərər], *s.* F: Vieux gaga *m.*
dodecagon [dou'dekagən], *s. Geom: Cryst:* Dodécagone *m.*
dodecahedron [doudekə'hiːdrən], *s.* Dodécaèdre *m.*
dodge¹ [dɔdʒ], *s.* **1.** Mouvement de côté. *Box: Fb:* Esquive *f.* **2.** (a) Ruse *f,* artifice *m.* (b) Truc *m,* ficelle *f;* tour *m* de main. **Trade dodges,** recettes *f* de métier. **To be up to all the dodges,** connaître tous les trucs.
dodge². **1.** *v.i.* (a) Se jeter de côté. (b) *Box: Fb:* Esquiver, éviter. (c) Biaiser; user d'artifices. **2.** *v.tr.* Se jeter de côté pour éviter (un coup); esquiver (un coup); éviter (qn); esquiver, tourner' (une difficulté). **To dodge a question,** éluder une question.
dodger ['dɔdʒər], *s.* F: **An artful dodger,** un malin, un fin matois, un roublard.
dodo, *pl.* **-o(e)s** ['doudou,-ouz], *s. Orn:* Dodo *m.* F: **As dead as the dodo,** vieux comme Hérode.
doe [dou], *s. Z:* **1.** Daine *f.* **2.** (*Of rabbit*) Lapine *f;* (*of wild rabbit and hare*) hase *f.*
doer ['duːər], *s.* Faiseur, -euse; auteur *m* (d'une action).
does [dʌz], **doest** ['duəst]. See DO¹.
doeskin ['douskin], *s.* (a) Peau *f* de daim. (b) *Tex:* Simili-daim *m.*
doff [dɔf], *v.tr.* Enlever, ôter (un vêtement).
dog¹ [dɔg], *s.* **1.** Chien *m.* **House-dog,** chien de garde, d'attache. **Sporting dog,** chien de chasse. **Dog racing,** courses de lévriers. F: **To go to the dogs,** se dégrader, se débaucher; marcher à la ruine; (*of business*) aller à vau-l'eau. **To lead a dog's life,** mener une vie de chien. **To throw discretion to the dogs,** mettre de côté toute discrétion. **To help a lame dog over a stile,** tirer qn d'un mauvais pas. **To take a hair of the dog that bit you,** reprendre du poil de la bête. *Prov:* **Every dog has his day,** à chacun son tour. **Give a dog a**

bad name and hang him, qui veut noyer son chien l'accuse de la rage. Dog does not eat dog, les loups ne se mangent pas entre eux. **2.** Dog-fox, renard *m* mâle. Dog-hyena, hyène *f* mâle. **3.** *F:* Sly dog, rusé coquin, fin renard. Lucky dog! (le) veinard! Jolly dog, gai luron. Gay dog, (i) *Pej:* viveur *m*, noceur *m*; (ii) joyeux gaillard. *P:* Dirty dog, sale type *m*. **4.** (*a*) (*Pawl*) Chien, cliquet *m*, détente *f*. (*b*) (*Of lathe*) Toc *m* (d'entraînement). (*c*) *Aut:* Direct-drive dogs, griffes *f* de prise directe. **5.** Fire-dog, chenet *m*. 'dog-biscuit, *s.* Biscuit *m* de chien. 'dog-cart, *s.* *Veh:* Charrette anglaise. 'dog-clutch, *s.* *Aut:* Clabot *m*. 'dog-collar, *s.* **1.** Collier *m* de chien. **2.** *F:* Faux col d'ecclésiastique. 'dog-days, *s.pl.* (La) canicule. 'dog-faced, *a.* *Z:* Cynocéphale. 'dog-fight, *s.* **1.** Combat *m* de chiens. **2.** *F:* Mêlée générale. 'dog-fish, *s.* *Ich:* Chien *m* de mer; roussette *f*. 'dog-headed, *a.* Cynocéphale. 'dog-in-the-manger, *s.* *F:* Chien *m* du jardinier. dog-'Latin, *s.* Latin *m* de cuisine. 'dog-rose, *s.* *Bot:* **1.** Églantine *f*. **2.** (*Bush*) Rosier *m* sauvage; églantier *m*. 'dog's-ear¹, *s.* Corne (faite à la page d'un livre). 'dog's-ear², *v.tr.* Corner (la page d'un livre). 'dog-show, *s.* Exposition canine. 'dog's meat, *s.* **1.** Pâtée *f* (pour chiens). **2.** Déchets *mpl* de viande. 'dog-spike, *s.* **1.** Clou *m* à large tête. **2.** *Rail:* Crampon *m*. 'Dog-star (the), *s.* *Astr:* La Canicule. 'dog-'tired, *a.* *F:* Éreinté, vanné, fourbu. 'dog-watch, *s.* *Nau:* Petit quart; quart de deux heures.

dog², *v.tr.* (dogged [dɔgd]) Suivre (qn) à la piste; ·filer (qn). To dog s.o.'s footsteps, s'attacher aux pas de qn; marcher sur les pas de qn. Dogged by ill fortune, poursuivi par la guigne.

dogberry ['dɔgbəri], *s.* *Bot:* Cornouille *f*.

doge [doudʒ], *s.* *Hist:* Doge *m*.

dogged ['dɔgid], *a.* Obstiné, résolu, tenace. *F:* It's dogged (as) does it, il faut persévérer. -ly, *adv.* Avec ténacité; opiniâtrement.

doggedness ['dɔgidnəs], *s.* Courage *m* tenace; persévérance *f*.

doggerel ['dɔgərəl], *a. & s.* (i) (Poésie *f*) burlesque; (ii) (vers *mpl*) de mirliton.

doggie ['dɔgi], *s.* *F:* Toutou *m*.

doggo ['dɔgo], *adv.* *F:* To lie doggo, se tenir coi; faire le mort.

doggy ['dɔgi]. **1.** *a.* (*a*) Canin; de chien. (*b*) *F:* Chic. (*c*) With a d. air, avec un petit air crâne. **2.** *s.* *F:* = DOGGIE.

dogma, *pl.* -as ['dɔgma, -əz], *s.* Dogme *m*.

dogmatic [dɔg'matik], *a.* **1.** Dogmatique. **2.** *F:* Autoritaire, tranchant. -ally, *adv.* D'un ton autoritaire, tranchant.

dogmatize ['dɔgmətaiz], *v.i.* Dogmatiser.

dogwood ['dɔgwud], *s.* *Bot:* Cornouiller *m*.

doily ['dɔili], *s.* **1.** Petit napperon. **2.** Dessus *m* d'assiette.

doldrums ['dɔldrəmz], *s.pl.* The doldrums, (i) le cafard; (ii) *Nau:* la zone des calmes; le pot au noir. To be in the doldrums, (i) *F:* (of pers.) avoir le cafard; (ii) *Nau:* être dans les calmes équatoriaux; (iii) *F:* (of business) être dans le marasme.

dole¹ [doul], *s.* **1.** *A:* Portion échue en partage. **2.** (*a*) Aumône *f*. (*b*) *Adm:* *F:* Unemployment dole, secours *m*, allocation *f*, ou indemnité *f* de chômage. To go on the dole, s'inscrire au chômage.

dole², *v.tr.* To dole out sth., distribuer parcimonieusement qch.

doleful ['doulful], *a.* (Mine) lugubre; (cri) dolent, douloureux; (of pers.) triste, larmoyant. -fully, *adv.* Tristement, douloureusement.

dolichocephalic [dɔlikose'falik], *a.* *Anthr:* Dolichocéphale.

doll¹ [dɔl], *s.* Poupée *f*. Dutch doll, poupée de bois. Doll's house, maison de poupée. *F:* Pretty d. of a woman, jolie poupée.

doll², *v.tr.* To doll up a child, a woman, poupiner un enfant, une femme. To doll oneself up, se bichonner, se pomponner.

dollar ['dɔlər], *s.* *Num:* **1.** *U.S:* Dollar *m*. **2.** *P:* (Pièce *f* de) cinq shillings.

dollop ['dɔləp], *s.* *P:* Morceau *m* (informe); motte *f* (de beurre, etc.).

dolly ['dɔli], *s.* **1.** *F:* (*a*) Poupée *f*. (*b*) (*Bandaged finger*) Poupée. **2.** Agitateur *m* (pour le linge). Dolly-tub, baquet *m* à lessive. **3.** *Metalw:* (*a*) Tas *m* à river. (*b*) Bouterolle *f* (de riveur).

dolman ['dɔlmən], *s.* *Cost:* Dolman *m*.

dolmen ['dɔlmen], *s.* *Archeol:* Dolmen *m*.

dolorous ['dɔlərəs], *a.* *A. & Poet:* **1.** Douloureux. **2.** Triste, plaintif. -ly, *adv.* Tristement, plaintivement.

dolphin ['dɔlfin], *s.* **1.** (*a*) *Z:* *Her:* Dauphin *m*. (*b*) *Ich:* Dorade *f*. **2.** *Nau:* (*a*) Baderne *f*; bourrelet *m* de défense (de mât). (*b*) Bouée *f* de corps-mort.

dolt [doult], *s.* Sot *m*, benêt *m*; lourdaud *m*; *P:* cruche *f*.

doltish ['doultiʃ], *a.* Sot, lourdaud.

domain [do'mein], *s.* Domaine *m*; terres *fpl*; propriété *f*. *F:* It does not come within my d., cela n'est pas de mon domaine.

dome [doum], *s.* **1.** *Arch:* Dôme *m*. **2.** *F:* Dôme, calotte *f* (des cieux, de verdure); calotte (du crâne).

domed [doumd], *a.* (*a*) (Édifice) à dôme. (*b*) En forme de dôme.

domestic [do'mestik], *a.* **1.** (Vertu) domestique; (charbon) de ménage. Domestic quarrels, scènes de ménage. Domestic life, la vie de famille. Domestic servant, *s.* domestique, domestique *mf*. Domestic arts, les arts ménagers. **2.** (*a*) (Commerce) intérieur. Domestic warfare, guerres intestines, domestiques. (*b*) Domestic animal, animal domestique. **3.** Domestic economy, l'économie domestique. **4.** (Of pers.) Casanier; (femme) d'intérieur. -ally, *adv.* Domestiquement.

domesticate [do'mestikeit], *v.tr.* **1.** Domestiquer, apprivoiser (un animal). **2.** Domesticated woman, femme d'intérieur.

domestication [dɔmesti'keiʃ(ə)n], *s.* **1.** Domestication *f* (d'un animal). **2.** Acclimatation *f*.

domesticity [dɔmes'tisiti], *s.* (*a*) Attachement *m* au foyer; goûts *m* domestiques. (*b*) Vie *f* de famille.

domicile¹ ['dɔmisail], *s.* Domicile *m*. To elect domicile at a place, élire domicile dans un endroit.

domicile², *v.tr.* *Com:* Domicilier (un effet).

domiciled, *a.* Domicilié, demeurant (at, à).

domiciliary [dɔmi'siljəri], *a.* (Visite) domiciliaire.

dominance ['dɔminəns], *s.* Dominance *f* (d'une maladie); prédominance *f* (d'une race).

dominant ['dɔminənt]. **1.** *a.* Dominant. **2.** *s.* *Mus:* Dominante *f*. Dominant seventh, septième *f* de dominante.

dominate ['dɔmineit], *v.tr. & i.* To dominate (over) s.o., a people, dominer (sur) qn, un peuple. *The fortress dominates the town*, la forteresse commande la ville. **dominating**, *a.* Dominant.

domination [dɔmi'neiʃ(ə)n], *s.* Domination *f.*

domineer [dɔmi'niːər], *v.i.* **1.** Se montrer autoritaire. **2.** To domineer over s.o., tyranniser qn ; régenter qn. **domineering,** *a.* Autoritaire.

dominical [dɔ'minik(ə)l], *a.* Dominical, -aux.

Dominican [dɔ'minikən], *a. & s.* Dominicain, -aine.

dominie ['dɔmini], *s.m. F:* Maître d'école.

dominion [dɔ'minjən], *s.* **1.** Domination *f*, maîtrise *f*, autorité *f*. To hold dominion over . . ., exercer son empire sur. . . . **2.** (*Often in pl.*) Possessions *fpl* (d'un État) ; colonie(s) *f* ; dominion(s) *m.* The Dominion of Canada, le Dominion du Canada.

domino, *pl.* **-oes** ['dɔmino, -ouz], *s.* **1.** Domino *m* (de bal masqué). **2.** *Games:* Domino. To play (at) dominoes, jouer aux dominos.

don[1] [dɔn], *s.m.* **1.** (*Spanish title*) Don. **2.** *Sch: F:* Professeur d'université). *F:* A great don at philology, grand docteur en philologie.

don[2], *v.tr.* (donned) Revêtir, endosser (un uniforme, etc.) ; mettre, coiffer (un chapeau).

donate [do'neit], *v.tr.* **1.** Faire un don de (qch.). **2.** *U.S:* Donner (to, à).

donation [do'neiʃ(ə)n], *s.* Donation *f*, don *m.*

done [dʌn]. *See* DO[1].

donkey ['dɔŋki], *s.* **1.** Ane, *f.* ânesse ; baudet *m.* To ride a donkey, aller à âne. Donkey ride, promenade à âne. *F:* She would talk the hindleg of a donkey, elle jase comme une pie borgne. Donkey work, travail de routine. **2.** *F:* Imbécile *mf*, âne *m.* '**donkey-boiler,** *s. Nau:* Chaudière *f* auxiliaire ; petite chaudière. '**donkeycart,** *s.* Charrette *f* à âne. '**donkey-driver,** *s.* Anier, -ière. '**donkey-engine,** *s. Mch:* Petit-cheval *m.* **2.** Treuil *m* à vapeur. '**donkeyman,** *pl.* **-men,** *s.m.* **1.** Anier. **2.** Homme de petite chaudière.

donor ['dounər], *s.* **1.** *Jur:* Donateur, -trice. **2.** *Surg:* Donor of blood, donneur, -euse, de sang.

don't [dount]. = do not.

doom[1] [duːm], *s.* **1.** Destin *m* (funeste) ; sort (malheureux). He met his doom at . . ., il trouva la mort à. . . . **2.** Perte *f*, ruine *f.* His doom is sealed, c'en est fait de lui. **3.** The Day of doom, le jugement dernier. Until the crack of doom, jusqu'au jugement dernier.

doom[2], *v.tr. Lit:* Condamner (to, à). Doomed man, homme perdu. Attempt doomed to failure, tentative condamnée à l'insuccès.

doomsday ['duːmzdei], *s.* Le (jour du) jugement dernier. Till doomsday, (i) jusqu'à la fin du monde ; (ii) *F:* indéfiniment.

door ['dɔːər], *s.* **1.** Porte *f.* Entrance-door, *usu.* street-door, front-door, porte d'entrée, porte de (la) rue. Side-door, porte latérale. *S.a.* BACKDOOR. Carriage-door, porte cochère. Double or folding door, porte brisée, à deux battants. Sliding door, porte à coulisse, à glissières. Two doors away, deux portes plus loin. To show s.o. the door, éconduire qn. To show s.o. to the door, conduire qn jusqu'à la porte ; reconduire qn. To keep within doors, se tenir chez soi ; rester à la maison. To turn s.o. out of doors, mettre qn à la porte. *To play out of doors,* jouer dehors, en plein air. To be denied the door, trouver porte close. *F:* To open a door to abuses, prêter aux abus. To open the door to a settlement, rendre possible un arrangement. To close the door to, against, s.o., fermer sa porte à qn. *F:* To close the door upon any discussion, empêcher, rendre impossible, aucune discussion. *F:* To lay a charge at s.o.'s door, imputer qch.

à qn. *The fault lies at my d.*, la faute en est à moi. **2.** Portière *f* (de wagon, d'auto, etc.). '**door-bell,** *s.* **1.** (*Swinging*) Sonnette *f.* **2.** (*Fixed*) Timbre *m.* '**door-frame,** *s.* Dormant *m*, bâti (dormant). '**door-handle,** *s.* Poignée *f* de porte, de portière. '**door-keeper,** *s.* Portier *m* ; concierge *mf.* '**door-knob,** *s.* Poignée (ronde) de porte ; bouton *m.* '**doormat,** *s.* Paillasson *m* ; essuie-pieds *m inv.* '**door-nail,** *s.* Clou *m* de porte. *S.a.* DEAD I. 1. '**door-post,** *s.* Montant *m* de porte. '**doorscraper,** *s.* Décrottoir *m* ; gratte-pieds *m inv.* '**door-step,** *s.* **1.** Seuil *m*, pas *m* (de la porte). **2.** *F:* Grosse tartine (de pain beurré).

doorway ['dɔːrwei], *s.* (Encadrement *m* de la) porte. In the doorway, sous la porte.

dope[1], *s.* **1.** *Av:* Enduit *m.* (de carrosserie). **2.** *F:* Stupéfiant *m*, narcotique *m.* Turf: Doping (administré à un cheval). **3.** *I.C.E:* Doping (du combustible). **4.** *U.S: P:* (*a*) Renseignement *m*, tuyau *m.* (*b*) Faux renseignements ; bourrage *m* de crâne. '**dopefiend,** *s.* Morphinomane *mf*, toxicomane *mf.* '**dope-habit,** *s.* Toxicomanie *f.*

dope[2], *v.tr.* **1.** *Av:* Enduire (les ailes). **2.** Administrer un narcotique à (qn). *Turf:* Doper (un cheval). *F:* To dope (oneself), prendre des stupéfiants. **3.** *Aut: Av:* Doper (le combustible). **4.** Mêler un narcotique à (un verre de vin) ; narcotiser (une cigarette).

dorado [do'raːdo], *s. Ich:* Dorade *f.*

Doric ['dɔrik], *a. & s. Arch:* Dorique (*m*).

dormant ['dɔːrmənt], *a.* (*a*) (*Of passion*) Assoupi, endormi. To lie dormant, sommeiller, dormir. (*b*) (Volcan) en repos, assoupi.

dormer(-window) ['dɔːrmər(windo)], *s.* Lucarne *f* ; (fenêtre *f* en) mansarde *f.*

dormitory ['dɔːrmitəri], *s.* Dortoir *m.*

dormouse, *pl.* **-mice** ['dɔːrmaus, -mais], *s. Z:* Loir *m.* Garden dormouse, lérot *m.*

dory ['dɔːri], *s. Ich:* (**John**) **Dory,** zée *m* forgeron.

dose[1] [dous], *s. Med: Pharm:* Dose *f* (de médecine).

dose[2], *v.tr.* **1.** Doser (un médicament). **2.** Médicamenter, droguer (qn).

doss[1] [dɔs], *s. P:* Lit *m* (dans un asile de nuit). '**doss-house,** *s. P:* Asile *m* de nuit.

doss[2], *v.i. P:* **1.** Coucher à l'asile de nuit. **2.** To doss down, se coucher.

dost [dʌst]. *See* DO[1].

dot[1] [dɔt], *s.* **1.** Point *m.* *Tg:* Dots and dashes, points et traits *m* ; brèves *f* et longues *f.* *F:* He arrived on the dot, il est arrivé à l'heure tapante. **2.** Mioche *mf.*

dot[2], *v.tr.* (dotted) **1.** Mettre un point sur (un i). *S.a.* I[1]. **2.** Marquer (une surface) avec des points ; pointiller. Dotted line, ligne en pointillé. *Hillside dotted with chalets,* coteau parsemé de chalets. **3.** *Mus:* Pointer (une note). **4.** To dot and carry one, (i) *Ar: A:* reporter un chiffre ; (ii) *F:* boiter (en marchant) ; clopiner. '**dotting-pen,** *s.* Traulet *m.*

dotage ['doutedʒ], *s.* Radotage *m* ; seconde enfance ; gâtisme *m.*

dotal ['doutəl], *a.* Dotal, -aux.

dotard ['doutərd], *s.* (Vieillard) radoteur ; *F:* gâteux *m.*

dote [dout], *v.i.* **1.** Radoter ; tomber dans la sénilité. **2.** To dote (up)on s.o., aimer qn à la folie. **doting,** *a.* **1.** Radoteur, -euse ; sénile. **2.** Qui montre une tendresse ou une indulgence ridicule.

doth [dʌθ]. *See* DO[1].

dott(e)rel ['dɔt(ə)rel], *s. Orn:* (Pluvier *m*) guignard *m*.

dottle [dɔtl], *s. F:* Culot *m* (de pipe).

dotty ['dɔti], *a.* **1.** Marqué de points ; moucheté. **2.** *P:* Toqué, piqué, maboul. **To go dotty,** perdre la boule.

double¹ [dʌbl]. I. *a.* **1.** (*a*) Double. **With a double meaning,** à deux sens, à double sens. **To give a double knock,** frapper d'un coup redoublé. **Double bedroom,** chambre à deux personnes. **'All' is spelt 'a, double l,'** "all" s'écrit "a, deux l." **To reach double figures,** atteindre les deux chiffres. **To play a double game,** jouer double jeu ; ménager la chèvre et le chou. **To lead a double life,** (i) (*of Raffles, etc.*) mener une vie double ; (ii) avoir deux ménages. (*b*) De grandeur ou de force double. **Double whisky,** double consommation *f* de whisky. **2.** *To fold a sheet d.,* plier une feuille en deux. (*Of pers.*) Bent **double,** courbé en deux. **3. Double the number,** le double ; deux fois autant. **I am double your age,** je suis deux fois plus âgé que vous. **4. Double time,** pas redoublé. II. **double,** *adv.* **1.** Double **as long as . . .,** deux fois plus long que. . . **2. To see double,** voir double. III. **double,** *s.* **1.** Double *m* ; deux fois autant. **To toss double or quits,** jouer (à) quitte ou double. **2.** (*Of pers.*) Double ; *F:* sosie *m*. **3.** Détour *m* (d'un animal poursuivi, d'un fleuve). **4.** *Mil:* **At the double,** au pas de course ; au pas gymnastique. **5.** *Ten:* Men's **doubles,** double *m* messieurs. **'double-'acting,** *a. Mec.E:* (Cylindre) à double effet. **'double-'barrelled,** *a.* (Fusil) à deux coups. **'double-bass** [beis], *s. Mus:* Contrebasse *f* (à cordes). **'double-'bedded,** *a.* (Chambre) à deux lits. **'double-'breasted,** *a.* (Gilet, pardessus) croisé. **double-'concave,** *a.* Biconcave. **'double-cross,** *v.tr. U.S: F:* Duper, tromper (un autre membre de sa bande). **'double-dealing,** *s.* Duplicité *f*, fourberie *f*. **'double-'decker,** *s.* **1.** *Av:* Biplan *m*. **2.** *Nau:* Deux-ponts *m inv.* **3.** *F:* Autobus *m* à double étage. **'double 'Dutch,** *s. F:* **To talk double Dutch,** baragouiner ; parler un langage inintelligible. **'double-dyed,** *a.* **1.** *Tex:* (Étoffe) bon teint *inv.* **2.** *F:* Double-dyed scoundrel, gredin fieffé. **'double-edged,** *a.* (Épée, argument) à deux tranchants. **'double-faced,** *a.* **1.** *Tex:* (Étoffe) sans envers, à double envers. **2.** (Homme) à deux visages, hypocrite. **'double-headed,** *a.* A deux têtes ; bicéphale. **double-'lock,** *v.tr.* Fermer (une porte) à double tour. **'double-quick,** *a. & adv.* **In double-quick time,** double-quick, (i) au pas gymnastique ; (ii) *F:* en moins de rien. **double-'scull¹,** *s. Nau:* Aviron *m* à couple. **double-'scull²,** *v.i.* Nager à, en, couple. **'double-'width,** *a.* Double-width cloth, étoffe grande largeur.

double². I. *v.tr.* **1.** Doubler (un nombre, etc.). *Mus:* **To double a note,** doubler, redoubler, une note (à l'octave). *Th:* **To double parts,** jouer deux rôles. **2.** *Nau:* **To double a cape,** doubler un cap. **3. To double (up) paper,** plier en deux, replier, doubler, du papier. **To double (up) one's fist,** serrer le poing. **4.** *Cards:* (At bridge) Contrer. II. **double,** *v.i.* **1.** (*Of population, etc.*) Doubler, se doubler. **2.** Prendre le pas gymnastique, le pas de course. **3.** (*Of hunted animal*) **To double (back),** faire un brusque crochet ; doubler ses voies. **double back,** *v.tr.* Replier, rabattre (une couverture, etc.). **double down,** *v.tr.* Plier, faire une corne à (une page) ; replier (une page). **double over. 1.** *v.i.* Se

plier. **2.** *v.tr.* Replier, rabattre. **double up. 1.** *v.i.* (*a*) Se plier (en deux) ; se replier. **To double up with laughter,** se tordre de rire. (*b*) Accourir au pas gymnastique. **2.** *v.tr.* (*a*) Replier (qch.). (*b*) (*Of blow, etc.*) Faire plier (qn) en deux.

doublet ['dʌblet], *s.* **1.** *A.Cost:* Pourpoint *m*, doublet *m*. **2.** *Ling:* Doublet. **3.** *Phot:* Doublet lens, (i) objectif *m* double ; (ii) objectif dédoublable.

doubly ['dʌbli], *adv.* Doublement.

doubt¹ [daut], *s.* Doute *m*. **To be in doubt,** être en doute, dans le doute. **To cast doubts on sth.,** mettre qch. en doute. **To have one's doubts about, as to, sth.,** avoir des doutes sur, au sujet de, à l'endroit de, qch. *I have my doubts whether he will come,* je doute qu'il vienne. **There is no room for doubt,** le doute n'est pas permis. **Beyond (a) doubt,** sans le moindre doute ; à n'en pas douter. **No doubt he will come,** sans doute qu'il viendra. *There seems to be no d.* (*but*) *that . . .,* il ne semble faire aucun doute que (ne) + *sub.,* more usu. que + *ind.* **Without (a) doubt,** sans aucun doute. **There is no doubt about it,** cela ne fait point de doute.

doubt². **1.** *v.tr.* Douter. **To doubt s.o., s.o.'s word,** douter de qn, de la parole de qn. *I d. whether he will come,* je doute qu'il vienne, s'il viendra. *I do not d. (but) that he will come,* je ne doute pas qu'il ne vienne. **2.** *v.i.* *He doubted no longer,* il n'hésita plus.

doubtful ['dautful], *a.* **1.** (*Of thg*) Douteux. *Com:* Doubtful debt, dette véreuse. **2.** (*Of pers.*) (*a*) Indécis, incertain. *I was still d. about speaking to him,* j'hésitais encore à lui parler. (*b*) *To be d. of, as to, sth.,* douter de qch. **3.** (Caractère) équivoque, suspect ; (question) discutable. **Doubtful society,** compagnie louche. **-fully,** *adv.* **1.** D'un air de doute. **2.** En hésitant. **3.** Vaguement.

doubtfulness ['dautfulnəs], *s.* **1.** Ambiguïté *f*. **2.** Incertitude *f* (du temps, de l'avenir). **3.** Irrésolution *f*, indécision *f*.

doubtless ['dautləs], *adv.* Sans doute ; très probablement.

douceur [du:'sə:r], *s.* **1.** Gratification *f*, pourboire *m*. **2.** *Pej:* Pot-de-vin *m*.

douche¹ [du:ʃ], *s. Esp. Med:* Douche *f*.

douche². **1.** *v.tr.* Doucher. **2.** *v.i.* Se doucher.

dough [dou], *s.* **1.** Pâte *f* (à pain). **2.** *U.S: P:* Argent *m* ; *P:* galette *f*.

doughnut ['dounʌt], *s. Cu:* Pet *m* de nonne.

doughty ['dauti], *a. A. & Hum:* Vaillant, preux. **Doughty deeds,** hauts faits. **-ily,** *adv.* Vaillamment.

doughy ['doui], *a.* **1.** (Pain) pâteux. **2.** *F:* (Visage) terreux.

dour [duər], *a. Scot:* **1.** Austère, froid, sévère. **2.** Obstiné ; buté. **-ly,** *adv.* **1.** Avec une austérité froide. **2.** Avec obstination.

douse¹ [daus], *v.tr. F:* **1.** Plonger, tremper, (qch.) dans l'eau. **2.** Arroser, asperger (qn) ; administrer une douche à (qn). **dousing,** *s.* (*a*) Plongeon *m*. (*b*) Douche *f*.

douse², *v.tr. Nau:* **1.** (*a*) Amener rondement (une voile). (*b*) Fermer (un sabord). **2.** *P:* Éteindre (la lumière).

dove [dʌv]. **1.** *s.* Colombe *f*. **2.** *a.* **Dove (-coloured, -grey),** colombin ; gorge-de-pigeon *inv.*

dovecot(e) ['dʌvkɔt], *s.* Colombier *m*, pigeonnier *m*.

Dover ['douvər]. *Pr.n. Geog:* Douvres *m*. **The Straits of Dover,** le Pas de Calais.

dovetail¹ ['dʌvteil], *s. Carp:* Queue-d'aronde *f*.

dovetail², *v.tr.* **1.** Assembler à queue-d'aronde. **Dovetailed joint**, assemblage endenté, à queue-d'aronde. **2.** (*a*) *F:* To *d. two schemes into each other*, opérer le raccord entre deux entreprises. (*b*) *v.i.* (*Of schemes, etc.*) Se rejoindre, se raccorder.

dowager ['dauədʒər], *s.f.* Douairière.

dowdiness ['daudinəs], *s.* Manque *m* d'élégance (dans la toilette).

dowdy ['daudi], *a.* (Femme ou toilette) peu élégante, sans élégance. *An old dowdy*, une vieille dame mal fagotée. **-ily**, *adv.* (Vêtue) sans élégance.

dowel¹ ['dauel], *s. Carp:* Goujon *m* (d'assemblage); cheville *f* (en bois).

dowel², *v.tr.* (dowelled) Goujonner.

dower¹ ['dauər], *s.* **1.** (*Widow's*) Douaire *m.* **2.** *A. & Lit:* = DOWRY.

dower², *v.tr.* **1.** Assigner un douaire à (une veuve). **2.** Doter (une jeune fille).

dowerless ['dauərləs], *a.* Sans dot.

down¹ [daun], *s.* **1.** Dune *f.* **2.** *pl.* (*In Sussex, etc.*) *The South Downs*, les hautes plaines crayeuses et accidentées; les Downs *m.* **3.** *Geog:* *The Downs*, la rade au large de Deal.

down², *s.* **1.** (*On birds*) Duvet *m.* *D. pillow*, oreiller de plume. **2.** (*On pers.*) Duvet; poil follet. **3.** (*On plants, fruit*) Duvet.

down³. **I.** *adv.* **1.** (*Motion*) Vers le bas; (de haut) en bas. *To go down*, aller en bas; descendre. *To lay down one's arms*, mettre bas les armes. *To fall down*, tomber (i) à terre, (ii) par terre. *Cash down*, argent (au) comptant, sur table. *Down with the traitors!* à bas les traîtres! (*To a dog*) *Down!* à bas! couché! **2.** (*Position*) *Down below*, en bas, en contre-bas. *Down there*, là-bas (en contre-bas). *Down in the country*, (au loin) à la campagne, en province. *Down here*, ici; dans ces parages. *Down under*, aux antipodes. *The blinds were down*, les stores étaient baissés. *The curtains are d.*, on a enlevé les rideaux. *Face down*, face en dessous. *Head down*, la tête en bas. *To be down*, (i) être tombé (par terre); (ii) (*of student*) être rentré chez soi (à la fin du trimestre); (iii) n'être plus à l'université. *He is not down (from his bedroom) yet*, il n'est pas encore descendu. *To hit a man when he is down*, frapper un homme à terre. *He is down for £20*, il est inscrit pour (une cotisation de) 20 livres. *He is £20 down*, il a un déficit de £20. *Down with fever*, alité, frappé, par la fièvre. *The sun is down*, le soleil est couché. *The wind is d.*, le vent est tombé. *The tide is d.*, la mer est basse. *Bread is down*, le pain a baissé. *Her hair is down*, ses cheveux sont dénoués, défaits. *Aut: etc:* *Your tyres are down*, vos pneus sont dégonflés, à plat. *Games:* *To be ten points down*, avoir dix points de moins. *Cards:* *To be two down*, avoir deux de chute. *Ship down by the head*, navire enfoncé par l'avant. **3.** *From prince down to pedlar*, du prince jusqu'au colporteur. *Down to recent times*, jusqu'au temps présent; jusqu'à présent. *D. to here*, (en descendant) jusqu'ici. **4.** *To be down on s.o.*, en vouloir à qn; être toujours sur le dos de qn. *To be down in the mouth*, être découragé, abattu. *F:* *To be down and out*, être ruiné, décavé, à bout de ressources. **II.** **down**, *prep.* *To lower s.o. down a precipice*, descendre qn le long d'un précipice. *Her hair is hanging down her back*, les cheveux lui pendent dans le dos. *To go down the street*, *down a hill*, descendre la rue, une colline. *Down the river*, en aval. *To fall down the stairs*, tomber en bas de l'escalier. *Down town*, en ville. *S.a.* UP¹ II. 2. III. **down**,

a. **1.** *Rail:* **Down train, down platform**, train montant, quai montant. **2.** *Mus:* **Down beat**, temps fort. **3.** *F:* = DOWN-HEARTED. **IV. down**, *s.* **1.** *In the phr.* **Ups and downs**, *q.v. under* UP¹ IV. **2.** *P:* *To have a down on s.o.*, en vouloir à qn; avoir une dent contre qn. **down-at-'heel**, *a.* (Soulier) éculé; (*of pers.*) râpé, *F:* décheux. **'down-draught**, *s.* Courant d'air descendant. *I.C.E:* **Down-draught carburettor**, carburateur inversé. **'down-grade**, *s.* **1.** *Rail:* Rampe descendante; descente *f.* **2.** *To be on the down-grade*, être sur le déclin, *F:* sur le retour. **down-'hearted**, *a.* Découragé; déprimé, abattu. **'down-'stage**, *adv.* & *a.* *Th:* Sur le devant (de la scène). **'down-'stream.** **1.** *adv.* En · aval. **2.** *a.* D'aval. **'down-stroke**, *s.* **1.** (*In writing*) Jambage *m*, plein *m.* **2.** *Mch:* Course descendante (du piston).

down⁴, *v.tr.* **1.** (*a*) *To down s.o.*, terrasser, abattre, qn. *To down an aeroplane*, 'descendre' un avion. (*b*) *P:* Battre, vaincre (qn). **2.** *Ind:* *To down tools*, mettre bas les outils; se mettre en grève.

downcast ['daunka:st], *a.* **1.** (*Of pers.*) Abattu, déprimé. **2.** (*Of look*) Baissé (vers la terre).

downfall ['daunfo:l], *s.* **1.** Chute *f* (de neige, etc.). **2.** Chute, ruine *f*; écroulement *m*, effondrement *m* (d'un empire, etc.).

downhill. **1.** ['daunhil], *a.* En pente; incliné. **2.** [daun'hil], *adv.* *To go downhill*, (*of road*) aller en descendant; (*of cart, etc.*) descendre (la côte); *F:* (*of pers.*) être sur le déclin.

downiness ['dauninəs], *s.* Duveté *m*; velouté *m.*

downmost ['daunmoust], *a.* Le plus bas, la plus basse.

downpour ['daunpɔ:ər], *s.* Forte pluie; grosse averse.

downright ['daunrait]. **1.** *adv.* (*a*) Tout à fait; complètement. (*b*) (Refuser) nettement, catégoriquement, carrément. **2.** *a.* (*a*) (*Of pers., language*) Direct; franc, *f.* franche; carré. (*b*) Absolu, véritable. **Downright lie**, mensonge éclatant. *D. swindle*, véritable escroquerie. *A d. no*, un non catégorique.

downstairs [daun'stɛərz], *adv.* En bas (de l'escalier). *To come, go, downstairs*, descendre (l'escalier).

downtrodden ['dauntrɔdn], *a.* Foulé aux pieds; (peuple) opprimé, tyrannisé.

downward ['daunwərd]. **1.** *a.* (Mouvement) descendant, de haut en bas; (regard) dirigé en bas. *F:* **The downward path**, la pente fatale. **2.** *adv.* = DOWNWARDS.

downwards ['daunwərdz], *adv.* (*a*) De haut en bas; en descendant; (*on river*) en aval. *Face d.*, face en dessous. (*b*) *From the twelfth century downwards*, à partir du douzième siècle.

downy ['dauni], *a.* **1.** (*a*) Duveteux; couvert de duvet. *Bot:* Lanugineux, pubescent. (*b*) (*Of fruit*) Velouté. (*c*) (*Lit*) douillet, moelleux. **2.** *F:* *A downy bird*, un malin, un rusé.

dowry ['dauri], *s.* Dot *f.*

dowse [dauz], *v.i.* Faire de l'hydroscopie, de la radiesthésie. **dowsing**, *s.* Hydroscopie *f.* **'dowsing-rod**, *s.* Baguette *f* divinatoire, de sourcier.

dowser ['dauzər], *s.* Sourcier *m*; hydroscope *m.*

doze¹ [do:uz], *s.* Petit somme. *To have a doze*, faire un petit somme.

doze², *v.i.* Sommeiller; être assoupi. *To doze off*, s'assoupir.

dozen [dʌzn], *s.* Douzaine *f.* **1.** (*Inv. in pl.*) *Half a d.*, une demi-douzaine. **Six dozen bottles**, six douzaines de bouteilles. **2.** (*pl.* dozens) To sell articles in (sets of) dozens, by the dozen, vendre des articles à la douzaine. Dozens and dozens of times, maintes et maintes fois. A long dozen, a baker's dozen, treize douze ; treize à la douzaine. *F :* To talk nineteen to the dozen, jaser comme une pie borgne.

drab¹ [drab], *s.f.* Souillon.

drab², *a. & s.* (*a*) Gris (*m*) ou brun (*m*) ; écru ; beige. (*b*) *F :* Drab existence, existence terne, décolorée.

drachm [dram], *s. Pharm.Meas :* Drachme *f.*

Draconian [dra'kounjən], *a.* Draconien, sévère.

draff [draf], *s. Brew :* Drêche *f.*

draft¹ [drɑːft], *s.* I. **1.** *Mil :* (*a*) Détachement *m* (de troupes) ; contingent *m* (de recrues). (*b*) Membre *m* d'un détachement, d'un contingent. **2.** *Com :* (*a*) Tirage *m* (d'un effet). (*b*) Traite *f* ; lettre *f* de change ; effet *m*. Draft at sight, effet à vue. **3.** Dessin *m* schématique ; plan *m*, tracé *m* ; ébauche *f.* **4.** Projet *m* (de contrat) ; brouillon *m* (de lettre). First d. of a novel, premier jet d'un roman. II. **draft**, *s.* = DRAUGHT¹ I.

draft², *v.tr.* **1.** *Mil :* Détacher, envoyer en détachement (des troupes). **2.** To draft s.o. to a post, désigner qn à, pour, un poste. **3.** Rédiger (un acte) ; faire le brouillon (d'une lettre).

drafter ['drɑːftər], *s.* Rédacteur *m* (d'un acte).

draftsman, *pl.* **-men** ['drɑːftsmən, -men], *s.* = DRAUGHTSMAN I.

drag¹ [drag], *s.* **1.** *Veh :* Drag *m*, mail-coach *m* (à quatre chevaux). **2.** (*a*) (*Dredging*) Drague *f.* (*b*) (*For retrieving lost object*) Araignée *f* ; *Nau :* grappin *m* à main. (*c*) *Fish :* = DRAG-NET. **3.** (*a*) Sabot *m*, patin *m* (d'enrayage). To put a drag on a wheel, enrayer une roue. *F :* (*Of pers.*) To put on the drag, enrayer. (*b*) Entrave *f.* To be a drag on s.o., entraver qn ; être un boulet au pied de qn. (*c*) *Nau :* = DRAG-ANCHOR. **4.** (*a*) Tirage *m*, résistance *f* (à l'avancement) ; frottement excessif. (*b*) *Av :* Traînance *f* ; effort *m* de traînée. (*c*) To walk with a drag, marcher en traînant la jambe. **'drag-anchor,** *s. Nau :* Ancre flottante, ancre de cape. **'drag-bar,** *s.* Barre *f* d'attelage, d'accouplement (de wagons, etc.). **'drag-link,** *s.* (*a*) = DRAG-BAR. (*b*) *Aut :* Bielle *f* de commande de direction. **'drag-net,** *s. Fish :* Drague *f*, chalut *m*, seine *f* ; filet *m* à la trôle.

drag², *v.* (dragged [dragd]) **I.** *v.tr.* (*a*) Traîner, tirer ; entraîner (qn) (contre sa volonté). To drag one's feet, traîner les pieds. (*b*) *Nau :* (*Of ship*) To drag her anchor, chasser sur ses ancres ; déraper. (*c*) Draguer *(un étang). **2.** *v.i.* (*a*) (*Of pers.*) Traîner, rester en arrière ; (*of thg*) traîner (à terre) ; (*of lawsuit, etc.*) traîner en longueur ; (*of conversation*) languir, s'éterniser. (*b*) Offrir de la résistance ; (*of brakes*) frotter (sur les roues). (*c*) *Nau :* (*Of anchor*) Raguer le fond, labourer le fond. (*d*) Draguer (*for sth.*, à la recherche de qch.). *Fish :* Pêcher à la drague. **drag about,** *v.tr.* Traîner, *F :* trimbaler (qn, qch.). **drag along,** *v.tr.* Traîner, entraîner (qn, qch.). **drag away,** *v.tr.* (*a*) Entraîner, emmener, (qn) de force. (*b*) Arracher (qn) (*from,* à, de). **drag down,** *v.tr.* Tirer, entraîner, (qn, qch.) en bas. He has dragged me down with him, il m'a entraîné dans sa chute. **drag in,** *v.tr.* Faire entrer de force (qn, qch.). **drag on,** *v.i.* (*Of affair, etc.*) Traîner en longueur ; s'éterniser. **drag out,** *v.tr.* **1.** To drag s.o. out of bed, tirer qn de son lit. To drag the truth out of s.o., arracher la vérité à qn. **2.** Faire traîner (une affaire). **3.** To

drag out a wretched existence, poursuivre, traîner, jusqu'à sa fin une existence misérable. **drag up,** *v.tr.* **1.** Entraîner, tirer, (qn, qch.) jusqu'en haut. **2.** Repêcher (un cadavre, etc.) à la drague. *F :* Why do you drag up that old story? pourquoi ressortir cette vieille histoire? **3.** *F :* (*Of child*) Dragged up, élevé à la va-comme-je-te-pousse, tant bien que mal. **dragging,** *s.* **1.** Traînage *m*, traînement *m* (d'un fardeau). *Nau :* Dragging of the anchor, dérapage *m*. **2.** Dragage *m* (d'un étang, etc.).

draggle [dragl]. **1.** *v.tr.* Traîner (sa jupe, etc.) dans la boue ; crotter (ses vêtements). **2.** *v.i.* Traîner ; rester en arrière. **'draggle-tail,** *s.f. F :* Souillon ; traînée.

dragon ['dragən], *s.* (*a*) Dragon *m.* (*b*) *A : F :* Duègne *f*, dragon. **'dragon-fly,** *s. Ent :* Libellule *f* ; *F :* demoiselle *f.*

dragoon¹ [dra'guːn], *s. Mil :* Dragon *m.*

dragoon², *v.tr.* **1.** *Hist :* Dragonner (le peuple). **2.** *F :* Tyranniser (qn). To dragoon s.o. into doing sth., contraindre qn à faire qch.

drain¹ [drein], *s.* **1.** Canal *m*, -aux (de décharge) ; tranchée *f*, caniveau *m*, rigole *f.* Open drain, tranchée à ciel ouvert. **2.** (*a*) Égout *m. F :* To throw money down the drain, jeter son argent par la fenêtre. (*b*) The drains of a house, la canalisation sanitaire d'une maison. **3.** (*a*) Tuyau *m* d'écoulement ou de vidange. (*b*) *Surg :* Drain *m.* **4.** Perte *f*, fuite *f* (d'énergie, etc.). Constant d. on the resources, saignée continuelle. **'drain-cock,** *s.* Robinet *m* de purge, de vidange. **'drain-pipe,** *s.* Tuyau *m* d'écoulement, d'échappement. **'drain-plug,** *s.* Bouchon *m* de vidange.

drain². **I.** *v.tr.* (*a*) To drain water (away, off), (i) évacuer, faire écouler, des eaux ; (ii) faire égoutter l'eau. (*b*) Boire (un liquide) jusqu'à la dernière goutte ; vider (un fût). (*c*) Assécher (un terrain) ; mettre à sec, vider (un étang) ; assécher, drainer, épuiser (une mine) ; (faire) égoutter (des bouteilles, des légumes). *I.C.E :* To drain the sump, vidanger le carter. (*d*) Épuiser, *F :* saigner (qn, la bourse). To drain a country of money, épuiser l'argent d'un pays. *F :* To drain s.o. dry, saigner qn à blanc. Writer who has drained himself dry, écrivain qui a épuisé sa veine. **2.** *v.i.* (*a*) (*Of water, etc.*) To drain (away), s'écouler. (*b*) (*Of thg*) (S')égoutter. **draining,** *s.* **1.** Écoulement *m* (des eaux) ; assèchement *m* (d'un marais) ; drainage *m* (d'un terrain) ; égouttage *m* (des bouteilles). **2.** *pl.* Drainings, égoutture *f* (d'un verre). **'draining-rack,** *s.* Égouttoir *m.*

drainage ['dreinedʒ], *s.* **1.** = DRAINING **1.** **2.** (i) Système *m* d'écoulement des eaux ; (ii) système *m* d'égouts. **'drainage-tube,** *s. Surg :* Drain *m.*

drainer ['dreinər], *s.* Égouttoir *m.*

drake [dreik], *s.* Canard *m* mâle.

dram [dram], *s.* **1.** = DRACHM. **2.** *F :* Goutte *f* (à boire) ; petit verre. **'dram-shop,** *s. P :* Débit *m* d'alcool ; *P :* bistrot *m.*

drama ['drɑːma], *s.* **1.** Drame *m.* **2.** The drama, l'art *m* dramatique ; le théâtre.

dramatic [dra'matik], *a.* Dramatique. The dramatic works of Corneille, le théâtre de Corneille. **-ally,** *adv.* Dramatiquement.

dramatist ['dramatist], *s.* Auteur *m* dramatique ; dramaturge *m.*

dramatize ['dramataiz], *v.tr.* Dramatiser ; adapter (un roman) à la scène.

drank [draŋk]. See DRINK².

drape [dreip], *v.tr.* (*a*) Draper, tendre (*with, in, de*). (*b*) *Art:* Draper (une étoffe).

draper ['dreipər], *s.* Marchand *m* d'étoffes, de nouveautés. **Draper's shop,** magasin de nouveautés. *S.a.* LINEN-DRAPER.

drapery ['dreipəri], *s.* Draperie *f.* **Drapery and fancy goods store,** magasin *m* de nouveautés.

drastic ['drastik], *a.* **1.** *Med:* Drastique. **2.** To take **drastic measures,** prendre des mesures énergiques, rigoureuses; *F:* trancher dans le vif. **-ally,** *adv.* Énergiquement, rigoureusement.

drat [drat], *v.tr.* *F:* (*Third pers. sub.*) D. the child! au diable cet enfant! quel sacré mioche! **dratted,** *a.* *F:* Maudit (mioche, etc.).

draught[1] [drɑːft], *s.* I. **1.** Traction *f*, tirage *m.* Draught animal, bête de trait. **2.** *Fish:* Coup *m* de filet; pêche *f.* **3.** (*Drinking*). Trait *m*, coup *m*, gorgée *f.* At a draught, d'un seul trait, d'un seul coup. **4.** *Med:* Potion *f*, breuvage *m.* Black draught, purgatif *m*, médecine noire. **5.** *Nau:* Tirant *m* d'eau (d'un vaisseau). Load draught, tirant d'eau en charge. Light draught, tirant d'eau en lège. **6.** *pl.* Draughts, (jeu *m* de) dames *fpl.* **Draught-board,** damier *m.* **7.** (*a*) (*In room*) Courant *m* d'air. (*b*) (Induced) draught (*of chimney*), tirage; appel *m* d'air. **8.** Beer on draught, **draught-beer,** bière au tonneau, à la pompe. II. **draught,** *s.* = DRAFT[1] I. **'draught-excluder,** *s.* = DRAUGHT-TUBE. **'draught-harness,** *s.* Harnais *m* d'attelage. **'draught-regulator,** *s.* *Mch: etc:* Registre (régulateur) de tirage. **'draught-screen,** *s.* Paravent *m.* **'draught-tube,** *s.* Bourrelet *m* de porte.

draught[2], *v.tr.* = DRAFT[2].

draughtsman, *pl.* -men ['drɑːftsmən, -men], *s.* **1.** *Ind:* Dessinateur *m*, traceur *m* (d'épures, etc.). **2.** *Games:* Pion *m* (du jeu de dames).

draughtsmanship ['drɑːftsmənʃip], *s.* **1.** L'art *m* du dessin industriel; *Ind:* le dessin. **2.** Talent *m* de dessinateur.

draughty ['drɑːfti], *a.* **1.** Plein de courants d'air. **2.** (Coin de rue, etc.) exposé à tous les vents.

draw[1] [drɔː], *s.* **1.** (*a*) Tirage *m.* (*b*) *F:* This was meant as a d., but he did not rise to it, ceci était dit pour l'attirer sur ce sujet, mais il n'a pas mordu. **2.** (*a*) Tirage au sort. (*b*) Loterie *f*, tombola *f.* **3.** *F:* Attraction *f*; clou *m* (de la fête, etc.). (*Of play, etc.*) To be a draw, faire recette. **-** *Sp:* Partie nulle; résultat nul.

draw[2], *v.* (drew [druː]; drawn [drɔːn]) I. *v.tr.* **1.** (*a*) Tirer (un verrou, un rideau); lever (un pont-levis). To d. the blinds, baisser les stores. To d. one's hand across one's forehead, passer la main sur son front. To draw a bow, bander, tendre, un arc. (*b*) Tirer, traîner (une voiture). Drawn by a locomotive, remorqué par une locomotive. **2.** (*a*) (*Take in*) Tirer, aspirer (l'air dans ses poumons). (*b*) (*Attract*) Attirer. To draw a crowd, crowds, attirer une foule; provoquer un rassemblement. *Abs.* To draw, attirer la foule, le public. To draw s.o. into the conversation, faire entrer qn dans la conversation. To d. s.o. into a conspiracy, engager, entraîner, qn dans une conspiration. To draw s.o. into doing sth., amener qn à faire qch. To feel drawn to s.o., se sentir attiré vers qn. I feel drawn to him, il m'est sympathique. **3.** (*a*) Tirer, retirer, ôter (*sth. from, out of, sth.*, qch. de qch.). To draw (one's sword), tirer l'épée; dégainer. To draw (lots) for sth., tirer qch. au sort. The number drawn, le numéro sortant. To draw a blank, (i) tirer un numéro blanc; (ii) *F:* éprouver une déception; faire chou blanc. *Cp.* 4 (*b*). To draw

straws, tirer à la courte paille. (*b*) Arracher (un clou, une dent, etc.). To draw tears from s.o., tirer, arracher, des larmes à qn. *F:* To draw s.o.'s teeth, mettre qn hors d'état de nuire. (*c*) To d. water from the river, puiser, tirer, de l'eau à la rivière. To draw wine (*from a barrel*), tirer du vin (d'un tonneau). To d. a conclusion from sth., tirer une conclusion de qch. (*d*) Toucher (de l'argent, un salaire). *Abs.* To draw upon one's savings, prendre sur ses économies. *F:* To draw upon one's memory, faire appel à sa mémoire. (*e*) *Tchn:* To d. the fire(s), mettre bas les feux. (*f*) *Ven:* To draw a fox, lancer, mettre sur pied, un renard. *Mil:* To draw the enemy's fire, attirer sur soi le feu de l'ennemi. *F:* To try to d. s.o., essayer de faire parler qn. **4.** (*a*) Vider (une volaille). *A:* To be hanged, drawn and quartered, être pendu, éviscéré et écartelé. (*b*) *Ven:* To draw a covert, battre un taillis. To draw a blank, (i) faire buisson creux; (ii) *F:* revenir bredouille. *Cp.* 3 (*a*). **5.** To draw the tea, faire infuser le thé. **6.** *Metall:* Étirer, tirer (des tubes, etc.); tréfiler (un métal). **7.** (*a*) (*Trace*) Tracer (un plan); tirer, mener (une ligne). (*b*) To draw a map, (i) (*of surveyor*) dresser une carte; (ii) (*of schoolboy*) faire, dessiner, une carte. (*c*) Dessiner (un paysage). To d. a picture of s.o., faire le portrait de qn. (*d*) Faire, établir (une distinction, des comparaisons). **8.** To d. a cheque on a bank, tirer un chèque sur une banque. To draw a bill, *abs.* to draw, (up)on s.o. for £ . . ., tirer sur qn pour £ . . . **9.** *Nau:* (*Of ship*) To d. twenty feet of water, tirer, jauger, vingt pieds d'eau. **10.** To draw (a game) with s.o., faire partie nulle, match nul, avec qn. The battle was drawn, la bataille resta indécise. II. **draw,** *v.i.* **1.** (*a*) To draw near to s.o., se rapprocher de qn; s'approcher de qn. The crowd drew to one side, la foule se rangea (de côté). The train drew into the station, le train entra en gare. To draw round the table, s'assembler autour de la table. (*b*) (*Of the day, etc.*) To draw to an end, tirer, toucher, à sa fin. **2.** (*Of chimney*) Tirer; (*of pump*) aspirer. **3.** To let the tea draw, laisser infuser le thé. **draw along,** *v.tr.* Traîner, entraîner (qn, qch.). **draw apart.** **1.** *v.tr.* Séparer, écarter. **2.** *v.i.* Se séparer, s'écarter. **draw aside.** **1.** *v.tr.* (*a*) Détourner, écarter (qch.); tirer (les rideaux). (*b*) Prendre (qn) à l'écart. **2.** *v.i.* S'écarter; se ranger. **draw away.** **1.** *v.tr.* (*a*) Entraîner (qn). (*b*) Détourner (s.o. *from sth.*, qn de qch.). **2.** *v.i.* S'éloigner. **draw back.** **1.** *v.tr.* (*a*) Tirer en arrière; retirer (sa main). (*b*) Tirer, ouvrir (les rideaux). **2.** *v.i.* (Se) reculer; se retirer en arrière. **draw down,** *v.tr.* Faire descendre (qch.); baisser (les stores). **draw in.** **1.** *v.tr.* (*a*) Faire entrer (qch.) en train; (*of cat*) rentrer, rétracter (ses griffes). (*b*) Aspirer (l'air) (à pleins poumons). (*c*) *Abs.* Réduire sa dépense; faire des économies. **2.** *v.i.* The day is drawing in, le jour baisse. The days are drawing in, les jours diminuent. **draw off,** *v.tr.* (*a*) Retirer, ôter (ses gants). (*b*) Détourner (l'attention). (*c*) Soutirer (un liquide). *Mch:* Draw-off plug, bouchon *m* de vidange. **draw on.** **1.** *v.tr.* (*a*) Mettre (ses gants); passer, enfiler (un vêtement). (*b*) To draw s.o. on to do sth., entraîner qn à faire qch. **2.** *v.i.* (*a*) S'avancer. (*b*) Evening was drawing on, la nuit approchait. **draw out,** *v.tr.* **1.** Sortir, retirer (qch. de qch.); arracher (un clou, une dent). **2.** *F:* Encourager (qn) à sortir de sa réserve; faire parler (qn). **3.** (*a*) Allonger (un cordage); étirer (le fer). (*b*) Prolonger (un

repas) ; tirer (une affaire) en longueur ; (faire) traîner (une affaire). **draw to,** *v.tr.* Tirer, fermer (les rideaux). **draw together,** *v.tr.* (*a*) Rassembler, réunir, rapprocher (des personnes, des choses). (*b*) = DRAW TO. **draw up. 1.** *v.tr.* (*a*) Tirer (qch.) en haut ; faire (re)monter (qch.) ; lever (un store) ; relever (ses manches) ; aspirer (de l'eau). To draw oneself up (to one's full height), se (re)dresser (de toute sa hauteur). (*b*) *To d. up a chair* (*to the table*), approcher une chaise (de la table). (*c*) Ranger, aligner (des troupes). (*d*) Dresser, rédiger, libeller (un document) ; établir (un compte) ; arrêter (un programme) ; élaborer (un projet). **2.** *v.i.* (*a*) *To d. up to the table*, s'approcher de la table. To draw up with s.o., arriver à la hauteur de qn. (*b*) (*Of carriage*) S'arrêter, stopper. (*c*) (*Of troops*) Se ranger, s'aligner. **drawn,** *a.* **1.** With drawn curtains, les rideaux tirés. **2.** With drawn swords, sabre au clair. **3.** (*a*) *Metalw :* Drawn tube, tube étiré. (*b*) Drawn features, traits tirés, contractés. **4.** Drawn battle, bataille indécise. *D. match*, partie égale, nulle. **drawing,** *s.* **1.** (*a*) Tirage *m* ; (*of water*) puisage *m*, puisement *m* ; (*of teeth, nails*) extraction *f.* (*b*) Attraction *f* (*towards*, vers). Drawing power, pouvoir attractif. (*c*) *Metalw :* Étirage *m.* **2.** (*a*) Dessin *m.* To learn drawing, apprendre le dessin. Freehand drawing, dessin à main levée. Out of drawing, mal dessiné. Mechanical drawing, dessin industriel. (*b*) Pencil drawing, dessin au crayon. Rough drawing, ébauche *f*, croquis *m.* *Sectional d.*, (vue *f* en) coupe *f.* (*c*) *Ind :* Épure *f.* Wash drawing, épure au lavis. **'drawing-board,** *s.* Planche *f* à dessin. **'drawing-knife,** *s. Tls :* Plane *f*, plaine *f* (de charron). **'drawing-master,** *s.m.* Professeur de dessin. **'drawing-mill,** *s. Metalw :* Tréfilerie *f.* **'drawing-paper,** *s.* Papier *m* à dessin. **'drawing-pen,** *s.* Tire-ligne *m.* **'drawing-pin,** *s.* Punaise *f* (pour papier à dessin).
draw⁻, *comb.fm.* **'draw-bar,** *s.* Barre *f* d'attelage, de tirage. **'draw-bench,** *s. Metalw :* Banc *m* à étirer, à tréfiler. **'draw-hole,** *s. Metall :* Trou *m* de coulée (de haut-fourneau). **'draw-hook,** *s.* Crochet *m* d'attelage. **'draw-knife,** *s. Tls :* = DRAWING-KNIFE. **'draw-slide, -tube,** *s. Opt :* Tube *m* à tirage (d'un microscope).
drawback ['drɔ:bak], *s.* **1.** Inconvénient *m*, désavantage *m.* **2.** *Cust :* Remboursement *m* (à la sortie) des droits d'importation ; drawback *m.*
drawbridge ['drɔ:bridʒ], *s.* **1.** Pont-levis *m.* **2.** *Civ.E :* Pont basculant.
drawee [drɔ:'i:], *s.* Tiré *m* (d'une lettre de change).
drawer ['drɔ:ər], *s.* **1.** (*Pers.*) (*a*) Tireur, -euse ; (*of water*) puiseur, -euse ; (*of teeth*) arracheur, -euse. (*b*) Tireur de vin, de bière. (*c*) Tireur, souscripteur *m* (d'une lettre de change). (*d*) Dessinateur *m*, traceur *m.* (*e*) Drawer (up), rédacteur *m* (d'un document). **2.** (*Device*) Extracteur *m.* **3.** (*a*) Tiroir *m.* Chest of drawers, commode *f.* Nest of drawers, classeur *m* à tiroirs. (*b*) Cash-drawer, tiroir-caisse *m.* **4.** *pl.* (*a*) (*Underwear*) (Pair of) drawers, (*for men*) caleçon *m* ; (*for women*) pantalon *m.* (*b*) Running drawers, culotte *f* (de coureur) ; short *m.*
drawing-room ['drɔ:iŋrum], *s.* **1.** Salon *m.* **2.** (*At Court*) Réception *f.*
drawl¹ [drɔ:l], *s.* Voix traînante *f.* débit traînant.
drawl². **1.** *v.i.* Parler d'une voix traînante.

2. *v.tr.* To drawl out sth., dire qch. avec une nonchalance affectée.
dray [drei], *s. Veh :* (*a*) Camion *m* (de brasseur). (*b*) Fardier *m.* **'dray-horse,** *s.* Cheval *m* de camion, de charrette.
drayman ['dreimən], *pl.* **-men** ['dreimən, -men], *s.m.* Livreur de brasserie ; camionneur.
dread¹ [dred], *s.* Crainte *f*, terreur *f*, épouvante *f* ; *F :* phobie *f.* In dread of doing sth., de crainte de faire qch. To be, stand, in dread of s.o., craindre, redouter, qn.
dread², *v.tr.* Redouter, craindre. To dread that . . ., redouter que (ne) + *sub.*
dread³, *a. Lit :* = DREADFUL 1.
dreadful ['dredful], *a.* **1.** Terrible, redoutable. **2.** Atroce, épouvantable. It is something dreadful, c'est quelque chose d'affreux. *F :* It's a d. bore! c'est assommant ! *I've been hearing d. things about you,* on m'a raconté des horreurs sur votre compte. *S.a.* PENNY DREADFUL. **-fully,** *adv.* **1.** Terriblement, affreusement, atrocement. **2.** *F :* (*Intensive*) Dreadfully ugly, affreusement laid. *I am d. sorry,* je regrette infiniment.
dreadnought ['drednɔ:t], *s.* **1.** (*a*) *Cost :* Paletot-pilote *m.* (*b*) *Tex :* Frise *f.* **2.** *Navy :* (Cuirassé *m* du type) Dreadnought *m.*
dream¹ [dri:m], *s.* Rêve *m.* (*a*) Songe *m.* To have a dream, faire un rêve, un songe. Sweet dreams! faites de beaux rêves ! To see sth. in a dream, voir qch. en songe. (*b*) Waking dream, day-dream, rêverie *f*, rêvasserie *f*, songerie *f.* To be in a dream, être dans un rêve. *F :* It's a dream of a hat! c'est le chapeau rêvé.
dream², *v.tr. & i.* (*p.t. & p.p.* dreamed [dri:md], *occ.* dreamt [dremt]) **1.** (*During sleep*) To dream of, about, sth., rêver de qch. **2.** Laisser vaguer ses pensées ; rêvasser. To dream empty dreams, rêver creux. **3.** I shouldn't dream of doing it, jamais je ne m'aviserais de faire cela. Little did I dream that . . ., je ne songeais guère que. . . .
dreaming, *s.* Rêves *mpl*, songes *mpl.*
dreamer ['dri:mər], *s.* **1.** Rêveur, -euse. **2.** *F :* Rêveur ; (*esprit*) songeur *m.* **3.** *Pej :* Cerveau creux ; songe-creux *m inv.*
dream-hole ['dri:mhoul], *s. Arch : A :* Rayère *f.*
dreaminess ['dri:minəs], *s.* (État *m* de) rêverie *f.*
dreamland ['dri:mland], *s.* Le pays des rêves.
dreamy ['dri:mi], *a.* Rêveur ; songeur ; langoureux.
drear ['driər], *a. Lit :* = DREARY.
dreariness ['driərinəs], *s.* Tristesse *f*, aspect *m* morne (d'un paysage, etc.).
dreary ['driəri], *a.* (Paysage) triste, morne ; (discours) morne, ennuyeux.
dredge¹ [dredʒ], *s. Fish :* Drague *f.*
dredge², *v.tr. & i.* Draguer, curer, dévaser (un chenal, un canal). To dredge for sth., draguer à la recherche de qch. **dredging¹,** *s.* Dragage *m.*
dredge³, *v.tr. Cu :* Saupoudrer. **dredging²,** *s.* Saupoudrage *m.*
dredger¹ ['dredʒər], *s.* **1.** (*Pers.*) (Ouvrier) dragueur *m.* **2.** (*Machine*) Drague *f* ; cure-môle *m.*
dredger², *s.* Saupoudroir *m* (à sucre, etc.).
dreg [dreg], *s.* (*Usu. pl.*) To drink the cup to the dregs, boire la coupe jusqu'à la lie. *F :* The very dregs of the population, la lie du peuple.
drench¹ [drenʃ], *s. Vet :* Breuvage *m*, purge *f.*
drench², *v.tr.* **1.** Tremper, mouiller (with, de). Drenched to the skin, trempé jusqu'aux os ; trempé comme une soupe. **2.** *Vet :* Administrer une médecine à (une bête). **drenching,** *a.* Drenching rain, pluie battante, diluvienne.
Dresden ['drezdən]. *Pr.n. Geog :* Dresde *f.* Dresden china, porcelaine *f* de Saxe.

dress¹ [dres], *s.* **I.** Habillement *m* ; habits *mpl* ; vêtements *mpl*. In full dress, en grande toilette ; en grand costume ; en grande tenue. **Morning dress,** (i) (*of women*) négligé *m* ; (ii) tenue de ville. **Evening dress,** tenue de soirée. **Faultless dress,** mise *f* irréprochable. **To talk dress,** causer chiffons. **Dress-materials,** étoffes *f* pour robes, pour costumes. **2.** Robe *f*, costume, toilette. **Ball dress,** robe de bal. **Bathing dress** = BATH-ING-COSTUME. *Com:* **Ladies' dresses,** modes *f*. **'dress-'circle,** *s. Th:* (Premier) balcon. **'dress-'coat,** *s.* Habit *m* (de soirée) ; frac *m*. **'dress-preserver, -shield,** *s. Cost:* Sous-bras *m inv.* **'dress-stand,** *s.* Mannequin *m* (de vitrine, etc.). **'dress-'suit,** *s.* Habit *m* (de soirée, de cérémonie).

dress², *v.tr.* (dressed [drest]) **I.** (*a*) Habiller, vêtir (qn). Well dressed, bien habillé, bien mis ; élégant. **To be plainly dressed,** avoir une mise simple. **Badly dressed,** mal habillé ; mal mis. *Th:* **To dress a play,** costumer une pièce. (*b*) *v.pr. & i.* **To dress (oneself),** s'habiller ; faire sa toilette. *To d. with taste,* se mettre avec goût. **To dress (for dinner),** (i) (*of man*) se mettre en habit ; (ii) se mettre en toilette du soir. **2.** Orner, parer (*with,* de). *Com:* **To dress the window,** faire la vitrine ; faire l'étalage. *Nau:* **To dress a ship,** pavoiser un navire. **3.** *Mil:* Aligner (des troupes). *v.i.* (*Of troops*) S'aligner. **Right dress!** à droite alignement ! **4.** *Med:* Panser (une blessure). **5.** (*a*) *Tchn:* Apprêter (une surface) ; dresser, tailler, parer (des pierres). **To dress timber roughly,** dégrossir le bois. **To dress cloth,** (i) apprêter, (ii) lainer, l'étoffe. (*b*) **To dress s.o.'s hair,** coiffer qn. *Cu:* Apprêter, accommoder (un mets) ; assaisonner, garnir (une salade). (*d*) *Agr:* Donner une façon à (un champ). **dress down,** *v.tr. F:* Chapitrer (qn) ; laver la tête à (qn). **dressing down,** *s. F:* Verte semonce. **dress out,** *v.tr.* Parer, orner (qn) ; *F:* attifer (qn). **dress up,** *v.tr.* Habiller, parer, *F:* attifer (qn). **To dress oneself up,** *v.i.* to dress up, **as a soldier,** s'habiller, se costumer en soldat. *P:* **To be dressed up to the nines,** être tiré à quatre épingles ; être sur son trente et un. **dressing,** *s.* **I.** (*a*) Habillement *m*, toilette *f*. (*b*) Arrangement *m* (des cheveux). (*c*) *Agr:* Façon *f*. (*d*) *Cu:* Accommodage *m*, apprêt *m* (des mets). (*e*) Pansement *m* (d'une blessure). (*f*) Alignement *m* (des troupes). (*g*) Pavoisement *m*. (*h*) *Tchn:* Apprêt *m*, apprê-tage *m* (des étoffes) ; dressage *m*, taille *f* (des pierres). **2.** (*a*) *Cu:* (Salad-)dressing, assaisonne-ment *m* (pour la salade) genre sauce mayonnaise. (*b*) Produit *m* d'entretien ; enduit *m* (pour cuirs, etc.) ; graisse *f* (pour courroies). *Agr:* Fuma-ges *mpl*. **Light dressing,** engrais légers. *Surface d.,* top d., couche *f* d'engrais. (*c*) *Med:* Pansement, appareil *m*. (*d*) *Tex:* Apprêt, . empois *m*. **'dressing-case,** *s.* Nécessaire *m*, sac *m* (de toilette, de voyage). **'dressing-gown,** *s.* Robe *f* de chambre ; (*for women*) peignoir *m*, saut-de-lit *m*. **'dressing-jacket,** *s.* Camisole *f*. **'dressing-room,** *s.* **I.** Cabinet *m* de toilette. **2.** *Th:* Loge *f* (d'acteur, d'actrice). **'dressing-station,** *s. Mil:* Poste *m* de secours. **'dress-ing-table,** *s.* (Table *f* de) toilette *f* ; coiffeuse *f*.

dresser¹ ['dresər], *s. Furn:* Buffet *m* de cuisine ; dressoir *m*.

dresser², *s.* **I.** *Ind:* Apprêteur, -euse. **2.** *Th:* Habilleur, -euse. **3.** Externe *m* (des hôpitaux) ; panseur, -euse.

dressiness ['dresinəs], *s.* Recherche *f* dans sa mise, dans sa toilette.

dressmaker ['dresmeikər], *s.* (*a*) Couturière *f*. (*b*) Couturier *m*.

dressmaking ['dresmeikiŋ], *s.* **I.** Couture *f*. **2.** Confections *fpl* pour dames ; confection de robes.

dressy ['dresi], *a.* **I.** (*Of pers.*) Mis avec re-cherche ; (*of woman*) qui aime la toilette ; coquette. **2.** (*Of clothes, etc.*) Chic, élégant.

drew [dru:]. *See* DRAW².

dribble¹ [dribl], *s.* **I.** (*a*) Dégouttement *m*, égouttage *m*. (*b*) (*Of child*) Bave *f*. **2.** *Fb:* Dribbling *m*, dribble *m*.

dribble². **I.** *v.i.* (*a*) Dégoutter ; tomber goutte à goutte. *F:* *The men came dribbling back,* les ouvriers revenaient par deux ou trois, par petits groupes. (*b*) (*Of child, idiot*) Baver. **2.** *v.tr. Fb:* Dribbler (le ballon).

drib(b)let ['driblet], *s.* Petite quantité ; chiquet *m*. *In, by, driblets,* *F:* chiquet à chiquet. *To pay in driblets,* payer sou par sou, petit à petit.

dried [draid]. *See* DRY².

drier, driest, *a. See* DRY¹.

drift¹ [drift], *s.* **I.** (*a*) Mouvement *m*. *Ph:* **Ether drift,** mouvement relatif de la terre et de l'éther. (*b*) (i) Direction *f*, sens *m* (d'un courant) ; (ii) vitesse *f* (d'un courant). (*c*) Cours *m*, marche *f* (des événements). **2.** (*a*) *Artil:* Dérivation *f* (d'un projectile). (*b*) *Av: Nau:* Dérive *f*. *Av:* **Drift indicator,** dérivomètre *m*. *F:* **Policy of drift,** politique de laisser-faire. **3.** But *m*, tendance *f*, sens général, portée *f*. *What is the d. of these questions?* où tendent ces questions? **4.** (*a*) Amoncellement *m* (de neige, de sable). (*b*) *Geol:* Apport(s) *m(pl)*. **Glacial drift,** mo-raine *f*. **5.** *Tls:* (*a*) **Drift (punch),** chasse-clef *m*, chasse-clavette *m* ; poinçon *m*. (*b*) (*For rivet-holes*) Broche *f* d'assemblage ; mandrin *m*. **'drift-boulder,** *s. Geol:* Caillou roulé. **'drift-ice,** *s.* **drift-net,** *s.* Filet traînant ; traîne *f*. **'drift-sand,** *s.* Sable mouvant. **'drift-wood,** *s.* Bois flotté, bois flotté.

drift². **I.** *v.i.* (*a*) Flotter ; être charrié, entraîné. *Nau:* Dériver, aller en dérive ; *Av:* déporter. *Nau: To d. to leeward,* être dépalé, dériver. *To drift on shore,* abattre à la côte. **To drift with the current,** se laisser aller au fil de l'eau. (*b*) **To drift into vice,** se laisser aller au vice. **To let oneself drift, to let things drift,** se laisser aller ; laisser aller les choses. (*c*) (*Of snow*) S'amon-celer, s'amasser. (*d*) (*Of questions, events*) Tendre (vers un but). **2.** *v.tr.* (*a*) Flotter (du bois) ; (*of current*) charrier, entraîner (qch.). (*b*) (*Of wind*) Amonceler, entasser (la neige, le sable). (*c*) Brocher, mandriner (un trou de rivet).

drifter ['driftər], *s. Nau:* (*a*) Pêcheur *m* au filet traînant ; chalutier *m*. (*b*) (*Boat*) Chalutier *m*.

drill¹ [dril], *s.* **I.** (*a*) *Tls:* Foret *m*, pointe *f* à forer, mèche *f* ; perforateur *m*. *Min:* Fleuret *m*. **Wall-drill** (*for plugging*), tamponnoir *m*. (*b*) *Tls:* Vilebrequin *m*. **Hand-drill,** drille *f*, perceuse *f* à main. **2.** *Mil: etc:* Exercice(s) *m(pl)*, manœu-vre(s) *f(pl)*. **Company drill,** école *f* de com-pagnie. **Company at drill,** compagnie à l'exercice. **To do punishment drill,** faire la pelote. *S.a.* GROUND² 5, PACK-DRILL, RECRUIT¹. **'drill-book,** *s. Mil:* Théorie *f* (du soldat). **'drill-hall,** *s. Mil:* Salle *f* d'exercice. **'drill-sergeant,** *s. Mil:* Sergent instructeur.

drill². **I.** *v.tr.* Forer (un puits) ; perforer (une plaque) ; percer (un trou). *Dent:* **To drill a tooth,** buriner une dent. **2.** *v.tr.* Faire faire l'exercice à (des hommes) ; instruire, faire

15

manœuvrer (des soldats). **3.** *v.i.* Faire l'exercice ; manœuvrer.

drill³, *s.* *Agr: Hort:* **1.** Ligne *f*, rayon *m*, sillon *m*. *To sow in drills,* semer par sillons. **2.** Semeuse *f* (à cuillers) ; semoir *m* en lignes. **'drill-plough,** *s.* *Agr:* Sillonneur *m*.

drill⁴, *v.tr.* *Agr:* Semer en lignes, par sillons.

drill⁵, *s.* *Tex:* Coutil *m*, treillis *m*.

drily ['draili], *adv.* = DRYLY.

drink¹ [driŋk], *s.* **1.** (*Liquid drunk*) (*a*) Boire *m*. Food and drink, (i) le boire et le manger ; (ii) à boire et à manger. (*b*) To give s.o. a drink, donner à boire à qn ; faire boire qn. To have a drink, se désaltérer. *To have a long d.,* boire un bon coup. *Give me a d. of water,* donnez-moi un peu d'eau à boire. (*c*) Consommation *f*. To have a drink, prendre quelque chose ; boire un coup. (Will you) have a drink? voulez-vous boire quelque chose? **2.** (*Beverage*) Boisson *f*, breuvage *m*. Strong drink, liqueurs fortes ; spiritueux *mpl*. **3.** Boisson ; ivrognerie *f*. To take to drink, s'adonner à la boisson. The drink question, la question de l'alcoolisme. To be in drink, the worse for drink, under the influence of drink, avoir trop bu ; être ivre, soûl ; *Jur:* être en état d'ébriété. To smell of drink, puer l'alcool.

drink², *v.tr.* (*p.t.* drank ; *p.p.* drunk) Boire. **1.** *To d.* water, wine, boire de l'eau, du vin. To drink the waters, prendre les eaux. Will you have something to drink? voulez-vous boire quelque chose? Fit to drink, bon à boire ; buvable, potable. To drink (of) the cup of joy, boire s'abreuver, à la coupe des plaisirs. To drink success to s.o., to s.o.'s success, boire au succès de qn. To drink oneself drunk, se soûler. *S.a.* DEATH, HEALTH. **2.** *Abs.* Être adonné à la boisson. To drink hard, heavily, (i) boire sec, raide ; (ii) s'alcooliser. To drink like a fish, boire comme une éponge. **drink away,** *v.tr.* Boire (sa fortune) ; noyer (ses soucis, etc.). **drink down,** *v.tr.* Boire, avaler (un breuvage). **drink in,** *v.tr.* **1.** Absorber, boire (l'eau) ; s'imbiber (d'eau). **2.** *F:* Boire (les paroles de qn). **3.** *F:* He drank it all in, il a avalé ça doux comme lait. **drink off,** *v.tr.* Boire (un verre) d'un coup, d'un trait. **drink up,** *v.tr.* **1.** Achever de boire ; vider (un verre). **2.** (*Of plants, etc.*) = DRINK IN 1. **drunk. 1.** *Pred. a.* (*a*) Ivre, gris ; soûl (*with,* de). To be drunk, être pris de boisson. To get drunk, s'enivrer, se griser, se soûler. Dead drunk, ivre-mort, *pl.* ivres-morts. Blind drunk, soûl perdu. As drunk as a fiddler, as a lord, soûl comme une prune. *Jur:* Drunk and disorderly, en état d'ivresse manifeste. (*b*) Enivré, grisé (*with success,* par le succès). Drunk with carnage, ivre de carnage. **2.** *s.* Homme pris de boisson ; ivrogne *m*. **3.** *s.* *F:* Ribote *f*.

drinking, *s.* **1.** After drinking, après boire. **2.** Ivrognerie *f*, alcoolisme *m*. **'drinking-bout,** *s.* Soûlerie *f*, ribote *f*. **'drinking-fountain,** *s.* Borne-fontaine *f*, *pl.* bornes-fontaines ; fontaine publique. **'drinking-song,** *s.* Chanson *f* à boire ; chanson bachique. **'drinking-trough,** *s.* Abreuvoir *m*. **'drinking-water,** *s.* Eau *f* potable.

drinkable ['driŋkəbl], *a.* (*a*) Buvable. (*b*) (Eau) potable.

drinker ['driŋkər], *s.* Buveur, -euse. **1.** *Water drinkers,* buveurs d'eau. **2.** Hard drinker, grand buveur ; alcoolique *m*.

drip¹ [drip], *s.* **1.** Dégouttement *m* ; égouttement *m* (d'un robinet). *Mch:* Drip receiver, godet *m*. **2.** Goutte *f* ; *pl.* égoutture *f*. **3.** *Arch:* Lar-

mier *m* (de corniche). **'drip-cock,** *s.* *Mch:* (Robinet) purgeur *m*. **'drip-feed,** *s.* *Mch:* Distributeur *m* compte-gouttes (d'huile). **'drip-stone,** *s.* *Arch:* Capucine *f* ; larmier *m*.

drip², *v.* (dripped) **I.** *v.i.* Dégoutter, s'égoutter ; tomber goutte à goutte. *Wall that drips,* mur qui suinte. **2.** *v.tr.* Laisser tomber (du liquide) goutte à goutte. **dripping¹,** *a.* Ruisselant ; (robinet) qui pleure. To be dripping wet, être trempé (comme une soupe). Dripping joint, joint qui jute. **dripping²,** *s.* **1.** Dégouttement *m*, égouttement *m*. **2.** *pl.* Égoutture *f* (des arbres) ; dégouttures *fpl* (du toit). **3.** *Cu:* Graisse *f* de rôti. Bread and dripping, tartine *f* à la graisse. **'dripping-pan,** *s.* *Cu:* Lèchefrite *f*. **'dripping-tube,** *s.* Pipette *f* compte-gouttes.

drive¹ ['draiv], *s.* **1.** Promenade *f* en voiture ; course *f*. To go for a drive, faire une promenade en voiture. **2.** *Ven:* Battue *f* (du gibier). **3.** *Mec.E:* (Mouvement *m* de) propulsion *f* ; (i) attaque *f* (d'un organe) ; (ii) commande *f* (par un organe) ; transmission *f*, actionnement *m*. Belt drive, entraînement *m* par courroie. *Aut:* Direct drive, prise directe, attaque directe. Car with front wheel drive, voiture à traction avant. Rear drive, pont *m* arrière. **4.** *Sp:* (*a*) *Golf:* Crossée *f* de départ. (*b*) *Ten:* Drive *m*. Fore-arm drive, drive de coup droit. **5.** (*a*) *D.* of business, urgence *f* des affaires. (*b*) (*Of pers.*) To have plenty of drive, avoir de l'énergie ; être très entreprenant. **6.** (*a*) Avenue *f* (dans une forêt). (*b*) = CARRIAGE-DRIVE. **7.** Bridge, whist, drive, tournoi *m* de bridge, de whist.

drive², *v.* (*p.t.* drove [drouv] ; *p.p.* driven [drivn]) **I.** *v.tr.* **1.** (*a*) Chasser, pousser, faire aller (devant soi). *To d.* cattle to the fields, conduire, mener, le bétail aux champs. To drive s.o. from, out of, the house, chasser qn de la maison. *F:* To drive sth. out of s.o.'s head, faire oublier qch. à qn. *To be driven out of one's course,* être entraîné hors de sa route. *To be driven ashore,* être drossé, poussé, à la côte. (*b*) *Ven:* To drive the game, rabattre le gibier. **2.** (*a*) Faire marcher (une machine) ; conduire (un cheval, une auto, une locomotive). *Abs.* Can you drive? savez-vous conduire? (*b*) To drive s.o. to the station, conduire qn à la gare. **3.** (*a*) Pousser (qn à une action) ; contraindre (qn à faire qch.). He was driven to it, on lui a forcé la main. *S.a.* NEEDS. (*b*) To drive s.o. out of his senses, rendre qn fou. **4.** Surcharger (qn) de travail ; exploiter (qn) ; surmener (ses employés). **5.** Enfoncer (un clou) ; foncer, battre, ficher (un pieu). **6.** Percer, forer, avancer (un tunnel). **7.** (*a*) To drive a trade, exercer un métier ; faire un métier. (*b*) To drive a bargain, faire, conclure, passer, un marché. **8.** *Sp:* To drive the ball, *abs.* to drive, *Ten:* jouer un drive ; *Golf:* jouer une crossée. **9.** (*a*) Actionner, faire marcher, commander (une machine). (*Of part*) *To d.* another part, actionner, entraîner, attaquer, un organe. (*b*) *F:* (*Of pers.*) To drive a pen, a quill, écrire ; manier la plume ; gratter le papier. **II.** drive, *v.i.* **1.** (*a*) (*Of clouds, etc.*) To drive before the wind, chasser, être charrié, devant le vent. To let drive at s.o., décocher un coup à qn. (*b*) (*Of snow*) S'amonceler. (*c*) *Nau:* (*Of ship*) Dériver. Driving ashore, dérivant à la côte. **2.** To drive along the road, rouler sur la route. To drive to a place, se rendre en voiture à un endroit. *I don't like to d. at night,* je n'aime pas conduire, voyager, la nuit. *To d.* on the right side of the road, circuler à droite ; tenir la droite. **drive along. 1.** *v.tr.* Chasser, pousser (qn, qch.). **2.** *v.i.* Cheminer (en voiture); rouler. **drive at,** *v.i.* **1.** Travailler à (qch.) sans relâche; *F:* bûcher (qch.). **2. What are you driving at?** à quoi voulez-vous en venir? où tendent ces questions? **drive away. 1.** (*a*) *v.tr.* Chasser, éloigner, repousser. (*b*) *v.i.* Partir, s'en aller, en voiture; *Aut:* démarrer. **2.** *v.i.* To drive away at one's work, travailler d'arrache-pied. **drive back. 1.** *v.tr.* (*a*) Repousser, refouler, faire reculer. (*b*) Reconduire, ramener, (qn) en voiture. **2.** *v.i.* Rentrer, revenir, retourner, en voiture. **drive down. 1.** *v.tr.* (*a*) *To d. s.o. down to, into, the country,* conduire qn (en voiture) à la campagne. (*b*) *To d. down an aeroplane,* forcer un avion à descendre. **2.** *v.i.* Se rendre en voiture (de la ville à la campagne, de Londres en province). **drive in. 1.** *v.tr.* (*a*) Enfoncer (un clou); visser (une vis). (*b*) (*Of chauffeur, etc.*) Faire entrer (qn). **2.** *v.i.* Entrer (en voiture). **drive off,** *v.tr. & i.* = DRIVE AWAY 1. **drive on. 1.** *v.tr.* Pousser, entraîner (qn). **2.** *v.i.* Continuer sa route. **drive out. 1.** *v.tr.* Chasser (qn, qch.); faire sortir (qn). **2.** *v.i.* Sortir (en voiture). **drive over,** *v.i.* Venir, se rendre, (à un endroit) en voiture. **drive through. 1.** *v.tr.* To drive one's sword through s.o.'s body, passer son sabre à travers le corps à qn. **2.** *v.i.* Traverser, passer par, (une ville) en voiture. **driven,** *a.* **1.** Tempest-driven ship, vaisseau battu par les tempêtes. *S.a.* SNOW[1] 2. *Mec.E:* Driven shaft, arbre commandé. Electrically driven, actionné par l'électricité; à commande électrique; (voiture) électromotrice. Belt-driven, à entraînement par courroie. **driving**[1], *a.* **1.** *Mec.E:* (*Of wheel, etc.*) Moteur, -trice. *S.a.* AXLE 1, SHAFT[1] 5. Driving force, force motrice. **2.** Driving rain, pluie battante. **driving**[2], *s.* Conduite *f* (d'une voiture, etc.). *Jur:* Driving to the public danger, infraction *f* au code de la route. **'driving-band, -belt,** *s.* Courroie *f* de commande, d'entraînement, de transmission. **'driving-chain,** *s.* *Mec.E:* Chaîne *f* de transmission. **'driving-gear,** *s.* *Mec.E:* (Engrenage(s) *m(pl)* de) transmission *f*; commande *f*. **'driving-iron,** *s.* *Golf:* Grand fer. **'driving-pulley,** *s.* Poulie conductrice, de commande. **'driving-test,** *s.* *Aut:* Examen *m* pour permis de conduire. **'driving-wheel,** *s.* Roue motrice (de locomotive, etc.). **drivel**[1] [drivl], *s.* **1.** Bave *f*. **2.** *F:* Radotage *m*; balivernes *fpl*. To talk drivel, radoter. **drivel**[2], *v.i.* (drivelled) **1.** Baver. **2.** *F:* Radoter. **driveller** ['drivələr], *s.* **1.** Baveur, -euse. **2.** *F:* Radoteur, -euse. **driver** ['draivər], *s.* **1.** (*a*) Mécanicien *m* (de locomotive); conducteur *m* (d'autobus); conducteur, -trice, chauffeur, -euse (d'automobile); cocher *m* (de voiture); voiturier *m* (de charrette). He is a good driver, il conduit bien. (*b*) Conducteur (de bestiaux). (*c*) Surveillant *m* (d'esclaves). **2.** *Tls:* (*a*) Poinçon *m*. (*b*) Chasse-clavette *m*. **3.** (*a*) = DRIVING-WHEEL. (*b*) = DRIVING-PULLEY. **drizzle**[1] [drizl], *s.* Bruine *f*, crachin *m*; pluie fine et pénétrante. **drizzle**[2], *v.i.* Bruiner, crachiner; pleuvoir à petites gouttes. **droll** [droul]. **1.** *s.* *A:* Bouffon *m*. **2.** *a.* Drôle, drolatique, bouffon, plaisant. *A d. fellow,* (i) un drôle de corps; (ii) un farceur. **drollery** ['drouləri], *s.* Drôlerie *f*, plaisanterie *f*, bouffonnerie *f*. **drollness** ['droulnəs], *s* Caractère *m* drôle (de qch.).

dromedary ['drʌmədəri, 'drɔm-], *s.* Dromadaire *m*. Racing dromedary, méhari *m*. **drone**[1] [droun], *s.* **1.** (*a*) *Ent:* Abeille *f* mâle; faux-bourdon. (*b*) *F:* Fainéant *m*, parasite *m*. The drones, les inutiles *m*. **2.** (*a*) Bourdonnement *m* (des abeilles). *F:* The parson's endless drone, le débit monotone du pasteur. *Av:* Drone of the engine, ronronnement *m*, vrombissement *m*, du moteur. (*b*) *Mus:* Bourdon *m* (de cornemuse). **drone**[2]. **1.** *v.i.* (*a*) (*Of bee, etc.*) Bourdonner. (*b*) Fainéanter. **2.** *v.tr.* To drone (out) sth., débiter (une prière, etc.) d'un ton monotone. **droop**[1] [dru:p], *s.* **1.** (*a*) Attitude penchée (de la tête). (*b*) Abaissement *m* (des paupières). **2.** Langueur *f*, abattement *m*, affaissement *m*. **droop**[2]. **1.** *v.i.* (*a*) (*Of head, etc.*) (Se) pencher; (*of eyelids*) s'abaisser; (*of feathers*) pendre, retomber. (*b*) (*Of flower*) Pencher, languir. (*c*) (*Of pers.*) Languir, s'affaiblir, s'affaisser. To revive s.o.'s drooping spirits, remonter le courage à qn. **2.** *v.tr.* Baisser, pencher (la tête); abaisser (les paupières); (*of bird*) laisser pendre (les ailes). **drop**[1] [drɔp], *s.* **1.** (*a*) Goutte *f*. *Water falling drop by drop,* eau qui tombe goutte à goutte. *F:* It's only a drop in the bucket, in the ocean, ce n'est qu'une goutte d'eau dans la mer. *F: A drop of wine,* une goutte, un doigt, de vin. *Cu:* A few drops of vinegar, un filet de vinaigre. *F:* To take a drop, boire la goutte. He has had a drop too much, il a bu un coup de trop. (*b*) (*Of necklace, chandelier, etc.*) Pendant *m*, pendeloque *f*. (*c*) Peppermint, chocolate, drop, pastille *f* de menthe, de chocolat. *S.a.* ACID 1. **2.** Chute *f*. *Surv:* Drop in the ground, dénivellation *f* du terrain. Drop in prices, chute, baisse *f*, de prix. *El.E:* Drop in voltage, perte *f* de charge. **3.** (*Of lock*) Cache-entrée *m inv.* (*b*) *Th:* = DROP-CURTAIN. (*c*) (*In gallows*) Bascule *f*, trappe *f*. **'drop-curtain,** *s.* *Th:* Rideau *m* d'entr'acte. **'drop-forge,** *v.tr.* *Metalw:* Étamper, estamper; emboutir; forger à la presse. **drop-forging,** *s.* **1.** Estampage *m*; matriçage *m*. **2.** Pièce emboutie, étampée; pièce matricée. **'drop-hammer,** *s.* Marteau-pilon à friction, *pl.* marteaux-pilons; mouton *m*. **'drop-head,** *s.* *Aut:* Capote *f* rabattable. **'drop-kick,** *s.* *Fb:* Coup tombé. **'drop-scene,** *s.* **1.** *Th:* (*a*) Toile *f* de fond. (*b*) = DROP-CURTAIN. **2.** *F:* Dernier acte (d'un drame de la vie réelle). **'drop-shutter,** *s.* *Phot:* Obturateur *m* à guillotine. **'drop-stitch,** *s.* *Tex:* Maille sautée. **'drop-valve,** *s.* *I.C.E:* Soupape renversée. **drop**[2], *v.* (dropped [drɔpt]) I. *v.i.* **1.** Tomber goutte à goutte, dégoutter (*from*, de); s'égoutter. **2.** Tomber; (*of pers.*) se laisser tomber; (*of ground*) s'abaisser. A remark dropped from him, il laissa échapper une remarque. To drop into a chair, s'écrouler sur une chaise; s'affaler dans un fauteuil. *F:* He almost dropped (*with surprise*), il pensa tomber de son haut. I am ready to drop, je tombe de fatigue (ou de sommeil). *S.a.* PIN[1] 1. **3.** (*Of prices, temperature*) Baisser; (*of wind*) tomber, se calmer. **4.** There the matter dropped, l'affaire en resta là. **5.** (*a*) To drop to the rear, rester en arrière; se laisser dépasser. (*Of pers., car*) To drop into place, prendre sa place (dans la file); prendre la file. (*b*) To drop into the habit, the way, of . . ., prendre l'habitude de. . . . **6.** (*a*) To drop into one's club, entrer en passant à son cercle. (*b*) To drop upon, across, s.o., rencontrer qn par hasard. *To d. on to a secret,* surprendre un secret. **7.** *F:* To drop (up)on s.o. (like a ton of bricks), attraper qn;

rembarrer qn. **II. drop,** *v.tr.* **1.** Verser (une larme). **To drop oil into sth.,** verser de l'huile goutte à goutte dans qch. **2.** (*a*) Laisser tomber; lâcher (qch.); baisser (un rideau); lancer, larguer (une bombe); (*in knitting*) sauter, laisser échapper (une maille). *Rugby:* **To drop a goal,** marquer un but sur coup tombé. *Nau:* **To drop the pilot,** débarquer le pilote. *Geom:* **To drop a perpendicular to, on, a line,** abaisser une perpendiculaire à une ligne. *S.a.* ANCHOR[1], BRICK[1] 1. (*b*) (*Of sheep, etc.*) Mettre bas (des petits). (*c*) Laisser échapper (une observation). **To drop a word in s.o.'s ear,** couler, glisser, un mot à l'oreille de qn. *S.a.* HINT[1]. (*d*) *To d. a letter into the pillar-box,* jeter une lettre à la poste. *F:* **To drop s.o. a line,** a card, envoyer, écrire, un mot, une carte, à qn. **3.** Perdre (de l'argent) (*over sth.,* sur qch.). **4.** (*Cause to drop*) Abattre (qn, une pièce de gibier, un avion) (d'un coup de feu). **5.** (*Set down*) I shall drop you at your door, je vous déposerai chez vous en passant. *Will you d. this parcel at Mrs Smith's,* voulez-vous avoir l'obligeance de remettre ce paquet chez madame Smith. **6.** (*a*) Omettre, supprimer (une lettre, une syllabe). (*b*) Ne pas prononcer (les r, etc.). *S.a.* AITCH. **7.** Baisser (les yeux); baisser, laisser tomber (la voix). **8.** (*a*) Abandonner, délaisser (un travail); cesser, lâcher (une poursuite); se départir (d'une habitude). **To drop the idea of doing sth.,** renoncer à (l'idée de) faire qch. **Let us drop the subject,** laissons ce sujet, qu'il n'en soit plus question. *F:* **Drop it!** finissez! en voilà assez! (*b*) **To drop s.o.'s acquaintance,** *F:* **to drop s.o.,** cesser de voir qn; cesser ses relations avec qn. **drop away,** *v.i.* **1.** *The members of the family have dropped away,* la famille s'est égrenée; les membres de la famille ont disparu un à un. **2.** (*Of members, receipts*) Diminuer. **drop behind,** *v.i.* Rester en arrière; se laisser dépasser; se laisser distancer. **drop in. 1.** *v.tr.* Ajouter (qch.) goutte à goutte; glisser, laisser tomber, (qch.) dedans. **2.** *v.i.* Entrer en passant. **To drop in on s.o.,** faire une petite visite, un bout de visite, à qn. **drop off,** *v.i.* **1.** (*Of leaves, etc.*) Tomber, se détacher. **2.** *F:* **To drop off to sleep,** s'assoupir, s'endormir. **3.** = DROP AWAY 2. **drop out. 1.** *v.tr.* Omettre, supprimer. **2.** *v.i.* (*a*) Tomber dehors. (*b*) *To drop out of a contest,* se retirer. *Two of the runners dropped out,* deux des coureurs ont renoncé. *Mil:* (*Of man unable to keep up with his troop*) Sortir des rangs; rester en arrière. **dropped,** *a. Aut: etc:* Dropped axle, *etc.,* essieu, etc., surbaissé. **dropping,** *s.* **1.** (*a*) Dégouttement *m* (d'un liquide). (*b*) Descente *f,* chute *f* (d'un objet); abaissement *m,* baisse *f,* chute (des prix); suppression *f* (d'un mot); abandon *m* (d'un projet). **2.** *pl.* Droppings, (*a*) Gouttes *fpl;* égoutture *f.* (*b*) (*Of animals*) Fiente *f;* (*of sheep*) crottes *fpl.* **'dropping-tube,** *s.* Pipette *f,* compte-gouttes *m inv.*

droplet ['drɔplet], *s.* Gouttelette *f.*

dropper ['drɔpər], *s.* **1.** Compte-gouttes *m inv.* **2.** *Fish:* Bout *m* de ligne.

dropsical ['drɔpsik(ə)l], *a. Med:* Hydropique.

dropsy ['drɔpsi], *s. Med:* Hydropisie *f.*

drosera ['drɔsərə], *s. Bot:* Drosère *m,* rossolis *m.*

dross [drɔs], *s.* **1.** *Metall:* Scories *fpl,* crasse *f,* laitier *m.* **2.** (*a*) Impuretés *fpl* (de toutes sortes); déchet *m.* (*b*) *F:* Rebut *m.*

drought [draut], *s.* (Période *f* de) sécheresse *f;* disette *f* d'eau.

drouth [drauθ, *Scot:* druθ], *s.* **1.** *A:* = DROUGHT. **2.** *Scot:* (*a*) Soif *f.* (*b*) Soif d'ivrogne.

drove[1] [drouːv], *s.* (*a*) Troupeau *m* (de bœufs) en marche. (*b*) *F:* Multitude *f,* foule *f* (de personnes en marche).

drove[2]. *See* DRIVE[2].

drover ['drouvər], *s.* Conducteur *m* de bestiaux; toucheur *m.*

drown [draun], *v.tr.* **1.** Noyer. **To drown oneself,** se noyer; se jeter à l'eau. **To be drowned,** *v.i.* to drown (*by accident*), se noyer; être noyé. **A drowning man,** un homme qui se noie. *Drowned at sea,* noyé en mer. *F:* **To drown one's sorrow in drink,** noyer son chagrin dans la boisson. **2.** (*a*) Inonder, submerger (une prairie). (*b*) **To be drowned out,** être chassé (de sa demeure, etc.) par l'inondation. **3.** Étouffer, couvrir (un son). **drowned,** *a.* **1.** Noyé. **A drowned man,** un noyé. **2. Drowned lands,** terrains noyés, inondés. **drowning,** *s.* **1. Death by drowning,** asphyxie *f* par submersion. **2.** Inondation *f* (de champs). **drowse** [drauz]. **1.** *v.i.* Somnoler, s'assoupir. **To drowse away, off,** s'assoupir. **2.** *v.tr.* **To drowse the time away,** passer le temps à dormir, à somnoler.

drowsiness ['drauzinəs], *s.* Somnolence *f.*

drowsy ['drauzi], *a.* Assoupi, somnolent. **To grow drowsy,** s'assoupir. **To be, feel, d.,** avoir envie de dormir; avoir sommeil. **To make s.o. drowsy,** assoupir qn. **Drowsy afternoon,** après-midi lourd.

drub [drʌb], *v.tr.* (drubbed) Battre, rosser (qn, l'ennemi); *F:* flanquer une raclée, une tripotée, à (qn). **drubbing,** *s.* (*a*) Volée *f* de coups (de bâton, de poing); *F:* tripotée *f.* (*b*) Défaite *f.*

drudge[1] ['drʌdʒ], *s.* Femme *f,* homme *m,* de peine. **The drudge of the household,** le souffre-douleur *inv* de la maison; la cendrillon.

drudge[2], *v.i.* Trimer, peiner. *F:* **To drudge and slave,** mener une vie de forçat, de galérien.

drudgery ['drʌdʒəri], *s.* Travail pénible, ingrat; besognes fastidieuses; métier d'esclave.

drug[1] [drʌg], *s.* **1.** Produit *m* pharmaceutique; drogue *f.* **2.** Narcotique *m,* stupéfiant *m.* *F:* **To take drugs,** faire usage de stupéfiants; s'adonner aux stupéfiants. **3.** *F:* (*Of goods*) **To be a drug in the market,** être invendable. **'drug-addict,** *s.* Morphinomane *mf* ou cocaïnomane *mf;* toxicomane *mf.* **'drug-fiend,** *s.* Morphinomane *mf* ou cocaïnomane *mf;* toxicomane *mf.* **'drug-store,** *s. U.S:* Pharmacie *f.*

drug[2], *v.tr.* (drugged) **1.** Donner, administrer, un narcotique, des stupéfiants, à (qn); *F:* endormir (qn). **To drug oneself,** faire usage de stupéfiants; s'adonner aux stupéfiants. **2. They had drugged his wine,** on avait mis, mêlé, un narcotique à son vin. **3.** *Lit: Drugged with pleasure,* rassasié de plaisirs.

druggist ['drʌgist], *s.* **1.** *Scot. & U.S:* Pharmacien *m.* **2. Wholesale druggist,** pharmacien en gros; droguiste *m.*

Druid ['druːid], *s.m.* Druide.

Druidess ['druːides], *s.f.* Druidesse.

drum[1] [drʌm], *s.* **1.** *Mus:* Tambour *m,* caisse *f.* Big drum, bass drum, grosse caisse. Long drum, tenor drum, caisse roulante. *Mil:* The drums, la batterie. **To play the drum,** battre du tambour. **To beat the drum,** battre le tambour. *F:* **To bang the big drum,** battre la (grosse) caisse; faire de la réclame. With drums beating, tambour(s) battant(s). **Beat on the drum,** coup *m* de tambour. **2.** Tambourinage *m.* **3.** *Anat:* (Caisse, membrane *f,* du) tympan *m.* **4.** Tonneau *m* en fer; tonnelet *m;* gonne *f* (à goudron); bidon *m,* tambour, estagnon *m* (à huile). **5.** (*a*) *Arch:* Tambour (d'une colonne); vase *m* (d'un chapiteau). (*b*) Tambour, touret *m* (de treuil). **Capstan**

drum, tambour, cloche *f*, de cabestan. **Cable drum**, tambour, bobine *f*, dévidoir *m* (de câble électrique). *Mch:* D. *of the pressure gauge*, barillet *m* de l'indicateur de pression. **Concrete mixing drum**, tonneau mélangeur à béton. **'drum-head,** *s.* **1.** Peau *f* de tambour. *Mil:* Drum-head service, office divin en plein air. **2.** Tête *f*, chapeau *m* (de cabestan). **drum-'major,** *s.* Tambour-major *m*.

drum², *v.* (drummed) **1.** *v.i.* (*a*) Tambouriner; battre du tambour. *F:* (*Of pers., rain*) To drum on the window-panes, tambouriner sur les vitres. (*b*) (*Of insects*) Bourdonner. (*c*) (*Of car, etc.*) Ferrailler, tambouriner. **2.** *v.tr.* (*a*) To d. *a tune on sth.*, tambouriner un air sur qch. To drum sth. into s.o.'s head, enfoncer, fourrer, qch. dans la tête de qn. (*b*) To drum together *the natives*, rassembler les indigènes au son du tambour. **drum out,** *v.tr. Mil:* To drum s.o. out, expulser qn au son du tambour; dégrader qn. **drum up,** *v.tr.* Racoler (des partisans). To d. *up recruits*, faire du recrutement. **drumming,** *s.* (*a*) Tambourinage *m*; bruit *m* de tambour. (*b*) Bourdonnement *m* (d'un insecte, des oreilles). (*c*) *F:* (*Of car*) Ferraillement *m*. tambourinement *m*.

drummer ['drʌmər], *s.* **1.** Tambour *m* (qui joue du tambour. **Big drummer,** joueur *m* de grosse caisse; *F:* la grosse caisse. **2.** *U.S:* Commis voyageur. **'drummer-boy,** *s.m.* Petit tambour.

drumstick ['drʌmstik], *s.* **1.** Baguette *f* de tambour. **Bass-drumstick,** tampon *m*, mailloche *f*. **Kettle-drumstick,** baguette *f* de timbale. **2.** *Cu:* Pilon *m* (d'une volaille).

drunk [drʌŋk]. *See* DRINK².

drunkard ['drʌŋkərd], *s.* Ivrogne, *f.* ivrognesse; *F:* pochard *m*.

drunken ['drʌŋk(ə)n], *a.* **1.** Ivrogne. **2.** D. state, état d'ivresse, d'ébriété. **-ly,** *adv.* En ivrogne; comme un ivrogne.

drunkenness ['drʌŋkənnəs], *s.* **1.** Ivresse *f.* **2.** Ivrognerie *f.*

drupe [dru:p], *s. Bot:* Drupe *m*.

dry¹ [drai], *a.* (drier, driest) Sec, *f.* sèche. **1.** (*a*) (*Of well, etc.*) Tari, à sec; (*of country*) aride. **Dry land,** terre ferme. *S.a.* DOCK³. **To pump a well dry,** épuiser l'eau d'un puits; assécher un puits. **To wring linen dry,** essorer le linge. **To run dry, to go dry,** (*of channel*) se dessécher, (s')assécher; (*of spring, well*) s'épuiser, (se) tarir. (*Of speaker, writer*) He soon runs dry, il a l'haleine courte. **Dry weather,** temps sec. *It has been dry* (*weather*) *for a week*, il fait sec depuis huit jours. *S.a.* HIGH I. 7. (*b*) *Ind:* etc: Dry process, procédé par voie sèche. **Dry crushing,** broyage à sec. **Dry masonry,** maçonnerie à sec. *S.a.* WALL¹. (*c*) *To put on dry clothing*, mettre des vêtements secs. *Dry bread*, pain sec. (*Of goods, etc.*) 'To be kept dry,' "craint l'humidité." (*d*) *F:* (*Of pers.*) To be, feel, dry, avoir le gosier sec; avoir soif. **Dry work,** travail qui donne soif. **2.** *U.S:* *F:* Dry country, pays "sec" (où les boissons alcooliques sont prohibées). **3.** Aride; sans intérêt. *A dry subject*, un sujet aride. **4.** (*a*) Dry smile, sourire teinté d'ironie. **Dry humour,** esprit caustique, mordant. *A man of dry humour*, un pince-sans-rire. (*b*) *Dry reception*, accueil peu cordial. **5.** *U.S:* Dry goods, articles *m* de nouveauté; étoffes *f*, tissus *m*; mercerie *f*. **-ly,** *adv.* **1.** D'un ton sec; sèchement. **2.** Avec une pointe d'ironie contenue. **'dry-bulb,** *attrib. a.* **Dry-bulb thermometer** (*of hygrometer*), thermomètre à boule sèche; thermomètre sec. **'dry-'clean,** *v.tr.* Nettoyer à sec; dégraisser

(des vêtements). **dry-cleaning,** *s.* Nettoyage *m* à sec; dégraissage *m*. **'dry-'dock. 1.** *v.tr.* Mettre (un navire) en cale sèche. **2.** *v.i.* (*Of ship*) Entrer, passer, en cale sèche. **'dry-'eyed,** *a.* To look on dry-eyed, regarder d'un œil sec. **'dry-foot(ed),** *a. & adv.* A pied sec. **'dry-'nurse¹,** *s.* Nourrice sèche; sevreuse *f.* **'dry-nurse²,** *v.tr.* **1.** Élever (un enfant) au biberon. **2.** *F:* Servir de mentor à (qn). **'dry-'plate,** *s. Phot:* Plaque sèche. **'dry-point,** *s. E gr:* **1.** *Tls:* Pointe sèche. **2.** (*Process or etched engraving*) Gravure *f* à la pointe sèche; pointe-sèche *f.* **'dry-'rot,** *s.* (*a*) Carie sèche, pourriture sèche (du bois). (*b*) *F:* Political dry-rot, désintégration *f.* **'dry-'shod,** *a. & adv.* A pied sec.

dry², *v.* (dried [draid]; drying) **1.** *v.tr.* Sécher (qch.); faire sécher (le linge); essorer. To dry sth. with a cloth, essuyer qch. avec un torchon. To dry (up) the dishes, essuyer la vaisselle, les plats. To dry one's eyes, s'essuyer les yeux. *Wind that dries* (*up*) *the skin*, vent qui dessèche, ratatine, la peau. **2.** *v.i.* (*a*) Sécher, se dessécher. To put sth. out to dry, mettre qch. à sécher dehors. (*b*) *Husb:* (*Of cow*) Tarir; se sécher. **dry off,** *U.S:* **dry out. 1.** *v.tr.* Faire évaporer (l'eau, etc.). **2.** *v.i.* (*Of moisture*) S'évaporer. **dry up,** *v.i.* **1.** (*Of well, pool*) Se dessécher, (s')assécher, tarir. **Little dried-up man,** petit homme sec. **2.** *F:* Cesser de parler; se taire; rester court. *P:* Dry up! la ferme! **dried,** *a.* Séché, desséché. **Dried fruits,** fruits secs. *D. apples, pears*, pommes, poires, tapées. **drying,** *s.* **1.** Séchage *m*; assèchement *m*, dessèchement *m*; essorage *m* (du linge); (*with a cloth*) essuyage *m.* *Ind:* Dessiccation *f.* **Drying ground, drying yard,** sécherie *f*, étendage *m*, étendoir *m. Laund:* Drying line, tendoir *m* (pour lessive); corde *f* à linge. *Ind:* Drying cupboard, drying closet, étuve *f*; chambre chaude. **2.** Drying quality (*of a varnish*), siccativité *f.*

dryad ['draiad], *s.f. Myth:* Dryade.

dryer ['draiər], *s.* **1.** *Ind:* Séchoir *m*; dessiccateur *m.* **Centrifugal dryer,** essoreuse *f* centrifuge. **2.** *Paint:* Siccatif *m.*

dryness ['drainəs], *s.* **1.** Sécheresse *f*; aridité *f* (du sol). **2.** Sécheresse, sévérité *f* (de ton); aridité (d'un discours); causticité *f* (de l'esprit).

drysalter ['draisɔltər], *s.* (*a*) Marchand *m* de conserves. (*b*) Marchand de couleurs; droguiste *m.*

D.T.'s [di:'ti:z], *s.pl. P:* Delirium *m* tremens.

dual ['djuəl]. **1.** *a.* Double. *I.C.E:* Dual ignition, double allumage. **Dual tyres,** pneus jumelés. *Psy:* Dual personality, dédoublement *m* de la personnalité. **2.** *a. & s. Gram:* Dual (number), duel (*m*).

dub¹ [dʌb], *v.tr.* (dubbed) **1.** (*a*) To dub s.o. (a) knight, armer, adouber, qn chevalier; donner l'accolade à qn. (*b*) *F:* To dub s.o. a quack, qualifier qn de charlatan. **2.** *Leath:* Préparer (le cuir) avec le dégras.

dub², *v.tr. Cin:* *U.S:* Doubler (un film) en langue étrangère.

dubbin ['dʌbin], *s. Leath:* Dégras *m.*

dubiety [dju'baiəti], *s.* (Sentiment *m* de) doute *m*; incertitude *f* (*regarding*, à l'égard de).

dubious ['djubiəs], *a.* **1.** Douteux. (*a*) Incertain, vague. D. result, résultat incertain. (*b*) Équivoque, louche. D. company, compagnie douteuse, louche. **2.** Hésitant; qui doute. Dubious expression, air de doute. **-ly,** *adv.* D'un air de doute ou d'un ton de doute.

dubiousness ['djubiəsnəs], *s.* **1.** Incertitude *f*

(du résultat, etc.). **2.** Caractère douteux, équivoque *f* (d'un compliment, etc.). **3.** = DUBIETY.

ducal ['dju:k(ə)l], *a.* Ducal, -aux ; de duc.

duchess ['dʌtʃes], *s.f.* **1.** Duchesse. **2.** *P :* (*a*) Grande dame. (*b*) My old duchess, my old dutch, ma femme ; *F :* ma vieille, la bourgeoise.

duchy ['dʌtʃi], *s.* **1.** Duché *m.* **2.** The Duchies, les duchés de Cornouaille et de Lancastre.

duck[1] [dʌk], *s.* **1.** *Orn :* (*a*) (*Female of drake*) Cane *f.* (*b*) (*Generic*) Canard *m.* Wild duck, canard sauvage. *Cu :* Duck and green peas, canard aux petits pois. To take to Latin like a duck to water, mordre au latin. To play at ducks and drakes, faire des ricochets (sur l'eau). To play ducks and drakes with one's money, with one's life, jeter son argent par les fenêtres ; gâcher sa vie. **2.** *F :* (*a*) A lame duck, (i) un(e) faible ; une épave (de la vie) ; (ii) personne *f* dont les affaires périclitent. (*b*) A duck of a child, of a hat, un enfant joli à croquer ; un amour de chapeau. (*c*) *Cr :* Duck, duck's egg, zéro *m.* **'duck-bill,** *s.* *Z :* Ornithor(h)ynque *m.* **'duck-boards,** *s.pl.* Caillebotis *m.* **'duck-gun,** *s.* *Sm.a:* Canardière *f.* **'duck-pond,** *s.* Canardière *f.* **'duck-shooting,** *s.* Chasse *f* aux canards (sauvages). **'duck-shot,** *s.* Plomb *m* à canard.

duck[2], *s.* *Tex:* Coutil *m* ; toile fine (pour voiles). Duck trousers, *pl.* *F :* ducks, pantalon blanc ; pantalon de coutil, de toile. *The crew were in ducks,* l'équipage était en blanc.

duck[3], *s.* **1.** Plongeon *m,* bain (inattendu ou involontaire). **2.** Mouvement instinctif de la tête (pour se dérober). *Box :* Esquive *f.*

duck[4]. **1.** *v.i.* (*a*) Plonger dans l'eau ; faire le plongeon. (*Of water-fowl*) Replonger. (*b*) Baisser la tête, se baisser (subitement, instinctivement). *Box :* Esquiver de la tête. **2.** *v.tr.* (*a*) Plonger (qn) dans l'eau ; faire faire le plongeon à (qn). (*b*) Baisser subitement (la tête). **ducking,** *s.* Plongeon *m* (involontaire) ; bain forcé. To give s.o. a ducking, *F :* faire boire une tasse à qn.

duckling ['dʌkliŋ], *s.* *Orn :* Canardeau *m* ; (*drake*) caneton *m* ; (*duck*) canette *f.*

duckweed ['dʌkwi:d], *s.* *Bot :* Lentille *f* d'eau ; lenticule *f.*

ducky ['dʌki]. **1.** *s.* *F :* (My) ducky, mon petit chat, ma petite chatte ; ma poupoule, ma cocotte. **2.** *a.* *F :* Mignon, -onne ; coquet, -ette.

duct [dʌkt], *s.* **1.** Conduit *m,* conduite *f* ; caniveau *m* ; *El.E :* canalisation *f* (pour câbles, etc.). **2.** *Anat :* Canal, -aux ; vaisseau *m,* voie *f.* Auditory d., conduit auditif. **3.** *Bot :* Trachée *f,* canal.

ductile ['dʌktail, -til], *a.* (*a*) Ductile ; malléable. (*b*) Ductile character, caractère docile, malléable, souple.

ductility [dʌk'tiliti], *s.* (*a*) Ductilité *f* ; malléabilité *f.* Ductility *f,* souplesse *f* (de caractère).

ductless ['dʌktləs], *a.* *Anat :* Ductless glands, glandes closes, endocrines.

dud [dʌd]. *P :* **1.** *s.pl.* Duds, frusques *fpl* ; nippes *fpl.* **2.** *s. & a.* (*a*) Incapable. He's a dud, (i) c'est un type nul ; (ii) c'est un raté. (*b*) Mauvais ; *P :* moche. *Artil :* Dud (shell), obus qui a raté. Dud cheque, chèque sans provision. *The note was a dud,* le billet était faux.

dudgeon ['dʌdʒən], *s.* Colère *f,* ressentiment *m.* In high, deep, dudgeon, fort en colère.

due[1] [dju:]. **I.** *a.* (*a*) (*Of debt*) Exigible ; (*of bill*) échéant, échu. Bill due on 1st May, effet payable le premier mai. *The balance due to us,* le solde qui nous revient. Balance due to us (*from Mr Smith*), redoit M. Smith. Debts due to us, to the firm, dettes actives ; créances *f.* Debts due

by us, by the firm, dettes passives. (*Of bill, etc.*) To fall due, échoir ; venir à (l')échéance. When due, à l'échéance. (*b*) Dû, *f.* due ; juste, mérité. *The first place is due to Milton,* la première place revient à Milton. *With due care,* avec tout le soin requis. In due form, dans les formes voulues ; en bonne forme ; en règle ; dans les règles. After due consideration, après mûre réflexion ; tout bien considéré. *S.a.* COURSE[1] 1, DEFERENCE, RESPECT[1] 3, TIME[1] 5. (*c*) (*In consequence of*) Due to . . ., dû à . . . ; occasionné, causé, par . . . ; attribuable à . . . . It is due to him, to his negligence, c'est lui, c'est sa négligence, qui en est (la) cause. What is it due to? à quoi cela tient-il ? (*d*) (*Expected*) The train is due (*to arrive*), is due in, at two o'clock, le train arrive à deux heures. **2.** *adv.* Due north, east, droit vers le nord, vers l'est ; nord franc, est franc.

due[2], *s.* **1.** Dû *m.* To give s.o. his due, donner à qn ce qui lui est dû, ce qui lui revient ; rendre justice à qn. To pay one's dues, payer ce qu'on doit. **2.** *pl.* Droits *mpl,* frais *mpl.* Taxes and dues, impôts *m* et taxes *f.* *Nau :* Port dues, droits de port.

duel[1] ['dju:əl], *s.* Duel *m* ; affaire *f* d'honneur ; rencontre *f.* To fight a duel, se battre en duel ; aller sur le terrain.

duel[2], *v.i.* (duelled) Se battre en duel. **duelling,** *s.* Le duel. *S.a.* PISTOL.

duellist ['dju:əlist], *s.* Duelliste *m.*

duenna [dju'enə], *s.f.* Duègne *f.*

duet [dju'et], *s.* Duo *m* ; (*for piano*) morceau *m* à quatre mains.

duettist [dju'etist], *s.* Duettiste *mf.*

duffel ['dʌfl], *s.* Drap molletonné ; molleton *m.*

duffer ['dʌfər], *s.* *F :* *Sch :* Cancre *m,* croûte *f.* *Sp :* Maladroit, -oite ; mazette *f.* To be a duffer at sth., n'entendre rien à qch. An old duffer, une ganache.

dug[1] [dʌg], *s.* (*a*) Mamelle *f* (d'un animal) ; pis *m* (de vache). (*b*) Trayon *m,* tétin *m.*

dug[2]. See DIG[2].

dug-out ['dʌgaut], *s.* **1.** Canot creusé dans un tronc d'arbre ; pirogue *f.* **2.** *Mil :* Abri (blindé). Deep dug-out, abri-caverne *m.*

duke [dju:k], *s.* Duc *m.* My Lord Duke, monsieur le duc.

dukedom ['dju:kdəm], *s.* **1.** Duché *m.* **2.** Dignité *f* de duc.

dulcet ['dʌlset], *a.* (Son) doux, suave, agréable.

dulcify ['dʌlsifai], *v.tr.* Dulcifier ; adoucir.

dulcimer ['dʌlsimər], *s.* *Mus :* Tympanon *m.*

Dulcinea [dʌlsi'ni:a]. *Pr.n.f.* Dulcinée.

dull[1] [dʌl], *a.* **1.** (*Of pers.*) Lent, lourd ; à l'esprit obtus, épais. Dull sense of touch, dull hearing, toucher *m,* ouïe *f,* peu sensible. To be dull of sight, of hearing, avoir la vue faible ; avoir l'oreille dure. *Sch :* The dull boys, les élèves peu brillants ; *F :* les cancres *m.* **2.** (*a*) A dull ache, une douleur sourde. (*b*) (Bruit) sourd, étouffé, mat. **3.** *Com :* (Marché) calme, inactif, lourd, inanimé. The dull season, la morte-saison. **4.** (*Depressed*) Triste, morne, déprimé. I feel dull, je m'ennuie ; j'ai le cafard. In a dull mood, maussade. **5.** Triste, ennuyeux, peu intéressant. As dull as ditch-water, ennuyeux comme un jour de pluie. A deadly d. task, une besogne abrutissante, assommante. A thoroughly dull evening, une soirée tout à fait assommante. **6.** (*Blunt*) Émoussé. (*Of tool, etc.*) To become d., s'émousser. **7.** (*Of colour, surface*) Terne, mat. Dull eyes, yeux morts, sans éclat. A dull fire, un feu triste ; un pauvre feu. **8.** (*Of weather*) Lourd,

triste, sombre. **-lly,** *adv.* **1.** Lourdement ;
ennuyeusement ; tristement. **2.** Sourdement,
faiblement ; sans éclat. **'dull-'brained,**
-'witted, *a.* A l'esprit lourd, obtus, épais.
'dull-'eyed, *a.* Au regard terne.
dull². I. *v.tr.* **1.** (*a*) Hébéter (qn). (*b*) Alourdir,
appesantir (l'esprit) ; émousser (les sens).
2. Émousser (un outil). **3.** (*a*) Amortir, assourdir
(le son) ; ternir (les couleurs, un miroir) ;
dépolir (une surface) ; mater (un métal).
(*b*) Amortir (une douleur) ; rendre moins vif
(le plaisir). II. **dull,** *v.i.* **1.** (*Of senses, etc.*)
S'engourdir, s'alourdir. **2.** (*Of colour*) Se ternir ;
(*of metal, etc.*) se dépolir.
dullard ['dʌlərd], *s.* Lourdaud *m.* *Sch:* Cancre *m,*
crétin *m.*
dul(l)ness ['dʌlnəs], *s.* **1.** Lenteur *f,* pesanteur *f,*
de l'esprit ; épaisseur *f* de l'intelligence ;
émoussement *m* (des sens). **Dul(l)ness of hear-**
ing, dureté *f* d'oreille. **2.** Matité *f* (d'un son).
3. Ennui *m,* tristesse *f* ; monotonie *f.* **4.** *Com:*
Stagnation *f,* marasme *m* (des affaires) ; peu *m*
d'activité (du marché). **5.** Manque *m* de tranchant, de fil (d'une lame) ; émoussement *m* (d'une
pointe, d'un tranchant). **6.** Manque d'éclat ;
faiblesse *f* (d'un son, d'une lumière) ; bruit
sourd (d'un coup).
duly ['dju:li], *adv.* **1.** Dûment, justement ;
comme de juste ; convenablement. **2.** En temps
voulu ; en temps utile.
dumb [dʌm], *a.* **1.** Muet, *f.* muette. **Deaf and**
dumb, sourd-muet, *f.* sourde-muette. **Born**
dumb, muet de naissance. *F:* **Dumb as a fish,**
as an oyster, muet comme un poisson, comme
une carpe. **Dumb animals,** les bêtes, les animaux.
To strike s.o. dumb, (i) frapper qn de mutisme ;
(ii) *F:* rendre qn muet ; abasourdir, *F:* sidérer,
qn. **Dumb show,** pantomime *f* ; jeu muet. *To act*
a scene in d. show, mimer une scène. **2.** (*Wanting*
some essential detail) **Dumb piano,** piano *m* sans
cordes ; clavier *m* (pour l'étude du doigté, etc.).
Nau: **Dumb craft,** bateaux *mpl* sans voiles ;
chalands *mpl.* **3.** *U.S:* Sot, *f.* sotte. **-ly,** *adv.*
Sans rien dire, sans mot dire ; en silence.
'dumb-bell, *s.* Haltère *m.* **'dumb-iron,** *s.*
Aut: Main *f* (de ressort). **'dumb-'waiter,** *s.*
1. *Furn:* Servante *f,* desserte *f.* **2.** *U.S:* Monte-
plats *m inv.*
dumbfound [dʌm'faund], *v.tr.* Abasourdir,
stupéfier, ahurir, confondre, ébahir. **dumb-**
founding, *a.* Abasourdissant ; ahurissant.
dumbness ['dʌmnəs], *s.* **1.** Mutisme *m.*
2. *F:* Silence *m.*
dummy ['dʌmi], *s.* **1.** Homme *m* de paille ;
prête-nom *m inv.* **2.** (*a*) *Dressm:* Mannequin *m* ;
(*in shop window*) figure *f* de cire. *Fb:* **To give,**
sell, the dummy, faire une feinte de passe.
(*b*) Chose *f* factice ; faux paquet. *Publ:* Maquette *f* (d'un livre). (*c*) (**Baby's**) **dummy,** sucette *f* ; tétine *f* sur anneau. **3.** *Cards:* Mort *m.*
To be, play, dummy, faire le mort. **Dummy**
bridge, bridge à trois (personnes). **4.** *Attrib.*
Postiche ; faux, *f.* fausse. **Dummy cartridge,**
fausse cartouche.
dump¹ [dʌmp], *s.* **1.** Coup sourd (d'une masse
qui tombe). **2.** Tas *m,* amas *m* (de déchets, de
déblais, de minerai, etc.). *Min:* Halde *f.*
3. Chantier de dépôt ; dépôt *m* des déblais ;
(lieu *m* de) décharge *f.* **Town (nightsoil) dump,**
dépotoir *m.* **4.** Dépôt (de vivres, de munitions).
dump², *v.tr.* **1.** (*a*) Décharger, déverser (une
charretée de sable, de matériau). (*b*) **To dump**
(**down**), déposer, jeter, culbuter, (qch). (avec un
bruit sourd) ; laisser tomber lourdement (un

ballot, etc.). **2.** Faire un dépôt (de vivres, etc.).
3. *Com:* **To dump goods on a foreign market,**
écouler à perte des marchandises à l'étranger ;
faire du dumping. **dumping,** *s.* **1.** (*a*) Déversement *m,* versage *m* (du contenu d'un chariot).
(*b*) Dépôt *m.* **Dumping-ground,** (lieu *m* de)
décharge *f* ; déversement ; (*for refuse*) dépotoir *m.* **2.** *Com:* Déversement au dehors
(même à perte) du trop-plein de la production ;
dumping *m.*
dumpling ['dʌmpliŋ], *s.* *Cu:* (*a*) Boulette (de
pâte) (servie avec le bœuf bouilli, etc.). (*b*) **Apple**
dumpling, pomme enrobée (cuite au four).
F: **Little dumpling,** petit boulot (d'enfant).
dumps [dʌmps], *s.pl.* *F:* Cafard *m* ; idées noires.
To be (down) in the dumps, to have the dumps,
broyer du noir ; avoir le cafard.
dumpy ['dʌmpi]. **1.** *a.* Trapu ; boulot, -otte ;
replet, -ète. *A d. little man,* un petit homme
replet ; un courtaud. **2.** *s.* (*a*) (*Umbrella*) Tom-
pouce *m.* (*b*) *Furn:* Pouf *m.*
dun¹ [dʌn]. **1.** *a.* (*a*) Brun foncé. (*b*) *Poet:*
Sombre, obscur. **2.** *a.* & *s.* (*Cheval*) gris louvet.
Yellow-dun, bai doré ; louvet.
dun², *s.* **1.** (*a*) Créancier importun. (*b*) Agent *m*
de recouvrement (de dettes). **2.** Demande
pressante (de payement).
dun³, *v.tr.* (**dunned**) Importuner, harceler,
relancer (un débiteur). **To be dunned on all**
sides, être accablé de dettes criardes.
dunce [dʌns], *s.* Ignorant, -ante, *F:* crétin,
-ine ; âne *m.* *Sch:* *F:* Cancre *m,* crétin.
Dunce's cap, bonnet *m* d'âne.
dunderhead ['dʌndərhed], *s.* *F:* (*a*) Lourdaud,
-aude. (*b*) Imbécile *mf.*
dune [dju:n], *s.* (**Sand-)dune,** dune *f.*
dung¹ [dʌŋ], *s.* **1.** Fiente *f,* crotte *f* ; bouse *f*
(de vache) ; crottin *m* (de cheval). *Dy:* Bouse.
2. *Agr:* Fumier *m,* engrais *m.* **'dung-beetle,**
s. *Ent:* Bousier *m* ; stercoraire *m.*
dung², *v.tr.* *Agr:* Fumer (un champ).
(*b*) *Dy:* Bouser (une étoffe).
dungaree [dʌŋgə'ri:], *s.* **1.** Étoffe de coton
grossière (de l'Inde) ; cotonnade *f,* treillis *m.*
2. *pl.* *Ind:* Dungarees, combinaison *f* ; *F:* salopette *f* ; bleus *mpl* (de mécanicien). *Mil:* (Jeu *m*
de) treillis.
dungeon ['dʌndʒən], *s.* Cachot *m* (d'un château
du moyen âge). **The deepest dungeon,** le cul de
basse-fosse.
dunghill ['dʌŋhil], *s.* Tas *m* de fumier ; pailler *m,*
fumier *m.* *F:* **To be on one's own dunghill,**
être sur son pailler. *S.a.* COCK¹ 1. **'dunghill-**
cock, -hen, *s.* Coq *m,* poule *f,* de basse-cour.
Dunkirk ['dʌn'kə:rk]. *Pr.n.* *Geog:* Dunkerque.
dunlin ['dʌnlin], *s.* *Orn:* Bécasseau *m* cincle ;
alouette *f* de mer.
dunnage ['dʌnedʒ], *s.* *Nau:* (*a*) Grenier *m* ;
parquet *m* de chargement. **Dunnage-mats,**
nattes *f* d'arrimage. (*b*) *F:* Effets personnels ;
sac *m* (de marin).
duodecimal [djuo'desim(ə)l], *a.* Duodécimal,
-aux.
duodecimo [djuo'desimo], *s.* *Typ:* In-douze
m inv.
duodenal [djuo'di:n(ə)l], *a.* Duodénal, -aux.
Duodenal ulcer, ulcère au duodénum.
duodenum [djuo'di:nəm], *s.* Duodénum *m.*
dupe¹ [dju:p], *s.* Dupe *f.*
dupe², *v.tr.* Duper, tromper.
dupery ['dju:pəri], *s.* Duperie *f.*
duple [dju:pl], *a.* *Mus:* **Duple time,** mesure *f* à
deux temps ; mesure binaire.
duplex ['dju:pleks], *a.* Double. **Duplex crank,**

manivelle double. **Duplex engine,** moteur bi-cylindrique. **Duplex pump,** pompe duplex *inv,* jumelle. **Duplex telegraphy,** télégraphie duplex.
duplicate[1] ['djupliket]. **I.** *a.* Double. *D. parts,* pièces de rechange. **Duplicate receipt,** reçu en duplicata. **2.** *s.* (*a*) Double *m,* répétition *f* (d'une œuvre d'art, etc.). (*b*) Duplicata *m* (d'un chèque égaré, etc.); double, contre-partie *f* (d'un écrit); ampliation *f* (d'un acte). **In duplicate,** en, par, duplicata; en double exemplaire, en double expédition. (*c*) Reconnaissance *f* (de prêteur sur gages).
duplicate[2] ['djuplikeit], *v.tr.* (*a*) Faire le double de (qch.); reproduire (un document) en double exemplaire. (*b*) Tirer un certain nombre de copies (d'un document) à l'autocopiste. **duplicating,** *s.* **I.** Duplication *f.* **2.** Reproduction *f* à l'autocopiste. **'duplicating-machine,** *s.* Duplicateur *m,* autocopiste *m.*
duplication [djupli'keiʃ(ə)n], *s.* **I.** Duplication *f,* reproduction *f.* **2.** *Opt:* Dédoublement *m.*
duplicator ['djuplikeitər], *s.* *Typewr:* etc: Duplicateur *m.*
duplicity [dju'plisiti], *s.* Duplicité *f;* mauvaise foi.
durability [djuərə'biliti], **durableness** ['djuə-rəblnəs], *s.* Durabilité *f;* durée *f* (d'une étoffe).
durable ['djuərəbl], *a.* Durable; résistant. **-ably,** *adv.* D'une façon durable.
duralumin [djuə'raljumin], *s.* *Metall:* Duralu-min *m,* duraluminium *m.*
duramen [djuə'reimən], *s.* Duramen *m;* cœur *m* du bois.
durance ['djuərəns], *s.* *Lit:* Captivité *f.* *Esp.* **In durance vile,** dans un vil cachot.
duration [dju'reiʃ(ə)n], *s.* Durée *f;* étendue *f* (de la vie).
duress [djuə'res], *s.* **I.** Emprisonnement *m.* **2.** *Jur:* Contrainte *f,* violence *f.* **To act under duress,** agir à son corps défendant; céder à la force.
during ['djuəriŋ], *prep.* Pendant, durant. **During his life,** pendant (toute) sa vie; sa vie durant. **During the winter,** au cours de l'hiver. **During that time,** (i) pendant ce temps; (ii) sur ces entrefaites.
durst [də:rst]. *See* DARE.
dusk [dʌsk]. **I.** *a.* It is growing dusk, la nuit tombe. **2.** *s.* (*a*) Obscurité *f,* ténèbres *fpl.* (*b*) Crépuscule *m.* **At dusk,** à la brune, à la nuit tombante; entre chien et loup.
duskiness ['dʌskinəs], *s.* **I.** Obscurité *f.* **2.** (*Of complexion*) (*a*) Teint brun, bistré. (*b*) Teint noiraud.
dusky ['dʌski], *a.* **I.** Sombre, obscur. **2.** (*a*) (*Of complexion*) Brun foncé *inv*; bistré. (*b*) Noirâtre; (*of pers.*) noiraud, moricaud.
dust[1] [dʌst], *s.* **I.** Poussière *f;* *Poet:* poudre *f.* **To raise the dust,** faire de la poussière. **To humble oneself in the dust,** s'humilier dans la poussière. **To reduce sth. to dust,** mettre, réduire, qch. en poussière. *Lit:* **To bite the dust,** mordre la poussière. *F:* **To throw dust in s.o.'s eyes,** jeter de la poudre aux yeux de qn. **To kick up a dust, to raise a dust,** faire une scène; *P:* faire du barouf. **Marble dust,** sciure *f* de marbre. **2.** Cendres *fpl* (d'un mort). *Ashes to ashes,* dust to dust, cendres aux cendres, poudre à la poudre. **'dust-cap,** *s.* **I.** *Cost:* Bonnet *m* anti-poussière. **2.** *Mec.E:* etc: Cache-poussière *m inv;* pare-poussière *m inv.* **'dust-cart,** *s.* Tom-bereau *m* aux ordures; voiture *f* de boueur. **'dust-coat,** *s.* *Cost:* Cache-poussière *m inv,*

pare-poussière *m inv.* **'dust-colour(ed),** *a.* Cendré. **'dust-cover,** *s.* **I.** *Bookb:* Chemise *f* (d'un livre); protège-livre *m.* **2.** *Mec.E:* etc: (*a*) = DUST-CAP 2. (*b*) Blindage *m* cache-poussière *inv.* *Aut:* Blindage de roue. **'dust-guard,** *s.* Pare-poussière *m inv.* *I.C.E:* Cache-soupape(s) *m inv.* **'dust-jacket,** *s.* = DUST-COVER I. **'dust-pan,** *s.* Pelle *f* à main; ramasse-poussière *m inv.* **'dust-proof,** *a.* Étanche, imperméable (à la poussière). **'dust-sheet,** *s.* Toile *f* de protection contre la poussière; housse *f.* **'dust-shoot,** *s.* Lieu *m* de décharge; dépotoir *m.* **'dust-shot,** *s.* *Sm.a:* Cendrée *f;* petit plomb.
dust[2], *v.tr.* **I.** (*a*) Saupoudrer (un gâteau, etc.) (*with,* de). (*b*) *Metall:* Tamponner (un moule, etc.). **2.** Épousseter (une pièce, un meuble). *F:* **To dust s.o.'s jacket,** flanquer une raclée, une frottée, à qn. **3.** *v.i.* (*Of bird*) S'é-brouer dans la poussière. **dusting,** *s.* **I.** (*a*) Saupoudrage *m;* *Phot:* poudrage *m.* (*b*) *Metall:* Tamponnement *m.* **2.** (*a*) Époussetage *m.* (*b*) *F:* Frottée *f,* raclée *f,* tripotée *f.* **3.** *Nau:* *F:* Gros temps; *F:* coup *m* de tabac. **dust-'up,** *s.* *F:* **I.** Querelle *f;* *F:* prise *f* de bec. **2.** *Sp:* Pointe *f* de vitesse.
dustbin ['dʌstbin], *s.* Boîte *f* ou bac *m* à ordures (ménagères); (*in France*) poubelle *f.*
duster ['dʌstər], *s.* Chiffon *m* (à épousseter); torchon *m.* **Feather duster,** plumeau *m,* épous-sette *f.*
dustman, *pl.* **-men** ['dʌstmən, -men], *s.m.* Boueur, boueux.
dusty ['dʌsti], *a.* **I.** Poussiéreux, poudreux; recouvert de poussière. **2.** Aride; dépourvu d'intérêt. **3.** *P:* It's not so dusty, ce n'est pas si mauvais; *F:* c'est pas mal du tout. **dusty 'miller,** *s.* *Bot:* Auricule *f.*
Dutch [dʌtʃ]. **I.** *a.* (*a*) Hollandais; de Hollande. *The D. Government,* le Gouvernement néer-landais. **Dutch cheese,** fromage de Hollande. *F:* **Dutch courage,** bravoure après boire; cou-rage puisé dans la bouteille. *S.a.* OVEN, UNCLE. (*b*) *U.S:* Allemand. **2.** *s.* (*a*) **The Dutch** (*people*) les Hollandais. (*b*) *Ling:* Le hollandais. (ii) *Hist:* **High Dutch,** haut allemand. **Low Dutch,** bas allemand.
Dutchman, *pl.* **-men** ['dʌtʃmən, -men], *s.* **I.** Hollandais *m.* **2.** (*a*) *U.S:* Allemand *m.* (*b*) *Nau:* Matelot étranger. *S.a.* FLYING[1] 5.
dutiable ['dju:tiəbl], *a.* (*Of goods*) Soumis aux droits de douane; taxable.
dutiful ['dju:tiful], *a.* (*Of child, etc.*) Respectueux, soumis. **A dutiful husband,** un mari plein d'égards pour sa femme. **-fully,** *adv.* Avec soumission; suivant son devoir.
duty ['dju:ti], *s.* **I.** Obéissance *f,* respect *m.* **To pay one's duty to s.o.,** présenter ses respects, ses hommages, à qn. **2.** Devoir *m* (*to,* envers). **To do one's duty,** s'acquitter de son devoir; faire son devoir. **Do your duty come what may,** fais ce que dois, advienne que pourra. *I shall make it my d.,* a point of d., *to help him,* je prendrai à tâche de l'aider. **As in duty bound,** comme il est de mon devoir. *S.a.* BOUND[6] 2. **From a sense of duty,** par devoir. **To pay a duty call,** faire une visite obligée, une visite de poli-tesse. (*Of mutineer, etc.*) **To return to duty,** rentrer dans le devoir. **3.** Fonction(s) *f(pl),* tâche *f.* **Duties of various officials,** attributions *fpl* de divers fonctionnaires. **To enter upon, take up, one's duties,** entrer en fonctions, en charge. **To do duty for s.o.,** remplacer qn. **4.** *Mil:* etc: Service *m.* **To be on duty,** être de service, de

garde f ; Nau : être de quart m. To be on sentry duty, être en faction f. Navy : Duty men, hommes de corvée. **5.** Droit m. (a) **Customs duty,** droit(s) de douane. **Liable to duty,** passible de droits ; soumis aux droits. **Duty paid,** franc de douane. (b) **Stamp duties,** droit de timbre. **6.** Mec.E : Heavy-duty engine, machine de grande puissance. **'duty-'free,** a. Cust : Exempt de droits ; (importé) en franchise.

dwarf[1] [dwɔ:rf], s. & a. Nain, -e ; nabot, -ote ; (of plant) (i) nain ; (ii) rabougri.

dwarf[2], v.tr. **1.** Empêcher de croître ; rabougrir ou naniser (une plante). **2.** Rapetisser (par contraste).

dwarfish ['dwɔ:rfiʃ], a. (De) nain ; chétif ; (of pers.) nabot, -ote.

dwell [dwel], v.i. (dwelt ; dwelt) **1.** To dwell in a place, habiter (dans) un lieu ; demeurer, résider, dans un lieu. **2.** Rester ; se fixer ; être fixé. Her memory dwells with me, son souvenir reste présent à ma mémoire. **3.** To dwell on sth., s'étendre sur, s'appesantir sur (un sujet) ; appuyer sur (une syllabe). We will not dwell on that, glissons là-dessus. Mus : To dwell on a note, appuyer (sur) une note. **dwelling,** s. **1.** (a) Séjour m, résidence f (dans un endroit). (b) Insistance f (sur un fait). **2.** Lieu m de séjour ; logis m, demeure f. **'dwelling-house,** s. Maison f d'habitation. **'dwelling-place,** s. Demeure f, résidence f.

dweller ['dwelər], s. Habitant, -ante (in, on, de).

dwindle [dwindl], v.i. To dwindle (away), diminuer, dépérir, s'affaiblir. **dwindling,** s. Diminution f, dépérissement m, affaiblissement m.

dye[1] [dai], s. **1.** (a) Dy : Teinture f, teint m. Fast dye, bon teint, grand teint. (b) Teinte f. Villain of the deepest dye, coquin fieffé ; triple coquin. **2.** Matière colorante ; teinture, colorant m. **'dye-works,** s. Teinturerie f.

dye[2], v.tr. (a) Teindre. To dye sth. black, teindre qch. en noir. To have a dress dyed, faire teindre une robe. (b) Teinter (un film, etc.). **Material that dyes well,** tissu qui prend bien la teinture. **dyeing,** s. **1.** (a) Teinture f (d'étoffes, des cheveux). (b) Teintage m. **2.** Dyeing(-trade), la teinturerie.

dyer ['daiər], s. Teinturier m. Bot : Dyer's moss, orseille f. Dyer's (green)weed, (réséda m) gaude (f).

dying. See DIE[2].

dyke[1], [2] [daik], s. & v.tr. = DIKE[1], [2].

dynamic [dai'namik], a. Dynamique. F : D. personality, caractère énergique.

dynamics [dai'namiks], s.pl. Dynamique f.

dynamite[1] ['dainəmait], s. Dynamite f.

dynamite[2], v.tr. Faire sauter (des roches, etc.) à la dynamite ; dynamiter (un édifice).

dynamiter ['dainəmaitər], s. Dynamiteur m.

dynamo, pl. **-os** ['dainəmo, -ouz], s. Dynamo f ; génératrice f, générateur m (de courant). **'dynamo-e'lectric,** a. Dynamo-électrique.

dynamometer [dainə'məmetər], s. Dynamomètre m.

dynamotor ['dainəmoutər], s. Aut : Dynamo-démarreur f, dynastart f.

dynastic [di'nastik], a. Dynastique.

dynasty ['dinəsti], s. Dynastie f.

dysenteric [disen'terik], a. Med : Dysentérique.

dysentery ['disntri], s. Dysenterie f.

dyspepsia [dis'pepsiə], s. Med : Dyspepsie f.

dyspeptic [dis'peptik], a. & s. Dyspepsique (mf), dyspeptique (mf).

dyspnoea [dis'pni:a], s. Med : Dyspnée f.

dytiscus [di'tiskəs], s. Ent : Dytique m.

E

' E, e [i:], s. **1.** (La lettre) E, e m. **2.** Mus : Mi m. Key of E flat, clef de mi bémol.

each [i:tʃ]. **1.** a. Chaque. **Each man,** chaque homme. E. day, chaque jour ; tous les jours. Each one of us, chacun, chacune, de nous, d'entre nous. **2.** pron. (a) Chacun, -une. Each of us, chacun de nous ; chacun d'entre nous. (b) We each earn one pound, we earn one pound each, nous gagnons une livre chacun. Peaches that cost a shilling e., pêches qui coûtent un shilling chacune, un shilling pièce. Three groups of ten men each, trois groupes de chacun dix hommes. (c) Each other, l'un l'autre, les uns les autres. For each other, l'un pour l'autre. Separated from each other, séparés l'un de l'autre. To fight each other, s'entre-battre. (d) Triangles equal each to each, triangles égaux chacun à chacun.

eager ['i:gər], a. (a) Ardent, passionné. **Eager for gain,** âpre au gain. E. for, after, fame, avide, assoiffé, de gloire. **Eager in pursuit of the enemy,** ardent à poursuivre l'ennemi. To be eager to do sth., être impatient de faire qch. ; désirer ardemment faire qch. ; F : brûler de faire qch. To be eager for sth., ambitionner qch. ; désirer ardemment qch. (b) Eager glance, œillade avide. Eager pursuit, âpre poursuite. E. desire, vif désir. **-ly,** adv. Ardemment, passionnément, avidement.

eagerness ['i:gərnəs], s. Ardeur f ; impatience f ; empressement m ; vif désir. E. for praise, soif f d'éloges.

eagle [i:gl], s. **1.** Orn : Aigle mf. Golden eagle, aigle royal. Eagle nose, F : eagle's beak, nez aquilin, en bec d'aigle. **2.** Her : Aigle f. **3.** Ecc : (Lectern) Aigle m. **4.** (a) The Roman Eagles, les aigles romaines. Fr.Hist : The Imperial Eagle, le drapeau impérial ; l'aigle impérial. **5.** U.S : (= 10 dollars) Aigle m. **'eagle-eyed,** a. Aux yeux d'aigle ; au regard d'aigle.

eaglet ['i:glet], s. **1.** Aiglon m. **2.** Her : Aiglette f.

eagre ['eigər, 'i:gər], s. = BORE[5].

ear[1] ['i:ər], s. **1.** Oreille f. Med : Ear specialist, auriste m. To wear rings in one's ears, porter des anneaux aux oreilles. Your ears must have burned, must have been tingling, les oreilles ont dû vous corner, vous tinter. F : To be up to the ears, over head and ears, in work, être accablé, débordé, de travail ; avoir du travail par-dessus la tête. S.a. DEBT, LOVE[1] 1. To set people by the ears, brouiller les gens ; mettre des personnes aux prises. To send s.o. away with a flea in his ear, (i) renvoyer qn avec un refus net et catégorique ; (ii) éconduire qn avec une verte semonce ; lui dire ses quatre vérités. He went off with a flea in his ear, il est parti l'oreille basse, tout penaud. S.a. BOX[5] 1. Prov : Walls have ears, les murs ont des oreilles. **To have sharp ears,** avoir l'oreille, l'ouïe, fine. **To have an ear, a fine ear, for music;** to have a good ear, avoir l'oreille musicienne, juste; avoir de l'oreille. **To play by ear,** jouer d'oreille. **To keep one's ears open,** être, se tenir, aux écoutes. **To have s.o.'s ear,** avoir, posséder, l'oreille de qn. **To gain s.o.'s ear,** s'assurer l'attention bienveillante de qn. **To give ear, lend an ear,** lend one's ear, to s.o., prêter l'oreille à qn. **To close one's ears to the truth,** fermer l'oreille à la vérité. *If it should come to the ears of . . .,* si cela parvient aux oreilles de. . . . *S.a.* DEAF. **2.** *Tchn:* Anse *f,* oreille (de vase); anse (de cloche); orillon *m* (d'une écuelle, etc.). **'ear-ache,** *s.* Mal *m,* maux *mpl,* d'oreille(s); *Med:* otalgie *f.* **To have ear-ache,** avoir mal à l'oreille, aux oreilles. **'ear-drop,** *s.* Pendant *m* d'oreille; pendeloque *f.* **'ear-drum,** *s.* (Caisse *f* du) tympan *m.* **'ear-flap,** *s.* **1.** Lobe *m* de l'oreille. **2.** Oreillette *f* (de casquette). **'ear-mark**[1], *s.* **1.** *Husb:* Marque à l'oreille (à laquelle on reconnaît les moutons). **2.** Marque particulière, distinctive. **'ear-mark**[2], *v.tr.* **1.** *Husb:* Marquer (les moutons, etc.) à l'oreille. **2.** **To ear-mark funds,** spécialiser des fonds. *To e.-m. funds for a purpose,* assigner, affecter, des fonds à un projet. **'ear-pendant,** *s.* Pendant *m* d'oreille. **'ear-phone,** *s.* *W.Tel:* = HEAD-PHONE. **'ear-piece,** *s.* *Tp:* Écouteur *m,* pavillon *m* (de récepteur). **'ear-protector,** *s.* **1.** Protège-tympan *m inv* (d'aviateur, etc.). **2.** *Fb:* Protège-oreilles *m inv.* **'ear-ring,** *s.* Boucle *f* d'oreille. Stud ear-ring, dormeuse *f.* **'ear-shot,** *s.* Within ear-shot, à portée de voix, de l'ouïe. Out of ear-shot, hors de portée de la voix. **'ear-splitting,** *a.* (Cri) qui vous fend les oreilles. Ear-splitting noise, bruit à briser le tympan, à fendre la tête. **'ear-trumpet,** *s.* Cornet *m* acoustique. **'ear-wax,** *s.* *Physiol:* Cérumen *m.*

ear[2], *v.tr.* Mettre une anse à (qch.). **eared**[1], *a.* Long-eared, short-eared, aux oreilles longues, courtes. **Quick-eared,** à l'oreille fine. **ear**[3], *s.* Épi *m* (de blé, de maïs). **Corn in the ear,** blé en épi.

ear[4], *v.i.* (*Of corn*) Monter en épi; épier. **eared**[2], *a.* À épis. Eared corn, blé en épi; blé épié. **Full-eared,** à épis pleins.

earing ['iːəriŋ], *s.* *Nau:* Empointure *f.* **Head earing,** raban *m* d'empointure.

earl [əːrl], *s.* (*f.* countess, *q.v.*) Comte *m.*

earldom ['əːrldəm], *s.* Comté *m*; titre *m* de comte.

earliness ['əːrlinəs], *s.* **1.** (*a*) Heure peu avancée (du jour). (*b*) Heure prématurée (de la mort de qn). **2.** Précocité *f* (d'un fruit).

early ['əːrli]. **I.** *a.* (**earlier, earliest**) **1.** Qui appartient au commencement (du jour, de l'année, de la vie). (*a*) The e. cock, le coq matinal. **In the early morning,** de bon matin; de grand matin. **In the early afternoon,** au commencement de l'après-midi. To have an e. dinner, dîner de bonne heure. **To be an early riser,** *F:* early bird, être (un) matineux; être toujours matinal; se lever (de bon) matin. *S.a.* BIRD 1. **To keep early hours,** se coucher tôt et se lever tôt. *A cold morning* in early spring, une froide matinée du début du printemps. *During the earlier months of the year,* pendant les premiers mois de l'année. *Com:* Early closing day, jour où les magasins sont fermés l'après-midi. **It is early days yet** *to make up one's mind,* il est encore trop tôt pour se décider. (*b*) Early ages,

premiers âges. *The earliest times,* les temps les plus reculés. **The early Church,** l'Église primitive. **An early Victorian,** un Victorien de la première époque. **In early days,** (i) dans l'ancien temps; (ii) de bonne heure (dans le passé). **At an early date,** de bonne heure (dans le passé). *Cp.* 3. *Hist. of Art:* The early masters, les primitifs. (*c*) Early youth, première jeunesse. *In his earliest youth,* dans sa prime jeunesse. Early age, âge tendre, bas âge, premier âge. *At an e. age,* tout jeune; dès l'enfance. **My earliest recollections,** mes souvenirs les plus lointains. **2.** Précoce, hâtif. Early death, mort prématurée. Early beans, (i) haricots précoces, hâtifs; (ii) haricots de primeur. *E. vegetables, e. fruit, e. produce,* primeurs *fpl.* **3.** Prochain, rapproché. **At an early date,** prochainement; sous peu; bientôt. *Cp.* 1 (*b*). *At an earlier date,* (i) à une date antérieure; (ii) à une date plus rapprochée. **At the earliest possible moment,** dans le plus bref délai possible; au plus tôt. *S.a.* CONVENIENCE 1. **II. early,** *adv.* **1.** (*a*) De bonne heure; tôt. **Earlier,** de meilleure heure; plus tôt. **Too early,** trop tôt; de trop bonne heure. *To arrive five minutes too e.,* arriver avec cinq minutes d'avance. **Too early in the morning,** trop matin. **Early in the morning,** le matin de bonne heure; de grand matin. *It was e. in the afternoon,* c'était au commencement de l'après-midi. **Early in the evening,** très tôt dans la soirée. **To rise early,** se lever de bonne heure; être matineux. **Early enough,** à temps. *E.* in the winter, dans, dès, les premiers jours de l'hiver; à l'entrée de l'hiver. *E.* in the year, au commencement, au début, de l'année. *E.* in (his) life, dans ses jeunes années; dans sa jeunesse. *E.* in his career, au début de sa carrière. **As early as the tenth century,** dès le dixième siècle. **As early as possible,** aussitôt que possible. (*b*) **To die early,** (i) mourir jeune; (ii) mourir prématurément. **2.** Early in the list, tout au commencement de la liste.

earn [əːrn], *v.tr.* **1.** Gagner (de l'argent). **To earn one's living by writing,** gagner sa vie à écrire, en écrivant. *Fin:* **Earning capacity,** productivité financière (d'une entreprise). **2.** Mériter, gagner (des éloges, l'affection de qn). **To earn a character for audacity,** se faire une réputation d'audace.

earnest[1] ['əːrnest]. **I.** *a.* (*a*) (*Of pers.*) Sérieux. E. worker, ouvrier consciencieux. (*b*) An e. Christian, un chrétien sincère et convaincu. (*c*) Earnest request, demande pressante. E. prayer, prière fervente. E. effort, sérieux effort; effort soutenu. **2.** *s.* In earnest, sérieusement; pour de bon. **To be in earnest,** être sérieux; ne pas plaisanter. **It is raining in real earnest,** il pleut pour (tout) de bon. **He is very much in earnest,** (i) il est terriblement convaincu; (ii) il prend son rôle à cœur. *S.a.* DEAD I. 5. **-ly,** *adv.* (Parler) sérieusement, d'un ton convaincu, d'un ton sérieux; (travailler) de bon cœur, avec ardeur, avec zèle. **To entreat s.o. earnestly,** prier qn instamment.

earnest[2], *s.* **1.** *Com:* etc: Arrhes *fpl.* **Earnest money,** dépôt *m* de garantie; arrhes. **2.** Gage *m,* garantie *f.* **An earnest of one's good intentions,** une preuve, un gage, de ses bonnes intentions.

earnestness ['əːrnestnəs], *s.* Gravité *f,* sérieux *m* (de ton); ardeur *f,* ferveur *f* (d'une prière).

earnings ['əːrniŋz], *s.pl.* **1.** Fruit *m* du travail; salaire *m,* gages *mpl.* **2.** Profits *mpl,* bénéfices *mpl* (d'une entreprise).

earth[1] [əːrθ], *s.* **1.** Terre *f.* (*a*) Le monde; le globe terrestre. He is just back **from the ends of**

the earth, il revient du bout du monde. On earth, sur terre. *F:* **Where on earth have you been?** où diable étiez-vous? **Why on earth . . .?** pourquoi diable . . .? *(b)* Le sol. *Av:* **To drop to earth,** atterrir. *F:* **To come back to earth,** retomber des nues; sortir de sa rêverie. **2.** *(a)* **To till the earth,** cultiver la terre. *Fat, heavy, e.,* terre(s) grasse(s); terroir gras. *(b) Ch:* **Aluminous earth,** terre d'alumine. **Alkaline earths,** terres alcalines. **3.** *El.E:* **Terre. Earth-cable,** câble de terre; prise de terre; *(in engine, car, etc.)* fil de masse. **Earth-leakage,** perte à la terre. **Earth to frame** *(of a car, etc.),* contact *m* à la masse. **4.** Terrier *m*, tanière *f* (de renard). *(Of fox)* **To go to earth,** se terrer. **To run to earth,** (i) chasser (un renard) jusqu'à son terrier; (ii) *F:* découvrir la source, l'origine (d'une citation, d'une erreur de calcul, etc.); dépister, dénicher (qn); découvrir la retraite de (qn). **'earth-closet,** *s. Hyg:* Garde-robe *f* à terre pulvérisée. **'earth-nut,** *s. Bot:* **1.** Gland *m* de terre; noix *f* de terre. **2.** = PEANUT.

earth², *v.tr. (a) Hort:* **To earth (up),** butter, terrer (une plante). *(b) El:* Mettre, relier, (le courant) à la terre, au sol; *(in car)* relier à la masse.

earthen ['ɔːrθən], *a.* De terre. *E. pot,* marmite en terre (cuite).

earthenware ['ɔːrθənwɛər], *s.* Poterie *f* (de terre); argile cuite. **Glazed earthenware,** (i) faïence *f*; (ii) grès flambé.

earthly ['ɔːrθli], *a.* **1.** Terrestre. **2.** *F:* **There is no earthly reason for . . .,** il n'y a pas la moindre raison du monde pour. . . . **For no earthly reason,** à propos de rien; à propos de bottes. **3. Earthly-minded,** attaché aux choses de ce monde; terre à terre *inv.*

earthquake ['ɔːrθkweik], *s.* **1.** Tremblement *m* de terre; séisme *m.* **2.** *F:* Convulsion *f*, bouleversement *m* (politique, etc.).

earthwork ['ɔːrθwɔːrk], *s.* **1.** (Travaux *mpl* de) terrassement *m.* **2.** *pl. Civ.E:* **Earthworks,** travaux en terre.

earthworm ['ɔːrθwɔːrm], *s. Ann:* Lombric *m*; ver *m* de terre.

earthy ['ɔːrθi], *a.* **1.** Terreux. **Earthy taste,** goût de terre. **2.** *(Of pers.)* **Of the earth earthy,** matériel, grossier; terre à terre *inv.*

earwig ['iːərwig], *s. Ent:* Forficule *f*; *F:* perce-oreille *m.*

ease¹ [iːz], *s.* **1.** *(a)* Tranquillité *f* (d'esprit); repos *m*, bien-être *m*, aise *f* (du corps). **To be at ease,** avoir l'esprit tranquille. *S.a.* ILL III. **3. To be at one's ease,** (i) être à son aise; (ii) être tranquille. **To set s.o. at ease,** (i) mettre qn à son aise; (ii) tranquilliser qn. **To set s.o.'s mind at ease,** tirer qn de son inquiétude. **To take one's ease,** prendre ses aises. *Mil:* **To stand at ease,** se mettre, se tenir, au repos. **Stand at ease!** (en place,) repos! *(b)* **Ease from pain,** adoucissement *m* de douleur; soulagement *m. S.a.* CHAPEL. **2.** *(a)* Loisir *m.* *(b)* Oisiveté *f.* **To live a life of ease,** vivre dans l'oisiveté, vivre une vie de loisirs. **3.** *(a)* Aisance *f* (de manières, etc.); moelleux *m* (des mouvements). *(b)* Simplicité *f* (de réglage); douceur *f*, facilité *f* (de manœuvre). **With ease,** facilement; aisément; avec aisance.

ease², *v.tr.* **1.** *(a)* Adoucir, calmer, alléger, atténuer (la souffrance); soulager (un malade). *v.i. The pain has eased,* la douleur s'est atténuée. *(b)* Calmer, tranquilliser (l'esprit). **2.** Débarrasser, délivrer *(s.o. of, from, sth.,* qn de qch.). *To e. oneself of a burden,* se soulager d'un fardeau. *F:* **To ease s.o. of his purse,** soulager qn de son

porte-monnaie. **3.** Détendre, relâcher, soulager (un cordage, un ressort); desserrer (une vis); *Nau:* mollir (une manœuvre); *Mch:* modérer, soulager (la pression); ralentir (la vitesse). **To ease (the strain on) a girder,** alléger, soulager, une poutre. *Nau:* **Ease the engines!** lentement la machine! **To ease the helm (down),** mettre moins de barre. *Row:* **Ease all!** stop(pe)! **ease off.** **1.** *v.tr. (a) Nau:* Filer, choquer (un cordage). *(b)* Dégager (une surface). **2.** *v.i. (a)* = EASE UP 2 *(a).* *(b) Nau:* S'éloigner un peu du rivage. **ease up.** **1.** *v.tr. Nau:* Soulager (un palan). **2.** *v.i. (a) F:* Se relâcher; moins travailler. *(b)* Diminuer la vitesse; ralentir.

easel [iːzl], *s.* Chevalet *m* (de peintre). **Easel-picture, -piece,** tableau *m* de chevalet.

easement ['iːzmənt], *s. Jur:* Servitude *f*; service foncier; droit *m* d'usage.

easiness ['iːzinəs], *s.* **1.** Bien-être *m*, commodité *f.* **2.** Aisance *f*, grâce *f* (des manières, du style). **3.** Indifférence *f*, insouciance *f.* **4.** Facilité *f* (d'un travail). **5.** *(a)* Complaisance *f*; humeur *f* facile. *(b)* Jeu *m* facile (d'une machine); douceur *f* (de roulement).

east [iːst], *s.* **1.** *(a)* Est *m*, orient *m*, levant *m.* *House facing (the) e.,* maison exposée à l'est. **On the east, to the east,** à l'est *(of,* de). *(b)* **The East,** l'Orient, le Levant. **The Far East,** l'extrême Orient. **2.** *adv.* A l'est, à l'orient. **To travel east,** voyager vers l'est. *Prov:* **Too far east is west,** les extrêmes se touchent. **3.** *adj.* (Vent) d'est; (pays) de l'est, oriental; (fenêtre) qui fait face à l'est. **The East Indies,** les Indes orientales. **'East-'End (the),** *s.* Quartiers pauvres et populeux de la partie est de Londres.

Easter ['iːstər], *s.* Pâques *m.* **Easter day,** le jour de Pâques. **Easter Monday,** le lundi de Pâques. **Easter egg,** œuf de Pâques.

easterly ['iːstərli]. **1.** *a.* **Easterly wind,** vent d'est. **E. current,** courant qui se dirige vers l'est. **2.** *adv.* Vers l'est.

eastern ['iːstərn], *a.* Est, de l'est; oriental, -aux. **The Eastern question,** la question d'Orient. **The Eastern Church,** l'Église d'Orient.

Eastertide ['iːstərtaid], *s.* Pâques *m.*

eastward ['iːstwərd]. **1.** *s.* **To the eastward,** vers l'est. **2.** *a. (a)* A l'est; dans l'est. *(b)* Du côté de l'est.

eastwards ['iːstwərdz], *adv.* A l'est; vers l'est; vers l'orient.

easy ['iːzi] (easier, easiest) **I.** *a.* **1.** *(a)* A l'aise. **To feel easier,** se sentir plus à son aise; se sentir mieux. *Mil:* **Stand easy!** (en place,) repos! *(b)* Tranquille; sans inquiétude. **To make one's mind e. about sth.,** se tranquilliser, se rassurer, sur qch. **Easy life,** vie sans souci, sans tracas. *S.a.* CIRCUMSTANCE 1. **2.** *(a) (Of manners, etc.)* Aisé, libre, dégagé. **Easy style,** style facile, coulant. *(b)* **Coat of an easy fit,** veston dans lequel on est à l'aise. *(c)* **Easy movement,** mouvement moelleux. *Nau:* **Easy rolling,** roulis doux. *Mec.E:* **Easy fit,** ajustage lâche. **3.** *(a)* **Easy task,** travail facile, aisé. **That is easy to see,** cela se voit; il y paraît. *It is e. for him to . . .,* il lui est facile de. . . . *It is e. to say . . .,* on a vite fait de dire. . . . *'House within easy distance,* maison à distance commode de. . . . *F:* **As easy as A B C,** as winking, simple comme bonjour. *P: Esp. U.S:* *(Of pers.)* **Easy mark,** jobard *m.* *(b) (Of pers.)* Facile, accommodant, complaisant; débonnaire. **Easy person to get on with,** personne d'un commerce facile. *S.a.* FREE¹ 5. *(c)* **To travel by easy stages,** voyager à petites étapes. **At an easy**

trot, au petit trot. *Com:* By easy payments, on easy terms, avec facilités de payement. *Sp: etc:* To come in an easy first, arriver bon premier. 4. *Com:* Easy market, marché tranquille, calme. Cotton was easier, le coton a accusé une détente. 5. *Cards:* Honours easy, honneurs partagés. -ily, *adv.* 1. Tranquillement, à son aise, paisiblement. To take things, life, easily, prendre le temps comme il vient ; se laisser vivre ; *F:* se la couler douce. 2. (a) Doucement ; sans secousse. The door shuts e., la porte se ferme sans effort. (b) Avec confort. The car holds six people e., on tient à l'aise six dans cette voiture. 3. Facilement, sans difficulté, avec aisance. To speak e., parler avec facilité. He came in easily first, il est arrivé bon premier. II. easy, *adv.* *F:* 1. I can do it easy, cela me sera facile. Easier said than done, c'est plus facile à dire qu'à faire ; c'est bon à dire. 2. (a) To take things easy, prendre les choses en douceur. To take it easy, en prendre tout à son aise. Take it easy! ne vous faites pas de bile ! To take life easy, se laisser vivre. To go easy with sth., ménager qch. (b) *Nau: Row:* Easy (ahead)! (en avant) doucement ! Easy all! stop(pe) ! (c) *Mil:* Stand easy! repos ! 'easy-'chair, s. Fauteuil m ; bergère f. 'easy-going, a. 1. (Of horse) A l'allure douce. 2. (Of pers.) (a) Qui prend les choses tranquillement ; insouciant ; qui ne se fait pas de bile. (b) Accommodant ; peu exigeant ; peu tracassier. (c) D'humeur facile. An easy-going man, une bonne pâte d'homme ; un homme de bonne composition ; un bon garçon.

eat [i:t], *v.tr.* (p.t. ate [et] ; p.p. eaten [i:tn]) (a) Manger. To eat one's breakfast, dinner, supper, déjeuner, dîner, souper. To ask for something to eat, demander à manger ; mangeable. Fit to eat, bon à manger ; mangeable. To eat like a wolf, manger comme un ogre ; dévorer. *S.a.* FILL¹ 1. To eat one's heart out, se ronger le cœur. Abs. To eat of a dish, manger d'un plat. *F:* He eats out of my hand, il m'obéit comme un chien. *F:* I thought he was going to eat me, j'ai cru qu'il allait m'avaler. To eat one's words, (i) se rétracter ; (ii) bafouiller ; manger ses mots. (Of insect, worm) To eat into wood, ronger, mouliner, le bois. (b) *U.S:* Prendre ses repas ; dîner. eat away, *v.tr.* (a) Ronger, éroder (une falaise) ; saper (des fondations). (b) (Of acid) Mordre, dissoudre, attaquer (un métal). eat off, *v.tr.* To eat its head off, (of horse, etc.) s'engraisser à ne rien faire ; (of factory) mâcher à vide. eat up, *v.tr.* 1. Manger jusqu'à la dernière miette (un gâteau, etc.) ; achever de manger (qch.). Eat up your bread! finis ton pain ! (Of motor car, etc.) To eat up the miles, dévorer la route. 2. Consumer (qch.) sans profit. Stove that eats up the coal, poêle qui mange beaucoup de charbon. 3. *F:* To be eaten up (with sth.), être dévoré (d'orgueil) ; être confit (de vanité) ; être consumé (par l'ambition). eating, s. Manger m. Pheasants are good eating, les faisans sont bons à manger. Eating chocolate, chocolat à croquer. 'eating-house, s. Restaurant m. Cheap e.-h., gargote f.

eatable ['i:təbl]. 1. a. Mangeable ; bon à manger. 2. s.pl. Eatables, provisions f de bouche ; comestibles m.

eater ['i:tər], s. Mangeur, -euse ; dîneur, -euse. Small e., great e., petit mangeur, gros mangeur.

eaves [i:vz], s.pl. *Const:* Avance f (du toit) ; avant-toit m.

eavesdrop ['i:vzdrɔp], *v.i.* (eavesdropped) Écouter aux portes, à la porte ; être aux écoutes.

eavesdropper ['i:vzdrɔpər], s. Écouteur, -euse ; aux portes ; indiscret, -ète.

ebb¹ [eb], s. 1. Reflux m, jusant m ; baisse f (de la marée). The ebb and flow, le flux et le reflux. Set of the ebb, direction f du jusant. Slack of the ebb, étale m du jusant. 2. *F:* Déclin m (de la fortune, de la vie). The patient is at a low ebb, le malade est très bas. 'ebb-'tide, s. Marée descendante ; marée de jusant ; reflux m.

ebb², *v.i.* 1. (Of tide) Baisser, refluer. To ebb and flow, monter et baisser. The tide is ebbing, la marée baisse. 2. *F:* (Of life, etc.) Décliner ; être sur le déclin ; décroître, baisser. To ebb away, s'écouler. Ebbing strength, forces qui s'en vont.

ebon ['ebən], a. *Poet:* D'ébène.

ebonite ['ebənait], s. Ébonite f ; vulcanite f.

ebony ['ebəni], s. (a) Ébène f ; bois m d'ébène. (b) (Plaqueminier) ébénier.

ebriety [i:'braiəti], :. Ébriété f, ivresse f.

Ebro ['i:bro]. *Pr.n. Geog:* L'Èbre m.

ebullience [i'bʌliəns], s. Bouillonnement m, effervescence f (de la colère, de la jeunesse).

ebullient [i'bʌliənt], a. 1. Bouillonnant. 2. *F:* (Sentiment) débordant, exubérant ; (homme) plein de vie.

ebullition [ebʌ'liʃ(ə)n], s. 1. Ébullition f, bouillonnement m. 2. Ebullition of feeling, transport m.

eccentric [ek'sentrik], a. & s. (a) Excentrique (m) ; désaxé. Eccentric load, charge décentrée. (b) *F:* (Of pers.) Excentrique (mf) ; original, -aux.

eccentricity [eksen'trisiti], s. (a) Excentricité f, désaxage m, décentrement m. (b) Excentricité (de caractère) ; bizarrerie f, originalité f.

ecclesiastic [ekli:zi'astik], a. & s. Ecclésiastique (m).

ecclesiastical [ekli:zi'astik(ə)l], a. Ecclésiastique. The ecclesiastical body, le sacerdoce. *Adm:* Ecclesiastical matters, les Cultes m.

echelon¹ ['eʃələn], s. *Mil:* Échelon m.

echelon², *v.tr.* *Mil:* Échelonner (des troupes). echeloned, a. *Mil:* En échelon.

echo¹ ['eko], s. (pl. echoes) Écho m. To applaud to the echo, applaudir à tout rompre.

echo². 1. *v.tr.* Répéter (en écho). To echo s.o.'s opinions, se faire l'écho des opinions de qn. To echo back a shout, faire écho à un cri. 2. *v.i.* (a) Faire écho. (b) Retentir. His voice echoed through the hall, sa voix retentit, résonna, dans le vestibule.

echoless ['ekoləs], a. Sans écho. *Cin:* Echoless studio, studio complètement sourd.

eclair [e'klɛər], s. *Cu:* Éclair m (à la crème, etc.).

eclampsia [e'klampsiə], s. *Med:* Éclampsie f.

éclat [e'kla:], s. Éclat m, gloire f.

eclectic [ek'lektik], a. & s. Éclectique (m). -ally, *adv.* Éclectiquement.

eclecticism [ek'lektisizm], s. Éclectisme m.

eclipse¹ [i'klips], s. Éclipse f (de soleil, de lune ; d'un phare). *F:* To be under an eclipse, être éclipsé ; se trouver relégué dans l'ombre.

eclipse², *v.tr.* Éclipser.

ecliptic [i'kliptik], a. & s. *Astr:* Écliptique (f).

eclogue ['eklɔg], s. *Lit:* Églogue f.

economic [i:ko'nɔmik], a. Qui se rapporte à l'économie politique ; (problème) économique. The e. system of Europe, l'économie f de l'Europe.

economical [i:ko'nɔmik(ə)l], a. (a) (Of pers.) Économe. (b) (Of method, apparatus, etc.) Économique. -ally, *adv.* Économiquement. To use sth. e., ménager qch.

economics [iːkoˈnɔmiks], *s.pl.* **1.** L'économie *f* politique. **2.** *The e. of a country*, le régime économique d'un pays.
economist [i(ː)ˈkɔnomist], *s.* (Political) economist, économiste *m.* **Rural economist**, économiste rural ; agronome *m.*
economization [i(ː)kɔnomiˈzeiʃ(ə)n], *s.* Économie *f* dans l'emploi (de qch.) ; ménagement *m* (des ressources, etc.).
economize [i(ː)ˈkɔnomaːiz], *v.tr.* Économiser, ménager (le temps, l'argent, etc.). *Abs.* Faire des économies.
economy [i(ː)ˈkɔnomi], *s.* **1.** Économie *f.* **To practise economy**, économiser. *Aut :* **Economy run**, concours *m* de consommation. **2.** **Political economy**, économie politique.
ecstasy [ˈekstəsi], *s.* **1.** Transport *m* (de joie) ; ravissement *m.* **To be in an ecstasy of joy**, se pâmer de joie. **To go into ecstasies over sth.**, s'extasier devant qch. **2.** Extase (religieuse, etc.).
ecstatic [ekˈstatik], *a.* Extatique. **-ally**, *adv.* *E. happy*, heureux jusqu'au ravissement. **To gaze ecstatically at s.o.**, tomber en extase devant qn.
ectropion [ekˈtroupiən], *s.* *Med :* Ectropion *m* ; éversion *f* (de la paupière).
Ecuador [ekwaˈdoːr]. *Pr.n. Geog :* (La République de) l'Équateur *m.*
eczema [ˈekzima], *s.* *Med :* Eczéma *m.*
eczematous [ekˈzemətəs], *a.* Eczémateux.
eddy[1] [ˈedi], *s.* **1.** Remous *m* ; tourbillon *m* ; tournoiement *m* ; *Nau :* revolin *m.* **2.** *El :* **Eddy currents**, courants de Foucault. **'eddy-wind**, *s. Nau :* Revolin *m.*
eddy[2], *v.i.* (*Of water*) Faire des remous ; (*of wind*) tourbillonner, tournoyer.
Eden [iːdn]. *Pr.n.* (**The Garden of**) **Eden**, l'Éden.
edentate [iˈdentet], *a. & s. Z :* Édenté (*m*).
edge[1] [edʒ], *s.* **1.** Fil *m*, tranchant *m* (d'une lame). *F :* **The thin edge of the wedge**, le premier pas (qui mène à une mauvaise habitude, etc.). *Knife with a keen e. on it*, couteau à tranchant aigu, acéré. **To put an edge on a blade**, (re)donner du fil à, aiguiser, affiler, une lame. **To take the edge off sth.**, émousser (un couteau, *F :* l'appétit, le plaisir). **Not to put too fine an edge upon it**, pour ne pas mâcher les mots. **2.** (*a*) Arête *f*, angle *m* (d'une pierre, etc.) ; crête *f* (d'une chaîne de montagnes). **Sharp edge**, arête vive. (*b*) *Tls :* **Straight edge**, limande *f.* **3.** Bord *m*, rebord *m* (de table) ; tranche *f*, champ (d'une planche) ; ourlet *m* (d'un cratère) ; tranche (d'une pièce de monnaie, d'un livre). *Bookb :* **Gilt edges**, tranches dorées. **With g. edges**, doré sur tranches. **On edge**, (i) (*of brick*) de champ ; (ii) *F :* (*of teeth*) agacé ; (*of pers.*) énervé. **It sets my teeth on edge**, cela m'agace les dents ; cela me crispe. **To have one's nerves on edge**, avoir les nerfs en pelote. *She is on e. to-day*, cela est nerveuse, elle a ses nerfs, aujourd'hui. **4.** Lisière *f*, bordure *f*, orée *f* (d'un bois) ; bord, rive *f* (d'une rivière) ; liséré *m*, bord (d'une étoffe, etc.). *At the e. of a precipice*, au bord d'un précipice. **'edge-'tool**, *s.* Outil tranchant, coupant.
edge[2], *v.tr. & i.* **1.** Affiler, aiguiser (un couteau) ; affûter (un outil). **2.** Border (une étoffe, la route) (*with*, de) ; lisérer (une jupe). **3.** **To edge (one's way) into a room** ; **to edge in**, se faufiler, se glisser, dans une pièce. **To edge in a word**, placer son mot ; glisser un mot. *To e. to(wards) the right*, obliquer vers la droite. **edge away**, *v.i.* S'éloigner, se reculer, s'écarter, tout doucement (*from*, de). **edged**, *a.* **1.** (*Of tool, etc.*) Tranchant, acéré. *F :* **To play with edged tools**, jouer avec le feu ; jouer un jeu dangereux. **2.** (*a*) A

tranchant. **Two-edged sword**, épée à deux tranchants, à double tranchant. (*b*) **Gilt-edged**, doré sur tranches. **edging**, *s. Dressm :* etc : Liséré *m*, cordonnet *m*, passement *m*, ganse *f* *Hort :* Bordure *f* (de parterre, etc.). **'edging-shears**, *s.pl. Hort :* Cisaille *f* à bordures.
edgeways [ˈedʒweiz], **edgewise** [ˈedʒwaiz], *adv.* **1.** (Vu) latéralement, de côté. **2.** (Placé) de champ, sur champ. *F :* **I can't get a word in edgeways**, impossible de glisser un mot (dans la conversation).
edible [ˈedibl]. **1.** *a.* Comestible ; bon à manger. **2.** *s.pl.* **Edibles**, comestibles *m.*
edict [ˈiːdikt], *s. Hist :* Édit *m.*
edification [edifiˈkeiʃ(ə)n], *s.* Édification *f*, instruction *f.*
edifice [ˈedifis], *s.* Édifice *m.*
edify [ˈedifai], *v.tr.* Édifier (qn).
Edinburgh [ˈedinb(ə)rə]. *Pr.n.* Édimbourg.
edit [ˈedit], *v.tr.* (*a*) Annoter, éditer (le texte d'un auteur) ; diriger (une série de textes, etc.). (*b*) Rédiger, diriger (un journal). **Edited by . . .**, (série, journal, etc.) sous la direction de. . . . **editing**, *s.* **1.** Préparation *f*, annotation *f* (d'un texte). **2.** Rédaction *f*, direction *f* (d'un journal).
edition [iˈdiʃ(ə)n], *s. Publ :* Édition *f.* **Limited edition**, édition à tirage limité. *Book in its fourth e.*, livre à sa quatrième édition.
editor [ˈeditər], *s.* **1.** Annotateur *m*, éditeur *m* (d'un texte) ; auteur *m* (d'une édition critique). **2.** (*a*) Surveillant *m* de la publication ; directeur *m* (d'une série, d'un dictionnaire). (*b*) Rédacteur *m* en chef, directeur (d'un journal). **Managing editor**, rédacteur gérant.
editorial [ediˈtɔːriəl]. **1.** *a.* Éditorial, -aux. *The e. staff*, la rédaction. **2.** *s. Journ :* Article *m* de fond, de tête ; éditorial *m.*
editorship [ˈeditərʃip], *s.* **1.** Rôle *m* d'annotateur (d'un texte). **2.** *Series published under the e. of . . .*, série publiée sous la direction de. . . . **3.** Direction *f* (d'un journal).
educate [ˈedjukeit], *v.tr.* **1.** (*a*) Donner de l'instruction à, instruire (qn). *He was educated in France*, il a fait ses études en France. (*b*) (i) Faire faire ses études à (un enfant) ; (ii) pourvoir à l'instruction de (son enfant). **To educate one's son for the bar**, diriger son fils vers le barreau. **2.** Former (qn, le goût de qn). **Educated man**, homme instruit ; esprit cultivé.
education [edjuˈkeiʃ(ə)n], *s.* **1.** Éducation *f.* **2.** Enseignement *m*, instruction *f.* **Board of Education** = Ministère *m* de l'Éducation nationale. *He has had a classical e.*, il a fait ses études classiques. *He has had a good e.*, il a fait de fortes études. **3.** Dressage *m* (des animaux).
educational [edjuˈkeiʃən(ə)l], *a.* (Maison, ouvrage) d'éducation, d'enseignement ; (procédé) éducatif, pédagogique. *E. film*, film éducatif.
educative [ˈedjukətiv], *a.* Éducatif.
educator [ˈedjukeitər], *s.* Éducateur, -trice.
Edward [ˈedwəd]. *Pr.n.m.* Édouard.
eel [iːl], *s.* **1.** Anguille *f.* *Cu :* **Stewed eel**, anguille à la matelote. **2.** **Electric eel**, gymnote *m.* **'eel-basket, -buck**, *s.* Nasse *f* à anguilles. **'eel-pout**, *s. Ich :* Lotte (commune) ; barbot *m.* **'eel-prong, -spear**, *s.* Foène *f.*
e'en [iːn], *adv. Poet :* = EVEN[3].
e'er [ɛər], *adv. Poet :* = EVER.
eerie, eery [ˈiːəri], *a.* Étrange, mystérieux ; qui donne le frisson. **-ily**, *adv.* Étrangement ; d'une façon à donner le frisson.
efface [eˈfeis], *v.tr.* (*a*) Effacer ; oblitérer. (*b*) **To efface oneself**, s'effacer.
effacement [eˈfeismənt], *s.* Effacement *m.*

effect[1] [e'fekt], s. **1.** (a) Effet m, action f, influence f; résultat m, conséquence f. The effect of heat upon metals, l'action de la chaleur sur les métaux. To feel the effects of an illness, ressentir les effets d'une maladie. To have an effect on s.o., produire de l'effet sur qn; affecter qn. To be of no effect; to have, produce, no effect, ne produire aucun effet; rester sans action. Nothing has any effect on it, rien n'y fait. It has little effect, cela ne fait pas grand'chose. To take effect, (i) faire (son) effet; (ii) (of regulation) entrer en vigueur; (iii) (of drugs) agir, opérer; (of vaccination) prendre; (iv) (of shot) porter. Of no effect, (i) sans effet, inutile, inefficace; (ii) Jur: non avenu. To no effect, en vain; sans résultat. To give effect to sth., exécuter (un décret); donner suite à (une décision). To carry into effect, mettre (qch.) à exécution. (b) Sens m, teneur f (d'un document). I received a telegram to the same effect, j'ai reçu une dépêche dans le même sens. That is what he said, or words to that effect, voilà ce qu'il a dit, ou quelque chose d'approchant. **2.** (a) Th: Stage effects, effets scéniques, jeux m scéniques. (b) Words meant for effect, phrases à effet. To do sth. for e., faire qch. pour se faire remarquer. **3.** In effect, en fait, en réalité. **4.** pl. (Personal) effects, effets, biens (personnels). Bank: 'No effects,' "défaut de provision."

effect[2], v.tr. Effectuer, accomplir, réaliser (qch.). To effect one's purpose, atteindre son but. To effect an entrance, forcer la porte. To effect a payment, effectuer un payement. To effect an insurance, a policy of insurance, prendre, souscrire, une police d'assurances.

effective [e'fektiv]. **1.** a. (a) Efficace. The medicine was e., la médecine a produit son effet. (b) (Actual) Effectif. Mec.E: Effective power, rendement m; puissance effective; effet m utile. (c) E. contrast, contraste frappant, saisissant. E. picture, tableau qui fait de l'effet. (d) Mil: Effective troops, troupes valides. (e) U.S: (Of decree, etc.) To become effective, entrer en vigueur. **2.** s.pl. Mil: Effectives, effectifs m. -ly, adv. **1.** Avec effet, efficacement, utilement. **2.** Effectivement; en réalité. **3.** D'une façon frappante.

effectiveness [e'fektivnəs], s. **1.** Efficacité f. **2.** L'impression frappante (produite par un tableau, etc.).

effectual [e'fektjuəl], a. **1.** Efficace. **2.** (Contrat) valide; (règlement) en vigueur. -ally, adv. Efficacement.

effeminacy [e'feminəsi], s. Caractère efféminé; mollesse f.

effeminate [e'feminet], a. & s. Efféminé (m).

effervesce [efər'ves], v.i. Être ou entrer en effervescence; (of drinks) mousser.

effervescence [efər'ves(ə)ns], s. Effervescence f (d'un liquide).

effervescent [efər'ves(ə)nt], a. Effervescent.

effete [e'fiːt], a. (Of method, etc.) Caduc, -uque.

efficacious [efi'keiʃəs], a. Efficace. -ly, adv. Efficacement; avec efficacité.

efficaciousness [efi'keiʃəsnəs], **efficacy** ['efikəsi], s. Efficacité f.

efficiency [e'fiʃənsi], s. **1.** Efficacité f (d'un remède, etc.). **2.** (a) Mec.E: Rendement (industriel) coefficient m de rendement, d'effet utile. High-efficiency engine, moteur à grand, bon, rendement. (b) Bon fonctionnement (d'une administration, etc.). **3.** (Of pers.) Capacité f; valeur f. Mil: Efficiency pay, prime payée aux hommes qui ont fait leurs classes.

efficient [e'fiʃənt], a. (a) Phil: Efficient cause, cause efficiente. (b) (Of method, work) Effectif, efficace. (c) Efficient machine, (i) machine à bon rendement; (ii) machine d'un fonctionnement sûr. (d) (Of pers.) Capable, compétent. -ly, adv. **1.** Efficacement. **2.** Work e. done, travail exécuté avec compétence.

effigy ['efidʒi], s. Effigie f. To burn, hang, s.o. in effigy, brûler, pendre, qn en effigie.

efflorescence [eflɔ'res(ə)ns], s. Efflorescence f.

efflorescent [eflɔ'res(ə)nt], a. Efflorescent.

effluence ['efluəns], s. Émanation f.

effluvium, pl. -ia [e'fluːviəm, -ia], s. (a) Effluve m, émanation f. (b) Pej: Émanation désagréable; exhalaison f.

efflux ['eflʌks], s. Flux m, écoulement m (de liquide).

effort ['efərt], s. **1.** (a) Effort m. To make an e. to do sth., faire (un) effort pour faire qch.; s'efforcer de faire qch. F: Make an effort! secouez-vous! He spares no effort, il ne s'épargne pas; rien ne lui coûte. Hospital financed by voluntary e., hôpital subventionné par l'initiative privée. (b) F: You've seen his last effort? vous avez vu son dernier ouvrage, sa dernière œuvre? **2.** Mec: Effort (de traction, etc.); poussée f, travail m.

effortless ['efərtləs], a. (a) Sans effort. (b) Facile.

effrontery [e'frʌntəri], s. Effronterie f.

effulgence [e'fʌldʒəns], s. Éclat m, splendeur f.

effulgent [e'fʌldʒənt], a. Resplendissant, éclatant.

effusion [e'fjuːʒ(ə)n], s. **1.** Effusion f, épanchement m (du sang, etc.). **2.** Effusion (de tendresse, etc.); épanchement de cœur. F: Have you ever read such an e.? avez-vous jamais lu une tartine pareille?

effusive [e'fjuːsiv], a. Démonstratif, expansif. To be e. in one's compliments, se répandre en compliments. To be effusive in one's thanks, se confondre en remercîments. -ly, adv. Avec effusion, avec expansion. To thank s.o. effusively, se confondre en remercîments auprès de qn.

effusiveness [e'fjuːsivnəs], s. Effusion f; volubilité f.

eft [eft], s. = NEWT.

egad [i'gad], int. A: Parbleu! morbleu!

egg[1] [eg], s. **1.** (a) Œuf m. Boiled egg, œuf à la coque. Hard-boiled egg, œuf dur. Soft-boiled egg, œuf mollet. Fried egg, œuf sur le plat. Poached egg, œuf poché. Scrambled eggs, œufs brouillés. The goose with the golden eggs, la poule aux œufs d'or. A bad egg, (i) un œuf pourri; (ii) P: un bon à rien, un vaurien. P: Good egg! bon! à la bonne heure! P: chouette! (b) Œuf (d'insecte); lente f (de pou). Silkworm's eggs, F: graines f de vers à soie. J: Needlew: Darning egg, œuf à repriser. 'egg-cosy, s. Cosy m (pour œufs à la coque). 'egg-cup, s. Coquetier m. 'egg-flip, s. Boisson chaude composée d'un œuf battu dans de la bière, de l'alcool; (non-alcoholic) lait m de poule. 'egg-fruit, s. Hort: Aubergine f. 'egg-man, pl. -men, 'egg-merchant, s.m. Coquetier; marchand d'œufs. 'egg-'nog, s. = EGG-FLIP. 'egg-plant, s. Bot: Hort: Aubergine f. 'egg-powder, s. Cu: Œufs mpl en poudre. 'egg-shaped, a. Ovoïde. 'egg-shell, s. Coquille f d'œuf. 'egg-spoon, s. Cuiller f à œufs. 'egg-stand, s. 'egg-timer, s. Cu: Sablier m. 'egg-whisk, s. Batteuse f, fouet m, à œufs.

egg[2], v.tr. To egg s.o. on (to do sth.), pousser, inciter, encourager, qn (à faire qch.).

eglantine ['egləntain], s. Bot: **1.** Églantine f. **2.** (Bush) Églantier m.

egoism ['egoizm], *s.* **1.** Culte *m* du moi. **2.** = EGOTISM.

egoist ['egoist], *s.* = EGOTIST.

egoistic(al) [ego'istik(əl)], *a.* **1.** Qui rapporte tout à soi. **2.** *F:* Entiché de sa personne; rempli de sa propre importance.

egotism ['egotizm], *s.* Égotisme *m.*

egotist ['egotist], *s.* Égotiste *mf.*

egregious [i'gri:dʒjəs], *a.* (Sot, etc.) insigne, fieffé. *E. blunder,* maladresse insigne. **-ly,** *adv.* D'une manière insigne.

egregiousness [i'gri:dʒjəsnəs], *s.* Énormité *f* (d'une maladresse).

egress ['i:gres], *s.* (*a*) Sortie *f*, issue *f.* (*b*) *Mch:* *etc:* Échappement *m.*

egret ['egret, 'i:gret], *s.* **1.** *Orn:* Aigrette *f*; héron argenté. **2.** *Bot:* Aigrette (de chardon).

Egypt ['i:dʒipt]. *Pr.n.* L'Égypte *f.*

Egyptian [i'dʒipʃ(ə)n], *a. & s.* Égyptien, -ienne.

Egyptology [i:dʒip'tolodʒi], *s.* Égyptologie *f.*

eh [ei], *int.* Eh! hé! hein?

eider(-duck) ['aicər(dʌk)], *s.* *Orn:* Eider *m.* '**eider-down,** *s.* **1.** Duvet *m* d'eider. **2.** Eider-down (quilt), édredon piqué.

eight [eit]. **1.** *num. a. & s.* Huit (*m*). *E. and twenty, twenty-e.,* vingt-huit. *E. and six* (*pence*), huit shillings six pence. **To be eight (years old),** avoir huit ans. *There were e. of us,* nous étions huit. *Page e.,* page huit. **Eight days,** huit jours; *F:* une huitaine. *P: He's had one over the eight,* il a bu un coup de trop. *Aut:* Eight-cylinder car, *F:* **an eight,** voiture *f* à huit cylindres; *F:* une huit-cylindres. **2.** *s.* *Sp:* (i) Équipe *f* de huit rameurs; (ii) canot *m* à huit rameurs; huit de pointe.

eighteen [ei'ti:n], *num. a. & s.* Dix-huit (*m*).

eighteenth [ei'ti:nθ], *num. a. & s.* (*a*) Dix-huitième. (*b*) (*On*) the e. (of May), le dix-huit (mai). **Louis the Eighteenth,** Louis Dix-huit.

eightfold ['eitfould]. **1.** *a.* Octuple. **2.** *adv.* Huit fois autant.

eighth [eitθ]. **1.** *num. a. & s.* (*a*) Huitième. *In the e. place,* huitièmement. (*b*) (*On*) the eighth (of April), le huit (avril). **Henry the Eighth,** Henri Huit. **2.** *s.* (*Fractional*) Huitième *m.*

eightieth ['eitiəθ], *num. a. & s.* Quatre-vingtième (*m*).

eighty ['eiti], *num. a. & s.* Quatre-vingts (*m*). Eighty-one, quatre-vingt-un. *E.-first,* quatre-vingt-unième. **Page eighty,** page quatre-vingt.

either ['aiðər, 'i:ðər]. **1.** *a. & pron.* (*a*) L'un(e) et l'autre, chaque, chacun(e). **On either side,** de chaque côté; des deux côtés. (*b*) L'un(e) ou l'autre. **Either of them,** soit l'un(e), soit l'autre. *I don't believe e.,* je ne vous crois ni l'un ni l'autre. *You can do it e. way,* vous pouvez le faire d'une manière ou de l'autre, des deux façons également. **Do you want this one or that one?**—Either, voulez-vous celui-ci ou celui-là?— L'un ou l'autre; n'importe lequel. **2.** *conj. & adv.* (*a*) Either . . . or . . . ou . . ., ou . . .; soit . . ., soit. . . . **Either come in or go out,** entrez ou sortez. (*b*) Not . . . either, ne . . . non plus. **Nor I either!** ni moi non plus.

ejaculate [i'dʒakjuleit], *v.tr.* *F:* Pousser (un cri); lancer (un juron, etc.). *"What a misfortune!" he ejaculated,* "quel malheur!" fit-il, s'écria-t-il.

ejaculation [idʒakju'leiʃ(ə)n], *s.* Cri *m*, exclamation *f.*

eject [i'dʒekt], *v.tr.* **1.** Jeter, émettre (des flammes, etc.); expulser, évacuer (de la bile). **2.** (*a*) Expulser (un agitateur d'une réunion). (*b*) *Jur:* Expulser (un locataire).

ejection [i'dʒekʃ(ə)n], *s.* (*a*) Jet *m* (de flammes); éjection *f* (de la vapeur, d'une cartouche); expulsion *f* (de qn); évacuation *f* (de la bile). (*b*) Éviction *f*, expulsion (d'un locataire).

ejector [i'dʒektər], *s.* *Sm.a:* *Mch:* Éjecteur *m.*

eke [i:k], *v.tr.* **To eke out,** suppléer à l'insuffisance de, augmenter (ses revenus, etc.); ménager, faire durer (les vivres). *To eke out the soup, the sauce (with water),* allonger la soupe, la sauce. **To eke out a livelihood,** gagner une maigre pitance.

elaborate[1] [i'laboret], *a.* (*Of mechanism*) Compliqué; (*of work*) soigné, fini; (*of style*) travaillé; (*of inspection*) minutieux. *E. toilet,* toilette recherchée, étudiée. **-ly,** *adv.* Avec soin; soigneusement; minutieusement.

elaborate[2] [i'laboreit], *v.tr.* (*a*) Élaborer (une théorie); fouiller, pousser (une œuvre d'art). (*b*) *Physiol:* Élaborer (un suc, etc.) (*into,* en).

elaborateness [i'laboretnəs], *s.* Complication *f* (d'un mécanisme); fini *m* (d'un travail); minutie *f* (de recherches).

elaboration [ilabo'reiʃ(ə)n], *s.* *Physiol:* *etc:* Élaboration *f.*

elapse [i'laps], *v.i.* (*Of time*) S'écouler; (se) passer.

elastic [i'lastik]. **1.** *a.* (*a*) Élastique; (bois, etc.) flexible. **To be elastic,** (i) faire ressort; (ii) *F:* (*of pers.*) avoir du ressort. (*b*) *F:* (Règlement, etc.) élastique. **2.** *s.* Élastique *m.*

elasticity [i:las'tisiti, el-], *s.* Élasticité *f*; ressort *m* (de caractère); souplesse *f* (de corps).

elate [i'leit], *v.tr.* Exalter, transporter. *To be elated with joy, with success,* être transporté de joie, enivré de succès.

elater ['elatər], *s.* *Ent:* Élatère *m*; *F:* taupin *m.*

elation [i'leiʃ(ə)n], *s.* **1.** Exaltation *f*; ivresse *f* (du succès). **2.** Joie *f*, gaîté *f.*

elbow[1] ['elbo], *s.* **1.** Coude *m* (du bras). *To rest one's e. on sth.,* s'accouder sur qch. **To be out at elbow(s),** (i) (*of coat*) être troué, percé, aux coudes; (ii) *F:* (*of pers.*) être loqueteux, déguenillé. *F:* **To crook the elbow, to lift one's elbow,** lever, hausser, le coude; être adonné à la boisson. **To rub elbows with s.o.,** coudoyer qn. **2.** (*a*) Coude, tournant *m* (d'une route). (*b*) Coude, genou *m*, jarret *m* (d'un tuyau). '**elbow-glove,** *s.* Passe-coude *m.* '**elbow-grease,** *s.* *F:* Huile *f* de bras. **Put a bit of elbow-grease into it,** mettez-y un peu de nerf. '**elbow-high,** *adv.* **1.** Jusqu'au coude. **2.** *Const:* A hauteur d'appui. '**elbow-joint,** *s.* **1.** *Anat:* Articulation *f* du coude. **2.** *Mec.E:* *etc:* Joint articulé; (joint à) genou *m.* '**elbow-rest,** *s.* Accoudoir *m*, accotoir *m.* '**elbow-room,** *s.* **To have elbow-room,** avoir ses coudées franches.

elbow[2]. **1.** *v.tr. & i.* (*a*) Coudoyer (qn); pousser (qn) du coude ou des coudes. **To elbow s.o. aside,** écarter qn d'un coup de coude. (*b*) **To elbow (one's way) through the crowd,** se frayer un passage à travers la foule; jouer des coudes. **2.** *v.i.* (*Of road*) Faire coude. **elbowing,** *s.* Coudoiement *m.*

elder[1] ['eldər]. **1.** *a.* Aîné, plus âgé (de deux personnes). **Pliny the Elder,** Pline l'Ancien. **The elder girls (of the school),** les grandes. **2.** *s.* (*a*) Aîné, -ée; plus âgé, -ée. (*b*) *pl.* **Obey your elders!** obéissez à vos aînés! (*c*) *Ecc:* Ancien *m.*

elder[2], *s.* *Bot:* Elder(-tree), sureau *m.* *Dwarf e.,* hièble *f.* '**elder-berry,** *s.* Baie *f* de sureau.

elderly ['eldərli], *a.* D'un certain âge; assez âgé.

eldest ['eldəst], *a.* Aîné.

eldritch ['el(d)ritʃ], *a.* *Scot:* Affreux, effrayant.

elect¹ [i'lekt], *a.* Élu. The Lord Mayor elect, le futur Lord Maire. *s. Theol:* The elect, les élus *m.*

elect², *v.tr.* **1.** To elect to do sth., choisir de faire qch.; se décider à faire qch. **2.** Élire. (*a*) To elect s.o. (a) member, s.o. to be a member, élire qn député. (*b*) *Jur:* To elect domicile, élire domicile.

election [i'lekʃ(ə)n], *s.* Élection *f.* Parliamentary elections, élections législatives.

electioneering [ilekʃə'niːəriŋ], *s.* Propagande électorale.

elective [i'lektiv], *a.* Électif.

elector [i'lektər], *s.* **1.** Électeur *m*, votant *m.* **2.** *Hist:* Électeur (de Brandebourg, de Saxe).

electoral [i'lektərəl], *a.* Électoral, -aux.

electorate [i'lektəret], *s.* **1.** *Hist:* Électorat *m.* **2.** *Pol:* Corps électoral; les votants *m.*

electric [i'lektrik], *a.* Électrique.

electrical [i'lektrik(ə)l], *a.* **1.** Électrique. **2.** Electrical fitter, monteur-électricien *m.* *S.a.* ENGINEER¹ 1, ENGINEERING. **-ally,** *adv.* Électriquement. *E.* driven, actionné par électromoteur.

electrician [ilek'triʃ(ə)n], *s. Ind:* Monteur-électricien *m*; *F:* électricien *m.*

electricity [ilek'trisiti], *s.* Électricité *f.* Electricity works, centrale *f* électrique

electrification [ilektrifi'keiʃ(ə)n], *s.* **1.** Électrisation *f* (d'un corps). **2.** Électrification *f* (d'un chemin de fer).

electrify [i'lektrifai], *v.tr.* **1.** Électriser (un corps, *F:* son auditoire). **2.** Électrifier (un chemin de fer). **electrifying¹**, *a.* Électrisant. **electrifying²**, *s.* **1.** Électrisation *f.* **2.** Électrification *f.*

electro [i'lektro], *s. & v.tr. F:* **1.** = ELECTROPLATE¹, ². **2.** = ELECTROTYPE¹, ².

electro-, *comb. fm.* **e'lectro-'chemistry,** *s.* Électrochimie *f.* **e'lectro-de'posit,** *s.* Dépôt *m* galvanoplastique; dépôt électrolytique. **e'lectro-'magnet,** *s.* Électro-aimant *m.* **e'lectro-plate¹,** *s.* (*a*) Articles plaqués. (*b*) Articles argentés; couverts *mpl* en ruolz. **e'lectro-plate²,** *v.tr.* (*a*) Plaquer (un métal). (*b*) Argenter. **electro-plating,** *s.* (*a*) Plaqué *m.* (*b*) Argenture *f* (galvanique). **e'lectro-'therapy,** *s. Med:* Électrothérapie *f.* **e'lectro-'thermic, -thermi'onic,** *a.* Électrothermique.

electrocute [i'lektrokjut], *v.tr.* Électrocuter.

electrocution [ilektro'kjuʃ(ə)n], *s.* Électrocution *f.*

electrode [i'lektroud], *s.* Électrode *f.* *W.Tel:* Three-electrode valve, lampe à trois électrodes.

electrodynamics [i'lektrodai'namiks], *s.pl.* Électrodynamique *f.*

electrolier [ilektro'liːər], *s.* Lustre *m* électrique; (*ceiling type*) plafonnier *m*; (*hanging*) suspension *f.* Three-light e., lustre à trois lampes.

electrolyse [i'lektrolaːiz], *v.tr.* Électrolyser.

electrolysis [ilek'trolisis], *s.* Électrolyse *f.*

electrolyte [i'lektrolait], *s. El:* Électrolyte *m*; liquide excitateur.

electromotive [i'lektro'moutiv], *a.* Electromotive force, force électromotrice.

electromotor [i'lektro'moutər], *s.* Électromoteur *m.*

electron [i'lektrɔn], *s.* Électron *m.*

electronic [ilek'trɔnik], *a.* Électronique.

electropathy [ilek'trɔpaθi], *s. Med:* Électrothérapie *f.*

electroscope [i'lektroskoup], *s.* Électroscope *m.*

electrotype¹ [i'lektrotaip], *s.* **1.** Électrotype *m*; cliché *m* galvano; *F:* galvano *m.* **2.** = ELECTROTYPING.

electrotype², *v.tr.* Clicher (par électrotypie).

electrotyping, *s.* Électrotypie *f*, galvanoplastie *f*; clichage *m.*

electuary [i'lektjuəri], *s. Pharm:* Électuaire *m.*

elegance [elegəns], *s.* Élégance *f.*

elegant ['elegənt], *a.* **1.** Élégant. **2.** *U.S. & P:* Excellent; de premier ordre. **-ly,** *adv.* Élégamment.

elegiac [ele'dʒaiək]. **1.** *a.* Élégiaque. **2.** *s.pl.* Elegiacs, vers *m* élégiaques.

elegist ['eledʒist], *s.* Poète *m* élégiaque.

elegy ['eledʒi], *s.* Élégie *f.*

element ['elemənt], *s.* Élément *m.* **1.** *F:* To brave the elements, braver les éléments. *F:* To be in one's element, être dans son élément. To be out of one's element, être hors de son élément; être dépaysé. **2.** (*a*) The personal element, le facteur humain. (*b*) Partie *f* (d'un tout). *Battery of fifty elements,* batterie de cinquante éléments. **3.** *Ch:* Corps *m* simple. **4.** *pl.* Elements, rudiments *m* (d'une science).

elemental [ele'ment(ə)l], *a.* **1.** (Culte, etc.) des éléments. **2.** (*Of substance*) Élémentaire. **3.** *E.* truths, vérités premières.

elementary [ele'mentəri], *a.* Élémentaire. Elementary school, école primaire. *Sch:* E. algebra, rudiments *mpl* d'algèbre. *E. prudence demands that . . .,* la simple prudence veut que. . . .

elephant ['elefənt], *s.* **1.** (Bull) elephant, éléphant *m* (mâle). Cow elephant, éléphant femelle. White elephant, (i) éléphant blanc; (ii) *F:* objet *m*, cadeau *m*, d'une certaine valeur mais inutile et encombrant. **'elephant-driver,** *s.* Cornac *m.* **'elephant's ear,** *s. Bot:* Bégonia *m.*

elephantine [ele'fantin], *a.* **1.** Éléphantin. Elephantine wit, esprit lourd. **2.** (*Of proportions, etc.*) Éléphantesque.

elevate ['eleveit], *v.tr.* Élever (l'hostie, etc.); relever (son style); hausser, élever (la voix). **elevated,** *a.* **1.** Élevé. *E.* style, haut style. *E. personage,* personnage éminent. *F:* To be slightly elevated, être un peu gris; avoir son plumet. **2.** (*Overhead*) Surélevé; (*of railway*) aérien. **elevating,** *a.* **1.** (*Of discourse, etc.*) Qui élève l'esprit. **2.** Élévatoire; élévateur; (*organe*) de relevage. Elevating screw (*of gun*), vis *f* de pointage en hauteur. *Av:* Elevating power, force ascensionnelle.

elevation [ele'veiʃ(ə)n], *s.* **1.** Élévation *f* (de qn à un rang supérieur, de l'hostie). **2.** (*a*) Elevation above sea-level, altitude *f*, hauteur *f*, au-dessus du niveau de la mer. (*b*) Élévation (d'un astre). (*c*) *Artil:* Élévation; hausse *f*; pointage *m* en hauteur. **3.** (*Hill*) Élévation, éminence *f.* **4.** *Geom.Draw: Arch:* Élévation (d'un édifice, etc.). Sectional elevation, coupe verticale. Front elevation, façade *f.* **5.** Élévation, noblesse *f*, grandeur *f.*

elevator ['eleveitər], *s.* **1.** (*a*) Élévateur *m*; monte-charge(s) *m inv.* (*b*) *U.S:* Ascenseur *m.* (*c*) *U.S:* Silo *m* à élévateur pneumatique. **2.** *Av:* Gouvernail *m* de profondeur, d'altitude.

eleven [e'levn]. **1.** *num. a. & s.* Onze (*m*). They are only e., ils ne sont que onze, *F:* qu'onze. (For other phrases see EIGHT.) **2.** *s. Sp: Cr:* Équipe *f* de onze joueurs.

eleventh [i'levnθ], *num. a. & s.* Onzième *m.* At the eleventh hour, (i) *B:* à la onzième heure; (ii) *F:* au dernier moment; à la dernière heure. (*For other phrases see* EIGHTH.)

elf, *pl.* **elves** [elf, elvz], *s.* Elfe *m*; lutin *m*, lutine *f*. **'elf-struck,** *a.* Ensorcelé.

elfin ['elfin], *a.* D'elfe, de lutin, de fée.

elfish ['elfi$], *a.* (*a*) Des elfes, de lutin. (*b*) (*Of child*) Espiègle.

elicit [i'lisit], *v.tr.* Faire jaillir (qch. de caché); découvrir (la vérité); déduire, mettre au jour (des vérités d'après des données). To e. *the facts,* tirer les faits au clair. To e. *a reply from s.o.,* tirer, obtenir, une réponse de qn.

elide [i'laid], *v.tr.* Élider (une voyelle, etc.).

eligible ['elid3ibl], *a.* **1.** Éligible (en droit) (*to,* à). **2.** *E. for an occupation,* admissible à un emploi. **Eligible young man,** jeune homme acceptable; bon parti; parti sortable.

Elijah [e'laid3a]. *Pr.n.m. B.Hist:* Élie.

eliminable [i'liminəbl], *a.* Éliminable.

eliminate [i'limineit], *v.tr.* Éliminer (des matières toxiques, *Mth:* une inconnue); supprimer, écarter (une éventualité). **eliminating,** *a.* Éliminateur, -trice. *Sp:* Eliminating heats, épreuves éliminatoires.

elimination [ilimi'nei$(ə)n], *s.* Élimination *f.*

eliminative [i'liminətiv], *a.* Éliminateur, -trice.

eliminator [i'liminейtər], *s.* **1.** Éliminateur *m.* **2.** *W.Tel:* Dispositif *m* de filtrage du courant du secteur.

Elisha [i'lai$a]. *Pr.n.m. B.Hist:* Élisée.

elision [i'li3(ə)n], *s.* Élision *f.*

elixir [i'liksər], *s.* Élixir *m.*

Elizabethan [ilizə'bi:θən], *a. & s.* Élisabéthain; du règne de la reine Élisabeth.

elk [elk], *s.* *Z:* Élan *m.* **Canadian elk,** orignac *m.*

ell [el], *s.* *Meas:* (*a*) Aune *f.* *S.a.* INCH. (*b*) Aunée *f* (de drap, etc.).

ellipse [e'lips], *s.* *Geom:* Ellipse *f.*

ellipsis, *pl.* **-ses** [e'lipsis, -siz], *s.* *Gram:* Ellipse *f.*

elliptic(al) [e'liptik(əl)], *a.* *Gram: Geom:* Elliptique.

elm [elm], *s.* Orme *m.* Young elm, ormeau *m.* **Wych-elm,** orme blanc. **Elm-grove,** ormaie *f.*

elocution [elo'kju:$(ə)n], *s.* Élocution *f,* diction *f.*

elongate ['i:lɔŋgeit]. **1.** *v.tr.* Allonger, étendre. **2.** *v.i.* S'allonger, s'étendre.

elongation [i:lɔŋ'gei$(ə)n], *s.* (*a*) Allongement *m.* (*b*) Allonge *f*; prolongement *m* (d'une ligne).

elope [i'loup], *v.i.* (*Of daughter, wife*) S'enfuir avec un amant; se faire enlever. **They eloped,** ils ont pris la fuite.

elopement [i'loupmənt], *s.* Fuite *f* (de la maison paternelle, du domicile conjugal); enlèvement (consenti).

eloquence ['elokwəns], *s.* Éloquence *f.*

eloquent ['elokwənt], *a.* Éloquent. **Eloquent look,** regard qui en dit long. *Action e. of a generous nature,* action qui annonce une nature généreuse. **-ly,** *adv.* Éloquemment.

else [els]. **1.** *adv.* Autrement; ou bien. *Come in or else* go out, entrez ou bien sortez. **2.** (*a*) *a. or adv.* Anyone else, anybody else, (i) toute autre personne; tout autre, n'importe qui d'autre. (ii) (*Interrog.*) Can I speak to anyone else? *Did you see anybody else?* avez-vous vu encore quelqu'un? **Anything else,** (i) n'importe quoi d'autre. (ii) (*Interrog.*) *Anything else, madam?* et avec cela, madame? **Someone else, somebody else,** quelqu'un d'autre, un autre. **Something else,** autre chose *m.* **No one else, nobody else,** personne *m* d'autre, aucun autre, nul autre. **Nothing else,** rien *m* d'autre. *Nothing else, thank you,* plus rien, merci. **Who else?** qui d'autre? qui

encore? **What else?** quoi encore? quoi de plus? *What else can I do?* que puis-je faire d'autre, de mieux? *Everything* **else,** tout le reste. *S.a.* EVERYONE. **Little else,** pas grand'chose *m* d'autre. *He eats little else than bread,* il ne mange guère que du pain. **Much else,** encore beaucoup. (*b*) **Where else?** (i) où encore? (ii) en quel autre lieu? **Everywhere else,** partout ailleurs. **Somewhere else,** autre part; ailleurs. **Nowhere else,** nulle part ailleurs; en aucun autre lieu. **Anywhere else,** (i) n'importe où (ailleurs); partout ailleurs. (ii) (*Interrog.*) *Can I find some anywhere else?* puis-je en trouver ailleurs?

elsewhere ['elshwɛər], *adv.* Ailleurs; autre part.

elucidate [i'lju:sideit], *v.tr.* Élucider, éclaircir; porter la lumière dans (une question).

elucidation [ilju:si'dei$(ə)n], *s.* Élucidation *f,* éclaircissement *m.*

elude [i'lju:d], *v.tr.* Éluder (une question); tourner (la loi); esquiver, éviter (un coup); échapper à (la poursuite); se soustraire à (la justice). **To elude s.o.'s grasp,** échapper aux mains de qn.

elusive [i'lju:siv], *a.* Insaisissable, intangible. **Elusive reply,** réponse évasive. **-ly,** *adv.* Évasivement.

elusory [i'lju:səri], *a.* Évasif.

elves [elvz]. *See* ELF.

Elysian [i'lizian], *a. Myth:* Élyséen. **The Elysian fields,** les Champs *m* Élysées.

Elysium [i'liziəm]. *Pr.n. Myth:* L'Élysée *m.*

elytron, *pl.* **-tra** ['elitrɔn, -tra], *s. Ent:* Élytre *m.*

em [em], *s.* (La lettre) m. *S.a.* QUADRAT.

emaciated [i'mei$ieitid], *a.* Émacié, amaigri, décharné.

emaciation [imei$i'ei$(ə)n], *s.* Amaigrissement *m,* émaciation *f.*

emanate ['eməneit], *v.i.* Émaner (*from,* de).

emanation [emə'nei$(ə)n], *s.* Émanation *f.*

emancipate [i'mansipeit], *v.tr.* Émanciper (un mineur, les femmes); affranchir (un esclave).

emancipation [imansi'pei$(ə)n], *s.* Émancipation *f* (d'un mineur); affranchissement *m* (d'un esclave).

emancipator [i'mansipeitər], *s.* Émancipateur, -trice; affranchisseur *m.*

emasculate [i'maskjuleit], *v.tr.* Émasculer, châtrer.

emasculation [imaskju'lei$(ə)n], *s.* Émasculation *f.*

embalm [em'ba:m], *v.tr.* **1.** Embaumer (un cadavre). **2.** Embaumer, parfumer (l'air). **embalming,** *s.* Embaumement *m.*

embank [em'baŋk], *v.tr.* Encaisser, endiguer (un fleuve); remblayer (une route). **embanking,** *s.* Endiguement *m*; remblayage *m.*

embankment [em'baŋkmənt], *s.* **1.** = EMBANKING. **2.** (*a*) Digue *f*; levée *f* de terre. (*b*) Talus *m*; remblai *m,* banquette *f* (d'une route). **River embankment,** berge *f*; quai *m,* rive *f* d'un fleuve.

embargo, *pl.* **-oes** [em'ba:rgo, -ouz], *s.* Embargo *m,* séquestre *m.* *To lay an e. on a ship,* mettre l'embargo, l'arrêt, sur un navire. (*Of ship, goods*) *To be under an embargo,* être séquestré. *F:* **To put an embargo on all public rejoicings,** défendre, interdire, toutes réjouissances publiques.

embark [em'ba:rk]. **1.** *v.tr.* Embarquer (des troupes, etc.). **2.** *v.i.* S'embarquer (à bord d'un navire, *F:* dans une affaire).

embarkation [embɑ:r'kei$(ə)n], *s.* Embarquement *m.*

embarrass [em'barəs], *v.tr.* Embarrasser, gener (qn, les mouvements de qn); déconcerter (qn).

embarrassed, *a.* Embarrasse; dans l'embar-

16

ras; gêné. **To be embarrassed,** être embarrassé; se sentir gêné. **Embarrassed estate,** propriété grevée d'hypothèques.

embarrassment [em'barəsmənt], s. Embarras *m*, gêne *f*.

embassy ['embəsi], s. Ambassade *f*.

embattled [em'batld], a. *Arch: Her:* Crénelé.

embed [em'bed], *v.tr.* (**embedded**) Enfoncer, noyer (un clou dans un mur); encastrer, enchâsser, sceller (une plaque dans un mur).

embellish [em'beliʃ], *v.tr.* Embellir, orner, agrémenter (qch.); enjoliver (une robe, un récit).

embellishment [em'beliʃmənt], s. Embellissement *m*, ornement *m*, agrément *m*; enjolivure *f* (de robe, etc.).

ember[1] ['embər], s. (*Usu. pl.*) Braise *f*; charbon (ardent); *pl.* cendres ardentes.

Ember[2], *attrib.* *Ecc:* **Ember days,** les Quatre-Temps *m.* **Ember eve,** vigile *f* des Quatre-Temps.

embezzle [em'bezl], *v.tr.* Détourner, distraire, s'approprier (des fonds).

embezzlement [em'bezlmənt], s. Détournement *m* de fonds.

embezzler [em'bezlər], s. Détourneur *m* de fonds; déprédateur, -trice.

embitter [em'bitər], *v.tr.* Remplir d'amertume, enfieller (qn); aigrir (le caractère); envenimer (une querelle, etc.). **embittered,** a. Aigri (*by*, par); *F:* (cœur) ulcéré. **embittering,** s. Aigrissement *m* (de qn); envenimement *m*, aggravation *f* (d'une querelle).

emblazon [em'bleiz(ə)n], *v.tr.* Blasonner.

emblem ['emblem], s. Emblème *m*, symbole *m*; insigne (sportif); *Her:* devise *f*.

emblematic(al) [emble'matik(əl)], a. Emblématique.

embodiment [em'bodimənt], s. Incorporation *f*; incarnation *f*; personnification *f*.

embody [em'bodi], *v.tr.* (**embodied; embodying**) 1. Incarner. 2. Réaliser (une conception); mettre en application (un principe); personnifier (une qualité). 3. Incorporer (un article dans une loi). 4. Réunir, rassembler, organiser (des troupes).

embolden [em'bouldən], *v.tr.* Enhardir (*s.o. to do sth.*, qn à faire qch.).

embolism ['embolizm], s. *Med:* Embolie *f*.

emboss [em'bos], *v.tr.* Graver en relief; travailler en relief, en bosse; repousser, estamper (le métal); frapper, gaufrer (le cuir). **embossing,** s. Bosselage *m* (du métal); estampage *m*, repoussage *m* (du métal, du cuir); gaufrage *m* (du cuir). **Embossing punch,** repoussoir *m*.

embower [em'bauər], *v.tr.* *Lit:* Abriter (dans un berceau de verdure).

embrace[1] [em'breis], s. Étreinte *f*, embrassement *m*.

embrace[2], *v.tr.* 1. Embrasser, étreindre. 2. Embrasser (une carrière); adopter (une cause); profiter de, saisir (une occasion). 3. Embrasser (*in*, dans); contenir, renfermer (*in*, dans); comporter, comprendre (des sujets). 4. **To embrace a situation,** envisager une situation sous tous ses aspects.

embrasure [em'breizjər], s. Embrasure *f*.

embroider [em'broidər], *v.tr.* 1. *Needlew:* Broder. 2. *F:* Broder, enjoliver (un récit). **To embroider the story,** broder l'histoire; broder sur le canevas.

embroiderer [em'broidərər], s. Brodeur, -euse.

embroideress [em'broidəres], s.f. Brodeuse.

embroidery [em'broidəri], s. 1. *Needlew:* Broderie *f.* 2. *F:* Broderie, enjolivure *f* (d'un récit).

embroil [em'broil], *v.tr.* 1. (*a*) Brouiller, em-

brouiller (une affaire). (*b*) **To embroil a nation in a war,** entraîner une nation dans une guerre. 2. **To embroil s.o. with s.o.,** brouiller qn avec qn.

embroilment [em'broilmənt], s. 1. Brouillement *m*, embrouillement *m* (d'une affaire). 2. Brouille *f* (entre deux personnes).

embryo, *pl.* **-os** ['embrio, -ouz], s. *Biol:* Embryon *m.* **In embryo,** (i) (à l'état) embryonnaire; (ii) *F:* (avocat) en herbe.

embryonic [embri'onik], a. 1. *Biol:* Embryonnaire. 2. *F:* En germe.

emend [i'mend], *v.tr.* Corriger (un texte).

emendation [iːmen'deiʃ(ə)n], s. Émendation *f*.

emerald ['emərəld], s. Émeraude *f.* **The Emerald Isle,** la verte Irlande. **'emerald-'green,** a. & s. Vert (*m*) d'émeraude.

emerge [i'məːrdʒ], *v.i.* 1. Émerger (*from*, de); surgir, s'élever (de l'eau, etc.). 2. Déboucher (*from*, de); apparaître à l'orée (d'un bois); sortir (d'un trou, de l'enfance). 3. (*a*) (*Of difficulty*) Se dresser; surgir. (*b*) *From these facts it emerges that . . .,* de ces faits il paraît, il ressort, que. . . .

emergence [i'məːrdʒəns], s. Émergence *f* (d'un rayon lumineux); émersion *f* (d'un rocher).

emergency [i'məːrdʒənsi], s. Circonstance *f* critique; cas urgent, cas imprévu. **To provide for emergencies,** parer aux éventualités, à l'imprévu. **To rise to the emergency,** être, se montrer, à la hauteur de la situation, des circonstances. **In this emergency,** en cette conjoncture; en cette occurrence. **In case of emergency,** au besoin; en cas d'urgence. **Emergency repairs,** réparations d'urgence. **Emergency-brake,** frein de secours. **Emergency-exit,** sortie éventuelle, de secours.

emeritus [iː'meritəs], a. (Professeur) honoraire.

emery ['eməri], s. Émeri *m.* **Emery paper,** papier émerisé; papier d'émeri. **Emery-cloth,** toile *f* (d')émeri. **Emery-wheel,** meule *f* en émeri.

emetic [i'metik], a. & s. Émétique (*m*).

emigrant ['emigrənt], a. & s. Émigrant, -ante.

emigrate ['emigreit], *v.i.* Émigrer.

emigration [emi'greiʃ(ə)n], s. Émigration *f*.

eminence ['eminəns], s. Éminence *f.* 1. (*a*) Élévation *f* (de terrain); monticule *m.* (*b*) *Anat:* Saillie *f.* 2. Grandeur *f*, distinction *f.* 3. *Ecc:* (*Title of cardinal*) Your E., votre Éminence.

eminent ['eminənt], a. Éminent. **-ly,** *adv.* Éminemment; par excellence. *An e. respectable family,* une famille des plus honorables.

emir [e'miːər], s. Émir *m*.

emissary ['emisəri], s. Émissaire *m*.

emission [i'miʃ(ə)n], s. Émission *f*.

emit [i'mit, iː-], *v.tr.* 1. Dégager, émettre (de la chaleur); exhaler, répandre (une odeur); lancer (des étincelles); rendre (un son). *W.Tel:* Emitting station, poste émetteur, d'émission. 2. Émettre (du papier-monnaie, un avis).

emitter [i'mitər, iː-], s. 1. (*Pers.*) Émetteur *m* (de papier-monnaie, etc.). 2. *W.Tel:* Dull emitter valve, lampe *f* de faible consommation, à filament obscur. **Emitter station** = *emitting station.*

emollient [i'moliənt], a. & s. Émollient (*m*).

emolument [i'moljumənt], s. (*Usu. pl.*) Émoluments *mpl*, appointements *mpl*, traitement *m*.

emotion [i'mouʃ(ə)n], s. Émotion *f*; trouble *m*, attendrissement *m.* **To appeal to the emotions,** faire appel aux sentiments; *F:* toucher la corde sensible. *Voice touched with e.,* voix émue.

emotional [i'mouʃən(ə)l], a. Émotionnable. *To be e.,* s'attendrir facilement.

empanel [em'pan(ə)l], *v.tr.* (**empanelled**) *Jur:*

To **empanel a jury,** dresser la liste du jury ; former un tableau.

empennage [em'penedʒ], s. *Av :* Empennage *m.*

emperor ['empərər], s. Empereur *m.*

emphasis ['emfəsis], s. **1.** Force *f* ; (énergie *f* d')accentuation *f.* **2.** *To ask with e.,* demander avec insistance. *To lay* emphasis on a fact, souligner, faire ressortir, un fait. **3.** *Ling :* Accent *m* d'insistance.

emphasize ['emfəsaiz], *v.tr.* Accentuer, appuyer sur, souligner (un fait) ; faire ressortir, mettre en relief (une qualité).

emphatic [em'fatik], *a.* (Manière) énergique (de s'exprimer) ; (dénégation) absolue, énergique ; (ton) autoritaire ; (refus) positif, net, absolu. **-ally,** *adv.* **1.** Énergiquement, positivement ; (refuser) carrément, catégoriquement. **2.** En termes pressants.

empire ['empaiər], s. Empire *m.* To establish one's empire over sth., établir son empire sur qch. **Empire day,** fête nationale de l'Empire britannique (le 24 mai).

empiric(al) [em'pirik(ə)l], *a.* Empirique. **-ally,** *adv.* Empiriquement.

empiricism [em'pirisizm], s. Empirisme *m.*

emplacement [em'pleismənt], s. *Mil :* Emplacement *m* (d'un canon).

emplane [em'plein]. **1.** *v.i.* Monter en avion. **2.** *v.tr.* Faire monter (des troupes) en avion.

employ¹ [em'plɔi], s. Emploi *m.* To be in s.o.'s e., être au service de qn.

employ², *v.tr.* **1.** Employer (qn, son temps, etc.) ; faire usage de (la force, etc.). **2.** To employ oneself (in doing sth.), s'occuper (à faire qch.). *To be employed in doing sth.,* être occupé à faire qch. *To keep s.o. well employed,* donner de quoi faire à qn.

employable [em'plɔiəbl], *a.* Employable.

employee [emplɔi'i:], s. Employé *m.*

employer [em'plɔiər], s. *Ind :* Patron, patronne ; maître, maîtresse. *The big employers of labour,* les grands employeurs de main-d'œuvre.

employment [em'plɔimənt], s. **1.** Emploi *m* (de l'argent, etc.). **2.** Emploi, travail *m* ; place *f,* situation *f* ; occupation *f.* To be out of employment, être sans emploi ; chômer. *To find e. for s.o.,* placer, caser, qn. Employment agency, bureau *m* de placement ; (*for workmen*) service *m* d'embauche.

emporium [em'pɔ:riəm], s. **1.** Entrepôt *m* ; marché *m.* **2.** *F :* Grand(s) magasin(s).

empower [em'pauər], *v.tr.* **1.** *Jur :* Donner pouvoir, donner procuration, à (qn). **2.** *To e. s.o. to do sth.,* autoriser qn à faire qch. ; donner, conférer, plein(s) pouvoir(s) à qn pour faire qch.

empress ['empres], *s.f.* Impératrice.

emptiness ['em(p)tinəs], s. **1.** Vide *m* (d'une chambre, etc.). **2.** Néant *m,* vanité *f* (des plaisirs).

empty¹ ['em(p)ti]. **1.** *a.* Vide (*of,* de). (*a*) *Building standing e.,* immeuble inoccupé. *E. stomach,* estomac creux. 'To be taken on an empty stomach,' "à prendre à jeun." (*b*) *F :* To go empty away, s'en aller les mains vides. (*c*) *E. head, mind,* tête vide ; esprit creux, nul. (*d*) *E. words,* vaines paroles. *E. threats,* menaces en l'air. **2.** *s.pl. Com :* Empties, caisses *f* vides ; bouteilles *f* vides. **empty-'handed,** *a.* Les mains vides. *To return empty-handed, F :* revenir bredouille. **empty-'headed,** *a.* A la tête creuse.

empty². 1. *v.tr.* Vider ; décharger (un wagon) ; débourrer (une pipe) ; vidanger (une fosse d'aisance, un carter). **2.** *v.i.* (*a*) (*Of river, etc.*)

Se décharger, se déverser (*into,* dans). (*b*) (*Of hall*) Se dégarnir, se vider.

empyrean [empi'ri:ən, em'piriən], *a. & s.* Empyrée (*m*).

emu ['i:mju:], s. *Orn :* Émeu *m.*

emulate ['emjuleit], *v.tr.* Être l'émule de (qn) ; rivaliser avec, imiter (qn).

emulation [emju'lei∫(ə)n], s. Émulation *f.*

emulative ['emjulətiv], *a.* **1.** Plein d'émulation. **2.** *E. of s.o.,* qui rivalise ou tente de rivaliser avec qn.

emulator ['emjuleitər], s. Émule *mf* (*of,* de) ; émulateur, -trice.

emulous ['emjuləs], *a.* Émulateur, -trice (*of,* de).

emulsify [i'mʌlsifai], *v.tr.* Émulsionner.

emulsion [i'mʌl∫(ə)n], s. Émulsion *f.*

en [en], s. (La lettre) n *m. S.a.* QUADRAT.

enable [e'neibl], *v.tr.* To enable s.o. to do sth. (i) rendre qn capable, mettre qn à même, de faire qch. ; (ii) *Jur :* habiliter qn à faire qch. ; donner pouvoir à qn de faire qch.

enact [e'nakt], *v.tr.* **1.** *Jur :* Rendre, décréter (une loi) ; ordonner, arrêter, décréter (une mesure). As by law enacted, aux termes de la loi. **2.** *Lit :* Jouer, représenter (une tragédie) ; procéder à, accomplir (une cérémonie).

enactment [e'naktmənt], s. **1.** Promulgation *f* (d'une loi). **2.** Loi, ordonnance *f* ; décret *m.*

enamel¹ [e'nam(ə)l], s. **1.** Émail *m, pl.* émaux. (*a*) Niello enamels, émaux de niellure. (*b*) *The e. of the teeth,* l'émail des dents. **2.** Vernis *m* ; émail, *pl.* émails ; laque *f.* Enamel paint, peinture *f* au vernis ; *F :* ripolin *m.* Baked(-on) enamel, émail au four. **e'namel-ware,** s. Ustensiles *mpl* en fer émaillé. **e'namel-work,** s. **1.** Émaillure *f.* **2.** Peinture *f* sur émail.

enamel². 1. *v.tr.* (enamelled) **1.** Émailler (la porcelaine, etc.). **2.** Peindre au ripolin ; *F :* ripoliner ; vernir, vernisser (le fer, le cuir) ; glacer (le papier) ; *Phot :* émailler, satiner (une épreuve). Enamelled saucepan, casserole en fer émaillé. Enamelled tile, carreau vernissé. **enamelling,** s. (*a*) Émaillage *m.* (*b*) (*Art of enamelling*) Émaillure *f.* (*c*) Vernissage *m* (du fer, du cuir, etc.) ; glaçage *m* (du papier, etc.).

enameller [e'namələr], s. Émailleur, -euse.

enamour [e'namər], *v.tr.* Enamourer (qn) ; rendre (qn) amoureux. To be enamoured of, with, s.o., être amoureux, épris, de qn. To be enamoured of, with, sth., être passionné pour qch., être féru de qch.

encamp [en'kamp]. **1.** *v.tr.* (Faire) camper (une armée). **2.** *v.i.* Camper.

encampment [en'kampmənt], s. Campement *m* ; camp *m.*

encase [en'keis], *v.tr.* **1.** Encaisser, enfermer (*in,* dans). **2.** (*a*) Munir (qch.) d'une enveloppe ; blinder (un mécanisme). (*b*) *F :* Revêtir, recouvrir (*s.o. in sth.,* qn de qch.).

encasement [en'keismənt], s. **1.** Revêtement *m* ; enveloppe *f.* **2.** *Anat :* Emboîtement *m* (de deux os).

encash [en'ka∫], *v.tr.* Encaisser (un chèque).

encashment [en'ka∫mənt], s. **1.** Encaissement *m.* **2.** Recette *f,* rentrée *f.*

encaustic [en'kɔ:stik], *a. & s.* Encaustique (*f*).

encephalitis [ensefə'laitis], s. *Med :* Encéphalite *f.*

enchain [en't∫ein], *v.tr. Lit :* Enchaîner.

enchant [en't∫a:nt], *v.tr.* **1.** Enchanter, ensorceler. **2.** *Lit :* Enchanter, charmer, ravir.

enchanting, *a. Lit :* Enchanteur, -eresse ; ravissant, charmant. **-ly,** *adv.* A ravir ; d'une manière ravissante.

enchanter [en't∫ɑːntər], *s.* Enchanteur *m.*
enchantment [en't∫ɑːntmənt], *s.* Enchantement *m.* **I.** Ensorcellement *m.* **2.** Ravissement *m.*
enchantress [en't∫ɑːntres], *s.f.* Enchanteresse.
encircle [en'səːrkl], *v.tr.* Ceindre, encercler; envelopper, cerner (une armée); entourer (une armée, la taille). **encircling,** *s.* Encerclement *m.*
enclave[1] [en'kleːiv], *s.* **I.** Enclave *f.* **2.** Pièce *f* de terre en hache.
enclave[2], *v.tr.* Enclaver.
enclitic [en'klitik], *a. & s. Gram:* Enclitique (*f*).
enclose [en'kloːuz], *v.tr.* **I.** (*a*) Enclore, clôturer, enceindre (un champ) (*with,* de); entourer (l'ennemi, une ville). (*b*) Blinder; enfermer (un mécanisme) dans un carter. **2.** *Ecc:* Cloîtrer (une femme). **3.** Inclure, renfermer, enfermer (*in,* dans). **Enclosed (herewith) please find . . .,** veuillez trouver ci-inclus, ci-joint, sous ce pli. . . .
enclosure [en'klouʒər], *s.* **I.** (*a*) Renfermement *m,* clôture *f. Ecc:* Clôture, claustration *f* (de religieuses). (*b*) Enceinte *f,* clôture. **2.** (*a*) Enclos *m,* clos *m.* (*b*) *Turf:* Le pesage. **The public enclosures,** la pelouse. *The royal e.,* l'enceinte réservée pour le roi. **3.** *Com:* Pièce annexée; annexe *f.*
encloud [en'klaud], *v.tr. Lit:* Voiler, assombrir (le ciel); envelopper de nuages.
encomium, *pl.* **-ums** [en'koumiəm(z)], *s.* Panégyrique *m,* éloge *m,* louange *f.*
encompass [en'kʌmpəs], *v.tr.* **I.** Entourer, environner, ceindre (*with,* de). **2.** Envelopper, renfermer (*with, within,* dans). **3.** Méditer, comploter, ou consommer (la mort de qn).
encore[1] [ɔŋ'koːər], *s. & int.* Bis *m.*
encore[2], *v.tr.* Bisser (un passage, un acteur).
encounter[1] [en'kauntər], *s.* **I.** Rencontre *f.* **2.** (*a*) Rencontre (hostile); combat *m.* (*b*) Duel *m.* (*c*) *F:* **Encounter of wits,** assaut *m* d'esprit.
encounter[2], *v.tr.* Rencontrer (un obstacle); éprouver, essuyer (des difficultés); affronter, aborder (l'ennemi).
encourage [en'kʌredʒ], *v.tr.* **I.** Encourager, enhardir (qn). **2.** Encourager, inciter (qn à faire qch.). **3.** Favoriser (les arts); encourager (une croyance). **encouraging,** *a.* Encourageant. **-ly,** *adv.* D'une manière encourageante.
encouragement [en'kʌredʒmənt], *s.* Encouragement *m.*
encroach [en'krout∫], *v.i.* To e. (up)on sth., empiéter sur (une terre, etc.); entamer (son capital). *The sea is encroaching upon the land,* la mer gagne du terrain. *To e. upon s.o.'s time,* abuser du temps de qn.
encroachment [en'krout∫mənt], *s.* Empiétement *m* (on, sur). (*a*) *E. upon s.o.'s rights,* usurpation *f* des droits de qn. (*b*) Anticipation *f* (sur la voie publique).
encrust [en'krʌst], *v.tr.* (*a*) Incruster. (*b*) Couvrir d'une croûte; encroûter (*with,* de).
encumber [en'kʌmbər], *v.tr.* **I.** Encombrer (*with,* de); embarrasser, gêner (qn, le mouvement); surcharger (le marché). **2. Encumbered estate,** propriété grevée de dettes, d'hypothèques.
encumbrance [en'kʌmbrəns], *s.* **I.** Embarras *m,* charge *f. To be an e. to s.o.,* être à charge à qn. *Without (family) encumbrances,* sans charges de famille. **2.** *Jur:* (*a*) Charges (d'une succession). *To free an estate from encumbrances,* dégrever une propriété. (*b*) Servitude *f.*
encyclic(al) [en'siklik(əl)], *a. & s. R.C.Ch:* Encyclique (*f*).
encyclopaedia [ensaiklo'piːdia], *s.* Encyclopédie *f.*

encyclopaedic [ensaiklo'piːdik], *a.* Encyclopédique.
encyclopaedist [ensaiklo'piːdist], *s.* Encyclopédiste *m.*
encysted [en'sistid], *a.* Enkysté.
end[1] [end], *s.* **I.** (*a*) Bout *m,* extrémité *f*; fin *f* (d'un livre); queue *f* (d'une procession). *The upper end of the table,* le haut bout de la table. *Fb: To change ends,* changer de camp. **The end house of the street,** la dernière maison de la rue. *F:* **To have the right end of the stick,** tenir le bon bout. **To get, have, hold of the wrong end of the stick,** comprendre de travers, à rebours. **To begin, start, at the wrong end,** brider l'âne par la queue. **To keep one's end up,** (i) *Cr:* maintenir son guichet intact; (ii) *F:* ne pas se laisser démonter; tenir bon. *Adv.phrs.* **End to end,** bout à bout. **From one end to end,** d'un bout à l'autre; de bout en bout. **On end.** (i) (*Of barrel, etc.*) Debout; sur bout. *S.a.* HAIR I. (ii) **Two hours on end,** (pendant) deux heures de suite, d'affilée. **Straight on end, right on end,** de suite; consécutivement. **End on,** bout à bout. *Nau:* (*Of ships*) **To meet end on,** se rencontrer nez à nez. *S.a.* DEAD-END, DEEP I. 1, LOOSE[1] 1. (*b*) *I.C.E:* **Big end,** tête *f* de bielle. **Small end,** pied *m* de bielle. (*c*) Tronçon *m* (de mât, etc.); tronche *f* (de câble). **Candle-end,** bout de chandelle. **2.** Limite *f,* borne *f. To the ends of the earth,* jusqu'au bout du monde. **3.** Bout, fin (du mois); issue *f* (d'une réunion); terme *m* (d'un procès, etc.). **We shall never hear the end of the matter,** cela va être des commérages sans fin. **And there's an end of it!** et voilà tout! **There's no end to it,** cela n'en finit pas. **To make an end of sth.; to put an end to sth.; to bring sth. to an end,** en finir avec qch.; achever qch.; mettre fin à (un abus, etc.). **To draw to an end,** tirer, toucher, à sa fin. **To come to an end,** prendre fin; arriver à son terme. **To be at an end,** (i) (*of resources*) être épuisé; (ii) (*of time*) être accompli; (iii) (*of action*) être terminé, fini, achevé. *To be at the end of one's resources,* être au bout de ses ressources. *At the end of (the) winter,* au sortir de l'hiver. *At the end of the six months allowed,* au délai de six mois. **In the end,** (i) à la longue, avec le temps; (ii) à la fin; enfin; en fin de compte. *F:* **No end,** à n'en plus finir. **No end of . . .,** infiniment de . . .; une infinité de. . . . **It'll do you no end of good,** ça vo〮s fera énormément de bien. *No end of books,* des livres sans nombre. *No end of money,* un argent fou. **To think no end of s.o.,** avoir une très haute idée de qn. *He thinks no end of himself,* il se gobe. **To make a good end,** avoir une belle mort; mourir en beauté. **To come to a bad end,** mal finir. **To meet one's end,** trouver la mort. **4.** Fin, but *m,* dessein *m.* **Private ends,** intérêt(s) personnel(s). *To gain, attain, one's ends,* en venir, parvenir, à ses fins. **With this end in view,** dans ce but; à cet effet. **For, to, this end,** à cet effet; dans ce dessein. **To the end that . . .,** afin que + *sub.* **To no end,** en vain; vainement. **'end-paper,** *s. Bookb:* Garde *f.* **'end-play,** *s. Mec.E:* Jeu longitudinal. **'end-thrust,** *s. Mec.E:* Poussée axiale. **'end-ways, 'end-wise,** *adv.* **I.** (*a*) De champ, debout. (*b*) End-ways on, avec le bout en avant. **2.** (*End to end*) Bout à bout. **3.** Longitudinalement.
end[2]. **I.** *v.tr.* Finir, achever, terminer (un ouvrage); conclure, clore (un discours). *To end war,* mettre un terme aux guerres. **To end off, up,** *a speech with a quotation,* conclure un discours avec une citation. **In order to end the matter,** pour en finir. **It is ended and done with,** (i) c'est

fini et bien fini ; (ii) il n'y a plus à revenir là-dessus. **2.** *v.i.* Finir, se terminer. *All stories end (up) like that,* toutes les histoires finissent de cette manière. *He ended by insulting me,* il finit par m'injurier. *To end in a point,* aboutir, se terminer, en pointe. *F:* **To end in smoke,** n'aboutir à rien ; s'en aller en fumée. **ended,** *a.* **1.** Fini, terminé. **2.** Round-ended, à bout rond. Two-ended, à deux bouts. **ending,** *s.* **1.** Terminaison *f*, achèvement *m.* **2.** Fin *f*, conclusion *f* (d'un ouvrage). **3.** *Gram:* Désinence *f*, terminaison.

endanger [en'deindʒər], *v.tr.* Mettre en danger ; exposer, hasarder, risquer (sa vie, etc.) ; compromettre (des intérêts).

endear [en'diːər], *v.tr.* Rendre cher (*to,* à). **endearing,** *a.* **1.** Qui inspire l'affection. **2.** (Mot) tendre, affectueux. **-ly,** *adv.* Tendrement, affectueusement.

endearments [en'diːərmənts], *s.pl.* Caresses *f* ; mots *m* tendres.

endeavour[1] [en'devər], *s.* Effort *m*, tentative *f*. **To use, make, every endeavour to . . .,** faire tous ses efforts, tout son possible, pour. . . .

endeavour[2], *v.i.* *To e. to do sth.,* s'efforcer, essayer, tâcher, de faire qch. ; chercher à faire qch.

endemic [en'demik]. **1.** *a.* Endémique. **2.** *s.* Endémie *f* ; maladie *f* endémique.

endive ['endiv], *s.* Chicorée *f* endive. **Curled endive,** chicorée frisée. **Broad-leaved endive,** endive *f*, (e)scarole *f*.

endless ['endləs], *a.* **1.** (*a*) (Vis, voyage) sans fin. (*b*) Sans bornes ; infini. **Endless conversations,** raisonnements à perte de vue. **2.** (*In time*) (*a*) Sans fin ; éternel. *It is an e. task,* c'est à n'en plus finir. (*b*) (*Of pain, etc.*) Continuel, incessant ; (*of chatter, etc.*) intarissable. **-ly,** *adv.* Sans fin ; sans cesse, éternellement ; perpétuellement, intarissablement.

endocarditis ['endokɑːr'daitis], *s.* *Med:* Endocardite *f*.

endocarp ['endokɑːrp], *s.* *Bot:* Endocarpe *m*.

endocrine ['endokrain], *a. & s.* (Glande *f*) endocrine, à sécrétion interne.

endogamy [en'dogəmi], *s.* *Anthr:* Endogamie *f*.

endorse [en'dɔːrs], *v.tr.* **1.** Endosser (un document) ; viser (un passeport). *To e. sth. on a document, to e. a document with sth.,* mentionner qch. au verso d'un document. *Com:* *To e. a bill,* avaliser un effet. **To endorse back a bill to drawer,** contre-passer un effet au tireur. **2.** Appuyer, venir à l'appui de (l'opinion de qn) ; souscrire à (une décision).

endorsee [endɔːr'siː], *s.* *Fin:* Endossataire *mf*.

endorsement [en'dɔːrsmənt], *s.* **1.** Endossement *m*, endos *m* (d'une lettre de change) ; (*on passport, etc.*) mention spéciale. **2.** Approbation *f* (d'une action) ; adhésion *f* (à une opinion).

endorser [en'dɔːrsər], *s.* *Fin:* Endosseur *m*.

endosmosis [endos'mousis], *s.* *Ph:* Endosmose *f*.

endow [en'dau], *v.tr.* Doter (qn, une église) (*with,* de). **To endow a bed in a hospital,** fonder un lit dans un hôpital. *Endowed with great talents,* doué de grands talents.

endowment [en'daumənt], *s.* **1.** (*a*) Dotation *f*. (*b*) Fondation (léguée à un hospice, etc.). (*c*) **Endowment assurance,** assurance *f* en cas de vie ; assurance à terme fixe, à dotation. **2.** Don (naturel).

endue [en'djuː], *v.tr.* *Lit:* Revêtir (qn d'une dignité, etc.). **To be endued with a quality,** être doué d'une qualité.

endurable [en'djuərəbl], *a.* Supportable, endurable.

endurance [en'djuərəns], *s.* **1.** (*a*) Endurance *f*, résistance *f*. **To have great powers of endurance,** être dur à la fatigue, au mal. **Beyond endurance,** insupportable, intolérable. (*b*) **Endurance test,** (i) *Mec.E:* essai *m* de durée ; (ii) *Sp:* épreuve *f* d'endurance. **2.** Patience *f*, longanimité *f*.

endure [en'djuər]. **1.** *v.tr.* Supporter, endurer (des insultes, etc.). *I can't e. being disturbed,* je ne peux pas souffrir qu'on vienne me déranger. **2.** *v.i.* Durer, rester. **enduring,** *a.* **1.** Durable, permanent. **Enduring evil,** mal qui persiste. **Enduring remorse,** remords vivace. **2.** Patient, longanime, endurant. **-ly,** *adv.* D'une manière durable.

enema ['enema, e'niːma], *s.* *Med:* **1.** Lavement *m*. **2.** Appareil *m* à lavements ; irrigateur *m*.

enemy ['enəmi, -ni-]. **1.** *s.* (*a*) Ennemi, -e. **To be one's own (worst) enemy,** se desservir soi-même. **To be an enemy to discipline,** être ennemi de la discipline. *F:* **How goes the enemy?** quelle heure est-il? (*b*) *Coll.* **The enemy,** l'ennemi, l'adversaire *m*. **2.** *a.* **The enemy fleet,** la flotte ennemie.

energetic [enər'dʒetik], *a.* Énergique. **-ally,** *adv.* Énergiquement.

energize ['enərdʒaiz], *v.tr.* (*a*) Donner de l'énergie à (qn) ; stimuler (qn). (*b*) *El:* Aimanter (l'âme d'une bobine, etc.) ; amorcer (une dynamo). **energizing,** *a.* **1.** Stimulant, activant ; (nourriture) énergétique. **2.** *El:* **Energizing circuit,** circuit d'aimantation ; circuit d'amorçage.

energumen [enər'gjuːmən], *s.* Énergumène *m*.

energy ['enərdʒi], *s.* **1.** Énergie *f*, force *f*, vigueur *f*. **2.** *Mec:* Énergie, travail *m*. **Kinetic energy,** force vive ; énergie cinétique.

enervate ['enərveit], *v.tr.* Affaiblir, amollir, énerver (le corps, la volonté).

enervation [enər'veiʃ(ə)n], *s.* **1.** Affaiblissement *m*, aveulissement *m*. **2.** Mollesse *f*.

enfeeble [en'fiːbl], *v.tr.* Affaiblir (qn).

enfeoff [en'fef], *v.tr.* *A:* **1.** Investir, ensaisiner, (qn) d'un fief. **2.** Inféoder (une terre).

enfilade[1] [enfi'leid], *s.* *Mil:* Enfilade *f*.

enfilade[2], *v.tr.* *Mil:* Enfiler (une tranchée, etc.). **enfilading,** *a.* (Tir) d'enfilade.

enfold [en'fould], *v.tr.* Envelopper (*in, with,* dans). **To enfold s.o. in one's arms,** étreindre, embrasser, qn.

enforce [en'fɔːrs], *v.tr.* **1.** Faire valoir (un argument) ; appuyer (une demande). **2.** Mettre en vigueur, exécuter (une loi). **To enforce one's rights,** faire valoir ses droits. **To enforce the law,** appliquer la loi. **To enforce the blockade,** rendre le blocus effectif. **3.** *To e. a rule,* faire observer un règlement. **To enforce obedience,** se faire obéir. *To e. one's will on s.o.,* imposer sa volonté à qn.

enforceable [en'fɔːrsəbl], *a.* (Contrat) exécutoire.

enforcement [en'fɔːrsmənt], *s.* *Jur:* Exécution *f*, mise *f* en vigueur, application *f* (d'une loi).

enfranchise [en'frantʃaiz], *v.tr.* Admettre au suffrage (un citoyen).

enfranchisement [en'frantʃizmənt], *s.* *Pol:* Admission *f* (d'un citoyen) au suffrage.

engage [en'geidʒ], *v.tr. & i.* **1.** Engager (sa parole, son honneur). **To engage (oneself) to do sth.,** s'engager, s'obliger, à faire qch. **2.** (*a*) Engager, prendre (un domestique) ; embaucher (des ouvriers). (*b*) Retenir, réserver (une chambre, etc.) ; louer (un taxi). **3.** Occuper (qn) ; fixer (l'attention) ; attirer, gagner (l'affection). **To engage s.o. in conversation,** lier conversation, entrer en conversation, avec qn. **4.** **To engage**

the enemy, en venir aux prises avec, attaquer, l'ennemi; donner. **5.** (*a*) Mettre en prise (un engrenage). (*b*) *v.i.* (*Of cog-wheel*) (S')engrener, se mettre en prise (*with*, avec). **engage in,** *v.i.* To engage in battle, engager le combat. To **engage in conversation with s.o.,** entrer en conversation avec qn. To engage in politics, s'embarquer, se lancer, dans la politique. **engaged,** *a.* **1.** Engaged (to be married), fiancé. *To become e.,* se fiancer. **2.** Occupé, pris. Are you engaged? êtes-vous occupé? (*to taxi-driver*) êtes-vous libre? **3.** This seat is engaged, cette place est retenue, prise. *Tp:* 'Line engaged,' "ligne occupée." **4.** *Mec.E:* (*Of gear-wheels, etc.*) En prise. **engaging,** *a.* Engageant, attrayant, séduisant. **engagement** [en'geidʒmənt], *s.* **1.** Engagement *m*, promesse *f*, obligation *f*. To enter into an **engagement,** prendre, contracter, un engagement. *Com:* **To meet one's engagements,** faire face à ses engagements. **Owing to a previous engagement,** à cause d'une promesse antérieure. Social **engagements,** invitations *fpl* dans le monde. To **have an engagement,** être pris. Engagement book, agenda *m*. **2.** (*a*) Engagement (de domestiques). (*b*) Poste *m*, situation *f* (de domestique, de secrétaire). **3.** Fiançailles *fpl*. Engagement ring, anneau *m*, bague, de fiançailles. **4.** *Mil:* *Navy:* Combat *m*, action *f*. **5.** *Mec.E:* Mise *f* en prise; embrayage *m*.
engender [en'dʒendər], *v.tr.* Faire naître (un effet); engendrer (un sentiment).
engine ['endʒin], *s.* **1.** Machine *f*, appareil *m*. Pumping engine, machine d'épuisement. *S.a.* FIRE-ENGINE. **2.** (*a*) (Steam-)engine, machine à vapeur. Double-expansion engine, machine à double détente. Auxiliary engine, petit cheval. *S.a.* DONKEY-ENGINE, TRACTION-ENGINE. (*b*) *Rail:* Locomotive *f*. To sit with one's face to the engine, s'asseoir dans le sens (de la marche) du train. **3.** Moteur *m*. Internal-combustion engine, moteur à combustion interne. Gas engine, moteur à gaz. Side-valve engine, moteur à soupapes en chapelle. Overhead-valve engine, moteur à soupapes en tête. **'engine-'bed,** *s.* Bâti *m* du moteur. **'engine-driver,** *s.* Mécanicien *m*. **'engine-house,** *s.* Bâtiment *m* des machines. **'engine-oil,** *s.* Huile *f* à graisser. **'engine-room,** *s.* **1.** Salle *f* des machines. **2.** *Nau:* Chambre *f* des machines. **'engine-shed,** *s.* Garage *m*, dépôt *m*, de locomotives. **'engine-turn,** *v.tr.* *Metalw:* Guillocher.
-engined ['endʒind], *a.* Twin-engined, (i) à deux machines; (ii) bimoteur. Three-engined, trimoteur.
engineer[1] [endʒi'ni:ər], *s.* **1.** Ingénieur *m*. Consulting engineer, ingénieur consultant. Mining engineer, ingénieur des mines. Electrical engineer, ingénieur électricien. Mechanical engineer, ingénieur mécanicien. Naval engineer, ingénieur maritime. **2.** *Nau:* Mécanicien *m*. **3.** *Mil:* Soldat *m* du génie. The Engineers, le génie. **4.** Combinateur, -trice; *Pej:* machinateur, -trice (d'un projet).
engineer[2], *v.tr.* Machiner (un coup); manigancer (une affaire). **engineering,** *s.* (i) Le génie; (ii) la construction mécanique. Mechanical engineering, l'industrie *f* mécanique. Electrical engineering, la technique électrique. Engineering college, école des arts et métiers.
England ['ingland]. *Pr.n.* L'Angleterre *f*. *In E.,* en Angleterre.
English ['ingliʃ]. **I.** *a. & s.* Anglais, -aise. *Typ:* Old English, gothique *f*. **2.** *s. Ling:* L'anglais *m*; la langue anglaise. *What is the E.*

for . . .? comment dit-on en anglais . . .? The **King's English,** l'anglais correct.
Englishman, *pl.* **-men** ['ingliʃmən, -men], *s.m.* Anglais.
Englishwoman, *pl.* **-women** ['ingliʃwumən, -wimen], *s.f.* Anglaise.
engraft [en'graːft], *v.tr.* **1.** Greffer (*into, upon,* sur). *Surg:* Implanter (de la peau). **2.** *Sound principles had been engrafted in him,* on lui avait inculqué de bons principes.
engrave [en'greiv], *v.tr.* Graver (des caractères). Engraved on the memory, gravé dans la mémoire.
engraving, *s.* (*Process or print*) Gravure *f*; (*print*) estampe *f*. Wood e., gravure sur bois. Half-tone engraving, similigravure *f*.
engraver [en'greivər], *s.* Graveur *m*.
engross [en'grous], *v.tr.* **1.** *Jur:* (*a*) Écrire (un document) en grosse. (*b*) Rédiger (un document). **2.** S'emparer de, accaparer (la conversation). **3.** Absorber, occuper (qn, l'attention). **To be engrossed in one's work,** être tout entier à son travail. *To become engrossed in sth.,* s'absorber dans qch.
engulf [en'gʌlf], *v.tr.* Engloutir, engouffrer. *To be engulfed (in the sea),* s'engouffrer, sombrer, dans les flots.
enhance [en'haːns], *v.tr.* Rehausser (le mérite de qch.); augmenter, accroître (le plaisir); mettre en valeur, relever (la beauté de qn).
enigma [e'nigma], *s.* Énigme *f*. **To solve the enigma,** trouver le mot de l'énigme.
enigmatic(al) [enig'matik(əl)], *a.* Énigmatique.
enjoin [en'dʒɔin], *v.tr.* Enjoindre, prescrire, imposer. To enjoin prudence (up)on s.o., recommander la prudence à qn. To enjoin (on) **s.o. to do sth.,** enjoindre, ordonner, à qn de faire qch.
enjoy [en'dʒɔi], *v.tr.* **1.** Aimer, goûter; prendre plaisir à (qch.). To enjoy one's dinner, trouver le dîner bon. To e. a pipe, savourer une pipe. How did you enjoy your holidays? avez-vous passé de bonnes vacances? **To enjoy oneself,** s'amuser, se divertir; s'en donner à cœur joie. He enjoys life, il sait jouir de la vie. **To enjoy doing sth.,** prendre plaisir, trouver (du) plaisir, à faire qch. **2.** Jouir de, posséder (une fortune, la confiance de qn). **To enjoy good health,** jouir d'une bonne santé.
enjoyable [en'dʒɔiəbl], *a.* (Séjour, etc.) agréable; (mets) savoureux. *We had a most e. evening,* nous avons passé une excellente soirée. **-ably,** *adv.* Agréablement; avec plaisir.
enjoyment [en'dʒɔimənt], *s.* **1.** *Jur:* Jouissance *f* (d'un droit, etc.). **2.** Plaisir *m*.
enlarge [en'laːdʒ]. **1.** *v.tr.* (*a*) Agrandir; accroître, augmenter (sa fortune); élargir (un trou). *Phot:* Agrandir (un cliché). *Med:* Enlarged heart, hypertrophie *f* du cœur. (*b*) Développer, élargir (l'intelligence, etc.); amplifier (une idée). **2.** *v.i.* (*a*) S'agrandir, s'étendre, s'élargir. (*b*) To enlarge upon . . ., s'étendre sur, discourir longuement sur (un sujet).
enlargement [en'laːdʒmənt], *s.* Agrandissement *m*; accroissement *m* (d'une fortune); élargissement *m* (d'un trou); augmentation *f*. *Phot:* Agrandissement. *Med:* Hypertrophie *f* (du cœur).
enlarger [en'laːdʒər], *s.* *Phot:* Agrandisseur *m*, amplificateur *m*.
enlighten [en'laitn], *v.tr.* To enlighten s.o. on a subject, éclairer une s.o. un sujet. **enlightened,** *a.* (*Of pers., mind*) Éclairé. *In these e. days,* en ce siècle de lumières.
enlightenment [en'laitnmənt], *s.* **1.** Éclaircisse-

ments *mpl* (*on*, sur). **2.** Age of enlightenment, siècle *m* de lumières.

enlist [en'list]. **I.** *v.tr.* (*a*) *Mil:* Enrôler (un soldat). (*b*) *F:* Enrôler, *F:* racoler (des partisans). To enlist the services of s.o., s'assurer le concours de qn. **2.** *v.i.* (*Of soldier*) S'engager, s'enrôler.

enlistment [en'listmənt], *s. Mil:* Engagement *m*, enrôlement *m*.

enliven [en'laiv(ə)n], *v.tr.* (*a*) Animer (qn, une discussion); stimuler (les affaires). (*b*) Égayer (un tableau, une fête).

enmity ['enmiti], *s.* Inimitié *f*, hostilité *f*. At enmity with s.o., en guerre ouverte avec qn.

ennoble [e'noubl], *v.tr.* **I.** Anoblir (un roturier). **2.** Ennoblir (qn, le caractère).

enormity [e'nɔːrmiti], *s.* Énormité *f* (d'un crime).

enormous [e'nɔːrməs], *a.* Énorme; colossal, -aux; (succès) fou. **-ly**, *adv.* Énormément.

enough [i'nʌf]. **I.** *a. & s.* Assez. E. money, money e., assez d'argent. E. to cover a sixpence, de quoi couvrir une pièce de six pence. *F:* I've had enough of it, j'en ai assez. *That's e.*, (i) cela suffit; (ii) en voilà assez! More than enough, plus qu'il n'en faut. Have you enough to pay the bill? avez-vous de quoi payer? Enough said! assez parlé! brisons là! *One word was e. to prove that . . .*, il a suffi d'un mot pour prouver que. . . . *It was e. to drive one crazy*, c'était à vous rendre fou. *S.a.* SPARE² 2. **2.** *adv.* (*a*) Good enough, assez bon. It's a good e. reason, c'est une raison comme une autre. (*b*) You know well enough what I mean, vous savez très bien ce que je veux dire. Curiously enough . . ., chose curieuse. . . . *S.a.* SURE 1. (*c*) (*Disparaging*) She sings well enough, elle chante passablement. It is well e. in its way, but . . ., ce n'est pas si mal en son genre, mais. . . .

enplane [en'plein], *v.i. & tr.* = EMPLANE.

enquire [en'kwaiər], *v.* = INQUIRE.

enquiry [en'kwaiəri], *s.* = INQUIRY.

enrage [en'reidʒ], *v.tr.* Rendre (qn) furieux; faire enrager (qn).

enrapture [en'raptjər], *v.tr.* Ravir, enchanter, transporter (un auditoire).

enrich [en'ritʃ], *v.tr.* Enrichir; amender (la terre). *Enriched with gold*, rehaussé d'or.

enrichment [en'ritʃmənt], *s.* Enrichissement *m*.

enrol(l) [en'roul], *v.tr.* (**enrolled**) Enrôler, encadrer (des recrues); embrigader, embaucher (des balayeurs); immatriculer (des étudiants). *To e.* (*oneself*) *in the army*, s'enrôler, s'engager, dans l'armée. *To e. for a course of lectures*, se faire inscrire pour un cours.

enrolment [en'roulmənt], *s.* Enrôlement *m* (de soldats); engagement *m*, embauche *f* (d'ouvriers).

ensconce [en'skɔns], *v.tr.* To ensconce oneself *in a corner, in an armchair*, se nicher dans un coin, se rencogner dans un angle; se camper dans un fauteuil.

enshrine [en'ʃrain], *v.tr.* Enchâsser (une relique, une image) (*in*, dans).

ensign ['ensain], *s.* **I.** Étendard *m*, drapeau *m*. *Nau:* Pavillon national; enseigne *f* de poupe. White ensign, pavillon de la Marine anglaise. Red ensign = pavillon marchand. **2.** *Mil: A:* Porte-drapeau *m inv*, enseigne *m*.

enslave [en'sleiv], *v.tr.* Réduire à l'esclavage; asservir. *F:* To enslave hearts, captiver, enjôler, les cœurs.

enslavement [en'sleivmənt], *s.* Asservissement *m*.

ensnare [en'snɛər], *v.tr.* Prendre (qn) au piège.

ensue [en'sjuː], *v.i.* S'ensuivre. *The evils that ensued on, from, this misunderstanding*, les maux qui se sont ensuivis, qui ont résulté, de ce malentendu. A long silence ensued, il se fit un long silence. **ensuing**, *a.* (An, jour) suivant; (événement) subséquent.

ensure [en'ʃuər], *v.tr.* **I.** Assurer (*against, from*, contre); garantir (de). **2.** (*a*) Assurer (le succès); réaliser (une guérison). (*b*) *To e. s.o. enough to live on*, assurer à qn de quoi vivre.

entablature [en'tablətjər], *s. Arch:* Entablement *m*.

entail¹ [en'teil], *s. Jur:* **I.** Substitution *f* (d'héritiers). **2.** Bien substitué.

entail², *v.tr.* **I.** *Jur:* To entail an estate (on s.o.), substituer un bien (au profit de qn). **2.** (*Of actions*) Amener, entraîner (des conséquences); occasionner (des dépenses); comporter (des difficultés).

entangle [en'taŋgl], *v.tr.* **I.** Empêtrer. *To get entangled in the seaweed*, s'empêtrer dans les algues. *To get entangled in a shady business*, se trouver entraîné dans une affaire louche. **2.** Emmêler (les cheveux, du fil); enchevêtrer; embrouiller.

entanglement [en'taŋglmənt], *s.* **I.** Embrouillement *m*, enchevêtrement *m*. *S.a.* WIRE¹ 1. **2.** Embarras *m* (de voitures, etc.).

enter ['entər], *v.* (**entered**) I. *v.i.* Entrer (*into, through*, dans, par). *Th:* Enter Hamlet, Hamlet entre. II. **enter**, *v.tr.* **I.** (*a*) Entrer, pénétrer, dans (une maison); monter dans (une voiture). *S.a.* HEAD¹ 1. (*b*) Faire entrer. *Artil:* To enter the charge, enfoncer la gargousse. **2.** To enter the Army, the Navy, entrer au service; se faire soldat, se faire marin. **3.** (*a*) To enter a name on a list, inscrire, porter, un nom sur une liste. To enter a horse for a race, engager un cheval dans une course. *Abs.* To enter for a race, se faire inscrire, s'engager, pour une course. *S.a.* EXAMINATION 2. (*b*) *Com:* To enter (up) an item in the ledger, porter un article au grand livre. E. that to me, mettez cela à mon compte. (*c*) To enter an action against s.o., intenter un procès à qn. To e. a protest, protester formellement.

enter into, *v.i.* **I.** (*a*) To enter into relations with s.o., entrer en relations, entamer des relations, avec qn. To enter into a bargain, a contract, conclure un marché; passer un contrat. To enter into explanations, fournir des explications; s'expliquer. (*b*) Prendre part à (un complot, etc.). **2.** To enter into s.o.'s feelings, partager les sentiments de qn. To e. into the spirit of the game, se laisser gagner par l'esprit du jeu. **enter on, upon**, *v.i.* Entrer en (fonctions, etc.); entreprendre (une tâche); débuter dans (une carrière); entamer (des négociations). *To e. upon one's sixtieth year*, entrer dans sa soixantième année.

enteric [en'terik], *a. Med:* Entérique. Enteric fever, fièvre *f* typhoïde.

enteritis [ente'raitis], *s. Med:* Entérite *f*.

enterprise ['entərpraiz], *s.* **I.** = UNDERTAKING 2. **2.** Esprit entreprenant; hardiesse *f*.

enterprising ['entərpraiziŋ], *a.* Entreprenant. **-ly**, *adv.* Hardiment, résolument.

entertain [entər'tein], *v.tr.* **I.** (*a*) Amuser, divertir (qn). *To e. s.o. with a story*, raconter une histoire à qn pour le distraire. (*b*) Faire la conversation à (qn). **2.** Régaler, fêter (qn). To entertain s.o. to dinner, offrir un dîner à qn. *Abs.* They entertain a great deal, ils reçoivent beaucoup. **3.** Admettre, accueillir (une proposition); faire bon accueil à (une demande).

4. Concevoir (une idée, des doutes); éprouver (des craintes); nourrir, caresser, choyer (un espoir); chérir (une illusion). **entertaining,** *a.* Amusant, divertissant.
entertainer [entər'teinər], *s.* **1.** Hôte *m*, hôtesse *f*. **2.** Diseur, -euse (de monologues, etc.); comique *m*.
entertainment [entər'teinmənt], *s.* **1.** (*a*) Divertissement *m. Much to the e. of the crowd,* au grand amusement de la foule. (*b*) *Th:* Spectacle *m.* **Entertainment tax,** taxe sur les spectacles. **2.** Hospitalité *f. Adm:* **Extra pay for entertainment,** frais de représentation.
enthral(l) [en'θrɔ:l], *v.tr.* **(enthralled)** Captiver, charmer, ensorceler.
enthrone [en'θroun], *v.tr.* (*a*) Introniser (un évêque). (*b*) Mettre (un roi) sur le trône. *To sit enthroned,* trôner.
enthuse [en'θju:z], *v.i. F:* S'enthousiasmer, se passionner (*over, about, sth.,* de, pour, qch.).
enthusiasm [en'θju:ziazm], *s.* Enthousiasme *m* (*for, about,* pour). *Book that arouses e.,* livre qui passionne.
enthusiast [en'θju:ziast], *s.* Enthousiaste *mf* (*for,* de). *Golf e.,* fervent(e) du golf; *F:* enragé(e) de golf.
enthusiastic [enθju:zi'astik], *a.* Enthousiaste. *E. fisherman,* pêcheur passionné, enragé. *To become, wax, e. over sth.,* s'enthousiasmer sur qch. **-ally,** *adv.* Avec enthousiasme; (travailler) avec élan.
entice [en'tais], *v.tr.* Attirer, séduire, allécher. *To e. s.o. to do sth.,* entraîner qn à faire qch. *To e. s.o. away,* entraîner qn à sa suite. *To e. s.o. into a place,* attirer qn dans un endroit. **enticing,** *a.* (*Of offer*) Séduisant, attrayant, alléchant; (*of dish*) affriandant, alléchant.
enticement [en'taismənt], *s.* **1.** Séduction *f.* **2.** Attrait *m*, charme *m.* **3.** Appât *m.*
entire [en'taiər], *a.* (*a*) Entier, tout. *The e. population,* la population (tout) entière. (*b*) Entier, complet. *Not a window was left entire,* pas une vitre ne restait entière, intacte. *An e. success,* un véritable succès. **-ly,** *adv.* Entièrement, tout à fait. *To agree e. with s.o.,* être entièrement d'accord avec qn; être tout à fait du même avis que qn. *E. unnecessary,* absolument inutile. *You are e. mistaken,* vous vous trompez du tout au tout.
entirety [en'taiərti], *s.* Intégralité *f. In its entirety,* en entier; totalement. *To fulfil an order in its e.,* exécuter intégralement une commande.
entitle [en'taitl], *v.tr.* **1.** Intituler (un livre). **2.** Donner à (qn) le titre de (duc, etc.). *To* **entitle oneself a baron,** se qualifier de baron. **3.** *To e. s.o. to do sth.,* donner à qn le droit de faire qch. **entitled,** *a.* **To be entitled to do sth.,** avoir droit à qch. **To be entitled to do sth.,** avoir qualité pour faire qch.; être en droit, avoir le droit, de faire qch. *To be e. to say that . . .,* pouvoir dire à juste titre que. . . . *Jur:* **To be entitled to inherit,** avoir habilité à hériter.
entity [en'titi], *s. Phil:* Entité *f.*
entomb [en'tu:m], *v.tr.* **1.** Mettre au tombeau; enterrer, ensevelir (un mort). **2.** Servir de tombeau à (un mort).
entomological [entomo'lɔdʒik(ə)l], *a.* Entomologique.
entomology [ento'mɔlodʒi], *s.* Entomologie *f.*
entrails [en'treilz], *s.pl.* Entrailles *f.*
entrain [en'trein]. **1.** *v.tr.* (Faire) embarquer (des troupes, etc.) en chemin de fer. **2.** *v.i.* S'embarquer (en chemin de fer).
entrance[1] [en'trəns], *s.* **1.** Entrée *f.* (*a*) *To make*

one's e., faire son entrée. **Actor's entrance (on the stage),** entrée en scène d'un acteur. **Entrance gate,** barrière *f*; grille *f* d'entrée. (*b*) Admission *f*, accès *m. To give e. to a room,* donner accès à une pièce. **2.** (*Way in*) **Main entrance,** entrée principale. **Side entrance,** entrée latérale; porte *f* de service. *S.a.* HALL **3.** **'entrance-fee,** *s.* (*a*) Prix *m* d'entrée. (*b*) Droit *m* d'inscription; cotisation *f* d'admission (à un club, etc.).
entrance[2] [en'trɑːns], *v.tr.* Extasier, ravir, transporter (qn). *To be entranced by . . .,* s'extasier sur. . . . **entrancing,** *a.* Enchanteur, -eresse; ravissant; (conte) passionnant; (paysage) d'une beauté féerique.
entrant [en'trənt], *s.* (*a*) Débutant, -ante (dans une profession, etc.). (*b*) Inscrit, -ite (pour une course).
entrap [en'trap], *v.tr.* **(entrapped)** Prendre (qn) au piège. *To e. s.o. into doing sth.,* user d'artifices pour faire faire qch. à qn.
entreat [en'tri:t], *v.tr.* **To entreat s.o. to do sth.,** prier, supplier, qn de faire qch.; demander instamment à qn de faire qch. **I entreat your indulgence,** je réclame votre indulgence. **entreating,** *a.* (Ton, regard) suppliant. **-ly,** *adv.* D'un air, d'un ton, suppliant.
entreaty [en'tri:ti], *s.* Prière *f*, supplication *f. At the urgent e. of s.o.,* sur les vives instances de qn. **Look of entreaty,** regard suppliant.
entrench [en'trenʃ], *v.tr. Mil:* Retrancher (un camp). *To e. oneself,* se retrancher, se terrer. **Entrenching tool,** pelle-bêche *f.*
entrenchment [en'trenʃmənt], *s. Mil:* Retranchement *m.*
entrust [en'trʌst], *v.tr.* **To entrust s.o. with sth.,** charger qn (d'une tâche, etc.); investir qn (d'une mission). **To entrust sth. to s.o.,** confier (un secret, un enfant) à qn. *To e. s.o. with the care of sth.,* s'en remettre à qn du soin de qch. *To e. a sum to s.o.,* remettre (en confiance) une somme à qn.
entry [en'tri], *s.* **1.** (*a*) Entrée *f.* (*One-way street*) **'No entry,'** "sens interdit." (*b*) **To make one's entry,** faire son entrée; *Th:* entrer en scène. (*c*) *Mus:* Entrée (d'un instrument). (*d*) Début *m* (dans la politique, etc.). **2.** (*a*) Enregistrement *m* (d'un acte, etc.); inscription *f* (d'un nom sur une liste). (*b*) *Book-k:* (i) Passation *f* d'écriture. **Single, double, entry,** comptabilité *f* en partie simple, en partie double. (ii) (*Item*) Article *m*, écriture *f.* *Nau:* **Entry in the log,** élément *m* du journal. **3.** *Sp:* Engagement *m*, inscription (d'un concurrent). **Entry-form,** feuille *f* d'inscription.
entwine [en'twain]. **1.** *v.tr.* (*a*) Entrelacer. (*b*) Enlacer (*with,* de). *The ivy entwines the elms,* le lierre enlace, embrasse, les ormes. **2.** *v.i.* S'entrelacer.
enucleate [i'nju:klieit], *v.tr. Surg:* Énucléer (les amygdales, une tumeur).
enucleation [inju:kli'eiʃ(ə)n], *s.* Énucléation *f.*
enumerate [i'nju:məreit], *v.tr.* Énumérer, détailler, dénombrer.
enumeration [inju:mə'reiʃ(ə)n], *s.* Énumération *f*, dénombrement *m.*
enunciate [i'nʌnʃieit], *v.tr.* **1.** Énoncer, exprimer (une opinion, etc.). **2.** Prononcer, articuler. **To enunciate clearly,** articuler distinctement.
enunciation [inʌnsi'eiʃ(ə)n], *s.* **1.** Énonciation *f* (d'une opinion). **2.** Articulation *f*, énonciation.
envelop [en'veləp], *v.tr.* **(enveloped)** Envelopper (*in,* dans, de).
envelope ['envəloup, 'ɔn-], *s.* **1.** (*Covering*) Enveloppe *f. Biol:* Tunique *f* (d'un organe). **2.** Enveloppe (d'une lettre). *To put a letter in*

an e., mettre une lettre sous enveloppe. In a sealed envelope, sous pli cacheté.

envenom [en'venəm], v.tr. Envenimer, aigrir (une discussion).

enviable ['enviəbl], a. Enviable; digne d'envie.

envious ['enviəs], a. Envieux. E. looks, regards d'envie. To be e. of s.o., porter envie à qn. To make s.o. e. of sth., faire envier qch. à qn. (Of thg) To make s.o. e., faire envie à qn. **-ly**, adv. Avec envie; (regarder qch.) d'un œil d'envie.

environment [en'vaiərənmənt], s. Milieu m, entourage m; ambiance f, environnement m.

environs [en'vaiərənz], s.pl. Environs m, alentours m.

envisage [en'vizedʒ], v.tr. **1.** Envisager (une difficulté, un danger). **2.** Faire face à (un danger, etc.).

envoy ['envoi], s. Envoyé m (diplomatique).

envy¹ ['envi], s. **1.** Envie f. To be green with envy, être dévoré d'envie. **2.** To be the envy of s.o., être l'objet d'envie de qn; faire envie à qn.

envy², v.tr. Envier, porter envie à (qn). To envy s.o. sth., envier qch. à qn. To be envied by s.o., s'attirer l'envie de qn.

enzyme ['enzaim], s. Ch: Enzyme f.

eocene ['i:osi:n], a. & s. Geol: Éocène (m).

eon ['i:ən], s. = AEON.

epaulet(te) ['epɔ:let], s. Épaulette f.

epergne [i'pəːrn], s. Surtout m (de table).

ephemeral [i'femərəl], a. Éphémère. E. passion, passion fugitive. Their beauty is e., leur beauté n'est que d'un jour.

ephemeris, pl. **ephemerides** [i'femeris, ife-'meridi:z], s. Astr: Éphéméride f.

epic ['epik]. **1.** a. Épique; F: (combat) légendaire. **2.** s. Poème m épique; épopée f.

epicentre ['episentər], s. Épicentre m (d'un séisme).

epicure ['epikjuər], s. Gourmet m, gastronome m.

epicurean [epikju'ri:ən], a. & s. Épicurien, -ienne.

epicureanism [epikju'ri:ənizm], **epicurism** ['epikjurizm], s. Épicurisme m.

epicycle ['episaikl], s. Astr: Épicycle m.

epicyclic [epi'saiklik], a. Mec.E: Épicycloïdal, -aux.

epicycloid [epi'saikloid], s. Geom: Épicycloïde f.

epidemic [epi'demik]. **1.** a. Épidémique. **2.** s. Épidémie f.

epidemical [epi'demik(ə)l], a. Épidémique.

epidermis [epi'dəːrmis], s. Anat: Épiderme m.

epigastrium [epi'gastriəm], s. Anat: Épigastre m.

epiglottis [epi'glɔtis], s. Anat: Épiglotte f.

epigram ['epigram], s. Épigramme f.

epigrammatic [epigra'matik], a. Épigrammatique. **-ally**, adv. Épigrammatiquement.

epilepsy ['epilepsi], s. Épilepsie f.

epileptic [epi'leptik], a. & s. Épileptique (mf). Epileptic fit, crise f d'épilepsie.

epilogue ['epilɔg], s. Épilogue m.

Epiphany [e'pifəni], s. Ecc: L'Épiphanie f; F: le jour, la fête, des Rois.

episcopal [e'piskəp(ə)l], a. Épiscopal, -aux. Episcopal ring, anneau pastoral.

episcopate [e'piskəpet], s. Épiscopat m.

episode ['episoud], s. Épisode m.

episodic(al) [epi'sɔdik(əl)], a. Épisodique.

epistle [e'pisl], s. Épître f.

epistolary [e'pistoləri], a. Épistolaire.

epistyle ['epistail], s. Arch: Épistyle m.

epitaph ['epitɑːf, -taf], s. Épitaphe f.

epithelial [epi'θi:liəl], a. Épithélial, -aux.

epithet ['epiθet], s. Épithète f. Gram: Epithet adjective, adjectif qualificatif.

epithetic(al) [epi'θetik(əl)], a. Épithétique.

epitome [e'pitomi], s. Épitomé m, abrégé m, résumé m (d'un livre); raccourci m.

epitomize [e'pitoma:iz], v.tr. Abréger, résumer (un discours, etc.).

epizootic [epizo'ɔtik], a. (Maladie) épizootique.

epoch ['i:pɔk], s. Époque f, âge m. To make, mark, an epoch, faire époque, faire date.

Epsom ['epsəm]. Pr.n. Epsom salts, sulfate m de magnésie; sels m d'Epsom, sels anglais.

equability [i:kwə'biliti], s. Uniformité f (de climat); égalité f, régularité f (d'humeur).

equable ['i:kwəbl], a. Uniforme, régulier; égal, -aux. Equable temperament, humeur égale.

equal¹ ['i:kwəl]. **1.** a. (a) Égal, -aux (to, with, à). To fight on e. terms, combattre à armes égales. To be on e. terms with s.o., être sur un pied d'égalité avec qn. All things being equal, toutes choses égales (d'ailleurs). Sp: Equal in points, à égalité (de points). F: To get equal with s.o., se venger de qn; prendre sa revanche. (b) To be equal to the occasion, to a task, être à la hauteur de la situation, d'une tâche. To be equal to doing sth., être de force à, de taille à, à même de, faire qch. I don't feel e. to (doing) it, je ne m'en sens pas le courage, la force. **2.** s. Égal, -ale; pair m. Your equals, vos pareils, vos égaux. You will not find his equal, vous ne trouverez pas son semblable. To treat s.o. as an equal, traiter qn d'égal à égal, F: de pair à compagnon. E. exhausted, tout aussi éreintés. Equally with s.o., à l'égal de qn. **-ally**, adv. Également, pareillement.

equal², v.tr. (equalled) Égaler (in, en). Not to be equalled, sans égal; qui n'a pas son égal.

equalitarian [ikwɔli'tɛəriən], a. & s. Pol: Égalitaire (mf).

equality [i'kwɔliti], s. Égalité f. On a footing of equality, on an equality, sur un pied d'égalité, d'égal à égal (with, avec).

equalization [i:kwəlai'zeiʃ(ə)n], s. **1.** Égalisation f. **2.** Compensation f; équilibrage m (de forces, etc.).

equalize ['i:kwəlaiz]. **1.** v.tr. (a) Égaliser. Fb: To equalize (the score), marquer égalité de points; égaliser (la marque). (b) Compenser, équilibrer (des forces, etc.). **2.** v.i. (a) S'égaliser. (b) Se compenser, s'équilibrer.

equanimity [i:kwə'nimiti], s. Égalité f d'âme, de caractère; tranquillité f d'esprit; équanimité f. To recover one's e., se ressaisir; se rasséréner.

equate [i'kweit], v.tr. Mth: Mettre (deux expressions, etc.) en équation. To equate an expression to zero, égaliser une expression à zéro.

equation [i'kweiʃ(ə)n], s. **1.** a. (a) Astr: Equation of time, équation f du temps. (b) Psy: Personal equation, équation personnelle. **2.** Mth: Simple, quadratic, equation, équation du premier, du deuxième, degré.

equator [i'kweitər], s. Équateur m. At the e., sous l'équateur.

equatorial [ekwa'tɔ:riəl, i:k-], a. Équatorial, -aux.

equerry ['ekwəri], s.m. **1.** Écuyer. **2.** Officier de la maison du roi.

equestrian [i'kwestriən]. **1.** a. (Statue, etc.) équestre. **2.** s. (a) Cavalier, -ière. (b) Écuyer, -ère (de cirque).

equidistant [i:kwi'distənt], a. Geom: Équidistant.

equilateral [i:kwi'latərəl], a. Geom: Équilatéral, -aux.

equilibrate [i:kwi'laibreit], s. **1.** v.tr. Équilibrer;

mettre en équilibre. **2.** *v.i.* S'équilibrer ; être en équilibre.

equilibration [i:kwilai'brei∫(ə)n], *s.* Équilibration *f* ; mise *f* en équilibre.

equilibrist [i:'kwilibrist], *s.* Équilibriste *mf* ; funambule *mf.*

equilibrium [i:kwi'libriəm], *s.* Équilibre *m*, aplomb *m.*

equine ['i:kwain, 'ekwain], *a.* Équin ; de cheval. *É. race*, race chevaline.

equinoctial [i:kwi'nɔk∫(ə)l, ekwi-], *a.* (*a*) Équinoxial, -aux. (*b*) **Equinoctial tides**, grandes marées.

equinox ['i:kwinɔks, 'ekwi-], *s.* Équinoxe *m.*

equip [i'kwip], *v.tr.* (**equipped**) **1.** Équiper, armer (un navire, un soldat). **2.** Meubler, monter (une maison) ; installer, doter (une ferme, etc.) ; outiller, monter (une usine). *To e. s.o. with sth.*, munir, pourvoir, qn de qch. *To e. a car with brakes*, munir une voiture de freins. **Well-equipped**, bien équipé ; (laboratoire) bien installé, bien agencé ; (ménage) bien monté.

equipage ['ekwipedʒ], *s.* Équipage *m.*

equipment [i'kwipmənt], *s.* **1.** Équipement *m* (d'une expédition) ; armement *m* (d'un navire) ; outillage *m* (d'une usine) ; installation *f* (d'un laboratoire). **2.** (Objets *mpl* d')équipement ; équipage *m. Electrical e. of a motor car*, appareillage *m* électrique d'une auto. **Camping equipment**, matériel *m* de campement. *A soldier's e.*, les effets *m*, le fourniment, d'un soldat. *Works with modern e.*, usine avec outillage moderne.

equipoise ['ekwipɔiz], *s.* (*a*) Équilibre *m. To preserve the e. of sth.*, maintenir qch. en équilibre. (*b*) Contrepoids *m.*

equitable ['ekwitəbl], *a.* Équitable, juste. **-ably**, *adv.* Équitablement ; avec justice.

equitation [ekwi'tei∫(ə)n], *s.* Équitation *f.*

equity ['ekwiti], *s.* **1.** Équité *f*, justice *f.* **2.** *Th:* Le syndicat des artistes de la scène.

equivalence [i'kwivələns], *s.* Équivalence *f. Fin:* **Equivalence of exchange**, parité *f* de change.

equivalent [i'kwivələnt]. **I.** *a.* Équivalent. **To be equivalent to sth.**, être équivalent, équivaloir, à qch. **2.** *s.* Équivalent *m. To drink the e. of a glass of wine*, boire la valeur d'un verre de vin.

equivocal [i'kwivok(ə)l], *a.* Équivoque. (*a*) Ambigu, -uë ; (mot) à double entente. *To give an e. answer*, répondre d'une façon équivoque. (*b*) Incertain, douteux. (*c*) Suspect, douteux ; louche. **-ally**, *adv.* D'une manière équivoque.

equivocate [i'kwivokeit], *v.i.* User d'équivoque ; équivoquer, tergiverser.

equivocation [ikwivo'kei∫(ə)n], *s.* Équivocation *f*, tergiversation *f.*

era ['i:ərə], *s.* Ère *f.* **To mark an era**, faire époque.

eradicate [i'radikeit], *v.tr.* (*a*) Déraciner (une plante). (*b*) *F:* Extirper, déraciner (des préjugés).

eradication [iradi'kei∫(ə)n], *s.* Déracinement *m* (d'un arbre). *F:* Extirpation *f* (d'un préjugé).

erase [i'reiz], *v.tr.* Effacer ; raturer ou gommer (un mot).

eraser [i'reizər], *s.* (*a*) Grattoir *m.* (*b*) Gomme *f* (à effacer). *Ink e.*, gomme à encre.

erasure [i'reiʒər], *s.* Rature *f* ; grattage *m.*

ere ['ɛər]. *A. & Poet:* **1.** *prep.* Avant. **Ere night**, avant la nuit. **Ere now**, auparavant, déjà. *S.a.* LONG[1] II. **2.** *conj.* Avant que + *sub.*

erect[1] [i'rekt], *a.* (*Of pers.*) Droit, debout. **With tail erect**, la queue levée, dressée. **With head e.**, la tête haute, le front haut. **To stand erect**, se tenir droit ; se redresser.

erect[2], *v.tr.* **1.** Dresser ; arborer (un mât, etc.). **2.** Ériger, construire (un édifice) ; élever, ériger (une statue) ; dresser (un échafaudage) ; monter, installer (une machine) ; imaginer, édifier (un système). **3.** *Opt:* Redresser (une image renversée). **erecting**, *s.* **1.** = ERECTION 1. **Erecting shop**, atelier de montage. **2.** *Opt:* Redressement *m* (d'une image). **Erecting prism**, prisme redresseur.

erection [i'rek∫(ə)n], *s.* **1.** (*a*) Dressage *m* (d'un mât, etc.). (*b*) Construction *f* (d'un édifice) ; érection *f* (d'une statue) ; montage *m*, installation *f* (d'une machine). **2.** Bâtisse *f*, construction, édifice *m.*

erg [ə:rg], *s. Ph.Meas:* Erg *m.*

erigeron [e'ridʒərən], *s. Bot:* Érigéron *m.*

Erin ['erin], *Pr.n. A. & Poet:* L'Irlande *f.*

ermine ['ə:rmin], *s.* **1.** *Z:* Hermine *f.* **2.** (*Fur*) Hermine, *Com:* roselet *m.* **Ermine tails**, mèches *f*, mouchetures *f*, d'hermine.

erne [ə:rn], *s. Orn:* Orfraie *f*, pygargue *m* ; grand aigle des mers.

erode [i'roud], *v.tr.* (*of acid*) corroder (le fer, etc.) ; (*of water*) éroder, affouiller (les berges, etc.).

erosion [i'rouʒ(ə)n], *s.* Érosion *f* ; affouillement *m* (par la mer, etc.) ; usure *f* (d'une chaudière).

erosive [i'rousiv], *a.* Érosif.

erotic [e'rɔtik], *a.* Érotique.

eroticism [e'rɔtisizm], *s.* Érotisme *m.*

err [ə:r], *v.i.* (*a*) S'égarer, s'écarter (*from*, de). (*b*) Pécher. **He does not err on the side of modesty**, il ne pèche pas par la modestie. *To err out of ignorance*, pécher par ignorance. (*c*) Errer ; être dans l'erreur ; faire erreur ; se tromper. **erring**, *a.* Dévoyé, égaré ; tombé dans l'erreur.

errand ['erənd], *s.* Commission *f*, course *f.* **To go, run, errands**, faire des commissions, des courses. **What is your errand?** qu'est-ce qui vous amène ? **'errand-boy**, *s.m.* Garçon de courses ; petit commissionnaire ; (*in lawyer's office*) F: saute-ruisseau *inv* ; (*in hotel*) chasseur. **'errand-girl**, *s.f.* Petit trottin ; *P:* arpette *f.*

errant ['erənt], *a.* (*a*) Errant. *S.a.* KNIGHT-ERRANT. (*b*) Tombé dans l'erreur ; dévoyé.

errantry ['erəntri], *s.* Vie errante (des chevaliers). *S.a.* KNIGHT-ERRANTRY.

erratic [e'ratik], *a.* **1.** *Geol: Med:* (Bloc, douleur) erratique. **2.** Irrégulier. *Aut: E. driving*, conduite mal assurée. **3.** (*Of pers.*) Excentrique, fantasque, velléitaire. *E. life*, vie désordonnée. **-ally**, *adv.* Sans méthode, sans règle ; (travailler) à bâtons rompus, par boutades.

erratum, *pl.* **-ta** [e'reitəm, -ta], *s.* Erratum *m*, *pl.* errata.

erroneous [e'rouniəs], *a.* Erroné ; faux, *f.* fausse. **-ly**, *adv.* Erronément ; par erreur.

error ['erər], *s.* **1.** Erreur *f*, faute *f*, méprise *f. E. of, in, judgment*, erreur de jugement. **Printer's error**, faute d'impression ; *F:* coquille *f.* **Clerical error**, erreur de plume, d'écriture. *Com:* **Errors and omissions excepted**, sauf erreur ou omission. *Mil: E. in range*, écart *m* en portée. **To make, commit, an error**, faire, commettre, une erreur ; se tromper. *It is an e. to suppose that . . .*, on aurait tort de croire que. . . . **2.** (*a*) **To be in error**, être dans l'erreur ; avoir tort. **To catch s.o. in error**, prendre qn en faute. **Goods sent in error**, marchandises envoyées par erreur. (*b*) **He has seen the error of his ways**, il est revenu de ses égarements. **3.** Écart (de conduite).

erstwhile ['ə:rstwhail], *adv. A. & Poet:* Autrefois, jadis.

eructation [i:rʌk'tei∫(ə)n], *s.* Éructation *f.*

erudite ['erudait], *a.* Érudit, savant.

erudition [eru′diʃ(ə)n], *s.* Érudition *f.*

erupt [e′rʌpt], *v.i.* **I.** (*Of teeth*) Percer. **2.** (*Of volcano*) Entrer en éruption ; faire éruption.

eruption [e′rʌpʃ(ə)n], *s.* **I.** (*a*) Éruption *f.* (*b*) Éclat *m*, accès *m* (de colère, etc.). **2.** Éruption, poussée *f* (de boutons) ; éruption (des dents).

erysipelas [eri′sipiləs], *s.* *Med:* Érysipèle *m*, érésipèle *m.*

escalade[1] [eska′leid], *s.* Escalade *f.*

escalade[2], *v.tr.* Escalader.

escalator [′eskəleitər], *s.* Escalier roulant, trottoir roulant ; *Rail:* escalator *m.*

escapade [eska′peid], *s.* Escapade *f* ; *F:* frasque *f*, fredaine *f.*

escape[1] [es′keip], *s.* **I.** (*a*) Fuite *f*, évasion *f.* To make one's escape, s'échapper, se sauver. To make good one's e., réussir, parvenir, à s'échapper. To have a narrow escape, l'échapper belle. He had a narrow e. from falling, il a failli tomber ; il s'en est fallu de peu qu'il ne tombât. Way of escape, issue *f.* (*b*) Échappement *m*, fuite, dégagement *m* (de gaz, d'eau, etc.). **2.** (Fire-) escape, échelle *f* de sauvetage. **es′cape-valve,** *s.* Soupape *f* d'échappement, de décharge.

escape[2]. **I.** *v.i.* (*a*) (S')échapper (*from, out of,* de)ʏ ; prendre la fuite. To e. from prison, s'évader. To e. to the mountains, gagner les montagnes. Escaped prisoner, évadé. (*b*) To escape by the skin of one's teeth, échapper, s'en tirer, tout juste. He escaped with a fright, il en a été quitte pour la peur. (*c*) (*Of gases, fluids*) Se dégager ; s'échapper, fuir. **2.** *v.tr.* (*a*) (*Of pers.*) Échapper à (un danger). To escape pursuit, se dérober aux poursuites. He narrowly escaped death, il a échappé tout juste à la mort. He just escaped being killed, il a manqué (de) se faire tuer. (*b*) (*Of thgs*) To escape notice, échapper à l'attention ; passer inaperçu. That fact escaped me, ce fait m'avait échappé. (*c*) An oath escaped him, il laissa échapper un juron. Not a word escaped his lips, pas un mot n'échappa de ses lèvres.

escapement [es′keipmənt], *s.* *Clockm: etc:* Échappement *m.*

escarp [es′kɑːrp], *s.* (*a*) *Fort:* Escarpe *f.* (*b*) Talus *m.*

escarpment [es′kɑːrpmənt], *s.* Escarpement *m.*

escheat[1] [es′tʃiːt], *s.* *Jur:* **I.** Déshérence *f* ; dévolution *f* d'héritage à l'État. **2.** Bien (tombé) en déshérence.

escheat[2], *v.i.* *Jur:* **I.** (*Of estate*) Tomber en déshérence ; revenir à l'État.

eschew [es′tʃuː], *v.tr.* Éviter (qch.) ; renoncer à (qch.) ; s'abstenir de (qch.).

escort[1] [′eskɔːrt], *s.* *Mil: etc:* Escorte *f* ; *F:* (*to a lady*) cavalier *m.* Under the escort of . . ., sous l'escorte de. . . . Under e., sous escorte.

escort[2] [es′kɔːrt], *v.tr.* Escorter, faire escorte à (un général, un convoi) ; servir de cavalier à (une dame). Escorted by the maid, sous la conduite de la bonne. I will e. you home, je vais vous reconduire.

escritoire [eskri′twɑːr], *s.* *Furn:* Secrétaire *m.*

esculent [′eskjulənt], *a.* Comestible.

escutcheon [es′kʌtʃ(ə)n], *s.* **I.** (*a*) *Her:* Écu *m*, écusson *m.* To sully one's e., ternir son blason. (*b*) *N.Arch:* Tableau *m.* **2.** *Tchn:* Écusson *m*, entrée *f* (de serrure).

Eskimo, *pl.* **-o(e)s** [′eskimo, -ouz], *a. & s.* (*pl. also* Eskimo) Esquimau (*m*), -aux. E. woman, femme esquimau.

esoteric [eso′terik], *a.* Ésotérique ; secret.

espalier [es′paljər], *s.* Espalier *m* ((i) treillis, (ii) arbre).

esparto(-grass) [es′pɑːrto(grɑːs)], *s.* Spart(e) *m* ; alfa *m.* E. products, sparterie *f.*

especial [es′peʃ(ə)l], *a.* Spécial, -aux ; particulier. In especial, surtout ; en particulier. **-ally,** *adv.* Surtout, particulièrement. (*More*) e. as, d'autant plus que.

espial [es′paiəl], *s.* Action *f* d'apercevoir (qn au loin).

espionage [′espionedʒ, espio′nɑːʒ], *s.* Espionnage *m.*

esplanade [espla′neid], *s.* Esplanade *f.*

espousal [es′pauz(ə)l], *s.* *A. & Lit:* **I.** *Usu. pl.* Épousailles *f.* **2.** Espousal of a cause, adhésion *f* à une cause.

espouse [es′pauz], *v.tr.* **I.** *Lit:* Épouser (une femme). **2.** *F:* Épouser, embrasser (une cause).

espy [es′pai], *v.tr.* Apercevoir, aviser, entrevoir (au loin).

esquire [es′kwaiər], *s.* Titre *m* honorifique d'un "gentleman." John W. Smith, Esq. = Monsieur John W. Smith.

essay[1] [′esei]. **I.** Essai *m*, effort *m* ; tentative *f* (at, de). **2.** (*a*) *Lit:* Essai. (*b*) *Sch:* Dissertation *f* ; composition *f* (littéraire).

essay[2] [e′sei], *v.tr.* *Lit:* **I.** Mettre à l'épreuve. **2.** Essayer (sth., to do sth., qch., de faire qch.).

essayist [′eseiist], *s.* *Lit:* Essayiste *mf* ; auteur *m* d'essais.

essence [′es(ə)ns], *s.* Essence *f.* The essence of the matter, le fond de l'affaire. *F:* The e. of a book, le suc, la moelle, d'un livre. Meat essence, extrait *m* de viande.

essential [e′senʃ(ə)l]. **I.** *a.* (*a*) Essentiel, indispensable ; capital, -aux. E. foodstuffs, denrées de première nécessité. E. oil, outil de première utilité. It is essential that . . ., il est indispensable que + sub. Prudence is e., la prudence s'impose. (*b*) See OIL[1] 3. **2.** *s.* *Usu. pl.* L'essentiel. **-ally,** *adv.* Essentiellement ; au premier chef.

establish [es′tabliʃ], *v.tr.* **I.** (*a*) Affermir (sa foi) ; asseoir (des fondements, son crédit). (*b*) *Jur:* To establish one's right, faire apparoir son bon droit. **2.** Établir (un gouvernement) ; édifier (un système) ; fonder (une maison de commerce) ; créer, instituer (une agence). To e. a reputation for scholarship, se faire une réputation de savant. To establish s.o., oneself (in business, etc.), établir qn, s'établir. To e. oneself (in the country), s'installer à la campagne. **3.** Établir, constater (un fait) ; démontrer (l'identité de qn). **established** [es′tabliʃt], *a.* Établi ; (réputation) solide ; (fait) avéré, acquis. Well-e. business, fortune, maison solide ; fortune bien assise. S.a. CHURCH 2.

establishment [es′tabliʃmənt], *s.* **I.** (*a*) Constatation *f* (d'un fait, etc.). (*b*) Établissement *m* (d'un gouvernement, d'une industrie) ; création *f* (d'un système) ; fondation *f* (d'une maison de commerce). **2.** Établissement, maison *f.* Business establishment, maison de commerce. To keep up an establishment, avoir un grand train de maison. **3.** (*a*) Personnel *m* (d'une maison). To be on the establishment, faire partie du personnel. (*b*) *Mil: Navy:* Effectif *m* (d'une unité, etc.). Peace establishment, effectifs (en temps) de paix. On a war e., sur le pied de guerre.

estate [es′teit], *s.* **I.** État *m*, condition *f.* Man's estate, l'âge d'homme. The holy estate of matrimony, le saint état de mariage. **2.** Rang *m*, condition. Of high, low, estate, de haut rang, d'humble condition. **3.** *Fr.Hist:* The Third Estate, le Tiers État, la bourgeoisie. **4.** *Jur:* (*a*) Bien *m*, domaine *m*, immeuble *m.* Personal estate, biens mobiliers, biens meubles. Life estate, biens en viager. S.a. REAL 2. (*b*) Succession f (d'un défunt). **Estate duty**, droits de succession. (c) **Actif** m (d'un failli). **5.** (a) Terre f, propriété f. (b) **Housing estate**, cité f. **es'tate-agency**, s. Agence f de location ; agence immobilière. **es'tate-agent**, s. Agent m de location ; agent immobilier.

esteem[1] [es'tiːm], s. Estime f, considération f. **To hold s.o. in high esteem**, avoir qn en haute estime. **Held in low e.**, peu estimé. **To rise, fall, in s.o.'s esteem**, monter, baisser, dans l'estime de qn.

esteem[2], v.tr. **I.** Estimer (qn) ; priser (qch.). **Man highly esteemed**, homme fort estimé. Com: **Your esteemed favour**, votre honorée. **2.** Estimer, considérer (as, comme). **To e. oneself happy**, s'estimer heureux.

estimable ['estiməbl], a. Estimable.

estimate[1] ['estimet], s. **I. I.** Appréciation f, évaluation f, calcul m (des pertes, du contenu de qch.). **To form a correct e. of sth.**, se faire une idée exacte de qch. **These figures are only a rough e.**, ces chiffres sont très approximatifs. **On, at, a rough estimate**, par aperçu ; F: à vue de nez. **At the lowest e.**, au bas mot. **2.** Com: Devis (estimatif). **Building e.**, devis de construction. **To put in an estimate**, soumissionner. **E. of expenditure**, chiffre prévu pour les dépenses. Pol: **The Estimates**, les prévisions f budgétaires ; les crédits m. **Navy estimates**, budget m de la marine.

estimate[2] ['estimeit], v.tr. Estimer, évaluer (les frais) ; apprécier (une distance, etc.). **His fortune is estimated at . . .**, on évalue sa fortune à. . . . **Estimated cost**, coût estimatif.

estimation [esti'meiʃ(ə)n], s. (a) Jugement m. **In my estimation**, à mon avis. (b) Estime f, considération f. **To hold s.o. in estimation**, tenir qn en grande estime.

estival ['estivəl, es'taivəl], a. = AESTIVAL.

estrange [es'treindʒ], v.tr. (a) **To estrange s.o.**, s'aliéner l'estime, l'affection, de qn. **To become estranged from s.o.**, se détacher de qn. **Estranged friends**, amis brouillés. (b) **To e. s.o. from s.o.**, indisposer qn contre qn.

estrangement [es'treindʒmənt], s. Aliénation f (de qn) ; éloignement m ; brouille f (between, entre).

estuary ['estjuəri], s. Estuaire m.

etch [etʃ], v.tr. **I.** Graver à l'eau-forte. **To etch away the metal**, enlever le métal à l'eau-forte. **2.** Abs. Faire de la gravure à l'eau-forte. **etching**, s. **I.** Gravure f à l'eau-forte. **Etching-needle**, pointe sèche (à graver). Ind: **Etching test**, essai m par corrosion. **2.** (Print) Gravure à l'eau-forte ; eau-forte f.

etcher ['etʃər], s. Graveur m à l'eau-forte ; aquafortiste mf.

eternal [i'təːrn(ə)l, iː-]. **I.** a. (a) Éternel. (b) F: Continuel ; sans fin ; sempiternel. **2.** s. **The Eternal**, l'Éternel m, Dieu m. **-ally**, adv. Éternellement.

eternity [i'təːrniti, iː-], s. (a) Éternité f. (b) pl. **The eternities**, les vérités éternelles.

eternize [i'təːrnaiz], v.tr. Éterniser.

Etesian [e'tiːʒən], a. Nau: (Vent) étésien.

ether ['iːθər], s. Ph: Ch: Med: Éther m.

ethereal [i'θiːəriəl], a. **I.** (Of regions, love) Éthéré ; (of form, vision) impalpable ; qui n'est pas de ce monde. **2.** Ch: (Of liquid) Éthéré, volatil.

etherize ['iːθəraiz], v.tr. Éthériser, endormir (un malade).

ethic(al) ['eθik(əl)], a. **I.** Moral. -aux. **2.** Gram: **Ethic dative**, datif m éthique.

ethics ['eθiks], s.pl. Éthique f, morale f.

Ethiopia [iːθi'oupiə]. Pr.n. L'Éthiopie f.

Ethiopian [iːθi'oupiən], a. & s. Éthiopien, -ienne.

ethnic(al) ['eθnik(əl)], a. Ethnique, ethnologique.

ethnographer [eθ'nɔgrəfər], s. Ethnographe mf.

ethnography [eθ'nɔgrəfi], s. Ethnographie f.

ethnologist [eθ'nɔlodʒist], s. Ethnologue mf.

ethnology [eθ'nɔlodʒi], s. Ethnologie f.

ethyl ['eθil], s. Ch: Éthyle m.

ethylene ['eθiliːn], s. Ch: Éthylène m.

etiolate ['iːtioleit]. **I.** v.tr. Étioler. **2.** v.i. (Of plants) S'étioler.

etiolation [iːtio'leiʃ(ə)n], s. Étiolement m.

etiquette ['etiket], s. (a) Étiquette f ; (les) convenances f ; Dipl: le protocole. **Court etiquette**, le cérémonial de cour. **It is not e. to . . .**, il n'est pas d'étiquette de. . . . (b) **The etiquette of the Bar**, les règles f du Barreau.

Eton ['iːtən]. Pr.n. **Eton College**, l'école d'Eton (une des grandes "public schools"). S.a. CROP[1] 4. **'Eton 'jacket**, s. Veste noire courte.

Etruscan [i'trʌskən], a. & s. Étrusque (mf).

etymological [etimo'lodʒik(ə)l], a. Étymologique. **-ally**, adv. Étymologiquement.

etymologist [eti'mɔlodʒist], s. Étymologiste mf.

etymology [eti'mɔlodʒi], s. Étymologie f.

eucalyptus [juka'liptəs], s. Eucalyptus m. **Eucalyptus oil**, essence f d'eucalyptus.

eucharist (the) [ðiˈjuːkarist], s. Ecc: L'eucharistie f.

Euclid ['juːklid]. **I.** Pr.n.m. Euclide. **2.** s. F: Géométrie f (d'Euclide).

eugenics [ju'dʒeniks], s.pl. (Usu. with sg. const.) Eugénisme m.

eulogist ['juːlodʒist], s. Panégyriste m.

eulogistic(al) [juːlo'dʒistik(əl)], a. Élogieux.

eulogize ['juːlodʒaiz], v.tr. (a) Faire l'éloge, le panégyrique, de (qn, qch.). (b) Adresser des éloges à (qn).

eulogy ['juːlodʒi], s. Panégyrique m.

eunuch ['juːnək], s. Eunuque m.

euphemism ['juːfemizm], s. Euphémisme m.

euphemistic [juːfe'mistik], a. Euphémique. **-ally**, adv. Euphémiquement ; par euphémisme.

euphonic [ju'fɔnik], a. Euphonique.

euphonium [ju'founjəm], s. Mus: Saxhorn m basse ; basse f (des cuivres).

euphony ['juːfoni], s. Euphonie f.

euphuism ['juːfjuizm], s. **I.** Lit.Hist: Euphuisme m. **2.** F: Préciosité f ; affectation f (de langage).

euphuistic [juːfju'istik], a. Euphuistique, euphuiste ; (parler) précieux, affecté.

eurhythmic [juˈriθmik]. **I.** a. Eurythmique. **2.** s.pl. **Eurhythmics**, gymnastique f rythmique.

eurhythmy [ju'riθmi], s. Eurythmie f.

Europe ['juərəp]. Pr.n. L'Europe f.

European [juərə'piːən], a. & s. Européen, -enne.

Eustachian [juːs'teikiən], a. Anat: **The Eustachian tube**, la trompe d'Eustache.

euthanasia [juːθə'neizia, -sia], s. Euthanasie f.

Euxine (the) [ðiˈjuːksain], s. A.Geog: Le Pont-Euxin.

evacuate [i'vakjueit], v.tr. **I.** (a) Évacuer (une forteresse, etc.). (b) Évacuer, décharger (le ventre). **2.** Évacuer (les blessés, etc.). **3.** Expulser, refouler (les gaz brûlés d'un moteur, etc.).

evacuation [ivakju'eiʃ(ə)n], s. **I.** Évacuation f (d'une ville, etc.). **2.** (a) Évacuation, décharge f (du ventre). (b) Usu. pl. Déjections f, selles f. **3.** Évacuation (des blessés, etc.).

evadable [i'veidəbl], *a.* Évitable; (*of question*) éludable.

evade [i'veid], *v.tr.* **1.** Éviter (un coup, un danger); esquiver (un coup); se soustraire à, éluder (un châtiment); tourner (une question, la loi); déjouer (la vigilance de qn). **2.** (*Of thgs*) Échapper à (l'intelligence).

evaluate [i'valjueit], *v.tr.* Évaluer; estimer le montant (des dommages).

evaluation [ivalju'eiʃ(ə)n], *s.* Évaluation *f.*

evanescent [eva'nes(ə)nt], *a.* Évanescent; (gloire, etc.) éphémère.

evangelic [iːvan'dʒelik, ev-], *a. Ecc:* Évangélique; conforme à l'Évangile.

evangelical [iːvan'dʒelik(ə)l, ev-]. **1.** *a.* = EVANGELIC. **2.** (*a*) *a.* Qui appartient à la religion réformée. (*b*) *s.* Protestant *m* évangélique.

evangelist [i'vandʒelist], *s.* Évangéliste *m.*

evangelize [i'vandʒelaːiz], *v.tr.* Évangéliser; prêcher l'Évangile à (qn).

evaporate [i'vaporeit]. **1.** *v.tr.* Faire évaporer (un liquide). **2.** *v.i.* (*Of liquid*) S'évaporer, se vaporiser; (*of acid*) se volatiliser.

evaporation [ivapo'reiʃ(ə)n], *s.* Évaporation *f*; volatilisation *f* (d'un acide).

evaporator [i'vaporeitər], *s. Ind:* Évaporateur *m*, vaporisateur *m*; bouilleur *m.*

evasion [i'veiʒ(ə)n], *s.* **1.** Évitement *m*; moyen *m* d'éluder (une question). **2.** Échappatoire *f*, faux-fuyant *m.* **To resort to evasions, to use evasions,** user de détours; biaiser. *Without e.*, sans détours.

evasive [i'veisiv], *a.* Évasif. **-ly,** *adv.* (Répondre) évasivement.

Eve¹ [iːv]. *Pr.n.f.* Ève.

eve², *s.* (*a*) *Ecc:* Vigile *f* (de fête). (*b*) Veille *f.* **Christmas Eve,** la veille de Noël. **On the eve of . . . ,** à la veille de. . . .

even¹ ['iːv(ə)n], *s. Poet:* Soir *m.* **At even,** le soir.

even², *a.* **1.** (*a*) (*Of surface*) Uni; plan; égal, -aux; uniforme. (*b*) **To be even with sth.,** être à fleur de, à ras de, qch.; affleurer qch. (*c*) (*Of spacing, weights, etc.*) Égal, -aux. **To make even,** aplanir (une surface); affleurer (deux planches), etc.; *Typ:* espacer (la composition). **2.** (Souffle, pouls) égal, régulier, uniforme. *Even pace,* allure uniforme. **Even temper,** humeur égale. **3.** (*a*) **Even bet,** pari avec enjeu égal. *To lay even odds,* F: **to lay evens,** parier à égalité. (*b*) *Games:* **To be even,** être manche à manche. *F:* **To get even with s.o.,** rendre la pareille à qn, se venger de qn. *I'll be even with him yet,* je le lui revaudrai; *F:* il ne l'emportera pas en paradis. (*c*) **Even bargain,** marché équitable, juste. **4.** (*a*) (Nombre) pair. **Odd or even,** pair ou impair. (*b*) **Even money,** compte rond. *To make up the e. money,* faire l'appoint. *S. Com:* **Of even date,** de même date. **-ly,** *adv.* **1.** Uniment. **2.** (*a*) Régulièrement; (diviser) également. (*b*) **Evenly matched,** de force égale. **'even-'handed,** *a.* Équitable; impartial, -aux.

even³, *adv.* **1.** Même; (*with comparative*) encore; (*with negative*) seulement, même. **Even the cleverest,** même les plus habiles. *Even the children knew,* les enfants mêmes le savaient. *To love even one's enemies,* aimer même ses ennemis. *To jest even on the scaffold,* plaisanter jusque sur l'échafaud. *I never even saw it,* je ne l'ai même pas vu. *That would be even worse,* ce serait encore pis. *Even sadder than usual,* encore plus triste que de coutume. *Without even speaking,* sans seulement parler. **Even if, even though,** he failed, même s'il échouait; alors même qu'il échouerait; quand même il échouerait. **If even** one could speak to

him, encore si on pouvait lui parler. **Even so,** mais cependant, quand même, encore. **2.** *A:* *It fell out even as he had foretold,* les choses se sont passées précisément comme il l'avait annoncé. **Even now,** à l'instant même. **Even then,** dès cette époque; déjà.

even⁴, *v.tr.* Aplanir, niveler, égaliser (une surface); affleurer (deux planches). **2.** Rendre égal. *Typ:* **To even (out) the spacing,** égaliser l'espacement. *F:* *That will even things up,* cela rétablira l'équilibre.

evening ['iːvniŋ], *s.* **1.** Soir *m*; (*duration of e.*) soirée *f.* **To-morrow evening,** demain (au) soir. **In the evening,** le soir, au soir. *At nine o'clock in the e.,* à neuf heures du soir. (*On*) *that e.,* ce soir-là. (*On*) *the previous e.,* la veille au soir. *On the e. of the next day,* le lendemain soir. *On the e. of the first of May,* le premier mai au soir. *One, on a, fine summer e.,* (par) un beau soir d'été. *Every e.,* tous les soirs. *Every Monday e.,* tous les lundis soir. *All the e.,* toute la soirée. *Long winter evenings,* longues veillées d'hiver. **Evening paper,** journal du soir. *Th:* **Evening performance,** représentation de soirée. **2.** **Musical evening,** soirée musicale. **'evening-'dress,** *s.* **1.** Habit *m* (à queue); tenue *f* de soirée. **In evening dress,** en tenue de soirée. **2.** Robe *f* du soir. **In evening dress,** en toilette de soirée. **In full evening-dress,** en grand décolleté.

evenness ['iːvənnəs], *s.* **1.** Égalité *f*; régularité *f* (de mouvement). **2.** Sérénité *f*, calme *m* (d'esprit); égalité (d'humeur).

evensong ['iːvənsɔŋ], *s. Ecc:* Vêpres *fpl* et salut *m*; office *m* du soir.

event [i'vent], *s.* **1.** Cas *m.* **In the event of** his refusing, au cas, dans le cas, où il refuserait. **2.** Événement *m.* (*a*) **In the course of events . . . ,** au cours des événements . . . , par la suite. (*b*) Issue *f*, résultat *m.* **In either event** *you will lose nothing,* dans l'un ou l'autre cas vous ne perdrez rien. **Wise after the event,** sage après coup. **At all events,** dans tous les cas; en tout cas; quoi qu'il arrive. **3.** *Sp:* (*a*) Réunion sportive. (*b*) Épreuve *f* (dans un programme).

eventful [i'ventful], *a.* (*Of story, life*) Plein d'événements; mouvementé; (jour) mémorable, qui fait époque; (semaine) fertile en événements.

eventide ['iːvəntaid], *s. Poet:* Soir *m*; *Poet:* chute du jour.

eventual [i'ventjuəl], *a.* **1.** (Profit, etc.) éventuel. **2.** (Destiny); final, -aux. *His prodigality and his e. ruin,* sa prodigalité et sa ruine finale. *He had foreseen these mistakes and the e. downfall of the government,* il avait prévu ces fautes, qui ne pouvaient aboutir qu'à la chute du ministère. **-ally,** *adv.* En fin de compte, par la suite, dans la suite. *He will do it,* il finira bien par le faire.

eventuality [iventju'aliti], *s.* Éventualité *f.*

eventuate [i'ventjueit], *v.i.* Se terminer (*in,* par); aboutir (*in,* à). *These plans will soon e.,* ces projets entreront bientôt en voie d'exécution.

ever ['evər], *adv.* **1.** Jamais. (*a*) *I read seldom if ever,* je lis jamais, ou rarement. **Now if ever** *is the time to . . . ,* c'est maintenant ou jamais le moment de. . . . **If ever** *I catch him,* si jamais je l'attrape. *Nothing ever happens,* il n'arrive jamais rien. *He hardly ever,* **scarcely ever,** smokes, il ne fume presque jamais. *Do you ever miss the train?* vous arrive-t-il (jamais) de manquer le train? *He is a liar if ever there was one,* c'est un menteur, s'il en fut jamais. *It started to rain faster than ever,* il se mit à pleuvoir de plus belle. *It is* **as warm as ever,** il fait toujours aussi chaud. *S.a.* WORSE 3. (*b*) *They lived happy ever after,* depuis lors, à partir de ce jour, ils vécurent toujours heureux. (c) **Ever since** (*then*), dès lors, depuis (lors). (d) **Ever and anon, ever and again,** de temps en temps ; de temps à autre. **2.** (a) Toujours. *The river grows ever wider,* le fleuve va s'élargissant. *Ever-increasing influence,* influence toujours plus étendue. *Corr :* **Yours ever,** à vous de cœur ; bien cordialement à vous ; tout(e) à vous. (b) **For ever,** pour toujours ; à jamais ; à perpétuité. *Gone for ever,* parti sans retour. **For ever and ever,** à tout jamais ; jusqu'à la fin des siècles. **Scotland for ever!** vive l'Écosse ! *To live for ever,* vivre éternellement. **He is for ever** grumbling, il grogne sans cesse. *To be for ever chopping and changing,* changer d'opinion à tout bout de champ. **3.** (*Intensive*) (a) **As quick as ever you can,** du plus vite que vous pourrez. *As soon as ever he comes home,* aussitôt qu'il rentrera. **We are the best friends ever,** nous sommes les meilleurs amis du monde. **Ever so difficult,** difficile au possible ; tout ce qu'il y a de plus difficile. *Ever so simple,* simple comme bonjour. *Ever so much easier,* infiniment plus facile. *Ever so long ago,* il y a bien, bien longtemps. *I waited ever so long,* j'ai attendu un temps infini. *Ever so many times,* je ne sais combien de fois. **Thank you ever so much,** merci mille fois ; merci infiniment. *I am ever so pleased* (*with it*)! j'en suis on ne peut plus content. **Be they ever so rich,** quelque riches, si riches, qu'ils soient. *No doctor, be he ever so skilful . . .,* aucun médecin, si habile soit-il. . . . (b) **How ever** *did you manage?* comment diable avez-vous fait? **What ever** *shall we do?* qu'est-ce que nous allons bien faire? *What ever's the matter with you?* mais qu'est-ce que vous avez donc? *What ever can it be?* qu'est-ce que ça peut bien être? *When ever will he come?* quand donc viendra-t-il? *Where ever can he be?* où peut-il bien être? *Who ever told you that?* qui est-ce qui a bien pu vous dire cela? *Why ever not?* pourquoi pas, grand Dieu !

evergreen ['evəgriːn]. **I.** *a.* Toujours vert ; *Bot :* à feuilles persistantes. *F :* **Evergreen topic,** question toujours d'actualité. **2.** *s.* Arbre (toujours) vert. **Evergreens,** plantes vertes.

everlasting [evər'lɑːstiŋ]. **I.** *a.* (a) Éternel. (b) **Everlasting pea,** pois vivace. (c) (*Of stuffs, etc.*) Inusable, solide. (d) *F :* Perpétuel, sempiternel. *E. complaints,* plaintes sans fin. **2.** *s.* (a) Éternité *f.* **From everlasting,** de toute éternité. *F : He is for e. on the grouse,* il grogne sans cesse. (b) *Bot :* Immortelle *f.* **-ly,** *adv.* **I.** Éternellement. **2.** *F :* Sempiternellement.

evermore [evər'mɔːr], *adv.* Toujours. **For evermore,** à jamais, pour toujours. *Their name liveth for e.,* leur nom vivra éternellement.

eversion [iˈvəːrʃ(ə)n], *s.* (a) *Surg :* Éversion *f,* retournement *m* (d'un organe). (b) **Eversion of the eyelid,** ectropion *m* ; éraillement *m* de la paupière.

every ['evri], *a.* (a) Chaque ; tout ; tous les. . . . **Every day,** chaque jour, tous les jours. *In e. Frenchman there is an idealist,* chez tout Français il y a un idéaliste. *His desire to meet* **your every** **wish,** son désir d'aller au-devant de chacun de vos désirs. **Every other day, every second day,** tous les deux jours ; un jour sur deux. *E. other Sunday,* un dimanche sur deux. *E. three days,* tous les trois jours ; un jour sur trois. *E. third man was chosen,* on choisissait un homme sur trois. *To do sth. e. quarter of an hour,* faire qch. tous les quarts d'heure. *S.a.* NOW I. **1.** **Every few minutes,** *F :* toutes les cinq minutes. *I expect him every minute,* je l'attends d'un instant à l'autre. (b) (*Intensive*) *F : He was every inch a*

republican, il était républicain jusqu'au bout des ongles, des doigts. **I have every reason to believe that . . .,** j'ai toute raison, tout lieu, de croire que. . . . *E. bit as good as . . .,* tout aussi bon que. . . . *I shall give you e. assistance,* je vous aiderai de tout mon pouvoir. (c) **Every** 'one, chacun, chacune ; tout le monde. *E. one of us,* tous tant que nous sommes. *Cf.* EVERYONE. **Every man for himself,** (i) chacun pour soi ; (ii) (*in danger*) sauve qui peut ! *F :* **Every man Jack** of them, tous sans exception.

everybody ['evribɒdi], *indef.pron.* = EVERYONE.

everyday ['evridei], *a.* **1.** Journalier, quotidien. *E. occurrence,* (i) fait journalier ; (ii) fait banal. **Everyday life,** la vie quotidienne. **2.** *My e. clothes,* mes vêtements de tous les jours. **3.** Banal, -aux ; ordinaire, commun. *Words in e. use,* mots d'usage courant ; mots très usités. *E. knowledge,* connaissances usuelles.

everyone ['evriwʌn], *indef.pron.* Chacun ; tout le monde ; tous. *As e. knows,* comme chacun le sait. *E. knows that,* le premier venu, n'importe qui, sait cela. **Everyone else knows it,** tous les autres le savent. *E. we know,* tout notre cercle de connaissances.

everything ['evriθiŋ], *indef.pron.* (a) Tout. *E. in its place,* chaque chose *f* à sa place. *We must show him e.,* il faut tout lui montrer. *E. good,* tout ce qu'il y a de bon. *They sell e.,* on y vend de tout. *Com : E. for cyclists,* tout ce qui concerne le cyclisme. (b) (*As predicate*) De première importance. **Money is everything,** l'argent fait tout. *She is very pretty.—Beauty isn't e.,* elle est très jolie.—Il n'y a pas que la beauté (qui compte).

everywhere ['evrihweər], *adv.* Partout ; en tout lieu ; en tous lieux. *To look e. for s.o.,* chercher qn partout, de tous côtés. **Everywhere you go,** partout où vous allez.

evict [iˈvikt], *v.tr.* Évincer, expulser (un locataire) (*from,* de) ; *F :* faire déguerpir (un locataire).

eviction [iˈvikʃ(ə)n], *s.* Éviction *f,* expulsion *f* (d'un locataire).

evidence[1] ['evidəns], *s.* **1.** Évidence *f.* (a) **To fly in the face of evidence,** se refuser à l'évidence. (b) *F :* **To be in evidence,** être en évidence. *A man much in e.,* un homme très en vue. **2.** Signe *m,* marque *f.* **To bear evidence(s) of, give evidence of, sth.,** porter la marque, les marques, de qch. *To give e. of intelligence,* (i) (*of action*) marquer l'intelligence ; (ii) (*of pers.*) faire preuve d'intelligence. **3.** (a) Preuve *f.* **Internal evidence,** preuves intrinsèques. (b) *Jur :* Preuve testimoniale ; témoignage *m.* **Documentary evidence, evidence in writing,** document probant ; preuve littérale. **To give evidence,** témoigner ; déposer (en justice) ; porter témoignage. *The e. was strongly against him,* les témoignages pesaient contre lui. *F :* **The evidence of the senses,** le témoignage des sens. *S.a.* CIRCUMSTANTIAL **1.** **4.** *Jur :* (*Pers.*) Témoin(s) *m(pl).* **The evidence for the prosecution, for the defence,** les témoins à charge, à décharge. **To turn King's evidence,** témoigner contre ses complices (sous promesse de pardon) ; dénoncer ses complices.

evidence[2], *v.tr.* Prouver, manifester, démontrer. *His genius was evidenced in his first attempts,* son génie se manifesta dès ses premiers essais.

evident ['evidənt], *a.* Évident. *E. truth,* vérité patente. *He had taken too much, as was e. from his gait,* il avait trop bu, et il y paraissait à sa démarche. **-ly,** *adv.* Évidemment, manifestement. *He was e. afraid,* il était manifeste qu'il avait peur.

evil ['i:v(i)l]. **I.** *a.* Mauvais. (*a*) *House of e. repute*, lieu mal famé. *E. tidings*, fâcheuses nouvelles. *E. omen*, présage de malheur. **Of evil omen,** de mauvais présage. **An evil day,** un jour malheureux. **To fall on evil days,** tomber dans l'infortune. (*b*) Méchant. *E. spirit*, esprit malfaisant, malin. **The Evil One**, l'Esprit malin, le Malin. *E. influence*, influence néfaste. **Evil eye,** mauvais œil; (*in Italy*) jettature *f*. **Evil tongue,** mauvaise langue. **2.** *s.* Mal *m, pl.* maux. (*a*) *A social e.*, une plaie sociale. **To speak evil of s.o.,** dire du mal de qn. (*b*) *F :* **The King's evil,** les écrouelles *f*, la scrofule. **evil-'doer,** *s.* Malfaiteur, -trice. **'evil-looking,** *a.* De mauvaise mine; qui ne dit rien de bon. **evil-'minded,** *a.* Porté au mal; malintentionné, malveillant. **evil-'smelling,** *a.* Nauséabond. **evil-'speaking, -'tongued,** *a.* Médisant. *An e.-t. person,* une mauvaise langue.

evince [i'vins], *v.tr.* Montrer, témoigner, faire preuve de (qch.). **To evince curiosity,** manifester de la curiosité. *To e. intelligence,* faire paraître de l'intelligence. *To evince a taste for . . .,* témoigner d'un goût pour. . . .

eviscerate [i'visəreit], *v.tr.* **I.** Éviscérer, éventrer. **2.** *F :* Émasculer (un ouvrage littéraire).

evocation [evo'keiʃ(ə)n], *s.* Évocation *f*.

evocative [e'vɔkətiv], *a.* Évocateur, -trice.

evocatory [e'vɔkətəri], *a.* Évocatoire.

evoke [i'vouk], *v.tr.* Évoquer. *F :* This remark **evoked** a smile, cette observation évoqua, suscita, un sourire.

evolution [i:vo'lju:ʃ(ə)n, ev-], *s.* **I.** (*a*) *Biol :* Évolution *f*, développement *m*. (*b*) *The e. of events*, le déroulement des événements. **2.** Évolution (d'un acrobate, d'une flotte). **3.** (*a*) *Geom :* Déroulement *m* (d'une courbe). (*b*) *Ar :* Extraction *f* de la racine. **4.** Dégagement *m* (de chaleur).

evolutionist [i:vo'lju:ʃənist, ev-], *s. Biol :* Évolutionniste *mf*.

evolve [i'vɔlv]. **I.** *v.tr.* (*a*) Dérouler, développer (des projets); élaborer (une méthode); développer, déduire (une théorie) (*from,* de). (*b*) *Ch :* Dégager (de la chaleur). **2.** *v.i.* (*a*) (*Of events*) Se dérouler. (*b*) (*Of race*) Se développer, évoluer.

ewe [ju:], *s.* Brebis *f*.

ewer ['ju:ər], *s.* Pot *m* à eau. *Com :* Broc *m* de toilette. *Ecc :* Aiguière *f*.

ex¹ [eks], *prep.* **I.** (*Out of*) *Com :* **Ex ship,** transbordé. **Ex store,** en magasin. **2.** *Fin :* **Shares quoted ex dividend,** actions citées ex-dividende, sans intérêt.

ex², *pref.* Ancien; ex-. *Ex-Minister,* ex-ministre. *Ex-schoolmistress,* ancienne institutrice.

exacerbate [eks'asərbeit], *v.tr.* Irriter, exaspérer (qn); aggraver (une douleur).

exact¹ [eg'zakt], *a.* Exact. **I.** (*a*) Précis. *To give e. details,* donner des précisions; préciser. **To be more exact . . .,** pour mieux dire. . . . *E. copy of a document,* copie textuelle d'un document. (*b*) **The exact word,** le mot juste. *The public must tender the e. amount,* le public est tenu de faire l'appoint. **2.** *To be e. in carrying out one's duties,* être exact à s'acquitter de ses devoirs. **-ly,** *adv.* Exactement; tout juste, justement. *I don't know e. what happened,* je ne sais pas au juste ce qui est arrivé. **Exactly! précisément! parfaitement!** *Three months e.,* trois mois jour pour jour. *He is not exactly a scholar,* il n'est pas à proprement parler un savant.

exact², *v.tr.* **I.** (*a*) Exiger (un impôt) (*from, of,*

de). (*b*) Extorquer (une rançon à qn). **2.** Exiger, réclamer (beaucoup de soins). **exacting,** *a.* (*Of pers.*) Exigeant; (*of work*) astreignant. **To be too e. with s.o.,** en demander trop à qn.

exaction [eg'zakʃ(ə)n], *s.* (*a*) Exaction *f* d'impôts. (*b*) Exaction, demande exorbitante (d'argent).

exactitude [eg'zaktitju:d], *s.* Exactitude *f*.

exactness [eg'zaktnəs], *s.* Exactitude *f*, précision *f*; justesse *f* (d'un calcul).

exaggerate [eg'zadʒəreit], *v.tr.* Exagérer; grandir (un incident); outrer (une mode, des éloges). *Abs.* Exagérer; forcer la note. **exaggerated,** *a.* Exagéré. *To attach e. importance to sth.,* prêter une importance excessive à qch.

exaggeration [egzadʒə'reiʃ(ə)n], *s.* Exagération *f*.

exalt [eg'zɔlt], *v.tr.* **I.** Élever (qn en rang, etc.). *To e. bribery to a system,* ériger la corruption en système. **2.** Exalter, louer (les vertus de qn). **To exalt s.o. to the skies,** porter, élever, qn jusqu'aux nues. **3.** Exciter, exalter (l'imagination). **exalted,** *a.* **I.** (*Rang*) élevé. **Exalted** personage, personnage haut placé. **2. To speak in an exalted strain,** parler d'un ton élevé.

exaltation [egzɔl'teiʃ(ə)n], *s.* **I.** Élévation *f* (*to a dignity,* à une dignité). **2.** Exaltation *f*.

exam [eg'zam], *s. F :* = EXAMINATION 2.

examination [egzami'neiʃ(ə)n], *s.* Examen *m*. **I.** Inspection *f*, visite *f* (des machines); vérification *f* (de comptes). **Under examination,** à l'examen. **To undergo a medical examination,** passer une visite médicale. **2.** *Sch :* **Entrance examination,** examen d'entrée. **Competitive examination,** concours *m*. **To go up, sit, enter, for an examination,** se présenter à un examen; passer, subir, un examen. **3.** *Jur :* Interrogatoire *m* (d'un accusé); audition *f* (de témoins). **Examination-in-chief,** interrogatoire d'un témoin par la partie qui l'a fait citer.

examine [eg'zamin], *v.tr.* Examiner. **I.** Inspecter (une machine); *Cust :* visiter (les bagages); vérifier (des comptes); contrôler (un passeport). *To e. a question thoroughly,* approfondir une question. *Nau :* *To stop and e. a ship,* arraisonner un navire. *v.i.* *To e. into a matter,* faire une enquête sur une affaire. **2.** Interroger (un témoin).

examinee [egzami'ni:], *s. Sch :* Candidat *m*.

examiner [eg'zaminər], *s.* **I.** Inspecteur, -trice (de machines, de bagages). **2.** *Sch :* Examinateur, -trice. **The examiners,** le jury (d'examen).

example [eg'za:mpl], *s.* Exemple *m*. **I.** *To quote sth. as an e.,* citer qch. en exemple. **Practical example,** cas concret. **For example,** **by way of example,** par exemple. **I.** Précédent *m*. **Beyond, without, example,** sans exemple, sans précédent. **3. To set an example,** donner l'exemple. *To take s.o. as an e.,* prendre exemple sur qn. **Following the example of . . .,** à l'exemple de. . . .

exasperate [eg'za:spəreit], *v.tr.* **I.** Exaspérer, aggraver (la haine, une douleur). **2.** Exaspérer, irriter (qn). **Exasperated at, by, his insolence,** exaspéré de son insolence. **exasperating,** *a.* (Ton) exaspérant, irritant.

exasperation [egza:spə'reiʃ(ə)n], *s.* **I.** Exaspération *f*, aggravation *f* (d'une douleur). **2.** (*Of pers.*) Exaspération, irritation *f*. **To drive s.o. to exasperation,** pousser qn à bout.

excavate ['ekskaveit], *v.tr.* Excaver, creuser (un tunnel); fouiller (la terre). *Abs.* Faire des fouilles (dans un endroit).

excavation [ekska'veiʃ(ə)n], *s.* Excavation *f*. **I.** Fouillement *m* (de la terre). **2.** Terrain excavé; fouille *f*. **The excavations at Pompeii,** les fouilles de Pompéi.

excavator ['ekskəveitər], s. Civ.E : Excavateur m ; machine f à creuser ; fouilleuse f.

exceed [ek'si:d]. **1.** v.tr. (a) Excéder, dépasser, outrepasser (ses droits). **Not exceeding ten pounds**, ne dépassant pas dix livres. **To e. one's instructions**, aller au delà de ses instructions. To e. one's powers, sortir de sa compétence. Aut : **To exceed the speed limit**, dépasser la vitesse légale. (b) Surpasser (in, en). It exceeded my expectations, cela a été au-dessus de mon attente. **2.** v.i. Manger, boire, à l'excès. **exceedingly,** adv. Très, extrêmement, excessivement.

excel [ek'sel], v. (excelled) **1.** v.i. Exceller (in, at, sth., à qch.). **To excel in an art**, être éminent dans un art. To e. at a game, exceller à un jeu. **2.** v.tr. Surpasser (qn). To e. all one's rivals, dépasser tous ses rivaux.

excellence ['eksələns], s. Excellence f. **1.** Perfection f (d'un ouvrage). **2.** Mérite m, qualité f (de qn).

excellency ['eksələnsi], s. **Your Excellency**, votre Excellence. It is I, your E., who . . ., c'est moi, Excellence, qui. . . .

excellent ['eksələnt], a. Excellent, parfait. E. business, affaire d'or. **-ly,** adv. Excellemment.

except[1] [ek'sept], v.tr. Excepter, exclure (from, de). **Present company excepted**, les présents exceptés.

except[2]. **1.** prep. (a) Excepté ; à l'exception de ; sauf. He does nothing e. eat and drink, il ne fait rien sinon manger et boire. Nobody heard it e. myself, il n'y a que moi qui l'aie entendu. E. by agreement between the parties . . ., sauf accord entre les parties. . . . (b) **Except for . . .,** à part . . . ; si ce n'est. . . . The dress is ready, e. for the buttons, la robe est prête, à l'exception des boutons. **2.** (a) conj. A. & Lit : A moins que. (b) Conj.phr. **Except that**, excepté que, hormis que.

exception [ek'sepʃ(ə)n], s. **1.** Exception f. **To be an exception to a rule**, faire exception à une règle. With that e. we are agreed, à cela près nous sommes d'accord. **Without exception**, sans exception. **With the exception of . . .,** à l'exception de . . ., exception faite de. . . . **With certain exceptions**, sauf exceptions. **2.** Objection f. **To take exception to sth.**, (i) trouver à redire à qch. ; (ii) s'offenser de qch. E. was taken to his youth, on lui objecta sa jeunesse. Jur : To take e. to a witness, récuser un témoin. To take e. to s.o.'s doing sth., trouver mauvais que qn fasse qch.

exceptionable [ek'sepʃ(ə)nəbl], a. Blâmable, répréhensible.

exceptional [ek'sepʃən(ə)l], a. Exceptionnel. **-ally,** adv. Exceptionnellement. **1.** Par exception. **2.** E. cheap, d'un bon marché exceptionnel.

excerpt ['eksə:rpt], s. Extrait m, citation f.

excess[1] [ek'ses], s. **1.** (a) Excès m (de lumière, etc.). E. of precaution, luxe m de précautions. **In excess, to excess**, (jusqu')à l'excès. **Indulgence carried to excess**, indulgence poussée trop loin. (b) **To commit excesses**, commettre des excès. **2.** Excédent m (de poids). **Excess weight**, surpoids m. Rail : **Excess fare**, supplément m. **Excess-profits tax**, contribution f sur les bénéfices de guerre.

excess[2], v.tr. Rail : Percevoir un supplément sur (un billet).

excessive [ek'sesiv], a. Excessif ; (of zeal) immodéré : (of thirst) extrême. **-ly,** adv. Excessivement ; (manger) à l'excès. To be e. generous, être par trop généreux.

exchange[1] [eks'tʃeindʒ], s. **1.** Échange m (de marchandises). **Exchange and barter**, troc m. **In exchange (for sth.)**, en échange (de qch.).

Prov : **Exchange is no robbery**, échange n'est pas vol. Car, etc., **taken in part exchange**, reprise f. **2.** Fin : (a) **Foreign exchange**, change (extérieur). Operations in foreign e., opérations de change. **(Rate of) exchange**, taux m du change. At the current rate of e., au change du jour. **(Foreign) exchange broker**, cambiste m, agent m de change. E. centre, place f cambiste. (b) **Bill of exchange**, effet m, traite f ; lettre f de change. **First of exchange**, première f de change. **3.** (a) Bourse f (des valeurs). (b) **Telephone exchange**, central m (téléphonique). **'Exchange, please!'** "la ville, s'il vous plaît."

exchange[2], v.tr. **To exchange sth. for sth.**, échanger, troquer, qch. pour, contre, qch. **To exchange glances**, échanger un regard. They had exchanged hats, ils avaient fait un échange de chapeaux. Adm : **To exchange (posts) with s.o.**, permuter avec qn.

exchangeable [eks'tʃeindʒəbl], a. Échangeable (for, pour, contre).

exchequer [eks'tʃekər], s. **1. The Exchequer**, (i) la Trésorerie, le fisc ; (ii) le Trésor public ; (iii) = le Ministère des Finances. **The Chancellor of the Exchequer** = le Ministre des Finances. **2.** F : Finances fpl (d'un particulier). My e. is empty, je ne suis pas en fonds.

excise[1] [ek'saiz], s. Contributions indirectes. **The Excise Office**, la Régie. **Excise Officer**, employé de la régie.

excise[2], v.tr. (a) Surg : Exciser, retrancher (un organe). (b) Retrancher (un passage d'un livre).

excised, a. Nat.Hist : Encoché, entaillé.

exciseman, pl. **-men** [ek'saizmən, -men], s.m. Employé de la régie.

excision [ek'siʒ(ə)n], s. **1.** Excision f, coupure f. **2.** Incision f, entaille f.

excitability [eksaitə'biliti], s. **1.** Promptitude f à s'émouvoir. **2.** El : Physiol : Excitabilité f.

excitable [ek'saitəbl], a. **1.** (Of pers.) Émotionnable, surexcitable. **2.** El : Physiol : Excitable.

excitant ['eksitənt, ek'saitənt], a. & s. Med : Excitant (m), stimulant (m).

excitation [eksi'teiʃ(ə)n], s. (a) Physiol : Excitation f. (b) El : Amorçage m (d'une dynamo).

excite [ek'sait], v.tr. **1.** (a) Provoquer, exciter (un sentiment) ; susciter (de l'intérêt). **To excite s.o.'s curiosity**, piquer la curiosité de qn. (b) Physiol : Exciter, stimuler (un nerf). (c) El : Exciter, amorcer (une dynamo). **2.** (a) Exciter, enflammer (une passion). (b) Agiter, émouvoir, surexciter (qn). To e. the mob, passionner la foule. **Easily excited**, surexcitable, émotionnable. **excited**, a. **1.** El : Physiol : Excité. **2.** (Of pers.) Agité, surexcité. **Don't get excited!** ne vous montez pas la tête ! F : ne vous frappez pas ! He gets e. over nothing, F : il s'emballe pour un rien. **-ly**, adv. D'une manière agitée ; avec agitation. **exciting,** a. **1.** Passionnant, émouvant. An e. novel, un roman palpitant d'intérêt. **2.** El : Excitateur. **Exciting dynamo**, excitatrice f. **Exciting battery**, batterie f d'excitation.

excitement [ek'saitmənt], s. **1.** Surexcitation f (d'un organe). **2.** Agitation f, surexcitation. The thirst for e., la soif des sensations fortes. The e. of departure, l'émoi m du départ. **To cause great excitement**, faire sensation. F : What's all the excitement about? qu'est-ce qui se passe donc ?

exclaim [eks'kleim]. **1.** v.i. S'écrier, s'exclamer. **To exclaim at, against, an injustice**, se récrier contre une injustice. **2.** v.tr. He exclaimed that he would rather die, il cria qu'il aimerait mieux mourir.

exclamation [eksklə'meiʃ(ə)n], s. Exclamation f.

Note of exclamation, *U.S:* exclamation mark, point *m* d'exclamation.

exclamative [eks′klamətiv], **exclamatory** [eks-klamətəri], *a.* Exclamatif.

exclude [eks′klu:d], *v.tr.* (*a*) Exclure (*from*, de). *To e. the sun*, empêcher le soleil d'entrer. *Aliens are excluded from these posts*, les étrangers ne sont pas admis à ces emplois. **Excluding . . .,** à l'exclusion de. . . . (*b*) Écarter (le doute). *This excludes all possibility of doubt*, le doute n'est plus admis.

exclusion [eks′klu:ʒ(ə)n], *s.* **1.** Exclusion *f* (*from*, de). **To the exclusion of . . .,** à l'exclusion de. **2.** Refus *m* d'admission (*from*, à).

xclusive [eks′klu:siv], *a.* **1.** Exclusif. *Two qualities that are mutually e.*, deux qualités qui s'excluent. **2.** (*a*) (Droit) exclusif. **To have exclusive rights in a production**, avoir l'exclusivité *f* d'une production. *Cin:* Exclusive film, film en exclusivité. (*b*) Seul, unique. *The e. work of . . .,* l'œuvre seule de. . . . (*c*) *U.S:* Choisi; de choix. (*d*) *E. profession*, profession très fermée. *Very e. club*, cercle très fermé. **3.** *Rent (of lodgings) fifteen shillings a week*, **exclusive**, loyer quinze shillings par semaine sans pension. *Price of the dinner e. of wine*, prix du dîner, vin non compris. **-ly,** *adv.* Exclusivement.

exclusiveness [eks′klu:sivnəs], *s.* Caractère exclusif (de qch.). *E. of mind*, esprit *m* de caste.

excogitate [eks′kɔdʒiteit], *v.tr.* Imaginer, combiner (un projet, etc.); machiner (un complot).

excommunicate [eksko′mjunikeit], *v.tr.* Excommunier.

excommunication [ekskomjuni′keiʃ(ə)n], *s.* Excommunication *f.*

excoriate [eks′kɔrieit], *v.tr.* Excorier.

excoriation [ekskɔri′eiʃ(ə)n], *s.* Excoriation *f.*

excrement [′ekskrəmənt], *s.* Excrément *m.*

excrescence [eks′kres(ə)ns], *s.* Excroissance *f.* *Bot:* (*On tree trunk*) Bourrelet *m*, loupe *f.*

excrete [eks′kri:t], *v.tr.* Excréter; (*of plant*) sécréter (un suc).

excretion [eks′kri:ʃ(ə)n], *s.* Excrétion *f.*

excruciate [eks′kru:ʃieit], *v.tr. Lit:* Mettre au supplice; torturer. **excruciating,** *a.* (*Of pain*) Atroce, affreux. **-ly,** *adv.* Atrocement, affreusement. *F: It's e. funny*, c'est à se tordre.

exculpate [′ekskʌlpeit], *v.tr.* Disculper (*from*, de).

exculpation [ekskʌl′peiʃ(ə)n], *s.* Disculpation *f.*

excursion [eks′kə:ʃ(ə)n], *s.* **1.** Excursion *f*; voyage *m* d'agrément; partie *f* de plaisir; sortie *f.* *Aut: Cy:* Randonnée *f.* *Rail:* **Excursion ticket**, billet d'excursion. **2.** *F:* Excursion, digression *f* (dans un discours).

excursionist [eks′kə:ʃənist], *s.* Excursionniste *mf.*

excusable [eks′kju:zəbl], *a.* Excusable, pardonnable. **-ably,** *adv.* Excusablement.

excuse[1] [eks′kju:s], *s.* **1.** Excuse *f.* *His conduct admits of no e.*, il est inexcusable. *Ignorance of the law is no excuse*, nul n'est censé ignorer la loi. **2.** Excuse, prétexte *m.* **To make excuses,** s'excuser. *By way of excuse he alleged that . .,* en guise d'excuse il allégua que. . . . *To offer a reasonable e.*, alléguer valablement une excuse.

excuse[2] [eks′kju:z], *v.tr.* (*a*) Excuser, pardonner. *E. my being late*, excusez-moi d'être en retard. *He may be excused for laughing*, il est excusable d'avoir ri. *If you will e. the expression*, si vous voulez me passer l'expression. **Excuse me!** (i) excusez-moi ! (ii) pardon ! (*b*) **To excuse s.o. from doing sth.**, excuser, dispenser, qn de faire qch. *To e. s.o. from attendance*, excuser qn.

F: E. me getting up, pardonnez-moi si je ne me lève pas. *Mil: Navy:* **To be excused a fatigue**, être exempté d'une corvée.

exeat [′eksiat], *s.* *Ecc: Sch:* Exeat *m.*

execrable [′eksikrəbl], *a.* Exécrable, détestable. **-ably,** *adv.* Détestablement.

execrate [′eksikreit], *v.tr.* **1.** Exécrer, détester. **2.** *Abs.* Proférer des imprécations.

execration [eksi′kreiʃ(ə)n], *s.* Exécration *f.*

executant [ek′sekjutənt, egz-], *s.* *Mus:* Exécutant, -ante.

execute [′eksikjut], *v.tr.* **1.** (*a*) Exécuter (un travail); s'acquitter (d'une tâche). *Fin:* Effectuer (un transfert). *To e. a deed*, souscrire un acte. (*b*) Exécuter, jouer (un morceau de musique). **2.** Exécuter (un criminel).

execution [eksi′kju:ʃ(ə)n], *s.* **1.** (*a*) Exécution *f* (d'un projet). **In the execution of one's duty,** dans l'exercice de ses fonctions. (*b*) *Jur:* Souscription *f* (d'un acte). (*c*) (i) Exécution (d'un morceau de musique); (ii) jeu *m* (d'un musicien). **2.** *Jur:* Saisie-exécution *f.* Writ of execution, exécutoire *m.* **3.** *Artil:* (*Of guns*) **To do execution**, causer des ravages. *F: To do great e. among the partridges*, faire un grand abattis de perdrix. **4.** Exécution (d'un criminel); exécution capitale.

executioner [eksi′kju:ʃənər], *s.* Bourreau *m*; exécuteur *m* des hautes œuvres.

executive [eg′zekjutiv]. **1.** *a.* Exécutif. *Adm: Mil:* **Executive duties**, service *m* de détail. **2.** *s.* (*a*) Pouvoir exécutif, exécutif *m* (d'un gouvernement). (*b*) Bureau *m* (d'une association).

executor, *s.* **1.** [′eksikjutər] Exécuteur *m* (d'un ordre). **2.** [eg′zekjutər] *Jur:* Exécuteur testamentaire (d'un testateur).

executory [ek′sekjutəri, egz-], *a.* *Jur:* (*a*) (Jugement) exécutoire. (*b*) = EXECUTIVE **1.**

executrix [eg′zekjutriks], *s.f.* *Jur:* Exécutrice testamentaire.

exegesis [eksi′dʒi:sis], *s.* *Theol:* Exégèse *f.*

exemplar [eg′zemplər], *s.* *Lit:* Exemplaire *m*, modèle *m.*

exemplary [eg′zempləri], *a.* Exemplaire. **1.** An exemplary husband, un époux modèle. **2.** (*Of punishment*) Infligé pour l'exemple. **3.** Qui fournit un exemple de qch.; typique. **-ily,** *adv.* Exemplairement.

exemplification [egzemplifi′keiʃ(ə)n], *s.* **1.** Démonstration *f* au moyen d'exemples. **2.** Exemple *m.*

exemplify [eg′zemplifai], *v.tr.* **1.** Démontrer par des exemples. *To e. a rule*, donner un exemple d'une règle. **2.** Servir d'exemple à (une règle).

exempt[1] [eg′zem(p)t], *a.* Exempt, dispensé. *E. from taxation*, franc, *f.* franche, d'impôts.

exempt[2], *v.tr.* **To exempt s.o. (from sth.),** exempter, exonérer, dispenser, qn (de qch.).

exemption [eg′zem(p)ʃ(ə)n], *s.* Exemption from sth., exemption *f*, exonération *f*, dispense *f*, de qch.

exercise[1] [′eksərsaiz], *s.* **1.** Exercice *m* (d'une faculté). **In the exercise of one's duties,** dans l'exercice de ses fonctions. **2.** (*a*) **Mental exercise**, exercice de l'esprit. **Outdoor e.**, exercice au grand air. **To take exercise**, prendre de l'exercice. (*b*) *Mil:* Tactical exercises, évolutions *f* tactiques. (*c*) School exercise, exercice scolaire. *Written e.*, exercice écrit; devoir *m.* (*d*) Religious exercises, exercices religieux. **'exercise-book**, *s.* Cahier *m* (de devoirs).

exercise[2], *v.tr.* **1.** Exercer (un droit); pratiquer (un métier). *To e. a right*, user d'un droit. *To e. an influence upon s.o.*, agir sur qn. **2.** (*a*) Exercer

(le corps, l'esprit). **To exercise oneself,** prendre de l'exercice. *To e.* troops, faire faire l'exercice à des troupes. *To e. a horse,* promener un cheval. **To exercise one's** wits *in order to do sth.,* s'ingénier à faire qch. (*b*) *v.i.* S'entraîner; *Mil:* faire l'exercice. **3.** *To e. s.o.'s patience,* mettre à l'épreuve la patience de qn. *The problem that is exercising our minds,* le problème qui nous préoccupe.
exergue ['eksə:rg, eg'zə:rg], *s. Num:* Exergue *m.*
exert [eg'zə:rt], *v.tr.* **I.** Employer (la force); mettre en œuvre (la force, son talent); déployer (son talent); exercer (une influence). **2. To exert oneself,** s'employer; se donner du mal. *To e. oneself to do sth.,* s'efforcer de faire qch.
exertion [eg'zə:rʃ(ə)n], *s.* **I.** Usage *m,* emploi *m* (de la force). **2.** Effort *m,* efforts. *Being now unequal to the e. of travelling,* n'étant plus à même de soutenir la fatigue d'un voyage.
exeunt ['eksiʌnt]. *Lt.v.i. Th:* (Un tel et un tel) sortent. **Exeunt omnes,** tous sortent.
exfoliate [eks'foulieit], *v.i.* (*Of bone, etc.*) S'exfolier; (*of rock*) se déliter.
exfoliation [eksfouli'eiʃ(ə)n], *s.* **I.** Exfoliation *f. Geol:* Délitation *f.* **2.** Squame *f.*
exhalation [eksə'leiʃ(ə)n], *s.* **I.** (*a*) Exhalation *f* (de vapeurs). (*b*) Expiration *f* (du souffle). **2.** Effluve *m,* exhalaison *f.*
exhale [eks'heil]. **I.** *v.tr.* Exhaler. **2.** *v.i.* (*Of vapour, etc.*) S'exhaler.
exhaust¹ [eg'zɔːst], *s.* **I.** *Mch:* I.C.E: (*a*) Échappement *m* (de la vapeur, des gaz). I.C.E: **Exhaust stroke,** échappement, évacuation *f.* (*b*) Gaz *m* d'échappement. **2.** Production *f* du vide (dans un cylindre). **Exhaust fan,** ventilateur aspirant. **3.** (*a*) (*Apparatus*) Aspirateur *m.* (*b*) = EXHAUST-PIPE. **ex'haust-pipe,** *s.* I.C.E: Tuyau *m* d'échappement.
exhaust², *v.tr.* (*a*) Aspirer (l'air). (*b*) Épuiser, tarir (une source, ses ressources). *To e. a bulb (of air),* faire le vide dans une ampoule. (*c*) Épuiser, éreinter, exténuer (qn). **exhausted,** *a.* **I.** (*Of bulb*) Vide d'air. **2.** (*a*) Épuisé. *E. land,* terre usée. (*b*) (*Of pers., animal*) Épuisé, exténué. *I am e.,* je n'en peux plus. **exhausting,** *a.* (Effort) épuisant.
exhauster [eg'zɔːstər], *s.* Aspirateur *m.*
exhaustion [eg'zɔːstʃ(ə)n], *s.* **I.** *Ph:* Aspiration *f,* exhaustion *f* (d'un gaz). **2.** Épuisement *m* (du sol). **3.** Épuisement; *F:* affalement *m. To be in a state of e.,* être à bout de forces.
exhaustive [eg'zɔːstiv], *a.* Qui épuise toutes les hypothèses. *E. enquiry,* enquête approfondie. **-ly,** *adv. To treat a subject e.,* traiter un sujet à fond.
exheredate [eks'heredeit], *v.tr. Jur:* Exhéréder.
exhibit¹ [eg'zibit], *s.* **I.** *Jur:* Pièce *f* à conviction (en procédure criminelle); pièce ou document *m* à l'appui. **2.** Objet exposé (à une exposition). *There are several interesting exhibits,* il y a plusieurs envois intéressants.
exhibit², *v.tr.* **I.** Exhiber, montrer (un objet); faire preuve (de courage). **2.** Offrir, présenter (qch. à la vue). **3.** *To e. goods in shop windows,* exposer des marchandises à l'étalage. **4.** *Jur:* Exhiber, produire (des pièces à l'appui).
exhibition [eksi'biʃ(ə)n], *s.* **I.** (*a*) Exposition *f,* étalage *m* (de marchandises). *F:* **To make an exhibition of oneself,** se donner en spectacle. (*b*) Démonstration *f* (d'un procédé). (*c*) *Jur:* **Exhibition of documents,** exhibition *f* des pièces. **2.** (*a*) Exposition. (*b*) *Com:* **Exhibition room,** salon d'exposition (d'automobiles). (*c*) *Cin:* Présentation *f* (d'un film). **3.** *Sch:* Bourse *f.*

exhibitioner [eksi'biʃənər], *s. Sch:* Boursier, -ière (à une université).
exhibitor [eg'zibitər], *s.* **I.** (*At exhibition*) Exposant, -ante. **2.** *Cin:* Exploitant *m* d'une salle.
exhilarate [eg'ziləreit], *v.tr.* Vivifier; mettre à (qn) la joie au cœur; *F:* émoustiller. **exhilarated,** *a.* Ragaillardi, émoustillé. **exhilarating,** *a.* Vivifiant, émoustillant. *E. wine,* vin capiteux.
exhilaration [egzilə'reiʃ(ə)n], *s.* Gaieté *f;* joie *f* de vivre.
exhort [eg'zɔːt], *v.tr.* Exhorter, encourager (*s.o. to* (*do*) *sth.,* qn à (faire) qch.).
exhortation [egzɔː'teiʃ(ə)n], *s.* Exhortation *f.*
exhumation [ekshju'meiʃ(ə)n], *s.* Exhumation *f.*
exhume [eks'hjuːm], *v.tr.* Exhumer.
exigence ['eksidʒəns], **exigency** ['eksidʒənsi], *s.* **I.** Exigence *f,* nécessité *f.* **2.** (*a*) Situation *f* critique; cas pressant. *In this e.,* dans cette extrémité. (*b*) **To be reduced to exigency,** être dans le besoin.
exigent ['eksidʒənt], *a.* **I.** Urgent. **2.** Exigeant.
exigible ['eksidʒibl], *a.* Exigible.
exiguity [eksi'gjuiti], *s.* Exiguïté *f* (d'un logement); modicité *f* (d'un revenu).
exiguous [eg'zigjuəs], *a.* Exigu, -uë.
exile¹ ['eksail], *s.* Exil *m,* bannissement *m.*
exile², *s.* Ex·lé, -ée; banni, -ie.
exile³, *v.tr.* Exiler, bannir (*from,* de).
exist [eg'zist], *v.i.* Exister. **I think, therefore I exist,** je pense, donc je suis. **To continue to exist,** subsister. *Wherever these conditions e.,* partout où règnent ces conditions. *How do you manage to e. here?* comment parvenez-vous à vivre ici?
existing, *a.* Existant, actuel, présent. *In e. circumstances,* dans les circonstances actuelles.
existence [eg'zistəns], *s.* **I.** Existence *f. The firm has been in e. for fifty years,* la maison existe depuis cinquante ans. **To come into existence,** naître. **2.** Existence, vie *f.*
existent [eg'zistənt], *a.* Existant.
exit¹ ['eksit], *s.* **I.** Sortie *f. Th:* **Sham exit,** fausse sortie. **To make one's exit,** quitter la scène. **2.** Sortie; (porte *f* de) dégagement *m* (d'un théâtre). *To provide for exits,* ménager des issues *f.* **Emergency exit,** sortie de secours. **Exit only,** porte exclusivement affectée à la sortie.
exit², *v.i.* (exited) **I.** *Th:* Exit Macbeth, Macbeth sort. **2.** *F:* Sortir; faire sa sortie.
exodus ['eksədəs], *s.* (**The Book of**) **Exodus,** l'Exode. *F: After the Chairman's speech there was a general exodus,* après le discours du président il y eut une sortie générale.
ex(-)officio [eksɔ'fiʃio], *adv.phr.* Ex(-)officio **member,** membre à titre d'office.
exonerate [eg'zonəreit], *v.tr.* **I.** Exonérer, dispenser (*from,* de). **2. To exonerate s.o.** (from blame), disculper qn. *Evidence that exonerates you,* témoignage à votre décharge.
exoneration [egzonə'reiʃ(ə)n], *s.* **I.** Exonération *f,* décharge *f,* dispense *f* (*from,* de). **2. Exoneration from blame,** disculpation *f.*
exorbitance [eg'zɔːbitəns], *s.* Exorbitance *f,* énormité *f,* extravagance *f* (des prix).
exorbitant [eg'zɔːbitənt], *a.* Exorbitant, extravagant. Exorbitant **price,** prix exorbitant.
exorcism ['eksɔːsizm], *s.* Exorcisme *m.*
exorcist ['eksɔːsist], *s.* Exorciste *m.*
exorcize ['eksɔːsaiz], *v.tr.* Exorciser (un démon); adjurer (un esprit). **exorcizing,** *s.* Exorcisation *f,* exorcisme *m.*
exorciser ['eksɔːsaizər], *s.* Exorciseur, -euse.
exordium [eg'zɔːdiəm], *s.* Exorde *m.*

exosmosis [eksɔs'mousis], s. Ph: Exosmose f.
exotic [ek'sɔtik], a. Exotique.
expand [eks'pand]. **1.** v.tr. (a) Dilater (un gaz);
développer (un abrégé); élargir (l'esprit). Mch:
Détendre (la vapeur). (b) Déployer (les ailes).
2. v.i. (a) (Of solid, air) Se dilater; (of steam) se
détendre; (of chest) se développer. His mind is
expanding, son intelligence se développe. (b) F:
(Of pers.) S'expansionner. **expanding,** a.
1. The e. universe, l'univers en expansion.
2. Expanding trunk, malle à soufflets. Expanding
bracelet, bracelet extensible.
expander [eks'pandər], s. Gym: (Chest) expander, extenseur m, sandow m.
expanse [eks'pans], s. Étendue f (de pays).
expansibility [ekspansi'biliti], s. Expansibilité f.
Ph: Dilatabilité f.
expansible [eks'pansibl], a. Expansible. Ph:
Dilatable.
expansion [eks'panʃ(ə)n], s. Dilatation f (d'un
gaz, d'un métal); développement m (d'un
abrégé, de la poitrine). Mch: Détente f (de la
vapeur). Mch: **Triple expansion engine,** machine
à triple détente.
expansive [eks'pansiv], a. **1.** (a) (Of force)
Expansif. (b) (Of gas) Expansible, dilatable.
2. (Of pers.) Expansif, démonstratif. **3.** Large,
étendu.
expansiveness [eks'pansivnəs], s. Expansibilité f.
ex parte [eks'pɑːrti], Lt.adv. & a.phr. Jur:
(Déclaration) émanant d'une seule partie; unilatéral, -aux.
expatiate [eks'peiʃieit], v.i. Discourir (longuement), s'étendre (on, upon, sur). To be for ever
expatiating on . . ., ne pas tarir sur. . . .
expatiation [ekspeiʃi'eiʃ(ə)n], s. Dissertation f;
long discours.
expatriate [eks'peitrieit], v.tr. Expatrier (qn).
expatriation [ekspeitri'eiʃ(ə)n], s. Expatriation f.
expect [eks'pekt], v.tr. **1.** Attendre (qn);
s'attendre à (un événement); compter sur
(l'arrivée de qn). I expected as much, je m'y
attendais. I knew what to e., je savais à quoi
m'attendre. As one might expect, F: comme de
raison. To e. that s.o. will do sth., s'attendre à
ce que qn fasse qch. It is to be expected that . . .,
il est vraisemblable que + ind. It is hardly to be
expected that . . ., il y a peu de chances (pour)
que + sub. To e. to do sth., compter faire qch.
Don't expect me till you see me, ne m'attendez
pas à date fixe. **2.** To expect sth. from s.o.,
attendre, exiger, qch. de qn. ¶ e. you to be
punctual, je vous demanderai d'être exact. What
do you e. me to do? qu'attendez-vous de moi?
How do you e. me to do it? comment voulez-vous
que je le fasse? It is not expected of you, vous
n'êtes pas tenu de le faire. **3.** F: I expect so, je
pense que oui. **expected,** a. Attendu, espéré.
s. It is not always the expected that happens, le
vraisemblable n'arrive pas toujours.
expectancy [eks'pektənsi], s. **1.** Attente f.
Awaited with eager e., attendu avec une vive
impatience. **2.** Expectative f (d'un héritage).
expectant [eks'pektənt], a. (a) Qui attend;
expectant. To be expectant of sth., attendre
qch.; avoir lieu d'espérer qch. (b) Jur: Expectant heir, héritier en expectative. -ly, adv. To
gaze at s.o. e., regarder qn avec un air d'attente.
expectation [ekspek'teiʃ(ə)n], s. **1.** (a) Attente f,
espérance f, prévision f. To. come up to, fall
short of, s.o.'s expectations, répondre à, tromper,
l'attente de qn. Contrary to all expectations,
contre toute attente. (b) With eager e., avec une

vive impatience. **2.** (a) Expectative f d'héritage.
(b) pl. Expectations, espérances. **3.** Probabilité f
(d'un événement). Ins: E. of life tables, tables
de survie.
expectative [eks'pektətiv], a. Expectatif.
expectorate [eks'pektəreit], v.tr. Expectorer.
expectoration [ekspektə'reiʃ(ə)n], s. Expectoration f; (i) crachement m; (ii) crachat m.
expediency [eks'piːdjənsi], s. Convenance f,
opportunité f (d'une mesure).
expedient [eks'piːdjənt]. **1.** a. Expédient, convenable, opportun. Do what you think e., faites
ce que vous jugerez à propos. **2.** s. Expédient m,
moyen m. Man fertile in expedients, homme de
ressources. -ly, adv. Convenablement.
expedite ['ekspedait], v.tr. **1.** Activer (une
mesure); accélérer (un procédé). **2.** Expédier,
dépêcher (une affaire).
expedition [ekspe'diʃ(ə)n], s. **1.** (a) Mil: etc:
Expédition f. To be on an expedition, être en
expédition. (b) Excursion f. **2.** Célérité f, promptitude f. To do sth. with (all) expedition, faire
qch. en toute diligence.
expeditionary [ekspe'diʃənəri], a. (Corps,
armée) expéditionnaire.
expeditious [ekspe'diʃəs], a. (Procédé) expéditif;
(trajet) rapide; (réponse) prompte. -ly, adv.
Avec célérité; promptement.
expel [eks'pel], v.tr. (expelled) Expulser (un locataire); chasser (l'ennemi). To e. s.o. from a
society, bannir qn d'une société. To e. a boy from
school, chasser un élève (de l'école).
expend [eks'pend], v.tr. **1.** (a) To expend
money, dépenser de l'argent. (b) To e. care, time,
in doing sth., employer du soin, du temps, à faire
qch. **2.** (a) Having expended all their car-
tridges . . ., ayant épuisé leurs cartouches. . . .
(b) To e. too much ammunition, consommer trop
de munitions.
expenditure [eks'penditjər], s. **1.** Dépense f
(d'argent); consommation f (de munitions).
2. Dépense(s). The national e., les dépenses
de l'État.
expense [eks'pens], s. **1.** (a) Dépense f, frais mpl.
Regardless of expense, sans regarder à la dépense.
Free of expense, sans frais; franco. To go to
great e., faire beaucoup de dépense. To put s.o.
to expense, occasionner des frais à qn. (b) pl.
Expenses, dépenses, frais; Com: sorties f.
Travelling expenses, frais de déplacement. Running expenses (of a car), dépenses d'utilisation.
Incidental expenses, faux frais. Household
expenses, dépenses du ménage. To have all
expenses paid, être défrayé de tout. **2.** Dépens m.
A laugh at my expense, un éclat de rire à mes
dépens. **3.** To be a great expense to s.o., être
une grande charge pour qn. **4.** pl. Expenses,
indemnité f (pour débours). Travelling expenses,
indemnité de voyage.
expensive [eks'pensiv], a. (Objet) coûteux,
cher; (procédé) dispendieux. Expensive car,
voiture de luxe. To be expensive, coûter cher inv.
Little places that are not too e., petits trous pas
chers. -ly, adv. (S'habiller) coûteusement. To
live e., mener la vie large.
expensiveness [eks'pensivnəs], s. Cherté f
(d'une denrée); prix élevé (de qch.).
experience[1] [eks'piːəriəns], s. Expérience f.
1. Épreuve personnelle. To go through painful
experiences, passer par de rudes épreuves. It was
a new e. for them, ce fut une nouveauté pour eux.
2. We profit by experience, l'expérience nous
rend habiles. Practical experience, la pratique.
Driving e., expérience de la route; habitude f de

conduire. **He still lacks experience,** il manque encore de pratique. **Facts within my experience,** faits à ma connaissance. *It is an account of actual e., F:* c'est du vécu. **Have you had any previous experience?** avez-vous déjà travaillé dans cette partie?

experience², *v.tr.* **1.** Éprouver; faire l'expérience de (qch.). *To e. difficult times,* passer par des temps difficiles. **2.** Apprendre (par expérience) *(that, que).* **experienced,** *a.* Qui a de l'expérience, du métier; expérimenté; (observateur) averti; (œil) exercé *(in, à). E. in business,* rompu aux affaires.

experiment¹ [eks'perimənt], *s.* Expérience *f;* essai *m. To carry out an e.,* procéder à une expérience. **As an experiment,** *by way of e.,* à titre d'essai.

experiment², *v.i.* Expérimenter, faire une expérience, des expériences *(on, with,* sur, avec). **experimenting,** *s.* Expérimentation *f.*

experimental [eksperi'ment(ə)l], *a.* **1.** (Savoir) expérimental, -aux. **2.** *Ind: The e. department,* le service des essais. **-ally,** *adv.* Expérimentalement.

experimentation [eksperimen'teiʃ(ə)n], *s.* Expérimentation *f.*

experimenter [eks'perimentər], *s.* Expérimentateur, -trice.

expert¹ [eks'pə:rt], *a.* Habile, expert. **-ly,** *adv.* Habilement, expertement.

expert² ['ekspə:rt], *s.* Expert *m;* spécialiste *m.* **The experts,** les gens *m* du métier, les techniciens *m.* **With the eye of an expert,** d'un regard connaisseur. **Expert's report,** expertise *f.*

expertness [eks'pə:rtnəs], *s.* Adresse *f,* habileté *f.*

expiable ['ekspiəbl], *a.* Expiable.

expiate ['ekspieit], *v.tr.* Expier.

expiation [ekspi'eiʃ(ə)n], *s.* Expiation *f.*

expiatory ['ekspiətəri], *a.* Expiatoire, piaculaire.

expiration [ekspi'reiʃ(ə)n], *s.* Expiration *f.* **1.** *E. of* air from the lungs, expiration de l'air des poumons. **2.** Cessation *f,* terme *m* (d'une concession); échéance *f* (d'un marché à prime). *Ins:* **Expiration of a policy,** déchéance *f* d'une police.

expire [eks'paiər]. **1.** *v.tr.* Expirer, exhaler (l'air des poumons). **2.** *v.i. (a)* Expirer, mourir; *(of fire)* s'éteindre; *(of hope)* s'évanouir. *(b)* Expirer, cesser, prendre fin. *Com:* **Expired bill,** effet périmé. *Ins: Expired policy,* police déchue.

expiry [eks'paiəri], *s.* Expiration *f,* terminaison *f;* terme *m.*

explain [eks'plein], *v.tr.* Expliquer, éclaircir. *That explains matters,* voilà qui explique tout. *That is easily explained,* cela s'explique facilement. **To explain oneself,** (i) s'expliquer; (ii) se justifier. **explain away,** *v.tr.* Donner une explication satisfaisante de (propos offensants).

explainable [eks'pleinəbl], *a.* Explicable; (conduite) justifiable.

explanation [ekspla'neiʃ(ə)n], *s.* Explication *f. To give an e. of* one's conduct, rendre raison de sa conduite.

explanatory [eks'planətəri], *a.* Explicatif.

expletive [eks'pli:tiv]. **1.** *a.* Explétif. **2.** *s. (a) Gram:* Explétif *m. (b) F:* Juron *m.*

explicable ['eksplikəbl], *a.* Explicable.

explicit [eks'plisit], *a.* Explicite; formel, catégorique. *To be more e. in* one's statements, préciser ses affirmations. *Mth:* **Explicit function,** fonction explicite. **-ly,** *adv.* Explicitement; catégoriquement.

explode [eks'ploud]. **1.** *v.tr. (a)* Démontrer la fausseté de (qch.): discréditer (une théorie).

(b) Faire éclater (un obus); faire sauter (une mine). **2.** *v.i.* Faire explosion. *(a) (Of shell)* Éclater; *(of mine)* sauter. *(b) (Of gunpowder)* Exploser, détoner. **exploded,** *a.* **1. Exploded theory,** théorie abandonnée. **2.** (Obus) éclaté; (mine) qui a sauté.

exploit¹ ['eksploit], *s.* Exploit *m;* haut fait.

exploit² [eks'ploit], *v.tr. (a)* Exploiter (une mine). *(b) F:* Exploiter (qn).

exploitable [eks'ploitəbl], *a.* Exploitable.

exploitation [eksploi'teiʃ(ə)n], *s.* Exploitation *f.*

exploration [eksplo'reiʃ(ə)n], *s.* Exploration *f.*

exploratory [eks'plo:rətəri], *a.* Exploratif; explorateur, -trice.

explore [eks'plo:ər], *v.tr. (a)* Explorer (une région). **To explore for coal,** rechercher un filon houiller. *(b) Med:* Explorer, sonder (une plaie).

explorer [eks'plo:rər], *s.* Explorateur, -trice.

explosion [eks'plou3(ə)n], *s.* **1.** Explosion *f. Min:* **Fire-damp explosion,** coup *m* de grisou. **To cause an explosion,** provoquer une explosion. *I.C.E:* **Explosion stroke,** détente *f.* **2.** Détonation *f.*

explosive [eks'plousiv]. **1.** *a.* (Matière) explosible; (mélange) explosif. *I.C.E:* **Explosive mixture,** mélange tonnant. **2.** *s.* Explosif *m,* détonant *m; F: (generic term)* poudre *f.* **High explosive,** explosif puissant, haut explosif.

exponent [eks'pounənt], *s.* **1.** Interprète *mf* (d'un système, etc.). *Mus:* Interprète, exécutant, -ante. **2.** *Mth:* Exposant *m* (d'une quantité).

exponential [ekspo'nenʃ(ə)l], *a. Mth:* Exponentiel.

export¹ ['ekspo:rt], *s.* **1.** *pl.* **Exports,** (i) articles *m* d'exportation; (ii) exportations *f.* **2. Export trade,** commerce d'exportation. **Export duty,** droit(s) de sortie.

export² [eks'po:rt], *v.tr.* Exporter.

exportation [ekspo:r'teiʃ(ə)n], *s.* Exportation *f.*

exporter [eks'po:rtər], *s.* Exportateur, -trice.

expose [eks'po:uz], *v.tr.* Exposer. **1.** *(a)* Laisser sans abri. *'Not to be exposed to the air,'* 'ne pas laisser à l'air.' *(b)* To expose oneself to danger, s'exposer au danger. *(c) Phot: I exposed two plates,* j'ai exposé deux plaques. **2.** *(a)* Mettre (qch.) à découvert, à nu, à jour, en évidence. **To expose one's ignorance,** afficher son ignorance. *(b) To e.* **goods for sale,** exposer, étaler, des marchandises pour la vente. **3.** Éventer (un secret); démasquer (un hypocrite); dévoiler (un crime).

exposed, *a.* **1.** Exposé (à la vue). *E. goods,* marchandises étalées, en montre. *Mil:* **Exposed position,** endroit exposé. *(Of troops)* **To be exposed,** être en l'air. *(b) (Laid bare)* A nu; *(of root)* déchaussé.

exposition [ekspo'ziʃ(ə)n], *s.* Exposition *f;* interprétation *f* (d'une œuvre littéraire).

expositor [eks'pozitər], *s.* Interprète *mf,* commentateur, -trice (d'une doctrine).

expostulate [eks'postjuleit], *v.i. To e. with s.o.,* faire des remontrances à qn.

expostulation [ekspostju'leiʃ(ə)n], *s. (a)* Remontrances *fpl. (b)* Remontrance. *E. proved useless,* j'ai eu beau le raisonner.

exposure [eks'pou3ər], *s.* **1.** *(a)* Exposition *f* (à l'air). **To die of exposure,** mourir de froid. *(b) Phot:* (Temps *m* de) pose *f.* **Time-exposure** pose. **To make an exposure,** exposer une plaque; prendre un cliché. **2.** *(a)* Exposition, étalage *m* (de marchandises) pour la vente. *(b)* Dévoilement *m* (d'un crime). *The fear of e.,* la crainte d'un éclat, d'un scandale. **3.** Exposition, orientation *f* (d'un lieu). *Southerly e.,* exposition au midi.

expound [eks'paund], *v.tr.* **1.** Exposer (une doctrine). **2.** Expliquer, interpréter.

express¹ [eks'pres]. **1.** *a.* (*a*) **Express image**, image exacte, fidèle (*of*, de). (*b*) (*Of order*) Exprès, formel. *For this e. purpose*, dans ce but même. (*c*) **Express train**, (train) express *m*, rapide *m*. *Post :* **By express messenger**, par exprès. (*d*) *U.S :* **Express company**, compagnie *f* de messageries. **2.** *adv.* (*a*) **To go express**, aller en toute hâte. (*b*) **Sans arrêt. 3.** *s.* (*a*) (Messager) exprès *m*. (*b*) *Rail :* Express *m*, rapide *m.* *U.S :* **Express agent**, agent *m* de messageries.

express², *v.tr.* **1.** Exprimer (le jus, l'huile) (*out of*, *from*, de). **2.** Énoncer (un principe) ; exprimer (ses sentiments, une pensée). **To express a wish**, formuler un souhait. *To e. one's appreciation*, témoigner son appréciation. *To e. one's thoughts on paper*, traduire ses pensées sur le papier. **3. To express oneself** *in French*, s'exprimer en français.

express³, *v.tr.* Envoyer (une lettre) par exprès.

expressible [eks'presibl], *a.* Exprimable.

expression [eks'preʃ(ə)n], *s.* **1.** Expression *f* (du jus d'une orange). **2.** Expression (d'une pensée). *Beyond expression*, inexprimable. *To give e. to one's gratitude*, témoigner sa reconnaissance. **3.** (*a*) Expression, locution *f.* *Unguarded expression*, mot malheureux. (*b*) *Algebraical expression*, expression, formule *f*, algébrique. **4.** (*a*) Expression (du visage). (*b*) *Mus :* **To sing with expression**, chanter avec expression.

expressionless [eks'preʃənləs], *a.* Sans expression ; (visage) impassible.

expressive [eks'presiv], *a.* (*a*) Expressif ; plein d'expression. (*b*) *Attitude e. of disdain*, attitude qui exprime le dédain. **-ly**, *adv.* Avec expression.

expressiveness [eks'presivnəs], *s.* Caractère expressif, force *f* d'expression (d'une langue, d'un mot).

expressly [eks'presli], *adv.* **1.** Expressément, formellement (défendu). **2.** *I did it e. to please you*, je l'ai fait dans le seul but de vous plaire.

expropriate [eks'prouprieit], *v.tr.* Exproprier.

expropriation [eksproupri'eiʃ(ə)n], *s.* Expropriation *f.*

expulsion [eks'pʌlʃ(ə)n], *s.* Expulsion *f.*

expulsive [eks'pʌlsiv], *a.* Expulsif.

expunge [eks'pʌndʒ], *v.tr.* Effacer, rayer (un nom d'une liste).

expurgate ['ekspərgeit], *v.tr.* Expurger (un livre).

expurgation [ekspər'geiʃ(ə)n], *s.* Expurgation *f.*

exquisite ['ekskwizit]. **1.** *a.* (*a*) (Plat) exquis. (*b*) (*Of pleasure*) Vif. *Exquisite torture*, supplice raffiné ; tourment atroce. *E. enjoyment*, jouissance délicieuse. (*c*) **To have an exquisite ear**, avoir l'oreille délicate. **2.** *s.* *A :* Élégant *m.* **-ly**, *adv.* D'une manière exquise.

ex-service-man, *pl.* **-men** [eks'sə:rvismən, -men], *s.m.* Ancien combattant ; ancien mobilisé.

extant ['ekstənt, ek'stant], *a.* Existant ; qui existe encore. *Still e.*, subsistant.

extemporaneous [ekstempo'reinjəs], *a.* Improvisé ; impromptu *inv.* **-ly**, *adv.* = EXTEMPORE 1.

extempore [eks'tempori]. **1.** *adv.* *To speak e.*, parler d'abondance, impromptu. **2.** *a.* Improvisé, impromptu *inv.* **To make an extempore speech**, improviser un discours.

extemporize [eks'tempora:iz]. **1.** *v.tr.* Improviser (un discours). **2.** *v.i.* (*a*) Improviser ; parler d'abondance. (*b*) *Mus :* Improviser.

extend [eks'tend]. **I.** *v.tr.* **1.** (*a*) Étendre,

allonger (le corps) ; prolonger (une ligne). (*b*) **To extend shorthand**, transcrire de la sténographie. (*c*) Étendre, déployer (des troupes). (*d*) *Sp : etc :* **To extend a horse**, pousser un cheval. **2.** Prolonger (une période de temps) ; *Com :* proroger (l'échéance d'un billet). **3.** Étendre, porter plus loin (les limites) ; accroître (un commerce) ; agrandir (son pouvoir). **4.** (*a*) Tendre (la main). (*b*) **To extend a welcome to s.o.**, souhaiter la bienvenue à qn. **II. extend**, *v.i.* **1.** S'étendre, s'allonger. *Estate that extends to the sea*, propriété qui s'étend jusqu'à la mer. **To extend beyond** *the wall*, saillir, faire saillie, au delà du mur. **2.** (*Of period of time*) Se prolonger, continuer.

extensibility [ekstensi'biliti], *s.* Extensibilité *f.*

extensible [eks'tensibl], *a.* Extensible.

extension [eks'tenʃ(ə)n], *s.* **1.** (*a*) Extension *f* (du bras) ; prolongement *m* (d'un canal) ; agrandissement *m* (d'une usine). **Extension ladder**, échelle *f* à coulisse. (*b*) *Phot :* Tirage *m* (du soufflet). **2.** Extension, accroissement *m* (des affaires). **3.** (*a*) (R)allonge *f* (de table). *Rail :* *Line with extensions to . . .*, ligne avec prolongements jusqu'à. . . . (*b*) *U.S :* Annexe *f* (d'un bâtiment). (*c*) *Gram :* Complément *m* (du sujet). **4.** Prolongation *f* (de congé). **To get an extension of time**, obtenir un délai. **5.** *Phil :* Étendue *f*, extension (de la matière).

extensive [eks'tensiv], *a.* **1.** Étendu, vaste, ample. *E. knowledge*, connaissances étendues. *E. researches*, travaux approfondis. **2.** *Extensive agriculture*, l'agriculture extensive. **-ly**, *adv.* **To use sth. extensively**, se servir beaucoup de qch. ; faire un usage considérable de qch.

extensor [eks'tensər], *s.* *Anat :* (Muscle) extenseur *m.*

extent [eks'tent], *s.* Étendue *f.* *What is the e. of the park?* jusqu'où va le parc? *Extent of the damage*, importance *f* du dommage. **To a certain extent**, jusqu'à un certain point ; dans une certaine mesure. **To such an extent that . . .**, à tel point que. **To some slight e.**, quelque peu. **To the full extent of his power**, de tout son pouvoir.

extenuate [eks'tenjueit], *v.tr.* **1.** *A :* Exténuer, amaigrir. *Extenuated by hunger*, amaigri par la faim. **2.** **To extenuate an offence**, atténuer une faute. **extenuating**, *a.* **Extenuating circumstance**, circonstance atténuante.

extenuation [ekstenju'eiʃ(ə)n], *s.* **1.** Exténuation *f*, affaiblissement *m* extrême (du corps). **2.** Atténuation *f* (d'une faute). *To plead sth.* **in extenuation** *of a crime*, alléguer qch. pour atténuer un crime.

exterior [eks'ti:əriər]. **1.** *a.* Extérieur (*to*, à) ; en dehors (*to*, de). *Geom :* **Exterior angle**, angle externe. **2.** *s.* Extérieur *m*, dehors *mpl.* **On the exterior**, à l'extérieur. *Man of pleasant e.*, homme aux dehors agréables.

exterminate [eks'tə:rmineit], *v.tr.* Exterminer. **exterminating**, *a.* Exterminateur, -trice.

extermination [ekstə:rmi'neiʃ(ə)n], *s.* Extermination *f.*

exterminator [eks'tə:rmineitər], *s.* Exterminateur, -trice.

external [eks'tə:rnəl]. **1.** *a.* (*a*) (Angle) externe. *Med :* **For external application**, pour l'usage externe. (*b*) Extérieur ; du dehors. *E. walls*, murs extérieurs. **External events**, affaires du dehors. **2.** *s.* (*Usu. in pl.*) Extérieur *m.* **To judge by externals**, juger les choses d'après les dehors. **-ally**, *adv.* Extérieurement ; à l'extérieur.

extinct [eks'tiŋ(k)t], *a.* (*a*) (*Of volcano, passion*)

Éteint. (b) (Of race) Disparu ; (of title) aboli, tombé en désuétude.

extinction [eks'tiŋ(k)ʃ(ə)n], s. Extinction f (d'un incendie, d'une race, d'une dette). Race threatened with e., race en passe de disparaître.

extinctive [eks'tiŋ(k)tiv], a. Extinctif.

extinguish [eks'tiŋgwiʃ], v.tr. Éteindre (le feu) ; souffler (la chandelle) ; abolir (un droit) ; amortir, éteindre (une dette). F : To be extinguished by s.o., être surpassé, éclipsé, par qn. **extinguishing**, a. Extincteur, -trice.

extinguisher [eks'tiŋgwiʃər], s. (a) (Appareil) extincteur m (d'incendie). (b) (For candle) Éteignoir m. F : To put the extinguisher on s.o., river le clou à qn.

extirpate ['ekstərpeit], v.tr. Extirper.

extirpation [ekstər'peiʃ(ə)n], s. Extirpation f.

extirpator ['ekstərpeitər], s. 1. (Pers.) Extirpateur, -trice. 2. (Machine) Extirpateur m.

extol [eks'tɔl], v.tr. (extolled) Exalter, prôner. To extol s.o. to the skies, porter qn aux nues.

extort [eks'tɔːrt], v.tr. Extorquer (une signature, etc.) (from, out of, s.o., à qn). To e. money out of s.o., extorquer de l'argent à qn. To e. a promise from s.o., arracher une promesse à qn.

extorter [eks'tɔːrtər], s. Exacteur m (of, de).

extortion [eks'tɔːrʃ(ə)n], s. Extorsion f, exaction f (d'impôts) ; arrachement m (d'une promesse).

extortionate [eks'tɔːrʃənet], a. (Prix) Extorsionnaire, exorbitant.

extortioner [eks'tɔːrʃənər], **extortionist** [eks'tɔːrʃənist], s. Extorqueur, -euse ; exacteur m.

extra ['ekstrə]. I. a. (a) En sus, de plus ; supplémentaire. E. dish, plat d'extra. E. charge, supplément m de prix. To make an e. charge, percevoir un supplément. **Extra pay**, surpaye f ; Mil : Navy : supplément de solde. E. horse, cheval de renfort. Rail : To put on an e. coach, rajouter une voiture. Sch : E. subject, matière facultative. (b) De qualité supérieure ; superfin. **Extra binding**, reliure de luxe. Rope of e. strength, corde d'une solidité exceptionnelle. 2. adv. (a) Plus que d'ordinaire ; extra-. E. strong binding, reliure extra-solide. E. smart, ultra-chic. (b) En plus. The wine is e., le vin est en plus. Packing e., emballage non compris. 3. s. (a) Supplément m (de menu) ; édition spéciale (d'un journal) ; numéro m supplémentaire (d'un programme varié). (b) pl. **Extras**, frais m ou dépenses f supplémentaires. Sch : Arts m d'agrément. Typ : Surcharge f. Little extras, les petits à-côtés.

extract¹ ['ekstrakt], s. Extrait m. (a) Beef extract, extrait de bœuf ; liebig m. (b) Lit : Sch : Extracts, morceaux choisis.

extract² [eks'trakt], v.tr. Extraire. To extract a tooth, extraire, arracher, une dent. To e. a bullet from a wound, retirer une balle d'une plaie. To e. a confession from s.o., arracher un aveu à qn.

extraction [eks'trakʃ(ə)n], s. Extraction f. 1. E. of stone from a quarry, tirage m de la pierre d'une carrière. E. of a nail, arrachage m d'un clou. Extraction of a tooth, arrachement m, extraction, d'une dent. 2. Origine f. To be of English e., être d'origine anglaise.

extractor [eks'traktər], s. Extracteur m. **Bullet extractor**, tire-balle m, pl. tire-balles.

extraditable [ekstra'daitəbl], a. 1. (Of pers.) Passible d'extradition. 2. E. crime, crime qui justifie l'extradition.

extradite ['ekstradait], v.tr. Jur : Extrader.

extradition [ekstra'diʃ(ə)n], s. Extradition f.

extrados [eks'treidɔs], s. Arch : Extrados m.

extrajudicial [ekstradʒu'diʃ(ə)l], a. Extrajudi-

ciaire ; en dehors des débats. **-ally**, adv. Extrajudiciairement.

extramural [ekstra'mjuərəl], a. (Quartier) extramuros inv.

extraneous [eks'treiniəs], a. Étranger (to, à). To be e. to the matter in hand, n'avoir rien à faire avec l'affaire.

extraordinary [eks'trɔːrdinəri], a. Extraordinaire. (a) To have e. ability, avoir des talents remarquables, extraordinaires. To call an e. meeting of the shareholders, convoquer d'urgence les sociétaires. (b) The e. thing is that . . ., ce qu'il y a d'étrange, c'est que. . . . (c) F : Prodigieux. **-ily**, adv. Extraordinairement.

extra-special [ekstra'speʃəl], a. F : E.-s. wine, du vin d'extra. Suit for e.-s. occasions, costume pour les grandes occasions.

extravagance [eks'travəgəns], s. 1. Extravagance f, exagération f. 2. Folles dépenses ; prodigalités fpl. A piece of e., une dépense inutile.

extravagant [eks'travəgənt], a. 1. Extravagant. E. praise, éloges outrés. 2. (Of pers.) Dépensier. E. tastes, goûts dispendieux. 3. (Of price) Exorbitant. **-ly**, adv. 1. D'une façon extravagante. To talk e., dire des folies. 2. Excessivement ; à l'excès. She dresses e., elle s'habille au delà de ses moyens.

extravaganza [ekstravə'ganza], s. Lit : Mus : Œuvre f d'une extravagance bouffonne ; fantaisie f.

extravasate [eks'travəseit], v.i. (Of blood) S'extravaser, s'épancher.

extreme [eks'triːm]. I. a. Extrême. At the e. end of the pier, tout au bout du quai. The extreme penalty, le dernier supplice. R.C.Ch : Extreme unction, extrême-onction. To hold extreme opinions, être outrancier dans ses opinions. E. old age, extrême vieillesse. E. youth, grande jeunesse. An extreme case, un cas exceptionnel. 2. s. To go from one extreme to the other, aller d'un extrême à l'autre. In the extreme, à l'excès ; au dernier degré. Extremes meet, les extrêmes se touchent. To go to extremes, pousser les choses à l'extrême. To drive s.o. to extremes, pousser qn à bout. To be reduced to extremes, être aux abois. **-ly**, adv. Extrêmement ; au dernier point. To be e. witty, avoir énormément d'esprit.

extremist [eks'triːmist], s. Extrémiste mf.

extremity [eks'tremiti], s. 1. Extrémité f ; point m extrême ; bout m (d'une corde) ; sommité f (d'une plante, d'une branche). 2. pl. The extremities, les extrémités (du corps). 3. They are in great e., ils sont dans une grande gêne.

extricate ['ekstrikeit], v.tr. Dégager. To e. a carriage from the mud, désembourber une voiture. To e. oneself from difficulties, se débrouiller.

extrinsic [eks'trinsik], a. Extrinsèque.

extrude [eks'truːd], v.tr. (a) Expulser (from, de). (b) Metalw : Refouler (un métal).

exuberance [eg'zjuːbərəns], s. Exubérance f.

exuberant [eg'zjuːbərənt], a. Exubérant. In e. health, débordant de santé. **-ly**, adv. Avec exubérance.

exudation [eksju'deiʃ(ə)n], s. 1. Exsudation f (de la résine). 2. Arb : E. of sap, écoulement m de la sève.

exude [ek'sjuːd], v.tr. & i. Exsuder.

exult [eg'zʌlt], v.i. 1. Exulter. 2. To e. over s o., triompher de qn.

exultant [eg'zʌltənt], a. Triomphant, exultant. To be e., exulter. **-ly**, adv. D'un air de triomphe. He spoke e., il exultait.

exultation [egzʌl'teiʃ(ə)n], s. Exultation f.

ex-voto [eks'vouto], *s. Ecc:* Ex-voto *m inv.*

eyas ['aiəs], *s. Orn:* Jeune faucon *m.*

eye[1] [ai], *s.* **1.** Œil *m, pl.* yeux. (*a*) *To have blue eyes*, avoir les yeux bleus. *To give s.o. a black eye*, pocher l'œil à qn. *To lose an eye*, perdre un œil; devenir borgne. *To put out s.o.'s eyes*, crever les yeux à qn. *To open one's eyes wide*, ouvrir de grands yeux; écarquiller les yeux. *F: That made him open his eyes*, ç'a été pour lui une révélation. *To screw up one's eyes*, faire les petits yeux. *To do sth. with one's eyes open*, faire qch. en connaissance de cause. *To keep one's eyes open*, *F:* skinned, avoir l'œil ouvert; avoir l'œil américain. *Keep your eyes open!* ouvrez l'œil! ayez l'œil! (*He was so sleepy that*) *he could not keep his eyes open*, il dormait debout. *To open s.o.'s eyes (to sth.)*, éclairer, désabuser, qn. *To shut one's eyes to the faults of s.o.*, être aveugle sur les défauts de qn. *To shut one's eyes to the truth*, se dissimuler la vérité. *To be up to the eyes in work*, avoir du travail par-dessus la tête. *To show the whites of one's eyes*, faire les yeux blancs. *With tears in one's eyes*, les larmes aux yeux. *To look on with dry eyes*, regarder d'un œil sec. *P:* My eye! mince (alors)! That's all my eye (and Betty Martin)! tout ça c'est de la blague. *Z:* Simple eye, ocelle *m*, stemmate *m*. (*b*) *To catch the eye*, frapper l'œil, les regards. *To catch s.o.'s eye*, attirer l'attention de qn. (*In Parliament*) *To catch the Speaker's eye*, obtenir la parole. He has eyes at the back of his head, il a des yeux d'Argus. *To set eyes on sth.*, apercevoir, voir, qch. *Where are your eyes?* êtes-vous aveugle? (*c*) *To make eyes at s.o.*, *F:* to give s.o. the glad eye, faire de l'œil à qn. *To make sheep's eyes at s.o.*, faire les yeux doux à qn. *To see eye to eye with s.o.*, voir les choses du même œil que qn. *You can see that with half an eye*, cela saute aux yeux. *Mil:* Eyes right! tête (à) droite! Eyes front! fixe! (*d*) *To give an eye to sth.*, veiller à qch. *To keep a strict eye on s.o.*, surveiller qn de près. *Golf:* To keep one's eye on the ball, fixer la balle. *Keep your eye on him!* ne le quittez pas des yeux! *Under the eye of . . .*, sous la surveillance de. . . *To have one's eye on a situation*, *F:* lorgner une place. *To work with an eye to the future*, travailler en vue de l'avenir. *To be all eyes*, être tout yeux. (*e*) *To have an eye for a horse*, s'y connaître en chevaux. *Sp:* To have one's eye well in, avoir l'œil exercé. (*f*) *To be very much in the public*

eye, occuper une position très en vue. **2.** (*a*) *Eyes in a peacock's tail*, yeux, miroirs *m*, de la queue d'un paon. (*b*) *Hort:* (i) Œil, bourgeon *m*. (ii) (*In grafting*) Œilleton *m*. **3.** (*a*) Chas *m* (d'une aiguille). *To pass through a needle's eye*, passer par le trou d'une aiguille. (*b*) Piton *m*. *S.a.* HOOK[1] **1.** **4.** (*a*) *Phot: etc:* Œilleton *m* (de viseur clair). (*b*) *El.E:* Electric eye, cellule *f* photo-électrique; œil électrique. **5.** In the eye of . . ., dans la direction opposée à. . . *Nau:* In the wind's eye, dans le lit, dans l'épi *m*, du vent. **'eye-ball**, *s.* Globe *m* de l'œil. **'eye-bath**, *s. Med:* Œillère *f*; bassin *m* oculaire. **'eye-bolt**, *s.* **1.** Boulon *m* à œil. **2.** Piton *m*. **'eye-bud**, *s. Hort:* Œilleton *m*. **'eye-glass**, *s.* (*a*) (*Single*) Monocle *m*. (*b*) (*Pair of*) eyeglasses, binocle *m*, lorgnon *m*, pince-nez *m inv.* **'eye-lash**, *s.* Cil *m*. **'eye-opener**, *s.* Révélation *f*; surprise *f*. **'eye-shade**, *s.* Visière *f*; protège-vue *m inv.* **'eye-strain**, *s.* *To suffer from eye-strain*, avoir les yeux fatigués. **'eye-tooth**, *s.* (Dent) œillère *f*. **'eye-wash**, *s.* **1.** *Pharm:* Collyre *m*. **2.** *F:* That's all eye-wash, tout ça c'est du boniment, de la poudre aux yeux.

eye[2], *v.tr.* (eyed; eyeing) Regarder, observer (d'un œil jaloux, etc.); mesurer (qn) des yeux; *F:* reluquer (qn). *To eye s.o. from head to foot*, toiser qn (de haut en bas).

eyebrow ['aibrau], *s.* Sourcil *m*. *To knit one's eyebrows*, froncer le(s) sourcil(s). *P: He's hanging on by his eyebrows*, il se maintient tout juste (dans son poste).

eyed [aid], *a.* **1.** A black-eyed boy, un garçon aux yeux noirs. Big-eyed, aux grands yeux. **2.** (Poinçon) à œil. **3.** (*Of feather*) Ocellé.

eyehole ['aihoul], *s.* **1.** Orbite *m* de l'œil. **2.** Petite ouverture; judas *m* (d'une porte). **3.** Œillet *m* (à lacet, etc.).

eyelet ['ailet], *s.* Œillet *m*; (*in rope*) cosse *f*.

eyelid ['ailid], *s.* Paupière *f*.

eyepiece ['aipiːs], *s.* (*a*) Oculaire *m* (de télescope). (*b*) Viseur *m* (de théodolite).

eyeshot ['aiʃɔt], *s.* Within, out of, eyeshot, à portée, hors de portée, de la vue.

eyesight ['aisait], *s.* Vue *f*. *To have good e.*, avoir la vue bonne. *My e. is failing*, ma vue baisse.

eyesore ['aisɔːr], *s.* Ce qui blesse la vue. *To be an e. to s.o.*, être la bête noire de qn.

eyewitness ['aiwitnəs], *s.* Témoin *m* oculaire.

eyot [eit], *s.* Ilot *m*.

eyrie, eyry ['ɛəri], *s.* Aire *f* (d'un aigle).

F

F, f [ef], *s.* **1.** (La lettre) F, f *f*. **2.** *Mus:* Fa *m*. F clef, clef *f* de fa. **'f-hole**, *s.* Esse *f* (de violon).

fable [feibl], *s.* **1.** Fable *f*, conte *m*. *The region of f.*, le domaine de la légende. *To sort out fact from f.*, séparer le réel de l'imaginaire. **2.** *Lit:* Fable, apologue *m*.

fabled [feibld], *a.* Légendaire, fabuleux.

fabric ['fabrik], *s.* **1.** (*a*) Édifice *m*, bâtiment *m*. The whole fabric of society, tout l'édifice social. (*b*) *Ecc:* Fabrique *f*. *Upkeep of the f.*, entretien de la fabrique. **2.** *Tex:* Tissu *m*; étoffe *f*. *Av:* Entoilage *m*. *Silk and woollen fabrics*, soieries *f* et lainages *m*. **3.** Structure *f*, fabrique (d'un édifice).

fabricate ['fabrikeit], *v.tr. F:* Inventer, fabriquer, forger (une nouvelle).

fabrication [fabri'keiʃ(ə)n], *s.* **1.** *F:* Invention *f* (d'une nouvelle); fabrication *f* (d'un passeport). It's pure f., c'est de la pure fabrication. **2.** (*a*) *A pure f.*, une pure invention. (*b*) Contrefaçon *f*.

fabricator ['fabrikeitər], *s. F:* Inventeur *m*, fabricateur, -trice (de calomnies); forgeur *m* (d'une histoire); contrefacteur *m* (d'un document).

fabulist ['fabjulist], *s.* Fabuliste *m*.

fabulous ['fabjuləs], *a.* **1.** Fabuleux; (personnage) légendaire, mythique. **2.** *F:* Prodigieux, excessif. A fabulous price, un prix fou. **-ly**, *adv.* Fabuleusement; prodigieusement.

façade [fa'sɑːd], s. Arch: Façade f.
face[1] [feis], s. **I.** Figure f, visage m, face f. *Pretty little f.*, joli minois. **To strike s.o. in the face**, frapper qn au visage. *He threw the inkpot in my f.*, il me jeta l'encrier au nez. *I can never look him in the f. again*, je me sentirai toujours honteux devant lui. **He won't show his face here again!** il ne se risquera pas à remettre les pieds ici! *To bring the two parties f. to f.*, mettre les deux parties en présence. **To fall on one's face**, tomber à plat (ventre). **To set one's face against sth.**, s'opposer résolument à qch. *The rain was beating full in our faces*, la pluie nous battait en plein visage. **In the face of danger**, en présence du danger. **To fly in the face of Providence**, porter un défi à la Providence. *To fly in the f. of facts*, aller contre l'évidence. *I told him so to his f., F:* je ne le lui ai pas envoyé dire. **In the face of all men**, au vu et au su de tous. **Face massage**, massage facial. **2.** (a) Mine f, physionomie f. *To be a good judge of faces*, être physionomiste. **To save (one's) face**, sauver la face; sauver les apparences. **To make, pull, faces** (at s.o.), faire des grimaces (à qn). **To keep a straight face**, garder son sérieux. **To put a good, a brave, face on a bad business**, faire bonne mine à mauvais jeu. (b) Audace f, front m. He had the face to tell me so, il a eu l'aplomb, le toupet, de me le dire. **3.** Apparence f, aspect m (de qch.). **On the face of things**, au premier aspect. *His evidence is false* on the face of it, son témoignage est manifestement faux. **4.** Surface f (de la terre). **5.** Surface frontale. (a) Face (d'une pièce de monnaie). (b) Devant m, façade f (d'un bâtiment); face (d'une falaise); parement m (d'un mur). (c) Cadran m (de montre). (d) Typ: Œil m (d'un caractère). **'face-ache**, s. Névralgie faciale. **'face-cream**, s. Toil: Crème f de beauté. **'face-lifting**, s. Ridectomie f. **'face-powder**, s. Poudre f de riz. **'face-towel**, s. Serviette f de toilette. **'face-value**, s. Fin: Valeur nominale.
face[2], v.tr. **I.** Affronter, faire face à, faire front à (un danger); envisager (les faits). *The problem that faces us*, le problème qui nous confronte. *To be faced with bankruptcy*, être acculé à la faillite. *F:* **To face the music**, tenir tête à l'orage. **2.** (a) v.tr. Faire face à, se tenir devant (qn, qch.). *Window that faces the garden*, fenêtre qui donne sur le jardin. *Hotel facing the square*, hôtel en façade sur la place. *The picture facing page 10*, la gravure en regard de la page 10. *Facing each other*, vis-à-vis l'un de l'autre. *Rail:* Seat facing the engine, place face à la route. (b) v.i. *The house faces north*, la maison est exposée au nord. *Face this way!* tournez-vous de ce côté! **3.** Cards: Retourner (une carte). **4.** Tchn: (a) Faced surface, surface dressée, usinée. Tex: Faced cloth, drap fin. (b) Revêtir (un mur). (c) *Coat faced with silk*, habit à revers de soie. **face about**, v.i. Mil: Faire volte-face. **'face-about**, s. Volte-face f. **face out**, v.tr. To face it out, payer d'audace. **facing**, s. **I.** F: Send him to me and I'll put him through his facings, envoyez-le-moi et je verrai ce qu'il sait faire. **2.** Surfaçage m; dressage m (d'une surface). **3.** (a) Revers m, parement m (d'un habit). *Mil:* Regimental facings, parement (de la manche ou du col) qui sert à distinguer les différents corps. (b) Perré m (d'un talus); revêtement m, parement (d'un mur).
facer ['feisər], s. F: **I.** Gifle f ou coup m au visage. **2.** Difficulté à laquelle il faut parer d'urgence; obstacle inopiné.

facet ['faset], s. Facette f (d'un diamant).
faceted ['fasetid], a. (Pierre) à facettes.
facetious [fa'siːʃəs], a. Facétieux, plaisant; (style) bouffon. **-ly**, adv. Facétieusement.
facial ['feiʃəl], a. (Nerf, etc.) facial, -aux.
facile ['fasil], a. Usu.Pej: **I.** (Of work, etc.) Facile; qui a coûté peu d'efforts. *To be a f. liar*, être habile à controuver des mensonges. **2.** (Of pers.) Accommodant, complaisant.
facilitate [fa'siliteit], v.tr. Faciliter.
facility [fa'siliti], s. Facilité f. **I.** (a) F. in speaking, facilité à parler. *F. with the pen*, souplesse f de plume. (b) *To enjoy facilities for doing sth.*, avoir la facilité de faire qch. *To assure full facilities . . .*, assurer toutes facilités. . . . *There are no bathing facilities*, les conditions ne sont pas favorables aux bains de mer. **2.** Souplesse de caractère; complaisance f.
facsimile [fak'simili], s. Fac-similé m. **Facsimile signature**, signature autographique.
fact [fakt], s. **I.** Fait m, action f. An accomplished fact, un fait accompli. **2.** *To bow before the facts*, s'incliner devant les faits; se rendre à l'évidence. **To look facts in the face**, voir les choses telles qu'elles sont. **Fact and fiction**, le réel et l'imaginaire. **To stick to facts**, s'en tenir aux faits. *Owing to the f. that these things are rare*, du fait que ces choses sont rares. *It is a f. that . . .*, il est de fait que. . . . **To accept a statement as fact**, ajouter foi à une déclaration. **Apart from the fact that . . .**, hormis que. . . . **To know for a fact that . . .**, savoir de science certaine que. . . . **The fact is**, I have no money, c'est que je n'ai pas d'argent. **In fact**, de fait. **In point of fact**, par le fait. **As a matter of fact**, (i) à vrai dire (il était ivre); (ii) en effet (le désastre se produisit).
faction ['fakʃ(ə)n], s. **I.** Faction f, cabale f. **2.** (Esprit m de) discorde f.
factious ['fakʃəs], a. Factieux. **-ly**, adv. Factieusement.
factitious [fak'tiʃəs], a. Factice, artificiel.
factor ['faktər], s. **I.** (Pers.) (a) Com: Agent m (dépositaire). (b) Scot: Régisseur m; intendant m (d'un domaine). **2.** (a) Mth: Facteur m, diviseur m. **Prime factor**, diviseur premier. **The greatest common factor**, le plus grand commun diviseur. (b) Mec.E: etc: Factor of safety, facteur, coefficient ı.ı, de sûreté, de sécurité. **3.** Facteur (concourant à un résultat). *One of the factors of happiness*, un des éléments constitutifs du bonheur. *The human f.*, l'élément humain.
factorize ['faktəraiz], v.tr. Mth: Décomposer (une quantité) en facteurs.
factory ['faktəri], s. **I.** Com: Factorerie f, comptoir m. **2.** Ind: Fabrique f, usine f. **Spinning factory**, filature f. **Factory inspector**, inspecteur du travail. **'factory-hand**, s. Ouvrier, -ière, d'usine.
factotum [fak'toutəm], s. Factotum m; homme m à tout faire.
facultative ['fakəlteitiv], a. **I.** (Optional) Facultatif. **2.** Contingent.
faculty ['fakəlti], s. **I.** (a) Faculté f. **To be in possession of all one's faculties**, jouir de toutes ses facultés. (b) Facilité f, talent m. *To have the f. of observation*, savoir bien observer. **2.** Sch: The four faculties, les facultés des lettres, des sciences, de droit et de médecine. *Abs.* **The (medical) Faculty**, la Faculté. *Jur:* Faculté, liberté f (to do sth., de faire qch.).
fad [fad], s. Marotte f, dada m. *All his fads*

toutes ses manies. **To be full of fads,** *F:* avoir un tas de marottes.

faddist ['fadist], *s. F:* Maniaque *mf;* homme, femme, à marotte.

faddy ['fadi], *a.* Capricieux, maniaque.

fade [feid]. **I.** *v.i.* (*a*) Se faner, se flétrir; (*of colour*) perdre son éclat; (*of material*) se déteindre. *Guaranteed not to f.,* garanti bon teint. (*b*) **To fade away, out,** s'évanouir, s'affaiblir. *Her smile faded away,* son sourire s'éteignit. *To f. from memory,* s'effacer de la mémoire. **She was fading away,** elle dépérissait. *W.Tel: To stop signals from fading away,* empêcher des signaux de s'évanouir. **2.** *v.tr.* (*a*) Faner, flétrir (une fleur); décolorer (une étoffe). *Curtains faded by the sun,* rideaux décolorés par le soleil. (*b*) *Cin:* **To fade one scene into another,** enchaîner deux scènes. **'fade-out, fading out,** *s. Cin: W.Tel:* Fondu *m; Cin:* fermeture *f* en fondu.

fader ['feidər], *s.* Potentiomètre *m.*

faecal ['fi:k(ə)l], *a.* Fécal, -aux.

fag¹ [fag], *s.* **I.** *F:* (*a*) Fatigue *f.* **What a fag!** quelle corvée! *It's too much fag,* ça prend trop de peine. (*b*) Surmenage *m.* **2.** *Sch:* "Petit" attaché au service d'un grand. **3.** *P:* Cigarette *f; P:* sèche *f.* **fag-'end,** *s.* **I.** (*a*) Bout *m* (d'un morceau d'étoffe, d'un cordage); *F:* restes *mpl* (d'un gigot). (*b*) Queue *f* (de l'hiver). **2.** *F:* Mégot *m.*

fag², *v.* (**fagged**) **I.** (*a*) *v.i. & pron.* **To tag (oneself),** trimer; *P:* s'échiner. **To fag (away) at sth.,** s'échiner à qch. **To fag oneself out,** s'éreinter. (*b*) *v.tr.* (*Of occupation*) Fatiguer, *F:* éreinter (qn). **2.** *v.i. Sch:* **To fag for a senior,** être au service d'un grand. **fagging,** *s.* **I.** *F:* Fatigue *f;* dur travail; turbin *m.* **2.** *Sch:* Système d'après lequel les jeunes élèves font le service des grands.

faggot ['fagət], *s.* **I.** (*a*) Fagot *m. Fort:* Fascine *f.* (*b*) *Metall:* Faisceau *m* (de fer en barres). **2.** *Cu:* Crépinette *f.*

Fahrenheit ['farənhait], *a.* (Thermomètre) Fahrenheit. (Degrés F. - 32) × ⁵⁄₉ = degrés centigrades.

fail¹ [feil]. *Adv.phr.* **Without fail,** (i) sans faute, sans remise; (ii) immanquablement, à coup sûr.

fail². **I.** *v.i.* (*a*) Manquer, faillir, faire défaut. **To fail in one's duty,** manquer, faillir, à son devoir. **To fail to do sth.,** faillir à faire qch. *He failed to come,* il n'est pas venu. *I failed to hear this remark,* ce propos m'a échappé. *Things that cannot f. to be seen,* choses qui ne sauraient échapper aux regards. **To fail s.o.,** manquer à ses engagements envers qn. *My strength is failing me,* mes forces m'abandonnent, me trahissent. *His heart failed him,* le cœur lui manqua. *His memory often fails him,* la mémoire lui fait souvent défaut. (*b*) (*Of car, etc.*) Rester en panne; flancher. *The engine failed,* le moteur a eu une panne. (*c*) Baisser. *Daylight is failing,* le jour baisse, s'éteint. *His sight is failing,* sa vue commence à baisser, à faiblir. *His memory is failing,* sa mémoire baisse. *He is failing,* sa santé baisse. (*d*) Ne pas réussir; échouer; manquer son coup; (*of enterprise*) échouer, *F:* rater; (*of play*) faire four; (*of negotiations*) ne pas aboutir. **I fail to see why . . .,** je ne vois pas pourquoi. . . . *Sch:* **To fail in an examination,** être refusé, échouer, à un examen. (*e*) *Com:* Faire faillite. *To f. for a million,* faire une faillite d'un million. **2.** *v.tr. Sch:* Refuser, coller (un candidat).

failing¹, *s.* **I.** (*a*) Manquement *m.* (*b*) Affaiblissement *m,* défaillance *f* (de forces, etc.); baisse *f*

(de la vue, etc.). (*c*) Non-réussite *f;* échec *m.* **2.** Faible *m,* faiblesse *f,* défaut *m.* **failing**², *prep.* A défaut de; faute de (paiement, etc.).

failure ['feiljər], *s.* **I.** (*a*) Manque *m,* manquement *m,* défaut *m. F. to observe a bye-law, to keep a promise,* inobservation *f* d'un règlement de police, manquement à une promesse. *F. to pay a bill,* défaut de paiement d'un effet. (*b*) Panne *f,* défaillance *f* (d'électricité, etc.). *S.a.* HEART-FAILURE. **2.** (*a*) Insuccès *m,* non-réussite *f;* avortement *m* (d'un projet, etc.); échec *m:* (dans un examen). *Th:* Four *m,* fiasco *m;* chute *f* (d'une pièce). **To court failure,** aller au-devant d'une défaite. (*b*) *Com:* Faillite *f,* déconfiture *f.* **3.** (*a*) (*Of pers.*) Raté, -ée; *F:* fruit sec. (*b*) *The play was a f.,* la pièce a fait four. *Apples are a complete f. this year,* cette année les pommes font absolument défaut.

fain [fein]. **I.** *Pred.q. A. & Lit:* Contraint par la nécessité (*to do sth.,* de faire qch.). **2.** *adv. A. & Lit:* Volontiers. *I would f. have stayed at home,* j'aurais bien voulu rester à la maison.

faint¹ [feint], *a.* **I.** **Faint heart,** cœur pusillanime. *Prov:* **Faint heart never won fair lady,** jamais honteux n'eut belle amie. **2.** (*a*) Faible, affaibli, alangui. *F. hope,* faible espoir. *F. voice,* voix faible, éteinte. (*b*) (*Of colour*) Pâle, délavé; (*of sound, breeze, etc.*) léger, à peine perceptible; (*of smell, etc.*) faible; (*of idea, etc.*) vague, peu précis. *F. inscription,* inscription indistincte. *I haven't the faintest idea,* je n'en ai pas la moindre idée. **3.** = FEINT¹. **4.** (*a*) **To feel faint,** se sentir mal; être pris d'une défaillance. (*b*) *F. perfume,* parfum fade, écœurant. **-ly,** *adv.* **I.** Faiblement; d'une voix éteinte. **2.** Légèrement; un peu. *F. reminiscent of . . .,* qui rappelle vaguement. . . . *F. sarcastic tone,* ton légèrement sarcastique. *F. visible,* à peine visible. **faint-'hearted,** *a.* Pusillanime, timide. **faint-'heartedness,** *s.* Pusillanimité *f,* timidité *f.*

faint², *s.* Évanouissement *m,* syncope *f,* défaillance *f.* **To be in a (dead) faint,** être évanoui. **To fall down in a faint,** tomber évanoui; tomber en défaillance.

faint³, *v.i.* **To faint (away),** s'évanouir, défaillir; tomber en faiblesse. **fainting,** *s.* Évanouissement *m,* défaillance *f.* **Fainting fit** = FAINT².

faintness ['feintnəs], *s.* **I.** (*Of voice*) Faiblesse *f;* (*of breeze*) légèreté *f.* **2.** Malaise *m,* faiblesse.

fair¹ ['feər], *s.* Foire *f.* **Horse-fair,** foire aux chevaux. **World fair,** exposition universelle. *F:* **To come a day after the fair,** arriver trop tard. **'fair-ground,** *s.* Champ *m* de foire.

fair². **I.** *a.* **I.** Beau, *f.* belle. **The fair sex,** le beau sexe. **My fair readers,** mes (aimables) lectrices *f.* **2.** Spécieux, plausible. **To put s.o. off with fair promises,** faire patienter qn avec de belles promesses. **3.** (*Of pers., hair*) Blond. **4.** (*a*) *F. writing,* écriture nette. **A fair name,** un nom sans tache. *S.a.* COPY¹ 2. (*b*) (*Intensive*) *F: It's a fair swindle,* c'est une pure, véritable, escroquerie. (*c*) Juste, équitable; loyal, -aux. **Fair play,** jeu loyal, franc jeu. *He is strict but f.,* il est sévère mais sans parti pris. *F:* **It's not fair!** ce n'est pas juste! **As is, was, only fair,** comme de juste. **By fair means or foul,** d'une manière ou d'une autre; de gré ou de force. *Jur:* **Fair and accurate report,** compte rendu loyal et exact. **5.** Passable; assez bon. *A f. number of . . .,* un nombre respectable de. . . . **He has a fair chance of success,** il a des chances de réussir. **To obtain a fair mark** (*in an exam, etc.*), obtenir une note passable. **It is fair to middling,** c'est entre les deux; c'est passable. **6.** (*a*) (*Of* *wind, etc.*) Propice, favorable. (*b*) **Fair weather,** beau temps. **Set fair,** beau (temps) fixe. **-ly,** *adv.* **1.** Impartialement, équitablement. **2.** Honnête-ment, loyalement, franchement. **3.** *F:* Com-plètement, absolument. *They f. screamed with delight,* ce fut une véritable explosion de cris de joie. **4.** Moyennement, passablement; assez (riche, habile, etc.). *To do sth. f. well,* faire qch. d'une façon passable. II. **fair,** *adv.* **1.** To speak **(s.o.)** fair, (i) parler courtoisement (à qn); (ii) *F:* faire patte de velours; (iii) faire (à qn) de belles promesses. **2.** *F:* (Agir) loyalement, de bonne foi. **To play fair,** jouer beau jeu. **3.** (Écrit) au net, bien lisiblement. *S.a.* BID² 2. **'fair and 'square. 1.** *a.* (*a*) (Coup de marteau) au beau milieu. (*b*) Loyal, honnête. *It's all fair and square,* c'est de bonne guerre. **2.** *adv.* (*a*) Struck fair(ly) and square(ly) by a shell, frappé au plein milieu par un obus. (*b*) Loyale-ment. **'fair-haired,** *a.* Blond; aux cheveux blonds. **'fair-'minded,** *a.* Équitable; impar-tial, -iaux. **'fair-'mindedness,** *s.* Impar-tialité *f.* **'fair-'sized,** *a.* Assez grand. **'fair-'spoken,** *a.* (*a*) A la parole courtoise. (*b*) A la parole mielleuse. **'fair-weather,** *attrib. a.* *F:* **Fair-weather friends,** amis des beaux jours.

fairing ['fɛəriŋ], *s.* **1.** *Av:* *Aut:* Profilage *m*; carénage *m*. **2.** Entoilage *m*.

fairness ['fɛənəs], *s.* **1.** Couleur blonde (des cheveux); blancheur *f*, fraîcheur *f* (du teint). **2.** Équité *f*, honnêteté *f*, impartialité *f*. **In all fairness,** en toute justice.

fairway ['fɛəwei], *s.* **1.** *Nau:* Chenal *m*, passe *f*, passage *m*. **2.** *Golf:* Parcours normal.

fairy ['fɛəri]. I. *s.* Fée *f*. **The wicked fairy,** la fée Carabosse. *Th:* **Fairy play,** féerie *f*. **2.** *a.* Féerique; de(s) fée(s). **Fairy godmother,** (i) marraine *f* fée; (ii) *F:* marraine gâteau. *F.* **footsteps,** pas légers. **'fairy-cycle,** *s.* Bi-cyclette *f* d'enfant. **'fairy-lamp, -light,** *s.* Lampion *m* (pour décorations). **'fairy-like,** *a.* Féerique. **fairy-'queen,** *s.f.* Reine des fées. **'fairy-ring,** *s.* Cercle *m*, rond *m*, des fées. **'fairy-tale,** *s.* **1.** Conte *m* de fées. **2.** *F:* (*a*) Conte invraisemblable. (*b*) Mensonge *m*; *F:* craque *f*.

fairyland ['fɛəriland], *s.* (*a*) Le royaume des fées. (*b*) Féerie *f*.

faith [feiθ], *s.* Foi *f*. **1.** (*a*) Confiance *f*, croyance *f*. **To have faith in s.o.,** avoir confiance en qn. *To have f. in God,* avoir foi en Dieu. **To pin one's faith on, to, s.o.,** se fier aveuglément à qn. **To give faith to a rumour,** donner croyance, ajouter foi, à un canard. (*b*) **The Christian faith,** la foi chrétienne. *To belong to the same f.,* appartenir à la même communion. **To die in the faith,** mourir en religion. *F:* **Political faith,** credo *m* politique. **2.** (*a*) Fidélité *f* à ses engage-ments. **To keep faith with s.o.,** tenir ses engage-ments envers qn. **To break faith with s.o.,** manquer de foi, de parole, à qn. (*b*) **Good faith,** bonne foi, fidélité, loyauté *f*. *To do sth. in all good f.,* faire qch. en tout honneur. **Bad faith,** perfidie *f*, déloyauté *f*. **'faith-healing,** *s.* Thérapeutique fondée sur la prière et sur la suggestion.

faithful ['feiθful]. I. *a.* Fidèle. (*a*) Loyal, -aux. (*b*) (*Of copy, etc.*) Exact, juste, vrai. *S.pl. Ecc:* **The faithful,** les fidèles *m*; (*Islam*) les croyants *m*. **-fully,** *adv.* **1.** Fidèlement, loyalement. *Corr:* **We remain yours faithfully,** agréez nos meilleures salutations. **He promised faithfully to come to-morrow,** il (nous) a donné sa parole qu'il

viendrait demain. **2.** (Traduire) exactement, fidèlement.

faithfulness ['feiθfulnəs], *s.* Fidélité *f.* **1.** Loyau-té *f* (*to,* envers). **2.** Exactitude *f.*

faithless ['feiθləs], *a.* **1.** Infidèle; sans foi. **2.** Déloyal, -aux; perfide. **-ly,** *adv.* Déloyale-ment, perfidement.

faithlessness ['feiθləsnəs], *s.* **1.** Infidélité *f* (*to,* à). **2.** Déloyauté *f.*

fake¹ [feik], *s.* *F:* Article truqué; maquillage *m*. *It's a f.,* c'est du trucage.

fake², *v.tr.* *F:* Truquer (des calculs); maquiller (un meuble, etc.); cuisiner (des nouvelles).

fake up, *v.tr.* Inventer (une histoire); fabriquer (un appareil) de pièces et de morceaux. **faking,** *s.* Trucage *m*, maquillage *m*.

faker ['feikər], *s.* Truqueur *m*; maquilleur *m*.

falcon ['fɔː(l)kən], *s.* *Orn:* Faucon *m*.

falconer ['fɔːkənər], *s.* Fauconnier *m*.

falconry ['fɔː(l)kənri], *s.* Fauconnerie *f.*

fall¹ [fɔːl], *s.* **1.** (*a*) Chute *f* (d'un corps); descente *f* (d'un marteau, etc.). *Th:* Chute, baisser *m* (du rideau). **To have a fall,** faire une chute; tomber. *F:* **To ride for a fall,** (i) aller en casse-cou; (ii) aller au-devant de la défaite; courir à un échec. (*b*) *Wr:* (i) Chute (d'un lutteur); (ii) reprise *f.* *F:* **To try a fall with s.o.,** lutter avec qn. (*c*) *There has been a heavy f. of snow,* il est tombé beaucoup de neige. **2.** (*a*) **The fall of day,** la chute du jour. **The fall of the year,** le déclin de l'année. (*b*) *U.S:* **The fall,** l'automne *m* or *f.* **3.** (*a*) *Usu. pl.* Chute (d'eau); cascade *f*, cataracte *f.* **The Victoria Falls,** les chutes de Victoria. (*b*) *Hyd.E:* Hauteur *f* de chute (d'un barrage). **4.** (*a*) Décrue *f*, baisse *f* (des eaux); reflux *m*, jusant *m* (de la marée); diminution *f* (de poids, etc.); baisse, descente *f*, chute (du baromètre, etc.); cadence *f* (de la voix). (*b*) Dé-nivellation *f*; pente *f*, inclinaison *f* (d'un toit, etc.). (*c*) Baisse (des prix). *St.Exch:* **Dealing for a fall,** opération à la baisse. **5.** Perte *f*, ruine *f.* **Fall from grace,** déchéance *f.* **The Fall,** la chute de l'homme. **6.** Chute (d'une place forte), déchéance (d'un empire, etc.). **7.** Éboulement *m*, éboulis *m*, tombée *f* (de terre, de rocher). **8.** *Nau:* **The falls,** les garants *m* (des embarcations). **'fall-pipe,** *s.* *Const:* Descente *f* (de gouttière). **'fall-trap,** *s.* *Ven:* Assommoir *m*.

fall², *v.i.* **(fell** [fel]; **fallen** ['fɔːlən]) Tomber. **1.** (*a*) **To fall to the ground** (*from on high*), tomber à terre. **To fall off a ladder,** tomber d'une échelle, à bas d'une échelle. **To fall on one's feet,** (i) (re)tomber sur ses pieds; (ii) *F:* avoir de la chance, de la veine. **To fall into a trap,** donner dans un piège. **To fall into s.o.'s hands,** tomber entre les mains de qn. **To let fall,** (i) laisser tomber (une assiette); (ii) baisser (le rideau); (iii) abaisser (une perpendiculaire); (iv) laisser échapper (une larme, un mot). **Night is falling,** la nuit tombe; le soir fait nuit; le jour baisse. (*b*) *His hair fell over his shoulders,* ses cheveux lui pendaient, lui descendaient, jusqu'aux épaules. (*c*) *Christmas falls on a Thursday,* Noël tombe un jeudi. **2.** (*From standing position*) (*a*) **To fall to the ground,** tomber par terre. **To fall full length,** tomber de tout son long. **To fall on one's knees,** tomber à genoux. **To fall by the sword,** périr sous l'épée. **To fall (to temptation),** succomber à la tentation. (*b*) (*Of building*) Crouler, s'écrouler, s'effondrer. **To fall to pieces,** tomber en morceaux. (*c*) *When Liège fell,* lorsque Liège capitula. *The Government has fallen,* le Ministère est tombé, a été renversé. **3.** (*a*) (*Of tide, barometer*) Descendre, baisser; (*of wind*) tomber ; (of sea) (se) calmer ; (of price, etc.) baisser. F: His stock is falling, ses actions baissent. (b) (Of ground) Aller en pente ; s'incliner ; descendre, s'abaisser. Mth: (Of curve) Décroître. Her eyes fell, elle baissa les yeux. His face fell, sa figure s'allongea. (c) Nau: To fall to leeward, tomber sous le vent. (d) To fall from one's position, déchoir de sa position. To fall in esteem, déchoir dans l'estime (du public). 4. (a) The sunlight falls on the peaks, le soleil donne sur les cimes. A sound fell (up)on my ear, un son frappa mon oreille. (b) To fall upon s.o.'s neck, on one's food, se jeter au cou de qn, sur la nourriture. To fall (up)on the enemy, fondre sur, attaquer, l'ennemi. (c) (Of river) Déboucher, se jeter (dans la mer, etc.). 5. (a) To fall to s.o.'s share, échoir (en partage) à qn. The blame falls upon . . ., le blâme retombe sur. . . . The responsibility falls on me, toute la responsabilité retombe sur moi. It falls on me to . . ., c'est à moi qu'incombe la tâche de. . . . It fell to me to . . ., le devoir m'échut de. . . . It falls within article 10, cela rentre dans, relève de, l'article 10. (b) (Of pers.) To fall under suspicion, se trouver, devenir, l'objet des soupçons ; devenir suspect. To fall across s.o., rencontrer qn par hasard. To fall on a means of doing sth., trouver un moyen de faire qch. To fall on evil days, avoir des jours de malheur ; F: tomber dans la débine. (c) I soon fell into their ways, (i) je me suis vite accoutumé à leur manière de faire ; (ii) j'eus bientôt appris la routine. To fall into a habit, contracter une habitude. To fall out of a habit, perdre une habitude. To fall into error, être induit en erreur. 6. Pred. (a) To fall sick, devenir malade, tomber malade. (Of post) To fall vacant, se trouver vacant. (b) To fall a victim to . . ., devenir victime de. . . . 7. To fall to sth., to doing sth., se mettre à qch., à faire qch. I fell (to) thinking of the past, mes pensées se tournèrent vers le passé. **fall away,** v.i. 1. (Of ground, etc.) S'affaisser brusquement ; s'abaisser. 2. Déserter ; faire défection. Theol: Apostasier. **fall back,** v.i. 1. Tomber en arrière, à la renverse. 2. (a) (Of outpost) Se replier ; reculer. (b) To f. back on substitutes, se rabattre sur des succédanés. Sum put by to f. back upon, somme en réserve comme en-cas. To f. back on lies, avoir recours au mensonge. **fall behind,** v.i. Rester en arrière. Rac: Se laisser distancer. **fall down,** v.i. 1. Tomber à terre, par terre. To fall down before s.o., se prosterner devant qn. 2. (a) (Of building) Crouler, s'écrouler, s'effondrer. (b) U.S: F: (Of pers., plan) Échouer. **fall for,** v.i. U.S: F: 1. Tomber amoureux de (qn) ; adopter (un projet, etc.) avec enthousiasme. 2. He fell for the trick, il s'y laissa prendre. **fall in,** v.i. 1. (a) (Of roof, etc.) S'écrouler, s'effondrer ; (of trench) s'ébouler. (b) (Of cheeks) Se creuser. 2. Mil: (Of troops) Former les rangs ; (of man) rentrer dans les rangs. Fall in! à vos rangs ! 3. (a) (Of lease, etc.) Expirer ; (of land) devenir disponible. (b) (Of debt) Arriver à échéance. 4. (a) To fall in with s.o., rencontrer qn. (b) To fall in with s.o.'s opinion, se ranger, se conformer, à l'avis de qn. To f. in with a proposal, accepter une proposition. (c) (Of plan, etc.) To f. in with . . ., cadrer avec. . . . 'fall-in, s. Mil: Rassemblement m. **falling in,** s. 1. Écroulement m, effondrement m. 2. Mil: Rassemblement m. 3. Expiration f (d'un bail) ; échéance f (d'une dette). 4. (a) Rencontre f (with s.o., avec qn). (b) Acquiescement m

(with, à) ; acceptation f (with, de). **fall off,** v.i. 1. His hat fell off, son chapeau tomba. 2. Nau: Abattre sous le vent ; arriver. 3. (Of followers) Faire défection. 4. (a) (Of profits) Diminuer ; (of speed) ralentir, décroître ; (of zeal) se relâcher. (b) Décliner ; (of skill) baisser ; (of beauty) passer. **fall out,** v.i. 1. Tomber dehors. 2. (Of hair) Tomber. 3. Mil: Quitter les rangs. 4. Se brouiller, se fâcher (with, avec). 5. Things fell out well, les choses se sont bien passées. It (so) fell out that . . ., il advint que . . . ; il arriva que. . . . **fall over,** v.i. 1. (Of pers.) Tomber à la renverse ; (of thg) se renverser, être renversé. 2. To fall over an obstacle, buter contre un obstacle et tomber. F: Publishers were falling over each other for his new book, les éditeurs se disputaient avec acharnement son prochain livre. **fall through,** v.i. (Of scheme) Ne pas aboutir ; échouer, avorter. **fall to,** v.i. (a) Se mettre à l'œuvre, au travail. (b) Entamer la lutte. (c) S'attaquer au repas. **fallen.** 1. a. (a) F. leaves, feuilles tombées. (b) Fallen humanity, l'humanité déchue. 2. s. The fallen, les morts m (sur le champ de bataille). **falling,** a. Tombant. Ph: Falling body, corps en chute. F. temperature, température en baisse. Com: Falling market, marché orienté à la baisse.

fallacious [fa'leiʃəs], a. Fallacieux, trompeur, -euse. **-ly,** adv. Fallacieusement, trompeusement.

fallaciousness [fa'leiʃəsnəs], s. Fausseté f.

fallacy ['faləsi], s. Log: Sophisme m ; faux raisonnement. F: A current fallacy, une erreur courante.

fallibility [fali'biliti], s. Faillibilité f.

fallible ['falibl], a. Faillible.

fallow¹ ['falo]. Agr: 1. s. Jachère f, friche f. 2. a. (Of land) En friche ; en jachère. To lie fallow, être en jachère ; être, rester, en friche. F: Mind that lies f., esprit incultivé, F: resté en friche.

fallow², a. (Of colour) Fauve.

false ['fɔls], a. Faux, f. fausse. 1. False report, F: canard m. To take a false step, faire un faux pas. To be in a false position, se trouver dans une position fausse. To put a f. interpretation on sth., interpréter qch. à faux. S.a. ALARM¹ 1. 2. Perfide, infidèle ; (of promise) mensonger. F. balance-sheet, faux bilan. To be false to one's husband, tromper son mari. False witness, faux témoin. To bear false witness, rendre faux témoignage. adv. To play s.o. false, trahir qn ; faire une perfidie à qn. 3. (Of hair, etc.) Artificiel, postiche ; (of action, tears) feint, prétendu, simulé ; (of document, etc.) forgé ; (of coin, seal) contrefait. False bottom, double fond (d'une boîte). **-ly,** adv. Faussement. 1. To interpret sth. f., interpréter qch. à faux. 2. Menteusement ; perfidement.

falsehood ['fɔlshu:d], s. 1. (a) Fausseté f (d'un bruit, etc.). (b) To distinguish truth from f., distinguer le vrai d'avec le faux. 2. Mensonge m. To tell a f., mentir.

falseness ['fɔlsnəs], s. 1. Fausseté f. 2. Infidélité f (d'un amant, etc.).

falsetto [fɔl'seto], s. & attrib. Mus: Falsetto (voice), voix f de tête, de fausset.

falsification [fɔlsifi'keiʃ(ə)n], s. Falsification f.

falsifier ['fɔlsifaiər], s. Falsificateur, -trice.

falsify ['fɔlsifai], v.tr. (falsified ; falsifying) 1. Falsifier (un document) ; fausser (un bilan). 2. (a) Prouver la fausseté de (qch.). (b) Tromper (un espoir).

falsity ['fɔlsiti], s. Fausseté f (d'une doctrine).

falter ['fɔltər]. **I.** *v.i.* (*a*) (*Of voice*) Hésiter, trembler, s'altérer. (*b*) (*Of pers.*) Vaciller, chanceler. (*c*) (*Of pers. or courage*) Défaillir ; *F:* flancher. **2.** *v.tr.* Dire (qch.) d'une voix hésitante, tremblante. **faltering,** *a.* **I.** (*Of voice, etc.*) Hésitant, tremblant, troublé. **2.** (*Of legs*) Vacillant, chancelant. **3.** (*Of courage, memory, etc.*) Défaillant. **-ly,** *adv.* **I.** (Parler) d'une voix tremblante, troublée. **2.** (Marcher) d'un pas mal assuré.

fame [feim], *s.* Renom *m*, renommée *f*. To win **fame,** se faire un grand nom. **Of good, ill, fame,** bien, mal, famé.

famed [feimd], *a.* Célèbre, renommé, fameux. To be **famed for sth.,** être renommé, bien connu, pour qch.

familiar [fə'miljər]. **I.** *a.* (*a*) Familier, intime. To be **familiar, on familiar terms,** with s.o., être familier, avoir des rapports d'intimité, avec qn. *You are rather too f.,* vous prenez trop de privautés. (*b*) **Familiar spirit,** démon familier. (*c*) (*Of thg*) Familier ; bien connu. *Amid f. surroundings,* en pays de connaissance. **Familiar phrase,** cliché *m*. To be on familiar ground, être sur son terrain. **His voice sounded familiar to me,** il me sembla reconnaître sa voix. (*d*) (*Of pers.*) To be **familiar with sth.,** être familier avec qch. ; connaître qch. *To make oneself f. with a language,* se familiariser avec une langue. **2.** *s.* Démon familier. **-ly,** *adv.* Familièrement, intimement.

familiarity [famili'ariti], *s.* Familiarité *f*. **I.** Intimité *f*. *Prov:* **Familiarity breeds contempt,** la familiarité engendre, fait naître, le mépris. **2.** Connaissance *f* (*with*, de).

familiarize [fə'miljəra:iz], *v.tr.* **I.** Familiariser (qch.) ; rendre (qch.) familier. **2.** To **familiarize s.o. with sth.,** habituer qn à qch.

family ['famili], *s.* Famille *f*. To be one of the **family,** être de la maison. **Man of good family,** homme de famille. **It runs in the family,** cela tient de famille. **A family dinner,** un dîner en famille. **Family hotel,** hôtel de famille. **Family butcher,** boucher qui livre à domicile. **Family life,** vie familiale. **Family man,** (i) père de famille ; (ii) homme d'intérieur.

famine ['famin], *s.* (*a*) Famine *f*. To die of **famine,** mourir de faim. (*b*) Disette *f*. **At famine prices,** à des prix de famine.

famished ['famiʃt], *a.* Affamé. *F.-looking,* (à l'aspect) famélique.

famishing ['famiʃiŋ], *a.* Qui a grand'faim. *To be f.,* *F:* avoir une faim de loup.

famous ['feiməs], *a.* **I.** Célèbre, renommé, fameux (*for,* pour, par). **2.** *F:* **That's famous!** excellent ! à la bonne heure ! **-ly,** *adv.* *F:* Fameusement ; à merveille.

fan¹ [fan], *s.* **I.** *Husb:* Tarare *m*. **2.** Éventail *m*. **3.** Ventilateur (rotatif, à ailes). **'fan-cooled,** *a.* *I.C.E:* (Radiateur) soufflé. **'fan-light,** *s.* Fenêtre *f* en éventail ; vasistas *m*. **'fan-shaped,** *a.* En éventail. **'fan-tracery,** *s.* *Arch:* Réseau *m* en éventail (d'une voûte).

fan², *v.tr.* (fanned) **I.** (*a*) Vanner (le grain). **2.** Éventer (qn). **To fan away the dust,** chasser la poussière avec un éventail, avec un journal. **To fan** (up) **the fire,** aviver le feu. **To fan a quarrel,** attiser, envenimer, une querelle. **3.** (*Of punkah, etc.*) Agiter (l'air).

fan³, *s.* *F:* Passionné, -ée, enragé, -ée, fervent *m* (du sport, etc.). **Film-fan,** cinéphile *mf*. **Fan mail,** courrier *m* des admirateurs et admiratrices (d'une vedette, etc.).

fanatic [fə'natik], *a. & s.* Fanatique (*m*).

fanatical [fə'natik(ə)l], *a.* Fanatique. **-ally,** *adv.* Fanatiquement.

fanaticism [fə'natisizm], *s.* Fanatisme *m*.

fancier ['fansiər], *s.* Amateur, -trice (de fleurs, etc.). **Dog-fancier,** (i) amateur de chiens ; (ii) éleveur *m* de chiens. *S.a.* BIRD-FANCIER, PIGEON-FANCIER.

fanciful ['fansiful], *a.* **I.** (*a*) (*Of pers.*) Capricieux, fantasque. (*b*) (*Travail*) fantaisiste. **2.** (Projet) chimérique ; (conte) imaginaire.

fancy¹ ['fansi]. **I.** *s.* **I.** (*a*) Imagination *f*, fantaisie *f*. **The land of fancy,** le pays des chimères. **In fancy I saw . . .,** en esprit, en imagination, je voyais. . . . (*b*) *It's only f.!* c'est pure imagination ! idées que tout cela ! (*c*) Idée *f.* **I have a fancy that . . .,** j'ai idée que. . . . **2.** (*a*) Fantaisie, caprice *m*. *Just as the f. takes me,* comme l'idée me prend. (*b*) Fantaisie, goût *m*. **To take a fancy to sth.,** prendre goût à qch. **To take a fancy to s.o.,** prendre qn en affection ; s'éprendre, s'enticher, de qn. *It took my f. at once,* cela m'a séduit du premier coup. **That suits my fancy,** cela me va. **A house after my fancy,** une maison à mon goût. *We must let her marry according to her fancy,* il faut la laisser se marier à son idée. **To have a** (passing) **fancy for s.o.,** avoir un caprice, un petit béguin, pour qn. **3.** The fancy. (*a*) (i) Les amateurs *m* de la boxe ; (ii) la boxe. (*b*) Les éleveurs *m* d'animaux ou oiseaux d'agrément. **II. fancy,** *a.* (*a*) (Pain, etc.) de fantaisie. **Fancy goods,** nouveautés *f*. **Fancy dress,** travesti *m*, déguisement *m*. **Fancy-dress ball,** bal travesti. (*b*) **Fancy dog, fancy breed,** chien, race, d'agrément, de luxe. **'fancy-'free,** *a.* (Cœur) inoccupé. **'fancy work,** *s.* Ouvrage(s) *m(pl)* d'agrément ; travaux *mpl* pour dames.

fancy², *v.tr.* **I.** (*a*) S'imaginer, se figurer (qch.). *He fancies he knows everything,* il se figure tout savoir. *F:* **Fancy now! fancy** (that)! figurez-vous ça ! conçoit-on ! (*b*) Croire, penser. *I f. he is out,* je crois bien, j'ai (l')idée, qu'il est sorti. *He fancied he heard footsteps,* il crut entendre des pas. **2.** (*a*) To **fancy sth.,** se sentir attiré vers qch. *I don't f. his offer,* son offre ne me dit rien. *Let him eat anything he fancies,* il peut manger tout ce qui lui dira. (*b*) To **fancy s.o.,** se sentir attiré vers qn ; être épris, entiché, de qn. (*c*) To **fancy oneself,** s'en faire accroire ; *F:* se gober. *He fancies his tennis,* il se croit de première force au tennis. **fancied,** *a.* Imaginaire, imaginé.

fane [fein], *s.* *Poet:* Temple *m*.

fanfare ['fanfɛər], *s.* Fanfare *f* (de cors) ; sonnerie *f* (de trompettes).

fang [faŋ], *s.* **I.** (*a*) Croc *m* (de chien, etc.) ; défense *f* (de sanglier). (*b*) Crochet *m* (de vipère). **2.** Soie *f* (d'un outil). **3.** Racine *f* (d'une dent).

fantasia [fanta'ziːa, fan'tɔːzia], *s.* *Mus:* Fantaisie *f*.

fantastic [fan'tastik], *a.* Fantasque, bizarre, excentrique ; capricieux.

fantasy ['fantəzi], *s.* **I.** Fantaisie *f*. (*a*) Imagination capricieuse. (*b*) Caprice *m*. (*a*) Vision *f*, idée *f*, bizarre, fantastique. (*b*) Idée fantasque.

far¹ [fɑːr], *adv.* (farther, -est, further, -est, *q.v.*) Loin. **I.** (*a*) *To go far,* aller loin. *'Not so 'far,* pas si loin. (*Cp.* 2.) *To advance far into Africa,* pénétrer très avant dans l'Afrique. *To carry a canal as far as the sea,* conduire un canal jusqu'à la mer. **How far is it from . . . to . . . ?** combien y a-t-il de . . . à . . . ? *'So far and no farther,* jusque-là et pas plus loin. **Thus far,** jusqu'ici ; jusque-là. **As far as the eye can reach,** à perte de vue. *To live far away, far off,* demeurer au loin. **Far and wide,** de tous côtés ; partout.

Stake driven far into the ground, pieu enfoncé profondément dans la terre. Far from . . ., loin de. . . . Not far from . . ., à peu de distance de . . .; non loin de. . . . (b) That will go far towards making up for our loss, cela aidera beaucoup à nous dédommager. To make one's money go far, faire bon usage de son argent. To go so far as to do sth., aller jusqu'à faire qch. He has gone too far to withdraw, il est trop engagé pour reculer. That is going too far, cela passe la mesure, les bornes. To carry a joke too far, pousser trop loin une plaisanterie. How far have you got (in your reading, etc.)? où en êtes-vous (de votre lecture, etc.)? As far as I know, autant que je sache. As far as that goes . . ., pour ce qui est de cela. . . I will help you as far as I can, je vous aiderai dans la mesure de mes moyens. So far so good, c'est fort bien jusque-là; jusqu'ici ça va bien. In so far as . . ., dans la mesure où . . .; pour autant que. . . . To be far from believing sth., être à mille lieues de croire qch. Far from admiring him I loathe him, bien loin de l'admirer je le déteste. He is far from happy, il s'en faut de beaucoup qu'il soit heureux. Far from it, tant s'en faut; loin de là. Not far from it, peu s'en faut. Far be it from me to put pressure on you! loin de moi l'idée de vous influencer! He is not far off sixty, il approche de la soixantaine. By far the best, de beaucoup le meilleur. 2. (Of time) 'So far, jusqu'ici. Not 'so far, pas encore. (Cp. 1 (a).) As far back as I can remember, aussi loin, du plus loin, qu'il me souvienne. As far back as 1900, déjà en 1900. As far as I can tell, autant que je puisse prévoir. He did not look so far into the future, il ne regardait pas si avant (dans l'avenir). Far into the night, bien avant dans la nuit. 3. (With qualifying adjectives, adverbs, etc.) Beaucoup, bien, fort. It is far better, c'est beaucoup mieux. It is far more serious, c'est bien autrement sérieux. Far and away the best, de beaucoup le meilleur. The night was far advanced, far spent, la nuit était fort avancée. 'far-away, a. Lointain, éloigné. Far-away look, regard perdu dans le vague. F.-a. voice, voix éteinte. 'far-be'tween, pred. a. Visits few and far-between, visites rares et espacées. 'far-'famed, a. Dont la renommée s'est étendue au loin; célèbre. 'far-'fetched, a. (Of example, comparison) Forcé, outré; tiré par les cheveux. 'far-flung, a. (Of empire, etc.) Très étendu; vaste. 'far-'off, a. = FAR-AWAY. 'far-reaching, a. De grande envergure; d'une grande portée. 'far-'seeing, a. Prévoyant, clairvoyant, perspicace. 'far-'sighted, a. 1. = FAR-SEEING. 2. Presbyte; à la vue longue. far-'sightedness, s. 1. Prescience f; perspicacité f. 2. Presbytie f.

far², a. (farther, -est, further, -est, q.v.) 1. Lointain, éloigné, reculé. 2. At the far end of the street, à l'autre bout de la rue.

farce [fɑːrs], s. Th: Farce f. F: His examination was a farce, on lui fit passer un examen pour rire.

farcical ['fɑːrsik(ə)l], a. Risible, bouffon, grotesque. A f. examination, un examen pour rire.

fare¹ ['feər], s. 1. (a) Prix m du voyage, de la place; prix de la course (en taxi, etc.). Single fare, prix du billet simple. Return fare, billet et retour m. Excess fare, supplément m. (In bus, etc.) Fares, please! les places, s'il vous plaît! (b) (In hired vehicle) Client m; voyageur, -euse. 2. Chère f, manger m. Prison f, régime m de prison. To be fond of good f., aimer la table.

fare², v.i. 1. A. & Lit: Voyager. To fare forth, partir. 2. (a) To fare well, ill, aller bien, mal;

se trouver dans une bonne, mauvaise, situation. To fare alike, partager le même sort. A. & Poet: Fare thee well! adieu! (b) Impers. How fares it (with you)? est-ce que ça marche? 3. Manger, se nourrir. We fared well, nous avons fait bonne chère.

farewell [feər'wel], int. & s. Adieu (m). To bid farewell to s.o., to take one's farewell of s.o., dire adieu, faire ses adieux, à qn.

farinaceous [fari'neiʃəs], a. Farinacé.

farm¹ [fɑːrm], s. (a) Ferme f (d'exploitation agricole). Sheep-farm, élevage m de moutons. S.a. BABY-FARM, MUSSEL-FARM, OYSTER-FARM, POULTRY-FARM, SEWAGE. (b) = FARM-HOUSE. 'farm-hand, -labourer, s. Valet m de ferme. 'farm-house, s. (Maison f de) ferme f. 'farm-stead, s. Ferme f. 'farm-yard, s. Cour f de ferme; basse-cour f.

farm², v.tr. 1. To farm (out). (a) Donner à ferme, affermer (des impôts). (b) Mettre (des enfants) en nourrice. 2. (a) Cultiver, faire valoir (une propriété). (b) Abs. Être fermier. farming, s. 1. Affermage m (d'une propriété, des impôts). 2. Exploitation f agricole; agriculture f. Stock farming, élevage m. Farming lease, bail m à ferme. S.a. DAIRY-FARMING.

farmer ['fɑːrmər], s. 1. Farmer of revenues, fermier m des impôts. 2. Fermier, cultivateur m. The farmer's wife, la fermière. Stock farmer éleveur m. S.a. BABY-FARMER.

faro ['feərəʊ], s. Cards: Pharaon m.

Faroe Islands ['feərəʊailəndz, 'fɑːr-]. Pr.n.pl. Les îles f Féroé.

farrago [fə'reigəʊ], s. Pej: Méli-mélo m, macédoine f; fatras m (de connaissances).

farrier ['fariər], s. 1. Maréchal (ferrant). 2. Vétérinaire m.

farriery ['fariəri], s. 1. Maréchalerie f. 2. Art m vétérinaire.

farrow ['farəʊ], s. Portée f (de cochons).

farther ['fɑːrðər]. (Comp. of FAR) 1. adv. (a) Plus loin (than, que). Farther off, plus éloigné. Farther on, plus en avant; plus loin; plus avancé. Nothing is farther from my thoughts, rien n'est plus éloigné de ma pensée. F: To wish s.o. farther, envoyer qn au diable. (b) Farther back, plus en arrière. 2. a. (a) Plus lointain, plus éloigné. At the f. end of the room, à l'autre bout de la salle; au fond de la salle. (b) Farther back, antérieur (than, à).

farthermost ['fɑːrðəmoust], a. Le plus lointain, le plus éloigné, le plus reculé.

farthest ['fɑːrðəst]. (Sup. of FAR) 1. a. (a) Farthest (off), le plus lointain, le plus éloigné. In f. Siberia, au fin fond de la Sibérie. (b) (Of way, etc.) Le plus long. (c) The men f. in his confidence, les hommes les plus avancés dans sa confiance. 2. adv. Le plus loin.

farthing ['fɑːrðiŋ], s. Quart m d'un penny. F: Not to have a farthing, n'avoir pas le sou. To pay to the uttermost farthing, payer jusqu'au dernier sou. Not to be worth a brass farthing, ne pas valoir un centime, un rouge liard.

fascia, pl. -iae ['faʃiə, -ii], s. 1. (a) Arch: Fasce f, bandelette f, bande f. (b) Com: Enseigne f en forme d'entablement. 2. Anat: Fascia m.

fascicle ['fasikl], fascicule ['fasikjul], s. Nat. Hist: Fascicule m.

fascinate ['fasineit], v.tr. (a) (Of serpent) Fasciner, charmer (sa proie). (b) F: Fasciner, enchanter, séduire. fascinating, a. Enchanteur, -eresse; séduisant.

fascination [fasi'neiʃ(ə)n], s. 1. Fascination f

(d'une proie). **2.** *F:* Fascination, charme *m*, attrait *m*.

fascine [fa'si:n], *s.* Fascine *f*.

fashion[1] ['faʃ(ə)n], *s.* **1.** Façon *f* (d'un habit, etc.); forme *f* (d'un objet); manière *f* (de faire qch.). (*In the) French f.*, à la française. *Everyone does it in his own f.*, chacun le fait à sa mode, à sa façon. **After the fashion of . . .**, à la façon, à la manière, de. **. . . After a fashion**, tant bien que mal. **2.** Habitude *f*, coutume *f*. *As was his f.*, selon sa coutume. **3.** (*Of clothes, etc.*) Mode *f*, vogue *f*. In (the) fashion, à la mode, de mode, en vogue. **Out of fashion**, passé de mode; démodé. **To bring sth. into fashion**, mettre qch. à la mode; lancer la mode de qch. **To come into fashion**, entrer en vogue. **To lead, set, the fashion**, donner la note, le ton; fixer, mener, la mode. *A man of fashion*, un élégant. *A woman of f.*, une mondaine. *People of f.*, gens de condition; le beau monde. **'fashion-book**, *s.* Journal *m* de modes. **'fashion-plate**, *s.* Gravure *f* de modes.

fashion[2], *v.tr.* Façonner, former (une poterie, etc.); confectionner (une robe, etc.).

fashioned, *a.* **1.** (*Of wood, etc.*) Façonné, travaillé, ouvré. **2.** New-fashioned, de nouvelle mode; à la mode (du jour). *S.a.* OLD-FASHIONED.

fashionable ['faʃənəbl], *a.* A la mode, élégant, fashionable, en vogue. *The f. world*, le beau monde. *A f. resort*, un endroit mondain. **-ably**, *adv.* Élégamment; à la mode.

fast[1] [fɑːst], *s.* Jeûne *m*. **To break one's fast**, (i) rompre le jeûne; (ii) déjeuner. *I have not yet broken my f.*, je suis encore à jeun. **'fast-day**, *s.* *Ecc:* Jour *m* de jeûne; jour maigre.

fast[2], *v.i.* (*a*) Jeûner; s'abstenir (*from*, de). *Med:* 'To be taken fasting,' " à prendre le matin à jeun." (*b*) *Ecc:* Jeûner; faire maigre. **fasting**, *s.* Jeûne *m*.

fast[3]. **I.** *a.* **1.** (*a*) Ferme, fixe, solide; (*of grip, hold*) tenace; (*of knot*) serré. **Fast pulley**, poulie fixe. **Feet f. in the mud**, pieds collés dans la boue. **To make a rope fast**, amarrer un cordage. **To have fast hold of sth.**, tenir qch. serré. **To hold a prisoner f.**, tenir ferme un prisonnier. **Fast friends**, des amis sûrs, solides. (*b*) *Nau:* Amarré. *To make a boat f.*, amarrer un bateau. **To make fast**, prendre le corps-mort; s'amarrer. (*c*) (*Of door, etc.*) (Bien) assujetti; bien fermé. (*d*) (*Of colour*) Solide, résistant; bon teint *inv*. **2.** (*a*) Rapide, vite. *Fb:* *F. forwards*, avants très vites. *Rail:* **Fast train**, rapide *m*. **To send goods by fast train**, expédier des marchandises en grande vitesse. (*b*) **Fast billiard-table**, billard qui rend bien. **3.** (*Of clock, watch*) En avance. *My watch is five minutes f.*, ma montre avance de cinq minutes. **4.** *F:* (*Of pers.*) (*a*) Dissipé; de mœurs légères. **The fast set**, les viveurs *m*. (*b*) (Trop) émancipé. *F. girl*, jeune fille d'allures très libres. **II. fast**, *adv.* **1.** Ferme, solidement. **To hold fast**, tenir ferme; tenir bon. **To stand fast**, tenir bon; rester inébranlable. **To stick fast**, (i) bien tenir; (ii) rester pris, rester collé. **To sleep fast**, dormir d'un profond sommeil. *F:* **To play fast and loose**, agir avec inconstance; jouer double jeu (*with s.o.*, avec qn). **2.** Vite, rapidement. **Not so fast!** pas si vite! doucement! *It is raining f.*, il pleut à verse. *He drew back as f. as I advanced*, (au fur et) à mesure que j'avançais il reculait.

fasten [fɑːsn]. **1.** *v.tr.* (*a*) Attacher (*to, on*, à). *To f. a boat to a post*, amarrer un bateau à un pieu. **To fasten one's eyes on s.o.**, attacher, fixer, les yeux sur qn. **To fasten a crime on s.o.**,

imputer un crime à qn. *To f. the responsibility on s.o.*, mettre, rejeter, la responsabilité sur le dos de qn. (*b*) Fixer, assurer, assujettir (la porte, etc.). **To fasten (up) a parcel with string**, lier un colis avec une ficelle. *To f. (up) a garment*, agrafer, boutonner, un vêtement. **2.** *v.i.* S'attacher, se fixer. *His opponent fastened on to his leg*, son adversaire se cramponna à sa jambe. *My eyes fastened on the statue*, mes yeux s'arrêtèrent, s'attachèrent, sur la statue. **He fastened on me as an easy prey**, il s'attacha à moi, flairant un jobard. *To f. (up)on a pretext*, saisir un prétexte. **fasten down**, *v.tr.* Assujettir, fixer, (qch.) à terre ou en place; sceller (une lettre). **fastening**, *s.* **1.** Attache *f*, attachement *m*; assujettissement *m*; agrafage *m*. **2.** = FASTENER.

fastener ['fɑːsnər], *s.* Attache *f*; (*of garment*) agrafe *f*; (*of book, purse*) fermoir *m*; (*of window, etc.*) fermeture *f*. **Patent fastener, snap fastener**, bouton *m* (à) pression. *S.a.* PAPER-FASTENER, ZIP[1] 3.

fastidious [fas'tidiəs], *a.* Difficile (à satisfaire); délicat (*about sth.*, sur qch.). **-ly**, *adv.* D'un air de dégoût; dédaigneusement.

fastness ['fɑːstnəs], *s.* **1.** (*a*) Fermeté *f*, stabilité *f* (d'un pieu); solidité *f* (d'une couleur). (*b*) Rapidité *f*, vitesse *f*. (*c*) Légèreté *f* de conduite. **2.** *Lit:* Place forte. **Mountain fastness**, repaire *m* (de brigands).

fat[1] [fat], *a.* (**fatter**; **fattest**) **1.** Gras, *f.* grasse. *To get, grow, fat*, engraisser; prendre de l'embonpoint. *F:* *To give a fat laugh*, rire gras. **Fat volume**, gros tome. *Aut:* **Fat spark**, étincelle nourrie. **Fat coal**, houille grasse, bitumineuse. **2.** (*Of land*) Riche, fertile, gras. *F:* **Fat salary**, de gros appointements. **'fat-head**, *s.* *F:* Imbécile *m*, nigaud *m*. **'fat-headed**, *a.* *F:* A l'esprit bouché; sot, *f.* sotte. *That f.-h. postman*, cet imbécile de facteur.

fat[2], *s.* **1.** Graisse *f*. *Mutton fat*, suif *m* de mouton. *Pharm:* Hog's fat, axonge *f*. *F:* **The fat is in the fire**, le feu est aux poudres! gare la bombe! **2.** Gras *m* (de viande). *F:* **To live on the fat of the land**, vivre comme un coq en pâte; vivre grassement. *P:* **A bit of fat**, un coup de chance; un peu de beurre dans les épinards.

fat[3], *v.tr. & i. Husb:* = FATTEN. **fatted**, *a.* *A:* Engraissé. **To kill the fatted calf**, tuer le veau gras.

fatal ['feit(ə)l], *a.* Fatal, -als. **1.** *The f. hour*, l'heure fatale; l'heure de la mort. **2.** (*a*) Fatal blow, coup fatal, mortel. **Fatal disease**, maladie mortelle. (*b*) *Reef f. to navigation*, écueil fatal, funeste, à la navigation. *A f. influence*, influence néfaste. *A f. mistake*, une faute capitale. **-ally**, *adv.* **1.** Fatalement, inévitablement. **2.** Mortellement (blessé, etc.).

fatalism ['feitəlizm], *s.* Fatalisme *m*.

fatalist ['feitəlist], *s.* Fataliste *mf*.

fatalistic [feitə'listik], *a.* Fataliste.

fatality [fa'taliti], *s.* **1.** (*Fate*) Fatalité *f*. **2.** Caractère *m* funeste, influence *f* néfaste (*of*, de). **3.** Accident mortel; sinistre *m*. *Bathing fatalities*, baignades tragiques, mortelles.

fate [feit], *s.* Destin *m*, sort *m*. *Myth:* **The Fates**, les Parques *f*. **To leave s.o. to his fate**, abandonner qn à son sort. *He met his f. in 1915*, il trouva la mort en 1915.

fated ['feitid], *a.* **1.** (*Of day, occurrence*) Fatal, -als; inévitable. **2.** Destiné, condamné (*to do sth.*, à faire qch.). **3.** Voué à la destruction; condamné.

fateful ['feitful], *a.* **1.** (Voix, etc.) prophétique. **Fateful word**, parole fatidique. **2.** (Jour, etc.)

décisif, fatal, -als. **3.** (Événement, etc.) fatal, inévitable.

father[1] ['fɑːðər], *s.* **I.** Père *m.* From father to son, de père en fils. Like a father, paternellement; en père. *F:* To talk to s.o. like a f., sermonner qn. Yes, Father, oui, (mon) père. *Th:* Heavy father, père noble. **2.** *pl.* Our fathers, nos ancêtres *m*, nos pères. **3.** (a) *F:* Père, fondateur *m*, créateur *m* (d'un art, etc.). (b) The Fathers of the Church, les Pères de l'Église. **7.** *Theol:* God the Father, Dieu le Père. **5.** *Ecc:* (a) The Holy Father, le Saint-Père, le père des fidèles. Father confessor, père spirituel; directeur *m* (de conscience). (b) Father O'Malley, (i) le Père O'Malley; (ii) l'abbé O'Malley. The Capuchin fathers, les pères capucins. **6.** Doyen *m* (d'une société, etc.). *Rom.Hist:* The City Fathers, les Édiles *m.* **'father-in-law,** *s.m.* Beau-père.

father[2], *v.tr.* **I.** Engendrer (un enfant); *F:* inventer, produire (qch.); concevoir (un projet). **2.** Adopter (un enfant). **3.** To father a child, *F:* a book, (up)on s.o., attribuer à qn la paternité d'un enfant, *F:* d'un livre. To f. the fault on s.o., imputer la faute à qn.

fatherhood ['fɑːðərhud], *s.* Paternité *f.*

fatherland ['fɑːðərlænd], *s.* Patrie *f.*

fatherless ['fɑːðərləs], *a.* Sans père; orphelin, -ine, de père.

fatherly ['fɑːðərli], *a.* Paternel.

fathom[1] ['fæðəm], *s. Nau:* Brasse *f* (= 1 m. 829). Harbour four fathom deep, port avec un brassiage de quatre toises *f.*

fathom[2], *v.tr. Nau:* Sonder. *F:* To fathom the mystery, approfondir, pénétrer, sonder, le mystère.

fathomless ['fæðəmləs], *a.* (Abîme) sans fond, insondable.

fatidical [fei'tidik(ə)l], *a.* Fatidique.

fatigue[1] [fə'tiːg], *s.* **I.** Fatigue *f.* **2.** *Mil:* Corvée *f.* To be on fatigue, être de corvée. Fatigue party, (détachement *m* de) corvée. **fa'tigue-cap,** *s. Mil:* Bonnet *m* de police. **fa'tigue-dress,** *s. Mil:* Tenue *f* de corvée; (jeu *m* de) treillis *m.*

fatigue[2], *v.tr.* **I.** Fatiguer, lasser (qn). **2.** *Tchn:* Fatiguer (un métal, un mât). **fatiguing,** *a.* Fatigant, épuisant.

fatness ['fætnəs], *s.* **I.** Adiposité *f*; embonpoint *m*, corpulence *f.* **2.** Onctuosité *f* (de l'argile).

fatten [fætn]. **I.** *v.tr.* To fatten (up), engraisser (des moutons, etc.); empâter (la volaille). **2.** *v.i.* Engraisser; devenir gras. **fattening**[1], *a.* (Of food, etc.) Engraissant. **fattening**[2], *s.* Engraissement *m.*

fatty ['fæti]. **I.** *a.* (a) Graisseux, onctueux, cléagineux. *Ch:* Fatty acid, acide gras. (b) (Of tissue, etc.) Adipeux. *Med:* Fatty heart, dégénérescence graisseuse du cœur. **2.** *s. P:* Gros enfant; gros bonhomme.

fatuity [fə'tjuiti], **fatuousness** ['fætjuəsnəs], *s.* Sottise *f*; imbécillité *f* (d'une observation).

fatuous ['fætjuəs], *a.* Sot, imbécile, idiot; (sourire) béat. **-ly,** *adv.* Sottement; d'un air idiot.

faucet ['fɔːset], *s.* (a) *Dial:* Cannelle *f* (de tonneau). (b) *U.S:* Robinet *m.*

faugh [fɔː], *int.* Pouah !

fault [fɔːlt], *s.* **I.** Défaut *m*, travers *m*; imperfection *f*; vice *m* de construction. In spite of all his faults, malgré tous ses travers. His f. is excessive shyness, il pèche par trop de timidité. Scrupulous to a fault, scrupuleux à l'excès. To find fault with s.o., sth., trouver à redire contre qn, à qch. I can find no f. with him, je ne trouve rien à lui reprocher. **2.** Faute *f.* To be in fault, at fault, être en défaut; être fautif, coupable. To find, catch, s.o. in fault, trouver, prendre, qn en faute. Whose fault is it? à qui la faute? It is nobody's f. but your own, il ne faut vous en prendre qu'à vous-même. **3.** *Ten:* Faute. **4.** *Ven:* (Of hounds) To bark at fault, aboyer à faux. To be at fault, être en défaut. Memory at fault, mémoire en défaut; mémoire fautive. To be at fault for an answer, être embarrassé pour répondre. **5.** *Geol:* Faille *f*; cassure *f* avec rejet. **'fault-finder,** *s.* **I.** (Pers.) Épilogueur, -euse; critiqueur, -euse; mécontent *m.* **2.** *El.E:* (Device) Déceleur *m* de fuites. **'fault-finding**[1], *a.* Censeur, -euse; chicanier, -ière. **'fault-finding**[2], *s.* Disposition *f* à critiquer.

faultiness ['fɔːltinəs], *s.* Incorrection *f* (de style, etc.); défectuosité *f*, imperfection *f.*

faultless ['fɔːltləs], *a.* Sans défaut, sans faute; impeccable, irréprochable. **-ly,** *adv.* Parfaitement, irréprochablement. *F.* dressed, d'une mise impeccable.

faulty ['fɔːlti], *a.* (Of work, etc.) Défectueux, imparfait; (of style, etc.) incorrect; (of reasoning, etc.) erroné, inexact. *F.* expression, locution vicieuse. **-ily,** *adv.* Défectueusement, incorrectement.

faun [fɔːn], *s. Myth:* Faune *m.*

fauna ['fɔːnə], *s.* Faune *f* (d'un pays).

favour[1] ['feivər], *s.* Faveur *f.* **I.** Approbation *f*; bonnes grâces. To find favour with s.o., to gain s.o.'s favour, gagner la faveur de qn; se faire bien voir de qn. To be in favour with s.o., être en faveur auprès de qn; jouir de la faveur de qn. To be restored, to return, to f., rentrer en faveur. To be out of favour, (i) être mal en cour; (ii) (of fashion) n'être plus en vogue. To bring sth. into f., mettre qch. à la mode. **2.** Grâce *f*, bonté *f.* To ask a favour of s.o., solliciter une grâce, une faveur, de qn. To do s.o. a favour, faire une faveur à qn; obliger qn. Will you do me a f.? voulez-vous me faire plaisir? As a favour, à titre gracieux. (On letter) By favour of . . ., par bonté de. . . . *Com:* Your favour of the 15th, votre lettre, votre honorée, du 15. **3.** (a) Partialité *f*, préférence *f.* To show favour towards s.o., favoriser qn; accorder à qn un traitement de faveur. To administer justice without fear or favour, rendre la justice sans distinction de personnes. (b) Appui *m*, protection *f.* Under favour of the night, à la faveur de la nuit. **4.** *Prep.phr.* In favour of . . ., en faveur de . . .; à l'avantage de. . . . To have everything in one's favour, avoir tout pour soi. To decide in f. of s.o., in s.o.'s f., donner gain de cause à qn; donner raison à qn. To be in favour of sth., être partisan de qch.; tenir pour qch. **5.** Faveur *f*; nœud *m* de ruban.

favour[2], *v.tr.* Favoriser. **I.** Approuver, préférer. To f. a scheme, se prêter à un projet; approuver un projet; être en faveur d'un projet. I don't favour the idea, l'idée ne me sourit pas. **2.** Gratifier, obliger (qn); accorder une grâce à (qn). To favour s.o. with an interview, accorder un rendez-vous à qn. To be favoured with an order, être honoré d'une commande. **3.** (a) Avantager (qn); montrer la partialité pour (qn). (b) Faciliter (qch.). Favoured by fortune, secondé par le sort. Device that favours combustion, dispositif qui active la combustion. **4.** (a) (Of fact) Confirmer (un rapport). (b) Every indication favoured rain, toutes les indications étaient à la pluie. **5.** *F:* Ressembler à (qn). **favoured**, *a.* (Of pers.) **I.** Favorisé. *F:* The favoured few, les élus. **2.** **Well-favoured,** beau, *f.* belle. *S.a.* ILL-FAVOURED.

favourable ['feivərəbl], *a.* Favorable; (*of weather*) propice; (*of reception*) bienveillant; (*of terms*) bon, avantageux; (*of report*) rassurant. **To look on s.o. with a favourable eye,** regarder qn d'un œil favorable. *Com: Specially f. rate,* taux de faveur. **-ably,** *adv.* Favorablement, avantageusement. *S.a.* PROGRESS².

favourite ['feivərit]. **I.** *s.* Favori, *f.* favorite. *To be a f. with, of, s.o.; to be s.o.'s f.,* être le bien vu, la bien vue, de qn. **He is a universal favourite,** tout le monde l'aime. *Rac:* **To back the favourite,** jouer le favori. **2.** *a.* (Fils, auteur, etc.) favori, préféré. *F. event,* réunion (sportive) très courue.

favouritism ['feivəritizm], *s.* Favoritisme *m.*

fawn¹ [fɔːn]. **I.** *s.* *Z:* Faon *m.* **2.** *a.* **Fawn (-coloured),** fauve.

fawn², *v.ind.tr.* **To fawn (up)on s.o.,** (i) (*of dog*) caresser qn; se coucher devant qn; (ii) (*of pers.*) faire le chien couchant, le plat valet, auprès de qn; ramper devant qn. **fawning¹,** *a.* (*Of dog*) Caressant; *F:* (*of pers.*) servile; flagorneur, -euse. **fawning²,** *s.* Flagornerie *f*; servilité *f.*

fawner ['fɔːnər], *s.* Adulateur, -trice; flagorneur, -euse.

fealty ['fiːəlti], *s.* féauté *f*; fidélité *f.*

fear¹ ['fiːər], *s.* **I.** Crainte *f,* peur *f.* **Deadly fear,** effroi *m.* *Have no f.,* ne craignez rien! n'ayez pas peur! **To be, stand, go, in fear of s.o.,** redouter, craindre, qn. **To go in fear of one's life,** craindre pour sa vie. **For fear of mistakes, of making a mistake,** de crainte d'erreur. *For f. we should forget,* de peur que nous (n')oubliions. **To have fears for s.o., for s.o.'s safety,** craindre pour qn. *F:* **No fear!** pas de danger! **2.** Respect *m,* crainte (de Dieu, etc.). *F:* **To put the fear of God into s.o.,** faire à qn une semonce dont il se souviendra.

fear², *v.tr.* **I.** Craindre, avoir peur de, redouter. **2.** Appréhender, craindre (un événement). **To fear for s.o.,** s'inquiéter au sujet de qn. *I f. it is too late,* j'ai peur, je crains, qu'il ne soit trop tard. *F:* **Never (you) fear! don't you fear!** pas de danger! soyez tranquille! **3.** Avoir la crainte de (Dieu, etc.).

fearful ['fiːərful], *a.* **I.** Affreux, effrayant, redoutable. *F:* **A fearful mess,** un désordre effrayant. **2.** (*a*) Peureux, craintif, timide. (*b*) *I was f. of wakening him, lest I should waken him,* je tremblais de le réveiller. **-fully,** *adv.* **I.** Affreusement, terriblement. **2.** Peureusement, craintivement, timidement.

fearfulness ['fiːərfulnəs], *s.* **I.** Caractère épouvantable, terrifiant (de qch.). **2.** Crainte *f,* timidité *f.*

fearless ['fiːərləs], *a.* Intrépide, courageux; sans peur (*of,* de). **-ly,** *adv.* Intrépidement; sans peur, sans hésitation.

fearlessness ['fiːərləsnəs], *s.* Intrépidité *f.*

fearnought ['fiːərnɔːt], *s.* *Tex:* Frise *f.*

fearsome ['fiːərsəm], *a.* Redoutable, *F:* formidable.

feasibility [fiːzi'biliti], **feasibleness** ['fiːziblnəs], *s.* **I.** Praticabilité *f,* possibilité *f.* **2.** Plausibilité *f,* vraisemblance *f.*

feasible ['fiːzibl], *a.* **I.** Faisable, possible, praticable. **2.** Vraisemblable, probable.

feast¹ [fiːst], *s.* **I.** *Ecc: etc:* Fête *f.* **Movable feast,** fête mobile. **2.** Festin *m,* banquet *m*; régal *m,* -als. **'feast-day,** *s.* (Jour *m* de) fête *f*; jour férié.

feast². **I.** *v.i.* Faire festin; banqueter, se régaler. *To f. (up)on sth.,* se régaler de qch. **2.** *v.tr.* Ré-

galer, fêter (qn). **To feast one's eyes on sth., feasting,** *s.* Festoiement *m*; bonne chère.

feat [fiːt], *s.* **I.** Exploit *m,* haut fait; prouesse *f.* **Feat of arms,** fait d'armes. **2.** (*a*) Tour *m* de force. (*b*) Feat of skill, tour d'adresse.

feather¹ ['feðər], *s.* **I.** Plume *f*; (*of tail, wing*) penne *f.* *F:* **To show the white feather,** voir qu'on a peur; *P:* caner, caler. *I tried to smooth his ruffled feathers,* j'ai essayé de le remettre de bonne humeur. **You could have knocked me down with a feather,** j'ai pensé tomber de mon haut. *Prov:* **Fine feathers make fine birds,** la belle plume fait le bel oiseau. **2.** Plumage *m.* **To be in full feather,** (i) (*of bird*) avoir tout son plumage; (ii) *F:* (*of pers.*) être en grande toilette. **To be in high feather,** être gai et dispos. **They are birds of a feather,** ce sont gens de (la) même farine. *Prov:* **Birds of a feather flock together,** qui se ressemble s'assemble. **3.** *Mil:* Plumet *m.* *F:* **That's a feather in his cap,** c'est pour lui un titre de vanité. **4.** *Mec.E:* Clavette plate. **'feather-'bed,** *s.* Lit *m* de plume. **'feather-brain,** *s.* Hurluberlu *m*; évaporée *f*; tête *f* de linotte. **'feather-brained,** *a.* Écervelé, étourdi; à tête de linotte. **'feather-'brush, -'duster,** *s.* Plumeau *m.* **'feather-stitch,** *s.* *Needlew:* Point *m* d'arêtes. **'feather-weight,** *s.* *Box:* Poids *m* plume.

feather². **I.** *v.tr.* (*a*) Empenner (une flèche): emplumer (un chapeau). **To tar and feather s.o.,** emplumer qn. *F:* **To feather one's nest,** faire sa pelote, ses choux gras; mettre du foin dans ses bottes. (*b*) *Row:* Ramener (l'aviron) à plat; *abs.* nager plat. **2.** *v.i.* (*a*) (*Of young bird*) **To feather (out),** s'emplumer. (*b*) *The snow comes feathering down,* la neige tombe en flocons légers.

featherless ['feðərləs], *a.* **I.** Sans plumes. **2.** Déplumé.

feathery ['feðəri], *a.* Plumeux.

feature¹ ['fiːtjər], *s.* **I.** Trait *m* (du visage). **The features,** la physionomie. **2.** (*a*) Trait, caractéristique *f,* particularité *f* (d'un paysage, d'un édifice). **Main features,** grands traits. **Feature of the ground,** accident *m* de terrain. (*b*) *Shop that makes a f. of its China tea,* boutique qui a pour spécialité les thés de Chine. *Cin:* **The feature film,** le grand film du programme.

feature², *v.tr.* **I.** Caractériser, marquer, distinguer (qch.). **2.** *Cin:* (i) Représenter (qn); tourner (un rôle). (ii) **Film featuring George Arliss,** film avec George Arliss en vedette. **3.** *Journ:* To feature a piece of news, mettre une nouvelle en manchette. **-featured,** *a.* Rugged-featured, aux traits rudes. **Pleasant-featured,** à la physionomie agréable.

febrifuge ['febrifjuːdʒ], *s.* *Med:* Fébrifuge *m.*

febrile ['fiːbrail], *a.* Fébrile, fiévreux.

February ['februəri], *s.* Février *m.* *In F.,* au mois de février. (*On) the fifth of F.,* le cinq février.

feckless ['fekləs], *a.* *Dial:* **I.** Veule; sans énergie. **2.** Incapable.

fecund ['fekənd], *a.* *Lit:* **I.** Fécond. **2.** Fécondant, fertilisant.

fecundate ['fekəndeit], *v.tr.* Féconder.

fecundation [fekən'deiʃ(ə)n], *s.* Fécondation *f.*

fecundity [fe'kʌnditi], *s.* Fécondité *f.*

fed [fed]. *See* FEED².

federal ['fedərəl]. **I.** *a.* Fédéral, -aux. **2.** *a.* *U.S.Hist:* Fédéral *m,* nordiste *m.*

federalism ['fedərəlizm], *s.* Fédéralisme *m.*

federalist ['fedərəlist], *s.* Fédéraliste *mf.*

federate¹ ['fedərət], *a.* Fédéré.

federate² ['fedəreit]. **1.** *v.tr.* Fédérer. **2.** *v.i.* Se fédérer.

federation [fedə'reiʃ(ə)n], *s.* Fédération *f.*

fee¹ [fiː], *s.* **1.** (*a*) *Hist:* Fief *m.* (*b*) *Jur:* Propriété *f* héréditaire. **2.** (*a*) Honoraires *mpl* (d'un médecin consultant, d'un avocat); cachet *m* (d'un précepteur); jeton *m* de présence (d'un administrateur). **To draw one's fees,** toucher ses honoraires, ses cachets; (*of director*) toucher ses jetons. (*b*) **School fees,** rétribution *f* scolaire; frais *mpl* de scolarité. *Boarding-school fees,* pension *f.* **Examination fee,** droit *m* d'examen. *Th:* **Author's fee,** droit d'exécution. *Post:* **Registration fee,** droit de recommandation. **Late fee,** taxe *f* supplémentaire. *S.a.* ENTRANCE-FEE. **'fee-simple,** *s.* (Property held in) **fee-simple,** propriété *f* sans conditions; bien *m* en toute propriété.

fee², *v.tr.* (**fee'd**) **1.** Payer des honoraires à (qn). **To fee a lawyer,** retenir un avocat. **2.** Donner une gratification à (qn).

feeble [fiːbl], *a.* Faible, infirme, débile. **Feeble pulse,** pouls déprimé. *F. work,* travail médiocre. *F:* **He's a feeble sort of chap,** c'est un garçon sans caractère. **-bly,** *adv.* Faiblement. **'feeble-'minded,** *a.* D'esprit faible.

feebleness ['fiːblnəs], *s.* Faiblesse *f.*

feed¹ [fiːd], *s.* **1.** (*a*) Alimentation *f.* (*b*) Nourriture *f,* pâture *f*; fourrage *m* (pour les chevaux, etc.). *To give the horse a f.,* donner à manger au cheval. *F:* **To be off one's feed,** bouder sur la nourriture. (*c*) Mesure *f,* ration *f.* **Feed of oats,** picotin *m* d'avoine. (*d*) *F:* Repas *m,* festin *m.* **To have a good feed,** bien manger; faire bonne chère. **2.** *Tchn:* (*a*) Alimentation *f* (d'une chaudière, etc.); avance *f* (d'une machine-outil). **Gravity feed,** alimentation par (la) pesanteur. **Forced feed, pressure feed** (*of oil*), graissage *m* sous pression. (*b*) Conduit *m* (d'alimentation). **feed-'back,** *s.* *El.E:* *W.Tel:* Rétroaction *f.* **'feed-engine,** *s.* Machine *f* auxiliaire. **'feed-motion,** *s.* *Mec.E:* Mouvement *m* d'avancement, d'entraînement. **'feed-pump,** *s.* *Mch:* Pompe *f* alimentaire, d'alimentation. **'feed-screw,** *s.* *Mec.E:* Vis *f* d'avance. **'feed-tank,** *s.* *Mch:* Bâche *f* d'alimentation; réservoir *m* alimentaire.

feed², *v.* (**fed** [fed]; **fed**) I. *v.tr.* **1.** (*a*) Nourrir; donner à manger à (qn); alimenter (une famille, etc.); approvisionner (un pays, etc.); ravitailler (une armée); allaiter (un enfant); (*of mother bird*) donner la becquée à (ses petits). **To feed s.o. on, with, sth.,** nourrir qn de qch. (*b*) *Field that feeds three cows,* champ qui nourrit trois vaches. **2.** (*a*) Alimenter (une machine, le feu); charger (un fourneau). *Tchn:* **To feed a machine with raw materials,** introduire les matières premières dans une machine. *Mec.E:* **To feed the tool to the work,** (faire) avancer l'outil à la pièce. (*b*) *Fb:* **To feed the forwards,** alimenter les avants. (*c*) *Th:* **To feed an actor,** donner la réplique à un acteur; soutenir un acteur. II. *v.i.* Manger. (*Of cattle, sheep*) Paître, brouter. **To feed (up)on sth.,** se nourrir, s'alimenter, se repaître, de qch. (*Of animal*) **To feed out of s.o.'s hand,** manger dans la main de qn. **feed up,** *v.tr.* Engraisser (une bête); suralimenter (qn). *P:* **To be fed up,** en avoir assez; en avoir soupé; en avoir plein le dos. **feeding,** *s.* **1.** Alimentation *f.* **Forcible feeding,** gavage *m.* *Med.E:* Amenage *m,* avance *f,* avancement *m* (du travail à l'outil, etc.). **'feeding-bottle,** *s.* Biberon *m.*

feeder ['fiːdər], *s.* **1.** (*a*) *Husb:* Nourrisseur *m* (de bestiaux). (*b*) = EATER. **Heavy f.,** gros mangeur. **2.** (*a*) Bavette *f*; serviette *f* d'enfant. (*b*) Biberon *m.* **3.** *Hyd.E:* Canal *m* d'alimentation, d'amenée. *El.E:* **Feeder(-cable),** conducteur *m* alimentaire. **4.** *Ind:* *Mechanical f.,* chargeur *m* mécanique.

feel¹ [fiːl], *s.* **1.** Toucher *m,* tact *m.* **Rough to the feel,** rude au toucher. **2.** (*a*) Toucher, manier *m,* main *f* (du papier, etc.). **To know sth. by the feel of it,** reconnaître qch. au toucher. (*b*) Sensation *f.* *The f. of his clammy hand,* la sensation de sa main froide et moite.

feel², *v.* (**felt** [felt]; **felt**) **1.** (*a*) *v.tr.* Toucher, palper (qch. avec la main); promener les doigts sur (qch.); tâter (le pouls, etc.); manier (une étoffe). (*b*) *v.tr. & i.* **To feel (about) for sth., to feel after sth.,** chercher qch. à tâtons. **To feel about in the dark,** tâtonner dans l'obscurité. **To feel one's way,** (i) avancer, aller, marcher, à tâtons; (ii) *F:* sonder, explorer, le terrain. **To feel in one's pockets for sth.,** fouiller dans ses poches pour trouver qch. **2.** (*a*) *v.tr.* Sentir (qch.). **I felt the floor tremble,** je sentis trembler le plancher. *She felt her feet to be stone-cold,* elle se sentait les pieds gelés. (*b*) *v.tr. & i.* (Res)sentir, éprouver (de la douleur, etc.). *The effect will be felt,* l'effet se fera sentir. **To feel the heat,** être incommodé par la chaleur. **To feel the cold,** être sensible au froid; être frileux. **To make one's authority felt,** affirmer son autorité. **To feel a kindly interest towards s.o.,** éprouver de la sympathie pour qn. **To feel for s.o.,** être plein de pitié pour qn. **To feel for, with, s.o. in his sorrow,** partager la douleur de qn. *How did you f.?* quels sentiments avez-vous éprouvés? (*c*) *v.tr.* Avoir conscience de (qch.). **I feel it in my bones that I shall succeed,** un sentiment intime me dit que je réussirai. **I felt it necessary to interfere,** j'ai jugé nécessaire d'intervenir. **3.** *v.i.* (*Of pers.*) (*a*) *Pred:* **To feel cold,** avoir froid. **To feel ill, tired,** se sentir malade, fatigué. **To feel all the better for it,** s'en trouver mieux. **He doesn't feel quite himself,** il n'est pas dans son assiette. **To feel up to sth., to doing sth.,** se sentir (i) assez bien pour faire qch., (ii) de taille à faire qch. **To feel certain that . . .,** être certain que. . . . (*b*) **I feel as if . . .,** j'ai comme si . . ., il me semble que. . . . *F:* **To feel like doing sth.,** être en humeur de faire qch. *I felt like crying,* j'avais envie de pleurer. **4.** *v.i.* **To feel hard, soft,** être dur, doux, au toucher. *The room feels damp,* la salle donne une impression d'humidité. **It feels like . . .,** cela donne la sensation de. . . .

feeling¹, *a.* **1.** (*Of pers.*) Sensible. **2.** (*Of language, etc.*) Ému. **-ly,** *adv.* **To speak feelingly** of sth., parler (i) d'une voix émue, (ii) sympathiquement, (iii) avec chaleur, de qch. **feeling²,** *s.* **1.** Tâtage *m* (de qch. avec les mains); maniement *m.* **2.** (*Sense of*) feeling, toucher *m,* tact *m.* **To have no feeling in one's arm,** avoir le bras mort. **3.** Sensation (douloureuse, etc.). **4.** Sentiment *m.* (*a*) *To have kindly feelings towards s.o.,* éprouver de la sympathie pour qn. *The f. of the meeting,* l'opinion *f,* le sentiment, de l'assemblée. *Public f.,* le sentiment populaire. (*b*) **I had a feeling of danger,** j'avais le sentiment d'être en danger. **There is a general feeling that . . .,** l'impression règne dans le public que. . . . (*c*) Sensibilité *f,* émotion *f.* **To have no feelings,** être dépourvu de toute sensibilité; n'avoir point de cœur. *To speak with f.,* parler (i) avec enthousiasme, (ii) avec émotion, (iii) avec chaleur.

feeler ['fiːlər], *s.* **1.** Antenne *f,* palpe *f* (d'un insecte) ; corne *f* (d'escargot) ; moustache *f* (d'un chat, etc.) ; tentacule *m* (d'un mollusque). **2.** F: To throw out a feeler, lancer un ballon d'essai ; tâter le terrain. **3.** *Mec.E:* Feuille *f* d'épaisseur.

feet [fiːt], *s.pl.* *See* FOOT¹.

feign [fein]. **I.** *v.tr.* Feindre, simuler. **To feign surprise**, affecter, jouer, la surprise. *To f. death,* faire, contrefaire, le mort. *To f. to do sth.,* feindre, faire semblant, de faire qch. **2.** *v.i.* **To feign sick,** faire semblant d'être malade. **feigned**, *a.* Feint, simulé. **Feigned name,** nom d'emprunt.

feigning, *s.* Feinte *f* ; (dis)simulation *f.*

feint¹ [feint], *s.* (*a*) *Mil:* Fausse attaque. (*b*) *Box: Fenc:* Feinte *f.* (*c*) F: **To make a feint of doing sth.,** feindre, faire semblant, de faire qch.

feint², *v.i.* (*a*) *Mil:* Faire une fausse attaque. (*b*) *Box: Fenc:* Feinter.

feint³, *a. & adv.* *A:* = FAINT¹. **Feint-ruled paper,** papier réglé (en bleu clair).

fel(d)spar ['fel(d)spɑːr], *s.* *Miner:* Feldspath *m.*

felicitations [filisi'teiʃ(ə)nz], *s.pl.* Félicitations *f.*

felicitous [fi'lisitəs], *a.* Heureux. (*a*) (*Of word, etc.*) Bien trouvé ; à propos. (*b*) (*Of pers.*) *F. in his choice of words,* heureux dans le choix de ses mots.

felicity [fi'lisiti], *s.* **I.** Félicité *f,* bonheur *m.* **2.** A-propos *m,* bien-trouvé *m* (d'une observation).

feline ['fiːlain]. **I.** *a.* Félin. **Feline grace,** grâce féline. **2.** *s.* Félin *m.*

fell¹ [fel], *s.* **I.** Fourrure *f* ; peau *f* (de bête). **2.** Toison *f.*

fell², *s.* **I.** *A:* Colline ou montagne rocheuse. **2.** *pl.* Fells, hauteurs *f,* crêtes *f.*

fell³, *v.tr.* **I.** (*a*) Abattre (un adversaire) ; assommer (un bœuf, etc.). (*b*) Abattre (un arbre). **2.** Rabattre (une couture). **felling**, *s.* Abattage *m.*

fell⁴, *a.* *Lit:* **I.** Féroce, cruel. **2.** (*Of thg*) Funeste, désolant. **Fell disease,** maladie redoutable, impitoyable. *F. design,* projet sinistre.

fell⁵. *See* FALL².

felloe ['felou], *s.* **I.** Jante *f* (de roue). **2.** Section *f* de la jante.

fellow ['felo], *s.* **I.** Camarade *m,* compagnon *m,* confrère *m,* collègue *m.* **Fellow-sufferer,** compagnon de misère. **Fellow-being, fellow-creature,** semblable *m.* **Fellow-citizen,** concitoyen, -enne. **Fellow-countryman, -woman,** compatriote *mf,* concitoyen, -enne. **Fellow-student,** camarade *mf* d'études ; condisciple *m.* **Fellow-worker,** (i) compagnon (d'un ouvrier) ; (ii) collaborateur, -trice ; (iii) confrère *m.* **2.** (*Of pers.*) Semblable *m,* pareil *m* ; (*of thg*) pendant *m.* **3.** (*a*) *Sch:* (i) Membre *m* de la corporation (d'une université) ; (ii) boursier chargé de cours. (*b*) Membre, associé, -ée (d'une société savante). **4.** F: (*a*) Homme *m,* garçon *m.* **A good fellow,** un brave garçon, un brave type. *He's a queer f.,* c'est un drôle de type. *The poor little f.,* le pauvre petit. *That old f.,* ce vieux bonhomme. *Congratulations, my good f.,* je vous félicite, mon brave, mon vieux. (*b*) *Pej:* Individu *m.* **These editor fellows,** ces journalistes. *There's a f. downstairs who wants to speak to you,* il y a un individu, un particulier, en bas qui désirerait vous parler. (*c*) **Why can't you let a fellow alone!** laissez-moi donc tranquille ! *A f. doesn't like to be treated like that,* on n'aime pas à être traité comme ça. **fellow-'feeling,** *s.* Sympathie *f.*

fellowship ['feloʃip], *s.* **I.** Communion *f,* communauté *f.* **2.** (**Good**) **fellowship,** amitié *f,* camaraderie *f.* **3.** Association *f,* corporation *f,*

(con)fraternité *f.* **4.** (*a*) (i) Dignité *f* de membre (d'une corporation universitaire) ; (ii) bourse *f* universitaire (avec obligation de faire un cours, des recherches). (*b*) Titre *m* de membre, d'associé (d'une société savante).

felo-de-se ['fiːloudiːˈsiː], *s.* *Jur:* **I.** Suicidé, -ée. **2.** Suicide *m.*

felon¹ ['felən], *s.* *Jur:* Criminel, -elle.

felon², *s.* *Med:* Panaris *m.*

felonious [fe'lounjəs], *a.* *Jur:* Criminel. **-ly,** *adv.* Criminellement.

felony ['feləni], *s.* *Jur:* Crime *m.*

felt¹ [felt], *s.* **I.** Feutre *m.* **2. Roofing felt, tarred felt,** carton bitumé, goudronné.

felt². **I.** *v.tr.* (*a*) *Tex:* Feutrer. (*b*) Couvrir (un toit, etc.) de carton bitumé. **2.** *v.i.* (*Of wool, etc.*) Se feutrer. **felting,** *s.* Feutrage *m.*

felt³. *See* FEEL².

felucca [fe'lʌka], *s.* *Nau:* Felouque *f.*

female ['fiːmeil]. **I.** *a.* (*a*) (*Of pers.*) Féminin ; (de) femme. **Female child,** enfant du sexe féminin. **Male and f. candidates,** candidats et candidates. **Male and female patients,** malades hommes et femmes. *F. education,* l'éducation des femmes. (*b*) (*Of animals, plants, etc.*) Femelle. (*c*) *Tchn:* **Female screw,** vis *f* femelle ; écrou *m.* **2.** *s.f.* (*a*) (*Of pers.*) Femme. (*b*) (*Of animals, plants*) Femelle.

feminine ['feminin], *a.* Féminin. *Gram:* **In the feminine (gender),** au féminin.

femoral ['femərəl], *a.* *Anat:* Fémoral, -aux.

femur, *pl.* **femurs, femora** ['fiːmər(z), 'femora], *s.* *Anat: Ent:* Fémur *m.*

fen [fen], *s.* Marais *m,* marécage *m.* *Geog:* **The Fens,** les plaines marécageuses de l'Est-Anglie.

'fen-man, *pl.* **-men,** *s.m.* Habitant des Fens.

fence¹ [fens], *s.* **I.** = FENCING I. **2.** Clôture *f,* barrière *f,* palissade *f.* **Wire fence,** clôture en fil métallique. **Sunk fence,** saut *m* de loup. *Sp:* **To put a horse over the fences,** mettre un cheval sur les obstacles. F: **To sit on the fence,** ménager la chèvre et le chou ; se réserver. **3.** *Ind:* Garde *f* (d'une machine-outil, etc.) ; garde-corps *m inv.* **4.** *P:* Receleur, -euse (d'objets volés).

fence². **I.** *v.i.* Faire de l'escrime ; tirer des armes ; *abs.* tirer. **2.** *v.tr.* **To fence** (in), clôturer, palissader (un terrain). **To fence off** *one corner of a field,* séparer un coin d'un champ par une clôture. **To fence a town** (about, round) **with walls,** enceindre une ville de murailles. **To fence (in) machinery,** munir la machine d'un garde-corps. **3.** *Abs.* Faire le recel. **fencing,** *s.* **I.** Escrime *f.* **2. Fencing (in),** clôture *f,* palissadement *m* (d'un terrain). **3.** Clôture, barrière *f,* palissade *f,* enceinte *f.* **4.** *Ind:* Garde-corps *m inv* (de machine) ; garde *f.* **'fencing-bout,** *s.* Assaut *m* d'armes. **'fencing-master,** *s.m.* Maître d'escrime, d'armes. **'fencing-match,** *s.* Assaut *m* d'armes. **'fencing-school,** *s.* Salle *f* d'armes.

fencer ['fensər], *s.* **I.** Escrimeur *m* ; tireur *m* (d'armes). **2.** Cheval sauteur de haies.

fend [fend]. **I.** *v.tr.* **To fend off,** parer, détourner (un coup, etc.). **2.** *v.i.* **To fend for s.o.,** pourvoir aux besoins de qn. **To fend for oneself,** se débrouiller ; voler de ses propres ailes.

fender ['fendər], *s.* **I.** (*a*) *Aut:* Pare-choc(s) *m inv.* *Nau:* Défense *f* ; baderne *f.* (*b*) Bouteroue *f,* borne *f.* *Civ.E:* Éperon *m* (de pile de pont). **2.** *Furn:* Galerie *f* de foyer; garde-feu *m inv.* **3.** *Veh:* Garde-boue *m inv* ; pare-boue *m inv.*

fennel [fenl], *s.* *Bot:* **I.** Fenouil *m* ; anet(h) doux. **2. Giant fennel,** férule *f.*

fenny ['feni], a. **1.** Marécageux. **2.** Des marais.
feoff [fef], s. = FIEF.
ferment[1] ['fə:rmənt], s. **1.** Ferment m. **2.** Fermentation f (des liquides); F: agitation f (populaire). *The whole town was in a (state of)* f., toute la ville était en effervescence f.
ferment[2] [fər'ment]. **1.** v.i. (a) Fermenter; (of wine) travailler. (b) (Of cereals) S'échauffer. (c) F: (Of sedition, etc.) Fermenter; (of the people) être en effervescence. **2.** v.tr. Faire fermenter (un liquide, etc.). To ferment wine, cuver le vin.
fermentation [fə:rmen'teiʃ(ə)n], s. (a) Fermentation f; travail m (du vin). (b) Échauffement m (des céréales). (c) F: The town was in a state of f., la ville était en effervescence f.
fern [fə:rn], s. Bot: Fougère f. **'fern-owl,** s. Orn: Engoulevent m.
fernery ['fə:rnəri], s. Fougeraie f.
ferocious [fe'rouʃəs], a. Féroce. **-ly,** adv. Avec férocité.
ferocity [fe'rɔsiti], s. Férocité f.
ferrate ['fereit], s. Ch: Ferrate m.
ferret[1] ['feret], s. Z: Furet m.
ferret[2], v. (ferreted) **1.** v.i. Fureter; chasser au furet. F: To ferret about, fureter, fouiner, partout. **2.** v.tr. Chasser, prendre, (les lapins) au furet. F: To ferret out (sth.), dénicher (qch.).
ferreting, s. Furetage m; chasse f au furet. To go ferreting, chasser au furet.
ferret[3], s. Tex: Padou m, fleuret m.
ferrety ['fereti], a. **1.** De furet. Esp. **Ferrety eyes,** yeux de furet, de fouine. **2.** (Of pers.) Fureteur, -euse; P: fouinard.
ferric ['ferik], a. Ch: Ferrique.
ferrocerium [fero'si:əriəm], s. Ferrocérium m (pour pierre à briquet).
ferro-chrome ['ferokroum], s. Metall: Ferrochrome m.
ferro-concrete [fero'kɔnkri:t], s. Béton armé.
ferrocyanide [fero'saianaid], s. Ferrocyanure m.
ferroglass ['feroɡlɑ:s], s. Ind: Cristal armé.
ferrotype ['ferotaip], s. Phot: Ferrotypie f.
ferrous ['ferəs], a. (Oxyde) ferreux. **Ferrous sulphide,** pyrite f de fer.
ferruginous [fe'rudʒinəs], a. Ferrugineux.
ferrule ['ferəl, 'ferju:l], s. Virole f, frette f (d'un manche d'outil, etc.); bout ferré, embout m (de canne).
ferry[1] ['feri], s. **1.** Endroit m où l'on peut passer la rivière en bac; passage m; F: le bac. To cross the ferry, passer le bac. Ferry dues, droits de passage. **2.** = FERRY-BOAT. Chain ferry, toue f. Train ferry, transbordeur m de trains. **3.** Aerial ferry, (pont) transbordeur m. **'ferryboat,** s. Bac m; bateau m de passage; va-et-vient m inv. **'ferry-bridge,** s. Bac transbordeur.
ferry[2]. **1.** v.i. To ferry across, over, the river, passer la rivière en bac. **2.** v.tr. To f. the car across the river, passer la voiture en bac; transborder la voiture. Will you f. me across?, voulez-vous me passer?
ferryman, pl. **-men** ['ferimən, -men], s.m. Passeur.
fertile ['fə:rtil, -tail], a. Fertile, fécond (in, en).
fertility [fə:r'tiliti], s. Fertilité f, fécondité f.
fertilization [fə:rtilai'zeiʃ(ə)n], s. **1.** Fertilisation f, fécondation f (d'un œuf). Bot: Pollinisation f. **2.** Fertilisation, amendement m (du sol).
fertilize ['fə:rtilaiz], v.tr. **1.** Fertiliser, féconder (un œuf). **2.** Fertiliser (le sol); (with manure) amender (le sol).

fertilizer ['fə:rtilaizər], s. Engrais m, fertilisant m. Artificial fertilizers, engrais chimiques.
fervency ['fə:rvənsi], s. Ferveur f (d'une prière).
fervent ['fə:rvənt], a. Ardent, fervent. **-ly,** adv. (Prier) avec ferveur.
fervid ['fə:rvid], a. (Of preacher) Fervent.
fervour ['fə:rvər], s. Passion f, ferveur f, ardeur f; zèle m.
fescue ['feskju:], s. Bot: Fétuque f.
fess(e) [fes], s. Her: Fasce f.
festal ['fest(ə)l], a. **1.** (Jour, air) de fête. **2.** (Gens) en fête, joyeux.
fester[1] ['festər], s. Med: Inflammation f, écorchure f, avec suppuration.
fester[2]. **1.** v.i. (a) (Of wound) Suppurer, s'envenimer. (b) Se putréfier, pourrir. (c) (Of resentment) Couver. **2.** v.tr. (a) Ulcérer (une plaie). (b) Putréfier. **festering**[1], a. (a) (Of wound) Ulcéreux, suppurant. (b) Putrescent, pourrissant. **festering**[2], s. (a) Suppuration f, ulcération f. (b) Putréfaction f.
festival ['festivəl], s. (a) Fête f. F: To hold high festival, faire fête. (b) Mus: Festival m, -als.
festive ['festiv], a. **1.** (Jour) de fête; (table) du festin. The festive season, Noël. **2.** To be in f. mood, avoir le cœur en fête.
festivity [fes'tiviti], s. Fête f, réjouissance f.
festoon[1] [fes'tu:n], s. Feston m, guirlande f.
festoon[2], v.tr. (a) Festonner (with, de). (b) Disposer (des fleurs, etc.) en festons.
fetch[1] [fetʃ], s. Nau: (a) Virage m. (b) Chemin m à faire, distance f à parcourir. F: It was still a far fetch to London, il y avait encore un bon bout jusqu'à Londres.
fetch[2], v.tr. **1.** (a) Aller chercher (qn, qch.). Go and f. him, allez le chercher. To f. water from the river, aller puiser de l'eau à la rivière. (b) Apporter (qch.); amener (qn). F. it here, apportez-le-moi. To fetch and carry for s.o., (of dog) rapporter; F: (of pers.) faire les commissions de qn. **2.** Rapporter. It fetched a high price, cela se vendit cher. **3.** F: Faire de l'effet sur (le public, etc.). That'll fetch him! voilà qui le séduira, qui l'allumera! **4.** To fetch a sigh, a groan, pousser un soupir, un gémissement. **5.** F: To fetch s.o. a blow, flanquer un coup à qn. **6.** Nau: Gagner, atteindre (le rivage). v.i. To fetch into port, gagner le port. **fetch about,** v.i. Nau: Tirer des bordées. **fetch back,** v.tr. Ramener; rapporter. **fetch down,** v.tr. Faire descendre (qn); descendre (qch.). **fetch up. 1.** v.tr. (a) Faire monter. (b) Vomir (des aliments). **2.** v.i. Nau: To fetch up at a port, parvenir, arriver, à un port. **fetching,** a. (Sourire, air) séduisant, attrayant. There's something f. about her, elle a du ça.
fête[1] [feit], s. Fête f. Village f., fête communale.
fête[2], v.tr. Fêter (un événement); faire fête à (qn).
fetid ['fetid, 'fi:tid], a. Fétide, puant.
fetidity [fe'tiditi, fi:'tiditi], **fetidness** ['fetidnəs, 'fi:tidnəs], s. Fétidité f, puanteur f.
fetish ['fi:tiʃ, 'fe-], s. Fétiche m.
fetlock ['fetlok], s. Fanon m (du cheval). Fetlock joint, boulet m.
fetter[1] ['fetər], s. **1.** Lien m; pl. chaînes f, fers m; entrave f (d'un cheval). In fetters, dans les fers. To burst one's fetters, rompre ses liens, ses fers.
fetter[2], v.tr. Enchaîner (qn); charger (qn) de fers; entraver (un cheval, la pensée).
fettle [fetl], s. Condition f. To be in fine, in good, fettle, être en condition, en forme, en train.
feu [fju:], s. (Scot.) (a) Bail perpétuel moyennant une redevance fixe. (b) Petite propriété assujettie à une redevance.

feud [fju:d], *s.* Inimitié *f* (entre familles, clans). Family blood feud, vendetta *f.* *Family feuds,* dissensions *f* domestiques. To be at feud with s.o., être à couteaux tirés avec qn.

feudal ['fju:dəl], *a.* Féodal, -aux.

feudalism ['fju:dəlizm], *s.* Le régime féodal; la féodalité.

fever[1] ['fi:vər], *s.* Med: Fièvre *f.* Low *f.,* fièvre lente. High *f.,* forte fièvre; fièvre de cheval. To be in a fever, avoir la fièvre. To throw s.o. into a fever, donner la fièvre à qn. *F:* A fever of excitement, une agitation fébrile. **'fever-hospital,** *s.* Hôpital *m* des maladies contagieuses. **'fever-patient,** *s.* Fiévreux, -euse. **'fever-swamp,** *s.* Marécage impaludé.

fever[2], *v.tr.* Enfiévrer; donner la fièvre à (qn). **fevered,** *a.* Enfiévré, fiévreux.

feverfew ['fi:vərfju:], *s.* Bot: Matricaire *f*; pyrèthre *m.*

feverish ['fi:vəriʃ], *a.* **1.** (État) fiévreux, fébrile. To make s.o. *f.,* donner la fièvre à qn. **2.** (Of climate) Fiévreux, malsain. **-ly,** *adv.* Fiévreusement, fébrilement.

feverishness ['fi:vəriʃnəs], *s.* État fiévreux.

few [fju:], *a.* **1.** (a) Peu de (personnes). He has (but) few friends, il a peu d'amis. One of the few people who . . ., une des rares personnes qui. . . . During the last (or next) few days, ces jours-ci. With few exceptions, à de rares exceptions près. Every few days, tous les deux ou trois jours. (b) A few, quelques. A few more, encore quelques-uns. He had a good few enemies, il avait pas mal d'ennemis. In a few minutes, dans quelques minutes. (c) (Pred. use) Peu nombreux. Our days are few, nos jours sont comptés. Such occasions are few, de telles occasions sont rares. **2.** (With noun function) (a) Peu (de gens, etc.). Few of them had travelled, peu d'entre eux avaient voyagé. There are very few of us, nous sommes peu nombreux. The fortunate few, une minorité de gens heureux. (b) Quelques-uns, -unes. A few thought otherwise, quelques-uns pensaient autrement. Some few of the survivors, quelques-uns des survivants. F: There were a good few of them, il y en avait pas mal.

fewer ['fju:ər], *a.* (Comp. of FEW) **1.** Moins (de). He has fewer debts (than you), il a moins de dettes (que vous). **2.** (Pred. use) Plus rares; moins nombreux.

fewest ['fju:əst], *a.* (Sup. of FEW) **1.** Le moins (de). **2.** There the houses are fewest, c'est là que les maisons sont le moins nombreuses, le plus rares.

fewness ['fju:nəs], *s.* Rareté *f*; petit nombre.

fey [fei], *a.* Scot: **1.** (a) Destiné à mourir. (b) Qui est doué de seconde vue. **2.** Fou, *f.* folle.

fez [fez], *s.* Cost: Fez *m.*

fiasco [fi'asko], *s.* Fiasco *m*; F: four *m.*

fiat ['faiat], *s.* **1.** Consentement *m*, autorisation *f.* **2.** Décret *m*, ordre *m.*

fib[1] [fib], *s.* F: Petit mensonge; F: colle *f*, craque *f*, blague *f.*

fib[2], *v.i.* (fibbed) F: Blaguer, craquer; en conter (à qn).

fibre ['faibər], *s.* **1.** Fibre *f*; filament *m.* (a) Muscle *f.,* fibre musculaire. (b) F: Our moral fibre, notre nature *f*; notre composition *f.* A man of coarse fibre, un homme d'une trempe grossière. **2.** Com: Fibre trunk, malle en fibre. Wood fibre, laine *f* de bois.

fibril ['faibril], *s.* Fibrille *f.*

fibrin ['faibrin], *s.* Ch: Physiol: Fibrine *f.*

fibroid ['faibrɔid]. **1.** *a.* (Tumeur) fibroïde. **2.** *s.* Fibrome *m.*

fibroma, *pl.* -mata [fai'broumə(ta)], *s.* Med: Fibrome *m.*

fibrous ['faibrəs], *a.* Fibreux.

fibula ['fibjula], *s.* **1.** Rom.Ant: Fibule *f.* **2.** Anat: Péroné *m.*

fichu ['fi:ʃu], *s.* Cost: Fichu *m.*

fickle [fikl], *a.* Inconstant, volage.

fickleness ['fiklnəs], *s.* Inconstance *f.*

fiction ['fikʃ(ə)n], *s.* **1.** Fiction *f*; création *f* de l'imagination. *Jur:* Legal fiction, fiction légale. **2.** (Works of) fiction, romans *m*; ouvrages *m* d'imagination. Light *f.,* romans de lecture facile.

fictitious [fik'tiʃəs], *a.* (a) Fictif. F. being, être imaginaire. (b) (Of fight, etc.) Simulé, feint. **-ly,** *adv.* Fictivement.

fid [fid], *s.* **1.** Nau: Clef *f* (de mât). **2.** Épissoir *m.* **3.** Cale *f*, coin *m* (pour caler ou obturer).

fiddle[1] [fidl], *s.* **1.** F: (a) Violon *m*, P: crincrin *m.* (b) (Joueur m de) violon. First *f.,* premier violon. F: To play second fiddle (to s.o.), jouer un rôle secondaire (auprès de qn). **2.** Nau: Violon de mer; fiche *f* de roulis. **'fiddle-block,** *s.* Nau: (Poulie *f* à) violon *m.* **'fiddle-string,** *s.* Corde *f* de violon.

fiddle[2], *v.i.* F: **1.** (i) Jouer du violon; (ii) Pej: violoner; racler du violon. **2.** S'amuser à des niaiseries; tripoter, bricoler. Don't *f.* with the mechanism, laissez le mécanisme tranquille. To *f.* over a job, fignoler un travail. To fiddle away one's time, passer son temps à des niaiseries.

fiddling, *a.* F: Futile, insignifiant, niais.

fiddlededee ['fidldi'di:], *int.* F: Bah! turlututu! turlurette! quelle blague!

fiddle-faddle[1] ['fidl'fadl]. **1.** *s.* Bagatelles *fpl*, balivernes *fpl*, niaiseries *fpl.* **2.** *a.* Chipotier, musard.

fiddle-faddle[2], *v.i.* Muser, musarder, baguenauder.

fiddler ['fidlər], *s.* (a) Joueur *m* de violon. (b) Strolling *f.,* ménétrier *m*, violoneux *m.*

fiddlestick ['fidlstik], *s.* **1.** *s.* Archet *m* (de violon). F: I don't care a *f.,* je m'en moque comme d'une guigne. **2.** *int.* Fiddlesticks = FIDDLEDEDEE.

fidelity [fai'deliti, fi-], *s.* **1.** Fidélité *f*, loyauté *f.* **2.** The *f.* of a translation, l'exactitude *f* d'une traduction.

fidget[1] ['fidʒet], *s.* **1.** To have the fidgets, to be in a fidget, ne pas tenir en place; se trémousser (sur sa chaise); avoir des impatiences dans les jambes; P: avoir la bougeotte. It gives me the fidgets, cela m'énerve. **2.** He's a fidget, c'est un énervé.

fidget[2], *v.i.* (fidgeted) (a) To fidget (about), remuer continuellement; se trémousser. (To child) Don't *f.!* tiens-toi tranquille! To *f.* with one's watch-chain, tripoter sa chaine de montre. (b) S'inquiéter, se tourmenter. **fidgeting,** *s.* Agitation nerveuse; nervosité *f.*

fidgety ['fidʒeti], *a.* **1.** Qui remue continuellement. **2.** Nerveux impatient.

fiduciary [fai'dju:ʃiəri], *a.* Fiduciaire.

fie [fai], *int.* Fie (upon you)! fi (donc)!

fief [fi:f], *s.* Hist: Fief *m.*

field[1] [fi:ld], *s.* **1.** Champ *m.* (a) In the fields, dans les champs. The beasts of the field, les bêtes sauvages. (b) District *m*, région *f.* Mine field, champ de mines. S.a. GOLD-FIELD, etc. (c) Mil: Field of battle, champ de bataille. To take the field, entrer en campagne. Attrib. Field service, service en campagne. **2.** Cr: Fb: (a) Terrain *m.* Baseball: Champ. (b) Cr: To place the field, disposer l'équipe. **3.** Turf: The field, les chevaux courants (à l'exception du favori). To bet

against the field, parier contre le champ. *F: On this subject there are already several books in the f.,* plusieurs livres ont déjà paru sur ce sujet. **4.** (a) Étendue *f*, espace *m*. **Field of ice,** banc *m* de glace; banquise. *f*. (b) *Her:* Champ, sol *m*. **5.** (a) Théâtre *m*, champ (d'opération); domaine *m* (d'une science). **Field of conjecture,** champ des hypothèses. **To have a clear field before one,** avoir le champ libre. (b) *Com:* **There is a great field for . . .,** il y a un excellent marché pour. . . . **6.** (a) *Opt:* **Field of vision,** champ de vision. (b) *El: Magn:* Champ (magnétique). **field-ar'tillery,** *s.* Artillerie *f* de campagne. **'field-coil,** *s. El:* Bobine *f* de champ. **'field-day,** *s.* **I.** *Mil:* Jour *m* de grandes manœuvres. **2.** *F:* Grande occasion; grand jour. **'field-'dressing,** *s. Mil:* **I.** Paquet (individuel) de pansement. **2.** Pansement *m* sommaire. **'field-glass,** *s.* (a) Lunette *f* d'approche. (b) *Usu. pl.* Jumelle(s) *f*. **'field-grey,** *a. & s.* Gris (*m*) des troupes allemandes; feldgrau (*m*) *inv.* **'field-gun,** *s.* Canon *m* de campagne. **'field-'hospital,** *s. Mil:* Ambulance *f* divisionnaire. **'field-ice,** *s.* Glace *f* de banquise. **'field-'marshal,** *s.* (Feld-)maréchal *m, pl.* -aux. **'field-mouse,** *pl.* -mice, *s.* Mulot *m*. **'field-officer,** *s. Mil:* Officier supérieur. **'field-sports,** *s.pl.* Sports *m* au grand air; la chasse et la pêche. **field-winding,** *s. El:* Bobinage inducteur.

field², *Cr:* **I.** *v.i.* Tenir le champ (pour relancer la balle). **2.** *v.tr.* **To field the ball,** arrêter (et relancer) la balle.

fielder ['fi:ldər], *s. Cr:* Membre *m* de l'équipe du bôleur.

fieldfare ['fi:ldfɛər], *s. Orn:* Litorne *f*.

fiend [fi:nd], *s.* **I.** (a) Démon *m*, diable *m*. (b) Monstre *m* (de cruauté). *F: He's a perfect f.,* c'est un vrai suppôt de Satan. **2.** *F:* **These** *interviewer fiends,* ces pestes *f* de journalistes qui viennent vous relancer. *S.a.* DRUG-FIEND, OPIUM-FIEND.

fiendish ['fi:ndiʃ], *a.* Diabolique, satanique. **To take a fiendish delight in . . .,** prendre un plaisir diabolique à. . . . **-ly,** *adv.* Diaboliquement.

fiendishness ['fi:ndiʃnəs], *s.* Méchanceté *f* ou cruauté *f* diabolique.

fierce ['fiərs], *a.* (a) Féroce; (*of desire*) ardent; (*of battle*) acharné; (*of wind*) furieux, violent. (b) *Aut:* **Fierce brake,** frein brutal. **-ly,** *adv.* **I.** Férocement. **2.** Violemment; avec acharnement.

fierceness ['fiərsnəs], *s.* Violence *f*, véhémence *f* (de qn); férocité *f* (d'un animal); ardeur *f* (du feu); acharnement *m* (de la bataille); fureur *f* (du vent). *Aut:* Brutalité *f* (de l'embrayage).

fieriness ['faiərinəs], *s.* **I.** Ardeur *f* (du soleil). **2.** Ardeur, fougue *f*.

fiery ['faiəri], *a.* **I.** Ardent, brûlant, enflammé. *F. red,* rouge ardent, rouge feu. *F. sky,* ciel embrasé. *S.a.* CROSS¹ **I.** *F. taste,* saveur cuisante. *Cr:* **Fiery pitch, wicket,** terrain très sec. **2.** (*Of pers.*) (i) Fougueux, ardent, impétueux; (ii) colérique, bouillant. **Fiery steed,** cheval ardent, coursier fougueux. **3.** (*Of gas*) Inflammable; (*of mine*) grisouteux, à grisou. **-ily,** *adv.* Ardemment, impétueusement; avec feu.

fife [faif], *s. Mus:* Fifre *m*.

fifteen [fif'ti:n], *num. a. & s.* Quinze (*m*). **A Rugby fifteen,** une équipe de rugby.

fifteenth [fif'ti:nθ], **I.** *num. a. & s.* Quinzième. **Louis the Fifteenth,** Louis Quinze. **2.** *s.* (*Fractional*) Quinzième *m*.

fifth [fifθ]. **I.** *num. a. & s.* Cinquième. **Henry the Fifth,** Henri Cinq. **Charles the Fifth** (*of Germany*), Charles-Quint. *Sch:* **Fifth form,** (*approx.* =) classe *f* de seconde. **2.** *s.* (a) (*Fractional*) Cinquième *m*. (b) *Mus:* Quinte *f*. **Diminished fifth,** fausse quinte. **-ly,** *adv.* Cinquièmement; en cinquième lieu.

fiftieth ['fiftiəθ], *num. a. & s.* Cinquantième.

fifty ['fifti], *num. a. & s.* Cinquante (*m*). **To go fifty-fifty with s.o.,** se mettre de moitié avec qn; mettre qn de compte à demi dans l'affaire. *About f. books,* une cinquantaine de livres. **She is in the fifties,** elle a passé la cinquantaine.

fig¹ [fig], *s.* Figue *f*. *Green figs,* figues fraîches. *F:* **A fig for Smith!** zut pour Smith! **Fig-tree,** figuier *m*. **'fig-leaf,** *s.* **I.** Feuille *f* de figuier. **2.** *Art:* Feuille de vigne.

fig², *s. F:* **I.** In full fig, en grande tenue; en grand costume. **2.** In good fig, bien en train.

fight¹ [fait], *s.* **I.** (a) Combat *m*, bataille *f*. **Sham fight,** petite guerre; simulacre *m* de combat. (b) *Box:* Assaut *m*. **Hand-to-hand fight,** corps-à-corps *m*. **Fight to the death,** combat à outrance. **Free fight,** mêlée générale. **2.** (a) Lutte *f*. *To carry on a stubborn f. against s.o.,* soutenir une lutte opiniâtre contre qn. (b) **'To show fight,** résister; *F:* montrer les dents; *P:* rouspéter. *Sp: etc:* **To put up a good fight,** se bien acquitter. **There was no fight left in him,** il n'avait plus de cœur à se battre.

fight², *v.* (**fought** [fɔːt]; **fought**) **I.** *v.i.* Se battre; combattre; lutter. *To f. against disease,* combattre la maladie. *To f. against sleep,* lutter contre le sommeil. *F:* To *f. for one's own hand,* défendre ses propres intérêts. *Two dogs fighting over a bone,* deux chiens qui se disputent un os. *F:* **To fight with the gloves off,** ne pas ménager qn. **To fight fair,** se battre loyalement. *They began to f.,* ils en vinrent aux mains. **To fight a battle,** livrer une bataille. **To fight one's way (out),** se frayer un passage (pour sortir). **To fight an action** (at law), se défendre dans un procès. **2.** *v.tr.* (a) **To fight s.o.,** se battre avec, contre, qn; combattre qn. **To fight a fire,** combattre un incendie. (b) **To fight one's ships** (*in battle*), manœuvrer ses vaisseaux. **fight down,** *v.tr.* Vaincre (une passion). **fight off,** *v.tr.* **I.** Résister à (une maladie). **2.** To *f. off the enemy,* repousser l'ennemi. **fight out,** *v.tr.* **To fight it out,** se battre jusqu'à une décision; lutter jusqu'au bout.

fighting¹, *a.* **Fighting men,** combattants *m*; *Mil:* hommes disponibles. **Fighting forces,** forces sous les armes. **fighting²,** *s.* Combat *m*. *Box:* Pugilat *m*, boxe *f*. *Close f.,* lutte *f* corps à corps. **Fighting line,** ligne de combat. *There's just a f. chance for his recovery,* il a une chance sur dix de s'en tirer. **'fighting-cock,** *s.* Coq *m* de combat. *F:* **To live like a fighting-cock,** vivre comme un coq en pâte. **'fighting-top,** *s. Navy:* Hune *f* militaire.

fighter ['faitər], *s.* **I.** Combattant *m*. *F. for an idea,* militant *m* d'une idée. **2.** *Av:* Appareil *m* de combat; avion *m* de chasse.

figment ['figmənt], *s.* Fiction *f*, invention *f*.

figuration [figju'rei∫(ə)n], *s.* **I.** (a) Figuration *f* (d'une idée). (b) Configuration *f* (d'un objet). **2.** Représentation figurative.

figurative ['figjurətiv], *a.* **I.** Figuratif, emblématique. **2.** (*Of language*) Figuré, métaphorique. **-ly,** *adv.* **I.** Figurativement. **2.** Au figuré; par métaphore.

figure¹ ['figər], *s.* **I.** (a) Figure *f*; forme extérieure. (b) (*Of pers.*) Taille *f*, tournure *f*. **To have**

figure] 278 [fillet

a fine **figure**, être bien fait de sa personne ; (*esp. of woman*) être bien prise; avoir du galbe. *His commanding f.*, son port imposant. **2.** (*a*) Personne *f*, être *m*. **A magnificent figure of a man,** un homme magnifique. *A fine f. of a woman*, une belle femme. *What a f. of fun!* quelle caricature l (*b*) Personnage *m*. **The central figure** (*of a drama*), le pivot de l'action. (*c*) Figure, apparence *f*. **To cut a sorry figure,** faire piètre figure. **3.** *Art:* Lay figure, mannequin *m*. *Anatomical f.*, pièce *f* d'anatomie. **4.** (*a*) Geometrical **figure**, figure géométrique. (*b*) Dessin *m* (sur une étoffe). **5.** (*a*) Chiffre *m*. **To work out the figures,** effectuer les calculs. **In round figures,** en chiffres ronds. *A mistake in the figures,* une erreur de calcul. *To go into figures,* aligner des chiffres. **To be quick at figures,** calculer vite et bien. **To fetch a high figure,** se vendre cher. *Tchn:* **Dimensional figures,** cotes *f* (d'une machine). *Med:* **Figure of eight bandage,** bandage en huit-de-chiffre. *F:* **What's the figure?** ça coûte combien? (*b*) *pl.* **Figures,** détails chiffrés (d'un projet). **6.** Figure of speech, (i) figure *f* de rhétorique ; métaphore *f* ; (ii) façon *f* de parler. **'figure-head,** s. **1.** *N.Arch:* Figure *f* de proue. **2.** *F:* (*a*) Prête-nom *m*. (*b*) Personnage purement décoratif.

figure². 1. *v.tr.* (*a*) Figurer, représenter. (*b*) **To figure sth.** (to oneself), se représenter, se figurer, qch. (*c*) *U.S:* *F:* Estimer, évaluer. (*d*) Brocher, gaufrer, ouvrager (la soie). (*e*) *Mus:* Chiffrer (la basse). **2.** *v.i.* (*a*) Chiffrer, calculer ; faire des chiffres. (*b*) *U.S:* **To figure on a success,** compter sur un succès. (*c*) **His name figures on the list,** son nom figure, se trouve, sur la liste. **figure out. 1.** *v.i.* Se chiffrer. *The total figures out at £50,* le total se monte à cinquante livres. **2.** *v.tr.* **To figure out the expense,** supputer les dépenses ; aligner des chiffres. *F:* **That's how I figure it out,** voilà mon calcul.

figurine [figju'ri:n], s. Figurine *f*.

filament ['filəmənt], s. **1.** Filament *m*, cil *m*. *Bot:* Filet *m* (de l'étamine). *A fine f.*, Fil *m*, filament (d'une lampe). **3.** *Ph:* Filet (d'air, d'eau).

filbert ['filbərt], s. Aveline *f*.

filch [fil(t)ʃ], *v.tr.* Chiper, filouter, escamoter.

file¹ [fail], s. **1.** *Tls:* Lime *f*. **Three-cornered f., triangular f.,** tiers-point *m*. **To gnaw, bite, a file,** s'en prendre à plus dur que soi. **2.** *F:* **He's a sly old file,** c'est un fin matois.

file², *v.tr.* Limer (le métal, etc.). **To file down,** enlever (une saillie, etc.) à la lime ; adoucir (une surface) à la lime ; *Farr:* raboter (le sabot d'un cheval). **To file away, off,** enlever (une saillie) à la lime. **filing¹,** s. **1.** Limage *m* (d'un métal). Filing down, adoucissement *m* à la lime. **2.** *pl.* Filings, limaille *f*. **'filing-machine,** s. Limeuse *f*.

file³, s. **1.** (*a*) Bill file, spike file, pique-notes *m inv.* (*b*) Classeur *m*, cartonnier *m*. Card-index file, fichier *m*. **2.** Collection *f*, liasse *f* (de papiers). *Adm:* Dossier *m*. **'file-case,** s. Cartonnier *m*. **'file-copy,** s. *Publ:* Exemplaire *m* des archives.

file⁴, *v.tr.* **1.** Enfiler (des reçus) ; classer (des fiches) ; ranger (des lettres, etc.). *To f. a document,* joindre une pièce au dossier (d'une affaire). **2.** *Jur:* **To file a petition,** enregistrer une requête. **To file one's petition (in bankruptcy),** déposer son bilan. **filing²,** s. **1.** Classement *m*. **Filing-case,** cartonnier *m*. **Filing-cabinet,** classeur *m*. **Filing-clerk,** archiviste *mf*. **2.** *Jur:* Enregistrement *m* (d'une requête).

file⁵, s. File *f*. **In single, Indian, file,** en file indienne; *F:* à la queue leu leu. *To walk in single f.,* marcher à la file, en file indienne. *Mil:* **To form single file,** dédoubler les rangs. **Blank file,** file creuse. **'file-closer,** s. *Mil:* Serre-file *m inv*. **'file-leader,** s. *Mil:* Chef *m* de file.

file⁶, *v.i.* **To file off,** défiler. **To file past a catafalque,** défiler devant un catafalque. **To file in, out,** entrer, sortir, un à un.

filial ['filjəl], *a.* Filial, -als, -aux. **-ally,** *adv.* Filialement.

filiation [fili'eiʃ(ə)n], s. Filiation *f*.

filibuster¹ ['filibʌstər], s. *Hist:* Flibustier *m*.

filibuster², *v.i.* **1.** *Hist:* Flibuster. **2.** *Pol:* *U.S:* Faire de l'obstruction.

filigree ['filigri:], s. Filigrane *m*.

fill¹ [fil], s. **1.** **To have one's fill of sth.,** avoir sa suffisance, son content, de qch. **To eat one's fill,** manger à sa faim ; *F:* manger tout son soûl. *When he had taken his f. . . . ,* quand il se fut contenté. **. . . To drink one's fill,** boire à sa soif. **2.** Charge *f*, plein *m*. **A fill of tobacco,** une pipe de tabac.

fill². I. *v.tr.* **1.** (*a*) Remplir, emplir (*with*, de). **To fill s.o.'s glass,** verser à boire à qn ; (*to the brim*) verser une rasade à qn. **To fill a truck,** charger un wagon. **To fill a lamp,** garnir une lampe. **To fill one's pipe,** charger, bourrer, sa pipe. *Well-filled pockets,* poches bien bourrées. **To fill (up)** the boilers, faire le plein des chaudières. (*b*) **To fill the air with one's cries,** remplir l'air de ses cris. *He is filled with despair,* il est en proie au désespoir. **2.** (*a*) Combler (une lacune) (*with*, de). **To fill a tooth,** plomber une dent. (*b*) **To fill (up) a vacancy,** suppléer, pourvoir, à une vacance. **3.** Occuper. (*a*) *A post he has filled for some time,* un poste qu'il occupe depuis quelque temps. *Th:* **To fill a part,** remplir, tenir, un rôle. (*b*) *The thoughts that filled his mind,* les pensées qui occupaient son esprit. **4.** *U.S:* **To fill every requirement,** répondre à tous les besoins. *Com:* **To fill an order,** exécuter un ordre. **II. fill,** *v.i.* **1.** Se remplir, s'emplir. *The hall is beginning to f.,* la salle commence à se garnir. **2.** *Nau:* (*Of sails*) S'enfler, porter. **fill in,** *v.tr.* **1.** Combler, remplir (un trou); condamner (une porte); remblayer (un fossé). **2.** Combler (des vides); remplir (une formule); libeller (un chèque). **To fill in the date,** insérer la date. **fill out. 1.** *v.tr.* (*a*) Enfler, gonfler (un ballon). (*b*) Étoffer (un discours). **2.** *v.i.* (*a*) S'enfler, se gonfler. (*b*) Prendre de l'embonpoint ; se remplumer. *Her cheeks are filling out,* ses joues se remplissent. **fill up. 1.** *v.tr.* (*a*) Remplir jusqu'au bord ; combler (une mesure). *Abs.* **To fill up with petrol,** faire le plein d'essence. (*b*) Boucher (un trou avec du mastic); condamner (une porte); remblayer (un fossé). (*c*) Remplir (une formule); libeller (un chèque). **2.** *v.i.* Se remplir, s'emplir, se combler. **filling¹,** *a.* (*Of food*) Rassasiant. **filling²,** s. **1.** (*a*) (R)emplissage *m* (d'une mesure); chargement *m* (d'un wagon). (*b*) Peuplement *m* (d'un étang). **2.** (*a*) Comblement *m* (d'une brèche). *Dent:* Plombage *m*. (*b*) Filling of a vacancy, nomination *f* de quelqu'un à un poste. **3.** Occupation *f* (d'un poste). **4.** Matière *f* de remplissage. *Dent: Carp:* Mastic *m*. **'filling-station,** s. *Aut:* Poste *m* d'essence.

filler ['filər], s. (*a*) (*Pers.*) Remplisseur, -euse. (*b*) (*Thg*) Remplisseur. **Fountain-pen filler,** compte-gouttes *m inv*.

fillet¹ ['filet], s. *a.* **1.** *Cost:* Filet *m*, bandelette *f* (pour maintenir les cheveux). **2.** *Cu:* (*a*) Filet (de bœuf). (*b*) Rouelle *f* (de veau). **3.** (*a*) *Arch:* Nervure *f*, filet. (*b*) *Join:* Baguette *f*, listel *m* (de panneau). (*c*) *Mec.E:* Bourrelet *m*, boudin *m* (sur un tuyau). *Metalw:* Fillet(-border), suage *m*. **4.** (*a*) *Her:* Filet. (*b*) *Bookb: Typ:*. Filet.

fillet², *v.tr.* (filleted) **I.** Orner (qch.) d'un filet, d'une baguette. **Filleted ceiling,** plafond à nervures. **2.** *Cu:* Détacher, lever, les filets. **Filleted sole,** filets de sole.

fillip ['filip], *s.* **I.** Chiquenaude *f*; *F:* pichenette *f*. **2.** Coup de fouet (donné au système nerveux). *To give a f. to business,* stimuler les affaires.

filly ['fili], *s.* Pouliche *f*.

film¹ [film], *s.* **I.** (*a*) Pellicule *f*, couche *f* (de glace, d'huile); peau *f* (du lait bouilli). **Film over the eye,** taie *f* sur l'œil. (*b*) *F:* Voile *m* (de brume). **2.** *Phot:* (*a*) Pellicule. (*b*) Couche sensible (de la plaque ou de la pellicule). **3.** *Cin:* (*a*) Film *m*, bande *f*. **Silent film,** film muet. **Talking film,** film parlant. **News film,** film d'actualité. **To shoot a film,** tourner un film; prendre les vues. **To act in a film,** jouer dans, *F:* tourner, un film. (*b*) **The films,** le cinématographe; *F:* le ciné. **Silent films,** l'écran muet. **Sound films,** le cinématographe sonore. **He acts for the films,** il fait du ciné. **To put a novel on the films,** filmer un roman. **To have a film face,** être photogénique. **Film rights,** droits d'adaptation cinématographique. **Film-star,** vedette *f* de l'écran, du ciné.

film². **I.** *v.tr. Cin:* Filmer, *F:* tourner (une scène). **He films well,** il est photogénique. **2.** *v.i.* To film (over), (i) (*of lake*) se couvrir d'une pellicule; (ii) (*of the eyes*) se couvrir d'une taie.

filmy ['filmi], *a.* **I.** (*a*) Couvert d'une pellicule; (*of eye*) couvert d'une taie. (*b*) Voilé (de brume). **2.** (*Of lace, cloud*) Léger, transparent.

filter¹ ['filtər], *s.* **I.** Filtre *m*; épurateur *m* (d'essence). *Phot:* Écran (coloré, orthochromatique). **'filter-paper,** *s.* Papier *m* filtre.

filter². **I.** *v.tr.* Filtrer (l'eau); épurer, tamiser (l'air). **2.** *v.i.* (*Of water*) Filtrer, s'infiltrer (*through*, à travers).

filterable ['filtərəbl], *a.* (Virus) filtrant.

filth [filθ], *s.* **I.** (*a*) Ordure *f*; immondices *mpl.* (*b*) **These races live in f.,** ces races vivent dans la saleté. **2.** (*a*) Corruption morale. (*b*) **To talk filth,** dire des saletés.

filthiness ['filθinəs], *s.* **I.** Saleté *f*. **2.** Corruption morale; obscénité *f*.

filthy ['filθi], *a.* **I.** Sale, immonde, dégoûtant. **A filthy hovel,** un taudis infect. **2.** (*Of talk*) Ordurier; (*of pers.*) crapuleux. **-ily,** *adv.* D'une manière ordurière.

filtrate ['filtreit], *s. Ch: etc:* Filtrat *m*.

filtration [fil'treiʃ(ə)n], *s.* Filtration *f*, filtrage *m*.

fin [fin], *s.* **I.** (*a*) Nageoire *f* (d'un poisson); aileron *m* (d'un requin). (*b*) *P:* **Tip us your fin,** donne-moi ta pince que je la serre. **2.** Plan fixe vertical (d'un avion); empennage *m* (de dirigeable). **3.** (*a*) Ailette *f* (de radiateur d'automobile). (*b*) Bavure *f* (d'une pièce coulée). **'fin-back,** *s. Z:* Rorqual *m*, -als.

final ['fain(ə)l]. **I.** *a.* Final, -als. (*a*) Dernier. **To put the final touches to sth.,** mettre la dernière main à qch. *Com:* **Final date** (for payment), terme fatal, de rigueur. (*b*) Définitif, decisif. *Jur:* **Final judgment,** jugement définitif; jugement souverain. *The umpire's decision is f.,* la décision de l'arbitre est sans appel. **Am I to consider that as final?** c'est votre dernier mot?

(*c*) *Phil:* **Final cause,** cause finale. *Gram:* **Final clause,** proposition finale. **2.** *s. Sp:* **The finals,** les (épreuves) finales. **-ally,** *adv.* Finalement. **I.** Enfin. **2.** Définitivement. **3.** En somme, en définitive.

finale [fi'nɑːle], *s.* **I.** *Mus:* Final(e) *m*. **2.** *F:* Conclusion *f*. *Th:* **Grand finale,** apothéose *f*.

finalist ['fainəlist], *s. Sp:* Finaliste *mf*.

finality [fai'naliti], *s.* **I.** *Phil:* Finalité *f*. **2.** Caractère définitif; irrévocabilité *f*.

finance¹ [fi'nans, fai-], *s.* **I.** Finance *f*. **High finance,** la haute finance. **2.** *pl. F:* **His finances are low,** ses finances en baisse; ses fonds sont bas.

finance², *v.tr.* Financer, commanditer (une entreprise). **financing,** *s.* Financement *m* (d'une entreprise).

financial [fi'nanʃ(ə)l, fai-], *a.* Financier. *F:* **statement,** état des finances. *Adm:* **Financial year,** exercice (financier).

financier [fi'nansiər], *s.* **I.** Financier *m*. **2.** Bailleur *m* de fonds.

finch [fin(t)ʃ], *s. Orn:* Pinson *m*. **Thistle finch, yellow finch,** chardonneret *m*. *S.a.* BULLFINCH, CHAFFINCH, GOLDFINCH.

find¹ [faind], *s.* **I.** Découverte *f*. **2.** Trouvaille *f*.

find², *v.tr.* (found [faund]; found) Trouver. **I.** (*a*) Rencontrer, découvrir. **It is found everywhere,** cela se trouve, se rencontre, partout. **To find some difficulty in doing sth.,** éprouver quelque difficulté à faire qch. (*b*) **To leave everything as one finds it,** tout laisser tel quel. *I found myself crying,* je me surpris à pleurer. **2.** (*By searching*) (*a*) **The (lost) key has been found,** la clef s'est retrouvée. **To try to find sth.,** chercher qch. **He is not to be found,** il est introuvable. **To find a leak in a main,** localiser une fuite dans une conduite. **To find one's way home,** trouver le chemin pour rentrer chez soi. **I can't find time to . . .,** je n'ai pas le temps de. . . . **He found courage to . . .,** il eut le courage de. . . . **To find it in one's heart to do sth.,** avoir le cœur de faire qch. (*b*) Obtenir (une sûreté, une caution). (*c*) *Abs. Ven:* **To find,** découvrir le renard, etc. **3.** (*a*) Constater. **It has been found that . . .,** on a constaté que. . . . *I found she had left the house,* j'appris, je vis, qu'elle avait quitté la maison. *I f. it is time to go,* je m'aperçois qu'il est temps de partir. *This letter, I find, arrived yesterday,* cette lettre, à ce que je vois, à ce que j'apprends, est arrivée hier. (*b*) **They will find it easy,** cela leur sera facile. **To find it impossible to . . .,** se trouver dans l'impossibilité de. . . . **4.** *Jur:* (*a*) **To find s.o. guilty,** déclarer qn coupable. (*b*) Rendre (un verdict). **To find for s.o.,** prononcer un verdict en faveur de qn. **5.** (*a*) **To find the money for an undertaking,** procurer les capitaux, fournir l'argent, pour une entreprise. *X finds half the money,* X baille les fonds pour moitié. (*b*) **Wages £20,** **all found,** gages £20, nourri, logé, chauffé, et blanchi; gages £20, tout fourni. **To find oneself,** se pourvoir soi-même. *To f. oneself in clothes,* se vêtir à ses frais. **find out,** *v.tr.* (*a*) Deviner (une énigme); découvrir (un secret); constater (une erreur). *Abs.* **To find out about sth.,** se renseigner sur qch. *What have you done with it?*—**Find out!** qu'en avez-vous fait?—A vous de trouver. (*b*) **To find s.o. out,** (i) découvrir le vrai caractère de qn; (ii) trouver qn en défaut. **finding,** *s.* **I.** (*a*) Découverte *f* (d'un pays); invention *f* (d'un système). (*b*) Fourniture *f* (de fonds). **2.** Trouvaille *f*. **3.** *The findings* *of an official report*, les constatations *f*, les conclusions *f*, d'un procès-verbal.

finder ['faindər], *s.* **I.** Trouveur, -euse; *Jur:* inventeur, -trice (d'un objet perdu). **2.** *(a) Opt:* *(Of telescope)* Chercheur *m*, trouveur *m*. *(b) Phot:* **(View-)finder**, viseur *m*; *Cin:* oculaire *m*. *(c) El:* **Short-circuit finder**, détecteur *m* de courts-circuits.

fine[1] [fain], *s.* **I.** In **fine**, enfin, finalement. **2.** *Jur:* *(a)* Arrhes (payées par le locataire pour compenser la modicité du loyer). *(b)* Amende *f*. *To impose a f. on s.o.*, infliger une amende à qn.

fine[2], *v.tr.* Condamner (qn) à une amende; frapper (qn) d'une amende.

fine[3], *a.* **I.** *(a)* Fin, pur. *Gold twenty-two carats f.*, or à vingt-deux carats de fin. *(b)* Fin, subtil, raffiné. *F. distinction*, distinction subtile. **2.** Beau, bel, belle, beaux. *(a) A f. statue*, une belle statue. *F. woman*, belle femme. **The fine arts**, ·les beaux-arts *m*. *(b)* **Fine sentiments**, de beaux sentiments. **To appeal to s.o.'s finer feelings**, faire appel aux sentiments élevés de qn. **3.** *(a) Meat of the finest quality*, viande de premier choix. *(b)* Excellent, magnifique. *F. display*, étalage superbe. *F. piece of business*, affaire d'or. *F. future*, bel avenir. **We had a fine time**, nous nous sommes bien amusés. **That's fine!** voilà qui est parfait. *(c) Iron:* **That's all very fine, but . . .**, tout cela est bel et bon, est fort beau, mais . . . **4.** Beau. *When the weather is f.*, quand il fait beau. *F:* **One of these fine days**, un de ces beaux jours; un de ces quatre matins. **5.** *(a) (Of texture)* Fin; *(of dust)* menu, subtil. **To chop (meat) fine**, hacher menu. *(b)* Effilé; *(of writing, thread)* délié, mince. **Fine edge**, tranchant affilé, aigu. **Fine nib**, plume pointue. *F:* **Not to put too fine a point on it . . .**, pour parler franc, carrément. . . . **6.** *F:* **To cut it fine, to run it fine**, faire qch. tout juste; réussir tout juste; arriver de justesse. **Prices are cut very fine**, les prix sont au plus bas. *Sp:* **To train a horse too fine**, pousser trop loin l'entraînement d'un cheval. **-ly**, *adv.* **I.** Finement. *(a)* Habilement; on ne peut mieux. *(b)* Délicatement, subtilement. *(c) F. powdered*, finement pulvérisé. *F. chopped*, haché menu. **2.** Admirablement, magnifiquement. **'fine-'darn**, *v.tr. Needlew:* Stopper. **'fine-'darning**, *s.* Stoppage *m*. **'fine-'darner**, *s.* Stoppeur, -euse. **'fine-'drawn**, *a.* **I.** *(a) Needlew:* **Fine-drawn seam**, rentraiture *f*. *(b) (Of wire)* Finement étiré; *(of thread)* délié, ténu. **2.** *F.-d. arguments, distinctions*, arguments subtils, distinctions subtiles. **'fine-'spun**, *a. Tex:* Au fil ténu, délié.

fineness ['fainnəs], *s.* **I.** Titre *m*, aloi *m* (de l'or). **2.** Qualité supérieure, excellence *f* (d'un article). **3.** Splendeur *f*, élégance *f* (d'un costume). **4.** Finesse *f* (d'une étoffe); ténuité (d'un fil); délicatesse *f* (des sentiments).

finery ['fainəri], *s. Iron:* Parure *f*; fanfreluches *fpl.* **Decked out in all her finery**, parée de ses plus beaux atours.

finesse[1] [fi'nes], *s.* Finesse *f*.

finesse[2]. **I.** *v.i. (a)* User de finesse; ruser. *(b) Cards:* Faire une impasse. **2.** *v.tr. Cards:* **To finesse the queen**, faire une impasse à la dame.

finger[1] ['fingər], *s.* **I.** Doigt *m* (de la main). **First finger**, index *m*. **Middle finger, second finger**, médius *m*, doigt du milieu. **Third finger, ring finger**, annulaire *m*. **Little finger**, petit doigt; auriculaire *m*. *F:* **I forbid you to lay a finger on him**, je vous défends de le toucher. **To lay, put, one's finger on the cause of the evil**, mettre le doigt sur la source du mal. **He wouldn't lift a**

finger to help you, il ne remuerait pas le petit doigt pour vous aider. **To point the finger of scorn at s.o.**, montrer qn au doigt. *He has a f. in every pie*, il est mêlé à tout. **He is a Frenchman to the finger tips**, il est Français jusqu'au bout des ongles. **He has the whole business at his fingers' ends**, il est au courant de toute l'affaire. **2.** *Mec.E:* Doigt (de guidage). **'finger-board**, *s.* *(a)* Touche *f* (de violon). *(b)* Clavier *m* (de piano). **'finger-bowl**, *s.* Rince-doigts *m inv.* **'finger-hold**, *s.* Prise *f* pour les doigts. **'finger-nail**, *s.* Ongle *m* (de la main). **'finger-plate**, *s.* Plaque *f* de propreté (d'une porte). **'finger-post**, *s.* Poteau *m* indicateur. **'finger-print**, *s.* *Adm:* Empreinte digitale. *F.-p.* **identification**, dactyloscopie *f.* **'finger-stall**, *s.* *Med:* Doigtier *m*.

finger[2], *v.tr.* **I.** Manier, tâter, *F:* tripoter (qch.). *F:* **To finger s.o.'s money**, palper l'argent de qn. **2.** *Mus:* Doigter (un morceau). **fingering**, *s.* **I.** *(a)* Maniement *m*. *(b)* Action *f* de palper qch. **2.** *Mus:* Doigter *m*, doigté *m* (du piano).

finial ['finiəl], *s. Arch:* Fleuron *m* (de faîte).

finical ['finik(ə)l], **finicking** ['finikiŋ], **finicky** ['finiki], *a.* Méticuleux, vétilleux; *(of pers.)* fignoleur, -euse.

finis ['fainis], *s. (At end of book, story)* Fin *f*.

finish[1] ['finiʃ], *s.* **I.** Fin *f*. *Sp:* Arrivée *f* (d'une course). **To fight (it out) to a finish**, se battre jusqu'à une décision. **To be in at the finish**, (i) *Sp:* *Turf:* assister à l'arrivée; (ii) *F:* voir la fin de l'aventure. **2.** *(a)* Fini *m*, achevé *m* (d'un travail); finesse *f* de l'exécution (d'un travail). *(b)* Apprêt *m* (d'un drap).

finish[2]. **I.** *v.tr.* Finir; terminer, achever. *To f. doing sth.*, achever, finir, de faire qch. **To finish off** *a piece of work*, mettre la dernière main à un travail. **To finish off a wounded beast**, expédier une bête blessée. *He's finished! P:* il est flambé! *F. up your soup!* finis ta soupe! **2.** *v.i.* Finir. *(a)* Cesser, se terminer. *His engagement finishes this week*, son engagement prend fin cette semaine. *(b)* **To finish in a point**, se terminer, finir, en pointe. *(c)* **He finished by calling me a liar**, il finit par me traiter de menteur. *(d) F:* **I have finished with you!** tout est fini entre nous! *(e) Wait till I've finished with him!* attendez que je lui aie réglé son compte! *(f)* **To finish fourth**, finir, arriver, quatrième (dans une course). **finished**, *a.* **I.** *(Article)* fini, apprêté. **2.** *(Of appearance)* Soigné, parfait. **A finished speaker**, un parfait orateur; un orateur accompli. **A finished portrait**, un portrait achevé. **finishing**, *s.* **I.** *(a)* Achèvement *m*. *(b) Tchn:* Finissage *m* (d'un article de commerce); apprêt *m* (des tissus). **2.** *Sp:* **Finishing line**, ligne *f* d'arrivée. **'finishing-rolls**, *s.pl. Metall:* Laminoir *m* de finissage. **'finishing-school**, *s.* École *f* d'arts d'agrément.

finisher ['finiʃər], *s.* **I.** *Ind:* Finisseur, -euse. *Dressm:* Retoucheuse *f*. **2.** *F:* Coup *m* de grâce.

finite ['fainait], *a.* *(a)* Fini, limité, borné. *(b) Gram:* **Finite moods**, modes finis. **Finite verb**, verbe à un mode fini.

Finland ['finlənd], *Pr.n. Geog:* La Finlande.

Finlander ['finləndər], **Finn** [fin], *s.* Finlandais, -aise; Finnois, -oise.

finned [find], *a.* **I.** *Ich:* A nageoires. **2.** *Tchn:* A ailettes.

Finnish ['finiʃ]. **I.** *a.* Finlandais. **2.** *s. Ling:* Le finnois.

fiord ['fjɔːrd], *s.* Fiord *m*, fjord *m*.

fir [fəːr], *s.* **I.** **Fir(-tree)**, sapin *m*. **Silver fir**,

sapin blanc, argenté. **Scotch fir,** pin *m* sylvestre ; pin d'Écosse ; sapin du nord. **Fir plantation,** sapinière *f*. **2.** (Bois *m* de) sapin. **'fir-cone,** *s.* Pomme *f*, cône *m*, de sapin ; pigne *f*.
fire¹ ['faiǝr], *s.* **I.** Feu *m*. (*a*) **He has gone through the fire(s) of adversity,** il s'est retrempé dans l'adversité. (*b*) **To light, make, a fire,** faire du feu. **To lay a fire,** préparer le feu. *To make up the f.,* charger, arranger, le feu. **To cook sth. on a slow fire,** faire cuire qch. à petit feu, à feu doux. *F:* **To pull the chestnuts out of the fire for s.o.,** tirer les marrons du feu pour qn. *F:* **To keep the fire warm,** garder les tisons. *Before a rousing, a roaring, f.,* devant une belle flambée. **Electric fire,** radiateur *m* électrique. (*c*) Incendie *m*, sinistre *m*. *The sufferers from the f.,* les incendiés, les sinistrés. *An outbreak of f.* **took place,** un incendie s'est déclaré. **Fire!** au feu ! **To catch fire,** prendre feu ; s'enflammer. *Her dress caught f.,* le feu a pris à sa robe. **To set fire to sth.,** to **set sth. on fire,** mettre le feu à qch. **On fire,** en feu, en flammes. *A forest on f.,* une forêt embrasée. *A chimney on f.,* un feu de cheminée. *F:* **To get on like a house on fire,** avancer à pas de géant. *F:* **To add fuel to the fire,** jeter de l'huile sur le feu. **To put a town to fire and sword,** mettre une ville à feu et à sang. (*d*) **Greek fire,** feu grégeois. (*e*) Lumière *f*, éclat *m*. *The f. of a diamond,* les feux d'un diamant. *Nau:* **St Elmo's fire,** feu de Saint-Elme. **2.** *Aut:* Allumage *m*. **3.** *F:* Ardeur *f*, zèle *m*. *The f. of youth,* l'enthousiasme *m* de la jeunesse. **4.** *Mil:* Feu, tir *m* ; coups *mpl* de feu. **Individual fire,** tir à volonté. *F:* **Rapid fire of questions,** feu roulant de questions. **To be under fire,** essuyer le feu. *To be steady under f.,* être ferme au feu. **To be between two fires,** être pris entre deux feux.
'fire-alarm, *s.* (Appareil) avertisseur *m* d'incendie. **'fire-arm,** *s.* Arme *f* à feu. **'fireball,** *s.* *Meteor:* (*a*) Bolide *m*. (*b*) Globe *m* de feu. **'fire-bar,** *s.* Barreau *m* de grille (de foyer). **'fire-basket,** *s.* Brasier *m*, braséro *m*. **'fire-box,** *s.* Foyer *m*, boîte *f* à feu (d'une locomotive). **'fire-brand,** *s.* **I.** Tison *m*, brandon *m*. **2.** (Pers.) *F:* Brandon de discorde. **'fire-brick,** *s.* Brique *f* réfractaire. **'firebrigade,** *s.* (Corps *m* de) sapeurs-pompiers *mpl* ; *F:* les pompiers. **'fire-bucket,** *s.* Seau *m* à incendie. **'fire-clay,** *s.* Argile *f* réfractaire. **'fire-damp,** *s.* *Min:* Grisou *m* ; méthane *m*. **'fire-dog,** *s.* *Furn:* Chenet *m* ; (*large*) landier *m*. **'fire-drill,** *s.* Exercices *mpl* de sauvetage. **'fire-eater,** *s.* **I.** (Saltimbanque) avaleur *m* de feu. **2.** Tranche-montagne *m*, matamore *m*. **'fire-engine,** *s.* Pompe *f* à incendie. **'fireescape,** *s.* Échelle *f* de sauvetage ; échelle à incendie. **'fire-extinguisher,** *s.* Extincteur *m* d'incendie ; grenade *f* ignifuge. **'fire-fighting,** *s.* Précautions *fpl* contre l'incendie ; service *m* d'incendie. **'fire-float,** *s.* Ponton *m* d'incendie. **'fire-fly,** *s.* *Ent:* Luciole *f*; *F:* mouche *f* à feu. **'fire-guard,** *s.* **I.** Pare-étincelles *m inv* ; garde-feu *m inv*. **2.** (Pers.) *U.S:* Garde-feu *m* (de forêt), *pl*. gardes-feu. **'fire-hose,** *s.* Tuyau *m*, manche *f*, d'incendie. **'fire-insurance,** *s.* Assurance *f* contre l'incendie. **'fire-iron,** *s.* **I.** Ringard *m* (de fourneau). **2.** *pl.* Fire-irons, garniture *f* de foyer. **'fire-lighter,** *s.* Allumefeu *m inv*. **'fire-line,** *s.* *For:* Tranchée *f* garde-feu. **'fire-place,** *s.* Cheminée *f*, foyer *m*. **'fire-plug,** *s.* Prise *f* d'eau ; bouche *f* d'incendie. **'fire-proof¹,** *a.* (*a*) Incombustible, ignifuge. *F.-p. door,* porte à revêtement calorifuge. *To make a door f.-p.,* ignifuger une porte.

(*b*) *Cer:* Réfractaire. *F.-p. dish,* plat allant au feu. **'fire-proof²,** *v.tr.* Ignifuger (un tissu). **'fire-quarters,** *s.pl.* *Nau:* Postes *m* d'incendie. **'fire-raiser,** *s.* Incendiaire *mf*. **'fireraising,** *s.* *Jur:* Incendie *m* volontaire, par malveillance. **'fire-resisting,** *a.* **I.** Ignifuge. **2.** *Cer:* Réfractaire. **'fire-screen,** *s.* (*a*) Devant *m* de cheminée. (*b*) Écran *m* ignifuge. **'firestation,** *s.* Poste *m* d'incendie, de (sapeurs-) pompiers. **'fire-wood,** *s.* Bois *m* de chauffage ; bois à brûler. *Bundle of f.-w.,* margotin *m*. **'fire-worship,** *s.* *Anthr:* Culte *m* du feu.
fire², *v.* **I.** *v.tr.* **I.** (*a*) Mettre feu à, embraser (qch.). (*b*) Mettre le feu à, incendier (une maison). (*c*) Animer, *F:* emballer (qn) ; enflammer (les passions). **2.** Cuire (de la poterie). **3.** *Mch:* Chauffer (une locomotive). **4.** (*a*) **To fire a mine,** faire jouer la mine. *I.C.E:* **To fire the mixture,** enflammer le mélange (gazeux). (*b*) **To fire a torpedo,** lancer une torpille. (*c*) *Abs.* **To fire at, on, s.o.,** tirer sur qn. *To f. a gun at s.o.,* lâcher un coup de fusil à qn. *F:* **To fire a question at s.o.,** poser à qn une question à brûle-pourpoint. **To fire (off)** *a gun,* décharger un canon ; faire feu d'une pièce. (*With passive force*) *Guns were firing,* on tirait le canon. *Without firing a shot,* sans brûler une amorce. **5.** *F:* Renvoyer, *F:* flanquer à la porte (un employé, etc.) ; balancer (un fonctionnaire). **II. fire,** *v.i.* (*a*) *The revolver failed to f.,* le revolver fit long feu. (*b*) *I.C.E:* (*Of mixture*) Exploser. *The engine fires evenly,* le moteur tourne régulièrement. *Engine firing badly,* moteur qui donne mal. **fire away,** *v.tr.* **I.** Gaspiller (ses munitions). **2.** *Abs. F:* **Fire away!** allez-y ! allez, racontez ! **fire off,** *v.tr.* **I.** Tirer, faire partir (un coup de fusil). **2.** *To f. off an epigram,* décocher une épigramme. **fire up.** **I.** *v.i. F:* (*Of pers.*) S'emporter. *To f. up in a moment,* monter comme une soupe au lait. **2.** *v.tr. Mch: etc:* (*a*) Mettre (une chaudière) en feu. (*b*) *Abs.* Activer la chauffe. **firing,** *s.* **I.** *Brickm: Cer:* Cuite *f*, cuisson *f*. **2.** Chauffage *m*, chauffe *f* (d'un four, d'une locomotive). **3.** (*a*) *Min:* Allumage *m* (d'un coup de mine). (*b*) *I.C.E:* Allumage. (*c*) *Mil: etc:* Tir *m*, feu *m*. *Artil:* Barrage *f*., tir de barrage. **Firing party,** peloton *m* d'exécution. **4.** Combustible *m*. *To gather f.,* ramasser du bois (mort), du petit bois. **'firing-pin,** *s.* Percuteur *m* (de mitrailleuse) ; aiguille *f* (de fusil).
firelock ['faiǝrlɔk], *s.* *Sm.a:* *A:* Fusil *m* à pierre.
fireman, *pl.* **-men** ['faiǝrmǝn, -men], *s.m.* **I.** Chauffeur (d'une machine à vapeur). **2.** (Sapeur-)pompier.
fireside [faiǝr'said], *s.* Foyer *m* ; coin *m* du feu. Fireside tales, contes du foyer.
firework ['faiǝrwǝːrk], *s.* **I.** Pièce *f* d'artifice. **2.** *pl.* Fireworks, feu *m* d'artifice. **Grand display of fireworks,** grand feu d'artifice. *F:* *His speech was all fireworks,* son discours n'a été qu'un feu d'artifice.
firkin ['fǝːrkin], *s.* Tonnelet *m*, barillet *m* (pour poisson ou liquides) ; tinette *f* (pour beurre).
firm¹ [fǝːrm], *s. Com:* **I.** Raison sociale ; firme *f*. **2.** Maison *f* (de commerce). *Name, style, of the f.,* raison sociale. *F. of solicitors,* bureau *m* d'affaires.
firm², *a.* Ferme. **I.** (*Of substance*) Consistant, compact ; (*of post, nail*) solide, fixe ; (*of touch*) vigoureux, assuré. *As firm as a rock,* inébranlable. **To rule with a firm, hand,** gouverner d'une main ferme. **2.** (*Of friendship, etc.*) Constant ; (*of intention*) résolu, déterminé ; (*of character*) décidé, résolu. *Firm chin,* menton qui dénote la fermeté. **To be firm as to sth.,** tenir bon sur qch. **To have**

a **firm** belief that . . ., être fermement convaincu que. . . . **3.** *Com: Fin:* (*Of offer, sale*) Ferme. **4.** *adv.* To stand firm, tenir bon ; tenir ferme. **-ly,** *adv.* **I.** Fermement, solidement. *To hold the reins f.*, tenir les rênes d'une main ferme. **2.** D'un ton ferme.

firmament ['fə:rməmənt], *s.* Firmament *m.*

firmness ['fə:rmnəs], *s.* Fermeté *f* ; solidité *f.*

first [fə:rst]. I. *a.* **I.** Premier. (*a*) *The f. of April*, le premier avril. *The f. two acts*, les deux premiers actes. To live on the first floor, (i) demeurer au premier (étage) ; (ii) *U.S:* demeurer au rez-de-chaussée. **Charles the First**, Charles Premier. At first sight, at the first blush, de prime abord ; au premier abord. In the first place, d'abord ; en premier lieu. *To succeed the very f. time*, réussir du premier coup. *To wear a new dress for the f. time*, étrenner une robe. To fall head first, tomber la tête la première. *To come out f.*, passer le premier (dans un examen). *I'll do it to-morrow f.* thing, je le ferai dès demain matin. *Th:* First night, première *f. Typ:* First edition, édition princeps, édition originale. *Aut:* First speed, première vitesse. *Box:* First round, round initial. *S.a.* FORM[1] 5. (*b*) First lieutenant, lieutenant en premier. (*c*) *To have got news at first hand*, tenir une nouvelle de première main. **2.** Unième. **Twenty-first**, vingt et unième. **Seventy-first**, soixante et onzième. **-ly,** *adv.* Premièrement ; en premier lieu. II. **first,** *s.* **I.** (Le) premier, (la) première. *He was among the very f.*, il est arrivé tout des premiers. To come in an easy first, arriver bon premier. *Sch: F:* To get a double first, être rangé dans la première classe dans chacune des deux parties de l'examen. **2.** Commencement *m. From f. to last*, depuis le début jusqu'à la fin. From the first, dès le premier jour. At first, au commencement ; d'abord. **3.** *F:* (= *first class*) I always travel first, je voyage toujours en première. III. **first,** *adv.* **I.** Premièrement, au commencement, d'abord. **First of all,** *F:* **first and foremost,** pour commencer ; en premier lieu. *U.S:* First off, de prime abord. First and last, en tout et pour tout. To say first one thing and then another, *F:* dire tantôt blanc tantôt noir. **2.** Pour la première fois. **3.** Plutôt. I'd die first, plutôt mourir. **4.** He arrived first, il arriva le premier. You go first! allez devant ! First come first served, les premiers vont devant. Ladies first! place aux dames ! Women and children first! les femmes et les enfants d'abord ! **'first-'aid,** *s.* Premiers secours ; soins *mpl* d'urgence. First-aid outfit, trousse de pansement. First-aid station *or* post, poste de (premiers) secours. Hints on first-aid, notions de secourisme. **'first-born,** *a. & s.* (Enfant) premier-né, *pl.* premiers-nés. **'first-class,** *a.* (Wagon) de première classe ; (marchandises) de première qualité, de (premier) choix ; (hôtel) de premier ordre. *F: F.-c. dinner*, chic dîner. *F.-c. player*, joueur de premier ordre. That's **'first-'class!** à la bonne heure ! **'first-fruits,** *s.pl.* Prémices *f* (d'un travail). **'first-'hand,** *a.* (Nouvelle) de première main. **'first-'rate,** *a.* Excellent ; de première classe. *Of f.-r. quality*, de toute première qualité. *F.-r. dinner*, dîner soigné ; *F:* chic dîner. *F.-r. idea*, fameuse idée. *He is a f.-r. man*, c'est un homme supérieur. *adv. F:* It is going first-rate, ça marche à merveille. **'first-'rater,** *s. F:* As *m.*

firth [fə:rθ], *s.* (*Scot.*) Estuaire *m* ; bras *m* de mer.

fiscal ['fisk(ə)l]. **I.** *a.* Fiscal, -aux. F. year, année d'exercice. **2.** *s. Scot.* = PROCURATOR-FISCAL.

fish[1], *pl.* **fishes,** coll. **fish** [fiʃ, -iz], *s.* **I.** Poisson *m.*

Fresh-water f., poisson d'eau douce. *Salt-water f.*, poisson de mer. *F:* He is like a fish out of water, il est comme un poisson sur la paille ; il se sent dépaysé. All is fish that comes to his net. tout lui est bon. I've other fish to fry, j'ai d'autres chats à fouetter. To feed the fishes, (i) se noyer ; (ii) avoir le mal de mer. Neither fish, flesh nor fowl, ni chair ni poisson. *Prov:* There's as good fish in the sea as ever came out of it, il, elle, n'est pas unique au monde. *F:* He's a queer fish, c'est un drôle de corps, c'est un type à part. **2.** *Astr:* The Fish(es), les Poissons. **'fish-ball,** *s. Cu:* Boulette *f*, rissole *f*, de poisson. **'fish-basket,** *s.* **I.** Panier *m* de pêche. **2.** Bourriche *f* à poissons. **'fish-bone,** *s.* Arête *f* (de poisson). **'fish-cake,** *s.* = FISH-BALL. **'fish-eating,** *a.* Ichtyophage. **'fish-glue,** *s.* Colle *f* de poisson. **'fish-hook,** *s.* Hameçon *m.* **'fish-kettle,** *s. Cu:* Poissonnière *f.* **'fish-market,** *s.* Marché *m* au poisson ; poissonnerie *f.* **'fish-slice,** *s.* Truelle *f* à poisson. **'fish-spear,** *s.* Foène *f*, trident *m.* **'fish-train,** *s.* Train *m* de marée.

fish[2]. **I.** *v.i.* Pêcher. *To f. for trout*, pêcher la truite. **2.** *v.tr.* (*a*) To fish up a dead body, (re)pêcher un cadavre. (*b*) To fish a river, pêcher une rivière. **fishing,** *s.* **I.** La pêche. Trout-fishing, la pêche à la truite. Deep-sea fishing, la grande pêche. Pearl-fishing, la pêche des perles. **2.** Fishing up, out (again), *of sth.*, repêchage *m* de qch. **'fishing-boat,** *s.* Bateau *m* de pêche **'fishing-ground,** *s.* Pêcherie *f.* **'fishing-line,** *s.* Ligne *f* de pêche. **'fishing-net,** *s.* Filet *m* de pêche. **'fishing-rod,** *s.* Canne *f* à pêche. **'fishing-smack,** *s.* = FISHING-BOAT. **'fishing-tackle,** *s.* Appareil *m*, attirail *m*, de pêche.

fish[3], *pl.* **fishes,** *s. Rail: Const:* Éclisse *f.* **'fish-plate,** *s. Rail:* Éclisse *f.*

fish[4], *pl.* **fish,** *s. Games:* Fiche *f.*

fisherman, *pl.* **-men** ['fiʃərmən, -men], *s.m.* Pêcheur.

fishery ['fiʃəri], *s.* **I.** Pêche *f.* Cod, whale, *f.*, pêche à la morue, à la baleine. *Coral f.*, la pêche du corail. High-sea(s) fishery, la grande pêche. Fishery-protection vessel, garde-pêche *m inv.* **2.** (*Fishing-ground*) Pêcherie *f.*

fishmonger ['fiʃmʌŋgər], *s.* Marchand *m* de poisson.

fishpond ['fiʃpɔnd], *s.* Vivier *m.*

fishwife, *pl.* **-wives** ['fiʃwaif, -waivz], *s.f.* Marchande de poisson ; *F:* poissarde.

fishy ['fiʃi], *a.* **I.** (Odeur, goût) de poisson. *F:* Fishy eyes, yeux ternes, vitreux. **2.** *F:* (*Of pers., affair*) Véreux ; (*of pers., conduct*) louche. *It looks, sounds, f.*, ce n'est pas catholique.

fissile ['fisail], *a.* Fissile, lamellé.

fissiparous [fi'sipərəs], *a. Biol:* Fissipare.

fissure[1] ['fiʃər], *s.* Fissure *f*, fente *f*, crevasse *f.* **fissure**[2]. **I.** *v.tr.* Fissurer, fendre. **2.** *v.i.* (*Of rock*) Se fissurer ; se crevasser.

fist [fist], *s.* **I.** Poing *m.* To fight with one's fists, se battre à coups de poing. *To shake one's fist at s.o.*, menacer qn du poing. **2.** *F:* To make a good first of a job, bien réussir une besogne. **3.** *F:* He writes a first-class fist, il a une jolie écriture. **4.** *P:* Main *f.*

fistful ['fistful], *s.* Poignée *f* (d'argent, etc.).

fisticuffs ['fistikʌfs], *s.pl.* Coups *m* de poing. *To resort to f.*, se battre à coups de poing.

fistula ['fistjula], *s. Med:* Fistule *f.*

fit[1] [fit], *s.* **I.** (*a*) Accès *m*, attaque *f* (de fièvre, etc.). *Fit of madness*, accès de folie. Fit of

coughing, quinte *f* de toux. (*b*) **Fainting fit,**
évanouissement *m*, s.,ncope *f*. **To fall into a fit,**
tomber en convulsions. *F:* **He will have a fit
when he knows,** il en aura une congestion quand
il le saura. **To frighten s.o. into fits,** convulser
qn. **2.** Accès, mouvement *m* (de mauvaise
humeur). *To answer in a fit of temper,* répondre
sous le coup de la colère. *Fit of crying,* crise *f* de
larmes. **To be in fits of laughter,** avoir le fou
rire. *To have sudden fits of energy,* avoir des élans
d'énergie. **To work by fits and starts,** travailler
à bâtons rompus.

fit², *a.* (fitter; fittest) **I.** Bon, propre, convenable
(*for sth.,* à qch.). Fit to + *inf.,* bon à, propre
à + *inf.* **Fit to drink,** buvable, potable. **Fit to
wear,** mettable. **I am not fit to be seen,** je ne suis
pas présentable. *At a fitter moment,* à un moment
plus opportun. **To think fit, see fit, to do sth.,**
juger convenable, trouver bon, de faire qch. *Do
as you think fit,* faites comme bon vous semblera.
She cried fit to break her heart, elle pleurait à
gros sanglots. **2.** (*a*) Capable. **Fit for sth.,** en
état de faire qch.; apte à qch. *Mil:* **Fit for
service,** bon pour le service. **To be fit for one's
job,** être à la hauteur de sa tâche. **He is not fit
to live,** il n'est pas digne de vivre. **He is fit for
nothing,** il n'est propre à rien; c'est un propre à
rien. (*b*) *F:* Disposé, prêt (à faire qch.). **I felt
fit to drop,** je n'en pouvais plus. **3.** *Med: Sp:*
To be (bodily) fit, être en bonne santé; être
dispos. *F:* **To be as fit as a fiddle,** être en parfaite
santé. **-ly,** *adv.* Convenablement.

fit³, *s.* (*a*) Ajustement *m.* *Your coat is a perfect fit,*
votre pardessus est juste à votre taille. **It was a
tight fit,** on tenait tout juste. (*b*) *Mec.E:* Ajustage *m* (d'un assemblage); frottement *m* (d'organes mobiles). *Easy fit,* frottement doux.

fit⁴, *v.* (fitted) **I.** *v.tr.* **I.** (*Of clothes, etc.*) Aller à
(qn); être à la taille de (qn). *Key that fits the
lock,* clef qui va à la serrure. *Shoes that fit well,*
souliers qui chaussent bien. **It fits you like a
glove,** cela vous va comme un gant. **2.** (*a*) Adapter, ajuster, accommoder (*sth. to sth.,* qch. à
qch.). **To make the punishment fit the crime,**
proportionner le châtiment à l'offense. *To fit a
garment on s.o.,* ajuster un vêtement à qn. *To
fit a handle to a broom,* emmancher un balai. *To
fit the key in the lock,* engager la clef dans la
serrure. (*b*) **To fit parts** (*together*), monter,
assembler, des pièces. **3. To fit s.o. for sth.,**
préparer qn à qch. **4. To fit sth. with sth.,**
garnir, munir, qch. de qch. *Fitted with two
propellers,* pourvu de deux hélices. **II. fit,** *v.i.*
(*a*) **To fit** (*together*), s'ajuster, s'adapter, se
raccorder. *To fit on sth.,* s'adapter sur qch. *To
fit into sth.,* s'emboîter, s'enclaver, dans qch.
(*b*) *Your dress fits well,* votre robe (vous) va bien.
fit in. I. *v.tr.* (*a*) Emboîter (des tubes). (*b*) Faire
concorder (des témoignages). **2.** *v.i.* (*a*) *To fit in
between two things,* s'emboîter entre deux choses.
(*b*) **To fit in with sth.,** être en harmonie avec qch.
Your plans do not fit in with mine, vos projets
ne cadrent pas avec les miens. **fit on,** *v.tr.*
I. Essayer (un vêtement, etc.). **2.** Monter (un
pneu) (*to,* sur). **fit out,** *v.tr.* Équiper (*sth. with
sth.,* qch. de qch.); garnir (un coffret); outiller
(une usine); *Nau:* armer (un vaisseau). **To fit
s.o. out** (*with clothing, etc.*), équiper qn. **fit-'out,**
s. (*a*) Trousseau *m.* (*b*) Équipement *m.* **fit up,**
v.tr. Monter (une machine); appareiller (un
poste de T.S.F.). **fitted,** *a.* **I.** Ajusté, monté.
(*Of case, chest*) Fitted (up), garni. **2.** *He is f. for
the post,* il est apte à occuper le poste. **fitting¹,** *a.*
I. Convenable, bienséant; approprié (*to,* à).

F. remark, remarque à propos. **2. Well-fitting
garment,** vêtement qui va bien. **Easy-fitting,**
commode. **-ly,** *adv.* Convenablement; à
propos. **fitting²,** *s.* **I.** (*a*) Ajustage *m* (d'une
pièce). **Fitting (up, together)** *of a machine,*
montage *m* d'une machine. *Fitting on of a tyre,*
montage d'un pneu. (*b*) Fitting (on) (*of clothes*),
essayage *m,* ajustage (de vêtements). **Fitting
room,** salon d'essayage. **2.** *Usu. pl.* Agencements *m,*
installations *f* (d'un atelier); armement *m* (d'une
machine); garniture *f* (d'une chambre); appareillage *m* (pour lumière électrique). **Metal fittings,** ferrures *f.* **Brass fittings,** garnitures en cuivre.

fitch [fitʃ], *s.* Brosse *f* en putois.

fitchet ['fitʃit], **fitchew** ['fitʃuː], *s.* Putois *m.*

fitful ['fitful], *a.* Irrégulier, capricieux; d'humeur changeante. **-fully,** *adv.* Irrégulièrement;
par à-coups.

fitment ['fitmənt], *s.* Montage *m*; monture *f.*

fitness ['fitnəs], *s.* **I.** Aptitude *f* (*for,* à, pour).
Aut: F. to drive, aptitude à conduire. **2.** (*a*) A-
propos *m,* justesse *f* (d'une remarque). (*b*) Convenance *f,* bienséance *f.* **3. Physical fitness,**
santé *f* physique.

fitter ['fitər], *s.* **I.** *Mec.E: Aut:* Ajusteur *m,*
(re)monteur *m.* **2.** *Tail:* Essayeur, -euse.

five [faiv], *num. a. & s.* Cinq (*m*). **A five-pound
note,** un billet de cinq livres. **Five-Year Plan,**
Plan quinquennal. (*For other phrases see* EIGHT.)

fivefold ['faivfould]. **I.** *a.* Quintuple. **2.** *adv.*
Cinq fois autant; au quintuple.

fiver ['faivər], *s.* *F:* Billet *m* de cinq livres,
U.S: de cinq dollars.

fives [faivz], *s.* *Games:* = Balle *f* au mur.

fix¹ [fiks], *s.* *F:* Embarras *m,* difficulté *f,* mauvais
pas. **To be in a fix,** être dans une situation
embarrassante; se trouver dans une impasse;
être dans le pétrin. *To get into a fix,* se mettre
dans le pétrin.

fix², *v.tr.* Fixer. **I.** Caler, monter (une poulie,
etc.); assujettir (une poutre); ancrer (un
tirant); arrêter, assurer (une planche). *To fix
a stake into the ground,* ficher un pieu en terre.
F: **To fix sth. in one's memory,** se graver qch.
dans la mémoire. *To fix one's eye(s) on s.o.,* fixer
qn (du regard). *F:* **To fix s.o. with one's eye,**
fixer qn des yeux. **2.** (*a*) *Phot: etc:* Fixer (une
épreuve). (*b*) *Med: F:* Stériliser (une
préparation microscopique). **3.** Établir. *To fix a
camp,* établir un camp. **4.** (*a*) Fixer, établir (une
limite); arrêter, nommer (un jour). *The date is
not yet fixed,* la date n'est pas encore arrêtée.
On the date fixed, à la date prescrite. **There is
nothing fixed yet,** il n'y a encore rien d'assuré,
rien d'arrêté. (*b*) **To fix (up)on sth.,** se décider
pour qch. **5.** *U.S:* *F:* (*a*) Mettre (qn) dans
l'impossibilité de nuire. *I've fixed him!* il a
son compte! (*b*) Graisser la patte à (qn). **fix
up,** *v.tr.* **I.** *F:* Placer, mettre, installer (qch.).
2. *F:* Arranger, régler, conclure (une affaire).
I've fixed it up, j'ai conclu l'affaire. *It is all fixed
up,* c'est une affaire réglée. **fixed,** *a.* Fixe,
arrêté. **I.** (Vitrage, etc.) dormant. *F. wheel,* roue
calée. *Ind:* **Fixed plant,** matériel fixe. **2.** (*a*) Lever arm of f. length,* bras de levier de longueur
constante. *Com:* Fixed prices, prix fixes. *F. rule,*
règle établie. *F:* Fixed idea, idée fixe. **Fixed
smile,** sourire figé. (*b*) *F. point,* point fixe. *Astr:*
Fixed star, étoile fixe. **Fixed assets,** immobilisations *f.* **3. How are we fixed for time?** de
combien de temps disposons-nous? **fixing,** *s.*
Fixage *m,* pose *f* (de rails); fixage (d'une épreuve
photographique); ancrage *m* (de crampons).
'fixing-bath, *s.* *Phot:* Bain *m* de fixage.

fixative ['fiksətiv], s. Fixatif m (de dessins au pastel ou au fusain).

fixature ['fiksətjuər], s. Fixatif m (pour les cheveux).

fixedly ['fiksidli], adv. Fixement.

fixer ['fiksər], s. (a) = FIXATIVE. (b) Phot: Bain m de fixage.

fixity ['fiksiti], s. Fixité f. F. of purpose, détermination f.

fixture ['fikstjər], s. **1.** Appareil m fixe; partie f fixe (d'une machine, etc.); meuble m à demeure. To make sth. a f., ancrer qch. en place. **2.** Usu. pl. Choses fixées à demeure; meubles à demeure fixe; agencements m inamovibles. **3.** Sp: Engagement m; match (prévu). List of fixtures, programme m.

fizz[1] [fiz], s. **1.** Pétillement m (du champagne, etc.); crachement m, sifflement m (de la vapeur). **2.** P: Champagne m.

fizz[2], v.i. (Of champagne, etc.) Pétiller; (of escape of steam) fuser, siffler.

fizzle[1] [fizl], s. Pétillement m (du champagne, etc.); sifflement m (d'un bec de gaz); grésillement m (de la graisse bouillonnante).

fizzle[2], v.i. (Of wine, etc.) Pétiller; (of gas-burner) siffler; (of boiling fat) grésiller. **fizzle out**, v.i. P: (Of affair, etc.) Ne pas aboutir; avorter; faire fiasco; s'en aller en eau de boudin.

fizzy ['fizi], a. (Of mineral water, etc.) Gazeux, effervescent; (of wine) mousseux.

flabbergast ['flabərgɑːst], v.tr. F: Épater, abasourdir, ahurir (qn). **flabbergasting**, a. Ahurissant, abasourdissant.

flabbiness ['flabinəs], s. Flaccidité f, manque m de fermeté (de la chair, etc.); avachissement m, mollesse f (de caractère).

flabby ['flabi], a. (Of muscles, etc.) Flasque mou, f. molle; (of cheeks) mollasse; (of pers character) mollasse, avachi. **-ily,** adv. Mollement.

flaccid ['flaksid], a. **1.** Mou, f. molle; (chair) flasque. **2.** F. (Volonté) flasque, mollasse.

flag[1] [flag], s. Bot: Iris m. Water flag, glaïeul m des marais.

flag[2], s. Const: (Paving-)flag, carreau m (en pierre); dalle f. Flag pavement, carrelage m, dallage m.

flag[3], v.tr. Daller, carreler (un trottoir, etc.). **flagging**[1], s. Carrelage m, dallage m.

flag[4], s. **1.** (a) Drapeau m. Flag of truce, white flag, drapeau parlementaire. With flags flying, enseignes déployées. (b) Nau: Pavillon m. Black flag, pavillon noir (des pirates). To fly a flag, (i) battre pavillon; (ii) arborer un pavillon. F: To keep the flag flying, maintenir l'honneur de la maison, etc. F: To lower one's flag, baisser pavillon. (c) Flags (for dressing a ship), pavois m. To deck a ship with flags, pavoiser un vaisseau. **2.** Ven: (Of dog) Queue f (de setter). **3.** Drapeau (de taximètre). Taxi with the flag up, taxi libre. '**flag-captain**, s. Navy: Capitaine m de pavillon. '**flag-day**, s. Jour m de vente d'insignes pour une œuvre de bienfaisance. '**flag-lieutenant**, s. Navy: Officier m d'ordonnance. '**flag-wagger**, s. **1.** Mil: F: Signaleur m. **2.** P: Patriotard m, chauvin m. '**flag-waving**, s. Chauvinisme m; patriotisme m de façade.

flag[5], v.tr. **1.** Pavoiser (un vaisseau). **2.** Transmettre des signaux à (qn) au moyen de fanions.

flag[6], v.i. (Of plant) Languir; (of pers.) s'alanguir; (of conversation) se ralentir, traîner; (of attention) faiblir, fléchir; (of zeal) se relâcher. **flagging**[2], s. Amollissement m (du courage); ralentissement m (du zèle).

flagellate ['fladʒeleit], v.tr. Flageller; fouetter.

flagellation [fladʒe'leiʃ(ə)n], s. Flagellation f.

flageolet [fladʒo'let], s. Mus: Flageolet m.

flagitious [fla'dʒiʃəs], a. Infâme, abominable.

flagon ['flagən], s. **1.** Flacon m. Ecc: Burette f. **2.** Grosse bouteille ventrue.

flagrancy ['fleigrənsi], s. Énormité f (d'un crime, etc.).

flagrant ['fleigrənt], a. (Of offence) Flagrant, énorme. A f. case, un cas notoire. **-ly,** adv. Scandaleusement; d'une manière flagrante.

flagrante delicto [fla'grantidi'likto], Lt. adv.phr. En flagrant délit.

flagship ['flagʃip], s. (Vaisseau m) amiral m.

flagstaff ['flagstɑːf], s. **1.** (i) Mât m de drapeau; (ii) lance f, hampe f, de drapeau. **2.** Nau: (a) Mât de pavillon. (b) Gaule f (d'enseigne).

flagstone ['flagstoun], s. = FLAG[2].

flail [fleil], s. Husb: Fléau m.

flair ['fleər], s. Flair m, perspicacité f. To have a flair for bargains, avoir du flair pour les occasions.

flake[1] [fleik], s. (a) Flocon m (de neige, etc.). (b) Flammèche f. (c) Écaille f, éclat m, paillette f (de métal, etc.).

flake[2], v.i. (a) (Of snow, etc.) Tomber en flocons. (b) (Of metal, mineral, etc.) To flake (away, off), s'écailler, se feuilleter; (of stone) s'épaufrer.

flaky ['fleiki], a. **1.** (Of snow, etc.) Floconneux. **2.** (Of metal, etc.) Écailleux, lamellé, lamelleux. Flaky pastry, pâte feuilletée.

flamboyant [flam'bɔiənt], a. Flamboyant.

flame[1] [fleim], s. **1.** Flamme f. In flames, en flammes, en feu. To burst, break, into flame(s), s'enflammer brusquement. **2.** F: (a) Passion f, ardeur f, flamme. (b) Hum: An old f. of mine, une de mes anciennes flammes, de mes anciennes amours. '**flame-projector, -thrower**, s. Mil: Lance-flammes m inv; projecteur m de flammes. '**flame-'red**, a. Rouge feu inv.

flame[2], v.i. (Of fire, etc.) Flamber, jeter des flammes; F: (of passions, etc.) s'enflammer. **flame up**, v.i. (a) S'enflammer. (b) F: (Of pers.) S'enflammer de colère; s'emporter. **flaming**[1], a. **1.** (Feu) flambant, flamboyant; (maison, etc.) en flammes. **2.** F: F. sun, soleil ardent, flamboyant. Flaming red, rouge feu inv. **flaming**[2], s. Flamboiement m, embrasement m.

flamingo [fla'mingo], s. Orn: Flamant m.

flan [flan], s. Cu: Tarte f aux fruits.

Flanders ['flɑːndərz], Pr.n. Geog: La Flandre.

flange[1] [flandʒ], s. **1.** Collet m, collerette f, saillie f; bride f, bourrelet m (d'un tuyau, etc.); boudin m, rebord m (d'une roue). Flange coupling, flange joint, joint m ou raccordement m à brides. **2.** Cooling flange, ailette f ou nervure f de refroidissement.

flange[2], v.tr. Tchn: Brider, faire une bride à (un tube, etc.). To f. a plate, border une tôle. **flanged**, a. (Tube, etc.) à bride(s); (roue, etc.) à boudin, à rebord. F. plate, tôle à bord tombé.

flank[1] [flank], s. **1.** (a) Flanc m. (b) Cu: Flanchet m (de bœuf). **2.** (a) F: Côté m, flanc (d'une montagne, etc.). (b) Mil: To take the enemy in flank, prendre l'ennemi de flanc.

flank[2], v.tr. Flanquer. **1.** To f. sth. with, by, sth., flanquer qch. de qch. **2.** Mil: Prendre (l'ennemi) de flanc.

flannel ['flan(ə)l], s. (a) Flanelle f. (b) pl. To wear flannels, porter un costume en flanelle; porter un costume de cricket, etc.

flannelette [flanəl'et], s. Flanelle f de coton.

flap[1] [flap], s. **1.** (a) Battement m, coup m (d'aile, etc.); clapotement m, claquement m (d'une voile).

(b) Coup léger (de la main) ; tape f. **2.** (a) Patte f (d'une enveloppe, d'une poche, etc.) ; rabat m (d'une casquette). (b) Abattant m, battant m (de table) ; trappe f (de cave). *Phot :* Flap-shutter, obturateur m à volet. (c) *Av :* Volet m. **'flap-eared,** a. (Chien, etc.) aux oreilles pendantes. **'flap-seat,** s. **1.** Strapontin m. **2.** Abattant m (de cuvette de cabinet d'aisances). **'flap-valve,** s. (Soupape f à) clapet m. **flap²,** v. (flapped) **1.** v.tr. (a) Battre (des ailes). To flap one's arms about, battre des bras. (b) Frapper (qch.) légèrement. To flap away the flies, chasser les mouches. **2.** v.i. (Of sail, etc.) Battre, fouetter, claquer ; (of wings) battre ; (of shutter) ballotter. **flapdoodle** [flap'duːdl], s. *P :* Balivernes fpl ; boniments mpl oiseux. **flapper** ['flapər], s. **1.** Balai m tue-mouches ; tapette f. **2.** (a) = FLIPPER **1.** (b) *Crust :* Telson m. **3.** *P :* Fillette f ; jeune fille qui n'a pas encore débuté. **flare¹** ['flɛər], s. **1.** (a) Flamboiement irrégulier ; flamme vacillante. (b) Feu m (de signal). *Mil :* Artifice éclairant ; fusée éclairante. *Av :* Landing flare, feu d'atterrissage. (c) *Phot :* Flare(-spot), tache f par réflexion ; spectre m secondaire. **2.** Évasement m, godet m (d'une jupe) ; pavillon m (d'un entonnoir). **flare².** **1.** v.i. (a) Flamboyer, vaciller. (b) (Of skirt) S'évaser. **2.** v.tr. Évaser (une jupe, une embrasure). **flare up,** v.i. (a) S'enflammer brusquement ; lancer des flammes. (b) *F :* (Of pers.) S'emporter ; se mettre en colère. **flare-'up,** s. (a) Flambée soudaine. (b) *F :* (i) Altercation f, scène f ; (ii) bagarre f. **flash¹** [flaʃ], a. *F :* **1.** Fastueux, voyant. **2.** (Of money) Contrefait, faux. **3.** *F. gentry,* les filous m, les escrocs m ; la haute pègre. **flash²,** s. **1.** Éclair m ; éclat m (de flamme). *El :* *F. across the terminals,* jaillissement m d'étincelles entre les bornes. *F :* A flash in the pan, un feu de paille. Flash of wit, saillie f, boutade f. In a flash, en un rien de temps ; en un clin d'œil. **2.** *F :* Faste m, ostentation f ; *P :* épate f. **'flash-lamp,** s. **1.** Lanterne f de signalisation. **2.** Lampe électrique portative ; lampe de poche. **'flash-light,** s. **1.** (Of lighthouse) Feu m à éclats. **2.** *Phot :* Lumière-éclair f. Flash-light powder = FLASH-POWDER. **'flash-point,** s. = FLASHING-POINT. **'flash-powder,** s. *Phot :* Poudre-éclair f, photopoudre f. **flash³.** **1.** v.i. (a) Jeter des éclairs ; lancer des étincelles ; flamboyer ; (of diamonds) éclater, briller, étinceler. His eyes flashed fire, ses yeux jetèrent des éclairs. To flash in the pan, (i) *A :* (of gun) faire long feu ; (ii) *F :* (of undertaking, etc.) faire feu de paille. (b) To flash past, passer comme un éclair. It flashed upon me, across my mind, that . . ., l'idée me vint tout d'un coup que. . . . **2.** v.tr. (a) Faire flamboyer (un sabre, etc.) ; faire étinceler (ses bijoux). (b) Projeter (un rayon de lumière). He flashed his lantern on to . . ., il dirigea les rayons de sa lanterne sur . . . He flashed a glance of hatred at me, il darda sur moi un regard chargé de haine. (c) Répandre (une nouvelle) par le télégraphe ou par la radio. **flash back,** v.i. (Of Bunsen burner) Avoir un retour de flamme. **'flashback,** s. **1.** Retour m de flamme. **2.** *Cin :* Scène f de rappel (du passé). **flashing¹,** a. Éclatant, flamboyant. *Nau :* Flashing light, feu m à éclats. **flashing²,** s. Flamboiement m (du feu) ; éclat m, étincellement m (d'un diamant) ; clignotement m (d'un signal). **'flashing-point,**

s. Point m d'éclair, point d'ignition (d'une huile lourde). **flashiness** ['flaʃinəs], s. Éclat superficiel ; faux brillant. **flashy** ['flaʃi], a. (Of speech, etc.) (D'un éclat) superficiel ; d'un faux brillant ; (of dress, etc.) voyant, éclatant, tapageur. **-ily,** adv. Flashily-dressed, à toilette tapageuse. **flask** [flɑːsk], s. (a) Flacon m ; gourde f (d'eau-de-vie). (b) *Ch :* (i) Fiole f. (ii) Ballon m. Flat-bottomed f., ballon à fond plat. **flat¹** [flat], s. Appartement m. Service-flat, appartement avec service compris et repas à volonté. **flat².** **I.** a. Plat. **1.** (a) Horizontal, -aux ; posé à plat. (b) (Of curve, etc.) Aplati. (c) Étendu à plat. To fall flat on one's face, tomber, se jeter, à plat ventre. To fall f. on one's back, tomber sur le dos. To lie down flat on the ground, s'aplatir par terre. To place sth. f. against a wall, mettre qch. à plat contre un mur. *Aut :* To go flat out, filer à toute allure. (d) (Of surface) Plat, uni. Flat (bar-)iron, fer m éplati. Flat nose, nez épaté, aplati, camus. Flat tyre, pneu à plat. To beat, make, sth. f., aplatir qch. *Sp :* Flat race, course plate. *Geom :* Flat projection, plan géométral. *F :* As flat as a pancake, plat comme une galette. (e) *I.C.E :* Flat spot (of a carburettor), "trou" m (dans le passage du ralenti à la marche normale. (f) *Paint :* Flat colour, surface mate, couleur mate. **2.** *F :* Net, f. nette ; positif. *F.* refusal, refus net, catégorique. *F :* That's flat! voilà qui est net ! **3.** (a) Monotone, ennuyeux ; (of style, etc.) fade, insipide. *F.* voice, voix terne, blanche. I was feeling a bit flat, je me sentais déprimé, à plat. *Com :* Flat market, marché calme, languissant. *F :* To fall flat, (of joke, etc.) rater, manquer, son effet ; (of play) faire tour. (b) (Of drink) Éventé, plat. **4.** Invariable, uniforme. Flat rate of pay, taux uniforme de salaires. **5.** (a) (Son, etc.) sourd. (b) *Mus :* Bémol inv. To sing flat, chanter faux. **-ly,** adv. *F :* Nettement, carrément. To deny sth. f., nier absolument qch. To refuse f., refuser carrément. *F.* opposed, en contradiction directe. **II.** flat, adv. *F :* Nettement, positivement. **III.** flat, s. **1.** Plat m (d'un sabre, etc.). Blow with the f. of the hand, coup donné avec la main plate. **2.** (a) Plaine f ; bas-fond m ; marécage m. (b) *Nau :* Bas-fond. **3.** *Rail :* Track on the f., voie en palier. *Rac :* On the flat, sur le plat. **4.** (a) *Nau :* = FLAT-BOAT. (b) *Th :* Châssis m ou ferme f ; paroi f (d'une scène). **5.** *Mus :* Bémol m. **'flat-boat,** s. *Nau :* Bateau plat ; plate f. **flat-'bottom(ed),** a. (Bateau) à fond plat. **'flat-fish,** s. *Ich :* Poisson plat. **'flat-footed,** a. *Med :* Pied plat. **flat-'footed,** a. A pied plat, aux pieds plats. **'flat-iron,** s. *Laund :* Fer m à repasser. **flat-'nosed,** a. Au nez épaté, camard, camus. **flatness** ['flatnəs], s. **1.** Égalité f (d'une surface) ; manque m de relief. *Opt :* Absence f de distorsion (du champ d'une lentille). **2.** Aplatissement m (d'une courbe, etc.). **3.** *F :* Netteté f (d'un refus). **4.** *F :* Monotonie f (de l'existence, etc.) ; engourdissement m, langueur f (du marché, etc.) ; platitude f, insipidité f (du style, etc.). **flatten** [flatn]. **I.** v.tr. (a) To flatten (down, out), aplatir, aplanir (qch.). *F :* To flatten oneself against a wall, se plaquer, se coller, contre un mur. To flatten (out) s.o., aplatir, écraser, qn. (b) *Mus :* Bémoliser (une note). (c) Rendre mat ; amatir, amortir (une couleur). **2.** v.i. (a) S'aplatir, s'aplanir. (b) *Av :* To flatten out, (i) se redresser (après un vol piqué) ; (i) allonger le vol. **flat-**

tening, *s.* **1.** (*a*) Aplatissement *m*, aplatissage *m* (d'une courbe, d'un pneu, etc.); affaissement *m*, écrasement *m* (en charge). (*b*) Amortissement *m* (d'une couleur). **2.** *Av:* **Flattening out** (*after dive*), ressource *f*, redressement *m*.

flatter ['flatər], *v.tr.* **1.** Flatter. *To f. oneself on one's cleverness, on being clever*, se flatter de son habileté, d'être habile. **2.** Charmer, flatter (les yeux, l'oreille). **flattering**, *a.* (*Of words, portrait*) Flatteur, -euse. **-ly**, *adv.* Flatteusement.

flatterer ['flatərər], *s.* Flatteur, -euse; flagorneur, -euse. *F:* **Mealy-mouthed flatterer**, patelin *m*; patelineur, -euse.

flattery ['flatəri], *s.* Flatterie *f.*

flatulence ['flatjuləns], **flatulency** ['flatjulənsi], *s.* **1.** *Med:* Flatulence *f*, flatuosité *f.* **2.** *F:* (*a*) Prétention *f*, vanité *f.* (*b*) Emphase *f.*

flatulent ['flatjulənt], *a.* **1.** *Med:* Flatulent. **2.** (*a*) Bouffi d'orgueil. (*b*) (Style) emphatique.

flaunt [flɔ:nt]. **1.** *v.i.* (*a*) (*Of flag*) Flotter (fièrement). (*b*) (*Of pers.*) Se pavaner, s'afficher. **2.** *v.tr. To f. one's wealth*, faire montre, faire étalage, de son opulence; étaler tout son luxe. *To f. advanced opinions*, afficher des opinions avancées.

flautist ['flɔ:tist], *s. Mus:* Flûtiste *mf.*

flavescent [flei'ves(ə)nt], *a.* (Blé, etc.) flavescent, qui tourne au jaune.

flavour¹ ['fleivər], *s.* Saveur *f*, goût *m. Latest flavours in ices*, glaces *f* parfums du jour.

flavour². **1.** *v.tr.* Assaisonner, parfumer. *To f. a sauce with garlic*, relever une sauce avec de l'ail. **2.** *v.i. To flavour of sth.*, (i) avoir un goût de qch.; (ii) tenir de qch. **flavouring**, *s.* **1.** Assaisonnement *m* (d'un mets). **2.** Assaisonnement, condiment *m.*

flavourless ['fleivərləs], *a.* Sans saveur; insipide.

flaw [flɔ:], *s.* **1.** Défaut *m*, défectuosité *f*, imperfection *f*; (*in china, etc.*) fêlure *f*; (*in wood, etc.*) fissure *f*, fente *f*, crevasse *f*; (*in metal*) brisure *f*, paille *f*, soufflure *f. F:* (*In reputation, etc.*) Flétrissure *f*, tache *f. F. in a scheme*, point *m* faible d'un projet. **2.** *Jur:* (*In deed, etc.*) Vice *m* de forme (entraînant la nullité).

flawed [flɔ:d], *a.* Défectueux; (*of timber*) gercé; (*of iron*) pailleux.

flawless ['flɔ:ləs], *a.* Sans défaut; parfait; (technique) impeccable. **-ly**, *adv.* Parfaitement.

flax [flaks], *s. Bot:* Lin *m.* **Flax field**, linière *f.*

flaxen ['flaks(ə)n], *a.* **1.** (Toile, etc.) de lin. **2.** *F:* (*Of hair*) Blond filasse *inv.* **flaxen-haired**, *a.* (*Of pers.*) Aux cheveux très blonds; blondasse.

flay [flei], *v.tr.* (*a*) Écorcher (un animal, etc.). **To be flayed alive**, être écorché vif. (*b*) *F:* Fouetter, rosser, étriller (qn). (*c*) (*Of shop-keeper*) Écorcher (un client). **flaying**, *s.* Écorchement *m.*

flayer ['fleiər], *s.* (*Pers.*) Écorcheur *m.*

flea [fli:], *s. Ent:* Puce *f. S.a.* EAR¹ **1.** **'flea-bag**, *s. Mil: P:* Sac *m* de couchage; *P:* pucier *m.* **'flea-bite**, *s.* **1.** Morsure *f* de puce. **2.** *F:* Vétille *f*, bagatelle *f*, rien *m.* **'flea-bitten**, *a.* **1.** Mordu par les puces. **2.** (*Of horse's coat*) Moucheté, truité.

fleck¹ [flek], *s.* **1.** Petite tache (de lumière, etc.); moucheture *f* (de couleur). **2.** Particule *f* (de poussière, etc.).

fleck², *v.tr.* Tacheter, moucheter (*with*, de).

fled [fled]. *See* FLEE.

fledged [fledʒd], *a.* (Oiseau) qui a toutes ses plumes.

fledg(e)ling ['fledʒliŋ], *s.* **1.** Oisillon *m.* **2.** *F:* Béjaune *m*, novice *mf.*

flee [fli:], *v.* (**fled** [fled]; **fled**) **1.** *v.i.* (*a*) (*Of pers.*)

Fuir, s'enfuir, se sauver. (*b*) *Time was fleeing* (*away*), le temps s'écoulait vite; le temps fuyait. **2.** *v.tr.* S'enfuir de (qn, la ville, etc.); fuir, éviter (la tentation, etc.). **fleeing**, *a.* (*Of army, etc.*) En fuite.

fleece¹ [fli:s], *s.* **1.** Toison *f.* **2.** *Tex:* Molleton *m.*

fleece², *v.tr. F:* Tondre, écorcher, plumer. *I have been fleeced*, je me suis fait tondre; j'ai essuyé le coup de fusil. **-fleeced**, *a.* **Golden-fleeced**, à la toison d'or.

fleecer ['fli:sər], *s. F:* Écorcheur, -euse.

fleecy ['fli:si], *a.* (*Of wool*) Floconneux; (*of hair, etc.*) laineux; (*of cloud*) moutonné, cotonneux.

fleed [fli:d], *s. Cu:* Lard *m* (de porc).

fleer [fliːr], *v.i.* Railler, se moquer, ricaner. *To f. at s.o.*, se moquer de qn; railler qn.

fleet¹ [fli:t], *s.* **1.** Flotte *f* (de vaisseaux). **2.** **Air-fleet**, flotte aérienne. *Large f. of motor cars*, vaste train *m* de voitures automobiles.

fleet², *a. Lit:* **Fleet of foot**, léger à la course; au pied léger. **'fleet-'footed**, *a.* Au pied léger.

fleet³, *v.i.* (*Of time, etc.*) Passer rapidement; s'enfuir. **fleeting**, *a.* (*Of time*) Fugitif, fugace; (*of beauty*) passager, éphémère. *The f. years*, les années qui passent. *To pay s.o. a f. visit*, faire une courte visite à qn.

fleetness ['fli:tnəs], *s.* Vitesse *f*, rapidité *f* (à la course).

Fleming ['flemiŋ], *s.* Flamand, -ande.

Flemish ['flemiʃ]. **1.** *a.* Flamand. **2.** *s. Ling:* Le flamand.

flesh [fleʃ], *s.* Chair *f.* **1.** (*a*) **To make s.o.'s flesh creep**, donner la chair de poule à qn. **To put on flesh**, (*of animal*) prendre chair; (*of pers.*) engraisser; prendre de l'embonpoint. **To lose flesh**, maigrir, s'amaigrir. (*b*) *Occ.* Viande *f. Ecc:* **To eat flesh**, faire gras. *S.a.* FISH¹, HORSE-FLESH. (*c*) Chair (d'un fruit). **2. To mortify the flesh**, mortifier, châtier, son corps. **It was he in the flesh, in flesh and blood**, c'était lui en chair et en os. **His own flesh and blood**, la chair de sa chair; les siens. **It is more than flesh and blood can stand**, c'est plus que la nature humaine ne saurait endurer. **To go the way of all flesh**, payer sa dette à la nature. **'flesh-colour**, *s.* Couleur *f* (de) chair; *Art:* carnation *f.* **'flesh-coloured**, *a.* De couleur chair. **'flesh-eating**, *a. Z:* Carnassier. **'flesh-fly**, *s. Ent: F:* Mouche *f* à viande. **'flesh-glove**, *s. Toil:* Gant *m* de crin. **'flesh-pink**, *a.* (Teint) carné; rose incarnat *inv.* **'flesh-pots**, *s.pl. B:* Potées *f* de chair (d'Égypte). **To sigh for the flesh-pots of Egypt**, regretter les oignons d'Égypte. **'flesh-tints**, *s.pl. Art:* Carnations *f*, chairs *f.* **'flesh-wound**, *s.* Blessure *f* dans les chairs.

fleshiness ['fleʃinəs], *s.* État charnu (du corps, du nez, etc.).

fleshless ['fleʃləs], *a.* Décharné.

fleshy ['fleʃi], *a.* Charnu.

fleur-de-lis ['flɔ:rdə'li:], *pl.* **fleurs-de-lis** ['flɔ:rdə'li:z], *s.* **1.** *Bot:* Iris *m.* **2.** *Her:* Fleur *f* de lis.

flew [flu:]. *See* FLY³.

flex¹ [fleks]. **1.** *v.tr.* Fléchir (le bras). **2.** *v.i.* (*Of spring*) Fléchir; (*of stratum*) se plier. **flexing**, *s.* Fléchissement *m*; flexion *f.*

flex², *s. El:* Câble *m* souple, flexible *m.*

flexibility [fleksi'biliti], *s.* Flexibilité *f*; élasticité *f*; souplesse *f. Aut: F. of the engine*, souplesse du moteur.

flexible ['fleksibl], *a.* Flexible, souple, pliant. *Aut: F. engine*, moteur souple, nerveux. *F. character*, caractère (i) liant, souple, (ii) complaisant. *El: F. wire*, cordon *m* souple; flexible *m.*

flexion ['flekʃ(ə)n], *s.* **1.** Flexion *f*, courbure *f* (d'un ressort, etc.). **2.** Courbe *f*. **3.** *Gram:* = INFLEXION 2.

flexional ['flekʃənəl], *a. Ling:* Flexionnel. **Flexional ending**, désinence *f*.

flick[1] [flik], *s.* **1.** Petit coup (de fouet, etc.); (*with finger*) chiquenaude *f*, *F:* pichenette *f*. **A flick of the wrist**, un tour de main. **2.** *P:* (= *flickers*) **The flicks**, le ciné.

flick[2], *v.tr.* (*With whip, etc.*) Effleurer (un cheval); (*with finger*) donner une chiquenaude, *F:* une pichenette, à (un grain de poussière). **To flick sth. away, off, with a duster**, faire envoler qch. d'un coup de torchon.

flicker[1] ['flikər], *s.* (*a*) Tremblotement *m*. *F. of the eyelids*, battement *m*, clignement *m*, de paupière. (*b*) *A f. of light*, une petite lueur tremblotante. (*c*) *Cin:* Scintillation *f* (de la reproduction).

flicker[2], *v.i.* (*Of flame, etc.*) Trembloter, vaciller; (*of light*) papilloter, clignoter; (*of speedometer needle, etc.*) osciller. *Cin:* (*Of reproduction*) Scintiller. *The candle flickered out*, la bougie vacilla en s'éteignit. **flickering**, *s.* (*a*) Tremblotement *m*, vacillement *m*, papillotement *m*, clignotement *m*. (*b*) *Cin:* Scintillation *f*.

flier ['flaiər], *s.* = FLYER.

flight[1] [flait], *s.* **1.** (*a*) Vol *m* (d'un oiseau, d'un avion). *Av:* **Trial flight**, vol d'essai. (*b*) Course *f* (d'un projectile, des nuages, etc.). *The f. of time*, le cours du temps. (*c*) Envol *m* (d'un oiseau, d'un avion). (*Of bird*) **To take its flight**, prendre son vol, son essor; s'envoler. *F:* **Flight of fancy**, élan *m*, essor *m*, de l'imagination. (*d*) Migration *f* (d'oiseaux, d'insectes). **2.** Volée *f*, distance parcourue (par un oiseau, etc.); trajectoire *f* (d'un projectile). **3.** (*a*) **Flight of stairs**, volée *f* d'escalier; escalier *m*. (*b*) *Rac:* *F. of hurdles*, série *f* de haies. **4.** (*a*) Bande *f*, vol, volée d'oiseaux, etc.). *F:* **To be in the first flight**, être parmi les premiers. (*b*) *Av:* Escadrille *f* (d'avions). **'flight-lieutenant**, *s. Av:* Capitaine aviateur.

flight[2], *s.* Fuite *f*. **To take to flight**, prendre la fuite. **To put the enemy to flight**, mettre l'ennemi en fuite, en déroute. **In full flight**, en pleine déroute.

flightiness ['flaitinəs], *s.* Inconstance *f*; instabilité *f* (de caractère); légèreté *f*, étourderie *f*.

flighty ['flaiti], *a.* (*a*) Frivole, écervelé, étourdi. (*b*) Volage. *F. imagination*, imagination vagabonde.

flimsiness ['flimzinəs], *s.* Manque *m* de solidité. (*a*) Légèreté *f* (d'une étoffe, du papier, etc.). (*b*) Futilité *f*, faiblesse *f* (d'une excuse).

flimsy ['flimzi]. **1.** *a.* Sans solidité. (*a*) (*Of material, etc.*) Léger; peu résistant; peu solide; sans consistance. (*b*) *F:* (*Of excuse, etc.*) Pauvre. **2.** *s.* (*a*) Papier *m* pelliculé; papier pelure. (*b*) *P:* Billet *m* de banque.

flinch [flinʃ], *v.i.* **1.** Reculer, fléchir, défaillir. **2.** Faire une grimace; tressaillir (de douleur). **Without flinching**, sans broncher, sans sourciller.

fling[1] [fliŋ], *s.* **1.** (*a*) Jet *m*; (*of horse*) ruade *f*. **To have a fling at s.o.**, (i) (*of horse*) lancer un coup de pied à qn; (ii) *F:* (*of pers.*) envoyer, lancer, un trait à qn. (*b*) *F:* Essai *m*, tentative *f*. *To have a f. at an appointment*, se mettre sur les rangs à tout hasard. **2.** *Danc:* Highland-fling, pas seul écossais. **3.** *F:* **To have one's fling**, jeter sa gourme. *Youth will have its f.*, il faut que jeunesse se passe.

fling[2], *v.* (flung [flʌŋ]; flung) **I.** *v.tr.* Jeter (qch.); lancer (une balle, etc.). *F:* **To fling one's money out of the window**, jeter son argent par la fenêtre.

To f. one's arms round s.o.'s neck, se jeter, sauter, au cou de qn. *To f. abuse at s.o.*, lancer des injures, des sottises, à qn. **2.** *v.i.* Se précipiter, s'élancer. **fling about**, *v.tr.* Jeter (des objets) de côté et d'autre. *To f. one's arms about*, gesticuler violemment. *To f. oneself about like a madman*, se démener comme un possédé. **fling aside**, *v.tr.* Rejeter (qch.); jeter (qch.) de côté. **fling away**, *v.tr.* Jeter de côté (qch.). *To f. away one's money*, prodiguer, gaspiller, son argent. **fling back**, *v.tr.* Repousser ou renvoyer violemment (qch.). *To f. back defiance*, riposter par un défi. **fling down**, *v.tr.* Jeter (qch.) à terre. **fling off**, *v.tr.* Se débarrasser de (ses vêtements, etc.); secouer (le joug). **fling open**, *v.tr.* Ouvrir toute grande (la fenêtre, etc.). **fling out.** **I.** *v.tr.* (*a*) Jeter dehors; *F:* flanquer (qn) à la porte. (*b*) **To fling out one's arm**, étendre le bras d'un grand geste. **2.** *v.i.* (*Of horse*) Lancer une ruade; ruer. *F:* **To fling out at s.o.**, faire une algarade à qn. **fling up**, *v.tr.* **1.** Jeter (qch.) en l'air; ouvrir, relever, brusquement (la fenêtre). *To f. up one's hands*, jeter les bras aux cieux. (*Of horse*) **To fling up its heels**, ruer. **2.** *F:* Abandonner, renoncer à (une tâche); lâcher (sa situation).

flint [flint], *s.* **1.** *Miner:* Silex *m*. *F:* **Heart of flint**, cœur de pierre. **2.** Pierre *f* à briquet; pierre à feu. **Flint and steel**, briquet *m* à silex. *F:* **To skin, flay, a flint**, tondre (sur) un œuf. **'flint-glass**, *s. Glassm: Opt:* Flint(-glass) *m*; verre *m* de plomb. **'flint-lock**, *s. A:* Fusil *m* à pierre. **'flint-ware**, *s. Cer: U.S:* Grès fin.

flinty ['flinti], *a.* **1.** (*a*) De silex. (*b*) Caillouteux, rocailleux. **2.** *F:* (*Cœur*) dur, insensible.

flip[1] [flip], *s.* **1.** Chiquenaude *f*, pichenette *f*. **2.** Petite secousse vive. *F. of the tail*, coup *m* de queue. **3.** *Av:* Petit tour de vol.

flip[2], *v.* (flipped) **I.** *v.tr.* = FLICK. **2.** *v.i. Av: P:* **To flip around**, faire un petit tour de vol.

flippancy ['flipənsi], *s.* Légèreté *f*, irrévérence *f*, désinvolture *f*.

flippant ['flipənt], *a.* Léger, désinvolte, irrévérencieux. **-ly**, *adv.* Légèrement, irrévérencieusement.

flipper ['flipər], *s.* **1.** Nageoire *f* (de cétacé); aileron *m* (de requin). **2.** *P:* Main *f*; *P:* patte *f*, pince *f*.

flirt[1] [flərt], *s.* Flirteur *m*; (*woman*) coquette *f*.

flirt[2]. **1.** *v.tr.* **To flirt a fan**, jouer de l'éventail. **2.** *v.i.* Flirter. *To f. with s.o.*, (*of woman*) coqueter; faire la coquette, avec qn; (*of man*) conter fleurette à (une jeune fille). **flirting**, *s.* Flirt *m*, flirtage *m*.

flirtation [flər'teiʃ(ə)n], *s.* Flirt *m*, flirtage *m*. *To carry on a (little) f. with a woman*, faire un doigt de cour à une femme.

flit[1] [flit], *s. Scot:* Déménagement *m*. **Moonlight flit**, déménagement à la cloche de bois.

flit[2], *v.i.* (flitted) **I.** *To flit (away)*, partir. **2.** *Scot:* Déménager. **3.** (*Of pers., bird, etc.*) **To flit by**, passer comme une ombre. **To flit about**, to flit to and fro**, aller et venir sans bruit. **To flit into the room**, se glisser (vivement) dans la salle. *A smile flitted across his face*, un sourire fugitif passa sur son visage. **flitting**, *s.* **1.** Départ *m*. **2.** *Scot:* Déménagement *m*. **3.** Volettement *m*, voltigement *m*.

flitch [flitʃ], *s.* **1.** Flèche *f* (de lard). **2.** Dalle *f* (de baleine, de flétan).

flitter ['flitər], *v.i.* Voleter, voltiger. **'flitter-mouse**, *s. Z:* Chauve-souris *f*, *pl.* chauves-souris.

flivver ['flivər], *s.* *P:* Bagnole *f*; auto *f* à bon marché.
float[1] [flout], *s.* **1.** (*a*) Flot *m*, train *m* (de bois). (*b*) Radeau *m*. **2.** Flotteur *m* (de chaudière, de carburateur, d'hydravion). *Fish:* Flotteur, flotte*f*, bouchon *m*. **3.** *Th:* (*Lighting*) **The float(s),** la rampe. **4. Float(-board),** aube*f*, palette *f* (de roue hydraulique). **5.** Charrette basse à essieu brisé. **'float-chamber,** *s.* *I.C.E:* Chambre *f* du flotteur (du carburateur). **'float-needle,** *s.* *I.C.E:* Pointeau *m* (du carburateur).
float[2]. I. *v.i.* **1.** (*a*) Flotter, nager (sur un liquide) ; surnager. (*b*) *Swim:* Faire la planche. **2.** *The animalcules that f. about in the water,* les animalcules qui nagent dans l'eau. *Corpse that floats to the surface,* cadavre qui revient sur l'eau. *To f. about in the air,* planer dans l'air. *F: A rumour is floating about, around, that . . .,* le bruit court que. . . . II. **float,** *v.tr.* (*a*) Flotter (des bois, etc.). (*b*) *F:* To float a rumour, faire circuler un bruit. (*c*) *Com:* Lancer, créer, fonder (une compagnie). *Fin:* To float a loan, émettre un emprunt. **float off,** *v.tr.* Renflouer, déséchouer (une épave). **floating off,** *s.* *Nau:* Renflouage *m*, renflouement *m*. **floating**[1], *a.* **1.** Flottant, à flot. **2.** (*a*) Libre, mobile. **Floating ribs,** fausses côtes, côtes flottantes. *F:* population, population flottante, instable. (*b*) *Com:* Floating capital, capital circulant, fonds *mpl* de roulement, capitaux roulants. **floating**[2], *s.* **1.** (*a*) Flottement *m*. (*b*) *Swim:* La planche. **2.** (*a*) Mise *f* à flot (d'un vaisseau). (*b*) Flottage *m* (à bûches perdues). (*c*) *Com:* Lancement *m* (d'une société commerciale, etc.). *Fin:* Émission *f* (d'un emprunt).
flo(a)tation [flo'teiʃ(ə)n], *s.* **1.** *Nau:* Flottaison*f*. **2.** *Com:* Lancement *m* (d'une compagnie) ; émission *f* (d'un emprunt).
flocculent ['flɔkjulənt], *a.* Floconneux.
flock[1] [flɔk], *s.* Bourre *f* de laine.
flock[2], *s.* Bande *f*, troupe *f* (d'animaux) ; troupeau *m* (de moutons, d'oies). **Flocks and herds,** le menu et le gros bétail. *F: A pastor and his f.,* un pasteur et ses ouailles *f*. **Those who have strayed from the flock,** ceux qui se sont écartés du bercail. **They arrived in flocks,** ils arrivaient en bandes, en foule.
flock[3], *v.i.* **To flock (together),** s'attrouper, s'assembler. **To flock about s.o.,** s'attrouper, faire foule, autour de qn. **To flock in,** entrer en masse.
floe [flou], *s.* Glaçon flottant ; banc *m* de glace ; banquise *f*.
flog [flɔg], *v.tr.* (**flogged**) Fustiger, flageller (qn). *To f. a horse,* (i) fouetter, (ii) cravacher, un cheval. *F:* **To flog a dead horse,** se dépenser en pure perte. **To flog oneself,** s'éreinter. **To flog a competitor,** battre un concurrent à plates coutures. **flogging,** *s.* Fustigation *f*, flagellation *f*. *Sch:* La punition du fouet ou des verges.
flong [flɔŋ], *s.* *Typ:* Flan *m*.
flood[1] [flʌd], *s.* **1.** *Nau:* Flot *m*, flux *m* (de la marée) ; marée montante. **Ebb and flood,** flux et reflux. **2.** (*a*) Déluge *m*, inondation *f*. **The Flood,** le Déluge. (*b*) **A flood of light,** des flots de lumière. *F:* **Floods of tears,** un torrent de larmes. (*c*) Crue *f* (d'une rivière). **'flood-gate,** *s.* Vanne *f* (de décharge) ; porte *f* d'écluse. **To open, close, the flood-gates,** lever, mettre, les vannes. **'flood-light,**[1] *s.* **1.** Lumière *f* à grands flots. **2. Flood-light (projector),** projecteur *m* à flots de lumière ; phare *m* d'éclairage. **'flood-light,**[2] *v.tr.* Illuminer (un bâtiment, etc.) par projecteurs. **flood-lighting,** *s.* Éclairage diffusé ; illumination *f* par projecteurs (à flots de

lumière). **'flood-tide,** *s.* Marée montante flux *m*.
flood[2]. **1.** *v.tr.* (*a*) Inonder, submerger. *Agr:* Irriguer, noyer (une prairie). (*Of house, etc.*) *T be flooded,* être envahi par l'eau. *I.C.E:* To floo **the carburettor,** noyer le carburateur. *F:* To b **flooded with letters,** être inondé, submergé, d lettres. (*b*) (*Of rain, etc.*) Faire déborder (un rivière). **2.** *v.i.* (*a*) (*Of river, etc.*) Déborder *I.C.E:* (*Of carburettor*) Se noyer. (*b*) (*Of river* Être en crue. **flooding,** *s.* **1.** Inondation *f* irrigation *f* (d'une prairie). **2.** Débordement *r* (d'une rivière, etc.).
floor[1] ['flɔ:ər], *s.* **1.** (*a*) Plancher *m*, parquet *m* Tile(*d*) *f.*, carrelage *m* ; dallage *m* en tuiles. *T throw sth. on the f.,* jeter qch. à terre, par terre *P:* To mop, wipe, the floor with s.o., battre q à plate couture. (*b*) *N.Arch:* Plafond *m* (d cale). Floor-frame,-timber, varangue*f*. (*c*) Fond *n* (de l'océan) ; tablier *m*, aire *f* (d'un pont) sole *f* (d'une galerie de mine). (*d*) Parquet (à l Bourse) ; parquet, prétoire *m* (d'un tribunal) *U.S:* **To have, take, the floor,** avoir, prendre la parole. **2.** Étage *m* (de maison). **Ground-floor** rez-de-chaussée *m*. *House on two floors,* maiso avec étage. *To live on the second f.,* (i) demeure au second ; (ii) *U.S:* demeurer au premier *We live on the same f.,* nous habitons sur 1 même palier. **3.** Aire (d'une grange, etc.) **'floor-board,** *s.* **1.** Planche *f* (du plancher) **2.** *N.Arch:* Varangue *f*. **'floor-cloth,** **1.** Linoléum *m*. **2.** Torchon *m* à laver. **'floor polish,** *s.* Encaustique *f* ; cire *f* à parquet.
floor[2], *v.tr.* **1.** *Const:* (i) Planchéier, (ii) par queter (iii) carreler (une pièce). **2.** (*a*) Terrasse (un adversaire). (*b*) *F:* Mettre, réduire, (qn) quia ; clouer le bec à (qn) ; aplatir (qn) *Sch:* Coller (un candidat, etc.). **flooring,** *r* **1.** (*a*) (i) Planchéiage *m*, (ii) parquetage *n* (iii) carrelage *m*, dallage *m*. (*b*) Renversement *n* (d'un adversaire). **2.** (*a*) Plancher *m*. (*b*) Car reau *m*, dallage.
flop[1] [flɔp], *s.* *F:* **1.** Coup mat ; bruit sourc (d'un rat qui plonge, etc.). **2.** Four *m*, fiasco *m*
flop[2], *int. & adv.* *F:* **1.** Plouf ! patapouf ! floc **To fall flop,** faire patapouf. **2. To go flop,** (o *play*) faire four ; (*of business, etc.*) aller à vau l'eau ; (*of pers.*) s'effondrer.
flop[3], *v.i.* (**flopped**) *F:* **1. To flop (down),** s laisser tomber ; s'affaler. **To flop about,** faire de sauts de carpe. **2.** = *to go flop, q.v. under* FLOP[2]
floppy ['flɔpi], *a.* (*Of hat, etc.*) Pendant, flasque souple ; (*of garment*) lâche, trop large.
flora ['flɔ:ra], *s.* Flore *f* (d'une région).
floral ['flɔ:rəl], *a.* Floral, -aux. *Dress with a bol f. design,* robe à grands ramages.
florescence [flɔ:'res(ə)ns], *s.* Fleuraison *f* floraison *f*.
floret ['flɔ:ret], *s.* *Bot:* Fleuron *m*.
florid ['flɔrid], *a.* (*Of style, etc.*) Fleuri ; orné l'excès ; (*of architecture, etc.*) flamboyant ; (*o countenance*) rubicond, fleuri. **To have a flori complexion,** être haut en couleur.
florin ['flɔrin], *s.* *Num:* Florin *m* ; pièce *f* d deux shillings.
florist ['flɔrist], *s.* Fleuriste *mf*.
floss [flɔs], *s.* Floss(-silk), bourre *f* de soie filoselle *f* ; soie *f* floche.
flotation [flo'teiʃ(ə)n], *s.* = FLOATATION.
flotilla [flo'tila], *s.* Flottille *f*.
flotsam ['flɔtsəm], *s.* *Jur:* Épave(s) flottante(s) **Flotsam and jetsam,** choses *f* de flot et de mer.
flounce[1] [flauns], *s.* Mouvement vif (d'indigna tion, d'impatience).

flounce[2], *v.i.* To flounce in, out, entrer, sortir, dans un mouvement d'indignation.

flounce[3], *s. Dressm:* Volant *m.*

flounder[1] ['flaundər], *s. Ich:* Flet *m*, carrelet *m.*

flounder[2], *v.i.* **1.** Patauger, barboter, patouiller (dans la boue, etc.). **To flounder about in the water**, se débattre dans l'eau. **To flounder along**, avancer en trébuchant. *F:* **To flounder in a speech**, patauger dans un discours. **2.** (*Of horse*) (*a*) Se débattre (par terre). (*b*) Faire feu des quatre fers (pour ne pas tomber). **floundering**, *s.* Barbotage *m*, débattement *m*, pataugeage *m.*

flour[1] ['flauər], *s.* Farine *f. Pure wheaten f.*, fleur *f* de farine. *To cover, dust, sth. with f.*, (en)fariner qch. **'flour-box, -dredger**, *s.* Saupoudroir *m* à farine. **'flour-factor**, *s.* Minotier *m.* **'flour-mill**, *s.* Moulin *m* à farine; (*large*) minoterie *f.* **'flour-milling**, *s.* Minoterie *f*, meunerie *f.*

flour[2], *v.tr.* (En)fariner (qn, qch.); saupoudrer de farine.

flourish[1] ['flʌriʃ], *s.* **1.** (*a*) Trait *m* de plume, enjolivure *f*; (*after signature*) parafe *m.* (*b*) Fleur *f* (de rhétorique); fioriture *f* (de style). **2.** Geste prétentieux; brandissement *m* (d'épée). **3.** *Mus:* (*a*) Fanfare *f* (de trompettes). (*b*) Fioriture, ornement *m.*

flourish[2]. **1.** *v.i.* (*a*) (*Of plant*) Bien venir. *To f. in a sandy soil*, se plaire dans un terrain sablonneux. (*b*) (*Of pers., commerce, etc.*) Être florissant; prospérer. (*c*) Être dans sa fleur, dans tout son éclat; battre son plein; (*of arts*) fleurir. **2.** *v.tr.* Brandir (une épée, un bâton). *To f. one's stick*, (i) agiter sa canne; (ii) faire des moulinets avec sa canne. **flourishing**, *a.* Florissant; (commerce) prospère.

floury ['flauəri], *a.* **1.** Enfariné. **2.** (*Of potatoes*) Farineux.

flout (flaut], *v.tr.* Faire fi de (l'autorité de qn); se moquer (d'un ordre). **flouting**, *s.* Moquerie *f*, raillerie *f.*

flow[1] [flou], *s.* **1.** (*a*) Coulement *m*; écoulement *m.* (*b*) *Mch:* Courant *m*, flux *m* (de vapeur). (*c*) *El:* Passage *m* (du courant). *El.E:* **Parallel-flow condenser**, condensateur à courants dans le même sens. (*d*) Courant, cours *m*, affluence *f* (d'eau). (*e*) Passage, arrivée *f* (d'air, *I.C.E:* d'essence, etc.). (*f*) **Flow of the tide**, flot *m*, flux *m*, de la marée. *S.a.* EBB[1] 1. **2.** Volume *m* (de liquide débité). *Hyd.E:* Débit *m* (d'un lac, d'une pompe). **3.** Flot, flux (de sang, de paroles, etc.). **To have a ready flow of language**, avoir de la faconde; être disert. **4.** Lignes tombantes (d'une robe); drapé *m* (d'un vêtement).

flow[2], *v.i.* **1.** (*a*) Couler, s'écouler. (*Of river*) **To flow into the sea**, déboucher, se verser, dans la mer. (*b*) (*Of tide*) Monter, remonter. (*c*) (*Of blood, electric current, etc.*) Circuler. (*d*) (*Of drapery, etc.*) Flotter. **2.** (*Of stream, blood, tears, etc.*) Se répandre; jaillir. **3.** Dériver, découler, provenir (*from*, de). **4.** *Lit:* Abonder. **Land flowing with milk and honey**, pays découlant de lait et de miel. **flow away**, *v.i.* (*Of liquid*) S'écouler. **flow back**, *v.i.* Refluer. **flow in**, *v.i.* (*a*) (*Of liquid*) Entrer. (*b*) (*Of people, money*) Affluer. **flow out**, *v.i.* Sortir, s'écouler. **flowing**, *a.* **1.** Coulant; (*of tide*) montant. **2.** (*Of style, etc.*) Coulant, fluide, facile; (*of movement*) gracieux, aisé. **3.** (*Of draperies*) Flottant. **Flowing beard**, barbe longue, fleurie. **-ly**, *adv.* D'une manière coulante; avec facilité.

flower[1] ['flauər], *s.* **1.** Fleur *f.* **Bunch of flowers**, bouquet *m. He had a f. in his buttonhole*, il avait la boutonnière fleurie. **Flower show**, exposition *f* horticole. **2.** *pl. A:* Fleur(s) (de soufre, etc.). **3.** (*a*) *Typ:* Fleuron *m.* (*b*) **Flowers of speech**, fleurs de rhétorique. **4.** *F:* Fine fleur, élite *f* (de l'armée, etc.). **5.** Fleuraison *f.* **In flower, en fleur.** *In full f.*, en plein épanouissement. **To burst into flower**, fleurir. *F:* **To be in the flower of one's age**, être dans la fleur de l'âge. **'flower-bed**, *s.* Parterre *m*; plate-bande *f*, *pl.* plates-bandes. **'flower-garden**, *s.* Jardin *m* d'agrément. **'flower-girl**, *s.f.* Bouquetière. **'flower-pot**, *s.* Pot *m* à fleurs; (*ornamental*) cache-pot *m inv.* **'flower-shop**, *s.* Boutique *f* de fleuriste. **'flower-stand**, *s.* Jardinière *f.*

flower[2], *v.i.* Fleurir. **flowered**, *a. Tex:* Flowered material, étoffe à fleurs, à ramages. **flowering**[1], *a.* **1.** Fleuri; en fleur. **2.** **Flowering plant**, plante à fleurs. **flowering**[2], *s.* Fleuraison *f.*

floweret ['flauərət], *s.* Fleurette *f.*

flowery ['flauəri], *a.* **1.** (Pré, etc.) fleuri; (tapis, etc.) orné de fleurs, de ramages. **2.** (*Of speech, style*) Fleuri.

flown [floun]. *See* FLY[3], HIGH-FLOWN.

flu [flu:], *s. Med: P:* = INFLUENZA.

fluctuate ['flʌktjueit], *v.i.* Fluctuer. **1.** (*Of conditions*) Varier; (*of markets, values*) osciller. **2.** (*Of pers.*) Flotter, vaciller, hésiter. **fluctuating**, *a.* (*Of temperature, etc.*) Variable; (*of prices, etc.*) oscillant.

fluctuation [flʌktju'eiʃ(ə)n], *s.* Oscillation *f*; variations *fpl* (de température); fluctuation *f* (du marché).

flue [flu:], *s.* **1.** Conduite *f*, tuyau *m*, de cheminée. **2.** *Mus:* Bouche *f* (de tuyau d'orgue). **'flue-brush**, *s.* Hérisson *m.* **'flue-pipe**, *s.* **1.** *Mus:* Tuyau *m* à bouche (d'un orgue). **2.** *Const:* Tuyau de poêle.

fluency ['flu:ənsi], *s.* Facilité *f* (de parole).

fluent ['flu:ənt], *a.* (*Of speech, etc.*) Coulant, facile, fluide. *To be a f. speaker*, avoir la parole facile; être disert. *He is a f. speaker of French*, il parle le français couramment. **-ly**, *adv.* Couramment; (s'exprimer) avec facilité.

fluff[1] [flʌf], *s.* **1.** Duvet *m* (d'étoffe); peluches *fpl.* (*Of cloth*) **To lose, shed, its f.**, pelucher; jeter son coton. *F:* **A little bit of fluff**, une petite femme, une jeunesse. **2.** Fourrure douce (d'un jeune animal). **3.** *Th: F:* Loup *m.*

fluff[2], *v.tr.* **1.** Lainer (un drap, etc.). **To fluff (out) one's hair**, faire bouffer ses cheveux. *Bird that fluffs (up) its feathers*, oiseau qui hérisse ses plumes. **2.** *Th: F:* **To fluff one's entrance**, louper, manquer, son entrée.

fluffy ['flʌfi], *a.* (Drap) pelucheux; (poussin, etc.) duveteux. *F. hair*, cheveux flous.

fluid ['flu:id]. **1.** *a. & s.* (*a*) Fluide (*m*). (*b*) Liquide (*m*). **Fluid measures**, mesures *f* pour les liquides. **2.** *a. F:* (*a*) (*Of style, etc.*) Fluide, coulant, facile. (*b*) (*Of opinions, etc.*) Inconstant, changeant.

fluidity [flu'iditi], *s.* **1.** Fluidité *f.* **2.** (*a*) Fluidité, facilité *f* (de style, etc.). (*b*) Caractère changeant; inconstance *f.*

fluke[1] [flu:k], *s. Vet:* Fluke(-worm), douve *f* (du foie).

fluke[2], *s.* **1.** *Nau:* Patte *f* (d'ancre). **2.** *pl.* Queue *f* (de baleine).

fluke[3], *s.* (*a*) *Bill:* (Coup *m* de) raccroc *m. By a f.*, par raccroc. (*b*) *F:* Coup de veine, de hasard; chance *f.*

fluky ['flu:ki], *a.* (Coup, etc.) de raccroc; (jeu) hasardeux, incertain. *F. wind*, vent incertain.

flummery ['flʌməri], *s.* **1.** *Cu:* Crème *f* aux œufs. **2.** *F:* (*a*) Flagornerie *f.* (*b*) **That's all**

flummery, tout ça, c'est du boniment, de la blague.

flummox ['flʌməks], *v.tr.* F: Réduire (qn) à quia; démonter (qn). *Sch:* Coller (un élève).

flung [flʌŋ]. *See* FLING².

flunkey ['flʌŋki], *s.* Laquais *m*, F: larbin *m*.

fluoresce [fluɔ'res], *v.i.* Entrer en fluorescence.

fluorescence [fluɔ'res(ə)ns], *s.* Fluorescence *f*.

fluorescent [fluɔ'res(ə)nt], *a.* Fluorescent.

fluorine ['fluɔri:n, -in], *s.* *Ch:* Fluor *m*.

fluor-spar [fluɔ:r'spɑ:r], *s.* *Miner:* Spath *m* fluor.

flurry¹ ['flʌri], *s.* **1.** (*a*) *Nau:* Risée *f*, grain *m* (de vent); brise folle. (*b*) *U.S:* (i) Averse *f*; (ii) rafale *f* de neige. **2.** Agitation *f*, bouleversement *m*, émoi *m*. All in a flurry, tout effaré, tout en émoi. **3.** The death flurry, les dernières convulsions (de la baleine expirante, etc.).

flurry², *v.tr.* Agiter, étourdir, effarer (qn). To get flurried, perdre la tête.

flush¹ [flʌʃ], *s.* *Ven:* Envolée *f* (d'oiseaux).

flush², *v.tr.* *Ven:* (Faire) lever, faire partir (des perdrix).

flush³, *s.* **1.** *Hyd.E:* Chasse *f* (d'eau). **2.** F: Accès *m*, élan *m* (d'émotion, de passion, etc.). In the first flush of victory, dans l'ivresse de la victoire. **3.** (*a*) Éclat *m* (de lumière, F: de la beauté). To be in the full flush of health, jouir d'une santé florissante. (*b*) Rougeur *f*, flux *m* de sang (au visage); (*in fever*) bouffée *f* de chaleur.

flush⁴, *v.* **1.** (*a*) *v.i.* (*Of stream*) To flush (forth, out, up), jaillir. To flush over, déborder. (*b*) *v.tr.* To flush (out) a drain, donner une chasse à un égout; balayer un égout à grande eau. **2.** *v.i.* (*Of pers.*) Rougir; (*of blood*) monter (au visage). His face flushed, he flushed up, le sang, le pourpre, lui monta au visage. **flushed**, *a.* (Visage) enfiévré, empourpré. Face f. with drink, visage allumé par la boisson. F. with success, ivre de succès.

flush⁵, *s.* *Cards:* (*At poker*) Floch(e) *m*, flush *m*.

flush⁶, *a.* **1.** (*a*) (*Of stream*, etc.) Très plein; débordant. (*b*) (*Of pers.*) To be flush (of money), être en fonds. (*c*) *Cards:* To be flush, être à flux. **2.** (*Of surfaces*, etc.) Ras; de niveau; affleurant. Flush joint, assemblage affleuré. To be flush with sth., être à fleur, au ras, de qch. Houses built f. with the pavement, maisons bâties à même le trottoir.

Flushing ['flʌʃiŋ], *Pr.n. Geog:* Flessingue *f*.

fluster¹ ['flʌstər], *s.* Agitation *f*, trouble *m*. In a fluster, tout en émoi.

fluster², **1.** *v.tr.* Agiter, bouleverser (qn); faire perdre la tête à (qn). To be, get, flustered, se troubler; être démonté, effaré. **2.** *v.i.* S'agiter, s'énerver.

flute¹ [flu:t], *s.* **1.** Flûte *f*. Concert flute, grande flûte. **2.** Flute(-player), (joueur *m* de) flûte. **3.** (*a*) Rainure *f*; cannelure *f* (de colonne). (*b*) *Laund:* Tuyau *m*.

flute², *v.tr.* (*a*) Rainer, rainurer (une planche); canneler (une colonne). (*b*) *Laund:* Tuyauter, rucher, gaufrer. **fluted**, *a.* **1.** (*Of notes, voice*) Flûté. **2.** (*a*) A rainure(s); à cannelures; (*of column*) cannelé, strié. (*b*) (*Linge*) tuyauté, à godets. **fluting**, *s.* **1.** Fluting machine, machine *f* à canneler. *Laund:* Fluting iron, fer *m* à tuyauter. **2.** *Coll.* Rainures *fpl*, cannelures *fpl*. *Laund:* Tuyaux *mpl*, godrons *mpl*.

flutter¹ ['flʌtər], *s.* **1.** Volètement *m*, voltigement *m*, trémoussement *m* (d'un oiseau); battement *m* (des ailes); palpitation *f* (du cœur); flottement *m*, voltigement *m* (d'un drapeau). *Av:* Vibration *f* (de l'hélice). **2.** Agitation *f*, trouble *m*, émoi *m*.

To be (all) in a flutter, être tout troublé, tout en émoi. **3.** *Fin:* F: Petite spéculation. *Cards: Turf:* To have a little flutter, risquer de petites sommes.

flutter², **1.** *v.i.* (*a*) (*Of birds*) Trémousser des ailes, battre des ailes; (*of flag, ribbon, etc.*) flotter, s'agiter (au vent); (*of heart*) palpiter, battre; (*of pulse*) battre irrégulièrement. (*b*) (*Of pers.*) Trembler, frémir. **2.** *v.tr.* (*a*) Agiter, secouer (un drapeau, etc.); jouer de (l'éventail). (*Of bird*) To f. its wings, battre des ailes; trémousser des ailes. (*b*) F: Agiter, troubler (qn). To flutter the dovecotes, porter l'alarme dans le camp.

fluty ['flu:ti], *a.* (*Of voice, etc.*) Flûté.

fluvial ['flu:viəl], *a.* Fluvial, -aux.

flux [flʌks], *s.* **1.** *Med:* Flux *m* (de sang, etc.); flux de ventre. **2.** (*a*) Flux; changement continuel. To be in a state of flux, être sujet à des changements fréquents. (*b*) *Ph:* Flux (magnétique, etc.). **3.** (*a*) *Metall:* Fondant *m*, flux. (*b*) *Metalw:* Décapant *m*; fondant de brasage.

fly¹, *pl.* **flies** [flai(z)], *s.* (*a*) *Ent:* Mouche *f*. House fly, mouche commune. Spanish fly, blister(ing) fly, mouche d'Espagne; cantharide *f*. Horse fly, taon *m*. Blow fly, mouche à viande. Black fly (*sg. & pl.*), thrips *m*. (*In S. Africa*) Tsetse fly, la tsétsé. *S.a.* GREEN-FLY. F: In the hold they died like flies, dans la cale on mourait dru, comme des mouches. F: To play the fly on the wheel, faire la mouche du coche. There's a fly in the ointment, P: il y a un cheveu. That's the fly in the ointment, voilà le chiendent. To catch flies, bayer aux corneilles. There are no flies on him, il n'est pas bête. *Box:* Fly-weight, poids *m* mouche. (*b*) *Fish:* Mouche. To rise to the fly, (i) (*of fish*) mordre à l'appât; (ii) F: (*of pers.*) gober la mouche. **'fly-blow**, *s.* **1.** Œufs *mpl* de mouche (dans la viande). **2.** F: Chiures *fpl* de mouche. **'fly-blown**, *a.* **1.** Couvert d'œufs de mouches; (viande) gâtée. F: (*Of reputation, etc.*) Souillé, entaché. **2.** F: Couvert de chiures de mouche. **'fly-catcher**, *s.* **1.** Piège *m* à mouches; attrape-mouche(s) *m*. **2.** *Orn:* Gobe-mouches *m inv.* **'fly-fishing**, *s.* *Fish:* Pêche *f* à la mouche. **'fly-paper**, *s.* Papier *m* attrape-mouche(s) *m*. **'fly-speck, -spot**, *s.* Chiure *f* de mouche.

fly², *s.* **1.** Vol *m*. On the fly, en vol. **2.** *A:* (*pl. usu.* flys) Fiacre *m*; voiture *f* de place. **3.** (*a*) Patte *f* (d'habit); braguette *f*, brayette *f* (de pantalon). (*b*) Battant *m* (d'un drapeau). **4.** *pl. Th:* The flies, les cintres *m*, les dessus *m*. **5.** *Tchn:* Moulinet *m* (d'anémomètre, etc.); régulateur *m*, volant *m* (de sonnerie d'horloge). **'fly-bill**, *s.* Feuille volante; prospectus *m*. **2.** (*Poster*) Papillon *m*. **'fly-half**, *s.* *Rugby Fb:* Demi *m* d'ouverture. **'fly-leaf**, *s.* (Feuille *f* de) garde *f* (d'un livre broché). **'fly-nut**, *s.* Écrou ailé, à oreilles; papillon *m*. **'fly-press**, *s.* Presse *f* à vis à balancier. **'fly-wheel**, *s.* *Mec.E:* Volant *m*. To act as a fly-wheel, faire volant.

fly³, *v.* (flew [flu:]; flown [floun]) I. *v.i.* **1.** (*a*) (*Of bird*) Voler. To catch sth. flying, saisir qch. au vol. F: To find the birds flown, trouver buisson creux. To fly high, (i) voler haut; (ii) F: avoir de hautes visées. F: My watch has flown, on m'a escamoté ma montre. **2.** *Av:* Voler. To fly to Paris, se rendre à Paris en avion. To fly over London, survoler Londres. **2.** (*Of flag, etc.*) Flotter. **3.** (*a*) (*Of pers.*) Courir, aller à toute vitesse; (*of time*) fuir. To fly to s.o.'s assistance, voler à l'aide de qn. To fly at s.o., (i) s'élancer

sur qn; (ii) faire une algarade à qn. *To fly at
s.o.'s throat*, sauter à la gorge de qn. **To fly into
a rage,** s'emporter; **prendre la mouche. The
door flew open,** la porte s'ouvrit brusquement,
en coup de vent. **The branch flew back,** la
branche fit ressort. (*b*) (*Of cork, etc.*) Voler;
sauter en l'air; (*of sparks*) jaillir. *F:* **To make
the money fly,** prodiguer son argent. **To fly off
the handle,** (i) (*of axe-head, etc.*) se démancher,
s'envoler; (ii) *P:* s'emporter; sortir des gonds.
F: **To send s.o. flying,** envoyer rouler qn (sur le
carreau). *To send a plate flying,* envoyer, lancer,
une assiette à la volée. (*c*) **To fly in pieces,** voler
en éclats. **4. To let fly,** lancer (un projectile,
une flèche). **To let fly at s.o.,** (i) tirer sur qn;
(ii) *F:* flanquer un coup à qn; (*of horse*)
détacher une ruade à qn; (iii) s'en prendre à qn.
5. (= FLEE, *in pres. tenses only*) (*a*) Fuir, s'enfuir.
To send the enemy flying, mettre l'ennemi en
fuite. **To fly from a place,** s'enfuir d'un endroit.
To fly from danger, fuir le danger, se dérober au
danger. **To fly for one's life,** chercher son salut
dans la fuite. (*b*) *v.tr.* **To fly the country,** s'exiler
du pays; émigrer. II. **fly,** *v.tr.* **1.** *Nau:* To fly
a flag, battre un pavillon. **2.** *Ven:* Lancer, faire
voler (un faucon, etc.). **3.** *Av:* **To fly a kite,** faire
voler un cerf-volant. **3.** *Av:* (*a*) Piloter (un
appareil). **To fly s.o. to Paris,** conduire qn en
avion à Paris. (*b*) **To fly the Channel,** passer la
Manche en avion; survoler la Manche. **fly
away,** *v.i.* **1.** (*Of bird, etc.*) S'envoler; prendre
son vol. **2.** (*Of pers.*) S'enfuir. **fly back,** *v.i.*
1. Revenir (i) en volant, (ii) au plus vite. **2.** (*Of
steel rod, etc.*) Faire ressort. **fly by,** *v.i.* Passer
très rapidement, comme un éclair. **fly off,** *v.i.*
1. (*Of bird, etc.*) = FLY AWAY 1. **2.** (*Of pers.*)
S'en aller en coup de vent. **3.** (*Of button, etc.*)
Sauter. **fly up,** *v.i.* Se projeter en l'air. **flying**[1],
a. **1.** (Oiseau) volant. *Av:* **Flying man,** aviateur *m*.
Flying corps, corps *m* d'aviation (militaire).
2. (Voile, ruban) volant, flottant, léger. *S.a.*
COLOUR[1] 4. **3.** (*a*) (Course, etc.) rapide. *Mil:*
Flying column, colonne *f* mobile; camp volant.
F: **To take a flying shot at sth.,** tirer (un oiseau,
etc.) au vol. (*b*) Court, passager. **To pay a flying
visit to London,** passer quelques heures, quelques
jours, à Londres (pour affaires, etc.). (*c*) *Sp:* Fly-
ing start, départ lancé. *Fb:* **Flying kick,** coup de
pied donné en pleine course. **4. Flying scaffold-
(ing),** échafaudage volant. **5.** En fuite. **The
Flying Dutchman,** le Vaisseau fantôme. **'flying-
'buttress,** *s. Arch:* Arc-boutant *m*, *pl.* arcs-
boutants. **'flying-'fish,** *s. Ich:* Poisson volant.
flying[2], *s.* **1.** (*a*) Vol *m* (d'un oiseau, etc.).
(*b*) Aviation *f*, vol. **Trick flying,** vol d'acrobatie.
Flying machine, avion *m*. **Flying ground,** terrain *m*
d'aviation. **Flying suit,** combinaison *f* (d'aviateur). **Flying school,** école *f* de pilotage. **Flying
sickness,** mal *m* des aviateurs. **2.** Sautage *m* (d'un
rivet, etc.); jaillissement *m* (d'étincelles). **Flying
asunder,** éclatement *m* (d'un verre). **3.** Fuite *f*.
4. (*a*) Lancement *m* (de pigeons, d'un cerf-volant).
(*b*) Déploiement *m* (d'un drapeau). **'flying-
boat,** *s.* Hydravion *m* à coque. **'flying-club,**
s. Aéro-club *m*. **'flying-height,** *s. Av:* Altitude *f*. **Maximum flying-height,** (valeur *f* de)
plafond *m*. **'fly-by-night,** *s. F:* **1.** Oiseau *m*
de nuit; noctambule *mf*. **2.** Déménageur *m* à
la cloche de bois.

fly[4], *a. F:* Astucieux; *F:* ficelle.

flyer ['flaiər], *s.* **1.** (*a*) Oiseau *m*, insecte *m*, qui
vole. (*b*) Aviateur, -trice. **2.** (*a*) Aile *f*, volant *m*
(de moulin à vent). (*b*) Balancier *m* (de tournebroche, etc.). **3.** *Cy: F:* **To take a flyer over the**

handle-bars, se trouver lancé, projeté, par-dessus
le guidon.
foal[1] [foul], *s.* Poulain *m* (de cheval); ânon *m*,
bourriquet *m* (d'âne). **Mare in, with, foal,**
jument pleine.
foal[2], *v.tr.* (*Of mare, etc.*) Mettre bas (un
poulain, etc.); *abs.* pouliner.
foam[1] [foum], *s.* **1.** Écume *f*; (*on beer*) mousse *f*.
His horse was in a foam, son cheval écumait.
2. (*a*) (*Slaver*) Bave *f*. (*b*) Écume (à la bouche).
foam[2], *v.i.* (*Of sea, etc.*) Écumer, moutonner;
(*of beer, etc.*) mousser. **To foam at the mouth,**
avoir l'écume aux lèvres; (*of dog, etc.*) baver.
F: **To foam with rage,** écumer; être furieux.
fob[1] [fob], *s.* Gousset *m* (de pantalon). **Fob-chain,**
régence *f*.
fob[2], *v.tr.* (fobbed) **To fob s.o.** (off), tromper,
duper, qn. **To fob s.o. off with sth., to fob sth.
off on s.o.,** *F:* refiler qch. à qn.
focal ['fouk(ə)l], *a.* Focal, -aux.
foc's'le [fouksl], *s. F:* = FORECASTLE.
focus[1], *pl.* **foci, focuses** ['foukəs, 'fousai,
'fouksaiz], *s.* **1.** Foyer *m* (de lentille, de miroir,
de courbe). **Opt: In focus, au point. Out of
focus,** (i) (*of image*) pas au point; brouillé;
(ii) (*of head-lamp bulb, etc.*) mal centré ou mal
réglé. **To bring sth. into focus,** mettre qch. au
point. **2.** Siège *m*, foyer (d'une maladie, etc.).
focus[2], *v.tr.* (focused ['foukəst]) **1.** Concentrer
(les rayons de lumière, l'observation, etc.) (*in, on,
dans, sur*); faire converger (des rayons). *v.i.* (*Of
light, sound, etc.*) Converger (*on, sur*). *F:* **All
eyes were focused on him,** il était le point de
mire de tous les yeux. **2.** Mettre au point (un
microscope, une lunette, etc.). **focusing,** *s.* **1.** Concentration *f*, convergence *f* (de rayons, etc.).
2. Mise *f* au point (d'une jumelle, etc.). *Phot:*
Focusing cloth, voile noir de mise au point.
Focusing screen, verre dépoli.
fodder[1] ['fodər], *s.* Fourrage *m*. *S.a.* CANNON-
FODDER.
fodder[2], *v.tr.* Affour(r)ager.
foe [fou], *s. Lit:* Ennemi *m*, adversaire *m*.
foeman, *pl.* **-men** ['foumən, -men], *s.m. A. &
Lit:* Ennemi, adversaire.
foetus, *pl.* **-uses** ['fi:təs, -əsiz], *s.* Fœtus *m*.
fog[1] [fog], *s.* (*a*) Brouillard *m*; *Nau:* brume *f*. *F:*
I'm in a fog, je ne sais plus où j'en suis. (*b*) *Phot:*
(*On negative*) Voile *m*. **'fog-bound,** *a. Nau:*
Arrêté par le brouillard; pris dans la brume.
'fog-horn, *s. Nau:* Corne *f*, trompe *f*, de
brume; sirène *f*. **fog-signal.** (*a*) *Nau:*
Signal *m*, -aux, de brume, de brouillard. (*b*) *Rail:*
Pétard *m*, détonateur *m*.
fog[2], *v.* (fogged [fogd]) **1.** *v.tr.* (*a*) Embrumer (un
endroit). *F:* Brouiller (les idées); embrouiller
(qn). (*b*) *Phot:* Voiler (un cliché). **2.** *v.i.* (*Of
negative*) Se voiler. **fogging,** *s. Phot:* Voile *m*.
fogey ['fougi], *s.* = FOGY.
foggy ['fogi], *a.* **1.** Brumeux. **On a f. day,** par
un jour de brouillard. **It is foggy,** il y a, il fait,
du brouillard. **2.** *F:* (*Of photograph, etc.*) Voilé,
brouillé; (esprit, etc.) confus. **I haven't the
foggiest (idea)** je n'en ai pas la moindre idée!
fogy ['fougi], *s. F:* **Old fogy,** vieille baderne,
vieille barbe.
foible ['foibl], *a.* Côté *m* faible, point *m* faible;
faible *m* (de qn).
foil[1] [foil], *s.* **1.** *Arch:* Lobe *m* (d'un arc, etc.).
2. *Metalw:* (*a*) Feuille *f*, lame *f* (d'or, etc.);
clinquant *m*. **Brass foil,** oripeau *m*. *S.a.* LEAD-
FOIL, SILVER-FOIL, TINFOIL. (*b*) Tain *m* (d'une
glace). **3. To serve as a foil to s.o.'s beauty,**
servir de repoussoir *m* à la beauté de qn.

foil², *s. Fenc:* Fleuret *m.*

foil³, *s. Ven:* Foulée *f*, piste *f*.

foil⁴, *v.tr.* Faire échouer, faire manquer (une tentative, etc.); déjouer (qn, un complot).

foiled [fɔild], *a. Arch:* (Arc, etc.) à lobes.

foist [fɔist], *v.tr.* Refiler (*sth. on s.o.*, qch. à qn). *To f. a bad coin on s.o.*, repasser une fausse pièce à qn. **To foist oneself on s.o.**, s'implanter chez qn; s'imposer à qn, chez qn.

fold¹ [fould], *s.* I. Sheep-fold, parc *m* à moutons; bergerie *f*. 2. *F:* Sein *m* de l'Église; bercail *m*.

fold², *v.tr. Husb:* Parquer, emparquer (les moutons).

fold³, *s.* (*a*) Pli *m*, repli *m*; accident *m* (de terrain). **Box folds, inverted folds,** plis rentrés. (*b*) *Metalw:* Repli, agrafe *f* (d'une tôle). (*c*) Battant *m*, vantail *m*, -aux (d'une porte); feuille *f* (de paravent). (*d*) *Geol:* Flexure *f*, plissement *m*.

fold⁴. I. *v.tr.* (*a*) Plier (une feuille de papier, etc.). **To fold back**, rabattre (un col, etc.). **To fold back, down,** *the blankets*, retourner les couvertures. **To fold sth. up (again)**, (re)plier qch. (*b*) **To fold sth. in sth.**, envelopper qch. de, dans, qch. **To fold s.o. in one's arms**, enlacer, serrer, qn dans ses bras. (*c*) **To fold one's arms**, (se) croiser les bras. **To fold one's hands,** (i) joindre les mains; (ii) *F:* se croiser les bras. 2. *v.i.* Se (re)plier, se briser. **To fold back, down,** se rabattre. **folding¹**, *a.* Pliant, repliable, rabattable. **Folding camera**, appareil pliant; folding *m*. **'folding-'chair,** *s.* Chaise pliante. **'folding-'ladder,** *s.* Échelle brisée. **folding²**, *s.* I. (*a*) Pliage *m* (de l'étoffe, etc.). **Folding up, down,** repliage *m*, repliement *m*, rabattement *m*. (*b*) *Metalw:* Agrafage *m* (de tôles). 2. *Geol:* Plissement *m* (du terrain).

-fold⁵, *a.suff.* -uple. **Fourfold**, quadruple. *To repay s.o.* **tenfold**, rendre à qn au décuple ce qu'on lui doit.

folder ['fouldər], *s.* I. (*Pers.*) Plieur, -euse (de journaux, etc.). 2. *Tls: Bookb:* Plioir *m*. 3. *Com:* Prospectus (plié).

foliage ['fouliedʒ], *s.* Feuillage *m.*

foliated ['foulieitid], *a. Miner: Geol: etc:* Feuilleté, lamellaire.

foliation [fouli'eiʃ(ə)n], *s.* I. Foliation *f*, frondaison *f* (d'une plante). 2. Foliotage *m* (d'un livre).

folio¹, *pl.* **-os** ['foulio, -ouz], *s.* I. (*a*) Folio *m*, feuille *f*, feuillet *m* (de manuscrit). (*b*) *Typ: etc:* Numéro *m* (d'une page); folio. 2. (Livre *m*) in-folio *m*.

folio², *v.tr.* Folioter (les feuilles d'un livre).

folk [fouk], *s.* I. *A:* Race *f*, peuple *m*, nation *f*. 2. *pl.* **Folk(s),** gens *mf*, personnes *f*. **Country folk,** campagnards *m*. **My folks,** les miens, ma famille. **'folk-dance,** *s.* Danse villageoise, rustique. **'folk-lore,** *s.* Folklore *m*; tradition *f*. **'folk-song,** *s.* Chanson *f* populaire.

follow ['fɔlo]. I. *v.tr.* I. Suivre. (*a*) **To follow s.o. about,** suivre qn partout. *A master followed by his servant*, un maître suivi de son domestique. **To follow s.o. in,** entrer à la suite de, après, qn. **To follow the hounds,** chasser à courre. *F:* **To follow the plough,** être laboureur. *F:* **To follow one's nose,** aller tout droit devant soi. (*b*) **To follow a road,** suivre un chemin. *Boat that follows the coast*, bateau qui longe la côte. (*c*) Succéder à (qn, qch.). *The years f. one another*, les années se succèdent, se suivent. (*Of action*) **To be followed by consequences,** entraîner des conséquences. 2. Être le disciple, le partisan, de (qn). 3. Poursuivre (l'ennemi). 4. Suivre, se conformer à (la mode, etc.). **To follow s.o.'s**

advice, example, suivre le conseil, l'exemple, de qn. 5. Exercer, suivre (une profession); s'attacher à, poursuivre (une carrière). **To follow the sea,** être marin. 6. (*a*) Suivre, comprendre (une explication, etc.). (*b*) Prêter attention à, suivre (un discours). 7. *To f. a tragedy with a light comedy*, faire suivre une tragédie d'une comédie légère. II. **follow,** *v.i.* I. **To follow (after),** suivre; aller ou venir à la suite. **As follows,** ainsi qu'il suit. *Our method is as follows*, notre méthode est la suivante. 2. **To follow in s.o.'s footsteps,** marcher sur les traces de qn. **To follow close behind s.o.,** emboîter le pas à qn. 3. S'ensuivre, résulter (*from*, de). **Hence it follows that . . .**, il s'ensuit que . . ., il suit de là que. . . . **It does not follow that . . .**, ce n'est pas à dire que + *sub.* **follow on,** *v.i.* Continuer (dans la même direction). **follow out,** *v.tr.* Poursuivre (une idée, etc.) jusqu'à sa conclusion. **follow through,** *v.i. Sp:* Suivre la balle (avec la batte, la raquette, etc.). **follow up,** *v.tr.* I. Suivre (qn, qch.) de près. 2. (*a*) Poursuivre (avec énergie). *Com:* Suivre, *F:* chauffer (une affaire). **To follow up a clue,** s'attacher à une indication. **To follow up an advantage,** poursuivre un avantage. (*b*) Donner suite immédiate à (une menace, etc.). **following¹,** *a.* I. Qui suit. *Nau:* **Following sea,** mer *f* de l'arrière. *N.Arch: Av:* **Following edge,** bord *m* de sortie (de l'hélice). 2. (*a*) Suivant. **On the following day,** le jour suivant; le lendemain. (*b*) *The f.* **resolution,** la résolution énoncée ci-après, la résolution que voici. (*c*) **Two days following,** deux jours de suite. **following²,** *s.* (*a*) Suite *f* (d'un prince). (*b*) *Pol: etc:* Parti *m* (d'un chef). **'follow-my-'leader,** *s. Games:* Jeu *m* de la queue leu leu.

follower ['fɔloər], *s.* (*a*) Serviteur *m*, satellite *m*, affidé, -ée (d'un prince, etc.). (*b*) Partisan *m*, disciple *m*, sectateur, -trice. (*c*) *F:* Amoureux *m*, admirateur *m* (d'une domestique).

folly ['fɔli], *s.* I. Folie *f*, sottise *f*, déraison *f*. *To pay for one's f.*, être victime de sa propre folie. 2. Édifice coûteux et inutile.

foment [fo'ment], *v.tr.* Fomenter (une plaie, la discorde).

fomentation [foumen'teiʃ(ə)n], *s.* Fomentation *f*.

fomenter [fo'mentər], *s.* Fomentateur, -trice, fauteur, -trice (de troubles, etc.).

fond [fɔnd], *a.* I. *A:* Crédule, naïf. **Fond hope,** espoir dont on se flatte. 2. (*a*) (Parent) follement dévoué, trop indulgent. (*b*) Affectueux, tendre, aimant. 3. (*a*) **To be fond of s.o.**, aimer, affectionner, avoir de l'attachement pour, qn. *They are f. of each other*, ils s'aiment. (*b*) *F:* **To be fond of music, of novelty,** être amateur de musique, de nouveauté. *F. of sweets*, friand de sucreries. **To be fond of doing sth.**, aimer faire qch.; faire volontiers qch. **-ly,** *adv.* I. Crédulement, naïvement. *He fondly hoped to . . .*, il se flattait de. . . . 2. Tendrement, affectueusement.

fondle [fɔndl], *v.tr.* Caresser, câliner, *F:* chouchouter (qn); faire des mamours à (qn).

fondness ['fɔndnəs], *s.* I. Indulgence excessive (d'une mère, etc.). 2. Affection *f*, tendresse *f* (*for*, pour, envers). 3. Penchant *m*, prédilection *f*, goût *m* (*for sth.*, pour qch.).

font [fɔnt], *s.* Fonts baptismaux.

food [fu:d], *s.* I. (*a*) Nourriture *f*; aliments *mpl*; vivres *mpl*. *To offer s.o. f.*, offrir à manger à qn. **Food and clothing,** le vivre et le vêtement. **Plain food,** aliments simples. *Hotel where the f. is good*, hôtel où la cuisine, la table, est bonne. **To be**

off one's food, n'avoir pas d'appétit. **Food-stuffs, articles of food,** comestibles *m* ou denrées *f*. **Food products,** produits *m* alimentaires. **Food value,** valeur nutritive. (*b*) *Physiol:* Complete food, aliment complet. *Toil:* **Skin food,** aliment pour la peau. (*c*) *Husb:* Pâture *f* (d'animaux); mangeaille *f* (de volaille). **Soft food** (*for poultry*), pâtée *f*. (*d*) **Mental, intellectual, food,** nourriture de l'esprit; pâture intellectuelle. **To give s.o. food for thought,** donner à penser, à réfléchir, à qn. **2. Food and drink,** le boire et le manger.

fool¹ [fuːl], *s.* **1.** Imbécile *mf*; idiot, -ote; niais, -aise; sot, *f.* sotte. **To play, act, the fool,** faire l'imbécile; faire des bêtises, des sottises. **To make a fool of oneself,** se rendre ridicule. **Silly fool!** *P:* espèce d'idiot! **Some fool of a politician,** quelque imbécile d'homme politique. **2.** Fou *m*, bouffon *m*. **To play the f.,** faire le bouffon, le pitre. (*Cf.* 1.) **3.** Dupe *f.* **To make a fool of s.o.,** berner qn, mystifier qn. *S.a.* ALL FOOL'S DAY, APRIL. **'fool-proof,** *a.* A l'épreuve des imbéciles; (mécanisme) indéréglable, indétraquable. **'fool's-cap,** *s.* **1.** Bonnet *m* de fou. **2.** Bonnet *m* d'âne.

fool². **1.** *v.i.* Faire la bête. *Stop fooling!* assez de bêtises! **To fool about, around,** flâner; baguenauder; gâcher son temps; courir la ville (*with,* avec). **2.** *v.tr.* Berner, mystifier, duper (qn); *F:* se payer la tête de (qn). **fooling,** *s.* **1.** Bouffonnerie *f*; (*in school, etc.*) dissipation *f.* **2.** Bernement *m*, duperie *f* (de qn).

fool³, *s. Cu:* **Gooseberry fool,** marmelade *f* de groseilles (à maquereau) à la crème.

foolery ['fuːləri], *s.* **1.** Sottise *f*, bêtise *f.* **2.** Bouffonnerie *f*; pitrerie *f.*

foolhardiness ['fuːlhɑːdinəs], *s.* Témérité *f*, imprudence *f.*

foolhardy ['fuːlhɑːdi], *a.* Téméraire, imprudent. **-ily,** *adv.* Témérairement, imprudemment.

foolish ['fuːliʃ], *a.* **1.** (*a*) Insensé; fou, *f.* folle; étourdi. (*b*) Sot, *f.* sotte; bête. **2.** Absurde, ridicule. **To look foolish,** avoir l'air penaud. **To feel foolish,** rester penaud. **-ly,** *adv.* **1.** Follement, étourdiment. **2.** Sottement, bêtement.

foolishness ['fuːliʃnəs], *s.* **1.** Folie *f*, étourderie *f.* **2.** Sottise *f*, bêtise *f.*

foolscap ['fuːlskap], *s.* Papier *m* ministre.

foot¹, *pl.* **feet** [fut, fiːt], *s.* **1.** Pied *m.* (*a*) *He gets under your feet,* il se met dans vos jambes. **To put one's best foot foremost,** (i) presser, allonger, le pas; (ii) pousser la besogne; faire de son mieux. **To sit at s.o.'s feet,** (i) s'asseoir aux pieds de qn; (ii) être le disciple de qn. **To set foot on an island,** mettre pied sur une île. **To knock s.o. off his feet,** faire perdre l'équilibre à qn; renverser qn. *F:* **To carry s.o. off his feet,** transporter qn d'admiration, d'enthousiasme. **To keep one's feet,** (i) tenir pied, rester debout; (ii) *F:* tenir bon, tenir ferme. **To rise to one's feet (again),** se (re)lever; se (re)mettre debout. **To be on one's feet,** se tenir debout. *He is on his feet again,* il est de nouveau sur pied; le voilà remis. **To set s.o. on his feet,** (i) (re)mettre qn sur pied, (r)établir qn; (ii) lancer qn (dans les affaires, etc.). **To find one's feet,** voler de ses propres ailes; se débrouiller. **To begin to feel one's feet,** (*of pers.*) commencer à se sentir. **To put one's foot down upon sth.,** réprimer énergiquement (un abus); opposer un refus formel à (un projet, etc.). **To put one's foot down,** faire acte d'autorité. **To put one's foot in,** s'implanter, s'impatroniser (chez qn, etc.). **To put one's foot in it,** mettre les pieds dans le plat. *P:* **To have, get, cold feet,** caner, capponner. (*b*) Marche *f*,

allure *f*. **To have a light foot, a heavy foot,** avoir le pied léger, lourd. **Swift of foot,** léger à la course. (*c*) *Adv.phr.* **On foot.** (i) A pied; pédestrement. (ii) Debout. **To buy cattle on foot,** acheter du bétail sur pied. (iii) Sur pied, en train. **To set a business on foot,** mettre sur pied une affaire. **Under foot, underfoot,** sous les pieds. **To trample, tread, sth. under foot,** fouler qch. aux pieds. **2.** Pied (d'animaux à sabot); patte *f* (de chien, de chat, d'insecte, d'oiseau). *Equit:* **The fore feet,** le bipède antérieur (du cheval). **3.** *Coll. Mil:* Infanterie *f.* **Foot and horse,** infanterie et cavalerie. *Twenty thousand foot,* vingt mille hommes d'infanterie. **4.** (*a*) Pied, semelle *f* (d'un bas). (i) Bas bout (d'une table); pied (d'un lit); extrémité inférieure (d'un lac). (*c*) Base *f* (de colonne, d'échelle); patte *f* (de verre à boire). (*d*) Bas *m* (d'échelle, de page); départ *m* (d'un escalier). **At the foot of the page,** au bas de la page. **At the foot of the list,** of the class, à la queue de la liste, de la classe. **5.** (*a*) *Pros:* Pied. (*b*) *Meas:* Pied anglais (de 30 cm. 48). **foot-and-'mouth disease,** *s.* Fièvre aphteuse; *F:* cocotte *f.* **'foot-bath,** *s.* Bain *m* de pieds. **'foot-brake,** *s.* Frein *m* à pédale; frein au pied. **'foot-bridge,** *s.* Passerelle *f*; pont *m* pour piétons. **'foot-fault,** *s. Ten:* Faute *f* de pied. **'foot-gear,** *s.* = FOOT-WEAR. **'foot-guards,** *s.pl. Mil:* Gardes *m* à pied; garde *f* à pied. **'foot-hills,** *s.pl.* Contreforts *m* (d'un massif). **'foot-lathe,** *s. Tls:* Tour *m* à pédale. **'foot-mark,** *s.* Empreinte *f* de pied. **'foot-muff,** *s.* Chancelière *f.* **'foot-note,** *s.* Note *f* au bas de la page; renvoi *m* en bas de page. **'foot-pace,** *s.* **To go, ride, at a foot-pace,** aller au pas. **'foot-passenger,** *s.* Piéton *m.* **'foot-plate,** *s. Mch:* Plate-forme *f*, tablier *m* (de locomotive). **'foot-race,** *s.* Course *f* à pied. **'foot-rot,** *s. Vet:* Fourchet *m*, piétin *m.* **'foot-rule,** *s.* Règle *f* (d'un pied). **'foot-slogger,** *s. Mil: P:* Pousse-caillou *m inv*; *F:* troubade *m.* **'foot-soldier,** *s.* Fantassin *m*; soldat *m* d'infanterie. **'foot-warmer,** *s.* (*a*) *Rail:* Bouillotte *f.* (*b*) Chaufferette *f.* **'foot-wear,** *s.* Chaussures *fpl.* **'foot-work,** *s. Sp:* Jeu *m* de pieds, de jambes.

foot², *v.tr.* **1.** (*a*) Danser (un quadrille). (*b*) *F:* **To foot it,** (i) danser; (ii) faire le trajet à pied. **2.** *F:* **To foot the bill,** payer la note. **-footed,** *a.* Flat-footed, aux pieds plats. Sure-footed, au pied sûr. **footing,** *s.* **1.** (*a*) *Fenc: Danc: etc:* Pose *f* des pieds. (*b*) = FOOTHOLD. **To lose one's footing,** perdre pied. *I missed my f.,* le pied me manqua. **2.** (*a*) Situation sûre. **To gain a footing,** s'implanter, prendre pied. (*b*) Position *f*, condition *f.* **On a war footing,** sur le pied de guerre. **To be on an equal footing (with . . .),** être de pair, sur un pied d'égalité (avec . . .). (*c*) Admission *f* (à une société). **To pay one's footing,** payer sa bienvenue; *Mil:* arroser ses galons. **3.** *Const:* Empattement *m.*

football ['futbɔːl], *s.* **1.** Ballon *m.* **2.** Le football. **Rugby football,** le rugby. **Football ground,** terrain *m* de football.

footballer ['futbɔːlər], *s.* Joueur *m* de football; footballeur *m.*

footboard ['futbɔːrd], *s. Veh:* (Planche *f*) marchepied *m*; (*in front of driver*) coquille *f.*

footer ['futər], *s. F:* = FOOTBALL 2.

footfall ['futfɔːl], *s.* (Bruit *m* de) pas *m.*

foothold ['futhould], *s.* Assiette *f* de pied. To **get a foothold,** prendre pied. **To keep one's f.,** préserver l'équilibre. **To lose one's foothold,** perdre pied.

footle [fu:tl], *v.i.* F: To footle about, s'occuper à des bagatelles. To footle away one's time, gâcher son temps. **footling,** *a.* F: Insignifiant, futile.

footlights ['futlaits], *s.pl.* Th: Rampe *f*.

footman, *pl.* **-men** ['futmən, -men], *s.m.* Valet de pied ; laquais.

footpad ['futpad], *s. A :* Voleur *m* ; détrousseur *m* de grand chemin.

footpath ['futpɑːθ], *s.* Sentier *m* (pour piétons) ; *(in street)* trottoir *m*.

footprint ['futprint], *s.* Empreinte *f* de pas.

footsore ['futsɔːər], *a.* Aux pieds endoloris.

footstep ['futstep], *s,* **I.** Pas *m*. **2.** To follow, tread, walk, in s.o.'s footsteps, suivre les brisées de qn.

footstool ['futstuːl], *s.* Tabouret *m*.

footway ['futwei], *s.* = FOOTPATH.

foozle [fuːzl], *v.tr. & abs.* Golf : To foozle (a shot), rater, manquer (un coup).

fop [fɔp], *s.* F: Bellâtre *m*, fat *m*.

foppish ['fɔpiʃ], *a.* F: (Homme) bellâtre, fat. **-ly,** *adv.* Avec une élégance affectée.

foppishness ['fɔpiʃnəs], *s.* Élégance affectée.

for[1] [fɔːr, *unstressed* fər, for], *prep.* Pour. I. **I.** (a) (i) *(Representing)* Member for Liverpool, député de Liverpool. Tp : A for Andrew, A comme André. (ii) *(Instead of)* To act for s.o., agir pour qn, au nom de qn. He is writing for me, il écrit à ma place. (b) They want her for his wife, il la veut pour femme. He was sold for a slave, il fut vendu comme esclave. (c) To be paid for one's services, recevoir des gages pour ses services. (d) To exchange one thing for another, échanger une chose contre une autre. To sell sth. for ten francs, vendre qch. dix francs. He'll do it for a fiver, il le fera pour cinq livres. **2.** (a) *(In favour of)* He is for free trade, il est pour le libre-échange. The exchange is for us, le change nous est favorable. (b) It is not for you to blame him, cé n'est pas à vous de le critiquer. **3.** (a) What for? 'pourquoi (faire)? What's that gadget for? à quoi sert ce truc-là? Garments for men, vêtements pour hommes. For sale, à vendre. For example, par exemple. P: He's for it ['fɔːrit], he's in for it ['infɔːrit], son affaire est bonne. (b) To marry s.o. for his money, épouser qn pour son argent. To choose s.o. for his ability, choisir qn en raison de sa compétence. To jump for joy, sauter de joie. **4.** (a) Ship bound for America, vaisseau en partance pour l'Amérique. The trains for Orleans, les trains pour, sur, Orléans. 'Train for London,' "train direction de Londres." (b) His feelings for you, ses sentiments envers vous. **5.** The road is lined with trees for two miles, la route est bordée d'arbres pendant deux milles. **6.** (a) *(Future)* I am going away for a fortnight, je pars pour quinze jours. He will be away for a year, il sera absent pendant un an. He won't be back for a week, il ne reviendra pas d'ici à huit jours. (b) *(Past)* He was away for a fortnight, il fut absent pendant quinze jours. I have not seen him for three years, voilà, il y a, trois ans que je ne l'ai vu. (c) I have been here for three days, il y a trois jours que je suis ici ; je suis ici depuis trois jours. I had known him for years, je le connaissais depuis des années. **7.** (a) This box is for you, cette boîte est pour vous. A cake had been set aside for me, on avait mis de côté un gâteau à mon intention. To make a name for oneself, se faire un nom. Here is news for you! voici une nouvelle qui vous intéressera ! To write for the papers, écrire dans les journaux. (b) Your task for to-morrow, votre devoir pour demain. **8.** To care

for s.o., aimer qn. Eager for praise, avide d'éloges. Fit for nothing, bon à rien. Oh, for a muse of fire ! que n'ai-je une muse enflammée ! Now for it ! allons-y ! **9.** (a) As for him . . ., quant à lui. . . . As for that . . ., pour ce qui est de cela. . . . See for yourself ! voyez par vous-même ! (b) For all that, malgré tout ; ce nonobstant. For all that, you should have let me know, encore auriez-vous dû me prévenir. For all that he is so wealthy . . ., tout riche qu'il est. . . . (c) But for her I should have died, n'eût été elle, sans elle, je serais mort. (d) Translate word for word, traduisez mot à mot. For one enemy he has a hundred friends, pour un ennemi il a cent amis. II. **for** introducing an infinitive clause. **I.** It is easy for him to come, il lui est facile de venir. For this to be feasible, pour que cela se puisse. **2.** I have brought it for you to see, je l'ai apporté pour que vous le voyiez. It is not for me to decide, ce n'est pas à moi de décider. **3.** It s no good for Mr X to talk, M. X a beau dire. **4.** He gave orders for the boxes to be packed, il donna l'ordre de faire les malles. **5.** To arrange for sth. to be done, prendre des dispositions pour que qch. se fasse. To wait for sth. to be done, attendre que qch. se fasse. **6.** The best plan will be for you to go away for a time, le mieux sera que vous vous absentiez pour quelque temps. For you to back out now would be a disgrace, vous retirer maintenant serait honteux.

for[2], *conj.* Car.

forage[1] ['fɔredʒ], *s.* **I.** Fourrage(s) *m(pl).* **2.** To go on the forage, aller au fourrage. **'forage-cap,** *s. Mil:* Bonnet *m* de police ; calot *m*. **'forage-waggon,** *s.* Fourragère *f.*

forage[2]. **I.** *v.i.* Fourrager ; aller au fourrage. F: To forage for sth., fouiller pour trouver qch. **2.** *v.tr.* (a) Ravager, saccager, fourrager (un pays). (b) Donner du fourrage à (un cheval, etc.).

forager ['fɔredʒər], *s.* Fourrageur *m.*

forasmuch [fɔraz'mʌtʃ], *adv. A :* Forasmuch as . . ., d'autant que, vu que, attendu que.

foray[1] ['fɔrei], *s.* Razzia *f*, incursion *f*, raid *m.*

foray[2], *v.i.* Faire des incursions, des raids.

forbade [fɔr'bad]. See FORBID.

forbear[1] ['fɔːrbɛər], *s.* Aïeul, -eux *m* ; ancêtre *m.*

forbear[2] [fɔr'bɛər], *v. (p.t.* forbore [fɔr'bɔːr] ; *p.p.* forborne [fɔr'bɔːrn] **I.** *v.tr.* S'abstenir de (qch.). **2.** *v.i.* (a) S'abstenir. To forbear from doing sth., s'abstenir de, se garder de, faire qch. (b) To bear and forbear ['fɔːrbɛər], se montrer patient et indulgent. **forbearing,** *a.* Patient, endurant.

forbearance [fɔr'bɛərəns], *s.* **I.** Forbearance from, of, sth., abstention *f* de qch. **2.** Patience *f*, longanimité *f.*

forbid [fɔr'bid], *v.tr.* (forbade [fɔr'bad] ; forbidden) **I.** Défendre, interdire ; *Jur:* prohiber. 'Smoking forbidden,' "défense de fumer." Forbidden fruit, fruit défendu. Forbidden subjects, sujets tabous. *Mil:* Forbidden weapons, armes prohibées. To forbid s.o. sth., défendre, interdire, qch. à qn. To forbid s.o. the house, interdire, défendre, l'entrée de) sa maison à qn. To forbid s.o. to do sth., défendre à qn de faire qch. **2.** F: Empêcher (qch.). My health forbids my coming, ma santé m'empêche de venir. God forbid (that . . .)! à Dieu ne plaise (que + sub.)!

forbidding, *a.* (Visage) sinistre, rébarbatif ; (ciel, temps) sombre.

forbore [fɔr'bɔːər], **forborne** [fɔr'bɔːrn]. See FORBEAR[2].

forby(e) [fɔr'bai]. *Scot:* **I.** *prep.* En outre de. **2.** *adv.* D'ailleurs.

orce¹ [fɔːrs], s. Force f. **I.** (a) Violence f, contrainte f. **By sheer force**, de vive force. *By sheer f. of will*, à force de volonté. *The f. of circumstances*, la force, la contrainte, des circonstances. **To resort to force**, (i) faire appel à la force; (ii) se porter à des voies de fait. **To yield to force**, céder à la force. (b) Influence f, autorité f. *F. of example*, influence de l'exemple. **2.** (a) Énergie f (d'un coup); effort(s) m(pl), intensité f (du vent). *He argued with much f. that . . .*, il a représenté avec insistance que. . . . (b) *Mec:* Force, effort. **Force of gravity**, (force de la) pesanteur. *Impulsive f.*, force d'impulsion. **3.** Puissance f (militaire); force (au service de l'État). **The allied forces**, les puissances alliées. **Home forces**, armée métropolitaine. *Land and sea forces*, armées de terre et de mer. **The police force**, *F:* **the Force**, la force publique; la police. **A strong force of police**, un fort détachement de police. **In (full) force**, en force. **4.** (a) Vertu f, efficacité f (d'un remède). **There is force in what you say**, votre argument n'est pas sans valeur. *I can't see the f. of working for nothing*, je ne vois pas pourquoi je travaillerais pour rien. (b) Signification f (d'un mot). **Verb used with passive force**, verbe employé avec la valeur d'un passif. **5.** (*Of law*) **To be in force**, être en vigueur. **The methods in force**, les méthodes appliquées actuellement. **'force-pump**, s. *Hyd.E:* Pompe (re)foulante.

orce², v.tr. Forcer. **I.** (a) **To force s.o.'s hand**, forcer la main à qn. **To force the pace**, forcer l'allure. *She forced a smile*, elle eut un sourire contraint. *Cards:* **To force an ace**, forcer un as. (b) Prendre (qn, qch.) par force; desceller (un coffre-fort). **To force one's way**, se frayer un chemin. *To f. one's way into a house*, pénétrer de force dans une maison. (c) **To force sth. into sth.**, faire entrer qch. de force dans qch. (d) **To force a plant**, forcer, hâter, une plante. *Aut: etc:* *To f. the engine*, trop pousser le moteur. **2.** (a) Contraindre, obliger. *The town was forced to capitulate*, la ville fut obligée de capituler. *I am forced to conclude that . . .*, je suis forcé de conclure que. . . . (b) *To f. a nation into war*, forcer une nation à entrer en guerre. (c) *To f. an action on the enemy*, contraindre l'ennemi à la bataille. (d) **To force sth. from s.o.**, extorquer, arracher, (une promesse, etc.) à qn. **force back**, v.tr. **I.** Repousser; faire reculer. **2.** Refouler (l'air, l'eau). **forced**, a. Forcé. **I.** Inévitable, obligatoire. **Forced loan**, emprunt forcé. **2.** Contraint. **Forced laugh**, rire forcé. *To give a f. laugh*, rire faux. **forcing**, s. **I.** Forcement m (d'une serrure); descellement m (d'un coffre-fort); enfoncement m (d'une porte). **2.** *Hort:* Forçage m; culture forcée. **'forcing-house**, s. *Hort:* Forcerie f.

forceful ['fɔːrsful], a. (*Of pers., speech*) Plein de force; énergique. **-fully**, adv. Avec force.

force-meat ['fɔːrsmiːt], s. *Cu:* Farce f, hachis m. **Force-meat ball**, boulette f, quenelle f.

forceps ['fɔːrseps], s. sg. & pl. *Surg:* Pince f. *Dent:* Davier m. *Ent:* Pince (de forficule).

forcible ['fɔːrsibl], a. **I.** (Entrée) de, par, force. **2.** (Langage) énergique, vigoureux. **-ibly**, adv. **I.** Par force, de force. **2.** Énergiquement.

ford¹ [fɔːrd], s. Gué m.

ford², v.tr. Guéer, traverser à gué (une rivière).

fordable ['fɔːrdəbl], a. Guéable.

fore¹ [fɔːr]. I. a. (a) Antérieur, -eure; de devant. (b) *Nau:* (De l')avant. II. **fore**, s. (a) *Nau:* Avant m. **At the fore**, au mât de misaine. (b) **To the fore**, (i) en vue, en évidence; (ii) présent. **'fore(-)and(-)'aft**, a. & adv. *Nau:* De l'avant à l'arrière. *F.-and-a. sail*, voile f aurique. **'fore-cabin**, s. *Nau:* Cabine f de l'avant. **'fore-carriage**, s. Avant-train m (d'une voiture). **'fore-court**, s. Avant-cour f. **'fore-deck**, s. *Nau:* Avant-pont m. **'fore-edge**, s. *Bookb:* Gouttière f (d'un livre). **'fore-foot**, s. pl. **-feet**, s. Pied antérieur; patte f de devant. **'fore(-)part**, s. Avant m, devant m; avant-corps m inv (d'un bâtiment); tête f (d'un train). *The f.-p. of the ship*, la partie avant du navire. **'fore-quarter**, s. Quartier m de devant (de bœuf). *Fore-quarters of a horse*, avant-main m, avant-train m, d'un cheval. **'fore-sail**, s. *Nau:* (Voile f de) misaine f. **'fore-stage**, s. *Th:* Avant-scène f. **'fore-tooth**, pl. **-teeth**, s. (Dent) incisive f; dent du devant.

fore², int. *Golf:* Attention devant! gare devant!

forearm ['fɔːrɑːrm], s. Avant-bras m inv.

forearmed [fɔːr'ɑːrmd], a. See FOREWARN.

forebode [fɔr'boud], v.tr. **I.** (*Of thg*) Présager, augurer (le malheur). **2.** (*Of pers.*) Pressentir (un malheur). **foreboding**, s. **I.** Mauvais augure; présage m (sinistre). **2.** (Mauvais) pressentiment.

forecast¹ ['fɔːrkɑːst], s. Prévision f. *Racing f.*, betting f., pronostic m (des courses).

forecast² [fɔr'kɑːst], v.tr. (p.t. & p.p. **forecast** or **forecasted**) Calculer, prévoir (les événements).

forecastle [fouksl], s. *Nau:* **I.** Gaillard m (d'avant). **2.** (*In merchant vessel*) Poste m de l'équipage.

foreclose [fɔr'klouz], v.r. **To foreclose (the mortgage)**, saisir l'immeuble hypothéqué.

foreclosure [fɔr'klouʒər], s. *Jur:* Saisie f (d'une hypothèque).

foreconscious [fɔr'kɔnʃəs], s. *Psy:* Préconscient m.

foredoomed [fɔr'duːmd], a. Condamné d'avance (to, à). *Plan f. to failure*, projet mort-né, voué à l'insuccès.

forefather ['fɔːrfɑːðər], s. Aïeul m, ancêtre m. *Our forefathers*, nos aïeux.

forefinger ['fɔːrfiŋgər], s. Index m.

forefront ['fɔːrfrʌnt], s. *F:* Premier rang, premier plan.

foregather [fɔr'gæðər], v.i. = FORGATHER.

forego [fɔr'gou], v.tr. = FORGO.

foregoing [fɔr'gouiŋ], a. Précédent, antérieur; déjà cité. **The foregoing**, ce qui précède.

foregone [fɔr'gɔn], a. (*Of conclusion*) Décidé d'avance; prévu.

foreground ['fɔːrgraund], s. *Art: Phot:* Premier plan; avant-plan m.

forehand ['fɔːrhænd]. **I.** s. (*Of horse*) Avant-main m. **2.** a. *Ten:* **Forehand stroke**, coup m d'avant-main; coup droit.

forehead ['fɔred], s. *Anat:* Front m.

foreign ['fɔrin], a. Étranger. **I.** **Foreign to**, **from** (sth.), étranger à, éloigné de, sans rapport avec (qch.). *Med: etc:* **Foreign body**, corps étranger. **2.** Qui n'est pas du pays. (a) (Situated abroad) **Foreign countries**, **foreign parts**, pays étrangers; l'étranger m. *He has been in f. parts*, il a été à l'étranger. *Our relations with f. countries*, nos rapports avec l'extérieur. (b) (Dealing with foreign countries) **Foreign trade**, commerce extérieur; *Nau:* long cours. **Foreign money order**, mandat international. **The Foreign Office** = le Ministère des Affaires étrangères. **The Foreign Secretary** = le Ministre des Affaires

foreigner ['fɔrinər], s. **I.** Étranger, -ère. **2.** *F:* Homme m, etc., qui n'est pas d'ici.

foreknowledge [fɔər'nɔledʒ], s. Préconnaissance f ; prescience f.

foreland ['fɔːrlənd], s. Cap m, promontoire m ; pointe f (de terre) ; falaise f à pic.

foreleg ['fɔːrleg], s. Jambe antérieure, de devant (d'un cheval) ; patte f de devant (d'un chien).

forelock ['fɔːrlɔk], s. (Of pers.) Mèche f (de cheveux) sur le front ; (of pers., horse) toupet m. F : To take time by the forelock, saisir l'occasion aux cheveux.

foreman, pl. **-men** ['fɔːrmən, -men], s.m. **I.** Jur : Chef du jury. **2.** (a) Ind : Contremaître ; chef d'équipe. Works f., conducteur des travaux. (b) Printer's foreman, prote m.

foremast ['fɔːrmɑːst], s. Mât m de misaine ; (arbre m de) trinquet m.

foremost ['fɔːrmoust]. **I.** a. Premier ; le plus avancé. In the f. rank, au tout premier rang. To come f., venir tout en tête. **2.** adv. First and foremost, tout d'abord ; d'abord et avant tout.

forenoon [fɔːr'nuːn], s. Matinée f.

forensic [fɔ'rensik], a. (Éloquence) judiciaire, du barreau. Forensic medicine, médecine légale.

forerunner ['fɔːrɛrʌnər], s. Avant-coureur m, avant-courrier, -ière ; précurseur m.

foresee [fɔr'siː], v.tr. (foresaw [fɔr'sɔː] ; foreseen [fɔr'siːn]) Prévoir, entrevoir (des difficultés, l'avenir). **foreseeing**, a. Prévoyant.

foreshadow [fɔr'ʃadou], v.tr. Présager, annoncer, laisser prévoir (un événement).

foreshore ['fɔːrʃɔːr], s. **I.** Plage f. **2.** Partie f de la plage qui découvre à marée basse.

foreshorten [fɔr'ʃɔːrtn], v.tr. Art : Dessiner, présenter, (un objet) en raccourci, en perspective. **foreshortened**, a. Art : Raccourci, en raccourci. **foreshortening**, s. Art : Raccourci m.

foresight ['fɔːrsait], s. **I.** (a) Prévision f (de l'avenir). (b) Prévoyance f. Want of foresight, imprévoyance f, imprévision f. **2.** Sm.a : Guidon m.

forest ['fɔrest], s. Forêt f. F. of timber trees, open forest, forêt de haute futaie. The national forests, le domaine forestier. 'forest-'guard, -'ranger, s. Garde forestier. 'forest-tree, s. Arbre forestier ; arbre de haute futaie.

forestall [fɔr'stɔːl], v.tr. Anticiper, devancer, prévenir (qn, un événement). **forestalling**, s. Anticipation f (des désirs de qn) ; devancement m (d'un concurrent).

forester ['fɔrestər], s. (Garde) forestier m.

forestry ['fɔrestri], s. Sylviculture f.

foretaste ['fɔːrteist], s. Avant-goût m.

foretell [fɔr'tel], v.tr. (foretold [fɔr'tould] ; foretold) **I.** (Of pers.) Prédire. **2.** Présager. **foretelling**, s. Prédiction f.

forethought ['fɔːrθɔːt], s. **I.** Préméditation f. **2.** Prévoyance f.

foretold [fɔr'tould]. See FORETELL.

foretop ['fɔːrtɔp], s. Nau : Hune f de misaine.

forever [fɔ'revər], adv. See EVER 2 (b).

forevermore [fɔrevər'mɔːər], adv. See EVERMORE.

forewarn [fɔr'wɔːrn], v.tr. Prévenir, avertir. Forewarned is forearmed, un homme averti en vaut deux.

forewoman, pl. **-women** ['fɔːrwumən, -wimen], s.f. Contremaîtresse ; première ouvrière ; "première."

foreword ['fɔːrwəːrd], s. Avant-propos m inv, préface f ; avis m au lecteur ; avertissement m.

forfeit[1] ['fɔːrfit], a. Hist : Jur : Confisqué ; perdu.

forfeit[2], s. (a) Amende f. Turf : Forfait m.

Forfeit clause (of a contract), clause f de dédit (b) Games : Gage m, punition f.

forfeit[3], v.tr. **I.** Perdre (qch.) par confiscation To f. a right, être déchu d'un droit ; laisse[ ] périmer un droit. **2.** Perdre (qch.). To f. one' life, payer de sa vie. To f. one's honour, forfair[ ] à l'honneur.

forfeiture ['fɔːrfitjər], s. Perte f (de biens) pa[ ] confiscation ; perte (de l'honneur, etc.). Jur[ ] Fin : Déchéance f, forfaiture f (d'un droit).

forfend [fɔr'fend], v.tr. God forfend! à Dieu n[ ] plaise ! Dieu m'en préserve !

forgather [fɔr'gaðər], v.i. Esp. Scot : **I.** S'as sembler ; se réunir. **2.** To f. with s.o., rencontre[ ] qn.

forgave [fɔr'geiv]. See FORGIVE.

forge[1] [fɔ'rdʒ], s. Forge f. **I.** Blacksmith's forge forge de maréchalerie. **2.** (a) Atelier m de for geron. (b) Metall : Atelier de forge.

forge[2], v.tr. **I.** (a) Forger (un fer à cheval). (b) Metall : Forger, cingler (le fer). **2.** Forger (une excuse) ; contrefaire (une signature). Abs. Commettre un faux. **forged**, a. **I.** (Fer[ ] forgé. **2.** (Document) faux, contrefait. Jur : To produce a f. will, supposer un testament. Production of f. documents, supposition f. **forging**, s. **I.** Metalw : Travail m de forge. **2.** Pièce forgée. **3.** Falsification f (de documents).

forge[3], v.i. To forge ahead. (a) (Of ship) Couri[ ] sur son erre. (b) (i) Nau : Voguer à pleines voiles ; (ii) gagner les devants ; (iii) (in business) pousser de l'avant.

forger ['fɔːrdʒər], s. **I.** Metall : Forgeron m. **2.** (Of signature) Faussaire mf ; falsificateur, -trice.

forgery ['fɔːrdʒəri], s. **I.** Contrefaçon f (de billets de banque) ; falsification f (de documents) ; supposition f (de testament). Jur : Plea of forgery, inscription f de faux. **2.** Faux m. The signature was a f., la signature était contrefaite.

forget [fɔr'get], v.tr. (forgot [fɔr'gɔt] ; forgotten [fɔr'gɔtn] ; forgetting) Oublier. **I.** Perdre le souvenir, la mémoire, de (qch.). To f. a fact, oublier un fait. To f. one's Latin, désapprendre son latin. Forget about it! n'y pensez plus ! F : And don't you forget it! faites-y bien attention ! To f. how time goes, perdre la notion de l'heure, du temps. That is easily forgotten, cela s'oublie facilement. Never to be forgotten, inoubliable. **2.** (a) Omettre, oublier (un nom sur une liste). Don't forget to . . ., ne manquez pas de. . . . (b) Oublier (son mouchoir). (c) Négliger (son devoir). **3.** F : To forget oneself, s'oublier. (a) Manquer à soi-même ou aux bienséances. I think you are forgetting yourself! vous vous oubliez, je pense ! (b) Ne plus penser à ce qu'on fait. I forgot myself! ça m'a échappé ! **forgetting**, s. Oubli m. **for'get-me-not**, s. Bot : Myosotis m ; F : ne m'oubliez pas m inv.

forgetful [fɔr'getful], a. **I.** Oublieux (of, de). He is very f., il a très mauvaise mémoire. **2.** Négligent.

forgetfulness [fɔr'getfulnəs], s. **I.** (a) Manque (habituel) de mémoire. (b) A moment of forgetfulness, un moment d'oubli m. **2.** Négligence f.

forgivable [fɔr'givəbl], a. Pardonnable.

forgive [fɔr'giv], v.tr. (forgave [fɔr'geiv] ; forgiven [fɔr'givn]) **I.** (a) Pardonner (une injure). F. this whim of mine, passez-moi ce caprice. (b) To f. s.o. a debt, faire grâce d'une dette à qn. **2.** To f. s.o., pardonner à qn. I have never been forgiven for this joke, on ne m'a jamais pardonné cette plaisanterie. **forgiving**, a. Indulgent ; peu rancunier.

forgiveness [fɔr'givnəs], *s*. **I.** (*a*) Pardon *m*. (*b*) Remise *f* (d'une dette). **2.** Indulgence *f*, clémence *f*.

forgo [fɔr'gou], *v.tr.* (forwent [fɔr'went] ; forgone [fɔr'gɔn]) Renoncer à (qch.) ; s'abstenir de (qch.).

forgot [fɔr'gɔt], **forgotten** [fɔr'gɔtn]. *See* FORGET.

fork¹ [fɔːrk], *s*. **I.** *Agr* : Fourche *f*. Two-pronged *f*., fourchet *m*. **2.** Fourchette *f* (de table). Carving fork, fourchette à découper. **3.** (*a*) (*Prop*) Poteau fourchu ; (*of incandescent mantle*) potence *f*. (*b*) *Arb* : Branche fourchue. **4.** (*a*) *Cy* : Front fork(s), fourche de direction. *Mec.E* : Cardan fork, chape *f* de cardan. (*b*) *Mus* : Tuning-fork, diapason *m*. **5.** (*a*) Bifurcation *f*, fourche (de routes). (*b*) (En)fourchure *f*, fourchement *m* (de branches) ; enfourchure (des jambes).

fork². **I.** *v.i.* (*Of tree, etc.*) Fourcher ; (*of road*) fourcher, faire la fourche, (se) bifurquer. *Aut* : Fork right for York, 'prenez à droite pour York." **2.** *v.tr.* Remuer (le foin, le sol) à la fourche. **fork out, up,** *v.tr. P* : Allonger, abouler (de l'argent). *Abs.* S'exécuter, *P* : casquer. **forked,** *a*. Fourchu, bifurqué. **forking,** *s*. Bifurcation *f*, fourchement *m*.

forlorn [fɔr'lɔːrn], *a*. *Lit* : **I.** (*Of undertaking*) Désespéré. Forlorn hope, (i) *Mil* : enfants perdus ; (ii) *F* : aventure désespérée. **2.** (*a*) Abandonné, délaissé. (*b*) *F. appearance*, mine triste, désolée.

form¹ [fɔːrm], *s*. **I.** (*a*) Forme *f*. *Statistics* in tabular form, statistique sous forme de tableau. (*b*) Figure *f*, silhouette *f*. **In the form of a dog,** sous la forme d'un chien. **The form and the substance,** la forme et le fond. **2.** (*a*) Forme, formalité *f*. *F* : To go through the form of refusing, *F* : faire la simagrée de refuser. For form's sake, **as a matter of form,** pour la forme ; par manière d'acquit. *It is a mere matter of f.*, c'est une pure formalité. (*b*) Les convenances *f* ; l'étiquette *f*. *It is good f.*, c'est de bon ton. **It is not good form, it is bad form,** c'est de mauvais ton ; cela ne se fait pas. **3.** (*a*) Formule *f*, forme. *Correct f. of words*, tournure correcte de phrase. *It is only a f. of speech*, ce n'est qu'une façon de parler. (*b*) *Adm* : Formule. Printed form, imprimé *m*. *F. of tender*, modèle *m* de soumission. Inquiry form, bulletin *m* de demande de renseignements. Form of return, feuille *f* de déclaration (de revenu). **To fill in, fill up, a form,** remplir une formule, un formulaire. **4.** (*a*) *Sp* : (*Of horse, athlete*) Forme ; état *m*, condition *f*. To be in form, out of form, être, ne pas être, en forme. *To be in good f.*, être en haleine. (*b*) (*Of pers.*) Verve *f*. *To be in capital f.*, être fort en verve, en train. **5.** *Sch* : Classe *f*. First form, approx. = (classe de) sixième *f*. Sixth form, approx. = (classe de) première *f*. Form master, professeur principal. **6.** Banc *m*, banquette *f*. **7.** (*a*) *Metall* : Forme, moule *m*. (*b*) *Typ* : Forme. **8.** Gîte *m* (du lièvre). **'form-room,** *s*. *Sch* : Salle *f* de classe ; la classe.

form². **I.** *v.tr.* **I.** Former, faire, façonner. **To form sth. from, out of, sth.,** faire qch. de qch. **To form a child's mind,** façonner l'esprit d'un enfant. **2.** (*a*) Former, organiser (une société). *They formed themselves into a committee*, ils se constituèrent en comité. (*b*) Former, contracter (une habitude). (*c*) Former, arrêter (un plan). **3.** (*a*) *The coastline forms a series of curves*, le littoral dessine une série de courbes. *Mil* : **To form fours,** se mettre sur quatre. (*b*) **To form part of sth.,** faire partie de qch. *The ministers who f. the cabinet*, les ministres qui composent le gou-

vernement. **II. form,** *v.i.* Prendre forme ; se former. *His style is forming*, son style se fait. *Mil* : To form into line, se mettre en ligne. To f. into a square, se former en carré ; former le carré.

formal [ˈfɔːrm(ə)l], *a*. **I.** *Log* : *Theol* : Formel. **2.** (*Of procedure*) Formel, en règle ; (*of order*) formel, positif. *F. denial*, démenti formel. *F. contract*, contrat en due forme. **3.** Formal bow, salut cérémonieux. **Format dinner,** dîner prié. *F. style*, style empesé. **4.** (*a*) (*Of pers.*) Formaliste, cérémonieux. *He is always very f.*, il est toujours très compassé. *She is very f.*, elle est très collet monté. (*b*) (Style) conventionnel. **-ally,** *adv.* **I.** Formellement. **2.** Cérémonieusement.

formaldehyde [fɔːrˈmaldihaid], *s*. *Ch* : Formaldéhyde *f*.

formalin(e) [ˈfɔːrməlin], *s*. *Ch* : Formaline *f*.

formalism [ˈfɔːrməlizm], *s*. Formalisme *m*.

formalist [ˈfɔːrməlist], *s*. Formaliste *mf*.

formality [fɔrˈmaliti], *s*. **I.** Formalité *f*. **A mere formality,** une pure formalité. **2.** (*a*) Compassement *m* (d'un discours). (*b*) Cérémonie *f*, formalité(s).

format [ˈfɔːrma], *s*. Format *m* (d'un livre).

formation [fɔrˈmeiʃ(ə)n], *s*. **I.** Formation *f*. **2.** Formation, disposition *f* (des troupes). Battle formation, formation de combat. Close formation, ordre serré. In open formation, en formation ouverte. **3.** *Geol* : Granite *f*, formation, terrain *m*, granitique.

former¹ [ˈfɔːrmər], *a*. **I.** Antérieur, -eure, précédent, ancien. *My f. pupils*, mes anciens élèves. *His f. letters*, ses lettres précédentes. **Former times,** le passé. *In f. times*, autrefois. **2.** The former. (*a*) *I prefer the f. alternative to the latter*, je préfère la première alternative à la seconde. (*b*) *pron*. Celui-là, celle-là ; ceux-là, celles-là. *Of the two methods I prefer the f.*, des deux méthodes je préfère celle-là. **-ly,** *adv.* Autrefois, jadis.

former², *s*. *Ind* : Gabarit *m*, calibre *m* (de forme) ; matrice *f*. *El.E* : Winding former. gabarit de bobinage.

formidable [ˈfɔːrmidəbl], *a*. Formidable, redoutable. **-ably,** *adv.* Formidablement.

formless [ˈfɔːrmləs], *a*. Informe.

formlessness [ˈfɔːrmləsnəs], *s*. Absence *f* de forme.

formula, *pl*. **-as, -ae** [ˈfɔːrmjula, -əz, -iː], *s*. Formule *f*.

formulary [ˈfɔːrmjuləri], *s*. Formulaire *m*.

formulate [ˈfɔːrmjuleit], *v.tr.* Formuler.

forsake [fɔrˈseik], *v.tr.* (forsook [fɔrˈsuk] ; forsaken [fɔrˈseikn]) **I.** Abandonner, délaisser (qn). *His confidence forsook him*, la confiance lui fit défaut. **2.** Renoncer à, abandonner (une habitude).

forsooth [fɔrˈsuːθ], *adv.* *A. & Lit* : **I.** En vérité. **2.** *Iron* : Par exemple ! ma foi !

forswear [fɔrˈswɛər], *v.tr.* (forswore [fɔrˈswɔːər] ; forsworn [fɔrˈswɔːrn]) **I.** Abjurer, renier (qch.). **2.** To forswear oneself, se parjurer. **forsworn,** *a*. Parjure.

fort [fɔːrt], *s*. *Mil* : **I.** Fort *m*. Small *f*., fortin *m*. **2.** Place fortifiée ; forteresse *f*.

forte [fɔːrt], *s*. *Singing is not his f.*, le chant n'est pas son fort.

forte² [ˈfɔːrte], *a., adv. & s*. *Mus* : Forte (*m inv*).

forth [fɔːrθ], *adv.* **I.** En avant. To go, sally, forth, sortir ; se mettre en route. **To stretch forth one's hand,** avancer la main. **2.** From this time forth, dès maintenant ; désormais. **3.** And so forth, et ainsi de suite.

forthcoming [fɔːrθˈkʌmiŋ], *a*. **I.** (*a*) Qui arrive. *Help is f.*, des secours sont en route. (*b*) Prochain, à venir. **2.** (Livre) prêt à paraître. **3.** To be forthcoming, paraître. *The answer is always f.,* la réponse ne se fait jamais attendre.

forthright [fɔːrθˈrait]. *A. & Lit*: **1.** *adv.* Tout droit; carrément. **2.** *a.* [ˈfɔːrθrait] = DOWN-RIGHT 2 (*a*).

forthwith [fɔːrθˈwiθ, -wið], *adv.* Sur-le-champ; tout de suite.

fortieth [ˈfɔːrtiəθ], *num. a. & s.* Quarantième.

fortifiable [ˈfɔːrtifaiəbl], *a.* Fortifiable.

fortification [fɔːrtifiˈkeiʃ(ə)n], *s.* **1.** (*a*) Fortification *f* (d'une ville); renforcement *m* (d'une barricade). (*b*) Fortification, affermissement *m* (du courage). **2.** *pl.* Fortifications, fortifications.

fortify [ˈfɔːrtifai], *v.tr.* **1.** (*a*) Renforcer, fortifier (un navire). (*b*) Fortifier (l'estomac); affermir, fortifier (qn). *Courage fortified against dangers,* courage armé contre les dangers. **2.** Remonter (un vin) en alcool. **3.** *Mil*: Fortifier (une place). *Fortified area,* camp fortifié.

fortitude [ˈfɔːrtitjuːd], *s.* Force *f* d'âme; courage *m.*

fortnight [ˈfɔːrtnait], *s.* Quinzaine *f*; quinze jours. *This day, to-day, fortnight,* d'aujourd'hui en quinze. *To adjourn a case for a f.,* remettre une cause à quinzaine.

fortnightly [ˈfɔːrtnaitli]. **1.** *a.* Bimensuel. **2.** *adv.* Tous les quinze jours.

fortress [ˈfɔːrtres], *s.* Forteresse *f*; place forte.

fortuitous [fɔːrˈtjuitəs], *a.* Fortuit, imprévu. **-ly,** *adv.* Fortuitement; par hasard.

fortunate [ˈfɔːrtjunet], *a.* **1.** Heureux, fortuné. *To be fortunate,* avoir de la chance. **2.** Propice, heureux. *How f.!* quel bonheur! quelle chance! **-ly,** *adv.* **1.** Heureusement. **2.** Par bonheur.

fortune [ˈfɔːrtjun], *s.* Fortune *f*. **1.** (*a*) Hasard *m,* chance *f.* *By good fortune,* par bonheur. *To try one's fortune,* tenter la chance. *Fortune favours him,* la fortune lui sourit. (*b*) Destinée *f,* sort *m.* *The fortune of war,* le sort des armes. *To tell fortunes,* dire la bonne aventure. *To tell s.o.'s f. by cards,* tirer les cartes à qn. **2.** (*a*) Prospérité *f,* richesse *f.* *A man of fortune,* un homme riche. *Born to fortune,* né coiffé. (*c*) Richesses *fpl,* biens *mpl.* *To make a fortune,* faire fortune. *To come into a fortune,* hériter d'une fortune; faire un gros héritage. *F*: **It has cost me a fortune,** cela m'a coûté un argent fou. (*d*) *To marry a fortune,* épouser une grosse dot. **'fortune-hunter,** *s.* Coureur *m* de dots. **'fortune-teller,** *s.* Diseur, -euse, de bonne aventure; (*with cards*) tireur, -euse, de cartes. **'fortune-telling,** *s.* La bonne aventure; (*with cards*) cartomancie *f.*

forty [ˈfɔːrti], *num. a. & s.* Quarante (*m*). *About f. guests,* une quarantaine d'invités. *She'll never see f. again,* elle a passé la quarantaine. **forty-'eightmo,** *a. & s.* *Typ*: In-quarante-huit (*m inv*).

forward¹ [ˈfɔːrwərd]. **I.** *a.* **1.** (*a*) De devant, d'avant. *Nau*: De l'avant, sur l'avant, avant. (*b*) (Mouvement) progressif, en avant. *F. motion,* marche (en) avant. *The f. journey,* l'aller *m.* *Fb*: Forward pass, passe en avant. **2.** (*Of plants, child*) Avancé; précoce. **3.** (*Of opinions*) Avancé. **4.** Effronté. **5.** *Com*: (*Of price, delivery*) A terme. **II. forward,** *s.* *Fb*: (*Pers.*) Avant *m.* **III. forward,** *occ.* **forwards** [ˈfɔːrwərdz], *adv.* **1.** (*a*) From that day forward, à partir de ce jour-là. *To look forward to sth.,* attendre qch. avec plaisir. (*b*) *Bank*: 'Forward' rates, taux *m* pour les opérations à terme. **2.** (*a*) En avant. *To move forward,* avancer. *To go straight forward,* aller tout droit. *To rush forward, se* précipiter (en avant). **Forward!** en avant! (*b*) (*Position*) A l'avant. *The seat is too far f.,* la banquette est trop avancée. *Fb*: To play forward, jouer comme avant. *The crew's quarters are f.,* le logement de l'équipage est à l'avant. (*c*) *Com*: (Carried) forward, à reporter; report *m.* **3.** *To come forward,* se proposer, s'offrir. *To thrust, push, oneself forward,* se mettre en évidence.

forward², *v.tr.* **1.** Avancer, favoriser, seconder (un projet). **2.** (*a*) Expédier, envoyer (des marchandises). *To f. sth. to s.o.,* faire parvenir qch. à qn. (*b*) 'To be forwarded,' 'please forward,' "prière de faire suivre"; "à faire suivre."

forwarding, *s.* **1.** Avancement *m* (d'une affaire). **2.** (*a*) Expédition *f,* envoi *m* (d'un colis). (*b*) Transmission *f* (d'une lettre).

forwardness [ˈfɔːrwərdnəs], *s.* **1.** Avancement *m,* progrès *m* (d'un travail). **2.** État avancé; précocité *f* (de la récolte, d'un élève). **3.** Hardiesse *f,* effronterie *f.*

fossa, *pl.* **-ae** [ˈfɒsa, -iː], *s.* *Anat*: Fosse (nasale).

fossil [ˈfɒsil]. **1.** *s.* Fossile *m.* *F*: An old fossil, une vieille baderne; une croûte. **2.** *a.* Fossile.

fossilize [ˈfɒsilaiz]. **1.** *v.tr.* Fossiliser. **2.** *v.i.* Se fossiliser. *F*: (*Of pers.*) S'encroûter.

fossorial [fɒˈsɔːriəl], *a.* (Animal, insecte) fouisseur.

foster¹ [ˈfɒstər], *v.tr.* **1.** Élever, nourrir (un enfant). **2.** Entretenir, nourrir (une idée). *To f. friendship between peoples,* développer, stimuler, l'amitié entre les peuples.

foster-², *comb.fm.* Qui se rapporte à l'élevage, à l'alimentation. **'foster-brother,** *s.m.* **1.** Frère de lait. **2.** Frère adoptif. **'foster-child,** *s.* **1.** Nourrisson, -onne. **2.** Enfant adopté. **'foster-father,** *s.m.* **1.** Père nourricier. **2.** Père adoptif. **'foster-mother,** *s.f.* **1.** (Mère) nourricière; (mère) nourrice. **2.** Mère adoptive. **'foster-sister,** *s.f.* **1.** Sœur de lait. **2.** Sœur adoptive.

fought [fɔːt]. *See* FIGHT².

foul¹ [faul]. **I.** *a.* **1.** (*a*) Infect, nauséabond; méphitique. *F. air,* air vicié. *F. gas,* gaz toxique. (*b*) (*Of thoughts*) Immonde, impur; (*of language*) ordurier. *F. word,* gros mot. (*c*) (*Of deed*) Noir, infâme. Foul deed, infamie *f.* (*d*) *F*: What f. weather! quel sale temps! **2.** (*a*) (Linge) sale. Foul water, eau croupie. (*b*) (*Of sparking-plug*) Encrassé; (*of pump*) engorgé. *Nau*: (*Of ship*) Foul bottom, carène *f* sale. **3.** *Nau*: (*a*) (*Of anchor*) Engagé. Foul cable, tour *m* de chaîne. *To run foul of another ship,* aborder, entrer en collision avec, un autre navire. *F*: To fall foul of the law, tomber sous le coup de la loi. (*b*) Foul weather, gros temps. **4.** *Sp*: *etc*: Déloyal, -aux; illicite. Foul play, (i) *Sp*: jeu déloyal; (ii) malveillance *f.* Box: Foul blow, coup bas. **-lly,** *adv.* **1.** Salement. **2.** Abominablement, méchamment. *He was f. murdered,* il fut ignoblement assassiné. **II. foul,** *s.* *Sp*: Faute *f*; coup illicite, déloyal. *Fb*: Poussée irrégulière. *Box*: Coup bas. **foul-'mouthed,** *a.* (*Of pers.*) Mal embouché; grossier.

foul². **1.** *v.tr.* **1.** (*a*) Salir, souiller (sa réputation). (*b*) Encrasser (un canon de fusil). **2.** (*a*) Embarrasser, obstruer (une ligne de chemin de fer). *Nau*: Engager (une ancre). (*b*) *Nau*: (*Of ship*) Entrer en collision avec, aborder (un autre vaisseau). **II. foul,** *v.i.* **1.** (*Of gun-barrel*) S'encrasser; (*of pump*) s'engorger. **2.** *Nau*: (*Of anchor*) *To foul,* to become fouled, s'engager.

foulard [ˈfuːlaːr, fuˈlaːrd], *s.* *Tex*: *Cost*: Foulard *m.*

foulness ['faulnəs], s. **1.** (a) Impureté f (de l'air). (b) Saleté f, malpropreté f. **2.** Obscénité f (de langage). **3.** Infamie f, noirceur f (d'un acte).

found[1] [faund]. *See* FIND[2].

found[2], v.tr. (a) Fonder (une ville). (b) Fonder, créer (un collège); établir (une maison de commerce). **To found a family**, faire souche; faire tige. (c) Baser, fonder, appuyer (ses soupçons) (on, sur). (Of novel) **Founded on fact**, reposant sur des faits véridiques.

found[3], v.tr. Metall: Fondre (les métaux); mouler (la fonte).

foundation [faun'deiʃ(ə)n], s. **1.** (a) Fondation f (d'une ville); établissement m (d'une maison de commerce). (b) Fondation et dotation f (d'un hôpital). **2.** (a) Fondement m, fondation (d'un édifice); assiette f (d'une chaussée); assise f (d'une machine). *The foundations of a building*, les fondements d'un édifice. *To dig the foundations*, creuser les fondations. (b) *The foundations of music*, les bases f de la musique. *The foundations of modern society*, les assises f de la société moderne. **3.** *Embroidery on a silk f.*, broderie sur fond m de soie. **4.** Fondement, base (d'une théorie). *Statement wholly devoid of f.*, assertion de pure imagination. **5.** Institution dotée; fondation. *Sch:* Scholar on the foundation, élève boursier. **foun'dation-stone**, s. *Const:* Pierre fondamentale. **To lay the foundation-stone**, poser la première pierre.

founder[1] ['faundər], s. Fondateur m (d'une institution); souche f (d'une famille).

founder[2], s. Metall: Fondeur m.

founder[3], v.i. (a) (Of horse) (i) S'effondrer. (ii) *To f. in the mire*, s'embourber. (iii) Devenir fourbu. (b) Nau: (Of ship) Sombrer (en pleine mer); couler (bas, au fond). **foundered**, a. **1.** Vet: (Cheval) fourbu. **2.** (Navire) qui a sombré.

foundling ['faundliŋ], s. Enfant trouvé, -ée. *Adm:* Foundlings, enfants assistés. **Foundling hospital**, hospice m des enfants trouvés.

foundry ['faundri], s. Metalw: Fonderie f.

fount[1] [faunt], s. Poet: Lit: Source f (d'eau). F: **He is a fount of knowledge**, c'est un puits de science.

fount[2], s. Typ: Fonte f. **Wrong fount**, lettre f d'un autre œil.

fountain ['fauntən], s. **1.** Fontaine f. (a) A. & Lit: Source f (d'eau). F: Fountain of wisdom, source f de sagesse. (b) Jet m d'eau (de jardin public). **2.** Réservoir m (d'une lampe). **'fountain-head**, s. Source f (d'une rivière). F: **To go to the fountain-head**, puiser à la source. **'fountain-pen**, s. Porte-plume m inv (à) réservoir; stylographe m, F: stylo m.

four ['fɔːr], num. a. & s. Quatre (m). *Twenty is four times as much as five*, vingt est le quadruple de cinq. *Scattered to the four corners of the earth*, éparpillés aux quatre coins du monde. *Mil:* (Move) to the right in fours! à droite par quatre! *To run on all fours*, courir à quatre pattes. F: *To be on all fours with* . ., aller de pair avec. . . (For other phrases see EIGHT.) **'four-cleft**, a. Bot: Quadrifide. **four-'engined**, a. Av: Quadrimoteur. **four-figure**, attrib.a. Four-figure logarithms, logarithmes à quatre décimales. **'four-footed**, a. Quadrupède; à quatre pattes. **four-'handed**, a. **1.** (Singe) à quatre mains, quadrumane. **2.** (Jeu) à quatre (personnes). **four-'horse(d)**, a. (Véhicule) à quatre chevaux. **'four-in-hand**. **1.** s. Attelage m à quatre. **2.** adv. **To drive four-in-hand**, conduire à grandes guides. **'four-leaved**, a. Bot: Quadrifolié.

four-'master, s. Nau: Quatre-mâts m inv. **'four-oared**, a. (Canot) à quatre avirons. **'four-place**, attrib.a. (Logarithmes) à quatre décimales. **four-'poster**, s. Lit m à colonnes. **four-'seater**, s. Aut: Voiture f à quatre places. **'four-'square**, a. & adv. Solide(ment). **'four-wheel(ed)**, a. (Véhicule) à quatre roues. **fourfold** ['fɔːrfould]. **1.** a. (a) Quadruple. (b) Fourfold draught-screen, paravent à quatre feuilles. **2.** adv. Quatre fois autant; au quadruple.

fourscore ['fɔːrskɔːr], a. A. & Lit: Quatre-vingts.

foursome ['fɔːrsəm]. **1.** a. A quatre. Danc: Foursome reel, "reel" dansé à quatre. **2.** s. Golf: Partie f (de) double, à deux contre deux.

fourteen [fɔːr'tiːn], num. a. & s. Quatorze (m).

fourteenth [fɔːr'tiːnθ], num. a. & s. Quatorzième. **Louis the Fourteenth**, Louis Quatorze.

fourth ['fɔːrθ]. **1.** num. a. & s. Quatrième. *He arrived fourth or fifth*, il est arrivé quatre ou cinquième. *Sch:* The f. form, approx. = la classe de troisième. *Cards:* To make a fourth, faire le quatrième. **2.** s. (a) (Fractional) Quart m. (b) Mus: Quarte f. **-ly**, adv. Quatrièmement: en quatrième lieu.

fowl [faul], s. **1.** (a) Lit: Oiseau m; volatile m. **The fowls of the air**, les oiseaux des cieux. (b) Coll. Oiseaux. **Wild fowl**, gibier m d'eau. **2.** (a) Poule f, coq m; volaille f. **To keep fowls**, élever de la volaille. (b) Cu: Poulet m, volaille. **'fowl-house**, s. Poulailler m.

fowler ['faulər], s. Oiseleur m.

fowling ['fauliŋ], s. Chasse f aux oiseaux. **'fowling-piece**, s. Fusil m de chasse (à petit plomb).

fox[1] [fɔks], s. **1.** (*The female is* VIXEN, q.v.) Renard m. **She-fox**, renarde f. *Cost:* Fox fur, (fourrure f en) renard. F: **A sly fox**, un madré, un fin matois. **'fox-cub**, s. Renardeau m. **'fox-evil**, s. Med: Pelade f. **'fox-glove**, s. Bot: Digitale (pourprée). **'fox-hound**, s. Ven: Chien courant. **'fox-hunt**, s. Chasse f au renard. **'fox-hunter**, s. Chasseur m de renards. **'fox-hunting**, s. La chasse au renard. **fox-terrier**, s. F: Fox m.

fox[2]. **1.** v.tr. (a) Maculer, piquer (une gravure). (b) P: Mystifier, tromper (qn). **2.** v.i. F: Feindre; ruser. **foxed**, a. (Livre, papier) piqué; (estampe) maculée. **foxing**, s. **1.** Décoloration f, piqûre f (du papier). **2.** Piqûres; macules fpl (d'une estampe).

foxiness ['fɔksinəs], s. Astuce f, roublardise f.

foxtail ['fɔksteil], s. **1.** Queue f de renard. **2.** Bot: Vulpin m.

foxy ['fɔksi], a. **1.** Ruse, madré. **2.** (Of hair, complexion) Roux, f. rousse.

foyer ['twaje], s. **1.** Th: Foyer m (du public). **2.** Med: Foyer (d'infection).

fraction ['frakʃ(ə)n], s. **1.** Petite portion; fragment m. **2.** Mth: Fraction f; nombre m fractionnaire. **Vulgar fraction**, fraction ordinaire. **Improper fraction**, expression f fractionnaire.

fractional ['frakʃən(ə)l], a. **1.** Mth: etc: Fractionnaire. **F. part**, fraction f. **2.** Fractional distillation, distillation fractionnée.

fractious ['frakʃəs], a. (a) Difficile de caractère; revêche. (b) A f. baby, un bébé pleurnicheur. (c) (Cheval) difficile, rétif.

fractiousness ['frakʃəsnəs], s. (a) Humeur hargneuse; (of a baby) pleurnicherie f. (b) Rétivité f (d'un animal).

fracture[1] ['fraktiər], s. **1.** Fracture f (d'un os,

etc.). *Surg:* Compound fracture, fracture compliquée. **To set a fracture,** réduire une fracture. **2.** *Geol:* Cassure *f*, fracture.

fracture². **1.** *v.tr.* Casser, briser (qch.). *Surg:* Fracturer (un os). **2.** *v.i.* Se casser, se briser; (*of limb*) se fracturer.

fraenum ['fri:nʌm], *s.* *Anat:* Frein *m*, filet *m* (de la langue).

fragile ['fradʒail], *a.* Fragile; (*of pers.*) faible, miévre.

fragility [fra'dʒiliti], *s.* Fragilité *f*; (*of pers.*) faiblesse *f*; délicatesse *f* (de santé).

fragment ['fragmənt], *s.* Fragment *m*, morceau *m* (de papier, etc.); éclat *m* (d'obus); brin *m* (de papier). **Smashed to fragments,** réduit en fragments; brisé en mille morceaux.

fragmentary ['fragməntəri], *a.* Fragmentaire.

fragrance ['freigrəns], *s.* Parfum *m*; odeur *f* suave.

fragrant ['freigrənt], *a.* Parfumé, odorant.

frail¹ [freil], *a.* **1.** Fragile; frêle. **2.** (*a*) (*Of pers.*, *health*) Faible, délicat. **She's getting very frail,** elle commence à se casser. (*b*) (Femme) de vertu fragile.

frail², *s.* *Com:* Cabas *m*; panier *m* de jonc.

frailty ['freilti], *s.* Faiblesse morale; fragilité humaine.

frame¹ [freim], *s.* **1.** (*a*) Construction *f*, structure *f*, forme *f*. **Frame of mind,** disposition *f* d'esprit. (*b*) Système *m*, forme (de gouvernement). **2.** (*a*) Ossature *f* (d'un animal). **Man of gigantic *f.*,** homme d'une taille colossale. **Sobs shook her frame,** des sanglots lui secouaient le corps. (*b*) Charpente *f* (d'un bâtiment); bâti *m* (d'un moteur); cadre *m* (d'une bicyclette); châssis *m* (d'une automobile); monture (d'un parapluie); armature *f* (d'une raquette). (*c*) *N.Arch:* Membrure *f*, carcasse *f* (d'un navire). **3.** (*a*) Cadre, encadrement *m* (d'un tableau); (*b*) Chambranle *m*, châssis (d'une fenêtre). (*c*) *Cin:* Image *f* (de film). **Televis: Emission at 25 frames per second,** émission de 25 images par seconde. **4.** (*a*) Métier *m* (à broder, etc.); tambour *m* (à broder). (*b*) *Tex:* Métier (à filer). **5.** *Hort:* Châssis de couches. **'frame-saw,** *s.* *Tls:* Scie montée; scie à châssis.

frame², *v.tr.* **1.** Former, régler (ses pensées). *v.i.* **He is framing well,** il montre des dispositions. **2.** (*a*) Projeter (un dessein); charpenter (un roman, etc.). (*b*) Articuler, prononcer (un mot). **3.** (*a*) Imaginer, concevoir (une idée); se faire (une opinion). (*b*) Ourdir (un complot). *U.S:* *F:* **To frame s.o.,** monter une accusation contre qn. **4.** Encadrer (un tableau). **'frame-up,** *s.* *U.S:* *F:* Coup monté. **framing,** *s.* (*a*) Construction *f*, formation *f* (de qch.). (*b*) Composition *f* (d'un poème); conception *f* (d'une idée). (*c*) Articulation *f* (d'un mot). (*d*) Fabrication *f* (d'une fausse accusation). (*e*) Encadrement *m* (d'un tableau).

framer ['freimər], *s.* (**Picture-)framer,** encadreur *m*.

framework ['freimwə:rk], *s.* (*a*) Charpente *f*, ossature *f*, carcasse *f*. (*b*) Construction *f* en cloisonnage; coffrage *m* (de travaux en béton).

France [frɑ:ns]. *Pr.n.* *Geog:* La France. **In France,** en France.

Frances ['frɑ:nses]. *Pr.n.f.* Françoise.

franchise ['frantʃaiz], *s.* **1.** *Hist:* *Jur:* Franchise *f*, immunité *f*, privilège *m*. **2.** *Pol:* Droit *m* de vote.

Francis [frɑ:nsis]. *Pr.n.m.* François.

frangible ['frandʒibl], *a.* Cassant, fragile.

Frank¹ [fraŋk], *s.* *Hist:* Franc, *f.* Franque.

---

frank², *a.* Franc, *f.* franche; sincère. *To be quite f.,* parler franchement, à cœur ouvert. **-ly,** *adv.* Franchement; ouvertement.

frank³, *s.* *Post:* Marque *f* d'affranchissement.

frank⁴, *v.tr.* *Post:* Affranchir (une lettre). **franking,** *s.* Affranchissement *m.* **Franking machine,** machine à affranchir (les lettres).

Frank⁵. *Pr.n.m.* (*Dim. of Francis*) François.

frankincense ['fraŋkinsens], *s.* Encens *m* (mâle).

Frankish ['fraŋkiʃ], *a.* *Hist:* Franc, *f.* franque.

frankness ['fraŋknəs], *s.* Franchise *f*, sincérité *f.*

frantic ['frantik], *a.* **1.** Frénétique, forcené. **Frantic efforts, efforts effrénés.** *F.* **with joy,** fou de joie. *It drives him f.,* cela le met hors de lui. **2.** *P:* **Frantic toothache,** mal de dents affreux. **-ally,** *adv.* Frénétiquement.

fraternal [fra'tə:rn(ə)l], *a.* Fraternel. **-ally,** *adv.* Fraternellement.

fraternity [fra'tə:rniti], *s.* **1.** Fraternité *f.* **2.** Confrérie *f.*

fraternize ['fratərna:iz], *v.i.* Fraterniser (*with,* avec). **fraternizing,** *s.* Fraternisation *f* (*with,* avec).

fratricidal [fratri'said(ə)l], *a.* (Guerre) fratricide.

fratricide¹ ['fratrisaid], *s.* Fratricide *mf.*

fratricide², *s.* (Crime *m* de) fratricide *m.*

fraud [frɔ:d], *s.* **1.** (*a*) *Jur:* Fraude *f*, dol *m.* (*b*) Supercherie *f*, tromperie *f.* **Pious fraud,** pieux mensonge. **2.** *F:* (*a*) Imposteur *m.* **He's a fraud,** c'est un fumiste. (*b*) Chose *f* qui ne répond pas à l'attente.

fraudulence ['frɔ:djuləns], *s.* (*a*) Caractère frauduleux (d'une transaction). (*b*) Infidélité *f* (d'un dépositaire).

fraudulent ['frɔ:djulənt], *a.* Frauduleux. **-ly,** *adv.* Frauduleusement.

fraught [frɔ:t], *a.* **1.** *A:* Pourvu, muni (*with,* de). **2.** *Lit:* (*a*) *Remarks f.* **with malice,** observations pleines de méchanceté. (*b*) *Decision f.* **with far-reaching consequences,** décision grosse de conséquences.

fray¹ [frei], *s.* **1.** Bagarre *f*, échauffouree *f.* **2.** *Lit:* Combat *m.* **Always ready for the fray,** toujours prêt à se battre.

fray². **1.** *v.tr.* Érailler, effiler (un tissu). *F:* **My nerves are frayed out,** je suis à bout de nerfs. **2.** *v.i.* (*Of tissue*) S'érailler, s'effiler.

frazzle ['frazl], *s.* *P:* **To beat s.o. to a frazzle,** battre qn à plates coutures.

freak [fri:k], *s.* **1.** Caprice *m*; *F:* lubie *f.* **Freaks of fashion,** caprices de la mode. **Freak of fortune,** jeu *m* de la fortune, du hasard. **2.** Tour *m*, farce *f*, fredaine *f*, frasque *f.* **3.** **Freak** (**of nature**), (i) *Nat.Hist:* variation sportive; (ii) *F:* phénomène *m*, curiosité *f.* **4.** *Attrib.* *F:* **Freak religion,** religion de fantaisie.

freakish ['fri:kiʃ], *a.* Capricieux, fantasque, bizarre. *F.* **notion,** fantaisie *f.* **-ly,** *adv.* Capricieusement, bizarrement.

freakishness ['fri:kiʃnəs], *s.* Caractère *m* fantasque, baroque, bizarre (de qch.).

freckle ['frekl], *s.* Tache *f* de rousseur.

freckle². **1.** *v.tr.* Marquer (la peau) de taches de rousseur. **2.** *v.i.* Se couvrir de taches de rousseur. **freckled,** *a.* Taché de rousseur; *F:* taché de son.

free¹ [fri:], *a. & adv.* **1.** (*a*) Libre. *Nau:* **Free port,** port franc. **Thought is f.,** on ne saurait entraver la pensée. **Man is a free agent,** l'homme est libre. (*b*) En liberté. *To set a slave f.,* affranchir un esclave. *To set a bird f.,* laisser envoler un oiseau. *To set f. a prisoner,* élargir un prisonnier. **She offered to set him free,** elle lui proposa de lui rendre sa parole. **2.** (*Unoccupied*) Libre. **Is**

this table free? est-ce que cette table est libre? *Tg : Tp :* **Free line**, ligne dégagée. **3.** (*a*) **Free speech**, libre parole. **Right of free entry**, droit de passer librement les frontières. **To have a free hand**, avoir ses coudées franches (*to, pour*). **To give s.o. a free hand**, donner carte blanche à qn. *You are f. to do so*, libre à vous de le faire. *He is not f. to act*, il a les mains liées. **Fishing is free**, la pêche est autorisée. (*b*) (*Of touch, style, etc.*) Franc, *f.* franche ; sans raideur ; souple. (*c*) *Mec.E :* **Free motion** *of a piece*, jeu *m* d'une pièce. (*d*) **Free from sth., of sth.**, débarrassé, exempt, de qch. *To be f. from care*, être sans souci. *F. from all preoccupations*, affranchi de toute préoccupation. **Place free from dust**, endroit exempt de poussière. **Style free from affectation**, style dénué de toute recherche. **At last I am free of him**, enfin je suis débarrassé de lui. **To break free from an influence**, s'affranchir d'une influence. (*e*) Franc (*of, de*). *Cust :* **Free of duty, duty-free**, exempt de droits d'entrée. *To import free.* *f. of duty*, faire entrer qch. en franchise. **Free list**, liste d'exemptions. **4.** (*a*) *Ch : etc :* (*Of gas, etc.*) (A l'état) libre, non-combiné. **Free gold**, or à l'état natif. (*b*) (*Of power, energy*) Libre, disponible. **5.** (*a*) **Free offer**, offre spontanée. **Free choice**, choix arbitraire. **As a free gift**, en pur don. *Pros :* **Free verse**, vers libres. *You are very f. in blaming others*, vous blâmez volontiers les autres. (*b*) Libéral, généreux. *To be f. with sth.*, donner libéralement de qch. **To be free with one's money**, ne pas regarder à l'argent. **To be free with one's hands**, avoir la main leste. (*c*) (*Of pers., manner*) Franc, ouvert, aisé. **Free and easy**, désinvolte ; sans gêne. *F. and easy tone*, ton dégagé. (*d*) **To make free with s.o.**, prendre des libertés avec qn. **To make free with sth.**, user librement de qch. (*e*) (*Of language*) Libre, licencieux. **6.** **To be free of s.o.'s house**, avoir ses entrées libres chez qn. **7.** Gratuit ; franco *inv.* **Admission free**, entrée gratuite, gratis. *Th : etc :* **Free ticket**, billet de faveur. *Com :* **Delivery free**, livré franco. **Post free**, franco de port. **Free on rail**, franco gare. **Free alongside ship**, franco quai. **Free on board** (*abbr.* f.o.b.), franco à bord. **8.** *adv.* (*a*) **Catalogue sent free on request**, catalogue franco sur demande. *The gallery is open free on Saturdays*, l'entrée du musée est gratuite le samedi. (*b*) *Vessel running f.*, navire courant largue. **-ly**, *adv.* **I.** Librement, volontairement. *To give f. to s.o.*, faire des libéralités à qn. **2.** (Parler) franchement, sans contrainte. **'free-board**, *s.* *Nau :* Franc-bord *m.* **'free-born**, *a.* Né libre. **'Free 'Church**, *s.* Église *f* non-conformiste ; Église libre. **'free-hand**, *a. & s.* Free-hand (drawing), dessin *m* à main levée. **free-'handed**, *a.* Généreux. **'free 'lance**, *s.* Journaliste ou politicien indépendant. **free-'spoken**, *a.* Franc, *f.* franche ; qui a son franc-parler. **free-'thinker**, *s.* Libre penseur ; esprit fort. **free-'thinking, free-'thought**, *s.* Libre pensée *f.* **free 'trade**, *s.* Libre-échange *m.* **free-'trader**, *s.* Libre-échangiste *m.* **'free 'wheel**, *s.* *Cy :* Roue *f* libre. **'free-'wheel**, *v.i.* **I.** *Cy :* Faire roue libre. **2.** *Aut :* Marcher, rouler, en roue libre. **'free 'will**, *s.* Libre arbitre *m.* **Of one's own free will**, de (son) propre gré. **Free-will offering**, don volontaire.

free², *v.tr.* (freed ; freeing) (*a*) Affranchir (un peuple) ; libérer, élargir (un prisonnier). *To f. oneself from s.o.'s grasp*, se dégager des mains de qn. *To f. oneself from one's commitments*, se délier de tous ses engagements. (*b*) Débarrasser (*from,*

of, de) ; dégager (un sentier). (*c*) *Mec.E :* Dégager (une pièce). (*d*) Décolmater, désobstruer (un filtre). (*e*) **To free a property (from mortgage)**, déshypothéquer une propriété.

freebooter ['fri:bu:tər], *s.* **I.** *Hist :* Flibustier *m.* **2.** *F :* Maraudeur *m* ; pillard *m.*

freedom ['fri:dəm], *s.* **I.** (*a*) Liberté *f*, indépendance *f.* (*b*) Liberté d'action ; liberté d'agir, de penser. **Freedom of speech**, le franc-parler. **2.** (*a*) Franchise *f*, familiarité *f* (d'une conversation, du style). (*b*) Sans-gêne *m.* **To take freedoms with s.o.**, prendre des libertés avec qn. **3.** (*Of action*) Facilité *f*, souplesse *f.* **4.** (*a*) Exemption *f*, immunité *f* (*from*, de). (*b*) **Freedom of the city**, droit *m* de cité. **5.** Jouissance *f*, libre usage *m* (de qch.).

freehold ['fri:hould]. **I.** *a.* Tenu en propriété perpétuelle et libre. **2.** *s.* Propriété foncière libre.

freeholder ['fri:houldər], *s.* Propriétaire foncier (à perpétuité).

freeman, *pl.* **-men** ['fri:mən, -men], *s.m.* **I.** Homme libre. **2.** Citoyen.

freemason [fri:'meisn], *s.* Franc-maçon *m*, *pl.* francs-maçons.

freemasonry [fri:'meisnri], *s.* Franc-maçonnerie *f.*

freestone ['fri:stoun], *s.* Pierre *f* de taille ; grès *m* à bâtir.

freeze [fri:z], *v.* (froze [fro:uz] ; frozen [fro:uzn]) Geler. **I.** *v.i.* (*a*) *Impers :* **It is freezing hard**, il gèle à pierre fendre. (*b*) (Se) geler ; se congeler ; prendre. **The river has, is, frozen (up)**, la rivière est prise. *The radiator froze (up)*, le radiateur s'est congelé. *U.S :* *F :* **To freeze on to s.o.**, (i) se coller, se cramponner, à qn ; (ii) s'attacher à qn. **The smile froze on his lips**, le sourire se figea sur les lèvres. (*c*) **To freeze to death**, mourir de froid. **2.** *v.tr.* (*a*) Geler, congeler (qch.). **To freeze the blood (in one's veins)**, glacer le sang, le cœur. (*b*) *Fin :* "Geler" (des crédits, des devises). **freeze out**, *v.tr.* *F :* Évincer (qn) ; supplanter (un rival). (*b*) Boycotter (qn). **frozen**, *a.* Gelé, glacé. *Com :* **Frozen meat**, viande congelée. *Fin :* *F :* **Frozen assets**, fonds non liquides. *F :* **Credits**, crédits gelés, congelés. *F :* *I am f. to death*, je meurs de froid. **freezing**, *s.* **I.** Congélation *f* ; gel *m.* *Ph :* **Freezing-point**, point *m* de congélation. **2.** Réfrigération *f.* **'freezing-mixture**, *s.* Mélange réfrigérant.

freight¹ [freit], *s.* **I.** (*a*) Fret *m* ; nolis *m* (d'un navire). (*b*) Transport *m* (de marchandises). **2.** (*a*) Fret, cargaison *f.* *To take in f.*, prendre du fret. (*b*) *U.S :* **Freight train**, train de marchandises. **3.** Fret ; prix *m* du louage d'un bâtiment, du transport de marchandises.

freight², *v.tr.* Fréter, affréter, noliser (un navire).

freightage ['freitedʒ], *s.* **I.** Affrètement *m.* **2.** Fret *m*, cargaison *f.* **3.** Transport *m* des marchandises par voie d'eau.

freighter ['freitər], *s.* **I.** Affréteur *m* (d'un vaisseau). **2.** Cargo *m* ; vapeur *m* de charge.

French [frenʃ]. **I.** *a.* **I.** (*a*) Français. *F. king*, roi de France. *F. emperor*, empereur des Français. (*b*) (*Of fashion, etc.*) A la française. (*c*) *Sch :* **French lesson**, leçon *f* de français. **French master**, professeur de français. **To take French leave**, filer à l'anglaise ; brûler la politesse à qn. **II.** **French**, *s.* **I.** Le français ; la langue française. *To speak F.*, parler français. *Say it in F.*, dites-le en français. **2.** *pl.* **The French**, les Français. **'french 'chalk**, *s.* Talc *m* ; craie *f* de tailleur. **'french 'polish¹**, *s.* Vernis *m* au

tampon, à l'alcool. 'french-'polish², *v.tr.* Vernir (un meuble) au tampon. 'French 'window, *s.* Porte-fenêtre *f*, *pl.* portes-fenêtres. **Frenchify** ['frenʃifai], *v.tr.* Franciser (son style, etc.). *Frenchified ways*, manières à la française. **Frenchman,** *pl.* -men ['frenʃmən, -men], *s.m.* Français. **Frenchwoman,** *pl.* -women ['frenʃwumən, -wimen], *s.f.* Française. **frenzied** ['frenzid], *a.* (*Of pers.*) Affolé, forcené ; (*of joy*) frénétique, délirant. **frenzy** ['frenzi], *s.* **1.** Frénésie *f.* Frenzy of joy, transport *m* de joie. *Poetic f.*, fureur *f* poétique. **2.** *Med :* Délire *m.* **frequency** ['fri:kwənsi], *s.* Fréquence *f. W.Tel :* To change the frequency, changer la fréquence. **frequent¹** ['fri:kwənt], *a.* **1.** (*a*) Nombreux, abondant. *It is quite a f. practice*, c'est une coutume assez répandue. (*b*) *Med :* Frequent pulse, pouls rapide. **2.** Fréquent ; qui arrive souvent. -ly, *adv.* Fréquemment. **frequent²** [fri'kwent], *v.tr.* Fréquenter, hanter, courir (les théâtres). *A much frequented road*, une route très passante. To frequent the sacraments, fréquenter les sacrements. **frequentation** [fri:kwən'teiʃ(ə)n], *s.* Fréquentation *f* (de qn, des sacrements). **frequenter** [fri'kwentər], *s.* Habitué *m*, familier *m* (d'une maison). **fresco,** *pl.* -o(e)s ['fresko(z)], *s. Art :* Fresque *f.* To paint in fresco, peindre à fresque. Fresco painting, (peinture *f* à) fresque. **fresh** [freʃ]. I. *a.* **1.** (*a*) Nouveau, -el, -elle. Fresh paragraph, nouveau paragraphe. Fresh horses, chevaux frais. To put fresh courage into s.o., ranimer le courage de qn. To admit fresh air into a room, renouveler l'air d'une salle. He has had a fresh attack of gout, la goutte l'a repris. (*b*) Frais, *f.* fraîche ; récent. *It is still f. in my memory*, j'en ai le souvenir tout frais. Fresh from London, nouvellement arrivé de Londres. The bread was fresh from the oven, le pain sortait du four. **2.** Inexpérimenté, novice. **3.** (*a*) (Beurre) frais ; (légume) vert. (*b*) (Air) frais, pur. Fresh water, (i) (*newly drawn*) eau fraîche ; (ii) (*not salt*) eau douce. In the fresh air, au grand air, en plein air. **4.** (*a*) (Teint) frais, fleuri. As fresh as a daisy, frais comme une rose. (*b*) (*Of pers.*) Vigoureux, alerte ; (*of horse*) fougueux. (*c*) *U.S :* F: Outrecuidant, effronté. **5.** *Nau :* Fresh breeze, jolie brise. *adv.* It blows fresh, il vente frais. **6.** F: (*Of pers.*) Éméché ; un peu gris. -ly, *adv.* Nouvellement. II. fresh, *adv.* Fraîchement, nouvellement, récemment. Fresh-cut flowers, fleurs nouvellement cueillies. Fresh-shaven, rasé de frais. III. fresh, *s.* (*a*) Crue *f.* (*b*) Descente *f* d'eau (de fonte des neiges, etc.) ; avalaison *f.* 'fresh-'coloured, *a.* (Visage) au teint frais. 'fresh-'killed, *a.* (Bétail) fraîchement tué. **freshen** ['freʃ(ə)n]. **1.** *v.i.* (*a*) (*Of temperature*) (Se) rafraîchir. (*b*) (*Of wind*) Fraîchir. **2.** *v.tr.* Rafraîchir (la mémoire). *F:* To freshen s.o. up, requinquer qn. **fresher** ['freʃər], *s. F:* = FRESHMAN. **freshet** ['freʃet], *s.* Avalaison *f.* **freshman,** *pl.* -men ['freʃmən, -men], *s.m. & f.* (*At university*) Étudiant de première année. **freshness** ['freʃnəs], *s.* **1.** Caractère récent (d'un événement). **2.** Fraîcheur *f.* **3.** (*Of pers.*) (*a*) Vigueur *f*, vivacité *f.* (*b*) Naïveté *f*, inexpérience *f.* (*c*) *U.S :* F: Effronterie *f*, toupet *m.* **freshwater** ['freʃwɔːtər], *attrib.a.* (Poisson)

d'eau douce. *F :* Freshwater sailor, marin d'eau douce. **fret¹** [fret], *s.* **1.** *Arch :* (Greek) fret, grecque *f* ; frette *f.* **2.** *Her :* Frette. 'fret-saw, *s.* Scie *f* à découper. **fret²,** *s. Mus :* Touchette *f*, touche *f* (de guitare). **fret³,** *s.* Irritation *f* ; état *m* d'agacement. To be in a fret, se faire du mauvais sang ; se tracasser. **fret⁴,** *v.* (fretted) **1.** *v.tr.* (*a*) Ronger (qch.). Horse that frets its bit, cheval qui ronge son mors. *The stream has fretted a channel through the rock*, le ruisseau a creusé un chenal dans le roc. (*b*) Inquiéter, tracasser (qn). (*c*) Faire bouillonner (un ruisseau). **2.** *v.pr. & i.* (*a*) To fret (oneself), se tourmenter ; se faire du mauvais sang. *Don't f.!* ne vous faites pas de bile ! *Child fretting for its mother*, enfant qui pleurniche après sa mère, qui demande sa mère. To fret and fume, enrager ; se faire du mauvais sang. (*b*) (*Of stream*) S'agiter, bouillonner. **fretful** ['fretful], *a.* Chagrin ; irritable. *F. old age*, vieillesse chagrine. *F. baby*, bébé agité. -fully, *adv.* Chagrinement ; avec irritation. **fretfulness** ['fretfulnəs], *s.* Irritabilité *f.* **fretwork** ['fretwəːk], *s. Woodw :* Travail ajouré ; bois découpé. **friability** [fraiə'biliti], **friableness** ['fraiəblnəs], *s.* Friabilité *f.* **friable** ['fraiəbl], *a.* Friable. **friar** ['fraiər], *s.* Moine *m*, frère *m*, religieux *m.* 'friar's 'balsam, *s. Pharm :* Baume *m* de benjoin. **friary** ['fraiəri], *s.* Monastère *m* ; couvent *m* (de moines). **fricassee¹** [frika'siː], *s. Cu :* Fricassée *f.* **fricassee²,** *v.tr.* Fricasser. **friction** ['frikʃ(ə)n], *s.* **1.** *Med : Toil :* Friction *f.* **2.** Frottement *m* (de deux corps). *Av :* Friction of the air, frottement de l'air. **3.** *F :* Désaccord *m.* There is friction between them, il y a du tirage entre eux. 'friction-clutch, *s. Mec.E :* Embrayage *m* à friction. **Friday** ['fraidi], *s.* Vendredi *m. He is coming on F.*, il viendra vendredi. *He comes on Fridays*, il vient le vendredi. Good Friday, (le) Vendredi saint. **fried** [fraid]. *See* FRY³. **friend** [frend], *s.* **1.** Ami, *f.* amie. Bosom friend, un(e) ami(e) de cœur ; un(e) intime. *F :* To be friends with s.o., être lié (d'amitié) avec qn ; *F :* être ami avec qn. To be out of friends, not to be friends, with s.o., bouder qn. To make friends with s.o., se lier d'amitié avec qn. *F :* You'd better keep friends with them, vous ferez bien de ne pas vous brouiller avec eux. He is no friend of mine, (i) il n'est pas de mes amis ; (ii) il ne me veut pas de bien. *Prov :* The best of friends must part, il n'est si bonne compagnie qui ne se sépare. A friend in need is a friend indeed, c'est dans le besoin qu'on connaît ses véritables amis. **2.** Connaissance *f. F :* A friend at court, un ami en haut lieu. To have friends at court, avoir de la protection, des protections. *To dine with a few friends*, dîner en petit comité. Friend Robinson, notre ami Robinson. *Parl :* My honourable friend, *Jur :* my learned friend, mon (cher) confrère. **3.** (*a*) Friend of the poor, bienfaiteur, -trice, des pauvres. (*b*) Ami, partisan *m* (de l'ordre, etc.) ; patron, -onne (des arts, etc.). **4.** The Society of Friends, la Société des Amis ; les Quakers. **friendless** ['frendləs], *a.* Délaissé ; sans amis.

friendliness ['frendlinəs], *s.* Bienveillance *f*, bonté *f* (*to, towards*, envers).

friendly ['frendli], *a.* **1.** (Ton, sentiment) amical, -aux ; sympathique. *F. gathering*, réunion d'amis. *To be f. with s.o.*, être ami avec qn. *In a f. manner*, amicalement. **To be on friendly terms with s.o.**, être en bons rapports, en relations d'amitié, avec qn. *Sp: F. match*, match amical. **2.** (*Of pers.*) Bienveillant, favorablement disposé ; favorable. *F. winds*, vents propices. **3.** *Friendly society*, association *f* de bienfaisance.

friendship ['frendʃip], *s.* Amitié *f. I did it out of f.*, je l'ai fait par amitié.

Friesian ['friːziən], *a. & s.* = FRISIAN.

Friesland ['friːzlənd]. *Pr.n. Geog:* La Frise.

frieze¹ [friːz], *s. Tex:* Frise *f*, ratine *f.*

frieze², *s.* **1.** *Arch:* Frise *f.* **2.** Bordure *f* (de papier ou de tenture).

frigate ['friget], *s. Navy: Orn:* Frégate *f.*

fright [frait], *s.* **1.** Peur *f*, effroi *m.* **To take fright**, s'effrayer, s'effarer (*at*, de). **To give s.o. a fright**, faire peur à qn. **2.** *F: (Esp. of woman)* Personne *f* laide, grotesque ; épouvantail *m*, -ails.

frighten [fraitn], *v.tr.* Effrayer (qn) ; faire peur à (qn). *F:* **To frighten s.o. out of his wits**, faire une peur bleue à qn. **To frighten s.o. into doing sth.**, faire faire qch. à qn sous le coup de la peur. **frighten away, off**, *v.tr. The dog frightened the thieves away*, le chien a fait décamper les voleurs. *Don't f. away the birds*, n'effarouchez pas les oiseaux. **frightened**, *a. (Of pers., etc.)* Apeuré, épeuré. **Easily frightened**, peureux, poltron. **To be, feel, frightened**, avoir peur. **To be frightened to death**, mourir de peur. **To be frightened at, of, sth.**, avoir peur de qch.

frightening, *a.* Effrayant.

frightful ['fraitful], *a.* Terrible, effroyable, affreux, épouvantable. *F: To have a f. headache*, avoir un mal de tête affreux. **-fully**, *adv.* Terriblement, effroyablement, affreusement. *F:* I am frightfully sorry, je regrette énormément.

frightfulness ['fraitfulnəs], *s.* **1.** Horreur *f*, atrocité *f* (d'un crime, etc.). **2.** *Policy of* "frightfulness," politique de terrorisme *m*.

frigid ['fridʒid], *a. (a)* Glacial, -als ; (très) froid. *(b) F. answer*, réponse glacée. **-ly**, *adv.* Glacialement ; très froidement.

frigidity [fri'dʒiditi], *s.* Frigidité *f* ; grande froideur.

frigorific [frigo'rifik], *a.* Frigorifique.

frill¹ [fril], *s. (a) Cost:* Volant *m*, ruche *f.* Toby frill, collerette plissée ; fraise *f.* **Shirt frill**, jabot *m. Cu: (Cutlet, ham)* frill, papillote *f.* *(b) pl. F:* **To put on frills**, faire des façons ; poser.

frill², *v.tr.* Plisser, froncer, tuyauter (le linge).

fringe¹ [frindʒ], *s.* **1.** *Tex:* Frange *f.* **2.** *(a)* Bordure *f*, bord *m.* **The outer fringe(s) of London**, la banlieue excentrique de Londres. **To live on the fringe of society**, vivre en marge de la société. *(b) Toil:* (Grecian) fringe, devant *m* de cheveux ; cheveux *mpl* à la chien.

fringe², *v.tr.* Franger (un tapis, etc.). *Eyes fringed with black lashes*, yeux bordés, frangés, de cils noirs. **fringing**, *a.* Marginal, -aux ; (récif, etc.) en bordure.

frippery ['fripəri], *s.* Parure *f* sans valeur ; camelote *f* ; (*of style, etc.*) clinquant *m.*

Frisian ['friziən], *a. & s. Geog:* Frison, -onne.

frisk [frisk]. **1.** *v.i.* **To frisk** (about), (*of lambs, etc.*) s'ébattre ; faire des cabrioles. **2.** *v.tr. (Of dog, etc.)* **To frisk its tail**, frétiller de la queue.

friskiness ['friskinəs], *s.* Folâtrerie *f*, vivacité *f.*

frisky ['friski], *a.* Vif, folâtre ; (cheval) fringant. **-ily**, *adv.* Folâtrement.

fritillary [fri'tiləri], *s.* **1.** *Bot:* Fritillaire *f.* **2.** *Ent:* Damier *m.*

fritter¹ ['fritər], *s. Cu:* Beignet *m*, roussette *f.*

fritter², *v.tr.* **To fritter** (sth.) away, down, morceler (qch.) ; réduire (qch.) à rien. *To f. away one's money*, gaspiller son argent.

frivol ['friv(ə)l], *v.* (frivolled) *F:* **1.** *v.i.* Baguenauder, muser. **2.** *v.tr.* **To frivol away one's time**, gaspiller son temps.

frivolity [fri'vɔliti], *s.* Frivolité *f.*

frivolous ['frivələs], *a.* Frivole ; (*of claim, etc.*) vain, futile ; (*of pers.*) baguenaudier, évaporé. **-ly**, *adv.* Frivolement.

frizz [friz]. **1.** *v.tr.* Crêper, bichonner (les cheveux). **2.** *v.i. (Of hair)* Frisotter.

frizziness ['frizinəs], *s.* Crêpelure *f* (des cheveux).

frizzle [frizl]. **1.** *v.i. (a)* Grésiller, chanter (dans la poêle). *(b)* Crépiter. **2.** *v.tr. Cu: (a)* Faire frire (le lard, etc.). *(b)* Griller (le lard, etc.).

frizzy ['frizi], *a. (Of hair)* Crêpelé, frisotté.

fro [frou], *adv.* **To and fro**, *see* TO III. 2.

frock [frɔk], *s. Cost:* **1.** Robe *f* (d'enfant, de femme). **2.** *(a)* Froc *m* (de moine). *(b)* Blouse *f*, sarrau *m* (de paysan, d'ouvrier). **'frock-'coat,** *s.* Redingote *f.*

frog¹ [frog], *s.* **1.** Grenouille *f.* **2.** *Med:* Aphte *m. F:* **To have a frog in one's throat**, avoir un chat dans la gorge, dans le gosier. **'frog('s)-march,** *v.tr.* Porter (qn) à quatre, le derrière en l'air.

frog², *s. Farr:* Fourchette *f* (du sabot).

frog³, *s. Mil: etc:* **1.** Porte-épée *m inv* ; porte-baïonnette *m inv.* **2.** *Cost:* Soutache *f*, olive *f.*

frog⁴, *s. Rail:* (Cœur *m* de) croisement *m.*

frogged [frogd], *a. Cost:* A brandebourgs.

frolic¹ ['frɔlik], *s. (a)* Ébats *mpl*, gambades *fpl.* *(b)* Fredaine *f*, divertissement *m.*

frolic², *v.i.* (frolicked) Se divertir, s'ébattre, folâtrer. **frolicking**, *s.* Divertissement *m*, ébats *mpl.*

frolicsome ['frɔliksəm], *a.* Gai, joyeux, folâtre.

from [frɔm], *prep.* **1.** De. *To go f. home*, partir de chez soi ; quitter la maison. *From . . . to . . ., de . . . à . . .* ; depuis . . . jusqu'à . . . *F. flower to flower*, de fleur en fleur. *Wines from one franc a bottle*, vins depuis, à partir de, un franc la bouteille. **2.** Depuis, dès, à partir de. *From the earliest records onward*, à partir des plus anciens documents. *As from . . .*, à partir de . . . . *F. his childhood*, *f. a child*, depuis, dès, son enfance. *From time to time*, de temps en temps. **3.** *He is* (away, absent) *from home*, il est absent, sorti, en voyage. *Not far f. . . .*, pas loin de . . . **4.** *(a)* De, à. *Take that knife f. that child*, ôtez ce couteau à cet enfant. *He stole a pound f. her*, il lui a volé une livre. *To dissuade s.o. f. doing sth.*, dissuader qn de faire qch. *(b)* **To shelter f. the rain**, s'abriter contre la pluie. **5.** *(a)* **From bad to worse**, de mal en pis. *The price has been increased from sixpence to a shilling*, on a augmenté le prix de six pence à un shilling. *(b)* D'avec, de. *To distinguish the good f. the bad*, distinguer le bon d'avec le mauvais. *(c)* **To pick s.o. out from the crowd**, démêler qn parmi la foule. *To drink f. the brook*, boire au ruisseau. **6.** *(a) He is, comes, f. Manchester*, il est natif de, originaire de, Manchester. *Air-lines to and from the Continent*, lignes aériennes à destination ou en provenance du Continent. *Broadcast commentary (on the Derby) f. Epsom*, radio-reportage émanant d'Epsom, depuis Epsom. *A quotation f. Shakespeare*, une citation tirée de Shakespeare. **To**

draw a conclusion from sth., tirer une conclusion de qch. *To write f. s.o.'s dictation*, écrire sous la dictée de qn. *From your point of view*, à votre point de vue. *(b) A letter f. my father*, une lettre de mon père. *The petition is f. . . .*, la pétition émane de. . . . *A dispatch f. the colonel*, une dépêche de la part du colonel. *Tell him that from 'me*, dites-lui cela de ma part. *(On parcel)* *From . . .*, envoi de. . . . *(c) Painted from life, from nature*, peint d'après nature. **7.** *To act from conviction*, agir par conviction. *To die from fatigue*, mourir de fatigue. *From what I heard . . .*, d'après ce que j'ai entendu dire. . . . *From what I can see . . .*, à ce que je vois. . . . **8.** *(With adv., prep.) From above*, d'en haut. *I saw him from afar*, je l'ai vu de loin. *He went from hence, from thence*, il est parti d'ici, de là. *From henceforth*, à partir d'aujourd'hui. *To look at s.o. f. under, f. over, one's spectacles*, regarder qn par-dessous, par-dessus, ses lunettes. *From of old*, du temps jadis, du vieux temps.

frond [frɔnd], *s. Bot:* **1.** Fronde *f* (de fougère). **2.** *F:* Feuille *f* (de palmier).

front¹ [frʌnt]. I. *s.* **1.** *(a)* Front *m*, contenance *f*. *Front to front*, face à face. *To put a bold front on it*, faire bonne contenance. *(b)* **To have the front to do sth.**, avoir l'effronterie, le front, de faire qch. **2.** *Mil:* Front (d'une armée). *To present an unbroken front*, présenter un front inentamé. *At the Front*, au front, sur le front. **3.** *(a)* Devant *m*, partie antérieure ; façade *f*, face *f* (d'un bâtiment) ; montre *f* (d'un orgue) ; devant, plastron *m* (de chemise). *Carriage in the f. of the train*, voiture en tête du train. *To look at the f. of sth.*, regarder qch. de face. *Fenc:* To show less front, s'effacer. *(b)* = SEA-FRONT. *House on the front*, maison faisant face à la mer. **4.** *To push one's way to the f.*, se frayer un chemin jusqu'au premier rang. *F:* **To come to the front**, arriver au premier rang ; percer ; se'faire connaître. **5.** *Adv.phr.* **In front**, devant, en avant. *To send s.o. on in front*, envoyer qn en avant. *Attacked in front and rear*, attaqué par devant et par derrière. **In front of**, (i) en face de, vis-à-vis de ; (ii) devant. *Look in f. of you*, regardez devant vous. II. **front**, *a.* Antérieur, de devant, d'avant, de face. *F. seat*, siège au premier rang. *In the f. part of the train*, en tête du train. **Front rank**, premier rang. **Front-line soldiers**, soldats du front. **'front-brake**, *s. Cy:* Frein *m* avant. **'front-'door**, *s.* Porte *f* d'entrée (principale) ; porte sur la rue. **'front 'page**, *s. Journ:* Première page. **'front-room**, *s.* Chambre *f* sur le devant, sur la rue. **'front-'view**, *s.* Vue *f* de face. *Arch:* Élévation *f*.

front². **1.** *v.tr. & i.* *To front sth.; to front (up)on, to(wards)*, sth., faire face à qch. ; être tourné vers qch. *Windows that f. the street*, fenêtres qui donnent sur la rue. **2.** *v.tr.* *To front s.o. with sth.*, confronter qn avec qn. **3.** *v.tr.* Donner une (nouvelle) façade à (un édifice). *House fronted with stone*, maison avec façade en pierre. **4.** *Mil:* *(a) v.i.* Faire front. *Left front!* à gauche front ! *(b) v.tr.* Établir le front de (l'armée, etc.).

frontage ['frʌnted̥ʒ], *s.* **1.** Terrain *m* en bordure (d'une chaussée, etc.). **2.** *(a)* Étendue *f* du devant (d'un édifice, etc.) ; devanture *f* (d'un magasin). *(b)* Façade *f* (sur la rue).

frontal ['frʌnt(ə)l], *a.* **1.** *Anat:* Frontal, -aux. **2.** *Mil:* (Attaque, etc.) de front. **-ally**, *adv.* De front.

frontier ['frʌntiər, frɔnt-], *s.* Frontière *f.*

Frontier town, ville *f* frontière. **Frontier districts**, régions frontalières, de la frontière.

frontier(s)man, *pl.* **-men** ['frʌntiər(z)mən, frɔn-, -men], *s.m.* Frontalier.

frontispiece ['frʌntispiːs], *s. Typ:* Frontispice *m.*

fronton ['frʌntən], *s. Arch:* Fronton *m.*

frost¹ [frɔst], *s.* **1.** *(a)* Gelée *f*, gel *m.* *Ground frost, white frost*, gelée blanche. *F:* **Jack Frost**, le bonhomme Hiver. *Ten degrees of f.*, dix degrés de froid. *(b)* (Hoar) frost, givre *m* ; *Lit:* frimas *m.* Glazed frost, verglas *m.* **2.** *F:* Four *m*, fiasco *m.* *The play was a dead frost*, ç'a été un four noir. **'frost-bite**, *s.* **1.** *Med:* Gelure *f.* **2.** *Agr: Hort:* Brûlure *f* par la gelée. **'frost-bitten**, *a.* **1.** *(Of nose, etc.)* Gelé. **2.** *(Of plants)* Brûlé par le froid. **'frost-shoe¹**, *s.* *Farr:* Fer *m* à glace, à crampons. **'frost-shoe²**, *v.tr.* *Farr:* Ferrer (un cheval) à glace. **'frost-work**, *s.* Fleurs *fpl* de givre.

frost², *v.tr.* **1.** Geler (un arbre fruitier). **2.** *(a)* Givrer (les vitres, etc.). *(b)* Saupoudrer de sucre. **3.** Dépolir (le verre). **frosted**, *a.* **1.** Givré. **2.** *(Of glass)* Dépoli.

frostiness ['frɔstinəs], *s.* **1.** Froid glacial (du temps). **2.** Manière glaciale (de qn).

frosty ['frɔsti], *a.* **1.** Gelé ; glacial, -als. *F. day*, jour de gelée. *F:* **Frosty reception**, accueil glacial. **2.** (Carreaux) couverts de givre ; (arbre) givré. **-ily**, *adv.* *F:* Glacialement.

froth¹ [frɔθ], *s.* **1.** Écume *f* (du bouillon) ; mousse *f* (de la bière) ; faux col (d'un verre de bière). **2.** *F:* Futilités *fpl* ; paroles creuses.

froth², *v.i.* Écumer, mousser. **To froth up**, mousser fortement. **To froth over**, déborder (en moussant). *He was frothing at the mouth*, sa bouche écumait.

frothy ['frɔθi], *a.* Écumeux, écumant ; mousseux.

froward ['frouwərd], *a.* *A:* *(Of pers.)* Obstiné, indocile.

frown¹ [fraun], *s.* Froncement *m* de sourcils ; regard sévère, désapprobateur.

frown², *v.i.* *(a)* *(Of pers.)* Froncer les sourcils ; se renfrogner. *To frown at, (up)on, s.o.*, regarder qn de travers, en fronçant les sourcils. *To f. upon a suggestion*, désapprouver une suggestion. *(b)* *(Of thgs)* Avoir l'air sombre, menaçant. **frowning**, *a.* *(Of looks, face, etc.)* Renfrogné ; *(of brow)* sourcilleux ; *(of thgs)* sombre, menaçant. **-ly**, *adv.* En fronçant les sourcils.

frowstiness ['fraustinəs], *s* *F:* Odeur *f* de renfermé.

frowsty ['frausti], *a.* *F:* Qui sent le renfermé.

frowzy ['frauzi], *a.* **1.** Qui sent le renfermé. **2.** *(Of pers., clothes)* Sale, mal tenu, peu soigné.

froze(n) [frouz(n)]. *See* FREEZE.

fructification [frʌktifi'keiʃ(ə)n], *s.* Fructification *f.*

fructify ['frʌktifai], *v.i.* Fructifier.

frugal ['fruːg(ə)l], *a.* **1.** *(Of pers.)* Frugal, -aux ; économe. *To be frugal of sth.*, ménager qch. **2.** *(Of meal)* Frugal, simple. *F. eater*, homme sobre. **-ally**, *adv.* Frugalement, sobrement.

frugality [fru'galiti], *s.* Frugalité *f.*

fruit [fruːt], *s.* **1.** Fruit *m.* Stone fruit, fruit à noyau. *Eat more fruit*, mangez plus de fruits. Dried fruit, fruits secs. Stewed fruit, compote *f* de fruits. *To bear fruit*, porter fruit. **2.** *The fruits of the earth*, les fruits de la terre. *His knowledge is the f. of much study*, son savoir est le fruit de longues études. **'fruit-cake**, *s.* Gâteau *m* aux fruits ; gâteau anglais. **'fruit-dish, -stand**, *s.* Compotier *m.* **'fruit-knife**, *s.*

Couteau *m* à fruit(s) ; pèle-fruits *m inv.* **'fruit-tree,** s. Arbre fruitier.

fruiterer ['fru:tərər], s. (*Pers.*) Fruitier, -ière.

fruitful ['fru:tful], *a.* (*Of tree, etc.*) Fructueux, productif ; (*of soil, etc.*) fertile, fécond. **F :** Action fruitful of, in, consequences, action fertile en conséquences. **-fully,** *adv.* Fructueusement, utilement.

fruitfulness ['fru:tfulnəs], s. Productivité *f* (d'un arbre, etc.) ; fertilité *f* (du sol, etc.).

fruition [fru'i\(ə)n], s. **I.** Jouissance *f* (d'un bien). **2.** Réalisation *f* (d'un projet) ; fructification *f* (d'une idée). To come to fruition, fructifier.

fruitless ['fru:tləs], *a.* (*Of plant, work*) Stérile. Fruitless efforts, vains efforts. **-ly,** *adv.* Vainement.

fruity ['fru:ti], *a.* **I.** (*a*) (Goût, etc.) de fruit. (*b*) (*Of wine*) Fruité, fruiteux. **2. F :** (Scandale, etc.) corsé.

frump [frʌmp], s.f. **F :** Old frump, vieille caricature, vieille toupie, vieille fée.

frumpish ['frʌmpiʃ], **frumpy** ['frʌmpi], *a.* **F :** Fagotée ; mal attifée.

frustrate [frʌs'treit, 'frʌstreit], *v.tr.* (*a*) Faire échouer, faire avorter (un projet, etc.). To f. s.o.'s hopes, frustrer qn dans son espoir ; frustrer l'espoir de qn. (*b*) Contrecarrer (qn).

frustration [frʌs'treiʃ(ə)n], s. Anéantissement *m* (des projets de qn) ; frustration *f* (d'un espoir).

frustum, *pl.* **-ta, -tums** ['frʌstəm, -ta, -təmz], s. Tronc *m* (de cône, de prisme, etc.) ; tronçon *m* (d'une colonne).

fry[1] [frai], s. Coll. **I.** Ich : Frai *m*, fretin *m*, alevin *m*. Small fry, menu fretin. **2. F :** The small fry, (i) le menu fretin, le menu peuple, les petites gens ; (ii) les gosses *m*.

fry[2], s. Cu : **I.** Plat *m* de viande frite ; friture *f*. **2.** Issues *fpl* ; fressure *f*.

fry[3], *v.* (fried [fraid]) **I.** *v.tr.* (Faire) frire (la viande, etc.). Fried eggs, œufs sur le plat. Fried potatoes, pommes de terre frites. **2.** *v.i.* (*Of meat, etc.*) Frire. **F :** To fry in one's own grease, cuire dans son jus. **'frying-pan,** s. Poêle *f* (à frire). **F :** To jump out of the frying-pan into the fire, tomber d'un mal dans un pire.

fuchsia ['fju:ʃjɑ], s. Bot : Fuchsia *m*.

fuddle [fʌdl], *v.tr.* **F :** (*a*) Soûler, griser. The wine had fuddled his brain, le vin lui avait enfumé le cerveau. (*b*) Brouiller les idées de (qn).

fuddled, *a.* **F :** **I.** Soûl ; pris de vin ; gris. To get fuddled, s'enivrer. **2.** Brouillé (dans ses idées) ; hébété.

fudge [fʌdʒ], s. **I.** Bêtise(s) *f*, sottise(s) *f*. **2.** Fondant américain.

fuel[1] ['fjuəl], s. (*a*) Combustible *m*, comburant *m*. Patent fuel, compressed fuel, aggloméré(s) *m(pl)*. **F :** To add fuel to the flame, to the fire, jeter de l'huile sur le feu. (*b*) I.C.E : Carburant *m*.

fuel[2], *v.tr.* (fuelled) (*a*) Charger (un fourneau, etc.). Oil-fuelled, chauffé au pétrole. (*b*) Pourvoir (la flotte, etc.) de combustibles. **fuelling,** s. Alimentation *f*, approvisionnement *m*, en combustibles.

fug [fʌg], s. **F :** Forte odeur de renfermé ; touffeur *f*.

fugacious [fju'geiʃəs], *a.* Fugace.

fugacity [fju'gasiti], s. Fugacité *f*.

fugginess ['fʌginəs], s. **F :** Touffeur *f* de l'air.

fuggy ['fʌgi], *a.* **F :** (Salle) qui sent le renfermé.

fugitive ['fju:dʒitiv]. **I.** *a.* (*a*) Fugitif, fuyard. (*b*) (*Of happiness, etc.*) Fugitif, fugace, éphémère. **2.** s. (*a*) Fugitif, -ive ; fuyard *m*. (*b*) Exilé, -ée ; réfugié, -ée.

fugue [fju:g], s. Mus : Fugue *f*

fulcrum, *pl.* **-cra** ['fʌlkrəm, -kra], s. Mec : (Point *m*, axe *m*, d')appui *m*, centre *m*, pivot *m* (d'un levier).

fulfil [ful'fil], *v.tr.* (fulfilled) **I.** (*a*) Accomplir (une prophétie) ; répondre à, remplir (l'attente de qn). (*b*) Satisfaire (un désir) ; exaucer (une prière). (*c*) Accomplir (une tâche). To f. a duty, s'acquitter d'un devoir ; acquitter, remplir, un devoir. (*d*) Remplir (les conditions requises, etc.). (*e*) Obéir à (un commandement). **2.** Achever, compléter.

fulfilment [ful'filmənt], s. **I.** (*a*) Accomplissement *m* (d'un devoir, etc.). (*b*) Exaucement *m* (d'une prière) ; accomplissement (d'un désir). (*c*) Exécution *f* (d'une condition, d'un projet). **2.** Achèvement *m* (d'une période de temps).

fuliginous [fju'lidʒinəs], *a.* Fuligineux.

full[1] [ful]. **I.** *a.* **I.** Plein, rempli, comble. **Full to overflowing,** plein à déborder. **Full day,** jour chargé. **F :** His heart was full, il avait le cœur gros, gonflé. **Full of holes,** plein de trous. *Look f. of gratitude,* regard chargé de reconnaissance. **To be full of hope,** être rempli d'espoir. **2.** (*Of bus, etc.*) Plein, complet. **To be full up,** avoir son plein. **Full up!** complet ! **Full house,** salle *f* comble. **Full session** (*of a committee, etc.*), réunion, assemblée, plénière. **3.** To be full of one's own importance, être pénétré de sa propre importance. **4.** (*Of facts, etc.*) Ample, abondant, copieux. **Full particulars,** tous les détails. *Until fuller information is available . . .,* jusqu'à plus ample informé. **5.** Complet, entier. (*a*) **Full meal,** repas complet. **Full pay,** paye entière ; solde entière. *Th :* To pay f. price, Rail : to pay full fare, payer place entière. **Full weight,** full measure, poids juste ; mesure comble. **Full text,** texte intégral. **Battalion at full strength,** bataillon au grand complet. (*b*) **In full flower,** en pleine fleur. **Roses in full bloom,** roses larges épanouies. **In full uniform,** en grande tenue. **In full flight,** en pleine déroute. (*c*) **I waited two full hours,** j'ai attendu deux bonnes heures, deux grandes heures. **It is a full five miles from here,** c'est à au moins deux lieues d'ici. (*d*) **Full brother, full sister,** frère germain, sœur germaine. **6.** (*a*) (*Of face*) Plein ; (*of figure*) rond, replet ; (*of chin*) renflé. **Full lips,** lèvres grosses, fortes. (*b*) (*Of sleeve, etc.*) Ample, large, bouffant. (*c*) **Full voice,** voix pleine, ronde, étoffée. **7.** Nau : (*Of sail*) Plein, gonflé. **To keep her full,** porter plein. **Full and by,** près et plein. **F :** Taking it full by . . .,** à tout prendre. . . . **-lly,** *adv.* **I.** (*a*) Pleinement, entièrement, complètement, amplement. **Fully armed,** armé de toutes pièces. **Fully paid,** payé intégralement. (*b*) *To treat a subject, develop a negative,* f., traiter un sujet, développer un cliché, à fond. **2.** It takes fully two hours, cela prend bien, au moins, deux heures. **II. full,** s. **I.** The moon is at the full, la lune est dans son plein. **2.** adv.phr. (a) In full. *To publish a letter in f.,* publier une lettre intégralement. *Account given in f.,* compte rendu in extenso. Fin : Capital paid in f., capital entièrement versé. Name in full, (i) nom *m* et prénoms ; (ii) nom en toutes lettres. (b) To the full, complètement, tout à fait, dans toute son étendue. **III. full,** *adv.* **I.** A. & Lit : Full many a time, bien des fois. I know it full well, je le sais bien, parfaitement. It is full five miles from here, c'est au moins deux lieues d'ici. **2.** Précisément, justement, en plein. Full in the middle, au beau milieu. Hit f. in the face, atteint en pleine figure. **'full-back,** s. Fb : Arrière *m*. **'full-'blooded,** *a.* **I.** (*a*) (*Of brother, sister*)

Germain. (*b*) De race pure ; (cheval) pur sang
inv. **2.** Vigoureux ; robuste. **3.** (Tempérament)
sanguin. **'full-'blown,** *a.* **1.** (*Of rose, etc.*)
Épanoui ; en pleine fleur. **2.** *F:* He is a full-
blown doctor, il a (obtenu) tous ses diplômes.
'full-bodied, *a.* **1.** Corpulent. **2.** (Vin) corsé,
qui a du corps. **'full-bred,** *a.* De race pure ;
(cheval) pur sang *inv.* **'full-chested,** *a.* A
forte poitrine. **'full-dress,** *attrib.a.* Full-dress
clothes, tenue *f* de cérémonie. *F:* Full-dress
debate, débat solennel. *Th:* Full-dress rehearsal,
répétition générale, en costume. **'full-fledged,**
a. **1.** (*Of bird*) Qui a toutes ses plumes. **2.** *F:*
= FULL-BLOWN 2. **'full-length,** *a.* (Portrait)
en pied. **'full-page,** *attrib.a.* (Illustration)
hors texte. **'full-rigged,** *a.* *Nau:* Gréé en
trois-mâts carré. **'full-size(d),** *a.* (Dessin, etc.)
(i) de grandeur naturelle, (ii) *Ind:* à la dimension
exacte, à la cote. **'full 'stop,** *s.* (*In punctuation*)
Point (final). *F:* He came to a *f. s.*, il est resté
court (dans son discours). **'full-'throated,** *a.*
(Chant, etc.) à plein gosier, à pleine gorge.
'full-time. *Ind:* **1.** *a.* (Emploi) de toute la
journée, (ii) pour toute la semaine. **2.** *adv.* To
work full time, travailler à pleines journées.
full², *v.tr.* Fouler (l'étoffe, le cuir). **fulling,** *s.*
Foulage *m*, foulement *m* (des draps).
fuller¹ ['fulər], *s.* *Tex:* Fouleur, -euse ; foulon *m.*
Fuller's earth, terre savonneuse ; terre à foulon.
Bot: Fuller's teasel, cardère *f* à foulon ;
chardon *m* à foulon.
fuller², *s.* **1.** *Tls:* Dégorgeoir *m.* **2.** Gouttière *f*
(de baïonnette) ; onglet *m* (d'épée).
ful(l)ness ['fulnəs], *s.* **1.** État plein (d'un réceptacle) ; plénitude *f* (de l'estomac). Out of the
fullness of his heart he told us . . ., comme son
cœur débordait il nous raconta . . . **2.** Plénitude, totalité *f* (de la force, etc.). In the fullness
of time, quand les temps furent, seront, révolus.
3. Ampleur *f* (d'un vêtement, d'un compte
rendu) ; abondance *f* (de détail) ; rondeur *f* (de
la forme) ; richesse *f* (du style, d'une couleur).
fulminate¹ ['fʌlmineit], *s.* *Ch:* Fulminate *m* (de
mercure, etc.).
fulminate². **1.** *v.i.* Fulminer ; faire explosion.
2. *v.tr. & i.* *Ecc:* Fulminer (une excommunication). *F:* To fulminate against s.o., fulminer
contre qn.
fulness ['fulnəs], *s.* See FUL(L)NESS.
fulsome ['fulsəm], *a.* (*Of praise, etc.*) Écœurant,
excessif. Fulsome flattery, flagornerie *f*, adulation *f*.
fulsomeness ['fulsəmnəs], *s.* Bassesse *f*, platitude *f* (des louanges, etc.).
fulvous ['fʌlvəs], *a.* Fauve.
fumble [fʌmbl]. **1.** *v.i.* Fouiller (au hasard) ;
tâtonner. To fumble (*in a drawer, etc.*) for sth.,
(far)fouiller (dans un tiroir, etc.) pour trouver
qch. To fumble for words, chercher ses mots.
To fumble with sth., manier qch. maladroitement. **2.** *v.tr.* Manier (qch.) maladroitement,
gauchement ; tripoter (qch.). *Sp:* To fumble
the ball, arrêter, attraper, la balle maladroitement.
fumbling, *a.* Maladroit, gauche.
fumbler ['fʌmblər], *s.* Maladroit, -e.
fume¹ [fjuːm], *s.* **1.** Fumée *f*, vapeur *f*, exhalaison *f.*
Ind: Factory fumes, fumée d'usine. **2.** *F:* In
a fume, hors de soi ; en rage. **'fume-chamber,**
-cupboard, *s.* *Ch:* Sorbonne *f* (de laboratoire).
fume². **1.** *v.tr.* Exposer (qch.) à la fumée, à une
vapeur, à un gaz. Fumed oak, chêne patiné.
2. *v.i.* (*a*) Fumer ; émettre de la fumée, des

vapeurs. (*b*) (*Of smoke, vapour*) Monter, s'exhaler.
(*c*) *F:* (*Of pers.*) Rager ; se faire du mauvais sang.
fumigate ['fjuːmigeit], *v.tr.* Fumiger (qch.) ;
désinfecter (un appartement) par fumigation.·
fumigation [fjumi'geiʃ(ə)n], *s.* Fumigation *f* ;
désinfection *f.*
fumitory ['fjuːmitəri], *s.* *Bot:* Fumeterre *f.*
fun [fʌn], *s.* *F:* Amusement *m*, gaieté *f* ; plaisanterie *f.* To make fun of, poke fun at, s.o., se
moquer, se railler, de qn. For fun, in fun, (i) pour
rire ; par plaisanterie ; (ii) pour se distraire.
I did it for the fun of the thing, je l'ai fait histoire
de m'amuser. He is great fun, full of fun, il est
très gai, il a toujours le mot pour rire. It was
great fun, c'était fort amusant. It's poor fun to . . .,
ce n'est guère amusant de. . . . To have fun,
s'amuser, se divertir. It was only my fun, c'était
pour rire. *P:* He went at it like fun, il s'y est
mis énergiquement, vigoureusement. **'fun fair,**
s. *F:* Foire *f* aux plaisirs.
funambulist [fjuˈnambjulist], *s.* Funambule *mf* ;
danseur, -euse, de corde.
function¹ ['fʌŋ(k)ʃ(ə)n], *s.* **1.** Fonction *f.* Vital
functions, fonctions vitales. **2.** (*a*) (*Of office-
holder, etc.*) Fonction, charge *f.* In his *f.* as a
magistrate, en sa qualité de magistrat. (*b*) *pl.* To
discharge one's functions, s'acquitter de ses
fonctions. It is part of my functions to . . .,
c'est à moi qu'il appartient de. . . . **3.** (*a*) Réception *f*, soirée *f*, réunion *f.* (*b*) Cérémonie
publique ; solennité *f.* **4.** *Mth:* Fonction. As a
function of . . ., en fonction de. . . .
function², *v.i.* **1.** Fonctionner, marcher. **2.** *Adjective that functions as an adverb,* adjectif qui
fait fonction d'adverbe.
functional ['fʌŋ(k)ʃən(ə)l], *a.* Fonctionnel.
functionary ['fʌŋ(k)ʃənəri], *s.* Fonctionnaire *m.*
fund¹ [fʌnd], *s.* **1.** Fonds *m* (d'érudition, etc.).
He has a rare *f.* of perseverance, il est doué d'une
persévérance rare. *Fin: etc:* (*a*) Fonds *m*,
caisse *f.* Old-age pension fund, caisse des retraites
pour la vieillesse. To start a fund, lancer une
souscription. (*b*) *pl.* Funds, fonds, masse *f* ;
ressources *f* pécuniaires. (*Of company*) To make
a call for funds, faire un appel de capital. To be
in funds, être en fonds. *Bank:* 'No funds,'
"défaut *m* de provision," "manque *m* de fonds."
To misappropriate public funds, détourner les
deniers de l'État, les deniers publics. (*c*) *pl.*
Funds, la Dette publique ; les fonds publics ; la
rente sur l'État. **'fund-holder,** *s.* Rentier, -ière.
fund², *v.tr.* *Fin:* **1.** Consolider, fonder (une
dette publique). **2.** Placer (de l'argent) dans les
fonds publics. Funded property, biens en rentes.
fundament ['fʌndəmənt], *s.* *Anat:* Fondement *m* ; *F:* le derrière.
fundamental [fʌndəˈment(ə)l]. **I.** *a.* **1.** (*a*) Fondamental, -aux ; essentiel. *F.* question, question
de fond. *F.* qualities of s.o., qualités foncières de
qn. (*b*) (*Of colours, etc.*) Primitif ; original, -aux.
2. *Mus:* (*Of note, etc.*) Fondamental. **-ally,**
adv. Fondamentalement, foncièrement. *His
argument is f. wrong,* son raisonnement pèche
par la base. **II. fundamental,** *s.* **1.** *pl.* Fundamentals, principe *m*, partie essentielle (d'un
système, etc.). **2.** *Mus:* Note fondamentale ;
fondamentale *f.*
funeral ['fjuːnərəl], *s.* **1.** (*a*) Funérailles *fpl.* ;
obsèques *fpl.* ; enterrement *m.* To attend s.o.'s
funeral, assister à l'enterrement de qn. *U.S:* *F:*
That's your funeral! ça c'est votre affaire ! (*b*)
(*b*) Convoi *m* funèbre ; cortège *m* funèbre.
2. Funeral expenses, frais funéraires. *F:* At a
funeral pace, à un pas d'enterrement.

funereal [fju'niːəriəl], a. **1.** *Poet:* Funèbre, funéraire. **2.** *F:* Lugubre, funèbre, triste ; (*of voice*) sépulcral, -aux. **-ally,** *adv.* Funèbrement, lugubrement.

fungous ['fʌŋgəs], a. Fongueux, fongoïde.

fungus, *pl.* **-uses, -i** ['fʌŋgəs, -əsiz, 'fʌndʒai], *s.* (*a*) *Bot:* (i) Mycète *m* ; (ii) champignon véné-neux. (*b*) *F: Fungus towns,* villes *f* champignons.

funicular [fju'nikjulər], a. *&* s. Funiculaire (*m*).

funk¹ [fʌŋk], *s. P:* **1.** Frousse *f*, trac *m*, venette *f*. **To be in a** (blue) funk, avoir une peur bleue ; avoir le trac, la frousse. **2.** Froussard, -arde ; caneur, -euse. **'funk-hole,** *s. F:* **1.** *Mil:* Abri enterré. **2.** (*For shirkers*) Nid *m* d'embusqués.

funk², *v.tr. & i. P:* **To funk** (it), caner. **To funk s.o., sth.,** to funk doing sth., to funk at sth., avoir peur de qn, de qch., de faire qch.

funky ['fʌŋki], *a. P:* Froussard.

funnel [fʌnl], *s.* **1.** (*a*) Entonnoir *m*. (*b*) *Ind:* (Charging, loading) funnel, trémie *f*, hotte *f*. **2.** (*a*) Tuyau *m* (d'aérage). (*b*) Cheminée *f* (d'une locomotive, d'un bateau à vapeur).

funniness ['fʌninəs], *s.* **1.** Drôlerie *f*. **2.** Bizarrerie *f*.

funny ['fʌni], *a.* Drôle. **1.** Comique, amusant, facétieux. **None of your funny tricks!** I don't want any funny business! pas de vos farces ! He is trying to be funny, il veut faire de l'esprit. *Th:* **Funny man,** bouffon *m*. **2.** Curieux, bizarre. **He was funny that way,** il était comme ça. **A funny idea,** une drôle d'idée. *This butter tastes funny,* ce beurre a un drôle de goût. **3.** *P:* I came over all funny, je me suis senti(e) tout(e) chose. **-ily,** *adv.* Drôlement. **1.** Comiquement. **2.** Curieusement. **Funnily enough . . .,** chose curieuse. . . **'funny-bone,** *s. F:* Le "petit Juif" (à l'articulation du coude).

fur¹ [fəːr], *s.* **1.** (*a*) Fourrure *f*, pelleterie *f*. **Fur coat,** manteau *m* de fourrure. (*b*) Poil *m*, pelage *m* (de lapin, etc.). *F:* **To make the fur fly,** se battre avec acharnement. (*c*) *pl.* Furs, peaux *fpl* (d'animaux). **2.** *Her:* Fourrure. **3.** (*a*) (*In boiler*) Incrustations *fpl*, tartre *m*, calcin *m*. (*b*) *Med:* (*On tongue*) Enduit *m* (blanchâtre, noirâtre). **'fur-lined,** *a.* Doublé de fourrure ; fourré. **'fur-trade,** *s.* Pelleterie *f*. **'fur-trader,** *s.* Pelletier *m*.

fur², *v.* (furred) I. *v.tr.* **1.** Entartrer, incruster (une chaudière, etc.). *Med:* Charger (la langue). **2.** Désincruster, détartrer (une chaudière). II. **fur,** *v.i.* **To fur up,** (*of boiler, etc.*) s'incruster, s'entartrer ; (*of tongue*) se charger, s'empâter. **furred,** *a.* **1.** (*a*) (*Of pers.*) Habillé de fourrures. *To be f. to the eyes,* être emmitouflé de fourrures jusqu'aux yeux. (*b*) (Animal) à poil. **2.** (*Of boiler, etc.*) Entartré, incrusté. *Med:* **Furred tongue,** langue chargée. **furring,** *s.* **1.** (*a*) Entartrage *m*, incrustation *f* (d'une chaudière, etc.). *Med:* Chargement *m* (de la langue). (*b*) Détartrage *m*, décrassage *m* (des chaudières). **2.** (*In boiler*) Calcin *m*, tartre *m*.

furbelow ['fəːbilo], *s.* **1.** *A:* Falbala *m*. **2.** *F:* Furbelows, fanfreluches *f*.

furbish ['fəːbiʃ], *v.tr.* **To furbish** (up). **1.** Fourbir, polir, astiquer. **2.** (Re)mettre à neuf, retaper (des meubles, etc.).

furcate ['fəːkeit], *a.* (*Of road, etc.*) En bifurca-, tion ; (*of hoof*) fourchu.

furious ['fjuəriəs], *a.* Furieux ; (*of look*) furibond ; (*of battle*) acharné. *At a f. pace,* à une allure folle ; (*of horseman*) à bride abattue. *F. at having failed,* furieux d'avoir manqué son coup. **To get furious,** entrer en fureur. **To be furious with s.o.,** être furieux contre qn. **Furious driving,** con-

duite folle (d'une voiture). **-ly,** *adv.* Furieuse-ment ; (combattre, etc.) avec acharnement, avec furie ; (conduire) à une allure folle ; (*of horseman*) (courir) à bride abattue.

furiousness ['fjuəriəsnəs], *s.* Fureur *f* ; acharne-ment *m* (d'un combat, etc.) ; furie *f* (du vent).

furl [fəːrl], *v.tr.* (*a*) *Nau:* Serrer, ferler (une voile). (*b*) Rouler (un parapluie, etc.) ; serrer (une tente). *Mil:* (*Of flag*) Furled and craped, en berne.

furlong ['fəːrlɔŋ], *s. Meas:* Furlong *m* (220 yards = 201 mètres).

furlough ['fəːrlou], *s. Mil:* Congé *m*, permis-sion *f*. **To be, go, on furlough,** être, aller, en permission.

furnace ['fəːrnes], *s.* **1.** (*a*) *Metall: etc:* Four-neau *m*, four *m*. *S.a.* BLAST-FURNACE.. (*b*) (*Hot place*) Fournaise *f*. **Fiery furnace,** fournaise ardente. *The burning houses were a glowing f.,* l'incendie formait un vaste brasier. **2.** (*a*) **House-heating furnace,** calorifère *m*. (*b*) *Mch:* Foyer *m* (de chaudière).

furnish ['fəːrniʃ], *v.tr.* **1.** (*a*) Fournir, donner (des renseignements, etc.) ; pourvoir (les fonds nécessaires, etc.) ; alléguer (des raisons, etc.). (*b*) **To furnish s.o. with sth.,** fournir, pourvoir, munir, qn de qch. **2.** Meubler, garnir (une maison, etc.). **Furnished flat,** appartement meublé. *To live in furnished apartments,* loger en garni, en meublé. **furnishing,** *s.* **1.** House-furnishing firm, maison *f* d'ameublement. **2.** *pl.* Furnishings, ameublement *m* (d'une maison).

furnisher ['fəːrniʃər], *s.* Fournisseur *m* (*of*, de) ; *esp.* marchand *m* d'ameublement.

furniture ['fəːrnitʃər], *s.* **1.** Meubles *mpl*, ameublement *m*, mobilier *m* ; matériel *m* (d'une école). **Piece of furniture,** meuble. **Suite, set, of furniture,** mobilier ; meuble (de salon, etc.). **2.** Ferrures *fpl* (d'une porte, etc.). **'furniture-polish,** *s.* Encaustique *f*. **'furniture-re-mover,** *s.* Déménageur *m* ; entrepreneur *m* de déménagements. **'furniture-shop,** *s.* Maison *f* d'ameublement. **'furniture-van,** *s.* Voi-ture *f* de déménagement. **2.** *Com:* Tapissière *f*.

furrier ['fʌriər], *s.* Pelletier, -ière ; fourreur *m*.

furriery ['fʌriəri], *s.* Pelleterie *f*.

furrow¹ ['fʌro], *s.* **1.** (*a*) *Agr:* (i) (Open) furrow, sillon *m* ; (ii) billon *m* ; tranche *f* (de terre) re-tournée par la charrue. *F:* **To plough a lonely fur-row,** poursuivre seul une idée. (*b*) *Lit:* Sillage *m* (d'un navire). **2.** Cannelure *f*, rainure *f*. **3.** *On face, etc.*) Ride profonde ; sillon.

furrow², *v.tr.* **1.** Labourer (la terre). *F:* (*Of ship*) Sillonner (les mers, etc.). **2.** Canneler, rainer (une pianche, etc.). **3.** Rider profondé-ment. *Age has furrowed his face,* l'âge a sillonné, labouré, son visage.

furry ['fʌri], *a.* **1.** = FURRED. **2.** Qui ressemble à (de) la fourrure.

further¹ ['fəːrðər], *a.* (*Comp. of* far) I. *adv.* **1.** = FARTHER 1. (*a*) Davantage, plus. *I did not question him any f.,* je ne l'interrogeai pas davantage. *Without troubling any f.,* sans plus se tracasser. **Until you hear further,** jusqu'à nouvel avis. (*b*) **To go further into sth.,** entrer plus avant dans qch. (*c*) (*In time*) Further back, à une période plus reculée. (*d*) D'ailleurs, en outre, de plus, aussi, du reste. II. **further,** *a.* **1.** = FARTHER 2 (*a*). **2.** Nouveau, additionnel, supplémentaire. **To remand a case for further enquiry,** renvoyer une cause à plus ample informé. **Without further loss of time,** sans autre perte de temps. **Without further ado . . .,**

sans plus de cérémonie . . . ; sans plus. . . .
Upon further consideration, après plus ample réflexion. *One or two f. details,* encore un ou deux détails. *Com:* **Further orders,** commandes ultérieures. **Awaiting your further orders,** dans l'attente de vos nouvelles commandes.

further², *v.tr.* Avancer, favoriser, servir (les intérêts de qn, etc.).

furtherance ['fəːrðərəns], *s.* Avancement *m* (d'un travail, etc.). **For the furtherance of, in furtherance of (sth.),** pour avancer, pour servir (qch.).

furthermore ['fəːrðərmɔːr], *adv.* En outre, outre cela, de plus, par ailleurs.

furthermost ['fəːrðərmoust], *a.* = FARTHERMOST.

furthest ['fəːrðəst], *a. & adv.* = FARTHEST.

furtive ['fəːrtiv], *a.* (*Of action, etc.*) Furtif; (*of pers.*) sournois. **-ly,** *adv.* Furtivement; à la dérobée.

furuncle ['fjuːrʌŋkl], *s. Med:* Furoncle *m.*

fury ['fjuːri], *s.* **1.** Furie *f*, fureur *f*, emportement *m*; acharnement *m* (d'un combat). **To get into a fury,** entrer en fureur, en furie; s'emporter. *F:* **To work like fury,** travailler avec acharnement. **2.** *pl. Myth:* **The Furies,** les Furies *f.*

furze [fəːrz], *s. Bot:* Ajonc *m.*

fuse¹ [fjuːz], *s.* **1.** Fusée *f* (d'obus); amorce *f. Min:* (Safety-)fuse, étoupille *f*, cordeau *m.*

fuse², *s. El.E:* (Safety-)fuse, (coupe-circuit *m* à) fusible *m*; (*in private house*) plomb *m.* **'fuse-box,** *s.* Boîte *f* à fusibles. **'fuse-wire,** *s.* Fil *m* fusible.

fuse³. **1.** *v.tr.* (*a*) Fondre, mettre en fusion (un métal, etc.). (*b*) *F:* Fusionner, amalgamer, réunir (deux partis, etc.). **2.** *v.i.* (*a*) (*Of metals, etc.*) Fondre. *F:* **The light has fused,** les plombs ont sauté. (*b*) *F:* Fusionner; s'amalgamer; s'unir par la fusion.

fusee [fjuːˈziː], *s.* Allumette-tison *f.*

fuselage ['fjuːzledʒ], *s. Av:* Fuselage *m.*

fusel oil ['fjuːzlˈɔil], *s.* Huile *f* de fusel, de pomme de terre.

fusibility [fjuːziˈbiliti], *s.* Fusibilité *f.*

fusible ['fjuːzibl], *a.* Fusible.

fusilier [fjuːziˈliːər], *s. Mil:* Fusilier *m.*

fusillade [fjuːziˈleid], *s. Mil:* Fusillade *f.*

fusion ['fjuːʒ(ə)n], *s.* Fusion *f.* **1.** Fondage *m*, fonte *f* (d'un métal, etc.). **2.** Fusionnement *m* (de plusieurs banques, etc.). *Pol:* Fusion (de deux partis, etc.).

fuss¹ [fʌs], *s.* **1.** Bruit exagéré. *A lot of f. over a trifle, about nothing,* bien du tapage pour peu de chose; beaucoup de bruit pour rien. **To make, kick up, a fuss,** faire un tas d'histoires. **To be in a fine fuss,** être dans tous ses états.

2. Embarras *mpl*; façons *fpl.* **To make a fuss** faire des cérémonies, des embarras. **To make a fuss of s.o.,** (i) être aux petits soins pour qn; (ii) mettre qn en avant. **Fuss and feathers,** l'esbrouf(f)e *f.* **'fuss-pot,** *s. P:* Tatillon, -onne.

fuss². **1.** *v.i.* Tatillonner; faire des embarras; faire des histoires; se tracasser. **To fuss about, to fuss round,** faire l'affairé; s'affairer. **To fuss over, around, s.o.,** être aux petits soins pour qn; faire l'empressé auprès de qn. **2.** *v.tr.* Tracasser, agiter (qn).

fussiness ['fʌsinəs], *s.* Tatillonnage *m*; façons *fpl,* embarras *mpl.*

fussy ['fʌsi], *a.* **1.** (*Of pers.*) Tatillon, -onne; tracassier, méticuleux. **2.** (*Of dress, etc.*) Qui a trop de façon; trop pomponné. **-ily,** *adv.* (*a*) D'une manière tatillonne. (*b*) D'un air important; en faisant des embarras.

fustian ['fʌstjən], *s.* **1.** *Tex:* Futaine *f.* **2.** Grandiloquence *f*, emphase *f.*

fustigate ['fʌstigeit], *v.tr. Hum:* Fustiger (qn).

fustiness ['fʌstinəs], *s.* **1.** Odeur *f* de renfermé. **2.** Caractère suranné, démodé.

fusty ['fʌsti], *a.* Fusty smell, odeur de renfermé. *F:* Fusty ideas, idées surannées, démodées.

futile ['fjuːtil, -tail], *a.* **1.** Futile, vain. **2.** Puéril.

futility [fjuːˈtiliti], *s.* **1.** Futilité *f.* **2.** Puérilité *f.*

futtock ['fʌtək], *s. N.Arch:* Genou-allonge *m*, *pl.* genoux-allonges; allonge *f.* **'futtock-plate,** *s.* Latte *f* de hune. **'futtock-shroud,** *s.* Gambe *f* (de revers); jambe *f* de hune.

future ['fjuːtjər], *s.* **1.** *a.* (*a*) (*Of life, etc.*) Futur; (*of events*) à venir; (*of prospects, etc.*) d'avenir. **My future wife,** ma future. **Future delivery,** livraison à terme. (*b*) *Gram:* **Future tense,** temps futur. **2.** *s.* (*a*) Avenir *m.* **In (the) future, for the future,** à l'avenir. **In the near future,** dans un avenir peu éloigné; à brève échéance. (*b*) *Gram:* (Temps) futur *m.* Verb in the future, verbe au futur. (*c*) **To ruin one's future,** briser son avenir.

futurity [fjuːˈtjuəriti], *s.* **1.** L'avenir *m.* **2.** *pl.* Événements *m* à venir.

fuze [fjuːz], *s.* = FUSE¹.

fuzz¹ [fʌz], *s.* **1.** (*On blankets, etc.*) Peluches *fpl*, bourre *f*, duvet *m.* **A fuzz of hair,** cheveux bouffants, crêpelus. **2.** *Phot:* Flou *m.*

fuzz², *v.* To fuzz (out). **1.** *v.i.* (*Of hair, etc.*) Bouffer, frisotter. **2.** *v.tr.* Faire bouffer, frisotter (les cheveux).

fuzziness ['fʌzinəs], *s.* **1.** Crêpelure *f* (des cheveux). **2.** *Phot:* Flou *m*; manque *m* de netteté.

fuzzy ['fʌzi], *a.* **1.** (*Of hair*) (i) Bouffant, flou; (ii) crêpelu, frisotté, moutonné. **2.** (*a*) *Phot:* Flou. (*b*) *P:* Un peu ivre; gris.

fylfot ['filfɔt], *s.* Croix gammée; svastika *m.*

G

G, g [dʒiː], *s.* **1.** (La lettre) G, g *m.* **2.** *Mus:* Sol *m.* G clef, clef de sol.

gab [gab], *s. F:* (*a*) Faconde *f.* (*b*) Bagou(t) *m. Esp.* **To have the gift of the gab,** (i) avoir la langue bien pendue; avoir de la faconde; (ii) avoir du bagout.

gabble¹ ['gabl], *s.* **1.** Bredouillement *m.* **2.** Caquet *m*, jacasserie *f.*

gabble². **1.** *v.i.* (*a*) Bredouiller. *Don't g.!* ne parlez pas si vite! (*b*) (*Of pers., birds*) Caqueter, jacasser. **2.** *v.tr.* To gabble out a speech, débiter un discours à toute vitesse. **To gabble off a mass,** dire sa messe au galop.

gabion ['geibiən], *s.* Gabion *m.*

gabion², *v.tr.* Gabionner.

gable [geibl], *s. Arch: Const:* Pignon *m.* **Gable**

roof, comble *m* sur pignon(s). **Stepped gable,** pignon à redans. **'gable-'end,** *s.* Pignon *m.*

gabled [geibld], *a.* (*Of house*) A pignon(s); (*of wall*) en pignon; (*of roof*) sur pignon(s).

gad[1] [gad], *v.i.* (gadded) To gad (about), courir le monde, la ville, les rues.

Gad[2], *int.* (= GOD) (By) Gad! ma foi! parbleu! sapristi!

gadabout ['gadabaut], *s.* Coureur, -euse.

gad-fly ['gadflai], *s.* Ent: (*a*) Taon *m.* (*b*) Œstre *m.*

gadget ['gadʒet], *s.* P: (*a*) Accessoire *m* (de machine); dispositif *m.* (*b*) Chose *m*, machin *m*, truc *m.*

gadroon [ga'druːn], *s.* Arch: etc: Godron *m.*

Gaelic ['geilik]. **1.** *a.* Gaélique. **2.** *s.* Le gaélique.

gaff[1] [gaf], *s.* **1.** Fish: Gaffe *f.* **2.** Nau: Corne *f.* **'gaff-hook,** *s.* Fish: Gaffeau *m.* **'gaff-sail,** *s.* Nau: Voile *f* à corne.

gaff[2], *v.tr.* Gaffer (un saumon, etc.).

gaff[3], *s.* P: To blow the gaff, vendre la mèche.

gaff[4], *s.* P: (Penny-)gaff, théâtre *m* de bas étage.

gaffer ['gafər], *s.* F: **1.** A: L'ancien; vieux bonhomme. **2.** Contremaître *m*; chef *m* d'équipe.

gag[1] [gag], *s.* **1.** Bâillon *m.* **2.** Parl: Clôture *f* (des débats). **3.** Th: F: Interpolation faite par l'acteur; F: cascade *f.*

gag[2], *v.tr.* (gagged) **1.** Bâillonner; mettre un bâillon à (qn). **2.** Parl: Clôturer (un débat). **3.** Th: P: To gag one's part, abs. to gag, cascader.

gage[1] [geidʒ], *s.* **1.** Gage *m*, garantie *f.* Jur: Nantissement *m.* To give sth. in gage, donner qch. en gage. **2.** Gage of battle, gage de bataille, de combat. To throw down the gage to s.o., F: lancer un défi à qn.

gage[2], *v.tr.* Mettre, donner, (qch.) en gage.

gage[3], *s.* & *v.tr.* = GAUGE[1, 2].

gaggle [gagl], *v.i.* (*Of goose*) Cacarder.

gaiety ['geiəti], *s.* **1.** Gaîté *f*, gaieté *f.* **2.** Usu. pl. Amusement *m*, fête *f*, réjouissances *fpl.* **3.** G. in dress, couleurs gaies.

gaily, *adv.* See GAY.

gain[1] [gein], *s.* **1.** Gain *m*, profit *m*, avantage *m*, bénéfice *m.* Prov: No gains without pains, nul bien sans peine. Ill-gotten gains seldom prosper, bien mal acquis ne profite jamais. **2.** Accroissement *m*, augmentation *f.*

gain[2], *v.tr.* Gagner. **I.** Acquérir (une réputation, des faveurs). To gain money, one's living, gagner de l'argent, sa vie. To gain strength, (re)prendre des forces. To gain a hearing, (i) obtenir une audience; (ii) se faire écouter. You will gain nothing by it, vous n'y gagnerez rien. To g. by doing sth., gagner à faire qch. **2.** To gain (s.o.) over, gagner (qn) à sa cause; gagner (un partisan). **3.** He is gaining in weight, il prend du poids. To gain in popularity, gagner de la popularité. **4.** (*a*) To gain a battle, the day, gagner une bataille; remporter la victoire. To gain the upper hand, prendre le dessus. (*b*) (*Of sea*) To gain (ground) on the land, empiéter sur la terre. To gain (ground) on s.o., gagner (du terrain) sur qn. Sp: To gain on a competitor, prendre de l'avance sur un concurrent. A bad habit gains on one, une mauvaise habitude s'impose, s'enracine, peu à peu. (*c*) To gain the further shore, gagner, atteindre, l'autre rive. S.a. END[1] 4. **5.** (*Of clock*) To gain five minutes a day, avancer de cinq minutes par jour. Abs. To gain, avancer; prendre de l'avance.

gainer ['geinər], *s.* **1.** Gagnant (d'une victoire). **2.** To be the gainer by sth., gagner à qch.

gainsay [gein'sei], *v.tr.* (gainsaid [gein'sed]) Contredire, démentir; nier (un fait). Facts that cannot be gainsaid, faits indéniables.

gait [geit], *s.* (*a*) Allure *f*, démarche *f.* Unsteady gait, pas chancelant, mal assuré. To know s.o. by his gait, reconnaître qn à son allure. His awkward gait, sa dégaine. (*b*) Allures, train *m* (d'un cheval). To break up, ruin, a horse's gait, détraquer un cheval.

gaiter ['geitər], *s.* **1.** Guêtre *f.* **2.** (*a*) Guêtre, emplâtre *m* (pour pneu). (*b*) Aut: Spring gaiter, gaine *f* de ressort.

gala ['geilə], *s.* Fête *f*, gala *m.* Swimming gala, grand concours de natation. Gala day, jour de gala, de fête. In gala dress, in gala, en habits de gala.

galalith ['galaliθ], *s.* Ind: Galalithe *f.*

galantine [galan'tiːn], *s.* Cu: Galantine *f.*

galaxy ['galaksi], *s.* **1.** Astr: The Galaxy, la Voie lactée. **2.** F: Assemblée brillante (de belles femmes, etc.); constellation *f* (d'hommes illustres, etc.).

gale[1] [geil], *s.* **1.** Nau: etc: Coup *m* de vent; grand vent, vent fort. Fresh gale, brisk gale, vent frais. Moderate gale, forte brise. **2.** Tempête *f.* (*Of wind*) To blow a gale, souffler en tempête; faire rage.

gale[2], *s.* Bot: (Sweet) gale, galé *m*; myrte *m* des marais.

galena [ga'liːna], *s.* Miner: Galène *f.*

Galilee [galiliː]. Pr.n. La Galilée.

Galileo [gali'liːo]. Pr.n.m. Hist. of Astr: Galilée.

galingale ['galiŋgeil], *s.* Bot: Souchet long; souchet odorant.

galipot ['galipot], *s.* Galipot *m.*

gall[1] [gɔːl], *s.* **1.** Fiel *m.* F: To vent one's gall on s.o., épancher sa bile contre qn. Pen dipped in gall, plume trempée dans le fiel. **2.** Anat: Vésicule *f* biliaire. **'gall-bladder,** *s.* Anat: Vésicule *f* biliaire. **'gall-stone,** *s.* Med: Calcul *m* biliaire.

gall[2], *s.* Bot: Galle *f.* S.a. OAK-GALL, ROSE-GALL. **'gall-fly,** *s.* Cynips *m.* **'gall-nut,** *s.* Noix *f* de galle.

gall[3], *s.* (*a*) Écorchure, excoriation (causée par le frottement). (*b*) F: Froissement *m*, humiliation *f*; blessure (faite à l'amour-propre).

gall[4], *v.tr.* (*a*) Écorcher (par le frottement); mettre le talon, etc.) à vif. (*b*) F: Irriter, exaspérer; froisser, blesser, humilier. **galling,** *a.* (*Of restrictions*) Irritant, exaspérant; (*of remark*) blessant, humiliant. Galling experience, expérience amère.

gallant ['galənt]. **I.** *a.* **1.** (*a*) Brave, vaillant; chevaleresque. (*b*) (*Of ship, etc.*) Beau, *f.* belle; noble, fier, superbe. Gallant display, étalage superbe. **2.** [ga'lant] Galant (auprès des femmes). **-ly,** *adv.* Galamment. **1.** Bravement, vaillamment. **2.** Élégamment, magnifiquement. **3.** [ga'lantli] En homme galant; avec empressement (auprès d'une femme). **II.** gallant, *s.* **1.** *A:* Galant *m*, élégant *m.* **2.** [ga'lant] *A:* Galant; amoureux *m.*

gallantry ['galəntri]; *s.* **1.** Vaillance *f*, bravoure *f.* **2.** Galanterie *f* (auprès des femmes).

galleon ['galjən], *s.* Nau: A: Galion *m.*

gallery ['galəri], *s.* **1.** Galerie *f.* Parl: Public gallery, strangers' gallery, tribune réservée au public; tribune publique. (*b*) The gallery, Th: la (troisième) galerie; F: le poulailler, le paradis. Sp: etc: F: To play to the gallery, jouer pour la galerie. **2.** Art-gallery, (i) galerie (ii) musée *m* (d'art).

galley ['gali], *s.* **1.** Nau: (*a*) *A:* Galère *f.*

(b) Yole f (d'amiral). **2.** *Nau:* Cuisine f, coquerie f. **3.** *Typ:* Galée f. **'galley-proof,** s. Épreuve f en placard. **'galley-slave,** s. Galérien m.

Gallic[1] ['galik], a. Gallique, gaulois.

gallic[2], a. *Ch:* (Acide) gallique.

gallicism ['galısizm], s. Gallicisme m.

gallinaceae [gali'neisii:], s.pl. *Orn:* Gallinacés m.

gallinaceous [gali'neiʃəs], a. *Orn:* Gallinacé.

gallivant [gali'vant], v.i. Fréquenter la société des femmes ; courir la prétentaine.

gallon ['galən], s. Gallon m (= 4 lit. 54).

gallop[1] ['galəp], s. **1.** Galop m. (At) full gallop, au grand galop ; à fond de train ; (of horse) ventre à terre ; (of rider) à bride abattue. To break into a gallop, prendre le galop. **2.** To have, go for, a gallop, faire une galopade.

gallop[2], v. (galloped) **1.** v.i. (a) (Of horse) Galoper. (b) (Of rider) Aller au galop, à bride abattue. To gallop away, partir, s'éloigner, au galop. To gallop back, revenir au galop. **2.** v.tr. Faire aller (un cheval) au (grand) galop ; galoper (un cheval). **galloping,** a. **1.** (Of horse, etc.) Au galop. **2.** *Med:* Galloping consumption, phtisie galopante.

Gallo-Roman [galo'roumən], a. Gallo-romain.

gallows ['galouz], s. (Often with sg. const.) **1.** Potence f, gibet m. To have a gallows look, avoir une mine patibulaire ; sentir la potence. **2.** Portique m (de gymnastique). **'gallows-bird,** s. F: Gibier m de potence ; pendard m. **'gallows-bitts,** s.pl. *Nau:* Potence f de drome. **'gallows-tree,** s. Gibet m ; potence f.

galop ['galəp], s. *Danc:* Galop m.

galore [gə'lɔːr], s. & adv. F: (In) galore, en abondance, à foison, à profusion.

galosh [gə'lɔʃ], s. **1.** A: Galoche f. **2.** Caoutchouc m ; couvre-chaussure m.

galvanic [gal'vanik], a. Galvanique.

galvanism ['galvanizm], s. Galvanisme m.

galvanization [galvanai'zeiʃ(ə)n], s. **1.** Galvanisation f (du corps humain, etc.). **2.** *Metalw:* Galvanisation ; galvanisage m ; (i) métallisation f électrique ; (ii) zingage m au trempé.

galvanize ['galvana:iz], v.tr. **1.** Galvaniser (un cadavre, etc.). F: To galvanize sth. into life, donner à qch. une animation passagère ; galvaniser qch. **2.** *Metalw:* Galvaniser ; (i) plaquer par galvanoplastie ; (ii) zinguer. Galvanized iron, tôle zinguée.

galvanometer [galva'nɔmetər], s. Galvanomètre m.

galvanoplasty ['galvano'plasti], s. Galvanoplastie f.

gamble[1] [gambl], s. F: (a) Jeu m de hasard. (b) Pure gamble, pure spéculation ; affaire f de chance.

gamble[2]. **1.** v.i. Jouer de l'argent. To g. on a throw of the dice, miser sur un coup de dé(s). To gamble on the Stock Exchange, agioter. To g. on a rise in prices, jouer à la hausse. F: You may gamble on that, vous pouvez compter là-dessus. **2.** v.tr. To gamble away, perdre (sa fortune, etc.) au jeu. **gambling,** s. Le jeu. Gambling-debts, dettes f de jeu. Gambling-den, -house, maison f de jeu ; tripot m.

gambler ['gamblər], s. Joueur, -euse (pour de l'argent). Gambler on the Stock Exchange, spéculateur, -trice ; agioteur, -euse.

gamboge [gam'buːʒ, -'buudʒ], s. Gomme-gutte f.

gambol[1] ['gamb(ə)l], s. (a) Gambade f, cabriole f. (b) pl. F: Ébats m.

gambol[2], v.i. (gambolled) (a) Gambader, cabrioler ; faire des gambades. (b) S'ébattre.

game[1] [geim], s. **1.** (a) Amusement m, divertissement m, jeu m. To make game of s.o., se moquer de qn ; se jouer de qn. (b) Jeu. Game of skill, of chance, jeu d'adresse, de hasard. Out-door games, jeux de plein air. *Sch:* Games master, maître qui organise et surveille les sports. Olympic games, jeux olympiques. F: It's all in the game, c'est dans la règle du jeu. (c) To play a good game, être bon joueur. To play the game, jouer franc jeu ; jouer, agir, loyalement. That's not playing the game, ce n'est pas loyal ; ce n'est pas de jeu. To play s.o.'s game, faire le jeu de qn. To beat s.o. at his own game, battre qn avec ses propres armes. Two can play at that game, à bon chat bon rat. To be on one's game, être bien en forme. (d) F: What's his game? où veut-il en venir? quel but poursuit-il? I was watching their little g., j'observais leur manège. To spoil s.o.'s game, déjouer les plans de qn. The game's up, l'affaire est dans l'eau ; il n'y a plus rien à faire. (e) Partie f (de cartes, de billard, etc.) ; manche f (d'une partie de cartes). To have, play, a game of cricket, faire une partie de cricket. How goes the g.? (i) comment marche la partie? (ii) où en est la partie? To be game, avoir gagné la partie. The odd game, the deciding game, la belle. Ten: Game, set, and match, jeu, set, et partie. F: To have, hold, the game in one's hands, tenir le succès entre ses mains. **2.** (a) Gibier m. Big game, (i) gros gibier ; (ii) les grands fauves. Big-game shooting, la chasse aux grands fauves. Small game, menu gibier. F: Fair game, (gibier) de bonne prise. He is fair game, on a bien le droit de se moquer de lui. (b) *Cu:* Gibier. Game pie, pâté m de gibier. **'game-bag,** s. Carnassière f, gibecière f. **'game-cock,** s. Coq m de combat. **'game-licence,** s. Permis m de chasse. **'game-preserve,** s. Parc m à gibier.

game[2]. **1.** v.i. Jouer (de l'argent). **2.** v.tr. To game away a fortune, dissiper une fortune au jeu. **gaming,** s. Jeu m. Gaming debt, dette de jeu. Gaming-house = gambling-house. Gaming-losses, pertes au jeu. Gaming-table, table de jeu.

game[3], a. Courageux, résolu. To be game, (i) avoir du cran ; (ii) être d'attaque. He is game for anything, il est prêt à tout, capable de tout. To die game, mourir crânement.

game[4], a. Game arm, bras estropié. Game leg, jambe boiteuse, percluse. **game-'legged,** a. Estropié, boiteux.

gamekeeper ['geimki:pər], s. Garde-chasse m, pl. gardes-chasse(s).

gameness ['geimnəs], s. Courage m, crânerie f.

gammer ['gamər], s. F: A: Vieille (bonne) femme.

gammon[1] ['gamən], s. (a) Quartier m de derrière (du porc). (b) Quartier de lard fumé. F: That's all gammon and spinach, tout ça c'est de la blague.

gammon[2], s. P: Blague f ; bourrage m de crâne. Cf. GAMMON[1] (b).

gammon[3], v.tr. P: Blaguer (qn) ; monter un bateau à (qn). To gammon s.o. into doing sth., monter le coup à qn pour lui faire faire qch.

gamp [gamp], s. **1.** *Pej:* Garde-malade f ou sage-femme f. **2.** F: Parapluie de coton mal roulé (comme celui que portait Sarah Gamp) ; P: riflard m, pépin m.

gamut ['gamət], s. **1.** *Mus:* (a) Gamme f. (b) Étendue f (de la voix). **2.** Gamme (de couleurs, etc.).

gamy ['geimi], a. *Cu:* Faisandé, avancé.

gander ['gandər], *s.* **I.** Jars *m. S.a.* SAUCE[1] I. **2.** *F:* Niais *m*, sot *m*, imbécile *m*.

gang [gaŋ], *s.* **I.** (*a*) Groupe *m*, troupe *f* (de personnes); équipe *f*, escouade *f*, atelier *m* (d'ouvriers). *Civ.E: Itinerant g.* (*of roadmen*), brigade ambulante. (*b*) Bande *f* (de voleurs, de faussaires, etc.). *Pej:* **One of the gang,** un de la clique. **The whole gang,** toute la bande. **2.** (*a*) Série *f* (d'outils qui vont ensemble). (*b*) *W.Tel:* **Two-gang condenser,** condensateur à deux blocs. **'gang-board, -plank,** *s. Nau:* Planche *f* à débarquer; appontement *m*.

ganged [gaŋd], *a.* **I.** (Outils) multiples ou montés ensemble. **2.** *W.Tel:* **Ganged condensers,** condensateurs à blocs combinés.

ganger ['gaŋər], *s. Rail:* Chef *m* d'équipe. *Civ.E:* Brigadier *m* cantonnier.

ganglion, -ia ['gaŋliən, -ia], *s.* (*a*) *Anat:* Ganglion *m*. (*b*) *F:* Centre *m*, foyer *m*, d'activité.

gangrene[1] ['gaŋgriːn], *s. Med:* Gangrène *f*, mortification *f*, sphacèle *m*. **Hospital gangrene,** ulcère rongeant; pourriture *f* d'hôpital.

gangrene[2]. I. *v.tr.* Gangrener, mortifier. **2.** *v.i.* Se gangrener.

gangrenous ['gaŋgrenəs], *a.* Gangreneux, sphacélé.

gangster ['gaŋstər], *s. U.S: F:* Bandit *m*; gangster *m*.

gangway ['gaŋwei], *s.* **I.** Passage *m*; couloir central (d'autobus, etc.). **2.** *Nau:* (*a*) Passerelle *f* de service. (*b*) (*Opening*) Coupée *f* (dans la muraille). (*c*) (**Fore-and-aft**) **gangway,** passavant *m*.

gannet ['ganet], *s. Orn:* Gannet *m*, fou *m*.

gantry ['gantri], *s.* **I.** Chantier *m* (pour fûts); porte-fût(s) *m inv.* **2.** *Ind:* (*a*) Portique *m*; pont roulant (pour grue roulante). *Rail:* Signal gantry, pont à signaux. (*b*) **Gantry(-crane),** grue *f* à portique.

gaol[1] [dʒeil], *s.* Prison *f*; maison *f* d'arrêt. **The County gaol** = la maison centrale. **To be in gaol,** être en prison. **'gaol-bird,** *s. F:* Échappé, -ée, de prison; gibier *m* de potence. **'gaol-delivery,** *s.* Levée *f* d'écrou (de prisonniers).

gaol[2], *v.tr.* Mettre (qn) en prison; écrouer (qn).

gaoler ['dʒeilər], *s.* Gardien *m* de prison.

gap [gap], *s.* **I.** (*a*) Trou *m*; trouée *f*, ouverture *f*, vide *m* (dans une haie, etc.); brèche *f* (dans un mur, etc.); solution *f* de continuité (d'une surface). **To fill (in), fill up, a gap; to stop a gap,** boucher un trou, une brèche; combler un vide. *S.a.* STOP-GAP. (*b*) *U.S:* Col *m* (de montagne). (*c*) Interstice *m*; jour *m* (entre les planches, etc.); distance *f*, intervalle *m* (entre les électrodes). *Gap between the curtains,* interstice entre les rideaux; bâillement *m* des rideaux. **Armature gap,** ouverture, entrefer *m*, d'induit. (*e*) Trou, lacune *f*, vide (dans des souvenirs, etc.). **2.** *Mec.E:* Coupure *f*, rompu *m* (d'un banc de tour). **'gap-toothed,** *a.* Aux dents écartées.

gape[1] [geip], *s.* Bâillement *m. F:* **To give s.o. the gapes,** faire bâiller qn.

gape[2], *v.i.* **I.** (*a*) (*Of pers.*) (i) Ouvrir la bouche toute grande; (ii) bâiller (d'ennui). (*b*) (*Of bird*) Ouvrir un large bec. (*c*) (*Of thg*) To gape (open), s'ouvrir (tout grand); (*of hole*) être béant; (*of seam, etc.*) bâiller. **2.** (*Of pers.*) Être, rester, bouche bée; bayer aux corneilles. **To gape at s.o., sth.,** regarder qn, qch., bouche bée, d'un air hébété. **gaping[1],** *a.* Béant. **gaping[2],** *s.* **I.** Contemplation *f* bouche bée. **2.** Bâillement *m*.

garage[1] ['garɑːʒ, 'garedʒ], *s. Aut:* Garage *m*. **Open garage,** hall *m* de garage. **Lock-up garage,**

box *m*. **Garage keeper, garage proprietor,** garagiste *m*.

garage[2], *v.tr.* (i) Garer, (ii) remiser (une automobile).

garb[1] [gɑːrb], *s.* Vêtement *m*, costume *m*. **In Turkish garb,** vêtu à la turque. *F:* **His usual garb of indifference,** ses dehors habituels d'indifférence.

garb[2], *v.tr.* Habiller, vêtir (*in, de*).

garbage ['gɑːrbedʒ], *s.* **I.** Tripaille *f*, entrailles *fpl*; issues *fpl* (de boucherie). **2.** Im-. mondices *fpl*, détritus *mpl*; ordures (ménagères). **Garbage heap,** tas *m* d'ordures; voirie *f. F:* **Literary garbage,** rebut *m* de la littérature.

garble [gɑːrbl], *v.tr.* Tronquer, fausser (une citation, des comptes, etc.); dénaturer (les faits); mutiler, altérer (un texte). **Garbled account,** compte rendu mensonger.

garbler ['gɑːrblər], *s.* Mutilateur, -trice (d'un texte, etc.); faussaire *m* (de faits, etc.).

garden[1] [gɑːrdn], *s.* (*a*) Jardin *m. Small g.,* jardinet *m.* **Kitchen garden, vegetable garden,** (jardin) potager *m.* **Market garden,** jardin maraîcher. **Strawberry garden,** champ *m* de fraises. **Winter garden,** (i) jardin d'hiver; grande serre; (ii) (*in hotel, etc.*) hall vitré. *S.a.* BEAR-GARDEN, LANDSCAPE-GARDEN, ROCK-GARDEN, TEA-GARDEN. (*b*) *pl.* Jardin public ou parc *m.* (*c*) *pl.* Rue avec jardins. **'garden-'hose,** *s.* Tuyau *m* d'arrosage. **'garden-'party,** *s.* Réception (mondaine) en plein air. **'garden-'produce, -'stuff,** *s.* Jardinage *m*; produits maraîchers; denrées potagères.

garden[2], *v.i.* Jardiner. **gardening,** *s.* Jardinage *m*; horticulture *f*.

gardener ['gɑːrdnər], *s.* Jardinier *m. S.a.* LANDSCAPE-GARDENER, MARKET-GARDENER, NURSERY-GARDENER.

gargantuan [gɑːr'gantjuən], *a.* Gargantuesque.

gargle[1] ['gɑːrgl], *s. Med:* Gargarisme *m*.

gargle[2]. I. *v.i.* Se gargariser. **2.** *v.tr.* To gargle one's throat, se gargariser la gorge. **gargling,** *s.* Gargarisme *m*.

gargoyle ['gɑːrgɔil], *s. Arch:* Gargouille *f*.

garish ['gɛəriʃ], *a.* (*Of dress, etc.*) Voyant; d'un luxe criard. **I.** (*Of light*) Cru. **2.** (*G. light,* lumière crue, aveuglante. **-ly,** *adv.* (Meublé, etc.) avec un luxe criard.

garishness ['gɛəriʃnəs], *s.* **I.** Luxe criard; faste *m*. **2.** Éclat excessif; crudité *f* (d'une couleur).

garland[1] ['gɑːrlənd], *s.* Guirlande *f*; couronne *f* (de fleurs). **To hang sth. with garlands,** orner, parer, qch. de guirlandes.

garland[2], *v.tr.* (En)guirlander.

garlic ['gɑːrlik], *s. Bot:* Ail *m.* **Clove of garlic,** gousse *f* d'ail; caïeu *m* d'ail.

garment ['gɑːrmənt], *s. Lit:* Vêtement *m*.

garner[1] ['gɑːrnər], *s. Lit:* Grenier *m*.

garner[2], *v.tr. Lit:* Mettre (le grain) en grenier, en grange; engranger, rentrer (le blé, etc.). **garnering,** *s.* Engrangement *m* (du blé, etc.).

garnet ['gɑːrnet], *s. Miner:* Grenat *m*.

garnish[1] ['gɑːrniʃ], *s. Cu: etc:* Garniture *f*.

garnish[2], *v.tr.* Garnir, orner, embellir (*with, de*). **garnishing,** *s.* **I.** Garnissage *m*, garnissement *m*. **2.** Garniture *f* (d'un plat).

garret ['garet], *s.* Mansarde *f*, galetas *m*, soupente *f*. **From cellar to garret,** de la cave au grenier. **'garret-'window,** *s.* (Fenêtre *f* en) mansarde *f*.

garrison[1] ['garisən], *s.* Garnison *f*. **To be in garrison in a town,** être en garnison dans une ville. *Attrib.* **Garrison duty,** service de place,

de garnison. **Garrison troops,** troupes sédentaires. **Garrison artillery,** artillerie de place.
garrison², *v.tr.* **1.** To garrison a town, (i) placer,
mettre, une garnison dans une ville ; (ii) (*of
troops*) être en garnison dans une ville. *To g. a
stronghold,* garnir une place de guerre. **2.** Mettre
(des troupes) en garnison.
gar(r)otte¹ [ga'rɔt], *s.* **1.** Supplice *m* du garrot.
2. Strangulation *f.*
gar(r)otte², *v.tr.* **1.** Garrotter (qn). **2.** Étrangler
(qn) ; *P:* serrer le quiqui à (qn). **garrotting,**
s. **1.** Garrottage *m.* **2.** Strangulation *f.*
garrotter [ga'rɔtər], *s.* Étrangleur *m.*
garrulity [ga'ruːliti], **garrulousness** ['garu-
ləsnəs], *s.* **1.** Loquacité *f* ; garrulité *f.* **2.** Verbosité *f* (de style).
garrulous ['garuləs], *a.* **1.** Loquace, bavard.
2. (Discours, style) verbeux. **-ly,** *adv.* Avec
volubilité ; verbeusement.
garter¹ ['gɑːrtər], *s.* (*a*) Jarretière *f. To put on
one's garters,* mettre ses jarretières ; (se) jarreter.
(*b*) **Arm-garter,** bracelet *m* (pour retenir les
manches de chemise). **'garter-stitch,** *s.
Knitting:* Tricot uni.
garter², *v.tr.* Jarreter (sa jambe, ses bas).
gas¹, *pl.* **gases** [gas, 'gasiz], *s.* **1.** Gaz *m.* (*a*) *Ch:
Ind:* Nitrogen gas, gaz azote. (*b*) **Lighting gas,
coal gas,** gaz d'éclairage, de houille. **The gas is
laid on,** les conduites de gaz sont posées ; *F:* le
gaz est posé. **The gas industry,** l'industrie
gazière. (*c*) *Med: Dent:* **Laughing gas,** *F:* gas,
gaz hilarant, gaz nitreux. *F: To have gas,* se
faire anesthésier. (*d*) *Mil:* **Asphyxiating gas,**
F: **poison-gas,** gaz asphyxiants, toxiques.
2. *U.S: F: =* GASOLINE (*b*). *S.a.* STEP ON.
3. *P:* Verbiage *m,* bavardage *m,* jaserie *f.*
'gas-attack, *s. Mil:* Attaque *f* par les gaz, aux
gaz. **'gas-bacillus,** *s. Med:* Vibrion *m*
septique. **'gas-bag,** *s.* **1.** *F:* Grand parleur ;
vantard *m.* **2.** *Aer:* (*a*) Enveloppe *f* (à gaz).
(*b*) Ballonnet *m* (de dirigeable, etc.). **'gas-
burner,** *s.* Bec *m* de gaz. **'gas-coke,** *s.* Coke *m*
de gaz. **'gas-company,** *s.* Compagnie *f* du
gaz. **'gas-'cooker,** *s.* **1.** Réchaud *m* à gaz.
2. *=* GAS-OVEN. **'gas-engine,** *s. I.C.E:* Moteur *m* à gaz ; machine *f* à gaz. **'gas-filled,** *a.
El.E:* (Lampe) gazeuse. **'gas-'fire,** *s.* Radiateur *m* à gaz. **'gas-fitter,** *s.* Gazier *m.*
'gas-fitting, *s.* **1.** Pose *f* des appareils à gaz.
2. *pl.* Gas-fittings, appareillage *m* pour le gaz.
'gas-generator, *s.* Générateur *m* de gaz ;
gazogène *m.* **'gas-holder,** *s.* Gazomètre *m.*
'gas-lamp, *s.* (*In street*) Bec *m* de gaz ;
réverbère *m.* **'gas-light,** *s.* Lumière *f* du gaz.
Phot: Gas-light paper, papier au gélatino-
chlorure. **'gas-lighting,** *s.* Éclairage *m* au gaz.
'gas-main, *s.* (Tuyau *m* de) conduite *f* de gaz.
'gas-man, *pl.* **-men,** *s.m. F:* Employé du gaz ;
(i) le gazier ; (ii) l'encaisseur (de la Compagnie).
'gas-mantle, *s.* Manchon *m* (de bec de gaz).
'gas-mask, *s.* Masque *m* à gaz, contre les
gaz ; masque respiratoire. **'gas-meter,** *s.*
Compteur *m* (à gaz). **'gas-oven,** *s.* (*a*) Four *m*
à gaz. (*b*) Fourneau *m* à gaz ; poêle *m,*
cuisinière *f,* réchaud *m,* à gaz. **To put one's
head in the gas-oven,** s'asphyxier par le gaz
d'éclairage. **'gas-pipe,** *s.* Tuyau *m* à gaz ;
conduite *f* de, du, gaz. **'gas-producer,** *s.
Ind:* Gazogène *m.* **'gas-proof,** *a. Mil:* (Abri,
etc.) à l'épreuve des gaz. **'gas-range,** *s. Cu:*
Fourneau *m* à gaz ; cuisinière *f* à gaz. **'gas-
ring,** *s.* **1.** *Cu:* Réchaud *m* à gaz à un feu.
2. (Brûleur *m* à) couronne *f.* **'gas-shell,** *s.
Mil:* Obus *m* à gaz (de combat). **'gas-stove,** *s.*

1. *=* GAS-FIRE. **2.** *=* GAS-OVEN. **'gas-works,**
s.pl. (*Usu. with sg.const.*) Usine *f* à gaz.
gas², *v.* (gassed) **1.** *v.tr.* (*a*) *Ch: Ind:* Passer
(un produit) au gaz. (*b*) Asphyxier, intoxiquer.
Mil: Gazer. **Gassed,** atteint par les gaz asphyxiants ; gazé. **2.** *v.i. P:* Jaser ; (*of public
speaker, etc.*) pérorer.
Gascon ['gaskən], *a. & s. Geog:* Gascon, -onne.
Gascony ['gaskəni]. *Pr.n. Geog:* La Gascogne.
gaseous ['geisiəs, gasiəs], *a.* Gazeux.
gash¹ [gaʃ], *s.* Coupure *f,* entaille *f* (faite dans la
chair) ; taillade *f* ; (*on face*) balafre *f.*
gash², *v.tr.* Entailler, couper ; balafrer (le
visage). **To gash one's chin** (*in shaving*), se faire
une entaille au menton.
gasify ['gasifai], *v.tr.* Gazéifier.
gasket ['gaskit], *s.* **1.** *Nau:* Garcette *f,* raban *m*
(de ris, de ferlage). **2.** *Mec.E:* Joint *m* métallo-
plastique, en papier huilé, en étoupe, à l'amiante ;
I.C.E: obturateur *m* de joint.
gasogene ['gasodʒiːn], *s.* Gazogène *m.*
gasolene, gasoline ['gasoliːn], *s.* (*a*) Gazoline *f.*
(*b*) *U.S:* Essence *f* de pétrole ; *Aut:* essence.
gasometer [ga'sɔmətər], *s.* Gazomètre *m* ; réservoir *m* à gaz (d'éclairage).
gasp¹ [gɑːsp], *s.* Hoquet *m,* sursaut *m* (de surprise, etc.). **To be at one's last gasp,** agoniser.
To defend sth. to the last gasp, défendre qch.
jusqu'à son dernier souffle. **To give one's last
gasp,** rendre le dernier soupir.
gasp², *v.i. & tr.* (*a*) Avoir un hoquet de surprise,
etc.). **To gasp with fright, with astonishment,**
sursauter. **To make s.o.** gasp, couper la respiration, le souffle, à qn. (*b*) **To gasp for breath, for
air,** haleter, suffoquer. *P:* **I'm gasping for a
drink,** je meurs de soif. **gasping¹,** *a.* (*a*) Haletant. (*b*) Agonisant ; à la dernière extrémité.
gasping², *s.* Halètement *m.*
gasper ['gaspər], *s. P:* Cigarette *f* (de mauvaise
qualité) ; *P:* sèche *f.*
gassy ['gasi], *a.* **1.** Gazeux ; (*of wine*) mousseux,
crémant. **2.** *P:* Verbeux, bavard.
gast(e)ropod, *pl.* **-ods, -opoda** ['gast(ə)rɔpɔd,
-ɔdz, gast(ə)'rɔpoda], *s. Moll:* Gastéropode *m.*
gast(e)ropodous [gastə'rɔpodəs, gas'trɔpodəs],
a. Moll: Gastéropode.
gastric ['gastrik], *a.* Gastrique. *G.* trouble(s),
embarras gastriques, gastrique. **Gastric ulcer,** *m*
simple de l'estomac ; gastrite ulcéreuse.
gastritis [gas'traitis], *s. Med:* Gastrite *f.*
gastronome ['gastronom], **gastronomer**
[gas'trɔnəmər], *s.* Gastronome *m.*
gastronomic(al) [gastro'nɔmik(əl)], *a.* Gastronomique.
gastronomy [gas'trɔnomi], *s.* Gastronomie *f.*
gastrotomy [gas'trɔtomi], *s. Surg:* Gastrotomie *f.*
gate¹ [geit], *s.* **1.** Porte *f* (d'une ville, etc.). **Main
gates** (*of exhibition, etc.*), entrée principale.
U.S: P: **To give s.o. the gate,** congédier qn.
2. (*a*) (Wooden) gate, barrière *f* ; porte à claire-
voie. (*Wrought-iron*) **entrance gate** (*to grounds*),
grille *f* d'entrée. *Sp:* (i) Le public (à un
match) ; (ii) *=* GATE-MONEY. **3.** *Aut:* Gate
(quadrant), grille *f* (de changement de vitesse).
'gate-crasher, *s. F:* Resquilleur, -euse.
'gate-crashing, *s.* Resquillage *m.* **'gate-
house,** *s.* **1.** Loge *f* de garde (à l'entrée d'un
parc). **2.** Corps-de-garde *m inv* (d'un château
fort). **'gate-keeper,** *s.* **1.** Portier, -ière.
2. *Rail:* Garde-barrière *mf, pl.* gardes-barrière(s).
'gate-legged, *a. F:* **Gate-legged** table, table à
abattants. **'gate-money,** *s. Sp:* Recette *f* ;
les entrées *f.* **'gate-post,** *s.* Montant *m* (de
barrière, de porte).

gate², *v.tr.* Consigner (un etudiant). **gating**, *s.* *Sch:* Consigne *f.*

gate³, *s. Scot:* Chemin *m.* **To take the gate,** se mettre en route. **To let s.o. gang his own gate,** laisser qn se débrouiller.

gateway ['geitwei], *s.* **1.** Porte *f*, entrée *f.* **Carriage gateway,** porte cochère. **2.** Porte monumentale ; portail *m.*

gather ['gaðər]. I. *v.tr.* **1.** (*a*) Assembler, rassembler (des personnes) ; rassembler, recueillir (des choses). **To gather one's thoughts,** recueillir ses esprits. **To gather all one's strength** *in order to* . . ., recueillir, rassembler, ramasser, toutes ses forces pour. . . . (*b*) Ramasser (ses papiers, etc.). **To gather (up) one's hair into a knot,** tordre ses cheveux en chignon. **To gather up one's skirts,** retrousser ses jupes. (*c*) Cueillir (des fleurs) ; recueillir (du blé)· **To gather (in) the harvest,** rentrer la récolte. *To g. the strawberries,* faire la cueillette des fraises. *To g.* sticks (*for firewood*), ramasser du bois. **To gather taxes, rents,** percevoir les contributions, les loyers. (*d*) **To gather oneself,** se mettre en boule. **To gather (oneself) together for a spring,** se ramasser pour sauter. **2. To gather speed,** acquérir, prendre, de la vitesse. (*Of invalid*) **To gather strength,** reprendre des forces. **To gather volume,** croître en volume. **3.** (*a*) Serrer. **To gather one's shawl about oneself,** serrer son châle. (*b*) *Needlew: To g. a skirt,* froncer une jupe. **4.** Conclure. **I gather from the papers that he has . . .,** à en croire les journaux il aurait. . . . *As will be gathered from the enclosed letter,* comme il ressort de la lettre ci-jointe. II. **gather,** *v.i.* **1.** (*Of pers.*) (*a*) Se réunir, se rassembler. **To gather round the fire,** se grouper autour du feu. **Gather round!** approchez-vous ! faites cercle ! (*b*) Affluer, s'attrouper (en foule). **2.** (*Of thgs*) S'accumuler, s'amonceler, s'amasser. (*a*) **A storm is gathering,** un orage se prépare. (*b*) **In the gathering darkness,** dans la nuit grandissante. *The story gathered like a snowball,* l'histoire faisait boule de neige. **3.** *Med:* (*Of wound*) Abcéder. (*Of abscess*) **To gather to a head,** aboutir, mûrir. **gathered,** *a.* (*a*) (Front) sourcilleux. (*b*) *Needlew:* (Volant, etc.) froncé, à fronces. (*c*) **To have a gathered finger,** avoir un abcès au doigt. **gathering,** *s.* **1.** (*a*) Rassemblement *m*, attroupement *m* (d'une foule). (*b*) Accumulation *f* (de choses). (*c*) Cueillette *f* (des fruits, etc.). **Gathering (in) of the crop,** (rentrage *m* de la) récolte. (*d*) Froncement *m* (des sourcils). *Needlew:* Fronçure *f* (d'une robe, etc.). (*e*) Accumulation, amoncellement *m* (de nuages). (*f*) *Med:* Collection *f* (du pus). **2.** (*a*) Assemblée *f*, réunion *f*, compagnie *f* (dans une salle) ; assemblage *m*, rassemblement, attroupement (dans les rues). **Family gathering,** réunion de famille. (*b*) *Needlew:* Froncis *m*, fronces *fpl.* (*c*) *Med:* Abcès *m*; *F:* bobo *m.*

gatherer ['gaðərər], *s.* (Pers.) (*a*) (R)amasseur, -euse. (*b*) Cueilleur, -euse (de fruits, etc.). **Tax-gatherer,** percepteur *m* des contributions.

gathers ['gaðərz], *s.pl. Needlew:* Fronces *f.*

gaudery ['gɔːdəri], *s.* Oripeaux *mpl*, clinquant *m.*

gaudiness ['gɔːdinəs], *s.* Ostentation *f*; clinquant *m.*

gaudy ['gɔːdi], *a.* (*Of colours, etc.*) Voyant, criard, éclatant ; (*of display, etc.*) fastueux. **-ily,** *adv.* De manière voyante ; fastueusement ; (peint) en couleurs criardes.

gauge¹ [geidʒ], *s.* **1.** (*a*) Calibre *m* (d'un écrou, etc.) ; jauge *f* (d'une futaille, etc.). *F:* **To take**

s.o.'s gauge, mesurer les capacités de qn. (*b*) *Veh:* (Cart-)gauge, voie (charretière). *Rail:* **Gauge of the track,** largeur *f*, écartement *m*, de la voie. **2.** (*a*) (Appareil *m*) vérificateur *m* ; calibre, jauge (pour mesurer qch.). *Mec.E:* **Thickness-gauge, feeler-gauge,** calibre d'épaisseur. **Slide gauge,** (i) calibre à curseur ; pied *m*, compas *m*, à coulisse ; (ii) vernier *m.* **Calliper gauge,** calibre de précision. **Cylindrical gauge,** plug gauge, tampon vérificateur. *Rail:* **Loading gauge,** tunnel gauge, gabarit *m* de chargement. (*b*) *Carp:* (Marking) gauge, trusquin *m.* **3.** Indicateur *m*, contrôleur *m.* (*a*) **Vacuum gauge,** indicateur, jauge, du vide. (*b*) *Mch: etc:* **Water gauge, oil gauge,** (indicateur d') niveau *m* d'eau, d'huile. *Aut:* **Petrol gauge,** indicateur jauge d'essence. (*c*) *Av:* **Height gauge,** altimètre *m.* *S.a.* PRESSURE-GAUGE, RAIN-GAUGE, TYRE-GAUGE. **4.** *Const:* Dose *f* (de ciment). **5.** *Nau:* (Often gage) (*a*) Tirant *m* d'eau (d'un navire). (*b*) **Weather gauge,** avantage *m* du vent. *S.a.* LEE-GAUGE.

gauge², *v.tr.* **1.** Calibrer, étalonner (un écrou, etc.) ; jauger, mesurer (le vent, etc.). *To g. sth. by the eye,* mesurer qch. à l'œil, à la vue. *F:* **To gauge s.o.'s capacities,** estimer, jauger, les capacités de qn. **2.** *Carp:* Trusquiner (le bois). **3.** Doser (le ciment). **4.** *Dressm:* Bouillonner (une jupe, etc.). **Gauged sleeves,** manches à bouillons. **gauging,** *s.* **1.** Calibrage *m* ; étalonnage *m* ; jaugeage *m.* **2.** Dosage *m* (du ciment). **3.** *Dressm:* Bouillon *m.*

Gaul [gɔːl]. **1.** *Pr.n. A.Geog:* La Gaule. **2.** *s.* Gaulois, -oise.

gaunt [gɔːnt], *a.* **1.** Maigre, décharné. **2.** (*a*) D'aspect redoutable, farouche. (*b*) Lugubre, désolé.

gauntlet¹ ['gɔːntlet], *s.* **1.** *Archeol:* Gantelet *m*, gant *m.* **To throw down the gauntlet to s.o.,** jeter le gant à qn. **To take up the gauntlet,** relever le gant. **2.** **Gauntlet glove,** gant à crispins, à manchette ; gant à la mousquetaire.

gauntlet², *s. Mil:* **To run the gauntlet,** passer par les bretelles, par les baguettes. *F:* **To run the gauntlet of adverse criticism,** soutenir un feu roulant de critiques adverses.

gauze [gɔːz], *s.* **1.** Gaze *f.* (*b*) **Wire gauze,** toile *f* métallique, tissu *m* métallique.

gauzy ['gɔːzi], *a.* Diaphane ; léger.

gave [geiv]. *See* GIVE².

gavel ['gav(ə)l], *s. U.S:* Marteau *m* (de commissaire-priseur, etc.).

gawk [gɔːk], *s. G. of a man,* escogriffe *m* ; grand dadais *m.* *G. of a woman,* grande godiche ; grande bringue.

gawkiness ['gɔːkinəs], *s.* Gaucherie *f.*

gawky ['gɔːki], *a.* Dégingandé, gauche ; *F:* empoté, godiche. **-ily,** *adv.* Gauchement.

gay [gei], *a.* (gayest) **1.** (*a*) Gai, allègre. **To become gay,** s'égayer. (*b*) **To lead a gay life,** mener une vie de plaisir(s). **To have a gay time,** s'amuser follement. *S.a.* DOG¹ 3. (*c*) **Gay woman,** femme galante. **2.** Gai, splendide, brillant. **Scene gay with lights,** scène égayée, resplendissante, de lumières. **gaily,** *adv.* **1.** Gaiement, allègrement. **2.** (Habillé) de couleurs gaies.

gaze¹ [geiz], *s.* Regard *m* fixe. *A horrible sight met his g.,* un spectacle horrible s'offrit à sa vue, à ses regards.

gaze², *v.i.* Regarder fixement. **To gaze into space,** regarder dans le vide. **To gaze at, on, upon,** s.o., fixer, contempler, considérer, qn. **gazing,** *a.* (*Of crowd, etc.*) Curieux.

gazelle [ga'zel], *s. Z:* Gazelle *f.*

gazer ['geizər], *s.* Contemplateur, -trice (*at, upon, de*); curieux, -euse.

gazette[1] [ga'zet], *s.* **1.** *A:* Gazette *f.* **2.** Journal officiel. **To be, appear, in the Gazette,** figurer (à la *Gazette*) dans les déclarations de faillite. **3.** *Cin:* Topical Gazette, film *m* d'actualité; actualités *fpl.*

gazette[2], *v.tr.* Annoncer, publier, (une faillite, une nomination, etc.) dans un journal officiel. (*Of officer, etc.*) **To be gazetted,** être à la *London Gazette* (= à l'Officiel).

gazetteer [gazə'ti:ər], *s.* **1.** (*Pers.*) *A:* (*a*) Gazetier (officiel). (*b*) Nouvelliste *m.* **2.** Répertoire *m* géographique.

gean [gi:n], *s.* *Bot:* **1.** Merise *f.* **2.** Gean(-tree), merisier *m.*

gear[1] ['gi:ər], *s.* **1.** (*a*) *A:* Accoutrement *m.* (*Still used in compounds*) Foot-gear, chaussures *fpl.* (*b*) Harnais *m,* harnachement *m* (de cheval de trait). **2.** (*a*) Effets (personnels). Household gear, ustensiles *m* de ménage. (*b*) Attirail *m,* appareil *m*; *Nau:* apparaux *mpl.* Fishing gear, attirail de pêche. Pump gear, garniture *f,* gréement *m,* d'une pompe. **3.** *Mec.E:* (*a*) Appareil, mécanisme *m.* Control gear, (i) appareil de commande; (ii) *Av:* dispositif *m* de manœuvre. (*b*) (Driving-, transmission-)gear, transmission *f,* commande *f.* Wheel gear, transmission, commande, par engrenage. Belt gear, commande par courroie. Crank gear, pédalier *m* (d'une bicyclette, etc.). Train of gears, train *m* d'engrenages. Reversing gear, (appareil de) changement *m* de marche. *Aut:* Sliding gear, throw-over gear, (train) bal(l)adeur *m.* In gear, (i) engrené, en prise; (ii) (*of machine*) en action, en jeu. To come into gear, s'enclencher (*with, avec*). To throw (sth.) into gear, embrayer, enclencher, engrener (les roues); mettre (une machine) en marche, en jeu. Out of gear, (i) débrayé, désengrené; (ii) (*of machine*) hors d'action; (iii) hors de service; détraqué; (iv) *F:* (*of organization, etc.*) dérangé, déréglé. To throw (sth.) out of gear, (i) débrayer, déclencher (des roues); mettre (une machine) au repos; (ii) détraquer (une machine); (iii) *F:* disloquer, déranger (les plans de qn, etc.). (*c*) (i) Multiplication *f,* démultiplication *f* (d'un engrenage, etc.). Bicycle with a 66 inch gear, bicyclette avec un développement de 5 m. 25, qui développe 5 m. 25. (ii) *Aut:* Vitesse *f.* High gear, low gear, grande, petite, vitesse; grande, petite, multiplication. First, low, bottom, gear, première vitesse. To change gear, changer de vitesse. *To engage the first g.,* mettre en première (vitesse). **'gear-box,** *s.* **1.** *Mec.E:* Carter *m,* couvre-engrenages *m inv.* **2.** *Aut:* Boîte *f* de vitesses. **'gear-case,** *s.* **1.** *Mec.E:* = GEAR-BOX 1. **2.** *Cy:* Carter *m.* **'gear-ratio,** *s.* *Mec.E:* Rapport *m* d'engrenage; (i) multiplication *f*; (ii) (reduction) gear-ratio, démultiplication *f.* **'gear-wheel,** *s.* (*a*) *Mec.E:* (Roue *f* d')engrenage *m*; roue dentée; rouage *m.* (*b*) *Cy:* Pignon *m.*

gear[2]. **1.** *v.tr.* (*a*) Gréer (une machine). (*b*) Embrayer, enclencher, engrener (un pignon, etc.). **2.** *v.i.* S'embrayer, s'enclencher, s'engrener. **3.** *v.tr.* To gear up, down, multiplier, démultiplier (la vitesse de révolution). **geared,** *a.* *Mec.E:* (Tour, etc.) à engrenage(s). **gearing,** *s.* **1.** (*a*) Engrenage *m,* embrayage *m,* enclenchement *m.* (*b*) Gearing up, multiplication *f*; *Cy:* développement *m.* Gearing down, démultiplication *f,* réduction *f.* **2.** Transmission *f,* commande *f.*

(Train of) gearing, système *m,* jeu *m,* train *m,* d'engrenages.

gee[1] [dʒi:], *s.* La lettre g.

gee[2]. **1.** *int.* Gee-up! hue! huhau! **2.** *s.* = GEE-GEE.

gee-gee ['dʒi:dʒi:], *s.* (*Child's speech*) Cheval *m*; dada *m.*

geese [gi:s]. *See* GOOSE.

geezer ['gi:zər], *s.* *P:* Old geezer, bonhomme ou bonne femme légèrement grotesque.

Gehenna [gi'hena]. *Pr.n.* *B.Hist:* La Géhenne, l'Enfer.

gel[1] [dʒel], *s.* *Ch:* Colloïde (coagulé).

gel[2], *v.i.* (gelled) (*Of colloid*) Se coaguler.

gelatine ['dʒelatin, -ti:n], *s.* (*a*) Gélatine *f.* (*b*) *Biol:* Gelatine meat-broth, bouillon *m* de culture. (*c*) *Exp:* Blasting gelatine, explosive gelatine, gélatine détonante; dynamite *f* gomme.

gelatinous [dʒe'latinəs], *a.* Gélatineux.

geld [geld], *v.tr.* Hongrer (un cheval).

gelding ['geldiŋ], *s.* Cheval *m* hongre.

gem [dʒem], *s.* **1.** (*a*) Pierre précieuse; gemme *f,* joyau *m.* (*b*) *F:* The gem of the collection, le joyau de la collection. **2.** Pierre gravée; intaille *f,* camée *m.*

geminate ['dʒeminet], *a.* (*Of leaves, etc.*) Géminé, accouplé.

gemmed [dʒemd], *a.* Orné de pierres précieuses, de pierreries; gemmé.

gender ['dʒendər], *s.* **1.** *Gram:* Genre *m.* **2.** *F:* Sexe *m.*

genealogical [dʒi:niə'lɔdʒik(ə)l], *a.* Généalogique. **-ally,** *adv.* Généalogiquement.

genealogist [dʒi:ni'alodʒist], *s.* Généalogiste *m.*

genealogy [dʒi:ni'alodʒi], *s.* Généalogie *f.*

genera ['dʒenərə]. *See* GENUS.

general ['dʒenərəl]. **I.** *a.* Général, -aux. **1.** *G.* drawing or sketch, dessin d'ensemble (d'une machine, etc.). **2.** (*a*) General meeting, assemblée générale. *Adm:* General holiday, fête publique; jour férié. *Mil:* General headquarters, grand quartier général. *Ecc:* General confession, confession en commun. (*b*) The use of it is pretty general, l'usage en est assez commun, assez général. **As a general rule,** en règle générale. **Speaking in a general way;** *F:* as a general thing, en thèse générale. **The general public,** le grand public. **The general reader,** le commun des lecteurs; le public (qui lit). (*c*) General knowledge, connaissances générales. General store, grand magasin; bazar *m.* General shop, petite boutique pour toutes sortes d'approvisionnements. General bookseller, librairie *f* d'assortiment. General servant, bonne *f* à tout faire. (*d*) General resemblance, ressemblance générale, vague. **3.** Inspector-general, inspecteur général, en chef. **4.** *adv.phr.* In general, en général; universellement. **2.** Généralement; en général. **Generally speaking,** (parlant) d'une manière générale; en général. **3.** *He g. comes on Thursdays,* en règle générale il vient le jeudi. **II.** *general,* *s.* **1.** To argue from the general to the particular, arguer du général au particulier. **2.** *A:* The general, le gros public. **3.** *Mil:* Général *m.* General Smith, Monsieur le général Smith. Yes, General, (i) oui (monsieur le) général; (ii) (*from subordinate*) oui, mon général. *F:* He's no general, il n'est pas tacticien, stratégiste. **4.** *F:* = General servant.

generalissimo [dʒenərə'lisimo], *s.* Généralissime *m.*

generality [dʒenə'raliti], *s.* Généralité *f.* (*a*) *G. of a statement,* portée générale d'une affirmation.

(b) Considération générale. **To confine oneself to generalities,** s'en tenir aux généralités. (c) **The generality of mankind,** la généralité, la plupart, des hommes.
generalization [dʒenərəlai'zeiʃ(ə)n], s. Généralisation f.
generalize ['dʒenərəla:iz], v.tr. **1.** Généraliser (des faits). **2.** Répandre, populariser (un usage, etc.). **generalizing**[1], a. Généralisateur, -trice; généralisant. **generalizing**[2], s. Généralisation f.
generalship ['dʒenərəlʃip], s. **1.** Généralat m. **2.** Stratégie f, tactique f.
generate ['dʒenəreit], v.tr. **1.** A: Engendrer (des êtres vivants, des plantes, etc.). **2.** Générer, produire (de la vapeur); produire, engendrer (de la chaleur, etc.). **3.** Geom: Engendrer (une surface, etc.). **4.** Amener, produire (un résultat).
generating, a. Générateur, -trice. **Generating station,** station, usine, génératrice; centrale f électrique.
generation [dʒenə'reiʃ(ə)n], s. Génération f. **1.** Génération, production f (de la chaleur, etc.). **2.** (a) **From generation to generation,** de génération en génération; de père en fils. F: **It is generations since anybody did such a thing,** on n'a pas fait une telle chose depuis des siècles. (b) **The rising generation,** la jeune, la nouvelle, génération.
generative ['dʒenəreitiv, -ətiv], a. Génératif; générateur, -trice; producteur, -trice.
generator ['dʒenəreitər], s. **1.** (Pers.) Générateur, -trice (d'une idée, etc.). **2.** (Apparatus, plant) (a) Générateur (de vapeur, de gaz, etc.); appareil producteur (de gaz). (b) El.E: Générateur; génératrice. **3.** Mus: Son fondamental; son générateur (d'un accord).
generic(al) [dʒe'nerik(ə)l], a. Générique. **-ally,** adv. Génériquement.
generosity [dʒenə'rɔsiti], s. Générosité f. (a) Magnanimité f. (b) Libéralité f.
generous ['dʒenərəs], a. Généreux. (a) Magnanime. (b) Libéral, -aux. (c) **Generous soil,** sol généreux, fertile. G. living, bonne chère. G. colour, couleur riche. (d) F: G. meal, repas copieux. **-ly,** adv. Généreusement. **1.** Avec magnanimité. **2.** Libéralement.
genesis ['dʒenesis], s. **1.** Genèse f; origine f. **2.** B: (The Book of) Genesis, la Genèse.
Geneva[1] [dʒi'ni:va]. Pr.n. Geog: Genève f. **The Lake of Geneva,** le lac Léman. Attrib. **Geneva gown,** robe noire (des prédicateurs calvinistes).
geneva[2], s. (Eau-de-vie f de) genièvre m.
genial ['dʒi:nial], a. **1.** (a) (Of climate, etc.) Doux, f. douce; clément; (of fire, etc.) réconfortant. (b) Plein de bienveillance; plein de bonne humeur; sympathique. **2.** Génial, -aux; de génie. **-ally,** adv. Affablement, cordialement.
geniality [dʒi:ni'aliti], s. (a) Douceur f, clémence f (d'un climat). (b) Bienveillance f; bonne humeur.
genie, pl. usu. **genii** ['dʒi:ni, dʒi:niai], s. Myth: Djinn m, génie m.
genital ['dʒenit(ə)l], a. Génital, -aux. **2.** s.pl. **Genitals,** organes génitaux externes; F: les parties.
genitive ['dʒenitiv], a. & s. Gram: Génitif (m).
genius ['dʒi:niəs], s. **1.** (a) (Only in sg.) Génie m; esprit m tutélaire. (b) (With pl. genii ['dʒi:niai]) Génie, démon m, esprit, djinn m. **2.** (No pl.) Génie particulier, esprit (d'une époque, etc.). **3.** (No pl.) (Ability) (a) Aptitudes naturelles. **To have a genius for mathematics,** avoir le don, F: la bosse, des mathématiques. **To have a**

genius for doing sth., avoir le don de faire qch. (b) **Man of genius,** homme de génie. **Work of genius,** œuvre géniale, de génie. **4.** (Pers.) (pl. geniuses ['dʒi:niəsiz]) **To be a genius,** être un génie. F: **He's no genius,** ce n'est pas un aigle.
Genoa [dʒenoua]. Pr.n. Geog: Gênes f.
Genoese [dʒenou'i:z], a. & s. Geog: Génois, -oise.
gent [dʒent], s. P. & Com: = GENTLEMAN. **Gents' footwear,** chaussures pour hommes.
genteel [dʒen'ti:l], a. (Now usu. Iron:) De bon ton; comme il faut; qui affecte de la distinction. G. tone of voice, ton maniéré.
gentian ['dʒenʃən], s. Bot: Gentiane f.
Gentile ['dʒentail], a. & s. B.Hist: Gentil.
gentilitial [dʒenti'liʃəl], a. **Gentilitial name** (i) nom m générique, de famille; (ii) gentilé m.
gentility [dʒen'tiliti], s. **1.** Prétention f à la distinction, au bon ton. **Shabby gentility,** la misère en habit noir. **2.** Coll. **The aristocracy and the gentility,** l'aristocratie et la meilleure bourgeoisie.
gentle [dʒentl]. I. a. **1.** (a) Bien né; A: gentil. Of gentle birth, de bonne naissance; de bonne extraction. F: **The gentle art,** la pêche à la ligne. (b) **Gentle reader,** cher lecteur; aimable lectrice. **2.** Doux, f. douce. **Gentle as a lamb,** doux comme un agneau. **The gentle(r) sex,** le sexe faible. G. exercise, exercice physique modéré. G. medicine, médicament bénin. **-tly,** adv. **1.** A: **Gently born,** bien né. **2.** Doucement. **Gently (does it)!** allez-y doucement, F: en douceur. II. **gentle,** s. **1.** pl. A: **Gentles** = GENTLEFOLK. **2.** Fish: Asticot m.
gentlefolk(s) ['dʒentlfouk(s)], s.pl. (a) Gens m comme il faut. (b) Personnes f de bonne famille.
gentleman, pl. **-men** ['dʒentlmən, -men], s.m. **1.** A: Gentilhomme, pl. gentilshommes. **Gentleman in waiting,** gentilhomme servant, de service (près du roi). **Gentleman-at-arms,** gentilhomme de la garde. **2.** Galant homme; homme comme il faut. **A fine old English gentleman,** un gentleman de la vieille roche. F: **To be no gentleman,** être un goujat, un malotru. **3.** (a) Jur: **Gentleman (of independent means),** homme sans profession; rentier. F: **To be a gentleman of leisure,** vivre de ses rentes. (b) Sp: Amateur. **4.** Monsieur. (To audience) **Ladies and gentlemen!** mesdames et messieurs! mesdames, messieurs! **Young gentleman,** jeune homme, jeune monsieur. F: **The old gentleman** (in black), le diable. Com: **Gentlemen's hairdresser,** coiffeur pour hommes, d'hommes. **5.** Danc: Cavalier. (Of a lady) **To dance, take, gentleman,** faire le cavalier; conduire. **gentleman-'commoner,** s.m. Sch: A: (At Oxford and Cambridge) Étudiant privilégié. pl. Gentlemen-commoners. **'gentleman-'farmer,** s.m. Propriétaire qui fait lui-même valoir ses terres. **gentleman-'usher,** s.m. Huissier (d'une grande maison).
gentlemanlike ['dʒentlmənlaik], a. = GENTLEMANLY.
gentlemanliness ['dʒentlmənlinəs], s. Bonnes manières; savoir-vivre m.
gentlemanly ['dʒentlmənli], a. Comme il faut; bien élevé. G. bearing, (i) tenue convenable; (ii) air distingué.
gentleness ['dʒentlnəs], s. **1.** A: Bonne naissance. **2.** Douceur f.
gentlewoman, pl. **-women** ['dʒentlwumən, -wimen], s.f. **1.** (a) Dame ou demoiselle bien née. (b) Personne comme il faut, tout à fait bien. (c) Jur: Dame sans profession, qui vit de

ses rentes. **2.** *A:* Dame d'honneur ; dame de compagnie (à la Cour).

gently [ˈdʒentli], *adv. See* GENTLE I.

gentry [ˈdʒentri], *s. Coll.* **I.** *(a)* Petite noblesse. The nobility and gentry, la haute et la petite noblesse. *(b) F:* **The gentry,** la gentilhommerie. **2.** *Pej:* Gens *mpl* ; individus *mpl.*

genuflection, genuflexion [dʒenjuˈflekʃ(ə)n], *s.* Génuflexion *f.*

genuine [ˈdʒenjuin], *a.* *(a)* Authentique, véritable. *G. coin,* pièce de bon aloi. *A g. diamond,* un diamant véritable. *(b)* Véritable, sincère ; franc, *f.* franche. *Com:* G. purchaser, acheteur sérieux. **-ly,** *adv.* **I.** Authentiquement. **2.** Franchement, véritablement.

genuineness [ˈdʒenjuinnəs], *s.* **I.** Authenticité *f* (d'un manuscrit, etc.) ; véritabilité *f* (d'un événement). **2.** Sincérité *f,* loyauté *f.*

genus, *pl.* **genera** [ˈdʒiːnəs, ˈdʒenərə], *s.* **I.** *Log:* Genre *m.* **The genus and differentia,** le genre et la différence. **2.** *(a) Nat.Hist:* Genre. *(b) F:* Genre, espèce *f.*

geodesy [dʒiːˈɔdesi], *s. Mth:* Géodésie *f.*

geodetic(al) [dʒiːoˈdetik(ə)l], *a.* Géodésique.

geographer [dʒiːˈɔɡrəfər], *s.* Géographe *m.*

geographic(al) [dʒiːoˈɡrafik(ə)l], *a.* Géographique. **-ally,** *adv.* Géographiquement.

geography [dʒiːˈɔɡrəfi], *s.* Géographie *f. F: To study the g. of the place,* étudier la disposition du terrain.

geological [dʒiːoˈlɔdʒik(ə)l], *a.* Géologique. **-ally,** *adv.* Géologiquement.

geologist [dʒiːˈɔlɔdʒist], *s.* Géologue *m.*

geology [dʒiːˈɔlɔdʒi], *s.* Géologie *f.*

geometer [dʒiːˈɔmetər], *s.* **I.** Géomètre *m.* **2.** *Ent:* *(a)* (Chenille) arpenteuse *f.* *(b)* (Moth) Géomètre *f.*

geometric(al) [dʒiːoˈmetrik(ə)l], *a.* Géométrique. **-ally,** *adv.* Géométriquement.

geometrician [dʒiːomeˈtriʃ(ə)n], *s.* Géomètre *m.*

geometry [dʒiˈɔmetri], *s.* Géométrie *f.* **Solid geometry,** géométrie dans l'espace.

George [dʒɔːrdʒ]. *Pr.n.m.* Georges. *F: By George!* sapristi !

georgette [dʒɔːrˈʒet], *s. Tex:* (Crêpe *m*) georgette *f.*

geranium [dʒəˈreinjəm], *s.* **I.** *Bot:* Géranium *m.* **2.** *Hort: F:* Pélargonium *m ; F:* géranium.

gerb(e) [dʒəːrb], *s. Pyr:* Gerbe *f.*

gerfalcon [dʒəːrfɔː(l)kən], *s. Orn:* Gerfaut *m.*

germ [dʒəːrm], *s.* **I.** *Biol:* Germe *m* (d'un organisme). **2.** *Med: F:* Germe, microbe *m* (d'une maladie) ; bacille *m.* **ˈgerm-carrier,** *s. Med:* Porteur *m* de bacilles. **ˈgerm-killer,** *s.* Microbicide *m.* **ˈgerm-killing,** *a.* = GERMICIDAL.

german[1] [ˈdʒəːrmən], *a.* Germain ; (apparenté) au premier degré.

German[2], *a. & s.* **I.** *(a) Geog:* Allemand, -ande. **The German Ocean,** la mer du Nord. **The German Empire,** l'empire d'Allemagne ; l'empire germanique. *(b) A.Hist:* Germain, -aine. **2.** *Ling:* L'allemand *m.*

germander [dʒərˈmandər], *s. Bot:* Germandrée *f.*

germane [dʒərˈmein], *a.* **I.** *A:* = GERMAN[1]. **2.** Approprié *(to,* à) ; en rapport *(to,* avec) ; se rapportant *(to,* à).

Germanic [dʒərˈmanik], *a.* **I.** Allemand. **2.** *Hist:* Germanique, germain.

Germany [ˈdʒəːrməni]. *Pr.n. Geog:* L'Allemagne *f.*

germicidal [dʒəːrmiˈsaid(ə)l], *a.* Microbicide.

germicide [ˈdʒəːrmisaid], *s.* Microbicide *m.*

germinate [ˈdʒəːrmineit], *v.i.* Germer.

germination [dʒəːrmiˈneiʃ(ə)n], *s. Biol:* Germination *f.*

gerrymander[1] [ɡeriˈmandər], *s.* Truquage électoral ; tripatouillage *m.*

gerrymander[2], *v.tr.* To gerrymander an election, truquer, manigancer, une élection.

gerund [ˈdʒerʌnd], *s. Gram:* Gérondif *m. F:* Gerund-grinder, pédant *m,* pédagogue *m.*

gerundive [dʒeˈrʌndiv], *a. Gram:* Du gérondif.

gestation [dʒesˈteiʃ(ə)n], *s. Physiol:* Gestation *f.*

gesticulate [dʒesˈtikjuleit]. **I.** *v.i.* Gesticuler. **2.** *v.tr.* Exprimer, manifester, (des sentiments, etc.) par des gestes.

gesticulation [dʒestikjuˈleiʃ(ə)n], *s.* Gesticulation *f.*

gesticulator [dʒesˈtikjuleitər], *s.* Gesticulateur, -trice.

gesticulatory [dʒesˈtikjulətəri], *a.* Gesticulaire.

gesture[1] [ˈdʒestjər], *s.* **I.** Geste *m,* signe *m.* **To make a gesture,** faire un geste. **By gestures,** par gestes ; à la muette. **2.** Le geste. *To signal by g.,* mimer un signal.

gesture[2]. **I.** *v.i.* Faire des gestes. **2.** *v.tr.* Exprimer par gestes.

get [get], *v.* *(p.t.* got [gɔt] ; *p.p.* got, *A. & U.S:* gotten [gɔtn] ; *pr.p.* getting) I. *v.tr.* **I.** Procurer, obtenir. *(a)* To get sth. (for oneself), se procurer qch. To get sth. for s.o., obtenir qch. à qn. *To get sth. to eat,* (i) trouver de quoi manger ; (ii) manger quelque chose (au buffet, etc.). *Where can I get . . . ?* où trouverai-je . . . ? *I got this horse cheap,* j'ai eu ce cheval à bon marché. *(b)* Acquérir, gagner. **To get (oneself) a name,** se faire un nom. **To get a wife,** prendre femme. **To get the prize,** gagner, remporter, avoir, le prix. I will see what I can get for it, je verrai ce qu'on m'en donnera. *To get nothing by it,* out of it, n'y rien gagner. *F:* **Don't you wish, think, you may get it!** je vous en souhaite ! *(c)* To get leave (of, from, s.o.) to do sth., obtenir la permission (de qn) de faire qch. To get one's own way, faire valoir sa volonté. *S.a.* WAY[1] 6. If I get the time, si j'ai le temps. *To get a fine view of sth.,* avoir une belle vue de qch. *(d) W.Tel:* To get a station, accrocher un poste émetteur. **2.** *(a)* Recevoir (un cadeau, une lettre, etc.). *He gets his timidity from his mother,* il tient sa timidité de sa mère. *(b)* Attraper (une maladie) ; recevoir, attraper, un coup. *F:* To get religion, se convertir. He got ten years (in prison), il a été condamné à, *F:* il a attrapé, dix ans de prison. **3.** *(a)* Prendre, attraper (une bête fauve, etc.). *F: We'll get them yet!* on les aura ! *The play didn't really get me,* la pièce ne m'a pas emballé. **What's got him?** qu'est-ce qu'il a ? *(b) U.S: F:* **I don't get your meaning,** je ne saisis pas bien. **Got me?** vous comprenez ? **4.** Aller chercher (son chapeau, un médecin, etc.). **5.** *(a)* Faire parvenir. **To get s.o. home,** conduire ou transporter qn chez lui. **To get s.o. upstairs,** aider qn à monter l'escalier. **To get s.o. on to a subject,** amener qn sur un sujet. *(b)* To get sth. (off) by heart, apprendre qch. par cœur. **To get the breakfast (ready),** préparer le déjeuner. **To get s.o. into trouble,** (i) attirer des histoires à qn ; (ii) mettre (une femme) à mal. **6.** *(a)* To get sth. done *(by s.o.),* faire faire qch. (à, par, qn). *To get oneself appointed,* se faire nommer. *(b)* To get one's work finished, finir son travail. **To get one's arm broken,** se (faire) casser le bras. *(c)* To get s.o. to do sth., faire faire qch. à qn. *Get him to read it,* faites-le-lui lire. *To get a plant to grow,* réussir à faire pousser une plante. *(d) U.S:* That got him guessing, ça l'a intrigue. **7.** *F:* (*Only in perf.*) Have got. (*a*) Avoir. *I haven't got any,* je n'en ai pas. *What's that got to do with it?* qu'est-ce que cela y fait? *He's got measles,* il a la rougeole. *F:* **You've got it!** vous avez deviné! vous y êtes! (*b*) **You have got to do it,** il faut absolument que vous le fassiez. *It has got to be done,* il faut que cela se fasse. **8.** *Min:* Exploiter, extraire (du charbon, etc.). **9.** *v.pr. A:* **Get thee gone,** va-t'en. II. **get,** *v.i.* **1.** (*a*) Devenir (riche, gras, etc.). **To get old,** devenir vieux, se faire vieux, vieillir. **To get angry,** se mettre en colère. *Flowers are getting scarce,* les fleurs se font rares. *It is getting late,* il se fait tard. (*b*) **To get dressed,** s'habiller. **To get married,** (i) se marier ; (ii) faire épouser. *To get killed,* se faire tuer. *To get drowned,* se noyer. *Everything gets known,* tout se sait. (*c*) **To get doing sth.,** se mettre à faire qch. **To get talking with s.o.,** entrer en conversation avec qn. **2.** (*a*) Aller, arriver, se rendre (*to a place, etc.*, à un endroit, etc.). *He'll get here to-morrow,* il arrivera (ici) demain. *U.S: F:* **To get there,** arriver, réussir. *F:* **We're not getting anywhere,** nous n'aboutissons à rien. *Where have you got to with your work?* où en êtes-vous dans votre travail? *Where has that book got to?* où est-ce que ce livre a passé? (*b*) Se mettre. *To get behind a tree,* se mettre derrière un arbre. **To get to work,** se mettre à l'œuvre. **To get to bed,** aller se coucher. (*c*) **To get to do sth.,** finir par, en arriver à, faire qch. *To get to know sth.,* apprendre qch. **get about,** *v.i.* **1.** (*Of pers.*) Circuler. (*Of invalid*) **To get about again,** être de nouveau sur pied. **2.** (*Of news*) Se répandre, circuler, s'ébruiter. *It's sure to get about,* cela se saura certainement. **get across. 1.** *v.i.* Traverser (une plaine) ; passer (une rivière). *Th: F:* **The play failed to get across (the footlights),** la pièce n'a pas passé la rampe. **2.** *v.tr.* Faire passer (qch.). **get along. 1.** *v.i.* (*a*) S'avancer (dans son chemin). *F:* **Get along (with you)!** (i) allez-vous-en ! (ii) allons donc ! (*b*) Faire des progrès ; faire du chemin. **To get along without s.o.,** sth., se passer de qn, de qch. (*c*) **To get along with s.o.,** faire bon ménage avec qn. **2.** Faire avancer (qn, qch.). **get at,** *v.i.* **1.** Parvenir à, atteindre (un endroit). **Difficult to get at,** (endroit) peu accessible. **To get at the root of the trouble,** trouver la racine du mal. *F:* **What are you getting at?** (i) où voulez-vous en venir? (ii) qu'est-ce que vous voulez insinuer? **Let me get at him!** si jamais il me tombe sous les pattes ! **2.** (*a*) Accéder jusqu'à (qn). (*b*) *F:* **To get at a witness,** suborner, travailler, un témoin. **3.** *F:* Faire des sorties contre (qn). *Who are you getting at?* à qui en avez-vous? **get away. 1.** *v.i.* (*a*) Partir, déloger. *To get away for the holidays,* partir en vacances. *F:* **Get away with you!** allons donc ! (*b*) (*Of prisoner, etc.*) S'échapper, se sauver. **To get away from one's environment,** échapper, se soustraire, à son entourage. *F:* **There's no getting away from it,** il n'y a pas à sortir de là. (*c*) *Aut:* Démarrer. (*d*) *The burglars got away with* £1000, les cambrioleurs ont raflé £1000. *F:* **To get away with it,** faire accepter la chose. **2.** *v.tr.* (*a*) Arracher (*sth. from s.o.,* qch. à qn). (*b*) Éloigner (qn). **'get-away,** *s.* **1.** *U.S:* Fuite *f.* **To make one's get-away,** s'enfuir, s'évader. **2.** (*a*) *Rac:* Départ *m* ; démarrage *m* (d'un coureur). (*b*) *Aut:* Démarrage. **get back. 1.** *v.i.* (*a*) Reculer. (*b*) Revenir, retourner. **To get back home,** rentrer chez soi. **2.** *v.tr.* (*a*) Se faire rendre (qch.) ; rentrer en possession de (qch.) ; retrouver (un

objet perdu) ; regagner (le temps perdu, etc.) ; recouvrer (ses biens) ; reprendre (ses forces). *I got my money back,* on m'a remboursé. **To get one's own back,** (i) recouvrer ce qui vous appartient ; (ii) *F:* prendre sa revanche. (*b*) Faire revenir (qn). (*c*) **To get sth. back into its box,** faire rentrer qch. dans sa boite. **get beyond,** *v.i.* Dépasser (qch.). **get by,** *v.i.* Passer. **get down.** **1.** *v.i.* (*a*) Descendre (*from, off,* de). **To get down on one's knees,** se mettre à genoux. (*b*) *F:* **To get down to one's work,** se mettre à l'ouvrage pour de bon. **To get down to the facts,** en venir aux faits. (*c*) (*To dog*) **Get down!** à bas les pattes ! **2.** *v.tr.* (*a*) Descendre (un livre d'un rayon, etc.) ; décrocher (son chapeau). *Nau:* Amener (une voile). (*b*) **To get sth. down** (*on paper*), noter qch. par écrit. (*c*) Abattre, descendre (une perdrix). (*d*) Avaler (une bouchée, etc.). **get in.** I. *v.i.* **1.** *F:* = GET INTO 1 (*a*). **2.** (*a*) Entrer ; monter (en wagon, en voiture). *The water had got in everywhere,* l'eau avait pénétré partout. *If the train gets in in time,* si le train arrive à l'heure. (*b*) *To get in between two people,* s'introduire, se glisser, entre deux personnes. (*c*) *F:* **To get in with s.o.,** s'insinuer dans les bonnes grâces de qn. (*d*) *Pol:* **To get in for a constituency,** être élu député pour une circonscription. II. **get in,** *v.tr.* **1.** Rentrer. **To get in the crops,** rentrer la moisson. **To get in debts,** recouvrer des dettes. *To get money in,* faire rentrer ses fonds. *To get a man in to mend the window,* faire venir un homme pour réparer la fenêtre. **2.** **To get a blow in,** placer un coup. **To get a word in,** placer un mot. *If I can get it in* (*in the time*), si je trouve le temps nécessaire pour le faire. **3.** **To get one's hand in,** se faire la main. **4.** Planter, semer (des graines, etc.). **getting in,** *s.* Rentrage *m* (de la moisson) ; rentrée *f* (d'impôts). **get into. 1.** *v.i.* (*a*) Entrer dans (une maison) ; pénétrer dans (un bois, etc.) ; monter dans (une voiture). **To get into a club,** se faire élire membre d'un club. *To get into bad company,* faire de mauvaises connaissances. (*b*) Mettre (ses habits). **To get into a rage,** se mettre en rage. **To get into a bad habit,** acquérir une mauvaise habitude. **To get into the way of doing sth.,** (i) apprendre à faire qch. ; (ii) prendre l'habitude de faire qch. **2.** *v.tr.* **To get sth. into sth.,** (faire) (r)entrer, enfoncer, qch. dans qch. **To get s.o. into the way of doing sth.,** faire prendre à qn l'habitude de faire qch. **get off.** I. *v.i.* **1.** (*a*) Descendre de (la table). (*b*) **To get off a duty,** se faire exempter d'une tâche. **2.** (*a*) Se tirer d'affaire ; être acquitté. **To get off with a fine,** en être quitte pour une amende. (*b*) *F:* (*Of girl*) **To get off,** attraper, décrocher, un mari. (*c*) *Av:* S'élever, décoller. (*d*) **To get off to sleep,** s'endormir. II. **get off,** *v.tr.* **1.** **To get off one's clothes,** ôter ses vêtements. *To get a nut off,* desserrer un écrou. **To get stains off** (sth.), ôter, enlever, des taches (de qch.). **2.** **To get a shot off,** faire partir un coup de fusil. **3.** Expédier (un colis). **4.** **To get sth. off one's hands,** se débarrasser de qch. **To get one's daughter off** (one's hands), marier sa fille. **5.** Faire acquitter (un prévenu) ; tirer (qn) d'affaire. **6.** Renflouer, déséchouer (un navire). **7.** Apprendre (sa leçon) par cœur. **get on.** I. *v.tr.* **1.** Mettre (ses souliers, etc.). **2.** **To get a good speed on,** prendre de la vitesse. **3.** Faire faire des progrès à (un élève). II. **get on,** *v.i.* **1.** Monter, se mettre, sur (une chaise, etc.) ; enfourcher (une bicyclette). **2.** (*a*) S'avancer (vers un endroit). **To be getting on for forty, approcher de, friser, la quarantaine. **To be getting on (in years)**, prendre de l'âge ; avancer en âge. *Time is getting on*, allons, l'heure s'avance. *It is getting on for twelve*, il approche de minuit. *Getting on for* 300 *boys*, pas loin de 300 élèves. (*b*) Faire des progrès. **To get on in** life, réussir dans la vie. *He will get on (in the world)*, il fera son chemin (dans le monde) ; il arrivera. *How to get on*, le moyen de parvenir. **To get on with the job**, pousser la besogne. *How are you getting on?* comment allez-vous? *How did you get on with your examination?* comment votre examen a-t-il marché? **To get on without s.o., sth.**, se passer de qn, de qch. (*c*) **To get on (well) with s.o.**, s'accorder, s'entendre, s'accommoder, avec qn. *Easy to get on with*, commode à vivre. (*d*) *P :* **Get on with you!** allons donc ! (*e*) *U.S :* *F :* **To get on to the trick**, découvrir le truc. **get out.** I. *v.tr.* (*a*) Arracher (une dent) ; tirer, retirer (un bouchon) ; enlever, faire disparaître (une tache). **To get sth. out of sth.**, faire sortir, tirer, qch. de qch. **To get a secret out of s.o.**, arracher un secret à qn. *To get money out of s.o.*, tirer, *Pej :* soutirer, de l'argent à qn. *F :* **To get sth. out of it**, y gagner qch. ; y trouver son compte. **To get s.o. out of a fix**, tirer qn d'embarras, d'un mauvais pas. **To get s.o. out of a habit**, défaire qn d'une habitude. (*b*) Sortir (ses outils). **To get out one's car**, (faire) sortir sa voiture. **To get out a boat**, mettre une embarcation au dehors, à la mer. **To get out a book**, (i) (*of publisher*) publier un livre ; (ii) (*of library-member*) emprunter un livre. **To get out a scheme**, préparer un devis. *To get out plans*, dresser, lever, les plans. *Com :* **To get out a balance-sheet**, établir, dresser, un bilan. (*c*) Résoudre (un problème). 2. *v.i.* (*a*) **To get out of sth.**, sortir de qch. *The lion got out of its cage*, le lion s'échappa de sa cage. *The secret got out*, le secret se fit jour. **To get out of s.o.'s way**, faire place à qn. **Get out (of here)!** fichez-moi le camp ! *You must either do it or get out, F :* il faut passer par là ou par la porte. (*b*) **To get out of a difficulty**, se soustraire à une difficulté. **To get out of a duty, of doing sth.**, se faire exempter, se faire dispenser, d'une corvée, de faire qch. *Com :* *F :* **To get out without loss**, couvrir ses frais. (*c*) **To get out of the habit of doing sth.**, se désaccoutumer de faire qch. **get over.** I. *v.i.* (*a*) Franchir, escalader, passer par-dessus (un mur, etc.). *Th :* *F :* **The play failed to get over**, la pièce n'a pas passé la rampe. (*b*) **To get over an illness**, se remettre, guérir, revenir, d'une maladie. *She cannot get over her loss*, elle est inconsolable de sa perte. *To get over one's shyness*, vaincre, revenir de, sa timidité. *To get over one's surprise*, revenir de sa surprise. *He can't get over it*, il n'en revient pas ; il en reste tout ahuri. (*c*) *F :* **To get over s.o.**, enjôler qn. 2. *v.tr.* (*a*) Faire passer (qch.) par-dessus (un mur, etc.). (*b*) **To get sth. over**, en finir avec qch. **get round.** I. *v.i.* (*a*) Tourner (un coin). *To get round to every boy in a class*, interroger, voir le travail de, chaque élève dans une classe. (*b*) = GET ABOUT 2. (*c*) Tourner (une difficulté) ; contourner, tromper (la loi). *F :* **To get round s.o.**, enjôler qn. *To know how to get round s.o.*, savoir prendre qn. 2. *v.tr.* **To get s.o. round**, faire reprendre connaissance à qn. **get through.** I. *v.i.* I. (*a*) Passer par (un trou) ; se frayer un chemin à travers (la foule). (*b*) Accomplir, arriver au bout de (sa tâche, etc.) ; achever (un livre). **To get through the day**, faire passer la journée. **To get through an**

examination, être reçu, admis, à un examen. 2. (*a*) Parvenir à franchir un obstacle. *The news got through to them*, la nouvelle leur est parvenue. (*b*) (*Of candidate*) Passer ; être reçu. (*c*) *Pol :* Bill that will never get through, projet de loi qui ne passera jamais. (*d*) *Tp :* **To get through (to s.o.)**, obtenir la communication (avec qn). II. **get through**, *v.tr.* To get a bill through (Parliament), faire adopter un projet de loi. **get together.** I. *v.i.* Se réunir, se rassembler. 2. *v.tr.* Rassembler, ramasser (des objets) ; rassembler, réunir (des amis, etc.). **get under.** I. *v.i.* **To get under sth.**, (i) passer par-dessous qch. ; (ii) se mettre, se glisser, sous qch. 2. *v.tr.* Maîtriser (un adversaire, un incendie). **get up.** I. *v.i.* I. **To get up a ladder**, monter à une échelle. 2. (*a*) **To get up behind s.o.** (*on horse*), monter en croupe derrière qn. (*b*) **To get up to s.o.**, arriver à la hauteur de qn. *Where have you got up to?* où en êtes-vous ? (*c*) Se mettre debout ; se lever. *Get up!* debout ! levez-vous ! (*d*) Se lever (du lit). (*e*) **To get up to mischief**, faire des malices. (*f*) (*Of wind*) Se lever, s'élever ; (*of sea*) grossir. II. **get up**, *v.tr.* I. *To get s.o. up a tree, up a hill*, faire monter qn à un arbre ; faire gravir une colline à qn. 2. (*a*) Monter (une malle au grenier) ; relever (un navire coulé). (*b*) Faire lever (qn). (*c*) Organiser, arranger (une fête, etc.) ; monter (une pièce de théâtre) ; concerter (un complot) ; fomenter (une querelle) ; fabriquer (une histoire, etc.). (*d*) Apprêter (un article de commerce, etc.). *Com :* **To get up an article for sale**, habiller un article pour la vente. *Laund :* **To get up a shirt**, blanchir, apprêter, une chemise. (*e*) Préparer, travailler (un sujet d'examen). *To get up a lecture*, préparer une conférence. (*f*) **To get oneself up**, se faire beau, belle ; s'endimancher. **To get oneself up as a woman**, se déguiser, s'habiller, en femme. **'get-up**, *s.* I. (*a*) Habillement *m*, toilette *f*. *What a get-up!* comme la voilà attifée ! (*b*) Déguisement *m*. (*c*) Maquillage *m*. 2. Apprêt *m* (de linge, etc.) ; facture *f*, façon *f*, présentation *f*, aspect *m* (d'un livre). *Th :* Get-up of a play, mise *f* en scène, présentation *f*, d'une pièce. **got-up**, *a.* I. *F :* = PUT-UP. 2. (*Of pers.*) (*a*) Attifé. (*b*) Maquillé. **getting up**, *s.* I. Lever *m*. The getting-up bell, la cloche du lever. 2. *Nau :* Gréage *m* (d'un mât). 3. (*a*) Organisation *f* (d'une fête) ; montage *m* (d'une pièce de théâtre) ; fabrication *f* (d'une histoire). (*b*) Préparation *f* (d'une conférence). (*c*) Apprêt *m* (d'un article de commerce) ; présentation *f* (d'un livre). 4. (*a*) Attifage *m*. (*b*) Maquillage *m*.

getter ['getər], *s.* I. (*a*) Acquéreur *m*. (*b*) *Min :* Piqueur *m*. 2. **Getter-up.** (*a*) Organisateur, -trice ; promoteur, -trice. (*b*) Compilateur, -trice.

gewgaw ['gju:gɔ:], *s.* Bagatelle *f*, babiole *f*.

geyser ['geizər, 'gaizər, 'gi:zər], *s.* I. *Geol :* Geyser *m*. 2. *Chauffe-bain(s) *m* ; chauffe-eau *m inv* à gaz.

ghastliness ['gɑ:stlinəs], *s.* I. Horreur *f* (d'un crime). 2. Pâleur mortelle.

ghastly ['gɑ:stli]. I. *a.* (*a*) Horrible, effroyable, affreux. (*b*) Blême. *G. light*, lumière spectrale, blafarde. **Ghastly smile**, sourire affreux à voir. 2. *adv.* (*a*) Horriblement, effroyablement, affreusement. (*b*) **Ghastly pale**, blême.

Ghent [gent]. *Pr.n. Geog :* Gand *m*.

gherkin ['gə:rkin], *s.* Cornichon *m*.

Ghibelline ['gibelain], *s. Hist :* Gibelin *m*.

ghost [goust], *s.* I. *A :* Ame *f*. **To give up the ghost**, rendre l'âme. 2. **The Holy Ghost**, le Saint-Esprit. 3. (*a*) Fantôme *m*, spectre *m*, revenant *m*, ombre *f*, apparition *f*. **To raise a ghost**, évoquer un esprit. **To lay a ghost**, conjurer, exorciser, un esprit. *Attrib.* **Ghost ship**, vaisseau fantôme. (*b*) *F :* **To be the mere ghost of one's former self**, n'être plus que l'ombre de soi-même. **Not the ghost of a chance**, pas la moindre chance. **4.** *F :* Nègre *m* (d'un auteur, etc.). **'ghost-story,** *s.* Histoire *f* de revenants.

ghostlike ['goustlaik]. **I.** *a.* Spectral, -aux; de spectre. **2.** *adv.* Comme un spectre.

ghostly ['goustli], *a.* **I.** *A :* (Conseil, directeur) spirituel. **2.** Spectral, -aux; de fantôme.

ghoul [guːl], *s. Myth :* Goule *f*, vampire *m*.

ghoulish ['guːliʃ], *a.* De goule ; *F :* vampirique.

giant ['dʒaiənt]. **I.** *s.* Géant *m* ; *F :* colosse *m*. **2.** *a.* (Chêne, etc.) géant, gigantesque.

giantess ['dʒaiəntes], *s.f.* Géante.

gibber¹ ['dʒibər], *s.* (*a*) Sons inarticulés. (*b*) Baragouin *m*.

gibber², *v.i.* (*a*) Produire des sons inarticulés (comme un singe, un idiot). (*b*) Baragouiner.

gibbering¹, *a.* **Gibbering idiot,** (i) idiot aphasique ; (ii) *F :* espèce *m* d'idiot. **gibbering²,** *s.* Baragouinage *m*.

gibberish ['gibəriʃ], *s.* Baragouin *m*.

gibbet ['dʒibet], *s.* Gibet *m*, potence *f*.

gibbose [gi'bous], **gibbous** ['gibəs], *a.* **I.** Gibbeux, convexe. **2.** (*Of pers.*) Bossu.

gibbosity [gi'bɔsiti], *s.* Gibbosité *f*, bosse *f*.

gibe¹ [dʒaib], *s.* Raillerie *f* ; moquerie *f* ; sarcasme *m* ; quolibet *m*, brocard *m*.

gibe², *v.tr. & i.* **To gibe (at)** s.o., railler qn ; se moquer de qn. **gibing,** *a.* Railleur, moqueur. **-ly,** *adv.* D'un ton de sarcasme.

giblets ['dʒiblets], *s.pl.* Abatis *m* (de volaille).

giddiness ['gidinəs], *s.* **I.** Étourdissement *m*, vertige *m* ; tournement *m* de tête. **2.** (*a*) Étourderie *f*. (*b*) Frivolité *f* ; légèreté *f*.

giddy¹ ['gidi], *a.* **I.** (*a*) Étourdi. **To be, feel, turn, giddy,** être pris de vertige. *I feel g.*, la tête me tourne. (*b*) Vertigineux ; qui donne le vertige. **2.** Frivole, étourdi, écervelé. *She's a g. young thing*, c'est une évaporée. **-ily,** *adv.* **I.** D'une manière vertigineuse. **2.** Étourdiment ; à l'étourdie.

giddy², *v.tr.* Étourdir (qn) ; donner le vertige à (qn).

gift [gift], *s.* Don *m*. (*a*) **To make a gift of sth. to s.o.,** faire don de qch. à qn. **To acquire sth. by free gift,** acquérir qch. à titre gratuit. (*b*) Cadeau *m*, présent *m*. **It was a gift,** (i) on me l'a offert ; (ii) *F :* c'était donné. (*c*) (*On presentation of coupons*) Prime *f*. (*d*) **To have a gift for mathematics,** avoir le don, le génie, des mathématiques. **'gift-horse,** *s. Prov :* (You must) **never look a gift-horse in the mouth**, à cheval donné on ne regarde pas à la bride, à la bouche.

gifted ['giftid], *a.* Bien doué ; (artiste) de valeur, de talent.

gig¹ [gig], *s.* **I.** Cabriolet *m*. **2.** *Nau :* Petit canot ; yole *f*.

gig², *s. Fish :* Foëne *f*, foène *f*.

gigantic [dʒai'gantik], *a.* Géant, gigantesque ; (bâtiment, etc.) colossal, -aux, *F :* babélique. **-ally,** *adv.* Gigantesquement.

giggle¹ [gigl], *s.* (*Esp. of girls*) Petit rire nerveux.

giggle², *v.i.* (*Esp. of girls*) Rire nerveusement ; pousser des petits rires. **giggling,** *s.* Rires nerveux ; petits rires bêtes.

gild [gild], *v.tr.* (*p.t.* gilded ; *p.p.* gilded, *occ.* gilt [gilt]) Dorer. **To gild sth. over,** couvrir qch. d'une couche de dorure. *F :* **To gild the lily,** faire œuvre de superfétation. **gilded,** *a.* Doré.

gilt¹, *a.* Doré. **gilt²,** *s.* Dorure *f*, doré *m*.

Imitation gilt, similor *m*. *S.a.* SILVER-GILT. **'gilt-bronze,** *s.* Vermeil *m*. **'gilt-'edged,** *a.* **I.** (*Of book, card, etc.*) Doré sur tranche. **2.** *Fin :* **Gilt-edged stock**, valeurs de tout repos. **gild-ing,** *s.* Dorure *f*. **Leaf gilding**, dorure à la feuille.

gill¹ [gil], *s.* **I.** *Usu. pl.* Ouïe(s) *f*, branchie(s) *f* (de poisson). **2.** *pl.* **Gills.** (*a*) Caroncules *f*, fanons *m* (d'un oiseau). (*b*) Lames *f*, lamelles *f* (d'un champignon). (*c*) *F :* Bajoues *f* (de qn). **To look green about the gills**, avoir le teint vert. **3.** *Mch :* *Ind :* Ailette *f* (de cylindre, etc.). **'gill-cover,** *s. Ich :* Opercule (branchial).

gill² [dʒil], *s.* Gill *m* = canon *m* (d'eau-de-vie).

gilled [gild], *a.* **I.** *Biol :* Pourvu de branchies, de caroncules, de lames. **2.** *Mch : etc :* **Gilled radiator,** radiateur à ailettes.

gillie ['gili], *s. Scot :* **I.** *Hist :* Suivant *m* (d'un chef). **2.** *Ven : Fish :* Serviteur *m*.

gillyflower ['dʒiliflauər], *s. Bot :* **I.** (**Clove-**) **gillyflower**, œillet *m* giroflée ; œillet des fleuristes. **2.** *Dial :* = WALLFLOWER I.

gilt¹,² [gilt], *a. & s.* See GILD.

gimcrack ['dʒimkrak], *a.* (Meubles, etc.) de pacotille ; (maison) de carton ; (bijoux) en toc.

gimlet ['gimlet], *s. Tls : Carp :* Vrille *f* ; foret *m* à bois ; perçoir *m*. *Attrib.* **Gimlet eyes,** (i) yeux percés en vrille ; (ii) yeux louches.

gimp [gimp], *s. Furn :* Ganse *f*, galon *m*.

gin¹ [dʒin], *s.* **I.** *Ven :* Piège *m*, trébuchet *m*. **2.** *Mec.E :* *Ind :* Chèvre *f*, engin *m*.

gin², *s.* Genièvre *m*. *S.a.* SLOE. **'gin-soaked,** *a.* (*Of pers.*) Abruti par la boisson.

ginger¹ ['dʒindʒər]. **I.** *s.* (*a*) Gingembre *m*. (*b*) *F :* Entrain *m*, énergie *f*, vitalité *f*. **2.** *a.* (*Of hair*) Roux, *f.* rousse ; *P :* rouquin. **ginger-'ale, -'beer,** *s.* Variétés de boissons gazeuses au gingembre. **'ginger-'haired,** *a.* Aux cheveux roux ; rouquin. **'ginger-nut,** *s.* Biscuit *m* au gingembre.

ginger², *v.tr.* **I.** Aromatiser (une boisson, etc.) au gingembre. **2.** *F :* **To ginger s.o. up,** mettre du cœur au ventre de qn ; secouer, remonter, exciter, qn.

gingerbread ['dʒindʒərbred]. **I.** *s.* Pain *m* d'épice. **2.** *a. F :* En clinquant ; de mauvais aloi.

gingerly ['dʒindʒərli], *adv. & a.* In a gingerly fashion, gingerly, délicatement, doucement, avec précaution.

gingham ['giŋəm], *s.* **I.** *Tex :* Guingan *m*. **2.** *F :* Parapluie *m* (de coton) ; *F :* riflard *m*.

gipsy ['dʒipsi], *s.* Bohémien, -ienne ; nomade *mf* ; romanichel, -elle.

giraffe [dʒi'raf, -'raːf], *s. Z :* Girafe *f*.

gird¹ [gəːrd], *v.tr.* (*p.t. & p.p.* girded, girt) **I.** Ceindre, (*a*) *Lit :* **To gird up one's loins,** se ceindre les reins. *F :* **To gird oneself for the tray**, se préparer à la lutte. (*b*) **To gird s.o. with sth.**, to gird sth. on s.o., ceindre qn de qch. **To gird (on) one's sword,** ceindre son épée. **2.** Entourer, encercler, (*with*, de). (*Of pers.*) **With girded loins,** les reins ceints. **girt,** *a.* (*a*) = GIRDED. (*b*) Entouré, ceint (*with*, de).

gird², *s.* = GIBE¹.

gird³, *v.i.* **To gird at s.o.**, railler qn ; se moquer de qn.

girder ['gəːrdər], *s.* Support *m*. (*a*) *Const :* Solive *f*, longrine *f* (de plancher). (*b*) Poutre *f*. **Plate-girder,** poutre à âme pleine. **Trussed girder,** poutre armée ; ferme *f*.

girdle¹ ['gəːrdl], *s.* Ceinture *f*. **Dressing-gown g.**, cordelière *f* de robe de chambre.

girdle², *v.tr.* Ceinturer, ceindre, encercler.

girdle³, s. Scot: Tôle circulaire sur laquelle on cuit des galettes. **'girdle-cake,** s. Galette f.

girl [gə:rl], s.f. **1.** Jeune fille. (a) Little girl, young girl, fillette. Girl's name, prénom féminin. Poor little g., pauvre petite. (b) (School)girl, élève, écolière. Girls' school, pensionnat de jeunes filles. Old girl, ancienne élève. **2.** Jeune personne, jeune femme, jeune fille. (a) His wife is a charming g., sa femme est une jeune personne charmante. (Often best translated by jeune.) A French g., une jeune Française. Blind g., jeune aveugle. The Smith girls, les demoiselles Smith. Attrib. Girl typist, jeune dactylographe f. Girl friend, (jeune) amie. (b) P: His (best) girl, his girl friend, sa bonne amie. The girl I left behind me, la petite, celle, que j'ai laissée au pays. My dear girl! ma chère amie! (c) My eldest girl, ma fille aînée, mon aînée. **3.** (Shop-)girl, demoiselle de magasin; employée (de magasin); vendeuse. (Servant-)girl, domestique; bonne. Work-girl, (jeune) ouvrière.

girlhood ['gə:rlhud], s. Jeunesse f ou adolescence f (d'une femme). In her girlhood, quand elle était (i) petite fille, (ii) jeune fille.

girlish ['gə:rliʃ], a. **1.** (Of behaviour, figure, etc.) De petite fille ou de jeune fille. **2.** (Of boy, etc.) Mou, efféminé. **-ly,** adv. **1.** En jeune fille, en petite fille. **2.** Comme une jeune fille.

girt¹ [gə:rt]. See GIRD¹.

girt², s. = GIRTH 2.

girth [gə:rθ], s. **1.** Harn: Sangle f; sous-ventrière f (de harnais de trait). Saddle-girth, sangle de selle. **2.** Circonférence f (d'un arbre, etc.); tour m (de poitrine).

gist [dʒist], s. **1.** Jur: Principal motif (d'une action). **2.** Fond m, substance f, essence f (d'une conversation, etc.); point essentiel (d'une question).

give¹ [giv], s. Élasticité f.

give², v. (p.t. gave [geiv]; p.p. given [givn]) I. v.tr. Donner. **1.** (a) To give sth. to s.o., to give s.o. sth., donner qch. à qn. It was given to me, on me l'a offert. To give alms, faire l'aumône. God give me courage! que Dieu me donne du courage! It is not given to all to gather fame, il n'appartient pas, il n'est pas donné, à tous de se rendre célèbres. F: Give me the good old days! parlez-moi du bon vieux temps! (b) To give and take, y mettre chacun du sien. **2.** (a) To g. s.o. sth. to eat, to drink, donner à manger, à boire, à qn. To give a child a name, imposer, donner, un nom à un enfant. To g. s.o. a job, assigner une tâche, un rôle, à qn. (b) To give sth. into s.o.'s hands, remettre qch. entre les mains de qn. (c) To give one's compliments to s.o., présenter ses compliments à qn. Give him my love, faites-lui mes amitiés. (d) Engager (son honneur, etc.). To give one's word, donner sa parole. **3.** To g. a good price for sth., donner, payer, un bon prix pour qch. What did you give for it? combien l'avez-vous payé? **4.** To give one's life to God, donner, consacrer, sa vie à Dieu. To g. one's mind, oneself, to study, s'adonner, s'appliquer, à l'étude. **5.** Faire (une action). To give a jump, faire un saut; tressauter. To g. a laugh, laisser échapper un rire. To g. a sigh, pousser un soupir. To give s.o. a blow, porter un coup à qn. To g. s.o. a smile, adresser un sourire à qn. He gave a queer look, il eut un regard singulier. To give orders, (i) donner des ordres; (ii) (at shop) faire des commandes. **6.** (a) To give s.o. one's hand, donner, tendre, la main à qn. (b) To give (one's) attention to s.o., faire attention à qn. I will g. the matter every

care, j'y mettrai tous mes soins. **7.** (a) To g. particulars, donner, fournir, des détails. To give a decision, (i) donner, faire connaître, sa décision; (ii) Jur: prononcer, rendre, un arrêt. F: I'll give you best, je vous donne gagné. (b) To give no sign(s) of life, ne donner aucun signe de vie. To g. an average of . . ., rendre une moyenne de. . . . (c) To give an example, donner un exemple. Given any two points, étant donné(s) deux points quelconques. (d) To give a recitation, réciter; dire des vers. (e) To give a toast, boire à la santé de qn. I give you our host, je bois à la santé de notre hôte. **8.** (a) Motion given by the handle, mouvement imprimé par la manivelle. (b) To give pain, pleasure, faire, causer, de la peine, du plaisir. To g. oneself trouble, se donner du mal. (c) To give s.o. to suppose, believe, sth., faire supposer, faire croire, qch. à qn. To give s.o. to understand that . . ., donner à entendre à qn que. . . . (d) Rendre. Investment that gives 10%, placement qui rend, rapporte, 10%. **9.** (a) P: To give it (to) s.o., (i) semoncer vertement qn; P: laver la tête à qn; (ii) rosser qn. I gave him what for! je l'ai arrangé de la belle façon! (b) F: To give as good as one gets, rendre coup pour coup. **10.** To give way. (a) (Abs. to give) Céder, fléchir, succomber; (of ladder, etc.) se casser, se rompre; (of cable) partir. The ground gave way under our feet, le sol s'affaissa, se déroba, sous nos pieds; le sol nous manqua sous les pieds. To feel one's legs give (way) beneath one, sentir ses jambes (se) fléchir, mollir, se dérober, se ployer, sous soi. (b) Lâcher pied, céder au découragement; (of elastic, etc.) céder, prêter. (b) (Of colour) Passer; (of frost) Commencer à dégeler; (of weather) s'adoucir. **2.** The window gives (up)on the garden, la fenêtre donne sur le jardin. **give away,** v.tr. **1.** Donner (sth. to s.o., qch. à qn); se dénantir (ses possessions). I would rather g. it away, je préférerais en faire cadeau. **2.** To give away the bride, conduire, accompagner, la mariée à l'autel. **3.** F: To give s.o. away, trahir, vendre, dénoncer, qn. To give oneself away, se trahir. To give the show away, bavarder; vendre la mèche. **give back,** v.tr. Rendre, restituer. **giving back,** s. Restitution f. **give forth,** v.tr. **1.** = GIVE OFF. **2.** (a) Rendre, émettre, faire entendre (un son). (b) Publier (une nouvelle). **give in. 1.** v.tr. (a) To give in one's name, donner son nom; se faire inscrire. To g. in a parcel (at the door), délivrer, remettre, un paquet. (b) Com: Given in, ajouté en supplément. **2.** v.i. Céder; se rendre, se soumettre. **give off,** v.tr. Dégager, exhaler (une odeur, etc.); répandre (de la chaleur). **give out. 1.** v.tr. (a) Distribuer (les vivres, etc.). (b) = GIVE OFF. (c) Annoncer (un cantique, etc.). To give out a notice, faire une communication. To g. it out that . . ., annoncer que. . . . To g. oneself out for an expert, faire le savant. **2.** v.i. Manquer; faire défaut. My strength was giving out, j'étais à bout de forces. **give over,** v.tr. **1.** To give sth. over to s.o., remettre qch. entre les mains de qn; abandonner qch. à qn. **2.** F: Cesser; finir. **3.** To be given over to evil courses, être adonné au vice. **give up,** v.tr. **1.** (a) Rendre (sa proie); abandonner (ses biens, ses prétentions). **To give up one's seat to s.o.,** céder sa place à qn. (b) Remettre (un billet) (to, à). **2.** (a) Renoncer à (un projet, etc.); abandonner (un ami). **To give up the idea of doing sth.,** renoncer à faire qch. *To g. up a newspaper,* se désabonner à un journal. *To g. up business,* cesser, quitter, les affaires. **To give up the game, the struggle,** abandonner la partie. **To give up the race, etc.,** *abs.* to give up, abandonner, lâcher, renoncer. (*Of riddle*) **I give it up,** je donne ma langue au chat, aux chiens. **To give it up (as a bad job),** y renoncer. (b) **To give s.o. up (for lost),** considérer qn comme perdu. **I had given you up!** je ne vous espérais plus! **3.** (a) Livrer (qn à la justice, etc.); faire arrêter (qn). **To give oneself up,** se constituer prisonnier. (b) **To give oneself up to sth.,** se livrer (à un vice); s'absorber (dans la lecture d'un livre); s'appliquer, s'adonner (à l'étude); s'abandonner (à la paresse). **giving up,** *s.* Remise *f* (d'un billet); abandon *m* (d'une habitude, etc.). **given,** *a.* **I. In a given time,** dans un délai donné, convenu, déterminé. **At a g. point,** à un point donné. **2.** Porté, enclin (to, à). **Given to drink,** adonné à la boisson. **I am not given that way,** cela n'entre pas dans mes goûts, dans mes habitudes. **giving,** *s.* **I.** Don *m*, donation *f* (d'un cadeau, etc.); administration *f* (d'une potion, etc.); remise *f* (de qch. entre les mains de qn, etc.); engagement *m* (de sa parole). **2.** Prononciation *f*, prononcé *m* (d'un arrêt, etc.). **3. Giving way,** (i) affaissement *m*, fléchissement *m* (d'une poutre, etc.); altération *f* (de la santé, etc.); (ii) abandon *m* (à ses émotions). **'give- and-'take,** *a.* **Give-and-take policy,** politique d'accommodement, de concessions mutuelles.

giver ['givər], *s.* Donneur, -euse; donateur, -trice. *St. Exch:* Giver of stock, reporté *m*.

gizzard ['gizərd], *s.* Gésier *m*. *F:* **That sticks in my gizzard,** je ne peux pas avaler, digérer, ça.

glabrous ['gleibrəs], *a.* *Nat.Hist:* Glabre.

glacial ['glei(i)əl], *a.* **I.** *Geol:* Glaciaire. **2.** (Vent, etc.) glacial, -als. **3.** *Ch:* Cristallisé; en cristaux.

glacier ['glasiər, 'gleisiər], *s.* *Geol:* Glacier *m*. **Glacier-mud, -silt,** boue *f* glaciaire.

glacis ['glasi, 'gleisis], *s.* *Fort:* Glacis *m*.

glad [glad], *a.* (gladder) Heureux. **I.** Bien aise; content. **To be glad to hear sth.,** être heureux, bien content, d'apprendre qch. **I'm very glad of it,** j'en suis bien aise. **He is only too glad to help you,** il ne demande pas mieux que de vous aider. **It makes my heart glad to hear him,** cela me réjouit le cœur de l'entendre. **2. Glad tidings,** nouvelles joyeuses, heureuses; bonne nouvelle. **-ly,** *adv.* (a) Avec plaisir, volontiers, de bon cœur. (b) Avec joie.

gladden [gladn], *v.tr.* Réjouir.

glade [gleid], *s.* Clairière *f*, éclaircie *f* (dans une forêt).

gladiator ['gladieitər], *s.* Gladiateur *m*.

gladiatorial [gladiə'tɔːriəl], *a.* Gladiatorial, -aux.

gladiolus, *pl.* **-luses, -li** [gladi'ouləs, -ləsiz, -lai], *s.* *Bot:* Glaïeul *m*.

gladness ['gladnəs], *s.* Joie *f*, allégresse *f*.

glamorous ['glamərəs], *a.* Enchanteur, -eresse; charmeur, -euse.

glamour ['glamər], *s.* **I.** Enchantement *m*, charme *m*. **To cast a glamour over s.o.,** ensorceler qn. **2.** Fascination *f*; prestige *m* (d'un nom, etc.); éclat *m*.

glance¹ [glɑːns], *s.* **I.** Coup *m* qui ricoche; ricochet *m*. **2.** Regard *m*; coup d'œil. **At a**

glance, d'un coup d'œil. **At the first glance,** au premier coup d'œil. **Angry glance,** regard irrité.

glance², *v.i.* **I.** (a) (*Of bullet, etc.*) **To glance aside, glance off,** dévier, ricocher. (b) *v.tr.* **To glance back the rays of light,** réfléchir, refléter, les rayons de lumière. **2. To glance at s.o.,** at sth., jeter un regard sur qn, sur qch.; lancer un coup d'œil à qn. **To glance up, down,** jeter un coup d'œil en haut, en bas. **To glance through, over,** sth., parcourir, feuilleter (un livre). **glancing,** *a.* **I.** (*Of blow, etc.*) Oblique. **2.** Étincelant.

glance³, *s.* *A:* Minerai lustré, métallifère. (*Still used in compounds*) **Glance-coal,** houille éclatante; anthracite *m*.

gland¹ [gland], *s.* *Biol:* Glande *f*. **Swollen glands,** (i) glandes engorgées; (ii) (*in childhood*) états *m* ganglionnaires de l'enfance.

gland², *s.* *Mec.E:* *Mch:* Couronne *f*, gland *m*, chapeau *m*.

glandered ['glandərd], *a.* *Vet:* (Cheval) mor- veux, glandé.

glanders ['glandərz], *s.pl.* (*With sg. const.*) *Vet:* *Med:* Morve *f* (chez le cheval ou l'homme).

glare¹ ['gleər], *s.* **I.** (a) Éclat *m*, clarté *f*, rayonne- ment *m*. **In the full glare of the sun,** au grand soleil. *F:* **In the full glare of publicity,** sous les feux de la rampe. (b) Éblouissement *m*, aveugle- ment *m* (d'un phare, etc.). **2.** Clinquant *m*; faux éclat. **3.** Regard fixe et irrité.

glare², *v.i.* **I.** (*Of sun, etc.*) Briller d'un éclat éblouissant. **2. To glare at s.o.,** lancer un regard furieux, furibond, à qn. **glaring,** *a.* **I.** (a) (*Of light, etc.*) Éblouissant, éclatant; (soleil) aveu- glant. (b) (*Of costume, etc.*) Voyant, éclatant; (*of colour*) cru. **2.** (*Of fact, etc.*) Manifeste, patent; (*of injustice, etc.*) flagrant. **-ly,** *adv.* **I.** Avec un faux éclat ou avec trop d'éclat. **2.** Manifestement.

glaringness ['gleəriŋnəs], *s.* **I.** Éclat éblouissant, clarté crue (de la lumière). **2.** Évidence *f*, clarté; flagrance *f*.

glass [glɑːs], *s.* **I.** Verre *m*. **Pane of glass,** vitre *f*, carreau *m*. **Wired glass,** verre grillagé, armé; cristal armé. **Frosted glass,** verre dépoli. **Ground glass,** verre dépoli. **Ribbed glass,** verre strié. **Window glass, sheet glass,** verre à vitres. **Optical glass,** verre d'optique. **Cut glass,** cristal taillé. **Stained glass, coloured glass,** verre de couleur. **Stained glass window,** vitrail (peint); verrière *f*. **The (stained) g. of a church,** les vitraux, les verrières, d'une église. **Spun glass,** coton *m*, fil *m*, de verre. *Aut:* **Safety-glass,** verre de sûreté. **2.** (a) (**Drink- ing-)glass,** verre (à boire). **Wine glass,** verre à vin. **Glass of wine,** verre de vin. **Champagne glass,** flûte *f*, coupe *f*, à champagne. **A glass of brandy, etc.,** un petit verre. **To have had a glass too many,** avoir bu un coup de trop. *He's festive when he's had a g.,* il est d'humeur gaie après boire. (b) *Coll.* **Table glass,** verrerie *f* de table. **Oven glass,** verrerie allant au four. **Hollow glass,** gobeleterie *f*. **Glass and china shop,** magasin de verrerie et porcelaine. **3.** Vitre *f* (de fenêtre); glace *f* (de voiture); verre (de montre, de lampe). **4.** (a) Lentille *f* (d'un instrument d'optique). (b) (**Magnifying-, reading-)glass,** loupe *f*; verre grossissant. **5.** (**Looking-)glass,** glace, miroir *m*. **6.** *pl.* **Glasses,** (i) lunettes *f*; (ii) (*as opposed to spectacles*) lorgnon *m*, pince-nez *m inv.* **To wear glasses,** porter des lunettes. **7.** Longue-vue *f*, *pl.* longues-vues; lunette (d'approche); *pl.* ju- melles *f*. **8.** (**Weather-)glass,** baromètre *m* (à cadran). **The glass is falling,** le baromètre baisse. **9.** *Hort:* **Grown under glass,** cultivé sous verre.

10. Musical glasses, harmonica *m*. **11.** *Attrib.* De, en, verre. Glass bottle, bouteille de, en, verre. Glass door, porte vitrée. *Prov:* People who live in glass houses shouldn't throw stones, il faut être sans défauts pour critiquer autrui. **'glass-blower,** *s.* Souffleur *m* (de verre); verrier *m*. **'glass-blowing,** *s.* Soufflage *m* (du verre). **'glass-'case,** *s.* Vitrine *f*. To keep sth. in a glass-case, garder qch. sous verre. **'glass-cutter,** *s. Tls:* Coupe-verre *m inv*; (*circular*) tournette *f*. **'glass-house,** *s. Hort:* Serre *f*. **'glass-lined,** *a. Ind:* Glass-lined tank, cuve verrée. **'glass-paper,** *s.* Papier de verre; papier verré. **'glass-par'tition,** *s.* Vitrage *m*. **'glass-'rod,** *s.* Baguette *f* de, en, verre; *Ch:* agitateur *m*. **'glass-'roofing,** *s.* Vitrerie *f* de toit. **'glass-ware,** *s.* Articles *mpl* de verre; verrerie *f*. Small glass-ware, verroterie *f*. **'glass-'wool,** *s.* Coton *m* de verre. **'glass-work,** *s.* **1.** (*In church*) Vitrage *m*. **2.** *pl.* Glass-works, verrerie *f*. **'glass-worker,** *s.* Verrier *m*.

glassful ['glɑːsful], *s.* (Plein) verre.

glasswort ['glɑːswəːrt], *s. Bot:* (*a*) Jointed glasswort, salicorne *f*. (*b*) Prickly glasswort, soude *f*.

glassy ['glɑːsi], *a.* Vitreux.

Glaswegian [glas'wiːdʒiən], *a. & s.* (Natif, originaire) de Glasgow.

glaucous ['glɔːkəs], *a.* Glauque.

glaze¹ [gleːiz], *s.* **1.** Glace *f*, lustre *m*, vernissure *f* (du drap). **2.** *Cer:* Glaçure *f*, vernis (luisant), enduit *m*. **3.** *Cu:* Glace; dorure *f*. **4.** *Paint:* Glacis *m*.

glaze². I. *v.tr.* **1.** Vitrer(une fenêtre). **2.** (*a*) Glacer, lustrer (une étoffe); vernir (le cuir); lisser (le papier). *Phot:* Glacer, émailler (une épreuve). (*b*) To g. the eye, embuer l'œil. (*c*) *Cer:* Vernir, émailler (la poterie); plomber (la vaisselle de terre); vitrifier (les tuiles). (*d*) *Cu:* Glacer, dorer. II. **glaze,** *v.i.* To glaze (over), se glacer; (*of eye*) devenir vitreux. **glazed,** *a.* **1.** (*Of roof, door*) Vitré. (*Of picture*) Framed and g., encadré et sous verre. *Nau:* Glazed-in light, verrine *f*. **2.** (*a*) (*Tissu*) glacé, lustré; (papier) brillant, satiné. (*b*) *Cer:* Glacé, émaillé; (*of brick*) vitrifié. **glazing,** *s.* **1.** (*a*) Pose *f* des vitres. (*b*) Vernissage *m*. *Cer: Phot:* Émaillage *m*.

glazer ['gleizər], *s.* **1.** (*Pers.*) Vernisseur *m*; satineur *m*. **2.** *Phot:* (*Instrument*) Glaceur *m*, satineur.

glazier ['gleiziər], *s.* Vitrier *m*.

glaziery ['gleiziəri], *s.* Vitrerie *f*.

gleam¹ [gliːm], *s.* (*a*) Rayon *m*, lueur *f* (de lumière). The first gleams of the sun, les premières clartés du soleil. Gleam of hope, lueur d'espoir. (*b*) Reflet *m* (d'un couteau); miroitement *m* (d'un lac).

gleam², *v.i.* Luire, reluire; (*of water*) miroiter. **gleaming¹,** *a.* Luisant. **gleaming,** *s.* Miroitement *m*.

glean [gliːn], *v.tr.* **1.** Glaner (du blé). **2.** *Vit:* Grappiller. **gleaning,** *s.* **1.** (*a*) Glane *f*. (*b*) *Vit:* Grappillage *m*. **2.** *pl.* Gleanings, glanure(s) *f*.

gleaner ['gliːnər], *s.* **1.** Glaneur, -euse. **2.** *Vit:* Grappilleur, -euse.

glebe [gliːb], *s.* **1.** *Poet: A:* Glèbe *f*. **2.** *Ecc:* Terre assignée à un bénéfice.

glee [gliː], *s.* **1.** Joie *f*, allégresse *f*. In high glee, au comble de la joie; jubilant. **2.** *Mus:* Petit chant à trois ou quatre parties.

gleeful ['gliːful], *a.* Joyeux, allègre. **-fully,** *adv.* Joyeusement; allégrement.

glen [glen], *s.* Vallée étroite; vallon *m*.

glengarry [glen'gari], *s.* (Coiffure écossaise) Toque (haute sur le devant).

glib [glib], *a. Pej:* (*Of answer*) Spécieux, patelin. (*b*) (*Of speaker*) Qui a de la faconde. To have a glib tongue, avoir le débit facile. **-ly,** *adv.* (*a*) Spécieusement. (*b*) (Parler) avec aisance.

glibness ['glibnəs], *s.* **1.** Spéciosité *f* (d'une excuse). **2.** Faconde *f*; bagout *m*.

glide¹ [glaid], *s.* **1.** (*a*) Glissement *m*. (*b*) *Danc:* Glissade *f*. **2.** *Av:* Vol plané. **3.** *Mus:* Port *m* de voix. **4.** *Ling:* Son *m* transitoire.

glide², *v.i.* (*a*) (Se) glisser, couler. To glide past, passer tout doucement. The years glide past, les années coulent. (*b*) *Av:* Planer. **gliding,** *s.* (*a*) Glissement *m*. (*b*) Vol plané.

glider ['glaidər], *s. Av:* (*Machine*) Planeur *m*, glisseur *m*.

glimmer¹ ['glimər], *s.* Faible lueur *f* (d'une chandelle); miroitement *m* (de l'eau). *F:* Glimmer of hope, lueur d'espoir. *Not the slightest g. of intelligence,* pas la moindre trace d'intelligence.

glimmer², *v.i.* Jeter une faible lueur; (*of water*) miroiter.

glimpse¹ [glimps], *s.* Vision momentanée (de qch.). *G. of a subject,* aperçu *m* sur un sujet. To catch a glimpse of sth., entrevoir, aviser, apercevoir, qch. *I only caught a g. of him,* je n'ai fait que l'entrevoir.

glimpse², *v.tr.* To glimpse sth., avoir la vision fugitive de qch.; entrevoir qch.

glint¹ [glint], *s.* Trait *m*, éclair *m* (de lumière); reflet *m* (d'un couteau).

glint², *v.i.* Entreluire, étinceler.

glissade [gliˈsɑːd, -ˈseid], *s.* Glissade *f*.

glisten [glisn], *v.i.* Étinceler, reluire, scintiller. **glistening,** *a.* Étincelant, luisant, scintillant.

glitter¹ ['glitər], *s.* Étincellement *m*, scintillement *m*, éclat *m*, brillant *m*.

glitter², *v.i.* Scintiller, étinceler, (re)luire; (*of sea*) brasiller. *Prov:* All is not gold that glitters, tout ce qui brille n'est pas or. **glittering¹,** *a.* Brillant, étincelant, éclatant, reluisant, resplendissant. **glittering²,** *s.* Étincellement *m*, scintillement *m*.

gloaming ['gloumiŋ], *s.* Crépuscule *m* (du soir); *F:* l'heure *f* du berger. In the gloaming, entre chien et loup; à la brune.

gloat [glout], *v.i.* To gloat over sth., faire des gorges chaudes de qch.; savourer (un spectacle). *To g. over one's victim,* couver du regard sa victime. *To g. over the news,* se réjouir (méchamment) de la nouvelle. *To g. over s.o.'s misfortune,* triompher du malheur de qn. **gloating,** *a.* (Œil) avide; (sourire) d'exultation méchante. **-ly,** *adv.* Avec une satisfaction méchante.

globe [gloub], *s.* Globe *m*. (*a*) Sphère *f*. (*b*) (La) terre. (*c*) *Sch:* Terrestrial g., globe terrestre. (*d*) Globe (de lampe). *Aut:* Roof-light globe, coupe *f* en verre du plafonnier. (*e*) Bocal *m*, -aux (pour poissons rouges). **'globe-artichoke,** *s. Hort:* Artichaut *m*. **'globe-trotter,** *s.* Touriste *mf* qui court le monde.

globular ['glɔbjulər], *a.* Globulaire, globuleux.

globule ['glɔbjuːl], *s.* Globule *m*, gouttelette *f* (d'eau).

glomerule ['glɔməruːl], *s. Bot:* Glomérule *m*.

gloom [gluːm], *s.* **1.** Obscurité *f*, ténèbres *fpl*. **2.** Assombrissement *m*, mélancolie *f*. To cast a gloom over the company, attrister l'assemblée.

gloominess ['gluːminəs], *s.* Assombrissement *m*. (*a*) Obscurité *f* (du temps). (*b*) Tristesse *f* (de qn).

gloomy ['gluːmi], *a.* **1.** Sombre, obscur, ténébreux. **2.** Lugubre, morne, sombre. **The weather is gloomy,** il fait sombre. *G. picture,* tableau poussé au noir. **To see the gloomy side of things,** voir (tout en) noir. **-ily,** *adv.* Sombrement, lugubrement.

glorification [glɔːrifiˈkeiʃ(ə)n], *s.* Glorification *f.*

glorify [ˈglɔːrifai], *v.tr.* Glorifier. **glorified,** *a.* **1.** *Theol:* Glorifié. **2.** *F:* (*Of thg*) En plus grand; en mieux.

glorious [ˈglɔːriəs], *a.* **1.** (Règne) glorieux. **Glorious deed,** action éclatante. **2.** (*a*) Resplendissant, radieux. **A glorious day,** une journée radieuse. (*b*) *F:* Magnifique, superbe. **To have a glorious time,** s'amuser follement. *What a. weather!* quel temps superbe! **-ly,** *adv.* **1.** Glorieusement. **2.** Magnifiquement.

glory[1] [ˈglɔːri], *s.* Gloire *f.* **1.** (*a*) Honneur *m,* renommée *f.* **To cover oneself with glory,** se couvrir de gloire. **To crown s.o. with glory,** glorifier qn. (*b*) **Glory be to God!** gloire à Dieu! *F:* **Glory (be)!** grand Dieu! (*c*) **The saints in glory,** les glorieux. **To go to glory,** (i) mourir; (ii) *F:* (*of thg*) aller à la ruine. **2.** Splendeur *f,* éclat *m* (d'un spectacle). **To be in one's glory,** être dans son élément. **3.** *U.S:* *F:* **Old Glory,** la bannière étoilée (des États-Unis). **'gloryhole,** *s.* *F:* Capharnaüm *m*; (chambre *f* de) débarras *m.*

glory[2], *v.i.* **To glory in sth.,** se glorifier de qch.

gloss[1] [glɔs], *s.* **1.** (*a*) Glose *f.* (*b*) Glossaire *m,* commentaire *m.* **2.** Fausse interprétation.

gloss[2], *s.* **1.** Lustre *m,* vernis *m.* *Tex:* Cati *m.* **To take the gloss off sth.,** délustrer qch.; *Tex:* décatir (une étoffe). **2.** *F:* **To put a gloss on the truth,** farder la vérité.

gloss[3], *v.tr.* **1.** Lustrer, glacer. *Tex:* Catir (l'étoffe). **2.** *F:* **To g. over s.o.'s faults,** glisser sur les défauts de qn. *Do not g. over anything!* ne gazez rien!

glossary [ˈglɔsəri], *s.* Glossaire *m,* lexique *m.*

glossiness [ˈglɔsinəs], *s.* Lustre *m,* vernis *m*; éclat soyeux (des cheveux).

glossy [ˈglɔsi], *a.* Lustré, glacé, brillant. *Phot:* **Glossy paper,** papier brillant. **Glossy print,** épreuve glacée.

glottal [ˈglɔt(ə)l], *a.* *Ling:* **Glottal stop, glottal catch,** coup *m* de glotte.

glottis [ˈglɔtis], *s.* *Anat:* Glotte *f.*

glove[1] [glʌv], *s.* Gant *m.* (*a*) (*Lady's*) elbow-glove, passe-coude *m.* **The glove counter** (*in shop*), la ganterie. *El.E:* Wiring-gloves, moufles *f or m.* **To pull on one's gloves,** mettre ses gants; se ganter. **To take off one's gloves,** se déganter. (*b*) *Box:* (Boxing-)glove, gant (bourré). **To put on the gloves,** mettre les gants. *F:* **To handle s.o. with the gloves off,** traiter qn sans ménagement. **'glove-factory,** *s.* Ganterie *f.* **'glove-fastener,** *s.* Bouton *m* fermoir. **'glove-maker,** *s.* Gantier, -ière. **'glove-making,** *s.* Ganterie *f.* **'glove-shop,** *s.* Ganterie *f.* **'glove-stretcher,** *s.* Ouvre-gants *m* *inv.* **'glove-trade,** *s.* Ganterie *f.*

glove[3], *v.tr.* Ganter.

glover [ˈglʌvər], *s.* Gantier, -ière.

glow[1] [glou], *s.* **1.** Lueur *f* rouge; incandescence *f.* *To emit a lurid g.,* rougeoyer. **In a glow,** (i) incandescent, chauffé au rouge; (ii) (*of coal*) embrasé. **2.** (*a*) *Physiol:* Sensation *f* de douce chaleur. *F:* **The exercise had put me all in a glow,** l'exercice m'avait fouetté le sang. (*b*) Ardeur *f,* chaleur *f.* *In the first g. of enthusiasm,* dans l'exaltation première. **3.** **The g.** of health, l'éclat du teint dû à la santé. **'glow-lamp,** *s.* *El:* **1.** Lampe *f* à incandescence. **2.** *Cin:* Glow-

lamp recording, enregistrement par lampe à lueur. **'glow-worm,** *s.* *Ent:* (*a*) Ver luisant; lampyre *m*; *F:* bête *f* à feu. (*b*) Luciole *f.*

glow[2], *v.i.* **1.** Rougeoyer, *Lit:* rutiler. **To** (**begin to**) **glow,** (i) (*of metal*) rougir; (ii) (*of coal*) s'embraser; (iii) *El:* (*of lamp*) s'allumer. **2.** (*a*) Rayonner. (*b*) *His cheeks glowed,* il avait les joues en feu. **3.** **To make s.o. glow,** fouetter le sang à qn. **glowing,** *a.* **1.** Incandescent, rougeoyant; *Lit:* radieux. **2.** (*Of coal*) Embrasé. **3.** Rayonnant. **Glowing cheeks,** joues rouges, vermeilles. **Glowing with health,** rouge de santé. **4.** (*Of description, etc.*) Chaleureux; (*of pers.*) ardent. **To paint sth. in glowing colours,** présenter une affaire sous un jour des plus favorables. **To speak in glowing terms of s.o.,** dire merveille de qn.

glower [ˈglauər], *v.i.* **To glower at s.o.,** regarder qn d'un air fâché ou menaçant.

gloxinia [glɔkˈsinia], *s.* *Bot:* Gloxinie *f.*

gloze [glouz], *v.i.* **To gloze over (sth.),** glisser sur, pallier (les défauts).

glucose [ˈgluːkous], *s.* Glucose *f* (*in Ch. usu. m.*); sucre *m* de raisin.

glue[1] [gluː], *s.* Colle (forte). **Marine glue,** marine. **'glue-pot,** *s.* Pot *m* à colle.

glue[2], *v.tr.* (glued; gluing) (*a*) Coller (à la colle forte) (*to, on,* à). (*b*) *F:* *Her face was glued to the window,* son visage était collé à la vitre. *His eyes were glued on the door,* il ne détachait pas les yeux de la porte.

gluey [ˈgluːi], *a.* Gluant, poisseux.

glug-glug [ˈglʌgˈglʌg], *s.* Glouglou *m.*

glum [glʌm], *a.* (Visage) renfrogné, maussade. **To look glum,** se renfrogner. **-ly,** *adv.* D'un air maussade.

glume [gluːm], *s.* *Bot:* Glume *f,* bal(l)e *f.*

glumness [ˈglʌmnəs], *s.* Air *m* sombre.

glut[1] [glʌt], *s.* **1.** (*a*) Rassasiement *m* (de l'appétit). (*b*) Excès *m* (de nourriture). **2.** *Com:* (*a*) Encombrement *m* (du marché). (*b*) Surabondance *f* (d'une denrée). *There is a g. of pears in the market,* le marché regorge de poires.

glut[2], *v.tr.* (glutted) (*a*) **To glut oneself,** se rassasier, se gorger. **Glutted with food,** soûl de manger. (*b*) *Com:* Encombrer, inonder (le marché).

gluten [ˈgluːtən], *s.* Gluten *m.*

glutinous [ˈgluːtinəs], *a.* Glutineux.

glutton [ˈglʌt(ə)n], *s.* **1.** (*a*) Gourmand, -ande; glouton, -onne; goulu, -e. (*b*) *F:* **He's a glutton for work,** c'est un cheval à l'ouvrage. *Box:* **G. for punishment,** encaisseur *m.* **2.** *Z:* Glouton.

gluttonous [ˈglʌtənəs], *a.* Glouton, goulu. **-ly,** *adv.* Gloutonnement.

gluttony [ˈglʌtəni], *s.* Gloutonnerie *f,* gourmandise *f*; *F:* goinfrerie *f.*

glycerin(e) [ˈglisərin, -in], *s.* *Ch: etc:* Glycérine *f.* **To treat sth. with g.,** glycériner qch.

glycin(e) [ˈglisin], *s.* *Ch:* Glycine *f.*

glyph [glif], *s.* *Arch:* Glyphe *m.*

gnarl [nɑːrl], *s.* Loupe *f,* nœud *m,* broussin *m* (d'un arbre).

gnarled [nɑːrld], *a.* **1.** (*Of tree*) (*a*) Noueux, broussiné, rugueux. (*b*) Tortu, tordu. **2.** *F:* (*Of hands*) Noueux.

gnash [naʃ], *v.tr.* **To gnash one's teeth,** grincer des dents. **gnashing,** *s.* Grincement *m* (des dents).

gnat [nat], *s.* *Ent:* Cousin *m,* moustique *m.*

gnaw [nɔː], *v.tr.* & *i.* (*p.t.* gnawed; *p.p.* gnawed, gnawn) (*a*) **To gnaw** (*at, into*) sth., ronger qch. *F:* **To g. one's fingers with impatience,** se mordre les poings d'impatience. (*b*) Gnawed by hunger,

tenaillé par la faim. **gnawing,** s. (a) Ronge-
ment m. (b) Gnawings of hunger, tiraillements m
de la faim.

gneiss [(g)nais], s. Geol: Gneiss m.

gnome [noum], s. Myth: Gnome m.

gnomon ['noumon], s. Gnomon m.

gnostic ['nostik], a. & s. Gnostique (mf).

gnu [nu:], s. Z: Gnou m.

go¹ [gou], s. (pl. goes) **1.** Aller m. To be always
on the go, être toujours à trotter, à courir. To
keep s.o. on the go, faire trimer qn. **2.** To be
full of go, to have plenty of go, être plein d'entrain; avoir de l'allant. **3.** (a) Coup m, essai m.
To have a go at sth., (i) tenter l'aventure;
(ii) s'attaquer à (un rôti). Let's have a go!
essayons le coup! At one go, d'un (seul) coup;
tout d'une haleine. (b) Two more goes of port,
encore deux tournées de porto. **4.** P: Here's a
rum go, a pretty go! en voilà une farce! quelle
affaire! That was a near go! nous l'avons
échappé belle! No go! bernique! **5.** P: It's
all the go, c'est la grande vogue.

go², v.i. (thou goest, he goes; p.t. went [went];
p.p. gone [gon]. The aux. is 'have,' occ. 'be.')
Aller. **1.** (a) To go to a place, aller, se rendre,
à un endroit. To go to France, to Japan, aller en
France, au Japon. To go to church, aller à l'église.
What shall I go in? que vais-je mettre? To go to
prison, être mis en prison. To go to the window,
se mettre à la fenêtre. To come and go, aller et
venir. To go to s.o. for sth., aller trouver qn
pour avoir, obtenir, qch. To go (on) a journey,
faire un voyage. To go (for) a walk, faire une
promenade. To go on foot, on horseback, by
train, by car, aller à pied, à cheval, par le chemin
de fer, en auto. There he goes! le voilà qui passe!
Who goes there? qui va là? qui vive? To go the
shortest way, prendre par le plus court. To go (at)
ten miles an hour, faire dix milles à l'heure. You
go first! (i) partez en tête; (ii) à vous d'abord.
You go next! à vous ensuite. (b) Mountains that
go from east to west, montagnes qui courent de
l'est à l'ouest. (c) To go to school, (i) aller à
l'école; (ii) fréquenter l'école. To go on the
stage, monter sur les planches. To go to sea,
se faire marin. To go into the army, F: to go for
a soldier, se faire soldat; s'engager (dans
l'armée). Wine that goes to the head, vin qui
monte à la tête. (d) To go hungry, se serrer le
ventre. (e) To go one's own way, faire à sa guise.
(f) The names go in alphabetical order, les noms
sont rangés par ordre alphabétique. Promotion
goes by seniority, l'avancement se fait à l'ancienneté. **2.** Marcher. (a) To go by steam, marcher
à la vapeur. The table goes on wheels, la table
marche sur des roulettes. To be going, être en
marche. To set a machine going, mettre une
machine en marche. We must keep industry going,
il faut maintenir l'activité de l'industrie. To keep
the fire going, entretenir le feu. To make things
go, (i) faire marcher rondement les choses;
(ii) mettre de l'entrain dans la réunion. F: How
goes it? ça va bien? comment ça va? (Of play)
To go (well), réussir. The rehearsal went well,
la répétition a bien marché. Things are not going
well, cela ne marche pas. As things are going, du
train dont vont les choses. When he gets going
he never stops, une fois lancé, il ne s'arrête plus.
F: What I say, goes, c'est moi qui mène les
choses. (b) (i) It has just gone twelve, midi,
minuit, vient de sonner. It has gone six already,
il est déjà six heures passées. (ii) To go bang,
faire pan. (c) This is how the chorus goes, voici
les paroles du refrain. (d) (Of contest) Aboutir.

I don't know how matters will go, je ne sais pas
comment cela tournera. Judgment went for the
plaintiff, l'arrêt fut prononcé en faveur du demandeur. **3.** (a) (Of time) Passer. The time will soon
go, le temps passera vite. Ten minutes gone and
nothing done, dix minutes de passées et rien de
fait. F: How goes the time? quelle heure
est-il? (b) As the saying goes, selon l'adage. As
times go, par le temps qui court. That's not dear
as things go, ce n'est pas cher au prix où se
vendent les choses. (c) To go by a false name,
être connu sous un faux nom. (d) That goes
without saying, cela va sans dire. **4.** (a) Partir;
s'en aller. After I have gone, après mon départ.
Don't go yet, ne vous en allez pas encore. Let me
go! laissez-moi partir! (Cp. 12 (a).) Go, A: be
gone! allez-vous-en! Sp: Go! partez! F: From
the word go, dès le commencement. (b) A hundred employees to go, cent employés vont recevoir
leur congé. He must go, F: il faut le débarquer.
(c) Disparaître. My hat has gone, mon chapeau
a disparu. It has, is, all gone, il n'y en a plus.
The wine is all gone, le vin est épuisé. That's the
way the money goes, voilà comme l'argent file.
Her sight is going, sa vue baisse. His teeth are
all gone, il a perdu toutes ses dents. (d) (i) The
spring went, le ressort s'est cassé. El: A fuse
went, un plomb fondit, sauta. (ii) This stuff goes
at the folds, cette étoffe se coupe aux plis.
(e) These spoons are going for ten francs each, ces
cuillers sont en vente, en solde, à dix francs
pièce. Going! going! gone! une fois! deux
fois! adjugé! (f) If I hear of any job going, si
j'apprends qu'une situation se présente. (g) To
go the way of all things, P: to go west, mourir;
F: plier bagage. **5.** (a) To go to see s.o.; to
go and see s.o., aller voir qn; aller trouver qn.
Go and shut the door! allez fermer la porte!
P: Now you've (been and) gone and done it! vous
en avez fait une belle! (b) (Merely purpose) To
go to do sth., aller pour faire qch. (c) (Determination) I am going to have my own way, je veux
en faire à ma tête. (d) (Intention) I'm going to
spend my holidays abroad, je compte passer mes
vacances à l'étranger. (e) (Immediate future) I am
going to tell you a story, je vais vous raconter une
histoire. (f) To go motoring, aller se promener
en automobile. To go hunting, fishing, aller à la
chasse, à la pêche. F: There you go again!
vous voilà reparti! **6.** (a) To go to law, avoir
recours à la justice. To go to war, se mettre en
guerre. He will not go to the trouble of . . ., il ne
veut pas prendre, se donner, la peine de. . . .
(b) Cards: To go two, three, annoncer deux,
trois. To go one better, renchérir. **7.** (a)
(i) Trunk that will go under the berth, malle
qui se case sous la couchette. (ii) Where
does this book go? où est la place de ce livre?
(b) Six into twelve goes twice, douze divisé par six
fait deux. **8.** His title will go to his eldest son,
son titre (de noblesse) passera à son fils aîné. **9.** Contribuer (à qch.). The qualities that go to make a
great man, les qualités qui constituent un grand
homme. To go to prove sth., servir à prouver
qch. **10.** S'étendre. The estate goes down to the
river, la propriété s'étend jusqu'à la rivière. The
report is accurate as far as it goes, le rapport est
exact quant à ce qu'il dit. **11.** (a) Devenir. To
go mad, devenir fou. To go Bolshevist, se faire
bolcheviste. To go white, red, etc., blanchir,
rougir, etc. (See these adjectives.). (b) (Of house)
To go to ruin, tomber en ruine. His son has
gone to the bad, son fils a mal tourné. **12.** (a) To
let go, lâcher prise. To let go (one's hold of)

sth. lâcher, laisser échapper (une corde). **Let me go!** lâchez-moi! (*Cp.* 4 (*a*).) *Nau:* Let go forward! larguez devant! (*b*) To let oneself go, se laisser aller. *To let oneself go on a subject*, s'étendre, s'emballer, sur un sujet. (*c*) **Well, let it go at that!** passons! *We'll let it go at that*, tenons-nous-en là. **13.** *P:* (*a*) To go it, s'en donner à cœur joie; aller grand train. *He's going it!* il se lance! (*b*) **Go it!** vas-y, allez-y! allez toujours! **go about,** *v.i.* **1.** (*a*) Aller çà et là; circuler. *There is a rumour going about that . . .,* le bruit court que. . . . *He is going about again*, il est de nouveau sur pied. (*b*) *Nau:* Virer de bord. **2.** (*a*) *To go about the streets*, circuler dans les rues. (*b*) Se mettre à (une tâche). *How to go about it*, comment s'y prendre. (*c*) *In the morning I go about my work*, le matin je vaque à mes affaires. **go across,** *v.i.* Traverser, passer (la mer); franchir (le pont). **go after,** *v.i.* (*a*) Courir après (les femmes). (*b*) Solliciter, briguer (un emploi). **go against,** *v.i.* **1.** *If fate goes against us*, si la fortune nous est contraire. *His appearance goes against him*, il ne paye pas de mine. **2.** (*a*) To go against the tide, prendre le contresens de la marée. (*b*) Aller à l'encontre de, heurter (l'opinion publique). It goes against my conscience to . . ., il me répugne de. . . . **go along,** *v.i.* **1.** Passer par (une rue). **2.** Passer, suivre, son chemin. *F:* Go along with you! (i) allez, filez! (ii) dites cela à d'autres! **go at,** *v.i.* 'S'attaquer à (qn, qch.). To go at it hard, y aller de tout son cœur. **go away,** *v.i.* (*a*) *To go away on business*, s'absenter pour affaires. (*b*) To go away with sth., emporter, enlever, qch. **go back,** *v.i.* **1.** (*a*) *To go back to one's native land*, retourner dans sa patrie. (*b*) Rebrousser chemin. *To go back on one's steps*, revenir sur ses pas. (*c*) *To go back two paces*, reculer de deux pas. (*d*) *To go back to a subject*, revenir sur un sujet. *To go back to gas*, en revenir au gaz. **2.** *To go back to the* Flood, remonter (jusqu')au déluge. *We won't go back to the past*, ne revenons pas sur le passé. *His family goes back to the crusaders*, sa famille descend des croisés. **3.** (*a*) *To go back on a promise*, revenir sur sa promesse; se dédire. (*b*) *F: To go back on a friend*, planter là un ami. **going back,** *s.* **1.** (*a*) Retour *m.* Going back to school, rentrée *f* des classes. (*b*) *F:* There's no going back, il n'y a pas à reculer. **2.** (*a*) Going back on one's word, manque *m* de parole. (*b*) There's no going back on it, il n'y a pas à y revenir. (*c*) *F:* Going back on a friend, trahison *f* d'un ami. **go before,** *v.i.* **1.** (*a*) Devancer, précéder (qn). (*b*) Primer. *Might went before right*, la force primait le droit. **2.** (*a*) Partir en avant. (*b*) Marcher devant. **go behind,** *v.i.* (*a*) To go behind s.o.'s words, chercher une arrière-pensée. (*b*) To go behind a decision, revenir sur une décision. **go by,** *v.i.* **1.** Passer. As the years go by, à mesure que les années passent. *You must not let this chance go by*, il ne faut pas manquer cette occasion. **2.** (*a*) *He went by the shop*, il est passé devant la boutique. (*b*) *To go by s.o.*, se régler sur qn. *To go by the directions*, suivre les instructions. **To go by appearances**, juger d'après les apparences. *That is nothing to go by*, on ne peut fonder là-dessus. **'go-by,** *s.* To give s.o. the go-by. **1.** Dépasser, devancer, qn. **2.** *He gave me the go-by yesterday*, hier il a fait semblant de ne pas me reconnaître. **go down,** *v.i.* **1.** Descendre (l'escalier). **2.** (*a*) Descendre. *To go down to dinner*, descendre dîner. *Sch:* To go down (from the university), (i) quit-

ter l'université; (ii) partir en vacances. (*b*) *F: My dinner won't go down*, mon dîner a du mal à passer. That won't go down with me, ça ne prend pas avec moi. (*c*) (*Of sun*) Se coucher. (*d*) (*Of ship*) Couler à fond; sombrer. *To go down by the bows*, piquer de l'avant. (*e*) Tomber. To go down on one's knees, se mettre à genoux. (*f*) (*Of temperature*) Baisser, s'abaisser. The neighbourhood has gone down, ce quartier a déchu. *F:* He has gone down in the world, il a connu des jours meilleurs. (*g*) (*Of swelling*) Se désenfler; (*of balloon, tyre, etc.*) se dégonfler. (*h*) To go down to posterity, passer à la postérité. **go for,** *v.i.* **1.** Aller chercher (qn). **2.** (*a*) *F:* Tomber sur, fondre sur (qn). (*b*) *F:* S'en prendre à (qn); chercher noise à (qn). *To go for s.o. in the papers*, attaquer qn dans les journaux. **go forward,** *v.i.* **1.** Avancer. *Nau:* Aller devant. *The work is going forward*, le travail avance. **2.** *What is going forward?* qu'est-ce qui se passe? **go in,** *v.i.* **1.** *The key goes in the lock*, la clef entre dans cette serrure. **2.** (*a*) Entrer, rentrer. *I must go in to cook the dinner*, il faut que je rentre préparer le dîner. *F: The theatres were just going in*, c'était l'heure de l'ouverture des théâtres. (*b*) (*Of sun*) Se cacher. (*c*) To go in for (sth.), s'occuper de, se mêler de (qch.). *To go in for a course of lectures*, s'inscrire à un cours; suivre un cours. *To go in for sports*, s'adonner aux sports; faire du sport. *To go in for teaching*, entrer dans l'enseignement. *F:* To go in for a car, se payer une auto. To go in for an examination, se présenter à un examen. To go in for a competition, prendre part à un concours. *F:* Go in and win! bonne chance! To go in with s.o. in an undertaking, se joindre à qn dans une affaire. **go into,** *v.i.* **1.** (*a*) Entrer dans (une maison). To go into society, aller dans le monde. *To go into the army*, entrer dans l'armée. (*b*) To go into a lengthy explanation of sth., entrer dans de longues explications. (*c*) *To go into mourning*, prendre le deuil. *To go into fits of laughter*, éclater de rire. *To go into hysterics*, avoir une crise de nerfs. (*d*) *Aut:* To go into second gear, passer en deuxième (vitesse). **2.** Examiner, étudier (une question). *To go closely into a question*, approfondir une question. **go off,** *v.i.* **1.** (*a*) Partir, s'en aller. *Th:* Quitter la scène. (*b*) To go off with sth., emporter qch. (*c*) (*Of gun*) Partir. (*d*) To go off (into a faint), perdre connaissance; s'évanouir. (*Of feeling*) Passer. (*Of tennis player*) Perdre de sa forme; baisser. *Beauty that went off a little*, beauté défraîchie. (*f*) (*Of wine, etc.*) Se détériorer; perdre; (*of milk*) tourner. (*g*) *Everything went off well*, tout s'est bien passé. (*h*) *Com:* (*Of goods*) Se vendre. **2.** (*a*) (*Of train*) To go off the rails, dérailler. *F:* To go off the beaten track, s'écarter du chemin battu. (*b*) *I have gone off motoring*, je ne fais plus d'auto. **go on,** *v.i.* **1.** (*a*) (i) *Time goes on*, le temps marche. (ii) Continuer sa route; poursuivre sa course. (iii) He is going on for forty, il va sur la quarantaine. *It is going on for three o'clock*, il est près de trois heures. (*b*) Continuer (de faire qch.); reprendre la parole. *If you go on like this . . .*, si vous continuez. . . . *I've got enough to go on with*, j'ai de quoi marcher. (*c*) *I shall now go on to another matter*, je passe maintenant à une autre question. *He went on to give me all the details*, puis il me donna tous les détails. *F:* (*Iron:*) Go on! allons donc! dites ça à d'autres! (*d*) Marcher. *This has gone on for years*, cela dure depuis des années. *Preparations are going on*, les préparatifs se poursuivent. **What** is going on here? qu'est-ce qui se passe ici? How are you going on? comment cela marche-t-il? comment allez-vous? *To go on as before,* faire comme par le passé. (*e*) *F:* Se conduire. *I don't like the way she goes on,* je n'aime pas son manège. (*f*) **To go on at** s.o., gourmander qn. *She went on dreadfully,* elle nous a fait une scène terrible. (*g*) *Th:* **To go on,** monter en scène; entrer en scène. **2.** (*a*) *I went on that supposition,* je me suis fondé sur cette hypothèse. (*b*) *Those shoes won't go on* (*my feet*), ces souliers ne me vont pas. **goings-on,** *s.pl. F:* Conduite *f*; manège *m.* **go out,** *v.i.* **I.** (*a*) Sortir. **Out you go!** hors d'ici! *She was dressed to go out,* elle était en tenue de ville. **To go out** (**on strike**), se mettre en grève. *I am going out to dinner,* je dîne en ville. **My heart went out to him,** je ressentis de la pitié pour lui. (*b*) *To go out washing,* faire des journées de lessive. (*c*) Aller dans le monde; sortir. (*d*) *To go out to the colonies,* émigrer, ou aller servir, aux colonies. (*e*) Être mis en circulation. *This communiqué should never have gone out,* on n'aurait pas dû publier ce communiqué. **2. To go out of fashion,** passer de mode. **3.** Disparaître. *All the hatred had gone out of his voice,* toute la haine avait disparu de sa voix. **4.** *Pol:* Quitter le pouvoir. **5.** *Games: How many points do you want to go out?* combien de points vous faut-il pour gagner? **6. To go out of one's way,** s'écarter de son chemin. *S.a.* WAY¹ **2** (*a*). **7.** (*Of fire*) S'éteindre. **8.** (*Of tide*) Baisser. **going out,** *s.* **I.** Sortie *f.* **To like going out,** aimer à sortir. **2.** Baisse *f* (de la marée). **go over,** *v.i.* **I.** (*a*) Traverser, passer (la mer). (*b*) *To go over a drawing with ink,* passer un dessin à l'encre. (*c*) Examiner (un compte). *To go over a house,* visiter une maison. **To go over the ground,** reconnaître le terrain. (*d*) **To go over sth. in one's mind,** repasser qch. dans son esprit. **2. To go over to the enemy,** passer à l'ennemi. **go round,** *v.i.* **I.** (*a*) (i) Faire un détour, un circuit. *You'll have to go round,* il faudra faire le tour. (ii) *F:* **To go round to see** s.o., faire visite à qn. (*b*) (*Of wheel*) Tourner. **My head is going round,** la tête me tourne. (*c*) (*Of rumour*) Circuler, courir. (*d*) **There is not enough to go round,** il n'y en a pas pour tout le monde. **2.** *To go round the town,* faire le tour de la ville. **go through,** *v.i.* **I.** (*a*) Passer par (un trou); traverser (un pays). *A shiver went through me,* un frisson me parcourut. (*b*) Passer par, suivre en entier (un cours d'études). *To go through one's apprenticeship,* faire son apprentissage. *To go through the whole programme,* exécuter tout le programme. (*c*) *The book has gone through ten editions,* on a déjà tiré dix éditions de ce livre. (*d*) Remplir, accomplir (des formalités); subir, essuyer (de rudes épreuves). *F: I have gone through it,* j'ai passé par là. (*e*) Transpercer, percer. *This cold goes right through me,* ce froid me transit. (*f*) Examiner en détail. (i) Compulser (des documents). (ii) Fouiller dans (les poches de qn). (*g*) Manger (une fortune). **2.** (*a*) *The bill has gone through,* la loi a passé. *The deal did not go through,* le marché n'a pas été conclu. (*b*) **To go through with sth.,** aller jusqu'au bout (d'une épreuve). *We've got to go through with it, F:* le vin est tiré, il faut le boire. **go together,** *v.i.* (*a*) (*Of misfortunes*) Marcher ensemble. (*b*) (*Of colours*) S'accorder; aller bien ensemble. **go under,** *v.i.* Succomber, sombrer. **go up,** *v.i.* **I.** (*a*) Monter; aller en haut. **A cry went up** from the crowd, un cri s'éleva de la foule. *Sch:* **To go up a form,** monter d'une classe. (*b*) **To go up to the university,** entrer à l'univer-

sité. **To go up to** s.o., s'avancer vers qn; aborder qn. (*c*) (*Of price, temperature*) Monter, hausser. *Bread is going up* (*in price*), le pain renchérit. (*d*) (*Of mine*) Sauter. *To go up in flames,* se mettre à flamber. **2.** Monter (une colline). *To go up a ladder,* monter à une échelle. *To go up a river,* remonter une rivière. *Mil:* **To go up the line,** monter en ligne. **go with,** *v.i.* **I.** (*a*) Accompagner. (*b*) *Salary that goes with an office,* traitement applicable à une fonction. (*c*) *To go with the times,* marcher avec son époque. **2.** S'accorder avec (qch.); (*of colours*) se marier avec (une teinte). **go without,** *v.i.* (*a*) (*Do without*) Se passer de (qch.). **To go without food,** *F:* se serrer le ventre; se boucler la ceinture. (*b*) (*Be without*) Manquer de (qch.). **gone,** *a.* **I.** (*a*) Disparu, parti. **I won't be gone long,** je ne serai pas longtemps absent. (*b*) Mort. **2. Far gone in** drink, dans un état d'ivresse avancé. *He is too far g. to speak,* il est trop bas pour parler. **3.** *F:* **To be gone on** s.o., être amoureux, épris, de qn. **going¹,** *a.* **I.** Qui marche. *The business is a g. concern,* la maison est en pleine activité. **2. One of the best firms going,** une des meilleures maisons qui soient. **going²,** *s.* **I.** (*a*) **Goings and comings,** allées *f* et venues *f.* (*b*) *Eight miles in two hours, that's very good g.!* huit milles en deux heures, c'est bien marché! (*c*) *G. to law,* recours m à la justice. **2.** Départ *m.* **3.** Rough going, chemin rude. *F:* **To go while the going is good,** profiter de ce que les circonstances sont favorables. **'go-ahead,** *a.* Plein d'allant; entreprenant. *G.-a. times,* époque de progrès. **'go-as-you-'please,** *attrib.a.* **I.** (Vie) libre. **2.** (Travail) sans méthode. **'go-between,** *s.* Intermédiaire *mf*; entremetteur, -euse. **'go-cart,** *s.* Chaise pliante, charrette pliante (pour enfants).

goad¹ [goud], *s.* Aiguillon *m.*
goad², *v.tr.* Aiguillonner, piquer. **To goad** s.o. on, aiguillonner, inciter, qn.
goal [goul], *s.* But *m.* (*a*) *My goal is in sight,* j'approche de mon but. (*b*) *Fb:* **To score, kick, a goal,** marquer, réussir, un but. **To keep goal,** garder le but. **'goal-keeper,** *s. Fb: etc:* Gardien *m* de but; *F:* le goal. **'goal-post,** *s. Fb:* Montant *m* de but.
goat [gout], *s.* **I.** Chèvre *f.* **She-goat,** bique *f*, chèvre. **He-goat,** bouc *m.* *Old* (*he-*)*g.,* bouquin *m.* *Young g.,* chevreau, *f.* chevrette. *F:* **Don't play the goat,** ne faites pas l'imbécile. *U.S: P:* **To get** s.o.'s goat, irriter qn. **2.** *Astr:* The Goat, le Capricorne.
goatee [gou'ti:], *s.* Barbiche *f*, bouc *m.*
goatherd ['gouthə:rd], *s.* Chevrier, -ière.
goatskin ['goutskin], *s.* **I.** Peau *f* de chèvre; peau de bique. **2.** (*Bottle*) Outre *f.*
goatsucker ['goutsʌkər], *s. Orn:* Engoulevent *m*; *F:* tette-chèvre *m.*
gobble¹ [gobl], *v.tr.* **To gobble** (**up**) **sth.,** avaler qch. goulûment.
gobble², *v.i.* (*Of turkey-cock*) Glouglouter.
gobbler ['goblər], *s.* Dindon *m.*
goblet ['goblet], *s.* **I.** *A:* (*a*) Gobelet *m.* (*b*) *Lit:* Coupe *f.* **2.** *Com:* Verre *m* à pied.
goblin ['goblin], *s.* Gobelin *m*, lutin *m.*
goby ['goubi], *s. Ich:* Gobie *m.*
god [gɔd], *s.* **I.** (*a*) Dieu *m.* **Feast** (**fit**) **for the gods,** festin digne des dieux. **To make a** (**little tin**) **god of** s.o., se faire un dieu de qn. *F:* **Ye gods** (**and little fishes**)**!** grands dieux! (*b*) *Th:* *P:* **The gods,** le poulailler, le paradis. **2.** Dieu; *F:* le bon Dieu. **God willing,** s'il plaît à Dieu. **Would to God . . .,** plût à Dieu. . . . *What in*

God's name are you doing? que faites-vous là, grand Dieu ! **God Almighty !** Dieu tout-puissant ! **Thank God !** Dieu merci ! grâce au ciel ! **'god-child,** *pl.* **-children,** *s.* Filleul, *f.* filleule. **'god-forsaken,** *a. F:* God-for-saken place, endroit perdu. *What a g.-f. country !* quel fichu pays ! **'god-parent,** *s.* Parent spiri-tuel. **God's 'acre,** *s.* Le cimetière. **'God-speed,** *int.* Bon voyage ! adieu !

goddess ['gɔdes], *s.f.* Déesse.

godfather ['gɔdfɑːðər], *s.m.* Parrain.

godhead ['gɔdhed], *s.* The Godhead, Dieu *m.*

godless ['gɔdləs], *a.* Athée, impie.

godlessness ['gɔdləsnəs], *s.* Impiété *f.*

godliness ['gɔdlinəs], *s.* Piété *f.*

godly ['gɔdli], *a.* Dévot, pieux, saint.

godmother ['gɔdmʌðər], *s.f.* Marraine.

godown [gou'daun], *s. Com:* Comptoir *m,* entrepôt *m* (aux Indes).

godsend ['gɔdsend], *s.* Aubaine *f,* bénédiction *f ;* bienfait *m* du ciel.

godship ['gɔdʃip], *s.* Divinité *f.*

godson ['gɔdsʌn], *s.m.* Filleul.

goer ['gouər], *s.* (*Of horse*) Good goer, bad goer, bon, mauvais, marcheur.

goffer[1] ['gɔfər], *s.* **1.** *Cost:* Godron *m,* tuyau *m,* plissé *m.* **2.** Fer *m* à tuyauter, à gaufrer.

goffer[2], *v.tr. Laund:* Gaufrer ; tuyauter ; plisser.

goffering, *s. Laund:* Gaufrage *m ;* tuyautage *m ;* plissage *m.* **Goffering-tongs, goffering-iron(s),** fer *m* à tuyauter, à gaufrer.

goggle[1] [gɔgl], *v.i.* (*a*) Rouler de gros yeux. (*b*) (*Of the eyes*) Être saillants.

goggle[2], *a.* (Yeux) à fleur de tête. **'goggle-eyed,** *a.* Qui a des yeux à fleur de tête.

goggles [gɔglz], *s.pl. Ind:. Aut:* Lunettes (pro-tectrices).

goitre ['gɔitər], *s. Med:* Goitre *m.*

goitrous ['gɔitrəs], *a. Med:* Goitreux.

gold [gould], *s.* (*a*) Or *m.* **Gold in nuggets, or brut.** Ingot gold, or en barres. *F:* To speak words of gold, parler d'or. *St.Exch:* Gold shares, valeurs aurifères. *The Bank's g. reserve,* le stock d'or de la Banque. *U.S: P:* To sell s.o. a gold brick, escroquer, filouter, qn. (*b*) (Pièces *fpl* d')or. (*c*) Dutch gold, oripeau *m. Cost: Worked with g.,* lamé (d'or). (*d*) Couleur *f* de l'or. **Old-gold (colour),** vieil or *inv.* **'gold-bearing,** *a.* (Filon, etc.) aurifère. **'gold-beater,** *s.* Batteur, -euse, d'or. **Gold-beater's skin,** baudruche *f.* **gold-'cased,** *a.* Doublé d'or. **'gold-digger,** *s.* **1.** Chercheur *m* d'or. **2.** *U.S: P:* (*Of woman*) Exploiteuse *f* d'hommes riches. **'gold-digging,** *s.* (*a*) Exploitation *f* de quartz aurifère. (*b*) *pl.* Gold-diggings, placer *m.* **'gold-dust,** *s.* Poudre *f,* poussière *f,* d'or. **'gold-fever,** *s.* Fièvre *f* de l'or. **'gold-field,** *s.* Champ *m* aurifère. *pl.* Gold-fields, districts *m* aurifères, régions *f* aurifères. **'gold-fish,** *s.* Poisson *m* rouge. **'gold-foil,** *s.* Feuille *f* d'or. **gold-'laced,** *a.* Galonné d'or ; chamarré d'or. **'gold-leaf,** *s.* Feuille *f* d'or ; or *m* en feuille. **'gold-mine,** *s.* Mine *f* d'or. *F:* A regular gold-mine, une affaire d'or. **'gold-nibbed,** *a.* (Porte-plume) avec plume en or. **gold 'plate,** *s.* Vaisselle *f* d'or. **gold-'plated,** *a.* Doublé d'or. **'gold-rimmed,** *a.* (Monocle, etc.) cerclé d'or. **G.-r.** spectacles, lunettes à monture d'or. **'gold-rush,** *s.* Ruée *f* vers l'or. **'gold-tipped,** *a.* A bout doré. **'gold-washer,** *s.* Orpailleur *m.*

golden ['gould(ə)n], *a.* D'or. (*a*) The Golden Fleece, la Toison d'or. *U.S: F:* The Golden

City, San Francisco. (*b*) G. *hair,* cheveux d'or d'un blond doré. (*c*) Golden rule, règle d'or excellence, précieuse. **'golden-rod,** *s. Bot:* Solidage *f ;* verge *f* d'or. **'golden 'wedding,** *s.* Noces *fpl* d'or. To celebrate one's g. w., célébrer la cinquantaine.

goldfinch ['gouldfin(t)ʃ], *s.* Chardonneret *m.*

goldsmith ['gouldsmiθ], *s.* Orfèvre *m.* **Gold-smith's work,** orfèvrerie *f.*

golf[1] [gɔlf, gɔf], *s.* Golf *m.* **'golf-club,** *s.* **1.** Crosse *f* de golf ; club *m.* **2.** Club de golf. **'golf-course,** *s.,* **'golf-links,** *s.pl.* Terrain *m* de golf ; *F:* un golf.

golf[2], *v.i.* Jouer au golf.

golfer ['gɔlfər], *s.* Golfeur, -euse.

golly ['gɔli], *int.* Fichtre ! mince (alors) !

golosh [gɔ'lɔʃ], *s.* = GALOSH.

gonad ['gɔnad], *s. Biol:* Gonade *f.*

gondola ['gɔndola], *s.* **1.** *Nau:* Gondole *f.* **2.** Gondole, nacelle *f* (d'un dirigeable)

gondolier [gɔndo'liːər], *s.* Gondolier *m.*

gone [gɔn]. *See* GO[2].

goner ['gɔnər], *s. P:* **1.** Homme mort, femme morte. **2.** Homme fichu. *He's a g.,* c'en est fait de lui.

gong[1] [gɔŋ], *s.* (*a*) Gong *m.* (*b*) *Ind: Nau:* Alarm gong, timbre avertisseur. *Nau:* The fire gong, la cloche "feu."

gong[2], *v.tr. Aut:* To be gonged, être sommé de s'arrêter pour infraction au code.

goniometer [gouni'ɔmetər], *s.* Goniomètre *m.*

good [gud]. **I.** *a.* (better, best) Bon. **1.** (*a*) G. *wine,* bon vin ; vin de bonne qualité. G. *hand-writing,* belle écriture. G. *story,* bonne histoire. *F:* That's a good one ! en voilà une bonne ! **Good to eat,** bon à manger. *Give me something g.,* donnez-moi quelque chose de bien, de bon. **This is good enough for me,** cela fera mon affaire. **That's not good enough,** (i) je n'accepte pas cela ; (ii) *F:* ça, c'est un peu fort ! G. **business men,** excellents hommes d'affaires. **In good plain English,** en bon anglais. To have g. sight, avoir de bons yeux. (*b*) (*Of food*) To keep good, rester bon ; se conserver. (*c*) G. reason, excuse, raison, excuse, valable. G. debt, bonne créance. **Chit good for ten shillings,** bon *m* de dix shillings. **Ticket g. for two months,** billet valide, bon, pour deux mois. *He is g. for another ten years,* il en a encore bien pour dix ans à vivre. (*d*) Avantageux. G. marriage, mariage avantageux ; bon parti. G. op-portunity, bonne occasion. **They are people of good position,** ce sont des gens bien. **I thought good to do so,** il m'a semblé bon d'en faire ainsi. *A g. day (at the races),* un jour de veine. **To make a good thing out of sth.,** tirer bon parti de qch. **To earn good money,** gagner largement sa vie. (*e*) Heureux. G. news, bonnes, heureuses, nouvelles. **It is too good to be believed,** c'est trop beau pour y croire. **Good for you !** à la bonne heure ! Good (job) ! that's a good thing ! c'est bien heureux ! tant mieux ! à la bonne heure ! bon ! Very good ! très bien ! *It was a g. thing she called on him,* bien lui (en) a pris d'aller le voir. *How g. it is to . . . ,* comme il est agréable de. . . . (*f*) (*As salutation*) Good morn-ing ! good day ! good afternoon ! bonjour ! Good evening ! bonsoir ! Good night ! (i) bon-soir ! (ii) (*on retirement to bed*) bonne nuit ! To wish s.o. g. night, souhaiter bonsoir à qn. (*g*) Beer is not g. for me, la bière ne me vaut rien To drink more than is good for one, boire plus que de raison. (*h*) Good for nothing, bon à rien. *He is g. for nothing,* c'est un propre à rien. (*i*) Good at Latin, bon, fort, *F:* calé, en latin. *He is g. at* *all sports*, il excelle à tous les sports. (*j*) *U.S*: *F*: To feel good, se sentir gaillard, bien en train. **2**. (*a*) Good man, homme de bien. To lead a good life, vivre saintement. Good conduct, good behaviour, bonne conduite. Good men and true, hommes bons et braves. ⌐*F*: The good people, les fées *f*. *s*. The good and the bad, les bons et les méchants. *G*. old *John!* ce brave Jean! *A*. & *Lit*: The good ship Arethusa, l'Aréthuse *f*. (*b*) (*Of children*) Sage. As good as gold, sage comme une image. *Be a g. child!* sois sage! (*c*) Her good man, son mari. His good lady, sa femme. (*d*) Aimable. That's very good of you, c'est bien aimable à vous. *Will you be g. enough to* + *inf*., je vous prie de vouloir bien + *inf*. To be good to animals, être bon pour les animaux. He is a good sort, c'est un brave garçon. (*e*) Good Lord, deliver us! Seigneur, délivrez-nous! *F*: Good Lord! Good Heavens! grand Dieu! par exemple! **3**. (*Intensive*) (*a*) *To wait two g. hours*, attendre deux grandes heures. A good long time, a good while, pas mal de temps. You still have a good way to go, vous avez encore un bon bout de chemin à faire. A good deal, beaucoup. A good many people, a good few people, beaucoup de gens; pas mal de gens. After a good cry . . ., après avoir bien pleuré. . . . (*b*) *adv*. *U.S*: *F*: *To dress s.o. down* good (and proper), tancer qn de la belle manière. **4**. As good as. My family is as g. as his, ma famille vaut bien la sienne. To give s.o. as good as one gets, rendre la pareille à qn. It is as good as new, c'est comme neuf. It is as good as done, c'est une affaire faite ou autant vaut. *As g. as cured*, quasiment guéri. **5**. To make good. (*a*) Se rattraper de (ses pertes); remédier à (l'usure); réparer (une injustice). *I will make it g. to you*, je vous en dédommagerai. (*b*) Justifier (une affirmation); remplir (sa promesse). (*c*) Effectuer (sa retraite). *To make g. one's escape*, parvenir à s'échapper. (*d*) Assurer (sa position); faire prévaloir (ses droits). (*e*) *Abs.* (i) Prospérer. (ii) Racheter son passé. II. **good,** *s*. **I**. Bien *m*. (*a*) To do good (in the world), faire du bien. *He will never do any more g.*, il ne fera plus jamais rien de bon. He is up to no good, il prépare quelque mauvais coup. There's some good in him, il a du bon. (*b*) I did it for your good, je l'ai fait pour votre bien. *For the g. of one's health*, en vue de sa santé. *To labour for the common g.*, travailler pour le bien public. Much good may it do you! grand bien vous fasse! A lot of good that will do you! c'est ça qui vous fera une belle jambe! la belle avance! *That won't be much g.*, ça ne servira pas à grand'chose. *It is no g. saying* . . ., rien ne sert de dire. . . . No good talking about it, inutile d'en parler. He will come to no good, il tournera mal. He's no good, il est nul; c'est une non-valeur. (*c*) It is all to the good, c'est autant de gagné; tant mieux. (*d*) *Adv.phr. He is gone for good* (and all), il est parti définitivement, pour (tout) de bon. **2**. *pl*. Goods. (*a*) *Jur*: Biens, effets *m*. (*b*) (Comme singulier on emploie le mot COMMODITY.) Objets *m*, articles *m*; *Com*: marchandise(s) *f*. To deliver the goods, (i) livrer la marchandise; (ii) *P*: remplir ses engagements. *U.S*: *P*: To have the goods, être capable. *P*: That's the goods! à la bonne heure! *U.S*: To have the goods on s.o., avoir l'avantage sur qn. Goods lift, monte-charge *m inv*. Goods train, train *m* de marchandises. To send sth. by goods train, envoyer qch. en petite vitesse. **good-'class,** *a*. *A g.-c. article*, un article de choix. **good-'conduct,** *attrib.a.* *Sch*: Good-conduct

prize, prix *m* de sagesse. **good 'feeling,** *s*. Bonne entente. **good-'fellowship,** *s*. Camaraderie *f*. '**good-for-nothing. I**. *a*. (*Of pers*.) Qui n'est bon à rien; (*of thg*) sans valeur. **2**. *s*. (*a*) Propre *mf* à rien. (*b*) Vaurien, -ienne. **good-'hearted,** *a*. (Personne) qui a bon cœur. **good-'humoured,** *a*. (Personne) d'un caractère facile, facile à vivre; (sourire) de bonne humeur. -ly, *adv*. Avec bonhomie. **good-'looker,** *s*. Belle femme. **good-'looking,** *a*. Bien de sa personne; beau, *f*. belle; (*of girl*) jolie. He is a 'good-looking fellow, il est beau garçon. *She is rather g.-l.*, elle n'est pas mal. **good 'nature,** *s*. Bon naturel; bonhomie *f*. **good-'natured,** *a*. (*Of pers*.) Au bon naturel; accommodant. *G.-n. smile*, sourire bon enfant. -ly, *adv*. Avec bonhomie. 'good-sized, *attrib.a.* De belle taille. **good-'tempered,** *a*. De caractère facile, égal; facile à vivre. -ly, *adv*. (Répondre) sans se fâcher.

good-bye [gud'bai], *int*. & *s*. Adieu (*m*). *G.-b. for the present*, à bientôt, à tantôt. *To say g.-b. to s.o.*, faire ses adieux à qn. *G.-b. to hope!* plus d'espoir!

goodies ['gudiz], *s.pl*. Bonbons *m*, friandises *f*.

goodish ['gudiʃ], *a*. **I**. Assez bon. **2**. *It's a g. step from here*, c'est à un bon bout de chemin d'ici.

goodly ['gudli], *a*. *Lit*: **I**. D'une belle apparence; beau, *f*. belle. **2**. (*Of portion*) Large, ample. *G. heritage*, bel héritage.

goodman, *pl*. **-men** ['gudmən, -men], *s.m*. *A*. & *Lit*: Maître (de la maison).

goodness ['gudnəs], *s*. **I**. (*a*) Bonté *f* (de cœur). Have the goodness to step in, ayez la bonté d'entrer. (*b*) Bonne qualité (d'un article). **2**. To extract all the goodness out of sth., extraire de qch. tout ce qu'il y a de bon. **3**. Goodness gracious! bonté divine! miséricorde! My goodness! mon Dieu! Thank goodness! Dieu merci! Goodness (only) knows what I must do, Dieu seul sait ce que je dois faire.

goodwife, *pl*. **-wives** ['gudwaif, -waːivz], *s.f*. *A*. & *Scot*: Maîtresse (de la maison).

goodwill [gud'wil], *s*. **I**. Bonne volonté; bienveillance *f* (*towards*, pour, envers). *To retain s.o.'s g.*, conserver les bonnes grâces de qn. **2**. *Com*: Clientèle *f*; achalandage *m*.

goody ['gudi], *s.f*. *G. So-and-So*, la mère une telle.

goody(-goody) ['gudi(gudi)], *a*. *F*: (Personne) d'une piété outrée; (livre) édifiant.

goosander [guː'sandər], *s*. *Orn*: Merganser *m*.

goose, *pl*. **geese** [guːs, giːs], *s*. **I**. (*a*) (*Female of gander*) Oie *f*. (*b*) (*Generic*) Oie. Grey goose, oie cendrée. Green goose, oison *m* (de moins de quatre mois). *F*: All his geese are swans, tout ce qu'il fait tient du prodige. **2**. *F*: Niais, *f*. niaise. *She's a little g.*, c'est une petite sotte. **3**. *Mus*: *F*: Goose(-note), couac *m*. **4**. *Tail*: Carreau *m* (à repasser). 'goose-flesh, *s*. *F*: Chair *f* de poule. '**goose-foot,** *s*. **I**. *Bot*: (*pl*. goose-foots) Chénopode *m*; patte-d'oie *f*. **2**. *Mec.E*: *Aer*: (*pl*. goose-feet) Patte-d'oie, *pl*. pattes-d'oie. '**goose-girl,** *s.f*. Gardeuse d'oies. '**goose-grass,** *s*. *Bot*: **I**. Grateron *m*. **2**. Potentille *f* ansérine. '**goose-quill,** *s*. Plume *f* d'oie. '**goose-step,** *s*. *Mil*: Pas *m* de l'oie.

gooseberry ['guːzbəri], *s*. **I**. (*a*) Groseille *f* à maquereau, groseille verte. *P*: To play old gooseberry, faire les cent coups. (*b*) Gooseberry (-bush), groseillier *m* (à maquereau). **2**. *F*: To play gooseberry, se trouver en tiers (avec deux amoureux); *P*: faire sandwich.

gooseherd ['gu:shə:rd], *s* Gardeur, -euse, d'oies.
Gordian ['gɔ:rdiən], *a.* *A.Hist:* Gordien. **To cut the Gordian knot**, trancher le nœud gordien.
gore[1] ['gɔ:ər], *s.* **1.** (*a*) *Dressm:* (i) Soufflet *m*, (ii) godet *m.* (*b*) *Nau:* Pointe *f* (de voile). **2.** *Aer:* Fuseau *m* (d'un ballon). **3.** Langue *f* de terre; enclave *f.*
gore[2], *s.* *Lit:* **1.** Sang coagulé. **2.** Sang versé. *He lay in his g.*, il baignait dans son sang.
gore[3], *v.tr.* (*Of horned animal*) Blesser (qn) avec les cornes; découdre (qn).
gorge[1] [gɔ:rdʒ], *s.* **1.** *A. & Lit:* (*a*) Gorge *f*, gosier *m.* (*b*) *My gorge rises at it*, cela me soulève le cœur. **2.** *Geog:* Gorge, défilé *m.* **3.** *Mec.E:* Gorge (de poulie). **4.** *Arch:* Gorge (d'une moulure).
gorge[2], *s.* Repas plantureux; *P:* gueuleton *m.*
gorge[3]. **1.** *v.i.* **To gorge (oneself)**, se gorger; se rassasier; s'assouvir. **2.** *v.tr.* Assouvir, gorger, rassasier (qn). **gorging**, *s.* **1.** Rassasiement *m.* **2.** Bâfrerie *f.*
gorgeous ['gɔ:rdʒəs], *a.* (*a*) Magnifique, splendide. (*b*) *F:* Épatant, superbe. **-ly**, *adv.* Magnifiquement, splendidement.
gorgeousness ['gɔ:rdʒəsnəs], *s.* Splendeur *f*, magnificence *f.*
gorget ['gɔ:rdʒet], *s.* *Cost: A:* Gorgerette *f.*
gorgon ['gɔ:rgən], *s.* *Gr.Myth:* Gorgone *f.*
gorilla [gɔ'rilə], *s.* *Z:* Gorille *m.*
gormandize ['gɔ:rmandaiz]. **1.** *v.tr.* Manger goulûment. **2.** *v.i.* Bâfrer. **gormandizing**, *a.* Glouton, goulu.
gormandizer ['gɔ:rməndaizər], *s.* Glouton, -onne; *F:* bâfreur, -euse; goinfre *m.*
gorse [gɔ:rs], *s.* *Bot:* Ajonc(s) *m(pl)*; *F:* landier *m.*
gory ['gɔ:ri], *a.* Sanglant, ensanglanté.
gosh [gɔʃ], *int.* *F:* (**By**) **gosh!** sapristi !
goshawk ['gɔshɔ:k], *s.* *Orn:* Autour *m.*
gosling ['gɔzliŋ], *s.* Oison *m.*
gospel ['gɔspel], *s.* Évangile *m.* *F:* **To take sth. for gospel**, accepter qch. comme parole d'évangile, pour argent comptant. *F:* *To preach the g. of economy*, prêcher l'économie.
gossamer ['gɔsəmər]. **1.** *s.* (*a*) Fils *mpl* de la Vierge; filandres *fpl.* (*b*) *Tex:* Gaze légère. **2.** *a.* (Tissu) très léger.
gossip[1] ['gɔsip], *s.* **1.** (Pers.) (*a*) *A:* Compère *m*, commère *f.* (*b*) Bavard, -arde. (*c*) (*Ill-natured*) Cancanier, -ière. **2.** (*a*) Causerie *f.* *Journ:* Propos familiers. **Social gossip** (**column**), nouvelles *fpl* à la main. **To have a gossip with s.o.**, tailler une bavette avec qn. (*b*) (*Ill-natured*) Cancans *mpl*; commérage(s) *m(pl)*, clabaudage *m.* **Piece of gossip**, racontar *m*, cancan.
gossip[2], *v.i.* (*a*) Bavarder, papoter. (*b*) **To gossip about s.o.**, faire des cancans, des commérages sur qn.
got [gɔt]. *See* GET.
Gothic ['gɔθik]. **1.** *a.* (*Race*) gothique. **Gothic architecture**, architecture gothique, ogivale. **2.** *s.* *Art: Ling:* Le gothique.
gouache [guaʃ], *s.* *Art:* Gouache *f.* *To paint in g.*, peindre à la gouache.
gouge[1] [gaudʒ, gu:dʒ], *s.* *Tls: Carp:* Gouge *f.*
gouge[2], *v.tr.* **1.** Gouger (le bois). **2.** **To gouge out**, creuser (une cannelure) à la gouge. *Engr:* Échopper. *F:* **To gouge out s.o.'s eye**, faire sauter un œil à qn.
gourd ['gɔ:ərd, 'guərd], *s.* **1.** *Bot:* Courge *f*, gourde *f.* **2.** (*Bottle*) Gourde, calebasse *f.*
gourmand ['guərmənd]. **1.** *a.* Gourmand, glouton. **2.** *s.* ['gurmɑ̃] = GOURMET.

gourmet ['guərme], *s.* Gourmet *m*; *P:* fin bec.
gout [gaut], *s.* **1.** *Med:* Goutte *f*; (*of feet*) podagre *f.* **2.** *A. & Lit:* Goutte, caillot *m* (de sang).
gouty ['gauti], *a.* (*Of pers., joint*) Goutteux; (*of pers.*) podagre.
govern ['gʌvərn], *v.tr.* **1.** (*a*) Gouverner, régir (un État); administrer (une entreprise, une province). *Abs.* **To govern**, gouverner. (*b*) **Laws that govern chemical reactions**, lois qui régissent les réactions chimiques. (*c*) *Gram:* **To govern the accusative**, gouverner, régir, l'accusatif. **2.** Maîtriser, gouverner (ses passions). *To g. one's temper*, se maîtriser. **governing**[1], *a.* Gouvernant. **Governing body**, conseil *m* d'administration (d'une société). **governing**[2], *s.* (*a*) Gouvernement *m.* (*b*) Maîtrise *f* (des passions).
governess ['gʌvərnes], *s.f.* Institutrice. **Resident g.**, institutrice à demeure. **Daily g.**, institutrice à domicile. *S.a.* NURSERY-GOVERNESS. **'governess-car, -cart**, *s.* *Veh:* Tonneau *m*; (*of wicker*) panier *m.*
government ['gʌvərnmənt], *s.* Gouvernement *m.* (*a*) **Form of government**, régime *m.* **Monarchical g.**, régime monarchique. (*b*) **Government offices**, Ministères *m.* **Government loan**, emprunt public. (*c*) **To form a government**, former un ministère, un gouvernement. *The Government party*, le parti gouvernemental.
governmental [gʌvərn'ment(ə)l], *a.* Gouvernemental, -aux.
governor ['gʌvərnər], *s.* **1.** Gouvernant *m.* **2.** (*a*) Gouverneur *m* (d'une colonie, d'une banque). (*b*) Membre *m* du conseil d'administration (d'une école). (*c*) *P:* **The Governor.** (i) Le patron, le singe. *And what about something for myself, governor?* et le pourboire, mon bourgeois? (ii) Père *m*; le vieux. **3.** *Mec.E:* (*Device*) Régulateur *m*, modérateur *m* (de vitesse). **Governor-valve**, soupape régulatrice. **'governor-'general**, *s.* Gouverneur général, *pl.* gouverneurs généraux, *pl.* Governor-generals.
gown[1] [gaun], *s.* **1.** Robe *f* (de femme). **2.** Robe, toge *f* (de magistrat). *Judge in his g.*, juge en robe.
gown[2]. **1.** *v.tr.* Revêtir (qn) d'une robe, d'une toge. **2.** *v.i.* (*Of judge*) Revêtir sa robe.
gownsman, *pl.* **-men** ['gaunzmən, -men], *s.m.* Membre d'une université.
grab[1] [grab], *s.* Mouvement vif de la main pour saisir qch. *F:* **Policy of grab (and keep)**, politique rapace. **'grab-dredge(r)**, *s.* Grappin *m.*
grab[2], *v.tr. & i.* (**grabbed**) **To grab (hold of) sth.**, *s.o.*, saisir qch. (d'un geste brusque); se saisir de qch.; empoigner qn. *He grabbed a revolver from the table*, il saisit un revolver sur la table. *To g. at s.o.*, s'agripper à qn.
grabber ['grabər], *s.* Accapareur, -euse.
Gracchi (the) [ðə'grakai]. *Pr.n.m.pl. Rom.Hist:* Les Gracques.
grace[1] [greis], *s.* Grâce *f.* **1.** (*a*) *G. of style*, aménité *f* de style. (*b*) **To do sth. with a good grace**, faire qch. avec bonne grâce. *He had the g. to be ashamed*, il faut dire à son honneur qu'il se montra confus. (*c*) *Gr.Myth:* **The Graces**, les Grâces. **2.** (*a*) **Act of grace**, gracieuseté *f*, faveur *f.* *To get into s.o.'s good graces*, se mettre dans les bonnes grâces de qn. (*b*) *Theol:* **Saving grace**, grâce sanctifiante. *F:* **It has the saving grace that . . .**, cela a au moins ce mérite que. . . . **In the year of grace 1066**, en l'an de grâce 1066. **3.** (*a*) *A:* Grâce, pardon *m.* (*Still so used in*) **Act of grace**, (i) lettres *fpl* de grâce; (ii) loi *f* d'amnistie. (*b*) *Com:* **Days of grace**,

délai de trois jours (accordé pour le paiement d'un effet). **4. Grace**, (*before meal*) bénédicité *m* ; (*after meal*) grâces. **5. Your Grace**, votre Grandeur. **'grace-note**, *s. Mus:* Note *f* d'agrément.

grace², *v.tr.* (*a*) Honorer (*with*, de). (*b*) Embellir, orner.

graceful ['greisful], *a.* Gracieux. **-fully**, *adv.* Avec grâce ; avec élégance.

gracefulness ['greisfulnəs], *s.* Grâce *f*, élégance *f.*

graceless ['greisləs], *a. How's that g. nephew of yours getting on?* que devient votre garnement *m* de neveu?

gracile ['grasil], *a.* Gracile, grêle.

gracious ['greiʃəs], *a.* **1.** Gracieux, indulgent, bienveillant. *We were charmed with their g. reception*, l'aménité *f* de leur accueil nous charma. **2.** (*Of God*) Miséricordieux. **3. Gracious** (me)! **good(ness) gracious!** miséricorde! bonté divine! **-ly**, *adv.* **1.** Avec bienveillance. **To be graciously pleased to do sth.**, daigner faire qch. **2.** Miséricordieusement.

graciousness ['greiʃəsnəs], *s.* **1.** Grâce *f.* **2.** Condescendance *f*, bienveillance *f* (*to, towards*, envers). **3.** Bonté *f*, miséricorde *f* (de Dieu).

gradate [grə'deit]. **1.** *v.i.* (*Of colours*) Se dégrader, se fondre. **2.** *v.tr.* Dégrader (des teintes).

gradation [grə'deiʃ(ə)n], *s.* **1.** (*a*) Gradation *f.* *Aut:* **Gradation of speeds**, échelonnement *m* des vitesses. (*b*) *Art:* (Dé)gradation *f* (des teintes). **2.** *Ling:* (**Vowel) gradation**, alternance *f* de voyelles ; apophonie *f.*

grade¹ [greid], *s.* **1.** (*a*) Grade *m*, rang *m*, degré *m.* (*b*) Qualité *f* ; classe *f.* *G. of ore*, teneur *f* du minerai. **2.** *Civ.E: U.S:* (*a*) Pente *f*, rampe *f* ; montée *f* ou descente *f* (d'une voie ferrée). **To make the grade**, (i) parvenir au sommet ; (ii) *F:* surmonter ses difficultés. (*b*) Niveau *m.*

grade², *v.tr. & i.* **1.** Classer, trier (des marchandises). **2.** (*a*) Graduer (des exercices). **Graded tax**, impôt progressif. (*b*) *Art:* Dégrader, fondre (des teintes). **3.** *Civ.E: Rail:* (A)ménager, régulariser, la pente de (la voie). **4.** *Ling:* (*Of vowel*) S'altérer par apophonie. **grading**, *s.* **1.** Classement *m*, gradation *f* ; triage *m* (du minerai). **2.** (Dé)gradation *f* (des teintes). **3.** (A)ménagement *f* d'une pente).

gradient ['greidiənt], *s. Civ.E:* Rampe *f*, dénivellation *f*, pente *f.* **Upward gradient**, rampe. **Downward gradient**, pente. **Angle of gradient**, angle de déclivité. *Rail:* **Steep gradients**, lignes *f* à forte pente. **'gradient-indicator, -meter**, *s. Aut: Av:* Indicateur *m* de pente ; clinomètre *m.*

gradual ['gradjuəl]. **1.** *a.* Graduel ; progressif. *G. slope*, pente douce. *G. process*, gradation *f.* **2.** *s. Ecc:* Graduel *m.* **-ally**, *adv.* Graduellement ; peu à peu.

graduate¹ ['gradjuet], *s. Sch:* Gradué, -ée.

graduate² ['gradjueit]. **1.** *v.i. Sch:* Prendre ses grades ; (*in Fr.*) passer sa licence. **2.** *v.tr.* (*a*) Graduer (un thermomètre). *Graduated in inches*, gradué en pouces. (*b*) Graduer (des exercices). *Graduated taxation*, taxes imposées par paliers. *Graduated income-tax*, impôt progressif. (*c*) Dégrader (des teintes).

graduation [gradju'eiʃ(ə)n], *s.* **1.** *Sch:* (*a*) Collation *f* des grades. (*b*) (*By student*) Réception *f* d'un grade. **2.** Graduation *f* (d'un thermomètre). **3.** Gradation *f* (d'exercices).

graft¹ [grɑːft], *s. Arb: Surg:* Greffe *f.*

graft², *v.tr.* (*a*) *Arb:* Greffer, enter. (*b*) *Surg:* Greffer, implanter. **grafting**, *s.* (*a*) *Arb:*

Greffe *f*, greffage *m.* (*b*) *Surg:* Greffe (humaine) ; implantation *f.* **Skin grafting**, greffe épidermique. **'grafting-knife**, *s. Arb:* Greffoir *m*, entoir *m.*

graft³, *s. U.S: P:* Gratte *f*, corruption *f.*

grafter ['grɑːftər], *s. U.S: P:* Fonctionnaire ou politicien véreux, qui fait de la gratte.

grain¹ [grein], *s.* **1.** (*a*) Grain *m* (de blé). (*b*) *Coll.* **Grain crop**, récolte de grains, de céréales. **Refuse grain**, grenaille *f.* (*c*) (**Brewers') grains**, drêche *f.* **2.** (*a*) Grain (de poivre). (*b*) Grain (de sel, de sable). *Exp:* **Large grain, small grain, powder**, poudre à gros grains, à grains fins. *F:* **Grain of consolation**, brin *m* de consolation. **Not a grain of common sense**, pas un grain, pas un brin, pas l'ombre, de bon sens. (*c*) *Meas:* Grain (= 0 gr. 0648). **3.** (*a*) Grain (du bois) ; texture *f* (de la fonte). **Close grain**, grain fin, dense. *F:* **Man of coarse grain**, homme sans délicatesse. (*b*) Fil *m* (du bois, de la viande). **Against, across, the grain**, contre le fil ; à contre-fil. *F:* **It goes against the grain for me to do it**, c'est à contre-cœur que je le fais.

grain², *v.tr.* **1.** Chagriner, grainer (le cuir, le papier). **2.** *Paint:* Veiner (une surface) façon bois. **3.** *Tan:* Rebrousser (le cuir). **grained**, *a.* (*a*) Granulé, grenu. (*b*) *Paint:* Veiné ou marbré. **graining**, *s.* **1.** *Leath:* Rebroussement *m.* **2.** Veinage *m* (de la peinture).

graine [grein], *s.* Graines *fpl* (des vers à soie).

grains [greinz], *s. Fish:* Harpon *m* à trois branches.

gram [gram], *s. Meas:* = GRAMME.

graminaceous [grami'neiʃəs], *a. Bot:* Graminé. *G. plants*, graminées *f.*

gramineae [grə'minii], *s.pl. Bot:* Graminées *f.*

grammalogue ['gramalɔg], *s.* (*In shorthand*) Sténogramme *m.*

grammar ['gramər], *s.* (*a*) Grammaire *f.* *That's not (good) g.*, ce que vous dites là n'est pas grammatical. (*b*) (Livre *m*, traité *m*, de) grammaire. **'grammar-school**, *s.* École *f* secondaire ; *approx.* = collège communal.

grammarian [grə'mɛəriən], *s.* Grammairien *m.*

grammatical [grə'matik(ə)l], *a.* Grammatical, -aux. **-ally**, *adv.* Grammaticalement.

gramme [gram], *s. Meas:* Gramme *m.* (Poids en grammes × 0.035 = poids en onces.) **'gramme-'calory**, *s. Ph:* Petite calorie.

gramophone ['gramofoun], *s.* Gramophone *m.* **Gramophone recording**, phonographie *f.*

grampus ['grampəs], *s.* **1.** *Z:* Épaulard *m*, orque *f.* **2.** *F:* Gros bonhomme poussif.

granary ['granəri], *s.* Grenier *m.*

grand [grand], *a.* **1.** (*In titles*) Grand. **The Grand Vizier**, le grand vizir. **2.** (*a*) Grand ; principal, -aux. **The grand staircase**, l'escalier d'honneur. *Sp:* **The grand stand**, la tribune. (*b*) **Grand total**, total global. **3.** (*a*) *G. display of fireworks*, grand feu d'artifice. (*b*) **A grand piano**, *F:* a grand, un piano à queue. **4.** (*a*) Grandiose, magnifique. *G. panorama of mountains*, panorama magnifique de montagnes. **Grand style**, style grandiose. (*b*) **The grand air**, le grand air ; le panache. *s.* **They love to do the grand**, ils aiment à faire de l'épate. **5.** (*a*) *F:* Excellent; (*b*) *F:* épatant. *He's a g. fellow*, c'est un type épatant. (*b*) *F:* **I'm not over grand**, ça ne va qu'à moitié. **6.** *s. U.S: F:* Mille dollars. **-ly**, *adv.* (*a*) Grandement, magnifiquement. (*b*) Grandiosement. **'Grand 'Cross**, *s.* **1.** Grand'croix *f inv.* **2. Knight Grand Cross**, grand-croix *m*, *pl.* grands-croix. **'grand-dad**, *s.m. F:* Bon-papa, *pl.* bons-papas. **'grand-daughter**, *s.f.* Petite-fille, *pl.* petites-filles. **'Grand 'Duchess**, *s.f.* Grande-duchesse, *pl.* grandes-duchesses. **'Grand 'Duchy,** *s.* Grand-duché *m*, *pl.* grands-duchés. **'Grand 'Duke,** *s.m.* Grand-duc, *pl.* grands-ducs. **'grand-nephew,** *s.m.* Petit-neveu, *pl.* petits-neveux. **'grand-niece,** *s.f.* Petite-nièce, *pl.* petites-nièces.

grandchild, *pl.* **-children** ['gran(d)t∫aild, -t∫ildrən], *s.* Petit-fils *m* ou petite-fille *f*, *pl.* petits-enfants *m*.

grandee [gran'diː], *s.* (*a*) Grand *m* (d'Espagne). (*b*) *F:* Grand personnage.

grandeur ['grandjər], *s.* Grandeur *f.* (*a*) Noblesse *f*, éminence *f*. (*b*) Splendeur *f.* *The g. of the landscape,* la majesté du paysage.

grandfather ['gran(d)faːðər], *s.m.* Grand-père, *pl.* grands-pères; aïeul, *pl.* aïeuls.

grandiloquence [gran'dilokwəns], *s.* Grandiloquence *f*; emphase *f*.

grandiloquent [gran'dilokwənt], *a.* Grandiloquent; (ton) doctoral, -aux; (style) emphatique. **-ly,** *adv.* Avec emphase.

grandiose ['grandious], *a.* (*a*) Grandiose, magnifique. (*b*) Pompeux; qui vise à la majesté.

grandmamma, grandma ['gran(d)(ma)maː], *s.f.* Grand'maman, *pl.* grand'mamans.

grandmother ['gran(d)mʌðər], *s.f.* Grand'mère, *pl.* grand'mères; aïeule.

grandmotherly ['gran(d)mʌðərli], *a.* De grand'mère; *F:* (législation) qui pèche par trop de zèle.

grand(pa)pa ['gran(d)(pa)paː], *s.m.* Grand-papa, *pl.* grands-papas.

grandparent ['grandpɛərənt], *s.* Grand-père *m*, grand-mère *f*; aïeul, -e; *pl.* grands-parents *m*.

grandsire ['gran(d)saiər], *s.m.* *Lit:* **1.** Grand-père, *pl.* grands-pères. **2.** Aïeul. *Pl.* aeïux; ancêtre *m*.

grandson ['gran(d)sʌn], *s.m.* Petit-fils, *pl.* petits-fils.

grange [greindʒ], *s.* **1.** *A:* Grange *f.* **2.** Manoir *m* (avec ferme); château *m*.

grangerize ['greindʒəraiz], *v.tr.* To grangerize a book, truffer un exemplaire d'un livre.

granite ['granit], *s.* *Geol:* Granit(e) *m.* **Granite formation,** formation graniteuse, granitique.

granitic [gra'nitik], *a.* Granitique, graniteux.

grannie, granny ['grani], *s.f.* *F:* Bonne-maman, *pl.* bonnes-mamans.

grant¹ [graːnt], *s.* **1.** (*a*) Concession *f*, octroi *m* (d'une permission). (*b*) *Jur:* Don *m*, cession *f* (d'un bien). **Post in s.o.'s grant,** poste en la disposition de qn. (*c*) *Jur:* Acte *m* de transfert. **2.** Aide *f* pécuniaire; subvention *f.* **To receive a State grant,** être subventionné ou doté par l'État. *To put in a claim for a g.,* demander une allocation.

grant², *v.tr.* **1.** (*a*) Accorder, concéder, octroyer (un privilège, etc.). *He was granted permission to . . .,* il reçut la permission de. . . . **Heaven grant that . . .,** fasse le ciel que. . . . **God g. that . . .,** Dieu veuille que. . . . *F:* **I beg your pardon.**—**Granted!** je vous demande pardon.—Il n'y a pas de quoi; mais comment donc! (*b*) *Jur:* Exaucer (une prière); accéder à (une requête). **2.** Accorder (une subvention à qn). *To g. a loan,* consentir un pret (*to*, à). **3.** *To g. sth. as a fact,* admettre, reconnaître, qch. pour vrai. *I g. that you may be right,* je veux bien que vous ayez raison. **Granted that you are right,** admettons, *F:* mettons, que vous ayez raison. *I g. you that he is a rogue,* j'avoue que c'est un coquin. **To take sth. for granted,** présumer qch. pour avéré; présupposer qch. **You take too much for granted,** vous présumez trop. *I take it for granted you will come,*

c'est entendu que vous venez. **granting,** *s.* **1.** Concession *f*, octroiement *m*; octroi *m* (d'un droit). **2.** Don *m*, accord *m* (d'une subvention).

granular ['granjulər], *a.* (*a*) (*Of surface*) Granulaire, granuleux. (*b*) *Med:* (*Of fracture*) Grenu; (*of tumour*) granuleux.

granulate ['granjuleit], *v.tr.* Granuler; grener, grainer (la poudre); cristalliser (le sucre); grenailler (un métal). **granulated,** *a.* (*a*) Granulé, grené; (métal) en grenaille; (sucre) cristallisé. *Tp:* **Granulated carbon,** grenaille *f* de charbon. (*b*) (*Of surface*) Grenu.

granulation [granju'leiʃ(ə)n], *s.* **1.** Granulation *f*; grenaillement *m* (d'un métal). **2.** *pl. Med:* Granulations, bourgeonnement *m*.

granule ['granjuːl], *s.* Granule *m.* *Tp:* **Carbon granules,** grenaille *f* de charbon.

granulous ['granjuləs], *a.* Granuleux, granulaire.

grape [greip], *s.* (*a*) Grain *m* de raisin. (*b*) *pl.* **Bunch of grapes,** grappe *f* de raisin. **Dessert grapes,** raisin(s) de table. *For dessert I'll have grapes,* pour dessert je prendrai un raisin, du raisin. *F:* **Sour grapes!** ils sont trop verts! **'grape-fruit,** *s.* **1.** *Bot:* Pamplemousse *f.* **2.** *Com:* Grape-fruit *m.* **'grape-gatherer,** *s.* Vendangeur, -euse. **'grape-gathering,** *s.* Vendange *f.* **'grape-hyacinth,** *s.* *Bot:* Muscari *m.* **'grape-shot,** *s.* *Mil: A:* Mitraille *f.* **'grape-sugar,** *s.* Sucre *m* de raisin; glucose *f* (*in Ch: usu. m*).

graph¹ [graf, graːf], *s.* **1.** Graphique *m*, courbe *f*, tracé *m* (d'une équation, etc.). **Graph paper,** papier quadrillé. **2.** Abaque *m*; barème *m* graphique.

graph², *v.tr.* Tracer, figurer, (une courbe) graphiquement.

graphic ['grafik], *a.* **1.** *Mth: etc:* Graphique. **2.** (*Of description*) Pittoresque, vivant. **-ally,** *adv.* **1.** (Résoudre un problème) graphiquement. **2.** (Décrire) pittoresquement.

graphite ['grafait], *s.* Graphite *m*; mine *f* de plomb; plombagine *f*.

grapnel ['grapnel], *s.* *Nau:* Grappin *m.* *Hyd.E:* Araignée *f.* *Aer:* Ancre *f* (de ballon).

grapple ['grapl], *v.i.* To grapple with s.o., en venir aux prises avec qn; saisir qn à bras le corps; colleter qn. **To grapple with a difficulty,** en venir aux prises avec, s'attaquer à, une difficulté.

grasp¹ [graːsp], *s.* **1.** (*a*) Poigne *f.* To have a strong grasp, avoir la serre bonne. (*b*) Prise *f*; étreinte *f.* *To escape from s.o.'s g.,* échapper à l'étreinte de qn. **To have sth. within one's grasp,** avoir qch. à sa portée; tenir (le succès) entre ses mains. **Beyond one's grasp,** hors d'atteinte. (*c*) Compréhension *f.* *To have a good g. of modern life,* avoir une profonde connaissance de la vie moderne. **2.** Poignée *f* (d'un aviron, d'une épée).

grasp². **1.** *v.tr.* (*a*) Saisir; empoigner (un outil); serrer (qch.) dans sa main; étreindre (qch.). **To grasp s.o.'s hand,** serrer la main à qn. *F:* **To grasp the nettle,** y aller franchement; prendre le tison par où il brûle. (*b*) S'emparer se saisir, de (qch.). **To grasp the opportunity,** saisir l'occasion au vol. **Grasp all lose all,** qui trop embrasse mal étreint. **2.** *v.tr.* Comprendre (une difficulté, etc.); se rendre compte de (l'importance de qch.). *Argument difficult to g.,* raisonnement difficile à saisir. **3.** *v.i.* **To grasp at sth.** (*a*) Chercher à saisir qch. (*b*) Saisir avidement (une occasion). **grasping,** *a.* **1.** (*Of claws*) Tenace. **2.** To be g., être âpre au gain; *F:* avoir les dents longues.

grass¹ [grɑːs], s. Herbe f. **1.** (a) **Blade of grass,** brin d'herbe. F: **Not to let the grass grow under one's feet,** ne pas perdre de temps; ne pas traîner en affaires. (b) Bot: **The grasses,** les graminées f. **2.** (a) Herbage m, pâture f. F: **To turn, put, a horse out to grass,** mettre un cheval à l'herbe, au vert. **To put land under grass,** mettre du terrain en pré. (b) Gazon m. P.N: 'Please keep off the grass,' "défense de circuler sur le gazon," **'grass-green,** a. Vert pré inv. **'grass-grown,** a. Herbu, herbeux. **'grass-land,** s. Prairie f, pré m, herbage m. **'grass-plot,** s. Pelouse f; carré m de gazon. **'grass-snake,** s. Rept: Serpent m d'eau. **'grass 'widow,** s.f. F: Femme dont le mari est absent; veuve à titre temporaire. **'grass-'widower,** s.m. Mari dont la femme est absente; veuf à titre temporaire.

grass², v.tr. **1.** Mettre en herbe (un champ); gazonner (un terrain). **2.** Tex: Blanchir au pré (le lin). **3.** F: Étendre (un adversaire) par terre.

grasshopper ['grɑːshɔpər], s. Ent: Sauterelle f.

grassy ['grɑːsi], a. Herbu, herbeux.

grate¹ [greit], s. **1.** = GRATING¹ **1. 2.** (i) Grille f (de foyer); (ii) F: foyer m, âtre m. Mch: Grille, grillage m (de foyer de chaudière). **'grate-polish,** s. Noir m à fourneaux.

grate², v.tr. Griller (une fenêtre, etc.). **grated,** a. Grillé; à grille. **grating¹,** s. **1.** (a) Grille f, grillage m (de fenêtre, etc.); treillis m; (cloison f à) claire-voie f. Hyd.E: Crapaudine f (de débouché). (b) Nau: Caillebotis m. **2.** Opt: Diffraction grating, réseau m.

grate³. **I.** v.tr. Râper (de la muscade, etc.). **2.** To grate one's teeth, grincer des dents. **II.** **grate,** v.i. (a) (Of machinery) Grincer; (of chalk on blackboard) crisser. The door grated on its hinges, la porte cria sur ses gonds. (b) To grate on the ear, choquer, écorcher, l'oreille. **To grate on the nerves,** taper sur les nerfs; agacer les nerfs. **grating²,** a. (Of noise, etc.) Discordant, grinçant; qui écorche l'oreille. G. sound, grincement m, crissement m. **grating³,** s. **1.** (a) Râpage m. (b) pl. Gratings, râpure(s) f(pl). **2.** Grincement m, crissement m (d'un gond, etc.).

grateful ['greitful], a. **1.** (Of pers.) Reconnaissant. **To be grateful to s.o. for sth.,** savoir (bon) gré à qn de qch. I am g. to you for . . ., je vous suis très reconnaissant de. . . . **2.** (Of thg) Agréable; (repos) réconfortant, bienfaisant. **-fully,** adv. Avec reconnaissance.

gratefulness ['greitfulnəs], s. Reconnaissance f.

grater ['greitər], s. Râpe f (à muscade, etc.).

gratification [grætifi'keiʃ(ə)n], s. **1.** Satisfaction f, plaisir m. To do sth. for one's own g., faire qch. pour son propre contentement. **2.** Satisfaction, assouvissement m (des passions).

gratify ['grætifai], v.tr. **1.** Faire plaisir, être agréable, à (qn). **2.** Satisfaire, contenter (le désir de qn, etc.). To g. s.o.'s whims, flatter les caprices de qn. To g. one's fancy for sth., se passer la fantaisie de qch. **gratified,** a. Satisfait, content (with, de); flatté. **gratifying,** a. Agréable; flatteur. It is very g. to learn that . . ., c'est un réel plaisir d'apprendre que. . . .

gratis ['greitis]. **1.** a. Gratis, gratuit. **2.** adv. Gratis, gratuitement, à titre gratuit.

gratitude ['grætitjuːd], s. Gratitude f, reconnaissance f (to, envers).

gratuitous [grə'tjuːitəs], a. **1.** Gratuit; (service) bénévole. **2.** F: Gratuitous insult, insulte injustifiée, gratuite. G. lie, mensonge sans motif. **-ly,** adv. **1.** Gratuitement; à titre bénévole, gratuit. **2.** F: Sans motif.

gratuity [grə'tjuːiti], s. **1.** Gratification f, F: pourboire m; pot-de-vin m. 'No gratuities,' "défense de donner des pourboires." **2.** Mil: Navy: Prime f de démobilisation; pécule m.

gravamen [grə'veimen], s. Jur: Fond m, fondement m (d'une accusation). G. of a charge, matière f d'un crime.

grave¹ [greiv], s. (a) Tombe f, tombeau m, fosse f. The Paupers' grave, la fosse commune. **To be in one's grave,** être enterré. He just escaped a watery grave, il a failli être enseveli sous les ondes. F: He must have turned in his grave, il a dû crier dans la tombe. **To have one foot in the grave,** être au bord de la tombe. (b) From beyond the grave, d'outre-tombe. **'grave-digger,** s. Fossoyeur m. **'grave-digging,** s. Fossoyage m.

grave², v.tr. (graved; graven, graved) A: Graver, tailler, échopper (une inscription, etc.). Lit: Graven on his memory, gravé dans sa mémoire. B: Graven image, image taillée.

grave³, a. **1.** (a) Grave, sérieux. To look grave, avoir l'air sévère. (b) Grave news, de graves nouvelles. To make a g. mistake, se tromper lourdement. G. symptoms, symptômes graves, inquiétants. **2.** Gram: Grave accent, accent grave. **-ly,** adv. Gravement, sérieusement.

grave⁴, v.tr. Radouber (un navire). **graving,** s. Radoub m. S.a. DOCK³. **'graving-beach,** s. (Cale f d')échouage m.

gravel¹ ['grav(ə)l], s. **1.** Gravier m. **2.** Med: Gravelle f; F: graviers, sable m. **'gravel-'path,** s. Allée sablée, gravelée. **'gravel-pit,** s. Gravière f, sablière f.

gravel², v.tr. (gravelled) **1.** Graveler; sabler (un chemin). **2.** F: Mettre, réduire, (qn) à quia; P: coller (qn). To be gravelled, être à quia. **gravelling,** s. Gravelage m.

gravelly ['gravəli], a. Graveleux.

graveness ['greivnəs], s. Gravité f.

graver¹ ['greivər], s. **1.** (Pers.) Graveur m. **2.** Tls: Échoppe f, burin m, gravoir m.

graver², s.m. Nau: Radoubeur m.

gravestone ['greivstoun], s. = TOMBSTONE.

graveyard ['greivjɑːrd], s. Cimetière m.

gravid ['gravid], a. (Of woman) Gravide, enceinte; (of animal) pleine. F: Gravid with ideas, lourd d'idées.

gravitate ['graviteit], v.i. Graviter (towards, vers; round, autour de).

gravitation [gravi'teiʃ(ə)n], s. Gravitation f. The Law of gravitation, la loi de la pesanteur.

gravity ['graviti], s. Gravité f. **1.** (a) To preserve, lose, one's gravity, garder, perdre, son sérieux, sa gravité. (b) Gravité (d'une situation, d'une blessure). **2.** Ph: Gravité, pesanteur f. Centre of gravity, centre de gravité. Force of g., force de gravitation. Aut: Gravity feed, alimentation par la pesanteur, en charge. S.a. SPECIFIC **1.**

gravy ['greivi], s. Cu: (a) Jus m (qui sort de la viande). (b) Sauce f (au jus). **'gravy-beef,** s. Cu: Gîte m (à la noix); trumeau m. **'gravy-boat,** s. Saucière f.

gray [grei], a. & s. = GREY.

grayling ['greiliŋ], s. Ich: Ombre m.

graze¹ [greiz]. **1.** v.i. Paître, brouter. **2.** v.tr. (a) Paître, faire paître, mener paître (un troupeau). (b) (Of cattle, etc.) Pâturer (un champ); paître (l'herbe). **grazing,** s. Pâturage m (de troupeaux); élevage m (de moutons). **'grazing-ground, -land,** s. Pâturage m.

graze², s. Écorchure f, éraflure f.

graze³, v.tr. **1.** Écorcher, érafler (ses genoux,

etc.). **2.** Effleurer, raser, frôler. *The bullet grazed his shoulder, his ribs,* la balle lui rasa l'épaule, lui glissa sur les côtes. *Nau:* (*Of ship*) **To graze the bottom,** labourer le fond ; toucher.

ʒrazier ['greiziər], *s.* Herbager *m.*

grease[1] [gri:s], *s.* (*a*) Graisse *f.* **Carriage grease, cart grease,** (i) graisse pour voitures ; (ii) (*dirty*) cambouis *m. Mil:* **Rifle grease,** axonge *f. Mec.E:* **Belt-grease,** enduit *m* pour courroies. (*b*) **Wool grease,** suint *m.* **Wool in (the) grease,** laine en suint. **'grease-band,** *s. Arb:* Bande enduite de glu horticole. **'grease-box,** *s. Mch:* Boîte *f,* réservoir *m,* à graisse. **'grease-cap, -cup,** *s.* (Godet) graisseur *m.* **'grease-cock,** *s. Mec.E:* Robinet graisseur. **'grease-ʒun,** *s. Mec.E: Aut:* Graisseur *m* à graisse ; pompe *f* à graisse. **'grease-paint,** *s.* Fard *m. Th:* **Stick of grease-paint,** crayon gras (de maquillage). **'grease-proof,** *a.* (Papier) parcheminé, imperméable à la graisse.

grease[2] [gri:z], *v.tr.* **1.** Graisser, encrasser (ses habits). **2.** Graisser, lubrifier (une machine) ; suiffer (un mât). *To keep a mechanism well greased,* entretenir un mécanisme au gras. *S.a.* PALM[2] 1. **greasing,** *s.* Graissage *m* ; lubrification *f.*

greaser ['gri:zər], *s.* **1.** (*Pers.*) Graisseur *m.* **2.** = GREASE-CUP.

greasiness ['gri:zinəs, 'gri:sinəs], *s.* Onctuosité *f.*

greasy, *a.* **1.** ['gri:si] (*a*) Graisseux, huileux. *To taste g.,* sentir le graillon. (*b*) Taché d'huile, de graisse. **2.** ['gri:zi] Gras, *f.* grasse ; (chemin) gras, glissant. **Greasy pole,** mât *m* de cocagne.

great [greit], *a.* Grand. (*a*) **Great (big) man,** homme de grande taille. **Great toe,** gros orteil. **To grow greater (and greater),** augmenter, s'agrandir, grandir (de plus en plus). (*b*) **A great deal,** beaucoup, une quantité considérable (*of,* de). **A great many,** beaucoup (de + *pl.*). *There were not a g. many people there,* il n'y avait pas grand monde. **The great majority, the greater part,** la plupart, la majeure partie (*of,* de). **To a great extent,** en grande partie. *To reach a g. age,* parvenir à un âge avancé. *Of g. antiquity,* de haute antiquité. (*c*) *His greatest fault,* son plus grand défaut ; son défaut capital. *To take g. care,* prendre grand soin (*of,* de) ; prendre beaucoup de soin. *G. difference,* grande, forte, différence. *With the greatest pleasure,* avec le plus grand plaisir. **The Great War,** la Grande Guerre. (*d*) **The great men** (*of the age*), les grands hommes, les célébrités *f* (de l'époque). *F:* **Great Scott!** grands dieux ! **Alexander the Great,** Alexandre le Grand. (*e*) **Great eater,** grand, gros, mangeur. *They are g. friends,* ils sont grands amis. *F:* **To be great on dogs,** être grand amateur de chiens. **To be great at tennis,** être fort au tennis. (*f*) *It is no great matter,* ce n'est pas une grosse affaire. *To have no g. opinion of s.o.,* tenir qn en médiocre estime. *The g. thing is that . . .,* le grand avantage, le principal, c'est que. . . *It was a g. joke,* ça nous a joliment amusés. **It's great!** fameux ! c'est magnifique ! **-ly,** *adv.* Grandement ; beaucoup. *We were g. amused,* cela nous a beaucoup amusés. *G. irritated,* très irrité ; fortement irrité. *It is g. to be feared that . . .,* il est fort à craindre que. . . . **'great-aunt,** *s.f.* Grand'-tante. **'great-coat,** *s.* Pardessus *m. Mil:* Capote *f ;* (*hooded*) capot *m.* **great-'grand-child,** *pl.* **-children,** *s.* Arrière-petit-fils *m,* arrière-petite-fille *f, pl.* arrière-petits-enfants *m.* **great-'grand-daughter,** *s.f.* Arrière-petite-fille, *pl.* arrière-petites-filles. **great-'grand-father,** *s.m.* Arrière-grand-père, *pl.* arrière-

grands-pères ; bisaïeul. **great-'grandmother,** *s.f.* Arrière-grand'mère, *pl.* arrière-grand'mères ; bisaïeule. **great-'grandson,** *s.m.* Arrière-petit-fils, *pl.* arrière-petits-fils. **'great-great-'grandfather,** *s.m.* Trisaïeul. **'great-great-'grandmother,** *s.f.* Trisaïeule. **'great-'hearted,** *a.* Généreux ; magnanime. **great-'nephew,** *s.m.* Petit-neveu, *pl.* petits-neveux. **great-'niece,** *s.f.* Petite-nièce, *pl.* petites-nièces. **'great-uncle,** *s.m.* Grand-oncle, *pl.* grands-oncles.

greatness ['greitnəs], *s.* Grandeur *f.*

greave [gri:v], *s. Archeol:* Jambière *f.*

greaves [gri:vz], *s.pl. Cu:* Cretons *m,* rillons *m.*

grebe [gri:b], *s. Orn:* Grèbe *m.*

Grecian ['gri:ʃən], *a.* Grec, *f.* grecque. *In the G. style,* dans le style grec ; à la grecque.

Greece [gri:s], *Pr.n. Geog:* La Grèce.

greed [gri:d], *s.* = GREED.

greediness ['gri:dinəs], *s.* **1.** = GREED. **2.** Gourmandise *f,* gloutonnerie *f.*

greedy ['gri:di], *a.* **1.** Avide, cupide ; âpre (au gain). *G. of honours,* avide d'honneurs. **2.** Gourmand ; glouton, -onne ; goulu. **-ily,** *adv.* **1.** Avidement, cupidement. **2.** Avec gourmandise, gloutonnement ; (manger) à belles dents, goulûment.

Greek [gri:k], **1.** *a. & s.* Grec, *f.* grecque. *Art:* **Greek key pattern, Greek border,** grecque *f.* **The Greek Church,** l'Église grecque ; l'Église orthodoxe. **2.** *s. Ling:* Le grec. *F:* **It is all Greek to me,** c'est de l'hébreu pour moi.

green [gri:n], **1.** *a.* Vert. (*a*) **As green as grass,** vert comme pré. **To grow green,** verdir ; (*of grass, etc.*) verdoyer. *S.a.* SEA 2. (*b*) **G. arbour,** tonnelle de verdure. **Green winter,** hiver doux, clément. **Green stuff,** verdure *f,* herbages *mpl,* jardinage *m. Husb:* **Green food, green meat,** fourrages verts, frais. (*c*) **Green old age,** verte vieillesse. **To keep s.o.'s memory green,** entretenir, chérir, la mémoire de qn. *Memories still g.,* souvenirs encore vivaces. (*d*) **Green fruit,** fruits verts. **Green corn,** blé en herbe. *Tan:* **Green hide,** peau verte ; peau crue. **Green bacon,** lard salé et non fumé. (*e*) (*Of complexion*) **Blême. To go, turn, green,** blêmir. *S.a.* ENVY[1] 1. (*f*) (i) Jeune, inexpérimenté. (ii) Naïf, *f.* naïve. *He 'is g.!* il est bien de son village ! **He's not so green,** il n'est pas né d'hier. **2.** *s. & a.* (*In Fr. a.inv.*) **Grass-green,** vert pré *m.* **Sage-green,** vert cendré. *S.a.* BOTTLE-GREEN, OLIVE-GREEN. **3.** *s.* (*a*) **The greens of a picture,** les verts d'un tableau. *F:* **Do you see any green in my eye?** me prenez-vous pour une poire, pour un bleu ? (*b*) *pl.* **Greens,** légumes verts. (*c*) **Pelouse** *f,* gazon *m.* **Village green,** pelouse communale. *Golf:* **The** (putting-)**green,** la pelouse d'arrivée. *Turf:* **The green,** la pelouse. **'green-bottle,** *s. Ent:* Mouche dorée (de la viande). **'green-fly,** *s. Ent:* **1.** Puceron *m* (du rosier) ; aphis *m.* **2.** *Coll.* Aphidés *mpl,* aphidiens *mpl.* **'green-room,** *s. Th:* Foyer *m* des artistes. **'green-stick,** *s. & attrib. Med:* Green-stick (fracture), fracture incomplète. **'green-stone,** *s. Miner:* Néphrite *f.*

greenery ['gri:nəri], *s.* Verdure *f,* feuillage *m.*

greenfinch ['gri:nfinʃ], *s. Orn:* Verdier *m.*

greengage ['gri:ngeidʒ], *s.* Reine-Claude *f, pl.* reines-Claude.

greengrocer ['gri:ngrousər], *s.* Marchand, -ande, de légumes ; fruitier, -ière. **Greengrocer's shop,** boutique *f* de marchand de légumes ; fruiterie *f.*

greenhorn ['gri:nhɔ:rn], *s. F:* Blanc-bec *m,*

pl. blancs-becs ; *F:* bleu *m*, cornichon *m*, béjaune *m*.

greenhouse ['gri:nhaus], *s. Hort:* Serre *f* ; *esp.* serre chaude.

greenish ['gri:niʃ], *a.* Verdâtre.

Greenland ['gri:nlənd]. *Pr.n.* Le Groenland. *In G.,* au Groenland.

Greenlander ['gri:nləndər], *s.* Groenlandais, -aise.

greenness ['gri:nnəs], *s.* **1.** Verdeur *f.* (*a*) Couleur verte. (*b*) Immaturité *f* (d'un fruit, d'un projet, etc.). (*c*) (i) Inexpérience *f* ; (ii) naïveté *f*. (*d*) Verdeur, vigueur *f* (d'un vieillard). **2.** Verdure *f* (du paysage, etc.).

greensward ['gri:nswɔ:rd], *s.* Pelouse *f* ; (tapis *m* de) gazon *m* ; tapis de verdure.

greet[1] [gri:t], *v.tr.* (*a*) Saluer, aborder, ou accueillir (qn) avec quelques paroles aimables. To greet a speech with cheers, saluer un discours d'acclamations. (*b*) *F:* To greet the ear, the eye, frapper l'oreille, s'offrir aux regards. **greeting,** *s.* Salutation *f*, salut *m*. To send one's greetings to s.o., envoyer le bonjour à qn. New-year greetings, compliments *m* du jour de l'an.

greet[2], *v.i. Scot:* Pleurer.

gregarious [gre'gɛəriəs], *a.* Grégaire. *F: Men are g.,* les hommes aiment à vivre en société. **-ly,** *adv.* (Vivre) en troupes, par bandes.

Gregorian [gre'gɔ:riən], *a.* (Chant, etc.) grégorien.

Gregory ['gregəri]. *Pr.n.m.* Grégoire. *Pharm:* Gregory('s) powder, rhubarbe *f* en poudre.

grenade [gre'neid], *s.* **1.** *Mil:* Grenade *f*. *S.a.* HAND-GRENADE. **2.** (Fire-)grenade, grenade extinctrice.

grenadier [grena'di:ər], *s. Mil:* Grenadier *m*.

grenadine ['grenadi:n], *s.* **1.** *Tex:* Grenadine *f*. **2.** (*Syrup*) Grenadine. *Pharm:* Sirop grenadin.

grew [gru:]. *See* GROW.

grey [grei]. **1.** *a.* Gris. (*a*) *G. sky,* ciel gris. *Anat:* Grey matter, substance grise, cendrée (du cerveau). (*b*) (*Of hair*) Gris. To turn grey, go grey, grisonner. Grown grey in the service, *F:* in harness, blanchi sous le harnais. (*c*) (*Of complexion*) (Ashen) grey, blême. To turn (ashen) grey, blêmir. **2.** *s. & a.* (*In Fr. a.inv.*) Dull grey, gris mat. *S.a.* BLUE-GREY, DAPPLE-GREY, *etc.* **3.** *s.* (*a*) Gris. *m. Hair touched with g.,* cheveux grisonnants. (*b*) Cheval gris. **'grey-'haired, -'headed,** *a.* Aux cheveux gris ; grisonnant.

greybeard ['greibiərd], *s.* Grison *m* ; vieille barbe ; vieux barbon.

greyhound ['greihaund], *s.* Lévrier *m* ; (*bitch*) levrette *f*. Greyhound racing, courses de lévriers. *G.-racing track,* cynodrome *m*.

greyish ['greiiʃ], *a.* Grisâtre.

greylag (goose) ['greilag('gu:s)], *s. Orn:* Oie *f* sauvage, oie cendrée.

greyness ['greinəs], *s.* Teinte grise. *The g. of London,* la grisaille, la tonalité grise, de Londres.

grid [grid], *s.* **1.** (*a*) Grille *f*, grillage *m*. *El:* Accumulator grid, grille, grillage, d'accumulateur. (*b*) *W.Tel:* Valve grid, grille de lampe. Grid battery, pile de polarisation. Double-grid valve, valve bigrille. *S.a.* BIAS[1] 4, SCREENED 1. **2.** = GRIDIRON. **3.** *Surv:* Treillis *m*, graticule *m*. Grid-map, carte quadrillée. **4.** *F:* The grid, le réseau électrique national.

gridded ['gridid], *a.* (Carte) quadrillée.

gridiron ['gridaiərn], *s.* **1.** *Cu:* Gril *m*. *Ph:* Gridiron pendulum, balancier à gril. **2.** *P:* Bicyclette *f* ; *P:* bécane *f*.

grief [gri:f], *s.* Chagrin *m*, douleur *f*, peine *f*. *To die of g.,* mourir de chagrin. To come to

grief, (i) se voir accablé de malheurs ; (ii) (*of plan*) échouer, mal tourner ; (iii) avoir un accident ; faire une chute (de cheval, etc.). To bring s.o., sth., to grief, faire échouer qn, qch. **'grief-stricken,** *a.* Pénétré, accablé, de douleur.

grievance ['gri:vəns], *s.* **1.** Grief *m*. To air one's grievances, conter ses doléances. **2.** Injustice *f*. To redress a grievance, réparer un tort fait à qn.

grieve [gri:v]. **1.** *v.tr.* Chagriner, affliger, peiner (qn) ; faire de la peine à (qn). **2.** *v.i.* Se chagriner, s'affliger, se désoler (*over, about, sth.,* de qch.). **grieved,** *a.* Chagriné, affligé, désolé (*at, de*). *Deeply g.,* navré. *We are g. to learn . . . ,* nous apprenons avec peine. . . .

grievous ['gri:vəs], *a.* **1.** Douloureux, pénible. Grievous loss, perte cruelle. **2.** (Blessure) grave ; (erreur) grave, lamentable. **-ly,** *adv.* **1.** Douloureusement, péniblement. **2.** Gravement ; grièvement (blessé).

griffin ['grifin], *s. Myth:* Griffon *m*.

griffon[1] ['grifon], *s.* (Chien) griffon *m*.

griffon[2], *s.* Griffon(-vulture), (vautour *m*) griffon *m*.

grill[1] [gril], *s.* **1.** *Cu:* Grillade *f*. **2.** Grill(-room), grill-room *m* (de restaurant).

grill[2], *s. Dom.Ec:* Gril *m*.

grill[3], *v.tr. Cu:* Griller, brasiller (la viande). *U.S: P:* To grill a prisoner, cuisiner un détenu. **grilled,** *a.* Grillé. Grilled steak, bifteck *m* sur le gril ; grillade *f*.

grille [gril], *s.* Grille *f* (de couvent, etc.) ; judas *m* (de porte).

griller ['grilər], *s.* **1.** (*Pers.*) Grilleur, -euse. **2.** Gril de (de fourneau).

grim [grim], *a.* Menaçant, sinistre ; (sourire) de mauvais augure ; (humour) macabre ; (visage) sévère, rébarbatif ; (tyran) farouche. Grim Death, la Mort inexorable. *F:* To hold on like grim death, se cramponner avec acharnement. *G. necessity compelled him to . . . ,* la dure et sévère nécessité le força à. . . . *G. determination,* volonté inflexible. **-ly,** *adv.* Sinistrement ; (se battre) avec acharnement.

grimace[1] [gri'meis], *s.* **1.** Grimace *f*. To make a grimace, faire la grimace. **2.** Grimacerie *f*, affectation *f*. To make grimaces, faire des grimaceries des simagrées.

grimace[2], *v.i.* **1.** Grimacer ; faire la grimace. **2.** Faire des grimaceries, des mines, des simagrées. **grimacing,** *a.* Grimaçant, grimacier.

grimalkin [gri'mɔlkin], *s. F:* (Cat) Mistigri *m*.

grime[1] [graim], *s.* Saleté *f* ; poussière *f* de charbon, de suie (qui vous entre dans la peau).

grime[2], *v.tr.* (*Of coal-dust, etc.*) Salir, noircir (le visage, les mains).

grimness ['grimnəs], *s.* Caractère *m* sinistre, aspect *m* redoutable (de qch.) ; sévérité *f* (d'un visage) ; acharnement *m* (d'un combat).

grimy ['graimi], *a.* Sale, encrassé, noirci ; noir (de suie, etc.) ; (linge) crasseux ; (visage) barbouillé.

grin[1] [grin], *s.* Large sourire ; sourire épanoui. To give a broad grin, sourire à belles dents.

grin[2], *v.i.* (grinned) Sourire à belles dents. To grin at s.o., (i) adresser à qn un sourire de grosse gaieté (ii) regarder qn avec un sourire narquois. *He grinned broadly,* son visage s'épanouit en un large sourire. To grin and bear it, faire bonne mine à mauvais jeu. To grin like a Cheshire cat, rire à se fendre la bouche.

grind[1] [graind], *s.* **1.** Grincement *m*, crissement *m* (de roues, etc.). **2.** *F:* Labeur monotone et continu; *P:* turbin *m.* **The daily grind,** le boulot journalier; le train-train quotidien. *What a g.!* quelle corvée!

grind², *v.* (ground [graund]; ground) **I.** *v.tr.* (*a*) Moudre (du blé, du café); moudre, piler (du poivre); râper (le tabac à priser); broyer (des couleurs). **To grind sth. (down) to dust,** pulvériser qch.; réduire qch. en poudre. *To g. sth. between one's teeth,* broyer qch. entre ses dents. **To grind sth. under one's heel,** écraser qch. sous ses pieds. **To grind (down) the poor,** pressurer, opprimer, les pauvres. (*b*) Meuler (une pièce coulée); rectifier (une pièce) à la meule; dépolir (le verre). *Mec.E:* **To grind (in) a valve,** roder une soupape. **To grind down a lens,** meuler une lentille. (*c*) Aiguiser, émoudre, affûter (un outil); repasser (un couteau, un outil) (sur la meule). *S.a.* AXE I. (*d*) **To grind one's teeth,** grincer, crisser, des dents. (*e*) **To grind a barrel organ,** jouer d'un orgue de Barbarie. **To grind (out) a tune,** tourner, seriner, un air. **2.** *v.i.* (*a*) (*Of wheels, etc.*) Grincer, crisser. (*b*) *F:* Bûcher, turbiner; *Sch:* bachoter. **To grind for an exam,** potasser un examen. **ground,** *a.* **1.** Moulu, broyé, pilé. *S.a.* ALMOND, RICE. **2.** (Acier) meulé; (verre) dépoli. **Ground (glass) stopper,** bouchon *m* à l'émeri. **grinding¹,** *a.* **1. Grinding sound,** grincement *m,* crissement *m.* **2. Grinding poverty,** la misère écrasante. **grinding²,** *s.* **1.** Mouture *f* (du blé); broyage *m,* broiement *m* (des couleurs); pilage *m* (dans un mortier). **2.** Oppression *f,* écrasement *m* (du peuple). **3.** (*a*) Meulage *m;* rodage *m;* polissage *m* à la meule. **Grinding machine,** machine *f* à meuler. (*b*) Aiguisage *m,* affûtage *m,* émoulage *m,* repassage *m.* **4.** Grincement *m,* crissement *m.* **'grinding-wheel,** *s.* Roue *f* à meuler; meule *f* de rectification.

grinder ['graindər], *s.* **1.** (*a*) Pileur, -euse; broyeur, -euse. (*b*) Rémouleur *m* (de couteaux). *Itinerant g.,* repasseur ambulant. **2.** (*a*) (Dent) molaire *f.* (*b*) *pl. F:* **Grinders,** dents *f.* **3.** (*a*) Appareil broyeur. **Coffee-grinder,** moulin *m* à café. (*b*) *Mec.E:* Machine *f* à rectifier. (*c*) Machine à aiguiser; affûteuse *f.* **4.** *pl. W.Tel:* Grinders, crissements *m.*

grindstone ['graindstoun], *s.* Meule *f* (en grès) à aiguiser. *Geol:* **Grindstone grit,** (pierre) meulière *f. F:* **To keep one's nose to the grindstone,** travailler sans relâche, sans désemparer.

grip¹ [grip], *s.* **1.** Prise *f,* serrage *m;* serrement *m* (d'un outil, des mains); étreinte *f* (des mains). **To have a strong grip,** avoir bonne pince; avoir la serre bonne. **To be at grips with the enemy,** être aux prises avec l'ennemi. **To come to grips,** en venir aux mains, aux prises (*with,* avec). **To get a grip on sth.,** trouver prise à qch. *F:* **In the grip of a disease,** sous l'étreinte d'une maladie; en proie à une maladie. *The fever has him in its g.,* la fièvre le tient. **To have, get, a good grip of the situation,** avoir, prendre, la situation bien en main; *F:* empaumer l'affaire. *To have a good g. of a subject,* bien posséder un sujet. **2.** (*a*) Poignée *f* (d'aviron, etc.); poignée, crosse *f* (de pistolet). (*b*) *Ten:* Manchon *m,* couvre-manche *m* (pour raquette). *Cy:* Manchon, poignée (de guidon).

grip², *v.tr.* (gripped) (*a*) Saisir, empoigner, *F:* agripper, agripper (qch.); serrer, étreindre, (qch.) dans la main. *To g. sth. in a vice,* serrer, pincer, qch. dans un étau. (*b*) *Abs.* **The wheels are not gripping,** les roues n'adhèrent pas (sur la route). *Nau:* **The anchor grips,** l'ancre croche, mord,

prend fond. (*c*) *F:* **Fear gripped him,** la peur le saisit. *Play that grips the audience,* pièce qui empoigne les spectateurs. *Story that grips you,* histoire passionnante.

gripe [graip], *v.tr.* Donner la colique, des tranchées, à (qn). **Griping pains,** colique *f,* tranchées *fpl.*

gripes [graips], *s.pl.* Colique *f,* tranchées *fpl.*

grisly ['grizli], *a. Lit:* (*a*) Affreux, effroyable. (*b*) Effrayant, macabre. *G. shadow,* ombre monstrueuse.

grist [grist], *s.* **1.** Blé *m* à moudre. *F:* **That brings grist to the mill,** ça fait venir l'eau au moulin. **All is grist that comes to his mill,** il fait profit de tout. **2.** Blé moulu.

gristle [grisl], *s.* Cartilage *m,* croquant *m.*

gristly ['grisli], *a. F:* Cartilagineux.

grit¹ [grit], *s.* **1.** (*a*) Grès *m,* sable *m.* (*b*) *Mec.E: etc:* Corps étrangers; impuretés *fpl. F:* **To put grit in the bearings,** mettre des bâtons dans les roues. **2.** (*Gritstone*) Grès (dur). **Millstone grit,** grès à meule(s); (pierre) meulière *f.* **3.** Grain *m* (d'une pierre). **4.** Carrière *f* (d'une poire). **5.** *F:* Cran *m,* courage *m.* **Man of grit, who has plenty of grit,** homme qui a du cran, de l'étoffe.

grit², *v.* (gritted) **1.** *v.i.* Grincer, crisser. **2.** *v.tr.* **To grit one's teeth,** grincer des dents.

gritstone ['gritstoun], *s.* Grès (dur); pierre *f* de grès.

gritty ['griti], *a.* (Sol) sabionneux, cendreux; (crayon, etc.) graveleux. *G. pear,* poire graveleuse, sablonneuse.

grizzle¹ [grizl], *v.tr. & i.* Grisonner. **grizzled,** *a.* (*Of hair, pers.*) Grisonnant. *G. beard,* barbe poivre et sel.

grizzle², *s. P:* **1. To have a good grizzle,** raconter ses griefs. **2.** Pleurnicherie *f.*

grizzle³, *v.i. P:* **1.** Ronchonner; grognonner. **2.** Pleurnicher, geindre.

grizzler ['grizlər], *s. P:* **1.** Ronchonneur, -euse. **2.** Pleurnicheur, -euse.

grizzly ['grizli], *a.* **1.** = GRIZZLED. **2.** *Z:* **Grizzly (bear),** ours grizzlé.

groan¹ [groun], *s.* Gémissement *m,* plainte *f.*

groan², *v.i.* Gémir; pousser un gémissement. *To g. in pain,* gémir de douleur. **groaning,** *s.* Gémissement(s) *m(pl).*

groat [grout], *s. Num: A:* Pièce *f* de quatre pence.

groats [grouts], *s.pl.* Gruau *m* d'avoine.

grocer ['grousər], *s.* Épicier, -ière.

grocery ['grousəri], *s.* **1.** Épicerie *f.* **2.** *pl.* Groceries, (articles *m* d')épicerie.

grog [grɔg], *s.* Grog *m.* **'grog-blossom,** *s.* Bourgeon *m* (au nez d'un ivrogne).

groggy ['grɔgi], *a.* Chancelant, titubant, vacillant. **To feel groggy,** être peu solide sur ses jambes. *F: G. old table,* vieille table bancale.

groin [grɔin], *s.* **1.** *Anat:* Aine *f.* **2.** *Arch:* (*a*) Groin(-rib), arête *f* (de voûte). (*b*) Nervure *f* (d'arête).

groined [grɔind], *a. Arch:* (Voûte) à arêtes, d'arête.

grom(m)et ['grɔmet], *s.* = GRUMMET.

gromwell ['grɔmwəl], *s. Bot:* Grémil *m.*

groom¹ ['gruːm], *s.m.* **1.** Gentilhomme, valet (de la Chambre du Roi, etc.). **2.** (*a*) Palefrenier; valet d'écurie. (*b*) *Jockey,* laquais (dont on se fait suivre à cheval). **3.** = BRIDEGROOM.

groom², *v.tr.* Panser (un cheval). **groomed,** *a.* **Well-groomed,** (i) (cheval) bien entretenu, bien pansé; (ii) *F: (of pers.)* bien soigné, bien peigné.

groomsman, *pl.* **-men** ['gruːmzmən, -men], *s.m.* Garçon d'honneur (à un mariage).

groove¹ [gruːv], *s.* **1.** Rainure *f*; rayure *f* (d'un canon); cannelure *f* (d'une colonne); creux *m* (d'une vis); gouttière *f* (d'une épée); *Anat:* sillon *m*, gouttière (d'un os); *Carp:* (*notch*) encoche *f*; (*rabbet*) feuillure *f*. **Thumb-nail groove** (*of penknife*), onglet *m*. *G. for sliding part,* coulisse *f*, glissière *f*. *Carp:* **Groove and tongue joint,** assemblage à rainure et languette. *Gramophones:* **Sound groove,** sillon sonore. **2.** *F:* **To get into a groove,** s'encroûter; devenir routinier. **To get out of the groove,** sortir de l'ornière.

groove², *v.tr.* Rainer; rayer (un canon); canneler (une colonne). **To groove and tongue,** assembler à rainure et languette. **grooved,** *a.* Rayé, rainé, cannelé; à rayures, à rainures, à cannelures; (colonne) cannelée, striée; (pneu) cannelé; (roue) à gorge; (rail) à gorge, à ornière. **'grooving-plane,** *s. Tls:* Bouvet *m*; rabot *m* à languette.

grope [group], *v.i.* Tâtonner. **To grope for, after,** *sth.,* chercher qch. à tâtons; tâtonner en cherchant qch. **To grope one's way,** avancer à tâtons, à l'aveugle, à l'aveuglette. *To g. one's way in, out,* entrer, sortir, à tâtons. **groping,** *a.* Tâtonnant. **-ly,** *adv.* A tâtons; en tâtonnant.

grosbeak ['grousbiːk], *s. Orn:* Gros-bec *m*.

gross¹ [grous], *s. inv.* Douze douzaines *f*; grosse *f*. **Great gross,** douze grosses.

gross², *a.* **1.** Gras, *f.* grasse; gros, *f.* grosse; tout en chair. **2.** Grossier. (*a*) *G. ignorance,* ignorance crasse, grossière. *G. injustice,* injustice flagrante. *G. mistake,* grosse faute; faute grossière. (*b*) (*Of story*) Grivois, graveleux. **3.** (*Of amount*) Brut. *Nau:* **Gross displacement,** déplacement global. **Gross tonnage,** jauge brute. **-ly,** *adv.* Grossièrement. *G. exaggerated,* exagéré outre mesure.

grossness ['grousnəs], *s.* Grossièreté *f*; énormité *f* (d'un crime, etc.).

grotesque [gro'tesk]. *I. a. & s.* Grotesque (*m*). **2.** *a. F:* Absurde; saugrenu.

grotesqueness [gro'tesknəs], *s.* Caractère *m* grotesque.

grotto, *pl.* **-o(e)s** ['grɔto, -ouz], *s.* Grotte *f* (pittoresque).

ground¹ [graund]. *See* GRIND².

ground², *s.* **1.** Fond *m* (de la mer). (*Of ship*) **To touch ground,** talonner. **2.** *pl.* **Grounds,** marc *m* (du café); sédiment *m*. **3.** (*a*) Fond, champ *m* (d'un tableau). *Paint:* **Ground colour,** première couche. *Cin:* **Ground noise,** bruit de fond. (*b*) *Art:* **The middle ground,** le second plan. **4.** (*a*) Raison *f*, cause *f*, sujet *m*; base *f* (de soupçons, etc.). **Ground for complaint,** grief *m*. *There are grounds for supposing that . . .,* il y a lieu de supposer que. . . . *What grounds have you for saying that?* sur quoi vous fondez-vous pour affirmer cela? *I acted thus upon good grounds,* c'est à bon escient que j'ai agi de la sorte. *Upon what grounds?* à quel titre? *He has been retired on the g. of his infirmities,* on l'a mis à la retraite en raison de ses infirmités. *On legal grounds,* pour des raisons de droit. (*b*) *Jur:* *Grounds for divorce,* motifs *m* de divorce. *Grounds for appeal,* voies *f* de recours. **5.** (*a*) Sol *m*, terre *f*. *To sit down on the g.,* s'asseoir par terre. *To sleep on the* (*bare*) *g.,* coucher sur la dure. **To fall to the ground,** (i) tomber à, par, terre; (ii) *F:* (*of scheme*) tomber dans l'eau. *F:* **To dash s.o.'s hopes to the ground,** anéantir les espérances de qn. **Above ground,** sur terre; *Min:* au jour, à la surface. *F:* **He is still above**

ground, il est toujours de ce monde. **Burnt down to the ground,** brûlé de fond en comble. *F:* **That suits me down to the ground,** (i) cela me va à merveille, comme un gant; (ii) ça m'arrange le mieux du monde. (*Of building*) *To rest on firm g.,* reposer sur un terrain solide. *F:* **To be on sure, firm, ground,** connaître le terrain; être sûr de son fait. **To cut the ground from under s.o.'s feet,** couper l'herbe sous le pied à qn. (*b*) *Ven:* (*Of fox*) **To run, go, to ground,** se terrer. (*c*) **Terrain** *m. Mil:* **Drill-ground, parade-ground,** champ *m*, terrain, de manœuvres. **To find a common ground** *for negotiations,* s'accorder sur une base de négociation. **To change, shift, one's ground,** changer de terrain. **To gain ground,** gagner du terrain; (*of idea*) se répandre; prendre pied. **To give ground,** lâcher pied; (*of troops*) se replier. **To lose ground,** perdre, céder, du terrain. **To hold, stand, one's ground,** tenir bon, tenir ferme, tenir tête, tenir pied. **To tread on forbidden ground,** empiéter sur un terrain défendu. (*d*) *pl.* **Grounds,** terrains, parc *m*, jardin *m* (d'une maison). **'ground-bait,** *s. Fish:* Amorce *f* de fond. **'ground-'floor,** *s.* Rez-de-chaussée *m inv.* **On the ground-floor,** au rez-de-chaussée. *F:* **To get in on the ground-floor,** acheter des actions au plus bas prix. **'ground-game,** *s. Ven:* Gibier *m* à poil. **'ground-ivy,** *s. Bot:* Lierre *m* terrestre, rampant. **'ground-landlord,** *s.* Propriétaire foncier. **'ground-light,** *s.* Balise *f* (d'un aéroport). **'ground-line,** *s. Fish:* Ligne *f* de fond; trainée *f*. **'ground-plan,** *s. Const:* Plan *m* de fondation; plan horizontal; projection horizontale. *Fort:* Tracé *m* (d'une œuvre). **'ground-plot,** *s.* Terrain *m* à bâtir. **'ground-rent,** *s.* Loyer *m* de la terre; (*as source of income*) rente foncière. **'ground-sheet,** *s.* Bâche *f* de campement. **'ground-sill,** *s.* = GROUNDSEL². **'ground-swell,** *s. Nau:* Houle *f*, lame *f*, de fond.

ground³. **1.** *v.tr.* (*a*) Fonder, baser, appuyer (*on, in, sth.,* sur qch.). *To g. one's belief on . . .,* asseoir sa conviction sur. . . . (*b*) **To ground a pupil in Latin,** enseigner à fond les rudiments du latin à un élève. (*c*) Mettre (qch.) à terre. *Golf:* **To ground one's club,** asseoir sa crosse sur le sol. *Mil:* **Ground arms!** reposez armes! l'arme au pied! (*d*) *Nau:* Jeter (un navire) à la côte. **2.** *v.i.* (*a*) (*Of ship*) (i) (S')échouer (*on, sur*). (ii) Talonner. (*b*) (*Of balloon, etc.*) Atterrir. **grounded,** *a.* **1.** Well-, ill-grounded belief, croyance bien, mal, fondée. **2.** To be well grounded in Latin, posséder à fond les premiers principes du latin. **grounding,** *s.* **1.** (*a*) Assise (d'un argument sur qch.). (*b*) *Nau:* (i) Échouage *m.* (ii) Talonnement *m.* **2.** To have a good grounding in Latin, avoir une connaissance solide des rudiments du latin. *He has a good g.,* il connaît bien ses éléments.

groundless ['graundləs], *a.* (Soupçon, bruit) mal fondé, sans fondement. *My suspicions were g.,* mes soupçons n'étaient sans cause. **-ly,** *adv.* (S'alarmer) sans cause.

groundsel¹ ['graundsel], *s. Bot:* Senéçon *m*.

groundsel², *s. Const:* Sole *f*, semelle *f* (de cadre); seuil *m* (de dormant de porte).

groundsman, *pl.* **-men** ['graundzmən, -men], *s.m.* Préposé à l'entretien d'un terrain de jeux.

groundwork ['graundwɔːrk], *s.* **1.** Fond *m* (de tapisserie, etc.). **2.** (*a*) Fondement *m*; assise *f* (de la société, etc.). (*b*) Plan *m*, canevas *m* (d'un roman, etc.).

group¹ [gruːp], *s.* Groupe *m*; peloton *m* (de

personnes). **In groups,** par groupes. **To form a group,** se grouper. **L:terary group,** cercle *m*, cénacle *m*, littéraire. *To arrange articles in groups,* grouper des articles. *G. of mountains,* massif *m* de montagnes.

group². **I.** *v.tr.* Grouper, disposer en groupes, répartir par groupes ; combiner (des idées). **2.** *v.i.* Se grouper (*round,* autour de). **grouping,** *s.* Groupement *m* (de figures, etc.) ; combinaison *f* (de couleurs) ; agencement *m* (des figures d'un tableau).

grouse¹ [graus], *s. inv. Orn:* Tétras *m. Esp.* (Red) grouse, lagopède *m* rouge d'Écosse.

grouse², *s. P:* **I.** *He enjoys a good g.,* il aime à grogner. **2. To have a grouse against s.o.,** avoir un grief contre qn.

grouse³, *v.i. P:* Ronchonner, grogner, bougonner (*at, abou:,* contre). **grousing,** *s.* Grognonnerie *f.*

grout¹ [graut], *s. Const:* Coulis *m* ; mortier *m* liquide. **Cement grout,** lait *m* de ciment.

grout², *v.tr. Const:* To grout (in) stones, liaisonner, jointoyer, des pierres (avec du mortier liquide). **grouting,** *s.* **I.** Jointoiement *m* au mortier liquide. **2.** = GROUT¹.

grove [gro:uv], *s.* Bocage *m*, bosquet *m*. Beech-grove, hêtraie *f.* Orange-grove, orangerie *f.*

grovel [ˈgrɔv(ə)l], *v.i.* (grovelled) Ramper. *To g. in the dirt,* se vautrer, se traîner, dans la boue. *F:* **To grovel to, before, s.o.,** ramper, se mettre à plat ventre, devant qn. **grovelling,** *a.* Rampant ; *F:* vil, abject.

grow [grou], *v.* (grew [gru:] ; grown [groun]) **I.** *v.i.* **I.** (*a*) (*Of plant*) Croître, pousser. **To grow again,** repousser ; (*of plant, hair*) revenir. (*Of nail*) **To grow in,** s'incarner. (*b*) (*Of seeds*) Germer. *F: A feeling of hate grew* (up) *between them,* un sentiment de haine naissait entre eux. *This State grew out of a few small towns,* cet État est né de, doit son origine à, quelques bourgades. **2.** (*Of pers.*) Grandir. **To grow tall,** devenir grand ; se faire grand ; grandir. **To grow into a woman,** passer femme. **To grow up,** grandir ; atteindre l'âge d'homme. **To grow out of one's clothes,** devenir trop grand pour ses vêtements. He will grow out of it, cela passera avec l'âge. **3.** (*a*) S'accroître, croître, augmenter, grandir. *The crowd grew,* la foule grossissait. *The firm has grown considerably,* la maison a pris une extension considérable. **To grow in wisdom,** croître en sagesse. (*b*) *Habit that grows on one,* habitude qui vous gagne. (*c*) *That picture grows on me,* plus je regarde ce tableau plus il me plaît, plus il me dit. **4.** (*a*) Devenir. **To grow old,** devenir vieux ; se faire vieux ; vieillir. **To grow alarmed,** s'alarmer. **To grow rarer,** se faire plus rare. **It is growing dark,** il commence à faire sombre. (*b*) **I have grown to think that . . .,** j'en suis venu à penser que. . . . **II. grow,** *v.tr.* **I.** Cultiver (des roses) ; planter (des choux) ; faire venir (du blé). **2.** Laisser pousser (sa barbe, etc.). **grown,** *a.* **I.** (Full-)grown, grand ; qui a fini sa croissance. Grown(up-) man, homme fait. *When you are g. up,* quand tu seras grand. *s.* **The grown-ups,** les grands ; les grandes personnes. **2. Wall grown over with ivy,** mur couvert de lierre. **growing¹,** *a.* **I.** Croissant ; qui pousse. **Growing crops,** récoltes sur pied. **2.** Grandissant. *G. child,* enfant en cours de croissance. *G. debt,* dette grossissante. *There was a g. fear that . . .,* on craignait de plus en plus que. . . . **3. Corn-growing district,** région qui produit du blé ; région à blé. **growing²,** *s.* **I.** Croissance *f.* **The growing age,** l'âge

de croissance. **2.** .Culture *f,* éducation *f* (de plantes).

grower [ˈgrouər], *s.* Cultivateur, -trice (de roses, etc.). **Potato-grower,** planteur *m* de pommes de terre. **Vine-grower,** viticulteur *m.*

growl¹ [graul], *s.* Grondement *m,* grognement *m* (d'un chien, etc.).

growl², *v.i. & tr.* **I.** (*Of animal*) Grogner, gronder. **2.** *F:* (*Of pers.*) Gronder, grogner, grommeler ; *F:* ronchonner. *To g.* out oaths, maronner des jurons.

growler [ˈgraulər], *s.* **I.** (*Pers.*) Grogneur, -euse ; grognon *mf.* **2.** *F:* Fiacre *m.*

growth [grouθ], *s.* **I.** Croissance *f,* venue *f.* **To attain full growth,** atteindre l'âge de consistance ; (*of plant*) arriver à maturité. **2.** Accroissement *m* ; augmentation *f* (en quantité) ; extension *f* (des affaires). **3.** (*a*) **Yearly growth,** pousse annuelle. (*b*) Poussée *f* (de cheveux, etc.). **A week's growth on his chin,** le menton couver: d'une barbe de huit jours. **4.** *Med:* Grosseur *f,* tumeur *f.* Morbid growth, production *f* morbide.

groyne [grɔin], *s. Hyd.E:* Épi *m* à dent (d'une plage) ; éperon *m* (brise-lames).

grub¹ [grʌb], *s.* **I.** *Ent:* (*a*) Larve *f.* (*b*) *F:* Ver (blanc) ; asticot *m.* **2.** *F:* (*Pers.*) Écrivassier *m,* gratte-papier *m inv.* **3.** *P:* Mangeaille *f,* boustifaille *f.*

grub², *v.* (grubbed) **I.** *v.tr.* (*a*) Fouir, travailler superficiellement (la terre). (*b*) Défricher (un terrain). **2.** *v.i.* Fouiller (dans la terre). **grub up,** *v.tr.* Essoucher, essarter (un terrain) ; extirper (une racine) ; déraciner (une plante). **'grubbing-hoe,** *s., Tls:* Hoyau *m.*

grubby [ˈgrʌbi], *a.* Sale, malpropre.

grudge¹ [grʌdʒ], *s* Rancune *f.* **To bear, owe, s.o. a grudge ;** to have, nurse, a grudge against s.o., garder rancune à qn ; en vouloir à qn.

grudge², *v.tr.* **I.** Donner, accorder, (qch. à qn) à contre-cœur. *To g. s.o. the food he eats,* mesurer la nourriture à qn. *He does not g. his efforts,* il ne marchande pas sa peine. **2.** *To g. s.o. his pleasures,* voir d'un mauvais œil les plaisirs de qn. **grudging,** *a.* **I.** (*Of praise, gift*) Donné, accordé, à contre-cœur, en rechignant. **2.** *He is g. of praise,* il est avare de louanges. **-ly,** *adv.* (Faire qch.) à contre-cœur, à son corps défendant, en rechignant. *To praise s.o. g.,* marchander ses éloges à qn.

gruel [ˈgruəl], *s.* **I.** *Cu:* Gruau *m* (d'avoine) ; (thin) brouet *m.* **2.** *P:* **To give s.o. his gruel,** (i) battre qn comme plâtre ; (ii) éreinter, qn. **To take, get, one's gruel,** avaler sa médecine ; encaisser.

gruelling¹ [ˈgruəliŋ], *a.* Éreintant, épuisant ; (match) âprement disputé.

gruelling², *s.* Raclée *f* ; épreuve éreintante.

gruesome [ˈgruːsəm], *a.* Macabre, affreux ; qui donne le frisson.

gruff [grʌf], *a.* (Ton) bourru, revêche, rébarbatif, rude. *G. voice,* grosse voix. **-ly,** *adv.* D'un ton bourru, rébarbatif.

gruffness [ˈgrʌfnəs], *s.* Ton bourru, rébarbatif.

grumble¹ [ˈgrʌmbl], *s.* (*a*) Grommellement *m,* grognement *m.* (*b*) Murmure *m* (de mécontentement). *To obey without a g.,* obéir sans murmurer.

grumble², *v.i. & tr.* Grommeler, grogner, grognonner, murmurer ; *F:* ronchonner, bougonner. *To g. about the food,* trouver à redire à la nourriture. **To grumble at s.o.,** grommeler, gronder, contre qn. **grumbling¹,** *a.* Grognon, bougon ; grondeur, -euse. **-ly,** *adv.* En grommelant ; en murmurant. **grumbling²,** *s.* **I.** Grognonnerie *f.* **2.** Mécontentement *m.*

grumbler ['grʌmblər], *s.* **1.** Grognard, -arde, grognon, -onne, bougon, -onne. *An old g.*, un vieux ronchon. **2.** Mécontent, -ente.

grummet ['grʌmet], *s. Nau:* Estrope *f*; anneau *m* de corde ; bague *f* en corde.

grumpy ['grʌmpi], *a.* Maussade, renfrogné, grincheux. **-ily,** *adv.* Maussadement ; d'un ton maussade ou renfrogné.

Grundy ['grʌndi]. *Pr.n.* **Mrs Grundy,** personnification *f* du qu'en-dira-t-on ; les convenances (sociales). *I don't care what Mrs G. says,* je me moque du qu'en-dira-t-on.

grunt[1] [grʌnt], *s.* Grognement *m.*

grunt[2], *v.i.* (*Of pig, F: of pers.*) Grogner, grognonner ; pousser, faire entendre, un grognement.

grunting, *s.* Grognement(s) *m(pl).*

grunter ['grʌntər], *s.* **1.** Grogneur, -euse. **2.** *F:* Porc *m.*

guaiacum ['gwaiəkəm], *s.* Gaïac *m.*

guano ['gwɑːno], *s.* Guano *m.*

guarantee[1] [garən'tiː], *s.* **1.** Garant, -ante ; caution *f.* *To go guarantee for s.o.*, se rendre garant, se porter caution, pour qn. **2.** *Clock with g. for two years,* pendule avec une garantie de deux ans. **3.** *To leave sth.* as a guarantee, donner qch. pour caution, en garantie, pour gage.

guarantee[2], *v.tr.* Garantir, cautionner (qn, qch.) ; se porter garant, caution, pour (qn, qch.) ; garantir (une dette). *Watch guaranteed for two years,* montre garantie pour deux ans. *I g. his obedience,* je réponds de son obéissance. *F: He will come,* I guarantee, il viendra, je vous le garantis. **guaranteed,** *a. Com:* Avec garantie.

guarantor [garən'tɔːr], *s.* Garant, -ante ; caution *f*, répondant *m.* To stand as guarantor for s.o., appuyer qn de sa garantie ; cautionner qn.

guaranty ['garənti], *s.* = GUARANTEE[1] 2, 3.

guard[1] [gɑːrd], *s.* **1.** Garde *f.* (*a*) Posture *f* de défense. *Fenc: Box: To take one's g.*, se mettre en garde. On guard! en garde ! (*b*) To be, stand, on one's guard, être, se tenir, sur ses gardes ; se tenir pour averti. *To be on one's g. against sth.*, se méfier de qch. To put s.o. on (his) guard, mettre qn en garde (*against*, contre) ; donner l'éveil à qn. To throw s.o. off his guard, tromper la surveillance de qn ; endormir la vigilance de qn. To be caught off one's guard, être pris au dépourvu. (*c*) To be on guard (duty), être en faction ; être de garde, de faction. To go on guard, to mount guard, monter la garde. To come off guard, descendre de garde. To keep guard, faire la garde. *To keep a prisoner under* guard, garder un prisonnier à vue. **2.** *Coll.* (*a*) *Mil:* Garde *f.* Advanced g., avant-garde *f.* New guard, relieving guard, garde montante. *F:* One of the old guard, un vieux de la vieille. *To form a g. of honour,* faire, former, la haie. (*b*) To set a guard on a house, faire surveiller une maison. **3.** (*a*) *Rail:* Chef *m* de train. (*b*) *Mil:* The Guards, la Garde. **4.** (*a*) Dispositif protecteur ; protecteur *m* (d'une machine) ; carter *m* (d'engrenages). Fly-wheel guard, garde *f* du volant. Fire-guard, garde-feu *m inv*, pareétincelles *m inv.* Trigger-guard, pontet *m* (de fusil) ; sous-garde *f.* (*b*) (Hand-)guard *of a sword,* garde *f*, coquille *f*, d'une épée. (*c*) Cordon *m*, laisse *f* (de chapeau). *S.a.* WATCH-GUARD. (*d*) *Bookb:* Onglet *m.* **5.** *Med:* Correctif *m* (d'un médicament). **'guard-house,** *s. Mil:* Corps-de-garde *m inv.* **'guard-post, -stone,** *s.* Bouteroue *f* (de coin de rue, etc.). **'guard-rail,** *s.* Garde-corps *m*, garde-fou *m.* **'guard-room,** *s. Mil:* **1.** Corps-de-garde *m inv.* **2.** Poste *m* de police

guard[2]. **1.** *v.tr.* (*a*) Garder. To g. s.o. from, against, a danger, garder, protéger, qn d'un danger. (*b*) To guard one's tongue, surveiller sa langue. (*c*) *Ind:* Protéger (une courroie, etc.) ; grillager (une machine-outil). (*d*) *Cards:* To guard one's clubs, se garder en trèfle. *My king is guarded,* j'ai la garde au roi. (*e*) *Med:* Mêler un correctif à (un narcotique). **2.** *v.i.* To guard against sth., se garder, se mettre à l'abri, de qch. ; se précautionner contre qch. ; parer à qch. **guarded,** *a.* (*Of speech, etc.*) Prudent, mesuré. To be guarded in one's speech, surveiller ses paroles ; être réservé dans ses paroles. **-ly,** *adv.* Avec réserve, avec précaution.

guardian ['gɑːrdjən], *s.* **1.** Gardien, -ienne. **2.** Tuteur, -trice, curateur, -trice (de mineur, etc.). **3.** *A:* The (Board of) Guardians, le comité d'administration de l'Assistance publique. **4.** *Attrib.* Guardian angel, ange gardien, ange tutélaire.

guardianship ['gɑːrdjənʃip], *s.* **1.** Garde *f.* **2.** *Jur:* Gestion *f* tutélaire ; tutelle *f*, curatelle *f.* .Child under g., enfant en tutelle.

guardship ['gɑːrdʃip], *s. Navy:* Stationnaire *m.*

guardsman, *pl.* **-men** ['gɑːrdzmən, -men], *s.m.* Officier de la Garde.

guava ['gwɑːva], *s. Bot:* Goyave *f.* Guava(-tree), goyavier *m.*

gudgeon[1] ['gʌdʒən], *s. Ich:* Goujon *m.*

gudgeon[2], *s.* **1.** *Mec.E:* Goujon *m*, tourillon *m*, axe *m.* **2.** *Const:* Goujon (pour pierres). **'gudgeon-pin,** *s.* **1.** *I.C.E:* Axe *m* de pied de bielle. **2.** *Mch:* Tourillon *m* de la crosse.

guelder rose ['geldər'roːuz], *s. Bot:* Boule-de-neige *f.*

Guelph [gwelf], *s. Hist:* Guelfe *m.*

guerdon ['gɔːrdən], *s. Poet:* Récompense *f.*

Guernsey ['gɔːrnzi]. *Pr.n. Geog:* Guernesey.

guer(r)illa [ge'rila], *s. Mil:* **1.** Guérillero *m.* **2.** Guerilla (war), guerre *f* de guérillas, d'embuscades.

guess[1] [ges], *s.* Conjecture *f*, estimation *f.* To give, have, make, a guess, (i) hasarder une conjecture ; (ii) tâcher de deviner. *I give you three guesses,* je vous le donne en trois. It's pure guess-work, c'est pure conjecture. By guess (-work), à l'estime ; au jugé ; à vue de nez.

guess[2], *v.tr. & i.* **1.** To guess at sth., (tâcher de) deviner, conjecturer, qch. *To g.* (*at*) *the length* '*of sth.*, estimer la longueur de qch. *I guessed him to be twenty-five,* je lui donnai vingt-cinq ans. To keep an opponent guessing, mystifier un adversaire. **2.** To guess right, wrong, bien, mal, deviner. To guess a riddle, trouver le mot d'une énigme. You've guessed it! vous y êtes ! vous avez rencontré juste ! **3.** *U.S:* Croire, penser. *I g. you're right,* m'est avis que vous avez raison.

guest [gest], *s.* **1.** Convive *m*f ; invité, -ée ; hôte, -esse. **2.** (i) Pensionnaire *mf*, (ii) client, -ente (d'un hôtel). *S.a.* PAYING[1] 1. **'guest-house,** *s.* **1.** Hôtellerie *f* (d'un monastère). **2.** Pension *f* de famille.

guffaw[1] [gʌ'fɔː], *s.* Gros rire (bruyant) ; pouffement *m.*

guffaw[2], *v.i.* Pouffer, s'épouffer, de rire ; partir d'un gros rire.

Guiana [gi'ɑːna]. *Pr.n. Geog:* La Guyane.

guidance ['gaidəns], *s.* Direction *f*, gouverne *f*, conduite *f.* *I owe much to his g.*, je dois beaucoup à ses conseils. *This is for your guidance,* ceci est à titre d'indication ; ceci est pour votre gouverne. *Sch:* Vocational guidance, orientation professionnelle.

guide[1] [gaid], *s.* **1.** (*Pers.*) (*a*) Guide *m* ; pro-

meneur, -euse (de touristes). **Alpine guide,** guide alpin. **Guide, philosopher and friend,** mentor *m*. **To take sth. as a guide,** prendre qch. pour règle. *(b)* **Girl guide,** éclaireuse *f*; *(in Fr.)* guide *m* de France. **2. Guide(-book),** (livret-)guide *m*; itinéraire *m*. *G.* **to Switzerland,** guide de la Suisse. **Railway guide,** indicateur *m* des chemins de fer. **3.** *(a)* Indication *f*, exemple *m*. *Let this be a g. to you,* que ceci vous serve d'exemple. *(b) Mec.E:* **Belt-guide,** guide de courroie; guide-courroie *m*. *Mch:* **(Slipper-)guide,** glissière *f*. *Tex:* **Thread-guide,** distributeur *m* du fil. *(c)* **Guide-cards** *(of card-index)*, intercalaires *m*. **'guide-lines,** *s.pl.* Transparent (rayé) (pour écrire). **'guide-post,** *s.* Poteau indicateur (de route). **'guide-rope,** *s.* **1.** Câble *m* de guidage. **2.** *Aer:* Guide-rope *m*.
guide², *v.tr.* Guider, conduire, diriger. *To guide the way for s.o.,* guider qn. *All are guided by him,* tous se règlent sur lui. **guiding¹,** *a.* Qui sert de guide; directeur, -trice. *G. principle,* principe directeur. *Guiding star,* guide *m*. **guiding²,** *s.* Guidage *m*, conduite *f*, direction *f*.
guild [gild], *s.* **1.** *Hist:* Corporation *f*. **Trade guild,** corps *m* de métier. **2.** Association *f*, confrérie *f*. **Church guild,** cercle *m* (catholique, etc.).
guilder ['gildər], *s. Num:* Gulden *m*.
guildhall ['gildhɔ:l], *s.* Hôtel *m* de ville.
guile [gail], *s.* Artifice *m*, ruse *f*, astuce *f*. *She uses the g. of her sex,* elle use de la finesse de son sexe.
guileful ['gailful], *a.* Astucieux, artificieux, rusé; finassier, -ière.
guileless ['gailləs], *a.* **1.** Franc, *f.* franche; sincère, loyal; sans malice. **2.** Candide, naïf. **-ly,** *adv.* **1.** Franchement, sincèrement. **2.** Candidement.
guilelessness ['gailləsnəs], *s.* **1.** Franchise *f*, sincérité *f*. **2.** Candeur *f*, naïveté *f*.
guillemot ['gilimɔt], *s. Orn:* Guillemot *m*.
guilloche [gi'louʃ], *s.* Guillochis *m*.
guillotine¹ [gilo'ti:n], *s.* **1.** Guillotine *f*. **2.** *Bookb:* Massicot *m*; presse *f* à rogner.
guillotine², *v.tr.* Guillotiner, décapiter (qn). **guillotining,** *s.* Guillotinement *m*; exécution *f*.
guilt [gilt], *s.* Culpabilité *f*. *S.a.* ADMIT I.
guiltless ['giltləs], *a.* Innocent *(of sth.,* de qch.).
guiltlessness ['giltləsnəs], *s.* Innocence *f*.
guilty ['gilti], *a.* Coupable. *(a) G. of theft,* coupable de vol. *G. person,* coupable *mf. Jur:* **To plead guilty,** s'avouer coupable. *The accused pleads not g.,* l'accusé nie. *To find s.o. guilty, not guilty,* prononcer qn coupable, innocent. *He was found g.,* il fut reconnu coupable. *(b)* **Guilty conscience,** conscience coupable, chargée. *G. look,* regard confus. **-ily,** *adv.* Coupablement; d'un air coupable.
Guinea ['gini]. **I.** *Pr.n. Geog:* La Guinée. **2.** *s. A:* (Pièce *f* d'or d'une) guinée (= 21 shillings) (encore usitée comme monnaie de compte). **'guinea-cock,** *s.m.* Pintade *f* mâle. **'guinea-fowl,** *s.* Pintade *f*. **'guinea-pig,** *s.* Cobaye *m*; cochon *m* d'Inde.
guise [gaiz], *s.* **1.** *A:* Vêtements *mpl*, costume *m*. *In the g. of a pilgrim,* vêtu ou travesti en pèlerin. **2.** *She appeared* in the guise of *a nymph,* elle apparut sous la forme d'une nymphe. *F:* **Under, in, the guise of friendship,** sous l'apparence, sous le masque, de l'amitié.
guitar [gi'ta:r], *s. Mus:* Guitare *f*.
gulch [gʌltʃ], *s. U.S:* Ravin *m* (aurifère).
gules [gju:lz], *s. Her:* Gueules *m*.
gulf [gʌlf], *s.* **1.** *Geog:* Golfe *m*. **The Gulf**

Stream, le Courant du Golfe. **2.** Gouffre *m*, abîme *m*; abysse *m* (de la mer).
gull¹ [gʌl], *s. Orn:* Mouette *f*, goéland *m*.
gull², *s.* Gogo *m*, jobard *m*, gobeur *m*.
gull³, *v.tr.* Jobarder, flouer, rouler (qn). *He is easily gulled,* il se laisse facilement rouler.
gullet ['gʌlet], *s.* Œsophage *m*; *F:* gosier *m*.
gullibility [gʌli'biliti], *s.* Jobarderie *f*, jobardise *f*.
gullible ['gʌlibl], *a.* Facile à duper; jobard; qui s'en laisse conter.
gully¹ ['gʌli], *s.* **1.** *Geol:* (Petit) ravin; couloir *m*. **2.** *Civ.E:* Caniveau *m*; rigole *f*. **'gully-hole,** *s.* Bouche *f* d'égout.
gully², *v.tr.* Raviner; creuser.
gulp¹ [gʌlp], *s.* Coup *m* de gosier. **At one gulp,** (avaler qch.) d'un coup; (vider un verre) d'un (seul) trait, d'une lampée.
gulp². **1.** *v.tr.* *(a)* **To gulp sth. down,** avaler qch. à grosses bouchées; ingurgiter, gober (une huître); avaler (un verre de vin) à pleine gorge. *He gulped it down,* il n'en fit qu'une bouchée; *(of drink)* il n'en fit qu'une gorgée. *(b) F:* **To gulp down, back, one's tears,** avaler, refouler, ses larmes. *To g. down a sob,* ravaler un sanglot. **2.** *v.i.* Avoir un brusque serrement de gorge. *He gulped,* sa gorge se serra.
gum¹ [gʌm], *s.* **1.** Gomme *f* (soluble à l'eau). **2.** *(Mucilage)* Gomme, colle *f*. **3.** *(a)* **Gum resin,** gomme-résine *f*. *(b)* **Gum elastic,** *U.S:* gum, gomme élastique; caoutchouc *m*. **4.** *(a)* = CHEWING-GUM. *(b)* *(Sweetmeat)* Boule *f* de gomme. **5.** *(Of eye)* Chassie *f*. **6.** *Bot:* **Gum(-tree),** gommier *m*. *P:* **To be up a gum-tree,** être dans le pétrin. **gum-'arabic,** *s.* Gomme *f* arabique. **'gum-boots,** *s.pl. U.S:* Bottes *f* de caoutchouc. **'gum-shoes,** *s.pl. U.S:* Caoutchoucs *m*. **gum 'tragacanth,** *s. Com:* Gomme *f* adragante.
gum², *v.* (gummed) **I.** *v.tr.* *(a)* Gommer; encoller (le papier, la toile). *(b)* Coller (une page dans un livre, etc.). *(c)* **To gum (up),** gommer (un piston); encrasser (une lime). **2.** *v.i.* **To gum (up),** *(of piston)* (se) gommer; *(of file)* s'encrasser. **gummed,** *a.* **1.** *(Of label, etc.)* Gommé. **2.** *G. piston,* piston gommé. *G. oil,* huile goudronnée.
gum³, *s.* Gencive *f*.
gum⁴, *int. F: (Euphemism for* GOD) **By gum!** fichtre! mazette!
gumboil ['gʌmbɔil], *s.* Abcès *m* à la gencive; fluxion *f* à la joue.
gummy ['gʌmi], *a.* **1.** Gommeux, gluant, visqueux. *G. oil,* huile goudronneuse. **2.** *(Of eyes)* Chassieux.
gumption ['gʌm(p)ʃ(ə)n], *s. F:* Jugeotte *f*, gingin *m*. *He has plenty of g.,* c'est un débrouillard.
gun [gʌn], *s.* **1.** *(a)* Canon *m. Rifled gun,* canon rayé. **The guns,** le canon, l'artillerie *f*. *The big guns,* les gros canon. *Navy:* **Naval gun,** pièce *f* de bord. **Heavy gun,** grosse pièce. *After gun,* pièce de retraite. *F:* **He carries too many guns for me,** je ne suis pas de force à me mesurer avec lui. *(b)* **Salute of six guns,** salve de six coups de canon. **2.** *(a)* Fusil *m*; *esp.* fusil de chasse non rayé. *(Cp.* RIFLE² 2.) **Sporting gun, shot-gun,** fusil de chasse. *(b)* **A party of six guns,** une bande de six chasseurs. **3.** *U.S:* Revolver *m*; pistolet *m*. **4.** *Paint:* Spray gun, pistolet (vaporisateur). *S.a.* GREASE-GUN. **'gun-carriage,** *s. Artil:* Affût *m* de canon; *(at military funeral)* prolonge *f* d'artillerie. **'gun-cotton,** *s. Exp:* Coton azotique, fulminant; fulmicoton *m*, coton-poudre *m*. **'gun-fire,** *s. Artil:* Canonnade *f*; feu *m* (des pièces). **'gun-metal,** *s.* **1.** Bronze *m*

à canon. **2.** *Com: F:* Métal oxydé. **'gun-room,** *s. Navy:* Poste *m* des aspirants. **'gun-running,** *s.* Contrebande *f* d'armes.

gunboat ['gʌnbout], *s.* (Chaloupe) canonnière *f.*

gunman, *pl.* **-men** ['gʌnmən, -men], *s.m. U.S:* Voleur armé; bandit *m.*

gunnel ['gʌn(ə)l], *s.* = GUNWALE.

gunner ['gʌnər], *s.* (*a*) Artilleur *m*, canonnier *m.* (*b*) **(Machine-)gunner,** mitrailleur *m.*

gunnery ['gʌnəri], *s.* Artillerie *f*; tir *m* au canon. Gunnery drill, exercice des canons.

gunpowder ['gʌnpaudər], *s.* Poudre *f* (à canon). *Hist:* **The Gunpowder Plot,** la Conspiration des Poudres.

gunshot ['gʌnʃɔt], *s.* **I.** Coup *m* de fusil, de canon; coup de feu. Gunshot wound, blessure de balle, de boulet. **2.** Within gunshot, à (une) portée de fusil. Out of gunshot, hors de portée de fusil.

gunsmith ['gʌnsmiθ], *s.* Armurier *m.* Gun-smith's shop, armurerie *f.*

gunwale ['gʌn(ə)l], *s. Nau:* Plat-bord *m.* (*Of ship*) To roll gunwale under, engager; rouler à faire cuiller.

gurgle[1] [gə:rgl], *s.* (*a*) (*Of liquid*) Glouglou *m*; gargouillis *m* (de l'eau qui tombe). (*b*) *F:* (*Of pers.*) Gloussement *m*, roucoulement *m.*

gurgle[2]. **I.** *v.i.* (*Of liquid*) (*a*) Glouglouter; faire glouglou. (*b*) Gargouiller (en tombant). **2.** *v.i. & tr.* (*Of pers.*) Glousser, roucouler. *He gurgled with laughter*, il eut un rire gras. **gurgling,** *s.* **I.** (*a*) Glouglou *m.* (*b*) Gargouillement *m.* **2.** *F:* Roucoulement *m.*

gurnard ['gə:rnərd], **gurnet** ['gə:rnet], *s. Ich:* Red gurnet, grondin *m* rouge. Grey gurnet, grondin gris. Flying gurnet, rouget volant.

gush[1] [gʌʃ], *s.* **I.** Jaillissement *m*, effusion *f* (d'une source, de larmes). **2.** Jet *m*, flot *m* (de sang). **3.** Débordement sentimental.

gush[2], *v.i.* (*a*) To gush (forth, out), jaillir, saillir, couler à flots; (*of torrent*) bouillonner. *The blood was gushing out*, le sang sortait à gros bouillons. *The tears gushed into her eyes*, un flot de larmes lui monta aux yeux. (*b*) Faire de la sensiblerie; *F:* la faire au sentiment. *She gushed over their baby*, elle s'attendrissait sur leur bébé. **gushing**[1], *a.* **I.** (*Of water*) Jaillissant, vif; (*of torrent*) bouillonnant. Gushing spring, source d'eau vive. **2.** (*Of pers.*) Exubérant, expansif. G. compliments, compliments chaleureux. **-ly,** *adv.* Avec effusion. **gushing**[2], *s.* = GUSH[1].

gusher ['gʌʃər], *s.* (Mineral oil) gusher, puits jaillissant.

gusset ['gʌset], *s. Dressm: Tail:* Élargissure *f*, soufflet *m*; gousset *m* (de manche, etc.).

gust [gʌst], *s.* Gust of rain, ondée *f*, giboulée *f.* Gust of wind, coup *m* de vent; rafale *f*, bourrasque *f*, *Nau:* grain *m.* *F: G. of anger,* bouffée *f* de colère.

gustative ['gʌstətiv], *a.* Gustatif.

gustatory ['gʌstətəri], *a.* (Nerf, etc.) gustatif.

gusto ['gʌsto], *s.* To eat sth. with gusto, manger qch. savoureusement, en savourant. *F: To do sth. with g.,* faire qch. (i) avec plaisir, (ii) avec élan, avec entrain, avec brio.

gusty ['gʌsti], *a.* (Vent) à rafales, qui souffle par rafales; (journée) de grand vent.

gut[1] [gʌt], *s.* **I.** *Anat:* Boyau *m*, intestin *m.* Small gut, intestin grêle. **2.** *pl.* Guts. (*a*) Boyaux, intestins, entrailles *f*; vidure *f* (de volaille).

(*b*) *F:* To have guts, avoir du cran; avoir du cœur au ventre. **3.** Corde *f* à, de, boyau (pour violons, etc.). **4.** *Fish:* Silkworm gut, silk gut, racine (anglaise). **5.** Goulet *m* (dans un port, etc.); boyau, étranglement *m* (dans une rue).

gut[2], *v.tr.* (gutted) Étriper (un animal); vider (un poisson, une volaille). *F:* **The fire gutted the house,** le feu n'a laissé que les quatre murs, la carcasse, de la maison.

gutta-percha [gʌtə'pə:rtʃa], *s.* Gutta-percha *f.*

gutter[1] ['gʌtər], *s.* **I.** (Eaves-)gutter, gouttière *f*, chéneau *m* (de toit). **2.** Ruisseau *m* (de rue); caniveau *m* (de chaussée). Open g. (across road), cassis *m.* *F:* **Born in the gutter,** né dans la crasse. **Gutter-bred,** bercé dans la fange. *He rose from the g.,* il est sorti de la fange. Gutter wit, esprit voyou; verve voyoute. **3.** (*a*) Rigole *f*; sillon (creusé par la pluie). (*b*) Cannelure *f*, rainure *f* (dans une tôle, etc.). **'gutter-press,** *s.* *Journ:* Bas-fonds *mpl* du journalisme; la presse de bas étage. **'gutter-snipe,** *s.* Gamin, -ine, des rues; gavroche *m*; petit voyou, petite voyoute.

gutter[2]. **I.** *v.tr.* Sillonner, raviner (la terre). **2.** *v.i.* (*Of candle*) Couler. **guttering,** *s.* *Coll.* Gouttières *fpl* (d'une maison).

guttural ['gʌtərəl]. **I.** *a.* Guttural, -aux. **2.** *s. Ling:* Gutturale *f.* **-ally,** *adv.* Gutturalement; d'un ton guttural.

guy[1] [gai], *s.* **I.** Épouvantail *m.* She's a regular guy, elle est ficelée comme quatre sous. *What a guy!* comme la voilà fagotée! **2.** *U.S: P:* Type *m*, individu *m.*

guy[2], *v.tr.* (guyed) (*a*) Se moquer de (qn). (*b*) *Th:* Charger, travestir (un rôle).

guy[3], *s. Nau: etc:* (Câble *m* de) retenue *f*; hauban *m*, gui *m*, étai *m.* Funnel-guys, haubans de cheminée. **'guy-rope,** *s.* (*a*) Cordon *m* (de tente). (*b*) *Aer:* Corde *f* de manœuvre.

guy[4], *v.tr.* Hauban(n)er (un mât, etc.).

guzzle[1] ['gʌzl], *s.* Godaille *f*, bâfrée *f.*

guzzle[2], *v.tr. & i.* (*a*) Bâfrer, bouffer (la nourriture); s'empiffrer, goinfrer. (*b*) Boire avidement; lamper (la boisson). **guzzling,** *a.* Glouton, goulu.

guzzler ['gʌzlər], *s.* (*a*) Bâfreur, -euse; goinfre *m.* (*b*) Pochard, -arde; sac *m* à vin.

gymnasium [dʒim'neiziəm], *s.* Gymnase *m.* Gymnasium exercises, gymnastique *f* aux agrès.

gymnast ['dʒimnast], *s.* Gymnaste *m.*

gymnastic [dʒim'nastik]. **I.** *a.* Gymnastique. **2.** *s.pl.* (*Usu. with sg. const.*) Gymnastics, gymnastique *f.* To do g., faire de la gymnastique.

gymnotus, *pl.* **-i** [dʒim'noutəs, -ai], *s. Ich:* Gymnote *m.*

gynaeceum [dʒaini'si:əm], *s.* Gynécée *m.*

gypaetus [dʒi'pi:təs], *s. Orn:* Gypaète *m.*

gypsum[1] ['dʒipsəm], *s. Miner:* Gypse *m*; pierre *f* à plâtre. **'gypsum-quarry,** *s.* Plâtrière *f.*

gypsum[2], *v.tr. Agr:* Plâtrer (une terre).

gyrate [dʒai'reit], *v.i.* Tourner; tournoyer.

gyration [dʒai'rei(ə)n], *s.* Giration *f*, gyration *f.*

gyratory ['dʒaiərətəri], *a.* Giratoire, gyratoire. Gyratory traffic-system, sens *m* giro.

gyro-compass ['dʒaiəro'kʌmpəs], *s. Nau:* Gyro-compas *m.*

gyroscope ['dʒaiərəskoup], *s.* Gyroscope *m.*

gyroscopic [dʒaiərə'skɔpik], *a.* Gyroscopique.

H, h [eitʃ], s. **1.** (La lettre) H, h *mf.* Silent h, h muette. H aspirate, h aspirée. To drop one's h's [ˈeitʃiz], ne pas aspirer les h. **2.** H beam, H girder, poutre en H, en double T.

ha¹ [hɑː], *int.* Ha! ah!

ha², *v.i.* See HUM² I.

haberdasher [ˈhabərdaʃər], s. **1.** Chemisier *m.* **2.** Mercier *m.*

haberdashery [ˈhabərdaʃəri], s. **1.** Chemiserie *f.* **2.** Mercerie *f.*

habit [ˈhabit], s. **1.** Habitude *f,* coutume *f.* To be in the habit, to make a habit, of doing sth., avoir coutume, avoir l'habitude, avoir pour habitude, de faire qch. *I don't make a h. of it,* ce n'est pas une habitude chez moi. To get, grow, into the habit of doing sth., prendre, contracter, l'habitude de faire qch. *To get a dog into habits of obedience,* habituer un chien à obéir. To fall out, get out, of a habit, perdre une habitude ; se défaire d'une habitude. Out of (sheer) habit, *from* force of h., par habitude. Of gentle habits, de mœurs douces. **2.** (a) Habit of body, tempérament *m* ; constitution *f* physique. (b) Habit of mind, tournure *f* d'esprit. **3.** Cost: (a) Habit *m* (de religieuse). (b) (Lady's) riding-habit, amazone *f* ; habit de cheval.

habitable [ˈhabitəbl], *a.* Habitable.

habitat [ˈhabitat], s. *Nat.Hist:* Habitat *m.*

habitation [habiˈteiʃ(ə)n], s. **1.** Habitation *f* (d'une maison). Fit for habitation, en état d'être habité. **2.** Habitation, demeure *f* ; lieu *m* de séjour.

habitual [həˈbitjuəl], *a.* **1.** Habituel, d'habitude. **2.** (Ivrogne) invétéré. *He is a h. liar,* le mensonge lui est familier. **-ally,** *adv.* Habituellement. d'habitude, par habitude.

habituate [həˈbitjueit], *v.tr.* To habituate s.o, to sth., to doing sth., habituer, accoutumer, qn à qch., à faire qch.

hachure¹ [haˈʃjuər], s. *Mapm:* Hachure *f.*

hachure², *v.tr.* Hachurer.

hack¹ [hak], s. (a) Taillade *f,* entaille *f.* (b) *Fb:* Coup *m* de pied (sur le tibia). ˈhack-saw, s. Scie *f* à métaux.

hack², *v.tr. & i.* Hacher ; *Surg: F:* charcuter (un malade). To hack one's chin in shaving, se tailler, s'écharper, le menton en se rasant. To hack sth. to pieces, tailler qch. en pièces. To hack sth. down, abattre qch. à coups de pioche. Hacked out, taillé à coups de serpe, à coups de hache. To hack up the joint, *F:* massacrer le rôti. To hack one's way through, se frayer un chemin du tranchant et de la pointe. **hacking,** *a.* Hacking cough, toux sèche et pénible.

hack³, s. **1.** (a) Cheval *m* de louage. (b) *F:* Rosse *f,* haridelle *f.* (c) Cheval de selle à toutes fins. **2.** Homme *m* de peine. Literary hack, écrivain *m* à la tâche. ˈhack-work, s. Travail *m* d'écrivain à gages ; besogne *f* alimentaire.

hack⁴. 1. *v.tr.* (a) Banaliser (qch.). To hack an argument to death, ressasser un argument. (b) Louer (des chevaux). **2.** *v.i.* (a) To hack along the road, cheminer à cheval. (b) Monter des chevaux de louage.

hackle¹ [hakl], s. **1.** *Tex:* Peigne *m,* sérançoir *m.* **2.** *Orn:* Plume *f* de cou (des gallinacés). *pl.* Hackles, camail *m.* *F:* (Of pers.) When his hackles are up, quand il monte sur ses ergots.

hackle², *v.tr. Tex:* Peigner, sérancer (le lin, le chanvre).

hackney [ˈhakni], s. (a) Cheval *m* de louage. (b) Cheval de route ; bidet *m.* ˈhackney-ˈcarriage, s. Voiture *f* de place, de louage.

hackneyed [ˈhaknid], *a.* (Sujet) rebattu, usé, banal. Hackneyed phrase, expression devenue banale ; cliché *m.*

had [had]. See HAVE².

haddock [ˈhadək], s. *Ich:* Aiglefin *m.*

Hades [ˈheidiːz], s. *Gr.Myth:* Les Enfers *m.*

haematite [ˈhemətait, ˈhiː-], s. *Miner:* Hématite *f.* Red haema.ite, sanguine *f.*

haematuria [hiːməˈtjuəriə], s. *Med:* Hématurie *f.*

haemoglobin [hiːmoˈgloubin], s. Hémoglobine *f.*

haemophilia [hiːmoˈfiljə], s. *Med:* Hémophilie *f.*

haemorrhage [ˈhemoredʒ], s. Hémorragie *f.*

haemorrhoids [ˈhemorɔidz], *s.pl. Med:* Hémorroïdes *f.*

haft¹ [hɑːft], s. Manche *m,* poignée *f* (d'un poignard, d'un outil).

haft², *v.tr.* Emmancher, mettre un manche à (un outil, etc.).

hag¹ [hag], s. (Vieille) sorcière. *F:* Old hag, vieille fée, *P:* vieille taupe.

hag², s. *Scot:* (Moss-)hag, fondrière *f.*

haggard [ˈhagərd], *a.* (a) Hâve ; (visage) décharné. (b) (Visage) égaré, hagard, décomposé.

haggis [ˈhagis], s. *Cu:* Estomac de mouton bourré d'un hachis d'abats et de farine d'avoine. (Mets national écossais.)

haggle [hagl], *v.i.* Marchander, *F:* lésiner, chipoter. To haggle about, over, the price (of sth.), chicaner sur le prix de qch. ; marchander qch. ; débattre le prix.

hagiographer [hagiˈɔgrəfər], s. Hagiographe *m.*

hagiography [hagiˈɔgrəfi], s. Hagiographie *f.*

Hague (the) [ðəˈheig]. *Pr.n.* La Haye.

ha-ha [ˈhɑːˈhɑː], *int.* Ha, ha!

hail¹ [heil], s. Grêle *f.* ˈhail-stone, s. Grêlon *m.* ˈhail-storm, s. Orage accompagné de grêle.

hail², *v.i. & tr.* Grêler. Impers: It is hailing, il grêle. *F: Bullets were hailing on us,* les balles nous pleuvaient dru comme grêle. *F:* To hail down curses on s.o., faire pleuvoir des malédictions sur qn.

hail³. 1. *int.* Salut! **2.** s. Appel *m.* Within hail, à portée de (la) voix. To be hail-fellow-well-met with everyone, traiter les gens de pair à compagnon ; être à tu et à toi avec tout le monde. *F:* the Hail Mary, la salutation angélique.

hail⁴. 1. *v.tr.* (a) Saluer (qn). To hail s.o. (as) king, acclamer, saluer, qn roi. (b) Héler (qn, un navire). *Nau:* Arraisonner (un vaisseau). To hail a taxi, appeler, héler, un taxi. Within hailing distance, à portée de (la) voix. **2.** *v.i. Ship hailing from London,* (i) navire qui dépend du port de Londres ; (ii) navire en provenance de Londres.

hair [hɛər], s. **1.** (Of head) Cheveu *m. F:* To split hairs, fendre, couper, un cheveu en quatre ; pointiller ; vétiller. *S.a.* TURN² I. **2.** (b) Coll. The hair, les cheveux, la chevelure. Head of hair, chevelure. To do one's hair, se coiffer ; s'arranger les cheveux. It was enough to make your hair stand on end, c'était à faire dresser les cheveux sur la tête. *P:* Keep your hair on! ne vous emballez pas! **2.** (a). (Of body) (Usu. coll. sg.)

Poil *m.* **To remove s.o.'s superfluous hair(s),** épiler qn. (b) *Coll.* (*Of animal*) Poil, pelage *m.* **Against the hair,** à contre-poil ; à rebrousse-poil ; à rebours. (c) Crin *m* (de cheval) ; soie *f* (de porc). Hair-mattress, matelas de crin. **'hair-curler,** *s.* *Toil :* Frisoir *m* ; épingle *f* à onduler. **'hair-cut,** *s.* Taille *f*, coupe *f*, de cheveux. *To have a h.-c.,* se faire couper les cheveux. **'hair-drier,** *s.* Séchoir *m* (électrique). **'hair-line,** *s.* **1.** Délié *m.* **2.** *Typ :* Hair-line letter, capillaire *f.* **3.** *pl. Opt :* Fils croisés. **'hair-net,** *s.* Résille *f* ; filet *m* à cheveux. **'hair-raising,** *a.* Horripilant. horrifique. **'hair-restorer,** *s.* Régénérateur *m* des cheveux. **'hair's-breadth,** *s.* *To escape death by a h.-b.,* avoir été à deux doigts de la mort. *To be within a h.-b. of ruin,* être à un cheveu de la ruine. **'hair-'shirt,** *s.* Haire *f*, cilice *m.* **'hair-space,** *s.* *Typ :* Espace *f* d'un point. **'hair-splitting,** *s.* Ergotage *m*, ergoterie *f* ; distinctions subtiles. **'hair-spring,** *s.* *Clockm :* (Ressort) spiral *m.* **'hair-trigger,** *s.* *Sm.a :* Déclic *m* (de détente). Hair-trigger lock, platine *f* à double détente.

hairbreadth ['hɛərbredθ]. **I.** *s.* = HAIR'S-BREADTH. **2.** *Attrib.* **To have a hairbreadth escape,** l'échapper belle ; échapper comme par miracle.

hairbrush ['hɛərbrʌʃ], *s.* Brosse *f* à cheveux.

haircloth ['hɛərklɔθ], *s.* **1.** *A :* Cilice *m*, haire *f.* **2.** Étoffe *f* de crin ; étamine *f* de crin ; (*coarse*) thibaude *f.*

hairdresser ['hɛərdresər], *s.* Coiffeur, -euse.

hairdressing ['hɛərdresin], *s.* Coiffure *f. Style of h.,* coiffure.

-haired [hɛərd], *a.* **Long-haired, black-haired,** (*of pers.*) aux cheveux longs, noirs ; (*of animal*) à long pelage, à pelage noir.

hairless ['hɛərləs], *a.* Sans cheveux ; chauve ; (*of animal*) sans poils. *H. face,* visage glabre. *H. hide,* peau pelée.

hairpin ['hɛərpin], *s.* Épingle *f* à cheveux. *F :* **Hairpin bend** (*in road*), lacet *m.*

hairy ['hɛəri], *a.* **1.** Velu, poilu ; (*of scalp*) chevelu. **2.** *Bot :* Velu.

hake [heik], *s.* *Ich :* Merluche *f* ; *F :* colin *m.*

halation [ha'leiʃ(ə)n], *s.* *Phot :* Halo *m.*

halberd ['halbərd], **halbert** ['halbərt], *s.* Hallebarde *f.*

halberdier [halbər'di:ər], *s.m.* Hallebardier.

halcyon ['halsiən]. **1.** *s.* (a) *Myth :* Alcyon *m.* (b) *Orn :* Halcyon *m.* **2.** *Attrib. F :* Halcyon days, jours sereins ; jours de bonheur paisible.

hale [heil], *a.* (Vieillard) vigoureux, encore gaillard. **To be hale and hearty,** être frais et gaillard ; avoir bon pied bon œil.

half, *pl.* **halves** [hɑːf, hɑːvz]. **I.** *s.* (a) Moitié *f.* Half (of) his men, la moitié de ses hommes. *To take h. of sth.,* prendre la moitié de qch. *F :* **More than half** (of) the time, les trois quarts du temps. **To cut sth. in half, in halves,** couper qch. par moitié, en deux. **To go halves with s.o.,** se mettre de moitié, de compte à demi, avec qn. **Bigger by half,** plus grand de moitié. *F :* He is too clever by half, il est beaucoup trop malin. **To do things by halves,** faire les choses à demi. (b) Demi *m*, demie *f.* Two halves, deux demis. **Three and a half,** trois et demi. *I waited for* two hours and a half, j'ai attendu pendant deux heures et demie. (c) *F :* **My better half,** ma (chère) moitié, mon épouse. (d) *Rail :* Outward half, return half (*of ticket*), coupon *m* d'aller ; coupon de retour. (e) *Fb :* (i) **The first half** (*of the game*), la première mi-temps. **The second half,** la seconde mi-temps ; la reprise. (ii) = HALF-BACK.

Wing halves, demis aile. **2.** *a.* Demi. (a) Half an hour, une demi-heure. *F :* In h. a second, en moins de rien, d'un instant. **Half a dozen,** une demi-douzaine. **Half a cup,** une demi-tasse. *F :* Half one thing and half another, moitié figue moitié raisin. (b) H.-quadruped, h.-fish, mi-quadrupède, mi-poisson. **3.** *adv.* (a) *He only h. understands,* il ne comprend qu'à moitié. She h. got up, elle se releva à demi. He is not h. so formidable, il n'est pas de moitié si redoutable. Half laughing, half crying, moitié riant, moitié pleurant. *To do sth. h. willingly,* h. under compulsion, faire qch. mi de gré mi de force. Half done, à moitié fait. *H. undressed,* à demi dévêtu. Half asleep, à moitié endormi. *I was h. afraid that . . .* j'avais quelque crainte que + *sub. F :* It isn't half bad, (i) ce n'est pas mauvais du tout ; (ii) ce n'est pas si mal. *P :* (*Intensive*) She isn't half smart! elle est rien chic ! Not half! not half, tu parles ! (b) **It is half past two,** il est deux heures et demie. (c) **Half as big,** moitié aussi grand. *I got* half as much, half as many, j'en ai reçu la moitié autant, (la) moitié moins. **Half as big again,** plus grand de moitié. **Half as much again,** moitié plus. **'half-and-'half,** *adv.* Moitié l'un moitié l'autre. *How shall I mix them?* —H.-and-h., comment faut-il les mélanger?—A doses égales. **'half-'back,** *s. Fb :* Demi-arrière *m, pl.* demi-arrières ; demi *m.* **'half-'baked,** *a.* **1.** A moitié cuit. **2.** *F :* (a) (*Of pers.*) (i) Inexpérimenté, à peine dégrossi ; (ii) niais. (b) (Projet) bâclé, qui ne tient pas debout. **'half-belt,** *s. Tail :* Martingale *f.* **'half-'binding,** *s. Bookb :* Demi-reliure *f* à petits coins. **half-'boot,** *s.* Demi-botte *f, pl.* demi-bottes. **'half-'bred,** *a.* **1.** Métis, -isse. **half-'breed,** *s.* **1.** Métis, -isse. **2.** (Cheval *m*) demi-sang *inv.* **'half-'brother,** *s.m.* Demi-frère, *pl.* demi-frères. **'half-'caste,** *a. & s.* Métis, -isse. **'half-'closed,** *a.* Entre-clos ; entr'ouvert. **'half-'cock,** *s.* At half-cock, (fusil) au repos, au cran de sûreté. **'half-'crown,** *s. Num :* Demi-couronne *f* (deux shillings six pence). **'half-'dead,** *a.* A moitié mort ; à demi mort. Half-dead with fright, plus mort que vif. **'half-'dozen,** *s.* Demi-douzaine *f.* **'half-'dressed,** *a.* A moitié vêtu ; à demi vêtu. **'half-'empty'¹,** *a.* A moitié vide. **'half-'empty'²,** *v.tr.* Désemplir (une baignoire, etc.) ; vider à moitié (une bouteille). **'half-'fare,** *s. Rail : etc :* Demi-place *f.* Half-fare ticket, billet à demi-tarif. **'half-'hearted,** *a.* Tiède ; sans entrain ; (effort) timide. **-ly,** *adv.* Avec tiédeur ; sans enthousiasme. **'half-'holiday,** *s.* Demi-congé *m.* **'half-'hose,** *s.* Chaussettes *fpl* (d'hommes). **'half-'hour,** *s.* Demi-heure *f.* **'half-'hourly.** **1.** *adv.* De demi-heure en demi-heure. **2.** *a.* De toutes les demi-heures. **'half-'length,** *s.* Demi-longueur *f.* Half-length portrait, portrait en buste, portrait à mi-corps. **'half-'light,** *s.* Demi-jour *m* ; pénombre *f.* **'half-'mast,** *s.* At half-mast, à mi-mât ; (pavillon) en berne. **'half-'measure,** *s.* Demi-mesure *f.* To have done with half-measures, *F :* trancher dans le vif. **'half-'monthly,** *a.* Semi-mensuel. **'half-'moon,** *s.* **1.** Demi-lune *f.* **2.** Lunule *f* (des ongles). **'half-'mourning,** *s.* Demi-deuil *m.* **'half-'naked,** *a.* A demi nu *m* à demi nue. **'half-'pay,** *s.* Demi-solde *f* ; solde de non-activité. On half-pay, en demi-solde, en disponibilité. **'half-'price,** *s.* To sell sth. (at) h.-p., vendre qch. à moitié prix. *Th: etc:* Children half-price, les enfants paient demi-place. **'half-seas-'over,** *a. P:* A moitié ivre ; éméché. **'half-'shut,** *a.* Entre-clos. **'half-'sister,** *s.f.* Demi-sœur, *pl.* demi-sœurs. **'half-'term,** *s. Sch:* Congé *m* de mi-trimestre. **'half-'tide,** *s. Nau:* Mi-marée *f.* **'half-'time,** *s.* I. To work half-time, travailler à la demi-journée. 2. *Fb:* (La) mi-temps. **'half-tint,** *f.* Demi-teinte *f.* **'half-'title,** *s. Typ:* Faux titre ; avant-titre *m* (d'un livre). **'half-'tone,** *s. Art:* Demi-teinte *f. Phot.Engr:* Similigravure *f.* Half-tone block, *F:* simili *m.* **'half-turn,** *s.* I. Demi-tour *m.* 2. (*Of wheel*) Demi-révolution *f.* **'half-'way,** *adv.* A moitié chemin ; à mi-chemin. *H.-w. to Paris,* à mi-chemin de Paris. Half-way up, down, the hill, à mi-côte, à mi-pente. *F:* To meet s.o. half-'way, faire la moitié des avances ; *F:* couper la poire en deux. **'half-'witted,** *a.* Faible d'esprit ; *F:* à moitié idiot. **'half-'year,** *s.* Semestre *m.* **'half-'yearly.** I. *a.* Semestriel. 2. *ad.* Tous les six mois.

halfpenny ['heip(ə)ni], *s.* Demi-penny *m; F:* = sou *m.* I. (*pl.* halfpence, *F:* ha'pence ['heipəns]) *It will cost you three halfpence,* cela vous coûtera trois sous. 2. (*pl.* halfpennies) Pièce *f* d'un sou. *He gave me the change in halfpennies,* il me rendit la monnaie en sous.

halfpennyworth ['heip(ə)niwə:rθ, *F:* 'heipəθ], *s. To buy a h. of bread,* acheter (pour) un sou de pain.

halibut ['halibʌt], *s. Ich:* Flétan *m.*

halitosis [hali-tousis], *s. Med:* Mauvaise haleine.

hall [hɔ:l], *s.* I. Grande salle. (*a*) Dining-hall, (i) salle à manger ; (ii) (*of college*) réfectoire *m.* (*b*) The servants' hall, l'office *f* ; la salle commune (des domestiques). (*c*) Concert hall, salle de concert. Music-hall, music-hall *m.* 2. (*a*) Château *m, A:* manoir *m.* Born in marble halls, né sous des lambris dorés. (*b*) Maison *f* (d'un corps de métier, etc.). *S.a.* GUILDHALL, TOWN-HALL. 3. Entrance-hall, vestibule *m* (d'une maison) ; hall *m* (d'un hôtel). Hall porter, concierge *m.* **'hall-mark¹,** *s.* (Cachet *m* de) contrôle *m* (sur les objets d'orfèvrerie, apposé primitivement au "*Goldsmiths' Hall*"). *F:* The hall-mark of genius, le cachet, l'empreinte *f,* du génie. *Work bearing the h.-m. of genius,* ouvrage marqué au coin du génie. **'hall-mark²,** *v.tr.* Contrôler, poinçonner (l'orfèvrerie). **'hall-stand,** *s.* Porte-habit(s) *m inv.*

hallelujah [hali'lu:ja], *int. & s.* Alléluia *m.*

hallo [ha'lou], *int. & s.* Holà ! ohé ! *Cf.* HULLO.

halloo¹ [ha'lu:]. I. *s.* Cri *m* d'appel. *Ven:* Huée *f.* 2. *int. Ven:* Taïaut !

halloo² *v.i.* (*a*) Crier, appeler. To halloo to s.o., appeler qn (à grands cris). (*b*) *Ven:* Huer ; crier taïaut.

hallow ['halou], *v.tr.* Sanctifier, consacrer. Hallowed ['halouid] be thy name, que votre nom soit sanctifié. Hallowed ['haloud] ground, terre sainte.

Hallowe'en [halou'i:n], *s. Scot:* Veille *f* de la Toussaint.

hallucinate [ha'lju:sineit], *v.tr.* Halluciner.

hallucination [halju:si'nei∫(ə)n], *s.* Hallucination *f,* illusion *f.*

halo¹, *pl.* **-o(e)s** ['heilo, -ouz], *s.* I. *Astr: Opt:* Halo *m* ; auréole *f,* aréole *f* (de la lune). 2. Auréole, nimbe *m* (d'un saint).

halo², *v.tr.* Auréoler. *F:* Brow haloed with glory, front nimbé d'une auréole de gloire.

halogen ['halodʒen], *s. Ch:* Halogène *m.*

haloid ['halɔid], *a. & s. Ch:* Haloïde (*m*).

halt¹ [hɔlt], *s.* I. Halte *f,* arrêt *m. Ten minutes' h.,* dix minutes d'arrêt. To come to a halt, faire halte ; s'arrêter. *Mil:* At the halt, de pied ferme. *S.a.* CALL² I. 1. 2. *Rail:* (*Small station*) Halte.

halt², *v.i.* Faire halte ; s'arrêter. *Mil:* Halt ! halte !

halt³, *s.* To walk with a halt, boiter (en marchant). To speak with a h., hésiter en parlant.

halt⁴, *a. A. & B:* Boiteux. *s.pl.* The halt, les estropiés.

halt⁵, *v.i. A. & Lit:* (*Of pers., verse, etc.*) Boiter, clocher. **halting,** *a.* (Discours) hésitant ; (vers) qui boitent ; (style) heurté. **-ly,** *adv.* En hésitant.

halter ['hɔ:ltər], *s.* I. Licou *m,* longe *f* (pour chevaux). 2. Corde *f* (de pendaison) ; *A:* hart *f.*

halve [hɑ:v], *v.tr.* I. (*a*) Diviser en deux ; couper par (la) moitié ; partager (qch. en deux). *Golf:* Halved hole, trou partagé. (*b*) Réduire (des dépenses, etc.) de moitié. 2. *Carp:* Halved joint, assemblage *m* à mi-bois.

halves [hɑ:vz], *s.pl. See* HALF.

halyard ['hɔljərd, 'haljərd], *s. Nau:* Drisse *f.*

ham [ham], *s.* I. (*a*) *A:* Jarret *m.* (*b*) *pl. F:* The hams, les fesses *f,* le derrière. 2. *Cu:* Jambon *m.* Ham and eggs, œufs au jambon.

hamadryad [hama'draiad], *s.* Hamadryade *f.*

hame [heim], *s. Harn:* Attelle *f.*

hamlet ['hamlet], *s.* Hameau *m.*

hammer¹ ['hamər], *s.* I. *Tls:* Marteau *m* ; (*heavy*) masse *f. F:* To go at it hammer and tongs, y aller de toutes ses forces. *S.a.* CLAW-HAMMER, POWER-HAMMER, SLEDGE³, STEAM-HAMMER. 2. Marteau (de commissaire-priseur). To come under the hammer, passer sous le marteau ; être mis aux enchères. 3. Marteau (de piano). 4. Chien *m* ou percuteur *m* (d'une arme à feu). **'hammer-cloth,** *s. Veh:* Housse *f* (de siège de cocher). **'hammer-head,** *s.* I. Tête *f* de marteau ; pilon *m* (d'un marteau-pilon). 2. *Ich:* Hammer-head (shark), marteau *m.*

hammer². I. *v.tr.* (*a*) Marteler ; battre (le fer) ; travailler (le fer) au marteau. To hammer sth. into shape, (i) façonner qch. à coups de marteau ; (ii) *F:* mettre (un projet) au point. *F:* (*Of boxer*) To hammer one's opponent, cogner dur sur son adversaire. (*b*) *St.Exch:* To hammer a defaulter, exécuter un agent. 2. *v.i.* (*a*) Travailler avec le marteau. *F:* To hammer at, on, the door, heurter à la porte à coups redoublés. To hammer away at sth., travailler d'arrache-pied à qch. (*b*) (*Of machine part*) Tambouriner, cogner, marteler. **hammer down,** *v.tr.* Aplatir (un rivet) ; rabattre (une inégalité). **hammer in,** *v.tr.* Enfoncer (un clou) à coups de marteau. **hammer out,** *v.tr.* Étendre (l'or, etc.) sous le marteau. *F:* To hammer out lines of verse, (i) (*of reciter*) marteler des vers ; (ii) (*of poet*) forger des vers. To hammer out an excuse, se forger une excuse. **hammering,** *s.* I. (*a*) Martelage *m,* martèlement *m* ; battage *m* (du fer). (*b*) *P:* Dégelée *f* (de coups). To give s.o. a good hammering, cogner dur sur qn ; bourrer qn de coups. 2. *Mec.E:* Tambourinage *m,* cognement *m,* martèlement *m. Hyd.E:* (Water-)hammering in a pipe, coup(s) *m(pl)* de bélier dans une conduite.

hammerman, *pl.* **-men** ['hamərmən, -men], *s.* Marteleur *m* ; frappeur *m.*

hammersmith ['hamərsmiθ], *s.* Marteleur *m* ; frappeur *m.*

hammock ['hamək], *s.* Hamac *m.*

hamper[1] ['hampər], *s.* Manne *f*, banne *f*; bourriche *f* (d'huîtres, etc.); (*small*) banneau *m*, bannette *f*.

hamper[2], *v.tr.* Embarrasser, gêner, empêtrer (qn). *To h. the progress of business*, entraver la marche des affaires. *To h. oneself with luggage*, s'empêtrer de colis.

hamstring[1] ['hamstriŋ], *s. Anat:* Tendon *m* du jarret.

hamstring[2], *v.tr.* (*p.t. & p.p.* hamstringed *or* -strung) I. Couper les jarrets à (un cheval, etc.). 2. *F:* Couper les moyens à (qn).

hand[1] [hand], *s.* I. Main *f.* (*a*) To go on one's hands and knees, aller, marcher, à quatre pattes. *To vote by show of hands*, voter à main levée. *To hold* (*sth.*) *in one's h.*, tenir, avoir, (son chapeau) à la main, (des sous) dans la main, (le succès) entre les mains. **To take s.o.'s hand, to lead s.o. by the hand**, donner la main à qn. (*Of woman*) **To give her hand to a suitor**, donner, accorder, sa main à un prétendant. **To take sth. with, in, both hands**, prendre qch. à deux mains. **Here's my hand on it!** *F:* tope là! **To lay hands on sth.**, mettre la main sur qch.; s'emparer de qch. *If anyone should lay a h. on you*, si quelqu'un portait la main sur vous. **Hands off!** (i) n'y touchez pas! (ii) à bas les mains! **Hands up!** haut les mains! **To act with a high hand**, agir en despote, de haute main. **To rule with a firm hand**, gouverner d'une main ferme. *Believers in the strong hand*, partisans de la manière forte. *Fb:* **Hands**, faute *f* de mains. (*b*) *To set, put, one's h. to a task*, entreprendre, commencer, un travail. **He can turn his hand to anything**, c'est un homme à toute main. *What can you turn your h. to?* à quoi êtes-vous bon? **He never does a hand's turn**, il ne fait jamais œuvre de ses dix doigts. **To have a hand in sth.**, se mêler de qch.; tremper dans (un crime). *He has a h. in it*, il y est pour quelque chose. *I had no h. in it*, je n'y suis pour rien. **To take a hand in sth.**, se mêler de qch.; se mettre de la partie. **To lend, give, s.o. a hand**, aider qn; donner un coup de main, prêter la main, à qn. *I got a friend to bear a h.*, je me suis fait aider par un ami. (*c*) **To have one's hands full**, avoir fort à faire; avoir beaucoup de besogne sur les bras. **To have sth. on one's hands**, avoir qch. à sa charge, sur les bras. **To get sth. off one's hands**, se décharger de qch. *She is off my hands*, elle n'est plus à ma charge. *Com:* **Goods left on our hands**, marchandises invendues ou laissées pour compte. **To change hands**, (i) (*of pers.*) changer de main; passer qch. à l'autre main; (ii) (*of thg*) changer de propriétaire, de mains. **To fall into enemy hands**, tomber entre les mains de l'ennemi. *To be in good hands*, (i) être en bonnes mains; (ii) être à bonne école. *To put oneself in s.o.'s hands*, s'en remettre à qn. **To put a matter in the hands of a lawyer**, confier une affaire à un homme de loi. *My fate is in your hands*, mon sort est entre vos mains. **To have s.o. in the hollow of one's hand**, avoir qn sous sa coupe, à sa merci. 2. *Adv.phrs.* (*a*) **To be (near) at hand**, être sous la main, à portée de la main. *Spring is at h.*, voici venir le printemps. *Christmas was (close) at h.*, Noël était tout proche. *I have money at h.*, j'ai de l'argent tout prêt. (*b*) **Made by hand**, fait à la main. **To bring up a child by hand**, élever un enfant au biberon. **To send a letter by hand**, envoyer une lettre par porteur. (*c*) **Hat in hand**, chapeau bas. *Revolver in h.*, revolver au poing. *To have so much money in h.*, avoir tant d'argent disponible. **Stock in hand**, marchandises en magasin. *S.a.* CASH[1].

The matter in hand, la chose en question, dont il s'agit. *To take sth. in h.*, prendre qch. en main; se charger de qch. *To have a piece of work in h.*, avoir une œuvre sur le chantier, sur le métier. **Horse, situation, well in hand**, cheval, situation, bien en main. *To keep oneself well in h.*, se contenir. (*d*) **Work on hand**, travail en cours. *To take too much on h.*, trop entreprendre à la fois. **Supplies on hand**, ressources existantes. (*e*) **On the right hand**, du côté droit. **On every hand, on all hands**, partout; de toutes parts. **On the one hand . . ., d'une part. . . . On the other hand . . .**, d'autre part . . .; par contre. . . . (*f*) **To do sth. out of hand**, faire qch. sur-le-champ. *To shoot s.o. out of h.*, abattre qn sans autre forme de procès. **To get out of hand**, perdre toute discipline. *These children are quite out of h.*, on ne peut plus tenir ces enfants. (*g*) **Your parcel has come to hand**, votre envoi m'est parvenu. **Your favour of 4th inst. to hand**, nous avons bien reçu votre lettre du 4 ct. *F:* **The first excuse to hand**, le premier prétexte venu. (*h*) **To be hand and glove, hand in glove, with s.o.**, être d'intelligence, *P:* de mèche, avec qn. (*i*) **Hand in hand**, la main dans la main. *Here stock-raising goes h. in h. with agriculture*, ici l'élevage est en fonction de l'agriculture. (*j*) **Hand over hand, hand over fist**, main sur main (en grimpant). **To swim hand over hand**, faire la coupe. *F: To make money h. over fist*, faire des affaires d'or. (*k*) **Hand to hand**, (combattre) corps à corps. **Hand-to-hand fight**, corps-à-corps *m*. (*l*) **To live from hand to mouth**, vivre au jour le jour. (*m*) *Rac:* **To win hands down**, gagner haut la main. 3. (*Pers.*) (*a*) Ouvrier, -ière; manœuvre *m*. **To take on hands**, embaucher de la main-d'œuvre. *Nau: The ship's hands*, l'équipage *m*; les hommes. **All hands on deck!** tout le monde sur le pont! (*Of ship*) **To be lost with all hands**, périr corps et biens. *S.a.* DECK-HAND, FACTORY-HAND, *etc.* (*b*) **To be a good, a great, hand at doing sth.**, être adroit à faire qch.; avoir le talent de faire qch. *She is a good h. at making an omelet*, elle réussit bien une omelette. *S.a.* OLD 3. 4. (*a*) Écriture *f.* **Round hand, running hand**, écriture ronde, cursive. *To write (in) a small h.*, écrire en petits caractères. *He writes a good h.*, il a une belle main, une belle écriture. (*b*) **To set one's hand to a deed**, apposer sa signature à un acte. **Under your hand and seal**, signé et scellé de votre propre main. **Note of hand**, billet à ordre. 5. *Cards:* (*a*) Jeu *m.* *To have a good h.*, avoir beau jeu. *F:* **I am holding my hand**, je me réserve. (*b*) Partie *f.* **Let's have a hand at bridge**, faisons une partie de bridge. 6. *Farr:* Horse fifteen hands high, cheval de quinze paumes *f*. 7. (*a*) *Typ:* Index *m*, ☞. (*b*) (*Of sign-post*) Indicateur *m.* (*c*) Indicateur (de baromètre, etc.); aiguille *f* (de montre). 8. (*a*) **Hand of pork**, jambonneau *m.* (*b*) **Hand of bananas**, régime *m* de bananes. 9. *Dom.Ec:* Scotch hands, palettes *f* à beurre. 10. *Attrib.* **Hand luggage**, bagages à main, colis à la main. **Hand tool**, outil à main. **Hand lamp**, lampe portative. **Hand dynamo**, dynamo à manivelle. **'hand-bag**, *s.* Sac *m* à main; pochette *f*. **'hand-barrow**, *s.* Civière *f*, bard *m*; charrette *f* à bras. **'hand-cart**, *s.* Voiture *f* à bras, charrette *f* à bras. **'hand-grenade**, *s. Mil:* Grenade *f* à main. **'hand-lever**, *s.* Manette *f.* **'hand-made**, *a.* Fait, fabriqué, à la main. **'hand-'pick**, *v.tr.* Trier à la main. **'hand-rail**, *s.* Garde-fou *m*, garde-corps *m*; rampe *f*, main courante (d'escalier). **'hand-sewn**,

-stitched, *a.* Cousu à la main. **'hand-written,** *a.* Manuscrit.

hand², *v.tr.* **1.** To hand a lady into a carriage, donner la main à une dame pour l'aider à monter en voiture. **2.** Passer, remettre, donner (qch. à qn). *To h. one's card to s.o.*, tendre sa carte à qn. **hand down,** *v.tr.* **1.** Descendre (qch.) (et le remettre à qn). **2.** Transmettre (une tradition). **hand in,** *v.tr.* Remettre (un paquet, un télégramme). **hand on,** *v.tr.* Transmettre (une coutume). *To h. on news,* passer une nouvelle (*to,* à). **hand out,** *v.tr.* (a) Tendre, remettre (qch. à qn). (b) *To h. out the wages,* distribuer la paye. **hand over,** *v.tr.* Remettre (qch. à qn). (a) *To hand s.o. over to justice,* livrer, remettre, qn aux mains de la justice. (b) *To h. over one's authority,* transmettre ses pouvoirs (*to,* à). (c) *To h. over one's property to s.o.*, céder son bien à qn. **hand round,** *v.tr.* Passer, faire passer, (les gâteaux, etc.) à la ronde ; faire circuler (la bouteille).

handbell ['handbel], *s.* Sonnette *f*, clochette *f*.

handbill ['handbil], *s.* Prospectus *m*; programme *m* (de spectacle).

handbook ['handbuk], *s.* **1.** *Sch:* Manuel *m* (de sciences, etc.). **2.** Guide *m* (du touriste); livret *m* (d'un musée).

handcuff ['handkʌf], *v.tr.* Mettre les menottes à (qn).

handcuffs ['handkʌfs], *s.pl.* Menottes *f*.

handful ['handful], *s.* **1.** Poignée *f* (de noisettes, etc.). *To throw money away by the handful,* in handfuls, jeter l'argent à pleines mains, à poignées. **2.** *F:* That child is a handful, cet enfant-là me donne du fil à retordre. **3.** *Cards:* To have a h. of trumps, avoir de l'atout plein les mains.

handhold ['handhould], *s.* **1.** Prise *f*. *Crag with no h.* varappe où la main ne trouve pas de prise. **2.** (*On wall, etc.*) Main *f* de fer.

handicap¹ ['handikap], *s.* (a) *Sp:* Handicap *m*. Weight handicap (*of racehorse*), surcharge *f*. Time handicap, rendement *m* de temps. (b) *F:* Désavantage *m.* To be under a heavy handicap, être fort désavantagé.

handicap², *v.tr.* (handicapped) *Sp:* Handicaper. **handicapped,** *a.* **1.** Handicapé. **2.** Désavantage (*by,* par suite de).

handicraft ['handikraːft], *s.* **1.** Travail manuel ; habileté manuelle. **2.** Métier manuel.

handicraftsman, *pl.* -men ['handikraːftsmən, -men], *s.m.* Artisan.

handiness ['handinəs], *s.* **1.** Adresse *f*, dextérité *f* ; habileté (manuelle). **2.** (a) Commodité *f* (d'un outil). (b) Maniabilité *f* (d'un navire).

handiwork ['handiwəːrk], *s.* (a) Travail manuel. (b) Ouvrage *m*, œuvre *f*. *That is his h.*, c'est le travail de ses mains ; c'est son ouvrage.

handkerchief ['haŋkərtʃif], *s.* (**Pocket-**)hand-kerchief, mouchoir *m* (de poche). *Fancy h.*, pochette *f*.

handle¹ [handl], *s.* (a) Manche *m* (de balai, de couteau, etc.); balancier *m*, brimbale *f* (de pompe) ; brancard *m* (de civière); bras *m* (de brouette) ; queue *f* (de poêle) ; poignée *f* (de porte, de bicyclette, etc.); clef *f* (de robinet). *El.E:* Switch handle, manette *f* d'interrupteur. *F:* To have a handle to one's name, avoir un titre (de noblesse). To give a handle to, for, calumny, donner prise à la calomnie. (b) Anse *f* (de broc, de corbeille, de seau) ; portant *m* (de valise). (c) (*Crank-handle*) Manivelle *f*. *Aut:* Starting-handle, manivelle de mise en marche. **'handle-bar,** *s.* Guidon *m* (de bicyclette).

handle², *v.tr.* **1.** Tâter des mains. *To h. a material,* tâter une étoffe. **2.** (a) Manier, manipuler (qch.). *Ind:* Manutentionner (des pièces lourdes). *How to h. a gun,* comment se servir d'un fusil. To handle a ship, manœuvrer, gouverner, un navire. (b) Manier (qn, une affaire). He is hard to handle, il n'est pas commode. To handle s.o. roughly, malmener, rudoyer, qn. To handle a situation, prendre en main une situation. (c) To handle a lot of business, brasser beaucoup d'affaires. *To h. a lot of money,* remuer beaucoup d'argent. We don't h. those goods, nous ne tenons pas ces articles. **3.** *Fb:* To handle the ball, toucher le ballon. **handling,** *s.* (a) Maniement *m* (d'un outil) ; manutention *f* (de marchandises) ; manœuvre *f* (d'un navire). (b) Traitement *m* (de qn, d'un sujet). Rough handling, traitement brutal. (c) Maniement (de fonds).

handle³, *v.tr.* Emmancher (un outil). **Ivory-handled,** à manche d'ivoire. **Short-handled,** à manche court.

handmaid(en) ['handmeid(n)], *s.* *A:* Servante *f*.

handsel¹ ['hansl], *s.* Étrenne *f*.

handsel², *v.tr.* (handselled) **1.** Donner des étrennes à (qn). **2.** (*Use for the first time*) Étrenner, avoir l'étrenne de (qch.).

handshake ['handʃeik], *s.* Poignée *f* de main ; serrement *m* de main.

handsome ['hansəm], *a.* (a) Beau, *f.* belle. *H. young man,* jeune homme bien tourné, de belle mine. *H. furniture,* meubles élégants. *H. residence,* maison de belle apparence. (b) (*Of conduct*) Gracieux, généreux. *Prov:* Handsome is that handsome does, la naissance ne fait pas la noblesse. (c) Handsome fortune, belle fortune. *H. gift,* riche cadeau. To make a handsome profit, réaliser de beaux bénéfices. **-ly,** *adv.* **1.** (a) (S'habiller) élégamment, avec élégance. (b) (Agir) généreusement ; (se conduire) en galant homme ; (payer) libéralement. *P:* To come down handsomely, ouvrir largement sa bourse. **2.** *Nau:* Doucement.

handsomeness ['hansəmnəs], *s.* (a) Beauté *f*, élégance *f*. (b) Générosité *f* (d'une action) ; libéralité *f* (d'une récompense).

handspike ['handspaik], *s.* (a) *Nau:* Anspect *m* ; barre *f* de cabestan. (b) *Artil:* Levier *m* de manœuvre.

handwork ['handwəːrk], *s.* Travail *m* à la main, travail manuel.

handworker ['handwəːrkər], *s.* Ouvrier, -ière.

handwriting ['handraitiŋ], *s.* Écriture *f*. *This letter is in the h. of . . .*, cette lettre a été écrite par . . ., est de la main de. . . .

handy ['handi], *a.* **1.** (*Of pers.*) Adroit (de ses mains) ; débrouillard. Handy at doing sth., adroit à faire qch. *To be h. with a tool,* savoir se servir d'un outil. **2.** (*Of implement*) Maniable ; bien en main(s). *H. ship,* navire maniable. **3.** Commode. That would come in very handy, cela ferait bien l'affaire, viendrait bien à point. **4.** A portée (de la main). To keep sth. handy, tenir qch. sous la main. **-ily,** *adv.* **1.** Adroitement. **2.** (Placé) commodément, sous la main. **'handy-man,** *pl.* **-men,** *s.m.* Homme à tout faire, à toute main.

hang¹ [haŋ], *s.* **1.** (a) Pente *f*, inclinaison *f* (d'une falaise). (b) Ajustement *m* (d'un costume) ; drapement *m* (d'une étoffe). (c) *F:* To get the hang of sth., (i) attraper le coup, saisir le truc, pour faire qch. ; (ii) saisir le sens de qch. When you have got the hang of things, quand vous serez au courant. **2.** *F:* I don't care a hang, je m'en moque.

hang², v. (hung [hʌŋ]; hung) I. v.tr. **1.** Pendre, accrocher, suspendre (on, from, à). To h. one's hat on a peg, accrocher son chapeau à une patère. To hang a bell, poser une sonnette. To hang a door, monter une porte; mettre une porte sur ses gonds. Veh: Hung on springs, monté sur ressorts. Aut: Low-hung axle, essieu surbaissé. **2.** To hang (down) one's head, baisser la tête. **3.** Cu: Faire faisander, faire vener (le gibier). **4.** (a) To hang a room with tapestries, tendre une salle de tapisseries. Windows hung with lace curtains, fenêtres garnies de rideaux en dentelle. (b) To hang wall-paper, coller du papier à tapisser. **5.** To hang fire, (i) (of fire-crms) faire long feu; (ii) F: (of plan) traîner (en longueur). **6.** (p.t. & p.p. hanged, often F: hung) Pendre (un criminel). He hanged himself out of despair, il se pendit de désespoir. F: Hang the fellow! que le diable l'emporte! That be hanged for a tale! quelle blague! (I'll be) hanged if I know! je n'en sais fichtre rien! Hang it! sacristi! zut! Hang the expense! je me fiche pas mal de la dépense! S.a. DOG¹ I. II. **hang**, v.i. **1.** Pendre, être suspendu (on, from, à). Picture hanging on the wall, tableau pendu, accroché, au mur. Fruit hanging on a tree, fruits qui pendent à un arbre. To hang out of the window, (of pers.) se pencher par la fenêtre; (of thg) pendre à la fenêtre. **2.** A thick fog hangs over the town, un épais brouillard plane, pèse, sur la ville. The danger hanging over our heads, le danger suspendu sur nos têtes. A heavy silence hung over the meeting, un silence pesait sur l'assemblée. **3.** (a) To hang on s.o.'s arm, se pendre au bras de qn; se cramponner au bras de qn. To hang on s.o.'s words, boire les paroles de qn. (b) Everything hangs on his answer, tout dépend de sa réponse. **4.** Responsibility hangs heavy upon him, la responsabilité pèse sur lui. Time hangs heavy on my hands, le temps me pèse. **5.** He's always hanging around here, il est toujours à flâner, à rôder, par ici. To hang round a woman, tourner autour d'une femme. **6.** (Of drapery) Tomber, se draper. Her hair hangs down her back, ses cheveux lui tombent dans le dos. **7.** (Of criminal) Être pendu. **hang about**, v.i. **1.** Rôder, flâner. To keep s.o. hanging about, faire croquer le marmot à qn. **2.** To hang about a neighbourhood, rôder dans un voisinage. I have a cold hanging about me, j'ai un rhume dont je ne peux pas me débarrasser. **hang back**, v.i. **1.** Rester en arrière. **2.** F: Hésiter; montrer peu d'empressement. **hang down**, v.i. **1.** Pendre. **2.** Pencher. **hang on**, v.i. Se crampponner, s'accrocher (to, à). H. on to your job, ne lâchez pas votre situation. He is always hanging on to his mother, il est toujours dans les jupons de sa mère. **hang out.** **1.** v.tr. Pendre (qch.) au dehors; étendre (le linge); arborer (un pavillon). (Of dog) To hang out its tongue, tirer la langue. **2.** v.i. Pendre (au dehors). F: Where do you hang out? où nichez-vous? où juchez-vous? **hang over**, v.i. Surplomber. '**hang-over**, s. **1.** Reliquat m (d'une maladie, etc.). **2.** P: La gueule de bois. **hang together**, v.i. **1.** Rester unis. **2.** (Of statements) S'accorder. **hang up**, v.tr. (a) Accrocher, pendre (son chapeau, un tableau). Tp: To hang up the receiver, raccrocher (l'appareil). (b) Remettre (un projet) à plus tard. Parcels hung up in transit, colis en souffrance. We were hung up with a puncture, nous avons été retardés par une crevaison. **hanging¹**, a. **1.** (Pont) suspendu; (lustre) pendant; (échafaudage) volant. Hanging stair, escalier en encorbellement. Hanging door, porte battante. The h. gardens of Babylon, les jardins suspendus de Babylone. **2.** F: Hanging judge, juge qui condamne tous les accusés à la potence. **hanging²**, s. **1.** (a) Suspension f; pose f (d'une sonnette); montage m (d'une porte). (b) Pendaison f (d'un criminel). It's a hanging matter, c'est un cas pendable. (c) Hanging wardrobe, penderie f. **2.** pl. Hangings, tenture f; tapisserie f. Bed hangings, rideaux m de lit. '**hang-dog**, a. Hang-dog look, mine f patibulaire. '**hang-nail**, s. = AGNAIL.

hangar ['haŋər], s. Av: Hangar m.

hanger ['haŋər], s. **1.** (Pers.) Tendeur m (de tapisseries). Bell-hanger, poseur m de sonnettes. S.a. PAPER-HANGER. **2.** Crochet m (de suspension). (Coat-)hanger, cintre m; porte-vêtements m inv. **3.** (Pers.) Hanger-on, pl. hangers-on, (i) dépendant m; (ii) F: écumeur m de marmites; écornifleur m.

hangman, pl. **-men** ['haŋmən, -men], s.m. Bourreau.

hank [haŋk], s. **1.** Écheveau m (de laine, etc.). **2.** Nau: Anneau m, cosse f, bague f.

hanker ['haŋkər], v.i. To hanker after sth., désirer ardemment qch.; être talonné par le désir de qch. To h. after praise, être affamé de louanges. **hankering**, s. Vif désir, grande envie (after, for, de). To have a hankering for sth., soupirer après qch. H. after the stage, aspirations fpl à la scène. He had hankerings after the sea, (i) il avait la nostalgie de la mer; (ii) il avait des envies de se faire marin.

hanky-panky [haŋki'paŋki], s. F: Supercherie f; finasseries fpl. That's all hanky-panky, tout ça c'est du boniment.

Hannibal ['hanibal]. Pr.n.m. A.Hist: Annibal.

hanse [hans], s. Hist: Hanse f. The Hanse, la Ligue hanséatique.

hanseatic [hansi'atik], a. Hist: The Hanseatic League, la Ligue hanséatique.

hansom(-cab) ['hansəm('kab)], s. Cab (anglais).

hap¹ [hap], s. A: **1.** Hasard m, sort m, destin m. **2.** Hasard malencontreux.

hap², v.i. (happed) A: **1.** Arriver par hasard. **2.** (Of pers.) To hap on sth., trouver qch. par hasard.

ha'pence ['heipəns], s.pl., **ha'penny** ['heipni], s. F: See HALFPENNY, KICK¹ I.

haphazard [hap'hazərd]. **1.** s. At haphazard, au hasard; au petit bonheur. **2.** a. H. arrangement, disposition fortuite. To choose in a h. way, choisir à l'aveuglette. **3.** adv. To live haphazard, vivre à l'aventure.

hapless ['haplas], a. Infortuné, malheureux.

ha'p'orth ['heipərθ], s. F: (= HALFPENNY-WORTH) Give me a h., donnez-m'en pour un sou. He hasn't a h. of courage, il n'a pas pour deux sous de courage.

happen ['hapn], v.i. **1.** Arriver. (a) Se passer, se produire. An accident happens, un accident se produit; il arrive un accident. Don't let it happen again! que cela n'arrive plus! Just as if nothing had happened, comme si de rien n'était. Whatever happens, quoi qu'il advienne; quoi qu'il arrive. Happen what may, advienne que pourra. How does it happen that . . .? d'où vient que . . .? It might h. that . . ., il pourrait se faire que. . . . It so happened that . . ., le hasard a voulu que . . .; il se trouva que. . . . As it happens . . ., justement. . . . (b) What has happened to him? (i) qu'est-ce qui lui est arrivé? (ii) qu'est-ce qu'il est devenu? If any-

thing happened to you, si vous veniez à mourir. *Something has happened to him,* il lui est arrivé quelque malheur. **2. To happen to do sth.,** faire qch. accidentellement. *A carriage happened to be passing,* une voiture vint à passer. *The house happened to be empty,* la maison se trouvait vide. *Do you h. to know whether . . .?* sauriez-vous par hasard si . . .? *If I do h. to forget,* s'il m'advient, m'arrive, d'oublier. **3. To happen upon sth.,** tomber sur qch.; trouver qch. par hasard. **happening,** *s.* Événement *m.*

happiness ['hapinəs], *s.* Bonheur *m,* félicité *f.*

happy ['hapi], *a.* Heureux. **I.** (*a*) *In happier circumstances,* dans des circonstances plus favorables. *In a h. hour,* à un moment propice. (*b*) *To be as happy as the day is long, as a king, as a sand-boy,* être heureux et sans soucis; être heureux comme un roi; être heureux comme un poisson dans l'eau. *H. party of children,* bande joyeuse d'enfants. *I was happy in a son,* j'avais le bonheur de posséder un fils. *To make s.o. h.,* (i) rendre qn heureux; (ii) faire la joie de qn. *To be happy to do sth.,* être heureux, bien aise, content, de faire qch. **2. Happy phrase,** expression heureuse, à propos. **Happy thought!** bonne inspiration! **-ily,** *adv.* Heureusement. *To' live h.,* vivre heureux. **Happily, he did not die,** par bonheur il ne mourut pas. *She smiled h.,* elle eut un sourire de contentement.

happy-go-lucky ['hapigo'lʌki], *attrib.a.* Sans souci; insouciant. *To do sth. in a h.-go-l. fashion,* faire qch. au petit bonheur.

harangue[1] [ha'raŋ], *s.* Harangue *f.*

harangue[2]. **I.** *v.tr.* Haranguer (la foule). **2.** *v.i.* Prononcer, faire, une harangue; discourir (en public).

harass ['harəs], *v.tr.* **I.** *Mil:* Harceler, tenir en alerte (l'ennemi). **2.** Harasser, tracasser, tourmenter (qn).

harassment ['harəsmənt], *s.* **I.** Harcèlement *m,* harcelage *m* (de l'ennemi). **2.** Harassement *m,* tracasserie *f.*

harbinger ['ha:rbindʒər], *s.* Avant-coureur *m;* messager, -ère; annonciateur, -trice; précurseur *m.*

harbour[1] ['ha:rbər], *s.* **I.** (*a*) *A:* Abri *m,* asile *m.* (*b*) *Ven:* Lit *m* (d'un cerf). **2.** *Nau:* Port *m.* **Inner harbour,** arrière-port *m.* **Outer harbour,** avant-port *m.* **Tidal harbour,** port de, à, marée. **To enter harbour,** entrer au port, dans le port. **To leave harbour,** sortir du port. **To clear the harbour,** quitter le port. **'harbour-'dues,** *s.pl. Nau:* Droits *m* de mouillage. **'harbour-master,** *s.* Capitaine *m* de port. **'harbour-station,** *s.* Gare *f* maritime.

harbour[2], *v.tr.* Héberger; donner asile à (qn); recéler (un criminel). **To harbour dirt,** retenir la saleté. **To harbour a grudge against s.o.,** garder rancune à qn. *To h. suspicions,* entretenir, nourrir, des soupçons.

harbourage ['ha:rbərədʒ], *s.* **I.** Refuge *m,* abri *m,* asile *m.* **2.** *Nau:* To give good harbourage, offrir un bon mouillage, une rade sûre.

hard [ha:rd]. **I.** *a.* **I.** Dur. **To get hard,** durcir. *H. snow,* neige durcie. *H. muscles,* muscles fermes. *F:* **To be as hard as nails,** (i) être en bonne forme; (ii) être impitoyable. *Med:* **Hard tissues,** tissus scléreux. **2.** Difficile; (tâche) pénible. **To be hard to please,** être exigeant, difficile. **To be hard of hearing,** être dur d'oreille. *I.C.E:* The *engine is h. to start,* le moteur est dur à lancer. *I find it h. to believe that . . .,* j'ai peine à croire que + *sub.* **3.** (*a*) (*Of pers.*) Dur, sévère, rigoureux (*to, towards,* envers). **Hard master,** maître

sévère, exigeant. **To be hard on s.o.,** être sévère, user de rigueur, envers qn. **To be hard on one's clothes,** user rapidement ses vêtements. (*b*) **To call s.o. hard names,** qualifier durement qn. **Hard fact,** fait brutal. **Times are hard,** les temps sont rudes, durs. **To have a hard time of it,** en voir de dures. *F:* **Hard lines! hard luck!** pas de chance! quelle guigne! (*c*) *H. to the touch,* rude au toucher. **Hard water,** eau crue, dure. *U.S:* **Hard drinks,** boissons alcooliques. *Phot:* **Hard print,** épreuve heurtée. *H. paper,* papier à contrastes. **4. Hard work,** (i) travail assidu; (ii) travail ingrat. *It is h. work for me . . .,* j'ai beaucoup de peine, bien du mal, à. . . . **Hard drinker,** grand buveur. **Hard fight,** rude combat. *H. match,* match vivement disputé. *It is a h. blow for him,* c'est un rude coup pour lui. **To try one's hardest,** faire tout son possible, faire l'impossible. *S.a.* LABOUR[1] **I. 5.** (*a*) **Hard frost,** forte gelée. **Hard winter,** hiver rigoureux. (*b*) *W.Tel:* **Hard valve,** valve à vide très poussé. **-ly,** *adv.* **I.** (*a*) Sévèrement. *To deal h. with s.o.,* user de rigueur envers qn. (*b*) *H.* contested, vivement, chaudement, contesté. (*c*) Péniblement. *The victory was h.* won, la victoire a été remportée de haute lutte. **2.** (*a*) A peine; ne . . . guère. *She can h. read,* (c'est) à peine si elle sait lire. *He had h. escaped when . . .,* à peine s'était-il échappé que. . . . **You'll hardly believe it,** vous aurez (de la) peine, du mal, à le croire. **I hardly know,** je n'en sais trop rien. **I need hardly say . . .,** point besoin de dire. . . . **Hardly anyone,** presque personne. **Hardly ever,** presque jamais. (*b*) *He could h. have said that,* il n'aurait sûrement pas dit cela. **II. hard,** *adv.* **I.** (*a*) *Pull the bell h.,* tirez fort la sonnette. *As h. as one can,* de toutes ses forces. *To throw a stone h.,* lancer une pierre avec raideur. **To hit hard,** cogner dur; frapper raide. **To bite hard,** mordre serré. **To beg hard,** prier instamment. **To look h. at s.o.,** regarder fixement qn. **To think hard,** réfléchir profondément. **To work hard,** travailler dur, ferme. **To be hard at work,** être en plein travail. *He is always hard at it,* il est toujours attelé à son travail. *He studies h.,* il étudie sans relâche. *It is raining hard,* il pleut à verse. **To freeze hard,** geler dur. **To snow hard,** neiger dru. (*b*) **It will go hard with him if . . .,** il lui en cuira si. . . . (*c*) *Nau:* **Hard over!** la barre toute! *H. a-port!* tribord toute! *F:* **To be hard up (for money),** être à court (d'argent); *F:* être dans la dèche. **To be hard up for sth.,** avoir grand besoin de qch. **2.** Difficilement; avec peine. **Hard-earned wages,** salaire péniblement gagné. *S.a.* DIE[2] **I. 3. Hard by,** tout près, tout contre, tout à côté. **To follow hard (up)on s.o.,** suivre qn de près. *It was h. on twelve,* il était bientôt minuit. **'hard and 'fast,** *a.* **I.** *Nau:* (*Of ship*) A sec. **2.** *To lay down a hard and fast rule,* poser une règle absolue, rigoureuse. **'hard-'bitten,** *a.* **I.** (*Of dog*) Qui ne lâche pas. **2.** *F:* (*Of pers.*) Tenace; dur à cuire. **'hard-'boiled,** *a.* (Œuf) dur. **'hard-'fought,** *a.* Chaudement contesté; âprement disputé. **'hard-'headed,** *a.* (*Of pers.*) Positif, pratique. **'hard-'hearted,** *a.* Insensible, impitoyable, au cœur dur. **hard-'mouthed,** *a.* (Cheval) dur de bouche, sans bouche. **hard-'set,** *a.* **I.** (*Of pers.*) (*a*) Fort embarrassé; aux abois. (*b*) Qui a une faim de loup; affamé. **2.** *When the cement is hard-set,* lorsque le ciment a bien pris, a durci. **hard-'solder,** *v.tr. Metalw:* Braser; souder au cuivre. **hard-'wearing,** *a.* (Vêtement) de bon usage, de bon service; (étoffe) durable. **'hard-**

'won, *a. H.-w. trophy,* trophée chaudement disputé, remporté de haute lutte. **'hard-'working,** *a.* Laborieux; travailleur, -euse; assidu.

harden ['hɑːrdn]. **I.** *v.tr.* (*a*) Durcir; tremper (l'acier, *F:* les muscles); *Med:* indurer, scléroser. **To harden s.o.** to fatigue, aguerrir qn à, contre, la fatigue. **To harden s.o.'s heart,** endurcir le cœur de qn. (*b*) *Metall:* **To (case-) harden,** cémenter (l'acier). (*c*) *Phot:* Aluner (un cliché). **2.** *v.i.* (*a*) (*Of substance*) Durcir, s'affermir; (*of tissue*) s'ossifier. **His voice hardened,** sa voix devint dure. (*b*) (*Of shares*) **To harden (up),** se tendre. *Prices are hardening,* les prix sont en hausse. **hardened,** *a.* Durci; (acier) trempé; (criminel) endurci. **To be hardened against** *entreaties,* être cuirassé contre les supplications. **hardening,** *s.* (*a*) Durcissement *m,* affermissement *m. Metall:* Trempe *f.* **Air hardening,** (i) prise *f,* durcissement, (du ciment, etc.) à l'air; (ii) *Metall:* trempe à l'air. **Hardening steel,** acier de trempe. (*b*) *Metall:* (Case-) hardening, cémentation *f* (de l'acier). (*c*) *Phot:* Alunage *m. S.a.* BATH¹ 3.

hardihood ['hɑːrdihud], *s.* Hardiesse *f;* (i) intrépidité *f;* (ii) audace *f,* effronterie *f.*

hardness ['hɑːrdnəs], *s.* **I.** (*a*) Dureté *f;* trempe *f* (de l'acier). (*b*) Tons heurtés (d'un cliché). (*c*) Crudité *f* (de l'eau). **2.** Tension *f,* raffermissement *m* (du marché). **3.** (*a*) Difficulté *f* (d'un problème, etc.). (*b*) **Hardness of hearing,** dureté d'oreille. **4.** Sévérité *f,* rigueur *f,* dureté.

hardship ['hɑːrdʃip], *s.* Privation *f,* fatigue *f;* (dure) épreuve. *He has suffered great hardships,* il en a vu de dures.

hardware ['hɑːrdwɛər], *s.* Quincaillerie *f.* **Builders' hardware,** serrurerie *f* de bâtiments.

hardwareman, *pl.* **-men** ['hɑːrdwɛərmən, -men], *s.m.* Quincaillier.

hardwood ['hɑːrdwud], *s.* Bois dur.

hardy ['hɑːrdi], *a.* **I.** Hardi; audacieux, intrépide. **2.** (*a*) Robuste; endurci (à la fatigue). (*b*) *Bot:* Rustique, vivace; (plante) de pleine terre. **Hardy annual,** plante annuelle de pleine terre. **-ily,** *adv.* **I.** Hardiment, audacieusement. **2.** Vigoureusement.

hare¹ ['hɛər], *s.* **I.** Lièvre *m.* **Buck-hare,** bouquin *m.* **Doe-hare,** hase *f. Cu:* Jugged hare, civet *m* de lièvre. *F:* **To run with the hare and hunt with the hounds,** ménager la chèvre et le chou. **First catch your hare,** assurez-vous d'abord de l'essentiel. **2. Belgian hare,** léporide *m.* **'harebrained,** *a.* Écervelé, étourdi; (projet) insensé. Hare-brained fellow, (grand) braque; tocard *m;* cerveau brûlé. **'hare-lip,** *s.* Bec-de-lièvre *m.* **'hare-lipped,** *a.* A bec-de-lièvre.

hare², *v.i. F:* To h. back home, regagner la maison à toutes jambes. **To hare off,** se sauver à toutes jambes.

harebell ['hɛərbel], *s. Bot:* (*a*) Jacinthe *f* des prés. (*b*) Clochette *f.*

harem ['hɛərəm], *s.* Harem *m.*

haricot ['harikou], *s.* **I.** *Cu:* Haricot mutton, haricot *m* de mouton. **2.** *Bot:* Haricot (**bean**), haricot blanc.

hark [hɑːrk], *v.i.* **I.** **To hark to a sound,** prêter l'oreille à, écouter, un son. Hark! écoutez! **2.** *Ven:* Hark away! taïaut! *F:* (*Of pers.*) **To hark back to sth.,** en revenir à un sujet. He's always harking back to that, il y revient toujours.

harlequin ['hɑːrlikwin], *s. Th:* Arlequin *m.* Harlequin coat, habit bigarré ou mi-parti.

harlequinade [hɑːrlikwi'neid], *s.* Arlequinade *f.*

harlot ['hɑːrlət], *s.* Prostituée *f.*

harm¹ [hɑːrm], *s.* Mal *m,* tort *m.* **To do s.o. harm,** faire du tort à qn; nuire à qn. **To see no harm in sth.,** ne pas voir de mal, de malice, à qch. **You will come to harm,** il vous arrivera malheur. **Out of harm's way,** à l'abri du danger; en sûreté, en lieu sûr. **It will do more harm than good,** cela fera plus de mal que de bien. *That won't do any h.,* cela ne gâte rien; cela ne nuira en rien. **There's no harm in saying so,** il n'y a pas de mal à le dire. *S.a.* MEAN⁴ I.

harm². **I.** *v.tr.* Faire du mal, du tort, à (qn); nuire à (qn); léser (les intérêts de qn). **2.** *v.i. He will not h. for a little privation,* un peu de privation ne lui fera pas de mal.

harmful ['hɑːrmful], *a.* Malfaisant, pernicieux; nocif, nuisible (*to,* à).

harmfulness ['hɑːrmfulnəs], *s.* Nocivité *f.*

harmless ['hɑːrmləs], *a.* (Animal) inoffensif, pas méchant; (homme) sans malice; (passe-temps) innocent. **Harmless talk,** conversation anodine. **-ly,** *adv.* Sans (faire de) mal; (s'amuser) innocemment.

harmlessness ['hɑːrmləsnəs], *s.* Innocuité *f.*

harmonic [hɑːr'mɔnik]. **I.** *a.* Harmonique. **2.** *s.* Harmonique *m.* **-ally,** *adv.* Harmoniquement.

harmonious [hɑːr'mounjəs], *a.* Harmonieux. **I.** En bon accord. **2.** Mélodieux. **-ly,** *adv.* Harmonieusement; (vivre) en harmonie, en bon accord.

harmonist ['hɑːrmonist], *s.* Harmoniste *mf.*

harmonium [hɑːr'mounjəm], *s.* Harmonium *m.*

harmonize ['hɑːrmonaiz]. **I.** *v.tr.* (*a*) Harmoniser (des idées); concilier, faire accorder (des textes); allier (des couleurs). (*b*) *Mus:* Harmoniser (une mélodie). **2.** *v.i.* (*Of colours, etc.*) S'harmoniser, s'allier, s'assortir; (*of facts, pers.*) s'accorder. **To harmonize with sth.,** s'adapter harmonieusement à qch.; s'accorder, se marier, avec qch.

harmony ['hɑːrmoni], *s.* **I.** *Mus:* Harmonie *f.* **2.** Harmonie, accord *m. Colours in perfect h.,* assortiment parfait de couleurs. **To live in perfect harmony,** vivre en parfaite intelligence. **In harmony with . . .,** en rapport, en accord, avec. . . . *His tastes are in h. with mine,* ses goûts sont conformes aux miens.

harness¹ ['hɑːrnəs], *s.* **I.** Harnais *m,* harnachement *m. F:* **To get back into harness,** reprendre le collier. **To die in harness,** mourir à la besogne, à la peine. **To be out of harness,** être à la retraite. **2.** *Av:* Ignition harness, rampe *f* d'allumage. **'harness-maker,** *s.* Bourrelier *m.* **'harness-room,** *s.* Sellerie *f.*

harness², *v.tr.* **I.** Harnacher (un cheval). **To harness a horse to a carriage,** atteler un cheval à une voiture. **2.** Aménager (une chute d'eau); mettre (une chute d'eau) en valeur.

harp¹ [hɑːrp], *s. Mus:* Harpe *f.* **To play the harp,** pincer, jouer, de la harpe.

harp², *v.i.* Jouer de la harpe. *F:* **To be always harping on the same string,** rabâcher toujours la même chose; réciter toujours la même litanie. *He is always harping on that,* c'est toujours la même ritournelle.

harpings ['hɑːrpiŋz], *s.pl. N.Arch:* Lisses *f* de l'avant.

harpist ['hɑːrpist], *s. Mus:* Harpiste *mf.*

harpoon¹ [hɑːr'puːn], *s.* Harpon *m.*

harpoon², *v.tr.* Harponner.

harpooner [hɑːr'puːnər], *s.* Harponneur *m.*

harpsichord ['hɑːrpsikɔːrd], *s. Mus:* Clavecin *m.*

harpy ['hɑːrpi], *s.f. Myth:* Harpie. *F:* **Old**

harpy, vieille mégère, vieille harpie. **'harpy-eagle**, s. *Orn:* Harpie f.
harquebus ['hɑːrkwibəs], s. *A:* Arquebuse f.
harridan ['haridən], s.f. *F:* Vieille mégère; vieille chipie.
harrier[1] ['hariər], s. *Orn:* Busard m.
harrier[2], s. *Sp:* (Pers.) Harrier m, coureur m.
harrow[1] ['haro], s. *Agr:* Herse f. *F:* To be under the harrow, subir des tribulations, de dures épreuves.
harrow[2], v.tr. *Agr:* Herser (un terrain). *F:* To harrow s.o., s.o.'s feelings, agir sur la sensibilité de qn; déchirer le cœur à qn. **harrowing**, a. *F:* (Conte, etc.) poignant, navrant; (cri) déchirant.
Harry[1] ['hari]. *Pr.n.m.* **1.** Henri. **2.** *F:* Old Harry, le diable. *The climate has played old H. with his health*, le climat lui a détraqué la santé.
harry[2], v.tr. **1.** Dévaster, mettre à sac (un pays). **2.** Harceler (qn). To harry the enemy, ne laisser à l'ennemi aucun répit.
harsh [hɑːrʃ], a. **1.** Dur, rêche, rude (au toucher); âpre (au goût); aigre, strident (à l'oreille). Harsh voice, voix rude, rauque, éraillée. *H. style*, style dur. **2.** (Caractère) dur, bourru; (maître, réponse) rude. *To exchange h. words*, échanger des propos durs. **-ly**, adv. (Répondre, etc.) avec dureté, avec rudesse, d'un ton bourru; (traiter qn) sévèrement, avec rigueur.
harshness ['hɑːrʃnəs], s. **1.** Dureté f, rudesse f (au toucher); âpreté f (du vin); aigreur f (d'un son); aspérité f (du style, de la voix). **2.** Sévérité f, rudesse f (d'une punition); rigueur f (du destin).
hart [hɑːrt], s. *Cerf m.* Hart of ten, cerf dix cors.
'hart's-tongue, s. *Bot:* Langue-de-cerf f.
harum-scarum ['heərəm'skeərəm], a. & s. *F:* Étourdi, écervelé. *He is a h.-s.*, il a le cerveau brûlé. *She's a h.-s.*, c'est une évaporée.
harvest[1] ['hɑːrvest], s. **1.** Moisson f (du blé); récolte f (des fruits); fenaison f (du foin); vendange f (du vin). To get in, win, the harvest, faire la moisson. **2.** (Époque f de) la moisson. **'harvest-bug, -mite**, s. *Arach:* Lepte automnal; *F:* aoûtat m, rouget m. **'harvest-home**, s. (i) Fin f de la moisson; (ii) fête f de la moisson. **'harvest-spider**, s. *Arach:* Faucheur m, faucheux m.
harvest[2], v.tr. Moissonner (les blés); récolter (les fruits). *Abs.* Rentrer, faire, la moisson; faire les blés.
harvester ['hɑːrvestər], s. **1.** (Pers.) Moissonneur, -euse. **2.** (Machine) Moissonneuse f; esp. moissonneuse-lieuse. **3.** = HARVEST-BUG.
has [haz]. *See* HAVE[2].
has-been ['hazbiːn], s. *F:* Homme m vieux jeu; vieux ramolli. *His car's a good old has-been*, son tacot n'est plus de la première jeunesse.
hash[1] [haʃ], s. **1.** *Cu:* Hachis m. **2.** *F:* To make a hash of sth., gâcher un travail; faire un beau gâchis de qch. *To make a h. of it*, bousiller l'affaire. *P:* To settle s.o.'s hash, (i) régler son compte à qn; faire son affaire à qn; (ii) rabattre le caquet à qn. **3.** *F:* Hash-up, réchauffé m, ripopée f (de vieux contes, etc.).
hash[2], v.tr. To hash (up) meat, hacher la viande.
hasheesh, hashish ['haʃiːʃ], s. Hachisch m.
hasp [hɑːsp], s. **1.** (Staple-)hasp (for padlocking), moraillon m. **2.** (a) Loquet m (de porte). (b) Espagnolette f (de porte-fenêtre). (c) Fermoir m, agrafe f (d'album, etc.).
hassock ['hasək], s. Agenouilloir m; carreau m, coussin m (pour les genoux ou les pieds).
hastate ['hasteit], a. *Bot:* Hasté.
haste [heist], s. Hâte f, diligence f. To do sth.

in haste, (i) faire qch. à la hâte, en hâte; (ii) faire qch. à l'étourdie. *I am in h. to leave*, j'ai hâte de partir. In hot haste, en toute hâte. To make haste, se hâter, se dépêcher. Make haste! dépêchez-vous! More haste less speed, hâtez-vous lentement.
hasten [heisn]. **1.** v.tr. (a) Accélérer, hâter, presser (le pas, etc.); avancer (le départ de qn). *This action hastened his fall*, cette action précipita sa chute. (b) Activer (une réaction). **2.** v.i. Se hâter, se dépêcher, se presser (to do sth., de faire qch.). *We h. to assure you that . . .*, nous nous empressons de vous assurer que . . . *To h. downstairs*, se hâter de descendre. **hasten away**, v.i. Partir à la hâte. **hasten back**, v.i. Revenir en toute hâte. **hasten out**, v.i. Sortir à la hâte; se hâter de sortir.
hastiness ['heistinəs], s. **1.** Précipitation f, hâte f. **2.** (Of temper) Emportement m, vivacité f.
hasty ['heisti], a. **1.** (Départ) précipité; (croquis) fait à la hâte; (repas) sommaire. *Let us not be over-h.*, ne précipitons rien. **2.** (Aveu) irréfléchi. **3.** Emporté, vif. To be hasty-tempered, être d'humeur prompte. **4.** (Of growth) Rapide. **-ily**, adv. **1.** A la hâte; précipitamment. **2.** (Parler) sans réfléchir; (juger) à la légère.
hat [hat], s. Chapeau m. Top hat, silk hat, chapeau haut de forme. Soft felt hat, chapeau mou. Paper hat, coiffure f de cotillon. To raise one's hat to s.o., saluer qn (d'un coup de chapeau); donner à qn un coup de chapeau. Hat in hand, chapeau bas. To put on one's hat, mettre son chapeau; (of man) se couvrir. To take off one's hat, enlever son chapeau; (of man) se découvrir. *F:* To take off one's hat to s.o., reconnaître la supériorité de qn. *F:* To send, pass, the hat round on s.o.'s behalf, faire la quête au profit de qn. *P:* My hat! (i) pas possible! (ii) pigez-moi ça! *Keep it under your hat*, n'en dites pas un mot. *S.a.* TALK[2] I. **1.** **'hat-block**, s. Forme f à chapeaux. **'hat-box**, s. (i) Carton m à chapeaux (de modiste). (ii) Boîte f, étui m, à chapeau (de voyage). **'hat-peg**, s. Patère f. **'hat-pin**, s. Épingle f à chapeau. **'hat-shop**, s. **1.** (For men) Chapellerie f. **2.** (For women) Boutique f de modiste. *At the hat-shop*, chez la modiste. **'hat-stand**, s. Porte-chapeaux m inv. **'hat trick**, s. *Cr:* Mise f hors jeu de trois batteurs avec trois balles de suite.
hatband ['hatband], s. Ruban m de chapeau. Mourning hatband, crêpe m.
hatch[1] [hatʃ], s. **1.** *Nau:* (a) Hatch(way), descente f, écoutille f. (b) Hatch(-cover), panneau m de descente. Under hatches, dans la cale. *To close down the h.*, fermer le panneau. To (cover and) secure the hatches, condamner les descentes. **2.** Service hatch, buttery hatch, passe-plats m inv; guichet m de dépense.
hatch[2], s. *Husb:* **1.** Éclosion f (d'un œuf). **2.** Couvée f.
hatch[3]. **1.** v.tr. (a) Faire éclore (des poussins). To hatch out eggs, incuber, (faire) couver, des œufs. *F:* To hatch a plot, ourdir, tramer, couver, un complot. (b) *Pisc:* Incuber (les œufs). **2.** v.i. To hatch (out), (of chicks or eggs) éclore. *A plot is hatching*, il se trame quelque chose. *S.a.* CHICKEN I. **hatching**[1], s. **1.** (a) Éclosion f (d'une couvée); *Pisc:* incubation f (des œufs). (b) Machination f (d'un complot). **2.** Couvée f.
hatch[4], v.tr. *Engr:* Mapm: Hacher, hachurer. **hatching**[2], s. **1.** *Engr:* Mapm: Hachure f. **2.** Mapm: Liséré m (en couleur).
hatchet ['hatʃet], s. Hachette f, cognée f; hache f

à main. *F:* To bury the hatchet, enterrer la hache de guerre; faire la paix. **'hatchet-faced,** *a.* Au visage en lame de couteau.

hatchment ['hatʃmənt], *s. Her:* Écusson *m* funéraire.

hate[1] [heit], *s. Lit:* = HATRED.

hate[2], *v.tr.* **1.** Haïr, détester, exécrer; avoir (qn) en haine, en horreur. To hate s.o. like poison, like the plague, haïr qn comme la peste. **2.** To hate to do sth., détester (de) faire qch. *She hates to be contradicted,* elle ne peut pas souffrir qu'on la contredise. *I should hate to be late,* cela m'ennuierait fort d'être en retard. *I h. his going so far away,* cela me chagrine qu'il s'en aille si loin.

hateful ['heitful], *a.* Odieux, détestable.

hath [haθ]. *See* HAVE[2].

hatless ['hatləs], *a.* Sans chapeau, tête nue; (femme) en cheveux.

hatred ['heitred], *s.* Haine *f* (*of,* de, contre). To incur s.o.'s hatred, s'attirer la haine de qn. Out of hatred of sth., en haine de qch.

hatter ['hatər], *s.* Chapelier *m.*

hauberk ['hɔ:bə:rk], *s. Archeol:* Haubert *m.*

haughtiness ['hɔ:tinəs], *s.* Hauteur *f,* morgue *f.*

haughty ['hɔ:ti], *a.* Hautain, altier, sourcilleux. **-ily,** *adv.* Hautainement; avec hauteur.

haul[1] [hɔ:l], *s.* **1.** Amenée *f;* effort *m* (pour haler ou amener qch.). **2.** *Fish:* (*a*) At one haul (of the net), d'un seul coup de filet. (*b*) Prise *f,* pêche *f.* To make, get, a good haul, ramener un fameux coup de filet.

haul[2]. **1.** *v.tr.* (*a*) Tirer; traîner (une charge); remorquer (un bateau, un train). *Min:* To haul coal, rouler le charbon; hercher. (*b*) *Nau:* To haul the wind, serrer le vent (de près). **2.** *v.i. Nau:* (*a*) To haul on a rope, haler sur une manœuvre. (*b*) To haul upon the wind, haler le vent; se haler dans le vent. **haul down,** *v.tr. Nau:* Haler bas, rentrer, affaler (les voiles, etc.); rentrer (un pavillon); amener (un signal). **haul in,** *v.tr. Nau:* Haler, rentrer (une manœuvre). **haul up,** *v.tr. Nau:* Hisser (un pavillon). *To h. up a boat,* (*aboard ship*) rentrer une embarcation; (*on the beach*) haler une embarcation à sec.

hauling, *s.* (*a*) Traction *f; Min:* herchage *m.* (*b*) *Nau:* Halage *m.*

haulage ['hɔ:ledʒ], *s.* **1.** (*a*) (Transport *m* par) roulage *m,* charriage *m,* camionnage *m.* Haulage contractor, entrepreneur *m* de transports. (*b*) Traction *f,* remorquage *m,* halage *m. Min:* Herchage *m.* Man haulage, traction à bras. *Min:* Haulage man, rouleur *m,* hercheur *m.* **2.** Frais *mpl* de roulage, de transport.

haulier ['hɔ:liər], *s.m.* **1.** Camionneur. **2.** *Min:* Hercheur, rouleur.

haulm [hɔ:m, hɑ:m], *s. Bot:* **1.** Fane '*f* (de légume). **2.** *Coll.* Fanes; chaume *m.*

haunch [hɔ:nʃ, hɑ:nʃ], *s.* (*a*) *Anat:* Hanche *f.* (*b*) *Cu:* Cuissot *m,* quartier *m* (de chevreuil). (*c*) *pl.* Haunches, arrière-train *m.* Dog sitting on his haunches, chien assis sur son derrière.

haunt[1] [hɔ:nt], *s.* Lieu fréquenté (par qn, un animal); repaire *m* (de bêtes féroces, de voleurs). An evil haunt, un mauvais lieu.

haunt[2], *v.tr.* (*a*) (*Of pers., animal*) Fréquenter, hanter (un endroit). (*b*) (*Of ghost*) Hanter (une maison). **This place is haunted,** il y a des revenants ici. (*c*) (*Of thoughts*) Obséder, poursuivre (qn); troubler, hanter (l'esprit). **Haunted by memories,** assiégé, obsédé, par des souvenirs.

haunting, *a.* (Mélodie, etc.) qui vous hante, qui vous trotte dans la mémoire; (doute) obsédant.

Havana [ha'vana]. **1.** *Pr.n.* La Havane. **2.** *s.* A Havana (cigar), un havane; un londrès.

have[1] [hav], *s. P:* (*a*) (*Swindle*) Attrape *f;* escroquerie *f.* (*b*) (*Joke*) Attrape.

have[2], *v.tr.* (*pr.ind.* have, hast, has, *A. & B:* hath, *pl.* have; *pr. sub.* have; *past ind. & sub.* had, hadst; *pr.p.* having; *p.p.* had) **1.** (*a*) Avoir, posséder. *He had no friends,* il n'avait pas d'amis. All I have, tout ce que je possède, tout mon avoir. *He has a shop,* il tient une boutique. *My bag has no name on it,* ma valise ne porte pas de nom. *Have you any apples?* If you have . . ., avez-vous des pommes? Si vous en avez, . . . I have no words to express . . ., les mots me manquent pour exprimer. . . . I have no Latin, j'ignore le latin. I have it! j'y suis! (*b*) We don't have many visitors, nous ne recevons pas beaucoup de visites. **2.** To have a child, avoir un enfant. *Our cat has had kittens,* notre chatte a fait des petits. **3.** (*a*) *There was no work to be had,* on ne pouvait pas obtenir, se procurer, de travail. It is to be had at the chemist's, cela se trouve chez le pharmacien. (*b*) To have news from s.o., recevoir des nouvelles de qn. *I h. it on good authority that . . .,* je tiens de bonne source que. . . . (*c*) *I must h. them by to-morrow,* il me les faut pour demain. *I will let you h. it for £5,* je vous le céderai pour cinq livres. *Let me h. the money to-morrow,* envoyez-moi l'argent demain. Let me have your keys, donnez-moi, laissez-moi, vos clefs. *Let me h. an early reply,* répondez-moi sans retard. **4.** To have tea with s.o., prendre le thé avec qn. *Will you h. tea?* voulez-vous du thé? *What will you h., sir?—I'll h. a chop,* que prendra monsieur?—Donnez-moi une côtelette. *He is having his dinner,* il est en train de dîner. *I had some more,* j'en ai repris. To have a cigar, fumer un cigare. *P: I'm not having any!* on ne me la fait pas! ça ne prend pas! **5.** (*In verbal phrases; e.g.*) (*a*) To have measles, avoir la rougeole. To have an idea, avoir une idée. To have a right to sth., avoir droit à qch. (*b*) To have a dream, faire un rêve. To have a game, faire une partie. (*c*) To have a lesson, prendre une leçon. To have a bath, a shower-bath, prendre un bain, une douche. (*d*) To have a pleasant evening, passer une soirée agréable. I didn't have any trouble at all, cela ne m'a donné, ne m'a coûté, aucune peine. We had a rather strange adventure, il nous est arrivé une aventure assez étrange. *The only thing I ever had happen to me was . . .,* la seule chose qui me soit jamais arrivée, c'est. . . . **6.** (*a*) He 'will have it that Hamlet is mad, il soutient que Hamlet est fou. *Rumour has it that . . .,* le bruit court que. . . . (*b*) As Plato has it, comme dit Platon. (*c*) He will not have it that she is delicate, il n'admet pas qu'elle soit de santé délicate. **7.** (*a*) To have s.o. in one's power, avoir qn en son pouvoir. *He had me by the throat,* il me tenait à la gorge. (*b*) You have me there! voilà où vous me prenez en défaut! (*c*) *F:* (*Outwit*) Avoir, attraper (qn); mettre (qn) dedans. You been had! on vous a eu! vous avez été refait! I'm not to be had, on ne me la fait pas; ça ne prend pas. **8.** (*a*) (*Causative*) To have sth. done, faire faire qch. To have s.o. do sth., faire faire qch. à qn. *To h. one's hair cut,* se faire couper les cheveux. *H. it repaired,* faites-le réparer. He 'would have me come in, il a voulu à toute force me faire entrer. (*b*) He had his leg broken, il s'est cassé la jambe. *I had my watch stolen,* je me suis fait, laissé, voler ma montre. (*c*) I shall have everything ready, je veillerai à ce que tout soit prêt.

9. Will have. (a) **Which one will you have?** lequel voulez-vous? **She won't have him,** elle ne veut pas de lui. *What more would you h.?* que vous faut-il de plus? **As ill-luck would have it** *he arrived too late,* la malchance voulut qu'il arrivât trop tard. (b) **What would you have me do?** que voulez-vous que je fasse? *I would h. you know that . . .,* sachez que. . . . (c) **I will not have such conduct,** je ne supporterai pas une pareille conduite. *I won't h. him teased,* je ne veux pas qu'on le taquine. **10.** (a) **To have to do sth.,** devoir faire qch.; être obligé, forcé, de faire qch. *We shall h. to walk faster,* il nous faudra marcher plus vite. **I don't have to work,** moi je n'ai pas besoin de travailler. (b) *My shirt will h. to be ironed,* il va falloir me repasser ma chemise. **11.** (*Aux. use*) (a) **To have been, to have given,** avoir été, avoir donné. **To have come, to have hurt oneself,** être venu, s'être blessé. **When I had dined, I went out,** (i) quand j'avais dîné, je sortais; (ii) quand j'eus dîné, je sortis; (iii) quand j'ai eu dîné, je suis sorti. **I have lived in London for three years,** voilà trois ans que j'habite Londres. (*Emphatic*) *Well, you 'have grown!* ce que tu as grandi! (b) *You h. forgotten your gloves.*—So I have! vous avez oublié vos gants.—En effet! Tiens, c'est vrai! *You haven't swept the room.*—I have! vous n'avez pas balayé la chambre.—Si! Mais si! Si fait! *You h. been in prison before.*—I haven't! vous avez déjà fait de la prison.—C'est faux! **12.** (*Past sub.*) **I had better say nothing,** je ferai mieux de ne rien dire. **I had as soon, as lief, stay here,** j'aimerais autant rester ici. *I had much rather start at once,* j'aimerais bien mieux partir tout de suite. **have in,** *v.tr.* **To have s.o. in to dinner,** (i) inviter qn à dîner; (ii) avoir qn à dîner. *I had them in for a cup of tea,* je les ai fait entrer pour prendre une tasse de thé. *F:* **I had the doctor in,** j'ai fait venir le médecin. **have on,** *v.tr. See* ON II. **have out,** *v.tr.* **1. To have a tooth out,** se faire arracher une dent. **2.** *F:* **To have it out with s.o.,** vider une querelle avec qn; s'expliquer avec qn. **have up,** *v.tr. F:* (a) Citer, poursuivre, (qn) en justice. (b) (*Of magistrate*) Sommer (qn) de comparaître. **To be had up for an offence,** être cité devant les tribunaux pour un délit.

haven [heivn], *s.* (a) Havre *m*, port *m*. (b) *F:* Abri *m*, asile *m*. **Haven of refuge,** port de salut.

haversack ['havərsak], *s.* **1.** *Mil:* Musette *f.* **2.** Havresac *m* (de tourisme).

havoc ['havək], *s.* Ravage *m*, dégâts *mpl. The frosts have wrought havoc in, made havoc of, played havoc among, the vineyards,* les gelées ont fait de grands dégâts, des ravages, dans les vignobles.

haw[1] [hɔː], *s. Bot:* (a) Cenelle *f.* (b) = HAWTHORN.

haw[2], *v.i. See* HUM[2] 1.

Hawaiian [hɑːˈwaiiən], *a. & s.* Hawaïen, -ienne.

hawfinch ['hɔːfinʃ], *s. Orn:* Gros-bec *m.*

haw-haw[1] ['hɔːˈhɔː], *s.* **1.** Rire bruyant; gros rire. **2.** Prononciation affectée.

haw-haw[2], *v.i.* Rire bruyamment, bêtement.

hawk[1] [hɔːk], *s.* **1.** *Orn:* Faucon *m. F:* **To have eyes like a hawk,** avoir des yeux d'aigle. **2.** *F:* (*Of pers.*) Vautour *m*; homme *m* rapace. **'hawk-eyed,** *a.* Au regard d'aigle; qui a la vue perçante. **'hawk-moth,** *s. Ent:* Sphinx *m*; smérinthe *m.* **'hawk-nosed,** *a.* Au nez aquilin.

hawk[2], *v.i.* Chasser au faucon. **hawking**[1], *s.* Chasse *f* au faucon; faucon.nerie *f.* **To go hawking,** faire la chasse au faucon.

hawk[3], *s. F:* Graillement *m.*

hawk[4], *v.i. & tr. F:* Graillonner. **To hawk up phlegm,** expectorer des mucosités.

hawk[5], *v.tr.* Colporter, cameloter (des mar'chandises). **hawking**[2], *s.* Colportage *m.*

hawker ['hɔːkər], *s.* (a) Colporteur *m*, marchand ambulant, camelot *m.* (b) (*Of fruit, vegetables*) Marchand des quatre saisons.

hawkweed ['hɔːkwiːd], *s. Bot:* Épervière *f.*

hawse [hɔːz], *s.inv. Nau:* **1.** (a) *A:* = HAWSEHOLE. (b) *pl.* **The hawse,** les écubiers *m.* **2.** (a) Affourchage *m*, évitage *m.* (b) **Clear, open, hawse,** chaînes claires. **'hawse-hole,** *s.* Écubier *m.* **'hawse-pipe,** *s.* Manchon *m* d'écubier.

hawser ['hɔːzər, -s-], *s. Nau:* (a) Haussière *f*, aussière *f*, grelin *m.* (b) Amarre *f.* (c) Câble *m* de remorque.

hawthorn ['hɔːθɔːrn], *s.* Aubépine *f.*

hay[1] [hei], *s.* Foin *m.* **To make hay,** faire les foins; faner. *Prov:* **To make hay while the sun shines,** battre le fer pendant qu'il est chaud. *F:* **To make hay of sth.,** embrouiller qch.; démolir (un argument). **'hay-fever,** *s. Med:* Fièvre *f* des foins. **'hay-fork,** *s.* Fourche *f* à foin. **'hay-harvest,** *s.* Fenaison *f.* **'hayrack,** *s.* **1.** Râtelier *m* d'écurie. **2.** (*On cart*) Fausse ridelle. **'hay-seed,** *s.* **1.** Graine *f* de foin. **2.** *U.S: F:* Paysan *m*, rustaud *m.*

hay[2], *v.i.* Faire les foins. **haying,** *s.* Fenaison *f.*

haycock ['heikɔk], *s.* Meulette *f* de foin.

hayloft ['heilɔft], *s.* Fenil *m*; grenier *m* ou grange *f* à foin.

haymaker ['heimeikər], *s.* **1.** Faneur, -euse. **2.** (*Machine*) Faneuse *f*, tourne-foin *m inv.*

haymaking ['heimeikiŋ], *s.* Fenaison *f.*

hayrick ['heirik], **haystack** ['heistak], *s.* Meule *f* de foin.

hazard[1] ['hazərd], *s.* **1.** (a) Hasard *m.* **Game of hazard,** jeu de hasard. (b) Risque *m*, péril *m.* **At all hazards,** quoi qu'il en coûte. **2.** *Bill:* Coup *m* qui fait entrer une des billes dans la blouse. **To play a winning hazard,** blouser la bille sur laquelle on vise. **To play a losing hazard,** se blouser. **3.** *Golf:* Accident *m* de terrain.

hazard[2], *v.tr.* Hasarder, risquer, aventurer (sa vie, sa fortune); hasarder (une opinion).

hazardous ['hazərdəs], *a.* Hasardeux, chanceux, hasardé, risqué, périlleux.

haze [heiz], *s.* (a) Brume légère. (b) *F:* Obscurité *f*, incertitude *f* (de l'esprit).

hazel ['heizl], *s.* (a) Hazel(-tree), noisetier *m*, coudrier *m.* **Hazel-grove, -wood,** coudraie *f.* **Hazel eyes,** yeux couleur (de) noisette. **'hazel-nut,** *s.* Noisette *f.*

haziness ['heizinəs], *s.* État brumeux, nébuleux (du temps, de l'esprit). *The h. of his knowledge,* le vague, l'imprécision *f*, de son savoir.

hazy ['heizi], *a.* **1.** (*Of weather*) Brumeux, embrumé, gris. **2.** (a) (Contour, etc.) flou, estompé. (b) *F:* (*Of ideas*) Nébuleux, fumeux, vague. **-ily,** *adv.* Vaguement, indistinctement.

he [hi, hiː], *pers.pron.nom.m.* **1.** (*Unstressed*) Il. (a) *What did he say?* qu'a-t-il dit? (b) *Here he comes,* le voici qui vient. *He is an honest man,* c'est un honnête homme. **2.** (*Stressed*) (a) Lui. *He and I,* lui et moi. *I am as tall as he,* je suis aussi grand que lui. *It is he,* c'est lui. (*Emphatic*) *He knows nothing about it,* il n'en sait rien, lui; lui n'en sait rien. (b) (*Antecedent to a rel. pron.*) (i) Celui. **He that, he who, believes,** celui qui croit. (ii) **It is he who said so,** c'est lui qui l'a dit. **3.** (*As substantive*) Mâle. *Attrib:* He-bear, ours mâle. **He-goat,** bouc. **'he-man,** *pl.* -men, *s.m. U.S: F:* Homme dominateur, homme viril.

head[1] [hed], s. **1.** Tête *f.* (*a*) From head to foot, de la tête aux pieds, des pieds à la tête ; (armé) de pied en cap. **To walk with one's head (high) in the air**, marcher le front haut. **To sell a house over s.o.'s head**, vendre une maison sans donner au locataire l'occasion de l'acheter. **He gives orders over my head**, il donne des ordres sans me consulter. **Head down**, la tête baissée. **Head downwards**, la tête en bas. **Head first**, **head foremost**, la tête la première. **To stand on one's head**, se tenir sur sa tête. **To go, turn, head over heels**, faire la culbute. **To fall head over heels in love with s.o.**, devenir éperdument amoureux de qn. *He is taller than his brother by a h.*, il dépasse son frère de la tête. *Turf:* (*Of horse*) **To win by a head**, gagner d'une tête. **To win by a short head**, gagner de justesse. **To give a horse its head**, lâcher la bride, donner carrière, à un cheval. **His guilt be on his own head**, puisse son crime retomber sur lui. **To strike off s.o.'s head**, décapiter qn. *F:* **To talk s.o.'s head off**, étourdir qn ; rompre les oreilles à qn. **A fine head of hair**, une belle chevelure. (*b*) (*Pers.*) **Crowned head**, tête couronnée. (*c*) *Cu:* **Sheep's head**, tête de mouton. **Boar's head**, hure *f* de sanglier. **Potted head**, fromage *m* de tête, de hure. (*d*) *Ven:* (*Antlers*) Bois *m*, tête (de cerf). **2.** (*a*) (*Intellect, mind*) **He has a good head on his shoulders**, his head is screwed on the right way, c'est une forte tête, un homme de tête, de bon sens. **To have a good head for business**, avoir l'entente des affaires ; s'entendre aux affaires. **Idea running through my head**, idée qui me trotte dans la cervelle. **To reckon in one's head**, calculer de tête. **To get sth. into one's head**, se mettre qch. dans la tête, en tête, dans l'esprit. *I can't get that into his h.*, je ne peux pas lui enfoncer ça dans la tête, dans la cervelle. *He has got, taken, it into his h. that . . .*, il s'est mis dans la tête que. . . . **To take it into one's head to do sth.**, s'aviser, se mettre en tête, de faire qch. *It never entered my h. that . . .*, il ne me vint pas à l'idée, à l'esprit, que. . . . **What put that into your head?** où avez-vous pris cette idée-là ? **To put ideas into s.o.'s head**, donner des idées à qn. **His name has gone out of my head**, son nom m'est sorti de la mémoire. **We laid, put, our heads together**, nous avons conféré ensemble ; nous nous sommes concertés. *Prov:* **Two heads are better than one**, deux conseils, deux avis, valent mieux qu'un. *He gave an answer out of his own head*, il a donné une réponse de son cru. (*Of speech, etc.*) **To be over the heads of the audience**, dépasser l'entendement de l'auditoire. **To keep one's head**, conserver sa tête. **To lose one's head**, perdre la tête. **He is off his head**, il est timbré, il déménage ; il n'a plus sa tête à lui. **To go off one's head**, devenir fou. **Weak in the head**, faible d'esprit. (*b*) *F:* **To have a bad head, to have a head on one**, avoir mal à la tête, un mal de tête. **3.** (*a*) Tête (d'arbre, de fleur, de laitue) ; pomme *f* (de chou) ; pointe *f* (d'asperge) ; pied *m* (de céleri) ; épi *m* (de blé). (*b*) (*Knob-shaped end*) Tête (de violon, d'épingle, de clou) ; pomme (de canne) ; champignon *m* (de rail). (*c*) (*Top section*) Tête (de volcan, etc.) ; haut *m* (de page) ; chapiteau *m* (de colonne). *Nau:* Head of a sail, (i) têtière *f*, (ii) envergure *f*, d'une voile. (*d*) Haut (de l'escalier). (*e*) Tête, culasse *f*, fond *m* (de cylindre) ; chapiteau (d'alambic). *I.C.E:* **Combustion head**, culasse, calotte *f*. **Car with a folding head**, voiture décapotable. (*f*) Chevet *m*, tête (de lit) ; haut bout (de la table) ; source *f* (d'une rivière). *At the h. of the lake*, à l'amont du

lac. (*g*) (*Of abscess*) **To come to a head, to gather to a head**, mûrir, aboutir. *F:* **To bring a matter to a head**, faire aboutir une affaire. **4.** (*Category*) **On this head**, sur ce chapitre, sur ce point, sur cet article. *Under separate heads*, sous des rubriques différentes. *Jur:* Heads of a charge, chefs *m* d'accusation. **5.** (*a*) Nez *m*, avant *m*, cap *m* (de navire, etc.). **Head of a jetty, of a pier**, musoir *m*. **To collide with a ship head on** [hed'ɔn], aborder un navire par l'avant. **To be head to sea, head on to the sea**, présenter l'avant à la lame. **Head on to the wind**, cap au vent. **Ship (down) by the head**, vaisseau sur le nez. **How is her head?** où a-t-on le cap ? où est le cap ? (*b*) = HEADLAND 2. **Beachy Head**, le cap Beachy. **6.** (*a*) (*Front or chief place*) **At the head of a column** (*of troops*), **of a procession**, à la tête d'une colonne, d'un cortège. **To be at the head of the list**, venir en tête de liste. (*b*) (*Pers.*) Chef *m* (de la famille, d'une maison de commerce) ; directeur, -trice (d une école). **Head of a department, departmental head**, chef de service ; (*in stores*) chef de rayon. (*c*) *Attrib.* **Head clerk**, premier commis ; chef de bureau. **H. agent**, agent principal. **H. gardener**, jardinier en chef. **Head office**, bureau central, bureau principal. **7.** (*a*) (*Unit*) Usu. inv. **Six head of cattle**, six têtes, pièces *f*, de bétail. **Thirty h. of deer, of oxen**, trente cerfs, trente bœufs. (*b*) **To pay so much per head, so much a head**, payer tant par tête, par personne. **8.** Head of a coin, face *f*. **To toss heads or tails**, jouer à pile ou face. *F:* **I can't make head or tail of this**, je n'y comprends rien. **9.** *Hyd.E: etc:* Head of water, colonne *f* d'eau ; charge *f* d'eau. **Hydraulic head**, pression *f* en colonne d'eau. *Mch:* Head of steam, volant *m* de vapeur. **To gather head**, (i) (*of flood*) monter ; (*of discontentment*) augmenter, gagner de la force. **'head-dress**, s. **1.** (*Hairdressing*) Coiffure *f.* **2.** = HEAD-GEAR. **'head-gear**, s. Garniture *f* de tête ; coiffure *f* ; chapeau *m.* **'head-hunter**, s. *Anthr:* Chasseur *m* de têtes. **'head-lamp**, **'head-light**, s. Phare *m*, projecteur *m* (d'automobile, de locomotive) ; feu *m* d'avant (de locomotive). *Aut:* Nondazzle, anti-dazzle, head-light, phare-code *m*, *pl.* phares-code. **To dim, dip, the head-lights**, baisser les phares. **'head-line**, s. *Typ:* Ligne *f* de tête ; titre courant. *Journ:* Titre ou soustitre *m* (de rubrique, etc.-'. Sensational head-lines, manchette *f*. **head-'master**, s.m. Directeur (d'une école). (*In Fr.*) Principal (d'un collège) ; proviseur (d'un lycée). **head-'mastership**, s. Directorat *m* ; direction *f.* **head-'mistress**, s.f. Directrice. **'head-on**, a. De front. **Head-on collision**, collision frontale. *Cf.* HEAD[1] 5 (*a*). **'head-phone**, s. *W.Tel:* (*a*) Écouteur *m*, (*b*) *pl.* Head-phones, casque *m* (téléphonique). **'head-piece**, s. **1.** (*Helmet*) Casque *m*. **2.** *Typ:* Vignette *f* ou fleuron *m* de tête. **head-'quarters**, s.pl. **1.** *Mil:* Quartier général ; état-major *m.* **'Head-quarters staff**, état-major du général en chef. **2.** Centre *m*, siège social, bureau principal (d'une administration, d'une banque, etc.). **'head-race**, s. *Hyd.E:* Canal *m* de prise, d'amenée, de dérivation ; bief *m* d'amont (d'un moulin à eau) ; rayère *f* (d'une roue à auges). **'head-rest**, s. Appui-tête *m*, *pl.* appuis-tête ; support *m* de tête. **'head-rope**, s. Longe *f*, attache *f* (de cheval). **'head-splitting**, a. (*Bruit*) qui casse la tête. **H.-s. task**, casse-tête *m* inv. **'head-stall**, s. *Harn:* Têtière *f*, licou *m*, licol *m*. **'head voice**, s. *Mus:* Voix *f* de tête ; (voix de) fausset *m*.

'**head-wind**, *s. Nau:* Vent *m* contraire ; vent debout. '**head-work**, *s.* **1.** Travail *m* de tête ; travail intellectuel. **2.** *Fb:* Jeu *m* de tête. **head²**, *v.tr. & i.* **1.** To head (down) a tree, étêter, écimer, un arbre. **2.** (*Put a head on*) (*a*) Entêter, mettre une tête à (une épingle, un clou, etc.). ⌐(*b*) To head a chapter with certain words, mettre certains mots en tête d'un chapitre. **3.** (*a*) Conduire, mener (un cortège, un parti) ; être à la tête (d'un parti) ; venir en tête (d'un cortège). To head the poll, venir en tête du scrutin. To head the list, (i) s'inscrire en tête de la liste (de souscriptions, etc.) ; (ii) être, venir, en tête de (la) liste ; ouvrir la liste. (*b*) (*Of thg*) Surmonter, couronner, coiffer. **4.** *Fb:* To head the ball, jouer le ballon de la tête ; renvoyer d'un coup de tête. **5.** *v.i.* To head for a place, (i) *Nau:* piquer, gouverner, avoir le cap, mettre le cap, sur un endroit ; (ii) *F:* (s')avancer, se diriger, vers un endroit. The State is heading for ruin, l'État va tout droit vers la ruine, marche à la ruine. **6.** *v.i.* (*Of cabbage, etc.*) Pommer ; (*of grain*) épier. **head off,** *v.tr.* Barrer la route à (qn) ; détourner, intercepter (des fugitifs) ; rabattre (le gibier, l'ennemi) ; couper la retraite à (l'ennemi) ; parer à (une question embarrassante). **headed,** *a.* **1.** Muni (i) d'une tête, (ii) d'un en-tête. **2.** (*a*) Black-headed, aux cheveux noirs, à la chevelure noire ; (oiseau) à tête noire. (*b*) Gold-headed cane, canne à pomme d'or. **heading,** *s.* **1.** Écimage *m* (d'un arbre, d'une branche). **2.** *Fb:* Jeu *m* de tête. **3.** Intitulé *m* (d'un chapitre) ; rubrique *f* (d'un article) ; entête *m*, *pl.* en-têtes. *Book-k:* Poste *m*, rubrique. To come under the heading of . . ., ressortir à. . . .
headache ['hedeik], *s.* Mal *m* de tête, *pl.* maux de tête. Sick headache, migraine *f*. To have a h., avoir mal à la tête.
headband ['hedband], *s.* **1.** Bandeau *m*. **2.** *Bookb:* Tranchefile *f*, comète *f*.
header ['hedər], *s.* **1.** (*a*) To take a header, (i) plonger (dans l'eau) la tête la première ; piquer une tête ; (ii) *F:* tomber (par terre) la tête la première ; piquer une tête ; faire panache. (*b*) *Fb:* Coup *m* de tête. **2.** *Const:* Boutisse *f*.
headiness ['hedinəs], *s.* **1.** Emportement *m*, impétuosité *f*. **2.** Qualité capiteuse (d'un vin).
headland ['hedlənd], *s.* **1.** *Agr:* Tournière *f*, chaintre *m* or *f*. **2.** *Geog:* Cap *m*, promontoire *m*.
headlong ['hedloŋ]. **1.** *adv.* To fall headlong, tomber la tête la première. To rush headlong into the fight, se jeter tête baissée dans la mêlée. **2.** *a.* (*a*) H. fall, chute *f* la tête la première. (*b*) Précipité, irréfléchi, impétueux. Headlong flight, sauve-qui-peut *m inv* ; panique *f*.
headman, *pl.* **-men** ['hedmən, -men], *s.m.* Chef (d'une tribu).
headsman, *pl.* **-men** ['hedzmən, -men], *s.m.* Bourreau.
headstock ['hedstɔk], *s. Mec.E:* Poupée *f* (de tour, de machine-outil).
headstone ['hedstoun], *s.* **1.** Pierre tombale. **2.** *Arch:* (*a*) Clef *f* de voûte. (*b*) Pierre angulaire.
headstrong ['hedstrɔŋ], *a.* Volontaire, têtu, entêté, obstiné.
headway ['hedwei], *s.* **1.** Progrès *m. Nau:* Erre *f* ; marche *f* avant ; sillage *m*. To make headway, avancer ; faire des progrès ; (*of ship*) faire de la route. The enquiry is making no h., l'enquête piétine. *Nau:* To gather, fetch, headway, prendre de l'erre. **2.** *Civ.E:* Hauteur *f* libre, échappée *f* (d'un pont).
heady ['hedi], *a.* **1.** (*Of pers., action*) Impétueux,

emporté. **2.** (*Parfum, vin*) capiteux, entêtant, qui monte au cerveau.
heal [hiːl]. **1.** *v.tr.* Guérir (qn) ; guérir, cicatriser (une blessure). To heal the breach (*between two people*), amener une réconciliation (entre deux personnes). **2.** *v.i.* (*Of wound*) To heal (up), (se) guérir, se cicatriser, se refermer. **healing,** *s.* **1.** Guérison *f*. **2.** Cicatrisation *f* (d'une plaie).
'**heal-all,** *s.* **1.** Panacée *f*. **2.** *Bot:* Valériane *f*.
healer ['hiːlər], *s.* Guérisseur, -euse.
health [helθ], *s.* Santé *f*. **1.** (*a*) To restore s.o. to health, rendre la santé à qn. To regain health, recouvrer la santé. (*b*) To be in good health, être en bonne santé, bien portant ; se bien porter. To be in bad h., se mal porter, être mal portant. Public health, hygiène *f* ; salubrité publique. The Ministry of Health, le Ministère de l'hygiène. The Health Service, le Service de la santé. Medical officer of health, médecin *m* de la santé. Health insurance, assurance *f* maladie. Health certificate, certificat médical. **2.** To drink (to) the health of s.o., to propose s.o.'s health, porter la santé, boire à la santé, de qn.
healthful ['helθful], *a.* (Air) salubre ; (exercice) salutaire.
healthiness ['helθinəs], *s.* Salubrité *f* (d'un endroit, d'un climat).
healthy ['helθi], *a.* **1.** (*a*) (*Of pers.*) Sain ; en bonne santé ; bien portant. (*b*) (*Of climate, food, etc.*) Salubre. To make healthier, assainir (qch.). **2.** H. appetite, appétit robuste. H. criticism, critique vivifiante. **-ily,** *adv.* **1.** Sainement. **2.** Salubrement, salutairement.
heap¹ [hiːp], *s.* (*a*) Tas *m*, monceau *m*, amas *m*, amoncellement *m*. In a heap, en tas. *F:* (*Of pers.*) To fall in a heap, s'affaisser (sur soi-même) ; tomber comme une masse. To be struck all of a heap, en rester abasourdi, stupéfait, tout ébaubi. (*b*) *F:* A heap of people, un tas de gens. She had heaps of children, elle avait une ribambelle d'enfants. Heaps of times, bien des fois ; très souvent. Heaps of time, grandement le temps.
heap², *v.tr.* **1.** (*a*) To heap (up), entasser, amonceler ; amasser. (*b*) To heap praises, insults, on s.o., combler qn d'éloges ; accabler, charger, qn d'injures. **2.** To heap sth. with sth., combler qch. de qch. She heaped my plate with cherries, elle a rempli mon assiette de cerises. Heaped measure, mesure comble.
hear ['hiːər], *v.tr.* (heard [həːrd] ; heard) **1.** Entendre, *A:* ouïr. I h. you, je vous entends. A groan was heard, un gémissement se fit entendre. I heard my name (*mentioned*), j'entendis prononcer mon nom. To h. s.o. speak, entendre parler qn. I could hardly make myself heard, je pouvais à peine me faire entendre. He likes to hear himself talk, il aime à s'entendre parler. To hear sth. said (*or* told) to s.o., entendre dire qch. à qn. To hear s.o. say sth., entendre dire qch. à qn, par qn. I have heard it said, *F:* I have heard tell, that . . ., j'ai entendu dire que. . . . **2.** (*Listen to*) (*a*) Écouter. Hear me out, écoutez-moi, entendez-moi, jusqu'au bout. (*At meetings*) Hear! hear! très bien et très bien ! *Ecc:* To hear mass, assister à la messe. *Jur:* To hear a case, entendre une cause. (*b*) *Sch:* To hear a lesson, écouter une leçon. To hear a child his lesson, faire réciter, faire répéter, sa leçon à un enfant. (*c*) To hear a prayer, exaucer, écouter, une prière. **3.** (*Learn*) To hear a piece of news, apprendre une nouvelle. I have heard that . . ., j'ai appris, on m'a appris, que. . . . **4.** (*a*) To hear from s.o., recevoir des nouvelles, une lettre, de qn. You will h. from me, je vous écrirai.

23

(*As a threat*) You will hear from me later on! vous aurez de mes nouvelles! *Com:* Hoping to hear from you, dans l'attente de vous lire. (*b*) To hear of, about, s.o., avoir des nouvelles de qn, entendre parler de qn. *The explorers were never heard of again*, on n'a plus retrouvé trace des explorateurs. *This is the first I have heard of it*, c'est la première fois que j'en entends parler; en voici la première nouvelle. I never heard of such a thing! a-t-on jamais entendu une chose pareille! c'est inouï! I hear of nothing else, j'en ai les oreilles rebattues. Father won't hear of it, mon père ne veut pas en entendre parler, s'y oppose absolument. **hearing,** *s.* **1.** (*a*) Audition *f* (d'un son). (*b*) Audition, audience *f*. Trial hearing of a singer, audition d'un chanteur. Give me a hearing! veuillez m'entendre! To condemn s.o. without a hearing, condamner qn sans entendre sa défense. (*c*) *Jur:* Hearing of witnesses, audition des témoins. Hearing of the case, (i) l'audience; (ii) l'audition de la cause par le juge (sans jury). **2.** Ouïe *f.* To be quick of hearing, to have a keen sense of hearing, avoir l'oreille, l'ouïe, fine; avoir l'oreille sensible. Within hearing, à portée d'oreille, de la voix. Out of hearing, hors de portée de la voix. It was said in my hearing, on l'a dit devant moi, en ma présence.

hearer ['hiːərər], *s.* Auditeur, -trice. *pl.* Hearers, auditoire *m.*

hearken ['haːrk(ə)n], *v.i.* To hearken to s.o., to sth., écouter qn, qch.; prêter l'oreille à qn, à qch.

hearsay ['hiːərsei], *s.* Ouï-dire *m inv.* I know it, have it, only from hearsay, je ne le sais que par ouï-dire.

hearse [həːrs], *s.* **1.** *Ecc:* (Taper-)hearse, if *m*, herse *f.* **2.** Corbillard *m*; char *m* funèbre.

heart[1] [haːrt], *s.* Cœur *m.* **1.** With beating heart, le cœur battant. To have a weak heart, être cardiaque. *Med:* Heart attack, crise *f* cardiaque. Heart failure, défaillance *f* cardiaque. *F:* have one's heart in one's mouth, avoir un serrement de cœur; être angoissé. To have one's heart in one's boots, avoir une peur bleue; avoir un trac formidable. To press, clasp, s.o. to one's heart, serrer, presser, qn sur son cœur; étreindre qn. To break s.o.'s heart, briser le cœur à qn. He died of a broken heart, il est mort de chagrin; il mourut le cœur brisé. To break one's heart over sth., se ronger le cœur au sujet de qch. **2.** (*a*) Heart of gold, cœur d'or. Heart of steel, cœur de fer; cœur impénétrable. To have a heart of stone, avoir un cœur de roche. His heart is in the right place, il a le cœur bien placé. To wear one's heart on one's sleeve, avoir le cœur sur la main. (*Of thg*) To do one's heart good, réchauffer le cœur. Set your heart at rest, tranquillisez-vous; soyez tranquille. *His h. was full, heavy*, il avait le cœur gros. With a heavy h., le cœur serré, navré. Sight that goes to one's heart, cuts one to the heart, spectacle qui vous fend le cœur; spectacle navrant. *They were cut to the h.*, ils étaient navrés. In my heart of hearts, au plus profond de mon cœur; en mon for intérieur. From the bottom of my heart, de tout mon cœur. At heart *he is not a bad fellow*, au fond ce n'est pas un mauvais garçon. Searchings of the heart, inquiétudes *f* de l'âme. To learn sth. by heart, apprendre qch. par cœur. (*b*) To love s.o. with all one's heart, aimer qn de tout son cœur. To give, lose, one's heart to s.o., donner son cœur à qn; s'éprendre de qn. To win s.o.'s heart, gagner le cœur de qn; faire la conquête de qn. To have s.o.'s welfare at heart, avoir à cœur le

bonheur de qn. To take, lay, sth. to heart, prendre qch. à cœur. (*c*) To have set one's heart on sth., on doing sth., avoir qch. à cœur; avoir, prendre, à cœur de faire qch.; vouloir absolument avoir qch. *The thing he has set his h. on*, la chose qui lui tient au cœur. To one's heart's content, à cœur joie, à souhait. To eat, drink, to one's heart's content, manger, boire, tout son soûl, tout son content. (*d*) To have one's heart in one's work, avoir le cœur à l'ouvrage. With all my heart, du meilleur de mon cœur, de tout mon cœur. With heart and hand, with heart and soul, de cœur et d'âme; de tout cœur. (*e*) To put new heart into s.o.; to put s.o. in good heart, donner du courage, du cœur, à qn; réchauffer le cœur à qn; ragaillardir, encourager, qn. To pluck up, take, heart (of grace), (re)prendre courage. To be of good heart, avoir bon courage. To lose heart, perdre courage; se décourager, se rebuter. Not to find it in one's heart, not to have the heart, to do sth., ne pas avoir le cœur, le courage, de faire qch.; ne pouvoir se décider à faire qch. **3.** Cœur (d'un chou); cœur, vif *m* (d'un arbre). *F:* Heart of oak, homme courageux; cœur de chêne. *H. of a cable*, âme *f*, mèche *f*, d'un câble. The heart of the matter, le vif de l'affaire. In the heart of . . ., au cœur (d'une ville), au (beau) milieu (d'une forêt), au (fin) fond (d'un désert). **4.** *Cards:* Queen of hearts, dame *f* de cœur. Have you any hearts? avez-vous du cœur? 'heart-ache, *s.* Chagrin *m*, peine *f* de cœur, douleur *f.* 'heart-break, *s.* Déchirement *m* de cœur; chagrin poignant. 'heart-breaking, *a.* Navrant. *It was h.-b.*, c'était à fendre l'âme. 'heart-broken, *a.* To be heart-broken, avoir le cœur brisé; être navré. 'heart-disease, *s.* Maladie *f* de cœur. 'heart-failure, *s.* Arrêt *m* du cœur; syncope (mortelle). 'heart-felt, *a.* (Vœu) sincère; qui vient, part, du cœur. *H.-f.* words, paroles bien senties. *To make a h.-f. appeal*, mettre tout son cœur dans son plaidoyer. 'heart-piercing, -rending, *a.* (Soupir, nouvelle) à fendre le cœur, qui fend l'âme; (spectacle) navrant. *H.-r.* cries, cris déchirants. 'heart-searching, **1.** *a.* (Question) qui sonde le cœur. **2.** *s.* Examen *m* de conscience. 'heart's-ease, *s. Bot:* Pensée *f* sauvage. 'heart-shaped, *a.* Cordiforme; en (forme de) cœur. 'heart-sick, *a.* Écœuré. To be, feel, h.-s., être, se sentir, découragé; avoir la mort dans l'âme. 'heart-strings, *s.pl.* **1.** *A:* Fibres *f* du cœur. **2.** *F:* Tug at one's heart-strings, serrement *m* de cœur. 'heart to 'heart, *a. & adv.phr.* Heart-to-heart talk, conversation intime. *To talk with s.o. h. to h.*, parler avec qn à cœur ouvert. 'heart-whole, *a.* **1.** Qui a le cœur libre; qui n'a pas d'amour en tête. **2.** Heart-whole affection, affection sincère, vraie. **3.** Qui a conservé tout son courage. 'heart-wood, *s. Arb:* Bois *m* de cœur; cœur du bois.

heart[2], *v.i.* (*Of cabbage, lettuce*) To heart (up), pommer.

heartburn ['haːrtbəːrn], *s.* Aigreurs *fpl* (d'estomac); brûlures *fpl* d'estomac.

-hearted ['haːrtid], *a.* Evil-hearted, méchant; au cœur mauvais. Big-hearted, great-hearted, *fellow*, garçon de cœur. True-hearted, open-hearted, sincère. Warm-hearted, au cœur chaud, généreux. *Warm-h.* welcome, accueil chaleureux. Whole-hearted, (qui vient) du cœur; sincère. *Whole-h.* laugh, rire épanoui. *S.a.* BROKEN-HEARTED, CHICKEN-HEARTED, HARD-HEARTED, *etc.*

hearten [haːrtn]. **1.** *v.tr.* To hearten s.o. (up),

ranimer, relever, le courage de qn ; donner du cœur à qn. **2.** *v.i.* **To hearten up,** reprendre courage.
hearth, *pl.* **-ths** [hɑːrθ, -θs, -ðz], *s.* **1.** Foyer *m*, âtre *m*. **Without hearth or home,** sans feu ni lieu. **2.** (*a*) *Metall :* Aire *f*, foyer, sole *f* (de four à réverbère) ; creuset *m* (de haut-fourneau). (*b*) **Smith's hearth,** foyer de forge ; forge *f*. **'hearth-rug,** *s.* Tapis *m*, carpette *f*, de foyer ; devant *m* de foyer.
hearthstone ['hɑːrθstoun], *s.* **1.** Pierre *f* de la cheminée. **2.** *Dom.Ec :* Blanc *m* d'Espagne.
heartiness ['hɑːrtinəs], *s.* Cordialité *f*, chaleur *f* (d'un accueil) ; vigueur *f* (de l'appétit). *The h. which he puts into his work,* l'empressement *m* qu'il met dans son travail.
heartless ['hɑːrtləs], *a.* Sans cœur, insensible, sans pitié ; (traitement, mot) dur, cruel. *You will not be so h. as to do that,* vous n'aurez pas le cœur de faire cela. **-ly,** *adv.* Sans cœur, sans pitié.
heartlessness ['hɑːrtləsnəs], *s.* Manque *m* de cœur.
hearty ['hɑːrti], *a.* **1.** Cordial, -aux ; (sentiment) sincère, qui part du cœur. **2.** (*a*) Vigoureux, robuste, bien portant. *S.a.* HALE. (*b*) (Repas) copieux, abondant, solide. **Hearty appetite,** appétit bien ouvert. **3.** *s. Nau :* Now then, my hearties! allons, mes braves! **-ily,** *adv.* **1.** Cordialement ; chaleureusement ; (travailler, rire) de bon cœur ; (se réjouir) sincèrement. **2.** (Dîner) copieusement ; (manger) de bon appétit, avec appétit.
heat¹ [hiːt], *s.* **1.** (*a*) Chaleur *f* ; ardeur *f* (du soleil, d'un foyer). **In the heat of the day,** au plus chaud de la journée. *The h. and the cold should be avoided,* le chaud et le froid sont à éviter. (*b*) *Ph : etc :* Chaleur, calorique *m*. **Specific heat,** chaleur spécifique. **Heat efficiency,** rendement *m* calorifique. (*c*) *Metall :* Chaleur, chaude *f*. **Red heat,** chaude rouge. **White heat,** chaleur d'incandescence ; chaude blanche. **To raise iron to a white heat, to a red heat,** chauffer le fer à blanc, au rouge. (*d*) *Cu :* Intensité *f* de chauffe ; température *f*. **2.** (*Passion*) **To get into a heat,** s'échauffer, s'emporter. **To reply with some heat,** répondre avec une certaine vivacité. **Heat of youth,** fougue *f* de la jeunesse. **In the heat of the moment,** dans la chaleur du moment. **3.** *Med :* Rougeur *f* (sur la peau). *Esp.* **Prickly heat,** lichen *m* vésiculaire ; *F :* bourbouille *f*. **4.** *St : Rac :* Épreuve *f*, manche *f*. **Qualifying heat,** épreuve éliminatoire. **Dead heat,** manche nulle ; course nulle. **To run a dead heat,** courir à égalité. **'heat-engine,** *s.* Machine *f* thermique. **'heat-rash,** *s. Med :* Échauffaison *f*, échauffure *f*. **'heat-resisting,** *a.* **1.** Ignifuge, calorifuge. **2.** (Acier) indétrempable. **'heat-stroke,** *s. Med : Vet :* Coup *m* de chaleur. **'heat-wave,** *s.* (*a*) *Ph :* Onde *f* calorifique. (*b*) *Meteor :* Vague *f* de chaleur.
heat². **1.** *v.tr.* (*a*) Chauffer. (*b*) (*Abnormally*) Échauffer (le sang, etc.) ; enflammer (l'esprit). **To h. oneself running,** s'échauffer à courir. **2.** *v.i.* (*a*) (*Of water, etc.*) Chauffer. (*b*) (*Of bearing*) To heat (up), chauffer, s'échauffer. **heat up,** *v.tr.* (Faire) réchauffer (un plat). **heated,** *a.* **1.** Chaud, chauffé. **2.** (*a*) Heated bearing, palier échauffé, qui chauffe. (*b*) (*Of pers.*) To get heated, s'échauffer. **Heated debate,** discussion chaude, animée. **-ly,** *adv.* Avec chaleur, avec emportement. **heating¹,** *a.* **1.** Échauffant. **2.** *H. action of the sun,* action calorifiante du soleil. **heating²,** *s.* **1.** (*Making hot*) (*a*) Chauf-

fage *m*, chauffe *f* (des chaudières, etc.). **Central heating,** chauffage central. **Heating power,** puissance *f*, pouvoir *m*, calorifique ; rendement *m* calorique. **Heating apparatus,** calorifère *m*. (*b*) Réchauffage *m* (d'un plat, etc.). **2.** (*Becoming hot*) Échauffement *m* (d'un coussinet) ; échauffement, fermentation *f* (du foin).
heater ['hiːtər], *s.* (*a*) Radiateur *m*. **Electric heater,** radiateur électrique. (*b*) **Gas (water-) heater,** chauffe-bains *m inv*, chauffe-eau *m inv* (à gaz). (*c*) Réchaud *m*.
heath [hiːθ], *s.* **1.** Bruyère *f*, lande *f*, brande *f*. **2.** *Bot :* Bruyère, brande.
heathen ['hiːð(ə)n], *a. & s.* Païen, -ïenne. *Coll.* **The heathen,** les païens.
heathenish ['hiːðəniʃ], *a. A :* Païen ; idolâtre.
heather ['heðər], *s. Bot :* Bruyère *f*, brande *f*. **Scotch heather, bell heather,** bruyère cendrée. **'heather-'mixture,** *s. Tex :* Drap chiné bruyère.
heave¹ [hiːv], *s.* Soulèvement *m*. **1.** Effort *m* (pour soulever). **2.** (*a*) Haut-le-cœur *m inv* ; nausée *f*. (*b*) Palpitation *f* (du sein). **3.** *Nau :* **Heave of the sea,** poussée *f*, ondulation *f*, des lames ; houle *f*. **4.** *pl.* (*With sing. const.*) *Vet :* **The heaves,** la pousse.
heave², *v.* (*p.t. & p.p.* heaved *or* (*esp. Nau :*) hove [ho :uv]) **I.** *v.tr.* **1.** (*Lift*) Lever, soulever (un fardeau). *Nau :* **To heave (up) the anchor,** *abs.* **to heave up,** déraper ; lever l'ancre. **2.** Pousser (un soupir). **3.** (*a*) (*Pull, haul*) **To heave coal,** (i) porter, (ii) décharger, le charbon. (*b*) *Nau :* **To heave the ship ahead,** virer le navire de l'avant, de l'arrière. **4.** (*Throw*) Lancer, jeter (*sth. at s.o.*, qch. contre qn). *Nau :* **To heave the lead,** jeter la sonde, le plomb ; sonder. **II. heave,** *v.i.* **1.** (*a*) (*Swell*) (Se) gonfler, se soulever ; (*of sea*) se soulever ; (*of bosom*) palpiter. (*b*) (*Of pers.*) Avoir des haut-le-cœur. (*Of the stomach*) Se soulever, se retourner. (*c*) (*Of horse*) Battre du flanc. **2.** *Nau :* (*a*) **To heave at a rope,** haler sur une manœuvre. **To heave (away) at the capstan,** virer au cabestan. (*b*) **To heave ahead, astern,** virer de l'avant, de l'arrière. **3.** *Nau :* (*Of land, ship*) **To heave in sight,** paraître (à l'horizon) ; poindre. **heave in,** *v.tr. Nau :* Rentrer, virer (un cordage). **To h. in the lines,** rentrer les amarres. *Abs.* **To heave in,** virer au cabestan. **heave to,** *v.tr. & i. Nau :* (Se) mettre en panne, à la cape ; prendre la panne. **To be hove to,** être en panne, à la cape. **Hove to under bare poles,** en panne sèche.
heaven [hevn], *s.* Ciel *m*, *pl.* cieux. **In heaven,** au ciel. **To go to heaven,** aller au ciel, en paradis. **Good Heavens!** juste ciel ! bonté divine ! **Thank Heaven!** Dieu merci ! **For Heaven's sake!** pour l'amour de Dieu ! **'heaven-born,** *a.* **1.** Céleste ; divin. **2.** *F :* (Professeur, etc.) particulièrement doué. **'heaven-sent,** *a.* Providentiel.
heavenly ['hevnli], *a.* Céleste ; (don) du ciel. **Heavenly body,** astre *m*. **Our heavenly Father,** notre Père céleste.
heaviness ['hevinəs], *s.* (*a*) Lourdeur, *f*, pesanteur *f* ; poids *m* (d'un fardeau). (*b*) Engourdissement *m*, lassitude *f* (des membres, de l'esprit). **Heaviness of heart,** serrement *m* de cœur, tristesse *f*.
heavy ['hevi], *a.* **1.** Lourd. (*a*) *H. parcel,* paquet lourd, pesant. **To weigh heavy,** peser lourd. **To make a burden heavier,** alourdir, appesantir, un fardeau. *Ph :* **Heavy bodies,** corps graves. *Av :* **Heavier-than-air craft,** appareil plus lourd que l'air. **Heavy blow,** (i) coup violent ; (ii) rude coup (du sort, etc.). **Heavy wine,** gros vin ; vin

à forte teneur d'alcool. (b) **Heavy tread,** pas pesant, lourd. (c) (*Of animal*) **Heavy with young,** gravide. **2.** (a) **Heavy baggage,** gros bagages. *H. wire,* fil (de) grosse épaisseur. *Metall:* **Heavy castings,** grosses pièces.⌐ *Mil:* **Heavy guns,** artillerie lourde. **Heavy cavalry,** grosse cavalerie. *Navy:* **Heavy armament,** artillerie de gros calibre. (b) **Heavy features,** gros traits. **Heavy line,** gros trait. *Typ:* **Heavy type,** caractères gras. (c) *H. beard,* forte barbe. **Heavy crop,** grosse récolte ; récolte abondante. **Heavy meal,** repas copieux. *Mil:* **Heavy fire,** feu nourri ; feu vif ; feu intense. *H. shower,* grosse averse. *H. fog,* brouillard épais. **Heavy expenditure,** dépenses considérables ; grosses dépenses. *El:* **Heavy current,** courant intensif, intense. **Heavy cold,** gros rhume. (d) *H. silence,* silence profond. *H. sleep,* profond sommeil. **3.** **Heavy odour,** odeur lourde. *Air h. with scent,* air chargé de parfums. *S.a.* HEART[1] 2. **4.** **Heavy eyes,** yeux battus. *H. with sleep,* appesanti par le sommeil ; accablé de sommeil. **5.** (a) (Travail) pénible, difficile, dur, laborieux. *He did the h. work,* c'est lui qui a fait le gros de la besogne. **Heavy day,** journée chargée. *H. soil, h. ground,* terrain lourd ; sol gras ; sol fort. (b) **Heavy weather,** gros temps. **Heavy sea,** forte mer, grosse mer. *A h. sea was running,* il faisait une mer houleuse. **To ship a heavy sea,** embarquer un coup de mer. **6.** *Th:* **Heavy parts,** rôles sérieux, tragiques. *The h. villain,* le traître à gros effets de mélo. **7.** **Heavy eater,** gros mangeur. *H. drinker,* fort buveur. **To be a heavy sleeper,** avoir le sommeil dur. **-ily,** *adv.* **1.** Lourdement. **Time hangs heavily on his hands,** le temps lui pèse, lui dure. *He walked h.,* il avançait d'un pas pesant, à pas pesants. **2.** *H. underlined,* fortement souligné. **To lose heavily,** perdre une forte somme ; *F:* perdre gros. *To be h. taxed,* être fortement imposé. **3.** **To sigh heavily,** soupirer profondément. **To sleep heavily,** dormir profondément. **4.** (Respirer, se mouvoir) péniblement ; (se mouvoir) avec difficulté. 'heavy-'eyed, *a.* Aux yeux battus. 'heavy-'handed, *a.* **1.** A la main lourde. *H.-h. government,* gouvernement oppressif. **2.** Maladroit, gauche. 'heavy-'hearted, *a.* Abattu ; qui a le cœur gros. 'heavy-weight. **1.** *s.* *Box:* Poids lourd. **2.** *a.* *H.-w. materials,* étoffes lourdes.

Hebraic [hiː'breiik], *a.* Hébraïque.

Hebrew ['hiːbruː]. **1.** *B.Lit:* (a) *s.* Hébreu, *f.* Hébreue. (b) *a.* Hébreu, *f.* hébraïque. (The) **Hebrew** (language), l'hébreu *m.* *H. scholar,* hébraïste *m.* **2.** (*Modern use*) *a. & s.* Hébraïque (*mf*) ; Israélite (*mf*).

hecatomb ['hekatɔm, -tuːm], *s.* *Gr.Ant:* Hécatombe *f.*

heckle [hekl], *v.tr.* (*At public meetings*) Procéder à l'interrogatoire (d'un candidat) après son discours ; poser à (qn) des questions embarrassantes.

heckler ['heklər], *s.* *Pol: etc:* Questionneur *m* (à une réunion politique, etc.) ; adversaire *m* qui cherche à embarrasser le candidat.

hectic ['hektik], *a.* **1.** *Med:* (a) Hectique. (b) **Hectic cough,** toux de phtisique. **2.** *F:* Agité, fiévreux. *H. life,* existence trépidante. *We had a h. time,* (i) ç'a été à ne savoir où donner de la tête ; (ii) on a fait une de ces noces !

Hector[1] ['hektər]. **1.** *Pr.n.m.* *Gr.Lit:* Hector. **2.** *s.* *F:* Bravache *m,* matamore *m.*

hector[2], *v.tr. & i.* Faire de l'esbroufe ; faire le matamore ; intimider, rudoyer (qn). **hectoring,** *a.* (Ton, etc.) autoritaire, impérieux.

he'd [hiːd] = he had, he would.

heddles [hedlz], *s.pl.* *Tex:* Lices *f* (du métier).

hedge[1] [hedʒ], *s.* **1.** Haie *f.* **Quickset hedge,** haie vive. **Dead hedge,** haie morte, sèche. *F:* **To be on the hedge,** ménager la chèvre et le chou ; se réserver. **2.** Haie (d'agents de police, de troupes). **3.** *Attrib. Pej:* De bas étage ; interlope. **Hedge-priest, hedge-parson,** (i) prêtre ignorant ; (ii) prêtre interlope. **Hedge lawyer,** avocat marron. 'hedge-hopping, *s.* *Av:* *F:* Vol *m* à ras de terre ; rase-mottes *m inv.*

hedge[2]. **1.** *v.tr.* **To hedge in** *a piece of ground,* mettre une haie autour d'un terrain ; enfermer, enclore, un terrain. **Hedged in, hedged about, with difficulties,** entouré de difficultés. **2.** *v.i.* (a) *Turf:* Parier pour et contre. (b) *F:* (*In discussion*) Chercher des échappatoires ; se réserver ; s'échapper par la tangente. **hedging,** *s.* **1.** Entretien *m* des haies. **2.** Bordure *f.* **3.** *Turf:* Pari *m* pour et contre.

hedgehog ['hedʒhɔg], *s.* Hérisson *m.* *F:* **To curl up like a hedgehog,** se mettre en boule.

hedgerow ['hedʒrou], *s.* Bordure *f* de haies, d'arbres ou d'arbustes formant une haie.

hedonism ['hiːdonizm], *s.* *Phil:* Hédonisme *m.*

hedonist ['hiːdonist], *s.* *Phil:* Hédoniste *mf.*

heed[1] [hiːd], *s.* Attention *f,* garde *f,* soin *m.* **To give, pay, heed to sth., to s.o.,** faire attention à qch. ; prêter (son) attention à qn. **To take heed,** prendre garde. **To take no heed of sth.,** ne tenir aucun compte de qch. **To take heed to do sth.,** prendre garde, prendre soin, de faire qch.

heed[2], *v.tr.* Faire attention à, prendre garde à, tenir compte de (qch.).

heedful ['hiːdful], *a.* Vigilant, prudent. *H. of advice,* attentif aux conseils.

heedless ['hiːdləs], *a.* **1.** Étourdi, insouciant, imprudent. **2.** *To be h. of* (*sth.*), être inattentif à (ce qui se passe) ; être peu soucieux de (l'avenir, etc.). **-ly,** *adv.* Étourdiment.

heedlessness ['hiːdləsnəs], *s.* Inattention *f* (*of,* à) ; étourderie *f,* insouciance *f.*

hee-haw[1] [hiː'hɔː], *s.* Hi-han *m* ; braiment *m.*

hee-haw[2], *v.i.* Braire ; faire hi-han.

heel[1] [hiːl], *s.* **1.** (a) Talon *m* (du pied). **To be under the heel of the invader,** être sous la botte de l'envahisseur. **To tread on, be upon, s.o.'s heels,** marcher sur les talons de qn ; être aux trousses de qn. **To show a clean pair of heels, to take to one's heels,** prendre la fuite ; tourner les talons. *He showed us a clean pair of heels,* il nous a échappé. **To lay, clap, s.o. by the heels,** arrêter qn ; *F:* pincer qn ; mettre qn au bloc. *Nau:* *F:* **To have the heels of another ship,** dépasser, enganter, un autre navire. **To kick, cool, one's heels,** croquer le marmot ; faire le pied de grue. **To come to heel,** (*of dog*) venir derrière à l'ordre ; obéir à l'appel ; *F:* (*of pers.*) se soumettre. **To bring s.o. to heel,** mater qn ; mettre qn au pas. *S.a.* HEAD[1] 1. (b) Talon (d'un soulier, d'un bas). **Out at heels,** (bas) troués aux talons. *F:* (*Of pers.*) *To be out at heels,* (i) porter des bas percés ; être dans la dèche. **To be down at heel,** (i) porter des souliers éculés ; (ii) être dans la dèche. **2.** Talon (d'outil, de crosse de golf). *Nau:* Heel of the rudder, talon, talonnière *f,* du gouvernail. **3.** (a) Éperon *m,* ergot *m* (de coq). (b) Derrière *m* du sabot (d'un cheval, etc.). *F:* **To fling out its heels,** ruer. 'heel-and-'toe, *a.* **1.** A heel-and-toe dance, une gigue. **2.** *Sp:* H.-and-toe *walking,* marche *f* réglementaire (de concours athlétiques). 'heel-tap, *s.* **1.** *Bootm:* Hausse *f.* **2.** *pl.* Heel-taps, fonds *m* de verre. **To leave no heel-taps,** faire rubis sur l'ongle.

heel². **1.** *v.i.* Danser en frappant du talon. **2.** *v.tr.* (*a*) (i) Mettre un talon à (un soulier, un bas). (ii) Réparer le talon (d'un soulier) ; refaire le talon (d'un bas). (*b*) *Golf :* Talonner (la balle). (*c*) *Rugby Fb :* To heel (out), talonner. **heeled,** *a.* A talons. **High-heeled shoes,** souliers à hauts talons. **Low-heeled shoes,** souliers plats.

heel³, *s.* *Nau :* Bande *f*, gîte *f* (d'un navire). **On the heel,** à la bande.

heel⁴, *v.* *Nau :* To heel (over). **1.** *v.i.* (*Of ship*) Avoir, donner, de la bande ; prendre de la gîte. **2.** *v.tr.* Mettre (un navire) à la bande.

hefty ['hefti], *a.* *F :* (Homme) fort, solide, *P :* costaud.

heifer ['hefər], *s.* Génisse *f*.

heigh [hei], *int.* **1.** Hé ! **2.** Hé, là-bas !

height [hait], *s.* **1.** (*a*) Hauteur *f*, élévation *f*. **Wall six feet in height,** mur qui a six pieds de haut. (*b*) Taille *f*, grandeur *f*, stature *f* (de qn). **Full height,** taille debout. **Of average height,** de taille moyenne. **2.** Height above sea level, altitude *f* au-dessus du niveau de la mer. *Av :* Height gauge, altimètre *m*. **3.** (*Hill*) Hauteur ; éminence *f* (de terrain) ; colline *f*. **4.** Apogée *m* (de la fortune, de la gloire) ; faîte *m* (des grandeurs) ; comble *m* (de la folie). **At the height of the storm, of the action,** au (plus) fort de l'orage, du combat. **In the height of summer,** au cœur, au milieu, au fort, de l'été ; en plein été. **The season is at its height,** la saison bat son plein. **In the height of fashion,** à la dernière mode ; du dernier cri.

heighten [haitn]. **1.** *v.tr.* (*a*) Surélever, surhausser, rehausser (un mur, un immeuble). (*b*) Accroître, augmenter (un plaisir) ; aggraver (un mal) ; accentuer (un contraste) ; relever, faire ressortir (la beauté de qch.). **2.** *v.i.* S'élever ; se rehausser ; augmenter.

heinous ['heinəs], *a.* (*Crime*) odieux, atroce, abominable.

heinousness ['heinəsnəs], *s.* Énormité *f*, atrocité *f* (d'un crime).

heir ['ɛər], *s.* Héritier *m.* **To be heir to a relative, to an estate,** être l'héritier, le légataire, d'un parent, le légataire d'une propriété. *Jur :* **Heir apparent,** héritier présomptif. **Heir-at-law,** rightful heir, héritier légitime, naturel.

heiress ['ɛərəs], *s.f.* Héritière.

heirloom ['ɛərluːm], *s.* Meuble *m* ou bijou *m* de famille.

held [held]. *See* HOLD².

Helen ['helen]. *Pr.n.f.* Hélène.

heliacal [hiː'laiəkəl], *a.* *Astr :* Héliaque.

helianthus [hiːli'ænθəs], *s.* *Bot :* Hélianthe *m*, tournesol *m*.

helical ['helik(ə)l], *a.* **1.** *Conch :* Helical shell, hélice *f*, coquille contournée. **2.** *Mec.E :* (*Of gear, etc.*) Hélicoïdal, -aux ; (*of spring*) hélicoïde, en hélice. **Double helical gear,** engrenage à chevrons. **-ally,** *adv.* En spirale, en hélice.

helicoid ['helikɔid]. **1.** *a.* Hélicoïde ; hélicoïdal, -aux. **2.** *s.* Hélicoïde *m*.

helicoidal ['helikɔid(ə)l], *a.* = HELICOID 1.

helicopter ['helikɔptər], *s.* *Av :* Hélicoptère *m*.

heliograph¹ ['hiːliogrɑːf, -graf], *s.* **1.** Héliographe *m* ; héliostat *m*. **2.** *Phot.Engr :* Héliogravure *f*.

heliograph², *v.tr.* **1.** Communiquer (un message) par héliographe. **2.** Reproduire (un dessin) par héliogravure.

heliogravure [hiːliogra'vjuər], *s.* Héliogravure *f* ; photogravure *f*.

heliostat ['hiːliostat], *s.* Héliostat *m*.

heliotherapy [hiːlio'θerəpi], *s.* Héliothérapie *f*.

heliotrope ['hiːliotroup]. **1.** *s.* *Bot :* Héliotrope *m*. **2.** *a.* Héliotrope *inv*.

helium ['hiːliəm], *s.* *Ch :* Hélium *m*.

helix, *pl.* **helices** ['hiːliks, 'heliks, 'helisiːz], *s.* **1.** (*a*) *Geom :* Hélice *f*. (*b*) *Arch : etc :* Spirale *f* ; volute *f*. **2.** *Anat :* Hélix *m* (de l'oreille). **3.** *Moll :* (*Snail*) Hélice, colimaçon *m*.

hell [hel], *s.* **1.** *Myth :* Les enfers *m*. **2.** L'enfer. (*a*) In heaven and h., au ciel et en enfer. Hell is let loose, les diables sont déchaînés. **To raise hell** = to raise Cain, *q.v. under* CAIN. **To ride hell for leather,** galoper à bride abattue, à toute bride ; aller au triple galop. (*b*) *P :* **To make a hell of a noise,** faire un bruit d'enfer, un bruit infernal. **To work like hell,** travailler avec acharnement. **What the hell do you want?** que diable désirez-vous ? **3.** (*Gambling-den*) Tripot *m*. **'hell-'fire,** *s.* Feu *m*, tourments *mpl*, de l'enfer. **'hellhound,** *s.* Suppôt *m* de Satan.

he'll [hiːl] = *he will.*

hellebore ['helibɔːr], *s.* *Bot :* Ellébore *m*.

Hellene ['heliːn], *s.* Hellène *mf*.

Hellenic [he'liːnik], *a.* (*Race*) hellène ; (langue) hellénique.

hellish ['heliʃ], *a.* Infernal, -aux ; d'enfer ; diabolique. **-ly,** *adv.* D'une manière diabolique.

hello [he'lou], *int.* (*a*) (*Calling attention*) H. there, wake up ! holà ! debout ! hé, là-bas, debout ! (*b*) (*On the telephone*) Allô ! (*c*) (*Indicating surprise*) H., is that you? tiens ! c'est vous !

helm¹ [helm], *s.* *A :* Heaume *m*.

helm², *s.* *Nau :* Barre *f* (du gouvernail) ; gouvernail *m*, timon *m*. **The man at the helm,** (i) l'homme de barre ; (ii) *F :* l'homme qui tient le gouvernail, qui dirige l'entreprise. **Down (with the) helm!** la barre dessous ! **Up (with the) helm!** la barre au vent ! *F :* **The helm of the State,** le timon de l'État.

helmet ['helmet], *s.* Casque *m.* **Tropical helmet,** casque colonial.

helmsman, *pl.* **-men** ['helmzmən, -men], *s.m.* *Nau :* Homme de barre ; timonier.

helot ['helət, 'hiː-], *s.* *Gr.Hist :* Ilote *m*.

helotism ['helətizm], *s.* *Gr.Hist :* Ilotisme *m*.

help¹ [help], *s.* **1.** (*a*) Aide *f*, assistance *f*, secours *m.* With the h. of a friend, avec l'aide d'un ami. With the h. of a rope, à l'aide, au moyen, d'une corde. With God's h., Dieu aidant. **To cry for help,** crier au secours ; appeler à l'aide. Past help, perdu. To lend one's h., prêter son concours. **2.** To come to s.o.'s help, venir au secours de qn ; porter secours à qn. **3.** There's no help for it, il n'y a pas de remède ; il n'y a rien à faire. **4.** (*a*) To be a help to s.o., être d'un grand secours à qn, rendre grand service à qn. (*b*) (*Pers.*) Aide *mf.* Esp. *U.S:* Domestique *mf*, bonne *f* ; femme *f* de journée. **Mother's help,** jeune fille qui aide la mère dans le soin des enfants.

help², *v.tr.* **1.** (*a*) Aider, secourir, assister ; venir en aide à (qn) ; venir à l'aide de (qn). **To help s.o. to do sth.,** aider qn à faire qch. *That will not h. you,* cela ne vous servira à rien. **God help you!** Dieu vous soit en aide ! **So help me God!** que Dieu me juge si je ne dis pas la vérité ! *I got a friend to h. me,* je me suis fait aider par un ami. He knows how to help himself, il sait se tirer d'affaire. *Prov :* **God helps him who helps himself,** aide-toi et le ciel t'aidera. **Help!** au secours ! (*b*) Faciliter (la digestion, le progrès). **To help s.o. down, in, out, up,** aider qn à descendre, à entrer, à sortir, à monter. **2.** (*At table*) (*a*) Servir (qn). **To help s.o. to soup,**

servir du potage à qn. *To h. s.o. to wine, etc.,* verser à boire à qn. **Help yourself,** servez-vous. (*b*) **To help the soup, to help the fish,** servir le potage, le poisson. **3.** (*With negation expressed or implied*) (*a*) Empêcher. **Things we cannot help (happening),** choses qu'on ne saurait empêcher. **I can't help it,** je n'y peux rien. **It can't be helped,** tant pis! c'est sans remède. (*b*) S'empêcher, se défendre (de faire qch.). *I can't h. laughing,* je ne peux m'empêcher de rire. **I can't help it,** c'est plus fort que moi. (*c*) *F:* **Don't be away longer than you can help,** tâchez d'être absent le moins de temps possible. **helping**[1], *a.* **To lend a helping hand,** prêter son aide ; donner un coup d'épaule. **helping**[2], *s.* Portion *f* (de nourriture). *I had two helpings,* j'en ai repris.

helper ['helpər], *s.* Aide *mf.*

helpful ['helpful], *a.* **1.** (Personne) secourable, serviable. **2.** (Livre, etc.) utile ; (remède, etc.) salutaire. **-fully,** *adv.* Utilement ; salutairement.

helpless ['helpləs], *a.* **1.** Sans ressource, sans appui, délaissé. **2.** Faible, impuissant ; réduit à l'impuissance. *I am h. in the matter,* je n'y puis rien. **-ly,** *adv.* **1.** Sans ressource. **2.** Faiblement.

helplessness ['helpləsnəs], *s.* **1.** Abandon *m,* délaissement *m.* **2.** Faiblesse *f* ; manque *m* d'énergie, manque d'initiative.

helpmate ['helpmeit], *s.* **1.** Aide *mf,* collaborateur, -trice. **2.** = HELPMEET.

helpmeet ['helpmi:t], *s.* Compagnon *m* ou compagne *f* ; *esp.* épouse *f.*

helter-skelter ['heltər'skeltər]. **1.** *adv.* (Courir, fuir) pêle-mêle, à la débandade. **2.** *a.* **Helterskelter flight,** fuite désordonnée ; débandade *f* ; sauve-qui-peut *m inv.*

helve [helv], *s.* Manche *m* (d'une hache, d'un marteau). **To throw the helve after the hatchet,** jeter le manche après la cognée.

Helvetia [hel'vi:ʃiə]. *Pr.n.* L'Helvétie *f.*

Helvetian [hel'vi:ʃiən], *a.* & *s.* Helvétien, -ienne ; helvète.

Helvetic [hel'vetik], *a.* Helvétique.

hem[1] [hem], *s.* **1.** Bord *m* (d'un vêtement). **2.** Ourlet *m* (d'un mouchoir, etc.). **'hemstitch**[1], *s. Needlew:* Ourlet *m* à jour ; rivière *f.* **'hem-stitch**[2], *v.tr.* Ourler (un mouchoir) à jour.

hem[2], *v.tr.* **1.** *A:* Border, mettre un bord à (un vêtement). **2.** Ourler (un mouchoir, du drap). **3.** **To hem in,** entourer, cerner (l'ennemi) ; investir (une place).

hem[3], *v.i.* **1.** Faire hem, hum ; tousser un coup. **2. To hem and haw** = *to hum and haw, q.v. under* HUM[2] **1.**

hemicrania [hemi'kreinjə], *s. Med:* Hémicranie *f,* migraine *f.*

hemicycle ['hemisaikl], *s. Arch:* Hémicycle *m.*

hemiplegia [hemi'pli:dʒiə], *s. Med:* Hémiplégie *f.*

hemipter, *pl.* **-ers, -era** [he'miptər, -ərz, -ərə], *s. Ent:* Hémiptère *m.*

hemipterous ['hemiptərəs], *a. Ent:* Hémiptère.

hemisphere ['hemisfiːər], *s.* Hémisphère *m.*

hemispheric(al) [hemi'sferik(əl)], *a.* Hémisphérique.

hemistich ['hemistik], *s. Pros:* Hémistiche *m.*

hemlock ['hemlɔk], *s. Bot:* **1.** Ciguë *f.* **2.** **Hemlock fir, hemlock spruce,** sapin *m* du Canada ; sapin-ciguë *m.*

hemorrhage ['hemoredʒ], *s.* = HAEMORRHAGE.

hemp [hemp], *s.* **1.** (*a*) *Bot:* Chanvre *m.* (*b*) *Tex:* Chanvre, filasse *f.* **Hemp cloth,** tissu *m* de chanvre. **2.** *Pharm:* Hachisch *m,* bang(h) *m.* **'hemp-field,** *s.* Chènevière *f.*

hempen ['hempən], *a.* (Étoffe, corde, fil) de chanvre. *F:* **Hempen collar,** corde *f* de potence.

hempseed ['hempsi:d], *s.* Chènevis *m.*

hen [hen], *s.* **1.** Poule *f. Boiling hen,* poule à mettre au pot. *F:* **To take tea with a lot of old hens,** prendre le thé avec un tas de vieilles dindes. **2.** Femelle *f* (d'oiseau, etc.). **Henbird,** oiseau *m* femelle. **Hen-lobster,** homard *m* femelle. **'hen-coop,** *s.* Cage *f* à poules ; mue *f.* **'hen-house,** *s.* Poulailler *m.* **'hen-party,** *s. F:* Réunion *f* entre femmes. **'hen-pecked,** *a.* **Hen-pecked husband,** mari dont la femme porte la culotte, qui sa femme mène par le bout du nez. **'hen-roost,** *s.* (*a*) Juchoir *m,* perchoir *m.* (*b*) *F:* Poulailler *m.*

henbane ['henbein], *s. Bot:* Jusquiame *f.*

hence [hens], *adv.* **1.** *A.* & *Lit:* (From) hence, d'ici. *A:* (Get thee) hence! hors d'ici! **2.** (*Of time*) Dorénavant, désormais ; à partir d'aujourd'hui. **Five years hence,** dans cinq ans (d'ici). **3.** Hence his anger, de là sa fureur.

henceforth ['hensfɔ:rθ], **henceforward** ['hens'fɔ:rwərd], *adv.* Désormais, dorénavant ; à l'avenir.

henchman, *pl.* **-men** ['henʃmən, -men], *s.m.* (*a*) *Hist:* Écuyer ; (*b*) Partisan, acolyte.

hendecagon [hen'dekagən], *s. Geom:* Hendécagone *m.*

henna[1] ['hena], *s.* Henné *m.*

henna[2], *v.tr.* Teindre au henné. **To have one's hair hennaed,** se faire teindre les cheveux au henné.

Henrietta [henri'eta]. *Pr.n.f.* Henriette.

Henry ['henri]. *Pr.n.m.* Henri.

hepatic [he'patik], *a.* & *s. Anat: Pharm:* Hépatique (*m*).

heptagon ['heptagən], *s.* Heptagone *m.*

heptagonal [hep'tagon(ə)l], *a.* Heptagone, heptagonal, -aux.

heptameter [hep'tametər], *s. Pros:* Heptamètre *m.*

heptarchy ['heptɑ:rki], *s.* Heptarchie *f.*

her[1] [hər, ha:r], *pers. pron. f., objective case.* **1.** (*Unstressed*) (*a*) (Direct) La, (*before a vowel sound*) l' ; (*indirect*) lui. *Have you seen her?* l'avez-vous vue? *I obey her,* je lui obéis. *Look at her,* regardez-la. *Tell her,* dites-lui. (*b*) I am thinking of her, je pense à elle ; je ne l'oublie pas. *I remember her,* je me souviens d'elle. (*c*) (*Refl.*) Elle. *She took her parcel away with her,* elle emporta son paquet avec elle. **2.** (*Stressed*) (*a*) Elle. *I found him and her at the station,* je les ai trouvés lui et elle à la gare. *Her I can never forgive,* je ne lui pardonnerai jamais à elle. *I am thinking of 'her,* c'est à elle que je pense. (*b*) **To her who should take offence at this I would say . . .,** à celle qui s'en offenserait je dirais. . . . **3.** *F:* **It's her,** c'est elle. **That's her!** la voilà!

her[2], *poss.a.* (*denoting a f. possessor*) Son, *f.* sa, *pl.* ses. *Her friend, her friends,* son ami, *f.* son amie ; ses amis, *f.* ses amies. *The date and place of her birth,* ses date et lieu de naissance. *She has hurt her hand,* elle s'est fait mal à la main. (*Emphatic*) 'Her idea would be to . . ., son idée *f* à elle serait de. . . .

herald[1] ['herəld], *s.* (*a*) Héraut *m.* (*b*) *F:* Avant-coureur, précurseur *m* ; avant-courrier, messager. *The lark, h. of the morn,* l'alouette, avant-courrière du matin.

herald[2], *v.tr.* Annoncer, proclamer.

heraldic [he'raldik], a. Héraldique. **Heraldic bearing,** armoirie f, blason m.
heraldry ['herəldri], s. **I.** L'art m, la science, héraldique ; le blason. **Canting heraldry,** armes parlantes. **2.** Pompe f héraldique.
herb [həːrb], s. Bot: (a) Herbe f. (b) **Sweet herbs** (for seasoning), fines herbes. **Medicinal herbs,** herbes, plantes, médicinales ; simples m. **Herb-shop,** herboristerie f.
herbaceous [həːr'beiʃəs], a. Bot: Herbacé.
herbage ['həːrbedʒ], s. Herbes f pl ; herbage(s) m.
herbal ['həːrbəl]. **I.** s. Herbier m. **2.** a. (Breuvage) fait avec des herbes ; (infusion, tisane) d'herbes.
herbalist ['həːrbəlist], s. Herboriste mf.
herbarium [həːr'bɛəriəm], s. Herbier m.
herbivora [həːr'bivorə], s. pl. Z: Herbivores m.
herbivorous [həːr'bivorəs], a. Z: Herbivore.
Herculean [həːr'kjuːliən], a. (Travail, effort) herculéen ; (taille) d'Hercule.
Hercules ['həːrkjuliːz]. **I.** Pr.n.m. Hercule. **2.** s. F: Homme d'une grande force ; hercule m.
herd¹ [həːrd], s. (a) Troupeau m (de gros bétail, de porcs) ; harde f (de cerfs) ; troupe f, bande f (de chevaux, de baleines, etc.). **The herd instinct,** (i) l'instinct grégaire ; (ii) l'instinct qui gouverne le troupeau. S.a. FLOCK². (b) F: Troupeau, foule f (de gens). **The common, vulgar, herd,** la foule ; le commun des hommes. **'herd-boy,** s.m. Jeune pâtre ; aide de bouvier.
herd², v.i. (a) (Of animals) **To herd together,** (i) vivre en troupeaux ; (ii) s'assembler en troupeau. (b) (Of pers.) **To herd with . . .,** s'associer à, aller avec, fréquenter (un parti, une société).
herd³, s. Pâtre m, gardien m (de bêtes). See GOOSEHERD, SHEPHERD, SWINE-HERD, etc.
herd⁴, v.tr. Garder, surveiller, soigner (les bestiaux, les oies, etc.).
herdsman, pl. **-men** ['həːrdzmən, -men], s.m. Bouvier, pâtre.
here ['hiːər], adv. **I.** (a) Ici. **Stay h.,** restez ici. **In here,** ici. **Come in h., please,** venez par ici, s'il vous plaît. **Up to here, down to here,** jusqu'ici. **About here,** par ici. **Near here,** près d'ici. **From here to there,** d'ici là. **Between h. and London,** d'ici à Londres. **Christmas is h.!** voici Noël ! **I must have it here and now,** il me le faut sur-le-champ, séance tenante. **Here goes!** allons-y ! (b) Ci. (Only in) **This one here and that one there,** celui-ci et celui-là. **Here lies . . .,** ci-gît. . . . (c) (At roll-call) Présent ! (d) **Here below,** ici-bas. **2. Here's your hat,** voici votre chapeau. **H. I am,** me voici ! S.a. AGAIN **I. Here you are!** (i) vous voici ! (ii) tenez ! (ceci est pour vous). **3.** (In drinking a health) **Here's to you!** à votre santé ! F: à la vôtre ! **4. My friend here will tell you,** mon ami que voici vous le dira. **5.** (Exclamatory) **Here! I want you!** pst ! venez ici ! **6.** (a) **Here and there,** par-ci par-là ; çà et là. (b) **Here, there, and everywhere,** un peu partout. (c) F: **That's neither here nor there,** cela ne fait rien (à l'affaire) ; cela ne fait ni chaud ni froid.
hereabout(s) ['hiːərabaut(s)], adv. Près d'ici, par ici, dans ces parages, dans les environs.
hereafter [hiːər'aːftər]. **I.** adv. (a) (Of position) (In book, writings, etc.) Ci-après, ci-dessous. (b) (Of time) Dorénavant, à l'avenir, désormais. **2.** s. L'au-delà m ; l'autre monde m.
hereby [hiːər'bai, 'hiːərbai], adv. Jur: Par ces présentes. **The council hereby resolve, resolve**

hereby, that . . ., le conseil déclare par le présent acte que. . . .
hereditament [he'reditəmənt], s. Jur: **I.** Bien transmissible par héritage. Esp. pl. **Hereditaments,** biens composant la succession ; terres f et immeubles m. **2.** = INHERITANCE **I.**
hereditary [he'reditəri], a. Héréditaire.
heredity [he'rediti], s. Hérédité f.
herein [hiːər'in], adv. **I.** Ici, dans ce livre, dans ce lieu. **The letter enclosed h.,** la lettre ci-incluse. **2.** (In this matter) En ceci, sur ce point.
hereof [hiːər'ɔv], adv. A: De ceci.
heresy ['heresi], s. Hérésie f.
heretic ['heretik], s. Hérétique mf. **Relapsed heretic,** relaps, f. relapse.
heretical [he'retik(ə)l], a. Hérétique.
heretofore ['hiːərtu'fɔːr], adv. Jadis, autrefois ; jusqu'ici. **As heretofore,** comme auparavant.
hereupon ['hiːərə'pɔn], adv. Là-dessus ; sur ce.
herewith [hiːər'wiδ], adv. Avec ceci. Com: **I am sending you herewith . . .,** je vous envoie ci-joint, sous ce pli. . . .
heritable ['heritəbl], a. **I.** Biol: Héréditaire. **2.** Jur: (a) (Droit) héréditaire ; (propriété) héritable. (b) (Of pers.) Capable d'hériter.
heritage ['heritedʒ], s. Héritage m, patrimoine m.
Hermes ['həːrmiːz]. Pr.n.m. Gr.Myth: Hermès.
hermetic [həːr'metik], a. Hermétique. **I.** Hermetic philosophy, science, l'alchimie f. **2. Hermetic sealing, bouchage** m hermétique. **-ally,** adv. (Scellé) hermétiquement.
hermit ['həːrmit], s. Ermite m. **Hermit-crab,** bernard-l'ermite m.
hermitage ['həːrmitedʒ], s. Ermitage m.
hernia ['həːrnia], s. Hernie f. **Strangulated hernia,** hernie étranglée. **Suffering from hernia,** hernieux.
hernial ['həːrniəl], **herniary** ['həːrniəri], a. Herniaire.
herniated ['həːrnieitid], a. (Intestin) hernié.
hero, pl. **-oes** ['hiːərou, -ouz], s.m. Héros m. **To die like a hero,** se faire tuer en brave, en héros. **'hero-worship,** s. Culte m des héros.
Herod ['herəd]. Pr.n.m. Hist: Hérode.
heroic(al) [he'rouik(əl)]. **I.** a. Héroïque. H. **deed,** action d'éclat. **Heroic remedy,** remède héroïque. **Heroic poem,** poème épique. **Heroic verse,** vers décasyllabe, vers héroïque. **2.** s. (Usu. pl.) F: **Heroics,** déclamation f de sentiments outrés ; grandiloquence f. **-ally,** adv. Héroïquement.
heroi-comic [heroi'kɔmik], a. Héroï-comique.
heroin [he'rouin], s. Pharm: Héroïne f.
heroine ['herouin], s.f. Héroïne.
heroism ['herouizm], s. Héroïsme m.
heron ['herən], s. Orn: Héron m. **Young h.,** héronneau m.
heronry ['herənri], s. Héronnière f.
herpes ['həːrpiːz], s. Med: Herpès m ; dartres f pl.
herpetic [hər'petik], a. Med: Herpétique ; dartreux.
herring ['heriŋ], s. Ich: Hareng m. **Red herring,** hareng saur. **To draw a red herring across the track,** (i) dépister la meute ; (ii) F: faire dévier la conversation. **'herring-boat,** s. Harenguier m, trinquart m. **'herring-bone,** s. Arête f de hareng. **Herring-bone pattern,** dessin m ou tracé m en arête de hareng, en chevrons, à chevrons, à brin de fougère. **Herring-bone stitch,** point croisé ; point de chausson. **'herring-fisher,** s. Harenguier m. **'herring-harvest,** s. Harengaison f. **'Herring-pond (the),** s. F: L'Atlantique m.
hers [həːrz], poss.pron. Le sien, la sienne, les

siens, les siennes. *She took my pen and h.*, elle prit ma plume et la sienne. *This book is h.*, ce livre est à elle, lui appartient ; c'est son livre à elle. *A friend of hers*, un(e) de ses ami(e)s ; un(e) ami(e) à elle. *That pride of hers*, cet orgueil dont elle ne peut se défaire.
herself [hər'self], *pers.pron. See* SELF 4.
Hertzian ['hə:rtsiən], *a. El :* Hertzien. **Hertzian waves**, ondes hertziennes.
he's [hi:z] = *he is, he has*.
hesitancy ['hezitənsi], *s.* Hésitation *f*, incertitude *f*.
hesitant ['hezitənt], *a.* Hésitant, irrésolu.
hesitate ['heziteit], *v.i.* Hésiter. *To h. for a word*, hésiter pour trouver un mot. *To h. between two courses*, hésiter, balancer, entre deux partis. *He hesitates at nothing*, il n'hésite, ne recule, devant rien. *To hesitate to do sth.*, hésiter à faire qch. **hesitating**, *a.* Hésitant, incertain. **-ly**, *adv.* Avec hésitation ; en hésitant.
hesitation [hezi'teiʃ(ə)n], *s.* Hésitation *f*. **Without (the slightest) hesitation**, sans (la moindre) hésitation ; *F :* sans faire ni une ni deux.
Hesperus ['hespərəs]. *Pr.n. Poet :* Vesper *m* ; l'étoile *f* du soir.
Hessian ['hesiən]. **1.** *a. & s. Geog :* Hessois, -oise. **Hessian boots**, *F :* Hessians, bottes *f* à la Souwarov. **2.** *s. Tex :* Étoffe grossière de chanvre ; toile *f* d'emballage.
heteroclite ['hetəroklait], *a.* Hétéroclite.
heterodox ['hetərodɔks], *a.* Hétérodoxe.
heterodoxy ['hetərodɔksi], *s.* Hétérodoxie *f*.
heterodyne ['hetərodain], *a. & s. W.Tel :* (Récepteur) hétérodyne (*m*).
heterogeneous [hetəro'dʒi:niəs], *a.* Hétérogène.
hevea ['hi:via], *s. Bot :* Hévé *m*, hévéa *f*.
hew [hju:], *v.tr.* (*p.t.* hewed ; *p.p.* hewed, hewn [hju:n]) Couper, tailler (avec une hache, etc.). *To hew a stone*, tailler, dresser, équarrir, une pierre. *To hew coal*, piquer la houille. *To hew one's way*, se frayer, se tailler, un passage (à coups de hache). **hew away, down, off,** *v.tr.* Abattre. **hew out,** *v.tr.* **1.** Tailler, façonner (un trou, un passage). **2.** *To hew out a statue*, ciseler une statue. *F :* **To hew out a career for oneself**, se faire, se tailler, une carrière. **hewing,** *s.* Abattage *m* (d'un arbre) ; taille *f*, coupe *f*, équarrissage *m* (de pierres, de bois) ; piquage *m* (de la houille).
hewer ['hjuər], *s.* **1.** Tailleur *m* (de pierre). *Min :* Piqueur *m* (de houille) ; haveur *m*. **To be hewers of wood and drawers of water**, (i) *B :* être employé à couper le bois et à puiser l'eau ; (ii) *F :* mener une vie de forçat, de galérien. **2.** Abatteur *m* (d'arbres).
hewn [hju:n]. *See* HEW.
hexachord ['heksakɔ:rd], *s. Mus :* Hexacorde *m*.
hexad ['heksad], *a. & s. Ch :* (Corps simple, ou radical) hexavalent.
hexagon ['heksagən], *s. Geom :* Hexagone *m*.
hexagonal [hek'sagən(ə)l], *a.* Hexagone, hexagonal, -aux. *S.a.* NUT 2.
hexahedral [heksa'hi:drəl, -'hedrəl], *a. Geom :* Hexaèdre, hexaédrique.
hexahedron [heksa'hi:drən, -'hedrən], *s. Geom :* Hexaèdre *m*.
hexameter [hek'sametər], *s. Pros :* Hexamètre *m*.
hexametric(al) [heksa'metrik(əl)], *a.* Hexamètre.
hey [hei], *int.* **1.** Hé ! holà ! **2.** Hein ? **3.** Hey for the greenwoods! en route pour les bois ! **4.** Hey presto! passez muscade !
heyday ['heidei], *s.* Apogée *m*, beaux jours (de ses forces, de la prospérité). **To be in the heyday**

of youth, of life, être en pleine jeunesse, dans la fleur de l'âge, au midi de la vie.
Hezekiah [heze'kaia]. *Pr.n.m.* Ézéchias.
hi [hai], *int.* Hé, là-bas ! ohé !
hiatus, *pl.* **-uses** [hai'eitəs, -əsiz], *s.* **1.** Lacune *f* (dans une série, un récit, etc.). **2.** *Med : Gram :* Hiatus *m*.
hibernal [hai'bə:rn(ə)l], *a.* Hivernal, -aux ; (sommeil) hibernal.
hibernate ['haibərneit], *v.i.* (*a*) *Z :* (*Of animals*) Hiberner, hiverner. (*b*) (*Of pers.*) (*To winter*) Hiverner.
Hibernian [hai'bə:rniən], *a. & s.* Hibernien, -ienne ; irlandais, -aise.
Hibernianism [hai'bə:rniənizm], **Hibernicism** [hai'bə:rnisizm], *s. Ling :* Locution irlandaise ; tour de phrase irlandais.
hibiscus [hi'biskəs], *s. Bot :* Ketmie *f*, hibiscus *m*.
hiccough[1], **hiccup**[1] ['hikʌp], *s.* Hoquet *m*. *To have (got) the hiccups*, avoir le hoquet.
hiccough[2], **hiccup**[2]. **1.** *v.i.* Avoir le hoquet ; hoqueter. **2.** *v.tr.* He hiccuped out an apology, il s'excusa entre deux hoquets.
hickory ['hikəri], *s.* Noyer (blanc) d'Amérique ; hickory *m*.
hide[1] [haid], *v.* (*p.t.* hid ; *p.p.* hid, hidden [hidn]) **1.** *v.tr.* (*a*) Cacher (*from*, à) ; enfouir (qch. dans la terre). *Where has he gone and hidden himself?* où est-il allé se fourrer ? *To hide one's face*, se cacher la figure, se voiler la face. *I did not know where to hide my head*, je ne savais où me fourrer, où me mettre. *To hide sth. from s.o.*, (i) cacher qch. à qn ; (ii) taire qch. à qn. *To hide (away) a treasure*, mettre un trésor dans une cache. (*b*) *To hide sth. from sight*, dérober, soustraire, qch. aux regards. *Clouds hid the sun*, des nuages voilaient le soleil. *Small villa hidden in a wood*, petite villa tapie, nichée, dans un bois. *Carp : etc :* **Hidden joint**, joint dérobé. *F :* **Hidden hand**, influence *f* occulte. **2.** *v.i.* Se cacher ; (i) se tenir caché ; se blottir (dans un coin, etc.) ; (ii) aller se cacher. *I didn't know where to hide*, je ne savais où me fourrer. **hiding**[1], *s.* Dissimulation *f* (de la joie, etc.). *Jur :* Recel *m* (d'un criminel). **To go into hiding**, se cacher ; se soustraire aux regards. **To be in hiding**, se tenir caché. **'hiding-place**, *s.* Cachette *f* ; (lieu *m* de) retraite *f*. **'hide-and-'seek**, *s. Games :* Cache-cache *m*.
hide[2], *s.* Peau *f*, dépouille *f* (d'un animal). *Com :* Cuir *m*. **Hide rope**, corde en cuir. *F :* **To save one's hide**, sauver sa peau. **'hide-bound,** *a. F :* Aux vues étroites ; plein de préjugés. *H.-b.* opinions, idées étroites. *H.-b.* etiquette, étiquette rigide.
hide[3], *v.tr. P :* Tanner le cuir à (qn) ; administrer une tripotée à (qn). **hiding**[2], *s.* Raclée *f*, rossée *f*, volée *f*.
hideous ['hidiəs], *a.* **1.** Hideux, affreux, effroyable ; (crime) horrible, odieux. **2.** D'une laideur repoussante. **-ly**, *adv.* Hideusement, affreusement.
hideousness ['hidiəsnəs], *s.* Hideur *f*, laideur *f*, horreur *f*.
hie [hai], *v.i. & pr. Lit : To hie to a place*, se hâter de se rendre en un lieu.
hierarch ['haiərɑ:rk], *s. Ecc :* Hiérarque *m* ; grand prêtre.
hierarchic(al) ['haiə'rɑ:rkik(əl)], *a.* Hiérarchique. *In h. order*, par ordre hiérarchique. **-ally**, *adv.* Hiérarchiquement.
hierarchy ['haiərɑ:rki], *s.* Hiérarchie *f*.
hieroglyph ['haiəroglif], *s.* Hiéroglyphe *m*.

hieroglyphic(al) [haiəro'glifik(ə)l], *a.* Hiéroglyphique.

hieroglyphics [haiəro'glifiks], *s.pl.* Hiéroglyphes *m*; signes *m* hiéroglyphiques.

higgle [higl], *v.i.* Marchander.

higgledy-piggledy ['higldi'pigldi], *adv.* Sans ordre, en pagaïe, pêle-mêle.

high [hai]. I. *a.* Haut. **1.** (*a*) *H. mountain,* haute montagne. *The highest point of the range,* le point culminant de la chaîne. *Wall six feet high,* mur haut de six pieds; mur qui a six pieds de haut, de hauteur. *How h. is that tree?* quelle est la hauteur de cet arbre? (*b*) *Cost:* (Corsage, col) montant. **2.** Élevé. (*a*) *The sun is getting higher* (*with the lengthening days*), le soleil remonte. *Glory to God in the Highest,* gloire à Dieu au plus haut des cieux. *Higher up the river,* en amont. *To walk with one's head high,* marcher tête haute. *To hold one's head high,* porter la tête haute, porter haut la tête. *Equit:* High action, allure relevée (d'un cheval). (*b*) **To be high in office,** avoir un poste élevé, une haute situation. *H. official,* haut fonctionnaire. *Higher posts,* postes supérieurs. *Sch:* The high table, la table des professeurs (au réfectoire); la table d'honneur. High and mighty, haut et puissant. *F:* **To be high and mighty,** faire le grand seigneur; se donner de grands airs; le prendre de haut. *s.* The Most High(est), le Très-Haut, le Tout-Puissant. High and low, les grands et les petits. (*c*) High thoughts, grandes pensées. *H. mind,* esprit élevé, noble. *H. art,* le grand art. (*d*) *H. rate of interest,* taux élevé; gros intérêt. *It fetches a h. price,* cela se vend cher. *To buy at a h. figure,* acheter cher. *To set a high value on sth.,* estimer qch. haut. *To play for high stakes,* jouer gros (jeu). High percentage of moisture, forte proportion d'humidité. High temperature, température élevée. High speed, grande vitesse. (*e*) In the highest degree, au suprême degré, au plus haut degré; par excellence. In the highest sense of the word, dans toute l'acception du mot; par excellence. *H. respect,* respect profond. High fever, forte fièvre; grosse fièvre. High wind, vent fort, violent; grand vent; gros vent. A high sea is running, la mer est grosse, houleuse. (*f*) To have a high opinion of s.o., tenir qn en haute estime. (*g*) High colour, (i) couleur vive; (ii) vivacité *f* du teint. *Art:* High lights, (i) hautes lumières; rehauts *m*; accents *m*. clairs *m* (d'un tableau); (ii) *Phot:* blancs *m* (de l'image); grands noirs (du cliché). The high spot of the match, le point culminant du match. High diet, high feeding, forte nourriture. (*h*) High voice, (i) voix élevée, haute; (ii) voix grêle. **3.** *The high(er) industrial classes,* les classes élevées de l'industrie. *Sch:* The higher forms, les classes supérieures; *F:* les grandes classes. Higher mathematics, mathématiques supérieures. The higher animals, les animaux supérieurs. **4.** (*Principal*) The High Street, la Grand'rue, la Grande rue. *Ecc:* High mass, la grand'messe, la grande messe. **5.** High day, jour de fête. **6.** (*a*) High noon, plein midi. It is high time he went to school, il est grand temps, grandement temps, qu'il aille à l'école. (*b*) *Cu:* (Of meat) Avancé, gâté; (*of game*) faisandé. *H. butter,* beurre fort. **7.** *Nau:* (Of ship) High and dry, (échoué) à sec (sur le sable, sur la plage). *F:* To leave s.o. high and dry, laisser qn en plan. **8.** On high, en haut; dans le ciel. Glory be to God on High, gloire à Dieu dans les hauteurs. From on high, d'en haut; de là-haut. **-ly,** *adv.* **1.** (*a*) **Highly placed official,** haut fonctionnaire.

(*b*) To be highly descended, être de haute naissance. **2.** His services are highly paid, ses services sont largement rétribués. To think highly of s.o., avoir une haute opinion de qn. **3.** Fort, très, bien, fortement. Highly amusing, fort, très, amusant. Highly coloured, (tableau, style) haut en couleur; (récit) coloré. II. **high,** *adv.* **1.** Haut; en haut. *Higher and higher,* de plus en plus haut. *Higher up,* plus haut. *To aim, fly, high,* viser, voler, haut; avoir de hautes visées. *To rise high in public esteem,* monter très haut dans l'estime publique. *F:* To hunt high and low for sth.,* chercher qch. de haut en bas, de la cave au grenier. **2.** To go as high as £2000, aller jusqu'à 2000 livres. *Cards: etc:* To play, stake, high, jouer gros jeu. **3.** Fort, fortement, très. (*Of wind*) To blow high, souffler avec violence, en tempête. To run high, (i) (*of the sea*) être grosse, houleuse; (ii) (*of feeling, words*) s'échauffer; (iii) (*of prices*) être élevé. **4.** To live high, vivre largement, sur un grand pied. **'high-born,** *a.* De haute naissance. **'high-bred,** *a.* **1.** (*a*) De parentage noble, de haute naissance. (*b*) (Cheval) de race. **2.** Parfaitement élevé; élevé dans le grand monde. **'high-class,** *a.* *F:* De premier ordre, de première qualité. **'high-'coloured,** *a.* Haut en couleur. **'high-flown,** *a.* (Style, discours) ampoulé. *To write in a h.-f. style,* écrire avec emphase. **high-'frequency,** *attrib.a. El:* (Courant) à haute fréquence. **'high-grade,** *attrib.a.* (Minerai, etc.) à haute teneur, d'un haut titre. **'high-'handed,** *a.* (Action) arbitraire; (autorité) tyrannique. **-ly,** *adv.* Arbitrairement; tyranniquement. **high-'minded,** *a.* A l'esprit élevé; aux sentiments nobles. **high-'mindedness,** *s.* Élévation *f* d'esprit; grandeur *f* d'âme. **'high-necked,** *a.* High-necked dress, robe montante. **'high-pitched,** *a.* **1.** (*Of sound*) Aigu, -uë. **2.** High-pitched roof, comble à forte inclinaison, à forte pente. **'high-'power(ed),** *a.* (*a*) (Auto) de haute puissance. (*b*) (Jumelles) à fort grossissement. **'high-'pressure,** *attrib.a.* (Machine) à haute pression. **'high-'priced,** *a.* De grand prix; cher. **'high-'priest,** *s.m.* Grand-prêtre, *pl.* grands-prêtres. **'high-'souled,** *a.* Magnanime. **'high-sounding,** *a.* Pompeux, prétentieux. **'high-speed,** *attrib.a.* (*a*) (Locomotive) à grande vitesse. (*b*) *Ind:* (Machine) à mouvement accéléré, à bon rendement. **'high-'spirited,** *a.* Intrépide; plein d'ardeur, de feu; (cheval) fougueux, vif. **'high-'strung,** *a.* (Tempérament) nerveux, exalté.

highbrow ['haibrau], *s. F:* Intellectuel, -elle.

highfalutin(g) [haifə'lu:tin, -iŋ], *a. F:* (Style) ampoulé, prétentieux.

highland ['hailənd]. **1.** *s.pl.* Highlands, pays montagneux, hautes terres. *Geog:* The Highlands, la Haute Écosse. **2.** *Attrib.a.* (*a*) Des montagnes; montagnard. (*b*) De la Haute Écosse.

highlander ['hailəndər], **highlandman,** *pl.* **-men** ['hailəndmən, -men], *s.* **1.** Montagnard *m.* **2.** A Highlander, un Highlander; un montagnard écossais; un habitant de la Haute Écosse.

highness ['hainəs], *s.* **1.** (*a*) Élévation *f* (des prix, etc.). (*b*) Grandeur *f* (d'âme). **2.** (*Title*) Altesse *f.*

highway ['haiwei], *s.* (*a*) Chemin *m* de grande communication; grande route, grand'route *f.* Highways and by-ways, chemins et sentiers. The King's Highway, le grand chemin. **To take (to) the highway,** devenir un voleur de grand

chemin. **To be on the highway to success, to ruin,** être en bonne voie de réussir ; être sur la pente fatale de la ruine. (b) *Adm :* Voie publique. **The Highways Department,** les ponts et chaussées.
highwayman, *pl.* **-men** ['haiweimən, -men], *s.m.* Voleur de grand chemin.
hike[1] [haik], *s. F :* **1.** Vagabondage *m.* **To be on the hike,** vagabonder ; être sur le trimard. **2.** Excursion *f* à pied.
hike[2], *v.i. F : (a)* Vagabonder, trimarder. (b) Faire du tourisme à pied. **To hike it,** faire le trajet à pied. **hiking,** *s.* Excursions *fpl* à pied.
hiker ['haikər], *s.* Excursionniste *mf* à pied.
hilarious [hi'lɛəriəs], *a.* Gai, joyeux, hilare. **-ly,** *adv.* Gaiement, joyeusement.
hilarity [hi'lariti], *s.* Hilarité *f*, gaieté *f*.
Hilary ['hiləri]. *Pr.n.m.* Hilaire. *Jur :* **Hilary term,** session *f* de la Saint-Hilaire (commençant en janvier).
hill [hil], *s.* **1.** (a) Colline *f*, coteau *m*. **Up hill and down dale, over hill and dale,** par monts et par vaux. **Hill-country,** pays de montagne(s). (*In India*) **Hill station,** station de montagne. **Hill road,** chemin côtier. (b) Éminence *f* ; monticule *m. See* ANT-HILL, MOLE-HILL. **2.** (*On road*) Côte *f* ; (i) montée *f* ; (ii) descente *f. Aut :* **Speed up hill,** vitesse en côte. **To go down the hill,** (i) descendre la colline ; (ii) *F :* baisser, décliner.
hill-'side, *s.* Flanc *m* de coteau ; coteau *m*.
hilliness ['hilinəs], *s.* Montuosité *f*.
hillock ['hilək], *s.* Petite colline ; monticule *m*, butte *f*, tertre *m* ; (*rounded*) mamelon *m*. **Sand hillocks,** buttes de sable.
hilly ['hili], *a.* **1.** Montagneux ; (terrain) accidenté. **2.** (Chemin) montueux, à fortes pentes.
hilt [hilt], *s.* **1.** Poignée *f*, garde *f* (d'épée). **Up to the hilt,** jusqu'à la garde. **To prove an assertion up to the hilt,** démontrer surabondamment une assertion. **2.** Manche *m* (de dague, etc.) ; crosse *f* (de pistolet).
hilum ['hailəm], *s. Bot :* Hile *m*.
him [him], *pers.pron.m., objective case.* **1.** (*Unstressed*) (a) (*Direct*) Le, (*before a vowel sound*) l' ; (*indirect*) lui. *Do you love him?* l'aimez-vous ? *I obey him,* je lui obéis. *I shall tell him so,* je le lui dirai. (b) (*Refl.*) Lui, soi. *He took his luggage with him,* il prit ses bagages avec lui. (c) (*Refl.*) *A. & Lit : He laid him down to sleep,* il se coucha pour dormir. **2.** (*Stressed*) (a) Lui. *I found him and his friend in the park,* je les ai trouvés, lui et son ami, dans le parc. *Him I admire,* lui je l'admire. (b) *The prize goes to him who comes in first,* le prix est pour celui qui arrivera le premier. **3.** *F : It's him,* c'est lui. *That's him!* le voilà !
himself [him'self], *pers.pron. See* SELF 4.
hind[1] [haind], *s.* Biche *f*.
hind[2], *s.* **1.** Valet *m* de ferme. **2.** *F :* (a) Paysan *m*. (b) Rustre *m*.
hind[3], **hinder**[1] ['haindər], *a.* **1.** (*Usu.* hinder) *Hinder part,* partie postérieure, partie arrière. **2.** (*Always* hind) **Hind legs, feet,** jambes, pattes, de derrière. *F :* **To get on one's hind legs,** se mettre debout. **Hind quarters** (*of a horse*), arrière-main *m*, arrière-train *m*.
hinder[2] ['hindər], *v.tr.* **1.** Gêner, embarrasser (qn) ; retarder, entraver (qch.) ; faire obstacle à (un mouvement). **2.** (*Prevent*) Empêcher, retenir, arrêter (*s.o. from doing sth.,* qn de faire qch.).
hindmost ['haindmoust], *a.* Dernier. **Everyone for himself and the devil take the hindmost,** sauve qui peut.
Hindoo ['hin'du:], *a. & s. Ethn :* (H)indou, -oue.
hindrance ['hindrəns], *s.* Empêchement *m*,

obstacle *m*. **Without (let or) hindrance,** sans entrave(s) ; en toute liberté.
Hindu ['hin'du:] = HINDOO.
hinge[1] [hindʒ], *s.* **1.** (a) Gond *m* (de porte) ; paumelle *f*. **Hook and hinge,** penture *f* et gond. **Door off its hinges,** porte hors de ses gonds. (b) (Butt-)hinge, charnière *f*. **Pin hinge,** charnière à fiche, à broche. **2.** Pivot *m* (d'une entreprise) ; point principal, nœud *m* (d'un argument).
'hinge-pin, *s.* Broche *f*, cheville *f*, de charnière.
hinge[2]. **1.** *v.tr.* (i) Monter (une porte, etc.) sur ses gonds ; (ii) mettre les charnières à (une boîte, etc.). **2.** *v.i.* (a) *Tourner,* pivoter (*on, autour de*). (b) *F :* **Everything hinges on** *his* **answer,** tout dépend de sa réponse. **hinged,** *a.* (Couvercle) à charnière(s). **Hinged flap** (*of counter*), battant *m* relevable. **Hinged girder,** poutre articulée.
hinny[1] ['hini], *s. Z :* Bardot *m*, bardeau *m*.
hinny[2], *v.i.* (*Of horse*) Hennir.
hint[1] [hint], *s.* **1.** (a) Insinuation *f* ; allusion indirecte. **Broad hint,** (i) allusion évidente ; (ii) avis peu voilé. **To give, drop, s.o. a hint,** toucher un mot à qn. *I'll give, drop, him a gentle h.,* je vais lui en toucher un mot tout doucement. **To throw out, drop, let fall, a hint that . . .,** donner à entendre que. . . . **To know how to take a hint,** entendre (qn) à demi-mot. (b) (*Sign*) Signe *m*, indication *f*, suggestion *f*. **Not the slightest hint of . . .,** pas le moindre soupçon de. . . . **2.** Hints **for housewives,** conseils *m* aux ménagères. *Maintenance hints and tips,* conseils et indications pour l'entretien (d'un appareil, etc.).
hint[2], *v.tr. & i.* Insinuer (qch.) ; suggérer, dire, (qch.) à mots couverts. **To hint to s.o. that . . .,** faire entendre à qn que. . . . **To hint at sth.,** laisser entendre qch.
hinterland ['hintərland], *s.* Hinterland *m* ; arrière-pays *m*.
hip[1] [hip], *s.* **1.** *Anat :* Hanche *f*. **To smite s.o. hip and thigh,** anéantir qn. **2.** *Const :* Hip(-piece, -rafter), arêtier *m*, arête *f*. **'hip-bath,** *s.* Bain *m* de siège. **'hip-bone,** *s.* Os *m* de la hanche ; os iliaque. **'hip-disease,** *s.* Coxalgie *f*. **'hip-flask,** *s.* Flacon *m* à cognac. **'hip-joint,** *s.* Articulation *f* de la hanche. **'hip-'pocket,** *s.* Poche *f* sur la hanche ; poche (à) revolver. **'hip-roof,** *s. Arch :* Comble *m* en croupe.
hip[2], *s. Bot :* Cynorrhodon *m* ; *F :* gratte-cul *m inv.*
hip[3], *s. F :* **To have the hip,** avoir le cafard.
hip[4], *v.tr. F :* Attrister (qn) ; donner le cafard à (qn). **hipped,** *a.* Abattu, déprimé.
hip[5], *int.* **Hip! hip! hip! hurrah!** hip ! hip ! hip ! hourra !
hippodrome ['hipodroum], *s.* Hippodrome *m*.
hippopotamus, *pl.* **-muses, -mi** [hipo'potəməs, -məsiz, -mai], *s. Z :* Hippopotame *m*.
hircine ['hə:rsain], *a.* Hircin.
hire[1] ['haiər], *s.* **1.** Louage *m* (d'un domestique, d'une voiture) ; location *f* (d'une maison). **To let sth. (out) on hire,** louer qch. **2.** Salaire *m*, gages *mpl. 'hire-'purchase,** *s.* Vente *f* à tempérament ; location-vente *f*.
hire[2], *v.tr.* **1.** (a) Louer, engager (un domestique). **Hired assassin,** assassin à gages. (b) Louer (une voiture, etc.). **2. To hire out,** louer, donner en location (une voiture, etc.).
hireling ['haiərliŋ], *s. & a.* Mercenaire (*m*).
hirer ['haiərər], *s.* **1.** Locataire *m* (d'une charrette, etc.). **2. Hirer out,** loueur, -euse.
hirsute ['hə:rsju:t], *a.* Hirsute, velu.

his[1] [hiz], *poss.a.* (*denoting a m. possessor*) Son, *f.* sa, *pl.* ses. *One of his friends*, un de ses amis, un sien ami. *The date and place of his birth*, ses date et lieu de naissance. *He fell on his back*, il tomba sur le dos. (*Emphatic*) '*His idea would be to* . . ., son idée à lui serait de. . . .

his[2], *poss.pron.* (*denoting a m. possessor*) Le sien, la sienne, les siens, les siennes. *He took my pen and his*, il prit ma plume et la sienne. *This book is his*, ce livre est à lui, lui appartient ; c'est son livre à lui. *A friend of his*, un de ses amis. *That pride of his*, cet orgueil dont il ne peut se défaire.

Hispanic [his'panik], *a.* Hispanique.

hiss[1] [his], *s.* **1.** (*a*) Sifflement *m* (du gaz). (*b*) *Th :* etc : Sifflet *m.* **2.** *Ling :* Sifflante *f.*

hiss[2]. **1.** *v.i.* (*Of serpent, steam, etc.*) Siffler ; (*of arc-lamp*) bruire ; (*of steam, gas*) chuinter. **2.** *v.tr.* To hiss an actor, siffler un acteur.

hist [hist], *int.* **1.** (*To enjoin silence*) Chut ! **2.** (*To attract attention*) Pst !

histology ['his'tɔlɔdʒi], *s.* *Biol :* Histologie *f.*

historian [his'tɔ:riən], *s.* Historien *m.*

historiated [his'tɔ:rieitid], *a.* (Manuscrit) historié.

historic [his'tɔrik], *a.* Historique ; (événement) marquant.

historical [his'tɔrik(ə)l], *a.* **1.** (Fait) historique, de l'histoire. **2.** *H. painting, painter*, tableau, peintre, d'histoire. *H. novel*, roman historique. **-ally**, *adv.* Historiquement.

historiographer [histɔ:ri'ɔgrəfər], *s.* Historiographe *m.*

history ['histəri], *s.* **1.** L'histoire *f.* *F :* That's ancient history, c'est une vieille histoire. To know the inner history of an affair, connaître les dessous d'une affaire. History-book, manuel *m*, livre *m*, d'histoire. **2.** Natural history, histoire naturelle. **3.** *Mil :* Navy : History sheet, feuille *f* matriculaire.

histrionic(al) [histri'ɔnik(əl)], *a.* **1.** Théâtral, -aux. **2.** *Pej :* Histrionique ; (effusions) de cabotin.

histrionics [histri'ɔniks], *s.pl.* **1.** L'art *m* du théâtre. **2.** *Pej :* Démonstrations *f* peu sincères ; "la comédie."

hit[1] [hit], *s.* **1.** (*a*) Coup *m.* *F :* To have a sly hit at s.o., donner un coup de patte à qn. That's a hit at you, c'est vous qui êtes visé ; c'est une pierre dans votre jardin. (*b*) *Fenc :* Touche *f*, coup. To score a hit, toucher. (*c*) *Hockey :* Coup de crosse. *Free hit*, coup franc. (*d*) *Baseball :* Coup de batte ; frappe *f.* **2.** (*a*) Coup réussi ; succès *m.* Lucky hit, (i) coup heureux ; (ii) trouvaille *f.* To make a hit, (*of thg*) réussir. To make a big, a huge, hit, décrocher le grand succès. (*b*) *Th :* Pièce *f* à succès. It is a great hit, c'est un succès fou.

hit[2]. (*p.t.* & *p.p.* hit ; *pr.p.* hitting) **1.** *v.tr.* (*a*) Frapper. To hit s.o. a blow, porter, donner, un coup à qn. (*b*) *v.i.* To hit against sth., s'attraper à qch. ; se cogner contre qch. *His head hit against the pavement*, sa tête a porté, a donné, sur le trottoir. (*c*) Atteindre. *Fenc : Bill :* Toucher. To hit the mark, atteindre le but ; frapper juste. To be hit by a bullet, être atteint par une balle. *F :* To be hit in one's pride, être blessé dans son orgueil. (*Of allusion, etc.*) To hit home, porter (coup) ; piquer (qn) au vif. *F :* To be hard hit, être gravement atteint (par ses pertes, etc.). (*d*) *adj.* & *adv.phr.* To attempt sth. hit or miss, tenter qch. vaille que vaille. To strike out hit or miss, frapper au hasard. **2.** *v.tr.* & *i.* To hit (**up)on** sth., découvrir (un moyen) ;

rencontrer (un indice, etc.). You've hit it! vous avez deviné juste ! vous y êtes ! hit back, *v.tr.* & *i.* Se défendre ; rendre coup pour coup (à qn). hit off, *v.tr.* **1.** (*a*) To hit off a likeness, attraper une ressemblance. You have hit him off to a T, P : c'est lui tout craché. (*b*) To hit s.o. off, donner un portrait satirique de qn ; charger qn. **2.** To hit it off with s.o., s'accorder avec qn. hit out, *v.i.* To hit out at s.o., décocher un coup à qn.

hitch[1] [hitʃ], *s.* **1.** Saccade *f*, secousse *f.* To give one's trousers a h., remonter son pantalon. **2.** *Nau :* Nœud *m* ; amarrage *m* à demi-clefs ; clef *f.* **3.** Anicroche *f*, contretemps *m.* There is a hitch somewhere, il y a quelque chose qui cloche. Without a hitch, sans à-coup ; sans accroc.

hitch[2], *v.tr.* **1.** Remuer (qch.) par saccades. To hitch (up) one's trousers, remonter son pantalon. **2.** Accrocher, attacher, fixer. *F :* To hitch one's wagon to a star, attacher son char à une étoile.

hither ['hiðər]. **1.** *adv.* Ici (exprimant la venue). Hither and thither, çà et là. **2.** *a.* Le plus rapproché. *A.Geog :* Hither Gaul, la Gaule citérieure.

hitherto ['hiðər'tu:], *adv.* Jusqu'ici. As hitherto, comme le passé.

hitter ['hitər], *s.* Frappeur *m.* Box : Cogneur *m.*

hive[1] [haiv], *s.* **1.** Ruche *f.* **2.** (*Swarm*) Essaim *m.*

hive[2]. **1.** *v.tr.* Mettre (des abeilles) dans une ruche ; (re)cueillir (un essaim). **2.** *v.i.* (*a*) (*Of swarm*) Entrer dans la ruche. (*b*) *F :* Vivre ensemble (comme des abeilles dans une ruche).

ho [hou], *int.* **1.** (*Expressing surprise, mirth, etc.*) Ho ! **2.** (*To attract attention*) Hé ! ohé !

hoar ['hɔ:r], *s.* Hoar(-frost), gelée blanche ; givre *m*, *Lit :* frimas *m.*

hoard[1] [hɔ:rd], *s.* Amas *m*, accumulation secrète (de vivres, etc.). *H. of money*, trésor *m*, *F :* magot *m.*

hoard[2], *v.tr.* Amasser (le blé, etc.) ; accumuler (de l'argent). To hoard up tre~sure, ~bs. to hoard, thésauriser (des capitaux). **hoarding**[1], *s.* Resserre *f*, amassage *m* (de provisions) ; thésaurisation *f* (de capitaux).

hoarder ['hɔ:rdər], *s.* Amasseur, -euse. *H. of money*, thésauriseur, -euse.

hoarding[2] ['hɔ:rdiŋ], *s.* Clôture *f* en planches ; palissade *f.* Advertisement hoarding, panneau-réclame *m*, *pl.* panneaux-réclame.

hoarse [hɔ:rs], *a.* Enroué, rauque. To shout oneself hoarse, s'enrouer à force de crier. **-ly**, *adv.* D'une voix rauque, enrouée.

hoarseness ['hɔ:rsnəs], *s.* Enrouement *m.*

hoary ['hɔ:əri], *a.* **1.** (*Of hair*) Blanchi, chenu. **2.** Vénérable, séculaire. Of hoary antiquity, de la plus haute antiquité.

hoax[1] [houks], *s.* Mystification *f*, supercherie *f*, farce *f.* To play a hoax on s.o., (i) mystifier qn ; (ii) faire une farce à qn.

hoax[2], *v.tr.* Mystifier, attraper (qn) ; *P :* monter un bateau à (qn). **hoaxing**, *s.* Mystification *f.*

hob [hɔb], *s.* **1.** Plaque *f* de côté (d'une grille de cheminée, où l'on peut tenir des aliments au chaud). **2.** = HOBNAIL.

hobble[1] [hɔbl], *s.* **1.** Boitillement *m*, clochement *m.* **2.** (*a*) Entrave *f* (pour chevaux, etc.). (*b*) *F :* Embarras *m.* 'hobble-skirt, *s.* Cost : Jupe *f* fourreau.

hobble[2]. **1.** *v.i.* Boitiller, clocher, clopiner. To hobble along, avancer clopin-clopant ; traîner la jambe. **2.** *v.tr.* Entraver (un cheval, etc.).

hobbledehoy ['hɔbldi'hɔi], *s.* Jeune homme gauche ; grand dadais.

hobby ['hɔbi], s. .I. A: Bidet m; petit cheval de selle. 2. (a) Marotte f, dada m. To ride one's pet hobby, enfourcher son dada. (b) Passe-temps favori. To paint as a hobby, se distraire à faire de la peinture. **'hobby-horse,** s. Dada m; cheval m de bois.

hobgoblin ['hɔbgɔblin], s. Lutin m, farfadet m.

hobnail ['hɔbneil], s. Caboche f; clou m à ferrer (les souliers).

hobnailed ['hɔbneild], a. (Soulier) ferré, à gros clous.

hobnob ['hɔbnɔb], v.i. (hobnobbed) To hobnob with s.o., être de pair à compagnon avec qn.

hobo ['houbou], s. U.S: (a) Ouvrier ambulant. (b) F: Chemineau m, trimardeur m.

Hobson ['hɔbsən]. Pr.n.m. F: It's (a case of) Hobson's choice, il n'y a pas d'alternative.

hock[1] [hɔk], s. Jarret m (de quadrupède).

hock[2], s. Vin m du Rhin.

hockey ['hɔki], s. (Jeu m de) hockey m.

hocus ['houkəs], v.tr. (hocussed) I. Attraper (qn); F: monter un bateau à (qn). 2. Narcotiser, droguer (une boisson).

hocus-pocus[1] ['houkəs'poukəs], s. Tromperie f, supercherie f.

hocus-pocus[2], v.tr. (-pocussed) Berner, mystifier (qn).

hod [hɔd], s. I. Oiseau m, auge f, hotte f (de maçon). 2. Seau m à charbon.

hodman, pl. -men ['hɔdmən, -men], s. Aide maçon m, pl. aides-maçons.

hodometer [hɔ'dɔmetər], s. Odomètre m.

hoe[1] [hou], s. Hort: Houe f, binette f.

hoe[2], v.tr. (hoed; hoeing) Houer, biner (le sol); sarcler (les mauvaises herbes). F: A hard row to hoe, une tâche difficile, ingrate.

hog [hɔg], s. I. (a) Porc châtré. (b) Porc, cochon m, pourceau m. F: To go the whole hog, aller jusqu'au bout. 2. (Pers.) F: Goinfre m, glouton m; F: pourceau. 3. Nau: (Brush) Goret m. **'hog mane,** s. Crinière coupée en brosse. **'hog's back,** s. = HOGBACK. **'hog-wash,** s. (a) Eaux grasses (que l'on donne aux porcs). (b) F: Rinçures fpl, lavasse f.

hogback ['hɔgbak], s. Ph.Geog: Dos m d'âne; ligne f de crête; route f formant ligne de crête.

hogged ['hɔgd], a. I. (Navire) arqué, cassé. 2. (Crinière de cheval) en brosse.

hoggish ['hɔgiʃ], a. F: (Individu) glouton, grossier.

Hogmanay ['hɔgmaˈnei], s. Scot: La Saint-Sylvestre.

hogshead ['hɔgzhed], s. Tonneau m, barrique f.

hogweed ['hɔgwiːd], s. Bot: (a) Berce commune. (b) Centinode f; (renouée f) traînasse f.

hoi(c)k[1] [hɔik], s. Coup sec; saccade f.

hoi(c)k[2], v.tr. F: (a) Lever, tirer, d'un coup sec. (b) Faire monter (un avion) en chandelle. (c) Redresser (l'avion).

hoise [hɔːiz], v.tr. A: (p.p. hoist) = HOIST[2]. To be hoist with one's own petard, être pris à son propre piège.

hoist[1] [hɔist], s. I. (a) Coup m de treuil. To give sth. a hoist, hisser qch. (b) To give s.o. a hoist (up), aider qn à monter. 2. (a) Appareil m de levage; treuil m. (b) (For goods) Monte-charge m inv; ascenseur m (de marchandises).

hoist[2], v.tr. To hoist (up), hisser, guinder. To hoist a boat out, mettre un canot à la mer. F: To h. s.o. on to his horse, hisser qn sur son cheval. Hoisting gear, tackle, engine, appareil m de hissage, de levage.

hoist[3]. See HOISE.

hoity-toity ['hɔitiˈtɔiti]. I. int. Ta, ta, ta!

taratata! 2. a. Don't be so hoity-toity! prenez-le sur un autre ton!

hokey-pokey ['houki'pouki], s. F: (Crème f à la) glace (de marchand ambulant).

hokum ['houkəm], s. U.S: P: Boniments mpl à la noix de coco.

hold[1] [hould], s. I. (a) Prise f, étreinte f. To have hold of s.o., sth., tenir qn, qch. To catch, lay, take, hold of sth., saisir, empoigner, qch.; mettre la main sur qch. Where did you get hold of that? où vous êtes-vous procuré cela? F: où avez-vous pêché ça? To keep hold of sth., ne pas lâcher qch. To keep tight hold of, a firm hold on, sth., tenir qch. serré. To relax one's hold, relâcher son étreinte. To leave, lose, hold of sth., lâcher qch. To lose, let go, one's hold, lâcher prise. (b) To have a hold on, over, s.o., avoir prise sur qn. To gain a firm hold over s.o., acquérir un grand empire, un grand pouvoir, sur qn. (c) Box: Tenu m. Wr: Prise. 2. Soutien m; point m d'appui.

hold[2], v. (held [held]; held) I. v.tr. I. Tenir. (a) To hold sth. tight, serrer qch.; tenir qch. serré. To hold s.o. fast, tenir solidement qn. To hold hands, se donner la main. To hold one's sides with laughter, se tenir les côtes de rire. (b) To hold the key to the puzzle, tenir le mot de l'énigme. 2. (a) To hold sth. in position, tenir qch. en place. (b) To hold s.o. in check, tenir qn en échec. To hold s.o. prisoner, tenir, garder, qn prisonnier. To hold oneself ready, in readiness, se tenir prêt. To hold s.o. to his promise, obliger, contraindre, qn à tenir sa promesse. 3. To hold one's ground, tenir bon, tenir ferme. To hold one's own against all comers, maintenir sa position envers et contre tous. He can h. his own, il sait se défendre. F: To hold the fort, assurer la permanence (en l'absence des chefs). To hold the stage, (i) (of actor) retenir l'attention de l'auditoire; (ii) (of play) tenir l'affiche (pendant longtemps). Nau: To hold the course, tenir la route. Tp: Hold the line! ne quittez pas! 4. To hold one's head high, porter la tête haute. To h. oneself upright, se tenir droit. 5. (a) Contenir, renfermer (une quantité de qch.). Car that holds six people, voiture à six places. This car cannot h. five (persons), on ne tient pas cinq dans cette voiture. (b) What the future holds, ce que l'avenir nous réserve. 6. Tenir (une séance); avoir (une consultation); célébrer (une fête). The Motor Show is held in October, le Salon de l'automobile se tient au mois d'octobre. To hold a conversation with s.o., s'entretenir avec qn. 7. Retenir, arrêter, empêcher. (a) To hold (in) one's breath, retenir son haleine. There was no holding him, il n'y avait pas moyen de l'arrêter, de l'empêcher. Hold your hand! arrêtez! Abs. Hold (hard)! arrêtez! halte là! (b) To hold water, (i) (of cask, etc.) tenir l'eau, être étanche; (ii) F: (of theory, etc.) tenir debout. (c) Retenir (l'attention). (d) Mil: To hold the enemy, contenir l'ennemi. 8. Avoir, posséder (un emploi); détenir (une charge); occuper (une terre). To h. shares, détenir des actions. 9. (a) To hold sth. lightly, faire peu de cas de qch. This is held to be true, ceci passe pour vrai. To hold s.o. responsible, tenir qn responsable. To hold s.o. in respect, avoir du respect pour qn. (b) Avoir, professer (une opinion). He holds that . . ., il est d'avis que. . . . 10. (Sustain) Mus: To hold (on) a note, tenir, prolonger, une note. II. **hold,** v.i. I. (Of rope, nail, etc.) Tenir (bon); être solide. To hold tight, firm, fast, tenir bon, tenir ferme. **2.** (a) Durer, persister; continuer; (of weather) se maintenir. (b) To hold on one's way, suivre son chemin. **3.** To hold (good, true), être vrai, valable. Promise that still holds good, promesse qui est toujours valable. The objection holds, cette objection subsiste. **4.** To hold to a belief, rester attaché à une croyance. To hold by, to, one's opinion, adhérer à son opinion. **hold back.** **I.** v.tr. (a) Retenir (qn, ses larmes). (b) Cacher, dissimuler (la vérité). **2.** v.i. Rester en arrière; hésiter. To hold back from doing sth., se retenir de faire qch. To hold back for sth., se réserver pour qch. **hold down,** v.tr. **I.** Baisser (la tête). **2.** (a) To hold a man down, maintenir un homme à terre. (b) Opprimer (qn, le peuple). **hold forth,** v.i. Disserter, pérorer. To h. forth to the crowd, haranguer la foule. **hold in,** v.tr. Serrer la bride à (un cheval); F: réprimer (ses désirs); maîtriser (une passion). To hold oneself in, se contenir, se retenir. **hold off. I.** v.tr. Tenir (qn, qch.) à distance. **2.** v.i. (a) Se tenir à distance (from, de). (b) The rain is holding off, jusqu'ici il ne pleut pas. (c) S'abstenir; se réserver. **hold on. I.** v.tr. Maintenir. **2.** v.i. (a) To hold on to sth. (i) S'accrocher, se cramponner, à qch. (ii) Ne pas lâcher, ne pas abandonner, qch. Hold on! (i) tenez bon! tenez ferme! (ii) Tp: ne quittez pas! (iii) (attendez) un instant! How long can you h. on? combien de temps pouvez-vous tenir? (b) F: Hold on (a bit)! pas si vite! **hold out. I.** v.tr. Tendre, offrir, présenter (la main, etc.). F: To hold out a hand to s.o., tendre la perche à qn. **2.** v.i. Durer. To hold out against an attack, soutenir une attaque; tenir bon contre une attaque. To h. out to the end, tenir jusqu'au bout. **hold over,** v.tr. Remettre (à plus tard). **hold together. I.** v.tr. Maintenir (deux choses) ensemble. To h. one's staff together, assurer la cohésion de son personnel. **2.** v.i. Tenir (ensemble); garder de la cohésion. We must h. together, il faut rester unis. F: The story won't h. together, l'histoire ne tient pas debout. **hold up. I.** v.tr. (a) Soutenir (qn, qch.). (b) Lever (qch.) (en l'air). To h. up one's head (again), relever, redresser, la tête. To h. sth. up to the light, (i) exposer qch. à un bon jour; (ii) tenir qch. à contre-jour. (c) To hold s.o. up as a model, citer, offrir, proposer, qn comme modèle. To hold s.o. up to ridicule, tourner qn en ridicule. (d) Arrêter (un train, etc.); entraver, gêner (la circulation); immobiliser (l'ennemi). U.S: To hold up a train, arrêter un train (pour dévaliser les voyageurs). Goods held up at the custom house, marchandises en consigne, en souffrance, à la douane. **2.** v.i. (a) Se soutenir. (b) (Of weather) Se maintenir. (c) Ne pas tomber. **'hold-up,** s. **I.** (a) Arrêt m, embarras m (de voitures); suspension f de la circulation. (b) Panne f (du métro, etc.). **2.** Attaque f; coup m à main armée. **hold with,** v.i. To hold with s.o., tenir pour qn; être du parti de qn. **holding,** s. **I.** (a) Tenue f (d'une plume, etc.). (b) Tchn: Fixation f; serrage m. (c) Mil: H. of a captured position, conservation f d'une position. (d) Tenue (d'une séance, etc.). (e) Possession f (de terres); tenure f. **2.** (a) Agr: Terre affermée; ferme f. Small holdings, lopins m de terre. (b) Fin: Avoir m (en actions); effets mpl en portefeuille. **'hold-all,** s. Enveloppe f de voyage; (sac m) fourre-tout m inv. **hold³,** s. Nau: Cale f. The goods in the h., les marchandises à fond de cale.

holder ['houldər], s. **I.** (Pers.) (a) Teneur -euse (de qch.). Metalw: **Holder-on, -up,** teneur de tas. (b) Détenteur, -trice (Fin: de titres, d'une lettre de change); porteur, -euse (Fin: de titres, d'un effet); titulaire mf (d'un droit); propriétaire mf (d'une terre). Small **holder,** petit propriétaire. **2.** (Device) (a) Support m, monture f, patte f. (b) (Expressed by porte-, e.g.) Drillholder, bit-holder, porte-foret m. **Pen-holder,** porte-plume m inv. **3.** Récipient m. **Gas-holder,** cloche f à gaz; gazomètre m. **4.** Poignée f (pour fer à repasser, etc.).

holdfast ['houldfɑːst], s. Crampon m; serrejoint m. **Bench holdfast,** valet m.

hole¹ [houl], s. Trou m. **I.** (a) Creux m, cavité f. F: To be, find oneself, in a hole, être, se trouver, dans l'embarras, dans une impasse. To get s.o. out of a h., tirer qn d'un mauvais pas. (b) Terrier m (de lapin). (c) F: Dead and alive hole, petit trou mort. **2.** Orifice m, ouverture f; lumière f (de pinnule, etc.). Holes in a strap, points m d'une courroie. Mec.E: Inspection hole, orifice de visite; regard m (d'un fourneau, etc.). To bore a h., percer un trou. To wear a hole in a garment, trouer un vêtement. (Of garment) To wear, go, into holes, se trouer. Stockings in holes, full of holes, bas tout troués. To make a hole in sth., (i) faire un trou à qch.; percer qch.; (ii) F: faire une brèche à (son avoir). To knock holes in an argument, démolir un argument. **'hole-and-'corner,** attrib.a. Clandestin, secret.

hole². I. v.tr. (a) Trouer, percer (qch.); pratiquer, faire, un trou dans (qch.). (b) Golf: To h. the ball, abs. to hole (out), poter (la balle); mettre la balle dans le trou. **2.** v.i. Se trouer, se percer.

holiday ['hɔlidei], s. (a) (Jour m de) fête (religieuse); jour férié. To keep, make, holiday, faire fête. (b) (Jour de) congé m; jour de sortie. To take a holiday, prendre un congé; chômer. (c) The holidays, les vacances. A month's holiday, un mois de vacances. To be on holiday, on one's holidays, (i) être en congé, en vacance(s); (ii) être en villégiature. **'holiday-maker,** s. **I.** Fêteur, -euse. **2.** Villégiateur m.

holiness ['houlinəs], s. Sainteté f.

Holland ['hɔlənd]. **I.** Pr.n. La Hollande. **2.** s. Toile f de Hollande; toile bise, toile écrue.

hollands ['hɔləndz], s. Genièvre m de Hollande.

hollow¹ ['hɔlou]. **I.** a. **I.** Creux, caverneux, évidé. H. eyes, yeux caves, enfoncés. H. road, chemin creux. F: To feel hollow, avoir un creux dans l'estomac; avoir faim. **2.** (Son) sourd. In a hollow voice, d'une voix caverneuse. **3.** F: (Of friendship, etc.) Faux, f. fausse; trompeur, -euse; vain. **II. hollow,** adv. **I.** To sound hollow, sonner creux. **2.** To beat s.o. hollow, battre qn à plate couture. **III. hollow,** s. (a) Creux m (de la main, etc.); cavité f (d'une dent); excavation f. (b) Enfoncement m, dépression f (du sol). Ph.Geog: Bas-fond m. **hollow-'cheeked,** a. Aux joues creuses. **hollow-'eyed,** a. Aux yeux caves, enfoncés. **'hollow-ground,** a. (Rasoir) évidé. **'hollow-ware,** s. **I.** Boissellerie f. **2.** Articles mpl de ménage en faïence ou en fer battu.

hollow². I. v.tr. To hollow (out), creuser, évider. **2.** v.i. Se creuser; s'évider.

hollowness ['hɔlonəs], s. **I.** Creux m, concavité f. **2.** Timbre caverneux (de la voix). **3.** F: Manque m de sincérité (d'une promesse, etc.); fausseté f (de cœur).

holly ['hɔli], s. Bot: Houx m. **Holly grove, plantation,** houssaie f.

hollyhock ['hɔlihɔk], s. Rose trémière.

holm [houm], *s.* **1.** Ilot *m* (de rivière). **2.** Terrain *m* d'alluvion.

holm-oak ['houmouk], *s.* *Bot:* Yeuse *f*; chêne vert.

holocaust ['hɔlokɔːst], *s.* Holocauste *m*.

holograph ['hɔlɔgrɑːf]. **1.** *a.* (Document) olographe. **2.** *s.* Olographie *f*; testament *m* olographe.

holothurian [hɔlo'θjuəriən], *s.* *Echin:* Holothurie *f*; *F:* concombre *m* de mer.

holster ['houlstər], *s.* Fonte *f* (de selle); étui *m* de revolver (de selle ou de ceinturon).

holy ['houli]. **1.** *a.* (holiest) (*a*) Saint, sacré. **The Holy Ghost**, le Saint-Esprit. **The Holy Father**, le Saint-Père. **Holy Writ**, les Écritures saintes. **Holy bread, water**, pain bénit, eau bénite. **To keep the Sabbath day holy**, sanctifier le dimanche. **To swear by all that is holy**, jurer ses grands dieux. (*b*) (*Of pers.*) Saint, pieux. **2.** *s.* **The Holy of Holies**, le saint des saints. **-ily**, *adv.* Saintement.

holy-stone¹ ['houlistoun], *s.* *Nau:* Brique *f* à pont.

holy-stone², *v.tr.* *Nau:* Briquer (le pont).

homage ['homedʒ], *s.* Hommage *m*. **To pay, do, homage to s.o.**, rendre, faire, hommage à qn.

home [houm]. **I.** *s.* **1.** (*a*) Chez-soi *m inv*; foyer (familial, domestique). *The few houses near his h.*, les quelques maisons voisines de chez lui. *Hamlet of fifty homes*, hameau de cinquante feux. **The Ideal Home Exhibition**, le Salon des arts ménagers. **To have a home of one's own**, avoir un chez-soi. **To give s.o. a home, to make a home for s.o.**, recueillir qn; recevoir qn chez soi. **It's a home from home**, c'est un second chez-soi. *F:* **To go to one's last home**, partir pour sa dernière demeure. (*b*) **Le chez-soi**, la maison, le foyer. **Be it ever so humble there's no place like home**, il n'y a pas de petit chez-soi; à tout oiseau son nid est beau. **At home**, (i) à la maison, chez soi; (ii) *Sp:* (jouer) sur le terrain du club. *Jeweller working at h.*, bijoutier en chambre. *To stay at h.*, garder la maison. **Is Mr X at home?** M. X est-il chez lui? est-ce que monsieur y est? *Mrs X is not at h. to-day*, Mme X (i) est en ville, (ii) ne reçoit pas, aujourd'hui. *She is at h. on Tuesdays*, elle reçoit le mardi; son jour est le mardi. **To be 'not at home' to anyone**, consigner la porte à tout le monde. **To feel at home with s.o.**, se sentir à l'aise avec qn. **He is at home on, in, with, any topic**, tous les sujets lui sont familiers. **To make oneself at home**, faire comme chez soi. **To be (away, absent) from home**, ne pas être à la maison. **To go from home**, (i) partir, aller, en voyage; faire un voyage; (ii) sortir. **To leave home**, (i) partir (définitivement); (ii) quitter sa famille. **2.** Patrie *f*; pays (natal); terre natale. **At home and abroad**, chez nous, dans notre pays, et à l'étranger. *Adm: Mil: Navy:* **Service at home**, le service dans la métropole. **3.** *F:* **Nearer home**. *To take an example nearer h. . . .*, sans aller chercher si loin. . . . *When the question comes nearer h.*, they will think differently, quand la question les touchera de plus près, ils changeront d'avis. **4.** (*a*) *Nat.Hist:* Habitat *m*. (*b*) *Greece was the h. of fine arts*, la Grèce fut la patrie des beaux-arts. **5.** Asile *m*, refuge *m*. **Sailors' home**, foyer, abri *m*, du marin. **Home for the blind**, hospice *m* d'aveugles. **Home of rest**, maison de repos. *S.a.* MENTAL, NURSING HOME. **6.** (*a*) (*In games*) Le but. (*b*) *Rac:* L'arrivée *f*. **II. home**, *adv.* (Indique mouvement vers . . ., ou arrivée à. . . .) **1.** (*a*) A la maison; chez soi. **To go,**

come, home, (i) rentrer (à la maison); (ii) rentrer dans sa famille. **To get home, regagner la maison, son chez-soi. (*b*) **To go, come, home**, retourner au pays; (*of soldier, etc.*) rentrer dans ses foyers. (*c*) **To be home**, être de retour **2.** (*a*) (*Of bullet, etc.*) **To go home**, porter (coup) *The reproach went h.*, le reproche le toucha au vif; le reproche porta (coup). **To strike home**, trapper juste; porter coup. **To bring sth. home to s.o.**, faire sentir qch. à qn. **To bring a charge home to s.o.**, prouver une accusation contre qn. (*b*) **To screw a piece home**, visser, serrer, une pièce à fond, à bloc. **III. home**, *attrib.* **1.** (*a*) **Home circle**, cercle de famille. **Home training**, éducation familiale. **Home address**, adresse personnelle. *Sch:* **Home lessons** = HOMEWORK. (*b*) *Ven:* **The home coverts**, les fourrés les plus près du château. (*c*) **The home counties**, les comtés avoisinant Londres. *Sp:* **Home ground**, terrain du club. **The home side**, les locaux *m*. (*d*) **Home journey**, voyage de retour. *S.a.* TRUTH. **2.** **Home trade**, commerce intérieur. **Home products**, produits nationaux, du pays. **Home news**, nouvelles de l'intérieur. **The Home Fleet**, la flotte métropolitaine. **The Home Office** = le Ministère de l'Intérieur. **The Home Secretary** = le Ministre de l'Intérieur. **'home-baked'**, *a.* (Pain, gâteau) fait à la maison. **'home-bird'**, *s.* *F:* (*Of pers.*) Casanier, -ière. **'home-brewed'**, *a.* (Bière) brassée, fabriquée, à la maison; (cidre) de ménage. **'homecoming'**, *s.* Retour *m* au foyer, à la maison. **home-de'fence**, *s.* Défense nationale. **'home-farm'**, *s.* Ferme attachée au domaine. **'home-folk(s)**, *s.* (i) Parents *mpl*, famille *f*; (ii) gens *m* du village. **'home-grown'**, *a.* (Denrée) du pays; (produit) indigène; (vin) du crû. **Home-Guard (the)**, *s.* Les Territoriaux *m*. **'home-'made'**, *a.* Fait à la maison; (pain) de ménage. **'Home 'Rule'**, *s.* Autonomie *f*. **'home-thrust'**, *s.* (*a*) *Fenc:* Botte *f*; grand coup. (*b*) *F:* Pointe *f*, critique *f*, qui va droit au but. **That was a home-thrust**, cela l'a touché au vif. **'home-work'**, *s.* *Sch:* Devoirs *mpl* du soir.

homeless ['houmləs], *a.* Sans foyer; sans feu ni lieu.

homelike ['houmlaik], *a.* Qui rappelle le chez-soi.

homeliness ['houmlinəs], *s.* **1.** Simplicité *f* (de manières). **2.** Manque *m* de beauté.

homely ['houmli], *a.* **1.** (Nourriture) simple, ordinaire; (goûts) bourgeois, modestes; (gens) tout à fait simples. **2.** (*Of pers.*) Sans beauté.

Homer¹ ['houmər]. *Pr.n.m.* Homère.

homer², *s.* *Orn:* Pigeon voyageur.

Homeric [ho'merik], *a.* Homérique.

homesick ['houmsik], *a.* Qui a le mal du pays.

homesickness ['houmsiknəs], *s.* Mal *m* du pays; nostalgie *f*.

homespun ['houmspʌn]. **1.** *a.* (*a*) (Étoffe de laine) de fabrication domestique. *H. linen*, toile *f* de ménage. (*b*) *F:* Simple, sans apprêt. **2.** *s.* Étoffe faite à la maison.

homestead ['houmsted], *s.* Ferme *f* (avec dépendances).

homeward ['houmwərd]. **1.** *a.* Qui se dirige (i) vers sa maison, vers sa demeure; (ii) (*from abroad*) vers son pays. **2.** *adv.* = HOMEWARDS. **'homeward-'bound**, *a.* (Vaisseau) à destination de son port d'attache; (cargaison) de retour.

homewards ['houmwərdz], *adv.* Vers sa maison, vers sa demeure; (*from abroad*) vers son pays. *To hasten h.*, se presser de rentrer. **Cargo homewards**, cargaison de retour.

homicidal [hɔmi'said(ə)l], *a.* Homicide, meurtrier
homicide[1] ['hɔmisaid], *s.* (*Pers.*) Homicide *mf*, meurtrier *m*.
homicide[2], *s.* (*Crime*) Homicide *m. Jur :* Felonious homicide, homicide prémédité ; assassinat *m.* Justifiable homicide, homicide par légitime défense.
homily ['hɔmili], *s.* Homélie *f. F :* To read s.o. a homily, sermonner qn.
homing ['houmiŋ], *a.* **Homing pigeon,** pigeon voyageur.
homocentric [hɔmo'sentrik], *a.* Homocentrique.
homoeopath ['houmiopaθ], *s. Med :* Homéopathe *m.*
homoeopathic [houmio'paθik], *a.* (Traitement) homéopathique ; (médecin) homéopathe.
homoeopathy [houmi'ɔpaθi], *s. Med :* Homéopathie *f.*
homogeneity [hɔmodʒe'ni:iti], *s.* Homogénéité *f.*
homogeneous [hɔmo'dʒi:njəs], *a.* Homogène.
homologous [hɔ'mɔlogəs], *a.* Homologue.
homology [hɔ'mɔlodʒi], *s.* Homologie *f.*
homonym ['hɔmonim], *s.* Homonyme *m.*
homonymous [hɔ'mɔniməs], *a.* Homonyme.
hone[1] [houn], *s.* Pierre *f* à aiguiser, à affiler, pierre à rasoir.
hone[2], *v.tr.* Aiguiser, affiler ; repasser (un rasoir).
honest ['ɔnest], *a.* **I.** (*a*) (*Of pers.*) Honnête, probe ; loyal, -aux (en affaires) ; (juge) intègre. (*b*) Vrai, sincère. **The honest truth,** la pure vérité. *Tell us your h. opinion,* dites-nous de bonne foi votre opinion. (*c*) *H. means,* moyens légitimes. *To give h. weight,* donner bon poids. **2.** (*a*) *A :* (*Of woman*) Honnête, chaste. **To make an honest woman of s.o.,** rendre l'honnête à une femme (en l'épousant). (*b*) (*Respectable*) They are h. folk, ce sont de braves gens. **-ly,** *adv.* (*a*) Honnêtement, loyalement. (*b*) Sincèrement. **Honestly speaking,** à vrai dire.
honesty ['ɔnesti], *s.* **I.** (*a*) Honnêteté *f,* probité *f* ; loyauté *f* (en affaires) ; intégrité *f.* (*b*) Véracité *f,* sincérité *f* ; franchise *f.* **In all honesty,** en toute sincérité. **2.** *Bot :* Lunaire *f* ; monnaie *f* du pape.
honey ['hʌni], *s.* **I.** (*a*) Miel *m. Clear h.,* miel liquide. **Comb honey,** miel en rayon. (*b*) Douceur *f* (de mots, de caresses). **He was all honey,** il a été tout sucre et tout miel. **2.** *F :* Chéri, *f.* chérie ; mon petit chou. **'honey-bee,** *s. Ent :* Abeille *f* domestique ; *F :* mouche *f* à miel. **'honey-cake,** *s.* Pain *m* d'épice au miel ; nonnette *f.* **'honey-dew,** *s.* **I.** Miellée *f,* miellure *f.* **2.** Tabac sucré à la mélasse ; honeydew *m.* **'honey-eating,** *a. Z :* Mellivore.
honeycomb[1] ['hʌnikoum], *s.* Rayon *m* de miel. *Tex :* **Honeycomb-weave towel,** serviette nid d'abeilles.
honeycomb[2], *v.tr.* Cribler (de petits trous). *F : The army was honeycombed with disaffection,* la désaffection ravageait l'armée. **honeycombed,** *a.* **I.** Alvéolé. **2.** (Métal) chambré, crevassé.
honeyed ['hʌnid], *a.* (*a*) (Em)miellé ; couvert de miel. (*b*) *F :* **Honeyed words,** paroles doucereuses, mielleuses.
honeymoon ['hʌnimu:n], *s.* Lune *f* de miel. **Honeymoon trip,** voyage *m* de noces.
honeysuckle ['hʌnisʌkl], *s.* Chèvrefeuille *m.*
honied ['hʌnid], *a.* = HONEYED.
honk[1] [hɔŋk], *s. Aut :* Cornement *m* (de l'avertisseur). *Honk! honk!* couin ! couin !
honk[2], *v.i. Aut :* Corner.
honorarium, *pl.* **-ia, -iums** [ɔnə'rɛəriəm, -ia, -iəmz], *s.* Honoraires *mpl.*

honorary ['ɔnərəri], *a.* (*a*) (Emploi, service) honoraire, non rétribué, bénévole. (*b*) **Honorary member,** membre honoraire. (*c*) **Honorary degree,** grade honorifique, grade honoris causa.
honorific [ɔnə'rifik], *a.* (Épithète) honorifique.
honour[1] ['ɔnər], *s.* Honneur *m.* **I. To hold s.o. in great honour,** honorer qn. **The seat of honour,** la place d'honneur. *To put up a statue* in honour of s.o., ériger une statue à la gloire de qn. **To pay, do, honour to s.o.,** faire honneur à qn. **All honour to him!** honneur à lui ! *Prov :* **Honour where honour is due,** à tout seigneur tout honneur. **2.** (*a*) **To consider it an honour to do sth.,** tenir à honneur de faire qch. **To whom have I the honour of speaking?** à qui ai-je l'honneur de parler ? (*b*) *Games :* (*at bowls*) avoir la boule ; (*at golf*) avoir l'honneur. **3.** *To lose one's h.,* perdre son honneur ; se déshonorer. **To make** (it) **a point of honour to do sth.,** se piquer d'honneur de faire qch. **To be in honour bound to . . .,** être obligé par l'honneur à. . . . **He is the soul of honour,** il est l'honneur incarné, personnifié ; il est la probité même. *I cannot in honour accept this money,* je ne peux pas, en tout honneur, accepter cet argent. *To state* on one's honour that . . ., déclarer sur l'honneur que. . . . **Word of honour,** parole *f* d'honneur. **To be on one's honour,** être engagé d'honneur. **4.** Distinction *f* honorifique. **Academic honours,** distinctions académiques. **To carry off the honours,** remporter la palme. *Sch :* **Honours list,** palmarès *m.* **5.** *Sch :* **Honours degree,** grade obtenu après spécialisation. **To take honours in mathematics,** passer l'examen supérieur de mathématiques. **6.** (*a*) *Usu. pl.* **To receive s.o. with full honours,** recevoir qn avec tous les honneurs qui lui sont dus. **To do the honours** (*of one's house*), faire les honneurs (de sa maison). (*b*) *pl. Cards :* Honours are even, (i) les honneurs sont partagés ; (ii) *F :* nous sommes à deux de jeux. **7.** (*Of pers.*) (*a*) **To be an honour to one's country,** faire honneur à sa patrie. *An h. to his native town,* la gloire de sa ville natale. (*b*) **Your Honour, his Honour,** Monsieur le juge, Monsieur le président. **8.** *Com :* **Acceptance for honour,** acceptation *f* par honneur, sous protêt ; intervention *f* à protêt.
honour[2], *v.tr.* **I.** (*a*) Honorer. *I h. you for it,* cela vous fait honneur. (*b*) **To honour s.o. with one's confidence,** honorer qn de sa confiance. **2.** **To h. one's signature,** faire honneur à sa signature. *Com :* **To honour a bill,** faire honneur à un effet. **honoured,** *a.* Honoré. **To bear an honoured name,** porter un grand nom, un nom honorable.
honourable ['ɔnərəbl], *a.* **I.** (Conduite, famille) honorable. **2. The Honourable,** *abbrev.* the Hon., l'honorable. . . . **The Hon. member for Caithness,** l'honorable membre représentant Caithness. **The Most Honourable,** le très honorable. **The Right Honourable,** le très honorable. **-ably,** *adv.* Honorablement.
hood [hud], *s.* **I.** *Cost :* (*a*) Capuchon *m* (de moine) ; cagoule *f* (de pénitent) ; capeline *f* (de femme, d'enfant). (*b*) *Sch :* Chaperon *m* (de toge universitaire). (*c*) *Nat.Hist :* Capuchon *m* (de cobra). **2.** (*a*) *Veh : etc :* (Folding, extensible) hood, capote *f. Car with folding h.,* auto décapotable, à capote rabattable. (*b*) *Phot :* Parasoleil *m* (d'objectif). (*c*) Hotte *f* (de forge) ; chapeau *m* (de lampe, de pieu).
hooded ['hudid], *a.* (*a*) (*Of pers.*) Encapuchonné. (*b*) (Vêtement, fleur) à capuchon.

hoodlum ['hu:dləm], s. U.S: P: Voyou m, chenapan m.

hoodoo ['hu:du:], s. U.S: (a) = VOODOO¹. (b) Confusion f, agitation f.

hoodwink ['hudwiŋk], v.tr. F: Tromper, donner le change à (qn).

hoof¹, pl. **-s, hooves** [hu:f, -s, hu:vz], s. (a) Sabot m (de cheval). **Beef on the hoof,** bétail m sur pied. (b) F: Pied m.

hoof², v.tr. & i. P: **I.** To hoof (it), aller à pied, à pattes. **2.** v.tr. To hoof s.o. out, chasser qn à coups de pied.

hoofed [hu:ft], a. Z: Ongulé; à sabots.

hook¹ [huk], s. **I.** Crochet m, croc m. (a) Chimney hook, crémaillère f. **Hat and coat hook,** patère f. **Curtain-loop hook,** rinceau m. **Hook nail,** (i) clou m à croc, à crochet; (ii) clou barbelé. (b) **Bench hook,** crochet d'établi. Mec.E: **Pawl hook,** croc à déclic. F: **By hook or (by) crook,** d'une manière ou d'une autre. S.a. BOAT-HOOK, BUTTON-HOOK. (c) Cost: Agrafe f. **Hook and eye,** agrafe et œillet m; crochet et porte f. (d) **Hook and hinge,** gond m et penture f. F: **To go off the hooks,** sortir de ses gonds; se fâcher. **2.** (Fish-)hook, hameçon m. F: **To do sth. on one's own hook,** faire qch. pour son propre compte. **3.** (Reaping-)hook, faucille f. **4.** (a) Box: **Right hook, left hook,** crochet du droit, du gauche. (b) Golf: Cr: Coup tourné à gauche; Golf: coup tiré. **5.** Cap m; pointe f de terre. **6.** P: **To sling, take, one's hook,** décamper; plier bagage. **'hook-nose,** s. **I.** Nez crochu. **2.** Nez busqué.

hook², v.tr. **I.** Courber (le doigt). **2.** To hook sth. (on, up) to sth., accrocher qch. à qch. F: I hooked my arm in his, je l'ai croché (amicalement). **3.** To hook up a curtain, agrafer un rideau. Dress that hooks up at the back, robe qui s'agrafe par derrière. **4.** Crocher, gaffer (un objet flottant). **5.** (a) Fish: Prendre (un poisson) à l'hameçon; accrocher (un poisson). (b) F: Amorcer, attraper (un mari, etc.). **hooked,** a. **I.** Crochu, recourbé. **2.** Muni de crochets, d'hameçons.

hookah ['huka], s. Narguilé m.

hooligan ['hu:ligən], s. Voyou m; gouape f.

hooliganism ['hu:ligənizm], s. Voyouterie f.

hoop¹ [hu:p], s. **I.** (a) Cercle m (de tonneau). (b) Cercle, cerceau m (de mât, etc.); frette f (de pieu); virole f (de moyeu, etc.). (c) Jante f, bandage m (de roue). **2.** Cerceau (d'enfant, de cirque). **To trundle, drive, a hoop,** faire courir, faire rouler, un cerceau. **3.** (Half-hoop) (a) Cerceau (de tente de voiture, etc.). (b) Croquet: Arceau m, arche f. **'hoop-iron,** s. Fer m feuillard; fer plat.

hoop², v.tr. (a) Coop: Cercler (un tonneau). (b) Fretter, cercler (un canon, un mât, etc.).

hoop³, ⁴, int., s., & v.i. = WHOOP¹, ².

hoopoe ['hu:pu:], s. Orn: Huppe f.

hoot¹ [hu:t], s. **I.** Ululation f, (h)ululement m (de hibou). **2.** (Of pers.) Huée f. **3.** (a) Cornement m (de trompe d'automobile). (b) Coup m de sirène (de bateau).

hoot². **I.** v.i. (a) (Of owl) (H)ululer, huer. (b) (Of pers.) Huer. **To hoot after s.o.,** conspuer qn. (c) Aut: Corner; (of driver) donner un coup de klaxon. (d) (Of siren) Mugir; (of ship) lancer un coup de sirène. **2.** v.tr. Huer, conspuer (qn); siffler (une pièce de théâtre). **To hoot s.o. down,** faire taire qn (par des huées). **To hoot a play off the stage,** faire tomber une pièce. **hooting,** s. **I.** (H)ululement m (de hibou). **2.** (Of pers.)

Huées fpl. **3.** (a) Aut: Cornement m; coups mpl de klaxon. (b) Mugissement m (d'une sirène).

hooter ['hu:tər], s. **I.** Nau: Ind: Sirène f; sifflet m. **2.** Avertisseur m; trompe f (d'auto).

hoot(s) [hu:t(s)], **hoot-toot** ['hu:t'tu:t], int. Scot: Allons donc! c'est de la blague.

hooves [hu:vz], s.pl. See HOOF¹.

hop¹ [hɔp], s. Bot: Houblon m. **'hop-field, -garden,** s. Houblonnière f. **'hop-grower,** s. Houblonnier m. **'hop-kiln,** s. Four m à houblon. **'hop-picker,** s. Cueilleur, -euse, de houblon. **'hop-picking,** s. Cueillette f de houblon. **'hop-pole,** s. **I.** Perche f à houblon. **2.** F: (Pers.) Grande perche.

hop², s. **I.** (a) Petit saut; sautillement m. (b) Saut à cloche-pied. F: He went off with a hop, skip and a jump, il s'en alla en gambadant. **To catch s.o. on the hop,** prendre qn au pied levé. (c) Av: Flight in five hops, voyage avec quatre escales, en cinq étapes. **2.** F: (Dance) Sauterie f. P: Shilling hop, bal m musette.

hop³. (hopped) **I.** v.i. (a) Sauter, sautiller. **To hop away,** (i) s'éloigner à cloche-pied; (ii) (of sparrow) s'éloigner en sautillant. F: **To hop off,** filer; ficher le camp. (b) To hop over a ditch, sauter un fossé. **To hop out of bed,** sauter à bas de son lit. **2.** v.tr. F: Sauter (un obstacle). P: **To hop it,** filer; ficher le camp. **hopping¹,** s. Sautillement m, sauts mpl. **'Hop-o'-my- 'thumb.** Pr.n. Le Petit Poucet.

hope¹ [houp], s. **I.** (a) Espérance f, espoir m. **To be full of h.,** avoir bon espoir. **Past all hope,** perdu sans espoir. **To put one's hope in the future,** compter sur l'avenir. **To set all one's hopes on s.o.,** mettre tout son espoir en qn. Geog: **The Cape of Good Hope,** le cap de Bonne Espérance. (b) In the hope of . . ., dans l'espoir de . . ., dans l'espoir de . . . **To be, live, in hope of doing sth.,** avoir l'espoir de faire qch. **2.** He is the hope of his country, il est l'espoir de son pays. **My last hope,** ma dernière planche de salut. **To have hopes of sth.,** avoir qch. en vue; avoir l'espoir de faire qch. **To live, be, in hopes that . . .,** caresser l'espoir, avoir l'espoir, que . . .

hope². **I.** v.i. Espérer. **We must hope against hope,** il faut espérer quand même. **To hope for sth.,** espérer qch. **Hoped-for victory,** victoire attendue. **To hope in God,** mettre son espoir en Dieu. **2.** v.tr. I hope and expect that . . ., j'espère avec confiance que . . . **I only hope you may get it!** je vous en souhaite! Corr: **Hoping to hear from you,** dans l'espoir de vous lire.

hope³, s. Troupe f. S.a. FORLORN I.

hopeful ['houpful], a. **I.** Plein d'espoir. **To be hopeful that . . .,** avoir bon espoir que . . . **2.** (a) (Avenir) qui donne de belles espérances, qui promet. (b) **The situation looks more hopeful,** la situation s'annonce meilleure. **-fully,** adv. (Travailler, etc.) avec bon espoir, avec confiance.

hopefulness ['houpfulnəs], s. **I.** Bon espoir; confiance f. **2.** Bons indices (de la situation, etc.).

hopeless ['houpləs], a. **I.** Sans espoir; désespéré. **2.** (a) Qui ne permet aucun espoir; (maladie, etc.) incurable; (situation) désespérée, sans issue. It's a h. job, c'est désespérant. **To give sth. up as hopeless,** renoncer à faire qch. (b) F: **Hopeless drunkard,** ivrogne incorrigible. **-ly,** adv. **I.** (Vivre) sans espoir; (regarder qn) avec désespoir. **2.** (Vaincu) irrémédiablement. H. drunk, soûl perdu.

hopelessness ['houpləsnəs], s. État désespéré.

hopper¹ ['hɔpər], s. **1.** Sauteur, -euse. **2.** Trémie f, huche f, hotte f (de moulin).

hopper², s. F: = HOP-PICKER.

hopping² ['hɔpiŋ], s. Cueillette f du houblon.

hopscotch ['hɔpskɔtʃ], s. Games: La marelle.

horde [hɔːrd], s. Horde f.

horehound ['hɔːərhaund], s. Bot: Marrube m.

horizon [hoʹraizən], s. Horizon m. On the horizon, à l'horizon.

horizontal [hɔriʹzɔnt(ə)l], a. Horizontal, -aux. **-ally**, adv. Horizontalement.

hormone ['hɔːrmoun], s. Physiol: Hormone f.

horn [hɔːrn], s. **1.** (a) Corne f. Horns of a stag, bois m d'un cerf. (Of stag) To shed, cast, its horns, muer. F: Wind fit to blow the horns off an ox, vent à écorner les bœufs. (b) Nat.Hist: Antenne f (de cerf-volant); corne, F: antenne (d'un limaçon). F: To draw in one's horns, (i) rentrer les cornes; (ii) rabattre (de) ses prétentions; en rabattre. (c) Corne (d'un croissant); antenne (de mine sous-marine). (d) F: On the horns of a dilemma, enfermé dans un dilemme. **2.** (Horny matter) Corne. Horn comb, peigne en corne. **3.** Mus: (a) Cor m. French horn, cor d'harmonie. Hunting horn, cor, trompe f, de chasse. Coach horn, buccin m de mail-coach. (b) English horn (tenor oboe), cor anglais. **4.** Pavillon m (de haut-parleur). **5.** Aut: Cornet (avertisseur); corne (d'appel); trompe (d'auto). To sound, blow, one's horn, corner. **6.** A: Drinking horn, corne à boire. Horn of plenty, corne d'abondance. **'horn-handled**, a. (Couteau) à manche de corne. **'horn-rimmed**, a. (Lunettes) à monture en corne.

hornbeam ['hɔːrnbiːm], s. Bot: Charme m; hêtre blanc.

hornbill ['hɔːrnbil], s. Orn: Calao m.

horned [hɔːrnd, 'hɔːrnid], a. (a) (Animal) à cornes, cornu. (b) Orn: Horned owl, duc m. Great h. owl, grand-duc m.

hornet ['hɔːrnet], s. Ent: Frelon m. F: To bring a hornet's nest about one's ears, donner, se fourrer, dans un guêpier.

horniness ['hɔːrninəs], s. (a) Nature cornée (d'une substance). (b) Callosité f (des mains).

hornpipe ['hɔːrnpaip], s. Danc: Matelote f.

horny ['hɔːrni], a. (a) Corné; en corne. (b) (Of hand, etc.) Calleux.

horology [hoʹrɔlodʒi], s. **1.** Horlogerie f. **2.** Horométrie f.

horoscope ['hɔroskoup], s. Horoscope m. To cast s.o.'s horoscope, tirer l'horoscope de qn.

horrible ['hɔribl], a. Horrible, affreux. **-ibly**, adv. Horriblement, affreusement.

horrid ['hɔrid], a. **1.** Horrible, affreux. **2.** F: To be horrid to s.o., être méchant envers qn. Don't be horrid! (i) ne dites pas des horreurs pareilles! (ii) ne faites pas le vilain! You horrid thing! oh, le vilain! oh, la vilaine! **-ly**, adv. **1.** Affreusement. **2.** F: Méchamment, abominablement.

horrific [hoʹrifik], a. Lit: Horrifique.

horrify ['hɔrifai], v.tr. (a) Horrifier (qn); faire horreur à (qn). (b) F: Scandaliser (qn). To be horrified, être saisi, pénétré, d'horreur.

horror ['hɔrər], s. **1.** Horreur f. To have a horror of s.o., of sth., of doing sth., avoir horreur de qn, de qch., de faire qch. **2.** (a) Chose horrible, affreuse; horreur. Chamber of Horrors, Chambre f des Horreurs (d'un musée). (b) F: To have the horrors, grelotter de peur. It gives me the horrors, cela me donne le frisson; ça me met les nerfs en pelote. **'horror-stricken**,

-struck, a. Saisi d'horreur; pénétré, glacé, frappé, d'horreur.

hors-d'œuvre [hɔːrʹdəːvr], s. (pl. hors-d'œuvres) Cu: Hors-d'œuvre m inv.

horse [hɔːrs], s. **1.** Cheval m, -aux. (a) Draughthorse, cheval de trait. To mount, get on, a horse, monter, enfourcher, un cheval. To horse! à cheval! F: To ride the high horse, to get on one's high horse, monter sur ses grands chevaux. To change horses, relayer; prendre des relais. Change of horses, relais m. To talk horse, parler chevaux; parler courses. Prov: It's a good horse that never stumbles, il n'y a si bon cheval qui ne bronche. (b) Breed: Cheval mâle. (c) Nau: White horses, vagues f à crêtes d'écume; moutons m. **2.** Coll. Mil: Cavalerie f; troupes montées. Light horse, cavalerie légère. **3.** (a) Wooden horse, (i) (toy) cheval de bois; (ii) Ind: chevalet m de montage. (b) Gym: (Vaulting) horse, cheval de bois. (c) F: Iron horse, (i) bicyclette f, (ii) locomotive f. **4.** Towel horse, porte-serviette(s) m inv (mobile). **'horse-artillery**, s. Artillerie montée. **'horse-block**, s. Montoir m. **'horse-box**, s. (a) Rail: Wagon m à chevaux. (b) Veh: Fourgon m pour le transport des chevaux. **'horse-butcher**, s. Boucher m qui vend de la viande de cheval. Horse-butcher's, boucherie chevaline. **'horse-chestnut**, s. **1.** Marron m d'Inde. **2.** (Tree) Marronnier m d'Inde. **'horse-cloth**, s. Couverture f de cheval. **'horse-coper**, **-dealer**, s. Maquignon m. **'horse-doctor**, s. F: Vétérinaire m. **'horse-drawn**, a. (Véhicule) hippomobile. **'horse-flesh**, s. **1.** Viande f de cheval; boucherie chevaline. **2.** Coll. Chevaux mpl. **'horse-fly**, s. Ent: **1.** Taon m. **2.** Œstre m. **'horse-gear**, s. Manège m (actionnant une machine). **'Horse Guards**, s.pl. The (Royal) Horse Guards, la Garde du corps (à cheval). **'horse-hide**, s. Peau f, cuir m, de cheval. **'horse-laugh**, **-laughter**, s. Gros rire bruyant. **'horse-marines**, s.pl. Hum: He's in the horse-marines, c'est un amiral suisse. **'horse pistol**, s. Pistolet m d'arçon. **'horse-play**, s. Jeu brutal, jeu de main(s). **'horse-pond**, s. Abreuvoir m. **'horse-power**, s. (Abbr. h.p.) Mec: (i) Puissance f en chevaux; (ii) Meas: cheval-vapeur m (britannique = 1.0139 ch.-v. français). A forty horse-power car, une automobile de quarante chevaux; F: une quarante chevaux. **'horse-race**, s. Course f de chevaux. **'horse-racing**, s. Hippisme m; courses fpl de chevaux. **'horse-radish**, s. Bot: Raifort m. **'horse-show**, s. Exposition chevaline; concours m hippique. **'horse-tail**, s. **1.** Queue f de cheval. **2.** Bot: Prêle f (des marais). **'horse-towel**, s. Essuie-main(s) m inv à rouleau. **'horse-trough**, s. Abreuvoir m; auge f (à chevaux).

horseback ['hɔːrsbak], s. On horseback, à (dos de) cheval. F: A beggar on horseback, un parvenu.

horsehair ['hɔːrshɛər], s. Crin m (de cheval).

horseman, pl. **-men** ['hɔːrsmən, -men], s.m. Cavalier, écuyer.

horsemanship ['hɔːrsmənʃip], s. Équitation f.

horseshoe ['hɔːrsʃuː], s. (a) Fer m à cheval. (b) Attrib. (Table, etc.) en fer à cheval.

horsewhip¹ ['hɔːrshwip], s. Cravache f.

horsewhip², v.tr. (horsewhipped) Cravacher, sangler (qn). **horsewhipping**, s. Cravachée f.

horsewoman, pl. **-women** ['hɔːrswumən, -wimen], s.f. Amazone f, cavalière, écuyère.

24

horsiness ['hɔːrsinəs], s. Affectation *f* du genre jockey, du genre palefrenier.

horsy ['hɔːrsi], a. Qui affecte le langage, le costume, des grooms et des jockeys.

horticultural [hɔːrti'kʌltjurəl], a. (Outil) horticole. Horticultural show, exposition *f* d'horticulture.

horticulture ['hɔːrtikʌltjər], s. Horticulture *f*.

horticulturist [hɔːrti'kʌltjurist], s. Horticulteur *m*.

hose [houz], s. **1.** Coll. pl. (a) A : (i) Chausses *fpl*. (ii) Haut-de-chausses *m*, pl. hauts-de-chausses. (b) Com : Bas *mpl*. **2.** (pl. hoses) Manche *f* à eau ; tuyau *m*. Rubber hose, tuyau en caoutchouc. **'hose-pipe,** s. Tuyau *m* (de lavage, d'incendie, etc.). **'hose-reel,** s. Hort : Chariot *m* à tuyaux.

hosier ['houziər, -ʒiər], s. Bonnetier, -ière.

hosiery ['houziəri, -ʒiəri], s. Bonneterie *f*.

hospitable ['hɔspitəbl], a. Hospitalier. **-ably,** adv. Hospitalièrement.

hospital ['hɔspit(ə)l], s. **1.** Hôpital *m*, -aux. Patient in hospital, hospitalisé, -ée. (Of medical student) To walk the hospitals, assister aux leçons cliniques ; faire les hôpitaux. Hospital nurse, infirmière *f*. Hospital train, train sanitaire. Hospital ship, vaisseau hôpital. **2.** (a) Hist : Hospice *m* (des hospitaliers). (b) Occ. Asile *m*, hospice.

hospitality [hɔspi'taliti], s. Hospitalité *f*. To show s.o. hospitality, héberger qn ; faire à qn un accueil hospitalier.

hospital(l)er ['hɔspitələr], s. Hist : Hospitalier *m*.

host¹ [houst], s. (a) A. & Poet : Armée *f*. The Lord God of Hosts, le Dieu des armées. (b) F : A (whole) host of servants, (toute) une foule, (toute) une armée, de domestiques. A h. of gnats, une légion, une nuée, de moucherons.

host², s. (a) Hôte *m* ; F : amphitryon *m*. (b) Hôtelier *m*, aubergiste *m*. F : To reckon without one's host, compter sans son hôte.

host³, s. Ecc : Hostie *f*.

hostage ['hɔstedʒ], s. **1.** Otage *m*. As (a) hostage, en otage, pour otage. **2.** F : Gage *m*.

hostel ['hɔstəl], s. **1.** A : Hôtellerie *f*. **2.** (a) Pension *f*, foyer *m* (sous la direction d'une œuvre sociale). (b) Youth Hostels, auberges *f* de la jeunesse.

hostelry ['hɔstəlri], s. A. & Lit : Hôtellerie *f*.

hostess ['houstes], s.f. (a) Hôtesse. (b) Hôtelière, aubergiste *f*.

hostile ['hɔstail], a. (a) Hostile, adverse, ennemi. (b) Hostile, opposé (to, à) ; ennemi (to, de). To be hostile to s.o., être hostile à, envers, qn. **-ely,** adv. Hostilement.

hostility [hɔs'tiliti], s. **1.** Hostilité *f* (to, contre) ; animosité *f*. **2.** pl. Hostilities, hostilités ; état *m* de guerre.

hostler ['ɔslər], s. = OSTLER.

hot [hɔt], a. (hotter) **1.** (a) Chaud. Boiling hot, (tout) bouillant. Burning hot, brûlant. To be very hot, (of thg) être très chaud ; (of pers.) avoir très chaud ; (of weather) faire très chaud. To get hot, (i) (of thg) devenir chaud ; chauffer ; (ii) (of weather) commencer à faire chaud ; (iii) (of pers., contest) s'échauffer. Hot fire, feu vif. F : To be in hot water, être dans le pétrin, dans l'embarras. To get into hot water, s'attirer, se créer, des ennuis. F : To let off hot air, parler pour ne rien dire. It was hot work, on s'y échauffait. To blow hot and cold, (i) souffler le chaud et le froid ; (ii) F : parler, agir, de façons contradictoires. F : To get all hot and bothered, s'échauffer ; se faire du mauvais sang. To go hot and cold all

over, avoir le frisson. (b) Brûlant, cuisant. Hot tears, larmes cuisantes. (c) (Poivre) cuisant ; (moutarde) piquante ; (assaisonnement) épicé. F : He's hot stuff at tennis, au tennis c'est un as. **2.** (a) News hot from the press, nouvelles sortant tout droit de la presse. (b) Ven : Hot trail, voie chaude. To be hot on the scent, on the trail, être sur la bonne piste. Games : You are getting hot, tu brûles. **3.** (a) Violent. To have a hot temper, s'emporter facilement. (b) Acharné. Hot contest, chaude dispute. At the hottest of the fray, au plus fort du combat. To be in hot pursuit of s.o., presser qn de près. The resistance was hot and strong, la résistance a été vigoureuse. Adv.phr. They went at it hot and strong, ils y allaient avec acharnement, de toutes leurs forces. Turf : Hot favourite, grand favori. **4.** F : To make a place too hot for s.o., rendre la situation intenable à qn (dans un endroit). To make things too hot for s.o., rendre la vie intolérable, intenable, à qn. To give it (to) s.o. hot, laver la tête à qn ; semoncer qn d'importance. We are going to have a hot time, il va y avoir du grabuge ; ça va chauffer. **-ly,** adv. **1.** (Répondre, protester) vivement, avec chaleur. **2.** (Poursuivi) avec acharnement, de près. **'hot-'blooded,** a. Emporté, ardent, passionné. **'hot 'dog,** s. U.S : Petit pain fourré d'une saucisse chaude. **'hot-'foot,** adv. A toute vitesse, en (toute) hâte, précipitamment. **'hot-head,** s. (Pers.) Tête chaude ; impétueux *m*. **'hot-'headed,** a. **1.** Exalté, impétueux. **2.** Emporté, violent ; qui a la tête près du bonnet. **'hot-plate,** s. Chauffe-assiette *m*, réchaud *m*. **'hot-pot,** s. Cu : Ragoût de bœuf ou de mouton aux pommes de terre, cuit à l'étuvée. **'hot-press,** s. Étuve *f* à linge. **'hot-spot,** s. I.C.E : **1.** Point *m* d'inflammation. **2.** Réchauffeur *m* (des gaz). **'hot-'tempered,** a. Colérique ; emporté. **hot-'water bottle,** s. (a) Bouillotte *f* (en caoutchouc, etc.). (b) Cruchon *m*, F : moine *m*.

hotbed ['hɔtbed], s. **1.** Hort : Couche *f* (de fumier). **2.** F : Hotbed of corruption, foyer (ardent) de corruption.

hotchpotch ['hɔtʃpɔtʃ], s. **1.** Cu : Hochepot *m*, salmigondis *m*. Vegetable h., macédoine *f* de légumes. **2.** F : Mélange confus ; méli-mélo *m*.

hotel [ho'tel], s. **1.** Hôtel *m* (pour voyageurs). Private hotel, hôtel de famille. Residential hotel, pension *f* de famille, pension bourgeoise. Hotel-keeper, hôtelier, -ière.

hothouse ['hɔthaus], s. Serre chaude. Hothouse plant, plante de serre chaude. H. grapes, raisin de serre.

hound¹ [haund], s. Chien *m* de meute, chien courant. The (pack of) hounds, la meute, l'équipage *m*. Master of hounds, maître d'équipage. To ride to hounds, chasser à courre. S.a. HARE¹ **1.** (Of pers.) You miserable hound! misérable !

hound², v.tr. **1.** To hound s.o. down, poursuivre qn avec acharnement, sans relâche ; traquer qn. Hounded from place to place, pourchassé d'un lieu à l'autre. **2.** To hound the dogs on, exciter les chiens à la poursuite.

hound³, s. Nau : (Usu. pl.) Hounds, jottereaux *mpl* (de mât).

hour [auər], s. Heure *f*. **1.** An hour and a half, une heure et demie. Half an hour, une demi-heure. A quarter of an hour, un quart d'heure. Hour by hour, d'une heure à l'autre. To pay s.o. by the hour, payer qn à l'heure. Five miles an hour, cinq milles à l'heure. Ind : Output per hour, puissance horaire. F : To take hours over sth., mettre un temps interminable à faire qch. **Office hours,** heures de bureau. **After hours,** après l'heure de fermeture. **To work long hours,** faire de longues journées (de travail). **2.** (a) **At the hour of seven,** à sept heures. **At the h. stated,** à l'heure dite. **Thé questions of the hour,** les questions de l'heure (actuelle); les actualités f. **In the hour of need,** à l'heure du besoin. **In a happy h.,** à un moment heureux. **The hour has come,** le moment est venu; il est l'heure. (b) **In the small hours (of the morning),** fort avant dans la nuit. **To keep late hours,** (i) rentrer à des heures indues; (ii) veiller tard. (c) **Ecc:** **Book of Hours,** livre d'heures. **'hour-circle,** s. **Astr:** Cercle m horaire. **'hour-glass,** s. Sablier m. **'hour-hand,** s. Petite aiguille (de montre, de pendule).

hourly ['auərli]. **I.** a. (a) De toutes les heures; (service de trains, etc.) à chaque heure. (b) (Rendement) par heure, à l'heure; (salaire) à l'heure. (c) De chaque instant. **His h. dread of death,** sa crainte perpétuelle de la mort. **2.** adv. (a) Toutes les heures; d'heure en heure. (b) **We expect him h.,** nous l'attendons d'un moment à l'autre.

house¹, pl. -ses [haus, 'hauziz], s. **I.** Maison f, logis m, demeure f. **Town house,** hôtel (particulier). **Country house,** château m; maison de campagne. **Small h.,** maisonnette f. **Private house,** maison particulière. **At, to, in, my house,** chez moi. **To be confined to the h.,** être confiné au logis. **To keep (to) the house,** rester chez soi; garder la maison. **To keep house for s.o.,** tenir le ménage de qn; tenir, diriger, la maison de qn. **To keep house together,** faire ménage ensemble. **To set up house,** monter, se mettre, en ménage. **To move house,** déménager. **To keep a good house,** vivre bien; faire bonne chère. **House of cards,** château de cartes. **Attrib. House coal,** charbon de ménage. **House work,** travaux domestiques, de ménage. **S.a.** DOG¹ 1. **2.** (a) **The house of God,** la maison de Dieu. **House of prayer,** église f, temple m. **The House of Commons,** la Chambre des Communes. (b) **Business house,** maison de commerce. (c) **F: The House.** (i) **Parl:** La Chambre des Communes ou des Lords. **Bill before the H.,** loi en cours de vote. (ii) **Fin:** La Bourse. (d) **Sch: =** BOARDING-HOUSE 2. **3.** (a) **Carriage house,** remise f. **Fowl-house,** poulailler m. **S.a.** GATE-HOUSE, GLASS-HOUSE, etc. (b) **Tchn:** Cabine f, guérite f (d'une grue); **Nau:** Rouf m (sur le pont); kiosque m (de la barre, etc.). (c) **Com: Ind:** Salle f, bâtiment m. **S.a.** COUNTING-HOUSE, ENGINE-HOUSE, etc. **4.** (a) (Members of household) Maison, **F:** maisonnée f. (b) **Famille** f, maison, dynastie f. **The House of Bourbon,** les Bourbons m, la Maison des Bourbons. **5.** **Th:** Auditoire m, assistance f. **A good house,** une salle pleine. **To play to an empty house,** jouer devant les banquettes. **'house-agent,** s. Agent m de location; courtier m en immeubles. **'house-boat,** s. Bateau-maison m. **'house-flag,** s. **Nau:** Pavillon m de compagnie. **'house-fly,** s. Mouche f domestique. **'house-party,** s. Les invités réunis au château pour quelques jours (ouverture de la chasse, etc.). **'house-phy'si-cian,** s. Interne m en médecine (d'un hôpital). **'house-porter,** s. Concierge m; portier m. **'house-property,** s. Immeubles mpl. **'house-room,** s. Place f (pour loger qn, qch.); logement m. **'house-surgeon,** s. Interne m en chirurgie (d'un hôpital). **'house-top,** s. Toit m. **F:** To proclaim sth. from the house-tops, crier qch. sur les toits. **'house-warming,** s. Pen-

daison f de la crémaillère. **To have a house-warming,** pendre la crémaillère. **house²** [hauz], v.tr. (a) Loger, héberger (qn); pourvoir au logement de (la population). (b) Faire rentrer (les troupeaux); rentrer, engranger (le blé). (c) Mettre à l'abri, à couvert (une locomotive, etc.); garer (une voiture); loger, caser (un ustensile). (d) Enchâsser (un essieu, etc.). **Nau:** Caler (un mât). **housing¹,** s. **I.** (a) Logement m. **The housing problem,** la crise du logement. (b) Rentrée f (des troupeaux, du blé, etc.). (c) Mise f à l'abri; garage m (d'une auto). **2.** Enchâssure f (d'un essieu, etc.). **Nau:** Calage m (d'un mât). **3.** Logement, bâti m, cage f; carter m, boîte f. **Chain housing,** logement de chaîne. **Flexible housing,** gaine f flexible.

housebreaker ['hausbreikər], s. **I.** Cambrioleur m. **2.** **Const:** Démolisseur m. **House-breaker's yard,** chantier m de démolitions. **housebreaking** ['hausbreikiŋ], s. **I.** Effraction f, cambriolage m. **2.** Démolition f. **houseful** ['hausful], s. Maisonnée f; pleine maison (d'invités, etc.). **household** ['haushould], s. **I.** (Membres mpl de) la maison; le ménage; la famille. **Household expenses,** frais de ménage. **Household bread,** pain de ménage. **Household gods,** dieux domestiques. **Household word,** mot d'usage courant. **2.** (a) Les domestiques. **To have a large h.,** avoir une nombreuse domesticité. (b) **The Household,** la Maison du roi. **householder** ['haushouldər], s. **I.** Chef m de famille, de maison. **2.** **Adm:** Celui qui occupe une maison à titre de propriétaire ou de locataire **housekeeper** ['hauski:pər], s. **I.** Homme ou femme chargé(e) du soin d'un bâtiment; concierge mf. **2.** Femme f de charge; gouvernante f (d'un prêtre, etc.). **3.** **My wife is a good h.,** ma femme est bonne ménagère, s'entend bien aux affaires du ménage. **housekeeping** ['hauski:piŋ], s. **I.** Le ménage. **To set up housekeeping,** se mettre, entrer, en ménage. **2.** Économie f domestique; les soins m du ménage. **houseleek** ['hausli:k], s. **Bot:** Joubarbe f. **housemaid** ['hausmeid], s.f. Bonne; femme de chambre. **F: Housemaid's knee,** hygroma m du genou. **housemaster** ['hausmɑ:stər], s.m. **Sch:** Professeur chargé de la surveillance d'une des "maisons" où logent les élèves. **housewife,** pl. -wives. **I.** s.f. ['hauswaif, -waivz] Maîtresse de maison; ménagère. **2.** s. ['hazif, -vz] Trousse f de couture; nécessaire m à ouvrage. **housewifery** ['hazifri, hauswaifri], s Économie f domestique; soin m du ménage. **housing²** ['hauziŋ], s. Usu. pl. Housse f de cheval. **hove** [houv]. See HEAVE². **hovel** ['hovl], s. Taudis m, bouge m, masure f. **hover** ['hovər], v.i. **I.** (Of bird, etc.) Planer. **F:** A smile hovered over her lips, un sourire pointait, errait, sur ses lèvres. **2.** (Of pers.) (a) **To hover about s.o.,** errer, rôder, autour de qn. (b) **To hover between two courses,** hésiter entre deux partis. **how** [hau], adv. **I.** Comment. Tell me how he did it, dites-moi comment il l'a fait. Look how he holds his bow, regardez de quelle façon il tient son archet. **How are you?** comment allez-vous? **How is it that . . .?** comment se fait-il que . . .? **d'où vient que . . .? How so?** **how's that?** comment ça? **I see how it is,** je vois ce qui en est. *I fail to see how this affects you,* je ne vois pas en quoi cela vous intéresse. *How 'could you!* vous n'avez pas eu honte? **To learn how to do** sth., apprendre à faire qch. *I know how to swim,* je sais nager. **2.** (*a*) **How much, how many,** combien (de). *You see how little he cares,* vous voyez combien peu il s'en soucie. *You can imagine how angry I was,* songez si j'étais furieux! **How wide?** de quelle largeur? *How long is this room?* quelle est la longueur de cette pièce? **How old are you?** quel âge avez-vous? *S.a.* FAR[1] I, LONG[1] III. I, OFTEN, SOON I. (*b*) *How pretty she is!* comme elle est jolie! qu'elle est jolie! *How kind!* quelle bonté! *How she has changed!* ce qu'elle a changé! *You know how I love you,* vous savez si je vous aime. How I wish I could! si seulement je pouvais! **how-d'y(e)-do** ['haudi'du:], *s. F:* Here's a (pretty) how-d'ye-do! en voilà une affaire! en voilà du joli!

howbeit [hau'bi:it], *adv. A:* Néanmoins; quoi qu'il en soit.

however [hau'evər], *adv.* **I.** (*a*) **However he may do it,** de quelque manière qu'il le fasse. **However that may be,** quoi qu'il en soit. *Cp.* 'how ever' under EVER 3. (*b*) *H. artful she may be,* (i) si rusée qu'elle soit; (ii) toute rusée qu'elle est. *H. good his work is,* quelque excellent que soit son ouvrage. **However much** *he may admire you,* si fort qu'il vous admire. *H. much money you spend,* quelque argent que vous dépensiez. **However little,** si peu que ce soit. **2.** Toutefois, cependant, pourtant. *The scheme h. failed,* pourtant le projet échoua. *If h. you don't agree,* si toutefois cela ne vous convient pas.

howitzer ['hauitsər], *s. Artil:* Obusier *m.*

howl[1] [haul], *s.* (*a*) Hurlement *m*; mugissement *m* (du vent). **To give a howl of rage,** pousser un hurlement de rage. (*b*) Huée *f.*

howl[2], *v.i. & tr.* **I.** Hurler; pousser des hurlements; (*of wind*) mugir, rugir. *F:* **To h. with** *laughter,* rire à gorge déployée. **2.** *W.Tel:* (*Of set*) Rayonner dans l'antenne. **howl down,** *v.tr.* Faire taire (un orateur) en poussant des huées.

howling[1], *a.* **I.** Hurleur, -euse. *H. tempest,* tempête furieuse. **2.** *F:* (*Intensive*) **Howling mistake,** bourde énorme. (*Cf.* HOWLER 2.) *H. success,* succès fou. *H. injustice,* injustice criante.

howling[2], *s.* **I.** Hurlement *m*; mugissement *m* (du vent). **2.** *W.Tel:* Réaction *f* dans l'antenne.

howler ['haulər], *s.* **I.** (*a*) Hurleur, -euse. (*b*) *Z:* (*Monkey*) Hurleur *m.* **2.** *F:* Grosse gaffe, bourde *f* énorme. **Schoolboy howler,** bourde d'écolier; bévue *f* risible.

howsoever [hauso'evər], *adv.* = HOWEVER I.

hoyden ['hɔidn], *s.f.* Jeune fille à allures de garçon. *She's a regular h.,* c'est un garçon manqué.

hub [hʌb], *s.* **I.** Moyeu *m* (de roue). **2.** *F:* Centre *m* d'activité. **The hub of the universe,** le pivot, le centre, de l'univers. **'hub-cap,** *s.* Couvre-moyeu *m.* *Aut:* Chapeau *m* de moyeu; enjoliveur *m.*

hubbub ['hʌbʌb], *s.* Remue-ménage *m*, vacarme *m*, tohu-bohu *m.* *H. of voices,* brouhaha *m* de voix.

hubby ['hʌbi], *s. P:* Mari *m.*

huckaback ['hʌkəbak], *s.* **Huckaback (linen),** (grosse) toile ouvrée; toile à grain d'orge.

huckleberry ['hʌklbəri], *s. Bot: U.S:* Airelle *f* myrtille.

huckster[1] ['hʌkstər], *s.* **I.** Regrattier, -ière; revendeur, -euse. **Huckster's wares,** regratterie *f.* **2.** Mercanti *m*; trafiqueur *m* (politique).

huckster[2]. **I.** *v.i.* (*a*) Marchander. (*b*) Regratter; faire du regrat. **2.** *v.tr.* (*a*) Revendre.

(*b*) Faire trafic de (son influence, etc.). **huckstering,** *s.* **I.** Marchandage *m.* **2.** (*a*) Regratterie *f.* (*b*) Political huckstering, politicailleries *fpl.*

huddle[1] [hʌdl], *s.* Tas confus; fouillis *m*, ramassis *m.* *A h. of roofs,* un enchevêtrement de toits.

huddle[2], *v.tr. & i.* **I.** Entasser pêle-mêle, sans ordre. *Houses huddled together in the valley,* maisons serrées dans la vallée. *Passengers huddled on the after-deck,* passagers entassés sur l'arrière-pont. **To h. together,** se tasser; se serrer les uns contre les autres. **2.** **To huddle (oneself) up,** se pelotonner. *Huddled (up) in bed,* couché en chien de fusil. *Huddled (up) in a corner,* blotti dans un coin. **3.** **To huddle on one's clothes,** s'habiller à la hâte, à la va-vite.

hue[1] [hju:], *s.* Teinte *f*, nuance *f.* *Thoughts of a sombre hue,* pensées d'un coloris sombre.

hue[2] **and cry** ['hju:ən(d)'krai], *s.* Clameur *f* de haro. **To raise a hue and cry against** s.o., crier haro sur qn; crier tollé contre qn.

huff[1] [hʌf], *s.* **I.** **To be in a huff,** être froissé, fâché. **To take (the) huff,** s'offusquer; prendre la mouche. **2.** *Draughts:* Soufflage *m* (d'un pion).

huff[2]. **I.** *v.i.* Souffler, haleter. **2.** *v.tr.* (*a*) Froisser (qn). **To be, feel, huffed,** être froissé, fâché. (*b*) *Draughts:* Souffler (un pion).

huffiness ['hʌfinəs], *s.* **I.** Susceptibilité *f.* **2.** Mauvaise humeur.

huffy ['hʌfi], *a.* **I.** Susceptible. *In a h. tone of voice,* d'un ton pincé. **2.** Fâché, vexé. *He was very h. about it,* il a très mal pris la chose. **-ily,** *adv.* Avec (mauvaise) humeur; d'un ton de dépit.

hug[1] [hʌg], *s.* Étreinte *f.* **To give s.o. a hug,** étreindre qn.

hug[2], *v.tr.* (hugged) **I.** (*a*) Étreindre, embrasser (qn); serrer (qn) entre ses bras, sur son cœur. (*b*) (*Of bear*) Étouffer, enserrer (sa victime). (*c*) Chérir (ses défauts); choyer, tenir à (un préjugé). **2.** (*a*) *Nau:* **To hug the shore,** serrer la terre (de près); raser, ranger, longer, la côte. **To hug the wind,** serrer, pincer, le vent. (*b*) **To hug the wall,** raser, longer, serrer, le mur. *Aut:* **To hug the kerb,** tenir le bord du trottoir. *F:* **To hug the chimney-corner,** se blottir au coin du feu.

huge [hju:dʒ], *a.* Énorme, vaste; (*succès*) immense, formidable, colossal, -aux. **-ly,** *adv.* Énormément; immensément.

hugeness ['hju:dʒnəs], *s.* Énormité *f*, immensité *f.*

hugger-mugger ['hʌgərmʌgər]. **I.** *s.* Désordre *m*, confusion *f.* *To live in a h.-m. fashion,* vivre dans le désordre matériel. **2.** *adv.* En désordre, confusément, pêle-mêle.

Huguenot ['hju:gənɔt, -nou], *s. Hist:* Huguenot, -ote.

hulk [hʌlk], *s.* **I.** *Nau:* (*a*) Carcasse *f* de navire; ponton *m.* **Mooring-hulk,** ponton d'amarrage. (*b*) *pl. A:* Hulks, bagne flottant; pontons. **2.** *F:* (*Of pers.*) Gros pataud.

hulking ['hʌlkiŋ], *a.* Gros, lourd. **Big hulking creature,** gros pataud.

hull[1] [hʌl], *s.* **I.** Cosse *f*, gousse *f* (de pois, de fève); coquille *f*, écale *f* (de noix). **2.** Coque *f* (de navire, d'hydroplane). *Nau:* **Hull down,** coque noyée sous l'horizon.

hull[2], *v.tr.* Écosser (des pois); écaler (des noix); décortiquer (le riz). **Hulled barley,** orge mondé.

hullabaloo [hʌləbə'lu:], *s.* Tintamarre *m*, vacarme *m.* **To make a hullabaloo,** faire du vacarme.

hullo(a) [hʌ'lou], *int.* (*a*) (*Calling attention*) Ohé! holà! *Hullo* you! hé, là-bas! (*b*) (*Expressing surprise*) *H., old chap!* tiens, c'est toi, mon vieux! *H.! that's curious!* tiens! tiens! c'est curieux. (c) **Hullo everybody!** salut à tous! (d) *Tp:* Allô!

hum¹ [hʌm], *s.* Bourdonnement *m* (d'abeille); ronflement *m* (de machine, de toupie); ronron *m* (d'un moteur); vrombissement *m* (d'un avion). *W.Tel:* Ronronnement *m*, ronflement. *Hum of conversation,* brouhaha *m* de conversation.

hum², *v.* (hummed) **I.** *v.i.* (a) *(Of insect)* Bourdonner; *(of top)* ronfler; *(of aeroplane)* vrombir. *W.Tel:* Ronfler. *F:* **To make things hum,** faire marcher rondement les choses. (b) *(Of pers.)* **To hum and ha(w),** (i) toussoter (en commençant un discours); *F:* bafouiller; (ii) tourner autour du pot; *F:* barguigner. **2.** *v.tr.* Fredonner, chantonner (un air). *Mus:* **Hummed accompaniment,** accompagnement (de voix) en sourdine; accompagnement à bouche fermée. **'humming-bird,** *s.* Oiseau-mouche *m, pl.* oiseaux-mouches; colibri *m.*

human ['hju:mən]. **I.** *a.* Humain. **Human nature,** la nature humaine. *One can tell the h. hand,* on reconnaît la main de l'homme. *S.a.* BEING² **2. 2.** *s.* Être humain. **Humans,** les humains. **-ly,** *adv.* Humainement; en être humain. **Humanly speaking,** humainement parlant.

humane [hju'mein], *a.* (a) Humain, compatissant. *H. task,* œuvre humanitaire. (b) Clément; qui évite de faire souffrir. **-ly,** *adv.* Humainement; avec humanité.

humaneness [hju'meinnəs], *s.* Bonté *f,* humanité *f.*

humanist ['hju:mənist], *s.* Humaniste *m.*

humanitarian [hjumani'teəriən], *a. & s.* Humanitaire (*mf*).

humanity [hju'maniti], *s.* Humanité *f.* **I.** (a) Nature humaine. (b) Le genre humain. **2.** **To treat s.o. with humanity,** traiter qn avec humanité. **3.** *pl. Lit: Sch:* **The humanities,** les humanités, les lettres *f.*

humanize ['hju:mənaiz], *v.tr.* Humaniser.

humankind [hju:mən'kaind], *s.* Le genre humain.

humble¹ [hʌmbl], *a.* Humble. **I.** *H. prayer,* humble prière. **In my humble opinion,** à mon humble avis. **Humble-hearted,** au cœur humble. *S.a.* SERVANT **I. 2.** Modeste. **To spring from h. stock,** être de modeste souche, d'humble extraction. **-bly,** *adv.* **I.** (Parler) humblement, avec humilité. *Most h.,* en toute humilité. **2.** (Vivre) modestement. *H. clad,* pauvrement vêtu.

humble², *v.tr.* Humilier, mortifier (qn). **To humble oneself,** s'abaisser, *F:* s'aplatir (*before,* devant). *To h. s.o.'s pride,* (r)abattre, rabaisser, l'orgueil de qn.

humble-bee ['hʌmblbi:], *s. Ent:* = BUMBLE-BEE.

humble pie [hʌmbl'pai], *s. F:* **To eat humble pie,** s'humilier (devant qn); se rétracter; faire amende honorable. **To make s.o. eat humble pie,** forcer qn à se rétracter.

humbug¹ ['hʌmbʌg], *s.* **I.** Charlatanisme *m; F:* blagues *fpl. There's no h. about him,* c'est un homme franc et sincère. **(That's all) humbug!** tout cela c'est de la blague! **2.** *(Pers.)* (a) Charlatan *m;* blagueur *m.* (b) Enjôleur, -euse. **3.** Bonbon *m* à la menthe.

humbug², *v.tr.* (humbugged) Conter des blagues à (qn); enjôler (qn); mettre (qn) dedans; mystifier (le public). *Abs.* Blaguer.

humdrum ['hʌmdrʌm], *a.* (Travail, existence) monotone; banal, -aux; peu intéressant, ennuyeux. *H. daily life,* le train-train quotidien.

humeral ['hju:mərəl], *a. Anat:* Huméral, -aux.

humerus, *pl.* **-i** ['hju:mərəs, -ai], *s. Anat:* Humérus *m.*

humid ['hju:mid], *a.* Humide; *(of heat skin)* moite.

humidity [hju'miditi], *s.* Humidité *f.*

humiliate [hju'milieit], *v.tr.* Humilier, mortifier.

humiliation [hjumili'eiʃ(ə)n], *s.* Humiliation *f,* affront *m,* mortification *f.*

humility [hju'militi], *s.* Humilité *f.* **With all humility,** en toute humilité.

hummock ['hʌmək], *s.* **I.** Tertre *m,* mamelon *m* (de terre); monticule *m.* **2.** Monticule de glace; hummock *m.*

humorist ['(h)ju:mərist], *s.* **I.** Farceur *m,* plaisant *m.* **2.** *(At concert)* Comique *m;* diseur, -euse, de chansonnettes. **3.** Écrivain *m* humoristique; humoriste *m.*

humorous ['(h)ju:mərəs], *a.* *(Of pers.)* Plein d'humour; comique, drôle; *(of writer)* humoriste, humoristique.

humour¹ ['(h)ju:mər], *s.* **I.** (a) *A.Med:* Humeur *f.* (b) *Anat:* Aqueous h., vitreous h., humeur aqueuse, vitrée (de l'œil). **2.** Humeur, disposition *f.* **To be in the humour to do sth.,** être en humeur de faire qch., être disposé à faire qch. **Good humour,** bonne humeur. **To be in a good, bad, humour,** être de bonne, de mauvaise, humeur; être bien, mal, disposé. *To be in no laughing h.,* ne pas se sentir d'humeur à rire. **To be out of humour,** être maussade. **3.** (a) Humour *m.* **Broad humour,** grosse gaieté. (b) **The humour of the situation,** le côté plaisant, le comique, de la situation. (c) *To be lacking in h.,* n'avoir pas le sens de l'humour.

humour², *v.tr.* To humour s.o., se prêter aux caprices de qn; ménager qn. *To h. s.o.'s fancy,* passer une fantaisie à qn.

humoursome ['(h)ju:mərsəm], *a.* **I.** Capricieux, fantasque. **2.** D'humeur incertaine.

hump¹ [hʌmp], *s.* **I.** Bosse *f* (de bossu, de chameau). **To have a hump,** être bossu. **2.** *F:* **To have the hump,** avoir le cafard; broyer du noir. *That gives me the h.,* cela m'embête.

hump², *v.tr.* To hump the back, arquer, bomber, le dos; faire le gros dos. **To hump up one's shoulders,** rentrer la tête dans les épaules. **humped,** *a.* (Dos, animal) bossu; (dos) voûté; (toit) en bosse.

humpback ['hʌmpbak], *s.* Bossu, -ue.

humpbacked ['hʌmpbakt], *a.* Bossu.

humus ['hju:məs], *s. Hort:* Humus *m;* terreau *m;* terre végétale.

hunch¹ [hʌnʃ], *s.* **I.** Bosse *f.* **2.** Gros morceau (de fromage). **Hunch of bread,** quignon *m* de pain. **3.** *U.S: P:* **To have a hunch that . . .,** soupçonner que. . . .

hunch², *v.tr.* Arrondir (le dos); voûter (les épaules). **To sit hunched up,** se tenir accroupi le menton sur les genoux.

hunchback ['hʌnʃbak], *s.* = HUMPBACK.

hundred ['hʌndrəd], *num. a. & s.* Cent (*m*). *A h. and one,* cent un. *About a h. houses,* une centaine de maisons. *Two h. apples,* deux cents pommes. *Two h. and one pounds,* deux cent une livres. *In nineteen hundred,* en dix-neuf cent. *To live to be a h.,* atteindre la centaine. *They died in hundreds, in hundreds of thousands,* ils mouraient par centaines, par centaines de mille. **Hundreds and thousands of people,** des milliers *m* de gens. **To have three hundred a year,** avoir trois cents livres de rente. **A hundred per cent,** cent pour cent. *Com: A h. eggs,* un cent d'œufs. *To sell bv the h.,* vendre au cent.

hundredfold ['hʌndrədfould]. **1.** *a.* Centuple. **2.** *adv.phr.* **A hundredfold,** cent fois autant. *To be repaid a h.,* être payé au centuple.

hundredth ['hʌndrədθ], *num.a. & s.* Centième (*m*).

hundredweight ['hʌndrədweit], *s.* (*a*) Poids *m* de 112 livres, = 50 kg 802; (*approx* =) quintal *m.* (*b*) *U.S:* Poids de 100 livres, = 45 kg 359.

hung [hʌŋ]. *See* HANG².

Hungarian [hʌŋ'gɛəriən], *a. & s.* Hongrois, -oise.

Hungary ['hʌŋgəri]. *Pr.n. Geog:* La Hongrie.

hunger¹ ['hʌŋgər], *s.* Faim *f.* **Hunger is the best sauce,** il n'est sauce que d'appétit. *Pang of hunger,* fringale *f. F:* **Hunger for sth.,** ardent désir de qch.; soif *f* de qch. **'hunger-strike,** *s.* Grève *f* de la faim.

hunger², *v.i.* (*a*) Avoir faim. (*b*) **To hunger after, for,** sth., être affamé de, avoir soif de, qch.; désirer ardemment qch. **hungering,** *s.* Faim *f*, soif *f* (*after, for,* de).

hungry ['hʌŋgri], *a.* **1.** Affamé. **To be, feel, hungry,** avoir faim; se sentir faim. **To be ravenously hungry,** avoir une faim de loup. *To make s.o. h.,* donner faim à qn. **To go hungry,** souffrir de la faim. **To look hungry,** avoir l'air famélique. **2.** (Regard, œil) avide. **-ily,** *adv.* Avidement, voracement; (regarder) d'un œil avide.

hunk [hʌŋk], *s.* = HUNCH¹ 1.

hunks [hʌŋks], *s. F:* Stingy old hunks, vieil avare; grippe-sou *m, pl.* grippe-sou(s); ladre *m.*

hunt¹ [hʌnt], *s.* **1.** (*a*) Chasse *f; esp.* chasse à courre, aux fauves. **Tiger-hunt,** chasse au tigre. (*b*) Équipage *m* de chasse. **2.** Recherche *f. There was a h. for the missing book,** on cherchait le livre qui manquait.

hunt². **1.** *v.i.* (*a*) *Ven:* Chasser au chien courant; chasser à courre. (*b*) **To hunt (about) for sth.,** chercher (à découvrir) qch. (*Of engine, alternator*) Pomper; s'affoler par instants. **2.** *v.tr.* (*a*) Chasser (le cerf, etc.). *To h. whales,* pêcher la baleine. (*b*) **To hunt a thief,** poursuivre un voleur. (*c*) Parcourir, battre (un terrain). (*d*) **To hunt a horse,** monter un cheval à la chasse. **hunt down,** *v.tr.* Traquer (une bête); *F:* mettre (qn) aux abois, à l'accul. **hunt out,** *v.tr. F:* Déterrer, dénicher (qch.) (à force de recherches). **hunt up,** *v.tr.* **1.** Déterrer (des faits). **2.** Aller relancer (qn). **hunting,** *s.* **1.** (*a*) Chasse *f* (à courre). **Fox-hunting,** chasse au renard. **To go a-hunting,** aller à la chasse. **Hunting knife,** couteau de chasse. **Hunting terms,** termes de vénerie. (*b*) *F:* **Bargain-hunting,** chasse aux soldes. **To go house-hunting,** se mettre en quête d'un domicile. **2.** *Mch:* Mouvement *m* de galop (de locomotive). *Magn:* Affolement *m* (de l'aiguille aimantée). **'hunting-box,** *s.* Pavillon *m* de chasse. **'hunting-ground,** *s.* **1.** Terrain *m* de chasse. **2.** *F:* A happy hunting-ground for collectors (*of curios*), un endroit propice aux collectionneurs, un paradis pour les collectionneurs. **'hunting-horn,** *s.* Cor *m* de chasse. **'hunt-the-'slipper,** *s. Games:* Jeu *m* du furet.

hunter ['hʌntər], *s.* **1.** (*a*) Chasseur *m*; tueur *m* (de lions, etc.). (*b*) *F:* Pourchasseur *m* (*of,* de). **Curio-hunter,** dénicheur m d'antiquités. **2.** Cheval *m* de chasse. **3.** (Montre *f* à) savonnette *f.*

huntress ['hʌntres], *s.f.* Chasseuse; *Poet:* chasseresse.

huntsman, *pl.* **-men** ['hʌntsmən, -men], *s.m.* **1.** Chasseur (à courre). **2.** Veneur, piqueur.

hurdle¹ [həːrdl], *s.* **1.** Claie *f.* **2.** *Sp:* Barrière *f*, obstacle *m. Turf:* Haie *f.* **'hurdle-race,** *s.*

Sp: Course *f* d'obstacles. *Turf:* (*Short*) Course de haies; (*long*) steeple-chase *m.*

hurdle². **1.** *v.tr.* Garnir, entourer, (qch.) de claies. **2.** *v.i. Sp:* Courir une course d'obstacles; *Turf:* courir une course de haies. **hurdling,** *s. Sp:* Saut *m* d'obstacles, de haies.

hurdler ['həːrdlər], *s.* **1.** Fabricant *m* de claies. **2.** *Sp:* Sauteur *m* d'obstacles; *Turf:* jockey *m* de courses à obstacles.

hurdy-gurdy ['həːrdigəːrdi], *s.* **1.** *A:* Vielle *f.* **2.** *F:* Orgue *m* de Barbarie.

hurl [həːrl], *v.tr.* Lancer (qch.) avec violence (*at, contre*). *The explosion hurled them far and wide,* l'explosion les projeta au loin. **To hurl oneself at s.o.,** se ruer sur qn. *To h. oneself into the fray,* se jeter à corps perdu dans la mêlée. *Hurled into the chasm,* précipité dans le gouffre. *F:* **To hurl reproaches at s.o.,** cribler, accabler, qn de reproches. **hurl back,** *v.tr.* Refouler, rejeter (l'ennemi); rétorquer (une accusation). **hurl down,** *v.tr.* Précipiter; jeter bas.

hurly-burly ['həːrlibəːrli], *s.* Tohu-bohu *m.*

hurrah¹ [hu'rɑː], **hurray** [hu'rei], *int. & s.* Hourra (*m*). *H. for the holidays!* vive(nt) les vacances!

hurrah², *v.i.* Pousser un hourra, des hourras.

hurricane ['hʌrikən], *s.* Ouragan *m; Nau:* tempête *f. It was blowing a h.,* le vent soufflait en tempête. **'hurricane-lamp,** *s.* Lanterne-tempête *f.*

hurry¹ ['hʌri], *s.* Hâte *f*, précipitation *f.* **To write in a hurry,** écrire à la hâte. *To be in a h. to do sth.,* avoir hâte de faire qch. **To be in a hurry,** être pressé. **To be in no hurry,** ne pas être pressé; avoir le temps. *F:* **What's your hurry?** qu'est-ce qui vous presse? **Is there any hurry?** est-ce pressé? est-ce que cela presse? *There's no (special) h.,* rien ne presse. *F: I shan't do it again in a h.,* on ne m'y reprendra pas de sitôt.

hurry². **1.** *v.tr.* (*a*) Hâter, presser (qn). **To hurry oneself,** se hâter, se dépêcher, se presser. (*b*) Hâter, activer (le travail). *Work that cannot be hurried,* travail qui demande du temps. (*c*) *Troops were hurried to the spot,* on amena au plus vite, en toute hâte, des troupes sur les lieux. **2.** *v.i.* (*a*) Se hâter, se presser; se dépêcher. *To h. through, over, one's lunch,* expédier son déjeuner. **Don't hurry,** ne vous pressez pas. (*b*) Presser le pas. *To h. to a place,* se rendre en toute hâte à un endroit. *She hurried home,* elle se dépêcha, s'empressa, de rentrer. (*c*) **To hurry into one's clothes,** passer ses vêtements en toute hâte. **hurry along.** **1.** *v.tr.* Entraîner (qn) précipitamment. **2.** *v.i.* Marcher d'un pas pressé. **hurry away, off.** **1.** *v.tr.* Emmener (qn) précipitamment. **2.** *v.i.* Partir précipitamment. *I must h. away,* il faut que je me sauve. **hurry back,** *v.i.* Revenir à la hâte; se presser de revenir. **hurry on.** **1.** *v.tr.* Faire hâter le pas à (qn); activer, pousser (la besogne); presser (le départ de qn). **2.** *v.i.* Presser le pas; continuer sa route à vive allure. **hurry out,** *v.i.* Sortir vivement, précipitamment. **hurry up,** *v.i. F:* Se dépêcher, se hâter. **Hurry up!** dépêchez-vous! plus vite que ça! **hurried,** *a.* (Pas) pressé, précipité; (ouvrage) fait à la hâte. *A few h. words,* quelques paroles dites à la hâte. *To take a h. luncheon,* déjeuner à la hâte. **-ly,** *adv.* A la hâte, en toute hâte; précipitamment, vivement.

hurt¹ [həːrt], *s.* Mal *m.* **1.** Blessure *f.* **To do s.o. a hurt,** faire du mal à qn; blesser qn. **2.** Tort *m*, dommage *m. What h. can it do you?* en quoi cela peut-il vous nuire?

hurt², *v.tr.* (hurt; hurt) **I.** Faire (du) mal à, blesser (qn). *To h. oneself*, se faire (du) mal. *To h. one's foot*, se blesser au pied. **To get hurt**, être blessé ; recevoir une blessure. *My wound hurts (me)*, ma blessure me fait mal. *That hurts*, ça fait mal. **2.** Faire de la peine à (qn). **To hurt s.o.'s feelings**, blesser, froisser, peiner, qn. **3.** (*Of thg*) Nuire à, abîmer (qch.). **To hurt s.o.'s interests**, léser les intérêts de qn.

hurtful ['hɔːrtful], *a.* **I.** (*a*) Nuisible, nocif. (*b*) Préjudiciable (*to*, à). *It is h. to my interests*, cela porte atteinte à mes intérêts. **2.** Hurtful to the feelings, froissant, blessant.

hurtle [hɔːrtl], *v.i.* Se précipiter, s'élancer (avec bruit, comme un bolide). (*Of car, etc.*) **To hurtle along**, dévorer la route. *The rocks hurtled, came hurtling, down*, les rochers dévalaient avec fracas. *The shells hurtled through the air*, les obus passaient en trombe.

husband¹ ['hʌzbənd], *s.* Mari *m*, époux *m*. *H. and wife*, les (deux) époux, les conjoints *m*. *To live as h. and wife*, vivre maritalement.

husband², *v.tr.* **I.** *A:* Cultiver (la terre, etc.). **2.** Ménager, épargner, économiser (son argent, ses forces) ; bien gouverner (ses ressources).

husbandman, *pl.* **-men** ['hʌzbəndmən, -men], *s.m.* **I.** Cultivateur. **2.** Laboureur.

husbandry ['hʌzbəndri], *s.* **I.** Agronomie *f* ; industrie *f* agricole. **2.** Good husbandry, bonne gestion ; sage administration *f* (de son bien).

hush¹ [hʌʃ], *s.* Silence *m*, calme *m*. **The hush before the storm**, l'accalmie *f* avant la tempête.

hush². **I.** *v.tr.* (*a*) Apaiser, faire taire (un enfant) ; imposer silence à (qn). *All nature is hushed*, toute la nature se tait. (*b*) Hushed conversation, conversation étouffée, discrète. **2.** *v.i.* Se taire ; faire silence. **hush up**, *v.tr.* Étouffer (un scandale). **'hush-money**, *s.* Argent donné à qn pour acheter son silence ; pot-de-vin *m*.

hush³, *int.* Chut ! silence ! **hush-'hush**, *a.* *F:* Secret, -ète. Hush-hush ship, navire dont la construction a été tenue secrète, dont on fait mystère.

husk¹ [hʌsk], *s.* Cosse *f*, gousse *f* (de pois, etc.) ; brou *m*, écale *f* (de noix) ; bogue *f* (de châtaigne) ; coque *f* (de grain de café) ; tégument *m*, balle *f* (de grain). **Rice in the husk**, riz non décortiqué.

husk², *v.tr.* Décortiquer ; écaler, cerner (des noix) ; écorcer, perler, monder (le riz, l'orge) ; vanner (le grain).

huskiness ['hʌskinəs], *s.* Enrouement *m*, empâtement *m* (de la voix).

husky¹ ['hʌski], *a.* Husky voice, (i) voix enrouée, voilée ; (*of drunkard*) voix de rogomme ; (ii) voix altérée (par l'émotion).

husky², *s.* Chien *m* esquimau, chien de traîneau.

hussar [hu'zɑːr], *s.* *Mil:* Hussard *m*.

hussy ['hʌzi], *s.f.* *F:* **I.** Coquine, friponne. *You little h.!* petite effrontée ! **2.** Drôlesse, garce.

hustle¹ [hʌsl], *s.* **I.** Bousculade *f*. **2.** Hâte *f* ; activité *f* énergique.

hustle². **I.** *v.tr.* (*a*) Bousculer, pousser, presser (qn). **To hustle things on**, pousser le travail ; *F:* mener les choses tambour battant. (*b*) **To hustle s.o. into a decision**, forcer qn à se décider sans lui donner le temps de respirer. (*c*) (*Of pickpocket*) Bousculer (qn) ; voler (qn) à l'esbroufe. **2.** *v.i.* Se dépêcher, se presser. **hustling**, *s.* **I.** = HUSTLE¹. **2.** Vol *m* à l'esbroufe.

hustler ['hʌslər], *s.* **I.** (*a*) Bousculeur, -euse. (*b*) Esbroufeur *m*. **2.** *U.S:* Débrouillard *m* ; brasseur *m* d'affaires.

hut [hʌt], *s.* Hutte *f*, cabane *f*. *Mil:* Baraquement *m*, Alpine hut, chalet-refuge *m*.

hutch [hʌtʃ], *s.* **I.** Coffre *m*, huche *f*. **2.** (Rabbit-) hutch, clapier *m*, lapinière *f*. **3.** (*a*) (Baker's) hutch, pétrin *m*, huche. (*b*) *Min:* Benne (roulante) ; wagonnet *m*.

hutments ['hʌtmənts], *s.pl.* *Mil: etc:* Baraquements *m* ; camp *m* de baraques.

hyacinth ['haiəsinθ], *s.* **I.** *Lap:* Hyacinthe *f*. **2.** *Bot:* Jacinthe *f*. Wood, wild, hyacinth, jacinthe des prés. **3.** *a. & s.* (*Colour*) (*a*) Rouge orangé *inv* (de l'hyacinthe). (*b*) Bleu jacinthe *inv*.

hyaena [hai'iːna], *s.* = HYENA.

hyaline ['haiəlin], *a.* Hyalin, transparent.

hyaloid ['haiələid], *a.* *Anat: etc:* Hyaloïde.

hybrid ['haibrid], *a. & s.* *Biol: Ling: etc:* Hybride (*m*). *H. plant*, plante hybride, métisse.

hybridize ['haibridaiz], *v.tr.* Hybrider.

hydra ['haidrə], *s.* Hydre *f*. **Hydra-headed**, à têtes d'hydre, à sept têtes.

hydrangea [hai'dreindʒa], *s.* *Bot:* Hortensia *m*.

hydrant ['haidrənt], *s.* Prise *f* d'eau ; bouche *f* d'eau. *Esp.* **Fire-hydrant**, bouche d'incendie.

hydrarthrosis [haidrɑːr'θrousis], *s.* *Med:* Hydarthrose *f*.

hydrate¹ ['haidret], *s.* *Ch:* Hydrate *m*.

hydrate² ['haidreit], *v.tr.* *Ch:* Hydrater.

hydration [hai'drei(ə)n], *s.* *Ch:* Hydratation *f*.

hydraulic [hai'drɔːlik], *a.* Hydraulique. **Hydraulic engineering**, hydraulique *f*.

hydraulics [hai'drɔːliks], *s.pl.* Hydraulique *f*.

hydride ['haidraid], *s.* *Ch:* Hydrure *m*.

hydro ['haidro], *s.* *F:* = HYDROPATHIC 2.

hydrocarbon [haidro'kɑːrbən], *s.* *Ch:* Hydrocarbure *m* ; carbure *m* d'hydrogène.

hydrocephalic [haidrose'falik], **hydrocephalous** [haidro'sefaləs], *a.* *Med:* Hydrocéphale.

hydrocephalus [haidro'sefaləs], **hydrocephaly** [haidro'sefali], *s.* *Med:* Hydrocéphalie *f*, hydrocéphalie *f*.

hydrochloric [haidro'klɔ(ː)rik], *a.* *Ch:* (Acide) chlorhydrique.

hydrocyanic [haidrosai'anik], *a.* *Ch:* Cyanhydrique.

hydro-electric [haidroi'lektrik], *a.* Hydro-électrique.

hydrofluoric [haidroflu'ɔrik], *a.* *Ch:* Fluorhydrique.

hydrogen ['haidrodʒen], *s.* *Ch:* Hydrogène *m*.

hydrogenate [hai'drɔdʒeneit], **hydrogenize** [hai'drɔdʒenaːiz], *v.tr.* Hydrogéner.

hydrographer [hai'drɔgrəfər], *s.* (Ingénieur) hydrographe *m*.

hydrographic(al) [haidro'grafik(əl)], *a.* Hydrographique.

hydrography [hai'drɔgrəfi], *s.* Hydrographie *f*.

hydrolysis [hai'drɔlisis], *s.* *Ch:* Hydrolyse *f*.

hydrometer [hai'drɔmetər], *s.* *Ph:* Aréomètre *m* ; hydromètre *m*. **Acid hydrometer**, pèse-acide *m inv*, acidimètre *m*.

hydropathic [haidro'paθik], *Med:* **I.** *a.* (*a*) (Établissement) hydrothérapique. (*b*) (Médecin) hydropathe. **2.** *s.* Établissement *m* hydrothérapique ; établissement thermal.

hydrophobia [haidro'foubia], *s.* *Med:* Hydrophobie *f* ; *F:* la rage.

hydrophobic [haidro'foubik], *a.* Hydrophobe. *H. patient*, hydrophobe *mf*.

hydroplane ['haidroplein], *s.* **I.** *Av:* Hydravion *m* ; hydroplane *m*. **2.** (*Motor boat*) Hydroglisseur *m*. **3.** *pl.* Barres *f* de plongée (d'un sous-marin).

hydroquinone [haidrokwi'noun], *s.* *Phot:* Hydroquinone *f*.

hydrosphere ['haidrosfiːər], *s.* Hydrosphère *f*.

hydrostatic(al) [haidro'statik(əl)], *a.* Hydro-statique.

hydrostatics [haidro'statiks], *s.pl.* Hydro-statique *f.*

hydrosulphide [haidro'sʌlfaid], *s. Ch:* Sulf-hydrate *m.*

hydrotherapeutic [haidroθerə'pju:tik], *a. Med:* Hydrothérapique.

hydrotherapeutics [haidroθerə'pju:tiks], *s.pl.*, **hydrotherapy** [haidro'θerəpi], *s. Med:* Hy-drothérapie *f.*

hyena [hai'i:na], *s. Z:* Hyène *f.*

hygiene ['haidʒi:n], *s.* Hygiène *f.*

hygienic [hai'dʒi:nik], *a.* Hygiénique. **-ally,** *adv.* Hygiéniquement.

hygienist ['haidʒi:nist], *s.* Hygiéniste *mf.*

hygrometer [hai'grɔmetər], *s. Ph:* Hygro-mètre *m.*

hygrometric(al) [haigro'metrik(əl)], *a.* Hygro-métrique.

hygrometry [hai'grɔmetri], *s.* Hygrométrie *f.*

hygroscope ['haigroskoup], *s. Ph:* Hygro-scope *m.*

hymenoptera [haimen'ɔptərə], *s.pl. Ent:* Hy-ménoptères *m.*

hymn [him], *s. Ecc:* Hymne *f,* cantique *m.* **'hymn-book,** *s.* Recueil *m* de cantiques; hymnaire *m.*

hymnal ['himnəl], *s.* Recueil *m* de cantiques; hymnaire *m.*

hyoid ['haiɔid], *a. & s. Anat:* (Os *m*) hyoïde *m.*

hyperaesthesia [haipəres'θi:sia], *s.* Hyper-esthésie *f.*

hyperbola [hai'pə:rbola], *s. Geom:* Hyperbole *f.*

hyperbole [hai'pə:rboli], *s. Rh:* Hyperbole *f.*

hyperbolic(al) [haipər'bɔlik(əl)], *a. Geom: Rh:* Hyperbolique.

hypercritical [haipər'kritik(ə)l], *a.* Qui outre la critique. *To be h.,* (i) chercher la petite bête; (ii) se montrer d'un rigorisme exagéré.

hyperfocal [haipər'fouk(ə)l], *a. Phot:* Hyper-focal, -aux.

hypermetropia [haipərme'troupiə], *s. Med:* Hypermétropie *f.*

hyphen¹ ['haif(ə)n], *s.* Trait *m* d'union.

hyphen², **hyphenate** ['haifəneit], *v.tr.* Mettre un trait d'union à (un mot). **Hyphenated word,** mot à trait d'union.

hypnosis [hip'nousis], *s.* Hypnose *f.*

hypnotic [hip'nɔtik], *a.* Hypnotique. **Hypnotic state,** état *m* d'hypnose; somnambulisme provoqué.

hypnotism ['hipnɔtizm], *s.* Hypnotisme *m.*

hypnotist ['hipnɔtist], *s.* Hypnotiste *mf.*

hypnotize ['hipnɔta:iz], *v.tr.* Hypnotiser.

hypo ['haipo], *s. Phot: F:* = HYPOSULPHITE.

hypochondria [haipo'kɔndria], *s.* Hypocon-drie *f.*

hypochondriac [haipo'kɔndriak], *a. & s.* Hypocondriaque (*mf*); *s.* hypocondre *mf.*

hypocrisy [hi'pɔkrisi], *s.* Hypocrisie *f.*

hypocrite ['hipokrit], *s.* Hypocrite *mf; F:* tar-tufe *m.*

hypocritical [hipo'kritik(ə)l], *a.* Hypocrite. **-ally,** *adv.* Hypocritement.

hypodermic [haipo'də:rmik], *a. Med:* **Hypo-dermic syringe,** seringue *f* hypodermique, seringue de Pravaz.

hypogastric [haipo'gastrik], *a. Anat:* Hypo-gastrique.

hypogastrium [haipo'gastriəm], *s. Anat:* Hy-pogastre *m.*

hypogeum, -a [haipo'dʒi:əm, -a], *s. Archeol:* Hypogée *m.*

hypophosphate [haipo'fɔsfet], *s. Ch:* Hypo-phosphate *m.*

hypophysis [hai'pɔfisis], *s. Anat:* Hypophyse *f.*

hypostyle ['haipostail], *a. Arch:* Hypostyle.

hyposulphite [haipo'sʌlfait], *s. Ch:* Hypo-sulfite *m. Phot:* **Hyposulphite of soda,** *F:* hypo, hyposulfite de soude.

hypotenuse [hai'pɔtenju:s], *s. Geom:* Hypo-ténuse *f.*

hypothesis [hai'pɔθesis], *s.* Hypothèse *f.*

hypothetic(al) [haipo'θetik(ə)l], *a.* Hypothé-tique, supposé. **-ally,** *adv.* Par hypothèse.

hypsometric(al) [hipso'metrik(ə)l], *a.* Hypso-métrique.

hypsometry [hip'sɔmetri], *s. Surv:* Hypso-métrie *f.*

hyssop ['hisəp], *s. Bot:* Hysope *f.*

hysteresis [histə'ri:sis], *s.* Hystérèse *f* (magné-tique); traînée *f* magnétique.

hysteria [his'ti:əria], *s. Med:* Hystérie *f.*

hysterical [his'terik(ə)l], *a.* **1.** *Med:* Hystérique. **2.** (*a*) Sujet à des attaques de nerfs. *H. sobs,* sanglots convulsifs. *H. laugh,* rire nerveux, énervé. (*b*) To become hysterical, avoir une attaque de nerfs. **-ally,** *adv. To weep h.,* avoir une crise de larmes. *To laugh h.,* rire nerveuse-ment; avoir le fou rire.

hysterics [his'teriks], *s.pl.* Attaque *f* de nerfs; crise *f* de nerfs. *To go, fall, into hysterics,* avoir une crise de nerfs.

I

I¹, i [ai], *s.* (La lettre) I, i *m. To dot one's i's,* mettre les points sur les i.

I², *pers. pron.* (*a*) Je, j'. *I sing,* je chante. *I accuse,* j'accuse. *Here I am,* me voici. *What have I said?* qu'ai-je dit? (*b*) Moi *mf. He and I are great friends,* lui et moi, nous sommes de grands amis. *It is I,* c'est moi. *I .oo,* moi aussi. (*Stressed*) *'I'll see you home,* c'est moi qui vais vous reconduire.

iamb ['aiamb], *s.* = IAMBUS.

iambic [ai'ambik].↑ *Pros:* **1.** *a.* Iambique. **2.** *s.* Vers *m* iambique; iambe *m.*

iambus [ai'ambəs], *s. Pros:* Iambe *m.*

Iberia [ai'bi:əria]. *Pr.n. A.Geog:* L'Ibérie *f.*

Iberian [ai'bi:əriən]. **1.** *a.* (Péninsule) ibérique; (peuple) ibérien. **2.** *s:* Ibérien, -ienne. *The Iberians,* les Ibères *m.*

ibex ['aibeks], *s. Z:* Bouquetin *m,* ibex *m.*

ibis ['aibis], *s. Orn:* Ibis *m.*

ice¹ [ais], *s.* Glace *f.* **1.** The ice age, la période glaciaire. Granular ice, névé *m.* Anchor ice, ground ice, glaces de fond. My feet are like ice, j'ai les pieds glacés. *F:* To break the ice, rompre la glace; (i) faire cesser la contrainte; (ii) en-tamer un sujet, une affaire. *F:* To skate over thin ice, toucher à un sujet délicat. *U.S:* To cut no ice with s.o., ne faire aucune impression sur

qn. **2.** *Cu:* Strawberry ice, glace à la fraise. *Mixed ice,* glace panachée. **'ice-axe,** *s.* Piolet *m.*
'ice-bag, *s. Med:* Vessie *f,* sac *m,* à glace.
'ice-bank, *s.* Banquise *f.* **'ice-bound,** *a.* (i) (Navire) retenu par les glaces, pris dans les glaces; (ii) (port) fermé, bâclé, par les glaces.
'ice-box, -chest, *s.* Glacière *f* (domestique); sorbétière *f.* **'ice-breaker,** *s. Nau:* Brise-glace(s) *m inv.* **ice-'cream,** *s. Cu:* (Crème *f* à la) glace. **Ice-cream man,** glacier *m.* **'ice-field,** *s.* Champ *m* de glace. **'ice-floe,** *s.* Banquise *f;* banc *m* de glace. **'ice-hockey,** *s. Sp:* Hockey *m* sur glace. **'ice-house,** *s.* Glacière *f.* **'ice-pack,** *s.* (a) Embâcle *m.* (b) Banquise *f.* **'ice-period,** *s. Geol:* Époque *f* glaciaire. **'ice-plant,** *s. Bot:* (Ficoïde) glaciale *f.* **ice-'pudding,** *s. Cu:* Bombe glacée. **'ice-water,** *s.* **I.** Eau glacée, frappée. **2.** Eau de glace fondue.
ice², *v.tr.* **I.** Congeler, geler. **The pond was soon iced over,** l'étang eut, fut, bientôt gelé d'un bout à l'autre. **2.** Rafraîchir (l'eau, etc.) avec de la glace; frapper (du champagne). **3.** Glacer (un gâteau). **iced,** *a.* **I.** (Crème) glacée, à la glace; (melon) rafraîchi; (champagne) frappé. *I. coffee,* café glacé. **2. Iced cake,** gâteau glacé.
iceberg ['aisbə:rg], *s.* Iceberg *m;* montagne *f* de glace.
Iceland ['aislənd]. *Pr.n. Geog:* L'Islande *f.*
Icelander ['aisləndər], *s.* Islandais, -aise.
Icelandic [ais'landik]. **I.** *a.* Islandais; d'Islande. **2.** *s. Ling:* L'islandais *m.*
ichneumon [ik'nju:mən], *s.* **I.** *Z:* Ichneumon *m;* *F:* rat *m* de Pharaon. **2.** *Ent:* Ichneumon (-fly), ichneumon.
ichthyologic(al) [ikθio'lɔdʒik(əl)], *a.* Ichtyologique.
ichthyology [ikθi'ɔlodʒi], *s.* Ichtyologie *f.*
ichthyophagous [ikθi'ɔfagəs], *a.* Ichtyophage.
ichthyophagy [ikθi'ɔfadʒi], *s.* Ichtyophagie *f.*
ichthyosaurus [ikθio'sɔ:rəs], *s. Paleont:* Ichtyosaure *m.*
icicle ['aisikl], *s.* Petit glaçon; chandelle *f* de glace.
iciness ['aisinəs], *s.* **I.** Froid glacial. **2.** Froideur glaciale (d'un accueil).
icon ['aikon], *s. Ecc:* Icone *f.*
iconoclasm [ai'kɔnoklazm], *s.* Iconoclasie *f,* iconoclasme *m.*
iconoclast [ai'kɔnoklast], *s.* Iconoclaste *mf.*
iconoclastic [aikɔno'klastik], *a.* Iconoclaste.
icteric(al) [ik'terik(əl)], *a. Med:* Ictérique.
icy ['aisi], *a.* **I.** Couvert de glace; glacial, -als. **2.** (Vent, accueil) glacial. **Icy hands,** mains glacées. *This room is icy cold,* on gèle dans cette salle. **-ily,** *adv.* (Accueillir qn) d'un air glacial.
idea [ai'di:ə], *s.* Idée *f.* **What a funny idea!** quelle drôle d'idée! *To give a general i. of a book,* donner un aperçu d'un livre. **I can't bear the idea,** l'idée m'en est trop pénible. **Man of ideas,** homme à idées. **To hit upon the idea of doing sth.,** avoir la bonne inspiration, avoir l'idée, de faire qch. **I have an idea that . . .,** j'ai idée que. . . . **I had no idea that . . .,** j'étais loin de me douter que . . .; j'ignorais absolument que . . .; je n'avais aucune idée que. . . . *To have a clear i. of sth.,* se représenter clairement qch. par la pensée. **He has some idea of chemistry,** il a des notions de chimie. **To get ideas into one's head,** se faire des idées. *F:* **What an idea!** en voilà une idée! y pensez-vous! **The idea!** quelle idée! par exemple!
ideal [ai'di:əl]. **I.** *a.* Idéal, -aux. *F:* **It is ideal!** c'est le rêve! **2.** *s.* Idéal *m,* -aux, -als. **The ideal**

of beauty, le beau idéal, la beauté idéale. **-ally,** *adv.* Idéalement (beau, etc.).
idealist [ai'di:əlist], *s.* Idéaliste *mf.*
idealize [ai'di:əla:iz], *v.tr.* Idéaliser.
identical [ai'dentik(ə)l], *a.* Identique (with, à). *Our tastes are i.,* ses goûts sont conformes aux miens. **-ally,** *adv.* Identiquement.
identification [aidentifi'kei∫(ə)n], *s.* Identification *f.* **Identification papers, card, carte *f* d'identité.** *Aut:* **Identification plate,** plaque *f* d'identité, plaque matricule.
identify [ai'dentifai], *v.tr.* **I.** Identifier (sth. with sth., qch. avec qch.). *To i. oneself, become identified, with a party,* s'identifier à, avec, s'assimiler à, un parti. **2. To identify s.o.,** constater, établir, l'identité de qn.
identity [ai'dentiti], *s.* Identité *f.* **Identity card,** carte *f* d'identité. **Mistaken identity,** erreur *f* sur la personne. **To prove one's identity,** établir son identité.
ideologic(al) [aidio'lɔdʒik(əl)], *a.* Idéologique.
ideologist [aidi'ɔlodʒist], **ideologue** ['aidiolɔg], *s.* Idéologue *mf.*
ideology [aidi'ɔlodʒi], *s.* Idéologie *f.*
ides [aidz], *s.pl. Rom.Ant:* Ides *f.*
idiocy ['idiosi], *s.* **I.** Idiotie (congénitale). **2.** *F:* The i. of this plan, la bêtise sans nom de ce projet.
idiom ['idiəm], *s.* **I.** (a) Dialecte *m;* idiome *m* (d'une région). (b) Langue *f,* idiome (d'un pays). **2.** Idiotisme *m,* locution *f* (d'une langue).
idiomatic(al) [idio'matik(əl)], *a.* **I.** Idiomatique. *I. phrase,* idiotisme *m.* **2.** Qui appartient à la langue courante ou à la langue familière. **-ally,** *adv.* (S'exprimer) d'une façon idiomatique, en se servant d'idiotismes.
idiosyncrasy [idio'siŋkrəsi], *s.* **I.** Idiosyncrasie *f.* **2.** *F:* Habitude *f* propre à qn; petite manie; particularité *f* (de style).
idiot ['idiət], *s.* (a) *Med:* Idiot, -ote; imbécile *mf.* **The village idiot,** l'innocent *m* du village. (b) *F:* Imbécile. **You idiot!** espèce d'imbécile, d'idiot!
idiotic [idi'ɔtik], *a. F:* Bête. *That's i.,* c'est stupide; *F:* c'est bête comme chou. **-ally,** *adv.* Bêtement; (se conduire) en imbécile.
idle¹ [aidl], *a.* **I.** (a) (Of pers.) Inoccupé, oisif, désœuvré. *In my i. moments,* à mes heures perdues. (b) (Of machinery, workmen) Qui chôme, en chômage; (of. machine) au repos. *Factory standing i.,* usine qui chôme. **To run idle,** (i) (of machine) marcher à vide; (ii) *Aut:* (of engine) tourner au ralenti. *Capital lying i.,* fonds dormants, inemployés. (c) *Mec.E:* Idle motion, mouvement perdu. *Idle period (in cycle, etc.),* temps mort. *El:* Idle current, courant déwatté. (d) *Mec.E:* Idle wheel, roue folle, décalée. **2.** (Of pers.) Paresseux, fainéant. **The idle rich,** les riches désœuvrés. **3.** Inutile, oiseux, futile. *I. wish,* vain désir. *I. threats,* menaces en l'air. **Out of idle curiosity,** par curiosité désœuvrée.
idly, *adv.* **I.** Sans travailler. *To stand i. by,* rester là à ne rien faire. **2.** Inutilement; (parler) en l'air. **3.** Paresseusement. **idle-'pulley,** *s. Mec.E:* **I.** Poulie-guide *f.* **2.** Galet *m* de renvoi.
idle² [aidl], *v.i.* **I.** Fainéanter; paresser. *To i. about the streets,* flâner dans les rues. *v.tr.* **To idle one's time away,** perdre son temps à ne rien faire; à paresser, à flâner. **2.** *Aut:* (Of engine) **To idle (over),** tourner au ralenti.
idleness ['aidlnəs], *s.* **I.** (a) Oisiveté *f,* désœuvrement *m.* (b) Chômage *m* (involontaire). **2.** Futilité *f* (d'une menace, etc.). **3.** (Of pers.) Paresse *f,*

fa=néantise f. To live in idleness, to eat the bread of idleness, vivre dans l'oisiveté.

idler ['aidlər], s. **1.** (a) Oisif, -ive ; désœuvré, -ée ; flâneur, -euse. (b) Fainéant, -ante ; paresseux, -euse. **2.** *Mec.E:* (a) Roue folle ; pignon *m* libre. (b) (Pignon de) renvoi *m.* (c) Poulie *f* de tension.

idol ['aid(ə)l], s. Idole *f.* *F:* The idol of the day, l'idole du jour.

idolater [ai'dɔlətər], *f.* **idolatress** [ai'dɔlətres], s. Idolâtre *mf.*

idolatrous [ai'dɔlətrəs], a. Idolâtre.

idolatry [ai'dɔlətri], s. Idolâtrie *f.*

idolize ['aidəlaiz], *v.tr.* Idolâtrer, adorer (qn, qch.) ; faire une idole (de l'argent).

idyll ['aidil], s. *Lit:* Idylle *f.*

idyllic [ai'dilik], a. Idyllique.

if [if], *conj.* Si **1.** (a) *If I wanted him, I rang,* si j'avais besoin de lui, je sonnais. *This lapse, if lapse it be* . . ., cette faute, si faute il y a. . . . (b) *If he does it, he will be punished,* s'il le fait, il sera puni. *If he did it, he would be punished,* s'il le faisait, il serait puni. *If the weather is fine and (if) I am free, I shall go out,* s'il fait beau et si je suis libre, je sortirai. *If it is fine, and (if it is) not too windy, we shall go for a walk,* s'il fait beau et qu'il ne fasse pas trop de vent, nous irons en promenade. *If they are to be believed,* not a soul was saved, à les en croire, pas une âme n'aurait survécu. *If you hesitate (at all),* pour peu que vous hésitiez. **If (it is) necessary,** s'il est nécessaire ; s'il le faut ; au besoin. **If (it be) so,** s'il en est ainsi. *The water was warm, if anything,* l'eau était plutôt tiède. *He will give you a shilling for it, if that,* il vous en donnera un shilling, et encore ! **If not,** sinon ; si ce n'est. . . . *Go and see him, if only to please me,* allez le voir, ne fût-ce, ne serait-ce, que pour me faire plaisir. *S.a.* ANY I. 1, EVER 1 (c) **If I were you . . .,** si j'étais vous . . . ; à votre place. . . . *Even if he did say so,* quand même il l'aurait dit. *(Even) if I were given a hundred pounds, I would not do it,* on me donnerait cent livres que je ne le ferais pas ; quand même on me donnerait cent livres je ne le ferais pas. (d) *(Exclamatory)* **If I had only known!** si seulement je l'avais su ! *If only he comes in time!* pourvu qu'il vienne à temps ! (e) *As if,* comme si ; comme. *He talks as if he were drunk,* il parle comme s'il était ivre. *He stood as if thunderstruck,* il demeurait comme foudroyé. **As if by chance,** comme par hasard. **As if I would allow it!** comme si je le permettrais ! *S.a.* LOOK² 3. **2.** *(Concessive) If they are poor, they are at any rate happy,* s'ils sont pauvres, du moins sont-ils heureux. *F: Pleasant weather, if rather cold,* temps agréable, bien qu'un peu froid, encore qu'un peu froid. **3.** (= WHETHER 1.) *Do you know if he is at home?* savez-vous s'il est chez lui? **4.** s. *Your ifs and buts,* vos si et vos mais.

igloo ['iglu:], s. Hutte *f* d'Esquimau ; igloo *m.*

Ignatius [ig'nei∫əs]. *Pr.n.m.* Ignace.

igneous ['igniəs], a. *rock,* roche pyrogène, ignée.

ignite [ig'nait]. **1.** *v.tr.* Mettre le feu à (qch.) ; enflammer (un mélange explosif). **2.** *v.i.* Prendre feu ; s'enflammer.

igniter [ig'naitər], s. Dispositif *m* d'allumage ; *Artil: Min:* allumeur *m* ; *I.C.E:* (inter)rupteur *m.*

ignition [ig'ni∫(ə)n], s. **1.** Ignition *f,* inflammation *f* (d'une charge de mine). **2.** *I.C.E:* Allumage *m.* Ignition coil, circuit, bobine *f,* circuit *m,* d'allumage. Ignition (advance-)lever, levier *m* d'avance (à l'allumage).

ignoble [ig'noubl], a. **1.** Plébéien, roturier. **2.** Ignoble ; infâme, vil, indigne.

ignominious [igno'minjəs], a. Ignominieux ; honteux. **-ly,** adv. Ignominieusement ; avec ignominie.

ignominy ['ignomini], s. Ignominie *f,* honte *f.*

ignoramus [igno'reiməs], s. Ignorant, -ante ; ignare *mf* ; *F:* bourrique *f,* maître aliboron, âne bâté.

ignorance ['ignorəns], s. Ignorance *f.* To keep s.o. in ignorance of sth., laisser ignorer qch. à qn. *I am in complete i. of his intentions,* j'ignore tout de ses intentions.

ignorant ['ignorənt], a. (a) Ignorant. To be ignorant of a fact, ignorer un fait. *To be i. of history,* être ignorant en histoire ; connaître fort mal l'histoire. *He is i. of the world,* il ne connaît pas le monde. (b) *An i. question,* une question qui trahit l'ignorance. **-ly,** adv. **1.** (Se tromper) par ignorance. **2.** (Discourir) avec ignorance.

ignore [ig'nɔ:ər], *v.tr.* **1.** Ne tenir aucun compte de (qch.) ; passer (qch.) sous silence. **To ignore s.o., s.o.'s existence,** ne pas vouloir reconnaître qn ; feindre de ne pas voir qn. **To ignore the facts,** méconnaître les faits. **To i. an invitation,** ne pas répondre à une invitation. **To i. a rule,** sortir d'une règle. **To i. a prohibition,** passer outre à une interdiction. **2.** *Jur:* To ignore a bill, rendre une fin de non-recevoir. *To i. a complaint,* rejeter une plainte.

iguana [i'gwa:na], s. *Rept:* Iguane *m.*

ikon ['aikon], s. = ICON.

ilex, *pl.* **-exes** ['aileks, -eksiz], s. *Bot:* Ilex *m.* **1.** Yeuse *f* ; chêne vert. **2.** Houx *m.*

iliac ['iliak], a. *Anat:* Iliaque.

Iliad (the) [ði'iliad], s. *Gr.Lit:* L'Iliade *f.*

ilium ['iliəm], s. *Anat:* Ilion *m* ; os *m* iliaque.

ilk [ilk], a. *Scot:* Wemyss [wi:mz] of that ilk = Wemyss of Wemyss, Wemyss du domaine qui porte le même nom. *F:* And others of that ilk, et d'autres du même genre.

I'll [ail] = I will, I shall.

ill [il]. **I.** a. *(worse;* worst, *q.v.)* **1.** (a) Mauvais. Ill effects, effets pernicieux. *Prov:* 'Tis an ill wind that blows nobody good, à quelque chose malheur est bon. **To do s.o. an ill turn,** desservir qn. (b) Méchant, mauvais. *Ill deed,* mauvaise action, méchante action ; méfait *m.* **2.** Malade, souffrant. **To be, feel, ill,** être malade ; se sentir souffrant. **To fall ill, be taken ill,** tomber malade. *To be ill with a fever,* souffrir d'un accès de fièvre. **3.** *Scot:* Ill to please, difficile à contenter. **II. ill,** s. **1.** Mal *m.* *I know no ill of him,* je ne sais rien contre lui. **To do ill,** faire le mal. **To speak ill of s.o.,** dire du mal de qn. **2.** (a) Dommage *m,* tort *m.* (b) Maux *m,* malheurs *m.* *To suffer great ills,* souffrir de grands maux, de grandes misères. **III. ill,** *adv. (worse,* worst) Mal. **1.** To take sth. ill, prendre qch. en mauvaise part ; savoir mauvais gré à qn de qch. It will go ill with them, il leur en cuira. **2.** *I can ill afford the expense,* je peux difficilement supporter cette dépense. It ill becomes you to . . ., il vous sied mal, il vous messied, de. . . . **3. To be ill at ease,** (i) être mal à l'aise ; (ii) être inquiet. **ill-ad'vised,** a. **1.** *(Of pers.)* Malavisé. **2.** *(Of action)* Peu judicieux, mal assorti. **ill-as'sorted,** a. Mal assorti ; disparate. **ill-'bred,** a. Mal élevé ; malappris. **ill-'breeding,** s. Manque *m* de savoir-vivre. **ill-con'sidered,** a. Peu réfléchi. *I.-c. measures,* mesures hâtives. **ill-de'served,** a. Peu mérité. **ill-dis'posed,** a. **1.** Malintentionné, malveillant. *Ill-d. towards s.o.,* mal disposé envers qn. **2. To be ill-disposed to do**

sth., être peu disposé à faire qch. **ill-'doer,** s. Malfaiteur, -trice. **ill-'fated,** a. (Prince) infortuné; (effort) malheureux; (jour) fatal, néfaste. **ill-'favoured,** a. (Of pers.) Laid; de mauvaise mine. *He's an i.-f. fellow,* il ne paye pas de mine. **ill-'feeling,** s. Ressentiment m, rancune f. F: No ill-feeling! sans rancune! **ill-'founded,** a. (Bruit) mal fondé, sans fondement. **ill-'gotten,** a. (Bien) mal acquis. S.a. GAIN[1] **I. ill-'health,** s. Mauvaise santé; manque m de santé. **ill-'humoured,** a. De mauvaise humeur; maussade, grincheux. **ill-in'formed,** a. **1.** Mal renseigné. **2.** Peu instruit; ignorant. **ill-in'tentioned,** a. Malintentionné (*towards,* envers). **ill-'judged,** a. (Of action) Malavisé; peu sage. **'ill-(-)'luck,** s. Mauvaise fortune; malchance f; F: guigne f. By ill-luck, as ill-luck would have it, par malheur, par malchance; le malheur a voulu que + sub. **ill-'mannered,** a. Malhonnête, grossier, malappris. **ill-'matched,** a. Mal assorti; disparate. **ill(-)'nature,** s. Méchant caractère; méchanceté f. **ill-'natured,** a. D'un mauvais caractère; méchant; désagréable. **-ly,** adv. Méchamment; avec méchanceté. **ill-'omened,** a. De mauvais présage; de mauvais augure. **ill-'pleased,** a. Mécontent. **ill-'qualified,** a. Incompétent; peu qualifié (pour faire qch.). **ill-re'pute,** s. Mauvaise réputation. *Man of ill-r.,* homme taré. **ill-'sounding,** a. Malsonnant. **ill-'starred,** a. Né sous une mauvaise étoile; (prince) infortuné; (jour) malheureux, néfaste. *I.-s. adventure,* entreprise vouée à l'insuccès. **ill-suc'cess,** s. Insuccès m; mauvaise réussite; déconvenue f. **ill(-)'temper,** s. Mauvais caractère; humeur f acariâtre. **ill-'tempered,** a. De mauvais caractère; maussade, grincheux, de mauvaise humeur. **ill-'thriven,** a. Rabougri; mal venu. **ill-'timed,** a. Mal à propos; malencontreux. *Ill-t. arrival,* arrivée inopportune, intempestive. **ill-'treat,** v.tr. Maltraiter, brutaliser. **ill-'treatment,** s. Mauvais traitements. **ill-'use** [ju:z], v.tr. (a) Maltraiter (un enfant); malmener (un adversaire). *The dog had been ill-used,* le chien avait subi de mauvais traitements. (b) Mal agir envers (qn); faire une injustice à (qn). **ill-'will,** s. Mauvais vouloir; malveillance f, rancune f. To bear s.o. ill-will, garder rancune, en vouloir, à qn.

illegal [i'li:gəl], a. Illégal, -aux. **-ally,** adv. Illégalement.

illegality [ili'galiti], s. Illégalité f.

illegible [i'ledʒibl], a. Illisible. **-ibly,** adv. Illisiblement.

illegitimacy [ile'dʒitiməsi], s. Illégitimité f.

illegitimate [ile'dʒitimet], a. Illégitime. **-ly,** adv. Illégitimement.

illicit [i'lisit, il'l-], a. Illicite. *I. betting,* paris clandestins.

illimitable [i'limitəbl, il'l-], a. Illimitable, illimité; sans bornes.

illiteracy [i'litərəsi], s. Manque m d'instruction.

illiterate [i'litərət], a. & s. Illettré, -ée.

illness ['ilnəs], s. Maladie f. To have a long i., faire une longue maladie.

illogical [i'lɔdʒik(ə)l, il'l-], a. Illogique; peu logique. **-ally,** adv. Illogiquement.

illuminant [i'lju:minənt], a. & s. Illuminant (m), éclairant (m).

illuminate [i'lju:mineit], v.tr. **1.** Éclairer (une salle, l'esprit). **2.** Illuminer, embraser (un édifice à l'occasion d'une fête). *Illuminated sign,* enseigne lumineuse. **3.** Enluminer (un manu-

scrit). *Illuminated capitals,* lettres f d'apparat. **4.** Éclairer, élucider (un sujet).

illumination [iljumi'neiʃ(ə)n], s. **1.** (a) Éclairage m. (b) Illumination f, embrasement m (d'un édifice). **2.** (a) To go out to see the illuminations, sortir voir les illuminations. (b) pl. Enluminures f (d'un manuscrit). **3.** Opt: Éclat m (d'un objectif).

illuminator [i'lju:mineitər], s. **1.** (Pers.) (a) Illuminateur m. (b) Art: Enlumineur, -euse. **2.** Dispositif m d'éclairage.

illumine [i'lju:min], v.tr. = ILLUMINATE.

illusion [i'lju:ʒ(ə)n], s. Illusion f; tromperie f. Optical illusion, (i) illusion d'optique; (ii) truc m d'optique. To be under an illusion, être le jouet d'une illusion. I have no illusions, I am under no illusions, on this point, je ne me fais aucune illusion sur ce point.

illusionist [i'lju:ʒənist], s. **1.** Prestidigitateur m, illusionniste mf. **2.** Rêveur, -euse; songe-creux m inv.

illusive [i'lju:siv], a. Illusoire, trompeur, mensonger.

illusory [i'lju:səri], a. Illusoire; sans effet.

illustrate ['iləstreit], v.tr. **1.** Éclairer, expliquer, démontrer par des exemples (une règle). **2.** Illustrer; orner de gravures, de dessins (le texte d'un livre). Illustrated paper, journal illustré.

illustration [iləs'treiʃ(ə)n], s. **1.** Explication f, exemple m (d'une règle). By way of illustration, à titre d'exemple. **2.** Illustration f, gravure f, image f. Text illustration, vignette f.

illustrative ['iləstrətiv], a. Qui sert à éclaircir ou à expliquer. Illustrative of sth., qui fournit un exemple de qch.

illustrator ['iləstreitər], s. Illustrateur m (d'un ouvrage).

illustrious [i'lʌstriəs], a. Illustre, célèbre. **-ly,** adv. Avec éclat.

image[1] ['imedʒ], s. Image f. **1.** Image sculptée; représentation f (d'un dieu); idole f. **2.** Opt: Real image, image réelle. Virtual image, image virtuelle. **3.** God created man in his own i., Dieu créa l'homme à son image. He is the living image of his father, c'est le portrait vivant de son père; F: c'est son père tout craché. **4.** Style full of images, style imagé. To speak in images, s'exprimer par métaphores.

image[2], v.tr. **1.** (a) Représenter (qch.) par une image. (b) The mountains are imaged in the lake, les montagnes se reflètent dans le lac. **2.** To image sth. to oneself, se figurer, se représenter, qch.

imagery ['imedʒəri], s. **1.** Coll. Images sculptées; idoles fpl. **2.** Figures fpl de rhétorique; images. Style full of i., style imagé.

imaginable [i'madʒinəbl], a. Imaginable. The finest thing imaginable, la plus belle chose qu'on puisse imaginer; tout ce qu'on peut imaginer de plus beau.

imaginary [i'madʒinəri], a. Imaginaire.

imagination [imadʒi'neiʃ(ə)n], s. Imagination f. To see one's youth in imagination, revoir sa jeunesse en imagination, en idée. F: It's your imagination! vous l'avez rêvé!

imaginative [i'madʒineitiv, -ətiv], a. **1.** (Of pers.) Imaginatif. **2.** I. poem, poème d'imagination.

imagine [i'madʒin], v.tr. **1.** (a) Imaginer, concevoir (qch.); se figurer, se représenter (qch.). Try to i. our position, essayez de vous faire une idée de notre position. I. yourself in Paris, as a soldier, supposez-vous à Paris, figurez-vous que vous soyez soldat. As may (well) be imagined, comme on peut (se) l'imaginer. Just imagine my *despair*, figurez-vous, imaginez(-vous) un peu, mon désespoir. **You can imagine** *how angry I was!* pensez, songez, si j'étais furieux ! *You can't i. it!* on ne s'en fait pas idée ! (*b*) *I i. them to be fairly rich,* je les crois assez riches. *I know something about it,* **I imagine!** j'en sais quelque chose, peut-être ! *Do not i. that I am satisfied,* n'allez pas croire que je sois satisfait. **2. To be always imagining things,** se faire des imaginations, des idées. *I imagined I heard a knock at the door,* j'ai cru entendre frapper à la porte.

imago [i'meigo], *s. Ent:* Imago *f*; insecte parfait.

imbecile ['imbesi:l]. **I.** *a.* Imbécile; faible d'esprit. *F:* D'une stupidité crasse. **2.** *s.* Imbécile *mf. F:* **You imbecile!** espèce d'idiot !

imbecility [imbe'siliti], *s.* Imbécillité *f*; faiblesse *f* d'esprit.

imbibe [im'baib], *v.tr.* (*a*) Absorber, s'assimiler (des connaissances). (*b*) Boire, avaler (une boisson); absorber (de la bière); aspirer (l'air frais). (*c*) (*Of thg*) Imbiber (qch.); s'imprégner, se pénétrer, de (créosote, etc.).

imbricate ['imbriket], **imbricated** ['imbrikeitid], *a.* Imbriqué; (structure) à écailles.

imbrication [imbri'keiʃ(ə)n], *s.* Imbrication *f*, chevauchement *m*.

imbroglio [im'brouljo], *s.* Imbroglio *m*.

imbrue [im'bru:], *v.tr. Lit:* Imbrued in, with, *blood*, ensanglanté.

imbue [im'bju:], *v.tr.* **To imbue s.o. with** ən idea, pénétrer qn d'une idée. Imbued with prejudices, imbu de préjugés.

imitate ['imiteit], *v.tr.* (*a*) Imiter, copier. *To i. s.o.'s style,* pasticher le style de qn. (*b*) Contrefaire (le cri d'un oiseau).

imitation [imi'teiʃ(ə)n], *s.* **I.** Imitation *f.* In imitation of sth., à l'imitation de qch. **2.** (*a*) Copie *f*, imitation. *Com:* Beware of imitations, méfiez-vous des contrefaçons *f*. (*b*) *Attrib.* Factice; simili-. *I. morocco,* genre maroquin. *I. gold,* similor *m. I. marble,* similimarbre *m.* Imitation jewellery, bijouterie fausse ; bijoux *mpl* en toc.

imitative ['imiteitiv], *a.* **I.** (Son) imitatif. **2.** (*Of pers.*) Imitateur, -trice.

imitator ['imiteitər], *s.* (*a*) Imitateur, -trice. (*b*) *Com:* Contrefacteur *m*.

immaculate [i'makjulet], *a.* **I.** Immaculé ; sans tache. **2.** *F:* (*Of dress*) Irréprochable, impeccable. **-ly,** *adv.* **I.** Sans tache ; sans défaut. **2.** (Vêtu) irréprochablement.

immanent ['imanənt], *a. Phil:* Immanent.

immaterial [ima'ti:əriəl], *a.* **I.** (Esprit) immatériel. **2.** (*a*) Peu important. That is quite immaterial to me, cela m'est indifférent. (*b*) Immaterial to the subject, qui n'a aucun rapport avec la question.

immateriality [imati:əri'aliti], *s.* Immatérialité *f*.

immature [ima'tju:ər], *a.* (*a*) (Qui n'est) pas mûr. (*b*) *The project is i.,* le projet n'est pas suffisamment mûri.

immatureness [ima'tju:ərnəs], **immaturity** [ima'tju:əriti], *s.* Immaturité *f*.

immeasurable [i(m)'meʒərəbl], *a.* (Espace) incommensurable ; (temps) immesurable, immense. *F: To my i. delight,* à ma joie infinie. **-ably,** *adv.* Démesurément ; outre mesure.

immediate [i'mi:djet], *a.* Immédiat. **I.** (*a*) Sans intermédiaire ; direct. My immediate object, mon premier but. The immediate future, l'avenir prochain. (*b*) In the immediate vicinity, dans le voisinage immédiat. **2.** Instantané ; sans retard. 'For immediate delivery,' "à livrer de suite." **3.** (Besoin) pressant, urgent. **-ly.**

I. *adv.* Immédiatement. (*a*) *It does not affect me i.,* cela ne me touche pas directement. (*b*) Tout de suite. *Please answer i.,* veuillez nous répondre incessamment. Immediately on his return *I wrote to him,* dès son retour je lui ai écrit. Immediately after, aussitôt après. **2.** *conj.* Immediately he received the money, *he paid me,* dès qu'il eut reçu l'argent il me paya.

immemorial [ime'mɔ:riəl], *a.* Immémorial, -aux. From time immemorial, *F:* de toute éternité.

immense [i'mens], *a.* **I.** (Étendue) immense, vaste. **2.** *F:* Épatant. **-ly,** *adv.* Immensément. *F: To enjoy oneself immensely,* s'amuser énormément.

immensity [i'mensiti], *s.* Immensité *f*.

immerse [i'mə:rs], *v.tr.* **I.** Immerger, submerger, plonger (qn, qch.) (dans un liquide). **2. To be immersed in one's work,** être absorbé dans son travail.

immersion [i'mə:rʃ(ə)n], *s.* **I.** Immersion *f*, submersion *f*. **2.** Absorption *f* (d'esprit) (*in,* dans).

immigrant ['imigrənt], *a. & s.* Immigrant, -ante ; immigré, -ée.

immigrate ['imigreit], *v.i.* Immigrer.

immigration [imi'greiʃ(ə)n], *s.* Immigration *f*.

imminence ['iminəns], *s.* Imminence *f*, proximité *f* (*of,* de).

imminent ['iminənt], *a.* (Danger) imminent.

immitigable [i'mitigəbl], *a.* **I.** Implacable. **2.** Que l'on ne saurait adoucir.

immixture [i'mikstʃər], *s.* Mélange *m*.

immobility [imo'biliti], *s.* Immobilité *f*.

immobilize [i'moubilaiz], *v.tr.* **I.** Immobiliser, arrêter (une armée). **2.** *Fin:* To immobilize capital, specie, rendre des capitaux indisponibles ; immobiliser des espèces monnayées.

immoderate [i'modəret], *a.* Immodéré, intempéré. *I. thirst,* soif démesurée. **-ly,** *adv.* Immodérément.

immodest [i'modest], *a.* Immodeste, impudique. **-ly,** *adv.* Immodestement, impudiquement.

immodesty [i'modesti], *s.* Immodestie *f*, impudeur *f*.

immolate ['imoleit], *v.tr.* Immoler.

immolation [imo'leiʃ(ə)n], *s.* Immolation *f*.

immoral [i'morəl], *a.* Immoral, -aux. (*Of pers.*) Dissolu. **-ally,** *adv.* Immoralement.

immorality [imo'raliti], *s.* Immoralité *f*.

immortal [i'mɔ:rtəl], *a. & s.* Immortel (*m*). The immortals, les (dieux) immortels.

immortality [imɔ:r'taliti], *s.* Immortalité *f*.

immortalize [i'mɔ:rtəlaiz], *v.tr.* Immortaliser.

immortelle [i(m)mɔ:r'tel], *s. Bot:* Immortelle *f*.

immovable [i'mu:vəbl], *a.* **I.** Fixe ; à demeure. **2.** (Volonté) inébranlable. **3.** (Visage) impassible. **-ably,** *adv.* **I.** Sans bouger. **2.** Immuablement, inébranlablement. **3.** Sans s'émouvoir.

immune [i'mju:n], *a. Med:* Immune from contagion, à l'abri de la contagion. Immune against a poison, immunisé contre un poison.

immunity [i'mju:niti], *s.* **I.** Exemption *f* (*from,* de). **2.** Immunity from a disease, immunité *f* contre une maladie.

immunization [imjuni'zeiʃ(ə)n], *s. Med:* Immunisation *f* (*from,* contre).

immunize ['imjunaiz], *v.tr. Med:* Immuniser.

immure [i'mju:ər], *v.tr.* Enfermer, cloîtrer (qn).

immutability [imjutə'biliti], *s.* Immu(t)abilité *f*.

immutable [i'mju:təbl], *a.* Immuable ; inaltérable. **-ably,** *adv.* Immuablement.

imp [imp], *s.* (*a*) Diablotin *m*, lutin *m*. (*b*) *F:* (*Of child*) Petit espiègle.

impact ['impakt], *s. Mec.E:* Choc *m*, impact *m*.
impair [im'pɛːər], *v.tr.* Affaiblir (la vue, l'esprit) ; altérer, abîmer (la santé) ; diminuer (les forces) ; ébrécher (sa fortune). *Impaired digestion,* estomac délabré.
impairment [im'pɛːərmənt], *s.* Affaiblissement *m* ; altération *f* (de la santé) ; délabrement *m* (de l'estomac).
impale [im'peil], *v.tr.* **I.** *Her:* Accoler (deux blasons). **2.** Empaler (un criminel).
impalement [im'peilmənt], *s.* Supplice *m* du pal.
impalpable [im'palpəbl], *a.* Impalpable.
impaludism [im'paljudizm], *s.* (Im)paludisme *m*.
impanel [im'pan(ə)l], *v.tr.* = EMPANEL.
impart [im'paːrt], *v.tr.* **I.** (*a*) Donner (du courage) ; communiquer (un mouvement) (*to*, à). (*b*) *Body that imparts heat,* corps qui transmet de la chaleur. **2.** Communiquer (des connaissances) ; faire connaître (une nouvelle) (*to*, à).
impartial [im'paːrʃ(ə)l], *a.* (*Of pers., conduct*) Impartial, -aux. **-ally,** *adv.* Impartialement.
impartiality [impaːrʃi'aliti], *s.* Impartialité *f*.
impassable [im'paːsəbl], *a.* Infranchissable ; (chemin) impraticable.
impassibility [impasi'biliti], **impassibleness** [im'pasiblnəs], *s.* Impassibilité *f*.
impassion [im'paʃ(ə)n], *v.tr.* Passionner. **impassioned,** *a.* (Discours) passionné, exalté.
impassive [im'pasiv], *a.* Impassible ; (visage) composé. **-ly,** *adv.* Sans s'émouvoir.
impassiveness [im'pasivnəs], *s.* Impassibilité *f* ; insensibilité *f*.
impatience [im'peiʃ(ə)ns], *s.* (*a*) Impatience *f*. (*b*) **Impatience of sth.,** intolérance *f* de qch. (*c*) **Impatience to do sth.,** désir impatient de faire qch.
impatient [im'peiʃ(ə)nt], *a.* (*a*) Impatient. *To get, grow, i.,* s'impatienter. (*b*) **To be impatient of advice,** souffrir difficilement les conseils. (*c*) **To be impatient to do sth.,** être impatient de faire qch. **-ly,** *adv.* Avec impatience ; impatiemment.
impeach [im'piːtʃ], *v.tr.* **I.** (*a*) Attaquer, mettre en doute (la probité de qn). (*b*) *Jur:* Révoquer (un témoignage) en doute. **2.** *Jur:* **To impeach s.o. for high treason,** accuser qn de haute trahison.
impeachable [im'piːtʃəbl], *a.* **I.** (*a*) (*Of motive*) Attaquable ; susceptible de blâme. (*b*) (Témoin, témoignage) sujet à caution. **2.** *Jur:* (*Of pers.*) Susceptible d'être mis en accusation.
impeachment [im'piːtʃmənt], *s.* (*a*) Accusation *f*. *F:* **I own the soft impeachment,** (que je sois amoureux, etc.) j'en conviens. (*b*) Mise *f* en accusation (d'un ministre, etc.) par la Chambre des Communes.
impeccability [impekə'biliti], *s.* Impeccabilité *f*.
impeccable [im'pekəbl], *a.* Impeccable. **-ably,** *adv.* De façon irréprochable.
impecuniosity [impekjuni'ɔsiti], *s.* Manque *m* d'argent.
impecunious [impe'kjuːnjəs], *a.* Impécunieux, besogneux.
impedance [im'piːdəns], *s.* *El:* Impédance *f*. **Impedance coil,** bobine de self.
impede [im'piːd], *v.tr.* Mettre obstacle à, empêcher, entraver, gêner (le progrès). *To i. the traffic,* entraver la circulation.
impediment [im'pedimənt], *s.* **I.** (*a*) Entrave *f*, empêchement *m*, obstacle *m* (*to*, à). *I. to traffic,* gêne *f* pour la circulation. (*b*) **Impediment of speech,** empêchement de la langue. **2.** *pl.* = IMPEDIMENTA.
impedimenta [impedi'menta], *s.pl.* Impedimenta *mpl* ; *F:* bagag es *m*.

impel [im'pel], *v.tr.* (impelled) **I.** Pousser, forcer (*s.o. to do sth.,* qn à faire qch.). **2.** Pousser (en avant). *Ship impelled by the wind,* navire chassé par le vent. **impelling,** *a.* Impulsif ; moteur, -trice.
impend [im'pend], *v.i.* **I.** Être suspendu (*over,* sur). **2.** *War was impending,* la guerre était imminente. **impending,** *a.* (Danger) imminent. *Her i. arrival,* son arrivée prochaine.
impenetrability [impenetrə'biliti], *s.* Impénétrabilité *f*.
impenetrable [im'penetrəbl], *a.* Impénétrable (*to, by,* à). *I. mystery,* mystère insondable. **-ably,** *adv.* Impénétrablement.
impenitence [im'penitəns], *s.* Impénitence *f*.
impenitent [im'penitənt], *a. & s.* Impénitent, -ente. **-ly,** *adv.* Sans contrition.
imperative [im'perətiv]. **I.** *a. & s. Gram: In the i.* (*mood*), à l'impératif *m*, au mode impératif. **2.** *a.* (*a*) Impérieux, péremptoire. (*b*) Urgent, impérieux. *Discretion is i.,* la discrétion s'impose. *It is imperative for us all to . . . ,* il nous incombe à tous de. . . . **-ly,** *adv.* Impérativement ; impérieusement.
imperceptible [impər'septibl], *a.* Imperceptible ; (bruit) insaisissable. *An i. difference,* une différence insensible. *I. to the eye,* inappréciable à l'œil. **-ibly,** *adv.* Imperceptiblement, insensiblement.
imperfect [im'pəːrfekt]. **I.** *a.* Imparfait, incomplet, défectueux. **2.** *a. & s. Gram:* **Imperfect** (**tense**), (temps) imparfait *m*. **-ly,** *adv.* Imparfaitement.
imperfection [impər'fekʃ(ə)n], *s.* **I.** Imperfection *f*, défectuosité *f*. **2.** État incomplet.
imperial [im'piːriəl], *a.* (*a*) Impérial, -aux. (*b*) *I. trade,* commerce de l'Empire britannique. (*c*) (Poids et mesures) qui ont cours légal dans le Royaume-Uni. (*d*) *F:* Majestueux, auguste. **-ally,** *adv.* Impérialement ; *F:* majestueusement.
imperialism [im'piːriəlizm], *s.* Impérialisme *m*.
imperil [im'peril], *v.tr.* (imperilled) Mettre en péril, en danger. *To i. one's good name,* compromettre sa réputation.
imperious [im'piːriəs], *a.* **I.** Impérieux, arrogant. **2.** Urgent. *I. necessity,* besoin impératif. **-ly,** *adv.* Impérieusement.
imperishable [im'periʃəbl], *a.* Impérissable.
impermeability [impəːrmiə'biliti], *s.* Imperméabilité *f*.
impermeable [im'pəːrmiəbl], *a.* Imperméable, étanche.
impersonal [im'pəːrsən(ə)l], *a.* **I.** (Style) impersonnel. **2.** *Gram:* **Impersonal verb,** verbe impersonnel, unipersonnel. **-ally,** *adv.* Impersonnellement.
impersonate [im'pəːrsəneit], *v.tr.* **I.** Personnifier (qch.). **2.** (*a*) *Th:* Représenter (qn). (*b*) Se faire passer pour (qn).
impersonation [impəːrsə'neiʃ(ə)n], *s.* **I.** Personnification *f*. **2.** *Th:* (*a*) Création *f*, interprétation *f* (d'un rôle). (*b*) *To give impersonations of the actors of the day,* donner des imitations *f* des acteurs du jour. **3.** *Jur:* Supposition *f* de personne.
impertinence [im'pəːrtinəns], *s.* **I.** (*a*) Impertinence *f*, insolence *f*. *It's the height of i.,* c'est se moquer du monde. (*b*) *An i.,* **a piece of impertinence,** une impertinence. **2.** *Jur:* Manque *m* de rapport avec la question.
impertinent [im'pəːrtinənt], *a.* **I.** Impertinent, insolent. *An i. fellow,* un impertinent. **To be impertinent to s.o.,** être insolent envers qn.

2. *Jur:* Hors de propos ; sans rapport avec la cause. **-ly,** *adv.* **I.** Avec impertinence ; d'un ton insolent. **2.** (Répondre) en dehors de la question.
imperturbability [impərtəːrbəˈbiliti], *s.* Imperturbabilité *f;* flegme *m;* sang-froid *m.*
imperturbable [impərˈtəːrbəbl], *a.* Imperturbable. **-ably,** *adv.* Imperturbablement ; sans se déconcerter.
impervious [imˈpəːrviəs], *a.* **I.** (*a*) (Forêt) impénétrable. (*b*) **Impervious (to water),** imperméable, étanche. **2. Person impervious to reason,** personne inaccessible à la raison.
imperviousness [imˈpəːrviəsnəs], *s.* (*a*) Impénétrabilité *f.* (*b*) **Imperviousness to damp,** imperméabilité *f;* étanchéité *f* (à l'humidité).
impetigo [impeˈtaigo], *s.* *Med:* Impétigo *m;* (*in children*) gourme *f;* croûtes *fpl* de lait.
impetuosity [impetjuˈɔsiti], *s.* Impétuosité *f.*
impetuous [imˈpetjuəs], *a.* Impétueux. **-ly,** *adv.* Impétueusement.
impetus [ˈimpetəs], *s.* Vitesse acquise ; élan *m.* **To give an impetus to sth.,** donner l'impulsion à qch.
impiety [imˈpaiəti], *s.* Impiété *f.*
impinge [imˈpindʒ], *v.ind.tr.* **To impinge on sth.,** entrer en collision avec qch. ; se heurter à qch.
impingement [imˈpindʒmənt], *s.* Collision *f,* heurt *m.*
impious [ˈimpiəs], *a.* Impie. **-ly,** *adv.* Avec impiété ; sacrilègement.
impish [ˈimpiʃ], *a.* De petit diable. *I. laughter,* rire espiègle, malicieux. **-ly,** *adv.* En espiègle.
impishness [ˈimpiʃnəs], *s.* Espièglerie *f.*
implacability [implakəˈbiliti], *s.* Implacabilité *f.*
implacable [imˈplakəbl], *a.* Implacable (*towards,* à, pour). **-ably,** *adv.* Implacablement.
implant [imˈplɑːnt], *v.tr.* **I. To be implanted,** être implanté (*in,* dans). **2.** Implanter (*an idea in s.o.,* une idée dans la tête de qn). *To i. in s.o.'s breast the desire to . . .,* inspirer à qn le désir de. . . .
implement¹ [ˈimplimənt], *s.* Outil *m,* instrument *m,* ustensile *m. Fishing implements,* attirail *m* de pêche. *Implements of war,* matériel *m* de guerre.
implement², *v.tr.* *Scot:* Rendre effectif (un contrat) ; exécuter, remplir (un engagement). *To i. one's promise,* accomplir sa promesse.
implicate [ˈimplikeit], *v.tr.* Impliquer. *To implicate s.o. in a crime,* impliquer qn dans un crime. *Without implicating anyone,* sans mettre personne en cause.
implication [impliˈkeiʃ(ə)n], *s.* **I. By implication,** implicitement. *He did not realize the full i. of these words,* il ne se rendait pas compte de la portée de ces paroles. **2.** Insinuation *f.*
implicit [imˈplisit], *a.* **I.** (Condition) implicite. *I. recognition of . . .,* reconnaissance tacite de. . . . **2. Implicit faith,** confiance aveugle, sans réserve (*in,* dans). **Implicit obedience,** obéissance absolue. **-ly,** *adv.* **I.** Implicitement, tacitement. **2. To obey implicitly,** obéir aveuglément.
implore [imˈplɔːr], *v.tr.* Implorer. *I implored his forgiveness,* je le suppliai de me pardonner. *To i. s.o. to do sth.,* conjurer, supplier, qn de faire qch. **imploring,** *a.* (Regard) suppliant.
imply [imˈplai], *v.tr.* **I.** Impliquer. *Smoke implies a fire,* la fumée ne va pas sans feu. *That implies courage on his part,* cela lui suppose du courage. *The questions implied,* les questions en jeu. **2. Do you mean to imply that . . .?** est-ce à dire que . . .? *You seem to i. that . . .,* ce

que vous dites fait supposer que. . . . **implied,** *a.* (Consentement) implicite; tacite.
impolite [impoˈlait], *a.* Impoli (*to, towards,* envers). *I. answer,* réponse malhonnête. **-ly,** *adv.* (Répondre) impoliment.
impoliteness [impoˈlaitnəs], *s.* Impolitesse *f.*
impolitic [imˈpɔlitik], *a.* Impolitique ; peu politique.
imponderable [imˈpondərəbl], *a.* Impondérable.
import¹ [ˈimpɔːrt], *s.* **I.** Sens *m,* signification *f* (d'un mot) ; teneur *f* (d'un document). **2.** *I had not grasped the full i. of these words,* je ne m'étais pas rendu compte de toute la portée de ces mots. *Matter of great import,* affaire de haute importance. **3.** *Com:* (*Usu. pl.*) Imports, (i) articles *m* d'importation ; (ii) importations *f.* **Import duty,** droit *m* d'entrée.
import² [imˈpɔːrt], *v.tr.* **I.** *Com:* Importer (des marchandises). *Imported goods,* importations *f.* **2.** Indiquer. (*a*) Signifier ; vouloir dire. (*b*) Déclarer, faire savoir (*that,* que). **importing¹,** *a.* Importateur, -trice. **importing²,** *s.* Importation *f* (de marchandises).
importable [imˈpɔːrtəbl], *a.* Importable.
importance [imˈpɔːrtəns], *s.* (*a*) Importance *f. To give i. to a word,* mettre un mot en valeur. **To be of importance,** avoir de l'importance. **Question of first, capital, importance,** question d'importance primordiale, capitale. *Business of first i.,* affaire majeure **It is of importance to . . .,** il importe de. . . . *It is of no great i.,* cela importe peu. *To attach the greatest i. to a fact,* tenir le plus grand compte d'un fait. (*b*) (*Of pers.*) Importance, F: conséquence *f.* **People of importance,** personnages importants. *To set up for a person of i.,* faire l'important.
important [imˈpɔːrtənt], *a.* (*a*) Important. *It is i. for you to know that . . .,* il importe que vous sachiez que. . . . (*b*) F: (*Of pers.*) Important ; plein d'importance. **To look important,** prendre, se donner, des airs d'importance. **-ly,** *adv.* (*a*) D'une manière importante. (*b*) F: D'un air, d'un ton, d'importance.
importation [impɔːrˈteiʃ(ə)n], *s.* Importation *f.*
importer [imˈpɔːrtər], *s.* Importateur, -trice.
importunate [imˈpɔːrtjunət], *a.* (Créancier) importun ; (visiteur) ennuyeux. **-ly,** *adv.* Importunément.
importune [impɔrˈtjuːn], *v.tr.* Importuner (qn).
importunity [impɔrˈtjuːniti], *s.* Importunité *f.*
impose [imˈpouz]. **I.** *v.tr.* *Typ:* Imposer (une feuille) ; mettre (la matière) en pages. **2.** *v.tr.* (*a*) **To impose conditions (up)on s.o.,** imposer des conditions à qn. (*b*) *To i. a tax on sugar,* imposer, taxer, le sucre ; frapper le sucre d'un impôt. *To i. a penalty on s.o.,* infliger une peine à qn ; frapper qn d'une peine. **3.** *v.i.* **To impose (up)on s.o.,** en imposer à qn ; en faire accroire à qn ; abuser de l'amabilité de qn. **imposing,** *a.* (Air, ton) imposant ; (spectacle) grandiose. **-ly,** *adv.* D'une manière imposante.
imposition [impoˈziʃ(ə)n], *s.* **I.** (*a*) *Typ:* Imposition *f* (d'une feuille). (*b*) Imposition (d'une tâche). **2.** Imposition, impôt *m; pl.* contributions *f.* **3.** *Sch:* Pensum *m.* **5.** Tromperie *f,* imposture *f.*
impossibility [impɔsiˈbiliti], *s.* **I.** Impossibilité *f* (de qch.). **2.** Chose *f* impossible. **Physical impossibility,** chose matériellement impossible. *No one is expected to perform impossibilities,* à l'impossible nul n'est tenu.
impossible [imˈpɔsibl]. **I.** *a.* (*a*) Impossible. *To make it i. for s.o. to do sth.,* mettre qn dans

l'impossibilité de faire qch. (*b*) (Histoire, récit) invraisemblable. **Impossible person,** personne difficile à vivre. **You are impossible!** vous êtes impossible! vous êtes ridicule! **2.** *s.* **The impossible,** l'impossible *m.* *If, to suppose the i.,* . . ., si, par impossible. . . .

impost¹ ['impoust], *s.* *Hist:* (*a*) Impôt *m.* (*b*) Tribut *m.*

impost², *s.* *Arch:* Imposte *f.*

impostor [im'pɔstər], *s.* Imposteur *m.*

imposture [im'pɔstjər], *s.* Imposture *f.*

impotence ['impotəns], **impotency** ['impotənsi], *s.* (*a*) Impuissance *f.* (*b*) Faiblesse *f,* impotence *f.*

impotent ['impotənt], *a.* (*a*) Impuissant. (*b*) Impotent, décrépit. **-ly,** *adv.* Sans force; en vain.

impound [im'paund], *v.tr.* **1.** (*a*) Mettre (une bête) en fourrière. (*b*) *Hyd.E:* Endiguer, capter (les eaux). **2.** *Jur:* Confisquer, saisir.

impoverish [im'pɔvəriʃ], *v.tr.* Appauvrir.

impoverishment [im'pɔvəriʃmənt], *s.* Appauvrissement *m* (d'un pays, du sang).

impracticability [impraktikə'biliti], *s.* Impraticabilité *f,* impossibilité *f.*

impracticable [im'praktikəbl], *a.* **1.** Infaisable, impraticable. **2.** (*Of pers.*) Intraitable.

imprecation [impre'keiʃ(ə)n], *s.* Imprécation *f.*

imprecatory ['imprekeitəri], *a.* Imprécatoire.

impregnable [im'pregnəbl], *a.* (Forteresse) imprenable, inexpugnable.

impregnate [im'pregneit], *v.tr.* **1.** *Biol:* Imprégner, féconder. **2.** Imprégner, imbiber (*sth. with sth.*, qch. de qch.).

impregnation [impreg'neiʃ(ə)n], *s.* **1.** *Biol:* Fécondation *f.* **2.** Imprégnation *f* (d'un tissu).

impresario [impre'zɑːrio], *s.* Imprésario *m.*

imprescriptible [impre'skriptibl], *a.* *Jur:* (Droit) imprescriptible.

impress¹ ['impres], *s.* (*a*) Impression *f,* empreinte *f.* *I. of the fingers,* empreintes digitales. (*b*) Marque distinctive; cachet *m.* *Work that bears the i. of genius,* œuvre qui porte le cachet du génie.

impress² [im'pres], *v.tr.* **1.** (*a*) *To i. a seal upon wax,* imprimer un sceau sur la cire. *To i. a kiss on s.o.'s forehead,* appliquer un baiser sur le front de qn. (*b*) **To impress motion (up)on a body,** imprimer un mouvement à un corps. **2.** *F:* **To impress sth. upon s.o.,** faire bien comprendre qch. à qn. *I must i. upon you that* . . ., mettez-vous bien dans la tête que. . . . **3.** *F: To i. s.o. with the idea that* . . ., pénétrer qn de l'idée que. . . . **4.** (*a*) *He impressed me favourably,* il m'a fait une impression favorable. (*b*) **To impress s.o.,** faire impression sur qn; impressionner qn. *His firmness impressed them,* sa fermeté leur en a imposé. *F:* **I am not impressed,** cela me laisse froid.

impress³ [im'pres], *v.tr.* (*a*) Réquisitionner (des hommes en âge de servir). *Esp. Navy: A:* Presser, enrôler de force (des marins). *To i. the railwaymen into military service,* militariser les cheminots. (*b*) Réquisitionner (des vivres).

impression [im'preʃ(ə)n], *s.* **1.** Impression *f* (d'un cachet sur la cire). *Typ:* Impression (d'un livre). **2.** Empreinte *f,* impression (d'un cachet). **3.** *Typ:* Empreinte (des caractères sur le papier); foulage *m.* **4.** *Publ:* Tirage *m,* édition *f* (d'un livre). *Second i.,* deuxième tirage. **5.** (*a*) **To make a good, bad, impression on s.o.,** faire une bonne, une mauvaise, impression sur qn. *His speech created a great i.,* son discours fit une grande impression. (*b*) **I am under the impression**

that . . ., j'ai l'impression que . . ., j'ai dans l'idée que. . . .

impressionable [im'preʃənəbl], *a.* Impressionnable, sensible. *To be i.,* avoir la fibre sensible.

impressionism [im'preʃənizm], *s.* *Art:* Impressionnisme *m.*

impressive [im'presiv], *a.* (Spectacle) impressionnant. *I. silence,* silence impressionnant, solennel. **-ly,** *adv.* D'une manière impressionnante; (parler) d'un ton émouvant.

imprest ['imprest], *s.* *Adm:* Avance *f* de fonds (à un fournisseur du Gouvernement).

imprint¹ ['imprint], *s.* **1.** Empreinte *f* (d'un cachet). **2.** **Publisher's imprint,** firme *f,* rubrique *f,* de l'éditeur.

imprint² [im'print], *v.tr.* Imprimer. (*a*) **To imprint sth. on sth.,** imprimer, empreindre, qch. sur qch. (*b*) *Sand imprinted with footmarks,* sable qui porte des empreintes de pas.

imprison [im'prizən], *v.tr.* Emprisonner. *To keep s.o. imprisoned,* tenir qn en prison.

imprisonment [im'prizənmənt], *s.* Emprisonnement *m.* *Ten days' i.,* dix jours de prison. **To serve a sentence of imprisonment,** faire de la prison.

improbability [imprɔbə'biliti], *s.* Improbabilité *f*; invraisemblance *f.*

improbable [im'prɔbəbl], *a.* Improbable; (histoire) invraisemblable.

impromptu [im'prɔm(p)tju]. **1.** *adv.* (Faire qch.) sans préparation; (à l')impromptu. **2.** *a.* (Discours) impromptu *inv.* *To get up an i. dance,* improviser un bal. **3.** *s.* *Lit: Mus:* Impromptu *m.*

improper [im'prɔpər], *a.* **1.** (Partage) incorrect; (expression) impropre; (terme) inexact. **2.** Malhonnête, inconvenant; (conte) scabreux. *There's nothing i. in the play,* la pièce n'a rien d'inconvenant. **3.** Déplacé. **-ly,** *adv.* **1.** (Se servir d'une expression) improprement. *Word i. used,* mot employé abusivement. **2.** (Se conduire) d'une manière malséante; malhonnêtement. **3.** Contrairement à la bonne règle.

impropriate [im'prouprieit], *v.tr.* *Ecc:* Séculariser (un bénéfice, un bien d'Église).

impropriety [imprɔ'praiəti], *s.* **1.** (*a*) Impropriété *f* (de langage). (*b*) Inconvenance *f* (de conduite). **2.** *To commit improprieties,* (i) commettre des maladresses; (ii) commettre des inconvenances.

improve [im'pruːv]. **I.** *v.tr.* (*a*) Améliorer (qch.); perfectionner (une invention). *Agr:* Bonifier, amender (le sol). *To i. the appearance of sth.,* embellir qch. (*b*) **To improve the occasion,** *F:* **the shining hour,** tirer parti de l'occasion. (*c*) *v.ind.tr.* **To improve (up)on sth.,** améliorer qch.; remédier aux imperfections de qch. *Com:* **To improve on s.o.'s offer,** enchérir sur l'offre de qn. **2.** *v.i.* S'améliorer; (*of wine*) se bonifier. **To improve with use,** s'améliorer à l'usage. *He has greatly improved,* il a fait de grands progrès. *Business is improving,* les affaires reprennent. *She has greatly improved in looks,* elle a beaucoup embelli, elle est beaucoup embellie. **improving,** *a.* **1.** (Livre) instructif, édifiant. **2.** *Santé:* en voie de rétablissement.

improvement [im'pruːvmənt], *s.* **1.** Amélioration *f* (de la situation); perfectionnement *m* (d'une invention); embellissement *m* (d'une ville). **Open to improvement,** susceptible d'amélioration. **2.** (*a*) (*Usu. pl.*) **Improvements,** améliorations, embellissements. *All these so-called improvements,* tous ces prétendus progrès. (*b*) **To**

be an improvement on sth., surpasser qch.; valoir mieux que qch.

improvidence [im'prɔvidəns],s. Imprévoyance f.

improvident [im'prɔvidənt], a. (a) Imprévoyant. (b) Prodigue. **-ly,** adv. Sans prévoyance.

improvisation [improvai'zeiʃ(ə)n], s. Improvisation f.

improvise ['improvaiz], v.tr. Improviser (des vers, de la musique, un abri).

imprudence [im'pru:dəns], s. Imprudence f.

imprudent [im'pru:dənt], a. Imprudent. How i. of you! quelle imprudence de votre part! **-ly,** adv. Imprudemment.

impudence ['impjudəns], s. Impudence f, effronterie f, audace f. **To have the impudence to say sth.**, avoir l'aplomb de dire qch. A piece of impudence, une insolence.

impudent ['impjudənt], a. Effronté, insolent. You i. hussy! (i) petite effrontée! (ii) insolente! I. fellow, insolent. **-ly,** adv. Effrontément.

impudicity [impju'disiti], s. Impudicité f, impudeur f.

impugn [im'pju:n], v.tr. Attaquer, contester (une proposition); mettre en doute (la véracité de qch.). Jur: To impugn a piece of evidence, récuser un témoignage.

impugnment [im'pju:nmənt], s. Mise f en doute (d'une affirmation). Jur: Récusation f (d'un témoin).

impulse ['impʌls], s. **1.** (a) Impulsion f; poussée motrice. (b) F: To give an impulse to sth., donner une impulsion, de l'impulsion (au commerce, etc.). **2.** Impulsion; mouvement spontané; élan m. Stray impulse, velléité f. His first i. was to . . ., son premier mouvement fut de. . . . Rash, sudden, i., coup m de tête. To yield to i., céder à l'entraînement du moment.

impulsive [im'pʌlsiv], a. **1.** Impulsive force, force impulsive. **2.** (Of pers., action) Impulsif, velléitaire; prime-sautier, pl. prime-sautiers. I. action, coup m de tête. **-ly,** adv. (Agir) par impulsion.

impunity [im'pju:niti], s. Impunité f. With impunity, impunément.

impure [im'pju:ər], a. Impur.

impurity [im'pjuəriti], s. Impureté f.

imputable [im'pju:təbl], a. Imputable, attribuable (to, à).

imputation [impju'teiʃ(ə)n], s. Imputation f. (a) Attribution f (d'un crime à qn). (b) Chose imputée à qn.

impute [im'pju:t], v.tr. Imputer. To impute an action to s.o., imputer, attribuer, une action à qn.

imputrescible [impju'tresibl], a. Imputrescible.

in [in]. I. prep. **1.** (Of place) (a) En, à, dans. In Europe, en Europe. In Japan, au Japon. In India, dans l'Inde, aux Indes. In such and such a latitude, sous telle ou telle latitude. In Paris, à Paris. The streets in Paris, les rues de Paris. To be in town, être en ville. To spend a week in town, passer une semaine à la ville. In the country, à la campagne. Mil: In the field, en campagne. In the press, sous presse. In prison, en prison. In school, in church, à l'école, à l'église. In bed, au lit. In one's house, chez soi. In the second chapter, au deuxième chapitre. My fate is in your hands, mon sort est entre vos mains. In the distance, au loin. In your place, à votre place. Wounded in the shoulder, blessé à l'épaule. (b) (Among) In the crowd, dans la foule. It is not done in our circle, cela ne se fait pas parmi nous. He is in the sixties, il a passé la soixantaine. **2.** (In respect of) Blind in one eye, aveugle d'un

œil. Strong in logic, fort en logique. Two feet in length, long de deux pieds. The books, three in number, ces livres, au nombre de trois. **3.** (Of ratio) One in ten, un sur dix. To pay two shillings in the pound, payer deux shillings par livre sterling. Once in ten years, une fois tous les dix ans. **4.** (Of time) (a) In those days, en ce temps-là. In the reign of Queen Victoria, sous le règne de la reine Victoria. In the night, pendant la nuit; de nuit. In the afternoon, dans l'après-midi. At four o'clock in the afternoon, à quatre heures de l'après-midi. In the evening, le soir, pendant la soirée. In summer, autumn, winter, en été, en automne, en hiver. In spring, au printemps. In August, au mois d'août. In the future, à l'avenir. In the past, par le passé. Never in my life, jamais de ma vie. (b) To do sth. in three hours, faire qch. en trois heures. He'll be here in three hours, il sera là dans trois heures. In a little while, sous peu. (c) In crossing the river, en traversant la rivière. **5.** In tears, en larmes. In despair, au désespoir. Any man in his senses, tout homme jouissant de son bon sens. **6.** (Clothed in) In his shirt, en chemise. In slippers, en pantoufles. Dressed in white, habillé de blanc. **7.** To go out in the rain, sortir par la pluie. To work in the rain, travailler sous la pluie. In the sun, au soleil. In the dark(ness), dans l'obscurité. **8.** To be in the motor business, être dans les autos. **9.** In my opinion, à mon avis. In justice, en toute justice. **10.** (a) (Of manner) In a gentle voice, d'une voix douce. In the French style, à la française. To be in (the) fashion, être à la mode. (b) To write in French, écrire en français. To write in ink, écrire à l'encre. In writing, par écrit. To talk in whispers, parler en chuchotant. (c) To walk in groups, se promener par groupes. To stand in a row, se tenir en ligne. In alphabetical order, par ordre alphabétique. Packed in dozens, en paquets de douze. (d) (Of material) Dress in green velvet, robe en velours vert. (e) In the form of . . ., sous forme de. . . . (f) To die in hundreds, mourir par centaines. In part, en partie. In places, par endroits. **11.** (a) Equation true in itself, équation vraie par elle-même. This product is not a poison in itself, ce produit n'est pas un poison en lui-même. (b) A peculiarity in young people, une particularité chez les jeunes gens. (c) F: His rivals are not in it with him, ses rivaux ne sont pas de sa taille. You are not in it, vous n'avez aucune chance. II. in, adv. **1.** (a) (At home) A la maison, chez soi. Mr Smith is in, F: M. Smith y est. (b) The harvest is in, la moisson est rentrée. (c) The train is in, le train est en gare, à quai. (d) Is the fire still in? est-ce que le feu brûle encore? (e) In with it! rentrez-le! **2.** (a) The Liberals were in, le parti libéral était au pouvoir. (b) Strawberries are in, c'est la saison des fraises. (c) My hand is in, je suis bien en train. (d) To be (well) in with s.o., être en bons termes avec qn. (e) My luck is in, je suis en veine. **3.** We are in for a storm, nous aurons sûrement de l'orage. He is in for it! son affaire est bonne! le voilà dans de beaux draps! **4.** Phrases. (a) Day in, day out, tout le long du jour. (b) All in. (i) The prices quoted are all in, les prix cotés s'entendent tous frais compris. (ii) F: I'm absolutely all in, je suis absolument éreinté. III. in, s. F: To know the ins and outs of a matter, connaître tous les coins et recoins d'une affaire. The ins and outs of a house, les aîtres m d'une maison. **'in-going,** a. Qui entre: entrant. **In-going tenant,** nouveau

locataire. **'in-patient,** *s.* (Malade) hospitalisé, -ée. **in-'shore,** *adv. Nau:* To keep close in-shore, naviguer près de terre ; serrer la terre.

inability [inaˈbiliti], *s.* Incapacité *f (to do sth.,* de faire qch.) ; impuissance *f (to do sth.,* à faire qch.).

inaccessibility [inaksesiˈbiliti], *s.* Inaccessibilité *f.*

inaccessible [inakˈsesibl], *a.* Inaccessible *(to,* à) ; (personne) inabordable.

inaccuracy [inˈakjurəsi], *s.* Inexactitude *f,* imprécision *f.*

inaccurate [inˈakjuret], *a.* (Calcul) inexact ; (esprit) imprécis ; (sens) incorrect. **-ly,** *adv.* (Calculer) inexactement ; (citer) incorrectement.

inactinic [inakˈtinik], *a. Ph :* Inactinique.

inaction [inˈakʃ(ə)n], *s.* Inaction *f.* **Policy of inaction,** politique de laisser-faire.

inactive [inˈaktiv], *a.* Inactif ; (esprit) inerte. **-ly,** *adv.* Inactivement.

inactivity [inakˈtiviti], *s.* Inactivité *f.* **Masterly inactivity,** sage politique *f* de laisser-faire.

inadaptability [inadaptəˈbiliti], *s.* Incapacité *f* de s'adapter *(to,* à).

inadequacy [inˈadikwəsi], *s.* Insuffisance *f* (d'un revenu) ; imperfection *f* (de notre langage).

inadequate [inˈadikwet], *a.* Inadequat, insuffisant. *(Of thg)* To be inadequate to do sth., être insuffisant pour faire qch. **-ly,** *adv.* Insuffisamment.

inadmissibility [inadmisiˈbiliti], *s.* Inadmissibilité *f* (d'une supposition, d'une preuve).

inadmissible [inadˈmisibl], *a.* (Prétention) inadmissible ; (témoignage) irrecevable.

inadvertence [inadˈvəːrtəns], **inadvertency** [inadˈvəːrtənsi], *s.* Inadvertance *f,* étourderie *f.*

inadvertent [inadˈvəːrtənt], *a.* Commis par inadvertance, par mégarde. **-ly,** *adv.* Par inadvertance, par mégarde ; par étourderie.

inadvisability [inadvaizəˈbiliti], *s.* Imprudence *f,* inopportunité *f* (d'une action).

inalienable [inˈeiljənəbl], *a.* (Bien, droit) inaliénable.

inamorato [inamoˈraːto], *s.m.* Amant, amoureux.

inane [inˈein], *a.* Inepte, stupide. *I. remark,* ineptie *f.* **-ly,** *adv.* Bêtement, stupidement.

inanimate [inˈanimet], *a.* Inanimé.

inanition [inaˈniʃ(ə)n], *s.* Inanition *f.*

inanity [inˈaniti], *s.* Inanité *f,* niaiserie *f.*

inappeasable [inaˈpiːzəbl], *a.* Inapaisable.

inapplicable [inˈaplikəbl, inaˈplikəbl], *a.* Inapplicable *(to,* à).

inappreciable [inaˈpriːʃəbl], *a.* Inappréciable (à l'œil, etc.).

inappropriate [inaˈproupriet], *a.* Qui ne convient pas *(to,* à) ; *(of word)* impropre. **-ly,** *adv.* D'une façon impropre.

inapt [inˈapt], *a.* Inapte. **I.** *(a)* Incapable. *(b)* Inhabile, inexpert. **2.** Peu approprié *(to,* à). **-ly,** *adv.* Improprement.

inaptitude [inˈaptitjuːd], *s.* Inaptitude *f (for,* à).

inarticulate [inaːrˈtikjulet], *a.* **I.** *Nat.Hist:* Inarticulé ; sans articulations. **2.** *(a)* (Son) inarticulé, imparfaitement prononcé. *(b)* Muet, -ette ; incapable de parler. **Inarticulate with rage,** bégayant de colère. **-ly,** *adv.* Indistinctement.

inartistic [inaːrˈtistik], *a.* Peu artistique ; sans valeur artistique. *(of pers.)* dépourvu de sens artistique. **-ally,** *adv.* Sans art.

inasmuch as [inazˈmʌtʃaz], *conj.phr.* **I.** Attendu que, vu que. **2.** *A :* Dans la mesure que ; en tant que.

inattention [inaˈtenʃ(ə)n], *s.* Inattention *f.*

inattentive [inaˈtentiv], *a.* **I.** Inattentif, distrait. **2.** Négligent *(to,* de). **-ly,** *adv.* Sans attention ; distraitement

inaudible [inˈɔːdibl], *a.* (Son) imperceptible. *l. voice,* voix faible. **-ibly,** *adv.* Sans bruit ; (parler) de manière à ne pas être entendu.

inaugural [inˈɔːgjurəl], *a.* Inaugural, -aux. *l. address,* discours d'inauguration.

inaugurate [inˈɔːgjureit], *v.tr.* Inaugurer (un monument) ; introniser (un évêque) ; inaugurer, commencer (une ère nouvelle) ; mettre en application (un nouveau système).

inauguration [inɔːgjuˈreiʃ(ə)n], *s.* Inauguration *f* ; intronisation *f* (d'un évêque) ; mise *f* en application (d'un nouveau système).

inauspicious [inɔːˈspiʃəs], *a.* Peu propice. *At an i. moment,* à un moment malencontreux.

inborn [ˈinbɔːrn], *a.* (Instinct) inné, infus.

inbred [ˈinbred], *a.* **I.** Inné, naturel. **2.** *Breed :* (Of horses, etc.) Consanguin.

incalculable [inˈkalkjuləbl], *a.* **I.** Incalculable. **2.** **Incalculable temper,** humeur sur laquelle on ne peut compter. **-ably,** *adv.* Incalculablement.

incandescence [inkanˈdes(ə)ns], *s.* Incandescence *f* ; *Metall :* chaleur blanche.

incandescent [inkanˈdes(ə)nt], *a.* Incandescent. **Incandescent light,** lumière à incandescence.

incantation [inkanˈteiʃ(ə)n], *s.* Incantation *f,* conjuration *f,* charme *m.*

incapability [inkeipəˈbiliti], *s.* Incapacité *f.*

incapable [inˈkeipəbl], *a.* **I.** Incapable *(of,* de). **Incapable of speech,** incapable de parler. *I. of proof,* non susceptible de preuve. *I. of pity,* inaccessible à la pitié. **2.** (Homme) incapable, incompétent.

incapacitate [inkaˈpasiteit], *v.tr.* Rendre (qn) incapable *(from, for,* de).

incapacity [inkaˈpasiti], *s.* **I.** Incapacité *f,* incompétence *f.* **The incapacity of the staff,** la nullité du personnel. **2.** *Jur :* Incapacité légale ; inhabilité *f (to inherit,* à succéder).

incarcerate [inˈkaːrsəreit], *v.tr.* Incarcérer, mettre en prison, emprisonner.

incarceration [inkaːrsəˈreiʃ(ə)n], *s.* Incarcération *f,* emprisonnement *m.*

incarnadine [inˈkaːrnadain], *a.* *(a)* Incarnadin ; couleur de chair. *(b)* Rouge sang *inv.*

incarnate¹ [inˈkaːrnet], *a.* *(Of Christ)* To become incarnate, s'incarner. *F :* A devil incarnate, un démon incarné.

incarnate² [inˈkaːrneit], *v.tr.* Incarner (une idée).

incarnation [inkaːrˈneiʃ(ə)n], *s.* **I.** Incarnation *f* (du Christ, d'une idée). **2.** *(Of pers.)* To be the incarnation of wisdom, être la sagesse incarnée.

incautious [inˈkɔːʃəs], *a.* Imprudent ; inconsidéré. **-ly,** *adv.* Imprudemment ; sans réflexion.

incendiarism [inˈsendjərizm], *s.* **I.** Incendie *m* par malveillance. **2.** Politique *f* de dévastation par le feu.

incendiary [inˈsendjəri]. **I.** *a.* (Matériel) incendiaire. **2.** *s.* Incendiaire *m.*

incense¹ [ˈinsens], *s.* Encens *m.* **'incense-bearer,** *s. Ecc :* Thuriféraire *m.* **'incense-boat,** *s. Ecc :* Navette *f.*

incense² [inˈsens], *v.tr.* Exaspérer, courroucer. **incensed,** *a.* Enflammé de colère ; courroucé.

incentive [inˈsentiv]. **I.** *a.* *(a)* Provocant, excitant. *(b)* Stimulant. **2.** *s.* Stimulant *m,* aiguillon *m,* encouragement *m.* **Unemployment is an incentive to crime,** le chômage pousse au crime.

inception [inˈsepʃ(ə)n], *s.* Commencement *m,* début *m* (d'une entreprise, etc.).

25

incertitude [in'sə:rtitju:d], *s.* Incertitude *f.*

incessant [in'ses(ə)nt], *a.* (Bruit) incessant, continuel. **-ly,** *adv.* Sans cesse ; incessamment.

incest ['insest], *s.* Inceste *m.*

incestuous [in'sestjuəs], *a.* Incestueux.

inch [inʃ], *s. Meas :* Pouce *m* (= 1/36 du yard ; = 2 centimètres 54). *F : A man of your inches,* un homme de votre taille. *He couldn't see an inch before him,* il n'y voyait pas à deux pas devant lui. *Not to give way an inch,* ne pas reculer d'une semelle. *By inches, inch by inch,* peu à peu, petit à petit. *I know every inch of the neighbourhood,* je connais la région comme ma poche. *Give him an inch and he'll take an ell,* donnez-lui-en grand comme le doigt et il en prendra long comme le bras.

inchoate ['inkoet], *a.* **1.** Rudimentaire, fruste. **2.** Incomplet, imparfait.

inchoative [in'kouətiv, 'inkoeitiv], *a.* **1.** Initial, -aux ; premier. **2.** *Gram :* (Verbe) inchoatif.

incidence ['insidəns], *s.* **1.** Incidence *f* (d'un impôt). **2.** *Opt :* Angle of incidence, angle *m* d'incidence.

incident¹ ['insidənt], *s.* Incident *m. Journey full of incidents,* voyage mouvementé.

incident², *a.* **1.** Qui appartient, qui tient (*to,* à). *Dangers incident to travel,* dangers que comporte un voyage. **2.** *Opt :* (Rayon) incident.

incidental [insi'dent(ə)l], **1.** *a. (a)* (Événement) fortuit, accidentel ; (*of observation*) incident. *Incidental expenses,* faux frais. *Gram :* Incidental clause, incidente *f,* incise *f. (b)* Incidental to sth., qui est inséparable de qch. *Fatigues i. to a journey,* fatigues que comporte un voyage. **2.** *s.* Chose fortuite ; éventualité *f.* **-ally,** *adv.* **1.** Accessoirement. **2.** *Be it said i.,* soit dit en passant.

incinerate [in'sinəreit], *v.tr.* Incinérer, réduire en cendres, carboniser.

incineration [insinə'reiʃ(ə)n], *s.* Incinération *f.*

incinerator [in'sinəreitər], *s.* Incinérateur *m.*

incipient [in'sipiənt], *a.* Naissant ; qui commence. *Incipient beard,* barbe naissante.

incise [in'saiz], *v.tr.* **1.** Inciser, faire une incision dans (qch.). **2.** *Art :* Graver en creux.

incision [in'siʒ(ə)n], *s.* Incision *f,* entaille *f.*

incisive [in'saisiv], *a.* Incisif, tranchant ; (ton) mordant ; (esprit, jugement) pénétrant. **-ly,** *adv.* Incisivement.

incisiveness [in'saisivnəs], *s.* Ton incisif, tranchant. *The i. of his style,* son style tranchant.

incisor [in'saizər], *s.* (Dent) incisive *f.*

incite [in'sait], *v.tr.* Inciter, aiguillonner, pousser (*to sth.,* à qch.). *To i. s.o. to revolt,* exciter qn à la révolte. *To i. s.o. to work,* stimuler qn au travail. **inciting,** *a.* Incitateur, -trice.

incitement [in'saitmənt], *s.* **1.** Incitation *f,* excitation *f* (*to,* à). **2.** Stimulant *m,* aiguillon *m.*

inciter, -tress [in'saitər, -tres], *s.* Incitateur, -trice (*to,* à).

incivility [insi'viliti], *s.* Incivilité *f,* malhonnêteté *f. Piece of incivility,* incivilité.

inclemency [in'klemənsi], *s.* Inclémence *f,* rigueur *f* (de climat). *I. of the weather,* intempérie *f.*

inclement [in'klemənt], *a.* (Juge) inclément ; (climat) rigoureux, rude.

inclination [inkli'neiʃ(ə)n], *s.* **1.** Inclination *f* (de la tête). **2.** Inclinaison *f,* pente *f* (d'un coteau) ; dévers *m* (d'un mur). **3.** *(a)* Inclination, penchant *m* (*to, for,* à, pour). *To follow one's own i.,* en faire à sa tête. *(b)* Inclination to stoutness, tendance *f* à l'embonpoint.

incline¹ ['inklain], *s.* Pente *f,* déclivité *f,* inclinaison *f* (du terrain). *Civ.E :* (*Acclivity*) Rampe *f.*

incline² [in'klain], *v.* Incliner. **1.** *v.tr. (a)* Pencher (la tête). *(b)* To incline the heart to do sth., incliner, porter, le cœur à faire qch. *(c)* To incline one's steps to a place, diriger ses pas vers un lieu. **2.** *v.i. (a)* Incliner, pencher (*to, towards,* à, vers). *Inclined at an angle of* 45°, incliné à un angle de 45°. *(b)* Avoir un penchant (*to,* pour qch., à faire qch.) ; être enclin, porté (*to,* à). *To i. to pity,* incliner à la pitié. *To i. to the belief that . . .,* incliner à croire que. . . . *(c)* To incline to corpulence, avoir une tendance à la corpulence. *(d)* To incline to the left, obliquer à gauche. **inclined,** *a.* **1.** (Plan) incliné. **2.** Enclin, porté (*to,* à). *To be inclined to do sth.,* avoir de l'inclination à faire qch. *If you feel inclined,* si le cœur vous en dit. *If ever you should feel so inclined,* si jamais l'envie vous en prenait. *He is that way inclined,* il penche dans ce sens.

inclinometer [inkli'nɔmetər], *s. Av : etc :* Clinomètre *m,* inclinomètre *m.*

include [in'klu:d], *v.tr.* Comprendre, renfermer, embrasser. *He included them all in his contempt,* il les englobait tous dans son mépris. *His property was sold, his house included,* ses biens furent vendus, y compris sa maison. *We were six including our host,* nous étions six y compris notre hôte. *Up to and including 31st December,* jusqu'au 31 décembre inclus.

inclusion [in'klu:ʒ(ə)n], *s.* Inclusion *f.*

inclusive [in'klu:siv], *a.* Qui comprend, qui renferme. *Inclusive sum,* somme globale. *Inclusive terms* (*at hotel*), conditions, tout compris. **-ly,** *adv.* Inclusivement.

incognito [in'kɔgnito]. **1.** *adv.* Incognito. **2.** *s.* To preserve one's incognito, garder l'incognito *m.*

incoherence [inko'hiːərəns], **incoherency** [inko'hiːərənsi], *s.* Incohérence *f.*

incoherent [inko'hiːərənt], *a.* Incohérent. *Incoherent style,* style décousu. **-ly,** *adv.* Incohérence, sans suite.

incombustible [inkɔm'bʌstibl], *a.* Incombustible.

income ['inkəm], *s.* Revenu *m,* revenus *mpl. Private income,* rente(s) *f(pl).* *To live up to one's income,* dépenser (i) tout ce qu'on gagne, (ii) tout son revenu. **'income-tax,** *s.* Impôt *m* sur le revenu. *Income-tax return,* déclaration *f* de revenu.

incomer ['inkʌmər], *s. Incomers and outgoers,* (les) entrants *m* et (les) sortants *m.*

incoming¹ ['inkʌmin], *a.* Qui entre, qui arrive ; (locataire) entrant. *Incoming tide,* marée montante.

incoming², *s.* **1.** Entrée *f,* arrivée *f.* **2.** *pl. Incomings,* recettes *f,* revenus *m.*

incommensurable [inko'menʃərəbl], *a. Mth : (a)* Incommensurable (*with,* avec). *(b)* Incommensurable number, nombre irrationnel.

incommensurate [inko'menʃəret], *a.* Pas en rapport, pas en proportion (*with,* avec) ; disproportionné (*with,* à).

incommode [inko'moud], *v.tr.* Incommoder, gêner.

incommodious [inko'moudjəs], *a.* Incommode ; (appartement) où l'on est à l'étroit.

incommodiousness [inko'moudjəsnəs], *s.* Incommodité *f* (d'une maison).

incommunicable [inko'mju:nikəbl], *a.* Incommunicable.

incomparable [in'kɔmpərəbl], *a.* Incomparable (*to, with,* à). *I. artist,* artiste hors ligne. **-ably,** *adv.* Incomparablement.

incompatibility [inkɔmpati'biliti], *s.* Incom-

patibilité *f*; inconciliabilité *f* (de deux théories). **Incompatibility of temper,** opposition *f* d'humeur.
incompatible [inkom'patibl], *a.* Incompatible, inconciliable, inassociable (*with,* avec).
incompetence [in'kɔmpetəns], **incompetency** [in'kɔmpetənsi], *s.* **1.** *Jur:* Incompétence *f*, incapacité *f* (d'une personne). **Incompetency to succeed,** inhabilité *f* à succéder. **2.** Incompétence (de qn); manque *m* de capacité.
incompetent [in'kɔmpetənt], *a.* **1.** *Jur:* Incompétent. *I. to make a will,* inhabile à tester. *I am i. to act,* je n'ai pas qualité pour agir. **2.** Incapable. *s. To weed out the incompetents,* éliminer les incapables.
incomplete [iñkom'pli:t], *a.* Incomplet, -ète; inachevé. **-ly,** *adv.* Incomplètement.
incompleteness [inkom'pli:tnəs], *s.* Imperfection *f*, inachèvement *m.*
incomprehensibility [in'kɔmprihensi'biliti], *s.* Incompréhensibilité *f.*
incomprehensible [inkɔmpri'hensibl], *a.* Incompréhensible; indéchiffrable. **-ibly,** *adv.* Incompréhensiblement.
incompressible [inkom'presibl], *a.* Incompressible.
inconceivable [inkon'si:vəbl], *a.* Inconcevable. **-ably,** *adv.* Inconcevablement.
inconclusive [inkon'klu:siv], *a.* Peu concluant. **-ly,** *adv.* D'une manière peu concluante.
incongruity [inkon'gruiti], *s.* **1.** Désaccord *m*; manque *m* d'harmonie (*with,* avec). *I. of terms,* disconvenance *f* de mots. **2.** Absurdité *f*, incongruité *f.* **3.** Inconvenance *f.*
incongruous [in'kɔŋgruəs], *a.* **1.** Inassociable (*with,* avec); sans rapport (*to, with,* avec). **Incongruous colours,** couleurs qui jurent ensemble. **2.** (*Of remark*) Incongru, déplacé. **-ly,** *adv.* Sans harmonie; incongrûment.
inconsequence [in'kɔnsekwəns], *s.* Inconséquence *f.*
inconsequent [in'kɔnsekwənt], *a.* Inconséquent, illogique. *I. reasoning,* F: raisonnement biscornu. **-ly,** *adv.* Inconséquemment.
inconsiderable [inkon'sidərəbl], *a.* Peu considérable; insignifiant.
inconsiderate [inkon'sidəret], *a.* **1.** Inconsidéré, étourdi. *I. opinion,* opinion peu réfléchie. **2.** (Personne) sans égards pour les autres. *It was most i. of you,* vous avez manqué d'égards. **-ly,** *adv.* **1.** Sans considération, sans réflexion. **2.** To behave **inconsiderately to s.o.,** manquer d'égards envers qn.
inconsistency [inkon'sistənsi], *s.* **1.** Inconsistance *f*, contradiction *f.* **2.** Inconséquence *f*, illogisme *m.*
inconsistent [inkon'sistənt], *a.* **1.** Incompatible, en contradiction (*with,* avec); contradictoire (*with,* à). *His words are i. with his conduct,* il y a désaccord entre ses paroles et sa conduite. **2.** (*Of pers.*) Inconstant, inconséquent. *To be i. in one's replies,* varier dans ses réponses. **3.** (Histoire) qui ne tient pas debout.
inconsolable [inkon'soulǝbl], *a.* Inconsolable. **-ably,** *adv.* Inconsolablement.
inconspicuous [inkon'spikjuəs], *a.* Peu en vue; peu apparent; peu frappant. **-ly,** *adv.* (Vêtu) d'une manière discrète.
inconstancy [in'kɔnstənsi], *s.* Inconstance *f*; instabilité *f* (du temps).
inconstant [in'kɔnstənt], *a.* Inconstant, volage.
incontestable [inkon'testəbl], *a.* (Preuve) incontestable, indéniable. **-ably,** *adv.* Incontestablement.
incontinence [in'kɔntinəns], *s.* Incontinence *f.*

incontinent [in'kɔntinənt], *a.* (*a*) (*Unchaste*) Incontinent. (*b*) *Med:* Qui ne peut se retenir. (*c*) *I. of speech,* bavard.
incontinently [in'kɔntinəntli], *adv.* Sur-le-champ; incontinent.
incontrovertible [inkɔntro'və:rtibl], *a.* (Vérité) incontestable; (preuve) irrécusable. **-ibly,** *adv.* Sans contredit.
inconvenience[1] [inkon'vi:njəns], *s.* (*a*) Incommodité *f*, contretemps *m.* **I am putting you to a lot of inconvenience,** je vous donne beaucoup de dérangement. **Without the slightest inconvenience,** sans le moindre inconvénient. (*b*) *The i. of living so far from town,* les inconvénients qu'il y a à vivre si loin de la ville.
inconvenience[2], *v.tr.* Déranger, incommoder, gêner (qn).
inconvenient [inkon'vi:njənt], *a.* (*Of house*) Incommode; (*of time*) inopportun. *It is very i.,* c'est très gênant. **-ly,** *adv.* Incommodément.
incorporate [in'kɔ:rporeit]. **1.** *v.tr.* (*a*) Incorporer, unir (*with,* à, avec). (*b*) *Com:* Constituer (une association) en société commerciale. **2.** *v.i.* S'incorporer (*with others,* avec, à, d'autres).
incorporated, *a.* **1.** Incorporé; faisant corps (*with others,* avec d'autres). **2.** *Com:* **Incorporated company,** (i) société constituée; (ii) *U.S:* société anonyme.
incorporation [inkɔ:rpo'rei∫(ə)n], *s.* **1.** Incorporation *f* (in, *with,* into, à, avec, dans). **2.** *Com:* Constitution *f* (d'une association) en société commerciale.
incorporeal [inkɔ:r'pɔ:riəl], *a.* Incorporel.
incorrect [inko'rekt], *a.* **1.** (*a*) (*Of statement*) Inexact. (*b*) *I. expression,* locution vicieuse; incorrection *f* de langage. (*c*) *I. text,* texte fautif. **2.** (*Of behaviour*) Incorrect. **Incorrect act,** incorrection *f.* **It is incorrect to . . .,** il est de mauvais ton de. . . . **-ly,** *adv.* **1.** Inexactement. *Letter i. addressed,* lettre mal adressée. *I. printed,* imprimé fautivement. **2.** Incorrectement.
incorrectness [inko'rektnəs], *s.* **1.** Inexactitude *f* (d'un calcul). **2.** Incorrection *f.*
incorrigible [in'kɔridʒibl], *a.* Incorrigible.
incorrodible [inko'roudibl], *a.* Inattaquable (par les acides, aux acides).
incorruptible [inko'rʌptibl], *a.* Incorruptible.
increase[1] ['inkri:s], *s.* (*a*) Augmentation *f* (de prix); accroissement *m* (de vitesse); surcroît *m* (de besogne); redoublement *m* (d'efforts). **The increase in crime,** la multiplication des crimes. **increase in value** (*of property*), plus-value *f.* (*b*) *Adv. phr. To be on the increase,* être en augmentation; aller croissant. **Unemployment is on the i.,** le chômage s'accentue.
increase[2] [in'kri:s]. **1.** *v.i.* (*a*) Augmenter; grandir, s'agrandir; croître, s'accroître. *The rain increased,* la pluie redoubla. *To i. in price,* renchérir. *To go on increasing,* aller toujours croissant. (*b*) Se multiplier. *The population increases,* la population grossit, se multiplie. **2.** *v.tr.* Augmenter (la production); grossir (le nombre); accroître (sa fortune). *To i. the cost of goods,* renchérir des marchandises. **To increase s.o.'s salary,** augmenter les appointements de) qn. **To increase speed,** forcer la vitesse. *Nau:* **To increase speed to twenty knots,** pousser l'allure à vingt nœuds. *To i. one's vigilance,* redoubler de vigilance. **Increased cost of living,** renchérissement *m* de la vie. **increasing,** *a.* Croissant. *Mth:* **Increasing series,** progression ascendante. **-ly,** *adv.* De plus en plus (difficile).
incredible [in'kredibl], *a.* Incroyable. **-ibly,** *adv.* Incroyablement.

incredulity [inkre'dju:liti], s. Incrédulité f.
incredulous [in'kredjuləs], a. Incrédule. Incredulous smile, sourire d'incrédulité.
increment ['inkrimənt], s. **1.** Augmentation f.
Mth: **Increment of a function,** incrément m
d'une fonction. **2.** Profit m. **Unearned increment**
(of land), plus-value f.
incriminate [in'krimineit], v.tr. **1.** Incriminer
(qn). **2.** Impliquer (qn) (dans une accusation).
Incriminating documents, pièces f à conviction.
incrimination [inkrimi'nei∫(ə)n], s. Incrimination f, accusation f (de qn).
incrustation [inkrʌs'tei∫(ə)n], s. **1.** (a) Incrustation f; action f d'incruster. (b) *Mch:* Entartrage m
(des chaudières). **2.** (a) Incrustation (de nacre).
(b) *Mch:* Tartre m.
incubate ['inkjubeit]. **1.** v.tr. Couver (des œufs).
2. v.i. (Of eggs, of disease) Couver.
incubation [inkju'bei∫(ə)n], s. Incubation f.
Med: **Incubation period,** période f d'incubation
(d'une maladie).
incubator ['inkjubeitər], s. *Husb:* Éleveuse f;
couveuse artificielle.
incubus ['inkjubəs], s. **1.** *Myth:* Incube m.
2. F: (a) (Of pers.) To be an incubus on s.o.,
être un cauchemar pour qn. (b) Fardeau m,
poids m (des impôts).
inculcate ['inkʌlkeit], v.tr. Inculquer (une leçon).
inculpate ['inkʌlpeit], v.tr. **1.** Inculper, incriminer (qn). **2.** = INCRIMINATE 2.
inculpation [inkʌl'pei∫(ə)n], s. Inculpation f.
incumbency [in'kʌmbənsi], s. *Ecc:* **1.** (a) Possession f d'un bénéfice. (b) Charge f. **2.** Période f
d'exercice (d'une charge).
incumbent[1] [in'kʌmbənt], s. *Ecc:* Bénéficier m;
titulaire m (d'une charge).
incumbent[2], a. To be incumbent on s.o. to do
sth., incomber, appartenir, à qn de faire qch.
incumbrance [in'kʌmbrəns], s. = ENCUM-
BRANCE.
incunabulum, pl. -a [inkju'nabjuləm, -a], s.
Incunable m.
incur [in'kə:r], v.tr. (incurred) Courir (un risque);
encourir (un blâme); s'attirer (le courroux de
qn); contracter (des dettes). To incur expenses,
encourir des frais.
incurable [in'kjuərəbl], a. & s. Incurable.
-ably, adv. To be incurably lazy, être d'une
paresse incurable.
incurious [in'kjuəriəs], a. Incurieux; sans
curiosité. **-ly,** adv. Avec indifférence.
incursion [in'kə:r∫(ə)n], s. Incursion f.
incurvate [in'kə:rveit], v.tr. Incurver.
incurve [in'kə:rv]. **1.** v.tr. = INCURVATE. **2.** v.i.
S'incurver; se courber en dedans.
indebted [in'detid], a. **1.** Endetté. **2.** Redevable
(to s.o. for sth., à qn de qch.).
indebtedness [in'detidnəs], s. **1.** Dette(s) f(pl).
The amount of my i., le montant de ma dette.
2. Our i. to Greece, ce dont nous sommes rede-
vables à la Grèce.
indecency [in'di:sənsi], s. Indécence f, inconvenance f.
indecent [in'di:sənt], a. Peu décent, indécent,
inconvenant. **-ly,** adv. Indécemment.
indecipherable [indi'saifərəbl], a. Indéchiffrable.
indecision [indi'siʒ(ə)n], s. Indécision f, irrésolution f.
indecisive [indi'saisiv], a. **1.** (Of argument)
Indécisif, peu concluant; (of battle) indécis.
2. (Homme) indécis, irrésolu.
indeclinable [indi'klainəbl], a. *Gram:* Indéclinable.

indecorous [inde'kɔ:rəs, in'dekərəs], a. Inconvenant; peu convenable. **-ly,** adv. D'une
manière peu convenable.
indecorousness [in'dekərəsnəs], s. (a) Inconvenance f. (b) Manque m de décorum, de
maintien.
indeed [in'di:d], adv. **1.** (a) En effet; vraiment.
One may i. say so, on peut bien le dire. Praise
which i. was well deserved, éloges qui de fait
étaient bien mérités. (b) (Intensive) I am very
glad indeed, je suis très très content. Thank you
very much i., merci infiniment. (c) I may i. be
wrong, il se peut toutefois que j'aie tort.
2. Même; à vrai dire. I think so, i. I am sure of
it, je le pense et même j'en suis sûr. I forget his
name, if indeed I ever knew it, son nom m'échappe,
si tant est que je l'aie jamais su. **3.** (a) Yes
indeed! (i) mais certainement! F: pour sûr!
(ii) (contradicting) si fait! (b) I have lived in
Paris.—Indeed? j'ai vécu à Paris.—Vraiment?
indefatigable [indi'fatigəbl], a. Infatigable
inlassable. **-ably,** adv. Infatigablement.
indefeasible [indi'fi:zibl], a. (Droit) irrévocable,
imprescriptible.
indefensible [indi'fensibl], a. (Théorie) indéfendable; (argument) insoutenable. **-ibly,** adv.
D'une manière inexcusable.
indefinable [indi'fainəbl], a. **1.** Indéfinissable.
2. (Sentiment) vague (de . . .).
indefinite [in'definit], a. Indéfini. **1.** (a) (Nombre)
indéterminé. **Indefinite leave,** congé illimité.
(b) *Gram:* **Past indefinite,** passé indéfini. **Indefinite pronoun,** pronom indéfini. **-ly,** adv.
1. (Promettre) vaguement. **2.** To postpone sth.
indefinitely, remettre qch. indéfiniment.
indelible [in'delibl], a. Indélébile, ineffaçable.
Indelible pencil, crayon à copier. **-ibly,** adv.
Ineffaçablement.
indelicacy [in'delikəsi], s. (a) Indélicatesse f;
manque m de délicatesse. (b) Inconvenance f.
indelicate [in'deliket], a. (a) Indélicat; peu
délicat. I. action, indélicatesse f. (b) Inconvenant.
indemnification [indemnifi'kei∫(ə)n], s. **1.** Indemnisation f (for, de). **2.** Indemnité f.
indemnify [in'demnifai], v.tr. **1.** Garantir (qn)
(from, against, contre). **2.** Indemniser, dédommager (qn) (for a loss, d'une perte).
indemnity [in'demniti], s. **1.** Garantie f, assurance f (contre une perte, etc.). *Pol:* Bill, act, of
indemnity, bill m d'indemnité. *Com:* (Letter of)
indemnity, décharge f. **2.** Indemnité f, dédommagement m.
indent[1] ['indent, in'dent], s. (a) *Adm:* Ordre m
de réquisition (pour approvisionnements).
(b) *Com:* Commande f de marchandises (reçue
de l'étranger).
indent[2] [in'dent]. **1.** v.tr. (a) Denteler, découper
(le bord de qch.). (b) *Typ:* Renfoncer, faire
rentrer (une ligne). **2.** v.i. To indent on s.o. for
sth., (i) réquisitionner qch. de qn; (ii) passer
une commande à qn pour (une marchandise).
indented, a. **1.** (Bord) dentelé; (littoral)
échancré. **2.** *Typ:* **Indented line,** ligne en
alinéa, en retrait.
indent[3] [in'dent], v.tr. Empreindre (en creux);
bosseler, bossuer.
indentation [inden'tei∫(ə)n], s. **1.** Impression f,
foulage m (du sable par les roues, etc.). **2.** Dentelure f; découpure f; échancrure f (du littoral).
3. Empreinte creuse.
indention [in'den∫(ə)n], s. *Typ:* Renfoncement m
(d'une ligne).
indenture[1] [in'dentjər], s. *Jur:* (a) Contrat m

synallagmatique. *To be bound by an i.*, être lié par un engagement. (*b*) *pl.* **Indentures**, contrat d'apprentissage.

indenture², *v.tr.* Mettre (qn) en apprentissage (*to s.o.*, chez qn).

independence [indi'pendəns], *s.* **I.** Indépendance *f* (*of*, à l'égard de). *To show i.*, faire preuve d'indépendance. **2.** *He had acquired a modest independence*, il s'était acquis une modeste indépendance.

independent [indi'pendənt], *a.* (*a*) Indépendant. *To be i.*, être son maître. *To become i.*, s'affranchir. **Independent witness**, témoin volontaire. *Mil:* **Independent firing**, tir à volonté. (*b*) **A man of independent means**, un rentier. *To be i.*, avoir une fortune personnelle; vivre de ses rentes. (*c*) (Caractère, air) indépendant. **-ly**, *adv.* **I.** Indépendamment (*of*, de). **2.** Avec indépendance; d'un air indépendant.

indescribable [indis'kraibəbl], *a.* Indescriptible; (joie) indicible. **-ably**, *adv.* Indescriptiblement, indiciblement.

indestructible [indis'trʌktibl], *a.* Indestructible. **-ibly**, *adv.* Indestructiblement.

indeterminable [indi'tə:rminəbl], *a.* **I.** (Distance) indéterminable. **2.** (Dispute) qu'on ne saurait terminer.

indeterminate [indi'tə:rminet], *a.* Indéterminé; (*of thought*) vague.

indetermination [inditə:rmi'neiʃ(ə)n], *s.* Indétermination *f.* irrésolution *f.*

index¹, *pl.* **indexes, indices** ['indeks, 'indeksiz, 'indisi:z], *s.* **I.** (*pl.* **indexes**) Index *m*; premier doigt. **2.** *Tchn:* (*pl.* **indexes**) Aiguille *f* (de balance). **Index correction**, correction du zéro. **3.** (*pl.* **indices**) Indice *m*; signe (indicateur). **4.** (*pl.* **indexes**) Index, table *f* alphabétique, répertoire *m* (d'un livre). **Index-book**, livre *m* répertoire. **5.** (*pl.* **indices**) (*a*) *Alg:* Exposant *m.* (*b*) *Opt:* **Index of refraction**, indice de réfraction. **'index-finger**, *s.* Index *m.*

index², *v.tr.* (*a*) Faire, dresser, l'index (d'un livre). (*b*) Répertorier, classer (un article).

India ['indjə]. *Pr.n.* L'Inde *f.* **British India**, l'Inde anglaise. **The East India Company**, la Compagnie anglaise des Indes. **india-'rubber**, *s. See* RUBBER¹ 3.

Indiaman, *pl.* **-men** ['indjəmən, -men], *s.* Navire *m* qui fait le service des Indes orientales.

Indian ['indjən]. **I.** (*a*) *a.* De l'Inde; des Indes; indien. **The Indian Ocean**, la mer des Indes; l'océan Indien. (*b*) *s.* Indien, -ienne; *F:* Hindou, -oue. **2.** *a. & s.* Indien, -ienne (d'Amérique). **Red Indians**, (les) Peaux-Rouges *m.*

indicate ['indikeit], *v.tr.* **I.** (*a*) Indiquer, montrer. *To i. sth. with the hand*, indiquer qch. de la main. (*b*) *At the hour indicated*, à l'heure dite, indiquée. (*c*) *Med:* **Case in which a certain treatment is indicated**, cas pour lequel un certain traitement est indiqué. **2.** Indiquer, dénoter (qch.). *Face that indicates energy*, visage qui dénote l'énergie.

indication [indi'keiʃ(ə)n], *s.* **I.** Indication *f* (de qch. à qn). **2.** (*a*) Indice *m*, signe *m. Not the least i. of . . .*, aucune apparence de. . . . *There are many indications that . . .*, tout porte à croire que. . . . (*b*) **To give clear indication of one's intentions**, faire connaître clairement ses intentions.

indicative [in'dikətiv]. **I.** *a. & s. Gram:* **Indicative (mood)**, (mode) indicatif *m.* **2.** *a.* Indicatif (*of*, de).

indicator ['indikeitər], *s.* (*a*) Table *f* d'orientation. (*b*) Index *m*, aiguille *f* (de baromètre). *Aut:*

Wing-indicator, repère *m* d'aile. (*c*) **Pressure indicator**, indicateur *m* de pression. (*d*) *El.E: etc:* **Indicator (board)**, tableau indicateur; *Tp:* annonciateur *m. Rail:* **Train indicator**, tableau indicateur du service des quais.

indicatory ['indikeitəri], *a.* **I.** Indicateur, -trice; qui indique. **2.** (Symptôme) indicatif (*of*, de).

indices ['indisi:z], *s.pl. See* INDEX¹.

indict [in'dait], *v.tr.* Accuser, inculper (qn) (*for*, de); mettre (qn) en accusation; traduire, poursuivre, (qn) en justice (*for*, pour).

indictable [in'daitəbl], *a.* **I.** (Personne) attaquable, traduisible, en justice. **2.** (Action) qui tombe sous le coup de la loi. **Indictable offence**, délit *m.*

indictment [in'daitmənt], *s. Jur:* **I.** Accusation *f*; (*by public prosecutor*) réquisitoire *m. I. for theft*, inculpation *f* de vol. **2.** *To draw up an i.*, rédiger un acte d'accusation.

Indies (the) [ði'indiz]. *Pr.n.pl.* Les Indes *f.* **The East Indies**, les Indes (orientales), les Grandes Indes. **The West Indies**, les Antilles *f.*

indifference [in'difərəns], *s.* **I.** Indifférence *f*, manque *m* d'intérêt (*to, towards, sth., s.o.*, pour qch., à l'égard de qn). *It is a matter of perfect i. to me*, cela m'est parfaitement indifférent. **2.** Médiocrité *f* (de talent, etc.).

indifferent [in'difərənt], *a.* **I.** Indifférent (*to*, à). *His praise is i. to me, F:* ses éloges ne me font ni chaud ni froid. *He is i. to everything*, tout lui est indifférent, égal. **2.** Médiocre, passable. *Very i. quality*, qualité très médiocre. *To be an i. painter*, peindre pauvrement. **3.** *To converse on i. topics*, causer de choses sans importance. **-ly**, *adv.* **I.** Indifféremment; avec indifférence. **2.** Médiocrement.

indigence ['indidʒəns], **indigency** ['indidʒənsi], *s.* Indigence *f*, pauvreté *f.*

indigenous [in'didʒənəs], *a.* Indigène (*to*, de); du pays.

indigent ['indidʒənt], *a. & s.* Indigent, pauvre; nécessiteux.

indigestible [indi'dʒestibl], *a.* Indigeste.

indigestion [indi'dʒestʃ(ə)n], *s.* Dyspepsie *f*; mauvaise digestion. **An attack of indigestion**, une indigestion.

indignant [in'dignənt], *a.* (Air) indigné; (cri) d'indignation. **To be, feel, indignant at sth.**, être indigné, s'indigner, de qch. **To make s.o. indignant**, indigner qn. **-ly**, *adv.* Avec indignation; d'un air indigné.

indignation [indig'neiʃ(ə)n], *s.* Indignation *f.* **Indignation meeting**, meeting *m*, réunion *f*, de protestation.

indignity [in'digniti], *s.* Indignité *f*, affront *m. To treat s.o. with i.*, faire affront à qn.

indigo ['indigo], *s. Dy: Com:* Indigo *m.* **'indigo-'blue**, *a. & s.* (Bleu) indigo *m inv.*

indirect [indi'rekt], *a.* **I.** Indirect. **2.** (Moyen, etc.) détourné, oblique. **-ly**, *adv.* Indirectement.

indiscernible [indi'zə:rnibl, -'sə:r-], *a.* **I.** Indiscernable. **2.** Imperceptible.

indiscipline [in'disiplin], *s.* Indiscipline *f.*

indiscreet [indis'kri:t], *a.* **I.** Indiscret, -ète. **2.** Peu judicieux; imprudent, inconsidéré. **-ly**, *adv.* **I.** Indiscrètement. **2.** Imprudemment; sans considération.

indiscretion [indis'kreʃ(ə)n], *s.* **I.** (*a*) Manque *m* de discrétion. (*b*) Indiscrétion *f.* **2.** (*a*) Action inconsidérée; imprudence *f.* (*b*) *F:* Écart *m* de conduite; faux pas.

indiscriminable [indis'kriminəbl], *a.* Indiscernable (*from*, de).

indiscriminate [indis'kriminet], *a.* (Charité, admirateur) aveugle. *I. blows*, coups frappés à tort et à travers. **-ly,** *adv.* Sans faire de distinction ; au hasard ; (louer) aveuglément.

indiscrimination [indiskrimi'neiʃ(ə)n], *s.* Manque *m* de discernement.

indispensability [indispensə'biliti], **indispensableness** [indis'pensəblnəs], *s.* Indispensabilité *f.*

indispensable [indis'pensəbl], *a.* **1.** (Loi, devoir) obligatoire. **2.** Indispensable, de première nécessité (*to s.o.*, à qn). *To make oneself i. to s.o.*, se rendre indispensable à qn. **-ably,** *adv.* Indispensablement.

indispose [indis'poːuz], *v.tr.* **1.** To indispose s.o. towards s.o., indisposer, prévenir, qn contre qn. **2.** To indispose s.o. for sth., for doing sth., rendre qn incapable, hors d'état, de faire qch. **3.** Rendre (qn) malade. **indisposed,** *a.* **1.** Peu enclin, peu disposé (*to do sth.*, à faire qch.). **2.** To be, feel, indisposed, être indisposé, souffrant ; n'être pas dans son assiette.

indisposition [indispo'ziʃ(ə)n], *s.* **1.** Peu *m* d'inclination (*to do sth.*, à faire qch.). **2.** Indisposition *f*, malaise *m*.

indisputable [in'dispjutəbl, indis'pjuːtəbl], *a.* Incontestable, indiscutable. **-ably,** *adv.* Indiscutablement, incontestablement.

indissoluble [indi'sɔljubl], *a.* (Union) indissoluble. **-bly,** *adv.* Indissolublement.

indistinct [indis'tiŋ(k)t], *a.* (Objet) indistinct ; (bruit) confus ; (souvenir) vague. **-ly,** *adv.* (Voir, parler) indistinctement ; (sentir) vaguement.

indistinctness [indis'tiŋ(k)tnəs], *s.* Indistinction *f* ; manque *m* de netteté.

indistinguishable [indis'tiŋgwiʃəbl], *a.* **1.** Indistinguible, indiscernable (*from*, de). **2.** (Bruit) insaisissable. *I. to the naked eye*, imperceptible à l'œil nu.

indite [in'dait], *v.tr.* A. & Hum: Composer (un poème) ; rédiger (une lettre, une dépêche).

individual [indi'vidjuəl], *a.* **1.** *a.* (*a*) Individuel. (*b*) Particulier. **2.** *s.* Individu *m.* A private individual, un simple particulier. **-ally,** *adv.* **1.** Individuellement. **2.** Personnellement.

individuality [individju'aliti], *s.* Individualité *f.*

indivisibility [indivizi'biliti], *s.* Indivisibilité *f.*

indivisible [indi'vizibl], *a.* Indivisible, insécable. **-ibly,** *adv.* Indivisiblement.

Indo-China [indo't'ʃaina]. *Pr.n.* L'Indo-Chine *f*, l'Indochine *f.*

indocile [in'dousail], *a.* Indocile.

indocility [indo'siliti], *s.* Indocilité *f.*

Indo-European [indojuərə'piːən], *a. & s.* *Ethn: Ling:* Indo-européen, -enne ; aryen, -enne.

indolence ['indoləns], *s.* Indolence *f*, paresse *f.*

indolent ['indolənt], *a.* Indolent, paresseux. **-ly,** *adv.* Indolemment, paresseusement.

indomitable [in'dɔmitəbl], *a.* Indomptable. **-ably,** *adv.* Indomptablement.

indoor ['indoːər], *a.* (Robe) d'intérieur ; (décoration) d'appartement. Indoor games, (i) jeux de salle ; (ii) jeux de salon, de société. Indoor servants, gens de maison.

indoors [in'doːərz], *adv.* A la maison. Indoors and out, dans la maison et dehors. *To go i.*, entrer, rentrer (dans la maison). To keep indoors, garder la maison.

indorse, *v.tr.*, **indorsement,** *s.* = ENDORSE, *etc.*

indubitable [in'djuːbitəbl], *a.* Indubitable ; incontestable. **-ably,** *adv.* Indubitablement ; incontestablement. (

induce [in'djuːs], *v.tr.* **1.** To induce s.o. to do sth., persuader à qn de faire qch. ; décider qn à faire qch. **2.** (*a*) Amener, produire, occasionner. To induce sleep, provoquer le sommeil. To induce the belief, the hope, that . . ., porter à croire, faire espérer, que. . . . (*b*) *El:* *etc:* Amorcer (un courant, etc.) ; induire (un courant). **3.** Induire, conclure (que . . .). **induced,** *a.* Induced draught, tirage induit par aspiration ; tirage par induction. *El:* Induced current, courant induit. **inducing,** *a.* *El:* (*Of wire, etc.*) Inducteur, -trice.

inducement [in'djuːsmənt], *s.* Motif *m*, mobile *m*, raison *f*, cause *f*, qui encourage qn à faire qch. *I. to sleep*, provocation *f* au sommeil. To hold out an inducement to s.o. to do sth., encourager qn à faire qch. par des offres attrayantes. *The inducements of a large town*, (i) les attraits *m*, (ii) les tentations *f*, d'une grande ville.

induct [in'dʌkt], *v.tr.* *Ecc:* Installer (un ecclésiastique) dans sa paroisse.

inductance [in'dʌktəns], *s.* *El:* **1.** Inductance *f* ; coefficient *m* de self-induction. **2.** Inductance (-ooil), (bobine *f* de) self(-induction) *f.*

induction [in'dʌkʃ(ə)n], *s.* **1.** Installation *f* (d'un ecclésiastique, d'un fonctionnaire). **2.** Induction of facts, énumération *f* des faits ; apport *m* de preuves. **3.** *Log:* *Mth:* Induction *f.* **4.** *El:* Induction. *S.a.* SELF-INDUCTION. **5.** *Mch:* *I.C.E:* Admission *f*, entrée *f* (de la vapeur, des gaz) ; aspiration *f* (des gaz). **in'duction-coil,** *s.* *El:* Bobine *f* d'induction. **in'duction-pipe,** *s.* *I.C.E:* Tuyau *m* d'admission.

inductive [in'dʌktiv], *a.* **1.** *Log:* *I. reasoning*, raisonnement inductif. **2.** *El:* (*a*) (*Of current, etc.*) Inducteur, -trice. (*b*) (*Of charge, etc.*) Inductif. **-ly,** *adv.* *Log:* *El:* Par induction.

inductor [in'dʌktər], *s.* **1.** *Ecc:* Installateur *m* (d'un ecclésiastique). **2.** *El.E:* Inducteur *m.*

indulge [in'dʌldʒ]. **1.** *v.tr.* (*a*) Avoir, montrer, trop d'indulgence pour (qn) ; gâter (qn). To indulge oneself, s'écouter ; ne rien se refuser. (*b*) S'abandonner à (une fantaisie) ; se laisser aller à (un penchant) ; nourrir (un espoir). **2.** *v.i.* To indulge in a practice, s'adonner, se livrer, à une habitude. To indulge too freely in sth., faire abus de qch., abuser de qch. *To i. in sin*, s'adonner au péché. *To i. in tobacco*, être adonné au tabac. *To i. in a cigar*, se permettre un cigare.

indulgence [in'dʌldʒəns], *s.* **1.** Indulgence *f*, complaisance *f* (*to*, envers). **2.** (*a*) Indulgence in sin, abandon *m* au péché. (*b*) *These are my only indulgences*, ce sont là mes seules petites douceurs. **3.** *R.C.Ch:* Indulgence.

indulgent [in'dʌldʒənt], *a.* **1.** Indulgent (*to s.o.*, envers, pour, à, qn). **2.** Indulgent, faible. **-ly,** *adv.* Avec indulgence.

indurate ['indjureit]. **1.** *v.tr.* (*a*) Durcir (l'argile) ; *F:* endurcir (l'âme, le cœur). (*b*) *Med:* Indurer (les tissus). **2.** *v.i.* (*a*) Se durcir, durcir ; (*of feelings, etc.*) s'endurcir. (*b*) *Med:* S'indurer.

induration [indju'reiʃ(ə)n], *s.* **1.** *Geol:* *etc:* Durcissement *m* (de l'argile, etc.). *F:* Endurcissement *m* (du cœur, de la conscience). **2.** *Med:* Induration *f.*

industrial [in'dʌstriəl], *a.* Industriel. Industrial school, (i) école professionnelle ; (ii) école pour enfants moralement abandonnés. **-ally,** *adv.* Industriellement.

industrialism [in'dʌstriəlizm], *s.* Industrialisme *m.*

industrialist [in'dʌstriəlist], *s.* Industrialiste *m*, industriel *m.*

industrialize [in'dʌstriəlaːiz], *v.tr.* Industrialiser.

industrious [in'dʌstriəs], *a.* Travailleur, laborieux, assidu, industrieux. **-ly,** *adv.* Laborieusement, industrieusement, assidûment.

industry ['indəstri], *s.* **1.** Application *f*; assiduité *f* au travail; diligence *f*, zèle *m*. **2.** Industrie *f*. The heavy industries, les fonderies *f* et forges *f*; la sidérurgie.

inebriate[1] [in'iːbriet], *s.* Ivrogne, *f.* ivrognesse; alcoolique *mf*.

inebriate[2] [in'iːbrieit], *v.tr.* Enivrer, griser. To *i.* oneself with (sth.), s'enivrer de (vin, etc.); se griser de (popularité). **inebriated,** *a.* Ivre, gris. *F: I.* by success, grisé par son succès.

inebriation [iniːbri'eiʃ(ə)n], *s.* **1.** Enivrement *m*. **2.** = INEBRIETY I.

inebriety [iniː'braiəti], *s.* **1.** Ivresse *f*, ébriété *f*. **2.** Ivrognerie *f*, alcoolisme *m*.

ineffable [in'efəbl], *a.* Ineffable, indicible.

ineffaceable [ine'feisəbl], *a.* Ineffaçable, indélébile. **-ably,** *adv.* Ineffaçablement, indélébilement.

ineffective [ine'fektiv], *a.* **1.** Inefficace, sans effet, sans résultat. **2.** (Architecture) qui manque d'effet artistique. *I.* retort, réplique qui ne porte pas. *I.* style, style plat, terne. **3.** (Of pers.) Incapable. **-ly,** *adv.* Inefficacement, vainement.

ineffectiveness [ine'fektivnəs], *s.* **1.** Inefficacité *f*. **2.** Manque *m* de force (d'un argument, etc.).

ineffectual [ine'fektjuəl], *a.* **1.** (a) (Effort, raisonnement) inefficace. (b) Qui donne une impression de faiblesse; terne. **2.** *I. person,* personne incapable; velléitaire *mf*. **-ally,** *adv.* Inefficacement.

ineffectualness [ine'fektjuəlnəs], *s.* Inefficacité *f*.

inefficacious [inefi'keiʃəs], *a.* (Remède) inefficace, sans effet.

inefficacy [in'efikəsi], *s.* Inefficacité *f*.

inefficiency [ine'fiʃənsi], *s.* **1.** Inefficacité *f* (des mesures qu'on avait prises, etc.). **2.** Incapacité (professionnelle); incompétence *f*, insuffisance *f*.

inefficient [ine'fiʃənt], *a.* **1.** (Of a measure, etc.) Inefficace. **2.** (Of pers.) Incapable, incompétent. **-ly,** *adv.* **1.** Inefficacement. **2.** Sans compétence.

inelastic [ini'lastik], *a.* Inélastique; raide; qui ne prête pas.

inelasticity [inilas'tisiti], *s.* **1.** Inélasticité *f*. **2.** Raideur *f* (d'esprit, de caractère).

inelegance [in'elegəns], *s.* Inélégance *f*.

inelegant [in'elegənt], *a.* **1.** Inélégant; sans élégance. **2.** (Goût, etc.) peu délicat, fruste. **-ly,** *adv.* Sans élégance.

ineligible [in'elidʒibl], *a.* (a) (Candidat) inéligible. (b) Indigne d'être choisi; *F:* peu acceptable, peu désirable, inacceptable.

ineluctable [ine'lʌktəbl], *a.* Inéluctable, inévitable. **-ably,** *adv.* Inéluctablement.

inept [in'ept], *a.* **1.** Déplacé; mal à propos. **2.** (Of remark, etc.) Inepte, absurde. **-ly,** *adv.* Ineptement; stupidement.

ineptitude [in'eptitjuːd], *s.* **1.** Manque *m* de justesse, d'à-propos (d'une observation). **2.** Ineptitude for sth., to do sth., inaptitude *f* à qch., à faire qch. **3.** Ineptie *f*, sottise *f*.

ineptness [in'eptnəs], *s.* = INEPTITUDE I, 2.

inequality [iniː'kwɔliti], *s.* **1.** Inégalité *f*. **2.** Irrégularité *f* (*pl*), rugosité *f* (du sol); variabilité *f* (du climat).

inequitable [in'ekwitəbl], *a.* Inéquitable; peu équitable. **-ably,** *adv.* Inéquitablement, injustement.

ineradicable [ini'radikəbl], *a.* Indéracinable, inextirpable.

inert [in'əːrt], *a.* **1.** Inerte. **2.** *Ch:* (Gaz) inactif, inerte.

inertia [i'nəːrʃja], *s.* **1.** *Ph:* (a) Inertie *f*. Moment of inertia, moment *m* d'inertie. (b) Force *f* d'inertie. **2.** (Of pers.) Inertie; paresse *f*.

inertness [i'nəːrtnəs], *s.* Inertie *f*, inactivité *f*.

inescapable [ines'keipəbl], *a.* Inéluctable.

inestimable [in'estiməbl], *a.* Inestimable, incalculable, inappréciable.

inevitable [in'evitəbl], *a.* (a) Inévitable, inéluctable. (b) Fatal, -als; obligé. The *i.* hour, l'heure fatale. **-ably,** *adv.* Inévitablement, inéluctablement; fatalement.

inexact [ineg'zakt], *a.* Inexact. **-ly,** *adv.* Inexactement.

inexactitude [ineg'zaktitjuːd], *s.* **1.** Inexactitude *f*. **2.** Erreur *f*.

inexcusable [ineks'kjuːzəbl], *a.* Inexcusable; sans excuse; impardonnable. **-ably,** *adv.* Inexcusablement.

inexhaustible [ineg'zɔːstibl], *a.* Inépuisable; (source) intarissable. **-ibly,** *adv.* Inépuisablement, intarissablement.

inexorable [in'eksɔrəbl], *a.* Inexorable. **-ably,** *adv.* Inexorablement.

inexpedience [ineks'piːdiəns], **inexpediency** [ineks'piːdiənsi], *s.* Inopportunité *f* (of, de).

inexpedient [ineks'piːdiənt], *a.* Inopportun, malavisé.

inexpensive [ineks'pensiv], *a.* Peu coûteux; bon marché; (qui ne coûte) pas cher. **-ly,** *adv.* (A) bon marché; à bon compte.

inexpensiveness [ineks'pensivnəs], *s.* Bon marché, bas prix (de qch.).

inexperience [ineks'piəriəns], *s.* Inexpérience *f*.

inexperienced [ineks'piəriənst], *a.* **1.** Inexpérimenté. *I. in doing sth.,* malhabile à faire qch. **2.** Inaverti. *I. eye,* œil inexercé.

inexpert [ineks'pəːrt], *a.* Inexpert, maladroit; peu habile (in, à). **-ly,** *adv.* Maladroitement.

inexpiable [in'ekspiəbl], *a.* Inexpiable.

inexplicable [in'eksplikəbl], *a.* Inexplicable. **-ably,** *adv.* Inexplicablement.

inexpressible [ineks'presibl], *a.* Inexprimable; (charme) indicible. **-ibly,** *adv.* Indiciblement.

inexpressive [ineks'presiv], *a.* (Geste, mot) inexpressif; sans expression; (visage) fermé.

inexpugnable [ineks'pʌgnəbl], *a.* (Forteresse) inexpugnable.

inextinguishable [ineks'tiŋgwiʃəbl], *a.* Inextinguible.

inextricable [in'ekstrikəbl], *a.* Inextricable. **-ably,** *adv.* Inextricablement.

infallibility [infali'biliti], *s.* Infaillibilité *f*.

infallible [in'falibl], *a.* Infaiilible. **-bly,** *adv.* Infailliblement.

infamous ['infəməs], *a.* **1.** Infâme; (conduite) abominable; (homme) noté d'infamie. **2.** *Jur:* Infamant.

infamy ['infəmi], *s.* Infamie *f*.

infancy ['infənsi], *s.* **1.** (a) Première enfance; bas âge. (b) *F:* Débuts *mpl*, première période, enfance (d'un art). **2.** *Jur:* Minorité *f*.

infant ['infənt], *s.* **1.** Enfant *mf* en bas âge; tout(e) petit(e) enfant; nourrisson *m*. Newly-born *i.,* nouveau-né *m*, nouveau-née *f*. Infant mortality, mortalité infantile. *Sch:* Infant class, the infants, classe enfantine. **2.** *Jur:* Mineur, -eure.

infanticide[1] [in'fantisaid], *s.* (Pers.) Infanticide *mf*.

infanticide[2], *s.* (Crime *m* d')infanticide *m*.

infantile ['infəntail], *a.* **1.** (Esprit) d'enfant; (raisonnement) enfantin. **2.** (Maladie) infantile.

infantry ['infəntri], s. Infanterie f. *Four hundred infantry*, quatre cents fantassins.

infantryman, pl. **-men** ['infəntrimən, -men], s.m. Soldat d'infanterie ; fantassin.

infatuate [in'fatjueit], v.tr. **1.** Infatuer, affoler (qn). **2.** Enticher, engouer (qn) *(with,* de).

infatuated, a. Infatué, entiché. *To become, be, infatuated with* s.o., s'infatuer, s'engouer, s'enticher, de qn ; avoir un béguin pour qn.

infatuation [infatju'eiʃ(ə)n], s. Infatuation f, engouement m.

infect [in'fekt], v.tr. **1.** Infecter, corrompre, vicier (l'air, les mœurs, etc.). **2.** *Med:* Contaminer, contagionner. *Infected with the plague,* atteint de la peste. *F: To infect* s.o. *with an opinion,* inculquer une opinion à qn.

infection [in'fekʃ(ə)n], s. Infection f, contagion f ; *Med:* contamination f.

infectious [in'fekʃəs], a. **1.** (Air) infect, pestilentiel. **2.** (a) *(Of disease)* Infectieux. (b) *F: I. laughter,* rire contagieux, communicatif.

infectiousness [in'fekʃəsnəs], s. Nature infectieuse (d'une maladie) ; *F:* contagion f (du rire, etc.).

infelicitous [infi'lisitəs], a. *(Of event, expression, etc.)* Malheureux ; fâcheux.

infer [in'fəːr], v.tr. (inferred) **1.** To infer sth. from sth., inférer, déduire, arguer, qch. de qch. It is inferred that . . ., on suppose que. . . . **2.** Impliquer.

inference ['infərəns], s. *Log:* **1.** Inférence f. By inference, par induction. **2.** Déduction f, conclusion f. To draw an inference from sth., tirer une conclusion, une conséquence, de qch.

inferential [infə'renʃ(ə)l], a. Déductif.

inferior [in'fiəriər], **1.** a. Inférieur. To be inferior to s.o. in learning, in merit, être inférieur à qn en science, par le mérite. To be in no way inferior to s.o., ne le céder en rien à qn. *Typ:* Inferior letter, petite lettre inférieure. **2.** s. (a) Inférieur m. (b) *Adm: etc:* Subordonné, -ée ; subalterne m. **-ly,** adv. Inférieurement.

inferiority [infiːəri'ɔriti], s. Infériorité f *(to,* par rapport à).

infernal [in'fəːrnəl], a. **1.** Infernal, -aux ; des enfers. The infernal regions, les régions infernales ; l'enfer m. **2.** *F:* (a) Infernal, abominable, diabolique. (b) *(Intensive)* (Chaleur, etc.) d'enfer. Infernal row, bruit infernal. **-ally,** adv. *F: It is i. hot,* il fait une chaleur d'enfer. *It is i. lonely here,* on se sent diablement seul ici.

inferno, pl. **-os** [in'fəːrno, -ouz], s. Enfer m.

infertile [in'fəːrtail], a. (a) (Terrain) infertile, infécond ; (esprit) stérile. (b) (Œuf) clair.

infertility [infər'tiliti], s. Infertilité f, infécondité f.

infest [in'fest], v.tr. *(Of vermin, etc.)* Infester.

infidel ['infidəl], a. & s. **1.** *Hist:* Infidèle (mf). **2.** *Pej:* Incroyant, -ante.

infidelity [infi'deliti], s. **1.** Infidélité f (en matière de religion). **2.** Infidélité, déloyauté f (d'un serviteur, etc.).

infiltrate [in'filtreit], **1.** v.tr. (a) Infiltrer (un fluide) *(into,* dans). (b) *(Of liquid)* Infiltrer, imprégner (une substance) ; pénétrer dans (une substance). **2.** v.i. S'infiltrer.

infiltration [infil'treiʃ(ə)n], s. Infiltration f *(through,* à travers). *(Of troops, etc.) To advance, progress, by i.,* s'infiltrer.

infinite ['infinit]. **1.** a. Infini. (a) Illimite ; sans bornes. *Mth:* Infinite series, série infinie. (b) *To have* **i.** *trouble in doing sth.,* avoir une peine infinie, infiniment de peine, à faire qch. (c) [in'fainait] *Gram:* Verb infinite, formes

substantives du verbe. **2.** s. The Infinite, l'infini m. **-ly,** adv. Infiniment.

infinitesimal [infini'tesiməl], a. Infinitésimal, -aux. Infinitesimal calculus, calcul infinitésimal. *F: I. majority,* majorité infime.

infinitive [in'finitiv], a. & s. *Gram:* Infinitive (mood), (mode) infinitif (m). In the infinitive, à l'infinitif.

infinitude [in'finitjuːd], s. = INFINITY I.

infinity [in'finiti], s. **1.** Infinité f, infinitude f (de l'espace, etc.). **2.** *Mth: etc:* Infini m. To infinity, à l'infini.

infirm [in'fəːrm], a. **1.** *(Of pers.)* Infirme, débile. **2.** (Esprit) irrésolu, flottant. To be infirm of purpose, avoir une volonté flottante, débile.

infirmary [in'fəːrməri], s. **1.** Infirmerie f (d'une école, etc.). **2.** Hôpital m, -aux.

infirmity [in'fəːrmiti], s. **1.** (a) Infirmité f, débilité f. (b) Infirmité ; affection particulière. **2.** Infirmity of purpose, faiblesse f de caractère ; irrésolution f.

inflame [in'fleim]. **1.** v.tr. Mettre le feu à, enflammer ; allumer (les désirs). *Med:* Enflammer (une plaie). **2.** v.i. (a) S'enflammer ; prendre feu. (b) *Med:* S'enflammer.

inflammability [inflamə'biliti], s. Inflammabilité f.

inflammable [in'flaməbl], a. (a) Inflammable. (b) *(Of pers., crowd)* Prompt à s'échauffer.

inflammation [inflə'meiʃ(ə)n], s. **1.** (a) Inflammation f (d'un combustible). (b) Inflammation, excitation f (des esprits). **2.** *Med:* Inflammation. Inflammation of the lungs, fluxion f de poitrine.

inflammatory [in'flamətəri], a. (Discours) incendiaire.

inflate [in'fleit], v.tr. **1.** Gonfler. **2.** (a) *Com:* Grossir, charger (un compte). (b) Hausser, faire monter (les prix). (c) *Pol.Ec:* To inflate the currency, recourir à l'inflation. **inflated,** a. **1.** (Ballon, etc.) gonflé. *F: (Of pers.)* Inflated with pride, bouffi, gonflé, d'orgueil. **2.** (Prix) exagéré. **3.** *F:* (Style) enflé, boursouflé, bouffi.

inflater [in'fleitər], s. Pompe f (pour pneus).

inflation [in'fleiʃ(ə)n], s. **1.** (a) Gonflement m. (b) Hausse f (des prix). (c) Inflation of the currency, inflation f fiduciaire. **2.** Enflure f (du style).

inflect [in'flekt], v.tr. **1.** Fléchir, courber (en dedans). To i. a ray, infléchir un rayon. **2.** *Gram:* Donner des inflexions à (un mot). **3.** (a) Moduler (la voix). (b) *Mus:* Altérer (une note).

inflection [in'flekʃ(ə)n], s. = INFLEXION.

inflexibility [infleksi'biliti], s. Inflexibilité f.

inflexible [in'fleksibl], a. Inflexible ; (courage) inébranlable ; (morale) rigide. **-ibly,** adv. Inflexiblement, rigidement.

inflexion [in'flekʃ(ə)n], s. **1.** Inflexion f ; fléchissement m (du corps, d'un ressort). **2.** *Gram:* Inflexion, flexion f (d'un mot). **3.** (a) Inflexion (de la voix). (b) *Mus:* Altération f (d'une note).

inflexional [in'flekʃən(ə)l], a. *(Of language)* Flexionnel.

inflict [in'flikt], v.tr. To inflict a wound on s.o., faire une blessure à qn. To i. suffering on s.o., faire subir, occasionner, du chagrin à qn. *Jur:* To inflict a punishment, a fine, on s.o., infliger une punition, une amende, à qn. *F: To inflict oneself, one's company, on s.o.,* imposer sa compagnie à qn.

infliction [in'flikʃ(ə)n], s. **1.** *Jur:* Infliction f (d'une peine). **2.** Peine infligée ; châtiment m.

inflorescence [inflɔ'resəns], s. *Bot:* **1.** Inflorescence f. **2.** (a) Floraison f. (b) Fleurs fpl (d'un arbre, etc.).

inflow ['inflou], *s.* = INFLUX. Inflow pipe, arrivée *f* d'eau.

inflowing ['inflouiŋ], *a.* Entrant; qui entre.

influence[1] ['influəns], *s.* (*a*) Influence *f* (*upon, sur*). **To exert an influence, to bring influence to bear, on** s.o., exercer une influence sur qn; agir sur qn. **To bring every influence to bear,** mettre tout en jeu (*in order to,* pour). **To have great influence over** s.o., avoir beaucoup d'influence sur qn. (*Of thg*) **To have an influence on** sth., agir, influer, sur qch. **Under the influence of** fear, sous le coup de la peur. **Under the influence of drink,** sous l'empire de la boisson. *Jur :* Undue influence, intimidation *f.* (*b*) (*Of pers.*) **To have influence,** (i) avoir de l'influence, de l'autorité; (ii) avoir de la protection, du crédit. **To have far-reaching** i., *F :* avoir le bras long. **Man of influence,** homme influent.

influence[2], *v.tr.* (*Of pers.*) Influencer (qn); (*of thg*) influer sur (qch.).

influential [influ'enʃ(ə)l], *a.* Influent. **To be** i., avoir de l'influence; *F :* avoir le bras long.

influenza [influ'enza], *s. Med :* Grippe *f*, influenza *f.*

influx ['inflʌks], *s.* (*a*) Entrée *f*, affluence *f* (d'un cours d'eau, etc.). (*b*) Affluence (de gens); invasion *f* (d'idées nouvelles).

inform [in'fɔ:rm]. **I.** *v.tr.* (*a*) **To inform** s.o. of sth., informer, avertir, aviser, qn de qch.; faire savoir qch. à qn; faire part de qch. à qn. **To keep** s.o. **informed of what is happening,** tenir qn au courant de ce qui se passe. **To** i. **the police,** avertir la police. *I regret to have to* i. *you that* . . ., j'ai le regret de vous annoncer, de vous faire savoir, que. . . . (*b*) **To inform** s.o. **on, about,** sth., renseigner qn sur qch. *Until we are better informed,* jusqu'à plus ample informé. **2.** *v.i. Jur :* **To inform against** s.o., dénoncer qn.

informal [in'fɔ:rməl], *a.* **I.** (*a*) *Jur :* En dehors des règles; irrégulier. (*b*) (Réunion, séance) en dehors des statuts; (renseignement) officieux. **2.** (Dîner, etc.) sans cérémonie, en famille. **-ally,** *adv.* **I.** (*a*) En dehors des règles; irrégulièrement. (*b*) A titre non-officiel. **2.** Sans cérémonie; sans formalités.

informality [infɔr'maliti], *s.* Absence *f* de formalité, de cérémonie.

informant [in'fɔ:rmənt], *s.* **I.** Informateur, -trice. **2.** *Jur : Adm :* Déclarant, -ante.

information [infɔr'meiʃ(ə)n], *s.* **I.** Renseignements *mpl,* informations *fpl.* *To give* s.o. i. *on* sth., renseigner qn sur qch. *I am sending you for your information* . . ., je vous envoie à titre d'information. . . . **To get information about** sth., se renseigner sur qch. **Piece of information,** indication *f,* renseignement. **Information bureau,** bureau de renseignements. **2.** Instruction *f,* savoir *m,* connaissances *fpl.* **3.** Dénonciation *f* (*against* s.o., contre qn); délation *f* (de qn). **To lay an information against** s.o. **with the police,** dénoncer qn à la police; informer contre qn.

informative [in'fɔ:rmətiv], **informatory** [in'fɔ:rmətəri], *a.* Instructif. *Cards :* **Informatory bid,** annonce *f* d'indication.

informer [in'fɔ:rmər], *s.* Dénonciateur, -trice; *F :* mouchard *m. Jur :* **Common informer,** délateur *m.* **To turn informer,** dénoncer ses complices.

infraction [in'frakʃ(ə)n], *s.* Infraction *f* (d'un droit); transgression *f.* **Infraction of the law,** violation *f* de la loi, infraction à la loi.

infra dig ['infra'dig], *adj.phr. F :* Au-dessous de la dignité de (qn); au-dessous de soi. **It would be infra dig to** . . ., ce serait se manquer à soi-même que de. . . .

infra-red [infra'red], *a. Opt :* Infra-rouge.

infrequent [in'fri:kwənt], *a.* Rare; peu fréquent. **-ly,** *adv.* Rarement.

infringe [in'frindʒ]. **I.** *v.tr.* Enfreindre, violer (une loi, un serment); transgresser (une règle). **To infringe a patent,** (i) contrefaire un objet breveté; (ii) empiéter sur un brevet. **2.** *v.ind.tr.* **To infringe upon** s.o.'s rights, empiéter sur les droits de qn.

infringement [in'frindʒmənt], *s.* **I.** Infraction *f* (d'un règlement); violation *f* (d'une loi, d'un droit). **2. Infringement of a patent, of copyright,** contrefaçon *f.*

infuriate [in'fjuərieit], *v.tr.* Rendre furieux. **infuriated,** *a.* Furieux; en fureur.

infuse [in'fju:z], *v.tr.* **I. To infuse courage into** s.o., infuser du courage à qn. **2.** Infuser, faire infuser (le thé, des herbes).

infuser [in'fju:zər], *s.* (*Device*) Infusoir *m.* **Tea infuser,** œuf *m* à thé.

infusible [in'fju:zibl], *a.* Infusible; non fusible.

infusion [in'fju:ʒ(ə)n], *s.* (*a*) Infusion *f* (d'une tisane). (*b*) Tisane *f,* infusé *m,* infusion.

infusoria [infju'sɔ:ria], *s.pl. Prot :* Infusoires *m.*

infusorial [infju'sɔ:riəl], *a.* **Infusorial earth,** (i) *Geol :* terre *f* à infusoires; (ii) *Com :* terre d'infusoires.

infusorian [infju'sɔ:riən], *s. Prot :* Infusoire *m.*

ingenious [in'dʒi:njəs], *a.* Ingénieux. **-ly,** *adv.* Ingénieusement.

ingeniousness [in'dʒi:njəsnəs], *s.* = INGENUITY.

ingenuity [indʒe'nju:iti], *s.* Ingéniosité *f.*

ingenuous [in'dʒenjuəs], *a.* **I.** Franc, *f.* franche; sincère. **2.** (Regard) ingénu, candide; naïf, *f.* naïve. **-ly,** *adv.* **I.** Franchement, sincèrement. **2.** Ingénument, naïvement.

ingenuousness [in'dʒenjuəsnəs], *s.* Ingénuité *f,* naïveté *f,* candeur *f.*

ingle [iŋgl], *s. Lit :* Foyer *m* (domestique). **The ingle-nook,** le coin du feu.

inglorious [in'glɔ:riəs], *a.* **I.** (*Of pers.*) Humble, obscur. **2.** (Combat) honteux, inglorieux. **-ly,** *adv.* Inglorieusement.

ingot ['ingət], *s.* Lingot *m* (d'or); saumon *m* (d'étain).

ingrained [in'greind], *a.* (*a*) **Hands ingrained with coal-dust,** mains encrassées de poussier de charbon. *I. dirt,* charbon, etc., qui est entré dans les pores. (*b*) **Ingrained prejudices,** préjugés enracinés.

ingratiate [in'greiʃieit], *v.tr.* **To ingratiate oneself with** s.o., s'insinuer dans les bonnes grâces de qn. **ingratiating,** *a.* Insinuant, prévenant.

ingratiatory [in'greiʃiətəri], *a.* (Sourire, ton) insinuant.

ingratitude [in'gratitju:d], *s.* Ingratitude *f.*

ingredient [in'gri:diənt], *s.* Ingrédient *m;* élément *m.*

ingress ['ingres], *s.* Entrée *f. Jur :* **Free ingress,** droit *m* de libre accès.

ingression [in'greʃ(ə)n], *s.* Ingression *f,* incursion *f.*

ingrowing[1] ['ingrouiŋ], *a.* (Ongle) incarné.

ingrowing[2], *a. Med :* Incarnation *f* (des ongles).

ingrown ['ingroun], *a.* **I.** (Ongle) incarné. **2.** (Préjugé) invétéré.

inguinal ['iŋgwinəl], *a.* Inguinal, -aux.

ingulf [in'gʌlf], *v.tr.* = ENGULF.

ingurgitate [in'gə:rdʒiteit], *v.tr.* Ingurgiter, avaler.

inhabit [in'habit], *v.tr.* Habiter, habiter dans (une maison).

inhabitable [in'habitəbl], *a.* Habitable.

inhabitant [in'habitənt], *s.* Habitant, -ante.
inhalation [inha'leiʃ(ə)n], *s.* (*a*) Inhalation *f.*
(*b*) Aspiration *f.*
inhale [in'heil], *v.tr.* (*a*) *Med:* Inhaler (de
l'éther, etc.). (*b*) Aspirer, humer (un parfum);
F: avaler (la fumée d'une cigarette).
inhaler [in'heilər], *s.* (*Device*) Inhalateur *m.*
inharmonious [inhɑːr'mounjəs], *a.* Inharmonieux; peu harmonieux.
inherent [in'hiːərənt], *a.* Inhérent, naturel (*in,*
à). *I. defect,* vice propre. **-ly,** *adv.* Par
inhérence. *I. lazy,* né paresseux.
inherit [in'herit], *v.tr.* (*a*) Hériter de (qch.);
succéder à (une fortune). (*b*) *To i. sth. from s.o.,*
hériter qch. de qn. *To i. a characteristic from
one's father,* tenir un trait caractéristique de son
père. *Inherited taint,* tache héréditaire.
inheritable [in'heritəbl], *a.* (*a*) (Titre) dont on
peut hériter. (*b*) (Maladie) transmissible à ses
descendants.
inheritance [in'heritəns], *s.* 1. Succession *f.*
Law of inheritance, droit successif. 2. Patrimoine *m,* héritage *m.*
inheritor [in'heritər], *s.* Héritier *m.*
inhibit [in'hibit], *v.tr.* (*a*) *To inhibit s.o. from
doing sth.,* interdire, défendre, à qn de faire qch.
(*b*) *Ecc:* Suspendre, interdire (un prêtre).
2. *Psy:* Inhiber (un sentiment).
inhibition [inhi'biʃ(ə)n], *s.* 1. (*a*) Défense
expresse; prohibition *f.* (*b*) *Ecc:* Interdiction *f*
(d'un prêtre). 2. *Psy:* Inhibition *f.*
inhibitory [in'hibitəri], *a.* 1. (Mandat) prohibitif. 2. *Psy: Physiol:* Inhibitory reflex,
réflexe inhibiteur.
inhospitable [in'hɔspitəbl], *a.* Inhospitalier.
inhuman [in'hjuːmən], *a.* Inhumain; brutal,
-aux. **-ly,** *adv.* Inhumainement.
inhumanity [inhju'maniti], *s.* Inhumanité *f,*
cruauté *f.*
inhumation [inhju'meiʃ(ə)n], *s.* Inhumation *f;*
enterrement *m.*
inhume [in'hjuːm], *v.tr.* Inhumer, enterrer.
inimical [i'nimik(ə)l], *a.* (*a*) Ennemi, hostile.
(*b*) Défavorable, contraire (*to,* à).
inimitable [i'nimitəbl], *a.* Inimitable.
iniquitous [i'nikwitəs], *a.* Inique. **-ly,** *adv.*
Iniquement.
iniquity [i'nikwiti], *s.* Iniquité *f.*
initial[1] [i'niʃəl]. 1. *a.* (*a*) Initial, -aux; premier.
Disease in the initial stages, maladie au début de
son évolution. (*b*) *Typ:* Initial letter, lettre
initiale; (*ornamental*) lettrine *f.* 2. *s.* (*Usu. pl.*)
Initials, initiales *f;* parafe *m;* (*of supervisor, etc.*)
visa *m.* **-ally,** *adv.* Au commencement; au début.
initial[2], *v.tr.* (initialled) Parafer (une correction);
viser (un acte, etc.).
initiate[1] [i'niʃiet], *a. & s.* Initié, -ée.
initiate[2] [i'niʃieit], *v.tr.* 1. Commencer, ouvrir
(des négociations); lancer, amorcer (une mode).
To i. a reform, prendre l'initiative d'une réforme.
Jur: To initiate proceedings against s.o., instituer des poursuites contre qn. 2. Initier. To
initiate s.o. into a secret, initier qn à un secret.
initiation [iniʃi'eiʃ(ə)n], *s.* 1. Commence-
ment(s) *m,* début(s) *m* (d'une entreprise). 2. Initiation *f* (*into,* à).
initiative [i'niʃiətiv], *s.* Initiative *f.* To take the
initiative in doing sth., prendre l'initiative pour
faire qch. To do sth. on one's own initiative,
faire qch. de sa propre initiative, par soi-même.
initiator [i'niʃieitər], *s.* Initiateur, -trice; lanceur *m* (d'une mode, etc.).
initiatory [i'niʃiətəri], *a.* (*Of rite*) Initiateur,
-trice.

inject [in'dʒekt], *v.tr.* Injecter. *To i. s.o.'s arm
with morphia,* faire une piqûre de morphine au
bras de qn.
injection [in'dʒekʃ(ə)n], *s.* Injection *f.* To give
s.o. a hypodermic injection, faire à qn une
injection sous-cutanée, une piqûre. Rectal
injection, lavement *m.*
injector [in'dʒektər], *s.* *Mch:* Injecteur *m;*
appareil *m* alimentaire.
injudicious [indʒu'diʃəs], *a.* Peu judicieux;
malavisé.
injunction [in'dʒʌŋkʃ(ə)n], *s.* 1. Injonction *f,*
ordre *m.* To give s.o. strict injunctions to do sth.,
enjoindre strictement, formellement, à qn de
faire qch. 2. *Jur:* Arrêt *m* de suspension; arrêt
de sursis.
injure ['indʒər], *v.tr.* 1. Nuire à, faire tort à
(qn); endommager (la réputation de qn); léser
(qn). *To i. s.o.'s interests,* compromettre, léser, les
intérêts de qn. 2. (*a*) Blesser (qn); faire mal à
(qn). *To i. oneself,* se blesser; se faire du mal.
Fatally injured, blessé mortellement. (*b*) Endommager, gâter (qch.). *To i. one's health,* altérer sa
santé. *To i. one's eyes,* se gâter la vue. **injured,**
a. 1. (*Of pers.*) Offensé. The injured party,
l'offensé, -ée; *Jur:* la partie lésée. In an injured
tone (of voice), d'une voix offensée. 2. (Bras,
etc.) blessé ou estropié. *s.* The injured, les
blessés *m;* (*from accident*) les accidentés *m.*
injurious [in'dʒuəriəs], *a.* 1. Nuisible, pernicieux (*to,* à). Injurious to the health, nocif;
nuisible à la santé. 2. (Langage) injurieux,
offensant.
injuriousness [in'dʒuəriəsnəs], *s.* Nocivité *f.*
injury ['indʒəri], *s.* 1. Tort *m,* mal *m.* *Jur:*
Lésion *f.* To do s.o. an injury, faire du tort
à qn. To the injury of s.o., au détriment de qn.
2. (*a*) Blessure *f* (au corps); *Med:* Lésion. To
do oneself an injury, se blesser; se faire du mal.
There were no personal injuries, il n'y a pas eu
d'accident de personne. (*b*) Dommage *m,* dé-
gât *m;* *Nau: Mch:* avarie *f.* To do injury to
sth., faire subir une avarie à (une machine, etc.).
injustice [in'dʒʌstis], *s.* 1. Injustice *f.* *Flagrant
cases of injustice,* des injustices flagrantes. 2. *You
do him an i.,* vous êtes injuste envers lui.
ink[1] [iŋk], *s.* 1. Encre *f.* Copying ink, encre à
copier. Copying-ink pencil, crayon *m* à copier.
Printing ink, printer's ink, encre d'impression.
Indian ink, encre de Chine. Written in ink, écrit
à l'encre. 2. Noir *m* (de seiche); sépia *f.*
'ink-bag, *s.* *Moll:* Glande *f* du noir (de la
seiche). 'ink-bottle, *s.* Bouteille *f* à encre.
'ink-feed, *s.* Conduit *m* (de stylo). 'ink-
well, *s.* Encrier *m* (pour pupitre).
ink[2], *v.tr.* 1. Noircir d'encre; tacher d'encre.
2. *Typ:* Encrer (les lettres). **ink in, over,** *v.tr.*
Tracer à l'encre (des lignes faites au crayon).
inking, *s.* *Typ:* Encrage *m* (des rouleaux).
inkling ['iŋkliŋ], *s.* Soupçon *m.* To give s.o. an
inkling of sth., faire entrevoir qch. à qn. *He
had an i. of the truth,* il entrevit, entrevoyait, la
vérité. *Without having the least i. of . . .,* sans
se douter le moins du monde de. . . .
inkpot ['iŋkpɔt], *s.* Encrier *m.*
inkstand ['iŋkstand], *s.* Grand encrier (avec
pose-plumes).
inky ['iŋki], *a.* 1. Taché d'encre; (doigt) barbouillé d'encre. 2. Noir comme (de) l'encre.
inlaid ['inleid], *a.* See INLAY[2].
inland ['inland]. 1. *s.* (L')intérieur *m* (d'un pays).
2. *Attrib.* Intérieur. Inland sea, mer intérieure.
Inland trade, commerce intérieur. Inland produce, produits indigènes, produits du pays.

Inland money order, mandat sur l'intérieur. The
Inland Revenue, le fisc. 3. adv. To go, march, i.,
pénétrer dans les terres.

inlay[1] ['inlei, in'lei], s. **I.** Incrustation f (de
nacre, etc.). Marquetry inlay, marqueterie f.
2. Bookb: Encartage m.

inlay[2] [in'lei], v.tr. (inlaid) **I.** Incruster (with, de);
marqueter (une table, etc.). Metalw: Damas-
quiner (une épée, etc.). **2.** Bookb: Encarter
(des illustrations).

inlet ['inlet], s. **I.** Arrivée f, admission f (de
vapeur, I.C.E: d'essence, etc.). Inlet valve,
soupape f d'admission. **2.** (a) Orifice m d'admission (de vapeur, etc.); ouïe f (de ventilateur).
(b) Inlets into a lake, débouchés m d'un lac.

inmate ['inmeit], s. (a) Habitant, -ante (d'une
maison). (b) Pensionnaire mf (d'un asile, etc.);
hôte m (d'un hospice).

inmost ['inmoust], a. Le plus profond. Our
inmost thoughts, nos pensées les plus secrètes.

inn [in], s. **I.** Auberge f; (in town) hôtellerie f.
2. Jur: The Inns of Court, les (quatre) Écoles f
de droit.

innate [i(n)'neit], a. Inné, infus; (bon sens)
foncier, naturel.

innavigable [i(n)'navigəbl], a. (Mer) innavigable.

inner ['inər]. **I.** a. Intérieur; (écorce, etc.)
interne, de dedans. On the inner side, à l'intérieur, en dedans. Inner meaning, sens intime
(d'un passage). To belong to the i. circle, compter
parmi les initiés. **2.** s. Premier cercle autour de
la mouche (d'une cible).

innermost ['inərmoust], a. = INMOST.

innings ['ininz], s.sg. (pl. inv.) Cr: Tour m de
batte. He had a long innings, (i) il est resté
longtemps au guichet; (ii) F: il a fourni une
longue carrière. F: My innings now! à mon
tour!

innkeeper ['inki:pər], s. Aubergiste mf; hôtelier,
-ière.

innocence ['inosəns], s. (a) Innocence f (d'un
accusé). (b) Naïveté f, innocence, candeur f. To
pretend innocence, faire l'innocent. F: To pose
as Miss Innocence, faire sa petite sainte nitouche.

innocent ['inosənt], a. **I.** (a) Innocent; pas
coupable. (b) F: Dépourvu, vierge (of, de). To
be quite i. of Latin, ne pas savoir un mot de latin.
2. (a) Pur; sans péché; innocent. s. The Holy
Innocents, les (Saints) Innocents. (b) Naïf,
f. naïve; sans malice; innocent. To put on an
innocent air, faire l'innocent; avoir l'air de
ne pas y toucher. **-ly,** adv. Innocemment.

innocuity [ino'kju:iti], s. Innocuité f.

innocuous [i'nokjuəs], a. Inoffensif. **-ly,** adv.
Inoffensivement.

innocuousness [i'nokjuəsnəs], s. Innocuité f.

innovate ['inoveit], v.i. Innover (in, à, en, dans).

innovating, a. Innovateur, -trice.

innovation [ino'veiʃ(ə)n], s. **I.** Innovation f,
changement m. To make innovations in sth.,
apporter des changements à qch.

innovator ['inoveitər], s. (In)novateur, -trice.

innoxious [i(n)'nokʃəs], a. Inoffensif.

innuendo, pl. **-oes** [inju'endo, -ouz], s. Allusion
(malveillante). To throw out innuendoes against
s.o., F: jeter des pierres dans le jardin de qn.

innumerable [i(n)'nju:mərəbl], a. Innombrable;
sans nombre.

inobservance [inob'zə:rvəns], s. **I.** Inattention f.
2. Inobservance f (d'une loi, etc.); inobservation f (d'une promesse).

inoccupation [inokju'peiʃ(ə)n], s. Inoccupation f.

inoculable [i'nokjuləbl], a. Med: Inoculable.

inoculate [i'nokjuleit], v.tr. Med: (a) To i. s.o.
with a germ, to i. a germ into s.o., inoculer un
germe à qn. (b) To i. s.o. against a disease, F: to
inoculate s.o., inoculer, vacciner, qn (contre une
maladie).

inoculation [inokju'leiʃ(ə)n], s. Med: Inoculation f.

inodorous [in'oudərəs], a. (Gaz, etc.) inodore.

inoffensive [ino'fensiv], a. **I.** (Homme) inoffensif. **2.** (Odeur, etc.) sans rien de désagréable;
(observation, etc.) qui n'a rien d'offensant. **-ly,**
adv. Inoffensivement.

inoperative [in'opərativ], a. Jur: etc: Inopérant.

inopportune [in'opɔrtju:n], a. Inopportun;
intempestif; (propos) hors de saison. **-ly,** adv.
Inopportunément; mal à propos. To come i.,
tomber mal.

inopportuneness [in'opɔrtju:nnəs], **inoppor-**
tunity [inopər'tju:niti], s. Inopportunité f.

inordinate [in'ɔ:rdinet], a. **I.** Démesuré, excessif, immodéré. **2.** To keep i. hours, rentrer à
des heures indues. **-ly,** adv. Démesurément,
excessivement.

inorganic [inɔ:r'ganik], a. Inorganique.

inoxidizable [inoksi'daizəbl], a. Inoxydable.

input ['input], s. **I.** Mch: Input of steam,
prise f de vapeur. **2.** Énergie ou puissance
absorbée; consommation f (d'une machine).
W.Tel: Aerial input, puissance reçue, collectée,
par l'antenne.

inquest ['inkwest], s. Enquête f. Esp. Coroner's
inquest, enquête judiciaire par-devant jury (en
cas de mort violente ou suspecte).

inquire [in'kwaiər], v.tr. & i. **I.** To i. the price
of sth., s'informer du prix de qch. To i. the way
of s.o., demander son chemin à qn. 'Inquire
within,' "s'adresser ici." **2.** To inquire about
sth., s'enquérir de, se renseigner sur, qch.; aller
aux informations. To inquire after s.o., after
s.o.'s health, s'informer de la santé de qn; demander des nouvelles de qn. To inquire for s.o.,
demander qn, demander si qn est là. To inquire
into sth., faire des recherches, des investigations,
sur qch.; examiner (une question). **inquiring,**
a. Investigateur, -trice; curieux. **-ly,** adv.
D'un air, d'un ton, interrogateur. To glance i. at
s.o., interroger qn du regard.

inquiry [in'kwaiəri], s. **I.** Enquête f. To conduct, hold, an inquiry, procéder à une enquête.
To set up an inquiry regarding sth., ouvrir une
enquête sur qch. To open a judicial inquiry,
ouvrir une instruction. To remand a case for
further inquiry, renvoyer une affaire à plus
ample informé. **2.** Demande f de renseignements.
To make inquiries, aller aux informations, aux
renseignements. To make inquiries about s.o.,
s'informer de, se renseigner sur, qn. To make
inquiries after s.o., s'enquérir de qn. Inquiry
office, bureau m de renseignements.

inquisition [inkwi'ziʃ(ə)n], s. (a) Recherche f,
investigation f. (b) The Inquisition, l'Inquisition f.

inquisitive [in'kwizitiv], a. Curieux; questionneur, -euse. **-ly,** adv. Avec curiosité.

inquisitiveness [in'kwizitivnəs], s. Curiosité f
indiscrète.

inquisitor [in'kwizitər], s. Rel.H: Inquisiteur m.

inquisitorial [inkwizi'tɔ:riəl], a. Inquisitorial,
-aux.

inroad ['inroud], s. (a) Mil: Incursion f,

invasion *f*, irruption *f*. (b) *F:* Empiétement *m* (sur la liberté, les droits, de qn). **To make inroads upon one's capital,** entamer, ébrécher, son capital.

inrush ['inrʌʃ], *s.* Irruption *f* (d'eau, *F:* de voyageurs, etc.); entrée soudaine (d'air).

insalubrious [insa'l(j)u:briəs], *a.* Insalubre; malsain.

insalubrity [insa'l(j)u:briti], *s.* Insalubrité *f.*

insane [in'sein], *a.* **1.** (*Of pers.*) Fou, *f.* folle; (esprit) dérangé, aliéné. *To become i.,* tomber en démence; perdre la raison. **2.** *F:* (Désir, etc.) insensé, fou. **-ly,** *adv.* Follement; comme un insensé.

insanitary [in'sanitəri], *a.* Insalubre; malsain.

insanity [in'saniti], *s. Med:* Folie *f*, démence *f*, aliénation mentale.

insatiability [inseiʃə'biliti], **insatiableness** [in'seiʃəblnəs], *s.* Insatiabilité *f.*

insatiable [in'seiʃəbl], *a.* Insatiable. **-ably,** *adv.* Insatiablement.

inscribable [in'skraibəbl], *a Geom:* Inscriptible (*in,* dans).

inscribe [in'skraib], *v.tr.* **1.** Inscrire, graver. **2.** Dédier (une œuvre littéraire). **3.** *Geom:* Inscrire (un polygone) (*in,* dans). **4. Inscribed stock,** rente inscrite (au Grand-Livre).

inscription [in'skripʃ(ə)n], *s.* **1.** Inscription *f* (sur un monument, etc.); légende *f* (d'une pièce de monnaie). **2.** Dédicace *f* (d'un livre, etc.).

inscrutable [in'skru:təbl], *a.* (Dessein) impénétrable, inscrutable; (visage) fermé.

insect ['insekt], *s.* Insecte *m.* **'insect-eater,** *s.* *Z:* Insectivore *m.* **'insect-powder,** *s.* Poudre *f* insecticide.

insecticidal [insekti'said(ə)l], *a.* Insecticide.

insecticide [in'sektisaid], *a. & s.* Insecticide (*m*).

insectivorous [insek'tivorəs], *a.* Insectivore.

insecure [insi'kjuər], *a.* **1.** (Verrou, etc.) peu sûr; (glace, etc.) peu solide; (pont) mal affermi; (espoir) incertain. **2.** Exposé au danger. **-ly,** *adv.* Peu solidement; sans sûreté; sans sécurité.

insecurity [insi'kjuəriti], *s.* Insécurité *f.*

insensate [in'senset], *a.* **1.** (Corps) insensible. **2.** (Désir) insensé.

insensibility [insensi'biliti], *s.* **1.** Défaillance *f.* **2.** Insensibilité *f* (*to,* à); indifférence *f* (*to,* pour).

insensible [in'sensibl], *a.* **1.** Insensible, imperceptible. **2.** Sans connaissance. *To become i.,* perdre connaissance; s'évanouir; tomber en syncope. **3.** Insensible, indifférent (à la douleur, etc.). **-ibly,** *adv.* Insensiblement, imperceptiblement; petit à petit; peu à peu.

insensitive [in'sensitiv], *a.* Insensible (*to,* à).

inseparable [in'sepərəbl], *a.* Inséparable (*from,* de).

insert [in'sə:rt], *v.tr.* **1.** Insérer. *To i. a clause in an act,* insérer, introduire, une clause dans un acte. *El.E:* *To i. a condenser in the circuit,* intercaler un condensateur dans le circuit. **2.** Introduire, enfoncer (la clef dans la serrure). **Wheel with inserted teeth,** roue à dents rapportées.

insertion [in'sə:rʃ(ə)n], *s.* **1.** Insertion *f*, introduction *f* (de qch. dans qch.). **2.** (*a*) *Typ:* Insertion. Insertion mark, renvoi *m.* (*b*) *Needlew:* Entre-deux *m inv*, entretoile *f* (de dentelle, etc.). (*c*) *Dressm:* Incrustation *f.*

inset¹ ['inset], *s.* **1.** Flux *m* (de la marée). **2.** *Bookb:* (*a*) Encart *m*, carton *m* (de 4 ou 8 pages). (*b*) (*Leaf*) Encartage *m.* **3.** *Typ:* Gravure *f* hors texte; hors-texte *m inv*; médaillon *m* (en coin de page). **4.** *Dressm:* Incrustation *f.*

inset² [in'set], *v.tr.* (*p.p. & p.t.* inset: insetting)

1. *Bookb:* Encarter (des feuillets). **2.** *Typ:* Insérer en cartouche, en médaillon. **'Inset map** (*in corner of larger one*), cartouche *m*, papillon *m.* **'Inset portrait** (*in corner of larger illustration*), portrait en médaillon. **3.** *Dressm:* Insérer (une pièce d'étoffe, etc.). **4.** *Typ:* Renfoncer (les lignes, un alinéa).

inside ['in'said]. **I.** *s.* (*a*) Dedans *m*, (côté) intérieur *m* (d'un habit, etc.). *The door opens from the inside,* la porte s'ouvre de dedans. *On the inside,* en dedans, au dedans. *To walk on the i. of the pavement,* prendre le haut du pavé. *F:* **To know the inside of an affair,** connaître les dessous d'une affaire. *To turn sth. inside out,* retourner qch. comme un gant. *F:* **To turn everything inside out,** mettre tout sens dessus dessous. *The wind has blown my umbrella i. out,* le vent a retourné mon parapluie. *F:* **To know sth. inside out,** savoir qch. à fond; connaître qch. comme sa poche. (*b*) Intérieur (d'une maison, etc.). (*c*) *F:* **To have pains in one's inside,** avoir des douleurs d'entrailles; avoir mal au ventre ou à l'estomac. (*d*) *Fb:* **The insides,** les centres *m.* **2.** *a.* ['insaid] Intérieur, d'intérieur; (mesure, etc.) dans œuvre. **Inside-drive car,** voiture à conduite intérieure. **To be on the inside track,** (i) *Rac:* tenir la corde; (ii) *F:* être avantagé. *Fb:* **Inside left,** intérieur *m* gauche. *F:* **Inside information,** renseignements privés. **I speak with inside knowledge,** ce que je dis, je le sais de bonne source. **3.** *adv.* [in'said] (*a*) Intérieurement; (fermé) en dedans. *There is nothing i.,* il n'y a rien dedans. *F:* **Walk inside!** entrez! **Inside and out** ['inside'aut], any place (*b*) *F. & U.S:* **To do sth. inside of three hours,** faire qch. en moins de trois heures. **4.** *prep.* A l'intérieur de; dans l'intérieur de; dans.

insidious [in'sidiəs], *a.* Insidieux; (raisonnement) captieux, astucieux. **-ly,** *adv.* Insidieusement, astucieusement.

insidiousness [in'sidiəsnəs], *s.* Caractère insidieux (d'une maladie, etc.); astuce *f* (d'une question, etc.).

insight ['insait], *s.* **1.** Perspicacité *f*; pénétration *f.* **2.** Aperçu *m.* **To get an insight into sth.,** prendre un aperçu de qch.

insignia [in'signiə], *s.pl.* Insignes *m* (de la royauté, etc.).

insignificance [insig'nifikəns], *s.* Insignifiance *f.*

insignificant [insig'nifikənt], *a.* Insignifiant; de peu d'importance; (personne) sans importance.

insincere [insin'si:ər], *a.* (*a*) Peu sincère; de mauvaise foi. (*b*) (*Of smile, etc.*) Faux, *f.* fausse. **-ly,** *adv.* Sans sincérité.

insincerity [insin'seriti], *s.* Manque *m* de sincérité; fausseté *f.*

insinuate [in'sinjueit], *v.tr.* Insinuer. **1.** *To insinuate oneself into s.o.'s favour,* s'insinuer dans les bonnes grâces de qn. **2.** Donner adroitement à entendre, à comprendre (que); laisser entendre (que). **insinuating,** *a.* Insinuant.

insinuation [insinju'eiʃ(ə)n], *s.* Insinuation *f.*

insinuative [in'sinjueitiv], *a.* Insinuant.

insipid [in'sipid], *a.* Insipide, fade; (sourire) bête. **-ly,** *adv.* Insipidement, fadement.

insipidity [insi'piditi], *s.* Insipidité *f*; fadeur *f.*

insist [in'sist], *v.i.* Insister. **1.** *To insist (up)on a point,* insister, appuyer, sur un point. *To i. upon one's innocence,* affirmer son innocence avec insistance. *He insisted that it was so,* il maintenait, soutenait, qu'il en était ainsi. **2. To insist**

on doing sth., insister pour faire qch. ; vouloir absolument faire qch. **To insist that s.o. shall do** sth., on s.o.'s **doing sth.**, exiger de qn qu'il fasse qch. *He insists on your coming*, il insiste pour que vous veniez. I **insist upon it**, je le veux absolument. I **insist on obedience**, je veux être obéi.

insistence [in'sistəns], **insistency** [in sistənsi], s. Insistance *f*. (a) **His insistence upon his innocence**, ses protestations *f* d'innocence. (b) **Insistence in doing sth.**, insistance à faire qch.

insistent [in'sistənt], a. Qui insiste ; (créancier) importun. *Don't be too i.*, n'appuyez pas trop, n'insistez pas trop. **-ly,** adv. Instamment ; avec insistance.

insobriety [inso'braiəti], s. Insobriété *f*.

insociable [in'souʃəbl], a. = UNSOCIABLE.

insolation [inso'leiʃ(ə)n], s. 1. *Phot :* Insolation *f*. 2. *Med :* Coup *m* de soleil ; insolation.

insolence ['insoləns], s. Insolence *f* (to, envers).

insolent ['insolənt], a. Insolent (to, envers). **-ly,** adv. Insolemment.

insolubility [insolju'biliti], s. 1. Insolubilité *f*, indissolubilité *f*. 2. Insolubilité (d'un problème).

insoluble [in'soljubl], a. 1. (Sel) insoluble, indissoluble. 2. (Problème) insoluble, irrésoluble.

insolvency [in'solvənsi], s. (a) Insolvabilité *f*. (b) Déconfiture *f* ; faillite *f*.

insolvent [in'solvənt]. 1. a. (Débiteur) insolvable, en (état de) faillite **To become insolvent,** faire faillite. **To declare oneself insolvent,** *Com :* déposer son bilan. 2. s. Débiteur *m* insolvable ; *Com :* failli *m*.

insomnia [in'somniə], s. Insomnie *f*.

insomuch [inso'mʌtʃ], adv. *Lit :* 1. **Insomuch as** = INASMUCH AS. 2. **Insomuch that . . .,** à un tel point que. . . .

inspan [in'span], v.tr. (In S. Africa) Atteler (un wagon, une paire de bœufs).

inspect [in'spekt], v.tr. 1. Examiner de près (qch.) ; inspecter (une école, une fabrique) ; contrôler (les livres d'un négociant) ; vérifier, inspecter (une machine, etc.). 2. Faire l'inspection (d'un régiment) ; passer (un régiment) en revue.

inspection [in'spekʃ(ə)n], s. 1. Inspection *f* ; vérification *f*, examen *m* (de documents) ; contrôle *m* (de billets). **To subject sth. to a close inspection,** soumettre qch. à un examen minutieux. **Inspection hole,** orifice *m* de visite. 2. *Mil :* Revue *f*. **Kit inspection,** revue d'effets, de détail.

inspector [in'spektər], s. Inspecteur *m* (des écoles, de police, etc.). **Woman inspector,** inspectrice *f*. **Road inspector,** (agent) voyer *m*. **Inspector of weights and measures,** vérificateur *m* des poids et mesures. **Inspector general,** inspecteur général. *S.a.* FACTORY, SANITARY, TICKET-INSPECTOR.

inspectorate [in'spektəret], s. Corps *m* d'inspecteurs ; ''l'inspection *f*.''

inspectorship [in'spektərʃip], s. Inspectorat *m*.

inspectress [in'spektres], s.f. Inspectrice.

inspiration [inspi'reiʃ(ə)n], s. 1. Aspiration *f*, inspiration *f* (d'air). *To take a deep i.*, respirer profondément. 2. Inspiration. *Divine i.*, inspiration divine. *To do sth.* **by inspiration,** faire qch. d'inspiration. *To take one's i. from s.o.*, s'inspirer de qn. **To have a sudden inspiration,** avoir une inspiration subite.

inspire [in'spaiər], v.tr. 1. Aspirer, inspirer (l'air, etc.). 2. *To be inspired to do sth.*, être inspiré de faire qch. **To inspire a feeling in,**

into, s.o., inspirer un sentiment à qn. **To inspire** s.o. **with confidence, with fear,** inspirer (de la) confiance, de la terreur, à qn. *To i. s.o. with respect*, imposer le respect à qn. **To inspire** respect, inspirer, imprimer, le respect. *Journ :* Inspired paragraph, note *f* d'origine officieuse.

inspirit [in'spirit], v.tr. Animer, encourager.

inspiriting, a. Encourageant ; qui donne du courage ; (musique) entraînante ; (air) vivifiant.

instability [insta'biliti], s. Instabilité *f*.

install [in'stɔːl], v.tr. 1. Installer (un évêque, qn dans une fonction). *F : To i. oneself in a place*, s'installer dans un endroit. 2. (a) Installer (l'électricité, etc.). (b) Monter (un atelier, etc.).

installation [instə'leiʃ(ə)n], s. 1. Installation *f* (d'un évêque, etc.). 2. Installation (de l'éclairage électrique, de l'eau à tous les étages) ; montage *m* (d'un poste de T.S.F., etc.).

instalment [in'stɔːlmənt], s. 1. Acompte *m* ; versement partiel. *To pay an i.*, verser un acompte, faire un versement. **To pay in, by, instalments,** échelonner les payements. **To buy on the instalment system,** acheter à tempérament. 2. **Instalment of a publication,** livraison *f* d'un ouvrage qui paraît en fascicules.

instance¹ ['instəns], s. 1. **At the instance of . . .,** sur l'instance de . . ., à la demande de. . . . 2. Exemple *m*, cas *m*. *An isolated i.*, un cas isolé. **In many instances,** dans bien des cas. **For instance,** par exemple. *As an i. of his honesty, I may mention . . .*, en témoignage de son intégrité je pourrais citer. . . . 3. (a) **Court of first instance,** tribunal *m* de première instance. (b) **In the first instance,** en (tout) premier lieu. *In the present i., in this i.*, dans le cas actuel ; dans cette circonstance.

instance², v.tr. 1. Citer en exemple. 2. **To be instanced in . . .,** être illustré par. . . . *This instinct is instanced in young children*, cet instinct se retrouve chez les jeunes enfants.

instancy ['instənsi], s. Urgence *f* (d'un besoin) ; imminence *f* (du danger).

instant¹ ['instənt], a. 1. Instant, pressant, urgent. 2. (*Abbr.* inst.) Courant ; de ce mois. **On the 5th instant,** le 5 courant. 3. (a) Immédiat. *This calls for i. remedy*, il faut y remédier sur-le-champ. (b) Imminent. **-ly,** adv. Tout de suite ; sur-le-champ ; à l'instant.

instant², s. Instant *m*, moment *m*. *I expect him every i.*, je l'attends d'un instant à l'autre. **Come this instant,** venez à l'instant, sur-le-champ. **The instant he arrived,** (i) au moment où il arriva ; (ii) dès, aussitôt, qu'il fut arrivé.

instantaneous [instən'teinjəs], a. Instantané. *Phot :* Instantaneous exposure, instantané *m*. **-ly,** adv. Instantanément.

instanter [in'stantər], adv. *F :* Immédiatement ; sur-le-champ.

instauration [instɔː'reiʃ(ə)n], s. Restauration *f*, rénovation *f*.

instead [in'sted]. 1. *Prep.phr.* **Instead of sth.,** au lieu de qch. *To stand i. of sth.*, tenir lieu de qch. **Instead of s.o.,** à la place de qn. **Instead of doing sth.,** au lieu de faire qch. *I. of our having profited by it . . .*, au lieu que nous y ayons gagné quelque chose. . . . 2. adv. Au lieu de cela. *If he can't come*, **take me instead,** s'il ne peut pas venir, prenez-moi à sa place.

instep ['instep], s. 1. Cou-de-pied *m*. 2. *Bootm :* Cambrure *f* (d'un soulier).

instigate ['instigeit], v.tr. 1. Instiguer, inciter, provoquer (*to do sth.*, à faire qch. de mal). 2. *To i. revolt*, provoquer, susciter, la révolte.

instigation [insti'geiʃ(ə)n], s. Instigation *f*,

incitation *f.* **At, by, the instigation of s.o.,** à l'instigation de qn.

instigator ['instigeitər], *s.* **1.** Instigateur, -trice (d'un meurtre, etc.). **2.** Fauteur *m*, auteur *m* (de troubles).

instil(l) [in'stil], *v.tr.* (instilled) **1.** Instiller (un liquide) (*into*, dans). **2.** Faire pénétrer ("goutte à goutte"). **To instil an idea into s.o.,** infiltrer une idée dans l'esprit de qn.

instillation [insti'leiʃ(ə)n], *s.* **1.** Instillation *f* (d'un liquide). **2.** Inspiration *f* (d'une idée); inculcation *f* (d'une vertu).

instinct[1] ['instiŋkt], *s.* Instinct *m.* **By instinct, from instinct,** par instinct.

instinct[2] [in'stiŋkt], *a.* **Instinct with life,** doué, plein, de vie.

instinctive [in'stiŋktiv], *a.* Instinctif. **-ly,** *adv.* D'instinct; instinctivement.

institute[1] ['institjuːt], *s.* Institut *m.*

institute[2], *v.tr.* **1.** Instituer, établir. *Newly instituted office,* poste de création récente. **2.** *Jur:* Ordonner, instituer (une enquête); procéder à (une enquête). **To institute (legal) proceedings, an action, against s.o.,** intenter un procès à qn.

institution [insti'tjuːʃ(ə)n], *s.* **1.** Institution *f*, établissement *m* (d'une loi, etc.). **2.** Institution; chose établie. *Afternoon tea has become an i.,* the five-o'clock est passé dans les mœurs. **3. Charitable institution,** institution, établissement, œuvre *f*, de charité.

instruct [in'strʌkt], *v.tr.* **1.** Instruire (qn). **To instruct s.o. in sth., how to do sth.,** instruire qn en, dans, qch.; enseigner qch. à qn. **2.** (*a*) **To instruct s.o. of a fact, of what is going on,** instruire qn d'un fait, de ce qui se passe. (*b*) *Jur:* **To instruct a solicitor,** donner ses instructions à un avoué. **3. To instruct s.o. to do sth.,** charger qn de faire qch.; mander à qn de faire qch.

instruction [in'strʌkʃ(ə)n], *s.* **1.** Instruction *f*, enseignement *m.* *Aut:* **Driving instruction,** leçons *fpl* de conduite. **2.** *Usu. pl.* Indications *f*, instructions, ordres *m*; (*to sentry, etc.*) consigne *f.* *To give s.o. instructions how to use sth.,* donner des indications, des conseils *m*, à qn sur le mode d'emploi de qch. *To go beyond one's instructions,* aller au delà des ordres reçus. *Mil: To act according to instructions,* se conformer à la consigne. *Adm: etc:* **Book of standing instructions,** règlement *m*; *F:* guide-âne *m.*

instructive [in'strʌktiv], *a.* Instructif. **-ly,** *adv.* D'une manière instructive.

instructor [in'strʌktər], *s.* Maître (enseignant). *Mil:* Instructeur *m.* *Aut:* **Driving instructor,** professeur *m* de conduite.

instrument[1] ['instrumənt], *s.* Instrument *m.* **1.** *The Government, through its instruments . . .,* le Gouvernement, par ses intermédiaires *m* . . ., par ses organes *m.* . . . **2.** (*a*) Instrument, appareil *m*, mécanisme *m.* (*b*) **Musical instrument,** instrument de musique. *Wind, stringed, i.,* instrument à vent, à cordes. **3.** (*a*) *Jur:* Acte *m* juridique; instrument; document officiel. (*b*) *Com:* **Negotiable instrument,** effet *m* de commerce; titre *m* au porteur.

instrument[2], *v.tr.* *Mus:* Orchestrer, instrumenter (un opéra, etc.).

instrumental [instru'ment(ə)l], *a.* **1.** Contributif (*to*, à). **To be instrumental to a purpose, in doing sth.,** contribuer à un but, à faire qch. **2. Instrumental music,** musique instrumentale. **Instrumental performer,** instrumentiste *m.*

instrumentalist [instru'mentəlist], *s.* *Mus:* Instrumentiste *m.*

instrumentality [instrumen'taliti], *s.* **Through the instrumentality of s.o.,** avec le concours de qn, par l'intermédiaire de qn, à l'aide de qn.

instrumentation [instrumen'teiʃ(ə)n], *s.* *Mus:* Instrumentation *f.*

insubmersible [insʌb'məːrsibl], *a.* Insubmersible.

insubordinate [insʌ'bɔːrdinet], *a.* Insubordonné.

insubordination [insʌbɔːrdi'neiʃ(ə)n], *s.* Insubordination *f*, insoumission *f.*

insubstantial [insʌb'stanʃəl], *a.* Insubstantiel. **1.** Imaginaire. **2.** (*a*) (Corps) immatériel. (*b*) *I. food,* aliments creux.

insuccess [insʌk'ses], *s.* Insuccès *m.*

insufferable [in'sʌfərəbl], *a.* Insupportable, intolérable. **-ably,** *adv.* Insupportablement, intolérablement.

insufficiency [insʌ'fiʃənsi], *s.* Insuffisance *f.*

insufficient [insʌ'fiʃənt], *a.* Insuffisant. **-ly,** *adv.* Insuffisamment.

insular ['insjulər]. **1.** *a.* (*a*) (Climat) insulaire. (*b*) D'insulaire. *F:* **Insular mind,** esprit étroit, borné, rétréci. **2.** *s.* Insulaire *mf.*

insularism ['insjularizm], **insularity** [insju'lariti], *s.* Étroitesse *f* de vues.

insulate ['insjuleit], *v.tr.* **1.** Faire une île, un îlot, de (qch.). *To i. sth. from its proper surroundings,* isoler qch. de son (propre) milieu. **2.** (*a*) *El:* Isoler (un fil, etc.). (*b*) Calorifuger (une chaudière). (*c*) *Cin:* Insonoriser (la camera).

insulating, *a.* **1.** *El:* Isolant; isolateur, -trice. **Insulating tape,** ruban *m* d'isolement; chatterton *m.* **2.** *Mch: etc:* (Enveloppe) calorifuge.

insulation [insju'leiʃ(ə)n], *s.* **1.** Détachement *m* (d'une île d'avec un continent, etc.); isolement *m* (*from*, de). **2.** *El:* (*a*) Isolement, isolation *f* (des câbles). (*b*) Isolant *m.* Bakelite i., isolant bakélisé. **3. Heat insulation,** isolation calorifuge. **4.** *Cin:* Insonorisation *f* (de la camera, etc.).

insulator ['insjuleitər], *s.* **1.** *El:* (*a*) (Material) Isolant *m.* (*b*) (Device) Isolateur *m*, isoloir *m.* **2. Heat insulator,** matière isolante, calorifuge. **3.** (*a*) Tampon amortisseur (de moteur, etc.). (*b*) Godet *m* de support (de piano).

insulin ['insjulin], *s.* *Med:* Insuline *f.*

insult[1] ['insʌlt], *s.* Insulte *f*, affront *m*, indignité *f.* **To suffer, pocket, an insult,** boire un affront. **To add insult to injury,** doubler ses torts d'un affront.

insult[2] [in'sʌlt], *v.tr.* Insulter (qn); faire (une) insulte à (qn); faire affront, faire injure, à (qn).

insulting, *a.* Offensant, injurieux. *To use i. language to s.o.,* dire des injures, lancer des insultes, à qn.

insuperable [in'sjuːpərəbl], *a.* (Difficulté, etc.) insurmontable; (obstacle) infranchissable.

insurable [in'ʃuərəbl], *a.* Assurable.

insurance [in'ʃuərəns], *s.* **1.** (*a*) Assurance *f.* **Life insurance,** assurance sur la vie; assurance-vie *f.* **Third-party insurance,** assurance au tiers. **Employers' liability insurance,** assurance des patrons contre les accidents du travail. **Burglary insurance,** assurance-vol *f.* **To effect an insurance,** passer une assurance (*on*, sur). **To take out an insurance,** se faire assurer, s'assurer (*against*, contre). **Insurance company,** compagnie *f*, société *f*, d'assurance(s). (*b*) *F:* Prime *f* d'assurance. **2.** *Adm:* **State insurance,** prévoyance sociale; assurances sociales.

insure [in'ʃuər], *v.tr.* **1.** (i) Assurer, (ii) faire assurer (un navire, un mobilier). **To insure one's life,** s'assurer, se faire assurer, sur la vie.

2. (*a*) Garantir, assurer (le succès, etc.). (*b*) *To i. against a danger*, parer à un danger.

insurer [in'ʃuərər], *s. Com:* Assureur *m.*

insurgent [in'sə:rdʒənt], *a. & s.* Insurgé, -ée, révolté, -ée.

insurmountable [insər'mauntəbl], *a.* Insurmontable; (obstacle) infranchissable.

insurrection [insə'rekʃ(ə)n], *s.* Insurrection *f*, soulèvement *m*, émeute *f*. **To rise in insurrection**, s'insurger, se soulever.

insurrectionist [insə'rekʃənist], *s.* Émeutier *m*, insurgé, -ée.

insusceptible [insʌ'septibl], *a.* Insensible (*to*, à). *A mind i. to flattery*, un esprit insensible à la flatterie.

insweep ['inswi:p], *s.* Courbure *f* en dedans. *Aut:* Étranglement *m* (du châssis).

inswept ['inswept], *a. Aut:* (Châssis) étranglé, à avant rétréci.

intact [in'takt], *a.* Intact.

intaglio [in'taljo], *s. Lap:* Intaille *f*; (gravure) en creux.

intake ['inteik], *s.* **1.** Prise *f*, appel *m* (d'air); prise (d'eau, *El:* de courant); adduction *f*, admission *f* (de vapeur). **Intake valve**, soupape *f* d'admission. **2.** = INPUT 2.

intangibility [intandʒi'biliti], *s.* Intangibilité *f.*

intangible [in'tandʒibl], *a.* Intangible, impalpable. *Com:* **Intangible assets**, valeurs immatérielles.

integer ['intedʒər], *s. Mth:* Nombre entier.

integral ['integrəl]. **1.** *a.* (*a*) Intégrant. **To be an integral part of sth.**, faire corps avec qch. (*b*) *Mth:* **Integral calculus**, calcul intégral. (*c*) *Mec.E:* (Tige, etc.) solidaire (*with*, de). **Forged integral with . . .**, forgé d'une seule pièce avec. . . . **2.** *s. Mth:* Intégrale *f.* **-ally,** *adv.* Intégralement; en totalité.

integrate¹ ['integret], *a.* Intégral, -aux; entier.

integrate² ['integreit], *v.tr.* **1.** Compléter, rendre entier (qch. d'incomplet). **2.** *Mth:* Intégrer (une fonction).

integration [inte'greiʃ(ə)n], *s. Mth:* Intégration *f.*

integrity [in'tegriti], *s.* Intégrité *f.* **1. In its integrity**, en entier. **2.** Honnêteté *f*, probité *f.*

intellect ['intelekt], *s.* Intelligence *f*, esprit *m.* **Man of intellect**, homme intelligent, à l'esprit éclairé.

intellectual [inte'lektjuəl], *a. & s.* Intellectuel, -elle. **-ally,** *adv.* Intellectuellement.

intelligence [in'telidʒəns], *s.* **1.** Intelligence *f.* (*a*) Entendement *m*, sagacité *f.* (*b*) **To exchange a look of intelligence**, échanger un regard d'intelligence. **2.** Renseignement(s) *m(pl)*, avis *m*, nouvelle(s) *f(pl).* *Journ:* **Latest intelligence**, dernières nouvelles; informations *fpl* de la dernière heure. **Shipping intelligence**, mouvement *m* maritime. *Mil:* **Intelligence department, service**, service *m* des renseignements, des informations.

intelligent [in'telidʒənt], *a.* Intelligent; avisé. **-ly,** *adv.* Intelligemment; avec intelligence.

intelligentsia [inteli'dʒentsia, -'gen-], *s. Coll.* L'intelligence *f*, les gens intelligents.

intelligibility [intelidʒi'biliti] *s.* Intelligibilité *f.*

intelligible [in'telidʒibl], *a.* Intelligible. **-ibly,** *adv.* Intelligiblement.

intemperance [in'tempərəns], *s.* **1.** Intempérance *f.* **2.** Alcoolisme *m.*

intemperate [in'tempəret], *a.* **1.** (*Of pers.*) Intempérant, immodéré. **2.** Adonné à la boisson. **-ly,** *adv.* (Rire) immodérément; (boire) à l'excès.

intend [in'tend], *v.tr.* **1.** (*a*) **To intend doing sth.**,

to do sth.; **to intend sth.**, avoir l'intention de faire qch. **We intend no harm**, nous l'avons fait sans mauvaise intention. *I do not i. you any harm*, je ne vous veux pas de mal. **Was that intended?** était-ce fait avec intention, à dessein? (*b*) *I i. to be obeyed*, je veux être obéi. **2. To intend sth. for sth.**, destiner qch. à qch. *This remark is intended for you*, c'est à vous que cette observation s'adresse. **3.** (*a*) *I intended it for a compliment*, mon intention était de vous faire un compliment. (*b*) Vouloir dire; entendre. **intended,** *a.* **1.** (*a*) (Voyage, etc.) projeté. *My i. husband*, *F:* my intended, mon fiancé, mon prétendu. (*b*) **The intended effect**, l'effet voulu. **2.** Intentionnel; fait avec intention.

intendant [in'tendənt], *s.* Intendant *m.*

intense [in'tens], *a.* (*a*) Vif, *f.* vive; fort, intense. (*b*) *I. expression*, expression d'intérêt profond. (*c*) *F:* D'un sérieux exagéré. **-ly,** *adv.* (*a*) Excessivement. *I. blue eyes*, yeux d'un bleu très vif. *To hate s.o. i.*, haïr qn profondément. (*b*) (Vivre, regarder) avec intensité.

intenseness [in'tensnəs], *s.* Intensité *f* (du froid); force *f* (d'une passion); violence *f* (d'une douleur).

intensify [in'tensifai]. **1.** *v.tr.* Intensifier, augmenter; rendre plus fort, plus vif (un son); renforcer (une couleur). *Phot:* Renforcer (un cliché faible). **2.** *v.i.* Devenir plus intense.

intensity [in'tensiti], *s.* **1.** = INTENSENESS. **2.** *Ph: El: etc:* Intensité *f*, puissance *f* (de son, de courant). *Phot:* **Intensity of a negative**, densité *f* d'un cliché.

intensive [in'tensiv], *a.* Intensif. **-ly,** *adv.* Intensivement.

intent¹ [in'tent], *s.* Intention *f*, dessein *m*, but *m.* **With good intent**, dans une bonne intention. **With intent to defraud**, dans l'intention, dans le but, de frauder. **To do sth. with intent**, faire qch. de propos délibéré. **To all intents and purposes**, virtuellement; en fait.

intent², *a.* **1.** (*a*) **To be intent on sth.**, être tout entier à qch., être absorbé par qch. **To be intent on doing sth.**, être résolu, déterminé, à faire qch. (*b*) *To stand silent and i.*, se tenir silencieux et attentif. **2.** *Mind i. on learning*, esprit acharné à l'étude. **Intent gaze**, regard fixe, profond. **-ly,** *adv.* (Écouter) attentivement; (regarder) fixement, avec une attention soutenue.

intention [in'tenʃ(ə)n], *s.* Intention *f.* **1.** (*a*) Dessein *m.* *I have not the slightest i. to . . .*, je n'ai pas la moindre intention de . . ., je n'ai garde de. . . . **With the intention of being . . .**, dans l'intention d'être. . . . **To do sth. with the best (of) intentions**, faire qch. dans la meilleure intention. (*b*) But *m.* **With the intention of . . .**, dans le but de. . . . (*c*) *pl. F:* **To court a woman with honourable intentions**, courtiser une femme pour le bon motif. **To make known one's intentions**, se déclarer. **2.** *Surg:* Healing by the first, second, intention, réunion *f* par première, deuxième, intention.

intentional [in'tenʃən(ə)l], *a.* Intentionnel, voulu; fait exprès. **-ally,** *adv.* A dessein; exprès; intentionnellement; de propos délibéré.

-intentioned [in'tenʃənd], *a.* **Well-intentioned**, bien intentionné. **Ill-intentioned**, mal intentionné.

intentness [in'tentnəs], *s.* Contention *f* d'esprit; tension *f* d'esprit; attention soutenue (du regard).

inter [in'tə:r], *v.tr.* (interred) Enterrer, ensevelir (un mort).

interact [intər'akt], *v.i.* Réagir réciproquement. **interacting**, *a.* A action réciproque; à action conjuguée.

interallied [intər'alaid], *a.* Interallié.
interbreed [intər'bri:d]. **1.** *v.tr.* Croiser, entre-croiser (des races). **2.** *v.i.* S'entre-croiser.
intercalary [in'tə:rkələri], *a.* Intercalaire.
intercalate [in'tə:rkəleit], *v.tr.* Intercaler.
intercalation [intərkə'leiʃ(ə)n], *s.* Intercalation *f.*
intercede [intər'si:d], *v.i.* To intercede (with s.o.) for s.o., intercéder (auprès de qn) en faveur de qn, pour qn.
intercellular [intər'seljulər], *a.* Intercellulaire.
intercept [intər'sept], *v.tr.* Intercepter (la lumière, une lettre); arrêter (qn) au passage. *Tg: Tp:* Capter, intercepter (un message).
interception [intər'sepʃ(ə)n], *s.* Interception *f.* *Tg: Tp:* Captation *f* (de messages).
intercession [intər'seʃ(ə)n], *s.* Intercession *f.*
intercessor [intər'sesər], *s.* Intercesseur *m.*
interchange[1] ['intərtʃeindʒ], *s.* **1.** Échange *m* (de compliments); communication *f* (d'idées). *Rail:* Interchange service, correspondance *f.* **2.** Succession alternative, alternance *f* (du jour et de la nuit, etc.).
interchange[2] [intər'tʃeindʒ], *v.tr.* Échanger (des parties d'une machine, etc.). To *i.* the position of two things, changer deux choses de place; mettre l'une à la place de l'autre.
interchangeable [intər'tʃeindʒəbl], *a.* Inter-changeable, permutable.
intercommunicate [intərko'mju:nikeit], *v.i.* Communiquer. The prisoners *i.*, les prisonniers communiquent entre eux.
intercommunication [intərkomju:ni'keiʃ(ə)n], *s.* Communication *f* réciproque. (a) Échange mutuel. (b) Rapports *mpl* (entre prisonniers, etc.).
interconnected [intərko'nektid], *a.* **1.** (Chambres, etc.) en communication réciproque. *Av:* Interconnected rudders, gouvernails con-jugués. **2.** (Faits) intimement liés.
intercourse ['intərkɔ:rs], *s.* Commerce *m*, rela-tions *fpl*, rapports *mpl*. Business *i.*, rapports de commerce. Human *i.*, commerce du monde; relations humaines. To have, hold, intercourse with s.o., avoir des relations, des rapports, avec qn.
intercross [intər'krɔs]. **1.** *v.tr.* Entrecroiser. **2.** *v.i.* S'entrecroiser; s'entrelacer.
interdependent [intərdi'pendənt], *a.* Solidaire (with, de).
interdict[1] ['intərdikt], *s.* **1.** *Jur:* Défense *f*, interdiction *f.* **2.** *Ecc:* Interdit *m.* To lay a priest under an interdict, frapper d'interdit un prêtre.
interdict[2] [intər'dikt], *v.tr.* **1.** *Jur:* Interdire, prohiber. To *i.* s.o. from doing sth., interdire à qn de faire qch. **2.** *Ecc:* Frapper d'interdiction, interdire (un prêtre).
interdiction [intər'dikʃ(ə)n], *s.* Interdiction *f.*
interest[1] ['int(ə)rest], *s.* Intérêt *m.* **1.** *Com: etc:* (a) Participation *f.* To have an interest in the profits, participer aux bénéfices. To have a financial, a money, interest in sth., avoir des capitaux, être intéressé, dans qch. To give s.o. a joint *i.* in an affair, coïntéresser qn dans une affaire. (b) The shipping interest, les armateurs *m*; le commerce maritime. The Conservative in-terest, le parti conservateur. The landed in-terest, les propriétaires terriens. **2.** Avantage *m*, profit *m.* To act for, in, one's own interest(s), agir dans son intérêt. To act in s.o.'s interest(s), agir pour le compte de qn. To promote s.o.'s in-terest, prendre les intérêts de qn. **3.** *A:* Crédit *m*, influence *f.* **4.** To take, feel, an interest in s.o., in sth., s'intéresser à qn; prendre de l'intérêt

à qch. To take no (further) *i.* in sth., se désin-téresser de qch. Questions of public interest, questions qui agitent le grand public. **5.** To bear interest at 5%, porter intérêt à cinq pour cent. Simple, compound, interest, intérêts simples, composés. Shares that yield high *i.*, actions à gros rendement. *F:* To repay an injury with interest, rendre le mal avec usure.
interest[2], *v.tr.* **1.** Intéresser (s.o. in a business, qn à, dans, une affaire). **2.** Éveiller l'intérêt de (qn). To interest oneself, to be interested, in s.o., in doing sth., s'intéresser à qn, à faire qch. To be interested in painting, in music, s'occuper de peinture, de musique. **interested,** *a.* **1.** The interested parties, les parties intéressées; les intéressés *m.* *Jur:* Interested party, ayant droit *m*, *pl.* ayants droit. **2.** Interested motives, motifs intéressés. **3.** With an *i.* look, avec un regard d'intérêt; d'un air intéressé. **-ly,** *adv.* Avec intérêt. **interesting,** *a.* Intéressant.
interfere [intər'fiːər], *v.i.* **1.** (a) (Of pers.) S'in-gérer, s'immiscer, intervenir (dans une affaire); s'interposer (dans une querelle). Don't *i.* with, in, what does not concern you, ne vous mêlez pas de ce qui ne vous regarde pas. (b) Toucher (with, à). Don't *i.* (with it)! n'y touchez pas! Don't *i.* with the children! laissez les enfants tranquilles! (c) (Of thg) To interfere with (sth.), gêner (la circulation, etc.). Nothing must *i.* with the course of justice, rien ne doit entraver le cours de la justice. It interferes with my plans, cela dérange mes plans. **2.** *Ph:* (Of light-waves, etc.) Inter-férer. *W.Tel:* Brouiller. **interfering,** *a.* **1.** (a) (Of pers.) Importun, tracassier. (b) He is so *i.!* il est si tatillon! il fourre son nez partout! **2.** *Ph:* (Of rays, etc.) Interférent.
interference [intər'fiːərəns], *s.* **1.** Intervention *f*; intrusion *f*, ingérence *f* (in, dans). **2.** *Ph:* Interfé-rence *f.* *W.Tel:* Effet *m* parasitaire; brouil-lage *m.*
interim ['intərim]. **1.** *adv.* Entre temps; en attendant. Ad interim, par intérim, provisoire-ment. **2.** *s.* Intérim *m.* In the *i.*, dans l'intérim; sur ces entrefaites. **3.** *a.* (Rapport, professeur) intérimaire. *S.a.* DIVIDEND.
interior [in'tiːəriər]. **1.** *a.* (a) Intérieur. *Geom:* Interior angle, angle interne. (b) *I.* feelings, sentiments intimes. **2.** *s.* (a) Intérieur *m* (du pays, des terres). (b) *Art:* (Tableau *m* d')intérieur.
interject [intər'dʒekt], *v.tr.* To *i.* a remark, lancer une remarque. "Nonsense!" he interjected, "quelle bêtise!" s'écria-t-il.
interjection [intər'dʒekʃ(ə)n], *s.* Interjection *f.*
interlace [intər'leis]. **1.** *v.tr.* (a) Entrelacer; entrecroiser (des fils). (b) Entremêler (with, de). **2.** *v.i.* S'entrelacer, s'entrecroiser.
interlard [intər'lɑːrd], *v.tr.* (Entre)larder, en-tremêler (un discours, ses récits) (with, de).
interleaf, *pl.* **-leaves** ['intərliːf, -liːvz], *s.* Feuille blanche (intercalée dans un livre); page inter-foliée.
interleave [intər'liːv], *v.tr.* Interfolier (un livre).
interline [intər'lain], *v.tr.* **1.** (a) Interligner, entre-ligner. (b) Écrire (une traduction, etc.) entre les lignes. **2.** Mettre une doublure inter-médiaire (à un vêtement, etc.).
interlinear [intər'liniər], *a.* (Traduction) inter-linéaire.
interlink [intər'liŋk]. **1.** *v.tr.* Enchaîner, relier, rattacher (with, à). With hands interlinked, les mains entrelacées. **2.** *v.i.* Se relier; s'agrafer.
interlinking, *s.* Raccordement *m*; jonction *f.*
interlock [intər'lɔk]. **1.** *v.tr.* Emboîter. *Rail:* Enclencher (des aiguilles). **2.** *v.i.* (a) S'entre-

mêler, s'entrelacer, s'entrecroiser. (*b*) *Mec.E*: S'enclencher; s'emboîter. **interlocking,** *s.* Enclenchement *m*, emboîtement *m*; engrènement *m*.

interlocutor [intər'lɔkjutər], *s.* Interlocuteur *m*.

interlocutory [intər'lɔkjutəri], *a. Jur:* (Arrêt) interlocutoire, préjudiciel.

interlocutress [intər'lɔkjutres], **interlocutrix** [intər'lɔkjutriks], *s.f.* Interlocutrice.

interloper ['intərloupər], *s.* (*a*) Intrus, -use. (*b*) Commerçant *m* marron.

interlude ['intərlju:d], *s.* Intermède *m.*

intermarriage [intər'maredʒ], *s.* Intermariage *m.*

intermarry [intər'mari], *v.i.* (*a*) Se marier les uns avec les autres, entre eux. (*b*) Se marier entre parents.

intermediary [intər'mi:djəri], *a. & s.* Intermédiaire (*m*).

intermediate [intər'mi:djet]. **I.** *a.* (*a*) Intermédiaire; (*of time*) intermédiat. *Sch:* Intermediate course, cours moyen (d'algèbre, etc.). (*b*) *Sch:* Intermediate examination in arts, examen *m* intermédiaire (entre la "matriculation" et l'examen du diplôme). **2.** *s.* (*Pers.*) Intermédiaire *m*.

interment [in'tə:rmənt], *s.* Enterrement *m*, inhumation *f.*

interminable [in'tə:rminəbl], *a.* Interminable; sans fin. **-ably,** *adv.* Interminablement; sans fin.

intermingle [intər'miŋgl]. **I.** *v.tr.* Entremêler; mélanger. **2.** *v.i.* S'entremêler, se mêler, se confondre (*with*, avec).

intermission [intər'miʃ(ə)n], *s.* **I.** Interruption *f*, trêve *f.* *Med:* Intermission *f* (de la fièvre). **2.** *Th:* *U.S:* Entr'acte *m.*

intermit [intər'mit], *v.tr.* (**intermitted**) Interrompre, suspendre (ses travaux, etc.).

intermittence [intər'mitəns], *s.* **I.** Intermittence *f* (d'une source, etc.). **2.** Pause *f*; arrêt momentané.

intermittent [intər'mitənt], *a.* Intermittent. **-ly,** *adv.* Par intervalles, par intermittence.

intern [in'tə:rn], *v.tr.* Interner (des troupes, des étrangers).

internal [in'tə:rn(ə)l], *a.* **I.** (Puits, circuit) intérieur; (angle, maladie) interne. **2.** (*a*) (Valeur) intrinsèque; (preuve) intime. (*b*) Secret, intime. **3.** (*a*) *I. trade*, commerce intérieur. *A prey to i. wars*, en proie aux guerres intestines. (*b*) *Sch:* Internal student, étudiant interne. **-ally,** *adv.* Intérieurement.

international [intər'naʃən(ə)l]. **I.** *a.* International, -aux. International law, droit international; droit des gens. **2.** *s. Sp:* (Joueur) international. **-ally,** *adv.* Internationalement.

internecine [intər'ni:sain], *a.* **Internecine war,** guerre *f* d'extermination réciproque.

internee [intə:r'ni:], *s.* Interné, -ée.

internment [in'tə:rnmənt], *s.* Internement *m.*

interphone ['intərfoun], *s.* Téléphone *m* de communication entre les services (d'une usine).

interplanetary [intər'planetəri], *a.* Interplanétaire.

interplay ['intərplei], *s.* Effet *m* réciproque.

interpolate [in'tə:rpoleit], *v.tr.* Interpoler; intercaler.

interpolation [intə:rpo'leiʃ(ə)n], *s.* Interpolation *f.*

interpose [intər'po:uz]. **I.** *v.tr.* Interposer. **2.** *v.i.* S'interposer, intervenir.

interposition [intərpo'ziʃ(ə)n], *s.* **I.** Interposition *f.* **2.** Intervention *f.*

interpret [in'tə:rpret], *v.tr.* **I.** Interpréter,

expliquer (un texte); déchiffrer (des signaux). **2.** *Th: Mus:*ʼ Interpréter (un rôle, une composition). **3.** Interpréter, traduire. *Abs.* Faire l'interprète.

interpretation [intə:rpre'teiʃ(ə)n], *s.* Interprétation *f.*

interpreter [in'tə:rpretər], *s.* Interprète *mf.*

interregnum, *pl.* **-ums, -a** [intər'regnəm, -əmz, -a], *s.* Interrègne *m.*

interrelated [intərri'leitid], *a.* (Faits) intimement reliés, en relation mutuelle, en corrélation.

interrelation [intərri'leiʃ(ə)n], *s.* Relation mutuelle; corrélation *f.*

interrogate [in'terogeit], *v.tr.* Interroger, questionner (qn).

interrogation [intero'goiʃ(ə)n], *s.* Interrogation *f*; interrogatoire *m* (d'un prévenu). **Point, mark, note, of interrogation,** point *m* d'interrogation.

interrogative [intə'rɔgətiv], *a.* Interrogateur, -trice. **Interrogative pronoun,** pronom interrogatif. **-ly,** *adv.* D'un air interrogateur.

interrogatory [intə'rɔgətəri]. **I.** *a.* Interrogateur, -trice. **2.** *s. Jur:* Interrogatoire *m.*

interrupt [intə'rʌpt], *v.tr.* **I.** Interrompre; couper la parole à (qn). *Abs.* Don't interrupt! n'interrompez pas! **2.** Interrompre (la circulation, un circuit électrique); rompre (la cadence).

interrupter [intə'rʌptər], *s.* **I.** (*Pers.*) Interrupteur, -trice. *El:* Interrupteur *m*; coupecircuit *m inv*; (*switch*) disjoncteur *m.*

interruption [intə'rʌpʃ(ə)n], *s.* Interruption *f*; dérangement *m* (de qn). *To work six hours without interruption*, travailler six heures d'arrache-pied.

intersect [intər'sekt]. **I.** *v.tr.* Entrecouper, intersecter, entrecroiser (*with, by*, de). **2.** *v.i.* (*Of lines*) Se couper, s'intersecter, se croiser.

intersection [intər'sekʃ(ə)n], *s.* **I.** *Geom:* Intersection *f.* **2.** Carrefour *m*; croisement *m* de chemins.

interspace [intər'speis], *v.tr.* Espacer (ses visites).

intersperse [intər'spə:rs], *v.tr.* Entremêler (*between, among*, parmi; *with*, de). *Poppies interspersed among the wheat*, coquelicots répandus parmi les blés. *Pages interspersed with witty sayings*, pages émaillées de bons mots.

interstice [in'tə:rstis, 'intərstis], *s.* (*a*) Interstice *m.* (*b*) Alvéole *m or f* (de grillage d'accu, etc.).

intertwine [intər'twain]. **I.** *v.tr.* Entrelacer. **2.** *v.i.* S'entrelacer, s'accoler. **intertwining,** *a.* Entrelacé(s).

interurban [intər'ə:rbən], *a. Rail:* **I.** Interurbain. **2.** (Ligne de) banlieue.

interval ['intərv(ə)l], *s.* Intervalle *m.* **I.** (*a*) **At intervals,** par intervalles; par à-coups. *Meetings held at short intervals*, séances très rapprochées. *Meteor:* **Bright intervals,** belles éclaircies. (*b*) *Sch:* Récréation *f.* (*c*) *Th:* Entr'acte *m.* *Fb:* La mi-temps; la pause. **2.** *I. between beams,* écartement *m* de deux poutres. *To place objects at regular intervals,* échelonner des objets.

intervene [intər'vi:n], *v.i.* **I.** Intervenir, s'interposer. **2.** (*Of event*) Survenir, arriver. **3.** *Ten years intervened,* dix ans s'écoulèrent. *Ten miles intervened between the two towns,* dix milles séparaient les deux villes.

intervention [intər'venʃ(ə)n], *s.* Intervention *f.*

interview[1] ['intərvju:], *s.* **I.** Entrevue *f.* *Adm:* *To invite s.o. to an i.,* convoquer qn. **2.** *Journ:* Interview *m or f.*)

interview[2], *v.tr.* **I.** Avoir une entrevue avec (qn). **2.** *Journ:* Interviewer (qn).

interweave [intər'wi:v], *v.* (*p.t.* **interwove**

[intər'woːuv]; *p.p.* interwoven [intər'wouvn]) **I.** *v.tr.* (*a*) Tisser ensemble (des fils d'or et de laine, etc.); entrelacer (des branches). (*b*) Entremêler (des idées, etc.). **2.** *v.i.* S'entrelacer, s'entremêler.

intestacy [in'testəsi], *s. Jur:* Fait *m* de mourir intestat; absence *f* de testament.

intestate [in'testet], *a.* **I. To die intestate,** mourir intestat *inv.* **2. Intestate estate,** succession ab intestat.

intestinal [in'testinəl, intes'tainəl], *a.* Intestinal, -aux.

intestine¹ [in'testin], *a.* Intestin.

intestine², *s. Anat:* Intestin *m.* **The large intestine,** le gros intestin. **The small intestine,** l'intestin grêle.

intimacy ['intiməsi], *s.* Intimité *f.*

intimate¹ ['intimet]. **I.** *a.* Intime. (*a*) **To become intimate with s.o.,** se lier (d'amitié) avec qn. (*b*) **To have an intimate knowledge of sth.,** avoir une connaissance approfondie de qch. *I. connexion,* rapport intime, étroit. **2.** *s.* His **intimates,** ses intimes *mf*, ses familiers *m.* **-ly,** *adv.* Intimement; à fond. *The question is i. connected with . . .,* la question a un rapport très étroit avec. . . .

intimate² ['intimeit], *v.tr.* **I. To intimate sth. to s.o.,** signifier, notifier, qch. à qn. **2.** Donner à entendre, indiquer (que).

intimation [inti'meiʃ(ə)n], *s.* **I.** Avis *m* (de décès, etc.). **2.** (*a*) Avis à mots couverts; suggestion *f.* (*b*) **Intimations of immortality,** indications *f*, signes *m*, de l'immortalité.

intimidate [in'timideit], *v.tr.* Intimider. **intimidating,** *a.* Intimidateur, -trice; intimidant.

intimidation [intimi'deiʃ(ə)n], *s.* Intimidation *f*; *Jur:* menaces *fpl.*

intimity [in'timiti], *s.* **I.** (Sentiment *m* d')intimité *f.* **2.** La vie privée; le privé.

into ['intu], *prep.* Dans, en. **I.** *To go into a house,* entrer dans une maison. *To go into France,* passer en France. *To fall into the hands of the enemy,* tomber entre les mains de l'ennemi. *To work far into the night,* travailler bien avant dans la nuit. *To look into the future,* voir dans l'avenir. **2. To change sth. into sth.,** changer qch. en qch. *To grow into a man,* devenir un homme. *To divide into four,* diviser en quatre. *To burst into tears,* fondre en larmes.

intolerable [in'tɔlərəbl], *a.* Intolérable, insupportable. **-ably,** *adv.* Insupportablement.

intolerance [in'tɔlərəns], *s.* Intolérance *f* (*of*, de).

intolerant [in'tɔlərənt], *a.* **I.** Intolérant. **2.** *Med:* **To be intolerant of a drug,** ne pas supporter un médicament. **-ly,** *adv.* Avec intolérance.

intonation [intə'neiʃ(ə)n], *s.* Intonation *f*, ton *m* (de la voix).

intone [in'toun], *v.tr. Ecc.Mus:* **I.** Psalmodier (les litanies). **2.** Entonner (le chant).

intoxicant [in'tɔksikənt], **I.** *a.* Enivrant, grisant. **2.** *s.* Boisson *f* alcoolique.

intoxicate [in'tɔksikeit], *v.tr.* Enivrer, griser. **intoxicated,** *a.* Ivre; gris; pris de boisson. *Jur:* En état d'ébriété. *F:* **Intoxicated with praise,** grisé d'éloges. **intoxicating,** *a.* Enivrant, grisant. **Intoxicating liquors,** boissons *f* alcooliques.

intoxication [intɔksi'keiʃ(ə)n], *s.* (*a*) Ivresse *f.* (*b*) *F:* Griserie *f*, enivrement *m* (du plaisir, etc.).

intractability [intræktə'biliti], *s.* Indocilité *f.*

intractable [in'træktəbl], *a.* (Enfant, animal) intraitable, insoumis, indocile; (maladie) opiniâtre; (bois, etc.) difficile à travailler. **-ably,** *adv.* D'une façon intraitable.

intrados [in'treidɔs], *s. Arch:* Intrados *m.*

intramural [intra'mjuərəl], *a.* Intra-muros *inv.*

intransigency [in'transidʒənsi], *s.* Intransigeance *f.*

intransigent [in'transidʒənt], *a. & s.* Intransigeant, -e.

intransitive [in'trɑːnsitiv], *a. Gram:* Intransitif. **-ly,** *adv.* Intransitivement.

intrepid [in'trepid], *a.* Intrépide. **-ly,** *adv.* Intrépidement.

intrepidity [intre'piditi], *s.* Intrépidité *f.*

intricacy ['intrikəsi], *s.* Complexité *f* (d'un mécanisme, d'un problème). *The intricacies of the law,* les dédales *m* de la loi.

intricate ['intrikət], *a.* (*a*) (Mécanisme) compliqué. (*b*) (*Of statements*) Embrouillé, confus. *I. details,* détails compliqués.

intrigue¹ [in'triːg], *s.* Intrigue *f.*

intrigue². **I.** *v.i* Intriguer; mener des intrigues. **To intrigue against s.o.,** travailler contre qn. **2.** *v.tr. F:* Intriguer (qn); éveiller, piquer, la curiosité de (qn). **intriguing¹,** *a.* **I.** (Politicien, etc.) intrigant. **2.** *F:* **All this is very intriguing,** tout cela nous intrigue beaucoup. **intriguing²,** *s.* Machinations *fpl*, intrigues *fpl.*

intriguer [in'triːgər], *s.* Intrigant, -ante.

intrinsic [in'trinsik], *a.* Intrinsèque. **-ally,** *adv.* Intrinsèquement.

introduce [intrə'djuːs], *v.tr.* **I.** Introduire. (*a*) Faire entrer. *To i. a subject, a question,* amener un sujet, une question. (*b*) **To introduce s.o. into s.o.'s presence,** introduire qn auprès de qn. (*c*) Établir, faire adopter (un usage). **2. To introduce s.o. to s.o.,** présenter qn à qn. *To i. oneself to s.o.,* se présenter à qn. **3. To introduce s.o. to a process,** initier qn à un procédé.

introducer [intrə'djuːsər], *s.* Introducteur, -trice.

introduction [intrə'dʌkʃ(ə)n], *s.* **I.** Introduction *f.* **2.** Présentation *f* (*of s.o. to s.o.,* de qn à qn). **To give s.o. an introduction to s.o.,** donner à qn une lettre de recommandation auprès de qn. **3.** Avant-propos *m inv*; introduction (d'un livre, d'une symphonie). **4.** Manuel *m* élémentaire; introduction (*to,* à).

introductive [intrə'dʌktiv], **introductory** [intrə'dʌktəri], *a.* Introductoire. **After a few introductory words,** après quelques mots d'introduction.

introit [in'trouit], *s. Ecc:* Introït *m.*

introspection [intrə'spekʃ(ə)n], *s.* Introspection *f.*

introspective [intrə'spektiv], *a.* Introspectif.

introvert ['introvəːrt], *s. Psy:* Introverti, -ie.

introverted [intrə'vəːrtid], *a.* (Esprit) recueilli, *Psy:* introverti.

intrude [in'truːd], **I.** *v.tr.* (*a*) **To intrude sth. into sth.,** introduire qch. de force dans qch. **To i. oneself into a business,** s'ingérer dans une affaire. (*b*) **To intrude sth. on, upon, s.o.,** imposer qch. à qn. **2.** *v.i.* Faire intrusion (*on s.o.,* auprès de qn). **I am afraid of intruding,** je crains de vous être importun, d'être de trop. *I don't want to i. into your affairs,* je ne voudrais pas m'ingérer dans vos affaires. *To i. on s.o.'s privacy,* empiéter sur la solitude de qn.

intruder [in'truːdər], *s.* Intrus, -use; *F:* (*at reception, etc.*) resquilleur, -euse.

intrusion [in'truːʒ(ə)n], *s.* **I.** Intrusion *f.* *I hope I am not guilty of an i.,* j'espère que je ne suis pas indiscret. **2.** *Geol:* Intrusion, injection *f* (volcanique).

intrusive [in'truːsiv], *a.* Importun, indiscret. **-ly,** *adv.* Importunément; en importun.

intrusiveness [in'truːsivnəs], *s.* Indiscrétion *f*; importunité *f*.

intuition [intju'iʃ(ə)n], *s.* Intuition *f*. **To have an intuition of sth.**, avoir l'intuition de qch.

intuitive [in'tjuitiv], *a.* Intuitif. **-ly**, *adv.* Intuitivement; par intuition.

intumescence [intju'mes(ə)ns], *s.* Intumescence *f*; enflure *f*; boursouflure *f*.

intumescent [intju'mes(ə)nt], *a.* Intumescent; boursouflé; enflé.

inulin ['injulin], *s. Ch:* Inuline *f*.

inundate ['inʌndeit], *v.tr.* Inonder (*with*, de). *F:* **To be inundated with requests** être débordé de requêtes.

inundation [inʌn'deiʃ(ə)n], *s.* Inondation *f*.

inure [in'juər], *v.tr.* Accoutumer, habituer, rompre, endurcir (*to*, à). **Inured to hardships, to fatigue**, habitué aux privations; dur à la fatigue.

invade [in'veid], *v.tr.* **1.** Envahir. *F:* **To i. s.o.'s house**, faire invasion chez qn. **To i. s.o.'s privacy**, violer la retraite de qn. **2.** Empiéter sur (les droits de qn).

invader [in'veidər], *s.* Envahisseur *m*.

invagination [invadʒi'neiʃ(ə)n], *s. Surg:* Invagination *f*.

invalid¹ [in'valid], *a. Jur:* (Mariage) invalide; (arrêt) nul et non avenu. **-ly**, *adv.* Sans validité; illégalement.

invalid² ['invalid, -liːd], *a. & s.* (*Suffering from illness*) Malade (*mf*); (*from infirmity or disability*) infirme (*mf*); (*from ill-health*) valétudinaire (*mf*). **Invalid chair**, (i) fauteuil *m* de malade; (ii) voiture *f* d'infirme.

invalid³ [in'valiːd], *v.tr.* (*a*) Rendre malade ou infirme. (*b*) **To invalid a man out of the army**, réformer un homme. **Invalided home**, renvoyé dans ses foyers.

invalidate [in'valideit], *v.tr. Jur:* **1.** Invalider, rendre nul (un testament); vicier (un contrat). **2.** Casser, infirmer (un jugement).

invalidation [invali'deiʃ(ə)n], *s. Jur:* **1.** Invalidation *f* (d'un document). **2.** Infirmation *f* (d'un jugement).

invaluable [in'valjuəbl], *a.* Inestimable; (trésor) d'un prix incalculable.

invariability [inveəriə'biliti], **invariableness** [in'veəriəblnəs], *s.* Invariabilité *f*.

invariable [in'veəriəbl], *a.* Invariable. **-ably**, *adv.* Invariablement, immanquablement.

invasion [in'veiʒ(ə)n], *s.* **1.** Invasion *f*, envahissement *m*. **These invasions of my privacy**, ces intrusions *f* dans mon intimité. **2.** *Med:* Invasion, début *m* (d'une maladie). **3.** **Invasion of s.o.'s rights**, violation *f* des droits, atteinte *f* aux droits, de qn.

invective [in'vektiv], *s.* Invective *f*. *Coll.* **A torrent of invective**, un flot d'invectives, d'injures *f*.

inveigh [in'vei], *v.i.* Invectiver, tonner, fulminer (*against*, contre).

inveigle [in'viːgl], *v.tr.* Attirer, séduire, enjôler (qn). **To i. s.o. into doing sth.**, entraîner qn à faire qch.

inveiglement [in'viːglmənt], *s.* **1.** Séduction *f*, enjôlement *m*. **2.** Leurre *m*.

inveigler [in'viːglər], *s.* Séducteur, -trice; enjôleur, -euse.

invent [in'vent], *v.tr.* Inventer. **Newly invented process**, procédé d'invention récente.

invention [in'venʃ(ə)n], *s.* Invention *f*. **A story of his own invention**, une histoire de son cru.

inventive [in'ventiv], *a.* Inventif.

inventiveness [in'ventivnəs], *s.* Fécondité *f* d'invention; don *m* d'invention; imagination *f*.

inventor [in'ventər], *s.* Inventeur, *occ. f.* -trice.

inventory ['invənt(ə)ri], *s. Com:* Inventaire *m*. **To take, draw up, an inventory**, faire, dresser, un inventaire.

inverse [in'vəːs], *a. I. a.* Inverse. **In inverse order**, en sens inverse. *In i. ratio*, en raison inverse (*to*, de). **2.** *s.* Inverse *m*, contraire *m* (*of*, de). **-ly**, *adv.* Inversement.

inversion [in'vəːʃ(ə)n], *s.* **1.** Renversement *m*. **2.** *Gram:* Inversion *f* (du sujet, etc.).

invert [in'vəːrt], *v.tr.* **1.** Renverser, retourner (un objet) (le haut en bas). *Mus:* **To invert a chord**, renverser un accord. **2.** Invertir, intervertir, renverser (l'ordre, les positions). **3.** Retourner; mettre à l'envers.

invertebrate [in'vəːrtebret], *a. & s. Z:* Invertébré (*m*).

invest [in'vest], *v.tr.* **1.** Revêtir (*with, in*, de). **To invest a subject with interest**, rendre un sujet intéressant. **2.** **To invest s.o. with an office**, investir qn d'une fonction. **3.** *Mil:* Investir, cerner (une place forte). **4.** *Fin:* Placer, investir (des fonds). **To invest money**, faire des placements. *To i. one's money in real estate*, mettre son argent en fonds de terre. *Abs.* **To invest in house property**, faire des placements en immeubles. *F:* *To i. in a new suite of furniture*, se payer un nouveau mobilier.

investigate [in'vestigeit], *v.tr.* Examiner, étudier, sonder (une question). *To i. a crime*, faire une enquête sur un crime; informer sur un crime. **Investigating committee**, commission *f* d'enquête.

investigation [investi'geiʃ(ə)n], *s.* Investigation *f*; enquête *f* (*of*, sur). **Question under investigation**, question à l'étude. *Preliminary investigations with a view to ...*, études *f* préparatoires en vue de.... **Scientific investigation**, enquête scientifique. **On further investigation ...**, en poursuivant mes recherches. ...

investigator [in'vestigeitər], *s.* Investigateur, -trice.

investiture [in'vestitjər], *s.* (*a*) Investiture *f* (d'un évêque, etc.). (*b*) Remise *f* de décorations.

investment [in'vestmənt], *s.* **1.** *Mil:* Investissement *m* (d'une place forte). **2.** *Fin:* Placement *m* (de fonds); mise *f* de fonds. **Safe investment**, valeur *f* de tout repos.

investor [in'vestər], *s.* Actionnaire *mf*, capitaliste *mf*. **Small investors**, petits capitalistes, petits rentiers.

inveterate [in'vetəret], *a.* (*a*) Invétéré. (*b*) (*Of smoker, etc.*) Obstiné, acharné. **Inveterate hatred**, haine implacable, vivace.

invidious [in'vidiəs], *a.* **1.** Haïssable, odieux. *I. task*, tâche ingrate. **2.** (*a*) Qui excite l'envie, la haine. (*b*) Qui suscite la jalousie. **Invidious comparison**, comparaison désobligeante. **-ly**, *adv.* Odieusement, désobligeamment.

invigilate [in'vidʒileit], *v.i. Sch:* Surveiller les candidats (à un examen).

invigilation [invidʒi'leiʃ(ə)n], *s. Sch:* Surveillance *f* (des candidats).

invigilator [in'vidʒileitər], *s. Sch:* Surveillant, -ante.

invigorate [in'vigəreit], *v.tr.* (*a*) Fortifier (qn); donner de la vigueur à (qn). (*b*) (*Of the air, etc.*) Vivifier, tonifier.

invincibility [invinsi'biliti], *s.* Invincibilité *f*.

invincible [in'vinsibl], *a.* Invincible. **-ibly**, *adv.* Invinciblement.

inviolability [invaiələ'biliti], *s.* Inviolabilité *f*.

inviolable [in'vaiələbl], *a.* Inviolable. **-ably**, *adv.* Inviolablement.

invisibility [invizi'biliti], **invisibleness** [in-'viziblnəs], s. Invisibilité f.
invisible [in'vizibl], a. Invisible. Invisible ink, encre sympathique. S.a. MENDING. **-ibly,** adv. Invisiblement.
invitation [invi'teiʃ(ə)n], s. Invitation f (to do sth., à faire qch.). To come at s.o.'s invitation, venir sur l'invitation de qn.
invite [in'vait], v.tr. **1.** Inviter; convier (des amis à dîner). To invite s.o. in, prier qn d'é trer. **2.** Engager, inviter, appeler (s.o. to do sᵗ qn à faire qch.). **3.** Provoquer (le malheuᵣ, la critique). **inviting,** a. Invitant, attrayant; (mets) appétissant, ragoûtant. Not very i., peu ragoûtant. **-ly,** adv. D'une manière attrayante, tentante.
invocation [invo'keiʃ(ə)n], s. Invocation f.
invoice¹ ['invɔis], s. Com: Facture f (d'achat). As per invoice, suivant la facture. Invoice clerk, facturier m.
invoice², v.tr. Facturer (des marchandises)
invoke [in'vouk], v.tr. **1.** (a) Invoquer (Dieu). (b) To invoke s.o.'s aid, appeler qn à son secours. **2.** Évoquer (un esprit) par des incantations.
invoker [in'voukər], s. Invocateur, -trice.
involuntary [in'vɔləntəri], a. Involontaire. **-ily,** adv. Involontairement.
involute ['invɔljuːt]. **1.** a. (a) Bot: (Feuille) involutée, involutive. (b) (Arc) de développante; (engrenage) à développante. **2.** s. Geom: Développante f.
involution [invo'ljuːʃ(ə)n], s. **1.** (a) Complication f; tours mpl et détours. (b) Enchevêtrement m, embrouillement m. **2.** Nat.Hist: etc: Involution f.
involve [in'vɔlv], v.tr. **1.** (a) Envelopper, entortiller. To get involved with a rope, s'empêtrer dans un cordage. (b) Compliquer, entortiller (un récit). **2.** To involve s.o. in a quarrel, engager qn dans une querelle. To i. s.o. in a charge, impliquer qn dans une accusation. He involved his friend in his ruin, il entraîna son ami dans sa ruine. To involve oneself in trouble, se créer des ennuis. To be involved in a failure, être enveloppé, entraîné, dans une faillite. He is involved in the plot, il est compromis, il a trempé, dans le complot. The vehicle involved, le véhicule en cause (dans l'accident). His honour is involved, son honneur est engagé. The forces involved, les forces en jeu. **3.** Comporter, entraîner. To involve much expense, nécessiter, entraîner, de grands frais. It would i. living in London, cela nécessiterait que j'aille vivre à Londres. **involved,** a. **1.** (Style) embrouillé, compliqué, touffu. **2.** (Domaine) grevé de dettes. To be in involved circumstances, être dans la gêne.
invulnerable [in'vʌlnərəbl], a. Invulnérable.
inward ['inwərd]. **1.** a. (a) Intérieur, interne. (b) Vers l'intérieur. **2.** s.pl. Inwards, entrailles f, viscères m. **3.** adv. = INWARDS. **-ly,** adv. En dedans; intérieurement.
inwardness ['inwərdnəs], s. Essence f, signification f intime (de qch.).
inwards ['inwərdz], adv. Vers l'intérieur; en dedans.
iodate¹ ['aiodeit], s. Ch: Iodate m.
iodate², v.tr. Med: Phot: Ioder, iodurer.
iodide ['aiodaid], s. Ch: Iodure m.
iodine ['aiodiːn], s. Iode m. Tincture of iodine, teinture f d'iode.
iodize ['aiodaiz], v.tr. Ioder, iodurer.
iodoform [ai'oudofɔːrm], s. Pharm: Iodoforme m.
ion ['aiən], s. El: Ph: Ch: Ion m.

Ionic [ai'ɔnik], a. Arch: Ionique.
ionization [aionai'zeiʃ(ə)n], s. El: Ph: Ionisation f.
ionize ['aionaiz], v.tr. El: Ph: Ioniser (l'air, un gaz).
iota [ai'outa], s. **1.** Gr.Alph: Iota m. **2.** F: Not one iota, pas un iota.
I.O.U. [aiou'juː], s. (pl. I.O.U's) (I owe you) Reconnaissance f (de dette).
ipecacuanha [ipikakju'ana], F: **ipecac** ['ipi-kak], s. Bot: Ipécacuana m, F: ipéca m.
Irak, Iraq [iə'rɑːk]. Pr.n. Geog: Irak m.
Iran [iə'rɑːn]. Pr.n. Geog: L'Iran m.
Iraqi [iə'rɑːki], a. & s. Geog: Irakien, -ienne.
irascibility [airasi'biliti, iras-], s. Irascibilité f.
irascible [ai'rasibl, i'ras-], a. (Homme) irascible, coléreux; (tempérament) colérique.
irate [ai'reit], a. Courroucé; en colère.
ire ['aiər], s. Lit: Courroux m, colère f.
Ireland ['aiərlənd]. Pr.n. L'Irlande f.
iridescence [iri'desəns], s. Irisation f, iridescence f; chatoiement m (d'un plumage, etc.).
iridescent [iri'desənt], a. Irisé, iridescent; chatoyant.
iridium [ai'ridiəm], s. Ch: Iridium m.
Iris ['aiəris]. **1.** Pr.n.f. Myth: Iris. **2.** s. (pl. irides ['airidiːz]) Anat: Iris m (de l'œil). **3.** s. (pl. irises ['airisiz]) Bot: Iris m. Yellow iris, iris jaune, iris des marais. **4.** s. (pl. irises) Reflets irisés; chatoiement m. **'iris-'diaphragm,** Phot: Diaphragme m iris.
irisation [airi'seiʃ(ə)n], s. Irisage m, irisation f.
Irish ['airiʃ]. **1.** a. Irlandais; (toile) d'Irlande. **2.** s. (a) Ling: L'irlandais m. (b) pl. The Irish, les Irlandais m. **'Irish Free 'State (the).** Pr.n. L'État m libre d'Irlande.
Irishman, pl. **-men** ['airiʃmən, -men], s.m. Irlandais. F: He has had an Irishman's rise, d'évêque il s'est fait meunier.
Irishwoman, pl. **-women** ['airiʃwumən, -wi-men], s.f. Irlandaise.
irk [əːrk], v.tr. A: Ennuyer. Impers. It irks me to . . ., cela m'est pénible de . . .; il m'en coûte de. . . .
irksome ['əːrksəm], a. (Travail) ennuyeux, ingrat.
irksomeness ['əːrksəmnəs], s. Caractère ennuyeux, ingrat (d'une tâche, etc.).
iron¹ ['aiərn, 'aiərn], s. **1.** Fer m. Cast iron, fer de fonte; fonte f (de fer). Pig iron, fonte en saumon, en gueuse(s). Wrought iron, fer forgé. Com: Bar iron, fer marchand, fer méplat. Corrugated iron, tôle ondulée. Old iron, ferraille f. Iron mounting, fitting ferrure f. Iron ore, minerai de fer. Red iron ore, hématite f rouge. F: Iron will, volonté de fer. To have an iron constitution, avoir un corps de fer. Man of iron, homme dur, sans pitié; cœur m de fer. **2.** (a) Tls: Curling iron, fer à friser. F: To have too many irons in the fire, mener trop d'affaires de front; avoir trop d'affaires en main. (b) Plane iron, fer de rabot. **3.** Golf: (Crosse f en) fer. **4.** Dom.Ec: (Flat-)iron, laundry iron, fer à repasser. **5.** pl. (a) Fers, chaînes f. Nau: etc: To put a man in irons, mettre un homme aux fers. (b) (Of ship) To be in irons, faire chapelle.
'iron-bound, a. **1.** Cerclé de fer, fretté de fer. **2.** Iron-bound coast, côte f à pic; littoral hérissé de rochers. **3.** Inflexible, compassé.
'iron-clad. 1. a. (Navire) cuirassé; (puits) blindé. **2.** s. Navy: Cuirassé m.
'iron-'filings, s.pl. Limaille f de fer. **'iron-foundry,** s. Fonderie f de fonte; usine f métallurgique. **'iron-'grey,** a. & s. Gris (de) fer (m inv). **'iron-holder,** s. Dom.Ec: Poi-

gnée _f_ (de fer à repasser). **'iron-mould,** _s._ Tache _f_ de rouille. **'iron-shod,** _a._ Ferré.

iron², _v.tr._ Repasser (le linge). **To iron (up) a** hat, donner un coup de fer à un chapeau. **To iron out a crease** (_in a frock, etc._), faire disparaître un faux pl au fer chaud. **ironing,** _s._ Repassage _m._

ironer [ˈaiərnər], _s._ Repasseur, -euse.

ironic(al) [aiˈrɔnik(əl)], _a._ Ironique. **-ally,** _adv._ Ironiquement; par ironie.

ironmaster [ˈaiərnmɑːstər], _s.m._ Maître de forges; métallurgiste.

ironmonger [ˈaiərnmʌŋgər], _s._ Quincaillier _m,_ ferronnier _m._

ironmongery [ˈaiərnmʌŋgəri], **ironware** [ˈaiərnwɛər], _s._ Quincaillerie _f,_ ferronnerie _f._

ironwork [ˈaiərnwəːrk], _s._ **1.** (_a_) Serrurerie _f;_ (travail _m_ de) ferronnerie _f._ Ironwork constructor, contractor, serrurier _m_ en bâtiments. (_b_) Heavy ironwork, constructional ironwork, charpente _f_ en fer, grosse serrurerie, profilés _mpl_ pour constructions. (_c_) (_Parts made of iron_) Ferrure(s) _f(pl)._ **2.** _pl._ Ironworks, usine _f_ sidérurgique; forges _fpl._

ironworker [ˈaiərnwəːrkər], _s._ **1.** (_In wrought iron_) (Ouvrier) serrurier _m_ **2.** (_In heavy iron_) Charpentier _m_ en fer.

irony [ˈaironi], _s._ Ironie _f._

irradiance [iˈreidjəns], _s._ Rayonnement _m,_ éclat _m._

irradiant [iˈreidjənt], _a._ Rayonnant.

irradiate [iˈreidieit], _v.tr._ **1.** (_Of light, heat_) Irradier, rayonner sur (la terre); (_of light rays_) illuminer (une surface). **2.** Émettre comme des rayons. _Presence that irradiates strength,_ présence d'où irradie la force. **3.** _Good humour irradiated his face,_ la bonne humeur faisait rayonner son visage.

irradiation [ireidiˈeiʃ(ə)n], _s._ **1.** Irradiation _f._ **2.** Rayonnement _m_ (d'une source de lumière).

irrational [iˈraʃən(ə)l], _a._ (_a_) Dépourvu de raison. (_b_) Déraisonnable, absurde. (_c_) _Mth:_ (Nombre) irrationnel. **-ally,** _adv._ Déraisonnablement; irrationnellement.

irreclaimable [iriˈkleiməbl], _a._ **1.** Incorrigible; (ivrogne) invétéré. **2.** (Terrain) incultivable.

irreconcilable [irekənˈsailəbl], _a._ **1.** (Ennemi) irréconciliable; (haine) implacable. **2.** (Croyance) incompatible, inconciliable (_with,_ avec). **-ably,** _adv._ **1.** Irréconciliablement. **2.** Inconciliablement.

irrecoverable [iriˈkʌvərəbl], _a._ (Créance) irrécouvrable; (perte) irréparable.

irrecusable [iriˈkjuːzəbl], _a._ (Témoignage) irrécusable.

irredeemable [iriˈdiːməbl], _a._ **1.** Irredeemable bonds, obligations non amortissables. **2.** (_a_) (Désastre) irrémédiable. (_b_) (Coquin) incorrigible. **-ably,** _adv._ (Condamné) sans recours.

irreducible [iriˈdjuːsibl], _a._ (Fraction, hernie) irréductible.

irreformable [iriˈfɔːrməbl], _a._ Irréformable.

irrefragable [iˈrefragəbl], _a._ Irréfragable.

irrefutable [iˈrefjutəbl], _a._ Irréfutable; (témoignage) irrécusable. **-ably,** _adv._ Irréfutablement.

irregular [iˈregjulər], _a._ Irrégulier. **1.** (_a_) Contraire aux règles. _I._ life, vie déréglée. (_b_) _Nat. Hist:_ Anormal, -aux. **2.** Asymétrique; (_of surface_) inégal, -aux. **3.** _Mil:_ Irregular troops, _s.pl._ irregulars, troupes irrégulières; irréguliers _m._ **-ly,** _adv._ Irrégulièrement.

irregularity [iregjuˈlariti], _s._ **1.** (_a_) Irrégularité _f_ (de conduite, etc.) (_b_) _Adm: Com:_ To

commit irregularities, commettre des irrégularités. **2.** Irregularity of ground, aspérités _fpl,_ accidents _mpl,_ de terrain.

irrelevance [iˈreləvəns], **irrelevancy** [iˈreləvənsi], _s._ **1.** Inapplicabilité _f_ (_to,_ à). **2.** Manque _m_ d'à-propos. _Speech full of irrelevancies,_ discours rempli d'à-côtés qui n'ont rien à voir avec la question.

irrelevant [iˈreləvənt], _a._ Non pertinent; (_of remark, etc._) hors de propos. _To make i. remarks,_ divaguer. _That is i.,_ cela n'a rien à voir avec la question. **-ly,** _adv._ Mal à propos; hors de propos.

irreligious [iriˈlidʒəs], _a._ Irréligieux, indévot. **-ly,** _adv._ Irréligieusement.

irremediable [iriˈmiːdiəbl], _a._ Irrémédiable; sans remède. **-ably,** _adv._ Irrémédiablement: sans remède.

irremissible [iriˈmisibl], _a._ (Faute) irrémissible; (péché) impardonnable.

irremovable [iriˈmuːvəbl], _a._ (Fonctionnaire) inamovible.

irreparable [iˈrepərəbl], _a._ Irréparable; (perte) irrémédiable. **-ably,** _adv._ Irréparablement; irrémédiablement.

irrepressible [iriˈpresibl], _a._ (Bâillement) irrésistible, irréprimable; (force) irrépressible. _F:_ Irrepressible child, enfant qui a le diable au corps. **-ibly,** _adv._ Irrésistiblement.

irreproachable [iriˈproutʃəbl], _a._ Irréprochable; (vêtement) impeccable. **-ably,** _adv_ Irréprochablement.

irresistible [iriˈzistibl], _a._ Irrésistible. **-ibly,** _adv._ Irrésistiblement.

irresolute [iˈrezoljut], _a._ **1.** Indécis. **2.** (Caractère) irrésolu; (esprit) vacillant, hésitant. **-ly,** _adv._ Irrésolument.

irresoluteness [iˈrezoljutnəs], **irresolution** [irezoˈljuːʃ(ə)n], _s._ Indécision _f_ (de caractère); irrésolution _f._

irresolvable [iriˈzɔlvəbl], _a._ **1.** Insoluble. **2.** (Corps) indécomposable, irréductible.

irrespective [iriˈspektiv]. **1.** _a._ Indépendant (_of,_ de). **2.** _adv._ Irrespective of sth., indépendamment, sans tenir compte, de qch.

irresponsibility [irispɔnsiˈbiliti], _s._ Étourderie _f;_ manque _m_ de sérieux; irréflexion _f._

irresponsible [iriˈspɔnsibl], _a._ (_a_) (Of pers.) Étourdi, irréfléchi; évaporé; à la tête légère. (_b_) (Of action) Irréfléchi. **-ibly,** _adv._ Étourdiment. _To act i.,_ agir à l'étourdie, à la légère.

irresponsive [iriˈspɔnsiv], _a._ (Of pers.) Flegmatique, froid; (visage) fermé. _I. to entreaties,_ sourd aux prières.

irresponsiveness [iriˈspɔnsivnəs], _s._ Flegme _m,_ réserve _f,_ froideur _f._

irretrievable [iriˈtriːvəbl], _a._ Irréparable, irrémédiable. **-ably,** _adv._ Irréparablement; irrémédiablement.

irreverence [iˈrevərəns], _s._ Irrévérence _f;_ manque _m_ de respect (_towards,_ envers, pour).

irreverent [iˈrevərənt], _a._ **1.** (_In religious matters_) Irrévérent. **2.** (_In social intercourse_) Irrévérencieux. **-ly,** _adv._ **1.** Irrévéremment. **2.** Irrévérencieusement.

irreversible [iriˈvəːrsibl], _a._ **1.** (Décision) irrévocable. **2.** _Mec.E:_ Irréversible.

irrevocability [irevokəˈbiliti], _s._ Irrévocabilité _f._

irrevocable [iˈrevokəbl], _a._ Irrévocable. **-ably,** _adv._ Irrévocablement.

irrigable [ˈirigəbl], _a._ (Terre) irrigable.

irrigate [ˈirigeit], _v.tr._ (_a_) _Agr:_ Irriguer (des champs). (_b_) (Of river) Arroser (une région).

irrigation [iriˈgeiʃ(ə)n], _s._ Irrigation _f._

irritability [iritə'biliti], **irritableness** ['iri-təblnəs], s. Irritabilité f.
irritable ['iritəbl], a. Irritable, irascible, atrabilaire.
irritate ['iriteit], v.tr. **1.** Irriter, agacer. **2.** Med: Irriter (un organe); aviver, envenimer (une plaie). **irritating,** a. **1.** Irritant, agaçant. **2.** Med: Irritant, irritatif.
irritation [iri'teiʃ(ə)n], s. **1.** Irritation f. Nervous irritation, énervement m. **2.** Med: Irritation.
irruption [i'rʌpʃ(ə)n], s. Irruption f.
is [iz]. See BE.
Isaiah [ai'zaiə]. Pr.n.m. B.Hist: Isaïe.
isinglass ['aizɪŋglɑːs], s. (a) Colle f de poisson; ichtyocolle f. (b) Gélatine f (pour gelées, etc.).
Islamic [is'lamik, iz-], a. Islamique.
Islamism ['islamizm, 'iz-], s. Islamisme m.
Islamist ['islamist, 'iz-], s. Islamite mf.
island ['ailənd], s. **1.** Île f. Small i., îlot m. Cu: Floating islands, œufs m à la neige. **2.** (a) F: Îlot (de maisons, etc.). (b) (Street-) island, refuge m (pour piétons).
islander ['ailəndər], s. Insulaire mf.
isle [ail], s. Île f. Esp. Geog: The British Isles, les Îles britanniques. The Isle of Man, l'île de Man.
islet ['ailet], s. Îlot m.
isobar ['aisobɑːr], s. Meteor: Isobare f.
isobaric [aiso'barik], a. (Ligne) isobare; (carte) isobarique, isobarométrique.
isochromatic [aisokro'matik], a. Isochromatique.
isochronal [ai'sɔkrənəl], **isochronic** [aiso-'krɔnik], **isochronous** [ai'sɔkrənəs], a. Mec: Isochrone, isochronique.
isolable ['aisoləbl], a. Ch: etc: Isolable.
isolate ['aisoleit], v.tr. (a) Isoler (un malade) (from, de, d'avec); cantonner (des bestiaux). (b) F: Faire le vide autour de (qn). **isolated,** a. (Hameau) isolé, écarté. I. instance, cas isolé.
isolation [aiso'leiʃ(ə)n], s. **1.** Isolement m (d'un malade). Isolation hospital, hôpital d'isolement; hôpital de contagieux. **2.** Isolement, solitude f.
isolator ['aisoleitər], s. El: Isolateur m, isoloir m; tabouret isolant.
isomer ['aisomər], s. Ch: Isomère m.
isomeric [aiso'merik], a. Ch: Isomère, isomérique.
isomerism [ai'sɔmerizm], s. Ch: Isomérisme m.
isomorph ['aisomɔːrf], s. Cryst: Isomorphe m.
isomorphic [aiso'mɔːrfik], **isomorphous** [aiso-'mɔːrfəs], a. Isomorphe.
isosceles [ai'sɔsiliːz], a. (Triangle) iso(s)cèle.
isotherm ['aisoθəːrm], s. Meteor: Isotherme f.
isothermal [aiso'θəːrm(ə)l], a. (Ligne) isotherme.
isotopes ['aisotoups], s.pl. Ch: (Composés) isotopes m.
Israel ['izreəl]. Pr.n.m. B.Hist: Israël.
Israelite ['izreəlait], a. & s. Israélite (mf).
issue¹ ['iʃjuː, 'isjuː], s. **1.** Écoulement m. Med: Épanchement m, perte f, décharge f, saillie f (de sang, etc.); décharge (de pus). **2.** (a) Issue f, sortie f, débouché m (out of, de). To find an i. out of . . ., trouver un moyen de sortir de. . . . (b) Embouchure f (d'un fleuve); déversoir m (d'un barrage, etc.). **3.** Issue, résultat m, dénouement m. To wait the issue, attendre la fin, le résultat. In the issue . . ., à la fin . . ., en fin de compte. . . . To bring a matter to an issue, faire aboutir une question; en finir avec une question. Favourable i., unfavourable i., bon,

mauvais, succès. **4.** Progéniture f, descendance f, postérité f. To die without issue, mourir sans enfants. **5.** Jur: Issue (of fact, of law), (i) question f de fait, de droit; (ii) conclusion f. Main issue of a suit, fond m d'un procès. S.a. SIDE¹ 6. To join issue, accepter les conclusions. F: To join issue with s.o. about sth., discuter l'opinion, le dire, de qn au sujet de qch. The point at issue, la question pendante, en litige. To be at issue with s.o., être (i) en désaccord, (ii) en contestation, avec qn. To obscure the issue, (i) obscurcir la question; (ii) F: faire du camouflage autour de la question. To evade the issue, user de faux-fuyants. **6.** (a) Fin: Émission f (de billets de banque, d'actions). Issue price, prix d'émission. (b) Parution f, publication f (d'un livre); lancement m (d'un prospectus, etc.). In course of issue, en cours de publication. (c) Délivrance f (de billets, de passeports). (d) Mil: Distribution f, versement m (de vivres, etc.). Issue shirt, chemise réglementaire, d'ordonnance. **7.** Édition f (d'un livre); édition, numéro m (d'un journal).
issue². **1.** v.i. (a) To issue (out, forth), (of pers.) sortir; (of blood) jaillir, s'écouler (from, de); (of smell, gas) se dégager (from, de). (b) Provenir, dériver (from, de). **2.** v.tr. (a) Émettre, mettre en circulation (des billets de banque, etc.). (b) Publier, donner (une nouvelle édition); lancer (un prospectus, etc.). Jur: To issue a warrant for the arrest of s.o., décerner, lancer, un mandat d'arrêt contre qn. Mil: To issue an order, publier, donner, un ordre. (c) Verser, distribuer (des provisions, etc.); délivrer (des passeports, etc.). (d) To issue the ship's company with rum, distribuer du rhum à l'équipage.
issueless ['iʃjuləs, 'isjuləs], a. Sans enfants; sans descendance.
Istanbul [istan'buːl]. Pr.n. Geog: Istamboul m.
isthmus, pl. **-uses** ['is(θ)məs(iz)], s. Geog: Anat: Isthme m.
it [it], pers.pron. **1.** (a) (Nom.) Il, f. elle. The house is small but it is my own, la maison est petite mais elle est à moi. (b) (Acc.) Le, f. la. He took her hand and pressed it, il lui prit la main et la serra. And my cake, have you tasted it? et mon gâteau, y avez-vous goûté? (c) (Dat.) Lui mf. Bring the child and give it a drink, amenez l'enfant et donnez-lui à boire. (d) (Reflexive) The Committee has devoted great care to the task before it, le comité a donné beaucoup d'attention à la tâche qui lui incombait. (e) F: He thinks he's it [hiːz'it], il se croit sorti de la cuisse de Jupiter. This book is absolutely 'it! c'est un livre épatant! She's got 'it, elle a de ça. **2.** To face it, faire front. Hang it! zut! I haven't got it in me to . . ., je ne suis pas capable de. . . . Now for it! et maintenant allons-y! There is nothing for it but to run, il n'y a qu'une chose à faire, c'est de filer. To have a bad time of it, en voir de dures. The worst of it is that . . ., le plus mauvais de la chose c'est que. . . . **3.** Ce, cela, il. Who is it? qui est-ce? That's it, c'est ça; (ii) ça y est! It doesn't matter, cela ne fait rien. It is raining, il pleut. It is Monday, c'est aujourd'hui lundi. **4.** It only remains to thank the reader, il ne me reste qu'à remercier le lecteur. It's nonsense talking like that, c'est absurde de parler comme ça. It makes one shudder to look down, cela vous fait frémir de regarder en bas. How is it that . . .? d'où vient que . . .? It is said that . . ., on dit que. . . . It is written that . . ., il est écrit que. . . . The fog made it difficult to calculate the distance, le brouillard

rendait difficile l'estimation des distances. *I thought it well to warn you,* j'ai jugé bon de vous avertir. **5.** **At it, in it, to it,** y. *To consent to it,* y consentir. *To fall in it,* y tomber. **Above it,** over it, au-dessus ; dessus. **Below it, under(neath) it,** au-dessous ; dessous. **For it,** en ; pour lui, pour elle, pour cela. *I feel the better for it,* je m'en trouve mieux. **From it,** en. **Far from it,** tant s'en faut, il s'en faut. **Of it,** en. *Give me half of it,* donnez-m'en la moitié. **On it,** y, dessus.

Italian [i'taljən]. **1.** *a.* (*a*) Italien, d'Italie. (*b*) **Italian cloth,** satin *m* de Chine ; brillantine *f.* **2.** *s.* (*a*) Italien, -ienne. (*b*) *Ling :* L'italien *m.*

Italianize [i'taljənaiz], *v.tr.* Italianiser.

Italic [i'talik]. **1.** *a.* *A.Geog :* Italique. **2.** *s.* *Typ : Usu. pl.* **To print in italic(s),** imprimer en italique *m.*

italicize [i'talisaiz], *v.tr.* *Typ :* Imprimer, mettre, en italique.

Italy ['itəli]. *Pr.n.* L'Italie *f.*

itch[1] [it∫], *s.* **1.** Démangeaison *f.* *F :* **To have an itch to do sth.,** avoir une démangeaison de faire qch. ; brûler de faire qch. **2.** *Med : Vet :* Gale *f.* **'itch-mite,** *s.* Sarcopte *m* de la gale ; acare *m.*

itch[2], *v.i.* **1.** Démanger ; (*of pers.*) éprouver des démangeaisons. *My hand itches,* la main me démange. **2.** *F :* **To itch to do sth.,** brûler, griller d'envie, de faire qch. *I was itching to speak,* j'avais une démangeaison de parler. **He's itching for trouble,** la peau lui démange. **itching,** *s.* Démangeaison *f.*

itchiness ['it∫inəs], *s.* Démangeaison *f,* picotement *m* (à la peau).

itchy ['it∫i], *a.* **1.** *Med :* Galeux. **2.** *F :* Qui démange.

item ['aitem]. **1.** *adv.* Item ; de plus. . . .

2. *s.* *Com : etc :* Article *m* ; détail *m* ; rubrique *f.* *Book-k :* Écriture *f,* poste *m.* **Expense item,** chef *m* de dépense. **To give the items,** donner les détails. *Items of expenditure,* articles de dépense. **News items** (*in a paper*), faits divers ; échos *m.* **Items on the agenda,** questions *f* à l'ordre du jour. **The last item on the programme,** le dernier numéro du programme.

iterate ['itəreit], *v.tr.* Réitérer.

iteration [itə'rei∫(ə)n], *s.* (Ré)itération *f.*

iterative ['itərətiv], *a.* Itératif.

itineracy [ai'tinərəsi], **itinerancy** [ai'tinərənsi], *s.* **1.** Vie ambulante. **2.** Itinerancy, ambulance *f* (d'un juge, d'un prédicateur).

itinerant [ai'tinərənt], *a.* **1.** (Musicien) ambulant. *I. vendor,* marchand forain. **2.** (Prédicateur) itinérant.

itinerary [ai'tinərəri], *a. & s.* Itinéraire (*m*).

itinerate [ai'tinəreit], *v.i.* Voyager.

its [its], *poss.a.* Son ; *f.* sa, (*before vowel sound*) son ; *pl.* ses. *I cut off its head,* je lui ai coupé la tête.

it's [its]. *F : = it is.*

itself [it'self], *pers.pron.* *See* SELF 4.

I've [aiv]. *F : = I have.*

ivied ['aivid], *a.* Couvert de lierre.

ivory ['aivəri], *s.* **1.** (*a*) Ivoire *m.* **Raw ivory, live ivory,** ivoire vert. **Worker in ivory,** ivoirier *m.* *F :* **Black ivory,** les esclaves noirs. **The black ivory trade,** la traite des noirs. (*b*) (Objet *m* d')ivoire. **2.** *Attrib.* (*a*) D'ivoire, en ivoire. (*b*) *Geog :* **The Ivory Coast,** la Côte d'Ivoire. **'ivory-'black,** *s.* Noir *m* d'ivoire.

ivy ['aivi], *s.* *Bot :* **1.** Lierre *m.* **2.** **Poison ivy,** sumac vénéneux. *S.a.* GROUND-IVY.

izard ['izərd], *s.* *Z :* Isard *m,* izard *m.*

J

J, j [dʒei], *s.* (La lettre) J, j *m.*

jab[1] [dʒab], *s.* **1.** Coup *m* du bout de quelque chose ; coup de pointe. **2.** *Box :* Coup sec.

jab[2], *v.tr. & i.* (jabbed) To jab (at) s.o. with sth., piquer qn du bout de qch. *To jab s.o.'s eye out with an umbrella,* crever un œil à qn avec un parapluie.

jabber[1] ['dʒabər], *s.* **1.** Baragouin *m,* baragouinage *m.* **2.** Bavardage *m,* jacasserie *f.*

jabber[2]. **1.** *v.i.* (*a*) Bredouiller, baràgouiner. (*b*) Jacasser. **2.** *v.tr.* Baragouiner (le français).

jacinth ['dʒasinθ], *s.* *Miner : Lap :* Jacinthe *f.*

Jack[1] [dʒak]. **I.** *Pr.n.m.* (*Dim. of John*) **1.** Jean, Jack. *F : He was off before you could say Jack Robinson,* il est parti sans qu'on ait le temps de faire ouf, de dire ouf. **Jack Ketch,** le bourreau. **2.** (*Sailor*) *When Jack is ashore . . .,* quand le marin tire une bordée. . . . **II. jack,** *s.* **1.** (*Pers.*) (*a*) (i) Valet *m* ; (ii) manœuvre *m.* (*b*) **Cheap Jack,** camelot *m.* **Jack in office,** bureaucrate *m* (qui fait l'important). **Jack of all trades,** maître Jacques. **2.** *Cards :* Valet. **3.** *Clockm :* Jaquemart *m.* **4.** *Ich :* Brocheton *m.* **III. jack,** *s.* (Outil, dispositif) *s.* **1.** (*Roasting-*)**jack,** tournebroche *m.* **2.** (*a*) **Sawyer's jack,** chevalet *m* (de scieur). (*b*) Cric *m,* vérin *m.* **Wheel jack,** lève-roue *m inv.* **Car jack,** cric pour autos. (*c*) *See* BOOT-JACK. **3.** *U.S :* **Black jack,** matraque *f,* assommoir *m.* **4.** *El.E :* *Tp :* Jack *m* ;

fiche *f* femelle. **5.** *Games :* (At bowls) Cochonnet *m.* **'jack-boots,** *s.pl.* Bottes *f* de cavalier. **'Jack-in-the-box,** *s.* **1.** *Toys :* Diable *m* (à ressort) ; boîte *f* à surprise. **2.** *F :* (*Of pers.*) Fantoche *m.* **'jack-knife,** *s.* Couteau *m* de poche ; couteau pliant. **jack-o'-'lantern,** *s.* Feu follet. **'jack-plane,** *s.* *Tl :* Riflard *m* ; demi-varlope *f.* **'jack-shaft,** *s.* *Aut :* Arbre *m* secondaire, arbre de renvoi. **'jack-'tar,** *s.* Marin ; *F :* mathurin. **An old jack-tar,** un oup de mer. **'jack-'towel,** *s.* Essuie-main(s) *m inv* à rouleau ; touaille *f.*

jack[2] **up,** *v.tr.* Soulever (une charrette, etc.) avec un cric, avec un vérin.

jack[3], *s.* *Nau :* Pavillon *m* de beaupré. *S.a.* UNION JACK. **'jack-staff,** *s.* *Nau :* Mât *m,* bâton *m,* de pavillon de beaupré.

jack[4], *s.* *Archeol :* **1.** *Cost :* Jaque *f,* hoqueton *m.* **2.** Broc *m* en cuir.

jackal ['dʒakɔ:l], *s.* Chacal *m,* -als.

jackanapes ['dʒakəneips], *s.* **1.** *A :* Singe *m.* **2.** *F :* (*a*) Impertinent *m,* fat *m.* (*b*) Petit vaurien.

jackass ['dʒakas], *s.* **1.** (*a*) *Z :* Ane (mâle) *m* ; baudet *m.* (*b*) *F :* Idiot *m,* imbécile *m.* **2.** *Orn :* **Laughing jackass,** martin-pêcheur géant d'Australie.

jackdaw ['dʒakdɔ:], *s.* Choucas *m* ; corneille *f* d'église. *F :* **Jackdaw in peacock's feathers,** geai paré des plumes du paon.

jacket¹ ['dʒaket], *s.* **1.** (*a*) *Cost:* Veston *m* (d'homme); jaquette *f* (de femme); veste *f* (de garçon de café); casaque *f* (de jockey). **Bed-jacket,** liseuse *f.* **Single-breasted jacket,** veston droit. *Double-breasted j.,* veston croisé. *S.a.* BLUE JACKET, DINNER-JACKET, ETON JACKET. (*b*) Robe *f* (d'un animal); pelure *f* (de fruit, etc.). **Potatoes cooked in their jackets,** pommes de terre en robe de chambre. **2.** (*a*) Chemise *f* (de documents). **Filing jacket,** garde-notes *m inv*; classeur *m.* (*b*) Couverture *f* (mobile) (de livre). *S.a.* DUST-JACKET. (*c*) *I.C.E:* etc: **Water-jacket, cooling-jacket,** chemise d'eau; manchon *m* de refroidissement.

jacket², *v.tr.* Garnir, envelopper, (une chaudière, etc.) d'une chemise. **jacketing,** *s.* Chemisage *m* (d'un cylindre, etc.).

jackstay ['dʒakstei], *s. Nau:* Filière *f* d'envergure.

Jacob ['dʒeikəb]. *Pr.n.m.* Jacob. **Jacob's ladder,** l'échelle *f* de Jacob.

Jacobean [dʒakoˈbiːən], *a.* (*a*) *Arch:* De l'époque de Jacques Iᵉʳ. (*b*) *Furn:* En chêne patiné.

Jacobite ['dʒakobait], *a. & s. Eng.Hist:* Jacobite (*mf*); partisan *m* de Jacques II, des Stuarts (après 1688).

jaconet ['dʒakonet], *s. Tex:* **1.** Jaconas *m.* **2. Glazed jaconet,** brillanté *m* (pour doublures).

jade¹ [dʒeid], *s.* **1.** (*Of horse*) Rosse *f,* haridelle *f.* **2.** (*Of woman*) (*a*) Drôlesse *f.* (*b*) *F:* **You little jade!** petite coquine! petite effrontée! **She's a fickle jade,** c'est un oiseau volage.

jade², *s. Miner:* **1.** Jade *m.* **2.** Jade(-green), vert *m* de jade.

jaded ['dʒeidid], *a.* (*a*) (*Of horse*) Surmené, éreinté, excédé. (*b*) (*Of pers.*) Fatigué, excédé. **Jaded palate,** goût blasé.

jag¹ [dʒag], *s.* Pointe *f,* saillie *f,* dent *f* (de rocher).

jag², *v.tr.* (jagged [dʒagd]) Déchiqueter (une robe, etc.); denteler (le bord d'une étoffe); ébrécher (un couteau). **jagged** ['dʒagid], *a.* Déchiqueté, dentelé, ébréché; (feuille) découpée. **Jagged stone,** pierre aux arêtes vives.

jaguar ['dʒagwar, 'dʒagjuar], *s.* Jaguar *m.*

jail [dʒeil], *s.,* **jailer** ['dʒeilər], *s.* = GAOL¹, GAOLER.

jalap ['dʒaləp], *s. Bot: Pharm:* Jalap *m.*

jam¹ [dʒam], *s.* (*a*) Foule *f,* presse *f* (de gens). (*b*) **Traffic-jam,** embouteillage *m* (de la circulation). (*c*) Embâcle *m* (de glaçons, de bûches, dans une rivière).

jam², *v.* (jammed) **1.** *v.tr.* (*a*) Serrer, presser. **To jam sth. into a box,** fourrer, enfoncer de force, qch. dans une boîte. (*b*) **To get one's finger jammed,** avoir le doigt coincé, écrasé. **To jam one's hat on one's head,** enfoncer son chapeau sur sa tête. **To jam on the brakes,** freiner brusquement; serrer les freins à bloc. (*c*) Coincer, caler (une machine, etc.); enrayer (une roue, etc.). **To get jammed,** (se) coincer. (*d*) *W.Tg:* Brouiller (un message). **2.** *v.i.* (*Of machine part*) (Se) coincer, s'engager; (*of rifle*) s'enrayer; (*of wheel*) se caler; (*of brake*) se bloquer.

jam³. **1.** *pred.a.* Serré. **To stand jam (up) against the wall,** se tenir collé au mur. **2.** *adv. The bus was jam full,** l'autobus était comble. **To screw up a nut jam tight,** serrer un écrou à refus.

jam⁴, *s.* Confiture(s) *f(pl). P:* Bit of jam, coup *m* de veine. **'jam-dish,** *s.* Confiturier *m.* **'jam-jar, -pot,** *s.* Pot *m* à confitures. **'jam-'puff,** *s. Cu:* Puits *m* d'amour.

Jamaica [dʒaˈmeika]. *Pr.n.* La Jamaïque.

jamb [dʒam], *s.* Jambage *m,* montant *m* (de porte, de cheminée).

jamboree [dʒamboˈriː], *s.* Grande réunion de boy-scouts; jamboree *m.*

James [dʒeimz]. *Pr.n.m.* Jacques.

Jane [dʒein]. *Pr.n.f.* Jeanne.

Janet ['dʒanet]. *Pr.n.f.* (*Dim. of Jane*) Jeannette.

jangle¹ [dʒangl], *s.* Sons discordants; cliquetis *m.*

jangle². **1.** *v.i.* Rendre des sons discordants; cliqueter; s'entre-choquer. **2.** *v.tr.* Faire entre-choquer (des clefs, etc.). *F:* **Jangled nerves,** nerfs ébranlés, agacés. **jangling,** *a.* Aux sons discordants; cacophonique.

janissary ['dʒanisəri], *s.* = JANIZARY.

janitor ['dʒanitər], *s.* Portier *m,* concierge *m.*

janitress ['dʒanitres], *s.f.* Portière; concierge *f.*

janizary ['dʒanizəri], *s.* Janissaire *m.*

January ['dʒanjuəri], *s.* Janvier *m.* **In January,** en janvier. (*On*) **the first, the seventh, of J.,** le premier, le sept, janvier.

Jap [dʒap], *s. F:* Japonais, -aise.

Japan¹ [dʒaˈpan]. *Pr.n.* Le Japon. **In J.,** au Japon. **2.** *s.* (*a*) Laque *m* (de Chine); vernis japonais. (*b*) **Black japan,** vernis à l'asphalte.

japan², *v.tr.* (japanned) Laquer (un métal, etc.); vernisser avec du laque. **Japanned leather,** cuir verni.

Japanese [dʒapaˈniːz]. **1.** *a. & s.* Japonais, -aise. **2.** *s. Ling:* Le japonais.

japonica [dʒaˈpɔnika], *s. Bot:* **1.** Cognassier *m* du Japon. **2.** (**Camellia) japonica,** camélia *m*; rose *f* du Japon.

jar¹ [dʒɑːr], *s.* **1.** Son discordant. **2.** (*a*) Ébranlement *m*; choc *m*; secousse *f.* **Jars of a machine,** à-coups *m,* secousses *f,* battements *m,* d'une machine. **His fall gave him a nasty jar,** sa chute l'a fortement ébranlé. **Jar to the nerves,** secousse nerveuse. (*b*) Manque *m* d'accord; choc (d'intérêts, etc.). (*c*) *Family jars,* discordes familiales.

jar², *v.* (jarred) **1.** *v.i.* (*a*) Rendre un son discordant, dur. (*b*) Heurter, cogner. **To jar on s.o.'s feelings,** froisser, choquer, les sentiments de qn. **The noise jarred on my nerves,** le bruit m'agaçait, m'ébranlait, les nerfs; le bruit me portait sur les nerfs; le bruit me crispait les nerfs. (*c*) (*Of window, etc.*) Vibrer, trembler; (*of machine*) marcher par à-coups. (*d*) Être en désaccord (*with sth.,* avec qch.). **Colours that jar,** couleurs qui jurent (*with,* avec). (*e*) *Mus:* (*Of note*) Détonner. **2.** *v.tr.* (*a*) Faire vibrer. *Machine that jars the whole house,* machine qui ébranle toute la maison. (*b*) Choquer (l'oreille, etc.); agacer (les nerfs, etc.). **jarring,** *a.* **1.** (*Of sound*) Discordant, dur. **2.** (*Of blow, etc.*) Qui ébranle tout le corps; (*of incident, etc.*) qui produit une impression désagréable. **3.** (*Of door, window, etc.*) Vibrant, tremblant. **4.** En désaccord; opposé. **Jarring colours,** couleurs disparates.

jar³, *s.* **1.** Récipient *m*; pot *m* (à confitures, etc.); bocal *m,* -aux. *El:* Verre *m,* vase *m* (de pile). **2.** *El:* **Leyden jar,** bouteille *f* de Leyde.

jar⁴, *s. Used only in the phr.* **On the jar, on (a) jar,** (porte) entr'ouverte, entrebâillée.

jargon ['dʒɑːrgən], *s.* **1.** Jargon *m,* langage *m* (d'une profession, etc.). **2.** Baragouin *m* (intelligible); charabia *m.*

jarvey ['dʒɑːrvi], *s. F:* Cocher *m* (de fiacre); *P:* collignon *m.*

jasmin(e) ['dʒasmin], *s. Bot:* Jasmin *m.*

jasper ['dʒaspər], *s. Miner:* Jaspe *m.*

jaundice ['dʒɔːndis], *s. Med:* Jaunisse *f,* ictère *m.*

jaundiced ['dʒɔːndist], *a. Med:* Ictérique, bilieux. *F:* **To look on the world with a jaundiced eye,** voir tout en noir; voir jaune.

'**aunt** [dʒɔːnt], s. Petite excursion balade f, sortie f, randonnée f.

jauntiness ['dʒɔːntinəs], s. (a) Désinvolture f, insouciance f. (b) Air effronté; suffisance f.

jaunty ['dʒɔːnti], a. **1.** (a) Insouciant, désinvolte. (b) Effronté, suffisant. **2.** Enjoué, vif. Jaunty gait, démarche vive, preste. **-ily,** adv. **1.** Avec insouciance; cavalièrement. **2.** D'un air effronté ou suffisant.

Javanese [dʒɔːvaˈniːz], a. & s. Javanais, -aise.

javelin ['dʒavəlin], s. Javelot m, javeline f.

jaw[1] [dʒɔː], s. **1.** (a) Mâchoire f. The jaws, la mâchoire, les mâchoires. P: I'll break your jaw! je vais te casser la gueule! F: Jaws of a chasm, gueule f d'un gouffre. (b) Tchn: Mâchoire, mors m, mords m (d'un étau, etc.); bec m (d'une clef anglaise). **2.** P: (a) Caquet m, bavardage m. Hold your jaw! ferme ça! (b) Causette f, conversation f. (c) Discours (édifiant); F: laïus m. (d) Sermon m, semonce f. '**jaw-bone,** s. Os m maxillaire; mâchoire f. '**jaw-breaker,** s. F: Mot m à vous décrocher la mâchoire.

jaw[2]. **1.** v.i. P: (a) Caqueter, bavarder, jaser (b) Laïusser. **2.** v.tr. P: Sermonner, chapitrer (qn).

-jawed [dʒɔːd], a. **Heavy-jawed,** à forte mâchoire. S.a. LANTERN-JAWED.

jay [dʒei], s. **1.** Orn: Geai m. **2.** P: (a) Jobard m, P: gogo m. (b) Aut: **Jay(-walker),** piéton distrait ou imprudent.

jazz[1] [dʒaz], s. (a) Jazz m. (b) Tex: Étoffe bariolée. '**jazz-'band,** s. Jazz-band m.

jazz[2]. **1.** v.i. Danser le jazz. **2.** v.tr. To jazz a tune, tourner une mélodie en jazz.

jealous ['dʒeləs], a. **1.** Jaloux (of, de). To be jealous of, for, one's good name, être jaloux de sa réputation. **2.** Jealous care, soin jaloux. **-ly,** adv. **1.** Jalousement. **2.** Soigneusement.

jealousy ['dʒeləsi], s. Jalousie f.

Jean[1] [dʒiːn]. Pr.n.f. Scot: Jeanne.

jean[2], s. **1.** Tex: Coutil m, treillis m. **2.** pl. Cost: Jeu m de treillis.

jeer[1] ['dʒiːər], s. **1.** Raillerie f, gausserie f. **2.** Huée f.

jeer[2], v.i. **1.** To jeer at sth., se moquer de qch. **2.** To jeer at s.o., (i) se moquer de qn; F: se gausser de qn; (ii) huer, conspuer, qn. **jeering**[1], a. Railleur, -euse, moqueur, -euse.

jeering[2], s. Raillerie f, moquerie f.

Jehovah [dʒiˈhouvə]. Pr.n.m. Jéhovah.

Jehu ['dʒiːhjuː]. **1.** Pr.n.m. Jéhu. **2.** s. (a) Cocher qui va un train d'enfer. (b) Automédon m.

jejune [dʒiˈdʒuːn], a. Stérile, aride.

jejuneness [dʒiˈdʒuːnnəs], s. Stérilité f, aridité f.

jell [dʒel], v.i. Esp. U.S: = JELLY[2].

jelly[1] ['dʒeli], s. **1.** Cu: Gelée f. F: To pound s.o. to a jelly, réduire qn en marmelade. **2.** Hectograph jelly, pâte f à copier. '**jelly-bag,** s. Cu: Chausse f (à filtrer la gelée). '**jelly-fish,** s. Coel: Méduse f.

jelly[2]. **1.** v.tr. Faire prendre (un jus) en gelée. Cold jellied chicken, chaud-froid m de poulet. **2.** v.i. Se prendre en gelée.

jemmy ['dʒemi], s. (Burglar's) jemmy, pince f monseigneur.

jennet ['dʒenet], s. (Horse) Genet m.

Jenny ['dʒeni]. **1.** Pr.n.f. (Dim. of Jane) Jeannette. **2.** s. (a) Jenny wren, roitelet m. (b) (Indicating the female) Jenny owl, hibou m femelle. Jenny(-ass), ânesse f. **3.** s. Tex: (Spinning-) jenny, machine f à filer.

jeopardize ['dʒepərdaiz], v.tr. Exposer au danger; mettre en péril. To j. one's life, com-promettre sa vie To j. one's business, laisser péricliter ses affaires.

jeopardy ['dʒepərdi], s. Danger m, péril m. To be in jeopardy, (of life) être en danger; (of happiness) être compromis; (of business) péricliter.

jerboa ['dʒɔːrboa, dʒɔr'boua], s. Z: Gerboise f.

jeremiad [dʒeri'maiəd], s. Jérémiade f.

Jeremiah [dʒeri'maiə]. **1.** Pr.n.m. Jérémie. **2.** s.m. F: Geigneur, geignard; prophète de malheur.

Jericho ['dʒeriko]. Pr.n. Jéricho m. F: To send s.o. to Jericho, envoyer promener, envoyer paître, qn. Go to Jericho! va t'asseoir! fiche-moi le camp!

jerk[1] [dʒɔːrk], s. **1.** Saccade f, secousse f (d'une corde). With one jerk, tout d'une tire. To move by jerks, avancer par saccades, par à-coups. **2.** Med: Réflexe tendineux.

jerk[2]. **1.** v.tr. (a) Donner une secousse, une saccade, des saccades, à (qch.); tirer (qch.) d'un coup sec. He jerked himself free, il se dégagea d'une secousse. (b) Lancer brusquement (une pierre). **2.** v.i. Se mouvoir soudainement, par saccades.

jerked [dʒɔːkt], a. (Of meat) Charqué.

jerkin ['dʒɔːrkin], s. A.Cost: Justaucorps m.

jerky ['dʒɔːrki], a. Saccadé; (of style) coupé. **-ily,** adv. Par saccades; par à-coups.

Jerry ['dʒeri]. **1.** Pr.n.m. Jérémie. **2.** s. P: (a) Mil: Boche m. (b) Pot de chambre. '**jerry(-built),** a. Jerry(-built) house, maison de pacotille, de camelote. '**jerry-builder,** s. Constructeur m de maisons de pacotille.

jersey ['dʒɔːrzi], s. Cost: Jersey m; tricot m (de laine). Sailor's jersey, vareuse f. Football jersey, maillot m.

jessamine ['dʒesəmin], s. = JASMIN(E).

jest[1] [dʒest], s. **1.** Raillerie f, plaisanterie f, badinage m. To say sth. in jest, dire qch. en plaisantant. Half in jest, half in earnest, moitié plaisantant, moitié sérieux. **2.** Bon mot; facétie f.

jest[2], v.i. Plaisanter (about sth., sur qch.); badiner. **jesting,** s. Raillerie f, plaisanterie f, badinage m.

jester ['dʒestər], s. Hist: Bouffon m.

Jesuit ['dʒezjuit], s. Jésuite m.

Jesuitical [dʒezju'itik(ə)l], a. Jésuitique.

Jesus ['dʒiːzəs]. Pr.n.m. Jésus.

jet[1] [dʒet], s. Miner: Jais m. '**jet-'black,** a. Noir comme du jais.

jet[2], s. **1.** Jet m (d'eau, de vapeur). **2.** (a) Ajutage m, jet (de tuyau d'arrosage). (b) I.C.E: (Carburetter) jet, gicleur m. (c) Brûleur m (à gaz, de foyer à mazout).

jetsam ['dʒetsəm], s. Jur: **1.** Marchandise jetée à la mer (pour alléger le navire). **2.** Épaves jetées à la côte.

jettison ['dʒetis(ə)n], v.tr. (jettisoned) Nau: To jettison the cargo, jeter la cargaison à la mer; se délester de la cargaison.

jetty ['dʒeti], s. Jetée f, digue f; (on piles) estacade f, appontement m. '**jetty-'head,** s. Musoir m (de jetée).

Jew [dʒuː], s.m. Juif. The wandering Jew, le Juif errant. **Jew's-'harp,** s. Guimbarde f.

jewel ['dʒuəl], s. **1.** (a) Bijou m, joyau m. F: She's a jewel of a servant, cette servante est une perle. (b) pl. Pierres précieuses; pierreries f. '**jewel-case,** s. Coffret m à bijoux; écrin m. '**jewel-stand,** s. Porte-bijoux m inv.

jewelled ['dʒuəld], a. **1.** Orné de bijoux. **2.** Clockm: Monté sur rubis.

jeweller ['dʒuələr], s. Bijoutier m, joaillier m.

jewel(le)ry ['dʒuəlri], s. Bijouterie f, joaillerie f.

Jewess ['dʒues], s.f. Juive.

jewing ['dʒuiŋ], s Morilles fpl (du bec d'un pigeon).

Jewish ['dʒuiʃ], a. Juif, f. juive.

Jewry ['dʒuəri], s. La Juiverie.

Jezebel ['dʒezəbl]. Pr.n.f. **1.** B.Hist: Jézabel. **2.** F: (a) Femme éhontée. (b) **Painted Jezebel**, vieille femme fardée.

jib¹ [dʒib], s. **1.** Nau: Foc m. **Main jib**, grand foc. **Flying jib**, clinfoc m. P: I know him by the cut of his jib, je le reconnais à sa tournure. **2.** Mec.E: (Crane-)jib, derrick-jib, volée f, flèche f, potence f (de grue). **jib-'boom**, s. Nau: Bout-dehors m de foc. **Flying jib-boom**, baïonnette f de clinfoc.

jib², v.i. (jibbed) (a) (Of horse) Refuser; se dérober. (b) F: (Of pers.) Regimber. **To jib at doing sth.**, rechigner à faire qch. **jibbing**, a. (Cheval) quinteux.

jiffy ['dʒifi], s. F: In a jiffy, en, dans, un instant; F: en cinq sec.

jig¹ [dʒig], s. **1.** Danc: Mus: Gigue f. **2.** Mec.E: Calibre m, gabarit m (de réglage, d'usinage). **3.** Min: Plan automoteur (de crible à minerai); jig m.

jig², v. (jigged) **1.** v.i. (a) Danser la gigue. (b) F: To jig up and down, se trémousser (en dansant). **2.** v.tr. Min: Sasser (le minerai); laver (le minerai) au jig. **'jig-saw**, s. Scie f à chantourner. Games: **Jig-saw puzzle**, (jeu m de) patience f.

jigger¹ ['dʒigər], s. **1.** (a) Bill: Chevalet m. (b) El: W.Tel: Transformateur m d'oscillations. (c) Golf: Fer m à face renversée. **2.** Nau: (Sail) Tapecul m.

jigger², v.tr. P: I'm jiggered if I'll do it, du diable si je le fais. **Well, I'm jiggered!** pas possible! zut alors!

jilt¹ [dʒilt], s.f. Coquette (qui plaque ses amoureux).

jilt², v.tr. Laisser là, F: planter (là) (un amoureux).

Jim [dʒim], **Jimmy** ['dʒimi]. Pr.n.m. (Dim. of James) Jim, Jimmy. **'jim-'crow**, s. U.S: Nègre m.

jingle¹ ['dʒiŋgl], s. Tintement m (d'un grelot); bruit m d'anneaux; cliquetis m.

jingle². **1.** v.i. (Of bells) Tinter; (of keys) cliqueter. **2.** v.tr. Faire tinter (des grelots); faire sonner (son argent, ses clefs). **jingling**, s. Tintement m (de clochettes); cliquetis m (de clefs).

jingo ['dʒiŋgo]. **1.** int. (a) By jingo! nom de nom! (b) By j., you're right! tiens! mais vous avez raison! **2.** s. (pl. jingoes) Chauvin, -ine.

jingoism ['dʒiŋgoizm], s. Chauvinisme m.

jinks [dʒiŋks], s.pl. F: High jinks, (i) A: soirée f folâtre; (ii) folichonneries fpl. **To hold high jinks**, s'amuser bruyamment.

jinnee, pl. **jinn, F: jinns** ['dʒini; dʒin, dʒinz], s. Djinn m.

jinricksha [dʒin'rikʃa], s. Pousse-pousse m inv.

Joan [dʒoun]. Pr.n.f. Jeanne.

job [dʒɔb], s. **1.** (a) Tâche f, besogne f, travail m. **To do a job**, exécuter un travail. I have a little job, F: a job of work, for you, j'ai de quoi vous occuper un peu. F: To be on the job, travailler avec acharnement. **Odd jobs**, (i) petits travaux; (ii) les métiers m à part. **To do odd jobs**, bricoler. **Odd-job man**, homme à tout faire. **To work by the job**, travailler à la tâche, à la pièce. F: To make a (good) job of sth., réussir qch. **It's a good job that . . .**, il est fort heureux que. . . **That's a good job!** ce n'est pas malheureux! à la bonne heure! **It's a bad job!** c'est une triste affaire! **To give sth. up as a bad job**, y renoncer. (b) Tâche difficile; corvée f. I had a job to do it, j'ai eu du mal à le faire. It's quite a job to get there, c'est toute une affaire que d'y aller. **2.** F: Emploi m. He has a fine job, il a une belle situation. He likes his job, F: il aime son boulot. **To be out of a job**, être sans ouvrage; chômer. This trade is not anybody's job, ce métier n'est pas l'affaire de tout le monde. He knows his job, il connaît son affaire. **Every man to his job**, chacun son métier. **3.** Intrigue f, tripotage m. **'job-line**, s. Com: Solde(s) m(pl); marchandises fpl d'occasion. **'job 'lot**, s. Com: (Lot m de) soldes mpl. **To buy a job lot of books**, acheter des livres en vrac. **'job-master**, s. Loueur m de chevaux et de voitures. **'job-work**, s. (a) Travail m à la pièce, aux pièces, à la tâche. (b) Travail à forfait.

jobber ['dʒɔbər], s. **1.** = JOB-MASTER. **2.** Intermédiaire m revendeur. **3.** St.Exch: (Stock-)jobber, marchand m de titres. **4.** Pej: Tripoteur m.

jobbery ['dʒɔbəri], s. Tripotages mpl; prévarication f.

jobbing¹ ['dʒɔbiŋ], a. Jobbing workman, ouvrier à la tâche. J. tailor, tailleur à façon. **Jobbing gardener**, jardinier à la journée.

jobbing². s. **1.** Louage m de voitures, de chevaux. **2.** Ind: Com: Commerce m d'intermédiaire.

jockey ['dʒɔki], s. Jockey m.

jockey², v.tr. To jockey s.o. into doing sth., amener sournoisement qn à faire qch.

jocose [dʒo'kous], a. Facétieux; goguenard, gouailleur. **-ly**, adv. Facétieusement; d'un ton goguenard; en plaisantant.

jocoseness [dʒo'kousnəs], s. Humeur joviale.

jocular ['dʒɔkjulər], a. Facétieux. With a j. air, d'un air rieur. **-ly**, adv. Facétieusement.

jocularity [dʒɔkju'læriti], s. Jovialité f.

jocund ['dʒoukənd, 'dʒɔkənd], a. Lit: Jovial, -aux; enjoué.

jodhpurs ['dʒɔdpərz], s.pl. Cost: Pantalon m d'équitation (serré du genou à la cheville).

jog¹ [dʒɔg], s. **1.** (a) Coup m (de coude). F: To give s.o.'s memory a jog, rafraîchir la mémoire de qn. (b) Secousse f, cahot m. **2.** Petit trot. **'jog-trot**, s. Petit trot. At a jog-trot, au petit trot. The jog-trot of the office, le train-train du bureau.

jog², v. (jogged) **1.** v.tr. To jog s.o.'s elbow, pousser le coude à qn. **To jog s.o.'s memory**, rafraîchir la mémoire à qn. **2.** v.i. To jog along, aller son petit bonhomme de chemin. We are jogging along, les choses vont leur train.

joggle¹ ['dʒɔgl], v.tr. F: Secouer légèrement.

joggle², s. **1.** Joint m à goujon, à embrèvement. **2.** Carp: etc: Goujon m.

joggle³, v.tr. Carp: (a) Goujonner (deux pièces). (b) Embrever (deux pièces).

John [dʒɔn]. Pr.n.m. Jean. **St John the Baptist**, saint Jean-Baptiste.

Johnnie, Johnny ['dʒɔni]. **1.** Pr.n.m. Jeannot. Mil: P: Johnny Raw, bleu m, morveux m. **2.** s. P: Type m, individu m. **3.** s. Orn: F: Manchot m.

join¹ [dʒɔin], s. Joint m, jointure f; ligne f de jonction (de deux feuilles d'une carte, etc.).

join². **1.** v.tr. **1.** (a) Joindre, unir, réunir. **To join (together) the broken ends of a cord**, (re)nouer les bouts cassés d'un cordon. **To join sth. with sth.**, réunir qch. à qch. **To join hands (with s.o.)**, s'unir à qn, se joindre à qn (pour faire qch.); se donner la main. **To join forces with s.o., to join company with s.o.**, se joindre à qn. *(b)* Ajouter. *To j. threats with, to, remonstrances,* ajouter les menaces aux remontrances. *(c) Straight line that joins two points,* droite *f* qui joint deux points. *The road that joins Paris to Trouville,* la route qui relie Paris et Trouville. **2.** *(a)* Se joindre à, s'unir à (qn); rejoindre (qn). *He joined us on our way,* il nous a rejoints en route. **Will you join us, join our party?** voulez-vous vous mettre des nôtres? *To j. the procession,* se mêler au cortège. *(b) Mil:* **To join one's unit,** rallier son unité. *Navy:* **To join one's ship,** rallier le bord. *(c)* Entrer dans (un club, un régiment). *To j. a party,* s'affilier à un parti. **3.** Se joindre, s'unir, à (qch.). *The footpath joins the road,* le sentier rejoint la route. II. **join,** *v.i.* Se (re)joindre, s'unir *(with,* à). **To join together,** *(of bone)* se souder; *(of pers.)* se réunir. **join in,** *v.i.* **1.** *To j. in the protests,* prendre part, joindre sa voix, aux protestations. **2.** Se mettre de la partie. **join up. 1.** *v.tr.* *(a)* Assembler (deux choses); embrancher (des tuyaux). *(b) El:* Connecter, (ac)coupler (des piles). **2.** *v.i. Mil:* *F:* -S'engager; entrer au service. **joining,** *s.* **1.** Jonction *f,* assemblage *m*; liaison *f* (de sons). **2.** Entrée *f* (dans un club); engagement *m* (dans l'armée).

joiner ['dʒɔinər], *s.* Menuisier *m.* **Joiner's shop,** menuiserie *f.*

joinery ['dʒɔinəri], *s.* Menuiserie *f.*

joint¹ [dʒɔint], *s.* **1.** *(a)* Joint *m,* jointure *f. F:* **To find the joint in the armour,** trouver le défaut de la cuirasse. **Soldered joint,** soudure *f.* **Universal joint, Cardan joint,** joint articulé; joint de Cardan. *(b) Bookb:* Mors *m. (c) Carp: etc:* Assemblage *m.* **Mortise-and-tenon joint,** assemblage à tenon et (à) mortaise; assemblage à emboîtement. **Scarf-joint,** assemblage à mi-bois. **2.** *Anat:* Joint, jointure (du genou). **Elbow-joint,** articulation *f* du coude. *Rheumatism in, of, the joints,* rhumatisme articulaire. **Out of joint,** (bras) disloqué, déboîté. **3.** *(a)* Partie *f* entre deux articulations; phalange *f* (du doigt). **Three-joint fishing-rod,** canne à pêche à trois corps. *(b) Cu:* Morceau *m,* quartier *m,* pièce *f,* de viande. **Cut off the joint,** tranche *f* de rôti. **4.** *U.S: P:* Gambling joint, tripot *m.* **Opium joint,** fumerie *f* d'opium.

joint², *a.* **1.** (En) commun; combiné. **Joint action,** action collective. **Joint commission,** commission mixte. **Joint undertaking,** entreprise en participation. *Fin:* **Joint shares,** actions indivises. **Joint stock,** capital social. **Joint-stock bank,** société *f* de dépôt. **2.** Co-, associé. **Joint heir,** cohéritier. *J. management,* codirection *f.* **-ly,** *adv.* Ensemble, conjointement. *Jur:* **Jointly liable, responsible,** solidaire. **Jointly and severally liable,** responsables conjointement et solidairement.

jointed ['dʒɔintid], *a.* Articulé. *Mec.E:* **Jointed coupling,** accouplement à articulation.

jointure ['dʒɔintjər], *s.* Douaire *m.*

joist [dʒɔist], *s. Const:* Solive *f,* poutre *f,* poutrelle *f.*

joke¹ [dʒouk], *s.* *(a)* Plaisanterie *f,* farce *f, F:* blague *f.* *I did it for a j.,* je l'ai fait histoire de rire. *The joke is that ...,* le comique de l'histoire, c'est que ... *F: It will be no j. to ...,* ce ne sera pas une petite affaire (que) de ... *Practical joke,* mystification *f,* farce. *That's a good j.!* en voilà une bonne! *He knows how to take a j.,* il entend la plaisanterie. *(b)* Bon

mot; facétie *f,* plaisanterie. *He must have his little j.,* il aime à plaisanter.

joke², *v.i.* Plaisanter, badiner. **To joke at, about,** sth., plaisanter de qch. *I was only joking,* je l'ai dit histoire de rire. *You're joking!* vous voulez rire! *I'm not joking,* je ne plaisante pas. **joking¹,** *a.* (Ton, air) moqueur, de plaisanterie. **-ly,** *adv.* En plaisantant; pour rire. **joking²,** *s.* Plaisanterie *f,* badinage *m, F:* blague *f.*

joker ['dʒoukər], *s.* **1.** Farceur, -euse; plaisant *m; F:* loustic *m.* **Practical joker,** mauvais plaisant. **2.** *P:* Type *m,* individu *m.* **3.** *Cards:* Joker *m.*

jollification [dʒɔlifi'keiʃ(ə)n], *s. F:* Partie *f* de plaisir; rigolade *f*; petite noce. *To have a j.,* faire la noce.

jollity ['dʒɔliti], *s.* **1.** Gaieté *f.* **2.** Réjouissance *f.*

jolly¹ ['dʒɔli]. **I.** *a.* *(a)* Joyeux, gai, gaillard. *To have a j. evening,* passer une soirée joyeuse. *(b) F:* Éméché; légèrement pris de boisson. *(c) J. little room,* gentille petite chambre. *(d) P:* (Intensifying) *I got a j. hiding,* j'ai reçu une fameuse raclée. *It's a j. shame,* pour sûr que c'est pas chic. **2.** *adv. P:* Rudement, fameusement. **Jolly glad,** rudement content. *I'll take j. good care,* je ferai rudement attention.

jolly²-boat ['dʒɔli(bout)], *s. Nau:* (Petit) canot (à bord d'un navire).

jolt¹ [dʒoult], *s.* *(a)* Cahot *m,* secousse *f.* *(b) Mec.E:* A-coup *m, pl.* à-coups.

jolt². **1.** *v.tr.* Cahoter, secouer. **2.** *v.i.* *(a)* Cahoter, tressauter. *The carriage jolted terribly,* la voiture avait des cahots terribles. *(b) Mec.E:* Avoir, donner, des à-coups, des coups de raquette.

Jonah ['dʒouna]. **1.** *Pr.n.m.* Jonas. **2.** *s. F:* Guignard *m.* *A Jonah aboard,* un porte-malheur *inv.*

jonquil ['dʒɔŋkwil], *s. Bot:* Jonquille *f.*

Jordan ['dʒɔːrdən]. *Pr.n. Geog:* Le Jourdain. *F:* **This side of Jordan,** de ce côté de la tombe.

jorum ['dʒɔːrəm], *s.* Bol *m,* bolée *f* (de punch).

Joshua ['dʒɔʃjuə]. *Pr.n.m. B.Hist:* Josué.

joss [dʒɔs], *s.* *(In China)* Idole *f.* **'joss-house,** *s.* Temple *m.* **'joss-stick,** *s.* Bâton *m* d'encens.

josser ['dʒɔsər], *s. P:* Type *m,* individu *m.* **Old josser,** vieille baderne.

jostle [dʒɔsl]. **1.** *v.i.* Jouer des coudes. **To jostle against s.o. in the crowd,** bousculer qn dans la foule. **2.** *v.tr.* *(a)* Bousculer, coudoyer (qn). **To be jostled about,** être houspillé. *(b) Rac:* Serrer (un concurrent). **jostling,** *s.* **1.** Bousculade *f.* **2.** *Rac:* Action *f* de serrer un concurrent.

jot¹ [dʒɔt], *s. F:* **Not a jot, not one jot or tittle,** pas un iota. *Not a jot of truth,* pas un atome de vérité.

jot², *v.tr.* (jotted) **To jot sth. down,** noter qch.; prendre note de qch.; jeter qch. sur le papier. **jotting,** *s.* **1.** Jotting down *(of a note),* prise *f* (d'une note). **2.** *pl.* Jottings, notes *f.*

journal ['dʒəːrn(ə)l], *s.* **1.** Journal *m,* -aux. *Nau:* Journal de bord; livre *m* de loch. **2.** *Mec.E:* Tourillon *m* (d'arbre). *Main journals of the crank-shaft,* portées *fpl* du vilebrequin. **'journal-box,** *s. Mec.E:* Boîte *f* des coussinets.

journalese [dʒəː'rəˈliːz], *s. F:* Style *m* de journaliste, de journal.

journalism ['dʒəːrnəlizm], *s.* Journalisme *m.*

journalist ['dʒəːrnəlist], *s.* Journaliste *mf.*

journey¹, *pl.* **-eys** ['dʒəːrni, -iz], *s.* Voyage *m*; trajet *m.* *To set out on one's j.,* se mettre en route. **On a journey,** en voyage. **Pleasant journey!** bon voyage! *He talked the whole j.,* il a parlé pendant tout le parcours. *Aut:* The *j. across the Sahara,* la traversée du Sahara.

journey², *v.i.* (journeyed) Voyager.

journeyman, *pl.* **-men** ['dʒə:rnimən, -men], *s.* I. Journeyman carpenter, compagnon charpentier. Journeyman baker, ouvrier boulanger. 2. *F:* Homme *m* de peine.

joust¹ [dʒu:st, dʒaust], *s. A. & Lit:* Joute *f.*

joust², *v.i. A. & Lit:* Jouter.

Jove [dʒo:uv]. *Pr.n.m.* Jupiter. Jove's thunderbolts, les traits *m* de Jupiter. *F:* By Jove! mâtin! By *J.,* it is cold! bigre, qu'il fait froid!

jovial ['dʒouvjəl], *a.* Jovial, -aux. **-ally,** *adv.* Jovialement.

joviality [dʒouvi'aliti], *s.* Jovialité *f,* gaîté *f.*

jowl [dʒaul], *s.* (a) Mâchoire *f.* (b) Joue *f,* bajoue *f* (d'homme, de porc). (c) Hure *f,* tête *f* (de saumon).

joy [dʒɔi], *s.* Joie *f,* allégresse *f.* To leap for joy, sauter de joie. Oh joy! quel bonheur! To wish s.o. joy (of sth.), féliciter qn (de qch.). *The joys of the countryside,* les charmes *m* de la campagne. **'joy-bells,** *s.pl.* Carillon *m* (de fête). *The joy-bells were ringing,* les cloches carillonnaient. **'joy-ride,** *s.* I. Balade en auto (faite à l'insu du propriétaire). 2. *Av:* Vol *m* de plaisir. **'joy-stick,** *s. Av: F:* Levier *m* de commande; *F:* manche *m* à balai.

joyful ['dʒɔiful], *a.* Joyeux, heureux. **-fully,** *adv.* Joyeusement.

joyfulness ['dʒɔifulnəs], *s.* Joie *f,* allégresse *f.*

joyless ['dʒɔiləs], *a.* Sans joie; triste.

joylessness ['dʒɔiləsnəs], *s.* Absence *f* de joie; tristesse *f.*

joyous ['dʒɔiəs], *a. Lit:* Joyeux, heureux. **-ly,** *adv.* Joyeusement.

joyousness ['dʒɔiəsnəs], *s.* Joie *f,* allégresse *f.*

jubilant ['dʒubilənt], *a.* (a) (*Of pers.*) Réjoui (at sth., de qch.); *F:* dans la jubilation. (b) (Cri) joyeux. *J. face,* visage épanoui. **-ly,** *adv.* Avec joie; *F:* dans la jubilation.

jubilate ['dʒubileit], *v.i.* Se réjouir; exulter.

jubilation [dʒubi'leiʃ(ə)n], *s.* (a) Joie *f,* allégresse *f; F:* jubilation. (b) *F:* Réjouissance *f,* fête *f.*

jubilee ['dʒubili:], *s.* Jubilé *m;* cinquantième anniversaire *m.* Silver jubilee, fête *f* du vingt-cinquième anniversaire. Diamond jubilee, fête du soixantième anniversaire.

Judaic(al) [dʒu'deiik(əl)], *a.* Judaïque.

Judaism ['dʒu:deizm], *s.* Judaïsme *m.*

Judas ['dʒu:dəs]. I. *Pr.n.m.* Judas. Judas kiss, baiser *m* de Judas. 2. *s.* Judas(-hole, -trap), judas *m* (dans une porte).

judge¹ [dʒʌdʒ], *s.* I. Juge *m.* Presiding judge, président *m* du tribunal. 2. *Sp: etc:* Arbitre *m,* juge. 3. Connaisseur, -euse. *To be a good j. of wine,* s'y connaître en vin.

judge², *v.tr.* I. (a) Juger (un prisonnier, une affaire). *A man is judged by his actions,* un homme se juge par ses actions. (b) *To j. others by oneself,* mesurer les autres à son aune. Judging by . . ., à en juger par. . . . (c) Arbitrer (à un comice agricole, etc.). 2. Apprécier, estimer (une distance). 3. To judge it necessary to do sth., juger nécessaire de faire qch. It is for you to judge, c'est à vous d'en juger. 4. *v.ind.tr.* Judge of my surprise! jugez de ma surprise!

judg(e)ment ['dʒʌdʒmənt], *s.* I. (a) The Last Judgment, le jugement dernier. *F:* To sit in judgment on s.o., se poser en juge de qn. (b) Décision *f* judiciaire; arrêt *m,* sentence *f. J. by consent,* jugement d'accord. To pronounce, deliver, judgment, rendre un arrêt;

statuer sur une affaire. *F:* It is a judgment on you, c'est un châtiment de Dieu. 2. Opinion *f,* avis *m.* To give one's judgment on sth., exprimer son avis, son sentiment, sur qch. 3. Bon sens; discernement *m.* To have sound, good, judgment, avoir le jugement sain. *To use j. in sth.,* faire preuve de discernement. **'judg(e)ment-day,** *s.* (Jour *m* du) jugement dernier.

judicature ['dʒu:dikətjər], *s.* I. Judicature *f.* 2. *Coll.* La magistrature.

judicial [dʒu'diʃəl], *a.* I. (a) Juridique. Judicial enquiry, enquête judiciaire. *J. proof,* preuves en justice. (b) *To be invested with j. powers,* être investi de pouvoirs judiciaires. *A:* Judicial combat, combat judiciaire. 2. Judicial faculty, faculté judiciaire; sens critique. **-ally,** *adv.* I. Judiciairement. 2. Impartialement.

judiciary [dʒu'diʃəri]. I. *a.* Judiciaire. 2. *s.* = JUDICATURE 2.

judicious [dʒu'diʃəs], *a.* Judicieux. **-ly,** *adv.* Judicieusement.

judiciousness [dʒu'diʃəsnəs], *s.* Discernement *m;* bon sens.

jug¹ [dʒʌg], *s.* I. Cruche *f,* broc *m;* (*for milk*) pot *m.* Small jug, cruchon *m.* 2. *P:* Prison *f.*

jug², *v.tr.* (jugged) I. *Cu:* Étuver; faire cuire en civet. *Esp.* Jugged hare, civet *m* de lièvre. 2. *P:* Emprisonner, *P:* coffrer (qn).

jugful ['dʒʌgful], *s.* Cruchée *f;* plein pot (of, de).

juggins ['dʒʌginz], *s. F:* Niais *m,* jobard *m.*

juggle [dʒʌgl]. I. *v.i.* (a) Jongler (avec des boules). (b) Faire des tours de passe-passe. *F:* To juggle with figures, jongler avec les chiffres. *To j. with s.o.'s feelings,* jouer avec les sentiments de qn. 2. *v.tr.* To juggle sth. away, escamoter qch. **juggling,** *s.* = JUGGLERY.

juggler ['dʒʌglər], *s.* (a) Jongleur, -euse; bateleur *m.* (b) Escamoteur, -euse; prestidigitateur *m.*

jugglery ['dʒʌgləri], *s.* I. (a) Jonglerie *f.* (b) Tours *mpl* de passe-passe; escamotage *m.* 2. *F:* Fourberie *f;* mauvaise foi.

Jugoslav [jugo'sla:v], *a. & s.* Yougoslave (*mf*).

Jugoslavia [jugo'sla:via]. *Pr.n.* La Yougoslavie.

jugular ['dʒʌgjulər], *a. & s. Anat:* Jugulaire (*f*).

jugulate ['dʒʌgjuleit], *v.tr.* I. Égorger. 2. (a) Étrangler. (b) *F:* Juguler (une maladie, une épidémie).

juice [dʒu:s], *s.* I. Jus *m,* suc *m* (de la viande, d'un fruit). 2. *P:* (a) *Aut:* Essence *f, P:* jus. (b) *El.E:* Courant *m, P:* jus.

juiciness ['dʒu:sinəs], *s.* Succulence *f.*

juicy ['dʒu:si], *a.* Succulent, juteux; plein de jus. *F:* Juicy pipe, pipe qui supe.

jujube ['dʒu:dʒu:b], *s.* I. *Bot:* Jujube *f.* 2. Boule *f* de gomme.

Julian ['dʒu:ljən], *a.* Julien; de Jules César. *Chr:* Julian year, année julienne.

Juliet ['dʒu:ljet]. *Pr.n.f.* Juliette.

July, *pl.* **-s** [dʒu'lai, -a:iz], *s.* Juillet *m.* In July, in the month of July, en juillet, au mois de juillet.

jumble [dʒʌmbl], *s.* Méli-mélo *m,* fouillis *m,* fatras *m.* **'jumble-sale,** *s.* Vente *f* d'objets usagés, etc. (pour une œuvre de charité).

jumble², *v.tr.* Brouiller, mêler. *To j. everything up, F:* tout mettre en salade.

jump¹ [dʒʌmp], *s.* I. (a) Saut *m,* bond *m.* To take a jump, faire un saut; sauter. *Sp:* High jump, saut en hauteur. Long jump, saut en longueur. *F:* Jump in prices, sauté *f* dans les prix. (b) Lacune *f,* vide *m* (dans une série). 2. Sursaut *m,* haut-le-corps *m inv.* That gave

me a jump, cela m'a fait sursauter. *F:* To keep
s.o. on the jump, ne pas laisser le temps de
souffler à qn. **3.** *Turf: Equit:* Obstacle *m.* To
put a horse over a jump, faire sauter un obstacle
à son cheval. *Race-course with jumps,* piste *f* à
obstacles.
jump². I. *v.i.* **1.** Sauter, bondir. To jump off a
wall, sauter à bas d'un mur. *F:* To jump down
s.o.'s throat, rembarrer, rabrouer, qn. *F:* To
jump at an offer, saisir une occasion ; s'empresser
d'accepter une offre. To jump to a conclusion,
conclure à la légère. **2.** (*a*) Sursauter, tressauter.
The price mentioned made me j., l'énoncé du prix
me fit sauter. (*b*) (*Of tool*) Brouter. (*c*) (*Of gun*)
Se cabrer. II. **jump,** *v.tr.* **1.** Franchir, sauter
(une haie). *To i. a flight of stairs,* sauter du haut
en bas d'un escalier. *Rail:* (*Of engine, etc.*) To
jump the metals, sortir des rails ; dérailler. (*Of
gramophone needle*) To jump the sound-groove,
dérailler. **2.** (*a*) To jump a horse, faire sauter
un cheval. (*b*) *Bill:* To jump a ball off the table,
faire sauter une bille. **3.** Saisir (qch.) à l'improviste. *Min: U.S:* To jump a claim, s'emparer d'une concession (en l'absence de celui qui
l'a délimitée). **jump about,** *v.i.* Sautiller.
jump across, *v.tr.* Franchir (qch.) d'un bond.
jump in, *v.i.* **1.** Entrer d'un bond. *Aut: Rail:*
Jump in! montez vite ! **2.** Se jeter à l'eau (pour
sauver qn). **jump out,** *v.i.* Sortir d'un bond.
To jump out of bed, sauter à bas du lit. *F:* I
nearly jumped out of my skin, cela m'a fait
sursauter. **jump up,** *v.i.* **1.** Sauter sur ses
pieds. **2.** Bondir. **jumped-up,** *a. F:* (Bourgeois) parvenu. **'jumping-bar,** *s. Sp:* Sautoir *m.* **jumping-'off place,** *s.* Base avancée
(d'une expédition, d'un raid aérien). **'jumping-
pole,** *s. Sp:* Perche *f* à sauter.
jumper¹ ['dʒʌmpər], *s.* Sauteur, -euse. *Equit:*
High jumper, grand sauteur.
jumper², *s.* **1.** Vareuse *f,* chemise *f* (de marin).
2. Casaquin *m,* casaque *f* (de femme). *Knitted j.,*
tricot *m.*
jumpiness ['dʒʌmpinəs], *s.* Nervosité *f,* agitation *f.*
jumpy ['dʒʌmpi], *a. F:* Agité, nerveux. To be
jumpy, avoir les nerfs agacés, à vif.
junction ['dʒʌŋ(k)ʃ(ə)n], *s.* **1.** Jonction *f,* confluent *m* (de deux rivières) ; raccordement *m* (de
tuyaux). *Anat: Bot: etc:* Line of junction,
commissure *f.* **2.** (*a*) (Point *m* de) jonction ;
(em)branchement *m,* bifurcation *f* (de route, de
voie de chemin de fer). (*b*) *Rail:* Gare *f* de
bifurcation, d'embranchement.
juncture ['dʒʌŋ(k)tjər], *s.* **1.** Jointure *f* (de deux
plaques). **2.** Conjoncture *f* (de circonstances).
At this juncture, à ce moment critique.
June [dʒuːn], *s.* Juin *m.* In June, in the month
of June, en juin, au mois de juin.
jungle ['dʒʌŋgl], *s.* Jungle *f,* fourré *m,* brousse *f.*
junior ['dʒuːnjər], *a. & s.* **1.** Cadet, -ette ; plus
jeune. He is my junior by three years, il est plus
jeune que moi de trois ans. W. Smith Junior
(*abbr.* Jun.), W. Smith (i) le jeune, (ii) fils. *Sch:*
The juniors, the junior school, les petits. *
Sp:* Junior event, épreuve *f* des cadets. **2.** Moins
ancien ; subalterne (*m*). *Jur:* Junior counsel,
avocat *m* en second.
juniper ['dʒuːnipər], *s. Bot:* Genévrier *m,*
genièvre *m.* **'juniper-berry,** *s.* Baie *f* de
genièvre.
junk¹ [dʒʌŋk], *s.* **1.** (*a*) Vieux cordages ; vieux
filin ; étoupe *f.* (*b*) *Com:* Piece of junk, rossignol *m.* **2.** *Nau:* Bœuf salé.

junk², *s. Nau:* Jonque *f.*
junket¹ ['dʒʌŋket], *s.* **1.** *Cu:* Lait caillé.
2. *F:* Festin *m,* bombance *f.*
junket², *v.i.* Faire bombance ; festoyer.
Juno ['dʒuːno]. *Pr.n.f. Myth:* Junon.
junta ['dʒʌnta], *s.* **1.** *Hist:* Junte *f.* **2.** = JUNTO.
junto, *pl.* **-os** ['dʒʌnto, -ouz], *s.* Cabale *f,*
faction *f.*
Jupiter ['dʒuːpitər]. *Pr.n.m. Myth:* Jupiter.
juridical [dʒuˈridik(ə)l], *a.* Juridique.
jurisdiction [dʒuərisˈdikʃ(ə)n], *s.* Juridiction *f.*
Area within the jurisdiction of . . ., territoire
soumis à la juridiction de . . ., territoire relevant
de. . . . To come within the jurisdiction of a
court, rentrer dans la juridiction d'une cour ;
être du ressort d'une cour. *This matter does not
come within our j.,* cette matière n'est pas de
notre compétence.
jurisprudence [dʒuərisˈpruːdəns], *s.* Jurisprudence *f. Medical j.,* médecine légale.
jurist ['dʒuərist], *s.* Juriste *m,* légiste *m.*
juror ['dʒuərər], *s.* Juré *m* ; membre *m* du jury.
jury¹ ['dʒuəri], *s.* Jury *m* ; jurés *mpl.* To serve
on the jury, être du jury. Foreman of the jury,
chef *m* du jury. Gentlemen of the jury! messieurs
les jurés ! **'jury-box,** *s.* Banc(s) *m(pl)* du
jury.
jury², *a. Nau:* Improvisé. Jury-mast, -rudder,
mât *m,* gouvernail *m,* de fortune.
juryman, *pl.* **-men** ['dʒuərimən, -men], *s.*
= JUROR.
just [dʒʌst]. I. **1.** *a.* (*a*) Juste, équitable. It is
only just, ce n'est que justice. As was only just,
comme de juste. To show just cause for . . .,
donner une raison valable de. . . . (*b*) A just
remark, une observation juste, judicieuse.
2. *s.pl.* To sleep the sleep of the just, dormir du
sommeil du juste. **-ly,** *adv.* Justement. **1.** Avec
justice. To deal j. with s.o., faire justice à qn.
Famous and j. so, célèbre à juste titre. **2.** Avec
justesse ; avec juste raison. II. **just,** *adv.*
1. (*a*) Juste, justement. Just here, tout juste ici.
J. by the gate, tout près de la porte. Not ready
just yet, pas encore tout à fait prêt. Just how
many are there? combien y en a-t-il au juste?
I thought you were French.—That's j. what I am,
je pensais que vous étiez Français.—Je le suis
précisément. That's just it, (i) c'est bien cela ;
(ii) justement ! Just so! c'est bien cela ! parfaitement ! It's just the same, c'est tout un ;
F: c'est tout comme. *He did it j. for a joke,* il
l'a fait simplement histoire de rire. Just when
the door was opening, au moment même où la
porte s'ouvrait. (*b*) Just as. (i) *I can do it j. as
well as he,* je peux le faire tout aussi bien que lui.
It would be just as well if he came, il y aurait
avantage à ce qu'il vienne. Just as you please!
comme vous voudrez ! à votre aise ! *Leave my
things j. as they are,* laissez mes affaires telles
quelles. Just as . . . so . . ., de même que . . .
de même. . . . (ii) Just as he was starting out,
au moment où il partait. (*c*) Just now. (i) *Business
is bad j. now,* actuellement les affaires vont mal.
(ii) *I can't do it j. now,* je ne peux pas le faire pour
le moment. (iii) *I saw him j. now,* je l'ai vu tout
à l'heure. (*d*) *It was j. splendid,* c'était ni plus ni
moins que merveilleux. *P:* Won't you just
catch it! tu (ne) vas rien écoper ! *You remember?*
—Don't I just! vous vous en souvenez?—Si je
m'en souviens ! **2.** (*a*) Just before *I came,*
immédiatement avant mon arrivée. (*b*) He has
just written to you, il vient de vous écrire. *He
has (only) j. come,* il ne fait que d'arriver. *I have*

only *j. heard of it*, je l'apprends à l'instant même.
I have j. dined, je sors de table. **Just cooked,**
fraîchement cuit. *(Of book)* **Just out,** vient de
paraître. **3.** *He was j. beginning*, il ne faisait que
de commencer. *I was j. finishing my dinner,*
j'achevais de dîner. *I am j. coming!* j'arrive!
He is j. going out, il est sur le point de sortir.
4. **He just managed to do it,** c'est à peine s'il
a pu le faire. *I was only j. saved from drowning,*
j'ai failli me noyer. *I've got only j. enough to live
on*, j'ai tout juste de quoi vivre. **You are just in
time to . . .,** vous arrivez juste à temps pour. . . .
5. *(a)* Seulement. **Just once,** rien qu'une fois.
Just one, un seul. **Just a little bit,** un tout petit
peu. *J. give her a pair of gloves*, donnez-lui tout
simplement une paire de gants. *I j. told him
that . . .,* je lui ai dit tout bonnement que. . . .
(b) *F:* **Just sit down, please,** veuillez donc vous
asseoir. *J. listen!* écoutez donc! *J. look!* regardez-moi ça!
justice ['dʒʌstis], *s.* **I.** Justice *f.* *(a) To dispute
the j. of a sentence*, contester le bien-fondé, la
justice, d'un jugement. *(b) I am bound in j.
to . . .*, je suis obligé, pour être juste, de. . . .
Poetical justice, justice idéale. **To do justice to
one's talent,** faire valoir son talent. *F:* **To do
justice to a meal,** faire honneur à un repas.
(c) **To bring s.o. to justice,** traduire qn en justice.
2. Magistrat *m.* *(a)* Juge *m.* **The Lord Chief**

Justice, le président du Tribunal du Banc du Roi.
(b) **The Justices,** les magistrats (de la justice
de paix).
justifiable ['dʒʌstifaiəbl], *a.* (Crime) justifiable;
(colère) légitime. *J. refusal*, refus motivé. **-ably,**
adv. Justifiablement, légitimement.
justification [dʒʌstifi'keiʃ(ə)n], *s.* Justification *f.*
justify ['dʒʌstifai], *v.tr.* **I.** Justifier (qn, sa
conduite); légitimer, motiver (une action).
2. *Typ:* Justifier (une ligne). **justified,** *a.*
Justifié. *Fully j. decision*, décision bien fondée.
To be justified in doing sth., être fondé, justifié,
à faire qch. **He was justified in the event,**
l'événement lui donna raison.
justness ['dʒʌstnəs], *s.* **I.** Justice *f* (d'une cause).
2. Justesse *f* (d'une observation).
jut [dʒʌt], *v.i.* (jutted) **To jut (out),** être en saillie;
faire saillie, (s')avancer. *To jut out over sth.,*
surplomber qch. **jutting(-out),** *a.* Saillant; en
saillie.
jute [dʒuːt], *s.* *Bot:* *Tex:* Jute *m.*
juvenile ['dʒuːvinail]. **I.** *a.* Juvénile. *J. books,*
livres pour la jeunesse. *J. literature,* littérature
enfantine. *J. offender*, accusé mineur. **2.** *s.*
Jeune *mf.*
juxtapose [dʒʌksta'pouz], *v.tr.* Juxtaposer.
juxtaposed, *a.* Juxtaposé; en juxtaposition.
juxtaposition [dʒʌkstapo'ziʃ(ə)n], *s.* Juxtaposition *f.* *To be in j.*, se juxtaposer.

K

K, k [kei], *s.* (La lettre) K, k *m.*
Kaffir ['kafər], *a. & s. Ethn:* Cafre (*mf*).
kail [keil], *s.* = KALE.
kailyard ['keiljɑːrd], *s. Scot:* Jardin potager.
kainite ['kainait], *s. Miner:* Kaïnite *f.*
kale [keil], *s.* **I.** Curly kale, chou frisé. **Scotch
kale,** chou rouge. **2.** *Scot:* Soupe *f* aux choux.
kaleidoscope [ka'laidəskoup], *s.* Kaléidoscope *m.*
kaleidoscopic(al) [kalaido'skɔpik(əl)], *a.* Kaléidoscopique; toujours changeant.
kalends ['kalǝndz], *s.pl.* = CALENDS.
kangaroo [kaŋgə'ruː], *s. Z:* Kangourou *m.*
kaolin ['keiolin, 'kao-], *s. Cer:* Kaolin *m.*
kapok ['kɑːpɔk], *s. Furn:* Capoc *m*, kapok *m.*
Kashmir [kaʃ'miːǝr]. *Pr.n.* Le Cachemire.
Kate, Katie ['keit(i)]. *Pr.n.f.* Catherine.
Katherine ['kaθǝrin]. *Pr.n.f.* Catherine.
katydid ['keitidid], *s. U.S:* *Ent:* Sauterelle
verte d'Amérique.
kauri ['kauri],'*s.* Kauri (pine), kauri *m.*
kedge[1] [kedʒ], *s. Nau:* Kedge(-anchor), ancre *f*
de touée; ancre à jet.
kedge[2], *v.tr. Nau:* Haler (un navire) sur une
ancre à jet.
keel [kiːl], *s.* **I.** *(a) N.Arch:* Quille *f.* **Even keel,**
tirant d'eau égal. **On an even keel,** sans différence
de calaison. *(b) Aer:* (Quille de) dérive *f.*
2. *Poet:* Navire *m.* **3.** *Nat.Hist:* Carène *f* (de
pétale). **'keel-blocks,** *s.pl. N.Arch:* Tins *m*
(de cale sèche).
keelhaul ['kiːlhɔːl], *v.tr. Nau:* *A:* Donner la
cale humide à (un matelot).
keelson ['kiːlsən, 'kelsən], *s. N.Arch:* Carlingue *f.*
keen [kiːn], *a.* **I.** (Couteau) affilé, aiguisé. *K.
edge*, fil tranchant. **2.** (Froid, vent) vif, perçant.

3. *K. pleasure*, vif plaisir. *K. appetite*, appétit
vorace. *K. satire*, satire mordante. **4.** *(a)* Ardent,
zélé. *K. golfer*, enragé *m* de golf. *F:* *He is* **as
keen as mustard**, il brûle de zèle. *F:* **To be keen
on sth.**, être enthousiaste de qch.; être emballé
pour qch. *He is not k. on it*, il n'y tient pas
beaucoup. *I'm not very k. on it*, ça ne me dit pas
grand'chose. *(b)* **Keen competition,** concurrence
acharnée. *Com:* **Keen prices,** prix de concurrence. **5.** (Œil, regard) perçant, vif. **To have a
keen eye for a bargain,** être prompt à reconnaître
une bonne affaire. **To have a keen ear,** avoir
l'ouïe fine. **6.** (Esprit) fin, pénétrant. **-ly,** *adv.*
Aprement, vivement. *To be k. interested in . . .,*
s'intéresser vivement à. . . . **'keen-'set,** *a.*
Qui se sent de l'appétit (*for*, pour). **'keen-
'sighted,** *a.* A la vue perçante. **'keen-
'witted,** *a.* A l'esprit perçant.
keenness ['kiːnnəs], *s.* **I.** Finesse *f*, acuité *f* (du
tranchant d'un outil). **2.** Apreté *f* (du froid).
3. Ardeur *f*, zèle *m.* **Keenness on doing sth.,**
grand désir de faire qch. **4.** **Keenness of sight,**
acuité de la vision.
keep[1] [kiːp], *s.* **I.** *Hist:* Donjon *m*, réduit *m* (du
château fort). **2.** Nourriture *f*; frais *mpl* de
subsistance. **To earn one's keep,** gagner de quoi
vivre. *Ten francs a day and his k.*, dix francs par
jour logé et nourri. *He isn't worth his keep*, il
ne gagne pas sa nourriture. *F:* **For keeps,**
pour de bon.
keep[2], *v.* (kept [kept]; kept) **I.** *v.tr.* **I.** Observer,
suivre (une règle); tenir (une promesse). **To
keep an appointment,** ne pas manquer à un
rendez-vous. **2.** Célébrer (une fête). *To k. Lent,*
observer le carême. *To k. Christmas in the old
style*, fêter Noël à l'ancienne mode. **3.** *(a)* God

keep you! Dieu vous garde! (*b*) Préserver (*s.o. from evil*, qn du mal). (*c*) *Sp:* To keep (the) goal, garder le but. **4.** (*a*) Garder (des moutons). (*b*) *Badly kept road*, route mal entretenue. (*c*) Tenir (un journal, des comptes). **To keep note of sth.**, tenir note de qch. (*d*) Subvenir aux besoins de (qn); faire vivre (qn). *He has his parents to k.*, il a ses parents à sa charge. **To keep s.o. in clothes**, fournir le vêtement à qn. (*e*) Avoir (une voiture); élever (de la volaille). (*f*) Tenir (une école, une boutique). **5.** (*a*) Maintenir (l'ordre); garder (le silence). (*b*) **To keep a good table**, faire habituellement bonne chère. **6.** (*De-tain*) *To k. s.o. in prison*, retenir, détenir, qn en prison. *To k. s.o. at home*, faire rester qn à la maison. *To k. s.o. for dinner*, retenir qn à dîner. *Don't let me keep you!* je ne vous retiens pas! **7.** *Banks to k. the river within its bed*, digues pour contenir la rivière dans son lit. *The noise keeps him from sleeping*, le bruit l'empêche de dormir. **8.** Garder (*sth. for s.o.*, qch. pour qn). **9.** Garder (des provisions). *The place where I k. my clothes*, l'endroit où je mets mes habits. **10.** Conserver; retenir (l'attention de qn). **11.** **To keep sth. from s.o.**, cacher, taire, qch. à qn. **12.** **To keep one's course**, poursuivre sa route. **13.** **To keep one's bed**, garder le lit. **14.** (*a*) **To keep the stage**, tenir la scène. **To keep the saddle**, rester en selle. (*b*) **To keep one's seat**, rester assis. (*c*) **To keep one's figure**, conserver sa sveltesse. **15.** (*a*) **To keep sth. clean, warm**, tenir qch. propre, chaud. **To keep s.o. waiting**, faire attendre qn. (*b*) **To keep one's eyes fixed on sth.**, fixer qch. du regard. *F:* **To keep s.o. at it**, serrer les côtes à qn. *Nau:* **Keep her so!** gouvernez comme ça. **II. keep,** *v.i.* **1.** Rester, se tenir. *To k. standing*, se tenir debout. *How are you keeping?* comment allez-vous? *To k. quiet*, se tenir tranquille, rester tranquille. **To keep smiling**, rester souriant; *F:* garder le sourire. **2.** Continuer. (*a*) **To keep at work**, continuer son travail. *F:* **To keep at it**, travailler, *F:* piocher, sans relâche. **To keep straight on**, suivre tout droit. (*b*) **To keep doing sth.**, ne pas cesser de faire qch. **3.** (*Of food, etc.*) Se garder, se conserver. *Butter that will k.*, beurre conservable. *My revenge will k.*, il ne perdra rien pour attendre. **keep away. I.** *v.tr.* Éloigner; tenir éloigné. **2.** *v.i.* Se tenir éloigné; se tenir à l'écart. **keep back. I.** *v.tr.* (*a*) Arrêter (une armée); contenir, retenir (la foule). (*b*) Retenir, détenir (l'argent de qn); dissimuler (la vérité). **To keep things back** (*from s.o.*), faire des cachotteries à qn). **2.** *v.i.* Se tenir en arrière ou à l'écart. **Keep back!** n'avancez pas! **keep down. 1.** *v.tr.* (*a*) Empêcher (qch.) de monter. (*b*) *She kept her head down*, elle se tenait la tête baissée. (*c*) Contenir, réprimer (une révolte); comprimer (sa colère). (*d*) **To keep prices down**, maintenir les prix bas. **2.** *v.i.* Se tapir. **keep from,** *v.i.* S'abstenir de (faire qch.). **keep in. 1.** *v.tr.* (*a*) Retenir (qn) à la maison. *Sch:* **To keep a pupil in**, mettre un élève en retenue; consigner un élève. (*b*) Contenir (sa colère). (*c*) Entretenir (le feu). (*d*) *F:* **To keep one's hand in**, s'entretenir la main. **2.** *v.i.* (*1*) Garder la maison. (*b*) (*Of fire*) Rester allumé. (*c*) *F:* **To keep in with s.o.**, rester bien avec qn; cultiver qn. **keep off. 1.** *v.tr.* (*a*) Ne pas mettre (son chapeau). (*b*) **Keep your hands off!** n'y touchez pas! (*c*) Éloigner (qn, la foule). *The wind will k. the rain off*, le vent empêchera la pluie. **2.** *v.i.* (*Of pers.*) Se tenir éloigné. *If the rain keeps off*, si nous n'avons pas de pluie. **keep on. 1.** *v.tr.*

(*a*) Garder (son chapeau). *K. your hat on*, restez couvert. (*b*) *I hope I'll be kept on*, j'espère garder ma place. **2.** *v.i.* (*a*) *Buttons that do not k. on*, boutons qui ne tiennent pas. (*b*) Avancer; aller toujours. (*c*) **To keep on doing sth.**, continuer de, à, faire qch.; ne pas cesser de faire qch. *The dog keeps on barking*, le chien ne fait qu'aboyer. *He keeps on hoping*, il s'obstine à espérer. *F:* **To keep on at s.o.**, harceler qn; être toujours sur le dos de qn. **keep out. 1.** (*a*) *v.tr.* Empêcher d'entrer. (*b*) *v.i.* Se tenir dehors. **2.** **To keep out of.** (*a*) *v.tr.* Landlord kept out of his rents, propriétaire frustré de ses loyers. (*b*) *v.i. To k. out of a quarrel*, ne pas se mêler d'une querelle. *To k. out of danger*, se tenir à l'abri du danger. **keep to.** (*a*) *v.tr. To k. s.o. to his promise*, exiger de qn qu'il tienne sa promesse. (*b*) *v.i.* S'en tenir à (une résolution). *To k. to the pattern*, se conformer au modèle. **To keep to one's bed**, garder le lit. **To keep to the left**, tenir la gauche. **They keep to themselves**, ils font bande à part. **keep together. 1.** *v.tr.* Tenir ensemble, unir (des personnes). **2.** *v.i.* (*a*) Rester ensemble. (*b*) Rester unis. **keep under,** *v.tr.* Tenir (qn) dans la soumission; maîtriser (ses passions); contenir (un incendie). **keep up. 1.** *v.tr.* (*a*) Empêcher de tomber; soutenir (qn). (*b*) Tenir (la tête) haute. (*c*) **To keep prices up**, maintenir les prix. (*d*) Entretenir (un bâtiment, une route); maintenir (une maison) en bon état. (*e*) Conserver (un usage); entretenir (une correspondance, son grec). *To k. up the pace*, conserver l'allure. *F:* **Keep it up!** allez toujours! continuez! (*f*) Soutenir (l'intérêt). **Keep up your courage!** haut les cœurs! **To keep up appearances**, sauver les apparences. (*g*) **To keep s.o. up (at night)**, faire veiller qn. **2.** *v.i.* (*a*) Ne pas se laisser abattre; (*of weather*) se maintenir. (*b*) **To keep up with s.o.**, aller de pair avec qn. **To keep up with the times**, *F:* se maintenir à la page. **keeping,** *s.* **1.** (*a*) Observation *f* (d'une règle). (*b*) Célébration *f* (d'une fête). **Keeping of the Sabbath**, sanctification *f* du dimanche. **2.** Garde *f*. **To be in s.o.'s keeping**, être sous la garde de qn. **3. In keeping with . . .**, en accord, en rapport, avec. . . . *Their action was in k.*, ils se sont conduits à l'avenant. *Out of keeping with . . .*, en désaccord avec. . . . **4.** Keeping up, entretien *m* (d'un bâtiment); conservation *f* (d'un usage).

keeper ['ki:pər], *s.* **1.** (*a*) Garde *m*, gardien *m*; surveillant *m*; conservateur *m* (de musée). **Park-keeper, lighthouse-keeper**, gardien de parc, de phare. **The Keeper of the Seals**, le Garde des sceaux. (*b*) = GAMEKEEPER. (*c*) **Boarding-house keeper**, patron, -onne, d'une pension de famille. **2.** Bague *f* de sûreté (portée au doigt).

keepsake ['ki:pseik], *s.* Souvenir (donné à qn).

keg [keg], *s.* Caque *f* (de harengs); barillet *m* (d'eau-de-vie). *Nau:* Tonnelet *m* (d'eau potable).

kelp [kelp], *s.* Varech *m*.

kelpie ['kelpi], *s.* *Scot:* (**Water-)kelpie**, esprit *m* dès eaux.

ken [ken], *s.* **Within s.o.'s ken**, dans les connaissances de qn.

kennel [kenl], *s.* **1.** Chenil *m* (de chiens de chasse). **The hunt kennel(s)**, le chenil de la meute. **2.** Niche *f* (de chien de garde).

Kentish ['kentiʃ], *a.* Du comté de Kent. *F:* **Kentish fire**, applaudissements prolongés (souvent ironiques); ovation *f* ou huées *fpl*.

kentledge ['kentledʒ] *s.* *Nau:* Lest *m* en gueuses.

Kenya ['ki:nja]. *Pr.n. Geog:* Kenia *m*.

kept [kept]. *See* KEEP².
kerb [kə:rb], *s.* = CURB¹ 2.
kerchief ['kə:rtʃif], *s.* I. (*a*) (*For head*) Fanchon *f*; mouchoir *m* de tête. (*b*) Fichu *m*. 2. *Poet:* = HANDKERCHIEF.
kerf [kə:rf], *s.* Trait *m* de scie; voie *f* de scie.
kermes ['kə:rmiz], *s.* (*a*) *Ent: Dy:* Kermès *m.* (*b*) *Bot:* **Kermes** (oak), chêne *m* kermès.
kernel ['kə:rnəl], *s.* I. (*a*) Amande *f* (de noisette); pignon *m* (de pomme de pin). (*b*) Grain *m* (de céréale). 2. *F:* **The kernel of the matter,** le fond, l'essentiel m, de l'affaire.
kerosene ['kerosi:n], *s.* *U.S:* Pétrole *m.*
kestrel ['kestrəl], *s.* *Orn:* Crécerelle *f*; émouchet *m.*
ketch [ketʃ], *s.* *Nau:* I. *A:* Ketch *m.* 2. Dundee *m.*
ketchup ['ketʃəp], *s.* Sauce piquante (en bouteille) à base de tomates, de champignons.
kettle [ketl], *s.* (*a*) Bouilloire *f.* (*b*) *Mil:* Campkettle, marmite *f.* **Mess-kettle,** gamelle *f.* *F:* **Here's a pretty kettle of fish!** en voilà une belle besogne, une jolie affaire, un beau gâchis! **'kettle-drum,** *s.* *Mus:* Timbale *f.* **'kettle-drummer,** *s.* Timbalier *m.* **'kettle-holder,** *s.* Poignée *f* de bouilloire (en drap).
key¹ [ki:], *s.* I. Clef *f*, clé *f* (de serrure). *To leave the key in the door,* laisser la clef sur la porte. 2. (*a*) Clef (d'une énigme). *I hold the key to the puzzle,* je tiens le mot de l'énigme. (*b*) **Key numbers** (*on a squared map*), numéros *m* de repérage. (*c*) *Sch:* Corrigé *m*; solutions *fpl* (des problèmes). 3. *Mus:* Major key, ton majeur. *The key of C,* le ton d'ut. *F:* **To speak in a high key,** parler sur un ton haut; avoir le verbe haut. 4. (*a*) Touche *f* (de piano). *F:* **To touch the right key,** toucher la corde sensible. (*b*) Touche (de machine à écrire). *Tg:* **Morse key,** manipulateur *m.* (*c*) Clef (d'instrument à vent). 5. (*a*) Clef à écrous. (*b*) Remontoir *m* (de pendule, de locomotive d'enfant). 6. (*a*) Clavette *f*, cale *f*, coin *m.* (*b*) *El:* Fiche *f.* 7. *Bot:* Samare *f* (de frêne, d'érable). **'key-note,** *s.* (*a*) *Mus:* Tonique *f.* (*b*) *F:* Note dominante (d'un discours). **'key-ring,** *s.* Anneau brisé (pour clefs); porte-clefs *m inv.* **'key-'signature,** *s.* *Mus:* Armature *f* (de la clef). *To put the k.-s. to a piece of music,* armer la clef. **'keyway,** *s.* I. Entrée *f* de serrure. 2. Rainure *f* de clavette, de clavetage. **'key-word,** *s.* Mot-clé *m*, *pl.* mots-clés.
key², *v.tr.* I. *Mec.E:* Clavet(t)er, caler (*a pulley on a spindle*), une poulie sur un arbre). 2. *Mus:* To key (up), accorder (un piano). *F:* **To key s.o. up,** mettre du cœur au ventre à qn. *Crowd keyed up for the match,* foule tendue dans l'attente du match.
key³, *s.* *Geog:* Caye *f*; îlot *m* à fleur d'eau.
keyboard ['ki:bɔ:rd], *s.* I. Clavier *m* (de piano). 2. (*In hotel*) Porte-clefs *m inv*; tableau *m.*
keyhole ['ki:houl], *s.* Trou *m* de (la) serrure.
keystone ['ki:stoun], *s.* Clef *f* de voûte; claveau droit.
khaki ['ka:ki]. I. *s.* *Tex:* Kaki *m.* *F:* **To get into khaki,** se faire soldat. 2. *a.* Kaki *inv.*
kibble¹ [kibl], *s.* *Min:* Benne *f.*
kibble², *v.tr.* Égruger (le blé, etc.).
kibosh ['kaibɔʃ, ki'bɔʃ], *s.* *P:* Bêtises *fpl.* 2. **To put the kibosh on s.o.,** on sth., faire son affaire à qn; mettre fin à qch.
kick¹ [kik], *s.* I. (*a*) Coup *m* de pied. *Fb:* **Free kick,** coup de pied franc. *F:* **To get more kicks than ha'pence,** recevoir plus de coups que de pain, que de caresses. (*b*) Ruade *f* (d'un cheval).

2. (*a*) *F:* **He has no kick left in him,** il est à plat (*b*) *F:* **A drink with a kick in it,** une boisson qu vous remonte. 3. (*a*) Recul *m*, réaction (d'un fusil). (*b*) *I.C.E:* = KICK-BACK. **'kick-start(er),** *s.* *Motor Cy:* Démarreur *m* a pied; *F:* kick *m.*
kick². I. *v.i.* (*a*) Donner un coup de pied *F:* gigoter; (*of animals*) ruer. (*b*) (*Of pers.*) T kick at, against, sth., regimber contre qch (*c*) (*Of gun*) Reculer, repousser. 2. *v.tr.* (*a*) Donner un coup de pied à (qn); pousser (qn) d pied; (*of horse*) détacher un coup de sabot (qn). *I felt like kicking myself,* je me serais donné des claques. **To kick s.o. downstairs,** fai dégringoler l'escalier à qn. *F:* **To kick s.o.'** bottom, botter qn. *P:* **To kick the bucke** mourir; *P:* casser sa pipe. (*b*) **The gun kicke** my shoulder, j'ai reçu le recul du fusil sur l'épaule (*c*) *Fb:* **To kick the ball,** botter le ballon. **T kick a goal,** marquer un but. **kick about I.** *v.i.* *F:* (*Of books*) To lie kicking about th house, traîner partout dans la maison. 2. *v.tr They were kicking the ball about,* ils se relançaien le ballon. **kick away,** *v.tr.* Repousser (qch du pied. **kick back.** *v.i.* *I.C.E:* (*Of engine* Donner des retours en arrière. 2. *v.tr.* *Fb:* Re lancer (le ballon). **'kick-back,** *s.* *I.C.E:* Start ing-handle k.-b., retour *m* de manivelle. **kicl off,** *v.tr.* I. Enlever (qch.) d'un coup de pied 2. *Abs. Fb:* Donner le coup d'envoi. **kick-'off** *s.* *Fb:* Coup d'envoi. K.-o. at two o'clock, partie commence à deux heures. **kick-'out,** *s Fb:* Renvoi *m.* **kicking,** *s.* I. Coups *mpl* d pied; (*of animal*) ruades *fpl.* 2. *F:* Recul *m* repoussement *m* (d'un fusil).
kid¹ [kid], *s.* I. *Z:* Chevreau *m*, *f.* chevrette (*a*) (Peau *f* de) chevreau. **Kid gloves,** gants (e peau) de chevreau. **Glacé-kid gloves,** gants glacés *F:* **To handle s.o. with kid gloves,** ménager qn (qn). 2. *F:* Mioche *mf*, gosse *mf*; *P:* loupiot *m.*
kid², *s.* *P:* Blague *f.* **No kid!** sans blague!
kid³, *v.tr.* *P:* **To kid s.o.,** conter à (qn); faire marche (qn). *No kidding!* sans blague! *To kid onese that . . .,* se faire accroire que. . . .
kid⁴, *s.* *Nau:* (*Mess-*)kid, gamelle *f*, écuelle *f.*
kidnap ['kidnap], *v.tr.* (kidnapped) Enlever (qn de vive force; voler (un enfant). **kidnapping** *s.* Vol *m* (d'enfant); *Jur:* (délit *m* de) rapt *m.*
kidnapper ['kidnapər], *s.* Auteur *m* de l'enlève ment; voleur, -euse, ravisseur, -euse (d'enfant).
kidney ['kidni], *s.* I. (*a*) *Anat:* Rein *m* (*b*) *F:* **Two people of the same kidney,** deu personnes du même acabit. 2. *Cu:* Rognon *m* (de mouton). **'kidney-bean,** *s.* (*a*) *Harico* nain. (*b*) Haricot d'Espagne. **'kidney-po'tato** *s.* Vitelotte *f.* **'kidney-stone,** *s.* *Geol:* Ro gnon *m* de silex.
kill¹, *s.* *Ven:* (*a*) Mise *f* à mort (du renard, etc.) (*b*) Gibier tué; le tableau.
kill², *v.tr.* (*a*) Tuer, faire mourir; abattr (une bête). **Kill or cure remedy,** remède héroïque **To be hard to kill,** avoir la vie dure. *To kill tw* birds with one stone, faire d'une pierre deu coups. **To kill s.o. with kindness,** faire du mal qn par excès de bonté. **You are killing me** inches, vous me faites mourir à petit feu. He wa laughing fit to kill himself, il crevait de rire. T be dressed to kill, porter une toilette irrésistible être en grand tralala. (*b*) (*Of butcher*) Abattr tuer (un bœuf). *Abs. The butcher kills on Friday* le boucher tue le vendredi. 2. **To kill time,** tue le temps. 3. (*a*) Amortir (le son). (*b*) **To kill lime** éteindre la chaux. (*c*) *Phot:* **To kill the hypo** éliminer l'hyposulfite. 4. *Ten:* Tuer, massacre

(la balle). **kill off,** v.tr. Exterminer. **killing**[1], a. **1.** (a) Meurtrier. F: **Killing glance,** œillade assassine. (b) (In compounds) **Germ-killing,** microbicide. **2.** (Métier) assommant. **3.** F: **It is too killing for words,** c'est à mourir de rire. **killing**[2], s. **1.** Tuerie f, massacre m, abattage m (d'animaux). **2.** Meurtre m. **'kill-joy,** s. Rabat-joie m inv. K.-j. countenance, face f de carême, d'enterrement. **'killer** ['kilər], s. **1.**(a) Tueur, -euse; meurtrier m. (b) Z: **Killer-whale,** épaulard m. **2.** **Vermin-killer,** insecticide m. **kiln** [kiln], s. **1.** (a) Four m (céramique). (b) Séchoir m, étuve f. **2.** **Charcoal-kiln,** meule f. **kilogram(me)** ['kilogram], s. Kilogramme m; F: kilo m. **kilometre** ['kilomi:tər], s. Kilomètre m. **kilowatt** ['kilowɔt], s. El.Meas: Kilowatt m. **kilt**[1] [kilt], s. Scot: Jupon court et plissé (des montagnards); kilt m. **kilt**[2], v.tr. To kilt (up) one's skirts, retrousser ses jupes. **kilted,** a. **1.** Portant le kilt. **2.** (a) (Of skirt) Retroussé. (b) (Of cloth, garment) Plissé. **kimono** [ki'mouno, 'kimono], s. Cost: Kimono m. **kin** [kin], s. (a) Parents mpl. His kin, ses parents, sa parenté. (b) To be of kin to s.o., être apparenté avec qn. To inform the next of kin, prévenir la famille. **kind**[1] [kaind], s. **1.** (Race) Espèce f, genre m. The human kind, l'espèce humaine; le genre humain. **2.** (a) (Sort) Genre, espèce, sorte f. Of what k. is it? de quelle sorte est-ce? What k. of man is he? quel genre d'homme est-ce? He is the k. of man who will hit back, il est homme à se défendre. Facts of a k. to astonish us, faits de nature à nous étonner. Perfect of its kind, parfait dans son genre. Something of the kind, quelque chose de semblable, de ce genre. Nothing of the kind, rien de la sorte. Coffee of a kind, quelque chose qui pouvait passer pour du café. In a kind of a way, en quelque façon. That's the k. of thing I mean, c'est à peu près ce que je veux dire. He felt a kind of compunction, il ressentait comme des remords. She was with them as a k. of maid, elle était comme qui dirait leur bonne. (b) F: These kinds of men, ce genre d'hommes; les hommes de cette sorte. **3.** In kind. (a) Discovery new in k., découverte d'une espèce entièrement nouvelle. They differ in k., ils diffèrent en nature. Difference in kind, différence spécifique. (b) Payment in kind, paiement en nature. F: To repay s.o. in kind, payer qn de la même monnaie. **kind**[2], a. **1.** Bon, aimable, bienveillant. To give s.o. a k. reception, faire bon accueil à qn. Give him my kind regards, faites-lui mes amitiés. S.a. REGARD[1] 3. To be kind to s.o., se montrer bon pour, envers, qn. It is very kind of you, c'est bien aimable de votre part. Be so kind as to . . ., soyez assez bon pour . . .; voulez-vous être assez aimable pour . . .; voulez-vous avoir l'amabilité de. . . . **2.** (Of metals, etc.) Facile à travailler. **-ly**[1], adv. Avec bonté, avec bienveillance, avec douceur. He spoke very k. of you, il m'a dit des choses très obligeantes à votre égard. To be kindly disposed towards s.o., être plein de bienveillance pour qn. Will you kindly . . .? voulez-vous avoir la bonté de . . .; je vous prie de vouloir bien. . . . Com: Kindly remit by cheque, prière de nous couvrir par chèque. I thank you kindly, je vous remercie bien. To take sth. kindly, prendre qch. en bonne part. **kind-'hearted,** a. Bon, bienveillant. **kindergarten** ['kindərgɑːrtn], s. Jardin m d'enfants; école maternelle.

kindle [kindl]. **1.** v.tr. (a) Allumer; enflammer, embraser. (b) Faire naître, susciter (les passions); enflammer (les désirs); embraser (le cœur); exciter (le zèle). **2.** v.i. S'allumer, s'enflammer, prendre feu. **kindling,** s. **1.** Allumage m, embrasement m, enflammement m. **2.** Petit bois (pour allumer); bois d'allumage. **kindliness** ['kaindlinəs], s. **1.** Bonté f, bienveillance f, bienfaisance f. **2.** Douceur f (de climat). **kindly**[1] ['kaindli], adv. See KIND[2]. **kindly**[2], a. (a) Bon, bienveillant. K. feeling, sentiment de bonté. (b) (Climat) doux; (terrain) favorable. **kindness** ['kaindnəs], s. **1.** Bonté f (towards s.o., pour qn); bienveillance f, amabilité f (envers); prévenance f. Will you have the kindness to . . .? voulez-vous avoir la bonté de . . .? **2.** A kindness, un service (rendu). To do s.o. a kindness, rendre service à qn. To shower kindnesses on s.o., combler qn de bienfaits, de bontés. **kindred** ['kindred]. **1.** s. (a) (i) Parenté f. The ties of k., les liens m du sang. (ii) Affinité f (with, avec). (b) Coll. Parents mpl. **2.** a. (a) De la même famille. (b) De la même nature; analogue. Kindred souls, âmes f sœurs. **kine** [kain], s.pl. A: See COW[1]. **kinematic** [kaini'matik], a. Cinématique. **kinematics** [kaini'matiks], s.pl. Cinématique f. **kinetic** [kai'netik], a. Cinétique. **kinetics** [kai'netiks], s.pl. Cinétique f. **king** [kiːŋ], s. **1.** (a) Roi m. (a) King Albert, le roi Albert. B: The three Kings, les (trois) Rois Mages. F: Dish fit for a king, morceau m de roi. He wouldn't call the king his cousin, le roi n'est pas un oncle, son cousin. (b) F: Gros bonnet (de la finance, etc.). One of the oil kings, un des rois du pétrole. **2.** (a) (At chess, cards) Roi. (b) (At draughts) Dame f. **'king-bolt,** s. Cheville ouvrière; pivot central. **'king-cup,** s. Bot: Bouton m d'or. **King-of-'Arms,** s. Her: Roi m d'armes. **'king-pin,** s. = KING-BOLT. **'king-post,** s. Const: Poinçon m (d'une ferme de comble). **kingdom** ['kiːŋdəm], s. **1.** Royaume m. The United Kingdom, le Royaume-Uni. **2.** Biol: Règne (animal, végétal). **3.** Thy kingdom come, que votre règne arrive. **kingdom-come,** s. F: Le paradis. To send s.o. to kingdom-come, expédier qn dans l'autre monde. **kingfisher** ['kiːŋfiʃər], s. Orn: Martin-pêcheur m. **kinglike** ['kiːŋlaik]. **1.** a. De roi. **2.** adv. En roi. **kingly** ['kiːŋli], a. De roi; royal, -aux. **kingship** ['kiːŋʃip], s. Royauté f. **kink**[1] [kiŋk], s. **1.** Nœud m, tortillement m (dans une corde); faux pli (dans le fil de fer). Nau: Coque f (dans un cordage). **2.** F: Faux pli (dans l'esprit); point m faible (de qn). **kink**[2]. **1.** v.i. (Of rope) Se nouer, se tortiller; Nau: former une coque. **2.** v.tr. Faire une coque à (un cordage). **kinkajou** ['kiŋkadʒuː], s. Z: Kinkajou m. **kinsfolk** ['kinzfouk], s.pl. Parents et alliés mpl; famille f. **kinship** ['kinʃip], s. Parenté f. **kinsman,** pl. **-men** ['kinzmən, -men], s.m. Parent; Jur: affin. **kinswoman,** pl. **-women** ['kinzwumən, -wimen], s.f. Parente f. **kiosk** [ki'ɔsk], s. Kiosque m. **kipper** ['kipər], s. Com: Hareng légèrement salé et fumé; hareng doux; craquelot m. **kirk** [kəːrk], s. Scot: Église f.

27

kirkyard [kə:rk'jɑːrd], *s. Scot:* Cimetière *m.*
kismet ['kismet], *s. F:* Le sort; le destin.
kiss¹ [kis], *s.* **I.** Baiser *m*; accolade *f.* **To give s.o. a kiss,** donner un baiser à qn. **To blow s.o. a kiss,** envoyer un baiser à qn du bout des doigts. **2.** *Bill:* Contre-coup *m.* **'kiss-'curl,** *s.* Accroche-cœur *m.*
kiss². **I.** *v.tr.* Donner un baiser à, embrasser (qn); baiser (le front, la main, de qn). *They kissed (each other),* ils se sont embrassés. *F:* **To kiss and be friends,** se réconcilier. **To kiss the Pope's toe,** baiser la mule du Pape. *Lit:* **To kiss the dust,** mordre la poussière. **To kiss the rod,** lécher, baiser, la main qui vous frappe. **To kiss one's hand to s.o.,** envoyer de la main un baiser à qn. **2.** *v.i. Bill:* (*Of balls*) Se frapper par contre-coup. **'kiss-in-the-'ring,** *s.* Ronde enfantine (avec embrassades).
kit¹ [kit], *s.* **I.** (*a*) *Mil:* *Navy:* Petit équipement; fourniment *m*; *F:* fourbi *m.* **Kit inspection,** revue *f* de détail. **To pack up one's kit,** plier bagage. (*b*) Sac *m* (de marin). (*c*) *F:* Effets *mpl* (de voyageur). **2.** *Tchn:* Trousseau *m*, trousse *f* (d'outils). *Repair kit,* nécessaire *m* de réparation. **'kit-bag,** *s.* **I.** Sac *m* (de voyage). **2.** *Mil:* Ballot *m*, musette *f*; sac d'ordonnance.
kit², *s.* *Mus:* *A:* Pochette *f* (de maître de danse).
kitchen ['kitʃən], *s.* Cuisine *f.* **Communal kitchen,** soup-kitchen, fourneau *m* économique; "soupe" *f* populaire. **Thieves' kitchen,** retraite *f* de voleurs. **Kitchen table,** table de cuisine. **'kitchen-'gardener,** *s.* Maraîcher *m.* **'kitchen-maid,** *s.f.* Fille de cuisine. **'kitchen-'range,** *s.* Fourneau *m* de cuisine; cuisinière anglaise. **'kitchen-utensils,** *s.pl.,* **'kitchen-ware,** *s.* Batterie *f* de cuisine.
kitchener ['kitʃənər], *s.* Fourneau *m* de cuisine; cuisinière *f.*
kite [kait], *s.* **I.** (*a*) *Orn:* Milan *m.* (*b*) *F:* (*Of pers.*) Vautour *m*, usurier *m.* **2.** Cerf-volant *m*, *pl.* cerfs-volants. **To fly, send up, a kite,** (i) lancer, enlever, un cerf-volant; (ii) *F:* tâter le terrain; lancer un ballon d'essai. **3.** *Navy:* Mine-sweeping kites, panneaux *m* de dragage. **'kite-balloon,** *s.* Ballon captif; *F:* saucisse *f.*
kith [kiθ], *s.* *A:* Amis *mpl*, voisins *mpl* et connaissances *fpl.* *Used in* **Our kith and kin,** nos amis et parents.
kitten [kitn], *s.* Chaton *m*; petit(e) chat(te).
kittenish ['kitəniʃ], *a.* (*Of girl*) (*a*) Coquette, aguichante. (*b*) Enjouée.
kittiwake ['kitiweik], *s.* *Orn:* Mouette *f* tri-dactyle.
kittle [kitl], *a.* Difficile à manier. **Kittle cattle,** gens d'humeur difficile.
kitty¹ ['kiti], *s.* *Cards:* Cagnotte *f.*
Kitty². *Pr.n.f.* (*Dim. of Catherine*) Catherine.
kiwi ['kiːwi], *s.* *Orn:* Aptéryx *m.*
kleptomania [klepto'meinia], *s.* Kleptomanie *f.*
kleptomaniac [klepto'meiniak], *a. & s.* Kleptomane (*mf*).
knack [nak], *s.* Tour *m* de main; *F:* truc *m.* **To have the knack of doing sth., a knack for doing sth.,** avoir le coup, le tour de main, pour faire qch.; savoir s'y prendre pour faire qch. **To acquire, get into, the knack of sth.,** attraper le coup pour faire qch. *He has a happy k. of saying the right thing,* il a le don de l'à-propos.
knacker ['nakər], *s.* Équarrisseur *m.*
knapsack ['napsak], *s.* Havresac *m*, sac *m* (porté sur le dos); sac alpin (de boy-scout). (*b*) *Mil:* Sac d'ordonnance.
knapweed ['napwiːd], *s.* *Bot:* Centaurée (noire).

knave [neiv], *s.* **I.** Fripon *m*, coquin *m.* **2.** *Cards* Valet *m.*
knavery ['neivəri], *s.* Friponnerie *f*, coquinerie
knavish ['neiviʃ], *a.* De fripon; fourbe, malin
K. trick, coquinerie *f*, friponnerie *f.*
knead [niːd], *v.tr.* **I.** Pétrir, malaxer, travailler (la pâte, l'argile). **2.** *Med:* Masser, pétrir (les muscles). **kneading,** *s.* **I.** Pétrissage *m* (de la pâte); malaxage *m* (de l'argile, etc.). **2.** *Med* Massage *m.* **'kneading-trough,** *s.* Pétrin *m.*
knee [niː], *s.* **I.** (*a*) Genou *m*, -oux. *The future* on the knees of the gods, pour l'avenir il fau s'en remettre au destin. **To bend, bow, the kne to, before, s.o.,** mettre un genou en terre devan qn. **On one's (bended) knees,** à genoux. **On on knee,** un genou à terre. **To go down, fall, drop on one's knees,** s'agenouiller; se mettre, se jeter à genoux. **To go down on one's knees to s.o** se jeter aux genoux de qn. **To bring s.o. to hi knees,** (i) forcer qn à s'agenouiller; (ii) *F:* obli ger qn à capituler. **To learn sth. at one's mother' knee,** apprendre qch. auprès de sa mère (*b*) *Vet:* (*Of horse*) Broken knees, couronnement *m* **To break its knees,** se couronner. (*c*) *F:* 'Knees (in trousers), poches *f*, ronds *m*, aux genoux **2.** *Mec.E:* *Const:* Genou, équerre *f.* **Knee bracket,** console-équerre *f.* **'knee-breeches,** *s.pl.* Culotte courte. **'knee-cap,** *s.* *Anat* Rotule *f.* **'knee-'deep,** *a.* Jusqu'aux genoux à hauteur du genou. **'knee-hole,** *s.* Trou *m* (dans un bureau) pour l'entrée des genoux Knee-hole writing-table, bureau *m* ministre **'knee-holly,** *s.* *Bot:* Petit houx; housson *m* faux buis. **'knee-joint,** *s.* **I.** Articulation *f* d genou. **2.** *Mec.E:* Joint articulé; rotule *f* etc.). **'knee-pad,** *s.* Genouillère *f* (de parqueteur etc.). **'knee-pipe,** *s.* Genou *m* (de tuyau).
kneed [niːd], *a.* **I.** Weak-kneed, faible de genoux, du jarret. *S.a.* BROKEN-KNEED, KNOCK KNEED. **2.** *Tchn:* Coudé.
kneel [niːl], *v.i.* (*p.t. & p.p.* knelt [nelt]) To knee (down), s'agenouiller; se mettre à genoux. **To kneel to s.o.,** se mettre à genoux devant qn **kneeling¹,** *a.* Agenouillé; à genoux. **kneel-ing²,** *s.* Agenouillement *m.* **'kneeling-chair,** *s* Prie-Dieu *m inv.*
knell [nel], *s.* Glas *m.* **Death knell,** glas funèbre **To toll the knell,** sonner le glas.
knelt [nelt]. *See* KNEEL.
knew [njuː]. *See* KNOW².
knickerbockers ['nikərbokərz], *s.pl.* Culotte (bouffante).
knickers ['nikərz], *s.pl.* Pantalon *m*, culotte *f* (de femme).
knick-knack ['niknak], *s.* Colifichet *m*, bibelot *m.*
knife¹ ['naif], *s.* *pl.* knives [naif, na:ivz], *s.* **I.** (*a*) Cou-teau *m.* **Table-knife,** couteau de table. **Carving-knife,** couteau à découper. **To lay a knife and fork for s.o.,** mettre un couvert pour qn. (*b*) Pocket-knife, couteau de poche. **Pen-knife,** canif. *S.a.* CLASP-KNIFE, JACK-KNIFE. (*c*) Cou-teau, poignard *m*; *P:* surin *m.* **War to the knife,** guerre à couteaux tirés. *F:* **To have one's knife** in s.o., s'acharner après, contre, sur, qn. **2.** Cou-teau, lame *f* (d'un hache-paille, etc.); couperet *m* (de la guillotine). **3.** *Surg:* The knife, le bistouri, le scalpel. **To resort to the k.,** avoir recours au fer; trancher dans le vif. **To have a horror of the k.,** trembler à l'idée d'être opéré. **'knife-board,** *s.* **I.** Planche *f* à couteaux. **2.** *A:* (*Of omnibus*) Banquette *f* de l'impériale. **'knife-edge,** *s.* **I.** (*a*) Arête *f* en lame de couteau. (*b*) *Ph:* Couteau *m* de balance. **2.** *W.Tel:* Knife-edge tuning, réglage *m* à sélectivité très

poussée. **'knife-grinder**, s. Rémouleur m; repasseur m de couteaux. **'knife-rest**, s. Porte-couteau m. **'knife-switch**, s. El: Interrupteur m à couteau.

knife², v.tr. Donner un coup de couteau à (qn); poignarder (qn); P: suriner (qn).

knight¹ [nait], s. **I.** Chevalier m. F: Knight of the pestle, apothicaire m. Knight of the road, commis voyageur. **2.** (At chess) Cavalier m. **knight-'errant**, pl. **knights-'errant**, s.m. Chevalier errant; paladin. **knight-'errantry**, s. Chevalerie errante.

knight², v.tr. Hist: Armer chevalier (un écuyer, etc.). **2.** Faire, créer, (qn) chevalier; donner l'accolade à (qn).

knighthood ['naithud], s. **I.** Chevalerie f. **2.** Titre m de chevalier.

knightly ['naitli], a. Chevaleresque; de chevalier.

knit¹ [nit], v. (p.t. & p.p. knitted or knit; pr.p. knitting) **I.** v.tr. (a) Tricoter. (b) Knit two, purl two, deux à l'endroit, deux à l'envers. (c) To knit one's brows, froncer les sourcils. (d) Joindre, unir, lier. **2.** v.i. (Of bones) Se souder, se nouer, se recoller. **knit²**, **knitted**, a. **I.** Knitted scarf, écharpe tricotée; écharpe de, en, tricot. Knitted wear, tricot m. Knitted goods, bonneterie f. **2.** Knitted eye-brows, sourcils froncés. **3.** Closely knit sentences, phrases d'une structure serrée. **knitting**, s. **I.** (a) Tricotage m. (b) Union f. (c) Soudure f (des os). **2.** Tricot m. Plain knitting, tricot à l'endroit. **'knitting-machine**, s. Tricoteuse f. **'knitting-needle**, s. Aiguille f à tricoter.

knitter ['nitər], s. Tricoteur, -euse.

knob [nɔb], s. **I.** (a) Bosse f, protubérance f. (b) Pomme f (de canne); bouton m, olive f (de porte, de tiroir); bouton de réglage, de mise en marche, etc. (c) P: Tête f, caboche f. **2.** Morceau m (de charbon, de sucre).

knobstick ['nɔbstik], s. (a) Canne f à pommeau. (b) Gourdin m.

knock¹ [nɔk], s. **I.** Coup m, heurt m, choc m. To give s.o. a knock on the head, (i) porter à qn un coup à la tête; (ii) assommer qn. To get a nasty knock, attraper un vilain coup. **2.** (a) Knock at the door, coup à la porte; coup de marteau. There was a knock (at the door), on frappa à la porte. (b) Knock, knock! toc, toc! pan, pan! **3.** I.C.E: Engine-knock, cognement m du moteur. **4.** Cr: = INNINGS.

knock². **I.** v.tr. (a) Frapper, heurter, cogner. To knock s.o. on the head, (i) frapper qn sur la tête; (ii) assommer qn. To knock one's head against sth., (i) se cogner la tête contre qch.; (ii) F: se heurter à un obstacle. To knock sth. out of s.o.'s hand, faire tomber qch. de la main de qn. (b) To knock a hole in, through, sth., faire un trou dans qch.; percer qch. (c) P: Épater, ébaubir (qn). **2.** v.i. (a) Frapper, heurter (at, à); taper (at, sur). (b) To knock against sth., se donner un coup, se heurter, se cogner, contre qch. (c) I.C.E: (Of engine) Cogner, pilonner. **knock about. I.** v.tr. Bousculer, maltraiter, malmener (qn). Ship that has been terribly knocked about (in battle), vaisseau affreusement ravagé. **2.** v.i. To knock about (the world), parcourir le monde; rouler sa bosse; vadrouiller par le monde. **'knock-about**, attrib.a. (a) (Jeu, etc.) violent, bruyant. Th: Knock-about comedian, bateleur m; clown m. (b) Knock-about life, vie errante; F: vie de bâton de chaise. (Habits) de tous les jours. **knock down**, v.tr. **I.** Renverser; jeter (qch.) par terre; étendre (qn) par terre d'un coup de poing; abattre (une muraille,

des pommes, etc.). He was knocked down by a motor car, il a été renversé par une auto. **2.** (At auction) To knock sth. down to s.o., adjuger qch. à qn. **'knock-down**, attrib.a. **I.** Knock-down blow, coup d'assommoir. **2.** Knock-down price, (i) (at auction) prix minimum; (ii) Com: prix de réclame. **knock in**, v.tr. **I.** (R)enfoncer (un clou). **2.** Défoncer (une malle). **knock off**. **I.** v.tr. **I.** (a) To k. the book off the table, faire tomber le livre de la table. To k. the handle off the jug, faire sauter l'anse de la cruche. (b) To knock something off the price, rabattre quelque chose du prix. **2.** (a) Faire tomber (le chapeau de qn, etc.). (b) Achever (un travail); expédier (une besogne). (c) To k. off the odd pence, rabattre les quelques sous d'appoint. **II.** knock off, v.i. Cesser le travail. **knock out**, v.tr. **I.** Faire sortir, faire tomber (qch.); chasser, repousser (un rivet). To knock s.o.'s brains out, faire sauter la cervelle à qn. **2.** Box: To knock s.o. out, mettre (l'adversaire) knock-out; knockouter qn. **3.** (a) Supprimer (un mot d'un passage, etc.). (b) Ten: To be knocked out in a tournament, être éliminé. **knock-'out**. **I.** Attrib.a. (a) (Coup) de grâce. (b) (Prix) qui défie la concurrence. **2.** s. (a) Box: Knock-out m. (b) Sp: Élimination progressive des concurrents ou des équipes. **knock over**, v.tr. Faire tomber, renverser (qn, qch.); abattre (un arbre, etc.). **knock up**. **I.** v.tr. (a) To k. s.o.'s hand up, faire sauter la main de qn. (b) To knock up the ball, faire une chandelle. Ten: F: To knock up the balls, faire quelques balles avant la partie. (c) Cr: To knock up a century, totaliser cent points. (d) Construire (un édifice) à la hâte. (e) Réveiller, faire lever (qn). (f) Éreinter, épuiser, échiner (qn); mettre (un cheval, qn) sur le flanc. **2.** v.i. (a) To knock up against sth., se heurter contre qch. F: To knock up against s.o., rencontrer qn par hasard, à l'improviste. (b) S'effondrer de fatigue, etc.). **knocking**, s. **I.** Coups mpl. **2.** (Of engine) Pilonnage m; cognement m. **'knock-'kneed**, a. Cagneux.

knocker ['nɔkər], s. (a) (Door-)knocker, marteau m (de porte); heurtoir m. (b) P: Dressed up to the knocker, sur son trente et un.

knoll [noul], s. Tertre m, monticule m, butte f.

knot¹ [nɔt], s. **I.** (a) Nœud m. To tie a knot, faire un nœud. To untie a knot, défaire un nœud. Running knot, slip-knot, nœud coulant. Granny's knot, nœud mal fait; nœud de vache, d'ajust. (b) Nœud (de rubans). Sailor's knot, nœud régate. (c) Knot of hair, chignon m. **2.** Nau: (a) Nœud, division f, de la ligne de loch. (b) (Of ship) To make ten knots, filer dix nœuds. **3.** Nœud (d'un problème). **4.** The marriage knot, les nœuds du mariage; le lien conjugal. **5.** Nœud (d'une tige, du bois). Knot-hole, trou m provenant d'un nœud. **6.** Groupe m (de personnes, d'objets). K. of trees, bouquet m d'arbres. **'knot-grass**, s. Bot: Renouée f des oiseaux; centinode f.

knot², v. (knotted) **I.** v.tr. Nouer; faire un nœud, des nœuds, à (une ficelle). To k. together two ropes, attacher deux cordages ensemble. **2.** v.i. Se nouer; faire des nœuds. **knotted**, a. **I.** (Corde, fouet) à nœuds. **2.** = KNOTTY 3.

knottiness ['nɔtinəs], s. **I.** Nodosité f (d'une plante). **2.** Difficulté f, complexité f (d'un problème).

knotty ['nɔti], a. **I.** (Of rope, etc.) Plein de nœuds. **2.** F: Knotty point, question difficile, épineuse. **3.** (a) (Of plank, etc.) Noueux, raboteux. (b) Knotty hands, mains noueuses.

knout¹ [naut], s. Knout m.

knout², *v.tr.* Knouter.

know¹ [nou], *s.* F: To be in the know, avoir le mot de l'affaire ; être dans le secret. *Those who are in the k.,* les initiés.

know², *v.tr.* (knew [njuː]; known [noun]) **1.** (*a*) Reconnaître. *I knew him by his walk,* je l'ai reconnu à son allure, à sa démarche. **I knew him for a German,** je l'ai reconnu comme Allemand. (*b*) Distinguer (*from,* de, d'avec). To know good from evil, connaître le bien d'avec le mal. **2.** (*a*) Connaître (qn, un lieu). **To get, come, to know s.o.,** faire la connaissance de qn. *To get to k. s.o.* better, faire plus ample connaissance avec qn. **To be in surroundings one knows,** être en pays de connaissance. (*b*) *He knows no fear,* il ne sait pas ce que c'est que d'avoir peur. *His zeal knows no bounds,* son zèle ne connaît pas de bornes. **3.** Connaître, fréquenter (qn). *They are neighbours of ours but we do not k. them,* ils sont nos voisins mais nous ne les fréquentons pas. **4.** Savoir, connaître, posséder (un sujet). **To know sth. by heart,** savoir qch. par cœur. **To know how to do sth.,** savoir faire qch. *To k. how to read,* savoir lire. F: *They ran all they knew,* ils coururent de toutes leurs forces. **5.** (*a*) **To know more than one says,** en savoir plus long qu'on n'en dit. *I know that well enough,* je ne le sais que trop. **As far as I know,** for all I know, autant que je sache. **Not to know sth.,** ne pas savoir qch. ; ignorer qch. *He doesn't seem to k.* the value of time, il semble ignorer le prix du temps. *Is his father rich?*—**I don't know,** son père est-il riche?—Je n'en sais rien. **How do I know?** est-ce que je sais? **As everyone knows,** comme tout le monde le sait. **He knows his own mind,** il sait ce qu'il veut. **I would have you know that . . .,** sachez que. . . . *I don't know that he understands much about it,* je doute qu'il y entende grand'chose. *I knew (that) he had talent,* je lui connaissais, savais, du talent. *He didn't quite k. what to say,* il ne savait trop que dire. **He knows what he is talking about,** il est sûr de son fait. **I know not what,** je ne sais quoi. (*b*) *I k. him to be a liar,* je sais que c'est un menteur. **I have known it (to) happen,** c'est une chose que j'ai vue se produire. *Have you ever known me (to) tell a lie?* m'avez-vous jamais entendu dire un mensonge? **He had never been known to laugh,** on ne l'avait jamais vu rire. **6. To get to know sth.,** apprendre qch. *I knew it yesterday,* je l'ai appris hier ; je l'ai su hier. **Please let us know whether . . .,** veuillez nous faire savoir si. . . . **Everything gets known,** tout se sait. **7.** F: **Don't I know it!** à quoi le dites-vous! **Not if I know it!** pour rien au monde! **8. To know better than to . . .,** se bien garder de. . . . *I k.* better (*than that),* (i) je sais le contraire ; (ii) je suis plus malin que ça. *He knows better than to do that,* il est trop fin, trop avisé, pour faire cela. **You ought to know better** at your age, vous devriez avoir plus de sagacité à votre âge. **You ought to have known better,** vous auriez dû être plus prudent. **You know best,** vous en êtes le meilleur juge. **know about,** *v.i.* **To know about sth.,** être informé de qch. ; être au courant. **He knows all about it,** il sait tout ; il est renseigné. **I know nothing about it,** je n'en sais rien, je n'en sais pas un mot. **I don't know about that!** je n'en suis pas bien sûr! **know of,** *v.i.* **To know of s.o.,** connaître qn de réputation. *I k. of a good watchmaker,* je connais un bon horloger. **To get to know of sth.,** apprendre qch. **known,** *a.* Connu, reconnu, su. *Such are the known facts,* tels sont les faits constatés. **A known thief,** un voleur avéré. (*Of news, etc.*) **To become known to s.o.,** arriver à la connaissance, aux oreilles, de qn. **To make sth. known to s.o.,** porter qch. à la connaissance de qn. **To make s.o.'s presence known,** divulguer la présence de qn. **To make one's wishes known,** déclarer ses volontés. **It is known to all that . . .,** il est notoire que. . . . **He is known to everyone,** known everywhere, il est connu partout. **Known as . . .,** connu sous le nom de. . . . **This is what is known as . . .,** c'est ce qu'on appelle. . . . (*Of author, etc.*) **To become known,** sortir de l'obscurité. **knowing¹,** *a.* Fin, malin, rusé. **A knowing smile,** un sourire entendu. **To put on a knowing look,** faire l'entendu. **-ly,** *adv.* **1.** Sciemment ; à bon escient. **2.** Finement, habilement ; d'un air rusé. **knowing²,** *s.* **1.** Compréhension *f,* connaissance *f (of,* de). **2. There is no knowing (how . . ., why . . .),** il n'y a pas moyen de savoir (comment . . ., pourquoi . . .).

knowable ['nouəbl], *a.* **1.** Connaissable. **2.** Reconnaissable (*by,* à).

knowledge ['nɔledʒ], *s.* **1.** (*a*) Connaissance *f* (d'un fait, d'une personne). **To get knowledge of sth.,** apprendre qch. **I had no knowledge of it,** je ne le savais pas ; je l'ignorais. **Lack of knowledge,** ignorance *f (of,* de). *This is within the k. of all,* cela, tout le monde le sait. **It is a matter of common knowledge that . . .,** il est notoire que. . . . **To the knowledge of everyone, to everyone's knowledge,** au su de tout le monde. **To my knowledge, to the best of my knowledge, as far as my knowledge goes,** à ma connaissance ; autant que je sache. **To my certain knowledge,** à mon vu et su. **Not to my knowledge,** pas que je sache. **Without my knowledge,** à mon insu. **To speak with full knowledge (of the facts),** parler en connaissance de cause. (*b*) *He had grown out of all knowledge,* il était tellement grandi qu'on ne le reconnaissait plus. **2.** Savoir *m,* science *f,* connaissances *f.* *To have a k. of several languages,* avoir l'intelligence de plusieurs langues. **To have a thorough knowledge of a subject,** connaître un sujet à fond. *His wide k.,* son savoir étendu ; ses vastes connaissances (*of,* en). **Knowledge of the world, of the heart,** la science du monde, du cœur. **Knowledge is power,** savoir c'est pouvoir. **The advance of knowledge,** les progrès *m* de la science.

knowledgeable ['nɔledʒəbl], *a.* F: Intelligent ; bien informé.

knuckle¹ [nʌkl], *s.* **1.** Articulation *f,* jointure *f,* du doigt. **To rap s.o. over the knuckles,** donner sur les ongles à qn. **2.** *Cu:* **Knuckle of a leg of mutton,** (i) (*bone*) manche *m* ; (ii) (*meat*) souris *f* (d'un gigot). **Knuckle of veal,** jarret *m* de veau. F: **That's getting rather near the knuckle,** cela frise l'indécence. **'knuckle-bone,** *s.* **1.** = KNUCKLE¹ 1. **2.** Osselet *m.* *To play at knuckle-bones,* jouer aux osselets. **'knuckle-duster,** *s.* Coup-de-poing américain. **'knuckle-'joint,** *s.* **1.** = KNUCKLE¹ 1. **2.** *Mec.E:* Articulation *f* à genouillère.

knuckle², *v.i.* **To knuckle down, under,** se soumettre ; céder ; mettre les pouces. *I won't k. down to him,* il ne va pas me faire la loi.

knur [nəːr], *s.* Nœud *m* (dans un tronc d'arbre).

knurl¹ [nəːrl], *s.* **1.** Nœud *m* (du bois). **2.** (*a*) *Tls:* Molette *f.* (*b*) Molet(t)age *m.*

knurl², *v.tr.* Molet(t)er, godronner.

kohlrabi [koul'rɑːbi], *s.* *Bot:* Chou-rave *m, pl.* choux-raves.

kola ['koulə], *s.* *Bot:* Cola *m,* kola *m.*

Koran (the) [ðə'kɔːran, ko'rɑːn], *s.* Le Koran ; le Coran.
Korea [ko'riːa]. *Pr.n. Geog:* La Corée.
kosher ['kouʃər], *a. Jew.Rel:* Cachir *inv* ; cacher, -ère.
ko(w)tow [kou'tau], *v.i.* **1.** Se prosterner, se courber (à la chinoise) (*to*, devant). **2.** *F:* To **kotow to** s.o., s'aplatir devant qn ; courber l'échine devant qn.

kraft [krɑːft], *s. Paperm:* Papier d'emballage fort.
Krakow ['krɑːkɔf]. *Pr.n. Geog:* Cracovie *f.*
kudos ['kjuːdɔs], *s. F:* La gloriole.
Kurd [kəːrd], *a. & s. Ethn:* K(o)urde.
Kurdish ['kəːrdiʃ]. **1.** *a.* K(o)urde. **2.** *s. Ling:* Le k(o)urde.
Kurdistan [kəːrdis'tɑːn]. *Pr.n.* Le K(o)urdistan.
kyle [kail], *s. Scot:* Détroit *m*, passe *f.*

L

L, l [el], *s.* **1.** (La lettre) L, l *m or f.* **2.** (*Abbr. of Lat.* libra, *pound*) Livre *f* sterling. *F:* **It is not merely a question of L.S.D.**, ce n'est pas simplement une question d'argent.
la [lɑː], *s. Mus:* **1.** (*Fixed la*) La *m.* **2.** (*Movable la*) La sus-dominante.
laager[1] ['lɑːgər], *s.* (*In S. Africa*) Laager *m* ; campement *m* avec rempart de chars à bœufs.
laager[2]. **1.** *v.tr.* Former (les chars à bœufs) en laager ; mettre (les gens) en laager. **2.** *v.i.* Se former en laager ; former le camp.
lab [lab], *s. F:* = LABORATORY.
label[1] [leibl], *s.* **1.** Étiquette *f.* Gummed label, stick-on label, étiquette gommée. **2.** *Jur:* Queue *f* (d'un document). **3.** *Arch:* = DRIP-STONE.
label[2], *v.tr.* (labelled) Étiqueter. Luggage labelled for London, bagages enregistrés pour Londres.
labial ['leibiəl]. **1.** *a.* Labial, -aux. **2.** *s. Ling:* Labiale *f.*
labiate ['leibiet]. *Bot:* **1.** *a.* Labié. **2.** *s.* Labiée *f.*
laboratory ['labərətəri, *often* la'bɔrətəri], *s.* Laboratoire *m.*
laborious [la'bɔːriəs], *a.* Laborieux. **1.** Travailleur, -euse. **2.** Pénible, fatigant. **-ly**, *adv.* Laborieusement, péniblement.
labour[1] ['leibər], *s.* **1.** (*a*) Travail *m*, labeur *m*, peine *f.* Material and labour, matière *f* et façon *f.* (*b*) *Jur:* Hard labour, réclusion *f* avec travail disciplinaire. **To be sentenced to two years (with) hard labour**, être condamné à deux ans de prison avec travail disciplinaire. **2.** (*a*) *Ind:* Main-d'œuvre *f* ; travailleurs *mpl.* **Manual labour**, main-d'œuvre. **Skilled labour**, main-d'œuvre spécialisée. **Capital and labour**, le capital et le travail. **Labour troubles**, conflits entre ouvriers et patrons ; troubles ouvriers. (*b*) *Coll:* Les travaillistes *m.* **The demands of l.**, les revendications ouvrières. **The Labour party**, le parti travailliste. **3.** **The twelve labours of Hercules**, les douze travaux d'Hercule. **Labour of love**, (i) travail gratuit ; (ii) travail fait avec plaisir. **4.** *Med:* Travail ; couches *fpl.* **Premature labour**, accouchement *m* avant terme. **Woman in labour**, femme en couches. **'labour-exchange**, *s.* Bureau *m* de placement(s) (pour ouvriers) ; Bourse *f* du Travail. **'labour-saving**, *a.* L.-s. device, économiseur *m* de travail. **L.-s. houses**, maisons construites pour parer à la crise domestique.
labour[2]. **1.** *v.i.* (*a*) Travailler, peiner. **To labour for sth.**, se donner de la peine pour obtenir qch. **To labour at, over, sth.**, travailler à qch. ; peiner sur qch. (*b*) **To labour along**, marcher, avancer, péniblement. **To labour up a hill**, gravir péniblement une pente. (*c*) **To labour under a burden**, être courbé sous un fardeau. **To l. under a sense of wrong**, nourrir un sentiment d'injustice. **To labour under a delusion**, être (la) victime d'une illusion ; se faire illusion. (*d*) (*Of engine*) Fatiguer, peiner. (*Of ship*) Bourlinguer, fatiguer. (*Of car*) To l. uphill, peiner en côte. **2.** *v.tr.* Élaborer (un ouvrage) ; travailler (son style). **I will not labour the point**, je ne m'étendrai pas là-dessus. **laboured**, *a.* **1.** (Style) travaillé. **2.** (Respiration) pénible. **labouring**, *a.* **1.** Labouring man, ouvrier *m.* **The labouring class**, la classe ouvrière. **2.** L. heart, cœur palpitant (d'émotion).
labourer ['leibərər], *s.* (*a*) Travailleur *m.* *Prov:* **The labourer is worthy of his hire**, toute peine, tout travail, mérite salaire. (*b*) *Ind:* Manœuvre *m* ; homme *m* de peine. *S.a.* DAY-LABOURER. (*c*) **Agricultural labourer**, ouvrier *m* agricole.
laburnum [la'bəːrnəm], *s. Bot:* Cytise *m* ; faux ébénier.
labyrinth ['labirinθ], *s.* Labyrinthe *m*, dédale *m.*
lac[1] [lak], *s.* Gomme *f* laque ; laque *f.*
lac[2], *s.* Lack *m* (de roupies).
lace[1] [leis], *s.* **1.** Lacet *m* (de corset, de soulier) ; cordon *m* (de soulier). **2.** Gold lace, galon *m*, ganse *f*, passement *m*, d'or. **3.** Dentelle *f*, point *m.* Bobbin lace, pillow lace, dentelle aux fuseaux ; guipure *f.* Alençon l., point d'Alençon. **'lace-maker**, *s.* **1.** Fabricant, -ante, de dentelles. **2.** Dentellière *f.* **'lace-making**, *s.* Dentellerie *f.* **'lace-work**, *s.* (*a*) Dentelles *fpl* ; dentellerie *f.* (*b*) Passementerie *f.*
lace[2], *v.tr.* **1.** To lace (up) one's boots, lacer ses bottines. **To l. oneself, one's waist, too tightly**, se serrer trop. **To lace oneself in**, se lacer. **Lace-up shoes**, chaussures à lacets. **2.** To lace sth. with sth., entrelacer qch. de, avec, qch. **3.** Garnir, border, de dentelles. **4.** Glass of milk laced with rum, lait *m* au rhum. **lacing**, *s.* **1.** Lacement *m*, laçage *m.* **2.** (*a*) Lacet *m.* (*b*) Galon *m*, passement *m.*
lacerate ['lasəreit], *v.tr.* Lacérer ; *F:* déchirer (la chair, le cœur).
laceration [lasə'reiʃ(ə)n], *s.* **1.** Lacération *f*, déchirement *m.* **2.** *Med:* Déchirure *f.*
lachrymal ['lakrim(ə)l], *a.* Lacrymal, -aux.
lachrymatory ['lakrimətəri], *a.* **1.** (Urne) lacrymatoire. **2.** (Gaz) lacrymogène.
lachrymose ['lakrimous], *a.* Larmoyant.
lack[1] [lak], *s.* Manque *m*, absence *f*, défaut *m* (of, de). **There was no lack of people**, il ne manquait pas de monde. **For lack of . . .**, faute de . . . .
lack[2], *v.tr. & i.* To lack (for) sth., manquer de qch. ; ne pas avoir qch. **lacking**, *a.* Qui manque ; manquant. **Money was l.**, l'argent

manquait, faisait défaut. **He is lacking in courage,** il manque de courage. *L. in meaning,* dépourvu, dénué, de sens. **'lack-lustre,** *attrib.a.* (Œil) terne, éteint.

lackadaisical [lakǝ'deizik(ǝ)l], *a.* Affecté, affété, minaudier.

lackaday [lakǝ'dei], *int. A :* Hélas !

lackey ['laki], *s.* Laquais *m.*

laconic [lǝ'kɔnik], *a.* Laconique. **-ally,** *adv.* Laconiquement.

lacquer¹ ['lakǝr], *s.* **1.** Vernis-laque *m inv ;* vernis *m* de Chine ; laque *m.* **Gold lacquer,** batture *f.* **2.** *F :* Peinture laquée. **Cellulose lacquer,** laque cellulosique.

lacquer², *v.tr.* **1.** Laquer. **2.** *F :* Vernir (des meubles, etc.).

lacrosse [lǝ'krɔs], *s. Games :* Crosse canadienne.

lacteal ['laktiǝl], *a.* Lacté ; (suc) laiteux.

lacteous ['laktiǝs], *a.* Laiteux.

lactic ['laktik], *a. Ch :* Lactique.

lactiferous [lak'tifǝrǝs], *a.* (Conduit, etc.) lactifère.

lactometer [lak'tɔmetǝr], *s.* Lactomètre *m,* pèse-lait *m inv.*

lacuna, *pl.* **-ae, -as** [lǝ'kju:nǝ, -i:, -ǝz], *s.* Lacune *f ;* hiatus *m.*

lacustrian [lǝ'kʌstriǝn], *a.* (Cité) lacustre.

lacustrine [lǝ'kʌstrin], *a.* (Plante) lacustre.

lad [lad], *s.m. (a)* Jeune homme ; (jeune) garçon. *A servant lad,* un jeune domestique. **Now then, my lads!** allons, mes garçons ! allons, les gars ! *(b) F :* **He's a regular lad !** c'est un gaillard !

ladder¹ ['ladǝr], *s.* **1.** Échelle *f.* **Folding ladder,** échelle pliante, brisée. *F :* **The social ladder,** l'échelle sociale. **To be at the top of the ladder,** être au haut de l'échelle. **2.** *Hyd.E :* **Ladder of locks,** suite *f* de biefs. **3.** *(In silk stockings)* Maille partie, maille lâchée ; éraillure *f,* échelle. *To mend ladders in a stocking,* rem(m)ailler un bas. **'ladder-proof,** *a.* (Bas) indémaillable.

ladder², *v.i. (Of stocking)* Se démailler.

laddie ['ladi], *s.m. Scot : F : (a)* = LAD. *(b)* Mon petit gars.

lade¹ [leid], *s.* (Mill-)lade, courant *m* de moulin ; bief *m.*

lade², *v.tr.* (laded ; laden) *Nau : (a)* Charger (un navire) *(with,* de). *(b)* Embarquer (des marchandises). **laden,** *a.* Chargé. **Fully laden ship,** navire en pleine charge. **Well-laden tree,** arbre chargé de fruits. **lading,** *s.* Chargement *m* (d'un navire). *S.a.* BILL¹ 4.

la-di-da ['lɑ:di'dɑ:], *a. F :* **La-di-da manner,** air affecté.

ladified ['leidifaid], *a.* (Airs) de grande dame ; (personne) qui fait la grande dame.

ladle¹ ['leidl], *s.* **1.** Cuiller *f* à pot. **Soup ladle,** cuiller à potage ; louche *f.* **2.** *(a) Ind :* Puisoir *m,* puchet *m. (b) Metall :* **Foundry ladle,** poche *f* de fonderie.

ladle², *v.tr.* **To ladle (out) the soup,** servir le potage (avec la louche). *F :* **To l. out facts,** sortir des faits à n'en plus finir.

ladleful ['leidlful], *s.* Pleine cuiller à pot, pleine louche (de) ; grande cuillerée (de).

lady ['leidi], *s.f.* Dame. **1.** *(a) (At court)* **Lady-in-waiting,** dame d'honneur. *(b)* Femme bien élevée. **She looks a l.,** elle a l'air distingué ; elle a l'air très bien. **To play the fine lady,** trancher de la grande dame. *(c) (Woman)* **A lady and a gentleman,** un monsieur et une dame. **An English l.,** une Anglaise. **Young lady,** *(married)* jeune dame ; *(unmarried)* demoiselle, jeune fille. **Old lady,** vieille dame. **This lady, this young lady,** cette dame, cette demoiselle ; *(when speaking in*

their *presence)* madame, mademoiselle. **Ladies and gentlemen!** Mesdames, mesdemoiselles, messieurs ! *F :* messieurs-dames ! *(d)* **Lady's watch,** montre de dame. **Ladies' tailor,** tailleur pour dames. **A ladies' man, a lady's man,** un galant. **Lady cashier,** caissière ; dame, demoiselle, de comptoir. **Lady doctor,** femme médecin ; docteur *m* femme. **2.** *Ecc :* **Our Lady,** Notre-Dame ; la sainte Vierge. **3.** *(As title, without Fr. equivalent)* Lady, *F :* milady. **My lady,** madame (la comtesse, etc.). **The lady of the manor,** la châtelaine. **4.** *P :* **My young lady,** (i) ma bonne amie ; (ii) ma future. **'lady-bird,** *s. Ent :* Coccinelle *f ; F :* bête *f* à bon Dieu. **'lady-chair,** *s.* Entrecroisement *m* de mains (de deux porteurs) (pour le transport d'un blessé). **To carry s.o. in a lady-chair,** porter qn en chaise. **'lady chapel,** *s. Ecc :* Chapelle *f* de la Vierge. **'Lady day,** *s. Ecc :* La fête de l'Annonciation. **'lady-killer,** *s.m. F :* Bourreau des cœurs. **lady's 'slipper,** *s. Bot :* Sabot *m* de la Vierge, de Vénus.

ladylike ['leidilaik], *a.* (Air) distingué, de dame ; *(of pers.)* comme il faut ; bien élevée. *L.* costume, costume de bon ton ; costume seyant.

ladyship ['leidiʃip], *s.* **Her ladyship, your ladyship,** madame (la comtesse, etc.).

laevulose ['li:vjulous], *s. Ch :* Lévulose *m ;* sucre *m* de fruit.

lag¹ [lag], *s. Ph :* Retard *m ;* décalage *m* (entre deux opérations). **Magnetic lag,** retard d'aimantation ; hystérèse *f.* **Lag of the brushes,** décalage des balais (d'une dynamo, etc.). **Phase lag,** retard de phase ; déphasage *m* en arrière.

lag², *v.i.* (lagged) **1.** *(Of pers.)* **To lag (behind),** rester en arrière ; traîner. **2.** *Tchn : (Of tides, etc.)* Retarder. *El.E : (Of current)* Être déphasé en arrière.

lag³, *s. P :* Condamné *m,* forçat *m.* **An old lag,** un repris de justice ; un récidiviste.

lag⁴, *v.tr.* Garnir, envelopper, revêtir, (une chaudière) d'un calorifuge. **Air-lagged,** à chemise d'air. **lagging,** *s.* **1.** Garnissage *m.* **2.** Garniture *f,* revêtement *m* calorifuge (d'une chaudière).

lager ['lɑ:gǝr], *s.* **Lager (beer),** bière blonde allemande.

laggard ['lagǝrd], **1.** *a.* Lent, paresseux. **2.** *s.* Traînard *m ;* lambin, -ine.

lagoon [lǝ'gu:n], *s.* **1.** *(In Adriatic)* Lagune *f.* **2.** Lagon *m* (d'atoll).

laicization [le(i)isai'zeiʃ(ǝ)n], *s.* Laïcisation *f.*

laicize ['le(i)isaiz], *v.tr.* Laïciser.

laid [leid]. *See* LAY⁴.

lain [lein]. *See* LIE⁴.

lair ['lɛǝr], *s.* Tanière *f,* repaire *m* (de bête fauve) ; lit *m* (du cerf) ; bauge *f* (du sanglier). *F :* **Brigands' lair,** repaire, caverne *f,* de brigands.

laird ['lɛǝrd], *s. Scot :* Propriétaire (foncier). **The laird,** le châtelain de l'endroit.

laity ['le(i)iti], *s. Coll.* Les laïques *m ; F :* les profanes *m.*

lake¹ [leik], *s.* Lac *m.* **Ornamental lake,** bassin *m ;* pièce *f* d'eau décorative. **'lake-dwelling,** *s.* Habitation *f* lacustre. **Lake-dwellings,** cité *f* lacustre.

lake², *s. Paint :* Laque *f.* **Crimson lake,** laque carminée.

lakh [lak], *s.* = LAC².

lam [lam], *v.tr. & i.* (lammed) *P :* **To lam (into)** s.o., rosser, étriller, qn.

lama¹ ['lɑ:mǝ], *s. Buddhist Rel :* Lama *m.*

lama², *s.* = LLAMA.

lamb¹ [lam], *s.* Agneau *m.* **Ewe lamb,** agnelle *f. F :* **My one ewe lamb,** mon seul trésor. *Theol :*

The lamb (of God), l'Agneau (de Dieu). *F:* He took it like a lamb, il s'est laissé faire ; il n'a pas protesté. *Cu:* L. *cutlet,* côtelette *f* d'agneau. **'lamb-like,** *a.* Doux, *f.* douce, comme un agneau. **'lamb's 'lettuce,** *s.* *Bot:* Mâche *f.* **'lambs' 'tails,** *s.pl.* *Bot:* Chatons *m* (du noyer).

lamb², *v.i.* (*Of ewe*) Agneler, mettre bas.

lambing, *s.* Agnelage *m.*

lambency ['lambənsi], *s.* **1.** Lueur blafarde (d'une flamme). **2.** Chatoiement *m* (de l'esprit).

lambent ['lambənt], *a.* **1.** Blafard. **2.** (Esprit, style) chatoyant.

lame¹ [leim], *a.* **1.** (*a*) Boiteux ; (*through accident*) estropié ; *F:* éclopé. **To be lame of, in, one leg,** boiter d'une jambe. **To walk lame,** boiter, clocher ; traîner la jambe. **To go lame, se mettre à boiter.** (*b*) *Pros:* Lame verses, vers boiteux ; vers qui clochent. **2. Lame excuse,** faible, pauvre, excuse. Lame story, histoire qui ne tient pas debout. **-ly,** *adv.* **1.** (Marcher) en boitant. **2.** (S'excuser, etc.) imparfaitement, faiblement.

lame², *v.tr.* (*a*) (*Of pers.*) Rendre (qn) boiteux ; écloper (qn, un cheval) ; (*of blister, etc.*) faire boiter (qn). (*b*) Estropier.

lamella, *pl.* **-ae** [lə'mela, -iː], *s.* Lamelle *f.*

lamellar [lə'melər], *a.* Lamellaire.

lamellate ['lamelet], *a.* Lamellé, feuilleté.

lameness ['leimnəs], *s.* **1.** (*a*) Claudication *f* ; boitement *m.* (*b*) Boiterie *f* (d'un cheval) **2.** Faiblesse *f* (d'une excuse, etc.).

lament¹ [lə'ment], *s.* **1.** Lamentation *f.* **2.** *Mus:* *A:* Complainte *f.*

lament², *v.tr. & i.* To lament (for, over) sth., s.o., se lamenter sur qch. ; pleurer qch., qn. **lamented,** *a.* The late lamented X, le regretté X.

lamentable ['lamontabl], *a.* (Perte) lamentable, déplorable. **-ably,** *adv.* Lamentablement, déplorablement.

lamentation [lamən'teiʃ(ə)n], *s.* Lamentation *f.*

lamina, *pl.* **-ae** ['lamina, -iː], *s.* Lame *f,* lamelle *f,* feuillet *m.*

laminar ['laminər], *a.* Laminaire.

laminate¹ ['lamineit], **1.** *v.tr.* (*a*) Laminer. (*b*) Diviser en lamelles ; feuilleter. **2.** *v.i.* Se feuilleter. **laminated,** *a.* **1.** (Ressort, etc.) feuilleté, à feuilles, à lames. **2.** (Bois) contreplaqué.

laminate² ['laminet], *a.* *Nat.Hist:* Lamineux ; à lamelles.

lamination [lami'neiʃ(ə)n], *s.* **1.** (*a*) Laminage *m.* (*b*) Feuilletage *m.* **2.** Lamelle *f.*

Lammas ['laməs], *s.* Lammas(-day, -tide), le premier août (en Écosse, terme de loyers) ; la Saint-Pierre aux Liens.

lammergeyer ['lamərgaiər], *s.* *Orn:* Gypaète barbu.

lamp [lamp], *s.* **1.** (*a*) Lampe *f.* *F:* (*Of work*) To smell of the lamp, sentir la lampe ; sentir l'huile. Portable lamp, inspection lamp (*of garage, etc.*), baladeuse *f.* Stable lamp, falot *m.* Pocket lamp, torche *f* ; lanterne *f* de poche. *Min:* Safety lamp, lampe de sûreté. (*b*) Lanterne (de voiture, de bicyclette). *Aut:* Head-lamp, phare *m.* Side lamps, feux *m* de côté. **2.** Table lamp, lampe de table ; lampe portative. Standard lamp, torchère *f* ; lampadaire *m.* Hanging lamp, suspension *f.* Ceiling lamp, plafonnier *m.* *S.a.* GAS-LAMP, READING-LAMP, STREET-LAMP. **3.** *El:* (*Bulb*) Lampe, ampoule *f.* *S.a.* ARC-LAMP. **'lamp-black,** *s.* Noir *m* de fumée. **'lamp-bracket,** *s.* *Aut:* *etc:* Porte-lanterne *m inv* ; (*for head-lamp*) porte-phare *m inv.* **'lamp-holder,** *s.*

El: Douille *f* (de lampe) ; porte-ampoule *m inv.* **'lamp-man,** *pl.* **-men,** *s.m.* Lampiste. **'lamp-oil,** *s.* **1.** Huile *f* d'éclairage ; huile lampante. **2.** Pétrole lampant. **'lamp-post,** *s.* (*In street*) (*a*) Montant *m* de réverbère. (*b*) *F:* Réverbère *m.* **'lamp-shade,** *s.* Abat-jour *m inv.*

lamplight ['lamplait], *s.* Lumière *f* de la lampe. To work by lamplight, travailler à la lampe.

lamplighter ['lamplaitər], *s.* Allumeur *m* de réverbères.

lampoon¹ [lam'puːn], *s.* Pasquinade *f,* libelle *m,* satire *f,* brocard *m.*

lampoon², *v.tr.* Lancer des satires, des libelles, des brocards, contre (qn) ; chansonner (qn).

lampooner [lam'puːnər], **lampoonist** [lam'puːnist], *s.* Libelliste *m,* satiriste *m.*

lampoonery [lam'puːnəri], *s.* Satire *f* ; esprit *m* satirique.

lamprey ['lampri], *s.* *Ich:* Lamproie *f.*

Lancaster ['laŋkastər]. *Pr.n.* *Geog:* Lancastre.

Lancastrian [laŋ'kastriən], *a. & s.* *Hist:* Lancastrien, -ienne.

lance¹ [lɑːns], *s.* **1.** Lance *f.* *F:* To break a lance with s.o., rompre une lance avec qn ; croiser le fer avec qn. **2.** (*Pers.*) *Hist:* Lance. *S.a.* FREE LANCE. **'lance-'corporal,** *s.* *Mil:* Soldat *m* de première classe.

lance², *v.tr.* *Med:* Donner un coup de bistouri, de lancette, à (un abcès) ; percer, inciser (un abcès).

lanceolate ['lɑːnsiolet], *a.* *Bot:* Lancéolé ; en fer de lance.

lancer ['lɑːnsər], *s.* **1.** *Mil:* Lancier *m.* **2.** *pl.* Lancers, (quadrille *m* des) lanciers.

lancet ['lɑːnset], *s.* **1.** *Med:* Lancette *f,* bistouri *m.* **2.** *Arch:* (Ogive *f* à) lancette.

lancinating ['lɑːnsineitiŋ], *a.* Lancinant. L. pains, élancements *m.*

land¹ [land], *s.* **1.** (*a*) (*Opposed to sea*) Terre *f.* Dry land, terre ferme. **To travel by land,** voyager par voie de terre. **By land and sea, on land and at sea,** sur terre et sur mer. **To see how the land lies,** (i) *Nau:* prendre le gisement de la côte ; (ii) *F:* sonder, tâter, le terrain. **To make, sight, land,** atterrir ; arriver en vue de la terre. **To touch land,** toucher terre ; aborder, atterrir. (*b*) (*Soil*) Terre, terrain *m,* sol *m.* **Back to the land!** le retour aux champs, à la terre ! Waste l., terre inculte ; terrain vague. **The land question,** la question agraire. **2.** Terre, pays *m,* contrée *f.* Distant lands, pays lointains. The Holy Land, la Terre Sainte. *F:* Theatreland, le quartier des spectacles. **3.** Terre(s) ; fonds *m* de terre ; terrain(s). **4.** Plat *m,* intervalle *m* (entre cannelures ou gorges). **'land-act,** *s.* *Jur:* Loi *f* agraire. **'land-agency,** *s.* **1.** Intendance *f.* **2.** Agence foncière. **'land-agent,** *s.* **1.** Intendant *m,* régisseur *f,* d'un domaine. **2.** Courtier en immeubles. **'land-breeze,** *s.* *Nau:* Brise *f* de terre. **'land-girl,** *s.f.* Jeune fille qui s'est offerte pour travailler la terre (p.ex. en temps de guerre). **'land-lubber,** *s.* *F:* Marin *m* d'eau douce. **'Land's End.** *Pr.n.* *Geog:* La pointe de Cornouaille. **'land-slide,** *s.* **1.** = LANDSLIP. **2.** *Pol:* Débâcle *f,* défaite accablante (d'un parti politique aux élections). **'land-steward,** *s.* = LAND-AGENT 1. **'land-surveying,** *s.* Arpentage *m* ; géodésie *f.* **'land-surveyor,** *s.* See SURVEYOR 1. **'land-worker,** *s.* Travailleur *m* agricole.

land². **1.** *v.tr.* (*a*) Mettre, faire descendre, (qn) à terre ; mettre (qch.) à terre ; débarquer (qn, qch.). To land an aeroplane, atterrir un avion. (*b*) To land a fish, amener un poisson à terre. *F:* To land a prize, remporter un prix.

(c) Amener. *F:* That will land you in prison, cela vous vaudra de la prison. *You have landed us in a nice fix!* vous nous avez mis dans de beaux draps! *I was landed with an encyclopaedia I didn't want,* je me suis trouvé empêtré d'une encyclopédie dont je n'avais que faire. (d) *F:* To land s.o. a blow in the face, allonger, porter, flanquer, à qn un coup au visage. **2.** *v.i.* (a) *(Of pers.)* Descendre à terre; débarquer; *(of aeroplane)* atterrir. *Av:* To 'land' on the sea, amerrir. (b) Tomber (à terre). (c) *(After jumping)* Retomber. *To l. on one's feet,* retomber sur ses pieds; retomber d'aplomb. *F:* He always lands on his feet, il retombe toujours sur ses pattes.

landed, *a.* Landed property, propriété foncière; bien-fonds *m, pl.* biens-fonds. Landed proprietor, propriétaire terrien. **landing¹,** *a.* Landing force, troupes *fpl* de débarquement. **landing²,** *s.* **I.** (a) *Nau:* Débarquement *m*; mise *f* à terre. (b) *Mil: Navy:* Descente *f.* (c) *Av:* (i) Atterrissage *m*; (ii) *(on sea)* amerrissage *m.* To make a forced landing, faire un atterrissage forcé. Landing light, phare *m* d'atterrissage. **2.** (a) *Const:* Palier *m* (de repos) (d'un escalier); repos *m*, carré *m.* (b) *Min:* Recette *f.* **'landing-ground,** *s. Av:* Terrain *m* d'atterrissage. **'landing-net,** *s. Fish:* Épuisette *f.* **'landing-stage,** *s.* Débarcadère *m*, embarcadère *m* (flottant); ponton *m.*

landau ['landɔː], *s. Veh:* Landau *m*, -aus.

landfall ['landfɔːl], *s. Nau: Av:* Arrivée *f* en vue de terre; atterrissage *m.* To make a landfall, atterrir.

landlady ['landleidi], *s.f.* **I.** Propriétaire *f* (d'un immeuble). **2.** Logeuse (en garni). **3.** Hôtelière, hôtesse; *F:* patronne.

landlocked ['landlɔkt], *a. Geog:* Enfermé entre les terres; entouré de terre. L. sea, mer intérieure.

landlord ['landlɔːd], *s.* **I.** Propriétaire (foncier). **2.** Propriétaire (d'un immeuble). **3.** Aubergiste *m*, hôtelier *m*, hôte *m.*

landmark ['landmɑːk], *s.* **I.** Borne *f* limite. **2.** (a) (Point *m* de) repère *m. Nau:* Amer *m.* (b) Point coté (sur une carte, etc.). **3.** Point décisif, événement marquant (dans l'histoire, etc.). *(Of event)* To be a landmark, faire époque.

landowner ['landounər], *s.* Propriétaire foncier.

landscape ['landskeip], *s.* Paysage *m.* **'landscape-'garden,** *s.* Jardin *m* à l'anglaise; jardin paysager. **'landscape-'gardener,** *s.* Jardiniste *m*; architecte *m* paysagiste. **'landscape-'painter,** *s.* Paysagiste *m.*

landslip ['landslip], *s.* Éboulement *m*, glissement *m*, de terrain.

landsman, *pl.* **-men** ['landzmən, -men], *s.m.* Terrien.

landward ['landwərd]. **I.** *adv.* Du côté de la terre; vers la terre. **2.** *a.* (Population) de l'intérieur; (côté) de la terre.

landwards ['landwərdz], *adv.* Du côté de la terre; vers la terre.

lane [lein], *s.* **I.** *(In country)* Chemin vicinal, rural; *(in town)* ruelle *f*, passage *m.* *(Of troops, etc.)* To form a lane, faire la haie. **2.** *(In ice-field)* Fissure *f*, passage. **3.** *Nau:* Route *f* de navigation.

lang syne ['laŋ'sain]. *Scot:* **I.** *adv.* Autrefois, jadis. **2.** *s.* Le temps jadis. *S.a.* AULD.

language ['laŋgwedʒ], *s.* **I.** Langue *f* (d'un peuple). *Dead, living, languages,* langues mortes, vivantes. **2.** Langage *m. Have animals a l.?* les animaux ont-ils un langage? Strong language, langage violent, expressions vives. Bad language, langage grossier; grossièretés *fpl*; gros mots.

languid ['laŋgwid], *a.* Languissant, langoureux; mou, *f.* molle. To be l. about sth., avoir peu d'enthousiasme pour qch. *L. voice,* voix traînante. **-ly,** *adv.* Languissamment, langoureusement; mollement, sans animation.

languidness ['laŋgwidnəs], *s.* Langueur *f*, mollesse *f.*

languish ['laŋgwiʃ], *v.i.* Languir. To languish after, for, s.o., sth., languir après, pour, qn, qch.

languishing¹, *a.* Languissant, langoureux; (regard) plein de langueur. **languishing²,** *s.* **I.** Dépérissement *m*; étiolement *m.* **2.** Langueur *f.*

languor ['laŋg(w)ər], *s.* Langueur *f.*

languorous ['laŋg(w)ərəs], *a.* Langoureux. **-ly,** *adv.* Langoureusement.

laniard ['lanjərd], *s.* = LANYARD.

laniferous [la'nifərəs], **lanigerous** [la'nidʒərəs], *a.* Lanifère, lanigère.

lank [laŋk], *a.* **I.** *(Of pers.)* Maigre; sec, *f.* sèche; *(of animal)* efflanqué. *L. cheeks,* joues creuses. **2.** Lank hair, cheveux plats.

lankiness ['laŋkinəs], *s.* Taille grande et maigre.

lanky ['laŋki], *a.* Grand et maigre; grand et sec. *A great l. fellow,* a lanky-legs, un grand maigre; un grand efflanqué.

lansquenet ['lanskənet], *s.* Lansquenet *m.*

lantern ['lantərn], *s.* **I.** (a) Lanterne *f*, falot *m. Nau:* Fanal *m*, -aux. Dark lantern, bull's-eye lantern, lanterne sourde. Chinese lantern, lanterne vénitienne. (b) Magic lantern, lanterne magique; lanterne à projections. **2.** *Arch:* Lanterne, lanterneau *m* (de dôme). **'lantern-jawed,** *a.* Aux joues creuses; à la figure émaciée. **'lantern-jaws,** *s.pl.* Joues creuses. **'lantern-light,** *s. Arch:* = LANTERN 2.

lanyard ['lanjərd], *s.* **I.** *Nau:* Aiguillette *f*; ride *f* (de hauban); *(of knife)* amarrage *m.* **2.** *Artil:* (Cordon *m*) tire-feu *m inv.*

lap¹ [lap], *s.* **I.** Pan *m*, basque *f* (d'un vêtement). **2.** Genoux *mpl*; *A:* giron *m.* To sit in, on, s.o.'s lap, s'asseoir sur les genoux de qn. To catch sth. in one's lap, attraper qch. dans son tablier, dans sa jupe. *It is in the lap of the gods,* Dieu seul le sait. *S.a.* LUXURY. **'lap-dog,** *s.* Bichon *m*; chien *m* de salon.

lap², *s.* **I.** *Const:* Chevauchement *m*, recouvrement *m* (des ardoises, etc.). **2.** *El:* Guipage *m* (de coton); couche isolante. **3.** (a) Tour *m* (d'une corde autour d'un cylindre, etc.). (b) *Sp:* Tour (de piste); boucle *f*, circuit *m.* To cover a lap in six minutes, boucler le circuit en six minutes. **'lap-joint¹,** *s.* **I.** *Carp: etc:* Assemblage *m* à recouvrement. **2.** *Metalw:* Ourlet *m* à clin. **'lap-joint²,** *v.tr.* **I.** (a) Assembler (des planches) à clin. (b) Assembler (des poutres) (i) à mi-fer, (ii) à mi-bois. **2.** Ourler (une tôle). **'lap-jointed,** *a.* A recouvrement, à clin.

lap³, *v.* (lapped [lapt]) **I.** *v.tr.* (a) *To lap sth. round sth.,* enrouler qch. autour de qch. (b) *Const:* Enchevaucher (des planches). (c) *El.E:* Guiper (un câble, etc.). (d) *Sp:* (i) Boucler (un concurrent). (ii) To lap the course, boucler le circuit. **2.** *v.i.* **To lap over sth.,** retomber, se rabattre, sur qch.; dépasser, chevaucher, qch.

lapped, *a.* **I.** *Carp: Mec.E: etc:* (Joint) à recouvrement. *Lapped tiles,* tuiles chevauchées. **2.** *El.E:* Single-lapped wire, double-lapped wire, fil à guipage simple, double. **3.** Lapped in luxury, entouré de luxe. **lapping,** *s.* **I.** Recouvrement *m*, chevauchement *m.* **2.** *El:* (i) Guipage *m*, (ii) guipure *f* (d'un câble, etc.).

lap⁴, *s.* **I.** Gorgée *f* (de lait, etc.). **2.** Clapotement *m*, clapotis *m* (de vagues).

lap⁵. 1. *v.tr.* (*Of animal*) To lap (up) milk, laper du lait. *F:* He laps up, down, everything you tell him, il avale, gobe, tout ce qu'on lui dit. **2.** *v.i.* (*Of waves*) Clapoter.

lapel [la'pel], *s. Tail:* Revers *m* (d'un habit)

lapelled [la'peld], *a. Tail:* A revers.

lapidate ['lapideit], *v.tr:* Lapider.

lapidation [lapi'deiʃ(ə)n], *s.* Lapidation *f.*

lapis lazuli ['lapis'lazjulai], *s. Miner:* Lazulite *m*; lapis(-lazuli) *m inv.*

Lapland ['lapland]. *Pr.n.* La Laponie.

Laplander ['laplandər], *s.* Lapon, -one.

Lapp [lap]. **1.** *a. & s.* Lapon, -one. **2.** *s. Ling:* Le lapon.

lapse¹ [laps], *s.* **1.** (*a*) (*Mistake*) Erreur *f*, faute *f*. Lapse of the tongue, lapsus *m* linguæ. Lapse of memory, défaillance *f*, lapsus, de mémoire. (*b*) Faute; faux pas; écart *m* de conduite. *L. from one's duty*, manquement *m* à son devoir. **2.** *Jur:* Déchéance *f* (d'un droit). **3.** Cours *m*, marche *f* (du temps); laps *m* de temps. *After a l. of three months*, après un délai de trois mois; au bout de trois mois.

lapse², *v.i.* **1.** (*a*) Déchoir (*from the faith*, de la foi). *To l. from duty*, manquer au devoir; s'écarter de son devoir. **To lapse (back)** *into idleness*, (re)tomber dans la paresse. *To l. into silence*, rentrer dans le silence. (*b*) *Abs.* Manquer à ses devoirs; être coupable d'un écart de conduite; faire un faux pas. **2.** *Jur:* (*Of right, etc.*) (Se) périmer; tomber en désuétude; (*of law*) s'abroger. *Ins:* (*Of policy, etc.*) Cesser d'être en vigueur. (*Of right, estate, etc.*) To lapse to s.o., passer à qn. **lapsed,** *a.* **1.** Déchu. **2.** (Billet) périmé. *Jur:* (Droit) périmé; (legs) tombé en dévolu; (contrat) caduc, *f.* caduque.

lapwing ['lapwiŋ], *s. Orn:* Vanneau *m*.

lar, *pl.* **lares** [lɑːr, 'leəriːz], *s. Rom.Ant:* Lare *m*. *Esp. pl.* Dieux lares.

larboard ['lɑːrbɔːrd, 'lɑːrbərd], *s. Nau: A:* = PORT³.

larceny ['lɑːrsəni], *s.* Larcin *m*; vol insignifiant. *Jur:* Petty larceny, vol simple.

larch [lɑːrtʃ], *s. Bot:* Mélèze *m*. Larch-wood, bois *m* de mélèze.

lard¹ [lɑːrd], *s.* (*a*) Saindoux *m*; graisse *f* de porc. (*b*) *Pharm: Ind:* Axonge *f.*

lard², *v.tr. Cu:* Larder, piquer (la viande). Larding-needle, -pin, lardoire *f. F:* To lard one's writings with quotations, larder, entrelarder, ses écrits de citations.

larder ['lɑːrdər], *s.* Garde-manger *m inv.*

large [lɑːrdʒ]. **I.** *a.* **1.** (*a*) De grandes dimensions; grand; gros, fort. *L. book, parcel*, gros livre; gros paquet, paquet volumineux. *The largest hall*, la salle la plus vaste. *To grow l., larger*, grossir, grandir. **As large as life,** (i) (*of statue, etc.*) de grandeur naturelle; (ii) *F. & Hum:* (*of pers.*) aucunement rabaissé dans sa propre estime. (*b*) *A l. sum*, une grosse, forte, somme; une somme considérable. *L. fortune*, grande, belle, fortune. *To incur l. losses*, éprouver, subir, de fortes pertes. *L. family*, famille nombreuse. *L. meal*, repas copieux. **In a large measure,** en grande partie. **Criminal on a large scale,** criminel de grande envergure. *To open a business on a l. scale*, établir une maison (de commerce) sur un grand pied. *To do things on a l. scale*, faire les choses en grand, sur une grande échelle. **Large** farmer, gros fermier. **2.** (*a*) Large views, idées larges. (*b*) **Large powers,** pouvoirs larges, étendus. **-ly,** *adv.* **1.** En grande partie; pour une grande part. *They come very l. from round about Birmingham*, ils viennent pour une grande

---

part des environs de Birmingham. **2.** *That is l. sufficient*, cela suffit grandement. **II. large,** *adv. Nau:* To sail large, courir largue; naviguer vent largue. *S.a.* BY II. 1. **III. large,** *s.* **(a) To set a** prisoner at large, élargir, relaxer, un prisonnier. **To be at large,** être libre, en liberté. (*b*) **Society,** the people, at large, le grand public. **'large-'hearted,** *a.* **1.** Magnanime. **2.** Généreux. **'large-'heartedness,** *s.* **1.** Magnanimité *f.* **2.** Générosité *f.* **'large-'minded,** *a.* A l'esprit large. **'large-'mindedness,** *s.* Largeur *f* d'esprit; tolérance *f.* **'large-'sized,** *a.* De grandes dimensions; (livre) de grand format.

largeness ['lɑːrdʒnəs], *s.* **1.** (*a*) Grosseur *f* (du corps). (*b*) Grandeur *f* (d'une majorité); ampleur *f* (d'un repas). **2.** (*a*) Étendue *f* (d'un pouvoir). (*b*) Largeur *f* (d'idées).

largess(e) ['lɑːrdʒes], *s. A. & Lit:* Largesse *f.*

lariat ['lariət], *s.* **1.** Corde *f* à piquet. **2.** Lasso *m*.

lark¹ [lɑːrk], *s. Orn:* Alouette *f. F:* To rise with the lark, se lever au chant du coq. She sings like a lark, elle chante comme une fauvette.

lark², *s. F:* Farce *f*, rigolade *f*, blague *f.* **To do** sth. for a lark, faire qch. pour rire, histoire de rigoler.

lark³, *v.i. F:* Faire des farces; folichonner, rigoler.

larkspur ['lɑːrkspər], *s. Bot:* Pied-d'alouette *m*, delphinium *m*.

larky ['lɑːrki], *a. F:* Folichon; espiègle.

larrikin ['larikin], *s. F:* (*In Austr.*) Gavroche *m*; gamin *m* (des rues).

larva, *pl.* **-vae** ['lɑːrva, -viː], *s.* Larve *f.*

larval ['lɑːrvəl], *a.* **1.** *Ent:* Larvaire. **2.** (*Of disease*) Latent, larvé.

laryngeal [la'rindʒəl], *a.* **1.** (Muscle, nerf) laryngé. **2.** *L. cavity*, cavité laryngienne.

laryngitis [larin'dʒaitis], *s. Med:* Laryngite *f.*

laryngoscope [la'riŋgoskoup], *s. Med:* Laryngoscope *m*.

larynx ['lariŋks], *s. Anat:* Larynx *m*.

lascar ['laskər], *s.* Lascar *m*.

lascivious [la'siviəs], *a.* Lascif. **-ly,** *adv.* Lascivement.

lasciviousness [la'siviəsnəs], *s.* Lasciveté *f.*

lash¹ [laʃ], *s.* **1.** (*a*) Coup *m* de fouet; sanglade *f*, cinglon *m.* (*b*) Lanière *f* (de fouet). (*c*) (The penalty of) the lash, le supplice du fouet. *F:* To be under the lash of criticism, être exposé aux coups de la critique; être flagellé par la critique. **2.** *Mec.E:* Jeu *m.* Side lash, jeu latéral. *S.a.* BACK-LASH. **3.** = EYE-LASH.

lash², *v.tr. & i.* **1.** (*a*) Fouailler, cingler (un cheval, etc.). (*Of rain*) To lash (against) the windows, the face, fouetter les vitres, cingler le visage. *F:* To lash oneself into a fury, entrer dans une violente colère. (*b*) (*Of animal*) To lash its tail, se battre les flancs avec la queue. (*c*) Flageller, fouailler, cingler (les vices, etc.). **2.** *v.i. Mec.E:* (*Of running part*) Fouetter. **lash out,** *v.i.* **1.** (*Of horse*) Ruer. (*Of pers.*) To lash out at s.o., (i) lâcher un coup (de poing, etc.) à qn (ii) lancer un coup de langue à qn. **2.** (*a*) Décocher un coup de fouet (à un cheval). (*b*) To lash out into expenditure, se livrer à de folles dépenses. **lashing¹,** *a.* (*Of rain*) Cinglant. **lashing²,** *s.* **1.** (*a*) Coups *mpl* de fouet; le fouet. (*b*) Fouettée *f*; sanglade *f.* (*c*) *Mec.E:* Fouettement *m*. **2.** *pl. F:* Lashings, profusion *f* (of, de).

lash³, *v.tr.* Lier, attacher; *Nau:* amarrer; saisir (l'ancre). **To lash down** the load on a waggon, lier, brider, brêler, la charge sur un chariot. *Nau:* To lash a pulley, aiguilleter une poulie. **lashing³,** *s. Nau:* **1.** Amarrage *m*, aiguilletage *m*. **2.** Amarre *f*; point *m* d'amarrage; aiguillette *f*.

lass [las], *s.f. Esp. Scot:* Jeune fille.

lassie ['lasi], *s.f. Esp. Scot:* Fillette, gamine.

lassitude ['lasitjuːd], *s.* Lassitude *f*.

lasso¹ ['laso], *s.* Lasso *m*.

lasso², *v.tr.* Prendre au lasso.

last¹ [lɑːst], *s. Bootm:* Forme *f* (à chaussure). *Prov:* Let the shoemaker stick to his last, à chacun son métier.

last². **I.** *a.* Dernier. **1.** (*a*) **The last two,** *F:* the two last, les deux derniers. **She was the last to arrive,** elle arriva la dernière. **The last but one,** the second last, l'avant-dernier. *I should be the l. to believe it,* je serais le dernier à le croire. *That's the l. thing that's worrying me,* c'est le cadet de mes soucis. **In the last resort, as a last resource,** en dernier ressort; en désespoir de cause. **To have the last word,** avoir le dernier mot. *He has said the l. word on the matter,* il a dit le mot final là-dessus. *F:* **The last word in hats,** chapeau dernier cri. **Last thing at night,** tard dans la soirée. *s. U.S:* **The last of the week, month, year,** *etc.,* le dernier jour, la fin, de la semaine, du mois, de l'année, etc. *Com:* **In my last,** dans ma dernière lettre. (*b*) **A matter of the last importance,** une affaire de la plus haute importance, de la dernière importance. **2. Last Tuesday, Tuesday last,** mardi dernier. **Last week,** la semaine dernière; la semaine passée. **Last evening,** hier (au) soir. **Last night,** (i) la nuit dernière; (ii) hier soir. **The night before last,** avant-hier (au) soir. *I have not seen him for the l. four days,* il y a quatre jours que je ne l'ai vu. *In the l. fifty years,* dans les cinquante ans qui viennent de s'écouler. **This day last week,** il y a aujourd'hui huit jours. **This day last year,** l'an dernier à pareil jour. **-ly,** *adv.* Pour finir . . .; en dernier lieu. **II. last,** *s.* **1. This last,** ce dernier, cette dernière. **2.** (*a*) **We shall never hear the last of it,** on ne nous le laissera pas oublier. *We haven't heard the l. of it,* tout n'est pas dit. *That is the l. I saw of him,* je ne l'ai pas revu depuis. *This is the l. of it,* c'est la fin. (*b*) **To, till, the last,** jusqu'au bout, jusqu'à la fin, jusqu'au dernier moment. *S.a.* FIRST II. 2. (*c*) **At last, at long last,** enfin; à la fin (des fins). (*d*) **To look one's last on sth.,** jeter un dernier regard sur qch.; voir qch. pour la dernière fois. (*e*) **To be near one's last,** toucher à sa fin. **III. last,** *adv.* (*a*) **When I saw him l.,** la dernière fois que je l'ai vu. (*b*) **He spoke, came, last,** il a parlé, est arrivé, le dernier. **'last-'ditcher,** *s. Pol:* Jusqu'au-boutiste *mf*.

last³. **1.** *v.i.* Durer, se maintenir. **It's too good to last,** c'est trop beau pour durer. *How long does your leave l.?* quelle est la durée de votre congé? *The supplies will not last (out) two months,* les vivres n'iront pas deux mois. *This soap lasts longer,* ce savon est plus durable. *Stuff that will not l. long,* étoffe qui ne tiendra pas. *Dress which will l. me two years,* robe qui me fera deux ans. *It will l. me a lifetime,* j'en ai pour la vie. *F:* **He won't last (out) long,** il n'ira pas loin. **2.** *v.tr.* **To last s.o. out,** (i) (*of pers.*) survivre à qn; (ii) (*of thg*) durer autant que qn. *My overcoat will l. the winter out,* mon pardessus fera encore l'hiver.

lasting, *a.* (*a*) Durable; (*of material, etc.*) résistant, d'un bon user. **Lasting peace,** paix durable. (*b*) (Parfum) durable, persistant.

lastingness ['lɑːstiŋnəs], *s.* Durabilité *f*, permanence *f*.

latakia [lata'kiːa], *s.* Tabac *m* de Latakieh *m* lattaquié *m*.

latch¹ [latʃ], *s.* (*a*) Loquet *m*, clenche *f*. (*b*) Serrure de sûreté (avec clef de maison). **To leave the door on the latch,** (i) fermer la porte au loquet (ii) fermer la porte à demi-tour. **'latch-key,** *s.* Clef *f* de maison; passe-partout *m inv.*

latch², *v.tr.* **1.** Fermer (la porte) au loquet ou à demi-tour. **2.** Fermer (la porte) sans mettre le verrou.

latchet ['latʃet], *s. B:* Cordon *m* (de soulier).

late [leit]. **I.** *a.* (later; latest; *see also* LATTER *and* LAST²) **1.** (*a*) En retard. **To be late (for sth.),** être en retard (pour qch.); se faire attendre. *I don't want to make you l.,* je ne veux pas vous mettre en retard. **Number of minutes l.,** importance *f* du retard (d'un train). (*b*) (*Delayed*) Retardé. **2.** (*a*) Tard. **It is getting late,** il se fait tard. *I was too l.,* je ne suis pas arrivé à temps. *I did not think it was so l.,* je ne pensais pas qu'il fût si tard. *F:* **It is late in the day to change your mind,** il est un peu tard pour changer d'avis. *I was l. (in) going to bed,* je me suis couché tard. **At a late hour (in the day),** bien avant, très avant, fort avant, dans la journée. **In the late afternoon,** tard dans l'après-midi. **In late summer, in late autumn,** vers la fin de l'été, de l'automne. **Easter is late this year,** Pâques est tard cette année. **Later events proved that . . .,** la suite des événements a démontré que. . . . *At a later meeting,* dans une séance ultérieure. *It is twelve o'clock at (the) latest,* c'est tout au plus s'il est midi. *Com:* **Latest date,** terme fatal; terme de rigueur, délai *m* de rigueur. (*b*) **In the late eighties,** dans les années approchant 1890. **3.** (Fruit, etc.) tardif. **Late frosts,** gelées tardives, printanières. **4.** (*a*) Ancien, ex. *The l. minister,* l'ancien ministre, l'ex-ministre. (*b*) **My late father,** feu mon père, mon père décédé. **The l. queen,** feu la reine, la feue reine. **5.** Récent, dernier. **Of late years,** (dans) ces dernières années; depuis quelques années. **Of late,** dernièrement; depuis peu. *This author's latest work,* le dernier ouvrage de cet auteur. **Latest novelties,** dernières nouveautés. *Journ:* **Latest intelligence, latest news,** informations *fpl* de la dernière heure; dernières nouvelles. **That is the latest,** (i) c'est ce qu'il y a de plus nouveau; (ii) *F:* ça c'est le comble! **X's latest,** (i) la dernière plaisanterie de X; (ii) le dernier exploit de X. **-ly,** *adv.* Dernièrement, récemment; il y a peu de temps; depuis peu. **Till lately,** jusqu'à ces derniers temps. **As lately as yesterday,** hier encore; pas plus tard qu'hier. **II. late,** *adv.* (later; latest; *see also* LAST²) **1.** En retard. **To arrive too late,** arriver trop tard. *Prov:* **Better late than never,** mieux vaut tard que jamais. **2.** Tard. **Early and late,** à toute heure du jour; du matin au soir. **Early or late, sooner or later,** tôt ou tard. **To keep s.o. up late,** attarder qn. **Very late at night,** bien avant, fort avant, dans la nuit. **Late into the night,** jusqu'à une heure avancée de la nuit. **L. in the afternoon,** vers la fin de l'après-midi. **Late in life,** à un âge avancé. **As late as yesterday,** pas plus tard qu'hier. **Later,** later encore; pas plus tard qu'hier. **A moment later,** l'instant d'après. *This happened later (on),* cela est arrivé après, plus tard. *A few days later on,* à quelques jours de là. *F:* **See you later!** à plus tard! **3. Late of London,** dernièrement domicilié à Londres. **'late-comer,** *s.* Retardataire *mf*.

lateen [la'tiːn], *a. Nau:* Lateen sail, voile latine. **Lateen yard,** antenne *f*.

lateness ['leitnəs], *s.* **1.** Arrivée tardive (de qn);

tardiveté *f* (d'un fruit). **2.** The lateness of the hour, l'heure avancée. **3.** Date récente, époque peu reculée (d'un événement).

latent ['leitənt], *a.* Latent; caché. *Ph:* Latent heat, chaleur latente.

lateral ['latər(ə)l], *a.* Latéral, -aux. **-ally,** *adv.* Latéralement.

lath¹ [lɑ:θ, *pl.* lɑ:ðz], *s.* **I.** *Const:* (*a*) Latte *f.* Lath and plaster partition, cloison lattée et plâtrée. (*b*) Slate-lath, volige *f.* **2.** Lame *f* (de jalousie). **3.** Batte *f*, latte (d'Arlequin). **lath²,** *v.tr.* (*a*) Latter (une cloison). (*b*) Voliger (un toit).

lathe [le:ið], *s. Tls:* Tour *m.* **I.** Treadle lathe, tour à pédale. *Power l.,* tour à la mécanique. Bench lathe, tour à banc. Gap lathe, tour à banc rompu. *Screw-cutting l.,* tour à fileter, à décolleter. Capstan lathe, turret lathe, tour à revolver. Polishing lathe, touret *m* à polir. Made on the lathe, fait au tour. **2.** Potter's lathe, tour de potier. **'lathe-bed,** *s.* Banc *m* de tour ; bâti *m* de tour. **'lathe-'centre,** *s.* Pointe *f* (de tour). **lathe-'head,** *s.* Poupée *f.* **'lathe-turned,** *a.* Fait au tour ; tourné.

lather¹ [lɑðər], *s.* **I.** Mousse *f* de savon. **2.** (*On horse*) Écume *f.* *Horse all in a lather,* cheval couvert d'écume. **lather²** **I.** *v.tr.* (*a*) Savonner (le menton). (*b*) *F:* Rosser (qn) ; fouailler (un cheval). **2.** *v.i.* (*a*) (*Of soap*) Mousser. (*b*) (*Of horse*) Jeter de l'écume. **lathering,** *s.* **I.** Savonnage *m.* **2.** *F:* Rossée *f* ; fouaillée *f.*

Latin ['latin]. **I.** *a. & s.* Latin, -ine. **2.** (*a*) *s. Ling:* Le latin. Low Latin, bas latin. Late Latin, latin de la décadence. (*b*) *a. Typ:* Latin characters, lettres romaines. *S.a.* DOG-LATIN

Latinity [la'tiniti], *s.* Latinité *f.*

latish ['leitiʃ], *a. & adv.* (*a*) Un peu en retard. (*b*) Un peu tard. At a latish hour, latish in the day, à une heure plutôt avancée ; sur le tard.

latitude ['latitju:d], *s.* **I.** To allow s.o. the greatest latitude, laisser à qn la plus grande latitude, la plus grande liberté d'action. **2.** *Geog: Nau:* Latitude *f.* In the latitude of . . ., sous, par, la latitude de. . . . *In l.* 30° *north,* par 30° (de) latitude nord. In these latitudes, (i) sous ces latitudes ; (ii) *F:* dans ces parages.

latitudinal [lati'tju:dinəl], *a.* Latitudinal, -aux ; transversal, -aux.

latrines [la'tri:nz], *s.pl.* Latrines *f.*

latter ['latər], *a.* **I.** Dernier (des deux). The latter, ce, le, dernier ; celui-ci, ceux-ci. **2.** The latter half of the story, la dernière moitié de l'histoire. Latter end, (i) fin *f* (d'une époque) ; (ii) mort *f*, fin (de qn). **-ly,** *adv.* **I.** (*a*) Dans les derniers temps. (*b*) Dans la suite. **2.**=LATELY. **'latter-day,** *attrib.a.* Récent, moderne, d'aujourd'hui.

lattice¹ ['latis], *s.* Treillis *m*, treillage *m.* Lattice frame, lattice girder, poutre *f* en treillis, à croisillons. Lattice mast, pylône *m* métallique. **'lattice-'window,** *s.* **I.** Fenêtre treillagée, jalousée. **2.** Fenêtre à losanges. **'lattice-work,** *s.* Treillage *m*, treillis *m* ; (*metal*) grillage *m.* **lattice²,** *v.tr.* Treillager, treillisser.

Latvia ['latviə]. *Pr.n.* La Lettonie ; la Latvie.

Latvian ['latviən], *a. & s.* **I.** *Geog:* Letton, -one. **2.** *Ling:* Le lette.

laud [lɔ:d], *v.tr.* Louer ; chanter les louanges de (qn).

laudable ['lɔ:dəbl], *a.* Louable ; digne d'éloges. **-ably,** *adv.* Louablement.

laudanum ['lɔ:d(ə)nəm], *s.* Laudanum *m.*

laudatory ['lɔ:dətəri], *a.* Élogieux.

laugh¹ [lɑ:f], *s.* Rire *m.* To burst into a laugh, éclater de rire. To force a laugh, to give a forced laugh, rire du bout des dents ; rire jaune. With a laugh, en riant. To raise a laugh, faire rire. *F:* To have, get, the laugh of s.o., mettre les rieurs de son côté. To have the laugh on one's side, avoir les rieurs de son côté. **laugh².** **I.** *v.i.* Rire. (*a*) *To l.* heartily, rire de bon cœur. *To l.* immoderately, uproariously, rire à gorge déployée ; *P:* se crever de rire. To laugh till one cries, rire (jusqu')aux larmes. To laugh to oneself, rire en soi-même ; rire tout bas. To laugh in, up, one's sleeve, inwardly, rire sous cape, en dedans. *F:* I soon made him laugh on the wrong side of his face, on the wrong side of his mouth, je lui ai bientôt fait passer son envie de rire. (*b*) To laugh at, over, sth., rire de qch. There is nothing to laugh at, il n'y a pas de quoi rire. To laugh at s.o., se moquer, (se) rire, de qn. To get laughed at, se faire moquer de soi. **2.** *v.tr.* (*a*) *With cogn.acc.* He laughed a bitter laugh, il eut un rire amer. (*b*) *We laughed him out of it,* nous nous sommes tellement moqués de lui qu'il a y renoncé. To laugh down a proposal, tuer une proposition par le ridicule. To laugh s.o. out of court, se moquer des prétentions de qn. To laugh s.o. to scorn, accabler qn de ridicule. He laughed the matter off, il tourna la chose en plaisanterie. **laughing¹,** *a.* Riant ; rieur. **-ly,** *adv.* En riant. **laughing²,** *s.* Rires *mpl.* In a laughing mood, en humeur de rire. It is no laughing matter, il n'y a pas de quoi rire. **'laughing gas,** *s.* Gaz hilarant. **'laughing-stock,** *s.* To make a laughing-stock of oneself, se faire moquer de soi.

laughable ['lɑ:fəbl], *a.* Risible, ridicule. *L.* offer, offre dérisoire. **-ably,** *adv.* Risiblement.

laugher ['lɑ:fər], *s.* Rieur, -euse.

laughter ['lɑ:ftər], *s.* Rire(s) *m(pl).* He made us cry with laughter, il nous a fait rire aux larmes. To be convulsed, to shake, with laughter, se tordre de rire ; se tenir les côtes de rire. To roar with laughter, rire aux éclats ; rire à gorge déployée. *F:* To split, die, with laughter, crever de rire.

launch¹ [lɔ:nʃ, lɑ:nʃ], *s.* Chaloupe *f.* Motor launch, bateau *m* automobile ; vedette *f.*

launch², *s.* = LAUNCHING I.

launch³. **I.** *v.tr.* (*a*) Lancer (un projectile, un coup). (*b*) *Nau:* Lancer (un navire) ; mettre (une embarcation) à l'eau, à la mer. *To l.* a torpedo, lancer une torpille. *F:* To launch s.o. into eternity, envoyer qn ad patres. (*c*) *F:* Lancer (qn, une affaire). *Mil:* To launch an offensive, déclencher une offensive. **2.** *v.i.* (*a*) To launch out, against, s.o., (i) lancer un coup à qn ; (ii) faire une sortie à, contre, qn. (*b*) To launch out, mettre à la mer. To launch out, forth, on an enterprise, se lancer dans une affaire. *Once he is launched on this subject . . .,* une fois lancé sur ce sujet. . . . To launch out (into expense), se lancer dans la dépense ; se mettre en frais. **launching,** *s.* **I.** *Nau:* Lancement *m*, mise *f* à l'eau (d'un navire). **2.** Lancement (d'une affaire).

launder ['lɔ:ndər], *v.tr.* Blanchir (le linge).

laundering, *s.* Blanchissage *m.*

laundress ['lɔ:ndres], *s.f.* Blanchisseuse.

laundry ['lɔ:ndri], *s.* **I.** Laundry(-works), blanchisserie *f.* **2.** Linge blanchi ou à blanchir (d'une affaire).

lauraceae [lɔ:'reisii:], *s.pl. Bot:* Lauracées *f.*

lauraceous [lɔ:'reiʃəs], *a. Bot:* Lauracé.

laureate ['lɔ:riet], *a. & s.* Lauréat, -ate.

laurel ['lɔrəl], s. Bot: Laurier m. Noble laurel, laurier commun. Crowned with laurel(s), couronné, ceint, de lauriers. F: To reap, win, laurels, cueillir, moissonner, des lauriers. To rest on one's laurels, se reposer sur ses lauriers.

lava ['lɑːva], s. Lave f. Cellular lava, scories f volcaniques.

lavatory ['lavət(ə)ri], s. **1.** Cabinet m de toilette; lavabo m. **2.** Water-closet m, cabinets mpl; (in street) cabinets sous terre; (on train) toilette f.

lave [leːiv], v.tr. **1.** Lit: Laver (les mains, etc.); (of stream) baigner, laver (un pré). **2.** Med: Bassiner (une plaie).

lavender ['lavəndər]. **1.** s. Lavande f. French lavender, spike lavender, lavande commune, mâle; F: aspic m, spic m. Sea lavender, statice m. **2.** a. (Colour) Lavande inv. '**lavender-water**, s. Eau f de lavande.

lavish[1] ['laviʃ], a. **1.** Prodigue (in, of, de). To be lavish in, of, praises, prodiguer des louanges; se prodiguer en éloges. **2.** Somptueux; abondant. L. meal, repas plantureux. L. expenditure, dépenses folles. -**ly**, adv. Avec prodigalité. To spend l., dépenser de l'argent à profusion, à pleine(s) main(s).

lavish[2], v.tr. Prodiguer, répandre (son argent). To lavish sth. on s.o., prodiguer qch. à qn.

lavishness ['laviʃnəs], s. Prodigalité f.

law [lɔː], s. **1.** Loi f. The laws in force, la législation en vigueur. Law of nature, loi de la nature. Laws of a game, règles f d'un jeu. **2.** The law, la loi. To keep the law, observer la loi. To break the law(s), enfreindre la loi, les lois. F: His word is law, sa parole fait loi. To lay down the law, faire la loi (to s.o., à qn). He thinks he's above the law, il se croit tout permis. To be a law unto oneself, n'en faire qu'à sa tête. **3.** Droit m. Civil law, le droit civil. Common law, (i) le droit commun; (ii) le droit civil. Commercial law, mercantile law, le droit commercial; le code de commerce. To read, study, law, étudier le droit; faire son droit. To practise law, exercer le droit. To be in the law, avoir une étude. Law-student, étudiant en droit. Doctor of Laws, docteur en droit. **4.** Court of law, cour f de justice; tribunal m, -aux. To go to law, avoir recours à la justice. To settle a matter without going to law, arranger une affaire à l'amiable. To go to law with s.o., F: to have the law of s.o., citer, poursuivre, qn en justice. Action at law, action f en justice. To be at law, être en procès. To take the law into one's own hands, se faire justice à soi-même. F: Limb of the law, suppôt m de justice. **5.** (a) Sp: Ven: To give (fair) law to . . ., donner de l'avance à . . .; laisser . . . prendre du champ. (b) To give s.o. three days' law, accorder à qn trois jours de grâce. '**law-abiding**, a. Respectueux des lois; ami de l'ordre. '**law-breaker**, s. Transgresseur m, violateur m, de la loi. '**law-lord**, s.m. Pol: Membre juriste de la Chambre des Lords. '**law-maker**, s. Législateur m.

lawful ['lɔːful], a. Légal, -aux. **1.** Permis, licite; loisible. **2.** (Droit, enfant) légitime; (contrat) valide. Lawful currency, cours légal. **3.** (Revendication, etc.) juste. -**fully**, adv. Légalement, légitimement.

lawgiver ['lɔːgivər], s. Législateur m.

lawless ['lɔːləs], a. **1.** Sans loi; (temps) d'anarchie. **2.** Déréglé, désordonné.

lawlessness ['lɔːləsnəs], s. Dérèglement m, désordre m, anarchie f.

lawn[1] [lɔːn], s. Tex: Batiste f; (fine) linon m.

lawn[2], s. Pelouse f; (parterre m de) gazon m.

'**lawn-mower**, s. Tondeuse f (de gazon).

'**lawn-'tennis**, s. See TENNIS 1.

Lawrence ['lɔrəns]. Pr.n.m. Laurent.

lawsuit ['lɔːsjuːt], s. Procès m; F: affaire f. To bring a lawsuit against s.o., intenter un procès à qn.

lawyer ['lɔːjər], s. **1.** Homme m de loi; juriste m; jurisconsulte m. Common-lawyer, jurisconsulte en droit coutumier. **2.** = (i) SOLICITOR, (ii) BARRISTER.

lax [laks], a. **1.** (a) (Of conduct) Relâché; (of pers.) négligent, inexact; (gouvernement) mou. Lax morals, morale facile. To be lax in (carrying out) one's duties, être inexact à remplir ses devoirs. Lax attendance, irrégularité f de présence. (b) Vague; peu exact. Lax use of a word, emploi peu précis d'un mot. **2.** (Limp) Mou, f. molle; flasque. **3.** Med: (Ventre) lâche, relâché.

laxative ['laksətiv], a. & s. Laxatif (m).

laxity ['laksiti], s. **1.** (a) Relâchement m (des mœurs); inexactitude f à remplir ses devoirs. (b) Vague m, imprécision f (de langage, etc.). **2.** Flaccidité f, mollesse f (de tissu, etc.).

lay[1] [lei], s. **1.** Lai m, chanson f. **2.** Poème m (lyrique); chant m.

lay[2], a. Laïque, lai. (a) Ecc: Lay brother, frère lai, frère convers. Lay sister, sœur converse. Lay clerk, chantre m. (b) F: To the lay mind . . ., aux yeux du profane. . .

lay[3], s. **1.** F: Genre m d'affaires; spécialité f. **2.** Commettage m (d'un cordage). **3.** Lay of the land, configuration f du terrain. **4.** Typ: To mark the lay on a page, repérer une page. Lay-mark, repère m.

lay[4], v.tr. (laid [leid]; laid) **1.** Coucher. (a) To lay s.o. low, flat, (i) coucher, étendre, qn (par terre); (ii) terrasser, abattre, qn. To lay a building in ashes, réduire un bâtiment en cendres. To lay low an empire, mettre à bas un empire. (b) (Of wind) Coucher, verser, abattre (le blé). **2.** (a) Abattre (la poussière, les vagues, etc.). Prov: Small rain lays great dust, petite pluie abat grand vent. (b) Exorciser, conjurer (un esprit). To lay s.o.'s fears, dissiper les craintes de qn. **3.** Mettre, placer, poser (sth. on sth., qch. sur qch.). To lay one's hand on s.o.'s shoulder, mettre la main sur l'épaule de qn. To lay one's head on the pillow, mettre, poser, sa tête sur l'oreiller. To have nowhere to lay one's head, n'avoir pas où reposer la tête. To lay s.o. to rest, in the grave, mettre, coucher, qn au tombeau. **4.** (Of bird) Pondre (un œuf). **5.** Faire (un pari); parier (une somme); mettre (un enjeu). To lay so much on a horse, mettre, parier, miser, tant sur un cheval. To lay 5 francs on a colour, miser 5 francs sur une couleur. To lay that . . ., parier que. . . **6.** (a) To lay a spark to the train, mettre le feu aux poudres. To lay a ship alongside (the quay), amener, accoster, un navire le long du quai. (b) Artil: Pointer (un canon). **7.** Soumettre (une demande). Jur: To lay a complaint, déposer une plainte; porter plainte. To lay an information, présenter une information. S.a. CLAIM[1] 2. **8.** (a) Imposer (une peine, une charge) (upon s.o., à qn); infliger (une amende, etc.). (b) To lay a tax on sth., mettre un impôt sur qch.; frapper qch. d'un impôt. (c) To lay a stick on s.o.'s back, F: to lay into s.o., rosser qn. To lay about one, frapper de tous côtés; frapper, taper, comme un sourd. **9.** (a) Poser, jeter, asseoir (des fondements); ranger (des briques); poser, immerger (un câble). To lay the table, the cloth, mettre, dresser, le couvert; mettre la nappe. **To lay for three,** mettre trois couverts. **To lay a carpet,** poser, tendre, un tapis. **To lay the fire,** préparer le feu. *Navy:* **To lay a mine,** poser, mouiller, une mine. (*b*) Dresser, tendre (un piège, une embuscade). (*c*) Ourdir, tramer (un complot). **To lay a scheme to do sth.,** combiner de faire qch. (*d*) *Th:* **The scene is laid in Paris,** la scène se passe à Paris. (*e*) *Nau:* **To lay the course,** tracer, donner, la route. **10.** *Ropem:* Commettre (un cordage). **lay aside,** *v.tr.* Enlever, quitter (un vêtement); se dépouiller de (ses vêtements, ses préjugés); abandonner, mettre de côté (un travail); écarter (un papier); épargner (de l'argent); déposer (la couronne). **lay away,** *v.tr.* Mettre (qch.) de côté; ranger, serrer (qch.). **lay by,** *v.tr* Mettre (qch.) de côté; réserver (qch.). **She had laid by a tidy sum,** elle avait fait sa petite pelote. **lay down,** *v.tr.* **1.** (*a*) Déposer, poser (qch.). **To lay down one's arms,** mettre bas, rendre, ies armes. *Cards:* **To lay down one's hand,** étaler, abattre, son jeu. (*b*) Coucher, étendre (qn). **To lay oneself down,** se coucher. (*c*) Quitter, se démettre de, résigner (ses fonctions). (*d*) **To lay down one's life,** donner, sacrifier, sa vie (*for,* pour). **2.** (*a*) **To lay down a ship,** mettre un navire en chantier. **To lay down a railway,** asseoir, poser, une voie ferrée. *To lay down mains, a cable,* poser une canalisation, un câble. (*b*) Poser, imposer, établir, instituer (un principe, une règle); fixer (des conditions); tracer, prescrire (une ligne de conduite). **To lay it down (as a principle) that . . .,** poser en principe que. . . . *To lay down that . . .,* stipuler que . . .; spécifier que. . . . **To lay down conditions to s.o.,** imposer des conditions à qn. **3.** Mettre (du vin) en cave, sur chantier. **lay in,** *v.tr.* Faire provision, s'approvisionner, de (qch.). **lay off,** *v.tr.* **1.** Débaucher, congédier (des ouvriers). **2.** *Nau:* **To lay off a bearing,** porter un relèvement (sur la carte). **3.** *Turf: etc:* **To lay off a bet,** faire la contre-partie d'un pari. **lay on,** *v.tr.* **1.** Imposer (des impôts). **2.** Étendre, coucher, appliquer (un enduit). *F:* **To lay it on thick, with a trowel,** (i) flatter qn grossièrement; (ii) exagérer. **3.** (*a*) **To lay on the lash,** appliquer le fouet. (*b*) *Abs.* **He laid on with a will,** il frappait, il y allait, de bon cœur. **4.** Installer (le gaz, l'électricité). *Bedroom with water laid on,* chambre avec eau courante. **lay out,** *v.tr.* **1.** Arranger, disposer (des objets); étaler, déployer (des marchandises). **2.** (*a*) Ensuairer (un mort); faire la toilette (d'un mort). (*b*) *F:* Étendre (qn) d'un coup; coucher (qn) par terre, sur le carreau. **3.** Dépenser, débourser (de l'argent). **4.** Dresser, tracer, aligner (un camp); dessiner, disposer (un jardin); tracer (une route); faire le tracé (d'une route). **5.** **To lay oneself out to please,** chercher à plaire; se mettre en frais pour plaire. **'lay-out,** *s.* Tracé *m* (d'une ville, etc.); dessin *m* (d'un jardin); disposition *f* typographique (d'une annonce, etc.); agencement *m* (d'une boîte de vitesses). **lay to.** **1.** *v.tr. Nau:* Mettre (un navire) à la cape. **2.** *v.i.* (*Of ship*) Prendre la cape. **lay up,** *v.tr.* **1.** Mettre (qch.) en réserve; accumuler, amasser (des provisions, etc.). **To lay up trouble for oneself,** s'apprêter bien des ennuis. **2.** Désarmer, déséquiper (un navire). **To lay up a car,** remiser une voiture (p.ex. pour l'hiver). **3.** **To be laid up,** être alité, au lit. **laid,** *a.* **1.** *Paperm:* Vergé. **Cream-laid paper,** vergé blanc. **2.** *Nau:* **Cable-laid rope,** cordage commis en grelin. **laying¹,** *a.* **Laying hen,** poule pondeuse. **laying²,** *s.* **1.** Pose *f* (de rails, de tuyaux, de câbles, etc.);

assise *f* (de fondements); commettage *m* (d'un cordage); mouillage *m* (d'une mine). **2.** Ponte *f* (des œufs). **3.** *Artil:* Pointage *m* (d'un canon). **'lay-days,** *s.pl.* *Com: Nau:* Jours *m* de planche. **Extra lay-days,** jours de surestarie. **'lay-shaft,** *s. Mec.E:* *Aut:* Arbre *m* intermédiaire (de changement de vitesse); arbre de couche; arbre de renvoi.

lay⁵. *See* LIE⁴.

layer¹ ['leiər], *s.* **1.** (*a*) Poseur *m* (de tuyaux, etc.); tendeur *m* (de pièges). (*b*) *Artil:* Pointeur *m*. **2.** (*Of hen*) **Good layer,** bonne pondeuse. **3.** Couche *f* (de peinture, etc.); *Const:* assise *f* (de béton, etc.). **4.** *Hort:* Marcotte *f*. **layer-'out,** *s.* **1.** Dessinateur *m* (de jardins, etc.). **2.** Ensuaireuse *f*, ensevelisseuse *f*. **layer²,** *v.tr.* (*a*) Poser, disposer, en couches. (*b*) *Hort:* Marcotter.

lay-figure ['leifigər], *s.* *Art:* Mannequin *m* (en bois, etc.).

layman, *pl.* **-men** ['leimən, -men], *s.* **1.** *Ecc:* Laïque *m*, séculier *m*. **2.** Profane *m*, civil *m*.

lazaret(to) [laza'ret(o)], *s.* *Nau:* Lazaret *m* (de quarantaine).

laze [le:iz], *v.tr. & i.* **1.** *To laze;* **to laze away one's time,** paresser, fainéanter. **To laze about,** baguenauder.

laziness ['leizinəs], *s.* Paresse *f*, fainéantise *f*.

lazy ['leizi], *a.* **1.** Paresseux, fainéant. **Lazy over one's lessons,** paresseux à apprendre ses leçons. **2.** *L. moments,* moments de paresse. *Nau:* **Lazy guy, sheet,** fausse écoute. **-ily,** *adv.* Paresseusement. **'lazy-bones, 'lazy-boots,** *s.* Paresseux, -euse; fainéant, -ante. **'lazy-tongs,** *s.pl.* Zigzag *m*, ciseaux *mpl*; pantographe *m*.

lea [li:], *s.* *Poet:* Prairie *f*, pâturage *m*.

leach [li:tʃ]. **1.** *v.tr.* Filtrer (un liquide). **2.** *v.i.* (*Of liquid*) Filtrer (*through,* à travers). **leaching,** *s.* Filtration *f*.

lead¹ [led], *s.* **1.** Plomb *m.* (*a*) **Sheet lead,** plomb laminé, en feuilles. *Sm.a:* **Lead shot,** grenaille *f* de plomb; petit plomb. (*b*) **White lead,** blanc *m* de plomb; céruse *f*. **Yellow lead,** massicot *m.* **Red oxide of lead,** red lead, minium *m.* *S.a.* BLACK-LEAD I. (*c*) **Window-leads,** plombs de vitrail; plombure *f*. **2.** Mine *f* (de crayon). **3.** *Nau:* (Plomb de) sonde *f*. **Deep-sea lead,** grande sonde. *Nau. & Mil: P:* **To swing the lead,** tirer au flanc. **4.** *Typ:* Interligne *f*; entre-ligne *m.* **'lead-colic,** *s.* Colique *f* de plomb, colique saturnine. **'lead-covered,** *a.* (Câble) sous gaine de plomb. **lead-'foil,** *s.* Papier *m* de plomb. **'lead-line,** *s.* Ligne *f* de sonde. **'lead-poisoning,** *s.* Intoxication *f* saturnine; saturnisme *m.* **'lead-works,** *s.pl.* Fonderie *f* de plomb; plomberie *f*.

lead² [led], *v.tr.* (**leaded** ['ledid]; **leading** ['ledin]) (*a*) Plomber (un toit); couvrir, garnir, (un objet) de plomb. (*b*) *Fish:* Plomber, caler (une ligne, un filet). (*c*) *Typ:* Interligner (des lignes). **To lead out matter,** blanchir la composition. **leading¹,** *s.* **1.** (*a*) Plombage *m.* (*b*) *Coll.* Plombs *mpl.* **2.** *Typ:* Interlignage *m*.

lead³ [li:d], *s.* **1.** Conduite *f* (action de conduire). (*a*) **To follow s.o.'s lead,** se laisser conduire par qn; suivre l'exemple de qn. **To give the lead,** *F:* donner le ton. **To give s.o. a lead,** (i) amener qn (sur un sujet); (ii) mettre qn sur la voie. (*b*) **To take the lead,** (i) prendre la tête; (ii) prendre la direction. **To take the lead of, over, s.o.,** prendre le pas, gagner les devants, sur qn. *To have one minute's l. over s.o.,* avoir une minute d'avance sur qn. *Cards:* **To have the lead,** (i) jouer le premier; avoir la main; (ii) être le premier en cartes. **Your lead!** à vous de jouer (le premier). **To return a lead,** renvoyer de la couleur demandée ; répondre à l'invite de qn. **3.** *Th*: Premier rôle ; (rôle de) vedette *f*. **To play juvenile leads,** jouer les jeunes premiers, les jeunes premières. **4.** (*a*) *Mec*.*E*: Hauteur *f* du pas (d'une vis). (*b*) *Mch*: *I.C.E*: Avance *f* (du tiroir, de l'allumage, etc.). (*c*) *El*.*E*: **(Angle of) lead of brushes,** décalage *m* en avant, avance, des balais. **5.** (*For dog*) Laisse *f*. **On a lead,** en laisse. **6.** *El*.*E*: Câble *m*, branchement *m*, de canalisation. *Battery l.*, connexion *f* de batterie.

lead⁴ [li:d], *v*. (led [led] ; led) I. *v*.*tr*. **1.** (*a*) Mener, conduire, guider. **To lead s.o. into temptation,** entraîner qn dans la tentation ; induire qn en tentation. (*b*) **To lead the way, to lead the van,** montrer le chemin ; marcher le premier ; aller devant. **2.** Conduire, guider, (un aveugle) par la main ; mener (un cheval) par la bride ; tenir (un chien) en laisse. **Led horse,** cheval à main, de main. **He is easily led,** il va comme on le mène. **To lead a woman to the altar,** conduire une femme à l'autel. **3.** Induire, porter, pousser (*s.o. to do sth.*, qn à faire qch.). **That leads us to believe that . . .,** cela nous mène à croire que. . . . **I was led to the conclusion that . . .,** je fus amené à conclure que. . . . **4.** (*a*) Mener, couler (une vie heureuse) ; mener (une existence misérable). (*b*) **To lead s.o. a wretched life, a dog's life,** faire une vie d'enfer, une vie de chien, à qn. **5.** (*a*)₊Commander (une armée). (*b*) Mener (la danse). **To lead an orchestra,** faire fonction de chef d'attaque. **To lead a movement,** être à la tête d'un mouvement. **6.** (*In race, etc.*) **To lead the field,** *Abs*. to lead, mener le champ ; tenir la tête. **7.** *Cards*: **To lead a card,** entamer, attaquer, d'une carte. *Abs*. **To lead,** ouvrir le jeu ; jouer le premier. II. **lead,** *v.i.* **1.** (*Of road*) Mener, conduire (*to*, à). **Which street leads to the station?** quel est le chemin de la gare ? **Door that leads into the garden,** porte qui donne accès au jardin. **2. To lead to a good result,** aboutir à un bon résultat ; produire un heureux effet. **To lead to a discovery,** conduire à une découverte. **Everything leads to the belief that . . .,** tout porte à croire que. . . . *This incident led to a breach,* cet incident amena une rupture. **To lead to nothing,** n'aboutir, ne mener, à rien. **lead away,** *v.tr.* **1.** Emmener. **2.** Entraîner, détourner (qn). *Esp. in passive.* **To be led away,** se laisser détourner (*from*, de) ; se laisser entraîner. **lead back,** *v.tr.* Ramener, reconduire. **lead in,** *v.tr.* **1.** Faire entrer, introduire (qn). **2.** (*Of electrical conductor*) Amener (le courant). **lead-'in,** *s.* (*a*) *W.Tel*: *Tp*: Fil *m* d'entrée de poste. (*b*) *W.Tel*: Descente *f* d'antenne. **lead off. 1.** *v.tr.* Emmener, entraîner (qn). **2.** *v.i.* (*a*) Commencer, débuter (*with*, par). (*b*) Entamer les débats ; *F*: ouvrir le bal. **lead on,** *v.tr.* Conduire, entraîner (qn) ; montrer le chemin à (qn). **Lead on!** en avant ! **To lead s.o. on to talk,** encourager qn à parler. *F*: **To lead s.o. on,** (i) aider qn à s'enferrer ; (ii) faire des agaceries à qn ; agacer qn ; faire des coquetteries à qn. **lead out,** *v.tr.* Emmener, reconduire, faire sortir (qn) ; conduire (qch.) dehors. **lead up. 1.** *v.tr.* (*a*) Faire monter (qn) ; conduire (qn) en haut. (*b*) Amener, faire avancer (qn). **2.** *v.i.* (*a*) (*Of ladder, etc.*) Conduire, donner accès (au toit, etc.). (*b*) **To lead up to a subject,** amener un sujet. **leading²,** *a*. **1.** (*a*) *Jur*: **Leading question,** question tendancieuse. **Leading cases,** cas d'espèce qui font

autorité. (*b*) *Mus*: **Leading note,** note sensible. **2.** (*Chief*) Premier ; principal, -aux. **A leading man,** un homme important ; une notabilité. *The l. surgeon in Manchester,* le premier chirurgien de Manchester. **A leading shareholder,** un des principaux actionnaires. **To be had from l. jewellers,** en vente chez les principaux bijoutiers. **Leading idea,** idée dominante, directrice, maîtresse (d'une œuvre, etc.). **Leading article,** (i) *Journ*: = LEADER 5 ; (ii) *Com*: spécialité *f* de réclame. *Th*: **Leading part,** premier rôle. **Leading man, lady,** premier rôle ; vedette *f*. *F*: **To play a leading part** *in an affair,* jouer un rôle prépondérant dans une affaire. *Mus*: **Leading violin,** violon principal. **3.** (*a*) **Leading car in a race,** voiture de tête dans une course. (*b*) *Av*: **Leading edge** (of wing), bord *m* d'attaque (de l'aile). **leading³,** *s.* **1.** Conduite *f*, menage *m* (de chevaux, etc.). *Harn*: **Leading-rein,** longe *f*. **2.** (*a*) *Mil*: Commandement *m*. (*b*) Direction *f* (d'une entreprise, etc.). **'leading-strings,** *s.pl.* Lisière *f*. *F*: **To be in leading-strings,** être à la lisière, en brassières.

leaden [ledn], *a*. (Teint, ciel) de plomb. **Leaden-eyed,** aux yeux ternes. **Leaden-footed,** à la démarche pesante.

leader ['li:dər], *s.* **1.** (*a*) Conducteur, -trice ; guide *m*. (*b*) *Mil*: Chef *m*. (*c*) Chef, directeur *m* (d'un parti) ; meneur *m* (d'une émeute). (*d*) *Mus*: Chef d'attaque. **2.** Cheval *m* de volée, de tête. **3.** Observation faite pour orienter la conversation. **4.** *Anat*: = TENDON. **5.** *Journ*: Article principal ; article de fond, de tête ; éditorial, -aux *m*.

leaderless ['li:dərləs], *a*. Sans chef, sans guide.

leadership ['li:dərʃip], *s.* **1. To be under s.o.'s leadership,** être sous la conduite de qn. **2.** (*a*) *Mil*: Commandement *m*. (*b*) Fonctions *fpl* de chef ; direction *f*.

leadless ['ledləs], *a*. *Cer*: (Glaçure) sans plomb.

leadsman, *pl.* **-men** ['ledzmən, -men], *s.m. Nau*: Sondeur ; homme de sonde.

leaf¹, *pl.* **leaves** [li:f, li:vz], *s.* **1.** (*a*) Feuille *f*. (*Of tree*) **To shed its leaves,** s'effeuiller. **In leaf,** (arbre) couvert de feuilles, en feuilles. **Fall of the leaf,** chute *f* des feuilles. (*b*) *F*: Pétale *m* (de fleur). **2.** (*a*) Feuillet *m* (de livre). **To turn over the leaves of a book,** feuilleter un livre. *F*: **To turn over a new leaf,** changer de conduite ; faire peau neuve. **To take a leaf out of s.o.'s book,** prendre exemple sur qn. (*b*) **Counterfoil and leaf,** talon *m* et volant *m* (d'un carnet de chèques, etc.). **3.** Feuille (d'or, etc.). **4.** Battant *m*, vantail *m*, -aux (de porte) ; feuille (de paravent) ; lame *f*, feuille, feuillet (de ressort). **Leaf of a table,** (*inserted*) (r)allonge *f* ; (*hinged*) battant. **'leaf-insect,** *s.* *Ent*: Phyllie *f* feuille sèche. **'leaf-mould,** *s.* *Hort*: Terreau *m* de feuilles.

leaf², *v.i.* (Se) feuiller ; pousser des feuilles.

leafless ['li:fləs], *a*. Sans feuilles ; dépourvu de feuilles.

leaflet ['li:flet], *s.* **1.** *Bot*: Foliole *f*. **2.** Feuillet *m* (de papier) ; feuille volante, feuille mobile ; papillon *m* (de publicité).

leafy ['li:fi], *a*. Feuillu ; couvert de feuilles.

league¹ [li:g], *s.* *Meas*: Lieue *f*.

league², *s.* Ligue *f*. **To form a league against s.o.,** se liguer contre qn. **He was in league with them,** il était ligué, d'intelligence, avec eux. **The League of Nations,** la Société des Nations. *Fb*: **The League matches,** les matchs de championnat (professionnels).

league³, *v.i.* **To league** (together), se liguer.

leak¹ [li:k], *s.* **1.** (*a*) Fuite *f*, écoulement *m* (d'un liquide) ; perte *f* d'eau. (*b*) Infiltration *f*, rentrée *f* (d'eau, etc.). *Nau:* Voie *f* d'eau. *(Of ship)* To spring a leak, faire une voie d'eau. To stop a leak, (i) aveugler, boucher, une voie d'eau ; (ii) remédier à, étancher, une fuite (d'eau, etc.). **2.** *W.Tel:* Grid-leak, résistance *f* de fuite de la grille. **'leak-detector,** *s. El:* Indicateur *m* de pertes à la terre ; déceleur *m* de fuites. **'leak-proof,** *a.* Étanche.

leak², *v.i.* **1.** *(Of tank, etc.)* Avoir une fuite ; fuir, couler ; *(of liquid)* fuir, couler. To leak away, se perdre. **2.** *(Of ship)* Faire eau. **leak out,** *v.i. (Of news, etc.)* S'ébruiter, transpirer.

leakage ['liːkedӡ], *s.* **1.** *(a)* Fuite *f* (d'eau, de gaz) ; perte *f*, fuite, déperdition *f* (d'électricité) (par dispersion). *Surface l. of insulator,* décharge superficielle sur l'isolateur. *(b)* Fuites, pertes, coulage *m.* **2.** *F:* Leakage of official secrets, fuite de secrets officiels.

leakiness ['liːkinəs], *s.* Manque *m* d'étanchéité.

leaky ['liːki], *a.* *(a)* (Tonneau) qui coule, qui perd, qui fuit. Leaky shoes, souliers qui prennent l'eau. *(b)* (Bateau) qui fait eau.

leal ['iːl], *a. Scot:* Loyal, -aux ; fidèle.

lean¹ [liːn]. **1.** *a.* Maigre. *(a)* Amaigri, décharné ; *(of animal)* efflanqué. *(b)* Lean meat, viande maigre. *(c)* Lean years, années maigres, déficitaires. Lean diet, maigre régime ; régime frugal. **2.** *s.* Maigre *m* (de la viande).

lean², *s.* Inclinaison *f.*

lean³, *v. (p.t. & p.p.* leant [lent]) **1.** *v.i. (a)* S'appuyer *(against, on, sth.,* contre, sur, qch.). To lean on one's elbow *or* on one's elbows, s'accouder. To lean (up) against the wall, with one's back against the wall ; to lean back against the wall, s'adosser au mur, contre le mur. *F:* To lean on s.o. (for aid), s'appuyer sur qn. To lean on a broken reed, s'appuyer sur un roseau. *(b)* Se pencher *(over,* sur) ; *(of wall, etc.)* incliner, pencher. *(c)* To *l.* to, *towards, mercy,* incliner vers la clémence. **2.** *v.tr.* To *l.* a *ladder against the wall,* appuyer une échelle contre le mur. To lean sth. (with its back) against sth., adosser qch. à qch. **lean back,** *v.i.* Se pencher en arrière. To lean back in one's chair, se renverser dans son fauteuil. **lean forward. 1.** *v.i.* Se pencher en avant. **2.** *v.tr.* Pencher (la tête) en avant. **lean out,** *v.i.* Se pencher au dehors. *To l. out of the window,* se pencher à, par, la fenêtre. **leaning¹,** *a.* Penché, penchant ; hors d'aplomb. **2.** Inclination *f (towards,* pour) ; penchant *m (towards,* pour, vers) ; tendance *f (towards,* à). **lean-'to. 1.** *Attrib.a.* Lean-to roof, comble *m* en appentis. **2.** *s.* Appentis *m* ; hangar *m.*

leanness ['liːnnəs], *s.* Maigreur *f.*

leant [lent]. *See* LEAN³.

leap¹ [liːp], *s.* **1.** Saut *m,* bond *m.* To take a leap, faire un saut. To take a leap in the dark, faire un saut dans l'inconnu. His heart gave a leap, son cœur bondit. To advance by leaps and bounds, avancer par bonds et par sauts. **2.** Obstacle *m* (à sauter) ; saut. **'leap-frog,** *s. Games:* Saute-mouton *m.* **'leap-year,** *s.* Année *f* bissextile.

leap², *v. (p.t. & p.p.* leaped [liːpt] *or* leapt [lept]) **1.** *v.i. (a)* Sauter, bondir. To leap to one's feet, se lever brusquement. *To l. over the ditch,* sauter le fossé ; franchir le fossé (d'un bond). *F:* To leap at an offer, sauter sur une offre. To leap for joy, sauter de joie. To leap up with indignation, sursauter d'indignation. *(b) (Of flame, etc.)* To leap (up), jaillir. **2.** *v.tr.* Sauter (un fossé) ; franchir (un fossé) d'un saut.

leaper ['liːpər], *s.* Sauteur, -euse.

leapt [lept]. *See* LEAP²

learn [ləːrn], *v.tr. (p.t. & p.p.* learnt [ləːrnt] *or* learned [ləːrnd]) **1.** Apprendre. To learn to read, apprendre à lire. To learn up a lesson, apprendre une leçon par cœur. *F:* I have learnt better since then, j'en sais plus long maintenant. *Prov:* It is never too late to learn ; live and learn, on apprend à tout âge. **2.** Apprendre (une nouvelle, etc.). To learn sth. about s.o., apprendre qch. sur le compte de qn. **learned** ['ləːrnid], *a.* Savant, instruit, érudit, docte. Learned in the law, versé dans le droit. **-ly,** *adv.* Savamment. **learning,** *s.* **1.** Action *f* d'apprendre. *The l. of the lessons,* l'étude *f* des leçons. **2.** Science *f,* instruction *f,* érudition *f.* Seat of learning, centre intellectuel. Man of great learning, homme d'un grand savoir. *S.a.* BOOK-LEARNING.

learnedness ['ləːrnidnəs], *s.* Érudition *f.*

learner ['ləːrnər], *s.* **1.** *To be a quick l.,* apprendre facilement. **2.** Élève *mf,* commençant, -ante, débutant, -ante.

lease¹ [liːs], *s. Jur: (a)* Bail *m, pl.* baux. Lease of a farm, of ground, of land, bail à ferme. To take land on lease, louer une terre à bail ; affermer une terre. To take a new lease of a house, renouveler le bail d'une maison. *F:* To take (on) a new lease of life, renaître, se reprendre, à la vie ; faire corps neuf. *(b)* Concession *f* (d'une source d'énergie, etc.).

lease², *v.tr.* **1.** To lease (out), louer ; donner (une maison) à bail ; affermer (une terre). **2.** Prendre (une maison) à bail ; louer (une maison) ; affermer (une terre). **leasing,** *s.* Location *f* à bail ; affermage *m.*

leasehold ['liːshould]. **1.** *s. (a)* Tenure *f* à bail. *(b)* Propriété *f,* immeuble *m,* loué(e) à bail. **2.** *a.* Maison louée à bail.

leaseholder ['liːshouldər], *s.* Locataire *mf* ou affermataire *mf* à bail.

leash¹ [liːʃ], *s.* **1.** Laisse *f,* attache *f.* On the leash, (chien) en laisse, à l'attache. To hold a dog on a short leash, tenir un chien de court. **2.** *(a) Ven:* Harde *f* (de trois chiens, etc.). *(b) F:* A leash of . . ., un trio de . . .

leash², *v.tr.* **1.** Mettre (un chien) à l'attache ; attacher la laisse à (un chien). **2.** *Ven:* Leashed hounds, chiens à l'accouple.

least [liːst]. **1.** *a. (a)* (The) least, (le, la) moindre ; (le, la) plus petit(e). *Arith:* The least common multiple, le plus petit commun multiple. *(b) A:* Le moins important. This was not the least of his services, ce n'est pas le moindre des services qu'il nous a rendus. *F:* That is the least of my cares, ça, c'est le dernier, le cadet, de mes soucis. **2.** *s.* (The) least, (le) moins. To say the least (of it), pour ne pas dire plus ; pour ne pas mieux dire. At least, (tout) au moins, à tout le moins. I can at least try, je peux toujours essayer. *It would at l. be advisable to . . .,* il conviendrait tout le moins de . . . *A hundred pounds* at the (very) least, (tout) au moins cent livres. Not in the least (degree), pas le moins du monde ; pas du tout. It does not matter in the least, cela n'a pas la moindre importance. *Prov:* (The) least said (the) soonest mended, trop gratter cuit, trop parler nuit. **3.** *adv.* (The) least, (le) moins. *The l. unhappy,* le moins malheureux. He deserves it least of all, il le mérite moins que tous les autres, moins que personne. *L. of all would I . . .,* je ne voudrais surtout pas. . . .

leastways ['liːstweiz], *adv. Dial. & P:* En tout cas . . . ; ou du moins. . . .

leat [liːt], *s. Hyd.E:* Canal *m* d'amenée ; (canal de) dérivation *f* ; bief *m.*

leather[1] ['leðər], s. **1.** Cuir m. **Russia leather,** cuir de Russie. Leather bottle, outre f. Leather shoes, chaussures en cuir. Fancy leather goods, maroquinerie f. Mil: Leather equipment, buffleterie f. Nothing like leather! = vous êtes orfèvre, Monsieur Josse! **2.** (a) Cuir (de pompe, de soupape, etc.). Hand-leather, manique f (de cordonnier); Nau: paumelle f (de voilier). Upper leather (of shoe), empeigne f. Sp: F: The leather, Cr: la balle; Fb: le ballon. (b) = STIR-RUP-LEATHER. **3.** Artificial leather, similicuir m. American leather, moleskine f. **'leather-jacket,** s. Ent: Larve f de la tipule. **'leather-work,** s. **1.** Travail m en cuir; travail du cuir. **2.** (a) Cuirs (d'une carrosserie, etc.). (b) Fancy leather-work, maroquinerie f.

leather[2], v.tr. **1.** Garnir (qch.) de cuir. **2.** F: Tanner le cuir à (qn); étriller, rosser (qn). **leathering,** s. F: To give s.o. a leathering, tanner le cuir à qn.

leatherette [leðə'ret], s. Similicuir m.

leathern ['leðərn], a. De cuir; en cuir.

leathery ['leðəri], a. Qui ressemble au cuir; (of food) coriace.

leave[1] [liːv], s. **1.** Permission f, autorisation f, permis m. **To beg leave to do sth.,** demander la permission de faire qch.; demander à faire qch. **By your leave, with your leave,** avec votre permission; si vous le voulez bien. **2.** (a) Mil: etc: **Leave** (of absence), (in months) congé m; (in days) permission f. Shore leave, sortie f à terre; permission d'aller à terre. To be on leave, être (i) en permission, (ii) en congé. Soldier, sailor, on l., permissionnaire m. **Absence without leave,** absence illégale. **To break leave,** s'absenter sans permission. (b) Release of prisoner on ticket of leave, libération conditionnelle. To break one's ticket of l., rompre son ban. **3.** To take one's leave, prendre congé; faire ses adieux. **To take leave of s.o.,** prendre congé de qn. **To take French leave,** (i) filer, s'en aller, à l'anglaise; (ii) agir sans attendre la permission. **4.** Bill: To give one's opponent a leave, livrer du jeu à son adversaire. **'leave-taking,** s. Adieux mpl.

leave[2], v.tr. (left [left]; left) **1.** Laisser. (a) F: Take it or leave it, c'est à prendre ou à laisser. (b) To l. a wife and three children, laisser une femme et trois enfants. To be well, badly, left, être laissé dans l'aisance, dans la gêne. (c) To leave one's money to s.o., laisser, léguer, sa fortune à qn. (d) To leave the door open, laisser la porte ouverte. To l. a page blank, laisser une page en blanc. To l. s.o. free to do what he wants, laisser qn libre de faire ce qu'il veut. Left to oneself, livré à soi-même. L. him to himself, laissez-le faire. Let us leave it at that, demeurons-en là. (e) To leave hold, F: leave go, of sth., lâcher qch. (f) To l. one's bag in the cloak-room, déposer sa valise à la consigne. Left-luggage office, consigne. Left-luggage ticket, bulletin m de consigne. To leave sth. with s.o., déposer qch. entre les mains de qn; confier qch. à qn. (g) To leave s.o. to do sth., laisser à qn le soin de faire qch. I leave it to you, je m'en remets à vous. Leave it to me, remettez-vous-en à moi; laissez-moi faire. Leave it to time, laissez faire au temps. I l. it to you whether I am right or wrong, je vous laisse à juger si j'ai tort ou raison. (h) Bill: To leave the balls in a good, bad, position, donner un bon, mauvais, acquit. (i) To be left, rester. There are three bottles left, il reste trois bouteilles. To stake what money one has left, jouer le reste de son argent. Nothing was left to me but to . . ., il ne me restait qu'à . . .

(j) Three from seven leaves four, trois ôté de sept reste quatre. **2.** (a) Quitter (un endroit, qn). He has left London, il est parti de Londres; il a quitté Londres. I l. home at eight o'clock, je pars de la maison à huit heures. To l. the room, sortir (de la salle). To leave one's bed, quitter le lit. You may l. us, vous pouvez nous laisser; vous pouvez vous retirer. To leave the table, se lever de table. To l. one's situation, quitter son emploi. On leaving school, au sortir du collège. Nau: To leave harbour, sortir du port. We leave to-morrow, nous partons demain. He has just left, il sort d'ici. (Just) as he was leaving, on leaving, au moment de son départ. (b) Abandonner. To l. one's wife, quitter sa femme; se séparer d'avec sa femme. (c) (Of train) To leave the track, the rails, dérailler. **leave about,** v.tr. Laisser traîner (des objets de valeur, etc.). **leave behind,** v.tr. **1.** Laisser, oublier (son parapluie). **2.** Laisser (des traces, etc.). **3.** Devancer, distancer, laisser en arrière (un rival). **leave off. 1.** v.tr. (a) Cesser de porter, ne plus mettre (un vêtement); quitter (un vêtement d'hiver). (b) Quitter, renoncer à (une habitude). (c) To leave off work, cesser le travail. Leaving-off time, heure f de la sortie des ateliers. To l. off crying, cesser de pleurer. **2.** v.i. Cesser, s'arrêter; en rester là. Where did we l. off? où en sommes-nous restés (de notre lecture)? Leave off! cessez donc! finissez! **leave out,** v.tr. **1.** Exclure (qn). **2.** (a) Omettre (qch.). (b) Oublier. To l. out a line (in copying), sauter une ligne. (c) Mus: To l. out notes, croquer des notes. **leave over,** v.tr **1.** Remettre (une affaire) à plus tard. **2.** To be left over, rester. **leaving,** s. **1.** Départ m. Sch: Leaving certificate, certificat m d'études (secondaires). **2.** pl. Leavings, restes m; débris m; reliefs m (d'un repas).

leaved [liːvd], a. **1.** Thick-leaved, aux feuilles épaisses. Three-leaved, (volet, paravent) à trois feuilles. **2.** (Porte) à deux battants; (table) à rallonges.

leaven[1] [levn], s. Levain m.

leaven[2], v.tr. **1.** Faire lever (le pain, la pâte). **2.** F: Modifier, transformer (with, par).

leaves [liːvz]. See LEAF[1].

Lebanon ['lebanən]. Pr.n. Geog: Le Liban.

lecherous ['letʃərəs], a. Lascif, lubrique, débauché. **-ly,** adv. Lascivement.

lecherousness ['letʃərəsnəs], **lechery** ['letʃəri], s. Lasciveté f, lubricité f, luxure f.

lectern ['lektərn], s. Ecc: Lutrin m, aigle m.

lecture[1] ['lektjər], s. **1.** Conférence f (on, sur); leçon f (on, de). Course of lectures on history, cours m d'histoire. To give, deliver, a lecture, faire une conférence. To attend lectures, suivre un cours. Lantern lecture, conférence avec projections. **2.** F: Sermon m, semonce f, mercuriale f. To read s.o. a lecture, sermonner qn; chapitrer qn. **'lecture-hall, -room,** s. Salle de conférences.

lecture[2]. **1.** v.i. Faire une conférence, des conférences; faire un cours. To lecture on history, faire un cours d'histoire. **2.** v.tr. F: Sermonner, semoncer, réprimander (qn); faire la morale à (qn). **lecturing,** s. Cours mpl; conférences fpl.

lecturer ['lektʃərər], s. **1.** Conférencier, -ière. **2.** (With permanent appointment) Maître m de conférences; (temporary) chargé m de cours.

lectureship ['lektʃərʃip], s. Sch: Maîtrise f de conférences.

led [led]. See LEAD[4].

ledge [ledʒ], s. **1.** Rebord m; saillie f; (on

building) corniche *f*, épaulement *m*, projecture *f*.
2. Banc *m* de récifs.
ledger ['ledʒər], *s.* **I.** (*a*) Book-k: Grand livre.
(*b*) *U.S:* Registre *m.* **2.** Ledger(-stone), dalle *f*
tumulaire ; pierre tombale. **'ledger-line,** *s.*
Mus: Ligne *f* postiche ; ligne supplémentaire
(ajoutée à la portée).
lee [li:], *s.* (*a*) *Nau:* Côté *m* sous le vent. Under
the lee of the land, sous le vent de la terre.
(*b*) Abri *m* (contre le vent). *Under the lee,* à l'abri
du vent. **'lee-board,** *s. Nau:* Aile *f* de dérive.
'lee-ga(u)ge, *s. Nau:* Dessous *m* du vent.
To have the lee-gauge of a ship, être sous le vent
d'un navire. **'lee-shore,** *s. Nau:* Terre *f* sous
le vent. **'lee-side,** *s. Nau:* Côté *m* sous le vent.
leech¹ [li:tʃ], *s.* **I.** Sangsue *f.* **2.** *F:* (*a*) Extorqueur *m*, sangsue. (*b*) Importun *m*, crampon *m.*
leech², *s. A. & Hum:* Médecin *m.*
leech³, *s. Nau:* Chute *f* arrière (de voile).
leek [li:k], *s.* Poireau *m. F:* To eat the leek,
filer doux ; *F:* avaler un crapaud.
leer¹ ['li:ər], *s.* (*a*) Œillade *f* en dessous ; mauvais
regard de côté. (*b*) Regard paillard, polisson.
leer², *v.t.* To leer at s.o., (i) lorgner, guigner, (qn)
d'un air méchant ; (ii) lancer des œillades à qn.
lees [li:z], *s.pl.* Lie *f* (de vin, etc.). *F:* The lees
of society, le rebut, la lie, de la société.
leeward ['li:wərd, 'luərd]. *Nau:* **I.** *a. & adv.*
Sous le vent. **2.** *s.* Côté *m* sous le vent. To drop,
fall, to leeward, tomber sous le vent. To (the)
leeward of . . ., sous le vent de. . . .
leeway ['li:wei], *s. Nau:* Dérive *f. F:* He has
considerable leeway to make up, il a un fort
retard à rattraper.
left¹ [left]. **I.** *a.* Gauche. On my left hand, à ma
gauche. **2.** *adv. Mil:* Eyes left! tête (à) gauche !
3. *s.* (*a*) (i) (*Left hand*) Gauche *f.* On. the left, to
the left, à gauche. (ii) *Box:* To feint with the l.,
feinter du gauche. (*b*) (*Left wing*) *Mil:* Gauche *f* ;
l'aile *f* gauche. (*c*) *Pol:* The Left, les gauches *m* ;
la gauche. **'left-hand,** *attrib.a.* On the left-
hand side, à gauche. The l.-h. drawer, le tiroir
de gauche. **left-'handed,** *a.* (*a*) (*Of pers.*)
Gaucher, -ère. (*b*) *F:* (*Of pers.*) Gauche, maladroit. (*c*) *F:* Left-handed compliment, compliment douteux. **left-'handedness,** *s.* Habitude *f* de se servir de la main gauche.
left-'hander, *s.* **I.** (*Pers.*) Gaucher, -ère.
2. *Box:* Coup *m* du gauche.
left². *See* LEAVE².
leg¹ [leg], *s.* **I.** Jambe *f* ; patte *f* (de chien,
d'oiseau, d'insecte, de reptile). *F:* To take to
one's legs, prendre ses jambes à son cou. I ran
as fast as my legs would carry me, j'ai couru à
toutes jambes. To stand on one leg, se tenir sur
un pied. To be on one's legs, être debout, être
sur pied. I have been on my legs all day, j'ai été
sur pied toute la journée. To get on one's legs
again, (i) se relever ; (ii) se rétablir. To set s.o.
on his legs again, (i) relever qn ; remettre qn
debout ; (ii) rétablir qn dans ses affaires ; tirer
qn d'affaire. To be on one's last legs, tirer vers
sa fin ; être à bout de ressources. To walk s.o.
off his legs, exténuer qn à force de le faire marcher. To be carried off one's legs, être emporté ;
perdre pied. To feel, find, one's legs, (i) se
trouver en état de se tenir debout ; (ii) prendre
conscience de ses forces ; (iii) se faire une
clientèle. To keep one's legs, se maintenir
debout. To give s.o. a leg up, (i) faire la courte
échelle à qn ; (ii) aider qn à monter en selle ;
(iii) *F:* donner à qn un coup d'épaule. *F:* To
pull s.o.'s leg, se payer la tête de qn ; faire
marcher qn. **2.** *Cu:* Leg of chicken, cuisse *f* de

volaille. **Leg of beef,** trumeau *m*, gîte *m.* **Leg of
veal,** cuisseau *m.* **Leg of pork,** jambon *m.* **Leg
of mutton,** gigot *m. Cost: F:* **Leg-of-mutton
sleeves,** manches à gigot. *Nau:* **Leg-of-mutton
sail,** voile triangulaire. **3.** Jambe (de pantalon) ;
tige *f* (de bas). **4.** Pied *m* (de table) ; branche *f*
(de compas) ; jambage *m*, montant *m* (de chevalet). To set a chair on its legs (again), relever
une chaise. **5.** *Nau:* Bordée *f.* **'leg-bone,** *s.*
Anat: Tibia *m.* **'leg-iron,** *s. Surg:* Attelle *f*
en fer. **'leg-pull,** *s. F:* Mystification *f*,
carotte *f.* **'leg-puller,** *s. F:* Farceur, mystificateur. **'leg-shields,** *s.pl.* Pare-jambes *m*
(de motocyclette).
leg², *v.tr.* (legged) *F:* To leg it, (i) faire la route
à pied ; *P:* prendre le train onze ; (ii) marcher
ou courir rapidement ; jouer des jambes.
legacy ['legəsi], *s.* Legs *m.* To leave a legacy to
s.o., faire un legs à qn. To come into a legacy,
faire un héritage. **'legacy-duty,** *s.* Droits *mpl*
de succession. **'legacy-hunter,** *s.* Coureur,
-euse, d'héritages.
legal ['li:g(ə)l], *a.* **I.** Légal, -aux ; licite.
2. (*a*) Légal ; judiciaire, juridique. By legal
process, par voies de droit. L. security, caution *f*
judiciaire. Legal document, acte *m* authentique.
(*Of corporation*) To acquire legal status, acquérir
la personnalité juridique, morale. (*b*) Legal year,
année civile. Legal department (*of bank, etc.*),
service *m* du contentieux. To go into the legal
profession, se faire une carrière dans le droit.
Legal practitioner, homme de loi. To take legal
advice, consulter un avocat. Legal term, terme
de pratique. The l. mind, l'esprit juridique.
-ally, *adv.* Légalement ; (i) licitement, (ii) judiciairement, juridiquement. L. responsible, responsable en droit.
legality [li'galiti], *s.* Légalité *f.*
legalize ['li:gəla:iz], *v.tr.* Rendre (un acte) légal ;
autoriser (un acte) ; légaliser, authentiquer (un
document).
legate ['leget], *s.* Légat *m.*
legatee [legə'ti:], *s.* Légataire *mf.* Residuary
legatee, légataire (à titre) universel.
legation [le'gei∫(ə)n], *s.* Légation *f.*
legend ['ledʒənd], *s.* **I.** Légende *f*, fable *f.*
2. (*a*) Inscription *f*, légende (sur une médaille,
etc.). (*b*) Explication *f*, légende (d'une carte, etc.).
legendary ['ledʒəndəri], *a.* Légendaire.
legerdemain ['ledʒərdə'mein], *s.* (Tours *mpl* de)
passe-passe *m* ; tour d'adresse ; escamotage *m.*
leggings ['legiŋz], *s.pl. Cost:* Jambières *f* ;
guêtres *f.*
leggy ['legi], *a.* Aux longues jambes ; dégingandé.
Leghorn ['legho:rn]. **I.** *Pr.n. Geog:* Livourne *f.*
2. *s.* Leghorn (hat), chapeau *m* de paille d'Italie.
legibility [ledʒi'biliti], *s.* Lisibilité *f*, netteté *f*
(d'une écriture).
legible ['ledʒibl], *a.* (Écriture) lisible, nette.
-ibly, *adv.* Lisiblement.
legion ['li:dʒ(ə)n], *s.* Légion *f. F:* Their name
is Legion, ils sont innombrables ; ils s'appellent
légion.
legionary ['li:dʒənəri], *a. & s.* Légionnaire (*m*).
legislate ['ledʒisleit], *v.i.* Faire les lois ; légiférer.
legislation [ledʒis'lei∫(ə)n], *s.* Législation *f.*
legislative ['ledʒislativ], *a.* Législatif. *Fr.Hist:*
The Legislative Assembly, l'Assemblée législative.
legislator ['ledʒisleitər], *s.* Législateur *m.*
legislature ['ledʒislətjər], *s.* Législature *f* ;
corps législatif.
legist ['li:dʒist], *s.* Légiste *m.*
legitimacy [le'dʒitiməsi], *s.pl.* Légitimité *f.*

28

legitimate¹ [le'dʒitimet], *a.* **1.** (*a*) (Enfant, autorité, etc.) légitime. (*b*) *The l. drama,* le vrai théâtre. **2.** (Raisonnement, etc.) légitime. **-ly,** *adv.* Légitimement.

legitimate² [le'dʒitimeit], *v.tr.* Légitimer (un enfant).

legitimation [ledʒiti'meiʃ(ə)n], *s.* Légitimation *f.*

legless ['legləs], *a.* Sans jambes. *L. cripple,* cul-de-jatte *m, pl.* culs-de-jatte.

legume ['legju:m], *s.,* **legumen** [le'gju:men], *s.* **1.** Fruit *m* d'une légumineuse. **2.** *pl.* Légumes *m.*

leguminous [le'gju:minəs], *a.* Légumineux.

leisure ['leʒər], *s.* Loisir(s) *m*(*pl*). **To have leisure for reading,** leisure to read, avoir le loisir, le temps, de lire. **Tọ be at leisure,** être de loisir; ne pas être occupé. **To do sth. at (one's) leisure,** faire qch. à loisir, à tête reposée. **People of leisure,** les désœuvrés *m.* **Leisure hours,** heures de loisir. **In my leisure moments,** à mes moments perdus.

leisured ['leʒərd], *a.* De loisir; désœuvré. **The leisured classes,** les désœuvrés *m.*

leisureliness ['leʒərlinəs], *s.* Absence *f* de hâte; lenteur *f* (*in doing sth.,* à faire qch.).

leisurely ['leʒərli]. **1.** *a.* (*Of pers.*) Qui n'est jamais pressé. **Leisurely pace,** allure mesurée, posée, tranquille. **Leisurely journey,** voyage par petites étapes. *To do sth. in a l. fashion,* faire qch. sans se presser. **2.** *adv.* (*a*) A tête reposée. (*b*) Posément; sans se presser.

lemon ['lemən]. **1.** *s. Bot:* (*a*) Citron *m,* limon *m.* (*b*) = LEMON-TREE. **2.** *a.* Jaune citron *inv.* **'lemon-cheese, -curd,** *s. Cu:* Pâte composée d'œufs, de beurre et de jus de citron. **'lemon-drop,** *s.* Bonbon acidulé. **'lemon-'squash,** *s.* Citron pressé; citronnade *f.* **'lemon-squeezer,** *s.* Presse-citrons *m inv.* **'lemon-tree,** *s. Bot:* Citronnier *m,* limonier *m.*

lemonade [lemə'neid], *s.* Limonade *f.* **Still lemonade,** citronnade *f*; citron pressé.

lemon-sole [lemən'soul], *s. Ich:* Plie *f* sole; limande *f* sole.

lemur ['li:mər, 'lemər], *s. Z:* Lémur *m.*

lend [lend], *v.tr.* (lent [lent]; lent) **1.** (*a*) Prêter. *L. me a pen,* prêtez-moi une plume. **To lend money at interest,** prêter de l'argent à intérêt. (*b*) **To lend (out) books,** louer des livres. **2.** **To lend s.o. aid,** prêter aide, prêter secours, à qn. **To lend an ear,** one's ear(s), **to . . . ,** prêter l'oreille à. . . . **3.** *v.pr.* **To lend oneself, itself, to sth.,** se prêter à qch. *Spot that lends itself to meditation,* lieu propice à la méditation. **lending¹,** *a.* Prêteur, -euse. **lending²,** *s.* Prêt *m*; *Fin:* prestation *f* (de capitaux). **Lending (out) of books,** location *f* de livres.

lender ['lendər], *s.* Prêteur, -euse.

length [leŋθ], *s.* **1.** Longueur *f.* **Length over all,** longueur hors tout. **To be two feet in length,** avoir deux pieds de longueur; être long de deux pieds. **Length of stroke,** course *f* (d'un outil); *Mch:* parcours *m* (du piston). (*Of ship, etc.*) To turn in its own length, virer sur place. *Row:* **To win by a length,** gagner d'une longueur. *F:* **Over the length and breadth of the country,** dans toute l'étendue du pays. **To go the length of the street,** aller jusqu'au bout de la rue. **I fell all my length** (*on the ground*), je suis tombé de tout mon long. **2.** *Stay of some length,* séjour assez prolongé, d'une certaine durée. **Length of service,** ancienneté *f.* **For some length of time,** pendant quelque temps. *To recite sth. at* (full) **length,** réciter qch. tout au long, d'un bout à l'autre. *To speak at some length on a subject,* parler assez longuement sur un sujet. *He lectured me at great length,* il m'a fait une longue semonce. *To recount sth. at greater l.,* raconter qch. plus en détail. *At length he gave his consent,* enfin, à la fin, il consentit. **3.** **To go to the length of asserting . . . ,** aller jusqu'à prétendre. . . . **He would go to any lengths,** rien ne l'arrêterait; ne reculerait devant rien (*to,* pour). **To go to great lengths,** aller bien loin, pousser les choses bien loin. **To go to all lengths,** to go the whole length, aller jusqu'au bout; se porter aux dernières extrémités (*against s.o.,* sur, contre, qn). **Have you got (to) that length with him?** en êtes-vous là avec lui? **4.** *Pros:* Longueur (d'une voyelle, d'une syllabe). **5.** *Ten:* **To keep a good length,** conserver une bonne longueur de balle. **6.** Morceau *m,* bout *m* (de ficelle, etc.); pièce *f,* coupon *m* (d'étoffe); tronçon *m* (de tuyau). *Dressm:* **Dress length,** coupon de robe.

lengthen ['leŋθən]. **1.** *v.tr.* Allonger, rallonger; prolonger (la vie, etc.). **2.** *v.i.* S'allonger, se rallonger; (*of days*) augmenter, croître, grandir. *F:* **His face lengthened,** son visage s'allongea.

lengthening, *s.* **1.** Allongement *m,* rallongement *m*; prolongation *f* (d'un séjour, etc.). **2.** Augmentation *f* (des jours).

lengthiness ['leŋθinəs], *s.* Longueurs *fpl*; prolixité *f* (d'un discours).

lengthways ['leŋθweiz], *adv.* Longitudinalement; en longueur; en long.

lengthwise ['leŋθwaiz]. **1.** *adv.* = LENGTHWAYS. **2.** *a.* (Coupe) en long, en longueur.

lengthy ['leŋθi], *a.* (Discours) assez long, prolixe. **-ily,** *adv.* (Parler) longuement, avec prolixité; (raconter) tout au long.

leniency ['li:njənsi], *s.* Clémence *f*; douceur *f,* indulgence *f* (*to, towards,* pour).

lenient ['li:njənt], *a.* Clément; doux, *f.* douce; indulgent (*to, towards,* envers, pour). **-ly,** *adv.* Avec clémence, avec douceur.

lenitive ['lenitiv]. **1.** *a. & s. Med:* Lénitif (*m*); adoucissant (*m*). **2.** *s. F:* Palliatif *m,* adoucissement *m.*

lens [lenz], *s.* **1.** *Opt:* (*a*) Lentille *f*; verre *m* (de lunettes). **Field lens** (*of surveying instrument*), verre de champ. *Phot:* **Front, back, lens,** système antérieur, postérieur (d'un objectif). (*b*) (*Magnifying glass*) Loupe *f*; verre grossissant. (*c*) *Phot:* Objectif *m.* **2.** *Anat:* Crystalline lens, cristallin *m* (de l'œil). **'lens-holder,** *s.* *Phot:* Porte-objectif *m inv.* **'lens-hood,** *s.* Parasoleil *m* (d'objectif).

Lent¹ [lent], *s. Ecc:* Le carême. **To keep Lent,** faire carême.

lent². *See* LEND.

lenten ['lentən], *a.* De carême.

lenticular [len'tikjulər], **lentiform** ['lenti-fɔ:rm], *a.* Lenticulaire, lentiforme.

lentigo, *pl.* **-tigines** [len'taigo, -'tidʒini:z], *s. Med:* Lentigo *m*; *F:* tache(s) *f*(*pl*) de rousseur.

lentil ['lentil], *s. Hort:* Lentille *f.*

leonine ['li:onain], *a.* De lion(s); léonin.

leopard ['lepərd], *s.* Léopard *m.* **American leopard,** jaguar *m.* **Leopard cat,** ocelot *m.*

leopardess ['lepərdes], *s.* Léopard *m* femelle.

leper ['lepər], *s.* Lépreux, -euse.

lepidopter, *pl.* **-ters, -tera** [lepi'dɔptər, -tərz, -tərə], *s. Ent:* Lépidoptère *m*; papillon *m.*

lepidopteran [lepi'dɔptərən], *a. & s. Ent:* Lépidoptère (*m*).

leporine ['lepərain], *a.* De lièvre.

leprechaun [lepre'kɔ:n, -'χɔ:n], *s. Irish Myth:* Farfadet *m,* lutin *m.*

leprosy ['leprosi], *s. Med:* Lèpre *f.*

leprous ['leprəs], a. Lépreux.
lesion ['li:ʒ(ə)n], s. Lésion f.
less [les]. **I.** 1. a. (a) Moindre. Of l. value, d'une moindre valeur; de moindre valeur. In a less degree, à un moindre degré, à un degré inférieur. Quantities, sums, less than . . ., quantités, sommes, au-dessous de . . . To grow less, s'amoindrir. (b) Eat less meat, mangez moins de viande. He does the less work, il n'en fait que moins de travail. With a few l. windows the house would be warmer, avec quelques fenêtres de moins la maison serait plus chaude. (c) A : Moins important. James the Less, Jacques le Mineur. 2. prep. Purchase price less 10%, prix d'achat moins 10%, sous déduction de 10%. 3. s. Moins m. In l. than an hour, en moins d'une heure. So much the less to do, d'autant moins à faire. I can't let you have it for l., je ne peux pas vous le laisser à moins (than, de). 4. adv. Less known, moins connu. One man less, un homme de moins. Less than six, moins de six. Less and less, de moins en moins. I was (all) the less surprised as . . ., j'en ai été d'autant moins surpris que. . . . Still less, even less, moins encore. He continued none the less, il n'en continua pas moins. None the less he came in first, néanmoins il arriva premier. 5. (a) Nothing less than. (i) Rien (de) moins que. It is nothing l. than monstrous, c'est absolument monstrueux. (ii) Rien moins que. He resembled nothing l. than a demagogue, il ne ressemblait à rien moins qu'à un démagogue. (b) No less. (i) To fight with no less daring than skill, se battre avec autant d'habileté que de courage. No less good, également bon. (ii) They have no l. than six servants, ils n'ont pas moins de six domestiques. (iii) It was no less a person than the duke, ce n'était rien moins que le duc. (iv) He fears it no less than I, il ne le craint pas moins que moi (je ne le crains). He fears him no less than me, il a aussi peur de lui que de moi.
lessee [le'si:], s. **I.** Locataire mf (à bail) (d'un immeuble, etc.); tenancier, -ière (d'un casino, etc.). 2. Concessionnaire mf.
lessen [lesn]. **I.** v.i. S'amoindrir, diminuer; (of symptoms, etc.) s'atténuer; (of receding object) (se) rapetisser. 2. v.tr. Amoindrir, diminuer; rapetisser; atténuer; ralentir (son activité). Artil : To lessen the range, raccourcir le tir. **lessening**, s. Amoindrissement m, diminution f; atténuation f, rapetissement m.
lesser ['lesər], attrib.a. **I.** Petit. Astr : The Lesser Bear, la Petite Ourse. Ph : The lesser calory, petite calorie. 2. To choose the lesser of two evils, the lesser evil, de deux maux choisir le moindre.
lesson[1] ['les(ə)n], s. Leçon f. **I.** To hear the lessons, faire réciter les leçons. Dancing lessons, leçons de danse; cours m de danse. To give, take, lessons in French, donner, prendre, des leçons de français. To draw a lesson from sth., tirer enseignement, tirer une leçon, de qch. F : Let that be a lesson to you! que cela vous serve d'exemple, de leçon! To read s.o. a lesson, faire la leçon à qn. 2. Ecc : The first, second, lesson, la première, la seconde, leçon.
lesson[2], v.tr. Faire la leçon à (qn).
lessor [le'sɔ:r], s. Bailleur, -eresse.
lest [lest], conj. **I.** De peur, de crainte, que . . . (ne) + sub. Lest we forget, de peur que nous n'oublions. 2. I feared l. he should fall, je craignais qu'il (ne) tombât. I feared l. I should fall, j'avais peur de tomber; je craignais de tomber.
let[1] [let], s. **I.** A : Empêchement m. S.a. HIN-

DRANCE. 2. Ten : Let (ball), coup m à remettre ; balle f de filet.
let[2], s. Location f. When I get a let for the season, quand je loue ma maison pour la saison.
let[3], v. (p.t. & p.p. let; pr.p. letting) I. v.tr. **I.** (a) Permettre ; laisser. To let s.o. do sth., laisser qn faire qch.; permettre à qn de faire qch. To let oneself be guided, se laisser guider. Let me tell you that . . ., permettez-moi de vous dire que. . . . To let fall, slip, laisser échapper (qch.). S.a. FALL[2] I, SLIP[2] I. 3. He let go the rope, il lâcha la corde. S.a. GO[2] 12. When can you let me have my coat? quand pourrai-je avoir mon habit? S.a. ALONE 2, FLY[3] I. 4, HAVE[2] 3, LOOSE[1] I. (b) To let s.o. know sth., about sth., faire savoir, faire connaître, qch. à qn ; faire part de qch. à qn. Let me hear the story, racontez-moi l'histoire. (c) The police would not let anyone along the street, la police ne laissait passer personne. To let s.o. through, laisser passer qn. (d) A.Med : To let blood, pratiquer une saignée ; saigner qn. 2. Louer (une maison, etc.). House to let, maison à louer. II. let, v.aux. (supplying 1st & 3rd pers. of imperative) Let us make haste! dépêchons-nous! Let us pray, prions. Don't let us start yet, ne partons pas encore. Let there be light, que la lumière soit. So let it be! soit! Let there be no mistake about it! qu'on ne s'y trompe pas! Let ABC be any angle, soit ABC un angle quelconque. Let me see! voyons! attendez un peu! Let them all come! qu'ils viennent tous! Let their love be ever so strong . . ., si grand que soit leur amour. . . . **let down**, v.tr. **I.** (a) Baisser (la glace, le marchepied) ; descendre (une barrique à la cave). (b) Baisser (un store) ; détrousser (son tablier) ; défaire, dénouer (ses cheveux). (c) Allonger (une robe, etc.). 2. (a) The chair let him down, la chaise le laissa tomber par terre. (b) F : To let s.o. down gently, user de tact pour faire comprendre à qn qu'il est dans son tort, pour lui refuser qch. (c) F : (i) Laisser (qn) en panne ; faire faux bond à (qn). (ii) faire une avanie à (qn). I won't let you down, vous pouvez compter sur moi. 3. Mch : etc : To let the fires down, laisser tomber les feux. 4. Détendre, débander (un ressort) ; dégonfler (un pneu). **'let-'down**, s. F : Désappointement m, déception f. **let in**, v.tr. **I.** (a) Laisser entrer (qn) ; faire entrer (qn) ; admettre (qn) ; laisser entrer (l'air, la pluie). Shoes that let in water, souliers qui prennent l'eau. (b) F : To let s.o. in on a secret, initier qn à un secret. 2. Encastrer (une plaque). Dressm : Tail : Ajouter, introduire (une pièce). 3. F : (a) Mettre (qn) dedans ; rouler, duper (qn). I've been let in for a thousand, j'y suis de mille livres. (b) I did not know what I was letting myself in for, je ne savais pas à quoi je m'engageais. **let into**, v.tr. (a) To let s.o. into the house, laisser entrer qn dans la maison. To let s.o. into a secret, mettre qn dans le secret. (b) To let a slab into a wall, encastrer une plaque dans un mur. To let a piece into a skirt, incruster une pièce dans une jupe. **let off**, v.tr. **I.** Tirer, faire partir (un feu d'artifice) ; décocher (une flèche sous épigramme). 2. Lâcher, laisser échapper (de la vapeur). 3. (a) To let s.o. off from sth., from doing sth., décharger qn d'une corvée, etc. ; dispenser qn de faire qch. (b) To let s.o. off, faire grâce à qn. To be let off with a fine, en être quitte pour une amende. **let on**, v.i. & tr. F : To let s.o. about sth. to s.o., rapporter, cafarder, qch. à qn. Don't go and let on that I was there, n'allez pas dire que j'y étais.

let out, *v.tr.* **1.** Laisser sortir (qn) ; ouvrir la porte à (qn) ; laisser échapper (un oiseau) ; élargir (un prisonnier). *To let out the air from sth.*, laisser échapper l'air de qch. ; dégonfler (un ballon, etc.). *F:* **To let out a yell**, laisser échapper un cri. **2.** (*a*) Rélargir (un vêtement). *To let a strap out one hole*, (re)lâcher une courroie d'un cran. (*b*) *Nau:* Lâcher (un cordage) ; larguer (une voile). **3.** **To let chairs out (on hire)**, louer des chaises. **4. To let out a secret**, laisser échapper, lâcher, un secret. **5.** *v.i. F:* **To let out at s.o.** with one's foot, décocher un coup de pied à qn. **letting**, *s.* Louage *m.* **Letting value**, valeur locative.

lethal ['liːθəl], *a.* Mortel. **Lethal weapon**, arme meurtrière, léthifère. **Lethal chamber**, salle *f* d'asphyxie (d'une fourrière).

lethargic(al) [le'θɑːrdʒik(əl)], *a.* Léthargique. **-ally**, *adv.* Lourdement, paresseusement.

lethargy ['leθərdʒi], *s.* Léthargie *f.*

Lett [let], *s.* **1.** *Ethn:* Letton, -one. **2.** *Ling:* Le lette, le letton.

letter[1] ['letər], *s.* **1.** Lettre *f*, caractère *m.* *Engr:* **Proof before letters**, épreuve *f* avant la lettre. *S.a.* BLACK LETTER, RED-LETTER. **To obey to the letter**, obéir à la lettre, au pied de la lettre. *S.a.* DEAD I. 1. **2.** (*a*) Lettre, missive *f.* **To open the letters**, dépouiller le courrier. (*b*) *Jur:* **Letters of administration**, lettres d'administration. **3.** *pl.* **Letters**, lettres ; belles-lettres ; littérature *f.* **Man of letters**, homme de lettres ; littérateur *m.* **'letter-balance**, *s.* Pèse-lettres *m inv.* **'letter-box**, *s.* Boîte *f* aux lettres. **'letter-card**, *s.* Carte-lettre *f*, *pl.* cartes-lettres. **'letter-case**, *s.* Porte-lettres *m inv*, portefeuille *m.* **'letter-file**, *s.* Classeur *m* de lettres. **'letter-opener**, *s.* Ouvre-lettres *m inv.* **'letter-pad**, *s.* Bloc *m* de papier à lettres ; bloc-notes *m.* **'letter-paper**, *s.* Papier *m* à lettres. **'letter-perfect**, *a.* To be letter-perfect in one's part, savoir son rôle par cœur. **'letter-press**, *s.* Presse *f* à copier. **'letter-scales**, *s.pl.* = LETTER-BALANCE. **'letter-writer**, *s.* Épistolier, -ière.

letter[2], *v.tr.* Marquer (un objet) avec des lettres ; graver des lettres sur (un objet) ; estampiller. **lettered**, *a.* **1.** Marqué avec des lettres. **2.** (Homme) lettré. **lettering**, *s.* **1.** Lettrage *m* ; estampillage *m.* *Typ:* **Lettering by hand**, repoussage *m.* **2.** Lettres *fpl* ; inscription *f* ; titre *m* (d'un livre).

letter[3], *s.* **1.** Loueur, -euse. **2. Letter of blood**, saigneur *m.*

letterpress ['letərpres], *s.* **1.** *Typ:* Impression *f* typographique. **2.** Texte *m* (accompagnant une illustration).

Lettic ['letik], **Lettish** ['letiʃ]. **1.** *a. & s. Ethn: Geog:* Letton, -one. **2.** *s. Ling:* Le lette, le letton.

lettuce ['letəs], *s.* Laitue *s.* **Cabbage lettuce**, laitue pommée. *S.a.* COS, LAMB'S LETTUCE.

Levant[1] [le'vant]. *Geog:* **1.** *Pr.n.* The Levant, le Levant. **2.** *Attrib.* Du Levant ; levantin.

levant[2], *v.i. F:* Partir sans payer ; (*esp. of bookmaker*) décamper sans payer.

Levantine [le'vantin, 'levantin], *a. & s. Geog:* Levantin, -ine.

levee ['levi], *s.* (*a*) *Hist:* Lever *m* (du roi). (*b*) Réception royale (tenue l'après-midi et pour hommes seulement).

level[1] [levl]. I. *s.* **1.** *Tls:* (*a*) Niveau *m* (de charpentier, etc.). **Plumb level**, niveau à plomb. *S.a.* SPIRIT-LEVEL. (*b*) *Mch:* **Water-level**, niveau d'eau. **2.** (*a*) Niveau (de la mer) ; niveau, étage *m*

(de la société). **Difference of level** *between two objects*, dénivellation *f* de deux objets. **At a higher level**, en contre-haut (*than*, de). **At eye level**, à la hauteur de l'œil ; à hauteur des yeux. **On a level with sth.**, de niveau avec qch. ; à la hauteur de qch. *Drawing-room on a l. with the garden*, salon de plain-pied avec le jardin. **To be on a level with s.o.**, être au niveau de qn ; être l'égal de qn. **To come down to s.o.'s level**, se mettre au niveau, à la portée, de qn. **To find one's level**, trouver son niveau (social, etc.). (*b*) (*Of billiard-table, etc.*) Out of level, dénivelé. **3.** (*a*) Surface *f* de niveau ; terrain *m* de niveau. *Aut: Rail:* Palier *m.* **On the level**, (i) à l'uni ; (ii) *F:* (*of pers.*) loyal, -aux ; de bonne foi ; (iii) *F:* en toute honnêteté, en toute sincérité. *Aut:* Speed on the level, vitesse en palier. (*b*) *Min:* (i) Niveau, étage ; (ii) galerie *f* (de niveau). (*c*) Bief *m* (d'un canal). II. **level**, *a.* **1.** (*a*) (*Not sloping*) (Terrain) de niveau, à niveau ; (route, etc.) en palier. (*b*) (*Flat*) Égal, -aux ; uni. (*c*) **Level with . . .**, de niveau avec . . . ; au niveau de . . . ; à (la) hauteur de . . . ; affleurant. . . . *L.* with the water, à fleur de l'eau ; à fleur d'eau ; au ras de l'eau. *L.* with the ground, à fleur du sol ; à ras de terre. **To lay a building** *l. with the ground*, raser un édifice. *Sp:* **To draw level with . . .**, arriver à (la) hauteur de . . . **2. Level tone**, ton soutenu. **To keep a level head**, garder sa tête, son sang-froid. *F:* **To do one's level best**, faire tout son possible. **'level-'headed**, *a.* Qui a la tête bien équilibrée ; pondéré. **level-'headedness**, *s.* Esprit bien équilibré ; pondération *f.*

level[2], *v.tr.* (levelled) **1.** (*a*) Niveler ; mettre (un billard, etc.) de niveau. (*b*) Niveler, aplanir, égaliser (une surface). **2.** Pointer (un fusil), braquer (un canon), diriger (une longue-vue) (*at*, sur). **To level one's gun at, against, s.o.**, coucher, mettre, qn en joue. *F:* **To level accusations against s.o.**, lancer des accusations contre qn. **To level a blow at s.o.**, porter un coup à qn. **level down**, *v.tr.* **1.** Araser (un mur). **2.** Abaisser (qn, qch.) à son niveau. **level up**, *v.tr.* **1.** To level sth. up to . . ., élever qch. au niveau de. . . . **2.** Égaliser (le terrain, etc.). **levelling**, *s.* **1.** Nivellement *m* ; (i) mise *f* à niveau, de niveau ; (ii) aplanissement *m* (d'une surface). **2.** Pointage *m*, braquage *m* (d'une arme à feu).

leveller ['lev(ə)lər], *s.* (*Pers.*) Niveleur, -euse.

lever[1] ['liːvər], *s. Mec:* Levier *m. Aut:* Gear lever, levier des vitesses. **Control lever** (*on steering-wheel*), manette *f.* **'lever 'watch**, *s. Clockm:* Montre *f* à ancre, à échappement.

lever[2]. **1.** *v.i.* Manœuvrer un levier. (*Of part, etc.*) To lever against sth., faire levier sur qch. **2.** *v.tr.* To lever sth. up, soulever qch. au moyen d'un levier.

leverage ['liːvərədʒ, - vrədʒ], *s.* **1.** (*a*) Force *f*, puissance *f*, de levier. (*b*) To bring leverage to bear on (*a door, etc.*), exercer des pesées *f* sur (une porte, etc.). **2.** Système *m* de leviers.

leveret ['levəret], *s.* Levraut *m.*

leviable ['leviəbl], *a.* (Impôt) percevable.

leviathan [le'vaiəθən], *s.* **1.** *B:* Léviathan *m.* **2.** *F:* Navire *m* monstre.

Leviticus [le'vitikəs], *s. B:* Le Lévitique.

levity ['leviti], *s.* Légèreté *f* ; manque *m* de sérieux.

levy[1] ['levi], *s.* **1.** (*a*) Levée *f* (d'un impôt). (*b*) *Mil:* Levée (des troupes) ; réquisition *f* (des chevaux, etc.). **2.** Impôt *m*, contribution *f.* *S.a.* CAPITAL[2] II. 1.

levy², *v.tr.* **1.** Lever, percevoir (un impôt); imposer (une amende). *To l. a fine on s.o.*, frapper qn d'une amende. **2.** *Mil:* (a) Lever (des troupes). (b) Mettre en réquisition, réquisitionner (des denrées, etc.). **3.** (a) *Jur:* To levy execution on s.o.'s goods, faire une saisie-exécution sur les biens de qn. (b) To levy war on s.o., faire la guerre à, contre, qn. To levy blackmail, faire du chantage.

lewd [lju:d], *a.* **1.** Impudique, lascif. **2.** *A. & B:* Bas, vil, ignoble. **-ly**, *adv.* Impudiquement, lascivement.

lewdness ['lju:dnəs], *s.* **1.** Impudicité *f*, lasciveté *f*. **2.** Luxure *f*, débauche *f*.

Lewis ['lu:is]. *Pr.n.m.* Louis. **Lewis gun**, *s. Mil:* Fusil mitrailleur. **'Lewis-'gunner**, *s.* Mitrailleur *m*.

lexicographer [leksi'kɔgrəfər], *s.* Lexicographe *m*.

lexicography [leksi'kɔgrəfi], *s.* Lexicographie *f*.

lexicology [leksi'kɔlodʒi], *s.* Lexicologie *f*.

lexicon ['leksikən], *s.* Lexique *m*.

Leyden ['laidən]. *Pr.n. Geog:* Leyde *f*. *S.a.* JAR³.

liability [laiə'biliti], *s.* **1.** *Jur:* Responsabilité *f*. Joint liability, responsabilité conjointe. Several liability, responsabilité séparée. Joint and several liability, responsabilité (conjointe et) solidaire. The Employers' Liability Act, la loi sur les accidents du travail. **2.** *pl. Com: Fin:* Liabilities, ensemble *m* des dettes; engagements *mpl*, obligations *fpl*; (*in bankruptcy*) masse passive. Assets and liabilities, actif *m* et passif *m*. To meet one's liabilities, faire face à ses engagements, à ses échéances. **3.** (a) Liability to a fine, risque *m* d'(encourir une) amende. (b) Disposition *f*, tendance *f* (*to sth., to do sth.*, à qch., à faire qch.). (c) (*Of product, etc.*) L. to explode, danger *m* d'explosion.

liable ['laiəbl], *a.* **1.** *Jur:* Responsable (*for*, de). **2.** *L. to a tax*, assujetti à un impôt; redevable, passible, d'un impôt. *Dividends l. to income-tax*, dividendes soumis à l'impôt sur le revenu. Liable to a fine, passible d'une amende. *L. to military service*, astreint au service militaire. **3.** Sujet, apte, exposé (*to*, à). *Car l. to overturn*, voiture sujette à verser. *Goods l. to go bad*, marchandises susceptibles de se corrompre. *To be l. to catch cold*, avoir une disposition à s'enrhumer. **4.** *Difficulties are l. to occur*, des difficultés sont susceptibles de se présenter. *Plan l. to modifications*, projet qui pourra subir des modifications.

liaison [li'eizən], *s.* Liaison *f*.

liana [li'a:na], *s. Bot:* Liane *f*.

liar ['laiər], *s.* Menteur, -euse.

libation [lai'beiʃ(ə)n], *s.* Libation *f*.

libel¹ ['laibl], *s.* (a) Diffamation *f*, calomnie *f*. (b) *Jur:* Diffamation par écrit; écrit *m* diffamatoire; libelle *m*. To bring an action for libel against s.o., intenter un procès en diffamation à qn.

libel², *v.tr* (libelled) *Jur:* Diffamer (qn) (par écrit); calomnier (qn).

libeller ['laibələr], *s.* Diffamateur, -trice.

libellous ['laibələs], *a.* (Écrit) diffamatoire, calomnieux. **-ly**, *adv.* Calomnieusement.

liberal ['libərəl], *a.* **1.** (a) Libéral, -aux. The liberal arts, les arts libéraux. (b) (*Of pers.*) D'esprit large; sans préjugés. *In the most l. sense of the word*, au sens le plus large du mot. **2.** (a) Libéral, généreux. *L. of advice*, prodigue de conseils. Liberal to s.o., généreux envers qn. *To be l. in business*, être large en affaires. Liberal

offer, offre généreuse. (b) Libéral, abondant. *L. provision of . . .*, ample provision de. . . . **3.** *a. & s. Pol:* Libéral (*m*). **-ally**, *adv.* Libéralement.

liberality [libə'raliti], *s.* Libéralité *f*. **1.** Largeur *f* (de vues). **2.** Générosité *f*.

liberate ['libəreit], *v.tr.* **1.** Libérer; mettre en liberté; lâcher (des pigeons). **2.** *Ch:* To liberate a gas, dégager un gaz. **liberating**, *a.* Libérateur, -trice.

liberation [libə'reiʃ(ə)n], *s.* **1.** Libération *f*; mise *f* en liberté. *L. from the yoke of . . .*, affranchissement *m* du joug de. . . . **2.** *L. of heat*, dégagement *m* de chaleur.

liberator ['libəreitər], *s.* Libérateur, -trice.

libertinage ['libətinedʒ], **libertinism** ['libətinizm], *s.* Libertinage *m*; débauche *f*.

libertine ['libətin], *a. & s.* Libertin (*m*); débauché (*m*). *S.a.* CHARTERED.

liberty ['libəti], *s.* Liberté *f*. (a) Liberty of conscience, liberté de conscience. At liberty, (i) en liberté; *Navy:* en permission; (ii) libre, disponible. To set s.o. at liberty, mettre qn en liberté. To be at liberty to do sth., être libre de faire qch. *You are at l. to believe me or not*, libre à vous de ne pas me croire. *The chauffeur is not always at l.*, le chauffeur n'est pas toujours disponible. *F: This is Liberty Hall*, vous êtes ici comme chez vous. *S.a.* CAP¹ 1. (b) To take the liberty of doing sth., se permettre de faire qch. (c) To take liberties with s.o., prendre des libertés, se permettre des privautés, avec qn. *He takes a good many liberties*, il se permet bien des choses. **'liberty-boat**, *s. Navy:* Vedette *f* des permissionnaires. **'liberty-man**, *pl.* **-men**, *s.m. Navy:* Permissionnaire.

libidinous [li'bidinəs], *a.* Libidineux.

librarian [lai'brɛəriən], *s.* Bibliothécaire *m*.

library ['laibrəri], *s.* Bibliothèque *f*. Lending library, cabinet *m* de lecture. Reference library, salle *f* de lecture. Free library, bibliothèque municipale. Library edition, édition grand format.

librettist [li'bretist], *s. Th:* Librettiste *m*.

libretto, *pl.* **-i**, **-os** [li'breto, -i, -ouz], *s.* Libretto *m*, livret *m* (d'opéra).

Libya ['libiə]. *Pr.n.* La Libye.

Libyan ['libiən], *a. & s.* Libyen, -enne. The Libyan Desert, le désert de Libye.

lice [lais]. *See* LOUSE.

licence ['laisəns], *s.* **1.** (a) Permission *f*, autorisation *f*. Under licence from the author, avec l'autorisation de l'auteur. (b) *Adm:* Permis *m*, autorisation; patente *f*, privilège *m*. Liquor licence, patente de débit de boissons. Pedlar's licence, autorisation de colportage. Printer's licence, brevet *m* d'imprimeur. Trades subject to a licence, requiring a licence, métiers patentables. Theatre licence, tabac licence, wireless licence, autorisation d'exploiter une salle de spectacles, un débit de tabac, d'avoir un poste de radio. Marriage licence, dispense *f* de bans. Gun licence, permis de port d'armes. To take out a licence, se faire inscrire à la patente. Licence holder, patenté, -ée. *Aut:* To take out a car licence, acquitter le droit de mise en circulation. Driving licence, permis de conduire; (*in Fr.*) carte *f* rose. **2.** (a) Licence *f*. Poetic licence, licence poétique. (b) = LICENTIOUSNESS.

license ['laisəns], *v.tr.* Accorder un permis, une patente à, (qn); patenter (qn). To be licensed to sell sth., avoir l'autorisation de vendre qch. To license a play, autoriser la représentation d'une pièce. Licensed dealer, patenté. Licensed house, débit *m* de boissons. *Av:* **Licensed pilot,** pilote breveté.

licensee [laisən'si:], *s.* Patenté, -ée; détenteur *m* d'une patente ou d'un permis.

licentiate [lai'senʃiet], *s.* Licencié, -ée.

licentious [lai'senʃəs], *a.* Licencieux, dévergondé.

licentiousness [lai'senʃəsnəs], *s.* Licence *f*, dérèglement *m*, dévergondage *m.*

lichen ['laikən], *s.* Lichen *m.*

lich-gate ['litʃgeit], *s.* Porche d'entrée de cimetière surmonté d'un appentis.

licit ['lisit], *a.* Licite. **-ly,** *adv.* Licitement.

lick¹ [lik], *s.* **1.** Coup *m* de langue. *F:* **To give oneself a lick and a promise,** se faire un brin de toilette. **2.** *F:* **At full lick,** à toute vitesse.

lick². **1.** *v.tr.* Lécher. **To lick one's lips,** *F:* **one's chops,** se (pour)lécher les babines. *F:* **To lick s.o.'s boots,** lécher les bottes à qn. **To lick a recruit into shape,** dégrossir une recrue. *Travel licks a young man into shape,* les voyages façonnent un jeune homme. *The cat licked up the spilt milk,* le chat a léché, lapé, le lait répandu. **2.** *v.tr.* *F:* Battre, rosser (qn); rouler (un concurrent). *This licks me,* ça me dépasse. **3.** *v.i.* *F:* **As hard as he could lick,** à toute vitesse. **lick off,** *v.tr.* Enlever (qch.) avec la langue. **licking,** *s.* **1.** Léchement *m.* **2.** *F:* (*a*) Raclée *f*, roulée *f.* **To give s.o. a good licking,** rosser qn d'importance. (*b*) Défaite *f.* **'lick-spittle,** *s.* Parasite *m,* flagorneur *m*, sycophante *m.*

lictor ['liktər], *s.* *Rom.Ant:* Licteur *m.*

lid [lid], *s.* **1.** Couvercle *m.* *P:* **That puts the lid on it!** ça, c'est le comble! il ne manquait plus que ça! **2.** = EYELID. **3.** *Nat.Hist:* Opercule *m.*

lie¹ [lai], *s.* (*a*) Mensonge *m.* **White lie,** mensonge innocent. **It's a pack of lies!** pure invention tout cela! **To tell lies,** mentir. **To act a lie,** agir faussement. (*b*) **To give s.o. the lie** (direct), donner un démenti (formel) à qn; démentir qn.

lie², *v.i.* (lied; lied; lying) Mentir (*to s.o.,* à qn). **lying¹,** *a.* Menteur, -euse; faux, *f.* fausse; (récit) mensonger. **lying²,** *s.* Le mensonge.

lie³, *s.* **1.** Disposition *f.* *Geol:* Gisement *m* (d'une couche). **Lie of the land,** configuration *f*, disposition, du terrain. *Nau:* **To know the lie of the coast,** connaître le gisement de la côte. *Civ.E:* **Lie of the ground,** site *m.* **2.** *Golf:* Position *f*, assiette *f* (de la balle). **3.** *Ven:* Retraite *f*, gîte *m* (d'une bête).

lie⁴, *v.i.* (lay [lei]; lain [lein]; lying) **1.** (*a*) Être couché (à plat). *To lie on the ground,* être couché sur le sol. *He was lying* (*helpless*) *on the ground,* il gisait sur le sol. *To be lying ill in bed,* être alité. **To lie asleep,** être endormi. *To lie at the point of death,* être à l'article de la mort. **To lie dead,** être étendu mort. *The body was lying in state,* le corps reposait sur son lit de parade. (*On gravestone*) **Here lies . . .,** ci-gît. . . . (*b*) Être, rester, se tenir. *To lie in bed,* rester au lit. **To lie in prison,** être en prison. **To lie in ambush,** se tenir en embuscade. **To lie still,** rester tranquille. **To lie under suspicion,** être soupçonné. *Mil:* *A large force lay to the south,* une forte armée se trouvait au sud. **2.** (*Of thg*) Être, se trouver. *His clothes were lying on the ground,* ses habits gisaient par terre. *The snow lies deep,* la neige est épaisse. *To lie open,* être ouvert. *The obstacles that lie in our way,* les obstacles dont notre chemin est jonché. *Nau:* **Ship lying at her berth,** navire mouillé ou amarré à son poste. (*Of money*) **To lie at the bank,** être déposé à la banque. *The snow never lies there,* la neige n'y

séjourne jamais. *S.a.* IDLE¹ 1. **Time lies heavy on my hands,** le temps me pèse. *The onus of proof lies upon, with, them,* c'est à eux qu'incombe le soin de faire la preuve. *Town lying in a plain,* ville située dans une plaine. *His house lies on our way,* sa maison se trouve sur notre chemin. *Nau:* **The coast lies east and west,** la côte s'étend à l'est et à l'ouest. *To know how the coast lies,* connaître le gisement de la côte. *The island lies N.N.E.,* l'île gît à N.N.E. *S.a.* LAND¹ 1. **The difference lies in this, that . . .,** la différence réside en ceci que. . . . **The fault lies with you,** la faute en est à vous. **As far as in me lies,** autant qu'il m'est possible. *A vast plain lay before us,* une vaste plaine s'étendait devant nous. *F:* *A brilliant future lies before him,* un brillant avenir s'ouvre devant lui. *Road that lies between two mountains,* route qui passe entre deux montagnes. *Our road lay along the valley,* notre route longeait la vallée. **3.** *Jur:* *It was decided that the action would not lie,* l'action fut jugée non recevable. *No appeal lies against the decision,* la décision ne souffre pas d'appel. **lie about,** *v.i.* Traîner. *To leave one's papers lying about,* laisser traîner ses papiers. **lie back,** *v.i.* Se laisser retomber. **lie by,** *v.i.* *To have sth. lying by,* avoir qch. en réserve. **lie down,** *v.i.* **1.** Se coucher, s'étendre. *Lie down for a little,* reposez-vous un peu. **2.** *F:* *He took it lying down,* il n'a pas dit mot; *P:* il a filé doux. *He won't take it lying down,* il ne se laissera pas faire. **lie in,** *v.i.* Être en couches. **lying in,** *s.* Accouchement *m.* **Lying-in hospital,** maternité *f.* **lie off,** *v.i.* **1.** *Nau:* (*Of ship*) Rester au large. **2.** *Ind:* Cesser de travailler; chômer. **lie over,** *v.i.* Rester en suspens. *The motion was allowed to lie over,* la motion a été ajournée. **To let a bill lie over,** différer l'échéance d'un effet. **lie to,** *v.i.* *Nau:* Être à la cape; tenir la cape. **lie up,** *v.i.* **1.** *F:* Garder le lit. **2.** (*Of ship*) Être désarmé. **lying³,** *a.* Couché, étendu.

lief [li:f], *adv. Lit:* Volontiers. (*Used in*) **I would, had, as lief . . .,** j'aimerais autant. . . . *I would liefer have died,* j'aurais préféré mourir.

liege [li:dʒ], *a. & s. Hist:* **1.** (Vassal *m*) lige. **2. Liege lord,** suzerain *m.*

lien ['li:ən], *s. Jur:* Privilège *m* (sur un meuble). **Lien on goods,** droit *m* de rétention de marchandises.

lieu [lju:], *s.* **In lieu of . . .,** au lieu de . . .; au lieu et place de. . . . *To stand in l. of . . .,* tenir lieu de. . . .

lieutenancy [lef'tenənsi], *s.* **1.** *Hist:* Lieutenance *f.* **2.** *Mil:* Grade *m* de lieutenant.

lieutenant [lef'tenənt], *s.* Lieutenant *m.* *Navy:* Lieutenant de vaisseau. **Second lieutenant,** sous-lieutenant *m.* **lieu'tenant-colonel,** *s.* Lieutenant-colonel *m.* **lieu'tenant-commander,** *s.* *Navy:* Capitaine *m* de corvette. **lieu'tenant-'general,** *s.* Général *m* de division.

life, *pl.* **lives** [laif, laːivz], *s.* **1.** Vie *f.* **To have life,** être en vie; vivre. **To come to life,** s'animer. **It is a matter of life and death,** il y va de la vie. **Life-and-death struggle,** lutte désespérée. **To take s.o.'s life,** tuer qn. **To take one's own life,** se suicider. **To save s.o.'s life,** sauver la vie à qn. *To beg for one's l.,* demander la vie. **To sell one's life dearly,** vendre cher sa peau. *He was carrying his life in his hands,* il risquait sa vie. *Without accident to l. or limb,* sans accident personnel. **To escape with one's life,** s'en tirer la vie sauve. *Many lives were lost,* beaucoup de personnes ont péri; les morts ont été nombreuses.

To fly, run, for one's life, for dear life, s'enfuir à toutes jambes. *Run for your lives!* ṣauve qui peut! *He was rowing for dear l.*, il ramait de toutes ses forces. *F: I cannot for the life of me understand* . . ., je ne comprends absolument pas. . . . *Not on your life!* jamais de la vie! **'Pon my life!** sur ma vie! **To have as many lives as a cat,** avoir l'âme chevillée au corps. **To give life to sth.,** animer (la conversation). **To put new life into sth.,** ranimer, *F:* galvaniser (une entreprise). **He is the life and soul of the party,** c'est le boute-en-train de la compagnie. **To draw from life,** dessiner sur le vif; dessiner d'après nature. **True to life,** (roman) vécu, senti. *His acting is absolutely true to l.,* son jeu est tout à fait naturel. *S.a.* LARGE I. 1. **Animal, vegetable, life,** la vie animale, végétale. **Bird life,** les oiseaux. *The water swarms with l.,* la vie pullule dans l'eau. *Art:* **Still life,** nature morte. 2. (*a*) **Vie,** vivant *m* (de qn). **Never in (all) my life,** jamais de la vie. **At my time of life,** à mon âge. **Early life,** enfance *f.* **Tired of life,** las de vivre. *Appointed for l.,* nommé à vie. **Life annuity,** rente viagère. *Penal servitude for l.,* travaux forcés à perpétuité. **Life senator,** sénateur inamovible. (*b*) *Ins:* **To be a good life,** être bon sujet d'assurance. (*c*) Biographie *f.* (*d*) Durée *f* (d'une lampe, etc.). 3. (*a*) **To depart this life,** quitter ce monde; mourir. (*b*) **Manner of life,** manière *f* de vivre; train *m* de vie. **High life,** le grand monde; la vie mondaine. **Low life,** le petit monde. *F:* **What a life!** quel métier! **Such is life!** c'est la vie! **He has seen life,** il a beaucoup vécu. **'life-belt,** *s.* Ceinture *f* de sauvetage. **'life-blood,** *s.* (*a*) *Lit:* Sang *m* (de qn). (*b*) *F:* Ame *f* (d'une entreprise). **'life-boat,** *s. Nau:* Canot *m* de sauvetage; (*on ship*) baleinière *f* de sauvetage. **'life-buoy,** *s.* Bouée *f* de sauvetage. **'life-estate,** *s.* Propriété viagère. **'life-guard,** *s. Mil:* Garde *f* du corps. **'life-guardsman,** *s.m.* Cavalier de la Garde. **'life-interest,** *s.* Usufruit *m* (*in an estate*, d'un bien). **'life-jacket,** *s.* Brassière *f* de sauvetage. **'life-line,** *s. Nau:* (*a*) Ligne *f* de sauvetage. (*b*) (*Aboard ship*) Sauvegarde *f.* (*c*) Corde *f* de communication (de scaphandrier). **'life-preserver,** *s.* Casse-tête *m inv*; assommoir *m*; porte-respect *m inv.* **'life-saver,** *s.* (*Pers.*) Sauveteur *m.* **'life-saving,** *s.* Sauvetage *m.* **Life-saving apparatus,** engins *mpl* de sauvetage. **Life-saving rocket,** fusée *f* porte-amarre. **'life-size,** *a.* (Portrait) de grandeur naturelle; (statue) en grand.

lifeless ['laifləs], *a.* Sans vie; (i) mort; (ii) sans vigueur; (style) inanimé; (soirée) sans entrain. **lifelessness** ['laifləsnəs], *s.* (i) Absence *f* de vie; (ii) manque *m* d'animation.

lifelike ['laiflaik], *a.* (Portrait) vivant.

lifelong ['laifloŋ], *a.* (Amitié) de toute la vie.

lifetime ['laiftaim], *s.* Vie *f.* **In his lifetime,** de son vivant. *It is the labour of a l.,* c'est le travail de toute une vie.

lift¹ [lift], *s.* 1. Haussement *m*; levée *f. Abrupt l.,* levée brusque. *F:* **To give s.o. a lift,** faire monter qn avec soi (dans sa voiture). *Can I give you a l.?* voulez-vous profiter de ma voiture? *I'll give you a l. (so far),* je vais vous conduire un bout. **To get a lift up in the world,** monter un degré de l'échelle sociale. 2. **Lift of a crane,** hauteur *f* de levage d'une grue. *Hyd.E:* **Lift of a canal-lock,** (hauteur *f*) chute *f* d'un bief. 3. *Aer:* Effort sustentateur, poussée *f* (de l'avion). *L. per unit of area,* portance *f.* 4. Ascenseur *m*, lift *m.* **'Lift to all floors,'** "ascenseur

à tous les étages." **Goods lift,** monte-charge *m inv*; élévateur *m.* **Dinner lift, service lift,** monte-plats *m inv.* 5. *Rail:* Rame *f* (de wagons). **'lift-attendant, -boy, -girl, -man,** *s.* Liftier, -ière.

lift². I. *v.tr.* 1. (*a*) Lever, soulever (un poids); lever (les yeux). *The tide will l. the boat,* la marée soulèvera le bateau. **To lift one's hand against s.o.,** lever la main sur qn. **To lift s.o. up,** (i) aider qn à se relever, à se mettre sur son séant; (ii) prendre un enfant dans ses bras. **To lift up one's head,** redresser la tête. **To lift up one's hands to heaven,** lever les bras au ciel. **To lift up one's voice,** élever la voix. **To lift sth. down** (*from a shelf*), descendre qch. *She lifted the child out of bed,* elle prit l'enfant dans son lit. *He lifted the spoon to his mouth,* il porta 'a cuiller à sa bouche. (*b*) *The church lifts its spire to the skies,* l'église dresse sa flèche vers le ciel. 2. *Agr:* Lever, arracher (les pommes de terre). 3. *Cr: Golf:* Donner de l'essor à (la balle). 4. *F:* (*a*) Voler, lever (qch.). *To l. cattle,* voler du bétail. **To lift a passage from an author,** plagier un auteur. (*b*) *Sp:* Remporter (une coupe). 5. Lever (un embargo). II. **lift,** *v.i.* 1. (*Of fog*) S'élever; se dissiper. 2. (*Of vessel*) S'élever à la lame.

lifting, *s.* 1. Levage *m*, relevage *m*, soulèvement *m* (d'un poids). **Lifting power, capacity,** puissance *f* de levée (d'une grue). *Av:* **Lifting force,** force de sustentation, force ascensionnelle, force sustentatrice. 2. *F:* Vol *m* (action de dérober qch.). **'lifting-gear,** *s.* Appareil *m* de levage. **'lifting-magnet,** *s.* Aimant *m* de suspension.

lifter ['liftər], *s.* 1. (*Pers.*) (*a*) Souleveur *m.* (*b*) *F:* Voleur, -euse. 2. (*a*) *I.C.E:* Exhaust (-valve) lifter, décompresseur *m.* (*b*) *Mec.E:* Came *f,* levée *f.*

ligament ['ligəmənt], *s. Anat:* Ligament *m.*

ligature¹ ['ligətjər], *s.* 1. *Surg: Typ:* Ligature *f.* 2. *Mus:* Liaison *f.*

ligature², *v.tr.* (*a*) *Surg:* Ligaturer, barrer (une veine). (*b*) Lier.

light¹ [lait], *s.* 1. Lumière *f.* (*a*) **By the light of the sun, of the moon,** à la lumière du soleil; au clair, à la clarté, de la lune. **Artificial light,** lumière artificielle. *Seen by the l. of a star-shell,* vu à la lueur d'un obus éclairant. *Ph:* **Light wave,** onde lumineuse. (*b*) **The light of day,** jour. *The first l. of dawn,* les premières lueurs, blancheurs, de l'aube. **It is light,** il fait jour. *F:* **I was beginning to see light,** le jour se faisait dans mon esprit. (*Of thing*) **To come to light,** se découvrir. *Some curious facts have come to l.,* quelques faits curieux se sont révélés. **To bring (sth.) to light,** mettre au jour (un crime); *F:* déterrer, exhumer (des objets anciens). (*c*) Éclairage *m. This lamp gives a bad l.,* cette lampe n'éclaire pas bien. *Seated in one's own light,* assis à contre-jour. **To stand in s.o.'s light,** cacher le jour à qn. *F:* **To stand in one's own light,** ne pas se faire valoir. *I do not look upon it in that light,* ce n'est pas ainsi que j'envisage la chose. *He does not see the matter in the right l.,* il ne voit pas la question sous son vrai jour. *His action appeared in the l. of a crime,* son action avait l'apparence d'un crime. (*d*) **To throw, shed, light on sth.,** jeter le jour sur qch.; éclairer qch. **To act according to one's lights,** agir selon ses lumières. 2. (*a*) Lumière, lampe *f*, bougie *f. To put out a l.,* éteindre une lumière. **To show s.o. a light,** éclairer qn. *Bring in a l.,* apportez de la lumière. *Aut:* **Dash-board light,** éclaireur *m* de tablier. *S.a.* NAKED 2. *F:* **One of the leading lights of the party,** une des lumières, un des hommes marquants, du parti. (b) The light, the lights, la lumière, l'éclairage ; l'électricité f, le gaz. (c) Feu m, phare m. Mil : Lights out, (sonnerie f de) l'extinction f des feux. Nau : Navigation lights, feux de route. Green l., red l., feu vert, feu rouge. F : To see the red light, se rendre compte du danger. Riding lights, feux de position. To steam without lights, naviguer à feux masqués. Adm : (Traffic) lights, feux de circulation. Aut : Rear light, tail light, feu d'arrière. Charged with driving without lights, inculpé d'avoir circulé avec absence totale d'éclairage. S.a. LANDING² I. (d) = LIGHTHOUSE. The Portland light, le phare de Portland. 3. (a) Give me a light, please, voudriez-vous bien me donner du feu? S.a. STRIKE² I. 2. (b) Feu, éclat m (du regard). I caught a l. in his eye, je vis passer une lueur dans ses yeux. 4. (a) Fenêtre f ; lucarne f. Aut : Glace f. Rear light, lunette f. (b) Jur : Right of light, droit de vues (et de jours). Ancient lights, fenêtres ou ouvertures existant depuis plus de vingt ans. 5. Art : Phot : Lumière, clair m. Light effects, effets de lumière. Light and shade, les clairs et les ombres. Mus : F : Lights and shades (of expression), nuances f. 'light-bath, s. Med : Bain m photothérapique. 'light-cure, s. Med : Photothérapie f. 'light-filter, s. Phot : Écran m orthochromatique. 'light-spot, s. (Of recording apparatus) Spot lumineux.

light², v. (p.t. & p.p. lighted or lit) I. v.tr. (a) Allumer. L. a fire in my room, faites du feu dans ma chambre. Abs. To light up, (i) allumer ; mettre la lumière ; (ii) Mch : Nau : mettre les feux ; (iii) F : allumer sa pipe. (b) Éclairer, illuminer (une chambre, les rues). (c) To light the way for s.o., éclairer qn. (d) A smile lighted (up) her face, un sourire illumina son visage. 2. v.i. (a) S'allumer ; prendre feu. The match will not l., l'allumette ne prend pas. (b) S'éclairer, s'illuminer. Her face lit up, son visage s'éclaira, s'ensoleilla. F : Lit up, un peu gris ; éméché, lighting, s. I. Allumage m. 2. Éclairage m. Electric l., éclairage à l'électricité. Adm : Lighting-up time, heure f d'éclairage. Th : Lighting effects, jeux m de lumière.

light³, a. I. Clair ; (bien) éclairé. 2. (Of hair) Blond ; (of colour) clair. Light blue, bleu clair inv. 'light-coloured, a. Clair ; F : clairet.

light⁴, a. I. (a) Léger. Light as a feather, aussi léger qu'une plume. Lighter than air, de moindre densité que l'air. Lighter-than-air craft, aérostats mpl. Light soil, terre meuble. To be light on one's feet, avoir le pas léger. L. breeze, brise faible, molle. (b) Light weight, poids faible. 2. (a) L. cannon, canon de petit calibre. S.a. DRAUGHT¹ I. 5, RAILWAY I. (b) To travel light, voyager avec peu de bagages. Rail : Light engine, locomotive haut-le-pied. (c) To be a light sleeper, avoir le sommeil léger. 3. (a) Light punishment, peine légère. (b) Light task, tâche facile ; travail peu fatigant. 4. Light comedy, comédie légère. Light reading, lecture(s) amusante(s). L. talk, propos frivoles. F : To make light of sth., traiter qch. à la légère To make l. of dangers, mépriser les dangers. 5. adv. To sleep light, avoir le sommeil léger. S.a. COME I (a). -ly, adv. I. Lightly clad, vêtu légèrement, à la légère. To walk, step, l., (i) marcher d'un pas léger ; (ii) étouffer son pas. To touch lightly on a delicate matter, couler sur un point délicat. His hand ran l. over the strings (of the harp), sa main effleura les cordes. His responsibilities sit lightly upon him, ses responsabilités ne lui pèsent

pas. 2. To get off lightly, s'en tirer à bon compte. 3. To speak lightly of sth., parler de qch. à la légère. light-'fingered, a. I. Aux doigts agiles. 2. The light-fingered gentry, messieurs les pickpockets ; les voleurs à la tire. light-'footed, a. Agile, leste ; au pied léger. light-'headed, a. I. To be light-headed, avoir le délire. 2. Étourdi, écervelé. light-'hearted, a. Au cœur léger ; allègre. -ly, adv. Gaiement ; de gaîté de cœur. light-'minded, a. Léger, étourdi, frivole. 'light-o'-love, s. A. & Lit : Femme légère. He is with his l.-o'-l., il est avec sa mie. 'light-weight. I. s. Box : Poids léger. 2. Attrib. Léger.

light⁵, v.i. (p.t. & p.p. lit or lighted) (a) (Of bird) S'abattre, se poser, (of thg) s'abattre, tomber. (b) To light on one's feet, tomber debout ; retomber sur ses pieds. (c) To light (up)on sth., rencontrer qch. ; trouver qch. par hasard. To light upon an interesting fact, tomber sur un fait intéressant.

lighten¹ [laitn]. I. v.tr. Alléger (un navire) ; réduire le poids de (qch.). To l. s.o.'s sorrow, alléger, soulager, une douleur. 2. v.i. My heart lightened, mon cœur fut soulagé. lightening, s. Allégement m.

lighten². I. v.tr. (a) Éclairer (le visage). (b) Éclaircir (une couleur). 2. v.i. (a) S'éclairer, s'illuminer. His eyes lightened (up), son regard s'éclaira. (b) It lightens, il fait des éclairs.

lighter¹ ['laitər], s. Nau : Allège f, pén che f, chaland m.

lighter², s. I. (Pers.) Allumeur-euse. 2. (Device) Allumeur, allumoir m (de becs de gaz). Petrol-lighter, briquet m à essence.

lighterage ['laitəredʒ], s. Nau : I. Déchargement m par allèges ; transport m par chalands. 2. Droits mpl ou frais mpl de chaland(s), d'allège.

lighterman, pl. -men ['laitərmən, -men], s.m. Nau : Gabarier, batelier.

lighthouse ['laithaus], s. Nau : Phare m. 'lighthouse-keeper, s. Gardien m de phare.

lightness ['laitnəs], s. Légèreté f.

lightning ['laitniŋ], s. Éclairs mpl, foudre f. A flash of lightning, un éclair. The l. has struck . . ., la foudre est tombée sur. . . . Struck by lightning, frappé de, par, la foudre. As quick as lightning, with lightning speed, F : like greased lightning, aussi vite que l'éclair. F : Lightning progress, progrès foudroyants. I.C.E. : Lightning pick-up, reprise foudroyante. 'lightning-ar'rester, s. Parafoudre m. 'lightning-con'ductor, s. I. Conducteur m de paratonnerre. 2. Paratonnerre m. 'lightning-rod, s. Tige f de paratonnerre ; paratonnerre m.

lights [laits], s.pl. Cu : Mou m (de veau).

lightship ['laitʃip], s. Nau : Bateau-feu m.

lightsome ['laitsəm], a. Poet : I. Léger, gracieux. 2. Au cœur léger, gai.

ligneous ['lignəs], a. Ligneux.

lignite ['lignait], s. Miner : Lignite m.

lignum vitae ['lignəm 'vaiti:], s. Bot : (Bois m de) gaïac m.

like¹ [laik]. I. a. Semblable, pareil, tel. I. (a) On this and the like subjects, sur ce sujet et les sujets similaires. Two plants of l. species, deux plantes de même espèce. Prov : Like master, like man, tel maître tel valet. Alg : Like terms, termes semblables. (b) The portrait is very like, le portrait est très ressemblant. They are as like as two peas, ils se ressemblent comme deux gouttes d'eau, à s'y méprendre. 2. (a) I want to find one l. it, je veux trouver le pareil, la pareille

A critic l. you, un critique tel que vous. *Pe1:* **Fellows like you,** des gens de votre sorte. *He is rather l. you,* il a de votre air. *Whom is he like? F: who is he like?* à qui ressemble-t-il? *What is he like?* comment est-il? *He was like a father to me,* il m'a servi de père. **Old people are like that,** les vieilles gens sont ainsi faits. **I never saw anything like it,** je n'ai jamais rien vu de pareil. **The sum amounts to something like ten pounds,** la somme s'élève à quelque dix livres. *That's something l. rain!* voilà qui s'appelle pleuvoir! **That's something like!** à la bonne heure! *There is nothing l. health,* rien de tel que la santé. *She is nothing like so pretty as you,* elle est bien loin d'être aussi jolie que vous. *S.a.* FEEL² 3, LOOK² 3. *(b)* **That's just like a woman!** voilà bien les femmes! *That's l. his impudence!* voilà bien son toupet! **Just like 'you!** tout comme vous! **3.** *A: He is l. to die,* il est en cas de mourir. **II. like,** *prep.* Comme. *I think l. you,* je pense comme vous. *Just l. anybody else,* tout comme un autre. *F: He ran like anything,* **like blazes,** **like the (very) devil, like mad,** il courait comme un dératé. *Don't talk l. that,* ne parlez pas comme ça, de la sorte. *He stood there l. a statue,* il se tenait debout telle une statue **To hate s.o. like poison,** haïr qn à l'égal de la peste. **III. like,** *adv.* **I.** *F:* **Like enough, very like;** (as) **like as not,** probablement, vraisemblablement. **2.** *(Incorrect use =as)* *I cannot knit like mother does,* je ne sais pas tricoter comme (le fait) ma mère. **IV. like,** *s.* Semblable *mf;* pareil, -eille. *We shall never look upon his like again,* nous ne reverrons plus son semblable, son pareil. *P: It is too good for the likes of me,* c'est trop bon pour des personnes comme moi. *I never heard the like (of it),* je n'ai jamais entendu chose pareille. **To do the like,** en faire autant; faire de même. **like²,** *s.* *(Usu. pl.)* Goût *m,* préférence *f.* **Likes and dislikes,** sympathies *f* et antipathies *f.* **like³,** *v.tr.* **I.** Aimer (qch.); avoir de la sympathie pour (qn). *I l. him,* je l'aime bien; il me plaît. *Do you l. him?* vous plaît-il? *I came to l. him,* il me devint sympathique. *I don't l. his looks,* son visage ne me revient pas. *How do you l. him?* comment le trouvez-vous? *I should l. time to consider it,* j'aimerais avoir le temps d'y réfléchir. **As much as ever you like,** tant que vous voudrez; *F:* en veux-tu en voilà. *Your father won't l. it,* votre père ne sera pas content. *Whether he likes it or not,* qu'il le veuille ou non; bon gré, mal gré. *These plants don't l. damp,* ces plantes craignent l'humidité. *F: I like your impudence!* vous êtes bon! **I like that!** en voilà une bonne! par exemple! **2.** *(a)* *I l. to see them,* j'aime à les voir. *I l. to be obeyed,* j'aime qu'on m'obéisse. *Your going out so often isn't liked,* on trouve à redire à ce que vous sortiez si souvent. *Would you l. to smoke?* voulez-vous fumer? *I should l. to be able to help you,* je souhaiterais (de) pouvoir vous aider. *I should like to have been there,* j'aurais aimé m'y trouver. *(b)* **As you like,** comme vous voudrez. **I can do as I like with him,** je fais de lui ce que je veux. *He is free to act as he likes,* il est libre d'agir à sa guise, comme il lui plaira. *To do just as one likes,* en faire à sa tête. **When I like,** quand je veux. *When you l.,* quand il vous plaira. *He thinks he can do anything he likes,* il se croit tout permis. **People may say what they like . . .,** on a beau dire. . . . **liking,** *s.* Goût *m,* penchant *m.* *To one's liking,* à souhait. *Is it to your l.?* cela est-il à votre gré *m?* *His l. for me,* son penchant pour moi. **To have a liking for s.o.,** se sentir de l'attrait

pour qn; affectionner qn. *I have taken a l. to it,* j'y ai pris goût. *I have taken a l. to him,* il m'est devenu sympathique. **likeable** ['laikəbl], *a.* Agréable, sympathique. **likelihood** ['laiklihud], *s.* Vraisemblance *f,* probabilité *f.* *There is little l. of his succeeding,* il y a peu de chances qu'il réussisse. **In all likelihood,** selon toute probabilité; vraisemblablement. **likely** ['laikli]. **I.** *a.* **I.** Vraisemblable, probable. *F: That's a l. story!* en voilà une bonne! *It is very l.,* c'est très probable. *He is not l. to betray you,* ce n'est pas un homme à vous trahir. *He is hardly l. to succeed,* il a peu de chances de réussir. **2.** *Incident l. to lead to a rupture,* incident susceptible d'entraîner une rupture. *This plan is most l. to succeed,* ce projet offre le plus de chances de succès. **The likeliest place for camping,** l'endroit le plus propre au camping. *The most l. candidates,* les candidats qui ont le plus de chances. **3.** *(a)* *A fine l. girl,* un beau brin de fille. *(b)* **A likely young man,** un jeune homme qui promet beaucoup. **II. likely,** *adv.* **Most likely, very likely,** vraisemblablement; très probablement. **As likely as not . . .,** (pour) autant que je sache. . . . *He will succeed as l. as not,* il se pourrait bien qu'il réussisse. *P: Not likely!* plus souvent! pas de danger! **liken** [laikn], *v.tr.* *Lit:* Comparer, assimiler (*to, with,* à. avec). **likeness** ['laiknəs], *s.* **I.** Ressemblance *f* (*to,* à). *Close l.,* ressemblance étroite. **2.** Apparence *f.* **3.** Portrait *m,* image *f.* **The picture is a good likeness,** le portrait est très ressemblant. **likewise** ['laikwaiz], *adv.* **I.** De plus, également, aussi. **2.** **To do likewise,** faire de même; en faire autant. **lilac** ['lailək]. **I.** *s.* Lilas *m.* **2.** *a.* Lilas *inv.* **liliaceae** [lili'eisii], *s.pl.* *Bot:* Liliacées *f.* **Lilliputian** [lili'pju:ʃən], *a. & s.* Lilliputien, -ienne. **lilt¹** [lilt], *s.* **I.** Chant (joyeux). **2.** Rythme *m,* cadence *f* (des vers). **lilt²,** *v.tr. & i.* Chanter mélodieusement, gaiement. **lily** ['lili], *s.* *Bot:* **I.** Lis *m.* *Lily hand,* main blanche comme le lis. *S.a.* GILD, ORANGE-LILY, TIGER-LILY, WATER-LILY. **2.** **Lily of the valley,** muguet *m.* **'lily-white,** *a.* Blanc, *f.* blanche, comme le lis; d'une blancheur de lis. **limb¹** [lim], *s.* **I.** Membre *m.* **To tear an animal limb from limb,** mettre un animal en pièces. *S.a.* LIFE I. **2.** *(a)* **Limb of Satan,** suppôt *m* de Satan. *(b)* *F:* Enfant *m* terrible; polisson *m.* **3.** (Grosse) branche (d'un arbre); bras *m* (d'une croix). **limb²,** *s.* *Astr: Bot: Mth:* Limbe *m,* bord *m.* **-limbed** [limd], *a.* **Large-limbed, strong-limbed,** membru; bien membré. **limber¹** ['limbər], *s.* *Artil:* Avant-train *m.* **limber²,** *v.tr.* *Artil:* Atteler à l'avant-train. *Abs.* **To limber up,** mettre l'avant-train. **limber³,** *a.* Souple, agile. **limbo** ['limbo], *s.* **I.** *Theol:* Les limbes *m.* *F:* **To descend into limbo,** tomber dans l'oubli. **2.** *F:* In limbo, en prison. **lime¹** [laim], *s.* **I.** = BIRD-LIME. **2.** Chaux *f.* *Slaked lime,* chaux éteinte. *S.a.* QUICKLIME. **'lime-burner,** *s.* Chaufournier *m,* chaulier *m.* **'lime-kiln,** *s.* Four à chaux. **'lime-pit,** *s.* Carrière *f* de pierre à chaux. **'lime-twig,** *s.* Gluau *m,* pipeau *m.* **'lime-water,** *s.* Eau *f* de chaux.

lime², *v.tr.* **1.** Gluer (des ramilles). *To l. birds,* prendre des oiseaux à la glu. **2.** *Agr:* Chauler (un terrain).

lime³, *s. Bot:* Lime *f.* **Sweet lime,** limette *f.* **Sour lime,** limon *m.* **'lime-juice,** *s.* Jus *m* de limon.

lime⁴, *s.* Lime(-tree), tilleul *m.*

limelight ['laimlait], *s.* Lumière *f* oxhydrique. *F:* **In the limelight,** sous les feux de la rampe; très en vue.

limerick ['limərik], *s.* Poème *m* en cinq vers, toujours comique et absurde, aux rimes a a b b a.

limestone ['laimstoun], *s. Miner:* Pierre *f* à chaux. *Geol:* Calcaire *m.* **Hard limestone,** liais *m.*

limit¹ ['limit], *s.* **1.** Limite *f,* borne *f. Within a three-mile l.,* dans un rayon de trois milles. *It is true within limits,* c'est vrai dans une certaine limite. *Without limit,* sans bornes. **Age limit,** limite d'âge. *F:* **That's the limit!** ça c'est le comble! ça c'est par trop fort! **He's the limit!** il est étonnant! il est impayable! **2.** *Mec.E:* Tolérance *f.* **Limit gauge,** calibre *m* de tolérance.

limit², *v.tr.* Limiter, borner, restreindre. **To limit oneself to . . .,** se borner à. . . . *Limited intelligence,* intelligence bornée. *People of limited views,* gens bornés dans leurs vues. *Publ:* **Limited edition,** édition à tirage restreint. *S.a.* COMPANY¹ **4. Limiting clause,** article limitatif.

limitation [limi'tei∫(ə)n], *s.* **1.** Limitation *f,* restriction *f.* **2.** He has his limitations, ses connaissances, ses capacités, sont bornées. **3.** *Jur:* Prescription (extinctive). **Time limitation** (*in a suit*), péremption *f.*

limitless ['limitləs], *a.* Sans bornes; illimité.

limitrophe ['limitrouf], *a.* Limitrophe (*to,* de).

limousine ['limuzi:n], *s. Aut:* Limousine *f.*

limp¹ [limp], *s.* Boitement *m,* clochement *m,* claudication *f.* **To walk with a limp,** boiter.

limp², *v.i.* Boiter, clocher, clopiner. **To limp along,** aller clopin-clopant. **limping,** *a.* Boiteux.

limp³, *a.* Mou, *f.* molle, flasque. *Bookb:* **Limp binding,** cartonnage *m* souple. *F:* **To feel as limp as a rag,** se sentir mou comme une chiffe. **-ly,** *adv.* **1.** Mollement, flasquement. **2.** Sans énergie.

limpet ['limpet], *s. Moll:* Patelle *f.*

limpid ['limpid], *a.* Limpide, clair.

limpidity [lim'piditi], *s.* Limpidité *f,* clarté *f.*

limpness ['limpnəs], *s.* Mollesse *f.*

linaria [lai'neəria], *s. Bot:* Muflier bâtard; linaire *f.*

linchpin ['lin∫pin], *s. Veh:* Esse *f;* clavette *f* de bout d'essieu.

linden(-tree) ['lindən(-tri:)], *s.* Tilleul *m.*

line¹ [lain], *s.* **1.** (*a*) *Nau: etc:* Ligne *f,* corde *f.* **Heaving-line,** passeresse *f,* touline *f.* (*b*) Ligne (de pêche). *To give a fish plenty of l.,* donner de la ligne à un poisson. (*c*) *Tg: Tp:* Ligne, fil *m. S.a.* HOLD² I. **3.** (*d*) *Const: Surv:* Cordeau *m.* **Laid out by rule and line,** tiré au cordeau. (*e*) *F:* **It's hard lines,** c'est dur; c'est de la mauvaise chance. *It's hard lines on you,* c'est bien malheureux pour vous. **Hard lines!** pas de chance! **2. Electric l.,** canalisation *f* électrique. **3.** (*a*) Ligne, trait *m,* raie *f.* **To draw a line,** tirer, tracer, une ligne. **Straight line,** ligne droite. **Broken line,** trait discontinu. *S.a* SIDE¹ 6, TOE² 2. (*b*) *Ph:* **Lines of the spectrum,** spectrum lines, raies noires du spectre. *The lines on his forehead,* les rides *f* de son front. (*c*) *Geog:* **The line,** la Ligne (équatoriale); l'équateur *m.* (*d*) *Ph:* **Line of force,** ligne de force. (*e*) *Art:* **Picture hung on the line,** tableau pendu sur la cimaise. (*f*) *U.S:* **To give s.o. a line on sth.,**

tuyauter qn sur qch. (*g*) **Ligne** (de l'horizon); contours *mpl* (du rivage). *The hard lines of his face,* ses traits durs. *N.Arch:* **Lines of a ship,** formes *f* d'un navire. **Clean lines,** formes fines. *Art:* **Boldness of line,** fermeté *f* des lignes. *The general lines of a party's policy,* les directives *f* politiques d'un parti. **To be working on the right lines,** être en bonne voie. (*h*) **Ligne** de démarcation. *F:* **One must draw the line somewhere,** il y a limite à tout. **I draw the line at . . .,** je ne vais pas jusqu'à (mentir, etc.), jusqu'au (mensonge, etc.). **4.** (*a*) **Ligne,** rangée *f* (de personnes, d'objets). *Const:* **To project beyond the building l.,** dépasser l'alignement. **To stand in a line,** se tenir en ligne, alignés. **March in line,** marche de front. *F:* **I must try to fall into line with your ideas,** je vais essayer de me conformer à vos idées. **To fall out of line,** se désaligner. (*b*) **File** *f;* queue *f.* **Ten carriages in a l.,** dix voitures à la file. **Line of moving traffic,** colonne *f* de véhicules en marche. **To stand in a line,** (i) se tenir à la file; (ii) faire queue. (*c*) *Mil: Nau:* **Line of battle,** ligne de bataille. **The front lines,** le front. **The back lines,** l'arrière *m. Navy:* **Ship of the line,** vaisseau de ligne. (*d*) *First l. of a paragraph,* alinéa *m.* (*In dictating*) **'Next line,'** "à la ligne." *F:* **To drop s.o. a line,** envoyer un (petit) mot à qn. **Line of poetry,** vers *m. F:* **Marriage lines,** acte *m* de mariage. **5.** **Ligne,** compagnie *f* (de paquebots, etc.). **Shipping line,** messageries *f* maritimes. **6.** Ligne de descendants. **In direct line,** en ligne directe. **7.** *Rail:* **Voie** *f,* ligne. **Up line,** voie descendante, paire. **Down line,** voie montante, impaire. **8. L. of thought,** suite *f* d'idées. **L. of argument,** raisonnement *m. The l. to be taken,** la conduite à tenir. **9.** (*a*) Genre *m* d'affaires; métier *m.* **What is his line (of business)?** quel est son genre d'affaires? *F:* **That's not in my line,** ce n'est pas (de) mon métier; ce n'est pas de mon ressort. *That's more in his l.,* c'est plus dans son genre. (*b*) *Com:* **Line of goods,** série *f* d'articles; article *m.* **Leading line,** article de réclame. *F: A rice pudding or something in that line,* du riz au lait ou quelque chose dans ce genre-là. **'line drawing,** *s.* Dessin *m* au trait. **'line engraving,** *s.* Gravure *f* au trait. **'line-fishing,** *s.* Pêche *f* à la ligne. **'line-space,** *s. Typ: Typewr:* Entre-ligne *m,* interligne *m.* **'line-spacer,** *s. Typewr:* Levier *m* d'interligne.

line², *v.tr.* **1.** Ligner, régler (une feuille de papier). (*Of face*) **To become lined,** se rider. **2.** *To l. a walk with poplars,* border une allée de peupliers. *The troops lined the streets,* les troupes formaient la haie. **line up. 1.** *v.tr.* Aligner. **2.** *v.i.* S'aligner. **To line up for the theatre,** faire queue devant le guichet (du théâtre).

line³, *v.tr.* **1.** Doubler (un vêtement) (*with,* de). **2.** Garnir à l'intérieur (*with,* de). *A membrane lines the stomach,* une membrane tapisse l'estomac. *Nest lined with moss,* nid garni de mousse. *Walls lined with wooden panelling,* murs revêtus de boiseries. *S.a.* POCKET¹ I. **lined,** *a.* (Habit) doublé; (gant) fourré. **Felt-lined,** garni de feutre. *F:* **Well-lined purse,** bourse bien garnie.

lining, *s.* **1.** Doublage *m,* garnissage *m.* **2.** (*a*) Doublure *f* (de robe); coiffe *f* (de chapeau). (*b*) Garniture *f,* fourrure *f* (de frein); chemise *f* (de fourneau).

lineage ['liniedʒ], *s.* Lignée *f,* lignage *m. Person of high l.,* personne de haut parage.

lineal ['liniəl], *a.* Linéal, -aux. **Lineal descendant,** descendant en ligne directe.

lineament ['liniəmənt], s. Trait m, linéament m.
linear ['liniər], a. Linéaire.
lineman, pl. **-men** ['lainmən, -men], s.m.
1. Rail: Garde-ligne. 2. Tg: Tp: Poseur de lignes.
linen ['linən], s. 1. Toile f (de lin). L. sheets, draps en toile de fil. Linen trade, commerce des toiles. Linen warehouse, magasin m de blanc. 2. Linge m, lingerie f. Table linen, body linen, linge de table, de corps. A piece of linen, a linen rag, un linge. F: Don't wash your dirty l. in public, il faut laver son linge sale en famille. **'linen-draper**, s. Marchand de blanc, de nouveautés. **'linen-press**, s. Armoire f à linge. **'linen-room**, s. Lingerie f.
linenette [linə'net], s. Tex: Lustrine f.
liner ['lainər], s. Nau: (Ocean) liner, paquebot m. Atlantic l., transatlantique m.
linesman, pl. **-men** ['lainzmən, -men], s.m.
1. = LINEMAN. 2. Fb: Ten: Arbitre de lignes; Fb: arbitre de touche.
ling[1] [liŋ], s. Ich: Morue longue.
ling[2], s. Bot: Bruyère commune.
linger ['liŋgər], v.i. (a) Tarder, s'attarder. To l. behind the others, traîner derrière les autres. To linger over a meal, s'attarder sur un repas. A doubt still lingered in his mind, un doute subsistait encore dans son esprit. (b) (Of invalid) To linger (on), languir, traîner. **lingering**, a. 1. Lingering look, regard prolongé. L. doubt, doute qui subsiste encore. 2. Lingering death, mort lente. **'lingerer** ['liŋgərər], s. Traînard m; retardataire mf.
lingerie [lɛʒ'riː], s. Lingerie f (pour femmes).
lingo ['liŋgo], s. (pl. lingoes ['liŋgouz]) F: (i) La langue du pays; (ii) baragouin m, jargon m.
lingua franca ['liŋgwa'fraŋka], s. Sabir m.
lingual ['liŋgwəl], a. Lingual, -aux.
linguiform ['liŋgwifɔːrm], a. Linguiforme.
linguist ['liŋgwist], s. Linguiste mf.
linguistic [liŋ'gwistik], a. Linguistique.
linguistics [liŋ'gwistiks], s.pl. Linguistique f.
liniment ['linimənt], s. Liniment m.
link[1] [liŋk], s. 1. (a) Chaînon m, maillon m, anneau m (d'une chaîne). (b) Sleeve-links, cuff-links, boutons (de manchettes) jumelés, à chaînettes. 2. Mec.E: Tige f d'assemblage. 3. Lien m, trait m d'union (between, entre). Missing link, (i) lacune f; (ii) Biol: forme intermédiaire disparue; F: (le) pithécanthrope. **'link-lever**, s. Mch: Levier m de changement de marche. **'link-pin**, s. Goujon m de chaîne.
link[2]. 1. v.tr. Enchaîner, (re)lier, attacher (with, to, à). Line that links (up) two towns, ligne (de chemin de fer) qui relie deux villes. F: To be linked for life to s.o., être uni à qn pour la vie. To link arms, se donner le bras. 2. v.i. To link on to sth., s'attacher, s'unir, à qch.
link[3], s. A: Torche f, flambeau m. **'link-boy**, s.m. Porte-flambeau m inv.
linkman, pl. **-men** ['liŋkmən, -men], s.m.
1. A: = LINK-BOY. 2. Th: Cin: Commissionnaire.
links [liŋks], s.pl. Scot: (a) Coteaux mpl sablonneux. (b) Terrain m de golf.
linnet ['linet], s. Orn: Linotte f, linot m. Green linnet, verdier m.
lino ['laino], s. F: 1. = LINOLEUM. 2. = LINOTYPE.
linoleum [li'nouljəm], s. Linoléum incrusté.
linotype ['lainotaip], s. Typ: Linotype f.
linseed ['linsiːd], s. Graine f de lin. Linseed meal, farine f de lin.

lint [lint], s. Med: Charpie anglaise; lint m. Boracic lint, lint boriqué.
lintel [lintl], s. Linteau m, sommier m (de porte ou de fenêtre). Arch: Lintel course, plate-bande f.
lion ['laiən], s. 1. (a) Lion m. Lion's cub, lion's whelp, lionceau m. F: The lion's share, la part du lion; la part léonine. (b) Mountain lion, puma m, couguar m. 2. F: Personnage marquant; lion. To make a lion of s.o., faire une célébrité de qn. 3. The Gulf of Lions, le golfe du Lion. **'lion-hearted**, a. Au cœur de lion.
lioness ['laiənes], s.f. Lionne.
lionize ['laiənaiz], v.tr. F: Faire une célébrité de (qn).
lip [lip], s. 1. (a) Lèvre f; babine f (d'un animal). Lower lip, lèvre inférieure. Upper lip, lèvre supérieure. F: To keep a stiff upper lip, ne pas se laisser abattre; faire bonne contenance. A cigar between his lips, un cigare aux lèvres. With parted lips, les lèvres entr'ouvertes. To bite one's lip(s), se mordre les lèvres. To smack one's lips over sth., se lécher les babines. He never opened his lips, il n'a pas desserré les dents. No complaint ever passes his lips, jamais il ne se plaint. Lip consonant, consonne labiale; labiale f. (b) F: Insolence f. None of your lip! en voilà assez! (c) Lèvre (d'une plaie). 2. (a) Bord m, rebord m (d'une tasse). (b) Pouring lip, bec m (de vase, d'éprouvette). (c) Rebord, saillie f. **'lip-deep**, a. (Sentiment) peu profond; peu sincère. **'lip-read**, v.i. (Of the deaf) Lire sur les lèvres. **'lip-reading**, s. Lecture f sur les lèvres. **'lip-service**, s. To pay lip-service to s.o., rendre à qn des hommages peu sincères.
lipped [lipt], a. 1. Thin-lipped, aux lèvres minces. 2. (Tuyau) à rebord; (cruche) à bec.
lipsalve ['lipsaːv], s. Pommade f pour les lèvres.
lipstick ['lipstik], s. Toil: Bâton m de rouge; F: raisin m.
liquefaction [likwi'fakʃ(ə)n], s. Liquéfaction f.
liquefiable ['likwifaiəbl], a. Liquéfiable.
liquefy ['likwifai]. 1. v.tr. Liquéfier. 2. v.i. (a) (Of gas) Se liquéfier. (b) (Of oil) Se défiger.
liqueur [li'kjuər], s. Liqueur f (de dessert). Liqueur brandy, fine champagne; F: fine f.
liquid ['likwid]. 1. a. (a) Liquide. To reduce sth. to a l. state, liquéfier qch. (b) (Œil) limpide. (c) (Son) doux. (d) Fin: Liquid assets, valeurs f disponibles. (e) Ling: (Consonne) liquide. 2. s. Liquide m. Liquid measure, mesure de capacité pour les liquides.
liquidate ['likwideit], v.tr. Com: Liquider (une société, une dette).
liquidation [likwi'deiʃ(ə)n], s. Com: Liquidation f. To go into liquidation, entrer en liquidation.
liquidator ['likwideitər], s. Liquidateur m.
liquor ['likər], s. 1. Boisson f alcoolique. Spirituous liquors, spiritueux m. F: To be in liquor, the worse for liquor, être ivre; être pris de boisson. 2. ['laikwɔːr] Ch: Pharm: Solution f, liqueur f.
liquorice ['likəris], s. Réglisse f.
Lisbon ['lizbən]. Pr.n. Geog: Lisbonne f.
lisle [lail], s. Lisle thread, fil m d'Écosse.
lisp[1] [lisp], s. Zézaiement m, blèsement m. To speak with a lisp, zézayer.
lisp[2], v.i. & tr. Zézayer; être blèse; F: zozoter.
lisping, a. Blèse. F: L. stream, ruisseau m susurrant.
lissom(e) ['lisəm], a. Souple, agile, leste.
list[1] [list], s. 1. Tex: Lisière f. List slippers,

chaussons *m* de lisière. **2.** *pl.* *A :* Lists, lice *f*; champ clos. *F :* To enter the lists, entrer en lice (contre qn) ; descendre dans l'arène *f*.

list², *s.* Liste *f*, rôle *m*, tableau *m*, état *m*. **Alphabetical list**, répertoire *m* alphabétique. **List of names**, état nominatif. **Wine list**, carte *f* des vins. (*In hospitals*) **To be on the danger list**, être dans un état grave. *F : Person on the black list*, personne notée ; suspect *m*. *St.Exch :* Official list, cote officielle. *S.a.* ACTIVE 4, HONOUR¹ 4.

list³. 1. *v.tr.* Cataloguer (des articles). **2.** *v.i.* *A :* = ENLIST 2.

list⁴, *s.* *Nau :* Faux bord ; bande *f*, gîte *f*. **To have, take, a list**, donner de la bande ; prendre de la gîte.

list⁵, *v.i.* *Nau :* Donner de la bande ; avoir un faux bord ; prendre de la gîte.

list⁶, *v.tr.* *A :* (*3rd pers. sg., pr.t.* list *or* listeth ; *p.t.* list *or* listed) (*a*) *Impers.* Plaire ; sembler bon. *He did as him list*, il a fait comme il lui a plu. (*b*) *Ye who list to hear*, vous qui voulez entendre.

list⁷, *v.* *A. & Poet :* = LISTEN.

listel ['list(ə)l], *s.* *Arch :* Listel *m*, *pl.* listeaux.

listen [lisn], *v.ind.tr.* **1.** Écouter. **To listen to sth.**, écouter qch. *To l. attentively to s.o.*, prêter une oreille attentive à qn. **2.** Faire attention ; écouter. *He would not l.* (*to us*), il a refusé de nous entendre. **listen in**, *v.i.* **1.** *Tg : Tp :* Capter un message. **2.** *W.Tel :* Se mettre à l'écoute ; faire l'écoute. **listening**, *s.* Écoute *f*. *Mil : Tp :* **Listening-post**, poste *m* d'écoute ; écoute *f*.

listener ['lisnər], *s.* (*a*) (i) Auditeur, -trice ; (ii) (*usu. Pej.*) écouteur, -euse. *He is a good l.*, il sait écouter. *Prov :* Listeners never hear good of themselves, qui écoute aux portes entend plus qu'il ne désire. (*b*) *Mil :* Écouteur.

listless ['listləs], *a.* Nonchalant, distrait ; apathique. **-ly**, *adv.* Nonchalamment.

listlessness ['listləsnəs], *s.* Nonchalance *f*, apathie *f* ; indifférence *f*.

lit [lit]. *See* LIGHT².

litany ['litəni], *s.* *Ecc :* Litanies *fpl*.

literal ['litərəl], *a.* **1.** (*a*) Littéral, -aux. *In the literal sense of the word*, au sens propre du mot. *To take sth. in a l. sense*, prendre qch. au pied de la lettre. (*b*) (*Of pers.*) Positif ; sans imagination. **2.** (*a*) *Alg :* (Coefficient) littéral. (*b*) *Typ :* **Literal error**, *s.* literal, coquille *f*. **-ally**, *adv.* Littéralement. *To take an article l.*, interpréter un article à la lettre. *Literally speaking . . .*, à proprement parler. . . .

literary ['litərəri], *a.* Littéraire. **Literary man**, homme *m* de lettres ; littérateur *m*.

literate ['litərət], *a.* (*a*) Qui sait lire et écrire. (*b*) Lettré.

literature ['litərətjər], *s.* **1.** Littérature *f*. (*a*) La carrière des lettres. (*b*) Œuvres *f* littéraires. *Light l.*, lectures amusantes. **2.** (*a*) *The l. of a subject*, les écrits traitant d'un sujet. (*b*) Prospectus *mpl*, brochures *fpl*.

litharge ['li'θɑːrdʒ], *s.* Litharge *f*.

lithe [laːið], *a.* Souple, agile.

litheness ['laiðnəs], *s.* Souplesse *f* ; agilité *f*.

lithium ['liθiəm], *s.* *Ch :* Lithium *m*.

lithograph¹ ['liθəgraf, -grɑːf], *s.* Lithographie *f* ; image lithographiée.

lithograph², *v.tr.* Lithographier.

lithographer [li'θɔgrəfər], *s.* Lithographe *m*.

lithographic [liθo'grafik], *a.* Lithographique.

lithography [li'θɔgrəfi], *s.* Lithographie *f* ; procédés *m* lithographiques.

lithotomy [li'θɔtəmi], *s.* *Surg :* Lithotomie *f*.

Lithuania [liθju'einjə]. *Pr.n.* La Lithuanie.

Lithuanian [liθju'einjən], *a. & s.* Lithuanien, -ienne.

litigant ['litigənt], *s.* Plaideur, -euse.

litigate ['litigeit], *v.i.* Plaider ; être en procès.

litigation [liti'geiʃ(ə)n], *s.* Litige *m*.

litigious [li'tidʒəs], *a.* **1.** (Cas) litigieux, contentieux. **2.** (Homme) litigieux, processif, procédurier.

litmus ['litməs], *s.* Tournesol *m*.

litotes ['laitotiːz], *s.* *Rh :* Litote *f*.

litre ['liːtər], *s.* *Meas :* Litre *m*.

litter¹ ['litər], *s.* **1.**(*a*) *Veh :* Litière *f*. (*b*) Civière *f* (pour le transport des blessés). **2.** *Husb :* (*a*) Litière (de paille). (*b*) Fumier *m* (d'écurie). **3.** (*a*) Papiers *m* et objets *m* malpropres (qui jonchent les rues). (*b*) Fouillis *m*, désordre *m*. **4.** Portée *f*, mise-bas *f* (d'un animal).

litter², *v.tr.* **1.** Mettre en désordre (une chambre). *Room littered with books*, chambre où des livres traînent partout. *Table littered over with papers*, table encombrée de papiers. **2.** (*Of animals*) Avoir une portée.

little [litl]. **I.** *a.* (*Comp. and sup.* **less, least**, smaller, smallest) **1.** Petit. *L. boy*, petit garçon ; garçonnet *m*. *L. girl*, petite fille ; fillette *f*. **Little ones**, (i) enfants *m*, *F :* mioches *m* ; (ii) petits *m* (d'une bête). **The little people**, les fées *f*. *The poor l. fellow, the poor l. girl*, le pauvre petit ; la pauvre petite. (*To child*) **Come here, my little man**, viens ici, mon petit. *F :* A tiny little house, une toute petite maison. *Wait a l. while!* attendez un petit moment ! **The little finger**, le petit doigt. **2.** Peu (de). **Little money**, peu d'argent. **A little money**, un peu d'argent. *She knows l. music*, elle sait quelque peu de musique. **Ever so little**, un tout petit peu (de). *I took ever so l. of it*, j'en ai pris moins que rien. **Be it ever so little**, si peu que ce soit. **3.** (Esprit) mesquin. **II. little**, *s.* (*Comp. and sup.* **less, least**) **1.** Peu *m*. **To eat little or nothing**, manger peu ou point. *He knows very l.*, il sait peu de chose. **I had little to do with it**, j'y ai été pour peu de chose. *I see very l. of him*, je ne le vois guère. **To think little of sth.**, faire peu de cas de qch. **Little by little**, petit à petit ; peu à peu. *Prov :* Every little helps, tout fait nombre. **2.** A little. (*a*) A little more, encore un peu. *A l. makes us laugh*, un rien nous fait rire. **For a little** (while), pendant un certain temps. (*b*) *He helped him a l.*, il l'a aidé un peu. *I was a l. afraid*, j'avais un peu peur. **III. little**, *adv.* Peu. *L. more than an hour ago*, il n'y a guère qu'une heure.

littleness ['litlnəs], *s.* Petitesse *f*.

littoral ['litorəl], *s.* Littoral *m*.

liturgic(al) [li'təːrdʒik(əl)], *a.* Liturgique.

liturgy ['litərdʒi], *s.* Liturgie *f*.

live¹ [laiv], *a.* **1.** (*a*) Vivant ; en vie. *F :* A real live burglar, un cambrioleur en chair et en os. (*b*) Live coals, charbons ardents. **2.** (*a*) **Live cartridge**, cartouche chargée. (*b*) *El.E :* Live wire, fil en charge ; fil sous tension. *F :* He's a (real) live wire, il est très entreprenant ; il a de l'allant. **3.** *Tchn :* Live weight, poids utile. **'live-'bait**, *s.* *Fish :* Amorce vive. *To fish with l.-b.*, pêcher au vif. **'live-'oak**, *s.* *Bot : U.S :* Chêne vert. **'live-stock**, *s.* *Husb :* Bétail *m*, bestiaux *mpl*. *Jur :* Cheptel *m*.

live² [liv]. **1.** *v.i.* Vivre. (*a*) *Is he still living?* vit-il encore ? *While my father lives, lived*, du vivant de mon père. **Long live the king!** vive e roi ! *He hasn't a year to l.*, *F :* il n'en a pas pour un an. **He will live to be a hundred**, il atteindra la centaine. **As long as I live**, tant que je vivrai. **He cannot live through the winter**, il ne passera pas l'hiver. *Prov:* **Live and learn,** (i) on apprend à tout âge ; (ii) qui vivra verra. **Live and let live,** il faut que tout le monde vive. (*b*) Durer. **His name will live,** son nom vivra, durera. (*c*) *To l.* on *vegetables,* se nourrir de légumes. *F :* **To live on hope,** vivre d'espérance. *He earns, gets, enough to l. upon,* il gagne de quoi vivre. **To live on one's capital,** manger son capital. *He lives by his pen,* il vit de sa plume. (*d*) *To l. honestly,* vivre honnêtement. **To live in style,** mener grand train. **To live well,** faire bonne chère. *To l. up to one's reputation,* faire honneur à sa réputation. (*e*) **Where do you live?** où demeurez-vous? *To l.* (*out*) *in the country,* demeurer à, habiter, la campagne. *I l. at number 36, Wilson Street,* je demeure rue Wilson, numéro 36. **House not fit to live in,** maison inhabitable. (*f*) *He is living with his grandparents,* il habite chez ses grands-parents. **2.** *v.tr.* (*a*) **To live a happy life,** mener, passer, une vie heureuse. (*b*) *Th :* **To live a part,** entrer dans la peau d'un personnage. **live down,** *v.tr.* **To live down a scandal,** faire oublier un scandale à la longue. **live in,** *v.i.* *The employees l. in,* les employés sont logés et nourris. **live on,** *v.i.* Continuer à vivre. **living¹,** *a.* Vivant, vif ; en vie. *A l. man,* un homme vivant. *While he was l.,* de son vivant. **Living or dead,** mort ou vif. **Not a living soul is to be seen,** on ne rencontre pas âme qui vive. **No living man could do better,** personne au monde ne pourrait mieux faire. *s.* **The living,** les vivants. **He is still in the land of the living,** il est toujours vivant, encore de ce monde. **A living death,** une vie pire que la mort. **living²,** *s.* **1.** Vie *f.* **Style of living,** train *m* de vie. **Standard of living,** niveau *m* de vie. **To be fond of good living,** aimer la bonne chère. **2.** **To earn one's living,** gagner sa vie. **To work for one's living,** travailler pour vivre. **To make a living,** gagner de quoi vivre. **3.** *Ecc:* Bénéfice *m,* cure *f.* **'living-room,** *s.* Salle familiale ; salle commune. **'living-'wage,** *s.* Salaire vital ; salaire de base.

-lived [livd], *a.* Tough-lived, à la vie dure. *S.a.* LONG-LIVED, SHORT-LIVED.

livelihood ['laivlihud], *s.* Vie *f ;* moyens *mpl* d'existence ; gagne-pain *m.* **To make a livelihood,** gagner sa vie.

liveliness ['laivlinəs], *s.* Vivacité *f,* animation *f,* entrain *m,* vie *f.*

livelong ['livlɔŋ, 'laiv-], *a.* **The livelong day,** toute la (sainte) journée ; tout le long du jour.

lively ['laivli], *a.* **1.** (*Lifelike*) *To give a l.* idea of *sth.,* exposer qch. d'une manière vivante. **2.** (*a*) Vif, animé ; plein d'entrain. **Lively imagination,** imagination vive. *L. conversation,* conversation animée. (*b*) *F :* **Things are getting l.,** ça chauffe. **To have a lively time of it,** en voir de toutes les couleurs. (*c*) **To take a lively interest in sth.,** s'intéresser vivement à qch. **3.** **As lively as a cricket,** plein d'entrain.

liven [laivn]. **1.** *v.tr.* **To liven** (*up*), animer. **2.** *v.i.* **To liven up,** s'animer.

liver¹ ['livər], *s.* *Anat:* Foie *m.* *F :* **To have a liver,** (i) être malade du foie ; (ii) être de mauvaise humeur.

liver², *s.* Personne *f* qui vit (de telle ou telle façon). **Loose liver, evil liver,** libertin *m,* dissolu *m,* débauché *m.*

liveried ['livərid], *a.* En livrée.

liverish ['livəriʃ], *a.* *F :* Qui a le foie dérangé.

liverwort ['livərwəːrt], *s.* *Bot:* Hépatique *f.*

livery ['livəri], *s.* **1.** (*a*) Livrée *f.* (*b*) **Livery company,** corporation *f* d'un corps de métier.

2. **To take, keep, horses at livery,** prendre, avoir, des chevaux en pension. **'livery-horse,** *s.* Cheval de louage. **'livery-stable,** *s.* Écuries *fpl* de (chevaux de) louage. **Livery-stable keeper,** loueur *m* de chevaux ; remiseur *m.*

lives laːivz]. *See* LIFE.

livid ['livid], *a.* (Teint) livide, blême ; (ciel) plombé. **To become livid with anger,** devenir blême de colère.

lividity [li'viditi], *s.* Lividité *f.*

Livy ['livi]. *Pr.n.m.* Tite-Live.

lixiviate [lik'sivieit], *v.tr.* Lixivier, lessiver.

lizard ['lizərd], *s.* Lézard *m.*

Lizzie, Lizzy ['lizi]. *Pr.n.f.* Lisette.

llama ['laːma], *s.* *Z :* Lama *m.*

Lloyd's [lɔidz], *s.* *Nau :* = Le (Bureau) Véritas. **Lloyd's list** = le Véritas.

lo [lou], *int.* *A.* & *Lit :* Voyez, voilà (que . . .).

loach [loutʃ], *s.* *Ich :* Loche *f ;* petit barbot.

load¹ [loud], *s.* **1.** (*a*) Fardeau *m ;* *Lit :* faix *m.* (*b*) **Load of a waggon,** charge *f* d'un wagon. (*c* Charretée *f* (de gravier, etc.). **2.** *Mec.E:* Charge. **Load per unit area,** taux *m* de charge. **3.** Charge (d'une arme à feu). **4.** **To have a load on one's mind,** avoir un fardeau, un poids, sur l'esprit. *That's a load off my mind!* quel soulagement ! **5.** *pl.* *F :* **Loads of . . .,** des tas *m,* des quantités *f,* de. . .

load². **1.** *v.tr.* (*a*) Charger (une voiture). **To load s.o. with sth.,** charger qn de qch. *F :* **To be loaded up with . . .,** être encombré de. . . . (*b*) **To load s.o. with favours,** combler qn de faveurs. *Loaded with cares,* accablé de soucis. (*c*) **To load a gun with ball-cartridge,** charger un fusil à balle. *Aut:* **To load the grease-gun,** armer le graisseur. **2.** *v.i.* (*Of ship*) **To load** (*up*), prendre charge ; faire la cargaison. **loaded,** *a.* **1.** (Wagon, etc.) chargé. **2.** **Loaded cane,** canne plombée. **Loaded dice,** dés pipés. **loading,** *s.* Chargement *m.* *Nau:* **Loading in bulk,** chargement en vrac.

loadstone ['loudstoun], *s.* Aimant naturel ; pierre *f* d'aimant.

loaf¹, *pl.* **loaves** [louf, louvz], *s.* Pain *m ;* miche *f* (de pain). **Cottage loaf,** pain de ménage. *Prov :* **Half a loaf is better than no bread,** faute de grives on mange des merles. **loaf-'sugar,** *s.* Sucre *m* en pains.

loaf², *v.i.* **To loaf** (*about*), flâner, fainéanter.

loafing, *s.* Flânerie *f,* fainéantise *f.*

loafer ['loufər], *s.* Flâneur *m ;* *F :* baguenaudier *m.* **Young loafer,** voyou *m.*

loam [loum], *s.* **1.** *Agr:* Terre grasse, végétale. **2.** *Metall:* Glaise *f ;* potée *f.* **3.** Torchis *m,* pisé *m.*

loan¹ [loun], *s.* **1.** Prêt *m ;* avance *f* (de fonds). **Short loan,** prêt à court terme. **Loan without security,** prêt à fonds perdu. **Loan bank,** caisse *f* de prêts. **2.** Emprunt *m.* *May I have the l. of . . .?* puis-je vous emprunter . . . ? *Fin:* **To raise a loan,** contracter un emprunt. **'loan-society,** *s.* Établissement *m* de crédit. **'loan-word,** *s.* *Ling:* Mot emprunté (à une autre langue).

loan², *v.tr.* *U.S:* Prêter.

loath [louθ], *a.* **To be loath to do sth.,** répugner à faire qch. ; faire qch. à contre-cœur. **To be loath for s.o. to do sth.,** ne pas vouloir que qn fasse qch. *He did it nothing loath.* il l'a fait très volontiers.

loathe [louð], *v.tr.* Détester, exécrer, *F :* abominer. *I l. doing it,* il me répugne de le faire. *He loathes being praised,* il abhorre qu'on lui fasse des éloges. **loathing,** s. Dégoût m, répugnance (for, pour).

loathsome ['louðsəm], a. Repoussant, écœurant, dégoûtant, répugnant. **-ly,** adv. D'une manière repoussante.

loaves. See LOAF¹.

lob¹ [lɔb], s. **1.** Cr: Balle lente bôlée en dessous. **2.** Ten: Chandelle f.

lob², v.tr. (a) Cr: Bôler (la balle) en dessous. (b) Ten: Lober (la balle); abs. lober.

lobate ['loubeit], a. Nat.Hist: Lobé, lobaire.

lobby ['lɔbi], s. (a) Vestibule m; promenoir m (d'un tribunal). (b) Parl: **The lobby of the House,** la salle des pas perdus. **The division lobbies,** les vestibules.

lobe [loub], s. Arch:- Nat.Hist: Lobe m.

lobed [loubd], a. Nat.Hist: Lobé.

lobelia [lo'bi:lja], s. Bot: Lobélie f.

lobscouse ['lɔbskaus], s. Nau: Ratatouille f, ragoût m.

lobster ['lɔbstər], s. Homard m. **Spiny lobster,** langouste f. **Norway lobster,** langoustine f. **'lobster-pot,** s. Casier m à homards.

lobule ['lɔbjuːl], s. Physiol: Lobule m.

lob-worm ['lɔbwəːrm], s. F: Ver m des pêcheurs; ver rouge.

local ['louk(ə)l], a. (a) Local, régional; de la localité. **Local authorities,** autorités locales. **Local railway,** chemin de fer d'intérêt local. **Local road,** route vicinale. **Local government,** administration décentralisée. (b) (On addresses) 'Local,' en ville, "E.V." (c) **Local remedy,** remède topique, local; topique m. **-ally,** adv. Localement. Staff engaged l., personnel engagé sur place. He is well known l., il est bien connu dans la région.

locale [lou'kaːl], s. Scène f, théâtre m (des événements).

locality [lo'kaliti], s. **1.** F: **To have the bump of locality,** avoir la bosse de l'orientation. **2.** Localité f. (a) Région f (d'une faune). (b) Endroit m, voisinage m. In this l., F: dans ces parages.

localize ['loukəlaiz], v.tr. Localiser (une épidémie, etc.).

locate [lo'keit], v.tr. **1.** Localiser (qch.); établir la situation de (qch.); découvrir, repérer (le siège du mal). El: **To locate a fault,** repérer, localiser, un dérangement. **2. To be located in a place,** être situé dans un endroit. **locating,** s. Détermination f (d'une fuite de gaz, etc.). Artil: etc: Repérage m (d'une batterie, etc.).

location [lo'keiʃ(ə)n], s. **1.** = LOCATING. **2.** (a) Établissement m (de qn) dans un lieu. (b) Situation f, emplacement m. **3.** (S. Africa) Réserve f indigène.

locative ['lɔkətiv], a. & s. Gram: Locatif (m). **In the locative,** au locatif.

loch [lɔx], s. Scot: **1.** Lac m. **2.** Sea loch, bras m de mer.

lock¹ [lɔk], s. **1.** (a) Mèche f, boucle f (de cheveux). (b) pl. His scanty **looks,** ses rares cheveux. **2.** Flocon m (de laine).

lock², s. **1.** Serrure f, fermeture f. **Double lock,** serrure à double tour. **Double-sided lock,** serrure bénarde. **To pick a lock,** crocheter une serrure. **Under lock and key,** sous clef; F: (of pers.) sous les verrous. **2.** (a) Enrayure f (de roue). (b) Verrouillage m; verrou m, -ous. Rail: **Lock and block system,** système m à bloc enclenché. **3.** Platine f (de fusil). F: **Lock, stock, and barrel,** tout sans exception. **4.** Wr: Étreinte f, clef f. **5.** Aut: (Steering) **lock,** angle m de braquage. **6.** Hyd.E: Écluse f. To pass a barge through a l.,

écluser, sasser, un chaland. **'lock-'gate,** s. Porte f d'écluse. **'lock-jaw,** s. Med: (i) Trisme m; (ii) F: tétanos m. **'lock-keeper,** s. Gardien m d'écluse; éclusier m. **'lock-nut,** s. = CHECK-NUT. **'lock-stitch,** s. Point m de navette (d'une machine à coudre); point indécousable; ¡ oint noué.

lock³. I. v.tr. **1.** (a) Fermer à clef; donner un tour de clef à (la porte). The door locks on the inside, la serrure joue à l'intérieur. (b) To lock s.o. in a room, enfermer qn dans une chambre. **2.** (a) Enrayer, caler (les roues); enclencher (les pièces d'un mécanisme); Sm.a: verrouiller (la culasse). Wheel rigidly locked with another, roue solidaire d'une autre. (b) (Of pers.) To be locked (together) in a struggle, être engagés corps à corps dans une lutte. To be locked in each other's arms, se tenir étroitement embrassés. (c) To lock one's teeth, serrer les dents. **3.** Hyd.E: To lock a boat, écluser, sasser, un bateau. II. lock, v.i. (a) (Of wheels, etc.) S'enrayer, se bloquer. (b) (Of machine parts) S'enclencher. **lock in,** v.tr. Enfermer (qn) à clef; mettre (qn) sous clef. **lock out,** v.tr. (a) Mettre (qn) dans l'impossibilité de rentrer (en fermant la porte à clef). (b) Ind: Fermer les ateliers contre (le personnel); lock-outer (le personnel). **'lock-out,** s. Ind: Lock-out m inv. **lock up,** v.tr. **1.** (a) Mettre, serrer, (qch.) sous clef; enfermer (qch.). (b) To lock s.o. up, enfermer qn; écrouer qn au dépôt. (c) To lock up a house, fermer une maison à clef. (d) Typ: To lock up the forms, serrer les formes. **2.** Fin: Immobiliser, bloquer, engager (des capitaux). **lock-'up,** s. **1.** Hangar m, etc., fermant à clef. **Look-up in a garage,** box m. Attrib. **Lock-up shop,** desk, magasin, pupitre, fermant à clef. **2.** F: Poste m de police. **locking,** s. **1.** Fermeture f à clef. **2.** Mec.E: Immobilisation f, verrouillage m; blocage m, enclenchement m; enrayement m (des roues). **3.** Hyd.E: Éclusage m, sassement m (d'un bateau).

locker ['lɔkər], s. **1.** Armoire f ou coffre m (fermant à clef). **2.** Nau: (a) Caisson m, coffre. (b) Soute f. S.a. SHOT² 1.

locket ['lɔket], s. Médaillon m (porté en parure).

locksmith ['lɔksmiθ], s. Serrurier m.

locomotion [louko'mouʃ(ə)n], s. Locomotion f.

locomotive ['loukəmoutiv, louko'moutiv]. **1.** a. Locomotif, locomobile. **2.** s. Locomotive f.

locum-tenens ['loukəm'tiːnenz], s. Remplaçant, -ante; suppléant, -ante (d'un médecin). **To act as locum-tenens for a doctor,** faire l'intérim d'un médecin.

locus, pl. **loci** ['loukəs, 'lousai], s. Geom: Lieu m géométrique.

locust ['loukəst], s. **1.** Grande sauterelle d'Orient; locuste f. **2.** Bot: Locust(-bean), caroube f. **'locust-tree,** s. Bot: **1.** Caroubier m. **2.** Robinier m; faux acacia.

locution [lo'kjuːʃ(ə)n], s. Locut on f.

lode [loud], s. Min: Filon m, veine f; gisement m.

lodestar ['loudstaːr], s. **1.** The lodestar, l'étoile f polaire. **2.** F: Point m de mire de (attention).

lodestone ['loudstoun], s. = LOADSTONE.

lodge¹ ['lɔdʒ], s. **1.** (a) Loge f (de concierge, etc.). (b) Keeper's lodge, maison f de garde-chasse. **(Gate-)lodge,** pavillon m d'entrée d'une propriété. **2.** Shooting lodge, pavillon de chasse. **3.** Loge, atelier m (des francs-maçons). **'lodge-keeper,** s. Concierge m.

lodge². I. v.tr. **1.** Loger (qn dans un endroit); avoir (qn) comme locataire (en garni). **To be**

lodged in a place, loger, être logé, dans un endroit. **2.** (*a*) To **lodge money with** s.o., consigner, déposer, remettre, de l'argent chez qn. (*b*) To **lodge a bullet on the target,** loger une balle dans la cible. (*c*) To **lodge a complaint,** porter plainte (*against,* contre). *S.a.* APPEAL¹ I. **II. lodge,** *v.i.* **I.** (*Of pers.*) (Se) loger (quelque part). To **lodge with** s.o., (i) demeurer chez qn (comme locataire en garni); (ii) être en pension chez qn. **2.** (*Of .hg*) Rester, se loger. *The bullet has lodged in the lung,* la balle s'est logée dans le poumon.
lodging, *s.* **I.** (*a*) Hébergement *m.* (*b*) Dépôt *m,* consignation *f* (d'argent, etc.). **2.** A **night's lodging,** le logement pour la nuit. *S.a.* BOARD¹ 2. **3.** (*Often in pl.*) Logement, logis *m,* appartement meublé. To **let lodgings,** louer des chambres, des appartements. To **let furnished lodgings,** louer en garni. To **live, be, in** (furnished) **lodgings,** loger, habiter, en garni, en hôtel meublé. To **take lodgings,** louer un appartement meublé; louer une chambre, des chambres. **'lodging-house,** *s.* **I.** Hôtel garni; maison meublée. **2.** Common lodging-house, dépôt *m* de mendicité. *L.-h. keeper,* logeur, -euse, à la nuit.
odger ['lɔdʒər], *s.* Locataire *mf* (en meublé) ou pensionnaire *mf* (à la semaine, au mois). To **take** (in) **lodgers,** tenir un meublé; prendre des pensionnaires.
oft¹ [lɔft], *s.* **I.** Grenier *m,* soupente *f.* **2.** (*a*) Pigeonnier *m,* colombier *m.* (*b*) A loft of pigeons, un vol de pigeons. **3.** Galerie *f,* tribune *f* (dans une église, etc.). **4.** *Ind:* Atelier *m.* *N.Arch:* Drawing loft, salle *f* de gabarits.
oft², *v.tr.* Golf: Donner de la hauteur à (la balle).
oftiness ['lɔftinəs], *s.* **I.** Hauteur *f,* élévation *f* (d'une salle). **2.** Hauteur; ton hautain. **3.** (*a*) Élévation (des sentiments). (*b*) Sublimité *f,* élévation (du style).
ofty ['lɔfti], *a.* **I.** Haut, élevé. **2.** (*a*) (*Of pers.*) Hautain, altier. (*b*) (Air) condescendant, protecteur. **3.** (*a*) Lofty soul, âme élevée, de haut vol, (*b*) (*Of style*) Élevé, relevé, sublime, soutenu. **-ily,** *adv.* **I.** (Situé) en haut. **2.** Fièrement, altièrement.
og¹ [lɔg], *s.* **I.** Grosse bûche; tronçon *m* de bois. Chopping log, billot *m.* *F:* To **stand like a log,** rester (là) comme une souche. To **fall like a log,** tomber comme une masse. A King Log, un roi Soliveau, un roi Solive. **2.** *Nau:* Loch *m.* **3.** *Nau:* = LOG-BOOK I. *Mil:* Log of a listening-post, journal *m* d'écoute. **'log-book,** *s.* **I.** *Nau:* (*a*) Livre *m* de loch. (*b*) Ship's log-(book), (i) (*at sea*) journal *m* de navigation; (ii) (*in harbour*) journal de bord. **2.** (*a*) *Aut: etc:* Carnet *m* de route. (*b*) *Av:* Livre de vol. (*c*) *Ind:* Journal de travail (d'une machine); registre *m.* *W.Tel:* Carnet d'écoute. **'log-'cabin, -'house, -'hut,** *s.* Cabane *f* de bois. **'log-jam,** *s.* Embâcle *m* de bûches. **'log-line,** *s.* *Nau:* Ligne *f* de loch. **'log-rolling,** *s.* *U.S:* (*a*) Alliance *f* politique dans un but intéressé. (*b*) Battage *m* littéraire, camaraderie *f* littéraire.
og², *v.tr.* **I.** (*a*) *Nau:* Porter (un fait) au journal. (*b*) *Ind:* Noter (des résultats, etc.) sur le regis re. **2.** *W.Tel:* Repérer, étalonner (une station).
•g³, *s.* *Mth:* = LOGARITHM.
•ganberry ['lougənberi], *s.* Ronce-framboise *f, pl.* ronces-framboises.
•gan(-stone) ['lougən(stoun)], *s.* Rocher branlant.

logarithm ['lɔgəriθm], *s.* Logarithme *m.*
logarithmic [lɔgə'riθmik], *a.* **I.** Logarithmique. **2.** Logarithmic table, table *f* des logarithmes.
loggerhead ['lɔgərhed], *s.* To **be at loggerheads with** s.o., être en bisbille, en désaccord, en brouille, avec qn. To **come to loggerheads with** s.o., entrer en conflit, en collision, avec qn. To **set people at loggerheads,** mettre a discorde, semer la dissension, entre les gens; brouiller les gens.
loggia ['lɔdʒ,a], *s.* Arch: Loge *f,* loggia *f.*
logic ['lɔdʒik], *s.* Logique *f.* **'logic-chopper,** *s.* *F:* Ergoteur, -euse.
logical ['lɔdʒik(ə)l], *a.* **I.** Logique. **2.** (*Of pers.*) Qui a de la logique; qui a de la suite dans les idées. **-ally,** *adv.* Logiquement.
logician [lo'dʒiʃən], *s.* Logicien, -ienne.
logwood ['lɔgwud], *s.* Bois *m* de Campêche.
loin [lɔin], *s.* **I.** *pl.* Loins, reins *m.* *Anat:* Lombes *m.* To **gird up one's loins,** se ceindre les reins. **2.** *Cu:* Filet *m* (de mouton, de veau); longe *f* (de veau); aloyau *m* et faux-filet (de bœuf). **loin-'chop,** *s.* Côtelette *f* de filet. **'loin-cloth,** *s.* Bande-culotte *f, pl.* bandesculottes; pagne *m.*
loiter ['lɔitər], *v.i.* **I.** Flâner, traîner. To **loiter on the way,** s'attarder en route; s'amuser en chemin. **2.** *Jur:* Rôder (d'une manière suspecte).
loitering¹, *a.* Flâneur, -euse; traînard.
loitering², *s.* **I.** Flânerie *f.* **2.** Vagabondage délictueux.
loiterer ['lɔitərər], *s.* **I.** Flâneur, -euse. **2.** Rôdeur *m.*
loll [lɔl]. **I.** *v.tr.* (*Of dog*) To **loll out its tongue,** laisser pendre la langue. **2.** *v.i.* (*a*) (*Of tongue*) To **loll out,** pendre. (*b*) (*Of pers.*) Être étendu (*F:* comme un veau). To **loll (back) in an armchair,** se renverser nonchalamment dans un fauteuil. (*c*) To **loll about,** flâner, fainéanter.
lollipop ['lɔlipɔp], *s.* Sucrerie *f;* sucre *m* d'orge. Lollipops, bonbons *m.*
Lombardy ['lʌmbərdi]. *Pr.n.* La Lombardie.
London ['lʌndən]. *Pr.n.* Londres. **'London 'pride,** *s.* *Bot:* Désespoir *m* des peintres.
Londoner ['lʌndənər], *s.* Londonien, -ienne; habitant, -ante, de Londres.
lone [loun], *a.* **I.** Solitaire, seul. **2.** To **play a lone hand,** (i) (*at cards*) faire la chouette; (ii) *F:* agir tout seul. **3.** *F:* I'm a poor l. woman, je suis un pauvre femme livrée à ses propres ressources.
loneliness ['lounlinəs], *s.* **I.** Solitude *f,* solement *m.* **2.** Sentiment *m* d'abandon.
lonely ['lounli], *a.* Solitaire, isolé. To **feel very l.,** se sentir bien seul.
lonesome ['lounsəm], *a.* *F:* Solitaire, seul.
long¹ [lɔŋ]. **I.** *a.* Long, *f.* longue. **I.** To **be six feet long,** avoir six pieds de long, de longueur; être long de six pieds. How long is the table? quelle est la longueur de la table? de quelle longueur est la table? To **make sth. longer,** allonger, rallonger, qch. To **take the longest way round,** prendre par le plus long. The best by a long way, de beaucoup le meilleur. Two long miles, deux bons milles. To **pull a long face,** avoir la mine longue; faire une tête. He pulled a l. face, il a fait la grimace; son visage s'allongea. Face as long as a fiddle, figure longue d'une aune, figure d'enterrement. To **have a long tongue,** être trop porté à bavarder. To be long in the arm, avoir les bras longs. **2.** (*In time*) How long are the holidays? quelle est la durée des vacances? **The long vacation,** les grandes vacances. **The days are getting longer,** les jours croissent. It

will take a long time, cela prendra longtemps ; ce sera long. **They are a long time, a long while,** (in) **coming,** ils se font attendre. **It is a long time since I saw him.** il y a longtemps que je ne l'ai vu. **A long time ago,** il y a (bien) longtemps. *It will be a l. time before the agitation dies down,* l'agitation n'est pas près de se calmer. **To wait for a long time,** attendre ongtemps. *For a l. time he was thought to be dead,* pendant longtemps on le crut mort. **For a long time past** *he had been contemplating this step,* depuis longtemps il méditait cette démarche. **It will not happen for a long time,** cela ne se fera pas de longtemps. **Three days at the longest,** trois jours (tout) au plus. *Mil: Navy:* **Long service men,** engagés à long terme. **3.** **Long price,** grand prix, prix élevé. **Long bill,** grand compte. **Long purse,** bourse bien garnie. *Com:* **Long hundred,** grand cent, cent vingt. **4.** **Long-stemmed,** longicaule. **Long-leaved,** longifolié. **II. long,** *s.* **I.** (*a*) *He knows the long and the short of the matter,* il sait le fort et le fin de l'affaire. *The l. and the short of it is that . . .,* en un mot comme en mille. . . . (*b*) *Pros:* **Longs and shorts,** longues *f* et brèves. (*c*) *Sch:* *F:* **The long,** les grandes vacances. **2. Before long, ere long,** avant peu ; sous peu. **For long,** pendant longtemps. **I haven't long to live,** je n'ai pas longtemps à vivre. **It will not take long,** cela ne prendra pas longtemps. **I had only long enough to . . .,** je n'ai eu que le temps nécessaire pour. . . . **III. long,** *adv.* **I.** (*a*) Longtemps. *Have you been here l.?* y a-t-il longtemps que vous êtes ici? *He has been gone ever so long,* il y a beau temps qu'il est parti. **Long live the King!** vive le roi ! **Stay as long as you like,** restez aussi longtemps que vous voudrez. **As long, so long, as I live,** tant que je vivrai. *You may do as you like so l. as you leave me alone,* faites tout ce que vous voudrez pourvu que vous me laissiez tranquille. **To be long (in) doing sth.,** être longtemps à faire qch. ; tarder à faire qch. **He was not long in, about, over, setting up a ladder,** il eut bientôt fait de dresser une échelle. **You aren't long about it,** vous allez vite en besogne. **He won't be long,** il ne tardera pas. **Now we shan't be long!** (i) nous n'en avons plus pour longtemps ; (ii) *F:* voilà qui va bien ! **It will be long before we see his like,** de longtemps on ne verra son pareil. **It is long since I saw him,** il y a longtemps que je ne l'ai vu. *F:* **So long!** au revoir, à bientôt ! (*b*) Depuis longtemps. **I have long been expecting him,** je l'attends depuis longtemps. (*c*) **How long? combien de temps?** *How l. have you been here?* depuis combien de temps êtes-vous ici? depuis quand êtes-vous ici? *How l. will it be until . . .?* combien de temps faudra-t-il pour que . . .? *How l. does your leave last?* quelle est la durée de votre congé? **2. Long before, after,** longtemps avant, après. **Not long before, after,** peu de temps avant, après. *He died long since,* **long ago,** il est mort depuis longtemps. *He died not long ago,* il n'y a pas longtemps qu'il est mort ; il est mort depuis peu. **3. All day long,** tout le long du jour ; pendant toute la journée. *His life long,* toute sa vie durant. **4.** *I could no longer see him,* je ne pouvais plus le voir. *I could not wait* **any longer,** je ne pouvais pas attendre plus longtemps. **How much longer** *will it last?* combien (de temps) cela durera-t-il encore? **5. Long extended line,** ligne fort étendue. **Long felt want,** besoin senti depuis longtemps. **'long-a'go. I.** *a.* D'autrefois, de jadis. **2.** *s.* Le temps jadis. **In the days of long-ago,** autrefois ; au temps jadis. **'long-'armed,** *a.*

Au(x) bras long(s). **'long-boat,** *s. Nau:* Grand canot ; chaloupe *f.* **'long-bow,** *s. Archeol:* Arc *m* d'homme d'armes. *F:* **To draw the long-bow,** exagérer, hâbler. **'long-'clothes,** *s.pl.* Maillot anglais (de nouveau-né). **'long-'dated,** *a. Fin:* A longue échéance. **'long-'distance,** *attrib.a.* (Téléphonie, etc.) à longue distance. *Sp:* **Long-distance runner,** coureur *m* de fond. **'long-'drawn(-'out),** *a.* Long-drawn(-out) sigh, long soupir ; soupir prolongé. **'long-hand,** *s.* Écriture ordinaire, courante. **'long-'headed,** *a.* **I.** A (la) tête allongée ; dolicho-céphale. **2.** Perspicace, avisé. **'long-'legged,** *a.* A longues jambes ; (*of bird*) à longues pattes. **'long-'lived,** *a.* (*a*) Qui a la vie longue ; *Nat.Hist:* vivace. (*b*) *L.-l.* error, erreur persistante, vivace. **'long-'lost,** *a.* Perdu depuis longtemps. **'long-'sighted,** *a.* **I.** Presbyte. **2.** Prévoyant. **'long-'standing,** *attrib.a.* Ancien ; de longue date. **'long-'suffering. I.** *s.* (*a*) Patience *f*, endurance *f.* (*b*) Longanimité *f*, indulgence *f.* **2.** *a.* (*a*) Patient, endurant. (*b*) Longanime, indulgent. **'long-'tailed,** *a.* A longue queue ; longicaude. **'long-'winded,** *a.* **I.** (Histoire) de longue haleine, interminable. **2.** (*Of speaker*) Verbeux, intarissable.

long², *v.i.* To long for sth., désirer qch. fortement, ardemment ; avoir grande envie de qch. ; soupirer pour, après, qch. **To long for home,** avoir la nostalgie du foyer. **To long to do sth.,** avoir bien envie de faire qch. ; être impatient de faire qch. ; brûler, rêver, de faire qch. **longing¹,** *a.* Qui désire ardemment, qui attend impatiemment. **-ly,** *adv.* Avec envie. *To look l. at sth.,* couver qch. des yeux. **longing²,** *s.* Désir ardent, grande envie (*for, after,* de).

longanimity [lɔŋgə'nimiti], *s. Lit:* Longanimité *f.*

longevity [lɔn'dʒeviti], *s.* Longévité *f.*

longish ['lɔŋ(g)iʃ], *a.* Assez long, plutôt long.

longitude ['lɔndʒitjuːd], *s.* Longitude *f.* *In* longitude 20°, par 20° de longitude. *In the l. of . . .,* sous, par, la longitude de. . . .

longitudinal [lɔndʒi'tjuːdinəl], *a.* Longitudinal -aux ; en long. **Longitudinal beam, girder** longrine *f*, longeron *m.*

longshoreman, *pl.* **-men** ['lɔŋʃɔːrmən, -men] *s.m. Nau:* Homme qui travaille dans le port débardeur.

longways ['lɔŋweiz], **longwise** ['lɔŋwaiz], *adv* En long, en longueur.

loofah ['luːfa], *s. Toil:* Loofa(h) *m* ; épong végétale.

look¹ [luk], *s.* **I.** Regard *m.* **To have a look a** sth., jeter un coup d'œil sur qch. ; regarder qch **To take a good look at s.o.,** (i) scruter qn d regard ; (ii) dévisager qn. **To have, take, a loo** round the town, faire un tour de ville. **2.** (*a*) A pect *m*, air *m*, apparence *f* (de qn, de qch.) mine *f* (de qn). *By her l. one can see that . . .* à sa mine on voit que. . . . **To judge by looks** juger d'après les apparences. **I don't like hi looks,** the look of him, sa figure ne me revien pas. **I don't like the look of the thing,** cela m paraît louche ; cela ne me dit rien de bon. B **the look(s) of it,** d'après l'apparence. **The portra** has a look of your mother, le portrait ressemble u peu à votre mère. (*b*) *pl.* (Good) **looks,** belle min bonne mine, beauté *f.*

look², *v.i. & tr.* **I.** *v.i.* Regarder. (*a*) **To loo** through, out of, *the window,* regarder par fenêtre. **To look in at the window,** regarder à fenêtre. **To look down a list,** parcourir une lis

To look the other way, (i) regarder de l'autre côté; (ii) détourner les yeux. To look in s.o.'s face, (i) regarder qn; (ii) dévisager qn. (b) Look (and see) what time it is, regardez quelle heure il est; *F:* regardez voir quelle heure il est. (c) *I had looked to find a stern master,* je m'attendais à trouver un maître sévère. (d) Which way does the house look? quelle est l'exposition de la maison? 2. *v.tr.* (a) To look s.o. (full, straight) in the face, in the eyes, regarder qn dans le blanc des yeux; dévisager qn. *I can never l. him in the face again,* je me sentirai toujours honteux devant lui. To look s.o. up and down, regarder qn de haut en bas; mesurer qn des yeux; toiser qn. (b) *He looked a query at me,* il me lança un regard interrogateur. To look one's last on sth., jeter un dernier regard sur qch. 3. *Pred.* Avoir l'air, paraître, sembler. To look happy, avoir l'air heureux, avoir la mine heureuse. *She looks tired,* elle a l'air bien fatigué(e). He looks young for his age, il porte bien son âge. She looks her age, elle paraît son âge. To look ill, avoir l'air malade; avoir mauvaise mine. To look well, (i) (*of pers.*) avoir bonne mine, bon visage; (ii) (*of thg*) faire bien; faire bon effet. *It doesn't l. well,* (i) cela manque de cachet; (ii) (*of conduct, etc.*) cela fait mauvais effet. Things are looking bad, black, nasty, ugly, les choses prennent une mauvaise tournure, une mauvaise allure. How did he look? quel air avait-il? quelle mine a-t-il faite? How does my hat look? quel effet fait mon chapeau? He looks as if, as though, he wanted to . . ., il a l'air de vouloir. . . . It looks as if he wouldn't go, il semble qu'il ne veuille pas y aller. *It does not l. to me as if . . .,* il ne me semble pas que + *sub.* What does he look like? comment est-il? à quoi ressemble-t-il? *The rock looks like granite,* la roche ressemble à du granit. This looks to me like a way in, ceci m'a l'air d'une entrée. He looks a rascal, il porte la mine d'un coquin, d'un fripon. *He looks a pukka Hindoo,* il a bien l'air hindou. He looks the part, il est fait pour ce rôle; il a le physique de l'emploi. To look like doing sth., avoir mine de vouloir faire qch. He looks like it, il en a l'air. It looks like it, cela en a l'air; on le dirait. It looks like rain, il a l'air de vouloir pleuvoir; on dirait qu'il va pleuvoir. 4. *F:* Look here! écoutez donc! dites donc! **look about,** *v.i.* 1. To look about one, regarder autour de soi. 2. To look about for ş.o., chercher qn des yeux. To look about for a post, être à la recherche d'un emploi. **look after,** *v.ind.tr.* Soigner (qn, qch.); s'occuper de, avoir soin de (qn, qch.); veiller sur (qn, qch.). He is able to look after himself, il sait se suffire; il peut marcher seul. To look after one's interests, one's rights, veiller à ses intérêts, à ses droits. *I l. after the car myself,* j'entretiens l'auto moi-même. **look at,** *v.ind.tr.* 1. Regarder, considérer (qn, qch.); porter ses regards sur (qn, qch.). *What are you looking at?* qu'est-ce que vous regardez? *Just look at this!* voyez donc! To look at one's watch, regarder à sa montre. *F:* She will not look at a man, elle dédaigne les hommes; les hommes lui sont indifférents. To look at him *one would say . . .,* à le voir on dirait. . . . What sort of a man is ṇe to look at? quel air a-t-il? *The hotel is not much to look at,* l'hôtel ne paye pas de mine. 2. *L. at the result,* voyez, considérez, le résultat. Way of looking at things, manière *f* de voir les choses. **look away,** *v.i.* Détourner les yeux. **look back,** *v.i.* (a) Regarder en arrière; se retourner, tourner la tête (*at sth.,* pour regarder

qch.). (b) To look back upon the past, faire un retour sur le passé. *What a day to l. back to!* quelle journée à se rappeler plus tard! **look down,** *v.i.* Regarder en bas, par terre; baisser les yeux. *Standing here you l. down on the whole plain,* de ce point on domine toute la plaine. *F:* To look down on s.o., regarder qn de haut en bas; dédaigner qn. **look for,** *v.ind.tr.* 1. Chercher (qn, qch.). To go and look for s.o., aller à la recherche de qn. 2. S'attendre à (qch.). **look forward,** *v.i.* To look forward to sth., (i) s'attendre à qch.; (ii) attendre qch. avec plaisir. **look in,** *v.i.* 1. To look in (up)on s.o., at s.o.'s house, entrer chez qn en passant; faire une petite visite à qn. To l. in at the office, prendre l'air du bureau. *I shall l. in again to-morrow,* je repasserai demain. 2. *W.Tel: F:* To look in to a transmission, recevoir une émission de télévision. '**look-in,** *s.* 1. To give s.o. a look-in, passer chez qn; faire une petite visite à qn. 2. *Sp: etc:* He won't get a look-in, il n'a pas la moindre chance. **look into,** *v.ind.tr.* (a) Examiner, étudier (une question); prendre (une question) en considération. I will look into it, j'en prendrai connaissance. (b) Feuilleter, parcourir (un livre). **look on,** *v.i.* 1. (a) = LOOK UPON. (b) (*Of building, etc.*) To look on (to) . . ., donner sur. . . . 2. Être spectateur; faire galerie. *Suppose you helped me instead of looking on,* si vous m'aidiez au lieu de me regarder faire. **look out.** 1. *v.i.* (a) Regarder au dehors. (b) *Room that looks out on the yard,* pièce qui prend jour, qui prend vue, sur la cour. (c) Veiller. To look out for s.o., être à la recherche de qn; guetter qn. (d) *F:* Prendre garde; être sur ses gardes. Look out! attention! prenez garde! 2. *v.tr.* Chefcher (qch.). *To l. out a train in the time-table,* chercher un train dans l'indicateur. '**look-'out,** *s.* 1. Guet *m,* surveillance *f; Nau:* veille *f.* To keep a look-out, avoir l'œil au guet; *Nau:* être en vigie. To keep a sharp look-out, guetter d'un œil attentif; faire bonne garde; avoir l'œil. To be on the look-out, (i) être en observation; *Nau:* être de veille; (ii) être sur ses gardes; être sur le qui-vive. To be on the look-out for s.o., être à l'affût de qn; guetter qn. 2. (a) *Mil:* Look-out (post), poste *m* d'observation. (b) Look-out (man), (i) *Mil:* guetteur *m;* (ii) *Nau:* homme *m* de veille, de bossoir; vigie *f.* 3. Perspective *f. F:* That's a bad look-out for him, c'est une triste perspective. That's his look-out! ça c'est son affaire! **look over,** *v.tr.* 1. Jeter un coup d'œil sur (qch.); parcourir (qch.) des yeux; examiner (qch.). To look over a house, visiter une maison. *To l. over some papers,* parcourir des papiers. To look over an account (again), repasser un compte. To look s.o. all over, toiser qn. 2. *To l. over one's neighbour's newspaper,* lire le journal par-dessus l'épaule de son voisin. **look round,** *v.i.* 1. Regarder autour de soi. To look round for s.o., chercher qn du regard. 2. Se retourner (pour voir); tourner la tête. Don't look round! ne regardez pas en arrière! **look through,** *v.tr.* 1. Parcourir, examiner (des papiers, etc.); repasser (une leçon). 2. To look s.o. through and through, transpercer qn du regard. **look to,** *v.i.* (a) To look to sth., s'occuper de qch.; voir à qch. Look to it that . . ., veillez, faites attention, que + *sub.* To look to the future, envisager l'avenir. (b) To look to s.o. to do sth., compter sur qn pour faire qch. *I l. to you for protection,* je compte sur votre protection. **look up.** 1. *v.i.* (a) Regarder en haut; lever les yeux. (b) *F:* To look up to s.o., respecter,

29

considérer, qn. (c) F: **Business is looking up,** les affaires reprennent, se relèvent, se raniment. *Things are looking up with him,* ses affaires vont mieux. **2.** v.tr. (a) **To look up the time-table,** consulter l'indicateur. *To l. up a word in the dictionary,* (re)chercher un mot dans le dictionnaire. (b) F: **To look s.o. up,** aller voir qn. **look upon,** v.ind.tr. **1.** Regarder (qn, qch.). **Fair to look upon,** de belle apparence. **2.** *To l. upon s.o. favourably,* voir qn d'un œil favorable. **Look upon that as done,** tenez cela pour fait. *I do not look upon it in that light,* ce n'est pas ainsi que j'envisage la chose. **-looking,** a. **Good-looking,** beau, f. belle; joli; de bonne mine. **Queer-looking,** à l'air bizarre; d'un aspect singulier. **Serious-looking,** d'apparence sérieuse. **'looking-glass,** s. Miroir m, glace f. Bot: **Venus's looking-glass,** miroir de Vénus. **looker** ['lukər], s. **Looker-on,** pl. **lookers-on,** spectateur, -trice (at, de); assistant m (at, à). *To be a l.-on,* faire galerie. **loom¹** [lu:m], s. Tex: Métier m à tisser. **loom²,** v.i. Nau. & F: Apparaître indistinctement; se dessiner, s'estomper, dans le lointain ou dans le brouillard. *A ship loomed up out of the fog,* un vaisseau surgit, sortit, du brouillard. *Dangers looming ahead,* dangers qui menacent, qui paraissent imminents. F: (Of event) **To loom large,** paraître imminent. **loon** [lu:n], s. Orn: (Grand) plongeon. **loony** ['lu:ni], a. & s. F: Fou, f. folle; timbré, maboul. **loop¹** [lu:p], s. **1.** Boucle f (de ruban, etc.); boucle, œil m, anse f, ganse f (d'un cordage); boucle, poche f (de lettre écrite). **Running loop,** boucle à nœud coulant. **Curtain-loop,** embrasse f de rideau. Cost: **Overcoat loop,** attache f de pardessus. **2.** (a) Méandre m, sinuosité f, boucle (de rivière). (b) Tour m, spire f (de spirale, de bobine). (c) Ph: Ventre m; antinœud m (d'une onde). (d) Rail: **Loop(-line),** (voie f de) dérivation f. **'loop-way,** s. Route f d'évitement. **loop².** **1.** v.tr. (a) Boucler (un ruban, etc.). (b) Enrouler (sth. with sth., qch. de qch.). (c) **To loop up the hair,** retrousser, relever, les cheveux. **To loop back** a curtain, retenir un rideau avec une embrasse. (d) Av: etc: **To loop the loop,** boucler la boucle. **2.** v.i. Faire une boucle; boucler. **loop-hole** ['lu:phoul], s. **1.** (a) Fort: Meurtrière f, créneau m. (b) Trou m, ouverture f. **2.** **To find a loop-hole of escape,** trouver une échappatoire; se ménager une issue. **loose¹** [lu:s], a. **1.** (a) Mal assujetti; branlant; (of page) détaché; (of knot) défait, délié. **L. horseshoe,** fer qui lâche. **L. tooth,** dent qui branle, qui remue. El: **L. connection,** raccord déconnecté, desserré. **To come loose, to get loose,** se dégager, se détacher; (of knot) se défaire; se délier; (of screw) se desserrer. (Of machine parts) **To work loose,** prendre du jeu. (Of chisel, etc.) **To be loose in the handle,** branler dans le manche. (b) (Of animal) Déchaîné, échappé, lâché. **To let a dog loose,** lâcher, détacher, un chien. *To let l. a torrent of abuse,* lâcher, déchaîner, un torrent d'injures. (c) Non assujetti; mobile. **L. sheets,** feuilles volantes. Mec.E: **Loose wheel,** roue folle, décalée. **Loose piece,** pièce rapportée, pièce de rapport. **Loose end** (of rope), bout pendant. F: **To be at a loose end,** se trouver désœuvré, sans occupation; avoir une heure à perdre. (Of rope, etc.) **To hang loose,** pendre, flotter. (d) The money was loose in his pocket, l'argent était à même sa poche. **Loose cash,** menue monnaie.

Com: **Loose goods,** marchandises en vrac. **2.** (Slack) (a) **L. rope,** câble mou, détendu. **L. knot,** nœud lâche. (Of shoe-lace) **To come loose,** se relâcher. **L.** draperies, draperies flottantes. (b) **Man of loose build,** homme dégingandé. Med: **Loose cough,** toux grasse. **Loose bowels,** ventre m lâche. **3. Loose earth,** soil, terre meuble; terrain sans consistance. Mil: **Loose order,** ordre dispersé. **4.** Vague, peu exact; (style) lâche, décousu. **L. translation,** traduction peu exacte. **5.** Dissolu, débauché, libertin, licencieux. **Loose living,** mauvaise vie; inconduite f. **L.** morals, mœurs relâchées. s. **To be on the loose,** être en bordée; mener une vie de polichinelle. **To go on the loose,** faire la vadrouille, aller en vadrouille. **-ly,** adv. **1.** (Tenir qch.) sans serrer. **L. clad,** habillé dans des vêtements amples. **2.** Vaguement, inexactement. Word **l.** employed, mot employé abusivement. **3.** (Se conduire) d'une manière dissolue. **'loose box,** s. Box m (d'écurie). **'loose-fitting,** a. Non ajusté; (vêtement) ample, large. **'loose-jointed, -limbed,** a. Démanché; dégingandé. **'loose-leaf,** attrib.a. (Album, etc.) à feuilles mobiles. **loose²,** v.tr. **1.** Délier, détacher. **To loose s.o. from his bonds,** libérer qn. **To loose one's hold,** lâcher prise. **To loose hold of sth.,** lâcher qch. **2.** Dénouer, défaire (un nœud, etc.); dénouer (ses cheveux). Nau: Larguer (une amarre). **3.** Décocher (une flèche). **loosen** ['lu:s(ə)n]. **1.** v.tr. (a) Relâcher (un nœud); desserrer (un écrou, etc.); relâcher, détendre (une corde, un ressort). *To l. s.o.'s bonds,* dénouer les liens de qn. *To l. one's grip,* relâcher son étreinte. *To l. s.o.'s tongue,* délier, dénouer, la langue à qn. Mec.E: *To l. a bearing,* dégripper un palier. Med: **To loosen the bowels,** relâcher le ventre; dégager les intestins. **To loosen the cough,** dégager la toux. (b) Détacher (sth. from sth., qch. de qch.). (c) Relâcher (la discipline). **2.** v.i. (Of knot, etc.) Se délier, se défaire; (of screw, etc.) se desserrer; (of guy-rope, etc.) se relâcher; (of machinery, etc.) prendre du jeu. Med: (Of cough) Se dégager. **looseness** ['lu:snəs], s. **1.** (a) État branlant (d'une dent); jeu m (d'une cheville, etc.). (b) Flaccidité f (de la peau). **2.** (a) Relâchement m (d'une corde); ampleur f (d'un vêtement). (b) Med: Looseness of the bowels, relâchement du ventre. **3.** Inconsistance f (du terrain). **4.** (a) Vague m (d'une pensée); imprécision f (de terminologie); décousu m (du style). (b) Relâchement (de la discipline). (c) Licence f (de conduite). **loosestrife** ['lu:sstraif], s. Bot: Lysimachie f, lysimaque f. **loot¹** [lu:t], s. **1.** Pillage m. **On the loot,** en maraude. **2.** Butin m. **loot²,** v.tr. **1.** Piller, saccager (une ville, etc.). **2.** Voler (du bétail, etc.). **looting,** s. Pillage m; sac m (d'une ville, etc.). **looter** ['lu:tər], s. Pillard m. **lop¹** [lɔp], v.tr. (lopped [lɔpt]) (a) Élaguer, tailler, émonder (un arbre). **To lop away, lop off,** a branch, couper, élaguer, une branche. (b) **To lop off a head,** abattre une tête. **lopping,** s. **1.** Élagage m (d'un arbre). **2.** pl. **Loppings,** élagage, émondes fpl. **lop²,** v.i. **1.** **To lop (over),** retomber; pendre flasque. **2. To lop about,** flâner. **3.** (Of animals) **To lop along,** avancer par bonds. **'lop-ear,** s. **1.** Oreille pendante. **2.** Lapin m aux oreilles pendantes. **'lop-eared,** a. Aux oreilles pendantes.

lope¹ [loup], *s.* Pas de course allongé.

lope², *v.i.* To lope along, courir à petits bonds.

lopsided [lɔp'saidid], *a.* Qui penche trop d'un côté ; déjeté, déversé ; de guingois.

loquacious [lo'kweiʃəs], *a.* Loquace. **-ly,** *adv.* Avec loquacité.

loquaciousness [lo'kweiʃəsnəs], **loquacity** [lo'kwasiti], *s.* Loquacité *f.*

lord¹ [lɔːrd], *s.m.* 1. Seigneur, maître. *Hist:* Lord of the manor, seigneur (foncier) ; châtelain. The cotton lords, les rois du coton. 2. *Ecc:* Lord God Almighty, Seigneur Dieu Tout-puissant. The Lord, le Seigneur ; Dieu. In the year of our Lord . . ., en l'an de grâce. . . . The Lord's Day, le jour du Seigneur ; le dimanche. *F:* (Good) Lord! Seigneur (Dieu)! 3. (a) Lord *m* (titre des barons vicomtes, comtes, et marquis). *F:* To live like a lord, mener une vie de grand seigneur. My lord, (i) monsieur le baron, le comte, etc. ; (ii) (*to bishop*) monseigneur ; (*to judge*) monsieur le juge. (b) Lord High Constable, grand connétable. **'lords and 'ladies,** *s. Bot:* Arum maculé ; gouet *m.*

lord², *v.i. F:* To lord it, faire l'important ; trancher du grand seigneur. To lord it over s.o., vouloir dominer qn ; vouloir en imposer à qn.

lordliness ['lɔːrdlinəs], *s.* 1. (a) Dignité *f.* (b) Magnificence *f* (d'un château, etc.). 2. Hauteur *f,* orgueil *m.*

lordling ['lɔːrdliŋ], *s.* Petit seigneur.

lordly ['lɔːrdli], *a.* 1. De grand seigneur ; noble, majestueux ; magnifique. 2. Hautain, altier.

lordship ['lɔːrdʃip], *s.* 1. Suzeraineté *f* (over, de). 2. Your lordship, votre Seigneurie ; (*to nobleman*) monsieur le comte, etc. ; (*to bishop*) monseigneur.

lore [lɔːr], *s.* Science *f,* savoir *m.* Bird-lore, ornithologie *f.*

lorgnette [lɔːr'njet], **lorgnon** ['lɔːrnjɔn], *s.* 1. Face-à-main *m.* 2. Jumelle *f* (de théâtre) à manche.

lorn [lɔːrn], *a. Poet:* Délaissé, solitaire.

lorry ['lɔri], *s. Veh:* Camion *m.*

lose [luːz], *v.tr.* (lost [lɔst] ; lost) 1. (a) Perdre, égarer (son parapluie, etc.). (b) Perdre (un droit, son argent, etc.). *I lost a clear thousand francs,* j'ai perdu mille francs. To stand to lose nothing, (i) n'avoir rien à perdre ; (ii) être en position de gagner de toutes les façons. The incident did not lose in the telling, cet incident ne perdit rien de son importance à être raconté. To lose in value, in interest, perdre de sa valeur, de son intérêt. *Rac:* To lose (ground) on a competitor, perdre sur un concurrent. (c) He has lost an arm, il lui manque un bras. To lose one's voice, avoir, attraper, une extinction de voix. To lose one's reason, perdre la raison. To lose one's character, se perdre de réputation. To lose strength, s'affaiblir. *The patient is losing strength,* le malade baisse. To lose weight, perdre de son poids. (d) Perdre (son père, etc.). (*Of doctor*) To lose a patient, ne pas réussir à sauver un malade. To be lost at sea, périr en mer, dans un naufrage. 2. To lose one's way, to lose oneself, to get lost, perdre son chemin ; se perdre, s'égarer. *To l. oneself, to be lost, in the crowd,* se perdre, se dissimuler, dans la foule. To lose oneself in a book, s'absorber dans la lecture d'un livre. Lost in amazement, perdu d'étonnement. To lose sight of s.o., perdre qn de vue. 3. Gaspiller, perdre (son temps) ; perdre (sa peine). *F:* The joke was lost on him, il n'a pas saisi la plaisanterie. 4. Clock that loses five minutes a day, pendule qui retarde de cinq minutes par jour. 5. (a) Manquer (le train, etc.). (b) *I lost several words of his*

answer, plusieurs mots de sa réponse m'ont échappé. 6. Perdre (une partie, un procès). (*In debate*) The motion was lost, la motion a été rejetée. 7. Faire perdre (qch. à qn). That mistake lost him the match, cette faute lui coûta la partie. **lost,** *a.* Perdu. Lost property office, service *m* des objets trouvés. To give s.o. up for lost, abandonner tout espoir de retrouver ou de sauver qn. I gave myself up for lost, je me crus perdu. Lost soul, âme perdue. To wander like a l. soul, errer comme une âme en peine. He seems lost, looks lost, il a l'air dépaysé. To be lost to all sense of shame, avoir perdu tout sentiment de honte. **losing,** *a.* Perdant. Losing game, partie perdue d'avance. To play a losing game, (i) jouer un jeu à perdre ; (ii) défendre une cause perdue.

loser ['luːzər], *s.* 1. I am the loser by it, j'y perds. 2. (a) To be the loser of a battle, être battu dans une bataille. *Prov:* The losers are always in the wrong, les battus payent l'amende. (b) *Sp:* Perdant, -ante. To be a bad loser, être mauvais joueur.

loss [lɔs], *s.* 1. (a) Perte *f* (d'un parapluie) ; égarement *m* (d'un document). (b) Loss of sight, perte, privation *f,* de la vue. Loss of voice, extinction *f* de voix. Without loss of time, sans perte de temps ; sans tarder. *Com:* Loss of custom, désachalandage *m. Jur:* Loss of a right, déchéance *f* d'un droit. 2. To meet with a loss, subir une perte. Dead loss, perte sèche. *Com:* To sell at a loss, vendre à perte ; mévendre. *F:* To cut one's losses, faire la part du feu. It is her loss, the loss is hers, c'est elle qui y perd. He, it, is no loss, la perte n'est pas grande. *M.Ins:* Constructive total loss, perte censée totale. 3. (a) Déperdition *f* (de chaleur, etc.). Loss in transit, déchet *m* de route (d'un liquide, etc.). (b) *Med:* Écoulement *m,* perte. 4. To be at a loss, être embarrassé, désorienté. *I am quite at a l.,* je ne sais que faire. To be at a loss to . . ., avoir de la peine à . . . ; être en peine de. . . . To be at a loss what to do, what to say, ne savoir que faire, que dire. I am at a loss for words to express . . ., les mots me manquent pour exprimer. . . .

lost [lɔst]. *See* LOSE.

lot [lɔt], *s.* 1. To draw, cast, lots for sth., tirer au sort pour qch. ; tirer qch. au sort. To throw in one's lot with s.o., partager le sort, la fortune, de qn ; unir sa destinée à celle de qn. Drawn by lot *from amongst* . . ., tiré au sort parmi. 2. (a) Sort, part *f,* partage *m.* The lot fell upon him, le sort tomba sur lui. To fall to s.o.'s lot, échoir, tomber, en partage à qn. It fell to my lot to . . ., le sort voulut que je + *sub. S.a.* PART¹ I. 2. (b) Destin *m,* destinée *f.* 3. (a) (At auction) Lot *m.* (b) *Com:* Lot, part, par parties. To buy in one lot, acheter en bloc. (c) *F:* A bad lot, une canaille ; un mauvais garnement. (d) *F:* The lot, le tout. That's the lot, c'est tout. The whole lot, all the lot, of you, tous tant que vous êtes. 4. *F:* Beaucoup. What a lot! en voilà-t-il ! *What a lot of people!* que de monde ! que de gens ! Such a lot, tellement. *I have quite a lot,* j'en ai une quantité considérable. He knows quite a lot about you, il en sait long sur votre compte. *I saw quite a lot of him in Paris,* je l'ai vu assez souvent pendant mon séjour à Paris. He would have given a lot to . . ., il aurait donné gros pour . . . *adv. Times have changed a lot,* les temps ont bien changé. (b) *pl.* Lots of good things, un tas de bonnes choses. *Lots of people,* quantité de gens ; des tas

de gens. *adv. I feel lots better*, je me sens infiniment mieux.
Lothario [lo'θɛərio]. *Pr.n.m.* **A gay Lothario**, un joyeux viveur, un Don Juan.
lotion ['louʃ(ə)n], *s. Pharm:* Lotion *f*.
lottery ['lɔtəri], *s.* Loterie *f*. **Charity lottery**, tombola *f*. **Lottery loan**, emprunt *m* à lots.
lotus ['loutəs], *s.* **1.** *Gr.Myth:* Lotus *m*. **2.** *Bot:* (*a*) Lotus *m*, lotier *m*. (*b*) **Egyptian lotus**, nélombo *m*; lis *m* du Nil. **'lotus-eater**, *s.* *Gr.Myth:* Lotophage *m*.
loud [laud]. **1.** *a.* (*a*) Bruyant, retentissant. *L. noise*, *l. cry*, grand bruit, grand cri. *L. laugh*, gros rire. *L. voice*, voix forte, voix haute. *In a loud voice*, à haute voix. **Loud cheers**, vifs applaudissements. **To be loud in one's praises of sth.**, louer qch. chaudement. (*b*) (*Of pers.*, *behaviour*) Bruyant, tapageur. (*c*) (*Of colour, etc.*) Criard, voyant; (*of costume*) tapageur. **2.** *adv.* (Crier) haut, à haute voix. **-ly**, *adv.* **1.** (Crier) haut, fort, à voix haute; (rire) bruyamment. *To call l. for sth.*, réclamer qch. à grands cris. **2.** *L. dressed*, à toilette tapageuse. **loud-'mouthed**, *a.* Au verbe haut. **'loud-'speaker**, *s. W.Tel:* Haut-parleur *m, pl.* haut-parleurs.
loudness ['laudnəs], *s.* **1.** Force *f* (d'un bruit, etc.); grand bruit (d'une cataracte, etc.). **2.** *The l. of her dress*, sa toilette tapageuse, criarde.
lough [lɔx], *s.* (*Irish*) **1.** Lac *m*. **2.** Bras *m* de mer.
lounge[1] [laundʒ], *s.* **1.** (*a*) Flânerie *f*. (*b*) Allure nonchalante. **2.** (*a*) Promenoir *m*; (*in hotel*) hall *m*; (*in boarding-house*) petit salon. (*b*) *Th:* Foyer *m* (du public). **'lounge-chair**, *s.* Chaise-longue *f*. **'lounge-suit**, *s.* Complet veston *m*.
lounge[2], *v.i.* **1.** Flâner. *To lounge about*, *F:* tirer sa flemme. *To lounge along*, avancer en se dandinant. **2.** S'étaler, s'étendre paresseusement (sur un canapé, etc.).
lounger ['laundʒər], *s.* Flâneur, -euse.
louring ['lauəriŋ], *a.* **1.** (Air) renfrogné, menaçant; (front) sombre. **2.** (Ciel) sombre, menaçant, orageux.
louse, *pl.* **lice** [laus, lais], *s.* Pou *m, pl.* poux.
lousewort ['lauswə:rt], *s. Bot:* Pédiculaire *f*; herbe *f* aux poux.
lousy ['lauzi], *a.* **1.** Pouilleux. **2.** *F:* Sale, ignoble. **Lousy trick**, sale coup *m*; cochonnerie *f*.
lout [laut], *s.* Rustre *m*, lourdaud *m*.
loutish ['lauti∫], *a.* Rustre, lourdaud.
louver, louvre ['lu:vər], *s.* **1.** *Arch: A:* Lucarne *f*. **2.** (*a*) *Arch:* Abat-vent *m inv*, abat-son *m* (de clocher). (*b*) *Aut:* Auvent *m*, persienne *f* (du capot, etc.). **'louver-board**, *s.* = LOUVER 2.
lovable ['lʌvəbl], *a.* Aimable; sympathique.
lovableness ['lʌvəblnəs], *s.* Caractère *m* aimable.
lovage ['lʌvedʒ], *s. Bot:* Livèche *f*.
love[1] [lʌv], *s.* **1.** Amour *m*. (*a*) Affection *f*, tendresse *f*. **Love of, for, towards, s.o.**, amour de, pour, envers, qn. *F:* **There is no love lost between them**, ils ne peuvent pas se sentir. **For the love of God**, pour l'amour de Dieu. *He learnt French* **for the love of it**, il apprit le français par attrait *m* pour cette langue. **To play for love**, jouer pour l'honneur. **To work for love**, travailler pour rien, *F:* pour le roi de Prusse. **Give my love to your parents**, faites mes amitiés à vos parents. *F:* **It cannot be had for love or money**, on ne peut se le procurer à aucun prix. (*b*) (*Between lovers*) Amour (*the pl. is fem. in Lit. & Poet. use*). **First love**, les premières amours. **To be in love with s.o.**, être amoureux, épris, de qn. **Head over ears in love**, féru d'amour. **To fall in love with s.o.**, s'éprendre, tomber amoureux, de qn. **To make love to s.o.**, faire la cour à qn. **Love in a cottage**, un cœur et une chaumière. **To marry for love**, faire un mariage d'inclination. **2.** (*Pers.*) **My love**, mon amour; mon ami, mon amie. **An old love of mine**, une de mes anciennes amours. **3.** (*a*) *Pr.n.m.* L'Amour, Cupidon. (*b*) **What a love of a child, of a hat!** quel amour d'enfant, de chapeau! **4.** (*At tennis, etc.*) Zéro *m*, rien *m*. **Love all**, égalité *f* à rien. **Love game**, jeu blanc. **'love-bird**, *s. Orn:* Psittacule *m*; inséparable *m*. **'love-child**, *s.* Enfant naturel; enfant d'amour. **'love-feast**, *s. Ecc.Hist:* Agape *f*. **'love-in-a-'mist**, *s. Bot:* Nigelle *f* (de Damas); cheveux *mpl* de Vénus. **'love-in-'idleness**, *s. Bot:* Pensée *f*. **'love-knot**, *s.* Lacs *m* d'amour. **'love-letter**, *s.* Billet doux. **'love-lies-(a-)'bleeding**, *s. Bot:* Amarante *f* à fleurs en queue. **'love-lorn**, *a.* Délaissé, abandonné. **'love-making**, *s.* Cour (amoureuse). **'love-match**, *s.* Mariage *m* d'amour, d'inclination. **'love-song**, *s.* (*a*) Chant *m* d'amour. (*b*) Chanson *f* d'amour; romance *f.* **'love-story**, *s.* Histoire *f* d'amour; roman *m* d'amour.
love[2], *v.tr.* **1.** (*a*) Aimer, affectionner (qn). *Prov:* **Love me love my dog**, qui m'aime aime mon chien. (*b*) Aimer d'amour. **2.** Aimer (passionnément) (son chez-soi, etc.). **As you love your life . . .**, si vous tenez à la vie. . . . *I l. horse-racing*, les courses de chevaux me passionnent. *I l. music*, j'adore la musique. **To love to do sth., to love doing sth.**, aimer à faire qch.; adorer faire qch. **Will you come with me?**—I should love to, voulez-vous m'accompagner?—Je ne demande pas mieux; très volontiers.
loving, *a.* **1.** Affectueux, affectionné, tendre. **2.** Money-loving, qui aime l'argent. **3.** **Loving cup**, coupe *f* de l'amitié. **-ly**, *adv.* Affectueusement, affectionnément.
Lovelace ['lʌvleis]. **1.** *Pr.n.m.* Lovelace. (Personnage de *Clarissa Harlowe* de Richardson.) **2.** *s.m.* Séducteur de filles; lovelace, libertin.
loveliness ['lʌvlinəs], *s.* Beauté *f*.
lovelock ['lʌvlɔk], *s.* Accroche-cœur *m*.
lovely ['lʌvli], *a.* (*a*) Beau, *f.* belle; ravissant. (*b*) *F: It's been just l. seeing you again!* ça a été charmant de vous revoir!
lover ['lʌvər], *s.* **1.** (*a*) Amoureux *m*, prétendant *m*. (*b*) Fiancé *m*. (*c*) *They were lovers*, ils s'aimaient. **2.** **Her lover**, son amant, *F:* son bon ami. **3.** Amateur *m*, ami(e) (de qch.). **Music-lover**, mélomane *mf.* **lovers' knot**, *s.* = LOVE-KNOT.
lovesick ['lʌvsik], *a.* Féru d'amour.
low[1] [lou]. I. *a.* **1.** Bas, *f.* basse. *Low wall*, mur bas, peu élevé. *Low stature*, petite taille. *Low relief*, bas-relief *m*. **Low dress**, robe décolletée. **Light turned low**, lumière en veilleuse. **Low tide, low water**, marée basse; basse mer. **My stocks are rather low**, mes stocks sont un peu dégarnis. **2.** (*a*) *Low ceiling*, plafond bas, peu élevé. *Low bow*, profonde révérence. *Geog:* **The Low Countries**, les Pays-Bas. *Aut:* **Low chassis**, châssis surbaissé. (*b*) **To bring s.o. low**, humilier, abaisser, ravaler, qn. **To lie low**, (i) se tapir; se tenir accroupi; (ii) *F:* se tenir coi; faire le mort. (*c*) **Lower part**, bas *m* (d'une échelle, etc.); aval *m* (d'un cours d'eau). **The Lower Alps**, les basses Alpes. **The lower world**, les régions infernaes. **The lower jaw**, la mâchoire inférieure. (*d*) *Ling:* **Low German**, le bas allemand. **Low Latin**, le bas latin. **3.** (*a*) *Low birth*, basse naissance. *There was something low about her*, elle avait un

je sais quoi de peuple, de canaille. **The lower orders**, les basses classes ; le bas peuple. **Lower court**, tribunal inférieur. *Lower end of the table*, bas bout de la table. *Sch:* **Lower forms**, petites classes ; (*in secondary schools*) classes de grammaire. (*b*) **The lower animals**, les animaux inférieurs. **Low comedy**, le bas comique. **Low comedian**, comédien à rôles chargés. (*c*) Bas vil, trivial, canaille. **A low fellow**, un voyou. **The 'owest of the low**, le dernier des derniers. *Low expression*, expression canaille. *That's a low trick!* ça c'est un sale coup! **4. Low diet**, régime peu substantiel ; régime débilitant. (*Of invalid*) **To be very low**, être bien bas. **To feel low, to be in low spirits**, être abattu ; *F:* avoir le cafard. **5. Low price**, bas prix ; prix faible. *The lowest price*, le dernier prix. *A hundred pounds at the very lowest*, cent livres au bas mot, pour le moins. *Low speed*, petite vitesse, faible vitesse. **Low-consumption lamp**, lampe à faible consommation. **Low fever**, fièvre lente. **Low latitudes**, basses latitudes. *Cards: The low cards*, les basses cartes. **6. Low note**, note basse. **Low sound**, (i) son bas, grave ; (ii) faible son. *In a low voice*, à voix basse, à mi-voix. *Sh. has a low voice*, elle a une voix basse, au timbre grave. **7.** *Ecc:* **Low mass**, la messe basse. **Low Sunday**, Pâques closes, (dimanche de) la Quasimodo. **-ly¹**, *adv.* **1. Lowly born**, (i) de basse naissance ; (ii) de naissance modeste. **2.** Humblement. **II. low**, *adv.* **1.** (Pendre, viser) bas. **To bow low**, s'incliner profondément ; saluer très bas. I cannot go so low as to do that, je ne peux pas descendre jusqu'à faire cela. *Dress cut low in the back*, robe décolletée dans le dos. **2. The lowest paid employees**, les employés les moins payés. **3.** (*a*) (Parler) à voix basse. (*b*) *Mus:* I cannot get so low as that, je ne peux pas descendre si bas (dans la gamme). *To set* (*a song, etc.*) *lower*, baisser (une chanson, etc.). **'low-born**, *a.* **1.** De basse naissance. **2.** D'humble naissance. **'low-bred**, *a.* Mal élevé ; grossier. **'low-brow**, *F:* **1.** *a.* Terre à terre *inv* ; peu intellectuel. **2.** *s.* Bourgeois, -oise ; philistin, -ine. **'low-built**, *a.* Bas ; peu élevé. *Aut:* **Low-built chassis**, châssis surbaissé. **'low-class**, *a.* De bas étage ; vulgaire, inférieur. **'low-down¹**, *a.* **1.** Bas, *f.* basse ; près du sol. **2.** Bas, vil, ignoble, canaille. *L.-d. trick*, coup rosse. **'low-down²**, *s. U.S:* *P:* **To give** s.o. **the low-down**, renseigner qn ; tuyauter qn (*on*, sur). **'low-grade**, *attrib.a.* De qualité inférieure ; (minerai) pauvre. **'low-level**, *attrib.a.* **1.** Bas, *f.* basse. **2.** En contre-bas. **'low-'lying**, *a.* Situé en bas ; (terrain) enfoncé. **'low-'necked**, *a.* (Robe) décolletée. **'low-'pitched**, *a.* **1.** (*a*) (Son) grave. (*b*) (Piano) accordé à un diapason bas. **2.** *Const:* (Comble) à faible pente ; (chambre) à plafond bas. **'low-powered**, *a.* (Auto) de faible puissance. **'low-pressure**, *attrib.a.* (Cylindre, machine) à basse pression, à basse tension. **'low-'spirited**, *a.* Abattu, triste, déprimé, découragé. **'low-'water**, *attrib.a.* **Low-water mark**, (*of river*) étiage *m* ; (*of sea*) (i) niveau *m* des basses eaux, (ii) laisse *f* de basse mer.

low², *s.* Meuglement *m* (d'une vache).

low³, *v.i.* (*Of cattle*) Meugler ; (*occ. of bull*) beugler.

lower ['louər], *v.tr.* (*a*) Baisser (la tête) ; abaisser (les paupières) ; abaisser, rabattre (son voile). (*b*) **To lower** s.o. **on a rope**, affaler, (faire) descendre, qn au bout d'une corde. **To lower a ladder**, descendre une échelle. *Nau:* **Lower away!** laissez aller! **To lower a boat**, amener une embarcation ; mettre une embarcation à la mer. (*c*) Abaisser (qch.) ; diminuer la hauteur de (qch.). (*d*) Baisser, rabaisser (un prix) ; réduire, abaisser (la pression) ; baisser (la lumière) ; amoindrir (un contraste). (*e*) Baisser (la voix, le ton). *To l. the enemy's morale*, déprimer le moral de l'ennemi. (*f*) (R)abaisser, faire baisser, (r)abattre (l'orgueil). **To lower oneself**, s'abaisser, se rabaisser, se ravaler (*to*, à) ; s'avilir. **lowering¹**, *a.* **1.** (*Of conduct*) Abaissant. **2.** *Med:* (Régime) débilitant. **lowering²**, *s.* **1.** (*a*) Abaissement *m* ; baissement *m* (de la tête, etc.). (*b*) Descente *f* (d'une échelle dans un puits, etc.) ; mise *f* à la mer (d'une embarcation). (*c*) Abaissement, diminution *f* de la hauteur (de qch.). **2.** Diminution (des prix) ; réduction *f* (de la pression).

lowermost ['louərmoust], *a.* Le plus bas.

lowland ['loulənd], *s.* (*a*) Plaine basse ; terre *f* en contre-bas. (*b*) *pl.* **Lowlands**, terres basses ; pays plat. *Geog:* **The Lowlands**, la Basse-Écosse.

lowliness ['loulinəs], *s.* Humilité *f*.

lowly² ['louli], *a.* *A. & Lit:* Humble, modeste, sans prétention. *s.pl.* **The lowly**, les humbles *m*. **-lily**, *adv.* Humblement.

lowness ['lounəs], *s.* **1.** Manque *m* de hauteur ; petitesse *f* (d'un arbre, etc.). **2.** (*a*) Gravité *f* (d'un son). (*b*) Faiblesse *f* (d'un bruit) ; peu *m* d'élévation (de la température). **3.** Bassesse *f* (de conduite). **4. Lowness (of spirits)**, abattement *m*, découragement *m*.

loxodromic [lɔksoˈdrɔmik], *a.* *Nau:* (Navigation, etc.) loxodromique.

loyal ['lɔiəl], *a.* **1.** (Ami, etc.) fidèle, dévoué (*to*, à) ; loyal, -aux (*to*, envers). **2.** Fidèle au roi, à la famille royale. *To drink the loyal toast*, boire le toast au roi. **-ally**, *adv.* Fidèlement.

loyalist ['lɔiəlist], *s.* Loyaliste *mf*.

loyalty ['lɔiəlti], *s.* **1.** *A:* Fidélité *f* à sa promesse, à son serment. **2.** Fidélité à la Couronne. *L. to one's party*, fidélité à son parti.

lozenge ['lɔzəndʒ], *s.* **1.** *Geom: Her:* Losange *m*. **2.** *Pharm:* Pastille *f*, tablette *f*.

lubber ['lʌbər], *s.* **1.** (*a*) Lourdaud *m*. (*b*) *Nau:* Maladroit *m*, empoté *m*. **2.** *Nau:* **Land-lubber**, marin m d'eau douce ; terrien *m*.

lubberliness ['lʌbərlinəs], *s.* Gaucherie *f*.

lubberly ['lʌbərli]. **1.** *a.* Lourdaud ; empoté, gauche. **2.** *adv.* Lourdement, gauchement.

lubricant ['lju:brikənt, 'lu:-], *a. & s.* Lubrifiant (*m*).

lubricate ['lju:brikeit, 'lu:-], *v.tr.* Lubrifier ; graisser. **Lubricating oil**, huile *f* de graissage.

lubrication [lju:briˈkeiʃ(ə)n, lu:-], *s.* Lubrification *f*.

lubricator ['lju:brikeitər, 'lu:-], *s.* Graisseur *m*. **Cap lubricator**, graisseur à chapeau. **Drop lubricator**, graisseur compte-gouttes.

lubricity [lju:ˈbrisiti, lu:-], *s.* Lubricité *f*.

Lucca ['lʌkə]. *Pr.n. Geog:* Lucques *f*. **Lucca oil**, huile *f* d'olives de Lucques.

lucency ['lju:sənsi], *s.* Brillance *f*, luminosité *f*.

lucent ['lju:sənt], *a.* **1.** Brillant, lumineux. **2.** Clair, transparent.

lucern(e)¹ [lju'sə:rn], *s. Bot:* Luzerne *f*.

Lucerne² [lu'sə:rn]. *Pr.n. Geog:* Lucerne *f*. **The Lake of Lucerne**, le lac des Quatre-Cantons.

lucid ['lju:sid, 'lu:-], *a.* **1.** Brillant, lumineux. **2.** (*a*) (Esprit, style) lucide. (*b*) *Med:* **Lucid interval**, intervalle *m* de lucidité. (*c*) *Poet:* Clair, transparent. **-ly**, *adv.* Lucidement.

lucidity [lju:ˈsiditi, lu:-], *s.* **1.** (*a*) Luminosité *f*. (*b*) Transparence *f*. **2.** Lucidité *f* (d'esprit).

lucifer ['lju:sifər, 'lu:-], s. Lucifer match, allumette f (chimique).

luck [lʌk], s. **1.** Hasard m, chance f, fortune f. Good luck, bonne chance, heureuse fortune, bonheur m. Ill luck, bad luck, mal(e)chance f, mauvaise fortune, malheur m; F: déveine f, guigne f. To be down on one's luck, avoir de la déveine, être dans la déveine; F: être dans la dèche. To turn a player's luck, F: dé(sen)guignonner un joueur. To try one's luck, tenter la fortune, la chance. To bring s.o. good, bad, luck, porter bonheur, porter malheur, à qn. Better luck next time! ça ira mieux, vous ferez mieux, une autre fois. Worse luck! tant pis! Hard luck! pas de chance! As luck would have it ..., le hasard voulut que + sub. **2.** Bonheur m, bonne fortune, (bonne) chance. To have the luck to ..., avoir la chance de ..., être assez heureux pour. ... To keep sth. for luck, garder qch. comme porte-bonheur. Bit, piece, stroke, of luck, coup m de fortune, coup de veine. To be in luck, avoir de la chance. To be out of luck, jouer de malheur. My luck's in! quelle veine! As luck would have it ..., par bonheur. ...

luckless ['lʌkləs], a. **1.** (Of pers.) Malheureux, infortuné. **2.** L. day, jour malencontreux.

lucky ['lʌki], a. (a) (Of pers.) Heureux, fortuné. F: Lucky dog! veinard que vous êtes! To be lucky, avoir de la chance; jouer de bonheur. (b) Lucky hit, shot, coup de bonheur. L. day, jour de veine. At a l. moment, à un moment propice. How lucky! quelle chance! (c) Lucky stone, pierre porte-bonheur. (Of thg) To be lucky, porter bonheur. -ily, adv. Heureusement; par bonheur. 'lucky-bag, -dip, -tub, s. = BRAN-PIE.

lucrative ['lju:krətiv, 'lu:-], a. Lucratif. -ly, adv. Lucrativement.

lucre ['lu:kər], s. Lucre m. To do sth. for (filthy) lucre, agir par amour du gain, du lucre.

ludicrous ['lju:dikrəs, 'lu:-], a. Risible, grotesque. -ly, adv. Risiblement, grotesquement.

ludicrousness ['lju:dikrəsnəs, 'lu:-], s. Absurdité f (d'une réclamation, etc.).

luff[1] [lʌf], s. Nau: Lof m, ralingue f du vent (d'une voile). (Of sail) To tear from luff to leech, se déchirer dans toute sa longueur, dans toute sa largeur.

luff[2], v.i. Nau: Lof(f)er; faire une aulof(f)ée.

lug[1] [lʌg], s. Lug(-worm) = LOB-WORM.

lug[2], s. **1.** Scot: F: (a) (Ear) Oreille f. (b) Oreillette f (de casquette). **2.** Tchn: Oreille, tenon m, mentonnet m. Fixing lug, patte f d'attache.

lug[3], s. Traction violente, subite.

lug[4], v.tr. (lugged) Traîner, tirer (qch. de pesant). To lug sth. along, away, entraîner qch. To lug sth. about with one, promener, trimbaler, qch. avec soi.

luggage ['lʌgedʒ], s. Bagage(s) m(pl). Heavy luggage, gros bagages; gros colis pl. Luggage in advance, bagages non accompagnés. 'luggage-carrier, -grid, s. Aut: Porte-bagages m inv. 'luggage-label, s. Étiquette f à bagages. 'luggage-porter, s. **1.** Rail: Facteur m. **2.** (At hotel) Bagagiste m. 'luggage-ticket, s. Bulletin m d'enregistrement de bagages. 'luggage-van, s. Rail: Fourgon m (aux bagages).

lugger ['lʌgər], s. Nau: Lougre m.

lugsail ['lʌgseil, lʌgsl], s. Nau: Voile f à bourcet; taille-vent m inv.

lugubrious [lju'gu:briəs, lu-], a. Lugubre. -ly, adv. Lugubrement.

Luke [lu:k], Pr.n.m. Luc.

lukewarm ['lju:kwɔːrm, 'lu:-], a. Tiède. To become l., s'attiédir.

lull[1] [lʌl], s. Moment m de calme. Nau: Accalmie f.

lull[2]. **1.** v.tr. (a) Bercer, endormir (qn). (b) Endormir (les soupçons); assoupir (une douleur). (c) Calmer, apaiser (la tempête). **2.** v.i. (Of tempest) Se calmer, s'apaiser.

lullaby ['lʌləbai], s. Mus: Berceuse f.

lum [lʌm], s. Scot: Cheminée f.

lumbago [lʌm'beigo], s. Med: Lumbago m.

lumbar ['lʌmbər], a. Lombaire.

lumber[1] ['lʌmbər], s. **1.** Vieux meubles; fatras m. **2.** U.S: Bois m de charpente; bois en grume. 'lumber-jack, s. U.S: Bûcheron m. 'lumber-mill, s. U.S: Scierie f. 'lumber-room, s. Cabinet m, chambre f, de débarras; F: capharnaüm m. 'lumber-yard, s. U.S: Chantier m de bois.

lumber[2], v.tr. (a) Encombrer, embarrasser (un lieu); remplir (un lieu) de fatras. (b) Entasser (des objets) pêle-mêle.

lumber[3], v.i. To lumber along, in, avancer, entrer, à pas pesants, lourdement. **lumbering**, a. Lourd, pesant.

lumberman, pl. -men ['lʌmbərmən, -men], s.m. U.S: (a) Exploiteur de forêts. (b) Bûcheron.

luminary ['lju:minəri, 'lu:-], s. **1.** Corps lumineux; luminaire m, astre m. **2.** F: (Of pers.) Lumière f; flambeau m (de la science, etc.).

luminescence [lju:mi'nes(ə)ns, lu:-], s. Luminescence f.

luminescent [lju:mi'nes(ə)nt, lu:-], a. Luminescent.

luminous ['lju:minəs, 'lu:-], a. Lumineux.

luminousness ['lju:minəsnəs, 'lu:-], s. Clarté f (d'une explication).

lump[1] [lʌmp], s. **1.** (a) Gros morceau, bloc m (de pierre); motte f (d'argile); morceau m (de sucre); masse f (de plomb, etc.); (in porridge, etc.) motton m. To sell sth. in the lump, vendre qch. en bloc, en gros, globalement. Lump sum, (i) somme grosse, globale; (ii) prix à forfait. F: To have a lump in one's throat, avoir un serrement de gorge; se sentir le cœur gros. (b) Bosse f (au front, etc.). **2.** F: (Of pers.) Empoté m, pataud m, lourdaud m. Big lump of a lass, grosse dondon.

lump[2]. **1.** v.tr. (a) Mettre en bloc, en masse, en tas. (b) To lump things together, réunir des choses ensemble. F: To lump (one's all) on a horse, parier son (va-)tout sur un cheval. **2.** v.i. (a) (Of earth) Former des mottes. (b) To lump along, marcher lourdement, à pas pesants.

lump[3], v.tr. P: In the phr. If he doesn't like it, he may lump it, si cela ne lui plaît pas, qu'il s'arrange.

lumper ['lʌmpər], s. Nau: Déchargeur m, débardeur m.

lumpish ['lʌmpiʃ], a. **1.** Lourd, pataud, godiche. **2.** À l'esprit lent; à l'intelligence peu ouverte.

lumpishness ['lʌmpiʃnəs], s. **1.** Lourdeur f. **2.** Stupidité f.

lumpy ['lʌmpi], a. (a) (Of earth) Rempli de mottes; (of sauce, etc.) grumeleux. (b) Lumpy sea, mer courte, clapoteuse. (c) Couvert de protubérances.

lunacy ['lu:nəsi], s. Aliénation mentale; folie f; Jur: démence f. F: It's sheer lunacy, c'est de la folie.

lunar ['lu:nər], a. Lunaire; de (la) lune. Lunar month, mois lunaire.

lunate ['lu:net], a. Nat.Hist: Luné, luniforme.

lunatic ['lu:nətik]. **1.** a. De fou(s), d'aliéné(s). L. behaviour, conduite folle, extravagante.

2. *s.* Fou, *f.* folle; aliéné, -ée; *Jur:* dément, -ente.

lunch[1] [lʌnʃ], *s.* *F:* = LUNCHEON. **Quick lunch**, petit repas, casse-croûte *m inv* (à un bar, etc.).

lunch[2]. **1.** *v.i.* Déjeuner, luncher. **2.** *v.tr.* Donner à déjeuner à (qn); faire déjeuner (qn).

luncheon ['lʌnʃ(ə)n], *s.* **1.** Déjeuner *m* (à la fourchette); lunch *m*; repas *m* de midi. *We take, have, l. at noon*, nous déjeunons à midi. *Rail:* **Second luncheon**, deuxième service *m*. **Luncheon-basket**, (i) panier *m* à provisions; (ii) *Rail:* panier-repas *m*, *pl.* paniers-repas. **2.** Collation (matinale).

lune [lu:n], *s.* *Geom:* Lunule *f*, croissant *m*.

lung [lʌŋ], *s.* (*a*) Poumon *m*. **Inflammation of the lungs**, congestion *f* pulmonaire; *F:* fluxion *f* de poitrine. **Lung trouble**, maladie *f* pulmonaire, *esp.* phtisie *f.* (*b*) (*Of slaughtered animal*) Mou *m.*

lunge[1] [lʌndʒ], *s.* *Equit:* Longe *f*, allonge *f*.

lunge[2], *v.tr.* *Equit:* Faire trotter (un cheval) à la longe. **Lunging-rein**, (al)longe *f*.

lunge[3], *s.* **1.** *Fenc:* Botte *f*; coup droit. **2.** (*a*) Mouvement (précipité) en avant. (*b*) *With each l. of the ship*, chaque fois que le navire tanguait.

lunge[4], *v.i.* **1.** (*a*) *Fenc:* Se fendre. *To l. at the adversary*, porter une botte à l'adversaire. (*b*) *To l. at s.o. with one's walking-stick*, lancer un coup de pointe à qn avec sa canne. **To lunge out at s.o.**, (i) (*of pers.*) allonger un coup de poing à qn; (ii) (*of horse*) lancer une ruade à qn. **2. To lunge forward**, se précipiter en avant; se jeter en avant.

lungwort ['lʌŋwəːrt], *s.* *Bot:* Pulmonaire *f*; herbe *f* aux poumons.

luniform ['lu:nifɔːrm], *a.* Luniforme, luné.

lunule ['lu:njuːl], *s.* *Anat:* *Geom:* *etc:* Lunule *f*.

lupin ['lju:pin, 'lu:-], *s.* *Bot:* Lupin *m*.

lurch[1] [ləːrtʃ], *s.* **To leave s.o. in the lurch**, laisser qn dans l'embarras; planter là qn; laisser qn le bec dans l'eau.

lurch[2], *s.* **1.** Embardée *f*, coup *m* de roulis (d'un navire). **2.** Cahot *m*, embardée (d'une voiture). **3.** Pas titubant (d'un ivrogne); titubation *f*.

lurch[3], *v.i.* **1.** (*a*) (*Of ship*) Faire une embardée; embarder. (*b*) *F:* (*Of carriage, etc.*) Embarder; avoir un fort cahot. **2.** (*Of pers.*) **To lurch along**, marcher en titubant. **To lurch in, out**, entrer, sortir, en titubant.

lurcher ['ləːrtʃər], *s.* Chien croisé d'un lévrier avec un chien de berger; chien de braconnier.

lure[1] ['ljuər, 'luər], *s.* **1.** *Ven:* *Fish:* Leurre *m*. **2.** *F:* (*a*) Piège *m*. *He fell a victim to her lures*, il se laissa séduire. (*b*) Attrait *m* (de la mer, etc.).

lure[2], *v.tr.* **1.** Leurrer (un faucon, un poisson, etc.). **2.** Attirer, séduire, allécher. **To lure s.o. away from a duty**, détourner qn d'un devoir. *To be lured on to destruction*, être entraîné à sa perte.

lurid ['ljuərid, 'lu-], *a.* **1.** (Ciel) blafard, fauve. *L. light*, lueur blafarde, sinistre. **2.** (*a*) Cuivré. *L. flames*, flammes rougeoyantes. (*b*) *F:* Corsé; (langage) haut en couleur. **-ly**, *adv.* **1.** Avec une lueur blafarde. **2.** (*a*) En rougeoyant. (*b*) En corsant les effets.

lurk [ləːrk], *v.i.* Se cacher; rester tapi (dans un endroit). **lurking**, *a.* Caché; secret, -ète. *A lurking suspicion*, un vague soupçon.

luscious ['lʌʃəs], *a.* **1.** Succulent, savoureux. **2.** *Pej:* (*a*) (Vin) liquoreux, trop sucré. (*b*) (Style) trop fleuri. (*c*) (Littérature) d'un charme trop voluptueux.

lusciousness ['lʌʃəsnəs], *s.* **1.** Succulence *f*. **2.** *Pej:* Douceur affadissante.

lush [lʌʃ], *a.* (*Of grass*) Plein de sève.

lushness ['lʌʃnəs], *s.* Surabondance *f*, luxuriance *f* (de l'herbe, etc.).

lust[1] [lʌst], *s.* **1.** (*a*) *Theol:* Appétit *m* (coupable); convoitise *f*. **Lusts of the flesh**, concupiscence *f*. (*b*) Luxure *f*; désir (libidineux). **2.** *Lit:* Soif *f* (des richesses, du pouvoir).

lust[2], *v.ind.tr.* *Lit:* **1.** (*a*) *To l. for, after, sth.*, convoiter qch. (*b*) *To l. after a woman*, désirer une femme. **2.** *To l. for riches*, avoir soif des richesses.

lustful ['lʌstful], *a.* *Lit:* Lascif, libidineux. **-fully**, *adv.* Lascivement, libidineusement.

lustiness ['lʌstinəs], *s.* Vigueur *f*.

lustre[1] ['lʌstər], *s.* **1.** Éclat *m*, brillant *m*, lustre *m*. *F:* **To shed lustre on a name**, donner du lustre à un nom. **2.** (*a*) Pendeloque *f* (de lustre). (*b*) Lustre (de plafond). **'lustre-ware**, *s.* *Cer:* Poterie *f* à reflets métalliques; poterie lustrée.

lustre[2], *v.tr.* *Tex:* Lustrer, catir (une étoffe).

lustre[3], *s.* *Rom.Ant:* Lustre *m* (espace de cinq ans).

lustreless ['lʌstrələs], *a.* Mat, terne.

lustrine ['lʌstrin], *s.* *Tex:* Lustrine *f*.

lustrous ['lʌstrəs], *a.* Brillant, éclatant; (*of material*) lustré.

lusty ['lʌsti], *a.* Vigoureux, fort, robuste; *F:* puissant (de corps). **-ily**, *adv.* Vigoureusement, de toutes ses forces; (chanter) à pleine poitrine, à pleine gorge.

lute[1] [l(j)uːt], *s.* *Mus:* Luth *m*.

lute[2], *s.* Lut *m*, mastic *m*.

lute[3], *v.tr.* Luter, mastiquer.

Lutheran ['l(j)uːθərən], *a.* & *s.* Luthérien, -ienne.

luxation [lʌk'seiʃ(ə)n], *s.* Luxation *f*; déboîtement *m*.

luxuriance [lʌk'sjuəriəns, lʌg'z-], *s.* Exubérance *f*, luxuriance *f*.

luxuriant [lʌk'sjuəriənt, lʌg'z-], *a.* Exubérant, luxuriant. **-ly**, *adv.* Avec exubérance; en abondance.

luxuriate [lʌk'sjuərieit, ʌg'z-], *v.i.* **1.** (*Of vegetation*) Croître avec exubérance. **2.** (*Of pers.*) (*a*) *To l. in opulence*, vivre dans l'opulence, dans le luxe. (*b*) *To l. in dreams*, se griser de rêves.

luxurious [lʌk'sjuəriəs, lʌg'z-], *a.* (Appartement) luxueux, somptueux. **-ly**, *adv.* Luxueusement; dans le luxe.

luxuriousness [lʌk'sjuəriəsnəs, lʌg'z-], *s.* Luxe *m*; somptuosité *f*.

luxury ['lʌkʃəri], *s.* **1.** Luxe *m*. **To live in (the lap of) luxury**, vivre dans le luxe. **2.** (Objet *m* de) luxe. **Luxury article**, objet de luxe. **Table luxuries**, friandises *f*. *It is quite a l. for us*, c'est du luxe pour nous.

Lyceum [lai'siːəm], *s.* *Gr.Ant:* The Lyceum, le Lycée.

lych-gate ['litʃgeit], *s.* = LICH-GATE.

lychnis ['liknis], *s.* *Bot:* Lychnide *f*, lychnis *m*.

lye [lai], *s.* Lessive *f* (de soude, de potasse). **Caustic soda lye**, lessive de soude caustique.

lying[1, 2, 3] ['laiiŋ], *a.* & *s.* See LIE[2, 3, 4].

lymph [limf], *s.* **1.** *Physiol:* Lymphe *f*. **2.** *Med:* Vaccin *m*.

lymphatic [lim'fætik], *a.* Lymphatique.

lynch [linʃ], *v.tr.* Luncher. **lynching**, *s.* Lynchage *m*.

lynx [liŋks], *s.* *Z:* Lynx *m*; loup-cervier *m*, *pl.* loups-cerviers.

Lyons ['laiənz]. *Pr.n. Geog:* Lyon *m*.
lyre ['laiər], *s. Mus:* Lyre *f.* **'lyre-bird,** *s. Orn:* Ménure *m*; oiseau-lyre *m*.
lyric ['lirik]. **I.** *a.* Lyrique. **2.** *s.* Poème *m* lyrique. *Th:* Morceau *m* lyrique; chanson *f.*

lyrical ['lirik(ə)l], *a.* Lyrique.
lyricism ['lirisizm], *s.* **I.** Lyrisme *m.* **2.** *F:* (Faux) lyrisme.
lyricist ['lirisist], *s.* Poète *m* yrique.
lysol ['laisɔl], *s. Pharm:* Lysol *m.*

M

M, m [em], *s.* (La lettre) M, m.
ma [mɑː], *s. P:* = MAMMA.
ma'am [mɑːm, mam], *s.* **I.** = MADAM. **2.** *U.S: F:* School-ma'am [mɑːm], maîtresse *f* d'école.
mac [mak], *s. F:* = MACKINTOSH I.
macadam [mə'kadəm], *s. Civ.E:* Macadam *m.* Tar macadam, macadam au goudron; tarmacadam *m.*
macadamize [mə'kadəmaːiz], *v.tr. Civ.E:* Empierrer, macadamiser, ferrer (une route).
macaque [mə'kɑːk], *s. Z:* Macaque *m*, magot *m.*
macaroni [makə'rouni], *s. Cu:* Macaron *m.* Macaroni cheese, macaroni au gratin.
macaronic [makə'rɔnik], *a.* Macaronique.
macaroon [makə'ruːn], *s. Cu:* Macaron *m.*
mace¹ [meis], *s.* **I.** *Hist:* Masse *f* d'armes. **2.** (*a*) Masse (portée par le massier devant un fonctionnaire). (*b*) = MACE-BEARER. **'mace-bearer,** *s.* Massier *m*; appariteur *m.*
mace², *s. Bot: Cu:* Macis *m*; fleur *f* de muscade.
Macedonia [mase'dounjə]. *Pr.n. Geog:* La Macédoine.
Macedonian [mase'dounjən], *a. & s Geog: Hist:* Macédonien, -ienne.
macerate ['masəreit], *v.tr. & ɩ.* Macérer.
maceration [masə'reiʃ(ə)n], *s.* Macération *f.*
Machiavelli [makia'veli]. *Pr.n.m.* Machiavel.
Machiavellian [makia'veliən], *a.* Machiavélique.
machicolation [matʃikо'leiʃ(ə)n], **machicoulis** [maʃi'kuːli], *s.* Mâchicoulis *m.*
machinate ['makineit], *v.i* Comploter; tramer des complots.
machination [maki'neiʃ(ə)n], *s.* Machination *f,* complot *m*, intrigue *f.*
machinator ['makineitər], *s.* Machinateur, -trice; intrigant, -ante.
machine¹ [mə'ʃiːn], *s.* **I.** Machine *f.* (*Of pers.*) To be a mere machine, n'être qu'un automate. Reaping-machine, moissonneuse *f.* Wringing-machine, essoreuse *f.* Rivet(t)ing-machine, riveuse *f.* Machine-winding, bobinage mécanique. *F:* The party machine, l'organisation *f* politique du parti. **2.** (*a*) Bicyclette *f.* (*b*) *Av:* Appareil *m*, avion *m.* (*c*) *A:* Bathing-machine, cabine (de bains) roulante; voiture *f* de bains. **ma'chine-gun,** *s.* Mitrailleuse *f.* **ma'chine-gunner,** *s.* Mitrailleur *m.* **ma'chine-made,** *a.* (Fait) à la mécanique, à la machine. **ma'chine-minder,** *s.* Surveillant *m*, soigneu. *m*, de machines. **ma'chine-shop,** *s.* **I.** Atelier *m* de construction mécanique. **2.** Atelier d'usinage. **3.** Atelier des machines. **ma'chine-tool,** *s.* Machine-outil *f, pl.* machines-outils. **ma'chine-turned,** *a.* Fait au tour.
machine², *v.tr.* **I.** *Ind:* (*a*) Façonner (une pièce). (*b*) Usiner, ajuster. **2.** *Dressm:* Coudre, piquer, à la machine. **machining,** *s.* **I.** Usinage *m*; ajustage *m* mécanique. **2.** *Typ:* Tirage *m* à la machine. **3.** Couture *f*, piquage *m*, à la machine (à coudre).

machinery [mə'ʃiːn(ə)ri], *s.* **I.** Mécanisme *m*; machines *fpl*, machinerie *f.* Done by machinery fait à la mécanique, à la machine. **2.** *F:* The intricate machinery of government, les rouages *m* du gouvernement. **3.** *Lit: Th:* Le merveilleux.
machinist [mə'ʃiːnist], *s.* **I.** Machiniste *m*; mécanicien *m.* **2.** *Ind:* (*At sewing-machine*) Mécanicienne *f.*
mackerel ['mak(ə)rel], *s. Ich:* Maquereau *m.* **'mackerel-'sky,** *s.* Ciel pommelé; nuages pommelés.
mackintosh ['makintɔʃ], *s.* **I.** (Manteau *m* en) caoutchouc *m*; imperméable *m*; waterprool *m.* Light-weight m., paraverse *m.* **2.** Étoffe *f* ou toile *f* imperméable.
macle [makl], *s. Cryst: Miner:* Macle *f.*
macramé [mə'krɑːmi], *s. Needlew:* Macramé *m.*
macroscopic [makro'skɔpik], *a.* Macroscopique.
macula, *pl.* **-ae** ['makjula, -iː], *s. Astr: Med:* Macule *f.*
macular ['makjulər], *a. Med:* Pigmentaire.
maculation [makiu'leiʃ(ə)n], *s.* Maculation *f,* maculage *m.*
mad [mad], *a.* (madder) **I.** Fou, *f.* folle; aliéné. Raving mad, fou ɩ urieux. *F:* As mad as a hatter, as mad as a March hare, fou à lier. To drive s.o. mad, rendre qn fou. To go mad, devenir fou; tomber en démence. *F:* Imperialism gone mad, impérialisme forcené. Mad with pain, fou, éperdu, de douleur. *A mad hope,* un fol espoir. *A mad plan,* un projet insensé. *A mad gallop,* un galop furieux, effréné. *F:* Like mad, comme un enragé; follement **2.** Mad ɩor revenge, assoiffé de revanche. To be mad about, on, sth., être fou de qch.; avoir la folie, la rage, la manie, de qch. **3.** *Dial. & F:* To be mad with s.o., être furieux contre qn. It made me mad only to see him, rien que de le voir me rendait furieux. **4.** Mad bull, taureau furieux. *Vet:* Mad dog, chien enragé. **-ly,** *adv.* **I.** Follement; en fou; comme un fou. **2.** (Aimer) à la folie, éperdument. **3.** Furieusement. **'mad-doctor,** *s. F:* Médecin aliéniste.
Madagascan [madə'gaskən], *a.* Malgache.
madam ['madəm], *s.f.* **I.** Madame, mademoiselle. (*In letters*) Dear Madam, Madame, Mademoiselle. **2.** *F:* She's a bit of a madam, elle aime à le prendre de haut.
madcap ['madkap], *a. & s.* Écervelé, -ée.
madden [madn], *v.tr.* Rendre fou; exaspérer. **maddening,** *a.* A rendre fou; exaspérant.
madder ['madər], *s. Bot: Dy:* Garance *f.* **'madder-root,** *s.* Garance *f.*
madding ['madiŋ], *a.* The madding crowd, la foule bruyante.
made [meid]. *See* MAKE².
Madeira [mə'diərə]. *Pr.n. Geog:* Madère *f.* Madeira wine, vin *m* de Madère; madère *m.* Madeira cake, gâteau *m* de Savoie.

madhouse ['madhaus], *s.* Maison *f* de fous ; asile *m* d'aliénés.
madman, *pl.* **-men** ['madmən, -men], *s.m.* Fou, aliéné. *To fight like a m.,* se battre comme un forcené.
madness ['madnəs], *s.* **1.** Folie *f*; *Jur:* démence *f*. *F:* **It is sheer madness** *to go out in this weather,* c'est de la folie de sortir par le temps qu'il fait. **Midsummer madness,** (i) le comble de la folie ; (ii) une aberration qui passera. **2.** (*Of animals*) Rage *f*; hydrophobie *f*.
madonna [ma'dɔnɑ], *s.f.* Madone.
madrepore ['madripɔːər], *s. Coel:* Madrépore *m*.
madrigal ['madrigəl], *s.* Madrigal *m*, -aux.
madwort ['madwɔːrt], *s. Bot:* Alysse *f*, alysson *m*.
Maecenas [miː'siːnas]. *Pr.n.m.* Mécène.
Maelstrom ['meilstrɔm], *s.* **1.** *Geog:* (Le) Maelström. **2.** *F: The m.* of society life, le tourbillon de la vie mondaine.
maenad ['miːnad], *s.f. Gr.Myth:* Ménade.
magazine [magə'ziːn], *s.* **1.** (*a*) *Mil:* Magasin *m* d'armes, de vivres, d'équipement ; dépôt *m* de munitions. **Powder magazine,** (i) *Mil:* poudrière *f*; (ii) *Navy:* soute *f* aux poudres. (*b*) Magasin (d'un fusil, etc.). **Magazine gun,** fusil à répétition. **2.** Revue *f* ou recueil *m* périodique ; périodique *m*. **Illustrated m.,** magazine *m*.
Magdalen(e) ['magdalen, 'magdaliːn, -'liːni]. *Pr.n.f.* Madeleine.
magenta [ma'dʒentə], *s. & a.* (*Colour*) Magenta (*m*) *inv.*
Maggie ['magi]. *Pr.n.f.* (*Dim. of Margaret*) Margot.
Maggiore [ma'dʒɔːre . *Pr.n.* **Lake Maggiore,** le ac Majeur.
maggot ['magət], *s.* **1.** Larve *f* apode ; *F:* ver *m*, asticot *m*. **2.** *F:* Caprice *m*, lubie *f*.
maggoty ['magəti], *a.* Plein de vers.
magic ['madʒik]. **1.** *s.* Magie *f*, enchantement *m*. **As if by magic, like magic,** comme par enchantement. **2.** *a.* Magique, enchanté. *S.a.* LANTERN 1.
magical ['madʒik(ə)l], *a.* Magique. **-ally,** *adv.* Magiquement ; par magie.
magician [ma'dʒiʃ(ə)n], *s.* Magicien, -ienne.
magisterial [madʒis'tiːəriəl], *a.* **1.** (Air, ton) magistral, -aux ; (air) de maître. **2.** De magistrat. **-ally,** *adv.* **1.** (*a*) Magistralement. (*b*) En maître. **2.** En qualité de magistrat.
magistracy ['madʒistrəsi], *s.* Magistrature *f*.
magistrate ['madʒistret], *s.* Magistrat *m*, juge *m*. **Police-court magistrate,** juge de paix.
magistrateship ['madʒistret.ʃip]; **magistrature** ['madʒistretjuər], *s.* Magistrature *f*.
Magna C(h)arta ['magnə'kɑːrta], *s. Engl.Hist:* La Grande Charte (de 1215).
magnanimity [magnə'nimiti], *s.* Magnanimité *f*.
magnanimous [mag'naniməs], *a.* Magnanime. **-ly,** *adv.* Magnanimement.
magnate ['magneit], *s.* Magnat *m, F:* gros bonnet (de l'industrie).
magnesia [mag'niːʃa], *s.* **1.** *Ch:* Magnésie *f*. **2.** *Pharm:* Magnésie blanche ; magnésie anglaise.
magnesium [mag'niːziəm], *s. Ch:* Magnésium *m*. **Magnesium light,** éclair *m* au magnésium.
magnet ['magnet], *s.* **1.** Aimant *m*. **Bar magnet,** barreau aimanté. **Horse-shoe magnet,** aimant en fer à cheval. **2.** Électro-aimant *m*.
magnetic [mag'netik], *a.* **1.** Magnétique ; aimanté. **Magnetic iron ore,** pierre *f* d'aimant.

2. (*Of pers., power*) Magnétique, hypnotique. **-ally,** *adv.* Magnétiquement.
magnetism ['magnetizm], *s.* **1.** **Animal magnetism,** magnétisme animal ; hypnotisme *m*. **2.** Aimantation *f*. **Residual magnetism,** magnétisme remanent.
magnetite ['magnetait], *s. Miner:* Magnétite *f*.
magnetize ['magnetaːiz], *v.tr.* **1.** *F:* Magnétiser, attirer (qn). **2.** (*a*) Aimanter (une aiguille, etc.). (*b*) (*With passive force*) (*Of iron*) S'aimanter.
magnetizing, *s.* **1.** Magnétisation *f* (de qn, des esprits). **2.** Aimantation *f*.
magneto [mag'niːto], *s. I.C.E:* etc : Magnéto *f*.
magnific [mag'nifik], *a. A. & Lit:* Sublime, grandiose.
magnification [magnifi'keiʃ(ə)n], *s.* **1.** *Opt:* Grossissement *m*, amplification *f*. **2.** Exaltation *f* (de qn).
magnificence [mag'nifis(ə)ns],*s.* Magnificence*f*.
magnificent [mag'nifis(ə)nt], *a.* Magnifique ; (repas) somptueux. **-ly,** *adv.* Magnifiquement.
magnifier ['magnifaiər], *s.* Verre grossissant ; oupe *f*.
magnify ['magnifai], *v.tr.* Grossir, agrandir (une image) ; amplifier, renforcer (un son). **Magnifying glass,** loupe *f*; verre grossissant. *F: To m. an incident,* grossir, exagérer, un incident.
magnifying, *s. Opt:* **Magnifying power,** grossissement *m*.
magniloquence [mag'nilokwəns],*s.* Emphase *f*; grandiloquence *f*.
magniloquent [mag'nilokwənt], *a.* Emphatique, grandiloquent.
magnitude [mag'nitjuːd], *s.* Grandeur *f. Astr:* Magnitude *f*.
magnolia [mag'noulja], *s. Bot:* Magnolia(-tree), magnolia *m*, magnolier *m*.
magnum opus ['magnəm'oupəs], *Lt.s.phr. F:* Grand ouvrage ; chef-d'œuvre *m*.
magpie ['magpai], *s. Orn:* Pie *f*.
magus, *pl.* **-gi** ['meigəs, -dʒai], *s.* Mage *m.* **The Three Magi,** les trois Mages.
Magyar ['magjɑːr, 'madʒɑːr], *a. & s. Ethn:* Ma(d)gyar, -are.
mahogany [ma'hɔgəni], *s.* Acajou *m*.
Mahomet [ma'hɔmet]. *Pr.n.m. Rel.H:* Mahomet.
Mahometan [ma'hɔmətən], *a. & s.* = MOHAM-MEDAN.
mahout [ma'haut], *s.* Cornac *m*, mahout *m*.
maid [meid], *s.f.* **1.** *Lit:* = MAIDEN 1 (*a*). **2.** *A. & Poet:* = MAIDEN 1 (*b*). **The Maid (of Orleans),** la Pucelle (d'Orléans). **3.** **Old maid,** vieille fille. **4.** Bonne, domestique, servante. **Lady's maid,** camériste ; femme de chambre. **5.** **Maid of honour,** (i) fille d'honneur (de la reine) ; (ii) *Cu:* petite tarte genre flan. **'maid-of-'all-work,** *F:* Bonne à tout faire.
maiden [meidn],*s.* **1.** (*a*) Jeune fille *f*. (*b*) Vierge *f*. **2.** *Attrib.* (*a*) **Maiden aunt,** tante non mariée. **Maiden lady,** demoiselle *f*. (*b*) **Maiden modesty,** modestie de jeune fille. **Maiden name,** nom de jeune fille ; nom de demoiselle. **Adm:** *Mary Robinson,* **maiden name Jones,** Mary Robinson, née Jones. (*c*) **Maiden voyage, maiden trip,** premier voyage (d'un vaisseau). **Maiden speech,** discours de début (d'un député).
maidenhair ['meidnhɛər], *s. Bot:* Maidenhair (fern), capillaire *m ; F:* cheveux *mpl* de Vénus.
maidenhood ['meidnhud], *s.* **1.** Célibat *m* (de fille) ; condition *f* de fille.
maidenlike ['meidnlaik], **maidenly** ['meidnli]. **1.** *a.* De jeune fille, virgina, -aux ; modeste. **2.** *adv.* Avec modestie, avec pudeur.

maidservant ['meidsɔːrvənt], s.f. Lit: Servante; bonne.

mail[1] [meil], s. Archeol: Mailles fpl.

mail[2], s. Post: 1. Courrier m; F: la poste. To open the mail, dépouiller le courrier. 2. La poste. The Royal Mail = le Service des postes. **'mail-bag,** s. Sac m de dépêches, sac de poste. **'mail-boat,** s. Courrier postal; paquebot-poste m, pl. paquebots-poste. **'mail-cart,** s. Chariot m d'enfant; F: poussette f. **'mail-coach,** s. 1. A: Malle-poste f. 2. Rail: = MAIL-VAN 1. **'mail-order,** s. Com: Commande faite par l'entremise de la poste. Mail-order business, achat m et vente f par correspondance. **'mail-packet,** s. = MAIL-BOAT. **'mail-train,** s. Train-poste m, pl. trains-poste. **'mail-van,** s. 1. Wagon-poste m, pl. wagons-poste. 2. Fourgon m des postes; fourgon postal.

mail[3], v.tr. Esp. U.S: Envoyer par la poste, expédier (des lettres, des paquets).

mailed [meild], a. Revêtu de mailles. F: The mailed fist, la main gantelée; la force armée.

maim [meim], v.tr. Estropier, mutiler.

main[1] [mein], s. 1. Vigueur f. In the phr. With might and main, de toutes mes, ses, forces. 2. Poet: Océan m; haute mer. S.a. SPANISH 1. 3. In the main, en général, en somme; à tout prendre. 4. Civ.E: Canalisation maîtresse. El: Conducteur principal; câble m de distribution. El: To take one's power from the mains, brancher sur le secteur. W.Tel: All-mains set, poste secteur tous courants.

main[2], a. 1. By main force, de vive force; à main armée. 2. Principal, -aux; premier, essentiel. (a) The main body, le gros (de l'armée, etc.). Agr: Main crop, culture principale. (b) The main point, the main thing, l'essentiel, le principal. Main idea, idée f mère (d'une œuvre). Main features of a speech, grands traits, points saillants, d'un discours. Gram: Main clause, proposition principale. Cu: Main dish, plat m de résistance. (c) Main road, main highway, grande route; route à grande circulation. Main street, rue principale. Rail: etc: Main line, voie principale, grande ligne. (d) Nau: The main masts, les mâts majeurs. Main boiler, chaudière principale. **-ly,** adv. 1. Principalement, surtout. 2. En grande partie. **'main-brace,** s. Nau: Grand bras (de vergue). F: To splice the main-brace, boire un coup. **'main-'deck,** s. Nau: Pont principal; premier pont. **'main-top,** s. Nau: Grand'hune f. **'main-yard,** s. Nau: Grand'vergue f.

mainland ['meinlənd], s. Continent m; terre f ferme.

mainmast ['meinmɑːst, -məst], s. Nau: Grand mât.

mainsail ['meinseil, meinsl], s. Nau: Grand'-voile f; (of boat) taille-vent m inv.

mainspring ['meinspriŋ], s. 1. Grand ressort; ressort moteur. 2. F: Mobile essentiel, cheville ouvrière (d'une situation).

mainstay ['meinstei], s. 1. Nau: Étai m de grand mât. 2. F: Soutien principal; point m d'appui (d'une cause, etc.).

maintain [men'tein], v.tr. 1. Maintenir (l'ordre); soutenir (un siège, la conversation); entretenir (des relations); conserver (la santé); garder, observer (une attitude, le silence); garder (son sang-froid). To m. s.o., sth., in a position, maintenir qn, qch., dans une position. The improvement is maintained, le mieux se soutient. 2. Entretenir, soutenir, faire subsister (une famille, etc.); Jur: subvenir aux besoins de (sa famille). 3. Entretenir (une armée, une route). 4. Soutenir, défendre (une cause). To maintain one's rights, défendre ses droits. 5. Garder (un avantage). F: I m. my ground, je n'en démords pas. 6. (S'obstiner à) soutenir (une opinion, un fait). To maintain that ..., maintenir, soutenir, prétendre, que. . . .

maintainable [men'teinəbl], a. 1. (Position) tenable. 2. (Opinion) soutenable.

maintenance ['meintənəns], s. 1. Maintien m (de l'ordre). 2. (a) Entretien m (d'une famille, des routes). (b) (Moyens mpl de) subsistance f; Jur: pension f alimentaire. Jur: Maintenance order, obligation f alimentaire. 3. M. of one's rights, défense f de ses droits. In maintenance of this opinion ..., à l'appui de cette opinion. . . .

maize [meiz], s. Maïs m.

majestic(al) [ma'dʒestik(əl)], a. Majestueux, auguste. **-ally,** adv. Majestueusement, augustement.

majesty ['madʒəsti], s. Majesté f. His Majesty, Her Majesty, Sa Majesté le Roi, Sa Majesté la Reine. On His Majesty's Service, abbr. O.H.M.S., (pour le) service de Sa Majesté (= service de l'État); Post: en franchise.

majolica [ma'dʒɔlika], s. Cer: Majolique f.

major[1] ['meidʒər], s. Mil: Commandant m; chef m de bataillon (d'infanterie); chef d'escadron (de cavalerie). **'major-'general,** s. Général m de brigade.

major[2]. 1. a. (a) The major portion, la majeure partie, la plus grande partie. Geom: Major axis, axe transverse, grand axe (d'une ellipse). Mus: Major key, ton majeur. Aut: Major road, route de priorité. Cards: (At bridge) The major suits, les couleurs principales (pique et cœur). (b) Drum-major, tambour-major m. S.a. SERGEANT-MAJOR. Sch: Smith major, Smith aîné (l'aîné de deux Smith). 2. s. (a) Jur: (Pers.) Majeur, -eure; personne majeure. (b) Log: Majeure f.

Majorca [ma'dʒɔːrka], Pr.n. Geog: Majorque f.

major-domo, pl. -os ['meidʒər'doumou, -ouz], s. Majordome m.

majority [ma'dʒɔriti], s. 1. Majorité f (des voix). (a) To be in a majority, in the majority, être en majorité, avoir la majorité. Decision taken by a majority, décision prise à la majorité (des voix). (b) La plus grande partie, le plus grand nombre (des hommes, etc.). F: To join the (great) majority, mourir; s'en aller ad patres. 2. Jur: To attain one's majority, atteindre sa majorité; devenir majeur. 3. Mil: = MAJORSHIP.

majorship ['meidʒərʃip], s. Mil: Grade m de commandant.

make[1] [meik], s. 1. (a) Façon f, fabrication f (d'une robe, etc.). (b) Com: Ind: Marque f (d'un produit). Of French m., de fabrication française, de construction française. 2. Taille f (de qn). Man of slight m., homme plutôt mince. 3. F: To be on the make, poursuivre un but intéressé. 4. El.E: Fermeture f (du circuit).

make[2], v. (made [meid]; made) I. v.tr. 1. Faire; construire (une machine, etc.); façonner (un vase, etc.); fabriquer (du papier, etc.); confectionner (des vêtements). You are made for this work, vous êtes fait pour ce travail. F: He's as cute as they make 'em, c'est un malin entre tous. Bread is made of corn, le pain est fait de blé. What is it made of? en quoi est-ce? To make a friend of s.o., faire de qn son ami. I don't know what to make of it, I can make nothing of it, je n'y comprends rien. To show what one is made of, donner sa mesure. To make one's will, faire son testament. *Fin:* **To make a promissory note, a bill of exchange,** souscrire un billet à ordre; libeller une lettre de change. **To make the bed, the tea,** faire le lit, le thé. *Cards:* **To make the cards,** battre les cartes. **To make trouble,** causer, occasionner, des désagréments. **To make a noise,** faire du bruit. **To make peace,** faire, conclure, la paix. **To make an opportunity for s.o. to do sth.,** ménager à qn l'occasion de faire qch. **To make a speech,** faire un discours. **To make a mistake,** faire, commettre, une faute. **To make war,** faire la guerre. **To make one's escape,** s'échapper, se sauver. **We made the whole distance in ten days,** nous avons couvert toute la distance en dix jours. **2.** (*a*) Établir, assurer (*a connection between* . . ., le raccordement de . . .). *El:* **To make the circuit,** fermer le circuit. (*b*) **Two and two make four,** deux et deux font, égalent, quatre. *This book makes pleasant reading,* ce livre est d'une lecture agréable. **To make a good husband, a good wife,** se montrer bon époux, bonne épouse. **Will you make one (of the party)?** voulez-vous être des nôtres? **3. To make three pounds a week,** gagner trois livres par semaine. **To make a fortune, one's fortune,** faire fortune; gagner une fortune. *F:* **To make a bit,** se faire un peu d'argent. *To make a name,* se faire un nom. **To make profits,** réaliser des bénéfices. **What will you make by it?** quel profit vous en reviendra-t-il? *Cards:* **To make a trick,** faire une levée. **To make one's contract,** réussir son contrat. *Abs.* (*Of card*) **To make,** faire la levée. *U.S:* *F:* **To make it,** réussir; y arriver. **4.** *To make* the fortune de (qn). *This book made him,* ce livre lui assura la célébrité, la renommée. **5.** *Pred.* **To make s.o. happy,** rendre qn heureux. *To m. s.o. hungry, sleepy,* donner faim, sommeil, à qn. *To m. a box too heavy,* rendre une boîte trop lourde. *To m. a dish hot,* (faire) chauffer un plat. *To m. s.o. a judge,* nommer qn juge. *He was made a knight,* il fut créé chevalier. **To make sth. known, felt, understood,** faire connaître, sentir, comprendre, qch. **To make oneself heard,** se faire entendre. *To m. oneself comfortable,* se mettre à l'aise. *To m. oneself ill,* se rendre malade. **To make it a rule, one's object, to** . . ., se faire une règle, un but, de. . . . *Can you come at six?*—**Make it half-past,** pouvez-vous venir à six heures?—Plutôt la demie. **6. The climate is not so bad as you make it,** le climat n'est pas si mauvais que vous le dites. **What do you make the time?** quelle heure avez-vous? **7. To make s.o. speak,** faire parler qn. **You should make him do it,** vous devriez le lui faire faire. *What made you go?* qu'est-ce qui vous a déterminé à partir? *What made you say that?* pourquoi avez-vous dit cela? **8.** *Nau:* (*a*) Arriver à (un port). **To make a headland,** (i) arriver en vue d'un cap; (ii) doubler, franchir, une pointe. (*b*) (*Of ship*) **To make twenty knots,** faire vingt nœuds, filer à vingt nœuds. *F:* **We made bad weather,** nous avons essuyé du mauvais temps. **II. make,** *v.i.* **1. To make for, towards, a place,** se diriger vers un endroit. **He made for, after, me like a madman,** il s'élança, se précipita, sur moi comme un fou. *Nau:* **To make for** . . ., faire route sur . . ., mettre le cap sur . . . **To make for the open sea,** prendre le large. *To m. for the anchorage,* se rendre au mouillage. **2.** *These agreements m. for peace,* ces accords tendent à maintenir la paix. *This fine weather makes for optimism,* ce beau temps favorise l'optimisme. **3. To make as if, as though, to do sth.,** faire

mine ou faire semblant de faire qch. **4.** (*Of tide*) Se faire; (*of flood-tide*) monter; (*of ebb*) baisser. **5.** *El.E:* (*Of current*) **To make and break,** s'interrompre et se rétablir. **make away,** *v.i.* (*a*) S'éloigner. (*b*) **To make away with sth.,** détruire, faire disparaître, enlever, qch.; dérober (de l'argent, etc.). **To make away with s.o.,** mettre qn à mort; se défaire de qn. **To make away with oneself,** se suicider; se donner la mort. **make off,** *v.i.* Se sauver; décamper, filer. *To m. off with the cash,* filer avec l'argent; lever le pied. **make out,** *v.tr.* **1.** Faire, établir, dresser (une liste, etc.); établir, dresser, relever (un compte); faire, tirer, créer (un chèque). **2.** (*a*) Établir, prouver (qch.). **How do you make that out?** comment arrivez-vous à ce résultat, à cette conclusion? (*b*) **To make s.o. out to be richer than he is,** faire qn plus riche qu'il ne l'est. **He is not such a fool as people make out,** il n'est pas aussi bête qu'on le dépeint, qu'on le fait. **3.** (*a*) Comprendre (une énigme); démêler (les raisons de qch.); déchiffrer, débrouiller (une écriture). **I can't make it out,** je n'y comprends rien. (*b*) Distinguer, discerner (qch.). *Nau:* **To m. out a light,** reconnaître un feu. **make over,** *v.tr.* Céder, transférer, transmettre (*sth. to s.o.,* qch. à qn). **make up.** **I.** *v.tr.* **1.** Compléter, parfaire (une somme); combler, suppléer à (un déficit). **To make up the even money,** faire l'appoint. **2. To make up lost ground,** regagner le terrain perdu. **To make it up to s.o. for sth.,** dédommager qn de qch.; indemniser qn. **3.** Faire (un paquet). *Pharm:* Composer, préparer (une ordonnance). **4.** (*a*) Faire, confectionner, façonner (des vêtements). 'Customers' own material made up,' ''on travaille à façon''; ''tailleur à façon.'' (*b*) Dresser (une liste). (*c*) Régler, établir, arrêter (un compte); régler, balancer (les livres). (*d*) Inventer, forger (une histoire, des excuses). **5.** (*a*) Rassembler, réunir (une compagnie); rassembler (une somme d'argent). *b*) **To make up the fire,** ajouter du combustible au feu; (re)charger le poêle. (*c*) *Typ:* **To make up,** mettre en pages. **6.** Former, composer (un ensemble). **7. To make (oneself) up,** se farder, se maquiller; *Th:* faire sa figure; (*of man*) se grimer. **8. To make up one's mind,** se décider; prendre son parti. **9.** Arranger, accommoder (un différend). **To make it up (again),** se réconcilier; se remettre bien ensemble. **II. make up,** *v.i.* **1.** (*a*) **To make up for lost time,** rattraper, réparer, le temps perdu. *To m. up for one's losses,* se rattraper de ses pertes. *That makes up for it,* c'est une compensation. (*b*) **To make up for the want of sth.,** suppléer au manque de qch. **2. To make up on a competitor,** gagner sur un concurrent. **3. To make up to s.o.,** (i) s'avancer vers qn, s'approcher de qn; (ii) *F:* faire des avances, faire la cour, à qn. **'make-up,** *s.* **1.** Composition *f* (de qch.). **2.** *Th:* Maquillage *m,* fard *m.* **3.** *Typ:* Mise *f* en pages. **4.** Invention *f;* histoire inventée (de toutes pièces). **5.** Appoint *m.* **Make-up length** (*of pipe, etc.*), pièce jointive; pièce de raccordement. **made-up,** *a.* **1.** Made-up box, caisse assemblée. *Rail:* Made-up train, rame *f* de wagons. **2.** Artificiel, factice; faux, *f.* fausse. Made-up story, histoire inventée de toutes pièces; histoire faite à plaisir. **making up,** *s.* **1.** Compensation *f* (*for losses,* de pertes). **2.** *Pharm:* Préparation *f,* composition *f* (d'un médicament). **3.** (*a*) Confection *f,* façon *f* (de vêtements). (*b*) Dressage *m* (d'une liste). (*c*) *Com:* *Fin:* Confection (d'un bilan); arrêté *m,* alignement *m* (des comptes). *St.Exch:* Making-up

price, cours *m* de compensation. (*d*) Invention *f* (d'une histoire). **4.** *Typ:* Making up and imposing, mise *f* en pages. **5.** Composition, formation *f* (d'un ensemble). **6.** *Th: etc:* Maquillage *m.* **7.** Arrangement *m*, raccommodement *m* (d'un différend). **made,** *a.* **1.** Fait, fabriqué, confectionné. **Foreign-made,** fait à l'étranger. **2.** *F:* **He is a made man,** son avenir, son sort, est assuré ; sa fortune est faite. **making,** *s.* **1.** (*a*) Fabrication *f* ; confection *f*, façon *f* (de vêtements) ; construction *f* (d'un pont) ; composition *f* (d'un poème) ; création *f* (du monde). **The material and the making,** le matériel et la main-d'œuvre. *The marriage was* **none of her making,** ce n'était pas elle qui avait arrangé le mariage. **This incident was the making of him,** c'est à cet incident qu'il dut sa fortune, tout son succès. **History in the making,** l'histoire en train de se faire. (*b*) **To have the makings of . . .,** avoir tout ce qu'il faut pour devenir. . . . **I have not the makings of a hero,** je n'ai rien du héros. **2.** *pl.* **Makings,** recettes *f* ; petits profits. **'make-and-'break,** *s.* *El:* Conjoncteur-disjoncteur *m* ; trembleur *m*, vibreur *m.* **Make-and-break coil,** bobine *f* à rupteur, à trembleur. **'make-believe¹.** **1.** *s.* Semblant *m*, feinte *f*, trompe-l'œil *m.* **The land of make-believe,** le pays des chimères. **2.** *a.* Make-believe **soldiers,** soldats pour rire. **make-be'lieve²,** *v.i.* (**made-believe**) (*Of children*) Jouer à faire semblant ; faire semblant. **'make-do,** *attrib.a.* **Make-do expedient,** moyen *m* de fortune. **'make-weight,** *s.* Complément *m* de poids ; supplément *m.*

makefast ['meikfɑːst], *s.* *Nau:* Amarre *f.*

maker ['meikər], *s.* **1.** Faiseur, -euse. *Com: Ind:* Fabricant *m* ; constructeur *m* (de machines). **2.** **Our Maker, the Maker of all,** le Créateur.

makeshift ['meikʃift], *s.* Pis-aller *m*, expédient *m* ; moyen *m* de fortune. *A m.* **dinner,** un dîner de fortune.

maladjustment [malə'dʒʌstmənt], *s.* Ajustement défectueux ; déréglage *m.*

maladministration [maladminis'treiʃ(ə)n], *s.* Mauvaise administration ; mauvaise gestion (des affaires publiques, etc.). *Jur:* Forfaiture *f.*

maladroit ['maladrɔit], *a.* Maladroit. **-ly,** *adv.* Maladroitement.

maladroitness ['maladrɔitnəs], *s.* Maladresse *f.*

malady ['maladi], *s.* Maladie *f*, mal *m.*

malapert ['malapəːrt], *a.* *A:* Insolent, impertinent.

malapropism ['malapropizm], *s.* Emploi *m* de mots savants déformés ou hors de propos ; incongruité *f.*

malaria [mə'lɛəriə], *s.* *Med:* Malaria *f* ; (im)paludisme *m.* **Malaria-stricken,** impaludé.

malarial [mə'lɛəriəl], *a.* (*Of infection, etc.*) Paludéen.

malarious [mə'lɛəriəs], *a.* (Marécage) impaludé.

Malay [mə'lei]. **1.** *a. & s.* *Geog:* Malais, -aise. **The Malay Archipelago,** la Malaisie. **2.** *s.* *Ling:* Le malais.

Malayan [mə'leijən], *a.* *Geog:* Malais.

malcontent ['malkɔntent], *a. & s.* Mécontent, -ente.

male [meil]. **1.** *a.* Mâle. **Male sex,** sexe masculin. *M. child,* enfant mâle. *A m.* **friend,** un ami. **2.** *s.m.* Mâle. **Male ward** (*in a hospital*), salle *f* pour hommes.

malediction [mali'dikʃ(ə)n], *s.* Malédiction *f.*

maledictory [mali'diktəri], *a.* De malédiction.

malefactor ['malifaktər], *s.* Malfaiteur, -trice.

malefic [mə'lefik], *a.* Maléfique.

maleficence [mə'lefis(ə)ns], *s.* Malfaisance *f.*

maleficent [mə'lefis(ə)nt], *a.* **1.** Malfaisant (*to,* envers). **2.** (*Of pers.*) Criminel.

malevolence [mə'levolans], *s.* Malveillance *f* (*towards,* envers).

malevolent [mə'levolənt], *a.* Malveillant. **-ly,** *adv.* Avec malveillance.

malfeasance [mal'fiːzəns], *s.* **1.** *Jur:* Agissements *m* coupables ; malversation *f.* **2.** Méfait *m.*

malformation [malfɔr'meiʃ(ə)n], *s.* Malformation *f* ; défaut *m*, vice *m*, de conformation.

malice ['malis], *s.* **1.** Malice *f*, malveillance *f*, méchanceté *f.* **Out of malice,** par malice, par méchanceté. **To bear malice to, towards, s.o.** ; **to bear s.o. malice,** en vouloir à qn ; avoir de la rancune contre qn. **2.** *Jur:* Intention criminelle ou délictueuse. **With, of, malice prepense, with malice aforethought,** avec intention criminelle ; avec préméditation.

malicious [mə'liʃəs], *a.* **1.** (*a*) Méchant, malveillant. (*b*) Rancunier. **2.** *Jur:* Fait avec intention criminelle ou délictueuse ; criminel. **-ly,** *adv.* **1.** (*a*) Avec méchanceté, avec malveillance. (*b*) Par rancune. **2.** *Jur:* Avec intention criminelle ; avec préméditation.

malign¹ [mə'lain], *a.* **1.** Pernicieux, nuisible. **2.** *Med:* = MALIGNANT 2.

malign², *v.tr.* Calomnier, diffamer.

malignancy [mə'lignənsi], *s.* **1.** Malignité *f*, méchanceté *f*, malveillance *f.* *Med:* Malignité, virulence *f* (d'une maladie).

malignant [mə'lignənt], *a.* **1.** Malin, *f.* maligne ; méchant. **2.** *Med:* Malin. **-ly,** *adv.* Avec malignité ; méchamment.

maligner [mə'lainər], *s.* Calomniateur, -trice ; diffamateur, -trice.

malignity [mə'ligniti], *s.* = MALIGNANCY.

malinger [mə'liŋgər], *v.i.* *Mil: Navy:* Faire le malade ; *P:* tirer au flanc. **malingering,** *s.* Simulation *f* (de maladie) ; *P:* tirage *m* au flanc.

malingerer [mə'liŋgərər], *s.* *Mil: Navy:* Faux malade ; *P:* tireur *m* au flanc.

mallard ['malərd], *s.* Malard *m* ; canard *m* sauvage.

malleability [maliə'biliti], *s.* Malléabilité *f.*

malleable ['maliəbl] *a.* Malléable ; forgeable.

mallet ['malet], *s.* **1.** *Tls:* Maillet *m*, mailloche *f.* **2.** *Games:* Maillet (de croquet, de polo).

mallow ['malo], *s.* *Bot:* **1.** Mauve *f.* **2.** = MARSH-MALLOW.

malmsey ['mɑːmzi], *s.* Vin *m* de Malvoisie.

malnutrition [malnju'triʃ(ə)n], *s.* **1.** Sous-alimentation *f.* **2.** Alimentation défectueuse.

malodorous [mə'loudərəs], *a.* Malodorant ; nauséabond.

malpractice [mal'praktis], *s.* **1.** Méfait *m.* **2.** *Jur:* (*a*) Négligence *f* (d'un médecin). (*b*) Malversation *f.*

malt [mɔlt], *s.* Malt *m.* **Malt liquor,** bière *f.* **'malt-house,** *s.* *Brew:* Malterie *f.*

Malta ['mɔltə]. *Pr.n. Geog:* Malte *f.*

malted ['mɔltid], *a.* **Malted milk,** farine lactée.

Maltese [mɔl'tiːz], *a. & s.* *Geog: Ethn:* Maltais, -aise. *Her: Mec.E:* **Maltese cross,** croix *f* de Malte.

malting ['mɔltiŋ], *s.* **1.** Maltage *m.* **2.** = MALT-HOUSE.

maltreat [mal'triːt], *v.tr.* Maltraiter, malmener.

maltreatment [mal'triːtmənt], *s.* Mauvais traitement.

maltster ['mɔltstər], *s.m.* Malteur.

malvaceae [mal'veisii], *s.pl.* *Bot:* Malvacées *f.*

malvaceous [mal'veiʃəs], *a.* *Bot:* Malvacé, malvé.

malversation [malvər'seiʃ(ə)n], s. **1.** Malversation f. **2.** Mauvaise administration; gestion f coupable.

mamilla [ma'milə], s. **1.** Anat: Bout m de sein. **2.** Anat: Bot: Mamelon m.

mamillary ['mamiləri], a. **1.** Mamillaire. **2.** = MAMMIFORM.

mamma [ma'mɑ:], s.f. F: Maman.

mammal ['maməl], s. Z: Mammifère m.

mammalia [ma'meilia], s.pl. Z: Mammifères m.

mammary ['maməri], a. Anat: Mammaire.

mammiform ['mamifɔ:rm], a. Mammiforme.

mammoth ['maməθ]. **1.** s. Mammouth m. **2.** Attrib.a. F: Géant, monstre.

mammy ['mami], s.f. **1.** A. & P: Maman. **2.** U.S: Négresse bonne d'enfants.

man¹, pl. **men** [man, men], s.m. **1.** (a) (Human being) Homme. **Entertainment for man and beast**, ici on loge à pied et à cheval. **Every man**, tout le monde; tous; chacun. **Any man**, quelqu'un; n'importe qui. **No man**, personne. **No man's land**, (i) terrains m vagues; (ii) Mil: (1914-18) zone f neutre. **Some men**, quelques personnes, quelques-uns. **Few men**, peu de gens. **Men say that . . .**, on dit que. . . . *Solitude changes a man*, la solitude, ça vous change. (b) (*Mankind*) L'homme. **Man proposes, God disposes**, l'homme propose et Dieu dispose. (c) Theol: **The old, the new, man**, le vieil homme, le nouvel homme. F. & Hum: **To satisfy the inner man**, se refaire, se restaurer, se réfectionner. **2.** (*Adult male*) Homme. (a) **Men and women**, les hommes et les femmes. **Between man and man**, d'homme à homme. *May I speak to you as man to man?* puis-je vous parler d'homme à homme? **They were killed to a man**, ils furent tués jusqu'au dernier. **To show oneself a man**, se montrer homme. **To make a man of s.o.**, faire un homme de qn. **To bear sth. like a man**, supporter qch. avec courage. **He is not the man to** (*refuse, etc.*), il n'est pas homme à (refuser, etc.). **I'm your man**, je suis votre homme; (ii) cela me va! *He is just the man for me*, c'est mon homme. **To be one's own man**, (i) être maître de soi; (ii) ne dépendre que de soi. **A man's man**, un vrai homme. F: *Come here, my little man!* viens ici, mon petit bonhomme! *What are you doing there*, **my (good) man?** que faites-vous là, mon brave (homme), mon ami? **Good man!** bravo! *Good-bye*, **old man!** adieu, mon vieux! (b) (*Often not translated*) *An old man*, un vieillard. *The dead man*, le mort. **The man Smith**, le nommé Smith, le dit Smith. *That man Smith*, (i) Smith que voilà; (ii) ce chenapan de Smith. (c) *The men of Somerset*, les habitants, les natifs, du Somerset. Sch: **He's an Oxford man**, (i) c'est un étudiant d'Oxford; (ii) il a fait ses études à l'Université d'Oxford; (d) Attrib. **Man cook**, cuisinier. (e) Oyster-man, marchand d'huîtres. **3.** (a) Scot: Her man, son mari. (b) Man and wife, mari et femme. (c) P: **My young man**, (i) mon bon ami; (ii) mon futur, mon fiancé. **4.** (a) Hist: (*Vassal*) Homme. (b) Domestique m, valet m. (c) Adm: Com: Employé m, garçon m. (d) Ind: **The masters and the men**, les patrons et les ouvriers. (e) Mil: Nau: (*Usu. pl.*) Homme. **Officers, N.C.O.'s, and men**, officiers, sous-officiers, et hommes de troupe. (f) Sp: Joueur m. **5.** (*At chess*) Pièce f; (*at draughts*) pion m. **man-at-'arms**, s.m. (pl. men-at-arms) A: Homme d'armes. **'man-child**, s.m. Enfant mâle. **'man-eater**, s. (pl. man-eaters) **1.** (*Of pers.*) Anthropophage m, cannibale m. **2.** (*Of animal*) Mangeur m d'hommes. **'man-eating**, a. **1.** (Tribu, etc.) anthropophage. **2.** (Tigre, etc.) mangeur d'hommes. **'man-handle**, v.tr. **1.** Manutentionner (des marchandises, etc.). **2.** F: Maltraiter, malmener (qn). **'man-hater**, s. Misanthrope m. **'man-hole**, s. Trou m d'homme (de.chaudière); trou de visite. **Man-hole cover**, (i) tampon m (d'un égout); (ii) Mch: autoclave m d'un trou d'homme. **'man-hunter**, s. (pl. man-hunters) Chasseur m de têtes. **man-of-'war**, s. (pl. men-of-war) Nau: Vaisseau m de guerre; vaisseau de ligne. **'man-power**, s. **1.** Mec.E: La force des bras. **2.** Coll. 'a) Coll: Main-d'œuvre f. (b) Mil: Effectifs mpl. **'man-servant**, s.m. (pl. men-servants) Domestique; valet de chambre). **'man-trap**, s. Piège m à hommes, à loups.

man², v.tr. (manned) Garnir d'hommes. (a) **To man a fort**, mettre une garnison dans un fort; garnir un fort. (b) Nau: Armer, équiper (un canot). **Fully manned boat**, canot à armement complet. *To man a rope*, se mettre à, sur, une manœuvre. *To man the yards*, monter les vergues.

manacle¹ ['manəkl], s. Menotte f.

manacle², v.tr. Mettre les menottes à (qn).

manage ['manedʒ], v.tr. **1.** Manier (un outil); diriger, manœuvrer (un navire); conduire (une auto, etc.). **2.** Conduire (une entreprise, etc.); diriger, gérer (une affaire, une banque, etc.); régir (une propriété); mener (une affaire). *To m. s.o.'s affairs*, gérer les affaires de qn. **3.** Gouverner, mater (qn); tenir (des enfants, etc.); maîtriser, dompter (un animal). **To know how to manage s.o.**, savoir prendre qn. **4.** Arranger, conduire (une affaire). **To manage a piece of work**, venir à bout du travail. **To manage to do sth.**, arriver, parvenir, à faire qch.; trouver moyen de faire qch. **I shall manage it**, j'en viendrai à bout. *How do you m. not to dirty your hands?* comment faites-vous pour ne pas vous salir les mains? **A hundred pounds is the most that I can manage**, cent livres, c'est tout ce que je peux faire (pour vous). *If you can m. to see him*, si vous pouvez vous arranger pour le voir. F: **Can you manage a few more cherries?** pouvez-vous manger encore quelques cerises? **5.** Abs. **She manages well**, (i) elle sait s'y prendre; (ii) elle est bonne ménagère. **Manage as best you can**, arrangez-vous comme vous pourrez. *He'll m. all right*, il saura bien se retourner; il se débrouillera. **How will you manage about the children?** et pour les enfants, comment ferez-vous? **managing**, a. **1.** Directeur, -trice; gérant. **Managing director**, administrateur délégué; administrateur gérant. **Managing clerk**, chef m de bureau; commis principal; Jur: premier clerc. **2. A managing man**, un homme énergique, entreprenant. **A managing woman**, une maîtresse femme.

manageable ['manedʒəbl], a. **1.** Maniable; (canot) manœuvrable. **2.** (*Of pers.*) Traitable.

management ['manedʒmənt], s. **1.** (a) Maniement m (d'un outil, des hommes). (b) Direction f, conduite f (d'une affaire); gérance f, gestion f (d'une propriété). **Ill management**, mauvaise organisation. **2.** Adresse f; savoir-faire m. **3.** Coll. Les administrateurs m; 'administration f, la direction.

manager ['manedʒər], s. **1.** Directeur m, administrateur m; gérant m; régisseur m (d'une propriété). Com: **Sales manager**, directeur commercial. **Departmental manager**, chef m de service. Rail: .tc: **Traffic manager**, chef du mouvement. *Ind:* **Works manager,** chef du service; directeur d'usine. **Business manager,** (i) directeur commercial; (ii) *Journ:* administrateur; (iii) *Th:* impresario *m* (d'une actrice, etc.). **2.** *She is a good m.,* elle est bonne ménagère, bonne maîtresse de maison.

manageress ['manedʒəres] *s.f.* Directrice, gérante.

managerial [mane'dʒiːəriəl],*a.* Directorial,-aux.

managership ['manedʒərʃip], *s.* Direction *f*, gérance *f*.

manatee [mana'tiː], *s. Z:* Lamantin *m.*

manchineel [mantʃi'niːl],*s. Bot:* Mancenillier *m.*

Manchuria [man'tʃuːəria]. *Pr.n.* La Mandchourie.

Manchurian [man'tʃuəriən], *a. & s.* Mandchou, -oue, *pl.* -ous, -oues.

mandarin[1] ['mandərin], *s.* Mandarin *m. Toys:* **Nodding mandarin,** branle-tête *m inv.*

mandarin[2], **mandarine** ['mandəriːn], *s. Bot:* Mandarine *f.*

mandatary ['mandətəri],*s. Jur:* Mandataire *mf.*

mandate[1] ['mandet], *s.* **I.** *Lit:* Commandement *m*, ordre *m.* **2.** *Pol:* Mandat *m. The m. for Palestine,* le mandat sur la Palestine.

mandate[2] [man'deit], *v.tr. To m. a country to one of the Powers,* attribuer sous mandat un pays à une des Puissances. **Mandated territories,** territoires sous mandat.

mandatory ['mandətəri]. **I.** *a.* (a) **Mandatory writ,** mandement *m.* (b) **Mandatory states,** états mandataires. **2.** *s.* = MANDATARY.

mandible ['mandibl], *s.* **I.** *Z:* Mandibule *f.* **2.** *Anat:* Mâchoire inférieure.

mandolin(e) ['mandolin], *s.* Mandoline *f.*

mandragora [man'dragora],**mandrake** ['mandreik], *s. Bot:* Mandragore *f.*

mandrel ['mandrel], **mandril** ['mandril], *s. Mec.E:* **I.** Mandrin *m*, arbre *m* (de tour). **2.** Mandrin (pour évaser les tubes).

mandrill ['mandril], *s. Z:* Mandrill *m.*

mane [mein], *s.* Crinière *f.*

manes ['meiniːz], *s.pl. Rom.Ant:* Mânes *m.*

manful ['manful], *a.* Vaillant, hardi, viril. **-fully,** *adv.* Vaillamment, hardiment.

manfulness ['manfulnəs], *s.* Vaillance *f*; hardiesse *f*, virilité *f.*

manganate ['maŋganet], *s. Ch:* Manganate *m.*

manganese [maŋga'niːz], *s.* **I.** *Miner:* (Oxyde noir de) manganèse *m.* **2.** *Ch:* Manganèse. **Manganese steel,** acier au manganèse.

mange [meindʒ], *s.* Gale *f* (du chien, etc.).

mangel-wurzel ['maŋg(ə)l'wəːrz(ə)l], *s.* Betterave fourragère.

manger ['meindʒər], *s.* Mangeoire *f*, crèche *f*; auge *f* d'écurie. *F:* **He is a dog in the manger,** il fait le chien du jardinier.

mangle[1] [maŋgl], *s. Laund:* Calandreuse *f*, calandre *f.*

mangle[2], *v.tr.* Calandrer, cylindrer (le linge).

mangling[1], *s.* Calandrage *m.*

mangle[3], *v.tr.* **I.** Déchirer, lacérer, mutiler; charcuter, massacrer (une volaille). **2.** Mutiler, déformer (un mot); estropier (une citation).

mangling[2], *s.* Lacération *f*; mutilation *f.*

mango, *pl.* **-oes** ['maŋgou, -ouz], *s. Bot:* **I.** Mangue *f.* **2.** Manguier *m.*

mangrove ['maŋgrouv], *s. Bot:* Manglier *m.*

mangy ['meindʒi], *a.* **I.** Galeux. **2.** (a) *F:* (*Of furniture, etc.*) Minable, miteux. (b) *P:* "Sale," moche.

manhood ['manhud], *s.* **I.** Humanité *f*; nature humaine. **2.** Age *m* d'homme; âge viril.

mania ['meinia], *s.* **I.** *Med:* Manie *f*; folie *f*;

délire *m*; (ii) folie furieuse. **2.** *F:* Manie passion *f* (de qch.). **To have a mania for sth.** for doing sth., avoir la manie de qch., de faire qch

maniac ['meiniak]. **I.** *a. & s.* Fou furieux, foll furieuse. **2.** *s. F:* Enragé, -ée (de qch.).

maniacal [ma'naiak(ə)l], *a. Med:* **I.** Fou *f.* folle. **2.** De fou.

manicure[1] ['manikjuər], *s.* **I.** Soin *m* des mains **Manicure set,** trousse *f* de manucure; onglier *m* **2.** = MANICURIST.

manicure[2], *v.tr.* **I.** Soigner les mains de (qn) **2.** Soigner (les mains). **To manicure one's nails** se faire les ongles.

manicurist ['manikjuərist], *s.* Manucure *mf.*

manifest[1] ['manifest], *a.* Manifeste, évident, clair. **-ly,** *adv.* Manifestement.

manifest[2], *s. Nau:* Manifeste *m* (de sortie).

manifest[3],*v.tr.* (a) Manifester, témoigner (qch.) (b) **To manifest itself,** se manifester.

manifestation [manifes'teiʃ(ə)n], *s.* Manifestation *f.*

manifesto [mani'festo], *s. Pol:* Manifeste *m*, proclamation *f.*

manifold[1] ['manifould]. **I.** *a.* (a) Divers, varié; de diverses sortes. (b) Multiple, nombreux. **2.** *s.* (a) *Com: etc:* Polycopie *f.* **Manifold paper,** papier à copies multiples. (b) *I.C.E: etc:* Tubulure *f*, tuyauterie *f*; collecteur *m.* **Exhaust manifold,** tubulure d'échappement. **-ly,** *adv.* **I.** Diversement. **2.** En nombre multiple.

manifold[2], *v.tr.* Polycopier, autocopier.

manifoldness ['manifouldnəs], *s.* Multiplicité *f*, diversité *f.*

manikin ['manikin], *s.* **I.** Petit bout d'homme; homuncule *m*, nabot *m.* **2.** *Art: etc:* Mannequin *m.*

Manil(l)a [ma'nila]. *Pr.n. Geog:* Manille *f.* **Manilla rope,** cordage *m* en manille; manille *f.* **Manilla paper,** papier *m* bulle.

manille [ma'nil], *s. Cards:* Manille *f.*

manipulate [ma'nipjuleit], *v.tr.* **I.** Manipuler (un objet); manœuvrer, actionner (un dispositif mécanique). **2.** *F:* **To manipulate accounts,** tripoter, cuisiner, les comptes.

manipulation [manipju'leiʃ(ə)n],*s.* **I.** Manipulation *f.* **2.** Manœuvre *f.* **3.** *Pej:* Tripotage *m.*

manipulator [ma'nipjuleitər], *s.* **I.** Manipulateur *m.* **2.** *Pej:* Tripoteur *m.*

mankind [man'kaind], *s.inv.* **I.** [man'kaind] Le genre humain; l'homme *m.* **2.** ['mankaind] Les hommes.

manliness ['manlinəs], *s.* Caractère mâle, viril; virilité *f.*

manly ['manli], *a.* D'homme; mâle, viril.

manna ['mana], *s.* **I.** *B:* Manne *f.* **2.** *Pharm:* Manne du frêne.

mannequin ['manikin], *s.* (*Pers.*) Mannequin *m.*

manner ['manər], *s.* **I.** Manière *f*, façon *f* (de faire qch.). **In, after, this manner,** de cette manière, de cette façon; ainsi. *The m. in which . . .,* la manière dont. *. . . After his own m.,* à sa façon. **In like manner,** de la même manière; de même. **In such manner that . . .,** de manière que, de sorte que + *ind. or sub.* **In the same manner as . . .,** de la même manière que. **. . . In a manner (of speaking),** en quelque sorte; pour ainsi dire. *It is a manner of speaking,* c'est une façon de parler. **Novel after the manner of Dickens,** roman à la manière de Dickens. **2.** *A. & Lit:* Manière, coutume *f*, habitude *f. After the m. of the kings of old,* à la manière, selon l'habitude, des rois d'autrefois. **As (if) to the manner born,** comme s'il était né pour cela. **3.** *pl.* Mœurs *f*, usages *m* (d'un peuple). **Manners change with the times,** autres temps, autres mœurs. **4.** Maintien *m*, tenue *f*, air *m*. *I do not like his m. to his teachers,* je n'aime pas son attitude envers ses professeurs. **5.** *pl.* (a) Manières. **Bad manners,** mauvaises manières ; manque *m* de savoir-vivre. *It is bad* **manners to stare,** c'est mal élevé de dévisager les gens. (b) **(Good) manners,** bonnes manières, savoir-vivre *m*, politesse *f*. **To teach s.o. manners,** donner à qn une leçon de politesse. **To forget one's manners,** oublier les convenances ; s'oublier. *Aut :* *Road manners,* politesse sur la route. **6.** Espèce *f*, sorte *f*. **What manner of man is he?** quel genre d'homme est-ce? **All manner of people, of things,** toutes sortes de gens, de choses. **No manner of doubt,** aucune espèce de doute, aucun doute.

mannered ['manərd], *a.* **1.** Rough-mannered, aux manières rudes ; (homme) brusque. **2.** Maniéré ; affecté ; (style) recherché, précieux.

mannerism ['manərizm], *s.* **1.** Maniérisme *m*, affectation *f*. **2.** Particularité *f* (d'un écrivain, etc.).

mannerless ['manərləs], *a.* Sans tenue ; qui manque de savoir-vivre.

mannerliness ['manərlinəs], *s.* Courtoisie *f* ; politesse *f*.

mannerly ['manərli], *a.* Poli ; courtois ; (enfant) bien élevé.

mannish ['maniʃ], *a.* **1.** Qui caractérise l'homme. **2.** (*Of woman*) Hommasse. *M. ways,* habitudes garçonnières.

manœuvre[1] [ma'nu:vər, -nju:-], *s.* **1.** *Mil :* Navy : Manœuvre *f*. **2.** *F :* (a) **A clever, a false,** *m.*, une manœuvre habile, une fausse manœuvre. (b) *pl. Pej :* **(Underhand) manœuvres,** menées *f*, intrigues *f*.

manœuvre[2]. **1.** *v.tr.* Manœuvrer, faire manœuvrer (une armée, une flotte). *F :* **To manœuvre s.o. into a corner,** acculer qn dans un coin ; amener adroitement qn dans un impasse. **2.** *v.i.* Manœuvrer.

manometer [ma'nɔmetər], *s.* Manomètre *m*.

manor ['manər], *s. Hist :* Seigneurie *f*. **'manor-house,** *s.* Château seigneurial ; mano r *m*.

manorial [ma'nɔ:riəl], *a.* Seigneurial, -aux.

mansard ['mansərd], *s.* **Mansard (roof),** toit *m*, comble *m*, en mansarde.

manse [mans], *s. Esp. Scot :* Presbytère *m* (résidence du pasteur).

mansion ['manʃ(ə)n], *s.* **1.** (*In country*) Château *m* ; (*in town*) hôtel particulier (m). **2.** *pl.* **Mansions,** maison *f* de rapport. **3. The Mansion House,** la résidence officielle du Lord Maire de Londres (dans la City).

manslaughter ['mansləːtər], *s. Jur :* (a) Homicide *m* involontaire, par imprudence. (b) Homicide sans préméditation.

mantelpiece ['mantlpiːs], *s.* **1.** Manteau *m*, chambranle *m*, de cheminée. **2.** Dessus *m*, tablette *f*, de cheminée.

mantelshelf ['mantlʃelf], *s.* = MANTELPIECE 2.

mantilla [man'tila], *s. Cost :* Mantille *f*.

mantis ['mantis], *s. Ent :* Mante *f*. **Praying mantis,** mante religieuse.

mantissa [man'tisa], *s Mth :* Mantisse *f* (d'un logarithme).

mantle[1] ['mantl], *s.* **1.** (a) Manteau *m* (sans manches) ; cape *f*. (b) Mante *f*, pèlerine *f* (de femme). **2.** Manteau (de neige, de lierre) ; voile *m* (de brume). **3.** Manchon *m* (de bec de gaz à incandescence).

mantle[2]. **1.** *v.tr.* (a) Couvrir, vêtir, envelopper, (qn) d'un manteau. (b) Jeter un manteau sur (qch.) ; voiler (qch.). (c) Couvrir, envelopper

---

(*with,* de). **2.** *v.i.* (*Of blush*) Se répandre (*over the cheeks,* sur les joues) ; (*of face, cheeks*) rougir, s'empourprer.

mantua[1] ['mantjuə], *s. A.Cost :* (a) Mante *f*. (b) Robe flottante. **'mantua-maker,** *s. A :* Couturière *f*.

Mantua[2]. *Pr.n. Geog :* Mantoue *f*.

manual ['manjuəl]. **1.** *a.* (a) Manuel. *M. labour,* travail manuel ; travail de manœuvre. **Manual fire-engine,** pompe *f* à bras. *S.a.* SIGN-MANUAL. (b) *Mil :* **Manual exercise,** maniement *m* des armes. **2.** *s.* (a) Manuel *m* ; aide-mémoire *m inv.* (b) *Mus :* Clavier *m* (d'un orgue). **Great-manual,** clavier du grand orgue. **-ally,** *adv.* Manuellement ; à la main.

manufactory [manju'faktəri], *s.* Fabrique *f*, usine *f*, manufacture *f*.

manufacture[1] [manju'faktʃər], *s.* **1.** (a) Fabrication *f*, élaboration *f* (d'un produit industriel) ; confection *f* (de vêtements, etc.). (b) *The woollen m.*, l'industrie de la laine ; l'industrie lainière. **2.** Produit manufacturé.

manufacture[2], *v.tr.* (a) Fabriquer, manufacturer (un produit industriel) ; confectionner (des vêtements, etc.). **Manufacturing town,** ville industrielle. (b) *F :* Forger, fabriquer (des nouvelles).

manufacturer [manju'faktʃərər], *s.* **1.** Fabricant *m*, industriel *m*, manufacturier *m*, usinier *m*. **2.** *Pej : F :* Fabricateur *m*, inventeur *m* (de mensonges).

manumission [manju'miʃ(ə)n], *s. Hist :* Manumission *f*, affranchissement *m*.

manumit [manju'mit], *v.tr.* (manumitted) *Hist :* Affranchir, émanciper.

manure[1] [ma'njuər], *s.* Engrais *m*. **Farmyard manure,** fumier *m* (d'étable). **Fish manure,** engrais de poisson. **Chemical manure, artificial manure,** engrais artificiel. **Manure heap,** tas *m* de fumier ; *F :* fumier.

manure[2], *v.tr.* Fumer, engraisser (la terre).

manuring, *s.* Fumage *m*, engraissement *m*.

manuscript ['manjuskript] **1.** *s.* Manuscrit *m*. **2.** *a.* Manuscrit ; écrit à la main.

Manx [manks]. **1.** *a. Geog :* Mannois ; manxois. **Manx cat,** chat sans queue de l'île de Man. **2.** *s. Ling :* Le mannois.

Manxman, *pl.* **-men** ['manksmən, -men], *s.* Mannois.

many ['meni]. **1.** *a. & s.* (more, most, *q.v.*) Un grand nombre (de) ; beaucoup (de) ; bien des ; plusieurs, maint. **Many a time, many and many a time,** mainte(s) fois ; mainte et mainte fois. **Many a man, many a one,** bien des gens. **Many's the time** *I've heard that song,* j'ai entendu cette chanson bien des fois. **Before many days time** passed, avant qu'il soit longtemps. **Of many kinds,** de toutes sortes. **In many instances,** dans bien des cas. **For many years,** pendant de longues années. **Ever so many times,** je ne sais combien de fois. **Many of us,** beaucoup, un grand nombre, d'entre nous. **Many have seen it,** beaucoup de personnes l'ont vu. **They were so many,** ils étaient si nombreux ; il y en avait tant. **So many men, so many minds,** (au)tant d'hommes, (au)tant d'avis. *He told me in so many words that . . .,* il m'a dit en propres termes que. **Too many people,** trop de monde. **A card too many,** une carte de trop. **How many horses have you?** combien de chevaux avez-vous? *I have as many books as you,* j'ai autant de livres que vous. **As many again, twice as many,** deux fois autant, encore autant. **As many as ten people** saw it, usqu'à dix personnes l'ont vu. **A great**

map] 464 [marital

many people, un grand nombre de personnes. A good many things, un assez grand nombre de choses ; pas mal de choses. **There are a good many**, il y en a pas mal. **2.** *Comb.fm.* **Many-voiced**, aux voix nombreuses. **Many-flowered**, **-lobed**, multiflore, multilobé. **many-'coloured**, *a.* Multicolore. **many-'sided**, *a.* **1.** (Figure) à plusieurs côtés, multilatère. **2.** (Problème) complexe. **3.** (Personne) aux talents variés.

map[1] [map], *s.* Carte *f* (géographique). **Map of a town**, plan *m* d'une ville. **Sketch map**, carte-croquis *f* ; *F:* topo *m*. **Map of the world**, mappemonde *f*. *F: Questions very much on the map*, questions d'actualité. **'map-maker**, *s.* Cartographe *m.* **'map-making**, *s.* Cartographie *f.*

map[2], *v.tr.* (mapped) **1.** Dresser une carte, un plan, de (la région, etc.). **2. To map out a route**, tracer un itinéraire. **To map out a course of action**, se tracer un plan d'action. **mapping**, *s.* Cartographie *f.*

maple [meipl], *s.* (a) Érable *m.* **English maple**, **common maple**, érable champêtre. **Sugar maple**, **rock maple**, érable à sucre. **Maple sugar**, sucre *m* d'érable. (b) **Great maple**, érable blanc ; (érable) faux platane.

mar [mɑːr], *v.tr.* (marred) Gâter (le plaisir de qn) ; troubler (la joie de qn) ; déparer (la beauté de qn). *F:* **To make or mar s.o.**, faire la fortune ou la ruine de qn.

marabou ['marabuː], *s.* **1.** *Orn:* Marabout *m* ; cigogne *f* à sac. **2.** *Coll.* Duvet *m* de marabout.

marabout ['marabuːt], *s.* *Rel:* Marabout (musulman).

maraschino [mara'skiːno], *s.* Marasquin *m.*

maraud [ma'rɔːd]. **1.** *v.i.* Marauder ; aller en maraude. **2.** *v.tr.* Piller, marauder (un village, etc.). **marauding**[1], *a.* Maraudeur, -euse. **marauding**[2], *s.* Maraude *f* ; *Jur:* maraudage *m.* **To go marauding**, aller à la maraude.

marauder [ma'rɔːdər], *s.* Maraudeur *m.*

marble[1] [mɑːrbl], *s.* **1.** Marbre *m.* (a) **Clouded marble**, marbre tacheté. **Imitation marble**, similimarbre *m.* **Marble pavement**, dallage *m* en marbre. **Marble quarry**, marbrière *f.* (b) *Art:* **The Elgin marbles**, les marbres d'Elgin. **2.** *Games :* Bille *f.* **To play marbles**, jouer aux billes. **'marble-'edged**, *a.* *Bookb:* Marbré sur tranche.

marble[2], *v.tr.* Marbrer (une boiserie, etc.). *Bookb:* Marbrer, raciner (les plats). **marbled**, *a.* **1.** Marbré. *Bookb:* (Of cover) Raciné, marbré ; (of edge) jaspé. **2.** (Salle, etc.) à revêtement de marbre. **marbling**, *s.* Marbrure *f.* *Bookb:* Racinage *m* (des plats) ; aspage *m*, jaspure *f* (des tranches).

marcel [mɑːr'sel], *s.* *Hairdr:* Marcel(-wave), ondulation *f.*

March[1] [mɑːrtʃ], *s.* Mars *m.* *In M.*, au mois de mars. *(On) the fifth of M.*, le cinq mars.

march[2], *s.* *Hist:* (Often in pl.) Marche *f* ; frontière *f* militaire. **'march-land**, *s.* Marches *fpl* ; pays *m* limitrophe.

march[3], *v.i.* (Of country, domain) **To march upon**, **with . .**, confiner à, être limitrophe de. . .

march[4], *s.* **1.** *Mil:* (a) Marche *f.* **On the march**, en marche. **To do a day's march**, faire, fournir, une étape. **March past**, défilé *m* (de revue, etc.). **Route march**, promenade *f* militaire. (b) **Pas** *m*, allure *f.* **Slow march**, parade march, pas ordinaire. **Quick march**, pas cadencé, accéléré. **Double march**, pas gymnastique. **2.** Marche, progrès *m* (des événements). **3.** *Mus :* Marche.

march[5]. **1.** *v.i.* *Mil:* etc: Marcher. **Quick march!** en avant, marche ! **March at ease!** pas de route ! **March at attention!** pas cadencé, marche ! **To march along**, marcher, avancer. **To march to**, **towards**, **a place**, s'acheminer sur, vers, un endroit. **To march in**, entrer. **To march out**, sortir. **To march away**, partir. **To march off**, (i) se mettre en marche ; (ii) *F:* décamper ; plier bagage. **To march by**, **past** (s.o.), défiler (devant qn). **2.** *v.tr.* (a) Faire marcher (des troupes). (b) *F:* **He was marched off**, **away**, **to gaol**, il a été emmené en prison. **marching**, *s.* *Mil:* Marche *f.* **Marching past**, défilé *m.* **Marching orders**, feuille *f* de route. *F:* **To give s.o. his marching orders**, signifier son congé à qn.

marchioness ['mɑːrʃənes], *s.f.* Marquise.

marchpane ['mɑːrtʃpein], *s.* = MARZIPAN.

marconigram [mɑːr'kouniɡram], *s.* *W.Tel:* Marconigramme *m* ; *F:* sans-fil *m inv.*

mare ['meər], *s.* Jument *f.* *F:* **The grey mare is the better horse**, c'est la femme qui porte la culotte. *The discovery turned out to be a* **mare's nest**, la découverte s'est avérée illusoire. **'mare's-tail**, *s.* **1.** *Bot:* (a) Pesse *f* d'eau. (b) Prêle *f.* **2.** *Nau:* (Nuage *m* en) queue-de-chat *f* ; cirrus *m.*

Margaret ['mɑːrɡəret]. *Pr.n.f.* Marguerite.

margarine ['mɑːrɡəriːn, 'mɑːrdʒəriːn], *s.* *Com:* Margarine *f.*

margin[1] ['mɑːrdʒin], *s.* **1.** (a) Marge *f* ; lisière *f* (d'un bois) ; bord *m*, rive *f* (d'une rivière). (b) Marge, écart *m.* **To allow s.o. some margin**, accorder quelque marge à qn. *To allow s.o. for mistakes*, faire la part des erreurs possibles. (c) *Com:* Marge, couverture *f*, provision *f.* *St.Exch:* Acompte (versé au courtier). (d) *Mec.E:* etc: **Margin (of error)**, tolérance *f*, limite *f.* **Margin for safety**, marge de sécurité. **2.** Marge, blanc *m* (d'une page). *Phot:* Liséré *m* (d'une épreuve). **On**, **in**, **the margin**, en marge. *Typewr:* **Margin stop**, margeur *m* ; régulateur *m* de marges.

margin[2], *v.tr.* **1.** Annoter en marge (un livre). **2.** (a) *Pages insufficiently margined*, pages à marges insuffisantes. (b) *River margined with grass*, rivière bordée d'herbe.

marginal ['mɑːrdʒin(ə)l], *a.* Marginal, -aux ; en marge. **Marginal note**, note marginale ; manchette *f.* *To make m. notes in a book*, émarger un livre.

margrave ['mɑːrɡreiv], *s.* *Hist:* Margrave *m.*

marguerite [mɑːrɡə'riːt], *s.* *Bot:* (a) (Ox-eye daisy) Leucanthème *m* vulgaire ; grande marguerite. (b) (Paris daisy) Marguerite en arbre.

Maria [ma'raia]. *Pr.n.f.* Maria. *F:* **Black Maria**, la voiture cellulaire.

marigold ['mariɡould], *s.* *Bot:* **1.** Souci *m.* **2. African marigold**, œillet *m* d'Inde. **3. Corn marigold**, **field marigold**, marguerite dorée.

marine [ma'riːn]. **1.** *a.* (a) (Animal) marin, pélagien. (b) **Marine insurance**, assurance *f* maritime. (c) **Marine forces**, troupes *f* de la marine ; forces navales. (d) **Marine engine**, machine *f* (de) marine. **2.** *s.* (a) Marine *f.* Mercantile marine, marine marchande. (b) Soldat *m* de l'infanterie de marine. *F:* **Tell that to the (horse-)marines!** à d'autres ! allez conter ça ailleurs !

mariner ['marinər], *s.* *Nau:* Marin *m* (officier ou matelot).

marionette [mario'net], *s.* Marionnette *f.*

marital ['marit(ə)l, ma'rait(ə)l], *a.* **1.** Marital, -aux. **2.** Matrimonial, -aux. **-ally**, *adv.* Maritalement.

maritime ['maritaim], *a.* Maritime.
marjoram ['mɑːrdʒorəm], *s. Bot:* Origan *m*, marjolaine *f.*
mark[1] [mɑːrk], *s.* **I.** (*a*) But *m*, cible *f.* **To hit the mark**, atteindre le but ; frapper juste ; *F :* mettre dans le noir. **To miss the mark**, manquer le but. *F :* **Beside the mark**, à côté de la question ; hors de propos. **To be wide of the mark**, être loin de la réalité, la vérité. (*b*) *F :* **He's an easy mark**, c'est un jobard, *P :* une poire. (*c*) *Box :* **Blow to the mark**, coup au creux de l'estomac. **2.** *Nau :* Marque *f* ; amer *m* ; (*on buoy*) voyant *m*. **3.** (*a*) Marque, preuve *f*, signe *m*, témoignage *m*. **As a mark of my esteem**, en témoignage de mon estime. *To bear the m. of a strong conviction*, porter l'empreinte *f* d'une forte conviction. (*b*) *Farr :* **Mark of mouth**, marque (d'âge). **4.** (*a*) Marque, tache *f*, signe, empreinte. **Marks of a blow**, marques d'un coup. **Marks of old age**, marques, traces *f*, de la vieillesse. **To leave one's mark upon sth.**, laisser sa marque, son empreinte, sur qch. **To make one's mark**, se faire une réputation ; arriver. **(God) save the mark!** Dieu me pardonne ! passez-moi le mot ! (*b*) **The mark of a foot**, la marque, l'empreinte, d'un pied. *Fb :* **To make a mark, one's mark**, faire une marque. **5.** (*a*) Marque, signe. *He cannot write ;* he makes his mark, il ne sait pas écrire ; il fait une croix. **Punctuation marks**, signes de ponctuation. **Interrogation mark**, point *m* d'interrogation. (*b*) *Sch :* Point *m* ; note *f* d'appréciation. **Good mark, bad mark**, bon, mauvais, point. *Examination marks*, notes d'examen. **6.** (*a*) Marque, repère *m*, trace *f.* **Guiding mark, guide-mark, lay-mark, reference mark**, (point *m* de) repère. (*b*) *Nau :* **Plimsoll's mark**, ligne *f* Plimsoll. *F :* (*Of pers.*) **To be up to the mark**, (i) (*in ability*) être à la hauteur ; (ii) (*in health*) être dans son assiette ; être en train. *I am below the mark*, je ne suis pas dans mon assiette. (*Of thg*) **To be, to come, up to the mark**, répondre à l'attente ; être à la hauteur. (*c*) *For :* (*Blaze*) Blanchi(s) *m.* (*d*) *Sp :* Ligne de départ. (*Of motor car*) **To be quick off the mark**, démarrer vivement. **7.** **Man of mark**, homme marquant.
mark[2], *v.tr.* **I.** (*a*) Marquer, chiffrer (du linge) ; estampiller (des marchandises). **To mark the cards**, biseauter, piper, piquer, maquiller, les cartes. (*b*) (*Usu. passive*) **To be marked with spots, stripes**, être marqué de taches, de raies. **2.** (*a*) Marquer (the price of) an article, mettre le prix à un article. (*b*) *Scn :* **To mark an exercise**, coter un devoir. **3.** **To mark s.o., sth., as . . .**, désigner, choisir, qn, qch., pour. . . . *If we are marked to die*, si nous sommes destinés à mourir. **4.** (*a*) Marquer, repérer, indiquer. **To mark the points in a game**, to mark the game, marquer les points du jeu. (*b*) *Stream that marks the bounds of the estate*, ruisseau qui marque la limite de la propriété. *Post marking the course*, poteau indicateur de piste. (*c*) Indiquer. *Such an answer marks the boor*, cette réponse est d'un rustre. **5.** (*a*) **To mark one's approval, one's displeasure (by . . .)**, témoigner, montrer, son approbation, son mécontentement (par . . . ; en faisant qch.). **To mark time**, (i) *Mil :* marquer le pas ; (ii) *F :* piétiner sur place. (*b*) *His reign was marked by great victories*, son règne fut marqué, signalé, par de grandes victoires. **To mark an era**, faire époque. **6.** (*a*) *Lit :* Observer, regarder, guetter. (*b*) *To mark the fall of a shell*, repérer le point de chute d'un obus. (*c*) Observer, remarquer, noter (qch.). **Mark me! mark you!**

mark my words! écoutez-moi b en ! **7.** *Fb :* Marquer (un adversaire). **mark down**, *v.tr.* **I.** **To mark down (the price of) an article**, baisser un article de prix ; démarquer, dévaloriser, un article. **2.** *F :* Inscrire (un article à l'inventaire, etc.). **mark off**, *v.tr.* **I.** (*a*) *Surv :* **To mark off a line, a road**, bornoyer, jalonner, une ligne, une route. (*b*) *To m. off a distance on the map*, (i) prendre, mesurer, (ii) rapporter, une distance sur la carte. **2.** **To mark sth. off from . . .**, distinguer, séparer, qch. de. . . **mark out**, *v.tr.* **I.** Délimiter, tracer (des frontières) ; borner, bornoyer (un champ) ; jalonner (une concession minière). **2.** (*a*) *His neat attire marked him out from the crowd*, sa mise soignée le distinguait de la foule. (*b*) **To mark s.o. out for . . .**, destiner qn à . . . ; désigner qn pour. . . . **mark up**, *v.tr.* Hausser, élever, le prix de (qch.). **marked**, *a.* **I.** **Marked card**, carte marquée, biseautée. **2.** **Marked man**, homme marqué (par ses ennemis). **3.** **Marked difference**, différence marquée, prononcée. **Marked improvement**, amélioration sensible. **Strongly marked features**, traits fortement accusés. **The change is becoming more marked**, le changement s'accentue. **marking**, *s.* **I.** (*a*) Marquage *m.* (*b*) *Mec.E :* Repérage *m* (du point mort, etc.). **2.** *pl.* **Markings**, marques *f* ; (*on animal*) taches *f*, rayures *f.* **'marking-board**, *s. Games :* Tableau *m* (pour marquer les points). **'marking-ink**, *s.* Encre *f* à marquer. **'marking-tool**, *s.* Rouanne *f* ; pointe *f* à tracer.
mark[3], *s. Num :* Mark *m*, marc *m.* *Gold marks*, marks or.
Mark[4]. *Pr.n.m.* Marc.
markedly ['mɑːrkidli], *adv.* D'une façon marquée. *M. polite*, d'une politesse marquée.
marker ['mɑːrkər], *s.* **I.** (*Pers.*) (*a*) Marqueur, -euse (de linge, etc.). (*b*) (*At games*) Marqueur *m*, pointeur *m* ; (*at butts*) marqueur. (*c*) *Mil :* Jalonneur *m.* **2.** (*a*) *Ten : etc :* (*Machine*) Court-marker, marqueur à chaux. (*b*) *Cards :* **Bridge marker**, carnet-bloc *m* (de bridge). (*c*) = BOOK-MARKER.
market[1] ['mɑːrket], *s.* (*a*) Marché *m.* **Covered market**, halle *f*, halles *fpl.* **The market square**, la place du marché. **In the market**, au marché, à la halle. *F :* **To take one's pigs to a bad market**, mal conduire ses affaires. (*b*) **Overseas markets**, marchés d'outre-mer. (*Of pers.*) **To be in the market for sth.**, être acheteur de qch. (*Of thg*) **To be on the market, to come into the market**, être mis en vente. **To find a market for sth.**, trouver un débouché, des acheteurs, pour qch. (*Of thg*) **To find a ready market**, être d'un débit facile ; se placer facilement. **The market has risen**, le marché a haussé ; les cours *m* sont en hausse. **'market-day**, *s.* Jour *m* de marché. **'market-'garden**, *s.* Jardin maraîcher. **'market-'gardener**, *s.* Maraîcher, -ère. **'market-'gardening**, *s.* Maraîchage *m.* **'market-house**, *s.* Halle *f.* **'market-penny**, *s. F :* Sou *m* du franc. **'market-place**, *s.* Place *f* du marché. **'market-price**, *s. Com :* Prix courant. **'market-'town**, *s.* Ville *f* où se tient un marché ; bourg *m*, bourgade *f.* **'market-woman**, *s.f.* Femme de la halle ; marchande.
market[2], *v.* (*marketed*) **I.** *v.i.* Faire son marché, faire ses emplettes. **To go marketing**, aller faire son marché ; aller aux provisions. **2.** *v.tr.* Trouver des débouchés pour (ses marchandises) ; lancer (un article) sur le marché.
marketable ['mɑːrketəbl], *a.* **I.** (*Of goods*) Vendable ; d'un débit facile. **2.** **Marketable value**, valeur marchande.

marksman, *pl.* **-men** ['mɑːrksmən, -men,, *s.* Bon tireur ; tireur d'élite.

marksmanship ['mɑːrksmənʃip], *s.* Adresse *f*, habileté *f*, au tir.

marl¹ [mɑːrl], *s. Agr:* Marne *f.* **'marl-pit,** *s.* Marnière *f.*

marl², *v.tr. Agr:* Marner (le sol). **marling,** *s. Agr:* Marnage *m.*

marline ['mɑːrlin], *s. Nau:* (*Two yarns*) Lusin *m* ; (*three yarns*) merlin *m.*

marline-spike, marlinspike ['mɑːrlinspaik], *s. Nau:* Épissoir *m.*

marly ['mɑːrli], *a.* (Sol) marneux, crayonneux.

marmalade ['mɑːrməleid], *s. Cu:* Confiture *f* d'oranges.

marmoreal [mɑːr'mɔːriəl], **marmorean** [mɑːr'mɔːriən], *a. Poet:* Marmoréen ; de marbre.

marmoset [mɑːrmo'zet], *s.* Ouistiti *m*, marmouset *m.*

marmot ['mɑːrmɔt], *s. Z:* Marmotte *f.*

maroon¹ [ma'ruːn]. **1.** *a. & s.* (*Colour*) Marron pourpré *inv.* **2.** *s. Pyr:* Marron *m* ; fusée *f* à pétard.

maroon², *s.* Nègre marron, négresse marronne.

maroon³, *v.tr.* (*a*) Abandonner (qn) dans une ile déserte. (*b*) *F: Villagers marooned by the floods,* villageois isolés par les inondations.

marplot ['mɑːrplɔt], *s.* Brouille-tout *m* .nv; gaffeur *m.*

marque [mɑːrk], *s.*ˈ*Hist:* **Letters of marque (and reprisal),** 'ettres *f* de marque ; lettres de représailles.

marquee [mɑːr'kiː], *s.* (Tente-)marquise *f.*

marquess ['mɑːrkwes], **marquis** ['mɑːrkwis], *s.* Marquis *m.*

marquetry ['mɑːrkətri], *s.* Marqueterie *f.*

marriage ['maridʒ], *s.* **1.** Mar age *m.* **To give s.o. in marriage,** donner qn en mariage. **To take s.o. in marriage,** épouser qn. **To seek s.o., s.o.'s hand, in marriage,** rechercher qn en mariage. **Uncle by marriage,** oncle par alliance. **Civil marriage,** mariage civil. **Marriage settlement,** conventions matrimoniales ; dispositions *fpl* entre époux. **Marriage certificate,** *F:* marriage lines, acte *m* de mariage. **Marriage ring,** (bague *f* d')alliance *f.* **The marriage service,** la bénédiction nuptiale. **2.** Mariage, union *f* (entre les choses).

marriageable ['maridʒəbl], *a.* (*a*) (Fille) nubile. *She is of m. age,* elle est d'âge à se marier. (*b*) *To have three m. daughters,* avoir trois filles à marier.

marrow ['maro], *s.* **1.** (*a*) Moelle *f. F: To be frozen to the marrow,* être glacé jusqu'à la moelle. (*b*) *F: To extract the m. of a book,* tirer, extraire, la moelle d'un livre. **2.** *Hort:* **Vegetable marrow,** courge *f* à la moelle.

marrowbone ['maroboun], *s.* Os *m* à moelle. *F:* On your marrowbones! à genoux!

marrowfat ['marofat], *s.* **1.** *U.S:* Graisse *f* de moelle. **2.** *Hort:* Pois carré.

marry¹ ['mari], *v.tr.* **1.** (*Of priest, parent*) Marier ; unir (en mariage). *She has three daughters to marry off,* elle a trois filles à marier, à caser. **2.** (*a*) Se marier avec, à (qn) ; épouser (qn). **To marry money,** faire un mariage d'argent. (*b*) *Abs.* **To marry,** se marier. **To marry again, a second time,** se remarier ; *Hum:* convoler en secondes noces. **To marry into a family,** s'allier, s'apparenter, à une famille. **To marry beneath one,** faire une mésalliance. **3.** *Nau:* Marier (deux cordages). **married,** *a.* **1. Married man,** homme marié. **A married couple,** un ménage.

To get married, se marier. **2. Married love,** l'amour conjugal.

marry², *int. A:* Par la sainte Vierge !

Marseilles [mɑːr'seilz]. *Pr.n.* Marse lle *f.*

marsh [mɑːrʃ], *s.* Marais *m*, marécage *m.* **'marsh-'fever,** *s.* (Im)paludisme *m* ; fièvre paludéenne. **'marsh-'gas,** *s.* Gaz *m* des marais. **'marsh-'hen,** *s.* Poule *f* d'eau. **'marsh-'mallow,** *s.* Guimauve *f.* **'marsh-'marigold,** *s.* Souci *m* d'eau.

marshal¹ ['mɑːrʃəl], *s.* **1.** *Hist:* Marécha *m*, -aux. **2.** (*a*) *Mil:* **Field-marshal,** (i) *Hist:* feldmaréchal *m* ; (ii) maréchal. (*b*) *Mil. Av:* **Airmarshal,** généra *m*, -aux. **3.** Maître *m* des cérémonies.

marshal², *v.tr.* (marshalled) (*a*) Placer (des personnes) en ordre, en rang. (*b*) *Mil:* Ranger (des troupes). (*c*) *F:* **To marshal facts,** rassembler des faits et les mettre en ordre. (*d*) *Her:* *To m. two coats of arms in one shield,* disposer deux blasons sur un écu. (*e*) *Rail:* Classer, trier (des wagons). (*f*) **To marshal s.o. in, out,** introduire, reconduire, qn cérémonieusement. **marshalling,** *s.* **1.** Disposition *f* en ordre (de personnes, de choses). **2.** *Rail:* Classement *m*, triage *m*, manœuvre *f* (des wagons). **Marshalling yard,** voies *fpl* de classement ; gare *f* de triage.

marshiness ['mɑːrʃinəs], *s.* État marécageux (du terrain).

marshland ['mɑːrʃland], *s.* Terrain marécageux.

marshy ['mɑːrʃi], *a.* Marécageux.

marsupial [mɑːr'sjuːpiəl], **1.** *a.* (Repli, etc.) marsupial, -aux. **2.** *s. Z:* Marsupial *m.*

mart [mɑːrt], *s.* **1.** = MARKET-PLACE. **2.** (Auction-)mart, salle *f* de vente. **3.** Centre *m* de commerce.

marten ['mɑːrten], *s. Z:* Mart(r)e *f.* **Beech-marten, stone-marten,** fouine *f.* **Pine-marten,** martre des pins.

martial ['mɑːrʃ(ə)l], *a.* Martial, -aux ; guerrier. *M. array,* ordre *m* de bataille. **Martial law,** loi martiale. **-ally,** *adv.* Martialement ; en guerrier.

Martin¹ ['mɑːrtin]. *Pr.n.m.* Martin. **St Martin's day,** la Saint-Martin.

martin², *s. Orn:* Martinet *m.* **House-m.,** hirondelle *f* de fenêtre.

martinet [mɑːrti'net], *s.* Officier *m* à cheval sur la discipline. *He is a regular martinet,* c'est un vrai garde-chiourme.

martingale ['mɑːrtiŋgeil], *s. Harn: etc:* Martingale *f.*

Martinmas ['mɑːrtinməs], *s.* La Saint-Martin.

martlet ['mɑːrtlet], *s.* **1.** *Orn:* Martinet *m.* **2.** *Her:* Merlette *f.*

martyr ['mɑːrtər], *s.* Martyr, *f.* martyre. *F:* **To be a martyr to gout,** être sujet à la goutte ; être torturé par la goutte. *He makes a perfect martyr of himself,* il se torture le cœur à plaisir.

martyr², *v.tr.* Martyriser.

martyrdom ['mɑːrtərdəm], *s.* Martyre *m.*

marvel¹ ['mɑːrv(ə)l], *s.* **1.** (*a*) Merveille *f.* (*b*) *F:* **It is a marvel to me that** .·.., cela m'étonne beaucoup que. . . . **No marvel then if** . . ., il n'est donc pas étonnant si. . . . **To work marvels,** accomplir des merveilles. **2.** *A:* Émerveillement *m.*

marvel², *v.i.* (marvelled [mɑːrvld]) S'émerveiller ; s'étonner (*at*, de). **marvelling,** *a.* Émerveillé.

marvellous ['mɑːrv(ə)ləs,. **1.** *a.* Merveilleux, étonnant. *It is marvellous to me that* . . ., je m'étonne que + *sub.* **2.** *s.* **It savours of the marvellous,** cela tient du prodige. **-ly,** *adv.* A merveille ; merveilleusement.

Mary ['mɛəri]. *Pr.n.f.* **1.** Marie. **2.** *P:* **Little Mary**, l'estomac *m*.

marzipan [mɑːrzi'pan], *s.* Massepain *m*.

mascot ['maskɔt], *s.* Mascotte *f*; porte-bonheur *m inv.*

masculine ['maskjulin], *a.* **1.** Masculin, mâle. **2.** *Gram:* (Nom) masculin. **In the masculine (gender)**, au masculin. *Pros:* **Masculine rhyme**, rime masculine.

mash[1] [maʃ], *s.* *Husb:* Mâche *f*, mash *m* (pour chevaux); pâtée *f* (pour chiens et volaille). **Bran-mash**, eau blanche; son mouillé. **2.** *F:* Purée *f* de pommes de terre. **3.** Mélange *m*; pâte *f*; bouillie *f*.

mash[2], *v.tr.* Brasser, broyer, écraser, qch. *Cu:* **To mash potatoes**, mettre en purée des pommes de terre. **Mashed potatoes**, purée *f* de pommes de terre; pommes *f* mousseline.

mash[3], *v.tr.* *F: A:* **To be mashed on s.o.**, avoir un béguin pour qn.

masher ['maʃər], *s.* *F:* Gommeux *m*, bellâtre *m*.

mashie ['maʃi], *s.* *Golf:* Mashie *m*.

mask[1] [mɑːsk], *s.* **1.** (*a*) Masque *m*; (*silk or velvet*) loup *m*. *F:* **Under the mask of devotion, of friendship**, sous le masque, sous le voile, de la dévotion, de l'amitié. **To throw off, drop, the mask**, lever le masque; se démasquer. (*b*) **Protective mask**, masque de protection. **2.** *Ven:* Face *f* (de renard, etc.). **3.** *See* DEATH-MASK. **4.** *Phot:* **Printing-mask**, cache *m*.

mask[2], *v.tr.* **1.** Masquer. **To mask one's face**, se masquer. **Masked ball**, bal masqué. **2.** *Mil:* Masquer (une batterie, une place forte). **3.** *Phot:* Poser un cache à (un cliché). **4.** *F:* Cacher, déguiser (ses pensées); voiler (un défaut).

mason ['meis(ə)n], *s.* **1.** Maçon *m*. **2.** = FREE-MASON.

masonic [ma'sɔnik], *a.* Maçonnique; de la franc-maçonnerie.

masonry ['meisənri], *s.* **1.** Maçonnerie *f*. **2.** = FREEMASONRY.

masque [mɑːsk], *s.* *A:* Masque *m* (pantomime ou féerie).

masquerade[1] [mɑːskə'reid], *s.* Mascarade *f*.

masquerade[2], *v.i.* Se masquer; aller en masque. **To masquerade as . . .**, se déguiser en . . ., se faire passer pour. . . .

masquerader [mɑːskə reidər], *s.* (*a*) Personne déguisée, masquée. (*b*) Imposteur *m*.

mass[1] [mas], *s.* *Ecc:* Messe *f*. **High mass**, la grand'messe. **Low mass**, messe basse. **Requiem mass**, messe des morts.

mass[2], *s.* **1.** (*a*) Masse *f*, amas *m*, agglomération *f*. (*b*) *Mec:* Masse (d'un corps). **Power per unit of mass**, puissance *f* unitaire massique. **2.** (*a*) **A mass of people**, une foule, une multitude, des masses, de gens. *To gather in masses*, se masser. *F:* **The exercise was a mass of mistakes**, e devoir était cousu de fautes. *He was a m. of bruises*, il était tout couvert de meurtrissures. **Mass executions**, exécutions *f* en masse. (*b*) **The great mass of the people**, la plus grande partie de la population. **The masses**, les masses; la foule. '**mass meeting,** *s.* Réunion *f* en masse; *F:* meeting *m* monstre. '**mass pro'duction,** *s.* Fabrication *f*, travail *m*, en (grande) série.

mass[3]. **1.** *v.tr.* Masser (des troupes, etc.); agglomérer (des individus). **2.** *v.i.* (*Of troops*) Se masser; (*of clouds*) s'amonceler.

massacre[1] ['masəkər], *s.* Massacre *m*, tuerie *f*.

massacre[2], *v.tr.* Massacrer (des hommes).

massage[1] [ma'sɑːʒ], *s.* Massage *m*. **Scalp massage**, friction *f*.

massage[2], *v.tr.* *Med:* Masser (le corps); malaxer (les muscles).

masseur, *f.* **masseuse** [ma'səːr, ma'səːz], *s.* *Med:* Masseur, -euse.

massive ['masiv], *a.* (*a*) Massif. (*b*) **Massive protest**, protestation *f* en masse. **-ly,** *adv.* Massivement.

massiveness ['masivnəs], *s.* Massiveté *f*; caractère ou aspect massif (d'un monument, etc.).

mast[1] [mɑːst], *s.* **1.** *Nau:* Mât *m*. **Masts**, mâts, mâture *f*. **Lower mast**, bas mât. *To take down the masts of a ship*, démâter un navire. **Before the mast**, en avant du grand mât; sur le gaillard d'avant. **To sail before the mast**, servir comme simple matelot. **2.** Pylône *m* (de T.S.F., etc.). '**mast-'head,** *s.* *Nau:* Tête *f*, ton *m*, de mât. (*Of pers.*) *To be at the m.-h.*, être en vigie. '**mast-'heel,** *s.* *Nau:* Pied *m* de mât.

mast[2], *v.tr.* Mâter (un bâtiment). **Three-masted, four-masted, ship**, navire à trois, à quatre, mâts.

mast[3], *s.* *Husb:* Faînes *fpl* (de hêtre); faînée *f*; glands *mpl* (de chêne); glandée *f*. **Mast-year**, année de glandée.

master[1] ['mɑːstər], *s.* **1.** (*Man in control*) (*a*) Maître *m*. **To be master in one's own house**, être maître chez soi. **To be master of oneself**, être maître de soi-même; avoir de 'empire sur soi. **To be one's own master**, s'appartenir; ne dépendre que de soi. **To be master of the situation**, être maître de la situation. **To remain master of the field**, rester maître du champ de bataille. **To meet one's master**, trouver son maître. (*b*) (*Employer*) Maître, patron *m*, chef *m*. **Like master like man**, tel maître tel valet. **My master**, *F:* the master, is not at home, monsieur n'y est pas. (*c*) (*At Oxford and Cambridge*) Directeur *m*, principal *m*, -aux (de certains collèges). (*d*) *Nau:* Patron, maître (d'un navire de commerce). (*e*) **Master of foxhounds**, maître d'équipage; grand veneur. **Master of Ceremonies**, maître des cérémonies. **Master of the Rolls**, garde *m* des archives (juge de la Chancellerie). *Th:* **Chorus master**, répétiteur *m*. **2.** *Sch:* (*a*) Maître; professeur *m* ou instituteur *m*. **Form master**, professeur principal (d'une classe). **Writing master**, maître d'écriture. (*b*) **Fencing master**, professeur d'escrime; maître d'armes. (*c*) **Master of Arts**, maître ès arts = licencié ès lettres. **M. of Science**, maître ès sciences. **3.** (*a*) *A:* Artisan établi à son compte, travaillant en chambre. (*b*) **Master of an art**, maître d'un art. **To be master of a subject**, posséder un sujet à fond. **To make oneself master of sth.**, se rendre maître de qch. *S.a.* PAST-MASTER. *Art:* **An old master**, un maître d'autrefois. **4.** (*As title*) (*a*) *A:* **My masters**, messieurs. (*b*) (*As title given to boys not out of their teens*) **Master John**, Monsieur Jean. **5.** *Attrib.* (*a*) **Master carpenter**, maître charpentier. **Master mariner**, capitaine au long cours; capitaine marchand. (*b*) **Master hand**, main *f* de maître. *He is a m. hand at (doing sth.)*, il est passé maître dans l'art de (faire qch.). (*c*) **Master mind**, esprit supérieur. *Cards:* **Master card**, carte maîtresse. '**master-at-'arms,** *s.* *Navy:* Capitaine *m* d'armes. '**master-key,** *s.* Passe-partout *m inv.* '**master-singer,** *s.* *Mus.Hist:* Maître chanteur. '**master-stroke,** *s.* Coup *m* de maître.

master[2], *v.tr.* **1.** Dompter, maîtriser (qn, un cheval). **2.** Maîtriser, dompter (ses passions); surmonter (sa colère); apprendre (un sujet) à fond. *To m. a difficulty*, surmonter une difficulté;

venir à bout d'une difficulté. *To have mastered a subject*, posséder un sujet à fond.
masterful ['mɑːstəful], *a.* Impérieux, autoritaire.
masterly ['mɑːstəli], *a.* De maître ; magistral, -aux. **In a masterly manner,** magistralement.
masterpiece ['mɑːstəpiːs], *s.* Chef-d'œuvre *m.*
mastery ['mɑːstəri], *s.* **I.** Maîtrise *f* (*of*, de) ; domination *f* (*over*, sur). **To gain the mastery,** avoir le dessus. **2.** Connaissance approfondie (d'un sujet).
mastic ['mastik], *s.* **I.** (*Resin*) Mastic *m.* **2.** (*Cement*) Mastic. **Tyre mastic,** pâte *f* bouche-trous. **'mastic(-tree),** *s.* Lentisque *m.*
masticate ['mastikeit], *v.tr.* Mâcher, mastiquer.
mastication [masti'keiʃ(ə)n], *s.* Mastication *f.*
mastiff ['mɑːstif], *s.* Mâtin *m* ; dogue anglais.
mastodon ['mastodon], *s.* *Paleont:* Mastodonte *m.*
mastoid ['mastɔid], *a.* *Anat:* Mastoïde *f.*
mat[1] [mat], *s.* **I.** (*a*) Natte *f* (de paille). (*b*) Paillasson *m.* *Fibre mat,* tapis-brosse *m.* (*c*) Carpette *f.* *S.a.* BATH-MAT. (*d*) Table-mat, dessous *m* de plat ; rond *m* de table. **2.** *Nau:* Collision mat, paillet *m* d'abordage.
mat[2], *v.tr.* (matted) (*a*) Natter, tresser (le jonc). (*b*) Emmêler (les cheveux). (*c*) (*Of hair*) **To mat,** s'emmêler, se coller ensemble. **Matted hair,** cheveux emmêlés. (*Of stuff*) **To become matted,** se feutrer. **matting,** *s.* Natte(s) *f*(*pl*), paillassons *mpl.*
mat[3], *a.* Mat. *Mat complexion,* teint mat. *Phot:* **Mat paper,** papier mat.
match[1] [matʃ], *s.* **I.** (*a*) (*Of pers.*) Égal, -ale ; pareil, -eille. **To meet one's match,** trouver à qui parler. *To meet more than one's m.,* s'attaquer à plus fort que soi. **To be a match for s.o.,** être de force à lutter avec qn. (*b*) (*Of thgs*) **To be a (good) match,** aller bien ensemble ; être bien assortis. *Perfect m. of colours,* assortiment parfait de couleurs. **2.** *Sp:* Lutte *f*, partie *f*, match *m.* **Tennis match,** partie de tennis. **Football match,** match de football. *To win the m.,* gagner la partie. **3.** Mariage *m*, alliance *f.* **To make a match of it,** se marier. **To make a good match,** se marier avantageusement. **'match-maker,** *s.* Marieur, -euse. *She's a regular m.-m.,* c'est une marieuse acharnée. **'match-making,** *s.* Manie *f* d'arranger des mariages. **'match-play,** *s.* **I.** *Ten:* Jeu *'m* de match. **2.** *Golf:* Partie *f* par trous. *M.-p. competition,* concours *m* par trous.
match[2]. **I.** *v.tr.* (*a*) Égaler (qn) ; être l'égal de (qn) ; rivaliser avec (qn). *Pretty evenly matched,* à peu près de force égale. (*b*) **To match s.o. against s.o.,** opposer qn à qn. (*c*) Apparier (des gants) ; appareiller (des chevaux) ; assortir (des couleurs). *Com: Articles difficult to m.,* rassortiments *m* difficiles à obtenir. **2.** *v.i.* S'assortir ; s'harmoniser. *Colours to match,* couleurs assorties. *Dress with hat to m.,* robe et un chapeau à l'avenant. **matching,** *s.* Assortiment *m* ; appariement *m.* **'match-boarding,** *s.* *Carp:* Planches bouvetées.
match[3], *s.* **I.** Allumette *f.* **Safety match,** allumette de sûreté. **Book-matches,** allumettes Jupiter. **To strike a match,** frotter, craquer, une allumette. **2.** *A.Artil:* Mèche *f.* **Slow-match,** corde *f* à feu. **'match-box,** *s.* Boîte *f* à allumettes. *Match-box holder,* porte-allumettes *m inv.*
matchless ['matʃləs], *a.* Incomparable, inimitable ; sans égal, sans pareil.
matchwood ['matʃwud], *s.* *F:* **Smashed to matchwood,** mis en miettes.
mate[1] [meit], *s.* *Chess:* = CHECKMATE[1].

mate[2], *v.tr.* *Chess:* Faire (le roi) échec et mat.
mate[3], *s.* **I.** Camarade *mf* ; compagnon, *f.* compagne. *Ind:* **Workman's mate,** compagnon. **2.** (*Of birds*) Mâle *m* ou femelle *f* ; pair *m* ; (*of persons*) époux, *f.* épouse. **3.** *Nau:* (*a*) (*On merchant vessel*) Officier *m.* **First mate, second m,** **Second mate,** lieutenant *m.* (*b*) *Navy:* Second maître.
mate[4]. **I.** *v.tr.* Accoupler (des oiseaux). **2.** *v.i.* (*a*) (*Of pers.*) **To mate with s.o.,** épouser qn. (*b*) (*Of birds*) S'accoupler. **mating,** *s.* Union *f* (de personnes) ; accouplement *m* (d'oiseaux). **The mating season,** la saison des amours.
maté ['mate], *s.* Maté *m* ; thé *m* du Paraguay.
mater ['meitər], *s.* *F:* **The mater,** ma mère maman.
material [mə'tiːəriəl]. **I.** *a.* **I.** (*a*) *Phil:* Matériel (*b*) Matériel, grossier. **To be engrossed in m things,** être enfoncé dans la matière. (*c*) **To have enough for one's material needs,** avoir de quo vivre matériellement. **2.** (*a*) Important, essentiel (*to,* pour). *It has been of m. service to me,* cela m'a rendu un service sensible. (*b*) (*Fait*) pertinent. **-ally,** *adv.* **I.** Matériellement, essentiellement. **2.** Sensiblement. II. **material,** *s.* **I.** (*a*) Matière *f*, matériaux *mpl.* **Raw materials,** matières premières. **Building materials,** matériaux de construction ; matériau *m.* **War material,** matériel *m* de guerre. *To provide m. for conversation,* fournir des sujets de conversation. (*b*)*pl.* **Materials,** fournitures *f*, accessoires *m.* **Writing materials,** de quoi écrire. *Office materials,* fournitures de bureau. **2.** *Tex:* Étoffe *f*, tissu *m.* **'Customers' own material made up,'** "on travaille à façon."
materialism [mə'tiːəriəlizm], *s.* Matérialisme *m.*
materialist [mə'tiːəriəlist], *s.* Matérialiste *m.*
materialistic [mətiːəriə'listik], *a.* **I.** Matérialiste. **2.** (*Of pleasures*) Matériel.
materialize [mə'tiːəriəlaiz]. **I.** *v.tr.* Matérialiser. **2.** *v.i.* (*a*) *Psychics:* Se matérialiser. (*b*) *F:* Se réaliser ; (*of plans*) aboutir.
materia medica [mə'tiːəriə 'medikə], *s.* *Med:* Matière médicale.
maternal [mə'təːrn(ə)l], *a.* Maternel. **-ally,** *adv.* Maternellement.
maternity [mə'təːrniti], *s.* Maternité *f.* **Maternity hospital,** maternité.
mathematical [maθe'matik(ə)l], *a.* **I.** Mathématique. **2.** (*Étudiant*) en mathématiques ; (professeur, livre) de mathématiques. *He is a m. genius,* c'est un mathématicien de génie. **-ally,** *adv.* Mathématiquement.
mathematician [maθemə'tiʃ(ə)n], *s.* Mathématicien, -ienne.
mathematics [maθe'matiks], *s.pl.* Mathématiques *fpl. Sch:* **Higher mathematics,** mathématiques spéciales. **Strong in m.** fort en mathématiques ; *F:* fort en X.
maths [maθs], *s.pl.* *F:* = MATHEMATICS.
matinée ['matinei], *s.* *Th:* Matinée *f.*
matins ['matinz], *s.pl.* *Ecc:* Matines *f.*
matriarchal ['meitriɑːrk(ə)l], *a.* Matriarca, -aux.
matric [mə'trik], *s.* *F:* = MATRICULATION. **To take, pass, one's matric** = passer son bachot.
matricide[1] ['meitrisaid, mə-], *s.* Matricide *mf*
matricide[2], *s.* (*Crime*) Matricide *m.*
matriculate [mə'trikjuleit], *v.i.* Passer l'examen d'entrée à l'université.
matriculation [mətrikju'leiʃ(ə)n], *s.* Examen *m* de fin d'études secondaires (qui admet à l'université). *Cf.* MATRIC.

matrimonial [matri'mounjəl], *a.* Matrimonial, -aux ; conjugal, -aux.

matrimony ['matriməni], *s.* (Holy) matrimony, le mariage ; la vie conjugale.

matrix, *pl.* **-ixes**, **-ices** ['meitriks, 'meitriksiz, ma'traisi:z, *in sense* 3 'matrisi:z], *s.* **1.** *Anat:* Matrice *f.* **2.** *Geol: Miner:* Matrice, gangue *f.* **3.** *Typ: etc:* Matrice, moule *m.*

natron ['meitrən], *s.f.* **1.** Matrone ; mère de famille. **2.** *(a)* Intendante (d'une institution). *(b)* Infirmière en chef (d'un hôpital).

matronly ['meitrənli], *a.* A kindly matronly woman, une brave maman.

natter¹ ['matər], *s.* **1.** Matière *f* ; substance *f.* *(a) Log:* **Form and matter,** la forme et le fond. *(b) Ph:* **The indestructibility of matter,** l'indestructibilité de la matière. *(c)* **Vegetable matter,** matières végétales. **Colouring m.,** matière colorante. **2.** *Med:* Matière (purulente) ; pus *m.* **3.** *(a)* Matière, sujet *m* (d'un discours). **Reading matter,** choses *f* à lire (dans un journal). *(b) Typ:* Matière, copie *f.* **Plain matter,** composition *f* en plein. *S.a.* PRINT² 2. **4. It makes no matter,** n'importe ; cela ne fait rien. **No matter how you do it,** de n'importe quelle manière que vous le fassiez. *No m. how fast you run, you will not catch him,* vous avez beau courir, vous ne le rattraperez pas. **What matter?** qu'importe ? **5.** **Affaire** *f*, chose, cas *m.* **The m. I speak of,** l'affaire dont je parle. **It is an easy matter,** c'est facile. **It is no great matter,** c'est peu de chose. **That's quite another matter,** c'est toute autre chose. **As matters stand,** au point où en sont les choses. **Money matters,** affaires d'intérêt. **Business matters,** affaires. **In the matter of . . .,** quant à . . . ; en ce qui concerne. . . . **In this matter . . .,** à cet égard. . . . **Matter of taste,** affaire de goût. *It will be a m. of ten days,* ce sera l'affaire de dix jours. **For that matter, for the matter of that,** pour ce qui est de cela ; quant à cela ; d'ailleurs. **What is the matter?** qu'est-ce qu'il y a ? qu'y a-t-il ? *Something must be the m.,* il doit y avoir quelque chose. *As if nothing was the m.,* comme si de rien n'était. *What is the m. with your finger?* qu'est-ce que vous avez au doigt ? *You don't like that book?* **what is the matter with it?** vous n'aimez pas ce livre ? qu'est-ce que vous y trouvez à redire ? *S.a.* COURSE¹ 1, FACT 2. **'matter-of-'course,** *a.* Naturel ; qui va de soi. **'matter-of-'fact,** *a.* Pratique, positif, prosaïque.

matter², *v.i.* Importer (*to s.o.,* à qn) ; avo r de l'importance. *It does not m.,* n'importe ; cela ne fait rien. *It doesn't m. whether . . .,* peu importe que + *sub.* *Nothing else matters,* tout le reste n'est rien. *It matters a good deal to me,* cela importe beaucoup pour moi.

Matterhorn (the) [ðə'matərhɔ:rn]. *Pr.n.* Le Mont Cervin.

Matthew ['maθju]. *Pr.n.m.* Mat(t)hieu.

mattock ['matək], *s. Tls:* Hoyau *m* ; pioche *f* ; p c *m* à tranche.

mattress ['matrəs], *s. (a)* Matelas *m.* *(b)* **Spring mattress, box mattress,** sommier *m* élastique.

maturation [matju'reiʃ(ə)n], *s.* Maturation *f* (d'un fruit, d'un abcès) ; développement *m* (de l'intelligence).

mature¹ [ma'tjuər], *a.* **1.** Mûr. *Person of m. years,* personne d'âge mûr. **2.** *Fin:* (Papier) échu. **-ly,** *adv.* Mûrement.

mature². **1.** *v.tr.* Mûrir ; affiner (le vin, le fromage). **2.** *v.i.* *(a)* Mûrir. *(b) Fin:* (Of bill) Échoir ; arriver à l'échéance.

maturity [ma'tjuəriti], *s.* **1.** Maturité *f.* **The**

years of maturity, l'âge mûr. **2.** *Com:* (Date of) maturity, échéance *f* (d'une traite).

matutinal [matju'tain(ə)l], *a.* Matutinal, -aux.

maudlin ['mɔ:dlin], *a.* **1.** Larmoyant, pleurard. **2.** Dans un état d'ivresse larmoyante.

maul¹ [mɔ:l], *s. Tls:* Maillet *m,* mail oche *f.*

maul², *v.tr.* Meurtrir, malmener (qn). **To be mauled by a tiger,** être écharpé par un tigre.

mauling, *s.* Tripotée *f* ; mauvais quart d'heure.

maulstick ['mɔ:lstik], *s. Art:* Appui-main *m, pl.* appuis-main.

maunder ['mɔ:ndər], *v.i.* To maunder (on), divaguer, radoter. **Maunderings,** divagations *f.*

Maundy Thursday ['mɔ:ndi'θə:rzdi], *s.* Le jeudi saint.

Mauritius [mɔ'riʃəs]. *Pr.n.* L'île *f* Maurice.

mausoleum, *pl.* **-lea, -leums** [mɔ:so'li:əm, -'li:a, -'li:əmz], *s.* Mausolée *m.*

mauve [mo:uv], *a. & s.* (Colour) Mauve (*m*).

mavis ['meivis], *s. Orn:* Grive (chanteuse).

maw [mɔ:], *s.* **1.** *F. & Hum:* Estomac *m.* **To fill one's maw,** se remplir la panse. **2.** Gueule *f* (du lion).

mawkish ['mɔ:kiʃ], *a.* *(a)* Fade, insipide. *(b)* D'une sensiblerie outrée. **-ly,** *adv.* *(a)* Fadement ; avec fadeur. *(b)* Sentimentalement.

mawworm ['mɔ:wə:rm], *s.* Ver intestinal.

maxillary [mak'silər], *a.* Maxillaire.

maxim ['maksim], *s.* Maxime *f,* dicton *m.*

maximum, *pl.* **-a** ['maksiməm, -a]. **1.** *s.* Maximum *m, pl.* maximums, -a. **Maximum thermometer,** thermomètre *m* à maxima. **2.** *a.* Maximum, *f. occ.* maxima. **M. price,** prix *m* maximum. **M. load,** charge *f* limite.

may¹ [mei], *v.aux.* (3rd pers. sing. he may ; *p.t.* might [mait] ; *no pres. or past participle*) **1.** *(a)* *With luck I may succeed,* avec de la chance je peux réussir. *He may not be hungry,* l n'a peut-être pas faim. *He may miss the train,* il se peut qu'il manque le train. *I may (possibly) have done so,* j'ai pu le faire. *(b) How old might she be?* quel âge peut-elle bien avoir ? *Who may 'you be?* qui êtes-vous, sans indiscrétion ? *Might it not be well to warn him?* est-ce qu'on ne ferait pas bien de l'avertir ? *(c)* **It may, might, be that . . .,** il se peut, se pourrait, bien que + *sub.* **Be that as it may,** quoi qu'il en soit. **That's as may be,** c'est selon. *As you may suppose,* comme vous (le) pensez bien. *Run as he might he could not overtake me,* il a eu beau courir, il n'a pas pu me rattraper. *(d)* **We may, might, as well stay where we are,** autant vaut, vaudrait, rester où nous sommes. *S.a.* WELL² I. 1. *(e)* **I say, you might shut the door!** dites donc, vous pourriez bien fermer la porte ! *He might have offered to help,* il aurait bien pu offrir son aide. **2. May I?** vous permettez ? **May I come in?** —**You may,** puis-je entrer ?—Mais parfaitement. *If I may say so,* si j'ose (le) dire ; si je l'ose dire. *The Council may decide . . .,* il appartient, au besoin, au Conseil de décider. . . . **3.** *Let the dog loose that he may have a run,* lâchez le chien pour qu'il coure un peu. *I hope it may be true,* pourvu que cela soit vrai ! *I hope he may succeed,* j'espère qu'il réussira. **4.** *May he rest in peace!* qu'il repose en paix ! **Much good may it do you!** grand bien vous fasse ! *Long may you live to enjoy it!* puissiez-vous vivre longtemps pour en jouir !

May², *s.* **1.** Mai *m.* *In (the month of) May,* en au mois de mai. *(On) the first, the seventh, of May,* le premier, le sept, mai. **Queen of the May, May queen,** reine *f* du premier mai. *F:* **May and December,** une jeune fille qui epouse un vieillard. **2.** *Bot:* **May(-bush, -tree),** aubépine *f.* May(-blossom), fleurs *fpl* d'aubépine. **'may-beetle, -bug,** *s.* Hanneton *m.* **'May-day,** *s.* Le premier mai. **'may-fly,** *s. Ent:* Éphémère *m* vulgaire ; phrygane *f.*

maybe ['meibi], *adv.* Peut-être.

mayhap ['meihap], *adv. A. & Lit :* = MAYBE.

mayonnaise [meio'neːiz], *s.* Mayonnaise *f.*

mayor ['meər], *s.m.* Maire. Deputy mayor, adjoint (au maire) ; (*in Belgium*) échevin.

mayoralty ['meərə.ti], *s.* Temps *m* d'exercice des fonctions de maire.

mayoress ['meəres], *s.f.* Femme du maire ; mairesse.

maypole ['meipoul], *s.* To set up a *m.*, planter un mai.

mazarine [maza'riːn], *a. & s.* Bleu foncé *inv.*

maze[1] [meːiz], *s.* Labyrinthe *m*, dédale *m.* *F :* To be in a maze, ne savoir où donner de la tête.

maze[2], *v.tr.* Embrouiller, désorienter, ahurir (qn).

mazurka [ma'zəːrka], *s.* Mazurka *f.*

me [mi, miː], *pers.pron., objective case.* **1.** (*a*) Me, (*before a vowel sound*) m' ; moi. They see me, ils me voient. They hear me, ils m'entendent. Hear me! écoutez-moi ! Give me some! donnez-m'en ! (*b*) (*Refl.*) Moi. I will take it with me, je le prendrai avec moi. **2.** (*Stressed*) Moi. Come to me, venez à moi. He loves me alone, il n'aime que moi. No one ever thought of poor little me, personne ne pensait à ma pauvre petite personne. **3.** (*Stressed ; as a nominative*) *F :* It's me, c'est moi. He is younger than me, il est plus jeune que moi. **4.** (*In interjections*) Ah me! poor me! pauvre de moi ! Dear me! mon Dieu ! vraiment ! par exemple !

mead[1] [miːd], *s.* Hydromel (vineux).

mead[2], *s. Poet:* = MEADOW.

meadow ['medou], *s.* Pré *m*, prairie *f.* **'meadow-grass,** *s. Bot:* Pâturin *m.* **'meadow-land,** *s.* Prairie(s) *f(pl)* ; pâturages *mpl.* **'meadow-sweet,** *s. Bot:* (Spirée *f*) ulmaire *f* ; reine *f* des prés.

meagre ['miːgər], *a.* Maigre ; peu copieux. *M. attendance at a meeting,* assistance peu nombreuse. **-ly,** *adv.* Maigrement.

meal[1] [miːl], *s.* (*a*) Farine *f* (d'avoine, de seigle, de maïs) ; *esp.* = OATMEAL. (*b*) Farine ou poudre *f* (de diverses substances). *S.a.* WHOLE-MEAL.

meal[2], *s.* Repas *m.* Square meal, hearty m., repas copieux ; ample repas. To make a meal of it, en faire son repas. I like to rest after a m., j'aime à me reposer après manger. *Pharm :* 'To be taken after meals,' "à prendre après les principaux repas." **'meal-time,** *s.* Heure *f* du repas. At meal-times, aux heures de repas.

mealies ['miːliz], *s.pl.* Maïs *m.*

mealy ['miːli], *a.* **1.** Farineux. *M. potatoes,* pommes de terre farineuses. **2.** (*a*) Saupoudré de blanc ; poudreux. (*b*) *F:* (Visage) terreux, farineux. **3.** Mealy(-mouthed), doucereux, mielleux, patelin.

mean[1] [miːn], *s.* **I.** (*a*) Milieu *m* ; moyen terme. The golden mean, the happy mean, le juste milieu. (*b*) *Mth:* Moyenne *f.* Geometrical mean, moyenne proportionnelle. **2.** *pl.* Means, moyen(s) *m(pl)*, voie(s) *f(pl)*. To find (a) means to do sth., trouver moyen de faire qch. There is no means of doing it, il n'y a pas moyen. He has been the means of . . ., c'est par lui que. . . . By all (manner of) means! mais certainement ! mais faites donc ! Do it by all means, que rien ne vous en empêche ! May I come in?—By all means! puis-je entrer?—Mais, comment donc ! By no (manner of) means, en aucune façon ; pas

du tout. He is not by any means a hero, il n'es rien moins qu'un héros. By some means or othe de manière ou d'autre. By means of s.o., pa l'entremise de qn. By means of sth., au moyer par le moyen, de qch. **3.** *pl.* Moyens (de vivre) ressources *fpl.* To live beyond one's mean dépenser plus que son revenu. This car is beyon my means, cette voiture est hors de ma portée Private means, ressources personnelles. He is man of means, il a une belle fortune. *Com :* H has ample means at his disposal, il dispose d capitaux considérables.

mean[2], *a.* Moyen. Mean time, temps moyen *Mth:* Mean proportional, moyenne propor tionnelle.

mean[3], *a.* **I.** (*a*) Misérable, minable. *M.* street rue à l'aspect misérable. *M. rank,* rang infíme Of mean birth, de basse extraction. The meanes citizen, le dernier des citoyens. That ought to b clear to the meanest intelligence, cela devrait êtr compris par l'esprit le plus borné. (*b*) He is n mean scholar, c'est un érudit estimable. He ha no mean opinion of himself, il ne se croyait pa peu de chose. **2.** Bas, méprisable, mesquin. *M* souls, âmes basses. A mean trick, un vilain tour un sale coup. To take a m. revenge, se venge petitement. To take a mean advantage of s.o. exploiter indignement qn. **3.** Avare, mesquin chiche. **-ly,** *adv.* **I.** Misérablement, pauvre ment. *M. clad,* pauvrement vêtu. To thin meanly of sth., avoir une piètre opinion de qch **2.** (Se conduire) bassement, platement. **3.** (Ré compenser qn) mesquinement, chichement **mean-'spirited,** *a.* A l'âme basse ; vil, abject

mean[4], *v.tr.* (meant [ment] ; meant) **I.** (*a*) Avoi l'intention (to do sth., de faire qch.) ; se propose (de faire qch.). What do you m. to do? que comptez-vous faire? He meant to do me a service H voulait me rendre service. He means no harm il n'y entend pas malice ; il ne pense pas à mal I mean him no harm, je ne lui veux pas de mal He meant no offence, il n'avait nullement l'in tention de vous offenser. He didn't mean (to do) it, il ne l'a pas fait exprès. Without meaning it sans le vouloir. (*b*) He means well, il a de bonnes intentions. (*c*) I mean to be obeyed, j'entends qu'on m'obéisse. I m. to succeed, je veux réussir. **2.** (*a*) I meant this purse for you, je vous destinai cette bourse. (*b*) The remark was meant for you, la remarque s'adressait à vous. He meant that for you, c'est pour vous qu'il a dit cela. (*c*) Do you mean me? est-ce de moi que vous parlez? Thi portrait is meant for Mr A., ce portrait est censé représenter Monsieur A. **3.** (*a*) (Of word, phrase) Vouloir dire ; signifier. What does that word mean? que signifie ce mot? The name means nothing to me, ce nom ne me dit rien. What is meant by . . .? que veut dire . . .? (*b*) (Of pers.) What do you mean? que voulez-vous dire? What do you mean by that? qu'entendez-vous par là? Does he mean what he says? dit-il réellement sa pensée? I meant the remark for a joke, j'ai dit cela par plaisanterie. He meant it as a kindness, il l'a fait par bonté. You don't mean it! vous voulez rire! vous plaisantez! *I* m. it, c'est sérieux. (*c*) His refusal means my ruin, son refus entraînera ma ruine. Ten pounds means a lot to him! dix livres, c'est une somme pour lui ! If you knew what it means to live alone! si vous saviez ce que c'est que de vivre seul ! **meaning**[1], *a.* **I.** (With adv. prefixed, e.g.) Well-meaning, bien intentionné. **2.** (Regard) significatif, (sourire) d'intelligence. **-ly,** *adv.* D'un air, d'un ton, significatif. **meaning**[2], *s.* (*a*) Signification *f*, sens *m*, acception *f* (d'un mot). *What is the m. of that word?* que signifie, que veut dire, ce mot? *F: What's the meaning of this?* qu'est-ce que cela signifie? que signifie? (*b*) *You mistake my m.*, vous me comprenez mal. (*c*) *Look full of meaning*, regard significatif.

meander[1] [mi'andər], *s.* Méandre *m*, repli *m*, sinuosité *f*. *The meanders of a stream*, les méandres d'un cours d'eau.

meander[2], *v.i.* (*Of river*) Serpenter, se replier. **meandering**, *a.* **1.** (Sentier, etc.) sinueux, serpentant. **2.** (Discours) sans suite.

meaningless ['mi:niŋləs], *a.* Dénué de sens; qui ne signifie rien.

meanness ['mi:nnəs], *s.* **1.** Médiocrité *f*, pauvreté *f*, petitesse *f* (de l'esprit.); bassesse *f* (d'esprit, de naissance). **2.** (*a*) Mesquinerie *f*, avarice *f*. (*b*) Vilenie *f*. *A piece of meanness*, (i) une mesquinerie; (ii) une vilenie.

meant [ment]. *See* MEAN[4].

meantime ['mi:ntaim], **meanwhile** ['mi:n-hwail], *s. & adv.* (In the) meantime, (in the) moanwhile, dans l'intervalle; en attendant.

measles [mi:zlz], *s.pl.* **1.** Rougeole *f*. **German measles**, rougeole bénigne; roséole *f*. **2.** Ladrerie *f* (des porcs).

measly ['mi:zli], *a.* **1.** *Vet:* (Porc) ladre. **2.** *F:* Insignifiant, misérable.

measurable ['meʒərəbl], *a.* Mesurable, mensurable. *F: Within measurable distance of success*, à deux doigts de la réussite.

measure[1] ['meʒər], *s.* Mesure *f*. **1.** (*a*) Linear measure, mesure de longueur. **Square measure**, mesure de surface. **Cubic measure**, mesure de volume. *Give me full measure*, faites-moi pleine mesure. (*b*) *To take s.o.'s measure for a suit*, prendre les mesures de qn pour un complet. *F: To take the measure of a man*, prendre la mesure d'un homme. **Made to measure**, fait sur mesure. **2.** (*Instrument for measuring*) (*a*) Mesure (à grain, etc.). (*b*) Mètre *m*. *S.a.* TAPE-MEASURE. **3.** Mesure, limite *f*. **Beyond measure**, outre mesure; démesurément. **In some measure**, en partie; jusqu'à un certain point. **4.** (*a*) Mesure, démarche *f*. *Precautionary m.*, mesure de précaution. *He took measures accordingly*, il a pris ses arrangements en conséquence. **To take extreme measures**, employer les grands moyens. (*b*) Projet *m* de loi. **5.** *Ar:* Facteur *m*, diviseur *m* (d'un nombre). **Greatest common measure**, plus grand commun diviseur. **6.** *pl. Geol:* Coal measures, gisements houillers.

measure[2], *v.tr.* **1.** (*a*) Mesurer; métre: (un mur); cuber (le bois). *To m. a piece of ground*, faire l'arpentage d'un terrain. *To be measured (for one's height)*, passer à la toise. *To m. the tonnage of a ship*, jauger un navire. *F: To measure one's length (on the ground)*, s'étaler par terre; tomber de tout son long. (*b*) *Tail:* Mesurer (qn); prendre la mesure de (qn). (*c*) *To measure one's strength with s.o.*, mesurer ses forces avec qn. (*d*) *To measure one's words*, mesurer, peser, ses paroles. **2.** *This book measures six inches by four*, ce livre a six pouces de long sur quatre de large. **measure out**, *v.tr.* **1.** Mesurer (un terrain de tennis, etc.). **2.** Distribuer (les parts qui reviennent à chacun); mesurer (du blé, etc.). **measured**, *a.* **1.** Mesuré, déterminé. *Nau: Measured ton*, tonneau *m* d'encombrement. *S.a.* MILE. **2.** (*a*) (Pas) cadencé. (*b*) **With measured steps**, à pas comptés. **3.** Measured language, langage modéré. *To speak in m. tones*, parler avec mesure. **'measuring-**

chain, *s.* Chaîne *f* d'arpenteur. **'measuring-glass**, *s.* Verre gradué.

measurement ['meʒərmənt], *s.* **1.** Mesurage *m*. **2.** Mesure *f*, dimension *f*. **Head-, hip-measurement**, tour *m* de tête, de hanches. **To take s.o.'s measurements**, prendre les mesures de qn. *Const:* **Inside measurement**, **outside measurement**, mesure dans œuvre, mesure hors d'œuvre.

meat [mi:t], *s.* **1.** Viande *f*. *Ecc:* **To abstain from meat**, faire maigre. **Meat diet**, régime carné. **Meat tea**, thé-collation *m* avec un plat de viande. *S.a.* OLIVE 3. **2.** Aliment *m*, nourriture *f*. **Meat and drink**, le manger et le boire. *F: This was meat and drink to them*, ils en faisaient des gorges chaudes. **To get the meat out of a book**, extraire la moelle d'un livre. *Prov:* **One man's meat is another man's poison**, ce qui guérit l'un tue l'autre. *S.a.* BROKEN. **3.** **Grace before meat**, prière *f* avant le repas; bénédicité *m*. **'meat-'broth**, *s.* *Cu:* Bouillon gras. **'meat-safe**, *s.* Garde-manger *m* inv. **'meat-saw**, *:.* *Tls:* Scie *f* de boucher.

meatless ['mi:tləs], *a.* (Repas) maigre.

Mecca ['meka]. *Pr.n. Geog:* La Mecque.

mechanic [me'kanik], *s.* **1.** Artisan *m*, ouvrier *m*. **2.** Motor mechanic, mécanicien *m* automobiliste.

mechanical [me'kanik(ə)l], *a.* **1.** Mécanique. **2.** **The six mechanical powers**, les six machines simples. **Mechanical transport**, transport automobile. *S.a.* DRAWING 2, ENGINEER[1] 1. **3.** (*Of personal actions*) Machinal, -aux; automatique. **-ally**, *adv.* **1.** Mécaniquement. *M. operated*, à commande mécanique. **2.** Machinalement.

mechanician [mekə'niʃ(ə)n], *s.* Mécanicien *m*.

mechanics [me'kaniks], *s.pl.* La mécanique.

mechanism ['mekənizm], *s.* **1.** Appareil *m*, dispositif *m*; mécanisme *m*. **2.** Mécanisme (d'un artiste); technique *f* (du piano).

mechanization [mekənai'zeiʃ(ə)n], *s.* Mécanisation *f*.

mechanize ['mekənaiz], *v.tr.* Mécaniser.

Mechlin ['meklin]. *Pr.n. Geog:* Malines *f*. **Mechlin lace**, dentelle *f* de Malines; malines *f*.

medal ['med(ə)l], *s.* Médaille *f*. *F: The reverse of the medal*, le revers de la médaille.

medallion [me'daljən], *s.* Médaillon *m*.

medallist ['medəlist], *s.* Médaillé, -ée. **Gold medallist**, titulaire *mf* d'une médaille d'or.

meddle [medl], *v.i.* **To meddle with sth.**, (i) se mêler de qch.; (ii) toucher à qch. **To meddle in sth.**, s'immiscer dans qch. *Don't m. with my tools!* ne touchez pas à mes outils! **meddling**, *s.* Intervention *f*, ingérence *f* (*in, with, a matter*, dans une affaire).

meddler ['medlər], *s.* Officieux, -euse; fâcheux *m*; intrigant, -ante; touche-à-tout *m* inv.

meddlesome ['medlsəm], *a.* Officieux, intrigant; qui se mêle de tout.

mediaeval [medi'i:v(ə)l], *a.* **1.** Du moyen âge; médiéval, -aux. **2.** *F: Pej:* Moyenâgeux.

mediaevalist [medi'i:vəlist], *s.* Médiéviste *mf*.

medial ['mi:diəl], *a.* **1.** *a.* (*Of letter*) Médial, -als, -aux. **2.** *s.* Médiale *f*. **-ally**, *adv.* Médialement.

median ['mi:diən], *a.* **1.** *a.* Médian. **2.** *s.* (*a*) Nerf médian; veine médiane. (*b*) (Ligne) médiane *f*.

mediate ['mi:dieit], *v.i.* S'entremettre, s'interposer; agir en médiateur.

mediation [mi:di'eiʃ(ə)n], *s.* Médiation *f*; intervention (amicale).

mediator ['mi:dieitər], *s.* Médiateur, -trice.

medical ['medik(ə)l], *a.* Médical, -aux. *The m. profession*, (i) le corps médical; (ii) la profession de médecin. **Medical school**, ἐcole *f* de médecine. **Medical student**, étudiant *m* en médecine;

P: carabin m. **Medical stores,** matériel m sanitaire. **Medical man,** médecin m. **Medical officer,** médecin sanitaire; Mil: major m; (in hospital) chef m de service. **Medical officer of health,** médecin d'état civil. **Medical board,** conseil m de santé. S.a. ADVICE 1, FACULTY 2. **-ally,** adv. M. speaking, médicalement parlant. **To be medically examined,** subir un examen médical.

medicament [me'dikəmənt], s. Médicament m.
medicate ['medikeit], v.tr. Médicamentor.
Medici ['meditʃi]. Pr.n.pl. Hist: The Medici, les Médicis.
medicinal [me'disin(ə)l], a. Médicinal. -aux. **-ally,** adv. Médicinalement.
medicine ['med(i)sin], s. **1.** La médecine. To study m., faire sa médecine. **2.** (a) Médicament m, médecine. F: To give s.o. a dose of his own medicine, rendre la pareille à qn. S.a. PATENT¹ 2. (b) F: To take medicine, se purger. **3.** (Chez les Peaux-Rouges) (i) Sorcellerie f; (ii) charme m. **'medicine-chest,** s. (Coffret m de) pharmacie f. **'medicine-glass,** s. Verre gradué. **'medicine-man,** s. (Sorcier) guérisseur m.
medick ['midik], s. Bot: (Purple medick, luzerne f. Black medick, (luzerne) lupuline f.
medico ['mediko], s. F: Médecin m ou chirurgien m; P: carabin m.
medieval [medi'i:v(ə)l] = MEDIAEVAL.
mediocre ['mi:dioukər], a. Médiocre.
mediocrity [mi:di'ɔkriti], s. Médiocrité f.
meditate ['mediteit]. **I.** v.tr. Méditer (un projet). **To meditate doing sth.,** méditer de faire qch. **2.** v.i. (a) Méditer (on, upon, sur). (b) Se recueillir.
meditation [medi'teiʃ(ə)n], s. Méditation f (upon, sur); recueillement m.
meditative ['meditətiv], a. Méditatif, recueilli.
Mediterranean [medite'reinjən], a. The Mediterranean (Sea), la (mer) Méditerranée.
medium, pl. -a, -ums ['mi:diəm, -a, -əmz]. **I.** s. **1.** Milieu m; moyen terme (between, entre). Happy medium, juste milieu. **2.** Milieu, véhicule m. Air is the m. of sound, l'air est le véhicule du son. **3.** Intermédiaire m, entremise f. The newspaper as a m. for advertising, le journal comme moyen de réclame. **Advertising medium,** organe m de publicité. **Circulating medium,** agent m de circulation. **4.** Psychics: Médium m. **II. medium,** a. Moyen. **Medium-sized,** de grandeur moyenne, de taille moyenne.
medlar ['medlər], s. Bot: (a) Nèfle f. (b) Néflier m.
medley ['medli], s. Mélange m, pêle-mêle m inv; bigarrure f (de couleurs). Lit: Macédoine f. Mus: Pot pourri.
medulla [me'dʌlə], s. Moelle (épinière). **The medulla oblongata,** la moelle allongée.
medullary [me'dʌləri], a. Médullaire.
Medusa [me'dju:zə]. **1.** Pr.n.f. Gr.Myth: Méduse. **2.** s. Coel: Méduse f.
meed [mi:d], s. Poet: Récompense f. Lit: **To offer one's meed of praise,** apporter sa part d'éloges.
meek [mi:k], a. Doux, f. douce; humble. **-ly,** adv. Avec douceur; humblement.
meekness ['mi:knəs], s. Douceur f de caractère; soumission f, humilité f, mansuétude f.
meerschaum ['miərʃəm], s. **1.** Magnésite f; écume de mer. **2.** Pipe f en écume de mer.
meet¹ [mi:t], a. A: & Lit: Convenable; à propos; séant. Diamonds m. for a queen, diamants dignes d'une reine. **As was meet,** comme il convenait. **-ly,** adv. Convenablement.

meet², s. (a) Rendez-vous m de chasse; assemblée f de chasseurs. (b) Réunion f (de cyclistes).
meet³, v. (met [met]; met) **I.** v.tr. **1.** Rencontrer (qn); se rencontrer avec (qn). To m. s.o. on the stairs, croiser qn dans l'escalier. **He met his death at . . .,** il trouva la mort à. . . . **2.** (a) Rencontrer (qn en duel). (b) Affronter (la mort); faire face à (une difficulté). **3.** Rejoindre, se rencontrer avec (qn). **To go to meet s.o.,** aller au-devant de (qn); aller à la rencontre de qn. The bus meets all trains, le service d'autobus est en correspondance avec tous les trains. **To arrange to meet s.o.,** donner (un) rendez-vous à qn. **4.** Faire la connaissance de (qn). U.S: **Meet Mr Smith,** je vous présente M. Smith. **Pleased to meet you,** enchanté de faire votre connaissance. **5.** The request was met by the reply that . . ., il a été répondu à cette demande que. . . . **What a scene met my eyes!** quel spectacle frappa mes regards! If this should m. the eye of . . ., si ceci tombe sous les yeux de. . . . There is more in it than meets the eye, on ne voit pas le dessous des cartes. My eye met his, nos regards se croisèrent. **I dared not meet his eye,** je n'osais pas le regarder en face. **6.** (a) To m. s.o.'s views, se conformer aux vues de qn. To m. s.o., faire des concessions à qn. (b) Satisfaire à (un besoin); faire face à (une demande). It does not m. my requirements, cela ne répond pas à mes besoins. (c) Com: Faire honneur à, accueillir (un effet). (d) **To meet expenses,** faire face aux dépenses. **II. meet,** v.i. (a) Se rencontrer, se voir. We have met before, nous nous sommes déjà vus. Until we meet again, au revoir. (b) To meet (together), se réunir (en session). The society meets at . . ., la société tient ses réunions à. . . . (c) Se joindre. Two rivers that m., deux rivières qui confluent. Prov: Extremes meet, les extrêmes se touchent. Our eyes met, nos regards se croisèrent. F: **To make both ends meet,** joindre les deux bouts. (d) **To meet with sth.,** rencontrer, trouver, qch. To m. with a kindly reception, être accueilli avec bonté. To m. with difficulties, éprouver des difficultés; rencontrer des obstacles. To m. with losses, faire des pertes. To m. with a refusal, essuyer un refus. He has met with an accident, il lui est arrivé un accident. **meeting,** s. **1.** Rencontre f (de personnes, de routes); confluent m (de rivières). **2.** (a) Assemblée f, réunion f; Pol: Sp: meeting m. The m. to be held to-morrow, la réunion prévue pour demain. **To hold a public meeting,** se réunir en assemblée publique. **To call a meeting of the shareholders,** convoquer les actionnaires. **Notice of meeting,** circulaire convocatrice. **To address the meeting,** prendre la parole. **To put a resolution to the meeting,** mettre une résolution aux voix. (b) Rel: To go to meeting, aller au temple. **'meeting-house,** s. Temple m (des Quakers). **'meeting-place,** s. Lieu m de réunion; rendez-vous m.
megalith ['megaliθ], s. Mégalithe m.
megalithic [mega'liθik], a. Mégalithique.
megalomania [megalo'meinia], s. Mégalomanie f.
megaphone ['megafoun], s. Porte-voix m inv. Sp: etc: Mégaphone m.
megilp [me'gilp], s. Art: Véhicule (de couleur) composé d'huile et de vernis.
megrim ['mi:grim], s. A: **1.** Migraine f. **2.** pl. Megrims, the spleen; vapeurs fpl.
melancholia [melən'koulja], s. Hypocondrie f.
melancholic [melən'kɔlik], a. Mélancolique.
melancholy ['melənkoli]. **1.** s. Mélancolie f.

2. *a.* *(a)* *(Of pers.)* Mélancolique; triste. *(b)* *M. news,* triste nouvelle.

melissa [me'lisa], *s.* *Bot:* Mélisse *f*; *F:* citronnelle *f*. *Melissa cordial,* eau *f* de mélisse.

mellifluous [me'liflu∍s], *a.* Mielleux; doucereux. *M. eloquence,* éloquence melliflue.

mellow[1] ['melou], *a.* **1.** (Fruit) fondant, mûr; (vin) moelleux. **2.** *(Of voice)* Moelleux; doux, *f.* douce. **3.** (Esprit) mûr. **To grow mellow,** mûrir; s'adoucir. **4.** *(Of pers.)* *F:* Un peu gris; *P:* mûr.

mellow[2]. **1.** *v.tr.* *(a)* (Faire) mûrir (des fruits); donner du moelleux à (un vin). *(b)* Mûrir, adoucir (le caractère de qn). **2.** *v.i.* *(a)* *(Of fruit, wine)* Mûrir; *(of colour)* prendre de la patine. *(b)* *(Of character)* S'adoucir. **mellowing,** *s.* Maturation *f* (des fruits, du vin); adoucissement *m* (de la voix, des couleurs).

mellowness ['melon∍s], *s.* Maturité *f* (des fruits); moelleux *m* (du vin); douceur *f* (du caractère).

melodic [me'lɔdik], *a.* *Mus:* (Progression) mélodique. *S.a.* PASSAGE 5.

melodious [me'loudj∍s], *a.* Mélodieux, harmonieux. **-ly,** *adv.* Mélodieusement.

melodrama ['melodrɑːmɑ], *s.* Mélodrame *m*.

melodramatic [melodrɑ'matik], *a.* Mélodramatique. **-ally,** *adv.* D'un air ou d'un ton de mélodrame.

melody ['melodi], *s.* Mélodie *f*, air *m*, chant *m*.

melon ['mel∍n], *s.* **1.** Melon *m*. **Sugary melon,** (melon) sucrin *m*. *S.a.* WATER-MELON. **2.** *St.Exch:* **To carve, cut up, the melon,** distribuer les bénéfices. **'melon-bed,** *s.* Melonnière *f*.

melt [melt], *v.* *(p.t.* melted; *p.p.* melted; *p.p. adj.* molten ['moult(∍)n]) I. *v.i.* **1.** Fondre; se fondre; *(of glass, metals)* entrer en fusion. *S.a.* BUTTER[1] **1.** **2.** *His heart melted with pity,* la pitié lui attendrissait le cœur. **To melt into tears,** fondre en larmes. **3.** *(Of solid in liquid)* Fondre, (se) dissoudre. II. **melt,** *v.tr.* **1.** (Faire) fondre. *S.a.* BUTTER[1] **1.** **2.** Attendrir, émouvoir (qn). **melt away,** *v.i.* Se dissiper; *(of crowd)* se disperser. **melt down,** *v.tr.* Fondre (de la ferraille). **molten,** *a.* *Metall:* *Glassm:* En fusion; fondu. **melting**[1], *a.* **1.** *(a)* *(Of snow)* Fondant. *(b)* *(Of voice)* Attendri. **Melting mood,** attendrissement *m*. **2.** *M. sun,* soleil brûlant, torride. **melting**[2], *s.* **1.** Fonte *f*, fusion *f*. **2.** Attendrissement *m* (des cœurs), fusion *f*. **'melting-point,** *s.* Point *m* de fusion. **'melting-pot,** *s.* Creuset *m*. *F:* **Everything is in the melting-pot,** on est en train de tout refondre.

member ['memb∍r], *s.* Membre *m*. **1.** *Nat.Hist:* Organe *m*. **2.** *(a)* *Carp:* Pièce *f* (d'une charpente). *(b)* *Gram:* *Mth:* Membre (de la phrase, d'une équation). **3.** *(a)* *He is a m. of the family,* il fait partie de la famille. *M. of the audience,* assistant, -ante. *(b)* **Member of Parliament,** *F:* **M.P.,** membre de la Chambre des Communes; *(in Fr.)* député *m*. **Our member,** notre représentant (à la Chambre).

membership ['memb∍rʃip], *s.* **1.** Qualité *f* de membre. *Qualifications for m.,* titres *m* d'éligibilité *(of,* à). **Membership card,** carte *f* de membre. **2.** Nombre *m* des membres (d'une société).

membrane ['membrein], *s.* Membrane *f*. *Investing m.,* enveloppe *f*; tunique *f* (d'un organe). *Med:* **Diphtheric membrane,** couenne *f*.

membraned ['membreind], *a.* (Doigt) membrané.

membranous ['membran∍s], *a.* Membraneux, membrané.

memento, *pl.* **-o(e)s** [me'mento, -ouz], *s.* Mémento *m*, souvenir *m*.

memo ['memo], *s.* *F:* = MEMORANDUM **1.**

memoir ['memwɑːr], *s.* *(a)* Mémoire *m*, étude *f* (scientifique, etc.). *(b)* (i) Notice *f* biographique; (ii) *Journ:* article *m* nécrologique. *(c)* *pl.* **Memoirs,** mémoires.

memorable ['memor∍bl], *a.* Mémorable. **-ably,** *adv.* Mémorablement.

memorandum, *pl.* **-da, -dums** [memo'rand∍m, -da, -d∍mz], *s.* **1.** Mémorandum *m*, *F:* mémo *m*. **To make a memorandum of sth.,** noter qch. **2.** *Jur:* **Memorandum of association,** acte *m* de société. **Memorandum and articles of association,** statuts *mpl.* **3.** *Com:* Bordereau *m*. **memo-'randum-book,** *s.* Carnet *m*, calepin *m*, agenda *m*. **memo'randum-pad,** *s.* Bloc-notes *m*.

memorial [me'mɔːri∍l]. **1.** *a.* Commémoratif. **2.** *s.* *(a)* Monument (commémoratif). **War memorial,** monument aux morts de la guerre. *(b)* Pétition (adressée à un gouvernement). *(c)* *Jur:* **Memorial of a deed,** extrait *m* pour enregistrement.

memorialist [me'mɔːri∍list], *s.* Pétitionnaire *mf*.

memorialize [me'mɔːri∍la:iz], *v.tr.* **1.** Commémorer. **2.** Pétitionner (qn).

memorization [memorai'zeiʃ(∍)n], *s.* Mémorisation *f*.

memorize ['memora:iz], *v.tr.* Apprendre (qch.) par cœur.

memory ['memori], *s.* **1.** Mémoire *f*. **To commit sth. to memory,** apprendre qch. par cœur. *F:* **Memory like a sieve,** mémoire de lièvre, cervelle *f* de lièvre. *I have a bad m. for names,* je n'ai pas la mémoire des noms. **Loss of memory,** perte *f* de mémoire; amnésie *f*. *The thing comes back to my m.,* la chose me revient en mémoire. **To the best of my memory . . .,** autant que je m'en souviens, que je m'en souvienne. . . . **Never within living memory,** jamais de mémoire d'homme. **To play sth. from memory,** jouer qch. de mémoire. **2.** Mémoire, souvenir *m*. **Childhood memories,** souvenirs d'enfance. **We shall keep his memory,** nous garderons son souvenir. *The late king, of blessed m.,* le feu roi, d'heureuse mémoire.

mem-sahib ['memsɑːib], *s.f.* *(In India)* Madame (titre de respect donné par les indigènes à une Européenne mariée).

men [men], *s.m.pl.* See MAN[1].

menace[1] ['menes], *s.* *Lit:* Menace *f*.

menace[2], *v.tr.* *Lit:* **1.** Menacer (qn). **2.** *Those who m. war,* ceux qui nous menacent de la guerre.

menacing, *a.* Menaçant. **-ly,** *adv.* D'un air menaçant.

menagerie [me'nadʒeri], *s.* Ménagerie *f*.

mend[1] [mend], *s.* **1.** *(In fabric)* Reprise *f*, raccommodage *m*. **2.** **To be on the mend,** être en voie de guérison. *Trade is on the m.,* les affaires reprennent.

mend[2]. **I.** *v.tr.* **1.** Raccommoder (un vêtement); réparer (un outil). **To mend invisibly,** stopper (un vêtement). **To mend the fire,** arranger le feu. **2.** Rectifier, corriger. **To mend one's ways,** changer de conduite. **3.** *(a)* Réparer (une faute). *Prov:* **Least said soonest mended,** trop gratter cuit, trop parler nuit. *(b)* **To mend matters,** arranger les choses. *(c)* **To mend one's pace,** hâter, presser, le pas. **II.** *v.i.* **1.** *(Of invalid)* Se remettre. *The weather is mending,* le temps se remet au beau. **2.** S'amender, se corriger. **3.** S'améliorer. **mending,** *s.* Raccom-

modage *m.* **Mending outfit,** trousse *f* de raccommodage. **Invisible mending,** stoppage *m.*
mendacious [men'dei∫əs], *a.* Menteur, mensonger. **-ly,** *adv.* Mensongèrement.
mendaciousness [men'dei∫əsnəs], **mendacity** [men'dasiti], *s.* **I.** Penchant *m* au mensonge. **2.** Fausseté *f.*
mender ['mendər], *s.* Raccommodeur, -euse; ravaudeur, -euse (de vêtements); repriseuse *f* (de dentelles). **Invisible mender,** stoppeur, -euse.
mendicancy ['mendikənsi], *s.* Mendicité *f.*
mendicant ['mendikənt]. **I.** *a.* Mendiant. **Mendicant orders,** ordres quêteurs. **2.** *s.* Mendiant, -ante.
mendicity [men'disiti], *s.* = MENDICANCY.
menfolk ['menfouk], *s.m.pl.* Les hommes (de la famille).
menhir ['menhiər], *s.* *Archeol:* Menhir *m.*
menial ['mi:njəl]. **I.** *a.* *(Of duties)* Servile; bas, *f.* basse. **2.** *s.* *Usu. Pej:* Domestique *mf*; laquais *m.*
meningitis [menin'dʒaitis], *s.* *Med:* Méningite *f.* **Spinal meningitis,** myélo-méningite *f.* **Cerebrospinal meningitis,** méningite cérébro-spinale.
meniscus [me'niskəs], *s.* *Ph:* Ménisque *m.*
menstruation [menstru'ei∫(ə)n], *s.* *Physiol:* Menstruation *f.*
mensurable ['mensjurəbl], *a.* Me(n)surable.
mensuration [mensju'rei∫(ə)n, men∫u-], *s.* **I.** Mesurage *m.* **2.** *Geom:* Mensuration *f.*
mental ['ment(ə)l], *a.* Mental, -aux; de l'esprit. **Mental reservation,** arrière-pensée *f*; sousentente *f.* **Mental arithmetic,** calcul *m* de tête. **Mental deficiency,** déficience mentale; idiotie *f.* **The mental defectives, the mental deficients,** les déficients *m*; les minus habens *m.* **A mental case,** *F:* **a mental,** un(e) aliéné(e). **Mental hospital, mental home,** asile *m* d'aliénés; maison *f* de santé. **Mental specialist,** médecin *m* aliéniste. **-ally,** *adv.* Mentalement. **Mentally defective, mentally deficient,** à petite mentalité.
mentality [men'taliti], *s.* Mentalité *f.*
menthol ['menθɔl], *s.* Menthol *m.*
mention¹ ['men∫(ə)n], *s.* **I.** Mention *f* (de qch.). *M. may be made of three churches . . .,* on peut citer trois églises. . . . **2.** *Sch: etc:* **Honourable mention,** mention (honorable); accessit *m.*
mention², *v.tr.* Mentionner, citer, faire mention de (qch.). *We need hardly m. that . . .,* il est bien entendu que. . . . *You never mentioned it,* vous ne m'en avez jamais rien dit. *I shall mention it to him,* je lui en toucherai un mot. *It must never be mentioned again,* il ne faut plus jamais en reparler. *Too numerous to m.,* trop nombreux pour les citer. *It isn't worth mentioning,* cela est sans importance. *He has no property worth mentioning,* il n'a aucun bien qui vaille. *Not to mention . . .,* sans parler de . . .; sans compter. . . . *I heard my name mentioned,* j'entendis prononcer mon nom. *He mentioned no names,* il n'a nommé personne. *To mention s.o. in one's will,* coucher qn sur son testament. *F:* **Don't mention it!** (i) cela ne vaut pas la peine d'en parler! (ii) il n'y a pas de quoi! *Thank you, madam.—Don't m. it, sir,* merci, madame.—De rien, monsieur.
mentor ['mentər], *s.* Mentor *m,* guide *m.*
menu ['menju], *s.* Menu *m.* **Menu card,** menu.
mephitic [me'fitik], *a.* Méphitique.
mercantile ['mə:rkəntail], *a.* **I.** Mercantile, marchand. *M. affairs,* affaires commerciales. *M. nation,* nation commerçante. *M. establishment,* maison *f* de commerce. **Mercantile broker,** agent *m* de change. **2.** *Pej:* (Esprit) mercantile, intéressé.

Mercator [mər'keitər]. *Pr.n.m.* Mercator. **Mercator's sailing,** navigation *f* loxodromique; navigation plane.
mercenary ['mə:rsenəri]. **I.** *a.* Mercenaire, intéressé. **2.** *s.* *(Soldier)* Mercenaire *m.*
mercer ['mə:rsər], *s.* **(Silk-)mercer,** marchand, -ande, de soieries.
mercerize ['mə:rsəra:iz], *v.tr.* Merceriser.
merchandise ['mə:rt∫əndaiz], *s.* Marchandise(s) *f(pl).*
merchant ['mə:rt∫ənt]. **I.** *s.* *(a)* Négociant; commerçant; marchand en gros. **Merchant prince,** prince *m* du commerce. *(b)* *Scot. & U.S:* Marchand, -ande; boutiquier, -ière. *(c)* *P:* **Speed merchant,** chauffard *m.* **2.** *a.* Marchand; de commerce, du commerce. **Merchant ship, merchant vessel,** navire marchand; navire de commerce. **'merchant-'seaman,** *pl.* **-men,** *s.m.* Marin du commerce. **'merchant-'service,** *s.* Marine marchande.
merchantable ['mə:rt∫əntəbl], *a.* **I.** Vendable. **2.** De débit facile, de bonne vente.
merchantman, *pl.* **-men** ['mə:rt∫əntmən, -men], *s.* Navire marchand, navire de commerce.
merciful ['mə:rsiful], *a.* Miséricordieux *(to,* pour); clément *(to,* envers). **Be merciful to me,** faites-moi miséricorde. **-fully,** *adv.* Miséricordieusement; avec clémence.
mercifulness ['mə:rsifulnəs], *s.* Miséricorde *f.*
merciless ['mə:rsiləs], *a.* Impitoyable; sans pitié. **-ly,** *adv.* Impitoyablement; sans merci.
mercilessness ['mə:rsiləsnəs], *s.* Caractère *m* impitoyable; manque *m* de pitié.
mercurial [mə:r'kjuəriəl], *a.* **I.** *(a)* Vif, éveillé. *(b)* Inconstant; d'humeur changeante. **2.** *Med: Pharm:* Mercuriel.
Mercury ['mə:rkjuri]. **I.** *Pr.n.m.* *Myth: Astr:* Mercure. **II. mercury,** *s.* **I.** *Ch:* Mercure *m, A:* vif-argent *m.* *F:* **The mercury is falling,** le baromètre baisse. **2.** *Bot:* Mercuriale *f.*
mercy ['mə:rsi], *s.* **I.** Miséricorde *f,* grâce *f,* merci *f,* pitié *f.* *(a)* *He has no m.,* il est sans pitié. **Without mercy,** impitoyable(ment); sans pitié. **To show mercy to s.o.,** faire miséricorde à qn. **To have mercy on s.o.,** avoir pitié de qn. **To call, beg, for mercy,** demander grâce. **To throw oneself on s.o.'s mercy,** s'abandonner à la merci de qn. **For mercy's sake,** de grâce; par pitié. *The jurymen recommended the murderer to m.,* les jurés ont signé le recours en grâce. *Int. F:* **Mercy (on us)!** grand Dieu! miséricorde! *(b)* **To be, lie, at s.o.'s mercy,** être à la merci de qn. **At the mercy of the waves,** au gré des flots; à la dérive. *Iron:* **Left to the tender mercies of . . .,** livré au bon vouloir de. . . . *(c)* **Thankful for small mercies,** reconnaissant des moindres bienfaits *m.* **What a mercy!** quel bonheur! quelle chance! *(d)* **Works of mercy,** œuvres *f* de charité. **Sister of Mercy,** sœur de Charité, fille *f* hospitalière.
mere¹ ['miər], *s.* Lac *m,* étang *m.*
mere², *a.* Simple, pur, seul; rien que. . . . *Out of m. spite,* par pure méchanceté. *It's m. chance,* c'est un pur hasard. *The m. sight of her,* sa seule vue. *I shudder at the m. thought of it,* je frissonne rien que d'y penser. *He's a m. boy,* ce n'est qu'un enfant. *S.a.* NOBODY 2, NOTHING II. 3. **-ly,** *adv.* Simplement, seulement; tout bonnement. *The invitation is m. formal,* l'invitation est de pure forme. *He m. smiled,* il se contenta de sourire. *I said it m. as a joke,* j'ai dit cela histoire de rire.
meretricious [meri'tri∫əs], *a.* **I.** De courtisane. **2.** (Style, etc.) factice, d'un éclat criard.

merganser [mər'gansər], s. Orn: Harle m.

merge [mə:rdʒ]. I. v.tr. Fondre, fusionner (deux systèmes). To merge sth. in, into, sth., fondre qch. dans qch.; amalgamer qch. avec qch. These states became merged in the Empire, ces États furent englobés dans l'Empire. 2. v.i. Se fondre, se confondre (in, into, dans); se confondre (in, into, avec); (of banks, etc.) s'amalgamer, fusionner.

merger ['mə:rdʒər], s. I. Fin: Fusion f, amalgamation f (de plusieurs sociétés). Industrial merger, unification industrielle. 2. Jur: Extinction f par consolidation ou fusion.

meridian [me'ridiən]. I. s. (a) Méridien m. (b) Point culminant (d'un astre). F: At the meridian of his glory, à l'apogée de sa gloire. 2. a. Meridian line, méridienne f.

meridional [me'ridiən(ə)l], a. & s. Méridional, -aux; du midi.

meringue [mə'ran], s. Cu: Meringue f.

merino [me'ri:no], s. Husb: Tex: Mérinos m.

merit[1] ['merit], s. I. (a) Mérite m. To make a merit of sth., se faire un mérite de qch. (b) To treat s.o. according to his merits, traiter qn selon ses mérites. (c) Jur: The merits of a case, le bien-fondé d'une cause. To judge a proposal on its merits, juger une proposition au fond. To go into the merits of sth., discuter le pour et le contre de qch. 2. Valeur f, mérite. Book of sterling m., livre de véritable valeur. Sch: Certificate of merit, accessit m.

merit[2], v.tr. Mériter.

meritorious [meri'to:riəs], a. (Of pers.) Méritant; (of deed) méritoire. Sch: Prize for meritorious work, prix m d'encouragement. -ly, adv. D'une façon méritoire.

merlin ['mə:rlin], s. Orn: Émerillon m.

mermaid ['mə:rmeid], s.f. Sirène.

merman, pl. -men ['mə:rmən, -men], s.m. Triton.

Merovingian [mero'vindʒiən], a. & s. Hist: Mérovingien, -ienne.

merriment ['merimənt], s. Gaieté f, hilarité f, réjouissance f, divertissement(s) m(pl).

merry ['meri], a. (merrier) I. (a) Joyeux, gai. Merry as a grig, gai comme un pinson. To be always merry and bright, être toujours plein d'entrain. To make merry, se réjouir. To make m. over sth., se divertir de qch. A merry Christmas! joyeux Noël! Prov: The more the merrier, plus on est de fous, plus on rit. (b) F: To be merry, être éméché; être un peu gris. To be merry in one's cups, avoir le vin gai. 2. A: (a) The merry month of May, le gentil mois de mai. (b) Robin Hood and his merry men, Robin des Bois et sa troupe de gaillards. -ily, adv. Gaiement, joyeusement. **merry- 'andrew**, s.m. Paillasse, bouffon, pitre. **'merry-go-round**, s. (Manège m de) chevaux mpl de bois; carrousel m. **'merry-maker**, s. (a) The merry-makers, la bande joyeuse. (b) Noceur, -euse. **'merry-making**, s. Réjouissances fpl, divertissement m.

merrythought ['meriθo:t], s. Lunette f, fourchette f (d'une volaille).

meseems [mi'si:mz], v.impers. A. & Lit: Il me semble; m'est avis (that, que).

mesentery ['mesəntəri, 'mez-], s. Anat: Mésentère m.

mesh[1] [meʃ], s. I. Maille f (d'un filet). To mend the meshes of a net, re(m)mailler un filet. F: To entangle s.o. in the meshes of intrigue, engager qn dans un réseau d'intrigues. 2. Mec.E: Prise f, engrènement m, engrenage m. Constant-mesh gear, pignons de prise constante. In mesh, en prise.

mesh[2]. I. v.tr. Mec.E: Endenter, engrener (des roues dentées). 2. v.i. (Of teeth of wheel) (S')engrener; être en prise. -**meshed**, a. Wide-meshed, à larges mailles.

mesmerism ['mezmərizm], s. Mesmérisme m, hypnotisme m.

mesmerist ['mezmərist], s. Hypnotiseur m.

mesmerize ['mezməra:iz], v.tr. Magnétiser; hypnotiser.

mesocarp ['mesoka:rp], s. Bot: Mésocarpe m.

mesoderm ['mesodə:rm], s. Biol: Mésoderme m.

Mesopotamia [mesopo'teimjə]. Pr.n. La Mésopotamie.

Mespot ['mespot]. Pr.n. Mil: P: = MESOPO- TAMIA.

mess[1] [mes], s. I. (a) A: Plat m, mets m. B: Mess of pottage = plat de lentilles. (b) Husb: (For animal) Pâtée f. 2. Saleté f. To make a mess of the table-cloth, salir la nappe. 3. Fouillis m, gâchis m. Everything is in a m., tout est en désordre. What a mess! here's a pretty mess! voilà du propre! F: (Of pers.) To get into a mess, se mettre dans le pétrin, dans de beaux draps. To make a mess of it, tout gâcher. 4. Mil: Navy: (For officers) Table f, mess m, F: popote f; (for men) Mil: ordinaire m, Navy: plat m. Mess-jacket, veston m de mess. Nau: F: To lose the number of one's mess, mourir; perdre le goût du pain. **'mess- kettle**, s. Navy: Gamelle f. **'mess-room**, s. I. Mil: Salle f de mess. 2. Navy: Carré m (des officiers). **'mess-tin**, s. Mil: Gamelle (individuelle). Navy: Quart m.

mess[2]. I. v.tr. (a) Salir, souiller. (b) To mess (up) a business, gâcher une affaire. 2. v.i. Mil: Navy: (Of officers) Faire table, (of men) faire plat; manger en commun. **mess about**, v.i. F: (a) Patauger, saloper (dans la boue). (b) Bricoler; gaspiller son temps. **'mess-up**, s. F: I. Gâchis m. 2. Embrouillement m, malentendu m; P: cafouillage m.

message ['mesedʒ], s. I. (a) Message m. To deliver messages for s.o., faire les messages de qn. To leave a message for s.o., laisser un mot pour qn. (b) Communication f (par téléphone). 2. Commission f, course f. To run messages, faire les commissions, les courses. 3. (a) Prédiction f; évangile m (d'un prophète). (b) Enseignement m (d'un écrivain).

messenger ['mesəndʒər], s. I. (a) Messager, -ère. (b) Commissionnaire m; garçon m de bureau. Hotel messenger, chasseur m. Telegraph messenger, facteur m des télégraphes; facteur- télégraphiste m. S.a. EXPRESS[1] I. (c) Courrier m (diplomatique). King's messenger = messager d'État. 2. (On kite-string) Postillon m.

Messiah [me'saiə]. Pr.n. Messie m.

messianic [mesi'ænik], a. Messianique.

messianism [me'saiənizm], s. Messianisme m.

messmate ['mesmeit], s. Camarade m de table; Navy: camarade de plat.

Messrs ['mesərz], s.m.pl. Com: etc: Messieurs, abbr. MM.

messuage ['meswedʒ], s. Jur: Ma on, dépendances et terres fpl.

messy ['mesi], a. F: I. (a) Sale, malpropre. (b) En désordre. 2. Qui salit; salissant.

met [met]. See MEET[3].

metabisulphite [metabai'sʌlfait], s. Ch: Méta- bisulfite m.

metabolism [me'tabolizm], s. Biol: Métabolisme *m.* *Constructive* *m.,* anabol.sme *m.* *Destructive* *m.,* catabolisme *m.*

metacarpus [meta'kɑːrpəs], *s.* *Anat:* Métacarpe *m.*

metacentre ['metasentər], *s.* Métacentre *m.*

metal¹ ['met(ə)l], *s.* **I.** Métal *m,* -aux. Base metal, métal commun. Sheet metal, tôle *f* mince. The metal industries, les industries métallurgiques. **2.** *Glassm:* Verre *m* en fusion. **3.** *Civ.E:* (Matériau *m* d')empierrement *m;* ballast *m* (de voie ferrée). Road metal, cailloutis *m,* pierraille *f.* **4.** *Typ:* Caractères *mpl.* Old metal, vieille matière. **5.** *pl.* *Rail:* (*Of engine*) To leave, jump, the metals, quitter les rails; dérailler. **'metal-bearing,** *a.* Métallifère. **'metal-'oxide,** *attrib.a.* *El:* (Valve) cuproxyde. **'metal-work,** *s.* **I.** Travail *m* des métaux; serrurerie *f.* **2.** Métal ouvré.

metal², *v.tr.* (metalled) Empierrer, caillouter (une route).

metallic [me'talik], *a.* Métallique.

metalliferous [meta'lifərəs], *a.* Métallifère.

metallize ['metalaːiz], *v.tr.* **I.** Métalliser (une surface). **2.** Vulcaniser (le caoutchouc).

metallography [meta'lɔgrəfi], *s.* Métallographie *f.*

metalloid ['metalɔid], *a.* *&* *s.* Métalloïde (*m*).

metallurgic(al) [meta'ləːrdʒik(əl)], *a.* Métallurgique.

metallurgist [me'talərdʒist], *s.* Métallurgiste *m.*

metallurgy [me'talərdʒi], *s.* Métallurgie *f.* The *m.* of iron, la sidérotechnie; la sidérurgie.

metamorphic [meta'mɔːrfik], **metamorphous** [meta'mɔːrfəs], *a.* Métamorphique.

metamorphism [meta'mɔːrfizm], *s.* Métamorphisme *m.*

metamorphose [meta'mɔːrfouz], *v.tr.* Métamorphoser, transformer (to, into, en).

metamorphosis, *pl.* **-oses** [meta'mɔːrfosis, -ɔsiːz], *s.* Métamorphose *f.*

metaphor ['metafər], *s.* Métaphore *f;* image *f.* Mixed metaphor, métaphore disparate.

metaphoric(al) [meta'fɔrik(əl)], *a.* Métaphorique. **-ally,** *adv.* Métaphoriquement.

metaphysical [meta'fizik(ə)l], *a.* Métaphysique. **-ally,** *adv.* Métaphysiquement.

metaphysician [metafi'ziʃ(ə)n], *s.* Métaphysicien *m.*

metaphysics [meta'fiziks], *s.pl.* La métaphysique; ontologie *f.*

metatarsus, *pl.* **-i** [meta'tɑːrsəs, -ai], *s.* *Anat:* *Nat.Hist:* Métatarse *m.*

metathesis, *pl.* **-eses** [me'taθesis, -esiːz], *s.* **I.** *Ling:* *Surg:* Métathèse *f.* **2.** *Ch:* Substitution *f.*

metazoon, *pl.* **-zoa** [meta'zouɔn, -'zouə], *s.* *Biol:* Métazoaire *m.*

mete [miːt], *v.tr.* *Lit:* To mete (out) punishments, rewards, assigner des punitions; distribuer, décerner, des récompenses.

metempsychosis [metempsi'kousis], *s.* Métempsyc(h)ose *f.*

meteor ['miːtiər], *s.* Météore *m.*

meteoric [miːti'ɔrik], *a.* **I.** Météorique. Meteoric iron, sidérolithe *f.* *F:* *M. rise in the social scale,* montée rapide de l'échelle sociale. **2.** Atmosphérique.

meteorite ['miːtiorait], *s.* Météorite *m* or *f;* aérolithe *m.*

meteorological [miːtioro'lɔdʒik(ə)l], *a.* Météorologique, aérologique.

meteorologist [miːtio'rɔlodʒist], *s.* Météorologiste *m,* météorologue *m.*

meteorology [miːtio'rɔlodʒi], *s.* Météorologie *f.*

meter¹ ['miːtər], *s.* Compteur *m;* jaugeur *m* Electric meter, compteur de courant. To turn off the gas at the meter, fermer le compteur.

meter², *s.* *U.S:* = METRE¹ ².

methane ['meθein], *s.* *Ch:* Méthane *m.* Pheny. methane, toluène *m.*

methinks [mi'θiŋks], *v.impers.* (*p.t.* methought [mi'θɔːt]) *A.* *&* *Lit:* Il me semble.

method ['meθəd], *s.* (*a*) Méthode *f;* manière *j* (*of doing sth.,* de faire qch.); procédé *m* (pour faire qch.). *Adm:* Methods of payment, modalités *f* de paiement. *Mil:* *Tactical methods* procédés de combat. (*b*) Man of method, homme d'ordre. *F:* There's method in his madness, il n'est pas si fou qu'il en a l'air.

methodical [me'θɔdik(ə)l], *a.* Méthodique. *M.* life, vie réglée, ordonnée. *He is very m.,* il a beaucoup de méthode. **-ally,** *adv.* Méthodiquement; avec méthode.

Methodist ['meθodist], *a.* *&* *s.* *Ecc:* Méthodiste *mf.*

methought [mi'θɔːt]. *See* METHINKS.

methyl ['meθil], *s.* *Ch:* Méthyle *m.*

methylate ['meθileit], *v.tr.* *Ch:* Méthyler. Methylated spirit, alcool dénaturé; alcool à brûler.

methylene ['meθiliːn], *s.* *Ch:* Méthylène *m;* esprit *m* de bois.

meticulosity [metikju'lɔsiti], *s.* Méticulosité *f.*

meticulous [me'tikjuləs], *a.* Méticuleux. **-ly,** *adv.* Méticuleusement. *To be always m. accurate,* avoir le souci de l'exactitude.

meticulousness [me'tikjuləsnəs], *s.* Méticulosité *f.*

metonymical [meto'nimik(ə)l], *a.* *Rh:* Métonymique.

metonymy [me'tɔnimi], *s.* *Rh:* Métonymie *f.*

metre¹ ['miːtər], *s.* *Pros:* Mètre *m,* mesure *f.* In metre, en vers.

metre², *s.* *Meas:* Mètre *m* (= 39.37 *inches*). Square metre, mètre carré. Cubic metre, mètre cube.

metric¹ ['metrik], *a.* *Meas:* Métrique. The metric system, le système métrique.

metric²(al) ['metrik(əl)], *a.* (Poésie) métrique.

metrics ['metriks], *s.pl.* *Pros:* Métrique *f.*

metronome ['metronoum], *s.* *Mus:* Métronome *m.*

metropolis [me'trɔpolis], *s.* Métropole *f.*

metropolitan [metro'pɔlitən]. **I.** *a.* Métropolitain. **2.** . *Ecc:* Métropolitain *m,* archevêque *m.*

mettle [metl], *s.* **I.** (*Of pers.*) Ardeur *f,* courage *m,* feu *m;* (*of horse*) fougue *f.* To put s.o. on his mettle, piquer qn d'honneur; exciter l'émulation de qn. *I was on my m.,* ;e m'étais piqué au jeu. **2.** Caractère *m,* tempérament *m.* To show one's mettle, faire ses preuves.

mettlesome ['metlsəm], *a.* (*Of pers.*) Ardent, vif; (*of horse*) fougueux.

mew¹ [mjuː], *s.* *Orn:* (Sea-)mew, mouette *f.*

mew², *s.* Mue *f,* cage *f* (pour les faucons).

mew³, *v.tr.* *F:* To mew s.o. (up), claquemurer, renfermer, qn.

mew⁴, *s.* (*Of cat, sea-gull*) Miaulement *m.*

mew⁵, *v.i.* (*Of cat, sea-gull*) Miauler. **mewing,** *s.* Miaulement *m.*

mewl [mjuːl], *v.i.* (*Of infant*) Vagir, piailler.

mews [mjuːz], *s.* **I.** Écuries *fpl.* **2.** Impasse *f* (sur laquelle donnaient des écuries).

Mexican ['meksikən], *a.* *&* *s.* Mexicain, -aine.

Mexico ['meksiko]. *Pr.n.* Le Mex:que.

mezzanine ['mezaniːn], *s.* *Arch:* Mezzanine (-floor), mezzanine *f,* entresol *m.*

mezzotint ['medzotint], *s. Engr :* **1.** Gravure *f* à la manière noire. **2.** Estampe *f* à la manière noire.

mi [mi:], *s. Mus :* Mi *m.*

miaow¹ [mjau], *s.* Miaulement *m*, miaou *m* (du chat).

miaow², *v.i.* (*Of cat*) Miauler.

miasma, *pl.* -**ata** [mai'azma, -əta], *s.* Miasme *m.*

miasmal [mai'azməl], **miasmatic** [maiaz'matik], *a.* Miasmatique.

miaul [mjaul], *v.i.* Miauler. **miauling,** *s.* Miaulement *m.*

mica ['maikə], *s.* Mica *m.*

micaceous [mai'kei∫əs], *a.* Micacé.

mice [mais]. *See* MOUSE¹.

Michael [maikl]. *Pr.n.m.* Michel.

Michaelmas ['miklməs], *s.* **1.** La Saint-Michel (jour de terme). **2.** *Bot :* Michaelmas daisy, marguerite *f* d'automne.

Michelangelo [maikəl'andʒəlo]. *Pr.n.m.* Michel-Ange.

mickle [mikl]. *A. & Scot :* **1.** *a.* (*a*) Beaucoup de. (*b*) Grand. **2.** *s. Prov :* Many a little makes a mickle, les petits ruisseaux font les grandes rivières.

microbe ['maikroub], *s.* Microbe *m.*

microbial [mai'kroubiəl],' **microbic** [mai'krobik], *a.* Microbien, microbique.

microbiology [maikrobai'ɔlodʒi], *s.* Microbiologie *f.*

microcephalous [maikro'sefələs], *a.* Microcéphale.

microcosm ['maikrokɔzm], *s.* Microcosme *m.*

microfarad [maikro'farad], *s. El.Meas :* Microfarad *m.*

micrometer [mai'krɔmetər], *s.* Micromètre *m.* Micrometer screw, vis *f* micrométrique.

micrometric(al) [maikro'metrik(əl)], *a.* Micrométrique.

micron ['maikrɔn], *s. Meas :* Micron *m*; millième *m* de millimètre.

micro-organism [maikro'ɔ:rgənizm], *s.* Micro-organisme *m.*

microphone ['maikrofoun], *s.* Microphone *m.* Concealed m., espion *m.*

microphotograph [maikro'foutograf, -gra:f], *s.* Microphotographie *f.*

microscope ['maikroskoup], *s.* Microscope *m.* Visible under the microscope, visible au microscope.

microscopic(al) [maikro'skɔpik(əl)], *a.* **1.** Microscopique. **2.** Microscopical examination, examen au microscope.

microtherm ['maikroθə:rm], *s. Ph.Meas :* Microthermie *f.*

microtome ['maikrotoum], *s.* Microtome *m.*

microzoa [maikro'zoua], *s.pl. Biol :* Microzoaires *m.*

micturate ['miktjureit], *v.i. Med :* Uriner.

micturition [miktju'ri∫(ə)n], *s.* **1.** *Med :* Micturition *f.* **2.** *F :* Miction *f.*

mid¹ [mid], *a.* Du milieu; mi-, moyen. *From mid June to mid August,* de la mi-juin à la mi-août. In mid air, entre ciel et terre; au milieu des airs. In mid channel, au milieu du chenal. 'mid-iron,' *s. Golf :* Fer moyen; crosse moyenne en fer. 'mid-'Lent, *s.* Mi-carême *f.* mid-'season, *s.* Demi-saison *f.*

mid², *prep. Poet :* = AMID.

midday ['midei], *s.* Midi *m.* Midday heat, chaleur de midi; chaleur méridienne.

midden [midn], *s. Dial :* Tas *m* de fumier.

middle [midl]. **1.** *Attrib.a.* Du milieu; central, -aux; moyen, intermédiaire. Middle wall, mur

mitoyen; mur de refend. To take a middle course, prendre un parti moyen. Middle size, grandeur moyenne. *Box :* Middle weight poids moyen. *Log :* Middle (term), moyen terme. **2.** *s.* (*a*) Milieu, centre *m.* The middle of life, l'âge mûr. In the middle of . . ., au milieu de. . . . *The ball hit him in the m. of the back,* la balle l'atteignit en plein dos. *About the m. of August,* à la mi-août. In the very middle of . . ., right in the middle of . . ., au beau milieu de. . . . *F :* I was in the middle of putting, j'étais en train de lire. (*b*) Taille *f*, ceinture *f. The water came up to his m.,* l'eau lui venait à mi-corps. **middle-'aged,** *a.* (*Of pers.*) En re deux certain âge, d'un certain âge. **middle 'class.** **1.** *s.* The middle class(es), la classe moyenne; la bourgeoisie. **2.** *a. It's horribly m.-c.!* c'est du dernier bourgeois! **middle-'sized,** *a.* De grandeur moyenne; de taille moyenne.

middleman, *pl.* -**men** ['midlmən, -men], *s.m. Com :* Intermédiaire, revendeur.

middlemost ['midlmoust], *a.* Le plus au milieu; central, -aux.

middling ['midliŋ]. **1.** *a.* (*a*) (i) Médiocre; (ii) passable, assez bon. How are you?—Middling, comment allez-vous?—Pas mal; comme ci comme ça. (*b*) *Of m. size,* de grandeur moyenne. (*c*) *Com :* Bon ordinaire; de qualité moyenne. **2.** *adv.* Assez bien; passablement; ni bien ni mal.

middy ['midi], *s.m. Nau : F :* = MIDSHIPMAN.

midge [midʒ], *s.* Moucheron *m*; cousin *m.*

midget ['midʒet], *s.* **1.** Nain, *f.* naine; nabot, -ote. **2.** *Phot :* Miniature *f.* **3.** *Attrib.* Minuscule.

midland ['midlənd]. **1.** *s.pl.* The Midlands, les comtés centraux (de l'Angleterre). **2.** *a.* Des comtés du centre.

midmost ['midmoust], *a.* Le plus près du milieu; central, -aux.

midnight ['midnait], *s.* Minuit *m. To arrive about m.,* arriver sur les minuit.

midriff ['midrif], *s. Anat :* Diaphragme *m. Blow on the m.,* coup au creux de l'estomac.

midship ['mid∫ip], *s. N.Arch :* Milieu *m* du navire. *Esp. attrib.* Midship frame, maître couple *m.*

midshipman, *pl.* -**men** ['mid∫ipmən, -men], *s.m. Nau :* Aspirant (de marine); midship.

midst [midst]. **1.** *s.* (*a*) In the midst of sth., au milieu de, parmi (la foule, etc.). *In the m. of winter,* en plein hiver; au cœur de l'hiver. In the midst of all this, sur ces entrefaites. *F :* I was in the midst of reading, j'étais en train de lire. (*b*) In our midst, au milieu de nous; parmi nous. **2.** *prep. Poet :* = AMID(ST).

midstream [mid'stri:m], *s.* **1.** Ligne médiane (d'un fleuve). **2.** In midstream, au milieu du courant.

midsummer ['midsʌmər], *s.* (*a*) Milieu *m* de l'été. (*b*) Le solstice d'été. Midsummer day, la Saint-Jean.

midway ['midwei], *adv.* A mi-chemin, à moitié chemin. Midway between . . . and . . ., à mi-distance entre . . . et . . .

midwife, *pl.* -**wives** ['midwaif, -wa:ivz], *s.f.* Sage-femme, *pl.* sages-femmes.

midwifery ['midwifri], *s.* Obstétrique *f.*

midwinter [mid'wintər], *s.* (*a*) Milieu *m* de l'hiver, fort *m* de l'hiver. (*b*) Le solstice d'hiver.

mien [mi:n], *s. Lit :* Mine *f*, air *m. Lofty m.,* port hautain.

might¹ [mait], *s.* Puissance *f*, force(s) *f(pl).* To work with all one's might, travailler de toute sa force. Might against right, la force contre le

droit. Might is right, la force prime le droit ; la raison du plus fort est toujours la meilleure. **might²,** v. See MAY¹.

mightiness ['maitinəs], s. Puissance f, force f ; grandeur f.

mighty ['maiti]. I. a. (a) Puissant, fort. S.a. HIGH I. 2. (b) Grand, vaste, grandiose. (c) F : You're in a m. hurry, vous êtes diablement pressé. **-ily,** adv. 1. Puissamment, fortement, vigoureusement. 2. F : Extrêmement, fameusement. II. **mighty,** adv. F : Fort, extrêmement, rudement (content, etc.).

mignonette [minjə'net], s. Réséda odorant.

migraine [mi'grein], s. Med : Migraine f.

migrant ['maigrənt]. 1. a. = MIGRATORY. 2. s. Migrateur, -trice.

migrate [mai'greit], v.i. Émigrer.

migration [mai'greiʃ(ə)n], s. Migration f.

migratory ['maigrətəri], a. (Peuple) migrateur, nomade ; (oiseau) migrateur, de passage.

mike¹ [maik], s. F : Microphone m, F : micro m.

mike², v.i. Mil : P : Tirer au flanc.

Mike³. Pr.n.m. (Dim. of Michael) Michel. F : For the love of Mike . . ., pour l'amour de Dieu. . . .

Milanese [milə'ni:z], a. & s. Geog : Milanais, -aise.

milch-cow ['miltʃkau], s. Vache laitière.

mild [maild], a. 1. (Of pers., word) Doux, f. douce. F : As mild as a dove, as milk, doux comme un agneau. 2. (Of rule) Doux, peu sévère, peu rigoureux. M. punishment, punition légère. 3. (Climat) doux, tempéré ; (hiver) doux, bénin. It is milder here, il fait meilleur ici. 4. (a) (Médicament) doux, bénin ; (tabac) doux. Mild beer, bière légère. F : Draw it mild ! tout doux ! n'exagérez pas ! (b) A mild form of measles, une forme bénigne de la rougeole. 5. (Exercice) modéré ; (amusement) innocent, anodin. 6. Mild steel, acier doux. **-ly,** adv. 1. Doucement ; avec douceur. 2. F : To put it mildly, pour m'exprimer avec modération.

mildew¹ ['mildju:], s. 1. (a) Rouille f (sur le froment, etc.). (b) Mildiou m, mildew m (sur les vignes, etc.). (c) Chancissure f (sur le pain, etc.). 2. Moisissure f ; taches fpl d'humidité.

mildew², v.tr. (a) Rouiller, moisir (une plante). (b) (Of damp) Piquer (le papier, etc.) ; chancir (le pain).

mildness ['maildnəs], s. 1. Douceur f, clémence f (de qn, du temps). 2. Bénignité f (d'une maladie). Laitier, crémier.

mile [mail], s. Mille m. Statute mile, English mile (= 1760 yards = 1609 m. 31), mille anglais, mille terrestre. Nautical mile, sea mile (= 2206 yards = 1852 m.), mille marin. Square mile (= 259 hectares), mille carré. Nau : Measured mile, base f (pour essais de vitesse). F : Not a hundred miles away, tout près. To be miles from believing sth., être à mille lieues de croire qch. Nobody comes within miles of him, personne ne lui monte à la cheville. **'mile-post,** s. Borne f milliaire.

mileage ['maileʤ], s. (a) Distance f en milles. Daily mileage, parcours journalier (d'une locomotive, etc.). Car with very small m., auto qui a très peu roulé. (b) Vitesse f (en milles).

milestone ['mailstoun], s. 1. Borne milliaire, routière ; (in Fr.) borne kilométrique. 2. F : Milestones in s.o.'s life, événements qui jalonnent la vie de qn.

milfoil ['milfɔil], s. Bot : Mil-e-feuille f.

miliary ['miliəri], a. Med : Miliaire.

militancy ['militənsi], s. Esprit militant ; activisme m.

militant ['militənt], a. Militant. Hist : **Militant suffragette,** suffragette activiste.

militarism ['militərizm], s. Militarisme m.

militarist ['militərist], s. Militariste m.

military ['militəri]. 1. a. Militaire. **Military man,** militaire m. **Of military age,** en âge de servir. **Military law,** le code (de justice) militaire. 2. s.pl. Coll. **The military,** les militaires m ; la troupe ; la force armée. **-ily,** adv. Militairement.

militate ['militeit], v.i. Militer (in favour of, against, en faveur de, contre).

militia [mi'liʃə], s. Milice f ; garde nationale.

militiaman, pl. **-men** [mi'liʃəmən, -men], s.m. Milicien ; garde national.

milk¹ [milk], s. 1. Lait m. **New milk,** lait (encore) chaud ; lait du jour. **Milk diet,** régime lacté. F : **To come home with the milk,** rentrer au grand jour. **Land of milk and honey,** pays de cocagne. S.a. FLOW² 4. **Milk and water,** (i) lait coupé (d'eau) ; (ii) discours ou littérature fade, insipide. **Complexion of milk and roses,** teint de lis et de roses. Prov : **It is no use crying over spilt milk,** à chose faite point de remède. 2. Lait, eau f (de noix de coco). **Milk of almonds, of lime,** lait d'amandes, de chaux. **'milk-and-'water,** a. F : Fade, insipide. **'milk-can,** s. Boîte f à lait. **'milk-gauge,** s. = MILK-TESTER. **'milk-jug,** s. Pot m à lait. **'milk 'pudding,** s. Cu : Riz m, sagou m, tapioca m, etc., au lait. **'milk-tester,** s. Pèse-lait m inv, lactomètre m. **'milk-tooth,** pl. **-teeth,** s. Dent f de lait. **'milk-white,** a. D'une blancheur de lait. **'milk-woman,** pl. **-women,** s.f. Laitière, crémière.

milk², v.tr. 1. Traire (une vache, etc.). 2. F : Dépouiller, exploiter (qn). **To milk the till,** F : barboter la caisse. 3. Tg : Tp : **To milk a message, to milk the wire,** capter une communication (à l'écoute). **milking,** s. Traite f (d'une vache, etc.).

milker ['milkər], s. 1. (a) (Pers.) Trayeur, -euse. (b) Mechanical milker, trayeuse mécanique. 2. (Of cow) Good milker, bonne laitière.

milkiness ['milkinəs], s. Couleur laiteuse ; lactescence f (d'un liquide, etc.).

milkmaid ['milkmeid], s.f. 1. Laitière, crémière. 2. Trayeuse ; fille de laiterie.

milkman, pl. **-men** ['milkmən, -men], s.m. Laitier, crémier.

milksop ['milksɔp], s. F : Poule mouillée.

milkweed ['milkwi:d], s. Bot : Laiteron m.

milky ['milki], a. Laiteux ; lactescent. Astr : **The Milky Way,** la Voie lactée. El : **Milky cell,** accumulateur perlé, laiteux.

mill¹ [mil], s. 1. (a) (Flour-)mill, moulin m (à farine). **Steam mill,** minoterie f. F : **To go, pass, through the mill,** passer par de dures épreuves. (b) Coffee-mill, pepper-mill, moulin à café, à poivre. (c) (Crushing-)mill, (moulin) broyeur m, concasseur m. 2. Metalw : Rolling-mill, laminoir m. 3. Tls : = MILLING-CUTTER. 4. Usine f ; manufacture f. **Cloth-mill,** fabrique f de drap. **Cotton-mill,** filature f de coton. S.a. PAPER-MILL, SAWMILL. 5. F : Combat m à coups de poing ; assaut m de boxe. **'mill-course,** s. Bief m de moulin. **'mill-'dam,** s. Barrage m de moulin. **'mill-dust,** s. Folle farine. **'mill-finishing,** s. Apprêt m, apprêtage m (du papier). **'mill-hand,** s. (a) Ouvrier, -ière d'usine, de fabrique, de filature. (b) Garçon meunier. **'mill-owner,** s. 1. Propriétaire m de moulin. 2. Industriel m ; usinier m ; manufacturier m ; filateur m. **'mill-pond,** s. 1. Ré-

servoir *m* de moulin ; retenue *f*. **2.** *F* : L'océan *m*
Atlantique. **'mill-race,** *s.* Bief *m* de moulin.
mill². **I.** *v.tr.* (*a*) Moudre (le blé). (*b*) Broyer
(du minerai). (*c*) Fouler (le drap). (*d*) Fraiser
(des engrenages, etc.). (*e*) Molet(t)er (la tête
d'une vis). *Num:* Créneler (une pièce de
monnaie). **Milled edge** (*on coin*), crénelage *m*,
grènetis *m*. **2.** *v.i. Esp. U.S :* (*a*) (*Of cattle*)
Tourner en masse. (*b*) (*Of crowd*) Fourmiller ;
tourner en rond. **milling,** *s.* **I.** Meunerie *f*,
minoterie *f*. **2.** (*a*) Mouture *f*, moulage *m* (du
grain). (*b*) Broyage *m*. (*c*) Foulage *m* (du drap).
3. *Metalw:* (*a*) Fraisage *m*. (*b*) Molet(t)age *m*
(d'une tête de vis). **4.** *F :* Coups *mpl* de poing ;
raclée *f*, rossée *f*. **'milling-cutter,** *s. Mec.E:*
Fraise *f* ; fraiseuse *f*.
millboard ['milbɔːrd], *s.* Carton-pâte *m inv* ;
fort carton ; carton épais.
millenary ['milenəri], *a. & s.* Millénaire (*m*).
millennial [mi'lenjəl]. **I.** *a.* Millénaire : qui
dure depuis mille ans. **2.** *s.* Millième anniversaire *m*.
millennium [mi'leniəm], *s.* **I.** *Rel.H :* Millénium *m*. **2.** Millénaire *m* ; mille ans *m*.
millepede ['milipiːd], *s. Myr :* Mille-pattes *m inv*,
mille-pieds *m inv*.
miller ['milər], *s.* **I.** Meunier *m* ; (*of steam mill*)
minotier *m*. **2.** *Mec.E:* (*a*) (*Pers.*) Fraiseur *m*.
(*b*) (*Machine*) Fraiseuse *f* ; machine *f* à fraiser.
millet ['milet], *s. Bot:* Millet *m*, mil *m*. **African,
Indian, millet,** sorgho *m*. **'millet-seed,** *s.*
Graine *f* de millet.
milliampere [mili'ampeər], *s. El.Meas:* Milliampère *m*.
milliard ['miljard], *s.* Milliard *m*.
milligram(me) ['miligram], *s.* Milligramme *m*.
millimetre ['milimiːtər], *s.* Millimètre *m*.
milliner ['milinər], *s.* Modiste *f*.
millinery ['milinəri], *s.* (Articles *mpl* de)
modes *fpl. M. shop,* magasin *m* de modes.
million ['miljən], *s.* **I.** Million *m*. **Two m. men,**
two millions of men, deux millions d'hommes.
2. *F:* **The million,** la foule, le commun.
millionaire [miljə'neər], *a. & s.* Millionnaire
(*mf*).
millionth ['miljənθ], *a. & s.* Millionième (*m*).
millstone ['milstoun], *s.* Meule *f* (de moulin).
Upper millstone, meule courante. **Lower millstone,** *A :* nether millstone, meule gisante.
F: **To be between the upper and the nether
millstone,** être entre l'enclume et le marteau.
It will be a millstone round his neck all his life,
c'est un boulet qu'il traînera toute sa vie.
'millstone-quarry, *s.* Meulière *f*.
millwright ['milrait], *s.* Constructeur *m* de
moulins.
milt [milt], *s.* **I.** Rate *f* (des mammifères).
2. Laitance *f*, laite *f* (des poissons).
mime¹ [maim], *s. Gr. & Lt.Ant:* Mime *m*.
mime². **I.** *v.tr.* Mimer (une scène). **2.** *v.i.* Jouer
par gestes.
mimetic [mai'metik], *a.* **I.** D'imitation ; imitatif. **2.** = MIMIC¹ **I**. **3.** (Papillon, etc.) mimé-
tique.
mimetism ['maimetizm], *s. Nat.Hist:* Mimétisme *m*.
mimic¹ ['mimik]. **I.** *a.* (*Of gesture, etc.*) Mimique ;
imitateur, -trice. **2.** *s.* (*a*) Mime *m*. (*b*) Imitateur,
-trice.
mimic², *v.tr.* (mimicked) **I.** Imiter, mimer,
contrefaire ; *F:* singer (qn). **2.** Imiter, contrefaire (la nature, etc.).
mimicker ['mimikər], *s.* Imitateur, -trice.
F: singe *m*.

mimicry ['mimikri], *s.* Mimique *f*, imitation *f*.
minaret ['minaret], *s.* Minaret *m*.
minatory ['minətəri], *a.* Menaçant ; *Jur:* comminatoire.
mince¹ [mins], *s. Cu:* Hachis *m*.
mince², *v.tr.* **I.** Hacher (menu) (de la viande,
etc.). **Minced meat,** hachis *m*. **2.** (*Always neg.*)
Not to mince matters, ne pas mâcher ses words, ne pas mâcher
ses mots ; parler net, parler sans phrase. **3.** To
mince (one's words), parler du bout des lèvres ;
(*of woman*) minauder. **mincing,** *a.* (*a*) Affecté,
minaudier, affété. (*b*) *To take m.* steps, marcher à
petits pas.
mincemeat ['minsmiːt], *s. Cu:* Compote de
raisins secs, de pommes, d'amandes, etc., liée
avec de la graisse et conservée avec du cognac ;
mincemeat *m. F:* **To make mincemeat of sth.,**
hacher menu qch. **To make mincemeat of s.o.,**
réduire qn en chair à pâté.
mince-pie [mins'pai], *s. Cu:* Petite tarte contenant du mincemeat.
mincer ['minsər], *s. Cu:* Hache-viande *m inv*.
mind¹ [maind], *s.* **I.** (*Remembrance*) (*a*) Souvenir *m*,
mémoire *f*. **To bear, keep, sth. in mind,** (i) se
souvenir de qch. ; garder la mémoire de qch. ; ne
pas oublier qch. ; (ii) tenir compte de qch. **Bear
him in m.,** songez à lui. **Bear in m. that she
is only a child,** n'oubliez pas que c'est une
enfant. **To bring, (re)call, sth. to s.o.'s mind,**
rappeler qch. à la mémoire de qn. **To call sth.
to mind,** évoquer le souvenir de qch. **To put
s.o. in mind of s.o.,** rappeler qn à qn. *He puts me
in m. of his father,* il me fait penser à son père.
There comes to my m. a curious story, il me souvient d'une histoire curieuse. **To go, pass, out
of mind,** tomber dans l'oubli. **It went out of my
mind,** cela m'est sorti de l'esprit. (*b*) *Ecc:*
Year's mind, service *m* du bout de l'an. **2.** (*a*) Pensée *f*, avis *m*, idée *f*. **To tell s.o. one's mind,** dire
sa façon de penser à qn. **To give s.o. a piece,
a bit, of one's mind,** dire son fait, ses vérités, à
qn. **To be of the same mind as s.o.,** être du
même avis que qn. (*Of several pers.*) **To be of
a mind, of one mind,** être du même avis ; être
d'accord. **To my mind,** à mon avis ; selon mon
avis ; à ce que je pense. (*b*) **To know one's own
mind,** savoir ce qu'on veut. **To make up one's
mind,** prendre son parti ; se décider. **To make
up one's mind to do sth.,** se décider, se résoudre,
à faire qch. *To make up one's m. about sth.,*
prendre une décision au sujet de qch. **To make
up one's mind to, for, sth.,** (i) se résigner à qch. ;
(ii) décider en faveur de qch. *She couldn't make
up her m. what to choose,* elle ne pouvait se
décider à choisir. **To be in two minds about sth.,
about doing sth.,** être indécis sur qch., pour faire
qch., quant au parti à prendre. **The bright
weather put me in the mind for walking,** le beau
temps me donna l'envie de faire une promenade.
To change, alter, one's mind, changer d'avis ;
se raviser. **I have a mind, a good mind, a great
mind, to . . . ,** j'ai (grande) envie, j'ai bien envie,
de. . . **To have half a mind to do sth.,** avoir
pas mal envie de faire qch. *To have no m. to do
sth.,* n'avoir aucun désir de faire qch. *Those who
have a m. can go,* ceux qui le désirent peuvent
y aller. (*c*) **To let one's mind run upon sth.,**
songer à qch. **To set one's mind on sth.,** désirer
qch. ardemment. **To have set one's mind on
doing sth.,** avoir à cœur de faire qch. *His m.
turned to . . . ,* il se mit à songer à . . . ; sa
pensée se tourna vers. . . . **To give one's mind
to sth.,** s'adonner, s'appliquer, à qch. *To give
one's whole m. to sth.,* appliquer toute son atten-

tion à qch. **To bring one's mind to bear on sth.**, porter son attention sur qch. **To have sth. in mind**, avoir qch. en vue. **To find sth. to one's mind**, trouver qch. à son goût, à son gré. **3.** Esprit *m*, âme *f*. **State of mind**, état *m* d'âme. **Turn of mind**, mentalité *f* (de qn). *He was not in a state of m. to* . . ., (i) il n'était pas disposé à . . .; (ii) il n'était pas en état de. . . . **Peace of mind**, tranquillité *f* d'esprit. *To disturb s.o.'s peace of m.*, troubler l'esprit de qn. **4.** (*a*) *Phil: Psy:* (*Opposed to body*) Ame; (*opposed to matter*) esprit; (*opposed to emotions*) intelligence *f*. (*b*) Esprit, idée. *It comes to my m. that* . . ., l'idée me vient que . . ., il me vient l'idée que . . ., il me vient à l'esprit que. . . . *She has something on her mind*, elle a quelque chose qui la préoccupe. **To take** s.o.'s **mind off his sorrow**, distraire qn de son chagrin. **To be easy, uneasy, in one's mind**, avoir, ne pas avoir, l'esprit tranquille. **To set one's mind to sth.**, réfléchir à qch. **To turn one's mind to a study**, appliquer son esprit à une étude. *That is a weight off my mind*, voilà qui me soulage l'esprit. *To get an idea fixed in one's m.*, se mettre qch. dans la cervelle. **Put it out of your mind**, n'y pensez plus. *I can't get that out of his mind*, je ne peux pas lui ôter cela de l'idée. (*c*) *A noble m.*, une belle âme. *Prov:* **Great minds think alike**, les beaux esprits, les grands esprits, se rencontrent. **5.** **To be out of one's mind**, avoir perdu la raison, la tête; n'avoir plus sa raison. **To go out of one's mind**, perdre la raison; tomber en démence. **To be in one's right mind**, être dans son bon sens; avoir toute sa raison. **Of sound mind, sound in mind**, sain d'esprit. '**mind-healer,** *s*. Psychiatre *m*. '**mind-picture,** *s*. Représentation mentale.

mind², *v.tr.* **1.** Faire attention à, prêter (son) attention à (qn, qch.). **Never mind him**, ne faites pas attention à lui. *Never m. that*, qu'à cela ne tienne. *Never m. the money!* ne regardez pas à l'argent! *Never m. the remainder*, je vous tiens quitte du reste. **Mind my words!** écoutez bien ce que je vous dis! **Mind you!** remarquez bien! **2.** S'occuper de, se mêler de (qch.). **Mind your own business!** occupez-vous, mêlez-vous, de ce qui vous regarde! **3.** (*a*) *Would you m. shutting the door?* voudriez-vous bien fermer la porte? *Do you m. coming?* cela vous est-il égal de venir? *F:* **D'you mind** *if I open the window?* ça ne vous fait rien que j'ouvre la fenêtre? *You don't m. my keeping you waiting?* cela ne vous ennuie pas que je vous fasse attendre? *You don't m. my smoking?* la fumée ne vous gêne pas? *You don't m. my mentioning it?* cela ne vous froisse pas que je vous le dise? **If you don't mind**, si cela vous est égal, ne vous fait rien. *I don't m.*, je veux bien. **I don't mind trying**, je veux bien essayer. **I shouldn't mind a cup of tea**, je prendrais volontiers une tasse de thé. *A glass of wine?*—**I don't mind**, un verre de vin?—Ce n'est pas de refus. (*b*) *Don't m. them*, ne vous inquiétez pas d'eux. **Never mind the consequences!** ne vous souciez pas des conséquences! **Never mind!** (i) n'importe! peu importe! (ii) ne vous inquiétez pas! *Who minds what he says?* qui s'occupe de ce qu'il dit? *I don't m. the cold*, le froid ne me gêne pas. *He doesn't m. expense*, il ne regarde pas à la dépense. **I don't mind**, cela m'est égal; peu (m')importe. **4.** *M. you're not late!* ayez soin de ne pas être en retard. *M. you write to him!* ne manquez pas de lui écrire! **Mind what you are about!** prenez garde à ce que vous faites! *M. your language!* observez

votre langage! **Mind you don't fall!** prenez garde de tomber! *F:* **Mind and don't be late!** ayez soin de ne pas être en retard! **Mind the step!** attention à la marche! **Mind yourself!** méfiez-vous! ayez l'œil! **5.** Soigner, avoir l'œil sur (des enfants); garder (des animaux, etc.). **To mind the house, the shop**, garder la maison; garder, tenir, la boutique.

minded ['maindid], *a.* **1.** (*a*) Disposé, enclin (*to do sth.*, à faire qch.). **If you are so minded**, si le cœur vous en dit. (*b*) (*With advs.*) Commercially *m.*, à l'esprit commercial. **2.** (*With sb. or adj. prefixed, e.g.*) **Bloody-, feeble-, healthy-minded**, à l'esprit sanguinaire, faible, sain. **The book-minded public**, le public liseur.

-mindedness ['maindidnəs], *s.* **Strong-mindedness**, force *f* de caractère. **Narrow-mindedness**, étroitesse *f* de vues, d'esprit.

minder ['maindər], *s.* (*a*) Gardeur, -euse (de bestiaux); surveillant, -ante (d'enfants). (*b*) *Ind:* = MACHINE-MINDER.

mindful ['maindful], *a.* **1.** Attentif (*of one's health*, à sa santé); soigneux (*of*, de). **To be m. of one's good name**, avoir soin de sa réputation. **2.** **To be mindful of an event**, se souvenir d'un événement. **To be mindful to do sth.**, se souvenir, ne pas oublier, de faire qch.

mindless ['maindləs], *a.* (*a*) Insouciant (*of*, de); indifférent (*of*, à). (*b*) Oublieux (*of*, de).

mine¹ [main], *s.* **1.** Mine *f* (de houille, d'or). *F:* **A mine of information**, une mine, un trésor, d'informations. **2.** (*a*) *Mil:* Mine. **To spring, touch off, a mine**, faire jouer une mine. (*b*) *Navy:* **Ground mine**, mine de fond; mine dormante. **Contact mine**, mine vigilante. *Floating m.*, mine flottante. **To lay a mine**, poser, mouiller, une mine. '**mine field,** *s.* **1.** Région minière. '**mine-layer,** *s. Navy:* Poseur *m*, mouilleur *m*, de mines. '**mine-laying,** *s. Navy:* Pose *f*, mouillage *m*, de mines. '**mine-shaft,** *s.* Puits *m* de mine. '**mine-sweeper,** *s. Navy:* Dragueur *m* de mines.

mine², *v.tr. & i.* **1.** (*a*) To mine (under) the earth, fouiller (sous) la terre, creuser la terre. (*b*) *Mil:* Miner, saper (une muraille). *F:* **Excesses which have mined his constitution**, excès qui lui ont miné le corps. (*c*) *Navy:* To mine a harbour, miner, semer des mines dans, un port. **2.** *Min:* To mine (for) coal, exploiter le charbon.

mining, *s.* **1.** *Mil:* Sape *f*. **2.** *Navy:* Pose *f* de mines. **3.** *Min:* Exploitation minière, des mines; l'industrie minière. **Mining industry**, industrie minière. **Mining village**, village minier. **Mining engineer**, ingénieur *m* des mines.

mine³. **1.** *poss.pron.* Le mien, la mienne, les miens, les miennes. (*a*) *Your country and m.*, votre patrie et la mienne. *This letter is m.*, (i) cette lettre est à moi, m'appartient; (ii) cette lettre est de moi. **A friend of mine**, un(e) de mes ami(e)s; un(e) ami(e) à moi; un(e) mien(ne) ami(e). **It is no business of mine**, ce n'est pas mon affaire. **No effort of mine**, aucun effort de ma part. (*b*) **Be good to me and mine**, soyez gentil pour moi et les miens. (*c*) **Mine and thine**, le mien et le tien. *What is m. is thine*, ce qui est à moi est à toi. **2.** *poss.a. A. & Poet:* Mon, *f.* ma, *pl.* mes.

miner ['mainər], *s.* (*a*) *Min:* (Ouvrier *m*) mineur *m*; ouvrier du fond. (*b*) *Mil:* Mineur, sapeur *m*.

mineral ['minərəl]. **1.** *a.* Minéral, -aux. **The mineral kingdom**, le règne minéral. **Mineral waters**, (i) eaux minérales; (ii) (*also s.pl.*) *F:*

minera1s) boissons (hygiéniques) gazeuses. **Min-eral spring,** source minérale. **2.** s. (a) Minéral m. (b) Min: Minerai m; (in coal-mining) charbon m, houil e f. **Mineral rights,** droits miniers.

mineralogist ˌmɪnə'ralodʒist], s. Minéralogiste m.

mineralogy [minə'ralodʒi], s. Minéralogie f.

mingle [mɪŋgl]. **1.** v.tr. Mêler, mélanger. **2.** v.i. (a) S mêler, se mélanger, se confondre (with, avec). (b) (Of pers.) To m. with the crowd, se mêler à, dans, la foule.

miniature ['miniatjər]. **1.** s. Miniature f. To paint in miniature, peindre en miniature. A Niagara in miniature, un Niagara en miniature, en petit. **Miniature painter,** peintre m de miniatures ; miniaturiste mf. **2.** a. En miniature, en raccourci. (a) A miniature edition of a book, une édition minuscule d'un livre. He's quite a m. Napoleon, c'est un Napoléon au petit pied. Phot: **Miniature camera,** appareil m de petit format. (b) Ind: **Miniature model,** maquette f.

miniaturist ['miniatjurist], s. Miniaturiste mf.

minim ['minim], s. **1.** Mus: Blanche f. **2.** Meas: Goutte f.

minimize ['minimaɪz], v.tr. Réduire au minimum.

minimum, pl. -a ['minimom, -a]. **1.** s. Minimum m, pl. minimums, minima. To reduce sth. to a minimum, réduire qch. au minimum. **Minimum thermometer,** thermomètre à minima. **2.** a. Minimum, f. occ. minima. **Minimum price,** prix minimum. Mth: M. value, valeur minima.

minion ['minjən], s. Pej: (a) Favori, -ite. (b) The minions of the law, les recors m de la justice.

minister[1] ['ministər], s. **1.** Adm: Ministre m. **Minister of War, for War,** Ministre de la guerre. **2.** Ecc: Ministre, pasteur m. **Minister of the Gospel,** ministre de l'Évangile.

minister[2], v.i. To minister to s.o., to s.o.'s needs, pourvoir, subvenir, aux besoins de qn. **ministering**[1], a. (Ange, etc.) secourable. **ministering**[2], Soins mpl, service m (to, de).

ministerial [minis'tiːəriəl], a. **1.** Exécutif. **2.** Accessoire, subsidiaire. To be ministerial to . . ., contribuer à . . .; aider à . . . . **3.** Ecc: (Of duties, life, etc.) De ministre ; sacerdotal, -aux. **4.** Pol: Ministériel ; gouvernemental, -aux ; du Gouvernement.

ministration [minis'treiʃ(ə)n], s. **1.** Service m ; ministère m, soins mpl. **2.** Ecc: To go about one's ministrations, vaquer à ses devoirs sacerdotaux. To receive the ministrations of a priest, être administré par un prêtre.

ministry ['ministri], s. **1.** (a) Pol: Ministère m, gouvernement m. (b) Adm: Ministère, département m. The Air Ministry, le Ministère de l'Air. **2.** Ecc: The ministry, le saint ministère. He was intended for the m., il fut destiné à l'Église. **3.** Ministère, entremise f (of, de).

mink [mɪŋk], s. Z: (American) mink, vison m.

minnow ['minoʊ], . Ich: Vairon m.

minor ['mainər]. **1.** a. (a) (Lesser) Petit, mineur. M. planets, petites planètes. Ecc: Minor orders, ordres mineurs. (b) Petit, menu, peu important. **Minor poet,** petit poète ; poète de second ordre. Of m. interest, d'intérêt secondaire. To play a m. part, jouer un rôle subalterne, accessoire. Med: **Minor operation,** opération d'importance secondaire. (c) Log: Minor term, s. minor, petit terme ; mineure f. (d) Mus: **Minor scale,** gamme mineure. In the minor (key), en mineur. In A minor, en la mineur. (e) Sch: Jones minor, le

plus jeune des Jones (qui sont deux). **2.** s. Jur: Mineur, -eure.

Minorca [mi'nɔːrka]. Pr.n. Geog: Minorque f.

minority [mi'nɔriti, mai-], s. **1.** Minorité f. To be in a minority, in the minority, être en minorité. To be in a minority of one, être seul de son opinion. **2.** Jur: Minorité (d'âge).

minster ['minstər], s. **1.** Cathédrale f. **2.** Ég.ise abbatiale.

minstrel ['minstrəl], s. **1.** (a) Hist: Ménestrel m. (b) F: Poète m, musicien m, chanteur m. **2.** Nigger minstrels, troupe f de chanteurs et de comiques déguisés en nègres.

minstrelsy ['minstrəlsi], s. Coll. Chants mpl (d'une nation).

mint[1] [mint], s. **1.** The Mint, (l'Hôtel m de) la Monnaie. (Of coin) Fresh from the mint, à fleur de coin. (Of medal, stamp, book, etc.) In mint state, in mint condition, à l'état (de) neuf. F: To be worth a mint of money, (i) (of pers.) rouler sur l'or ; (ii) (of thg) valoir une somme fabuleuse. I: costs a m. of money, cela coûte les yeux de la tête. **2.** Source f, origine f.

mint[2], v.tr. **1.** (a) To mint money, (i) frapper de la monnaie, battre monnaie ; (ii) F: amasser de l'argent à la pelle. (b) Monnayer (de l'or, etc.). **2.** Inventer, forger, fabriquer (un mot, une expression). '**minting-press,** . Presse f monétaire.

mint[3], s. Bot: Menthe f. **Garden mint,** baume vert. '**mint-'sauce,** s. Cu: Vinaigrette f à la menthe.

minuet [minju'et], s. Danc: Menuet m.

minus ['mainəs]. **1.** prep. Moins. Ten m. eight leaves two, dix moins huit égale deux. F: I got out of it m. one eye, je m'en tirai avec un œil en moins. Bond m. its coupons, titre démuni de coupons. **2.** a. Mth: **Minus sign,** s. minus, moins m. **Minus quantity,** quantité négative.

minuscule [mi'nʌskjul]. **1.** a. Minuscule. **2.** s. Pal: Minuscule f.

minute[1] ['minit], s. **1.** (a) Minute f (de temps). **Ten minutes to three, ten minutes past three,** trois heures moins dix ; trois heures dix. (b) F: A minute's rest, un moment de repos. **Wait a minute!** attendez un instant! He has come in this (very) minute, il rentre à l'instant (même). He was here a minute ago, il sort d'ici. I'll come in a minute, j'arriverai dans un instant. I shan't be a m., (i) je n'en ai pour une seconde ; (ii) je ne ferai qu'aller et (re)venir. **On the minute, to the minute,** ponctuel, exact. He appeared at nine to the m., F: il est arrivé à neuf heures tapant. **Punctual to a minute,** exact à une minute près. I expect him every minute, any minute, je l'attends à tout moment. I'll send him to you the minute (that) he arrives, je vous l'enverrai dès qu'il arrivera. **2.** Geom: Astr: Minute (de degré). **3.** Minute, projet m (d'un contrat, etc.). **4.** (a) Note f. To make a minute of sth., prendre note de qch. ; faire la m nute (d'une transaction, etc.). (b) pl. **Minutes of a meeting,** procès-verbal m d'une séance. (c) Treasury minute, communiqué m de la Trésorerie. '**minute-book,** s. Registre m des procès-verbaux ; registre des délibérations. '**minute-hand,** s. Grande aiguille f (d'horloge, etc.).

minute[2], v.tr. **1.** Faire la minute de, minuter (un contrat, etc.). (b) To minute sth. down, prendre note de qch. ; noter qch. (c) To minute (the proceedings of) a meeting, dresser le procès-verbal, le compte rendu, d'une séance.

minute[3] [mai'njuːt, mi'njuːt], a. **1.** (a) Tout petit ; menu, minuscule, minime. (b) The

31

minutest particulars, les moindres détails. **2**. Mi-nutieux ; (compte rendu) détaillé. **-ly**, *adv*. Minutieusement ; en détail ; dans les moindres détails.

minuteness [mai'nju tnəs, mi-], *s*. **1**. Petitesse *f*, exiguïté *f*. **2**. Minutie *f* ; exactitude minutieuse.

minx [miŋks], *s.f. Hum :* Friponne, coquine ; petite espiègle.

mirabelle [mira'bɛl], *s. Hort :* Mirabelle (plum), mirabelle *f*.

miracle ['mirəkl], *s*. **1**. (*a*) Miracle *m*. By a miracle, par miracle. (*b*) *F :* Miracle, prodige *m*. It is a miracle that . . ., c'est (un) miracle que + *sub*. **2**. *Lit.Hist :* Miracle play, miracle.

miraculous [mi'rakjuləs], *a*. (*a*) Miraculeux. (*b*) *F :* Extraordinaire, merveilleux. **-ly**, *adv*. Miraculeusement ; par m racle.

mirage ['mi'ra:ʒ], *s*. Mirage *m*.

mire ['maiər], *s*. (*a*) Bourbier *m* ; fondrière *f*. (*b*) Boue *f*, bourbe *f*, fange *f* ; (*river deposit*) vase *f*. To sink into the mire, (i) s'enfoncer dans la boue ; s'embourber ; (ii) *F :* s'avilir ; (iii) ʋe mettre dans le pétrin. *F :* To drag s.o.'s namo through the mire, traîner qn dans la fange.

mirror[1] ['mirər], *s*. Miroir *m*, glace *f*. Hand mirror, glace à main, miroir à main. *F :* To hold up a mirror to one's contemporaries, présenter le miroir à ses contemporains. *Aut :* Driving mirror, (miroir) rétroviseur *m*.

mirror[2], *v.tr*. Refléter.

mirth [mə:rθ], *s*. Gaieté *f*, allégresse *f* ; hilarité *f*. **'mirth-provoking**, *a*. Qui provoque le rire ; désopilant.

mirthful ['mə:rθful], *a*. **1**. Gai, joyeux. **2**. Amusant, désopilant. **-fully**, *adv*. Gaiement, joyeusement.

mirthless ['mə:rθləs], *a*. Sans gaieté ; triste. **-ly**, *adv*. Sans gaieté ; tristement.

miry ['maiəri], *a*. Fangeux, bourbeux ; vaseux.

misadjustment [misə'dʒʌstmənt], *s*. Mauvais ajustage ; déréglage *m*.

misadventure [misəd'ventʃər], *s*. Mésaventure *f*, contretemps *m*.

misadvise [misəd'vaiz], *v.tr*. Mal conseiller (qn).

misalliance [misə'laiəns], *s*. Mésalliance *f*.

misanthrope ['misənθroup, 'miz-], *s*. Misanthrope *m*.

misanthropic(al) [misən'θrɔpik(əl), miz-], *a*. (Personne) misanthrope ; (humeur) misanthropique.

misanthropist [mi'sanθrəpist, mi'z-], *s*. = MISANTHROPE.

misanthropy [mi'sanθrəpi, mi'z-], *s*. Misanthropie *f*.

misapplication [misəpli'keiʃ(ə)n], *s*. **1**. Mauvaise application, emploi abusif (d'un mot, etc.). **2**. Détournement *m* (de fonds).

misapply [misə'plai], *v.tr*. **1**. Mal appliquer (qch.) ; appliquer (qch.) mal à propos. **2**. Détourner (des fonds).

misappreciate [misə'pri:ʃieit], *v.tr*. Méconnaître.

misapprehend [misəpri'hend], *v.tr*. Mal comprendre ; se méprendre sur (les paroles de qn).

misapprehension [misəpri'henʃ(ə)n], *s*. Malentendu *m*, méprise *f* ; idée fausse (des faits). *To do* sth. under a misapprehension, faire qch. par méprise.

misappropriate [misə'prouprieit], *v.tr*. Détourner, distraire (des fonds).

misappropriation [misəproupri'eiʃ(ə)n], *s*. Détournement *m*, distraction *f*, déprédation *f* (de fonds).

misbecome [misbi'kʌm], *v.tr*. (*Conj. like* BECOME) Messeoir à (qn). **misbecoming**, *a*. Malséant.

misbegotten [misbi'gɔtn], *a*. **1**. (*a*) (Enfant) illégitime, bâtard. (*b*) *M. plant or animal*, avorton *m*. **2**. *F :* Vil, misérable. *Another of his m. plans !* encore un de ses projets biscornus !

misbehave [misbi'heiv], *v.i. & pr*. To misbehave (oneself), se mal conduire.

misbehaviour [misbi'heivjər], *s*. Mauvaise conduite ; inconduite *f*.

misbelief [misbi'li:f], *s*. (*a*) *Theol :* Fausse croyance. (*b*) Opinion erronée.

miscalculate [mis'kalkjuleit], *s*. **1**. *v.tr*. Mal calculer (une somme, etc.). **2**. *v.i. To m. about* sth., se tromper sur qch.

miscalculation [miskalkju'leiʃ(ə)n], *s*. Faux calcul ; mécompte *m*.

miscall [mis'kɔ:l], *v.tr*. **1**. Mal nommer ; attribuer un faux nom à (qn). **2**. *Dial :* Injurier (qn).

miscarriage [mis'karedʒ], *s*. **1**. Égarement *m*, perte *f* (d'une lettre). **2**. (*a*) Avortement *m*, insuccès *m* (d'un projet). (*b*) *Jur :* Miscarriage of justice, erreur *f* judiciaire. **3**. *Med :* Fausse couche.

miscarry [mis'kari], *v.i*. **1**. (*Of letter*) (i) S'égarer ; (ii) parvenir à une fausse adresse. **2**. (*Of scheme*) Avorter, échouer ; manquer, rater, mal tourner. **3**. *Med :* Faire une fausse couche.

miscellaneous [mise'leinjəs], *a*. Varié, mêlé, mélangé, divers. **-ly**, *adv*. Avec variété ; diversement ; de diverses façons. *To write m.*, écrire sur des sujets variés.

miscellaneousness [mise'leinjəsnəs], *s*. Variété *f*, diversité *f*.

miscellany [mi'selani], *s*. **1**. Mélange *m* ; collection *f* d'objets variés. **2**. *Lit :* (*a*) *pl*. Miscellanies, miscellanées *f*, mélanges *m*. (*b*) Mélange, recueil *m*, macédoine *f*.

mischance [mis'tʃɑ:ns], *s*. **1**. Mauvaise chance ; malchance *f*. **2**. Malheur *m*, mésaventure *f*, accident *m*.

mischief ['mistʃif], *s*. **1**. Mal *m*, tort *m*, dommage *m*, dégât(s) *m(pl)*. To do mischief, faire le mal. To do s.o. a mischief, faire du mal ou du tort à qn ; porter un mauvais coup à qn. To mean mischief, chercher à nuire ; méditer un mauvais coup. To make mischief, apporter le trouble ; semer la discorde. To make m. between two people, brouiller deux personnes. **2**. Malice *f*. Out of pure mischief, par pure malice ; (i) par pure espièglerie ; (ii) par pure méchanceté. (*Of child*) To be always getting into mischief, être toujours à faire des siennes. To keep s.o. out of mischief, empêcher de faire des sottises, des bêtises. *He is up to (some) m.*, (i) il médite une malice ; (ii) il médite quelque mauvais tour, un mauvais coup. **3**. (*Pers.*) Fripon, -onne ; malin, -igne. Little mischief, petit(e) espiègle, petit(e) coquin(e). **'mischief-maker,** *s*. Brandon *m* de discorde ; mauvaise langue.

mischievous ['mistʃivəs], *a*. **1**. Méchant, malfaisant ; (*of thg*) mauvais, nuisible, pernicieux. **2**. (Enfant) espiègle, malicieux. As mischievous as a monkey, malin, malicieux, comme un singe. **-ly**, *adv*. **1**. (*a*) Méchamment ; par malveillance. (*b*) Nuisiblement. **2**. Malicieusement ; par espièglerie.

mischievousness ['mistʃivəsnəs], *s*. **1**. (*a*) Méchanceté *f*. (*b*) Nature *f* nuisible (de qch.). **2**. Malice *f*, espièglerie *f*.

misconception [miskon'sepʃ(ə)n], *s*. **1**. Idée fausse. **2**. Malentendu *m*.

misconduct[1] [mis'kɔndʌkt], *s*. **1**. Mauvaise

administration, mauvaise gestion (d'une affaire). **2.** (*Of pers.*) Mauvaise conduite ; inconduite *f.*

misconduct² [miskon'dʌkt], *v.tr.* **1.** Mal diriger, mal gérer (une affaire). **2.** **To misconduct oneself,** se mal conduire.

misconstruction [miskon'strʌkʃ(ə)n], *s.* Fausse interprétation ; mésinterprétation *f.*

misconstrue [mis'konstru:, miskon'stru:], *v.tr.* Mal interpréter, mésinterpréter (qch.) ; prendre (qch.) à rebours. *You have misconstrued my words,* vous avez mal pris mes paroles.

miscount¹ [mis'kaunt], *s.* Erreur *f* d'addition ; *esp.* erreur dans le dépouillement du scrutin.

miscount², *v.tr.* Mal compter.

miscreant ['miskriənt], *s.* (*a*) Scélérat *m,* misérable *m,* gredin *m.* (*b*) *A:* Mécréant *m,* infidèle *m.*

mis-cue [mis'kju:], *v.i.* *Bill:* Faire fausse queue.

misdate [mis'deit], *v.tr.* Mal dater (une lettre).

misdating, *s.* Erreur *f* de date.

misdeal¹ [mis'di:l], *s.* *Cards:* Maldonne *f.*

misdeal², *v.tr.* (**misdealt** [mis'delt]) *Cards: To m. the cards, abs.* **to misdeal,** faire maldonne.

misdeed [mis'di:d], *s.* Méfait *m.*

misdelivery [misdi'livəri], *s.* Erreur *f* de livraison.

misdemean [misdi'mi:n], *v.pr.* **To misdemean** oneself, se mal comporter.

misdemeanant [misdi'mi:nənt], *s.* *Jur:* Délinquant, -ante.

misdemeanour [misdi'mi:nər], *s.* **1.** *Jur:* Délit contraventionnel. **2.** Écart *m* de conduite ; méfait *m.*

misdirect [misdai'rekt, misdi-], *v.tr.* **1.** Mal adresser (une lettre). **2.** Mal diriger (un coup) ; mal viser avec (un revolver, etc.). **3.** Mal diriger (une entreprise, etc.). **4.** Mal renseigner (qn). **5.** *Jur:* (*Of judge*) Mal instruire (le jury).

misdirection [misdai'rekʃ(ə)n, misdi-], *s.* **1.** (*On letter*) Erreur *f* d'adresse ; fausse adresse. **2.** Indication erronée ; renseignement erroné.

misdoing [mis'du:iŋ], *s.* Méfait *m,* faute *f.*

misentry [mis'entri], *s.* Inscription erronée. *Book-k:* Contre-position *f.*

miser ['maizər], *s.* Avare *mf.*

miserable ['mizərəbl], *a.* **1.** (*Of pers.*) Malheureux, triste. **To make s.o.'s life miserable,** rendre la vie dure à qn. **2.** Misérable, déplorable. *What m. weather! F:* quel chien de temps ! **3.** Misérable, pauvre, piteux. *M. speech,* piteux discours. *M. salary,* salaire dérisoire. **-ably,** *adv.* Misérablement. (*a*) Malheureusement, lamentablement. (*b*) Piètrement. **To be miserably paid,** avoir un salaire de misère.

miserliness ['maizərlinəs], *s.* Avarice *f.*

miserly ['maizərli], *a.* **1.** (*Of pers.*) Avare, pingre, ladre. **2.** (*Of habits, etc.*) D'avare ; sordide.

misery ['mizəri], *s.* **1.** Souffrance(s) *f* (*pl*), supplice *m.* **To put an animal out of its misery,** donner le coup de grâce à un animal. **2.** Misère *f,* détresse *f.*

misfire¹ [mis'faiər], *s.* (*a*) *Sm.a:* *Artil:* Raté *m.* (*b*) *I.C.E:* Raté d'allumage.

misfire², *v.i.* (*a*) (*Of gun*) Rater ; faire long feu. (*b*) *I.C.E:* (*Of engine*) Avoir des ratés ; rater. (*c*) *F:* (*Of joke, etc.*) Manquer son effet.

misfit [mis'fit], *s.* Vêtement manqué, mal réussi. *Com:* Laissé-pour-compte *m.* *F:* **The social misfits,** les inaptes *m.*

misfortune [mis'fɔ:rtjun], *s.* Infortune *f,* malheur *m,* calamité *f.* **It is more his misfortune than his fault,** il est plus à plaindre qu'à blâmer.

misgive [mis'giv], *v.tr.* (**misgave** [mis'geːiv] ; **misgiven** [mis'givn]) *My heart, my mind,* misgives me, j'ai de mauvais pressentiments.

misgiving, *s.* Doute *m,* crainte *f.* *Not without misgivings,* non sans hésitation. *I had a m. that . . .,* j'avais le pressentiment que. . . .

misgovern [mis'gʌvərn], *v.tr.* Mal gouverner.

misgovernment [mis'gʌvərnmənt], *s.* Mauvais gouvernement ; mauvaise administration.

misguided [mis'gaidid], *a.* **1.** (*Of pers.*) Dont l'enthousiasme porte à faux ; qui se fourvoie. *These m. people . . .,* ces malheureux. . . . **2.** (*Of conduct*) Peu judicieux ; (*of zeal*) hors de propos ; (*of attempt*) malencontreux.

mishap [mis'hap], *s.* (*a*) Mésaventure *f,* contretemps *m.* *Aut:* Panne *f.* (*b*) Fausse couche.

misinform [misin'fɔ:rm], *v.tr.* Mal renseigner.

misinformation [misinfɔr'meiʃ(ə)n], *s.* Fausse information, faux renseignement(s).

misinterpret [misin'tə:rpret], *v.tr.* Mal interpréter.

misinterpretation [misintə:rpre'teiʃ(ə)n], *s.* **1.** Fausse interprétation. **2.** (*In translating*) Contre-sens *m inv.*

misjudge [mis'dʒʌdʒ], *v.tr.* Mal juger ; se tromper sur le compte de (qn) ; méconnaître (qn).

misjudged, *a.* Erroné ; peu judicieux.

misjudg(e)ment [mis'dʒʌdʒmənt], *s.* Jugement erroné.

mislay [mis'lei], *v.tr.* (**mislaid** [mis'leid] ; **mislaid**) Égarer (son parapluie, etc.).

mislead [mis'li:d], *v.tr.* (**misled** [mis'led] ; **misled**) (*a*) Induire (qn) en erreur ; tromper (qn). (*b*) Égarer, fourvoyer (qn). **misleading,** *a.* Trompeur, -euse ; fallacieux.

mismanage [mis'manedʒ], *v.tr.* Mal conduire, mal administrer, mal gérer (une affaire).

mismanagement [mis'manedʒmənt], *s.* Mauvaise administration, mauvaise gestion.

misname [mis'neim], *v.tr.* Mal nommer ; nommer improprement.

misnomer [mis'noumər], *s.* **1.** *Jur:* Erreur *f* de nom. **2.** Faux nom ; fausse appellation ; nom mal approprié.

misogamist [mi'sɔgəmist], *s.* Misogame *mf.*

misogynist [mi'sɔdʒinist], *s.* Misogyne *m.*

misogyny [mi'sɔdʒini], *s.* Misogynie *f.*

misplace [mis'pleis], *v.tr.* **1.** Placer à faux (l'accent tonique, etc.). **2.** Mal placer (sa confiance). **3.** Déplacer (un livre, etc.). **misplaced,** *a.* **1.** (*Of confidence, etc.*) Mal placé. **2.** (*Mot*) déplacé ; (*observation*) hors de propos.

misprint [mis'print], *s.* Faute *f* d'impression ; erreur *f* typographique ; *F:* coquille *f.*

mispronounce [mispro'nauns], *v.tr.* Mal prononcer.

mispronunciation [mispronʌnsi'eiʃ(ə)n], *s.* Mauvaise prononciation.

misquotation [miskwo'teiʃ(ə)n], *s.* Fausse citation ; citation inexacte.

misquote [mis'kwout], *v.tr.* Citer (qch.) à faux, inexactement.

misread [mis'ri:d], *v.tr.* (**misread** [mis'red] ; **misread**) Mal lire, mal interpréter (un texte, etc.). *F:* **To misread s.o.'s feelings,** mal lire dans le cœur de qn.

misreckon [mis'rek(ə)n], *v.tr.* **1.** Mal calculer ; mal compter. **2.** *Abs.* Calculer à faux. **misreckoning,** *s.* **1.** Calcul erroné. **2.** Manque *m* de perspicacité.

misreport¹ [misri'pɔ:rt], *s.* Rapport inexact.

misreport², *v.tr.* Rapporter (les faits) inexactement.

misrepresent [misrepri'zent], *v.tr.* Mal représenter ; dénaturer, travestir (les faits).

misrepresentation [misreprizen'teiʃ(ə)n], *s.* Faux rapport, faux exposé. *Jur:* (i) Fausse déclaration ; (ii) réticence *f.*

misrule¹ [mis'ru:l], *s.* Mauvaise administration ; désordre *m*, confusion *f.* *Hist:* Lord, Abbot, of Misrule, pape *m* des fous.

misrule², *v.tr.* Mal gouverner.

miss¹ [mis], *s.* **I.** Coup manqué ; coup perdu. *Bill:* Manque *m* à toucher. *F:* To give (s.o., sth.) a miss, passer le tour de (qn) ; négliger de voir, de visiter (un monument) ; sécher (une conférence). **2.** *P:* He's no great miss, on peut se passer de lui.

miss², *v.tr.* **I.** (*a*) Manquer, *F:* rater (le but). To miss one's mark, one's aim, manquer son coup, son but ; frapper à faux, à vide. *Abs.* He never misses, il ne manque jamais son coup. To miss the point (*in one's answer*), répondre à côté. *Bill:* To miss, manquer à toucher ; manquer de touche. *Th:* (*Of actor*) To miss one's entrance, louper son entrée. (*b*) To miss one's way, se tromper de route. He missed his footing, le pied lui manqua. (*c*) Ne pas trouver, ne pas rencontrer (qn). (*d*) Manquer, *F:* rater (un train). To m. the train by three minutes, manquer le train de trois minutes. (*e*) Manquer, laisser échapper, *F:* rater (une occasion). An opportunity not to be missed, une occasion à saisir. *F:* You haven't missed much ! ce n'était pas bien intéressant. To miss the market, laisser échapper le moment favorable pour la vente. (*f*) Ne pas se voir décerner (une récompense). *I missed my holiday this year*, je n'ai pas eu de vacances cette année. (*g*) Manquer (une conférence, un rendez-vous) ; *F:* sécher (une classe, une conférence). *I never m. going there*, je ne manque jamais d'y aller. (*h*) He narrowly missed, just missed, being killed, il a failli se faire tuer. (*i*) To miss a remark, a joke, ne pas saisir une observation, une plaisanterie. *You can't m. the house*, vous ne pouvez pas manquer de reconnaître la maison. **2.** (*Omit*) To miss (out) a word, passer, sauter, un mot. (*At dinner*) To miss out the fish course, laisser passer le poisson. **3.** (*a*) Remarquer l'absence de (qn, qch.). *I m. several books*, je vois qu'il me manque plusieurs livres. *I missed my spectacles*, je ne trouvais plus mes lunettes. It will never be missed, on ne s'apercevra pas que cela n'y est plus. (*b*) Regretter (qn) ; regretter l'absence de (qn). *I miss you*, vous me manquez. They will miss one another, ils se manqueront. **missing¹**, *a.* Absent ; perdu ; disparu, manquant. One man is m., un homme manque. *s.pl. Mil: etc:* The missing, les disparus. **missing²**, *s. I.C.E:* Ratés *mpl* ; *P:* cafouillage *m.*

miss³, *s.f.* **I.** Miss Smith, *pl.* the Miss Smiths, the Misses Smith, mademoiselle Smith, Mlle Smith ; les demoiselles Smith ; (*on address*) Mademoiselle ; trois demoiselles Smith, Mesdemoiselles Smith. *Thank you, Miss Smith*, merci, mademoiselle. **2.** *V:* Yes, Miss ; three whiskeys, Miss, oui, mademoiselle ; trois whiskys, mademoiselle. **3.** *Hum:* Demoiselle. A modern miss, une jeune fille moderne.

missal [misəl], *s. Ecc:* Missel *m.*

missel(-thrush) ['mis(ə)l(θrʌʃ)], *s.* Draine *f* ; grosse grive.

mis-shapen [mis'ʃeipn], *a.* Difforme, contrefait ; (*of hat, figure, etc.*) déformé ; (*of building, mind*) biscornu.

missile ['misail, -il]. **I.** *a.* (Arme de jet, de trait. **2.** *s.* Projectile *m.*

mission ['miʃ(ə)n], *s.* Mission *f.* (*a*) To be sent on a mission to s.o., être envoyé en mission auprès de qn. (*b*) *Ecc:* Foreign missions, missions étrangères. **Mission (station)**, mission. (*c*) *She thinks her mission in life is to help lame dogs*, elle croit avoir mission de secourir les malheureux.

missionary ['miʃənəri]. **I.** *a.* (Prêtre) missionnaire ; (société) de missionnaires. The missionary field, les missions (étrangères). **2.** *s.* (*a*) Missionnaire *m.* (*b*) **Police-court missionary**, délégué(e) d'une œuvre de miséricorde auprès des tribunaux de simple police.

missis ['misiz], *s.f. P:* (*a*) *I say, Missis!* eh dites donc, la petite mère ! (*b*) The missis, my missis, ma femme ; *P:* ma légitime. *Your m.*, votre dame. (*c*) (The) missis is in the drawing-room, madame est au salon.

missive ['misiv], *s.* Lettre *f*, missive *f.*

mis-spell [mis'spel], *v.tr.* (mis-spelt [mis'spelt] ; mis-spelt) Mal épeler, mal orthographier. **mis-spelling**, *s.* Faute *f* d'orthographe.

mis-spent [mis'spent], *a.* A mis-spent youth, (i) une jeunesse mal employée ; (ii) une jeunesse passée dans la dissipation.

mis-state [mis'steit], *v.tr.* Exposer (qch.) incorrectement ; altérer (des faits).

mis-statement [mis'steitmənt], *s.* Exposé inexact ; erreur *f* de fait.

missus ['misəs], *s.f. P:* = MISSIS.

missy ['misi], *s.f. F:* Mademoiselle.

mist¹ [mist], *s.* **I.** Brume *f*, *F:* brouillasse *f.* Scotch mist, bruine *f*, crachin *m.* *F:* Lost in the mists of time, perdu dans la nuit des temps. **2.** Buée *f* (sur une glace, etc.) ; voile *m* (devant les yeux). To see things through a mist, voir trouble.

mist². **I.** *v.tr.* Couvrir (une glace, etc.) de buée. **2.** *v.i.* To mist over, (i) (*of landscape*) disparaître sous la brume ; (ii) (*of windscreen*) se couvrir de buée.

mistakable [mis'teikəbl], *a.* Sujet à méprise.

mistake¹ [mis'teik], *s.* Erreur *f*, méprise *f*, faute *f.* *M. in calculating*, faux calcul ; erreur de calcul. *Grammatical mistakes*, fautes de grammaire. To make a mistake, faire une faute ; être dans l'erreur ; se méprendre, se tromper. *You made me make a m.*, vous m'avez fait tromper. To make the mistake of doing sth., avoir le tort de faire qch. *To do sth. by mistake*, faire qch. par erreur, par méprise. To labour under a mistake, être dans l'erreur. To acknowledge one's m., avouer (être dans) son tort. There is some mistake ! il y a erreur ! *There is, can be, no m. about that*, il n'y a pas à s'y tromper, à s'y méprendre. Let there be no mistake about it ; make no mistake, que l'on ne s'y trompe pas. *F: I am unlucky* and no mistake ! décidément je n'ai pas de chance ! To take s.o.'s umbrella in mistake for one's own, prendre le parapluie de qn par erreur pour le sien.

mistake², *v.tr.* (mistook [mis'tuk] ; mistaken [mis'teik(ə)n]) **I.** Comprendre mal (les paroles de qn) ; se méprendre sur (les intentions de qn). *To m. the time, one's way*, se tromper d'heure, de route. *To m. the way*, faire fausse route. If I mistake not, si je ne me trompe. There is no mistaking the facts, on ne peut pas se tromper à cet égard. **2.** To mistake s.o. for s.o., confondre qn avec qn. **mistaken**, *a.* **I.** (*Of pers.*) To be mistaken, être dans l'erreur ; faire erreur. To be mistaken about s.o., se tromper sur le compte de qn. If I am not mistaken, si je ne me trompe ; sauf erreur. That is just where you are mistaken !

c'est justement ce qui vous trompe. **2.** **Mistaken opinion,** opinion erronée. *M. zeal,* zèle mal entendu, hors de propos. **3. Mistaken identity,** erreur *f* sur la personne. **Mistaken statement,** (i) déclaration mal comprise; (ii) déclaration erronée. **-ly,** *adv.* Par erreur, par méprise.

mister ['mistər], *s.* **1.** (*Always abbreviated to* Mr) **Mr Smith,** monsieur Smith; M. Smith; (*on address*) Monsieur Smith. **Mr Chairman,** monsieur le président. **2.** *V : What's the time, mister?* quelle heure est-il, monsieur?

mistime [mis'taim], *v.tr.* **1.** Faire (qch.) mal à propos. **2.** Mal calculer (un coup).

mistiness ['mistinəs], *s.* (*a*) État brumeux. (*b*) *Owing to the m. of the windscreen* . . ., à cause de la buée qui obscurcissait le pare-brise. . . .

mistletoe ['misltou], *s. Bot :* Gui *m.*

mistook [mis'tuk]. *See* MISTAKE².

mistranslate [mistraːns'leit], *v.tr.* Mal traduire.

mistranslation [mistraːns'leiʃ(ə)n], *s.* Traduction inexacte; erreur *f* de traduction; contresens *m inv.*

mistress ['mistres], *s.f.* **1.** (*a*) Maîtresse (qui exerce l'autorité). **To be mistress of oneself,** être maîtresse de soi-même; avoir de l'empire sur soi-même. **She is mistress of her subject,** elle possède son sujet à fond. (*b*) **Mistress of a household,** maîtresse de maison. (*To servant*) *Is your m. at home?* madame y est-elle? **The mistress is not at home,** madame n'y est pas. (*c*) *Com :* Patronne. (*d*) Maîtresse (qui enseigne); (*in elementary schools*) institutrice; (*in secondary schools*) professeur *m.* *The French m.,* la maîtresse de français, le professeur de français. *S.a.* HEAD-MISTRESS. **2.** (*a*) *A :* Amante, maîtresse (recherchée en mariage). (*b*) Maîtresse, concubine. **Kept mistress,** femme entretenue. **3.** (*In title.*) (*a*) *A :* **Mistress Quickly,** Madame Quickly. (*b*) (*Now always* **Mrs** ['misiz]) **Mrs Smith,** Madame Smith, Mme Smith.

mistrust¹ [mis'trʌst], *s.* Méfiance *f*, défiance *f* (*of, in,* de); soupçons *mpl* (*of, in,* à l'endroit de); manque *m* de confiance.

mistrust², *v.tr.* Se méfier de, ne pas avoir confiance en (qn).

mistrustful [mis'trʌstful], *a.* Méfiant, soupçonneux (*of,* à l'endroit de). **-fully,** *adv.* Avec méfiance.

mistune [mis'tjuːn], *v.tr.* Mal accorder (un piano, un circuit de T.S.F.).

misty ['misti], *a.* Brumeux, brumailleux, embrumé. *It is m.,* le temps est brumeux. *F :* **Misty outlines,** contours vagues, flous. *M. eyes,* yeux voilés de larmes. *M. recollection,* souvenir vague, confus.

misunderstand [misʌndər'stand], *v.tr.* (misunderstood [misʌndər'stud]; misunderstood) **1.** Mal comprendre; se méprendre sur (qch.); mal interpréter (une action). *If I have not misunderstood* . . ., si j'ai bien compris. . . . *We misunderstood each other,* il y a eu quiproquo. **2.** Méconnaître (qn); se méprendre sur le compte de (qn). **misunderstood,** *a.* **1.** Mal compris. **2.** (*Of pers.*) Incompris. **misunderstanding,** *s.* **1.** Malentendu *m*, quiproquo *m.* **2.** Mésintelligence *f*, mésentente *f*, brouille *f.*

misuse¹ [mis'juːs], *s.* Abus *m*; mauvais usage, mauvais emploi. *M. of authority,* abus d'autorité. *M. of words,* emploi abusif des mots. **Fraudulent misuse of funds,** détournement *m* de fonds.

misuse² [mis'juːz], *v.tr.* **1.** Faire (un) mauvais usage, (un) mauvais emploi, de (qch.); mésuser

de (qch.). *To m. a word,* employer un mot abusivement. **2.** Maltraiter, malmener (qn).

mite [mait], *s.* **1.** (*a*) **The widow's mite,** le den er, l'obole *f*, de la veuve. *F :* **To offer one's mite,** donner son obole. (*b*) **Mite of consolation,** brin *m* de consolation. *There's not a m. left,* il n'en reste plus une miette. **2.** Mioche *mf*, bambin, -ine. *Poor little m.!* pauvre petit! pauvre petite! **3.** Acarien *m*; mite *f.* **Cheese mite,** mite du fromage.

mitigate ['mitigeit], *v.tr.* **1.** Adoucir, atténuer (la souffrance, un mal); amoindrir (un mal); mitiger, atténuer (la sévérité d'une peine). **2.** Tempérer (la chaleur); adoucir (le froid). **3.** Atténuer (un crime, une faute). **Mitigating circumstances,** circonstances atténuantes.

mitigation [miti'geiʃ(ə)n], *s.* Adoucissement *m*; amoindrissement *m* (d'un mal); mitigation *f*, atténuation *f* (d'une peine). *Jur : Plea in m. of damage.,* demande *f* en réduction de dommages-intérêts.

mitre¹ ['maitər], *s. Ecc :* Mitre *f.*

mitre², *s.* **1.** Mitre-(joint), (assemblage *m* à) onglet *m.* **2.** = MITRE SQUARE. **'mitre-block, -board, -box,** *s. Carp :* Boîte *f* à onglet(s). **'mitre-gear,** *s. Mec.E :* Engrenage *m* à onglet, à 45°. **'mitre square,** *s. Tls :* Équerre *f* (à) onglet. **'mitre-wheel,** *s. Mec.E :* Roue *f* d'angle, roue (dentée) conique.

mitre³, *v.tr.* **1.** Tailler (une pièce) à onglet. *Bookb : To m. the fillets,* biseauter les filets. **2.** Assembler (deux pièces) à onglet.

mitred ['maitərd], *a.* **Mitred abbot,** abbé mitré.

mitten [mitn], *s.* **1.** Mitaine *f.* *F :* **To give a suitor the mitten,** éconduire un soupirant. **To get the mitten,** (i) être éconduit; (ii) (*of employee, etc.*) recevoir son congé. **2.** *pl. Box : F :* **The mittens,** les gants.

mity ['maiti], *a.* (Fromage) plein de mites.

mix [miks]. **I.** *v.tr.* (*a*) Mêler, mélanger (des métaux). *To mix good people with bad,* confondre les bons et les méchants. *To mix two races,* mêler deux races. (*b*) Composer (un breuvage). (*c*) Brasser (des billets de loterie, etc.); malaxer (le mortier, etc.). *To mix the salad,* faire la salade. (*d*) Confondre (des faits). **2.** *v.i.* Se mêler, se mélanger (*with,* à, avec); (*of fluids*) s'allier. (*Of colours, etc.*) **To mix well,** aller bien ensemble. **To mix in society, with people,** fréquenter la société, les gens. *To mix with the aristocracy,* frayer avec l'aristocratie. **mix up,** *v.tr.* **1.** Mêler, mélanger; embrouiller (ses papiers, etc.). **2.** *I was mixing you up with your brother,* je vous confondais avec votre frère. **3.** *To be mixed up in an affair,* être mêlé à une affaire; se trouver engagé dans une affaire. **4.** Embrouiller (qn). *I was getting all mixed up,* je ne savais plus où j'en étais. **'mix-up,** *s.* **1.** Confusion *f*, embrouillement *m*; emmêlement *m.* **2.** *F :* Bagarre *f.* **mixed,** *a.* **1.** Mêlé, mélangé, mixte. *M. sweets,* bonbons assortis. *M. ice,* m. salad, glace, salade, panachée. *M. metal,* alliage *m.* *M. company,* compagnie mêlée; milieu *m* hétéroclite. *M. society,* société hétérogène. **Mixed marriage,** mariage mixte. **Mixed feelings,** sentiments mixtes. *To act from m. motives,* agir pour des motifs complexes. *Mth :* **Mixed number,** nombre fractionnaire. *S.a.* META-PHOR. **2.** **Mixed school,** école géminée; école pour garçons et filles. **Mixed bathing,** bains *m* mixtes. *Ten :* **Mixed double,** double *m* mixte. **3.** (*Of pers.*) **To get mixed,** s'embrouiller; perdre la tête.

mixer ['miksər], *s.* **1.** Garçon *m* du bar des

cocktails. **2.** (*Machine*) (*a*) *Ind*: Malaxeur *m*, agitateur *m*. **Mortar mixer**, tonneau *m* à mortier. (*b*) *I.C.E*: Diffuseur *m*. **3.** *F*: **Good, bad, mixer**, personne qui sait, qui ne sait pas, s'adapter à son entourage. *He is a good m.*, il a du liant.

mixture ['mikstjər], *s*. **1.** Mélange *m*. **2.** *Pharm*: Mixtion *f*, mixture *f*. **3.** *Mus*: **Mixture-stop**, (jeu *m* de) fourniture *f* (d'un orgue).

miz(z)en [mizn], *s*. *Nau*: Miz(z)en(-sail), artimon *m*. **'miz(z)en-mast**, *s*. Mât *m* d'artimon. **'miz(z)en-top'gallant**, *attrib.a*. Mizzen-topgallant sail, perruche *f*. **'miz(z)en-'topsail**, *s*. Perroquet *m* de fougue.

mizzle[1] [mizl], *s*. Bruine *f*, crachin *m*.

mizzle[2], *v.i.* Bruiner, crachiner.

mnemonic [ni'mɔnik], *a*. Mnémonique.

mnemonics [ni'mɔniks], *s.pl*. Mnémonique *f*, mnémotechnie *f*.

moan[1] [moun], *s*. Gémissement *m*, plainte *f*.

moan[2]. **1.** *v.i.* Gémir; pousser des gémissements; se lamenter; (*of wind*) gémir. **2.** *v.tr.* Dire (qch.) en gémissant. **To moan out a prayer**, gémir une prière. **moaning**, *s*. Gémissement *m*.

moat [mout], *s*. Fossé *m*, douve *f* (de fortifications).

moated ['moutid], *a*. (*Château*) entouré d'un fossé, de fossés.

mob[1] [mɔb], *s*. **1.** **The mob**, la populace; le bas peuple. **Mob law**, la loi de la populace. **Mob oratory**, éloquence tribunitienne. *To join the mob*, descendre dans la · rue. **2.** Foule *f*, cohue *f*, ameutement *m*; bande *f* d'émeutiers. *To form a mob, to gather into a mob*, s'ameuter. *The army had become a mob*, l'armée n'était plus qu'une cohue. **3.** *P*: **The swell mob**, la haute pègre.

mob[2], *v.* (mobbed) **1.** *v.tr.* (*a*) (*Of angry crowd*) Houspiller, attaquer, malmener (qn). (*b*) (*Of admiring crowd*) Assiéger (qn); faire foule autour de (qn). **2.** *v.i.* S'attrouper; former un rassemblement.

mob-cap ['mɔb'kap], *s*. *Cost: A*: Bonnet *m* (de femme) s'attachant sous le menton; petite coiffe.

mobile ['moubail, -bil], *a*. **1.** Mobile. **2.** (*Of pers., character*) Changeant, versatile.

mobility [mo'biliti], *s*. Mobilité *f*.

mobilization [moubilai'zeiʃ(ə)n], *s*. Mobilisation *f* (des troupes, de capitaux).

mobilize ['moubilaːiz], **1.** *v.tr.* Mobiliser (des troupes, *Pol.Ec*: le capital). **2.** *v.i.* (*Of army*) Entrer en mobilisation.

mobsman, *pl.* **-men** ['mɔbzmən, -men], *s.m*. *P*: Filou chic. *The mobsmen*, la haute pègre.

moccasin ['mɔkasin], *s*. Mocassin *m*.

mocha[1] ['moukα], *s*. Pierre *f* de Moka; agate mousseuse.

mocha[2], *s*. (Café *m*) moka *m*. *Cu*: **Mocha cake**, moka.

mock[1] [mɔk], *attrib.a*. D'imitation; feint, contrefait; faux, *f*. fausse. **Mock tortoise-shell**, écaille imitation. **Mock modesty**, modestie feinte, contrefaite. **Mock king**, roi pour rire. **Mock tragedy**, tragédie burlesque. **Mock trial**, simulacre *m* de procès; procès dérisoire. **Mock fight**, simulacre de combat; petite guerre. **mock-he'roic**, *a*. Héroï-comique; burlesque. **'mock-'sun**, *s*. Parhélie *m*; faux soleil. **'mock 'turtle**, *s*. *Cu*: **Mock turtle soup**, potage *m* (à la) fausse tortue; potage à la tête de veau.

mock[2], *s*. To make a mock of s.o., se moquer de qn; tourner on en ridicule.

mock[3]. **1.** *v.tr. & i.* To mock (at) s.o., sth., se moquer de qn, de qch.; railler qn, qch.

2. *v.tr.* (*a*) Narguer (qn). (*b*) Se jouer de, tromper (qn). (*c*) Imiter, contrefaire, singer (qn, qch.). **mocking**[1], *a*. **1.** Moqueur, -euse, railleur, -euse. *M. irony*, ironie gouailleuse. **2.** (Ton) d'imitation, de singerie. **-ly**, *adv.* D'un ton moqueur, railleur; par moquerie, par dérision. **'mocking-bird**, *s*. *Orn*: *U.S*: Moqueur *m*. **mocking**[2], *s*. Moquerie *f*, raillerie *f*.

mocker ['mɔkər], *s*. Moqueur, -euse.

mockery ['mɔkəri], *s*. **1.** Moquerie *f*, raillerie *f*. **2.** Sujet *m* de moquerie, de raillerie; objet *m* de risée, de dérision. **3.** Semblant *m*, simulacre *m* (*of*, de). *His trial was a mere m.*, son procès fut une pure moquerie.

mock-up [mɔk'ʌp], *s*. *Ind*: Maquette *f* (d'un avion, etc.).

modal ['moud(ə)l], *a*. Modal, -aux. *Log*: **Modal proposition**, modale *f*.

modality [mo'daliti], *s*. Modalité *f*.

mode [moud], *s*. **1.** (*Manner*) Mode *m*, méthode *f*, manière *f*. *M. of life*, façon *f* de vivre; manière de vivre, train *m* de vie. **2.** (*Fashion*) Mode *f*. **3.** *Mus*: Mode *m*. **Major, minor, mode**, mode majeur, mineur. **Church mode**, ton *m* d'église. **4.** *Log*: *Phil*: Mode *m*.

model[1] ['mɔd(ə)l], *s*. **1.** (*a*) Modèle *m*. **Wax model** (*in shop*), figurine *f* de cire. *To make a m. of a monument*, etc., faire la maquette d'un monument, etc. **Model maker**, modelliste *m*. (*b*) *N.Arch*: Gabarit *m*. **2.** (*a*) *Art*: **Drawn from the m.**, dessiné d'après le modèle. **To draw without a model**, dessiner de chic. (*b*) **On the model of s.o.**, à l'imitation de qn. **To take s.o. as one's model**, prendre modèle sur qn. (*c*) *Art*: (*Pers.*) Modèle *mf*. *He married one of his models*, il a épousé un(e) de ses modèles. **3.** *Dressm*: (*a*) Modèle *m*, patron *m*. (*b*) Mannequin *m*. **4.** *Attrib*. **Model farm**, ferme modèle. *M. husband*, époux modèle; le modèle des époux.

model[2], *v.tr.* (modelled ['mɔd(ə)ld]) Modeler. **To model sth. after, upon, sth.**, modeler qch. sur qch. **To model oneself on s.o.**, se modeler sur qn; prendre exemple sur qn. **modelling**, *s*. (*a*) *Art*: Modelage *m*. (*b*) Facture *f* sur modèle, sur gabarit.

modeller ['mɔdələr], *s*. Modeleur *m*.

moderate[1] ['mɔdəret], *a*. Modéré; moyen, ordinaire, raisonnable; (travail) médiocre. *M. in one's desires*, modéré dans ses désirs. *M. drinker*, buveur plutôt sobre. *M. language*, langage mesuré. **Moderate price**, prix modéré, modique. *M. capacities*, talents ordinaires, moyens. *M. size*, grandeur moyenne. **Moderate opinions**, opinions modérées. *M. meal*, repas sobre, frugal. **-ly**, *adv.* Modérément; avec modération; sobrement; médiocrement. **'moderate-'sized**, *a*. De grandeur moyenne.

moderate[2] ['mɔdəreit]. **1.** (*a*) *v.tr.* Modérer; tempérer (l'ardeur du soleil). *To m. one's pretensions*, rabattre de ses prétentions. (*b*) *v.i.* (*Of tempest, etc.*) Se modérer. **2.** *v.i.* *Ecc*: (*Esp. Scot.*) Présider (une assemblée).

moderateness ['mɔdəretnəs], *s*. **1.** Modération *f*; modicité *f* (de prix). **2.** Médiocrité *f* (du travail, etc.).

moderation [mɔdə'reiʃ(ə)n], *s*. **1.** Modération *f*. mesure *f*, retenue *f*; sobriété *f* (de langage), avec modération, mesurément. **In moderation**, modérément. **2.** *pl. Sch*: (*At Oxford*) **Moderations**, *F*: **Mods**, premier examen pour le grade de *Bachelor of Arts*.

moderator ['mɔdəreitər], *s*. **1.** Président *m* (d'une assemblée). **2.** *A*: **Moderator lamp**, lampe *f* à modérateur.

modern [ˈmɔdərn], *a.* Moderne. *To build in the m. style*, bâtir à la moderne. *M. times*, le temps présent, les temps modernes. **Modern languages**, langues vivantes. *s. The ancients and the moderns*, les anciens *m* et les modernes *m*.

modernism [ˈmɔdərnizm], *s.* **1.** Goût *m* de ce qui est moderne. **2.** *(a)* Invention *f* moderne ; usage nouveau. *(b)* Néologisme *m*.

modernity [mɔˈdəːrniti], *s.* Modernité *f*.

modernize [ˈmɔdərnaːiz], *v.tr.* Moderniser ; rénover ; mettre (ses idées, etc.) à jour.

modest [ˈmɔdest], *a.* Modeste. *(a)* **To be modest about one's achievements**, être modeste au sujet dc ses succès. *(b)* *(Of woman)* Pudique, honnête, chaste. *(c)* **To be modest in one's requirements**, être modéré dans ses demandes. *M. fortune*, fortune modeste. *(d)* Sans prétentions. **-ly,** *adv.* **1.** Modestement ; avec modestie. **2.** Pudiquement, chastement. **3.** Modérément. **4.** Sans prétentions ; sans faste.

modesty [ˈmɔdesti], *s.* **1.** Modestie *f. Be it said with all due modesty*, soit dit sans vanité. **2.** Pudeur *f* ; honnêteté *f* (chez une femme). *To offend m.*, commettre un outrage à la pudeur. *Cost :* **Modesty-front, -vest**, plastron *m.* **3.** Modération *f* (d'une demande, etc.) ; modicité *f* (d'une dépense). **4.** Absence *f* de prétention ; simplicité *f*.

modicum [ˈmɔdikəm], *s.* **A (small) modicum of . . .**, une petite portion, une faible quantité, de. . . . *To live upon a very small m.*, vivre d'une maigre pitance.

modification [mɔdifiˈkeiʃ(ə)n], *s.* **1.** Modification *f. To make modifications in sth.*, apporter des modifications à qch. **2.** Atténuation *f*.

modify [ˈmɔdifai], *v.tr.* **1.** *(a)* Modifier ; apporter des modifications à (qch.). *(b)* Mitiger, atténuer (une peine). *To m. one's demands*, rabattre de ses prétentions. **2.** Modifier (le verbe, une voyelle).

modillion [mɔˈdiljən], *s. Arch :* Modillon *m*.

modish [ˈmoudiʃ], *a. Usu. Pej :* Qui se pique d'être à la mode ; qui suit les outrances de la mode ; *(of pers.)* faraud, faraude. *A m. hat*, un chapeau un peu criard. **-ly,** *adv.* (Habillé) très à la mode.

modishness [ˈmoudiʃnəs], *s.* Conformité *f* à la mode ; élégance affectée.

Mods [mɔdz]. *See* MODERATION 2.

modulate [ˈmɔdjuleit]. **1.** *v.tr.* *(a)* Moduler (sa voix). *W.Tel : Cin :* **Modulated output power**, puissance modulée ; watts modulés. *(b)* Ajuster, approprier *(to, à).* **2.** *v.i. Mus :* **To modulate from one key (in)to another**, passer d'un ton dans un autre ; moduler.

modulation [ˌmɔdjuˈleiʃ(ə)n], *s.* Modulation *f*.

modulus, *pl.* **-i** [ˈmɔdjuləs, -ai], *s. Mth : Mec :* Module *m*, coefficient *m. Mec :* **Young's modulus, modulus of elasticity**, module, coefficient, d'élasticité.

Mogul [mouˈgʌl], *s.* **The Great, Grand, Mogul**, le Grand Mogol.

mohair [ˈmouhɛər], *s. Tex :* Mohair *m*.

Mohammedan, moˈhamedən], *a. & s.* Mahométan, -ane.

moiety [ˈmɔiəti, -iti], *s. A. & Jur :* **1.** Moitié *f*. **2.** Part *f*, demi-portion *f*.

moil [mɔil], *v.i.* Peiner. *In the phr.* **To toil and moil**, *q.v. under* TOIL[2].

moire [mwaːr], *s. Tex :* Moire *f.* **Moire crêpe**, crêpe ondé.

moiré [mwaːre], *a. & s.* Moiré (*m*).

moist [mɔist], *a.* (Climat, chaleur) humide ; (peau, main, chaleur) moite. **Eyes moist with** tears, yeux mouillés de larmes. *To grow m.*, s'humecter, se mouiller. *Paint :* **Moist colours**, couleurs moites. •

moisten [ˈmɔis(ə)n]. **1.** *v.tr.* *(a)* Humecter, mouiller ; moitir, amoitir (la peau) ; arroser (la pâte, etc.). *Tchn :* Humidifier, madéfier. *(b)* **To moisten a rag, a sponge, with . . .**, imbiber un chiffon, une éponge, de. . . . **2.** *v.i.* S'humecter, se mouiller.

moistness [ˈmɔistnəs], *s.* Humidité *f* ; moiteur *f* (de la peau).

moisture [ˈmɔistjər], *s.* Humidité *f* ; buée *f* (sur une glace, etc.). *M. of plants*, suc *m* des plantes. **Moisture-proof**, à l'épreuve de l'humidité.

moke [mouk], *s. P :* Bourricot *m*, bourrique *f* ; âne *m*.

molar[1] [ˈmoulər]. **1.** *a.* (Dent) molaire. **2.** *s.* Molaire *f* ; grosse dent.

molar[2], *a.* Qui se rapporte à la masse ; (concrétion) molaire.

molasses [moˈlasiz], *s.pl.* Mélasse *f*.

mole[1] [moul], *s.* **1.** Grain *m* de beauté (au visage). **2.** Nævus *m*.

mole[2], *s. Z :* Taupe *f.* **'mole-catcher,** *s.* Taupier *m* ; preneur *m* de taupes. **'mole-cricket,** *s. Ent :* Taupe-grillon *f, pl.* taupes-grillons. **'mole-hill,** *s.* Taupinière *f. S.a.* MOUNTAIN. **'mole-trap,** *s.* Taupière *f*.

mole[3], *s.* Môle *m* ; brise-lames *m inv* ; digue *f* ; jetée *f*.

molecular [moˈlekjulər], *a.* Moléculaire

molecule [ˈmoulikjuːl, ˈmɔ-], *s.* **1.** *Ch :* Molécule *f.* **2.** *F :* Molécule, parcelle *f*.

moleskin [ˈmoulskin], *s.* **1.** (Peau *f* de) taupe *f. M. coat*, manteau *m* en taupe. **2.** *(a) Tex :* Velours *m* de coton. *(b) pl.* **Moleskins**, pantalon *m* en velours de coton (de garde-chasse, etc.).

molest [moˈlest], *v.tr.* **1.** *A. & Jur :* Molester, inquiéter (qn). **2.** Rudoyer ; se livrer à des voies de fait contre (qn).

molestation [moulesˈteiʃ(ə)n], *s.* **1.** Molestation *f.* **2.** Voies *fpl* de fait.

mollification [mɔlifiˈkeiʃ(ə)n], *s.* Apaisement *m*, adoucissement *m*.

mollify [ˈmɔlifai], *v.tr.* **To mollify s.o.**, adoucir, apaiser, qn ; calmer la colère de qn. *He refused to be mollified (by them)*, il leur tcnait rigueur.

mollusc [ˈmɔləsk], *s.* Mollusque *m*.

mollusca [moˈlʌskə], *s.pl.* Les mollusques *m*.

Molly [ˈmɔli]. *Pr.n.f.* *(Dim. of Mary)* Mariette, Manon. **'molly-coddle**[1], *s. F :* *(a)* Petit chéri à sa maman. *(b)* (Homme) douillet *m.* *(c)* Poule mouillée. **'molly(-coddle)**[2], *v.tr.* Dorloter (un enfant) ; élever (un enfant) dans du coton.

molten [ˈmoult(ə)n]. *See* MELT.

Molucca [moˈlʌkə]. *Pr.n.* **1. The Moluccas, the Molucca Islands**, lcs Moluques *f.* **2.** *Bot :* *(a)* **Molucca balm**, mélisse *f* des Moluques. *(b)* **Molucca bean**, bonduc *m* jaune.

moly [ˈmouli], *s.* **1.** *Myth :* Moly *m.* **2.** *Bot :* Ail doré ; moly.

molybdenum [mɔlibˈdiːnəm], *s. Ch :* Mo ybdène *m*.

moment [ˈmoumənt], *s.* **1.** Moment *m*, instant *m.* **Come this moment !** venez à l'instant, tout de suite ! **Wait a moment ! one moment !** *F :* **half a moment !** une minute ! **un moment ! un instant ! One moment, please !** (i) *Tp :* ne quittez pas ! (ii) *W.Tel :* ne quittez pas 'écoute ! **To expect s.o. every moment**, attendre qn d'un moment à l'autre, d'un instant à l'autre. *To interrupt at every m.*, interrompre à tout propos. *He may return at any moment*, il peut revenir d'un instant à l'autre. *His entry was* timed to the moment, son entrée était calculée à la minute. *I have just* this moment, only this moment, *heard of it,* je l'apprends à l'instant. *I saw him* a moment ago, je l'ai vu il y a un instant. **I came the (very) moment I heard of it,** je suis venu aussitôt que je l'ai appris. *The m. I saw him I recognized him,* je ne l'eus pas plus tôt vu que je le reconnus. **From the moment when . . .,** dès l'instant où. . . . **At this moment, at the present moment,** en ce moment; actuellement. *I am busy* at the moment, je suis occupé pour le moment. **At the last moment,** à la dernière minute. *The book appeared* just at the right moment, le livre parut à point nommé. *I will come* in a moment, je viendrai dans un instant. *It was all over in a m.,* cela s'est fait en un clin d'œil. *I want nothing for the moment,* je n'ai besoin de rien pour le moment. **Not for a moment!** jamais de la vie! **The man of the moment,** l'homme de l'heure. **2.** *Mec:* Moment (d'une force); couple moteur. **Moment of inertia,** moment d'inertie. **Bending moment,** effort *m* de flexion. *(Of piece)* **To carry the bending moment,** travailler à la flexion. **3.** *(Of fact, event)* **To be** of moment, être important. *Of great, little, m.,* de grande, de petite, importance. **It is of no moment whether . . .,** peu importe que + *sub.*

momentary ['moumantari], *a.* **1.** Momentané, passager. **2. In momentary expectation of his arrival,** attendant à chaque instant son arrivée. **-ily,** *adv.* **1.** Momentanément, passagèrement. **2.** D'un moment à l'autre.

momentous [mo'mentas , *a.* Important. *M. decision,* décision capitale.

momentousness [mo'mentasnas], *s.* Importance *f.*

momentum, *pl.* **-ta** [mo'mentam, -ta], *s.* **1.** *Mec: Ph:* Force vive; quantité *f* de mouvement (mv). **2.** *F: (Impetus)* Vitesse acquise. **Carried away by my own momentum,** emporté par mon propre élan.

monac(h)al ['monak(a)l], *a.* Monacal, -aux.

monachism ['monakizm], *s.* Monachisme *m.*

monad ['monad], *s.* Monade *f.*

monadelph ['monadelf], *s. Bot:* Plante *f* monadelphe.

monadelphous [mona'delfas], *a. Bot:* Monadelphe.

monandrous [mo'nandras], *a. Bot:* Monandre.

monarch ['monark], *s.* Monarque *m.*

monarchic(al) [mo'na:rkik(al)], *a.* Monarchique.

monarchism ['monarkizm], *s. Pol:* Monarchisme *m.*

monarchist ['monarkist], *s. Pol:* Monarchiste *m.*

monarchy ['monarki], *s.* Monarchie *f. Limited m.,* monarchie tempérée.

monastery ['monast(a)ri], *s.* Monastère *m.*

monastic [mo'nastik], *a.* Monastique; monacal, -aux; claustral, -aux.

Monday ['mʌndi], *s.* Lundi *m.* **To take Monday off,** faire le lundi. *(For other phrases cf.* FRIDAY.)

monetary ['mʌnetari], *a.* Monétaire.

monetize ['mʌneta:iz], *v.tr.* Monétiser, monnayer.

money ['mʌni], *s.* **1.** *(a)* Monnaie *f,* numéraire *m,* espèces monnayées; argent *m.* **Piece of money,** pièce de monnaie. *Silver m.,* monnaie d'argent; argent blanc. **Paper money,** papier-monnaie *m.* **Current money,** monnaie qui a cours. **Counterfeit money, base money,** fausse monnaie. *F:* **To throw good money after bad,** s'enfoncer davan-

tage dans une mauvaise affaire. **Ready money,** argent comptant, argent liquide. *To pay in ready m.,* payer (au) comptant. **Money payment,** paiement en numéraire. *(b) One's own m.,* deniers personnels. *Fin:* **Money is scarce,** l'argent est rare, les capitaux *m* sont rares. *Bank:* **Money at call,** dépôts *mpl* à vue. **To make money,** faire, gagner, de l'argent; *F:* faire sa pelote. *F:* **To be coining money,** être en train de faire fortune. **To come into money,** hériter d'une fortune. **To be made of money,** être cousu d'or. **He has a pot of money,** c'est le père aux écus. **To be rolling in money,** rouler sur l'or. **To part with one's money,** débourser, s'exécuter. *I want to get my m. back,* je voudrais rentrer dans mes fonds. **It is a bargain for the money,** c'est une occasion à ce prix-là. *F:* **They are the people for my money,** parlez-moi de ces gens-là! **There is money in it,** c'est une bonne affaire. **It will bring in big money,** cela rapportera gros. **You have had your money's worth,** vous en avez eu pour votre argent. **Money makes, begets, money,** un bien en acquiert un autre; un sou amène l'autre. **Your money or your life!** la bourse ou la vie! **Money interest,** intérêt pécuniaire. *Journ:* **Money article,** bulletin financier. **2.** *pl. A. & Jur:* **Moneys, monies,** argent, fonds *mpl. Moneys paid out,* versements opérés. *Moneys paid in,* recettes effectuées. **Public moneys,** deniers publics. *Sundry monies owing to him,* diverses sommes à lui dues. **'money-bag,** *s.* Sac *m* à argent; sacoche *f.* **'money-belt,** *s.* Ceinture *f* à porte-monnaie. **'money-bill,** *s.* Loi *f* de finance(s). **'money-box,** *s.* **1.** Tirelire *f.* **2.** Caisse *f,* cassette *f.* **'money-changer,** *s.* Changeur *m,* cambiste *m.* **'money-grubber,** *s.* Grippe-sou *m, pl.* grippesous; thésauriseur *m.* **'money-grubbing**[1], *s.* Cupide, avare. **'money-grubbing**[2], *s.* Thésaurisation *f.* **'money-lender,** *s.* **1.** Prêteur *m* d'argent; banquier usurier; maison *f* de prêt. **2.** *Com:* Bailleur *m* de fonds. **'money-market,** *s.* Marché monétaire, financier; place *f* de change; bourse *f.* **'money-wort,** *s. Bot:* Nummulaire *f;* herbe *f* aux écus.

moneyed ['mʌnid], *a.* **1.** Riche; qui a de l'argent. **Moneyed man,** richard *m.* **The moneyed classes,** les classes possédantes. **2. The moneyed interest,** les rentiers *m,* les capitalistes *m.*

monger ['mʌŋgər], *s. (Chiefly in combination)* **1.** Marchand, -ande. **Cheesemonger, fishmonger,** marchand de fromage, de poisson. **Ironmonger,** quincaillier *m.* **2.** *Pej:* **News-monger,** colporteur *m* de nouvelles. **Mystery-monger,** colporteur de mystères. **Slander-monger,** mauvaise langue; médisant, -ante. **Strike-monger,** gréviculteur *m. S.a.* PANIC-MONGER, SCANDAL-MONGER, WAR-MONGER.

Mongol ['moŋgol], *a. & s. Ethn:* Mongol, -ole.

Mongolia [moŋ'goulja]. *Pr.n.* La Mongolie.

mongoose ['mʌŋgu:s, 'moŋ-], *s. Z:* Mangouste *f;* ichneumon *m.*

mongrel ['mʌŋgrəl]. **1.** *s.* Métis, -isse; *(of dog)* bâtard, -arde. **2.** *a. (Animal)* métis; *(plante)* métisse. **Mongrel cur,** roquet *m.*

monial ['mounial], *s. Arch:* Meneau *m.*

monism ['monizm], *s. Phil:* Monisme *m.*

monition [mo'niʃ(ə)n], *s.* **1.** *(a)* Avertissement *m.* *(b) Ecc:* Monition *f.* **2.** *Jur:* Citation *f* (à comparaître).

monitor ['monitar], *s.* **1.** Moniteur, -trice. **2.** *Cin:* Projection-room monitor, haut-parleur *m* de cabine, de contrôle. **3.** *Navy: A: (Ironclad)* Monitor *m.* **'monitor 'roof,** *s. U.S:* Lanterneau *m* (d'atelier, de wagon). **'monitor**

room, *s. Cin:* Cabine *f* d'enregistrement sonore.

monitory ['mɔnitəri], *a.* (*a*) (Mot) d'admonition, d'avertissement. (*b*) *Ecc:* Monitoire ; monitorial, -aux.

monk [mʌŋk], *s.m.* Moine, religieux. *To be a m.*, porter le froc. **Black monk,** bénédictin. **White monk,** (moine) cistercien. **'monk's-hood,** *s. Bot:* (Aconit *m*) napel *m*; capuchon-de-moine *m*.

monkey[1] ['mʌŋki], *s.* **I.** *Z:* Singe *m*. **Female monkey, she-monkey,** guenon *f. F:* **You young monkey!** petit polisson ! petit garnement ! petit(e) espiègle ! *Roguish little* **monkey face,** petite frimousse espiègle. *P:* **To put s.o.'s monkey up,** mettre qn en colère ; faire sortir qn de ses gonds. **To get one's monkey up, se fâcher. I won't stand any monkey business!** vous n'allez pas me la faire ! *.2.* Alcarazas *m.* **3.** *Civ.E:* Mouton *m*, singe (de sonnette). **4.** *P:* (Somme *f* de) cinq cents livres, *U.S:* cinq cents dollars. **'monkey-block,** *s. Nau:* Retour *m* de palan. **'monkey-bread,** *s. Bot:* **I.** Pain *m* de singe. **2.** (*Tree*) Baobab *m.* **'monkey-gaff,** *s. Nau:* Corne *f* de pavillon. **'monkey-house,** *s.* Singerie *f*; pavillon *m* des singes. **'monkey-jacket,** *s.* Veston court, veste courte (de chasseur de café). **'monkey nut,** *s.* = PEANUT. **'monkey-puzzle,** *s. Bot:* Araucaria *m.* **'monkey-tricks,** *s.pl.* Singeries *f*, tours *m* de singe, chinoiseries *f*, espiègleries *f*. **'monkey-wrench,** *s.* Clé anglaise ; lé à molette.

monkey[2]. **I.** *v.tr.* Singer (qn). **2.** *v.i.* (*a*) Faire des tours de singe. (*b*) *P:* **To monkey (about) with sth.,** tripoter qch. ; toucher à qch. (qu'il faut laisser tranquille).

monkhood ['mʌŋkhud], *s.* **I.** Monachisme *m.* **2.** *Coll.* Moinerie *f.*

monkish ['mʌŋkiʃ], *a. Pej:* De moine ; monacal, -aux.

monobasic [mɔnɔ'beisik], *a. Ch:* Monobasique.

monocarp ['mɔnɔkɑːrp], *s. Bot:* Plante mono-carpienne.

monochromatic [mɔnɔkrɔ'matik], *a.* (Éclairage) monochromatique.

monochrome ['mɔnɔkroum]. *Art:* **I.** *a.* Mono-chrome. **2.** *s.* Peinture *f* monochrome ; mono-chrome *m.*

monocle ['mɔnɔkl], *s.* Monocle *m.*

monocotyledon [mɔnɔkɔti'liːdən], *s. Bot:* Monocotylédone *f.*

monogamic [mɔnɔ'gamik], *a.* **I.** (*Of rule, custom*) Monogamique. **2.** (*Of pers.*) = MONO-GAMOUS.

monogamist [mɔ'nɔgəmist], *s.* Monogame *mf.*

monogamous [mɔ'nɔgəməs], *a.* Monogame.

monogamy [mɔ'nɔgəmi], *s.* Monogamie *f.*

monogram ['mɔnɔgram], *s.* Monogramme *m*, chiffre *m.*

monograph ['mɔnɔgrɑːf, -graf], *s.* Mono-graphie *f.*

monolith ['mɔnɔliθ], *s.* Monolithe *m.*

monolithic [mɔnɔ'liθik], *a.* Monolithe.

monologue ['mɔnɔlɔg], *s.* Monologue *m.*

monomania [mɔnɔ'meiniə], *s.* Monomanie *f.*

monomaniac [mɔnɔ'meiniak], *s.* Monomane *mf*, monomaniaque *mf.*

monomaniacal [mɔnɔmə'naiək(ə)l], *a.* Mono-mane, monomaniaque.

monomial [mɔ'noumiəl], *a. & s. Mth:* Mo-nôme (*m*).

monophase ['mɔnɔfeːiz], *a. El.E:* (Courant) monophasé, uniphasé.

monoplane ['mɔnɔplein], *s. Av:* Monoplan *m.*

monopolist [mɔ'nɔpolist], *s.* Monopolisateur *m*; accapareur, -euse.

monopolization [mɔnɔpolai'zeiʃ(ə)n], *s.* Mono-polisation *f.*

monopolize [mɔ'nɔpolaːiz], *v.tr.* **I.** Monopoliser, accaparer (une denrée). **2.** *F:* Accaparer ; s'em-parer de (la conversation).

monopoly [mɔ'nɔpoli], *s.* Monopole *m.*

monorail ['mɔnɔreil], *a. & s.* Monorail (*m*).

monorefringent [mɔnɔri'frindʒənt], *a. Ph:* Monoréfringent, uniréfringent.

monosyllabic [mɔnɔsi'labik], *a.* Monosyllabe, monosyllabique.

monosyllable [mɔnɔ'siləbl], *s.* Monosyllabe *m.*

monotonous [mɔ'nɔtənəs], *a.* Monotone ; fasti-dieux. **-ly,** *adv.* Monotonement ; fastidieusement.

monotony [mɔ'nɔtəni], *s.* Monotonie *f.*

monotremata [mɔnɔ'triːmətə], *s.pl. Z:* Mono-trèmes *m.*

monotreme ['mɔnɔtriːm], *a. & s. Z:* Mono-trème (*m*).

monotype ['mɔnɔtaip], *s. Typ:* Monotype *f.*

monovalence, -valency [mɔnɔ'veiləns, -'veil-ənsi], *s. Ch:* Monovalence *f*, univalence *f.*

monovalent [mɔnɔ'veilənt], *a. Ch:* Monova-lent, univalent.

monoxide [mɔ'nɔksaid], *s. Ch:* Protoxyde *m.* Carbon *m.*, oxyde *m* de carbone.

monsoon [mɔn'suːn], *s. Meteor:* Mousson *f.*

monster ['mɔnstər], *s.* **I.** *s.* Monstre *m.* **2.** *a. F:* Monstre ; colossal, -aux ; énorme.

monstrance ['mɔnstrəns], *s. Ecc:* Ostensoir *m.*

monstrosity [mɔn'strɔsiti], *s.* Monstruosité *f.* **I.** Monstre *m.* **2.** Énormité *f* (d'un crime).

monstrous ['mɔnstrəs], *a.* Monstrueux. (*a*) Con-tre nature. (*b*) Odieux. *F:* **It is perfectly mon-strous that . . .,** c'est monstrueux que + *sub.* (*c*) Énorme ; colossal, -aux.

month [mʌnθ], *s.* **I.** Mois *m.* **Calendar month,** mois du calendrier ; mois civil, commun. *S.a.* LUNAR. *In the m. of August,* au mois d'août ; en août. *Current m.,* mois en cours. *At the end of the current m.,* fin courant. **What day of the month is this?** le quantième du mois avons-nous? *F:* le combien sommes-nous? *This day month,* dans un mois, jour pour jour. *To hire sth.* **by the month,** louer qch. au mois. *Once a month,* une fois par mois ; mensuellement. *To receive one's* **month's pay,** toucher son mois. *Fin:* **Bill at three months,** papier à trois mois (d'échéance).

monthly[1] ['mʌnθli]. **I.** *a.* (*a*) Mensuel. *Com:* **Monthly instalment,** mensualité *f.* (*b*) *Rail:* **Monthly return ticket,** billet d'aller et retour valable pour un mois. **2.** *s. F:* Revue mensuelle ; publication mensuelle. **3.** *s.pl. Physiol: F:* **Monthlies,** menstrues *f*; *F:* règles *f*, époques *f.*

monthly[2], *adv.* Mensuellement ; une fois par mois ; tous les mois.

monument ['mɔnjumənt], *s.* **I.** Monument *m.* **2.** Monument funéraire ; pierre tombale.

monumental [mɔnju'ment(ə)l], *a.* **I.** Monu-mental, -aux. *F:* **Monumental ignorance,** igno-rance monumentale, prodigieuse. **2.** **Monu-mental mason,** entrepreneur *m* de monuments funéraires ; marbrier *m.*

moo[1] [muː], *s.* Meuglement *m*, beuglement *m.*

moo[2], *v.i.* (mooed) Meugler, beugler.

mooch [muːtʃ], *v.i. P:* **To mooch about,** flâner, traîner ; se balader ; baguenauder.

mood[1] [muːd], *s. Gram: Log: Mus:* Mode *m.*

mood[2], *s.* **I.** Humeur *f*, disposition *f.* **To be in a good, bad, mood,** être bien, mal, disposé ; être de bonne, méchante, humeur. *To be in a generous* *m.*, être en veine de générosité. **To be in the mood to write,** être en disposition d'écrire. *To be in the m. for reading,* **in a reading mood,** être en humeur de lire. *To be in no m. for laughing,* **in no laughing mood,** ne pas avoir le cœur à rire ; n'avoir aucune envie de rire ; ne pas être d'humeur à rire. **2.** *pl.* **To have moods,** avoir des lunes, des lubies. **Man of moods,** lunatique *m.*

moodiness ['mu:dinəs], *s.* **1.** Humeur chagrine ; morosité *f.* **2.** Humeur changeante.

moody ['mu:di], *a.* **To be moody,** (i) être maussade ; (ii) être mal luné ; (iii) avoir des lunes, des lubies ; avoir ses mauvaises heures. **-ily,** *adv.* D'un air chagrin, morose ; maussadement.

moon¹ [mu:n], *s.* Lune *f.* **New moon,** nouvelle lune. **Full moon,** pleine lune. **There is a moon to-night,** il fait clair de lune ce soir. *F:* **To cry for the moon,** to ask for the moon and stars, faire des demandes par-dessus les maisons ; demander la lune. **Once in a blue moon,** tous les trente-six du mois ; une fois par extraordinaire. **'moon-eye,** *s.* Œil *m* lunatique (de cheval). **'moon-fish,** *s.* Vomer *m* ; poisson-lune *m.*

moon². **1.** *v.i.* **To moon about,** muser, musarder. **2.** *v.tr.* **To moon away two hours,** passer deux heures à musarder.

moonbeam ['mu:nbi:m], *s.* Rayon *m* de lune.

moonless ['mu:nləs], *a.* (Nuit, etc.) sans lune.

moonlight ['mu:nlait], *s.* Clair *m* de lune. **In the moonlight, by moonlight,** au clair de (la) lune ; à la clarté de la lune. **It was moonlight,** il y avait, il faisait, clair de lune.

moonlit ['mu:nlit], *a.* Éclairé par la lune.

moonrise ['mu:nraiz], *s.* Lever *m* de la lune.

moonshine ['mu:nʃain], *s.* **1.** Clair *m* de lune. **2.** *F:* Balivernes *fpl* ; contes *mpl* en l'air. *That's all m.,* tout ça c'est de la blague.

moonstone ['mu:nstoun], *s.* *Lap:* Feldspath nacré ; pierre *f* de lune.

moonstruck ['mu:nstrʌk], *a.* **1.** (*a*) A l'esprit dérangé ; toqué. (*b*) Halluciné. **2.** *F:* Abasourdi, médusé.

moor¹ [mu:ər], *s.* (*a*) Lande *f*, bruyère *f.* (*b*) *Scot:* Chasse réservée. **'moor-cock,** *s.* *Orn:* Lagopède *m* d'Écosse mâle. **'moor-hen,** *s.* *Orn:* **1.** Poule *f* d'eau. **2.** Poule lagopède d'Écosse.

moor², *v.* *Nau:* **1.** *v.tr.* Amarrer (un navire) ; mouiller (une bouée, une mine). *To m. a ship alongside (the quay),* accoster un navire le long du quai. **2.** *v.i.* S'amarrer ; prendre le corps-mort. **mooring,** *s.* **1.** Amarrage *m* (d'un navire) ; mouillage *m* (d'une bouée). **Mooring ring,** organeau *m* d'amarrage ; organeau *m.* **Mooring rope,** amarre *f* ; aussière *f* en filin. *Aer:* **Mooring mast,** mât *m* d'amarrage. **2.** *pl.* **Ship at her moorings,** navire sur ses amarres. **To pick up one's moorings,** prendre son coffre.

Moor³, *s.* Maure *m*, Mauresque *f.*

moorage ['mu:əredʒ], *s.* *Nau:* **1.** Amarrage *m*, mouillage *m.* **2.** Droits *mpl* de corps-mort ; droits d'attache ; (*in river*) droits de rivage.

Moorish ['mu:əriʃ], *a.* Mauresque, moresque, maure. *A Moorish woman,* une Mauresque.

moorland ['mu:ərlənd], *s.* = MOOR¹ (*a*).

moose [mu:s], *s.* *Z:* Élan *m*, orignac *m.*

moot¹ [mu:t], *s.* *Hist:* Assemblée *f* (du peuple).

moot², *a.* (*Of question*) Sujet à controverse ; discutable. *Jur:* **Moot point,** point *m* de droit.

moot³, *v.tr.* Soulever (une question). *This question is mooted again,* cette question est remise sur le tapis.

mop¹ [mɔp], *s.* **1.** (*a*) Balai *m* à laver ; balai à franges. **Dish-mop,** lavette *f* (à vaisselle). (*b*) *Nau:* Faubert *m.* **2.** *F:* **Mop of hair,** tignasse *f.*

mop², *v.tr.* (mopped) Éponger, essuyer (le parquet). *Nau:* Fauberder (le pont). *F:* **To mop one's brow,** s'éponger, se tamponner, le front (avec son mouchoir). *S.a.* FLOOR¹ 1. **mop up,** *v.tr.* (*a*) Éponger (de l'eau) ; essuyer (la transpiration, etc.). (*b*) Rafler, absorber (tous les bénéfices). (*c*) *Mil:* *F:* **To mop up the trenches** (*after an attack*), *abs.* **to mop up,** nettoyer les tranchées. **mopping up,** *s.* (*a*) Épongeage *m* ; essuyage *m.* (*b*) *Mil:* *F:* Nettoyage *m* des tranchées.

mope [moup], *v.i.* Être triste, mélancolique ; s'ennuyer ; *F:* broyer du noir. **To mope to death,** mourir d'ennui.

mopish ['moupiʃ], *a.* Triste, morose.

moquette [mɔ'ket], *s.* *Tex:* Moquette *f.*

moraine [mɔ'rein], *s.* *Geol:* Moraine *f.*

moral ['mɔrəl]. **I.** *a.* Moral, -aux. **1.** **Moral philosophy,** la morale, l'éthique *f.* *To raise the m. standard of the community,* relever les mœurs de la société. **2.** Conforme aux bonnes mœurs. *To live a m. life,* avoir de bonnes mœurs ; *F:* avoir des mœurs. **3.** **Moral courage,** courage moral. **Moral victory,** victoire morale. **4.** **Moral certainty,** (i) certitude morale ; (ii) *Turf:* *F:* gagnant sûr ; certitude. **-ally,** *adv.* Moralement. **II.** **moral,** *s.* **1.** Morale *f*, moralité *f* (d'un conte). *S.a.* POINT² I. 2. **2.** *pl.* **Morals,** moralité, mœurs *fpl.* **Man of loose morals,** homme de peu de moralité, qui manque de conduite. **3.** = MORALE.

morale [mɔ'rɑ:l], *s.* (*No pl.*) Moral *m* (d'une armée, etc.).

moralist ['mɔrəlist], *s.* Moraliste *mf.*

morality [mɔ'raliti], *s.* **1.** (*a*) Moralité *f* ; principes moraux ; sens moral. *Commercial m.,* probité commerciale. (*b*) Bonnes mœurs. **2.** Réflexion morale ; moralité. **3.** *Lit.Hist:* **Morality-play,** moralité.

moralize ['mɔrəlaiz], **1.** *v.i.* Moraliser, faire de la morale (*on,* sur). **2.** *v.tr.* Moraliser. **moralizing¹,** *a.* Moralisateur, -trice. **moralizing²,** *s.* *F:* None of your m. ! pas de morale !

morass [mɔ'ras], *s.* Marais *m* ; fondrière *f.*

moratorium [mɔrə'tɔ:riəm], *s.* *Fin:* Moratorium *m.*

moratory ['mɔrətəri], *a.* Moratoire.

morbid ['mɔ:rbid], *a.* **1.** Morbide. *M. curiosity,* curiosité malsaine, maladive. **2.** *Med:* **Morbid anatomy,** anatomie *f* pathologique. **-ly,** *adv.* Morbidement, maladivement.

morbidity [mɔ:r'biditi], **morbidness** ['mɔ:rbidnəs], *s.* (*a*) Morbidité *f* ; état maladif. (*b*) Tristesse maladive (des pensées).

mordacity [mɔ:r'dasiti], **mordancy** ['mɔ:rdənsi], *s.* Mordacité *f*, causticité *f* (d'une critique).

mordant ['mɔ:rdənt]. **1.** *a.* Mordant, caustique. **2.** *s.* *Dy: etc:* Mordant *m.*

more ['mɔ:ər]. **1.** *a.* Plus (de). *He has more patience than I,* il a plus de patience que moi. *He is afraid it means m. work,* il craint un surcroît de besogne. **More than ten men,** plus de dix hommes. **One more,** un de plus ; encore un. **One or more,** un ou plusieurs. (**Some**) **more bread,** *please!* encore du pain, s'il vous plaît ! **To have some more wine,** reprendre du vin. *Is there any more?* y en a-t-il encore ? en reste-t-il ? *Do you want any m., some m.?* en voulez-vous encore ? *A little more,* encore un peu. *Have you any more books?* avez-vous d'autres livres ? **A few more days,** quelques jours de plus. **Many**

more, beaucoup d'autres; encore beaucoup. **As many more,** encore autant. **2.** *s. or indef. pron. I cannot give m.,* je ne peux donner davantage. *That's more than enough,* c'est plus qu'il n'en faut (*to,* pour). *That hat costs m. than this one,* ce chapeau-là coûte plus cher que celui-ci. *He is thirty and more,* il a trente ans et même davantage. *This incident, of which more anon . . .,* cet incident, sur lequel nous reviendrons. . . . *What is more . . .,* qui plus est. . . . *She was m. of a tie than a companion,* elle était une attache plutôt qu'une compagne. **3.** *adv.* (*a*) Plus, davantage. *M. easily,* plus facilement. **More and more,** de plus en plus. *You are rich but he is more so,* vous êtes riche mais il l'est davantage. *He was more surprised than annoyed,* il était plutôt surpris que fâché. *His total debts are m. than covered by his assets,* le chiffre de ses dettes est couvert et au delà par son actif. **More or less,** plus ou moins. (*b*) **Once more,** encore une fois, une fois de plus. **Never more,** jamais plus, plus jamais. *If I see him any more,* si jamais je le revois. **4. The more.** (*a*) *a. He only does the m. harm,* il n'en fait que plus de mal. (The) **more's the pity,** c'est d'autant plus malheureux. (*b*) *s.* **The more one has the more one wants,** plus on a, plus on désire avoir. (*c*) *adv.* **All the more . . .,** à plus forte raison . . .; d'autant plus. . . . *It makes me all the m. proud,* je n'en suis que plus fier. **The more so as . . .,** d'autant plus que. . . . *The m. he drank the thirstier he got,* plus il buvait, plus il avait soif. **5. No more, not any more.** (*a*) *a. I have no m. money,* je n'ai plus d'argent. *No m. soup, thank you,* plus de potage, merci. (*b*) *s. I have no m.,* je n'en ai plus. **To say no more,** ne pas en dire davantage. *Let us say no m. about it,* qu'il n'en soit plus question; n'en parlons plus. (*c*) *adv.* (i) **The house is no more,** la maison n'existe plus. *I shall see her no m.,* je ne la verrai jamais plus. (ii) *He is no more a lord than I am,* il n'est pas plus, pas davantage, (un) lord que moi. *He thought you had no wish to see him?*—**No more I have,** il a pensé que vous ne vouliez pas le voir.—Ce qui est parfaitement juste. *I can't make out how it has come about.* —*No m. can I,* je ne m'explique pas comment c'est arrivé.—Ni moi non plus.

morel [mɔ'rel], *s. Bot: Morelle f.*
morel(le) [mɔ'rel], *s. Fung: Cu: Morille f.*
morello [mɔ'relo], *s. Hort: Griotte f.*
moreover [mɔːˈrouvər], *adv.* D'ailleurs; du reste; et qui plus est.
Moresque [mɔ'resk], *a. & s.f.* Mauresque, moresque.
morganatic [mɔːgə'natik], *a.* Morganatique. **-ally,** *adv.* Morganatiquement.
morgue [mɔːrg], *s. Esp. U.S:* Morgue f; dépôt m mortuaire.
moribund ['mɔribʌnd], *a.* Moribond.
morion ['mɔriən], *s. Archeol:* Morion m.
Mormon ['mɔːrmən], *a. & s.* Mormon, -one.
Mormonism ['mɔːrmənizm], *s.* Mormonisme m.
morn [mɔːrn], *s. Poet:* = MORNING.
morning ['mɔːrniŋ], *s.* **I.** (*a*) Matin m. *I saw him this morning,* je l'ai vu ce matin. **To-morrow morning,** demain matin. **The next morning,** the morning after, le lendemain matin. **The morning before,** la veille au matin. **Every Monday morning,** tous les lundis matins. **Four o'clock in the morning,** quatre heures du matin. **(The) first thing in the morning,** dès le matin; à la première heure. **Early in the morning,** matinalement; de grand matin. *What do you do in the m.?* que faites-vous le matin? **Good morning,** bonjour.

(*b*) **Matinée f. In the course of the morning,** dans la matinée. **Morning off,** matinée de congé. *A morning's work,* une matinée de travail. **2.** *Attrib.* Matinal, -aux; du matin. **Early morning tea,** tasse de thé prise avant de se lever.
'morning-'gun, *s.* Coup m de canon de diane.
'morning-room, *s.* Petit salon.
Moroccan [mɔ'rɔkən], *a. & s.* Marocain, -aine.
Morocco [mɔ'rɔko]. **I.** *Pr.n. Geog :* Le Maroc. **2.** *s.* **Morocco (leather),** maroquin m. *M.* (*leather*) *goods,* maroquinerie f.
moron ['mɔːərɔn], *s.* **I.** (Homme, femme) faible d'esprit. **2.** *F:* Idiot, -ote.
morose [mɔ'rous], *a.* Chagrin, morose. **-ly,** *adv.* D'un air chagrin, morose.
moroseness [mɔ'rousnəs], *s.* Morosité f; humeur chagrine.
Morpheus ['mɔːrfjuːs]. *Pr.n.m.* Morphée.
morphia ['mɔːrfja], **morphine** ['mɔːrfiːn], *s.* Morphine f. **The morphia habit,** la morphinomanie.
morphi(n)omania [mɔːrfi(n)o'meinia], *s.* Morphinomanie f.
morphi(n)omaniac [mɔːrfi(n)o'meiniak], *a. & s.* Morphinomane (*mf*).
morphology [mɔːr'fɔlɔdʒi], *s.* Morphologie f.
morris-dance ['mɔrisdɑːns], *s.* Danse champêtre travestie.
morrow ['mɔrou], *s. A. & Lit:* Lendemain m. **On the morrow,** le lendemain. *A:* **Good morrow,** bonjour.
morse¹ [mɔːrs], *s. Z:* Morse m.
Morse². *Pr.n.m. Tg:* **The Morse alphabet,** l'alphabet m Morse.
Morse³, *v.i. Tg:* Télégraphier en morse.
morsel ['mɔːrsəl], *s.* Petit morceau. **Choice morsel, dainty morsel,** morceau friand, de choix. *Not a m. of bread,* pas une bouchée de pain.
mort [mɔːrt], *s. Ven:* Hallali m.
mortal ['mɔːrt(ə)l], *a.* Mortel. **I. Mortal remains,** dépouille mortelle. *s.* **The mortals,** les mortels. *F:* **She's a queer mortal,** c'est une drôle de femme. **2.** (*a*) Funeste; fatal, -als (*to,* à). *M. blow,* coup mortel. (*b*) **Mortal sin,** péché mortel. *To commit a m. sin,* pécher mortellement. **3. Mortal enemy,** ennemi mortel, à mort. **Mortal combat,** combat à outrance, à mort. **4.** (*a*) **To be in m. anxiety,** avoir la mort dans l'âme. *To be in m. fear of . . .,* avoir une peur mortelle de. . . . (*b*) *F:* **Two mortal hours,** deux mortelles heures; deux heures interminables. (*c*) *P:* **Any mortal thing,** n'importe quoi. **-ally,** *adv.* Mortellement. **Mortally wounded,** blessé à mort.
mortality [mɔːr'taliti], *s.* Mortalité f. *Ins:* **Mortality tables,** tables de mortalité.
mortar¹ ['mɔːrtər], *s.* **I.** (*a*) Mortier m (pour piler); égrugeoir m. (*b*) *Artil:* Mortier, lance-bombes m inv. **2.** *Const:* (*a*) Mortier. **Cement mortar,** enduit m de ciment. (*b*) **Clay and straw mortar,** bauge f. **'mortar-board,** *s.* **I.** *Const:* Planche f à mortier. **2.** *Cost:* Mortier universitaire anglais.
mortar², *v.tr. Const:* Lier (les pierres) avec du mortier.
mortgage¹ ['mɔːrgedʒ], *s.* Hypothèque f. **Loan on mortgage,** prêt m hypothécaire. **To raise a mortgage,** prendre, lever, une hypothèque. *To secure a debt by m.,* hypothéquer une créance. **To pay off, redeem, a mortgage,** purger une hypothèque. **Mortgage-deed,** contrat m hypothécaire.
mortgage², *v.tr.* Hypothéquer, grever (une terre, des titres). *Mortgaged estate,* domaine affecté d'hypothèques.
mortgageable ['mɔːrgedʒəbl], *a.* Hypothécable.

mortgagee [mɔːrge'dʒiː], s. Créancier m hypothécaire.

mortgagor ['mɔːrgedʒər], s. Débiteur m hypothécaire.

mortification [mɔːrtifi'keiʃ(ə)n], s. **1.** Mortification (corporelle). **2.** Mortification, déconvenue f. **3.** *Med:* Mortification, sphacèle m, gangrène f.

mortify ['mɔːrtifai]. **1.** *v.tr.* Mortifier. (a) Châtier (son corps). (b) Humilier (qn). (c) *Med:* Gangrener, sphacéler. **2.** *v.i. Med:* Se gangrener, se mortifier.

mortise¹ ['mɔːrtis], s. *Carp:* Mortaise f. **'mortise gauge,** s. *Tls:* Trusquin m. **'mortise lock,** s. Serrure encastrée.

mortise², *v.tr.* Mortaiser. **mortised,** a. Assemblé à mortaise. **mortising,** s. Mortaisage m. **Mortising axe,** besaiguë f.

mortmain ['mɔːrtmein], s. *Jur:* Mainmorte f.

mortuary ['mɔːrtjuəri]. **1.** a. Mortuaire. **2.** s. (a) Dépôt m mortuaire ; salle f mortuaire (d'hôpital). (b) Morgue f.

mosaic¹ [mo'zeiik]. **1.** a. *M. flooring,* dallage m en mosaïque. **2.** s. Mosaïque f.

Mosaic², a. *B.Hist:* (Loi) mosaïque, de Moïse.

moschatel [mɔskə'tel], s. *Bot:* (Tuberous) moschatel, moscatelle f.

Moscow ['mɔskou]. *Pr.n.* Moscou m.

Moses ['mouziz]. *Pr.n.m.* Moïse. *P:* Holy Moses! grand Dieu !

Moslem ['mɔslem, 'mɔz-], a. & s. Mahométan, -ane, musulman, -ane.

mosque [mɔsk], s. Mosquée f.

mosquito, *pl.* **-oes** [mɔs'kiːto, -ouz], s. *Ent:* Moustique m. **mos'quito craft,** s. *Coll. Navy:* Bât'ments légers. **mos'quito-net,** s. Moustiquaire f.

moss [mɔs], s. **1.** Marais m, marécage m. (Peat-) moss, tourbière f. **2.** *Bot:* Mousse f. *S.a.* ROLLING¹ 1. **'moss-grown,** a. Couvert de mousse ; moussu. **'moss-hag,** s. *Scot:* Tourbière épuisée ; fondrière f. **'moss rose,** s. *Bot:* Rose mousseuse. **'moss stitch,** s. *Knitting:* Point m de riz.

mossy ['mɔsi], a. Moussu.

most [moust]. **1.** a. (a) *You have made (the) m. mistakes,* c'est vous qui avez fait le plus de fautes. (b) Most men, la plupart des hommes. For the most part, (i) pour la plupart, en majeure partie ; (ii) le plus souvent. **2.** s. & indef. pron. (a) *Do the m. you can,* faites tout ce que vous pourrez. At (the) (very) most, au maximum ; (tout) au plus. To make the most of sth., (i) tirer le meilleur parti possible de qch. ; faire valoir (son argent) ; bien employer (son temps) ; ménager le plus possible (ses provisions, etc.) ; (ii) représenter qch. sous son plus beau jour ou sous son plus vilain jour. (b) *M. of the work,* la plupart, la plus grande partie, la majeure partie, du travail. Most of them *have forgotten him,* la plupart d'entre eux l'ont oublié. **3.** *adv. as sup. of comparison.* What I desire most, ce que je désire le plus, surtout, par-dessus tout. *The m. intelligent child,* l'enfant le plus intelligent. *The m. beautiful woman,* la plus belle femme. *Those who have answered m. accurately,* ceux qui ont répondu la plus exactement. **4.** *adv.* (Intensive) Très, fort, bien. Most likely, très probablement. *A m. costly motor car,* une auto des plus coûteuses. *He has been m. rude,* il a été on ne peut plus grossier. *It is m. remarkable,* c'est tout ce qu'il y a de plus remarkable. The Most Honourable . . ., le Très Honorable. . . . **-ly,** *adv.* **1.** Pour la plupart ; principalement. **2.** Le plus souvent ; (pour) la plupart du temps.

mote [mout], s. Atome m de poussière. To behold the mote in one's brother's eye, voir la paille dans l'œil du prochain.

moth [mɔθ], s. *Ent:* Lépidoptère m. **1.** (a) (Clothes-)moth, mite f ; teigne f des draps. (b) *Coll.* Fur coat ruined by moth, manteau de fourrure abîmé par les mites. **2.** Papillon m nocturne, de nuit ; phalène f. Emperor moth, paon m de nuit. Death's-head moth, sphinx m tête de mort. **'moth-balls,** *s.pl.* Boules f de naphtaline. **'moth-eaten,** a. Rongé des mites, des vers ; mité.

mother¹ ['mʌðər], s.f. **1.** Mère. She is the m. of six, elle est mère de six enfants. *F:* Every mother's son, tous sans exception. *Attrib.* Mother goat, chèvre femelle. *M. hen,* mère poule. **2.** *A. & F:* Old Mother Brown, la mère Brown. Mother Goose stories, contes de ma mère l'Oie. **3.** *Ecc:* The Mother Superior, la Mère supérieure. **4.** Mother metal, métal m mère. Mother rock, roche f mère. **'mother 'country,** s. Mère-patrie f ; métropole f (d'une colonie). **'mother 'earth,** s. La terre notre mère, la terre nourricière. **'mother-in-law,** *s.f.* Belle-mère (mère du mari ou de la femme de qn). **'mother 'naked,** a. Nu comme un ver, comme la main. **'mother of 'pearl,** s. Nacre f. **'mother 'ship,** s. *Navy:* Ravitailleur m ; vaisseau m gigogne. **'mother 'tongue,** s. Langue maternelle. **'mother 'wit,** s. Bon sens ; sens commun.

mother², *v.tr.* **1.** (a) Donner des soins maternels à (qn) ; servir de mère à (qn). (b) Dorloter (qn). **2.** To mother a young wolf upon a bitch, faire élever un louveteau par une chienne. **mothering,** s. Soins maternels.

mothercraft ['mʌðərkrɑːft], s. Puériculture f.

motherhood ['mʌðərhud], s. Maternité f.

motherland ['mʌðərland], s. Patrie f ; pays natal.

motherless ['mʌðərləs], a. Sans mère ; orphelin (de mère).

motherly ['mʌðərli], a. Maternel.

motility [mo'tiliti], s. Mobilité f, motilité f.

motion¹ ['mouʃ(ə)n], s. **1.** Mouvement m, déplacement m. **In motion,** en mouvement ; en marche. To put, set, (sth.) in motion, imprimer un mouvement à (qch.) ; mettre (qch.) en mouvement, en jeu, en marche ; faire mouvoir (qch.) ; faire agir (la loi). **2.** (a) *To make a m. towards the door,* faire mine de sortir. (b) Signe m, geste m. To make motions to s.o. to do sth., faire signe à qn de faire qch. **3.** (a) *To do sth. of one's own motion,* faire qch. de sa propre initiative. (b) Motion f, proposition f. To propose, bring forward, a motion, faire une proposition ; présenter une motion. The m. was carried, la motion fut adoptée. (c) *Jur:* Demande f, requête f. **4.** (a) Mécanisme m. Planetary motion, engrenage m planétaire. (b) Mouvement (d'une montre). **5.** *Med:* Évacuation f, selle f. **'motion picture,** s. *Cin:* Projection animée. Motion(-picture) camera, (ciné-)caméra f.

motion², *v.tr. & i.* To motion (to) s.o. to do sth., faire signe à qn de faire qch. He motioned me to a chair, d'un geste il m'invita à m'asseoir.

motionless ['mouʃ(ə)nləs], a. Immobile ; immobilisé ; sans mouvement.

motivate ['moutiveit], *v.tr.* Motiver (une action).

motive ['moutiv]. **1.** a. (a) Moteur, -trice. Motive power, force motrice. **Motive energy,** énergie cinétique. **2.** s. (a) Motif m (for acting, d'action). From a religious m., poussé par un sentiment religieux. (b) Mobile m (d'une action).

Interest is a powerful m., l'intérêt est un puissant ressort.

notivity [mo'tiviti], *s.* **1.** Motilité *f.* **2.** Énergie *f* cinétique.

notley ['mɔtli]. **1.** *a.* (*a*) Bariolé, bigarré. (*b*) Divers mêlé. *M. crowd*, foule bigarrée, panachée. **2.** *s.* Couleurs bigarrées ; mélange *m* (de choses disparates). *To don the motley*, revêtir la livrée de bouffon ; faire le bouffon.

notor[1] ['moutər]. **1.** *a.* Moteur, -trice. **2.** *s.* (*a*) Moteur *m. Driven by a clockwork m.*, entraîné par un mouvement d'horogerie. (*b*) *El.E:* **Motor generator,** moteur générateur ; dynamo génératrice ; générateur *m.* (*c*) *I.C.E:* **Four-stroke, two-stroke, motor,** moteur à quatre, à deux, temps. (*d*) **Motor vehicle,** voiture *f* automobile. **Motor car,** *F:* motor, automobile *f*, *F:* auto *f*, voiture. **Motor show,** salon *m* de l'automobile. **'motor boat,** *s.* Canot *m* automobile ; vedette *f* à moteur. **'motor bus,** *s.* Autobus *m.* **'motor coach,** *s.* Autocar *m* ; car *m.* **'motor cycle,** *F:* **'motor bike,** *s.* Motocyclette *f*, *F:* moto *f.* **'motor-cycling,** *s.* Motocyclisme *m.* **'motor cyclist,** *s.* Motocycliste *mf.* **'motor-driven,** *a.* **1.** Actionné, commandé, par moteur. **2.** À électromoteur. **'motor lorry,** *s.* Auto-camion *m* ; camion *m* automobile ; (*light*) camionnette *f.* **'motor-road,** *s.* Autostrade *f.* **'motor thresher,** *s. Agr:* Motobatteuse *f.* **'motor tractor,** *s.* Auto-tracteur *m.*

notor[2]. **1.** *v.i.* Aller, voyager, en auto(mobile). *To motor over to see s.o.*, aller visiter qn en auto. **2.** *v.tr.* Conduire (qn) en auto(mobile). **motoring,** *s.* Automobilisme *m* ; tourisme *m* en automobile. *To go in for motoring*, faire de l'automobile. **School of motoring,** auto-école *f.*

notorist ['moutərist], *s.* Automobiliste *mf.*

notorization [moutərai'zeiʃ(ə)n], *s* Motorisation *f.*

notorize ['moutəraiz], *v.tr.* Motoriser (une voiture, l'armée). **Motorized bicycle,** bicyclette *f* à moteur ; vélomoteur *m.* **Motorized agriculture,** motoculture *f.*

notory ['moutəri], *a. Anat:* Moteur, -trice.

nottle[1] ['mɔtl], *s.* **1.** Tache *f*, tacheture *f*, moucheture *f.* **2.** Marbrure *f*, diaprure *f.*

nottle[2], *v.tr.* Tacheter, diaprer, marbrer ; moirer (le méta.) ; jasper (des outils, etc.). *The cold mottles the skin*, le froid marbre la peau.

nottled, *a.* Truité, marbré, pommelé ; (savon) marbré, madré ; (bois) madré ; (tissu) chiné.

notto, *pl.* **-oes** ['mɔto, -ouz], *s.* **1.** Devise *f.* **2.** *Her:* Mot *m*, âme *f* (d'une devise).

nould[1] [mould], *s.* Terre végétale. **Vegetable mould,** terreau *m*, humus *m.* **'mould(-board),** *s.* Versoir *m* (de charrue).

nould[2], *s.* **1.** (*Template*) Calibre *m*, profil *m.* *N.Arch:* Gabarit *m.* **2.** (*a*) *Art: Cer:* Moule *m.* *F:* **To be cast in heroic mould,** être de la pâte dont on fait les héros. *Man cast in a simple m.*, homme tout d'une pièce. *Cu:* **Jelly mould,** moule à gelée. (*b*) *Metall:* **Casting mould,** moule à fonte. **Box mould,** châssis *m* à mouler. (*c*) *Typ:* Matrice *f.* **3.** *Cu:* **Rice-mould,** gâteau *m* de riz. **'mould-loft,** *s. N.Arch:* Salle *f* des gabarits.

nould[3], *v.tr.* **1.** Mouler ; *F:* pétrir, former, façonner (le caractère de qn). **2.** *Bak:* Mettre (le pain) en forme. **3.** *N.Arch:* Gabarier (la quille, etc.). **4.** *Typ:* **To mould a page,** prendre l'empreinte d'une page. **moulding,** *s.* **1.** (*a*) Moulage *m.* (*b*) *N.Arch:* Gabariage *m.* (*c*) *F:* Formation *f* (du caractère). **2.** Moulure *f*,

moulage, profil mouluré. *Arch:* (*Small*) **square moulding,** baguette *f*, tringle *f.* **Plain moulding,** bandeau *m*, listeau *m*, listel *m.* **Grooved moulding,** moulure à gorge. **Com:** *Ind:* **Mouldings,** profilés *m* (en fer, etc.). **'moulding-plane,** *s.* Rabot *m* à moulures ; mouchette *f.*

nould[4], *s.* Moisi *m*, moisissure *f. S.a.* IRON-MOULD.

nould[5], *v.i.* Moisir. **Blue-moulded cheese,** fromage persillé.

noulder[1] ['mouldər], *v.i.* Tomber en poussière ; s'effriter. *To m. in idleness*, s'encroûter dans l'oisiveté.

noulder[2], *s. Cer: Metall:* Mouleur *m.*

nouldiness ['mouldinəs], *s.* État moisi ; moisissure *f.*

nouldy ['mouldi], *a.* Moisi ; (pain) chanci. *To go mouldy*, (se) moisir. *To smell m.*, sentir le moisi. *P:* *I feel pretty m.*, je me sens mal en train ; j'ai le cafard.

noult[1] [moult], *s.* Mue *f.*

noult[2]. **1.** *v.i.* (*Of bird, reptile*) Muer. **2.** *v.tr.* Perdre (ses plumes, sa peau, sa carapace). **moulting**[1], *a.* En mue. **moulting**[2], *s.* Mue *f.* Moulting-time, mue.

nound [maund], *s.* (*a*) Tertre *m*, monticule *m*, butte *f* ; motte *f* (d'un moulin à vent). *Civ.E:* Remblai *m.* **Sepulchral mound,** tumulus *m.* (*b*) Monceau *m*, tas *m* (de pierres, etc.).

nount[1] [maunt], *s.* Mont *m*, montagne *f.* **Mount Sinai,** le mont Sinaï.

nount[2], *s.* **1.** (*a*) Montage *m*, support *m* ; monture *f* (d'un éventail) ; armement *m* (d'une machine) ; affût *m*, pied *m* (de télescope). **Brass mounts,** ferrures *f* en cuivre. *M. of a lens*, monture d'une lentille. (*b*) **Picture mount,** carton *m* de montage. (*c*) **Stamp mount** (*in album*), charnière *f.* **2.** Monture (d'un cavalier). *My m. was a camel*, j'étais monté sur un chameau. **3.** *Turf:* Monte *f.*

nount[3]. **I.** *v.i.* **1.** Monter (en haut d'une colline, etc.). **2.** *Equit:* Se mettre en selle ; monter, sauter, à cheval. **3.** (*Of bill, etc.*) Se monter, s'élever (*to so much*, à tant). **II.** **mount,** *v.tr. & i.* **1. To mount (on, upon) a chair,** monter sur une chaise. *To m. the pulpit*, monter en chaire. (*Of motor car, etc.*) **To mount the pavement,** monter sur le trottoir. **2. To mount (on, upon) a horse, a bicycle,** monter sur, enfourcher, un cheval, une bicyclette ; sauter à cheval. **III.** **mount,** *v.tr.* **1.** Monter, gravir (l'escalier, une colline). *To m. a ladder*, monter à une échelle. **2. To mount s.o. (on a horse),** (i) hisser qn sur un cheval ; (ii) pourvoir (un soldat, etc.) d'un cheval. **Mounted police,** agents à cheval. **3.** (*a*) *Artil:* Affûter, armer (une pièce). (*b*) *Ship* **mounting twenty guns,** navire armé de vingt canons. (*c*) **To mount guard,** monter la garde (*over*, auprès de). **4.** (*a*) Monter (un diamant, une scie, un hameçon) ; installer (une machine) ; monter, entoiler (un tableau) ; entoiler, encoller (une carte). **Diamonds mounted in platinum,** diamants montés sur platine, sertis de platine. (*b*) *Th:* Mettre (une pièce) à la scène. **mount up,** *v.i.* (*Of costs*) Croître, monter, augmenter. **mounting,** *s.* **1.** (*a*) Montage *m*, installation *f* (d'une machine). (*b*) Entoilage *m*, encollage *m.* (*c*) *Th:* Mise *f* à la scène (d'une pièce). **2.** (*a*) Monture *f*, garniture *f* (de fusil, etc.). **Iron mounting,** ferrure *f* ; garniture de fer. (*b*) Affût *m* (de canon, de mitrailleuse). **Tripod mounting,** affût-trépied *m. S.a.* = MOUNT[3] **1.** **'mounting-block,** *s. Equit:* Montoir *m.*

mountain ['mauntən], *s.* Montagne *f.* **To make mountains out of mole-hills,** se faire d'une mouche un éléphant. **Mountain stream**, ruisseau de montagne. *M. scenery*, paysage montagneux. *M. flower*, fleur des montagnes. **Mountain tribe**, tribu montagnarde. **'mountain 'ash**, s. *Bot:* Sorbier *m* des oiseaux; sorbier commun, sauvage. **'mountain 'range**, s. Chaîne *f* de montagnes. **mountaineer¹** [mauntə'ni:ər], s. **1.** Montagnard *m*. **2.** Alpiniste *mf*, ascensionniste *mf*. **mountaineer²**, *v.i.* Faire des ascensions en montagne; faire de l'alpinisme. **mountaineering**, s. Alpinisme *m*.

mountainous ['mauntənəs], *a.* (Pays) montagneux. Mountainous seas, vagues hautes comme des montagnes.

mountebank ['mauntibaŋk], s. (*a*) Saltimbanque *m*, bateleur *m*. (*b*) Charlatan *m*. *Political m.*, polichinelle *m* de la politique.

mounter ['mauntər], s. Monteur, -euse (de diamants, de machines, etc.); metteur *m* en œuvre (de diamants, etc.).

mourn [mɔːrn], *v.i. & tr.* Pleurer, (se) lamenter, s'affliger. To mourn (for, over) sth., pleurer, déplorer, qch. To mourn for s.o., pleurer (la mort de) qn. *His death was universally mourned*, sa mort fut un deuil général. **mourning**, s. **1.** Affliction *f*, deuil *m*. **2.** (*a*) House of mourning, maison endeuillée. (*b*) Habits *mpl* de deuil. In deep mourning, en grand deuil. To go into mourning, se mettre en deuil; prendre le deuil. To be in mourning for s.o., être en deuil de qn. To go out of mourning, quitter le deuil. **'mourning-band**, s. Crêpe *m*; brassard *m* de deuil.

mourner ['mɔːrnər], s. **1.** Affligé, -ée. **2.** Personne qui suit le cortège funèbre. The mourners, le convoi; le cortège funèbre. To be chief mourner, mener, conduire, le deuil.

mournful ['mɔːrnful], *a.* Lugubre, mélancolique; *F:* (figure) d'enterrement; (voix) funèbre. **-fully**, *adv.* Lugubrement, mélancoliquement.

mouse¹, *pl.* mice [maus, mais], s. **1.** Souris *f*. *Little m.*, souriceau *m*. **2.** *Nau:* (*a*) Aiguilletage *m* (de croc). (*b*) Guirlande *f*, bouton *m* (d'un cordage). **'mouse-catcher**, s. (*Cat, etc.*) Souricier *m*. **'mouse-colour**, s. (Couleur *f*) gris *m* (de) souris. **'mouse-ear**, s. *Bot:* Oreille *f* de souris. **'mouse-hole**, s. Trou *m* de souris.

mouse² [mauz]. **1.** *v.i.* (*a*) (*Of cat, etc.*) Chasser aux souris; chasser les souris. (*b*) *F:* To mouse (about), rôder çà et là (à la recherche de qch.); fouiner. **2.** *v.tr. Nau:* (*a*) Faire une guirlande à (un cordage). (*b*) Moucheter, aiguilleter (un croc). **mousing**, s. **1.** Chasse *f* aux souris. **2.** *Nau:* Aiguilletage *m*.

mouser ['mauzər], s. Souricier *m*. Good mouser, chat bon souricier.

mousetrap ['maustrap], s. Souricière *f*.

moustache [mus'tɑːʃ], s. Moustache(s) *f* (*pl*). To wear a moustache, porter la moustache.

mouth¹ [mauθ], s. (*pl.* mouths [mauðz]) **1.** (*Of pers.*) Bouche *f*. To make s.o.'s mouth water, faire venir l'eau à la bouche à qn. To make a (wry) mouth, faire une vilaine moue. To make a pretty m., faire la bouche en cœur. To make a poor mouth, crier famine; crier misère. To make mouths at s.o., faire des grimaces à qn. *P:* To have a bad mouth, avoir la bouche mauvaise; (*after drinking*) avoir la gueule de bois. To put a speech into s.o.'s mouth, attribuer un discours à ·qn. Rumours in everybody's mouth, bruits qui courent les rues. To stop s.o.'s mouth, clore la bouche à qn. **2.** Bouche (de cheval, d'âne, de bœuf, de mouton, d'éléphant, de poisson); gueule *f* (de chien, d'animaux carnassiers, de gros poissons). *Equit:* Horse with a hard mouth,

cheval fort en bouche sans bouche. *Soft m.*, bouche tendre, sensible. *Ven:* (*Of hounds*) To give mouth, donner de la voix. **3.** (*a*) Bouche (de puits, de volcan); goulot *m* (de bouteille); pavillon *m* (d'entonnoir); guichet *m* (de boîte à lettres); gueule (de sac, de canon); ouverture *f*, entrée *f* (de tunnel, de caverne); bée *f* (de bief). (*b*) Embouchure *f* (de fleuve). **'mouth-organ**, s. Harmonica *m*. **'mouth-wash**, s. Eau *f* dentifrice; dentifrice *m*.

mouth² [mauð]. **1.** *v.tr.* To mouth (out) one's words, déclamer ses phrases. **2.** *v.i.* (*a*) Grimacer; faire des grimaces. (*b*) Déclamer. **mouthing**, s. **1.** Emphase *f* (dans le discours). Rhetorical mouthings, rhétorique ampoulée. **2.** Grimaces *fpl*.

-mouthed [mauðd], *a.* **1.** (*a*) Single-mouthed, à une seule bouche. (*b*) (*Of pers.*) Cleanmouthed, au langage honnête. **2.** Well-mouthed horse, cheval bien embouché.

mouthful ['mauθful], s. **1.** Bouchée *f*. To swallow sth. at one mouthful, ne faire qu'une bouchée de qch. *F: To take just a m. of soup*, prendre une goutte de soupe. *M. of wine*, gorgée *f* de vin. **2.** *F:* Mot long d'une aune.

mouthpiece ['mauθpiːs], s. **1.** (*a*) Embouchure *f* (de chalumeau, etc.); embout *m* (de porte-voix). (*b*) *Mus:* Bec *m*, embouchure (de clarinette); (embouchure en) bocal *m* (de cornet). (*c*) *Tp:* Embouchure, pavillon *m*. **2.** To be the mouthpiece of a party, être le porte-parole *inv* d'un parti.

mov(e)able ['muːvəbl]. **1.** *a.* (*a*) Mobile. Movable feast, fête mobile. *Typ:* Movable type, caractère (s) *m* mobile(s). (*b*) *Jur:* Mobilier, meuble. Movable effects, effets mobiliers. **2.** *s.pl.* Movables. (*a*) Mobilier *m*; agencements *m* amovibles. (*b*) *Jur:* Biens mobiliers, biens meubles.

move¹ [muːv], s. **1.** (*a*) *Chess: etc:* Coup *m*. Knight's move, marche *f* du cavalier. To have first move, avoir le trait. To make a move, jouer. Whose move is it? c'est à qui de jouer? (*b*) Coup, démarche *f*. What is the next m.? qu'est-ce qu'il faut faire maintenant? He must make the first m., c'est à lui d'agir le premier. *F:* He is up to every move (in the game), il sait parer à tous les coups. **2.** Mouvement *m. F:* We must make a move, il faut partir. To be always on the move, être toujours en mouvement; être toujours par voie et par chemin. *F:* To get a move on, se dépêcher; *P:* se grouiller. **3.** Déménagement *m.*

move². **I.** *v.tr.* **1.** (*a*) Déplacer (un meuble, des troupes, etc.). *To m. one's chair*, changer sa chaise de place. *Sch:* To be moved up, passer dans la classe supérieure. *Chess:* To move a piece, jouer une pièce. (*b*) To move house, *abs.* to move, déménager. *To m. into the country*, aller s'installer à la campagne. **2.** (*a*) Remuer, bouger (la tête, etc.). Not to move a muscle, ne pas sourciller. *The wind moving the trees*, le vent qui agite les arbres. (*b*) Mouvoir, animer (qch.); mettre (qch.) en mouvement; mettre en marche (une machine). (*c*) *Med:* To move the bowels, relâcher le ventre. **3.** (*a*) Faire changer d'avis (à qn). He is not to be moved, il est inébranlable. (*b*) To move s.o. to do sth., pousser, inciter, qn à faire qch. *F: I will do it when the spirit moves me*, je le ferai quand le cœur m'en dira. (*c*) Émouvoir, toucher, affecter (qn). *Easily moved*, émotionnable. To move s.o. to anger, provoquer la colère de qn. *To m. s.o. to laughter*, faire rire qn. To move s.o. to tears, émouvoir qn jusqu'aux larmes. To move s.o. to pity, exciter la pitié de qn; attendrir qn. *Tears* *will not m.* him (*to pity*), les larmes ne le fléchiront pas. **4.** **To move a resolution,** proposer une motion; mettre aux voix une résolution. To move that . . ., faire la proposition que . . , proposer que + *sub.* **II. move,** *v.i.* *a*) Se mouvoir, se déplacer. **Keep moving!** circulez! **Com:** *F:* This article is not moving, cet article est d'un écoulement difficile. (*Of pers.*) To move in high society, fréquenter la haute société. (*b*) To move (about), faire un mouvement; bouger, (se) remuer. **Don't move!** ne bougez pas! *Mec.E:* (*Of part*) To move freely, jouer librement; avoir du jeu. (*c*) Marcher, aller; s'avancer. *To m. towards a place,* se diriger vers un endroit. He moved with dignity, il avait une démarche digne. *F:* It is time we were moving, il est temps de partir. Chess: The bishop moves diagonally, le fou marche diagonalement. **move back.** **1.** *v.tr.* (*a*) Faire reculer. (*b*) Ramener (qch.) en arrière. **2.** *v.i.* (*a*) (Se) reculer. (*b*) Revenir en arrière. **move forward. 1.** *v.tr.* Avancer (un outil, etc.); faire avancer, porter en avant (des troupes). **2.** *v.i.*(S')avancer; (*of troops*) se porter en avant. **move in,** *v.i.* Emménager. **move off,** *v.i.* S'éloigner, s'en aller; (*of army, train*) se mettre en marche, s'ébranler; (*of motor car*) démarrer. **move on,** *v.i.* (*a*) Avancer; continuer son chemin. **Move on, please!** circulez, s'il vous plaît! (*b*) Se remettre en route. **move out,** *v.i.* Déménager. **moving,** *a.* **1.** (*a*) En mouvement; (tramway) en marche. (*b*) Mobile. **Moving staircase,** escalier roulant, à marches mobiles. **Moving coil,** bobine *f* mobile (de haut-parleur). **2.** (*Of force, etc.*) Moteur, -trice. The moving spirit, l'âme *f* (d'une entreprise). **3.** Émouvant, touchant, attendrissant.

movement ['mu:vmənt], *s.* Mouvement *m*. **1.** (*a*) Déplacement *m*. There was a general m. towards the door, tout le monde se dirigea vers la porte. (*b*) *pl.* To study s.o.'s movements, épier les mouvements de qn, les agissements *m* (d'un criminel). *Journ:* Movements of ships, déplacements. **2.** To make a m. of impatience, faire un geste d'impatience. **3.** Popular movement, mouvement populaire. **4.** Transport *m* (de marchandises). **5.** Clockwork movement, mouvement d'horlogerie; mécanisme *m* d'horlogerie. **6.** *Mus:* Symphony in **three** movements, symphonie *f* en trois mouvements.

mover ['mu:vər], *s.* **1.** Moteur *m*. Prime mover, premier mobile. **2.** Auteur *m* (d'une motion).

movie ['mu:vi], *s.* *F:* Film (muet). The movies, le cinéma, *F:* le ciné.

mow [mou], *v.tr.* (mowed; mown) **1.** Faucher, moissonner. *F:* To mow down the enemy, faucher l'ennemi. **2.** Tondre (le gazon).

'mowing-machine, *s.* **1.** Faucheuse *f*. **2.** Tondeuse *f* (de gazon).

mower ['mouər], *s.* **1.** (Pers.) Faucheur -euse. **2.** Motor mower, faucheuse à moteur. Lawn mower, tondeuse *f* (de gazon)

Mr ['mistər]. See MISTER 1.

Mrs ['misiz]. See MISTRESS 3 (*b*).

MS., *pl.* **MSS.** ['em·es, em·esiz], *s.* Manuscrit *m*.

mu [mju:], *s.* *Gr.Alph:* Mu *m*.

much [mʌtʃ]. **1.** *a.* (*a*) Beaucoup (de) ; bien (du, de la, des). *M.* care, beaucoup de soin ; bien des oins. (*b*) How much bread? combien de pain? How much is it? c'est combien? How m. is it a pound? cela se vend combien la livre? **2.** *adv.* Beaucoup, bien (Very) much better, beaucoup mieux. *M.* worse, bien pis. It doesn't matter much, cela ne fait pas grand'chose. He is not m.

richer than I, il n'est guère plus riche que moi. Ever so much more intelligent, infiniment plus intelligent. *M.* pleased, fort content. **Much the largest,** de beaucoup le plus grand. Thank you very much (for . . .), merci bien, je vous remercie infiniment (de. . .). **Much of an age,** à peu près du même âge. It is pretty much the same thing, c'est à peu près la même chose. **Much to my astonishment,** à mon grand étonnement. *I don't want two,* much less three, il ne m'en faut pas deux, encore moins trois. **3.** *s.* (*a*) *M.* still remains to be done, il reste encore beaucoup à faire. Do you see much of one another? vous voyez-vous souvent? There is not m. to see, il n'y a pas grand'chose à voir. *F:* It is not up to much, cela ne vaut pas grand'chose; ce n'est pas fameux. *F:* He wasn't much of a teacher, il ne valait pas grand'chose comme professeur. *I am not m.* of a playgoer, je ne vais guère au théâtre. Not m. of a dinner, un dîner médiocre. (*b*) This much, autant que ceci. That m. too big, trop grand de cela. Cut that m. off, coupez-en long comme ça. This m. is certain, that . . ., il y a ceci de certain que. . . . (*c*) To make much of sth., (i) faire grand cas de qch.; (ii) vanter qch. To make much of s.o., (i) faire fête à qn; (ii) câliner, choyer (un enfant, etc.). To make m. of a horse, faire des caresses à un cheval. I don't think much of it, j'en fais peu de cas; ça ne me dit pas grand'chose. **4.** (*a*) Much as. *M. as I like* him . . ., quelle que soit mon affection pour lui. . . . *M. as I dislike it* . . ., pour autant que cela me déplaise. . . . (*b*) As much, autant (de). As much again, encore autant. Give me half as m. again, donnez-m'en 'a moitié en plus. Twice as m. water, deux fois autant d'eau. *F:* I thought as much, je m'y attendais ; je m'en doutais bien. (*c*) As much as . . ., autant que. . . *I have three times as m. as I want,* j'en ai trois fois plus qu'il ne m'en faut. He hates you as m. as you like him, autant vous l'aimez, autant il vous déteste. *F:* It is as m. as he can do to read, c'est tout juste s'il sait lire. He looked at me as much as to say . . ., il me regarda avec l'air de vouloir dire. . . . (*d*) As much (as), so much (as), tant (que), autant (que). He does not like me as m. as her, il ne m'aime pas autant qu'il l'aime, elle. Oceans do not so m. divide the world as uni-e it, les océans ne divisent pas tant le monde qu'ils l'unissent. I haven't so much as my fare, je n'ai pas même, pas seulement, e prix de mon voyage. (*e*) So much, tant (de), autant (de). So m. money, tant d'argent. So m. exaggerated, tellement exagéré. So much the better, tant mieux. It will be so m. the less to pay, ce sera autant de moins à payer. So much so that . . ., à ce point, à tel point, que. . . . So m. for his friendship! et voilà ce qu'il appelle l'amitié! (*f*) So much per cent, tant pour cent. (*g*) Too much, trop (de). Ten pounds too much, dix livres de trop. Too much by half, trop de moitié. To make too much of sth., attacher trop d'importance à qch.

'much-admired, *a.* Admiré de tous **'much-loved,** *a.* Bien-aimé.

muchness ['mʌtʃnəs], *s.* *F:* It's much of a much-ness, c'est bonnet blanc et blanc bonnet; c'est chou vert et vert chou.

mucilage ['mju:sildʒ], *s.* Mucilage *m*.

mucilaginous [mju:si'ladʒinəs], *a.* Mucilagineux.

muck[1] [mʌk], *s.* **1.** (*a*) Fumi r *m*; (*from street*) crotte *f*, ordures *fpl*. To be all in a muck, être crotté jusqu'à l'échine. **2.** *F:* Choses dégoûtantes; saletés *fpl*. **'muck-heap,** *s.*

Tas *m* d'ordures; fumier *m*. **'muck-rake,** *s*. Racloir *m* à boue; râteau *m* à fumier.
muck². **I.** *v.tr.* (*a*) To muck (out) a ·stable, nettoyer une écurie. (*b*) Salir, crotter. (*c*) *P:* To muck (up) a job, gâcher, bousiller, une besogne. **2.** *v.i.* *P:* To muck about, flâner, flânocher.
muckiness ['mʌkinəs], *s*. Saleté *f*, malpropreté *f*.
muckle [mʌkl], *s*. *Scot:* = MICKLE.
mucky ['mʌki], *a*. Sale, crotté, souillé, ma.propre.
mucosity [mjuːˈkɔsiti], *s*. Mucosité *f*.
mucous ['mjuːkəs], *a*. Muqueux.
mucus ['mjuːkəs], *s*. Mucus *m*, mucosité *f*, glaire *f*.
mud [mʌd], *s*. (*a*) Boue *f*, bourbe *f*; *Lit:* fange *f*. River mud, limon *m*, vase *f*. (*Of ship*) To sink in the mud, s'envaser. *S.a.* STICK² II. 3. *F:* To drag s.o.'s name in the mud, traîner qn dans la boue. To fling, throw, mud at s.o., déblatérer contre qn. Mud hut, hutte *f* de terre; adobe *m*. Mud wall, mur en torchis, en pisé. (*b*) *Mch:* Boue; tartres boueux. **'mud-bank,** *s*. Banc *m* de sable, de vase. **'mud-barge,** *s*. Marie-salope *f*. **'mud-bath,** *s*. *Med:* Bain *m* de boues; illutation *f*. **'mud-cock,** *s*. *Mch:* Purgeur *m*; robinet *m* d'ébouage. **'mud-flat,** *s*. Plage *f* de vase. **'mud-pack,** *s*. *Toil:* Emplâtre *m* de boues. **'mud-slinging,** *s*. *F:* Calomnies *fpl*; médisance *f*.
muddied ['mʌdid], *a*. Crotté; couvert de boue.
muddiness ['mʌdinəs], *s*. **I.** État crotté; saleté *f*. **2.** Turbidité *f*, état *m* trouble (d'un liquide).
muddle¹ [mʌdl], *s*. Confusion *f*, emmêlement *m*, fouillis *m*. To be in a muddle, (i) (*of thgs*) être en confusion, en désordre, en pagaille; (ii) (*of pers.*) avoir les idées brouillées. To get into a muddle, s'embrouiller. **'muddle-headed,** *a*. A l'esprit confus; brouillon. *M.-h.* ideas, idées confuses, embrouillées.
muddle², *v.tr.* (*a*) Embrouiller, brouiller (qch.); emmêler (une histoire). To muddle things (up), embrouiller les choses; *F:* brouiller les fils. (*b*) Brouiller l'esprit à (qn); embrouiller (qn). **muddle through,** *v.i.* Se débrouiller; se tirer d'affaire tant bien que mal.
muddler ['mʌdlər], *s*. Brouillon, -onne; gâte-tout *m inv*.
muddy ['mʌdi], *a*. **I.** (*a*) Boueux, fangeux, bourbeux; (cours d'eau) vaseux, limoneux. *Nau:* Muddy bottom, fond *m* de vase. (*b*) (Vêtement) crotté, couvert de boue. **2.** (*a*) (Liquide) trouble. *M.* ink, encre pâteuse. (*b*) (Couleur) sale, enfumée. Muddy complexion, teint brouillé, terreux.
mudguard ['mʌdgɑːrd], *s*. *Veh:* Garde-boue *m inv*, garde-crotte *m inv*, parc-boue *m inv*.
mudlark ['mʌdlɑːrk], *s*. Gamin *m* des rues.
muezzin [muˈezin], *s*. Muezzin *m*.
muff¹ [mʌf], *s*. **I.** *Cost:* Manchon *m*. **2.** *Mec.E:* Manchon d'accouplement. **'muff-coupling,** *s*. Accouplement *m* à manchon.
muff², *s*. *F:* **I.** (*Pers.*) Empoté *m*; *P:* andouille *f*. **2.** *Sp:* Coup raté.
muff³, *v.tr.* *F:* Rater, bousiller, louper. *Sp:* To muff a shot, manquer, rater, un coup.
muffin ['mʌfin], *s*. Petit pain mollet (plat et rond; se mange à l'heure du thé, beurré à l'intérieur et rôti).
muffle¹ [mʌfl], *s*. Mufle *m* (de bœuf, de vache).
muffle², *s*. *Metall:* *Cer:* Moufle *m*. Muffle-furnace, (four *m* à) moufle.
muffle³, *v.tr.* **I.** Emmitoufler (*in*, de). To muffle oneself up, s'emmitoufler. **2.** (*a*) Envelopper (qch., pour amortir le son); assourdir (une

cloche). Muffled drums, tambours voilés. (*b*) *The* carpet muffles every footfall, le tapis éteint, étouffe, tout bruit de pas.
muffler ['mʌflər], *s*. **I.** Cache-nez *m inv*. **2.** (*a*) *Box:* Gant *m*. (*b*) *F:* Moufle *f*, mitaine *f*. **3.** *I.C.E:* Pot *m* d'échappement; silencieux *m*.
mufti ['mʌfti], *s*. *Mil:* *F:* Tenue bourgeoise; costume *m* de ville. In mufti, en civil, en bourgeois.
mug¹ [mʌg], *s*. (*For beer*) Chope *f*, pot *m*; (*for tea*) (grosse) tasse. Tin mug, timbale *f*, gobelet *m*.
mug², *s*. *P:* **I.** Jobard *m*, nigaud *m*. *He looks a bit of a mug,* il a l'air d'une poire. **2.** = MUFF² I.
mug³, *s*. *Sch:* *F:* Bûcheur, -euse; potasseur *m*.
mug⁴, *v.tr.* (mugged) *Sch:* *F:* To mug up a subject, bûcher, potasser, piocher, un sujet.
mug⁵, *s*. *P:* (*Face*) Binette *f*, fiole *f*. Ugly mug, vilaine binette; vilain museau.
mugger ['mʌgər], *s*. *Z:* Crocodile *m* des marais, de l'Inde.
muggy ['mʌgi], *a*. **I.** (Temps) mou, lourd; (temps) chaud et humide. **2.** (Salle) qui sent le renfermé.
mugwump ['mʌgwʌmp], *s*. *U.S:* *F:* Personnage important; gros bonnet.
mulatto [mjuˈlato], **I.** *a*. (*a*) Mulâtre. (*b*) (Teint) basané. **2.** *s*. Mulâtre, -esse.
mulberry ['mʌlbəri], *s*. *Bot:* **I.** Mûre *f*. **2.** Mûrier *m*.
mulch [mʌltʃ], *s*. *Hort:* Paillis *m*.
mulct¹ [mʌlkt], *s*. Amende *f*.
mulct², *v.tr.* **I.** *Jur:* Frapper (qn) d'une amende. *He was mulcted* (in) *five pounds,* on lui imposa une amende de cinq livres. **2.** Priver (*s.o. of sth.,* qn de qch.).
mule¹ [mjuːl], *s*. **I.** (He-)mule, mulet *m*. (She-) mule, mule *f*. On a mule, à dos de mulet. **2.** Métis, -isse; hybride *m*. Mule canary, arlequin *m*. **3.** *Tex:* Mule-jenny *f*; renvideur *m*. Self-acting *m.,* renvideur automatique. **'mule-driver,** *s*. Muletier *m*.
mule², *s*. (*Slipper*) Mule *f*.
muleteer [mjuːləˈtiːər], *s*. Muletier *m*.
mulish ['mjuːliʃ], *a*. **I.** De mulet. **2.** Entêté, têtu, comme un mulet. **-ly,** *adv.* Avec entêtement.
mull¹ [mʌl], *s*. Mousseline *f*. Bookb: Mousseline de relieur; organdi *m*.
mull², *v.tr.* Chauffer (du vin ou de la bière) avec des épices. Mulled wine, vin chaud épicé.
mull³, *s*. *Scot:* Cap *m*, promontoire *m*.
mullein ['mʌlen], *s*. *Bot:* Molène *f*.
muller ['mʌlər], *s*. Molette *f*, porphyre *m* (de broyeur de couleurs).
mullet ['mʌlet], *s*. *Ich:* **I.** Muge *m*. Grey mullet, mulet *m*. **2.** Red mullet, rouget *m*; surmulet *m*.
mulligatawny [mʌligaˈtɔːni], *s*. Potage *m* au curry.
mullion ['mʌljən], *s*. *Arch:* Meneau (vertical).
mullioned ['mʌljənd], *a*. (Fenêtre) à meneau(x).
multi-colour(ed) ['mʌltikʌlər(d)], *a*. Multicolore.
multi-engined [mʌltiˈendʒind], *a*. *Av:* Multi.moteur.
multifarious [mʌltiˈfɛəriəs], *a*. Varié, divers; multiple.
multiflorous [mʌltiˈflɔːrəs], *a*. *Bot:* Mu.tiflore.
multiform ['mʌltifɔːrm], *a*. Multiforme.
multimillionaire [mʌltimiljəˈnɛər], *a. & s.* Multimillionnaire (*mf*), milliardaire (*mf*).
multiparous [mʌlˈtipərəs], *a*. *Biol:* Multipare.
multiple ['mʌltipl]. **I.** *a*. Multiple. Multiple store, maison *f* à succursales ·(mu tiples).

2. s. Multiple m. Ar: Least common multiple, plus petit commun multiple.

multiplex ['mʌltipleks], a. (Télégraphe) multiplex.

multipliable ['mʌltip.aiəbl], a. Multipliable.

multiplicand [mʌltipli'kand], s. Mth: Mult.-plicande m.

multiplication [mʌltipli'keiʃ(ə)n], s. Multiplication f.

multiplicity mʌlti'p isiti], s. Multiplicité f.

multiplier ['mʌltiplaiər], s. Mth: El: Multiplicateur m.

multiply ['mʌltip.ai]. **I.** v.tr. Multip.ier. **2.** v.i. (Of species, etc.) Se multiplier.

multipolar [mʌlti'poulər], a. Multipolaire.

multitone ['mʌltitoun], attrib.a. Aut: (Trompe) à sons multiples.

multitubular [mʌlti'tju:bjulər], a. Mch: (Chaudière) multitubulaire.

multitude ['mʌltitju:d], s. **I.** Multitude f, multiplicité f (de raisons, etc.). **2.** Multitude, foule f.

multitudinous [mʌlti'tju:dinəs], a. **I.** Nombreux, innombrable. **2.** De toutes sortes; multiple.

multivalence [mʌlti'veiləns], s. Ch: Polyvalence f.

multivalent [mʌlti'veilənt], a. Ch: Polyva.en..

multi-wire ['mʌltiwaiər], attrib.a. W.Tel: (Antenne) multifilaire.

mum[1] [mʌm], int. & a. Chut! Mum's the word! motus! To keep mum (about sth.), ne pas souffler mot (de qch.).

mum[2], s. F: Maman f.

mumble [mʌmbl], v.tr. Marmotter, marmonner. Abs. Manger ses mots. He mumbled a few words, il prononça quelques mots entre ses dents.

mummer ['mʌmər], s. **I.** Acteur m de pantomimes. **2.** Pej: F: Cabotin, -ine.

mummification [mʌmifi'keiʃ(ə)n], s. Momification f.

mummify ['mʌmifai], v.tr. Momifier.

mummy[1] ['mʌmi], s. Momie f.

mummy[2], s. F: Maman f.

mumps [mʌmps], s.pl. Med: Oreillons mpl.

munch [mʌnʃ], v.tr. Mâcher, mâchonner.

mundane [mʌndein], a. Mondain. **I.** Terrestre, F: sublunaire. **2.** Mundane pleasures, plaisirs mondains.

municipal [mju'nisip(ə)l], a. Municipal, -aux. Municipal buildings, hôtel m de ville.

municipality [mju:nisi'paliti], s. Municipalité f.

munificence [mju'nifis(ə)ns], s. Munificence f.

munificent [mju'nifis(ə)nt], a. Munificent, généreux, libéral, -aux.

munition[1] [mju'niʃ(ə)n], s. Munition(s) of war, munitions f de guerre.

munition[2], v.tr. Approvisionner; ravitailler en munitions; armer (un vaisseau).

muraena [mju'ri:nə], s. Ich: Murène f.

mural ['mjuərəl], a. Mural, -aux.

murder[1] ['mə:rdər], s. Meurtre m. Premeditated murder, assassinat m. To commit (a) murder, to do murder, commettre un meurtre, un assassinat. Murder! au meurtre! à l'assassin! To cry murder, crier à l'assassin. Prov: Murder will out, tôt ou tard la vérité se fait jour.

murder[2], v.tr. **I.** Assassiner. **2.** F: Estropier (un vers); massacrer (une chanson); écorcher (le français).

murderer ['mə:rdərər], s.m. Meurtrier, assassin.

murderess ['mə:rdəres], s.f. Meurtrière, assassine.

murderous ['mə:rdərəs], a. Meurtrier, assassin. With m. intent, dans une intention homicide.

murk [mə:rk], s. Scot: (a) Obscurité f, ténèbres fpl. (b) Fumée f.

murkiness ['mə:rkinəs], s. Obscurité f; fuliginosité f.

murky ['mə:rki], a. Fuligineux, ténébreux; (ciel) brouillé. F: Murky past, passé obscur, ténébreux.

murmur[1] ['mə:rmər], s. **I.** (a) Murmure m; bruissement m. (b) Med: Cardiac murmur, murmure, bruit m, cardiaque. **2.** Murmure (d'approbation ou d'improbation). **3.** To converse in murmurs, s'entretenir à voix basse.

murmur[2], v.i. & tr. **I.** Murmurer, susurrer; (of brook) bruire. **2.** To murmur at sth., against s.o., murmurer contre qch., contre qn. **3.** He murmured a name, il prononça un nom à voix basse.

muscadine ['mʌskadain], a. & s. Vit: Muscadine (grape), (raisin m) muscat m.

muscat ['mʌskat], a. & s. Muscat (grape), (raisin m) muscat m. **Muscat (wine)**, (vin m) muscat.

muscatel [mʌska'tel], s. **I.** Vit: = MUSCAT. **2.** Muscatel raisins; muscatels, raisins secs de Malaga.

muscle [mʌsl], s. Muscle m. To have m., avoir du muscle. Man of m., homme musculeux, musclé.

muscular ['mʌskjulər], a. **I.** (Tissu, force) musculaire. **2.** (Homme) musculeux, musclé, bien découplé.

Muse[1] [mju:z], s.f. Muse. The Muses, les Muses, les arts libéraux.

muse[2], v.i. Méditer, rêver, rêvasser. To muse on, about, sth., méditer sur qch.; réfléchir à qch. "That's queer," he mused, "voilà qui est bien étrange," murmura-t-il d'un ton rêveur. **musing**[1], a. Rêveur, -euse. **-ly**, adv. D'un air songeur, rêveur. **musing**[2], s. Rêverie f (on, à); méditation f (on, sur). Idle musings, rêvasseries f.

museum [mju'zi:əm], s. Musée m (d'antiquités, d'arts et métiers). **Museum piece**, objet exposé ou digne d'être exposé.

mush [mʌʃ], s. **I.** F: (a) Bouillie f, panade f. (b) W.Tel: Cafouillage m; (bruits mpl de) friture f. **2.** P: Bêtises fpl, niaiseries fpl. **'mush-ice**, s. Glace à moitié prise.

mushroom[1] ['mʌʃrum], s. **I.** Champignon m (comestible, de couche). Cu: Mushroom ketchup, sauce f aux champignons. **2.** Darning mushroom, œuf m, boule f, à repriser. **'mushroom-'anchor**, s. Nau: Crapaud m de mouillage. **'mushroom-grower**, s. Champignonniste m f. **'mushroom-'insulator**, s. El.E: Isolateur m à cloche. **'mushroom-'valve**, s. I.C.E: (Soupape f en) champignon m.

mushroom[2], v.i. **I.** Faire la cueillette des champignons. **2.** (Of bullet, etc.) Faire champignon; s'aplatir.

mushy ['mʌʃi], a. **I.** (Of food, ground) Détrempé; (of medlar, etc.) blet, f. blette. **2.** F: Mushy sentimentality, sensiblerie f.

music ['mju:zik], s. Musique f. To set verses to music, mettre des vers en musique. A: The music of the spheres, l'harmonie f céleste. **'music-case**, s. Porte-musique m inv. **'music-hall**, s. Music-hall m. **'music-lover**, s. Musicomane m f; amateur, -trice, de musique. **'music-rest**, s. Tablette f de piano. **'music-roll**, s. **I.** (Carrier) Rouleau m à musique. **2.** Rouleau m, bande perforée (pour piano mécanique). **'music-stand**, s. Pupitre m à musique.

musical ['mju:zik(ə)l], *a.* **1.** Musical, -aux. Musical instrument, instrument *m* de musique. Musical box, boîte *f* à musique. **2.** (*Of pers.*) (*a*) (Bon) musicien, (bonne) musicienne. (*b*) Amateur, -trice, de bonne musique. **3.** (*Of sounds, verses*) Harmonieux, mélodieux, chantant.

musician [mju'ziʃ(ə)n], *s.* Musicien, -ienne.

musk [mʌsk], *s.* Musc *m.* To perfume with m., musquer. **'musk-deer,** *s.* Z: Musc *m.* **'musk-duck,** *s.* Canard turc, de Barbarie; canard musqué. **'musk-ox,** *s.* Z: Bœuf musqué. **'musk-rat,** *s.* Z: Rat musqué. **'musk-rose,** *s.* **1.** Rose musquée. **2.** (*Bush*) Rosier musqué.

musket ['mʌsket], *s. Sm.a:* Mousquet *m.*

musketeer [mʌske'ti:ər], *s. A:* Mousquetaire *m.*

musketry ['mʌsketri], *s. Mil:* Tir *m.* Musketry instruction, exercices *mpl* de tir; école *f* de tir.

musky ['mʌski], *a.* Musqué. Musky smell, odeur de musc.

muslin ['mʌzlin], *s.* **1.** Mousseline *f.* Cambric muslin, percale *f.* **2.** Muslin glass, (verre *m*) mousseline.

musquash ['mʌskwɔʃ], *s.* **1.** Z: Rat musqué. **2.** Com: Castor *m* du Canada.

mussel ['mʌs(ə)l], *s. Moll:* Cu: Moule *f.* **'mussel-bed, -farm,** *s.* Banc *m* de moules.

Mussulman, *pl.* **-mans** ['mʌslman, -manz], *a. & s.* Musulman, -ane.

must¹ [mʌst], *s. Vit:* Moût *m*; vin doux.

must², *s.* Moisi *m*; moisissure *f.*

must³, *modal aux. v.* (*pr.t. & p.t.* must *in all persons; no infin., pr.p., p.p., or future*) **1.** (*a*) (Obligation) You m. be ready at four o'clock, vous devrez être prêt, il faut, faudra, que vous soyez prêt, à quatre heures. You m. hurry up, il faut vous dépêcher. Plant that m. have continual attention, plante qui demande, qui réclame, des soins continuels. Motors m. slow down over the bridge, les automobiles sont tenues de ralentir en passant sur le pont. They 'must have new clothes, il leur faut absolument de nouveaux habits. He simply 'must come, il est de toute nécessité qu'il vienne. Do so if you must, faites-le s'il le faut. He is failing, I must say, il faut avouer qu'il baisse. (*b*) (Probability) There's a ring, it must be the doctor, on sonne, ce doit être le médecin. He m. have missed the train, il aura manqué le train. I must have made a mistake, je me serai trompé. You 'must know him, vous n'êtes pas sans le connaître. **2.** (Past Tense) (*a*) The matter was urgent, he 'must arrive in time, il y avait urgence, il fallait absolument qu'il arrivât à temps. I saw that I m. appear guilty, je me rendais compte que je ne pouvais que paraître coupable. I saw that he m. have suspected something, je vis bien qu'il avait dû se douter de quelque chose. Had he attempted the task he m. have failed, s'il eût tenté cette tâche il aurait forcément échoué. (*b*) As we were starting what m. he do but cut his finger! au moment de partir voilà qu'il se fait une entaille au doigt!

mustang ['mʌstaŋ], *s. Z:* Mustang *m.*

mustard ['mʌstərd], *s.* **1.** Cu: Med: (Flour of) mustard, (farine *f* de) moutarde *f.* **2.** Bot: Moutarde; sénevé *m.* Wild mustard, moutarde des champs; sanve *f.* Hort: Mustard and cress, moutarde blanche et cresson alénois. **'mustard-'bath,** *s. Med:* Bain sinapisé. **'mustard-'gas,** *s. Mil:* Ypérite *f*; gaz *m* moutarde. **'mustard-'leaf, -'plaster,** *s. Med:* Sinapisme *m*; papier rigollot. **'mustard-pot,** *s.* Moutardier *m.* **'mustard-'poultice,** *s.* Cataplasme sinapisé; cataplasme à la farine de

moutarde. **'mustard seed,** *s.* Graine *f* de moutarde. *B:* Grain of mustard seed, grain *m* de sénevé.

muster¹ ['mʌstər], *s.* **1.** (*a*) Rassemblement *m* (d'une tribu, etc.). (*b*) Mil: Revue *f.* To take a muster of the troops, passer les troupes en revue. *F:* To pass muster, passer; être passable; être à la hauteur. (*c*) Nau: Appel *m.* **2.** Assemblée *f*, réunion *f.* To turn out in full muster, se présenter au grand complet. **'muster-roll,** *s.* Feuille *f* d'appel. Mil: Contrôles *mpl.* Nau: Rôle *m* de l'équipage. To be on the m.-r., figurer sur les cadres.

muster², *I.* *v.tr.* (*a*) Rassembler (ses partisans, etc.). Society that musters a hundred (members), association qui compte cent membres. (*b*) Mil: Passer (des troupes) en revue. (*c*) Nau: Faire l'appel (des hommes). (*d*) To muster (up) one's strength, rassembler toutes ses forces. **2.** *v.i.* Se réunir, se rassembler.

mustiness ['mʌstinəs], *s.* Goût *m* ou odeur *f* de moisi; relent *m.*

musty ['mʌsti], *a.* **1.** (Goût, odeur) de moisi. To smell musty, sentir le moisi; (of room) sentir le renfermé; (of food) sentir l'évent. **2.** *F:* Suranné. M. old laws, vieilles lois désuètes.

mutability [mjutə'biliti], *s.* Mutabilité *f.*

mutable ['mjutəbl], *a.* **1.** Muable, variable. **2.** Ling: Sujet à la mutation.

mutation [mju'teiʃ(ə)n], *s.* Mutation *f.*

mute¹ [mju:t]. **I.** *a.* **1.** Muet, -ette. Jur: To stand mute (of malice), refuser de plaider ou de répondre. **2.** Ling: (*a*) H mute, h muet. (*b*) Mute consonant, consonne sourde. **II.** mute, *s.* **1.** (Pers.) (*a*) Muet, -ette. (*b*) Employé *m* des pompes funèbres; croque-mort *m.* (*c*) Th: Personnage muet. **2.** Ling: Consonne sourde. **3.** Mus: Sourdine *f.* With the mute on, en sourdine.

mute², *v.tr.* **1.** Amortir, étouffer, assourdir (un son). **2.** Mus: Mettre la sourdine à (un violon, etc.). **muted,** *a.* Mus: (Violon) en sourdine; (corde) sourde.

muteness ['mju:tnəs], *s.* Mutisme *m.*

mutilate ['mjutileit], *v.tr.* Mutiler, estropier (qn); mutiler (une statue); tronquer (un passage).

mutilation [mjuti'leiʃ(ə)n], *s.* Mutilation *f.*

mutineer [mjuti'ni:ər], *s. Mil:* Nau: Révolté *m*, mutiné *m*, mutin *m.*

mutinous ['mjutinəs], *a.* Rebelle, mutiné, mutin; (équipage) en révolte.

mutiny¹ ['mjutini], *s. Mil:* Nau: Révolte *f*, mutinerie *f.* Hist: The Indian Mutiny, la Révolte des cipayes.

mutiny², *v.i.* Se révolter, se mutiner (against, contre).

mutt [mʌt], *s. U.S:* P: = MUTTON-HEAD.

mutter ['mʌtər], *v.tr. & i.* Marmonner, marmotter. To mutter an oath, grommeler, maronner, un juron. To mutter against s.o., murmurer contre qn. **muttering,** *s.* Marmottage *m*; murmures *mpl.*

mutton ['mʌt(ə)n], *s. Cu:* Mouton *m.* Leg of mutton, gigot *m.* **'mutton-'chop,** *s. Cu:* Côtelette *f* de mouton. **'mutton-head,** *s. F:* Nigaud *m*, benêt *m.*

mutual ['mju:tjuəl], *a.* **1.** Mutuel, réciproque. Transaction on mutual terms, marché stipulant un échange de services. Governess engaged on m. terms, institutrice engagée au pair. Mutual benefit society, société *f* de secours mutuels. **2.** *F:* Mutual friend, ami commun. **-ally,** *adv.* Mutuellement, réciproquement.

mutuality [mju:tju'aliti], *s.* Mutualité *f.*

muzzle¹ [mʌzl], *s.* **1.** Museau *m* (d'un animal). **2.** Bouche *f*, gueule *f* (d'une arme à feu). **3.** Muselière *f* (pour chiens); bâillon *m* (pour chevaux). **To put a muzzle on ...** = MUZZLE². **'muzzle-'loading,** *a. Artil:* Se chargeant par la bouche. **'muzzle-ve'locity,** *s. Ball:* Vitesse *f* à la bouche.

muzzle², *v.tr.* Museler (un chien); *F:* museler, bâillonner (la presse).

muzzy ['mʌzi], *a.* (*a*) (*Of pers.*) Brouillé dans ses idées; au cerveau fumeux. (*b*) (*Of ideas*) Confus, vague; (*of outline*) flou, estompé. (*c*) (*Of weather*) Brumeux, embrumé.

my [mai], *poss.a.* Mon; *f.* ma, *pl.* mes. *One of my friends,* un de mes amis; *Lit:* un mien ami. *I have broken my arm,* je me suis cassé le bras. (*Emphatic*) '*My idea would be to ...,* mon idée à moi serait de.... *P:* **My!** sapristi! par exemple!

myalgia [mai'aldʒia], *s. Med:* Myodynie *f.*

mycology [mai'kɔlodʒi], *s. Bot:* Mycologie *f.*

myelo-meningitis ['maiəlomenin'dʒaitis], *s. Med:* Myélo-méningite *f.*

myology [mai'ɔlodʒi], *s. Anat:* Myologie *f.*

myopia [mai'oupia], *s. Med:* Myopie *f.*

myopic [mai'ɔpik], *a.* Myope.

myriad ['miriəd]. **1.** *s.* Myriade *f.* **2.** *a. Poet:* Innombrable.

myriapod ['miriapɔd], *a.&s. Z:* Myriapode (*m*); *F:* mille-pattes *m inv.*

myriapoda [miri'apɔda], *s.pl. Z:* Myriapodes *m.*

Myrmidon ['mɔːrmidən]. **1.** *Pr.n. Gr.Myth:* Myrmidon *m.* **2.** *s. F:* The myrmidons of the law, les sbires *m* de la police; les suppôts *m* de la loi.

myrrh [mɔːr], *s.* Myrrhe *f.*

myrtaceae [mɔːr'teisiː], *s.pl. Bot:* Myrtacées *f.*

myrtle [mɔːrtl], *s. Bot:* **1.** Myrte *m.* **2.** Bog myrtle, myrte des marais; trèfle *m* d'eau.

myself [mai'self], *pers.pron. See* SELF 4.

mysterious [mis'tiːriəs], *a.* **1.** Mystérieux. *A m. business,* une ténébreuse affaire. **2.** (*Of pers.*) Mystérieux. *There was m. talk of ...,* on parlait sourdement de.... **-ly,** *adv.* Mystérieuse-ment.

mystery ['mistəri], *s.* **1.** Mystère *m.* **To make a mystery of sth.,** faire mystère de qch. *It is a m. to me,* c'est lettre close pour moi. *The mysteries of science,* les arcanes *m* de la science. **2.** *A.Th:* Mystery(-play), mystère.

mystic ['mistik]. **1.** *a.* (*a*) (*Of rites, arts*) Ésotérique, mystique. (*b*) (*Of power*) Occulte; (*of formula*) magique. **2.** *a. & s. Theol:* Mystique (*mf*).

mystical ['mistik(ə)l], *a.* Mystique.

mysticism ['mistisizm], *s.* Mysticisme *m.*

mystification [mistifi'keiʃ(ə)n], *s.* **1.** Mystification *f*; *F:* fumisterie *f.* **2.** Embrouillement *m*, désorientation *f* (de l'esprit de qn).

mystify ['mistifai], *v.tr.* **1.** Mystifier (qn). *Mystified by ...,* intrigué par.... **2.** Embrouiller, désorienter, dérouter.

myth [miθ], *s.* Mythe *m.*

mythical ['miθik(ə)l], *a.* Mythique.

mythological [miθo'lɔdʒik(ə)l], *a.* Mythologique.

mythology [mi'θɔlodʒi], *s.* Mythologie *f.*

myxoedema [miksiː'diːma], *s.* Myxœdème *m.*

myxomycetes [miksomai'siːtiːz], *s.pl. Fung:* Myxomycètes *m.*

N

N, n [en], *s.* (*a*) (La lettre) N, n *m.* (*b*) *Mth:* To the nᵗʰ (power), à la nième puissance. (*c*) *Typ:* N(-quadrat), demi-cadratin *m.*

nab [nab], *v.tr.* (nabbed) *P:* **1.** (*a*) Saisir, arrêter, *P:* pincer, cueillir (qn). *The police nabbed the lot,* la police les a ratissés. *To get nabbed,* se faire pincer. (*b*) Prendre (qn) sur le fait, la main dans le sac. **2.** Escamoter, chiper, chaparder (qch.).

nabob ['neibɔb], *s.* Nabab *m.*

nacarat ['nakarat], *a. & s.* Nacarat (*m*) *inv.*

nacelle [na'sel], *s. Aer:* Nacelle *f.*

nacreous ['neikriəs], *a.* Nacré.

nadir ['neidər], *s. Astr:* Nadir *m.*

naevus, *pl.* **-i** ['niːvəs, -ai], *s.* Nævus *m*, *pl.* nævi.

nag¹ [nag], *s. F:* Petit cheval (de selle); bidet *m.*

nag², *v.tr. & i.* (nagged) Chamailler, quereller (qn); gronder (qn) sans cesse. *To be always nagging (at) s.o.,* être toujours sur le dos de qn.

nagging, *a.* **1.** (*Of pers.*) Querelleur, -euse, grondeur, -euse, hargneux, -euse. **2.** (*Of pain*) Agaçant, énervant.

naiad ['naiad], *s. Myth:* Naïade *f*; nymphe *f* des eaux.

nail¹ [neil], *s.* **1.** Ongle *m* (de doigt, d'orteil). **2.** Clou *m*, *pl.* clous. French nail, wire nail, clou de Paris; pointe *f* de Paris. Brass-headed nail, clou doré. *F:* To hit the (right) nail on the head, frapper juste, tomber juste; mettre le doigt

dessus. **3.** *F:* To pay on the nail, payer argent comptant; payer rubis sur l'ongle. **'nail-brush,** *s. Toil:* Brosse *f* à ongles. **'nail-claw, -drawer, -wrench,** *s. Tls:* Arrache-clou(s) *m inv*; tire-clou(s) *m inv*; pied-de-biche *m.* **'nail-file,** *s. Toil:* Lime *f* à ongles. **'nail-hole,** *s.* **1.** (*a*) (*In horseshoe, etc.*) Étampure *f.* (*b*) Clouure *f*; trou fait par un clou. **2.** (*On penknife*) Onglet *m.* **'nail-scissors,** *s.pl. Toil:* Ciseaux *m* à ongles; ongliers *m.* **'nail-set,** *s. Tls:* Chasse-clou *m.*

nail², *v.tr.* **1.** Clouer. *F:* To nail one's eyes on sth.,* clouer, fixer, les yeux sur qch. **To nail a lie to the counter, to the barn door,** démontrer la fausseté d'une affirmation. *S.a.* COLOUR¹ 4. **2.** Clouter (des chaussures, une porte). **3.** *P:* Attraper, saisir (qn). **nail down,** *v.tr.* **1.** Clouer (le couvercle d'une boîte). **2.** *F:* To nail s.o. down to his promise,** obliger qn à tenir sa promesse. **nail up,** *v.tr.* (*a*) Clouer (une caisse); condamner (une porte). (*b*) Palisser (un arbre fruitier). **nailed,** *a.* **1.** (*a*) Cloué. (*b*) Clouté; garni de clous. Heavily m. boot, porte garnie de gros clous. **2.** Long-nailed, aux ongles longs.

nainsook ['neinsuk], *s. Tex:* Nansouk *m.*

naïve [na'iːv], **naive** [neiv], *a.* Naïf, *f.* naïve; ingénu. **-ly,** *adv.* Naïvement, ingénument.

naivety [na'iːvti, 'neivti], *s.* Naïveté *f.*

naked ['neikid], *a.* Nu. **1.** (*a*) (*Of pers.*) Sans vêtements; *P:* à poil. **Stark naked, mother naked,** tout nu; *F:* nu comme un ver, comme la main. (*b*) (Dos) découvert, nu. *The toga left the right arm n.,* la toge laissait à découvert, à nu, le bras droit. (*c*) (Mur) nu, dégarni, sans ornement; (pays) dénudé, *F:* pelé; (arbre) dépouillé de ses feuilles. (*d*) *To ride on a n. horse,* monter un cheval à nu, à cru, à poil. **2.** (*a*) **Naked sword,** épée nue, sans fourreau. *To fight with* **naked fists,** se battre sans gants. **Naked light,** feu nu; *Min:* lampe *f* à feu libre. (*b*) **Visible to the naked eye,** visible à l'œil nu, à la vue simple. (*c*) **The naked truth,** la vérité toute nue, sans fard. *N. facts,* faits bruts.

nakedness ['neikidnǝs], *s.* Nudité *f.*

namby-pamby ['nambi'pambi]. **1.** *a.* (*Of style*) Affété, mignard, fade; (*of pers.*) maniéré, affecté; mignard, minaudier; gnan-gnan *inv.* **2.** *s. F:* (*Of pers.*) Poule mouillée.

name[1] [neim], *s.* **1.** Nom *m.* (*a*) Full name, nom et prénoms. **Christian name,** prénom *m*; nom de baptême. **My name is . . .,** je m'appelle. . . . Name of a ship, devise *f* d'un navire. **Name of a firm,** nom social; raison sociale. **A man, X by name,** un homme du nom de X; *Jur:* le dénommé X. **To go by the name of . . .,** être connu sous le nom de. . . . **To know s.o.** (only) **by name,** (ne) connaître qn (que) de nom. *F:* **To mention no names,** ne nommer personne. (*To caller*) **What name shall I say?** qui dois-je annoncer? **To send in one's name,** (i) se faire inscrire (dans un concours); (ii) se faire annoncer **To put one's name down (for sth.),** (i) poser sa candidature; (ii) s'inscrire (pour qch.). **List of names,** liste nominative. *F:* (*Of police*) **To take s.o.'s name and address,** dresser une contravention à qn. **In the name of . . .,** au nom de . . ., de la part de. . . . **In the n. of the king,** de par le roi. **A king in name only,** un roi de nom seulement. (*b*) Terme *m.* **Endearing names,** termes d'amitié. *S.a.* CALL[2] I. 3. **2.** Réputation *f,* renommée *f.* *To get a bad n.,* se faire un mauvais renom. *S.a.* DOG[1] I. **He has a name for honesty,** il passe pour honnête. **To make a name for oneself, to make one's name,** se faire un grand nom; se faire une réputation; s'illustrer. **'name-plate,** *s.* Plaque *f* (pour porte, etc.); écusson *m,* médaillon *m* (avec le nom).

name[2], *v.tr.* **1.** Nommer; dénommer (un nouveau produit). *He was named Peter,* (i) on lui a donné le nom de Pierre; (ii) il s'appelait, se nommait, Pierre. *A person named Jones,* un nommé Jones. **To name s.o. after s.o.,** donner à qn le nom de qn. **2. To name s.o. to an office,** nommer qn à un poste. **3.** Désigner (qn, qch.) par son nom. *N. the kings of England,* donnez les noms des rois d'Angleterre. **Afore-named,** précité, -ée. **The last-named,** celui-ci, celle-ci. **4.** (*a*) Citer (un exemple). (*b*) Fixer (le jour, l'heure).

nameless ['neimlǝs], *a.* **1.** Sans nom; inconnu. **2.** Anonyme. **A lady who shall be nameless,** une dame dont je tairai le nom. **3.** (*a*) (*Of dread, etc.*) Indicible, inexprimable. (*b*) (*Vice,* etc.) innommable.

namely ['neimli], *adv.* (A) savoir; c'est-à-dire.

namesake ['neimseik], *s.* Homonyme *m* (de qn). *He is my n.,* il s'appelle comme moi.

nankeen [nan'kiːn,], *s.* **1.** *Tex:* Nankin *m.* **2.** *pl.* Nankeens, pantalon *m* de nankin.

Nanny ['nani], *s.f.* (*Child's speech*) Nounou. **'nanny-goat,** *s.f. F:* Chèvre (femel e); bique.

nap[1] [nap], *s.* Petit somme. **Afternoon nap,**

sieste *f*; *F:* méridienne *f.* **To take, have, a nap,** faire un petit somme; (*after midday meal*) faire la sieste.

nap[2], *v.i.* (**napping**) Sommeiller. *F:* **To catch s.o. napping,** (i) surprendre la vigilance de qn; prendre qn au dépourvu; (ii) surprendre qn en faute.

nap[3], *s.* (*Of velvet, cloth, felt*) Poil *m*; (*of cloth*) duvet *m.* **Cloth with raised nap,** étoffe molletonnée. **Short-nap velvet,** velours ras. **Against the nap,** à contre-poil, à rebrousse-poil. *His overcoat had lost its nap,* son pardessus était râpé, élimé.

nap[4], *v.tr. Tex:* Garnir, gratter, lainer, rebrousser (le drap, etc.); molletonner (la laine, le coton).

nap[5], *s.* **1.** *Cards:* Napoléon *m*; nap *m.* *F:* **To go nap on a horse** jouer son va-tout sur un cheval. **To deal oneself a nap hand,** se donner un jeu parfait. . **2.** *Turf:* Tuyau certain.

nape [neip], *s.* The nape of the neck, la nuque.

napery ['neipǝri], *s. A. & Scot:* Linge *m* de table.

naphtha ['nafθa], *s.* (Huile *f* de) naphte *m.*

naphthalene ['nafθaliːn], *s.* Naphtaline *f.*

napierian [nei'piːǝriǝn], *a. Mth:* (Logarithme) népérien.

napkin ['napkin], *s.* **1.** (*a*) (Table-)napkin, serviette *f* (de table). (*b*) (*To protect table-cloth*) Napperon *m.* (*c*) *Ecc:* (For consecrated bread) Tavaiole *f.* **2.** (*For infant*) Couche *f,* pointe *f.*

Napoleon [na'poulian]. *Pr.n.m.* Napoléon.

Napoleonic [napouli'ɔnik], *a.* Napoléonien.

nappy ['napi], *a.* (Drap) poilu, pelucheux.

narcissism ['naːrsisizm], *s. Psy:* Narcissisme *m.*

Narcissus [naːr'sisǝs]. **1.** *Pr.n.m. Myth:* Narcisse. **2.** *s.* (*pl.* **narcissi** [naːr'sisai]) *Bot:* Narcisse *m,* genette *f.*

narcosis [naːr'kousis], *s. Med:* Narcose *f.*

narcotic [naːr'kɔtik], *a. & s.* Narcotique (*m*), stupéfiant (*m*); *s.* opiat *m.*

narcotize ['naːrkotaiz], *v.tr.* Donner un narcotique à (qn); narcotiser.

nard [naːrd], *s.* Nard *m.*

narghile ['naːrgile], *s.* Narghileh *m,* narguilé *m.*

narrate [na'reit], *v.tr.* Narrer, raconter, relater (qch.); faire le narré de (qch.).

narration [na'reiʃ(ǝ)n], *s.* **1.** Narration *f* (d'une histoire, etc.). **2.** = NARRATIVE[1].

narrative[1] ['narativ], *s.* Récit *m,* narration *f.*

narrative[2], *a.* Narratif.

narrator [na'reitǝr], *s.* (*a*) Narrateur, -trice. (*b*) (*In oratorio*) Récitant *m.*

narrow[1] ['narou, 'naro]. **1.** *a.* (*a*) (Chemin) étroit; (vallon) serré, resserré, encaissé; (passage) étranglé; (jupon) étriqué. **To grow narrow,** se rétrécir. **Narrow-gauge railway,** chemin de fer à voie étroite. *Nau:* **The narrow seas,** la Manche et la mer d'Irlande. (*b*) De faibles dimensions, de peu d'étendue; (esprit) étroit, borné. *N. limits,* limites restreintes. **In the narrowest sense,** dans le sens le plus étroit. (*c*) (*Examen*) minutieux, méticuleux. (*d*) **A narrow majority,** une faible majorité; une majorité bien juste. *S.a.* ESCAPE[1] I, SHAVE[1] 2. **2.** *s.pl.* **Narrows,** passe étroite (entre deux terres); goulet *m* (d'un port); étranglement *m* (de rivière). **-ly,** *adv.* **1.** (*a*) (Interpréter) strictement, étroitement, rigoureusement. (*b*) (Examiner) minutieusement, de près. **2.** Tout juste. **He narrowly missed being run over,** il faillit être écrasé. **narrow-'minded,** *a.* Borné; à l'esprit étroit. *N.-m. ideas,* idées étroites, mesquines. **narrow-'mindedness,** *s.* Étroitesse *f,* petitesse *f,* d'esprit.

narrow[2]. **1.** *v.tr.* (*a*) Resserrer, (r)étrécir,

Narrowed eyelids, paupières mi-closes. (*b*) Restreindre, limiter, borner ; rétrécir (un espace, les idées). **2.** *v.i.* Devenir plus étroit ; se resserrer, se rétrécir ; (*of channel*) s'étrangler.

arrowness ['narɔnəs], *s.* **1.** (*a*) Étroitesse *f* ; manque *m* de largeur. (*b*) Petitesse *f*, exiguïté *f* (d'un espace) ; limitation *f*, circonscription *f* (de la vie, de l'intelligence). **Narrowness of mind,** étroitesse d'esprit. **2.** Minutie *f* (d'un examen).

arwhal ['nɑːrwəl], *s. Z :* Narval *m*, -als.

asal ['neiz(ə)l]. **1.** *a.* Nasal, -als, -aux. **Nasal accent,** accent nasillard. **2.** *s.* (*a*) *Archeol :* Nasal *m* (de casque). (*b*) *Ling :* Nasale *f*.

asality [nei'zaliti], *s.* Nasalité *f*.

asalize ['neizəlaiz], *v.tr.* Nasaliser (une syllabe).

ascent ['nasənt], *a.* Naissant ; *Ch :* à l'état naissant.

asturtium [nas'təːr∫əm], *s. Hort :* Capucine *f*.

asty ['nɑːsti], *a.* **1.** (*a*) Désagréable, dégoûtant. *To smell n.,* sentir mauvais. (*b*) **Nasty weather,** sale, vilain, temps. *N. corner,* tournant dangereux. *N. accident,* accident sérieux. *N. wound,* vilaine blessure. **To receive a nasty blow,** recevoir un mauvais coup. *F : That's a n. one!* quelle tuile ! **2.** (*Of pers.*) Méchant, désagréable ; *P :* rosse. **To turn nasty,** prendre un air méchant. **To be nasty to s.o.,** faire des méchancetés à qn. **Nasty trick,** vilain tour ; rosserie *f.* **3.** *Esp. U.S:* (*a*) Sale, malpropre. (*b*) (*Of book, etc.*) Ordurier, malpropre.

atality [na'taliti], *s.* Natalité *f.*

atation [na'tei∫(ə)n], *s.* Natation *f.*

atatory ['neitatəri], *a. Nat.Hist :* Natatoire.

ation ['nei∫(ə)n], *s.* **1.** Nation *f. The nations of Europe,* les nations de l'Europe ; les peuples européens. *People of all nations,* des gens de toutes les nationalités. **2.** *The whole n. rose in arms,* tout le pays se souleva. **The voice of the nation,** la voix du peuple.

ational ['na∫ən(ə)l]. **1.** *a.* National, -aux ; de l'État. *Adm :* **National status,** nationalité *f. Nau :* National flag, pavillon *m* de nation. **2.** *s.pl.* **Nationals,** nationaux *m,* ressortissants *m* (d'un pays). **-ally,** *adv.* Nationalement ; du point de vue national.

ationalism ['na∫ənəlizm], *s.* Nationalisme *m.*

ationalist ['na∫ənəlist], *s.* Nationaliste *mf.*

ationality [na∫ə'naliti], *s.* Nationalité *f.*

ationalize ['na∫ənəlaiz], *v.tr.* **1.** Nationaliser. **2.** Naturaliser (un étranger).

ative ['neitiv]. **1.** *s.* **1.** (*a*) Natif, -ive (d'un pays, d'une ville) ; naturel, -elle (du Congo, etc.). *Native of Australia,* Australien de naissance. *He speaks English like a native,* il parle l'anglais comme un Anglais. (*b*) (*Of non-European country*) Indigène *mf.* **2.** (*Of plant, animal*) Indigène. *The elephant is a n. of Asia,* l'éléphant est originaire de l'Asie. **II. native,** *a.* **1.** (*Of qualities, etc.*) Naturel, inhérent, inné. **Native to s.o.,** inhérent à qn. *To behave with n. ease,* se conduire avec naturel. **2.** (*a*) (*Of place*) Natal, -als, -aux ; de naissance. **Native language,** langue maternelle. **Native land,** terre natale ; patrie *f,* pays *m.* (*b*) (Costume, huîtres) du pays. **3.** (*Of mineral*) A l'état natif. **4.** (*Of plant, pers.*) Indigène, originaire (*to,* de). **A native rising,** une insurrection des indigènes.

ativity [na'tiviti], *s.* **1.** *Ecc :* Nativité *f.* **2.** *Astrol :* Nativité, horoscope *m.* **To cast s.o.'s nativity,** tirer l'horoscope de qn. **na'tivity play,** *s. Th :* Mystère *m* de la Nativité.

atty ['nati], *a.* **1.** (*Of pers., dress*) Pimpant ;

coquet, -ette. **2.** (*a*) (*Of pers.*) To be natty with one's hands, être adroit de ses mains. (*b*) Habilement exécuté. **A natty little gadget,** un petit dispositif b en trouvé. **-ily,** *adv.* **1.** Coquettement. **2.** Avec adresse.

natural ['natjurəl]. **I.** *a.* Naturel. **1.** **Natural law,** loi de la nature. **Natural size,** grandeur naturelle ; de grandeur normale. **In the natural state,** à l'état de nature. *Tex :* Natural wool, laine beige. **2.** (*a*) Natif, inhérent, inné. *N. goodness,* bonté foncière. *It comes natural to him,* c'est un don chez lui. *It comes n. to him to . . .,* il a une facilité innée pour. . . . *Ph :* Natural oscillation, oscillation propre. (*b*) It is natural that . . ., il est (bien) naturel que + sub. **As is natural,** comme de raison. **3.** **Natural child,** enfant naturel, illégitime. **-ally,** *adv.* **1.** (*a*) *N. lazy,* paresseux de sa nature, par tempérament. *N. curly hair,* cheveux qui frisent naturellement. (*b*) (Parler) naturellement, sans affectation. *He writes n.,* son style coule de source. (*c*) To die naturally, mourir de sa belle mort. **2.** *He n. does not wish . . .,* naturellement, comme de raison, il ne veut pas. . . . *Did you answer him?—* Naturally, lui avez-vous répondu?—Naturellement. **II. natural,** *s.* **1.** *A :* Idiot, -ote (de naissance). **The village natural,** l'innocent *m* du village. **2.** *Mus :* (*a*) Note naturelle. (*b*) (*Sign*) Bécarre *m.*

naturalism ['natjurəlizm], *s.* Naturalisme *m.*

naturalist ['natjurəlist], *s.* Naturaliste *mf.*

naturalistic [natjurə'listik], *a.* **1.** Naturaliste. **2.** *Art : Lit :* Naturiste.

naturalization [natjurəlai'zei∫(ə)n], *s.* Naturalisation *f* (d'un étranger).

naturalize ['natjurəlaiz], *v.tr.* (*a*) Naturaliser (un étranger, un mot) (*to,* dans, en). *To become a naturalized Frenchman,* se faire naturaliser Français. (*b*) Acclimater (une plante, un animal)

naturalness ['natjurəlnəs], *s.* **1.** Caractère naturel (d'une action, etc.). **2.** Naturel *m* ; absence *f* d'affectation.

nature ['neitjər], *s.* Nature *f.* **1.** (*a*) (*Of thg*) Essence *f,* caractère *m.* **The nature of fish is to swim,** le propre des poissons est de nager. **It is in the nature of things that . . .,** il est dans l'ordre des choses que. . . . (*b*) (*Of pers.*) Naturel *m,* caractère, tempérament *m.* **It is not in his nature to . . .,** il n'est pas de sa nature de. . . . **By nature,** par tempérament ; naturellement. **It comes to him by nature,** il tient cela de nature. **2.** Espèce *f,* sorte *f,* genre *m.* **Something in the nature of a . . .,** une espèce, une sorte, de. . . . **Facts of a nature to astonish us,** faits de nature à nous étonner. **3.** (La) nature. **The laws of nature,** les lois de la nature. **Nature study,** histoire naturelle. **To draw from nature,** dessiner d'après nature. **Return to nature,** retour à la nature.

-natured ['neitjərd], *a.* Simple-natured, au cœur simple. *S.a.* GOOD-NATURED, ILL-NATURED.

naught [nɔːt], *s.* **1.** Rien *m,* néant *m.* **To come to naught,** échouer ; n'aboutir à rien. **To bring an attempt to naught,** faire échouer, faire avorter, une tentative. **To set the law at naught,** ne tenir aucun compte de la loi ; passer outre à la loi. **2.** *Ar :* Zéro *m.*

naughty ['nɔːti], *a.* **1.** (*Of child, F : of pers.*) Vilain, méchant. *You n. child!* petit méchant ! oh, le laid ! **2.** *F :* (Conte) risqué, grivois, polisson. **-ily,** *adv. To behave n.,* ne pas être sage ; être méchant.

nausea ['nɔːsiə], *s.* **1.** (*a*) Nausée *f* ; soulèvement *m* de cœur. *To be overcome with n.,* avoir mal au

cœur ; avoir des nausées. (b) Mal m de mer.
2. F : Dégoût m, nausée, écœurement m.
nauseate ['nɔ:sieit]. **1.** v.tr. (a) Prendre (qch.)
en dégoût. (b) Écœurer, dégoûter (qn) ; donner
des nausées à (qn). **2.** v.i. To n. at sth., avoir la
nausée de qch. **nauseating,** a. Nauséabond,
dégoûtant, écœurant. It is n., cela soulève le
cœur.
nauseous ['nɔ:siəs, - jəs], a. = NAUSEATING.
nautch-girl ['nɔ:tʃgə:rl], s.f. (India) Bayadère.
nautical ['nɔ:tik(ə)l], a. Nautique, marin. N.
chart, carte marine. N. term, terme de navigation,
de marine. **Nautical almanac,** almanach m
nautique ; éphémérides fpl.
nautilus, pl. **-i** ['nɔ:tiləs, -ai], s. Moll : Nautile m.
Paper nautilus, argonaute m.
naval ['neiv(ə)l], a. Naval, -als ; de marine (de
guerre). N. forces, marine f (de guerre, militaire) ;
armée navale. N. engagements, combats en mer.
Naval base, port m de guerre. **Naval officer,**
officier de marine, de la flotte. **Nava' college,**
école navale.
nave[1] [neiv], s. Moyeu m (de roue).
nave[2], s. Nef f, vaisseau m (d'église).
navel ['neiv(ə)l], s. Anat : Nombril m, ombilic m.
'navel-string, s. Cordon ombilical. **'navel-
wort,** s. Bot : Ombilic m ; nombril m de Vénus.
navigability [naviɡə'biliti], s. Navigabilité f.
navigable ['naviɡəbl], a. (Fleuve, vaisseau)
navigable ; (ballon) dirigeable. **Ship in navigable
condition,** vaisseau en bon état de navigabilité.
navigate ['naviɡeit]. **1.** v.i. Naviguer. **2.** v.tr.
(a) Parcourir (les mers) ; naviguer sur (les mers) ;
voyager dans (les airs). (b) Gouverner, diriger
(un navire). Aer : Piloter (un dirigeable).
navigation [navi'ɡeiʃ(ə)n], s. Navigation f ;
conduite f (d'un navire, d'un ballon). **The
Navigation Laws,** le Code maritime. S.a. LIGHT[1] 2.
navigator ['naviɡeitər], s. Navigateur m (d'un
navire, d'un dirigeable, etc.).
navvy ['navi], s. **1.** (Pers.) Terrassier m.
2. Steam-navvy, excavateur m à vapeur piocheuse f.
navvying ['naviiŋ], . Travaux mpl de terrassier,
de terrassement.
navy ['neivi], s. Marine f de guerre, marine
militaire. His son is in the n., son fils est dans la
flotte. **The Royal Navy,** la marine de l'État.
'navy 'blue, s. Bleu m marine inv ; bleu foncé
inv.
nay [nei]. **1.** adv. (a) A. & Lit : Non. (b) Lit :
Pour mieux dire. I am astounded, nay, disgusted,
j'en suis ahuri, et même révolté, voire révolté.
2. s. Non m. He will not take nay, il n'accepte
pas de refus. **I cannot say him nay,** je ne peux
pas le lui refuser.
Nazarene [nazə'ri:n], a. & s. B.Hist : Nazaréen,
-enne.
naze [neiz], s. Promontoire m, cap m, pointe f.
neap[1] [ni:p], a. & s. Neap tides, F : neaps,
mortes-eaux ; marées de morte eau, de quadrature.
neap[2]. **1.** v.i. (Of tides) Décroître. **2.** v.tr. (Of
ship) To be neaped, être retenu par manque
d'eau ; être amorti.
Neapolitan [niə'pɔlitən], a. & s. Napolitain,
-aine.
near[1] ['ni:ər]. I. adv. **1.** (a) Près, proche. To come
near, draw near, s'approcher (to, de). He drew
nearer, il s'approcha davantage. **Near at hand,**
à proximité, tout près, à portée de la main.
Keep n. to me, restez près de moi. (b) They are
near of kin, ce sont de proches parents. Those
near and dear to him, ceux qui lui touchent de

près. **2.** As near as I can remember, autant que
je puisse m'en souvenir ; autant qu'il m'en
souvienne. I came n. to crying, je fus sur le poin
de pleurer. **Near upon thirty men,** près de trent
hommes. II. **near,** prep. **1.** Près de, auprès de
The houses n. the mountains, les maisons dans l
voisinage des montagnes. Bring your chair near(er
the fire, (r)approchez votre chaise du feu. **2.** N
death, près de mourir ; sur le point de mourir
To be near the end, toucher à la fin. He cam
near being run over, il s'en est fallu de peu qu'il
n'ait été écrasé. **3. To be, to come, near s.o.,** s
rapprocher de qn (par la ressemblance) ; res
sembler à qn. III. **near,** a. **1.** (Of relative
Proche, (of friend) intime, cher. **Our near
relations,** nos proches (parents). **2. The near
side,** le côté gauche ; (of horse) côté (du) montoir
The near horse, le cheval de gauche. N. rein
rêne du dedans. **3.** The nearest inn, l'auberg
la plus voisine, la plus proche. **The hour is near
l'heure est proche. Mth : To the nearest plac
(of decimals),** au plus près. **To the nearest milli
gramme,** à un milligramme près. **4. To go by the
nearest road,** prendre par le plus court. **5. Nea
translation,** traduction qui serre le texte de près
Near resemblance, grande ressemblance. N. guess
conjecture à peu près juste. **It was a near thing,
nous l'avons échappé belle ; P :** il était moins
cinq. **6.** (Of pers.) Chiche, parcimonieux. **-ly,
adv. 1.** (De) près. We are n. related, nous
sommes proches parents. Nat.Hist : **Nearly
allied species,** espèces voisines. **2.** (a) Presque
à peu près, près de. It is n. midnight, il est
bientôt minuit. N. the whole of our resources, la
presque totalité de nos ressources. It is the same
thing or n. so, c'est la même chose ou peu s'en
faut. Is he dead?—Pretty nearly, est-il mort?—I
ne s'en faut guère. Very nearly, peu s'en faut.
I n. caught them, j'ai été près de les pincer. I n.
fell, je faillis tomber, j'ai manqué de tomber.
(b) She is not nearly so old as you, il s'en faut de
beaucoup qu'elle soit aussi âgée que vous ; elle
n'est pas si âgée que vous à beaucoup près.
'near 'by, adv. & prep. Tout près (de), tout
proche (de). **near-'sighted,** a. Myope.
near[2], v.tr. (S')approcher de (qn, qch.). The
road is nearing completion, la route est prè
d'être achevée. We are nearing the goal, nous
touchons au but.
nearness ['ni:ərnəs], s. **1.** (a) (Of time, place)
Proximité f. (b) (Of translation) Fidélité f,
exactitude f. **2.** Parcimonie f.
neat[1] [ni:t], s. **1.** Occ. Bête bovine. Neat's-foot
oil, huile f de pied de bœuf. **2.** Coll. Gros bétail.
neat[2], a. **1.** (Of spirits) Pur ; sans eau. To drink
one's whisky n., boire son whisky sec. **2.** (a) Simple et de bon goût ; (of room, drawer) bien rangé,
en ordre ; (of garden) bien tenu, coquet. N
handwriting, écriture nette. **Neat ankles,** fine
chevilles. His n. attire, sa mise soignée. **As neat
as a new pin,** tiré à quatre épingles. (b) (Of style)
Élégant, choisi ; (of phrase) bien tourné, adroit.
3. (Of pers.) Ordonné ; qui a de l'ordre. **-ly,** adv.
1. (Ranger) avec ordre. N. dressed, habillé avec
goût, avec soin. **2.** Adroitement. N. turned
compliment, compliment bien tourné.
neatness ['ni:tnəs], s. **1.** Simplicité f, bon goût
(dans la mise) ; apparence soignée (d'un jardin) ;
netteté f (d'écriture) ; bon ordre (d'un tiroir,
etc.) ; finesse f (de la cheville) ; tournure adroite
(d'une phrase). **2.** (Of pers.) (a) Ordre m.
(b) Adresse f, dextérité f.
Nebuchadnezzar [nebjukad'nezər]. Pr.n.m.
B.Hist : Nabuchodonosor.

nebula, *pl.* **-ae** ['nebjulə, -iː], *s. Astr :* Nébuleuse *f.*

nebular ['nebjulər], *a.* Nébulaire.

nebulosity [nebju'lɔsiti], *s.* Nébulosité *f.*

nebulous ['nebjuləs], *a.* Nébuleux. *N. character*, personnage flou.

necessary ['nesəsəri]. **I.** *a.* (*a*) Nécessaire, indispensable (*to, for*, à). It is necessary to (do sth.), il est nécessaire de (faire qch.); il faut (faire qch.). *It is n. for him to return*, il faut qu'il revienne. *I shall do everything n. to . . .*, je ferai tout ce qu'il faudra pour. . . . To make all necessary arrangements, prendre toutes dispositions utiles. To make it necessary for s.o. to do sth., mettre qn dans la nécessité de faire qch. *If necessary*, s'il le faut; s'il y a lieu; au besoin; en cas de besoin. *Not to do more than is absolutely n.*, ne faire que le strict nécessaire, l'indispensable. (*b*) (Résultat) inévitable, inéluctable. **2.** *s.* (*a*) *Usu. pl.* The necessaries of life, les nécessités *f* de la vie; la vie matérielle. *Bare necessaries*, le strict nécessaire. (*b*) *F:* To do the necessary, faire le nécessaire; *esp.* payer la note. **-ily**, *adv.* Nécessairement, de (toute) nécessité. *What he says is not n. what he thinks*, ce qu'il dit n'est pas forcément ce qu'il pense.

necessitate [ne'ses.teit], *v.tr.* Nécessiter (qch.); rendre (qch.) nécessaire. *Process that necessitates very high pressures*, procédé qui comporte des pressions très élevées.

necessitous [ne'sesitəs], *a.* Nécessiteux, besogneux. *To be in n. circumstances*, être dans le besoin.

necessity [ne'sesiti], *s.* **I.** Nécessité *f.* (*a*) Obligation *f*, contrainte *f. Dire n. compels me to . . .*, la dure nécessité me force à. . . . By, out of, necessity, par nécessité. Of necessity, de (toute) nécessité. To be under the necessity of doing sth., être dans la nécessité, se trouver dans l'obligation, de (faire qch.). Case of absolute necessity, cas de force majeure. *Prov:* Necessity is the mother of invention, nécessité est mère d'invention. (*b*) Besoin *m. The n. for sth.*, le besoin de qch. In case of necessity, au besoin, en cas de besoin. *There is no n. for you to come*, vous n'avez pas besoin de venir. **2.** = NECESSARY : (*a*). *A car is a n. nowadays*, de nos jours une auto est indispensable. **3.** Nécessité, indigence *f.* To be in necessity, être dans le besoin.

neck [nek], *s.* **I.** (*a* Cou *m. To have a stiff n.*, avoir un, le, torticolis. *F:* To be up to one's neck in work, avoir du travail par-dessus la tête. To fling one's arms round s.o.'s neck, sauter, se jeter, au cou de qn. To break one's neck, se casser le cou. *F:* To break the neck of a task, faire le plus gros d'un ouvrage. *P:* To get it in the neck, écoper. *Rac:* To win by a neck, gagner par une encolure. *To finish* neck and neck, arriver à égalité. *F:* Neck and crop, tout entier; à corps perdu. It is neck or nothing, il faut jouer le tout pour le tout. (*b*) *Cu:* Collet *m* (de mouton); collier *m* (de bœuf). (*c*) Encolure *f* (de robe). High neck, col montant. Low neck, décolleté *m.* **2.** (*a*) Goulot *m* (de bouteille); col (d'un vase); goulet *m* (d'un port); rétrécissement *m*, étranglement *m* (de tuyau); manchon *m* (de ballon). (*b*) Langue *f* (de terre); collet (de vis, etc.); manche *m*, collet (de violon). 'neckband, *s.* Tour-du-cou *m* (de chemise). Neckband 15½", 40 cm. d'encolure. 'neck-line, *s. Dressm:* Encolure *f*, échancrure *f*; (*low*) décolletage *m*, décolleté *m.* 'neck-tie, *s. Cost:*

'neck-wear, *s. Com:* Cols *mpl*, cravates *fpl*, foulards *mpl*, etc.

neckcloth ['nekklɔθ], *s. A:* Foulard *m*, cravate *f*, tour *m* de cou.

-necked [nekt], *a.* **I.** (*Of pers.*) Bull-necked, au cou de taureau. Short-necked, à col court. **2.** (*Of dress*) Square-necked, V-necked, à décolletage carré, en pointe.

neckerchief ['nekərtʃif], *s. A:* Foulard *m*; mouchoir *m* de cou; (*man's*) cache-col *m*; (*woman's*) fichu *m.*

necklace ['nekles], *s.* Collier *m* (de diamants, etc.). Chain necklace, chaîne *f* de cou; sautoir *m.*

necklet ['neklet], *s.* Collier *m* (de perles, etc.). Fur necklet, tour *m* de cou (en fourrure).

necrological [nekro'lɔdʒik(ə)l], *a.* Nécrologique.

necrology [ne'krɔlodʒi], *s.* Nécrologe *m* (d'une église, etc.).

necromancer ['nekromansər], *s.* Nécromancien, -ienne.

necromancy ['nekromansi], *s.* Nécromancie *f.*

necropolis [ne'krɔpolis], *s.* Nécropole *f.*

necrosis [ne'krousis], *s.* Nécrose *f*; gangrène *f* des os.

necrotize ['nekrotaːiz], *v.i.* Se nécroser.

nectar ['nektər], *s.* Nectar *m.*

nectarine ['nektəriːn, -iːn], *s.* Brugnon *m.*

nectary ['nektəri], *s. Bot:* Nectaire *m*

need[1] [niːd], *s.* **I.** Besoin *m.* (*a*) If need(s) be, in case of need, en cas de besoin, au besoin; si besoin est. There is no need to . . ., il n'est pas nécessaire, il n'est pas besoin, de . . . What need is there *to send for him?* à quoi bon le faire venir? *No n. to say that . . .*, inutile de dire, point n'est besoin de dire, que. . . . To have need (to) do sth., avoir besoin de, devoir, faire qch. *You had no n. to speak*, vous n'aviez que faire de parler. (*b*) To have need, stand in need, be in need, of sth., avoir besoin de qch.; manquer de qch. *Premises badly in n. of repairs*, local qui a grand besoin de réparations. *I have no n. of your assistance*, je n'ai que faire de votre aide. **2.** (*a*) Adversité *f*; embarras *m.* In times of need, aux moments difficiles. (*b*) Besoin, indigence *f*, dénûment *m. My n. is great*, je suis dans un grand dénûment. To be in need, être dans le besoin. **3.** *pl. My needs are few*, peu me suffit. To supply the needs of s.o., pourvoir aux besoins de qn.

need[2]. **I.** *v.tr.* (*3rd pers. sg. pr. ind.* needs; *p.t. & p.p.* needed) (*a*) (*Of pers.*) Avoir besoin de (qn, qch.); (*of thg*) réclamer, exiger, demander (qch.). *This will n. some explanation*, ceci demande à être expliqué. *These facts n. no comment*, ces faits ne se passent de commentaire. That needs no saying, cela va sans dire. To need a lot of asking, se faire prier. *A much needed lesson*, une leçon dont on avait grand besoin. (*b*) To need to do sth., être obligé, avoir besoin, de faire qch. *They n. to be told everything*, il faut qu'on leur dise tout. *My readers will not n. to be reminded that . . .*, point n'est besoin de rappeler à mes lecteurs que. . . . *You only needed to ask*, vous n'aviez qu'à demander. **2.** *Modal aux.* (*3rd pers. sg. pr. ind.* need; *p.t.* need) Need he go? a-t-il besoin, est-il obligé, d'y aller? He needn't go, need he? il n'est pas tenu d'y aller, n'est-ce pas? *You n. not wait*, inutile d'attendre. *I n. hardly tell you . . .*, point n'est besoin de vous dire. . . . *Why n. he bother us?* qu'a-t-il besoin de nous déranger? **3.** *Impers.* It needed the horrors of war to open our eyes, il a fallu les horreurs de la guerre pour nous ouvrir les yeux.

needful ['niːdful], *a.* Nécessaire (*to, for*, à, pour).

As much as is n., autant qu'il est besoin, autant qu'il en faut. *s. F:* **To do the needful,** faire le nécessaire. **To supply the needful,** fournir l'argent nécessaire; *P:* casquer.

needle ['ni:dl], *s.* Aiguille *f.* **1.** Aiguille à coudre, à tricoter, etc. *F:* **To look for a needle in a haystack,** chercher une aiguille dans une botte de foin. **2.** *Tchn:* (*a*) Aiguille (de phonographe). *I.C.E:* Pointeau *m* (de carburateur, de soupape). *Sm.a:* **Firing needle,** percuteur *m.* *Art:* **Engraving needle,** pointe *f* pour tailledouce. (*b*) Aiguille (de boussole, etc.); aiguille, languette *f* (de balance). **3.** **Cleopatra's Needle,** l'Obélisque *m* de Cléopâtre. **'needle-case,** *s.* Étui *m* à aiguilles; sachet *m* d'aiguilles. **'needle-gun,** *s.* *Sm.a:* Fusil *m* à aiguille. **'needle-lace,** *s.* Dentelle *f* à l'aiguille. **'needle-valve,** *s.* *I.C.E:* Soupape *f* à pointeau.

needleful ['ni:dlful], *s.* Aiguillée *f* (de fil).

needless ['ni:dləs], *a.* Inutile, peu nécessaire, superflu. (**It is**) **needless to say that . . .,** (il est) inutile de dire que . . ., point n'est besoin de dire que. . . . *She is n. to say very pleased,* il va sans dire qu'elle est très contente.

needlewoman, *pl.* **-women** ['ni:dlwumən, -wimen], *s.f.* **1.** *She is a good n.,* elle travaille adroitement à l'aiguille. **2.** Couturière à la journée; (*in institution*) lingère.

needlework ['ni:dlwə:rk], *s.* Travaux *mpl* à l'aiguille; ouvrages *mpl* de dames; (*as school subject*) couture *f.* *Bring your n.,* apportez votre ouvrage.

needs [ni:dz], *adv.* (*Used only with 'must'*) I must **needs obey,** I needs must obey, (i) force m'est d'obéir; (ii) force me fut d'obéir. *There is no train, so we must n. walk,* il n'y a pas de train, il (nous) faudra donc faire le trajet à pied. If needs must, s'il le faut. Needs must when the devil drives, nécessité n'a pas de loi.

needy ['ni:di], *a.* Nécessiteux, besogneux. *To be in n. circumstances,* être dans l'indigence.

ne'er [neər], *adv.* *Poet:* = NEVER. **'ne'er-do-well,** *a. & s.* Propre à rien.

nefarious [ne'fεəriəs], *a.* Infâme, scélérat.

negation [ne'geiʃ(ə)n], *s.* Négation *f.*

negative¹ ['negətiv]. I. *a.* Négatif. *Nau:* **Negative signal,** triangle *m* non. *El:* **Negative electrode,** cathode *f.* *Phot:* **Negative proof,** épreuve négative. **-ly,** *adv.* Négativement. II. **negative,** *s.* **1.** Négative *f.* *Gram:* Négation *f.* **To return a negative,** répondre par la négative. *The answer is in the n.,* la réponse est négative, est non. **2.** (*a*) *Phot:* Négatif *m,* cliché *m.* (*b*) (*Of gramophone record*) Poinçon *m.* (*c*) *El:* Plaque négative (de pile).

negative², *v.tr.* **1.** S'opposer à, rejeter (un projet); repousser (un amendement). **2.** Réfuter (une hypothèse); contredire, nier (un rapport); annuler (un signal). **3.** Neutraliser (un effet).

neglect¹ [ne'glekt], *s.* **1.** (*a*) Manque *m* d'égards (*of,* envers, pour). (*b*) Manque de soin(s). *To die in total n.,* mourir complètement abandonné. (*c*) Mauvais entretien (d'une machine). **2.** Négligence *f,* inattention *f.* *From neglect,* par négligence. *N. of one's duties,* inattention à ses devoirs.

neglect², *v.tr.* **1.** (*a*) Manquer d'égards envers (qn). (*b*) Manquer de soins pour (qn); ne prendre aucun soin de (ses enfants). **2.** Négliger, oublier (ses devoirs, un avis). *To n. an opportunity,* laisser échapper une occasion. **To neglect to do sth.,** négliger, omettre, de faire qch.. **neglected,** *a.* (*Of appearance, etc.*) Négligé.

N. garden, jardin mal tenu, à l'abandon. *N. wife,* épouse délaissée.

neglectful [ne'glektful], *a.* Négligent. **To be neglectful of sth.,** négliger qch. *N. of his interests,* insoucieux de ses intérêts.

negligence ['neglidʒəns], *s.* **1.** Négligence *f,* incurie *f;* manque *m* de soins. **Through negligence,** par négligence. *S.a.* CONTRIBUTORY. **2.** Nonchalance *f,* insouciance *f.*

negligent ['neglidʒənt], *a.* **1.** Négligent. **To be negligent of sth.,** négliger qch. **2.** (Air, ton) nonchalant, insouciant. *N. attire,* tenue négligée. **-ly,** *adv.* Négligemment; avec négligence.

negligible ['neglidʒibl], *a.* Négligeable.

negotiable [ne'gouʃiəbl], *a.* **1.** *Fin:* (Effet, titre) négociable. **Not negotiable,** non-négociable; (*of military pension, etc.*) incessible. *S.a.* INSTRUMENT 3. **2.** *F:* (Barrière) franchissable; (chemin) praticable.

negotiate [ne'gouʃieit]. **1.** *v.tr.* (*a*) Négocier (une affaire, un emprunt). (*b*) *To n. a bill,* négocier un effet. *To n a treaty,* (i) négocier, (ii) conclure, un traité. (*c*) *F:* Franchir (une haie); surmonter (une difficulté). *Aut: To n. a curve,* prendre un virage. **2.** *v.i.* **To be negotiating with s.o. for . . .,** être en traité, en marché, avec qn pour. . . . *To n. for peace,* entreprendre des pourparlers de paix.

negotiation [negouʃi'eiʃ(ə)n], *s.* **1.** Négociat on *f* (d'un traité, d'un emprunt). **Under negotiation,** en négociation. *By n.,* par voie de négociations. *Price a matter for n.,* prix à débattre. **To be in negotiation with s.o.,** être en pourparler(s) avec qn. **To enter into, upon, negotiations with s.o.,** engager, entamer, des négociations avec qn. **2.** *F:* Franchissement *m* (d'un obstacle); prise *f* (d'un virage).

negotiator [ne'gouʃieitər], *s.* Négociateur, -trice.

negress ['ni:gres], *s.f.* Négresse.

negro, *pl.* **-oes** ['ni:gro, -ouz], *a. & s.* Nègre (*m*). **The negro race,** la race nègre.

negroid ['ni:grɔid], *a.* *Ethn:* Négroïde.

neigh¹ [nei], *s.* Hennissement *m.*

neigh², *v.i.* Hennir. **neighing,** *s.* Hennissement *m.*

neighbour ['neibər], *s.* **1.** Voisin, -ine. *My right-, left-hand n.,* mon voisin de droite, de gauche. **2.** *B:* Prochain *m.* *One's duty towards one's n.,* le devoir envers son prochain, envers autrui.

neighbourhood ['neibərhud], *s.* **1.** *Good n.,* bons rapports entre voisins; rapports de bon voisinage. **2.** Voisinage *m,* proximité *f* (*of,* de). **To live in the neighbourhood of . . .,** demeurer à proximité de. . . . *F:* **Something in the neighbourhood of ten pounds,** une somme dans les dix livres. **3.** (*a*) Alentours *mpl,* environs *mpl* (d'un lieu). *In the n. of the town,* aux alentours de la ville. (*b*) *The fruit grown in that n.,* les fruits cultivés dans cette région, dans ces parages. *All the youth of the n.,* toute la jeunesse du voisinage.

neighbouring ['neibəriŋ], *a.* Avoisinant, voisin; proche.

neighbourly ['neibərli], *a.* (*Of pers.*) Obligeant; amical, -aux; (visites) de bon voisinage. *To act in a n. fashion,* agir en bon voisin

neither ['naiðər, 'ni:ðər]. **1.** *adv. & conj.* (*a*) Neither . . . nor . . ., ni . . . ni . . . . *He will n. eat nor drink,* il ne veut ni manger ni boire. (*b*) Non plus. *If you do not go,* neither shall I, si vous n'y allez pas, je n'irai pas non plus. (*c*) = NOR 2. **2.** *a. & pron.* Ni l'un(e) ni l'autre; aucun(e). **Neither (of them) knows,** ils ne le savent ni l'un ni l'autre ; ni l'un ni l'autre ne le sait. *On n. side*, n d'un côté ni de l'autre.

nematode ['nematoud], *s. Ann:* Nématode *m*.

nem. con. ['nem'kɔn]. *Lt.adv.phr.* (*nemine contradicente*) Unanimement ; à l'unanimité ; (voter une loi) sans opposition.

nenuphar ['nenjufɑːr], *s. Bot:* Nénuphar *m*.

neo-classicism (niːoˈklasisizm], *s.* Néo-classicisme *m*.

neo-Greek [niːoˈɡriːk], *a.* Néo-grec, *f* -grecqu..

neo-Latin [niːoˈlatin], *a.* Néo-latin.

neolithic [niːoˈliθik], *a.* Néolithique.

neologism [niˈɔlɔdʒizm], *s.* Néologisme *m*.

neon ['niːɔro], *s. Ch:* Néon *m. El.E:* **Neon tube,** glow-lamp, tube, lampe, au néon.

neophyte ['niːofait], *s.* Néophyte *mf* ; *F:* débutant, -ante.

nephew ['nevju], *s.m.* Neveu.

nephrite ['nefrait], *s. Miner:* Néphrite *f*.

nephritic [neˈfritik], *a. Med:* Néphrétique.

nephritis [neˈfraitis], *s. Med:* Néphrite *f*.

Nereid ['niːəriid], *s. Myth:* Néréide *f*.

Nero ['niːəro]. *Pr.n.m. Rom.Hist:* Néron.

nervate ['nɔːrvet], *a. Bot:* Nervé.

nerve[1] [nɔːrv], *s.* **1.** (*a*) *Anat:* Nerf *m. F:* **Fit of nerves,** attaque de nervosité. **To be in a state of nerves,** être énervé ; avoir ses nerfs. **To get on s.o.'s nerves,** porter, donner, sur les nerfs à qn. (*b*) *F:* Courage *m*, assurance *f*. **To lose one's nerve,** perdre son sang-froid ; avoir le trac. (*c*) *F:* Audace *f*, aplomb *m*. **To have the nerve to . . .,** avoir l'aplomb de. . . *P:* **You 'have got a nerve!** tu en as un toupet ! **2.** *Bot: Arch:* Nervure *f*. **3.** (*a*) *A:* Tendon *m. F:* **To strain every nerve to do sth.,** déployer tous ses efforts pour faire qch. (*b*) Force *f* (musculaire). **Man of nerve,** homme vigoureux. **'nerve-cell,** *s. Anat:* Cellule nerveuse. **'nerve-racking,** *a.* Énervant, horripilant.

nerve[2], *v.tr.* Fortifier ; donner du nerf, de la force, à (son bras) ; donner du courage à (qn). **To nerve oneself to do sth.,** s'armer de courage, faire appel à tout son courage, pour faire qch. ; s'enhardir (à parler).

nerveless ['nɔːrvləs], *a.* **1.** Inerte, sans force ; (style) sans vigueur, mou. **2.** (*a*) *Anat: Z:* Sans nerfs. (*b*) *Bot:* Sans nervures.

nervelessness ['nɔːrvləsnəs], *s.* Inertie *f* ; manque *m* de force, d'énergie.

nerviness ['nɔːrvinəs], *s. F:* Nervosité *f* ; énervement *m*.

nervous ['nɔːrvəs], *a.* **1.** (*Of pers.*) (*a*) Excitable, irritable. (*b*) Inquiet, -ète ; ému. (*c*) Timide, peureux. **To feel n. in s.o.'s presence,** se sentir intimidé en présence de qn. **To get nervous,** s'intimider. *I was n. on his account,* j'avais peur pour lui. **To be nervous of doing sth.,** éprouver une certaine timidité à faire qch. **2.** *A:* (Style) nerveux, énergique. **3.** *Anat:* **The nervous system,** le système nerveux. *S.a.* BREAK-DOWN 2, WRECK[1] I. **-ly,** *adv.* **1.** Timidement. **2.** Craintivement.

nervousness ['nɔːrvəsnəs], *s.* (*a*) Nervosité *f*, état nerveux, état d'agitation. (*b*) Timidité *f*.

nervy ['nɔːrvi], *a. F:* (*a*) Énervé, irritable. **To feel nervy,** être dans un état d'agacement, d'énervement ; avoir les nerfs agacés, en pelote. *She is n.,* elle est très nerveuse. (*b*) (Mouvement) nerveux, sec, saccadé.

nescience ['neʃjəns, 'nesiəns], *s.* Nescience *f* ; ignorance *f* (*of*, de).

ness [nes], *s.* Promontoire *m*, cap *m*.

nest[1] [nest], *s.* **1.** (*a*) Nid *m*. (*b*) Repaire *m*, nid (de brigands). **2.** Nichée *f* (d'oiseaux, etc.).

3. Série *f*, jeu *m* (d'objets). **Nest of tables,** table *f* gigogne. **Nest of drawers,** chiffonnier *m* ; (*for office*) classeur *m* (à tiroirs). **Nest of shelves,** casier *m. Mil: N. of machine-guns,** nid de mitrailleuses. **'nest-box,** *s.* Pondoir *m*. **'nest-egg,** *s.* **1.** Nichet *m* ; œuf *m* en faïence. **2.** *F:* Argent mis de côté ; pécule *m. To have a nice little n.-e.,* avoir un bas de laine bien garni.

nest[2]. **1.** *v.i.* (*a*) (*Of bird, etc.*) (Se) nicher ; faire son nid. (*b*) = BIRD'S-NEST[2]. **2.** *v.tr.* Emboîter (des tubes, etc.) les uns dans les autres. **Nested boxes,** caisses emboîtées. **nesting**[1], *a.* (Oiseau) nicheur. **nesting**[2], *s.* **1.** Nesting time, époque *f* de la couvaison. **2.** Emboîtage *m*.

nestful ['nestful], *s.* Nichée *f*.

nestle [nesl], *v.i.* Se nicher. **To nestle (down) in an armchair,** se blottir, se pelotonner, dans un fauteuil. **To nestle close (up) to s.o.,** se serrer contre qn. **Village nestling in a valley, in a wood,** village blotti, tapi, niché dans une vallée, niché dans un bois.

nestling ['nes(t)liŋ], *s.* Oisillon *m* ; petit oiseau (encore au nid).

net[1] [net], *s.* **1.** (*a*) Filet *m.* **Cast(ing) net,** épervier *m.* **Shrimp(ing) net,** filet à crevettes ; bichette *f.* **Butterfly net,** filet à papillons. (*b*) *Ven:* (Game) **net,** rets *m* ; panneau *m* ; filet. *F:* **To walk, fall, into the net,** tomber, donner, dans le panneau. **2.** (*a*) **Hair net,** filet, résille *f*, réseau *m* (pour cheveux). **Marketing net, net-bag,** filet à provisions. (*b*) *Veh:* **Parcel net,** filet à bagages ; filet porte-bagages. (*c*) *Ten:* **To go up to the net,** monter au filet. **Net play,** jeu au filet. **3.** *Tex:* Tulle *m.* **Spotted n.,** tulle à pois. **Foundation net,** mousseline forte. **'net-fishing,** *s.* Pêche *f* au filet. **'net-layer,** *s. Navy:* Mouilleur *m* de filets.

net[2], *v.* (netted) **I.** *v.tr.* (*a*) Prendre (des poissons, etc.) au filet. (*b*) Tendre des filets dans (une rivière). (*c*) Couvrir de filets (un groseillier). (*d*) *Sp:* Envoyer (le ballon, la balle) dans le filet. **2.** *v.i.* Faire du filet. **netted,** *a.* **1.** Couvert d'un filet, d'un réseau. **2.** (*Of veins, paths*) En lacis, en réseau. **3.** (Oiseau, etc.) pris au filet. **netting,** *s.* **1.** Fabrication *f* du filet. **2.** (*a*) Pêche *f* au filet. (*b*) Pose *f* de filets, de rets ; chasse *f* au filet. **3.** (*a*) Tulle *m*. (*b*) *Nau:* Nettings, bastingages *mpl*.

net[3], *a.* (*Of weight, price*) Net, *f*. nette. **'Terms strictly net cash,'** "sans déduction" ; "payable au comptant."

net[4], *v.tr.* (netted) **I.** (*Of pers.*) Toucher net (tant de bénéfices). **2.** (*Of enterprise*) Rapporter net (une certaine somme).

nether ['neðər], *a.* Inférieur, bas. **The nether lip,** la lèvre inférieure. **Nether garments,** pantalon *m.* **The nether regions,** l'enfer *m*.

Netherlander ['neðərlandər], *s.* Néerlandais, -aise.

Netherlands (the) [ðəˈneðərləndz]. *Pr.n.pl.* Les Pays-Bas *m*.

nethermost ['neðərmoust], *a.* Le plus bas ; le plus profond. *In the n. parts of the earth,* dans les profondeurs de la terre.

nett [net], *a.* = NET[3].

nettle[1] [netl], *s.* **1.** Ortie *f.* **Stinging nettle,** ortie brûlante. *S.a.* GRASP[2] I. **Dead nettle,** ortie blanche ; lamier (blanc). **'nettle-rash,** *Med:* Urticaire *f.* **'nettle-tree,** *s.* Micocoulier *m*.

nettle[2], *v.tr.* **1.** (*a*) Fustiger (qn) avec des orties. (*b*) **To nettle oneself,** se piquer à des orties. **2.** *F:* (*a*) Piquer, irriter (qn). *Greatly nettled* *by, at, this remark,* piqué au vif par cette parole. (*b*) Piquer (qn) d'honneur.

network ['netwə:rk], *s.* **1.** Ouvrag *m* en filet. **Wire network,** treillis *m* métallique. **2.** Réseau *m* (de veines, de voies ferrées); lacis *m* (de nerfs, de tranchées); système *m* (de routes).

neuralgia [njuə'raldʒ a], *s.* Névralgie *f.* **Facial neuralgia,** tic douloureux.

neuralgic [njuə'raldʒik], *a.* Névra gique.

neurasthenia [njuərəs'θi:n a], *s.* Neurasthenie *f.*

neurasthenic [njuərəs'θenik], *a. & s.* Neurasthénique (*mf*).

neuritis [nju'raitis], *s.* Névrite *f.*

neurologist [njuə'rɔlodʒist], *s.* Neurologue *m.*

neuropath ['njuəropaθ], *s.* Névropathe *mf.*

neurosis, *pl.* **-es** [nju'rousis, -i:z], *s. Med:* Névrose *f.*

neurotic [nju'rɔtik]. **1.** ☐. Névrosé, neurotique. **2.** *s.* Névrosé, -ée.

neuter ['nju:tər]. **1.** *a.* (*a*) *Gram:* Neutre. *This word is n.,* ce mot est du neutre. (*b*) *Biol:* Neutre, asexué. *N. bee,* abeille neutre. **2.** *s. Gram:* (Genre) neutre *m.* **In the neuter,** au neutre.

neutral ['nju:trəl]. **1.** *a.* (*a*) *Pol: etc:* Neutre. *To remain n.,* garder la neutralité. (*b*) Neutre; moyen, indéterminé; *Ch:* (sel) neutre, indifférent. **Neutral tint,** teinte *f* neutre; grisaille *f.* (*c*) *Aut:* **Neutral position of change-gear,** point mort. **2.** *s. Pol:* Neutre *m. Rights of neutrals,* droits des neutres.

neutrality [nju'traliti], *s. Pol: Ch:* Neutralité *f.*

neutralization [nju:trəlai'zeiʃ(ə)n], *s.* Neutralisation *f.*

neutralize ['nju:trəlaiz], *v.tr.* Neutraliser. (*Of forces*) **To n. one another,** se détruire.

neutron ['nju:trɔn], *s. El:* Neutron *m.*

never ['nevər], *adv.* (*a*) (Ne . . .) jamais. *I n. go there,* je n'y vais jamais. **Never again, never more,** jamais plus; plus jamais (. . . ne). *He n. came back,* il ne revint plus. *The thing had never before been seen,* jusqu'alors la chose ne s'était jamais vue. *I have never yet seen* . . ., je n'ai encore jamais vu. . . . **Never, never,** *shall I forget it,* jamais, au grand jamais, je ne l'oublierai. **Never in (all) my life,** jamais de la vie. *F:* **To-morrow come never,** (dans) la semaine des quatre jeudis; à la Saint-Glinglin. (*b*) (*Emphatic negative*) *I n. expected him to come,* je ne m'attendais aucunement à ce qu'il vînt. *He n. said a word to him about it,* il ne lui en a pas dit le moindre mot. **Never a one,** pas un seul. *F:* **You (surely) never left him all alone!** ne me dites pas que vous l'avez laissé tout seul! **Well I never!** par exemple! c'est formidable! (*c*) *Lit:* **Be he never so brave,** quelque courageux qu'il soit; si courageux soit-il. **never-'ceasing,** *a.* Incessant, continuel. *N.-c. complaints,* plaintes sempiternelles. **never-'ending,** *a.* Perpétuel, éternel; qui n'en finit plus. **never-'failing,** *a.* **1.** (Remède) infaillible. **2.** (Source) intarissable.

nevermore [nevər'mɔ:ər], *adv.* (Ne . . .) plus jamais; (ne . . .) jamais plus.

nevertheless [nevərðə'les], *adv.* Néanmoins, quand même, toutefois, pourtant. *It n. makes me anxious,* cela ne laisse pas (que) de m'inquiéter; toujours est-il que cela m'inquiète.

new [nju:], *a.* **1.** (*a*) Nouveau, -elle. *New fashion,* nouvelle mode; mode nouvelle. *Ever new topic,* sujet toujours nouveau. *Here's something new,* (i) voici quelque chose de nouveau; (ii) *F:* voici du nouveau! *New ideas,* idées nouvelles, idées neuves. *New ground,* terre vierge. *A district quite new to me,* une région qui est toute nouvelle pour moi. *That has made a new man of him,* cela

a fait de lui un autre homme. *New batteries cost sixpence,* les piles de rechange coûtent six pence. *Mil:* **The new guard,** la garde montante. *Sch:* **The new boys,** les nouveaux. (*b*) (*Of pers.*) **To be new to business,** être nouveau, neuf, aux affaires. *I was new to that kind of work,* je n'étais pas fait, je n'étais pas habitué, à ce genre de travail. **2.** Neuf, *f.* neuve; non usagé. **(Shop-) new garment,** vêtement neuf. **To be dressed in new clothes,** être habillé de neuf. *Com:* **As new,** à l'état (de) neuf. **To make sth. like new,** remettre qch. à neuf. *The subject is quite new,* ce sujet est neuf, n'a pas encore été traité. **3.** (Pain) frais; (vin) nouveau, jeune. **New potatoes,** pommes de terre nouvelles. *S.a.* MILK[1] **1.** **-ly,** *adv.* Récemment, nouvellement. **Newly shaven,** rasé de frais. *The newly-elected members,* les députés nouveaux élus. *N.-painted wall,* mur fraîchement peint. *N.-formed friendship,* amitié de fraîche date, de date récente. **'new-blown,** *a.* (*Of flower*) Frais éclos, *f.* fraîche éclose; frais épanoui, *f.* fraîche épanouie. **'new-born,** *a.* Nouveau-né. *N.-b. children,* enfants nouveau-nés. *N.-b. daughter,* fille nouveau-née. **'new-comer,** *s.* Nouveau venu, nouvel arrivé, *f.* nouvelle venue, etc. *The new-comers,* les nouveaux venus. **'new-drawn,** *a.* (Vin) nouvellement tiré, nouveau-tiré; (bière) nouveau-tirée. **'new-fallen,** *a.* Qui vient de tomber; (neige) fraîche tombée. **'new-'foot,** *v.tr.* Rempiéter (un bas). **'new-found,** *a.* Récemment découvert ou inventé. **New 'Guinea.** *Pr.n.* La Nouvelle-Guinée. **'new-laid,** *a.* (Œuf) frais pondu, du jour. **'new-made,** *a.* De facture récente; nouvellement construit. *N.-m. grave,* fosse fraîchement creusée. **New Or'leans.** *Pr.n.* La Nouvelle-Orléans. **'New South 'Wales.** *Pr.n.* La Nouvelle-Galles du Sud. **'New 'Year,** *s.* Nouvel an; nouvelle année. **New-Year's Day,** le jour de l'an. **New-Year's Eve,** la Saint-Sylvestre. **To see the New Year in,** faire la veillée, le réveillon, de la Saint-Sylvestre; réveillonner. **To wish s.o. a happy New Year,** souhaiter la bonne année à qn. **New-Year's gift,** étrennes *fpl;* cadeau *m* de jour de l'an. **New 'Zealand.** *Pr.n.* La Nouvelle-Zélande. **New 'Zealander,** *s.* Néo-Zélandais, -aise.

newel ['njuəl], *s.* **1.** Noyau *m* (d'escalier tournant). **2.** Newel(-post), pilastre *m* (de rampe d'escalier).

newfangled [nju:'faŋgld], *a. Pej:* D'une modernité outrée.

Newfoundland ['nju:fənd land]. **1.** *Pr.n. Geog:* Terre-Neuve. *The N. fishermen, the N. fishing-boats,* les terre-neuviens *m.* **2.** *s.* [nju:'faundlənd] (*Dog*) Terre-neuve *m inv.*

Newfoundlander [nju:'faundləndər], *s.* Terre-neuvien, -ienne.

newness ['nju:nəs], *s.* **1.** (*a*) Nouveauté *f* (d'une mode, d'une idée). (*b*) Inexpérience *f* (d'un employé). **2.** État neuf (d'un vêtement). **3.** Manque *m* de maturité (du vin, du fromage).

news [nju:z], *s.* Nouvelle(s) *f.* **1. What (is the) news?** quelles nouvelles? qu'est-ce qu'il y a de nouveau, de neuf? *I have n. for you,* il y a du neuf; j'ai appris du nouveau. *A sad piece of news,* une triste nouvelle. **To break the news to s.o.,** faire part d'une mauvaise nouvelle à qn. **No news is good news,** point de nouvelles, bonnes nouvelles. **2.** *Journ: Financial n.,* chronique financière. *'The Sporting News,'* "la Gazette du Turf." **News in brief** = faits divers. *F:* **To be in the news,** faire parler de soi. *W.Tel:* **(Broadcast) news,** journal parlé; informations *fpl;*

communiqué *m.* News cinema, ciné-actualités *m.* News film, reel, film *m* d'actualité. **'news-agency,** *s.* Agence *f* d'informations. **'news-agent,** *s.* Marchand *m* de journaux; dépositaire *m* de journaux. **'news-boy,** *s.m.* Vendeur de journaux; *F:* petit camelot. **'news-print,** *s.* Papier *m* de journal. **'news-room,** *s.* (*In library*) Salle *f* des journaux.

newsmonger ['njuːzmʌŋgər], *s.* Colporteur, -euse, de nouvelles.

newspaper ['njuːspeɪpər], *s.* Journal *m,* -aux. Daily newspaper, (journal) quotidien *m.* Weekly newspaper, (journal) hebdomadaire *m.* Newspaper man, marchand *m* de journaux.

newt [njuːt], *s.* Amph: Triton *m*; salamandre *f* aquatique; *F:* lézard *m* d'eau.

next [nekst]. I. *a.* **1.** (*Of place*) Prochain; le plus proche. The *n. room,* la chambre voisine. Her room is next to mine, sa chambre est contiguë à, avec, la mienne. The garden *n. to mine,* le jardin attenant au mien. Seated *n. to me,* assis à côté de moi. The *n. house,* la maison d'à côté. The next house but one, la deuxième maison à partir d'ici. **2.** (*Of time*) Prochain, suivant. The next day, le jour (d')après; le lendemain. The next day but one, le surlendemain. The *n. three days,* les trois jours suivants. (The) next morning, le lendemain matin. The *n. instant,* l'instant d'après. (*Future time*) Next year, l'année prochaine. By this time n. year, dans un an d'ici. The year after next, dans deux ans. On Friday next, next Friday, vendredi prochain. (*b*) (*Of order*) The *n. chapter,* le chapitre suivant. *Con-tinued in n. column,* la suite à la colonne suivante. To be continued in our next, (la) suite au prochain numéro. The next time I see him, la première fois que je le reverrai. *F:* What next! par exemple! (*In shop*) What next, please? et avec cela? et ensuite? *Sch:* Next (boy)! au suivant! Who comes next? à qui le tour? He is next before me, next after me, il me précède, me suit, immédiatement. (*c*) The next larger, smaller, size (*in shoes, etc.*), la pointure au-dessus, au-dessous. The next best thing would be to . . ., à défaut de cela, le mieux serait de. . . *F: I got it for* next to nothing, je l'ai eu pour presque rien. There is next to no evidence, il n'y a pour ainsi dire pas de preuves. There was next to nobody at the meeting, il n'y avait presque personne à la réunion. **3.** *Jur:* Next friend, ami le plus proche. *S.a.* KIN. II. next, *adv.* **1.** Ensuite, après. What shall we do n.? qu'est-ce que nous allons faire maintenant, après cela? **2.** When next you are that way, la prochaine fois que vous passerez par là. When I n. saw him, quand je le revins. III. next, *prep.* Auprès de, à côté de. The carriage n. the engine, la première voiture près de la locomotive. To wear flannel n. the skin, porter de la flanelle sur la peau, à même la peau. *F:* The thing next my heart, la chose la plus chère à mon cœur. **next door.** I. *s.* The girl from n. d.,* la jeune fille (de la maison) d'à côté. **2.** *adv.phr.* (*a*) He lives next door (to us), il habite dans la maison voisine; il habite à côté (de chez nous). (*b*) *F: Flattery is n. d. to lying,* de la flatterie au mensonge il n'y a qu'un pas. Ideas n. d. to madness, idées qui avoisinent, qui frisent, la folie. **3.** *adv.* The people next door, les gens d'à côté. **4.** *Attrib.* Next-door neighbours, voisins de porte à porte, d'à côté.

nib [nib], *s.* **1.** (Bec *m* de) plume *f.* Broad nib, grosse plume; plume à gros bec. **2.** See COCOA-NIB.

nibbed [nibd], *a.* Hard-nibbed pen, plume à bee dur; plume dure

nibble[1] [nibl], *s.* **1.** (*a*) Grignotement *m.* To have a n. at the cake, grignoter le gâteau. (*b*) Fish: Touche *f.* I never had a nibble all day, le poisson n'a pas mordu de toute la journée. **2.** Juste de quoi grignoter; petit morceau (de biscuit). **nibble**[2], *v.tr. & i.* Grignoter, mordiller (qch.); (*of sheep*) brouter (l'herbe). To nibble (at) a biscuit, grignoter un biscuit. (*Of fish, F: of pers.*) To nibble (at the bait), mordre à l'hameçon. To n. at an offer, être attiré par une offre (sans pouvoir se décider).

nice [nais], *a.* **1.** *Lit:* (*a*) (*Of pers.*) (i) Difficile, délicat, exigeant; (ii) scrupuleux, méticuleux. To be nice about, in, the choice of words, avoir des scrupules dans le choix des mots. (*b*) (*Of question, etc.*) Délicat; (*of distinction*) subtil, fin; (*of ear, eye*) sensible, juste. That's a n. point, voilà une question délicate. **2.** *F:* (*a*) (*Of pers.*) Gentil, *f.* gentille; sympathique. He was as n. as could be, il s'est montré aimable au possible. To be nice to s.o., se montrer gentil, aimable, avec qn. It is nice of you to . . ., vous êtes bien aimable de. . . (*b*) (*Of thg*) Joli, bon. N. dinner, bon dîner. N. evening, soirée agréable. N. car, jolie auto. A n. little sum, une somme rondelette. It is n. here, il fait bon ici. (*c*) (*Intensive*) It is nice and cool, le temps est d'une fraîcheur agréable. They are n. and warm in their cots, ils sont bien au chaud dans leurs petits lits. The tea was n. and sweet, le thé était bien sucré. (*d*) Nice people, des gens bien. Not nice, pas tout à fait convenable. (*e*) *Iron:* We are in a nice mess! nous sommes dans de beaux draps! That's a n. way to behave! voilà une jolie conduite! **-ly,** *adv.* **1.** *Lit:* Scrupuleusement, méticuleusement. N. turned epigram, épigramme joliment tournée. **2.** Joliment, gentiment, bien. N. situated house, maison agréablement située. Those will do n., ceux-là feront très bien l'affaire. *F:* How are you?—Nicely, comment allez-vous?—Bien.

Nicene ['naiˈsiːn], *a.* The Nicene creed, le symbole de Nicée.

nicety ['naisiti], *s.* **1.** (*a*) Justesse *f,* précision *f* (d'un calcul). To a nicety, exactement, à la perfection, à merveille. Roast done to a n., rôti cuit à point. (*b*) Subtilité *f,* délicatesse *f* (d'une question, etc.). **2.** *pl.* Niceties, minuties *f.* Niceties of a craft, finesses *f* d'un métier.

niche [nitʃ], *s.* Niche *f* (pour statue, etc.). Secret *n.,* resserre *f.*

Nicholas ['nikolas]. *Pr.n.m.* Nicolas.

Nick[1] [nik]. *Pr.n.m.* Nicolas. *F:* Old Nick, le diable.

nick[2], *s.* **1.** (*a*) Entaille *f,* encoche *f,* cran *m*; (*in tally-stick*) coche *f,* hoche *f*; (*screw-head*) fente *f.* (*b*) Saignée *f* (de graissage); onglet *m* (de lame de couteau). **2.** (Just) in the nick of time, à point nommé; juste à temps, juste à point. You have come just in the n. of time, vous tombez à pic.

nick[3], *v.tr.* (*a*) Entailler, encocher (un bâton, etc.); biseauter (les cartes). (*b*) Anglaiser (la queue d'un cheval). **2.** *v.tr.* (*a*) Deviner (la vérité, etc.). He has nicked it! il y est! (*b*) To nick the time, arriver à point nommé, juste à temps. **3.** *v.i.* *Rac:* To nick n, coupe. son concurrent; s'insinuer.

nickel[1] [nikl], *s.* Nickel *m.* *S.a.* SILVER[1] 1. **'nickel-bearing,** *a.* Miner: Nickélifère. **nickel-'plate,** *v.tr.* Nickeler.

nickel[2], *v.tr.* (nickelled) Nickeler. **nickelling,** *s.* **1.** (*Action*) Nickelage *m.* **2.** Nickelure *f.*

nicker-nut ['nikərnʌt], *s.* Bot: Œil-de-chat *m*

nick-nack ['nik'nak], *s.* = KNICK-KNACK.

nickname¹ ['nikneim], s. Surnom m; sobriquet m.

nickname², v.tr. Surnommer (qn); donner un sobriquet à (qn). *He was nicknamed the Hunchback*, il était connu sous le sobriquet du Bossu.

nicol ['nik(ə)l], s. *Opt:* Nicol m.

nicotine ['nikotiːn], s. *Ch:* Nicotine f.

nic(ti)tate ['nik(ti)teit], v.i. Cligner les yeux; ciller; *(of horse)* nicter. *Z:* Nictitating membrane, membrane nictitante; *F:* onglet m (d'oiseau, etc.).

nic(ti)tation [nik(ti)'teiʃ(ə)n], s.· Nic(ti)tation f.

niece [niːs], s.f. Nièce.

niellist [ni'elist], s. Nielleur, -euse.

niello ['niˌelo], s. *Metalw:* Nielle m. *To inlay with n.*, nieller. Niello-work, niellure f.

nigella [nai'dʒela], s. *Bot:* Nigelle f.

niggard ['nigərd], s. Grippe-sou m, pingre m.

niggardliness ['nigərdlinəs], s. Ladrerie ·f, pingrerie f; mesquinerie f.

niggardly ['nigərdli], a. *(Of pers.)* Chiche, ladre, pingre; mesquin; *(of sum, portion)* mesquin.

nigger ['nigər], s. *F:* (Contemptuous) Nègre m, f. négresse. *A little n. boy*, un négrillon. *U.S: F:* There's a nigger in the wood-pile, il y a (quelque) anguille sous roche. *Cf.* NEGRO. **'nigger-'brown,** a. (Colour) Tête-de-nègre inv.

niggle [nigl], v.i. Vétiller; tatillonner. *Art:* Fignoler, pignocher. *To n. over trifles*, s'attarder à des vétilles. **niggling,** a. *(Of details)* Insignifiant; de rien du tout; *(of work)* fignolé; léché; *(of pers.)* tatillon, -onne.

nigh [nai]. *Poet: Dial:* = NEAR. Nigh unto death, à l'article de la mort. *S.a.* WELL-NIGH.

night [nai¹ , s. **I.** (a) Nuit f, soir m. Last night, a nuit dernière; hier (au) soir. The night before last, avant-hier (au) soir. The night before, la veille (au soir). To-morrow night, demain soir. Ten o'clock at night, dix heures du soir. *To be accustomed to late nights*, être accoutumé aux veilles. To have a good, a bad, night('s rest), bien, mal, dormir. Good night! bonsoir! *(when retiring)* bonne nuit! *The servant's night out*, le soir de sortie de la bonne. At night, la nuit, à la nuit. In the night, (pendant) la nuit. By night, de nuit; nuitamment. Night attire, vêtement m, toilette f, de nuit. The night boat, le bateau de nuit. (b) *Th:* First night, première f. Wagner night, soirée musicale consacrée à Wagner. **2.** Obscurité f, ténèbres fpl. *N. is falling*, il commence à faire nuit. *To go forth into the n.*, s'en aller dans les ténèbres. **'night-bird,** s. Oiseau m de nuit; oiseau nocturne. **'night-cap,** s. **I.** Bonnet m de nuit (de femme); bonnet de coton (d'homme). **2.** *F:* Grog m (avant de se coucher). **'night-club,** s. Établissement m de nuit; *F:* boîte f de nuit. **'night-dress, -gown,** s. Chemise f de nuit (de femme). **'night-light,** s. Veilleuse f. **'night-shift,** s. *Ind:* Équipe f de nuit. To be on night-shift, être de nuit. **'night-shirt,** s. Chemise f de nuit (d'homme). **'night-soil,** s. *Hyg:* Matières fpl de vidange; vidanges fpl. **'night-time,** s. La nuit. At night-time, la nuit. In the night-time, de nuit; pendant la nuit. **'night-watch,** s. (a) Garde f de nuit; veille f. (b) *Nau:* Quart m de nuit. **'night-watchman,** pl. -men, s.m. *Ind:* Veilleur, gardien, de nuit.

nightfall ['naitfɔːl], s. Tombée f du jour, de la nuit. At nightfall, a la nuit tombante; à nuit close.

nightingale ['naitiŋgeil], s. *Orn:* Rossignol m.

nightjar ['naitdʒaːr], s. *Orn:* Engoulevent m.

nightly ['naitli]. **I.** a. (a) *(Happening at night)* D‹ nuit, de soir, nocturne. (b) Nightly performance représentation (de) tous les soirs; soirée quo tidienne. **2.** adv. Tous les soirs, toutes les nuits

nightman, pl. -men ['naitmən, -men], s.m Vidangeur.

nightmare ['naitmeər], s. Cauchemar m. T‹ have (a) n., avoir le cauchemar. *F: The prospec was a n. to me*, cette perspective me donnait l‹ cauchemar.

nightshade ['naitʃeid], s. *Bot:* (Black) night shade, morelle noire; raisin m de loup. Woody nightshade, douce-amère f. Deadly nightshade belladone f.

nihilism ['nai(h)ilizm], s. Nihilisme m.

nihilist ['nai(h)ilist], s. Nihiliste mf.

nil [nil], s. Rien m; *(on report-sheet, etc.)* néant m *Sp:* Zéro m. *The balance is nil*, le solde est nul

Nile (the) [ðənail]. *Pr.n.* Le Nil.

nilgai ['niːlgai], s. *Z:* Nilgau(t) m.

nimble [nimbl], a. *(Of pers.)* Agile, leste, preste *(of mind, etc.)* délié, subtil, prompt. *(Of old pers.* Still nimble, encore ingambe. **-bly,** adv Agilement; lestement, prestement. **nimble-'footed,** a. Aux pieds agiles. **nimble-'witted,** a. A l'esprit délié, subtil; l'espri‹ prompt.

nimbus, pl. -i, -uses ['nimbəs, -ai, -əsiz], s. **I.** (a) *Art:* Nimbe m, auréole f, gloire f. (b) *Meteor:* Aréole / (autour de la lune) **2.** *Meteor:* Nimbus m.

nincompoop ['ninkəmpuːp], s. *F:* Benêt m nigaud m, niais m.

nine [nain], num. a. & s. Neuf (m). To have nine lives *(like a cat)*, avoir l'âme chevillée au corps *Adv.phr. F:* To the nines, à la perfection *S.a.* DRESS UP. *(For other phrases see* EIGHT.)

ninefold ['nainfould]. **I.** a. Nonuple. **2.** adv Neuf fois autant; au nonuple.

ninepin ['nainpin], s. **I.** pl. Ninepins, (jeu m de quilles f. **2.** Quille. *F:* To go down like ninepins, tomber comme des capucins de cartes.

nineteen [nain'tiːn], num. a. & s. Dix-neuf (m) *S.a.* DOZEN. *(For other phrases see* EIGHT.)

nineteenth [nain'tiːnθ], num. a. & s. Dix-neu‹ vième.

ninetieth ['naintiəθ], num. a. & s. Quatre-vingt dixième.

ninety ['nainti], num. a. & s. Quatre-vingt-dix Ninety-one, ninety-nine, quatre-vingt-onze, quatre-vingt-dix-neuf. The nineties, les années entre 1890 et 1900.

ninny ['nini], s. *F:* Niais m, niaise f; nigaud m, nigaude f; *(of man)* benêt m.

ninth [nainθ], num. a. & s. Neuvième (m). *(For other phrases see* EIGHTH.)

nip¹ [nip], s. **I.** Pincement m. *To give s.o. a nip*, pincer qn. Morsure f (de la gelée, du froid); *Hort:* coup m de gelée. *There was a nip in the air*, l'air était piquant; l'air piquait. **nip²,** v. (nipped) I. v.tr. **I.** Pincer. *He nipped his finger*, il s'est pincé le doigt. *Aut:* To nip an inner tube, pincer, cisailler, une chambre à air. *Nau:* To nip a cable, étriver, étrangler, un cordage. **2.** *Hort:* Pincer (des bourgeons) *F:* To nip in the bud, écraser dans l'œuf; étouffer dans le germe; étrangler au nid. **3.** *(Of cold)* (a) Pincer, piquer, mordre (les doigts, etc.) (b) Brûler (les bourgeons). Frost-nipped, brûlé par la gelée. II. **nip,** v.i. *F: Just nip round to the baker's and get a loaf*, cours vite chez le boulanger prendre un pain. *To nip in and out of the traffic*, se faufiler adroitement parmi les voitures. **nip off.** I. *v.tr.* Enlever, couper, (qch.) en le pinçant. *Hort:* Pincer (un bourgeon). **2.** *v.i.* Filer, s'esquiver. **nipping,** *s.* **I.** Pincement *m.* *Aut:* Cisaillement *m* (de la chambre à air). **2.** *Nau:* Étrive *f*, étranglement *m* (d'un cordage). **3.** *Hort:* Pincement, pinçage *m.*

nip³, *s.* *F:* Goutte *f*, doigt *m* (d'eau-de-vie, etc.). To take a nip, boire une goutte.

nip⁴, *v.i.* (nipped) *F:* Boire la goutte ; siroter.

nipper ['nipər], *s.* **I.** (Pair of) nippers. (*a*) Pince(s) *f(pl)* (de serrage) ; pincette(s) *f(pl)*, tenaille(s) *f(pl).* *Spring nippers,* brucelles *f.* (*b*) Cisaille(s) *f(pl)* ; pince(s) coupante(s). **2.** Pince (d'un homard, etc.). **3.** *F:* Gamin *m*, gosse *m.* *My little n.,* mon mioche.

nipple [nipl], *s.* **I.** (*a*) *Anat:* Mamelon *m* ; bout *m* de sein. (*b*) Tétine *f* (de biberon). **2.** *Tchn:* Raccord *m* (d'une conduite de vapeur, etc.). *Cy: Aut:* Douille *f*, écrou *m* (d'un rayon de roue). **Grease nipple,** raccord de graissage ; embout *m.*

nippy ['nipi], *a.* *F:* **I.** Alerte, vif. *Tell him to be n. about it, P:* dites-lui de se grouiller. **2.** (Vent) coupant, âpre.

nisi ['naisai], *Lt.conj.* *Jur:* (*Of decree, order*) Provisoire ; (*of decision*) rendu sous condition.

nit [nit], *s.* Lente *f* ; œuf *m* de pou.

nitrate¹ ['naitret], *s.* *Ch:* Nitrate *m*, azotate *m.* Nitrate fertilizers, engrais azotés.

nitrate² ['naitreit], *v.tr.* Nitrer ; traiter une matière) à, par, l'acide azotique.

nitre ['naitər], *s.* Nitre *m*, salpêtre *m.* 'nitre-bed, *s.* Nitrière *f.*

nitric ['naitrik], *a.* *Ch:* Nitric acid, acide *m* nitrique, azotique ; *Com:* eau-forte *f.*

nitro-cellulose [naitro'seljulous], *s.* Nitro-cellulose *f.*

nitro-compound [naitro'kompaund], *s.* *Ch:* Dérivé nitré ; composé nitré.

nitrogen ['naitrodʒen], *s.* *Ch:* Azote *m*

nitrogenous [nai'trodʒenəs], *a.* *Ch:* Azoté.

nitroglycerin(e) [na.tro'glisəri:n], *s.* *Exp:* Nitroglycérine *f.*

nitrous ['naitrəs], *a.* Nitreux, azoteux.

nitwit ['nitwit], *s.* *U.S:* *P:* Imbécile *mf* ; crétin *m.*

nix [niks]. **I.** *s.* *P:* Rien (du tout). **2.** *int.* Paix ! vingt-deux !

nix(ie) ['niks(i)], *s.* *Myth:* Ondine *f.*

no [nou]. I. *a.* **I.** Nul, pas de, point de, aucun (with ne *expressed or understood*). *To have no heart,* n'avoir pas de cœur. *He made no reply,* il ne fit aucune réponse. *He spared no pains,* il n'est sorte de soins qu'il n'ait pris. *I have no room to write more,* la place me manque pour vous en écrire davantage. *It is no distance,* ce n'est pas loin. *No two men are alike,* il n'y a pas deux hommes qui se ressemblent. *Details of no interest,* détails de peu d'intérêt, sans intérêt. *No surrender!* on ne se rend pas ! *No nonsense!* pas de bêtises ! **No admittance,** entrée interdite, défense d'entrer. **No smoking,** défense de fumer. **2.** Peu ; ne . . . pas (du tout). (*a*) *Intentions of no honourable kind,* intentions peu honorables. *The task is no easy one,* ce n'est pas une tâche facile. *S.a.* SUCH I. (*b*) *He is no artist,* il n'est pas artiste. *He was no general,* il n'avait aucune des qualités d'un général. *King or no king, he has no right to interfere,* qu'il soit roi ou non, il n'a pas le droit d'intervenir. (*c*) (*With gerund*) *There is no pleasing him,* il n'y a pas moyen de le satisfaire. *There is no getting out of it,* impossible de s'en tirer. **3.** *No one* = NOBODY I (*a*). II. **no,** *adv.* **I.** *Or no,* ou non. *Whether or no,*

que cela soit ou non ; dans tous les cas. *Whether you want it or no,* que tu le veuilles ou non. **2.** (*With comp.*) *I am no richer than he,* je ne suis pas plus riche que lui. *He is* no longer *here,* il n'est plus ici. *S.a.* LESS 5 (*b*), MORE 5, SOON 2. III. **no.** **I.** *adv.* (*a*) Non. *Have you seen him?*—*No,* l'avez-vous vu?—Non. *No, no, you are mistaken!* mais non, mais non, vous vous trompez ! (*b*) *One man could not lift it, no, not half a dozen,* un homme seul ne saurait le soulever, ni même six, pas même six. **2.** *s.* (*pl.* noes) Non *m inv.* **Not to take** (a) **no for an answer,** ne pas admettre de refus. (*In voting*) **Ayes and noes,** voix pour et contre. *The noes have it,* les non l'emportent ; le vote est contre. **no-'load,** *attrib.a.* *Ind:* *Mec.E:* (*Marche*) à vide. **No-load release,** (i) déclenchement *m* à vide ; (ii) interrupteur *m* à vide, à zéro.

Noah ['nouə]. *Pr.n.m.* *B.Hist:* Noé.

nob¹ [nob], *s.* *P:* Tête *f* ; *P:* boule *f*, caboche *f*

nob², *s.* *P:* Aristo *m.* **The nobs,** les rupins *m.*

nobiliary [no'biljəri], *a.* Nobiliaire.

nobility [no'biliti], *s.* **I.** Noblesse *f* (de rang, de cœur). **2.** *Coll.* Noblesse ; (la classe des) nobles *m.* *The n. and gentry,* la haute et la petite noblesse.

noble [noubl]. **I.** *a.* (*a*) Noble. *To be of n. birth,* être noble de race. (*b*) (*Sentiment*) noble, sublime, relevé. *N. soul,* grande âme. (*c*) (*Of monument, etc.*) Empreint de grandeur. **2.** *s.* Noble *m.* **-bly,** *adv.* **I.** Noblement. *N. born,* noble de naissance. **2.** Magnifiquement, superbement. *You did n.!* vous avez été magnifique !

nobleman, *pl.* **-men** ['noublmən, -men], *s.m.* Noble ; gentilhomme, *pl.* gentilshommes.

nobody ['noubodi]. **I.** *pron.* (*a*) Personne *m*, nul *m*, aucun *m* (*with* ne *expressed or understood*). *N. spoke to me,* personne ne m'a parlé. *Who is there?*—*Nobody,* qui est là?—Personne. *N. is perfect,* nul n'est parfait. *N. is more expert at it than he is,* il s'y connaît comme personne, comme pas un. *There is n. better informed,* il n'y a personne de mieux renseigné. *There was nobody else on board,* personne de (d')autre n'était à bord. *N. that was there heard anything,* aucun de ceux qui étaient là n'a rien entendu. *There was nobody about,* il n'y avait pas âme qui vive ; l'endroit était désert. (*b*) *F:* *I knew him when he was nobody,* j'ai été en relations avec lui alors qu'il était encore inconnu. **2.** *s.* (*Pers.*) (i) Nullité *f*, zéro *m* ; (ii) parvenu, -ue. *They are (mere) nobodies,* ce ne sont des gens de rien.

nock¹ [nok], *s.* Encoche, coche *f* (d'une flèche, de l'arc).

nock², *v.tr.* **I.** Encocher (une flèche) ; tailler les coches (de l'arc). **2.** Ajuster (la flèche).

noctambulism [nok'tambjulizm], *s.* **I.** Noctambulisme *m.* **2.** Somnambulisme *m.*

noctambulist [nok'tambjulist], *s.* **I.** Noctambule *mf.* **2.** Somnambule *mf.*

noctua ['noktjuə], *s.* *Ent:* Noctuelle *f.*

nocturnal [nok'tə:rn(ə)l], *a.* Nocturne.

nocturne ['noktə:rn], *s.* *Mus:* Nocturne *m.*

nocuous ['nokjuəs], *a.* Nocif, nuisible.

nod¹ [nod], *s.* Inclination *f* de la tête. **I.** (*a*) Signe *m* de tête affirmatif. *In answer with a nod,* répondre d'une inclination de tête. *F:* *To get sth. on the nod,* avoir qch. à l'œil. (*b*) Signe de tête (impératif). *To have s.o. at one's nod,* avoir qn à ses ordres. *To obey* (s.o.) *on the nod,* obéir (à qn) au doigt et à l'œil. **2.** *He gave me a nod,* il me fit un petit signe de la tête (en guise de salut). **3. The land of Nod,** le pays des rêves.

nod², *v.tr. & i.* (nodded) **I.** To nod (one's head),

taire un signe do tête ; incliner la tête. **To nod to** s.o., (i) faire un signe de tête à qn (en guise d'ordre ou pour exprimer son consentement); (ii) saluer qn d'une inclination de tête. **To nod** assent, faire signe que oui; opiner de la tête. **2.** Dodeliner (de) la tête ; somnoler, sommeiller. *Even Homer sometimes nods,* Homère lui-même sommeille quelquefois. **nodding¹,** *a.* (Vieillard, etc.) à la tête dodelinante, branlante ; (fleur, panache) qui se balance (au vent, etc.). **nodding²,** *s.* Inclination *f* de tête. **To have a nodding acquaintance with** s.o., connaître qn vaguement.

nodal ['noud(ə)l], *a. Ph : Opt :* Nodal, -aux.

noddle [nɔdl], *s. P :* Tête *f* ; *P :* boule *f*, caboche *f*.

node [noud], *s.* **1.** *Astr : Ph : Geom :* Nœud *m.* *Potential node (in circuit, aerial),* nœud de potentiel, de tension. **2.** Nœud, nodosité *f* (d'un tronc d'arbre, etc.). *Bot :* Nœud, articulation *f* (des graminées).

nodosity [no'dɔsiti], *s.* Nodosite *f.*

nodule ['nɔdjuːl], *s. Geol : Med : Bot :* Nodule *m.* Flint nodule, rognon *m* de silex.

nog¹ [nɔg], *v.tr.* (nogged) *Const : Min :* Hourder (une cloison, un mur). **nogging,** *s. Const :* Hourdage *m*, hourdis *m.*

nog², *s.* Bière forte. *S.a.* EGG-NOG.

noggin ['nɔgin], *s.* **1.** (Petit) pot (en étain, etc.). **2.** *Meas :* Quart *m* de pinte.

nohow ['nouhau], *adv. F :* En aucune facon.

noise¹ [nɔiz], *s.* Bruit *m.* **1.** Tapage *m,* vacarme *m,* fracas *m.* **To make a noise,** faire du bruit, du tapage. *To make a lot of n. about a novel,* faire du tintamarre autour d'un roman. *P :* The big noise, le grand manitou (de l'entreprise). **2.** Son *m. Tinkling* n., tintement *m. Hammering* n., bruit de marteau. **To have noises in the ears,** avoir des bourdonnements *m* d'oreilles.

noise², *v.tr.* **To noise sth. abroad,** ébruiter, *F :* corner (une nouvelle); publier, crier, qch. sur les toits. *It was noised (abroad) on all sides that . . .,* le bruit se répandit de tous côtés que. . . .

noiseless ['nɔizləs], *a.* Sans bruit ; (appareil) silencieux. *With n. tread,* à pas feutrés. **-ly,** *adv.* Silencieusement ; sans bruit, à petit bruit.

noisome ['nɔisəm], *a.* **1.** *A :* Nocif, nuisible. **2.** (*Of smell, etc.*) Fétide, infect, méphitique. **3.** *F : N.* task, tâche désagréable, répugnante.

noisy ['nɔizi], *a.* Bruyant, tapageur ; (enfant) turbulent. (*Of pers.*) *To be n.,* faire du bruit, du tapage. **-ily,** *adv.* Bruyamment ; avec grand bruit.

nomad ['nɔmad, 'nou-], *a. & s.* Nomade (*mf*).

nomadic [no'madik], *a.* Nomade.

nomenclature ['noumenkleitjər], *s.* Nomenclature *f.*

nominal ['nɔmin(ə)l], *a.* Nominal, -aux. **1.** Qui n'a que le nom. **To be the nominal head,** n'être chef que de nom. *N. value,* valeur nominale, fictive. *N. rent,* loyer purement nominal. **2.** *Mil : etc :* Nominal roll, état nominatif. **-ally,** *adv.* **1.** Nominalement ; de nom. **2.** Nominativement.

nominate ['nɔmineit], *v.tr.* (*a*) Nommer, choisir, désigner (qn). **To nominate** s.o. **to, for, a post,** nommer qn à un emploi. (*b*) Proposer, présenter (un candidat).

nomination [nɔmi'neiʃ(ə)n], *s.* **1.** (*a*) Nomination *f* (de qn à un emploi). (*b*) Droit *m* de nommer qn à un poste. **2.** Présentation *f* (d'un candidat).

nominative ['nɔminətiv]. **1.** *Gram :* (*a*) *a. & s.* Nominatif (*m*). **In the nominative (case),** au

nominatif, au cas sujet. (*b*) *s.* Sujet *m* (de la phrase). **2.** *a.* (Candidat) désigné, nommé.

nominator ['nɔmineitər], *s.* Présentateur *m* (d'un candidat).

nominee [nɔmi'niː], *s.* **1.** (*For an annuity*) Personne dénommée. **2.** (*For a post*) Candidat désigné, choisi.

nomogram ['nɔmogram], **nomograph** ['nomograf, -grɑːf], *s. Mth :* Abaque *m*, nomogramme *m.*

nomography [no'mɔgrəfi], *s.* Nomographie *f.*

non- [nɔn], *pref.* **1.** Non-. *Non-admission,* non-admission. **2.** In-. *Non-compliance,* insoumission. **3.** Sans. *Non-alcoholic,* sans alcool.

non-acceptance, *s. Com :* Non-acceptat on *f,* refus *m* d'acceptation (d'un effet).

nonage ['nounedʒ], *s.* Minorité *f.* **To be still in** one's nonage, être encore mineur.

nonagenarian [nounədʒe'neəriən], *a. & s.* Nonagénaire (*mf*).

non-aggression, *s.* **Non-aggression pact,** pacte *m* de non-agression.

non-appearance, *s. Jur :* Défaut *m* (de comparution); non-comparution *f.*

non-arrival, *s.* Non-arrivée *f.*

non-attendance, *s.* Absence *f.*

nonce [nɔns], *s.* **For the nonce,** pour l'occasion. **'nonce-word,** *s.* Mot créé, forgé, pour l'occasion ; mot de circonstance.

nonchalance ['nɔnʃaləns], *s.* Nonchalance *f.*

nonchalant ['nɔnʃalənt], *a.* Nonchalant ; indifférent. **-ly,** *adv.* Nonchalamment ; avec nonchalance.

non-com. ['nɔn'kɔm], *s. Mil : F : =* non-commissioned officer.

non-combatant, *a. & s. Mil :* Non-combatant (*m*).

non-commissioned, *a. Mil :* Sans brevet. **Non-commissioned officer,** sous-officier *m* ; gradé *m.*

non-committal, *a.* (*Of answer, etc.*) Qui n'engage à rien. **To be** n.-c. (in answering, etc.), observer une prudente réserve.

non-completion, *s.* Non-achèvement *m* (d'un travail) ; non-exécution *f* (d'un contrat).

non compos mentis ['nɔn'kɔmpɔs'ment.s]. *Lt.phr.* Aliéné, fou.

non-condensing, *a.* (Machine) sans condensation, à échappement libre.

non-conducting, *a. Ph :* Non-conducteur, -trice ; mauvais conducteur ; (*heat*) calorifuge ; (*electricity*) isolant.

non-conductor, *s. Ph :* Non-conducteur *m,* mauvais conducteur ; (*of heat*) calorifuge *m* ; (*of electricity*) isolant *m.*

nonconformist [nɔnkon'fɔːrmist], *s. & a. Ecc :* Dissident, -ente.

non-content [nɔn'kɔntent], *s. Parl :* Voix *f* contre (à la Chambre des Lords).

non-dazzle, *a.* *Aut :* **Non-dazzle head-light,** phare-code *m, pl.* phares-code.

non-delivery, *s.* Non-livraison *f* ; défaut *m* de livraison ; non-remise *f* (de lettres).

nondescript ['nɔndiskript], *a.* Indéfinissable, inclassable ; (costume) hétéroclite.

none [nʌn]. **1.** *pron.* (*a*) Aucun. *N. of them is, are, known to us,* nous n'en connaissons aucun. *N. of you can tell me . . .,* personne d'entre vous, aucun d'entre vous, ne peut me dire. . . . *None of this concerns me,* rien de ceci ne me regarde. *No news to-day?—None,* pas de nouvelles aujourd'hui?—Aucune(s). *Strawberries !* there are none, des fraises ! il n'y en a pas. *Any occupation is better than none at all,* une occupation quelle qu'elle soit est préférable à pas d'occupation du

tout. None of your impudence! pas d'insolences de votre part! *His nature is n. of the calmest,* sa nature n'est pas des plus calmes. (b) **None can tell,** personne ne le sait; nul ne le sait. *He is aware, none better, that . . .,* il sait mieux que personne que. . . . **None but he** *knew of it,* lui seul le savait. *The visitor was* **none** *other than the king,* le visiteur n'était autre que le roi. (c) (*In schedules, etc.*) **'None,'** "néant." **2.** *a.* **Money I had none,** d'argent je n'en avais point. *Sounds there were* n., *save the barking of a dog,* de sons aucun, sauf les aboiements d'un chien. *Village there was* n., de village point. **3.** *adv.* (a) **He is none the happier for his wealth,** pour être riche, il n'en est pas plus heureux. **I like him none the worse for that,** je ne l'en aime pas moins. *S.a.* LESS 4, WORSE I. (b) **He was none too soon,** il arriva juste à temps. *They love each other* n. *too well,* ils ne sont pas fort épris l'un de l'autre. *The evening passed* n. *too gaily,* la soirée fut peu gaie. *His position is* n. *too secure,* sa position n'est rien moins qu'assurée.

nonentity [nɔn'entiti], *s.* Personne insignifiante, de peu d'importance; non-valeur *f*; nullité *f*.

non-essential, *a.* = UNESSENTIAL.

non-existence, *s.* Non-existence *f*.

non-existent, *a.* Non-existant; inex stant.

non-explosive, *a.* Inexplosible.

non-fading, *a.* (*Of colour*) Résistant à la lumière, au soleil; bon teint.

non-flam ['nɔnflam], *a.* (Film) ininflammable.

non-freezing, *a.* Incongelable.

non-fulfilment, *s.* Non-exécution *f*, inexécution *f*.

non-inflammable, *a.* Ininflammable, ignifuge.

non-intervention, *s.* Non-intervention *f*; laisser-faire *m*.

non-juring [nɔn'dʒuəriŋ], *a.* *Hist:* (Prêtre) inassermenté, non assermenté (en 1689).

non-member, *s.* (*At club*) Invité, -ée. **Open to non-members,** ouvert au public.

non-observance, *s.* Inobservance *f* (des lois).

nonpareil [nɔnpa'rel], *s.* (a) *Typ:* Nonpareille *f*; corps *m* six. (b) (*Apple, comfit*) Nonpareille.

non-payment, *s.* Non-payement *m*; défaut *m* de payement.

non-performance, *s.* Non-exécution *f*, inexécution *f* (d'un contrat, etc.).

nonplus ['nɔnplʌs], *v.tr.* (**nonplussed**) Embarrasser, interdire, interloquer (qn); mettre, réduire, (qn) à quia. **To be nonplussed,** être désemparé.

non-resident, *a. & s.* **I.** Non-résident (*m*). *Non-r.* landowner, propriétaire forain. **2.** *Sch:* Externe (*mf*).

non-reversible, *a.* *Mec.E:* Irréversible.

non-rigid, *a.* *Aer:* Souple.

nonsense ['nɔnsəns], *s.* **I.** Non-sens *m.* **2.** Absurdité *f*, déraison *f*. **A piece of nonsense,** une bêtise, une absurdité. **To talk nonsense,** déraisonner; dire des bêtises, des inepties. **This passage makes nonsense,** ce passage est inintelligible. **Nonsense!** pas possible! à d'autres! quelle blague! *It is* n. *to think that . . .,* c'est absurde de penser que. . . . **Now, no nonsense!** allons, pas de bêtises!

nonsensical [nɔn'sensik(ə)l], *a.* **I.** Absurde; qui n'a pas le sens commun. **2.** *Don't be* n.! ne dites pas de bêtises, d'absurdités.

non-skid(ding), *a.* *Aut:* *etc:* (Bandage) antidérapant.

non-stop [nɔn'stɔp]. **I.** *Attrib.a.* **Non-stop train,** train faisant le trajet sans arrêt; train

direct. *Av:* **Non-stop flight,** vol sans escale. **2.** *adv.* Sans arrêt; (voler) sans escale.

nonsuch ['nɔnsʌt͡ʃ], *s.* (a) *Bot:* Lupuline *f*; petit trèfle jaune. (b) **Nonsuch apple,** nonpareille *f*.

nonsuit¹ ['nɔnsjuːt], *s.* *Jur:* Débouté *m*; ordonnance *f* de non-lieu.

nonsuit², *v.tr.* Débouter (un plaideur) (de son appel); renvoyer (qn) de sa demande.

non-union, *attrib.a.* (Ouvrier) non-syndiqué.

non-unionist, *s.* Non-syndiqué(e).

noodle [nuːdl], *s.* Niais, -aise, nigaud, -aude; benêt *m*.

noodles [nuːdlz], *s.pl.* *Cu:* Nouilles *f*.

nook [nuk], *s.* (a) Coin *m*, recoin *m*. **Nooks and corners,** coins et recoins. (b) Renfoncement *m* (dans une salle).

noon [nuːn], *s.* Midi *m.* *The sun at* n., le soleil de midi. *Shadow at* n., ombre méridienne.

noonday ['nuːndei], **noontide** ['nuːntaid], *s.* Midi *m*; plein jour. **The noonday sun,** le soleil de midi.

noose¹ [nuːs], *s.* (a) Nœud coulant; (*for catching hares, etc.*) lacet *m*, lacs *m*, collet *m.* (b) **Hangman's noose,** corde *f* (de potence).

noose², *v.tr.* **I.** Faire un nœud coulant a (une corde). **2.** Prendre (un lièvre) au lacet.

nopal ['noup(ə)l], *s.* *Bot:* Nopal *m*, -als; cochenillier *m*.

nor [nɔːr, nɔr], *conj.* **I.** (Ne; ni . . .) ni. **Neither you nor I know,** ni vous ni moi ne savons. *He shall not go* **nor** *you either,* il n'ira pas, ni vous non plus. **2.** *I do not know,* **nor** *can I guess,* n'en sais rien et je ne peux pas le deviner. *Nor does it seem that . . .,* il ne semble pas non plus que . . ., d'ailleurs il ne semble pas que . . .

nor' [nɔːr]. *Nau:* **Nor'east, nor'west** = NORTHEAST, NORTH-WEST.

Nordic ['nɔːrdik], *a.* *Ethn:* Nordique, scandinave.

noria ['nɔːria], *s.* Noria *f*; (pompe *f* à) chapelet *m*.

norm [nɔːrm], *s.* Norme *f*.

normal ['nɔːrm(ə)l]. **I.** *a.* (a) *Geom:* Normal, -aux, perpendiculaire (*to,* à). (b) Normal, régulier, ordinaire. *N. speed,* vitesse de régime. *Med:* N. temperature, température moyenne, normale. (c) **Normal school,** école normale. **2.** *s.* (a) *Geom:* Normale *f*, perpendiculaire *f*. (b) Condition normale; état normal. *Temperature above* (**the**) **normal,** température au-dessus de la normale. **-ally,** *adv.* Normalement.

normality [nɔːr'maliti], *s.* Normalité *f*.

Norman ['nɔːrmən], *a. & s.* Normand, -ande. **Norman architecture,** (i) l'architecture normande; (ii) l'architecture romane (anglaise).

Normandy ['nɔːrməndi], *Pr.n.* La Normandie.

Norse [nɔːrs]. **I.** *a.* (a) Norvégien. (b) *Hist:* Nordique. **2.** *s.* *Ling:* Les langues *f* scandinaves; *esp.* le norvégien.

Norseman, *pl.* -men ['nɔːrsmən, -men], *s.* *Hist:* Norvégien *m*.

north [nɔːrθ]. **I.** *s.* Nord *m.* *On the north, to the north* (of), au nord (de). **To live in the north of England,** demeurer dans le nord de l'Angleterre. **2.** *adv.* Au nord. **To travel north,** voyager vers le nord. **3.** *a.* Nord *inv*; septentrional, -aux; (pays) du nord; (mur) exposé au nord. **The north wind,** le vent du nord; *Lit:* la bise. **North Britain,** l'Écosse *f*. **'North 'Cape (the),** *s.* Le Cap Nord. **'North 'Country (the),** *s.* L'Angleterre du nord. **north-'east. I.** *s.* Nord-est *m.* **2.** *a.* (Du) nord-est *inv.* **3.** *adv.* Vers e nord-est.

north-'easterly, *a.* Du nord-est. **north-**

'eastern, *a.* (Du) nord-est *inv.* **'North 'Sea (the),** *s.* La mer du Nord. **north-'west. 1.** *s.* Nord-ouest *m.* **2.** *a.* (Du) nord-ouest *inv.* **3.** *adv.* Vers le nord-ouest. **north-'westerly,** *a.* Du nord-ouest. **north-'western,** *a.* (Du) nord-ouest *inv.*

northerly ['nɔːrðərli], *a.* (*Of wind*) Du nord; (*of district*) (du, au) nord; (*of direction*) vers le nord. *N. aspect,* exposition au nord.

northern ['nɔːrðərn], *a.* (Du) nord; septentrional, -aux. **Northern Ireland,** l'Irlande du nord. **Northern lights,** aurore boréale.

northerner ['nɔːrðərnər], *s.* Habitant *m* du nord.

northward ['nɔːrθwərd]. **1.** *s.* To the northward, au nord. **2.** *a.* Au, du, nord; du côté du nord.

northwards ['nɔːrθwərdz], *adv.* Vers le nord.

Norway ['nɔːrwei]. *Pr.n. Geog:* La Norvège.

Norwegian [nɔːr'wiːdʒən]. **1.** *a. & s.* Norvégien, -ienne. **2.** *s. Ling:* Le norvégien.

nose[1] [noːuz], *s.* **1.** (*Of pers.*) Nez *m*; (*of many animals*) museau *m*; (*of dog*) nez. **To blow one's nose,** se moucher. **To hold one's nose,** se boucher le nez. **To speak through the nose,** nasiller; parler du nez. *F:* The parson's nose, le croupion (d'une volaille). *I did it under his* (very) *nose,* je l'ai fait à son nez, à sa barbe. *To poke one's n. into everything,* fourrer son nez partout. **To make a long nose at s.o.,** faire un pied de nez à qn. **To lead s.o. by the nose,** mener qn par le bout du nez. **2.** Odorat *m.* **Dog with a good nose,** chien qui a du flair, du nez. **3.** *Tchn:* Nez (d'un bateau, d'un avion); nez, bec *m* (d'un outil); ajutage *m* (d'un tuyau). *Mil:* Pointe *f* (d'une balle). *Navy:* Cône *m* de choc (d'une torpille). **'nose-bag,** *s.* Musette *f* (mangeoire) (de cheval); sac *m* à fourrages. **'nose-band,** *s. Harn:* Muserolle *f.* **'nose-bleeding,** *s.* Saignement *m* du nez. **'nose-dive**[1], *s. Av:* Vol piqué; piqué *m.* **'nose-dive**[2], *v.i. Av:* Piquer du nez; descendre en piqué. **'nose-lift,** *s. Av:* Cabrage *m.* **'nose-piece,** *s.* Ajutage *m,* bec *m* (de tuyau d'arrosage, etc.); buse *f,* tuyère *f* (de soufflet); porte-objectifs *m inv* (de microscope). **'nose-ring,** *s.* **1.** *Husb:* Anneau nasal, nasière *f* (de taureau, etc.). **2.** *Anthr:* Anneau porté au nez.

nose[2]. **1.** *v.tr.* Flairer, sentir (qch.). **2.** *v.i.* To nose at sth., flairer qch. **To nose about,** (a)round, fureter, fouiner; fourrer le nez partout. **The ship nosed** (her way) **through the fog,** le navire s'avançait à l'aveuglette à travers le brouillard. **nose out,** *v.tr.* (*Of dog*) To nose out the game, flairer le gibier. *F:* To nose out a secret, découvrir, éventer, un secret. *To n. s.o. out,* dépister, dénicher, qn. **-nosed,** *a.* Red-nosed, au nez rouge. *S.a.* FLAT-NOSED, *etc.* **nosing,** *s.* (a) (*Of stair-tread*) Nez *m,* profil *m.* (b) *Arch:* Arête *f* (de moulure).

nosegay ['nouzgei], *s.* Bouquet *m* (de fleurs odorantes).

nostalgia [nos'taldʒia], *s* Nostalgie *f.*

nostoc ['nɔstɔk], *s. Algae:* Nostoc *m,* nodulaire *f.*

nostril ['nɔstril], *s.* (*Of pers.*) Narine *f*; (*of horse, etc.*) naseau *m.*

nostrum ['nɔstrəm], *s.* Drogue *f,* orviétan *m*; remède *m* de charlatan.

nosy ['nouzi], *a. P:* **1.** Fouinard; fur teur, -euse. **A Nosy Parker,** un indiscret, *F:* un fouinard. **2.** Odorant.

not [nɔt], *adv.* (Ne) pas, (ne) point. **1.** *A. & Lit: I know not,* je ne sais pas. **Fear not,** n'ayez point de crainte. **2.** (a) He will not, wou't, come, il ne viendra pas. **Sho is not, isn't, there,** elle n'est pas là. **Do not, don't, stir,** ne bougez pas. *You understand, do you not, don't you?* vous comprenez, n'est-ce pas? *He is here, isn't he, is he not?* il est ici, n'est-ce pas? (b) (*Stressed*) I am ready.—*You are 'not ready,* je suis prêt.—Non, vous n'êtes pas prêt.. (c) *What is she like?—Not pretty,* comment est-elle?—Pas jolie. *Are you ill?—Not at all,* êtes-vous malade?—Pas du tout. *Thank you so much!—Not at all!* mille mercis!—Pas de rien (monsieur, madame)! *If fine, we shall go out if not,* not, s'il fait beau nous sortirons, sinon, pas. *Why not?* pourquoi pas? *I wish it we ë not (so),* je voudrais bien que non, que cela ne soit pas. *I don't care whether he comes or not,* qu'il vienne ou non, cela m'est égal. **I think not,** je crois que non. **Not even in France,** (non) pas même en France. **Not negotiable,** non-négociable. **3.** *Not wishing to be seen, I drew the curtain,* ne désirant pas être vu, comme je ne désirais pas être vu, je tirai le rideau. **Not including . . .,** sans compter. . . . *He begged me not to move,* il me pria de ne pas me déranger. **4.** **Not that . . .,** ce n'est pas que . . ., ce n'est point à dire que. . . . *Not that I fear him,* non (pas) que je le craigne. **5.** (*With pronoun*) Are you going to tell him?—Not I! allez-vous le lui dire?—Moi? Bien sûr que non! **Not everybody** *can be a Milton,* il n'est pas donné à tout le monde d'être un Milton. **6.** (*In litotes*) There were not a few *women amongst them,* il y avait pas mal de femmes parmi eux. *The news caused* not a little *surprise,* grande fut la surprise à cette nouvelle. *An air of dignity not unmingled with shyness,* un air digne qui n'allait pas sans une certaine timidité. **7.** Not a murmur *was heard,* pas un murmure ne se fit entendre.

notability [nouta'biliti], *s.* **1.** (*Pers.*) Notabilité *f,* notable *m*; personne *f* considérable. **2.** Notabilité, caractère *m* notable (d'un fait).

notable ['noutəbl], *a.* **1.** (c) Notable, considérable, insigne; (*of pers.*) éminent. (b) *s.* Notable *m.* **2.** *Ch:* (*Of quantity, etc.*) Perceptible, sensible. **-ably,** *adv.* **1.** Notablement, remarquablement. **2.** Notamment, particulièrement.

notary ['noutəri], *s. Jur:* Notary (public), notaire *m.*

notation [no'tei∫(ə)n], *s.* Notation *f.* *Ar:* Decimal notation, numération décimale.

notch[1] [nɔt∫], *s.* (a) Entaille *f,* encoche *f,* cran *m.* *Mec.E:* Stop-notch, cran d'arrêt. *Sm.a:* Sight notch, sighting notch, cran de mire. (b) Brèche *f* (dans une lame, etc.).

notch[2], *v.tr.* (a) Entailler, encocher (un bâton, etc.). **To notch a tally,** faire une coche à une taille. (b) Ébrécher (une lame, etc.).

note[1] [nout], *s.* **1.** (a) Note *f*; caractère *m* de musique. (b) Touche *f* (d'un piano). (c) Note, son *m. To sing, play, a false n.,* chanter une fausse note. *F: There was a note of impatience in his voice,* son ton indiquait une certaine impatience. *Speech that hits the right n.,* discours dans la note voulue. **2.** Marque *f,* signe *m,* indice *m.* *A: To set a n. of infamy on . . .,* marquer d'un stigmate, d'une note d'infamie. **Note of exclamation,** point *m* d'exclamation. **3.** (a) Note, mémorandum *m.* **To make, take (down), notes,** prendre des notes. *To make a n. of sth.,* noter qch.; prendre note de qch. (b) Note, annotation *f,* remarque *f* (sur un texte). **Notes on Tacitus,** commentaire *m* sur Tacite. (c) Billet *m*; petite lettre. *I wrote off a n. to her at once,* je lui ai tout de suite écrit un mot, un billet. **4.** *Com:* (a) Billet, bordereau *m.* **Note of hand,** reconnaissance *f* (de dette). **Credit note,** note, facture *f,* de crédit.

Advice note, note, lettre, d'avis. (b) (Bank) note, billet (de banque). Ten-franc notes, coupures f de dix francs. **5.** (a) Man of note, homme marquant, de renom, de marque. (b) It is worthy of note that . . ., il convient de noter que. Nothing of note, rien d'important. To take note of sth., retenir qch. dans sa mémoire; remarquer qch. S.a. COMPARE² **1.** 'note-book, s. Carnet m, calepin m; (for shorthand) bloc-notes m. 'note-case, s. Porte-billets m inv. 'note-paper, s. Papier m à lettres, à écrire. **note²**, v.tr. **1.** Noter, constater, remarquer, prendre note de (qch.); relever (une erreur). We duly note that . . ., ous prenons bonne note (de ce) que. . . . **2.** To note sth. (down), écrire, inscrire, qch. noted, a. (Of pers.) Distingué, éminent, illustre; (of thg) célèbre, remarquable (for sth., par qch.).
noteworthy ['noutwəːrði], a. Remarquable; digne d'attention, de remarque.
nothing ['nʌθiŋ]. I. s. or pron. Rien (with ne expressed or understood). (a) I see n. that I like, je ne vois rien qui me plaise. Nothing could be simpler, rien de plus simple; c'est tout ce qu'il y a de plus simple. You can't live on nothing, on ne peut pas vivre de rien. S.a. NEXT I. 2. To say nothing of . . ., sans parler de. . . . There's nothing in these rumours, ces bruits sont sans fondement. He was nothing if not discreet, il était discret avant tout. To create an army out of n., créer une armée de toutes pièces. (b) (Followed by adj.) Nothing new, rien de nouveau. That's n. unusual, cela n'a rien d'anormal. There is n. heroic about him, il n'a rien d'un héros. Nothing much, pas grand'chose. There is n. more to be said, il n'y a plus rien à dire. (c) To have nothing to do with sth., n'avoir rien à faire, n'avoir aucun rapport, avec qch.; n'avoir rien à voir à qch. I have n. to do with it, e n'y suis pour rien. That is nothing to do with you, ce n'est pas votre affaire; cela ne vous regarde pas. There is nothing to cry about, il n'y a pas de quoi pleurer. (d) He is nothing of a scholar, ce n'est pas du tout un savant. S.a. KIND¹ 2, SORT¹ 1. (e) Nothing else, rien d'autre. N. else could be done, (i) on ne pouvait rien faire de plus; (ii) on ne pouvait faire autrement. Nothing but the truth, rien que la vérité. He does n. but go in and out, il ne fait qu'entrer et sortir. There is nothing for it but to submit, il n'y a qu'à se soumettre. There was n. for it but to wait, force nous fut d'attendre. You walked back?—There was n. else for it, vous êtes revenu à pied?—Il a bien falu. (f) It is not for nothing that . . ., ce n'est pas sans raison que. . . . All that goes for nothing, tout cela ne compte pas. (g) She is nothing to him, elle lui est indifférente. It is n. to me whether he comes or not, qu'il vienne ou non, cela m'est égal. (h) To make, think, nothing of sth., n'attacher aucune importance à qch.; ne faire aucun cas de qch. He makes n. of walking twenty miles, il se fait un jeu de faire vingt milles à pied. He makes n. of borrowing from the till, il ne se fait pas scrupule d'emprunter à la caisse. II. **nothing**, s. **1.** Ar: Zéro m. **2.** Néant m; rien. To come to nothing, ne pas aboutir; (of hopes, etc.) s'anéantir. **3.** Airy nothings, des bagatelles f. S.a. SWEET I. 5. A hundred francs? A mere nothing! cent francs? Une misère! To punish a child for a mere n., punir un enfant pour une vétille. III. **nothing**, adv. Aucunement, nullement; pas du tout. Nothing loath, volontiers, sans hésiter. S.a. DAUNT. He is nothing the worse for it, il ne s'en porte pas plus mal.

It was nothing (like) so wonderful as one imagined, ce n'était nullement aussi merveilleux que l'on se le figurait. Nothing near so large, loin d'être aussi grand. It is nothing less than madness, c'est de la folie ni plus ni moins.
nothingness ['nʌθiŋnəs], s. Néant m.
notice¹ ['noutis], s. **1.** (a) Avis m, notification f. Notice of receipt. avis de réception. (b) Préavis m, avertissement m. To give s.o. notice of sth., prévenir qn de qch. I must have notice, il faudra m'en avertir. Without notice (given), he sold the house, sans avis préalable, sans en aviser personne, il a vendu la maison. To give out a notice, lire une communication; faire l'annonce de qch. Notice is hereby given that . . ., le public est avisé que . . .; on fait savoir que. . . Public notice, avis au public. Until further notice, jusqu'à nouvel avis; jusqu'à avis contraire. (c) Avis formel, instructions formelles. To give s.o. n. to do sth., aviser qn de faire qch. Jur: To receive n. to do sth., être mis en demeure de faire qch. Notice to pay, avertissement. To serve a notice on s.o., signifier un arrêt à qn. (d) At short notice, à court délai. Ready to start at short n., at a day's n., prêt à partir à l'instant, du jour au lendemain. At a moment's notice, à la minute, à l'instant; (renvoyer qn) sans avertissement préalable. To give six months' n. of sth., donner avis de qch. six mois d'avance; donner un préavis de six mois. Com: Can be delivered at three days' n., livrable dans un délai de trois jours. (e) Notice to quit, congé m; avis de congé. Jur: intimation f de vider les lieux. To give a tenant n. to quit, donner congé, signifier son congé, à un locataire. To give notice to an employee, donner, signifier, son congé à un employé. (Of master or servant) To give s.o. a week's notice, donner ses huit jours à qn. To give notice (to one's employer), donner sa démission. **2.** (a) Affiche f; indication f, avis (au public); (on card) écriteau m. N. of sale by auction, publication de vente aux enchères. (b) (In newspaper) Annonce f. To put a n. in the papers, faire passer une note dans les journaux. (c) Revue f (d'un ouvrage). **3.** To take notice of sth., tenir compte, prendre connaissance de qch. To take no notice of sth., ne faire aucune attention à qch.; passer outre à (une objection). I have never taken any n. of it, je n'y ai jamais pris garde. The fact came to his notice that . . ., son attention fut attirée par le fait que. . . . To attract notice, se faire remarquer. To come into notice, commencer à être connu. To avoid notice, se dérober aux regards. To bring, call, a matter to s.o.'s notice, porter une affaire à la connaissance de qn; faire observer qch. à qn. 'notice-board, s. **1.** (On house or field, etc.) Écriteau m; (in club, etc.) tableau m d'annonces; porte-affiches m inv. **2.** Panneau indicateur (de route).
notice², v.tr. Observer, remarquer, s'apercevoir de, tenir compte, prendre garde à (qn, qch.); faire la remarque de (qch.). I have never noticed it, je n'y ai jamais pris garde. I noticed her wipe away a tear, je vis qu'elle essuyait une larme. To get oneself noticed, attirer l'attention (sur soi).
noticeable ['noutisəbl], a. **1.** Digne d'attention, de remarque. To be n. on account of sth., se faire remarquer par qch. **2.** Perceptible, sensible. It is not noticeable, cela ne se voit pas. **-ably**, adv. Perceptiblement, sensiblement.
notifiable ['noutifaiəbl], a. (Maladie f) dont la déclaration aux autorités est obligatoire.
notification [noutifi'kei∫(ə)n], s. Avis m, notification f, annonce f; déclaration f (de naissance).

notify ['noutifai], *v.tr.* Annoncer, notifier (qch.) ; déclarer (une naissance). **To notify s.o. of sth.**, avertir, aviser, qn de qch. **To notify the police of sth.**, signaler qch. à la police.

notion ['nouʃ(ə)n], *s.* (*a*) Notion *f*, idée *f.* **To form a true notion of sth.**, se former une idée exacte de qch. **To have no notion of sth.**, n'avoir pas la moindre notion de qch. (*b*) Opinion *f*, pensée *f.* **I have a notion that . . .**, j'ai dans l'idée que . . . ; je me suis mis en tête que. . . . (*c*) Caprice *m.* **As the notion takes him**, selon son caprice. *To have a n. to do sth.*, s'aviser de faire qch.

notoriety [nouto'raiəti], *s.* **1.** Notoriété *f.* **To bring s.o. into notoriety**, faire connaître qn. **To seek notoriety**, chercher à se faire remarquer ; s'afficher. **2.** (*Pers.*) Notabilité *f.*

notorious [no'tɔːriəs], *a.* **1.** (Fait) notoire, bien connu, reconnu. **2.** *Pej:* D'une triste notoriété ; (menteur) insigne ; (malfaiteur) reconnu, notoire ; (endroit) mal famé. **-ly**, *adv.* Notoirement. *N. cruel*, connu pour sa cruauté.

notwithstanding [nɔtwið'standiŋ]. **1.** *prep.* Malgré ; en dépit de. **This notwithstanding**, ce nonobstant. **This rule notwithstanding**, par, en, dérogation à cette règle. **2.** *adv.* Quand même, tout de même ; néanmoins, pourtant.

nougat ['nuːgɑː], *s.* Nougat *m.*

nought [nɔːt], *s.* = NAUGHT.

noun [naun], *s. Gram:* Substantif *m*, nom *m.* **Noun clause**, proposition substantive.

nourish ['nʌriʃ], *v.tr.* **1.** Nourrir (qn, une plante) ; alimenter (qn) ; sustenter (le corps) ; entretenir (le cuir). **To nourish s.o. on, with, sth.**, nourrir qn de qch. **2.** *F:* Nourrir, entretenir (un espoir). **nourishing**, *a.* Nourrissant, nutritif. *Milk is n.*, le lait nourrit.

nourishment ['nʌriʃmənt], *s.* **1.** Alimentation *f*, nourriture *f.* **2.** Nourriture, aliments *mpl.*

nous [naus], *s. F:* Intelligence *f* ; *F:* jugeotte *f.*

Nova Scotia ['nouvə'skouʃjə]. *Pr.n. Geog:* La Nouvelle-Écosse.

novel¹ ['nɔv(ə)l], *s. Lit:* Roman *m.*

novel², *a.* Nouveau, -elle ; original, -aux ; singulier. *That's a n. idea!* voilà qui est original !

novelist ['nɔvəlist], *s.* Romancier, -ière.

novelty ['nɔvəlti], *s.* **1.** Chose nouvelle ; innovation *f. Com:* (Article *m* de) nouveauté *f.* **2.** Nouveauté (de qch.). *The charm of n.*, charme de la nouveauté.

November [no'vembər], *s.* Novembre *m. In N.*, au mois de novembre. (*On*) *the fifth of N.*, le cinq novembre.

novice ['nɔvis], *s.* **1.** *Ecc:* Novice *mf.* **2.** *F:* Novice, apprenti, -ie, débutant, -ante. **To be a novice in, at, sth.**, être novice dans, à, qch. *He is no n.*, il n'en est pas à son coup d'essai.

noviciate [no'viʃiet], *s.* (*a*) *Ecc:* Noviciat *m. To go through one's n.*, faire son noviciat. (*b*) *F:* Apprentissage *m.*

now [nau]. **I.** *adv.* **1.** Maintenant. (*a*) En ce moment, actuellement, à l'heure actuelle ; *F:* à l'heure qu'il est. *The now reigning emperor*, l'empereur qui règne actuellement. **Now or never**, now if ever, or the time to . . ., c'est le cas ou jamais de. . . . (*b*) *He won't be long now*, il ne tardera plus guère. *I cannot now very well refuse*, dans ces circonstances je ne peux guère refuser. (*c*) Tout de suite. *We will now hear the lessons*, nous allons maintenant réciter les leçons. *Now I'm ready*, me voilà prêt. *U.S:* **Right now**, tout de suite. (*d*) (*In narrative*) Alors ; à ce moment-là. *All was now ready*, dès lors tout était prêt. *He was even now on his way*, il était

déjà en route. (*e*) (Every) now and then, (every) now and again, de temps en temps, de temps à autre ; de loin en loin ; par moments. Now . . . now . . ., tantôt . . . tantôt. . . . **Even now**, même à cette heure tardive. *S.a.* JUST II. I. **2.** (*Without temporal significance*) (*a*) *Now Barabbas was a robber*, or Barabbas était un brigand. *Now this was little enough, but . . .*, c'était déjà peu, mais. . . . (*b*) *Now what's the matter with you?* qu'avez-vous donc ? voyons, qu'est-ce que vous avez ? **Come now!** *stop quarrelling!* voyons, voyons ! assez de querelles ! **Well now!** eh bien ! **Now then!** (i) attention ! (ii) voyons ! allons ! **II. now**, *conj.* Maintenant que, à présent que. **Now I am older** *I think otherwise*, maintenant que je suis plus âgé je pense autrement. **III. now**, *s. I shall see you between now and then*, je vous verrai d'ici là. **In three days from now**, d'ici trois jours. **By now**, à l'heure qu'il est. *He ought to be here by now*, *he ought to have been here before now*, il devrait déjà être arrivé. **Until now, up to now**, jusqu'ici, jusqu'à présent. **From now (on)**, dès maintenant, dès à présent, à partir de maintenant.

nowadays ['nauədeiz], *adv.* Aujourd'hui ; de nos jours ; à l'heure actuelle ; *F:* à l'heure qu'il est ; par le temps qui court.

nowhere ['nouhwɛər], *adv.* Nulle part ; en aucun lieu. *He is nowhere near as tall as you*, il n'est pas à beaucoup près aussi grand que vous ; il s'en faut de beaucoup qu'il soit aussi grand que vous.

nowise ['nouwaiz], *adv.* En aucune façon.

noxious ['nɔkʃəs], *a.* Nuisible, nocif ; malfaisant, malsain ; (plante) vireuse ; (gaz) délétère ; (air) contagieux.

nozzle [nɔzl], *s.* Ajutage *m* ; jet *m*, lance *f* (de tuyau) ; canule *f* (de seringue) ; bec *m*, tuyau *m*, buse *f* (de soufflet) ; ventouse *f*, buse aspiratrice (de nettoyeuse par le vide). **Spray-nozzle**, (i) ajutage d'arrosage ; (ii) *I.C.E:* gicleur *m.*

nubile ['njuːbil], *a.* Nubile.

nubility [njuːˈbiliti], *s.* Nubilité *f.*

nuclear ['njuːkliər], *a.* Nucléaire.

nucleole ['njuːklioul], *s.* Nucléole *m.*

nucleus, *pl.* **-ei** ['njuːkliəs, -iai], *s.* Noyau *m* (de cellule, de comète, etc.). *F: The n. of a library*, un commencement de bibliothèque. **Nucleus crew**, noyau d'équipage.

nude [njuːd]. **I.** *a.* Nu. *Art:* **To paint n. figures**, peindre des nus. *Com:* **Nude stockings**, bas couleur chair. **2.** *s. Art:* Nudité *f* ; figure nue. **To draw from the nude**, dessiner d'après le nu. **A study from the nude**, une académie ; un nu.

nudge¹ [nʌdʒ], *s.* Coup *m* de coude.

nudge², *v.tr.* Pousser (qn) du coude ; donner un coup de coude à (qn) (en guise d'avertissement).

nudism ['njuːdizm], *s.* Nudisme *m.*

nudist ['njuːdist], *s.* Nudiste *mf.*

nudity ['njuːditi], *s.* Nudité *f.*

nugget ['nʌgit], *s.* Pépite *f* (d'or).

nuisance ['njuːs(ə)ns], *s.* **1.** *Jur:* Dommage *m* ; atteinte portée aux droits du public. 'Commit no nuisance,' défense de déposer des immondices. **2.** *F: He is a perfect n.*, il est assommant. **Go away, you're a n.!** va-t-en, tu m'embêtes ! *Long skirts are a n.*, les jupes longues sont gênantes. *That's a nuisance!* voilà qui est bien ennuyeux ! **What a nuisance!** quel ennui !

null [nʌl], *a. Jur:* Nul, *f.* nulle ; (*of legacy*) caduc, *f.* caduque. **Null and void**, nul et de nul effet, nul et sans effet, nul et non avenu.

nullify ['nʌlifai], *v.tr.* Annuler, nullifier ; infirmer (un acte).

nullity ['nʌliti], s. **1.** *Jur:* Nullité *f*, invalidité *f* (d'un mariage, etc.). **2.** (*Pers.*) A nullity, une non-valeur; un homme nul.

numb[1] [nʌm], *a.* Engourdi. **Hands numb with cold,** mains engourdies par le froid. '**numb-fish,** s. *Ich:* Torpille *f*.

numb[2], *v.tr.* Engourdir. **Senses numbed with** *terror,* sens glacés d'effroi.

number[1] ['nʌmbər], s. **1.** (a) *Ar:* Nombre *m*. **Whole** n., nombre entier. (b) **The greater** n. **are of this opinion,** le plus grand nombre est de cette opinion. **Given equal numbers we should be the stronger,** à nombre égal nous serions les plus forts. **They were six in number,** ils étaient au nombre de six. **They are few in** n., ils sont en petit nombre, peu nombreux. **Books without number,** des livres innombrables. (c) A (**certain**) **number of** *persons,* un certain nombre de personnes; plusieurs personnes. A (**large**) **number of** men, **numbers of** men, *were killed,* nombre d'hommes furent tués. *F:* **Any number of . . .,** un grand nombre de . . . ; bon nombre de. . . . (d) *pl.* **Numbers.** *In small numbers,* en petit nombre. **To win by (force of) numbers,** l'emporter par le nombre. *To be overpowered by numbers,* succomber sous le nombre. (e) **One of their number,** (l')un d'entre eux. **He is not of our** n., il n'est pas des nôtres; il n'est pas de notre compagnie. **2.** Chiffre *m*. **To write the** n. **on a** *page,* mettre le chiffre en une page. **3.** Numéro *m* (d'une maison, d'une auto, etc.); (numéro) matricule *m* (d'un soldat, d'un fusil). **I live at number forty,** je demeure au numéro quarante. *F:* **His number is up,** son affaire est faite; *F:* il est fichu, flambé. **4.** *Gram:* Nombre. **5.** (a) *Th:* Numéro (du programme). (b) *Publ:* Numéro (d'un journal); livraison *f*, fascicule *m* (d'un ouvrage qui paraît par (fascicules). **6.** *pl. Lit:* (a) *Mus:* **Soft numbers,** doux accords. (b) Vers *mpl*, poésie *f*.

number[2], *v.tr.* **1.** Compter, dénombrer. **His days are numbered,** il n'a plus longtemps à vivre; ses jours sont comptés. **To number s.o. among one's friends,** compter qn parmi ses amis. **The army numbers thirty thousand,** l'armée compte trente mille hommes. **They n. several thousand,** ils sont au nombre de plusieurs mille; leur nombre se chiffre par milliers. **2.** (a) Numéroter (les maisons, etc.). (b) *v.i. Mil:* **To number** (**off**), se numéroter. '**numbering-machine,** **-stamp,** s. Numéroteur *m*.

numberless ['nʌmbərləs], *a.* Innombrable; sans nombre.

numbness ['nʌmnəs], s. Engourdissement *m*; torpeur *f* (de l'esprit).

numeral ['njumərəl]. **1.** *a.* Numéral, -aux. **2.** *s.* (a) Chiffre *m*, nombre *m*. (b) **The cardinal** numerals, les numéraux cardinaux.

numeration [njumə'reiʃ(ə)n], s. *Ar:* Numération *f*.

numerator ['njuməreitər], s. *Mth:* Numérateur *m*.

numerical [nju'merik(ə)l], *a.* Numérique. **-ally,** *adv.* Numériquement.

numerous ['njumərəs], *a.* Nombreux.

numismatic [njumiz'matik], *a.* Numismatique.

numismatics [njumiz'matiks], *s.pl.* La numismatique.

numismatist [nju'mizmətist], s. Numismate *m*.

numskull ['nʌmskʌl], s. *F:* Nigaud, -aude; *F:* buse *f*; idiot, -ote.

nun [nʌn], *s.f. Ecc:* Religieuse, *F:* nonne. *He was nursed by the nuns,* il a été soigné par les sœurs. '**nun's 'veiling,** s. *Tex:* Flanelle *f* mousseline.

nunciature ['nʌnʃiətjər], s. *Ecc:* Nonciature *f*.

nuncio ['nʌnʃio], s. **Papal nuncio,** nonce *m* du Pape.

nunnery ['nʌnəri], s. Couvent *m* (de religieuses).

nuptial ['nʌpʃəl]. **1.** *a.* Nuptial, -aux. **2.** *s.pl.* Nuptials, noces *f*.

nurse[1] [nə:rs], s. **1.** (a (Wet-)nurse, nourrice *f*. **To put a baby out to nurse,** mettre un bébé en nourrice. (b) *See* DRY-NURSE[1]. (c) Bonne *f* (d'enfants). **2.** (Sick-)nurse, garde-malade *f*, *pl.* gardes-malades. **Hospital nurse,** infirmière *f*. **Male nurse,** garde-malade *m*; infirmier *m*.

nurse[2], *v.tr.* **1.** Allaiter (un enfant). *F:* **To be** nursed in luxury, élevé dans le luxe. **2.** Soigner (un malade). **Sh₃ nursed him back to health,** elle lui fit recouvrer la santé grâce à ses soins. **3.** (a) Soigner, abriter (des plantes, etc.); ménager (un cheval, etc.) en vue du dernier effort à donner. **To nurse one's public,** soigner sa popularité. (b) Nourrir, entretenir (un chagrin, etc.); mitonner, mijoter (un projet). **4.** Bercer (un enfant); tenir (qn, qch.) dans ses bras. '**nursing**[1], *a.* **1.** **Nursing mother,** (i) mère qui nourrit (au sein); (ii) (mère) nourricière *f*. **2.** (*In hospital*) **The nursing staff,** le personnel des infirmières. **nursing**[2], s. **1.** Allaitement *m*. **2.** Culture assidue (des plantes, etc.); ménagement *m*, soin *m* (d'une affaire); entretien *m* (d'un sentiment). **3.** (a) Soins *mpl* (d'une garde-malade). (b) Profession *f* de garde-malade. **To go in for nursing,** se faire infirmière. '**nursing home,** s. (*For mental cases*) Maison *f* de santé; (*for surgical cases*) clinique *f*; hôpital privé.

nurseling ['nə:rsliŋ], s. = NURSLING.

nursemaid ['nə:rsmeid], *s.f.* Bonne d'enfants.

nursery ['nə:rsəri], s. **1.** (a) Chambre *f* des enfants; nursery *f*. **Night nursery,** dortoir *m* des enfants. **Nursery tale,** conte *m* de nourrice; conte de ma mère l'Oie. (b) Crèche *f*; garderie *f*. **Resident nurse,** pouponnière *f*. **Nursery school,** maternelle *f*. **2.** (a) Pépinière *f*. (b) *Pisc:* Alevinier *m*, vivier *m*. '**nursery-'gardener,** s. Pépiniériste *mf*. '**nursery-'governess,** *s.f.* Gouvernante pour jeunes enfants.

nurseryman, *pl.* **-men** ['nə:rsərimən, -men], *s.m.* Pépiniériste *m*.

nursling ['nə:rsliŋ], s. Nourrisson *m*.

nurture[1] ['nə:rtjər], s. Nourriture *f*. **1.** Éducation *f*; soins *mpl*. **N. of the mind,** nourriture de l'esprit. **2.** Aliments *mpl*.

nurture[2], *v.tr.* **1.** Nourrir (les enfants, etc.) (*on*, de). **2.** Élever, faire l'éducation de (qn).

nut [nʌt], s. **1.** (a) Noix *f*. Hazel-nut, noisette *f*. *F:* **Tough, hard, nut to crack,** (i) problème *m* difficile à résoudre; (ii) personne difficile, peu commode. **He can't sing for nuts,** il ne sait pas chanter du tout. **To be dead nuts on s.o., on sth.,** raffoler de qn ou qch. *S.a.* BEECH-NUT, EARTH-NUT, *etc.* (b) *P:* Tête *f*; *P:* ciboulot *m*, boule *f*, caboche *f*. **To be off one's nut,** être timbré, toqué, loufoque; avoir perdu la boule. **2.** Écrou *m*. **Wing-nut, butterfly-nut,** écrou à oreilles, à ailettes. **Hexagonal nut,** écrou à six pans. *S.a.* CASTLE-NUT, CHECK-NUT. **3.** *Mus:* (a) Sillet *m* (de violon). (b) Hausse *f* (d'archet). '**At, with, the nut,'** "du talon." **4.** *Com:* Nut coal, nuts, gailletin *m*. '**nut-brown,** *a.* (Couleur) noisette *inv.* **Nut-brown hair,** cheveux châtains. '**nut-cracker,** s. (Pair of) nut-crackers, casse-noisette(s) *m inv*, casse-noix *m inv*. *F:* **Nut-cracker chin,** menton en casse-noisette, en pince de homard. **'nut-tree,** s. Noisetier *m*; *F:* coudrier *m*.

nuthatch ['nʌthatʃ], *s. Orn:* (Sittelle *f*) torchepot *m*; casse-noisette *m inv.*

nutmeg ['nʌtmeg], *s.* (Noix *f*) muscade *f*.

nutria ['njutria], *s.* Fourrure *f* de coypou; *Com:* loutre *f* d'Amérique; nutria *m*.

nutriment ['njutrimənt], *s.* Nourriture *f*; aliments nourrissants.

nutrition [nju'triʃ(ə)n], *s.* Nutrition *f*.

nutritious [nju'triʃəs], *a.* Nutritif, nourrissant.

nutritive ['njutritiv], *a.* Nutritif, nourrissant.

nutshell ['nʌtʃel], *s.* Coquille *f* de noix. *F:* **That's the whole thing in a nutshell,** voilà

toute l'affaire (résumée) en un mot, en deux mots.

nutting ['nʌtiŋ], *s.* Cueillette *f* des noisettes.

nux vomica [nʌks'vɔmika], *s.* Noix *f* vomique. **Nux vomica tree,** vomiquier *m*.

nuzzle [nʌzl], *v.i.* **1.** (*Of pig, etc.*) Fouiller avec le groin. **2. To nuzzle against s.o.'s shoulder,** (*of dog, horse*) fourrer son nez contre l'épaule de qn; (*of pers.*) se blottir sur l'épaule de qn.

nyctalope ['niktaloup], *a. & s.* Nyctalope (*mf*).

nyctalopia [nikta'loupia], *s.* Nyctalopie *f*.

nymph [nimf]. **1.** *s.f. Myth:* Nymphe. **Woodnymph,** hamadryade. **2.** *s. Ent:* Nymphe *f*.

nystagmus [nis'tagməs], *s. Med:* Nystagmus *m*.

O

O¹, o, *pl.* **o's, oes** [ou, o:uz], *s.* **1.** (La lettre) O, o *m*. **2.** *Tp:* (*Nought*) Zéro *m*. **3.** Cercle *m*, rond *m*.

O², *int.* O, oh. *O how tired I am!* ah! que je suis fatigué! *O for a glass of water!* que ne donnerais-je pas pour un verre d'eau! *O to be in England!* que ne suis-je en Angleterre!

oaf, *pl.* **-s, oaves** [ouf, -s, o:uvz], *s.* **1.** Idiot, -ote (de naissance). **2.** (*a*) Lourdaud *m*, godiche *m*. (*b*) Bon *m* à rien.

oafish ['oufiʃ], *a.* Lourdaud, stupide.

oak [ouk], *s.* (*a*) *Bot:* Oak(-tree), chêne *m*. Evergreen oak, holm-oak, yeuse *f*; chêne vert. Oak-plantation, chênaie *f*. (*b*) (Bois *m* de) chêne. Dark oak, (couleur) vieux chêne. (*c*) (*At universities*) To sport one's oak, défendre sa porte. **'oak-apple, -gall,** *s.* Noix *f* de galle; pomme *f* de chêne: **'oak-mast,** *s.* Glands *mpl* de chêne; glandée *f*.

oakum ['oukəm], *s.* Étoupe *f*, filasse *f*. To pick oakum, (i) tirer de l'étoupe; faire de la filasse; (ii) *F:* (*as prison task* =) casser des cailloux.

oar¹ ['ɔːər], *s.* (*a*) Aviron *m*, rame *f*. To ply the oars, to pull at the oars, tirer à la rame; *Nau:* souquer ferme. *Nau:* Oars! lève rames! To rest, lie, on one's oars, (i) lever les avirons; (ii) *F:* dormir sur ses lauriers. *F:* To put in one's oar, intervenir (mal à propos). (*b*) (*Opposed to scull*) Aviron de pointe. (*c*) (*Oarsman*) Good oar, bon rameur.

oar². **1.** *v.i.* Ramer. **2.** *v.tr.* To oar a boat, faire aller une embarcation. *To oar one's way along,* avancer à la rame.

-oared ['ɔːərd], *a.* Four-oared, à quatre rames. Eight-oared boat, huit *m* de pointe.

oarsman, *pl.* **-men** ['ɔːzmən, -men], *s.m.* Rameur; tireur d'aviron; *Nau:* nageur.

oasis, *pl.* **oases** [o'eisis, -iːz], *s.* Oasis *f*.

oast(-house) [oust(haus)], *s.* Séchoir *m* (à houblon); four *m* à houblon.

oat [out], *s.* Avoine *f*. Wild oat(s), folle avoine. *F:* To sow one's wild oats, faire des fredaines; jeter sa gourme. *A field of oats,* un champ d'avoine. (*Of horse*) To feel its oats, être vif; être en l'air. To be off its oats, refuser de manger; être malade. **'oat-cake,** *s. Cu:* Galette *f* d'avoine. **'oat-grass,** *s.* Folle avoine.

oaten ['outən], *a.* (De farine) d'avoine.

oath, *pl.* **oaths** [ouθ, o:uðz], *s.* **1.** Serment *m*. To take the oath, prêter serment. I'll take my oath on it, j'en jurerais; *F:* j'en lève la main.

To put s.o. on his oath; to administer, tender, the oath to s.o., faire prêter serment à qn; déférer le serment à qn. On oath, sous (la foi du) serment. **2.** Juron *m*; gros mot. To rap out an oath, lâcher un juron.

oatmeal ['outmiːl], *s.* Farine *f* d'avoine.

obduracy ['ɔbdjurəsi], *s.* **1.** (*a*) Endurcissement *m* (de cœur); opiniâtreté *f*, entêtement *m*. (*b*) Inflexibilité *f*. **2.** *Theol:* Impénitence *f*.

obdurate ['ɔbdjuret], *a.* **1.** (*a*) Endurci; têtu, opiniâtre. (*b*) Inexorable, inflexible. **2.** Impénitent. **-ly,** *adv.* (*a*) Avec entêtement. (*b*) Inexorablement.

obedience [o'biːdjəns], *s.* **1.** Obéissance *f* (*to*, à). To enforce obedience to the law, faire respecter la loi. To compel obedience, se faire obéir. *Com:* In obedience to your orders . . ., conformément à vos ordres. . . . **2.** *Ecc:* Obédience *f*.

obedient [o'biːdjənt], *a.* Obéissant, soumis, docile. *To be o. to s.o.,* obéir à qn. *S.a.* SERVANT 1. **-ly,** *adv.* Avec obéissance, avec soumission. *Corr:* Yours obediently, agréez, Monsieur, mes salutations empressées; *Com:* toujours à vos ordres.

obeisance [o'beisəns], *s.* **1.** *A. & Lit:* Salut *m*, révérence *f*. To make (an) obeisance to s.o., s'incliner devant qn. **2.** Obéissance *f*, hommage *m*. To pay obeisance to s.o., rendre hommage à qn.

obelisk ['ɔbilisk], *s.* **1.** *Archeol:* Obélisque *m*. **2.** (*a*) *Pal:* Obèle *m*. (*b*) *Typ:* Croix *f*; obèle.

obelus, *pl.* **-li** ['ɔbiləs, -lai], *s.* = OBELISK 2.

obese [o'biːs], *a.* Obèse.

obesity [o'biːsiti], *s.* Obésité *f*.

obey [o'bei], *v.tr.* Obéir à (qn, un ordre). *He is obeyed,* il est obéi. *The orders must be obeyed,* il faut obéir aux ordres. I must obey orders, je ne connais que la consigne. To obey the law, obéir, se plier, aux lois. To obey a summons, obtempérer à une sommation.

obfuscate ['ɔbfʌskeit], *v.tr.* Obscurcir, offusquer (la vue, le jugement). *P:* To be obfuscated (*by drink*), être hébété, stupéfié, par la boisson.

obiter ['ɔbitər], *Lt.adv.* En passant. **'Obiter dicta,** opinions et propos (d'un écrivain).

obituary [o'bitjuəri], *a. & s.* Obituary(-list), nécrologe *m*. Obituary notice, notice nécrologique. *Journ:* Obituary column, nécrologie *f*.

object¹ ['ɔbdʒekt], *s.* **1.** (*a*) Objet *m*, chose *f*. (*b*) *O. of, for, pity,* objet ou sujet *m* de pitié. *To be an o. of ridicule,* être en butte au ridicule.

The o. of his studies, le sujet de ses études. **2.** *(a)* But *m,* objectif *m,* objet. **With this object (in view)** ..., dans ce but ...; à cette fin. ... *What is the o. of all this?* à quoi vise tout cela? **There's no object in doing that,** cela ne sert à rien de faire cela. *(b) (In applying for post)* Salary **no object,** les appointements importent peu. *F:* Expense is no object, on ne regarde pas à la dépense. **3.** *Gram:* Complément *m,* régime *m,* objet. **Object clause,** proposition complétive. **'object-glass, -lens,** *s.* *Opt:* Objectif *m.* *Photomicrographic o.-g.,* micro-objectif *m.* **'object-lesson,** *s.* *(a) Sch:* Leçon *f* de choses. *(b) His modesty is an o.-l. to others,* sa modestie doit servir d'exemple *m* aux autres. **'object-slide,** *s.* Porte-objet *m inv* (de microscope).

object² [ob'dʒekt]. **I.** *v.tr.* To object sth. to s.o., objecter qch. à qn. *It was objected that* ..., on a objecté que ...; on a fait valoir que. ... **2.** *v.i.* **To object to sth.,** faire objection, élever une objection, trouver à redire, à qch.; désapprouver qch. **To object to s.o.,** avoir des objections à faire contre qn; récuser (un témoin). **To object to doing sth.,** se refuser à faire qch. *I o. to his doing it,* je m'oppose à ce qu'il le fasse. *Do you o. to my smoking?* la fumée vous gêne-t-elle? *I don't o. to a glass of wine,* un verre de vin ne serait pas de refus.

objection [ob'dʒekʃ(ə)n], *s.* **I.** Objection *f.* **To raise an objection,** soulever, formuler, une objection. *The o. has been raised that* ..., on a objecté que. ... **To find, make, an objection to sth.,** trouver un empêchement à qch. **To take objection to sth.,** (i) faire des objections à qch.; (ii) se fâcher de qch. **To make no objection to sth.,** ne rien objecter contre qch. *I have no o. to his doing so,* je ne m'oppose pas à ce qu'il le fasse. *I have a strong o. to doing that,* il me répugne (fortement) de faire cela. **If you have no objection,** si cela ne vous fait rien. **2.** Obstacle *m,* inconvénient *m.* *There is no o. to your leaving at once,* il n'y a pas d'obstacle à ce que vous partiez immédiatement. *I see no o. (to it),* je n'y vois pas d'inconvénient.

objectionable [ob'dʒekʃ(ə)nəbl], *a.* **I.** A qui, à quoi, on peut trouver à redire; répréhensible. **2.** Désagréable. *Idea that is most o. to me,* idée qui me répugne. **To use o. language,** tenir des propos choquants.

objective [ob'dʒektiv]. **I.** *a. (a) Phil:* Objectif. *(b) Gram:* Objective case, cas régime, cas objectif. **2.** *s.* But *m,* objectif *m.* *(b) Opt:* Objectif.

objectivity [obdʒek'tiviti], *s.* Objectivité *f.*

objector [ob'dʒektər], *s.* Protestataire *m,* réclameur *m.* *S.a.* CONSCIENTIOUS 2.

objurgate ['obdʒərgeit], *v.tr.* Accabler (qn) de reproches.

objurgation [obdʒər'geiʃ(ə)n], *s.* Objurgation *f.*

oblate¹ ['obleit], *s. Ecc:* Oblat, -ate.

oblate² ['obleit, o'bleit], *a. Geom:* (Ellipsoïde, etc.) aplati (aux pôles).

oblation [o'bleiʃ(ə)n], *s. Ecc:* Oblation *f.*

obligation [obli'geiʃ(ə)n], *s.* Obligation *f.* *(a)* **To put, lay, s.o. under an obligation to do sth.,** imposer à qn l'obligation de faire qch. *To be under an o. to do sth.,* être dans l'obligation de, être astreint à, être tenu de, faire qch. *Ecc:* Day of obligation, fête *f* d'obligation. *(b)* Dette *f* de reconnaissance. **To be under an obligation to s.o.,** devoir de la reconnaissance à qn. **To lay, put, s.o. under an obligation,** obliger qn; créer une obligation à qn. *You are laying me under an o.,* c'est à charge de revanche. *(c) Com:* **To**

meet, to fail to meet, one's obligations, faire honneur, manquer, à ses engagements.

obligatory ['obligətəri], *a.* Obligatoire; de rigueur. **To make it obligatory (up)on s.o. to do sth.,** imposer à qn l'obligation de faire qch.

oblige [o'blaidʒ], *v.tr.* **I.** Obliger, astreindre (qn à faire qch.). **To be obliged to do sth.,** être obligé, tenu, de faire qch. *I was obliged to obey,* je fus contraint d'obéir; force me fut d'obéir. **2.** *(a)* **To oblige a friend,** rendre service à un ami. *You would greatly o. (me) by sending me* ..., vous m'obligeriez beaucoup en m'envoyant. ... *Can you o. me with a light?* auriez-vous l'amabilité de me donner du feu? *He did it to o. (us),* il l'a fait par pure complaisance. *In order to o. you* ..., pour vous être agréable. ... **An answer by bearer will oblige,** prière de vouloir bien confier la réponse au porteur. *(b)* **To be obliged to s.o.,** être obligé à qn. *I am much obliged to you for your kindness,* je vous suis infiniment reconnaissant, je vous sais infiniment gré, de votre bonté.

obliging, *a.* Obligeant, complaisant, serviable. **-ly,** *adv.* Obligeamment, complaisamment.

obligingness [o'blaidʒiŋnəs], *s.* Obligeance *f,* complaisance *f.*

oblique¹ [o'bli:k], *a. (a)* (Ligne, angle) oblique; (regard) de biais. *Mil:* Oblique fire, tir d'écharpe. *(b) F:* **Oblique ways,** moyens indirects, détournés. *(c) Gram:* **Oblique case,** cas indirect, oblique. **Oblique oration,** discours indirect. **-ly,** *adv.* Obliquement, de biais, en biais. *Carp:* En mouchoir.

oblique², *v.i. Mil: etc:* Obliquer.

obliterate [o'blitəreit], *v.tr.* **I.** *(a)* Faire disparaître, effacer (des chiffres, etc.). *(b)* Oblitérer, composter (un timbre). **2.** *Med:* Oblitérer (un conduit, etc.).

obliteration [oblitə'reiʃ(ə)n], *s.* **I.** *(a)* Effaçage *m.* *(b)* Rature *f.* **2.** Oblitération *f* (d'un timbre).

oblivion [o'bliviən], *s.* (État *m* d')oubli *m.* **To sink into oblivion,** tomber dans l'oubli.

oblivious [o'bliviəs], *a.* **I.** Oublieux *(of,* de). **2.** *F:* To be totally o. of sth., ignorer tout à fait qch.

oblong ['obloŋ]. **I.** *a.* Oblong, -ongue; (sphéroïde) allongé. **2.** *s.* Rectangle *m.*

obloquy ['obləkwi], *s. (a)* Calomnie *f.* **To cover s.o. with obloquy,** cribler qn d'attaques malveillantes. **Held up to public obloquy,** exposé à la vindicte publique. *(b)* Honte *f,* opprobre *m.*

obnoxious [ob'nokʃəs], *a. (a)* Haïssable, odieux; antipathique *(to s.o.,* à qn). *(b) O. smell,* odeur nauséabonde, désagréable.

oboe ['oubou], *s.* Hautbois *m.*

oboist ['oubouist], *s.* Hautboïste *mf,* oboïste *mf.*

obscene [ob'si:n], *a.* Obscène.

obscenity [ob'si:niti], *s.* Obscénité *f.*

obscurantism [ob'skjuərəntizm], *s.* Obscurantisme *m.*

obscurantist [ob'skjuərəntist], *a. & s.* Obscurantiste *(mf).*

obscuration [obskju'reiʃ(ə)n], *s.* **I.** Obscurcissement *m.* **2.** Obscuration *f* (d'un astre).

obscure¹ [ob'skjuər], *a.* **I.** Obscur, ténébreux, sombre. *Ph:* **Obscure rays,** rayons invisibles. **2.** (Discours, livre) obscur; (argument) peu clair. **3.** *O. birth,* naissance obscure. *O. author,* auteur peu connu. **-ly,** *adv.* Obscurément.

obscure², *v.tr.* Obscurcir. **To o. sth. from s.o.'s view,** cacher qch. à qn. *Clouds obscured the sun,* des nuages voilaient le soleil. *Nau:* **To o. the lights,** masquer les feux. *S.a.* ISSUE¹ 5.

obscurity [ob'skjuəriti], *s.* Obscurité *f* (de la

nuit, de style, de naissance). **To lapse into obscurity**, tomber dans l'obscurité. **To live in obscurity**, vivre dans l'obscurité. **To rise from o.**, sortir de l'obscurité.

obsequies ['ɔbsekwiz], *s.pl.* Obsèques *f*, funérailles *f*. **To attend the obsequies**, suivre le convoi.

obsequious [ɔb'si:kwiəs], *a*. Obséquieux. **-ly**, *adv.* Obséquieusement.

obsequiousness [ɔb'si:kwiəsnəs], *s*. Obséquiosité *f*.

observable [ɔb'zə:rvəbl], *a*. **1**. (Cérémonie, etc.) à observer. **2**. Visible; (changement) perceptible, sensible. **3.** Remarquable; digne de remarque, d'attention. **-ably**, *adv.* Sensiblement, perceptiblement.

observance [ɔb'zə:rvəns], *s*. **1**. (*a*) Observation *f*, observance *f* (de la loi, etc.); observance (du dimanche). (*b*) Règle *f*, observance (d'un ordre religieux). **2.** **Religious observances**, pratiques religieuses.

observant [ɔb'zə:rvənt], *a*. **1**. Observateur, -trice (*of a rule*, d'une règle). *He is always o. of his duty*, il est toujours très attentif à son devoir. **2.** *O.* **mind**, esprit observateur. *He is very o.*, rien ne lui échappe; *F:* il n'a pas les yeux dans sa poche.

observation [ɔbzər'veiʃ(ə)n], *s*. Observation *f*. **1**. (*a*) **To keep s.o. under observation**, tenir qn en observation; surveiller qn. *To come under s.o.'s o.*, tomber sous les yeux de qn. **To escape observation**, se dérober aux regards. *Mil:* **Observation post**, poste *m* d'observation; observatoire *m*. (*b*) *Astr:* *Surv:* Coup *m* de lunette. **To take an observation**, prendre, faire, une observation; *Nau:* faire le point. **2.** (*a*) Remarque *f*. (*b*) *pl.* *To publish one's observations on* . . ., publier ses observations sur. . . .

observatory [ɔb'zə:rvətəri], *s*. Observatoire *m*.

observe [ɔb'zə:rv], *v.tr.* **1**. Observer (la' loi, un jeûne); se conformer à (un ordre). **To observe silence**, observer le silence. *To o. care in doing sth.*, apporter des précautions à faire qch. **To observe the Sabbath**, observer le dimanche. **2.** Observer, regarder (les étoiles, etc.). **3.** Apercevoir, remarquer, noter (un fait). *I observed him draw the curtains*, je le vis tirer les rideaux. **4.** (*a*) Dire. *I observed (to him) that* . . ., je lui fis remarquer, je lui fis l'observation, que. . . . (*b*) *Abs.* *No one has observed on this fact*, personne n'a commenté ce fait. **observing**, *a*. = OBSERVANT.

observer [ɔb'zə:rvər], *s*. Observateur, -trice.

obsess [ɔb'ses], *v.tr.* Obséder. **To be obsessed with an idea**, être obsédé, hanté, par une idée; être en proie à une idée.

obsession [ɔb'seʃ(ə)n], *s*. Obsession *f*.

obsidian [ɔb'sidiən], *s*. *Miner:* Obsidienne *f*, obsidiane *f*.

obsolescent [ɔbso'les(ə)nt], *a*. Qui tombe en désuétude. *This word is o.*, ce mot a vieilli.

obsolete ['ɔbsoli:t], *a*. Désuet, -ète; hors d'usage; tombé en désuétude; (*of fashion, car*) suranné; (*of ship*) déclassé. *To grow o.*, passer de mode; tomber en désuétude.

obstacle ['ɔbstəkl], *s*. Obstacle *m*, empêchement *m*. **To put obstacles in s.o.'s way**, dresser, susciter, des obstacles à qn. *To be an o. to sth.*, faire obstacle à qch. *Sp:* **Obstacle-race**, course *f* d'obstacles.

obstetric(al) [ɔb'stetrik(əl)], *a*. Obstétrical, -aux; obstétrique.

obstetrician [ɔbste'triʃ(ə)n], *s*. Accoucheur *m*.

obstetrics [ɔb'stetriks], *s.pl.* Obstétrique *f*.

obstinacy ['ɔbstinəsi], *s*. Obstination *f*, entêtement *m*, opiniâtreté *f*. *To show o.*, s'obstiner.

obstinate ['ɔbstinet], *a*. Obstiné (*in doing sth.*, à faire qch.); opiniâtre. **Obstinate as a mule**, entêté, têtu, comme un mulet. *O. contest*, combat acharné. **-ly**, *adv.* Obstinément, opiniâtrement.

obstreperous [ɔb'strepərəs], *a*. Bruyant, tapageur; turbulent. (*Of arrested drunkard, etc.*) **To be obstreperous**, *P:* faire de la rouspétance; rouspéter.

obstruct [ɔb'strʌkt], *v.tr.* (*a*) Obstruer; encombrer (la rue); engorger, boucher (un tuyau). 'Do not obstruct the gangway,' "n'encombrez pas le passavant." **To obstruct the view**, incommoder, gêner, la vue. (*b*) Gêner, entraver (les mouvements de qn). *Parl:* **To obstruct a bill**, faire de l'obstruction. (*c*) **To obstruct the traffic**, embarrasser, entraver, la circulation.

obstruction [ɔb'strʌkʃ(ə)n], *s*. **1**. (*a*) Engorgement *m* (d'un tuyau). *Med:* *O. of the bowels*, occlusion, obstruction, intestinale. (*b*) Empêchement *m* (de qn dans ses affaires). (*c*) *Parl:* **To practise obstruction**, faire de l'obstruction. **2.** Encombrement *m*, embarras *m* (dans la rue); entrave *f* (à la navigation). *Rail:* *An o. on the line*, un obstacle sur la voie.

obstructive [ɔb'strʌktiv], *a*. Obstructif. *O. tactics, o. measures*, tactique d'obstruction; mesures vexatoires.

obtain [ɔb'tein]. **1**. *v.tr.* Obtenir; se procurer (des provisions, etc.). **To obtain sugar from beet**, retirer du sucre de la betterave. *His merit obtained him the appointment*, son mérite lui a valu sa nomination. *To o. first place*, remporter la première place (dans un concours). **2.** *v.i.* Avoir cours; prévaloir. *Practice that obtains among the rich*, pratique établie, qui règne, dans les classes riches. *System now obtaining*, régime actuellement en vigueur.

obtainable [ɔb'teinəbl], *a*. Procurable. *Where is that o.?* où cela s'obtient-il? où peut-on se procurer cela?

obtrude [ɔb'tru:d], *v.tr. & i.* Mettre (qch.) en avant. **To obtrude oneself**, s'imposer à l'attention. *To o. (oneself) on s.o.*, importuner qn.

obtrusion [ɔb'tru:ʒ(ə)n], *s*. Intrusion *f*; importunité *f*.

obtrusive [ɔb'tru:siv], *a*. **1**. Importun; indiscret, -ète. **2.** *O. smell*, odeur pénétrante.

obtrusiveness [ɔb'tru:sivnəs], *s*. Importunité *f*.

obturate ['ɔbtjureit], *v.tr.* Boucher, obturer.

obturating, *a*. Obturateur, -trice.

obturation [ɔbtju'reiʃ(ə)n], *s*. Obturation *f*.

obturator ['ɔbtjureitər], *s*. Obturateur *m*.

obtuse [ɔb'tju:s], *a*. **1**. Obtus, émoussé. *Geom:* **Obtuse angle**, angle obtus. **2.** (Esprit) obtus, peu intelligent. **ob'tuse-angled**, *a*. Obtusangle.

obverse ['ɔbvə:rs], *a. & s*. Obverse (side) of a medal, obvers(e) *m*, face *f*, d'une médaille. (*b*) Obverse of a truth, opposé *m* d'une vérité.

obviate ['ɔbvieit], *v.tr.* Éviter, parer à, obvier à (une difficulté); prévenir (des scrupules).

obvious ['ɔbviəs], *a*. Évident, clair, manifeste; de toute évidence. *O. fact*, fait patent, qui crève les yeux. **It was the obvious thing to do**, c'était indiqué. *O. tricks*, finesses cousues de fil blanc. **-ly**, *adv.* Évidemment, manifestement. *She is o. wrong*, il est clair qu'elle a tort.

obviousness ['ɔbviəsnəs], *s*. Évidence *f*, caractère *m* manifeste (*of*, de).

occasion[1] [o'keiʒ(ə)n], *s*. **1**. Cause *f*, occasion *f*. *You have no o. to be alarmed*, il n'y a pas lieu de vous inquiéter. *I have no o. for his help*, je n'ai que faire de son aide. *To give o. for scandal*, donner occasion à la médisance. *There's no o. to crow*, il n'y a pas de quoi chanter victoire. **Should the occasion arise**, s'il y a lieu ; le cas échéant. **2.** *pl.* **To go about one's lawful occasions**, vaquer à ses affaires (dans le cadre de la loi). **3.** Occasion, occurrence *f*. **On the occasion of . . .**, à l'occasion de . . . ; lors de. . . . **On one occasion**, une fois. **On several occasions**, à plusieurs reprises. *On such an o.*, en pareille occasion. **On occasion**, de temps à autre, de temps en temps. *She is an acrobat on o.*, elle est acrobate à l'occasion. **As occasion requires**, suivant l'occasion ; au besoin. *Play written for the occasion*, pièce de circonstance. **4.** (*Opportunity*) **To take occasion to do sth.**, saisir l'occasion de faire qch. **occasion²**, *v.tr.* Occasionner, entraîner, donner lieu à (qch.). *To o. emotion*, faire naître l'émotion. **occasional** [o'keiʒən(ə)l], *a.* **1.** (*a*) **Occasional verse**, vers de circonstance. (*b*) **Occasional table**, table de fantaisie, table volante. **2.** *An o. visitor*, un visiteur qui vient de temps en temps. **Occasional showers**, averses éparses. **3. Occasional cause**, cause occasionnelle. **-ally**, *adv.* De temps en temps ; par occasion ; par intervalles. **occident** ['ɔksidənt], *s.* Occident *m*. **occidental** [ɔksi'dent(ə)l], *a.* Occidental, -aux. **occipital** [ɔk'sipit(ə)l], *a.* Occipital, -aux. **occiput** ['ɔksipʌt], *s. Anat :* Occiput *m*. **occlude** [ɔ'kluːd], *v.tr.* Fermer, boucher (un conduit, etc.) ; occlure (les rayons de lumière). **occlusion** [ɔ'kluːʒ(ə)n], *s.* Occlusion *f*, bouchage *m*, fermeture *f* (d'un conduit, etc.). **occult¹** [ɔ'kʌlt], *a.* Occulte. **occult².** **1.** *v.tr. Astr :* Occulter, immerger (une planète, etc.). **2.** *v.i. Nau :* (*Of light*) S'éclipser. **occultation** [ɔkʌl'teiʃ(ə)n], *s. Astr :* Occultation *f*. **occultism** [ɔ'kʌltizm], *s.* Occultisme *m*. **occupancy** ['ɔkjupənsi], *s.* Occupation *f*, habitation *f* (d'un immeuble). **occupant** ['ɔkjupənt], *s.* **1.** Occupant, -ante (de terres) ; locataire *mf* (d'une maison) ; titulaire *mf* (d'un emploi). **2. The occupants of the car**, les voyageurs *m*. **occupation** [ɔkju'peiʃ(ə)n], *s.* Occupation *f*. **1.** (*a*) **To be in occupation** *of a house*, occuper une maison. **House fit for occupation**, maison habitable. (*b*) **Army of occupation**, armée d'occupation. **2.** (*a*) **To give s.o. occupation**, donner de l'occupation à qn. *To do sth. for want of o.*, faire qch. par désœuvrement. (*b*) Métier *m*, emploi *m*. **What is he by occupation?** qu'est-ce qu'il est de son métier ? **occupier** ['ɔkjupaiər], *s.* Occupant, -ante ; locataire *mf* ; habitant, -ante (d'une maison). **occupy** ['ɔkjupai], *v.tr.* **1.** Occuper. (*a*) Habiter (une maison). (*b*) Remplir (un emploi). (*c*) Garnir (une place de guerre) ; s'emparer (d'un point stratégique). **2.** Remplir (un espace) ; occuper (une place, le temps). *The table occupies half the floor space*, la table tient la moitié de la pièce. **To occupy one's time in doing sth.**, remplir, occuper, son temps à faire qch. **3.** Occuper (qn) ; donner du travail à (qn). **To keep one's mind occupied**, s'occuper l'esprit. **occur** [ɔ'kəːr], *v.i.* (**occurred**) **1.** (*Of event*) Avoir lieu ; survenir, arriver ; se produire. *Should the case occur*, le cas échéant. *If another opportunity occurs*, si une autre occasion se présente. *This seldom occurs*, ce fait est assez rare. *Don't let it occur again!* que cela n'arrive plus ! **2.** Se rencontrer, se trouver. *This word occurs twice in the letter*, ce mot se rencontre deux fois dans la lettre. **3. It occurs to me that . . .**, il me vient

à l'idée, à l'esprit, que . . . ; l'idée me vient que. . . . *Such an idea would never have occurred to me*, une pareille idée ne me serait jamais venue à l'esprit. **occurrence** [o'kʌrəns], *s.* **1. To be of frequent occurrence**, arriver souvent ; se produire, se renouveler, fréquemment. **2.** Événement *m*, occurrence *f*. **An everyday occurrence**, un fait journalier. **ocean** ['ouʃ(ə)n], *s.* Océan *m*. **Ocean currents**, courants océaniques. *F :* **An ocean of sand**, une mer de sable. **'ocean-going**, *a.* (Navire) au long cours, long-courrier. **'ocean-'lane**, *s. Nau :* Route *f* de navigation. **Oceania** [ouʃi'einjə]. *Pr.n.* L'Océanie *f*. **oceanic** [ouʃi'anik], *a.* (*a*) Océanique. (*b*) (*Of fauna*) Pélagique. **oceanography** [ouʃiən'ɔgrəfi], *s.* Océanographie *f*. **ocellus**, *pl.* **-i** [o'seləs, -ai], *s. Nat.Hist :* Ocelle *m*. **ocelot** ['ousilɔt], *s. Z :* Ocelot *m*. **ochre¹** ['oukər], *s. Miner :* Ocre *f*. **Red ochre**, ocre rouge. **Yellow ochre**, jaune *m* d'ocre. **ochre²**, *v.tr.* Ocrer. **o'clock** [o'klɔk], *adv.phr. See* CLOCK¹. **octagon** ['ɔktagən], *s. Geom :* Octagone *m*. **octagonal** [ɔk'tagən(ə)l], *a.* Octogonal, -aux ; (écrou) à huit pans. **octahedral** [ɔkta'hiːdrəl], *a.* Octaèdre, octaédrique. **octahedron** [ɔkta'hiːdrən], *s.* Octaèdre *m*. **octave** ['ɔktev, 'ɔkteːiv], *s.* Octave *f*. **octavo** [ɔk'teivo], *a. & s. Typ :* In-octavo (*m*). **octet(te)** [ɔk'tet], *s. Mus :* Octuor *m*. **October** [ɔk'toubər], *s.* Octobre *m*. *In O.*, au mois d'octobre. (*On*) *the fifth of O.*, le cinq octobre. **octogenarian** [ɔktodʒe'neəriən], *a. & s.* Octogénaire (*mf*). **octopus** ['ɔktɔpəs], *s.* Poulpe *m* ; *esp.* pieuvre *f*. **octosyllabic** [ɔktosi'labik], *a.* Octosyllabe, octosyllabique. **octuple** ['ɔktjupl], *a.* Octuple. **ocular** ['ɔkjulər]. **1.** *a.* Oculaire. **2.** *s. Opt :* Oculaire *m* (de microscope, etc.). **oculist** ['ɔkjulist], *s.* Oculiste *m*. **odalisque** ['oudalisk], *s.* Odalisque *f*. **odd** [ɔd], *a.* **1.** (*a*) (Nombre) impair. **Odd or even**, pair ou impair. (*b*) **A hundred odd sheep**, une centaine de moutons ; quelque cent moutons. **Fifty odd thousand**, cinquante à soixante mille. *A hundred odd yards*, cent et quelques mètres. **Twenty pounds odd**, vingt livres et quelques shillings. *The odd three halfpence*, les trois sous de reste. **To be odd man**, rester en surnombre. (*At cards, etc.*) **The odd game**, la belle. **To make up the odd money**, faire l'appoint *m*. **2.** (*a*) (*Of one of a set*) Dépareillé ; (*of one of a pair*) déparié. *The odd stockings*, bas qui ne vont pas ensemble. (*b*) **Odd moments**, moments de loisir, moments perdus. **At odd times**, par-ci par-là. **Odd man**, homme à tout faire. *S.a.* JOB 1. *Com :* **Odd lot**, solde *m*. **3.** (*a*) *Com :* **Odd size**, dimension spéciale, non courante. (*b*) Singulier, drôle ; (*of pers.*) excentrique, original, -aux. *The odd thing about it is that . . .*, le curieux de l'affaire, c'est que. . . . *Well, that's odd!* voilà qui est singulier ! c'est bizarre ! **-ly**, *adv.* Bizarrement, singulièrement. *Oddly enough nobody knew anything about it*, chose curieuse, personne n'en savait rien. **oddity** ['ɔditi], *s.* **1.** (*a*) Singularité *f*, bizarrerie *f*. (*b*) *He has some little oddities*, il a quelques petites manies. **2.** (a) Personne excentrique ; original, -ale. (b) Chose f bizarre ; curiosité f.

oddments ['ɔdmənts], s.pl. Com: Fonds m de boutique ; fins f de série.

oddness ['ɔdnəs], s. **1.** Imparité f. **2.** Singularité f, bizarrerie f.

odds [ɔdz], s.pl. (Occ. with sg. const.) **1.** (a) Avantage m ; chances fpl. **The odds are against him,** les chances sont contre lui. **To fight against (great, long) odds,** (i) lutter contre des forces supérieures ; (ii) avoir affaire à plus fort que soi. (b) Différence f. **What's the odds?** qu'est-ce que ça fait ? **It makes no odds,** ça ne fait rien. (c) Turf: **Odds on or against a horse,** cote f d'un cheval. **Long odds,** forte cote. **Short odds,** faible cote. **To give, take, odds,** faire un pari inégal. F: **The odds are that . . .,** il y a gros à parier que. . . . (d) Sp: **To give s.o. odds,** concéder des points à qn. **2. To be at odds with s.o.,** (i) ne pas être d'accord avec qn ; (ii) être brouillé avec qn. **3. Odds and ends,** petits bouts ; bribes f et morceaux m.

ode [oud], s. Lit: Ode f.

odious ['oudjəs], a. Odieux (to, à) ; détestable. **-ly,** adv. Odieusement, détestablement.

odiousness ['oudjəsnəs], s. Caractère odieux, l'odieux m (d'une action).

odium ['oudiəm], s. Réprobation f ; détestation f. **To bring o. upon s.o.,** rendre qn odieux.

odometer [ɔ'dɔmetər], s. = HODOMETER.

odoriferous [oudə'rifərəs], a. Odoriférant, parfumé.

odorous ['oudərəs], a. Odorant.

odour ['oudər], s. **1.** (a) Odeur (bonne ou mauvaise). (b) Parfum m. **2. To be in good, bad, odour,** être en bonne, mauvaise, odeur ; être, ne pas être, en faveur (with s.o., auprès de qn). **To die in (the) odour of sanctity,** mourir en odeur de sainteté.

odourless ['oudərləs], a. Inodore ; sans odeur.

Odyssey ['ɔdisi], s. Odyssée f.

oedema [iː'diːma], s. Œdème m.

Oedipus ['iːdipəs]. Pr.n.m. Œdipe.

oenometer [iː'nɔmetər], s. Pèse-vin m inv.

o'er [ɔːər], prep. Poet: = OVER I.

oesophagus [iː'sɔfagəs], s. Œsophage m.

oestrus ['iːstrəs], s. Ent: Œstre m.

of [ɔv, əv], prep. De. **1.** (a) (Separation) **South of,** au sud de. **Free of,** libre de. U.S: **Five minutes of one,** une heure moins cinq. (b) (i) (Origin) **To buy sth. of s.o.,** acheter qch. à, chez, qn. **'Of all booksellers,'** "chez tous les libraires." (For 'beg of,' 'inquire of,' etc., see the verbs.) (ii) (Cause) **Of necessity,** par nécessité. **The miracle came about of itself,** le miracle s'est accompli tout seul. **To die of a wound,** mourir (des suites) d'une blessure. (For 'to smell of,' 'to taste of,' etc., see the verbs.) **2.** (Agency) (a) A: **Beloved of all,** aimé de tout le monde. (b) **It is very kind of you,** c'est bien aimable de votre part, c'est très gentil à vous. **3.** (Material) **Made of wood,** fait de, en, bois. **4.** (a) (Introducing ind. obj. of verb) **To think of s.o.,** penser à qn. **Judge of my surprise,** jugez de ma surprise. (b) (After adjs) **Guilty of,** coupable de. (c) **Doctor of medicine,** docteur en médecine. **Master of arts,** A: maître ès arts. (d) F: **Well, what of it?** eh bien, et après? **5.** (Descriptive genitive) (a) (i) **Name of Jones,** nom de Jones. **The city of Rome,** la cité de Rome. **Trees of my planting,** arbres que j'ai plantés moi-même. **People of foreign appearance,** gens à l'air étranger. **Child of ten,** enfant (âgé) de dix ans. (ii) **Swift of foot,** aux pieds légers. **Hard of heart,** au cœur dur. (b) **A palace of a house,** une

maison qui est un vrai palais. **That fool of a sergeant,** cet imbécile de sergent. (c) **All of a tremble,** tout tremblant. **6.** (a) (Subjective genitive) **The love of a mother,** l'amour d'une mère. (b) (Objective genitive) **The fear of God,** la crainte de Dieu. **Hope of relief,** espoir de secours. **7.** (Partitive) (a) **How much of it do you want?** combien en voulez-vous? **Two of them died,** deux d'entre eux moururent. **There were several of us,** nous étions plusieurs. **Of the twenty only one was bad,** sur les vingt un seul était mauvais. (b) (After superlative) **The best of men,** le meilleur des hommes. **The one he loved most of all,** celui qu'il aimait entre tous. (c) (Out of) **He, of all men,** should have been grateful, lui entre tous aurait dû se montrer reconnaissant. **The one thing of all others that I want,** ce que je désire pardessus tout, avant tout. (d) (Intensive) **A fool of fools,** un triple sot. **He is a radical of radicals,** c'est un ultra-radical. **The virtue of all virtues is success,** la vertu qui prime toutes les autres, c'est de réussir. **8.** (Possession or dependence) (a) **The widow of a barrister,** la veuve d'un avocat. **The first of the month,** le premier du mois. **The first of June,** le premier juin. (b) (+ possessive) **He is a friend of mine,** of my father's, c'est un de mes amis ; c'est un ami de mon père. **It's no business of yours,** ce n'est pas votre affaire. **9.** (In temporal phrases) **What do you do of a Sunday?** que faites-vous le dimanche ?

off [ɔf]. **I.** adv. **1.** (Away) (a) **House a mile off,** maison à un mille de distance. **To keep s.o. off,** empêcher qn d'approcher. S.a. HOLD OFF, KEEP OFF. (b) (Departure) **To go off,** s'en aller, partir. F: **I'm off to church,** to London, je pars à la messe, je pars pour Londres. **It's getting late, I'm off,** il se fait tard, je me sauve, je file. **Be off!** allez-vous-en ! filez ! **They're off!** les voilà partis ! **Off we go!** (i) en route ! (ii) nous voilà partis ! **To go off (to sleep),** s'endormir. (c) Nau: **Au large.** (d) Th: **'Off,'** à la cantonade ; derrière la toile. **2.** (a) (Removal) **To take off one's coat,** ôter son habit. **Hats off!** chapeaux bas ! **Off with your boots!** ôtez vos souliers ! **Off with his head!** qu'on (me) le décapite ! **'Off,'** (steam heating, etc.) "fermé" ; (on electric oven, etc.) "zéro". I.C.E: **The ignition is off,** l'allumage est coupé. (In restaurant) **Dish that is off,** plat qui est épuisé. **The deal, the concert, is off,** le marché ne se fera pas ; le concert n'aura pas lieu. (b) **Qui n'est plus frais. Meat that is slightly off,** viande un peu avancée. F: **This beer's off,** cette bière est éventée. (c) (Idée d'achèvement) **To finish off a piece of work,** parachever un travail. **3. To be well off,** see WELL OFF. **To be badly, poorly, off,** être dans la gêne. **To be badly off for sth.,** avoir grand(ement) besoin de qch. **He is better off where he is,** il est bien mieux, dans une meilleure situation, où il est. **He is worse off,** sa situation a empiré. **4.** Adv.phr. **Off and on:** on and off, par intervalles ; à différentes reprises. **Right off, straight off,** immédiatement ; tout de suite. **II. off,** prep. **1.** (a) Usu. De. **To fall off sth.,** tomber de qch. **To fall off one's horse,** tomber à bas de son cheval. **To take sth. (from) off a shelf,** prendre qch. sur une tablette, de dessus une tablette. **To eat off silver plate,** manger dans des assiettes d'argent. **To dine off a leg of mutton,** dîner d'une tranche de gigot. **To take sth. off the price,** rabattre qch. du prix. adv. **To allow 2½% off for ready money,** faire une remise de 2½% pour paiement comptant. (b) Écarté de, éloigné de. **A yard off me,** à un mètre de moi. **Street off the main road,** (i) rue qui donne sur la grande route ; (ii) rue éloignée de la grande route. *Fb :* Player off side, joueur hors jeu. *S.a.* POINT¹ I. 3. *(c)* To be off one's food, n'avoir pas d'appétit. *I am off that work now,* je ne fais plus ce travail. *F :* To have time off (work), avoir du temps de libre. To have a day off, avoir un jour de congé. **2.** *Nau :* (a) Off the Cape, à la hauteur du Cap ; au large du Cap. Off Calais, devant Calais. *(b)* To sail off the wind, naviguer vent largue. **3.** Off-white, blanc légèrement teinté. III. **off,** *a.* **1.** *(a) Equit : etc :* Off rein, rêne du dehors. The off side, le côté extérieur ; le côté droit ;. *U.S :* le côté gauche ; *Equit :* le côté hors montoir. Off horse, (cheval de) sous-verge *m.* *(b) Bookb :* Off side, verso *m.* **2.** Subsidiaire ; (rue) secondaire. **3.** Off day, (i) jour de chômage, de liberté ; (ii) jour où l'on n'est pas en train. Off season, morte-saison *f.* **4.** Off consumption *(of intoxicants),* consommation à domicile. **off-'hand.** **1.** *adv.* (a) Sans préparation ; au pied levé. To speak *o.-h.,* parler impromptu. *(b)* Sans cérémonie, sans façon ; d'un air dégagé. **2.** *a.* (a) Spontané. 'Off-hand speech, discours impromptu, improvisé. *(b)* Brusque, cavalier ; dégagé, désinvolte. *To treat s.o. in an 'off-hand manner,* traiter qn à la cavalière, avec désinvolture. **off-'handed,** *a.* = OFF-HAND 2 (b). **-ly,** *adv.* = OFF-HAND 1 (b). **'off-'handedness,** *s.* Brusquerie *f,* sans-façon *m,* désinvolture *f.* 'off-'print, *s.* *Typ :* Tirage *m* à part. 'off(-)'shore. *Nau :* **1.** *adv.* Au large. **2.** *a.* (a) Du côté de la terre. *(b)* Éloigné de la côte. **offal** ['ɔfəl], *s.* **1.** *(a)* Rebut *m,* restes *mpl,* déchets *mpl.* *(b)* Ordures *fpl.* **2.** Déchets d'abattage (de boucherie) ; issues *fpl ;* *F :* tripaille *f.*

offence [o'fens], *s.* **1.** Blessure faite à la susceptibilité de qn ; sujet *m* de déplaisir. To take offence (at sth.), se formaliser, se froisser (de qch.) ; *F :* prendre la mouche. To give offence to s.o., offenser, blesser, froisser, qn. I meant no offence, je ne voulais offenser personne. **2.** *(a)* Offense *f,* faute *f.* Serious o., faute grave. To commit an offence against the law, *against propriety,* commettre une infraction à la loi ; faire outrage aux convenances. *(b) Jur :* Indictable offence, crime *m* ou délit *m ;* acte délictueux. Minor offence, contravention *f.* Second offence, récidive *f.*

offend [o'fend]. **1.** *v.i.* To offend against the law, violer, enfreindre, la loi. To o. against the laws of courtesy, pécher contre la politesse. To o. against grammar, offenser la grammaire. **2.** *v.tr.* (a) Offenser, blesser, froisser (qn). To be offended at, with, by, sth., se piquer, se fâcher, de qch. To be easily offended, être très susceptible. *(b)* (Of thg) To offend the eye, choquer les regards, la vue ; offusquer l'œil. *Word that offends the ear,* mot qui sonne mal. *It offends our sense of justice,* cela outrage notre sentiment de la justice. **offending,** *a.* Offensant, fautif.

offender [o'fendər], *s.* *Jur :* Délinquant, -ante, contrevenant, -ante. A first offender, un délinquant primaire. An old, a hardened, offender, un récidiviste, un repris de justice. The chief o., un grand coupable.

offensive [o'fensiv]. **1.** *a.* (a) *Mil : etc :* Offensif. *(b)* Offensant, choquant ; (spectacle) désagréable, repoussant ; (odeur) nauséabonde. *(c) (Of pers.)* To be offensive to s.o., insulter qn ; injurier qn ; dire des grossièretés à qn. **2.** *s.* *Mil :* To take the offensive, prendre l'offensive *f.* **-ly,** *adv.* **1.** *Mil : etc :* Offensivement. **2.** *(a)* Désagréablement ; d'une manière choquante. *(b)* D'un ton injurieux.

offer¹ ['ɔfər], *s.* Offre *f.* To make an offer of sth. to s.o., faire offre de qch. à qn. *Com :* To make an offer for sth., faire une offre pour qch. *That is the best o.* I can make, c'est le plus que je puis offrir. Offer of marriage, demande *f* en mariage. **offer²**. **1.** *v.tr.* (a) To o. s.o. sth., offrir qch. à qn. To offer (up) prayers to God, adresser des prières à Dieu. To o. oneself for a post, s'offrir, se présenter, à un emploi. To o. one's flank to the enemy, prêter le flanc à l'ennemi. To offer battle, inviter le combat. To offer to do sth., offrir de, s'offrir à, faire qch. *(b)* To offer a remark, an opinion, faire une remarque ; avancer une opinion. *(c) The fireworks offered a fine spectacle,* le feu d'artifice a présenté, a offert, un beau spectacle. *(d)* Essayer, tenter. To offer resistance, faire (de la) résistance. *He offered to strike me,* il fit mine de me frapper ; il voulut, essaya de, me frapper. *Th :* 'Offers to go,' "fausse sortie." **2.** *v.i.* S'offrir, se présenter. *If a good occasion offers,* s'il s'offre une belle occasion. **offering,** *s.* **1.** *(Action)* Offre *f.* **2.** *(Thg offered)* Offre ; *Ecc :* offrande *f.* Burnt offering, holocauste *m.* **offertory** ['ɔfərtəri], *s.* *Ecc :* **1.** Offertoire *m.* **2.** Quête *f* (de l'offrande).

office ['ɔfis], *s.* **1.** *(a)* Office *m,* service *m.* Through the good offices of . . ., grâce aux bons offices de . . ., par les soins de. . . . *(b)* Last offices *(to the dead),* derniers devoirs (rendus à un mort). **2.** *(a)* Fonctions *fpl.* To perform the office of secretary, faire l'office de secrétaire. It is my office to . . ., il est de mon devoir de . . . ; il rentre dans mes fonctions de. . . . *(b)* Charge *f,* emploi *m.* To be in office, to hold office, (i) remplir un emploi ; (ii) *(of government)* être au pouvoir. To take office, to come into office, (i) entrer en fonctions ; (ii) *(of government)* prendre le pouvoir. To leave office, se démettre (de ses fonctions). **3.** *Ecc :* Office for the Dead, office des morts. **4.** *(a)* Bureau *m ;* *(lawyer's)* étude *f.* Head office, registered office *(of company),* bureau central ; siège (social). Office supplies, articles *m* de bureau. *(b)* Private office, cabinet particulier. *(c)* The Home Office = le ministère de l'Intérieur.' The Foreign Office = le ministère des Affaires Étrangères. *(d) pl.* Offices *(of a house),* communs *m* et dépendances *f.* **'office-boy,** *s.m.* Saute-ruisseau *inv.* **'office-work,** *s.* Travail *m* de bureau.

officer¹ ['ɔfisər], *s.* **1.** *(a)* Fonctionnaire *m,* officier *m.* Police officer, agent *m* de police, de la sûreté. Sheriff's officer, huissier *m.* *(b)* Officers of a society, membres *m* du bureau d'une société. **2.** *Mil :* Regimental officer, officier de corps, de troupe. Staff officer, officier d'état-major. *Sch :* Officers' training corps, bataillon *m* scolaire. *(b) Navy :* Executive officer, deck officer, officier de pont. Engineer-officer, officier mécanicien. *S.a.* NAVAL, PETTY 3. **3.** High officer *(of an Order),* grand dignitaire. **officer²,** *v.tr.* *Mil :* Fournir des officiers à (un corps) ; encadrer (un bataillon). A well-officered battalion, un bataillon bien commandé.

official [o'fiʃəl]. **1.** *a.* (a) Officiel. O. seal, cachet *m* réglementaire, de service. To act in one's o. capacity, agir dans l'exercice de ses fonctions. *(b)* Official news, nouvelles authentiques, officielles. *(c)* An o. organist, le titulaire de l'orgue. **2.** *s.* Fonctionnaire *m.* Railway official, employé *m* des chemins de fer. **-ally,** *adv.* Officiellement. **officialdom** [o'fiʃəldəm], *s.* Bureaucratie *f,* fonctionnarisme *m.* **officiate** [o'fiʃieit], *v.i.* **1.** *Ecc :* To o. at a service, officier à un office. To o. at a church, desservir

une église. **Officiating minister**, officiant *m*.
2. F: To officiate as host, remplir, exercer, les
fonctions d'hôte. *To o. at table*, officier à table.
officinal [ɔ'fisinəl], *a. Pharm:* Officinal, -aux.
officious [ɔ'fiʃəs], *a.* **1.** Empressé; trop zélé.
2. *(Unofficial) Adm:* Officieux.
officiousness [ɔ'fiʃəsnəs], *s.* Excès *m* de zèle.
offing ['ɔfiŋ], *s. Nau:* The offing, le large; la
pleine mer. **In the offing**, au large. **To get an
offing**, gagner au large. *F:* **I have a job in the
offing**, j'ai une place en perspective.
offset¹ ['ɔfset], *s.* **1.** *Occ.* = OUTSET. **2.** *Hort:*
Rejeton *m*, œilleton *m*, stolon *m*. **3.** Repoussoir *m*.
To serve as an offset to s.o.'s beauty, faire
ressortir la beauté de qn. **4.** Compensation *f*,
dédommagement *m*. *As an o. to my losses*, en
compensation de mes pertes. **5.** (a) *Arch:* Ressaut *m*, saillie *f*. (b) *Mec.E:* Désaxage *m*, décalage *m*, déport *m*. **6.** *Surv:* Perpendiculaire *f*.
7. (a) *Typ:* Maculage *m*. (b) *Phot.Engr:* **Offset
process**, tirage *m* par report.
offset², *v.* (*Conj.* like SET) **1.** *v.tr.* (a) Compenser
(ses pertes, etc.). (b) *Mec.E:* Désaxer, décentrer
(une roue); déporter, décaler (un organe).
2. *v.i.* (a) *Hort:* (Of plant) Pousser des rejetons.
(b) *Typ:* Faire du maculage. **offset³**, *a.*
Mec.E: Désaxé, déporté; en porte-à-faux.
offshoot ['ɔfʃuːt], *s.* **1.** Rejeton *m* (d'un arbre,
d'une famille). **2.** *Geol:* Caprice *m* (d'un filon).
offspring ['ɔfspriŋ], *s.* **1.** *Coll.* Progéniture *f*,
descendance *f*; descendants *mpl*. **2.** Descendant,
rejeton *m*.
oft [ɔft], *adv. Poet:* Souvent. **Many a time and
oft**, mainte(s) et mainte(s) fois. **'oft-times**, *adv.*
Souvent, *A:* souventefois.
often [ɔfn], *adv.* Souvent, fréquemment, mainte(s)
fois. *I see him o.*, *I o. see him*, je le vois souvent.
How often? (i) combien de fois? (ii) tous les
combien? **As often as . . .**, toutes les fois,
chaque fois, que. . . . *F:* **As often as not**, **more
often than not**, le plus souvent. *It cannot be too
o. repeated* . . ., on ne saurait trop répéter. . . .
ogee ['oudʒiː, ou'dʒiː], *s. Arch:* Ogee(-moulding),
doucine *f*, cimaise *f*. *Tls:* **Ogee plane**, doucine.
ogival [ou'dʒaiv(ə)l], *a.* Ogival, -aux. **Ogival
arch**, arc en ogive.
ogle¹ [ougl], *s.* Œillade (amoureuse); lorgnade *f*.
ogle². **1.** *v.tr.* Lorgner, guigner (qn); lancer des
œillades à (qn); reluquer (qn); *P:* faire de
l'œil à (qn). **2.** *v.i.* Jouer de la prunelle.
Ogpu ['ɔgpuː], *s. Russian Adm:* Le Guépéou.
ogre, *f.* **ogress** ['ougər, 'ougres], *s.* Ogre,
f. ogresse.
oh [ou], *int.* = O².
ohm [oum], *s. El.Meas:* Ohm *m*.
oidium ['ou'idiəm], *s. Fung:* Oïdium *m*.
oil¹ [ɔil], *s.* **1.** Huile *f*. **2.** *Ecc:* **The holy oil**, les
saintes huiles. **Lubricating oil**, huile de graissage.
Lamp oil, (i) huile à brûler; huile lampante;
(ii) pétrole lampant. *F:* **To burn the midnight
oil**, travailler fort avant dans la nuit. *Work that
smells of the midnight oil*, ouvrage qui sent l'huile,
l'étude. **To pour oil on troubled waters**, apaiser
le désordre par des paroles de conciliation. **Vegetable oil**, huile végétale. *Fried in oil*, frit à l'huile.
Linseed oil, huile de (graine de) lin. **Painting in
oil(s)**, peinture à l'huile. *S.a.* CASTOR OIL,
OLIVE-OIL, etc. **2. Mineral oil**, huile minérale.
Paraffin oil, pétrole (lampant). **Fuel oil**, **crude oil**,
mazout *m*. **Oil gas**, gaz *m* de pétrole. *The oil
industry*, l'industrie pétrolière. **3. Essential oil**,
huile essentielle; essence *f*. **Oil of cloves**, huile
de girofle. **'oil-bath**, *s. Mec.E:* Bain *m*

d'huile. **'oil-bearing**, *a.* **1.** *Bot:* Oléagineux,
oléifère. **2.** *Geol:* Pétrolifère. **'oil-can**, *s.*
1. Bidon *m* à huile. **2.** = OILER 2. **'oil-
colour**, *s.* Couleur *f* à l'huile. **'oil-cruet**, *s.*
Huilier *m* (domestique). **'oil-engine**, *s.* Moteur *m* à pétrole. **Heavy oil-engine**, moteur à
huile lourde. **'oil-field**, *s. Geol:* Gisement *m*
pétrolifère. **'oil-fired**, *a.* (*Of engine, etc.*)
Chauffé au mazout. **'oil-gauge**, *s.* Jauge *f* de
niveau d'huile. **'oil-groove**, *s.* Saignée *f* de
graissage. **Oil-grooves of a bearing**, pattes *f*
d'araignée d'un palier graisseur. **'oil-hole**, *s.*
Trou *m* de graissage. **'oil-lamp**, *s.* Lampe *f*
à huile ou à pétrole. **'oil-merchant**, *s.* = OIL-
MAN 1. **'oil-paint**, *s.* = OIL-COLOUR. **'oil-
painting**, *s.* **1.** Peinture *f* à l'huile. **2.** Tableau
peint à l'huile. **'oil-producing**, *a.* = OIL-
BEARING 1. **'oil-ring**, *s.* **1.** *Mec.E:* Anneau
graisseur. **2.** Cartel *m* du pétrole. **'oil shop**, *s.*
Huilerie *f*; boutique *f* de marchand d'huile.
'oil-stove, *s.* Réchaud *m* ou fourneau *m* à
pétrole. **'oil-tracks**, *s.pl. Mec.E:* Araignée *f*
(d'un palier). **'oil-varnish**, *s.* Vernis *m* à
l'huile; vernis gras. **'oil-well**, *s.* Puits *m*
pétrolifère; puits de, à, pétrole. **'oil-works**,
s.pl. Huilerie *f*; fabrique *f* d'huile.
oil². **1.** *v.tr.* (a) Huiler, graisser, lubrifier (une
machine, etc.). **To oil the wheels**, graisser les
roues; *F:* faciliter les choses. **To oil s.o.'s
palm**, graisser la patte à qn. (b) **To oil a pool**
(*against mosquitoes*), pétroler une mare. **2.** *v.i.
Nau:* Faire le plein de mazout. **oil up**, *v.tr.*
(a) Encrasser (d'huile). (b) (*With passive force*)
S'encrasser (d'huile). **oiled**, *a.* (a) Graissé. **To
keep one's tools slightly o.**, tenir ses outils un peu
gras. *F:* **Well-oiled tongue**, langue bien pendue.
(b) **Oiled silk**, taffetas *m* imperméable. **Oiled
raincoat**, imperméable *m* en toile huilée. **oiling**,
s. **1.** (a) Graissage *m*, huilage *m*, lubrification *f*.
(b) Onction *f* (d'un athlète). **2.** Pétrolage *m* (d'une
mare).
oilcake ['ɔilkeik], *s.* Tourteau *m* (pour bétail).
oilcloth ['ɔilklɔθ], *s.* **1.** (*For waterproofs, etc.*)
Tissu huilé. **2.** (*For tables, etc.*) Toile cirée.
3. (*For floors*) Linoléum imprimé.
oiler ['ɔilər], *s.* **1.** (*Pers.*) Graisseur *m*. **2.** Burette *f* à huile; burette de graissage. **Hand oiler**,
coup-de-poing *m*.
oiliness ['ɔilinəs], *s.* État ou aspect graisseux;
onctuosité *f*.
oilman, *pl.* **-men** ['ɔilmən, -men], *s.m.*
1. (a) Huilier *m*; marchand d'huile. (b) Marchand
de couleurs; droguiste. **2.** Graisseur (de
machines).
oilskin ['ɔilskin], *s.* **1.** Toile cirée, vernie, huilée.
2. *Nau:* (*Suit of*) oilskins, blouse *f* et pantalon *m*
en toile huilée; cirage *m*, ciré *m*.
oilstone¹ ['ɔilstoun], *s. Tls:* Pierre *f* à huile
(pour affûter); pierre à morfiler, à repasser.
oilstone², *v.tr.* Passer (un outil) à la pierre à
huile.
oily ['ɔili], *a.* **1.** Huileux; gras, *f.* grasse;
graisseux. **2.** *F:* (*Of manner*) Onctueux.
ointment ['ɔintmənt], *s.* Onguent *m*, pommade *f*.
Zinc ointment, pommade à l'oxyde de zinc.
S.a. FLY¹.
O.K.¹ [ou'kei], *a. F:* (a) (*Spoken*) Très bien!
ça va! d'accord! (b) (*Written*) "Vu et approuvé."
Everything is O.K., tout est en règle.
O.K.², *v.tr.* (O.K'd) *F:* Passer, approuver (une
commande).
okapi [o'kaːpi], *s. Z:* Okapi *m*.
old [ould], *a.* **1.** (a) (*Aged*) Vieux, *f.* vieille; âgé.
My old friend, mon vieil ami, mon vieux ami. **To**

be growing old, tirer sur l'âge ; se faire vieux ; vieillir. An old man, un homme âgé, un vieillard, *F :* un vieux. *F :* Old as Methuselah, vieux comme Hérode. An old woman, une vieille femme, *F :* une vieille. *Old John,* le père Jean. *Old Mrs Brown,* la mère Brown. *Old folk(s),* les vieux. Old wives' tale, conte de bonne femme. *s.pl.* Old and young, grands et petits. Old age, la vieillesse. *To die at a good old age,* mourir à un âge avancé, à un bel âge. *To live to be old,* vivre vieux, vieille. *(b) Old clothes,* vieux habits. *Old bread,* pain rassis. *Old wine,* vin vieux. 2. *(S.a.* ELDER[1] I, ELDEST.) How old are you? quel âge avez-vous? To be five years old, avoir cinq ans ; être âgé de cinq ans. *He is older than I,* il est plus âgé que moi ; il est mon aîné. *To be ten years older than . . .,* avoir dix ans de plus que . . . ; être plus âgé de dix ans que. . . . A two-year-old (child), un enfant (âgé) de deux ans. *To be old enough to do sth.,* être d'âge à faire qch. ; être en âge de faire qch. 3. *(a)(Long-established)* Vieux, ancien ; (famille) de vieille souche ; (dette) d'ancienne date. *He's an old friend of mine,* c'est un de mes vieux amis. That's an old dodge, c'est un coup classique. That's as old as the hills, c'est vieux comme le Pont-Neuf, comme Hérode, comme les rues. It's as old as Adam, cela remonte au déluge. *(b)* Old hand, ouvrier expérimenté ; *Nau: etc:* vétéran *m.* He's an old hand (at it), il possède la pratique du métier ; il n'en est pas à son coup d'essai. Ho is old in sin, c'est un pécheur endurci. 4. *(Former)* Ancien. *(a)* Old boy, old pupil, ancien élève. *Old customs,* anciennes coutumes. *We did so in the old days,* nous l'avons fait dans le temps. *(b)* The Old World, l'ancien monde. The Old Country, la mère-patrie. The Old Testament, l'Ancien Testament. 5. *F:* (a) Any old thing, la première chose venue ; n'importe quoi. *Take any old hat,* prenez un chapeau quelconque. *(b)* Old man, old chap, mon vieux, mon brave. *P:* The old man, (i) papa ; (ii) le patron, *P:* le singe. *P:* My old man, mon homme. My old woman, ma femme ; la bourgeoise. 6. Of old. *(a) Adj.phr.* Ancien, d'autrefois. *The knights of old,* les chevaliers de jadis. *(b) Adv.phr.* (i) Jadis, autrefois. (ii) I know him of old, je le connais depuis longtemps. 'old-'clothes-man, *pl.* -men *s.m.* Marchand d'habits ; fripier. 'old-'clothes-shop, *s.* Boutique *f* d'habits d'occasion ; friperie *f.* 'old-'clothes-woman, *pl.* -women, *s.f.* Marchande d'habits ; fripière. 'old-es'tablished, *a.* Ancien ; établi depuis longtemps. old-'fashioned, *a.* 1. (i) A l'ancienne mode ; (ii) démodé ; passé de mode ; suranné. 2. (i) *(Of pers.)* Partisan des anciens usages ; *(of manner)* de l'ancien temps ; (of ideas) arriéré, vieilli, vieux jeu. old-'maidish, *a.* (Façons) de vieille fille. *She is rather old-m.,* elle est un peu collet monté. 'old-'world, attrib.a. *I.* De l'ancien temps. 2. Du temps jadis.

olden ['ouldən], *a.* In olden time(s), au temps jadis ; autrefois ; du temps que Berthe filait.

oldish ['ouldiʃ], *a.* Vieillot, -otte.

oleaginous [ouli'adʒinəs], *a.* Oléagineux, huileux.

oleander [ouli'andər], *s. Bot:* Oléandre *m* ; laurier-rose *m.*

oleiferous [ouli'ifərəs], *a.* Oléifère, oléagineux.

olfactive [ɔl'faktiv], olfactory [ɔl'faktəri], *a.* Olfactif.

oligarchic(al) [ɔli'gɑ:rkik(əl)], *a.* Oligarchique.

oligarchy ['ɔligɑ:rki], *s.* Oligarchie *f.*

olio ['oulio], *s. F:* Pot pourri, mélange *m* (de mélodies, etc.).

oliphant ['ɔlifənt], *s. Mediev. Lit:* Olifant *m* ; cor *m* d'ivoire.

olivaceous [ɔli'veiʃəs], *a.* Olivacé, olivâtre.

olive ['ɔliv], *s.* I. Olive(-tree), olivier *m. B.Hist:* The Mount, Garden, of Olives, le Mont, le Jardin, des Oliviers. 2. Olive *f.* Pickled olive, picholine *f.* 3. *Cu:* (Meat-)olive, paupiette *f.* 'olive-branch, *s.* Rameau *m* d'olivier. *F:* To hold out the olive-branch, se présenter l'olivier à la main ; faire les premières avances (pour une réconciliation). 'olive-'green, *a.* (Couleur d')olive *inv.* ; olivacé. *O.-g.* ribbons, rubans olive. 'olive-grove, -plantation, *s.* Olivette *f,* olivaie *f.* 'olive-grower, *s.* Oléiculteur *m.* 'olive-moulding, *s. Arch:* Olive *f.* olive-'oil, *s.* Huile *f* d'olive.

Oliver ['ɔlivər]. *Pr.n.m.* Olivier.

olla podrida ['ɔlapo'dri:da], *s.* = OLIO.

olympiad [o'limpiad], *s.* Olympiade *f.*

Olympian [o'limpiən], *a. & s.* Olympien, -ienne. *The O.* gods, les dieux de l'Olympe.

Olympic [o'limpik], *a.* The Olympic games, les jeux olympiques.

Olympus [o'limpəs]. *Pr.n.* L'Olympe *m.*

omelet(te) ['ɔmlet], *s. Cu:* Omelette *f.* Savoury o., omelette aux fines herbes. *Sweet o.,* omelette aux confitures.

omen[1] ['oumen], *s.* Présage *m,* augure *m.* It is of good omen that . . ., il est de bon augure que. . . . Bird of ill omen, oiseau de sinistre présage, de mauvais augure ; porte-malheur *m inv.* omen[2], *v.tr.* Augurer, présager. Ill-omened, de mauvais augure.

ominous ['ɔminəs], *a.* De mauvais augure ; sinistre ; inquiétant. An o. silence, un silence lourd de menaces. -ly, *adv.* Sinistrement ; d'une façon menaçante, inquiétante.

omission [o'miʃ(ə)n], *s.* I. Omission *f.* 2. Négligence *f.* To rectify an o., réparer un oubli. *Theol:* Sin of omission, péché *m,* faute *f,* d'omission. 3. *Typ:* Bourdon *m.*

omit [o'mit], *v.tr.* (omitted) I. *(a)* Omettre ; passer sous silence. *(b) Typ:* Bourdonner (un mot). 2. To omit to do sth., oublier, omettre, de faire qch. *Not to o. to do sth.,* ne pas manquer de faire qch.

omnibus, *pl.* omnibuses ['ɔmnibəs, -əsiz]. I. *s.* (i) (Horse-)omnibus, omnibus *m* ; (ii) (motor) omnibus, autobus *m. Private o.,* (i) omnibus de famille ; (ii) autobus réservé. 2. *a.* Omnibus book, gros recueil (de contes, etc.). Omnibus bill, projet de loi embrassant des mesures diverses.

omnipotence [ɔm'nipotəns], *s.* Omnipotence *f* ; toute-puissance *f.*

omnipotent [ɔm'nipotənt], *a.* Omnipotent ; tout-puissant, *pl.* tout-puissants ; *f.* toute-puissante.

omnipresence [ɔmni'prez(ə)ns], *s.* Omniprésence *f.*

omnipresent [ɔmni'prez(ə)nt], *a.* Omniprésent.

omnivorous [ɔm'nivərəs], *a.* Omnivore.

on [ɔn]. I. *prep.* I. *(a) Usu.* Sur. *To tread on sth.,* marcher sur qch. *Do not tread on it,* ne marchez pas dessus. *On the Continent,* sur le Continent. *On the high seas,* en haute mer. *Dinner on the train,* dîner dans le train. *(b) On shore,* à terre. *On foot,* à pied. *On horseback,* à cheval. *(c)* To be on the committee, être membre du comité. *To be on the staff,* faire partie du personnel. 2. *(a) Hanging on the wall,* pendu au mur, contre le mur. *On the ceiling,* au plafond. *Shoes on his feet,* des souliers aux pieds. *His hat on his head,* son chapeau sur la tête. Have you any money on you? avez-vous de l'argent (sur vous)? **To play on the violin,** jouer du violon. *He played it on his violin,* il l'a joué sur son violon. *On page four,* à la page quatre. *Journ: Continued on page four,* la suite en quatrième page. (b) (*Proximity*) (i) *House on the main road,* maison sur la grande route. (ii) **Just on a year ago,** il y a près d'un an. **3.** (a) **On (to),** sur, à. *To drift on to the shore,* dériver sur la terre, vers la terre. (b) *On the right, left,* à droite, à gauche. *On this side,* de ce côté. (c) **To march on London,** avancer vers, sur, Londres. **To smile on s.o.,** sourire à qn. (d) **To serve a writ on s.o.,** signifier un arrêt à qn. *To leave one's card on s.o.,* déposer une carte chez qn. **4.** *Based on a fact,* fondé sur un fait. *To have sth. on good authority,* savoir qch. de source certaine, de bonne part. *Arrested on a charge of murder,* arrêté sous l'inculpation de meurtre. **On pain, penalty, of death,** sous peine de mort. *On an average,* en moyenne. *To borrow money on security,* emprunter de l'argent sur nantissement. *To retire on a pension of £500 a year,* prendre sa retraite avec une pension de cinq cents livres par an. *Dependent on circumstances,* qui dépend des circonstances. *On condition that . . .,* à condition que. . . . *To buy sth. on good terms,* acheter qch. à d'excellentes conditions. **5.** (a) **On Sunday,** dimanche (prochain ou dernier). **On Sundays,** le(s) dimanche(s). *On the following day,* le lendemain. **On April 3rd,** le trois avril. *On the evening of the first of June,* le premier juin au soir. (b) *On a warm day like this,* par une chaleur comme celle-ci. *On certain days,* à (de) certains jours. **On and after the fifteenth,** à partir, à dater, du quinze. **On or about the twelfth,** vers le douze. *On that occasion,* à, dans, cette occasion. *On his majority,* lors de, sa majorité. *On my arrival,* à mon arrivée. *On application,* sur demande. *On examination,* après examen. *On delivery of the letter,* lors de la remise de la lettre. (c) On (my) *entering the room . . .,* à, dès, mon entrée dans la salle. . . . **6.** (*With adjs*) **On the cheap,** à bon marché. **On the sly,** en sourdine, en catimini. **7. On sale,** en vente. **On tap,** en perce. **8.** (*Concerning*) *A lecture on history,* une conférence d'histoire. *Inquiry on sth.,* enquête sur qch. *Hume Brown on John Knox,* l'appréciation f de John Knox par Hume Brown. *To congratulate s.o. on his success,* féliciter qn de son succès. *Mad on s.o.,* fou, entiché, de qn. **9.** *I am here on business,* je suis ici pour affaires. *On tour,* en tournée. *On holiday,* en congé, en vacances. *To be (working) on sth.,* travailler à qch. **10.** *To have pity on s.o.,* avoir pitié de qn. *Attack on s.o.,* attaque contre qn. *F:* **This round (of drinks)** is **on me,** c'est moi qui paie cette tournée. **11. To live on one's** *private income,* vivre de ses rentes. *Many live on less than that,* beaucoup vivent avec moins que ça. **12.** (*Added to*) *Disaster on disaster,* désastre sur désastre. **II. on,** *adv.* **1.** (a) *To put on the cloth,* mettre la nappe. *To put the kettle on,* mettre la bouilloire à chauffer. *Th:* (*Of actor*) **To be on,** être en scène. (b) *To put on one's clothes,* mettre ses habits. *To put on one's gloves,* se ganter. *To have one's boots on,* avoir ses bottines aux pieds; être chaussé. **What had he got on?** qu'est-ce qu'il portait? **On with your coat,** mettez votre veston! **2.** *To fly on, go on, ride on, work on,* continuer son vol, son chemin, sa chevauchée, son travail. *To crawl on, drive on, talk on, wander on,* continuer à ramper, à rouler, à parler, à errer. **Go on!** continuez! allez toujours! **On, Stanley, on!** en avant, Stanley,

en avant! *To toil on and on,* peiner sans fin. **And so on,** et ainsi de suite. **3.** *To be broadside on to the shore,* présenter le côté à la terre. **4.** (a) **Later on,** plus tard. **From that day on,** à dater de ce jour. *S.a.* NOW III. **Well on in April,** fort avant dans le mois d'avril. **Well on in years,** d'un âge avancé. (b) *P:* **To be a bit on,** être un peu parti, un peu gris. (c) *P:* **To have s.o. on,** monter un bateau à qn. **5.** *To turn on the tap,* ouvrir le robinet. **'On,'** "ouvert"; (*of electric circuit*) "fermé." *The machine was on,* la machine était en marche. *The brakes are on,* les freins sont serrés. *The performance is now on,* la représentation est commencée. **On with the show!** **que le spectacle commence! What is on (at the theatre) just now?** qu'est-ce qui se joue actuellement? *I see Hamlet is on again,* je vois qu'on redonne Hamlet. **What's on to-night?** (i) qu'est-ce qui se passe ce soir? (ii) que fait-on ce soir? **Have you anything on this evening?** êtes-vous occupé, invité, ce soir? **6.** *F:* (a) **I'm on (for it)!** ça me va! (b) **To be on to sth.,** comprendre, saisir, qch. *They were on to him at once,* ils ont tout de suite vu clair dans son jeu. (c) *I was on to him on the phone this morning,* je lui ai parlé au téléphone ce matin. *The police are on to him,* la police est sur sa piste. (d) *He is always on to me,* il s'en prend toujours à moi. **7. On and off.** *See* OFF I. 4. **'on-coming**[1]**,** *a.* (a) Approchant (en sens inverse); (*danger*) imminent. (b) *Ind:* **On-coming shift,** poste entrant. **'on-coming**[2]**,** *s.* Approche f (de l'hiver, etc.). **'on-shore,** *a.* (Vent) du large.

onager ['onadʒər], *s.* *Z:* Onagre *m.*

once [wʌns], *adv.* **1.** (a) *To* **Once only,** une seule fois. **Once a week,** tous les huit jours. **Once more, once again,** encore une fois. **Once in a while,** une fois en passant. **Once (and) for all,** une (bonne) fois pour toutes. (b) (*If*) **once . . .,** *(when)* **once . . .,** dès que . . ., pour peu que. . . . *O. grasp this fact and everything becomes plain,* comprenez bien cela et tout s'éclaircit. **2.** Autrefois. **Once (upon a time) there was . . .,** il était une fois . . ., il y avait jadis. . . . *I knew him once,* je l'ai connu autrefois, dans le temps. *A collar that had o. been white,* un faux col jadis blanc. *O. when I was young . . .,* il arriva un jour, quand j'étais petit, que. . . . **3. At once.** (a) Tout de suite; à l'instant; sur-le-champ. (b) **Don't all speak at once,** ne parlez pas tous à la fois, en même temps. **At once a food and a tonic,** à la fois un aliment et un fortifiant. *To do a great deal at o.,* faire beaucoup (d'un coup) à la fois. *S.a.* ALL I. 3. **'once-over,** *s.* *U.S:* *F:* To give sth. the **once-over,** jeter un seul coup d'œil scrutateur sur qch.

one [wʌn]. **I.** *num.a.* **1.** (a) Un. *Twenty-one apples, one and twenty apples,* vingt et une pommes. *A hundred and one,* cent un. **The Thousand and one Nights,** les Mille et une Nuits. (b) *He comes one day out of two,* il vient un jour sur deux, de deux jours l'un. *F:* **That's one way of doing it,** c'est une manière comme une autre de le faire. **That's one comfort,** c'est déjà une consolation. *S.a.* ANOTHER 4. **2.** (a) Seul, unique. *My one and only collar,* mon seul et unique faux col. *The one way to do it,* la seule façon de le faire. **No 'one man can do it,** il n'y a pas d'homme qui puisse le faire à lui seul. (b) *They cried out with one voice,* ils s'écrièrent d'une seule voix, d'une commune voix. **To advance like one man,** avancer comme un seul homme. (c) Même. *All in one* *direction*, tous dans la même direction. **One and the same** *thought came into our minds*, une seule et même pensée nous vint à l'esprit. *F :* **It's all one**, cela revient au même ; c'est tout un. **It's all one to me**, cela m'est égal ; cela ne me fait ni chaud ni froid. (*d*) *God is one*, Dieu est un. **To become one, to be made one**, s'unir, se marier. **To be one with sth.**, ne faire qu'une pièce avec qch. ; faire corps avec qch. II. **one**, *s*. **1.** *Eleven is written with two ones*, onze s'écrit avec deux un. *Chapter one*, chapitre un, chapitre premier. *P :* **To look after number one**, soigner sa petite personne ; mettre ses intérêts en premier lieu. **2.** (*a*) *There is only one left*, il n'en reste qu'un. **The topmost stair but one**, l'avant-dernière marche. *S.a.* LAST² I. 1, NEXT I. 1, 2. *Goods that are sold in ones*, marchandises qui se vendent à la pièce. *Price of one*, prix de l'unité. **Garment all in one**, vêtement en une pièce. **To be at one with s.o.**, être d'accord avec qn. (*b*) **One and sixpence**, un shilling (et) six pence. **One (o'clock)**, une heure. *P :* **I fetched, landed, him one**, je lui ai flanqué un marron. **To call at the pub for a quick one**, entrer au cabaret pour s'en enfiler une. **That is one (up) for us!** et d'un dans nos filets ! III. **one**, *dem.pron.* (*a*) *This one*, celui-ci, *f.* celle-ci. *That one*, celui-là, *f.* celle-là. *Which one do you prefer?* lequel, laquelle, préférez-vous? *The one on the table*, celui, celle, qui est sur la table. *She is the one who helped Louise*, c'est elle qui a aidé Louise. (*b*) *To pick the ripe plums and leave the green ones*, cueillir les prunes mûres et laisser les vertes. *The portraits on the walls*, *especially the full-length ones* . . ., les portraits pendus aux murs, surtout les portraits en pied.... **That's a good one!** celle-là est bonne ! *He's a knowing one*, c'est un malin. *Our dear ones*, ceux qui nous sont chers. *The little ones*, les petits enfants ; (*of animals*) les petits. **The Evil One**, le Malin, l'Esprit malin. IV. **one**, *indef.a.* **One day**, un jour. *One stormy evening in January*, par une soirée orageuse de janvier. V. **one**, *indef. pron.* **1.** (*pl.* **some**, **any**) *I haven't a pencil, have you got one?* je n'ai pas de crayon, en avez-vous un? *The idea is one which occurs in primitive societies*, cette idée est de celles que l'on rencontre dans les sociétés primitives. **One of them**, l'un d'entre eux ; l'un d'eux. **He is one of the family**, il fait partie de la famille ; il est de la famille. *Will you make one of us?* voulez-vous vous mettre de la partie? voulez-vous être des nôtres? **Any one** of us, l'un quelconque d'entre nous ; n'importe lequel d'entre nous. *S.a.* EVERY (*c*). **Never a one**, pas un. **One and all**, tous sans exception. **(The) one . . . the other**, l'un . . . l'autre. *You can't have one without the other*, l'un ne va pas sans l'autre. **One after the other**, l'un après l'autre. *To enter by* **one or other** *of the doors*, entrer par l'une quelconque des portes. **One another**, *see* ANOTHER 4. **One by one**, un à un, une à une. **2.** *I want the opinion of one better able to judge*, je voudrais avoir l'opinion de quelqu'un qui soit plus capable de juger. *He looked like* **one dead**, il avait l'air d'un mort. *To one who can read between the lines, it is evident that* . . ., à qui sait lire entre les lignes, il est évident que. . . . *One Mr Jenkins*, un certain M. Jenkins ; un nommé Jenkins. **I am not (the) one to** . . ., je ne suis point homme à . . ., je ne suis pas de ceux qui . . . . *F :* **I'm not much of a one for sweets**, je ne suis pas grand amateur de plats sucrés. **3.** *Lit :* (*a*) (*Nom.*) On. *One cannot always be right*, on ne peut pas toujours avoir raison. (*b*) (*Acc.*) Vous. *It is enough to kill one*,

il y a de quoi vous faire mourir. **4.** **One's**, son, *f.* sa, *pl.* ses ; votre, *pl.* vos. *To give one's opinion*, donner son avis. *When one is allowed to see one's friends*, quand il nous est permis de voir nos amis. *To cut one's finger*, se couper le doigt. **'one-armed**, *a.* À un seul bras ; (*of pers.*) manchot. **'one-celled**, *a.* *Biol :* Unicellulaire. **'one-cylinder**, *attrib.a.* *I.C.E :* (Moteur) à cylindre unique, monocylindrique. **'one-eyed**, *a.* (*a*) *Z :* Unioculé. (*b*) (*Of pers.*) Borgne. **'one-horse**, *attrib.a.* *U.S :* *F :* **A one-horse show**, (i) un spectacle de deux sous ; (ii) une affaire de quatre sous. **One-horse town**, petit bourg de rien du tout. **'one-legged**, *a.* Qui n'a qu'une jambe ; amputé de la jambe. **'one-'price**, *attrib.a.* (Article, magasin) à prix unique ; (magasin) uniprix. **'one-'sided**, *a.* **1.** (*Of contract*) Unilatéral, -aux. **2.** (*Of shape*) Asymétrique. **3.** (*a*) (*Of bargain*) Inégal, -aux ; inéquitable. (*b*) (*Of judgment*) Partial, -aux ; injuste. **'one-storied**, *a.* (Maison) sans étage. **'one-way**, *attrib.a.* **One-way street**, rue à sens unique, à sens interdit. **One-way traffic**, circulation en sens unique.

oner ['wʌnər], *s.* *F :* Personne *f* unique, qui n'a pas sa pareille ; *P :* type épatant.

onerous ['ɔnərəs], *a.* **1.** Onéreux ; (tâche) pénible. **2.** *Jur :* (*Scot.*) (Contrat) à titre onéreux.

oneself [wʌn'self], *pron.* *See* SELF 4.

onion ['ʌnjən], *s.* O(i)gnon *m.* **Spring onion**, ciboule *f* ; petit oignon. *O.-stew*, fricassée *f* aux oignons. **String of onions**, chapelet *m* d'oignons. **'onion-'sauce**, *s.* *Cu :* Sauce blanche à l'oignon. **'onion-skin**, *s.* Pelure *f* d'oignon.

onlooker ['ɔnlukər], *s.* Spectateur, -trice. *The onlookers*, l'assistance *f* ; les assistants *m.*

only ['ounli]. I. *a.* Seul, unique. **Only son**, fils unique. *His one and only hope*, son seul et unique espoir. *His o. answer was to burst out laughing*, pour toute réponse il éclata de rire. *He was the o. one who noticed it*, il fut le seul à s'en apercevoir. **You are not the only one**, vous n'êtes pas le seul ; il n'y a pas que vous. II. **only**, *adv.* Seulement, ne . . . que. *I have o. three.* —*Only three?* je n'en ai que trois.—Que trois? **'Ladies only,'** "dames seules." *O. he can say*, lui seul saurait le dire. *O. the binding is damaged*, il n'y a que la reliure d'abîmée. *I o. touched it*, je n'ai fait que le toucher. *He has only to ask for it*, il n'a qu'à le demander. *I will o. say* . . ., je me bornerai à dire. . . . **Only to think of it**, rien que d'y penser. *If only I knew where he is!* si seulement je savais où il est ! **Not only** . . . **but** also . . ., non seulement . . . mais aussi, mais encore. . . . **Only yesterday**, hier encore ; pas plus tard qu'hier. *S.a.* JUST II. 2, 4. III. **only**, *conj.* Mais. *The book is interesting, o. rather too long*, le livre est intéressant, mais un peu trop long, seulement un peu long. *I would do it only that* . . ., je le ferais (si ce) n'était que. . . .

onomatopoeia [ɔnəmato'pi:a], *s.* Onomatopée *f.*

onrush ['ɔnrʌʃ], *s.* Ruée *f* ; attaque *f.* *The o. of water*, l'eau qui se précipite.

onset ['ɔnset], *s.* **1.** Assaut *m,* attaque *f.* *To withstand the o. of the enemy*, soutenir le choc de l'ennemi. **2.** At the (first) onset, d'emblée, de prime abord, au premier abord. **From the onset**, dès l'abord.

onslaught ['ɔnslɔ:t], *s.* = ONSET 1. *To make a savage o. on the Prime Minister*, attaquer véhémentement le Premier ministre.

onto ['ɔntu], *prep.* = on to, *q.v. under* ON I. 3.

ontogenesis [ɔnto'dʒenəsis], *s.* *Biol :* Ontogénèse *f.*

ontological [ɔntoˈlɔdʒik(ə)l], *a.* Ontologique.
ontology [ɔnˈtɔlodʒi], *s.* Ontologie *f.*
onus [ˈounəs], *s.* Responsabilité *f*, charge *f.* The onus **ies** upon the government to . . ., il incombe au gouvernement de. . . . *Jur:* Onus **probandi** [proˈbandai], charge de la preuve.
onward [ˈɔnwərd]. **1.** *adv.* = ONWARDS. **2.** *a.* En avant. *The o.* march *of ideas*, la marche progressive des idées.
onwards [ˈɔnwərdz], *adv.* (*a*) En avant. (*b*) From to-morrow onwards, à partir de demain. **From this time onwards**, désormais, dorénavant.
onyx [ˈɔniks], *s.* **1.** *Miner:* Onyx *m.* Black onyx, jais artificiel. **2.** *Med:* Ongle *m* (à l'œil).
oof [uːf], *s.* *P:* De l'argent; *P:* galette *f,* pognon *m.*
oolite [ˈoulait], *s.* *Miner: Geol:* Oolithe *m.*
oolitic [ouoˈlitik], *a.* *Miner: Geol:* Oolithique.
ooze¹ [uːz], *s.* **1.** Vase *f,* limon *m.* **2.** Suintement *m,* dégouttement *m* (d'un liquide).
ooze², *v.i.* (*a*) Suinter; dégoutter. *Waters that o.* out *from the rock*, eau qui sourd de la roche. *F:* His courage is oozing away, son courage l'abandonne. (*b*) (*With cogn. acc.*) Suer, suinter (de l'eau, etc.); laisser dégoutter (l'eau). *F: He* is oozing self-conceit, il sue l'orgueil par tous les pores. **oozing,** *s.* Suintement *m,* fuite *f* (de l'eau, etc.).
opacity [oˈpasiti], *s.* **1.** Opacité *f.* **2.** Lourdeur *f* (d'intelligence); esprit obtus.
opal [ˈoup(ə)l], *s.* **1.** *Lap:* Opale *f.* **2.** *Glassm:* Opal glass, verre opalin; verre opale.
opalescence [oupaˈles(ə)ns], *s.* Opalescence *f.*
opalescent [oupaˈles(ə)nt], *a.* Opalescent.
opaque [oˈpeik], *a.* **1.** Opaque. **2.** (*Of pers.*) Peu intelligent; à l'esprit épais, obtus.
opaqueness [oˈpeiknəs], *s.* = OPACITY.
open¹ [ˈoup(ə)n], *a.* Ouvert. **1.** (*a*) *O. window,* fenêtre ouverte. *To push the door o.,* ouvrir la porte d'une poussée. *Half open*, entr'ouvert, entrebâillé. *S.a.* WIDE OPEN. **To keep open house, an** open board, tenir table ouverte. (*b*) (*Of box*) Ouvert; (*of bottle*) débouché; (*of parcel*) défait. Open grave, tombe qui attend son cercueil. *El:* Open circuit, circuit ouvert, coupé. **To break open**, smash *open, a box*, éventrer une boîte. **To cut open**, couper, ouvrir. (*c*) **Open to the public**, ouvert, accessible, au public. (*d*) In (the) open court, en plein tribunal. **Open trial,** jugement public. (*e*) Posts open to all, charges accessibles à tout le monde. *Sp:* Open race, omnium *m.* **2.** Sans limites; sans bornes. **In the open air,** *s.* in the open, au grand air, en plein air. *To sleep in the o.* (*air*), coucher à la belle étoile. **Open country**, pays découvert. *In the o.* country, en pleine campagne, en rase campagne. *The house stands in the o.,* la maison est située en pleine campagne. **The** open sea, la haute mer; le large. *In the o. sea,* en pleine mer. **3.** (*a*) **Open carriage**, voiture découverte. **Open boat**, bateau non ponté. **Open light**, feu nu. (*b*) *Nau:* Open roadstead, rade foraine. (*c*) *O.* to every wind, exposé à tous les vents. (*d*) **To lay oneself open** to criticism, prêter le flanc, donner prise, à la critique. *O.* to ridicule, qui prête au ridicule. *O.* to doubt, exposé au doute. (*e*) To be open to conviction, être accessible à la conviction. **To be open to advice**, être tout prêt à accueillir des conseils. *Invention o.* to improvement, invention susceptible d'amélioration. **4.** (*a*) Manifeste; public, -ique. **Open secret**, secret de Polichinelle. **Open letter**, lettre ouverte (communiquée à la presse). **Fact open to all**, fait patent. (*b*) Franc. *O.* admiration, franche admiration. *O.* enemy of

the Government, ennemi déclaré du Gouvernement. **To be open with s.o.**, parler franchement à qn; ne rien cacher à qn. **5.** Open wound, plaie (i) béante, (ii) non cicatrisée. *Dress o.* at the neck, robe échancrée au col. Open pores, pores dilatés. **6.** Non serré. *Mil: To attack in* open order, attaquer en ordre dispersé. **Open fence,** clôture à claire-voie. *O. tissue,* tissu à jour. **7.** (*a*) Non obstrué. **Open road**, chemin libre. *Rail:* Open signal, signal effacé. **Open view,** vue dégagée. *Aut:* Open corner, virage découvert. **To keep the bowels open**, tenir le ventre libre. *Mus:* Open string, corde à vide. (*b*) To keep a day open for s.o., réserver un jour pour qn. *The* job is still *o.,* la place est toujours vacante. *Two courses are o. to us,* deux moyens s'offrent à nous. It is open to you to object, il vous est permis, loisible, de faire des objections. **8.** Non résolu. **Open question**, question discutable, indécise. **To keep an open mind on sth.**, rester sans parti pris; réserver son opinion sur qch. *S.a.* VERDICT 1. **9.** *Com:* Open account, compte ouvert; compte courant. *O. credit,* crédit à découvert; crédit en blanc. **Open cheque**, chèque ouvert, non barré. **-ly,** *adv.* Ouvertement, franchement, en toute franchise; au vu (et au su) de tous. *To act o.,* agir à découvert; jouer franc jeu. **'open-air,** *attrib.a.* Au grand air, en plein air. Open-air life, la vie des champs. **Open-air meeting**, assemblée en plein vent. **open-'eyed**, *a.* **1.** Qui voit clair; qui ne se laisse pas duper. **2.** To look at s.o. **with open-eyed astonishment**, regarder qn les yeux écarquillés de surprise. **open-'faced**, *a.* Au visage franc. **open-'handed**, *a.* Libéral, -aux; généreux. **-ly,** *adv.* Libéralement. **open-'handedness**, *s.* Libéralité *f.* **open-'hearted**, *a.* **1.** Franc, *f.* franche; expansif. *O.-h. welcome*, accueil cordial. **2.** Au cœur tendre, compatissant. **open-'minded**, *a.* Qui a l'esprit ouvert, large; impartial, -aux. *To be* o.-m. (*on a subject*), n'avoir pas de parti pris, d'idée préconçue, avoir l'esprit libre (sur un sujet). **open-'mouthed**, *a.* To remain open-mouthed with astonishment, rester bouche bée. **open-'necked**, *a.* (Chemise) avec col (à la) Danton; (robe) décolletée. **'open-work**, *s.* (*a*) Ouvrage *m* à jour. *O.-w. stockings*, bas ajourés, à jour. (*b*) Ajours *mpl*, jours *mpl.*
open². I. *v.tr.* **1.** (*a*) Ouvrir (une porte, etc.); baisser (une glace). **To half o.** the door, entrebâiller, entr'ouvrir, la porte. *S.a.* DOOR 1. (*b*) Déboucher, entamer (une bouteille); écailler (une huître); décacheter (une lettre); défaire (un paquet); lâcher (une écluse). **To open the mail,** dépouiller le courrier. *El:* To open the circuit, (inter)rompre, couper, le courant. *Med:* To open the bowels, relâcher les intestins. (*c*) To o. a new shop, ouvrir, fonder, monter, un nouveau magasin. **To open a road** (*to traffic*), livrer une route à la circulation. (*d*) Inaugurer (une fête, un établissement). **5.** Écarter (les jambes); ouvrir (la main, etc.). *I have not opened my* mouth all day, je n'ai pas desserré les dents de la journée. *To open o.'s eyes,* entr'ouvrir les yeux. *S.a.* EYE¹ 1. **3.** To open a hole *in a wall*, pratiquer, percer, un trou dans un mur. *To open a road*, ouvrir, frayer, un chemin. (*Cp.* I (*c*).) **4.** Découvrir, exposer, révéler. **To open one's** heart, to open oneself, (i) épancher son cœur; (ii) ouvrir son cœur, s'ouvrir (*to s.o.*, à qn). **5.** Commencer; entamer, engager (une conversation, un débat). *Com:* To open an account in s.o.'s name, ouvrir un compte en faveur de qn. *Jur:* To open the case, ouvrir l'affaire; exposer

les faits. *Cards :* To open clubs, attaquer trèfle ; entamer trèfle. II. **open,** *v.i.* S'ouvrir. **I.** (*a*) (*Of door, etc.*) To half open, to open a little, s'entrebâiller, s'entr'ouvrir. Door that opens into, on to, the garden, porte qui donne sur, dans, le jardin, qui ouvre sur le jardin. *The exits o. on to the street,* les sorties donnent accès à la rue. (*b*) The bank opens at ten, la banque ouvre, ouvre ses portes, à dix heures. *As soon as the season opens,* dès l'ouverture de la saison. **2.** (*a*) (*Of view, etc.*) S'étendre. (*b*) (*Of flower*) S'épanouir, s'ouvrir. **3.** Commencer. *Play that opens with a brawl,* pièce qui débute par une rixe. **open out. I.** *v.tr.* (*a*) Ouvrir, déplier (une feuille de papier, etc.). (*b*) Développer (une entreprise, etc.). (*c*) Élargir, agrandir (un trou) ; évaser (un tuyau). **2.** *v.i.* (*a*) (*Of view, etc.*) S'ouvrir, s'étendre. (*b*) *Aut :* Mettre, ouvrir, les gaz. **open up. I.** *v.tr.* Ouvrir (une mine, etc.) ; exposer, révéler (une perspective) ; frayer, pratiquer (un chemin). To open up a country to trade, ouvrir un pays au commerce. **2.** *v.i. Com :* Ouvrir une succursale (dans un endroit) ; entamer des affaires (dans un pays). **opening,** *s.* **1.** (*a*) Ouverture *f* ; débouchement *m* (d'une bouteille) ; dépouillement *m* (du courrier). (*b*) Formal opening. inauguration *f.* The opening of the courts, la rentrée des tribunaux. (*c*) Commencement *m* (d'une conversation, etc.). *Jur :* Exposition *f* des faits. (*d*) *Cards :* Attaque *f.* Chess openings, débuts *m* de partie. **2.** Trou *m,* ouverture, orifice *m* ; embouchure *f* (d'un sac) ; percée *f* (dans une forêt, un mur) ; éclaircie *f* (dans les nuages) ; clairière *f* (dans un bois). **3.** Occasion *f* favorable. *Com :* Débouché *m* (pour une marchandise). *Fine o. for a young man,* beau débouché pour un jeune homme. To give an adversary an opening, prêter le flanc à un adversaire. **4.** *Attrib.* D'ouverture ; inaugural, -aux. *O. sentence,* phrase de début. *St.Exch :* Opening price, cours de début, d'ouverture ; premier cours. *Cards :* (*At bridge*) Opening bid, annonce d'entrée.

opener ['oup(ə)nər], *s.* **1.** (*Pers.*) Ouvreur, -euse. **2.** (*Device*) *See* CASE-OPENER, EYE-OPENER, TIN-OPENER.

openness ['oupənnəs], *s.* **1.** Situation exposée (d'une côte) ; aspect découvert (du terrain). **2.** Franchise *f* ; ouverture *f* de cœur.

opera ['opərə], *s.* Opéra *m.* Grand opera, grand opéra. Comic opera, opéra bouffe. **'opera-cloak,** *s.* Sortie *f* de bal, de théâtre. **'opera-glass(es),** *s.(pl.)* Jumelle(s) *f* (de théâtre). **'opera-hat,** *s.* (Chapeau *m*) claque *m* ; gibus *m.* **'opera-house,** *s.* (Théâtre *m* de l')opéra *m* ; théâtre lyrique.

operable ['opərəbl], *a. Surg :* Opérable.

operate ['opəreit]. I. *v.i.* **1.** (*a*) Opérer. (*Of physic*) Agir ; produire son effet. (*b*) *Mch :* *U.S:* Fonctionner. **2.** *St.Exch :* To operate for a rise, for a fall, jouer, spéculer, à la hausse, à la baisse. **3.** To operate on s.o., on an appendix, opérer qn, un appendice. To o. (on s.o.) for appendicitis, faire (à qn) l'opération de l'appendicite. To be operated (up)on, subir une opération. II. **operate,** *v.tr.* **1.** Opérer, effectuer, accomplir (une guérison, etc.). **2.** (*a*) *Esp. U.S:* (*Of pers.*) Faire manœuvrer (une machine) ; faire jouer (un mécanisme). To o. (*Of part of machine*) To o. another part, commander, actionner, attaquer, un autre organe. *Operated by electricity,* actionné par l'électricité. **'operating-lever,** *s. U.S:* Levier de manœuvre, de commande. **'operating-table,** *s. Surg :* Table *f* d'opération.

'operating-theatre, *s. Surg :* Salle *f* d'opération.

operatic [opə'ratik]. **1.** *a.* D'opéra. Operatic singer, chanteur dramatique d'opéra. **2.** *s.pl. F :* Operatics, opéra *m* d'amateurs.

operation [opə'rei∫(ə)n], *s.* **1.** Fonctionnement *m,* action *f.* (*Of law*) To come into operation, entrer en vigueur. To be in operation, fonctionner, jouer. In full operation, en pleine activité. *Restrictions at present in o.,* restrictions actuellement en vigueur. Mode of operation, mode *m* opératoire. **2.** *Mth : Mil : etc :* Opération. **3.** *Surg :* To perform an o., on s.o. for cataract, faire subir à qn l'opération de la cataracte. To undergo an o., subir une opération, une intervention chirurgicale.

operative ['opərətiv]. **I.** *a.* (*a*) Opératif, actif. (*Of law, etc.*) To become operative, entrer en vigueur ; prendre effet. (*b*) *Surg :* Operative field, champ opératoire ; champ d'opération. **2.** *a. & s.* Ouvrier, -ière ; artisan *m.*

operator ['opəreitər], *s.* **I.** Opérateur, -trice. *Tg :* Télégraphiste *mf.* Wireless operator, opérateur de T.S.F. ; sans-filiste *mf. Tp :* To call the operator, appeler la téléphoniste. **2.** *St.Exch :* Operator for a fall, for a rise, opérateur, joueur *m,* à la baisse, à la hausse. **3.** *Surg :* Opérateur.

operculum, *pl.* **-la** [o'pə:rkjuləm, -la], *s. Nat.Hist :* Opercule *m.*

operetta [opə'retə], *s. Mus :* Opérette *f.*

ophidia [o'fidiə], *s.pl. Rept :* Ophidiens *m.*

ophidian [o'fidiən], *a. & s. Rept :* Ophidien (*m*).

ophite ['ofait], *s. Miner :* Ophite *m* ; marbre serpentin.

ophthalmia [of'θalmiə], *s. Med :* Ophtalmie *f.*

ophthalmic [of'θalmik], *a.* **I.** Ophtalmique. **2.** (Hôpital) ophtalmologique, pour les maladies des yeux.

ophthalmoscope [of'θalmoskoup], *s. Med :* Ophtalmoscope *m.*

opiate[1] ['oupiet], *s. Pharm :* Opiacé *m,* opiat *m,* narcotique *m.*

opiate[2] ['oupieit], *v.tr.* Opiacer (un médicament).

opine [o'pain]. **I.** *v.tr.* (*a*) Être d'avis (*that,* que). (*b*) Émettre l'avis (*that,* que). **2.** *v.i.* Opiner.

opinion [o'pinjən], *s.* (*a*) Opinion *f,* avis *m.* In my opinion, à, selon, mon avis ; à mon sens. *In the o. of experts,* de l'avis, au dire, au jugement, des experts. To be of (the) opinion that . . ., être d'avis, estimer, que. . . . To be entirely of 's.o.'s opinion, abonder dans le sens de qn. Matter of opinion, affaire d'opinion. To give one's opinion, dire, émettre son opinion. To ask s.o.'s opinion, se référer à qn ; consulter qn. To form an o. on sth., se faire une opinion sur, de, qch. *What is your o. of him?* que pensez-vous de lui ? To have, hold, a high opinion of s.o., avoir une bonne opinion de qn ; tenir qn en haute estime. To have no opinion of sth., ne pas faire grand cas de qch. Public opinion, l'opinion (publique). (*b*) Consultation *f* (de médecin, etc.). *Jur :* Counsel's opinion, avis motivé. *To take counsel's o.,* consulter un avocat.

opinionated [o'pinjəneitid], *a.* Opiniâtre ; entier (dans ses opinions) ; imbu de ses opinions.

opium ['oupjəm], *s.* Opium *m.* **'opium den,** *s.* Fumerie *f* d'opium. **'opium-fiend,** *s. F :* Opiomane *mf.* **'opium-smoker,** *s.* Fumeur *m* d'opium.

opodeldoc [opo'deldok], *s. Pharm :* Opodeldoch *m.*

Oporto [o'po:rto]. *Pr.n. Geog :* Porto *m.*

opossum [o'posəm], s. Z: Opossum m; sarigue m.
opponent [o'pounənt], s. Adversaire m, antagoniste mf (of, de). (
opportune ['opɔrtjuːn], a. (Of time) Opportun, convenable, commode; (of action) à propos. You have come at an o. moment, vous tombez bien. This cheque is most o., ce chèque tombe à merveille. **-ly**, adv. Opportunément, en temps opportun, à propos. It happens most o., cela arrive à point (nommé); F: cela arrive comme marée en carême.
opportuneness ['opɔrtjuːnnəs], s. Opportunité f; à-propos m.
opportunism ['opɔrtjunizm], s. Opportunisme m.
opportunist ['opɔrtjunist], s. Opportuniste mf.
opportunity [opɔr'tjuniti], s. **1.** Occasion f (favorable). A golden o., une occasion magnifique. At the first, earliest, o., à la première occasion. When the o. occurs, offers, à l'occasion. If I get an opportunity . . ., si l'occasion se présente. . . . To take the opportunity to do sth., profiter de l'occasion pour faire qch. To miss an opportunity, laisser passer une occasion. To make an opportunity of doing sth., se ménager une occasion de faire qch. **2.** = OPPORTUNENESS.
oppose [o'pouz], v.tr. **1.** Opposer (deux choses); mettre (deux couleurs) en opposition. **2.** S'opposer à (qn, qch.); aller au contraire de (qch.); mettre obstacle, opposition, à (qch.); résister à (qn, qch.). To oppose the motion, soutenir la contre-partie; parler contre. **opposed**, a. **1.** Opposé, hostile. **2.** What he says is o. to all reason, ce qu'il dit est le rebours, l'envers, du bon sens. Country life as opposed to town life, la vie à la campagne à la différence de, par opposition à, celle dans les grandes villes. **3.** Horizontally opposed cylinders, cylindres opposés. **opposing**, a. (Of armies, characters, etc.) Opposé; (of party, etc.) opposant.
opposer [o'pouzər], s. **1.** Opposant m, contradicteur m. **2.** = OPPONENT.
opposite [o'pozit]. **1.** a. (a) Opposé (to, à); vis-à-vis (to, de); en face (to, de). See the diagram on the o. page, voir la figure ci-contre. Text with illustration on the o. page, texte avec illustration en regard. The house o., la maison qui fait vis-à-vis; la maison (d')en face. Mil: Navy: etc: Opposite number, correspondant m en grade; F: similaire m. (b) Contraire (to, from, à). The opposite sex, l'autre sexe. Magn: Opposite po'es, pôles contraires, de nom contraire. To take the o. course, the o. view, to . . ., prendre le contre-pied de. . . . In the opposite direction, en sens inverse; dans le sens opposé. Ships going in o. directions, navires allant à contre-bord. **2.** s. Opposé m; le contre-pied; l'opposite m. Just the o. of what he says, tout le contraire de ce qu'il dit. **3.** adv. Vis-à-vis; en face. **4.** prep. En face de, vis-à-vis (de). To stand, sit, opposite s.o., faire vis-à-vis à qn. Stop o. number 128, arrêtez-vous à la hauteur du numéro 128.
opposition [opo'ziʃ(ə)n], s. Opposition f. (a) To act in o. to public opinion, agir contrairement à l'opinion publique. Parties in o., partis qui se combattent. (b) Résistance f. (c) (Le) camp adverse. Pol: The party in opposition, F: the opposition, (le parti de) l'opposition. (d) Com: To star in oppos.tion to s.o., ouvrir un magasin en concurrence avec qn.
oppress [o'pres], v.tr. (a) Opprimer. (b) Oppresser, accabler (l'esprit).
oppression [o'preʃ(ə)n], s. (a) Oppression f. Jur: Abus m d'autorité. (b) Accablement m (de l'esprit, etc.); resserrement m (de cœur).

oppressive [o'presiv], a. **1.** (Of law, etc.) Oppressif, opprimant, tyrannique. **2.** (a) (Of atmosphere, etc.) Lourd, étouffant. (b) (Of mental burden) Accablant. **-ly**, adv. **1.** Tyranniquement. **2.** D'une manière accablante.
oppressiveness [o'presivnəs], s. **1.** Caractère oppressif (d'un gouvernement, etc.). **2.** Lourdeur f (du temps).
oppressor [o'presər], s. (a) Oppresseur m. (b) Oppressors and oppressed, les opprimants m et les opprimés m.
opprobrious [o'proubriəs], a. Injurieux, outrageant. **-ly**, adv. Injurieusement.
opprobrium [o'proubriəm], s. Opprobre m.
opt [opt], v.i. Opter (for, pour; between, entre).
optative [op'teitiv, 'optativ], a. & s. Gram: Optatif (m).
optic ['optik], a. Optic nerve, nerf optique.
optical ['optik(ə)l], a. **1.** Optique. **2.** (Instrument) d'optique. Optica illusion, illusion d'optique.
optician [op'tiʃ(ə)n], s. Opticien m.
optics ['optiks], s.pl. L'optique f.
optimism ['optimizm], s. Optimisme m.
optimist ['optimist], s. Optimiste mf.
optimistic [opti'mistik], a. Optimiste. **-ally**, adv. Avec optimisme.
option [op'ʃ(ə)n], s. **1.** Option f, choix m. (a) To make one's option, faire son choix; opter (between, entre). Lease renewable at the option of the tenant, bail renouvelable au gré du locataire. (b) To have the option of doing sth., avoir la faculté, le choix, de faire qch. Jur: Imprisonment without the option of a fine, emprisonnement sans substitution d'amende. **2.** (a) To take an o. on sth., prendre une option sur qch. (b) St.Exch: Option; (marché m à) prime f. Option dealing(s), opérations fpl à prime.
optional [op'ʃənəl], a. Facultatif. It is o. for you to go or stay, vous avez le choix de partir ou de rester.
opulence ['opjuləns], s. Opulence f, richesse f. To live in o., vivre dans l'opulence.
opulent ['opjulənt], a. Opulent. **-ly**, adv. Avec opulence.
opuscule [o'pʌskjul], s. Opuscule m.
or [oːr], conj. (a) Ou; (with neg.) ni. Will you have beef or ham? voulez-vous du bœuf ou du jambon? Either one or the other, soit l'un soit l'autre; l'un ou l'autre. S.a. ELSE 1. Either you or he has done it; he or you have done it, c'est vous ou (c'est) lui, c'est l'un de vous deux, qui l'a fait. I cannot (either) read or write, je ne sais ni lire ni écrire. Without money or luggage, sans argent ni bagages. In a day or two, dans un ou deux jours. A mile or so, environ un mille. (b) Don't move, or I'll shoot, ne bougez pas, sinon je tire.
orach ['orɑtʃ], s. Bot: Arroche f.
oracle ['orəkl], s. Oracle m. To pronounce an o., rendre un oracle. P: To work the oracle, (i) faire agir certaines influences; (ii) arriver à ses fins. To be Sir Oracle, trancher sur tout.
oracular [o'rakjulər], a. **1.** Équivoque, obscur; (réponse, etc.) en style d'oracle. **2.** Our o. press, nos journaux qui tranchent sur tout. **-ly**, adv. En (style d')oracle.
oral ['oːrəl], a. **1.** Oral, -aux. Sch: Oral examination, s. F: oral, (examen) oral m. **2.** (a) Oral cavity, cavité orale, buccale. (b) O. administration (of a drug), administration par la bouche. **-ally**, adv. **1.** Oralement; de vive voix. **2.** Med: Par la bouche.
orange ['orəndʒ], s. **1.** Orange f. Bitter orange, Seville orange, orange amère; bigarade f.

Valencia orange, valence *f.* **China orange,** orange
douce. **2. Orange(-tree),** oranger *m.* **3.** *a. & s.*
(Colour) Orangé (*m*) ; orange (*m*) *inv.* **Orang-**
ed, rouge orange (*m*) *inv.* **'orange-blossom,**
s. Fleurs *fpl* d'oranger. **'orange-flower,** *s.*
Fleur *f* d'oranger. **Orange-flower water,** eau *f* de
fleur(s) d'oranger. **'orange-house,** *s.* Orangerie *f.* **'orange-lily,** *s. Bot:* Lis orangé.
'orange-stick, *s. Toil:* Bâtonnet *m* ; bâton *m*
d'oranger.

orangeman, *pl.* **-men** ['ɔrəndʒmən, -men], *s.m.*
Orangiste (du parti protestant de l'Irlande du
Nord).

orangery ['ɔrəndʒəri], *s.* Orangerie *f.*

orang-(o)utang [oˈraŋuˈtaŋ], *s. Z:* Orang-
outan(g) *m, pl.* orangs-outangs.

orate [ɔˈreit], *v.i. Hum:* Pérorer ; *P:* laïusser.

oration [ɔˈreiʃ(ə)n], *s.* **1.** Allocution *f,* discours *m* ;
morceau *m* oratoire ; *Hum. & Pej:* harangue *f* ;
Sch: *F:* laïus *m.* **Funeral oration,** oraison *f*
funèbre. **2.** *Gram:* Direct, indirect, oration,
discours direct, indirect.

orator ['ɔrətər], *s.* Orateur *m.*

oratorical [ɔrəˈtɔrik(ə)l], *a.* **1.** *(a)* (Style) oratoire. *(b)* (Discours) verbeux, ampoulé. **2.** *(Of*
pers.) *(a)* Grand parleur : disert. *(b)* Phraseur.

oratorio [ɔrəˈtɔːrio], *s. Mus:* Oratorio *m.*

oratory[1] ['ɔrətəri], *s.* L'art *m* oratoire ; l'éloquence *f.* **Flight** of o., envolée éloquente. *Pulpit*
o., forensic o., parliamentary o., éloquence de la
chaire, du barreau, de la tribune.

oratory[2], *s.* Oratoire *m* ; chapelle privée.

orb [ɔːrb], *s.* Orbe *m.* *(a)* Globe *m,* sphère *f.* *The*
orb of the sun, le globe du soleil. *(b)* *Poet:*
Corps *m* céleste ; astre *m.* *(c)* *(Of regalia)* Globe.

orbit ['ɔːrbit], *s.* **1.** Orbite *f* (d'une planète).
2. *Anat:* Orbite (de l'œil) ; fosse *f* orbitaire.

orc [ɔːrk], *s. Z:* Épaulard *m* ; orque *f.*

orchard ['ɔːrtʃərd], *s.* Verger *m.*

orchestra ['ɔːrkestra], *s.* **1.** Orchestre *m.*
Orchestra stalls, fauteuils *m* d'orchestre. **2.** *(Band)*
String orchestra, orchestre d'archets.

orchestral [ɔːrˈkestrəl], *a.* Orchestral, -aux.

orchestrate ['ɔːrkestreit], *v.tr. Mus:* Orchestrer, instrumenter.

orchestration [ɔːrkesˈtreiʃ(ə)n], *s.* Orchestration *f,* instrumentation *f.*

orchid ['ɔːrkid], *s.* Orchidée *f.* **Wild orchid,**
orchis *m.*

orchil ['ɔːrtʃil], *s. Bot:* Dy: Orseille *f.*

orchis ['ɔːrkis], *s. Bot:* Orchis *m.*

ordain [ɔːrˈdein], *v.tr.* Ordonner. **1.** *Ecc:* Conférer les ordres à (un prêtre). **To ordain s.o.**
deacon, ordonner qn diacre. **To be ordained,**
recevoir les ordres. **2.** *(Of the Deity, of fate)*
(a) Destiner. *Ordained of God to be judge,* destiné
de Dieu pour être juge. *(b)* Ordonner, fixer.
(c) *(Of pers.)* Prescrire, décréter (une mesure).
To ordain that . . ., statuer que + *ind.*

ordeal [ɔːrˈdiː(ə)l], *s.* **1.** *Hist:* Épreuve *f* judiciaire ; *A:* ordalie *f* ; jugement *m* de Dieu.
Ordeal by fire, épreuve du feu. **2.** *To go through*
a terrible o., passer par une rude épreuve.

order[1] ['ɔːrdər], *s.* Ordre *m.* **1.** *(a)* The higher,
lower, orders *(of society),* les classes supérieures ;
les classes inférieures. **Talents of the first order,**
of a high order, talents du premier ordre, d'un
ordre élevé. *(b)* *pl. Ecc:* Holy orders, ordres
sacrés, ordres majeurs. **Minor orders,** ordres
mineurs. **To take holy orders,** *F:* to take orders,
prendre les ordres ; recevoir les ordres. **To be**
in holy orders, être prêtre. *(c)* Monastic order,
ordre religieux ; communauté *f.* **The Order of**
knighthood, ordre de chevalerie. **The Order of**

the Garter, l'Ordre de la Jarretière. *S.a.* BOOT[1] 1.
(d) *To be wearing all one's orders,* porter tous ses
ordres, toutes ses décorations. *(e)* *Arch:* Ionic
order, Doric order, ordre ionique, ordre dorique.
2. Succession *f,* suite *f.* **In alphabetical order,**
par ordre alphabétique. *In chronological o.,* par
ordre de dates. *In o. of age,* par rang d'âge.
Out of (its) order, hors de son rang. *I.C.E:* Order
of firing, rythme *m* d'allumage. **3.** *Mil:* *(a)* Close
order, ordre serré. **Order of battle,** *Mil:* ordre
de bataille ; *Navy:* ordre tactique. *(b)* In marching order, en tenue de route. *In review o.,* in
gala o., en grande tenue. **4.** The old order of
things, l'ancien régime. *The present o.* of things,
le régime actuel. **5.** *(a)* To put a matter in order,
mettre une question en règle ; mettre ordre à une
affaire. *The matter is now in o.,* l'affaire est dès
maintenant en règle. **To set one's house in order,**
(i) remettre de l'ordre dans son ménage ;
(ii) *F:* remettre de l'ordre dans ses affaires. **Is**
your passport in order? votre passeport est-il en
règle ? **Cargo received in good order,** chargement
reçu en bon état. **Machine in good (working)**
order, machine en bon état (de fonctionnement).
S.a. WORKING[2] 3. **Out of order,** en mauvais état ;
(of room, business affairs) en désordre ; *(of*
machinery) détraqué. **To get out of order,** se
dérégler, se détraquer. *(b)* *Parl: etc:* In order,
dans les règles. *It is not in o.,* ce n'est pas
réglementaire. **To rule a question out of order,**
statuer qu'une interpellation n'est pas dans les
règles, n'est pas pertinente. **To rise to (a point**
of) order, se lever pour demander le rappel à
l'ordre. **To call s.o. to order,** rappeler qn à
l'ordre. **Order! order!** à l'ordre ! **Order of the**
day, ordre du jour. **6.** **Law and order,** l'ordre
public. **To keep order in a town, in a class-room,**
maintenir, assurer, l'ordre dans une ville ; maintenir la discipline dans une classe. **To keep the**
children in order, (i) soumettre les enfants à la
discipline ; (ii) avoir les enfants bien en main.
7. *Ecc:* Order of service, office *m.* **8.** *Mil:* Arms
at the order, l'arme au pied. **9. In order to do**
sth., afin de, pour, faire qch. **In order that . . .,**
afin que, pour que, + *sub.* **10.** *(a)* Commandement *m,* instruction *f. Mil: Navy:* Consigne *f.*
To give orders for sth. to be done, that sth.
should be done, ordonner qu'on fasse qch., que
qch. se fasse. *He gave me orders to do it,* il m'a
donné (l')ordre de le faire. **Orders are orders,** je
ne connais que la consigne. **Standing orders,**
ordres permanents ; règlement(s) *m.* **Until fur-**
ther orders, jusqu'à nouvel ordre. **By order**
of . . ., par ordre de. . . . *By o. of the king,*
de par le roi. *(b)* *Com:* **Pay to the order of . . .,**
payez à l'ordre de. . . . **Pay X or order,** payez
à X ou à son ordre. **Bill to order,** billet à ordre.
Cheque to order, order cheque, chèque à ordre.
(c) *Com:* **Commande** *f.* *(Of tradesman)* **To call**
for orders, passer prendre les commandes. **To**
place an order with s.o., to give an order to s.o.,
(i) faire, confier, passer, une commande à qn ;
(ii) commander qch. à qn. **To put goods on**
order, commander des marchandises ; mettre
des marchandises en commande. **By order and**
for account of . . ., d'ordre et pour compte
de . . . . **Made to order,** fabriqué sur commande,
à la demande. *Suit made to o.,* complet fait sur
mesure. *P:* That's (rather) a tall, large, order !
ça c'est une grosse affaire ! c'est demander un
peu trop ! **11.** *(a)* **Written order,** ordre par écrit.
Adm: General order, arrêt *m.* **Departmental**
order, arrêté ministériel. **Order to pay, order for**
payment, ordonnance *f* de payement. **Order in**

Council = décret présidentiel, arrêté ministériel ;
décret-loi *m*, *pl.* décrets-lois. *Jur:* Judge's order,
ordonnance. **Deportation order,** arrêté d'expulsion. **Order of the court,** injonction *f* de la cour.
Mil: **Regimental orders,** décisions *f.* **Mention in
orders,** citation *f* (à l'ordre du jour). *Navy:*
Sailing orders, instructions *f* pour la marche. **To
be under sailing orders,** avoir reçu l'ordre d'appareiller. **Sealed orders,** ordres cachetés ; pli
secret. *S.a.* MARCHING. (*b*) **Order on a bank,**
mandat *m* sur une banque. **Money order,**
F: post-office order, mandat de poste ; mandat-
poste, *pl.* mandats-poste. *Foreign, international,
money* o., mandat-poste international, sur
l'étranger. **Postal order,** bon *m* de poste. **'order-
book,** *s.* Carnet *m* de commandes.
order², *v.tr.* **1.** (*a*) Arranger, ranger, ordonner
(des papiers, des meubles) ; régler (sa vie).
(*b*) *Mil:* Order arms! reposez armes! **2.** = OR-
DAIN 2. **3.** (*a*) **To order s.o. to do sth.,** ordonner,
commander, à qn de faire qch. *They ordered him
to be hanged,* ils ordonnèrent qu'on le pendît.
Jur: **To be ordered to pay costs,** être condamné
aux dépens. *To o. an officer to Plymouth,* désigner
un officier pour Plymouth. (*b*) *Med:* Prescrire,
ordonner (un traitement, un remède, à qn).
(*c*) *Com:* Commander (qch.) ; mettre (qch.) en
commande. *To o. a suit of clothes,* commander
un complet ; se faire faire un complet. **order
about,** *v.tr.* Envoyer (qn) de côté et d'autre,
à droite et à gauche ; *F:* faire marcher, faire
aller (qn). **order in,** *v.tr.* **1.** Ordonner à (qn)
d'entrer ; faire entrer (qn). **2. To order in
supplies,** commander des approvisionnements.
order off, *v.tr.* Ordonner à (qn) de s'éloigner,
de s'en aller. *Fb:* **To order a player off (the
field),** ordonner à un joueur de quitter la partie
(pour brutalité). **order out,** *v.tr.* Ordonner à
(qn) de sortir. **To order out troops,** faire sortir
des troupes ; appeler la troupe. **ordering,** *s.*
Mise *f* en ordre ; agencement *m* (d'un appartement, etc.) ; disposition *f* (de troupes, de sa
maison,'etc.) ; règlement *m*.
orderliness ['ɔːrdərlinəs], *s.* **1.** Bon ordre ;
méthode *f.* **2.** Habitudes *fpl* d'ordre. **3.** Discipline *f* ; calme *m*.
orderly ['ɔːrdərli]. **1.** *a.* (*a*) Ordonné, méthodique ; (*of life*) réglé, rangé, régulier. (*Of pers.*)
To be very o., avoir beaucoup de méthode,
beaucoup de soin. (*b*) (*Of crowd, etc.*) Tranquille,
discipliné. (*c*) *Mil:* **Orderly officer,** officier *m* de
service ; officier de semaine. **2.** *s.* (*a*) *Mil:* Planton *m*. **Mounted orderly,** estafette *f.* **Hospital
orderly, medical orderly,** infirmier *m*, ambulancier *m*. (*b*) **Street orderly,** balayeur *m*,
arroseur *m* (de rues) ; boueur *m*.
ordinal ['ɔːrdinəl], *a. & s.* Ordinal, -aux.
ordinance ['ɔːrdinəns], *s.* **1.** Ordonnance *f*,
décret *m*, règlement *m*. **Police ordinance,** ordonnance, arrêté *m*, de police. **2.** *Ecc:* (*a*) Rite *m*,
cérémonie *f* (du culte). (*b*) **The (sacred) Ordinance,** l'Eucharistie *f*.
ordinary ['ɔːrdinəri]. **I.** *a.* **1.** (*a*) Ordinaire ; (*of
routine, etc.*) coutumier ; normal, -aux ; courant.
Dipl: **Ordinary ambassador,** ambassadeur ordinaire. *Fin:* **Ordinary share,** action ordinaire.
Ordinary agent, agent attitré. *S.a.* BICYCLE¹,
SEAMAN 1. (*b*) *O. Englishman,* Anglais moyen,
typique. *The o. reader,* le commun des lecteurs.
2. *Pej:* **A very ordinary kind of man,** un homme
tout à fait quelconque. *A small and very o. room,*
une petite chambre banale. **-ily,** *adv.* Ordinairement, normalement ; d'ordinaire, d'habitude ;
à l'ordinaire. **II. ordinary,** *s.* **1.** Ordinaire *m*.

Out of the ordinary, exceptionnel ; peu ordinaire.
Man above the ordinary, homme à part, au-
dessus du commun. **Physician-in-ordinary to the
king,** médecin ordinaire du roi. **2.** (*In restaurant*)
Table *f* d'hôte ; ordinaire *m*. **3.** *Her:* Pièce *f*
honorable. **4.** (*Pers.*) (*a*) (*Scot.*) Juge *m*. (*b*) *Ecc:*
Ordinaire (archevêque ou évêque). **5.** *Ecc:* **The
Ordinary (of the mass),** l'Ordinaire (de la messe).
ordinate ['ɔːrdinet], *s. Mth:* Ordonnée *f.*
ordination [ɔːrdi'neiʃ(ə)n], *s.* **1.** Arrangement *m* ;
classification *f* (des plantes, etc.). **2.** Ordonnance *f* (de Dieu). **3.** *Ecc:* Ordination *f.*
ordnance ['ɔːrdnəns], *s.* **1.** Artillerie *f.* **Piece of
ordnance,** bouche *f* à feu ; pièce *f* d'artillerie.
2. *Mil:* (*a*) Service *m* du matériel, des dépôts.
Ordnance and supplies, ravitaillement *m*. (*b*) **Ordnance Survey,** (i) service topographique, cartographique ; (ii) corps *m* des ingénieurs-géo-
graphes.
ordure ['ɔːrdjuər], *s.* Ordure *f*. (*a*) Excrément *m*.
(*b*) Immondice *f*, saleté *f.*
ore ['ɔːər], *s.* Minerai *m*. **Iron ore,** minerai de fer.
oread ['ɔːriad], *s.f. Gr.Myth:* Oréade.
organ ['ɔːrgən], *s.* **1.** *Mus:* (*a*) Orgue *m*, orgues
fpl. **Grand organ** (*in organ-loft*), grand orgue ;
grandes orgues. *To be, preside, at the o.,* tenir
l'orgue, les orgues. (*b*) **American organ,** orgue
de salon. (*c*) **Street organ,** orgue de Barbarie.
2. (*a*) Organe *m* (de la vue, etc.). **Organ of
hearing,** organe de l'ouïe. **The vocal organs,**
l'appareil vocal. (*b*) Journal *m*, bulletin *m*,
organe, porte-parole *m inv* (d'un parti politique,
etc.). **'organ-blower,** *s.* **1.** Souffleur *m*
(d'orgue). **2.** La soufflerie. **'organ-builder,** *s.*
Facteur *m* d'orgues. **'organ-case, -chest,** *s.*
Buffet *m* d'orgue. **'organ-grinder,** *s.* Joueur
d'orgue de Barbarie. **'organ-loft,** *s.* Tribune *f*
(de l'orgue). **'organ-pipe,** *s.* Tuyau *m* d'orgue.
'organ-screen, *s.* Jubé *m* (formant tribune
d'orgue). **'organ-stop,** *s.* Jeu *m* d'orgue.
organdi(e) ['ɔːrgəndi], *s. Tex:* Organdi *m*.
organic [ɔːr'ganik], *a.* **1.** (Maladie, fonction)
organique. **2.** (*a*) *O. beings,* êtres organisés. *The
law of o. growth,* la loi de croissance organisée.
(*b*) **Organic chemistry,** chimie organique.
organism ['ɔːrgəniz(ə)m], *s.* Organisme *m*.
organist ['ɔːrgənist], *s.* Organiste *mf*.
organization [ɔːrgənai'zeiʃ(ə)n], *s.* **1.** Organisation *f*. **2.** Organisme *m* (politique ,etc.). *Charity
o.,* œuvre *f* de charité.
organize ['ɔːrgənaiz], *v.tr.* **1.** Organiser.
2. Arranger (un concert) ; aménager (ses loisirs).
organizer ['ɔːrgənaizər], *s.* Organisateur, -trice.
The o. of the festivities, l'ordonnateur *m* de la fête.
orgiac ['ɔːrdʒiak], **orgiastic** [ɔːrdʒi'astik], *a.*
Orgiaque.
orgy ['ɔːrdʒi], *s.* Orgie *f*; *F:* bacchanale *f.*
F: O. of colour, orgie, profusion *f*, de couleurs.
oriel ['ɔːriəl], *s.* (i) Fenêtre *f* en saillie ; (ii) fenêtre
en encorbellement.
orielled ['ɔːriəld], *a.* A fenêtres en encorbellement.
orient¹ ['ɔːriənt]. **I.** *s.* **1.** (*a*) Orient *m*. *Geog:* **The
Orient,** l'Orient. (*b*) **Pearl of a fine orient,** perle
d'un bel orient. **2.** *a.* Oriental, -aux ; de l'orient
ou de l'Orient.
orient² [ɔːri'ent], *v.tr.* = ORIENTATE.
oriental [ɔːri'entəl]. **1.** *a.* Oriental, -aux ;
d'Orient. **2.** *s.* Indigène *mf* de l'Orient ; Oriental,
-ale.
orientate ['ɔːrienteit], *v.tr.* Orienter (une église).
orientation [ɔːrien'teiʃ(ə)n], *s.* Orientation *f*.
orifice ['ɔːrifis], *s.* Orifice *m*, ouverture *f*, trou *m*.
origin ['ɔːridʒin], *s.* Origine *f*. **1.** *The o. of the*

universe, la genèse des mondes. **2.** *Word of Greek o.*, mot d'origine grecque. (*Of pers.*) *To be of noble, humble, o.*, être d'origine illustre, d'humble extraction *f.* *Com:* Country of origin, pays de provenance. *Cust:* Certificate of origin, certificat d'origine.

original [o'ridʒinəl]. **I.** *a.* (*a*) Originaire, primordial, -aux, primitif. *O. meaning of a word*, sens premier d'un mot. *O. idea of a work*, idée mère d'une œuvre. *O. member of a club*, membre originaire d'un club. *Theol:* Original sin, péché originel. (*b*) *O. edition*, édition princeps. *The o. picture is at . . .*, le tableau original est au musée de. . . . (*c*) (Style, manière) original; (spectacle, etc.) inédit. *The scheme is not an o. one*, ce projet n'est pas inédit. **2.** *s.* Original *m* (d'un tableau, d'une facture). **3.** *s.* Personne originale; original, -ale; *F:* un type à part; un type. **-ally,** *adv.* **I.** (*a*) Originairement; à l'origine, dans l'origine. (*b*) Originellement; dès l'origine. **2.** Originalement.

originality [oridʒi'naliti], *s.* Originalité *f.*

originate [o'ridʒineit]. **I.** *v.tr.* Faire naître, donner naissance à, être l'auteur de (qch.). **2.** *v.i.* Tirer son origine, dériver, provenir (*from, in, de*); avoir son origine (dans). *The fire originated under the floor*, le feu a pris naissance sous le plancher.

origination [oridʒi'neiʃ(ə)n], *s.* (*a*) Source *f*, origine *f.* (*b*) Création *f*, invention *f* (d'une machine, etc.). (*c*) Naissance *f* (d'une rumeur).

originator [o'ridʒineitər], *s.* Créateur, -trice; auteur *m*; initiateur, -trice; promoteur *m* (d'une industrie).

oriole [o'rioul], *s.* *Orn:* Loriot *m.*

orison [o'rizon], *s.* *A:* Oraison *f*, prière *f.* *Esp.pl.* *She was at her orisons*, elle était en prière.

Orkneys (the) [ði'ɔ:rkniz]. *Pr.n.pl.* *Geog:* Les Orcades *f.*

orlop [o:rlɔp], *s.* *Nau:* Faux-pont *m.*

ormolu [o:rmolu:], *s.* **I.** Or moulu. Ormolu clock, pendule en or moulu. **2.** Similor *m.*

ornament[1] [o:rnəmənt], *s.* Ornement *m.* *The altar ornaments*, le parement d'autel.

ornament[2] [o:rnəmənt, o:rnə'ment], *v.tr.* Orner, ornementer, décorer; agrémenter (une robe).

ornamental [o:rnə'ment(ə)l], *a.* Ornemental, -aux; d'ornement, d'agrément. *O. piece*, enjolivement *m.* **-ally,** *adv.* **I.** Pour servir d'ornement. **2.** Décorativement.

ornamentation [o:rnəmen'teiʃ(ə)n], *s.* **I.** Ornementation *f*, embellissement *m*, décoration *f.* **2.** Les ornements *n.*

ornate [o:r'neit], *a.* Orné; surchargé d'ornements. *O. style*, style imagé, fleuri. **-ly,** *adv.* Avec une surabondance d'ornements; en style trop fleuri.

ornithological [o:rniθo'lɔdʒik(ə)l], *a.* Ornithologique.

ornithologist [o:rni'θɔlɔdʒist], *s.* Ornithologue *m*, ornithologiste *m.*

ornithology [o:rni'θɔlɔdʒi], *s.* Ornithologie *f.*

ornithorhynchus [o:rniθo'riŋkəs], *s.* *Z:* Ornithorynque *m.*

orography [o'rɔgrəfi], *s.* Orographie *f.*

orotund [orotʌnd], *a.* **I.** (Style, discours) sonore, mâle. **2.** (Style) emphatique, ampoulé.

orphan [o:rfən]. **I.** *s.* (*a*) Orphelin, -ine. *To be left an o.*, rester, devenir, orphelin. (*b*) *Adm:* Pupille *mf* de l'assistance publique; enfant assisté. Orphan home, orphelinat *m.* **2.** *a.* An orphan child, un(e) orphelin(e).

orphanage [o:rfəned̮ʒ], *s.* **I.** État *m* d'orphelin.

2. Orphelinat *m.* *To place a child in an o.*, mettre un enfant aux Orphelins.

orphaned [o:rfənd], *a.* Orphelin, -ine. *O. both of father and mother*, orphelin de père et (de) mère.

Orpheus [o:rfju:s]. *Pr.n.m.* Orphée.

orpiment [o:rpimənt], *s.* *Miner:* Orpiment *m*, orpin *m*; sulfure *m* jaune d'arsenic.

orrery [orəri], *s.* *Astr:* Planétaire *m.*

orris [oris], *s.* *Bot:* Iris *m.* *Pharm:* Orris-root, racine *f* d'iris. **Orris-powder,** poudre *f* d'iris.

orthocentre [o:rθo'sentər], *s.* *Geom:* Orthocentre *m.*

orthochromatic [o:rθokro'matik], *a.* Orthochromatique.

orthodox [o:rθodɔks], *a.* Orthodoxe.

orthodoxy [o:rθodɔksi], *s.* Orthodoxie *f.*

orthogonal [o:r'θɔgonəl], *a.* *Geom:* Orthogonal, -aux; orthographique. **-ally,** *adv.* Orthogonalement; à angle droit.

orthographic(al) [o:rθo'grafik(əl)], *a.* **I.** *Gram:* Orthographique. **2.** *Geom:* = ORTHOGONAL.

orthography [o:r'θɔgrəfi], *s.* **I.** Orthographe *f.* **2.** *Geom:* Coupe *f* perpendiculaire; projection orthogonale.

orthopaedic [o:rθo'pi:dik], *a.* Orthopédique.

orthopaedist [o:rθo'pi:dist], *s.* Orthopédiste *m.*

orthopaedy [o:rθopi:di], *s.* Orthopédie *f.*

ortolan [o:rtolən], *s.* *Orn:* Ortolan *m.*

oscillate [osileit]. **I.** *v.i.* Osciller. (*Of indicator needle*) *To o. violently*, s'affoler. **2.** *v.tr.* Balancer; faire osciller. **oscillating,** *a.* (*a*) Oscillant. (*b*) *El:* Oscillating current, courant oscillatoire. (*c*) *W.Tel:* Oscillating coil, bobine oscillatrice; bobinage oscillateur.

oscillation [osi'leiʃ(ə)n], *s.* *Ph: etc:* Oscillation *f* (d'un pendule, etc.). *W.Tel: etc:* **Damped oscillations, sustained oscillations,** oscillations amorties, entretenues.

oscillator [osileitər], *s.* *W.Tel:* (*a*) Oscillateur *m*; bobine oscillatrice. (*b*) Lampe oscillatrice.

oscillatory [osilətəri], *a.* Oscillatoire. *El:* O. discharge, décharge oscillante. *W.Tel:* Oscillatory circuit, circuit *m* vibratoire.

osculate [oskjuleit], *v.i.* *Geom:* (*Of curve*) To osculate with a line, baiser une ligne.

osculation [oskju'leiʃ(ə)n], *s.* *Geom:* Osculation *f.*

osculatory [oskjulətəri], *a.* *Geom:* Osculateur, -trice.

osier [ouʒər], *s.* Osier *m.* **Common osier, velvet osier,** osier blanc, vert; saule *m* des vanniers. **osier-bed, -holt,** *s.* Oseraie *f.*

Osmanli [os'manli], *a. & s.* *Hist:* Osmanli, -ie; Turc d'Europe.

osmium [osmiəm, oz-], *s.* *Ch:* Osmium *m.*

osmosis [os'mousis], *s.* *Ph:* Osmose *f.*

osmotic [os'mɔtik], *a.* *Ph:* (Pression) osmotique.

osprey [osprei], *s.* **I.** *Orn:* Orfraie *f*, pygargue *m.* **2.** *Cost:* Aigrette *f.*

osseous [osiəs], *a.* Osseux.

Ossianic [osi'anik], *a.* *Lit.Hist:* Ossianique.

ossicle [osikl], *s.* *Anat:* Osselet *m*; ossicule *m.*

ossification [osifi'keiʃ(ə)n], *s.* *Physiol:* Ossification *f.*

ossify [osifai]. **I.** *v.i.* S'ossifier. **2.** *v.tr.* Ossifier (un cartilage, *F:* le cœur, etc.).

ossuary [osjuəri], *s.* Ossuaire *m.*

Ostend [os'tend]. *Pr.n.* *Geog:* Ostende.

ostensible [os'tensibl], *a.* Prétendu; qui sert de prétexte; soi-disant; feint. *He went out with the o. object of . . .*, il est sorti sous prétexte de. . . . **-ibly,** *adv.* En apparence; *F:* censément.

ostensory [os'tensəri], *s.* *Ecc:* Ostensoir *m.*

ostentation [ɔsten'teiʃ(ə)n], *s.* Ostentation *f*, faste *m*, apparat *m*, parade *f*.

ostentatious [ɔsten'teiʃəs], *a.* Fastueux ; plein d'ostentation, qui fait de l'ostentation ; (luxe) affichant. **-ly**, *adv.* Avec ostentation ; avec faste.

osteology [ɔsti'ɔlodʒi], *s.* Ostéologie *f*.

osteopath ['ɔstiopæθ], *s.* Praticien manipulateur des os et des articulations.

osteopathy [ɔsti'ɔpæθi], *s. Med :* Traitement *m* des affections de la santé par la manipulation des os et des articulations.

ostler ['ɔslər], *s.m.* Valet d'écurie ; garçon d'écurie ; palefrenier.

ostracism ['ɔstrəsizm], *s.* Ostracisme *m*.

ostracize ['ɔstrəsa:iz], *v.tr.* **1.** *Gr.Ant :* Ostraciser, exiler, bannir. **2.** *F :* Ostraciser ; mettre (qn) au ban de la société.

ostreiculture ['ɔstriikʌltjər], *s.* Ostréiculture *f*.

ostrich ['ɔstritʃ], *s.* Autruche *f*. **'ostrich-feather**, *s.* Plume *f* d'autruche. **'ostrich-plume**, *s.* Plume *f* ou plumes d'autruche.

otalgia [o'taldʒia], *s. Med :* Otalgie *f* ; douleur *f* d'oreille.

other ['ʌðər]. **I.** *a.* Autre. *(a)* **The other one**, l'autre. *I saw him* **the other day**, je l'ai vu l'autre jour. *S.a.* EVERY. **The other world**, l'autre monde ; l'au-delà *m*. *S.a.* HAND[1] **2.** *(b)* **The other four**, les quatre autres. *Potatoes and (all)* o. *vegetables*, les pommes de terre et autres légumes. **Other things being equal**, toutes choses égales (d'ailleurs). *(c) Potatoes and (some)* o. *vegetables*, les pommes de terre et d'autres légumes. *Other people have seen it*, d'autres l'ont vu. *O. people's property*, le bien d'autrui. *No one other than he knows it*, nul autre que lui, personne d'autre, ne le sait ; il est seul à le savoir. *Prov :* **Other days, other ways**, autres temps, autres mœurs. *S.a.* SOME I. **1.** *(d) (Different)* **I do not wish him other than he is**, je ne le souhaite pas autre qu'il n'est. **2.** *pron.* Autre. *(a)* **One after the other**, l'un après l'autre. *S.a.* EACH 2, ONE V. **1.** *(b) pl.* **The others**, les autres, le reste. *(c)* **Some . . . others . . .**, les uns . . . les autres. . . . *Have you any others?* (i) en avez-vous encore ? (ii) en avez-vous d'autres ? *There are three others*, (i) il y en a encore trois ; (ii) il y en a trois autres. *I have no o.*, je n'en ai pas d'autre. **He and no other told me so**, lui et nul autre me l'a dit. **One or other of us** *will see to it*, l'un de nous s'en occupera. *This day of all others*, ce jour entre tous. *S.a.* SOMETHING I. **1.** *(d) pl. (Of pers.)* **Others**, d'autres ; *(in oblique cases also)* autrui *m*. *I find my happiness in that of others*, je trouve mon bonheur dans celui d'autrui. *(e)* **I could not do other than . . ., I could do no other than . . .**, (i) je n'ai pu faire autrement que . . . ; (ii) je n'ai pu m'empêcher de. . . . **3.** *adv.* Autrement. *To see things o. than they are*, voir les choses autrement qu'elles ne sont.

otherwise ['ʌðəwa:iz], *adv.* **1.** Autrement *(than, que)*. *To see things o. than (as) they are*, voir les choses autrement qu'elles ne sont. **He could not do otherwise, could do no otherwise, than obey**, il n'a pu faire autrement que d'obéir. **If he is not otherwise engaged**, s'il n'est pas occupé à autre chose. **Except where otherwise stated . . .**, sauf indication contraire. . . . **Tales moral and otherwise**, histoires morales et autres. *Poquelin*, **otherwise Molière**, Poquelin, (autrement) dit Molière. **2.** Autrement ; sans quoi, sans cela ; dans le cas contraire. *Work, o. you shall not eat*, travaille, sans quoi tu ne mangeras pas. **3.** Sous d'autres rapports ; par ailleurs. *O. he is quite*

sane, à d'autres égards, *F :* à part ça, il est complètement sain d'esprit.

otherworldly [ʌðər'wə:rldli], *a.* Détaché de ce monde.

otic ['outik, 'ɔ-], *a. Anat :* **Otic bone**, os pétreux ; rocher *m*. *The o. bones*, les osselets *m* de l'oreille.

otiose ['ouʃious], *a.* Inutile, superflu, oiseux. *O. epithet*, épithète oiseuse.

otology [ou'tɔlodʒi], *s. Med :* Otologie *f*.

otter ['ɔtər], *s. Z :* Loutre *f*. **'otter-skin**, *s.* Loutre *f*. **Otter-skin cap**, casquette *f* en loutre.

Otto ['ɔto]. *Pr.n.m.* Othon.

Ottoman[1] ['ɔtomən], *a. & s.* Ottoman, -ane ; turc, *f*. turque.

ottoman[2], *s. Furn :* Divan *m*, ottomane *f*.

ought[1] [ɔ:t], *v.aux.* (*With present and past meaning; inv. except for A :* oughtest *or* oughtst) (*Parts of*) devoir, falloir. **1.** (*Obligation*) **One o. never to be unkind**, il ne faut, on ne doit, jamais être malveillant. *To behave as one o.*, se conduire comme il convient. *I thought I o. to let you know about it*, j'ai cru devoir vous en faire part. **2.** (*Vague desirability or advantage*) **You o. to go and see the Exhibition**, vous devriez aller voir l'Exposition. *You o. not to have waited*, vous n'auriez pas dû attendre. *You o. to have said so*, il fallait le dire. **You ought to have seen it!** il fallait voir ça ! **3.** (*Probability*) *Your horse o. to win*, votre cheval a de grandes chances de gagner. *That o. to do*, je crois que cela suffira.

ought[2], *s.* = AUGHT.

ought[3], *s. F :* = NAUGHT.

ouija(-board) ['wi:ja(bɔ:rd), 'wi:dʒa], *s. Psychics :* Oui-ja *m*.

ounce[1] [auns], *s. Meas :* Once *f*. **1.** Avoirdupois ounce = 28gr. 35 ; Troy ounce = 31gr. 1035. *F :* **He hasn't an ounce of courage**, il n'a pas pour deux sous de courage. **2. Fluid ounce** = 28cm³, 4.

ounce[2], *s. Z :* Once *f* ; léopard *m* des neiges.

our ['auər], *poss.a.* Notre, *pl.* nos. *Our house and garden*, notre maison et notre jardin. *Our friends*, nos ami(e)s. *Let us look after our own*, (i) soignons le nôtre ; (ii) occupons-nous des nôtres. *Com :* **Our Mr Jones**, M. Jones de notre maison ; notre sieur Jones.

ours ['auərz], *poss.pron.* *(a)* Le nôtre, la nôtre, les nôtres. *Your house is larger than ours*, votre maison est plus grande que la nôtre. **This is ours**, ceci est à nous ; ceci nous appartient. **A friend of ours**, un(e) de nos ami(e)s ; un(e) ami(e) à nous. *(b)* **It is not ours to praise him**, ce n'est pas à nous de le louer.

ourself [auər'self], *pers.pron.* (*Of monarch, editor*) Nous-même. (*Cf.* WE 2.)

ourselves [auər'selvz], *pers.pron.pl.* See SELF 4.

oust [aust], *v.tr.* **1.** *(a) Jur :* Déposséder, évincer (qn) (of, de). *(b) To oust s.o. from his post*, déloger qn de son poste. **2.** Prendre la place de (qn) ; évincer, supplanter (qn).

out [aut]. **I.** *adv.* **1.** Dehors. *(a) (With motion) To go out, walk out*, sortir. *To run out*, sortir en courant ; courir dehors. **Out you go!** hors d'ici ! **Put him out!** out with him! mettez-le dehors ! emmenez-le ! *My daughter goes out a great deal*, ma fille sort beaucoup. **The voyage out**, l'aller *m*. *Voyage out and home*, **out-and-home voyage**, voyage d'aller et retour. *S.a.* CALL OUT, DRIVE OUT, GO OUT, SHOW OUT, *etc.* *(b) (Without motion) My father is out*, mon père est sorti. *My daughter is out a great deal*, ma fille sort beaucoup. **He is out and about again**, il est de nouveau sur pied. **Day out**, jour de sortie (d'une domestique). *F :* **To have a night out**, passer la nuit à faire la bombe. **The workmen are out**, les ouvriers sont en grève. **The troops are out,** les troupes sont sur pied. *He does not live far out (of the town),* il ne demeure pas loin de la ville. **Out at sea,** en mer, au large. **Out there,** là-bas. **The tide is out,** la marée est basse. *Fish: Nau:* **Our lines** *were out,* nos lignes étaient dehors. **2.** (a) **To turn one's toes out,** tourner les pieds en dehors. *S.a.* INSIDE 1. (b) **To ean out** (*of the window, etc.*), se pencher au dehors. *S.a.* HANG OUT, HIT OUT, STICK OUT, *etc.* **3.** (a) Au clair ; découvert, exposé ; (*of bird*) éclos ; (*of sword*) tiré, au clair. **The sun is out,** il fait du soleil. **The book is out, is already out, is just out,** le livre est paru, a déjà paru, vient de paraître. **The secret is out,** le secret est connu, éventé. (b) (*With motion*) *To whip out a revolver,* tirer, sortir, vivement un revolver. *F:* **Out with it!** achevez donc ! allons, dites-le ! expliquez-vous ! *S.a.* GIVE OUT 1, MURDER[1], TRUTH. (c) (*Of sail, etc.*) Déployé ; (*of flower, etc.*) épanoui. **The may is out,** l'aubépine est en fleur. (d) *F:* **To be out after s.o.,** être à la recherche de qn. **I am not out to reform the world,** je n'ai pas entrepris, je n'ai pas à tâche, de réformer le monde. **To go all out for sth.,** mettre toute son énergie à, se donner corps et âme pour, faire aboutir qch. ; mettre tout en œuvre pour obtenir qch. (e) *Sp:* *Aut: etc:* **All out,** à toute vitesse, à toute allure ; à plein rendement. (f) **Out loud,** tout haut, à haute voix. **To tell s.o. sth. straight out, right out,** dire qch. à qn carrément, franchement, sans détours, sans ambages. *S.a.* CALL OUT 2, CRY OUT, SHOUT OUT. **4. Shoulder out** (*of joint*), épaule luxée. **My hand is out** (*of practice*), je n'ai plus la main ; je suis rouillé. **The Tories are out** (*of power*), les Tories ne sont plus au pouvoir. *Cr:* (*Of batsman*) **Out,** hors jeu. (*Of boxer*) **To be out for seven seconds,** rester sur le plancher pendant sept secondes. *S.a.* KNOCK OUT 2. **5. To be out in one's calculations,** être loin de compte ; avoir dépassé ses prévisions. **He is five pounds out** (*in his accounts*), il a une erreur de cinq livres dans ses comptes. *I was not far out,* je ne me trompais pas de beaucoup. *You have put me out,* vous m'avez fait tromper. **6.** *The fire, gas, is out,* le feu, le gaz, est éteint. *Mil:* **Lights out,** extinction *f* des feux. **7.** (a) A bout ; achevé. **My patience is out,** ma patience est à bout. *My pipe is smoked out,* j'ai fini ma pipe. **Before the week is out,** avant la fin de la semaine ; avant que la semaine soit achevée. *S.a.* DIE OUT, GIVE OUT 2, YEAR. (b) **Hear me out,** entendez-moi, écoutez-moi, jusqu'à la fin, jusqu'au bout. **To have one's sleep out,** dormir tout son soûl ; finir de dormir. *S.a.* FIGHT OUT, HAVE OUT 2, *etc.* **8.** *Prep.phr.* **From out.** *From out the open window came bursts of laughter,* par la fenêtre ouverte arrivaient des éclats de rire. **9. Out of.** (a) Hors de, au dehors de, en dehors de. *That is out of our power,* cela n'est pas en notre pouvoir. **Out of danger,** (i) hors de danger ; (ii) à l'abri du danger. **Out of sight,** hors de vue. *S.a.* MIND[1] 1, SIGHT[1] 2. *To live out of the world,* vivre retiré du monde. **He is well out of the whole business,** il en est quitte, il s'en est tiré, à bon marché. **To be out of it,** (i) n'être pas de la partie (de plaisir, de chasse, etc.) ; (ii) n'être pas de connivence ; (iii) être laissé à l'écart. **To feel out of it,** se sentir dépaysé ; se sentir de trop. *S.a.* PLACE[1] 2, REACH[1] 2. (b) **Out of season,** hors de saison. *S.a.* SEASON[1] 2. **Times out of number,** maintes et maintes fois. **Out of measure,** outre mesure. **To be out of one's mind,** avoir perdu la raison. *S.a.* MIND[1] 5. **Out of spirits,** mal en train. (c) (*With motion*) *To go out of the house,*

sortir de la maison. *To throw sth. out of the window,* jeter qch. par la fenêtre. *To turn s.o. out of the house,* mettre, *F:* flanquer, qn à la porte. *To get money out of s.o.,* obtenir de l'argent de qn ; soutirer ou extorquer de l'argent à qn. (d) Dans, à, par. **To drink out of a glass,** boire dans un verre. **To drink out of the bottle,** boire à (même) la bouteille. *To eat out of the same dish,* manger au même plat. **To copy sth. out of a book,** copier qch. dans un livre. (e) Parmi, d'entre. *Choose one out of these ten,* choisissez-en un parmi les dix. *One out of every three,* un sur trois ; de trois l'un. (f) *Hut* **made out of** *a few old planks,* cabane faite de quelques vieilles planches. (g) **Out of respect for you,** par respect pour vous. *To do sth. out of friendship,* out of curiosity, faire qch. par amitié, par curiosité. (h) **To be out of tea,** ne plus avoir de thé ; être démuni, dépourvu, à court, de thé ; manquer de thé. *Com:* **This article is out of stock, I am out of this article,** je suis désassorti de cet article. *S.a.* BREATH, POCKET[1] 1, WORK[1] 4. **II. out,** *attrib.a.* **1.** Extérieur, à l'extérieur. *S.a.* OUT-GUARD, OUT-PATIENT, *etc.* **2.** Hors de l'ordinaire. *See* OUT SIZE. **III. out,** *s.* **1. Ins and outs.** *See* IN III. **2.** *Typ:* Bourdon *m*. **To make an out,** sauter un mot. **'out and 'out.** **1.** *adv.phr.* Complètement, absolument, sans restriction. **2.** *a.* **Out-and-out** *liar,* menteur fieffé, achevé. *Out-and-out nationalist,* nationaliste intransigeant. **'out-bound,** *a. Nau:* (Navire) sortant. **'out-building,** *s.* Bâtiment extérieur ; annexe *f*. **Out-buildings,** communs *m*, dépendances *f*. **'out-guard,** *s. Mil:* Garde avancée. **'out-of-'date,** *adj.phr.* **1.** Suranné, vieilli ; passé de mode ; démodé. *S.a.* DATE[2]. **2.** (Billet, passeport) périmé. **'out-of-the-'way,** *a.* **1.** (*Of house, etc.*) Écarté. **2.** Peu ordinaire, peu commun. **'out-patient,** *s.* (a) Malade qui est soigné(e) à domicile (par l'assistance publique). (b) Malade qui vient consulter à la clinique. **Out-patients' department** (*of hospital*), policlinique *f*, dispensaire *m*. **'out size,** *s. Com:* Dimension *f* ou pointure *f* hors série ; taille exceptionnelle. **Out-size dress,** robe en taille exceptionnelle. **'out-worker,** *s.* Ouvrier, -ière, à domicile.

outbid [aut'bid], *v.tr.* (*p.t.* outbade, outbid ; *p.p.* outbid, -bidden) **1.** (*At auction*) (R)enchérir, surenchérir, sur (qn). **2.** *F:* Surpasser.

outboard ['autbɔːd]. **1.** *a. Esp. Nau:* (*Of rigging, etc.*) Extérieur. **Outboard motor,** moteur hors bord. **Outboard motor boat,** hors-bord *m inv.* **2.** *adv. Esp. Nau:* Au dehors ; hors bord.

outbreak ['autbreik], *s.* **1.** Éruption *f* ; début *m*, ouverture *f* (des hostilités, etc.) ; débordement *m* (des sentiments). *O. of temper,* explosion *f*, bouffée *f*, accès *m*, de colère. *O. of an epidemic,* première manifestation d'une épidémie. *O. of pimples,* poussée *f* de boutons ; éruption. *O. of fire,* incendie *m*. **New outbreak,** recrudescence *f* (d'une épidémie, du feu, etc.). **2.** Révolte *f*, émeute *f*.

outburst ['autbəːst], *s.* Éruption *f*, explosion *f* ; éclat *m* (de rire, etc.) ; élan *m* (de générosité) ; déchaînement *m* (de colère).

outcast ['autkɑːst], *a. & s.* Expulsé, -ée, exilé, -ée, proscrit, -ite, banni, -ie. *Social outcasts,* les déchus *m* de la société.

outcaste ['autkɑːst]. **1.** *a.* Qui n'appartient à aucune caste ; hors caste. **2.** *s.* Hors-caste *mf inv* ; paria *m*.

outclass [aut'klɑːs], *v.tr. Sp:* Surclasser.

outcome [ˈautkʌm], s. Issue f, résultat m, aboutissement m, dénouement m.

outcrop[1] [ˈautkrɔp], s. Geol: Affleurement m.

outcrop[2], v.i. (outcropped) Geol: (Of seam) Affleurer.

outcry [ˈautkrai], s. (a) Cri m, cris (de réprobation, d'indignation); clameur f. **To raise an outcry against** s.o., crier haro, tollé, sur qn. (b) Réclamations indignées (against, contre).

outdistance [autˈdistəns], v.tr. Distancer, dépasser (un concurrent).

outdo [autˈduː], v.tr. (p.t. **outdid** [autˈdid]; p.p. **outdone** [autˈdʌn]) Surpasser (s.o. in sth., qn en qch.); l'emporter sur (qn).

outdoor [ˈautdɔːər], a. **1.** Extérieur, -eure; au dehors; (vie, jeux) au grand air, en plein air. **Outdoor clothes,** vêtements de ville. **2.** Adm: (a) (Of pauper) Externe. (b) **Outdoor relief,** secours m pl à domicile.

outdoors [autˈdɔːərz], adv. Dehors; hors de la maison; en plein air. **To sleep** o., coucher à la belle étoile.

outer [ˈautər]. **1.** a. Extérieur, -eure; externe. The o. side of . . ., le côté extérieur, externe, de. . . . **Outer garments,** vêtements de dessus. S.a. PORT[1]. **2.** s. (In range-shooting) Balle f hors zone.

outermost [ˈautərmoust], a. **1.** Le plus à l'extérieur; le plus en dehors. **2.** Le plus écarté; extrême.

outface [autˈfeis], v.tr. Faire baisser les yeux à (qn); dévisager, décontenancer (qn).

outfall [ˈautfɔːl], s. Embouchure f (d'une rivière); déversoir m, déchargeoir m, débouché m (d'un égout).

outfit [ˈautfit], s. **1.** Équipement m, équipage m; attirail m (de chasse, etc.). Nau: Armement m (d'un navire). O. of tools, jeu m d'outils; outillage m. **First aid outfit,** trousse f de premiers secours. **Repairing outfit,** nécessaire m, trousse, de réparation, à réparations. **2.** (Of clothes) Trousseau m; effets mpl. Mil: Équipement m.

outfitter [ˈautfitər], s. Com: Fournisseur m d'articles d'habillement; confectionneur m.

outfitting [ˈautfitiŋ], s. **1.** Équipement m; armement m (d'un navire). **2.** Com: **Outfitting department,** rayon de confection f.

outflank [autˈflaŋk], v.tr. (a) Mil: Déborder (l'ennemi, etc.). (b) F: Circonvenir (qn).

outflow [ˈautflou], s. Écoulement m, dépense f (d'eau, de gaz, etc.); coulée f (de lave, etc.); décharge f (d'un égout, d'un bief, etc.).

outgeneral [autˈdʒenərəl], v.tr. (-generalled) Surpasser (qn) en tactique.

outgoing[1] [ˈautgouiŋ], a. (Of tenant, etc.) Sortant; (of train) en partance. **Outgoing tide,** marée descendante. O. ministry, ministère démissionnaire. **Outgoing mail,** courrier à expédier.

outgoing[2], s. **1.** Sortie f (de qn). **2.** pl. **Outgoings,** dépenses f, débours m; sorties de fonds.

outgrow [autˈgrou], v.tr. (**outgrew** [autˈgruː]; **outgrown**) **1.** Croître plus vite, devenir plus grand, que (qn, qch.). **2.** (a) Devenir trop grand pour (ses vêtements, etc.). (b) **To outgrow a habit,** perdre une habitude avec le temps, en grandissant.

outgrowth [ˈautgrouθ], s. Excroissance f.

outhouse [ˈauthaus], s. (a) Dépendance f. **Outhouses,** communs m. (b) Appentis m, hangar m.

outing [ˈautiŋ], s. (a) Promenade f. (b) Excursion f, sortie f; partie f de plaisir.

outlandish [autˈlandiʃ], a. (a) (Of manner, costume) Baroque, bizarre, étrange; (langage) barbare. (b) (Of place) Retiré, écarté.

outlast [autˈlɑːst], v.tr. Durer plus longtemps que (qch.); survivre à (qn).

outlaw[1] [ˈautlɔː], s. Hors-la-loi m inv; proscrit; banni.

outlaw[2], v.tr. Mettre (qn) hors la loi; proscrire (qn).

outlawry [ˈautlɔːri], s. Mise f hors la loi; proscription f.

outlay [ˈautlei], s. Débours mpl, frais mpl, dépenses fpl. Ind: etc: **First outlay,** initial outlay, première mise de fonds; frais de premier établissement. **To get back, recover, one's outlay,** rentrer dans ses débours.

outlet [ˈautlet], s. **1.** Orifice m d'émission; issue f (de tunnel, etc.); sortie f, départ m (d'air, de gaz); échappement m (de vapeur); débouché m (de tuyau). To give sth. an o., donner issue à qch. **2.** Com: Débouché (pour marchandises).

outline[1] [ˈautlain], s. **1.** Outline(s), contour(s) m, profil m (d'une colline, etc.); configuration f (de la terre); silhouette f (de qn, d'un édifice). **2.** Dessin m au trait; tracé m; argument m, canevas m (d'une pièce, d'un roman). **Main outlines, general outline, broad outlines, of a scheme,** grandes lignes, données générales, aperçu m, d'un projet. **Outlines of astronomy,** éléments m d'astronomie.

outline[2], v.tr. **1.** Contourner, silhouetter (le profil de qch.). **2.** Exposer à grands traits, dans ses lignes générales (une théorie, etc.); esquisser (un roman, un projet); ébaucher, indiquer (un plan d'action). **3.** Draw: Esquisser à grands traits.

outlive [autˈliv], v.tr. Survivre à (qn, une défaite).

outlook [ˈautluk], s. **1.** Guet m. **To be on the outlook for sth.,** guetter qch. **2.** Vue f, perspective f. The o. is none too promising, la perspective n'est pas des plus rassurantes. **Breadth of outlook,** largeur f de vues.

outlying [ˈautlaiiŋ], a. Éloigné, écarté. O. quarter, quartier excentrique.

outmanœuvre [autməˈnuːvər], v.tr. L'emporter sur (l'ennemi) en tactique; F: déjouer (qn, les plans de qn); rouler (qn).

outmarch [autˈmɑːrtʃ], v.tr. Devancer, dépasser (l'ennemi, etc.).

outmost [ˈautmoust], a. = OUTERMOST.

outnumber [autˈnʌmbər], v.tr. L'emporter en nombre sur, surpasser en nombre, être plus nombreux que (l'ennemi, etc.).

outpace [autˈpeis], v.tr. Dépasser, devancer, distancer (un concurrent, etc.); gagner (qn) de vitesse.

outpost [ˈautpoust], s. Avant-poste m, poste avancé.

outpouring [ˈautpɔːəriŋ], s. Épanchement m, effusion f (de sentiments); débordement m (d'injures).

output [ˈautput], s. **1.** Rendement m (d'une machine, etc.); production f (d'une mine); débit m (d'un générateur, d'une pompe). **2.** W.Tel: **Output valve,** lampe f de sortie.

outrage[1] [ˈautreidʒ], s. (a) Outrage m, atteinte f. **To commit an outrage on, against, s.o.,** faire outrage à qn. (b) **Bomb outrage,** attentat m avec machine infernale.

outrage[2], v.tr. Outrager, faire outrage à (la religion, etc.); violenter (une femme).

outrageous [autˈreidʒəs], a. (a) Immodéré, indigne; (of price) excessif. (b) (Of statement, accusation) Outrageant, outrageux; (of conduct, *etc.*) outrageux, atroce, indigne. (*c*) *F:* *O. hat,* chapeau impossible. **-ly,** *adv.* (*a*) Immodérément ; outre mesure. (*b*) D'une façon scandaleuse, indigne..

outrageousness [aut′reidʒəsnəs], *s.* **I.** Caractère outrageant, outrageux. **2.** *The o. of his conduct,* l'indignité *f* de sa conduite.

outrange [aut′reindʒ], *v.tr.* (*Of gun*) Avoir une portée plus grande que. . . . .

outride [aut′raid], *v.tr.* (outrode [aut′roud] ; outridden [aut′ridn]) **I.** Chevaucher plus vite que (qn) ; dépasser, devancer, (qn) à cheval. **2.** *Nau:* Étaler (une tempête).

outrider [′autraidər], *s.* Piqueur *m* (de carrosse, de diligence).

outrigger [′autrigər], *s.* **I.** *Row:* (*a*) Porte-nage *m inv* en dehors ; porte-en-dehors *m inv* ; dame *f* de nage. (*b*) (*Boat*) Outrigger *m.* **2.** *Nau:* Balancier *m* (d'un prao).

outright [aut′rait]. **I.** *adv.* **I.** (*a*) Complètement. *To buy sth. outright,* acheter qch. comptant, à forfait. (*b*) Du premier coup ; sur le coup. *To kill s.o. outright,* tuer qn raide. **2.** Sans ménagement ; franchement, carrément. *To laugh outright* (*at s.o.*), partir d'un franc rire (au nez de qn) ; éclater de rire. **II. outright,** *a.* (*Attrib.* [′autrait]) **I.** Outright sale, vente *f* à forfait. *O. purchase,* marché *m* forfaitaire. **2.** (*Of manner*) Franc, *f.* franche ; carré.

outrun [aut′rʌn], *v.tr.* (*p.t.* outran [aut′ran] ; *p.p.* outrun ; *pr.p.* outrunning) **I.** Dépasser ; gagner (qn) de vitesse ; distancer (un concurrent). **2.** *His zeal outruns his discretion,* son ardeur l'emporte sur son jugement.

outset [′autset], *s.* Commencement *m.* *At the outset,* au début ; tout d'abord. *From the outset,* dès le début, dès l'origine, dès l'abord.

outshine [aut′ʃain], *v.tr.* (outshone [aut′ʃɔn] ; outshone) Surpasser en éclat ; dépasser, éclipser.

outside [aut′said]. **I.** *s.* (*a*) Extérieur *m,* dehors *m* (d'une maison, d'un livre). *On the outside of sth.,* à l'extérieur de qch. *To open a door from the o.,* ouvrir une porte du dehors. *The window opens to the o.,* la fenêtre s'ouvre en dehors. *To turn a skin outside in,* retourner une peau (de lapin, etc.). (*b*)′ *At the outside,* tout au plus ; au maximum. (*c*) Impériale *f* (d'un omnibus) ; banquette *f* (d'une diligence). **2.** *Attrib.a.* [′autsaid] (*a*) Du dehors ; extérieur, -eure. *Outside seat,* (i) (*on omnibus*) banquette de l'impériale ; (ii) (*of a row of seats*) place du bout. (*b*) **Outside porter,** commissionnaire messager. **Outside worker,** ouvrier, -ière, à domicile. (*c*) *To get an outside opinion,* obtenir un avis du dehors, un avis étranger. (*d*) **Outside prices,** les plus hauts prix ; prix maximum. (*e*) *F:* **It was an outside chance,** il y avait tout juste une chance (de réussite). **3.** *adv.* (*a*) Dehors, à l'extérieur en dehors. *I've left my dog o.,* j'ai laissé mon chien dehors, à la porte. *To put s.o. outside,* mettre qn dehors. *Seen from o.,* vu de dehors. *To ride outside,* voyager sur l'impériale. (*b*) **Outside of,** hors de, à l'extérieur de, en dehors de. **4.** *prep.* En dehors de, hors de, à l'extérieur de. *O. my bedroom,* (i) à la porte de, (ii) sous les fenêtres de, ma chambre. *Garden lying o. my grounds,* jardin extérieur à ma propriété. *That's outside the question,* c'est en dehors du sujet. (*Of artist*) *To go o. his range,* sortir de son talent.

outsider [aut′saidər], *s.* *F:* **I.** Étranger, -ère ; profane *mf.* *He's an outsider,* (i) il n'est pas du métier, de la partie ; (ii) il n'est pas de notre monde ; c'est un intrus. **2.** *St.Exch:* Courtier

marron. **3.** *Turf:* Cheval non classé ; outsider *m.* **4.** *Fb:* Ailier *m.*

outskirts [′autskə:rts], *s.pl.* Abords *m* ; lisière *f* (d'une forêt) ; faubourgs *m* (d'une ville) ; banlieue *f* (d'une grande ville).

outspan [′autspan], *v.* (outspanned) (*In S. Africa*) **I.** *v.i.* (*a*) Dételer. (*b*) Camper à l'étape. **2.** *v.tr.* Dételer (les bœufs).

outspoken [aut′spoukən], *a.* (*Of pers.*) Franc, *f.* franche ; carré, rond. *To be o.,* avoir son franc-parler. **-ly,** *adv.* Carrément, rondement.

outspokenness [aut′spoukənnəs], *s.* Franchise *f* un peu brusque ; franc-parler *m.*

outspread [′autspred], *a.* Étendu, étalé. *With o. wings,* les ailes déployées.

outstanding [aut′standiŋ], *a.* **I.** (*Of detail, feature, etc.*) Saillant ; (*of pers., incident*) marquant ; (*of artist, etc.*) hors ligne, éminent. **2.** (*Affaire*) en suspens, en cours de règlement ; (compte) impayé, dû ; (paiement) arriéré, en retard ; (intérêt) échu. *Fin:* *O. coupons,* coupons en souffrance. **-ly,** *adv.* Éminemment.

outstare [aut′steər], *v.tr.* Fixer (qn) jusqu'à ce qu'il détourne son regard ; faire baisser les yeux à (qn).

outstay [aut′stei], *v.tr.* **I.** Rester plus longtemps que (qn). **2.** *To outstay one's welcome,* lasser l'amabilité de ses hôtes.

outstretched [′autstretʃt], *a.* Déployé, étendu ; (bras) tendu. *With outstretched arms,* les bras ouverts.

outstrip [aut′strip], *v.tr.* (outstripped) (*a*) Devancer, dépasser (qn à la course) ; gagner (qn) de vitesse. (*b*) Surpasser.

outvie [aut′vai], *v.tr.* Surpasser (qn en splendeur, etc.) ; l'emporter sur (un concurrent).

outward [′autwərd]. **I.** *a.* (*a*) En dehors. *Nau:* Pour l'étranger. *The o. and the homeward voyages,* l'aller et le retour. *Rail:* **Outward half** (*of ticket*), billet *m* d'aller. (*b*) Extérieur ; de dehors. **Outward form,** extérieur *m,* dehors *m.* *Pharm:* **For outward application,** pour l'usage externe. **2.** *adv.* = OUTWARDS. **-ly,** *adv.* **I.** A l'extérieur, au dehors. **2.** En apparence. **′outward-′bound,** *a.* *Nau:* **I.** (Navire) en partance, sortant. **2.** (Navire) faisant route pour l'étranger.

outwards [′autwərdz], *adv.* Au dehors ; vers l'extérieur. *To turn one's feet o.,* tourner les pieds en dehors.

outwear [aut′weər], *v.tr.* (outwore [aut′wo:ər] ; outworn [aut′wo:rn]) **I.** User complètement. *Outworn shibboleth,* doctrine désuète. **2.** Durer plus longtemps que (qch.) ; faire plus d'usage que (qch.).

outweigh [aut′wei], *v.tr.* **I.** Peser plus que (qch.). **2.** *F:* Avoir plus d'influence, plus de poids, que (qn) ; l'emporter sur (qch.).

outwit [aut′wit], *v.tr.* (outwitted) **I.** Circonvenir (qn) ; déjouer les intentions, les menées, de (qn) ; duper (qn). **2.** Dépister (les chiens, la police).

outwork [′autwərk], *s.* **I.** *Fort:* Ouvrage avancé. *Arch:* Hors-d'œuvre *m inv.* **2.** *Ind:* (*Also* out-work) Travail fait à domicile.

ouzel [u:zl], *s.* *Orn:* **I.** (*a*) Ring ouzel, merle *m* à plastron. (*b*) Water ouzel, merle d'eau. **2.** *A. & Lit:* = BLACKBIRD.

oval [′ouv(ə)l]. **I.** *a.* Ovale ; en ovale. **2.** *s.* Ovale *m.*

ovalize [′ouvəlaiz]. *Mec.E:* **I.** *v.tr.* Ovaliser. **2.** *v.i.* (*Of cylinder, etc.*) S'ovaliser.

ovary [′ouvəri], *s.* Ovaire *m.*

ovate [′ouvet], *a.* *Nat.Hist:* Ové.

ovation [o′veiʃ(ə)n], *s.* Ovation *f.* *To give s.o. an o.,* faire une ovation à qn.

oven [ˈʌv(ə)n], s. **1.** (Cooking) oven, four m. *In the o.*, au four. Dutch oven, cuisinière f, rôtissoire f. *F: This room is a regular o.*, cette salle est une fournaise. *S.a.* GAS-OVEN. **2.** Drying oven, étuve f.

over [ˈouvər]. I. *prep.* **1.** (a) Sur, dessus, par-dessus. *To spread a cloth over sth.*, étendre une toile sur, par-dessus, qch. (b) All over *the north of England*, sur toute l'étendue du nord de l'Angleterre. *Famous all over the world*, célèbre dans le monde entier, par tout le monde. *Measured over its widest part*, mesuré sur la partie la plus large. *S.a.* OVER-ALL, OVERALL. *P:* To be all over s.o., (i) faire l'empressé auprès de qn; (ii) s'enthousiasmer pour qn. (c) Over (the top of) sth., par-dessus (qch.). *S.a.* TOP[1] I. 1. *To throw sth. over the wall*, jeter qch. par-dessus le mur. *We heard voices over the wall*, nous entendîmes des voix de l'autre côté du mur. *To fall over a cliff*, tomber du haut d'une falaise. To stumble, trip, over sth., buter contre qch.; trébucher sur qch. **2.** (a) *Jutting out over the street*, faisant saillie sur la rue, au-dessus de la rue. *His name is over the door*, il a son nom au-dessus de la porte. *Hanging over our heads*, suspendu au-dessus de, sur, nos têtes. *With his hat over his eyes*, le chapeau enfoncé jusqu'aux yeux. *His hat over one ear*, le chapeau sur l'oreille. To be over one's ankles in water, avoir de l'eau par-dessus la cheville. *S.a.* EAR[1] I, HAND[1] 2. (b) *To have an advantage over s.o.*, avoir un avantage sur qn. *To reign over a land*, régner sur un pays. *He is over me*, il est au-dessus de moi. (c) *Bending over his work*, courbé sur son travail. *Sitting over the fire*, assis tout près du feu; *F:* couvant le feu. **3.** (*Across*) (a) **The house over the way**, la maison d'en face; la maison vis-à-vis. Over the border, au delà de la frontière. To live over the river, demeurer de l'autre côté de la rivière. (b) **The bridge over the river**, le pont qui traverse la rivière. **4.** (*In excess of*) Numbers over a hundred, numéros au-dessus de cent. Over fifty pounds, plus de cinquante livres. Over five (years of age), au-dessus de cinq ans. *He is over fifty*, il a (dé)passé la cinquantaine. *He receives tips over and above his salary*, il reçoit des pourboires en sus de ses gages. **5.** Over the last three years wages have diminished, au cours des trois dernières années les salaires ont diminué. *Over the summer*, pendant tout l'été. II. over, *adv.* **1.** (a) Sur toute la surface. *To search Paris over*, chercher par tout Paris. To be all over dust, être tout couvert de poussière. To ache all over, avoir mal partout; souffrir de partout. (b) *To read a letter over*, lire une lettre en entier. *I have had to do it all over again*, j'ai dû le refaire d'un bout à l'autre. *S.a.* GO OVER 1, LOOK OVER. (c) (*Repetition*) Ten times over, dix fois de suite. Twice over, à deux reprises. Over and over (again), à plusieurs reprises; maintes et maintes fois. **2.** (a) Par-dessus (qch.). *To look over into a garden*, regarder dans un jardin par-dessus le mur. *The milk boiled over*, le lait s'est sauvé. (b) *To lean over*, (i) (*of pers.*) se pencher (à la fenêtre, etc.); (ii) (*of thg*) pencher. **3.** (a) To fall over, (i) (*of pers.*) tomber à la renverse; (ii) (*of thg*) se renverser; être renversé. To knock sth. over, renverser qch. (b) **Please turn over, P.T.O.**, voir au dos; tournez, s'il vous plaît; T.S.V.P. To turn sth. over and over, tourner et retourner qch. *S.a.* TURN OVER. To bend sth. over, replier qch. (c) *Nau:* Hard over! la barre toute! **4.** To cross over, (i) traverser (la rue, etc.); (ii) faire la traversée (de la Manche, etc.).

Over there, over yonder, là-bas. Over here, ici; de ce côté. Over against sth., vis-à-vis de qch.; en face de qch. He is over from France, il vient de France. *S.a.* GET OVER, GIVE OVER 1, etc. **5.** En plus, en excès. (a) Children of fourteen and over, les enfants qui ont quatorze ans et davantage, et au delà. *Three into seven goes twice and one over*, sept divisé par trois donne deux, et il reste un. *He is six foot and a bit over*, il a six pieds et le pouce. (b) *You will keep what is (left) over*, vous garderez l'excédent, le surplus. *I have a card over*, j'ai une carte de trop, en trop. *And over and above*, il est younger than you, et en outre, et d'ailleurs, il est moins âgé que vous. (c) (*Till later*) To hold over a decision, ajourner une décision. *The question is held over*, la question est différée. (d) (*Compounded with adjs. and advs.*) Trop; à l'excès. Over-abundant, surabondant. *Do not be over-shy*, ne vous montrez pas timide à l'excès. To be over-particular, être (par) trop exigeant, trop méticuleux. Over-scrupulous, scrupuleux (jusqu')à l'excès. Not over-gay, peu gai. (e) (*Compounded with a noun*) Excès de. Over-confidence, excès de confiance. (f) (*Compounded with a verb*) (i) Trop, sur-. To over-stretch a spring, trop tendre, surtendre, un ressort. (ii) To overpass, overstep, outrepasser. **6.** Fini, achevé. *The storm, danger, is over*, l'orage est passé, est dissipé; le danger est passé. It is all over, c'est fini; tout est fini. It is all over with me, c'en est fait de moi. *S.a.* GIVE OVER 2. III. over, s. **1.** *Cr:* Série f (de six ou huit balles). **2.** *Typ:* Overs, main f de passe; simple passe f. Double overs, double passe. **3.** *Knitting:* Single over, double over, jeté m simple, jeté double. **'over-all**, a. Over-all length, longueur hors tout. *Cp.* OVERALL. **'over-'bold**, a. **1.** Téméraire. **2.** Présomptueux. **over-'confidence**, s. **1.** Confiance exagérée (*in*, en). **2.** Suffisance f, présomption f, témérité f. **over-'confident**, a. **1.** Trop confiant (*in s.o.*, en qn). Suffisant, présomptueux, téméraire. **over-de'vel p**, v.tr. Développer à l'excès. *Phot:* Over-developed negative, négatif trop poussé. **over-elaborate** [ouvərˈlaboret], a. Trop compliqué; (*of literary style*) trop fouillé, tourmenté. **over-estimate**[1] [ouvərˈestimet], s. Surestimation f. **over-estimate**[2] [ouvərˈestimeit], v.tr. Surestimer; exagérer (le danger, etc.). **over-ex'pose**, v.tr. *Phot:* Surexposer; donner trop de pose à (une plaque, etc.). **over-ex'posure**, s. *Phot:* Surexposition f; excès m de pose. **over-fa'miliar**, a. To be over-familiar with s.o., se montrer trop familier avec qn; prendre des libertés, des privautés, avec qn. **over-fa'tigue**[1], s. Surmenage m. **over-fa'tigue**[2], v.tr. Surmener (qn). **over-in-'dulge**. **1.** v.tr. (a) Montrer trop d'indulgence envers (qn); gâter (qn). (b) Se laisser aller trop librement à (une passion, etc.). **2.** v.i. To over-indulge in metaphor, faire abus des métaphores. **over-in'dulgence**, s. **1.** Indulgence excessive (*of s.o.*, envers qn). **2.** Abus m (*in wine*, etc., du vin, etc.). **over-'nice**, a. Trop exigeant; renchéri. *O.-n. distinction*, distinction vétilleuse. **over night, overnight** [ouvərˈnait]. **1.** adv. (a) La veille (au soir). (b) (Pendant) la nuit. (*Of food*) To keep overnight, se conserver jusqu'au lendemain. **2.** [ˈouvərnait], attrib.a. De la veille. **over-'populated**, a. Surpeuplé. **'over-print**[1], s. Surcharge f (de timbre-poste). **over-'print**[2], v.tr. **1.** Surcharger (un timbre-poste). **2.** *Typ:* Tirer trop d'exemplaires de (qch.). **3.** *Phot:* Trop pousser

'over-proof, attrib.a. (Of spirits) Au-dessus de preuve. **over-re'fine-ment,** s. (a) Afféterie f, affectation f. (b) Alambiquage m, préciosité f (du style). **over-'ripe,** a. Trop mûr; (of cheese) trop fait; (of pear) blet, f. blette. **over-'train,** v.tr. & i. Sp: (S')épuiser par un entraînement trop sévère; "claquer." **'over-trick,** s. Cards: Levée f en plus de la demande. **over-'zealous,** a. Trop zélé. To be o.-z., pécher par excès de zèle.

overact [ouvər'akt], v.tr. Th: Outrer, charger (un rôle).

overall ['ouvərɔːl], s. (a) Blouse f (d'écolière, etc.); (child's, carter's) sarrau m, -aus, -aux; (lady's) tablier-blouse m. (b) Ind: **Overalls,** salopette f; combinaison f; F: bleus mpl.

overarm ['ouvərɑːrm], attrib.a. Swim: Overarm (side-)stroke, brasse indienne; nage (à l')indienne.

overawe [ouvər'ɔː], v.tr. Intimider; en imposer à (qn).

overbalance [ouvər'baləns]. I. v.tr. (a) Peser plus que (qch.). (b) Surpasser, l'emporter sur (qch.). (c) Renverser (qch.). 2. v.i. & pr. To overbalance (oneself), perdre l'équilibre. 3. v.i. (Of thg) Se renverser; tomber.

overbear [ouvər'bɛər], v.tr. (Conj. like BEAR) I. Renverser, terrasser (son adversaire). 2.(a) To overbear s.o., s.o.'s will, passer outre aux volontés de qn. (b) Intimider (qn). **overbearing,** a. Arrogant, impérieux, autoritaire.

overbid [ouvər'bid], v.tr. (Conj. like BID) Enchérir sur (qn).

overboard ['ouvərbɔːrd], adv. Nau: Hors du bord; par-dessus (le) bord. To fall overboard, tomber à la mer. Man overboard! un homme à la mer!

overburden [ouvər'bəːrdn], v.tr. Surcharger, accabler (with, de). F: Not overburdened with principles, peu encombré de principes.

overcapitalization ['ouvərkapitəlai'zeiʃ(ə)n], s. Fin: Surcapitalisation f.

overcast [ouvər'kɑːst], v.tr. (overcast; overcast) I. Obscurcir, assombrir (le ciel, l'esprit); couvrir (le ciel). 2. Needlew: Surjeter, surfiler. **overcast,** a. I. (a) Obscurci, assombri, couvert (with, de). Minds o. with fear, esprits sous le coup de la peur. (b) Overcast sky, ciel couvert, sombre. O. weather, temps bouché. 2. Needlew: Overcast stitch, (point m de) surjet m. S.a. SEAM¹ I.

overcharge¹ ['ouvərtʃɑːrdʒ], s. I. Surcharge f (d'un accumulateur, etc.). 2. (a) Prix excessif; prix surfait. (b) Majoration f (d'un compte).

overcharge² [ouvər'tʃɑːrdʒ], v.tr. I. Surcharger. 2. To overcharge goods, surfaire des marchandises. To overcharge s.o., faire payer trop cher un article à qn; F: écorcher qn.

overcloud [ouvər'klaud]. I. v.tr. (a) Couvrir de nuages. (b) Obscurcir, assombrir. 2. v.i. (Of sky) Se couvrir de nuages.

overcoat ['ouvərkout], s. Pardessus m; Mil: capote f.

overcome [ouvər'kʌm], v.tr. (overcame [ouvər-'keim]; overcome) Triompher de, vaincre (ses adversaires, etc.); venir à bout de, avoir raison de (qn, qch.); dominer, maîtriser, surmonter (son émotion, etc.). **overcome,** a. To be overcome with, by (sth.), être accablé de (douleur, etc.); être transi de (peur); être gagné par (le sommeil, les larmes). To be o. by a spectacle, être fortement ému par un spectacle. To be overcome by the heat, by emotion, succomber à la chaleur, à l'émotion.

overcrowd [ouvər'kraud], v.tr. (a) Trop remplir

(un autobus, etc.). To o. a shelf with ornaments, surcharger une planche d'ornements. (b) Surpeupler (une ville, une forêt). **overcrowded,** a. (a) Trop rempli (with, de);((appartement, autobus) bondé (with people, de monde). (b) (Ville) surpeuplée; (forêt) trop dense, surpeuplée. **overcrowding,** s. I. Encombrement m. 2. Surpeuplement m.

overdo [ouvər'duː], v.tr. (Conj. like DO) I. Outrer (les choses); charger (un rôle, etc.). F: To overdo it, forcer la note; exagérer. 2. To overdo oneself, F: to overdo it, se surmener. Don't overdo it! pas de zèle! 3. Cu: Trop cuire (la viande).

overdose ['ouvərdous], s. Trop forte dose; dose (i) nuisible, (ii) mortelle.

overdraft ['ouvərdrɑːft], s. Bank: Découvert m; solde débiteur.

overdraw [ouvər'drɔː], v.tr. (Conj. like DRAW) I. Charger (le portrait de qn); trop colorer (un récit). 2. To overdraw one's account, mettre son compte à découvert; tirer à découvert. Overdrawn account, compte découvert.

overdress [ouvər'dres], v.tr. Habiller avec trop de recherche. She is rather overdressed, sa toilette manque de simplicité et de bon ton.

overdrive [ouvər'draiv], v.tr. (Conj. like DRIVE) Surmener, F: éreinter (un cheval); surmener, fatiguer (une machine, etc.).

overdue [ouvər'djuː], a. (a) (Of account) Arriéré, échu, en retard, en souffrance. (b) Train ten minutes overdue, train en retard de dix minutes.

overeat [ouvər'iːt], v.pr. & i. To overeat (oneself), trop manger.

overexcite [ouvərek'sait], v.tr. Surexciter.

overexcitement [ouvərek'saitmənt], s. Surexcitation f.

overexertion [ouvəregzə:r'ʃ(ə)n], s. Surmenage m; abus m de ses forces.

overfeed [ouvər'fiːd], v. (overfed; overfed) I. v.tr. Suralimenter, F: surnourrir (on, de). 2. v.i. & pr. Trop manger. **overfed,** a. I. Suralimenté. 2. F: Pansu, ventru.

overflow¹ ['ouvərflou], s. I. (a) Débordement m, épanchement m (d'un liquide). (b) Inondation f. 2. Trop-plein m inv. Overflow-pipe, (tuyau m de) trop-plein; déversoir m (d'une citerne). 3. Overflow meeting, réunion f supplémentaire (pour ceux qui en arrivant ont trouvé salle comble).

overflow² [ouvər'flou]. I. v.tr. (a) (Of liquid) Déborder de (la coupe, etc.). (b) (Of river, etc.) Inonder (un champ). 2. v.i. (Of cup, heart, etc.) Déborder. Room overflowing with people, salle qui regorge de monde. (b) (Of liquid) Déborder, s'épancher; (of gutter, stream) dégorger. **overflowing¹,** a. Débordant; plein à déborder; (of kindness) surabondant. **overflowing²,** s. Débordement m. Full to overflowing, plein à déborder.

overfree [ouvər'friː], a. Trop familier (with, avec). To be o. in one's conduct, se conduire trop librement.

overgarment ['ouvərgɑːrmənt], s. Vêtement m de dessus.

overgrow [ouvər'grou], v.tr. (Conj. like GROW) (Of plants, etc.) Couvrir, recouvrir (un mur, etc.); envahir (un terrain, etc.). **overgrown,** a. I. Couvert (with sth., de qch.). Garden, road, overgrown with weeds, jardin envahi par les mauvaises herbes; route mangée d'herbes. 2. (Of child) Qui a grandi trop vite.

overgrowth ['ouvərgrouθ], s. I. Surcroissance f; croissance excessive. 2. Couverture f (d'herbes, de ronces, de poils, etc.).

overhang¹ ['ouvərhaŋ], *s.* Surplomb *m*; porte-à-faux *m inv*, saillie *f*.

overhang² [ouvər'haŋ], *v.tr.* (overhung [ouvər'hʌŋ]; overhung) Surplomber; faire saillie au-dessus de, pencher sur (qch.). **overhung,** *a.* 1. (*a*) En surplomb; en saillie; (*of crank, etc.*) en porte-à-faux. (*b*) Eyes overhung with beetling brows, yeux surplombés par des sourcils touffus. 2. *Cu*: (*Of meat*) Trop attendu. **overhanging,** *a.* Surplombant, en surplomb, en porte-à-faux.

overhaul¹ ['ouvərhɔːl], *s.* (*a*) Examen détaillé (d'un malade, etc.); révision *f* (d'une machine, etc.); visite *f* (pour réparations). (*b*) Remise *f* en état.

overhaul² [ouvər'hɔːl], *v.tr.* 1. Examiner en détail (un malade, une machine); réviser, remettre en état, réparer, réfectionner. *Nau:* Radouber (un navire). 2. *Nau:* Rattraper, dépasser (un autre navire).

overhead [ouvər'hed]. 1. *adv.* Au-dessus (de la tête); en haut, en l'air. 2. *Attrib.a.* ['ouvərhed] (*a*) Overhead cable, câble aérien. *O.* (*cable*) transport, transport *m* par trolley; telphérage *m. S.a.* CRANE¹ 2. (*b*) *I.C.E:* Overhead valves, soupapes en dessus, en tête. *S.a.* ENGINE 3. (*c*) *Com:* Overhead expenses, *s. F:* overhead(s), frais généraux; dépenses générales. (*d*) *Art:* Phot: Overhead lighting, éclairage vertical.

overhear [ouvər'hiːər], *v.tr.* (*Conj. like* HEAR) Surprendre (une conversation, etc.).

overheat [ouvər'hiːt], *v.tr.* (*a*) Surchauffer, trop chauffer. (*b*) To overheat oneself, s'échauffer (trop). **overheated,** *a.* (*Of engine, etc.*) Surchauffé. **To get overheated,** (i) (*of pers.*) s'échauffer, prendre chaud; (ii) (*of engine, brakes*) chauffer.

overjoyed [ouvər'dʒɔid], *a.* Transporté de joie. **To be overjoyed,** être au comble de la joie, rempli de joie. *To be o. to see s.o.,* être ravi de voir qn.

overladen [ouvər'leidn], *a.* Surchargé (with, de).

overland [ouvər'land]. 1. *adv.* Par voie de terre. 2. *Attrib.a.* ['ouvərland] Qui voyage par voie de terre. Overland route, voie *f* de terre.

overlap¹ ['ouvərlap], *s.* Recouvrement *m*; chevauchement *m*; (*of slates, etc.*) chevauchure *f*, imbrication *f. Carp:* Overlap joint, joint à recouvrement.

overlap² [ouvər'lap], *v.tr. & i.* (overlapped [-lapt]) 1. Recouvrir (partiellement). (*Of tiles, slates*) To overlap (one another), chevaucher. 2. Dépasser, outrepasser (l'extrémité de qch.). 3. (*Of categories, etc.*) Se chevaucher. Catalogue that overlaps another, catalogue qui fait double emploi avec un autre. **overlapping, s.** 1. Recouvrement *m*, chevauchement *m*. 2. Double emploi *m*.

overlay¹ ['ouvərlei], *s.* 1. *Furn:* (*a*) Matelas *m*. (*b*) Couvre-lit *m*. 2. *Typ:* Hausse *f*.

overlay² [ouvər'lei], *v.tr.* (*Conj. like* LAY) 1. Recouvrir, couvrir (with, de). Overlaid with mud, enduit (d'une couche) de boue. 2. *Typ:* Mettre des hausses sur (le tympan).

overlay³. See OVERLIE.

overleaf [ouvər'liːf], *adv.* Au dos, au verso (de la page). 'See overleaf,' "voir au verso."

overlie [ouvər'lai], *v.tr.* (overlay) overlain) Recouvrir, couvrir. **overlying,** *a.* Superposé.

overload¹ ['ouvərloud], *s.* 1. Poids *m* en surcharge; surcharge *f*. 2. *Mch:* Overload running, marche *f* en surcharge.

overload² [ouvər'loud], *v.tr.* 1. Surcharger. 2. Surmener (une machine).

overlook [ouvər'luk], *v.tr.* 1. Avoir vue sur (qch.); (*of building*) dominer, commander (un vallon, etc.); (*of window*) donner sur (la rue). 2. (*a*) Oublier, laisser passer (l'heure, etc.); négliger, laisser échapper (une occasion). I overlooked the fact, ce fait m'a échappé. (*b*) Fermer les yeux sur (qch.); passer sur (qch.); laisser passer (une erreur). Overlook it this time, passez-le-moi cette fois. 3. Surveiller (un travail).

overlord ['ouvərlɔːrd], *s.* Suzerain *m.*

overlordship [ouvər'lɔːrdʃip], *s.* Suzeraineté *f.*

overmantel ['ouvərmant(ə)l], *s.* Étagère *f* de cheminée.

overmaster [ouvər'maːstər], *v.tr.* Maîtriser, subjuguer. **overmastering,** *a.* (*a*) (*Of will*) Dominateur, -trice. (*b*) (*Of passion*) Irrésistible.

overmuch [ouvər'mʌtʃ]. 1. *adv.* (Par) trop; à l'excès; outre mesure. 2. *s.* Excès *m*; le trop.

overpass [ouvər'paːs], *v.tr.* 1. Surmonter, vaincre (un obstacle). 2. Surpasser (*s.o. in sth.,* qn en qch.). 3. Outrepasser (les bornes de . . .).

overpayment [ouvər'peimənt], *s.* 1. Surpaye *f*; paiement *m* en trop. 2. Rétribution excessive.

overplus ['ouvərplʌs], *s.* Excédent *m*, surplus *m.*

overpower [ouvər'pauər], *v.tr.* Maîtriser, dominer, vaincre, accabler. **Overpowered with** grief, accablé de douleur. **overpowering,** *a.* (*Of emotion*) Accablant; (*of desire*) tout-puissant, irrésistible. **Overpowering heat,** chaleur accablante.

overpraise [ouvər'preiz], *v.tr.* Trop louer.

overproduction [ouvərpro'dʌkʃ(ə)n], *s.* Surproduction *f.*

overrate [ouvər'reit], *v.tr.* Surestimer, surfaire; faire trop de cas de (qch.). **To overrate one's** strength, trop présumer de ses forces.

overreach [ouvər'riːtʃ], *v.tr.* 1. Dépasser. 2. Tromper, duper (qn). 3. **To overreach oneself,** (i) se donner un effort; (ii) être victime de sa propre fourberie.

override [ouvər'raid], *v.tr.* (*Conj. like* RIDE) 1. (*a*) Outrepasser (ses ordres, etc.); fouler aux pieds (les droits de qn). (*b*) Avoir plus d'importance que (qch.). *Considerations that o. all others,* considérations qui l'emportent sur toutes les autres. 2. Surmener (un cheval). 3. *v.i.* (*Of ends of fractured bone, of the toes, etc.*) Chevaucher. **overriding,** *a.* **Overriding principle,** principe auquel il ne saurait être dérogé. *Jur:* **Overriding** clause, clause dérogatoire.

overrule [ouvər'ruːl], *v.tr.* 1. Gouverner, diriger (avec une autorité supérieure). 2. (*a*) Décider contre l'avis de (qn). (*b*) *Jur:* Annuler, casser (un arrêt); rejeter (une réclamation). (*c*) Passer outre à (une difficulté); passer à l'ordre du jour sur (une objection).

overrun [ouvər'rʌn], *v.* (*Conj. like* RUN) I. *v.tr.* 1. (*a*) (*Of invaders*) (i) Se répandre sur, envahir (un pays); (ii) dévaster, ravager (un pays). (*b*) *These eastern towns are overrun with soldiers,* ces villes de l'est grouillent de soldats. **House** overrun with mice, maison infestée de souris. 2. Dépasser, aller au delà de (la limite). 3. Surmener, fatiguer (une machine); *El:* survolter (une lampe). 4. *Typ:* Reporter (un mot) à la ligne ou à la page suivante. II. **overrun,** *v.i.* (*Of liquid, of river*) Déborder.

oversea ['ouvərsiː]. 1. *Attrib.a.* (Colonie, commerce) d'outre-mer; (région) transmarine. 2. *adv.* Par delà les mers.

overseas [ouvər'siːz], *adv.* = OVERSEA 2. **Visitors** from overseas, visiteurs d'outre-mer.

oversee [ouvər'siː], *v.tr.* (*Conj. like* SEE) Surveiller. *F:* avoir l'œil sur (un atelier, etc.).

overseer ['ouvərsiːər], s. Surveillant, -ante; inspecteur, -trice; *Ind:* contremaître, -tresse; chef *m* d'atelier.

overset [ouvər'set], v.tr. & i. (overset: overset) = UPSET².

oversew ['ouvərsou], v.tr. (p.p. oversewn ['ouvərsoun]) *Needlew:* Surjeter; assembler au point de surjet.

overshadow [ouvər'ʃado], v.tr. **1.** Ombrager; couvrir de son ombre. **2.** Éclipser (qn); surpasser en éclat.

overshoe ['ouvərʃuː], s. Couvre-chaussure *m*; galoche *f*. **Rubber overshoes,** caoutchoucs *m*.

overshoot [ouvər'ʃuːt], v.tr. (Conj. like SHOOT) **1.** Dépasser, outrepasser (le point d'arrêt, etc.); (of shot, gun) porter au delà de (qch.). *F:* **To overshoot the mark,** dépasser le but. **2.** Trop chasser sur (une terre); dépeupler (une chasse). **'overshot,** a. Hyd.E: **Overshot wheel,** roue (à augets) en dessus.

oversight ['ouvərsait], s. **1.** Oubli *m*, omission *f*, inadvertance *f*. **Through, by, an oversight,** par mégarde; par inadvertance. **2.** Surveillance *f*.

oversize ['ouvərsaːiz], s. (a) Mec.E: etc: Surépaisseur *f*. (b) Dimensions *fpl* (i) au-dessus de la moyenne, (ii) Mec.E: au-dessus de la cote. **Oversize tyre,** bandage surprofilé. *I.C.E:* **Oversize piston,** piston à cote de réalésage.

oversleep [ouvər'sliːp], v.i. & pron. (Conj. like SLEEP) **To oversleep (oneself),** dormir trop longtemps.

oversleeve ['ouvərsliːv], s. Fausse manche.

overspread [ouvər'spred], v.tr. (Conj. like SPREAD) **1.** Couvrir (with, de). **2.** Se répandre, s'étendre, sur (qch.); (of floods, light, etc.) inonder.

overstate [ouvər'steit], v.tr. Exagérer (les faits, etc.).

overstatement [ouvər'steitmənt], s. **1.** Exagération *f*. **2.** Récit exagéré.

overstay [ouvər'stei], v.tr. Dépasser (son congé, etc.). *S.a.* WELCOME².

overstep [ouvər'step], v.tr. (Conj. like STEP) Outrepasser, dépasser (les bornes).

overstock [ouvər'stɔk], v.tr. (a) Encombrer (le marché, etc.) (with, de). (b) Trop meubler (une ferme) de bétail; surcharger (un étang) de poissons.

overstrain¹ ['ouvərstrein], s. **1.** Tension excessive. **2.** Surmenage *m*.

overstrain² [ouvər'strein], v.tr. **1.** Surtendre (un câble). **2.** (a) Surmener. (b) *To o. an argument,* pousser trop loin un argument.

overstress¹ ['ouvərstres], s. Mec.E: Surcharge *f*.

overstress² [ouvər'stres], v.tr. **1.** Mec.E: Surcharger (une transmission). **2.** Trop insister sur (un détail).

overt ['ouvərt], a. Patent, évident. *Jur:* **Overt act,** acte manifeste. **Market overt,** marché public.

overtake [ouvər'teik], v.tr. (Conj. like TAKE) **1.** (a) Rattraper, atteindre (qn). *F:* **To overtake arrears of work,** rattraper le retard dans son travail. (b) Doubler, dépasser, gagner de vitesse (un concurrent, une voiture, un bateau). **2.** (Of accident) Arriver à (qn); (of misfortune, etc.) s'abattre sur (qn). *Overtaken by a storm,* surpris par un orage. **overtaking,** s. Aut: 'Overtaking and passing forbidden; no overtaking,' "défense de doubler." **Overtaking signal,** signal *m* pour dépasser.

overtax [ouvər'taks], v.tr. (a) Pressurer (le peuple). (b) Trop exiger de (qn). **To overtax one's strength,** se surmener; abuser de ses forces.

overthrow¹ ['ouvərθrou], s. Renversement *m* (d'un empire); ruine *f*, défaite *f* (de qn, d'un projet).

overthrow² [ouvər'θrou], v.tr. (Conj. like THROW) **1.** Renverser. **2.** Défaire, vaincre (qn); mettre à bas (un empire); renverser, culbuter (un ministère, etc.); ruiner, réduire à néant (les projets de qn).

overtime ['ouvərtaim]. **1.** s. Ind: Heures *f* supplémentaires (de travail); heures hors cloche. **2.** adv. **To work overtime,** faire des heures supplémentaires.

overtone ['ouvərtoun], s. Mus: Harmonique *m*.

overtop [ouvər'tɔp], v.tr. (overtopped) **1.** Dépasser en hauteur. **2.** Surpasser (qn).

overtrump [ouvər'trʌmp], v.tr. Cards: Surcouper. **overtrumping,** s. Surcoupe *f*.

overture ['ouvərtjuər], s. **1.** Ouverture *f*, offre *f*. **To make overtures to s.o.,** faire des ouvertures à qn. **2.** Mus: Ouverture.

overturn [ouvər'təːrn]. **1.** v.tr. Renverser; mettre (qch.) sens dessus dessous; faire verser (une voiture); (faire) chavirer (un canot). **2.** v.i. (a) Se renverser; (of carriage) verser; (of boat) chavirer. (b) (Turn turtle) Aut: Av: Capoter.

overvaluation [ouvərvalju'eiʃ(ə)n], s. Surestimation *f*.

overvalue [ouvər'valju], v.tr. **1.** Com: Surestimer. **2.** Faire trop de cas de (qch.).

overvoltage [ouvər'voultedʒ], s. El: Surtension *f*.

overweening [ouvər'wiːniŋ], a. Outrecuidant, présomptueux, suffisant.

overweight¹ ['ouvərweit]. **1.** s. (a) Surpoids *m*; excédent *m* (de poids). (b) Excédent (de bagages). **2.** a. **Parcel two pounds overweight,** colis qui excède, dépasse, de deux livres le poids réglementaire.

overweight² [ouvər'weit], v.tr. Surcharger (with, de).

overwhelm [ouvər'hwelm], v.tr. **1.** Ensevelir (une ville dans la lave, etc.); submerger. **2.** (a) Écraser, accabler (l'ennemi, etc.). (b) *To be overwhelmed with work,* être accablé, débordé, de travail. (c) Combler (qn de bontés); confondre (qn de honte). *I am overwhelmed by your kindness,* je suis confus de vos bontés. *Overwhelmed with joy,* au comble de la joie. **overwhelming,** a. Irrésistible; accablant. **Overwhelming majority,** majorité écrasante.

overwork¹ ['ouvərwəːrk], s. **1.** Travail *m* en plus. **2.** Surmenage *m*.

overwork² [ouvər'wəːrk]. **1.** v.tr. (a) Surmener; surcharger (qn) de travail. (b) *To o. a literary device,* abuser d'un truc. **2.** v.i. Se surmener; travailler outre mesure.

overwrought [ouvər'rɔːt], a. (a) (Of pers.) Excédé (de fatigue); surmené. (b) O. senses, sens surexcités.

ovibos ['ouvibɔs], s. Ovibos *m*; bœuf musqué.

oviform ['ouvifɔːrm], a. Oviforme, ovoïde.

ovine ['ouvain], a. (Race *f*) ovine.

oviparous [ou'vipərəs], a. Ovipare.

ovoid ['ouvɔid], a. Ovoïde.

ovolo, pl. **-li** ['ouvolo, -lai], s. Arch: Boudin *m* (de base de colonne); quart *m* de rond.

ovule ['ouvjuːl], s. Biol: Ovule *m*.

ovum, pl. **ova** ['ouvəm, 'ouva], s. Biol: Ovule *m*; œuf *m*.

owe [ou], v.tr. (owed [oud]) Devoir. **1.** (a) **To owe s.o. sth., to owe sth. to s.o.,** devoir qch. à qn. *Abs.* I still owe you for the petrol, je vous dois encore l'essence. (b) *The duties that I owe him*, les devoirs auxquels je suis tenu envers lui. **To owe allegiance to s.o.**, devoir obéissance à qn. *I owe it to my friends to spare them this sorrow*, je dois à mes amis de leur éviter ce chagrin. **2.** I **owe my life to you**, je vous dois la vie. *He owes his ability to his mother*, il tient sa capacité de sa mère. **To what do I owe this honour?** qu'est-ce qui me vaut cet honneur? **owing. 1.** *Pred.a.* Dû, *f.* due. **All the money owing to me**, tout l'argent qui m'est dû. **2. Owing to**, à cause de, par suite de. **Owing to a recent bereavement . . .**, en raison d'un deuil récent. . . .

owl [aul], *s. Orn:* Hibou *m*, -oux. *The owl*, le hibou. **Brown owl, wood owl, tawny owl**, chat-huant *m*; chouette *f* des bois; hulotte *f*. **Barn owl, screech owl**, effraie *f*; chouette des clochers. **Horn(ed) owl**, duc *m*.

owlet [ˈaulet], *s. Orn:* Jeune hibou. **'owlet-moth**, *s. Ent:* Noctuelle *f*.

owlish [ˈauliʃ], *a.* De hibou. *O. air of wisdom*, air de profonde sagesse.

own[1] [oun], *v.tr.* **1.** Posséder. *Who owns this land?* quel est le propriétaire de cette terre? **2.** Reconnaître. (a) **To own a child**, avouer un enfant. *Dog nobody will own*, chien que personne ne réclame. **To own s.o. as one's brother**, avouer qn pour frère. (b) Avouer (qch). **I own I was wrong**, j'ai eu tort, je l'avoue, j'en conviens. *To own oneself beaten*, se reconnaître vaincu. (c) Reconnaître l'autorité de (qn). **3.** *v.ind.tr.* **To own to a mistake**, reconnaître, avouer, une erreur; convenir d'une erreur. *She owns (up) to (being) thirty*, elle accuse trente ans. **To own up to a crime**, faire l'aveu d'un crime. *To own up to having done sth.*, avouer avoir fait qch. *Abs. F:* **To own up**, faire des aveux.

own[2]. **1.** *a.* (a) *Attrib.* Propre. *Her own money*, son propre argent; son argent à elle. **Own brother, sister**, frère germain, sœur germaine. *I had my own table*, j'avais ma table à part. *I do my own cooking*, je fais la cuisine moi-même; je fais ma propre cuisine. (b) *Pred.* Le mien, le tien, etc.; à moi, à toi, etc. *The house is my own*, la maison est à moi; la maison m'appartient (en propre). *My money and your own*, mon argent et le vôtre. *My time is my own*, mon temps est à moi; je suis libre de mon temps. **2.** *s.* **My own**, **his own**, *etc.* (a) Le mien, le sien, etc. **I have money of my own**, j'ai de l'argent à moi. *He has a copy of his own*, il a un exemplaire à lui, en propre. **For reasons of his own**, pour des raisons particulières. **A style all one's own**, un style original. *May I have it for my (very) own?* est-ce que je peux l'avoir pour moi seul? **To come into one's own**, entrer en possession de son bien. (b) **To do sth. on one's own**, faire qch. (i) de sa propre initiative, de son chef; (ii) indépendam-

ment, à soi tout seul. *F:* **I am (all) on my own to-day**, je suis seul aujourd'hui.

owner [ˈounər], *s.* Propriétaire *mf*, possesseur *m*; patron *m* (d'une maison de commerce). *Cars parked here at owner's risk*, garage pour autos aux risques et périls de leurs propriétaires. *Aut:* **Owner-driver**, conducteur *m* propriétaire.

ownership [ˈounərʃip], *s.* (Droit *m* de) propriété *f*; possession *f*. **Bare ownership**, nue propriété. *'Under new ownership,'* "changement *m* de propriétaire."

ox, *pl.* **oxen** [ɔks, ˈɔks(ə)n], *s.* Bœuf *m*. **Wild oxen**, bovidés *m* sauvages. **'ox-cart**, *s.* Char *m* à bœufs. **'ox-eye**, *s. Bot:* Ox-eye daisy, grande marguerite; œil-de-bœuf *m*, *pl.* œils-de-bœuf. **'ox-tail**, *s. Cu:* Queue *f* de bœuf. **Ox-tail soup**, oxtail *m*. **'ox-tongue**, *s.* Langue *f* de bœuf.

oxalate [ˈɔksalet], *s. Ch:* Oxalate *m*.

oxalic [ɔkˈsalik], *a. Ch:* Oxalique.

oxide [ˈɔksaid], *s. Ch:* Oxyde *m*.

oxidizable [ɔksiˈdaizəbl], *a. Ch:* Oxydable.

oxidization [ɔksidaiˈzeiʃ(ə)n], *s. Ch:* Oxyda-tion *f*. *Metall:* Calcination *f*.

oxidize [ˈɔksidaiz], **1.** *v.tr. Ch:* Oxyder. *Metall:* Calciner. **2.** *v.i.* S'oxyder. **oxidizing**, *s.* Oxydation *f*.

oxidizer [ˈɔksidaizər], *s. Ch:* Oxydant *m*.

Oxonian [ɔkˈsounjən]. **1.** *a.* Oxonien, -ienne. **2.** *s.* Membre *m* de l'Université d'Oxford.

oxyacetylene [ɔksiaˈsetilin], *attrib.a. Metalw:* Oxyacétylénique. *S.a.* WELDING.

oxygen [ˈɔksidʒen], *s. Ch:* Oxygène *m*.

oxygenate [ɔkˈsidʒəneit], *v.tr. Ch:* Oxygéner.

oxyhydrogen [ɔksiˈhaidrɔdʒən], *attrib.a.* (Of blow-pipe, light) Oxhydrique.

oxylith [ˈɔksiliθ], *s.* Oxylithe *f* (pour appareils respiratoires).

oxytone [ˈɔksitoun], *s. Gr.Gram:* Oxyton *m*.

oyes! oyez! [ouˈjes], *int.* Oyez! [waje].

oyster [ˈɔistər], *s.* Huître *f*. **Pearl oyster**, huître perlière, à perle. **'oyster-bed**, *s.* Huîtrière *f*. (a) Banc *m* d'huîtres. (b) Parc *m* à huîtres. **'oyster-breeder**, *s.* Ostréiculteur *m*. **'oyster-breeding**, *s.* Ostréiculture *f*. **'oyster-dealer**, *s.* Écailler, -ère; marchand, -ande, d'huîtres. **'oyster-farm**, *s.* Parc *m* à huîtres; clayère *f*. **'oyster-farming**, *s.* L'industrie huîtrière, ostréicole. **'oyster-knife**, *s.* Ouvre-huîtres *m inv.* **'oyster-shell**, *s.* Écaille *f* d'huître.

ozocerite [oˈzɔsərait], **ozokerit(e)** [oˈzoukərit], *s. Miner:* Ozocérite *f*, ozokérite *f*; cire minérale.

ozone [ˈozoun], *s. Ch:* Ozone *m*.

ozonization [ouzonaiˈzeiʃ(ə)n], *s. Ch:* Ozonisa-tion *f*.

ozonize [ˈouzonaiz], *v.tr. Ch:* Ozoniser.

ozonizer [ˈouzonaizər], *s. Ch:* Ozoniseur *m*.

P

P, p [piː], *s.* (La lettre) P, p *m*. *F:* **To mind one's P's and Q's**, (i) se surveiller: (ii) faire bien attention.

pa [pɑː], *s.m. F:* Papa.

pabulum [ˈpabjuləm], *s.* Aliment *m*, nourriture *f*. *Esp. F:* **Mental pabulum**, nourriture de l'esprit.

pace[1] [peis], *s.* **1.** Pas *m*. **Ten paces off**, à dix pas

de distance. **2.** (a) **Paces of a horse**, allures *f* d'un cheval. **To put a horse through its paces**, faire parader un cheval. *F:* **To put s.o. through his paces**, mettre qn à l'épreuve. (b) (*Speed*) Vitesse *f*, train *m*, allure. **To gather pace**, prendre de la vitesse. **At a good, a smart, pace**, à vive allure. **At a walking pace**, au pas. *To walk at a* rapid *p.*, marcher d'un pas rapide. **To quicken one's pace**, hâter, presser, le pas. *Sp:* **To set, make, the pace**, donner l'allure ; mener le train. **To keep pace with s.o.**, marcher du même pas que qn ; marcher de pair avec qn. *F:* **To go the pace**, (i) mener la vie à grandes guides ; (ii) mener un train d'enfer. **3.** *Equit:* Amble *m.* **'pace-maker**, *s.* *Sp:* (*a*) Entraîneur *m.* (*b*) Meneur *m* de train.

pace². **1.** *v.i.* (*a*) Aller au pas ; marcher à pas mesurés. **To pace up and down**, faire les cent pas. (*b*) *Equit:* Ambler ; aller l'amble. **2.** *v.tr.* (*a*) Arpenter (la rue, etc.). (*b*) **To pace (off) a distance**, mesurer une distance au pas. (*c*) *Sp:* Entraîner (un cycliste, etc.). **-paced** [peist], *a.* **Even-paced**, à l'allure égale. **Easy-paced** *horse*, cheval au train doux.

pachyderm ['pakidə:rm], *s.* Pachyderme *m.*

pachydermatous [paki'də:rmatəs], *a.* Pachyderme ; à la peau épaisse.

pacific [pa'sifik], *a.* **1.** (*a*) Pacifique. (*b*) Paisible. **2.** *Geog:* **The Pacific (Ocean)**, l'océan *m* Pacifique ; le Pacifique.

pacification [pasifi'keiʃ(ə)n], *s.* Pacification *f* ; apaisement *m.*

pacifier ['pasifaiər], *s.* Pacificateur, -trice.

pacifism ['pasifizm], *s.* Pacifisme *m.*

pacifist ['pasifist], *s. & a.* Pacifiste (*mf*).

pacify ['pasifai], *v.tr.* Pacifier (une foule, un pays) ; apaiser, calmer (qn). **pacifying**, *a.* Pacificateur, -trice.

pack¹ [pak], *s.* **1.** (*a*) Paquet *m* ; balle *f* (de coton) ; ballot *m* (de colporteur) ; bât *m* (de bête de charge). *Mil:* Paquetage *m* ; sac *m* d'ordonnance. (*b*) *F: Pej:* **Pack of lies**, tissu *m*, tas *m*, de mensonges. **2.** (*a*) Bande *f* (de loups, *F:* de voleurs). *P. of fools*, tas d'imbéciles. (*b*) *Rugby Fb:* **The pack**, le pack. (*c*) *Ven:* **Pack of hounds**, meute *f.* **To lay on the pack**, laisser courre. **3.** Jeu *m* (de cartes, de dominos) ; paquet (de cartes). **4.** (Ice-)pack, embâcle *m* (de glaçons) ; pack. **5.** (*a*) *Med:* **Cold pack, wet pack**, enveloppement froid, humide. (*b*) *Toil:* Emplâtre *m.* **'pack-animal**, *s.* Bête *f* de charge, de somme. **'pack-cloth**, *s.* Toile *f* d'emballage ; serpillière *f.* **'pack-drill**, *s.* *Mil:* Punition *f* de l'exercice en tenue de route. **'pack-full**, *a.* Plein à déborder. **'pack-horse**, *s.* Cheval *m* de bât. **'pack-ice**, *s.* Glace *f* de banquise ; pack *m.* **'pack-mule**, *s.* Mulet *m* de bât, de somme. **'pack-road**, *s.* Chemin muletier. **'pack-saddle**, *s.* Bât *m.* **'pack-trail**, *s.* Piste muletière. **'pack-wool**, *s.* Laine *f* en balles.

pack². **1.** *v.tr.* (packed [pakt]) **1.** (*a*) Emballer, empaqueter. *Abs.* **To pack (up)**, (i) faire ses malles, *P:* faire son baluchon ; (ii) plier bagage, *F:* prendre ses cliques et ses claques. *Tent that packs (up) easily*, tente qui est facile à emballer. (*b*) *Com:* Conserver (la viande) en boîtes ; embariller (des harengs). **2.** Tasser (de la terre dans un trou, etc.) ; *F:* entasser, serrer (des voyageurs dans une voiture). **Packed (in) like herrings, like sardines in a box**, serrés comme des harengs en caque. **3.** Remplir, bourrer (*sth. with sth.*, qch. de qch.). **To pack one's trunk**, faire sa malle. **The train was packed** (*with people*), le train était bondé, le train regorgeait de monde. *Packed hall*, salle comble. *Book packed with facts*, livre bourré de faits. **4.** *Mch:* Garnir (un gland, un piston) ; étouper (un gland). **5.** (*a*) **To pack a jury**, se composer un jury favorable. **To pack a meeting**, s'assurer un nombre prépondérant de partisans à une réunion. **Packed meeting**, salle

faite d'avance. (*b*) *Cards:* Apprêter (les cartes). **6.** (*a*) **To pack a child off to bed**, envoyer un enfant au lit. (*b*) *F:* **To send s.o. packing**, envoyer promener qn. **II. pack**, *v.i.* **1.** (*Of earth*, etc.) Se tasser. **2.** (*Of people*) S'attrouper. *They packed round the speaker*, ils se pressaient autour de l'orateur. **packing**, *s.* **1.** (*a*) Emballage *m*, empaquetage *m.* **To do one's packing**, faire ses malles. (*b*) Conservation *f* (de la viande, etc.). **2.** Tassement *m*, agglomération *f* (de la terre, etc.). **3.** *Mch:* Garnissage *m* ; étoupage *m* (d'un gland). **4.** (*a*) Matière *f* pour garnitures, pour emballage. (*b*) *Mch:* Garniture *f* (d'un piston, etc.). **'packing-box**, *s.* *Mch:* Presseétoupe *m inv.* **'packing-case**, *s.* Caisse *f* ou boîte *f* d'emballage ; layette *f.* **Packing-case maker**, layetier *m.* **'packing-paper**, *s.* Papier *m* d'emballage ; papier gris. **'packing-ring**, *s.* **1.** *Mec.E:* Rondelle *f*, bague *f*, de garniture. **2.** *Mch:* Segment *m*, bague, garniture *f* (de piston). **'packing-sheet**, *s.* **1.** Drap *m* d'emballage. **2.** *Med:* Drap mouillé ; enveloppement froid.

package ['pakedʒ], *s.* **1.** Empaquetage *m*, emballage *m.* **2.** Paquet *m*, colis *m*, ballot *m.*

packer ['pakər], *s.* Emballeur *m.*

packet ['paket], *s.* **1.** (*a*) Paquet *m* ; pochette *f* (de papier photographique, etc.). **Packet teas**, thés en paquets. (*b*) *Colis m* ; article *m* de messagerie. **Postal packet**, colis postal. **2.** **Packet (-boat)**, paquebot *m.*

packman, *pl.* **-men** ['pakmən, -men], *s.m.* Colporteur, porteballe.

pact [pakt], *s.* Pacte *m*, convention *f*, contrat *m.* **To make a pact with s.o.**, faire, signer, un pacte avec qn.

pad¹ [pad], *s.* **1.** *Dial:* *P:* Chemin *m*, route *f.* **To be on the pad**, être sur le trimard. **2.** Bruit sourd des pas (d'un loup etc.).

pad², *v.tr. & i.* (padded) (*a*) *P:* Aller à pied. **To pad it**, **to pad the hoof**, trimarder. (*b*) (*Of wolf*, etc.) **To pad (along)**, trotter à pas sourds. (*Of pers.*) **To pad about the room**, aller et venir à pas feutrés, à pas de loup.

pad³, *s.* **1.** (*a*) Bourrelet *m*, coussinet *m.* *Fb:* **Ankle-pad**, protège-cheville *m inv.* (*b*) Tampon *m* (d'ouate, etc.). **Stamp pad**, tampon à timbrer. **Inking pad**, tampon encreur. **Engraver's pad**, tapette *f.* (*c*) *Toil:* **Hair-pad**, crêpé *m.* (*d*) *Harn:* Mantelet *m*, sellette *f* (de cheval de trait). (*e*) *Fenc:* Plastron *m.* **2.** (*a*) Pelote digitale ; pulpe *f* (du doigt, de l'orteil). (*b*) Patte *f* (de lapin, de chameau, etc.). **3.** (*a*) Bloc *m* (de papier). **Note-pad**, bloc-notes *m.* (*b*) Sous-main *m.* **4.** *Tls:* (*a*) Mandrin *m* (de vilebrequin). (*b*) Manche *m* porte-outils. **5.** Support *m*, amortisseur *m* ; cale *f* de support ; tampon amortisseur.

pad⁴, *v.tr.* (padded) **1.** Rembourrer (un coussin) ; matelasser (une porte) ; capitonner (un meuble) ; ouater (un vêtement). *Tls:* Garnir (les épaules d'un vêtement). **Padded cell**, cellule matelassée ; cabanon *m.* **2.** *F:* **To pad (out) a chapter**, tirer à la ligne. *To pad a speech*, délayer un discours. *To pad a line of verse*, cheviller un vers. **padding**, *s.* **1.** Remplissage *m*, rembourrage *m.* **2.** (*a*) Ouate *f*, bourre *f* ; coussin *m* (de cheval). (*b*) Remplissage (dans une œuvre littéraire).

paddle¹ ['padl], *s.* **1.** Pagaie *f.* **2.** (*a*) Aube *f*, pale *f*, palette *f* (de roue hydraulique). (*b*) = PADDLE-WHEEL. **3.** Nageoire *f* (de cétacé, de tortue) ; aileron *m* (de requin). **'paddleboat**, *s.* Bateau *m* à aubes, à roues. **'paddle-**

box, s. Tambour m de la roue à aubes. **'paddle-wheel,** s. Roue f à aubes, à palettes.

paddle², s. Row: (a) Allure douce. (b) Promenade f (en canot) à allure douce.

paddle³. (a) v.tr. Pagayer. F: To paddle one's own canoe, conduire seul sa barque. (b) v.i. Row: Tirer en douce.

paddle⁴, v.i. Barboter, F: grenouiller (dans l'eau); patauger (dans la boue). **'paddling-pool,** s. F: Grenouillère f (pour les enfants).

paddler ['padlər], s. **1.** Pagayeur, -euse. **2.** pl. Cost: Paddlers, barboteuse f (d'enfant).

paddock ['padək], s. (a) Parc m, enclos m (pour chevaux). To put a horse in the p., parquer un cheval. (b) Turf: Pesage m, paddock m.

paddy¹ ['padi], s. Com: Paddy m (riz non décortiqué).

Paddy². **1.** Pr.n.m. Patrice. **2.** s.m. P: To be in a paddy, être en colère.

padlock¹ ['padlɔk], s. Cadenas m.

padlock², v.tr. Cadenasser; fermer (une porte) au cadenas.

padre ['pɑːdre], s.m. Aumônier (militaire).

paean ['piːən], s. Gr.Ant: Péan m.

pagan ['peigən], a. & s. Païen, -ïenne.

paganism ['peigənizm], s. Paganisme m.

page¹ ['peidʒ], s. **1.** (a) A: Petit laquais. (b) Page m. Page of honour, page du roi, de la reine. **2.** Page(-boy), petit groom (d'hôtel); chasseur m.

page², s. Page f. Right-hand page, recto m. Left-hand page, verso m. On page 6, à la page 6. **'page-proof,** s. Typ: Épreuve f en pages.

page³, v.tr. **1.** Numéroter (les feuilles); paginer (un livre); folioter (un registre). **2.** Typ: Mettre (la composition) en pages. **paging,** s. **1.** Pagination f. foliotage m. **2.** Typ: Mise f en pages.

pageant ['padʒənt], s. **1.** Spectacle pompeux. An empty pageant, un pur spectacle. **2.** Grand spectacle historique donné en costume. **3.** Air pageant, fête f d'aviation.

pageantry ['padʒəntri], s. Apparat m, pompe f.

paginate ['padʒineit], v.tr. Paginer; folioter.

pagination [padʒi'neiʃ(ə)n], s. Pagination f.

pagoda [pa'goudə], s. Pagode f.

pah [pɑ], int. Pouah!

paid [peid]. See PAY².

pail [peil], s. **1.** Seau m; (wooden) seille f. Nau: Baille f. **2.** A p. of water, un seau d'eau.

pailful ['peilful], s. (Plein) seau (de lait, etc.).

pain¹ [pein]. **1.** (a) Douleur f, souffrance f; (mental) peine f. To give s.o. pain, (i) (of tooth, etc.) faire mal à qn, faire souffrir qn; (ii) (of incident, etc.) faire de la peine à qn. To be in great pain, souffrir beaucoup. To put a wounded animal out of its pain, achever un animal blessé. (b) A p. in the side, une douleur dans le côté; un point de côté. To have a p., pains, in one's head, souffrir de la tête. **2.** pl. Pains, peine. To take pains, be at great pains, to do sth., prendre, se donner, de la peine pour faire qch.; se donner du mal pour faire qch. To take pains over sth., s'appliquer à qch.; y mettre tous ses soins. To have one's labour for one's pains, en être pour sa peine, pour ses frais. A: Châtiment m. Still so used in On pain of death, sous peine de mort. **'pain-killer,** s. Anodin m, antalgique m.

pain², v.tr. Faire souffrir (qn) (physically) faire mal à (qn); (mentally) faire de la peine à (qn); peiner, affliger (qn). It pains me to say so, cela me coûte à dire; il m'en coûte de le dire.

pained, a. Attristé, peiné (at, de).

painful ['peinful], a. **1.** (Of wound) Douloureux. (Of limb, etc.) To become painful, s'endolorir. My knee was getting p., mon genou commençait à me faire mal. **2.** (Of spectacle, effort) Pénible. P. to behold, pénible à voir. It is p. to hear him, cela fait peine de l'entendre. **-fully,** adv. Douloureusement; péniblement.

painless ['peinləs], a. **1.** (Extraction, etc.) sans douleur. **2.** Painless tumour, tumeur indolente, indolore.

painstaking ['peinzteikiŋ], a. Soigneux, assidu; (élève) travailleur, appliqué; (travail) soigné.

paint¹ [peint], s. Peinture f. (a) Coat of paint, couche f de peinture. Give it a coat of p., il faut le peindre. 'Wet paint!' "attention à la peinture, à la couleur (fraîche)!" (b) Box of paints, boîte de couleurs. (c) (For the face) Fard m. **'paint-brush,** s. Pinceau m. **'paint-sprayer,** s. Pistolet m à peindre.

paint², v.tr. **1.** (a) To p. a portrait in oils, peindre un portrait à l'huile. To p. a sunset, peindre un coucher de soleil. (b) Abs. Faire de la peinture. **2.** Dépeindre. What words can p. the scene? comment dépeindre cette scène? **3.** (a) Enduire de peinture; peinturer. To p. a door green, peindre une porte en vert. Th: To p. the scenery for a play, brosser les décors d'une pièce. P: To paint the town red, faire une noce à tout casser. (b) To p. one's face, se farder; F: se plâtrer (le visage). (c) Med: Badigeonner (la gorge, etc.). To p. with iodine, badigeonner à la teinture d'iode. **painting,** s. Peinture f. **1.** (a) To study p., étudier la peinture. (b) Med: Badigeonnage m. (c) (Ornamental) painting, décoration f (en bâtiment, etc.). **2.** Tableau m (à l'huile ou à l'aquarelle).

painter¹ ['peintər], s. **1.** (a) Art: Peintre m. S.a. PORTRAIT-PAINTER, SCENE-PAINTER, etc. (b) Coloriste mf (de cartes postales, de jouets). **2.** (House-)painter, peintre en bâtiments; peintre décorateur.

painter², s. Nau: Amarre f. To slip the painter, (i) filer son amarre, son nœud; F: mourir. To cut the painter, (i) couper, trancher, l'amarre (ii) F: (of colony) se séparer de la mère-patrie.

pair¹ ['pɛər], s. **1.** (a) Paire f. Arranged in pairs, arrangés deux par deux, par paires. The p. of you, vous deux. (b) A pair of trousers, of drawers, un pantalon, un caleçon. (c) Carriage and pair, voiture f à deux chevaux. Pair of oxen, couple f de bœufs. (d) (Man and wife) Couple m. The happy pair, les deux conjoints m. P. of pigeons (cock and hen), couple m de pigeons. (e) These two pictures are a pair, ces deux tableaux se font pendant. (f) Where is the p. of this glove? où se trouve l'autre gant de cette paire? **2.** Pair of stairs, escalier m (en deux volées); étage m. To lodge on the three-pair front, back, loger au troisième (étage) sur la rue, sur la cour. Pair of steps, marchepied (volant); escabeau m.

pair². **1.** v.tr. (a) Appareiller, apparier, assortir (des gants, etc.). (b) Accoupler, apparier (des oiseaux, etc.). **2.** v.i. (a) Faire la paire (with sth., avec qch.). Two vases that p., deux vases qui (se) font pendant. (b) (Of birds, etc.) S'accoupler, s'apparier. (c) Parl: To pair (off), s'absenter après entente avec un adversaire qui désire aussi s'absenter. **pair off.** **1.** v.tr. Arranger, distribuer, deux par deux. **2.** v.i. S'en aller, défiler, deux par deux. **paired,** a. En couples; deux par deux. Artil: Guns paired on turret, canons conjugués.

pal[1] [pal], *s.* *P:* Camarade *mf*; *P:* copain, *f.* copine.

pal[2], *v.i.* *P:* (palled [pald]) To pal in, up, with s.o., se lier (d'amitié) avec qn; *P:* devenir copain avec qn.

palace [ˈpales], *s.* Palais *m.* Bishop's palace, évêché *m*; palais épiscopal.

paladin [ˈpaladin], *s.* Paladin *m.*

palaeographer [paliˈɔɡrəfər], *s.* Paléographe *m*; archiviste *m.*

palaeography [paliˈɔɡrəfi], *s.* Paléographie *f.*

palaeolithic [paliɔˈliθik], *a.* Paléolithique. The palaeolithic age, l'âge de la pierre taillée.

palaeontology [paliɔnˈtɔlɔdʒi], *s.* Paléontologie *f.*

palankeen, palanquin [palanˈkiːn], *s.* Palanquin *m.*

palatable [ˈpalətəbl], *a.* (*a*) Agréable au palais, au goût. (*b*) (*Of doctrine, etc.*) Agréable (*to*, à).

palatal [ˈpalat(ə)l], *Ling:* **1.** *a.* Palatal, -aux. Palatal l, l mouillée. **2.** *s.* Palatale *f.*

palate [ˈpalet], *s.* (*a*) *Anat:* (Hard) palate, palais *m.* Soft palate, voile *m* du palais. (*b*) *F:* To have a delicate palate, avoir le palais fin. To have no p. for broad humour, ne pas goûter les plaisanteries corsées.

palatial [paˈleiʃəl], *a.* (Édifice) qui ressemble à un palais; magnifique, grandiose.

palatinate [paˈlatinet], *s.* *Hist:* The Palatinate, le Palatinat.

palatine [ˈpalatain], *a. & s.* **1.** *Hist:* Palatin, -ine. **2.** *A.Geog:* The Palatine (Hill), le (mont) Palatin.

palaver[1] [paˈlɑːvər], *s.* **1.** Palabre *f*; conférence *f* (avec les indigènes). **2.** *F:* (*a*) Cajoleries *fpl*; flagornerie *f.* (*b*) Embarras *mpl.* None of your p.! pas tant d'histoires!

palaver[2], *v.i.* Palabrer.

pale[1] [peil], *s.* **1.** Pieu *m* (de clôture). **2.** *A:* Bornes *fpl*, limites *fpl.* Still so used in Outside the pale of society, beyond the pale, au ban de la société. Within the pale of the Church, dans le giron, dans le sein, de l'Église. **3.** *Her:* Pal *m.* Shield parted per pale, écu mi-parti.

pale[2], *a.* (*a*) Pâle, blême. Deadly pale, ghastly pale, pâle comme la mort, comme un mort; d'une pâleur mortelle. To grow, turn, pale, pâlir. (*b*) (*Of colour*) Pale blue dress, robe d'un bleu pâle; robe bleu clair. By the p. light of the moon, à la lumière blafarde de la lune. **'pale-face,** *s.* Blanc, *f.* blanche (dans le parler des Peaux-Rouges). **'pale-faced,** *a.* Au visage pâle ou blême.

pale[3], *v.i.* (*a*) Pâlir, blêmir. (*b*) *F:* My adventures p. beside yours, before yours, mes aventures pâlissent auprès des vôtres.

paleness [ˈpeilnəs], *s.* Pâleur *f.*

palette [ˈpalet], *s.* *Art:* Palette *f.* To set the palette, faire, charger, sa palette.

palfrey [ˈpɔːlfri], *s.* *Lit:* Palefroi *m.*

palikar [ˈpalikɑːr], *s.* *Gr.Hist:* Palikare *m.*

palimpsest [ˈpalimpsest], *a. & s.* Palimpseste (*m*).

palindrome [ˈpalindroum], *s.* Palindrome *m.*

paling(s) [ˈpeiliŋ(z)], *s.(pl.).* Clôture *f* à claire-voie; palissade *f*, palis *m.*

palinode [ˈpalinoud], *s.* *Lit: etc:* Palinodie *f.*

palisade[1] [paliˈseid], *s.* Palissade *f.*

palisade[2], *v.tr.* Palissader.

palish [ˈpeiliʃ], *a.* Un peu pâle; pâlot, -otte.

pall[1] [pɔːl], *s.* **1.** *Ecc:* Poêle *m*; drap *m* mortuaire. **2.** *F:* Manteau *m* (de neige, etc.); voile *m* (de fumée, etc.). **'pall-bearer,** *s.* Porteur *m* d'un cordon du poêle.

pall[2]. **1.** *v.i.* S'affadir; devenir fade, insipide (*on s.o.*, pour qn). These pleasures p., on se blase de ces plaisirs. Food, literature, that palls, nourriture, littérature, fastidieuse. It never palls on you, on ne s'en dégoûte jamais. **2.** *v.tr.* Blaser, émousser (les sens).

palladium [paˈleidiəm], *s.* *Ch:* Palladium *m.*

pallet [ˈpalet], *s.* (*a*) Paillasse *f.* (*b*) Grabat *m.*

palliasse [ˈpaljas], *s.* Paillasse *f.*

palliate [ˈpalieit], *v.tr.* Pallier; atténuer (un vice). Palliating circumstances, circonstances atténuantes.

palliation [paliˈeiʃ(ə)n], *s.* Palliation *f*; atténuation *f* (d'une faute).

palliative [ˈpaliətiv], *a. & s.* Palliatif (*m*), lénitif (*m*).

pallid [ˈpalid], *a.* (*a*) Pâle, décoloré. (*b*) (*Of light*) Blafard. (*c*) (*Of face*) Blême.

pallor [ˈpalər], *s.* Pâleur *f.*

pally [ˈpali], *a.* *P:* **1.** Qui se lie facilement (d'amitié); liant. **2.** To be p. with s.o., être lié, être copain, avec qn.

palm[1] [pɑːm], *s.* **1.** (*Tree*) Palmier *m.* Dwarf palm, palmette *f.* **2.** (*Branch*) Palme *f.* *Ecc:* Rameau *m.* Palm Sunday, le dimanche des Rameaux. *F:* To bear the palm, remporter la palme. To yield the palm to s.o., céder la palme à qn. **'palm-'cabbage,** *s.* (Chou *m*) palmiste *m.* **'palm-grove,** *s.* Palmeraie *f.* **'palm-house,** *s.* Serre *f* de palmiers. **'palm-oil,** *s.* Huile *f* de palme, de palmier.

palm[2], *s.* **1.** Paume *f* (de la main). *P:* To grease, oil, s.o.'s palm, graisser la patte de, à, qn. **2.** *Nau:* (*a*) Patte, oreille *f* (d'ancre). (*b*) *Tls:* Paumelle *f* (de voilier). **3.** *Ven:* Empaumure *f* (de bois de cerf).

palm[3], *v.tr.* **1.** To palm a card, escamoter une carte; filer la carte. **2.** *P:* Graisser la patte de, à (qn). **palm off,** *v.tr.* Faire passer, *F:* refiler (*sth. on s.o.*, qch. à qn). To p. off a bad coin on s.o., (re)passer une fausse pièce à qn.

palmate [ˈpalmet], *a.* *Nat.Hist:* Palmé.

palmer [ˈpɑːmər], *s.* Pèlerin *m* de retour de la Terre Sainte (en foi de quoi il portait un rameau).

palmetto [palˈmeto], *s.* *Bot:* (*a*) Palmier nain; palmette *f.* (*b*) (Chou *m*) palmiste *m.*

palmiped [ˈpalmiped], *a. & s.* Palmipède (*m*).

palmist [ˈpɑːmist], *s.* Chiromancien, -ienne.

palmistry [ˈpɑːmistri], *s.* Chiromancie *f.*

palmy [ˈpɑːmi], *a.* Palmy days, jours heureux; époque florissante (d'une nation, etc.).

palp [palp], *s.* *Nat.Hist:* Palpe *f.*

palpability [palpəˈbiliti], **palpableness** [ˈpalpəblnəs], *s.* **1.** Palpabilité *f.* **2.** Évidence *f* (d'un fait, etc.).

palpable [ˈpalpəbl], *a.* **1.** Palpable; que l'on peut toucher. **2.** Palpable, *F:* manifeste, clair, évident; (différence) sensible.

palpate [ˈpalpeit], *v.tr.* *Med:* Palper.

palpitate [ˈpalpiteit], *v.tr.* Palpiter.

palpitation [palpiˈteiʃ(ə)n], *s.* Palpitation *f.*

palsied [ˈpɔːlzid], *a.* Paralysé, paralytique.

palsy [ˈpɔːlzi], *s.* *Med:* Paralysie *f.*

palter [ˈpɔːltər], *v.i.* To palter (with s.o.), biaiser (avec qn). To p. with one's honour, transiger sur, avec, l'honneur. **paltering,** *s.* Compromission *f*; faux-fuyants *mpl.*

paltriness [ˈpɔːltrinəs], *s.* Mesquinerie *f* (d'un cadeau, etc.).

paltry [ˈpɔːltri], *a.* Misérable, mesquin. I had lost a p. five-franc piece, j'avais perdu une malheureuse pièce de cinq francs. P. excuses, plates excuses; pauvres excuses.

paludal [pa'lju:d(ə)l, 'paljud(ə)l], *a. Med :* Paludique ; paludéen, -enne.

paludism ['paljudizm], *s. Med :* (Im)paludisme *m.*

pampas ['pampəs], *s.pl.* Pampas *f.pl.* **'pampas-grass,** *s.* Gynérion argenté ; *F :* herbe *f* des pampas.

pamper ['pampər], *v.tr.* Choyer, dorloter, mignoter (un enfant).

pamphlet ['pamflet], *s.* Brochure *f* ; (*literary, scientific*) opuscule *m* ; (*scurrilous*) pamphlet *m.*

pamphleteer [pamfle'ti:ər], *s.* Auteur *m* de brochures ; (*scurrilous*) pamphlétaire *m.*

pan¹ [pan], *s.* **1.** (*a*) *Cu :* Casserole *f,* poêlon *m.* **Frying-pan,** poêle *f.* **Baking-pan,** plat *m* à rôtir. **Pots and pans,** batterie *f* de cuisine. (*b*) *Earthenware pan,* vaisseau *m* de terre. *Art :* **Moist colours in pans,** couleurs moites en godets. **2.** (*a*) (i) Plateau *m,* (ii) bassin *m* (d'une balance). (*b*) Carter *m,* tôle inférieure, cuvette *f* (de moteur, etc.). (*c*) *Hyg :* **Lavatory pan,** cuvette de garde-robe. **3.** *A :* (Priming-)pan, bassinet *m* (d'un fusil). *S.a.* FLASH² I, ³ I. **4.** *Geol :* Cuvette. *S.a.* SALT-PAN. **'pan-loaf,** *s.* Pain cuit au moule ; pain anglais.

pan², *v.* (panned) *Gold-min :* **1.** *v.tr.* To pan (out), laver (le gravier) à la bat(t)ée. **2.** *v.i. F :* **Things did not pan out as he intended,** les choses ne se sont pas passées comme il l'aurait voulu.

Pan³ [pan]. *Pr.n.m. Myth :* (Le dieu) Pan. **Pan's pipes, Pan-pipe,** flûte *f* de Pan.

panacea [panə'si:ə], *s.* Panacée *f* ; remède universel.

Panama [panə'mɑ:]. **1.** *Pr.n. Geog :* Le Panama. **2.** *s.* **Panama (hat),** panama *m.*

pan-American [panə'merikən], *a.* Panaméricain.

pancake¹ ['pankeik], *s.* **1.** *Cu :* Crêpe *f.* **Pancake day,** mardi gras. **2.** *Nau :* **Pancake ice,** gâteaux *mpl* de glace.

pancake², *v.i. Av :* **To pancake (to the ground),** asseoir l'appareil ; descendre à plat ; (se) plaquer.

panchromatic [pankro'matik], *a. Phot :* Panchromatique.

pancreas ['paŋkrias], *s. Anat :* Pancréas *m.*

pancreatic [paŋkri'atik], *a.* Pancréatique.

panda ['pandə], *s. Z :* Panda *m.*

pandemonium [pandi'mounjəm], *s.* Pandémonium *m. F :* **It's p.,** c'est une vraie tour de Babel. **To kick up a fearful pandemonium,** faire un bruit infernal ; faire un bacchanal de tous les diables.

pander ['pandər], *v.tr. & i.* Servir de proxénète à (qn). **To pander to a vice,** encourager, se prêter à, un vice.

Pandora [pan'dɔ:ra]. *Pr.n.f.* Pandore. **Pandora's box,** le coffret de Pandore.

pane [pein], *s.* Vitre *f,* carreau *m* (de fenêtre).

panegyric [pani'dʒirik], *a. & s.* Panégyrique (*m*).

panegyrist [pani'dʒirist], *s.* Panégyriste *m.*

panel¹ ['pan(ə)l], *s.* **1.** (*a*) Panneau *m* (de porte) ; caisson *m* (de plafond). **Sunk panel,** panneau en retrait. *Aut : Av :* **Instrument panel,** tableau *m* de manœuvre, de bord ; planche *f* de bord. (*b*) *Dressm :* Panneau ; (*shaped*) volant *m.* (*c*) *Arch : Civ.E :* Entre-deux *m inv.* **2.** (*a*) *Jur :* (i) Tableau, liste *f,* du jury. (ii) **The panel,** le jury. (*b*) *Adm :* (i) Tableau des médecins désignés pour le service des assurances sociales ; (ii) liste des assurés inscrits sur le rôle d'un certain médecin. (*c*) *Scot :* Commission *f* (d'enquête, etc.). **'panel-doctor,** *s.* Médecin désigné pour le service des assurances sociales. **'panel-patient,** *s.* Malade *mf* figurant sur la liste d'un '*panel-doctor.*'

panel², *v.tr.* (panelled) (*a*) Diviser (un mur, etc.) en panneaux. (*b*) Recouvrir de panneaux ; lambrisser (une paroi) ; plaquer (une surface).

panelled, *a.* Boisé, lambrissé ; revêtu de boiseries. **Oak-panelled,** à panneaux de chêne ; lambrissé de chêne. *P.* **door,** porte à panneaux.

panelling, *s.* **1.** (*a*) Division *f* (d'un mur) en panneaux. (*b*) Lambrissage *m* (d'une salle). **2.** Lambris *m,* boiserie *f.* **Oak panelling,** panneaux *mpl,* lambris *mpl,* de chêne.

pang [paŋ], *s.* Angoisse subite ; douleur *f* ; serrement *m* de cœur. **The pangs of death,** les affres *fpl,* les angoisses, de la mort. **To feel a pang,** sentir une petite pointe au cœur. **To feel the pangs of hunger,** entendre crier ses entrailles.

pan-Germanism [pan'dʒə:rmənizm], *s.* Pangermanisme *m.*

panic¹ ['panik], *a. & s.* **Panic (terror),** (terreur *f*) panique *f* ; affolement *m.* **To throw the crowd into a p.,** affoler la foule. **They fled in a p.,** pris de panique ils s'enfuirent. **'panic-monger,** *s.* Semeur, -euse, de panique ; *F :* paniquard *m.* **'panic-stricken,** *a.* Pris de panique ; affolé.

panic², *v.* (panicked ['panikt]) **1.** *v.tr.* Remplir de panique ; affoler (la foule, etc.). **2.** *v.i.* Être pris de panique ; s'affoler.

panic³(-grass) ['panik(grɑ:s)], *s.* Panic *m* (d'Italie) ; millet *m* des oiseaux.

panicky ['paniki], *a. F :* (*Of pers.*) Sujet à la panique ; (*of newspaper, etc.*) alarmiste. *Don't get p.,* ne vous impressionnez pas.

panicle ['panikl], *s. Bot :* Panicule *f.*

panjandrum [pan'dʒandrəm], *s. F :* Gros bonnet ; grand personnage. *Esp.* **Grand Panjandrum,** grand manitou.

pannier ['panjər], *s.* **1.** (*a*) (*Basket*) Panier *m.* (*b*) Panier de bât (d'une bête de somme). (*c*) Hotte *f* (de vendangeur). **2.** *A.Cost :* **Dress with panniers,** robe à paniers.

pannikin ['panikin], *s.* Écuelle *f* ou gobelet *m* (en fer blanc).

panoply ['panopli], *s.* Panoplie *f.*

panorama [panə'rɑ:mə], *s.* Panorama *m.*

panoramic [panə'ramik], *a.* Panoramique.

pansy ['panzi], *s. Bot :* Pensée *f.*

pant [pant], *v.i.* **1.** (*a*) Panteler ; (*of animal*) battre du flanc ; (*of heart*) palpiter. (*b*) Haleter. **To pant for breath,** chercher à reprendre haleine. **2.** **To pant to do sth.,** désirer ardemment faire qch. **To pant for, after, sth.,** soupirer après qch.

pant out, *v.tr.* Dire (qch.) en haletant.

panting, *s.* (*a*) Essoufflement *m,* halètement *m.* (*b*) Palpitation *f* (du cœur).

pantagruelic [pantagru'elik], *a.* (Repas, etc.) pantagruélique.

Pantaloon [pantə'lu:n], *s.* **1.** *A.Th :* (*Pers.*) Pantalon *m.* **2.** *Cost :* A. *& U.S :* (**Pair of**) pantaloons, pantalon.

pantechnicon [pan'teknikən], *s.* **1.** Garde-meuble *m.* **2.** **Pantechnicon(-van),** voiture *f* de déménagement.

pantheism ['panθiizm], *s.* Panthéisme *m.*

pantheist ['panθiist], *s.* Panthéiste *m.*

pantheistic(al) [panθi'istik(əl)], *a.* Panthéiste.

pantheon [pan'θi:ən, 'panθiən], *s.* Panthéon *m.*

panther ['panθər], *s.* **1.** *Z :* Panthère *f.* **2.** *U.S :* Couguar *m,* puma *m.*

pantile ['pantail], *s.* Tuile flamande, en S ; panne *f.*

pantograph ['pantogrɑ:f, -graf], *s.* **1.** *Draw :*

Pantographe *m*. **2.** *El.E:* Pantographe (de locomotive électrique, etc.).

pantomime ['pæntəmaim], *s. Th:* **1.** *Rom.Ant:* (*Pers.*) Pantomime *m*, mime *m*. **2.** (*a*) (*Dumb show*) Pantomime *f*. (*b*) Revue-féerie *f* à grand spectacle.

pantry ['pæntri], *s.* **1.** Garde-manger *m inv.* **2. Butler's pantry,** office *f*.

pants [pænts], *s.pl. Cost:* F: (Pair of pants, (i) *U.S:* pantalon *m*; (ii) *Com:* caleçon *m*.

pap[1] [pæp], *s.* **1.** *A. & Dial:* Mamelon *m*, tétin *m*, bout *m* de sein. **2.** Mamelon, piz *m*, pis *m* (de montagne).

pap[2], *s.* (*a*) Bouillie *f*. (*b*) Pulpe *f*, pâte *f* (très liquide).

papa [pə'pɑː], *s.m. F:* Papa ; petit père.

papacy ['peipəsi], *s.* **1.** Papauté *f*. **2.** = POPERY.

papal ['peip(ə)l], *a.* Papal, -aux. Papal legate, légat du Pape.

paper[1] ['peipər], *s.* **1.** Papier *m*. (*a*) Note-paper, papier à lettres. Art paper, coated paper, papier couché. Brown paper, papier gris. Cigarette paper, papier à cigarettes. *Phot:* Glossy p., papier brillant. *Soft p.*, papier pour effets doux. Blue-print paper, papier autocopiste. *S.a.* BLOTTING-PAPER, CARBON PAPER, EMERY, *etc.* (*b*) To put sth. down on paper, coucher qch. par écrit. The scheme is a good one on paper, ce projet est excellent en théorie. **Paper profits,** profits fictifs. **2.** (Morceau *m* de) papier. Curl-paper, papillote *f*. Paper of pins, carte *f* d'épingles. **3.** (*a*) Écrit *m*, document *m*, pièce *f*. *My private papers,* "mes papiers." (*Of officer*) To send in one's papers, donner sa démission. Ship's papers, papiers du bord. (*b*) *Com:* Valeurs *fpl*, papier(s). Negotiable paper, papier(s) négociable(s). (*c*) Voting-paper, bulletin *m* de vote. **4.** *Sch:* (Examination-)paper. (*a*) Composition *f* (d'examen); épreuve (écrite). History p., composition en histoire. To set a paper, choisir les sujets de composition. (*b*) *To do a good mathematics p.,* rendre une bonne copie de mathématiques. **5.** Étude *f*, mémoire *m* (sur un sujet scientifique, etc.). To read a paper, (i) faire une communication (à une société savante, etc.); (ii) faire une conférence, un exposé. **6.** Journal *m*, -aux. Weekly paper, hebdomadaire *m*. Fashion paper, journal de modes. To write in the papers, faire du journalisme. **'paper-backed,** *a. Bookb:* Broché. **'paper-chase,** *s. Sp:* Rallye-paper *m*. **'paper-clamp,** *s.* Pince-notes *m inv*, pince-feuilles *m inv*. **'paper-fastener,** *s.* Attache *f* métallique (à tête). **'paper-hanger,** *s.* Colleur *m* de papiers peints. **'paper-hanging,** *s.* Collage *m* de papiers peints. **'paper-knife,** *s.* **1.** Coupe-papier *m inv*; couteau *m* à papier. **2.** *Bookb:* Plioir *m*. **'paper-mill,** *s.* Fabrique *f* de papier; papeterie *f*. **'paper-trade,** *s.* Papeterie *f*. **'paper-weight,** *s.* Presse-papiers *m inv*.

paper[2], *v.tr.* **1.** Tapisser (une chambre). Room papered in blue, pièce tapissée de bleu, tendue de (papier) bleu. **2.** *Th:* P: Remplir (la salle) de billets de faveur.

paperer ['peipərər], *s.* = PAPER-HANGER.

papier mâché [pæpje'mɑːʃe], *s.* Carton-pâte *m*.

papilionaceae [pəpilio'neisiiː], *s.pl. Bot:* Papilionacées *f*.

papilla, *pl.* -ae [pə'pila, -iː], *s. Nat.Hist:* Papille *f*.

papillary [pə'piləri], *a.* Papillaire.

papist ['peipist], *s.* Papiste *mf*.

papistic(al) [pə'pistik(əl)], *a. Pej:* Qui sent le papisme ; papiste.

papistry ['peipistri], *s. Pej:* Papisme *m*.

papoose [pə'puːs], *s.* Enfant *mf* en bas âge (des Indiens de l'Amérique du Nord).

pappus ['pæpəs], *s. Bot:* Pappe *m*, aigrette *f*.

papula, *pl.* -ae ['pæpjula, -iː], *s. Med: Bot:* Papule *f*.

papyraceous [pæpi'reiʃəs], *a.* Papyracé.

papyrus, *pl.* -ri [pə'paiərəs, -rai], *s.* Papyrus *m*.

par[1] [pɑːr], *s.* Pair *m*, égalité *f*. (*a*) To be on a par with s.o., être au niveau de, aller de pair avec, qn. (*b*) *Fin:* Par of exchange, pair du change. Above par, below par, au-dessus, au-dessous, du pair. Exchange at par, change à (la) parité. (*c*) Below par, au-dessous de la moyenne; médiocre. F: To feel below par, n'être pas dans son assiette ; être mal en train.

par[2], *s.* (*Paragraph*) **1.** *Journ:* F: Entrefilet *m*; fait-divers *m*. Par writer, courriériste *m*, échotier *m*. **2.** Paragraphe *m*; alinéa *m*.

parable ['pærəbl], *s.* Parabole *f*. To speak in parables, parler par, en, paraboles.

parabola [pə'ræbolə], *s. Geom:* Parabole *f*.

parabolic(al) [pærə'bɔlik(əl)], *a.* Parabolique.

parachute[1] ['pærəʃuːt], *s. Aer:* Parachute *m*.

parachute[2], *v.i. Av:* To parachute down, descendre en parachute.

parachutist [pærə'ʃuːtist], *s.* Parachutiste *mf*.

parade[1] [pə'reid], *s.* **1.** Parade *f*. To make a parade of one's poverty, faire parade, étalage, de sa pauvreté ; afficher sa pauvreté. **2.** *Mil:* (*a*) Rassemblement *m*. (*b*) Exercice *m*. On parade, à l'exercice. To go on parade, parader. **Parade-ground,** terrain *m* de manœuvres ; place *f* d'armes. **3.** Défilé *m* (de troupes, etc.). **Mannequin parade,** défilé de mannequins. **4.** Esplanade *f*; promenade publique ; boulevard *m* (le long de la plage).

parade[2]. **1.** *v.tr.* (*a*) Faire parade, ostentation, étalage, de (ses richesses, etc.). *To p. one's poverty,* afficher sa pauvreté. (*b*) *Mil:* Faire l'inspection (des troupes) ; faire parader, faire défiler (les troupes). **2.** *v.i.* (*a*) *Mil:* Faire la parade ; parader (pour l'exercice, pour l'inspection). (*b*) To parade (through) the streets, défiler dans les rues.

paradigm ['pærədaim], *s. Gram:* Paradigme *m*.

paradise ['pærədais], *s.* Paradis *m*. **1.** The Earthly Paradise, le Paradis terrestre. An earthly p., un paradis sur terre. **2.** To go to paradise, aller en paradis. F: To live in a fool's paradise, se bercer d'un bonheur illusoire. Bird of paradise, oiseau *m* de paradis.

paradox ['pærədɔks], *s.* Paradoxe *m*.

paradoxical [pærə'dɔksik(ə)l], *a.* Paradoxal, -aux. **-ally,** *adv.* Paradoxalement.

paraffin[1] ['pærafin], **paraffine**[1] [pærə'fiːn], *s.* **1.** *Ch:* Paraffine *f*. *Pharm:* Liquid paraffin, huile *f* de vaseline, de paraffine ; vaseline *f* liquide. **2.** *Com:* F: = PARAFFIN OIL. **paraffin 'lamp,** *s.* Lampe *f* à pétrole. **paraffin 'oil,** *s.* (Huile *f* de) pétrole *m*; pétrole lampant. **paraffin 'wax,** *s.* Paraffine *f* solide.

paraffin(e)[2], *v.tr.* **1.** Paraffiner. **2.** Pétroler (un marais, etc.).

paragon ['pærəgən], *s.* Parangon *m*, modèle *m* (de vertu, etc.).

paragraph[1] ['pærəgrɑːf, -graf], *s.* **1.** Paragraphe *m*, alinéa *m*. To begin a new p., aller à la ligne. *Typ:* Paragraph (mark), pied *m* de mouche. **2.** *Journ:* Entrefilet *m*.

paragraph[2], *v.tr.* **1.** Diviser (une page) en paragraphes, en alinéas. **2.** *Journ:* Much para-

graphed actress, actrice très en vue dans les journaux.
parakeet ['parakiːt], s. Orn: Perruche f.
parallactic [para'laktik], a. Astr: Parallactique.
parallax ['paralaks], s. Astr: Parallaxe f.
parallel¹ ['paralel]. I. a. Parallèle (with, to, à).
I. In a p. direction with sth., parallèlement à qch. El: Parallel connection, accouplement m parallèle. Cells in parallel, piles en parallèle, en quantité, en dérivation. S.a. FLOW¹ I. **2.** Pareil, semblable; (cas) analogue (to, with, à). II. **parallel**, s. I. (a) (Ligne f) parallèle f. (b) Geog: Parallèle m (de latitude). **2.** Parallèle m, comparaison f. To draw a parallel between two things, établir un parallèle entre deux choses. Wickedness without parallel, méchanceté sans pareille. **3.** El.E: Dynamos out of parallel, dynamos déphasées, hors de phase.
parallel², v.tr. (paralleled) I. Mettre (deux choses) en parallèle. **2.** Égaler (qch.); être égal, pareil, à (qch.). **3.** El.E: Synchroniser (deux dynamos, etc.).
parallelepiped [parale'lepiped], s. Geom: Parallélépipède m.
parallelism ['paralelizm], s. Parallélisme m.
parallelogram [para'lelogram], s. Parallélogramme m.
paralogism [pa'ralodʒizm], s. Log: Paralogisme m.
paralyse ['paralaiz], v.tr. Paralyser. Paralysed in one leg, paralysé d'une jambe. F: Paralysed with fear, transi de peur; médusé. **paralysing**, a. Paralysant; paralysateur, -trice.
paralysis [pa'ralisis], s. Paralysie f. Creeping paralysis, paralysie progressive.
paralytic [para'litik], a. I. a. Paralytique. To have a p. stroke, tomber en paralysie. **2.** s. Paralytique mf.
parameter [pa'ramitər], s. Mth: Paramètre m.
paramount ['paramaunt], a. I. Éminent, souverain. Lord paramount, suzerain m. **2.** Of p. importance, d'une suprême importance. Duty is paramount (to everything) with him, chez lui le devoir l'emporte (sur tout).
paramour ['paramuər], s. (i) Amant m; (ii) maîtresse f, Lit: amante f.
parapet ['parapet], s. (a) Fort: Parapet m; berge f (de tranchée). (b) Civ.E: Parapet; garde-fou m, garde-corps m inv (d'un pont, etc.)
paraph ['paraf], s. Paraphe m, parafe m.
paraphernalia [parafər'neiljə], s.pl. F: (a) Effets m; affaires f. All the p., tout le bataclan. (b) Falbalas m (de toilette). (c) Attirail m, appareil m (de pêche, etc.).
paraphrase¹ ['parafreiz], s. Paraphrase f.
paraphrase², v.tr. Paraphraser.
paraphrastic [para'frastik], a. Paraphrastique.
paraplegia [para'pliːdʒiə], s. Med: Paraplégie f.
parasite ['parasait], s. Parasite m; (of pers.) écornifleur, -euse; pique-assiette m inv.
parasitic [para'sitik], a. (Of insect, etc.) Parasite (on, de). P. disease, maladie parasitaire.
parasitism ['parasaitizm], s. Parasitisme m.
parasol [para'sɔl], s. Ombrelle f, parasol m.
paratyphoid [para'taifɔid], s. Med: Paratyphoïde f.
paravane ['paravein], s. Navy: Paravane m; pare-mines m inv.
parboil ['paːrbɔil], v.tr. Cu: Faire cuire à demi (dans l'eau); faire bouillir à demi; étourdir (la viande).
Parcae (the) [ðə'paːrsiː]. Pr.n.f.pl. Myth: Les Parques.

parcel¹ ['paːrs(ə)l], s. I. (a) A: Partie f. S.a. PART¹ I. I. (b) Morceau m, parcelle f (de terrain). (c) St.Exch: etc: Parcel of shares, paquet m d'actions. P. of goods, (i) lot m, (ii) envoi m, de marchandises. Pej: Parcel of lies, tas m de mensonges. **2.** Paquet, colis m. Parcels office, bureau m de(s) messageries. **'parcel(s) de'livery**, s. Service m de messageries; remise f de colis à domicile. **'parcel-'gilt**, a. Doré à l'intérieur. Limander (un cordage). **'parcel 'post**, s. Service m des colis postaux; service de messageries. To send sth. by parcel post, envoyer qch. comme, par, colis postal.
parcel², v.tr. (parcelled) I. (a) To parcel (out), parceller, partager (un héritage); morceler (into, en); lotir (des terres, etc.). (b) Empaqueter (du thé, etc.). To parcel up a consignment of books, mettre en paquets, emballer, un envoi de livres. **2.** Nau: Limander (un cordage).
parch [paːrtʃ]. I. v.tr. (a) Rôtir, griller, sécher (des céréales). (b) F: (Of fever) Brûler (qn). Grass parched (up) by the wind, herbe desséchée par le vent. To be parched with thirst, avoir une soif ardente, dévorante. **2.** v.i. Se dessécher.
parchment ['paːrtʃmənt], s. (a) Parchemin m. (b) Parchment paper, vegetable parchment, papier parchemin; papier parcheminé.
pard [paːrd], s. A. & Poet: Léopard m.
pardon¹ ['paːrd(ə)n], s. I. Pardon m. I beg your pardon! je vous demande pardon! I beg your pardon? plaît-il? pardon? **2.** Ecc: Indulgence f. **3.** Jur: (a) Free pardon, grâce f. To receive the King's pardon, être gracié. General pardon, amnistie f. (b) Lettre f de grâce.
pardon², v.tr. I. Pardonner (une faute, etc.). P. my contradicting you, pardonnez(-moi) si je vous contredis. **2.** (a) To p. s.o., pardonner à qn. Pardon me! faites excuse! (b) To pardon s.o. sth., pardonner qch. à qn. **3.** Jur: Faire grâce à (qn); gracier, amnistier.
pardonable ['paːrdənəbl], a. I. Pardonnable, excusable. **2.** Graciable.
pare [peər], v.tr. Rogner (ses ongles, etc.); ébarber (la tranche d'un livre). Leath: Doler (les peaux). Farr: Parer (le sabot d'un cheval). **2.** Éplucher; peler (un fruit). **pare down**, v.tr. Rogner (ses ongles, F: les dépenses); amenuiser (un bâton). **paring**, s. I. (a) Rognage m, rognement m; ébarbage m (d'un livre). Leath: Dolage m (des peaux). (b) Épluchage m. **2.** Usu.pl. (a) Rognures f, Parings of metal, cisaille f. (b) Épluchures f, pelures f (de légumes, etc.). **'paring-knife**, s. Rognoir m. Bootm: Tranchet m. Farr: Rogne-pied m inv.
paregoric [pari'gɔrik], a. & s. Parégorique (m).
parent ['peərənt], s. I. Père m, mère f; pl. parents m, les père et mère. Parents and relations, les ascendants directs et les collatéraux. **2.** Parent rock, roche mère. Parent state (of colonies), mère patrie; métropole f. Com: Parent establishment, maison mère.
parentage ['peərəntedʒ], s. Parentage m, naissance f. Born of humble p., né de parents humbles.
parental [pa'rent(ə)l], a. (Autorité, etc.) des parents, des père et mère; (pouvoir) paternel.
parenthesis, pl. **-theses** [pa'renθesis, -θesiːz], s. Parenthèse f. In parentheses, entre parenthèses.
parenthetic(al) [paren'θetik(əl), a. I. Entre parenthèses. **2.** Gram: Parenthetical clause, incidente f. **-ally**, adv. Par parenthèse.
parget¹ ['paːrdʒet], s. Const: I. Plâtre m. **2.** Crépi m, crépissure f.
parget², v.tr. I. Recouvrir (un mur) d'une couche de plâtre. **2.** Crépir. **pargeting**, s. I. (a) Plâ-

trage m. (b) Crépissage m. **2.** (a) Plâtres mpl.
(b) Crépi m, crépissure f.
parhelion, pl. **-ia** [pɑ:r'hi:liən, -ia], s. Par(h)é-
lie m; faux soleil.
pariah ['pɛəria, 'paria], s. Paria m. **'pariah-
dog,** s. Chien métis des Indes; chien pariah.
parietal [pa'raiət(ə)l], a. Pariétal, -aux.
pari passu [pɛərai'pasju:]. Lt.phr. To go pari
passu with . . ., marcher de pair avec. . . .
Paris ['paris]. Pr.n. Geog: Paris m. Com: Paris
white, blanc m de Paris.
parish ['pariʃ], s. (a) Ecc: Paroisse f. Parish
church, église paroissiale. (b) Civil parish, commune f. Parish Council = conseil municipal.
Parish school, école communale. Parish boy,
enfant trouvé, enfant assisté. F: To come go,
on the parish, tomber à la charge de la commune.
parishioner [pa'riʃənər], s. (a) Paroissien,
-ienne. (b) Habitant, -ante, de la commune.
Parisian [pa'rizjən, -iʒ-], a. & s. Parisien,
-ienne.
parisyllabic [parisi'labik], a. Parisyllabe; pari-
syllabique.
parity ['pariti], s. **I.** (a) Égalité f (de rang, etc.);
parité f. (b) P. of reasoning, raisonnement m
analogue; analogie f de raisonnement. **2.** Exchange at parity, change à (la) parité; change
au pair.
park[1] [pɑ:rk], s. **I.** (a) Parc (clôturé). Deer-park,
chasse gardée pour le cerf. (b) Public park,
jardin public; parc. **2.** Car park, parc de
stationnement. Mil: Artillery-park, parc d'artillerie.
park[2], v.tr. **I.** (a) Enfermer (des moutons) dans
un parc. (b) Mettre (de l'artillerie) en parc.
2. (a) Parquer, garer (une auto). (b) Abs. Aut:
Stationner. **parking,** s. Parcage m. Aut: 'No
parking here,' "défense de stationner"; "stationnement interdit." Parking attendant, gardien m
d'autos. Parking lights, feux m de position.
parlance ['pɑ:rləns], s. Langage m, parler m.
In common parlance, en langage ordinaire. In
legal parlance, en termes de pratique.
parley[1] ['pɑ:rli], s. Conférence f. Mil: Pourparlers mpl (avec l'ennemi). To hold a parley,
parlementer (with, avec).
parley[2], v.i. Être ou entrer en pourparlers;
parlementer; entamer des négociations (avec
l'ennemi).
parliament [pɑ:rləmənt], s. Le Parlement; (in
Fr.) les Chambres f. The Houses of Parliament,
le palais du Parlement. In parliament, au
parlement.
parliamentarian [pɑ:rləmen'tɛəriən]. **I.** s. Parlementaire m; membre m du Parlement.
2. a. Parlementaire.
parliamentary [pɑ:rlə'mentəri], a. Parlementaire. Parliamentary election, élection législative.
P. eloquence, éloquence de la tribune.
parlour ['pɑ:rlər], s. Petit salon; parloir m (d'un
couvent, etc.). Bar parlour, arrière-salle f de la
taverne. Parlour games, petits jeux de salon, de
société. F: Parlour tricks, (i) arts m d'agrément;
(ii) talents m de société. **'parlour-maid,** s.f.
Bonne (affectée au service de table).
parlous ['pɑ:rləs], a. Lit: Périlleux, précaire.
The p. state of the finances, l'état alarmant des
finances.
Parmesan [pɑ:rmi'zan], s. Parmesan (cheese),
parmesan.
Parnassian [pɑ:r'nasiən], a. & s. Parnassien,
-ienne.
Parnassus [pɑ:r'nasəs]. Pr.n. Le Parnasse.
parochial [pa'roukjəl], a. (a) Ecc: Paroissial,

-aux. The p. hall, la salle d'œuvres de la paroisse.
(b) (Of civil parish) Communal, -aux. F: Parochial spirit, esprit de clocher.
parochialism [pa'roukjəlizm], s. Esprit m de
clocher.
parodist ['parodist], s. Parodiste m.
parody[1] ['parodi], s. Parodie f, pastiche m.
parody[2], v.tr. Parodier, pasticher.
parole [pa'roul], s. Esp.Mil: Parole f (d'honneur). Prisoner on parole, prisonnier sur parole.
To be put on parole, être libéré sur parole. To
break one's parole, manquer à sa parole.
parotid [pa'rɔtid], a. & s. Anat: (Glande f)
parotide.
paroxysm ['paroksizm], s. (a) Med: Paroxysme m
(d'une fièvre). (b) F: Crise f (de fou rire, de
larmes); accès m (de fureur). P. of toothache,
rage f de dents.
parpen ['pɑ:rpen], s. Const: Parpaing m. Parpen
wall, mur de parpaing.
parquet [pɑ:rke], s. Parquet (floor), parquet m
(en parquetage). Parquet flooring, parquetage m.
parquetry ['pɑ:rketri], s. Parquetage m, parqueterie f.
par(r) [pɑ:r], s. Ich: Saumoneau m.
parral, parrel ['parəl], s. Nau: Racage m.
parricidal [pari'said(ə)l], a. Parricide.
parricide[1] ['parisaid], s. (Pers.) Parricide mf.
parricide[2], s. (Crime m de) parricide m.
parrot ['parɔt], s. Orn: Perroquet m. Hen-
parrot, perruche f. **'parrot disease,** s. Med:
Psittacose f.
parry[1] ['pari], s. Fenc: Box: Parade f.
parry[2], v.tr. (a) Parer, détourner (un coup);
F: tourner, éviter (une difficulté); parer (une
question). (b) Abs. To p. with the riposte, riposter
du tac au tac.
parse [pɑ:rz], v.tr. Faire l'analyse (grammaticale)
(d'un mot). **parsing,** s. Analyse grammaticale.
Parsee [pɑ:r'si:], a. & s. Parsi, -ie.
parsimonious [pɑ:rsi'mounjəs], a. Parcimonieux. (a) Économe, F: regardant. (b) Pej:
Pingre. **-ly,** adv. Parcimonieusement.
parsimony ['pɑ:rsimoni], s. Parcimonie f.
(a) Épargne f. (b) Pej: Pingrerie f.
parsley ['pɑ:rsli], s. Bot: Persil m.
parsnip ['pɑ:rsnip], s. Panais m.
parson ['pɑ:rsɔn], s. Ecc: **I.** Titulaire m d'un
bénéfice. **2.** F: Prêtre m ou pasteur m. F: Parson's week, congé m de treize jours. S.a. NOSE[1] I.
parsonage ['pɑ:rsənedʒ], s. Presbytère m, cure f.
part[1] [pɑ:rt]. I. s. **I.** Partie f. (a) P. of the paper
is damaged, une partie du papier est avariée.
Good in parts, bon en partie. F: The funny
part (about it) is that . . . le comique de
l'histoire, ce qu'il y a de comique, c'est que. . . .
The greater part of the inhabitants, la plus grande
partie, la plupart, des habitants. To be, form,
part of sth., faire partie de qch. It is part and
parcel of . . ., c'est une partie intégrante, essentielle, de. . . . It is no part of my intentions
to . . . il n'entre pas dans mes intentions
de. . . . In (a) great part due to . . ., dû en
grande partie à. . . . To pay in part, payer
partiellement. S.a. MOST I. Ten parts of water
to one of milk, dix parties d'eau pour une partie
de lait. Results accurate to one p. in ten million,
résultats justes à un dix-millionième près.
F: Three parts drun.., aux trois quarts ivre.
(b) Ind: Pièce f, organe m. Machine part,
élément m de machine. Spare parts, pièces de
rechange. (c) Gram: Parts of speech, parties du
discours. Principal parts (of a verb), temps

principaux. (d) Fascicule m, livraison f (d'une œuvre littéraire). **2.** Part f. (a) To take (a) part in sth., prendre part à, participer à, qch. *To take p. in the conversation,* se mêler à la conversation. **To have neither part nor lot in sth.,** n'avoir aucune part dans (une affaire, etc.). *I had no p. in it,* je n'y suis pour rien. *Each one did his p.,* chacun s'acquitta de la tâche qui lui incombait. (b) *Th:* Rôle m, personnage m. *Small parts,* utilités f. *To play heroes' parts,* jouer les héros. *F:* He is **playing a part,** il joue la comédie ; c'est une comédie qu'il nous fait. **To play one's part,** remplir son rôle. *In all this imagination plays a large p.,* dans tout ceci l'imagination entre pour beaucoup. **It is not my part** *to speak about it,* ce n'est pas à moi d'en parler. **It is the part of prudence to . . .,** c'est agir avec sagesse que de. . . . (c) *Orchestral parts,* parties d'orchestre. **To sing in parts,** chanter à plusieurs parties, à plusieurs voix. **3.** (a) pl. **You don't belong to these parts?** vous n'êtes pas de ces parages ? vous n'êtes pas de ce pays ? (b) **On the one part . . .,** on the **other part . . .,** d'un côté . . ., de l'autre . . . ; d'une part . . ., d'autre part. . . . (c) **To take s.o.'s part,** prendre le parti de qn ; *F:* prendre fait et cause pour qn. (d) *An indiscretion on the* **part of . . .,** une indiscrétion de la part de. . . . **For my part . . .,** quant à moi, pour ma part. . . . **4. To take sth.** in good part, prendre qch. en bonne part, du bon côté. **5.** pl. **Man of (good) parts,** homme de valeur, de talent ; homme bien doué. **II. part,** adv. **P.** *eaten,* partiellement mangé ; mangé en partie. *Material p.* silk p. cotton, étoffe mi-soie et mi-coton. **Part one and part the other,** moitié l'un moitié l'autre. **'part-'owner,** s. Copropriétaire mf. **'part-song,** s. Chant m à plusieurs parties, à plusieurs voix. **'part-time,** s. & attrib.a. (Emploi) pour une partie de la journée. **To be on part-time,** être en chômage partiel. **part². I.** v.tr. (a) Séparer en deux ; fendre (la foule). **To part one's hair,** se faire une raie. *Her* Shield parted per pale, écu mi-parti. (b) Séparer (*from,* de). (c) Rompre (une amarre, etc.). *Nau:* To part one's cable, casser sa chaîne. **2.** v.i. (a) (*Of crowd, etc.*) Se diviser ; se ranger de part et d'autre. (b) (*Of two pers.*) Se quitter, se séparer ; (*of roads*) diverger. *Prov:* **The best of friends must part,** il n'y a si bonne compagnie qui ne se sépare. (c) (*Of cable, etc.*) (Se) rompre ; partir, céder. **part with,** v.i. Céder (qch.) ; se dessaisir, se départir de (qch.). *Jur:* Aliéner (un bien). *F:* He hates to part with his money, il n'aime pas à débourser ; il est dur à la détente. **parting¹,** a. **I.** Parting line, ligne de séparation. **2.** *A:* Partant. *Poet:* **The parting day,** le jour qui tombe. **parting²,** s. **I.** (a) Séparation f ; (*of waters*) partage m. *F:* **To be at the parting of the ways,** être au carrefour. (b) Départ m. Parting kiss, baiser d'adieu. *A few p. directions,* quelques dernières recommandations. **2.** Rupture f (d'un câble, etc.). **3.** (*Of the hair*) Raie f ; (*of horse's mane*) épi m. **partake** [pɑːrˈteik], v.i. (partook [pɑːrˈtuk] ; partaken) (a) To partake in, of, sth., prendre part, participer, à qch. *To p. of a meal,* (i) partager le repas de qn ; (ii) prendre un repas. *To p. of a dish,* goûter, manger, un mets. *Ecc:* **To partake of the Sacrament,** s'approcher des sacrements. (b) *Language that partakes of boastfulness,* langage qui participe, qui tient, de la jactance. **Parthian** [ˈpɑːrθiən], a. & s. *A.Geog:* Parthe (mf). *F:* **A Parthian shaft,** la flèche du Parthe. **partial** [ˈpɑːrʃ(ə)l], a. **I.** (a) (*Of judge*) Partial,

-aux ; injuste. (b) *F:* **To be partial to sth.,** avoir un faible, une prédilection, pour qch. *I am p. to a pipe after dinner,* je fume volontiers une pipe après dîner. **2.** Partiel ; en partie. *P.* board, demi-pension f. **-ally,** adv. **I.** Partiellement ; avec partialité. **2.** Partiellement ; en partie. **partiality** [pɑːrʃiˈaliti], s. **I.** Partialité f (*for, to,* pour, envers) ; injustice f. **2.** **To have a partiality for sth.,** marquer de la prédilection pour qch. *A p. for the bottle,* un penchant pour la boisson. **participant** [pɑːrˈtisipənt], a. & s. Participant, -ante (*in,* à). **participate** [pɑːrˈtisipeit], v.i. (a) To participate in sth., prendre part, participer, s'associer, à qch. (b) (*Of thg*) Participer, tenir (*of sth.,* de qch.). **participation** [pɑːrtisiˈpeiʃ(ə)n], s. Participation f (*in,* à). **participator** [pɑːrˈtisipeitər], s. Participant, -ante (*in,* de). **participial** [pɑːrtiˈsipiəl], a. *Gram:* Participial -aux. **participle** [ˈpɑːrtisipl], s. *Gram:* Participe m. **particle** [ˈpɑːrtikl], s. **I.** Particule f, parcelle f (de sable, etc.) ; paillette f (de métal). *F:* **There is not a particle of truth in this story,** il n'y a pas l'ombre de vérité dans ce récit. *Not a p. of evidence,* pas la moindre preuve, pas un semblant de preuve. **2.** *Gram:* Particule. **parti-coloured** [ˈpɑːrtikʌlərd], a. **I.** Mi-parti. **2.** Bigarré, bariolé, panaché. **particular** [pərˈtikjulər]. **I.** a. **I.** Particulier ; spécial, -aux. *A p.* object, un objet déterminé. *Our p. wrongs,* les torts dont nous avons à nous plaindre personnellement. **To take particular care over sth.,** faire qch. avec un soin particulier. **For no particular reason,** sans raison précise, sans raison bien définie. **In particular,** en particulier ; notamment, nommément. **2.** (*Of account, etc.*) Détaillé, circonstancié. **3.** (*Of pers.*) Méticuleux, minutieux ; pointilleux, vétilleux. **To be particular about one's food,** être difficile, exigeant, sur la nourriture. *To be p. about one's dress,* soigner sa mise. *P. on points of honour,* délicat sur le point d'honneur. *Don't be too p.,* ne vous montrez pas trop exigeant. **He is not particular to a few pounds,** il n'y regarde pas à quelques livres. **4.** *F:* I am not particular about it, je n'y tiens pas plus que ça. **-ly,** adv. Particulièrement. *Notice p. that . . .,* notez en particulier que. . . . *I want you to do this (most) particularly for to-morrow,* il me le faut absolument pour demain. *I p. asked him to be careful,* je lui priai instamment de faire attention. **II. particular,** s. Détail m, particularité f. *Alike in every particular,* semblables en tout point. **To give particulars of sth.,** donner les détails de qch. **For further particulars apply to . . .,** pour plus amples renseignements s'adresser à. . . . *Cust: etc:* Particulars of a car, signalement m d'une voiture. **particularity** [pərtikjuˈlariti], s. **I.** Particularité f. **2.** Méticulosité f ; minutie f (d'une description). **particularize** [pərˈtikjulərɑːiz], v.tr. (a) Particulariser, spécifier. (b) *Abs.* Entrer dans les détails ; préciser. **partisan¹** [ˈpɑːrtizan, pɑːrtiˈzan], s. Partisan m. **To act in a partisan spirit,** faire preuve (i) d'esprit de parti, (ii) de parti pris. **partisan²** [ˈpɑːrtizan], s. *Archeol:* Pertuisane f. **partisanship** [pɑːrtiˈzanʃip], s. Partialité f ; esprit m de parti. **partition¹** [pɑːrˈtiʃ(ə)n], s. **I.** Partage m (d'un pays) ; morcellement m (d'une terre). *Hist:* The

partition of Poland, le partage de la Pologne.
2. (a) Cloison f, cloisonnage m; entre-deux m inv.
Internal partition, mur m de refend. Wooden p.,
pan m de bois. Glass partition, vitrage m.
(b) Compartiment m (de cale, etc.).
partition², v.tr. **1.** Morceler (un domaine);
partager, démembrer (un pays vaincu). **2.** To
partition (off) a room, cloisonner une pièce.
partitive ['pɑːrtitiv], a. & s. Gram: Partitif (m).
partly ['pɑːrtli], adv. Partiellement; en partie.
P. by force p. by persuasion, moitié de force moitié
par persuasion.
partner¹ ['pɑːrtnər], s. (a) Associé, -ée. Partner
in life, époux ou épouse; conjoint ou conjointe.
Com: Senior partner associé principal. Sleeping
partner, (associé) commanditaire m. (b) Games:
Partenaire mf. (c) Danc: (Woman's p.) Cavalier m.
(Man's p.) Dame f. My partner, mon danseur,
ma danseuse.
partner², v.tr. **1.** (a) Être associé, s'associer, à
(qn). (b) Games: Être le partenaire de (qn).
(c) Danc: Mener (une dame). **2.** To partner s.o.
with s.o., donner qn à qn comme associé, comme
partenaire, comme cavalier ou comme danseuse.
partnership ['pɑːrtnərʃip], s. **1.** (a) P. in crime,
association f dans le crime. (b) Com: To enter,
go, into partnership with s.o., entrer en association avec qn; s'associer avec qn. To take s.o.
into partnership, prendre qn comme associé. To
give s.o. a p. in the business, intéresser qn dans son
commerce. **2.** Com: Ind: Société f. General
partnership, société en nom collectif. Limited
partnership, (société en) commandite f.
partridge ['pɑːrtridʒ], s. (a) Perdrix f. Young p.,
partridge poult, perdreau m. (b) Cu: Perdreau.
parturition [pɑːrtjuˈriʃ(ə)n], s. Parturition f.
party ['pɑːrti], s. **1.** Political parties, partis m
politiques. The Labour p., le parti travailliste.
Party warfare, guerre f de partis. **2.** (a) Pleasure
party, partie f de plaisir. Will you join our p.?
voulez-vous être des nôtres? We are a small
party, nous sommes peu nombreux. I was one
of the party, j'étais de la partie. (b) Private party,
réunion f intime; réception f. Evening party,
soirée f. To give a party, recevoir du monde. To
go to a p., aller en soirée. Party dress, toilette f de
soirée. **3.** (a) Bande f, groupe m (de voyageurs,
etc.). (b) Brigade f, équipe f (de mineurs, etc.);
atelier m (d'ouvriers). Rescue party, équipe de
secours. (c) Mil: Détachement m. The advance
party, les éléments m d'avant-garde. Firing party,
peloton m d'exécution. **4.** (a) Jur: Party to a
dispute, partie f. To be p. to a suit, être en cause.
(b) Com: To become a party to an agreement,
signer (à) un contrat. A third party, un tiers,
une tierce personne. Third-party insurance,
assurance f au tiers. (c) To be (a) party to a crime,
être complice d'un crime; tremper dans un
crime. To be no p. to sth., ne pas s'associer à qch.;
n'être pour rien dans qch. (d) P: A p. of the
name of Jones, un individu du nom de Jones.
'party line, s. Tp: Ligne f à postes groupées.
'party-'spirit, s. Esprit m de parti. **'party-
'wall,** s. Mur mitoyen.
parvis ['pɑːrvis], s. Parvis m (d'une cathédrale).
paschal ['pɑːsk(ə)l], a. Pascal, -aux.
pasha ['pɑːʃa, paˈʃɑː], s. Pacha m.
pasque-flower ['pɑːskflauər], s. (Anémone f)
pulsatille f; fleur f de Pâques; coquelourde f;
passe-fleur f.
pass¹ [pɑːs], s. **1.** Col m, défilé m (de montagne).
F: To hold the pass, tenir la clef d'une position.
To sell the pass, trahir son pays ou son parti.
2. Nau: Passe f (entre des hauts-fonds).

pass², s. **1.** (a) A. & Lit: To come to pass,
arriver, avoir lieu. S.a. BRING. (b) Things have
come to a pretty pass, les choses sont dans un
bel état. **2.** Sch: To obtain a pass, passer tout
juste. Pass-mark, moyenne f. **3.** (a) Passe f (de
prestidigitateur). (b) Fenc: Passe, botte f.
4. Passe, permission f. (Free) pass, (i) Rail:
titre m, carte f, de circulation; (ii) Th: billet m
de faveur. Police pass, coupe-file m inv. **5.** Fb:
Passe. **'pass-book,** s. Carnet m de banque.
'pass-key, s. (Clef f) passe-partout m inv.
pass³, v. (p.p. (in compound tenses) passed, (as adj.)
past [pɑːst]) I. v.i. Passer. **1.** (a) To pass into
a room, entrer dans une salle. Words passed
between them, il y eut un échange d'injures.
Mil: Pass friend! avance à l'ordre! (b) The
procession passed (by) slowly, le cortège défila
lentement. Everyone smiles as he passes, chacun
sourit à son passage. To let s.o. pass, livrer
passage à qn. Let it pass! passe pour cela!
Be it said in passing, (ceci) soit dit en passant.
2. (Of time) To pass (by), (se) passer, s'écouler.
When five minutes had passed, au bout de cinq
minutes. How time passes! comme le temps passe
vite! **3.** To pass (away), disparaître; (of clouds)
se dissiper. To p. into nothingness, rentrer dans
le néant. **4.** Arriver, avoir lieu. What was passing,
ce qui se passait, avait lieu. **5.** (a) Coin that
passes in England, pièce qui a cours en Angleterre.
That won't pass! (i) c'est inacceptable! (ii) ça ne
prend pas! (b) She passes for a great beauty, elle
passe pour une beauté. **6.** Jur: (Of verdict) Être
prononcé (for, en faveur de). II. pass, v.tr.
1. (a) Passer devant, près de (la fenêtre). To p.
s.o. on the stairs, croiser qn dans l'escalier.
(b) Rail: To pass a station, ne pas s'arrêter à une
station; F: brûler une station. (c) (Of company)
To pass a dividend, conclure un exercice sans
payer de dividende. (Cp. II. 2 (a).) (d) Passer,
franchir (la frontière). (e) Dépasser (le but);
outrepasser (les bornes de qch.). That passes my
comprehension, cela me dépasse. (f) Surpasser
(qn); gagner (qn) de vitesse; dépasser, rattraper
(qn). Sp: Devancer (un concurrent). (g) To p.
a test, subir une épreuve avec succès. (h) To pass
an examination, passer un examen; réussir à un
examen. (i) Abs. If the bill passes, si le projet
de loi est voté. (j) To pass the censor, être
accepté par la censure. **2.** Approuver. (a) Adm:
To p. an item of expenditure, allouer une dépense.
(Of company) To pass a dividend of 5%, approuver
un dividende de 5%. (Cp. II. 1 (c).) (b) Sch: To
pass a candidate, recevoir un candidat. (c) Parl:
To pass a bill, voter, adopter, un projet de loi.
3. (a) Transmettre, donner. To p. sth. from hand
to hand, passer qch. de main en main. Fb: To
pass the ball, abs. to pass, passer le ballon; faire
une passe. (b) (Faire) passer, écouler (un faux
billet de banque). **4.** To p. one's hand between
the bars, glisser, passer, sa main à travers les
barreaux. To p. a sponge over sth., passer l'éponge
sur qch. **5.** Mil: To pass troops in review,
passer les troupes en revue. **6.** To pass the
spring abroad, passer le printemps à l'étranger.
To pass (away) the time, passer le temps.
7. (a) Jur: To pass sentence, prononcer le
jugement. (b) F: To pass remarks on sth., faire
des remarques sur qch. S.a. TIME¹ 6. **8.** Abs.
Cards: etc: To pass (son tour). (At dominoes)
Bouder. **pass across,** v.i. Traverser (la rue).
pass along. 1. v.i. (a) Passer par (la rue).
Rail: Pass along the car! dégagez la portière!
(b) Pass along! (i) circulez! (ii) passez votre
chemin! **2.** v.tr. Faire passer (qch.) de main en

main. **pass away. I.** *v.i.* (*a*) *See* PASS³ I. 3.
(*b*) Trépasser. *He passed away in the night*, il est
mort pendant la nuit. **2.** *v.tr. See* PASS³ II. 6.
passing away, *s.* Mort *f*, trépas *m.* **pass
down,** *v.i.* Passer par, descendre (la rue). Pass
down the car! dégagez la portière! **pass off.**
I. *v.i.* (*a*) (*Of pain*) Se passer; disparaître.
(*b*) *Everything passed off smoothly*, tout s'est bien
passé. **2.** *v.tr.* (*a*) *To pass sth. off on s.o.*,
repasser qch. à qn. (*b*) *To pass oneself off for
an artist*, se faire passer pour artiste. (*c*) *To pass
sth. off as a joke*, (i) prendre qch. en riant;
(ii) dire que cela a été fait pour rire. **pass on.**
I. *v.i.* Passer son chemin; passer outre. *To p.
on to a new subject*, passer à un nouveau sujet.
2. *v.tr. Read this and p. it on*, lisez ceci et faites
circuler. **passing on,** *s.* Transmission *f* (d'un
ordre). **pass out,** *v.i.* **I.** Sortir (d'une salle).
2. (*a*) *U.S: F:* S'évanouir; se trouver mal. (*b*) *F:*
Mourir. **3.** *v.tr. To p. sth. out of the window*, sortir
qch. par la fenêtre. **pass-'out check,** *s.* *Th:*
Contremarque *f* de sortie. **pass over.** I. *v.i.*
I. (*a*) *To p. over a river*, traverser, franchir, une
rivière. (*b*) Passer (qch.) sous silence. *P. over
the details*, vous pouvez omettre les détails.
2. (*a*) *To pass over to the enemy*, passer à
l'ennemi. (*b*) (*Of storm*) Se dissiper, finir.
II. **pass over,** *v.tr.* **I.** Donner, transmettre
(qch. à qn). **2.** *To pass s.o. over* (*in making a
promotion*), passer par-dessus le dos à qn; faire
un passe-droit. **pass round. I.** *v.i.* (*a*) Contourner (un obstacle). (*b*) *The bottle passes round*,
la bouteille circule de main en main. **2.** *v.tr. To
p. round the wine*, faire circuler le vin. *S.a.* HAT.
pass through, *v.i.* **I.** *To p. through a country*,
traverser un pays. *To p. through a portal*,
franchir un portail. **2.** *To p. through a crisis*,
traverser une crise. **passing¹. I.** *a.* (*a*) (*Of pers.*)
Passant. *A p. cyclist*, un cycliste qui passait
par là. *Passing events*, actualités *f.* *P. remark*,
remarque en passant. (*b*) Passager, éphémère.
The p. hour, l'heure fugitive. **2.** *adv.* Extrêmement, fort (riche). *Passing fair*, de toute beauté.
passing², *s.* **I.** (*a*) Passage *m* (d'un train).
(*b*) Dépassement *m*, doublement *m* (d'une autre
voiture). **2.** (*a*) Écoulement *m* (du temps).
(*b*) Mort *f*, trépas *m.* **'passing-bell,** *s.* Glas *m.*
'passing-note, *s. Mus:* Note *f* de passage.
passable ['pɑːsəbl], *a.* **I.** (Rivière) traversable;
(route) praticable. *P. by vehicles*, carrossable.
2. Passable; assez bon. **-ably,** *adv.* Passablement, assez.
passage ['pæsedʒ], *s.* **I.** Passage *m. P. of birds*,
passe *f* d'oiseaux. **Bird of passage**, oiseau
passager. *Nau:* **To have a bad passage**, faire
une mauvaise traversée. **To work one's passage**,
gagner son passage. **2.** (*a*) Couloir *m*, corridor *m.*
(*b*) Passage, ruelle *f.* **3.** *Mec.E:* Air passage,
conduit *m* à air. **4.** *F:* Passage of arms, passe *f*
d'armes; échange *m* de mots vifs. **5.** Passage
(d'un texte). **The love passages**, les scènes
amoureuses (de la comédie). **Selected passages**,
morceaux choisis. *Mus:* Melodic passage, trait *m.*
'passage-way, *s.* **I.** *To leave a p.-w.*, laisser le
passage libre. **2.** Passage, ruelle *f.*
passenger ['pæs(ə)ndʒər], *s.* **I.** Voyageur, -euse;
(*by sea or air*) passager, -ère. **2.** *Sp:* *Ind:* *F:*
Non-valeur *f.* **'passenger coach,** *s.* **I.** Diligence *f.* **2.** *Rail:* Wagon *m* à voyageurs. **'pas-
senger-pigeon,** *s.* Pigeon *m* de passage.
'passenger train, *s.* Train *m* de voyageurs.
To send, forward, a box by passenger-train,
expédier un colis par grande vitesse.
passe-partout [pɑspɑr'tuː], *s.* **I.** (Clef *f*,

cadre *m*) passe-partout *m inv.* **2.** **Passe-partout**
framing, encadrement *m* en sous-verre.
passer(-by) ['pɑːsər('bai)], *s.* Passant, -ante.
passion ['pæʃ(ə)n], *s.* **I.** The Passion (*of Christ*).
la Passion. **2.** Passion. Ruling passion, passion
dominante. **To have a passion for painting**, avoir
la passion de la peinture. **3.** Colère *f*, emportement *m.* **Fit of passion**, accès de colère. **To be in
a passion**, être furieux. **4.** Amour *m*, passion.
To conceive a passion for s.o., se prendre d'amour
pour qn. **5.** *She burst into a p. of tears*, elle eut
une crise de larmes terrible. **'passion-flower,**
s. Fleur *f* de la Passion. **'passion-play,** *s.*
Lit.Hist: Mystère *m* de la Passion.
passionate ['pæʃənet], *a.* **I.** Emporté; (discours)
véhément. **2.** Passionné. **3.** *F: embrace*, étreinte
ardente. **-ly,** *adv.* **I.** Passionnément. **To be
passionately in love with s.o.**, aimer qn à la folie.
To be passionately fond of sth., être passionné
de qch. **2.** Avec colère, avec emportement.
passive ['pæsiv]. **I.** *a.* Passif. **Passive resistance**,
résistance passive, inerte. **2.** *a.* & *s.* *Gram:*
passive (voice), la voix passive; le passif. **-ly,**
adv. Passivement.
passiveness ['pæsivnəs], **passivity** [pæ'siviti], *s.*
Passivité *f*; inertie *f.*
passover ['pɑːsouvər], *s.* La Pâque.
passport ['pɑːspɔːrt], *s.* (*a*) Passeport *m.*
(*b*) Ship's passport, permis *m* de navigation.
password ['pɑːswɔːrd], *s.* Mot *m* de passe.
past¹ [pɑːst]. **I.** *a.* (*a*) Passé, ancien. *Those days
are p.*, ces jours sont passés. **In times past**,
autrefois; *F:* au temps jadis. (*b*) *Gram:* Past
participle, participe passé. **Verb in the past tense,**
verbe au passé. (*c*) *The p. few years*, ces dernières
années. **For some time past**, depuis quelque
temps. **2.** *s.* Passé *m.* (*a*) **In the past**, au temps
passé; autrefois. **As in the past**, comme par le
passé. *The old plan is a thing of the past*, l'ancien
projet (i) n'existe plus, (ii) est périmé. (*b*) **Town
with a past**, ville historique. **'past-'master,** *s.*
I. *A:* Maître passé (d'un corps de métier).
F: He is a p.-m. at it, il est expert dans la matière.
2. Ancien maître (d'une loge de francs-maçons).
past². **I.** *prep.* Au delà de. (*a*) *A little p. the
bridge*, un peu plus loin que le pont. *To walk p.
s.o.*, passer qn, passer devant qn. *The train ran
p. the signal*, le train brûla, dépassa, le signal.
(*b*) Plus de. *He is p. eighty*, il a quatre-vingts ans
passés. **A quarter past four**, quatre heures un
quart. (*c*) Past all understanding, hors de toute
compréhension. **Past endurance**, insupportable.
That is p. all belief, cela n'est pas à croire. **To be
past one's work**, n'être plus en état de travailler.
To be p. caring for sth., être revenu de qch.
F: I wouldn't put it past him *that he did it
himself*, je ne le croirais pas incapable de l'avoir
fait lui-même. *S.a.* PRAY I. **2.** *adv.* **To walk, go,
past**, passer. **To march past**, défiler.
paste¹ [peist], *s.* **I.** *Cu:* Pâte *f* (de pâtisserie).
2. Pâte. **Dental paste**, pâte dentifrice. **Bloater
paste**, beurre *m* de harengs. **Starch paste**, colle *f*
d'amidon. *S.a.* SCISSOR¹. **3.** *Lap:* Stras(s) *m*;
faux brillants; *F:* du toc. **'paste-board,** *s.*
Cu: Planche *f* à pâte. (*Cp.* PASTEBOARD I.)
paste², *v.tr.* **I.** Coller. **To paste (up) a placard,**
coller une affiche. **2.** Empâter (une plaque
d'accumulateur). *Pasted plate*, plaque tartinée.
pasteboard ['peistbɔːrd], *s.* **I.** Carton *m.*
Pasteboard box, carton. *F:* **To drop a p. on
s.o.**, déposer sa carte, un bristol, chez qn.
2. = PASTE-BOARD.
pastel¹ ['pæstəl], *s.* *Art:* Pastel *m*; crayon *m*
pastel. *P. drawing*, (dessin *m* au) pastel.

pastel², s. Bot: Dy: Pastel m, guède f.
pastern ['pastərn], s. Farr: Paturon m.
Pasteurize ['pastə:ra:iz], v.tr. Pasteuriser; stériliser.
pasticcio [pas'titʃo], **pastiche** [pas'ti:ʃ], s. Art: Lit: Mus: Pastiche m.
pastime ['pa:staim], s. Passe-temps m inv, amusement m, distraction f, divertissement m.
pastor ['pa:stər], s. Ecc: (a) Pasteur m, ministre m. (b) U.S: Prêtre m, ecclésiastique m.
pastoral ['pa:stərəl]. I. a. Pastoral, -aux. (a) Pastoral tribes, tribus pastorales; peuples pasteurs. (b) Ecc: Pastoral letter, s. pastoral, (lettre) pastorale. 2. s. Pastorale f. Lit: Poème pastoral; bergerie f. Mus: Pastoral song, pastourelle.
pastry ['peistri], s. I. Pâtisserie f. 2. Pâte f. **'pastry-cook**, s. Pâtissier, -ière. **'pastry-making**, s. Pâtisserie f. **'pastry-shop**, s. Pâtisserie f.
pasturage ['pa:stjuredʒ], s. I. Pâturage m, pacage m (du cheptel). 2. = PASTURE¹ I.
pasture¹ ['pa:stjər], s. I. Lieu m de pâture; pâturage m, pacage m. 2. = PASTURAGE I. **'pasture-land**, s. Pâturages mpl.
pasture². I. v.i. (Of animals) Paître, pacager. 2. v.tr. (Of shepherd) (Faire) paître (les bêtes).
pasturing, s. Pacage m.
pasty¹ ['peisti], a. I. Pâteux. 2. Pasty face, visage terreux; F: figure en papier mâché. **'pasty-faced**, a. Au teint brouillé, terreux.
pasty² ['pasti], s. Cu: Pâté m (de gibier, etc.) sans terrine.
pat¹ [pat], s. I. (a) Coup léger; petite tape f. (b) Caresse f. F: Pat on the back, éloge m; mot m d'encouragement. 2. (a) Rondelle f, pelote f (de beurre). (b) Motte f, pain m (de beurre).
pat², v.tr. (patted) (a) Taper, tapoter. (b) Caresser. To pat a dog on the back, flatter le dos d'un chien. To pat s.o. on the back, encourager qn. To pat oneself on the back over sth., s'applaudir de qch. **patting**, s. Tapotement m; caresses fpl.
pat³. I. adv. A propos. He answered pat, his answer came pat, il répliqua sur-le-champ. 2. a. Apte; à propos. He always has an excuse pat, il a toujours une excuse toute prête.
Pat⁴. Pr.n.m. (Dim. of Patrick) Patrice.
patch¹ [patʃ], s. I. (a) Pièce f (pour raccommoder). F: Not to be a patch on s.o., ne pas aller à la cheville de qn. (b) Pièce rapportée; Nau: placard m (de voile). 2. (a) Aut: etc: (Rubber) patch, (for inner tyre) pastille f; (for outer cover) guêtre f. (b) Eye-patch, couvre-œil m. (c) Toil: A: Mouche f. 3. Tache f (de couleur). Patch of blue sky, échappée f de ciel bleu. P. of snow on the mountain, flaque f de neige sur la montagne. F: To strike a bad patch, être en guigne, en déveine. 4. (a) Morceau m, parcelle f (de terre). (b) Carré m, plant m (de légumes).
patch², v.tr. Rapiécer, raccommoder (un vêtement); poser une pastille à (une chambre à air); mettre une pièce à (un pneu). **patch up**, v.tr. Rapetasser (de vieux vêtements); rafistoler (une machine). F: Patched-up peace, paix fourrée.
patchiness ['patʃinəs], s. Manque m d'harmonie (d'un paysage, etc.).
patchouli [pa'tʃu:li], s. Toil: Patchouli m.
patchwork ['patʃwə:rk], s. Ouvrage fait de pièces et de morceaux. P. of fields, campagne bigarrée.
patchy [patʃi], a. Inégal.
pate [peit], s. F: Tête f, caboche f.

patella [pa'telə], s. I. Anat: Rotule f (du genou). 2. Archeol: Moll: Bot: Patelle f.
paten ['pat(ə)n], s. Ecc: Patène f.
patent¹ ['peitənt]. I. a. I. Letters patent, lettres patentes; (i) brevet m d'invention; (ii) lettres de noblesse. 2. Breveté. Patent medicine, spécialité pharmaceutique. Patent leather, cuir verni. S.a. LOG¹ 2. 3. (Fait) patent, manifeste. **-ly**, adv. Manifestement; clairement. II. **patent**, s. I. Patent of nobility, lettres de noblesse. 2. (a) Brevet m d'invention. Infringement of a patent, contrefaçon f. Patent agent, agent en brevets (d'invention). Patent-rights, propriété industrielle. (b) Invention ou fabrication brevetée.
patent², v.tr. Faire breveter (une invention).
patentee [peitən'ti:], s. Breveté m.
pater (the) [ðə'peitər], s.m. P: Mon père; papa; F: le paternel.
paterfamilias [peitərfə'miliəs], s.m. Hum: Père de famille; chef m de maison.
paternal [pə'tə:rn(ə)l], a. Paternel. **-ally**, adv. Paternellement.
paternity [pə'tə:rniti], s. (a) Paternité f. (b) F: Origine f. Of doubtful p., de paternité douteuse.
paternoster [patər'nɔstər], s. Patenôtre f; pater m.
path, pl. **paths** [pɑ:θ, pɑ:ðz], s. I. (a) Chemin m; sentier m; (in garden) allée f. The beaten path, le chemin battu. The path of glory, le chemin de la gloire. S.a. DOWNWARD I. (b) = PATHWAY (b). 2: Course f (d'un corps en mouvement); route f (du soleil). **'path-finder**, s. Pionnier m.
pathetic [pə'θetik], a. (a) Pathétique, attendrissant. F: Isn't it pathetic? c'est tout de même triste! She's a p. creature, c'est une créature pitoyable. (b) Qui a rapport aux émotions. **-ally**, adv. Pathétiquement.
pathless ['pɑ:θləs], a. Sans chemin trayé.
pathological [paθə'lɔdʒik(ə)l], a. Pathologique.
pathologist [pə'θɔlɔdʒist], s. Pathologiste m.
pathology [pə'θɔlɔdʒi], s. Pathologie f.
pathos ['peiθɔs], s. (a) Pathétique m. Told with p., raconté d'une façon touchante. (b) Affected pathos, pathos m.
pathway ['pɑ:θwei], s. (a) Sentier m. (b) Trottoir m (de rue); accotement m (de grand chemin).
patience ['peiʃ(ə)ns], s. I. Patience f. To try, tax, s.o.'s patience, éprouver, exercer, la patience de qn. My p. is exhausted, je suis à bout de patience. To have patience with s.o., prendre patience avec qn. I have no patience with him, il m'impatiente. To possess one's soul in patience, patienter. 2. Cards: Réussite f. To play patience, faire des réussites.
patient ['peiʃənt]. I. a. Patient, endurant. To be p., patienter. **-ly**, adv. Patiemment. To wait p. for s.o., attendre qn avec patience. II. **patient**, s. Malade mf; (surgical case) -ente; (operated upon) opéré, -ée. A doctor's patients, les clients m d'un médecin.
patina ['patinə], s. Patine f.
patriarch ['peitriɑ:rk], s. Patriarche m.
patriarchal [peitri'ɑ:rk(ə)l], a. Patriarcal, -aux.
patrician [pə'triʃ(ə)n], a. & s. Patricien, -ienne.
Patrick ['patrik]. Pr.n.m. Patrice.
patrimonial [patri'mounjəl], a. Patrimonial, -aux.
patrimony ['patrimoni], s. I. Patrimoine m. 2. Biens-fonds mpl, revenu m, d'une église.
patriot ['peitriət, 'pa-], s. Patriote mf.

patriotic [peitri'ɔtik, pa-], a. **I.** (Of pers.) Patriote. **2.** (Discours, chanson) patriotique. **-ally,** adv. Patriotiquement ; en patriote.

patriotism ['peitriɔtizm, 'pa-], s. Patriotisme m.

patrol[1] [pa'troul], s. Patrouille f. (a) To go on patrol, faire la patrouille ; faire une ronde. (b) Mounted p., patrouille à cheval. Mil: Member of a p., patrouilleur m. Patrol leader, chef m de patrouille. **pa'trol-boat, -ship,** s. Patrouilleur m.

patrol[2], v. (patrolled) **I.** v.i. Patrouiller ; faire une ronde. **2.** v.tr. Faire la patrouille dans (un quartier).

patron ['peitrən]. **I.** s.m. (a) Protecteur (des arts) ; patron (d'une œuvre de charité). (b) Ecc: Patron saint, patron, -onne. (c) Ecc: Patron, présentateur (d'un bénéfice). **2.** s.m. & f. Com: Client, -ente (d'un magasin) ; habitué, -ée (d'un cinéma). The patrons of the drama, le public du théâtre.

patronage ['patrənedʒ], s. **I.** (a) Protection f, encouragement m (des arts) ; patronage m. To ɔxtend one's patronage to s.o., accorder sa protection à qn. Concert under the patronage of . . . concert honoré d'une souscription de. . . . (b) Pej: Air protecteur (of, envers). **2.** Clientèle f (d'un hôtel, etc.). **3.** Ecc: Droit m de présentation (of a living, à un bénéfice).

patronal [pa'troun(ə)l], a. Patronal, -aux.

patroness ['peitrɔnes],s.f. Protectrice (des arts) ; (dame) patronnesse (d'une œuvre de charité).

patronize ['patrənaiz], v.tr. **I.** (a) Patronner, protéger (un artiste). (b) Traiter (qn) d'un air protecteur. **2.** Accorder sa clientèle à (une maison). **patronizing,** a. (a) Protecteur, -trice. (b) Patronizing tone, ton de condescendance. To become p., prendre un air protecteur. **-ly,** adv. D'un air protecteur.

patronymic [patrɔ'nimik]. **I.** a. Patronymique. **2.** s. Nom m patronymique.

patten ['pat(ə)n], s. Socque m (pour garantir les chaussures contre la boue).

patter[1] ['patər], s. **I.** Boniment m (de charlatan) ; bagout m. **2.** Parlé m (dans une chansonnette).

patter[2]. **I.** v.tr. Bredouiller (ses prières) ; parler tant bien que mal (le français). **2.** v.i. They pattered on, elles continuèrent à caqueter.

patter[3],s. Petit bruit (de pas précipités) ; fouettement m (de la pluie).

patter[4], v.i. **I.** (Of footsteps) Sonner par petits coups ; (of hail, rain) crépiter, fouetter. (b) (Of pers.) To patter about, trottiner çà et là.

pattern ['patərn], s. **I.** Modèle m, type m. To take pattern by s.o., se modeler sur qn. **2.** (a) Modèle, dessin m. Garments of different patterns, vêtements de coupes différentes. (b) Dressm: etc: Patron m (en papier). To take a pattern, relever un patron. (c) Metall: Casting pattern, gabarit m, calibre m. **3.** Échantillon m. **4.** Dessin, motif m (de papier peint, etc.). **'pattern-book,** s. Com: Livre m d'échantillons. **'pattern-shop,** s. Ind: Atelier m de modelage.

patty ['pati], s. Cu: Petit pâté ; bouchée f à la reine.

paucity ['pɔːsiti],s. Manque m, disette f ; rareté f. P. of new plays, indigence f de la production théâtrale. There is a p. of news, il y a disette de nouvelles. P. of money, manque d'argent, rareté de l'argent. P. of words, sobriété f de mots.

Paul [pɔːl]. Pr.n.m. Paul.

paunch [pɔːnʃ], s. (a) Panse f, ventre m, F: bedaine f (de qn). (b) Panse (des ruminants).

pauper ['pɔːpər], s. **I.** Adm: Indigent, -ente.

Pauper children, enfants assistés. S.a. GRAVE[1]. **2.** Pauvre, -esse.

pauperism ['pɔːpərizm], s. Paupérisme m.

pauperization [pɔːpərai'zeiʃən], s. Réduction f à l'indigence.

pauperize ['pɔːpəraiz], v.tr. **I.** Réduire (qn) à l'indigence. **2.** Accoutumer (une famille) à compter sur les secours d'autrui.

pause[1] [pɔːz], s. **I.** (a) Pause f, arrêt m. (b) To give pause to s.o., faire hésiter qn. **2.** Pros: Repos m. **3.** Mus: Point m d'orgue.

pause[2], v.i. **I.** Faire une pause ; s'arrêter un instant ; marquer un temps. **2.** Hésiter. To make s.o. pause, donner à réfléchir à qn. **3.** To pause (up)on a word, s'arrêter sur un mot.

pave [peiv], v.tr. Paver (une rue) ; carreler (une cour). F: To pave the way, préparer le terrain ; frayer la voie. **paving,** s. **I.** Pavage m, dallage m, carrelage m. **2.** Pavé m, dalles fpl. **'paving-block, -stone,** s. Pierre f à paver ; pavé m.

pavement ['peivmənt], s. (a) Pavé m, pavage m, dallage m. (b) Trottoir m. **'pavement-artist,** s. Barbouilleur m de trottoir. **'pavement-glass, -light,** s. Dallage m en verre ; verdal. -als.

pavilion [pa'viljən], s. **I.** A: Pavillon m, tente f. **2.** Sp: Pavillon. **3.** Arch: Pavillon.

paviour ['peivjər], s. Paveur m, carreleur m.

paw[1] [pɔː], s. (a) Patte f (d'animal onguiculé). (b) P: Main f ; P: patte (de qn).

paw[2]. v.tr. (a) Donner des coups de patte à (qn, qch.). (b) (Of horse) To paw the ground, abs. to paw, piaffer ; gratter (la terre) du pied. **2.** (Of pers.) F: Tripoter (qn, qch.).

pawkiness ['pɔːkinəs], s. Scot: **I.** Malice f, finasserie f. **2.** Humour m de pince-sans-rire.

pawky ['pɔːki], a. Scot: **I.** Rusé, malicieux, finaud. **2.** A p. answer, une réponse normande. **-ily,** adv. Avec un grain de malice.

pawl [pɔːl], s. Mec.E: Linguet m (de cabestan) ; cliquet m (d'arrêt), chien m d'arrêt.

pawn[1] [pɔːn], s. **I.** Gage m, nantissement m. **2.** In pawn, en gage ; P: chez ma tante. To put one's watch in pawn, engager sa montre. To take sth. out of pawn, dégager qch. **'pawn-ticket,** s. Reconnaissance f (de dépôt de gage).

pawn[2], v.tr. Mettre (qch.) en gage ; engager (qch.) ; P: mettre (qch.) chez ma tante. **pawning,** s. Mise f en gage.

pawn[3], s. Chess: Pion m. F: To be s.o.'s pawn, être le jouet de qn.

pawnbroker ['pɔːnbroukər], s. Prêteur, -euse, sur gage(s).

pawnshop ['pɔːnʃɔp], s. Bureau m de prêt sur gage(s) ; maison f de prêt.

pax [paks]. **I.** s. Ecc: Patène f. **2.** int. Sch: Pouce !

pay[1] [pei], s. Paie f, salaire m (d'un ouvrier, d'un employé) ; gages mpl (d'un domestique) ; traitement m (d'un fonctionnaire). Mil: Navy: Solde f. Unemployed pay, solde de non-activité. Ind: Holidays with pay, congés payés. To be in s.o.'s pay, être à la solde, aux gages, de qn. **'pay-box, -desk,** s. Caisse f ; comptoir-caisse m. Th: Guichet m. **'pay-day,** s. Jour m de paie, de paiement. **'pay-dirt,** s. Gold-Min: Alluvion f exploitable. **'pay-office,** s. Caisse f, guichet m. **'pay-roll, -sheet,** s. Feuille f de paie. Adm: Feuille d'émargement. Mil: État m de solde.

pay[2], v.tr. (p.t. & p.p. paid [peid]) **I.** (a) To pay s.o. ten francs, payer, compter, dix francs à qn. To pay s.o. an annuity, servir une rente à qn. F: What's to pay? c'est combien ? Abs. To pay ready money, cash down, payer (argent) comptant. *To pay in advance,* payer d'avance. 'Pay at the gate,' "entrée payante." *F:* To pay through the nose, payer un prix excessif. *We had to pay through the nose,* on nous a salés. *S.a.* DEVIL¹ I. (b) Payer (un domestique); solder (des troupes); rétribuer (un employé). (c) To pay s.o. to do sth., payer qn pour faire qch. **2.** (a) Payer (une dette). To pay a bill, solder, régler, un compte. (*On receipted bill*) 'Paid,' "pour acquit." *F:* To pay s.o.'s account, régler son compte à qn. *Cust:* To pay the duty on sth., acquitter les droits sur qch. *S.a.* WAY¹ 2. (b) To pay honour to s.o., faire honneur à qn. To pay one's respects to s.o., présenter ses respects à qn. To pay s.o. a visit, faire, rendre, une visite à qn. To pay money into an account, verser une somme au compte de qn. **4.** It will pay you to . . ., vous y gagnerez à. . . . *It doesn't pay,* on n'y trouve pas son compte. *Prov:* It pays to advertise, la publicité rapporte. **pay away,** *v.tr.* Dépenser (de l'argent). **pay back,** *v.tr.* **I.** Rendre, restituer (de l'argent emprunté). **2.** Rembourser (qn). *F:* To pay s.o. back in his own coin, rendre la pareille à qn. **pay down,** *v.tr.* (a) Payer (qch.) comptant. (b) To pay something down, verser une provision. **pay for,** *v.tr.* **I.** (a) To pay (s.o.) for sth., payer qch. (à qn). *What do you pay for tea?* combien payez-vous le thé? *I had paid for his schooling,* j'avais subvenu aux frais de ses études. *To pay for services,* rémunérer des services. To pay s.o. for his trouble dédommager qn de sa peine. (b) *F:* To pay dear(ly) for one's happiness, payer cher son bonheur. *He paid for it up to the hilt,* il a expié durement sa faute. *He paid for his rashness with his life,* il a payé sa témérité de sa vie. I'll make him pay for this! il me le paiera! **2.** *He likes to invite people and to pay for them,* il aime à inviter les gens à ses frais. **pay in,** *v.tr.* To pay in a cheque, donner un chèque à l'encaissement. *Abs.* To pay in to a fund, contribuer à une caisse. **pay off,** *v.tr.* **I.** Solder, régler, acquitter (une dette); s'acquitter de (ses dettes). **2.** (a) Rembourser (un créancier); donner son compte à (un employé). (b) Congédier (un domestique); licencier (des troupes); désarmer (un navire). **3.** *Nau:* To pay off the ship's head, laisser arriver le navire. **pay out,** *v.tr.* **I.** Payer, débourser. **2.** I'll pay you out for that! je vous revaudrai cela! **3.** *Nau:* (Laisser) filer (un câble). **pay up,** *v.tr.* **I.** To pay up one's debts, *abs.* to pay up, se libérer (de ses dettes). Pay up! payez! **2.** *Fin:* Libérer (des actions). **paid,** *a.* (Domestique) à gages; (employé) rétribué. **paying¹,** *a.* **I.** (Élève, etc.) payant. Paying guest, pensionnaire *mf.* **2.** (*Of business*) Rémunérateur; qui rapporte. **paying²,** *s.* **I.** Paiement *m*, versement *m* (d'argent); remboursement *m* (d'un créancier). **2.** Règlement *m*, acquittement *m* (d'une dette).

payable ['peiəbl], *a.* Payable, acquittable. *Taxes p. by the tenant,* impôts à la charge du locataire. *Com:* Payable at sight, payable à vue. To make a bill payable to s.o., faire un billet à l'ordre de qn. *To make a cheque p. to bearer,* souscrire un chèque au porteur.

payee [pei'i:], *s.* Preneur, -euse, bénéficiaire *mf* (d'un bon de poste, etc.).

payer ['peiər], *s.* Payeur, -euse, payant, -ante.

paymaster ['peimɑ:stər], *s.* Payeur *m. Mil:* Trésorier *m. Navy:* Commissaire *m.*

payment ['peimənt], *s.* (a) Paiement *m*; versement *m.* On payment of *ten francs,* moyennant

paiement de dix francs. To stop payment of a cheque, frapper un chèque d'opposition. (*Of bank*) To stop payment, cesser les paiements. Method of payment, mode *m* de règlement. Cash payment, paiement comptant. Payment on account, versement à compte; acompte *m.* Payment in full, liquidation *f* (d'un compte). Payment of interest, service *m* de l'intérêt. 'Payment received,' "pour acquit." (b) Rémunération *f. As p. for your services,* en rémunération de vos services.

pea [pi:], *s.* **I.** *Hort:* Pois *m. Cu:* Green peas, petits pois. *S.a.* LIKE¹ I. **I. 2.** *Bot:* Sweet pea, pois de senteur. 'pea-'green, *a. & s.* Vert feuille (*m*) *inv.* 'pea-pod, -shell, *s.* Cosse *f*, gousse *f*, de pois. 'pea-shooter, *s.* Petite sarbacane de poche. 'pea-'soup, *s.* Soupe *f*, potage *m*, crème *f*, aux pois (cassés); (*thick*) purée *f* de pois. 'pea-'souper, *s.* *F:* Brouillard *m* (jaune) à couper au couteau.

peace [pi:s], *s.* **I.** (a) Paix *f. Country at peace with its enemies,* pays en paix avec ses ennemis. To make (one's) peace with s.o., faire la paix, se réconcilier, avec qn. Peace with honour, une paix honorable. (b) Traité *m* de paix. **2.** Peace and order, la paix et l'ordre public. *P. prevails in the town,* la paix règne dans la ville. To keep the peace, (i) ne pas troubler l'ordre public; (ii) veiller à l'ordre public. To break, disturb, the peace, troubler, violer, l'ordre public. Justice of the peace, juge *m* de paix (à titre bénévole). **3.** (a) Tranquillité *f* (de l'âme). To live in peace (and quietness), vivre en paix. *You may sleep in p.,* vous pouvez dormir tranquille. To give s.o. no peace, ne donner ni paix ni trêve à qn. *God rest his soul in p.!* que Dieu donne le repos à son âme! (b) To hold one's peace, se taire; garder le silence. 'peace-loving, *a*, Pacifique; qui aime la paix. 'peace-offering, *s.* **I.** *Jew.Rel:* Sacrifice *m* de propitiation. **2.** *F:* Cadeau *m* de réconciliation.

peaceable ['pi:səbl], *a.* **I.** Pacifique. P. man, homme de paix. **2.** = PEACEFUL 2. **-ably,** *adv.* **I.** Pacifiquement. **2.** En paix.

peaceful ['pi:sful], *a.* **I.** Paisible, calme, tranquille. *The p. countryside,* les campagnes paisibles. **2.** Pacifique. **-fully,** *adv.* **I.** Paisiblement. **2.** Pacifiquement.

peacefulness ['pi:sfulnəs], *s.* Tranquillité *f*, paix *f.*

peacemaker ['pi:smeikər], *s.* Pacificateur, -trice, conciliateur, -trice.

peach¹ [pi:tʃ], *s.* *Hort:* **I.** Pêche *f.* **2.** Peach (-tree), pêcher *m.* 'peach-blossom, *s.* Fleur *f* de pêcher.

peach², *v.i.* *P:* Cafarder, moucharder. *He peached to the boss,* il a rapporté ça au patron.

pea-chick ['pi:tʃik], *s.* *Orn:* Paonneau *m.*

peacock ['pi:kɔk], *s.* *Orn:* Paon *m.*

peafowl ['pi:faul], *s.* Paon *m*, paonne *f.*

peahen ['pi:hen], *s.* Paonne *f.*

pea-jacket ['pi:dʒaket], *s.* *Nau:* Vareuse *f*, caban *m.*

peak [pi:k], *s.* **I.** (a) Visière *f* (de casquette). (b) Bec *m* (d'une ancre). (c) Pointe *f* (de toit, etc.). **2.** *Nau:* (a) Coqueron *m* (de la cale). (b) Pic *m* (de voile). With the flag at the peak, le pavillon à la corne. **3.** (a) Pic, cime *f* (de montagne). *The highest peaks,* les plus hauts sommets. (b) *Mec: etc:* Pointe, apogée *m* (d'une courbe, d'une charge). *Ph:* Sommet *f* (d'une onde). Peak load, charge maximum (d'un générateur). *Rail: etc:* Peak hours, heures de pointe; heures d'affluence. **'peak-'halyard,** s. *Nau:* Drisse f de pic.

peaked [pi:kt], a. (a) (Casquette) à visière. (b) High-peaked hat, chapeau (haut et) pointu.

peaky ['pi:ki], a. F: To look peaky, avoir les traits tirés, hâves; (of child) être pâlot.

peal¹ [pi:l], s. **1.** Peal of bells, carillon m. **2.** (a) To ring a peal, carillonner. (b) Full peal of the bells, volée f de cloches. **3.** Retentissement m; grondement m (du tonnerre); coup m (de tonnerre).

peal². **1.** v.i. (a) (Of bells) Carillonner. (b) (Of thunder) Retentir, gronder. **2.** v.tr. Sonner (les cloches) à toute volée.

peanut ['pi:nʌt], s. B Pistache f de terre; arachide f. Com: Caca(h)ouette f.

pear ['pɛər], s. **1.** Poire f. S.a. PRICKLY I. **2.** Pear(-tree), poirier m. **'pear-shaped,** a. En forme de poire; piriforme. **'pear-switch,** s. El: Poire f de contact.

pearl¹ ['pɜːrl], s. **1.** Perle f. String of pearls, fil m de perles. **2.** (Mother-of-pearl) Nacre f (de perle). Pearl button, bouton de nacre. **'pearl-'barley,** s. Orge perlé. **'pearl-diver, -fisher,** s. Pêcheur m de perles. **'pearl-fishery,** s. Pêcherie f de perles. **'pearl-'grey,** a. & s. Gris perle inv. **'pearl-shell,** s. Coquille nacrée.

pearl². v.i. (Of moisture) Perler; former des gouttelettes; (of sugar) faire la perle.

pearlies ['pɜːrliz], s.pl. F: Boutons m de nacre.

pearly ['pɜːrli], a. Perlé; nacré. P. teeth, dents de perle; dents perlées.

peasant ['pezənt], s. Paysan, -anne; campagnard, -arde.

peasantry ['pezəntri], s. The peasantry, les paysans m; les campagnards m.

pease [pi:z], s. Pois mpl. **'pease-flour, -meal,** s. Farine f de pois cassés. **'pease-pudding,** s. Purée f de pois.

peat [pi:t], s. **1.** Coll. Tourbe f. Field of peat, cendrière f. To dig, cut, peat, extraire de la tourbe. **2.** (Turf, sod, block, of) peat, motte f de tourbe. **'peat-bog,** s. Tourbière f. **'peatmoss,** s. **1.** = PEAT-BOG. **2.** Bot: Sphaigne f. The peat mosses, les sphagnacées f.

pebble¹ [pebl], s. **1.** (a) Caillou m; (on sea-shore) galet m. F: You're not the only pebble on the beach, vous n'êtes pas unique au monde. (b) Scotch pebble, agate f (des ruisseaux d'Écosse). **2.** Opt: (a) Cristal m de roche. (b) Lentille f en cristal de roche. **3.** Leath: Maroquinage (communiqué au cuir).

pebble², v.tr. Leath: Crépir, maroquiner (le cuir).

pebbly ['pebli], a. Cailouteux; (plage) à galets.

peccadillo [peka'dilo], s. Peccadille f; vétille f.

peccant ['pekənt], a. Coupable; en faute.

peccary ['pekəri], s. Z: Pécari m.

peck¹ [pek], s. (a) Coup m de bec. (b) F: (Kiss) Bécot m. To give s.o. a peck, bécoter qn.

peck², v.tr. **1.** (a) (Of bird) Picoter, becqueter (qch.); donner un coup de bec à (qn). (b) F: (Kiss) Bécoter (qn). **2.** Abs. F: Manger du bout des dents. **peck at,** v.ind.tr. (a) Picoter; donner des coups de bec à (qn, qch.). (b) F: Chipoter (un plat). **peck out,** v.tr. Crever (les yeux) à coups de bec. **pecking,** s. Becquetage m.

peck³, s. Meas: **1.** (a) Approx. = Boisseau m. (b) Picotin m (d'avoine). **2.** F: She's had a p. of trouble, elle a eu bien des malheurs.

pecker ['pekər], s. F: Courage m; cran m. To keep one's pecker up, ne pas se laisser abattre.

peckish ['pekiʃ], a. F: To be, feel, peckish, se sentir le ventre creux.

pectinate ['pektinet], **pectinated** ['pektineitid], a. Nat.Hist: Pectiné.

pectoral ['pektərəl]. **1.** a. Pectoral, -aux. **2.** s. Jew.Rel: Anat: Pharm: Pectoral m.

peculate ['pekjuleit], v.i. Détourner des fonds.

peculation [pekju'leiʃ(ə)n], s. Péculat m, déprédation f; détournement m de fonds; prévarication f.

peculator ['pekjuleitər], s. Concussionnaire m, prévaricateur m.

peculiar [pi'kju:liər], a. (a) Particulier. The condor is p. to the Andes, le condor est particulier aux Andes. (b) Spécial, -aux; particulier. Of p. interest, d'un intérêt tout particulier. (c) (Of thg) Étrange; (of pers.) bizarre, singulier. He, she, is a little p., c'est un(e) excentrique. To be p. in one's dress, s'habiller singulièrement. **-ly,** adv. (a) Personnellement. (b) Particulièrement. (c) Étrangement; singulièrement.

peculiarity [pikju:li'ariti], s. **1.** Trait distinctif; particularité f. (On passport) Special peculiarities, signes particuliers. **2.** Bizarrerie f, singularité f.

pecuniary [pi'kju:niəri], a. Pécuniaire. P. difficulties, ennuis m d'argent.

pedagogic(al) [peda'gɔdʒik(əl)], a. Pédagogique.

pedagogue ['pedagɔg], s. Pej: Pédagogue m.

pedagogy ['pedagɔdʒi], s. Pédagogie f.

pedal¹ ['ped(ə)l], s. **1.** (a) Mec.E: Pédale f. Aut: Clutch pedal, pédale d'embrayage. (b) Cy: Pédale. **2.** (a) (Of piano) Soft pedal, petite pédale. Loud pedal, grande pédale. (b) (Of organ) Swell pedal, pédale expressive. (c) Pedal note, pédale. **'pedal-board,** s. Pédalier m (d'un orgue).

pedal² ['ped(ə)l], v.i. (pedalled) **1.** Cy: Pédaler. **2.** (Piano) Mettre la pédale.

pedant ['pedənt], s. Pédant, -ante.

pedantic [pe'dantik], a. Pédant, pédantesque. **-ally,** adv. Pédantesquement; en pédant.

pedantry ['pedəntri], s. Pédantisme m, pédanterie f.

peddle [pedl]. **1.** v.i. (a) Faire le colportage. (b) F: Chipoter. **2.** v.tr. Colporter (des marchandises). **peddling,** s. **1.** Colportage m. **2.** F: Chipotage m.

pedestal ['pedest(ə)l], s. **1.** Piédestal m, -aux; socle m; (small, for bust, etc.) piédouche m. F: To put s.o. on a pedestal, mettre qn sur un piédestal. **2.** (a) Socle (de pompe); support m, colonne f. (b) Mec.E: Palier m, chevalet m (de coussinet). **3.** (a) Pedestal(-cupboard), table f de nuit. (b) Pedestal writing-table, bureau ministre. **'pedestal-'table,** s. Guéridon m.

pedestrian [pe'destriən]. **1.** a. (a) Pédestre; (voyage) à pied. (b) (Style) prosaïque, terre à terre. **2.** s. Piéton m; voyageur, -euse, à pied.

pedicel ['pedisel], **pedicle** ['pedikl], s. Bot: Pédicelle m.

pedicular [pe'dikjulər], a. (Maladie) pédiculaire.

pedigree ['pedigri:], s. **1.** Arbre m généalogique. **2.** (a) Ascendance f, généalogie f (de qn). (b) Breed: Certificat m d'origine (d'un chien, etc.). Pedigree dog, chien de (pure) race, de bonne souche.

pediment ['pedimənt], s. Arch: Fronton m.

pedlar ['pedlər], s. Colporteur m, porteballe m.

pedometer [pe'dɔmetər], s. Podomètre m, compte-pas m inv.

peduncle [pe'dʌŋkl], s. Bot: Pédoncule m.

peel¹ [pi:l], s. Pelure f (de pomme); écorce f, peau f, Cu: zeste m (de citron). Candied peel, zeste confit.

peel². **I.** *v.tr.* (a) Peler (un fruit); éplucher (des pommes de terre); écorcer (un bâton). *Cu:* To p. the outer skin off a lemon, zester un citron. (b) *Sp:* F: **To peel**, se dépouiller de ses vêtements. **2.** *v.i.* (a) **To peel (off)**, (of paint) s'écailler; (of skin) se desquamer. (b) (Of the nose, etc.) Peler. **peeling,** *s.* **I.** (a) Épluchage *m*; écorçage *m*. (b) Peeling (off), écaillement *m*; *Med:* desquamation *f.* **2.** *pl.* **Peelings,** épluchures *f.*

peen [pi:n], *s.* *U.S:* Panne *f* (de marteau). **'peen-hammer,** *s.* *Tls:* Marteau *m* à panne. Ball-peen hammer, marteau à panne ronde; marteau de mécanicien.

peep¹ [pi:p], *s.* Piaulement *m*, pépiement *m* (d'oiseau); cri *m* (de souris).

peep², *v.i.* (Of bird) Piauler, pépier; (of mouse) crier.

peep³, *s.* **I.** Coup d'œil (furtif). To get a peep at sth., entrevoir qch. **2.** Filtrée *f* (de lumière); petite flamme (de gaz). At peep of day, au point du jour; dès l'aube. **'peep-bo,** *int.* Coucou! **'peep-hole,** *s.* **I.** Judas *m.* **2.** *Mec.E:* (Trou *m* de) regard *m.* **3.** *Sm.a:* Œilleton *m* (d'une hausse).

peep⁴, *v.i.* **I.** To peep at sth., regarder qch. à la dérobée. To p. round the corner, risquer un coup d'œil au coin de la rue. Peeping Tom, curieux *m*, indiscret *m.* **2.** To peep (out), se laisser entrevoir, se montrer.

peer¹ [pi:ər], *s.* **I.** Pair *m*; pareil, -eille. **2.** Peer of the realm, pair du Royaume-Uni.

peer², *v.i.* (a) To peer at s.o., sth., scruter qn, qch., du regard. (b) To p. over the wall, risquer un coup d'œil par-dessus le mur.

peerage ['pi:əredʒ], *s.* **I.** Pairie *f.* **2.** *Coll.* The peerage, (i) les pairs *m*; (ii) *F:* la noblesse. **3.** Peerage(-book), almanach *m* nobiliaire.

peeress ['pi:əres], *s.f.* Pairesse.

peerless ['pi:ərləs], *a.* Sans pareil, sans pair. *Hum:* Peerless beauty, beauté à nulle autre seconde.

peeved [pi:vd], *a.* Fâché, irrité, ennuyé.

peevish ['pi:viʃ], *a.* Irritable, geignard; maussade. **-ly,** *adv.* Maussadement.

peevishness ['pi:viʃnəs], *s.* Maussaderie *f*; mauvaise humeur.

peewit ['pi:wit], *s.* = PEWIT.

peg¹ [peg], *s.* **I.** (a) Cheville *f* (en bois); fiche *f.* F: He's a square peg in a round hole, il n'est pas dans son emploi. To take s.o. down a peg (or two), remettre qn à sa place. *S.a.* CLOTHES-PEG. (b) (Hat-)peg, patère *f.* Peg to hang a grievance on, prétexte *m* de plainte. (c) Piquet *m.* (At croquet) Finishing peg, piquet d'arrivée. **2.** (a) Pointe *f*, fer *m* (de toupie); pied *m*, pique *f* (de violoncelle). (b) P: Jambe *f*; P: quille *f.* **3.** Doigt *m* (de whisky, etc.). To mix oneself a stiff peg, se faire un grog bien tassé. **'peg-leg,** *s.* Jambe *f* de bois. **'peg-top,** *s.* Toupie *f.*

peg², *v.tr.* (pegged) **I.** Cheviller (un assemblage). To peg clothes on the line, accrocher le linge sur la corde. *Bootm:* Pegged soles, semelles chevillées. **2.** *Games:* Marquer (des points). **3.** *Fin:* To peg the exchange, stabiliser le cours du change. **4.** *v.i.* F: To peg away (at sth.), travailler ferme (à qch.), F: piocher (un sujet). **peg down,** *v.tr.* Fixer, assujettir, (un filet) avec des piquets. **peg out. I.** *v.tr.* To peg out a claim, piqueter, jalonner, une concession. **2.** *v.i.* (a) (Croquet) Toucher le piquet final (et se retirer de la partie). (b) P: Mourir; P: casser sa pipe.

pegamoid ['pegamɔid], *s.* Pégamoïd *m.*

Pegasus ['pegəsəs]. *Pr.n.* *Gr.Myth:* Pégase *m.* F: To mount one's Pegasus, enfourcher Pégase.

pejorative ['pi:dʒoreitiv, pi'dʒɔrətiv], *a. & s.* Péjoratif (*m*).

Pekinese, Pekingese ['pi:ki'ni:z, -ki'ŋi:z], *s.* (Épagneul *m*) pékinois *m.*

pelagian [pe'leidʒiən], **pelagic** [pe'ladʒik], *a.* *Oc:* Pélagien, pélagique.

pelargonium [pelər'gounjəm], *s.* *Bot:* Pélargonium *m*, *F:* géranium *m.*

pelf [pelf], *s.* *Pej:* Richesses *fpl*, lucre *m.*

pelican ['pelikən], *s.* Pélican *m.*

pelisse [pe'li:s], *s.* *Cost:* Pelisse *f.*

pellet ['pelet], *s.* (a) Boulette *f* (de papier); pelote *f* (d'argile). (b) *Sm.a:* Grain *m* de plomb. (c) *Pharm:* Pilule *f.*

pellicle ['pelikl], *s.* (a) Pellicule *f.* (b) Membrane *f.*

pellicular [pe'likjulər], *a.* Pelliculaire.

pellitory ['pelitəri], *s.* *Bot:* **I.** Pellitory of Spain, pyrèthre *m.* **2.** Wall-pellitory, pariétaire *f.*

pell-mell ['pel'mel]. **I.** *adv.* Pêle-mêle. **2.** *a.* Mis pêle-mêle; en confusion.

pellucid [pe'lju:sid], *a.* (a) Pellucide, transparent. (b) F: (Style) lucide, limpide. (c) (Esprit) clair.

pelmet ['pelmet], *s.* *Furn:* Lambrequin *m.*

pelota [pe'louta], *s.* *Games:* Pelote *f* basque.

pelt¹ [pelt], *s.* **I.** Peau *f*, fourrure *f* (de mouton). **2.** *Tan:* Peau verte.

pelt², *s.* **I.** Grêle *f* (de pierres). **2. (At) full pelt,** (courir) à toute vitesse.

pelt³. I. *v.tr.* To pelt s.o. with stones, lancer une volée de pierres à qn. **2.** *v.i.* (a) (Of rain) To pelt (down), tomber à verse, tomber à seaux. Pelting rain, pluie battante. (b) F: He was off as fast as he could pelt, il se sauva à toutes jambes.

peltry ['peltri], *s.* Pelleterie *f*; peaux *fpl.*

pelvic ['pelvik], *a.* *Anat:* Pelvien.

pelvis ['pelvis], *s.* *Anat:* Bassin *m.* False pelvis, pelvis *m.*

pen¹ [pen], *s.* Parc *m*, enclos *m* (à moutons).

pen², *v.tr.* (penned) To pen (up, in), parquer (des moutons); (r)enfermer, confiner (qn dans une chambre).

pen³, *s.* **I.** Plume *f* (pour écrire). Stroke of the pen, trait *m* de plume. To put one's pen to paper, mettre la main à la plume. To run one's pen through sth., biffer, rayer, qch. (d'un trait de plume). Pen-and-ink drawing, dessin à la plume. **2.** Pen(-nib), (bec *m* de) plume. Steel pen, plume métallique. **'pen-box,** *s.* Plumier *m.* **'pen-feather,** *s.* **I.** Penne *f.* **2.** = PIN-FEATHER. **'pen-name,** *s.* Nom *m* de plume; (of journalist) nom de guerre. **'pen-pusher,** *s.* F: Plumitif *m*; rond-de-cuir *m.* **'pen-rack, -rest,** *s.* Pose-plumes *m inv.* **'pen-tray,** *s.* Plumier (plat). **'pen-wiper,** *s.* Essuie-plume(s) *m inv.*

pen⁴, *v.tr.* (penned) Écrire (une lettre).

pen⁵, *s.* *Orn:* Cygne *m* femelle.

penal ['pi:n(ə)l], *a.* (a) (Of laws) Pénal, -aux; (of offence) qui comporte, entraîne, une pénalité. Penal servitude, travaux forcés. A: Penal colony, penal settlement, colonie *f* pénitentiaire.

penalize ['pi:nəla:iz], *v.tr.* **I.** Sanctionner (un délit) d'une peine. **2.** (a) Infliger une peine à (qn). (b) *Games:* Pénaliser (un joueur). (c) *Sp:* Handicaper.

penalty ['penəlti], *s.* **I.** (a) Peine *f*, pénalité *f.* *Com:* Amende *f* (pour retard de livraison). *Adm:* Sanction (pénale). Penalty clause (in contract), clause pénale (de dommages-intérêts). The death penalty, la peine de mort. **(Up)on, under, penalty of death,** sous peine de mort.

F: To pay the **penalty** of *one's foolishness,* être puni de sa sottise. (*b*) Désavantage *m.* To pay the *p.* of *fame,* payer la rançon de la gloire. **2.** *Sp:* (*a*) Pénalisation *f,* pénalité. *Golf:* Penalty stroke, coup *m* d'amende. *Fb:* **Penalty kick,** shot, coup de pied de réparation; penalty *m.* (*b*) Handicap *m.*

penance ['penəns], *s.* To do penance *for one's sins,* faire pénitence de, pour, ses péchés.

Penates [pe'neiti:z], *s.pl. Rom.Ant:* Pénates *m.*

pence [pens], *s.pl. See* PENNY.

pencil[1] ['pensil], *s.* **I.** Crayon *m.* (*a*) Lead **pencil,** crayon à mine de plomb. *Coloured p.,* crayon de couleur. *Indelible p.,* crayon à copier. Propelling **pencil,** porte-mine *m inv* à vis. **Written** in **pencil,** écrit au crayon. **Pencil drawing,** dessin *m* au crayon; crayonnage *m.* (*b*) Slate **pencil,** crayon d'ardoise. **2.** (*a*) *Opt:* **Pencil of light-rays, light pencil,** faisceau lumineux. (*b*) *Ball:* Pencil of trajectories, gerbe *f* de trajectoires. **'pencil-arm,** *s.* Branche *f* porte-mine (de compas). **'pencil-box,** *s.* Plumier *m.* **'pencil-case,** *s.* **I.** (*a*) Portecrayon *m.* (*b*) Porte-mine *m inv.* **2.** Plumier *m;* trousse *f* d'écolier. **'pencil-holder,** *s.* Portecrayon *m.* **'pencil-mark,** *s.* Trait *m* au crayon. **'pencil-sharpener,** *s.* Taille-crayon *m.*

pencil[2], *v.tr.* (pencilled) **I.** (*a*) Marquer (qch.) au crayon. (*b*) Dessiner au crayon. (*c*) (i) *To p. one's eyebrows,* se faire les sourcils (au crayon). (ii) *Delicately pencilled eyebrows,* sourcils d'un tracé délicat. **2.** *To p. a note,* crayonner un billet.

pendant ['pendənt], *s.* **I.** Pendentif *m* (de collier); pendeloque *f* (de lustre). *Arch:* Cul-de-lampe *m. Furn:* Gas pendant, lustre *m* à gaz; suspension *f.* **2.** *Nau:* (*a*) (*Rope*) Martinet *m.* (*b*) ['penənt] (*Flag*) Flamme *f,* guidon *m.* **3.** (*Also* [pãdã]) Pendant *m* (d'un tableau).

pendent ['pendənt], *a.* **I.** (*Of plant*) Pendant; (*of draperies*) retombant. **2.** *Jur:* (Procès) pendant, en instance.

pendentive [pen'dentiv], *s. Arch:* Pendentif *m.*

pending ['pendiŋ], *a.* **I.** *a.* = PENDENT 2. **2.** *prep.* (*a*) Pendant. *P. the negotiations,* pendant, durant, les négociations. (*b*) En attendant (le retour de qn).

pendulous ['pendjuləs], *a.* **I.** (*Of lip*) Pendant. **2.** Balançant, oscillant; (mouvement) pendulaire.

pendulum ['pendjuləm], *s.* Pendule *m,* balancier *m. S.a.* SWING[1] 2.

penetrable ['penitrəbl], *a.* Pénétrable.

penetrate ['penitreit]. **I.** *v.tr.* Pénétrer, percer. *The shell penetrated the hull,* l'obus a pénétré la coque. **2.** *v.i. The bayonet penetrated to the lung,* la baïonnette pénétra jusqu'au poumon. *The water is penetrating everywhere,* l'eau s'introduit partout. **penetrating,** *a.* **I.** (Vent) pénétrant; (son) mordant. **2.** (Esprit) clairvoyant, pénétrant.

penetration [peni'treiʃ(ə)n], *s.* (*a*) Pénétration *f. P. of poison gas,* venue *f* de gaz toxique. (*b*) Pénétration (de l'esprit); perspicacité *f.*

penetrative ['penitreitiv], *a.* Pénétrant.

penguin ['pengwin, 'peŋgwin], *s. Orn:* Manchot *m, F:* pingouin *m.*

penholder ['penhouldər], *s.* Porte-plume *m inv.*

peninsula [pe'ninsjula], *s. Geog:* Péninsule *f;* presqu'île *f.*

peninsular [pe'ninsjulər], *a.* Péninsulaire. *Hist:* The Peninsular War, la guerre d'Espagne.

penitence ['penitəns], *s.* Pénitence *f,* contrit on *f.*

penitent ['penitənt]. **I.** *a.* Pénitent, contrit. **2.** *s.* Pénitent, -ente. **-ly,** *adv.* D'un air contrit.

penitentiary [peni'tenʃəri]. **I.** *a. Ecc:* Penitentiary priest, pénitencier *m.* **2.** *s. U.S:* Prison *f.*

penknife ['pennaif], *s.* Canif *m.*

penmanship ['penmənʃip], *s.* **I.** L'art *m* d'écrire. **2.** Calligraphie *f.*

pennant ['penənt], *s.* **I.** *Nau:* = PENDANT 2. **2.** = PENNON 1.

pennate ['penet], *a. Nat.Hist:* Penné, pinné.

penniless ['peniləs], *a.* Sans le sou; sans ressources. *To be p.,* n'avoir pas le sou. *To leave oneself p.,* se dépouiller de ses biens.

pennon ['penən], *s.* **I.** Flamme *f,* banderole *f. Sp:* Fanion *m.* **2.** *Nau:* = PENNANT 2 (*b*).

penny ['peni], *s.* **I.** (*Coin*) (*pl.* pennies) Deux sous; gros sou. They haven't a penny (to bless themselves with), ils n'ont pas le sou. To look twice at every penny, prendre garde à un sou. To come back like a bad penny, revenir comme un mauvais sou. **2.** (*pl.* pence) (*a*) (*Value*) Nobody was a penny the worse, cela n'a fait de tort à personne. I'm not a p. the wiser, ʼe n'en sais pas plus qu'avant. *Prov:* In for a penny ʼn for a pound, qui a dit A doit dire B. *S.a.* SPEND 1, THOUGHT[1] 2. (*b*) *Coll. Prov:* Take care of the pence and the pounds will take care of themselves, il n'y a pas de petites économies. **3.** That will cost a pretty penny, cela coûtera cher *A thousand pounds is a pretty p.,* mille livres, c'est un beau denier. To earn an honest penny, gagner honnêtement de l'argent. **4.** *B:* Denier. **'penny-a-'liner,** *s. F:* Journaliste *m* à deux sous la ligne. **penny 'dreadful,** *s.* Roman *m* à deux sous; roman à sensation. **'penny-in-the-'slot,** *attrib.a.* Penny-in-the-slot machine, distributeur *m* automatique. **'penny-'piece,** *s. F:* Pièce *f* de deux sous. I haven't a penny-piece, je n'ai pas un sou vaillant. **'penny-'post,** *s. Post:* Affranchissement *m* à deux sous. **'penny-wise,** *a.* Qui fait des économies de bouts de chandelle. To be penny-wise and pound-foolish, économiser les sous et prodiguer les louis.

pennyroyal [peni'rɔiəl], *s. Bot:* Pouliot *m.*

pennyweight ['peniweit], *s. Approx.* = Un gramme et demi.

pennyworth ['peniwə:rθ], *s.* To buy a p. of bread, acheter (pour) deux sous de pain.

pension[1] ['penʃ(ə)n], *s.* **I.** Pension *f* (somme annuelle). Old age pension, retraite *f* de vieillesse. Retiring pension, pension de retraite; *Mil:* solde *f* de retraite; *F:* retraite. To retire on a pension, prendre sa retraite. To be discharged with a p., être mis à la retraite. **2.** [pãsjõ] Pension de famille.

pension[2], *v.tr.* Pensionner (qn). To pension s.o. off, mettre qn à la retraite.

pensioner ['penʃənər], *s.* Titulaire *mf* d'une pension. Army pensioner, (i) militaire retraité; (ii) (*in institution*) invalide *m.* State pensioner, pensionnaire *mf* de l'État.

pensive ['pensiv], *a.* Pensif, songeur. **-ly,** *adv.* Pensivement; d'un air pensif.

pensiveness ['pensivnəs], *s.* Air pensif; songerie *f.*

pent [pent], *a.* **I.** **Pent (in, up),** renfermé, parqué. **2. Pen:** up emotion, émotion refoulée, contenue.

pentagon ['pentagon], *s.* Pentagone *m.*

pentahedron [penta'hi:dron], *s.* Pentaèdre *m.*

pentameter [pen'tamətər], *s. Pros:* Pentamètre *m.*

pentane ['pentein], *s. Ch:* Pentane *m.*

pentasyllabic [pentasi'labik], *a.* Pentasyllabe.

Pentateuch (the) [ðə'pentatju:k], *s. B:* Le Pentateuque.

pentavalent [pen'tavələnt], *a. Ch:* Pentavalent.

Pentecost ['pentikɔst], *s.* La Pentecôte.

penthouse ['penthaus], *s. Const:* (*a*) Appentis *m*; hangar *m.* (*b*) (*Over door*) Auvent *m.*

pentode ['pentoud], *s. W.Tel:* Lampe *f* à cinq électrodes; lampe pent(h)ode.

pent-roof ['pentru:f], *s.* Comble *m* en appentis.

penult [pe'nʌlt], **penultimate** [pe'nʌltimet]. **1.** *a.* Pénultième; avant-dernier, -ière. **2.** *s.* Avant-dernière syllabe; pénultième *f.*

penumbra [pe'nʌmbrə], *s.* Pénombre *f.*

penurious [pe'nju̇əriəs], *a.* **1.** Pauvre. **2.** (*a*) Parcimonieux. (*b*) Mesquin. **-ly,** *adv.* **1.** Pauvrement. **2.** (*a*) Parcimonieusement. (*b*) Mesquinement.

penury ['penjuri], *s.* Pénurie *f.* **1.** Indigence *f*; dénuement *m*, misère *f.* **2.** Manque *m*, pauvreté *f* (*of*, de).

peony ['pi:ɔni], *s. Bot:* Pivoine *f.*

people[1] ['pi:pl], *s.* I. (*pl.* peoples) Peuple *m*, nation *f.* II. **people** (*Coll. with pl. const.*) **1.** (*a*) Peuple, habitants *mpl* (d'une ville). *The country p.*, les populations rurales. (*b*) **The King and his people**, le roi et ses sujets. (*c*) *F:* Parents *mpl.* **My people are abroad**, mes parents sont à l'étranger. **How are ꞏll your people?** comment va tout votre monde? **2.** (*a*) *Pol:* Citoyens *mpl* (d'un état). **Government by the people**, gouvernement par le peuple. **The people at large**, le grand public. (*b*) **The (common) people**, la populace; le (bas, menu, petit) peuple. **A man of the people**, un homme sorti du peuple. **3.** (*a*) Gens *mpl*, monde *m.* **Young people**, jeunes gens. **Old people**, les vieilles gens *m*, les vieux. **Fashionable people**, le beau monde. **Society people**, gens du monde. *All p. who are honest*, tous ceux qui sont honnêtes. **What do you people think?** qu'en pensez-vous, vous autres? (*b*) Personnes *fpl.* **On ꞏ thousand people**, mille personnes. (*c*) (*Nom.*) On; (*obl. cases*) vous. **People say**, on dit. *That's enough to alarm p.*, il y a de quoi vous alarmer. (*d*) *F: Hum:* **The feathered people**, la gent ailée. (*e*) *Myth:* **The little people, the good people**, les fées *f.*

people[2], *v.tr.* Peupler (*with*, de).

pep [pep], *s. U.S: P:* Entrain *m*, fougue *f.* **Full of pep**, plein de sève, d'allant.

pepper[1] ['pepər], *s.* **1.** Poivre *m.* **Pepper-and-salt cloth**, étoffe marengo *inv.* **Pepper-and-salt hair**, cheveux poivre et sel. *S.a.* CAYENNE 2. **2.** *Bot:* Black pepper, poivrier *m.* **'pepper-box, -castor,** *s.* **1.** Poivrière *f.* **2.** *Arch: F:* Pepper-box (turret), poivrière.

pepper[2], *v.tr.* **1.** Poivrer. **2.** *F:* (*a*) Cribler (l'ennemi) de balles. (*b*) Rosser (qn).

peppercorn ['pepəkɔ:rn], *s.* Grain *m* de poivre. **Peppercorn rent**, loyer nominal.

peppermint ['pepəmint], *s.* **1.** Menthe poivrée; menthe anglaise. **2.** Peppermint(-drop, -lozenge), pastille *f* de menthe.

peppery ['pepəri], *a.* **1.** Poivré. **2.** (*Of pers.*) Irascible, colérique.

pepsin ['pepsin], *s.* Pepsine *f.*

peptone ['peptoun], *s.* Peptone *f.*

per [pə:r], *prep.* **1.** (*a*) Par. **Sent per carrier**, envoyé par messageries. *Per Messrs Smith and Co.*, par l'entremise de MM. Smith et Cie. (*b*) **As per invoice**, suivant facture. **As per sample**, conformément à l'échantillon. (*c*) **One franc per pound**, un franc la livre. **Sixty miles per hour**, soixante milles à l'heure. **Per day**, par jour. **2.** **Per annum**, par an. **Per cent(um)**, pour cent. *Settlement* per contra, règlement par contre.

peradventure [pərad'ventjər], *adv. A:* **1.** Par aventure, par hasard. **2.** Peut-être. **Peradventure he s mistaken**, il a pu se tromper. **3.** *s.* **Beyond peradventurꞏ**, à n'en pas douter.

perambulate [pə'rambjuleit], *v.tr.* **1.** Parcourir, se promener dans (son jardin). **2. To perambulate the parish**, constater en procession solennelle les bornes de la commune; délimiter la commune.

perambulator [pə'rambjuleitər], *s.* Voiture *f* d'enfant.

perceive [pər'si:v], *v.tr.* **1.** Percevoir (la vérité). **2.** Percevoir (un son). **3.** S'apercevoir de (qch.). *He perceived that he was being watched*, il s'aperçut qu'on l'observait. **4.** *To p. s.o.*, apercevoir qn.

percentage [pər'sentedʒ], *s.* **1.** Pourcentage *m.* **To allow a percentage on all transactions**, allouer un tantième sur toutes opérations. *F:* **Only a small percentage of the pupils were successful**, la proportion des élèves admis a été faible. **2. Percentage of acid**, teneur *f* en acide. *P. of alcohol in a wine*, proportion *f* d'alcool dans un vin.

perceptible [pər'septibl], *a.* (*a*) Perceptible (à l'esprit). *P. difference*, différence sensible. (*b*) Perceptible to the eye visible. **-ibly,** *adv.* Sensiblement.

perception [pər'sepʃ(ə)n], *s.* (*a*) Perception *f.* (*b*) Sensibilité *f* (aux impressions extérieures).

perceptive [pər'septiv], *a.* Perceptif.

perch[1] [pə:rtʃ], *s.* **1.** Perchoir *m*; (*in cage*) bâton *m.* *F:* **To knock s.o. off his perch** déjucher qn. **2.** *Meas:* Perche *f* (de 5½ yards, *approx.* = 5 m.).

perch[2]. (*a*) *v.i.* (*Of bird, F: of pers.*) (Se) percher (*on*, sur); jucher. (*b*) *v.pr.* Se percher, se jucher (*on*, sur). **perching,** *a.* (Oiseau) percheur.

perch[3], *s. Ich:* Perche *f.*

perchance [pər'tʃɑ:ns], *adv. A:* = PERADVENTURE.

perchlorate [pər'klɔ:ret], *s. Ch:* Perchlorate *m.*

percipient [pər'sipiənt]. **1.** *a.* Percepteur, -trice (de sensations); conscient. **2.** *s.* Sujet *m* télépathique.

percolate ['pə:rkoleit]. **1.** *v.i.* S'infiltrer; (*of coffee*) filtrer. **2.** *v.tr.* To percolate the coffee, passer le café.

percolation [pə:rko'leiʃ(ə)n], *s.* **1.** Infiltration *f.* **2.** Filtration *f*, filtrage *m.*

percolator ['pə:rkoleitər], *s.* Filtre *m*; *esp.* filtre à café.

percuss [pər'kʌs], *v.tr.* Percuter (la poitrine).

percussion [pər'kʌʃ(ə)n], *s.* **1.** Percussion *f*; choc *m.* *Mus:* Percussion instruments, instruments *m* de, à, percussion; batterie *f.* *Sm.a:* Percussion cap, capsule *f* de fulminate. **2.** *Med:* Percussion (d'un organe). **per'cussion-fuse,** *s. Artil:* Fusée percutante. **per'cussion-pin,** *s. Artil:* Rugueux *m* (de fusée).

percussive [pər'kʌsiv], *a.* Percutant.

perdition [pər'diʃ(ə)n], *s.* Perte *f*, ruine *f*, *Theol:* perdition *f.*

peregrination [perigri'neiʃ(ə)n], *s.* Pérégrination *f*, voyage *m.*

peregrine ['perigrin], *a. Ven:* **Peregrine falcon**, faucon pèlerin.

peremptory ['perəm(p)təri], *a.* Péremptoire. (*a*) (*Of refusal*) Absolu, décisif. *P. necessity*, nécessité absolue. (*b*) (*Of tone*) Tranchant, impératif, absolu. **-ily,** *adv.* (*a*) Péremptoirement, absolument. (*b*) Impérieusement.

perennial [pə'renjəl]. **1.** *a.* (*a*) Éternel, perpétuel. (*b*) *Bot:* Vivace, persistant. **2.** *s.* Plante *f* vivace. **-ally,** *adv.* A perpétuité; éternellement.

perfect[1] ['pə:rfekt], *a.* **1.** (*a*) Parfait; (ouvrage) achevé. **Perfect specimen**, spécimen parfait. **To be perfect**, avoir toutes les perfections. *To have a p. knowledge of sth.*, savoir qch. à fond. *F:* **It's**

perfect, c'est perlé. (b) F: **Perfect idiot**, parfait imbécile. **She is a perfect fright**, c'est un véritable épouvantail. *He is a p. stranger to me*, il m'est parfaitement étranger. **2.** (a) *Mth:* **Perfect square**, carré parfait. (b) *Mus:* **Perfect fourth**, quarte *f* juste. **3.** *Nat.Hist:* (*Of plant, insect*) Complet, -ète. **4.** *Gram:* **The perfect tense**, *s.* **the perfect**, le parfait. **Future perfect**, futur antérieur. **Verb in the perfect**, verbe au parfait. **-ly**, *adv.* Parfaitement.

perfect[2] [pər'fekt, 'pɔːrfekt], *v.tr.* **1.** Achever, parachever (une besogne). **2.** Rendre parfait, parfaire (une méthode). **3.** *Typ:* Imprimer (une feuille) en retiration. **perfecting**, *s.* **1.** Achèvement *m*, accomplissement *m*. **2.** Perfectionnement *m*. **3.** *Typ:* (Impression *f* en) retiration *f*.

perfectible [pər'fektibl], *a.* Perfectible.

perfection [pər'fekʃ(ə)n], *s.* Perfection *f*. **1.** (a) Achèvement *m*, accomplissement *m* (d'une tâche). (b) Perfectionnement *m* (d'un projet). **2.** (a) **To succeed to perfection**, réussir à souhait. **With rare perfection**, dans une rare perfection. **Perfection of detail**, achevé *m* (d'un objet d'art). *S.a.* COUNSEL[1] 2. (b) Développement complet (d'une plante).

perfervid [pər'fəːrvid], *a.* Ardent, exalté. **-ly**, *adv.* Avec exaltation.

perfidious [pər'fidjəs], *a.* Perfide; traître, -esse. **-ly**, *adv.* Perfidement, traîtreusement.

perfidiousness [pər'fidjəsnəs], **perfidy** ['pəːrfidi], *s.* Perfidie *f*, traîtrise *f*.

perforate ['pəːrforeit]. **1.** *v.tr.* Perforer, percer, transpercer. **Perforating machine**, machine à perforer; perforatrice *f*. **2.** *v.i.* Pénétrer (*into, dans*). **To perforate through sth.**, perforer qch.

perforated, *a.* Perforé, troué, ajouré.

perforation [pəːrfo'reiʃ(ə)n], *s.* Perforation *f*. **1.** Perçage *m*, percement *m*. **2.** (a) Petit trou. (b) *Coll.* Trous *mpl*, perforation.

perforator ['pəːrforeitər], *s.* **1.** Machine *f* à perforer; perforateur *m*. *Min:* Perforatrice *f*. **2.** *Surg:* Tréphine *f*.

perforce [pər'fɔːrs], *adv. A. & Lit:* Forcément.

perform [pər'fɔːrm], *v.tr.* **1.** Exécuter (un mouvement); accomplir (une tâche); effectuer (une addition); célébrer (un rite); s'acquitter de, remplir (son devoir). **2.** (a) Jouer, représenter (une pièce de théâtre); exécuter (une danse); remplir (un rôle). (b) *Abs.* **To perform in a play**, jouer, tenir un rôle, dans une pièce. *To p. on the flute*, jouer de la flûte. **Performing dogs**, chiens savants. **performing**, *s.* **1.** Accomplissement *m* (*of*, de). **2.** *Th:* Représentation *f* (d'une pièce).

performance [pər'fɔːrməns], *s.* **1.** Exécution *f* (d'un opéra); accomplissement *m* (d'une tâche); célébration *f* (d'un rite). **2.** (a) Acte *m*, exploit *m*. (b) Marche *f*, fonctionnement *m* (d'une machine). (c) *Sp:* *Aut:* Performance *f* (d'un coureur, d'une voiture). **To put up a good performance**, bien s'acquitter. **3.** Représentation *f* (d'une pièce); séance *f* (de cinéma, etc.). **Evening performance**, soirée *f*. **Afternoon performance**, matinée *f*. **No performance to-night**, ce soir relâche.

performer [pər'fɔːrmər], *s.* Artiste *mf*. **1.** *Mus:* Exécutant, -ante. **2.** *Th:* Acteur, -trice.

perfume[1] ['pəːrfjuːm], *s.* Parfum *m*. (a) Odeur *f*. (b) Bottle of perfume, flacon *m* de parfum.

perfume[2] [pər'fjuːm], *v.tr.* Parfumer.

perfumer [pər'fjuːmər], *s.* Parfumeur, -euse.

perfumery [pər'fjuːməri], *s.* Parfumerie *f*.

perfunctory [pər'fʌŋktəri], *a.* **1.** (*Of examination*) Fait pour la forme. *P. glance*, coup d'œil

superficiel. *P. enquiry*, enquête peu poussée renseignements pris par manière d'acquit. **2.** (*Of pers.*) Négligent; peu zélé. **-ily**, *adv.* Par manière d'acquit; superficiellement; pour la forme.

pergola ['pəːrgolə], *s.* Treille *f* à l'italienne tonnelle *f*.

perhaps [pər'haps], *adv.* Peut-être. **Perhaps so perhaps not**, peut-être (bien) que oui, que non *P. I have it*, il se peut que je l'aie. *I am giving up this work, but may p. resume it later*, j'abandonne ce travail, quitte à le reprendre plus tard.

peri ['piːəri], *s. Myth:* Péri *mf*.

perianth ['perianθ], *s. Bot:* Périanthe *m*.

pericardium [peri'kɑːrdiəm], *s. Anat:* Péricarde *m*.

pericarp ['perikɑːrp], *s. Bot:* Péricarpe *m*.

perigee ['peridʒiː], *s. Astr:* Périgée *m*.

perihelion [peri'hiːliən], *s. Astr:* Périhélie *m*.

peril ['peril], *s.* Péril *m*, danger *m*. **In peril of one's life**, en danger de mort. *Touch him at your p.*, gare à vous si vous le touchez.

perilous ['periləs], *a.* Périlleux, dangereux. **-ly** *adv.* Périlleusement, dangereusement.

perimeter [pe'rimətər], *s.* Périmètre *m*.

perineum [peri'niːəm], *s. Anat:* Périnée *m*.

period ['piːəriəd], *s.* Période *f*. **1.** (a) Durée *f* délai *m*. **Within the agreed period**, dans le délai fixé. **Deposit for a fixed period**, dépôt à terme fixe. (b) *Astr: etc:* **Period of planet's revolution** cycle *m*, période, de la révolution d'une planète (c) *Med:* **Periods of a disease**, stades *m*, phases *f* d'une maladie. **2.** Époque *f*, âge *m*. *Cost:* **Period dress**, robe de style. **3.** (a) *Rh:* Phrase *f*. **Well rounded periods**, phrases, périodes, bien tournées (b) *Mus:* Phrase complète. **4.** *Gram:* Typ Point *m* (de ponctuation). **5.** *Ar:* Tranche (de trois chiffres). **6.** *pl.* **Periods** = MONTHLY 3.

periodic [piːəri'ɔdik], *a.* **1.** Périodique. **2.** *Lit* **Periodic style**, style riche en périodes; styl ample.

periodical [piːəri'ɔdik(ə)l]. **1.** *a.* Périodique **2.** *s.* Publication *f* périodique; périodique *m* **-ally**, *adv.* Périodiquement.

periosteum [peri'ɔstiəm], *s. Anat:* Périoste *m*

peripatetic [peripa'tetik], *a.* (a) *A.Phil:* Péripatéticien, péripatétique. (b) *F:* Ambulant.

peripheral [pe'rifərəl], *a.* Périphérique, péri métrique. *P. speed*, vitesse circonférentielle.

periphery [pe'rifəri], *s.* Périphérie *f*, pourtour *m*

periphrasis, *pl.* **-es** [pe'rifrasis, -iːz], *s.* Péri phrase *f*; circonlocution *f*.

periphrastic [peri'frastik], *a.* Périphrastique.

periscope ['periskoup], *s.* **1.** Périscope *m* **2.** *Phot:* Objectif *m* périscopique.

periscopic [peri'skopik], *a.* Périscopique.

perish ['periʃ]. **1.** *v.i.* (a) Périr, mourir. *I shall do it or perish in the attempt*, je le ferai ou j'y perdrai la vie. *Lit:* **Perish the thought!** loin de nous cette pensée! *F:* **I'm perishing with cold** je meurs de froid. (*Of rubber, etc.*) Se détériorer. **2.** *v.tr.* (a) Détériorer. (b) (*Of frost*) Faire mourir, brûler (la végétation). **perished** *a.* **1.** (*Of rubber*) Détérioré. **2.** **To be** perished with cold, être transi de froid.

perishable ['periʃəbl]. **1.** *a.* (a) Périssable sujet à s'altérer. (b) De courte durée; éphémère **2.** *s.pl.* **Perishables**, marchandises *f* périssables.

peristaltic [peri'staltik], *a.* Péristaltique.

peristyle ['peristail], *s.* Péristyle *m*.

peritoneum [perito'niːəm], *s.* Péritoine *m*.

peritonitis [perito'naitis], *s.* Péritonite *f*.

periwig ['periwig], *s. A:* Perruque *f*.

periwinkle[1] ['periwiŋkl], *s. Bot:* Pervenche *f*.

periwinkle², s. Moll: Bigorneau m.

perjure ['pɔːrdʒər], v.pr. To perjure oneself, (i) se parjurer ; (ii) commettre un parjure ; violer son serment. **perjured,** a. (Of pers.) Parjure.

perjurer ['pɔːrdʒərər], s. Parjure mf.

perjury ['pɔːrdʒəri], s. 1. (As a moral offence) Parjure m. 2. Jur: (a) To commit perjury, faire un faux serment. (b) Faux témoignage.

perk [pɔːrk]. 1. v.i. To perk (up), redresser la tête ; se ranimer. 2. v.tr. (a) To perk up one's head, redresser la tête. (b) To perk s.o. up, (i) parer, requinquer, qn ; (ii) (of drink, etc.) ravigoter qn.

perkiness ['pɔːrkinəs], s. 1. Allure(s) dégagée(s). 2. Air éveillé, alerte ; ton guilleret.

perks [pɔːrks], s.pl. See PERQUISITE.

perky ['pɔːrki], a. (a) Éveillé, guilleret. (b) (Ton) dégagé, désinvolte. **-ily,** adv. (a) D'un air éveillé. (b) D'un air dégagé.

perm¹ [pɔːrm], s. F: Hairdr: (Ondulation) permanente f, indéfrisable f.

perm², v.tr. F: To have one's ..air permed, se faire faire une indéfrisable.

permanence ['pɔːrmanəns], s. Permanence f; stabilité f (d'une conquête).

permanency ['pɔːrmanənsi], s. 1. = PERMANENCE. 2. Emploi permanent.

permanent ['pɔːrmanənt], a. Permanent. **Permanent post,** place inamovible ; poste fixe. **Permanen. establishment,** établissement à demeure. **Permanent abode, permanent address,** résidence fixe. Rail: The permanent way, la superstructure ; la voie ferrée. Hairdr: **Permanent wave,** ondulation permanente. **-ly,** adv. D'une façon permanente. **To be permanently appointed,** être nommé à titre définitif; être titularisé.

permanganate [pɔːr'maŋganet], s Ch: Permanganate m.

permeability ['pɔːrmiə'biliti], s. Perméabilité f.

permeable ['pɔːrmiəbl], a. Perméable.

permeate ['pɔːrmieit], v.tr. & i. To permeate (through) sth., filtrer à travers qch. **Water permeates everywhere,** l'eau s'insinue partout. The soil was permeated with water, le sol était saturé d'eau.

permeation [pɔːrmi'eiʃ(ə)n], s. Pénétration f, infiltration f.

permissible ['pɔːr'misibl], a. Tolérable, permis. Would it be p. to say that . . .? serait-on reçu à dire que . . .?

permission [pɔːr'miʃ(ə)n], s. Permission f. (a) To give s.o. permissio to do sth., donner à qn la permission de faire qch. With your kind p., si vous voulez bien (me) le permettre. (b) Permis m, autorisation f.

permissive [pɔːr'misiv], a. 1. Qui permet. Permissive leg slation législation facultative. 2. Permis, toléré.

permit¹ ['pɔːrmit], s. 1. (For pers.) Permis m, autorisation f. To take out a permit, se faire délivrer un permis. 2. Cust: (For goods) (a) Passavant m ; passe-debout m inv. (b) Export permit, autorisation d'exporter.

permit² [pɔːr'mit]. 1. v.tr. (permitted) Permettre. To permit s.o. to do sth., permettre à qn de faire qch. I was permitted to visit the works, j'ai été autorisé à visiter l'usine. P. me to tell you the truth, souffrez que je vous dise la vérité. 2. v.ind.tr. Tone which permitted of no reply, ton qui n'admettait pas, ne souffrait pas, de réplique.

permutable [pɔːr'mjutəbl], a. Permutable.

permutation [pɔːrmju'teiʃ(ə)n], s. Mth: Ling: Permutation f.

permute [pɔːr'mjut], v.tr. Mth: Permuter.

pernicious [pɔːr'niʃəs], a. Pernicieux; malsain, délétère. **-ly,** adv. Pernicieusement.

pernickety [pɔːr'nikəti], a. F: 1. Vétilleux, pointilleux. P. about one's food, difficile au sujet de sa nourriture. 2. (Of task) Délicat, minutieux.

peroration [pero'reiʃ(ə)n], s. Péroraison f.

peroxide [pe'rɔksaid], s. Ch: Peroxyde m. **Hydrogen peroxide,** eau oxygénée.

perpendicular [pɔːrpen'dikjulər]. 1. a. (a) Perpendiculaire ; (of cliff) vertical, -aux. (b) Arch: (Style) perpendiculaire. 2. s. (a) Fil m à plomb. (b) Geom: Perpendiculaire f. (c) Out of (the, perpendiculaire, hors d'aplomb ; hors d'équerre. **-ly,** adv. Perpendiculairement ; verticalement.

perpetrate ['pɔːrpetreit], v.tr. Commettre, perpétrer (un crime). To p. a breach of good taste, se rendre coupable d'un manque de bon goût.

perpetration [pɔːrpe'treiʃ(ə)n], s. 1. Perpétration f (d'un crime). 2. Péché m, crime m.

perpetrator ['pɔːrpetreitər], s. Auteur m (d'un crime). The p. of the joke, l'auteur de la farce.

perpetual [pɔːr'petjuəl], a. (a) Perpétuel, éternel. (b) F: Sans fin; continuel. **-ally,** adv. (a) Perpétuellement. (b) Sans cesse.

perpetuate [pɔːr'petjueit], v.tr. 1. Perpétuer, éterniser. 2. This invention has perpetuated his name, cette invention a préservé son nom de l'oubli.

perpetuation [pɔːrpetju'eiʃ(ə)n], s. 1. Perpétuation f, éternisation f. 2. Préservation f de l'oubli.

perpetuity [pɔːrpe'tjuiti], s. 1. Perpétuité f. In, to, for, perpetuity, à perpétuité. 2. Rente perpétuelle.

perplex [pɔːr'pleks], v.tr. Embarrasser (qn); mettre (qn) dans la perplexité. **perplexed,** a. 1. (Of pers.) Perplexe, embarrassé. 2. (Air) confus, perplexe. **perplexing,** a. Embarrassant, troublant.

perplexity [pɔːr'pleksiti], s. Perplexité f, embarras m.

perquisite ['pɔːrkwizit], s. (a) Casuel m. (b) F: Pourboire (auquel l'on a droit). (c) pl. **Perquisites,** F: perks; gratte f. These are the perquisites of the trade, c'est le revenant-bon du métier.

perron ['perən], s. Arch: Perron m.

perry ['peri], s. Poiré m.

persecute ['pɔːrsekjut], v.tr. 1. Persécuter (les hérétiques). 2. Tourmenter ; harceler.

persecution [pɔːrse'kjuʃ(ə)n], s. Persécution f.

persecutor ['pɔːrsekjutər], s. Persécuteur, -trice.

perseverance [pɔːrse'viːərəns], s. Persévérance f; constance f (dans le travail).

persevere [pɔːrse'viːər], v.i. Persévérer. To persevere with one's work, persévérer dans son travail. **persevering,** a. Persévérant, assidu (in doing sth., à faire qch.); constant (dans le travail). **-ly,** adv. Avec persévérance.

Persia ['pɔːrʃʌ]. Pr.n. Geog: La Perse.

Persian ['pɔːrʃ(ə)n]. 1. a. & s. Geog: (i) Persan, -ane; (ii) A.Hist: perse. (iii) The Persian Gulf, le Golfe Persique. Com: Persian carpet, tapis m de Perse. 2. s. Ling: Le persan.

persimmon [pɔːr'simən], s. Bot: 1. Plaquemine f. **Chinese persimmon,** kaki m. 2. Persimmon(-tree) plaqueminier m (de Virginie).

persist [pɔːr'sist], v.i. 1. To persist. o persis. in one's opinion, s'obstiner dans son opinion. To persist in doing sth., persister, s'obstiner, à faire qch. 2. Continuer. The fever persists, la fièvre persiste.

persistence [pɔːr'sistəns], **persistency** [pɔːr'sis_

tǝnsi], *s.* Persistance *f.* **1.** Obstination *f.*
2. Continuité *f. P. of matter,* permanence *f* de
la matière.
persistent [pǝr'sistǝnt], *a.* Persistant. **1.** *P. rain,*
pluie qui s'obstine. **2.** Continu. **-ly,** *adv.* Avec
persistance.
person ['pǝːrs(ǝ)n], *s.* Personne *f.* **1.** *(a)* Individu *m; pl.* gens *m. Foolish p.,* sot personnage.
Private person, simple particulier *m.* **To be no
respecter of persons,** ne pas faire cas des personnalités *f. Jur :* Some person or persons unknown,
un certain quidam. *(b)* **In** (one's own) person
en (propre) personne. **'To be delivered to the
addressee in person,'** "à remettre en mains
propres." *(c)* **To have a commanding person,**
posséder un extérieur imposant. *(d) Th : Lit :*
Personnage (d'un drame). **2.** *Gram :* **Verb in
the first person,** verbe à la première personne.
personable ['pǝːrsǝnǝbl], *a.* Bien (fait) de sa
personne ; beau, *f.* belle.
personage ['pǝːrsǝnedʒ], *s.* **1.** Personnage *m,*
personne *f,* personnalité *f.* **2.** *Th :* Personnage.
personal ['pǝːrsǝn(ǝ)l], *a.* Personnel. **1.** *(a)* Personal liberty, liberté individuelle. **Personal rights,**
droits du citoyen. *This is p. to myself,* cela m'est
propre. *Cust :* Articles for personal use, effets
usagers. *Journ :* Personal column, petite correspondance. *(b)* **Don't be personal,** ne faites pas
de personnalités. *(c) To make a p. application,* se
présenter en personne. *I have p. knowledge of this
kind of life,* j'ai connu cette existence par moi-
même. **2.** *Jur :* Personal property, biens mobiliers. **3.** *Gram :* **Personal pronoun,** pronom
personnel. **-ally,** *adv.* Personnellement. **Personally I think . . .,** quant à moi, je pense. . . .
P., I am willing, moi, je veux bien. *Don't take
that remark p.,* ne prenez pas cette remarque
pour vous. **To deliver sth. to s.o. personally,**
remettre qch. à qn en main(s) propre(s).
personality [pǝːrsǝ'naliti], *s.* **1.** *(a)* Personnalité *f,* personnage *m. (b)* Caractère *m* propre (de
qn). *To be lacking in p.,* manquer de personnalité.
2. **To indulge in personalities,** dire des personnalités (à qn).
personalty ['pǝːrsǝnǝlti], *s. Jur :* **1.** Objet
mobilier. **2.** Biens meubles ; fortune mobilière.
personate ['pǝːrsǝneit], *v.tr.* **1.** *Th :* Jouer (un
personnage). **2.** Se faire passer pour (qn).
personation [pǝːrsǝ'neiʃ(ǝ)n], *s.* **1.** *Th :* Représentation *f* (d'un personnage). **2.** *Jur :* (False)
personation, usurpation *f* de nom, d'état civil.
personification [pǝrsonifi'keiʃ(ǝ)n], *s.* Personnification *f.*
personify [pǝr'sonifai], *v.tr.* Personnifier. *He is
avarice personified,* il est, c'est, l'avarice même.
personnel [pǝːrso'nel], *s. Ind : etc :* Personnel *m.*
perspective [pǝr'spektiv]. **1.** *s. (a)* Perspective *f.
F :* **To see a matter in its true perspective,** voir
une affaire sous son vrai jour. *(b) A fine p. opened
out before his eyes,* une belle perspective, une belle
vue, s'ouvrit devant ses yeux. **2.** *a.* (Dessin)
perspectif, en perspective.
perspicacious [pǝːrspi'keiʃǝs], *a.* Perspicace.
He is very p., F : il a du nez.
perspicacity [pǝːrspi'kasiti], *s.* Perspicacité *f,*
pénétration *f,* clairvoyance *f,* discernement *m.*
perspicuity [pǝːrspi'kjuiti], *s.* Clarté *f,* netteté *f,*
lucidité *f* (de l'expression).
perspicuous [pǝr'spikjuǝs], *a.* *(Of style)* Clair,
lucide ; *(of reason)* évident.
perspiration [pǝːrspi'reiʃ(ǝ)n], *s. (a)* Transpiration *f.* **To break into perspiration,** entrer en
moiteur. *(b)* Sueur *f.* Bathed in perspiration,
trempé de sueur ; *F :* en nage.

perspire [pǝr'spaiǝr], *v.i.* Transpirer, suer
perspiring, *a.* En sueur.
persuade [pǝr'sweid], *v.tr.* *(a)* **To persuade s.o.
of sth.,** persuader, convaincre, qn de qch.
persuader qch. à qn. *To p. s.o. that he ought t
do sth.,* persuader à qn qu'il doit faire qch
(b) **To persuade s.o. to do sth.,** persuader à q
de faire qch. ; amener qn à faire qch. *P. you
brother to come!* déterminez, décidez, votre frèr
à venir! *(c) He persuaded me not to,* il m'en
dissuadé.
persuasion [pǝr'sweiʒ(ǝ)n], *s.* **1.** Persuasion *f
(a) The art of p.,* l'art de persuader. *(b)* Convic
tion *f.* **It is my persuasion that he is mad,** j'en
suis convaincu, j'ai la conviction, qu'il est fou
2. *(a)* (Religious) persuasion, religion *f,* con
fession *f. They are both of the same p.,* ils ont l
même religion. *(b)* **The Methodist p.,** la sect
méthodiste.
persuasive [pǝr'sweisiv], *a.* Persuasif ; per
suadant. **-ly,** *adv.* D'un ton persuasif.
persulphate [pǝr'sʌlfet], *s. Ch :* Persulfate *m.*
pert [pǝːrt], *a.* Mutin ; effronté, hardi. **-ly,** *adv
Avec mutinerie ; d'un air effronté.
pertain [pǝr'tein], *v.i.* Appartenir *(to sth.,* à qch.'
Subjects pertaining to religion, sujets qui ont rap
port à la religion. *This does not p. to my office
cela n'est pas de mon ressort.
pertinacious [pǝːrti'neiʃǝs], *a.* Obstiné, entêté
opiniâtre. **-ly,** *adv.* Obstinément, opiniâtre
ment.
pertinaciousness [pǝːrti'neiʃǝsnǝs], **pertinacity** [pǝːrti'nasiti], *s.* Obstination *f,* opiniâtreté *f*
entêtement *m (in doing sth.,* à faire qch.).
pertinence ['pǝːrtinǝns], **pertinency** ['pǝːrti
nǝnsi], *s.* Pertinence *f* (d'une raison) ; à-propos *m*
justesse *f* (d'une observation).
pertinent ['pǝːrtinǝnt], *a. (a)* Pertinent,
propos, juste. *(b)* **Books pertinent to the question**
livres qui ont rapport à la question. **-ly,** *adv
D'une manière pertinente ; à propos.
pertness ['pǝːrtnǝs], *s.* Mutinerie *f,* effronterie *f*
perturb [pǝr'tǝːrb], *v.tr.* Troubler, inquiéter
agiter.
perturbation [pǝːrtǝːr'beiʃ(ǝ)n], *s.* Agitation *f*
inquiétude *f,* trouble *m* (de l'esprit).
Peru [pe'ruː]. *Pr.n. Geog :* Le Pérou.
perusal [pe'ruːz(ǝ)l], *s.* Lecture *f. To give sth.
careful p.,* lire qch. attentivement.
peruse [pe'ruːz], *v.tr.* Lire attentivement
prendre connaissance (de (qch.).
pervade [pǝr'veid], *v.tr.* S'infiltrer dans (qch.).
The religious feeling that pervades the book, l
sentiment religieux qui anime tout ce livre. T
become pervaded, se pénétrer *(with,* de). (All-
porvading, qui se répand partout ; régnan
dominant.
pervasive [pǝr'veisiv], *a.* Qui se répand partout
pénétrant.
perverse [pǝr'vǝːrs], *a. (a)* Pervers, méchan
(b) Entêté dans le mal. *(c)* Contrariant. *(d)* Re
vêche. **-ly,** *adv. (a)* Perversement ; ave
perversité. *(b)* D'une manière contrariante.
perverseness [pǝr'vǝːrsnǝs], *s. (a)* Perversité *f
(b)* Esprit *m* contraire. *(c)* Caractère *m* revêche.
perversion [pǝr'vǝːrʃ(ǝ)n], *s.* Perversion *f.* A *p
of the truth,* un travestissement de la vérité.
perversity [pǝr'vǝːrsiti], *s.* = PERVERSENESS.
pervert[1] ['pǝːrvǝːrt], *s. (a)* Perverti, -ie. *(b)* Apos
tat *m.*
pervert[2] [pǝr'vǝːrt], *v.tr.* **1.** Détourner (qch. d
son but). **2.** Pervertir (qn) ; dépraver (le goût
3. Fausser (les faits).
perverter [pǝr'vǝːrtǝr], *s.* Pervertisseur, -euse.

ervious ['pəːviəs], a. Perméable (à l'eau, etc.).
erviousness ['pəːrviəsnəs], s. Perméabilité f (to, à).
essimism ['pesimizm], s. Pessimisme m.
essimist ['pesimist], s. Pessimiste mf.
essimistic [pesi'mistik], a. Pessimiste. To feel p. about a matter, augurer mal d'une affaire. **-ally,** adv. Avec pessimisme.
est [pest], s. (a) Insecte m ou plante f nuisible. Here the rabbits are a p., ici les lapins sont un fléau. (b) F: Peste f, fléau. That child is a perfect p.! quelle peste que cet enfant !
ester ['pestər], v.tr. **I.** Tourmenter, importuner. To p. s.o. with questions, assommer qn de (ses) questions. To pester s.o. to do sth., importuner qn pour lui faire faire qch. **2.** House pestered with rats, maison infestée de rats.
estiferous [pes'tifərəs], a. (a) (Of air) Pestifère. (b) (Of insects, etc.) Nuisible. (c) F: (Of doctrine) Pernicieux.
estilence ['pestiləns], s. Peste f.
estilent ['pestilənt], a. (a) (Of doctrine) Pestilentiel; pernicieux. (b) F: Assommant, empoisonnant.
estilential [pesti'lenʃ(ə)l], a. Pestilentiel. (a) (Of disease) Contagieux, pestifère. (b) P. smell, odeur infecte. (c) (Of doctrine) Pernicieux.
estle¹ [pesl], s. Pilon m (pour mortier).
estle², v.tr. Piler, broyer (au mortier).
et¹ [pet]. **I.** s. (a) Animal familier, favori. To make a pet of an animal, choyer un animal. 'No pets,' "pas de bêtes." (b) He is his mother's pet, c'est l'enfant gâté de sa mère. My pet! mon chouchou ! **2.** Attrib. Choyé, favori ; de prédilection. He's on his pet subject again, le revoilà sur son dada. Pet name, diminutif m ; nom m d'amitié. S.a. AVERSION 2.
et², v.tr. (petted) **I.** Choyer, mignoter, chouchouter. **2.** Esp. U.S: Caresser, câliner (qn).
et³, s. Accès m de mauvaise humeur. To take the pet, prendre la mouche. To be in a pet, bouder ; être de mauvaise humeur.
etal ['pet(ə)l], s. Bot: Pétale m. (Of flower) To shed its petals, s'effeuiller.
etard [pe'tɑːrd], s. Mil: A: Pétard m. S.a. HOISE.
Peter¹ ['piːtər]. **I.** Pr.n.m. Pierre. R.C.Ch: Peter's pence, le denier de Saint-Pierre. **2.** s. Nau: Blue Peter, pavillon m de partance.
peter² out [piːtə'raut], v.i. F: **I.** (a) Min: (Of seam) Mourir ; s'épuiser. (b) (Of stream) Disparaître. **2.** (Of scheme) Tomber dans l'eau. **3.** Aut: (Of engine) S'arrêter (faute d'essence).
petersham ['piːtərʃ(ə)m], s. **I.** Gros drap (à pardessus) ; ratine f. **2.** Petersham ribbon, ruban m gros grain.
etiole ['petioul], s. Bot: Pétiole m.
etition¹ [pe'tiʃ(ə)n], s. (a) Prière f (à Dieu). (b) Pétition f, supplique f, requête f. (c) Jur: Petition for a reprieve, recours m en grâce. Petition for a divorce, demande f en divorce. Petition in bankruptcy, (i) requête des créanciers ; (ii) requête du négociant insolvable. S.a. FILE⁴ 2.
etition², v.tr. Adresser, présenter, une pétition, une requête, à (la cour, un souverain). To petition the court for sth., réclamer qch. au tribunal.
etitioner [pe'tiʃənər], s. Pétitionnaire mf, solliciteur, -euse. Jur: Requérant, -ante.
etrel ['petrəl], s. Orn: Pétrel m. Stormy petrel, (i) oiseau m des tempêtes ; (ii) F: émissaire m de discorde.
etrifaction [petri'fakʃ(ə)n], s. Pétrification f.
etrify ['petrifai]. **I.** v.tr. (a) Pétrifier (le bois).

(b) F: Pétrifier, méduser (qn de peur). **2.** v.i. Se pétrifier.
petrol ['petrəl, -trɔl], s. Essence f (de pétrole). **'petrol-can,** s. Bidon m à essence. **'petrol tap,** s. Robinet m d'arrivée d'essence.
petroleum [pe'trouljəm], s. Pétrole m.
petticoat ['petikout], s. (a) A: Jupe f, cotillon m. Petticoat government, régime m de cotillons. He is under p. government, c'est sa femme qui porte la culotte. (b) Jupe de dessous ; jupon m.
pettifog ['petifɔg], v.i. (pettifogged) Avocasser. Pettifogging lawyer, attorney, homme de loi de bas étage.
pettiness ['petinəs], s. Petitesse f, mesquinerie f.
pettish ['petiʃ], a. De mauvaise humeur ; maussade ; irritable. **-ly,** adv. Avec humeur.
pettishness ['petiʃnəs], s. Mauvaise humeur ; irritabilité f ; maussaderie f.
petty ['peti], a. **I.** (a) Petit, insignifiant, sans importance. Petty monarch, roitelet m. Petty expenses, menus frais. S.a. LARCENY, SESSION 4. (b) Petty(-minded), mesquin. **2.** Com: Petty cash, petite caisse. **3.** Navy: Petty officer, contremaître m ; F: gradé m. The petty officers, la maistrance. **petty-'mindedness,** s. = PETTINESS.
petulance ['petjuləns], s. Irritabilité f, vivacité f. Outburst of p., mouvement m d'humeur.
petulant ['petjulənt], a. Irritable, susceptible, vif. **-ly,** adv. Avec irritation.
petunia [pe'tjuːnjə], s. Bot: Pétunia m.
pew [pjuː], s. Banc d'église (fermé). **'pewopener,** s. (Aide mf du) bedeau. **'pew-rent,** s. Abonnement m à un banc d'église.
pewit ['piːwit], s. Orn: Vanneau (huppé).
pewter ['pjutər], s. **I.** Étain m, potin m. Pewter ware, vaisselle f d'étain. **2.** Pot m d'étain.
pewterer ['pjutərər], s. Potier m d'étain.
phagocyte ['fagosait], s. Biol: Phagocyte m.
phalanges [fa'landʒiːz], s.pl. See PHALANX 2.
phalanx ['falaŋks], s. **I.** Gr.Ant: (pl. usu. phalanxes ['falaŋksiz]) Phalange f. **2.** Anat: Bot: (pl. usu. phalanges [fa'landʒiːz]) Phalange.
phanerogam ['fanərogam], s. Bot: Phanérogame f.
phantasm ['fantazm], s. **I.** Chimère f, illusion f. **2.** (a) Med: Phantasme m. (b) Psychics: Apparition f.
phantasmagoric [fantazma'gɔrik], a. Fantasmagorique.
phantom ['fantəm], s. Fantôme m, spectre m.
Pharaoh ['fɛəro], s. A.Hist: Pharaon m.
Pharisaic(al) [fari'seiik(ə)l], a. Pharisaïque. **-ally,** adv. Pharisaïquement ; en pharisien.
Pharisee ['farisiː], s. Pharisien m.
pharmaceutic(al) [fɑːrmə'sjuːtik(ə)l], a. Pharmaceutique.
pharmaceutics [fɑːrmə'sjuːtiks], s.pl. La pharmaceutique ; la pharmacie.
pharmacopœia [fɑːrmako'piːa], s. (a) Pharmacopée f ; codex m. (b) (Medicine chest) Pharmacie f.
pharmacy ['fɑːrmasi], s. **I.** Pharmacie f. **2.** Com: Pharmacie ; boutique f de pharmacien.
pharyngeal [fa'rindʒiəl], a. Anat: Pharyngien m.
pharyngitis [farin'dʒaitis], s. Med: Pharyngite f.
pharynx ['fariŋks], s. Anat: Pharynx m.
phase [feiz], s.tr. **I.** Phase f. Phases of an illness, phases, périodes f, d'une maladie. **2.** El.E: Phase. Three-phase, triphasé. W.Tel: Waves out of p., ondes décalées.
pheasant ['fez(ə)nt], s. (Cook-)pheasant, (coq)

faisan *m.* **Hen-pheasan**., faisane *f.* **Pheasant preserve,** faisanderie *f.*

phenacetin [fe'nasitin], *s.* Phénacétine *f.*

phenol ['fi:nɔl], *s. Ch :* Phénol *m.*

phenomena [fe'nɔməna], *s.pl. See* PHENOMENON.

phenomenal [fe'nɔmən(ə)l], *a.* Phénoménal, -aux. **I.** *Phil :* Aperceptible. **2.** *F :* Extraordinaire, prodigieux. **-ally,** *adv. F :* Phénoménalement.

phenomenon, *pl.* **-ena** [fe'nɔmənən, -əna], *s.* **I.** Phénomène *m.* Atmospheric phenomenon, phénomène météorologique. **2.** *F :* Phénomène ; chose *f* remarquable ; (*of pers.*) prodige *m.*

phew [fju:], *int.* **I.** Pouf ! **2.** (*Disgust*) Pouah !

phial ['faiəl], *s.* Fiole,*f*, flacon *m.*

philander [fi'landər], *v.i.* Flirter. *To p. with s.o.,* conter fleurette à (une femme).

philanderer [fi'landərər], *s.* Flirteur *m* ; galant *m.*

philanthropic(al) [filan'θrɔpik(əl)], *a.* Philanthropique ; (*of pers.*) philanthrope.

philanthropist [fi'lanθropist], *s.* Philanthrope *m.*

philanthropy [fi'lanθropi], *s.* Philanthropie *f.*

philatelic [fila'telik], *a.* Philatélique, philatéliste.

philatelist [fi'latəlist], *s.* Philatéliste *mf.*

philately [fi'latəli], *s.* Philatélie *f*, philatélisme *m.*

philharmonic [filha:r'mɔnik], *a.* (Société, etc.) philharmonique.

Philip ['filip]. *Pr.n.m.* Philippe.

philippic [fi'lipik], *s.* (*a*) *A.Lit :* The Philippics, les Philippiques *f.* (*b*) *F :* Philippique.

Philistine ['filistain], *a. & s.* (*a*) *B.Hist :* Philistin (*m*). (*b*) *F :* Philistin ; affreux bourgeois.

Philistinism ['filistinizm], *s.* Philistinisme *m* ; esprit bourgeois.

philological [filo'lɔdʒik(ə)l], *a.* Philologique. **-ally,** *adv.* Philologiquement.

philologist [fi'lɔlodʒist], *s.* Philologue *m.*

philology [fi'lɔlodʒi], *s.* Philologie *f.*

philosopher [fi'lɔsofər], *s.* Philosophe *m.* Moral philosopher, moraliste *m.* Natural philosopher, physicien *m.* The philosophers' stone, la pierre philosophale.

philosophical [filo'sɔfik(ə)l], *a.* **I.** Philosophique. **2.** (*Of pers.*) Philosophe, calme, modéré. **-ally,** *adv.* Philosophiquement.

philosophize [fi'lɔsofa:iz], *v.i.* Philosopher.

philosophy [fi'lɔsofi], *s.* Philosophie *f.* Moral philosophy, la morale. Natura. philosophy, la physique.

philtre ['filtər], *s.* Philtre *m.*

phiz [fiz], *s. P. & Hum :* Visage *m* ; *P :* binette *f. I know that* (*man's*) *p.,* je connais cette tête-là. *A funny p.,* une drôle de tête.

phlebitis [fle'baitis], *s. Med :* Phlébite *f.*

phlebotomy [fle'bɔtomi], *s.* Phlébotomie *f.*

phlegm [flem], *s.* **I.** Flegme *m. To cough up p.,* tousser gras. **2.** Flegme, calme *m.*

phlegmatic [fleg'matik], *a.* Flegmatique. **-ally,** *adv.* Flegmatiquement.

phlogiston [flo'dʒistɔn], *s. A.Ch :* Phlogistique *m.*

phlox [flɔks], *s. Bot :* Phlox *m.*

phobia ['foubia], *s.* Phobie *f.*

Phœnicia [fi:'niʃja]. *Pr.n. A.Geog :* La Phénicie.

Phœnician [fi:'niʃjən], *a. & s.* Phénicien, -ienne.

phœnix ['fi:niks], *s.* Phénix *m.*

phone[1] [foun], *s. F :* Téléphone *m. Who is on the p.?* qui est-ce qui est au bout du fil? *He is not on the phone,* il n'a pas le téléphone.

phone[2], *v.tr. & i. F :* To phone (up) s.o ,

téléphoner à qn. *To p. for sth., for s.o.,* demande qch., qn, par téléphone.

phonetic [fo'netik], *a.* Phonétique. **Phoneti** spelling, écriture *f* phonétique. **-ally,** *adv* Phonétiquement.

phonetician [foune'tiʃ(ə)n], *s.* Phonéticien *m.*

phonetics [fo'netiks], *s.pl.* Phonétique *f.*

phoney ['founi], *a. U.S : F :* Faux, *f.* fausse (bijouterie) en toc.

phonic ['founik, 'fɔnik], *a.* Phonique.

phonograph ['founogra:f, -graf], *s.* Phono graphe *m.*

phosgene ['fɔsdʒi:n], *s. Ch :* Phosgène *m.*

phosphate ['fɔsfeit], *s. Ch :* Phosphate *m.*

phosphene ['fɔsfi:n], *s.* Phosphène *m.*

phosphide ['fɔsfaid], *s. Ch :* Phosphure *m.*

phosphorescence [fɔsfo'res(ə)ns], *s.* Phos phorescence *f.*

phosphorescent [fɔsfo'res(ə)nt], *a.* Phosphores cent.

phosphoric [fɔs'fɔrik], *a. Ch :* (Acide) phos phorique.

phosphorous ['fɔsfɔrəs], *a.* Phosphoreux.

phosphorus ['fɔsfɔrəs], *s. Ch :* Phosphore *m* Yellow phosphorus, phosphore blanc. **'phos phorus ne'crosis,** *s.* Nécrose phosphorée (d la mâchoire).

phosphuretted ['fɔsfjuretid], *a.* Phosphuré Phosphuretted hydrogen, hydrogène phosphoré.

photo ['fouto], *s. F : =* PHOTOGRAPH[1].

photochemistry [fouto'kemistri], *s.* Photo chimie *f.*

photo-electric ['foutoi'lektrik], *a.* (Cellule photo-électrique.

photo-engraver ['foutoen'greivər], *s.* Photo graveur *m.*

photo-engraving ['foutoen'greiviŋ], *s.* Photo gravure industrielle.

photograph[1] ['foutogra:f, -graf], *s.* Photogra phie *f.* To have one's photograph taken, s faire photographier.

photograph[2], *v.tr.* **I.** Photographier ; prendr une photographie de (qn). **2.** (*With passive force* To photograph well, faire bien en photographie *Cin :* être photogénique.

photographer [fo'tɔgrəfər], *s.* Photographe *m.*

photographic [fouto grafik], *a.* Photographique **-ally,** *adv.* Photographiquement.

photography [fo'tɔgrəfi], *s.* Photographie *f* prise *f* de vue(s). Colour photography, hélio chromie *f.*

photogravure [foutogra'vjuər], *s.* Héliogra vure *f.*

photolysis [fou'tɔlisis], *s. Biol :* Photolyse *f.*

photometer [fo'tɔmetər], *s.* Photomètre *m. Shadow p.,* photomètre de Rumford. *Grease-spo p.,* photomètre à tache d'huile ; photomètre d Bunsen.

photometry [fo'tɔmetri], *s.* Photométrie *f.*

photomicrograph [fouto'maikrogra:f, -graf], *s* Photomicrographie *f.*

photomicrography [foutomai'krɔgrəfi], *s* Photomicrographie *f* (n procédé).

photosphere ['foutosfi:ər], *s. Astr :* Photo sphère *f.*

phototelegraphy [foutote'legrəfi], *s.* Télé photographie *f*, photo-télégraphie *f.*

phototherapy [fouto'θerəpi], *s.* Photothérapie *f*

phototype ['foutotaip], *s.* Phototype *m* ; (*from tracing*) photocalque *m.*

phototypography [foutotai'pɔgrəfi], *s.* Photo typographie *f.*

phrase¹ [freːiz], s. **I.** (a) Locution f, expression f; tour m de phrase. *Technical p.*, locution technique. As the phrase goes, selon l'expression consacrée. (b) *Felicity of p.*, bonheur m d'expression. (c) *Gram:* Locution; membre m de phrase. **2.** *Mus:* Phrase f, période f.

phrase², v.tr. **I.** Exprimer (sa pensée). *Well-phrased letter*, lettre bien rédigée. *That is how he phrased it*, voilà comment il s'est exprimé. **2.** *Mus:* Phraser.

phraseology [freizi'ɔlodʒi], s. Phraséologie f.

phrenological [freno'lɔdʒik(ə)l], a. Phrénologique.

phrenologist [fre'nɔlodʒist], s. Phrénologiste m.

phrenology [fre'nɔiodʒi], s. Phrénologie f.

phthisical ['tizik(ə)l, 'tai-], a. *Med:* Phtisique.

phthisis ['θaisis, 'fθisis], s. *Med:* Phtisie f.

phut [fʌt], adv. *P:* To go phut, (of electric lamp) griller; (of one's business, an engine) claquer.

phylactery [fi'laktəri], s. Phylactère m.

phylloxera [filo'ksi:əra], s. Phylloxéra m.

physic¹ ['fizik], s. Médecine f, médicaments mpl, F: drogues fpl.

physic², v.tr. (physicked) F: Médicamenter (qn). To p. oneself, se droguer.

physical ['fizik(ə)l], a. Physique. **I.** Physical impossibility, impossibilité matérielle. **2.** (Piece of) physical apparatus, appareil m de physique. **3.** *P. force*, force physique. *Gym:* Physical exercises, exercices physiques; exercices d'assouplissement. *S.a.* DEFECT 2. **-ally**, adv. Physiquement. *Thing p. impossible*, chose matériellement impossible.

physician [fi'ziʃ(ə)n], s. Médecin m.

physicist ['fizisist], s. Physicien, -ienne.

physics ['fiziks], s.pl. La physique.

physiognomy [fizi'ɔ(g)nomi], s. Physionomie f.

physiological [fizio'lɔdʒik(ə)l], a. Physiologique.

physiologist [fizi'ɔlodʒist], s. Physiologiste m.

physiology [fizi'ɔlodʒi], s. Physiologie f.

physique [fi'ziːk], s. **I.** Physique m (de qn). To have a fine physique, avoir un beau physique. To be of poor b., être d'apparence malingre. **2.** Structure f du corps.

phytozoon, pl. **-zoa** [faitə'zouɔn, -'zouɑ], s. Zoophyte m.

pi¹ [pai], s. Gr.Alph: Pi m.

pi², a. P: Pieux.

piacular [pai'akjulər], a. **I.** Piaculaire, expiatoire. **2.** (Of deed) Coupable, criminel.

pia mater ['paiə'meitər], s. Anat: Pie-mère f.

pianist ['piːanist], s. Pianiste mf.

piano¹ ['pjɑːno], adv. Mus: Piano (signe d'expression).

piano² [pi'ano], **pianoforte** [piano'fɔːrte], s. Mus: Piano m. (Concert) grand piano, piano à queue. Baby-grand piano, F: crapaud m. Upright piano, piano droit. To play (on) the piano, jouer du piano. **pi'ano-maker**, s. Facteur m de pianos. **pi'ano-wire**, s. Corde f à piano.

pianola [piːa'noulə], s. Mus: Pianola m.

piastre, piaster [pi'astər], s. Num: Piastre f.

piazza [pi'aza], s. **I.** Place publique (en Italie). **2.** U.S: Véranda f.

pibroch ['piːbrɔx], s. Pibroch m (air de cornemuse avec variations, martial ou funèbre).

pica ['paikə], s. Typ: Cicéro m; corps m 12. Double pica, gros parangon; corps 22.

Picardy ['pikərdi]. Pr.n. La Picardie.

piccalilli ['pikalili], s. Cu: Cornichons, etc., confits au vinaigre et à la moutarde.

piccaninny ['pikanini], s. **I.** Négrillon, -onne. **2.** U.S: F: Mioche mf; bambin, -ine.

piccolo ['pikolo], s. Mus: Petite flûte.

pick¹ [pik], s. **I.** Pic m, pioche f. Min: Rivelaine f. **2.** Tooth-pick, cure-dents m inv. **'pick-hammer**, s. Picot m.

pick², s. Choix m, élite f. F: The pick of the basket, of the bunch, le dessus du panier. The p. of the army, la (fine) fleur de l'armée.

pick³, v.tr. **I.** (a) Piocher (la terre). (b) F: To pick holes in sth., trouver à redire à qch.; F: chercher la petite bête. **2.** To pick one's teeth, se curer les dents. **3.** Éplucher (des groseilles); plumer (une volaille). To pick a bone, ôter, enlever, la chair d'un os. F: To have a bone, a crow, to pick with s.o., avoir maille à partir avec qn. **4.** (Of birds) Picoter, becqueter (le blé). F: (Of pers.) To pick (at) one's food, manger du bout des dents. **5.** (a) Choisir. To pick one's steps, marcher avec précaution. To pick and choose, se montrer difficile. Games: To pick sides, tirer les camps. S.a. QUARREL². (b) Trier (du minerai). **6.** (a) Cueillir (des fleurs, des fruits). (b) To pick rags, chiffonner. (c) To pick acquaintance with s.o., lier connaissance avec qn. **7.** (a) To pick pockets, pratiquer le vol à la tire. (b) Crocheter (une serrure). To pick s.o.'s brains, exploiter l'intelligence, les connaissances, de qn. **8.** Défaire, détisser, effilocher (des chiffons). S.a. OAKUM, PIECE¹. **pick off**, v.tr. **I.** Enlever, ôter; égrener (des raisins). **2.** A sniper in a tree picked off the three officers, un tireur posté dans un arbre descendit un à un les trois officiers. **pick out**, v.tr. **I.** (a) Extirper, enlever (qch.). (b) Faire le tri de (qch.); choisir. P. out the best! choisissez les meilleurs! To pick s.o. out from the crowd, repérer qn parmi la foule. **2.** Paint: Échampir. Picked out in gold, à filets d'or. **pick over**, v.tr. Trier (un panier de fruits). **pick up. I.** v.tr. **I.** Prendre; (off the ground) ramasser, relever. To p. up a shilling, (i) ramasser un shilling (par terre); (ii) se faire un shilling. To pick s.o. up in passing, prendre qn en passant. I will p. you up at Basle, je vous rejoindrai à Bâle. To p. up shipwrecked men, recueillir des naufragés. Nau: To p. up an anchor, relever une ancre. Knitting: To pick up a stitch, relever une maille. Cards: To p. up a trick, ramasser les cartes. **2.** Apprendre (un tour). To pick up a language, s'initier rapidement à une langue. **3.** Trouver, retrouver. To p. up one's path, retrouver son chemin. To pick up sth. cheap, acheter qch. à bon marché. It is a curio that I picked up, c'est un bibelot de rencontre. To pick up a livelihood, gagner péniblement sa vie. **4.** (a) (Of searchlight) To pick up an aeroplane, repérer un avion. (b) El: Prendre, capter (le courant). W.Tel: Capter (un message). To p. up Paris, avoir Paris. **5.** That will pick you up, voilà qui vous requinquera. **6.** (a) I.C.E: (Of engine) To pick up speed, abs. to pick up strength, reprendre des forces. II. pick up, v.i. **I.** Retrouver ses forces; se rétablir. To pick up with s.o., faire la connaissance de qn. **'pick-up**, s. **I.** Chose ramassée; connaissance f de rencontre. **2.** I.C.E: Reprise f (du moteur). **3.** Gramophones: Pick-up m. **4.** W.Tel: Captage m (des ondes). **picking**, s. **I.** (a) Épluchage m (d'une salade). (b) Picotage m (du fruit par les oiseaux). (c) Choix m (des mots); triage m (du minerai). (d) Cueillage m, cueillaison f (de fruits). (e) Picking and stealing grappillage m. (f) Crochetage m (d'une serrure). **2.** pl. Pickings.

(a) Épluchures f, rognures f. (b) F: Bénéfices m, gratte f. **'pick-me-up,** s. F: Cordial m, -aux ; réconfortant m ; remontant m. That's a rare pick-me-up! voilà qui vous remonte !

pick-a-back ['pikabak], adv. (Porter qn) sur le dos, sur les épaules.

pickax(e) ['pikaks], s. Tls: Pioche f. Min: Hoyau m.

picker ['pikər], s. **1.** Cueilleur, -euse (de fleurs, etc.). **2.** Crocheteur m (de serrures).

picket¹ ['piket], s. **1.** (a) Piquet m. Mil: Alignment picket, jalon m. (b) Piquet d'attache (pour chevaux). **2.** (a) Mil: etc: Piquet, poste m (d'hommes). Fire picket, piquet d'incendie. Outpost picket, grand'garde f. (b) Ind: Strike pickets, piquets de grève. **'picket-boat,** s. Vedette f (à vapeur). **'picket-fence,** s. Palis m.

picket², v.tr. (picketed) **1.** Mettre (des chevaux) au(x) piquet(s). **2.** Ind: To picket a factory, installer des piquets de grève. **picketing,** s. **1.** Mise f (des chevaux) au piquet. **2.** Ind: Constitution f de piquets de grève.

pickle¹ [pikl], s. **1.** Marinade f ; saumure f ou vinaigre m. In pickle, en train de mariner. S.a. ROD 2. **2.** pl. Pickles, conserves f au vinaigre. **3.** F: (a) To be in a (nice, sorry) pickle, être dans de beaux draps. What a p. you're in! vous voilà bien ! (b) Enfant mf terrible. **4.** Metalw: Solution f de décapage.

pickle², v.tr. **1.** Mariner ; conserver (au vinaigre ou à la saumure). **2.** Metalw: Décaper.

picklock ['piklɔk], s. **1.** (Pers.) Crocheteur m de serrures. **2.** Crochet m (de serrurier) ; rossignol m (de cambrioleur).

pickman, pl. **-men** ['pikmən, -men], s.m. Piocheur.

pickpocket ['pikpɔket], s. Voleur m à la tire ; pickpocket m.

picnic¹ ['piknik], s. Partie f de plaisir ; pique-nique m ; dînette f sur l'herbe.

picnic², v.i. (picnicked) Faire un pique-nique ; dîner sur l'herbe.

picrate ['pikret], s. Ch: Picrate m.

picric ['pikrik], a. Ch: (Acide m) picrique.

Pict [pikt], s. Ethn: Hist: Picte m.

pictorial [pik'tɔ:riəl], a. (a) (Écriture) en images. (b) (Périodique) illustré. (c) (Description) pittoresque. **-ally,** adv. Au moyen d'illustrations.

picture¹ ['piktjər], s. **1.** Image f ou tableau m ; peinture f ou gravure f. He is the picture of his father, c'est le portrait de son père. He is the picture of health, il respire la santé. She is a perfect picture, elle est à peindre. To draw a mental picture of sth., se représenter qch. (Of pers., thg) To be in, out of, the picture, compter, ne pas compter. **2.** Th: Living pictures, tableaux vivants. **3.** Cin: Film m. F: The pictures, le ciné. Sound picture, film sonore. Talking pictures, le cinéma parlant. **'picture-book,** s. Livre m d'images. **'picture-card,** s. Cards: Figure f. **'picture-goer,** s. Habitué, -ée, du cinéma. **'picture-palace,** s. Cinéma m, F: ciné m. **'picture-rail,** s. Moulure f pour accrocher les tableaux (au mur).

picture², v.tr. **1.** Dépeindre, représenter (qn, qch.). **2.** To picture to oneself, s'imaginer, se figurer (qch.).

picturesque [piktjə'resk], a. Pittoresque. P. phrases, expressions qui font image. **-ly,** adv. Pittoresquement.

picturesqueness [piktjə'resknəs], s. Pittoresque m.

piddle [pidl], v.i. F: Faire pipi.

pidgin ['pidʒin], s. **1.** Pidgin English, jargon commercial anglo-chinois. F: To talk pidgin = parler petit nègre. **2.** P: That's my pidgin, ça c'est mon affaire.

pie¹ [pai], s. Orn: = MAGPIE.

pie², s. (a) Meat pie, pâté m. Shepherd's pie, hachis m aux pommes de terre. S.a. FINGER¹ 1. (b) Fruit pie, tourte f. **'pie-dish,** s. Terrine f (à pâtés) ; tourtière f, timbale f.

pie³, s. Typ: (Composition tombée en) pâte f ; pâté m.

piebald ['paibɔ:ld], a. & s. (a) (Cheval) pie m. (b) F: Bigarré, disparate.

piece¹ [pi:s], s. **1.** (a) Morceau m (de pain) ; bout m (de ruban) ; parcelle f (de terrain). (b) Fragment m. To come, fall, go, to pieces, s'en aller en morceaux. Garment falling to pieces, vêtement qui ne tient plus (ensemble). F: He went to pieces in the second set, il s'est écroulé au second set. To fly in, into, to pieces, voler en éclats. F: To pick s.o. to pieces, déchirer qn à belles dents. To pull, tear, to pieces, déchirer, défaire (qch.). F: To tear an argument to pieces, démolir un argument. F: To pull s.o. to pieces, critiquer qn sévèrement ; P: éreinter qn. **2.** Partie f (d'une machine). To take a machine to pieces, démonter une machine. To take a dress to pieces, défaire une robe. **3.** Com: Pièce (de drap) ; rouleau m (de papier peint). To pay workmen by the piece, payer des ouvriers à la pièce, à la tâche. **4.** In one piece, tout d'une pièce. **5.** (a) A p. of my work, un échantillon de mon travail. Piece of water, pièce d'eau. P. out of a book, passage m d'un livre. (b) Piece of folly, acte m de folie. Piece of wit, trait m d'esprit. (c) A piece of advice, un conseil. A piece of carelessness, une étourderie. A ridiculous p. of affectation, une affectation bête. A piece of (good) luck, une chance (heureuse). A piece of news, une nouvelle. A piece of luggage, un colis. A piece of furniture, un meuble. A piece of clothing, un vêtement. **6.** (a) (i) Artil: Pièce (d'artillerie). (ii) To load one's p., charger son fusil. (b) Pièce (de monnaie). Five-shilling piece, pièce de cinq shillings. **7.** Morceau (de musique, de poésie) ; pièce (de théâtre). **8.** Chess: Pieces and pawns, pièces et pions. **'piece-work,** s. Travail m à la tâche, à la pièce. **'piece-worker,** s. Ouvrier, -ière, à la tâche, à la pièce.

piece², v.tr. **1.** Rapiécer, raccommoder. **2.** To p. ropes, joindre des cordages. **piece together,** v.tr. Joindre, unir (des fragments). To piece facts together, concorder des faits.

piecemeal ['pi:smi:l], adv. Par morceaux ; pièce à pièce.

piecrust ['paikrʌst], s. Croûte f, chapeau m, de pâté.

pied [paid], a. Mi-parti ; bariolé, bigarré.

pieman, pl. **-men** ['paimən, -men], s.m. Marchand de petits pâtés.

pier ['piər], s. **1.** (a) (Of stone) Jetée f, digue f. (b) (On piles) Estacade f. (Landing) pier, quai m. Pier dues, droits m de quai. **2.** Civ.E: Pilier m (de maçonnerie). **3.** Arch: (a) Pilastre m, pied-droit m (de porte). (b) Trumeau m (de mur). **'pier-glass,** s. Furn: Trumeau m. **'pier-head,** s. Extrémité f de la jetée ; musoir m.

pierce ['piərs], s. **1.** v.tr. Percer, transpercer, pénétrer. A thorn pierced his finger, une épine lui est entrée dans le doigt. Wall pierced with loop-holes, mur troué de meurtrières. (Of light)

To pierce the darkness, percer les ténèbres.
2. *v.i.* **To** *p.* **through the enemy's lines**, pénétrer les lignes de l'ennemi. **pierce through**, *v.tr.* Transpercer. **To** *p.* **through and through**, percer de part en part. **piercing**, *a.* (Cri) aigu, perçant ; (froid) pénétrant.
pierrot ['piːərɔ], *s.m.* *Th :* Pierrot.
pietism ['paiətizm], *s.* Piétisme *m.*
piety ['paiəti], *s.* Piété *f.*
piezometer [paiə'zɔmetər], *s.* *Ph :* Piézomètre *m.*
piffle[1] [pifl], *s.* *F :* Futilités *fpl*, balivernes *fpl.* **To talk** *p.*, dire des futilités.
piffle[2], *v.i.* *F :* **1.** Dire des niaiseries, des sottises. **2.** S'occuper à des futilités. **piffling**, *a.* *F :* Futile.
pig[1] [pig], *s.* **1.** (*a*) Porc *m*, cochon *m*, pourceau *m.* **To eat like a** *pig*, manger gloutonnement. **Pig farm**, porcherie *f.* **Pig breeding**, l'industrie porcine. *F :* **To buy a pig in a poke**, acheter chat en poche. **To bring one's pigs to the wrong market**, faire une mauvaise affaire ; rater son affaire. **To look at one another like stuck pigs**, se regarder en chiens de faïence. *S.a.* CLOVER. (*b*) *Cu :* Roast pig, rôti de cochon de lait. *S.a.* COLD[1] I. (*c*) *P :* (i) Grossier personnage. (ii) *You dirty little pig!* petit sale ! (iii) **To make a pig of oneself**, manger gloutonnement. (iv) *Don't be a pig!* voyons, sois chic ! **2.** *Metall :* Gueuse *f* (de fonte) ; saumon *m* (de plomb). **'pig-eyed**, *a.* A petits yeux (de porc). **'pig-iron**, *s.* *Metall :* Fer *m* en fonte, en gueuse. **'pig-nut**, *s.* *Bot :* = EARTH-NUT I. **'pig-pail, -tub**, *s.* Seau *m* aux déchets (de cuisine), aux eaux grasses.
pig[2], *v.i.* (pigged) (*a*) *F :* **To pig (it)**, vivre comme dans une étable. (*b*) *P :* **To pig together**, partager la même chambre.
pigeon ['pidʒən], *s.* **1.** Pigeon *m.* **Hen-pigeon**, pigeonne *f.* **Young** *p.*, pigeonneau *m.* **Pigeon-club**, société *f* colombophile. *Sp :* **Clay pigeon**, pigeon artificiel. *S.a.* CAPE[2], STOOL PIGEON. **2.** *F :* Pigeon, dupe *f.* **3.** = PIDGIN. **'pigeon-breasted, -chested**, *a.* Qui a la poitrine en saillie. **'pigeon-fancier**, *s.* Colombophile *mf.* **'pigeon-hole**[1], *s.* Case *f*, alvéole *m or f* (de bureau). **Set of** *pigeon-holes*, casier *m*, serre-papiers *m inv.* **'pigeon-hole**[2], *v.tr.* (*a*) Caser, classer (des papiers). (*b*) *Adm :* Classer (une réclamation). **'pigeon-house, -loft**, *s.* Colombier *m*, pigeonnier *m.* **'pigeon-post**, *s.* Transport *m* de dépêches par pigeons voyageurs. **'pigeon-toed**, *a.* Qui marche les pieds tournés en dedans.
piggery ['pigəri], *s.* (*a*) Porcherie *f.* (*b*) *F :* Endroit *m* sale ; vraie bauge.
piggish ['pigiʃ], *a.* (*a*) Sale, malpropre, grossier. (*b*) Goinfre. (*c*) Égoïste, désagréable.
piggishness ['pigiʃnəs], *s.* (*a*) Saleté *f*, malpropreté *f.* (*b*) Goinfrerie *f.*
pigheaded [pig'hedid], *a.* Têtu comme un âne ; obstiné, entêté.
pigheadedness [pig'hedidnəs], *s.* Obstination *f*, entêtement *m.*
piglet ['piglet], **pigling** ['piglin], *s.* Cochonnet *m*, cochon *m* de lait, porcelet *m.*
pigman, *pl.* **-men** ['pigmən, -men], *s.m.* Porcher.
pigment ['pigmənt], *s.* **1.** *Art :* Matière colorante ; colorant *m.* **2.** *Physiol : etc :* Pigment *m.* **'pigment-cell**, *s.* Cellule *f* pigmentaire.
pigmentary ['pigməntəri], *a.* *Physiol :* Pigmentaire.
pigmentation [pigmən'teiʃ(ə)n], *s.* Pigmentation *f.*

pigmented ['pigməntid], *a.* Pigmenté.
pigmy ['pigmi], *s.* = PYGMY.
pigskin ['pigskin], *s.* Peau *f* de porc, de truie. *Imitation* *p.*, cuir *m* façon porc.
pigsticker ['pigstikər], *s.* **1.** (*a*) Chasseur *m* de sangliers (à courre avec épieu). (*b*) Égorgeur *m*, saigneur *m*, de porcs. **2.** *F :* Gros couteau ; eustache *m.*
pigsticking ['pigstikin], *s.* **1.** Chasse *f* au sanglier. **2.** Égorgement *m* de porcs.
pigsty ['pigstai], *s.* **1.** Porcherie *f* ; étable *f* à porcs. **2.** *P :* Bauge *f* ; (sale) taudis *m.*
pigtail ['pigteil], *s.* **1.** Tabac *m* en corde. **2.** Queue *f*, natte *f* (de cheveux).
pigwash ['pigwɔʃ], *s.* **1.** Pâtée *f* pour les porcs ; eaux grasses. **2.** *P :* Lavasse *f.*
pike[1] [pai̇k], *s.* **1.** *Archeol :* Pique *f.* **2.** *Geog :* Pic *m* (de montagne).
pike[2], *s.* *Ich :* Brochet *m.*
pike[3], *s.* Barrière *f* de péage. *S.a.* TURNPIKE.
pikestaff ['paikstɑːf], *s.* Bois *m*, hampe *f*, de pique. *S.a.* PLAIN I. 1.
pilaster [pi'lastər], *s.* *Arch :* Pilastre *m.*
pilau, pilaw [pi'lau, -'lɔː], *s.* *Cu :* Pilau *m*, pilaf *m.*
pilchard ['piltʃərd], *s.* *Ich :* Sardine *f.*
pile[1] [pail], *s.* Pieu *m*, pilot *m.* *Row of piles*, pilotis *m.* **To drive in a pile**, enfoncer, battre, un pieu. **Built on piles**, bâti sur pilotis. **'pile-driver**, *s.* *Civ.E :* Sonnette *f.*
pile[2], *s.* **1.** (*a*) Tas *m*, monceau *m* ; pile *f* (d'obus). (*b*) *El :* **Voltaic pile**, pile de Volta. (*c*) *Mil :* Faisceau *m* (d'armes). (*d*) *F :* Magot *m.* **To make one's pile**, faire fortune ; faire sa pelote. **2.** (*a*) Masse *f* (d'un édifice). (*b*) Édifice.
pile[3]. **1.** *v.tr.* (*a*) **To pile (up)**, (i) entasser, amonceler ; amasser (une fortune) ; (ii) empiler (du bois). *F :* *Ship piled up on the rocks*, vaisseau échoué sur les rochers. **To pile on the agony**, accumuler les détails pénibles. **To pile it on**, exagérer, *P :* charrier. (*b*) *Mil :* **To pile arms**, former les faisceaux. **2.** *v.i.* **To pile up**, s'amonceler, s'entasser.
pile[4], *s.* *Tex :* Poil *m* (d'un tapis). **Pile fabrics**, tissus *m* à poil.
pile[5], *s.* *Med :* usu. *pl.* **Piles**, hémorroïdes *f.*
pilewort ['pailwəːrt], *s.* *Bot :* Ficaire *f.*
pilfer ['pilfər], *v.tr.* Chaparder, chiper (*sth. from s.o.*, qch. à qn). *Abs.* Faire de petits vols ; grappiller. **pilfering**, *s.* Petits vols ; chapardage *m.*
pilferer ['pilfərər], *s.* Chapardeur, -euse, chipeur, -euse ; grappilleur, -euse.
pilgrim ['pilgrim], *s.* **1.** Pèlerin, -ine. *Lit :* **The Pilgrim's Progress**, le Voyage du Pèlerin. **2.** **The Pilgrim Fathers**, les Pèlerins (colons anglais qui fondèrent New Plymouth).
pilgrimage ['pilgrimedʒ], *s.* (*a*) Pèlerinage *m.* (*b*) *F :* Long voyage.
piliferous [pai'lifərəs], *a.* *Bot :* Pilifère.
pill [pil], *s.* Pilule *f.* *F :* **It is a bitter pill**, la dragée est amère. **'pill-box**, *s.* **1.** Boîte *f* à pilules. **2.** *Mil :* *P :* Réduit *m* en béton pour mitrailleuse.
pillage[1] ['pilidʒ], *s.* Pillage *m.*
pillage[2], *v.tr.* Piller, saccager. *Abs.* Se livrer au pillage. **pillaging**, *a.* Pillard.
pillager ['pilidʒər], *s.* Pilleur, -euse ; pillard, -arde ; saccageur, -euse.
pillar ['pilər], *s.* **1.** Pilier *m* ; colonne *f.* *F :* *He is a p. of the Church*, c'est un pilier d'église. **To drive s.o. from pillar to post**, renvoyer qn de Caïphe à Pilate. **2.** (*a*) *Mec.E :* Colonne,

montant *m* (d'une machine). (*b*) *Aut:* **Steering pillar,** colonne de direction. (*c*) *Cy:* **Saddle pillar,** tige *f* de selle. (*d*) *N.Arch:* Épontille *f*, étançon *m*. **'pillar-box,** *s.* Boîte *f* aux lettres en forme de borne ; borne postale.
pillion ['piljən], *s.* **1.** *Harn:* (*a*) Selle *f* de femme. (*b*) Coussinet *m* de cheval. **To ride pillion,** monter en croupe. **2.** *Motor Cy:* **Pillion (-seat),** siège *m* arrière. **To ride pillion,** monter derrière. **Pillion-rider,** passager, -ère (de derrière).
pillory[1] ['piləri], *s.* Pilori *m*.
pillory[2], *v.tr.* (pilloried) Mettre (qn) au pilori.
pillow[1] ['pilou, 'pilə], *s.* **1.** (*a*) Oreiller *m*. **To take counsel of one's pillow,** consulter son chevet ; prendre conseil de son oreiller. *Take counsel of your p.,* dormez là-dessus. ·(*b*) **Lace-pillow,** coussin *m* (pour dentelle). **2.** *Mec.E:* **Coussinet** *m*. **'pillow-block,** *s.* *Mec.E:* Palier *m* (d'arbre). **'pillow-case, -slip,** *s.* Taie *f* d'oreiller. **'pillow-lace,** *s.* Dentelle *f* aux fuseaux.
pillow[2], *v.tr.* **To pillow one's head on one's arms,** reposer sa tête sur ses bras.
pilose ['pailous], *a.* *Nat.Hist:* Pileux, poilu.
pilot[1] ['pailət], *s.* **1.** (*a*) Pilote *m*. **Deep-sea pilot,** pilote hauturier. **Coast pilot, in-shore pilot, branch-pilot,** pilote côtier ; lamaneur *m*. (*b*) *F:* Guide *m*, mentor *m*. (*c*) *Av:* Pilote (aviateur). **2.** *Rail:* = PILOT-ENGINE. **3.** **Pilot(-lamp),** lampe *f* témoin. **'pilot-balloon,** *s.* Ballon *m* d'essai ; ballon pilote. **'pilot-boat,** *s.* Bateau *m* pilote. **'pilot-coat,** *s.* *Nau:* Vareuse *f*, caban *m*. **'pilot-engine,** *s.* *Rail:* Locomotive *f* estafette. **'pilot-fish,** *s.* *Ich:* Pilote *m* (de requin). **'pilot-flame,** *s.* Veilleuse *f* (d'un bec de gaz). **'pilot-jet,** *s.* *Aut:* Gicleur *m* de ralenti. **'pilot-print,** *s.* *Phot:* Épreuve *f* témoin.
pilot[2], *v.tr.* (*a*) Piloter (un navire, un avion). (*b*) Mener, conduire (qn à travers des obstacles).
piloting, *s.* Pilotage *m*.
pilotage ['pailətədʒ], *s.* **1.** Pilotage *m*. **2.** **Pilotage (dues),** (droits *m*, frais *m*, de) pilotage.
pilule ['pilju:l], *s.* Petite pilule.
pimento [pi'mento], *s.* *Bot:* *Cu:* Piment *m*.
pimp [pimp], *s.* Entremetteur, -euse ; proxénète *mf*.
pimpernel ['pimpərnel], *s.* *Bot:* Mouron *m*. **Scarlet pimpernel,** mouron rouge.
pimple [pimpl], *s.* Pustule *f*, bouton *m*. **To come out in pimples,** avoir une poussée de boutons.
pimply ['pimpli], *a.* Pustuleux, boutonneux.
pin[1] [pin], *s.* **1.** (*a*) Épingle *f*. **Curling-pins, waving-pins,** épingles à friser, à onduler. **Tie-pin,** épingle de cravate. *S.a.* BROOCH, DRAWING-PIN. *F:* **You could have heard a pin drop,** on aurait entendu trotter une souris. **For two pins** *I would* **box his ears,** pour un peu je lui flanquerais une gifle. **To be on pins and needles,** être sur des charbons. (*b*) **Pins and needles,** fourmillements *m*. **2.** (*a*) Goupille *f*, cheville *f*. **Axle pin,** clavette *f* d'essieu. **Split pin,** goupille fendue. *Mil:* **Safety pin** (*of fuse*), goupille de sûreté. (*b*) **Centre pin,** pivot central (de plaque tournante). (*c*) **Hinge** *f* (d'une charnière). *El:* **Fiche de prise de courant.** (*d*) *Nau:* **Thole-pin,** tolet *m*, dame *f*. **3.** *Cu:* **Rolling-pin,** rouleau *m* à pâte. **4.** (*a*) *Surv:* Fiche de jalonneur. (*b*) *Golf:* Drapeau *m* de trou. **5.** (*a*) (*At ninepins*) Quille *f*. (*b*) *pl.* *P:* Jambes *f*, *P:* guibolles *f*, quilles. **'pin-feather,** *s.* Plume naissante (de jeune oiseau). **'pin-fire,** *attrib.a.* *Sm.a:* (Cartouche, fusil) à broche. **'pin-head,** *s.* Tête *f* d'épingle. *Tex:* **Pin-head grey,** drap *m* gris pointillé. **'pin-hole,** *s.*

(*a*) Trou *m* d'épingle. (*b*) *Opt:* Très petit ouverture (dans un écran). *Phot:* Sténopé *m*. **'pin-money,** *s.* (*a*) Argent (donné à une femme) pour ses frais de toilette. (*b*) Argent de poche (d'une jeune fille). **'pin-point,** *s.* *T* turn down the gas to a pin-point,* mettre le gaz en veilleuse. **'pin-prick,** *s.* Piqûre *f* d'épingle *pl.* *F:* **Pin-pricks,** coups *m* d'épingle. **'pin-tray,** *s.* Épinglier *m*. **'pin-wheel,** *s* **1.** *Clockm:* Roue *f* des chevilles. **2.** *Mec.E* Roue à fuseaux. **3.** *Pyr:* Soleil *m*.
pin[2], *v.tr.* (pinned) **1.** (*a*) Épingler ; attacher avec une épingle. **To pin clothes on a line,** épingler du linge sur une corde. **To pin the paper to the board,** fixer le papier sur la planchette (avec des punaises). (*b*) *Mec.E:* Cheviller, goupiller **2.** Fixer, clouer. **To pin s.o.'s arms to his sides** (i) coller les bras à qn ; (ii) ligoter qn. **To be pinned** (*down*) *under a fallen tree,* se trouver pris sous un arbre déraciné. **To pin s.o.** (**down**) to facts,** obliger qn à s'en tenir aux faits, à reconnaître les faits. *Chess:* **To pin a piece,** cloue une pièce. **3.** Étayer, étançonner (un mur) une pièce. **pin on,** *v.tr.* Épingler (qch.), attacher (qch. avec une épingle (*to sth.,* à qch.). **pin up,** *v.tr* Épingler (ses cheveux).
pinafore ['pinəfɔ:r], *s.* Tablier *m* (d'enfant).
pinaster [pai'næstər], *s.* *Bot:* Pinastre *m* ; pin *m* maritime.
pincers ['pinsərz], *s.pl.* **1.** (**Pair of**) **pincers** pince *f*, tenaille(s) *f* (*pl*). **2.** Pince (de crustacé).
pinch[1] [pinʃ], *s.* **1.** (*a*) Action *f* de pincer pinçade *f*. **To give s.o. a pinch,** pincer qn (*b*) *F:* **The pinch of poverty,** la gêne. **The pinch of hunger,** la morsure de la faim ; la faim. **To feel the pinch,** tirer le diable par la queue (*c*) **At a pinch,** au besoin. *F:* **It was a close pinch,** il était moins cinq. **2.** Pincée *f* (de sel etc.). *To take a p. of snuff,* humer une prise.
pinch[2], *v.tr.* **1.** Pincer. *Cy:* **Pinched inner tube** chambre à air cisaillée. *Prov:* **Everyone knows best where his own shoe pinches,** chacun sai où le soulier le blesse. **2.** Serrer, gêner. **To pinch oneself,** *abs.* to pinch, se priver (du nécessaire). *To p. and scrape for one's children, F:* s saigner aux quatre veines pour ses enfants **3.** *P:* (*a*) Chiper, choper, chaparder. *Someone has pinched my matches,* on m'a chauffé mes allumettes. *My watch has been pinched,* on m'a refait ma montre. (*b*) Arrêter (un malfaiteur) **To get pinched,** se faire pincer. **pinch off,** *v.tr Hort:* **To pinch off a bud,** épincer un bourgeon **pinched,** *a.* **1.** (*Of face*) Tiré, hâve, amaigri *Face p. with hunger,* traits tirés par la faim **2.** Étroit. **Pinched for money,** à court d'argent dans la gêne. **To be pinched for room,** être à l'étroit.
pinchbeck ['pinʃbek], *s.* **1.** Chrysocale *m* similor *m*. **2.** *Attrib.* (*a*) En chrysocale, er similor. (*b*) *F:* En toc.
pincushion ['pinkuʃ(ə)n], *s.* Pelote *f* à épingles
pine[1] [pain], *s.* **1.** Pine(-tree), pin *m*. **Norway pine,** pin sylvestre ; pin suisse. **Parasol pine, stone-pine,** pin pignon ; pin (en) parasol **2.** (Bois *m* de) pin. **'pine-apple,** *s.* Ananas *m*. **'pine-cone,** *s.* Pomme *f* de pin. **'pine-grove,** *s.* Pinière *f*, pineraie *f*. **'pine-kernel,** *s.* Pigne *f*, pignon *m*. **'pine-wood,** *s.* **1.** (Bois *m* de) pin *m*. **2.** Pinière *f*, pineraie *f*.
pine[2], *v.i.* **1.** To pine (away), languir, dépérir **2.** To pine for s.o., for sth., languir pour, après qn, qch. *He is pining for home,* il a la nostalgie du foyer.

ineal ['piniəl], a. Anat: Pinéal, -aux.

inetum [pai'ni:təm], s. Sapinière f; pineraie f.

ing[1] [piŋ], s. Cinglement m, fouettement m (d'une balle de fusil).

ing[2], v.i. (Of bullet) Cingler, fouetter.

inion[1] ['pinjən], s. I. (a) Bout m d'aile; aileron m. (b) Poet: Aile f. 2. Penne f, rémige f.

inion[2], v.tr. I. Rogner les ailes à (un oiseau). 2. Lier les bras à, ligoter (qn). To p. s.o.'s arms to his sides, lier les bras de qn.

inion[3], s. Mec.E: Pignon m. Sliding pinion, pignon baladeur. Pinion wheel, roue à pignon.

ink[1] [piŋk], s. I. s. (a) Bot: Œillet m. Garden pink, (œillet) mignardise f. Sea pink, œillet maritime. (b) The pink of perfection, la perfection même. The p. of politeness, la fine fleur de la politesse. In the pink (of condition), en excellente condition; en parfaite santé. 2. a. & s. (a) Rose (m); couleur f de rose. P. cheeks, joues roses. The p. eyes of the albinos, les yeux rouges des albinos. (b) Ven: To wear pink, porter la tunique rouge, écarlate. (c) P: Strike me pink! pas possible!

ink[2], v.tr. I. Toucher (son adversaire avec l'épée). 2. Dressm: To pink (out), (i) denteler les bords de (qch.); (ii) travailler à jour. 3. To pink out, orner, parer.

ink[3], v.i. I.C.E: (Of engine) Cliqueter. **pinking**, s. Cliquetis (produit par les auto-allumages).

inkish ['piŋkiʃ], a. Rosé, rosâtre.

inkness ['piŋknəs], s. Couleur f rose; rose m.

innace ['pines], s. Navy: Grand canot.

innacle ['pinəkl], s. I. Arch: (a) Pinacle m, clocheton m. (b) Couronnement m (de faîte). 2. (a) Cime f (d'une montagne); pic m. (b) Rock pinnacle, gendarme m. 3. F: The pinnacle of glory, le faîte de la gloire. On the highest p. of fame, à l'apogée de la gloire.

innate ['pinet], **pinnated** ['pineitid], a. Nat.Hist: Penné, pinné.

innule ['pinjul], s. I. Pinnule f (d'une alidade). 2. Bot: Foliole f.

int [paint], s. Meas: Pinte f (= o l. 568). Imperial pint, pinte légale. Reputed pint, bouteille f d'environ une pinte.

intail ['pinteil], s. Orn: (Canard) pilet m.

intle [pintl], s. (a) Pivot central; goujon m (d'une charnière). Veh: Cheville ouvrière. (b) Nau: Aiguillot m (de gouvernail).

ioneer [paiə'ni:ər], s. Pionnier m.

ious ['paiəs], a. (a) Pieux. (b) Pious deeds, œuvres f pies. **-ly**, adv. Pieusement; avec piété.

ip[1] [pip], s. Pépie f (de la volaille). F: To give s.o. the pip, donner le cafard à qn.

ip[2], s. I. Point m (d'une carte, d'un dé). 2. Mil: F: = STAR[1] 2 (b). 3. W.Tel: F: Top m. The pips, le signal horaire.

ip[3], v.tr. (pipped) P: I. Vaincre, battre (qn). 2. Atteindre (qn) d'une balle.

ip[4], s. Pépin m (de fruit).

ip[5], s. Mil. Tg. & Tp: (La lettre) P. Pip emma (= p.m.), (six heures, etc.) du soir.

ipe[1] [paip], s. I. (a) Tuyau m, tube m, conduit m. To lay pipes, poser des tuyaux; canaliser. (b) Anat: Tube; esp. tube respiratoire. S.a. WINDPIPE. (c) Mus: Pipeau m, chalumeau m (d'une clef). 2. (a) Mus: Pipeau m, chalumeau m. (Bag)pipes, cornemuse f. S.a. PAN[3]. (b) Nau: Sifflet m (du maître d'équipage). 3. Filet m de voix; chant m (d'oiseau). 4. Pipe f. I am a pipe-smoker, je fume la pipe. Pipe of peace, calumet m de paix. To smoke the p. of peace with

s.o., fumer le calumet de paix avec qn. P: Put that in your pipe and smoke it! mettez cela dans votre poche et votre mouchoir dessus! mettez ça dans votre pipe! To put s.o.'s pipe out, faire échouer qn. 'pipe-clay'[1], s. Terre f de pipe; blanc m de terre à pipe (pour astiquage). 'pipe-clay'[2], v.tr. Astiquer (qch.) au blanc de terre à pipe. 'pipe-cleaner, s. Cure-pipe m (pour fumeurs). 'pipe-key, s. Clef forée. 'pipe-lighter, s. Briquet m (à essence). 'pipe-line, s. Conduite f, canalisation f; (for petrol) pipe-line m, pl. pipe-lines. 'pipe-organ, s. Mus: Grand orgue. 'pipe-rack, s. Râtelier m à pipes. 'pipe-stopper, s. Bourre-pipe m.

pipe[2]. I. v.i. (a) (i) Poet: Jouer du chalumeau ou de la flûte. (ii) Jouer du fifre ou de la cornemuse. (b) (Of wind) Siffler. (c) Nau: Donner un coup de sifflet. II. pipe, v.tr. I. (a) Jouer (un air) (sur le fifre ou sur la cornemuse). (b) Navy: Siffler (un commandement). To pipe all hands down, siffler en bas tout le monde. 2. F: To pipe one's eye(s), pleurer, pleurnicher. 3. Dressm: etc: Lisérer, ganser. pipe up. I. v.i. F: Here a little voice piped up, à ce moment une petite voix se fit entendre. 2. v.tr. Navy: Appeler (la bordée) au son du sifflet. **piped**, a. A tuyau(x); à tube(s). **piping**[1], a. I. Lit: Piping times of peace, heureuse époque de paix. 2. Piping hot, tout chaud, tout bouillant. **piping**[2], s. I. (a) Son m du chalumeau, du fifre, de la cornemuse. (b) Sifflement m (du vent); gazouillement m (d'oiseaux). (c) Navy: Commandement m au sifflet. 2. (a) Canalisation f (de l'eau). (b) Coll. Tuyauterie f, conduites fpl. 3. Laund: Tuyautage m. 4. Dressm: (a) Liséré m. Piping cord, ganse f. (b) Passepoil m; (on trousers) baguette f.

pipe[3], s. Pipe f (de vin); grande futaille.

pipeful ['paipful], s. Pipe f (de tabac).

piper ['paipər], s. Joueur m de chalumeau, de cornemuse. F: To pay the piper, payer les violons. He who pays the piper calls the tune, qui paye a bien le droit de choisir.

pipette [pi'pet], s. Pipette f.

pipit ['pipit], s. Orn: Pipi m, pipit m. Meadow pipit, farlouse f.

pipkin ['pipkin], s. Casserole f en terre; poêlon m.

pippin ['pipin], s. (Pomme f) reinette f.

piquancy ['pi:kənsi], s. I. Goût piquant (d'un mets). 2. Sel m, piquant m (d'un conte). The p. of the situation, le piquant de l'affaire.

piquant ['pi:kənt], a. (Of flavour, etc.) Piquant. **-ly**, adv. D'une manière piquante.

pique[1] [pi:k], s. Pique f, ressentiment m. In a fit of pique, dans un accès de pique. Feeling of p., sentiment m de rancune.

pique[2], v.tr. I. Piquer, dépiter (qn). 2. Piquer, exciter (la curiosité de qn). 3. To pique oneself on sth., se piquer de qch.

piquet [pi'ket], s. Cards: Piquet m.

piracy ['pairəsi], s. I. Piraterie f. 2. Contrefaçon f (d'un livre); pillage m des idées.

Piraeus (the) [ðə pai'ri:əs]. Pr.n. Geog: Le Pirée.

pirate[1] ['pairet], s. I. Pirate m, forban m, flibustier m. 2. Contrefacteur m (d'un ouvrage littéraire); voleur m (d'idées).

pirate[2], v.tr. Contrefaire ou démarquer (un livre); s'approprier (une invention).

piratical [pai'ratik(ə)l], a. De pirate.

pirn [pə:rn], s. I. Tex: Cannette f. 2. Bobine f (de fil à coudre, etc.).

pirogue [pi'roug], s. Pirogue f.

pirouette[1] [piru'et], s. Danc: Pirouette f.
pirouette[2], v.i. Pirouetter; faire la pirouette.
piscatorial [piskə'tɔːriəl], **piscatory** ['piskətəri], a. Qui se rapporte à la pêche.
pisciculture ['pisikʌltjər], s. Pisciculture f.
piscina, pl. -as, -ae [pi'siːna, pi'saina, -əz, -iː], s. 1. Rom. Ant: Ecc: Piscine f. 2. Vivier m.
pish[1] [piʃ], int. Fi! zut! bah!
pish[2], v.i. Dire fi.
piss[1] [pis], s. Urine f; (of animals) pissat m.
piss[2]. 1. v.i. Uriner, pisser; F: faire pipi. 2. v.tr. Pisser (du sang, etc.).
pistachio [pis'taːʃjo], s. 1. (Nut) Pistache f. 2. (Tree) Pistachier m.
pistil ['pistil], s. Bot: Pistil m.
pistol ['pist(ə)l], s. 1. Sm.a: Pistolet m. Duelling-pistols, pistolets de combat. 2. Tls: Pistolet (d'un outil pneumatique). 'pistol-shot, s. Coup m de pistolet. Within pistol-shot, à portée de pistolet.
piston ['pistən], s. Piston m (d'une machine à vapeur, Mus: d'un cornet à pistons); sabot m (de pompe). 'piston-ring, s. I.C.E: Segment m de piston. 'piston-rod, s. Tige f, verge f, de piston. 'piston-stroke, s. 1. Coup m de piston. 2. Course f du piston.
pit[1] [pit], s. 1. (a) Fosse f, trou m. Aut: etc: Inspection pit, fosse (à réparations). Gun-pit, emplacement m de pièce. Husb: Store-pit, silo m. (b) The pit, l'enfer m, les enfers. (c) Trappe f, piège m (à animaux). F: To dig a pit for s.o., tendre un piège à qn. (d) (i) Carrière f (à chaux). (ii) Puits m (d'une mine de charbon). (iii) Mine f (de charbon). 2. (a) Th: Parterre m. (b) U.S: The (Chicago) wheat pit, la Bourse des blés. 3. (a) Petite cavité, piqûre f (dans un métal). (b) Med: Cicatrice f (de la petite vérole). 4. Anat: The pit of the stomach, le creux de l'estomac. S.a. ARMPIT. 'pit-boy, -lad, s. Min: Galibot m. 'pit-coal, s. Houille f. pit-'head, s. Min: Bouche f de puits; carreau m (de la mine). 'Pit-head price, prix (du charbon) sur le carreau. 'pit-prop, s. Min: Poteau m, étai m, de mine. Pit-props, bois m de soutènement. 'pit-saw, s. Tls: Scie f de long. pit-'stall, s. Th: Fauteuil m de parterre.
pit[2], v.tr. (pitted) 1. (a) Mettre (deux coqs) en parc. (b) To pit s.o. against s.o., opposer qn à qn. To pit oneself against s.o., se mesurer contre qn. 2. (a) (Of acids) Piquer, trouer (le métal). (b) Med: (Of smallpox) Grêler, marquer (le visage). **pitted**, a. 1. (Of metal) Piqué (par un acide). 2. (Of pers.) Grêlé (par la petite vérole).
pit-(a-)pat ['pit(ə)pat], adv. To go pit-a-pat, (of rain) crépiter; (of feet) trottiner; (of the heart) battre, palpiter.
pitch[1] [pitʃ], s. Poix f; brai m. Minera pitch, bitume m; asphalte minéral. Navy pitch, goudron m à calfater. 'pitch-'black, a. 1. Noir comme poix. 2. = PITCH-DARK. 'pitch-'dark, a. It is pitch-dark, il fait nuit noire; il fait noir comme dans un four. 'pitch-'pine, s. Pitchpin m; faux sapin.
pitch[2], v.tr. Brayer; enduire (qch.) de brai.
pitch[3], s. 1. Lancement m, jet m (d'une pierre, etc.). F: The stone came full pitch at my head, la pierre vint droit à ma tête. 2. Nau: Tangage m. 3. (a) Place f (dans un marché); place habituelle (d'un camelot). S.a. QUEER[2]. (b) Cr: Terrain m entre les guichets. 4. (a) Arch: Hauteur f sous clef (d'un arc). (b) Mus: Hauteur (d'un son); diapason m (d'un instrument). To give the orchestra the pitch, donner l'accord à l'orchestre. (c) Degré m (d'élévation). To excite

s.o.'s interest to the highest pitch, porte l'intérêt de qn à son comble. To such a pitc that . . ., à tel point que. . . . 5. Degré pente (d'un toit). 6. (i) Avancement m, pas (d'une vis); (ii) espacement m, pas, de la dentu (d'une roue); (iii) angle m des dents (d'une scie 'pitch-accent, s. Ling: Accent m de hauteu 'pitch-pipe, s. Mus: Diapason m de bouche.
pitch[4]. 1. v.tr. 1. Dresser (une tente; Cr: le guichets). Abs. Camper. 2. Civ.E: (i) Empierre (ii) paver (une chaussée). 3. Mus: To pitch one voice higher, lower, hausser, baisser, le ton c sa voix. To p. one's aspirations too high, viser tro haut. 4. Lancer (une balle). To p. the hay on the cart, jeter le foin sur la charrette. Cr: Ful pitched ball, balle à toute volée. To be pitche off one's horse, être désarçonné. 5. P: To pitc it strong, exagérer; y aller fort. II. pitch, v. 1. To pitch on one's head, tomber sur la têt 2. (Of ship) Tanguer; F: canarder. 3. To pitc (up)on sth., arrêter son choix sur qch. pitc in, v.i. P: Se mettre à la besogne. pitc into, v.i. 1. F: (a) Taper sur (qn); s'attaqu à (qn). Pitch into him! tapez dessus! (b) T p. into the work, s'attaquer au travail. 2. Tomb la tête la première dans (la mare, etc.). pitche a. 1. Pitched battle, bataille rangée. 2. (Of roa (i) Empierré; (ii) (with square setts) pave 'pitch-and-'toss, s. Jeu m de pile ou face.
pitchblende ['pitʃblend], s. Miner: Pec blende f.
pitcher[1] ['pitʃər], s. 1. Cruche f (de grès) broc m. 2. Bot: F: Ascidie f. 'pitcher plant, s. Népenthès m.
pitcher[2], s. (At baseball) Lanceur m (de balle).
pitchfork[1] ['pitʃfɔːrk], s. Mus: Diapason m (de acier).
pitchfork[2], s. Fourche f (à foin).
pitchfork[3], v.tr. 1. Lancer (une gerbe) avec fourche. 2. F: Bombarder (qn dans un poste
piteous ['pitjəs], a. Pitoyable, piteux. -ly, ad Pitoyablement.
pitfall ['pitfɔːl], s. Trappe f, fosse f; piège F: The pitfalls of the law, les traquenards m d la procédure.
pith [piθ], s. 1. (a) Moelle f. Pith helmet, casqu (colonial) m in sola. (b) Peau blanche (d'un orange). 2. (a) Vigueur f, sève f, ardeur (b) Moelle, essence f (d'un livre).
pithecanthrope [piθe'kanθroup], s. Paleont Pithécanthrope m.
pithiness ['piθinəs], s. Concision f; styl nerveux.
pithy ['piθi], a. 1. (Of stem) Plein de moelle 2. (Of style) (i) Nerveux, concis, vigoureux (ii) substantiel. -ily, adv. En un style concis, dense; avec concision.
pitiable ['pitiəbl], a. Pitoyable, piteux; (c appearance) minable. It is pitiable! c'est à faire pitié! -ably, adv. Pitoyablement; à faire pitié
pitiful ['pitiful], a. 1. Compatissant; plein d pitié. 2. Pitoyable, lamentable. It is p., to see him, il fait pitié. (b) Pej: Lamentabl -fully, adv. 1. Avec compassion. 2. (a) Pi toyablement. To cry pitifully, pleurer à fendr l'âme. (b) Pej: Lamentablement.
pitiless ['pitiləs], a. Impitoyable; sans pitié (froid) cruel. -ly, adv. Sans pitié.
pitman, pl. -men ['pitmən, -men], s. 1. Min Mineur m, esp. houilleur m. 2. Scieur m de long
pittance ['pitəns], s. Maigre salaire m. To b reduced to a mere pittance, être réduit à l portion congrue.

ituitary [pi'tjuːitəri], *a.* *Anat:* Pituitaire.
ity[1] ['piti], *s.* Pitié *f.* (*a*) Compassion *f*, apitoiement *m.* To take pity on s.o., prendre pitié de qn. To feel pity for s.o., s'apitoyer sur qn. To move s.o. to pity, exciter la compassion de qn ; apitoyer qn. To do sth. out of pity for s.o., faire qch. par pitié pour qn. For pity's sake, par pitié ; de grâce. (*b*) What a pity! quel dommage ! .t is a great pity, c'est bien dommage. *S.a.* MORE 4.
ity[2], *v.tr.* Plaindre (qn) ; avoir pitié de, s'apitoyer sur (qn). He is to be pitied, il est à plaindre. **pitying,** *a.* Compatissant ; (regard) de pitié.
ivot[1] ['pivət], *s.* **I.** Pivot *m* ; tourillon *m* ; axe *m* (de rotation). Ball pivot, pivot à rotule. **2.** *Mil:* Pivot(-man), pivot, guide *m.*
ivot[2], *v.* (pivoted) **I.** *v.tr.* (*a*) Monter (une pièce) sur pivot. (*b*) To pivot a fleet, faire pivoter une flotte. **2.** *v.i.* Pivoter, tourner. **pivoting,** *a.* Pivotant ; à pivot.
ixie, pixy ['piksi], *s.* (i) Lutin *m*, farfadet *m* ; (ii) fée *f.*
lacard[1] ['plakɑːrd], *s.* Écriteau *m* ; affiche *f.*
lacard[2], *v.tr.* **I.** Couvrir (un mur) d'affiches. **2.** Placarder, afficher (une annonce).
lacate [plə'keit], *v.tr.* Apaiser, calmer (qn).
lace[1] [pleis], *s.* **I.** (*a*) Lieu *m*, endroit *m*, localité *f.* To come to a p., arriver dans un lieu. This is the place, c'est ici. A native of the place, quelqu'un du pays. Fortified place, place forte. Place of refuge, lieu de refûge. Watering place, ville *f* d'eaux ; station *f* balnéaire. A small country place, un petit coin rustique. From place to place, de-ci de-là. To move from p. to p., se déplacer souvent. Books all over the place, des livres dans tous les coins. In another place, autre part ; ailleurs. This is no place for you, vous n'avez que faire ici. *S.a.* HOME I. 1. (*b*) Place of amusement, lieu de divertissement. Place of worship, édifice *m* du culte. Place of business, maison *f* de commerce ; établissement *m.* Place of residence, demeure *f*, résidence *f.* You can all come and lunch at our p., venez tous déjeuner chez nous. A low place, un endroit mal fréquenté. In high places, en haut lieu. (*c*) (*In street names*) Cour *f*, ruelle *f.* (*d*) Market place, place *f* du marché. **2.** Place. To put a book back in its p., remettre un livre à sa place. To lay a place (*at table*), mettre un couvert. To change places with s.o., changer de place avec qn. If I were in your place, *I should go*, à votre place, j'irais. In (the) place of . . ., au lieu de. . . . Out of (its) place, (*volume*) déplacé ; (*fiche*) déclassée. Remark out of place, observation hors de propos, déplacée. (*Of pers.*) To look (sadly) out of place, avoir l'air dépaysé. To take place, avoir lieu ; se passer ; arriver. The marriage will not take p., le mariage ne se fera pas. While this was taking place, sur ces entrefaites. **3.** Place, rang *m.* (*a*) To attain to a high p., atteindre à un rang élevé. To put s.o. in his place, remettre qn à sa place. To keep one's place, observer les distances. In the first place, d'abord. In the second place, en second lieu. In the next place . . ., ensuite . . ., puis. . . . *Rac:* To back a horse for a place, jouer un cheval placé. (*b*) *Mth:* Answer to three places of decimals, solution *f* à trois décimales. **4.** Place, poste *m*, emploi *m*, situation *f.* To take, fill, s.o.'s place, remplacer qn. It is not my place to do it, ce n'est pas à moi de le faire. **5.** (*a*) Weak p. in a beam, endroit défectueux d'une poutre. (*b*) To find one's place (*in a book*), se retrouver. To lose one's place, ne plus retrouver où on en est resté. To laugh at the right p., rire au bon

endroit. **'place-kick,** *s.* *Fb:* Coup *m* d'envoi.
'place-name, *s.* Nom *m* de lieu.
place[2], *v.tr.* **I.** Placer, mettre. (*a*) To p. a board edgeways, poser une planche de champ. To be awkwardly placed, se trouver dans une situation difficile. The house is well placed, la maison est bien située. (*b*) To place a book with a publisher, faire accepter un livre par un éditeur. *Com:* Difficult to place, de vente difficile. (*c*) To place a matter in s.o.'s hands, remettre une affaire entre les mains de qn. To place an order (*for goods*), passer (une) commande. To place a child under s.o.'s care, mettre un enfant sous la garde de qn. *S.a.* CONTRACT[1] 2. (*d*) *Rugby:* To place a goal, marquer un but sur coup de pied placé. **2.** Donner un rang à (qn). To be well placed (*on a class list*), avoir une bonne place. *Sp:* To be placed third, se classer troisième. *Turf:* A placed horse, un placé. **3.** *F:* I can't p. you, je ne vous remets pas.
placer ['pleisər], *s.* *Geol: Min:* Placer *m* ; gisement *m* aurifère.
placid ['plasid], *a.* Placide, calme, tranquille, serein. **-ly,** *adv.* Avec calme ; tranquillement.
placidity [plə'siditi], *s.* Placidité *f*, calme *m*, tranquillité *f.*
placket(-hole) ['plaket(houl)], *s.* *Dressm:* Fente *f* de jupe.
plagiarism ['pleidʒiərizm], *s.* **I.** Plagiarisme *m* ; démarquage *m.* **2.** Plagiat *m.*
plagiarist ['pleidʒiərist], *s.* Plagiaire *m* ; démarqueur *m.*
plagiarize ['pleidʒiəraiz], *v.tr.* Plagier (un auteur) ; faire un plagiat à, contrefaire (une œuvre).
plague[1] [pleig], *s.* **I.** Fléau *m.* The ten plagues of Egypt, les dix plaies *f* d'Égypte. *F:* What a plague the child is! quelle petite peste que cet enfant ! **2.** Peste *f.* Cattle plague, peste bovine. *A:* A plague on him! la (male)peste soit de lui ! **'plague-spot,** *s.* Foyer *m* d'infection. **'plague-stricken,** *a.* **I.** (Pays) frappé de la peste. **2.** (*Of pers.*) Pestiféré.
plague[2], *v.tr.* *F:* Tourmenter, harceler (qn) ; *P:* embêter, raser (qn). To plague s.o.'s life out, être le fléau de qn. To plague s.o. with questions, assommer qn de questions.
plaguy ['pleigi], *a.* *F:* Fâcheux, assommant. *adv.* A plaguy long time, rudiment longtemps.
plaice [pleis], *s.* *Ich:* Carrelet *m* ; plie *f.*
plaid [plad, pleid], *s.* **I.** Couverture *f* servant de manteau (des Écossais). **2.** *Tex:* Tartan *m.*
plain [plein]. I. *a.* **I.** Clair, évident. To make sth. p. to s.o., faire comprendre qch. à qn. *F:* It is as plain as a pikestaff, as plain as daylight, c'est clair comme le jour ; cela saute aux yeux. To make one's meaning perfectly plain, bien se faire comprendre. In plain English . . ., pour parler clairement. *Goods* marked in plain figures, articles marqués en chiffres connus. *Tg: etc:* Message in plain, message en clair. **2.** (*a*) *P. style,* style simple. In plain clothes, en civil ; *Adm:* en costume de ville. Plain-clothes policeman, agent en bourgeois, en civil. *Knitting:* Plain stitch, maille à l'endroit. Plain and purl, mailles endroit, mailles envers. *S.a.* SAILING[1] 1. (*b*) Uni, lisse. Plain material, étoffe unie. (*c*) Plain cooking, cuisine bourgeoise. (*d*) Plain truth, vérité pure, simple. He was called plain John, il s'appelait Jean tout court. Plain answer, réponse carrée. Plain speech, le franc-parler ; la rondeur. To be plain with s.o., être franc avec qn. To use plain language, parler franchement. Plain dealing, procédés *m* honnêtes. Plain country-folk, de

simples villageois. **3.** (*Of pers.*) To be plain, manquer de beauté. *She looks plainer than ever*, elle a enlaidi. **-ly,** *adv.* **1.** Clairement, manifestement, évidemment. *I can see it p.*, cela saute aux yeux. **Plainly I was not wanted**, il était évident que j'étais de trop. **2.** (*a*) Simplement. *To dress p.*, s'habiller sans recherche. (*b*) Franchement, carrément. **To put it plainly,** *you refuse*, pour parler clair, vous refusez. **To speak plainly**, user du franc-parler. II. **plain,** *adv.* Clairement, distinctement. *I can't speak any plainer*, je ne peux pas m'exprimer plus clairement. III. **plain,** *s.* Plaine *f.* **In the open plain**, en rase campagne. **'plain-'speaking,** *s.* Franchise *f*; franc-parler *m.* **'plain-'spoken,** *a.* Qui a son franc-parler; carré, rond.

plainness ['pleinnəs], *s.* **1.** Clarté *f* (de langage); netteté *f* (des objets lointains). **2.** (*a*) Simplicité *f* (de vie, etc.). (*b*) Franchise *f* (de langage). **3.** Manque *m* de beauté.

plainsong ['pleinsɔŋ], *s.* *Mus:* Plain-chant *m.*

plaint [pleint], *s.* **1.** *Jur:* Plainte *f.* **2.** *Poet:* Plainte, lamentation *f.*

plaintiff ['pleintif], *s.* *Jur:* Demandeur, -eresse; plaignant, -ante.

plaintive ['pleintiv], *a.* Plaintif. **-ly,** *adv.* Plaintivement; d'un ton plaintif.

plait¹ [plat], *s.* **1.** *Usu.* [pliːt] = PLEAT. **2.** Natte *f*, tresse *f* (de cheveux).

plait², *v.tr.* **1.** *Usu.* [pliːt] = PLEAT². **2.** Natter, tresser. *Hatm:* Ourdir (la paille).

plan¹ [plan], *s.* **1.** (*a*) Plan *m* (d'une maison); cadre *m*, plan (d'une œuvre littéraire). *To draw a p.*, tracer un plan. (*b*) *Mth: Arch:* Plan, projection *f.* *Surv:* Levé *m* (d'un terrain). **2.** Projet *m*, plan; *F:* combinaison *f.* **Plan of campaign**, plan de campagne. **Preliminary plan,** avant-projet *m.* **To draw up a plan**, dresser un plan. **To change one's plans**, prendre d'autres dispositions. **To have no fixed plans**, ne pas être fixé. **To upset s.o.'s plans**, déranger les combinaisons de qn. **Everything went according to plan**, tout a marché selon les prévisions. *F:* **The best plan would be to . . .**, le mieux serait de. . . .

plan², *v.tr.* (planned) **1.** (*a*) Faire, tracer, le plan de (qch.). (*b*) Arrêter le plan (d'un roman). **2.** Projeter, se proposer (un voyage); combiner (une attaque); tramer, ourdir (un complot). *To p. for the future*, songer à l'avenir. **To plan to do sth.**, se proposer, former le projet, de faire qch. **Well-planned**, (ouvrage) bien conçu.

planchette [plan'ʃet], *s.* *Psychics:* Planchette *f.*

plane¹ [plein], *a.* (*a*) Plan, uni; plat. (*b*) *Geom:* Plan. *S.a.* TRIGONOMETRY. **'plane-table,** *s.* *Surv:* Planchette *f.*

plane², *s.* **1.** (*a*) Plan *m* (d'un cristal, etc.). **Horizontal plane**, plan horizontal. *Art:* **Planes that build up the face**, méplats *m* du visage. *Arch:* **Curved plane**, rampe hélicoïdale (d'accès). (*b*) *F:* **A high plane of intelligence**, un niveau élevé de capacité intellectuelle. **2.** *Mec:* **Inclined plane**, plan incliné. **3.** *Av:* (*a*) Plan, aile *f*; surface portante. (*b*) *F:* = AEROPLANE, AIRPLANE.

plane³, *v.i.* *Av:* (*a*) (*Of machine*) **To plane down**, descendre en vol plané. (*b*) (*Of hydroplane*) **To plane along the water**, courir sur le redan.

plane⁴, *s.* *Tls:* Rabot *m.* **Long plane**, grande varlope. **Curved plane**, sabot *m.* **Tongue plane**, rabot à languette. **Rabbet(ing) plane**, guillaume *m.* *To run the p. over a plank*, passer le rabot sur une planche. **'plane-iron,** *s.* Fer *m* de rabot. **'plane-stock,** *s.* Fût *m* de rabot.

plane⁵, *v.tr.* Raboter (le bois); aplanir, planer (le bois, le métal). *To p. a board even*, araser une

planche. **To rough-plane**, corroyer. *To p. dow* *a board*, menuiser une planche.

plane⁶, *s.* Plane(-tree), platane *m.*

planet ['planet], *s.* *Astr:* Planète *f.* **'planet gear,** *s.* *Mec.E:* (Sun-and-)planet-gear, engre nage *m* planétaire. **'planet-pinion, -wheel, s** (Roue *f*) satellite *m.*

planetary ['planetəri], *a.* *Astr:* (Système planétaire.

planimeter [pla'nimetər], *s.* Planimètre *m.*

planish ['planiʃ], *v.tr.* **1.** Dresser au marteau aplanir (le métal). **2.** Polir. *Phot:* Satiner (un épreuve).

planisphere ['planisfiːər], *s.* Planisphère *m* mappemonde *f* céleste.

plank¹ [plaŋk], *s.* Planche (épaisse); madrier *m* ais *m.* *Wood in planks*, bois méplat. *Nau: A:* **T** **walk the plank**, passer à la planche.

plank², *v.tr.* Planchéier (un plancher). **plank down,** *v.tr.* *P:* Jeter, déposer. *To p. down th money*, allonger l'argent. *To p. oneself down on* seat, se camper sur un banc. **planking,** *s* **1.** Planchéiage *m.* **2.** *Coll.* Planches *f pl*; revête ment *m.*

plankton ['plaŋktɔn], *s.* *Oc:* Plancton *m.*

plano-convex ['pleino'kɔnveks], *a.* *Opt:* Plan convexe.

plant¹ [plɑːnt], *s.* **1.** Plante *f.* **Plant life,** (i) l vie végétale; (ii) flore *f* (d'une région). **2.** *Ind* Appareil(s) *m(pl)*; installation *f* (d'éclairage) matériel, outillage *m* (d'une usine). **The plant** la machinerie. *Heavy p.*, grosses machines **3.** *P:* Coup monté. **'plant-eating,** *a* *Z:* Phytophage. **'plant-louse,** *s.* Aphis *m* puceron *m.*

plant², *v.tr.* **1.** (*a*) Planter (un arbre); enterre (des oignons). **To plant a field with corn** mettre une terre en blé. (*b*) *P:* Enterrer (qn) **2.** (*a*) Planter (un piquet dans la terre). *To fin* oneself planted on a desert island, se trouve délaissé sur une île déserte. **To plant an idea i** *s.o.'s mind*, implanter une idée dans l'esprit d qn. (*b*) *F:* To plant a bullet in the target, loge une balle dans la cible. A well-planted blow, u coup bien asséné. (*c*) **To plant oneself in front o** s.o., se planter, se camper, devant qn. *F:* **T** **plant oneself on s.o.**, s'implanter chez qn **3.** *F:* Mettre en sûreté (des objets volés) **plant out,** *v.tr.* *Hort:* Repiquer, dépoter (de semis).

plantain¹ ['plantein, -tən], *s.* *Bot:* Plantain *m*

plantain², *s.* **1.** Banane *f* des Antilles. **2.** Plan tain(-tree), bananier *m* du paradis.

plantation [plɑːn'teiʃ(ə)n], *s.* (*a*) *For:* Planta tion *f*, bosquet *m*; peuplement *m* (d'arbres) (*b*) Plantation (de coton, de café, etc.).

planter ['plɑːntər], *s.* (*a*) Planteur *m* (de choux etc.); cultivateur *m.* (*b*) (*In colonies*) Planteur propriétaire *m* d'une plantation.

plantigrade ['plantigreid], *a. & s.* *Z:* Planti grade (*m*).

plaque [plɑːk], *s.* Plaque *f* (de bronze, etc.).

plaquette [pla'ket], *s.* Plaquette *f.*

plash¹ [plaʃ], *s.* Flaque *f* d'eau.

plash², *s.* **1.** (*a*) Clapotement *m* (des vagues) bruissement *m* (de la pluie). (*b*) Flac *m* (d'un corp qui tombe dans l'eau). **2.** Tache *f* (de couleur de couleur).

plash³, *v.i.* **1.** (*a*) Clapoter; (*of brook*) bruire babiller. (*b*) Faire flac (sur l'eau).

plasm [plazm], *s.* *Biol:* Protoplasme *m.*

plasma ['plazmə], *s.* *Biol:* (*a*) Plasma *m* (d sang). (*b*) = PLASM.

●**laster**[1] ['plɑːstər], s. **I.** *Med:* Emplâtre *m*. Adhesive plaster, sparadrap *m*. Court plaster, taffetas gommé. **2.** Plâtre *m*. Wall-plaster, enduit *m* de mur. Plaster of Paris, plâtre de moulage. *S.a.* LATH[1] I. '**plaster-work,** *s*. Plâtrage *m*, plâtrerie *f*. ●**laster**[2], *v.tr.* **I.** *Med:* Mettre un emplâtre sur (une plaie). **2.** To plaster (over) a wall, plâtrer un mur; enduire un mur de plâtre. *F:* To be plastered (over) with mud, être tout couvert de boue. Plastered (over) with decorations, chamarré de décorations. **plaster up,** *v.tr.* **I.** Plâtrer, boucher (une fente). **2.** *F:* Réparer sommairement; rabibocher (qch.). ●**lasterer** ['plɑːstərər], *s*. Plâtrier *m*. ●**lastic** ['plastik], *a*. **I.** (Art) plastique. Plastic surgery, chirurgie plastique. **2.** Plastique; qui se laisse mouler ou modeler. Plastic clay, terre *f* à modeler. *F: P. mind,* esprit malléable. ●**lasticine** ['plastisiːn], *s*. Plasticine *f*. ●**lasticity** [plas'tisiti], *s*. Plasticité *f*. ●**lastron** ['plastrən], *s. Fenc:* Plastron *m*. ●**late**[1] [pleit], *s*. **I.** Plaque *f*, lame *f*, feuille *f* (de métal). **2.** (a) Plate iron, tôlerie *f*, tôle *f*. *Mch:* Bottom plates, tôles, plaques, de fond (de chaudière). (b) Plateau *m* (de machine); platine *f* (de serrure); paumelle *f* (de gond de porte). *Cu:* Hot plate, plaque chauffante (de poêle). *Aut:* Clutch-plate, plateau d'embrayage. *El:* Terminal plate, socle *m*, tablette *f*, à bornes. Accumulator plate, plaque d'accumulateur. *W.Tel:* Valve plate, plaque, anode *f*, de lampe. Plate battery, batterie de plaque. (c) *Aut:* Number plate, plaque matricule; plaque de police. (d) *Dent:* Dentier *m*; pièce *f* dentaire. **3.** (a) Plaque de verre. (b) *Phot:* Plaque. Sensitive p., plaque sensible. Whole-plate, plaque et format *m* 16 cm 5 × 21 cm 5. Half-plate, plaque et format 12 cm × 16 cm 5. **4.** (a) *Engr:* Planche *f*. (b) *Engr:* Gravure *f*, estampe *f*. Full-page plate, gravure hors texte. Book of plates, atlas *m*. (c) *Typ:* (Stereotype) plate, cliché *m*. **5.** *Const:* Roof plate, sablière *f* de comble. **6.** (a) Orfèvrerie *f*; vaisselle *f* d'or, d'argent. (b) *Rac:* Coupe donnée en prix. *S.a.* SELLING. **7.** (a) Assiette *f*. Dinner plate, assiette plate. Soup plate, assiette creuse. (b) *Ecc:* (Collection-)plate, plateau *m* de quête. *S.a.* TAKE ROUND. '**plate-armour,** *s*. **I.** (a) Plaque *f* de blindage. (b) Blindage *m*. **2.** *Archeol:* Armure *f* à plates. '**plate-basket,** *s*. Ramasse-couverts *m inv*. '**plate-carrier,** *s*. = PLATE-HOLDER. '**plate-clutch,** *s. Aut:* Embrayage *m* à disques. **plate-'glass,** *s*. Glace *f* sans tain; glace de vitrage; verre *m* à glaces. '**plate-holder,** *s. Phot:* **I.** Châssis (négatif); porte-plaque *m*. **2.** Intermédiaire *m* pour plaques. '**plate-layer,** *s. Rail:* (a) Poseur *m* de rails, de voie. (b) Ouvrier *m* de la voie. Foreman p.-l., piqueur *m* de voie. '**plate-laying,** *s. Rail:* Pose *f* de voies. '**plate-mark,** *s*. **I.** = HALL-MARK[1]. **2.** *Engr: Phot:* Coup *m* de planche. '**plate-mill,** *s. Metall:* Laminoir *m* à tôle. '**plate-powder,** *s*. Poudre *f* à polir l'argenterie. '**plate-rack,** *s*. (a) *Dom.Ec:* Porte-assiettes *m inv*, égouttoir *m*. (b) *Phot:* Égouttoir. '**plate-tester,** *s. Phot:* Opacimètre *m*. '**plate-warmer,** *s*. Chauffe-assiette *m*, réchaud *m*. ●**late**[2], *v.tr.* **I.** Plaquer. To p. with gold, silver, dorer, argenter. **2.** *Typ:* Clicher (les pages). ●**plated,** *a*. **I.** Recouvert, garni, de plaques; blindé. **2.** Gold-plated, doublé d'or. Nickel-plated, nickelé. *Com:* Plated ware, plaqué *m*.

plating, *s*. **I.** (a) Revêtement *m* en tôle. (b) Tôles *fpl.* Steel-plating, blindage *m*. **2.** Placage *m*. **3.** *Typ:* Clichage *m*. **plateau,** *pl.* -x, -s ['platou, -z], *s. Ph.Geog:* Plateau *m*. **plateful** ['pleitful], *s*. Assiettée *f*. **platen** ['plat(ə)n], *s*. **I.** Plateau *m*, table *f* (de machine-outil). **2.** (Of printing-press) Platine *f*. **3.** *Typewr:* Rouleau *m* porte-papier. **plater** ['pleitər], *s*. **I.** *Metalw:* Plaqueur *m*. **2.** *Turf:* (a) Cheval *m* à réclamer. (b) Cheval de second ordre. **platform** ['platfɔːrm], *s*. **I.** Terrasse *f*. *Fort:* Plate-forme *f* (en terre). **2.** (a) Plate-forme; tablier *m* (de bascule). Entrance p. of a bus, plate-forme d'entrée. *Artil:* Loading p., plateau chargeur. *Navy:* Flying(-off) platform, plate-forme d'envol (pour avions). (b) *Nau:* Engine-room p., parquet *m* de la machine. (c) *Rail:* Quai *m*, trottoir *m*. Departure platform, (quai de) départ *m*; embarcadère *m*. Arrival platform, débarcadère *m*. From what p. does the train start? sur quel quai part le train? *S.a.* TICKET[1] I. **3.** (a) Estrade *f*, tribune *f* (de réunion publique). (b) *Pol:* Plate-forme, programme *m* (d'un parti). **platinize** ['platinaiz], *v.tr.* Platiner. **platinum** ['platinəm], *s*. Platine *m*. Platinum sponge, mousse *f* de platine. Platinum foil, platine laminé. '**platinum-'blond,** *a*. (Cheveux *mpl*) blond platine. *s.* A platinum-blonde, une blonde-platine. '**platinum (contact-)point,** *s*. Grain platiné. **platitude** ['platitjuːd], *s*. **I.** Platitude *f*, insipidité *f* (d'un discours). **2.** Platitude; lieu commun. **platitudinize** [plati'tjuːdinaiz], *v.i.* Débiter des platitudes, des banalités. **Plato** ['pleitou], *Pr.n.m.* Platon. **Platonic** [pla'tɔnik], *a*. (a) (Philosophe) platonicien. (b) (Amour) platonique. **platoon** [pla'tuːn], *s. Mil:* Section *f* (de combat). **platter** ['platər], *s*. Plat *m* (de bois); écuelle *f*. **platypus** ['platipəs], *s*. Ornithor(h)ynque *m*. **plaudits** ['plɔːdits], *s.pl.* (Salve *f* d')applaudissements *mpl*. **plausibility** [plɔːzi'biliti], *s*. Plausibilité *f*. **plausible** ['plɔːzibl], *a*. **I.** (a) Plausible, vraisemblable. (b) Spécieux. **2.** (Of pers.) Enjôleur; aux belles paroles. **-ibly,** *adv.* Plausiblement. **play**[1] [plei], *s*. **I.** (a) Jeu *m* (de lumière). Play of light on a jewel, chatoiement *m* d'un bijou. (b) Jeu, maniement *m* (d'armes). To make play with one's stick, s'escrimer de sa canne. (c) Jeu, activité *f*. To come into play, entrer en jeu. To call sth. into play, mettre qch. en jeu, en œuvre. To keep s.o. in play, tenir qn en haleine. Play of fancy, essor *m* de la fantaisie. To give full play to one's imagination, donner libre cours à son imagination. (d) Jeu, fonctionnement *m* (d'une pièce de mécanisme). (e) *Mec.E: etc:* Jeu, liberté *f*. **2.** (a) Jeu, amusement *m*. Schoolboys at p., élèves en récréation. (b) To say sth. in play, dire qch. pour plaisanter. Play on words, calembour *m*, équivoque *f*. **3.** (a) Jeu (de hasard). To be ruined by p., s'être ruiné au jeu. The play runs high, on joue gros jeu. (b) Games: P. began at one o'clock, la partie a commencé à une heure. Ball in play, out of play, balle *f* en jeu; balle hors jeu. **4.** (a) Pièce *f* de théâtre. Short play, piécette *f*, saynète *f*. Shakespeare's plays, théâtre de Shakespeare. (b) Spectacle *m*. To go to the play, aller au spectacle, au théâtre. '**play-acting,** *s*. = ACTING[2] 2 (b), (c). '**play-**

actor, *f.* **-actress,** *s.* (*a*) Acteur, -trice. (*b*) *Pej:* Cabotin, -ine. **'play-bill,** *s.* Affiche *f* (de théâtre); annonce *f* de spectacle. **'play-boy,** *s.* *F:* Cerveau brûlé; luron *m*; farceur *m*. **'play-pen,** *s.* Parc *m* pour enfants. **'play-room,** *s.* *U.S:* Chambre *f* des enfants.

play². I. *v.i.* **1.** Se mouvoir vivement; (*of animals*) gambader, folâtrer; (*of light*) jouer, chatoyer. *The sun plays on the water,* le soleil se joue sur l'eau. **2.** (*a*) (*Of fountain*) Jouer. (*b*) *The organ is playing,* les orgues donnent. *v.tr. The band played the troops past,* la musique accompagna le défilé des troupes. (*c*) (*Of part of mechanism*) Jouer; fonctionner librement. **3.** (*a*) Jouer, s'amuser, se divertir. **Run away and play!** allez jouer (et laissez-moi tranquille)! (*b*) *To p. with one's stick,* badiner avec sa canne. (*c*) **To play with fire,** jouer avec le feu. **He's not a man to be played with,** ce n'est pas un homme avec qui on plaisante. II. **play,** *v.tr. or ind.tr.* **1.** To play (at) billiards, chess, jouer au billard, aux échecs. **Play!** y êtes-vous? *Ten:* play ! To play fair, jouer franc jeu; agir loyalement. *F:* To play for one's own hand, jouer un jeu intéressé. **To play into the hands of s.o.,** faire, jouer, le jeu de qn. *They play into each other's hands,* ils sont d'intelligence. *S.a.* TIME¹ 3. **2.** To play (on) the piano, the flute, jouer du piano, de la flûte. *Won't you p. for us?* voulez-vous nous faire un peu de musique? III. **play,** *v.tr.* **1.** *Th:* (*a*) To play a part, jouer un rôle, To p. Macbeth, tenir le rôle de Macbeth. **To play in a film,** tourner un film. *F:* T**o** play the idiot. faire l'imbécile. **To play the man,** se conduire en homme. *S.a.* TRUANT. (*b*) *To p. a tragedy,* jouer, représenter, une tragédie. **2.** To play a joke, a trick, on s.o., jouer un tour à qn. **3.** (*a*) *Cards:* To play a card, jouer une carte. (*b*) *Games:* To p. the ball too high, renvoyer la balle trop haut. *Abs. Who plays first?* à qui d'entamer? *Bowls:* à qui la boule? *Golf:* à qui l'honneur? **4.** (*a*) To play a game of tennis, faire une partie de tennis. *S.a.* GAME¹ 1. To play a match, disputer un match. (*b*) To play s.o. at chess, faire une partie d'échecs avec qn. *I'll p. you for the drinks,* je vous joue les consommations. (*c*) *Sp:* Inclure (qn) dans son équipe. **5.** To play s.o. false, trahir qn. **6.** To play a fish, épuiser un poisson. **7.** To play water on the fire, diriger de l'eau sur l'incendie. *Abs. The fire-engine played on the house,* la pompe à incendie donna contre la maison. **To play on s.o.'s feelings,** agir sur les sentiments de qn. *To p. on s.o.'s credulity,* abuser de la crédulité de qn. **play away,** *v.tr.* Perdre (son argent) au jeu. **play off,** *v.tr.* **1.** To play off s.o. against s.o., opposer qn à qn. **2.** *Sp:* Rejouer (un match nul). **play on,** *v.i.* Continuer de jouer. **play out,** *v.tr.* **1.** Jouer (une pièce de théâtre) jusqu'au bout. **2.** *The organ played the people out,* l'orgue a joué la sortie. **3.** *F:* To be played out, être à bout de forces. **play up. 1.** *v.i.* (*a*) *F:* Faire de son mieux. **Play up!** allez-y ! (*b*) To play up to s.o., (i) *Th:* donner la réplique à qn; (ii) *F:* flatter, aduler, qn. **2.** *v.tr. F:* To play s.o. up, agacer qn, chahuter qn. *She plays him up,* elle le fait marcher. **playing,** *s.* **1.** Jeu *m.* **2.** *Th:* (*a*) Interprétation *f* (d'un rôle); jeu (d'un acteur). (*b*) Représentation *f* (d'une pièce). **3.** *Mus:* Exécution *f* (d'un morceau). **'playing-card,** *s.* Carte *f* à jouer. **'playing-field,** *s.* Terrain de jeux, de sports. **player** [ˈpleiǝr], *s.* Joueur, -euse. **1.** *Mus:* Exécutant, -ante. **2.** *Th:* Acteur, -trice. **3.** *Sp:* (*a*) Équipier *m.* (*b*) **Gentlemen versus players,**

amateurs contre professionnels. **4.** *Cards:* First *p.,* premier en cartes. **'player-piano,** *s.* Piano *m* mécanique (à rouleau).

playfellow [ˈpleifelo], *s.* Camarade *mf* de jeu.

playful [ˈpleiful], *a.* Enjoué, badin, folâtre. **-fully,** *adv.* Gaiement; en badinant.

playfulness [ˈpleifulnǝs], *s.* Enjouement *m,* badinage *m,* folâtrerie *f.*

playgoer [ˈpleigouǝr], *s.* Habitué, -ée, des spectacles.

playground [ˈpleigraund], *s.* **1.** *Sch:* Cour *f* de récréation ou terrain *m* de jeu(x). **2.** *F:* Lieu *m* de divertissement.

playhouse [ˈpleihaus], *s.* *A:* Théâtre *m.*

playmate [ˈpleimeit], *s.* = PLAYFELLOW.

plaything [ˈpleiθiŋ], *s.* Jouet *m;* *F:* joujou *m.*

playtime [ˈpleitaim], *s.* *Sch:* (Heure *f* de la) récréation; heures de récréation ou de sports.

playwright [ˈpleirait], *s.* Auteur *m* dramatique; dramaturge *m.*

plea [pli:], *s.* **1.** *Jur:* (*a*) *A. & Scot:* Procès *m.* (*b*) Défense *f.* **Plea in bar, special plea,** exception *f* péremptoire; fin *f* de non-recevoir. *To submit the p. that . . .,* plaider que + *ind.* **2.** (*a*) Excuse *f,* prétexte *m.* **On the plea of . . .,** sous prétexte de. . . . (*b*) *P. for mercy,* appel *m* à la clémence.

plead [pli:d]. **1.** *v.i.* Plaider (*for,* pour; *against,* contre). To plead guilty, s'avouer coupable. **To plead not guilty,** nier sa culpabilité. **2.** *v.tr.* (*a*) Plaider (une cause). *F:* To plead s.o.'s cause with s.o., intercéder pour qn auprès de qn. (*b*) *F:* Invoquer, alléguer (une excuse). *To p. ignorance,* prétexter l'ignorance. **pleading,** *s.* **1.** L'art *m* de plaider. **2.** (*a*) Plaidoirie *f.* (*b*) Special pleading, arguments spécieux. **3.** Prières *fpl,* intercession *f* (*for,* en faveur de).

pleader [ˈpli:dǝr], *s.* Avocat (plaidant); défenseur *m.* Special pleader, (i) *Jur:* avocat consultant; (ii) *F:* plaideur *m* pour son saint; casuiste *m.*

pleasance [ˈplezǝns], *s.* *A:* **1.** Plaisir *m,* délice *m.* **2.** Jardin *m* d'agrément.

pleasant [ˈplezǝnt], *a.* **1.** Agréable, charmant, aimable. *Story that makes p. reading,* histoire agréable à lire. *P. breeze,* brise douce. *Life is p. here,* il fait bon vivre ici. *Good night, pleasant dreams,* bonne nuit, faites de beaux rêves. **2.** (*Of pers.*) Affable. **To make oneself pleasant (to s.o.),** faire l'agréable (auprès de qn). **-ly,** *adv.* **1.** Agréablement. **2.** Avec affabilité.

pleasantness [ˈplezǝntnǝs], *s.* **1.** Agrément *m,* charme *m* (d'un endroit). **2.** (*Of pers.*) Affabilité *f.*

pleasantry [ˈplezǝntri], *s.* Plaisanterie *f.*

please [pli:z], *v.tr.* **1.** (i) Plaire à (qn); faire plaisir à (qn); (ii) contenter (qn). *To be easily pleased,* s'arranger de tout. **There is no pleasing him,** il n'y a pas moyen de lui plaire. **He is hard to please,** il est difficile. *In order to p. s.o.,* pour faire plaisir, pour être agréable, à qn. *The plan pleases him,* le projet lui sourit. *Music that pleases the ear,* musique qui flatte l'oreille. **Please yourself!** faites à votre guise. *Abs.* To lay oneself out to please, se mettre en frais. **2.** (*a*) *Impers.* Please God! plaise à Dieu! Dieu le veuille! (*b*) (If you) please, s'il vous plaît. **P. don't cry,** de grâce, ne pleurez pas. *P. tell me . . .,* ayez la bonté de me dire. *. . . May I?*—**Please do!** vous permettez?—Faites donc! **Please be seated,** veuillez (donc) vous asseoir. **Please to return this book,** prière de retourner ce livre. **3.** *Abs.* To do as one pleases, agir à sa guise. **Do as you please,** faites comme vous voudrez, comme bon vous semblera. *He will do just as he pleases,* il

n'en fera qu'à sa tête. *S.a.* COOL¹ I. **pleased,** *a.*
I. Satisfait, content. **To be pleased with sth.**
être satisfait de qch. *F:* He is very well pleased
with himself, il est fort satisfait de sa petite
personne. *I am p. at the news,* je suis heureux
d'apprendre cette nouvelle. **To be anything but
pleased,** n'être pas du tout content. *F:* He
is as pleased as Punch, il est heureux comme
un roi ; il est aux anges. *I shall be p. to come,*
j'aurai grand plaisir à venir. *He will be very
p. to do it,* il le fera volontiers. *Com: I am p. to
inform you that . . .,* je m'empresse de vous
aviser que. . . . **2.** His Majesty has been
graciously **pleased to . . .,** il a plu à sa gracieuse
Majesté de. . . . **Be pleased to accept** *these few
flowers,* daignez accepter ces quelques fleurs.
pleasing, *a.* Agréable. *P. countenance,* visage
avenant, sympathique. **-ly,** *adv.* Agréablement.
pleasurable [ˈpleʒərəbl], *a.* Agréable. **-ably,**
adv. Agréablement.
pleasure [ˈpleʒər], *s.* I. Plaisir *m.* **To take, find,**
(a) **pleasure** in doing sth., éprouver du plaisir à
faire qch. **I have much pleasure in informing you**
that . . ., je suis très heureux de vous faire
savoir que. . . . **It would afford us great pleasure
to . . .,** nous aurions grand plaisir à . . . **Mrs
X requests the pleasure of Mrs Y's company
at . . .,** Mme X prie Mme Y de lui faire le
plaisir d'assister à. . . . **With pleasure,** avec
plaisir ; volontiers. **2.** (a) Plaisir(s) jouissances
fpl. To be fond of p., aimer la joie, le plaisir. **Pleasure trip,** voyage d'agrément. **Pleasure resort,** ville
de plaisir. (b) *Sensual p.,* volupté *f,* débauche *f.*
3. Volonté *f ;* bon plaisir. **Without consulting
my pleasure,** sans me consulter. **At pleasure,** à
volonté. **At s.o.'s pleasure,** au gré de qn. **Office
held during pleasure,** emploi amovible. **During
the King's pleasure,** pendant le bon plaisir du
roi. *Com:* **What is your pleasure, madam?**
qu'y a-t-il pour votre service, madame? **'pleasure-boat,** *s.* Bateau *m* de plaisance. **'pleas-
ure-loving,** *a.* Amoureux des plaisirs.
pleat¹ [pliːt], *s. Dressm:* Pli *m*
pleat², *v.tr.* Plisser (une jupe).
plebeian [pleˈbiːən], *a.* Plébéien ; du peuple.
P. name, nom bourgeois ; nom de roturier.
plebiscite [ˈplebisait], *s.* Plébiscite *m.*
plebs (the) [ðəplebz], *s.* La plèbe ; les classes
inférieures.
plectrum [ˈplektrəm], *s. Mus:* Plectre *m,*
médiator *m.*
pledge¹ [pledʒ], *s.* I. (a) Gage *m,* nantissement *m.*
(b) To put sth. in pledge, mettre qch. en gage.
To take sth. out of pledge, dégager qch. **2. Pledge
of good faith,** garantie *f* de bonne foi. **3.** (a) Promesse *f,* vœu *m. I am under a pledge of secrecy,*
j'ai fait vœu de garder le secret. (b) **To take, sign,
the pledge,** promettre de s'abstenir d'alcool ; faire
vœu de tempérance. **4.** Toast *m ;* santé (portée
à qn).
pledge², *v.tr.* I. Mettre (qch.) en gage ; engager
(une montre). *To p. one's property,* engager son
bien. **2.** Engager (sa parole). **To be pledged to
do sth.,** avoir pris l'engagement de faire qch.
To pledge one's allegiance to the king, vouer
obéissance au roi. **3.** Boire à a santé de (qn) ;
porter un toast à (qn).
pledget [ˈpledʒet], *s. Surg:* Tampon *m* de
charpie ; bourdonnet *m,* plumasseau *m.*
Pleiad, *pl.* **-ads, -ades** [ˈplaiad, -ədz, -ədiːz].
Pr.n. I. *pl. Astr:* Les Pléiades *f.* **2.** *Fr.Lit:* (La)
Pléiade.
pleistocene [ˈplaistosiːn], *a. & s. Geol:* Pléistocène (*m*).

plenary [ˈpliːnəri], *a.* Complet, -ète ; entier.
P. power, pouvoir absolu. **Plenary assembly,**
assemblée plénière.
plenipotentiary [plenipoˈten əri], *a. & s.*
Plénipotentiaire (*m*).
plenitude [ˈplenitjuːd], *s.* Plénitude *f.*
plenteous [ˈplentjəs], *a. Poet:* I. Abondant,
copieux. **2.** Fertile, riche (*in,* en). **-ly,** *adv.* En
abondance.
plentiful [ˈplentiful], *a.* Abondant, copieux.
-fully, *adv.* Abondamment ; copieusement.
plenty [ˈplenti]. I. *s.* Abondance *f.* (a) *He has
p. of everything,* il a de tout en suffisance. **Plenty
of money,** une ample provision d'argent. *To have
p. of courage,* ne pas manquer de courage. *You
have p. of time,* vous avez largement le temps.
To have plenty to live upon, avoir grandement de
quoi vivre. **He has plenty to go upon,** il peut
tailler en plein drap. (b) **To live in plenty,** vivre
à l'aise, grassement. **Land of plenty,** pays de
cocagne. **2.** *adv. F:* **Plenty big enough,** bien
assez gros.
plenum [ˈpliːnəm], *s. Ph:* Plein *m.* **Plenum fan,**
ventilateur, ventilateur positif, soufflant.
pleonasm [ˈpliːonazm], *s.* Pléonasme *m.*
pleonastic [pliːoˈnastik], *a.* Pléonastique, redondant. **-ally,** *adv.* Par pléonasme.
plesiosaurus, *pl.* **-ri** [pliːsioˈsɔːrəs, -rai], *s.*
Plésiosaure *m.*
plethora [ˈpleθora], *s.* I. *Med:* Pléthore *f.*
2. Pléthore, surabondance *f* (de bien, etc.).
plethoric [pleˈθɔrik], *a.* Pléthorique.
pleura, *pl.* **-ae** [ˈpluərə, -iː], *s. Anat:* Plèvre *f.*
pleural [ˈpluərəl], *a. Anat:* Pleural, -aux.
pleurisy [ˈpluərisi], *s. Med:* Pleurésie *f.*
pleuritic [pluəˈritik], *a.* Pleurétique.
pleuro-pneumonia [pluərɔnjuˈmounjə], *s.
Med:* Pleuropneumonie *f.*
plexus [ˈpleksəs], *s. Anat:* Plexus *m.*
pliability [plaiəˈbiliti], *s.* (a) Flexibilité *f.*
(b) Docilité *f,* souplesse *f* (de caractère).
pliable [ˈplaiəbl], *a.* I. (a) Flexible ; (cuir)
souple. (b) (Voix) flexible. **2.** (Caractère) docile,
complaisant.
pliant [ˈplaiənt], *a.* = PLIABLE. **-ly,** *adv.* (a) Avec
souplesse. (b) Docilement.
pliers [ˈplaiərz], *s.pl. Tls:* Pince(s) *f(pl),* te-
naille(s) *f(pl).* *Insulated p.,* pince isolante. *Gas
p.,* pince de plombier.
plight¹ [plait], *s.* Condition *f,* état *m.* **To be in
a sorry plight,** (i) *F:* être dans de beaux draps,
en mauvais arroi ; (ii) être dans un triste état.
plight², *v.tr. Lit:* To plight one's troth, promettre, engager, sa foi. **Plighted word,** parole
engagée. **Plighted lovers,** fiancés *m.*
Plimsoll [ˈplimsəl]. I. *Pr.n. Nau:* Plimsoll line,
ligne *f* de Plimsoll ; ligne de flottaison en charge.
2. *s.pl.* Plimsolls, souliers *m* bain de mer (en toile).
plinth [plinθ], *s. Arch:* Plinthe *f ;* socle *m* (d'une
colonne).
Pliny [ˈplini]. *Pr.n.m. Lt.Lit:* Pline.
plod [plɔd], *v.i.* (plodded) I. Marcher lourdement,
péniblement. **To plod along,** cheminer d'un pas
pesant. **To plod on,** persévérer. **2.** To plod
(away), travailler laborieusement (*at,* à). **plod-
ding¹,** *a.* (a) (Pas) pesant, lourd. (b) Persévérant. **plodding²,** *s.* Labeur assidu.
plodder [ˈplɔdər], *s.* Travailleur persévérant.
Sch: F: Bûcheur *m.*
plop¹ [plɔp], *s., adv., & int.* I. Flac (*m*), plouf (*m*)
(de qch. tombant dans l'eau). **2.** *He sits down p.,*
pouf ! il s'assoit.
plop², *v.i.* (plopped [plɔpt]) I. Faire flac, plouf.
2. Tomber en faisant pouf.

plosive ['plousiv], *a. & s.* (Consonne) plosive.
plot¹ [plɔt], *s.* **I.** (Parcelle *f*, lot *m*, de) terrain *m*; quartier *m* (de terre). **Building plot**, terrain à bâtir. **2.** Intrigue *f*, action *f*, plan *m* (d'une pièce, d'un roman). **The plot thickens**, l'intrigue se noue; *F:* l'affaire *f* se corse. *Unravelling of the p.*, dénouement *m*. **3.** *Mth: etc:* Tracé *m*, graphique *m*. **4.** Complot *m*, conspiration *f*. **To hatch a plot**, ourdir un complot. *To discover the p.*, *F:* éventer la mèche.
plot², *v.tr.* (plotted) **I.** (*a*) Relever (un terrain, etc.). (*b*) Tracer, rapporter (un levé de terrain). *To p. a diagram*, relever un diagramme. **2.** *Mth:* To plot the graph of an equation, tracer le graphique d'une équation. **3.** (*a*) Comploter, conspirer, tramer (la ruine de qn). (*b*) *Abs.* Comploter, conspirer (*against s.o.*, contre qn).
plotting, *s.* **1.** Levé *m* (d'un terrain). **2.** Tracé *m*, graphique *m*. **3.** Complots *mpl*, machinations *fpl*.
plotter ['plɔtər], *s.* **1.** (*a*) (*Pers.*) Traceur *m* (d'un cadastre). (*b*) (*Device*) Abaque *m*. **2.** Conspirateur, -trice.
plough¹ [plau], *s.* **I.** Charrue *f*. **Steam plough**, tractor plough, laboureuse *f*. **Multiple plough**, gang plough, (charrue) polysoc *m*. *F:* To put, set, one's hand to the plough, mettre la main à la pâte. **To follow the plough**, être laboureur. **2.** *Astr:* The Plough, le Chariot. **3.** *Bookb:* Rognoir *m*. **'plough-boy**, *s.m.* Valet de charrue. **'plough-horse**, *s.* Cheval, -aux *m*, de labour. **'plough-land**, *s.* (*a*) Terre *f* de labour; labours *mpl*. (*b*) Terre arable.
plough², *v.tr.* **I.** (*a*) Labourer (un champ); tracer, creuser (un sillon). *Abs.* To plough, labourer la terre. *Ploughed lands*, labours *m*. *F:* To plough the sands, battre l'eau avec un bâton. *S.a.* FURROW¹ 1. (*b*) (*Of ship*) Fendre, sillonner (les flots). **2.** *Bookb:* Rogner (le papier). **3.** *Sch: F:* Refuser, retoquer, recaler (un candidat). **To be ploughed**, échouer (à un examen); être refusé. *Ploughed in the oral examination*, collé à l'oral. **plough in**, *v.tr.* Enterrer, enfouir, (le fumier, etc.) dans le sol en labourant. **plough through**, *v.tr. & i. F:* To plough (one's way) through the mud, avancer péniblement dans la boue. **plough up**, *v.tr.* **I.** (*a*) Faire passer la charrue dans (un champ). (*b*) (*Of shells*) Effondrer (le terrain). **2.** Extirper (des mauvaises herbes, etc.) avec la charrue. **ploughing,** *s.* Labourage *m*, labour *m*.
ploughman, *pl.* **-men** ['plaumən, -men], *s.m.* Laboureur.
ploughshare ['plauʃɛər], *s.* Soc *m* de charrue.
plover ['plʌvər], *s.* **I.** *Orn:* Pluvier *m*. **2.** *Cu:* Plovers' eggs, œufs *m* de vanneau.
plow [plau], *s. & v. U.S:* = PLOUGH.
ploy [plɔi], *s. Scot:* **I.** Occupation *f*, passetemps *m inv.* **2.** Espièglerie *f*.
pluck¹ [plʌk], *s.* **I.** To give a pluck at sth., tirer qch. d'un petit coup sec. **2.** *Cu:* Fressure *f* (de veau). **3.** *F:* Courage *m*, cran *m*. *He has plenty of p.*, il a du cran; il a du cœur au ventre.
pluck², *v.tr.* **I.** Arracher (des plumes); cueillir (une fleur); épiler (les sourcils). **2.** To pluck s.o. by the sleeve, tirer qn par la manche. **3.** *Sch: F:* = PLOUGH² 3. **4.** Plumer (une volaille). **pluck off**, *v.tr.* Détacher (une feuille d'une plante). **pluck out**, *v.tr.* Arracher (des cheveux). **pluck up**, *v.tr.* To pluck up (one's) courage, s'armer de courage.
plucky ['plʌki], *a.* Courageux, *F:* crâne. *To be p.*, *F:* avoir du chien, du cran. *He's a p. one,*

c'est un rude lapin. **-ily,** *adv.* Courageusement; sans se laisser abattre.
plug¹ [plʌg], *s.* **I.** (*a*) Tampon *m*, bouchon *m*, bonde *f*. **Plug of a boat**, bouchon de nable d'une embarcation. (*b*) *Dent:* Tampon d'ouate. *Surg:* Bourdonnet *m*. **2.** (*a*) Cheville *f*. *El:* Fiche *f* de connexion. **Two-pin plug**, fiche à deux broches. **Wall plug**, prise *f* de courant. (*b*) *I.C.E:* Sparking plug, bougie *f* (d'allumage). **3.** (*a*) Firehydrant plug, bouche *f* d'incendie. (*b*) *Plumb:* Effet *m* d'eau (de cabinet d'aisances). **To pull the plug**, tirer la chaînette du réservoir de chasse. **4.** (*a*) = PLUG-TOBACCO. (*b*) **Plug of tobacco**, chique *f* de tabac. **5.** *U.S:* (*a*) Vieux cheval; rosse *f*. (*b*) *Publ:* Ouvrage *m* difficile à placer; ours *m*. **6.** *P:* Coup *m* de poing. *A p. on the ear*, un pain sur l'oreille. **'plug-hole,** *s.* Bonde *f*; trou *m* d'écoulement (de baignoire); *Nau:* nable *m* (d'embarcation). **'plug-switch,** *s. El:* Prise *f* de courant à fiche; interrupteur *m* à fiche. **'plug-to'bacco,** *s.* Tabac *m* en carotte.
plug², *v.* (plugged) I. *v.tr.* **I.** To plug (up) *an opening*, boucher, tamponner, une ouverture. To plug a wound, tamponner une plaie. **2.** *P:* (*a*) Flanquer une balle dans la peau à (qn). (*b*) Flanquer un coup à (qn). II. **plug,** *v.i. F:* To plug away, persévérer, s'acharner; bûcher. **plug in,** *v.tr. El.E:* (*a*) Intercaler (une résistance). (*b*) *Abs.* Mettre la fiche dans la prise de courant.
plum [plʌm], *s.* **I.** Prune *f*. **Plum tree**, prunier *m*. **2.** (*a*) *A:* Raisin sec. *Still so used in* PLUM-CAKE, PLUM-DUFF. (*b*) French plums, pruneaux *m* d'Agen ou de Tours. **3.** *F:* Fin morceau; morceau de choix. **The plums**, les meilleurs postes. **'plum-'cake,** *s.* Gâteau *m* aux raisins. **'plum-'duff,** *s.* Pudding *m* aux raisins.
plumage ['plu:medʒ], *s.* Plumage *m*.
plumb¹ [plʌm], *s.* **I.** Plomb *m* (de fil à plomb). **2.** Aplomb *m*. **Out of plumb**, hors d'aplomb; (mur) qui porte à faux. **3.** *Nau:* (Ligne *f* de) sonde *f*. **'plumb-bob,** *s.* Plomb *m* (de fil à plomb). **'plumb-line,** *s.* **I.** Fil *m* à plomb. **2.** *Nau:* Ligne *f* de sonde. **'plumb-rule,** *s.* Niveau vertical; niveau à plomb.
plumb², *v.tr.* **I.** Sonder (la mer). **2.** Vérifier l'aplomb de (qch.). **3.** *Plumb:* Plomber (une canalisation). **plumbing,** *s.* **I.** Plomberie *f*. **2.** *Coll.* Tuyauterie *f*.
plumb³. **I.** *a.* Droit; vertical, -aux; d'aplomb. **2.** *adv. F:* Plumb in the centre, juste au milieu. *U.S: P:* Plumb crazy, complètement fou.
plumbago [plʌm'beigo], *s.* Plombagine *f*.
plumber ['plʌmər], *s.* Plombier *m*.
plume¹ [plu:m], *s.* **I.** *A. & Lit:* Plume *f*. **2.** Panache *m*, aigrette *f*; plumet *m* (de casque).
plume². **I.** *v.tr.* Orner de plumes. **Blackplumed**, aux plumes noires. **2.** *v.pr.* (*a*) (*Of bird*) To plume itself, se lisser les plumes. (*b*) *F:* (*Of pers.*) To plume oneself on sth., se glorifier de qch.
plummer-block, -box ['plʌmərblɔk, -bɔks], *s. Mec. E:* Palier *m*.
plummet ['plʌmet], *s.* **I.** Plomb *m* (de fil à plomb). **2.** *Nau:* Sonde *f*.
plump¹ [plʌmp], *a.* (*Of pers.*) Rebondi, grassouillet, dodu; (*of chicken*) bien en chair.
plump². **I.** *s.* (*a*) Bruit sourd (de chute). (*b*) **Summer plump**, ondée *f*. **2.** *adv.* To fall plump into the mud, tomber dans la boue avec un floc.
plump³. **I.** *v.tr.* Jeter brusquement; flanquer. *To p. oneself into an armchair*, se laisser tomber dans un fauteuil. **2.** *v.i.* (*a*) Tomber lourdement; faire plouf. (*b*) *Pol: etc:* To plump for a candidate, donner tous ses votes à un candidat.

plumpness ['plʌmpnəs], s. Embonpoint m, rondeur f.

plumule ['plu:mju:l], s. Orn: etc: Plumule f.

plunder[1] ['plʌndər], s. **1.** Pillage m (d'une ville). **2.** (a) Butin m. (b) F: Petits bénéfices.

plunder[2], v.tr. Piller, dépouiller (un pays).

plunderer ['plʌndərər], s. Pillard m, ravisseur m.

plunge[1] [plʌndʒ], s. Plongeon m. F: To take the plunge, sauter le pas; faire le plongeon. To be about to take the p., être sur le tremplin.

plunge[2]. **1.** v.tr. Plonger, immerger (le linge dans la lessive). Plunged in darkness, plongé dans l'obscurité. **2.** v.i. (a) Plonger, F: piquer une tête (dans l'eau, etc.); s'enfoncer (dans un bois); se jeter (à corps perdu) (dans une affaire). (b) To plunge forward, s'élancer en avant. (c) (Of horse) (Se cabrer et) ruer. (d) (Of ship) Tanguer; piquer du nez. (e) Gaming: Jouer ou parier sans compter. St.Exch: Risquer de grosses sommes. **plunging**, s. **1.** Plongée f, plongement m. **2.** Tangage m (d'un bateau).

plunger ['plʌndʒər], s. **1.** F: Joueur effréné. St.Exch: (Spéculateur) risque-tout m inv. **2.** (a) Plongeur m (de pompe). Plunger-piston, (piston) plongeur. Grease-gun plunger, piston compresseur de pompe de graissage. (b) Husb: Batte f à beurre (de baratte). (c) Navy: Plunger of a mine, plongeur.

pluperfect [plu:'pə:rfekt], a. & s. Gram: Plus-que-parfait (m).

plural ['pluərəl]. **1.** a. & s. Gram: Pluriel (m). In the plural, au pluriel. **2.** a. Pol: Plural vote, vote plural.

pluralism ['pluərəlizm], s. **1.** Cumul m de fonctions (quelconques). **2.** Phil: Pluralisme m.

plurality [pluə'raliti], s. **1.** Pluralité f. **2.** Plurality of offices, cumul m de fonctions.

plus [plʌs]. **1.** prep. Plus. Courage plus sense, le courage plus le bon sens. **2.** a. (a) (Of quantity) Positif. (b) On the plus side of the account, à l'actif du compte. (c) Sp: Plus player, joueur qui rend des points. **3.** s. (pl. plusses ['plʌsiz]) (a) Plus m; signe m de l'addition. (b) Quantité positive. **'plus-'fours**, s.pl. Cost: Culotte bouffante pour le golf; culotte de golf.

plush [plʌʃ], s. Tex: Peluche f, panne f.

plutocracy [plu'tɔkrəsi], s. Ploutocratie f.

plutocrat ['plu:tokrat], s. Ploutocrate m.

pluvial ['plu:viəl]. a. Geol: Pluvial, -aux.

pluviometer [plu:vi'ɔmetər], s. Pluviomètre m.

ply[1] [plai], s. **1.** (a) Pli m (de tissu en plusieurs plis). (b) Pli, épaisseur f (de contre-plaqué). Five-ply wood, contre-plaqué m en cinq épaisseurs. **2.** Brin m, fil m (de corde, de laine); toron m (de corde). Three-ply wool, laine trois fils.

ply[2]. **1.** v.tr. (a) Manier vigoureusement. To ply the oars, (i) manier les avirons; (ii) faire force de rames. To ply the needle, faire courir l'aiguille. (b) To ply a trade, exercer un métier. (c) To ply s.o. with questions, presser qn de questions. To ply s.o. with drink, verser force rasades à qn. **2.** v.i. (a) (Of bus) Faire le service, le va-et-vient (between . . . and . . . entre . . . et . . .). (b) Car plying for hire, automobile de place.

plywood ['plaiwud], s. (Bois) contre-plaqué m.

pneumatic [nju'matik]. **1.** a. Pneumatique. Pneumatic tyre, (bandage) pneumatique m, F: pneu m. Pneumatic pick, pic à air comprimé. **2.** s. F: Pneu.

pneumonia [nju'moun a], s. Med: Pneumonie f; fluxion f de poitrine.

pneumothorax [(p)nju:mo'θɔ:rəks], s. *Med: Pneumothorax m.

po [pou], s. F: Pot m de chambre.

poach[1] [poutʃ], v.tr. Cu: Pocher (des œufs).

poach[2], v.tr. (a) Braconner dans (un bois). (b) Braconner (le gibier). (c) Abs. Braconner. F: To poach on s.o.'s preserves, empiéter sur les prérogatives de qn; piquer dans l'assiette de qn. (d) Ten: To poach a ball, chiper une balle à son partenaire. **poaching**, s. Braconnage m.

poacher ['poutʃər], s. **1.** Braconnier m. Tail: Poacher-pocket, poche f carnier (de costume de chasse). **2.** Ten: F: Chipeur, -euse.

pochard ['poutʃərd, 'pɔkərd], s. Orn: Milouin m.

pocket[1] ['pɔket], s. **1.** (a) Poche f (de vêtement). Trouser-pocket, poche de pantalon. Waistcoat-pocket, gousset m. To have empty pockets, avoir la poche vide. F: To line one's pockets, faire sa pelote. F: To have s.o. in one's pocket, avoir qn dans sa manche. S.a. BURN[2] I, PICK[3] 7. Pocket edition, édition de poche. Phot: Pocket camera, appareil de poche. (b) He always has his hand in his pocket, il est toujours à débourser. To be in pocket, être en bénéfice. I am out of pocket by it, 'y suis de ma poche. **2.** (a) Sac m (de houblon). (b) Bill: Blouse f. (c) Aut: Leather pocket (in door), fonte f; poche intérieure. (d) Pockets under the eyes, poches sous les yeux. **3.** Mec.E: Retrait m (pour recevoir un organe). **4.** (a) Min: Poche, sac (de minerai). (b) Cavité remplie d'eau, de gaz. (c) See AIR-POCKET. **'pocket-book**, s. (a) Carnet m de poche; calepin m. (b) Portefeuille m. **pocket-'handkerchief**, s. Mouchoir m de poche. **'pocket-knife**, s. Couteau m de poche. **'pocket-money**, s. Argent m de poche. **'pocket-picking**, s. Vol m à la tire. **'pocket-pistol**, s. **1.** Pistolet m de poche. **2.** F: Gourde f de poche (pour eau-de-vie).

pocket[2], v.tr. (pocketed) **1.** (a) Empocher; mettre (qch.) dans sa poche. (b) Pej: Soustraire (de l'argent); chiper (qch.). **2.** Avaler (un affront). **3.** Refouler (sa colère). To pocket one's pride, mettre son orgueil dans sa poche. **4.** Bill: Blouser (la bille). **pocketed**, a. (Électrode, soupape) en retrait.

pocketful ['pɔketful], s. Pleine poche; pochée f.

pock-mark ['pɔkmɑ:rk], s. Marque f de la petite vérole.

pock-marked ['pɔkmɑ:rkt], a. Marqué de la petite vérole; (visage) grêlé.

pod[1] [pɔd], s. (a) Cosse f, gousse f (de fèves); écale f (de pois). (b) Senna pods, follicules m de séné.

pod[2], v. (podded) **1.** v.i. (Of plant) Former des cosses. **2.** v.tr. Écosser, écaler (des pois, etc.).

podginess ['pɔdʒinəs], s. Embonpoint m, rondeur f.

podgy ['pɔdʒi], a. Boulot, -otte, replet, -ète.

poem ['pouem], s. Poème m; (short) poésie f.

poet ['pouet], s.m. Poète.

poetaster ['poue'tastər], s. Méchant poète.

poetess ['pouetes], s.f. Femme poète; poétesse.

poetic(al) [pou'etik(əl)], a. Poétique. S.a. JUSTICE I. **-ally**, adv. Poétiquement.

poetics [pou'etiks], s.pl. L'art m poétique.

poetry ['pouetri], s. Poésie f. To write poetry, écrire des vers. Piece of poetry, poésie.

poignancy ['pɔinənsi], s. (a) Piquant m (d'une sauce); mordant m (d'une satire). (b) Violence f (d'une émotion); acuité f (d'une douleur).

poignant ['pɔinənt], a. (a) Piquant, âpre. (b) (Of emotion) Poignant, vif; (of thought) angoissant. **-ly**, adv. D'une façon poignante.

point[1] [pɔint], s. **I.** Point m. **1.** Decimal point, virgule f. Three point five (3·5) = trois virgule cinq (3,5). **2.** (a) **Point of departure,** point de départ. *Astr:* The cardinal points, les points cardinaux. **At all points,** sous tous rapports; **en tout point.** Armed **at all points,** armé de toutes pièces. (b) **Point of view, view-point,** point de vue. *To consider sth. from all points of view,* considérer qch. sous tous ses aspects. **3.** (a) **Point,** détail m (d'un raisonnement). **Figures that give point** to his argument, chiffres qui ajoutent du poids à sa thèse. **To differ on a point,** ne pas être d'accord sur un point, sur un détail. *On that p. we disagree,* là-dessus nous ne sommes pas d'accord. **To pursue one's point,** poursuivre son idée. **To maintain one's point,** maintenir son dire. **To make a point,** faire ressortir un argument. **Points to be remembered,** considérations f à se appeler. **A point of conscience,** un cas de conscience. **To make a point of doing sth.,** se faire un devoir de faire qch. **Point of grammar,** question de grammaire. **In point of fact,** par le fait. *We are the stronger* **in point of numbers,** nous sommes les plus forts sous le rapport du nombre. *In p. of intelligence,* sous le rapport de l'intelligence. *S.a.* CARRY² 4, HONOUR¹ 3, POSSESSION 1, STRETCH² 1. (b) **The point,** le sujet, la question. **Here is the point,** voici ce dont il s'agit. **Off the point,** étranger à la question. **On this point,** à cet égard. **Argument to the point,** argument topique. *This is very much to the p.,* c'est bien parlé; c'est bien dit. *Your remark is not to the p.,* votre observation manque d'à-propos. **Let us get back to the point,** revenons à nos moutons. (c) **What would be the point of** (doing sth.)? à quoi bon (faire qch.)? *I don't see the p. of the story,* je ne vois pas où cette histoire veut en venir. *S:a.* MISS¹ 1. (d) **Point of interest,** détail intéressant. **To have one's good points,** avoir ses qualités. *S.a.* STRONG 2. **4.** (a) **To be on the point of doing sth.,** être sur le point de faire qch. *I was on the p. of jumping,* j'allais sauter. (b) **Matters are at such a point that . . .,** les choses en sont là que. . . . **To come to the point,** arriver au fait. **Severe to the point of cruelty,** sévère jusqu'à la cruauté. **5.** *Games:* **To score so many points,** marquer, faire, tant de points. **What points shall we play?** (i) en combien jouons-nous la partie? (ii) à combien le point? *Box:* **To win on points,** gagner aux points. **To give points to s.o.,** donner des points à qn. **6.** (a) **The thermometer went up two points,** le thermomètre est, a, monté de deux divisions. *St.Exch:* **To rise a point,** hausser d'un point. (b) *Typ:* Point. **Set up in twelve-point** (body), composé en corps douze. **II.** **point,** s. Pointe f. **1.** (a) **Pointe,** extrémité f (d'une épingle); bec m (d'une plume à écrire). *Box:* **Blow to the point,** coup sur la pointe de la mâchoire. **Five-point star,** étoile f à cinq rayons. **Point of a joke,** piquant m, sel m, d'une plaisanterie. *S.a.* FINE² 5. (b) *Farr:* Bay horse with black points, cheval bai aux extrémités noires. (c) *pl. Ven:* **Buck of ten points,** cerf dix cors. (d) *Geog:* Pointe, promontoire m. *Nau:* **To double a point,** doubler une pointe. **2.** *Tls:* Pointe, poinçon m. **3.** *El:* (a) Platinum point, contact platiné. (b) (Point de) prise f de courant (sur le secteur). **4.** *Rail:* Points, aiguillage m; aiguille f de raccordement. **To throw over the points,** aiguiller; changer l'aiguille. **5.** Point of the compass, aire f de vent. *Nau:* **To alter (the) course two points to the west,** changer la route de deux quarts vers l'ouest. **6.** *Lacem:* = POINT-LACE. **7.** *Cr:* Station f à droite dans le prolongement du guichet. **III.** **point,** s. **1.** Action f de montrer du doigt. **2.** *Ven:* **Dog making a point,**

chien qui tombe en arrêt. **'point-'blank.** **1.** a. (a) *Ball:* (Tir) direct, sans corrections (b) *F:* (Question) de but en blanc; (refus) net **2.** adv. **To fire point-blank at** s.o., tirer sur qn à bout portant. *F: He asked me p.-b. whether . . .* il m'a demandé à brûle-pourpoint si. . . . **To refuse point-blank,** refuser catégoriquement (tout) net. **'point-duty,** s. Policeman on point-duty, agent vigie. *To be on p.-d.,* être de service à poste fixe. **'point-'lace,** s. Dentelle f à l'aiguille; guipure f. **'point-to-'point,** a. Point-to-point race, course f au clocher. **point².** **I.** v.tr. **1.** (a) Marquer (qch.) de points (b) *Gram:* Ponctuer (la phrase). **2.** (a) Tailler f en pointe (un bâton, etc.); aiguiser (un outil) (b) Donner du piquant à (des remarques). **To point a moral,** inculquer une leçon (en soulignant la conclusion de l'histoire). **3.** **To point a gun,** a telescope, braquer un canon, une longue-vue (at, sur). *S.a.* FINGER¹ 1. **4.** **To point the way,** indiquer, montrer, le chemin. **5.** *Const:* Jointoyer (un mur). **6.** *Abs. Ven:* (Of hound) Tomber en arrêt. **II.** **point,** v.i. **1.** **To point at s.o.,** montrer qn du doigt, etc. **2.** (a) *The magnetic needle always points north,* l'aiguille aimantée est toujours tournée vers le nord. *The clock pointed to ten,* la pendule marquait dix heures. (b) *This points to the fact that . . .,* cette circonstance (i) laisse supposer que . . ., (ii) fait ressortir que. . . . *Everything seems to p. to success,* tout semble annoncer le succès. *Everything points to him as the culprit,* tout indique que c'est lui le coupable. **point out,** v.tr. **1.** **To point out sth. to s.o.** (with one's finger), désigner, montrer qch. du doigt à qn. **2.** **To point out sth. to s.o.,** signaler, faire remarquer, qch. à qn. **To point out the mistakes,** signaler les erreurs. **To point out a fact,** faire ressortir un fait. *To p. out to s.o. the advantages of . . .,* représenter à qn les avantages de. . . . **Might I point out that . . .,** permettez-moi de vous faire observer que. . . . **pointed,** a. **1.** Pointu; à pointe. *P. beard,* barbe en pointe. *S.a.* ARCH¹ 1. **2.** (a) (Réplique) mordante. (b) (Allusion) peu équivoque. **-ly,** adv. (a) Sarcastiquement; d'un ton mordant. (b) Explicitement, nettement. (c) D'une manière marquée.

pointedness ['pɔintidnəs], s. **1.** Mordant m (d'une remarque). **2.** Caractère m explicite (d'une allusion).

pointer ['pɔintər], s. **1.** *Ven:* Chien m d'arrêt. **2.** (a) Aiguille f, index m (d'une balance). (b) *Sch:* Baguette f (du tableau noir). **3.** *pl. Astr:* The Pointers, les Gardes f (de la Grande Ourse). **4.** *F: U.S:* Renseignement m; *F:* tuyau m.

pointless ['pɔintləs], a. **1.** Épointé, émoussé. **2.** (a) (Plaisanterie) fade, sans sel. (b) (Observation) qui ne rime à rien.

pointsman, pl. **-men** ['pɔintsmən, -men], s.m. *Rail:* Aiguilleur.

poise¹ [pɔiz], s. **1.** Equal, even, just) poise, équilibre m, aplomb m. **A man of poise,** un homme pondéré. **2.** Port m (de la tête, du corps).

poise². **1.** v.tr. (a) Équilibrer. (b) Balancer (un javelot). **To poise sth. in the hand,** soupeser qch. (c) The way he poises his head, son port de tête. **2.** v.i. **To poise in the air,** planer en l'air.

poison¹ ['pɔizn], s. Poison m, toxique m. Rank poison, (i) poison violent; (ii) *F:* un vrai poison. **To take poison,** s'empoisonner. *S.a.* HATE¹ 1, MEAT 2. **'poison-'gas,** s. Gaz toxique, asphyxiant; gaz de combat. **'poison-gland,** s. *Z:* Glande f à venin.

poison², *v.tr.* (*a*) Empoisonner, intoxiquer. Poisoned wound, plaie envenimée (*b*) Corrompre, pervertir (l'esprit). **poisoning,** *s.* Empoisonnement *m*; intoxication *f.*

poisoner ['pɔizənər], *s.* Empoisonneur, -euse.

poisonous ['pɔizənəs], *a.* Toxique, intoxicant; empoisonné; (*of animal*) venimeux; (*of plant*) vénéneux. *F:* **Poisonous doctrine,** doctrine pernicieuse.

poisonousness ['pɔizənəsnəs], *s.* Toxicité *f*; caractère pernicieux (d'une doctrine).

poke¹ [pouk], *s. Dial:* Sac *m*; poche *f. S.a.* PIG¹ I.

poke², *s.* Bord *m* (de chapeau capote). **'poke-'bonnet,** *s.* Chapeau *m* capote (à bord évasé); cabas *m.*

poke³, *s.* Poussée *f*; coup *m* de coude; coup du bout du doigt; coup de tisonnier; coup du bout de sa canne. To give s.o. a poke in the ribs, enfoncer son doigt, son coude, dans les côtes de qn.

poke⁴. I. *v.tr.* I. Pousser (qn, qch.) du bras, du coude; piquer (qch.) du bout d'un bâton. **To poke s.o. in the ribs,** donner une bourrade (amicale) à qn. **To poke a hole in sth.,** faire un trou dans qch.; crever qch. (avec le doigt, etc.). **2.** Tisonner, attiser, fourgonner (le feu); ringarder (un fourneau). **3. To poke sth. up the chimney, down a pipe,** passer qch. dans la cheminée, dans un tuyau. *To p. one's head round the corner,* porter la tête en avant pour regarder au coin; passer la tête au coin de la rue. *S.a.* NOSE¹ I. **4. To poke rubbish into a corner,** fourrer des saletés dans un coin. **5. To poke fun at s.o.,** (i) plaisanter amicalement qn; (ii) tourner qn en ridicule; se moquer de qn; *F:* se payer la tête de qn. II. **poke,** *v.i.* I. **To poke at sth. with one's umbrella,** tâter, tourmenter, qch. du bout de son parapluie. **2. To poke (about) in every corner,** fouiller, farfouiller, fureter, dans tous les coins. **To poke into other people's business,** fourrer son nez dans les affaires d'autrui. **poke out,** *v.tr.* (*a*) To poke s.o.'s eye out, éborgner qn. *To p. the fire out,* (i) éteindre le feu à coups de tisonnier; (ii) éteindre le feu à trop le fourgonner. (*b*) To poke one's head out (of the window), passer, sortir, la tête par la fenêtre.

poker¹ ['poukər], *s.* I. Tisonnier *m*; *Ind:* fourgon *m*; (*for furnace*) ringard *m. F:* He looks as if he had swallowed a poker, il est raide comme un pieu; on dirait qu'il a avalé sa canne. **2.** Pointe *f* métallique (pour pyrogravure). **3.** *Bot:* Red-hot poker, tritome *m.* **'poker-work,** *s.* Pyrogravure *f.*

poker², *s. Cards:* Poker *m.* **'poker-face,** *s. F:* Visage ne trahit aucune émotion (comme celui du joueur de poker); visage impassible.

poky ['pouki], *a.* (*Of room*) Exigu; misérable; (*of occupation*) mesquin. A poky little room, une petite pièce de rien du tout.

Poland ['poulənd]. *Pr.n.* La Pologne.

polar ['poulər]. **I.** *a.* Polaire. Polar lights, aurore boréale ou australe. Polar circle, cercle polaire. *S.a.* BEAR¹ I. **2.** *s. Mth:* Polaire *f.*

polarimeter [poulə'rimetər], *s. Ph:* Polarimètre *m.*

polariscope [pou'lariskoup], *s. Ph:* Polariscope *m.*

polarity [po'lariti], *s.* Polarité *f.*

polarization [poulərai'zei∫(ə)n], *s. Ph:* Polarisation *f.*

polarize ['pouləra:iz], *v.tr.* (*a*) Polariser (la lumière, une barre de fer, etc.). (*b*) (*With passive force*) Se polariser. **polarizing,** *a.* Polarisant, polarisateur.

polarizer ['pouləraizər], *s. Opt:* Polariseur *m.*

polder ['pouldər], *s.* Polder *m.*

pole¹ [poul], *s.* **I.** (*a*) Perche *f*; échalas *m*; baliveau *m*, mât *m* (d'échafaudage); hampe *f* (d'un drapeau); balancier *m* (de danseur de corde). Tent pole, mât, montant *m*, de tente. Boundary pole, poteau *m* de borne. Telegraph pole, poteau télégraphique. *P:* **To be up the pole,** (i) être timbré, piqué, maboul; (ii) être dans le pétrin. *S.a.* BARBER, GREASY **2.** (*b*) Timon *m*, flèche *f* (de voiture); bras *m* (de civière). (*c*) Curtain-pole, monture *f*, bâton *m*, pour rideaux. (*d*) *Nau:* Flèche (de mât). *S.a.* BARE¹ I. **2.** *Meas:* (*a*) Perche *f* (de 5½ yards = 5 m. 03). (*b*) Perche carrée. **'pole-horse,** *s.* Cheval *m* de timon; timonier *m.* **'pole-jump(ing),** *s.* Saut *m* à la perche.

pole², *v.tr.* Conduire, pousser, (un bateau) à la perche.

pole³, *s.* Pôle *m.* **I.** *Geog:* South Pole, Pôle sud. North Pole, Pôle nord. *S.a.* STAR¹ I. **2.** *El:* Positive pole, anode *f*; électrode positive. Negative pole, cathode *f*; électrode négative. *Opposite poles,* pôles de noms contraires. Double-pole switch, interrupteur bipolaire.

Pole⁴, *s. Geog:* Polonais, -aise.

pole-ax(e)¹ ['poulaks], *s.* **I.** *Archeol:* Hache *f* d'armes. **2.** Merlin *m*; assommoir *m* (de boucher).

pole-axe², *v.tr.* Assommer; abattre (une bête) avec le merlin.

polecat ['poulkat], *s. Z:* Putois *m.*

polemic [po'lemik]. **I.** *a.* Polémique. **2.** *s.* Polémique *f.*

polemics [po'lemiks], *s.pl. Theol:* La polémique-

police¹ [po'li:s], *s.inv.* Police *f* (de sûreté). (*a*) Police magistrate, juge *m* de tribunal de simple police. Police inspector = officier *m* de paix. Police office = commissariat central de police. Police station, poste *m* de police, commissariat de police. *Adm:* Police form (*to be filled up by travellers*), feuille *f*, fiche *f*, de police. *Journ:* Police intelligence, nouvelles judiciaires. *S.a.* COURT¹ 3, OFFICER¹ I, PASS² 4. (*b*) (*With pl. const.*) The police, la Sûreté. The civil police, la force publique. The River police, la police fluviale. The police are after you, la police est à vos trousses. **po'lice-van,** *s.* Voiture *f* cellulaire; *F:* panier *m* à salade.

police², *v.tr.* Policer; maintenir l'ordre dans (le pays, etc.).

policeman, *pl.* **-men** [po'li:smən, -men], *s.m. Adm:* Policeman; = (*in Fr.*) gardien de la paix, *F:* agent *m* (de police), sergent de ville. **Traffic policeman,** agent pivot. **Rural policeman** = garde champêtre.

policewoman, *pl.* **-women** [po'li:swumən, -wimen], *s.f.* Femme-agent *m* (de police), *pl.* femmes-agents.

policy¹ ['pɔlisi], *s.* **I.** Politique *f*; ligne *f* de conduite. **Foreign policy,** politique extérieure. *Our p. is to satisfy our customers,* notre seul but, notre objectif, est de satisfaire nos clients. *Jur:* Public policy, l'intérêt public. *Contrary to public p.,* contraire à l'ordre public. **2.** Diplomatie *f. To deem it p. to . . . ,* considérer comme de bonne politique, juger prudent, de. . . . **3.** *Scot:* Domaine *m* (d'un château).

policy², *s.* Police *f* (d'assurance(s)). **Floating policy,** police flottante; police d'abonnement. **To take out a policy,** prendre une police.

'**policy-holder,** s. Titulaire mf d'une police d'assurance ; assuré, -ée.

poliomyelitis ['pɔliɔmaiɔ'laitis], s. Med: Poliomyélite f ; paralysie spinale.

polish[1] ['pɔliʃ], s. **1.** Poli m, brillant m, lustre m (d'une surface, etc.) ; brunissure f (des métaux). **High polish,** poli brillant. **To lose its polish,** se dépolir. **To take the polish off** sth., dépolir, ternir, qch. **2.** Stove polish, pâte f pour fourneaux. **Floor polish,** encaustique f ; cire f à parquet. **Boot polish, shoe polish,** (i) cirage m ; (ii) crème f, pâte, pour chaussures. **Nail polish,** brillant, vernis m, pour les ongles. **3.** Politesse f ; belles manières ; le vernis de la société. **To have a certain polish,** avoir l'usage du monde.

polish[2], v.tr. **1.** Polir (le bois, le fer) ; brunir (l'or, l'argent) ; cirer (des chaussures) ; astiquer (le cuir) ; lisser (une pierre) ; encaustiquer, faire reluire (les meubles) ; cirer (le parquet). **2.** Polir, civiliser (qn). **polish off,** v.tr. (i) Terminer v te expédier, F: bâcler (un travail) ; (ii) vider, F: siffler (un verre) ; ne rien laisser (d'un plat) ; (iii) régler e compte de, en finir avec (qn). **polish up,** v.tr. **1.** Faire reluire (qch.) ; astiquer, brunir (des objets en métal). **2.** To polish up one's French, dérouiller son français. To polish up a poem, etc., polir un poème, etc. To p. up one's style, châtier son style. **polished,** a. **1.** Poli, brillant. **Polished oak,** chêne ciré. **2. Polished manners,** manières polies, distinguées. **3. Polished style,** sty.e châtié. '**polishing-cream,** s. Crème f à astiquer, à lustrer, à nettoyer.

Polish[3] ['pouliʃ], a. Geog: Polonais.

polisher ['pɔliʃər], s. **1.** (Pers.) Polisseur, -euse ; cireur, -euse (de parquet, de chaussures) ; astiqueur m (de cuivres). **2.** Tls: Polissoir m ; (for gold, silver) brunisso'r m. Toil: Nail-polisher, polissoir.

polite [pɔ'lait], a. **1. Polite society,** (i) le beau monde ; (ii) les gens instruits, cultivés. **Polite letters, polite learning,** belles-lettres fpl. **2.** Poli, courtois, civil, honnête (to s.o., envers, avec, qn). **To be polite,** être poli. **-ly,** adv. Poliment ; avec politesse.

politeness [pɔ'laitnəs], s. Politesse f, courtoisie f, civilité f.

politic ['pɔlitik], a. **1.** (Of pers., conduct) (a) Politique, avisé. (b) Adroit, habile. **2. The body politic,** le corps politique.

political [pɔ'litik(ə)l], a. Politique. **1.** Qui se rapporte au gouvernement de l'État. P. parties, partis politiques. **2.** Qui se rapporte aux peuples. **Political geography,** géographie politique. **Political-ally,** adv. Politiquement.

politician [pɔli'tiʃ(ə)n], s. **1.** Homme politique. **2.** Esp. U.S: Pej: Politicien m, politiqueur m.

politics ['pɔlitiks], s.pl. La politique. **To talk politics,** parler politique. **To study politics,** étudier la politique. **Foreign politics,** politique extérieure, étrangère. **Internal politics,** politique intérieure. **To go into politics,** se lancer dans la politique.

polity ['pɔliti], s. **1.** Administration f politique. **2.** (a) Constitution f politique ; régime m. (b) État m.

polka ['poulka, 'pɔl-] s. Polka f. '**polka-dot,** s. Tex: Pois m. Blue p.-d. tie, cravate bleue à pois.

poll[1] [poul], s. **1.** A: Dial: (a) Tête f (d'une personne, d'un animal). (b) Sommet m, haut m, de la tête ; nuque f (d'un cheval). **2.** (i) Votation f par tête ; (ii) vote m (par bulletins) ; scrutin m. A p. was demanded, on demanda le (vote par) scrutin. **To go to the poll,** prendre part au vote.

To declare the poll, déclarer, proclamer, le résultat du scrutin. **To head the poll,** venir en tête de liste. '**poll-tax,** s. Hist: Capitation f.

poll[2] [poul]. I. v.tr. **1.** (a) A: Tondre (qn); (b) = POLLARD[2]. (c) Écorner décorner (un taureau). **2.** (a) (Of polling-clerk) Faire voter (qn) ; recueillir le bullet.n de vote de (qn). (b) (Of candidate) Réunir (tant de voix). II. **poll,** v.i. Voter (à une élection). **polled,** a. (Of ox, etc.) **1.** Sans cornes. **2.** Décorné. **polling,** s. Vote m ; élections fpl. '**polling-booth,** s. Isoloir m ; bureau m de scrutin.

Poll[3] [pɔl]. Pr.n.f. (Dim. of Mary) **1.** Marie. **2.** (Pretty) Poll, Jacquot m (nom de perroquet).

pollack ['pɔlak], s. Ich: Merlan m jaune. **Green pollack,** colin m.

pollard[1] ['pɔlərd], s. a) Arb: Têtard m ; arbre étêté. (b) Animal m sans cornes. '**pollard-willow,** s. Arb: Saule étêté.

pollard[2], v.tr. Arb: Étêter, écimer un arbre).

pollen ['pɔlen], s. Bot: Pollen m.

pollinate ['pɔlineit], v.tr. Bot: Émettre du pollen sur (le stigmate).

pollination [pɔli'neiʃ(ə)n], s. Bot: Pollin(is)ation f, fécondation f.

pollute [pɔ'lju:t], v.tr. **1.** Polluer, souiller, rendre impur, corrompre. **2.** Profaner, violer (un lieu saint).

polluter [pɔ'lju:tər], s. **1.** Corrupteur, -tr:ce. **2.** Profanateur, -trice (d'un temple).

pollution [pɔ'lju:ʃ(ə)n], s. **1.** Pollution f, souilure f. **2.** Profanation f.

Polly ['pɔli]. Pr.n.f. = POLL[3]. **2.** s. P: (Eau minérale d')Apollinaris f.

polo ['poulo], s. Sp: Polo m. **Polo stick, mallet,** ma llet m. S.a. WATER-POLO.

polony [pɔ'louni], s. Polony sausage, (petit) saucisson ; cervelas m (sans ail).

poltergeist ['pɔltərgaist], s. Esprit frappeur.

poltroon [pɔl'tru:n], s. Poltron m.

poltroonery [pɔl'tru:nəri], s. Poltronnerie f.

polyandrous [pɔli'andrəs], a. Anthr: Bot: Polyandre.

polyandry ['pɔliandri], s. Anthr: Po yandrie f.

polyanthus [pɔli'anθəs], s. **1.** s. Primevère des jardins. **2.** Attrib. (Fleur, narcisse) à bouquets.

polychroism [pɔli'krɔuizm], s. Cryst: Polychroïsme m.

polychromatic [pɔlikrɔ'matik **polychrome** ['pɔlikroum], a. Polychrome.

polygamist [pɔ'ligəmist], s. Polygame m.

polygamous [pɔ'ligəməs], a. Polygame.

polygamy [pɔ'ligəmi], s. - Polygamie f.

polyglot ['pɔliglɔt], a. & s. Polyglotte (mf)

polygon ['pɔligɔn], s. Polygone m.

polygonal [pɔ'ligən(ə)l], a. Polygonal, -aux.

polygonum [pɔ'ligɔnəm], s. Bot: Renouée f.

polyhedral [pɔli'hi:drəl, -'hedrəl], **polyhedric** [pɔli'hedrik], a. Polyédrique, polyèdre.

polyhedron [pɔli'hi:drɔn, -'hedrɔn], s. Polyèdre m.

polymeric [pɔli'merik], a. Ch: Polymère.

polymerism [pɔ'limərizm], s. Ch: Polymérie f.

polymorphic [pɔli'mɔ:rfik], **polymorphous** [pɔli'mɔ:rfəs], a. Polymorphe.

polymorphism [pɔli'mɔ:rfizm], s. Polymorphisme m, polymorphie f.

Polynesia [pɔli'ni:ziə]. Pr.n, La Polynésie.

Polynesian [pɔli'ni:ziən], a. & s. Po ynésien, -ienne.

polynomial [pɔli'noumiəl], s. Alg: Polynôme m.

polyp ['pɔlip], s. Coel: Polype m.

polypetalous [pɔli'petələs], a. Bot: Polypétale.

polyphase ['pɔlifeːiz], a. El.E: **1.** Polyphase

current, courant polyphasé. **2.** (Alternateur, etc.) à courant polyphasé.

polypod ['pɔlipɔd], *a & s. Z:* Polypode (*m*); à pattes multiples.

polypoid ['pɔlipɔid], *a. Z: Med:* Polypoïde.

polypus ['pɔlipəs], *s. Med:* Polype *m*.

polysyllabic [pɔlisi'labik], *a.* Polysyllabe, polysyllabique.

polysyllable [pɔli'siləbl], *s.* Po ysy labe *m*.

polytechnic [pɔli'teknik], *a.* Polytechnique ; (école) d'arts et métiers, d'enseignement technique.

polytheism ['pɔliθiːizm], *s.* Polythéisme *m*.

polyvalency [pɔli'veilənsi], *s. Ch:* Polyvalence*f*.

polyvalent [pɔ'livələnt], *a. Ch:* Polyvalent.

pom [pɔm], *s. F:* Loulou *m* de Poméranie.

pomade [po'mɑːd], **pomatum** [po'meitəm], *s. Toil:* Pommade *f*.

pomegranate ['pɔmgranet, pɔm'granet] *s. Bot:* **1.** Grenade *f*. **2.** Pomegranate(-tree), grenadier *m*.

Pomeranian [pɔmə're.n ən] *a. & s.* (*a*) Poméranien, -ienne. (*b*) Pomeranian (dog), loulou *m* de Poméranie.

pommel¹ [pʌml], *s.* **1.** Pommeau *m* (d'épée). **2.** *Harn:* Arçon *m* de devant ; pommeau (de selle).

pommel², *v.tr.* (pommelled) Bourrer (qn) de coups.

Pomona [po'mounə]. *Pr.n.f. Myth:* Pomone.

pomp [pɔmp], *s.* Pompe *f*, éclat *m*, faste *m*, splendeur*f*, appareil *m*, apparat *m*. **To like pomp,** aimer le cérémonia.. **Pomp and circumstance,** grand apparat. **To renounce the pomps and vanities of this world,** renoncer aux pompes du siècle.

Pompeii [pɔm'piːai]. *Pr.n. A.Geog:* Pompéi.

pom-pom ['pɔm'pɔm], *s.* Canon-revolver *m*, canon-mitrailleuse *m* (système Maxim).

pompon ['pɔmpɔn], *s.* **1.** *Cost: etc:* Pompon *m*. **2.** *Hort:* (*a*) Rose *f* pompon. (*b*) Chrysanthème nain.

pomposity [pɔm'pɔsiti], *s.* Prudhommerie *f*, emphase *f*, suffisance *f*

pompous ['pɔmpəs], *a.* **1.** Pompeux, fastueux. **2.** (*a*) A pompous man, un homme suffisant, qui fait l'important. (*b*) **Pompous style,** style emphatique, ampoulé. **Pompousement.** **-ly,** *adv.*

pompousness ['pɔmpəsnəs], *s.* **1.** Pompe *f*, faste *m*. **2.** = POMPOSITY.

poncho ['pɔn(t)ʃo], *s. Cost:* Poncho *m*.

pond [pɔnd], *s.* Étang *m* ; bassin *m*, pièce *f* d'eau (de parc) ; mare *f*, abreuvoir *m* (de village) ; vivier *m*, réservoir *m* (pour le poisson) ; réservoir (de moulin). **Pond life,** vie animale des eaux stagnantes.

ponder ['pɔndər]. **1.** *v.tr.* Réfléchir sur (une question) ; considérer, peser (un avis) ; ruminer (une idée). **2.** *v.i.* Méditer. **To ponder on, over,** sth., réfléchir à. méditer sur, qch. **pondering,** *s.* Méditation *f*.

ponderable ['pɔndərəbl], *a.* Pondérable ; (gaz) pesant.

ponderous ['pɔndərəs], *a* **1.** Massif, lourd, pesant. **2.** (Style) lourd, pesant, ampoulé. **-ly,** *adv.* (Écrire, etc.) avec lourdeur.

pondweed ['pɔndwiːd], *s. Bot:* Potamot luisant ; épi *m* d'eau

pongee [pʌn'dʒiː], *s. Tex:* Pongée *m*.

poniard¹ ['pɔnjərd], *s.* Poignard *m*.

poniard², *v.tr.* Poignarder.

pontiff ['pɔntif], *s* Pontife *m. Ecc:* Évêque *m*, prélat *m. Esp:* **The sovereign pontiff,** le souverain pontife, le pape.

pontifical [pɔn'tifik(ə)l]. **1.** *a.* Pontifical, -aux ; épiscopal, -aux. *F: Pej:* **Pontifical airs, airs de pontife. 2.** *s.* Pontifical *m* (livre du rituel des évêques). **3.** *s.pl.* **Pontificals.** (*a*) Vêtements ou ornements sacerdotaux. (*b` F:* Vêtements de gala, de grande cérémonie.

pontificate¹ [pɔn'tifiket], *s.* Pontificat *m*.

pontificate² [pɔn'tifikeit], *v.i.* Pontifier ; officier en qualité de pontife ou d'évêque.

pontify ['pɔntifai], *v.i F:* Pontifier ; -faire l'important.

Pontius Pilate ['pɔnʃəs'pai.et]. *Pr.n.m.* Ponce Pilate.

pontoneer [pɔnto'niːər], *s.* Pontonn.er *m*.

pontoon¹ [pɔn'tuːn], *s.* **1.** Ponton *m*, bac *m*. **2.** *Mil.E:* Ponton (de pont de bateaux). **pon'toon-bridge,** *s.* Pont *m* de bateaux. **pon'toon-corps,** *s. Mil:* Corps *m* de pontonniers.

pontoon², *s. Cards:* Vingt et un.

pony ['pouni], *s.* **1.** Poney *m*. **2.** *P:* Vingt-cinq livres sterling. **'pony-carriage,** *s. Veh:* Panier *m*. **'pony-skin,** *s. Com:* (Fourrure *f*) poulain *m*. **'pony-truck,** *s.* Bissel *m* (de locomotive)

poodle [puːdl], *s.* Caniche *mf*.

pooh [puː], *int.* Bah ! peuh ! **Pooh, is that all!** la belle affaire !

Pooh-Bah ['puː'bɑː], *s. F: Pej:* Cumulard *m* ; *F:* homme-orchestre *m*. Personnage du *Mikado* de W. S. Gilbert.

pooh-pooh ['puː'puː], *v.tr.* Traiter légèrement, ridiculiser (une idée, etc.) ; se moquer, faire peu de ca، d'un avertissement) ; repousser (un conseil) avec mépris.

pool¹ [puːl], *s.* **1.** (*a*) (*Of running water*) Fontaine*f*. (*b* (*Stagnant*) Mare *f*. (*c*) (*For wimming*) Piscine *f*. (*d*) Flaque (d'eau, etc.) ; mare (de sang). **2.** (*a*) (*In river*) Trou *m* d'eau. (*b*) **The Pool,** le mouillage sur la Tamise en aval de London Bridge.

pool², *s.* **1.** (*a` Games:* Poule *f*, cagnotte *f*. (*b*) *Bill:* Fenc:* Poule. (*c*) Football pool, concours *m* de pronostics sportifs. **2.** *Com:* (*a*) Fonds communs ; masse commune. (*b*) Syndicat *m* de placement (de marchandises) ; syndicat de répartition des commandes.

pool³, *v.tr.* (*a*) Mettre en commun (des capitaux, etc.). (*b*) *Com:* Mettre en syndicat (les commandes) ; *Rail:* répartir l'exploitation (des ۱ignes, etc.).

poop¹ ،puːp], *s. Nau:* **1.** Poupe *f*. **2.** **Poop (-deck),** (pont *m* de) dunette *f*. **'poop-rail,** *s. Nau:* Rambarde *f*

poop², *v.tr. Nau:* **1.** (*Of wave*) To poop a ship, balayer la poupe d'un navire. **To be pooped,** embarquer une vague par l'arrière. **2.** (*Of ship*) Recevoir, embarquer, un paquet de mer) par l'arrière.

poor ['puər], *a.* Pauvre. **I.** (*a*) Besogneux, ma'heureux ; *Adm:* indigent. **A poor man,** un pauvre. A p. woman, une pauvresse. **The poorer classes,** les classes pauvres. *F:* **As poor as a church-mouse.** as Job, gueux comme un rat d'ég'ise, pauvre comme Job. *S.a.* MOUTH¹ I. (*b*) *s.pl.* **The poor,** les pauvres *m*, les malheureux, les ۱ndigents. **2.** De piètre qua ité ; médiocre. (*a*) **Poor soil,** so. maigre, peu fertile. *P. cattle,* bétai ۱ maigre. *P. wine,* vin g.nguet ; p quette*f*. *P. blood* sang vicié. *Ore poor in metal,* minerai pauvre en métal. (*b*) *P. excuse,* piètre excuse. **He** *sells* **poor stuff,** il vend de la camelote. **Poor quality,** basse qualité ; qualité inférieure. *P.* *health,* santé débile **My poor memory,** mon peu de mémoire. **To have a poor opinion of s.o.,** avoir une pauvre, piètre, triste, opinion de qn. **To cut a poor figure,** faire piètre figure. **In my poor opinion,** à mon humble avis. *He is a p. driver,* il n'est pas fameux comme chauffeur. **To be poor at mathematics,** être faible en mathématiques. **3. Poor creature! poor thing!** pauvre petit! pauvre petite! **Poor fellow!** le pauvre homme! le pauvre garçon! *Iron: P. fellow!* **poor you!** vous voi à bien ma ade! **Poor me!** pauvre de moi! **-ly. 1.** *adv.* Pauvrement, médiocrement, piètrement, maigrement. *S.a.* OFF I. 3. **2.** *pred.a.* **To be poorly,** être souffrant, ndisposé. *He is looking very p.,* il a bien mauvaise mine. **'poor-law,** *s.* Lois *fpl* sur l'assistance publique. **Poor-law administration,** l'assistance publique. **'poor-rate,** *s. Adm:* Taxe des pauvres. **'poor-relief,** *s. Adm:* Aide *f* ass stance(s) *f(pl),* aux pauvres, aux indigents. **'poor-'spirited,** *a.* Pusillanime.

poorhouse ['puəhaus], *s.* Hospice *m*; asile *m* des pauvres.

poorness ['puənəs], *s.* **1.** Pauvreté *f*, insuffisance *f*. **2.** Infériorité *f*; peu *m* de valeur.

pop¹ [pɔp]. **1.** *int.* Crac! pan! **To go pop,** éclater, crever. **Pop goes the cork!** on entend péter le bouchon. **2.** *s.* (a) Bruit sec, soudain (de bouchon qui saute, etc.). (b) Boisson pétillante, gazeuse, mousseuse; *esp.* champagne *m.* (c) *P:* (*Of jewelry, etc.*) **To be in pop,** être au clou, chez ma tante. **'pop-corn,** *s.* Maïs grillé et éclaté. **'pop-eyed,** *a. U.S: F:* Aux yeux en boules de loto. **'pop-gun,** *s. Toys:* Canonnière *f*, pétoire *f*; pistolet *m* à bouchon. **'pop-shop,** *s. P:* Maison *f* de prêt sur gages; *P:* clou *m.*

pop², *v.* (popped) **1.** *v.i.* Faire entendre une petite explosion; éclater, péter; (*of cork*) sauter, péter; (*of toy balloon*) crever. *I.C.E:* (*Of engine*) **To pop back** *in the carburettor,* donner des retours de flamme (au carburateur); pétarader. **2.** *v.tr.* (a) Crever (un ballon); faire sauter (un bouchon). *U.S:* **To pop corn,** faire éclater le maïs (devant le feu). (b) *P:* **To pop one's watch,** mettre sa montre au clou, chez ma tante. **3.** (*In familiar speech*) (a) (= 'come' or 'go') **To pop over,** **pop round,** *to the grocer's,* faire un saut jusque chez l'épicier. (b) (= 'put') **To pop sth. behind a screen,** fourrer qch. derrière un écran. *To pop one's head out of the window,* sortir (tout à coup) sa tête par la fenêtre. *F:* **To pop the question,** faire sa déclaration; faire la demande en mariage. **pop in,** *v.i. F:* Entrer à l'improviste; entrer en passant. **pop off,** *v.i.* (a) *F:* Filer, déguerpir. (b) *P:* Mourir subitement. **pop up,** *v.i. F:* Apparaître, surgir. (*Of swimmer, etc.*) **To pop up out of the water,** émerger brusquement à la surface de l'eau.

pop³, *s. U.S: P:* Papa *m.*

pop⁴, *s. F:* (*Abbr. for 'popular concert'*) Concert *m* populaire.

pope¹ [poup], *s.* **1.** Pape *m*; le Saint-Père. **Pope Joan,** (i) la papesse Jeanne; (ii) *Cards:* le Nain jaune. **2.** *Cu:* **Pope's eye,** noix *f* (de veau, de gigot). **3.** (*Brush*) **Pope's head,** tête-de-loup *f.*

pope², *s. Ecc:* Pope *m* (de 'Église orthodoxe).

popedom ['poupdəm], *s.* Papauté *f.*

popery ['poupəri], *s. Pej:* Papisme *m.*

popinjay ['pɔpindʒei], *s. A:* **1.** (a) Perroquet *m.* (b) *Sp:* Papega *m.* **2.** Fat *m*, freluquet *m.*

popish ['poupiʃ], *a. Pej:* Papiste.

poplar ['pɔplər], *s. Bot:* Peuplier *m.* **White poplar, silver poplar,** peuplier blanc; ypréau *m.* *S.a.* TREMBLING¹.

poplin ['pɔplin], *s Tex:* Popeline *f*

popliteal [pɔ'plitiəl], *a Anat:* Poplité; du jarret.

poppet ['pɔpet], *s.* **1.** *F:* **My poppet,** mon chéri; ma chérie. **2.** *Nau:* (a) Colombier *m* (de lancement). (b) (Rowlock-)poppets, portières *f* de dames. **3.** *Mec.E:* **Poppet(-head),** poupée *f* (de tour). **'poppet-valve,** *s. I.C.E:* Soupape soulevante, à déclic; clapet *m*; (soupape en) champignon *m.*

popple¹ [pɔpl], *s.* Clapotement *m.*

popple², *v.i.* (*Of water*) Clapoter, s'agiter.

poppy ['pɔpi], *s.* Pavot *m.* **Corn poppy, field poppy,** coquelicot *m.* **Opium poppy,** pavot somnifère; œillette *f.* **Poppy(-seed) oil,** huile *f* d'œillette. **'poppy-head,** *s.* Tête *f* de pavot.

populace ['pɔpjules], *s.* **The populace,** (i) e peuple, la foule; (ii) *Pej:* la populace.

popular ['pɔpjulər], *a.* Populaire. (a) Du peuple. **Popular phrase,** expression populaire. *P. insurrection,* insurrection du peuple; nsurrection populaire. (b) (Prédicateur, opéra) à la mode, goûté du public, qui a de la vogue; (prédicateur) très couru. (c) Compréhensible pour tout le monde. **Popular book on wireless,** ouvrage de vulgarisation sur la T.S.F. (d) **Popular error,** erreur courante. **-ly,** *adv.* Populairement.

popularity [pɔpju'lariti], *s.* Popularité *f.*

popularize ['pɔpjulərɑiz], *v.tr.* (a) Populariser, vulgariser (des connaissances, etc.). (b) Rendre (qn) populaire.

populate ['pɔpjuleit], *v.tr.* Peupler. *Thickly populated,* très peuplé.

population [pɔpju'leiʃ(ə)n,,, *s.* Population *f.* **Fall in population,** décroissance *f* de la population; dépopulation *f*

populous ['pɔpjuləs], *a.* Populeux; très peuplé.

populousness ['pɔpjuləsnəs], *s* Densité *f* de population (d'une région).

porcelain ['pɔːsələn], *s.* Porcelaine *f.* **'porcelain-clay,** *s.* Terre *f* à porcelaine; kaolin *m.* **'porcelain-shell,** *s. Moll:* Porcelaine *f*; coquille *f* de Vénus.

porch [pɔːtʃ], *s.* (a) Porche *m*, portique *m.* (b) Marquise *f* (d'hôtel etc.) (c) **Porch roof,** auvent *m.*

porcine ['pɔːsain], *a.* De porc; (race) porcine.

porcupine ['pɔːkjupain], *s.* **1.** *Z:* Porc-épic *m*, *pl.* porcs-épics. **2.** **Porcupine fish,** hérisson *m* de mer.

pore¹ ['pɔːər], *s. Anat: Bot:* Pore *m.*

pore², *v.i.* **To pore over a book,** s'absorber dans la lecture, dans l'étude, d'un livre; être plongé dans un livre. *He is always poring over his books,* il est toujours absorbé dans, courbé sur, ses livres. **To pore over a subject,** méditer longuement un sujet.

pork [pɔːk,, *s. Cu:* (Viande *f* de) porc *m.* **Salt pork,** petit salé. **Pork chop,** côtelette *f* de porc. **'pork-butcher,** *s.* Charcutier *m.* **'pork-'pie,** .. Pâté *m* de porc (en croûte). **Pork-pie hat,** chapeau *m* de feutre à forme aplatie en rond.

porker ['pɔːkər], *s.* Porc (destiné à l'engraissement); goret *m.*

porkling ['pɔːkliŋ], *s.* Goret *m*, porcelet *m.*

porky ['pɔːki], *a.* **1.** Qui tient du porc. **2.** Gras, obèse.

pornography [pɔː'nɔgrəfi], *s.* Pornographie *f.*

porosity [pɔː'rɔsiti], *s.* Porosité *f.*

porous ['pɔːrəs], *a.* Poreux, perméable

porphyry ['pɔːfiri], *s.* Porphyre *m*

porpoise ['pɔːpəs], *s. Z:* Marsouin *m.*

porridge ['pɔridʒ], *s.* Bouillie *f* d'avo ne.

porringer ['pɔrindʒər], *s.* Écuelle *f* (pour *porridge,* etc.); jatte *f.*

port¹ [pɔːrt], s. Port m. Sea port, port de mer. Outer port, avant-port m. Naval port, port miliaire ; port de guerre. Commercial p., trading p., port marchand ; port de commerce. Navy : Homo port, port d'attache. Port of registry, port d'armement. F : Any port in a storm, nécessité n'a pas de loi. Port charges, droits m de port. To come into p., entrer au port. To get safe into port, to reach port safely, arriver à bon port. To put into port, relâcher. To leave port, quitter le port. S.a. CALL¹ 3. **port-'admiral,** s. Amiral m du port ; = préfet m maritime. **'port-town,** s. Port m de mer.

port², s. I. Nau : Sabord m. Port-lid, mantelet m de sabord. Coaling port, sabord à charbon. 2. Mch : Or'fice m, umière f, fenêtre f (de cylindre). Inlet port, admission port, um'ère d'adm:ss:on. **'port-hole,** Nau : Sabord m, hub'ot m.

port³, s. Nau : Bâbord m. The port side, le côté de bâbord. On the p. side, to port, à bâbord. Land to port! (la) terre par bâbord ! Port tack, bâbord amures. Hard a-port! à gauche toute !

port⁴. Nau : I. v.tr. To port the helm, mettre la barre à bâbord. 2. v.i. (Of ship) Venir sur bâbord.

port⁵, v.tr. Mil : To port arms, présenter les armes (obliquement) pour l'inspection ; porter (le sabre).

port⁶(-wine), s. Vin m de Porto ; porto m.

portable ['pɔːrtəbl], a. Portatif ; transportable ; mobile. Portable (steam-)boiler, chaudière locomobile. Nau : Portable winch, cabestan volant. Portable wireless set, poste transportable.

portage ['pɔːrtedʒ], s. I. Transport m, port m (de marchandises). 2. Frais mpl de port, de transport. 3. Portage m (de bateaux entre deux cours d'eau, etc.)

portal¹ ['pɔːrt(ə)l], s. (a) Portail m (de cathédrale). (b) Entrée f (de tunnel). (c) Portique m.

portal², a. Anat : Portal vein, veine f porte.

portcrayon [pɔːrt'kreiɔn], s. Porte-fusain m.

portcullis [pɔːrt'kʌlis], s. Fort : Herse f.

Porte [pɔːrt], s. The Sublime Porte, the Ottoman Porte, la sublime Porte.

portend [pɔr'tend], v.tr. Présager, augurer, faire pressentir (qch.). Clouds that p. a storm, nuages qui annoncent un orage.

portent ['pɔːrtent], s. I. Présage m de malheur. 2. Prodige m.

portentous [pɔr'tentəs], a. I. De mauvais présage, de mauvais augure ; sinistre. 2. Monstrueux, prodigieux. **-ly,** adv. I. Sinistrement. 2. Prodigieusement.

porter¹ ['pɔːrtər], s. Portier m, concierge m ; tourier m (d'un monastère). Porter's lodge, (i) loge f de concierge ; (ii) maisonnette f, pavillon m, du portier (à l'entrée d'une grande propriété).

porter², s. I. Portefaix m ; chasseur m, garçon m (d'hôtel) ; garçon (de magasin) ; (at railway station) porteur m. Market porter = fort m de la Halle. Bank-porter, garçon de recette. 2. Bière brune (anglaise) ; porter m.

porterage ['pɔːrtəredʒ], s. I. Transport m, manutention f, factage m (de marchandises, de colis). 2. Prix m de transport ; factage.

portfolio [pɔːrt'foulio], s. I. (a) Serviette f (pour documents, etc.). (b) Chemise f de carton ; carton m (à dessins). Portfolio stand, porte-cartons m inv. Book in portfolio form, livre en carton. (c) Minister's portfolio, portefeuille m de ministre. Minister without portfolio, ministre sans portefeuille. 2. Securities in portfolio, valeurs en portefeuille.

portico, pl. **-o(e)s** ['pɔːrtiko, -ouz], s. Arch : Portique m.

portion¹ ['pɔːrʃ(ə)n], s. I. (a) Partie f ; part f (dans un partage) ; lot m (de terre). A p. of my money, une partie de mon argent. (b) Portion f, ration f (de viande) ; quartier m (de gâteau). (c) Jur : Portion (of inheritance), part d'héritage. (d) (Marriage) portion, dot f. (e) Rail : Rame f, tranche f (de wagons). The through-portion for Aberdeen, la rame directe pour Aberdeen. 2. Destinée f, destin m, sort m. Suffering is our p. here below, la souffrance est notre lot ici-bas.

portion², v.tr. I. To portion (out), partager (un bien, etc.) ; répartir (une somme) ; distribuer (les parts). 2. Doter (sa fille).

portionless ['pɔːrʃ(ə)nləs], a. Sans dot.

Portland ['pɔːrtlənd]. Pr.n. I. Portland m. Portland cement, (ciment m de) Portland. Portland stone, calcaire portlandien. 2. F : La prison de Portland.

portliness ['pɔːrtlinəs], s. I. Prestance f, port majestueux ; air imposant. 2. Corpulence f, embonpoint m.

portly ['pɔːrtli], a. I. Majestueux ; de noble prestance. P. matron, matrone imposante. 2. Corpulent, ventru.

portmanteau [pɔːrt'mantou], s. Valise f.

portrait ['pɔːrtret], s. Portrait m. Full-length, half-length, portrait, portrait en pied, en buste. To have one's portrait taken, to sit for one's portrait, poser pour son portrait ; (i) se faire faire son portrait, (ii) se faire photographier. **'portrait-painter,** s. Portraitiste m ; peintre m de portraits.

portraiture ['pɔːrtretjər], s. I. Portrait m. 2. L'art du portrait. 3. Description f (d'une société, etc.).

portray [pɔr'trei], v.tr. I. A. & Lit : Peindre (qn) ; faire le portrait de (qn). 2. Dépeindre, décrire (une scène, etc.). To portray character, peindre les caractères.

portrayal [pɔr'treiəl], s. Peinture f, représentation f, description f (d'une scène). P. of manners, peinture de mœurs.

portrayer [pɔr'treiər], s. Peintre m (des événements, etc.).

portress ['pɔːrtres], s.f. Portière, tourière (de couvent).

Portugal ['pɔːrtjug(ə)l]. Pr.n. Le Portugal.

Portuguese [pɔːrtju'giːz]. I. a. & s.inv. Portugais, -aise. 2. s. Ling : Le portugais.

pose¹ [pouz], s. I. Pose f, attitude f (du corps). 2. Pose, affectation f. Without pose, sans affectation.

pose². I. v.tr. I. (a) Poser (une question). (b) Émettre, énoncer (une opinion) ; citer (un exemple). 2. Art : Faire prendre une pose à (qn) ; poser un modèle. II. pose, v.i. I. (a) Poser (comme modèle). (b) F : Poser ; se donner des airs (affectés, prétentieux). 2. To pose as a Frenchman, se faire passer pour Français. I don't p. as a scholar, je ne prétends pas être un savant, je ne m'érige pas en savant. **posing,** s. Pose f.

poser ['pouzər], s. Question embarrassante ; F : colle f. To give s.o. a poser, poser une colle à qn.

posh¹ [pɔʃ], a. P : Chic, bath, chouette. It looks posh, ça fait riche.

posh², v.tr. P : To posh oneself up, se faire beau, belle. All poshed up, sur son trente et un.

posit ['pɔzit], v.tr. (posited) Log : Phil : Avancer

(une proposition); énoncer (un postulat, etc.); poser en principe (*that*, que). **position**[1] [po'ziʃ(ə)n], *s.* **1.** (*a*) Posture *f*, position *f*, attitude *f* (du corps, etc.). **To bring a gun to the firing position,** mettre une pièce en batterie. (*b*) Attitude, disposition *f* (de l'esprit). **To take up a position on a question,** prendre position sur une question. **2.** Position. (*a*) Place *f*; situation *f* (d'un objet, d'une ville). **Vertical position,** station verticale. **In position,** en place. **Out of position,** hors de sa place; déplacé, dérangé. **To place sth. in position,** mettre qch. en place. *Navy:* **To take up position ahead, astern,** prendre poste en tête, derrière. (*b*) *Nau:* **Ship's position,** lieu *m* du navire. *To determine the ship's p.,* to fix one's position, faire le point. (*c*) **To storm the enemy's positions,** prendre d'assaut les positions de l'ennemi. **To manœuvre for position,** manœuvrer pour s'assurer l'avantage. **3.** (*a*) État *m*, condition *f*, situation *f*. **Put yourself in my position,** mettez-vous à ma place. **To be in a position to do sth.,** être en état, à même, de faire qch. *You are in a better p. to judge,* vous êtes mieux placé que moi pour en juger. **Cash position,** situation de (la) caisse. *Customer's p. at the bank,* situation en banque d'un client. (*b*) **Rang social. In a high position,** haut placé; dans une haute situation. *In a good p.,* bien posé. **Youth of good social position,** fils de famille. *To fill one's p.,* tenir son rang. (*c*) *Sch:* **Position in class,** place *f* dans ta classe; rang, classement *m*. **4.** Emploi *m*, place, situation (dans un bureau, etc.). **To occupy, hold, a position,** remplir une fonction. **Position of trust,** poste *m* de confiance. **po'sition-light,** *s. Nau:* Feu *m* de position. **position**[2], *v.tr.* Déterminer la position de (qch.); situer (un lieu sur la carte). **positive** ['pozitiv], *a.* **1.** (*a*) Positif, affirmatif. *P. order,* ordre formel. **Positive proof,** preuve positive, manifeste. (*b*) **A positive miracle,** un pur, vrai, miracle. **It's a positive fact!** c'est un fait authentique, *F:* c'est positif! **2.** (*a*) Convaincu, assuré, sûr, certain (*of*, de). *He is p. of his facts,* il est sûr de ses faits. *I am quite p. on that point,* là-dessus je n'ai aucun doute. (*b*) **Positive tone of voice,** ton absolu, tranchant. **Positive person,** personne qui tranche sur tout. (*c*) **Positive turn of mind,** esprit positif, qui considère en tout l'intérêt. **Positive philosophy,** philosophie positive. **3.** (*a*) *Mth:* **Positive quantity,** quantité positive. (*b*) *El:* **Positive pole,** pôle positif. (*c*) *Mec.E:* **Positive drive,** commande positive; connexion directe. (*d*) *Opt:* **Positive optical system,** système optique convergent, positif. **4.** *a. & s. Phot:* Positif (*m*); photogramme *m*. *P. plate,* positif sur verre. **5.** *Gram:* **Positive (degree),** (degré) positif (*m*). **-ly,** *adv.* **1.** Positivement, affirmativement. **2.** (*a*) Assurément, certainement, sûrement. **I can't speak positively,** je ne puis rien affirmer. (*b*) D'un ton tranchant, absolu. **3.** *Mec.E:* **Positively connected,** solidarisé; à liaison rigide. **positiveness** ['pozitivnǝs], *s.* **1.** Certitude *f*, assurance *f*. **2.** Ton décisif, tranchant. **positivism** ['pozitivizm], *s. Phil:* Positivisme *m*. **positivist** ['pozitivist], *a. & s. Phil:* Positiviste (*mf*). **posse** ['posi], *s.* (*a*) Détachement *m* (d'agents de police). (*b*) Troupe *f*, bande *f* (de personnes). **possess** [po'zes], *v.tr.* **1.** (*a*) Posséder (un bien); être possesseur, être en possession, de (qch.). **All I possess,** tout mon avoir. (*b*) Avoir, posséder (une qualité, une faculté). **To be possessed of a quality,** être doué d'une

qualité. **2.** (*a*) **To possess oneself of sth.,** se rendre maître, s'emparer, de qch. (*b*) **To be possessed of a property,** posséder un bien. *Town possessed of many objects of interest,* ville recélant beaucoup de curiosités. **3.** **To possess oneself,** se posséder, se contenir. **To possess one's soul in peace,** posséder son âme en paix. *S.a.* SELF-POSSESSED. **4.** (*Of evil spirit*) Posséder (qn). **To be possessed by the devil,** être possédé du démon. **Possessed by fear,** sous le coup de l'effroi. *Possessed with doubt,* en proie au doute. **What possessed you to do that?** qu'est-ce qui vous a pris de faire cela? **To be possessed with an idea,** être obsédé, coiffé, d'une idée. **To possess s.o. with an idea,** pénétrer qn d'une idée. **To become possessed with an idea,** se pénétrer d'une idée. **possession** [po'zeʃ(ə)n], *s.* **1.** Possession *f*, jouissance *f* (*of*, de). **To have sth. in one's possession,** avoir qch. en sa possession. **To come, enter, into possession of an estate,** entrer en possession, en jouissance, d'un bien. **To take, get, possession of sth.,** s'emparer de qch. *To resume p. of one's domicile,* réintégrer son domicile. **To remain in possession of the field,** rester maître du champ de bataille. **To be in possession of a large fortune,** disposer d'une grande fortune. **In possession of a passport,** nanti d'un passeport. **In full possession of his faculties,** en pleine possession de toutes ses facultés. **Vacant possession,** libre possession (d'un immeuble). *House to let with vacant p.,* maison à louer avec jouissance immédiate. *Prov:* **Possession is nine points of the law,** possession vaut titre. *S.a.* SELF-POSSESSION. **2.** Possession (par le démon). **3.** (*a*) Objet possédé; possession. *A valued p. of my father's,* un objet auquel mon père attachait beaucoup de prix. (*b*) *pl.* **Possessions,** (i) possessions, biens, avoir *m*; (ii) possessions, conquêtes *f*, colonies *f*. **possessive** [po'zesiv], *a. Gram:* Possessive adjective, adjectif possessif. *a. & s.* The possessive (case), le (cas) possessif. **possessor** [po'zesər], *s.* Possesseur *m*; propriétaire *mf*. **possibility** [posi'biliti], *s.* **1.** Possibilité *f*. **To consider the possibility of an event,** considérer l'éventualité d'un événement. *The p. of severe penalties,* la perspective de peines graves. **There is no possibility** *of my going there,* il n'est pas possible que j'y aille. *If by any possibility I am not there,* si par hasard, par impossible, je n'y étais pas. **Within the range, the bounds, of possibility,** dans l'ordre des choses possibles; dans la limite du possible. **2.** Événement *m* possible; éventualité *f*. **To foresee all the possibilities,** envisager tout ce qui peut arriver, toutes les éventualités. **To allow for all possibilities,** parer à toute éventualité. *Life is full of possibilities,* tout est possible dans la vie. *The subject is full of possibilities,* c'est un sujet qui prête. *The plan has possibilities,* ce projet offre des chances de succès. **possible** ['posibl]. **1.** *a.* (*a*) Possible. **It is possible,** c'est possible; cela se peut bien. **It's just possible,** il y a une chance. *It is p. for you to . . .,* il vous est possible de. . . . **It is possible that . . .,** il se peut que + *sub. Is it p. that you know nothing?* se peut-il que vous n'en sachiez rien? **To give as many details as possible,** donner le plus de détails possible. *To give* all possible details, donner tous les détails possibles. *To do the utmost possible to get sth.,* faire tout son possible pour obtenir qch. *F:* **What possible interest can you have in it?** quel diable d'intérêt cela peut-il avoir pour vous? **If possible,** (i) (*if* *feasible*) si possible; si faire se peut; (ii) (*if imaginable*) si c'est possible. **As far as possible**, dans la mesure du possible; autant que faire se peut. **As early as possible**, le plus tôt possible. (*b*) **Possible in certain contingencies**, éventuel. *As a p. event*, à titre éventuel. **To insure against possible accidents**, s'assurer contre des accidents éventuels. (*c*) *F:* (*Of pers.*) Tolérable, acceptable. *They are quite p. people*, ce sont des gens que l'on peut très bien fréquenter. **2.** *s.* (*a*) **To do one's possible**, faire son possible (*to*, pour). (*b*) (*Shooting*) **To score a possible**, faire le maximum. **-ibly**, *adv.* **1.** **I cannot possibly do it**, il ne m'est pas possible de le faire. *How can I p. do it?* le moyen de le faire? **It can't possibly be!** pas possible! *I'll do all I possibly can*, je ferai tout mon possible. *I come as often as I p. can*, je viens aussi souvent que possible. **2.** Peut-être (bien). *P. he has heard of you*, peut-être a-t-il entendu parler de vous. **Possibly!** c'est possible; cela se peut.

possum ['pɔsəm], *s. U.S: F: =* OPOSSUM. **To play possum**, faire le mort; se tenir coi.

post¹ [poust], *s.* **1.** (*a*) Poteau *m*, pieu *m*, montant *m*, pilier *m.* **Trellis post**, pylône *m.* **Sign-post, finger-post**, poteau indicateur. *F:* **He stood there like a post**, il était planté là comme une borne, comme un piquet. (*b*) *Const:* Chandelle *f*; montant, dormant *m*, jambage *m.* (*c*) **Bed-post**, colonne *f* de lit. (*d*) *Arbre m*, fût *m* (de grue). (*e*) *Aut:* **Steering post**, arbre de direction. **2.** *El:* Borne *f* à vis. **3.** *Turf:* (*a*) (**Winning-**)**post**, (poteau d')arrivée *f*; but *m.* **To win on the post**, gagner de justesse. (**Starting-**)**post**, (poteau de) départ *m*; barrière *f.* **To go to the post**, prendre part à la course. (*Of horse*) *To refuse to leave the p.*, rester au poteau. **To be left at the post**, manquer le départ. (*b*) *Jalon m* (de la piste).

post², *v.tr.* **1. To post (up)**, placarder, coller (des affiches, etc.); afficher (un avis, etc.). *U.S:* **Post no bills**, défense *f* d'afficher. **2.** Inscrire (un vaisseau, etc.) comme disparu. (*At a club, etc.*) *To p. a member*, afficher le nom d'un membre en défaut.

post³, *s.* **1.** *A:* (**Malle-**)**post** *f.* **To travel post**, (i) voyager en poste; (ii) aller un train de poste. **2.** Courrier *m.* **By return of post**, par retour du courrier. *It is post-time*, c'est l'heure du courrier. **The post has come**, le facteur est passé. **To open one's post**, dépouiller son courrier. **The General Post** (delivery), la grande distribution (du matin). *Games:* **General post**, chassé-croisé *m.* *F:* **There has been a general post among the staff**, il y a eu un remaniement du personnel. **3.** Poste *f.* **To send sth. by post**, envoyer qch. par la poste. **4.** = POST-OFFICE. **To take a letter to the post**, porter une lettre à la poste. **'post-boy**, *s.m.* **1.** Courrier, messager. **2.** *F:* Postillon. **'post-chaise**, *s. A:* Chaise *f* de poste. **'post-'free**, *attrib. a.* Franc de port; en franchise; franco *inv.* **'post-'haste**, *adv.* En toute hâte. **To ride, travel, post-haste**, courir la poste; aller un train de poste. **'post-horn**, *s.* Trompe *f* (de la malle-poste). **'post-house**, *s. A:* Maison *f* de relais (de la malle-poste). **'post(-)office**, *s.* Bureau *m* de(s) poste(s); *F:* la poste. **The General Post Office**, la Grande Poste; les Postes et Télégraphes. **General post office**, head post office, hôtel *m* des postes. **District post office**, bureau postal de quartier. **Post-office clerk**, employé, -ée, commis *m*, des postes. **Post-office box**, boîte postale; case postale. **'post orderly**, *s. Mil:* Vaguemestre *m.* **'post-'paid**, *a.* Affranchi; port payé. **'post-paper**, *s.* *Appox.* = papier *m* écu.

post⁴. **1.** *v.i.* (*a*) Voyager par relais; voyager en poste. (*b*) *F:* Courir la poste; aller un train de poste. **2.** *v.tr.* (*a*) Mettre (une lettre) à la poste; jeter (une lettre) à la boîte. **To post sth. to s.o.**, envoyer qch. à qn (par la poste). (*b*) *Book-k:* **To post the books**, passer les écritures. **To post an entry**, passer écriture d'un article. **To post up the ledger**, mettre le grand-livre au courant, à jour. *F:* **To post s.o. up with sth.**, documenter qn sur qch.; mettre qn au courant de qch. *To p. oneself up on a matter*, se renseigner sur un sujet. *To keep s.o. posted up*, tenir qn à jour.

post⁵, *s.* **1.** (*a*) Poste *m* (de sentinelle, etc.). **Advanced post**, poste avancé. *Mil:* **To be on post**, être en faction. **Take post! posts!** à vos postes! *To die at one's p.*, mourir à son poste. (*b*) Poste (occupé par des troupes). (*c*) Troupes *fpl* (occupant un poste). **2.** *Hist:* **Trading-post**, station *f* de commerce; comptoir *m* (aux Indes, etc.). **3.** Poste, situation *f*, emploi *m.* **To take up one's post**, entrer en fonctions. **'post(-)captain**, *s. Hist: Navy:* Capitaine *m* de vaisseau.

post⁶, *v.tr.* **1.** Poster, mettre en faction (une sentinelle); aposter (un espion). *To p. a sentry at a door*, mettre un planton, un factionnaire, à une porte. **2.** *Mil: Navy:* **To be posted to a command, to a unit**, recevoir une affectation, être affecté à un commandement, à une unité. *Navy:* **To be posted to a ship**, être affecté à un navire. **To post s.o. as captain**, nommer qn capitaine de vaisseau.

post⁷, *s. Mil:* **Last post**, (i) la retraite (au clairon); (ii) la sonnerie aux morts. **To sound the last post** (*over the grave*), rendre les honneurs au mort (d'une sonnerie).

postage ['poustidʒ], *s.* Port *m*, affranchissement *m* (d'une lettre, d'un paquet). **Rates of postage**, taxes *fpl* d'affranchissement. **Postages**, ports de lettres; frais *m* de port. **Postage paid**, port payé. *S.a.* STAMP¹ 4.

postal ['poust(ə)l], *a.* Postal, -aux. **The Postal and Telegraph Service**, les Postes et Télégraphes. **Postal charges**, ports *m* de lettres. *S.a.* ORDER¹ 11.

postcard ['poustkɑːrd], *s.* Carte postale. **Picture postcard**, carte postale illustrée.

post-date [poust'deit], *v.tr.* Postdater (un chèque, etc.).

poster ['poustər], *s.* **1.** (*a*) Afficheur *m* (d'un avis, etc.). (*b*) = BILL-POSTER. **2.** Affiche murale; *esp.* affiche illustrée.

posterior [pɔs'tiːəriər]. **1.** *a.* Postérieur (*to*, à). **2.** *s. F:* Postérieur *m*, derrière *m* (de qn). **To kick s.o.'s p.**, enlever le ballon à qn. **-ly**, *adv.* Postérieurement.

posterity [pɔs'teriti], *s.* 'Postérité *f.* **1.** *To leave a large p.*, laisser une postérité nombreuse. **2.** **Posterity will be grateful to him**, la postérité lui sera reconnaissante.

postern ['poustərn], *s.* **1.** *Fort:* Poterne *f.* **2.** *A:* **Postern (door**), porte *f* de derrière; porte dérobée.

post-glacial [poust'gleiʃəl], *a. Geol:* Post-glaciaire.

posthumous ['pɔstjuməs], *a.* Posthume. **-ly**, *adv.* Posthumement; (paru) après la mort de l'auteur.

postil(l)ion [pɔs'tiljən], *s.* Postillon *m.*

post-impressionism [poustim'preʃənizm], *s. Art:* Néo-impressionnisme *m.*

postman, *pl.* **-men** ['poustmən, -men], *s.m.* **1.** Facteur. **Rural postman**, facteur rural. **2.** *Navy:* Vaguemestre.

postmark ['poustmɑːrk], *s.* Cachet *m* de la poste; timbre *m* de départ ou d'arrivée; timbre d'oblitération. *Letter bearing the London p.*, lettre timbrée de Londres, portant le timbre de Londres.

postmaster [poustmɑːstər], *s.m.* Receveur (des Postes). **The Postmaster General,** le ministre des Postes et Télégraphes.

postmeridian [poustmeˈridiən], *a.* Postméridien, de l'après-midi, du soir.

post meridiem [poustmeˈridiem], *Lt.phr.*(*Abbr.* **p.m.** [ˈpiːˈem]) De l'après-midi, du soir. *At four p.m.*, à quatre heures de l'après-midi.

postmistress [ˈpoustmistres], *s.f.* Receveuse des Postes.

post-mortem [poustˈmɔːrtem], *attrib. a. & s.* Après décès. *P.-m. rigidity,* rigidité cadavérique. **To hold a post-mortem (examination),** faire une autopsie (cadavérique).

postnuptial [poustˈnʌpʃ(ə)l], *a.* Postérieur au mariage.

post-obit [poustˈɔbit, -ˈoubit], *attrib. a. & s.* **Post-obit (bond),** contrat *m* exécutoire, obligation *f* réalisable, après le décès d'un tiers.

postpalatal [poustˈpalat(ə)l], *a.* Postpalatal, -aux; (consonne) vélaire.

postpone [pous(t)ˈpoun], *v.tr.* Remettre, ajourner, renvoyer à plus tard, reporter à plus tard, différer; reculer (un départ). *To p. a matter for a week,* remettre, renvoyer, une affaire à huitaine. *To p. a burial,* surseoir à une inhumation. *The sale has been postponed,* il a été sursis à la vente.

postponement [pous(t)ˈpounmənt], *s.* Remise *f* à plus tard; renvoi *m* (d'une cause) (*for a week,* à huitaine); ajournement *m.*

postprandial [poustˈprandiəl], *a. P.* eloquence, éloquence après dîner, au dessert. *P. nap,* sieste après le repas.

postscript [ˈpous(t)skript], *s.* (*Abbr.* **P.S.** [ˈpiːˈes]) **1.** Post-scriptum *m* inv. **2.** Postface *f* (d'un écrit).

postulate[1] [ˈpostjulet], *s. Geom: Log:* Postulat *m.*

postulate[2] [ˈpostjuleit]. **1.** *v.tr. & i.* **To postulate (for)** sth., postuler, demander, réclamer, qch. **2.** *v.tr.* Poser (qch.) en postulat; considérer (qch.) comme admis, comme établi. **3.** *v.tr. Ecc:* *To p. so and so for a bishop,* postuler un tel pour évêque.

posture[1] [ˈpostjər], *s.* (*a*) Posture *f*, pose *f*, attitude *f* (du corps). *To assume an easy p.,* prendre une posture commode. (*b*) Position *f*, situation *f*, état *m* (des affaires, etc.).

posture[2]. **1.** *v.tr.* Mettre (qn) dans une certaine posture; poser (un modèle). **2.** *v.i.* Prendre une posture, une pose. *F:* **To posture as a buffoon,** affecter la bouffonnerie; se poser en bouffon.

post-war [poustˈwɔːr], *attrib.a.* D'après guerre. **The post-war period,** l'après-guerre *m* inv.

posy [ˈpouzi], *s.* Bouquet *m* (de fleurs des champs).

pot[1] [pɔt], *s.* **1.** (*a*) Pot *m.* **(Flower-)pot,** pot à fleurs. *To drink a pot of beer,* boire un pot, un cruchon, de bière. **Chamber-pot,** pot de chambre; vase *m* de nuit. *El:* **Battery pot,** bac *m* de pile électrique. *S.a.* CHIMNEY-POT, COFFEE-POT, INKPOT, JAM-POT, TEA-POT. (*b*) Marmite *f.* **Pots and pans,** batterie *f* de cuisine. *P:* **To go to pot,** aller à la ruine, (s'en) aller à vau-l'eau. *Prov:* **The pot calls the kettle black,** la pelle se moque du fourgon. (*c*) **(Melting-)pot,** creuset *m.* *S.a.* MELTING-POT. (*d*) *Sp: F:* Coupe (remportée en prix). **2.** *Fish:* Casier *m. S.a.* CRAB-POT, LOBSTER-POT. **3.** (*a*) *F:* **Pots of money, a pot of money,** des tas *m* d'argent; de l'argent tant et plus. *To make pots of money,* gagner gros.

(*b*) *Cards:* **The pot,** la cagnotte. **4.** *F: (Of pers.)* **A big pot,** un gros bonnet; *P:* une grosse légume. **5.** *Paperm:* = POT-PAPER. **6.** = POT-SHOT. **ˈpot-bellied,** *a.* Ventru, pansu. *You are getting p.-b.,* tu commences à bedonner. **ˈpot-belly,** *s.* Panse *f*, bedon *m*, bedaine *f.* **ˈpot-boiler,** *s.* Œuvre *f* qui fait bouillir la marmite (de son auteur). *To write pot-boilers,* s'occuper de besognes alimentaires. **ˈpot-boy,** *s.m.* Garçon de cabaret. **ˈpot-herb,** *s.* Herbe potagère. **ˈpot-hole,** *s.* **1.** *Geol:* Marmite de géants; poche *f.* **2.** *F:* Trou *m*, flache *f* (dans une route). *Road full of pot-holes,* chemin défoncé. **ˈpot-hook,** *s.* **1.** Crémaillère *f* (de foyer). **2.** *Sch:* Bâton *m*, jambage *m* (de premier modèle d'écriture). **ˈpot-house,** *s.* Cabaret *m*, taverne *f.* **ˈpot-hunter,** *s. Sp:* Personne *f* qui prend part à tous les concours dans le seul but de remporter un prix. **ˈpot-luck,** *s.* **To take pot-luck,** manger (chez qn) à la fortune du pot. *Come and take p.-l. with us,* venez dîner chez nous sans cérémonie. **ˈpot-paper,** *s. Paperm:* Papier *m* pot. **ˈpot-shot,** *s. F:* **To take a pot-shot at sth.,** lâcher au petit bonheur un coup de fusil à qch. **ˈpot-valiant,** *a.* Brave après boire.

pot[2], *v.tr.* (potted) **1.** (*a*) Mettre en pot, conserver (le beurre, etc.). (*b*) Mettre en pot, empoter (une plante). (*c*) *Bill:* Blouser (une bille). **2.** *F:* (*a*) Tirer, tuer, abattre (du gibier, etc.). (*b*) *v.i.* **To pot at** (game, etc.), lâcher un coup de fusil à (une pièce de gibier); tirailler contre (l'ennemi); canarder (l'ennemi). *To pot at small game,* giboyer. **potted,** *a.* En pot, en terrine. **Potted foods,** conserves *fpl.*

potash [ˈpɔtaʃ], *s.* **1.** **(Carbonate of) potash,** carbonate *m* de potasse; *F:* potasse *f.* **2.** **Caustic potash,** potasse caustique. **3.** **Sulphate of potash,** potasse sulfatée. **ˈpotash-water,** *s.* Eau gazeuse bicarbonatée.

potassium [pɔˈtasiəm], *s. Ch:* Potassium *m.* **Potassium chlorate,** chlorate *m* de potasse. **Potassium carbonate,** carbonate *m* de potasse; *F:* potasse *f.*

potation [poˈteiʃ(ə)n], *s.* (*a*) Action *f* de boire; gorgée *f.* (*b*) *pl. F:* Libations *f.*

potato, *pl.* **-oes** [poˈteito, -ouz], *s.* **1.** Pomme *f* de terre. *Boiled potatoes,* pommes de terre à l'anglaise, à l'eau. *Baked potatoes,* pommes de terre au four, ou cuites sous la cendre. *Mashed potatoes,* purée *f* de pommes de terre; pommes de terre mousseline. *Chip potatoes,* pommes de terre frites. **2.** **Sweet potato, Spanish potato,** patate *f.* **Indian potato,** igname *f.* **poˈtato-ball,** *s. Cu:* Croquette *f* de pommes de terre. **poˈtato-beetle, -bug,** *s.* Doryphore *m.* **poˈtato-masher,** *s.* Presse-purée *m* inv. **poˈtato-spirit,** *s. Dist:* Alcool *m* amylique. **poˈtato-starch,** *s.* Fécule *f* (de pommes de terre).

poteen [pɔˈtiːn], **potheen** [pɔˈθiːn], *s.* Whisky irlandais distillé en fraude.

potency [ˈpoutənsi], *s.* **1.** Puissance *f*, autorité *f* (du monarque, etc.). **2.** Force *f*, puissance (d'un argument); efficacité *f* (d'un médicament); force (d'une boisson alcoolique).

potent [ˈpoutənt], *a.* **1.** *Lit:* Puissant. **2.** (*Of drug, etc.*) Efficace, puissant; (*of motive, etc.*) convaincant; plein de force. *P. drink,* boisson très forte. *P. poison,* poison violent. **-ly,** *adv.* Puissamment.

potentate [ˈpoutənteit], *s.* Potentat *m.*

potential [poˈtenʃəl]. **1.** *a.* (*a*) En puissance

virtuel ; latent. *P. danger,* danger possible, latent. *(b)* Potentiel. *The p. resources of Africa,* les ressources potentielles de l'Afrique. *(c) a. & s. Gram:* **The potential** (mood), le potentiel. **2.** *s.* Potentiel *m.* **Potential drop,** chute *f* de potentiel. *Operating p.,* voltage *m* de régime ; tension *f* de service. **-ally,** *adv.* Potentiellement, virtuellement, en puissance.

potentiality [poten∫i'aliti], *s.* Potentialité *f. Military ·potentialities of a country,* potentiel *m* militaire d'un pays. *Situation full of potentialities,* (i) situation où tout devient possible ; (ii) situation qui promet.

potentiometer [poten∫i'ɔmetər], *s. El:* Potentiomètre *m.*

pother ['poðər], *s.* **I.** Nuage *m* de fumée, de poussière. **2.** *(a)* Agitation *f,* confusion *f.* *(b)* Tapage *m,* tumulte *m,* vacarme *m.* *(c)* Tracas *m,* embarras *mpl.* **To make a pother,** faire des histoires. *All this p. about nothing!* tant d'histoires à propos de rien !

potion ['pou∫(ə)n], *s.* Potion *f ;* dose *f* (de médecine). *A :* Love-potion, philtre *m* (d'amour).

potman, *pl.* **-men** ['potmən, -men], *s.m.* = POT-BOY.

potsherd ['pot∫əːrd], *s. A :* Tesson *m* (de pot cassé) ; fragment *m* de vaisselle.

pottage ['potedʒ], *s. A :* **I.** Potée *f* (de viande et légumes). **2.** *See* MESS[1] I.

potter[1] ['potər], *s.* Potier *m.* **Potter's ciay,** terre *f* de potier ; argile *f* plastique. **Potter's wheel,** (i) tour *m* de potier ; (ii) disque *m* (du tour).

potter[2], *v.i.* **I.** S'occuper de bagatelles ; s'amuser à des riens. **To potter about at odd jobs,** bricoler. **2.** Traîner, flâner. *Aut :* **To potter along,** rouler à la papa ; aller son petit bonhomme de chemin. **To potter about the house** trottiner par la maison.

pottery ['potəri], *s.* **I.** Poterie *f.* *(a)* L'art *m* du potier. *(b)* La fabrique. **The Potteries,** les Poteries (du Staffordshire). **2.** Vaisselle *f* de terre. **A piece of** pottery, une poterie.

potty ['poti], *a. P :* **I.** *(a)* Petit, insignifiant. *A p. little state,* un petit État de rien du tout. *(b)* *(Of task, etc.)* Facile. **2.** *(a)* Toqué, timbré. *(b)* **To be potty on a ⸗irl,** être toqué d'une jeune fille.

pouch[1] [paut∫], *s.* **I.** Petit sac ; bourse *f, A :* escarcelle *f. S.a.* TOBACCO-POUCH. **2.** *Nat.Hist:* Poche ventrale (des marsupiaux) ; abajoue *f* (de singe). **3.** Poche (sous les yeux).

pouch[2]. **I.** *v.tr.* *(a)* Empocher. *(b)* *(Of fish, penguin, etc.)* Avaler. *(c)* *Dressm:* Faire bouffer (un vêtement). **2.** *v.i.* *(Of dress)* Former une poche ; bouffer.

pouf(e) [puːf], *s. Furn:* Pouf *m.*

poulp(e) [puːlp], *s. Moll:* Poulpe *m,* pieuvre *f.*

poult [poult], *s.* Jeune volaille *f* ; poulet *m* ; *(of turkey)* dindonneau *m.*

poulterer ['poultərər], *s.* Marchand *m* de volaille.

poultice[1] ['poultis], *s.* Cataplasme *m.* *F:* Poultice on a wooden leg, cautère *m* sur une jambe de bois. *S.a.* BREAD-POULTICE, MUSTARD-POULTICE.

poultice[2], *v.tr.* Mettre, appliquer, un cataplasme sur (qch.).

poultry ['poultri], *s. Coll.* Volaille *f.* **'poultry-farm,** *s.* Exploitation *f* agricole pour l'élevage de la volaille. **'poultry-show,** *s.* Concours *m* d'aviculture. **'poultry-yard,** *s.* Basse-cour *f,* *pl.* basses-cours.

pounce[1] [pauns], *s.* **To make a pounce on sth.,** (i) fondre, s'abattre, sur (sa proie) ; (ii) *(of pers.)* s'élancer pour saisir qch. ; se jeter sur qch.

pounce[2], *v.i.* *(a)* **To pounce on he prey,** fondre,

s'abattre, sur la proie. *(b)* *F :* Se précipiter, se jeter (*on,* sur). *All the tables are ·pounced upon,* toutes les tables sont prises d'assaut.

pounce[3], *s.* **I.** (Poudre *f* de) sandaraque *f.* **2.** Ponce *f.*

pounce[4], *v.tr.* **I.** Poncer ; polir, frotter, à la ponce. **2.** Copier, calquer (un dessin) à la ponce ; poncer (un dessin). **Pounced drawing,** poncif *m.*

pound[1] [paund], *s.* **I.** *(Abbr.* lb.) Livre *f* (de 453 gr, 6). *Coffee at three shillings a pound,* café à trois shillings la livre. *To sell sugar by the pound,* vendre le sucre à la livre. **2.** *(Symbol £)* Pound sterling, livre sterling (de 20 shillings). **Pound note,** billet *m* (de banque) d'une livre. *(Of bankrupt)* **To pay ten shillings in the pound,** payer dix shillings par livre. **A question of pounds, shillings and pence,** *F :* **a question of £. s. d.** [eles'diː], une question de gros sous. **'pound-foolish,** *a. See* PENNY-WISE.

pound[2], *s.* **I.** Fourrière *f* (pour animaux errants). **2.** Parc *m* (à moutons, etc.). **3.** *Fish:* Pound net, verveux *m.* **4.** Bief *m,* retenue *f* (entre deux écluses).

pound[3], *v.tr.* **I.** Mettre (des animaux) en fourrière. **2.** **To pound s.o. (up),** enfermer qn.

pound[4]. **I.** *v.tr.* *(a)* Broyer, piler, concasser ; égruger (du sucre) ; pilonner (la terre, une drogue). **Pounded sugar,** sucre en poudre. *(b)* Bourrer (qn) de coups de poing. *Mil:* **To pound a position,** pilonner, marteler, une position. *(c)* **To pound sth. to atoms,** réduire qch. en miettes. **To pound out a tune on the piano,** marteler un air sur le piano. **2.** *v.i.* *(a)* **To pound at, on, sth. ;** **to pound away at sth.,** cogner dur, frapper ferme, sur qch. *To p. (away) at the door,* frapper à la porte à coups redoublés. *Equit :* **To pound in the saddle,** *F :* piler du poivre. **To pound on the piano,** cogner sur le piano. *(b)* **To pound along,** avancer d'un pas lourd ; *(of steamer)* fendre les vagues avec difficulté. *I.C.E:* *(Of engine)* Cogner, marteler. *(d) The ship was pounding on the bottom,* le navire talonnait. *The hull was pounding on the rocks,* la coque se broyait sur les récifs.

poundage[1] ['paundedʒ], *s.* **I.** *(a)* Commission *f ;* remise *f* de tant par livre (sterling). *(b)* Part donnée au personnel sur les bénéfices réalisés. **2.** Taux *m* de tant par livre (de poids).

poundage[2], *s.* **I.** Mise *f* en fourrière. **2.** Frais *mpl* de fourrière.

pounder ['paundər], *s. Tls:* Pilon *m.*

-pounder ['paundər], *s.* *(With num. prefixed, e.g.)* **I.** Two-pounder, poisson, etc., de deux livres. **2.** *Artil:* **Thirty-pounder,** canon *m,* pièce *f,* de trente. **Eight-p.,** pièce de huit. **3.** *F :* **Thousandpounder,** billet *m* de banque de mille livres.

pour[1] ['poːər], *s.* **I.** Pluie abondante ; déluge *m* de pluie. **2.** *Metall:* Quantité *f* de métal coulée ; coulée *f.*

pour[2]. **I.** *v.tr.* *(a)* Verser (*into,* dans). *River that pours itself into the sea,* rivière qui se jette, se déverse, dans la mer. *To p. comfort into s.o.'s heart,* verser des consolations dans le cœur de qn. *(b)* *Metall:* **To pour the metal,** couler le métal. **2.** *v.i.* *(a)* *(Of rain)* Tomber à torrents, à verse. *It ·s pouring (with rain),* il pleut à verse. *The water was pouring into the cellar,* l'eau entrait à flots dans la cave. *The water was pouring from the roof,* l'eau ruisselait du toit. *(b)* *F :* **To pour into, out of, the theatre,** entrer dans le théâtre, sortir du théâtre, en foule, à flots. **pour in. I.** *v.tr.* **To pour in a broadside,** lâcher, envoyer, une bordée. **2.** *v.i.* **To pour in,** to come

pouring in, entrer à flots, en foule; arriver de toutes parts. *Invitations are pouring in on us,* il nous pleut des invitations. *Tourists p. in from all quarters,* les touristes affluent de toutes parts. **pour off,** *v.tr.* Décanter. **pour out. 1.** *v.tr.* (*a*) Verser (une tasse de thé, etc.). *He poured me out another glass,* il me versa encore à boire. *Abs.* To pour out, présider (à la table de thé). (*b*) Répandre, exhaler (sa colère); donner libre cours à (ses sentiments); émettre des flots de (musique, etc.); épancher (ses chagrins); décharger (son cœur). To pour out one's thanks, se confondre en remerciements. *To p. out threats,* se répandre en menaces. **2.** *v.i.* (*a*) Sortir à flots; ruisseler. (*b*) Sortir en foule. **pouring**[1], *a.* **Pouring rain,** pluie torrentielle; pluie battante. **A pouring wet evening,** une soirée ruisselante. **pouring**[2], *s.* *Metall:* Coulée *f.*

pourer ['pɔːrər], *s.* **1.** Entonnoir *m.* **2.** *Metall:* (Pers.) Couleur *m.*

pout[1] [paut], *s.* *Ich:* **(Whiting-)pout,** tacaud *m.* (Eel-)pout, lotte *f.*

pout[2], *s.* Moue *f.* *F:* **To have the pouts,** être d'humeur maussade; bouder.

pout[3], *v.i.* **1.** (*a*) Faire la moue, la lippe. *v.tr.* To pout the lips, faire la moue. (*b*) Bouder. **2.** (*Of pigeon*) Enfler le jabot; faire jabot.

pouter ['pautər], *s.* **1.** Pigeon *m* grosse-gorge; (pigeon) boulant *m.* **2.** *Ich:* Tacaud *m.*

poverty ['pɔvərti], *s.* **1.** Pauvreté *f.* *Adm:* Indigence *f.* **Extreme** *p.,* abject *p.,* misère *f.* *To live in p.,* vivre dans la gêne, dans la misère. To cry poverty, pleurer misère. *Prov:* Poverty is no sin, no vice, pauvreté n'est pas vice. **2.** Disette *f,* manque *m,* pénurie *f* (de denrées, etc.); stérilité *f,* pauvreté (du sol). *P. of ideas,* dénuement *m* d'idées. *I.C.E:* **Poverty of the mixture,** pauvreté du mélange. **'poverty-stricken,** *a.* **1.** Miséreux; indigent; dans la misère. **2.** *P.-s. quarter,* quartier misérable.

powder[1] ['paudər], *s.* Poudre *f.* (*a*) **To reduce sth. to powder,** (i) réduire qch. en poudre; pulvériser qch.; (ii) *F:* réduire qch. en poussière; anéantir qch. (*b*) **(Gun-)powder,** poudre (à canon). *Sporting p.,* poudre de chasse. **To smell powder for the first time,** recevoir le baptême du feu. *F:* **To keep one's powder dry,** parer aux événements. *It is not worth p. and shot,* le jeu n'en vaut pas la chandelle. **To waste one's powder and shot,** tirer sa poudre aux moineaux. (*c*) **Face-powder, toilet-powder,** poudre de riz. **'powder-flask, -horn,** *s.* *A:* Poire *f* cornet *m,* à poudre. **'powder-magazine,** *s.* Poudrière *f.* **'powder-mill,** *s.* Poudrerie *f;* manufacture *f* de poudre à canon. **'powder-monkey,** *s.* *Nau:* *A:* Moussaillon gargoussier.

powder[2], *v.tr.* **1.** Saupoudrer (*with,* de). **2.** Poudrer (à blanc) (les cheveux). **To powder one's face,** *abs.* **to powder,** se poudrer le visage. **3.** Réduire en poudre; pulvériser.

powderiness ['paudərinəs], *s.* Pulvérulence *f.*

powdery ['paudəri], *a.* (*a*) Poudreux. (*b*) Friable.

power ['pauər], *s.* **1.** Pouvoir *m.* I will do all in my power, je ferai tout ce qui est en mon pouvoir. **As far as lies within my power,** dans la mesure où cela m'est possible, où cela me sera possible. **To the utmost of my power,** de tout mon pouvoir. It is beyond my power, cela ne m'est pas possible. *It is beyond my p. to save him,* je suis impuissant à le sauver. **2.** (*a*) Faculté *f,* capacité *f,* talent *m.* **Mental powers,** facultés intellectuelles. *His powers are failing,* ses facultés baissent. (*b*) *Ph:* **Power of absorption,** capacité d'absorption. **3.** Vigueur *f,* force *f.* *F:* **More**

power to your elbow! (i) allez-y! (ii) puissiez-vous réussir! **4.** (*a*) Puissance *f* (d'une machine, d'un microscope); force (d'un aimant, d'une chute d'eau). **Attractive power,** force d'attraction. **Magnifying power,** pouvoir grossissant. *Mec:* **Power-to-weight ratio,** puissance massique (d'une machine). **Power delivered,** puissance développée. *S.a.* HORSE-POWER. (*b*) Énergie *f* (électrique, hydraulique). **Motive power,** force motrice. **Power unit,** unité motrice. **Generation of power,** production *f* d'énergie. **Power consumption,** énergie consommée. *P. supplied by a motor,* débit *m* d'un moteur. *The car came in under its own power,* l'auto est rentrée par ses propres moyens. *Nau:* **To work the engines at half power,** manœuvrer à petite vitesse. **Under power,** sous pression. (*c*) *P. has revolutionized modern industry,* le machinisme a transformé l'industrie moderne. **5.** (*a*) Pouvoir, influence *f,* autorité *f.* *Assumption of p.,* prise *f* de pouvoir. *Spain was then at the height of her p.,* l'Espagne était alors à l'apogée de sa puissance. **Absolute power,** le pouvoir absolu. **Executive power,** le pouvoir exécutif. **To have s.o. in one's power,** avoir qn sous sa coupe. **To fall into s.o.'s power,** tomber au pouvoir de qn. **To come into power,** arriver au pouvoir. **Power of life and death,** droit *m* de vie et de mort. (*b*) **To act with full powers,** agir de pleine autorité. *This lies within his powers,* cela rentre dans ses attributions. **To exceed, go beyond, one's powers,** outrepasser ses pouvoirs; sortir de sa compétence. (*c*) *Jur:* Procuration *f,* mandat *m,* pouvoir. **To furnish s.o. with full powers,** donner pleins pouvoirs à qn. *S.a.* ATTORNEY[2]. **6.** (*a*) **The powers that be,** les autorités constituées. **The powers of darkness,** les puissances des ténèbres. (*b*) **The Great Powers,** les Grandes Puissances. **7.** *P:* **A power of people,** une quantité de gens. *To make a p. of money,* gagner énormément d'argent. *To do a p. of work,* abattre de l'ouvrage tant et plus. **8.** *Mth:* Puissance (d'un nombre). **Three to the fourth power,** trois (à la) puissance quatre; trois à la quatrième puissance. *To the n*[th] *p.,* à la n[me] puissance. **The power of x,** l'exposant *m* de x. **'power-control,** *s.* Commande *f* mécanique. **'power-driven,** *a.* Mû par moteur. **'power-hammer,** *s.* Marteau-pilon *m.* **'power house,** *s.* = POWER STATION. **'power-installation,** *s.* Installation *f* de force, d'énergie. **'power-loom,** *s.* *Tex:* Métier *m* mécanique. **'power-petrol,** *s.* *Aut:* Essence *f* pour poids lourds. **'power-rail,** *s.* *El.Rail:* Rail conducteur; rail de contact. **'power station,** *s.* Station génératrice (d'électricité); centrale *f* électrique. **'power-stroke,** *s.* *Mch:* Temps moteur. **'power-tube, -valve,** *s.* *W.Tel:* Lampe émettrice, génératrice.

-powered ['pauərd], *a.* **High-powered car, low-powered car,** auto de haute, de faible, puissance.

powerful ['pauərful], *a.* **1.** (*a*) Puissant. *To have to deal with a p. adversary,* avoir affaire à forte partie. (*b*) Fort, vigoureux. *P. remedy,* remède énergique, efficace. **2.** *P:* **A powerful lot of people,** une masse de gens. **-fully,** *adv.* Puissamment; fortement. *P. built man,* homme puissamment charpenté.

powerless ['pauərləs], *a.* **1.** Impuissant. **To be powerless to do sth.,** se trouver impuissant à faire qch. *They are p. in the matter,* ils n'y peuvent rien. **2.** (Remède) inefficace, sans vertu.

powerlessness ['pauərləsnəs], *s.* **1.** Impuissance *f.* **2.** Inefficacité *f.*

pow-wow[1] ['pauwau], *s.* **1.** Sorcier guérisseur

(chez les Peaux-Rouges). **2.** Cérémonie *f* (avec rites magiques); assemblée *f*, orgie *f* (des Peaux-Rouges). **3.** (*a*) *U.S*: Conférence *f* politique. (*b*) *F*: Conférence, palabre *f*.

pow-wow² [pau'wau], *v.i.* **1.** (*Of N. American Indians*) Tenir une assemblée; se livrer à une orgie. **2.** *F*: Tenir un congrès; palabrer. **To pow-wow about sth.**, discuter qch.

pox [poks], *s.* **1.** *Med*: (*a*) Vérole *f*. (*b*) *See* CHICKEN-POX, SMALLPOX. **2.** Cow-pox, vaccine *f*; variole *f* des vaches.

practicability [praktikə'biliti], *s.* Praticabilité *f*.

practicable ['praktikəbl], *a.* **1.** Praticable; faisable. *This method is not so p.*, cette méthode n'est pas, du point de vue pratique, aussi satisfaisante. **2.** (*a*) (*Of road, ford*) Praticable. (*b*) *Th*: **Practicable window**, fenêtre praticable.

practical ['praktik(ə)l], *a.* **1.** Pratique. (*a*) **Practical mechanics, chemistry**, mécanique, chimie, appliquée. *Of no p. value*, inutilisable dans la pratique. *S.a.* JOKE¹. (*b*) **Practical proposal**, proposition d'ordre pratique. *P.* common sense, sens pratique. (*c*) **Practical shoemaker**, cordonnier à façon. (*d*) *Very p. little girl*, petite fille très entendue. **2.** **With practical unanimity**, d'un consentement pour ainsi dire unanime, quasi unanime. **-ally**, *adv.* **1.** Pratiquement, en pratique. **2.** Pour ainsi dire. *There has been p. no snow*, il n'y a pas eu de neige pour ainsi dire. *P. cured*, quasiment guéri. *P. the whole of the audience*, la quasi-totalité de l'auditoire.

practice ['praktis], *s.* **1.** Pratique *f*. *The p. of medicine*, l'exercice *m* de la médecine. **Doctor who is no longer in practice**, médecin qui ne pratique plus, qui n'exerce plus. *Jur*: *The practice of the courts*, la procédure, la pratique, du Palais. *To put, carry, a principle into practice*, mettre un principe en action, en pratique. **2.** (*a*) Habitude *f*, coutume *f*, usage *m*. **To make it a practice**, one's practice, to do sth.; to make a practice of doing sth., se faire une habitude, une règle, de faire qch. (*b*) **Shop practice**, tours *mpl* de main d'atelier; technique *f* d'atelier. **3.** Exercice(s). *Sp*: Entraînement *m*. *It can only be learnt by p.*, cela ne s'apprend que par l'usage. *Stroke that needs a lot of p.*, coup qui demande beaucoup d'application, de travail. **Out of practice**, rouillé. *To do sth. for p.*, faire qch. pour s'exercer. **Band practice, choir practice**, répétition *f*. *Mil*: **Target practice**, exercices de tir. *Prov*: **Practice makes perfect**, c'est en forgeant qu'on devient forgeron. *Sp*: **Practice match**, match d'entraînement. **4.** Pratique, clientèle *f* (de médecin); étude *f* (d'avoué). **To buy a practice**, acheter une clientèle. **5.** *Esp. in pl.* Pratiques, menées *fpl*, machinations *fpl*, intrigue *f*. **'practice-firing**, *s.* *Mil*: Exercice *m* de tir.

practician [prak'tiʃ(ə)n], *s.* Praticien *m*.

practise ['praktis], *v.tr.* **1.** Pratiquer (une vertu, etc.); suivre (une méthode); mettre en pratique, en action (un principe, une règle). **To practise what one preaches**, prêcher d'exemple. **2.** Pratiquer, exercer (une profession). **To p. medicine**, exercer la médecine. **3.** Étudier (le piano, etc.); s'exercer (au piano, sur la flûte, à l'escrime); répéter (un chœur, etc.). *Abs. Mus*: Faire des exercices. *To p. a shot* (*at tennis, billiards*), s'exercer à un coup. **practised**, *a.* Exercé, expérimenté; (joueur, etc.) averti. **Practised in sth.**, versé, habile, dans qch.; rompu à qch.

practitioner [prak'tiʃənər], *s.* Praticien *m*. **Medical practitioner**, médecin *m*. **General practitioner**, médecin et chirurgien; médecin ordinaire.

praetor ['priːtər], *s.* *Rom.Hist*: Préteur *m*.

praetorian [priː'tɔːriən], *a.* & *s.* Prétorien (*m*).

praetorium [priː'tɔːriəm], *s.* Prétoire *m*.

praetorship ['priːtərʃip], *s.* Préture *f*.

pragmatic [prag'matik], *a.* **1.** *Hist*: *Phil*: Pragmatique. **2.** = PRAGMATICAL.

pragmatical [prag'matik(ə)l], *a.* **1.** (i) Suffisant, important, infatué de soi-même; (ii) dogmatique, positif. **2.** *Phil*: Pragmatique.

pragmatism ['pragmatizm], *s.* **1.** *Phil*: Pragmatisme *m*. **2.** Pédanterie *f*.

prairie ['prɛəri], *s.* Prairie *f* (de l'Amérique du Nord); savane *f*. **'Prairie 'States (the)**. *Pr.n.pl.* La Prairie (Wisconsin, Iowa, Minnesota, etc.).

praisable ['preizəbl], *a.* Louable.

praise¹ [preiz], *s.* (i) (*Deserved*) Éloge(s) *m(pl)*; (ii) (*adulatory or of worship*) louange(s) *f(pl)*. **In praise of s.o.**, of sth., à la louange de qn, de qch. *To speak in p. of s.o.*, faire l'éloge de qn. *To sound one's own praises*, faire son propre éloge. *I am not given to p.*, je ne suis pas enclin à la louange. **To be loud, warm, in s.o.'s praise**, prodiguer les éloges à qn. *I have nothing but p. for him, for his conduct*, je n'ai qu'à me louer de lui, de sa conduite. **Beyond all praise**, au-dessus de tout éloge. **To the praise of God**, à la louange de Dieu. **Praise be to God!** Dieu soit loué!

praise², *v.tr.* **1.** Louer, faire l'éloge de (qn). *He was praised by everyone*, il s'attira les éloges de tout le monde. **2. To praise God**, glorifier Dieu; chanter les louanges de Dieu. **3.** *F*: **To praise up**, vanter, prôner.

praiseworthy ['preizwəːrði], *a.* Digne d'éloges; (travail) méritoire. **-ily**, *adv.* Louablement.

pram [pram], *s.* *F*: **1.** = PERAMBULATOR. **2.** Voiture *f* à bras (de laitier).

prance [prɑːns], *v.i.* **1.** (*Of horse*) Fringuer; piaffer. **To prance about**, caracoler. *F*: **To prance with rage**, trépigner de colère. **2.** (*Of pers.*) Se pavaner; se carrer. **prancing**, *s.* Allure fringante (d'un cheval); caracoles *fpl*.

prandial ['prandiəl], *a.* *Hum*: De, du, dîner. *P. excesses*, excès de table.

prank¹ [praŋk], *s.* **1.** Escapade *f*, folie *f*, frasque *f*, fredaine *f*. *To play pranks*, faire des joyeusetés. *To play one's pranks*, faire des siennes. **2.** Tour *m*, farce *f*, niche *f*, espièglerie *f*. **To play pranks on s.o.**, jouer des tours à qn; faire des espiègleries, des niches, à qn.

prank². **1.** *v.tr.* Parer, orner. *Field pranked with flowers*, champ émaillé de fleurs. **To prank oneself out, up**, se parer de ses plus beaux atours. **2.** *v.i.* Se pavaner; prendre des airs.

prankish ['praŋkiʃ], *a.* Espiègle, lutin.

prate [preit], *v.i.* (*a*) Dire des riens, des absurdités (d'un air important); jaser, bavarder, jacasser. (*b*) Rapporter des potins; jaser. **prating**, *a.* Babillard, bavard; jaseur, -euse.

pratique [pra'tiːk], *s.* *Nau*: Libre pratique *f*. *To admit a ship to p.*, donner libre pratique à un navire; lever la quarantaine.

prattle¹ [pratl], *s.* (*a*) Babil *m*, babillage *m* (d'enfants). (*b*) Bavardage *m*, papotage *m*.

prattle², *v.i.* (*a*) Babiller. (*b*) Jaser, bavarder, papoter.

prattler ['pratlər], *s.* (*a*) Babillard, -arde. (*b*) Jaseur, -euse; bavard, -arde.

prawn [prɔːn], *s.* Crevette *f* rose, rouge; bouquet *m*; (grande crevette) salicoque *f*.

pray [prei], *v.tr.* & *i.* **1.** Prier, implorer, supplier (*s.o. to do sth.*, qn de faire qch.). **To pray (to) God**, prier Dieu. **To pray for s.o.**, prier pour qn. **To pray for sth.**, prier le Seigneur qu'il nous accorde qch. *I p. that he may be safe,* je prie Dieu qu'il soit sain et sauf. *To p. for s.o.'s soul,* prier pour (le repos de) l'âme de qn. He's past praying for, (i) il est perdu sans retour ; (ii) *F :* il est incorrigible, indécrottable. **2.** (I) pray (you), je vous (en) prie ; de grâce. *What good will that do,* pray? à quoi bon, je vous demande un peu? *P. take a seat,* veuillez (bien) vous asseoir. **'praying-desk,** *s.* Prie-Dieu *m inv.*

prayer[1] ['prɛər], *s.* **1.** Prière *f* (à Dieu) ; oraison *f.* The Lord's Prayer, l'oraison dominicale ; le Pater. Prayer for the dead, requiem *m* ; prière pour les morts ; oraison des trépassés. To put up a prayer, to offer prayer, faire une prière. To say one's prayers, faire ses dévotions. To be at one's prayers, être en prières. To be at prayers, être à la prière (en commun). *Ecc :* Morning Prayer, Evening Prayer, office *m* du matin, du soir. **2.** Demande instante. *He did it at my p.,* il l'a fait à ma prière. **'prayer-book,** *s.* Livre *m* de prières ; livre d'heures. **'prayer-meeting,** *s. Ecc :* Service *m* de la semaine. **'prayer-stool,** *s.* Prie-Dieu *m inv.*

prayer[2] ['preiər], *s.* Suppliant, -ante.

preach [priːtʃ], *v.* Prêcher. **1.** *v.i.* Prononcer le sermon. *F :* To preach to s.o., sermonner qn ; prêcher qn. *F :* To preach at s.o., diriger un sermon contre qn (qui est présent, mais sans nommer personne). **2.** *v.tr.* (a) *To p. a sermon,* prononcer un sermon. (b) To preach the gospel, prêcher, annoncer, l'Évangile. (c) *F :* To preach up sth., prôner qch. **preaching**[1], *s.* Prêcheur.

preaching[2], *s.* **1.** Prédication *f.* **2.** *Pej :* Prêcherie *f.*

preacher ['priːtʃər], *s.* **1.** Prédicateur *m.* **2.** *Pej :* Prêcheur, -euse.

preachify ['priːtʃifai], *v.i. F :* Sermonner ; faire de la morale. **preachifying,** *s.* Prêcherie *f* ; prêchi-prêcha *m.*

preachy ['priːtʃi], *a. F :* Prêcheur, sermonneur.

pre-admission [priːəd'miʃ(ə)n], *s. Mch :* Admission prématurée (de la vapeur, etc.).

preamble [priː'ambl], *s.* **1.** (a) Préambule *m.* (b) Préliminaires *mpl* (d'un traité, etc.). **2.** *Jur :* Exposé *m* des motifs (d'un projet de loi).

preamplifier [priː'amplifaiər], *s. W.Tel :* Préamplificateur *m, F :* préampli *m.*

prebend ['prebənd], *s.* Prébende *f.*

prebendal [pri'bend(ə)l], *a. Ecc :* Attaché à la prébende. *P. stalls,* stalles canoniales.

prebendary ['prebəndəri], *s.* Prébendier *m,* chanoine *m.*

precarious [pri'kɛəriəs], *a.* **1.** *Jur :* (Possession) précaire. **2.** Précaire, incertain. To make a precarious living, gagner sa vie précairement. **-ly,** *adv.* Précairement.

precariousness [pri'kɛəriəsnəs], *s.* Précarité *f,* incertitude *f* (dans la possession) ; état *m* précaire (de la santé).

precaution [pri'kɔːʃ(ə)n], *s.* Précaution *f.* To take (one's) precautions against sth., prendre ses précautions, se précautionner, contre qch. By way of precaution, à tout événement.

precautionary [pri'kɔːʃ(ə)nəri], *a.* De précaution.

precede [pri'siːd], *v.tr.* **1.** (a) Précéder. *Formalities that p. the debate,* formalités préalables aux débats. *For a week preceding this occasion,* pendant une semaine avant cette occasion. (b) Faire précéder. *To p. a lecture with a few words of welcome,* préfacer une conférence de quelques mots de bienvenue. **2.** Avoir le pas, la préséance, sur (qn). **preceding,** *a.* Précédent. *The p. day,* la veille. *In the p. article,* dans l'article ci-dessus.

precedence ['presidəns, pri'siːdəns], *s.* (a) Préséance *f* ; priorité *f.* To have, take, precedence of s.o., avoir le pas, la préséance, sur qn ; prendre le pas sur qn. *Ladies take p.,* les dames passent avant. To yield precedence to s.o., céder le pas à qn. (b) Droit *m* de priorité.

precedent ['presidənt], *s.* **1.** Précédent *m.* To set, create, a precedent, créer un précédent. According to precedent, conformément à la tradition. **2.** *Jur :* Décision *f* judiciaire faisant jurisprudence.

precentor [pri'sentər], *s. Ecc :* **1.** (a) Premier chantre. (b) Maître *m* de chapelle. **2.** *A :* Chef *m* du chœur (dans l'église réformée).

precept ['priːsept], *s.* **1.** Précepte *m* ; commandement *m* (de Dieu). **2.** *Jur :* Mandat *m.*

preceptor [pri'septər], *s.* Précepteur *m.*

precession [pri'seʃ(ə)n], *s. Astr :* Précession *f* (des équinoxes).

precinct ['priːsiŋ(k)t], *s.* **1.** (a) Enceinte *f,* enclos *m.* (b) *pl.* Precincts, pourtour *m* (d'une cathédrale). **2.** Limite *f* (du pourtour).

preciosity [preʃi'ositi], *s.* Préciosité *f,* affectation *f.*

precious ['preʃəs]. **1.** *a.* (a) Précieux ; de grand prix. Precious stones, pierres précieuses. (b) *F :* Fameux, fier. A precious pair, une belle paire (de vauriens, etc.). *A p. fool he is!* c'est un fameux imbécile ! (c) (Style) précieux, recherché, affecté. **2.** *s.* My precious! mon trésor ! mon amour ! **3.** *adv. F :* To take precious good care of sth., prendre un soin particulier de qch. *There are p. few of them,* il n'y en a guère.

preciousness ['preʃəsnəs], *s.* **1.** Haute valeur (de qch.). **2.** *Art : Lit :* Préciosité *f.*

precipice ['presipis], *s.* Précipice *m.* *To fall over a p.,* tomber dans un précipice.

precipitable [pri'sipitəbl], *a. Ch :* Précipitable.

precipitance [pri'sipitəns], **precipitancy** [pri'sipitənsi], *s.* Précipitation *f ;* (i) empressement *m* ; (ii) manque *m* de réflexion.

precipitant [pri'sipitənt], *s. Ch :* Précipitant *m.*

precipitate[1] [pri'sipitet], *s.* **1.** *Ch :* Précipité *m.* To form a precipitate, (se) précipiter. **2.** *Meteor :* Eau *f* de condensation.

precipitate[2], *a.* Précipité. **1.** Fait à la hâte. *They escaped by a p. flight,* une fuite précipitée leur permit de s'échapper. **2.** Trop empressé ; irréfléchi. **-ly,** *adv.* Précipitamment ; avec précipitation.

precipitate[3] [pri'sipiteit]. **1.** *v.tr.* (a) Précipiter (into, dans). *To p. a country into war,* précipiter un pays dans la guerre. (b) (i) *Ch :* Précipiter (une substance). (ii) *Meteor :* Condenser ; faire tomber (la rosée). (c) Accélérer, hâter, précipiter (un événement). *To p. matters,* brusquer les choses. **2.** *v.i.* (a) *Ch : Ph :* (Se) précipiter. (b) *Meteor :* Se condenser.

precipitation [prisipi'teiʃ(ə)n], *s.* **1.** (a) *Ch : Ph :* Précipitation *f.* (b) *Meteor :* Précipitation. *Annual p.,* quantité *f* de pluie annuelle. **2.** To act with precipitation, agir avec précipitation, précipitamment.

precipitous [pri'sipitəs], *a.* Escarpé, abrupt ; à pic. **-ly,** *adv.* A pic.

precipitousness [pri'sipitəsnəs], *s.* Raideur *f* (d'une pente).

précis ['preisi], *pl.* **précis** ['preisiz], *s.* Précis *m,* analyse *f,* résumé *m,* abrégé *m. To make a p. of an affair,* rédiger un précis d'une affaire.

precise [pri'sais], *a.* **1.** (a) Précis ; exact. *P. movements,* mouvements exécutés avec précision. In order to be precise . . ., pour préciser. . . . (b) *At the p. moment when . . .,* au

moment précis où. . . . **2** (*Of pers.*) Formaliste ;
pointilleux ; méticuleux. **-ly,** *adv.* **1.** (*a*) Avec
précision. *To state the facts p.,* préciser les faits.
(*b*) *At six o'clock p.,* à six heures précises.
2. Precisely (so)! précisément ! parfaitement !
▸**reciseness** [pri'saisnəs], *s.* **1.** Précision *f.*
2. (*a*) Méticulosité *f.* (*b*) Formalisme *m.*
▸**recision** [pri'siʒ(ə)n], *s.* Précision *f.* *Lack of p.,*
imprécision *f.* **Precision instruments,** instruments
de précision.
▸**reclude** [pri'klu:d], *v.tr.* Empêcher, prévenir,
écarter (une objection, un malentendu, etc.). *In
order to p. any misunderstanding . . .,* pour
prévenir tout malentendu. . . . *To be precluded
from an opportunity,* être privé d'une occasion.
To be precluded from doing sth. être dans
l'impossibilité de faire qch.
▸**recocious** [pri'kouʃəs], *a.* Précoce, hâtif ; (enfant) précoce. **-ly,** *adv.* Précocement ; avec
précocité.
▸**recociousness** [pri'kouʃəsnəs], **precocity**
[pri'kɔsiti], *s.* Précocité *f.*
▸**recognition** [pri:kɔg'niʃ(ə)n], *s.* *Phil:* etc:
Préconnaissance *f* ; connaissance antérieure.
▸**reconceive** [pri:kon'si:v], *v.tr.* Préconcevoir.
Preconceived idea, idée préconçue.
▸**reconception** [pri:kon'sepʃ(ə)n], *s.* **1.** Préconception *f.* **2.** (*a*) Idée ou opinion préconçue.
(*b*) Préjugé *m.*
▸**reconcerted** [pri:kon'sə:rtid], *a.* Arrangé,
concerté, d'avance. **Following no preconcerted
plan,** sans plan arrêté.
▸**recursor** [pri'kə:rsər], *s.* Précurseur *m* ;
devancier *m,* avant-coureur *m.*
▸**recursory** [pri'kə:rsəri], *a.* (*a*) Précurseur ;
(symptôme) avant-coureur. (*b*) *P. remarks,*
observations préliminaires.
▸**redacious** [pre'deiʃəs], *a.* **1.** (Animal) rapace ;
(bête) de proie. **2.** *Dog with p. instincts,* chien
qui a des instincts de bête de proie.
▸**redate** [pri'deit], *v.tr.* **1.** Antidater (un document). **2.** Venir avant (un fait historique, etc.).
▸**redatory** ['predətəri], *a.* **1.** (*a*) Rapace, pillard,
(*b*) *P. animals,* bêtes de proie. **2.** *P. habits,*
habitudes de pillage, de rapine.
predecease¹ [pri:di'si:s], *s.* Prédécès *m.*
predecease², *v.tr.* Mourir avant (qn).
predecessor ['pri:disesər], *s.* **1.** Prédécesseur *m* ;
devancier, -ière. **2.** Ancêtre *m.*
predestinate [pri'destineit], *v.tr.* Prédestiner
(*to,* à).
predestination [pridesti'neiʃ(ə)n], *s.* Prédestination *f* (*to,* à).
predestine [pri'destin], *v.tr.* Destiner d'avance
(*to,* à) ; *Theol:* prédestiner (qn).
predetermination [pri:ditə:rmi'neiʃ(ə)n], *s.*
1. Détermination prise d'avance. **2.** *Theol:*
Prédétermination *f.*
predetermine [pri:di'tə:rmin], *v.tr.* **1.** Déterminer, arrêter, d'avance. **2.** *Theol: Phil:*
Prédéterminer ; préordonner.
▸**predicable** ['predikəbl]. *Log:* **1.** *a.* Prédicable.
2. *s.* Catégorème *m.* **The five predicables,** les
universaux *m.*
predicament [pri'dikəmənt], *s.* **1.** *Phil: Log:*
Prédicament *m,* catégorie *f.* **2.** Situation difficile,
fâcheuse. *To be in an awkward p.,* être en
mauvaise passe. *Iron:* **We're in a fine predicament!** nous voilà dans de beaux draps ! nous
voilà propres !
predicant ['predikənt], *a.* (Frère) prêcheur.
predicate ['predikeit], *s.* **1.** *Log:* Prédicat *m.*
2. *Gram:* Attribut *m.*
predicative [pre'dikətiv], *a.* Affirmatif. *Gram:*

Log: Prédicatif. **Predicative adjective.** adjectif
attribut.
predict [pri'dikt], *v.tr.* Prédire.
prediction [pri'dikʃ(ə)n], *s.* Prédiction *f.*
predictive [pri'diktiv], *a.* Prophétique.
predictor [pri'diktər], *s.* Prophète, -étesse.
predilection [pri:di'lekʃ(ə)n], *s.* Prédilection *f*
(*for,* pour). **To have a predilection for sth.,**
affectionner, affecter, qch.
predispose [pri:dis'pouz], *v.tr.* Prédisposer
(*to,* à).
predisposition [pri:dispo'ziʃ(ə)n], *s.* Prédisposition *f* (*to,* à).
predominant [pri'dɔminənt], *a.* Prédominant.
predominate [pri'dɔmineit], *v.i.* **1.** Prédominer.
2. L'emporter par le nombre, par la quantité.
predominating, *a.* Prédominant.
pre-eminence [pri'eminəns], *s.* Prééminence *f.*
pre-eminent [pri'eminənt], *a.* (*a*) Prééminent.
(*b*) Remarquable (*in,* par). **-ly,** *adv.* (*a*) A un
degré prééminent. (*b*) Souverainement ; par
excellence.
pre-emption [pri'em(p)ʃ(ə)n], *s.* (Droit *m* de)
préemption *f.*
pre-emptive [pri'em(p)tiv], *a.* **1.** (Titre, etc.)
préemptif. **2.** *Cards:* **Pre-emptive bid,** ouverture
préventive.
preen [pri:n], *v.tr.* **1.** (*Of bird*) Lisser, nettoyer
(ses plumes). **2. To preen oneself,** (i) se bichonner ; (ii) prendre un air avantageux ; (*of
girl*) faire des grâces.
pre-established [pri:es'tabliʃt], *a.* Préétabli.
pre-existent [pri:eg'zistənt], *a.* Préexistant.
preface¹ ['prefes], *s.* **1.** Préface *f* ; avant-propos
m. inv. **2.** Introduction *f,* préambule *m* (d'un
discours). **3.** *Ecc:* Préface.
preface², *v.tr.* **1.** Écrire une préface pour (un
ouvrage) ; préfacer (un ouvrage). **2.** Préluder à
(un discours).
prefatory ['prefətəri], *a.* Préliminaire.
prefect ['pri:fekt], *s.* *Rom.Ant: Fr.Adm:* Préfet *m.*
prefectorial [pri:fek'tɔ:riəl], **prefectoral** [pri-
'fektərəl], *a.* Préfectoral, -aux.
prefecture [pri:fektjər], *s.* *Rom.Ant: Fr.Adm:*
Préfecture *f.*
prefer [pri'fə:r], *v.tr.* (**preferred**) **1.** Nommer,
élever (qn à une dignité). **2.** *To p. a complaint,*
déposer une plainte, porter plainte (*against,*
contre). **3. To prefer sth. to sth.,** préférer qch.
à qch. *I p. meat well done,* je préfère la viande
bien cuite. *I would p. to go without,* j'aimerais
mieux m'en passer. **Preferred stock** = **preference
stock,** *q.v. under* PREFERENCE 3.
preferable ['prefərəbl], *a.* Préférable (*to,* à).
-ably, *adv.* Préférablement, par préférence
(*to,* à).
preference ['prefərəns], *s.* **1.** Préférence *f* (*for,*
pour). **In preference,** préférablement (*to,* à).
To give sth. preference, donner, accorder, la
préférence à qch. (*over,* sur). **2.** *Pol.Ec:* Tarif *m*
de faveur. **3.** *Fin:* **Preference stock,** actions
privilégiées ; actions de priorité.
preferential [prefə'renʃ(ə)l], *a.* (Traitement,
etc.) préférentiel ; (tarif) de faveur ; (créancier)
privilégié.
preferment [pri'fə:rmənt], *s.* Avancement *m* ;
promotion *f.*
prefix¹ ['pri:fiks], *s.* **1.** *Gram:* Préfixe *m.*
2. Titre *m* (précédant un nom propre).
prefix² [pri'fiks], *v.tr.* **1.** Mettre (qch.) comme
introduction (à un livre). **2.** *Gram:* Préfixer (une
particule à un mot). **prefixed,** *a.* (Particule)
préfixe.
pregnancy ['pregnənsi], *s.* **1.** Grossesse *f* ; (*of*

animal) gestation *f*. **2**. Richesse *f* de sens (d'un mot) ; grande portée (d'un événement).

pregnant ['pregnant], *a*. **I**. (*a*) (Femme) enceinte, grosse. (*b*) (*Of cow, etc*.) Pleine, gravide. **2**. Pregnant with consequences, gros de conséquences.

prehensile [pri'hensail], *a*. Préhensile.

prehistoric [pri:his'torik], *a*. Préhistorique.

prehistory [pri:'histori], *s*. Préhistoire *f*.

pre-ignition [pri:ig'niʃ(ə)n], *s*. *I.C.E:* Allumage prématuré ; auto-allumage *m*.

prejudge [pri:'dʒʌdʒ], *v.tr.* **I**. Préjuger (une question). **2**. Condamner (qn) d'avance.

prejudice¹ ['predʒudis], *s*. **I**. Préjudice *m*, tort *m*, dommage *m*. *Jur:* Without prejudice (to my rights), réservation faite de tous mes droits. (*In correspondence, etc.*) 'Without prejudice,' "sous toutes réserves." To the prejudice of . . ., au préjudice de. . . . **2**. Préjugé *m*, prévention *f*, préconception *f*. To have a prejudice against sth., être prévenu contre qch.

prejudice², *v.tr.* **I**. Nuire, porter préjudice, préjudicier, à (une réputation, etc.). **2**. Prévenir, prédisposer (*s.o. against s.o.*, qn contre qn).

prejudiced, *a*. (i) Prévenu (*against*, contre) ; (ii) à préjugés, à préventions. To be p., avoir des préjugés, des préventions.

prejudicial [predʒu'diʃ(ə)l], *a*. Préjudiciable, nuisible (*to*, à).

prelacy ['preləsi], *s*. (*a*) Prélature *f*, épiscopat *m*. (*b*) *Coll.* The prelacy, les prélats *m* ; l'épiscopat.

prelate ['prelet], *s*. Prélat *m*.

preliminary [pri'liminəri]. **I**. *a*. Préliminaire, préalable. *After a few p. remarks*, après quelques avant-propos. *Sch:* Preliminary examination, *s*. *F:* prelim, examen *m* préliminaire. *Jur:* Preliminary investigation, instruction *f* (d'une affaire). *Typ:* Preliminary matter, feuilles *f* liminaires. **2**. *s*. (*a*) Prélude *m* (à une conversation, etc.). By way of preliminary, à titre de mesure préalable. (*b*) *pl.* Preliminaries, préliminaires *m* (d'un traité, etc.). **-ily**, *adv*. (*a*) Préliminairement. (*b*) Préalablement ; au préalable.

prelude¹ ['prelju:d], *s*. **I**. Prélude *m* (*to*, de). **2**. *Mus:* Prélude.

prelude². **I**. *v.i. Mus: etc:* (*a*) Préluder. (*b*) Servir d'introduction, préluder (*to*, à). **2**. *v.tr.* (*a*) Faire présager (un événement, etc.). (*b*) Précéder.

premature ['prematjuər, pri:mə'tjuər], *a*. Prématuré. **-ly**, *adv*. Prématurément ; *Obst:* avant terme.

premeditate [pri'mediteit], *v.tr.* Préméditer. **premeditated**, *a*. Prémédité ; (crime) réfléchi. P. insolence, insolence calculée.

premeditation [primedi'teiʃ(ə)n], *s*. Préméditation *f*.

premier ['premjər, 'pri:miər]. **I**. *a*. Premier (en rang, en importance). **2**. *s*. Premier ministre ; (*in France*) président *m* du conseil des ministres.

premise¹ ['premis], *s*. **I**. *Log:* Prémisse *f*. **2**, *pl.* The premises, le local, les locaux ; l'immeuble *m*. On the premises, sur les lieux.

premise² [pri'maiz], *v.tr.* **I**. (*a*) *Log:* Poser en prémisse (*that*, que + *ind*.). (*b*) Poser en principe (*that*, que). **2**. Faire remarquer, citer, (qch.) en guise d'introduction.

premium ['pri:miəm], *s*. **I**. Pr x *m*, récompense *f*. To put a premium on laziness, donner une prime à la paresse. **2**. (*a*) Prix convenu, indemnité *f* (pour l'apprentissage d'une profession libérale). (*b*) Insurance premium, prime d'assurance. (*c*) Droit *m*, redevance *f* (à payer au début

d'un bail). **3**. *Fin:* (*a*) (Exchange) premium agio *m* ; prix du change. (*b*) Prime. Premium on redemption, prime de remboursement. Premium bonds, obligations à primes. To sell at a premium, vendre à prime. (*Of stock, F:* of dishonesty, etc.) To be at a premium, faire prime.

premonition [pri:mo'niʃ(ə)n], *s*. Prémonition *f*, pressentiment *m* (de malheur, etc.).

premonitory [pri'monitəri], *a*. Prémonitoire (signe) avant-coureur ; (indice) précurseur.

prenatal [pri:'neit(ə)l], *a*. Prénatal, -als, -aux.

prentice ['prentis]. **I**. *s*. *A:* = APPRENTICE¹. **2**. *Attrib.* Prentice hand, main de novice ; main inexpérimentée.

preoccupation [priokju'peiʃ(ə)n], *s*. (*a*) Préoccupation *f* (de l'esprit). (*b*) *My greatest p.*, ma plus grande préoccupation ; mon premier souci.

preoccupy [pri'okjupai], *v.tr.* Préoccuper, absorber (l'esprit). **preoccupied**, *a*. Préoccupé, absorbé (par un souci).

pre-ordain [pri:ɔːr'dein], *v.tr.* **I**. Ordonner, régler, d'avance. **2**. Préordonner, prédéterminer.

prep [prep], *s*. *Sch: F:* Étude *f* (du soir). Prep room, salle d'étude.

prepaid [pri'peid], *a*. *See* PREPAY.

preparation [prepə'reiʃ(ə)n], *s*. **I**. Préparation *f*. To do sth. without any preparation, faire qch sans apprêts, sans s'y être préparé, sans aucun préparatif. **2**. *Usu.pl.* Préparations *mpl*, apprêts *mpl*. To make (one's) preparations for sth., prendre ses dispositions, faire des préparatifs, en vue de qch. **3**. *Sch:* Étude *f* (du soir). **4**. Pharmaceutical preparation, préparation pharmaceutique.

preparative [pri'parətiv]. **I**. *a*. Préparatoire. **2**. *s.pl.* Preparatives, préparatifs *m*.

preparatory [pri'parətəri]. **I**. *a*. Préparatoire, préalable (*to*, à). Preparatory school, école préparatoire (aux grandes écoles secondaires). **2**. *adv*. Préalablement (*to*, à).

prepare [pri'pɛər]. **I**. *v.tr.* Préparer (un repas, etc.) ; accommoder, confectionner (un mets) ; apprêter (le cuir, etc.). To p. *s.o. for a piece of bad news*, préparer qn à une mauvaise nouvelle. To p. a surprise for s.o., ménager une surprise à qn. To p. the way for negotiations, amorcer des négociations. *Great events are preparing*, de grands événements se préparent. **2**. *v.i.* Se préparer, se disposer, s'apprêter (*for sth.*, to do sth., à qch., à faire qch.). To p. for departure, faire ses préparatifs de départ. To p. for an examination, préparer un examen. **prepared**, *a*. To be p. for anything, être prêt, s'attendre, à toute éventualité. Be p. to be coolly received, attendez-vous à être mal accueilli. (*Scouting*) Be prepared, soyez toujours sur le qui-vive.

preparer [pri'pɛərər], *s*. Préparateur, -trice.

prepay [pri:'pei], *v.tr.* (*p.t. & p.p.* prepaid) Payer (qch.) d'avance ; affranchir (une lettre, etc.). *Tg:* 'Answer prepaid,' "réponse payée."

prepayment [pri:'peimənt], *s*. Paiement *m* d'avance ; affranchissement *m* (d'une lettre).

prepense [pri'pens], *a*. *Jur:* Prémédité. *S.a.* MALICE 2.

preponderance [pri'pondərəns], *s*. Prépondérance *f* (*over*, sur).

preponderant [pri'pondərənt], *a*. Prépondérant.

preponderate [pri'pondəreit], *v.i.* Peser davantage ; emporter la balance, l'emporter (*over*, sur). **preponderating**, *a*. Prépondérant.

preposition [prepo'ziʃ(ə)n], *s*. Préposition *f*.

prepositional [prepo'ziʃən(ə)l], *a*. Prépositionnel, prépositif.

prepossess [pri:po'zes], *v.tr.* **I**. To p. *s.o. with* an idea, pénétrer qn d'une idée. **2.** (*Of idea, etc.*) Accaparer, posséder (qn) ; prendre possession de l'esprit de (qn). **3.** Prévenir (*in favour of*, en faveur de). **prepossessed,** *a.* **I.** Imbu, imprégné (*with*, de) ; pénétré (d'une opinion, etc.). **2.** Prévenu (contre qn). **prepossessing,** *a.* (Visage) agréable, prévenant. **Of prepossessing appearance,** de bonne mine. **-ly,** *adv.* D'une manière prévenante, attrayante, engageante.

prepossession [pri:pɔ'zeʃ(ə)n], *s.* Prévention *f* ; préjugé *m.*

preposterous [pri'pɔstərəs], *a.* Contraire au bon sens ; absurde.

preposterousness [pri'pɔstərəsnəs], *s.* Absurdité *f.*

prepotency [pri'poutənsi], *s.* **I.** Prédominance *f.* **2.** *Biol :* Prépotence *f.*

prepotent [pri'poutənt], *a.* **I.** Prédominant. **2.** *Biol :* (Caractère) dominant.

prepuce ['pri:pju:s], *s.* *Anat :* Prépuce *m.*

prerequisite [pri'rekwizit]. **I.** *a.* Nécessaire au préalable. **2.** *s.* Nécessité *f* préalable.

prerogative [pri'rɔgətiv], *s.* Prérogative *f*, privilège *m*, apanage *m.* *To exercise the royal p.,* faire acte de souverain.

presage[1] ['presedʒ], *s.* (*a*) Présage *m.* (*b*) Pressentiment *m.*

presage[2] ['presedʒ, pri'seidʒ], *v.tr.* (*a*) (*Of omen, etc.*) Présager, annoncer (une catastrophe, etc.). (*b*) (*Of pers.*) Augurer, prédire (qch.). **To presage sth. from sth.,** augurer qch. de qch.

presbyopia [prezbi'oupiə], *s.* *Med :* Presbytie *f.*

Presbyterian [prezbi'ti:əriən], *a. & s.* *Rel.H :* Presbytérien, -ienne.

presbytery ['prezbitəri], *s.* **I.** *Ecc.Arch :* Sanctuaire *m*, chœur *m.* **2.** *R.C.Ch :* Presbytère *m*, cure *f.* **3.** *Presbyterian Ch :* Consistoire *m.*

prescience ['preʃjəns], *s.* Prescience *f.*

prescient ['preʃjənt], *a.* Prescient.

prescribe [pri'skraib], *v.tr.* (*a*) Prescrire, ordonner. **Prescribed task,** tâche imposée. **In the prescribed time,** dans le délai prescrit. (*b*) *Med :* **To prescribe sth. for s.o.,** prescrire, ordonner, qch. à qn. *Abs.* **To prescribe for s.o.,** (i) indiquer un traitement pour qn ; (ii) rédiger une ordonnance pour qn.

prescription [pri'skripʃ(ə)n], *s.* Prescription *f.* **I.** (*a*) Ordre *m*, précepte *m.* (*b*) *Med :* Ordonnance *f.* **To write (out), make out, a prescription for s.o.,** rédiger une ordonnance pour qn. **2.** *Jur :* Positive prescription, acquisitive prescription, prescription acquisitive.

prescriptive [pri'skriptiv], *a.* Consacré par l'usage.

presence ['prez(ə)ns], *s.* Présence *f.* **I.** (*a*) **Your presence is requested at . . .,** (i) vous êtes prié d'assister à . . . ; (ii) *Adm :* vous êtes convoqué à. . . . **In the presence of,** en présence de. . . . (*b*) **To be admitted to the Presence,** être admis en présence du roi, etc. *F :* **Saving your presence,** sauf votre respect. **2. Presence of mind,** présence d'esprit. *To retain one's p. of mind,* conserver sa tête, son sang-froid. **3.** (*Of pers.*) Air *m*, mine *f*, extérieur *m*, maintien *m.* **To have a good presence,** avoir du maintien, une certaine prestance. *He is lacking in personal p.,* il ne représente pas bien ; il manque de prestance. **'presence-chamber,** *s.* Salle d'audience ; salle du trône.

present[1] ['prez(ə)nt]. **I.** *a.* **I.** *Usu.pred.* Présent (et non absent). **To be present at a ceremony,** être présent, assister, à une cérémonie. *All p.* *heard it,* toute l'assistance l'a entendu. *Nobody else was p.,* nul autre n'était là. *S.a.* COMPANY[1] 2. **2.** (*a*) Actuel. **Present fashions,** modes actuelles,

d'aujourd'hui. **Present year,** année courante. **At the present time,** à présent ; (i) en ce moment ; (ii) à l'époque actuelle ; aujourd'hui. **Present worth, present value,** valeur actuelle. (*b*) En question ; que voici. **The present writer,** l'auteur (c.-à-d. moi). *Com :* **On receipt of the present letter,** au reçu de la présente. (*c*) *Gram :* **The present tense,** *s.* **the present,** le (temps) présent. **In the present,** au présent. **-ly,** *adv.* (*Future*) Tout à l'heure ; bientôt ; dans un instant ; tout de suite. **II. present,** *s.* **I. The present,** le présent ; le temps présent. **Up to the present,** jusqu'à présent. **At present,** à présent ; actuellement. *As things are at p.,* (i) au point où en sont les choses ; (ii) par le temps qui court. **The present,** pour le moment. **2.** *Jur :* **Know all men by these presents that . . .,** savoir faisons par ces présentes que. . . . **'present-day,** *attrib.a.* Actuel ; d'aujourd'hui.

present[2], *s.* Don *m*, cadeau *m*, présent *m.* **To make s.o. a present of sth.,** faire présent, faire cadeau de qch. à qn ; offrir qch. à qn.

present[3] [pri'zent], *v.tr.* Présenter. **I.** (*a*) **To present s.o. to s.o.,** présenter qn à qn. **To present s.o. at court,** présenter qn à la cour. *Th :* **To present a play,** présenter, donner, une pièce. **To present oneself at, for, an examination,** se présenter à, pour, un examen. (*b*) **To present a fine spectacle to the oyes,** présenter, offrir, aux yeux un beau spectacle. **Affair that presents some difficulty,** affaire qui présente des difficultés. **A good opportunity presents itself** (*for doing sth.*), une bonne occasion se présente (de faire qch.). (*c*) **To present a pistol at s.o.'s head,** présenter un pistolet à la tête de qn. **2.** (*a*) **To present sth. to s.o.;** to present s.o. with sth., donner qch. à qn ; faire présent, faire cadeau, de qch. à qn. (*b*) **To present one's compliments to s.o.,** présenter ses compliments à qn. **3.** (*a*) *Com :* **To present a bill for payment,** présenter un billet à l'encaissement. (*b*) *Parl :* **To present a bill,** présenter, introduire, un projet de loi. **4.** *To p. a plan to a meeting,* soumettre un plan à une assemblée. **5.** *Mil :* **To present arms,** présenter les armes.

presentable [pri'zentəbl], *a.* ⟨*Of pers.*⟩ Présentable ; (*of garment*) portable.

presentation [prez(ə)n'teiʃ(ə)n], *s.* **I.** (*a*) Présentation *f* (d'une personne à la cour, etc.). (*b*) Présentation (de qn à un poste, *Ecc :* à un bénéfice). (*c*) Présentation, représentation *f* (d'une pièce à la scène). (*d*) *Com :* **Payable on presentation of the coupon,** payable contre remise du coupon. **2.** (*a*) Remise *f*, présentation (d'un cadeau à qn). (*b*) Souvenir (offert à un fonctionnaire, etc.). **presen'tation-copy,** *s.* (*a*) Exemplaire envoyé gracieusement, à titre gracieux ; spécimen (gratuit). (*b*) Exemplaire offert à titre d'hommage (par l'auteur).

presentient [pri'senʃjənt], *a.* Qui a un pressentiment (*of*, de).

presentiment [pri'zentimənt], *s.* Pressentiment *m.*

preservation [prezər'veiʃ(ə)n], *s.* **I.** Conservation *f* ; naturalisation *f* (d'une fleur). **In a state of good preservation, in a good state of preservation,** en bon état de conservation. **2.** Préservation *f* (*from*, de).

preservative [pri'zə:rvətiv]. **I.** *a.* Préservatif. **2.** *s.* (*a*) Préservatif *m* (contre un danger, etc.). (*b*) Antiseptique *m* ; agent *m* de conservation.

preserve[1] [pri'zə:rv], *s.* **I.** Confiture *f.* **2.** (*a*) *For :* Réserve *f.* (*b*) **Game preserve,** chasse

gardée. **Salmon preserve**, vivier *m* à saumons.
3. *pl.* Lunettes protectrices ; conserves *f.*
preserve[2], *v.tr.* **1.** Préserver, garantir (*from*, de). **2.** (*a*) Conserver (un bâtiment, etc.) ; maintenir (la paix) ; garder, observer (le silence). **To preserve appearances**, sauver les apparences, les dehors. (*b*) Conserver, mettre en conserve (des fruits, etc.) ; confire (des fruits). (*c*) Naturaliser (un spécimen botanique). **3.** (*a*) Élever (du gibier) dans une réserve. (*b*) Garder (une chasse). **preserved**, *a.* **1.** Conservé ; (*of fruit*) confit. **Preserved food**, conserves *fpl.* **Preserved meat**, conserve de viande. **2. Well preserved**, badly **preserved**, (bâtiment, etc.) en bon, mauvais, état de conservation. **pre'serving-pan**, *s.* Bassine *f* à confitures.
preserver [pri'zɔːrvər], *s.* **1.** (*Pers.*) Préservateur, -trice (*from*, de) ; sauveur *m.* **2.** *See* DRESS-PRESERVER, LIFE-PRESERVER.
preside [pri'zaid], *v.i.* Présider. (*a*) **To preside at, over, a meeting**, présider (à) une réunion. **To preside at the organ**, tenir l'orgue. (*b*) *Abs.* Exercer les fonctions de président ; occupe le fauteuil présidentiel ; présider (à table, etc.).
presidency ['prezidənsi], *s.* Présidence *f.*
president ['prezidənt], *s.* Président, -ente. **President of the Board of Trade** = Ministre *m* du Commerce.
presidential [prezi'denʃ(ə)l], *a.* Président.el.
press[1] [pres], *s.* **1.** (*a*) Pression *f* (sur qch.) ; serrement *m* (de main). (*b*) **Press of business**, presse *f*, urgence *f*, des affaires. (*c*) *A :* Presse, foule *f.* **To force one's way through the press**, fendre la foule. **In the press of the fight**, dans la mêlée. (*d*) *Nau :* **To carry a press of sail**, faire force de voiles. **2.** Presse. (*a*) **Letter-press, copying-press**, presse à copier. **Ten :** Racket press, presse à raquette. (*b*) **Hydraulic press**, presse hydraulique. *S.a.* FLY-PRESS, MINTING-PRESS, *etc.* (*c*) Linen-press, armoire *f* à linge. **3.** *Typ :* (*a*) **Printing-press**, presse d'imprimerie, à imprimer. **Rotary press**, presse rotative. (*b*) Imprimerie *f.* (*c*) *In time for p.*, à temps pour l'impression. **We are going to press**, nous mettons sous presse. **Ready for press**, prêt à mettre sous presse. **To pass a proof for press**, donner le bon à tirer. **In the press**, at press, sur le marbre ; sous presse. (*d*) La presse, les journaux *m.* **Liberty of the press**, liberté de la presse. (*Of book*) **To have a good press**, avoir une bonne presse. **Press photographer**, photographe de la presse. **'press-box**, *s. Sp :* Stand *m* de la presse. **'press-button**, *s.* **1.** Bouton *m* à pression ; bouton fermoir (de gant). **2.** = PUSH-BUTTON I. **'press-copy**, *s. Publ :* Exemplaire *m* de publicité. **'press-cutting**, *s.* Coupure *f* de journal, de presse. **'press-forged**, *a.* *Metalw :* Embouti. **'press-gallery**, *s.* Tribune *f* de la presse, des journalistes (à la Chambre, etc.). **'press-proof**, *s. Typ :* Épreuve *f* en bon à tirer. **'press-stud**, *s.* Bouton *m* (à) pression.
press[2]. **I.** *v.tr.* Presser. **1.** (*a*) Appuyer, peser, sur (qch.). **Press the button**, appuyez sur le bouton. **His face pressed close to the window**, son visage collé à la vitre. (*b*) Serrer. **To press s.o. to one's heart**, presser, serrer, qn sur son cœur. **To press the juice from, out of, a lemon**, exprimer le jus d'un citron. **2.** (*a*) *Tchn :* Mettre (qch.) sous presse ; emboutir (le métal) ; satiner, calandrer (le papier). (*b*) Pressurer (des pommes, etc.). (*c*) *Tail :* **To press a suit**, donner un coup de fer à un complet. **3.** (*a*) **To press the enemy hard**, serrer l'ennemi de près. *F :* **To press s.o. hard**, mettre qn aux abois. **Pressed by one's**

creditors, pressé, harcelé, par ses créanciers (*b*) **To press s.o. to do sth.**, presser qn de faire qch. **He did not need too much pressing**, il ne se fit pas trop prier. **To press for an answer**, insister pour avoir une réponse immédiate. (*c*) **To press a point, a claim**, insister sur un point, sur une demande. **To press one's advantage**, poursuivre son avantage. (*d*) **To press a gift on s.o.**, forcer qn à accepter un cadeau. **4.** *Abs.* **Time presses**, le temps presse. **II. press**, *v.i.* **1.** (*a*) Se serrer, se presser. **To press close against s.o.**, se serrer contre qn. (*b*) **To press on one's pen**, appuyer sur sa plume. **2. His responsibilities press heavily upon him**, ses responsabilités lui pèsent. **press down**, *v.tr.* (*a*) *Aut :* **To press the pedal down**, enfoncer la pédale. (*b*) **To press down a seam**, rabattre une couture. **press forward, press on. 1.** *v.i.* Presser, forcer, le pas ; brûler une étape. **2.** *v.tr.* Activer, hâter (le travail). **pressed**, *a.* **1.** (*a*) Pressé, serré, comprimé. **Pressed hay**, foin en balles. (*b*) *Metalw :* Embouti. **2. To be hard pressed**, (i) être serré de près ; (ii) être aux abois, à la dernière extrémité. **Pressed for space**, à court de place. **Pressed for time**, très pressé ; à court de temps. **We are very pressed**, nous sommes débordés (de commandes).
pressing[1], *a.* (Danger) pressant ; (travail) pressé, urgent. **The case is pressing**, il y a urgence. **Pressing invitation**, invitation instante. *Since you are so p. . . .*, puisque vous insistez. . . . **pressing**[2], *s.* **1.** (*a*) Pression *f* (sur qch.) ; pressurage *m* (des raisins) ; calandrage *m* (du papier, etc.). *Metalw :* Emboutissage *m.* **Pressing machine**, presse *f.* (*b*) *Tail :* Coup *m* de fer tailleur. **2.** (*a*) *Metalw :* Pièce emboutie. (*b*) *Usu. pl.* Pressing(s), pressée *f*, pressis *m* (de pommes, etc.) ; `uc exprimé.
press[3], *s.* *A :* Presse *f* (de matelots) ; enrôlement forcé. **'press-gang**, *s.* (Détachement *m* de la) presse.
press[4], *v.tr.* (*a*) *A :* Enrôler de force (un matelot). (*b*) *F :* **To press into service**, enrôler, faire appel à (qn) ; réquisitionner (qch.).
pressman, *pl.* **-men** ['presmən, -men], *s.m.* **1.** *Typ :* Pressier. **2.** Journaliste.
pressure ['preʃər], *s.* **1.** (*a*) *Ph : Mec :* Pression *f* ; poussée *f* (d'une charge, etc.). **High pressure**, haute pression. **P. of ten lbs to the square inch**, pression de dix livres par pouce carré ; pression de 06,8 atmosphères. **Water pressure**, poussée de l'eau ; charge *f* d'eau. *Aut :* **Table of tyre pressures**, tableau *m* de gonflages. *Mch :* **Test-pressure**, surcharge *f* d'épreuve ; timbre *m.* **At full pressure**, toute pression. (*b*) *El.E :* Tension *f* ; potentiel *m.* **Working p.**, tension de régime. (*c*) *Med :* **Blood pressure**, tension artérielle (du sang). **High blood pressure**, hypertension (artérielle). **2. To bring pressure to bear on s.o.**, exercer une pression sur qn ; agir sur, influencer, qn. **Under the pressure of necessity**, poussé par la nécessité. **To act under pressure**, agir par contrainte. **Pressure of business**, presse *f*, urgence *f*, des affaires. **To work at high pressure**, travailler fiévreusement. **'pressure-cooker**, *s.* *Cu :* Autoclave *m.* **'pressure-feed**, *s.* *Mec.E :* Alimentation *f* sous pression. **'pressure-gauge**, *s.* *Mch :* Manomètre *m* ; jauge *f* de pression. **Steam pressure-gauge**, manomètre à vapeur. *Aut :* **Tyre pressure-gauge**, contrôleur *m* de pression.
prestige [pres'tiːʒ], *s.* Prestige *m.* *It would mean loss of p.*, ce serait déchoir, déroger.
presto ['presto], *int.* Hey presto! passez muscade !

resumable [pri'zju:məbl], *a.* Présumable (*of s.o.*, de la part de qn). **-ably,** *adv.* Probablement. *P. he will come,* il est à croire qu'il viendra.

resume [pri'zju:m]. **1.** *v.tr.* (*a*) Présumer. *To p. s.o.* (*to be*) *innocent,* présumer qn innocent, que qn est innocent. **I presume that . . . ,** j'aime à croire que + *ind. You are Mr X,* I presume, vous êtes M. X, je suppose. (*b*) **To presume to do sth.,** prendre la liberté, présumer, de faire qch. *May I p. to advise you?* puis-je me permettre de vous conseiller? **2.** *v.i.* (*a*) **To presume too much,** trop présumer de soi. (*b*) *Abs.* Se montrer présomptueux. (*c*) **To presume on s.o.'s friendship,** abuser de l'amitié de qn. *To p. on one's birth,* se prévaloir de sa naissance. **presuming,** *a.* (*a*) Présomptueux. (*b*) Indiscret, -ète.

presumption [pri'zʌm(p)ʃ(ə)n], *s.* **1.** Présomption *f. The p. is that he is dead,* on présume, il est à présumer, qu'il est mort. **2.** Présomption, arrogance *f. Pardon my p.,* excusez mon audace.

presumptive [pri'zʌm(p)tiv], *a.* Presumptive evidence, preuve *f* par présomption ; présomption *f. M.Ins: The ship is a* **presumptive loss,** il y a présomption de perte.

presumptuous [pri'zʌm(p)tjuəs], *a.* Présomptueux, outrecuidant.

presumptuousness [pri'zʌm(p)tjuəsnəs], *s.* Présomption *f,* outrecuidance *f.*

presuppose [pri:sʌ'po:uz], *v.tr.* Présupposer.

pretence [pri'tens], *s.* **1.** (Faux) semblant ; simulation *f* ; prétexte *m.* **To make a pretence of doing sth.,** faire semblant de faire qch. *Under tho pretence of friendship,* sous prétexte, sous couleur, d'amitié. *Under, on, the p. of consulting me,* sous prétexte de me consulter. *Jur:* **To obtain sth. by, on, under, false pretences,** obtenir qch. par fraude *f,* par des moyens frauduleux. **2.** (*a*) Prétention *f,* vanité *f.* (*b*) *He makes no p. to wit,* il n'a aucune prétention à l'esprit.

pretend [pri'tend]. **1.** *v.tr.* (*a*) Feindre, simuler (qch.). **To pretend ignorance,** simuler l'ignorance ; faire l'ignorant. **To pretend to do sth.,** faire semblant, feindre, de faire qch. **Let's pretend we are kings and queens,** jouons au roi et à la reine. (*b*) Prétendre. *He does not pretend to be artistic,* il ne prétend pas être artiste. *I can't p. to advise you,* je n'ai pas la prétention de vous conseiller. **2.** *v.ind.tr.* **To pretend to intelligence,** avoir des prétentions, prétendre, à l'intelligence.

pretender [pri'tendər], *s.* **1.** Simulateur, -trice. **2.** Prétendant *m* (*to,* à). *Hist:* **The Young Pretender,** le Jeune Prétendant (Charles Stuart).

pretension [pri'tenʃ(ə)n], *s.* **1.** Prétention *f* (*to,* à). *To have no pretensions to the first rank,* n'avoir aucune prétention au premier rang. **Man of no pretension(s),** homme sans prétentions. **To have pretensions to literary taste,** se piquer de littérature. **2.** Droit *m,* titre *m. To have some pretensions to be considered a scholar,* revendiquer à bon droit le titre d'érudit.

pretentious [pri'tenʃəs], *a.* Prétentieux. **-ly,** *adv.* Prétentieusement.

pretentiousness [pri'tenʃəsnəs], *s.* Prétention *f* ; air prétentieux.

preterit(e) ['pretərit], *a. & s. Gram:* Preterite (tense), (temps) passé (*m*) ; prétérit *m.* **In the preterite,** au passé, au prétérit.

pretermission [pri:tər'miʃ(ə)n], *s.* **1.** Omission *f.* **2.** Interruption *f,* suspension *f,* cessation momentanée.

preternatural [pri:tər'natjurəl], *a.* Qui est en dehors de la nature ; surnaturel.

pretext¹ ['pri:tekst], *s.* Prétexte *m. To find a p. for refusing,* trouver prétexte à un refus. **Under,**

on, the pretext of *consulting me,* sous prétexte de me consulter.

pretext² [pri'tekst], *v.tr.* Alléguer (qch.) comme prétexte ; prétexter (qch.).

prettify ['pritifai], *v.tr.* Enjoliver.

prettiness ['pritinəs], *s.* (*a*) Gentillesse *f.* (*b*) Afféterie *f,* mignardise *f* (de style, etc.).

pretty ['priti]. **1.** *a.* (*a*) Joli ; beau, *f.* belle ; (*of manner, etc.*) gentil, -ille. **Sweetly pretty, pretty as a picture,** jolie comme un cœur ; gentille, jolie, à croquer. **My pretty (one),** ma mignonne. (*b*) *Iron:* **This s a pretty state of affairs!** (i) c'est du joli ! c'est du propre ! (ii) nous voilà dans de beaux draps ! *I have heard some p. tales about you,* j'en ai entendu de belles sur votre compte. **2.** *adv.* Assez, passablement. **I am pretty well,** cela ne va pas trop mal. **Pretty much the same,** à peu près la même chose. **New or p. nearly so,** neuf ou à peu de chose près. **-ily,** *adv.* Joliment ; gentiment. *To eat p.,* manger avec délicatesse. **'pretty-pretty,** *a* Affété, mignard.

prevail [pri'veil], *v.i.* **1.** To l revail over, against, s.o., prévaloir sur, contre, qn ; avoir l'avantage, l'emporter, sur qn. *The strong hand of the law prevailed,* force est restée à la loi. **2.** To prevail (up)on s.o. to do sth., amener, déterminer, décider, qn à faire qch. ; obtenir de qn qu'il fasse qch. *He was prevailed upon by his friends to . . . ,* il se laissa persuader par ses amis de. . . . **3.** Prédominer, régner. *Calm prevails,* le calme règne. *The conditions prevailing in France,* les conditions qui règnent en France. **prevailing,** *a.* Prevailing winds, vents régnants, dominants. *P. fashion,* mode en vogue. *P. opinion,* opinion prédominante, courante. *The p. cold,* le froid qui sévit en ce moment.

prevalence ['prevələns], *s.* Prédominance *f. P. of bribery,* généralité *f* de la corruption.

prevalent ['prevələnt], *a.* (Pré)dominant, répandu, général. *Disease that is p. in a place,* maladie qui est très répandue dans un lieu.

prevaricate [pri'varikeit], *v.i.* **1.** Équivoquer, biaiser, tergiverser. **2.** Mentir ; altérer la vérité.

prevarication [privari'keiʃ(ə)n], *s.* **1.** Équivoques *fpl* ; tergiversation *f.* **2.** Mensonge *m.*

prevent [pri'vent], *v.tr.* **1.** Empêcher, mettre obstacle à (qch.). **To prevent s.o. (from) doing sth.,** empêcher qn de faire qch. To be unavoidably prevented from doing sth., être dans l'impossibilité matérielle de faire qch. *F:* **That does not prevent her from being respectable,** cela n'empêche pas qu'elle soit honnête. **2.** (*a*) Prévenir, détourner (un malheur) ; parer à (un accident). *To p. any scandal,* pour obvier à tout scandale. (*b*) *You must p.* the machine from stalling, il faut éviter que l'appareil ne s'engage.

prevention [pri'venʃ(ə)n], *s.* **1.** Empêchement *m, P. of accidents,* précautions *fpl* contre les accidents. *To take measures for the p. of disease,* prendre des mesures préventives contre la maladie. **Rust prevention,** protection *f* contre la rouille.

preventive [pri'ventiv]. **1.** *a.* (*a*) (Médicament) préventif. *P. measure,* mesure imposée à titre préventif. (*b*) *Adm:* **The Preventive Service,** le Service des gardes-côtes (douaniers). **2.** *s.* (*a*) Empêchement *m* ; mesure préventive. (*b*) Médicament préventif. (*c*) Rust preventive, antirouille *m.*

preview [pri'vju:], *s.* Exhibition *f* préalable ; *Cin:* avant-première *f.*

previous ['pri:vjəs]. **1.** *a.* (*a*) Préalable ; antérieur, antécédent (*to,* à). *The p. day,* le jour précédent ; la veille. **Previous engagement,** engagement antérieur. *Parl:* **To move the**

previous question, demander la question préalable. (b) *U.S: F:* **You're a bi̇̇. (too) previous!** vous allez trop vite! **2.** *adv.* **Previous to** *my departure,* antérieurement à mon départ ; avant mon départ. **-ly,** *adv.* Préalablement, au préalable ; auparavant.

prevision [pri'viʒ(ə)n], *s.* Prévision *f.*

pre-war [pri:'wɔːr]. **1.** *attrib.a.* D'avant-guerre. **2.** *adv. For a long time pre-war,* pendant longtemps avant la guerre.

prey[1] [prei], *s.* Proie *f.* **Birds of prey,** oiseaux de proie. **To be ⌐ prey to sth.,** être en proie à, être dévoré, travaillé, par (la peur, etc.). **To fall a prey to temptation,** tomber en proie à la tentation.

prey[2], *v.i.* **To prey upon sth.,** faire sa proie de qch. *F:* **Something is preying on his mind,** il y a quelque chose qui le travaille. *Mind preyed upon by care,* esprit rongé, miné, par le souci.

price[1] [prais], *s.* (a) Prix *m.* **Cost price,** prix coûtant, prix de revient. **Cash price,** prix au comptant. **To pay top price,** payer la forte somme. **At a reduced price,** au rabais. (*Of goods*) **To advance, rise, in price,** renchérir. **One-price store,** magasin à prix unique. *What p. is that article?* quel est le prix de cet article? **His pictures fetch huge prices,** ses tableaux se vendent à prix d'or. **Beyond price,** without price, sans prix ; hors de prix. **You can buy it at a price,** vous pouvez l'acheter si vous y mettez le prix. *This must be done at any price,* il faut que cela se fasse à tout prix, coûte que coûte. **Not at any price,** pour rien au monde. **To set a high price on sth.,** faire grand cas de qch. **To set a price on s.o.'s head,** mettre à prix la tête de qn. (b) *Turf:* Cote *f.* **Long price, short price,** forte, faible, cote. *P:* **What price my new bike?** et ma nouvelle bécane, qu'est-ce que tu en dis? (c) **Issue price** *of shares,* taux *m* d'émission d'actions. *St.Exch:* **Market prices,** cours *m* du marché. **To make a price,** fixer un cours. **'price-list,** *s.* Prix-courant *m* ; bordereau *m* des prix ; tarif *m.*

price[2], *v.tr.* **1.** Mettre un prix à (qch.). *The book is priced at four shillings net,* le livre se vend au prix net de quatre shillings. **2.** Estimer, évaluer. **To price sth. high, low,** faire grand, peu de, cas de qch. **priced,** *a.* **1.** High-priced, de haut prix. **2.** *Everything in the window is p.,* à l'étalage tous les prix sont marqués.

priceless ['praisləs], *a.* (a) Hors de prix ; inestimable. (b) *P:* (*Of joke, pers.*) Impayable.

prick[1] [prik], *s.* **1.** Piqûre *f* (d'une aiguille, etc.). *F:* **Pricks of conscience,** remords *m* de conscience. **2.** *A:* Aiguillon *m. F:* **To kick against the pricks,** regimber. **'prick-eared,** *a.* **1.** (Chien) aux oreilles droites, pointues. **2.** (*Of pers.*) Aux oreilles dressées ; l'oreille aux aguets.

prick[2], *v.tr.* **1.** (a) Piquer ; faire une piqûre à (qch.). *To p. a blister,* crever, ponctionner, une ampoule. *F: His conscience pricks him,* sa conscience l'aiguillonne, le tourmente. (b) **To prick a hole in sth.,** faire un trou d'épingle dans qch. **To prick (off) a design on sth.,** piquer un dessin sur (une étoffe, etc.). **2. To prick (off) names on a list,** piquer, pointer, des noms sur une liste. *Nau:* **To prick a bearing** (*on the chart*), porter un relèvement sur la carte. **To prick the chart,** pointer la carte ; faire le point. **3.** *To p. one's horse with the spur,* appuyer l'éperon à son cheval ; (*lightly*) picoter son cheval. **prick out,** *v.tr. Hort:* Repiquer (des plants). **prick (up),** *v.tr.* **To prick (up) one's ears,** (i) (*of animal*) dresser les oreilles ; (ii) (*of pers.*) tendre, dresser, l'oreille. **With pricked ears,** l'oreille aux aguets.

pricking, *s.* **1.** (a) Piquage *m. Med:* Ponction (d'une ampoule). (b) Pointage *m* (d'une liste) *Nau:* de la carte). **2. Prickings of conscience** remords *mpl* (de conscience). **'pricking wheel,** *s.* Roulette *f* à piquer.

pricker ['prikər], *s. Tls:* (a) Poinçon *m,* pointe *f* nettoie-becs *m inv* (pour lanterne à acétylène) *Leath:* Tire-point *m. Metall: Mch:* Ringard *m* fourgon *m,* pique-feu *m inv.* (b) Tire-ligne *r* à pointiller.

pricket ['priket], *s.* **1.** *Ven:* Brocard *m* (d'ur an) ; daguet *m.* **2.** Broche *f* (de chandelier).

prickle[1] ['prikl], *s.* Piquant *m* (de plante, d'ani mal) ; épine *f,* aiguillon *m* (de plante).

prickle[2], *v.tr.* Piquer, picoter.

prickly ['prikli], *a.* **1.** (a) Hérissé ; armé de piquants ; épineux. *Bot:* **Prickly pear,** (i) figuier *m* de Barbarie ; raquette *f* ; (ii) figue *f* de Barbarie. (b) (*Of pers., question*) Épineux **2.** (Sensation) de picotement. *S.a.* HEAT[1] 3.

pride[1] [praid], *s.* **1.** Orgueil *m.* (a) Fierté *f* morgue *f.* **Puffed up with pride,** bouffi d'orgueil **False pride,** vanité *f.* **To take an empty pride ir sth.,** tirer vanité de qch. ; faire vanité de qch (b) **Proper pride,** orgueil légitime ; amour-propre *m.* **To take (a) pride in sth., in doing sth.,** êtr fier de qch. ; mettre son orgueil à faire qch **2. He is the pride of the family,** il fait l'orgueil de la famille. **3.** Comble *m,* apogée *m.* **May was ir its pride,** le mois de mai était dans toute sa splendeur. **In the pride of years,** à la fleur de l'âge.

pride[2], *v.pr.* **To pride oneself (up)on sth., (up)on doing sth.,** s'enorgueillir, se piquer, se vanter de qch., de faire qch.

priest [priːst], *s.m.* Prêtre. *The priests,* le c ergé. **Parish priest** = curé. **Priest in charge,** desservant (d'église succursale).

priestess ['priːstes], *s.f.* Prêtresse.

priesthood ['priːsthud], *s.* **1.** Prêtrise *f,* sacerdoce *m.* **To enter the priesthood,** se faire prêtre. **2.** *Coll.* **The priesthood,** le clergé.

priestly ['priːstli], *a.* Sacerdotal, -aux.

prig [prig], *s.* (a) Poseur *m* ; homme suffisant. **Don't be a prig!** *P:* ne fais pas ta poire! (b) Poseur à la vertu ; (*of boy*) petit saint de bois.

priggish ['prigiʃ], *a.* **1.** Poseur, suffisant. **2.** Collet monté *inv* ; bégueule.

priggishness ['prigiʃnəs], *s.* **1.** Pose *f,* suffisance *f* ; pédanterie *f.* **2.** Béguelerie *f.*

prim[1] [prim], *a.* (a) (*Of pers.*) Collet monté *inv* ; (*of manner*) guindé, compassé. *P. smile,* sourire pincé. (b) *P. garden,* jardin tracé au cordeau. **-ly,** *adv.* D'un air collet monté.

prim[2], *v.tr.* (primmed) **1. To prim (up) one's mouth,** *abs.* **to prim (up),** prendre un air pincé ; faire la bouche en cœur. **To prim oneself (up),** faire un brin de toilette.

primacy ['praiməsi]. *s.* **1.** Primauté *f.* **2.** *Ecc:* Primatie *f.*

primaeval [prai'miːv(ə)l], *a.* = PRIMEVAL.

prima facie [praimə'feiʃii], *adv. & a.* De prime abord, à première vue. *Jur:* **Prima facie case,** affaire qui d'après les premiers témoignages paraît bien fondée.

primary ['praiməri], *a.* **1.** Premier, primitif, originel. **Primary product,** produit de base. *Gram:* **Primary tenses,** temps primitifs. *P. colours,* couleurs primaires. **Primary education,** instruction primaire. *El:* **P. current,** courant primaire. **2.** Premier, principal, -aux, essentiel. **Primary cause,** cause première. **-ily,** *adv.* **1.** Primitivement ; dans le principe. **2.** Principalement, essentiellement.

rimate ['praimet], s. *Ecc:* Primat *m*; archevêque *m*.

rimates [prai'meiti:z], *s.pl.* *Z:* Primates *m*.

rime[1] [praim], a. **I.** Premier; principal, -aux; de premier ordre. Of prime importance, de toute première importance. **Prime necessity**, nécessité primordiale. **2.** De première qualité. *P. quality meat*, viande de surchoix. **3.** Premier, originel, primitif. **Prime cause**, cause première. *Mth:* **Prime number**, nombre premier. '**Prime 'Minister**, *v.tr.* Premier ministre.

rime[2], s. **I.** (*a*) Perfection *f*. In the prime of life, in one's prime, dans la force, dans la vigueur, de l'âge; à, dans, la fleur de l'âge. To be past one's prime, *F:* être sur le retour. (*b*) Le choix, le meilleur (d'un rôti, etc.). **2.** Premiers jours; commencement *m*. **3.** *Ecc:* Prime *f*. To sing the Prime, chanter prime. **4.** *Fenc:* Prime. **5.** *Mth:* N prime, n prime; n'.

rime[3], *v.tr.* **I.** Amorcer (une pompe, etc.). *Mch:* To prime the boilers, faire le plein des chaudières. **2.** *F:* (*a*) Faire la leçon à (un témoin, etc.). To p. s.o. with a speech, mettre qn au fait de ce qu'il devra dire. (*b*) To be well primed (with liquor), être bien parti; avoir son plumet. **3.** (*a*) *Paint:* Imprimer, apprêter (la surface à peindre). (*b*) Maroufler (la toile.

priming, s. **I.** (*a*) Amorçage *m* (d'une pompe). (*b*) Amorce *f* (de mine, etc.). **2.** (*a*) *Paint:* Apprêtage *m*, impression *f* (d'une toile sur châssis). (*b*) Première couche; couche d'impression.

primer ['primər, 'praimər], s. **I.** (*a*) Premier livre de lecture; alphabet *m*. (*b*) *P. of geography*, premier cours de géographie; premiers éléments de géographie. **2.** *Typ:* **Great primer**, gros romain; corps 16.

primeval [prai'mi:v(ə)l], a. Primordial, -aux; des premiers âges (du monde). **Primeval forest**, forêt vierge.

primitive ['primitiv], a. (*a*) Primitif. **Primitive rocks**, roches primitives, primaires. (*b*) (*Of method, etc.*) Primitif, rude, grossier.

primitiveness ['primitivnəs], s. Caractère primitif; rudesse *f* (d'un peuple, etc.).

primness ['primnəs], s. Air *m* collet monté. *The p. of her manners*, ses manières compassées.

primogeniture [praimo'dʒenitjər], s. Primogéniture *f*. **Right of primogeniture**, droit *m* d'aînesse.

primordial [prai'mɔːrdiəl], a. Primordial, -aux.

primrose ['primrouz], s. *Bot:* Primevère *f* à grandes fleurs. **Evening primrose**, onagre *f*; herbe *f* aux ânes. *F:* **The primrose path**, le chemin de velours.

primula ['primjulə], s. *Bot:* Primevère *f*.

prince [prins], *s.m.* (*a*) Prince. *S.a.* CROWN[1] I. (*b*) *F:* **The princes of this world**, les grands de ce monde. **The prince of darkness**, le prince des ténèbres; le diable.

princeling ['prinslin], *s.m.* Principicule.

princely ['prinsli], a. Princier; royal, -aux. *A p. gift*, un cadeau royal, magnifique.

princess ['prinses], *s.f.* Princesse. *P. royal*, princesse royale. *Cost:* **Princess petticoat**, combinaison-jupon *f*.

principal ['prinsip(ə)l]. I. a. Principal, -aux. *P. clerk*, commis en chef; premier commis. *Cu:* **Principal dish**, pièce *f* de résistance. *P. branch of a stream*, branche maîtresse (d'un cours d'eau. *Gram:* **Principal clause**, proposition principale. **-ally**, *adv.* Principalement. II. **principal**, s. **I.** (*Pers:*) (*a*) Directeur *m* (de fabrique, d'école); chef *m*, patron *m* d'une mai-

son de commerce). **Lady principal**, directrice *f*; patronne *f*. (*b*) (*In transaction*) Mandant *m*. *St.Exch:* Donneur *m* d'ordre. *Jur:* **Principal and agent**, employeur *m* et mandataire *m*; commettant et préposé *m*. (*c*) *Jur:* Auteur *m* (d'un crime). (*d*) **Principals in a duel**, combattants *m*, adversaires *m*, dans un duel. **2.** *Com:* Capital *m*, principal *m* (d'une dette).

principality [prinsi'paliti], s. Principauté *f*.

principle ['prinsipl], s. Principe *m*. **I.** **First principles of geometry**, premiers principes de la géométrie. **To lay sth. down as a principle**, poser qch. en principe. **2.** To have high principles, avoir des principes. **Man of high principles**, homme de haute moralité. *Laxity of p.*, morale relâchée. **To do sth. on principle, to make it a matter of principle to do sth.**, avoir pour principe de faire qch.; faire qch. par principe. **3.** *Ch:* **Active principle**, principe actif; élément actif.

principled ['prinsipld], a. **High-principled**, **low-principled**, qui a de bons, de mauvais, principes.

prink [prink]. **I.** *v.tr.* (*Of bird*) To p. its feathers, se lisser les plumes. **2.** *v.i.* Prendre des airs; *P:* faire de l'esbrouffe. **3.** *v.i. & pr.* To prink (oneself) up, s'attifer.

print[1] [print], s. **I.** (*a*) Empreinte *f*, impression *f*. *S.a.* FINGER-PRINT, FOOTPRINT. (*b*) **Butter print**, moule *m* à beurre, moule-beurre *m inv*. **2.** *Typ:* (*a*) Matière imprimée. **He likes to see himself in print**, il aime à se faire imprimer, à se voir imprimé. **The book is in print**, le livre est imprimé, a paru. **Out of print**, épuisé. (*b*) **Large print**, small print, gros, petits, caractères. (*c*) Édition *f*, impression. **3.** Estampe *f*, gravure *f*, image *f*. **4.** *Phot:* (*a*) Épreuve *f*; copie *f*. **To take a p. from a negative**, tirer une épreuve d'un cliché. (*b*) *Ind:* **Blue print**, dessin négatif; photocalque *m*; *F:* bleu *m*. **5.** *Tex:* Indienne *f*, cotonnade *f*. **Print dress**, robe d'indienne.

'**print-room**, s. Cabinet *m* d'estampes.
'**print-seller**, s. Marchand d'estampes, de gravures.

print[2], *v.tr.* **I.** Empreindre; imprimer; marquer (qch.) d'une empreinte. **2.** *Typ:* Imprimer. **To print (off)** a newspaper, tirer un journal. (*Of author*) To p. a book, to have a book printed, faire imprimer un livre; livrer un ouvrage à l'impression. **The book is now printing**, le livre est à l'impression. *Post:* 'Printed matter,' "imprimés" *mpl*. **3.** *Phot:* **To print (off, out)** a negative, tirer une épreuve d'un cliché. **4.** *Tex:* **Printed calico**, indienne imprimée. **printing**, s. **I.** (*a*) Impression *f*, tirage *m* (d'un livre). (*b*) (*Art of printing*) Imprimerie *f*, typographie *f*. **2.** *Phot:* Tirage. '**printing-frame**, s. *Phot:* Châssis (positif). '**printing-machine**, s. *Typ:* Machine *f* à imprimer; presse *f* mécanique. '**printing-office**, **-works**, s. Imprimerie *f*. '**printing-paper**, s. **I.** *Typ:* Papier *m* d'impression. **2.** *Phot:* (*a*) Printing(-out) paper, *usu.* P.O.P., papier à noircissement direct; papier au citrate. (*b*) *Ind:* Papier héliographique. '**printing-press**, s. *Typ:* See PRESS[1] 3.

printer ['printər], s. **I.** *Typ:* (i) Imprimeur *m* (typographique), typographe *m*; (ii) ouvrier *m* typographe. **Printer's error**, faute *f* d'impression; coquille *f*. **Printer's reader**, correcteur, -trice, d'épreuves. **2.** *Tex:* **Calico printer**, imprimeur d'indiennes.

prior[1] ['praiər]. **I.** a. Préalable, précédent; antérieur (*to sth.*, à qch.). **To have a p. claim**, être le premier en date. **2.** adv. **Prior to my departure**, antérieurement à mon départ.

prior[2], *s.m. Ecc.Hist:* Prieur.

prioress ['praiɔres], *s.f. Ecc. Hist:* Prieure.

priority [prai'ɔriti], *s.* Priorité *f*, antériorité *f*. Priority of invention, antériorité d'invention. To have priority over s.o., primer qn ; avoir le pas sur qn. According to priority, selon l'ordre de priorité. Priority rights, droits de priorité. *Fin :* Priority share, action privilégiée.

priory ['praiɔri], *s.* Prieuré *m* (le couvent).

prism [prizm], *s.* **1.** Prisme *m. Opt:* Erecting prism, prisme redresseur. Reflecting prism, prisme réflecteur. Polarizing prism, nicol *m.* **2.** (*a*) Spectre *m* (solaire). (*b*) *pl.* Prisms, couleurs *f* prismatiques. '**prism-bi'noculars,** *s.pl.* Jumelles *f* prismatiques.

prismatic [priz'matik], *a.* Prismatique. *Opt :* Prismatic sight, viseur à prisme.

prison ['priz(ə)n], *s.* Prison *f* ; maison *f* d'arrêt. To send s.o. to prison; to put s.o. in prison, mettre qn en prison ; (faire) emprisonner qn. He has been in p., il a fait de la prison. '**prison-breaker,** *s.* Échappé de prison. '**prison-van,** *s.* Voiture *f* cellulaire. '**prison-'yard,** *s.* Préau *m*, cour *f*, de prison.

prisoner ['priz(ə)nər], *s.* **1.** Pr:sonnier, -ière. They were taken prisoner, ils furent faits prisonniers. *F :* To be a prisoner to one's room, être cloué à sa chambre. **2.** *Jur :* (*a*) Prisoner at the bar, prévenu, -ue ; accusé, -ée. (*b*) (*After sentence*) Détenu, -ue ; coupable *mf.* **3.** *Games :* Prisoners' base, (jeu *m* de) barres *fpl.*

pristine ['pristain], *a.* Premier, primitif ; d'antan.

prithee ['priði], *int. A :* Je te prie.

privacy ['praivəsi], *s.* **1.** The privacy of one's home, l'intimité *f* du foyer. To live in privacy, mener une vie privée ; vivre dans la retraite. Desire for p., désir de se cacher aux regards indiscrets. **2.** Lack of privacy, manque de secret (dans une affaire).

private ['praivet]. I. *a.* Privé, particulier. **1.** Private persons, (simples) particuliers. In private life, dans le particulier, dans l'intimité *f. Pol :* Private member, simple député. **2.** Secret. To keep a matter private, empêcher qu'une affaire ne s'ébruite ; tenir une affaire secrète. P. entrance, (i) entrée secrète, dérobée ; (ii) entrée particulière. **3.** Private study, études particulières. P. motives, motifs personnels, particuliers. In my private opinion, à mon avis personnel. **4.** Private and confidential, secret et confidentiel. P. conversation, conversation intime ; aparté *m.* P. interview, entretien à huis clos. Private arrangement, accord à l'amiable. *Jur :* Private agreement, acte *m* sous seing privé. **5.** (*a*) (*Not business*) Private house, maison particulière. Private car, voiture particulière, privée. (*b*) P. room (in hotel, etc.), salon réservé. P. office, cabinet particulier. (*c*) P. dance, bal sur invitation. P. theatricals, comédie de salon. P. sitting, séance privée ; séance à huis clos. The funeral will be private, les obsèques auront lieu dans la plus stricte intimité. (*d*) Private education, enseignement par un précepteur. *S.a.* HOTEL, SCHOOL[1] I. **6.** Private property, propriété privée. 'Private,' "entrée interdite au public." Private income, rentes *fpl* ; fortune personnelle. **7.** (*Of place*) Loin des regards indiscrets ; retiré. **-ly,** *adv.* **1.** Privément ; en simple particulier. Privately owned, qui appartient à un particulier. **2.** To speak to s.o. p., parler à qn en particulier. To hear sth. p., entendre qch. à titre confidentiel. P. sold, vendu à l'amiable, de gré à gré. II. **private,** *s.* **1.** *Adv.phr.* In private. (*a*) To dine in p., dîner en famille. Married in p., marié dans

l'intimité. (*b*) (*Of assembly*) To sit in pr.vate, réunir en séance privée. To talk to s.o. in p parler à qn sans témoins. **2.** *Mil:* Simple so dat *m.* Fall out Private Smith! soldat Smith sortez des rangs !

privateer[1] [praivə'ti:ər], *s.* **1.** (Bâtiment arm en) corsaire *m.* **2.** (*Pers.*) Corsaire.

privateer[2], *v.i. Nau:* Faire la course. **pri vateering,** *s.* (Guerre *f* de) course *f.*

privation [prai'veiʃ(ə)n], *s.* Privation *f.* To liv in privation, vivre de privations.

privet ['privet], *s. Bot:* Troène *m.*

privilege[1] ['priviledʒ], *s.* **1.** Privilège *m*, préro gative *f.* To enjoy the privilege of doing sth jouir du privilège, avoir le privilège, de faire qc **2.** Immunité *f* contre .es poursuites en diffama tion. The Privilege, la prérogative royale Parliamentary privilege, prérogative, immunit parlementaire.

privilege[2], *v.tr.* Privilégier (qn). To p. s.o. t do sth., accorder à qn le privilège de faire qch A privileged few, quelques privilégiés. To b privileged to do sth., jouir du privilège de fair qch.

privy ['privi]. I. *a.* **1.** To be pr vy to sth., avoi connaissance de qch., être instruit de qch. t tremper dans (un complot). **2.** Privé. The Priv Council, le Conseil privé (du Roi). Lord Priv Seal, Garde *m* du petit Sceau. The Privy Purse la cassette du roi. **-ily,** *adv.* En secret II. **privy,** *s.* **1.** *Jur :* Partie intéressée ; ayan droit *m.* **2.** Lieux *mpl* d'aisances ; cabinets *mp*

prize[1] [praiz], *s.* **1.** Prix *m.* The Nobel prize le prix Nobel. To carry off the p., remporter l prix. Prize ox, bœuf primé, médaillé. **2.** (*In lottery*) Lot *m.* To draw the first p., gagner l gros lot. '**prize-book,** *s.* Livre *m* de prix '**prize-fighter,** *s.* Boxeur professionnel '**prize-fighting,** *s.* Boxe professionnelle '**prize-giving,** *s.* Distribution *f* de prix '**prize-list,** *s.* Palmarès *m.* '**prize-winner,** *s* Lauréat, -ate.

prize[2], *v.tr.* Évaluer, estimer, priser. To pr.z sth. highly, faire grand cas de qch.

prize[3], *s.* **1.** (*a*) *Navy:* Prise *f*, capture *f.* To b (a) lawful prize, être de bonne prise. Prize Court, Cour *f* des prises. (*b*) Butin *m* de guerre **2.** *F:* Aubaine *f.* '**prize-money,** *s. Navy Part *f* de prise.

prize[4], *s.* **1.** Force *f* de levier ; pesée *f* (au moyer d'un levier). **2.** Point *m* d'appui (pour exerce une pesée).

prize[5]. **1.** *v.tr.* To prize sth. up, soulever qch à l'aide d'un levier. To prize a lid open, force un couvercle avec un levier. **2.** *v.i.* To prize against sth., faire levier sur qch. ; exercer une pesée sur (une porte, etc.).

prizeman, *pl.* **-men** ['praizmən, -men], *s* Lauréat, -ate.

pro[1] [prou], *Lt.prep.* **1.** Pro forma, pour la forme Pro forma invoice, facture simulée. **2.** Pro rata au prorata ; au marc le franc. **3.** Pro tempore, *F:* pr> tem. (i) *Adv.phr.* Temporairement. (ii) *Adj.phr.* Temporaire. **4.** Pro and contra, *F:* pro and con., pour et contre. The pros and cons, le pour et le contre.

pro[2], *s. Sp :* Professionnel, -elle.

proa ['prouə], *s. Nau:* Prao *m* (malais).

probability [prɔbə'biliti], *s.* Probabilité *f* vraisemblance *f.* In al. probability, selon toute probabilité, selon toute vraisemblance. The p. is that . . , il est très probable que + *ind.*

probable ['prɔbəbl], *a.* **1.** Probable. It is p. that . . ., il est probable, vraisemblable, que +

ind.; il est à croire que + *ind.* **2.** *P. story,* histoire vraisemblable. **-ably,** *adv.* Probablement; vraisemblablement.

robate ['proubət], *s.* *Jur:* Validation *f*, homologation *f* (d'un testament). **To take out probate of a will,** faire homologuer un testament. **To grant probate of a will,** homologuer un testament. **'probate-duty,** *s.* Droits *mpl* de succession (par testament).

robation [pro'beiʃ(ə)n], *s.* **1.** Épreuve *f*, stage *m.* *Ecc:* Probation *f* (d'un novice). **To be on probation,** être à l'épreuve; faire son stage. *Period of p.,* période *f* stagiaire; stage. **2.** Mise *f* en liberté sous surveillance (d'un jeune condamné). **Probation officer,** délégué *m* à la liberté surveillée.

robationary [pro'beiʃ(ə)nəri], *a.* (Période) d'épreuve, de stage, stagiaire.

robationer [pro'beiʃ(ə)nər], *s.* **1.** Stagiaire *mf.* *Ecc:* Novice *mf.* **2.** Jeune condamné, -ée, qui bénéficie d'un sursis sous surveillance.

robative ['proubətiv], *a.* (*Of evidence, etc.*) Probant, probatoire.

robe¹ [proub], *s.* **1.** *Surg:* (*a*) Sonde *f.* (*b*) Coup *m* de sonde. **2.** Nettoie-becs *m inv* (pour lanterne à acétylène).

robe², *v.tr.* **1.** *Med:* Sonder, explorer; introduire une sonde dans (une plaie). **2.** *F:* (*a*) Sonder (qn) (*b*) Approfondir, fouiller (un mystère); scruter (des témoignages). **3.** *v.i.* **To probe into the past,** sonder le passé. *He has probed deep into the matter,* il a examiné l'affaire de près.

robity ['prɔbiti], *s.* Probité *f.*

roblem ['prɔbləm], *s.* Problème *m.* **The housing problem,** le problème, la crise, du logement. *It's a p. to know what to do,* c'est bien embarrassant de savoir quoi faire. *Th:* **Problem play,** pièce à thèse.

roblematic(al) [prɔblə'matik(ə)l], *a.* Problématique; *F:* douteux, incertain. *P. gain,* profit aléatoire.

roboscis [pro'bɔsis], *s.* Trompe *f* (d'éléphant, d'insecte).

rocedure [pro'si:djər], *s.* **1.** Procédé *m.* *I don't like his p.,* je n'aime pas sa manière d'agir, ses procédés. *The correct p.,* la (vraie) marche à suivre; la bonne méthode. **2.** (Mode *m* de) procédure *f* (du Parlement, etc.). **Order of procedure,** règles *fpl* de procédure.

roceed [pro'si:d], *v.i.* **1.** (*a*) **To proceed (on one's way),** continuer son chemin; poursuivre sa route. *Before we p. any farther,* avant d'aller plus loin. (*b*) **To proceed to(wards) a place,** se rendre à un endroit; diriger ses pas, s'acheminer, vers un endroit. **Let us proceed to the dining-room,** passons à la salle à manger. *Motor cars must p. at a moderate speed,* les autos sont tenues de prendre une allure modérée. (*Of ship*) **To p. at twenty knots,** filer à vingt nœuds. (*c*) **To p. cautiously,** agir, procéder, avec prudence. *How shall we proceed?* quelle est la marche à suivre? (*d*) **To proceed to do sth.,** se mettre à faire qch. **To p. to business,** se mettre à la besogne; passer aux affaires. *I will now p. to another matter,* je passe maintenant à une autre question. **To proceed to blows,** en venir aux coups. **To proceed to violence,** recourir à la violence. **2.** (*a*) (Se) continuer, se poursuivre. *The letter proceeds thus,* la lettre se poursuit, continue, dans ces termes. *After that things proceeded quickly,* après cela les choses ont marché rondement. (*b*) **The negotiations (now) proceeding,** les négociations en cours. *Things are proceeding as usual,* les choses vont leur train, suivent leur cours. *To pay as the work*

proceeds, payer au fur et à mesure de l'ouvrage. (*c*) **To proceed with sth.,** poursuivre, continuer (ses études, etc.). **Proceed!** allez toujours! continuez! **3. To proceed against s.o.,** procéder contre qn; intenter un procès à qn. **4.** *Sounds proceeding from a room,* sons qui sortent, proviennent, d'une chambre. *His conduct proceeds from most noble principles,* sa conduite découle, procède, des plus nobles principes. **proceeding,** *s.* **1.** Façon d'agir. *The best way of p.,* la meilleure marche à suivre. **2.** (*a*) Procédé *m*, action *f*; *pl.* faits et gestes *m.* **To note proceedings,** noter ce qui se passe. (*b*) *pl.* Débats *m* (d'une assemblée). **Proceedings of the Royal Society,** délibérations *f*, travaux *m*, de la Société Royale. *The proceedings will begin at eight p.m.,* la séance, la cérémonie, commencera à huit heures du soir. *The proceedings were orderly,* la réunion s'est déroulée dans le calme. (*c*) *Jur:* **To take, institute, proceedings against s.o.,** intenter un procès à qn; engager des poursuites contre qn. *To order proceedings to be taken against s.o.,* instrumenter contre qn.

proceeds ['prousi:dz], *s.pl.* Produit *m*, montant *m*, (d'une vente).

process¹ ['prouses], *s.* **1.** (*a*) Processus *m.* *Processes of the mind,* opérations *f* de l'esprit. *F:* **It's a slow process,** c'est un travail long; cela prend du temps. (*b*) Cours *m*, avancement *m*; marche *f* (des événements). *During the p. of dismantling,* au cours du démontage. **Building in process of construction,** bâtiment en cours, en voie, de construction. **To be in p. of removal,** être en train de déménager. *In p. of disappearing,* en passe de disparaître. **2.** Méthode *f*; procédé *m* (photographique); réaction *f* (chimique); opération (métallurgique). *Ch:* **Wet process, dry process,** voie humide, sèche. **3.** *Jur:* Action *f* en justice. **First process,** introduction *f* d'instance. **4.** *Anat:* Excroissance *f*, processus, procès *m*; (*of bone*) apophyse *f.* **'process-block,** *s.* Cliché *m* en similigravure, en simili. **'process-engraver,** *s.* Similigraveur *m.* **'process-engraving,** *s.* Similigravure *f.* **'process-server,** *s.* *Jur:* Huissier (exploitant). **'process-work,** *s.* *Typ:* Art: Similigravure *f*; *F:* simili *f.*

process², *v.tr.* **1.** *Ind:* Faire subir une opération à (qch.). *Tex:* Apprêter. **2.** *Typ:* Reproduire (un cliché) par similigravure.

procession [pro'seʃ(ə)n], *s.* Cortège *m*; défilé *m*; (*religious*) procession *f.* **To go, walk, in procession,** aller en cortège, en procession; défiler. *F:* **P. of motor cars,** défilé, file *f*, de voitures.

processional [pro'seʃənəl], *a.* Processionnel.

proclaim [pro'kleim], *v.tr.* **1.** Proclamer; déclarer (publiquement). **To proclaim s.o. king,** proclamer qn roi. *F:* *His face proclaims his guilt,* son visage crie, dénonce, sa culpabilité. **2.** *Irish Hist:* Mettre au ban, hors la loi.

proclamation [prɔklə'meiʃ(ə)n], *s.* Proclamation *f*; déclaration (publique). **To make, issue, a proclamation,** faire une proclamation. *To make sth. known by public p.,* annoncer qch. à cri public.

proclitic [pro'klitik], *a. & s.* *Ling:* Proclitique (*m*).

proclivity [pro'kliviti], *s.* Penchant *m*, tendance *f*, inclination *f* (*to sth.,* à qch.).

procrastinate [pro'krastineit], *v.i.* Remettre les affaires au lendemain, à plus tard; temporiser; *F:* lanterner.

procrastination [prokrasti'neiʃ(ə)n], *s.* Remise *f* des affaires à plus tard; temporisation *f.*

procrastinator [pro'krastineitər], *s.* Remetteur *m* au lendemain; temporisateur *m.*

procreate ['proukrieit], *v.tr.* Procréer, engendrer.
procreation [proukri'eiʃ(ə)n], *s.* Procréation *f*, engendrement *m.*
proctor ['prɔktər], *s.* **1.** *Sch:* Membre exécutif du conseil de discipline. **2.** *Jur:* **King's proctor**, procureur *m* du roi.
procumbent [pro'kʌmbənt], *a.* **1.** (*Of pers.*) Couché sur le ventre, la face contre terre. **2.** *Bot:* Rampant.
procurable [pro'kjuərəbl], *a.* Procurable.
procuration [prɔkju'reiʃ(ə)n], *s.* **1.** *Jur:* Procuration *f*. **To act by procuration**, agir par procuration. **2.** Acquisition *f*, obtention *f* (de qch. pour qn).
procurator ['prɔkjureitər], *s.* **1.** *Hist:* Procurateur *m.* **2.** *Jur:* Fondé *m* de pouvoir(s); procureur *m.* **'procurator-'fiscal**, *s.* (*Scot.*) Procureur général.
procure [pro'kjuər], *v.tr.* (*a*) Obtenir, procurer. *To p. sth. for s.o.*, procurer qch. à qn. (*b*) *To p. sth.* (*for oneself*), se procurer qch.
procurement [pro'kjuərmənt], *s.* Obtention *f*, acquisition *f* (*of*, de).
prod[1] [prɔd], *s.* Coup (donné avec qch. de pointu). *To give s.o. a p. with a bayonet*, donner un coup de baïonnette à qn. *F:* **Give him a prod**, aiguillonnez-le un peu.
prod[2], *v.tr.* (prodded) **1.** **To prod (at) sth.** (*with sth.*), tâter, pousser, qch. (du bout d'un bâton, du bout du doigt). **2.** *F:* Aiguillonner, stimuler, pousser (*s.o. into doing sth.*, qn à faire qch.). **To prod s.o. on**, presser, stimuler, qn.
prodigal ['prɔdig(ə)l], *a. & s.* Prodigue (*mf*); gaspilleur, -euse. **The Prodigal Son**, l'enfant prodigue. **To be prodigal of sth.**, être prodigue de qch.; prodiguer qch. **-ally**, *adv.* En prodigue. *To give p.*, donner à pleines mains.
prodigality [prɔdi'galiti], *s.* Prodigalité *f*.
prodigious [pro'didʒəs], *a.* Prodigieux; *F:* merveilleux, mirobolant.
prodigy ['prɔdidʒi], *s.* Prodige *m*; *F:* merveille *f*. **Infant prodigy**, enfant prodige.
prodrome ['prɔdrom], *s.* Prodrome *m.* **1.** Préambule *m* (d'un livre, etc.). **2.** Signe avant-coureur (d'une maladie).
produce[1] ['prɔdju:s], *s.* **1.** (*a*) Rendement *m* (d'un champ de blé, etc.). (*b*) Produit *m* (de son travail). **2.** *Coll.* Denrées *fpl*, produits. **Farm produce**, produits agricoles. **Colonial p.**, denrées coloniales.
produce[2] [pro'dju:s], *v.tr.* **1.** (*a*) Présenter, exhiber (son passeport). *Jur:* Représenter (des documents). *I can p. the documents*, je peux fournir les documents. (*b*) *Th:* **To produce a play**, mettre une pièce en scène. *Badly produced play*, pièce mal montée. **2.** (*a*) Créer. *El: To p. a spark*, faire jaillir une étincelle. *Current produced by a battery*, courant engendré par une pile. (*b*) *Ind:* Fabriquer. (*c*) Produire, éditer (un livre, un film). (*d*) Produire, causer, provoquer (un effet). **To produce a sensation**, faire sensation. **3.** Rapporter, rendre (un profit, etc.). **4.** *Geom:* Prolonger (une ligne).
producer [pro'dju:sər], *s* **1.**, Producteur, -trice. *Th:* Metteur *m* en scène. *Cin:* Directeur *m* de productions. **2.** *Ind:* (Gas-)**producer**, gazogène *m.*
producible [pro'dju:sibl], *a.* Productible.
product ['prɔdʌkt, -ɔkt], *s.* **1.** Produit *m.* *Products of a country*, produits, denrées *f*, d'un pays. *Ind:* **Secondary product**, sous-produit *m.* **2.** *Mth:* Produit.
production [pro'dʌkʃ(ə)n], *s.* **1.** (*a*) Production *f*, représentation *f*, communication *f* (de documents); présentation *f* (de son billet). (*b*) *Th:*

Mise *f* en scène (d'une pièce). **2.** (*a*) Génération (de la vapeur); production (d'un bruit, d'un effet, etc.). (*b*) Fabrication *f* (de marchandises). **Cost of production**, prix *m* de fabrique. *S.a.* MASS PRODUCTION. **3.** *Geom:* Prolongement *m* (d'une ligne). **4.** (*a*) Produit *m.* *Productions of a country* produits, denrées *f*, d'un pays. (*b*) Productio œuvre *f* (littéraire).
productive [pro'dʌktiv], *a.* **1.** (*a*) Producti générateur (*of sth.*, de qch.); (*of mine, etc.*) e rapport. (*b*) (*Of land*) Fécond. **2.** *Pol.Ec* (Travail) productif.
productiveness [pro'dʌktivnəs], **productivit** [proudʌk'tiviti, prɔd-], *s.* Productivité *f*. *Land i full p.*, terres en plein rapport, en plein rende ment.
pro-English [pro'ingliʃ], *a.* Anglophile.
profanation [prɔfa'neiʃ(ə)n], *s.* Profanation *f*.
profane[1] [pro'fein], *a.* Profane. (*a*) *Things sacre and p.*, le sacré et le profane. (*b*) (*Of pers.*) Non initié. (*c*) Païen, impie. (*d*) (Langage) impie blasphématoire. **Profane word**, juron *m*, blas phème *m. Don't be p.!* pas de jurons!
profane[2], *v.tr.* Profaner; polluer (une église) *To p. the Sabbath(-day)*, violer le repos dominical
profanity [pro'faniti], *s.* **1.** (*a*) Nature *f* profan (d'un écrit). (*b*) Impiété *f* (d'une action). **2.** T utter profanities, proférer des blasphèmes, de jurons.
profess [pro'fes], *v.tr.* **1.** (*a*) Professer, fair profession de (sa foi, etc.). *To p. oneself satisfie* se déclarer satisfait. (*b*) (*Falsely*) **To profes** (oneself) to be a social reformer, se dire, se fair passer pour, réformateur social. *I do not p. t be a scholar*, je ne prétends pas être savant. *Sh professes to be thirty*, elle se donne trente ans **2.** (*a*) Exercer (un métier, la médecine.). (*b*) *Sch* Professer (l'histoire, etc.). **professed** [pro'fest] *a.* **1.** (*Of monk, nun*) Profès, -esse. **2.** (*a*) P enemy of the Government, ennemi déclaré d gouvernement. (*b*) Prétendu, soi-disant.
professedly [pro'fesidli], *adv.* De son propre aveu; ouvertement. *He is p. ignorant on th subject*, il avoue son ignorance à ce sujet.
profession [pro'feʃ(ə)n], *s.* **1.** Profession *f*, dé claration *f.* **Profession of faith**, profession de foi *Ecc:* **To make one's profession**, faire professio (dans un ordre). **2.** (*a*) Profession, métier *m.* The (learned) professions, les carrières libérales. **B** profession he is a doctor, il est médecin d profession. (*b*) **The profession**, (i) les gens *m* d métier; *esp.* (ii) *F:* le théâtre. **To belong to th profession**, faire du théâtre.
professional [pro'feʃən(ə)l]. **I.** *a.* Professionne (*a*) *P.* practices, usages *m* du métier. **To tak professional advice on a matter**, (i) consulter u homme du métier sur qch.; (ii) consulter u médecin ou un avocat. (*b*) *The p. army*, l'armé de métier. *P. diplomatist*, diplomate de carrière *c*) Expert. (*d*) **The professional classes**, le membres *m* des professions libérales. **2.** *s.* (*a*) Expert *m.* *Professionals*, gens *m* de métier. (*b*) *Sp* Professionnel, -elle. **-ally**, *adv.* *To do sth. p.* faire qch. en homme du métier. *To act p.*, agi dans l'exercice de sa profession.
professor [pro'fesər], *s.* Professeur *m* (à un université). **Professor Smith,** (Monsieur) le pro fesseur Smith.
professorial [prɔfe'sɔ:riəl], *a.* Professoral, -aux
professoriate [prɔfe'sɔ:riet], *s.* **1.** Le corp professoral. **2.** = PROFESSORSHIP.
professorship [pro'fesərʃip], *s.* Professorat *m.* **To be appointed to a professorship**, être nommé à une chaire

proffer ['prɔfər], v.tr. (proffered) Offrir, présenter. To p. one's hand, tendre la main (à qn).

proficiency [prɔ'fiʃənsi], s. Capacité f, compétence f (in a subject, en une matière).

proficient [prɔ'fiʃənt], a. Capable, compétent; versé (in, dans). To be proficient in Latin, être fort en latin; posséder le latin à fond.

profile¹ ['proufail, -fi:l], s. I. (a) (i) Profil m; (ii) silhouette f. Drawn in profile, esquissé de profil. (b) Arch: etc: Profil; coupe f perpendiculaire. (c) Th: Ferme f (de décor). 2. Cer: etc: Calibre m (de tourneur, etc.).

profile², v.tr. I. Ind: Profiler, contourner, chantourner. 2. The trees are profiled against the horizon, les arbres se profilent sur l'horizon.

profit¹ ['prɔfit], s. Profit m, bénéfice m. (a) Avantage m. To turn sth. to profit, tirer profit de qch. (b) Com: Net profit(s), bénéfice net. To bring in, yield, show, a profit, donner un bénéfice. To sell sth. at a profit, vendre qch. à profit, à bénéfice. To make a profit on, out of, a transaction, retirer un profit d'une affaire. To make huge profits, gagner gros. Profit and loss, profits et pertes. 'profit-sharing, s. Ind: Participation f aux bénéfices.

profit², v. (profited) I. v.tr. Profiter à (qn); être avantageux à (qn). What will it profit you to go there? à quoi (cela) vous profitera-t-il d'y aller? 2. v.i. To profit by sth., profiter, bénéficier, de qch. To p. by s.o.'s advice, mettre à profit l'avis de qn. You don't p. by it, on n'y trouve pas son compte.

profitable ['prɔfitəbl], a. Profitable, avantageux; lucratif, rémunérateur. It is more p. to us to sell it, nous avons plus d'avantage à le vendre. **-ably**, adv. Profitablement, avantageusement. To study p., étudier avec fruit.

profiteer¹ [prɔfi'tiːər], s. F: Profiteur m, mercanti m.

profiteer², v.i. Faire des bénéfices excessifs.

profiteering, s. Mercantilisme m.

profitless ['prɔfitləs], a. Sans profit.

profligacy ['prɔfligəsi], s. I. Débauche f, libertinage m; crapule f, dévergondage m. 2. Prodigalité f.

profligate ['prɔfligit], a. & s. I. Débauché, -ée; libertin, -ine; dévergondé, -ée. 2. Prodigue.

profound [prɔ'faund], a. Profond. P. secret, secret absolu. P. scholar, érudit accompli, profond. P. study of a subject, étude approfondie d'un sujet. **-ly**, adv. Profondément.

profundity [prɔ'fʌnditi], s. Profondeur f.

profuse [prɔ'fjuːs], a. I. To be profuse in one's apologies, se montrer prodigue d'excuses; se confondre en excuses. To be profuse of praise, prodiguer les louanges. 2. Profus, abondant, excessif. P. bleeding, hémorragie abondante. **-ly**, adv. Profusément. To apologize p., se confondre en excuses. To perspire p., transpirer abondamment.

profuseness [prɔ'fjuːsnəs], s. Profusion f.

profusion [prɔ'fjuːʒ(ə)n], s. Profusion f; abondance f. Flowers in profusion, des fleurs à profusion, à foison.

progenitor [prɔ'dʒenitər], s. Aïeul m, pl. aïeux; ancêtre m.

progeniture [prɔ'dʒenitjər], s. Progéniture f.

progeny ['prɔdʒəni], s. I. Progéniture f. 2. Descendants mpl, lignée f, postérité f.

prognathic [prɔg'naθik], **prognathous** ['prɔgnaθəs], a. Anthr: Prognathe.

prognose [prɔg'nouz], v.tr. Med: Pronostiquer.

prognosis, pl. **-oses** [prɔg'nousis, -ousiːz], s. Med: I. Pronostic m. To give a very serious p.,

pronostiquer au plus grave. 2. (The art) Prognose f.

prognostic [prɔg'nɔstik], I. a. Med: (Signe) pro(g)nostique. Signs prognostic of sth., signes qui pronostiquent, présagent, qch. 2. s. (a) Pronostic m, présage m. (b) Med: Signe pronostique; symptôme m.

prognosticate [prɔg'nɔstikeit], v.tr. Pronostiquer, présager, prédire (qch.).

program(me) ['prougram], s. Programme m. Ball programme, carnet m de bal.

progress¹ ['prougres], s. (No pl.) I. (a) Marche f en avant; avancement m (d'un travail, etc.). The progress of events, le cours des événements. In progress of time, avec le temps. The work now in progress, le travail en cours. Harvesting in full progress, moisson qui bat son plein. (b) Progrès m. To make progress in one's studies, faire des progrès dans ses études. To make slow p., n'avancer que lentement. Negotiations are making good p., les négociations sont en bonne voie. 2. (a) A: Voyage m. (b) Tournée f (d'un juge). Royal progress, voyage d'apparat (du roi).

progress² [prɔ'gres], v.i. I. (a) S'avancer. As the year progresses, au cours de l'année. (b) To progress with one's studies, faire des progrès, avancer, dans ses études. The patient is progressing favourably, le malade fait des progrès satisfaisants. 2. (Of official) Faire une tournée.

progression [prɔ'greʃ(ə)n], s. I. Progression f. Mode of p., mode m de locomotion. 2. Mth: Arithmetical progression, progression arithmétique. 3. Mus: Harmonic p., marche f harmonique.

progressive [prɔ'gresiv], a. Progressif. (a) By progressive stages, par degrés. (b) P. age, siècle de progrès. To be p., être ami du progrès. **-ly**, adv. Progressivement; au fur et à mesure.

prohibit [prɔ'hibit], v.tr. I. Prohiber, défendre, interdire (qch.). Smoking is prohibited, il est défendu, interdit, de fumer; défense de fumer. To prohibit s.o. from doing sth., défendre, interdire, à qn de faire qch. 2. Empêcher (s.o. from doing sth., qn de faire qch.).

prohibition [prou(h)i'biʃ(ə)n], s. (a) Prohibition f, interdiction f, défense f (from doing sth., de faire qch.). (b) U.S: Régime sec.

prohibitionist [prou(h)i'biʃənist], a. & s. Partisan m de l'interdiction des boissons alcooliques. P. countries, pays secs.

prohibitive [prɔ'hibitiv], a. Prohibitive price, prix prohibitif, inabordable. The price of peaches is p., les pêches sont hors de prix.

project¹ ['prɔdʒekt, 'prou-], s. Projet m.

project² [prɔ'dʒekt]. I. v.tr. Projeter. I. To p. a journey, projeter un voyage. Projected buildings, édifices en projet. 2. Projeter, lancer, (un corps) en avant. To p. a picture on the screen, projeter une image sur l'écran. Art: Projected shadow, ombre portée. II. project, v.i. Faire saillie, faire ressaut; (s')avancer. Balcony projecting over the pavement, balcon surplombant le trottoir. To p. beyond the building line, déborder, dépasser, l'alignement. **projecting**, a. Saillant, en saillie; hors d'œuvre, en porte-à-faux. P. teeth, dents saillantes.

projectile [prɔ'dʒektail], a. & s. Projectile (m).

projection [prɔ'dʒekʃ(ə)n], s. I. (a) Lancement m (d'un projectile); projection f (d'un rayon de lumière). Cin: Projection room, cabine f de projection. (b) Conception f (d'un projet, etc.). 2. Geom: Projection. 3. Saillie f. (a) Avancement m (en dehors). (b) Arch: Partie f qui fait saillie ; ressaut *m* ; porte-à-faux *m*, portée *f* (d'un balcon).

projector [pro'dʒektər], *s.* Projecteur *m* (de rayons lumineux, etc.). Projector lantern, picture-projector, projecteur ; appareil *m* de projection.

prolate ['prouleit], *a.* Geom : (Ellipsoïde) allongé, prolongé.

prolegomena [proule'gɔmənə], *s.pl.* Prolégomènes *m* ; introduction *f.*

proletarian [prouli'tɛəriən]. **I.** *a.* Prolétarien, prolétaire. **2.** *s.* Prolétaire *mf.*

proletariat(e) [prouli'tɛəriət], *s.* Prolétariat *m.*

proliferation [prolifə'reiʃ(ə)n], *s.* Prolifération *f.*

proliferous [pro'lifərəs], *a.* Nat.Hist : Prolifère.

prolific [pro'lifik], *a* Prolifique ; fécond, fertile (*in, of,* en).

prolix ['prouliks], *a.* Prolixe, diffus ; (style) délayé.

prolixity [pro'liksiti], *s.* Prolixité *f.*

prologue ['proulɔg], *s.* Prologue *m* (*to,* de).

prolong [pro'lɔŋ], *v.tr.* Prolonger.

prolongation [proulɔŋ'gei∫(ə)n], *s.* Prolongation *f* ; délai accordé.

promenade[1] [prɔmə'nɑːd], *s.* **I.** Promenade *f* (en grande toilette). **2.** (*a*) (Lieu *m* de) promenade ; (*at seaside*) esplanade *f.* (*b*) Th : Promenoir *m*, pourtour *m* (du parterre). 'pro-menade 'concert, *s.* Concert *m* où l'auditoire peut circuler librement. 'promenade 'deck, *s.* Nau : Pont-promenade *m.*

promenade[2]. **I.** *v.i.* Se promener, parader (à pied, en voiture, etc.). **2.** *v.tr.* (*a*) Se promener dans (la salle) ; se promener sur (les boulevards). (*b*) Promener (qn).

promenader [prɔmə'nɑːdər], *s.* Promeneur, -euse.

prominence ['prɔminəns], *s.* **I.** (*a*) Proéminence *f* ; relief *m.* (*b*) Saillie *f*, protubérance *f.* **2.** Éminence *f.* To bring sth. into prominence, to give sth. prominence, faire ressortir qch. To come into prominence, (*of pers.*) percer ; arriver à un rang éminent ; (*of thg*) acquérir de l'importance.

prominent ['prɔminənt], *a.* **I.** Saillant ; en saillie ; proéminent. P. nose, nez prononcé. **2.** (*a*) Saillant ; remarquable ; (*of theory, etc.*) en évidence, très en avant. The most p. object on the hill, la chose la plus en vue sur la colline. (*Of idea, etc.*) To be prominent, ressortir. In a prominent position, très en vue. To play a p. part in an affair, jouer un rôle important dans une affaire. (*b*) Éminent. P. author, auteur en vue. -ly, adv. (*a*) Éminemment. (*b*) Goods p. displayed, marchandises bien en vue.

promiscuity [prɔmis'kjuːiti], *s.* Promiscuité *f.*

promiscuous [pro'miskjuəs], *a.* **I.** (*a*) Confus, mêlé. P. crowd, foule hétérogène. (*b*) Sans distinction de sexe. Promiscuous bathing, bains mixtes. **2.** P : Casuel, fortuit. -ly, adv. **I.** (*a*) Confusément, sans ordre ; en promiscuité. (*b*) Sans distinction de sexe. **2.** P : Casuellement, fortuitement.

promise[1] ['prɔmis], *s.* Promesse *f.* (*a*) To make a promise, faire une promesse. To keep one's promise, tenir sa promesse. To break one's promise, manquer à sa promesse ; manquer de parole. To release s.o. from his promise, rendre sa parole à qn. F : His promises are like piecrust, il a la promesse facile. B : The land of promise, la terre promise. (*b*) Child full of promise, enfant qui promet. To show great promise, donner de belles espérances. To hold out a promise to s.o. of sth., faire espérer qch. à qn.

promise[2], *v.tr.* (*a*) To promise s.o. sth., to

promise sth. to s.o., promettre qch. à qn. To promise s.o. one's daughter in marriage, promettre sa fille en mariage à qn. To promise (s.o. to do sth., promettre (à qn) de faire qch. To promise oneself sth., se promettre qch. F : You will be sorry for it, I promise you, vous le regretterez, je vous le promets, je vous en réponds (*b*) Action that promises trouble, action qui laisse prévoir des ennuis. Abs. The scheme promises well, le projet s'annonce bien ; l'affaire promet.

promising, *a.* Plein de promesses. Promising young man, jeune homme qui promet. The harvest looks promising, la moisson s'annonce bien.

promissory ['prɔmisəri], *a.* (Of oath) Promissoire. Com : Promissory note, billet *m* à ordre.

promontory ['prɔməntəri], *s.* Promontoire *m.*

promote [pro'mout], *v.tr.* **I.** Donner de l'avancement à (qn). To promote s.o. to an office, nommer qn à un poste. To be promoted, être promu ; avancer ; monter en grade. **2.** (*a*) Encourager (les arts, un projet) ; favoriser (le succès) ; faciliter (le progrès) ; avancer (les intérêts de qn) ; amener, contribuer à (un résultat, etc.). To promote good feeling between nations, encourager l'amitié entre les nations. (*b*) To promote a company, lancer une société anonyme.

promoter [pro'moutər], *s.* Instigateur, -trice, auteur *m* (d'un projet, etc.). Company promoter, promoteur *m*, fondateur *m*, de sociétés anonymes.

promotion [pro'mouʃ(ə)n], *s.* Promotion *f,* avancement *m.* Mil : Nomination *f* à un grade supérieur. To get promotion, obtenir de l'avancement.

prompt[1] [prɔm(p)t], *a.* **I.** Prompt. (*a*) Vif, rapide. (*b*) Immédiat. Prompt reply, réponse par retour du courrier. For prompt cash, argent comptant. Prompt delivery, livraison immédiate. (*c*) adv. To arrive prompt ..o the minute, arriver à l'heure exacte. **2.** Com : Prompt cotton, coton livrable sur-le-champ et comptant. -ly, adv. Promptement. (*a*) Avec empressement. (*b*) Sur-le-champ, immédiatement. To pay promptly, (i) payer argent comptant ; (ii) payer ponctuellement.

prompt[2], *s.* (*a*) Suggestion *f* ; F : inspiration *f,* tuyau *m.* *b*) Th : To give an actor a prompt, souffler un acteur. 'prompt-book, *s.* Th : Exemplaire *m* du souffleur. 'prompt-box, *s.* Th : Trou *m* du souffleur. 'prompt-side, F : 'P.S.', *s.* Th : Côté *m* de la scène à la droite des acteurs ; côté jardin.

prompt[3], *v.tr.* **I.** To prompt s.o. to sth., suggérer qch. à qn. To p. s.o. to do sth., inciter qn à faire qch. He felt prompted to speak, se sentit poussé à prendre la parole. To be prompted by a feeling of pity, être mû, avoir un sentiment de pitié. **2.** Souffler (un acteur, un élève). To prompt a witness, suggérer des jalons à un témoin.

prompting, *s.* **I.** Suggestion *f* ; incitation *f* (*to do sth.,* à faire qch.). **2.** Sch : No prompting! ne soufflez pas !

prompter ['prɔm(p)tər], *s.* **I.** Instigateur, -trice (*to a crime,* d'un crime) ; incitateur, -trice (*to,* à). **2.** Souffleur, -euse. Th : Opposite prompter, F : 'O.P.,' côté *m* de la scène à la gauche des acteurs ; côté cour. Prompter's box, trou *m* du souffleur.

promptitude ['prɔm(p)titjuːd], **promptness** ['prɔm(p)tnəs], *s.* Promptitude *f,* empressement *m.*

promulgate ['prɔməlgeit], *v.tr.* **I.** Promulguer (une loi). **2.** Disséminer, répandre (une idée) ; proclamer, répandre (une nouvelle).

▶romulgation [prɔmǝl'geiʃ(ǝ)n], s. **1.** Promulgation f (d'une loi). **2.** Dissémination f (d'une idée ; proclamation f (d'une nouvelle).

▶rone [proun], a. **1.** (a) (Of hand, etc.) En pronation. (b) (Of pers., etc.) Couché sur le ventre. **2.** To be pro:ne to sth., to do sth., être enclin, porte, a qch., à faire qch.

▶roneness ['prounnǝs], s. Disposition f, inclination f (to, à).

▶rong [prɔŋ], s. Fourchon m, dent f, branche f (de fourche) ; pointe f (d'andouiller, etc.).

▶ronged [prɔŋd], a. A fourchons, à dents. **Two-**pronged, a deux dents.

▶ronominal [pro'nɔmin(ǝ)l], a. Gram: Pronominal, -aux. **-ally,** adv. Pronominalement.

▶ronoun ['prounaun], s. Gram: Pronom m.

▶ronounce [pro'nauns], v.tr. **1.** (a) Déclarer. To p. the patient out of danger, déclarer que le malade est hors de danger. (b) Jur: Prononcer (une sentence, un jugement) ; rendre (un arrêt). **2.** Aos. To pronounce on a subject, prononcer sur un sujet. **To pronounce for s.o., in favour of s.o.**, se déclarer pour qn. **3.** Prononcer ; articuler (un mot, etc.). **pronounced,** a. Prononcé, marqué.

▶ronounceable [pro'naunsǝbl], a. Prononçable.

▶ronouncement [pro'naunsmǝnt], s. Déclaration f.

▶ronunciation [pronʌnsi'eiʃ(ǝ)n], s. Prononciation f.

▶roof¹ [pru:f], s. **1.** Preuve . **Positive proof,** preuve patente. F: **Cast-iron proof,** preuve rigide. **To give proof of sth.,** faire preuve de (bon voulo.r) ; annoncer (l'intelligence). To give, show, p. of goodwill, faire acte, témoigner, de bonne volonté. To give p. of one's gratitude to s.o., témoigner sa reconnaissance à qn. **This is proof that he is lying,** cela prouve qu'il ment. In proof of one's good faith, en preuve, en témoignage, de sa bonne foi. **Capable of proof,** susceptible de preuve, de démonstration. **To await proof of .th.,** attendre la confirmation de qch. **To produce proof to the contrary,** fournir la preuve contraire. **The onus of proof lies with . . .,** le soin de faire la preuve incombe à. . . . . Jur: Proo. of a right, constatation f d'un droit. **2.** (a) Épreuve f. **To bring, put, sth. to the proof,** mettre qch. à l'épreuve. **It has stood the proof,** cela a résisté à l'épreuve. (b) Spirit **30%** below proof (strength), alcool à 30% au-dessous de preuve. **3.** (a) Typ: Épreuve. **Slip proof,** épreuve en placard. **To pass the proofs,** donner le bon à tirer. (b) Engr: **Proof before the letter, before letters,** épreuve avant la lettre. **'proof-cutter,** s. Phot: Photocisaille f, coupe-épreuves m inv. **'proof-reader,** s. Typ: Correcteur, -trice (d'épreuves). **'proof-reading,** s. Typ: Correction f sur épreuves.

▶roof², a. **Proof against sth.,** résistant à qch. ; à l'épreuve de qch. ; à l'abri de qch. **Proof against damp, damp-proof,** étanche à l'eau, à l'humidité. **Bullet-proof,** à l'épreuve des balles. **To be proof against danger, against disease,** être à l'abri du danger, immunisé contre la maladie. **Proof against temptation, against flattery,** inaccessible, insensible, aux tentations, à la flatterie.

▶roof³, v.tr. **1.** Typ: Engr: Tirer une épreuve de (la page, etc.). **2.** (a) Imperméabiliser, caoutchouter (un tissu, etc.). (b) Rendre (qch.) étanche. (c) Rendre (qch.) résistant (aux acides, etc.). **To fire-proof a tissue,** ignifuger un tissu.

▶roofing, s. **1.** Imperméabilisation f. **2.** Enduit m imperméable.

prop¹ [prɔp], s. **1.** Appui m, support m, soutien m, étai m. Const: etc: Chandelle f, étançon m. S.a. PIT-PROP. **2.** Échalas m (de vigne, etc.) ; tuteur m·(d'un plant). **3.** F: One of the props of society, un des appuis, un des piliers, de la société.

prop², v.tr. (propped) (a) To prop (up), appuyer, soutenir. To p. a ladder (up) against the wall, appuyer une échelle contre le mur. **To prop up a piece of furniture,** placer des hausses sous les pieds d'un meuble. (b) Const: Étayer, chandeller, étançonner (un mur, etc.). (c) Échalasser (des vignes, etc.) ; ramer (des haricots, des pois).

propaganda [prɔpǝ'gandǝ], s. Propagande f.

propagandist [prɔpǝ'gandist], s. Propagandiste mf.

propagate ['prɔpǝgeit], **1.** v.tr. (a) Propager, faire reproduire (des animaux, etc.). (b) To propagate light, propager, répandre, la lumière. To propagate ideas, répandre, disséminer, propager, des idées. **2.** v.pr. & i. (Of animal, plant) Se propager, se reproduire, se multiplier.

propagation [prɔpǝ'geiʃ(ǝ)n], s. **1.** Propagation f, reproduction f. **2.** Propagation (de la lumière, etc.) ; dissémination f (d'une doctrine).

propel [pro'pel], v.tr. (propelled) Propulser ; pousser en avant ; donner une impulsion à (qch.). **Propelled by steam, by machinery,** mû par la vapeur, par une machine. **propelling,** a. Propulsif, propulseur, moteur, -trice. S.a. PENCIL¹ **1.**

propeller [pro'pelǝr], s. **1.** Propulseur m. **2.** Nau: Av: (Screw) propeller, (propulseur à) hélice f. **pro'peller-blade,** s. Aile f, pale f, branche f, d'hélice. **pro'peller-shaft,** s. **1.** Arbre m de l'hélice. **2.** Aut: etc: Arbre à Cardan ; arbre de propulsion, de transmission.

propensity [pro'pensiti], s. Propension f, penchant m, inclination f, tendance f (to, towards, sth., à, vers, qch. ; for doing sth., à faire qch.).

proper ['prɔpǝr], a. Propre. **1.** A: With my (own) proper eyes, de mes propres yeux. **2.** (a) Proper to sth., propre, particulier, à qch. (b) To paint s.o. in his p. colours, dépeindre qn sous son vrai jour. (c) Gram: Proper noun, nom propre. (d) Her: Lion proper, lion au naturel. **3.** (a) Vrai, juste, approprié. In a proper sense . . ., au sens propre. . . . (b) Mth: Proper fraction, fraction moindre que l'unité. **4.** P: He's a proper rogue, c'est un fripon dans toute l'acception du mot. To get a p. hiding, recevoir une belle volée (de coups), une belle raclée. **5.** (a) Convenable. **At the proper time,** en temps opportun ; en temps utile. **To deem it proper, to think proper, to . . .,** juger à propos de . . . ; juger bon de. . . . **Do as you think p.,** faites comme bon vous semblera. **To do the proper thing by s.o.,** agir loyalement avec qn. The p. way to do it, la meilleure manière de le faire. The p. tool to use, le bon outil ; l'outil approprié. **Proper receipt,** quittance régulière. **To keep sth. in proper condition,** tenir qch. en bon état. (b) Comme il faut ; (of language) bienséant, correct. **A very proper old lady,** une vieille dame (i) très comme il faut, (ii) très digne. **P. behaviour,** conduite bienséante. **-ly,** adv. **1.** (a) Word properly used, mot employé (i) correctement, (ii) au (sens) propre. **Properly so called,** proprement dit. (b) Bien ; de la bonne façon. **Do it properly or not at all,** faites-le comme il faut ou pas du tout. **2.** F: (Intensive) He was p. drunk, il était absolument gris. To tick s.o. off p., rembarrer vertement qn ; arranger qn de la belle manière. **3.** (a) Convenablement. **To**

behave properly, se conduire comme il faut. (b) *He very p. refused*, il a refusé, comme faire se devait.

property ['prɔpəti], s. **1.** (Droit m de) propriété f. **2.** (a) Propriété, biens mpl, avoir(s) m(pl). *Personal property*, biens personnels, mobiliers. *That's my property*, cela m'appartient; ça c'est à moi. *F: That's public property*, c'est un secret de Polichinelle. (b) Immeuble m, immeubles. *Property sale*, vente d'immeubles. *Man of property*, propriétaire m. **3.** *Th:* (a) Accessoire m. *Property sword*, épée de scène; épée pour rire. (b) *Properties*, réserve f de décors, de costumes, etc. **4.** Propriété; qualité f (propre). *Drug with antifebrile properties*, drogue qui a des qualités fébrifuges. *Inherent property*, attribut m. **'property-man**, pl. **-men**, s.m. *Th:* Garde, chef, des accessoires. **'property-room**, s. *Th:* Magasin m des accessoires. **'property-tax,** s. Impôt foncier.

prophecy ['prɔfisi], s. Prophétie f.

prophesy ['prɔfisai]. **1.** v.i. Parler en prophète; prophétiser, vaticiner. **2.** v.tr. Prophétiser, prédire (un événement). **prophesying**, s. Prophéties fpl; prédiction f.

prophet ['prɔfet], s. Prophète m. *Prov:* No man is a prophet in his own country, nul n'est prophète en son pays.

prophetess ['prɔfetes], s.f. Prophétesse.

prophetic(al) [prɔ'fetik(əl)], a. Prophétique. **-ally,** adv. Prophétiquement.

prophylactic [prɔfi'laktik], a. & s. *Med:* Prophylactique (m).

prophylaxis [prɔfi'laksis], s. *Med:* Prophylaxie f.

propinquity [prɔ'piŋkwiti], s. **1.** Proximité f (de lieu); voisinage m. **2.** (Proche) parenté f.

propitiate [prɔ'piʃieit], v.tr. **1.** Rendre propice, favorable. **2.** Apaiser (qn); se faire pardonner par (qn).

propitiation [prɔpiʃi'eiʃ(ə)n], s. **1.** Propitiation f. **2.** Apaisement m (des dieux courroucés, etc.). **3.** Expiation f.

propitious [prɔ'piʃəs], a. Propice, favorable. **-ly,** adv. D'une manière propice; favorablement.

proportion[1] [prɔ'pɔːrʃ(ə)n], s. **1.** Partie f (d'une surface); portion f; part f. *To divide expenses in equal proportions*, répartir les frais par parts égales. *Proportion of an ingredient in a mixture*, dose f d'un ingrédient dans un mélange. **2.** Rapport m, proportion f. (a) *P. of the net load to the gross load*, rapport du poids utile au poids mort. *Ch:* Law of multiple proportions, loi des proportions multiples. *Oil and vinegar in due proportion*, de l'huile et du vinaigre en proportions raisonnables, bien dosés. (b) *In proportion as* . . ., à mesure que. . . . *Payment in p. to work done*, rémunération au prorata du travail accompli. *His expenses are out of p. to, with, his income*, ses dépenses sont disproportionnées à son revenu. (c) *Out of proportion*, mal proportionné. *To have an eye for proportion*, avoir du coup d'œil. *F: To lose all sense of proportion*, ne garder aucune mesure. (d) *Mth:* The proportion that x bears to y, la proportionnalité entre x et y. *Arithmetical proportion*, proportion arithmétique. **3.** pl. *Proportions*, proportions (d'un édifice); *Ind:* dimensions f (d'une machine, etc.).

proportion[2], v.tr. **1.** Proportionner (la punition au crime, etc.). **2.** Doser (des ingrédients). **3.** *Ind:* (a) Déterminer les dimensions (d'une pièce). (b) Coter (un dessin). **4.** *Well-proportioned*, bien proportionné; taille bien prise.

proportional [prɔ'pɔːrʃən(ə)l]. **1.** a. Proportionnel; en proportion (to, de); proportionné (to, à). *Inversely proportional to* . . ., inversement proportionnel à . . .; en raison inverse de. . . . **2.** s. *Mth:* Proportionnelle f. **-ally,** adv. En proportion (to, de); proportionnellement (to, à).

proportionate [prɔ'pɔːrʃənet], a. Proportionné (to, à). **-ly,** adv. = PROPORTIONALLY.

proposal [prɔ'pouz(ə)l], s. **1.** (a) Proposition f, offre f. *To make a proposal*, faire, formuler, une proposition. (b) Demande f en mariage; offre de mariage. **2.** Dessein m, projet m.

propose [prɔ'pouz], v.tr. **1.** Proposer, poser (une question). **2.** (a) *To propose a course of action*, proposer une ligne de conduite. (b) *To propose a candidate*, proposer un candidat. *To propose a motion*, proposer une motion. *Will you p. m for your club?* voulez-vous me présenter à votre cercle? *To propose the health of s.o.*, porter un toast en l'honneur de qn. *To propose a toast*, porter un toast. (c) *To propose to do sth.*, doing sth., se proposer, avoir l'intention, de faire qch. *What do you p. to do now? what do you p. doing now?* que comptez-vous faire maintenant? **3.** *Abs.* Faire la demande en mariage; faire sa déclaration. *To propose to a girl*, demander sa main à une jeune fille.

proposer [prɔ'pouzər], s. Proposeur, -euse. *Proposer of a member*, parrain m d'un candidat (à un cercle).

proposition [prɔpo'ziʃ(ə)n], s. **1.** (a) = PROPOSAL 1 (a). (b) *F:* Affaire f. *Mining proposition*, entreprise minière. *Paying proposition*, affaire qui rapporte. *It's a tough proposition*, c'est une question difficile à résoudre. *P: He's a tough p.* (i) on ne sait par où le prendre; (ii) on ne sait qu'en faire. **2.** *Log: Geom:* Proposition f.

propound [prɔ'paund], v.tr. **1.** Proposer (une énigme); émettre (une idée); poser (une question, un problème); exposer (un programme). **2.** *Jur:* Soumettre (un testament) à la validation.

proprietary [prɔ'praiətəri], a. (a) De propriété, de propriétaire. *The p. rights of the Crown*, les droits de propriété de la Couronne. (b) *Proprietary classes*, classes possédantes. (c) *Proprietary chapel*, chapelle particulière, privée. *Com: Proprietary article*, spécialité f. *P. medicines*, spécialités médicales.

proprietor [prɔ'praiətər], s. Propriétaire mf. *Landed p.*, propriétaire foncier.

proprietorship [prɔ'praiətərʃip], s. **1.** Droit m de propriété. **2.** Propriété f, possession f.

proprietress [prɔ'praiətres], s.f. Propriétaire, patronne.

propriety [prɔ'praiəti], s. **1.** (a) Propriété f, justesse f, à-propos m (d'une expression, etc.); correction f (de langage); rectitude f (de conduite). *I doubt the p. of refusing*, je ne demande s'il convient de refuser. (b) Opportunité f (d'une démarche). **2.** (a) Bienséance f, décence f. *Marriage of propriety*, mariage de convenance. *Breach, lack, of propriety*, manque m de savoir-vivre. *To throw propriety to the winds*, se moquer de toutes les convenances. (b) *To observe the proprieties*, observer les convenances.

props [prɔps], s.pl. *Th: Cin:* = PROPERTIES.

propulsion [prɔ'pʌlʃ(ə)n], s. Propulsion f.

propulsive [prɔ'pʌlsiv], a. Propulsif, -ive; (effort) de propulsion.

prorogation [prouro'geiʃ(ə)n, prɔ-], s. Prorogation f.

prorogue [prɔ'roug], v.tr. Proroger (le Parlement).

rosaic [pro′zeiik], *a.* Prosaïque. **-ally,** *adv.* ′rosaïquement.

roscenium [pro′si:niəm], *s.* Th: Avan⁀-scène *f.* ′roscenium arch, manteau *m* d'Arlequin.

roscribe [pros′kraib], *v.tr.* Proscrire. **1.** Met⁀re hors la loi ; bannir. **2.** Interdire, défendre (un ısage, etc.).

roscript [′prouskript], *s.* Proscrit *m* ; hors-laɔi *m inv.*

roscription [pros′kripʃ(ə)n], *s.* Proscription *f* ; i) mise *f* (de qn) hors la loi ; (ii) interdiction *f* d'une pratique).

roscriptive [pros′kriptiv], *a.* **1.** (Lois, etc.) le proscription. **2.** (Décret) prohibitif.

rose[1] [pro:uz], *s.* **1.** Prose *f.* **2.** *Sch:* Latin *p.*, ′reek *p.*, thème latin, grec. **3.** Discours fastilieux, ennuyeux. **′prose-′poem,** *s.* Poème *m* ≀n prose. **′prose-writer,** *s.* Prosateur *m.*

rose[2], *v.i* F: Tenir des discours fastidieux, ennuyeux.

rosecute [′prosekjut], *v.tr.* **1.** (*a*) Poursuivre qn) (en justice répressive) ; engager ou exercer les poursuites contre (qn). **To be prosecuted** *or exceeding the speed limit,* attraper une contravention pour excès de vitesse. (*b*) **To prosecute ∍n action,** intenter une action. **To prosecute a ∍laim,** poursuivre une réclamation. **2.** (*a*) Effecuer (un voyage). (*b*) Poursuivre (des études) ; nener (une enquête). (*c*) Exercer (un métier).

rosecution [prose′kjuʃ(ə)n], *s.* **1.** *Jur:* (*a*) Poursuites *fpl* (en justice répressive) ; poursuites ɪudiciaires. **To start a prosecution against . . .,** ∍ngager des poursuites contre. . . . (*b*) Accusaɪon *f* ; action publique. (*c*) **The Prosecution,** les ɔlaignants *m* ; (*in Crown case*) le Ministère public. **Witness for the prosecution,** témoin à charge. **2.** (*a*) Continuation *f* (d'études, etc.). (*b*) Exerɔice *m* (d'un métier, etc.).

rosecutor [′prosekjutər], *s.* *Jur:* **1.** Plaignant *m,* ɔoursuivant *m,* demandeur *m.* **2. The Public Prosecutor,** (i) le procureur du Roi ; (ii) (*départ ment*) le Ministère public.

roselyte [′prosəlait], *s.* Prosélyte *mf.*

roselytism [′prosilitizm], *s.* Prosélytisme *m.*

rosiness [′prouzinəs], *s.* Prosaïsme *m* (d'une ɔonversation, etc.) ; terre à terre *m inv* (du style).

rosody [′prosodi], *s.* Prosodie *f* ; métrique *f.*

rospect[1] [′prospekt], *s.* **1.** Vue *f* ; point *m* de vue ; perspective *f.* *Wide p.,* horizon très étendu. **2.** (*a*) Perspective, expectative *f.* **To have sth. ɪn prospect,** avoir qch. en perspective, en ̈ vue. ′*b*) **There is no prospect** *of their leaving,* il n'y ∍ rien qui fasse prévoir leur départ. *No p. of ∍greement,* aucune perspective d'accord. **3.** *pl.* Avenir *m,* espérances *fpl.* *Future prospects of ∍n undertaking,* perspectives d'avenir d'une entreprise. *The prospects of the harvest are excellent,* la récolte s'annonce excellente. *His ɔrospects are brilliant,* un brillant avenir s'ouvre ɔevant lui. **′prospect-glass,** *s.* *A:* Lunette *f* d'approche.

rospect[2] [pro′spekt]. **1.** *v.i.* *Min:* Prospecter. **2.** *v.tr.* Prospecter (un terrain).

rospective [pro′spektiv], *a.* En perspective ; à venir ; ̈futur. *P. visit,* prochaine visite. *A p. buyer,* un acheteur éventuel.

rospector [pro′spektər], *s.* Chercheur *m* d'or ; prospecteur *m.*

rospectus [pro′spektəs], *s.* Prospectus *m*

rosper [′prospər]. **1.** *v.i.* Prospérer, réussir ; venir à bien. *He will p.,* il fera son chemin ; il arrivera. **2.** *v.tr.* Faire prospérer, faire réussir ; favoriser. **May God prosper you!** Dieu vous fasse prospérer !

prosperity [pros′periti], *s.* Prospérité *f.*

prosperous [′prospərəs], *a.* **1.** Prospère, florissant. **2.** Favorable, propice (*to,* à). *Esp.* **Prosperous winds,** vents favorables.

prosperousness [′prospərəsnəs], *s.* Prospérité *f.*

prostitute[1] [′prostitju:t], *s.f.* Prostituée *f.*

prostitute[2], *v.tr.* Prostituer.

prostitution [prosti′tju:ʃ(ə)n], *s.* Prostitution *f.*

prostrate[1] [′prostret], *a.* **1.** Prosterné ; couché (à terre) ; étendu. **2.** Abattu, accablé. *Med:* Prostré.

prostrate[2] [pros′treit], *v.tr.* **1. To prostrate oneself before s.o.,** se prosterner devant qn. **2.** *Med:* Abattre ; mettre dans un état de prostration. *Prostrated by the heat,* accablé par la chaleur.

prostration [pros′treiʃ(ə)n], *s.* **1.** Prosternation *f,* prosternement *m.* **2.** Abattement *m.* *Med:* Prostration *f.*

prosy [′prouzi], *a.* Prosaïque ; (*of pers.*) verbeux, ennuyeux. **-ily,** *adv.* Fastidieusement.

protagonist [pro′tagonist], *s.* Protagoniste *m.*

protect [pro′tekt], *v.tr.* **1.** (*a*) Protéger. **To protec⁀ s.o. from sth., against sth.,** protéger qn contre qch. ; préserver, défendre, qn de qch. **To p. sth. from the weather,** abriter qch. contre les intempéries. *To p. s.o. from s.o.'s wrath,* soustraire qn à la colère de qn. (*b*) Sauvegarder (les intérêts de qn, etc.). **2.** Patronner (qn) ; tenir (qn) en tutelle. **3.** *Pol.Ec:* Protéger (une industrie).

protecting, *a.* ̈Protecteur, -trice ; de protection, de garde.

protection [pro′tekʃ(ə)n], *s.* **1.** (*a*) Protection *f,* défense *f* (*against the weather, etc.,* contre le temps, etc.) ; sauvegarde *f* (des intérêts de qn, etc.). (*b*) **Under s.o.'s protection,** sous la sauvegarde de qn. *Com:* **Trade protection society,** agence *f* d'information(s). (*c*) Patronage *m.* **2.** *Pol.Ec:* Protectionnisme *m.* **3.** (*a*) Abri *m,* protection. (*b*) Blindage *m.* **4.** Sauf-conduit *m, pl.* sauf-conduits.

protectionist [pro′tekʃənist], *a. & s.* *Pol.Ec:* Protectionniste (*mf*). ̈

protective [pro′tektiv], *a.* Protecteur, -trice ; préservatif. *Pol.Ec:* **Protective tariff,** tarif protecteur, de protection.

protector [pro′tektər], *s.* **1.** (*Pers.*) (*a*) Protecteur *m.* (*b*) Patron *m.* **2.** (Dispositif) protecteur (d'un appareil, etc.). **Boot-protector,** ferrure *f* pour chaussures.

protectorate [pro′tektəret], *s.* Protectorat *m.*

protectress [pro′tektres], *s.f.* Protectrice ; patronne (des arts, etc.).

protein [′proutin], *s.* *Ch: Physiol:* Protéine *f.*

protest[1] [′proutest], *s.* **1.** Protestation *f.* **To make, set up, a protest,** protester ; faire des représentations. *To raise a strong p.,* élever des protestations ̈énergiques. **Under protest,** (i) (signer, etc.) sous réserve ; (ii) *F:* (faire qch.) à son corps défendant, en protestant. **2.** *Com:* Protêt *m.* **To make a protest,** lever protêt. **3.** *Nau:* **Ship's protest,** rapport *m* de mer ; procès-verbal *m* des avaries.

protest[2] [pro′test]. **1.** *v.tr.* (*a*) Protester. **To protest one's innocence,** protester de son innocence. (*b*) *Com:* **To protest a bill,** (faire) protester une lettre de change. **2.** *v.i.* Protester, réclamer, s'élever (*against,* contre).

protestant [′prostestənt], *a. & s.* *Rel.H:* Protestant, -ante.

protestantism [′protestəntizm], *s.* *Rel.H:* Protestantisme *m.*

protestation [protes′teiʃ(ə)n], *s.* **1.** Protestation *f* (*against,* contre). **2.** Protestation, déclaration *f* de sa foi, etc.).

protester, protestor [pro'testər], s. Protestateur, -trice; protestataire *mf*.

Proteus ['proutjus, -əs]. *Pr.n.m.* (a) *Myth:*
Protée. (b) *F:* A veritable P., un vrai Protée.

protocol ['proutokɔl], s. *Dipl:* Protocole *m*.

protoplasm ['proutoplazm], s. Protoplasme *m*,
protoplasma *m*.

prototype ['proutotaip], s. Prototype *m*, archétype *m*.

protozoa [prouto'zoua], s.pl. Protozoaires *m*.

protozoic [prouto'zouik], a. Protozoaire.

protract [pro'trakt], v.tr. **1.** Prolonger, allonger;
traîner (une affaire) en longueur. **2.** *Surv:*
Relever (un terrain).

protractile [pro'traktail, -til], a. *Z:* Extensile.

protraction [pro'trak§(ə)n], s. **1.** Prolongation *f*
(d'un procès, etc.). **2.** *Surv:* Relevé *m* (d'un
terrain).

protractor [pro'traktər], s. *Geom:* Rapporteur *m*.

protrude [pro'tru:d]. **1.** v.tr. Faire sortir;
pousser en avant. **2.** v.i. S'avancer, faire saillie,
déborder. **protruding,** a. En saillie; saillant.
Protruding forehead, front bombé. P. eyes, yeux
qui sortent de la tête. P. teeth, dents débordant
les lèvres.

protrusion [pro'tru:ʒ(ə)n], s. **1.** Saillie *f*. **2.** Protubérance *f*.

protuberance [pro'tju:bərəns], s. Protubérance *f*.

protuberant [pro'tju:bərənt], a. Protubérant.

proud [praud], a. **1.** (a) Fier, orgueilleux. As
proud as Lucifer, as a peacock, fier comme
Artaban. (b) To be proud of sth., of having done
sth., être fier de qch., d'avoir fait qch. House-
proud, orgueilleux de sa maison. (c) To be
proud to do sth., se faire honneur de faire qch.
F: To do s.o. proud, (i) faire beaucoup d'honneur à qn; (ii) se mettre en frais pour qn.
P: To do oneself proud, se bien soigner; ne se
priver de rien. **2.** *Poet:* (a) Altier, hautain,
superbe. (b) (Of view, etc.) Magnifique, superbe.
3. (a) Proud flesh, (i) *Med:* chair baveuse;
fongosité *f*; (ii) *Surg: Vet:* bouillon *m*.
(b) Proud nail, clou qui dépasse, qui fait saillie.
-ly, adv. Fièrement, orgueilleusement; avec
fierté.

provable ['pru:vəbl], a. Prouvable, démontrable.

prove [pru:v], v. (p.p. proved, A: proven ['pru:vn,
prouvn]) I. v.tr. **1.** (a) A. & Tchn: Éprouver;
mettre à l'épreuve; essayer (l'or, un cheval).
Proved remedy, remède éprouvé. To be proved
by adversity, passer par le creuset de l'adversité.
(b) Ar: Vérifier (un calcul); faire la preuve
(d'une opération). **2.** (a) Prouver, démontrer,
établir (la vérité, etc.). It remains to be proved,
cela n'est pas encore prouvé. To p. my case . . .,
comme preuve à l'appu. . . . All the evidence
goes to p. that . . ., les témoignages concourent
à prouver que. . . . *Jur:* (Scot.) Not proven
[nɔt 'prouvn], (verdict de) culpabilité non avérée;
non-lieu *m*. (b) *Jur:* Homologuer (un testament);
établir la validité (d'un testament). (c) To prove
oneself, faire ses preuves. II. **prove,** v.i. Se
montrer, se trouver, être. To p. useful, se trouver,
être reconnu, utile. The news proved false, la
nouvelle s'est avérée fausse. Their rashness proved
fatal to them, leur audace leur fut fatale. To p.
unequal to one's task, se révéler, se montrer,
au-dessous de sa tâche.

provender ['provendər], s. Fourrage *m*, aflour-
ragement *m*, provende *f*.

proverb ['provə:rb], s. Proverbe *m*

proverbial [pro'və:rbiəl], a. Proverbial, -au:
passé en proverbe. **-ally,** adv. Proverbialemen

provide [pro'vaid]. **1.** (a) v.i. To provide again
sth., se pourvoir, se prémunir, contre (un
attaque, etc.). To p. against a danger, parer à u
danger. Expenses provided for in the budg
dépenses prévues au budget. Com: To provi
for a bill, faire provision pour une lettre c
change. (b) v.tr. Stipuler (that, que + ind
2. (a) v.tr. To provide s.o. with sth., fourn
qch. à qn; pourvoir, munir, fournir, appr
visionner, qn de qch. To provide an exit, (i) (
passage) fournir une sortie; (ii) (of architec
ménager une sortie. (b) v.i. To provide for s.c
(i) pourvoir aux besoins, à l'entretien, de q
(ii) mettre qn à l'abri du besoin. To provide f
oneself, être pourvu de. To be provided for, être bie
nanti; être à l'abri du besoin. Abs. The Lo
will provide, Dieu nous viendra en a de. (c) v.i. F
provided for everything, il a subvenu à tou
provided. 1. a. Pourvu, muni (with, de). P. f
all eventualities, préparé à toute éventualit
2. conj. Provided (that) . . ., pourvu que + sub.
à condition que + ind. or sub.

providence ['providəns], s. **1.** (a) Prévoyance
prudence *f*. (b) = THRIFT I. **2.** Providenc
(divine). **3.** By a special providence . ., pa
une intervention providentielle. . . .

provident ['providənt], a. Prévoyant. Provider
society, société de prévoyance. P. scheme
œuvres *f* de prévoyance.

providential [provi'den§(ə)l], a. Providentie
-ally, adv. Providentiellement.

provider [pro'vaidər], s. Pourvoyeur, -euse
fournisseur, -euse.

province ['provins], s. **1.** Province *f*. In th
provinces, en province. **2.** *Jur: etc:* Juridictio
f, ressort *m*, compétence *f* (d'un tribunal
F: That is not (within) my province, ce n'es
pas, cela sort, de mon ressort, de ma compétence
cela ne rentre pas dans mes attributions *f*.

provincial [pro'vin§(ə)l], a. & s. Provincial, -ale
pl. -aux, -ales. Provincial theatre, théâtre d
province. **-ally,** adv. Provincialement.

provincialism [pro'vin§olizm], s. Provincia
lisme *m*.

provision[1] [pro'viʒ(ə)n], s. **1.** (a) Provision to
sth., against sth., prise *f* des dispositions néces
saires pour assurer qch., pour parer à qch. T
make provision for sth., pourvoir à qch. To mak
provision for one's family, (i) pourvoir au
besoins, (ii) assurer l'avenir, de sa famille. T
make provision against sth., se pourvoir, prendr
des mesures, contre qch. To make a provisio
for s.o., assurer une pension à qn. (b) Provisio
of the necessities of life, fourniture *f* des nécessité
de la vie. Com: Provision of capital, prestation
de capitaux. **2.** (a) Com: Provision *f*, réserve *f*
(b) Provisions, provisions (de bouche); vivres *m*
comestibles *m*. Provision merchant, marchan
de comestibles. **3.** Article *m* (d'un traité)
clause *f*, stipulation *f* (d'un contrat). There is n
provision to the contrary, il n'y a pas de clause
contraire. *F:* To come within the provisions
of the law, tomber sous le coup de la loi.

provision[2], v.tr. Approvisionner; ravitailler.

provisional [pro'viʒən(ə)l], a. Provisoire
-ally, adv. Provisoirement, intérimairement.

provisionment [pro'viʒənmənt], s. Approvisionnement *m*.

proviso, pl. **-oes** [pro'vaizo, -ouz], s. Clause
conditionnelle; condition *f* (d'un contrat)
stipulation *f*. With the proviso that . . ., à
condition que. . .

provisory [pro'vaizəri], *a.* **1.** (*Of clause, etc.*) Conditionnel. **2.** (Gouvernement) provisoire. **-ily,** *adv.* Provisoirement.
provocation [prɔvo'keiʃ(ə)n], *s.* Provocation *f.* To act under provocation, agir sous le coup de la colère.
provocative [pro'vɔkətiv], *a.* (*a*) Provocateur, -trice ; provocant. (*b*) (Sourire, etc.) agaçant, *F :* aguichant.
provoke [pro'vouk], *v.tr.* **1.** (*a*) Provoquer, pousser, inciter (*s.o. to do sth.*, qn à faire qch.). To provoke *s.o.* to anger, mettre qn en colère. (*b*) Irriter, fâcher, impatienter, contrarier, agacer, exaspérer (qn). **2.** (*a*) Exciter, faire naître (la curiosité, etc.) ; provoquer (la gaieté). To provoke a smile, faire naître un sourire. (*b*) To *p.* fermentation, provoquer la fermentation. **provoking,** *a.* Irritant, contrariant, exaspérant. How provoking! quel ennui ! **-ly,** *adv.* D'une manière irritante, contrariante, exaspérante.
provost ['prɔvəst], *s.* **1.** (*a*) Principal *m* (de certains collèges universitaires). (*b*) (Scot.) Maire *m.* (*c*) Hist : Prévôt *m.* **2.** [pro'vou] Mil : Provost-marshal, grand prévôt.
prow [prau], *s. A. & Lit :* Proue *f.*
prowess ['praues], *s.* Prouesse *f*, vaillance *f.*
prowl[1] [praul], *s.* (*Of lion, etc.*) To go on the prowl, partir en chasse. *F :* (*Of pers.*) To be for over on the prowl, être toujours à rôder.
prowl[2], *v.i.* (*a*) (*Of beast*) Rôder en quête de proie. (*b*) To *p.* about the streets, rôder par la ville.
prowler ['praulər], *s.* Rôdeur, -euse.
prox. [prɔks], *adv.* Com : = PROXIMO.
proximate ['prɔksimet], *a.* **1.** Proche, prochain, immédiat. **2.** Approximatif. **-ly,** *adv.* **1.** Immédiatement. **2.** Approximativement.
proximity [prɔk'simiti], *s.* Proximité *f.* In the proximity of a town, à proximité d'une ville. In proximity to the station, à proximité de la gare.
proximo ['prɔksimo], *adv.* (*Abbr.* prox.) (Du mois) prochain.
proxy ['prɔksi], *s. Jur :* **1.** Procuration *f* ; pouvoir *m* ; mandat *m.* To vote by proxy, voter par procuration. **2.** Mandataire *mf* ; fondé *m* de pouvoir(s) ; délégué, -ée.
prude [pru:d], *s.f.* Prude ; *F :* bégueule.
prudence ['pru:dəns], *s.* Prudence *f*, sagesse *f.*
prudent ['pru:dənt], *a.* Prudent, sage, judicieux. **-ly,** *adv.* Prudemment, sagement.
prudential [pru'denʃ(ə)l], *a.* De prudence ; dicté, commandé, par la prudence. Prudential insurance, assurance industrielle.
prudery ['pru:dəri], *s.* Pruderie *f* ; *F :* pudibonderie *f*, bégueulerie *f.*
prudish ['pru:diʃ], *a.* Prude ; *F :* pudibond, bégueule.
prudishness ['pru:diʃnəs], *s.* = PRUDERY.
prune[1] [pru:n], *s.* Pruneau *m.* *F :* Prunes and prisms, afféterie *f* de prononciation et de langage.
prune[2], *v.tr.* **1.** (*a*) Tailler (un rosier) ; rafraîchir (les racines d'un arbre). (*b*) Émonder (un arbre forestier). (*c*) To prune (off, away) a branch, élaguer une branche. **2.** *F :* Faire des coupures dans, élaguer (un article). **pruning,** *s.* (*a*) Taille *f* (d'un rosier, etc.). (*b*) Émondage *m.* (*c*) Pruning (off, away) of a branch, élagage *m* d'une branche. **'pruning-hook,** *s.* Émondoir *m*, ébranchoir *m.* **'pruning-knife,** *s.* Serpette *f.* **'pruning-shears,** *s.pl.* Sécateur *m.*
prurience ['pruəriəns], **pruriency** ['pruəriənsi], *s.* **1.** *A :* Démangeaison *f.* **2.** Lasciveté *f.*
prurient ['pruəriənt], *a.* Lascif.

Prussia ['prʌʃə]. *Pr.n.* La Prusse.
Prussian ['prʌʃ(ə)n], *a. & s.* Prussien, -ienne. Prussian blue, bleu *m* de Prusse.
prussic ['pr..sik], *a.* Prussic acid, acide *m* prussique.
pry[1] [prai], *s.* Curieux, -euse ; indiscret, -ète.
pry[2], *v.i.* (pried) Fureter ; fouiller, chercher à voir, *F :* fourrer le nez (*into sth.*, dans qch.). To *pry* into a secret, chercher à pénétrer un secret. **prying,** *a.* Curieux, indiscret ; *F :* fureteur.
pry[3], *v.tr.* (pried) Soulever, mouvoir, à l'aide d'un levier. To pry a door open, exercer des pesées sur une porte. The box had been pried open, on avait forcé la serrure du coffret.
psalm [sɑ:m], *s.* Psaume *m.*
psalmist ['sɑ:mist], *s.* Psalmiste *m.*
psalmody ['sɑ:modi, 'salm-], *s.* Psalmodie *f.*
psalter ['sɔ:ltər], *s.* Psautier *m.*
pseudo-archaic [(p)sju:dɔɑ:r'keiik], *a.* Pseudo-archaïque.
pseudo-membrane [(p)sju:dɔ'membrein], *s.* Med : Pseudo-membrane *f* ; fausse membrane.
pseudonym ['(p)sju:dɔnim], *s.* Pseudonyme *m.*
pshaw[1] [(p)ʃɔ:], *int.* F₁ (donc) ! peuh ! allons donc !
pshaw[2], *v.i.* Dire peuh ; pousser une exclamation de mépris ou d'impatience.
psht [pʃt], *int.* Chut !
psittacosis [(p)sita'kousis], *s.* Med : Psittacose *f.*
psora ['(p)sɔ:ra], *s.* Med : Psore *f* ; *F :* gale *f.*
psoriasis [(p)so'raiasis], *s.* Med : Psoriasis *m.*
Psyche ['(p)saiki]. *Pr.n.f.* Psyché.
psychiater [(p)sai'kaiətər], *s.* Psychiatre *m.*
psychiatric [(p)saiki'atrik], *a.* Psychiatrique.
psychiatry [(p)sai'kaiətri], *s.* Psychiatrie *f.*
psychic(al) ['(p)saikik(əl)]. **1.** *a.* Psychique ; métapsychique. **2.** *s.* Psychic, médium *m.*
psychics ['(p)saikiks], *s.pl.* La métapsychique ; le métapsychisme.
psychoanalysis [(p)saikoa'nalisis], *s.* Psychanalyse *f.*
psychoanalyst [(p)saiko'analist], *s.* Psychanalyste *m.*
psychological [(p)saiko'lɔdʒik(ə)l], *a.* Psychologique. *F :* The psychological moment, le moment psychologique. **-ally,** *adv.* Psychologiquement.
psychologist [(p)sai'kɔlodʒist], *s.* Psychologue *m.*
psychology [(p)sai'kɔlodʒi], *s.* Psychologie *f.*
psychosis, *pl.* **-oses** [(p)sai'kousis, -ousi:z], *s. Med :* Psychose *f.*
psychotherapy [(p)saiko'θerapi], *s.* Psychothérapie *f.*
psychrometer [(p)sai'krɔmetər], *s.* Meteor : Psychromètre *m.*
ptarmigan ['tɑ:rmigən], *s.* Orn : Lagopède alpin ; *F :* perdrix *f* des neiges.
Ptolemy ['tɔlemi]. *Pr.n.m.* Ptolémée.
ptomaine ['toumein, to'mein], *s. Ch :* Ptomaïne *f.* Ptomaine poisoning, intoxication *f* alimentaire (par les ptomaïnes).
pub [pʌb], *s. P :* (= public house) Cabaret *m* ; *P :* bistro *m.* **'pub-crawl,** *s. P :* Tournée *f* des cabarets. **'pub-crawler,** *s. P :* Coureur *m* de cabarets ; vadrouilleur *m.*
puberty ['pju:bərti], *s.* Puberté *f.*
pubescent [pju:'bes(ə)nt], *a.* **1.** *Bot :* Pubescent. **2.** *Physiol :* Pubère.
public ['pʌblik]. **1.** *a.* Public, *f.* publique. (*a*) Public holiday, fête légale. Public works, travaux publics. (*b*) Public library, bibliothèque municipale ou communale. (*c*) To make sth. public, rendre qch. public ; publier (une nouvelle). To make a public protest, protester

publiquement. (d) **Public ife,** vie publique. **Public spirit,** patriotisme m, civisme m. **2.** s. (a) Public m. **The general public, the public at large,** le grand public. (b) **In public,** en public; publiquement **-ly,** adv. Publiquement; en public; au grand jour. **public 'house,** s. **1.** Auberge f. **2.** Débit m de boissons. **public-'spirited,** a. Dévoué au bien public.

publican ['pʌblikən], s. **1.** Rom.Hist: B: Publicain m. **2.** (a) Aubergiste m. (b) Débitant m de boissons.

publication [pʌbli'keiʃ(ə)n], s. **1.** (a) Publication f; apparition f (d'un livre). (b) Publication (d'une nouvelle des bans); promulgation f (d'un décret). **2.** Ouvrage publié; publication.

publicist ['pʌblisist], s. Journaliste m, publiciste m.

publicity [pʌb'lisiti], s. **1.** Publicité f. **2.** Com: Publicité, réclame f. **The publicity department,** (i) Com: la publicité; (ii) Publ: le service de presse.

publish ['pʌbliʃ], v.tr. **1.** (a) Publier (un édit, etc.). (b) Publier, révéler (une nouvelle); F: crier (une nouvelle) sur les toits. **2.** Publier, faire paraître (un livre). **Just published,** (qui) vient de paraître. **publishing,** s. **1.** Publication f (des bans, etc.). **2.** Publication, mise f en vente (d'un livre). **Pub.ishing house,** maison d'édition.

publisher ['pʌbliʃər], s. Éditeur m; libraire-éditeur m.

puce [pju:s], a. & s. (Couleur) puce m inv.

Puck [pʌk]. **1.** Pr.n.m. (Le lutin) Puck. **2.** s. Lutin m, farfadet m.

puck², s. Galine f, palet m en caoutchouc (pour le hockey sur glace).

pucker¹ ['pʌkər], s. Ride f, pli m (du visage); fronce f, faux pli, godet m (d'une étoffe).

pucker². **1.** v.tr. Rider (le visage); plisser, froncer, faire goder (l'étoffe). **To pucker (up) one's brows, one's lips,** froncer les sourcils; plisser les lèvres. **2.** v.i. (a) (Of garment) **To pucker (up),** faire des plis, des fronces; se froncer. (b) His face puckered up, sa figure se crispa. **puckering,** s. Plissement m; froncement m.

puckish ['pʌkiʃ], a. Dévoué au lutin; malicieux, espiègle.

pudding ['pudiŋ], s. **1.** Cu: (a) Pudding m, pouding m. (b) **Milk pudding,** entremets sucré au lait. **Rice pudding,** riz m au lait. (c) **Black pudding,** boudin (noir). **White pudding,** boudin blanc. **2.** Nau: (a) Emboudinure f. (b) Bourrelet m de défense. **'pudding-face,** s. F: Visage empâté; P: tête de lard. **'pudding-head,** s. F: Nigaud m; P: cruche f. **'pudding-stone,** s. Miner: Poudingue m, conglomérat m.

puddle¹ ['pʌdl], s. **1.** (a) Flaque f d'eau, d'huile. (b) Petite mare. **2.** F: Gâchis m. **3.** Hyd.E: Corroi m, glaise f. **To line with puddle,** corroyer (un bassin, etc.).

puddle². **1.** v.i. **To puddle (about),** (i) patauger, barboter (dans la boue); (ii) F: faire du gâchis. **2.** v.tr. (a) Corroyer, malaxer (l'argile). (b) Metall: Puddler, brasser, corroyer (le fer). **'puddling-furnace,** s. Metall: Four m à puddler. **'puddle-ball,** s. Metall: Loupe f. **'puddle-'steel,** s. Acier puddlé.

puerile ['pjuərail], a. Puéril.

puerility [pjuə'riliti], s. Puérilité f.

puerperal [pju'ə:rpərəl], a. Med: Puerpéral, -aux.

puff¹ [pʌf], s. **1.** Souffle m (de la respiration, d'air); bouffée f (d'air, de tabac); échappement soudain (de vapeur). F: **Out o.** puff, essoufflé; à bout de souffle. **2.** Cost: (a) Bouillon m (de robe); bouffant m (d'une manche). **Puff sleeves,** manches bouffantes, ballonnées. (b) Bouffette f (de ruban); chou m, pl. choux. **3.** Toil: Powderpuff, houppe f, houppette f. **4.** Cu: Gâteau feuilleté (fourré de confiture, etc.). **5.** Réclame (tapageuse); puff m. **'puff-adder,** s. Vipère f clotho. **'puff-ball,** s. Fung: Vesse-de-loup f. **'puff-box,** s. Boîte f à poudre (de riz); boîte à houppe. **'puff-'pastry,** s. Cu: Pâte feuilletée.

puff². **1.** v.i. (a) Souffler. **To puff and blow,** haleter. **To puff (and blow) like a grampus,** souffler comme un phoque. (b) Lancer des bouffées (de fumée); émettre des jets (de vapeur). **To puff (away) at one's pipe,** tirer sur sa pipe. **2.** v.tr. (a) **To puff a cigar,** fumer un cigare par petites bouffées. (b) Gonfler (le riz, etc.). (c) F: Prôner, vanter, faire mousser (ses marchandises). **puff out. 1.** v.tr. (a) Gonfler (les joues); faire ballonner (une manche). (b) Émettre, lancer (des bouffées de fumée). **2.** v.i. (Of skirt) Bouffer. **puff up,** v.tr. (a) Gonfler ('es joues). (b) Bouffir, gonfler (d'orgueil). **To puff oneself up,** se rengorger. **puffed up,** a. **1.** (a) (Visage) enflé, bouffi. (b) (Style, langage) boursouflé. **2. Puffed up with pride,** bouffi, gonflé, d'orgueil.

puffed [pʌft], a. **1.** (a) **Puffed sleeves,** manches bouffantes. (b) **Puffed rice,** riz gonflé. **2.** F: (Of runner, etc.) Essoufflé; à bout de souffle.

puffer ['pʌfər], s. F: (In nursery speech) Locomotive f; teuf-teuf m inv.

puffin ['pʌfin], s. Orn: Macareux m.

puffiness ['pʌfinəs], s. Boursouflure f, enflure f. P. round the eyes, bouffissure f des yeux.

puffy ['pʌfi], a. **1.** (Vent) qui souffle par bouffées. **2.** (Of pers.) (i) A l'haleine courte; (ii) hors d'haleine. **3.** Bouffi, boursouflé; (of dress) bouffant.

pug¹ [pʌg], s. Pug(-dog), carlin m; petit dogue; roquet m. **'pug(-)'nose,** s. Nez épaté, nez camus. **'pug-'nosed,** a. Au nez épaté.

pug², s. Brickm: etc: Argile malaxée; glaise f.

pug³, v.tr. (pugged) **1.** Malaxer, corroyer, pétrir (l'argile). **2.** Const: Hourder (un plancher).

pug⁴, s. (Anglo-Indian) Empreinte f de pas (d'un tigre, etc.).

puggaree ['pʌgəri], s. Voile m (de casque colonial).

pugilism ['pju:dʒilizm], s. Pugilat m; la boxe.

pugilist ['pju:dʒilist], s. Pugiliste m; boxeur m.

pugnacious [pʌg'neiʃəs], a. Querelleur, -euse; batailleur, -euse.

pugnaciousness [pʌg'neiʃəsnəs], **pugnacity** [pʌg'nasiti], s. Humeur querelleuse, batailleuse.

puissant ['pjuis(ə)nt], a. A: Puissant.

puke [pju:k], v.tr. & i. Vomir.

pukka ['pʌka], a. (Anglo-Indian) F: Vrai, authentique. P. soldier, soldat de profession. A p. Englishman, un vrai Anglais d'Angleterre.

pule [pju:l], v.i. Piauler, piailler.

pull¹ [pul], s. **1.** (a) Traction f, tirage m. **To give a pull,** tirer. (b) Pull of a magnet, force f d'attraction d'un aimant; appel m, sollicitation f, d'un aimant. (c) Effort m de traction. **Up-hill pull,** effort à la montée. (d) Row: Coup m d'aviron); palade f. **To go for a pull on the water,** faire une promenade sur l'eau. **2.** Avantage m. **To have a pull,** (i) avoir le bras long; (ii) F: avoir du piston (with s.o., chez qn). **To have the pull of s.o., a pull over s.o.,** avoir l'avantage sur qn. **3.** F: (a) Gorgée f, P: lampée f (de bière, etc.). (b) To take a pull at one's pipe, tirer une bouffée

de sa pipe. **4.** Drawer pull, poignée *f* de tiroir.
5. *Typ: Engr:* Première épreuve.
pull², *v.tr.* **I.** (*a*) Tirer (les cheveux de qn, la sonnette, etc.). To pull the trigger, presser la détente. *Equit:* Horse that pulls, cheval qui gagne à la main. (*b*) *Row:* Manier (un aviron). To pull a boat, *abs.* to pull, ramer. *To p. hard,* souquer ferme. *To p. ashore,* ramer jusqu'au rivage. *S.a.* WEIGHT¹ I. (*c*) *Turf:* Retenir, tirer (un cheval) (pour l'empêcher de gagner). (*d*) *v.i.* To pull at a rope, tirer, agir, sur un cordage. To pull at one's pipe, tirer des bouffées de sa pipe. To pull at a bottle, boire un coup à même la bouteille. **2.** (*a*) Traîner, tirer (une charrette, etc.). *P. your chair near the fire,* approchez votre chaise du feu. Horse that pulls well, cheval qui tire bien. *Aut: etc: The engine is pulling heavily,* le moteur fatigue, peine. (*Of pers., car, etc.*) To pull slowly up the hill, gravir péniblement la colline. *F:* It is (a case of) pull devil pull baker, il faut les laisser se débrouiller. (*b*) Body pulled by a force, corps sollicité par une force. **3.** To pull a face, faire une grimace. To pull a wry face, faire la grimace. **4.** *F:* To pull a yarn, raconter, débiter, une histoire peu vraisemblable. **5.** *Typ: Engr:* Tirer (une épreuve). **6.** To pull the ball, *abs.* to pull, (i) *Cr:* renvoyer la balle d'un coup tiré à gauche ; (ii) *Golf:* faire un coup tiré. **pull about,** *v.tr.* (*a*) Tirailler ; traîner (qch.) çà et là. (*b*) *F:* Houspiller, malmener. **pull ahead,** *v.i. Sp:* Se détacher du peloton. **pull apart, asunder,** *v.tr* Séparer ; déchirer en deux. **pull away,** *v.tr.* Arracher, décoller (qch.). **pull back,** *v.tr.* **I.** Ramener en arrière. **2.** Empêcher (qn) de progresser. **'pull-back,** *s.* (*a*) Dispositif *m* de rappel. *Bill:* Effet *m* rétrograde ; rétro *m*. (*b*) Entrave *f.* **pull down,** *v.tr.* **I.** Baisser, faire descendre (un store, etc.) ; rabattre (son voile). **2.** (*a*) Démolir, abattre (une maison) ; raser (des fortifications) ; démonter (une cabane). (*b*) *F:* Renverser (un gouvernement). **3.** (*Of disease*) Abattre, affaiblir (qn). **pull in,** *v.tr.* (*a*) Rentrer (un filet, etc.). (*b*) Retenir (son cheval) ; tirer les rênes de (son cheval). (*c*) To pull oneself in, se serrer la taille. **pull off,** *v.tr.* **I.** To p. sth. off sth., enlever ou arracher qch. de qch. **2.** (*a*) Retirer, ôter (son chapeau) ; enlever (son pardessus). (*b*) *Sp:* Gagner, remporter, *F:* décrocher (un prix). (*c*) Réussir à faire (qch.) ; venir à bout de (qch.). **pull on,** *v.tr.* Enfiler, mettre (des bas, etc.). **pull out,** *v.tr.* **I.** (*a*) Sortir, re)tirer. *To p. s.o. out of qch.,* tirer qn de qch. (*b*) Arracher (une dent). **2.** *v.i.* (*a*) (*Of rower*) Ramer vers le large. (*b*) (*Of train*) Sortir de la gare ; démarrer. (*c*) *Aut:* To pull out from behind a vehicle, sortir de la file pour doubler. **pull over,** *v.tr.* **I.** (*a*) To pull one's hat over one's eyes, ramener son chapeau sur ses yeux. (*b*) Renverser (qch.) (en tirant dessus). **2.** *v.i.* (*Of car, etc.*) To pull over to one side, se ranger. **'pull-over,** *s.* Cost: Pull-over *m.* **pull round.** *F:* **I.** *v.tr.* (*a*) Ranimer (qn). (*b*) (*After illness*) Remettre (qn) sur pied. **2.** *v.i.* (*a*) (*After fainting*) Se ranimer. (*b*) (*After illness*) Se remettre. **pull through.** **I.** *v.tr.* Tirer (qn) d'embarras, d'affaire ; aid r (qn) à surmonter une difficulté. *To p. a thing through,* mener une chose à bien. **2.** *v.i.* Se tirer d'affaire ; s'en tirer. *He will never p. through,* il ne guérira pas ; il n'en reviendra pas. **pull to,** *v.tr.* Tirer, fermer (la porte). **pull together,** *v.tr.* **I.** To pull oneself together, se reprendre, se ressaisir ; reprendre ses esprits. *Come, p. yourself together!* voyons,

remettez-vous ! **2.** *Abs.* Tirer ensemble ; *F:* agir de concert ; s'accorder. *They are not pulling together,* ils ne s'entendent pas. *Nau:* Pull together! nage d'accord ! **pull up.** **I.** *v.tr.* (*a*) (Re)monter, hisser (qn, qch.). *Aut:* To pull up the brake, serrer le frein (à main). (*b*) Hausser, lever (un store) ; retrousser, relever (sa jupe). To pull up one's socks, (i) remonter ses chaussettes ; (ii) *F:* se dégourdir, s'activer ; faire appel à toute son énergie. (*c*) Arracher, extirper (les mauvaises herbes). (*d*) Arrêter (un cheval) ; arrêter brusquement (sa voiture). (*e*) *F:* Réprimander, rembarrer (qn). **2.** *v.i.* (*a*) S'arrêter. *To p. up at the corner,* arrêter (la voiture) au coin. *To p. up at the kerb,* se ranger le long du trottoir. (*b*) *Gym:* To pull up to the bar, faire une traction. **pull-'up,** *s.* **I.** Arrêt *m* (d'une voiture, etc.) ; *Mil:* à-coup *m* (dans une colonne, etc.). **2.** Auberge *f* où charretiers, cyclistes, etc., peuvent s'arrêter pour se rafraîchir. **pulling,** *s.* (*a*) Tirage *m.* *S.a.* WIRE-PULLING. (*b*) *Typ:* Tirage, impression *f* (d'épreuves). *c*) Pulling race, course *f* à l'aviron.

puller ['pu:ər], *s.* **I.** (*a*) Tireur, -euse. *S.a.* WIRE-PULLER. (*b*) Rameur, -euse. **2.** (*a*) (*Of horse*) To be a good p., tirer à plein collier. (*b*) *Equit:* Cheval fort en bouche, qui tire à la main. **3.** *Tls:* Extracteur *m* (pour roulements à billes).

pullet ['pulet], *s.* Poulette *f.* Fattened p., poularde *f,* gelinotte *f.*

pulley ['puli], *s.* **I.** Poulie *f.* Grooved pulley, poulie à gorge. Differential pulley, palan différentiel. *S.a.* TACKLE¹ 2. **2.** Belt-pulley, poulie ; roue *f* de courroie. Cable-pulley, roue à corde. Fixed pulley, poulie fixe. Loose pulley, dead pulley, poulie folle ; ga.op n *m.* Step-pulley, poulie à gradins. **'pulley-block,** *s.* (*a*) Moufle *f or m.* Three-strand pulley-block, moufle à trois brins. (*b*) Palan *m.* **'pulley-wheel,** *s.* Réa *m,* rouet *m.*

Pullman ['pulmən], *s.* *Rail:* Pullman car, voiture *f* Pullman.

pullulate ['pʌljuleit]. *v.i.* (*a*) (*Of seed*) Germer ; (*of bud*) pousser. (*b*) (*Of rats, heresy*) Pulluler ; (*of opinions*) proliférer. (*c*) *F:* (*Of vermin*) Grouiller.

pullulation [pʌlju'leiʃ(ə)n], *s.* (*a*) Germ.nation *f;* pousse *f* (des bourgeons, etc.). (*b*) Pullulat on *f.*

pulmonary ['pʌlmənəri], *a.* **I.** *Anat:* Pulmonaire. P. complaint, maladie des poumons. **2.** (*Of pers.*) Poitrinaire.

pulp¹ [pʌlp], *s.* **I.** Pulpe *f* (des doigts, dentaire) ; pulpe, chair *f* (des fruits). Paper-pulp, pâte *f,* pulpe à papier. To reduce sth. to a pulp, réduire qch. en pulpe. *F:* Arm crushed to p., bras réduit en marmelade, en bouillie.

pulp², *v.tr.* (*a*) Réduire en pulpe. To pulp books, mettre des livres au pilon. (*b*) Décortiquer.

pulping, *s.* Réduction *f* en pulpe. en pâte. Pulping machine, pilon *m.*

pulpit ['pulpit], *s.* Cha re *f* (du préd cateur). To ascend, mount, the pulpit, monter en chaire. The influence of the p., l' nfluence de la chaire.

pulpy ['pʌlpi], *a.* **I.** Pulpeux, charnu. **2.** *F:* Mou, *f.* molle ; flasque.

pulsate [pʌl'seit], *v.i.* (*a* (*Of heart, etc.* Battre. (*b*) Palpiter ; vibrer.

pulsatilla [pʌlsə'tilə], *s.* *Bot:* Pulsatille *f; F:* passe-fleur *f.*

pulsation [pʌl'seiʃ(ə)n], *s.* Pulsat on *f,* battement *m.*

pulse¹ [pʌls], . **I.** Pouls *m.* To feel s.o.'s pulse, tâter le pouls à qn. **2.** Pulsation *f,* battement *m* du cœur, etc.) ; vibration *f* (d'une corde).

pulse², *v.i.* Avoir des pulsations ; battre ; palpiter.

pulse³, *s.* Plantes légumineuses.

pulsimeter [pʌl'simetər], *s.* *Med:* Sphygmomètre *m.*

pulsometer [pʌl'sɔmetər], *s.* *Ind:* Pulsomètre *m.*

pulverizable ['pʌlvəraizəbl], *a.* Pulvérisable.

pulverization [pʌlvərai'zeiʃ(ə)n], *s.* Pulvérisation *f.*

pulverize ['pʌlvəraːiz]. **I.** *v.tr.* (*a*) Pulvériser ; réduire en poudre ; broyer. *F:* To pulverize an argument, réduire un argument en miettes, à néant. To pulverize s.o., pulvériser (l'orateur, etc.). (*b*) Atomiser (de la peinture, etc.). **2.** *v.i.* (*a*) Tomber en poussière. (*b*) Se vaporiser.

pulverulent [pʌl'verjulənt], *a.* Pulvérulent ; poudreux.

puma ['pjuːma], *s.* *Z:* Puma *m*, couguar *m.*

pumice ['pʌmis], *s.* Pumice(-stone), (pierre *f*) ponce *f.*

pummel ['pʌm(ə)l], *v.tr.* (pummelled) Bourrer (qn) de coups de poing.

pump¹ [pʌmp], *s.* (*a*) Pompe *f.* Hand pump, pompe à bras. *Aut:* Petrol pump, (i) (*of engine*) pompe à essence ; (ii) (*of service station*) poste *m* d'essence ; *F:* borne-fontaine *f.* (*b*) Pressure pump, force pump, pompe foulante. Bicycle pump, pompe à bicyclette. Foot pump, pompe à pied. *S.a.* AIR-PUMP. **'pump-brake,** *s.* *Nau:* Bringuebale *f.* **'pump-gear,** *s.* Garniture *f*, armature *f*, de pompe. **'pump-'handle,** *s.* Bras *m* de pompe. *F:* Pump-handle handshake, poignée *f* de main en coup de pompe. **'pump-room,** *s.* **I.** Chambre *f* des pompes. **2.** (*At a spa*) (*a*) Buvette *f* (où l'on prend les eaux). (*b*) Le Pavillon.

pump². **I.** *v.tr.* (*a*) To pump water, (i) pomper, extraire, de l'eau ; (ii) épuiser l'eau à la pompe. (*b*) To pump a well dry, assécher un puits. *F:* To pump s.o., sonder, faire causer, qn ; *F:* tirer les vers du nez de, à, qn. To pump a prisoner, cuisiner un prisonnier. (*c*) Refouler (l'eau dans une chaudière, l'air dans une mine). To p. air into the lungs, insuffler de l'air dans les poumons. **2.** *v.i.* (*Of heart, machine*) Pomper. **pump out,** *v.tr.* Dénoyer (une mine) ; épuiser l'eau (d'un puits) ; assécher (un puits). **pump up,** *v.tr.* **I.** Faire monter (l'eau) en la pompant ; pomper (l'eau). **2.** Gonfler (un pneu). **pumping,** *s.* Pompage *m*, extraction *f* (de l'eau). **'pumping-engine,** *s.* Machine *f* d'épuisement ; pompe *f* d'extraction. **'pumping-station,** *s.* *Min:* Station *f* d'épuisement.

pump³, *s.* Escarpin *m.*

pumpkin ['pʌm(p)kin], *s.* *Hort:* Potiron *m*, citrouille *f.*

pun¹ [pʌn], *s.* Calembour *m* ; jeu *m* de mots.

pun², *v.i.* (punned) Faire des calembours, des jeux de mots.

pun³, *v.tr.* Damer, pilonner (la terre, le pisé).

punch¹ [pʌnʃ], *s.* **I.** *Tls:* (*a*) (Centre-)punch, pointeau *m* (de mécanicien). (*b*) Chasse-goupilles *m inv*, chasse-clavettes *m inv.* Nail-punch, brad-punch, chasse-clou(s) *m inv.* (*c*) (*For piercing*) Perçoir *m.* (*d*) Hollow punch, emporte-pièce *m inv*, découpoir *m.* (*e*) Étampe *f*, poinçon *m.* **2.** Poinçon (de contrôleur de chemin de fer) ; pince *f* de contrôle. **'punch-mark,** *s.* Coup *m* de pointeau ; repère *m.*

punch², *s.* **I.** Coup *m* de poing ; horion *m.* **2.** *F:* Force *f*, énergie *f.* Style with p. in it, style énergique ; style à l'emporte-pièce. **'punch-ball,** *s.* = PUNCHING-BALL.

punch³, *v.tr.* **I.** (*a*) Percer ; découper (à l'em-

porte-pièce) ; poinçonner. (*b*) Poinçonner (un billet). (*c*) To p. an iron plate, estamper, étamper une plaque de fer. **2.** Donner un coup de poing à (qn) ; cogner sur (qn). **punch in,** *v.tr.* Enfoncer (un clou, etc.) au poinçon. **punch out,** *v.tr.* **I.** Découper à l'emporte-pièce. **2.** Chasser (une goupille). **punching,** *s.* **I.** (*a*) Perçage *m*, poinçonnage *m* ; découpage *m* à l'emporte-pièce. (*b*) Poinçonnement *m*, poinçonnage (des billets). **2.** *Metalw:* Pièce étampée. **'punching-ball,** *s.* *Box:* Punching-ball *m*, punching *m.* **'punching-machine,** *s.* **I.** Poinçonneuse *f* ; machine *f* à poinçonner. **2.** Découpeuse *f.*

punch⁴, *s.* (*Beverage*) Punch *m.* Milk punch, lait *m* au rhum. **'punch-bowl,** *s.* **I.** Bol *m* à punch. **2.** Cuvette *f* (entre collines).

Punch⁵. *Pr.n.m.* = Polichinelle ou Guignol. Punch and Judy show, (théâtre *m* de) Guignol *m.*

puncheon ['pʌnʃ(ə)n], *s.* Tonneau *m* (de 72 à 120 gallons). *P.* of rum, pièce *f* de rhum.

Punchinello [pʌn(t)ʃi'nelo]. *Pr.n.m.* *Ital.Th:* Polichinelle.

punctilio [pʌŋk'tiljo], *s.* **I.** Formalisme exagéré. **2.** Point *m* d'étiquette. To stand upon punctilios, s'attacher à des vétilles.

punctilious [pʌŋk'tiliəs], *a.* **I.** (*a*) Pointilleux, méticuleux. (*b*) *P.* on the point of honour, chatouilleux sur le point d'honneur. **2.** To be very *p.*, être à cheval sur le cérémonial ; être très soucieux du protocole. **-ly,** *adv.* **I.** Pointilleusement ; scrupuleusement. **2.** Cérémonieusement.

punctiliousness [pʌŋk'tiliəsnəs], *s.* **I.** Pointillerie *f* ; scrupule *m* des détails. **2.** Souci *m* du protocole.

punctual ['pʌŋktjuəl], *a.* Ponctue, exact. To be p. in one's payments, at the office, être exact, régulier, dans ses payements, au bureau. **-ally,** *adv.* Exactement, ponctuellement.

punctuality [pʌŋkt u'aliti], . Ponctualité *f*, exactitude *f.*

punctuate ['pʌŋktjueit], *v.tr.* Ponctuer.

punctuation [pʌŋktju'eiʃ(ə)n], *s.* Ponctuation *f.*

puncture¹ ['pʌŋktjər], *s.* **I.** (*a*) *Surg:* Ponction *f.* (*b*) Crevaison *f*, perforation *f* (d'un abcès, d'un pneu). **2.** (*Hole*) Piqûre *f*, perforation. **'puncture-proof,** *a.* (Pneu) increvable.

puncture², *v.tr.* (*a*) Ponctionner (un abcès). (*b*) Crever, perforer (un pneu). (*c*) (*With passive force*) (*Of tyre*) Crever.

pundit ['pʌndit], *s.* **I.** Pandit *m.* **2.** *F:* Pontife *m* (des lettres, etc.).

pungency ['pʌndʒənsi], *s.* **I.** Goût piquant ; odeur forte (d'un parfum). **2.** (*a*) Acuité *f* (d'une douleur) ; âcreté *f*, aigreur *f* (de paroles). (*b*) Saveur *f* (d'un récit) ; causticité *f* (d'une épigramme).

pungent ['pʌndʒənt], *a.* **I.** (*Of pain*) Cuisant ; aigu, -uë ; (*of sorrow, etc.*) poignant. **2.** (*Of style, etc.*) Mordant, caustique. **3.** (*Of smel, etc.*) Fort, âcre, piquant, irritant. **-ly,** *adv.* D'une manière piquante.

Punic ['pjuːnik], *a.* *Hist:* (Guerre, etc.) punique. Punic faith, la foi punique ; perfidie *f.*

puniness ['pjuːninəs], *s.* Chétiveté *f.*

punish ['pʌniʃ], *v.tr.* **I.** Punir ; châtier (qn) ; corriger (un enfant). To punish s.o. for sth., punir qn de qch. **2.** *F:* Taper dur sur (qn) ; malmener (qn, un adversaire, etc.). To punish s.o.'s cellar, ne pas épargner la cave de qn. To p. the roast beef, taper sur le rôti. *Aut: etc:* To punish the engine, fatiguer, forcer, le moteur.

punishable ['pʌniʃəbl], *a.* Punissable. *Jur:* Délictueux.

punishment ['pʌniʃmənt], s. Punition f, châtiment m. **Corporal punishment,** châtiment corporel. **Capital punishment,** peine capitale. **As a punishment,** par punition. *Mil:* **Summary punishment,** sanction f disciplinaire. *F:* **To take one's punishment like a man,** avaler sa médicine en homme.

punitive ['pjuːnitiv], **punitory** ['pjuːnitəri], a. Punitif; répressif.

punk [pʌŋk]. **I.** s. *U.S:* Amadou m. **2.** a. *P:* (*Of thg*) Mauvais; *P:* moche.

punka(h) ['pʌŋkə], s. (*Anglo-Indian*) Panka m, panca m.

punner ['pʌnər], s. *Tls:* Hie f, pilon m, dame f.

punster ['pʌnstər], s. Faiseur m de calembours.

punt¹ [pʌnt], s. (*a*) Bateau plat (conduit à la perche). (*b*) Bachot m, plate f, accon m. **'punt-gun,** s. Canardière f. **'punt-pole,** s. Gaffe f, perche f.

punt², v.tr. (*a*) Conduire (un bateau) à la perche. (*b*) Transporter (qn) dans un bateau plat.

punt³, s. *Rugby Fb:* Coup m (de pied) de volée.

punt⁴, v.tr. *Rugby Fb:* Envoyer (le ballon) d'un coup de pied de volée.

punt⁵, v.i. **I.** *Cards:* Ponter. **2.** (*a*) *Turf:* Parier. (*b*) *St.Exch:* Boursicoter.

punter ['pʌntər], s. **I.** *Cards:* Ponte m. **2.** (*a*) *Turf:* Parieur m. (*b*) *St.Exch:* Boursicoteur m.

puny ['pjuːni], a. **I.** (*a*) Petit, menu, grêlet. (*b*) Mesquin. **2.** (*Of pers.*) Chétif, faible, débile.

pup [pʌp], s. **I.** Petit chien, jeune chien; chiot m. *F:* **To sell** s.o. **a pup,** tromper, rouler, filouter, qn. **2.** *F:* = **PUPPY 2.**

pupa, pl. -ae ['pjuːpa, -iː], s. *Ent:* Nymphe f, chrysalide f.

pupil¹ ['pjuːpil], s. **I.** *Jur:* Pupille mf. **2.** *Sch:* Élève mf; écolier, -ière.

pupil², s. Pupille f (de l'œil).

pupil(l)age ['pjuːpiledʒ], s. *Jur:* (*a*) Minorité f. (*b*) Pupillarité f. **Child in pupil(l)age,** enfant en pupille, en tutelle.

puppet ['pʌpet], s. Marionnette f. *F:* (*Of pers.*) Mere puppet, pantin m. **'puppet-play,** s. = **PUPPET-SHOW I.** **'puppet-show,** s. **I.** Spectacle m de marionnettes. **2.** Théâtre m de marionnettes.

puppy ['pʌpi], s. **I.** Jeune chien; chiot m. **2.** (*Of pers.*) Freluquet m, fat m.

purblind ['pəːrblaind], a. **I.** (*a*) Myope. (*b*) Presque aveugle. **2.** À l'esprit épais, obtus.

purblindness ['pəːrblaindnəs], s. **I.** (*a*) Myopie f; vue basse. (*b*) Quasi-cécité f. **2.** Manque m d'intelligence, de vision.

purchase¹ ['pəːrtʃes], s. **I.** Achat m, acquisition f. **To make some purchases,** faire des emplettes, des achats. **2.** Loyer m. (*In the phr.*) **At so many years' purchase,** moyennant tant d'années de loyer. *F:* **His life would not be worth an hour's purchase,** on ne lui donnerait pas une heure à vivre. **3.** (*a*) Force f mécanique. (*b*) Prise f. **To get, secure, a purchase on** sth., trouver prise à qch. (*c*) Point m d'appui; appui m. **To take purchase on . . .,** prendre appui sur. . . . **4.** (*a*) (*Block*) Palan m, moufle m or f. (*b*) (*Tackle*) Appareil m (de levage). **'purchase-money, -price,** s. Prix m d'achat.

purchase², v.tr. Acheter, acquérir. *Abs.* Now is the time to purchase, c'est maintenant qu'il faut faire vos achats.

purchaser ['pəːrtʃesər], s. Acheteur, -euse, acquéreur, -euse.

purdah ['pəːrdaː], s. (*In India*) (*a*) Rideau destiné à soustraire les femmes à la vue; pur-

dah m. (*b*) Système m qui astreint à une vie retirée les femmes de haut rang.

pure ['pjuər], a. Pur. *P.* gold, or pur. *P.* alcohol, alcool rectifié. **Pure mathematics,** les mathématiques pures. **The pure and simple truth,** la vérité pure et simple. *P.* air, air pur. **-ly,** adv. Purement. **'pure-blood,** attrib. a. & s., **'pure-blooded,** a. (Personne f, animal m) de sang pur; (cheval m) de race. **'pure-bred,** a. (Chien) de race. **pure-'minded,** a. Pur d'esprit; chaste.

purgation [pər'geiʃ(ə)n], s. Purgation f.

purgative ['pəːrgətiv], a. & s. Purgatif (m).

purgatory ['pəːrgətəri], s. *Theol:* Le purgatoire. **The souls** in purgatory, les âmes du purgatoire, les âmes en peine. *F:* **It is** p. to me, cela me fait souffrir les peines du purgatoire.

purge¹ [pəːrdʒ], s. **I.** *Med:* Purgatif m, purge f. **2.** Purgation f. **3.** *Mch:* **Purge-cock,** robinet m de vidange.

purge², v.tr. **I.** Purger (un malade). **2.** Nettoyer (un égout); purifier (le sang); clarifier (un liquide); épurer (les mœurs). **To** p. **the finances of a country,** assainir les finances d'un pays. **3.** To purge away, purge out, one's sins, purger ses péchés. **4.** *Jur:* **To purge oneself of a charge,** se disculper, se justifier. **5.** *Jur:* **To purge an offence,** purger sa peine. **purging¹,** a. Purgatif. **purging²,** s. **I.** Purge f, purgation f (du corps). **2.** Nettoyage m; purification f.

purification [pjuərifi'keiʃ(ə)n], s. Purification f; épuration f.

purifier ['pjuərifaiər], s. **I.** (*Pers.*) Purificateur, -trice. **2.** (*Apparatus*) Épurateur m (de gaz, etc.).

purify ['pjuərifai], v.tr. Purifier (l'air, etc.); épurer (le gaz, l'huile, la langue); dépurer (le sang). **purifying¹,** a. Purifiant, purificateur. **purifying²,** s. Purification f; épuration f; dépuration f (du sang, etc.).

purist ['pjuərist], s. Puriste mf.

Puritan ['pjuəritən], a. & s. Puritain, -aine.

puritanical [pjuəri'tanik(ə)l], a. De puritain.

puritanism ['pjuəritənizm], s. Puritanisme m.

purity ['pjuəriti], s. Pureté f.

purl¹ [pəːrl], s. **I.** *Needlew:* (*Of twisted metal*) Cannetille f (à broder). **2.** Picot m, engrêlure f (de dentelle). **3.** *Knitting:* **Purl stitch,** maille f à l'envers.

purl², v.tr. **I.** Engrêler (la dentelle). **2.** *Knitting:* Faire des mailles à l'envers. **Knit one, purl one,** une maille à l'endroit, une maille à l'envers.

purl³, s. Doux murmure, gazouillement m (d'un ruisseau).

purl⁴, v.i. (*Of brook*) Murmurer, gazouiller.

purler ['pəːrlər], s. *F:* **To come a purler,** piquer une tête; *P:* ramasser une bûche.

purlieu ['pəːrljuː], s. **I.** *Jur:* Confins mpl (d'une forêt) soumis au régime du domaine forestier. **2.** Limites fpl, bornes fpl. **3.** pl. Purlieus, alentours mpl, environs mpl, abords mpl (d'une gare, etc.).

purlin ['pəːrlin], s. *Const:* Panne f, filière f. **'purlin-cleat,** s. Chantignol(l)e f.

purloin [pər'lɔin], v.tr. Soustraire, détourner; voler.

purloiner [pər'lɔinər], s. Détourneur m (d'une lettre, etc.); voleur, -euse.

purple [pəːrpl]. **I.** a. (*a*) *A:* Pourpre, pourpré. (*b*) Violet (tirant sur le rouge); mauve. *F:* **To get purple in the face** (*with anger*, etc.), devenir cramoisi, pourpre. *Lit:* **Purple passages, purple patches,** passages (d'un livre) qui frappent par leur coloris, par leur force; morceaux de bravoure. **II. purple,** s. **I.** (*a*) Pourpre f.

(b) Violet m, mauve m. (c) Born in the purple, né dans la pourpre ; né sous des lambris dorés. **2.** pl. Med: Purples, purpura m, pourpre m '**purple-wood,** s. Bot: Palissandre m.

purplish ['pəːrpliʃ], a. Violacé, violâtre : (of the face) cramoisi, vultueux.

purport[1] ['pəːrpərt, -pɔːrt], s. (a) Sens m, signification f, teneur f (d'un document). (b) Portée f, valeur f, force f (d'un mot).

purport[2] [pər'pɔːrt], v.tr. **1.** To purport to be sth., avoir la prétention d'être qch. ; être donné, présenté, comme étant qch. **2.** Impliquer ; tendre à démontrer, à établir (un fait).

purpose[1] ['pəːrpəs], s. **1.** (a) Dessein m, objet m ; but m, fin f, intention f. Fixed purpose, dessein bien arrêté. Novel with a purpose, roman à thèse. For, with, the purpose of doing sth., dans le but de, dans l'intention de, faire qch. To do sth. on purpose, faire qch. exprès, à dessein, de propos délibéré. Of set purpose, de propos délibéré, de parti pris. (b) Résolution f. Infirmity of purpose, manque m de volonté. Infirm of purpose, irrésolu ; sans caractère. Steadfastness of purpose, ténacité f de caractère ; détermination f. **2.** Destination f, fin (d'un bâtiment, d'un appareil). To answer, serve, various purposes, servir à plusieurs usages, à plusieurs fins. To answer the purpose, répondre au but. For this, that, purpose, dans ce but, dans cette intention ; à cet effet. For all purposes, à toutes fins, à tous usages. For all necessary purposes, pour tout ce qui est nécessaire. General purposes waggon, chariot à toutes fins. To retain a portion for purposes of analysis, en prélever une partie aux fins d'analyse. Jur: For the purpose of this convention . . ., pour l'application de la présente convention. . . . **3.** To speak to the purpose, parler à propos. Not to the p., hors de propos. It is nothing to the purpose, cela ne fait rien à l'affaire ; cela ne signifie rien. To come to the purpose, venir au fait. **4.** To work to good purpose, travailler avec fruit. He worked to such good purpose that . . ., il fit tant et si bien que. . . . To some purpose, utilement, avantageusement, efficacement. To work to no purpose, travailler en vain, en pure perte, inutilement.

purpose[2], v.tr. To purpose doing sth., to do sth., se proposer, avoir l'intention, de faire qch.

purposeful ['pəːrpəsful], a. (a) Prémédité ; (acte) réfléchi. (b) (Of pers.) Avisé. (c) Tenace. **-fully,** adv. Dans un but réfléchi.

purposeless ['pəːrpəsləs], a. Sans but ; inutile.

purposely ['pəːrpəsli], adv. **1.** (Insulter qn) à dessein, de propos délibéré. **2.** Exprès. I came p. to see him, je suis venu exprès pour le voir.

purpura ['pəːrpjura], s. Med: Pourpre m, purpura m.

purr[1] [pəːr], s. Ronron m (de chat).

purr[2], v.i. (Of cat, engine) Ronronner. **purring,** s. = PURR[1].

purse[1] [pəːrs], s. **1.** (a) Bourse f, porte-monnaie m inv. Chain purse, aumônière f. F: Well-lined purse, bourse bien garnie. Light purse, bourse plate, légère. I don't know the length of his purse, je ne sais pas si ses moyens le lui permettraient. To have a common purse, faire bourse commune. That car is beyond my p., cette voiture est au delà de mes moyens. You cannot make a silk purse out of a sow's ear, on ne peut tirer de la farine d'un sac de son. (b) The public purse, les finances f de l'État ; le Trésor. S.a. PRIVY I. 2. (c) Sp: To give, put up, a purse, constituer et offrir une somme d'argent pour une rencontre sportive, pour un match de boxe.

2. Nat.Hist: etc: Sac m, bourse, poche f '**purse-bearer,** s. Trésorier m. '**purse-proud,** a. Orgueilleux de sa fortune. '**purse-strings,** s.pl. Cordons m, tirants m, de bourse F: She holds the purse-strings, c'est elle qui tient les cordons de la bourse.

purse[2], v.tr. Plisser (le front) ; froncer (les sourcils). To purse (up) one's lips, pincer le lèvres ; faire la moue.

purser ['pəːrsər], s. Commissaire m (d'un paquebot).

purslane ['pəːrslen], s. Bot: Pourpier m.

pursuance [pər'sjuəns], s. Action f de poursuivre. In pursuance of your instructions, of our intention, conformément à vos instructions suivant notre intention. In p. of this decree, en vertu de ce décret.

pursuant [pər'sjuənt], adv. Pursuant to your instructions, conformément à vos instructions.

pursue [pər'sjuː]. **1.** v.tr. & ind.tr. To pursue (after) s.o., sth. (a) Poursuivre (qn). (b) Rechercher (le plaisir) ; être à la poursuite (du bonheur). **2.** v.tr. Continuer, suivre (son chemin) ; donner suite à, poursuivre (une enquête). To p. a line of conduct, suivre une ligne de conduite. To pursue a profession, suivre exercer, un métier.

pursuer [pər'sjuər], s. **1.** Poursuivant, -ante. **2.** Jur: (Scot.) = PLAINTIFF.

pursuit [pər'sjuːt], s. **1.** (a) Poursuite f. Pack in eager, hot, pursuit, meute acharnée à la poursuite. To set out in pursuit of s.o., se mettre à la poursuite de qn. (b) Recherche f (des richesses, etc.). In p. of happiness, à la recherche, en quête, du bonheur. In his p. of knowledge, dans ses efforts pour s'instruire. **2.** (a) Carrière f, profession f. To engage in scientific pursuits, s'adonner à des recherches scientifiques. His literary pursuits, ses travaux m littéraires. (b) Occupation f. Hunting is his favourite p., la chasse est son inclination dominante.

pursuivant ['pəːrswivənt], s. Her: Poursuivant m d'armes.

pursy ['pəːrsi], a. **1.** Poussif. **2.** Corpu.ent, bedonnant.

purulence ['pjuərulens], s. Med: **1.** Purulence f **2.** Pus m.

purulent ['pjuərulənt], a. Med: Purulent.

purvey [pər'vei], v.tr. Fournir (des provisions).

purveyance [pər'veiəns], s. Fourniture f de provisions ; approvisionnement m.

purveyor [pər'veiər], s. Fournisseur, -euse (de provisions).

purview ['pəːrvjuː], s. **1.** Jur: Corps m, texte m, articles mpl (d'un statut). **2.** (a) Limites fpl, portée f (d'un projet, d'un livre). (b) To lie, come, within the purview of s.o., (i) être à portée de la vue de qn ; (ii) être du ressort de qn, de la compétence de qn.

pus [pʌs], s. Med: Pus m ; sanie f.

push[1] [puʃ], s. **1.** Poussée f, impulsion f. To give sth. a p., pousser qch. At, with, one push, d'un seul coup. P: To give s.o. the push, flanquer qn à la porte ; donner son congé à qn. To give s.o. a (helping) push, pistonner qn. **2.** (a) Effort m. I must make a p. to get it done, il va falloir donner un coup de collier pour en finir. (b) Mil: Attaque f en masse. (c) To have plenty of push, avoir de l'entregent ; être un arriviste. **3.** At a push, dans une extrémité ; au besoin ; au moment critique. When it comes to the push, quand on en vient au fait et au prendre. **push-and-'pull,** attrib.a. El: Push-and-pull switch, interrupteur m à tirage. '**push-bicycle,** F: '**push-bike,** s.

Bicyclette *f*, *F:* bécane *f*. **'push-button,** *s*.
1. *El:* Bouton *m* de contact; poussoir *m*;
bouton-pressoir *m*. **2.** Poussoir (d'une montre
à répétit on). **'push-cart,** *s*. **1.** Charrette *f* à
bras. **2.** Charrette d'enfant; *F:* poussette *f*.
'push-pin, *s*. *Games:* Poussette *f*. **'push-
rod,** *s*. *I.C.E:* Poussoir *m* de soupape. **'push-
stroke,** *s*. *Bill:* Coup queuté. *To play a p.-s.*,
queuter.
push². I. *v.tr.* Pousser. **1.** *To push the button*,
appuyer sur e bouton. *To p. one's finger into
s.o.'s eye*, fourrer, enfoncer, le doigt dans l'œil de
qn. **2.** (*a*) *To push s.o. into the room*, faire entrer
qn d'une poussée. *Don't push* (me)! ne (me)
bousculez pas! (*b*) *To push oneself* (**forward**),
se mettre en avant; se pousser dans le monde.
3. (*a*) Poursuivre (son avantage). *To p. an attack
home*, pousser à fond une attaque. (*b*) Pousser la
vente de (sa marchandise); lancer (un article).
(*c*) *St.Exch:* *To push shares*, placer des valeurs
douteuses. **4.** *To push s.o. for payment*, presser,
importuner, qn pour se faire payer. *I am pushed
for time*, le temps me manque; je suis très
pressé. *To be pushed for money*, être à court
d'argent. II. **push,** *v.i.* **1.** Avancer (avec
difficulté). *To push* (**one's way**) *through the
crowd*, se frayer, s'ouvrir, un chemin à travers la
oule. **2.** Pousser; exercer une pression. **push
aside,** *v.tr.* Écarter (d'une poussée). **push
back,** *v.tr.* Repousser; faire reculer. **push in.**
1. *v.tr.* Enfoncer refouler, repousser. **2.** *v.i.* Entrer à toute force. **push off,** *v.i. Nau:* Pousser
au large. *F:* *Time to push off*, il est temps de se
mettre en route. **push on.** **1.** *v.tr.* Pousser
en avant; faire avancer. *To push on the work*,
pousser, hâter, activer, les travaux. **2.** *v.i.* (*a*) *To
push on to a place*, pousser jusqu'à un endroit.
(*b*) *It's time to push on*, i est emps de nous
remettre en route. **push out.** **1.** *v.tr.* (*a*) Pousser dehors; faire sortir. (*b*) *To p. a boat out*,
mettre une embarcation à l'eau. (*c*) (*Of plant*)
Pousser (des racines, etc.). (*Of snail*) *To push
out its horns*, sortir ses cornes. **2.** *v.i.* (*Of breakwater, etc.*) *To push out into the sea*, avancer dans
la mer. **push up,** *v.tr.* **1.** Relever (ses lunettes
sur son front, etc.). **2.** *F:* *He was pushed up*,
il est arrivé à coups de piston. **pushing,** *a*.
(*a*) Débrouillard, entreprenant. (*b*) *A pushing
man*, un arriviste, un ambitieux. (*c*) Indiscret.
pusillanimity [pjuːsila'nimiti], *s*. Pusillanimité *f*; manque *m* de cœur.
pusillanimous [pjuːsi'lanimas], *a*. Pusillanime.
puss [pus], *s*. **1.** Minet *m*, minette *f*; mimi *m*.
Puss in Boots, le Chat botté. *To play* (**at**) *puss
in the corner*, jouer aux quatre coins. **2.** *F:* (*To
little girl*) *You sly puss!* petite rusée!
pussy ['pusi], *s*. Pussy(-cat) = PUSS 1
pussyfoot ['pusifut], *s*. **1.** Patte-pelue *mf*.
2. = PROHIBITIONIST.
pustule ['pʌstjuːl], *s. Med:* Pustule *f*.
put¹ [put], *s*. *St.Exch:* Put (option), prime *f*
pour livrer; prime vendeur; option *f* de vente.
put², *v*. (put; put; putting) I. *v.tr.* Mettre. **1.** (*a*)
Put it on the mantelpiece, mettez-le, placez-le,
posez-le, sur la cheminée. *To put milk in one's tea*,
mettre du lait dans son thé. *To put one's lips to
one's glass*, remper ses lèvres dans son verre. *To
put s.o. in his place*, remettre qn à sa place; rembarrer qn. *To put one's signature to sth.*, apposer
sa signature sur, à, qch. *To put honour before
riches*, préférer l'honneur à l'argent. (*b*) *To put
the matter right*, arranger l'affaire. *To put s.o.
out of suspense*, tirer qn de doute. *To put the
law into operation*, appliquer la loi. *To put a*

field **under wheat**, mettre une terre en blé.
St.Exch: **To put stock at a certain price**, délivrer,
fournir, des actions à un certain prix. (*c*) *To put
a passage into Greek*, mettre, traduire, un passage
en grec. (*d* To put money into an undertaking*,
verser des fonds dans une affaire. *To put money
on a horse*, miser, parier, sur un cheval. **2.** *To
put a question to s.o.*, poser, faire, une question à
qn. *To put a resolution to the meeting*, présenter
une résolution à l'assemblée. *I put it to you
whether . . .*, je vous demande un peu si. . . .
Jur: I put it to you that . . ., n'est-il pas vrai
que. . . ? *Put it to him nicely*, présentez-lui la
chose gentiment. *To put the case clearly*, exposer
clairement la situation. *To put it bluntly*, pour
parler franc. **As Horace puts it**, comme dit
Horace. *If one may put it that way*, si l'on
peut s'exprimer ainsi. *All that can be put in two
words*, tout cela tient en deux mots. **3.** *To put
the population at* 10,000, estimer, évaluer, la
population à 10,000. **4.** *To put an end, a stop*,
to sth., mettre fin à qch. **5.** (*a*) *He is put to every
kind of work*, on lui fait faire toutes sortes de
besognes. *Put him to a trade*, apprenez-lui un
métier. *To put s.o. to bed*, mettre qn au lit;
coucher (un enfant). *To put a horse to, at,
a fence*, lancer un cheval sur une barrière.
To put s.o. through an ordeal, faire subir une
rude épreuve à qn. *F:* *To put s.o. through it*,
faire passer un mauvais quart d'heure à qn. (*b*)
To put the enemy to flight, mettre l'ennemi
en déroute. *To put s.o. to sleep*, endormir qn.
6. (*a*) *To put a bullet through s.o.'s head*, loger
une balle dans la tête de qn. *To put one's pen
through a word*, rayer, barrer, biffer, un mot.
(*b*) *Sp:* *To put the weight*, lancer le poids.
II. **put,** *v.i. Nau:* *To put* (out) *to sea*, mettre
à la voile, à la mer; prendre le large. *To put
into port*, relâcher; faire relâche. **put about**,
v.tr. **1.** Faire circuler (une rumeur). **2.** (*a*) Déranger (qn). (*b*) Mettre (qn) en émoi. *Don't put
yourself about*, n'allez pas vous inquiéter. **3.** *To
put a ship about*, *abs.* to put about, virer de bord.
put across, *v.tr.* *U.S:* *F:* *To put a deal
across*, boucler une affaire. *You can't put that
across me*, on ne me la fait pas. **put away**,
v.tr. **1.** (*a*) Serrer (qch. dans une armoire, etc.);
remiser (son auto). *Put away your books*, rangez
vos livres. (*b*) Mettre de côté (de l'argent).
2. Écarter, chasser (une pensée). **3.** *F:* Tuer,
assassiner (qn); tuer (un animal). **put back.**
1. *v.tr.* (*a*) Remettre (un livre) à sa place.
(*b*) Retarder (une horloge, l'arrivée de qn).
(*c*) *Mil:* Ajourner (une recrue). **2.** *v.i. Nau:*
Retourner, revenir (*to a port*, à un port); rentrer
au port. **put by,** *v.tr.* Mettre de côté (de
l'argent); mettre en réserve (des provisions).
To put by for the future, économiser pour
l'avenir. *To have money put by*, *F:* avoir du pain
sur la planche. **put down,** *v.tr.* **1.** Déposer,
poser. *Put it down!* laissez cela! (*Of bus*) *To
put down passengers*, débarquer, déposer, des
voyageurs. *Nau:* *To put down a buoy*, mouiller
une bouée. *S.a.* FOOT¹ 1. **2.** Supprimer, réprimer
(une révolte); vaincre (l'opposition); faire cesser,
mettre fin à (un abus). **3.** Fermer (un parapluie).
4. (*a*) Noter (sur papier); coucher par écrit. *To
put down one's name*, s'inscrire; se faire inscrire
(*for*, pour). *Put it down to my account*, inscrivez-
le, mettez-le, à mon compte. (*b*) *To put down a
number*, poser un chiffre. (*c*) *I put him down as,
for*, a Frenchman, je jugeai qu'il était Français.
I should put her down as thirty-five, e lui donne
trente-cinq ans. (*d*) *To put down sth. to sth.*,

attribuer, imputer, qch. à qch. **put forth**, *v.tr.*
1. Exercer, déployer (sa force). **2.** (*Of tree*)
Pousser (des feuilles). **put forward**, *v.tr.* **1.** (*a*)
Émettre, exprimer, avancer, proposer; mettre en
avant, en évidence; faire valoir (une théorie).
(*b*) **To put oneself forward**, se mettre en avant,
en évidence; se pousser, se produire. (*c*) *F:* **To
put one's best foot forward**, (i) presser le pas;
(ii) se mettre en devoir de faire de son mieux.
2. Avancer (la pendule, etc.). **put in. 1.** *v.tr.*
(*a*) *To put in one's head at the window*, passer sa
tête par la fenêtre. (*b*) Planter (un arbre).
(*c*) *F:* **To put a word in**, placer un mot (dans la
conversation). **To put in a (good) word for s.o.**,
dire un mot en faveur de qn. (*d*) *Jur:* Présenter,
produire, fournir (un document, un témoin).
S.a. CLAIM[1]. (*e*) **To put in an hour's work**, faire,
fournir, une heure de travail. *To put in one's time
reading*, passer son temps à lire. **2.** *v.i.* (*a*) *To
put in at a port*, entrer, relâcher, dans un port;
faire escale dans un port. (*b*) **To put in for a post**,
poser sa candidature à un poste. **put off.**
1. *v.tr.* (*a*) Retirer, ôter. **To put off the mask**,
déposer le masque. (*b*) Remettre, différer; ajourner, renvoyer. *To put off doing sth.*, différer de
faire qch.; tarder à faire qch. *Jur:* **To put off
a case for a week**, renvoyer, ajourner, une affaire
à huitaine. **To put off one's guests**, contremander
ses invités. (*c*) **To put s.o. off with an excuse**,
se débarrasser de qn, renvoyer qn, avec une excuse.
He is not to be put off with words, il ne se paie pas
de paroles. (*d*) Déconcerter, dérouter (qn). *You
put me off*, vous me faites tromper. (*e*) **To put
s.o. off doing sth.**, éloigner, dégoûter, décourager,
qn de faire qch.; faire passer à qn l'envie de
faire qch. **2.** *v.i.* *Nau:* Déborder du quai;
pousser au large; démarrer. **put on**, *v.tr.*
1. (*a*) **To put the kettle on**, mettre chauffer de
l'eau. **To put on a dish**, servir un plat. (*b*) **To
put a play on**, mettre sur la scène, monter, une
pièce de théâtre. **To put on a train**, mettre un
train en service. **2.** (*a*) Mettre (ses vêtements);
revêtir (un pardessus); enfiler (son pantalon);
chausser (ses pantoufles). **Put on your hat**,
couvrez-vous. *To put on one's shoes*, se chausser.
(*b*) **To put on an innocent air**, prendre, se donner,
un air innocent. *S.a.* AIR[1] III. *F:* **To put it on**,
poser; afficher de grands airs; *P:* faire sa poire.
3. **To put on weight**, grossir; prendre du poids.
To put on speed, prendre de la vitesse.
4. Avancer (la pendule). **5.** **To put on the light**,
mettre la lumière; allumer. **To put on steam**,
mettre la vapeur. **Put on the gramophone**, faites
marcher le gramophone. **6.** *To put s.o. on to a
job*, confier, donner, un travail à qn. **7.** *F:* *Who
put you on to it?* qui est-ce qui vous a donné le
tuyau? **8.** *Tp:* *Put me on to 'City'* 1380,
donnez-moi City 13,80. **put out**, *v.tr.* **1.** Avancer, tendre (la main); allonger, étendre (le bras).
2. (*a*) Mettre dehors **To put s.o. out** (*of the room*),
mettre qn à la porte. (*b*) *To put linen out to dry*,
mettre du linge à sécher. *Nau:* **To put out a
boat**, mettre un canot à l'eau. (*c*) **To put one's
tongue out**, tirer la langue (*at s.o.*, à qn). *To put
one's head out of the window*, passer sa tête par la
fenêtre; sortir la tête à la fenêtre. **3.** **To put out
(of joint)**, démettre, déboîter. *To put one's arm
out*, se démancher le bras. **4.** (*a*) Éte ndre (une
bougie, le feu). (*b*) **To put s.o.'s eyes out**, crever
les yeux à qn. *To put s.o.'s eye out with an
umbrella*, éborgner qn avec un parapluie.
5. (*a*) Déconcerter, interloquer (qn). *He never
gets put out*, il ne se démonte jamais; il ne
s'émeut de rien. (*b*) Ennuyer, contrarier (qn).

To be put out about sth., être contrarié de qch.
(*c*) Incommoder, gêner (qn). **To put oneself out
for s.o.**, se déranger, se mettre en frais, pour qn.
6. (*a*) **To put money out** (*to interest*), placer de
l'argent (à intérêt). (*b*) *All work done on the
premises, nothing put out*, tout est fait sur place,
rien n'est donné au dehors. **7.** Publier (un
ouvrage). **put through**, *v.tr.* **1.** Mener à bien
(un projet). **2.** *Tp:* **To put s.o. through to s.o.**,
mettre qn en communication avec qn. **put to**,
v.tr. **1.** Atte ler (un cheval); accrocher (une
.ocomotive). **2.** *He was hard put to it to find a
substitute*, il a eu fort à faire, il était très embarrassé, pour se faire remplacer. **put together**,
v.tr. **1.** Joindre; monter, assembler (une robe,
une machine). **2.** Rapprocher, comparer (des
faits). *S.a.* HEAD[1] 2, TWO. **put up**, *v.tr.*
1. (*a*) Lever (une glace de wagon); relever (le
col de son pardessus); ouvrir (un parapluie);
dresser (une échelle); accrocher (un tableau);
poser (un rideau). (*Of prisoner*) **To put up one's
hands**, lever, mettre, haut les mains. **To put up
one's hair**, se faire un chignon. (*b*) Apposer,
coller (une affiche); afficher (un avis). **2.** *Ven:*
(Faire) lever (une perdrix, etc.). **3.** Augmenter,
(faire) hausser, majorer (les prix). **4.** Offrir, faire
(une prière); présenter (une pétition). **5.** **To
put up a candidate**, proposer un candidat. *v.i.* (*Of
candidate*) **To put up for a seat**, poser sa candidature à un siège. **6.** **To put sth. up for sale**,
mettre qch. en vente. **7.** **To put up the money
for an undertaking**, faire les fonds d'une entreprise. **8.** Emballer, empaqueter (ses habits dans
une valise). *Com:* **This cream is put up in tubes**,
cette crème est présentée en tubes. **9.** Remettre
(l'épée) au fourreau; rengainer. **10.** **To put up
a stout resistance**, se défendre vaillamment.
S.a. FIGHT[1]. **11.** (*a*) Donner à coucher à (qn);
héberger (qn). *v.i.* **To put up at a hotel**,
(i) descendre, (ii) loger, à un hôtel. (*b*) Remiser
(une voiture); mettre à l'écurie (un cheval).
12. *Abs.* **To put up with sth.**, s'accommoder,
s'arranger, de qch.; se résigner à (des inconvénients); souffrir, endurer (les railleries).
13. (*a*) **To put s.o. up to sth.**, mettre qn au
courant, au fait, de qch.; *F:* tuyauter qn. (*b*) **To
put s.o. up to sth.**, **to do sth.**, pousser, inciter,
qn à qch., à faire qch. **14.** Construire, bâtir (une
maison); ériger (un monument). **'put-up**,
attrib. a. *F:* **A put-up job**, une affaire machinée
d'avance; un coup monté. **put upon**, *v.ind.tr.*
F: **To put upon s.o.**, en imposer à qn.

putative ['pju:tətiv], *a.* *Jur:* Putatif.
putrefaction [pju:tri'fakʃ(ə)n], *s.* Putréfaction *f.*
putrefactive [pju:tri'faktiv], *a.* Putréfactif. *P.
fermentation*, fermentation putride.
putrefy ['pju:trifai]. **1.** *v.tr.* Putréfier, pourrir.
2. *v.i.* (*a*) (*Of carrion*) Se putréfier, pourrir.
(*b*) (*Of living tissue*) (i) Suppurer, s'envenimer;
(ii) se gangrener.
putrescence [pju'tres(ə)ns], *s.* Putrescence *f.*
putrescent [pju'tres(ə)nt], *a.* En putréfaction;
en pourriture.
putrid ['pju:trid], *a.* **1.** Putride; en putréfaction;
infect. **2.** *P:* = ROTTEN 2.
putt[1] [pʌt], *s.* *Golf:* Coup roulé.
putt[2], *v.tr.* *Golf:* Poter (la balle). **'putting-
green**, *s.* *Golf:* Pelouse *f* du trou; pelouse
d'arrivée; le vert.
puttee ['pʌti, pʌ'ti:], *s.* Bande molletière.
putter ['pʌtər], *s.* *Golf:* **1.** (*Club*) Poteur *m.*
2. (*Pers.*) **Good putter**, joueur qui réussit bien
les coups roulés.

utty[1] ['pʌti], *s.* **I.** Mastic *m*, enduit *m*. **Glazier's putty**, mastic à vitres. **Plasterer's putty**, pâte *f* de chaux. **2.** Jeweller's putty, putty-powder, potée *f* (d'étain). **'putty-knife**, *s.* Spatule *f* de vitrier.

utty[2], *v.tr.* To putty (up) a hole, mastiquer un trou ; boucher un trou au mastic.

uzzle[1] [pʌzl], *s.* **I.** To be in a puzzle, être dans l'embarras ; être perplexe. **2.** Énigme *f*. *Your friend is a real p. to me*, votre ami est pour moi un vrai problème. **3.** (*a*) Chinese puzzle, casse-tête chinois. *S.a.* JIG-SAW. (*b*) Devinette *f*, problème *m*. **Pictorial puzzle**, rébus *m*. **Crossword puzzle**, problème de mots croisés.

uzzle[2]. **I.** *v.tr.* Embarrasser, intriguer. *I was somewhat puzzled how to answer*, j'étais assez embarrassé pour répondre. **To puzzle s.o. with a question**, poser à qn une question embarrassante. *It puzzles me what his plans are*, ses projets m'intriguent. **2.** *v.i.* To puzzle over sth., se creuser la tête pour comprendre qch. **puzzle out**, *v.tr.* Débrouiller, éclaircir (un mystère) ; déchiffrer (une écriture, un rébus). **puzzling**, *a.* Embarrassant, intriguant.

uzzler ['pʌzlər], *s.* Question embarrassante ; *Sch:* colle *f*.

ygmy ['pigmi]. **I.** *s.* Pygmée *m*. **2.** *Attrib.* Pygméen.

yjama [pi'dʒɑ:ma], *s.* Pyjama suit, *F:* pyjamas, pyjama *m*. **Pyjama-cord**, cordelière *f*.

ylon ['pailən], *s.* Pylône *m*.

ylorus [pai'lɔ:rəs], *s. Anat:* Pylore *m*.

yorrhea [paio'ri:a], *s. Med:* Pyorrhée *f*.

yracanth ['pairakanθ], *s. Bot:* Pyracanthe *f* ; *F:* buisson ardent.

yralis ['piralis], *s. Ent:* Pyrale *f*.

pyramid ['piramid], *s.* Pyramide *f*. **Pyramid-shaped**, en pyramide.

pyramidal [pi'ramid(ə)l], *a.* Pyramidal, -aux.

pyre ['paiər], *s.* Bûcher *m* (funéraire).

Pyrenean [pire'ni:ən], *a.* Pyrénéen ; des Pyrénées.

Pyrenees (the) [ðəpaire'ni:z]. *Pr.n.* Les Pyrénées *f*.

pyrethrum [pai'ri:θrəm], *s.* Pyrèthre *m*. **Pyrethrum powder**, poudre *f* de pyrèthre.

pyrexia [pai'reksia], *s. Med:* Pyrexie *f*.

pyrites [pai'raiti:z], *s.* Pyrite *f*. **Copper pyrites**, chalcopyrite *f*. **Iron pyrites**, sulfure *m* de fer ; fer sulfuré.

pyritic [pai'ritik], *a. Miner:* Pyriteux.

pyro [pairɔ], *s. Phot: F:* Pyrogallol *m* ; acide *m* pyrogallique.

pyrogallic [pairɔ'galik], *a. Ch:* **Pyrogallic acid**, acide *m* pyrogallique ; pyrogallol *m*.

pyrometer [pai'rɔmetər], *s.* Pyromètre *m*.

pyrotechnic(al) [pairɔ'teknik(əl)], *a.* Pyrotechnique.

pyrotechnics [pairɔ'tekniks], *s.pl.* Pyrotechnie *f*.

Pyrrhic[1] ['pirik], *a. & s.* (Danse) pyrrhique (*f*).

Pyrrhic[2], *a. Rom.Hist:* De Pyrrhus. *F:* **Pyrrhic victory**, victoire à la Pyrrhus ; victoire désastreuse.

Pythagoras [pai'θagorəs]. *Pr.n.m.* Pythagore.

python[1] ['paiθən], *s. Gr.Myth: Rept:* Python *m*

python[2], *s.* Démon *m* ; esprit familier.

pythoness ['paiθənes], *s.f.* Pythonisse.

pyx [piks], *s. Ecc:* Ciboire *m*. **'pyx-cloth**, *s. Ecc:* Custode *f*.

pyxidium [pik'sidiəm], *s. Bot:* Pyxide *f*.

pyxis, *pl.* **-ides** ['piksis, -idi:z], *s.* **I.** = PYXIDIUM. **2.** *Anat:* Cavité *f* cotyloïde.

Q

Q, q [kju:], *s.* (La lettre) Q, q *m*. *F:* On the q.t. [kju:'ti:] (= *quiet*), discrètement ; en confidence. On the strict q.t., en secret. *S.a.* P.

qua [kwei], *Lt.adv.* En tant que ; considéré comme. **Men qua men**, les hommes en tant qu'hommes.

quack[1] [kwak], *s. & int.* Couin-couin (*m*.

quack[2], *v.i.* (*Of duck*) Crier ; faire couin-couin.

quack[3], *s.* Quack (doctor), charlatan *m*. **Quack remedy**, remède *m* de charlatan.

quackery ['kwakəri], *s.* **I.** Charlatanisme *m* ; empirisme médical. **2.** Charlatanerie *f*, hâblerie *f*.

quad[1] [kwɔd], *s. Sch: F:* = QUADRANGLE 2.

quad[2], *s. Typ: F:* = QUADRAT.

quadragenarian [kwɔdrədʒe'neəriən], *a. & s.* Quadragénaire (*mf*).

Quadragesima [kwɔdrə'dʒesima], *s. Ecc:* La Quadragésime.

quadrangle ['kwɔdraŋgl], *s.* **I.** *Geom:* Quadrilatère *m*. **2.** Cour (carrée) (d'une école, etc.).

quadrangular [kwɔ'draŋgjulər], *a.* Quadrangulaire.

quadrant ['kwɔdrənt], *s.* **I.** *Astr: Mth:* Quart *m* de cercle ; quadrant *m*. **2.** *Mec.E:* Secteur denté. *Nau:* Steering quadrant, secteur du gouvernail.

quadrat ['kwɔdrət], *s. Typ:* Cadrat *m*, quadrat *m*. **Em-quadrat**, cadratin *m*. **En-quadrat**, demi-cadratin *m*.

quadrate ['kwɔ'dreit], *v.tr.* Réduire (une surface,

une expression) au carré équivalent. **To quadrate the circle**, faire la quadrature du cercle.

quadratic [kwɔ'dratik], *a.* **I.** **Quadratic equation**, équation du second degré. **2.** *Cryst:* Quadratique.

quadrature ['kwɔdrətjər], *s.* Quadrature *f*.

quadrennial [kwɔ'drenjəl], *a.* Quadriennal, -aux.

quadrifoliate [kwɔdri'fouliet], *a.* Quadrifolié.

quadrigeminal [kwɔdri'dʒemin(ə)l], *a. Anat:* The quadrigeminal bodies, les tubercules quadri-jumeaux.

quadrilateral [kwɔdri'latərəl]. **I.** *a.* Quadrilatéral, -aux ; quadrilatère. **2.** *s.* Quadrilatère *m*.

quadrille [kwa'dril, ka-], *s. Danc: etc:* Quadrille *m*.

quadrillion [kwɔ'driljən], *s.* **I.** Septillion *m* ; 10^{24}. **2.** *U.S:* Quadrillion *m*, quatrillion *m* ; 10^{15}.

quadrisyllabic [kwɔdrisi'labik], *a.* Quadrisyllabique.

quadrisyllable [kwɔdri'siləbl], *s.* Quadrisyllabe *m*.

quadroon [kwɔ'dru:n], *a. & s. Ethn:* Quarteron, -onne.

quadruped ['kwɔdruped], *a. & s.* Quadrupède (*m*).

quadruple[1] ['kwɔdrupl], *a. & s.* Quadruple (*m*).

quadruple[2], *v.tr. & i.* Quadrupler.

quadruplets ['kwɔdruplets], *s.pl.* Quatre enfants nés d'une seule couche.

quadruplicate [kwɔ'druːplikeit], *a.* Quadruplé, quadruple. In quadruplicate, en quatre exemplaires.

quaff [kwɑːf], *v.tr. Lit:* (*a*) Boire à longs traits, à plein verre. (*b*) Vider (une coupe) d'un trait ; *F:* lamper (son vin).

quagga ['kwaga], *s. Z:* Couagga *m.*

quagmire ['kwagmaiər], *s.* Fondrière *f* ; marécage *m. F:* To be in a quagmire, être dans le pétrin.

quail[1] [kweil], *s. Orn:* Caille *f. They shot six quail*, ils ont abattu six cailles.

quail[2], *v.i.* (*Of pers.*) Fléchir, faiblir (*before*, devant). *His heart quailed*, son cœur défaillit.

quaint [kweint], *a.* (*a*) Étrange, bizarre, falot, -ote, fantasque. (*b*) Qui a le pittoresque de l'ancienne mode. *Q. ideas*, idées (i) un peu surannées, (ii) baroques. *Q. style*, (i) style singulier, original ; (ii) style d'un archaïsme piquant.

quaintness ['kweintnəs], *s.* Bizarrerie *f*, singularité *f.*

quake [kweik], *v.i.* 1. (*Of thg*) Trembler, branler. 2. (*Of pers.*) Trembler, frémir, frissonner (*with fear*, de crainte). *He is quaking at the knees*, les jambes lui flageolent. *F:* To quake in one's shoes, trembler dans sa peau.

quaker ['kweikər], *s. Rel.H:* Quaker *m.*

quakeress ['kweikərəs], *s.f.* Quakeresse.

qualification [kwɔlifi'keiʃ(ə)n], *s.* 1. Réserve *f*, restriction *f. To accept* without qualification, accepter (i) sans réserve, (ii) sans conditions. 2. *Qualifications for an appointment*, titres *m* à un emploi. To have the necessary qualifications, avoir les qualités requises (pour un poste) ; avoir capacité (pour exercer un droit). *Qualifications for membership of a club*, titres d'éligibilité à un cercle. Property qualification (*to vote*), cens électoral.

qualificative ['kwɔlifikeitiv], **qualificatory** ['kwɔlifikeitəri], *a.* Qualificatif.

qualify ['kwɔlifai]. I. *v.tr.* 1. (*a*) To qualify sth. as sth., qualifier qch. de qch. (*b*) *Gram:* Qualifier. 2. To qualify s.o. for sth., to do sth., rendre qn apte, propre, à qch., à faire qch. ; *Jur:* donner qualité à qn pour faire qch. To qualify oneself for a job, acquérir les titres nécessaires pour remplir un emploi. 3. (*a*) Apporter des réserves à (un consentement, etc.) ; modifier, atténuer (une affirmation). (*b*) (*Of circumstance*) Modérer, diminuer (un plaisir). 4. (*a*) Étendre, couper (une boisson). (*b*) *F: A cup of tea qualified with brandy*, une tasse de thé renforcée de cognac. II. **qualify**, *v.i.* Acquérir les connaissances requises, se qualifier (*for*, pour). To qualify as (a) doctor, être reçu médecin. *Av:* To q. as a pilot, passer son brevet de pilote. **qualified**, *a.* 1. (*a*) To be qualified to do sth., avoir les capacités pour faire qch. ; avoir qualité pour faire qch. Qualified expert, expert diplômé. Qualified seaman, matelot breveté. (*b*) Autorisé. To be q. to vote, avoir qualité d'électeur. *Jur:* Qualified to inherit, habile à succéder. 2. Restreint, modéré. *Q. approval*, approbation modérée. *Com:* Qualified acceptance, acceptation conditionnelle, sous condition (d'une traite). **qualifying**, *a.* 1. *Gram:* (Adjectif) qualificatif ; (adverbe) modificatif. 2. (*a*) Qualifying examination, (i) examen pour certificat d'aptitude ; (ii) examen d'entrée (à une école). (*b*) *Ten: etc:* Qualifying round, série *f* éliminatoire. 3. Modificateur, -trice.

qualitative ['kwɔlitətiv], *a.* Qualitatif.

quality ['kwɔliti], *s.* Qualité *f.* 1. (*a*) *Of good, high, poor, q.*, de bonne qualité ; de qualité supérieure, inférieure. *Of the best q.*, de première qualité ; de premier choix. (*b*) *Wine that has q.*, vin qui a de la qualité. Quality car, voiture de qualité. 2. (*a*) (*Of pers.*) Qualité (distinctive). He has many good qualities, bad qualities, il a beaucoup de qualités, de défauts. (*b*) Heating quality, qualities, of a combustible, pouvoir *m*, valeur *f*, calorifique d'un combustible. 3. *A. & P:* People of quality, gens de qualité ; gens du monde. The quality, la noblesse. 4. To act in the quality of . . ., agir en qualité, en caractère, de. . . . 5. Qualité, timbre *m* (d'un son).

qualm [kwɑːm, kwɔːm], *s.* 1. Soulèvement *m* de cœur ; nausée *f.* 2. (*a*) Scrupule *m*, remords *m. To feel some qualms* (*about what one has done*), avoir des remords de conscience. To have no qualms about doing sth., ne pas se faire le moindre scrupule de faire qch. (*b*) Pressentiment *m* de malheur.

qualmish ['kwɑːmiʃ, 'kwɔː-], *a.* 1. Sujet aux nausées. 2. Mal à l'aise.

qualmishness ['kwɑːmiʃnəs, 'kwɔː-], *s.* 1. Soulèvement *m* de cœur. 2. Scrupules exagérés.

quandary ['kwɔndəri, kwɔn'dɛəri], *s.* To be in a quandary, (i) se trouver dans une impasse ; être dans l'embarras ; (ii) ne trop savoir que faire.

quanta ['kwɔntə], *s.pl. See* QUANTUM.

quantitative ['kwɔntitətiv], *a.* Quantitatif.

quantity ['kwɔntiti], *s.* 1. (*a*) Quantité *f.* To buy sth. in large quantities, acheter qch. par quantités considérables. In (great) quantities, en grande quantité. *Cust:* Q. permitted, tolérance permise (de tabac, etc.). (*b*) To survey a building for quantities, faire le toisé d'un immeuble. Bill of quantities, devis *m.* (*c*) *El:* Connected in quantity, couplé en quantité, en parallèle. 2. *Mth:* Quantity. Unknown quantity, inconnue *f.* 'quantity-surveying, *s.* Toisé *m* ; métrage *m.* 'quantity-surveyor, *s.* Métreur (vérificateur).

quantum, *pl.* -a ['kwɔntəm, -a], *s.* Quantum *m. Ph:* The quantum theory, la théorie des quanta.

quarantine[1] ['kwɔrɔntiːn], *s. Esp. Nau:* Quarantaine *f.* To be in quarantine, faire (la) quarantaine. To go into quarantine, se mettre en quarantaine. To be out of quarantine, avoir libre pratique. The quarantine flag, le pavillon de quarantaine ; le pavillon Q.

quarantine[2], *v.tr.* Mettre (qn, un navire) en quarantaine.

quarrel[1] ['kwɔrəl], *s. Archeol:* Carreau *m* (d'arbalète).

quarrel[2], *s.* (*a*) Querelle *f*, dispute *f*, brouille *f.* To pick a quarrel with s.o., faire (une) querelle à qn. To try to pick a q. with s.o., chercher querelle à qn. (*b*) I have no quarrel with, against, him, je n'ai rien à lui reprocher. *I have no q. with his behaviour*, je n'ai rien à redire à sa conduite. (*c*) To take up s.o.'s quarrel, épouser, embrasser, la querelle, la cause, de qn. To fight s.o.'s quarrels for him, prendre fait et cause pour qn.

quarrel[3], *v.i.* (quarrelled) 1. Se quereller, se disputer (*with s.o. over, about, sth.*, avec qn à propos de qch.) ; se brouiller (avec qn). 2. To quarrel with s.o. for doing sth., reprocher à qn de faire qch. To quarrel with sth., trouver à redire à qch. **quarrelling**, *s.* Querelle(s) *f*(*pl*), dispute(s) *f*(*pl*).

quarreller ['kwɔrələr], *s.* Querelleur, -euse.

quarrelsome ['kwɔrəsəm], *a.* Querelleur, batailleur. *Q. fellow, F:* mauvais coucheur.

quarrelsomeness ['kwɔrəlsəmnəs], *s.* Humeur querelleuse.

uarry[1] ['kwɔri], *s. Ven:* **1.** Proie *f*; gibier (poursuivi à courre). **2.** *A:* Curée *f*.

uarry[2], *s.* Carrière *f* (de pierres, etc.). *F: His book is a q. of facts*, son livre est une mine de faits. **'quarry-stone,** *s.* Moellon *m*.

uarry[3], *v.tr.* (quarried) **1.** Extraire, tirer, (la pierre) de la carrière. *Abs.* Exploiter une carrière. **2.** Creuser une carrière dans (une colline). **quarrying,** *s.* Exploitation *f* de carrières. *Q. of stone,* extraction *f*, tirage *m*, de la pierre.

uarryman, *pl.* **-men** ['kwɔrimən, -men], *s.m.* (Ouvrier) carrier.

uart [kwɔːrt], *s. Meas:* Un quart de *gallon*; *approx.* = litre *m*. (= 1 litre 136; *U.S:* = o litre 946.)

uart(e) [kɑːrt], *s. Fenc:* Quarte *f*. **To parry in quart,** parer en quarte.

uartan ['kwɔːrt(ə)n], *a.* **Quartan fever, quartan ague,** fièvre quarte.

uarter[1] ['kwɔːrtər], *s.* **1.** (*a*) Quart *m*. *To divide sth. in(to) quarters,* diviser qch. en quatre. **Bottle one quarter full,** bouteille au quart pleine. *It is (only) a q. as long,* c'est quatre fois moins long. (*b*) (i) *Cu:* Quartier *m* (de bœuf, d'agneau). **Fore-quarter, hind-quarter,** quartier de devant, de derrière. (ii) *pl.* (Hind-)quarters, arrière-train *m*, train *m* de derrière (d'une bête); arrière-main *m* or *f* (du cheval). (*c*) *Her:* Quartier, partition *f* (de l'écu). (*d*) *Nau:* Hanche *f*. **On the quarter,** par la hanche. *To fire on the q.,* tirer en retraite. (*e*) Loge *f*, tranche *f* (d'orange, etc.). (*f*) *To cut timber on the quarter,* débiter un tronc d'arbre sur quartier, sur maille. **2.** (*a*) *Nau:* Quart de brasse. (*b*) Trimestre *m*; terme *m* (de loyer). **A quarter's rent,** un terme, un trimestre (de loyer). (*c*) **Moon at the first quarter,** lune au premier quartier. **Moon in its last quarter,** lune sur son décroît. (*d*) **A quarter to six,** six heures moins le quart. **A quarter past six,** six heures et quart. **3.** (*a*) *Nau:* (i) Quart d'aire de vent (= 2° 48′ 45″); (ii) aire *f* de vent. *What quarter is the wind in?* de quel côté souffle le vent? *The wind is in the right q.,* le vent vient du bon côté. (*b*) **The four quarters of the globe,** les quatre parties du globe. *They arrived from all quarters,* ils arrivaient de tous côtés, de toutes parts. *I expect no more trouble from that quarter,* je n'attends plus aucune difficulté de ce côté-là. **In high quarters,** en haut lieu. **In responsible quarters,** dans les milieux autorisés. **4.** Quartier (d'une ville). **5.** *pl.* (*a*) **Living quarters,** appartements *m* (domestiques). *To shift one's quarters,* changer de résidence *f*. (*b*) *Mil:* Quartier, cantonnement *m*, logement *m*. **To take up one's quarters,** (*of troops*) prendre leurs quartiers; *F:* (*of pers.*) se loger, s'installer. *To return to quarters,* rentrer au quartier. *Navy:* **Sailors' quarters,** poste *m* d'équipage. **6.** *pl. Navy:* Postes de combat. **To beat, pipe, to quarters,** battre, sonner, le branle-bas. **All hands to quarters!** tout le monde à son poste! **7. To give quarter,** faire quartier. *To ask for q.,* **to cry quarter,** demander quartier; crier merci. **'quarter-day,** *s.* Le jour du terme; *F:* le terme. **'quarter-deck,** *s.* **1.** *Nau:* Gaillard *m* (d')arrière. *Navy:* Plage *f* arrière. **2.** *Coll. Navy:* **The quarter-deck,** les officiers *m*. **'quarter-plate,** *s. Phot:* Plaque *f* et format *m* 8.2 × 10.8 (cm.). **'quarter-round,** *s. Arch:* Quart *m* de rond. **quarter-'sessions,** *s.pl. Jur:* Assises trimestrielles.

quarter[2], *v.tr.* **1.** (*a*) Diviser (une pomme) en quatre; diviser (un bœuf) par quartiers; équarrir (un bœuf). **Quartered logs** (*of firewood*), bois *m* de quartier. (*b*) *A:* Écarteler (un condamné). (*c*) *Her:* Écarteler (l'écu). **2.** *Mil:* Cantonner, caserner (des troupes). **To quarter the troops on the inhabitants,** loger les troupes chez l'habitant. *To be quartered with s.o.,* loger chez qn.

quarterly ['kwɔːrtərli]. **1.** *a.* Trimestriel. **2.** *s.* Publication trimestrielle. **3.** *adv.* Trimestriellement; par trimestre.

quartermaster ['kwɔːrtərmɑːstər], *s.* **1.** *Nau:* Maître *m* de timonerie. **2.** *Mil:* **Quartermaster general,** *F:* Q.M.G., intendant général d'armée. **Quartermaster sergeant,** (*artillery, cavalry*) = maréchal *m* des logis chef; (*infantry*) = sergent chef.

quartern ['kwɔːrtərn], *s.* **1.** *Meas:* Quart *m* (de pinte, etc.). **2. Quartern loaf,** pain *m* de quatre livres.

quarterstaff ['kwɔːrtərstɑːf], *s. Sp:* **1.** Bâton *m* (à deux bouts). *To fence with quarterstaffs,* jouer du bâton. **2.** Escrime *f* au bâton.

quartet(te) [kwɔːr'tet], *s. Mus:* Quatuor *m*.

quarto ['kwɔːrto], *a. & s.* In-quarto (*m*) *inv.*

quartz [kwɔːrts], *s. Miner:* Quartz *m*; cristal *m* de roche. **Quartz sand,** sable quartzeux.

quash [kwɔʃ], *v.tr.* **1.** Casser, infirmer, annuler (un jugement); invalider (une élection). *To q. an action,* arrêter les poursuites. **2.** Étouffer (un sentiment, une révolte).

quasi ['kweisai], *pref.* Quasi, presque. **Quasi-contract,** quasi-contrat *m*. **Quasi-public,** quasi-public; soi-disant public.

quassia ['kwɔʃja], *s.* **1. Quassia(-tree),** quassier *m*; quassia *m*. **2.** *Pharm:* Quassia.

quaternary [kwo'tɜːrnəri], *a.* Quaternaire.

quatrain ['kwɔtrein], *s. Pros:* Quatrain *m*.

quaver[1] ['kweivər], *s.* **1.** *Mus:* Croche *f*. **2.** (*a*) *Mus:* Trille *m*, tremo o *m*. (*b* Tremblement *m*, chevrotement *m* (de la voix).

quaver[2], *v.i.* (*a*) (*Of singer*) Faire des trilles. (*b*) (*Of voice*) Chevroter, trembloter. **quavering,** *a. Q. voice,* voix tremblotante, chevrotante. **-ly,** *adv.* D'une voix mal assurée.

quay [kiː], *s.* Quai *m* ou appontement *m*. **Alongside the quay,** à quai. **Quay-side worker,** ouvrier de quai.

quayage ['kiːedʒ], *s.* **1.** Quayage *m*; droit(s) *m(pl)* de quai, de bassin. **2.** Quais *mpl*.

quean [kwiːn], *s.f.* **1.** *A:* Coquine, gueuse. **2.** *Scot:* Jeune fille; beau brin de fille.

queasy ['kwiːzi], *a.* (*a*) Sujet à des nausées. **To feel queasy,** *F:* avoir le cœur fade. *Q. stomach,* estomac délicat. (*b*) *F:* **Queasy conscience,** conscience scrupuleuse à l'excès.

queen[1] [kwiːn], *s.f.* **1.** Reine. **Queen Anne,** a reine Anne. *She was q. to Henry VIII,* elle fut l'épouse de Henri VIII. **2.** (*a*) *Cards:* Dame *f*. (*b*) *Chess:* Dame, reine. (*Of pawn*) **To go to queen,** aller à dame. **3.** *Ent:* Reine (des abeilles, des fourmis). **'queen-'bee,** *s.* Abeille *f* mère; reine *f*. **'queen-'mother,** *s.f.* Reine-mère. **'queen-post,** *s. Const:* Faux poinçon. **Queen-post truss,** arbalète *f* à deux poinçons.

queen[2]. **1.** *v.tr. Chess:* Damer (un pion). **2.** *v.i.* (*a*) *F:* **To queen it,** faire la reine. (*b*) *Chess:* (*Of pawn*) Aller à dame.

queenly ['kwiːnli], *a.* De reine; digne d'une reine.

queer[1] ['kwiːər], *a.* **1.** (*a* Bizarre, étrange, singulier. *A queer-looking chap,* une drôle de tête. *F:* **To be in Queer Street,** être dans une situation (financière) embarrassée. (*b*) Suspect. **On the queer,** par des moyens peu honnêtes; par des moyens louches. **2.** *F:* **I feel very queer,** je me sens tout chose, tout patraque. **-ly,** *adv.* Étrangement, bizarrement.

queer², *v.tr.* Déranger, détraquer. **To queer s.o.'s pitch**, bouleverser, faire échouer, les plans de qn; contrecarrer qn.

queerness ['kwiːərnəs], *s.* Étrangeté *f*, bizarrerie *f*.

quell [kwel], *v.tr. Lit:* Calmer, apaiser (une émotion); dompter, étouffer (une passion); réprimer, étouffer (une révolte).

quench [kwenʃ], *v.tr.* **1.** *Lit:* Éteindre (un feu). **2.** *Metalw:* Éteindre, tremper (le métal). **Quenched in oil**, refroidi à l'huile. **3.** (*a*) *Re-*primer, étouffer (un désir). (*b*) **To quench one's thirst**, apaiser, étancher, sa soif; se désaltérer. (*c*) *El:* (i) Étouffer (une étincelle). (ii) Amortir (des oscillations).

quern [kwəːrn], *s.* Moulin *m* à bras.

querulous ['kwer(j)uləs], *a.* Plaintif et maussade; chagrin, grognon. *Q. tone*, ton plaintif, dolent.

query¹ ['kwiːəri], *s.* **1.** (*a*) Question *f*, interrogation *f*. **He looked a query at me**, il me lança un regard interrogateur. (*b*) *Q. if the money was ever paid*, reste à savoir si la somme a jamais été versée. **2.** *Typ:* Point *m* d'interrogation.

query², *v.tr.* **1.** **To query if, whether . . .**, s'informer si . . . **2.** Marquer (qch.) d'un point d'interrogation; mettre (une affirmation) en question, en doute.

quest [kwest], *s.* (*a*) *Ven:* Quête *f* (par les chiens). (*b*) Recherche *f*. **To go in quest of s.o.**, se mettre à la recherche, en quête, de qn.

question¹ ['kwestʃ(ə)n], *s.* Question *f.* **1.** *A:* (*Torture*) **To put s.o. to the question**, mettre qn à la question; appliquer la question à qn. **2.** Mise *f* en doute. **Without question**, sans aucun doute; sans contredit; sans conteste. *To obey without q.*, obéir aveuglément. **Beyond (all) question**, past question, hors de doute; incontestable. **To call, bring, sth. in question**, mettre qch. en question, en doute; révoquer qch. en doute. *I make no q. but that it is so*, je ne doute aucunement qu'il n'en soit ainsi. **There is no question about it**, il n'y a pas de doute là-dessus. **3.** (*a*) **The matter in question**, l'affaire en question; l'affaire dont il s'agit. **There was some question of . . .**, il a été question de . . . *There is no q. of his returning so soon*, il n'est pas question qu'il revienne si promptement. (*b*) **That is not the question**, il ne s'agit pas de ce.a. *The q. is whether . . .*, il s'agit de savoir si. . . . **It is out of the question**, c'est impossible; il ne faut pas y songer. (*At meeting*) **To move the previous question**, demander la question préalable. **To put the question**, mettre la question aux voix. **Question!** (i) (revenez) au fait! (ii) (*erroneous use*) c'est à savoir! (*c*) *A vexed q.*, une question souvent débattue. *Success is merely a question of time*, le succès n'est qu'une question de temps. **4. To ask s.o. a question, to put a question to s.o.**, faire, poser, adresser, une question à qn. *Questions and answers*, demandes *f* et réponses. '**question-mark**, *s.* Point *m* d'interrogation.

uestion², *v.tr.* **1.** Questionner, interroger (qn). *To q. s.o. closely*, soumettre qn à un interrogatoire serré. *To be questioned*, subir un interrogatoire. **2.** Mettre (qch.) en question, en doute; révoquer (qch.) en doute. *Q. whether he will come*, je doute qu'il vienne. **It is not to be questioned that . . .**, il n'y a pas de doute que + *ind.* **questioning¹**, *a.* (Regard, etc.) interrogateur. **questioning²**, *s.* Questions *fpl*, interrogation *f*; interrogatoire *m* (de prisonniers).

questionable ['kwestʃənəbl], *a.* **1.** Contestable, discutable; problématique. **2.** *Pej:* (*Of conduct, etc.*) Équivoque. *In q. taste*, d'un goût douteux.

questioner ['kwestʃənər], *s.* Interrogateur, -trice

questionnaire [kestjo'nɛər, ˌkwestʃənɛər], s. Questionnaire *m*.

queue¹ [kjuː], *s.* **1.** Queue *f* (de cheveux) **2.** Queue (de personnes). **To form a queue, to stand in a queue**, faire (la) queue.

queue², *v.i.* **To queue (up)**, faire (la) queue (*of cars*) prendre la file.

quibble¹ ['kwibl], *s.* **1.** *A:* Calembour *m*; jeu *n* de mots. **2.** Argutie *f*; chicane *f* de mots faux-fuyant *m*.

quibble², *v.i.* **1.** Chicaner sur les mots; use d'équivoque. **2.** (*Split hairs*) Chicaner, vétiller

quibbling, *s.* Arguties *fpl*, évasions *fpl*; chicane *f* de mots.

quibbler ['kwiblər], *s.* Ergoteur, -euse; chicaneur, -euse.

quick [kwik]. **1.** *a.* (*a*) Rapide. *Q. pulse*, pouls fréquent. *The quickest way there*, le chemin le plus court pour y arriver. **Quick sale**, prompt débit; vente facile. **As quick as lightning**, comme un éclair; en un clin d'œil. **Be quick** (*about it*) faites vite! dépêchez-vous! *Try to be a little quicker*, tâchez d'y aller un peu plus vite. (*b*) *A q child*, un enfant vif, éveillé, qui a l'esprit prompt **Quick wit**, esprit prompt à la repartie. *Q. ear* oreille fine. *She has a q. temper*, elle s'emporte facilement; *F:* elle a la tête près du bonnet. **Quick to act**, prompt à agir. **Quick to anger**, prompt, vif, à se fâcher. **Quick of belief**, prompt à croire. **Quick of foot**, agile, leste, preste. (*c*) *Mus:* Éveillé. 'Quicker,' "animez." (*d*) *A:* Vif, vivant. **Quick hedge**, haie vive. *s.* **The quick and the dead**, les vivants et les morts. **To** *s.* Vif *m*; chair vive. **To bite one's nails to the quick**, ronger ses ongles jusqu'au vif. *F:* To sting, cut, s.o. to the quick, blesser, piquer, qn au vif. **3.** *adv.* Vite, rapidement. *To run quicker*, courir plus vite. **-ly**, *adv.* Vite, rapidement, vivement. '**quick-'acting**, *a.* (Mécanisme) à action rapide, immédiate. '**quick-'change**, attrib.a. *Th:* **Quick-change artist**, acteur à transformations rapides. **Quick-change part**, rôle à travestissements. '**quick-eared**, *a.* Qui a l'oreille fine. '**quick-eyed**, *a.* Aux yeux vifs, perçants. '**quick-firing**, *a.* (Canon) à tir rapide. '**quick-lunch**, attrib.a. **Quick-lunch bar**, casse-croûte *m inv.* '**quick-'tempered**, *a.* Emporté, irascible; prompt à la colère. '**quick-'witted**, *a.* A l'esprit prompt; vif, éveillé.

quicken ['kwik(ə)n]. **1.** *v.tr.* (*a*) *Lit:* Donner la vie à, (r)animer, vivifier. (*b*) Exciter, stimuler, aiguiser (le désir, l'appétit); animer (la conversation). (*c*) Hâter, presser, accélérer (*one's pace*, le pas). *Med:* Accélérer (le pouls). *Mus:* **To quicken the tempo**, presser la mesure. **2.** *v.i.* (*a*) (*Of nature, hope*) S'animer, se ranimer. (*b*) (*Of pace, etc.*) Devenir plus rapide; s'accélérer.

quicklime ['kwiklaim], *s.* Chaux vive.

quickness ['kwiknəs], *s.* **1.** Vitesse *f*, rapidité *f*, prestesse *f.* **2.** Acuité *f* (de vision); finesse *f* (d'oreille); promptitude *f*, vivacité *f* (d'esprit).

quicksand ['kwiksand], *s.* Sable(s) mouvant(s) (du bord de la mer); lise *f.* **To get caught in a quicksand**, s'enliser.

quickset ['kwikset]. **1.** *s.* Bouture *f* (d'aubépine, etc.). **2.** *a. & s.* **Quickset** (**hedge**), haie vive.

quicksilver¹ ['kwiksilvər], *s.* Vif-argent *m*, mercure *m.* *F:* **To have quicksilver in one's veins**, avoir du vif-argent dans les veines.

quicksilver², *v.tr.* Étamer (une glace).

quickstep ['kwikstep], *s.* **1.** *Mil:* Pas accéléré; pas redoublé. **2.** *Mus:* Pas redoublé.

quid¹ [kwid], s. P: Livre f (sterling). *Five quid,* cinq livres.

quid², s. Chique f (de tabac).

quid pro quo ['kwidprou'kwou], s. (a) Équivalent m, compensation f. (b) *To return a quid pro quo,* rendre la pareille à qn.

quiescence [kwai'es(ə)ns], s. Repos m, quiétude f, tranquillité f.

quiescent [kwai'es(ə)nt], a. En repos; tranquille.

quiet¹ ['kwaiət], s. Tranquillité f, repos m, quiétude f. *The quiet of the night,* le calme, la tranquillité, de la nuit.

quiet², a. **1.** Tranquille, calme, silencieux. Q. *running of a machine,* marche silencieuse d'une machine. *To keep quiet,* se tenir, rester, tranquille; se tenir coi. *Be quiet!* taisez-vous! *laissez-moi tranquille!* **2.** Q. *disposition,* caractère doux, calme. Q. *horse,* cheval doux, sage. **3.** (a) (Of dress, colours) Simple; discret, -ète; sobre. Q. *dinner,* dîner intime. Q. *wedding,* mariage célébré dans l'intimité. *To live in a quiet way,* avoir un train modeste. (b) Q. *irony,* ironie voilée. *To have a q. dig at s.o.,* faire une allusion discrète à qn. s. F: *To do sth.* **on the quiet,** faire qch. en cachette, à la dérobée. *I am telling you that on the q.,* F: je vous dis ça entre quat'z yeux. **4.** (a) Calme, tranquille, paisible. *To lead a q. life,* mener une vie calme. *He has had a q. sleep,* il a dormi tranquillement. *Business is very q.,* les affaires sont très calmes. (b) Sans inquiétude. *You may be q. on that score,* quant à cela vous pouvez être tranquille. **-ly,** adv. **1.** (a) Tranquillement, doucement. (b) Silencieusement, sans bruit; sans tambour ni trompette. **2.** Q. *and neatly dressed,* vêtu avec une simplicité de bon goût. *To get married q.,* se marier dans l'intimité.

quiet³, v. (quieted) **1.** v.tr. (a) Apaiser, calmer; tranquilliser (qn, sa conscience); faire taire (un enfant). (b) Apaiser, calmer (un tumulte); dissiper (les craintes). **2.** v.i. *To quiet down,* s'apaiser, se calmer.

quietness ['kwaiətnəs], s. **1.** Tranquillité f, repos m, calme m. **2.** Sobriété f (de tenue, etc.).

quietude ['kwaietju:d], s. Quiétude f.

quietus [kwai'i:təs], s. F: Coup m de grâce. *To give s.o.* his quietus, régler son compte à qn; envoyer qn dans l'autre monde.

quill¹ [kwil], s. **1.** (a) Orn: Tuyau m (de plume). (b) = QUILL-FEATHER. (c) = QUILL-PEN. **2.** Piquant m (de porc-épic, etc.). **3.** *Laund:* Tuyau. **'quill-bark,** s. Com: Quinquina m en tuyaux. **'quill-driver,** s. F: Gratte-papier m inv; plumitif m. **'quill-feather,** s. Orn: Penne f. **'quill-pen,** s. Plume f d'oie (pour écrire).

quill², v.tr. Tuyauter, rucher (une dentelle).

quillai [ki'lai], **quillaia** [kwi'leijə], s. Bot: Quillaja m. **Quillai(a)-bark,** bois m de Panama.

quilt¹ [kwilt], s. Couverture piquée, ouatée; édredon piqué; couvre-pied(s) m.

quilt², v.tr. Piquer, contre-pointer, capitonner, ouater (un vêtement). **quilting,** s. **1.** Piquage m, capitonnage m. **2.** Piqué m.

quince [kwins], s. **1.** Coing m. **2.** Quince(-tree), cognassier m.

quincunx ['kwinkʌŋks], s. Quinconce m.

quinine [kwi'ni:n], s. Ch: Quinine f. **Quinine wine,** (vin m de) quinquina m.

quinol ['kwinɔl], s. Ch: Hydroquinone f.

quinquagenarian [kwinkwadʒe'nɛəriən], a. & s. Quinquagénaire (mf).

quinquennial [kwin'kwenjəl], a. Quinquennal, -aux.

quinsy ['kwinzi], s. Med: Esquinancie f; angine (laryngée).

quintain ['kwint(ə)n], s. A: Quintaine f. *To tilt at the quintain,* courir la quintaine.

quintal ['kwint(ə)l], s. Meas: **1.** Quintal, -aux m (de 112 livres). **2.** Quintal métrique (de 100 kg.).

quintessence [kwin'tes(ə)ns], s. Quintessence f; F: suc m, moelle f (d'un livre).

quintet(te) [kwin'tet], s. Mus: Quintette m.

quintillion [kwin'tiljən], s. **1.** Dix à la trentième puissance; 10^{30}. **2.** U.S: Quintillion m; 10^{18}.

quintuple¹ ['kwintjupl], a. & s. Quintuple (m).

quintuple², v.tr. & i. Quintupler.

quintuplet ['kwintjuplet], s. **1.** Groupe m de cinq. **2.** pl. Quintuplets, cinq enfants nés d'une seule couche.

quip [kwip], s. Sarcasme m, repartie f; raillerie f; mot piquant; F: lardon m. **Quips and cranks,** pointes f et bons mots.

quire ['kwaiər], s. **1.** Q. *of paper* (24 sheets) = main f de papier (25 feuilles). **Quarter of a quire,** cahier m. **2.** Typ: In quires, en feuilles.

quirk [kwə:rk], s. **1.** = QUIP. **2.** Faux-fuyant m; équivoque f. *There's sure to be a q. in it,* on va encore être dupés. **3.** (a) Trait m de plume; arabesque f, fioriture f. (b) Parafe m. **4.** Arch: Gorge f.

quit¹ [kwit], a. Quitte. *The others can go quit,* les autres peuvent se considérer comme quittes. *To be quit for a fine,* en être quitte pour une amende. *To be quit of s.o.,* être débarrassé de qn. **'quit-rent,** s. Redevance f (minime).

quit², v.tr. (quitted, Dial. & U.S: quit) **1.** (a) Quitter (qn, un endroit). Abs. Vider les lieux; déménager. S.a. NOTICE¹ 1. (b) *To quit one's job,* U.S: to quit, quitter son emploi; démissionner. (c) *To quit hold of sth.,* lâcher qch.; lâcher prise. (d) U.S: *To quit doing sth.,* cesser de faire qch. **2.** A: (Acquit) **Quit you like men,** comportez-vous vaillamment.

quite [kwait], adv. **1.** Tout à fait; entièrement. Q. *new,* tout nouveau. Q. *recovered,* complètement rétabli. *It is q. five days ago,* il y a bien cinq jours de cela. **Quite as much,** tout autant. **Quite enough,** bien assez. **Quite right,** très bien; (of sum) parfaitement juste. **Quite so!** -F: *quite!* parfaitement! d'accord! *I do not q. know what he will do,* je ne sais pas trop ce qu'il fera. *I q. understand,* j'ai bien compris; je me rends parfaitement compte. **2.** *It is q. interesting,* cela ne manque pas d'intérêt. *His story is q. a romance,* son histoire est tout un roman. *It was q. a surprise,* ce fut une véritable surprise. *I q. believe that . . . ,* je veux bien croire que. . . . S.a. LOT 4.

quits [kwits], pred.a. Quitte(s). *We'll cry q.! now we're q.!* nous voilà quittes à quitte! *I am q. with you,* nous sommes quittes.

quitter ['kwitər], s. U.S: F: Tire-au-flanc m inv; lâcheur, -euse.

quiver¹ ['kwivər], s. Carquois m.

quiver², s. Tremblement m; (i) frisson m; (ii) frémissement m; (iii) palpitation f. *With a q. in his voice,* d'une voix frémissante. Q. *of the eyelid,* battement m de paupière.

quiver³, v.i. Trembler; frémir, tressaillir, frissonner; (of voice, light) trembloter; (of flesh) palpiter. *To q. with fear,* frémir de crainte. *Voice quivering with emotion,* voix vibrante d'émotion.

quiverful ['kwivərful], s. Plein carquois (de flèches). F: Q. *of children,* nombreuse famille.

Quixote (Don) [dɔn'kwiksot]. Pr.n.m. Don Quichotte.

quixotic [kwik'sɔtik], a. (a) Exalté, visionnaire.

(b)·Par trop chevaleresque. **-ally,** *adv.* En Don Quichotte.

quixotism ['kwiksotizm], *s.* (Don)quichottisme *m.*

quiz[1] [kwiz], *s.* **I.** Mystification *f*, farce *f.* **2.** *A:* (*a*) Une drôle de figure ; original *m.* (*b*) Railleur, -euse.

quiz[2], *v.tr.* (quizzed) **I.** Railler, persifler (qn). **2.** Lorgner, reluquer (qn).

quizzical ['kwizik(ə)l],· *a.* **I.** Risible, cocasse. **2.** Railleur, -euse ; plaisant.

quod [kwɔd], *s. P :* Prison *f* ; *P :* boîte *f*, bloc *m.* In quod, au bloc ; "à l'ombre."

quoin[1] [kɔin], *s.* **I.** *Const :* Pierre *f* d'angle ; encoignure *f.* **2.** *Mec.E :* Coin *m* (pour caler). *Artil :* Coussin *m* ; coin de mire. *Typ :* Coin, cale *f.* **'quoin-stone,** *s. Const :* Pierre *f* d'angle, d'arête.

quoin[2], *v.tr.* Caler, coincer. **To quoin up,** soulever avec des cales.

quoit [kɔit], *s. Games :* Palet *m.* **To play (at) quoits,** jouer au palet.

quondam ['kwɔndam], *a.* D'autrefois. *My· q. friends*, mes amis d'autrefois, de jadis.

quorum ['kwɔːrəm], *s.* Quorum *m* ; nombre voulu. **To form a quorum,** constituer un quorum.

quota ['kwoutə], *s.* (*a*) Quote-part *f*, quotité *f.* **To contribute one's quota,** payer, apporter, sa quote-part. (*b*) *Full q. of troops*, plein contingent de troupes. (*c*) *Electoral quota*, quotient électoral. (*d*) *Cin : etc :* **Quota system** (*of distribution*), contingentement *m.* **To fix quotas for an import,** contingenter une importation.

quotation [kwo'teiʃ(ə)n], *s.* **I.** Citation (empruntée à un auteur). **2.** *St.Exch :* Cote *f*, cours *m*, prix *m.* **The latest quotations,** les derniers cours faits. **3.** *Typ :* Cadrat creux. **quo'tation-marks,** *s.pl.* Guillemets *m.*

quote [kwout], *v.tr.* **I.** (*a*) Citer (un auteur, un passage). *Abs.* **To quote from an author,** tirer une citation d'un auteur. *To q. an instance of sth.*, fournir un exemple de qch. (*b*) *Com :* **In reply please quote this number,** prière de rappeler ce numéro. **2.** (*a*) *Com :* Établir, faire (un prix). **To quote s.o. a price for sth.**, fixer à qn un prix pour qch. (*b*) *St.Exch :* Coter (une valeur). **Shares quoted at 45/-,** actions qui se cotent à 45 shillings. **3.** *Typ :* Guillemeter (un passage). **Words quoted,** mots entre guillemets.

quoth [kwouθ], *v.tr. def. A :* 'No,' quoth I, "non," dis-je.

quotient ['kwouʃ(ə)nt], *s. Mth :* Quotient *m.*

R

R, r [ɑːr], *s.* (La lettre) R, r *f.* *F :* **The three R's** (*Reading*, (*w*)*Riting and* (*a*)*Rithmetic*), l'enseignement *m* primaire.

rabbet[1] ['rabet], *s. Carp :* Feuillure *f*, rainure *f.* **'rabbet-;oint,** *s.* Assemblage *m* à feuillure.

rabbet[2], *v.tr.* (*a*) Faire une feuillure, une rainure, à (une planche). (*b*) Assembler (deux planches) à feuillure. **rabbeting,** *s.* Assemblage *m* à feuillure.

rabbi ['rabai], *s. Jew.Rel :* Rabbin *m* ; (*voc. case and title*) rabbi *m.* **Chief rabbi,** grand rabbin.

rabbit[1] ['rabit], *s.* **I.** Lapin *m.* **Buck rabbit,** lapin mâle. **Doe rabbit,** lapine *f.* *Young r.*, lapereau *m.* *Tame r.*, lapin domestique, lapin de clapier. *Wild r.*, lapin de garenne. **2.** *Cu :* (*a*) **Stewed rabbit,** gibelotte *f* de lapin. (*b*) **Welsh rabbit,** fondue *f* au fromage sur canapé. **3.** *F :* (*a*) Poltron *m.* (*b*) *Sp :* Mazette *f* ; novice *mf.* **'rabbit-farm,** *s.* Élevage *m* de lapins. **'rabbit-hole,** *s.* Terrier *m* de lapin. **'rabbit-hutch,** *s.* Clapier *m.* **'rabbit-punch,** *s. Box :* Coup *m* sur la nuque. **'rabbit-warren,** *s.* Garenne *f.*

rabbit[2], *v.i.* **To go rabbiting,** faire la chasse au lapin.

rabble [rabl], *s.* **I.** Cohue *f* ; foule *f* (en désordre). **2.** **The rabble,** la populace, la canaille.

Rabelaisian [rabə'leiziən], *a.* Rabelaisien.

rabid ['rabid], *a.* **I.** (*a*) Furieux, féroce. *To be a r. enemy of s.o.*, être acharné contre, après, qn. (*b*) (Démagogue, etc.) outrancier, à outrance. *He had become a r. free-trader*, il s'était féru du libre-échange. **2.** *Vet :* (*a*) (Chien) enragé. (*b*) **Rabid virus,** virus rabique.

rabies ['reibiːz], *s. Med :* Rage *f*, hydrophobie *f.*

raccoon [ra'kuːn], *s.* = RACOON.

race[1] [reis], *s.* **I.** (*In sea*) Raz *m*, ras *m*, de courant. **2.** Carrière *f.* **His race is run,** il est arrivé au

terme de sa vie. **3.** (*a*) *Hyd.E :* Canal *m*, bief *m.* (*b*) *Mch :* Puits *m*, fosse *f* (du volant). **4.** *Mec.E :* **(Ball-)race,** (i) voie *f*, chemin *m*, de roulement ; (ii) cage *f* à billes. **5.** *Sp :* Course. **To run a race,** disputer une course. **Long-distance race,** course de (grand) fond ; marathon *m.* **Foot race,** course à pied. **Horse race,** course de chevaux. **Point-to-point race,** course au clocher. **To go to the races,** aller aux courses. **'race-card,** *s. Turf :* Programme *m* des courses. **'race-course,** *s.* Champ *m* de courses. **'race-goer,** *s.* Turfiste *m* ; habitué, -ée, du turf. **'race-horse,** *s.* Cheval *m*, -aux, de course. **'race-meeting,** *s.* Concours *m* hippique ; réunion *f* de courses.

race[2]. **I.** *v.i.* (*a*) Lutter de vitesse, faire une course (*with*, avec). (*b*) **To race along,** aller grand train ; filer à toute vitesse. *To r. down the street*, dévaler la rue à toute vitesse. (*c*) (*Of engine*) S'emballer ; (*of propeller*) s'affoler. (*d*) (*Of pulse*) Battre la fièvre. **2.** *v.tr.* (*a*) Lutter de vitesse avec (qn). *I'll r. you home !* au premier arrivé de nous deux à la maison ! *Abs.* **To race,** faire de l'hippisme ; monter en course. (*b*) Faire courir (un cheval) ; *abs.* faire courir. (*c*) *I.C.E :* **To race the engine** (*without a load*), emballer le moteur (à vide). (*d*) *F :* **To race a bill through the House,** faire voter une loi au grand galop.

racing, *s.* **I.** Courses *fpl.* **Road racing,** courses sur route. **Boat racing,** courses d'aviron. **Horse racing,** les courses (de chevaux) ; l'hippisme *m.* **Racing stable,** écurie de courses. **Racing car,** automobile de course. **Racing-track,** piste *f.* **2.** Emballement *m* (d'un moteur) ; affolement *m* (d'une hélice).

race[3], *s.* Race *f.* **I.** **Race-feeling,** conscience *f* de race. **The human race,** la race humaine. *F :* **The feathered race,** la race ailée ; *Hum :* la gent ailée. **2.** (*a*) Descendance *f.* *Of noble r.*, de sang noble. (*Of horse, etc.*) **True to race,** fortement racé.

(b) Lignée f. A long r. of seafaring men, une longue lignée de marins.
race⁴, s. Racine f (de gingembre).
raceme [ra'si:m], s. Bot: Racème m, grappe f.
racer ['reisər], s. **I.** (Pers.) Coureur, -euse.
2. (a) Cheval m, -aux, de course. (b) Bicyclette f, automobile f ou yacht m de course.
rachitic [ra'kitik], a. Med: Rachitique.
rachitis [ra'kaitis], s. Med: Rachitisme m.
racial ['reiʃəl]. **I.** a. De (la) race. R. minorities, minorités de race. **2.** s. Membre m d'une race (particulière). **-ally**, adv. Du point de vue de la race.
raciness ['reisinəs], s. **I.** (Of wine, fruit) Goût m de terroir ; (of wine) bouquet m. **2.** (Of style) Piquant m, verve f.
rack¹ [rak], s. (Cloud-)rack, légers nuages chassés par le vent.
rack², s. Only in the phr. To go to rack and ruin, aller à la ruine ; tomber en ruine.
rack³, s. **I.** (a) Husb: Râtelier m (d'écurie). F: To live at rack and manger, vivre dans l'abondance. (b) Arm-rack, râtelier d'armes. Tool-rack, porte-outils m inv. Music-rack, classeur m à musique. Hat-and-coat rack, porte-manteau m, vestiaire m. Av: Bomb rack, lance-bombes m inv. Rail: Luggage rack, porte-bagages m inv ; filet m (à bagages). (c) Veh: Ridelle f (de charrette). **2.** Mec.E: Rack and pinion, crémaillère f (et pignon). 'rack-'railway, s. Chemin m de fer à crémaillère. 'rack-wheel, s. Roue dentée.
rack⁴, s. Hist: Chevalet m (de torture). To put, submit, s.o. to the r., mettre qn à la torture, à la question. F: To be on the rack, être à la torture, au supplice ; être sur des charbons ardents.
rack⁵, v.tr. **I.** (a) Hist: Faire subir le supplice du chevalet à (qn). (b) (Of pain, etc.) Tourmenter, torturer (qn) ; faire souffrir le martyre à (qn). Racked by remorse, tenaillé par le remords. To rack a machine to pieces, détraquer une machine. S.a. BRAIN¹ 2. **2.** (a) Extorquer (un loyer) ; pressurer (un locataire). (b) Épuiser (le sol). **racking**, a. **I.** (Of pain) Atroce, déchirant. R. headache, mal de tête fou. **2.** (Impôt) exorbitant. 'rack(ing)-stick, s. Tordoir m, garrot m. 'rack-rent, s. Loyer exorbitant.
rack⁶, v.tr. To rack (off) wine, soutirer le vin.
racket¹ ['raket], s. **I.** (a) Raquette f (de tennis, etc.). (b) pl. Games: Rackets, la raquette. **2.** Raquette (pour la marche sur la neige).
racket², s. **I.** Tapage m, vacarme m, tintamarre m. To kick up a racket, faire du boucan. To kick up no end of a r., faire un charivari de tous les diables. To stand the racket, (i) subir les conséquences ; (ii) affronter la critique ; (iii) subvenir aux dépenses. **2.** Gaieté sociale ; dissipation f. To go on the racket, (i) s'adonner au plaisir ; (ii) faire la bombe ; tirer une bordée. **3.** P: (a) Genre m d'affaires, spécialité f (d'un escroc). (b) Entreprise f de gangsters ; affaire véreuse. Do you want to be in on this racket? voulez-vous être de la bande ?
racket³, v.i. (racketed) **I.** To racket (about), faire du tapage, P: du boucan. **2.** Faire la vie, faire la noce.
racketeer ['raketi:ər], s. **I.** Noceur m. **2.** U.S: Gangster m.
racoon [ra'ku:n], s. Z: Raton laveur.
racquet ['raket], s. = RACKET¹.
racy ['reisi], a. **I.** To be racy of the soil, sentir le terroir. **2.** (a) Racy anecdote, anecdote savoureuse. (b) (Of pers.) Vif, piquant. Racy

style, style plein de verve. **-ily**, adv. D'une façon piquante ; avec verve.
raddle¹ [radl], s. Ocre f rouge.
raddle², v.tr. (a) Peindre ou marquer à l'ocre. (b) Raddled face, visage au maquillage grossier.
radial¹ ['reidiəl], a. **I.** Mec.E : etc : Radial, -aux. I.C.E : Radial engine, moteur en étoile. Mec : Radial force, force centrifuge. **2.** Anat : Radial, du radius.
radial², a. Med : Du radium ; radique.
radian ['reidiən], s. Mth : Radian(t) m.
radiance ['reidjəns], s. **I.** Rayonnement m, splendeur f. In the full r. of her beauty, dans tout l'éclat de sa beauté. **2.** Ph : Rayonnement, radiation f.
radiant ['reidjənt]. **I.** a. (a) Radiant heat, Ph : chaleur rayonnante ; Med : chaleur radiante. (b) (Soleil, etc.) radieux. Face r. with smiles, visage souriant et radieux. R. eyes, yeux rayonnants de joie. **2.** s. (a) Ph : Foyer m de rayonnement. (b) Astr : Radiant m. **-ly**, adv. D'un air radieux. R. happy, rayonnant de joie.
radiate¹ ['reidiət], a. Nat.Hist : Radié.
radiate² ['reidieit]. **I.** v.i. Rayonner ; irradier. (a) Émettre des rayons. Happiness radiates from her eyes, ses yeux sont rayonnants de bonheur. (b) (Of lines) Partir d'un même centre. **2.** v.tr. (a) Émettre, dégager (de la chaleur, etc.). (b) (Radio)diffuser (un programme).
radiation [reidi'eiʃ(ə)n], s. **I.** Irradiation f ; rayonnement m. **2.** (Of radium, etc.) Radiation f.
radiator ['reidieitər], s. **I.** (a) Radiateur m (pour chauffage). (b) I.C.E : Radiateur, refroidisseur m. Fan-cooled r., radiateur soufflé. **2.** W.Tel : Antenne f d'émission. 'radiator-'cap, s. Aut : Bouchon m du radiateur. 'radiator-'muff, s. Aut : Couvre-radiateur m.
radical ['radik(ə)l]. **I.** a. Radical, -aux. (a) To make a r. alteration in sth., changer qch. radicalement. R. diversity, diversité radicale, foncière. (b) Pol : The Radical party, le parti radical ; les Gauches m. **2.** s. Ch : Ling : Mth : Radical. **-ally**, adv. Radicalement, foncièrement.
radicalism ['radikəlizm], s. Pol : Radicalisme m.
radicle ['radikl], s. Bot : (a) Radicule f (de l'embryon). (b) Radicelle f ; petite racine.
radio¹, ² ['reidio], s. & v.tr. = WIRELESS¹, ².
radio-active, a. Ph : Radio-actif.
radio-activity, s. Ph : Radio-activité f.
radiogoniometer [reidiogouni'ɔmetər], s. Radiogoniomètre m.
radiogram ['reidiogram], s. **I.** W.Tel : Radiogramme m. **2.** = RADIOGRAPH¹. **3.** F : Poste m de T.S.F. avec pick-up ; combiné m radio-phono.
radiograph¹ ['reidiogra:f, -graf], s. Med : etc : Radiogramme m, radiographie f.
radiograph², v.tr. Med : etc : Radiographier.
radiographic [reidio'grafik], a. Radiographique.
radiography [reidi'ɔgrəfi], s. Med : Radiographie f.
radiologist [reidi'ɔlodʒist], s. Med : Radiologue m.
radiology [reidi'ɔlodʒi], s. Med : Radiologie f.
radioscopy [reidi'ɔskopi], s. Radioscopie f.
radio-therapy, s. Radiothérapie f.
radish ['radiʃ], s. Radis m. S.a. HORSE-RADISH.
radium ['reidiəm], s. **I.** Radium m. Radium paint, incrustation f de radium.
radius ['reidiəs], pl. **-ii** ['reidiəs, -iai], s. **I.** Geom : Rayon m (de cercle). **2.** Aut : Steering radius, rayon de braquage. Radius of action of an aeroplane, rayon d'action d'un avion. Within a

radius of three miles, dans un rayon de trois milles. **2.** *Anat:* Radius *m* (de l'avant-bras).

radix, *pl.* **-ices** ['reidiks, -isi:z], *s.* **1.** *Mth:* Base *f* (d'un système de logarithmes). **2.** Racine *f*, source *f* (d'un mal).

raffia ['rafiǝ], *s. Bot:* Raphia *m.*

raffish ['rafiʃ], *a. F:* (*a*) Bravache, esbrouffeur. (*b*) (Air, etc.) canaille.

raffle[1] [rafl], *s.* Tombola *f* (à une vente de charité).

raffle[2], *v.tr.* Mettre (qch.) en tombola. **raffling**, *s.* Mise *f* en tombola (*of*, de).

raft [rɑ:ft], *s.* **1.** Radeau *m. Emergency r.*, radeau le fortune. **2.** Timber-raft, *U.S:* lumber raft, train *m* de bois, train de flottage. **3.** *Const:* Foundation raft, radier *m.* 'raft-wood, *s.* Bois flotté ; bois de flottage.

rafter ['rɑ:ftǝr], *s. Const:* Chevron *m* (d'un comble). Main rafter, arbalétrier *m.*

raftsman, *pl.* **-men** ['rɑ:ftsmǝn, -men], *s.m.* Flotteur (de bois).

rag[1] [rag], *s.* **1.** Chiffon *m* ; lambeau *m. F:* To feel like a rag, se sentir (mou) comme une chiffe. Meat cooked to rags, viande cuite et recuite. **2.** *pl.* Rags (and tatters), haillons *m*, guenilles *f*, loques *f*. To be in rags, être en guenilles, déguenillé. **3.** *Paperm:* Rag pulp, pâte *f* de chiffons. **4.** *Pej:* (*a*) (*Newspaper*) Feuille *f* de chou. (*b*) Mouchoir *m*, drapeau *m*, etc. ; "loque." 'rag-and-'bone, *attrib.a.* Rag-and-bone man, chiffonnier *m.* 'rag-bag, *s.* Sac *m* aux chiffons. 'rag-book, *s.* Livre d'images imprimé sur toile. 'rag-'doll, *s.* Poupée *f* en chiffons. 'rag-fair, *s.* Marché *m* aux vieux habits ; *F:* marché aux puces. 'rag-merchant, *s.* Marchand *m* de chiffons en gros. 'rag-paper, *s.* Papier *m* de chiffons. 'rag-picker, *s.* Chiffonnier, -ière. 'rag-tag, *s. F:* The rag-tag (and bob-tail), la canaille. 'rag-time, *s.* Musique nègre syncopée.

rag[2], *s. Sch: F:* **1.** Brimade *f* ; mauvais tour ; farce *f.* **2.** Chahut *m*, bacchanal *m.*

rag[3], *v.tr.* (ragged [ragd]) *F:* **1.** Brimer (un camarade). **2.** Chahuter (un professeur) ; chambarder les effets (d'un étudiant). *Abs.* To rag, chahuter ; faire du chahut. **3.** Gronder, tancer (qn).

ragamuffin ['ragǝmʌfin], *s.* **1.** (*a*) Gueux *m* ; va-nu-pieds *m inv.* (*b*) Mauvais garnement. **2.** Gamin *m* des rues.

rage[1] [reidʒ], *s.* **1.** Rage *f*, fureur *f*, emportement *m. Fit of rage*, accès *m* de fureur. To be in a rage with s.o., être furieux contre qn. To fly into a rage, se mettre en colère ; s'emporter. **2.** Fureur, furie *f* (des vents). **3.** Manie *f*, toquade *f.* To have a rage for sth., avoir la rage, la manie, de qch. (*Of thg*) To be all the rage, faire fureur, faire rage.

rage[2], *v.i.* **1.** To rage (and fume), être furieux ; rager. To rage against, at, s.o., tempêter contre qn. **2.** (*Of wind*) Fa`re rage ; (*of pestilence*) sévir.

raging[1], *a.* Furieux ; en fureur. To be in a raging temper, être furieux. *R. sea*, mer déchaînée, démontée. Raging fever, fièvre de cheval. *R. thirst*, soif ardente. Raging headache, mal de tête fou. **raging**[2], *s.* **1.** Rage *f*, fureur *f.* **2.** Fureur, furie *f* (de la mer).

ragged ['ragid], *a.* **1.** (*a*) En lambeaux, en loques. (*b*) (*Of pers.*) En haillons ; déguenillé. **2.** (*a*) (Nuage) déchiqueté ; (rocher) ébréché. (*b*) *Mus:* The execution is r., l'exécution manque d'ensemble. *Mil:* R. fire, feu désordonné. (*c*) *Bot:* Ragged Robin, lychnide *f* des prés.

raggedness ['ragidnǝs], *s.* **1.** Déguenillement *m*

(de qn) ; délabrement *m* (d'un vêtement). **2.** Inégalité *f* (d'un ouvrage) ; manque *m* d'ensemble (de l'exécution).

ragman, *pl.* **-men** ['ragmǝn, -men], *s.m.* Marchand de chiffons ; chiffonnier ; *F:* biffin.

ragout [ra'gu:], *s. Cu:* Ragoût *m.*

ragstone ['ragstoun], *s. Const:* Pierre bourrue ; souchet *m* (de carrière).

ragwort ['ragwɔ:rt], *s. Bot:* Jacobée *f.*

raid[1] [reid], *s.* (*a*) Razzia *f* (de bandits). (*b*) Police raid, descente *f* de police ; rafle *f.* (*c*) *Mil:* Raid *m* ; coup *m* de main. Air raid, raid aérien.

raid[2]. **1.** *v.i.* Faire une razzia ; *Mil:* faire un raid. **2.** *v.tr.* (*a*) Razzier (une tribu) ; (*of police*) faire une descente, une rafle, dans (une boîte de nuit, un quartier). (*b*) To r. orchards, marauder les fruits dans les vergers.

raider ['reidǝr], *s.* **1.** (*a*) Maraudeur *m* ; pillard *m.* (*b*) Soldat *m* en razzia ; aviateur *m* en raid. (*c*) *Nau: A:* Corsaire *m.* **2.** (*a*) Avion *m* en raid. (*b*) Navire *m* de course.

rail[1] [reil], *s.* **1.** (*a*) Barre *f*, barreau *m* (de barrière) ; bâton *m* (de chaise). (*b*) Barre d'appui ; garde-fou *m*, parapet *m* (de pont) ; balustrade *f* (de balcon) ; rampe *f* (d'escalier). (*c*) *Veh:* Ridelle *f* (de charrette). **2.** *pl.* (*Iron*) Grille *f* ; (*wood*) clôture *f*, palissade *f*, balustrade. *Rac:* The rails, la corde. **3.** *N.Arch:* (*a*) Lisse *f.* (*b*) *pl. F:* Bastingages *m* (d'un paquebot). **4.** *Rail:* (*a*) Rail *m.* Live rail, rail de contact. To leave the rails, dérailler. (*b*) Chemin *m* de fer ; voie ferrée. To travel by rail, voyager en chemin de fer. *Com:* Price on rail, prix sur `e wagon. 'rail-car, *s. Rail:* Automotrice *f*, autorail *m.* ; chaise *f* de rail. 'rail-chair, *s. Rail:* Coussinet *m* de rail ; chaise *f* de rail. 'rail-head, *s.* (*a*) *Rail:* Tête *f* de ligne. (*b*) *Mil:* Gare *f* de ravitaillement.

rail[2], *v.tr.* **1.** To rail sth. in, griller, palissader (un enclos). To rail sth. round, entourer (une pelouse) d'une grille. **2.** Envoyer (des marchandises) par chemin de fer. Railed(-in, -off) space, espace entouré d'une grille. **railing**(s), *s.*(*pl.*) **1.** Clôture *f* à claire-voie ; grille *f*, palissade *f.* **2.** Garde-fou *m*, parapet *m* (de pont) ; balustrade *f* (de balcon) ; rampe *f* (d'escalier).

rail[3], *s. Orn:* Râle *m.* Water-rail, râle d'eau.

rail[4], *v.i.* Se répandre en plaintes, en injures. To rail at, against s.o., crier contre qn ; s'en prendre à qn. To r. at fate, s'en prendre au sort.

raillery ['reilǝri], *s.* Raillerie *f.*

railroad ['reilroud], *s. U.S:* = RAILWAY 1.

railway ['reilwei], *s.* **1.** Railway (line), (ligne *f* de) chemin *m* de fer ; voie ferrée. Light railway, ligne d'intérêt local ; chemin de fer à voie étroite. Circle railway, chemin de fer de ceinture. *S.a.* SCENIC 2. Railway system, réseau ferré. Railway station, station *f* de chemin de fer ; gare *f.* Railway engineer, ingénieur des voies ferrées. Railway traffic, trafic ferroviaire. Railway parcels, articles *m* de messageries. Railway rug, couverture *f* de voyage. **2.** *Ind:* Overhead railway (*for shop use*), pont roulant. 'railway-cutting, *s.* (Voie *f* en) déblai *m* ; tranchée *f.* 'railway-em'bankment, *s.* (Voie *f* en) remblai *m.*

railwayman, *pl.* **-men** ['reilweimǝn, -men], *s.m.* Employé des chemins de fer ; *F:* cheminot.

raiment ['reimǝnt], *s. A. & Poet:* Habillement *m* ; vêtement(s) *m*(*pl*).

rain[1] [rein], *s.* Pluie *f.* **1.** Pelting r., driving r., pluie battante. It looks like rain, le temps est à la pluie, menace la p.uie. A walk in the rain, une promenade sous la pluie. **Come in out of the rain!** entrez donc, ne restez pas à la pluie! *P:* **To get out of the rain,** se défiler. *Pyr:* **Golden rain,** pluie d'or. *S.a.* RIGHT[1] I. 4. **2.** *pl.* **The rains** = *the rainy season.* **'rain-chart,** *s.* Carte *f* pluviométrique. **'rain-cloud,** *s.* Nimbus *m.* **'rain-coat,** *s.* Imperméable *m.* **'rain-gauge,** *s.* Pluviomètre *m.* **Recording rain-gauge,** pluviographe *m.* **'rain-pipe,** *s.* *Const:* (Tuyau *m* de) descente *f.* **'rain-water,** *s.* Eau *f* de p uie.

'ain², *v.tr.* & *i.* **I.** Pleuvoir. *It rains, it is raining,* il pleut; il tombe de la pluie. *It is raining fast,* il pleut à verse. *F:* **It is raining cats and dogs,** il pleut des hallebardes; il pleut à seaux. **It rained presents that day,** il pleuvait des cadeaux ce jour-là. *Prov:* **It never rains but it pours,** un malheur, un bonheur, ne vient jamais seul. **2.** *F:* **Blows rained upon him,** les coups pleuvaient sur lui. **To rain blows on s.o.,** faire pleuvoir des coups sur qn.

rainbow ['reinbou], *s.* Arc-en-ciel *m.* **Rainbow-hued,** irisé.

raindrop ['reindrop], *s.* Goutte *f* de pluie.

rainfall ['reinfɔ:l], *s.* **I.** *Meteor:* (*a*) Précipitation *f* (atmosphérique); chute *f* de pluie. (*b*) Quantité *f* d'eau tombée; pluviosité *f* (d'une région). **2.** Averse *f.*

rainproof ['reinpru:f], *a.* Imperméable (à la pluie); imbrifuge, hydrofuge.

rainy ['reini], *a.* Pluvieux. **Rainy season,** saison des pluies; saison pluvieuse. *The r. season has set in,* les pluies ont commencé. *F:* **We must put something by for a rainy day,** il faut garder une poire pour la soif.

raise [re:iz], *v.tr.* **I.** (*a*) Dresser, mettre debout (une échelle, un mât); relever (qch. qui est tombé). **To raise the standard of revolt,** arborer l'étendard de la révolte. (*b*) **To raise** (up) **s.o. from the dead,** ressusciter qn des morts. (*c*) **To raise game,** lever du gibier. **To raise the people,** soulever, exciter, le peuple (*against,* contre). **2.** Bâtir, élever (un palais); ériger (une statue). **3.** Élever (une famille, du bétail); cultiver (des légumes); faire l'élevage (du bétail). **4.** (*a*) Produire. **To raise a bump,** faire une bosse. **To raise steam,** produire de la vapeur; chauffer. *To r. a storm of laughter,* déchaîner une tempête de rires. *S.a.* WIND[1] I. **To raise a smile,** provoquer un sourire. (*b*) **To raise a hope,** faire naître une espérance. (*b*) **To raise a cry,** faire entendre, pousser, un cri. **No one raised his voice,** personne ne souffla mot. (*c*) **To raise an objection,** soulever une objection. **5.** (*a*) Lever (le bras, les yeux); soulever (un poids). *To r. one's glass to one's lips,* porter son verre à ses lèvres. *To raise a ship,* renflouer, renflouer, un navire. *S.a.* DUST[1] I, HAT. (*b*) **Élever. To raise s.o. to power,** élever qn au pouvoir. (*c*) **To raise** (up) **s.o. from poverty,** tirer qn de la misère. **To raise s.o.'s hopes,** exalter l'espoir de qn. **To raise s.o.'s spirits,** relever le courage de qn. **6.** (*a*) Hausser, relever (un store). (*b*) **To raise camp,** lever le camp. (*c*) **To raise one's voice,** élever, hausser, la voix. (*d*) *To r. the price of goods,* élever, (re)hausser, le prix des marchandises. *To r. production to a maximum,* porter la production au maximum. **To raise s.o.'s salary,** augmenter (les appointements de) qn. **7.** (*a*) **To raise an army,** lever, mettre sur pied, une armée. (*b*) **To raise money,** se procurer de l'argent; *F:* battre monnaie. *To r. funds by subscription,* réunir des fonds par souscription. **To raise money on an estate,** emprunter de l'argent

sur une terre. (*c*) (*Of the State*) **To raise a loan,** émettre un emprunt. **8. To raise a spirit,** évoquer un esprit. *S.a.* CAIN. **9.** *Nau:* **To raise the land,** hausser la terre. **10. To raise a siege,** (i) lever, (ii) faire lever, un siège. **raise up,** *v.tr.* **To raise up enemies,** se faire des ennemis. **raised,** *a.* **I.** (*a*) (*Of arm, etc.*) Levé; (*of head*) relevé. (*b*) **Raised deck,** pont surélevé. **2.** Saillant; en relief. **Raised work,** ouvrage relevé en bosse. **3. Raised voice,** voix élevée. **4.** *Cu:* **Raised pie,** pâté en croûte.

raisin [reizn], *s.* Raisin sec.

raj [rɑ:dʒ], *s.* (*Anglo-Indian*) Souveraineté *f.* **Under the British raj,** sous l'empire anglais.

raja(h) ['rɑ:dʒ.c], *s.m.* Raja(h).

rake¹ [reik], *s.* *Tls:* **I.** Râteau *m.* *Light r.,* ratissoire *f.* *Toil:* **Rake(-comb),** démêlo r *m.* **2.** (Fire-)rake. (*a*) Fourgon *m,* rouable *m* (de boulanger). (*b*) Croche: *m* à feu (de forgeron); râble *m.*

rake², *v.tr.* **I.** Ratisser (les feuilles). *To r. the hay,* râteler le foin. **2.** Râteler (le sol); ratisser (une allée). *To r. one's memory,* fouiller (dans) ses souvenirs. (*b*) Gratter, racler (une surface). **3. To rake a trench,** enfiler, prendre en enfilade, une tranchée. *To r. the enemy with machine-gun fire,* mitrailler l'ennemi. **rake in,** *v.tr.* (*a*) (*At casino*) Ratisser (les mises). (*b*) *P:* Amasser (de l'argent). **rake off,** *v.tr.* *F:* Prélever (une somme d'argent, un tantième). **'rake-off,** *s.* *F:* Gratte *f.* **rake out,** *v.tr.* **To rake out the fire,** (i) retirer, enlever, les cendres du feu; (ii) *Mch:* faire tomber le feu. **rake over,** *v.tr.* **I.** Égratigner (le sol). **2.** *To r. over a path,* repasser une allée. **rake up,** *v.tr.* Rassembler, attiser (le feu). **To rake up the past,** revenir sur le passé. *To rake up s.o.'s past,* fouiller dans le passé de qn. **raking¹,** *a.* (Feu) d'enfilade; (tir) en enfilade. **raking²,** *s.* **I.** Râtelage *m,* ratissage *m.* **2.** *pl.* Rakings, râtelures *f.*

rake³, *s.* Viveur *m,* roué *m.* **Old rake,** vieux marcheur.

rake⁴, *s.* **I.** Inclinaison *f* (d'un mât). *Nau:* **Rake of the stem, of the stern-post,** élancement *m* de l'étrave; quête *f* de l'étambot. **2.** *Th:* Pente *f* (du parterre, du plateau).

raking³ ['reikin], *a.* (Mât) incliné vers l'arrière.

rakish¹ ['reikiʃ], *a.* **I.** Libertin, dissolu. **2.** *R. appearance,* air bravache. *To wear one's hat at a r. angle,* porter avec désinvo'ture son chapeau sur l'oreille.

rakish², *a.* *N.Arch:* (Ayant) élancé; (navire) à formes élancées.

rakishness ['reikiʃnəs], *s.* Libertinage *m;* mœurs déréglées.

rally¹ ['rali], *s.* **I.** (*a*) Ralliement *m* (de partisans). (*b*) **Boy scouts' rally,** réunion de boy-scouts. **2.** (*a*) *Mil:* Reprise *f* en main. *Sp:* Dernier effort pour gagner le match; retour *m* d'énergie. (*b*) (i) Reprise des forces; (ii) mieux momentané. (*c*) *Com:* Reprise (des prix). **3.** *Box:* Reprise. **4.** *Ten:* (Belle) passe de jeu.

rally². **I.** *v.tr.* (*a*) Rallier (ses partisans) (*round,* autour de). (*b*) Battre le rappel de (ses partisans). **2.** *v.i.* (*a*) (*Of troops*) Se reformer. (*b*) Se rallier (*to a party,* à un parti). **His partisans rallied round him,** ses part sans se sont groupés autour de lui. (*c*) Reprendre des forces. **To rally from an illness,** se remettre d'une maladie. (*d*) (*Of team*) Se reprendre.

rally³, *v.tr.* Railler (*s.o. on sth.,* qn de qch.); se gausser de (qn). **rallying,** *s.* Raillerie *f.*

Ralph [reif, ralf]. *Pr.n.m.* Raoul, Rodolphe.

ram¹ [ram], *s.* **I.** (*a*) *Z:* Bélier *m.* (*b*) *Astr:* The

Ram, le Bélier. **2.** (Battering-)ram, bélier. **3.** *N.Arch:* Éperon *m* (d'étrave). **4.** Piston plongeur (de pompe refoulante, de presse). **5.** Mouton *m* pilon *m* (de marteau-pilon). **6.** = RAMMER 1. **'ram's-'horn**, *s.* Corne *f* de bélier.

ram², *v.tr.* (rammed) **1.** (*a*) Battre, damer, tasser (le sol). (*b*) *Min:* **To ram the charge home**, bourrer, refouler, la charge. (*c*) Enfoncer, damer (un pieu). **2.** (*a*) *Nau:* Éperonner (un navire). (*b*) *Aut:* **To ram a car**, tamponner une voiture. (*c*) Heurter, cogner (*against*, contre). **'ram-rod**, *s.* Baguette *f* (de fus.l). *Artil:* Écouvillon *m.* *S.a.* STRAIGHT I. 1.

ramble¹ [rambl], *s.* **1.** Promenade *f* (sans itinéraire bien arrêté). **To go for a r.**, *F:* faire une balade. **2.** Discours incohérent.

ramble², *v.i.* **1.** (*a*) Errer à l'aventure. (*b*) Faire des excursions à pied. **2.** Parler sans suite; (*in delirium*) battre la campagne. **To ramble on**, dire mille inconséquences. **rambling¹**, *a.* **1.** Errant, vagabond. **2.** (Discours) décousu, sans suite. **3.** **Rambling house**, maison pleine de coins et de recoins. **rambling²**, *s.* **1.** Promenades *fpl* à l'aventure; excursions *fpl* à pied. **2.** Divagations *fpl*, radotages *mpl.*

rambler ['ramblər], *s.* **1.** Promeneur *m*, excursionniste *m.* **2.** Rosier sarmenteux, grimpant.

ramekin, ramequin ['ramikin], *s.* *Cu:* Ramequin *m.*

ramification [ramifi'keiʃ(ə)n], *s.* Ramification *f.*

ramify ['ramifai], *v.i.* Se ramifier.

rammer ['ramər], *s.* **1.** Dame *f*, demoiselle *f*, pilon *m* (de paveur). **2.** *Artil:* Refouloir *m.* **3.** Mouton *m* (pour pieux).

ramose [ra'mous], *a.* Rameux, branchu.

ramp¹ [ramp], *s.* (*a*) Rampe *f*; pente *f*, talus *m.* **Approach-ramp** *of a bridge*, rampe d'accès d'un pont. (*b*) *Aut:* **Garage repair ramp**, ponton *m* de visite; pont élévateur. **ramp²**, *v.i.* (*Of pers.*) Rager, tempêter. **To ramp and rave**, crier comme un énergumène.

ramp³, *s.* *F:* **1.** Supercherie *f.* **2.** Majoration exorbitante des prix. **The housing ramp**, le scandale des loyers.

rampage¹ [ram'peidʒ], *s.* *F:* **To be on the rampage**, ne pas décolérer; se comporter comme un fou.

rampage², *v.i.* *F:* **To rampage (about)**, se conduire en énergumène, comme un fou.

rampageous [ram'peidʒəs], *a.* *F:* Violent, furieux, tapageur; rageur, -euse.

rampant ['rampənt], *a.* **1.** *Her:* (Lion) rampant. **2.** (*Of pers.*) Violent, effréné. **Vice is r.**, le vice s'étale. **3.** (*Of plant*) Exubérant. **4.** *Arch:* (*Of arch*) Rampant.

rampart ['rampɑːrt], *s.* *Fort:* Rempart *m.*

rampion ['rampiən], *s.* *Bot:* Raiponce *f.*

ramshackle ['ramʃakl], *a.* Délabré; qui tombe en ruines. **R. conveyance**, vieille guimbarde. **R. furniture**, meubles boiteux.

ran [ran]. *See* RUN².

ranch¹ [rɑːnʃ], *s.* *U.S:* Ranch *m*; prairie *f* d'élevage; ferme *f* d'élevage.

ranch², *v.i.* *U.S:* Faire de l'élevage.

rancher ['rɑːnʃər], *s.* Propriétaire *m* d'un ranch.

rancid ['ransid], *a.* Rance. **To smell rancid**, sentir le rance. **To grow rancid**, rancir.

rancidity [ran'siditi], **rancidness** ['ransidnəs], *s.* Rancidité *f.*

rancorous ['raŋkərəs], *a.* Rancunier, haineux, rancuneux. **-ly**, *adv.* Avec rancune; haineusement.

rancour ['raŋkər], *s.* Rancune *f*, rancœur *f.*

---

random ['randəm]. **1.** *s.* At random, au hasard; à l'aventure. **To speak at r.**, parler à tort et à travers. **To hit out at r.**, lancer des coups à l'aveuglette. **2.** *a.* Fait au hasard. **R. shot**, coup tiré au hasard.

randy ['randi], *a.* **1.** *Scot:* Grossièrement importun. **2.** (Taureau) farouche. **3.** (*Of pers.*) Lascif, émoustillé.

ranee ['rɑːni:], *s.f.* Rani (épouse du rajah); reine.

rang [raŋ]. *See* RING⁴.

range¹ [reindʒ], *s.* **1.** (*a*) Rangée *f* (de bâtiments). (*b*) Chaîne *f* (de montagnes). **2.** Direction *f*, alignement *m.* **3.** (*a*) Champ *m* libre. **He has free r.** *of the house*, la maison lui est ouverte. (*b*) *U.S:* Étendue *f* de terrain où les animaux paissent en liberté. (*c*) *Nat.Hist:* Région *f*, zone *f*; habitat *m* (d'une plante). **4.** (*a*) Étendue *f*, portée *f*, domaine *m.* **R.** *of knowledge*, étendue des connaissances. **Range of action**, champ d'activité. **Range of vision**, étendue de la vue. **R.** *of a telescope*, portée d'une lunette. **The whole r.** *of politics*, le champ entier de la politique. **Within my range**, à ma portée. (*Of writer*) **To go outside his range**, sortir de son talent. (*b*) **Range of the barometer**, variation *f* du baromètre. **Range of speeds**, gamme *f* de vitesses. *Av:* **Wide r.** *of speeds*, grand écart de vitesse. **Range of colours**, gamme de couleurs. **Wide r.** *of patterns*, ample assortiment *m* d'échantillons. (*c*) **The whole range of events**, la série complète des événements. **5.** *Ball:* (*a*) La distance. **At a range of . . .**, à une distance de. . . . **At long range**, à longue portée. **To correct the r.**, rectifier le tir. (*b*) Portée (d'une arme à feu). **Rifle that has a r.** *of a thousand yards*, fusil qui porte à mille mètres. **Within range**, à portée de tir. **At effective range**, à portée efficace. **Aeroplane out of range**, avion hors de portée, hors d'atteinte. **6.** **Shooting-range**, champ de tir. **Experimental range**, polygone *m.* **7.** *Dom.Ec:* Fourneau *m* de cuisine. **'range-finder**, *s.* Télémètre *m.* **'range-finding**, *s.* Télémétrie *f.*

range². I. *v.tr.* **1.** (*a*) Ranger, aligner (des troupes); disposer (des objets) en ordre, en ligne. (*b*) Ranger, classer. **To range oneself with s.o.**, se ranger du côté de qn. **2.** Parcourir (l'horizon); suivre (le bord d'un fleuve). **3.** (*a*) Braquer (un télescope). (*b*) *Abs. Artil:* Régler le tir. II. **range**, *v.i.* **1.** (*a*) S'étendre (*from one place to another*, d'un endroit à un autre). *Island that ranges along the mainland*, île qui longe la terre ferme. (*b*) *Our house ranges with the next building*, notre maison est à l'alignement du bâtiment voisin. **2.** Courir, errer. *To r. over the country*, parcourir le pays. *Researches ranging over a wide field*, recherches qui s'étendent sur un vaste terrain. **3.** *Temperatures ranging from ten to thirty degrees*, températures comprises, s'échelonnant, entre dix et trente degrés. **4.** *These guns r. over six miles*, ces pièces ont une portée de six milles.

ranger ['reindʒər], *s.* (*a*) *For:* (*In India*) Garde-général adjoint. (*b*) Grand maître des parcs royaux.

rank¹ [raŋk], *s.* **1.** *Mil:* (*a*) Rang *m.* **To close the ranks**, serrer les rangs. **To fall into rank**, se mettre en rangs. (*b*) *pl.* **To rise from the ranks**, sortir du rang; de simple soldat passer officier. *Reduction to the ranks*, dégradation *f* militaire. (*c*) **The rank and file**, les hommes de troupe (simples soldats et gradés); la troupe. **2.** (*a*) Rang (social); classe *f.* **The rank and fashion**, *F:* la haute gomme. **Dancer of the first rank**, *F:* danseuse de la première volée. (*b*) *Mil: Navy: etc:*

Grade *m. He had attained the r. of captain,* il était passé capitaine. *Officer of high r.,* officier supérieur. **Substantive rank,** grade effectif. **All ranks,** officiers et troupe. **3.** (Taxi-)rank, station *f* (de taxis) ; stationnement *m* (pour taxis).

rank². I. *v.tr.* To rank s.o. among the great writers, ranger, compter, qn parmi les grands écrivains. **2.** *v.i.* Se ranger, être classé (*among, parmi*). **To rank among the best,** compter parmi les meilleurs. **To rank above s.o.,** occuper un rang supérieur à qn. *Fin :* Shares that rank first in dividend rights, actions qui priment en fait de dividende. The shares will rank for the July dividend, les actions prendront part à la distribution de dividendes en juillet.

rank³, *a.* **I.** (Trop) luxuriant; exubérant. *R. vegetation,* végétation luxuriante. *Land too r. for corn,* sol trop fort pour le blé. **2.** (*a*) Rance ; fétide. **To smell rank,** sentir fort. (*b*) Grossier, répugnant. **3.** Rank poison, (i) vrai poison ; (ii) poison violent. *R.* duffer, parfait imbécile. *R. injustice,* injustice criante. **-ly,** *adv.* **I.** Fortement ; avec exubérance. **2.** Avec une odeur fétide. **3.** Grossièrement.

ranker ['raŋkər], *s.* **I.** Gentleman ranker, fils de famille qui s'est engagé dans les rangs. **2.** Officier sorti du rang.

rankle [raŋkl], *v.i.* **I.** *A :* S'envenimer, s'ulcérer. **2.** To rankle in s.o.'s mind, rester sur le cœur de qn. *This refusal rankles in his mind,* il garde de ce refus une rancœur. **rankling,** *a.* **I.** Envenimé, enflammé. **2.** Qui a laissé une rancœur.

rankness ['raŋknəs], *s.* **I.** Luxuriance *f,* exubérance *f* (des mauvaises, herbes). **2.** Goût fort et désagréable. **3.** Grossièreté *f* (d'une insulte).

ransack ['ransak], *v.tr.* **I.** Fouiller (un tiroir) ; fouiller dans (sa mémoire). **2.** Saccager, piller (une maison, etc.).

ransom¹ ['ransəm], *s.* **I.** Rachat *m* (d'un captif). **To hold s.o. to ransom,** mettre qn à rançon ; rançonner qn. **2.** Rançon *f.* **To pay ransom,** payer rançon. *F :* Furs at r. prices, fourrures hors de prix.

ransom², *v.tr.* **I.** (*a*) Racheter (qn) ; payer la rançon de (qn). (*b*) Racheter, expier (qch.). **2.** Mettre (qn) à rançon ; rançonner (qn).

rant¹ [rant], *s.* Rodomontades *fpl* ; discours *m* d'énergumène.

rant², *v.i.* Faire l'énergumène ; déclamer avec extravagance. **ranting¹,** *a.* Déclamatoire ; (discours) d'énergumène. **ranting²,** *s.* = RANT¹.

ranter ['rantər], *s.* Déclamateur, -trice ; énergumène *mf.*

ranunculus, *pl.* -uses, -i [ra'nʌŋkjuləs, -əsiz, -ai], *s.* Bot: Renoncule *f.*

rap¹ [rap], *s.* Petit coup sec et dur. **To give s.o. a rap on the knuckles,** donner sur les doigts à qn ; *F :* remettre qn à sa place. **A rap at the door,** un coup à la porte. *F :* To have a rap at s.o., donner sur les doigts à qn.

rap², *v.* (rapped) **I.** *v.tr.* Frapper (qch.) ; donner un coup sec à (qch.). **To rap s.o. on the knuckles,** donner sur les doigts à qn. **2.** *v.i. To rap at the door,* frapper un coup à la porte. **Rapping spirits,** esprits frappeurs. **rap out,** *v.tr.* **To rap out an oath,** lâcher un juron. **To rap out one's words,** parler sec. **rapping,** *s.* Coups frappés.

rap³, *s. A :* Sou *m,* liard *m. F :* I don't care a rap, je m'en moque comme de quatre sous.

rapacious [ra'peiʃəs], *a.* Rapace. **-ly,** *adv.* Avec rapacité.

rapaciousness [ra'peiʃəsnəs], **rapacity** [ra'pasiti], *s.* Rapacité *f.*

rape¹ [reip], *s.* **I.** *Poet:* Rapt *m,* ravissement *m.*

The rape of the Sabines, l'enlèvement *m* des Sabines. **2.** *Jur :* Viol *m.*

rape², *v.tr.* **I.** *Poet:* Ravir, enlever de force (une femme). **2.** *Jur :* Violer.

rape³, *s. Bot :* **I.** (Summer) rape, colza *m.* **2.** Navette *f.* '**rape-oil,** *s.* Huile ˊ de colza ; (huile de) navette *f.* '**rape-seed,** *s.* Graine *f* de colza.

rapid ['rapid], *a. & s.* Rapide (*m*). **-ly,** *adv.* Rapidement ; à grands pas. '**rapid-ˈfire,** *attrib.a.* (Canon) à tir rapide.

rapidity [ra'piditi], *s.* Rapidité *f.*

rapier ['reipiər], *s.* Rapière *f.*

rapine ['rapain], *s.* Rapine *f.*

rapscallion [rap'skaljən], *s.* Homme *m* de rien ; canaille *f,* vaurien *m,* propre *m* à rien.

rapt [rapt]. **I.** *p.p.* (*a*) Ravi, extasié (by, par). (*b*) Absorbé (in, dans). Rapt in contemplation, plongé dans la contemplation ; recueilli. **2.** *a.* (Of attention, interest) Profond.

raptores [rap'tɔ:ri:z], *s.pl. Orn :* Rapaces *m.*

raptorial [rap'tɔ:riəl], *a.* (Oiseau) de proie.

rapture ['raptjər], *s.* Ravissement *m,* extase *m.* **To be in raptures,** être ravi, enchanté (with, over, de). **To go into raptures,** s'extasier (over, sur).

rapturous ['raptjurəs], *a.* (Cris) de ravissement, d'extase. *R.* applause, applaudissements frénétiques. **-ly,** *adv.* Avec transport, avec frénésie.

rare¹ ['rɛər], *a.* **I.** (Atmosphère) rare, peu dense. **2.** *R.* occurrence, événement rare. **3.** *F :* Fameux. You gave me a r. fright, tu m'as fait une fière peur. **-ly,** *adv.* **I.** Rarement. **2.** *F :* Fameusement.

rare², *a.* Peu cuit ; (bifteck) saignant.

rarebit ['rɛərbit], *s.* Welsh rarebit = Welsh rabbit *q.v. under* RABBIT¹.

rarefaction [rɛəri'fakʃ(ə)n], *s.* Raréfaction *f.*

rarefy ['rɛərifai], *v.tr.* Raréfier (l'air). **rarefied,** *a.* (Air) raréfié. *To become r.,* se raréfier.

rareness ['rɛərnəs], *s.* Rareté *f.*

rarity ['rɛəriti], *s.* **I.** = RARENESS. **2.** Objet *m* rare ; événement *m* rare.

rascal ['rɑ:sk(ə)l], *s.* **I.** Coquin *m,* fripon . *m* ; mauvais sujet. *That r. of a nephew of mine,* mon polisson de neveu.

rascality [rɑ:s'kaliti], *s.* Coquinerie *f,* gredinerie *f.*

rascally ['rɑ:skəli], *a.* De coquin ; (homme de loi) retors. *These r. servants!* ces canailles de domestiques ! *Rascally trick,* méchant tour.

rase [reiz], *v.tr.* = RAZE.

rash¹ [raʃ], *s. Med :* Éruption *f* ; exanthème *m.* *S.a.* NETTLE-RASH.

rash², *a.* Téméraire ; irréfléchi, impétueux. *R. words,* paroles inconsidérées. **Rash act,** coup *m* de tête. **-ly,** *adv.* Témérairement ; inconsidérément. *To speak r.,* parler à la légère. *To act r.,* agir à l'étourdie.

rasher ['raʃər], *s. Cu:* Tranche *f* (de lard).

rashness ['raʃnəs], *s.* Témérité *f* ; étourderie *f.* *To pay for one's r., F :* payer la folle enchère.

rasp¹ ['rɑ:sp], *s.* **I.** *Tls:* Râpe *f.* **2.** Bruit *m* de râpe ; grincement *m.*

rasp², *v.* **I.** *v.tr.* (*a*) Râper (le bois). (*b*) Racler (une surface) ; écorcher (la peau). *Wine that rasps the throat,* vin qui racle, écorche, la gosier. **2.** *v.i.* Grincer, crisser. **3.** *v.tr.* **To rasp out an insult,** lâcher une insulte d'une voix âpre.

rasping, *a.* Rasping sound, son grinçant ; crissement *m.* **Rasping voice,** voix âpre ; *F :* voix de crécelle.

raspberry ['rɑ:zbəri], *s.* **I.** Framboise *f.* Raspberry bush, framboisier *m.* Raspberry vinegar, vinaigre framboisé. **2.** *P :* To get the raspberry, (i) essuyer une rebuffade ; (ii) se faire engueuler.

rat¹ [rat], s. I. Z: Rat m. **Sewer rat,** rat d'égout. **She-rat,** rate f. *To clear a place of rats,* dératiser un endroit. **Rat week,** semaine de dératisation. *F:* **To smell a rat,** soupçonner anguille sous roche. **To die like a rat in a hole,** mourir dans son trou, sans secours. *P:* **Rats!** *(in disbelief)* allons donc! **2.** (a) *Pol:* ·Transfuge m, renégat m. (b) *Ind:* Jaune m; renard m. **'rat-catcher,** s. Preneur m de rats. **'rat-poison,** s. Mort f aux rats; tord-boyaux m inv. **'rat's-tail,** s. (Lime f) queue-de-rat f. **'rat-tail,** s. Rat-tail file, queue-de-rat f. **'rat-trap,** s. Ratière f. *Cy:* Rat-trap pedals, pédales à scie(s).

rat², v.i. (ratted) *F:* (a) Tourner casaque; abandonner son parti. (b) *Ind:* Faire le jaune; faire le renard. (c) *To rat on a pal,* vendre un copain.

ratafia [rata'fi:a], s. Ratafia m.

ratchet ['ratʃet], s. I. Encliquetage m à dents. **2.** Cliquet m, rochet m. **'ratchet-brace,** s. Vilebrequin m ou foret m à rochet. **'ratchet-drill,** s. *Tls:* Drille f à rochet. **'ratchet-wheel,** s. Roue f à cliquet.

rate¹ [reit], s. I. Nombre proportionnel, quantité proportionnelle. **Rate per cent,** pourcentage m. **Birth, death, rate,** (taux m de la) ιtalité, mortalité. **2.** (a) Taux, raison f. **Rate of speed,** degré m de vitesse. **Rate of growth,** taux d'accroissement. *El:* **Rate of charging,** taux, régime m, de chargement (d'un accumulateur). (b) Allure f, vitesse f, train m. **At the rate of . . .,** à la vitesse de. . . . *Nau:* **At the r. of twenty knots,** à l'allure de vingt nœuds. *He was going at a tremendous r.,* il allait d'un train d'enfer. (c) Taux, cours m; tarif m. **R. of interest,** taux d'intérêt. **The Bank rate,** le taux de la Banque. **Market rate,** taux (de l'escompte) hors banque; taux du cours libre (du change). *Ind:* **Rate of wages,** taux du sa'aire. *Com:* **Market rates,** cours du marché. **Insurance rate,** prime f de l'assurance. **Harbour rates,** droits m de port. **Freight rate,** fret m maritime. **Railway rates,** tarifs des chemins de fer. *Advertising rates,* tarif de publicité. *To pay s.o. at the r. of . . .,* payer qn sur le pied de. . . . **Rate of living,** train m de vie. **At that rate,** sur ce pied-là; à ce compte-là. **At any rate,** dans tous les cas, en tout cas. **3.** *Adm:* Impôt local; contribution foncière. **Rates and taxes,** impôts et contributions. **Borough rates,** taxes municipales. *(Of pers.)* **To come upon the rates,** avoir recours à l'Assistance publique. **4.** Estimation f, évaluation f. *To value sth. at a low r.,* faire peu de cas de qch. **'rate-aided,** a. I. Assisté, secouru, par l'Assistance publique. **2.** Subventionné par la municipalité. **'rate-collector,** s. Percepteur m des impôts locaux; receveur municipal. **'rate-payer,** s. Contribuable m.

rate². I. v.tr. (a) Estimer, évaluer (qch.). *To r. sth. high,* assigner une haute valeur à qch.; faire grand cas de qch. (b) Considérer, regarder (as, comme). (c) Taxer (s.o. at a certain sum, qn à raison d'une certaine somme). (d) Classer, classifier (une auto); *Nau:* classer (un navire). **2.** v.i. Être classé (as, comme). **rating¹,** s. I. (a) Estimation f, évaluation f. (b) Répartition f des impôts locaux. (c) Classement m, classification f. **2.** *Mec.E:* Cheval nominal. **3.** *Navy:* (a) Spécialité f, classe f (d'un homme de l'équipage). (b) pl. **The ratings,** les matelots et gradés.

rate³, v.tr. Tancer, semoncer (qn) *(for doing sth.,* d'avoir fait qch.). **rating²,** s. Semonce f; verte réprimande.

ratel ['reitel], s. Z: Ratel m.

rather ['rɑːðər], adv. I. Plutôt. **Or rather,** ou plutôt, ou pour mieux dire. **2.** Un peu; quelque peu; assez. *R. pretty,* assez joli. *R. plain,* plutôt laid. **Rather a lot,** *F:* un peu beaucoup. *Do I look ill?—Well, you do r.,* est-ce que j'ai l'air malade?—Si tout de même. **I rather think you know him,** je crois bien que vous le connaissez. **3.** Plutôt (than, que); de préférence (than, à). **Anything rather than . . .,** tout plutôt que. . . . *I would r. be loved than feared,* j'aime mieux être aimé qu'être craint. *I had r. suffer than tell a lie,* plutôt souffrir que mentir. **I would rather not,** veuillez m'excuser. **4.** *F:* *Do you know him?—Rather!* le connaissez-vous?—Pour sûr!

ratification [ratifi'keiʃ(ə)n], s. Ratification f.

ratify ['ratifai], v.tr. Ratifier, entériner (un décret, etc.). *To r. a contract,* approuver un contrat. **ratifying¹,** a. Ratificatif. **ratifying²,** s. Ratification f, validation f.

ratio, pl. **-os** ['reiʃio, -ouz], s. Raison f, rapport m, proportion f. **Arithmetical ratio,** raison, proportion, arithmétique. **In the ratio of . . .,** dans le rapport de. . . . **In direct ratio to . . .,** en raison directe de. . . .

ratiocinate [rati'ɔsineit, raʃi-], v.i. *Lit. & Hum:* Raisonner, ratiociner.

ration¹ ['raʃ(ə)n], s. *Mil: etc:* Ration f. *To go and draw rations,* aller aux vivres. **Emergency ration,** *F:* iron ration, vivres m de réserve. **To put on (short) rations,** rationner (une garnison). *War Adm:* **Ration card,** carte f alimentaire. **Ration book,** carnet m de rations.

ration², v.tr. I. Rationner (qn); mettre (qn) à la ration. **2. To ration (out) bread,** rationner le pain. **rationing,** s. Rationnement m.

rational ['raʃən(ə)l], a. I. (a) Raisonnable; doué de raison. *To be quite r.,* avoir toute sa tête. (b) Raisonné; conforme à la raison. **Rational belief,** croyance fondée sur la raison. *F:* **Rational boating costume,** costume de canotage pratique. **2.** *Mth: Ph:* Rationnel. **-ally,** adv. Raisonnablement.

rationalize ['raʃənəlaiz], v.tr. Rationaliser.

ratlin(e) ['ratlin], s. *Nau:* Enfléchure f.

rat(t)an [ra'tan], s. *Bot:* Rotin m; jonc m d'Inde. **Rat(t)an walking-stick,** (canne f de) jonc.

rat(-)tat-tat ['rat(a)'tat]. Toc, toc. **To hear a rat-tat at the door,** entendre toc, toc, à la porte.

ratter ['ratər], s. I. (Chien) ratier m. **2.** = RAT² 1.

rattle¹ [ratl], s. I. (a) Hochet m (d'enfant). (b) Crécelle f (d'alarme). (c) pl. *Rept:* Rattles, sonnettes f (d'un crotale). **2.** (a) Bruit m, fracas m (d'une voiture); tapotis m (d'une machine à écrire); trictrac m (de dés); crépitement m (d'un fusillade). (b) *Med:* Râle m. (c) Bavardage m. **'rattle-brained,** a. *F:* Étourdi, écervelé.

rattle². I. v.i. (a) *(Of arms)* Cliqueter; (of car) ferrailler; *(of hail)* crépiter; *(of window)* trembler, branler. *To make the windows r.,* faire trembler les vitres. *Aut:* **The body rattles,** la carrosserie fait du bruit. (b) *(Of vehicle)* **To rattle along,** rouler avec fracas, à toute vitesse. (c) *Med:* Râler. **2.** v.tr. (a) Agiter (des chaînes) avec bruit; faire cliqueter (des clefs); faire sonner (son argent). **To rattle the dice,** agiter les dés (dans le cornet). (b) Consterner, bouleverser (qn). *He never gets rattled,* il ne s'épate jamais; il ne se laisse pas démonter. **rattle off,** v.tr. Réciter rapidement (une leçon); expédier (un travail). **rattle on,** v.i. Continuer à bavarder. **rattling¹,** a. I. Bruyant; crépitant. **2.** *F:* At a rattling pace, au grand trot. **3.** *F:* Rattling (good), excellent, épatant. **rattling²,** s. = RATTLE¹ 2.

rattler ['ratlər], s. I. *U.S:* = RATTLESNAKE.

2. Klaxon *m* d'alarme. **3.** *F:* Personne, chose, épatante.

rattlesnake ['ratlsneik], *s.* Serpent *m* à sonnettes ; crotale *m*.

rattletrap ['ratltrap], *s.* Vieille guimbarde ; tapecul *m*.

ratty ['rati], *a. F:* Fâché ; en rogne.

raucous ['rɔːkəs], *a.* Rauque. **-ly,** *adv.* D'une voix rauque, éraillée.

ravage[1] ['ravedʒ], *s.* Ravage *m. The ravage(s) wrought by torrents,* les dévastations *f* des torrents.

ravage[2], *v.tr.* Ravager, dévaster. **ravaging**[1], *a.* Ravageur. **ravaging**[2], *s.* Ravagement *m*.

ravager ['ravedʒər], *s.* Ravageur *m,* dévastateur *m*.

rave[1] [reiv], *s.* Ridelle *f* (de charrette).

rave[2], *v.i.* (*a*) Être en délire ; *F:* battre la campagne. *F:* **You're raving!** vous divaguez ! (*b*) **To rave and storm,** tempêter. **To rave at, against, s.o.,** pester contre qn. **Raving lunatic,** fou furieux. (*c*) (*Of wind*) Être en furie. (*d*) *F:* **To rave about sth.,** s'extasier sur qch.

raving, *s.* **1.** Délire *m,* divagation *f.* **2.** *pl.* Ravings, paroles incohérentes.

ravel[1] ['rav(ə)l], *s.* **1.** Emmêlement *m. Threads in a ravel,* fils enchevêtrés, emmêlés. **2.** Effilochure *f*.

ravel[2], *v.* (rave.led) I. *v.tr.* Embrouiller, emmêler (un écheveau). **2.** *v.i.* (*Of skein*) S'embrouiller, s'enchevêtrer. **ravel out.** (*a*) *v.tr.* Effilocher (un tissu). (*b*) *v.i.* S'effiler, s'effilocher.

raven[1] ['reiv(ə)n], *s. Orn:* (Grand) corbeau. **Raven locks,** boucles d'un noir de jais.

raven[2] ['rav(ə)n], *v.* **1.** *v.i.* Faire des ravages ; (*of animal*) chercher sa proie. **2.** *v.tr.* Dévorer (la proie). **ravening,** *a.* Vorace, rapace.

ravenous ['ravənəs], *a.* **1.** (Animal) vorace. **2.** (*a*) *R. appetite,* appétit vorace, féroce. (*b*) *F:* **To be ravenous,** avoir une faim dévorante. **-ly,** *adv.* Voracement. **To eat r.,** manger gloutonnement.

ravenousness ['ravənəsnəs], *s.* **1.** Voracité *f.* **2.** Faim *f* de loup ; faim dévorante.

ravine [ra'viːn], *s.* Ravin *m*.

ravish ['raviʃ], *v.tr.* **1.** (*a*) Ravir ; enlever (qn, qch.) de force. (*b*) Violer (une femme). **2.** Ravir (d'admiration) ; enchanter (qn). **ravishing,** *a.* Ravissant. **-ly,** *adv.* D'une manière ravissante.

ravisher ['raviʃər], *s.* Ravisseur *m*.

ravishment ['raviʃmənt], *s.* **1.** Enlèvement *m,* rapt *m.* **2.** Ravissement *m* ; transports *mpl* (de joie).

raw [rɔː]. I. *a.* **1.** Cru. **Raw meat,** viande crue, saignante. **2.** (*a*) **Raw material,** matière(s) première(s) ; matériaux bruts. **Raw hide,** cuir vert. **Raw silk,** soie grège. **Raw metal,** métal brut. *S.a.* SPIRIT[1] 6. (*b*) **Raw colouring,** coloris cru. **3.** Sans expérience ; inexpérimenté. **A raw hand,** un novice ; *F:* un bleu. **Raw troops,** troupes non aguerries. *S.a.* RECRUIT[1]. **4.** A vif. **Raw wound,** plaie vive. *My nerves are raw to-day,* j'ai les nerfs à fleur de peau aujourd'hui. **5.** Raw weather, temps gris et froid. *Raw winds,* vents aigres. II. **raw,** *s.* **To touch s.o. on the raw,** piquer qn au vif. **'raw-boned,** *a.* Maigre, décharné ; (cheval) efflanqué.

rawness ['rɔːnəs], *s.* **1.** Crudité *f* (des fruits, etc.). **2.** Inexpérience *f.* **3.** Écorchure *f.* **4.** Froid *m* humide ; âpreté *f* (du temps).

ray[1] [rei], *s.* **1.** *Ph:* Rayon *m. Ray of light,* rayon lumineux. *F:* **A ray of hope,** une lueur d'espoir. *S.a.* X-RAY[1]. **2.** Rayon (d'un animal ou d'une plante en étoile).

ray[2], *s. Ich:* Raie *f.* **Electric ray,** torpille *f*.

rayon ['reiɔn], *s. Tex:* Rayonne *f* ; tissu *m* de soie artificielle.

raze [reiz], *v.tr.* Raser (des fortifications). **To raze a building to the ground,** raser un édifice.

razor ['reizər], *s.* Rasoir *m.* **Safety razor,** rasoir de sûreté. **'razor-backed,** *a.* (Cheval) à dos tranchant. **'razor-bill,** *s. Orn:* Pingouin commun. **'razor-edge,** *s.* **1.** Fil *m,* tranchant *m,* de rasoir. **2.** Arête *f* (de montagne) en lame de couteau.

razzia ['razia], *s.* Razzia *f*.

razzle(-dazzle) ['razl(dazl)], *s. P:* **To go on the razzle(-dazzle),** faire la noce, faire a nouba.

re[1] [rei], *s. Mus:* Ré *m*.

re[2] [riː], *Lt. s. as prep. phr.* **1.** *Jur:* (In) **re** Smith v. Jones, (en l')affaire Smith contre Jones. **2.** *Com: F:* **Re your letter of June 10th,** relativement à, au sujet de, votre lettre du 10 juin.

reabsorb [riːab'sɔːrb], *v.tr.* Réabsorber.

reaccustom [riːa'kʌstəm], *v.tr.* Rhabituer, réaccoutumer (*to,* à).

reach[1] [riːtʃ], *s.* **1.** Extension *f* (de la main). *Box:* Allonge *f. Fenc:* **To have a long reach,** avoir beaucoup d'étendue. *Box:* **To have the longer r.,** être avantagé en allonge. **2.** (*a*) Portée *f,* atteinte *f.* **Within s.o.'s reach,** à la portée de qn. **Within r. of the hand,** à portée de la main ; *F:* sous la main. **Out of reach,** hors de portée. *Beyond the r. of all suspicion,* à l'abri de tout soupçon. *Cars within the r. of small purses,* voitures abordables aux petites bourses. *Posts within the r. of all,* emplois accessibles à tous. **The goal is within our reach,** nous touchons au but. (*b*) **Hotel within easy reach of the station,** hôtel à proximité de la gare. (*c*) Étendue *f* (de l'esprit). **3.** Reach of meadow, étendue de prairies. **4.** Partie droite (d'un fleuve) entre deux coudes ; bief *m* (d'un canal).

reach[2]. I. *v.tr.* **1.** To reach out, étendre ; tendre ; avancer (la main). **2.** Atteindre. *The law does not r. these cases,* la loi ne s'étend pas jusqu'à ces cas. **3.** (*a*) Arriver à, parvenir à. *To r. the summit of the mountain,* parvenir au haut de la montagne. *Windows reached by a flight of three steps,* fenêtres où l'on accède par trois marches. *To r. the age of sixty,* atteindre l'âge de soixante ans. **To reach perfection,** atteindre, toucher, à la perfection. *Your letter reached me to-day,* votre lettre m'est parvenue aujourd'hui. *These rumours reached him,* ces bruits vinrent jusqu'à lui. (*b*) Arriver à (une conclusion). **To reach an agreement,** aboutir à un accord. **4.** (*a*) **Reach me (over) my gloves,** passez-moi mes gants. (*b*) *R. me (down) that plate,* descendez-moi cette assiette. II. **reach,** *v.tr. & i.* Arriver, s'élever, monter, descendre (jusqu'à . . .). **To reach (down to) the bottom,** atteindre le fond ; descendre jusqu'au fond. *She scarcely reaches up to your shoulder,* c'est à peine si elle vous vient à l'épaule. III. **reach,** *v.i.* **1.** S'étendre. **As far as the eye could reach,** à perte de vue. **2.** **To reach out (with one's hand)** for sth., tendre, avancer, la main pour prendre qch. *He reached over to the table,* il étendit la main vers la table. **'reach-me-down,** *s. F:* Costume *m* de confection ; *P:* un décrochez-moi-ça.

react [ri'akt], *v.i.* **1.** Réagir (*upon,* sur ; *against,* contre). **2.** (*Of prices*) Réactionner.

reactance [ri'aktəns], *s. El:* Réactance *f*.

reaction [ri'akʃ(ə)n], *s.* Réaction *f.* **1.** (*a*) *The reactions of a policy,* les contre-coups *m* d'une politique. (*b*) *Physiol:* **Cutaneous r.,** réaction cutanée. (*c*) *Ph:* **Reaction wheel,** tourniquet *m* hydraulique. **2.** *Pol:* The forces of reaction, le parti réactionnaire.

reactionary [ri'akʃənəri], *a. & s. Pol:* Réactionnaire (*mf*).

reactive [ri'aktiv], *a.* Réactif.

reactor [ri'aktər], *s. El.E:* Bobine *f* de réactance.

read[1] [ri:d], *s.* Action *f* de lire. *He was having a quiet r.*, il lisait tranquillement.

read[2] [ri:d], *v.tr.* (*p.t. & p.p.* read [red]) **I.** (*a*) Lire. *To teach s.o. to r.*, enseigner la lecture à qn. To read to oneself, lire tout bas ; lire des yeux. *Adm:* **Read [red] and approved**, lu et approuvé. (*b*) *Typ:* To read proofs, corriger des épreuves. (*c*) To read up a subject, étudier un sujet. *He is reading for his examination*, il prépare son examen. To read law, *abs.* to read for the bar, faire son droit. **2.** To read sth. aloud, lire qch. à haute voix, tout haut. *To r. a report (to the meeting)*, donner lecture d'un rapport (à l'assemblée). To take the minutes as read, approuver le procès-verbal sans lecture. To read to s.o., faire la lecture à qn. *S.a.* LESSON[1] I, RIOT[1] I. **3.** To read s.o. to sleep, endormir qn en lui faisant la lecture. **4.** (*a*) Lire (la musique). (*b*) To read the future, lire dans l'avenir. To read s.o.'s hand, lire dans la main de qn. To read s.o.'s thoughts, lire dans la pensée de qn. I can read him like a book, je le connais comme le fond de ma poche. To read into a sentence what is not there, mettre dans une phrase ce qui n'y est pas. To read between the lines, lire entre les lignes ; *F:* aider à la lettre. *S.a.* RUN[2] I. I. **5.** Lire (l'horloge, le thermomètre) ; relever (un compteur à gaz). **6.** (*a*) The book reads like a translation, le livre fait l'effet d'une traduction. (*b*) *The clause reads both ways*, l'article peut s'interpréter dans les deux sens. **read out**, *v.tr.* Lire (qch.) à haute voix. To read out the agenda, donner lecture de l'ordre du jour. **read over**, *v.tr.* Relire (qch.). **read through**, *v.tr.* **I.** Parcourir (qch.). **2.** Lire (qch.) en entier.

read[3] [red], *a.* **I.** (Discours) lu. **2.** (*Of pers.*) Well-read, deeply-read, instruit, savant. **reading**[1], *a.* The reading public, le public qui lit. A reading man, un (grand) liseur. **reading**[2], *s.* **I.** (*a*) Lecture(s) *f(pl)*. To be fond of r., aimer la lecture. (*b*) Lecture à haute voix. R. of a will, lecture, ouverture *f*, d'un testament. *Parl:* Second reading, prise *f* en considération (d'un projet de loi). (*c*) Explication *f*, interprétation *f* (d'une énigme). **2.** (*a*) Lecture (d'un instrument de précision). (*b*) Relevé *m* (d'un compteur à gaz) ; observation (faite avec un instrument de précision) ; cote (donnée par l'instrument). **Barometer reading**, hauteur *f* barométrique. *W.Tel:* Dial readings, réglages *m* (du poste). **3.** (*a*) Façon *f* de lire. (*b*) Interprétation (d'un rôle). (*c*) Leçon *f*, variante *f* (d'un texte). **'reading-book**, *s.* Livre *m* de lecture. **'reading-desk**, *s.* Pupitre *m. Ecc:* Lutrin *m.* **'reading-glass**, *s.* Loupe *f.* **'reading-lamp**, *s.* Liseuse *f* ; lampe *f* de travail. **'reading-room**, *s.* Salle *f* de lecture (d'une bibliothèque).

readable ['ri:dəbl], *a.* Lisible. **I.** Qui se laisse lire ; *F:* lisable. **2.** *His handwriting is very r.*, son écriture est très lisible.

readdress [ri:ə'dres], *v.tr.* Changer l'adresse (d'une lettre) ; faire suivre (une lettre).

reader ['ri:dər], *s.* **I.** (*a*) Liseur, -euse ; lecteur, -trice. *He is not much of a r.*, il n'aime guère la lecture. (*b*) Publisher's reader, lecteur de manuscrits. (*c*) Proof-reader, correcteur d'épreuves. **2.** (*a*) Lecteur, -trice (à haute voix). (*b*) *Ecc:*

Lecteur *m.* (*c*) *Sch:* Chargé, -ée, de cours ; maître *m* de conférences. **3.** *Sch:* Livre *m* de lecture.

readiness ['redinəs], *s.* **I.** (*a*) Empressement *m*, alacrité *f* (à faire qch.). (*b*) Bonne volonté. **2.** Facilité *f*, vivacité *f* (d'esprit). R. of speech, facilit. de parole. **3.** To be in readiness, être prêt.

readjust [ri:ə'dʒʌst], *v.tr.* Rajuster ; remettre (un instrument) à point.

readjustment [ri:ə'dʒʌstmənt], *s.* Rajustement *m*, rectification *f. Nau:* Régulation *f* (des compas).

ready ['redi]. **I.** *a.* **I.** (*a*) Prêt. Are you ready? êtes-vous prêt? y êtes-vous? (*To racers*) Ready! go! préparez-vous ! partez ! To make ready, get ready, se préparer, s'apprêter, se disposer (*to, à*). R. for the fray, prêt au combat. (*Of book*) Now ready, sur le point de paraître. *To be r. to face s.o.*, attendre qn de pied ferme. *Nau:* All ready! on est paré ! *Typ:* To make ready, mettre en train. *Tg:* Ready signal, invitation *f* à transmettre. (*b*) Ready to hand, sous la main. Ready money, argent comptant. **2.** (*a*) Prêt, disposé (à faire qch.). He is a ready believer in miracles, il croit volontiers aux miracles. (*b*) Ready to die with hunger, sur le point de mourir de faim. **3.** Prompt, facile. (*a*) To have a ready wit, avoir l'esprit prompt. *To have a r. tongue*, avoir la langue agile, bien pendue. To have a ready pen, avoir la plume facile. To be ready with an answer, avoir la réplique prompte. (*b*) Goods that meet with a ready sale, marchandises de vente courante. **-ily**, *adv.* **I.** (Faire qch.) volontiers, avec empressement. **2.** (Imaginer qch.) aisément, facilement. **II.** *ready*, *adv.* Ready dressed, tout habillé. **III.** *ready*, *s.* **I.** *Mil:* To come to the ready, apprêter l'arme. *Artil:* Guns at the ready, pièces parées à faire feu. **2.** *P:* Argent comptant. **'ready-'cooked**, *a.* (Aliment) tout cuit. **'ready-'made**, *a.* (Article) tout fait. Ready-made clothes, vêtements de confection ; confections *f.* **'ready-'reckoner**, *s. Com:* Barème *m* (de comptes). **'ready-'witted**, *a.* A l'esprit prompt, vif.

reaffirm [ri:ə'fɔ:rm], *v.tr.* Réaffirmer (qch.).

reagent [ri'eidʒənt], *s. Ch:* Réactif *m.*

real ['ri:əl], *a.* **I.** (*a*) Vrai. R. silk, soie naturelle. Real old nobility, noblesse de bon aloi. (*b*) Véritable, réel. The r. world, le monde réel. The r. value of things, la véritable prix des choses. A r. friend, un vrai ami, un véritable ami. It is the real thing, (i) c'est authentique ; (ii) *F:* c'est ce qu'il nous faut. *s.* The real and the ideal, le réel et l'idéal. *Fin:* Real value, valeur effective. **2.** *Jur:* Real estate, real property, propriété immobilière ; biens-fonds *mpl.* **-lly**, *adv.* Vraiment ; réellement ; en effet. *It was r. my fault*, c'était vraiment, franchement, de ma faute. *You r. must go there*, il faut absolument que vous y alliez. *Has he r. gone?* est-il parti pour de vrai? *Is it r. true?* est-ce bien vrai? Really? vraiment? *F:* sans blague? Not really! pas possible !

realgar [ri'algər], *s. Miner:* Réalgar *m.*

realism ['ri:əlizm], *s.* Réalisme *m.*

realist ['ri:əlist], *a. & s.* Réaliste (*mf*).

realistic [riə'listik], *a.* Réaliste. **-ally**, *adv.* Avec réalisme.

reality [ri'aliti], *s.* **I.** La réalité ; le réel. In reality, en réalité. **2.** *We must stick to realities*, il faut s'en tenir aux réalités.

realizable [ri:ə'laizəbl], *a.* **I.** Réalisable. **2.** Imaginable ; dont on peut se rendre compte.

realization [ri:əlai'zeiʃ(ə)n], *s.* **I.** (*a*) Réalisation *f*

(d'un projet). (b) *Com:* Conversion *f* en espèces.
2. Conception nette (d'un fait).
realize ['ri:əla:iz], *v.tr.* **1.** (*a*) Réaliser (un projet).
(*b*) *Com:* Convertir (des biens) en espèces.
2. Concevoir nettement, bien comprendre (qch.);
se rendre compte de (qch.). *I realized it at the*
first glance, je m'en suis rendu compte au premier
coup d'œil.
really ['ri:əli], *adv. See* REAL.
realm [relm], *s.* Royaume *m. The realms of fancy,*
le domaine de l'imagination.
realty ['ri:əlti], *s. Jur:* Biens immobiliers;
immeubles *mpl.*
ream[1] [ri:m], *s. Paperm:* Rame *f. F:* He writes
reams, il écrit des pages et des pages.
ream[2], *v.tr.* **1.** To ream (out), aléser (un trou).
2. Fraiser, chanfreiner (un trou). **3.** Sertir
(une cartouche). **reaming,** *s.* **1.** Alésage *m.*
2. Fraisage *m.*
reamer(-bit) ['ri:mər(bit)], *s. Tls:* **1.** Alésoir *m,*
aléseuse *f.* **2.** Countersinking reamer, fraise *f.*
reanimate [ri:'animeit], *v.tr.* Ranimer, réanimer.
reap [ri:p], *v.tr.* (*a*) Moissonner (le blé, un
champ). *Abs.* Moissonner. *Prov:* We reap as
we sow, on recueille ce qu'on a semé. (*b*) Recueillir (le fruit de ses travaux). To reap laurels,
cueillir des lauriers. To reap profit from sth.,
tirer profit de qch. **reaping,** *s.* Moisson *f.*
'reaping-hook, *s.* Faucille *f.* **'reaping-**
machine *s.* Moissonneuse *f.*
reaper ['ri:pər], *s.* **1.** (*Pers.*) Moissonneur *m.*
Lit: The Reaper, la Mort. **2.** (*Machine*) Moissonneuse *f.*
reappear [ri:ə'pi:ər], *v.i.* Reparaître.
reappearance [ri:ə'pi:ərəns], *s.* (*a*) Réapparition *f.* (*b*) *Th:* Rentrée *f* (d'un acteur).
re-appoint [ri:ə'pɔint], *v.tr.* Réintégrer (qn) dans
ses fonctions.
rear[1] ['ri:ər]. I. *s.* **1.** *Mil:* (*a*) Arrière-garde *f,*
derrières *mpl* (d'une armée). *To remove a*
casualty to the r., transporter un blessé à l'arrière.
(*b*) *P:* The rear, les latrines *f,* les cabinets *m.*
2. (*a*) Arrière *m,* derrière *m* (d'une maison).
(*b*) Dernier rang, queue *f* (d'un cortège).
II. **rear,** *a.* D'arrière, de queue; postérieur.
Rear wheel, roue (d')arrière. *Mil:* Rear rank,
dernier rang; arrière-rang *m.* Rear-rank man,
serre-file *m.* **'rear-admiral,** *s.* Contre-amiral *m.*
'rear-drive, *s. Aut: etc:* Attaque *f* de
l'essieu arrière. **'rear-guard,** *s. Mil:* Arrière-
garde *f.* Rear-guard action, combat *m* en retraite.
'rear-light, *s. Aut:* Lanterne *f* arrière; feu *m*
arrière.
rear[2]. **1.** *v.tr.* (*a*) Élever (une cathédrale); ériger
(une statue). (*b*) Dresser (un mât). **2.** *v.tr.*
Élever (des animaux); cultiver (des plantes).
3. *v.i.* (*Of horse*) Se cabrer. **rearing,** *s.*
1. Élevage *m* (des animaux). Rearing of children,
puériculture *f.* **2.** Cabrement *m.*
rearm [ri:'ɑ:rm], *v.tr.* Réarmer.
rearmament [ri:'ɑ:rməmənt], *s.* Réarmement *m.*
rearmost ['ri:ərmoust], *a.* Dernier; de queue.
re-arrange [ri:ə'reindʒ], *v.tr.* (*a*) Arranger de
nouveau. (*b*) Remettre en ordre.
re-arrangement [ri:ə'reindʒmənt], *s.* (*a*) Nouvel arrangement. (*b*) Remise *f* en ordre.
rearwards ['ri:ərwərdz], *adv.* **1.** A l'arrière;
(par) derrière. **2.** Vers l'arrière.
reason[1] [ri:zn], *s.* **1.** Raison *f,* cause *f.* The
reason for my absence, la raison de mon absence.
To state one's reasons for a decision, motiver une
décision. *Jur:* Reasons adduced, les attendus *m*
(d'un jugement). For reasons best known to
myself, pour des raisons de moi seul connues.

For the same r. . . ., au même titre. . . . For
no reason at all, sans motif, sans cause. For the
very r. that . . ., précisément parce que. . . .
The reason why, le pourquoi. *What's the r. for*
it? à quoi cela tient-il? You have reason to be
glad, vous avez sujet à vous réjouir. I have
reason to believe that . . ., j'ai lieu de croire
que. . . . *He complains* with (good) reason, il
se plaint à bon droit. All the more reason for
going, raison de plus pour y aller. By reason
of . . ., à cause de. . . . **2.** Raison; faculté *f*
de raisonner. He lost his reason, il a perdu sa
raison. **3.** Raison; bon sens. To hear, listen
to, reason, entendre raison. It stands to reason,
c'est évident; cela va sans dire. I cannot in
reason do it, je ne peux pas, raisonnablement,
le faire. As in reason, comme de raison. Everything in reason, il y a mesure à tout.
reason[2]. **1.** *v.i.* To reason from premises, déduire
des conclusions des prémisses. To reason on,
about, a subject, raisonner sur un sujet. To
reason with s.o., raisonner qn, avec qn. **2.** *v.tr.*
(*a*) *To r. that* . . ., arguer que. . . . *To r.*
whether . . ., discuter pour savoir si. . . .
(*b*) **To** reason s.o. out of doing sth., faire
entendre raison à qn. **reasoned,** *a.* **1.** Raisonné; (refus) motivé. **2.** Raisonnable. **reason-**
ing[1], *a.* Doué de raison. **reasoning**[2], *s.*
Raisonnement *m;* dialectique *f.* There is no
reasoning with him, il n'y a pas moyen de lui
faire entendre raison.
reasonable ['ri:z(ə)nəbl], *a.* **1.** (*a*) Raisonnable;
équitable. *You must try to be r.,* il faut vous
raisonner. *R. offer,* offre acceptable, raisonnable.
(*b*) *R. suspicions,* soupçons bien fondés. **2.** *R.*
prices, prix modérés, raisonnables. **-ably,** *adv.*
Raisonnablement.
reasonableness ['ri:z(ə)nəblnəs], *s.* **1.** Caractère *m* raisonnable; raison *f.* **2.** Modération *f*
(des prix).
reasoner ['ri:z(ə)nər], *s.* Raisonneur, -euse.
reassemble [ri:ə'sembl]. **1.** *v.tr.* (*a*) Rassembler;
assembler de nouveau. (*b*) Remonter, remettre
en état (une machine); remboîter (un meuble).
2. *v.i.* Se rassembler.
reassurance [ri:ə'ʃuərəns], *s.* **1.** Action *f* de
rassurer (qn). **2.** *Ins:* Réassurance *f.*
reassure [ri:ə'ʃuər], *v.tr.* **1.** Rassurer, tranquilliser (qn) (*on, about,* sur). To feel reassured,
se rassurer. **2.** *Ins:* Réassurer. **reassuring,** *a.*
(*Of news*) Rassurant.
reave [ri:v], *v.tr.* (*p.t. & p.p.* reft [reft]) *A. &*
Poet: (*a*) Ravager; razzier (le bétail). (*b*) Enlever,
ravir. *The lands reft from the Crown,* les domaines
arrachés à la Couronne.
reaver ['ri:vər], *s. A. & Poet:* Pillard *m,*
brigand *m;* (*of a voleur m* de bétail.
reawaken [ri:ə'weik(ə)n]. **1.** *v.tr.* Réveiller (qn).
To r. s.o.'s love, ranimer l'amour de qn. **2.** *v.i.* Se
réveiller; se ranimer.
rebate ['ri:beit, 'ri:beit], *s. Com:* **1.** Rabais *m,*
escompte *m.* **2.** Ristourne *f;* remboursement *m.*
rebel[1] ['reb(ə)l]. **1.** *a.* Insurgé. **2.** *s.* Rebelle *mf;*
révolté, -ée; insurgé, -ée.
rebel[2] [ri'bel], *v.i.* (**rebelled**) Se rebeller, se
soulever (*against,* contre).
rebellion [ri'beljən], *s.* Rébellion *f,* révolte *f*
(*against,* contre); soulèvement *m.*
rebellious [ri'beljəs], *a.* Rebelle. *R. act,* acte de
rébellion. *F: Her r. locks,* sa chevelure rebelle.
-ly, *adv.* En rebelle; d'un ton de défi.
rebelliousness [ri'beljəsnəs], *s.* Esprit *m* de
rébellion; insubordination *f.*
rebind [ri:'baind], *v.tr.* (*p.t. & p.p.* rebound

[ri:'baund]) Relier (un livre) de nouveau, à neuf.

rebound[1] [ri'baund], *s.* Rebondissement *m*; retour *m* brusque; ricochet *m* (d'une balle). *F:* To take s.o. on the rebound, profiter du moment de détente de qn.

rebound[2], *v.i.* Rebondir.

rebound[3] [ri:'baund]. *See* REBIND.

rebuff[1] [ri'bʌf], *s.* Rebuffade *f*; échec *m.* To meet with a rebuff, essuyer un refus.

rebuff[2], *v.tr.* Repousser, rebuter.

rebuild [ri:'bild], *v.tr. (p.t. & p.p.* rebuilt [ri:'bilt]) Rebâtir, reconstruire. **rebuilding,** *s.* Reconstruction *f*; réfection *f* (d'un pont).

rebuke[1] [ri'bju:k], *s.* Réprimande *f*, blâme *m.*

rebuke[2], *v.tr.* Réprimander, blâmer (qn). **rebuking,** *a.* Plein de reproches; (regard) sévère. **-ly,** *adv.* D'un ton, d'un air, de reproche.

rebus ['ri:bəs], *s.* Rébus *m.*

rebut [ri'bʌt], *v.tr.* (rebutted) **1.** Réfuter (une accusation, une théorie). **2.** Rebuter, repousser (qn).

recalcitrance [ri'kalsitrəns], *s.* Récalcitrance *f*; esprit *m* réfractaire.

recalcitrant [ri'kalsitrənt], *a. & s.* Récalcitrant, réfractaire; *F:* regimbeur, -euse.

recall[1] [ri'kɔ:l], *s.* **1.** Rappel *m* (de qn). *Dipl:* Letters of recall, lettres de rappel. **2.** Rétractation *f*, révocation *f*. *Decision* past recall, décision irrévocable. *Lost* beyond recall, perdu irrévocablement.

recall[2], *v.tr.* **1.** Rappeler (un ambassadeur.) To recall s.o. to his duty, rappeler qn au devoir. **2.** (*a*) Rappeler (qch. à qn). *Legends that r. the past,* légendes évocatrices du passé. (*b*) *I don't r. his name,* je ne me souviens pas de son nom. *How vividly I r. the scene!* avec quelle netteté je revois ce spectacle! **3.** (*a*) Rétracter (une promesse). (*b*) Annuler (un jugement). **recalling,** *s.* **1.** Rappel *m.* **2.** Révocation *f*.

recant [ri'kant]. **1.** *v.tr.* Rétracter, revenir sur (une opinion); abjurer (une erreur de doctrine). **2.** *v.i.* Se rétracter.

recantation [ri:kan'teiʃ(ə)n], *s.* Rétractation *f*, abjuration *f* (*of*, de); *A:* palinodie *f*.

recapitulate [ri:ka'pitjuleit], *v.tr.* Récapituler.

recapitulation [ri:kapitju'leiʃ(ə)n], *s.* Récapitulation *f*.

recapture[1] [ri:'kaptjər], *s.* Reprise *f*.

recapture[2], *v.tr.* Reprendre, recapturer.

re-case [ri:'keis], *v.tr.* Remboîter (un livre). **re-casing,** *s.* Remboîtage *m*.

recast[1] [ri:'ka:st], *v.* **1.** Refonte *f*. **2.** Nouveau calcul. **3.** *Th:* Nouvelle distribution des rôles.

recast[2], *v.tr.* (recast; recast) **1.** *Metall:* Refondre (une cloche, etc.). **2.** Refaire le calcul de (ses dépenses). **3.** *Th:* Faire une nouvelle distribution des rôles de (la pièce).

recede [ri'si:d], *v.i.* **1.** (*a*) S'éloigner, reculer. *The coast recedes (from the ship),* les côtes s'enfuient. (*b*) (*Of forehead*) Fuir. **2.** *Art:* (*Of background*) Se renfoncer. **receding,** *a.* (*a*) Qui s'éloigne, qui recule. Receding tide, marée descendante. (*b*) Receding forehead, front fuyant.

receipt[1] [ri'si:t], *s.* **1.** = RECIPE. **2.** (*a*) *Com:* Recette *f*. Receipts and expenses, recettes et dépenses. (*b*) Perception *f* (des impôts). (*c*) Réception *f*. I am in receipt of your favour, j'ai bien reçu votre lettre. On receipt of this letter, au reçu de cette lettre. To pay on receipt, payer à la réception. To acknowledge receipt of a letter, accuser réception d'une lettre. **3.** (i) Reçu *m*, quittance *f*; (ii) récépissé *m*, accusé *m* de

réception. Receipt in full (discharge), quittance pour solde. To give a receipt for sth., donner acquit de qch. **re'ceipt-form,** *s.* Quittance *f* (à souche). **re'ceipt-stamp,** *s.* Timbre *m* de quittance.

receipt[2], *v.tr.* *Com:* Acquitter (une facture).

receivable [ri'si:vəbl], *a.* **1.** Recevable. **2.** *Com:* Bills receivable, effets *m* à recevoir.

receive [ri'si:v], *v.tr.* **1.** (*a*) Recevoir. On receiving your letter, au reçu de votre lettre. To receive money, recevoir, toucher, de l'argent. Received with thanks, pour acquit. (*b*) *Jur:* To receive stolen goods, receler (des objets volés). **2.** (*a*) Recevoir (des invités). To receive s.o. with open arms, accueillir qn à bras ouverts. *The proposal was well received,* la proposition reçut un accueil favorable. *Abs.* She is not receiving to-day, elle ne reçoit pas aujourd'hui. (*b*) To r. s.o. into the Church, admettre qn dans l'Église. **3.** (*a*) To receive sympathy, recevoir des marques de sympathie. (*b*) To r. a refusal, essuyer un refus. To r. a black eye, se faire pocher l'œil. **receiving**[1], *a.* Récepteur, -trice. **receiving**[2], *s.* Réception *f*; recel *m* (d'objets volés). **re'ceiving-order,** *s.* *Jur:* (*In bankruptcy*) Ordonnance *f* de mise sous séquestre. **re'ceiving-station,** *s.* *W.Tel:* Poste récepteur.

receiver [ri'si:vər], *s.* **1.** (*a*) Personne *f* qui reçoit (qch.); destinataire *mf* (d'une lettre). (*b*) *Adm:* Receveur *m* (des deniers publics). (*c*) Receiver in bankruptcy, (*in Eng.*) administrateur *m* judiciaire (en matière de faillite); (*in Fr.*) syndic *m* de faillite. (*d*) Receleur *m* (d'objets volés). **2.** (*a*) Récepteur *m* (de téléphone). To lift the receiver, décrocher le récepteur. (*b*) *Ch: Ind:* Récipient *m*.

recension [ri'senʃ(ə)n], *s.* **1.** Recension *f*, révision *f* (d'un texte). **2.** Texte révisé.

recent ['ri:sənt], *a.* Récent. Event of recent date, événement de fraîche date. **-ly,** *adv.* Récemment; tout dernièrement. As recently as yesterday, pas plus tard que d'hier. Until quite recently, jusque dans ces derniers temps.

receptacle [ri'septəkl], *s.* **1.** Réceptacle *m*. **2.** Récipient *m*.

reception [ri'sepʃ(ə)n], *s.* **1.** (*a*) Réception *f* (d'un candidat à une académie). (*b*) Reception office, reception desk (*of hotel*), la réception. *Adm:* Reception order, permis *m* de recevoir un aliéné (dans une maison de santé); permis d'internement. **2.** Accueil *m*. To give s.o. an unfriendly r., faire mauvais accueil à qn. Your r. of these people, la façon dont vous avez accueilli ces gens. **3.** Réception (officielle). We are going to a r., nous allons en soirée. Reception room, (i) salle *f* de réception; salon *m*; (ii) pièce *f* (par opposition à chambre à coucher). **4.** *W.Tel:* Réception.

receptionist [ri'sepʃənist], *s.* Préposé(e) à la réception (d'un hôtel).

receptive [ri'septiv], *a.* Réceptif.

recess [ri'ses], *s.* **1.** (*a*) Vacances *fpl* (des tribunaux); intersession *f* (parlementaire). (*b*) *Sch:* (L'heure *f* de) la récréation. **2.** (*a*) Recoin *m*. Mountain recesses, recoins, replis *m*, des montagnes. (*b*) Enfoncement *m*; rentrant *m* (de muraille); embrasure *f* (de fenêtre); niche *f*. R. under a staircase, soupente *f* d'escalier.

recession [ri'seʃ(ə)n], *s.* Recul *m*, retraite *f*, régression *f*.

recessional [ri'seʃənl], *a. & s.* *Ecc:* Recessional (hymn), hymne *m* de sortie du clergé.

recidivist [ri'sidivist], *s.* Récidiviste *mf*.

recipe ['resipi], *s.* **1.** *Cu:* Recette *f*. *Pharm:*

Formule *f*. *Med*: Ordonnance *f*. **2.** *F*: Re-cette; moyen *m* (de faire qch.).

recipient [ri'sipiənt]. **I.** *a*. Réceptif. **2.** *s*. Personne *f* qui reçoit (un don); destinataire *mf* (d'une lettre); bénéficiaire *mf* (d'un chèque); donataire *mf*.

reciprocal [ri'siprok(ə)l]. **I.** *a*. (*a*) Réciproque, mutuel. (*b*) *Gram*: (Verbe) réciproque. **2.** *s*. *Log*: Réciproque *f*, inverse *f*. **3.** *a*. *&* *s*. *Mth*: *Geom*: (Fonction *f*) inverse; (figure *f*) réciproque. **Reciprocal** ratio, raison *f* inverse. **-ally,** *adv*. **I.** Réciproquement, mutuellement. **2.** *Mth*: Inversement.

reciprocate [ri'siprokeit]. **I.** *v.tr.* (*a*) Se rendre mutuellement (des services). (*b*) Payer de retour (un sentiment). *To r. s.o.'s good wishes*, souhaiter la pareille à qn. **2.** *v.i.* (*a*) Retourner le compliment. (*b*) *Mec.E*: (*Of piston*) Avoir un mouvement alternatif, un mouvement de va-et-vient.

reciprocating, *a*. *Mec.E*: (Mouvement) alternatif; (machine) à mouvement alternatif.

reciprocity [resi'prositi], *s*. Réciprocité *f*.

recital [ri'sait(ə)l], *s*. **I.** Récit *m*, narration *f* (d'un incident); énumération *f* (des détails). **2.** Récitation *f* (d'une poésie). **3.** *Jur*: Exposé *m* (des faits). **4.** *Mus*: Audition *f*; récital *m*, -als.

recitation [resi'teiʃ(ə)n], *s*. Récitation *f*.

recitative [resitə'ti:v], *s*. *Mus*: Récitatif *m*.

recite [ri'sait], *v.tr.* **I.** (*a*) Réciter, déclamer (un poème). (*b*) *Abs*. Réciter une pièce. **2.** *Jur*: Exposer (les faits). **3.** Énumérer (des détails).

reciter [ri'saitər], *s*. **I.** Récitateur, -trice; déclamateur *m*. **2.** Livre *m* de récitations.

reck [rek], *v.tr.* *&* *i*. *Poet*: To reck but little of sth., se soucier peu de qch. **I reck not that . . .,** peu me chaut que. . . . **What recks it?** qu'importe?

reckless ['rekləs], *a*. Insouciant (*of*, de); téméraire. *R. gambler*, homme aventureux au jeu. *Aut*: Reckless driving, conduite imprudente, téméraire. **-ly,** *adv*. Témérairement; avec insouciance. *He spends r.*, il dépense sans compter.

recklessness ['rekləsnəs], *s*. Insouciance *f* (*of*, de); imprudence *f*, témérité *f*.

reckon ['rek(ə)n]. **I.** *v.tr.* (*a*) Compter, calculer. *Abs*. Reckoning from to-day, à compter d'aujourd'hui. **To reckon sth. among, with . . .,** compter, ranger, qch. parmi. . . . (*b*) Estimer, juger. **I reckon he is forty,** je lui donne quarante ans. (*c*) *To r. s.o. as . . .,* regarder qn comme. . . . **2.** *v.i.* (*a*) Compter, calculer. *To learn to r.*, apprendre le calcul. (*b*) **To reckon (up)on sth.,** compter sur qch. **reckon in,** *v.tr.* Faire entrer (qch.) en ligne de compte. *I've reckoned that in*, j'ai tenu compte de cela. **reckon up,** *v.tr.* Compter, calculer, supputer. *To r. up one's losses*, dresser le bilan de ses pertes. **reckon with,** *v.i.* **I.** To reckon with s.o., demander des comptes à qn. **2.** To have to reckon with s.o., avoir à compter avec qn. **reckoning,** *s*. **I.** (*a*) Compte *m*, calcul *m*. **To be out in one's reckoning,** s'être trompé dans son calcul. **Day of reckoning,** (i) jour de règlement; (ii) *Lit*: jour d'expiation. (*b*) Estimation *f*. **To the best of my reckoning,** autant que j'en puis juger. (*c*) *Nau*: (Dead) reckoning, estime *f* (du point). **By dead reckoning,** à l'estime. **2.** (*At hotel*) Note *f*; (*at restaurant*) addition *f*.

reclaim¹ [ri'kleim], *s*. *Used in the phr*. **Past reclaim, beyond reclaim,** qui ne se corrigera jamais.

reclaim², *v.tr.* (*a*) Réformer, corriger (qn). *To r. s.o. to a sense of duty*, ramener qn au devoir.

To reclaim s.o. from vice, tirer qn du vice. (*b*) Défricher ou assécher (du terrain); mettre (un marais) en valeur. **Reclaimed land,** terrain amendé. (*c*) Récupérer (un sous-produit).

reclaiming, *s*. = RECLAMATION.

reclamation [reklə'meiʃ(ə)n], *s*. **I.** Réforme *f* (de qn). **2.** Défrichement *m* (d'un terrain); assèchement *m*, mise *f* en valeur (des marais); récupération *f* (de sous-produits). **3.** Réclamation *f*.

recline [ri'klain]. **I.** *v.tr.* Reposer, appuyer, coucher (sa tête sur qch.). **2.** *v.i.* Être couché, se reposer (*on*, sur); (*of head*) reposer, être appuyé (*on*, sur). **Reclining on a couch,** étendu, à demi couché, sur un canapé.

reclose [ri:'klo:uz], *v.tr.* Refermer.

reclothe [ri:'klo:uð], *v.tr.* **I.** Rhabiller (qn). **2.** Fournir de nouveaux vêtements à (qn).

recluse [ri'klu:s]. **I.** *a*. Retiré du monde; reclus. **2.** *s*. Reclus, -use; solitaire *mf*; anachorète *m*. *F*: **To live the life of a recluse,** vivre en anachorète.

reclusion [ri'klu:ʒ(ə)n], *s*. Réclusion *f*.

recognition [rekog'niʃ(ə)n], *s*. Reconnaissance *f*. **I.** (*a*) *Fact which has obtained general r.*, fait qui a été reconnu de tous. (*b*) **In recognition of . . .,** en reconnaissance de. . . . **2. To alter sth. beyond, past, recognition,** changer qch. au point de le rendre méconnaissable. **Smile of recognition,** sourire de reconnaissance.

recognizable ['rekognaizəbl], *a*. Reconnaissable.

recognizance [ri'kɔ(g)nizəns], *s*. *Jur*: **I.** Caution personnelle; engagement *m* (par-devant le tribunal). **To enter into recognizances,** donner caution. **2.** Somme fournie à titre de cautionnement.

recognize ['rekognaiz], *v.tr.* **I.** To recognize a government, reconnaître un gouvernement. *To r. s.o. as king*, reconnaître qn pour roi. **2.** *He knows he is wrong but won't r. it*, il sait qu'il a tort mais ne veut pas l'admettre, le reconnaître. **To recognize a poor relation,** avouer un parent pauvre. **3.** (*a*) **To recognize s.o. by his walk,** reconnaître qn à sa démarche. *I do not r. you*, je ne vous remets pas. (*b*) *The duke recognized me*, le duc me fit un signe de connaissance. **recognized,** *a*. Reconnu, admis, reçu; (*of manner, etc.*) classique. *The r. term*, le terme consacré. *Com*: **Recognized agent,** agent accrédité, attitré.

recoil¹ [ri'kɔil], *s*. **I.** (*a*) Rebondissement *m*, détente *f* (d'un ressort). (*b*) Recul *m* (d'une arme à feu); contre-coup *m* (d'une explosion). **2.** Mouvement *m* de recul, de dégoût.

recoil², *v.i.* **I.** (*a*) (*Of spring*) Se détendre. (*b*) (*Of fire-arm*) Reculer, repousser. **2.** (*Of pers.*) Reculer (*from*, devant); se révolter (*from*, contre). **To recoil from doing sth.,** reculer devant l'idée de faire qch. **3.** (*Of evil*) Retomber, rejaillir (*on*, sur).

recollect [reko'lekt], *v.tr.* **I.** Se rappeler (qch.). **I don't recollect you,** je ne vous remets pas. **As far as I recollect . . .,** autant qu'il m'en souvienne. . . . **2. To recollect oneself,** se recueillir.

recollection [reko'lekʃ(ə)n], *s*. **I.** Souvenir *m*, mémoire *f*. *I have a dim r. of it*, j'en ai gardé un souvenir confus. **To the best of my recollection,** autant que je m'en souviens, que je m'en souvienne; autant qu'il m'en souvient, qu'il m'en souvienne. *It has never occurred within my recollection*, cela n'est jamais arrivé de mon temps. **2.** Recueillement *m*.

recommence [ri:ko'mens], *v.tr.* *&* *i*. Recommencer.

recommend [reko'mend], *v.tr.* **1.** To recommend s.o. to do sth., recommander, conseiller, à qn de faire qch. *I have been recommended (to come) to you*, on m'a adressé à vous. **2.** To recommend a candidate for a post, recommander un candidat pour un emploi. *The hotel is to be recommended for its cooking*, l'hôtel se recommande par sa cuisine. **3.** *To r. sth. to s.o.'s care*, commander qch. aux soins de qn.

recommendable [reko'mendəbl], *a.* Recommandable.

recommendation [rekomen'deiʃ(ə)n], *s.* Recommandation *f*. **1.** *To write* in recommendation of sth., écrire pour recommander qch. *Letter of recommendation*, (lettre *f* de) recommandation. **2.** The recommendations of the commission, les avis rendus par la commission.

recommission [ri:ko'miʃ(ə)n], *v.tr.* (*a*) Réarmer (un navire). (*b*) Réintégrer (un officier) dans les cadres.

recompense[1] ['rekompens], *s.* **1.** Récompense *f* (*for*, de). **2.** Dédommagement *m* (*for*, de). *As a r. for his trouble*, pour prix de sa peine.

recompense[2], *v.tr.* **1.** Récompenser (*s.o. for sth.*, qn de qch.). **2.** Dédommager (*s.o. for sth.*, qn de qch.). **3.** Compenser, réparer (un mal). **4.** Payer de retour (un service).

reconcilable [rekon'sailəbl], *a.* Conciliable, accordable (*with*, avec).

reconcile ['rekonsail], *v.tr.* **1.** Réconcilier, raccommoder, remettre bien ensemble (deux personnes). *To become reconciled*, se réconcilier. **2.** *To reconcile s.o. to sth.*, faire accepter qch. à qn. *To reconcile oneself to sth.*, se résigner à qch. **3.** Concilier, faire accorder (des faits); mettre d'accord (deux points de vue).

reconciliation [rekonsili'eiʃ(ə)n], *s.* **1.** Réconciliation *f*, rapprochement *m*. **2.** Conciliation *f* (d'opinions contraires).

recondite ['rekondait], *a.* (*Of knowledge*) Abstrus, profond; (*of style*) obscur.

reconditeness ['rekondaitnəs], *s.* Caractère abstrus (d'une science); sens profond, sens caché (d'un écrit); obscurité *f* (de style).

recondition [ri:kon'diʃ(ə)n], *v.tr.* Rénover; remettre à neuf, en état. *Reconditioned car*, voiture révisée.

reconnaissance [ri'konesəns], *s.* *Mil: etc:* Reconnaissance *f*. **Reconnaissance party**, détachement *m* d'exploration. *F: To make a r.*, explorer le terrain.

reconnoitre [reko'nɔitər], *v.tr.* *Mil: etc:* Reconnaître (le terrain). *Abs.* Faire une reconnaissance; éclairer le terrain. *Reconnoitring party*, détachement en reconnaissance. **reconnoitring**, *s.* Reconnaissance *f*.

reconquer [ri:'kɔnkər], *v.tr.* Reconquérir.

reconsider [ri:kon'sidər], *v.tr.* **1.** Considérer de nouveau, examiner à nouveau (une question); reviser, revoir (un jugement). **2.** Revenir sur (une décision).

reconsideration [ri:konsidə'reiʃ(ə)n], *s.* Examen *m* à nouveau; revision *f* (d'un jugement).

reconstituent [ri:kon'stitjuənt], *a. & s. Med:* Reconstituant (*m*).

reconstitute [ri:'konstitju:t], *v.tr.* Reconstituer.

reconstruct [ri:kon'strʌkt], *v.tr.* **1.** Reconstruire, rebâtir (un édifice); refaire (une comédie). **2.** *To r. a crime*, reconstituer un crime.

reconstruction [ri:kon'strʌkʃ(ə)n], *s.* **1.** Reconstruction *f*, réfection *f*. *Financial r.*, restauration financière. **2.** Reconstitution *f* (d'un crime).

reconvey [ri:kon'vei], *v.tr. Jur:* Rétrocéder.

reconveyance [ri:kon'veiəns], *s. Jur:* Rétrocession *f*.

recopy [ri:'kɔpi], *v.tr.* Recopier.

record[1] ['rekɔːrd], *s.* **1.** *Jur:* (*a*) Enregistrement *m* (d'un fait). (*Of judgment, fact*) To be on record, être enregistré, être authentique. *F: It is on record that . . .*, il est rapporté dans l'histoire que. . . . (*b*) Record of a court, feuille *f* d'audience. *F: To travel out of the record*, s'écarter de son sujet. (*c*) **Record of evidence**, procès-verbal *m* de témoignage. (*d*) Minute *f* (d'un acte). **2.** (*a*) Note *f*, mention *f*. To make, keep, a record of an observation, faire une note d'une observation; noter une observation. (*b*) Registre *m*. **Record of attendances**, registre de présence. **3.** *pl.* Archives *f*, annales *f*. *Com:* Archives. **The Public Records**, les Archives nationales. *Official record(s) of a society*, bulletin officiel d'une société. **The Record office**, les Archives. **4.** Monument *m*, document *m*, souvenir *m* (de qch.). **5.** Carrière *f*, dossier *m* (de qn). **Service record**, état *m* de service. *An employee's good r.*, les bonnes notes d'un employé. **His past record**, sa conduite passée. **Police record**, casier *m* judiciaire. *To have a clean record*, avoir un casier judiciaire intact, vierge. **6.** *Sp: etc:* Record *m*. **To break, beat, the record**, battre le record. **To hold a record**, détenir un record. *Ind:* **Record output**, production constituant un record. **At record speed**, à une vitesse record. **7.** Disque *m* (de gramophone). *To listen to records by . . .*, écouter des enregistrements par. . . .

record[2] [ri'kɔːrd], *v.tr.* **1.** (*a*) Enregistrer (un fait); consigner (qch.) par écrit; prendre acte de (qch.); minuter (un jugement, etc.). (*b*) Relater, narrer, rapporter (qch.). (*c*) (*Of instrument*) Enregistrer, marquer. **2.** *Gramophones:* Enregistrer (une chanson, etc.). *Singer who records for Pathé*, chanteur qui enregistre pour les disques Pathé. **recording**[1], *a.* **1.** **The recording angel**, l'ange qui tient le registre des actes de chacun. **2.** (Instrument) enregistreur. **recording**[2], *s.* **1.** (*a*) Enregistrement *m*; consignation *f* par écrit. (*b*) Narration *f*, relation *f*. **2.** *Gramophones:* Enregistrement. *Cin:* **Sound-and-picture recording**, enregistrement phono-visuel.

recorder [ri'kɔːrdər], *s.* **1.** *Jur:* Avocat nommé par la Couronne pour remplir certaines fonctions de juge. **2.** (*a*) *He was a faithful r. of what he saw*, il transcrivait fidèlement ce qu'il voyait. (*b*) Archiviste *m*. **3.** Appareil enregistreur. *Aut:* **Distance recorder**, enregistreur de distance. *Cin:* **Sound recorder**, appareil d'enregistrement du son.

recork [ri:'kɔːrk], *v.tr.* Reboucher (une bouteille).

recount[1] [ri'kaunt], *v.tr.* Raconter.

recount[2] [ri:'kaunt, 'ri:-], *s.* Nouveau dépouillement du scrutin.

recount[3] [ri:'kaunt], *v.tr.* Recompter.

recoup [ri'ku:p], *v.tr.* **1.** Dédommager (qn). *To recoup s.o. (for) his losses*, dédommager, indemniser, qn de ses pertes. *To recoup oneself for one's losses*, *abs. to recoup*, se récupérer, se dédommager, se rattraper de ses pertes. **2.** *Jur:* Défalquer.

recourse [ri'kɔːrs], *s.* **1.** Recours *m*. *To have recourse to sth.*, avoir recours à qch.; recourir à qch. **2.** Expédient *m*.

recover[1] [ri'kʌvər], *v.tr.* **1.** Recouvrer, retrouver (un objet perdu); retrouver (son appétit). *Ind:* **To recover by-products from coal**, récupérer, recueillir, capter, des sous-produits de la houille. **To recover one's breath**, reprendre haleine. **To**

recover consciousness, reprendre ses sens; revenir à soi. **2.** Regagner (de l'argent perdu); rentrer en possession de (ses biens); rentrer dans (ses droits, ses débours); recouvrer, récupérer (une créance). **To recover one's (fallen) fortunes,** se refaire une situation. **To recover lost time,** rattraper le temps perdu. **To recover lost ground,** reprendre du terrain perdu. **To recover sth. from s.o.,** reprendre qch. à qn. *Jur:* **To recover damages,** *abs.* to recover, **from s.o.,** obtenir des dommages-intérêts de qn. **3.** *To recover one's health, v.i.* to recover, guérir; recouvrer la santé; se rétablir. **To recover from an illness,** se remettre, guérir, d'une maladie. *To be quite recovered,* être tout à fait remis, rétabli. **To recover from one's astonishment,** revenir, se remettre, de son étonnement. **Prices have recovered,** les cours se sont relevés. **4. To recover oneself,** *abs.* to recover, se remettre, se ressaisir. **To recover one's balance,** se ressaisir; reprendre, retrouver, son équilibre. **5.** Réparer (une erreur). **6.** *Fenc:* **To recovers word,** *abs.* to recover, se remettre en garde.

recover², re-cover [riː'kʌvər], *v.tr.* Recouvrir; regarnir (des meubles).

recoverable [ri'kʌvərəbl], *a.* Recouvrable, récupérable.

recovery [ri'kʌvəri], *s.* **1.** Recouvrement *m* (d'un objet perdu). *Ind:* Récupération *f* (de sous-produits). **2.** *Jur:* Action for recovery of property, (action en) revendication *f.* **3.** (*a*) Rétablissement *m,* guérison *f* (de qn). **The patient is making a good recovery,** le malade est en bonne voie de guérison. **To be past recovery,** être dans un état désespéré. (*b*) Redressement *m* (économique); relèvement *m,* reprise *f* (des affaires). **4.** *Fenc:* Remise *f* en garde.

recreant ['rekriənt]. *Lit:* **1.** *a.* (*a*) Lâche. (*b*) Infidèle. **2.** *s.* (*a*) Lâche *m.* (*b*) Apostat *m.*

recreate¹ ['rekrieit], *v.tr.* Divertir, distraire (qn). **To recreate oneself,** se récréer, se divertir.

recreate² [riːkri'eit], *v.tr.* Recréer.

recreation [rekri'ei∫(ə)n], *s.* Récréation *f,* divertissement *m,* délassement *m.* **recre'ation-ground,** *s.* **1.** *Sch:* Cour *f* de récréation. **2.** Terrain *m* de jeux.

recreative ['rekrieitiv], *a.* Récréatif, divertissant.

recriminate [ri'krimineit], *v.i.* Récriminer.

recrimination [rikrimi'nei∫(ə)n], *s.* Récrimination *f.*

recriminatory [ri'kriminət(ə)ri], *a.* Récriminatoire.

recross [riː'krɔs], *v.tr.* Retraverser; repasser (une rivière).

recrudesce [riːkru'des], *v.i.* (*Of sore*) S'enflammer de nouveau; (*of fever, etc.*) reprendre.

recrudescence [riːkru'des(ə)ns], *s.* Recrudescence *f.* R. *of activity,* regain *m* d'activité.

recruit¹ [ri'kruːt], *s.* Recrue *f.* **A raw recruit,** *F:* un bleu. **Recruit drill,** école *f* du soldat.

recruit², *v.tr.* **1.** (*a*) Recruter (une armée, des partisans); racoler (des hommes pour l'armée). *The new party was largely recruited from the middle classes,* le nouveau parti faisait de nombreuses recrues dans la bourgeoisie. (*b*) **To recruit supplies,** se réapprovisionner. **2. To recruit one's health,** *abs.* to recruit, se restaurer, se remettre, se retremper. **recruiting,** *s. Mil:* Recrutement *m.* **Recruiting-sergeant,** sergent recruteur; racoleur *m.* **Recruiting station,** bureau *m* de recrutement.

rectal ['rekt(ə)l], *a. Anat:* Rectal, -aux. **Rectal injection,** lavement *m.*

rectangle ['rektaŋgl], *s.* Rectangle *m.*

rectangular [rek'taŋgjulər], *a.* Rectangulaire.

rectification [rektifi'kei∫(ə)n], *s.* **1. Rectification** *f.* **2.** *El.E:* Redressement *m* (du courant alternatif).

rectifier ['rektifaiər], *s.* **1.** *Dist:* Rectificateur *m.* **2.** *El:* Redresseur *m,* rectificateur (de courant). **Rectifier station,** poste *m* de redressement.

rectify ['rektifai], *v.tr.* **1.** (*a*) Rectifier, corriger (une erreur); réparer (un oubli). (*b*) *Dist:* Rectifier (l'alcool). **2.** *El.E:* Redresser (le courant). **rectifying,** *a.* Rectificatif. *W.Tel:* R. *device,* système redresseur.

rectilineal [rekti'liniəl], **rectilinear** [rekti'liniər], *a.* Rectiligne. *Phot:* **Rapid rectilinear lens,** objectif rectilinéaire.

rectitude ['rektitjuːd], *s.* Rectitude *f* (de conduite); droiture *f* (de caractère).

recto ['rekto], *s. Typ:* Recto *m* (de la page).

rector ['rektər], *s.m.* **1.** (*a*) *Ch. of Eng:* Ecclésiastique préposé à l'administration de la paroisse et titulaire du bénéfice et de la dîme. **Lay rector,** titulaire séculier d'un bénéfice (le préposé étant alors le *vicar,*). (*b*) *R.C.Ch:* Curé. **2.** (*a*) Recteur (d'une université). (*b*) *Scot:* Directeur (d'une école secondaire).

rectory ['rektəri], *s. Ecc:* Presbytère *m,* cure *f* (du rector, *q.v.*).

rectum ['rektəm], *s. Anat:* Rectum *m.*

recultivate [riː'kʌltiveit], *v.tr.* Remettre en valeur, en culture (des terres).

recumbent [ri'kʌmbənt], *a.* Couché, étendu.

recuperate [ri'kjuːpəreit]. **1.** *v.tr.* (*a*) Remettre, rétablir (qn). (*b*) *Ind:* To r. *waste heat,* récupérer la chaleur perdue. **2.** *v.i.* Se remettre, se rétablir; reprendre des forces.

recuperation [rikjuːpə'rei∫(ə)n], *s.* **1.** Rétablissement *m,* guérison *f.* **2.** *Ind:* Récupération *f.*

recuperator [ri'kjuːpəreitər], *s. Ind:* *Artil:* Récupérateur *m.*

recur [ri'kəːr], *v.i.* (**recurred**) **1.** Revenir (*to a subject,* sur un sujet). **2.** (*a*) To r. *to the memory,* revenir, se retracer, à la mémoire. (*b*) (*Of event, etc.*) Se reproduire, se renouveler; (*of occasion*) se représenter. **recurring,** *a.* Périodique. **Ever-recurring,** qui revient sans cesse. *Mth:* **Recurring decimal,** fraction décimale périodique.

recurrence [ri'kʌrəns], *s.* Réapparition *f,* renouvellement *m,* retour *m. Med:* Récidive *f* (d'une maladie). **To be of frequent recurrence,** revenir fréquemment.

recurrent [ri'kʌrənt], *a.* **1.** *Anat: Bot:* Récurrent. **2.** Périodique; qui revient souvent. *Mth:* **Recurrent series,** série récurrente.

recusant ['rekjuzənt, ri'kjuːzənt]. **1.** *s. Eng.Hist:* Catholique *mf* qui refusait d'assister à l'office divin dans une église anglicane. **2.** *a. & s.* Réfractaire (*mf*) (*against,* à).

recut [riː'kʌt], *v.tr.* Recouper; retailler (une lime).

red [red]. **1.** *a.* (**redder**) (*a*) Rouge; (*deep*) pourpre. **Red lips,** lèvres vermeilles. **Red (-rimmed) eyes,** yeux éraillés. **To turn, go, red,** rougir; (*of sky, etc.*) rougeoyer. *F:* **Red as a peony,** rouge comme une pivoine. **It makes him see red,** il voit rouge quand il entend dire cela. *Cu:* **Red meat,** viande saignante. **Red granite,** granit rose. **The Red Sea,** la Mer Rouge. *Art:* **Red chalk,** sanguine *f.* (*b*) (*Of hair*) Roux, *f.* rousse. (*c*) *Pol:* Rouge; de 'extrême gauche.' **2.** *a. & s.* (*In Fr. a.inv.*) **Cherry red,** rouge cerise. **Fiery red,** rouge feu. **3.** *s.* (*a*) Rouge *m.* **Dressed in red,** habillé de, en, rouge. *Pol:* Rouge *mf.* (*c*) *Bill:* **The red,** la bille rouge. **'red-blooded,** *a.* (*Of pers.*) Vigoureux, robuste. **'red-eyed,** *a.*

Aux yeux éraillés. **'red-faced**, *a.* Rougeaud, sanguin. **'red-haired**, *a.* Roux, *f.* rousse. **'red-'handed**, *a.* To be caught red-handed, être pris sur le fait, en flagrant délit. **'red-'hot**, *a.* **1.** (Chauffé au) rouge. *To make sth. red-hot*, porter qch. au rouge. **2.** *F:* Red hot Radical, ardent radical; radical à tous crins. **red lead** [led], *s.* Minium *m.* **'red-letter**, *attrib.a.* *F:* Red-letter day, (i) jour de fête; (ii) jour mémorable; jour pour lequel on fait une croix à la cheminée. **'red-shank(s)**, *s.* *Orn:* Chevalier *m*, gambette *m.* **'red-'short**, *a.* *Metall:* (Fer) cassant à chaud; (fer) rouverin. **red 'tape**, *s.* **1.** Bolduc *m* (rouge) (des documents officiels). **2.** *F:* Chinoiseries administratives; bureaucratie *f*, paperasserie *f.*

redan [ri'dan], *s.* *Fort:* Redan *m.*

redbreast ['redbrest], *s.* *See* ROBIN 2.

redcoat ['redkout], *s.* *Hist:* Soldat anglais.

redden [redn]. **1.** *v.tr.* Rougir (qch.). **2.** *v.i.* Devenir rouge; rougir; (*of sky*) rougeoyer; (*of leaves*) roussir.

reddish ['rediʃ], *a.* (*a*) Rougeâtre. (*b*) Roussâtre.

reddle[1] [redl], *s.* Ocre *f* rouge.

reddle[2], *v.tr.* Frotter (qch.) d'ocre rouge; marquer (qch.) à l'ocre rouge.

re-decorate [ri:'dekoreit], *v.tr.* Peindre et tapisser (un appartement) à nouveau.

redeem [ri'di:m], *v.tr.* **1.** Racheter, rembourser (une obligation); dégager (un nantissement); amortir (une dette); purger (une hypothèque). **To redeem one's watch** (from pawn), retirer, dégager, sa montre. **2.** Tenir, accomplir (sa promesse). **3.** (*a*) Libérer, racheter (un esclave). (*b*) His good points redeem his faults, ses qualités rachètent, compensent, ses défauts. **redeeming**, *a.* **1.** Rédempteur. **2.** Qui fait compensation. **Redeeming feature**, qualité *f* qui rachète les défauts.

redeemable [ri'di:məbl], *a.* (*Of stock*) Rachetable, remboursable, amortissable.

redeemer [ri'di:mər], *s.* *Theol:* The Redeemer, le rédempteur.

redemption [ri'dempʃ(ə)n], *s.* **1.** (*a*) Remboursement *m*, amortissement *m* (d'une obligation); rachat *m* (d'un emprunt); dégagement *m* (d'un nantissement); purge *f* (d'une hypothèque). Redemption fund, caisse *f* d'amortissement. (*b*) Sale with power of redemption, vente avec faculté de rachat. **2.** Rachat (d'un esclave). *Theol:* Rédemption *f* (du genre humain). **3.** Rachat (d'un crime, etc.). Crime past redemption, crime irréparable. *Spoilt* beyond (all hope of) redemption, abîmé irrémédiablement.

redhibitory [red'hibitəri], *a.* *Jur:* Rédhibitoire.

redirect [ri:dai'rekt, -di-], *v.tr.* Faire suivre (une lettre).

rediscover [ri:dis'kʌvər], *v.tr.* Redécouvrir; retrouver.

redistribute [ri:dis'tribjut], *v.tr.* (*a*) Redistribuer. (*b*) Répartir à nouveau.

redistribution [ri:distri'bju:ʃ(ə)n], *s.* (*a*) Redistribution *f.* (*b*) Nouvelle répartition.

redness ['rednəs], *s.* **1.** Rougeur *f.* **2.** Rousseur *f* (des cheveux).

redolence ['redoləns], *s.* **1.** Odeur *f* suave; parfum *m.* **2.** Odeur forte (*of*, de).

redolent ['redolənt], *a.* **1.** Odorant, parfumé. **Redolent of spring**, qui exhale une odeur de printemps, qui respire le printemps. **2.** Qui a une forte odeur (*of*, de). *To be r. of the soil*, sentir le cru. *Sauce r. of garlic*, sauce qui fleure l'ail.

redouble[1] [ri:'dʌbl], *s.* *Cards:* Surcontre *m.*

redouble[2] [ri:'dʌbl], *v.tr.* **1.** Replier (une étoffe, etc.); plier en quatre. **2.** *Cards:* To redouble spades, surcontrer pique.

redouble[3] [ri'dʌbl]. **1.** *v.tr.* Redoubler (ses cris, ses instances, etc.). **2.** *v.i.* Redoubler. **redoubling**, *s.* Redoublement *m* (de joie, de zèle).

redoubt [ri'daut], *s.* *Fort:* Redoute *f*, réduit *m.*

redoubtable [ri'dautəbl], *a.* Redoutable, formidable.

redound [ri'daund], *v.i.* **1.** Contribuer (*to*, à). This will redound to your credit, votre réputation y gagnera. **2.** Résulter; rejaillir (*to*, sur). The advantages that r. to us, les avantages qui en résultent pour nous.

redpoll ['redpoul], *s.* *Orn:* Linotte *f.*

redraft [ri'drɑ:ft], *v.tr.* Rédiger de nouveau.

re-draw [ri:'drɔ:], *v.tr.* (-drew [dru:]; -drawn) **1.** *Com:* Faire retraite (*on s.o.*, sur qn). **2.** Redessiner.

redress[1] [ri'dres], *s.* Redressement *m*, réparation *f* (d'un tort); réforme *f* (d'un abus). *Jur:* Legal redress, réparation légale. *Injury* beyond redress, past redress, tort irréparable.

redress[2] [ri'dres], *v.tr.* **1.** Rétablir (l'équilibre). **2.** Redresser, réparer (un tort); corriger, réformer (un abus).

redress[3] [ri:'dres], *v.tr.* *Th:* To redress a play. costumer une pièce à nouveau.

redressable [ri'dresəbl], *a.* (Tort) redressable, réparable.

redskin ['redskin], *s.* *Ethn:* Peau-Rouge *m.*

redstart ['redstɑ:rt], *s.* *Orn:* Rouge-queue *m.*

reduce [ri'dju:s], *v.tr.* **1.** (*a*) Réduire, rapetisser (un dessin); amincir, amaigrir (une planche); (*in length*) raccourcir. *v.i.* Do you wish to reduce? voulez-vous maigrir? (*b*) Réduire, abaisser (la température); (a)baisser, diminuer (le prix, etc.). **To reduce expenses**, diminuer la dépense; faire des économies. **To reduce speed**, diminuer de vitesse; ralentir la marche. *El:* To r. the voltage, abaisser la tension. (*c*) Atténuer (un contraste). *Phot:* Affaiblir, baisser (un cliché dur). (*d*) (*Of illness*) Affaiblir, amaigrir (qn). **2.** (*a*) To reduce sth. to ashes, to dust, réduire qch. en cendres, en poussière. *Clothes reduced to rags*, vêtements à l'état de guenilles. (*b*) To r. a fraction to its lowest terms, ramener une fraction à sa plus simple expression. *To r. yards to feet*, réduire des mètres en pieds. *To r. everything to a single principle*, tout ramener à un seul principe. (*c*) To r. bribery to a system, ériger la corruption en système. (*d*) To reduce sth. to writing, coucher, consigner, qch. par écrit. **3.** (*a*) To reduce s.o. to silence, faire taire qn. (*b*) *Mil:* Réduire (une ville révoltée). **4.** He was reduced to begging, il en était réduit à mendier son pain. **5.** (*a*) To r. s.o. to the level of beasts, ravaler qn au niveau des bêtes. (*b*) *Mil:* Réduire (une homme) à un grade inférieur; rétrograder (un sous-officier). **6.** *Ch:* Réduire (un oxyde). **7.** *Med:* Réduire (une fracture); remettre (une épaule démise). **reduced**, *a.* **1.** Réduit. At (greatly) reduced prices, au (grand) rabais; en solde. **2.** In reduced circumstances, dans l'indigence, dans la gêne.

reducer [ri'dju:sər], *s.* *Ch: etc:* Réducteur *m.*

reducible [ri'dju:sibl], *a.* Réductible (*to*, à).

reduction [ri'dʌkʃ(ə)n], *s.* **1.** Rapetissement *m* (d'un dessin, etc.); amincissement *m* (d'une planche, etc.). **Reduction compasses**, compas *m* de réduction. **2.** (*a*) Réduction *f*, diminution *f* (des prix); baisse *f* (de température). *Jur:* Relaxation *f* (d'une peine). *Phot:* Affaiblissement *m* (d'un cliché). *Mec.E:* Reduction of

gear ratio, démultiplication *f.* (*b*) *Com:* Rabais *m.* **To make a reduction on an article,** faire une remise sur un article. **3.** *Mil:* Réduction (d'une ville). **4.** *Mil:* Rétrogradation *f* (d'un sous-officier). **5.** *Ch:* Réduction (d'un oxyde). **6.** *Med:* Réduction (d'une fracture).

redundancy [ri'dʌndənsi], *s.* **1.** *Lit:* Redondance *f*, tautologie *f.* **2.** Surabondance *f.* **3.** Surplus *m*, excédent *m.*

redundant [ri'dʌndənt], *a.* **1.** *Lit:* (Mot) redondant, qui fait double emploi. **2.** Surabondant; superflu.

reduplicate [ri'dju:plikeit], *v.tr.* Redoubler, répéter.

reduplication [ridju:pli'keiʃ(ə)n], *s.* Redoublement *m.*

re-dye [ri:'dai], *v.tr.* (Faire) reteindre.

re-echo [ri:'eko]. **I.** *v.tr.* Répéter, renvoyer (un son). **2.** *v.i.* Retentir, résonner.

reed [ri:d], *s.* **I.** *Bot:* Roseau *m*; jonc *m* à balais. *F:* **To lean on a broken reed,** s'appuyer sur un roseau. **2.** *Poet:* Chalumeau *m*, pipeau *m.* **3.** *Mus:* (*a*) Anche *f* (de hautbois, etc.). (*b*) (*In orchestra*) **The reeds,** les instruments *m* à anche. **4.** Peigne *m* (de métier à tisser). **'reed-bed,** *s.* Roselière *f.* **'reed-mace,** *s.* *Bot:* Massette *f*; quenouille *f.* **'reed-stop,** *s.* *Organ:* Jeu *m* d'anches. **'reed-warbler,** *s.* *Orn:* Fauvette riveraine.

re-edit [ri:'edit], *v.tr.* Rééditer (d'anciens ouvrages); donner une nouvelle édition critique (d'un texte).

reedy ['ri:di], *a.* **1.** Abondant en roseaux; couvert de roseaux. **2.** *R. voice,* voix flûtée; voix ténue. *The r. oboe,* le hautbois nasillard.

reef[1] [ri:f], *s.* *Nau:* Ris *m.* **To take in a reef,** (i) prendre un ris; (ii) *F:* agir avec circonspection. **To shake out a reef,** larguer un ris. *P:* **To let out a reef,** relâcher sa ceinture (après dîner). **'reef-knot,** *s.* Nœud plat, nœud droit. **'reef-point,** *s.* Garcette *f* de ris.

reef[2], *v.tr.* **I.** **To reef a sail,** prendre un ris dans une voile. **2.** Rentrer (le beaupré, etc.). *S.a.* CLOSE-REEFED.

reef[3], *s.* **I.** Récif *m*, banc *m* de roches (à fleur d'eau). **Coral reef,** récif de corail. **Submerged reef,** récif sous-marin; écueil *m*, brisant *m.* **2.** *Gold-min:* Filon *m* de quartz aurifère; reef *m.*

reek[1] [ri:k], *s.* **I.** *Lit. & Scot:* (*a*) Fumée *f.* (*b*) Vapeur *f*, exhalaison *f.* **2.** (*a*) Odeur forte, âcre. *R. of tobacco,* relent *m* de tabac. (*b*) Atmosphère *f* fétide.

reek[2], *v.i.* **I.** *Scot:* (*Of chimney*) Fumer. **2.** *Lit:* Exhaler des vapeurs; fumer (*with sweat*, de sueur). (*Of street, etc.*) **To reek with crime,** suer le crime. **3.** Exhaler une mauvaise odeur. *To r. of garlic,* empester, puer, l'ail. *This room is reeking of* (*tobacco*), ça empoisonne le tabac ici.

Reekie ['ri:ki], *s.* *Scot:* **Auld Reekie,** la vieille Enfumée; Édimbourg.

reeky ['ri:ki], *a.* Enfumé; noirci de fumée.

reel[1] [ri:l], *s.* **I.** *Tex: etc:* Dévidoir *m*, bobine *f*; touret *m* (pour câbles). **2.** Moulinet *m* (de canne à pêche). *F:* (*Straight*) **off the reel,** d'arrachepied; (tout) d'une traite; d'affilée. **3.** Bobine (de coton). *R. of paper,* bobine de papier. **Paper in reels,** papier continu. *Cin:* **Film reel,** (i) bobine; (ii) bande *f*, rouleau *m*, de film.

reel[2], *v.tr.* (*a*) *Tex: etc:* Dévider ou bobiner (le fil, etc.). *F:* **To reel off verses,** réciter d'un trait, *P:* dégoiser, des vers. (*b*) *Nau:* **To reel in the log-line,** remonter la ligne de loch.

reel[3], *v.i.* **I.** Tournoyer. **To make s.o.'s senses reel,** donner le vertige à qn. *My head reels,* la

---

tête me tourne. **2.** Chanceler; (*of drunken man*) tituber. **He reeled out, back,** il sortit, il recula, en chancelant. *Reeling gai ,* marche chancelante, titubante. *The ship reeled under the force of the wave,* le navire s'abattit sous le coup de la vague.

reel[4], *s.* Danse écossaise (d'un mouvement très vif); branle écossais.

re-elect [ri:i'lekt], *v.tr.* Réélire.

re-election [ri:i'lekʃ(ə)n], *s.* Réélection *f.*

re-eligible [ri:'elidʒibl], *a.* Rééligible.

re-embark [ri:em'bɑ:rk], *v.tr. & i.* Rembarquer.

re-embarkation [ri:embɑ:r'keiʃ(ə)n], *s.* Rembarquement *m.*

re-emerge [ri:i'mə:rdʒ], *v.t.* Ressortir, reparaître (à la surface de l'eau).

re-enact [ri:e'nakt], *v.tr.* **I.** Remettre en vigueur (une loi). **2.** Reconstituer, reproduire (une scène).

re-engage [ri:en'ge:idʒ], *v.tr.* (*a*) Rengager (des troupes); réintégrer (des employés). (*b*) *Mec.E:* Rengrener (une roue dentée). *Aut:* **To re-engage** the clutch, rembrayer.

re-enlist [ri:en'list], *v.i.* Se rengager.

re-enter [ri:'entər]. **I.** *v.i.* (*a*) Rentrer. (*b*) *To re-enter for an examination,* se présenter de nouveau à un examen. **2.** *v.tr.* (*a*) Rentrer dans (un endroit). (*b*) Inscrire de nouveau (un article sur un compte).

re-entrant [ri:'entrənt], *a.* (Angle) rentrant.

re-entry [ri:'entri], *s.* Rentrée *f.*

re-establish [ri:es'tabliʃ], *v.tr.* **I.** Rétablir. *To re-establish s.o. in public esteem,* réhabiliter qn dans l'opinion. **2.** *To re-establish one's health,* se rétablir.

re-establishment [ri:es'tabliʃmənt], *s.* Rétablissement *m*; réintégration *f* (in, dans).

reeve[1] [ri:v], *s.* **I.** *Hist:* Premier magistrat; bailli *m.* **2.** (*In Canada*) Président *m* (du conseil municipal).

reeve[2], *v.tr.* (rove [ro:uv]; reeved, rove) *Nau:* **To reeve a rope,** passer un cordage (*through a block,* dans une poulie). *To r. a tackle,* passer les garants d'un palan. **To reeve a rope to a yard,** capeler un cordage sur une vergue.

re-examination [ri:egzami'neiʃ(ə)n], *s.* **I.** Nouvel examen. **2.** *Jur:* Nouvel interrogatoire.

re-examine [ri:eg'zamin], *v.tr.* **I.** Examiner de nouveau. **2.** *Jur:* Interroger de nouveau (un témoin).

re-export[1] [ri:'ekspo:rt], *s.* Réexportation *f.*

re-export[2] [ri:eks'po:rt], *v.tr.* Réexporter.

refashion [ri:'faʃ(ə)n], *v.tr.* Refaçonner.

refasten [ri:'fɑ:sn], *v.tr.* Rattacher; ragrafer.

refection [ri'fekʃ(ə)n], *s.* **I.** Réfection *f* (des forces, de l'esprit). **2.** Repas léger; collation *f.*

refectory [ri'fektəri], *s.* Réfectoire *m.*

refer [ri'fə:r], *v.* (referred) **I.** *v.tr.* (*a*) Rapporter, rattacher (un fait à une cause). *To r. ill temper to indigestion,* attribuer la mauvaise humeur à l'indigestion. (*b*) **To refer a matter to s.o.,** s'en référer à qn à une question. **To refer a question to s.o.'s decision,** s'en rapporter, s'en remettre, à la décision de qn. *To r. a matter to a tribunal,* soumettre une affaire à un tribunal. (*c*) **To refer s.o. to s.o.,** renvoyer, adresser, qn à qn. **'The reader is referred to . . .,'** "se reporter à . . . ." (*Of bank*) **To refer a cheque to drawer,** refuser d'honorer un chèque (faute de provision). (*d*) *Sch:* Ajourner (un candidat). **2.** *v.i.* (*a*) Se référer (à une autorité); se reporter (à un document). *Referring to your letter . . . ,* comme suite à votre lettre. . . . (*b*) (*Of statement*) **To refer to sth.,** se rapporter, avoir rapport, avoir trait, à qch. (*c*) (*Of pers.*) Faire allusion (à qn). *I am not referring to you,* ce n'est pas à vous que j'en ai. *To r. to a fact*, faire mention d'un fait ; signaler un fait. *We will not r. to it again*, n'en reparlons plus.

referee¹ [refə'ri:], *s. Sp: Jur:* Arbitre *m.* Board of referees, commission arbitrale.

referee², *v.i. & tr.* (refereed) *Sp:* To referee (at) a match, arbitrer un match.

reference ['refərəns], *s.* **I.** (*a*) Renvoi *m*, référence *f* (d'une question à une autorité). (*b*) Compétence *f*, pouvoirs *mpl* (d'un .ribunal). Terms of reference of a commission, mandat *m*, attributions *fpl*, d'une commission. *Outside the r. of the commission*, hors de la compétence de la commission. **2.** (*a*) With reference to *my letter of the* 20 *inst.* . . ., me référant à, comme suite à, ma lettre du 20 ct. . . . *Phot:* Reference plate, plaque témoin. *Surv: etc:* Reference mark, repère *m*. (*b*) Work of reference, ouvrage à consulter, ouvrage de référence. **3.** Rapport *m*. To have reference to sth., avoir rapport, avoir trait, se rapporter, à qch. In reference, with reference, to your letter . . ., en ce qui concerne votre lettre. . . . Without reference to . . ., sans tenir compte de. . . . **4.** To make reference to a fact, faire mention d'un fait, signaler un fait. (*A*) *r. was made to this conversation*, on a fait allusion à, on a parlé de, cette conversation. **5.** Renvoi (dans un livre). (*On map*) Reference point, point coté. Reference Bible, Bible avec parallèles. *Com.Corr:* Reference AB, rappeler dans la réponse AB ; mention AB. *Typ:* Reference mark, renvoi. Foot-note reference, appel *m* de note. **6.** (*a*) *To give a r. concerning s.o.*, fournir des renseignements sur qn. To take up s.o.'s references, prendre des renseignements sur qn. *To have good references*, avoir de bonnes références, de bonnes recommandations. (*b*) (*Pers.*) Référence *f. Jur:* répondant *m. To give s.o. as a r.*, se recommander de qn.

referendum [refə'rendəm], *s.* Referendum *m.*

refill¹ ['ri:fil], *s.* Pile *f* de rechange (pour lampe électrique) ; mine *f* de rechange (pour porte-mine) ; feuilles *fpl* de rechange (pour carnet à feuilles mobiles) ; etc.

refill² [ri:'fil], *v.tr.* (*a*) Remplir (qch.) (à nouveau). *To r. the tanks with water*, regarnir les réservoirs d'eau. *I refilled his glass*, je lui versai une nouvelle rasade. (*b*) *Abs*, Faire le plein (d'essence, etc.). *Aut:* Refilling station, relais *m* d'essence.

refine [ri'fain]. **I.** *v.tr.* (*a*) Raffiner, affiner (les métaux) ; purger (l'or) ; raffiner (le sucre). (*b*) Raffiner (les goûts) ; épurer, purifier (les mœurs). **2.** *v.i.* (*a*) Se raffiner. (*b*) (*Of pers.*) Renchérir (*on, upon*, sur). **refined,** *a.* **I.** (Or) fin, affiné ; (sucre) raffiné. **2.** (Goût) raffiné, délicat ; (homme) distingué, cultivé.

refinement [ri'fainmənt], *s.* **I.** Affinage *m* (des métaux) ; raffinage *m* (du sucre). **2.** Raffinement *m* (du goût, de qn). *A person of r.*, un(e) raffiné(e) ; un(e) délicat(e). **3.** Raffinement, subtilité *f* (de la pensée). *R. of cruelty*, raffinement de cruauté.

refiner [ri'fainər], *s.* Raffineur *m* (de sucre) ; affineur *m* (de métaux).

refinery [ri'fainəri], *s.* (Sugar-)refinery, raffinerie *f.*

refit [ri:'fit], *v.tr.* (refitted) **I.** *Nau:* (i) Radouber, (ii) réarmer (un vaisseau). *Abs.* (*Of ship*) (i) Entrer en radoub ; (ii) réarmer. **2.** Rajuster (une machine, etc.). **3.** Regarnir, remonter (une usine, etc.). **refitting,** *s.* **I.** *Nau:* (*a*) Radoub *m*. (*b*) Réarmement *m*. **2.** Rajustement *m* ; regarnissage *m* (d'une usine) ; remontage *m* (des organes d'une machine).

reflect [ri'flekt]. **I.** *v.tr.* (*a*) (*Of surface*) Ré-

fléchir, refléter (la lumière, une image) ; renvoye (la chaleur, la lumière). *Trees reflected in th water*, arbres qui se reflètent dans l'eau. (*b*) Actio that reflects credit on s.o., action qui fait honneu à qn. *Your glory will be reflected upon you children*, votre gloire rejaillira sur vos enfant **2.** *v.i.* (*a*) Méditer (*on, upon*, sur) ; réfléchir (à sur). To reflect that . . ., penser, se dire que. . . . *To r. how* . . ., se demander com ment. . . . (*b*) To reflect on s.o., adresser un critique, un reproche, à qn. To reflect on s.o.' honour, porter atteinte à l'honneur de qn (*c*) (*Of action*) Faire du tort (*on s.o.*, à qn) nuire à la réputation de (qn).

reflection [ri'flekʃ(ə)n], *s.* **I.** Réfléchissement *m* réflexion *f* (de la lumière, d'une image). *Opt* Angle of reflection, angle de réflexion. **2.** Ré flexion, reflet *m*, image *f. To see one's r. in mirror*, voir son image dans un miroir. **3.** To cas reflections on s.o., censurer, critiquer, qn. *Thi is a r. on your honour*, c'est une atteinte à votr honneur. **4.** On reflection, (toute) réflexion faite *To do sth. without due r.*, faire qch. sans avoi suffisamment réfléchi. **5.** *pl.* Reflections, con sidérations *f*, pensées *f.*

reflective [ri'flektiv], *a.* **I.** (*Of surface*) Qu réfléchit ; réfléchissant. **2.** (Homme, espri réfléchi. **-ly,** *adv.* D'un air réfléchi.

reflector [ri'flektər], *s.* Réflecteur *m. Cy:* Re reflector, cabochon *m* rouge.

reflex¹ ['ri:fleks], *s.* **I.** Reflet *m.* **2.** *Physiol* Réflexe *m.*

reflex², *a.* **I.** *Physiol:* (*Of movement*) Réflexe **2.** (*Of influence*) Indirect. **3.** (*Of thoughts* Introspectif.

reflexion [ri'flekʃ(ə)n], *s.* = REFLECTION.

reflexive [ri'fleksiv], *a. & s. Gram:* (Verbe pronom) réfléchi. **-ly,** *adv.* Au sens réfléchi.

refloat [ri:'flout], *v.tr.* Renflouer, (re)mettre flot (un navire échoué).

reflux ['ri:flʌks], *s.* **I.** Reflux *m* ; refluement *m* **2.** (*Tide*) Jusant *m.*

refoot [ri:'fut], *v.tr.* Rempiéter (un bas).

reform¹ [ri'fɔ:rm], *s.* **I.** Réforme *f* (d'un abus etc.). **2.** Réforme ; retour *m* au bien.

reform². **I.** *v.tr.* (*a*) Réformer (un abus) apporter des réformes à (une administration) (*b*) Réformer, corriger (qn) ; ramener (qn) a bien. **2.** *v.i.* Se réformer, se corriger. **reform ing,** *a.* Réformateur, -trice.

re(-)form [ri:'fɔ:rm]. **I.** *v.tr.* Reformer (ur bataillon, etc.). **2.** *v.i.* (*Of troops*) Se reformer.

reformation [refɔ:r'meiʃ(ə)n], *s.* Réformation *f* réforme *f. Rel.H:* The Reformation, la Réforme

reformatory [ri'fɔ:rmətəri]. **I.** *a.* (Mesures etc.) de réforme. **2.** *s.* École *f* de réforme maison *f* de correction ; prison *f* pour jeune détenus.

reformer [ri'fɔ:rmər], *s.* Réformateur, -trice.

refract [ri'frakt], *v.tr. Ph:* Réfracter, briser (ur rayon de lumière). *To be refracted*, se réfracter **refracting,** *a. Ph:* Réfringent. Double refracting, biréfringent. *S.a.* TELESCOPE¹.

refraction [ri'frakʃ(ə)n], *s. Ph:* Réfraction *f.*

refractive [ri'fraktiv], *a.* Réfractif, réfringent Refractive index, indice *m* de réfraction. Doubl refractive, biréfringent.

refractometer [rifrak'tɔmetər], *s.* Réfracto mètre *m.*

refractory [ri'fraktəri], *a.* **I.** (*Of pers.*) Réfrac taire, indocile, mutin, insoumis. **2.** *Ch:* Réfrac taire ; à l'épreuve du feu. **3.** (Toux, etc. opiniâtre.

refrain¹ [ri'frein], *s. Pros: Mus:* Refrain *m.*

efrain², *v.i.* Se retenir, s'abstenir (*from*, de). *He could not r. from smiling*, il ne put s'empêcher, se défendre, de sourire. *It is impossible to r. from admiring this work*, on ne peut laisser d'admirer ce travail.

efrangible [ri'frand3ibl], *a. Ph:* Réfrangible.

efresh [ri'freʃ], *v.tr.* (*a*) Rafraîchir; (*of rest*) délasser, récréer (qn). *To r. the eye*, reposer l'œil. *To awake refreshed*, s'éveiller bien reposé. *F:* **To refresh the inner man**, se refaire, se restaurer. (*b*) Rafraîchir (la mémoire). **refreshing**, *a.* Rafraîchissant; *F:* ravigotant. *R. sleep*, sommeil reposant, réparateur. *F:* **It was quite refreshing to hear him**, cela faisait du bien de l'entendre.

efresher [ri'freʃər], *s.* **I.** Chose *f* qui rafraîchit. *F:* **Let's have a r.**, on va boire quelque chose. **2.** *Sch:* **Refresher course**, cours *m* de rafraîchissement.

efreshment [ri'freʃmənt], *s.* **I.** (*a*) Rafraîchissement *m*, délassement *m*. (*b*) **To take some refreshment**, manger ou boire quelque chose; se rafraîchir. *Rail:* **Refreshment room**, buffet *m*. **2.** *pl.* **Refreshments**, rafraîchissements (servis au buffet, etc.).

refrigerate [ri'fridʒəreit], *v.tr. Ind:* Réfrigérer, frigorifier, refroidir. **Refrigerated meat**, viande frigorifiée. **refrigerating¹**, *a.* Réfrigérant, frigorifique. **refrigerating²**, *s.* Réfrigération *f*, frigorification *f*. **Refrigerating plant**, appareil *m* frigorifique.

refrigeration [rifridʒə'reiʃ(ə)n], *s.* Réfrigération *f*; frigorification *f*.

refrigerator [ri'fridʒəreitər], *s.* (*a*) Machine *f* frigorifique; congélateur *m*. (*b*) Chambre *f* frigorifique. **Refrigerator van**, wagon *m* frigorifique. (*c*) **(Cabinet-)refrigerator**, glacière *f* (frigorifique).

refringent [ri'frindʒənt], *a. Ph:* Réfringent.

reft [reft]. *See* REAVE.

refuel [ri:'fjuəl], *v.i.* (refuelled) *Nau: etc:* Se réapprovisionner, se ravitailler, en combustible. *Av:* Faire le plein d'essence.

refuge ['refju:dʒ], *s.* **I.** (*a*) Refuge *m*, abri *m* (*from*, contre). **Place of refuge**, lieu *m* de refuge, d'asile. **Haven of refuge**, port de salut. **To seek refuge**, chercher refuge. **To take refuge**, se réfugier (dans une église, etc.). (*b*) *God is my r.*, Dieu est mon recours, mon refuge. **2.** Lieu de refuge, d'asile. **Night refuge**, asile *m* de nuit. **Street-refuge**, refuge.

refugee [refju'dʒi:], *s.* Réfugié, -ée.

refulgence [ri'fʌldʒəns], *s.* Splendeur *f*, éclat *m*.

refulgent [ri'fʌldʒənt], *a.* Resplendissant, éclatant.

refund¹ [ri'fʌnd], *s.* (*a*) Remboursement *m*. (*b*) Ristourne *f*.

refund², *v.tr.* **I.** (*a*) Rembourser (de l'argent) (*to s.o.*, à qn). *To have money refunded*, rencaisser de l'argent. (*b*) Ristourner (un paiement en trop); restituer (de l'argent). **2.** **To refund s.o.**, rembourser qn. **refunding**, *s.* Remboursement *m*.

refundable [ri'fʌndəbl], *a.* Remboursable.

refurnish [ri:'fə:rniʃ], *v.tr.* Meubler de neuf (un appartement); remonter (sa maison).

refusal [ri'fju:z(ə)l], *s.* **I.** Refus *m*. **To give a flat refusal**, refuser (tout) net. **I will take no refusal**, je n'admets pas de refus. *Jur:* **Refusal of justice**, déni *m* de justice. **2.** Droit *m* de refuser. **To have the refusal of sth.**, avoir le droit d'accepter ou de refuser qch. **To have the first refusal of sth.**, avoir la première offre de qch.

refuse¹ ['refju:s]. **I.** *s.* Rebut *m* (de boucherie); déchets *mpl;* épluchures *fpl* (de légumes); ordures *fpl* (de marché). **Household refuse**, ordures ménagères. **Town refuse**, résidus urbains; gadoues *fpl.* **Garden refuse**, balayures *fpl*, détritus *m*, de jardin. **Refuse bin**, boîte *f* à ordures; (*in Fr.*) poubelle *f.* **Refuse dump**, voirie *f;* terrain *m* de décharge. **2.** *a.* De rebut. *Ind:* **Refuse water**, eaux vannes.

refuse² [ri'fju:z], *v.tr.* **I.** Refuser (une offre, un don). *That is not to be refused*, cela n'est pas de refus. **2.** (*a*) Rejeter, repousser (une requête). **To refuse s.o. sth.**, refuser qch. à qn. **He was refused a hearing**, on refusa de l'entendre. *I have never been refused*, on ne m'a jamais rien refusé. (*b*) **To refuse to do sth.**, refuser de faire qch. **se refuser à faire qch. 3.** **Horse that refuses the fences**, cheval qui refuse, qui se dérobe (devant les obstacles).

refutation [refju'teiʃ(ə)n], *s.* Réfutation *f.*

refute [ri'fju:t], *v.tr.* Réfuter (une opinion, qn). *To r. a statement*, démontrer la fausseté d'un dire.

refuter [ri'fju:tər], *s.* Réfutateur, -trice.

regain [ri:'gein, ri'gein], *v.tr.* **I.** Regagner; reconquérir (une province); recouvrer (la liberté). **To regain possession of sth.**, rentrer en possession de qch. **To regain consciousness**, reprendre connaissance, revenir à soi. **To regain one's footing**, reprendre pied. *To r. strength*, reprendre des forces. **2.** Regagner (un endroit).

regal ['ri:g(ə)l], *a.* Royal, -aux. **-ally**, *adv.* Royalement; en roi.

regale [ri'geil], *v.tr.* Régaler. **To regale s.o. with a cold collation, with a story**, régaler qn d'un repas froid, d'une anecdote.

regalia [ri'geilia], *s.pl.* (*a*) Insignes *m* de la royauté; joyaux *m* de la Couronne. (*b*) Insignes (de franc-maçon, etc.).

regard¹ [ri'gɑ:rd], *s.* **I. In this regard**, à cet égard, à ce point de vue. **With regard to . . .**, quant à . . .; pour ce qui concerne . . .; en ce qui se rattache à. . . . *Dispute with r. to a sale*, dispute à l'occasion d'une vente. **In regard to, of . . .**, en ce qui concerne. . . . **2.** Égard *m* (*to, for, à, pour*); attention *f* (*to, qch*). **To pay no regard to . . .**, ne faire aucune attention à. . . . *To have no r. for human life*, faire peu de cas de la vie humaine. *R. must be had, paid, to . . .*, on doit avoir égard à, faire attention à. . . . **Having regard to . . .**, si l'on tient compte de . . .; eu égard à. . . . **3.** (*a*) Égard, respect *m*, estime *f.* **To have (a) great regard for s.o., to hold s.o. in high regard**, tenir qn en haute estime. **To show regard for s.o.**, témoigner de l'estime, des égards, pour qn. **Out of regard for s.o.**, par égard pour qn. (*b*) *pl.* **To send s.o. one's kind regards**, envoyer le bonjour à qn. *Give my kind regards to your brother*, faites mes amitiés à votre frère. **With kind regards from . . .**, avec les sincères amitiés de . . .

regard², *v.tr.* **I.** *A. & Lit:* Regarder (*fixedly*, fixement). **2.** Faire attention, prendre garde, à (qn, qch). **To r. s.o.'s advice**, tenir compte des conseils de qn. **3.** (*a*) **To regard sth. as a crime**, regarder, considérer, qch. comme un crime. (*b*) *To r. sth. with horror*, regarder qch. avec horreur. *To r. sth. with suspicion*, avoir des soupçons au sujet de qch. **4.** Concerner. *That does not regard me*, cela ne me regarde pas. **As regards . . .**, pour ce qui regarde . . .; en ce qui concerne. . . . *As far as regards you*, en ce qui vous touche. **regarding**, *prep.* A l'égard de; concernant; quant à. *R. your enquiry*, en ce qui concerne votre demande. *To entertain* *suspicions r. s.o.*, avoir des soupçons à l'endroit de qn.

regardful [ri'gɑ:rdful], *a.* **1.** Soigneux (*of*, de); attentif (*of*, à). **2.** Plein d'égards (*of s.o.*, pour qn).

regardless [ri'gɑ:rdləs], *a.* Peu soigneux (*of*, de); inattentif (*of*, à). *R. of the consequences*, sans se soucier des conséquences. **Regardless of expense**, sans regarder à la dépense. *P: He was got up regardless*, il s'était mis sur son trente et un.

regatta [ri'gata], *s.* Régate(s) *f(pl)*.

regency ['ri:dʒənsi], *s.* Régence *f*.

regenerate [ri'dʒenəreit]. **1.** *v.tr.* Régénérer. **2.** *v.i.* Se régénérer. **regenerating**, *a.* **1.** Régénérateur, -trice. **2.** *Tchn:* **Regenerating furnace**, (four *m*) régénérateur *m*. **Regenerating plant**, régénérateur.

regeneration [ridʒenə'reiʃ(ə)n], *s.* Régénération *f*.

regenerative [ri'dʒenərətiv], *a.* = REGENERATING.

regenerator [ri'dʒenəreitər], *s.* **1.** (*Pers.*) Régénérateur, -trice. **2.** *Ind:* Régénérateur *m*, récupérateur *m*.

regent ['ri:dʒənt], *a. & s.* Régent, -ente. **Prince regent**, prince régent.

regicide[1] ['redʒisaid], *s. & a.* Régicide (*m*).

regicide[2], *s.* (Crime de) régicide *m*.

regime [re'ʒi:m], *s.* Régime *m*; forme *f* de gouvernement, d'administration.

regimen ['redʒimen], *s. Med: etc:* Régime *m*.

regiment ['redʒimənt], *s.* **1.** Régiment *m*. **2.** *A:* Régime *m*, gouvernement *m*.

regimental [redʒi'ment(ə)l]. **1.** *a.* Du régiment, de régiment; régimentaire. **2.** *s.pl.* **Regimentals**, uniforme *m*. *In full regimentals*, en grand uniforme, en grande tenue.

region ['ri:dʒ(ə)n], *s.* Région *f*. *The arctic regions*, les régions, les terres *f*, arctiques. **The nether regions**, les enfers *m*.

regional ['ri:dʒən(ə)l], *a.* Régional, -aux.

regionalism ['ri:dʒənəlizm], *s.* Régionalisme *m*.

register[1] ['redʒistər], *s.* **1.** (*a*) Registre *m*; matricule *f. Nau:* **Ship's register**, livre *m* de bord. *There are ten million (annuitants, etc.)* on the registers, il y a dix millions d'immatriculés. *The registers of births, marriages, and deaths*, les registres de l'état civil. **Register of voters**, liste électorale. **Trade Register**, registre du Commerce. (*b*) *Nau: Adm:* Lettre *f* de mer (d'un navire); acte *m* de nationalité. **2.** *Mus:* Registre (d'un instrument, de la voix); étendue *f* (de la voix). **3.** Registre (d'un fourneau); rideau *m*, trappe *f* (d'une cheminée). **4.** Compteur *m* (kilométrique, etc.). *S.a.* CASH-REGISTER. **5.** *Typ:* **In register**, en registre. **Out of register**, mal en registre. **'register office**, *s.* = REGISTRY OFFICE.

register[2]. **1.** *v.tr.* (*a*) Enregistrer; inscrire (un nom); immatriculer (une auto). **To register a birth**, déclarer une naissance. **To register a trade-mark**, déposer une marque de fabrique. **To register (oneself) with the police**, se faire inscrire à la police (pour permis de séjour, etc.). (*b*) **To register luggage**, enregistrer des bagages. **To register a letter**, (i) recommander une lettre; (ii) (valeur déclarée) charger une lettre. (*c*) (*Of thermometer, etc.*) Marquer (tant de degrés). (*d*) *Typ: Engr:* Repérer (les impressions). (*e*) *Cin: U.S:* Enregistrer (une émotion). *F: His face registered disappointment*, son visage a témoigné de la déception. **2.** *v.i.* (*a*) (*Of holes and pins, etc.*) Coïncider exactement. *Typ:* Être

en registre. (*b*) S'inscrire sur le registre (d'un hôtel, etc.).

registrar ['redʒistrɑ:r], *s.* **1.** *Jur:* Greffier *m*. **2.** Officier *m* de l'état civil. *The registrar's office*, le bureau de l'état civil. **The Registrar General**, le Conservateur des actes de l'état civil. *To get married before the r.*, se marier civilement. **3.** Secrétaire *m* et archiviste *m* (d'une université).

registration [redʒis'treiʃ(ə)n], *s.* **1.** Enregistrement *m*, inscription *f*; immatriculation *f* (d matériel roulant, etc.). *R. of a trade-mark*, dépôt *m* d'une marque de fabrique. **Registration of luggage**, inscription des bagages. **(Hotel) registration form**, fiche policière. **Registration number**, immatricule *f*; numéro *m* matricule. *Aut:* **Registration plate**, plaque de contrôle, de police **2.** *Engr: Typ:* Repérage *m*.

registry ['redʒistri], *s.* **1.** Enregistrement *m Nau:* **Certificate of registry**, lettre *f* de mer acte *m* de nationalité. **Port of registry**, por d'armement; port d'attache. **2.** **Registry (office)**. (*a*) Bureau *m* d'enregistrement; greffe *m* (*b*) Bureau de l'état civil. **To be married at registry (office)**, se marier civilement. (*c*) Bureau agence *f*, de placement (de domestiques).

reglet ['reglet], *s. Arch: Typ:* Réglet *m*.

regress[1] ['ri:gres], *s.* (*a*) Retour *m* en arrière rétrogression *f*. (*b*) *Astr:* Rétrogradation *f*.

regress[2] [ri'gres], *v.i. Astr:* Rétrograder.

regression [ri'greʃ(ə)n], *s.* **1.** = REGRESS[1] **2.** *Biol:* Régression *f*. **3.** *Mth:* Rebroussement *m* (d'une courbe).

regressive [ri'gresiv], *a.* Régressif.

regret[1] [ri'gret], *s.* Regret *m. To feel r.*, éprouve du regret. *To have no regrets*, n'avoir aucun regret. *I state the fact with r.*, je le dis à regret **Much to my regret**, *I find myself constrained to . . .*, à mon grand regret, je me vois force de. . . . *It is to be regretted that . . .*, il est à regretter, il est regrettable, que + *sub*.

regret[2], *v.tr.* (regretted) Regretter. *I r. having deceived him*, j'ai regret de l'avoir trompé. *I r. to have to leave you*, je regrette d'avoir à vous quitter. *I r. to have to inform you that . . .*, j'a le regret de vous annoncer que. . . . *We very much r. to hear . . .*, nous sommes désolés d'apprendre. . . . *It is to be regretted that . . .*, il est à regretter, il est regrettable, que + *sub*.

regretful [ri'gretful], *a.* (*Of pers.*) Plein de regrets. **-fully**, *adv.* Avec regret, à regret.

regrettable [ri'gretəbl], *a.* Regrettable; à regretter.

regroup [ri:'gru:p], *v.tr.* Reclasser, regrouper.

regular ['regjulər]. **I.** *a.* Régulier. **1.** *R. footsteps* pas réguliers, mesurés. *F:* **As regular as clock-work**, exact comme une horloge; réglé comme du papier à musique. **My regular time for going to bed**, l'heure habituelle à laquelle je me couche. **To do sth. as a regular thing**, faire qch. régulière-ment. *Rail:* **The regular travellers**, les abonnés *m. (At restaurant)* **Our regular waiter**, notre garçon habituel. **Regular staff**, employés per-manents. **2.** Réglé, rangé. **Man of regular habits**, homme rangé dans ses habitudes. **3.** (*a*) Dans les règles; réglementaire. *The r. expression*, l'expression consacrée. **To make regular**, régu-lariser (sa position, etc.). (*b*) Ordinaire; normal, -aux. *Ind:* **Regular model**, modèle courant; type courant. (*c*) *Gram:* (Verbe) régulier. (*d*) (*Cui-sinier*, médecin) de profession; (médecin, etc.) diplômé. (*e*) *Mil:* **Regular troops**, troupes régulières. **Regular officer**, officier de carrière. **4.** *F:* (*Intensive*) Vrai, véritable. *R. rascal*, vrai coquin. **Regular set-to**, bataille *f* en règle. **-ly**, *adv.* **1.** Régulièrement. **2.** *F:* Véritablement, franchement. **II. regular**, *s.* **I.** *Ecc :* Régulier *m* ; religieux *m.* **2.** *Mil :* Soldat *m* de l'armée permanente. **Regulars**, troupes régulières.

regularity [regju'lariti], *s.* Régularité *f.* **Regularity of attendance**, assiduité *f.*

regularize ['regjuləra:iz], *v.tr.* Régulariser.

regulate ['regjuleit], *v.tr.* **I.** Régler, ajuster (une machine, etc.). **2.** Régler, diriger (les affaires) ; réglementer (les affaires) ; fixer les règles pour (une procédure, etc.). **To regulate one's life by s.o.**, se régler sur qn.

regulation [regju'leiʃ(ə)n], *s.* **I.** (*a*) Réglage *m* (d'un chronomètre, etc.) ; *Nau :* régulation *f* (des compas). (*b*) Règlement *m*, réglementation *f* (des affaires, etc.). **To bring under regulation**, réglementer. **2.** (*a*) Règlement, arrêté *m*, ordonnance *f.* **Hospital regulations**, régime *m* des hôpitaux. (*b*) *Attrib.* Réglementaire. *Mil :* **Regulation revolver**, revolver d'ordonnance.

regulator ['regjuleitər], *s.* **I.** (*Pers.*) Régulateur, -trice ; régleur. **2.** (*Device*) Régulateur *m* ; modérateur *m* (de moteur). *Mch :* **Regulator-lever**, registre *m* (de prise de vapeur).

regurgitate [ri'gə:rdʒiteit]. **I.** *v.tr.* Régurgiter, regorger. **2.** *v.i.* (*Of liquid, etc.*) Refluer, regorger.

regurgitation [rigə:rdʒi'teiʃ(ə)n], *s.* Régurgitation *f.*

rehabilitate [ri:ha'biliteit], *v.tr.* Réhabiliter.

rehabilitating, *a.* (*Of order, etc.*) Réhabilitant, réhabilitoire.

rehabilitation [ri:nabili'teiʃ(ə)n], *s.* **I.** Réhabilitation *f.* **2.** Assainissement *m* (des finances).

rehandle¹ [ri:'handl], *v.tr.* Remmancher (un outil, etc.).

rehandle², *v.tr.* Traiter à nouveau (un sujet).

reharden [ri:'ha:rd(ə)n], *v.tr.* *Metall :* Retremper (le métal). **rehardening**, *s.* Retrempe *f.*

rehear [ri:'hi:ər], *v.tr.* (**reheard** [ri:'hə:rd]) Entendre (une cause, etc.) de nouveau.

rehearsal [ri'hə:rs(ə)l], *s.* **I.** Récit détaillé, relation *f* (des aventures de qn). **2.** *Th :* Répétition *f.* **The dress rehearsal**, la (répétition) générale ; l'avant-première *f.*

rehearse [ri'hə:rs], *v.tr.* **I.** Raconter tout au long ; énumérer (des faits) ; repasser (une liste) ; réciter (des prières). **2.** *Th :* Répéter (une pièce).

reheat [ri:'hi:t], *v.tr.* (*a*) Réchauffer. (*b*) *Metall :* Recuire, réchourir.

reign¹ [rein], *s.* Règne *m.* **In, under, the reign of . . .**, sous le règne de. . .

reign², *v.i.* Régner (*over*, sur).

reimbursable [ri:im'bə:rsəbl], *a.* Remboursable.

reimburse [ri:im'bə:rs], *v.tr.* **I.** Rembourser (une somme). **2. To reimburse s.o. (for) his costs**, rembourser qn de ses frais.

reimbursement [ri:im'bə:rsmənt], *s.* Remboursement *m.*

reimport [ri:im'pɔ:rt], *v.tr.* Réimporter.

reimportation [ri:impɔ:r'teiʃ(ə)n], *s.* Réimportation *f.*

reimpose [ri:im'pouz], *v.tr.* *Typ :* Réimposer (une feuille) ; remanier (les pages).

reimposition [ri:impo'ziʃ(ə)n], *s.* Réimposition *f.*

rein¹ [rein], *s.* Rêne *f* (de cheval monté) ; guide *f* (de cheval de voiture). **Bearing-rein, check-rein**, fausses rênes. **To hold the reins**, tenir les rênes ; tenir la bride ; *Veh :* tenir les guides. **With a loose rein, with a slack rein**, (i) (chevaucher) à bout de rênes ; (ii) *F :* (mener ses gens) mollement. **To give a horse the reins**, lâcher la bride à un cheval. **To give rein to one's anger**, lâcher la bride à sa colère. **To draw rein**, serrer

a bride ; s'arrêter. **To keep a tight rein on**, over, s.o., tenir la bride serrée, tenir la bride haute, à qn. **To drop the reins**, abandonner les rênes ; *F :* abandonner.

rein², *v.tr.* **To rein in a horse**, serrer la bride à un cheval. *Abs.* **To rein in**, ramener son cheval au pas. *F :* **To rein s.o. in**, ramener qn sous la discipline. **To rein up a horse**, arrêter un cheval.

reincarnation [ri:inka:r'neiʃ(ə)n], *s.* Réincarnation *f.*

reincorporate [ri:in'kɔ:rporeit], *v.tr.* Réincorporer.

reindeer ['reindi:ər], *s.* *Z :* Renne *m.* *A herd of reindeer*, un troupeau de rennes.

reinflate [ri:in'fleit], *v.tr.* Regonfler (un ballon).

reinforce [ri:in'fɔ:rs], *v.tr.* **I.** Renforcer (une armée, un son) ; appuyer (une demande). **2.** Renforcer (un mur, etc.) ; consolider (des fondations) ; entretoiser (un bâtiment) ; nervurer (une tôle, etc.). **Reinforced concrete**, béton armé.

reinforcement [ri:in'fɔ:rsmənt , *s.* **I.** (*a*) *Mil :* Renforcement *m* (d'une garnison). (*b*) *Const : etc :* Renforcement, renforçage *m* ; armature *f* (du béton). **2.** *Mil :* (*Usu. pl.*) **To await reinforcements**, attendre un renfort, des renforts.

reinsert [ri:in'sə:rt], *v.tr.* **I.** Réinsérer. **2.** Remettre (une pièce) en place.

reinstall [ri:in'stɔ:l], *v.tr.* Réinstaller.

reinstate [ri:in'steit], *v.tr.* **I.** Réintégrer (qn) (dans ses fonctions) ; rétablir (un fonctionnaire). **2.** Remettre, rétablir (qch.).

reinstatement [ri:in'steitmənt], *s.* **I.** Réintégration *f* (de qn dans ses fonctions). **2.** Rétablissement *m* (de qch.).

reinsurance [ri:in'ʃuərəns], *s.* *Ins :* Réassurance *f* ; contre-assurance *f.*

reinsure [ri:in'ʃuər], *v.tr.* *Ins :* Réassurer.

reinter [ri:in'tə:r], *v.tr.* (**reinterred**) Enterrer de nouveau.

reinvest [ri:in'vest], *v.tr.* Trouver un nouveau placement pour (des fonds).

reinvestment [ri:in'vestmənt], *s.* *Fin :* Nouveau placement.

reinvigorate [ri:in'vigəreit], *v.tr.* Redonner de la vigueur à (qn) ; *F :* retremper, ravigoter.

reissue¹ [ri:'iʃju:, -'isju:], *s.* **I.** Nouvelle émission (de billets de banque, etc.). **2.** *Publ :* Nouvelle édition ou nouveau tirage.

reissue², *v.tr.* **I.** *Fin :* Émettre de nouveau (des actions, etc.). **2.** Donner une nouvelle édition ou un nouveau tirage (d'un livre).

reiterate [ri:'itəreit], *v.tr.* Réitérer, répéter.

reiteration [ri:itə'reiʃ(ə)n], *s.* Réitération *f*, répétition *f.*

reiterative [ri:'itərativ], *a.* Réitératif.

reject¹ ['ri:dʒekt], *s.* Pièce *f* de rebut.

reject² [ri'dʒekt], *v.tr.* (*a*) Rejeter, repousser (une offre) ; rejeter (un projet de loi) ; réprouver (une doctrine). (*b*) Refuser (des marchandises, un candidat). *Ind :* **To r. a casting**, mettre une pièce au rebut.

rejection [ri'dʒekʃ(ə)n], *s.* **I.** Rejet *m* (d'un projet de loi, etc.) ; repoussement *m* (d'une mesure) ; refus *m* (d'une offre). **2.** *pl.* *Ind :* Rejections, pièces *f* de rebut ; rebuts *m.*

rejoice [ri'dʒɔis]. **I.** *v.tr.* Réjouir (qn). *I am rejoiced to hear it*, je me réjouis, je suis heureux, de l'entendre. **2.** *v.i.* (*a*) Se réjouir (*at, over*, de). (*b*) *F :* **To rejoice in sth.**, jouir de qch. ; posséder qch. **rejoicing¹**, *a.* **I.** (*Of news, etc.*) Réjouissant. **2.** Joyeux, jubilant ; qui se réjouit.

rejoicing², *s.* **I.** Réjouissance *f*, allégresse *f.* **2.** *pl.* **The rejoicings**, les réjouissances ; la fête.

rejoin[1] [ri'dʒɔin], *v.i.* Répliquer, répondre.
rejoin[2] [ri:'dʒɔin]. **I.** *v.tr.* (*a*) Rejoindre, réunir (*to, with*, à). (*b*) Rejoindre (qn, son régiment). *Mil: The scouts rejoined their unit*, les éclaireurs rallièrent leur unité. **To rejoin one's ship**, rallier le bord. **2.** *v.i.* (*Of lines. etc.*) Se réunir, se rejoindre.
rejoinder [ri'dʒɔindər], *s.* Réplique *f*, repartie *f*.
rejuvenate [ri'dʒu:veneit], *v.tr. & i.* Rajeunir.
rejuvenation [ridʒu:ve'neiʃ(ə)n], *s.* **I.** (*a*) Rajeunissement *m.* (*b*) *Med:* Régénérescence *f.* **2.** Cure *f* de rajeunissement.
rekindle [ri:'kindl]. **I.** *v.tr.* Rallumer (le feu); ranimer (l'espoir). **2.** *v.i.* Se rallumer.
relapse[1] [ri'laps], *s.* **I.** *R. into sin*, rechute *f* dans le péché. *R. into crime*, récidive *f.* **2.** *Med:* Rechute. **To have a relapse**, faire une rechute; rechuter.
relapse[2], *v.i.* **I.** *To r. into vice*, retomber dans le vice. *To r. into crime*, récidiver. *Theol: Relapsed heretic*, relaps, *f.* relapse. **2.** *Med:* Rechuter; avoir une rechute.
relate [ri'leit]. **I.** *v.tr.* Raconter, conter (une histoire); rapporter, *Jur:* relater (les faits). *To r. one's adventures*, faire le récit de ses aventures. **Strange to relate !** chose étonnante à dire ! **2.** (*a*) *v.tr. Nat.Hist: etc:* Rapporter, rattacher (une espèce à une famille); établir un rapport entre (deux faits). (*b*) *v.i.* Se rapporter, avoir rapport (*to*, à). *Agreement relating to . . .*, convention ayant trait à. . . . **related**, *a.* **I.** (*a*) Ayant rapport (*to*, à). (*b*) **Related ideas**, idées connexes. *Ch:* **Related elements**, éléments apparentés. *Mus:* **Related keys**, tons relatifs. **2.** (*Of pers.*) Apparenté (*to*, à); parent (*to*, de); (*by marriage*) allié (*to*, à). *He is r. to us*, il est notre parent. **They are nearly, closely, related**, ils sont proches parents. **They are very distantly related**, ils sont parents à un degré très éloigné; *F:* ils sont cousins à la mode de Bretagne. **relating**, *a.* **Relating to . . .**, relatif à . . .; qui se rapporte à. . . . *Information r. to a matter*, renseignements afférents à une affaire.
relater [ri'leitər], *s.* Conteur, -euse; narrateur, -trice.
relation [ri'leiʃ(ə)n], *s.* **I.** Relation *f*, récit *m* (d'événements). **2.** (*a*) Relation, rapport *m.* **In relation to . . .**, relativement à . . .; par rapport à. . . . **To bear a relation to . .**, avoir rapport à. . . . *That has no r. to the present situation*, cela n'a rien à faire, rien à voir, avec la situation actuelle. (*b*) *pl.* **To have (business) relations with s.o.**, être en relations (d'affaires) avec qn. **To enter into relations with s.o.**, entrer en rapport, en relations, avec qn; entamer des relations avec qn. **To break off all relations with s.o.**, rompre toutes relations, cesser tout rapport, avec qn. **3.** Parent, -ente. **Near relation**, proche parent. **Relation by marriage**, allié, -ée. *Distant r.*, parent éloigné. *Parents and relations*, ascendants directs et collatéraux. **What relation is he to you?** quelle est sa parenté avec vous? **Is he any relation to you?** est-il de vos parents?
relationship [ri'leiʃənʃip], *s.* **I.** (*a*) Rapport *m* (entre deux choses). (*b*) (*Of pers.*) **To be in relationship with s.o.**, avoir des relations avec qn; être en rapport avec qn. **2.** Parenté *f*; lien *m* de parenté. **Blood relationship**, proximité *f* de sang.
relative [ri'lətiv]. **I.** *a.* (*a*) Relatif, qui se rapporte (*to*, à). (*b*) (*Of terms, etc.*) Relatif. *R. positions of two parts*, positions relatives de deux organes. *They live in r. luxury*, par rapport aux autres ils vivent dans le luxe. (*c*) *Gram:* **Relative pronoun**, pronom relatif. **2.** *adv. F: I am writing

relative to the rent, je vous écris par rapport au loyer, au sujet du loyer. **3.** *s.* = RELATION 3.
-ly, *adv.* (*a*) Relativement (*to*, à); par rapport (à). (*b*) *F: She is r. happy*, somme toute elle est assez heureuse.
relativity [relə'tiviti], *s.* Relativité *f.*
relax [ri'laks]. **I.** *v.tr.* (*a*) Relâcher (les muscles, la discipline); détendre, délasser (l'esprit); détendre, débander (un arc). *The serpent relaxed its hold*, le serpent desserra son étreinte. (*b*) **To relax the bowels**, relâcher le ventre. (*c*) *Med:* **Relaxed throat**, pharyngite subaiguë. (*d*) Mitiger (une loi, une peine). **2.** *v.i.* (*a*) (*Of muscles, etc.*) Se relâcher, se détendre. **His face relaxed into a smile**, son visage se détendit dans un sourire. (*b*) (*Of pers.*) Se détendre. *To r. for an hour*, prendre une heure de délassement. **relaxing**, *a.* (Climat) énervant, débilitant, mou; (médicament) relâchant, laxatif.
relaxation [ri:lak'seiʃ(ə)n], *s.* **I.** (*a*) Relâchement *m* (des muscles, de la discipline). (*b*) Mitigation *f*, adoucissement *m* (d'une loi). **2.** Délassement *m*, repos *m*, détente *f.* **To take some relaxation**, se donner un peu de relâche; se délasser. *These little jobs come as a r.*, ces petits travaux me dissipent. **To seek relaxation in books**, se délasser dans les livres.
relay[1] [ri'lei], *s.* **I.** Relais *m* (d'hommes, de chevaux); relève *f* (d'ouvriers). **To work in relays**, se relayer. **Relay horse**, (i) cheval de relais; (ii) cheval de renfort. *Sp:* **Relay race**, course de, à, relais. **2.** (*a*) *El.E:* Relais; contacteur *m.* *Tg:* Répétiteur *m.* (*b*) Servo-moteur *m.* **3.** *W.Tel:* Radio-diffusion relayée. **re'lay station**, *s.* Relais *m*; poste amplificateur.
relay[2], *v.tr.* (relayed [ri'leid]) *Tg: W.Tel:* Relayer (un message, un programme); transmettre (un message) par relais.
re-lay [ri:'lei], *v.tr.* (re-laid [-leid]) **I.** Poser (un tapis, etc.) de nouveau; remettre (la nappe). **2.** Reposer (une voie ferrée); remanier (une canalisation).
release[1] [ri'li:s], *s.* **I.** (*a*) (*Of pers.*) Délivrance *f* (*from*, de); décharge *f*, libération *f* (*from an obligation*, d'une obligation). (*b*) Élargissement *m*, mise *f* en liberté, *Jur:* relaxation *f* (d'un prisonnier). **Order of release**, (ordre de) levée *f* d'écrou. (*c*) Mise *f* en vente (d'une nouvelle auto, etc.). *Cin:* Mise en circulation (d'un film). **2.** (*a*) *Ch:* Dégagement *m* (d'un gaz). *Mch:* Échappement *m* (de la vapeur). (*b*) *Av:* Lâchage *m* (d'une bombe); lancement *m* (d'un parachute). (*c*) *Mec.E: etc:* Mise en marche (d'un appareil); déclenchement *m* (d'un ressort); dégagement *m*, desserrage *m* (d'un frein). **Release gear**, déclancheur *m*, déclic *m.* *Phot:* **Shutter-release**, déclancheur *m.* **Bulb release**, déclancheur à poire. **Trigger release**, déclenchement au doigt. **3.** *El.E:* Disjoncteur *m*, interrupteur *m.* **4.** *Com:* Acquit *m*, quittance *f.* **5.** *Jur:* Cession *f* (de terres).
release[2], *v.tr.* **I.** (*a*) Décharger, acquitter, libérer (qn d'une obligation). **To release s.o. from his promise**, délier qn de sa promesse; rendre sa parole à qn. (*b*) Libérer, élargir, relâcher (un prisonnier). *Released on bail*, remis en liberté sous caution. (*c*) Lâcher (des pigeons voyageurs, *Mil:* des gaz asphyxiants). (*d*) Mettre en vente (une nouvelle auto, etc.). *Cin:* Mettre (un film) en circulation. **2.** (*a*) *Ch:* Dégager (un gaz); émettre (de la fumée). (*b*) *Av:* Lâcher (une bombe); lancer (un parachute). (*c*) Faire jouer (un ressort); déclinquer (un doigt d'encliquetage); déclancher, décoller (un organe). **To release one's hold**, lâcher prise. **To release

the brake, dégager, desserrer, le frein. *To r. the trigger* (*of a gun*), faire jouer la gâchette. *Phot :* **To release the shutter**, déclancher l'obturateur. **3.** *Jur :* (*a*) **To release a debt**, faire (à qn) la remise d'une dette. (*b*) Renoncer à (un droit). (*c*) Céder (une terre).

relegate ['relegeit], *v.tr.* **1.** Reléguer (un tableau au grenier, etc.). *To r. one's wife to the position of a servant*, ravaler sa femme au rôle de servante. **2.** *To r. a matter to s.o.*, (i) remettre une question à la décision de qn ; (ii) confier une affaire à qn.

relent [ri'lent], *v.i.* Se laisser attendrir ; revenir sur une décision (sévère). *He would not r.* (*towards me*), il me tenait-rigueur.

relentless [ri'lentləs], *a.* (*a*) Implacable, impitoyable. (*b*) *R. persecution*, persécution sans rémission. *To be r. in doing sth.*, mettre de l'acharnement à faire qch. **-ly**, *adv.* (*a*) Implacablement, impitoyablement. (*b*) Sans rémission.

relentlessness [ri'lentləsnəs], *s.* Inflexibilité *f*, implacabilité *f* ; acharnement *m*.

relevance ['reləvəns], **relevancy** ['reləvənsi], *s.* Pertinence *f*, à-propos *m* ; rapport *m* (*to*, avec).

relevant ['reləvənt], *a.* Qui a rapport (*to*, à) ; pertinent (*to*, à) ; à propos (*to*, de). *The r. documents*, les documents qui se rapportent à l'affaire. *All r. information*, tous renseignements utiles.

reliability [rilaiə'biliti], *s.* Sûreté *f* ; honnêteté *f*, véracité *f* (de qn) ; sécurité *f* du fonctionnement, régularité *f* de marche (d'une machine). *Aut :* **Reliability trial**, épreuve *f* de régularité, d'endurance.

reliable [ri'laiəbl], *a.* Sûr ; (homme) sérieux, digne de confiance ; (ami) solide ; (renseignement) sûr, digne de foi ; (machine) d'un fonctionnement sûr. *R. firm*, maison de confiance. *R. guarantee*, garantie solide. *Jur :* **R. witness**, témoin sans reproche.

reliance [ri'laiəns], *s.* Confiance *f.* **To place reliance in**, **(up)on**, **s.o.**, avoir confiance en qn ; se fier à qn ; compter sur qn. *I put little r. in him*, je fais peu de fond sur lui.

reliant [ri'laiənt], *a.* **To be reliant on . . .**, (i) avoir confiance en . . . ; compter sur . . . ; (ii) dépendre de (qn pour vivre). *S.a.* SELF-RELIANT.

relic ['relik], *s.* **1.** *Ecc :* Relique *f.* **2.** *pl.* **Relics**, restes *m.* (*a*) Dépouille mortelle. (*b*) *Relics of the past*, vestiges *m* du passé ; survivance *f* des temps passés.

relict ['relikt], *s.* *Jur :* Veuve *f* (*of*, de).

relief[1] [ri'li:f], *s.* **1.** (*a*) Soulagement *m* (d'une douleur) ; allégement *m* (d'une détresse). **To heave a sigh of relief**, pousser un soupir de soulagement. *It was a r. to me when . . .*, je fus soulagé quand. . . . (*b*) *Black costume without r.*, toilette noire sans agrément. *A comic scene follows by way of r.*, une scène comique suit pour détendre les esprits. (*c*) Décharge*f.* *Mch :* **Relief cock**, décompresseur *m.* **2.** (*a*) **To go to s.o.'s relief**, aller, se porter, au secours de qn, à l'aide de qn. **Relief fund**, caisse *f* de secours (en cas de sinistre). **Relief engine**, locomotive remorqueuse. (*b*) *Adm :* **(Poor-)relief**, secours, aide *f*, aux pauvres ; assistance publique. **Out(door) relief**, secours à domicile. **3.** *Mil :* (*a*) Dégagement *m* (d'une place forte). **Relief troops**, troupes de secours. (*b*) **Relève** (d'une garde, etc.). **Relief party, draft of reliefs**, détachement *m* de relève ; une relève. **4.** *Jur :* Réparation *f* (d'un grief) ; redressement *m* (d'un tort). **5.** *Mec.E :* Dégagement *m*, dépouille *f* (d'un foret, etc.).

relief-valve, *s.* *Mch :* Soupape *f* de sûreté, de décompression.

relief[2], *s.* *Art :* Relief *m* ; modelé *m.* **High relief**, **low relief**, haut-relief, bas-relief. **In relief**, **en relief**. *To stand out in r.*, ressortir, se détacher (*against*, sur). **To bring, throw, sth. into relief**, faire ressortir qch. ; mettre qch. en relief. **Relief map**, carte en relief.

relieve [ri'li:v], *v.tr.* **1.** (*a*) Soulager, alléger (les souffrances). **To relieve s.o.'s mind**, tranquilliser l'esprit de qn. **To relieve one's feelings**, se décharger le cœur. *F :* **To relieve nature**, faire ses besoins ; se soulager. (*b*) *Black bodice relieved with white lace*, corsage noir agrémenté de dentelle blanche. *To r. the tedium of the journey*, tromper, dissiper, l'ennui du voyage. (*c*) Soulager, décharger (une soupape, etc.). **To relieve congestion**, (i) faciliter la circulation (aux heures d'affluence) ; (ii) *Med :* décongestionner (les poumons). **2.** Secourir, aider, assister (qn) ; venir en aide à (qn). **3.** **To relieve s.o. of sth.**, soulager, délester, qn (d'un fardeau) ; débarrasser qn (de son manteau) ; dégager qn (d'une obligation) ; relever qn (de ses fonctions). *Relieved of anxiety*, hors d'inquiétude ; allégé de souci. *F :* **To relieve s.o. of his purse**, soulager qn de son porte-monnaie. **4.** (*a*) *Mil :* Dégager (une ville). (*b*) Relever (des troupes, une sentinelle) ; relayer (qn). *Nau :* **To relieve the watch**, faire la relève. **5.** *Mec.E :* Dépouiller, dégager (un foret, etc.). **6.** *Art :* Relever, mettre en relief, donner du relief à (un motif) ; faire ressortir (une couleur). *Relieved against a dark background*, qui se découpe, qui se détache, qui tranche, sur un fond noir. **relieving**, *a.* **1.** *Adm :* **Relieving officer**, commissaire *m* du bureau de bienfaisance. **2.** (*a*) *Mil :* (Armée) de secours. (*b*) (Équipe, etc.) de relève. **3.** *Arch :* **Relieving arch**, voûte *f* de décharge ; *Civ.E :* arche *f* de soutènement.

relievo [ri'li:vo], *s.* *Art :* Relief *m.* **Alto relievo**, haut-relief *m.* **Basso relievo**, bas-relief.

relight [ri:'lait], *v.tr.* Rallumer.

religion [ri'lidʒən], *s.* Religion *f* ; culte *m.* *Adm :* *Mil :* Confession *f.* **Established religion**, religion d'État. **To enter into religion**, entrer en religion. *F :* **To get religion**, (i) se convertir ; (ii) devenir bigot. **To make a religion of doing sth.**, se faire une religion de faire qch.

religious [ri'lidʒəs], **1.** *a.* (*a*) Religieux, pieux, dévot. (*b*) (Ordre) religieux. *R. book*, livre de piété, de dévotion. *R. minorities*, minorités de religion. (*c*) *F :* (Soin) religieux, scrupuleux. **2.** *s.* (*sing. in pl.*) *Ecc :* Religieux, -euse. **-ly**, *adv.* Religieusement. (*a*) Pieusement. (*b*) *F :* Scrupuleusement.

re-line [ri:'lain], *v.tr.* **1.** Remettre une doublure à (un manteau) ; rentoiler (un tableau, etc.). **2.** Regarnir (un frein, etc.).

relinquish [ri'liŋkwiʃ], *v.tr.* **1.** Abandonner (une habitude, tout espoir) ; renoncer à (un projet, un droit) ; se dessaisir de (ses biens). *Jur :* Délaisser (un droit, une succession). **2.** Lâcher (qch.).

relinquishment [ri'liŋkwiʃmənt], *s.* Abandon *m* (de ses biens) ; renonciation *f* (*of a right*, à un droit).

reliquary ['relikwəri], *s.* Reliquaire *m.*

relish[1] ['reliʃ], *s.* **1.** (*a*) Goût *m*, saveur *f* (d'un mets). *His food has no more r. for him*, il ne trouve plus de goût à sa nourriture. *F :* **The relish of novelty**, le ragoût, l'attrait de la nouveauté. (*b*) Assaisonnement *m.* *F :* **With hunger for a relish**, avec la faim pour assaisonnement. (*c*) *Cu :* Soupçon *m*, pointe *f* (de piment,

etc.). **2.** To eat sth. with relish, manger qch. de bon appétit. *He used to tell the story with great r.,* il se délectait à raconter cette histoire. **To have a relish for sth.,** avoir le goût de, avoir du goût pour, qch.
relish². **I.** *v.tr.* (*a*) Relever le goût de (qch.). (*b*) (*Of pers.*) Goûter, savourer (un mets). *F :* **To relish doing sth.,** trouver du plaisir à faire qch. *We did not r. the idea,* l'idée ne nous souriait pas. **2.** *v.i.* **To relish of sth.,** avoir un léger goût de qch. ; sentir (l'ail, etc.).
reload [ri:'loud], *v.tr.* Recharger.
reluctance [ri'lʌktəns], *s.* **I.** Répugnance (*to do sth.,* à faire qch.). **To do sth. with reluctance,** faire qch. à regret, à contre-cœur. **To affect reluctance,** faire des manières. **2.** *El :* Reluctance *f.*
reluctant [ri'lʌktənt], *a.* **I.** Qui agit à contre-cœur. **To be reluctant to do sth.,** être peu disposé, hésiter, à faire qch. *I feel r. to . . .,* il me répugne de. . . . **2.** (Consentement) accordé à contre-cœur. **-ly,** *adv.* Avec répugnance ; à contre-cœur. *I say it r.,* il m'en coûte de le dire.
reluctivity [relʌk'tiviti], *s. El :* Reluctivité *f.*
rely [ri'lai], *v.i.* To rely (up)on s.o., compter sur qn ; se fier à qn. *To r. on s.o.'s evidence,* faire fond sur le témoignage de qn. *We cannot r. on the weather,* le temps n'est pas sûr.
remain¹ [ri'mein], *s.* **I.** Reste *m.* **2.** *pl.* Restes (d'un repas, d'un édifice) ; vestiges *m* (d'une ancienne voie) ; œuvres *f* posthumes (d'un auteur). **Mortal remains,** restes mortels ; dépouille mortelle. *To discover* **human remains,** découvrir des ossements *m.*
remain², *v.i.* **I.** Rester. **This objection remains,** cette objection subsiste. **The fact remains that . . .,** il n'en est pas moins vrai que. . . . *Much yet remains to be done,* il reste encore beaucoup à faire. **It remains to be seen whether . . .,** reste à savoir si. . . . **2.** Demeurer, rester. (*a*) *To r. at home,* rester à la maison. *To r. sitting,* demeurer assis. **To remain beh·nd,** rester ; ne pas partir. (*b*) *Let it r. as it is,* laissez-le comme cela. **3.** (*a*) *The weather remains fine,* le temps se maintient au beau. (*b*) *Corr :* I **remain, Sir, yours truly,** agréez, Monsieur, mes salutations empressées. **remaining,** *a. I have four r.,* j'en ai quatre de reste. *The r.* **travellers,** le reste des voyageurs.
remainder¹ [ri'meindər], *s.* **I.** (*a*) Reste *m,* restant *m* (de fortune). *The r. of his life,* le reste de sa vie. (*b*) *Ar :* Division *with no r..* division sans reste. **2.** (*a*) *Coll.* **The remainder,** les autres *mf.* (*b*) *Publ :* Remainders, remainder line, fin *f* de série ; solde *m* d'édition. **3.** *The estate is left to A with r. to B,* la succession passe à A avec réversion sur B.
remainder², *v.tr.* Solder (une édition).
remake [ri:'meik], *v.tr.* (Conj. like MAKE) Refaire. **remaking,** *s.* Réfection *f.*
remand¹ [ri'mɑ:nd], *s. Jur :* Renvoi *m* (d'un prévenu) à une autre audience. **Detention under remand,** détention préventive.
remand², *v.tr. Jur :* Renvoyer (un prévenu) à une autre audience. *He was remanded for a week,* son cas a été remis à huitaine.
remanence ['remənəns], *s. Magn :* Remanence *f.*
remanent ['remənənt], *a.* (Magnétisme) remanent, résiduel.
remark¹ [ri'mɑ:rk], *s.* **I.** Remarque *f,* attention *f.* **Things worthy of remark,** choses dignes d'attention. **2.** Remarque, observation *f,* commentaire *m.* **To make a remark,** faire une observation **To venture a remark,** se permettre un mot. *After*

some preliminary remarks, après quelques avant-propos *m.* *F :* **To pass remarks upon s.o.,** faire des observations sur qn.
remark². **I.** *v.tr.* (*a*) Remarquer, observer. *It may be remarked that . . .,* constatons que. . . . (*b*) Faire la remarque (que . . .) ; faire observer (à qn que . . .). **2.** *v.i.* Faire une remarque, faire des remarques (*on,* sur). *I remarked upon it to my neighbour,* j'en fis l'observation à mon voisin.
remarkable [ri'mɑ:rkəbl], *a.* Remarquable ; frappant. *Our family has never been r.,* notre famille n'a jamais marqué. **-ably,** *adv.* Remarquablement.
remarry [ri:'mari], *v.i.* Se remarier ; (*of widow*) convoler en deuxièmes noces.
remediable [re'mi:diəbl], *a.* Remédiable.
remedial [re'mi:diəl], *a.* Réparateur, -trice ; (traitement, etc.) curatif.
remedy¹ ['remedi], *s.* **I.** Remède *m.* **Remedy for an ailment,** remède pour, contre, une maladie. *F :* **Old wives' remedy,** remède de bonne femme. **The evil is past remedy,** le mal est sans remède. **2.** *To have no remedy at law,* n'avoir aucun recours contre qn.
remedy², *v.tr.* Remédier à (qch.). *That cannot be remedied,* on ne saurait y remédier.
remelt [ri:'melt], *v.tr.* Refondre. **remelting,** *s.* Refonte *f.*
remember [ri'membər], *v.tr.* **I.** (*a*) Se souvenir de (qch.) ; se rappeler (qch.). *I r. seeing it,* je me souviens, il me souvient, de l'avoir vu. *I r. his going,* je me rappelle son départ. **If I remember aright,** si j'ai bonne mémoire. **As far as I remember.** autant qu'il m'en souvient, qu'il m'en souvienne. *I can't r. his name for the moment,* son nom m'échappe pour l'instant. **Don't you remember me?** est-ce que vous ne me remettez pas ? **It will be something to remember you by,** ce sera un souvenir de vous. (*b*) *One cannot r. everything,* on ne peut pas songer à tout. *That is worth remembering,* cela est à noter. (*c*) *He remembered me in his will,* il ne m'a pas oublié dans son testament. (*d*) *To remember oneself,* se ressaisir. **2. Remember me (kindly) to them,** rappelez-moi à leur bon souvenir.
remembrance [ri'membrəns], *s.* **I.** Souvenir *m,* mémoire *f.* **To have sth. in remembrance,** avoir qch. à la mémoire. **To the best of my remembrance,** autant qu'il m'en souvienne. **In remembrance of s.o.,** en souvenir, en mémoire, de qn. **2.** *pl.* **Give my kind remembrances to him,** rappelez-moi à son bon souvenir.
remind [ri'maind], *v.tr.* To remind s.o. of sth., rappeler, remémorer, qch. à qn ; faire souvenir qn de qch. *That reminds me of . . .,* cela me rappelle. . . . *That reminds me!* à propos ! *R. me to write to him,* faites-moi penser à lui écrire.
reminder [ri'maindər], *s.* (*a*) Mémento *m.* *As a r. that . . .,* pour rappeler que. . . . (*b*) *Com :* (Letter of) reminder, lettre de rappel. *I'll send him a r.,* je vais lui rafraîchir la mémoire. (*c*) *Com :* Rappel *m* de compte ; rappel d'échéance.
reminiscence [remi'nis(ə)ns], *s.* **I.** Réminiscence *f* ; souvenir *m* vague. **2.** To write one's reminiscences, écrire ses souvenirs.
reminiscent [remi'nis(ə)nt], *a.* **I.** Qui se souvient. **2.** Reminiscer t of sth., qui rappelle qch. ; qui fait penser à qch.
remiss [ri'mis], *a.* Négligent, insouciant ; inexact à remplir ses devoirs.
remission [ri'miʃ(ə)n], *s.* **I.** Remission of sins, pardon *m,* rémission *f,* des péchés. *To grant s.o. r. of his sins,* absoudre qn de ses péchés. **2.** Re-

mise *f* (d'une peine, d'une dette). **3.** (*a*) Relâchement *m* (du froid). (*b*) *Med:* Rémission (d'une fièvre).

remissness [ri'misnəs], *s.* Négligence *f*.

remit [ri'mit], *v.tr.* (**remitted**) **I.** (*a*) Remettre, pardonner (les péchés). (*b*) Remettre (une dette, une peine). **2.** Relâcher (son zèle). **3.** Renvoyer (un procès à un autre tribunal). **4.** *Com:* To remit a sum to s.o., remettre, envoyer, une somme à qn; faire tenir une somme à qn. *Abs.* Kindly remit, prière de nous couvrir.

remittal [ri'mit(ə)l], *s.* **I.** Remise *f* (*of a debt*, d'une dette). **2.** *Jur:* Renvoi *m* (d'un procès à un autre tribunal).

remittance [ri'mitəns], *s.* *Com:* Remise *f* (d'argent); envoi *m* de fonds. *F:* Remittance-man, propre à rien envoyé aux colonies, où il vit des fonds que lui envoie sa famille.

remitter [ri'mitər], *s.* *Com:* Remetteur *m*, remettant *m*.

remnant ['remnənt], *s.* **I.** Reste *m*, restant *m*. *I found a few remnants of food*, je trouvai quelques restes de nourriture. **2.** Vestige *m* (d'un usage). **3.** Coupon *m* (d'étoffe). **Remnants,** soldes *m*. Remnant sale, solde de coupons.

remodel [ri:'mɔd(ə)l], *v.tr.* (**remodelled**) Remodeler (une statue); remanier (un ouvrage); transformer (une machine).

remonstrance [ri'mɔnstrəns], *s.* Remontrance *f*.

remonstrate [ri'mɔnstreit]. **I.** *v.i.* To remonstrate with s.o., faire des remontrances à qn. To remonstrate against sth., protester contre qch. **2.** *v.tr.* To remonstrate that ..., protester que ....

remonstrative [ri'mɔnstrətiv], *a.* (Ton, lettre) de remontrance, de protestation.

remorse [ri'mɔ:rs], *s.* **I.** Remords *m*. **A feeling of remorse,** un remords. **2. Without remorse,** sans aucune componction; sans pitié.

remorseful [ri'mɔ:rsful], *a.* Plein de remords; repentant. **-fully,** *adv.* Avec remords.

remorseless [ri'mɔ:rsləs], *a.* **I.** Sans remords. **2.** Sans pitié; impitoyable. **-ly,** *adv.* **I.** Sans remords. **2.** Sans pitié.

remote [ri'mout], *a.* **I.** Éloigné, écarté. *Sciences r. from each other,* sciences qui n'ont rien en commun. **2.** Lointain; éloigné, écarté. **The house lies remote from the road,** la maison est située loin de la route. **In a remote future,** dans un avenir lointain, reculé. **Remote ancestors,** ancêtres reculés. **Remote causes,** causes lointaines. *S.a.* CONTROL[1] 2. **3.** *A r. resemblance,* une vague ressemblance. *Without the remotest chance of succeeding,* sans la moindre chance de réussir. **Remote prospect,** éventualité *f* peu probable. **-ly,** *adv.* **I.** Loin; au loin; dans le lointain. **2.** *We are r. related,* nous sommes parents de loin. **3.** Vaguement.

remoteness [ri'moutnəs], *s.* **I.** Éloignement *m*, lointaineté *f* (d'un village). **2.** (*a*) Degré éloigné (de parenté). (*b*) Faible degré (de ressemblance).

remount[1] [ri:'maunt, ri-], *s.* *Mil:* **I.** Remonte *f*. **2.** Cheval *m* de remonte. **Army remounts,** chevaux de troupe.

remount[2], *v.tr.* Remonter. *Esp.* To remount one's horse, *abs.* to remount, remonter à cheval; se remettre en selle.

removability [rimu:və'biliti], *s.* Amovibilité *f*.

removable [ri'mu:vəbl], *a.* **I.** Détachable; amovible. **2.** Transportable. **3.** (Fonctionnaire) amovible, révocable.

removal [ri'mu:v(ə)l], *s.* **I.** (*a*) Enlèvement *m* (d'une tache); suppression *f* (d'un abus). (*b*) Révocation *f* (d'un fonctionnaire); destitu-

tion *f* (d'un officier). (*c*) *F:* Assassinat *m* (de qn). **2.** Déplacement *m* (d'une épave); transport *m* (d'un colis). **3.** Démontage *m* (d'un pneu); levée *f* (de scellés). **4.** Déménagement *m*. *Adm:* Removal expenses, frais de déplacement.

remove[1] [ri'mu:v], *s.* **I.** *Cu:* Relevé *m*. **2.** *Sch:* (*a*) Passage *m* à une classe supérieure. (*b*) Classe *f* intermédiaire. **3. It is but one remove from ...,** cela est tout près de. . . .

remove[2], *v.tr.* **I.** (*a*) Enlever, effacer, ôter (une tache); écarter (un obstacle); résoudre (une objection); chasser (une appréhension); supprimer (un abus). *To r. s.o.'s name from a list,* rayer qn d'une liste. (*b*) Révoquer (un fonctionnaire); destituer (un officier). (*c*) Assassiner, *F:* supprimer (qn). **2.** (*a*) Déplacer (une machine); transporter (des colis); déménager (sa bibliothèque). **To remove oneself and all one's belongings,** *F:* faire place nette. *Abs.* **To remove,** déménager. (*b*) Éloigner (qch., qn). (*c*) Enlever, retirer (son chapeau); enlever (les assiettes, etc.). *Med: To r. a bandage,* lever un appareil. (*d*) Déplacer (un fonctionnaire).

removed, *a.* **I.** First cousin once removed, cousin(e) issu(e) de germain. **2.** Éloigné. **Far removed from ...,** bien loin de. . .

remover [ri'mu:vər], *s.* **I.** (*Pers.*) = FURNITURE-REMOVER. **2.** Varnish remover, décapant *m* pour vernis. **Superfluous hair remover,** pâte *f* dépilatoire.

remunerate ['ri'mju:nəreit], *v.tr.* Rémunérer.

remuneration [rimju:nə'reiʃ(ə)n], *s.* Rémunération *f* (*for,* de).

remunerative [ri'mju:nərətiv], *a.* (Travail, prix) rémunérateur, -trice.

renaissance [ri'neisəns], *s.* *Art: Lit:* Renaissance *f*. *R. style,* style (de la) Renaissance.

renal ['ri:n(ə)l], *a.* *Anat:* Rénal, -aux; des reins.

renascent [ri'nas(ə)nt], *a.* Renaissant.

rend [rend], *v.tr.* (rent; rent) Déchirer. **To rend sth. asunder,** in two, in twain, déchirer qch. en deux. **To rend one's garments,** déchirer ses vêtements. **A cry rent the air,** un cri fendit l'air. **To rend s.o.'s heart,** fendre, déchirer, le cœur à qn.

render ['rendər], *v.tr.* Rendre. **I.** (*a*) *To r. good for evil,* rendre le bien pour le mal. (*b*) *To r. thanks to s.o.,* remercier qn. *To r. thanks to God,* rendre grâce à Dieu. **2.** *Lit:* Rendre (une forteresse). **3.** *To render a service to s.o.,* rendre un service à qn. **4.** (*a*) To render an account of sth., rendre compte de qch. (*b*) *To render an account to s.o.,* remettre un compte à qn. 'As per account rendered,' 'to account rendered,' "suivant notre compte," "suivant compte remis." **5.** Interpréter (un morceau de musique); rendre, traduire (une phrase). **6.** Rendre; faire devenir. *His action renders it probable that ...,* son action fait pressentir que. . . . **7.** *Cu:* Fondre (la graisse); clarifier. **rendering,** *s.* **I.** (*a*) R. of thanks, of help, remerciements *mpl,* assistance *f*. (*b*) Reddition *f* (d'un compte, d'une forteresse). **2.** Rendu *m* (des traits de qn); interprétation *f* (d'un morceau de musique); traduction *f* (d'une phrase). **3.** Fonte *f,* extraction *f* (de la graisse); clarification *f*.

rendezvous [rɔndi'vu:], *s.* Rendez-vous *m*.

renegade ['renigeid], *s.* Renégat *m.* **Renegade Christian,** chrétien renié.

renew [ri'nju:]. **I.** *v.tr.* (*a*) Renouveler. **To renew one's youth,** rajeunir. **To renew a lease,** renouveler un bail. *To r. one's subscription,* se réabonner (*to,* à). *Com:* **To renew a bill,** prolonger une lettre de change. (*Of bill*) **Unless**

renewed, à moins de renouvellement. *Jur:* To renew a title, rénover un titre. (*b*) To renew one's acquaintance with s.o., renouer connaissance avec qn. To r. the combat, rengager le combat. To r. a promise, renouveler une promesse. (*c*) Remplacer (un organe de machine); renouveler (ses vêtements). **2.** *v.i.* Se renouveler.

renewable [ri'njuːəbl], *a.* Renouvelable.

renewal [ri'njuːəl], *s.* **1.** (*a*) Renouvellement *m*. R. of beauty, regain *m* de beauté. **Renewal of subscription**, réabonnement *m* (*to*, à). *Com:* **Renewal of a bill**, atermoiement *m*, prolongation *f*, d'une lettre de change. (*b*) **Renewal of acquaintance**, renouement *m* des relations. R. of negotiations, reprise *f* de négociations. **2.** Remplacement *m* (d'un pneu).

rennet[1] ['renet], *s.* Présure *f*.

rennet[2], *s. Hort:* (Pomme *f* de) rainette *f*.

renounce[1] [ri'nauns], *s. Cards:* Renonce *f*.

renounce[2], *v.tr.* **1.** Renoncer à, abandonner (une prétention); répudier (une succession). **2.** (*a*) Renoncer à un projet). (*b*) Dénoncer (une convention); répudier (un traité). To r. one's principles, renier ses principes. To r. one's faith, renoncer (à) sa foi; apostasier. **3.** *Abs. Cards:* Renoncer.

renouncement [ri'naunsmənt], *s.* Renoncement *m* (*of*, à). *Jur:* **Renouncement of a succession**, répudiation *f* d'une succession.

renovate ['renoveit], *v.tr.* **1.** Renouveler (l'air), **2.** Remettre à neuf (un vêtement); rénover (des pneus). **renovating**, *a.* Rénovateur, -trice.

renovation [reno'veiʃ(ə)n], *s.* Rénovation *f*, renouvellement *m*; remise *f* à neuf.

renown [ri'naun], *s.* Renommée *f*, renom *m*, célébrité *f*. To win r., se faire un grand nom.

renowned [ri'naund], *a.* Renommé (*for*, pour); célèbre (*for*, par); fameux, illustre.

rent[1] [rent]. *See* REND.

rent[2], *s.* **1.** Déchirure *f*, accroc *m* (à un vêtement); déchirure (dans les nuages). **2.** Fissure *f* (de terrain). **3.** Rupture *f*, schisme *m* (dans une société).

rent[3], *s.* Loyer *m*; (prix *m* de) location *f* (d'une maison); fermage *m* (d'une ferme). *Quarter's* r., terme *m*. **'rent-collector**, *s.* Receveur *m* de loyers. **'rent-day**, *s.* Jour *m* du terme. **'rent-free**, *a.* To live r.-f. in a house, habiter une maison sans payer de loyer. **'rent-roll**, *s.* État *m* des fermages (d'une propriété).

rent[4], *v.tr.* (*a*) (*Let*) Louer (une maison); affermer (une terre). (*b*) (*Hire*) Louer, prendre en location (une maison); affermer (une terre). To r. a house from the tenant, sous-louer une maison.

rental ['rent(ə)l], *s.* **1.** (*a*) Loyer *m*; valeur locative; montant *m* du loyer. *Yearly* r., redevance annuelle. (*b*) Revenu *m* provenant des loyers. **2.** *Tp:* **Fixed rental**, taux principal d'abonnement.

renunciation [rinʌnsi'eiʃ(ə)n], *s.* **1.** Renoncement *m*, renonciation *f* (*of rights*, aux droits). *Jur:* R. of a succession, répudiation *f* d'une succession. **Letter of renunciation**, lettre de renoncement. **2.** Reniement *m* (*of*, de). **Renunciation on oath**, abjuration *f* (*of*, de).

reopen [riː'oup(ə)n]. **1.** *v.tr.* (*a*) Rouvrir (un livre). *F:* To reopen an old sore, raviver une plaie. (*b*) Reprendre (les hostilités); recommencer (le feu). (*c*) The question cannot be reopened, il n'y a pas à y revenir. **2.** *v.i.* (*a*) (*Of wound*) Se rouvrir. (*b*) (*Of theatre*) Rouvrir; (*of school*) rentrer. **reopening**, *s.* **1.** Réouverture *f*

(d'un théâtre). **2.** Rentrée *f* (des classes, des tribunaux).

reorganization [riːɔːrgənai'zeiʃ(ə)n], *s.* Réorganisation *f*.

reorganize [riː'ɔːrgənaiz]. **1.** *v.tr.* Réorganiser. **2.** *v.i.* Se réorganiser.

rep [rep], *s. Tex:* Reps *m*.

repaid [ri'peid]. *See* REPAY.

repaint [riː'peint], *v.tr.* Repeindre.

repair[1] [ri'pɛər], *v.i.* To repair to a place, aller, se rendre, à un endroit; gagner un endroit.

repair[2], *s.* **1.** Réparation *f* (d'une machine); rétablissement *m* (d'un bâtiment); *Nau:* radoub *m* (d'une coque). **Road repairs**, réfection *f* des routes. **Road(side) repairs** (*to motor car*), dépannage *m*. To be under repair, subir des réparations. **Ship under** r., navire en radoub. **Ruined beyond** r., ruiné irréparablement. **2.** To be in (good) repair, être en bon état. **Keeping in** r., entretien *m*; réparations d'entretien. **re'pair outfit**, *s.* Nécessaire *m*, trousse *f*, de réparation.

repair[3], *v.tr.* **1.** Réparer, réfectionner, remettre en état (une machine); raccommoder (un vêtement); radouber (un filet, *Nau:* une coque). To repair one's fortunes, réparer, rétablir, sa fortune. **2.** Réparer (un tort). **3.** Rétablir (sa santé). **repairing**, *s.* Réparation *f*, raccommodage *m*. **Repairing shop, works**, atelier *m* de réparations.

repairer [ri'pɛərər], *s.* Réparateur, -trice. R. of clocks, horloger rhabilleur.

repaper [riː'peipər], *v.tr.* Retapisser (une pièce).

reparation [repə'reiʃ(ə)n], *s.* Réparation *f*.

repartee [repɑr'tiː], *s.* Repartie *f*. To be quick at repartee, avoir la repartie prompte; avoir des répliques spirituelles.

repartition [repɑr'tiʃ(ə)n, riː-], *s.* **1.** Répartition *f*. **2.** [riː-] Nouveau partage.

repass [riː'pɑːs]. **1.** *v.tr.* (*a*) Repasser, retraverser (la mer). (*b*) Passer de nouveau devant (la maison). **2.** *v.i.* Repasser.

repast [ri'pɑːst], *s.* Repas *m*.

repatriate [riː'patrieit], *v.tr.* Rapatrier.

repatriation [ripatri'eiʃ(ə)n], *s.* Rapatriement *m*.

repay [ri'pei], *v.tr.* (repaid [ri'peid]; repaid) **1.** Rendre (de l'argent). To r. an obligation, s'acquitter d'une obligation. To r. an injury, se venger d'un tort. To r. s.o.'s kindness, payer de retour la bonté de qn. I owe you more than I can repay, *F:* je vous dois une fière chandelle. **2.** (i) Rembourser (qn); (ii) récompenser (qn) (*for*, de). To repay s.o. in full, s'acquitter avec, envers, qn. To r. s.o. with ingratitude, payer qn d'ingratitude. How can I r. you? comment pourrai-je m'acquitter envers vous? **3.** Book that repays reading, livre qui vaut la peine d'être lu.

repayable [ri'peiəbl], *a.* Remboursable.

repayment [ri'peimənt], *s.* **1.** Remboursement *m*. **2.** Récompense *f* (d'un service).

repeal[1] [ri'piːl], *s.* Abrogation *f* (d'une loi); rappel *m*, révocation *f* (d'un décret).

repeal[2], *v.tr.* Rapporter, abroger, annuler (une loi); révoquer, rappeler (un décret).

repeat[1] [ri'piːt], *s.* **1.** *Mus:* **Repeat(-mark)**, (barre *f* de) reprise *f*; renvoi *m*. **2.** *Tg:* **Repeat signal**, invitation *f* à répéter. **3.** *Com:* **Repeat (order)**, commande renouvelée; "à nouveau" *m inv.*

repeat[2]. **1.** *v.tr.* (*a*) Répéter; réitérer (un ordre). (*After a line of a song*) 'Repeat,' "bis." To have a telegram repeated, faire collationner un télégramme. (*b*) *Pej:* Rapporter (un méfait). He repeats everything to the master, c'est un rapporteur. (*c*) Renouveler (ses efforts). *Com:* Re-

nouveler (une commande). (d) To repeat the lessons, réciter les leçons. 2. v.i. (a) (Of rifle) Être à répétition. (b) Ar : (Of figures) Se répéter. (c) (Of food) Revenir ; donner des renvois. **repeated,** a. Répété, réitéré, redoublé. R. requests, demandes réitérées. -ly, adv. A plusieurs reprises. **repeating,** a. 1. (Fusil) à répétition ; (montre) à sonnerie. 2. Mth: Repeating decimal, fraction f périodique.
repeater [ri'pi:tər], s. 1. (a) Montre f à répétition, à sonnerie. (b) Fusil m à répétition. 2. Mth: Fraction f périodique.
repel [ri'pel], v.tr. (repelled) 1. Repousser (une attaque). 2. Repousser (qn); répugner à (qn). To be repelled by s.o., éprouver de la répulsion pour qn. **repelling,** a. Répulsif.
repellent [ri'pelənt], a. 1. Répulsif. Ph: R. force, force répulsive. 2. Repoussant, répulsif, répugnant. He has a r. manner, il a l'abord antipathique.
repent [ri'pent]. 1. v.i. Se repentir (of, de). 2. v.tr. To repent having done sth., se repentir d'avoir fait qch. He has bitterly repented it, F: il s'en est mordu les doigts.
repentance [ri'pentəns], s. Repentir m. Stool of repentance, sellette f.
repentant [ri'pentənt], a. 1. Repentant, repenti. 2. (Soupir) de repentir.
repeople [ri:'pi:pl], v.tr. Repeupler. **re-peopling,** s. Repeuplement m.
repercussion [ri:pər'kʌʃ(ə)n], s. Répercussion f; conʧre-coup m (d'une explosion).
repertoire ['repərtwɑ:r], s. Th: Mus: Répertoire m.
repertory ['repərtəri], s. 1. Répertoire m (de renseignements). 2. Th: Répertoire. Repertory company, troupe f à demeure (dans une ville).
repetition [repe'tiʃ(ə)n], s. 1. (a) Répétition f (d'un mot) Mus: (In playing) Reprise f. Tg: Collationnement m. (b) Sch: Récitation f. 2. Répétition, réitération f (d'une action) ; renouvellement m (d'un effort).
repine [ri'pain], v.i. Être mécontent, se chagriner (at, against, de) ; exhaler des plaintes. **repin-ing**[1], a. 1. Disposé à se plaindre ; mécontent. 2. (Ton) dolent; (humeur) chagrine. **repin-ing**[2], s. Mécontentement m, plaintes fpl.
replace [ri'pleis], v.tr. 1. Replacer (qch.); remettre (qch.) en place. Tp: To replace the receiver, raccrocher le récepteur ; F: raccrocher. 2. Remplacer. I shall ask to be replaced, je demanderai à me faire remplacer. To r. coal by oil fuel, remplacer le charbon par le pétrole.
replaceable [ri'pleisəbl], a. Remplaçable.
replacement [ri'pleismənt], s. 1. Remise f en place ; remontage m (d'un pneu). 2. (a) Remplacement m, substitution f. (b) pl. Ind : Replacements, pièces f de rechange.
replant [ri:'plɑ:nt], v.tr. Replanter.
replaster [ri:'plɑ:stər], v.tr. Replâtrer.
replay[1] ['ri:plei], s. Games: Sp: Second match (après match nul).
replay[2] [ri:'plei], v.tr. Rejouer (un match).
replenish [ri'pleniʃ], v.tr. Remplir (de nouveau) (with, de). To r. one's wardrobe, remonter sa garde-robe. To r. one's supplies, se réapprovisionner (with, de). Aut: To r. the oil, rétablir le niveau d'huile.
replenishment[ri'pleniʃmənt],s. Remplissage m. R. of supplies, réapprovisionnement m, ravitaillement m.
replete [ri'pli:t], a. Rempli, plein (with, de).
repletion [ri'pli:ʃ(ə)n], s. Réplétion f. To eat to repletion, manger jusqu'à satiété.

replevin [ri'plevin], s. Mainlevée f de saisie.
replica ['replikə], s. (a) Reproduction f, copie f (d'un document). (b) Art : Réplique f, double m (d'une œuvre d'art).
reply[1] [ri'plai], s. 1. Réponse f. What have you to say in reply? qu'avez-vous à répondre? Tg : Reply paid, réponse payée. 2. Jur : Réplique f.
reply[2], v.i. & tr. (replied) Répondre, répliquer (to, à). Jur : Répliquer.
repolish [ri:'poliʃ], v.tr. Repolir.
report[1] [ri'pɔ:rt], s. 1. (a) Rapport m (on, sur) ; compte rendu ; exposé m (d'une affaire). Annual report (of a company), rapport de gestion. Policeman's report, procès-verbal. Sch : Terminal report, bulletin trimestriel. Examiners' report, notes fpl des examinateurs. Mil : Sick report, rôle m des malades. Law reports, Jur : recueil m de jurisprudence. S.a. EXPERT[2]. (b) Weather report, bulletin m météorologique. 2. (i) Bruit m qui court ; rumeur f ; (ii) nouvelle f. There was a r. that . . ., le bruit courait que. . . . To know of sth. by mere report, savoir qch. par ouï-dire. 3. Réputation f, renommée f. Man of good report, homme de bonne réputation, bien famé. 4. Détonation f (d'une arme à feu) ; coup m de fusil, de canon.
report[2]. I. v.tr. 1. (a) Rapporter (un fait) ; rendre compte de (qch.). To r. a speech, a meeting, faire le compte rendu d'un discours, d'une séance. To report progress, exposer l'état de l'affaire. Parl : To move to report progress, demander la clôture des débats. To r. to a superior, rendre compte à un supérieur. Parl : To report a bill (to the House), rapporter un projet de loi. S.a. SPEECH 5. (b) Journ : Faire le reportage de (qch.). (c) Rapporter, dire (qch.). It is reported that . . ., le bruit court, on dit, que. . . . Journ : It is reported from Paris that . . ., on mande de Paris que. . . . 2. (a) To r. an accident to the police, signaler un accident à la police. Adm : Mil : To report s.o. sick, porter qn malade. 'Nothing to report,' "rien à signaler." Cust : To report a vessel, déclarer un navire ; faire la déclaration d'entrée. (b) To report oneself to (s.o.), se présenter à, devant (un supérieur). II. **report,** v.ind.tr. To report (up)on sth., faire un rapport sur qch. ; rendre compte de qch. He is well reported on, il est bien noté. **reporting,** s. Reportage m ; comptes rendus. Journ : Reporting staff, service m des informations.
reporter [ri'pɔ:rtər], s. (a) Journaliste m, reporter m. (b) Sténographe mf (parlementaire). The Reporters' Gallery, la Tribune de la presse.
repose[1] [ri'pouz], v.tr. To repose one's trust in s.o., mettre sa confiance en qn.
repose[2], v.i. 1. Repos m. (b) To seek repose, chercher du repos. (b) Sommeil m. (c) Calme m, tranquillité f (d'esprit). Features in repose, traits au repos. 2. Civ.E: Angle of repose, angle d'éboulement (d'un talus).
repose[3], v.i. (a) Se reposer : (i) se délasser ; (ii) dormir. (b) Reposer (on, upon, sur). The foundations r. upon rock, les fondations reposent sur la roche.
repository [ri'pɔzitəri], s. 1. Dépôt m, entrepôt m, magasin m (de marchandises). Furniture repository, garde-meuble m. 2. Répertoire m (de renseignements). He is a r. of curious information, c'est une mine de renseignements curieux. 3. (Pers.) Dépositaire mf (d'un secret).
repossess [ri:po'zes], v.tr. To r. s.o. of sth., remettre qn en possession de qch. To r. oneself of sth., reprendre possession de qch.

repoussé [rə'puːse], *a. & s.* Repoussé (*m*). Repoussé work(ing), travail *m* de repoussé.

reprehend [repri'hend], *v.tr.* **1.** Reprendre, blâmer, réprimander (qn), **2.** *To r. s.o.'s conduct,* trouver répréhensible la conduite de qn.

reprehensible [repri'hensibl], *a.* Répréhensible, blâmable, condamnable. **-ibly,** *adv.* Répréhensiblement.

reprehension [repri'henʃ(ə)n], *s.* Réprimande *f.*

represent [repri'zent], *v.tr.* **1.** (*a*) Représenter (qch. à l'esprit). (*b*) *Th:* Représenter (une pièce); jouer (un personnage). (*c*) *The flag represents the nation,* le drapeau symbolise la nation. **2.** Faire remarquer, signaler (*sth. to s.o.*, qch. à qn). *May I r. that . . .?* puis-je vous faire observer que . . .? **3.** *He represents himself as a model of virtue,* il se donne pour un modèle de vertu. *Exactly as represented,* exactement conforme à la description. **4.** Représenter (une maison de commerce).

representation [reprizen'teiʃ(ə)n], *s.* **1.** (*a*) Représentation *f* (de qch. à l'esprit). (*b*) *Th:* Représentation (d'une pièce); interprétation *f* (d'un rôle). **2.** (*a*) *Pol:* Proportional representation, représentation proportionnelle. (*b*) *Coll.* Les représentants *m.* **3.** To make false representations to s.o., déguiser la vérité à qn. **4.** (i) Représentation; remontrance courtoise; (ii) exposé *m* des faits.

representative [repri'zentətiv]. **1.** *a.* (*a*) Representative govornment, gouvernement représentatif. (*b*) *Meeting of r. men from all classes,* réunion d'hommes représentant toutes les classes. **2.** *s.* (*a*) Représentant, -ante; délégué, -ée. (*b*) *Last r. of an illustrious race,* dernier rejeton d'une race illustre. (*c*) **District representative,** représentant régional. (*d*) *Pol:* Député *m.*

repress [ri'pres], *v.tr.* **1.** Réprimer (une sédition). **2.** Réprimer, retenir (ses désirs). *Psy:* Refouler (ses sentiments). *To r. a sneeze,* étouffer un éternûment. **repressed,** *a.* Réprimé, contenu.

repressible [ri'presibl], *a.* Réprimable.

repression [ri'preʃ(ə)n], *s.* Répression *f.*

repressive [ri'presiv], *a.* Répressif, réprimant.

reprieve¹ [ri'priːv], *s.* **1.** (*a*) Commutation *f* de la peine capitale. (*b*) Lettre(s) *f*(*pl*) de grâce. **2.** Répit *m,* délai *m.*

reprieve², *v.tr.* **1.** *Jur:* Accorder à (un condamné) une commutation de la peine capitale. **2.** Donner du répit à (un débiteur).

reprimand¹ [repri'maːnd], *s.* (*a*) Réprimande *f.* (*b*) *Adm. & Jur:* Blâme *m.*

reprimand², *v.tr.* (*a*) Réprimander. (*b*) *Adm. & Jur:* Blâmer publiquement (qn).

reprint¹ ['riːprint], *s.* Réimpression *f;* nouveau tirage. *Cheap r. of a book,* édition *f* populaire d'un ouvrage.

reprint² [riː'print], *v.tr.* Réimprimer.

reprisal [ri'praiz(ə)l], *s.* Usu.pl. Représaille *f.* To make reprisal(s), user de représailles.

reproach¹ [ri'proutʃ], *s.* **1.** (*a*) Motif *m* de honte. To be a reproach to . . ., être la honte, l'opprobre *m,* de . . . (*b*) Honte, opprobre. **2.** Reproche *m,* blâme *m. To abstain from r.,* s'abstenir de tout reproche. **Beyond reproach,** irréprochable. **Term of reproach,** terme injurieux.

reproach², *v.tr.* **1.** Faire, adresser, des reproches à (qn) (*about*, au sujet de). **To reproach s.o. with sth.,** reprocher qch. à qn. **2.** Blâmer (l'ignorance de qn).

reproachful [ri'proutʃful], *a.* Réprobateur,

-trice; plein de reproche(s). **-fully,** *adv.* D'un air, d'un ton, de reproche.

reprobate¹ ['reprobet], *s.* *F:* Chenapan *m* vaurien *m.* Old reprobate, vieux marcheur.

reprobate² ['reprobeit], *v.tr.* Réprouver (qn, un crime).

reprobation [repro'beiʃ(ə)n], *s.* Réprobation *f.*

reproduce [riːpro'djuːs]. **1.** *v.tr.* Reproduire. (*a*) Copier. *The features are well reproduced,* les traits sont bien rendus. (*b*) Multiplier (par génération). **2.** *v.i.* Se reproduire, se multiplier.

reproduction [riːpro'dʌkʃ(ə)n], *s.* **1.** Reproduction *f.* **2.** Copie *f,* imitation *f.*

reproductive [riːpro'dʌktiv], *a.* Reproductif; reproducteur, -trice.

reproof [ri'pruːf], *s.* **1.** Reproche *m,* blâme *m. Deserving of r.,* réprimandable. **2.** Réprimande *f.* de reproche.

reprove [ri'pruːv], *v.tr.* (*a*) Reprendre, réprimander (qn). (*b*) Condamner, réprouver (une action). **reproving,** *a.* Réprobateur, -trice; (ton) de reproche, de blâme. **-ly,** *adv.* D'un ton de reproche.

reptile ['reptail]. **1.** *s.* Reptile *m.* **2.** *a.* (*a*) Reptile, rampant. (*b*) *F:* (Caractère) rampant.

republic [ri'pʌblik], *s.* République *f.*

republican [ri'pʌblikən], *a. & s.* Républicain, -aine.

republicanism [ri'pʌblikənizm], *s.* Républicanisme *m.*

republication [riːpʌbli'keiʃ(ə)n], *s.* **1.** Nouvelle édition, réédition *f* (d'un livre). **2.** Nouvelle publication (d'une loi, d'un décret).

republish [riː'pʌbliʃ], *v.tr.* Rééditer (un livre).

repudiate [ri'pjuːdieit], *v.tr.* **1.** Répudier (une épouse). **2.** Répudier, désavouer (une opinion). (*Of government*) *To r. its debts,* répudier ses engagements.

repudiation [ripjuːdi'eiʃ(ə)n], *s.* **1.** Répudiation *f* (d'une épouse). **2.** Répudiation, désaveu *m* (d'une opinion); reniement *m* (d'une dette).

repugnance [ri'pʌgnəns], *s.* Répugnance *f,* antipathie *f* (*to, against,* pour). *To feel r. to doing sth.,* répugner à faire qch.

repugnant [ri'pʌgnənt], *a.* **1.** Incompatible (*to, with,* avec); contraire (*to, with,* à). **2.** Répugnant (*to,* à). *To be r. to s.o.,* répugner à qn.

repulse¹ [ri'pʌls], *s.* **1.** Échec *m;* défaite *f* (de l'ennemi). **2.** Rebuffade *f,* refus *m.*

repulse², *v.tr.* **1.** Repousser, refouler (un assaut, un ennemi). **2.** Repousser (les avances de qn, une demande); refuser, renvoyer (qn).

repulsion [ri'pʌlʃ(ə)n], *s.* **1.** *Ph:* Répulsion *f.* **2.** Répulsion, aversion *f,* répugnance *f.*

repulsive [ri'pʌlsiv], *a.* **1.** *Ph:* Répulsif. **2.** Répulsif, repoussant. **3.** (*Of pers.*) Qui repousse les avances; à l'abord difficile. **-ly,** *adv.* R. ugly, d'une laideur repoussante.

repulsiveness [ri'pʌlsivnəs], *s.* **1.** *Ph:* Force répulsive. **2.** Caractère repoussant.

repurchase¹ [riː'pəːrtʃes], *s.* Rachat *m. Jur:* Réméré *m.*

repurchase², *v.tr.* Racheter.

reputable ['repjutəbl], *a.* **1.** (*Of pers.*) Honorable, estimé, estimable. **2.** (Emploi) honorable. **-ably,** *adv.* Honorablement.

reputation [repju'teiʃ(ə)n], *s.* Réputation *f,* renom *m.* To have a reputation for courage, avoir une réputation de courage. Of bad reputation, de mauvaise réputation; *Adm:* mal noté. Of good reputation, de bon renom. *To ruin s.o.'s r.,* perdre qn de réputation.

repute¹ [ri'pjuːt], *s.* Réputation *f,* renom *m,* renommée *f.* To know s.o. by repute, connaître qn de réputation. **To be held in high repute,**

(i) avoir une haute réputation ; (ii) *Adm :* être bien noté. **Doctor of repute,** médecin réputé. *The family is of good r.,* la famille est honorablement connue. **Place of ill repute,** endroit mal famé. **Of no repute,** sans réputation.
repute², *v.tr.* To be reputed wealthy, avoir la réputation d'être riche. **reputed,** *a.* Réputé, censé, supposé. *A r.* Hogarth, un tableau attribué à Hogarth. *Jur :* Reputed father, père putatif. *S.a.* PINT. **-ly,** *adv.* Suivant l'opinion commune.
request¹ [ri'kwest], *s.* **1.** Demande *f*, requête *f*. *Earnest r.,* sollicitation *f*. *R. for money,* demande d'argent. At the request of s.o., à la demande, sur la demande, de qn. *At the urgent r. of . . .,* sur les instances pressantes de. . . . *Samples sent on request,* échantillons sur demande. To make a request, faire une demande. *To grant a r.,* accéder à un désir. To sing sth. by request, chanter qch. à la demande générale. 'Cars stop by request,' "arrêt facultatif." **2.** Recherche *f*, demande. To be in request, être recherché. *Com :* Article in great request, article très demandé. *He is very much in r.,* on se le dispute.
request², *v.tr.* **1.** To request sth. of s.o., demander qch. à qn ; solliciter qch. de qn. *S.a.* PLEASURE I. **2.** To request s.o. to do sth., demander à qn de faire qch. ; prier qn de faire qch. *The public is requested to keep off the grass,* prière au public de ne pas marcher sur le gazon. *Com :* As requested, conformément à vos instructions. **3.** To request permission to do sth., demander à faire qch.
requiem ['rekwiem], *s.* **1.** Requiem (mass), requiem *m* ; messe *f* des morts. **2.** *F :* Chant *m* funèbre.
require [ri'kwaiər], *v.tr.* **1.** To require sth. of s.o., demander, réclamer, qch. à qn ; exiger qch. de qn. *What do you r. of me?* que prétendez-vous de moi? To require s.o. to do sth., exiger de qn qu'il fasse qch. *I r. you to obey me,* je veux que vous m'obéissiez. *The court requires you to attend,* la cour requiert que vous comparaissiez. *Required to multiply x by y,* soit *x* à multiplier par *y*. **2.** Exiger, réclamer. *Work that requires great precision,* travail qui nécessite une grande précision. *Ore that requires special treatment,* minerai qui comporte des traitements particuliers. *The vine requires a chalky soil,* la vigne veut un terrain crayeux. *Have you got all you r.?* avez-vous tout ce qu'il vous faut? *You will not r. a coat,* vous n'aurez pas besoin d'un manteau. He did not require a second telling, he did not require twice telling, il ne se le fit pas dire deux fois. *I shall do whatever is required,* je ferai tout ce qu'il faudra. If required, s'il le faut ; si besoin est ; au besoin. As occasion shall require, selon les nécessités. **required,** *a.* Exigé, demandé, voulu. *To cut sth. to the r. length,* couper qch. à la longueur voulue. *In the r. time,* dans le délai prescrit. *To have the money r.,* avoir l'argent nécessaire. *The qualities r. for this post,* les qualités requises pour ce poste.
requirement [ri'kwaiərmənt], *s.* **1.** Demande *f*, réclamation *f*. **2.** Exigence *f*, besoin *m*. To meet s.o.'s requirements, satisfaire les exigences de qn. *To make one's requirements known,* faire connaître ses besoins. **3.** Condition requise ; nécessité *f*.
requisite ['rekwizit]. **1.** *a.* Requis (*to*, pour) ; nécessaire (*to*, à) ; indispensable (*to*, pour) ; voulu. **2.** *s.* (*a*) Condition requise (*for*, pour). (*b*) Chose *f* nécessaire. **Toilet requisites,** accessoires *m* de toilette. **Office requisites,** fourni-

tures *f* de bureau. **Travelling requisites,** articles *m* de voyage.
requisition¹ [rekwi'ziʃ(ə)n], *s.* **1.** Demande *f*. *Upon a r. by ten members,* sur la demande de dix membres. *Com :* R. for materials, for supplies, demande de matériaux ; commande *f* pour fournitures. **Requisition number,** numéro de référence. **2.** *Mil :* Réquisition *f*. *F :* His services were in constant r.,* on avait constamment recours à ses services.
requisition², *v.tr.* **1.** Réquisitionner (des vivres) ; mettre (des chevaux) en réquisition. *To r. s.o.'s services,* avoir recours aux services de qn. **2.** Faire des réquisitions dans (une ville).
requital [ri'kwait(ə)l], *s.* **1.** Récompense *f*, retour *m*. In requital for, en récompense, en retour, de. **2.** Revanche *f*, représailles *fpl*.
requite [ri'kwait], *v.tr.* **1.** Récompenser, payer de retour (un service). To requite s.o.'s love, répondre à l'amour de qn. Requited love, amour partagé. **2.** To requite s.o. for a service, récompenser qn d'un service. *He requites me with ingratitude,* il me paie d'ingratitude.
reredos ['riərdɔs], *s.* *Ecc :* Retable *m*, rétable *m*.
res [riːz], *s.* *Jur :* Chose *f*. **Res judicata,** chose jugée.
resaddle [riː'sadl], *v.tr.* Reseller (un cheval).
resale [riː'seil], *s.* Revente *f*.
rescind [ri'sind], *v.tr.* Rescinder (un acte) ; annuler (un vote) ; abroger (une loi). **rescinding,** *a.* (Clause) abrogatoire.
rescission [ri'siʒ(ə)n], *s.* Rescision *f*, abrogation *f* (d'un acte) ; annulation *f* (d'un contrat).
rescript ['riːskript], *s.* Rescrit *m*.
rescue¹ [reskjuː], *s.* Délivrance *f* ; (*from shipwreck, fire*) sauvetage *m*. To the rescue! au secours! *A :* à la rescousse! **Rescue party,** équipe *f* de sauvetage.
rescue², *v.tr.* **1.** Sauver, délivrer, secourir. To r. s.o. from death, dérober qn à la mort. To r. s.o. from drowning, sauver qn qui se noie. The rescued men, *s.* the rescued, les rescapés *m*. To r. s.o. from a scrape, tirer qn d'un mauvais pas. **2.** *Jur :* Arracher (un prisonnier) aux mains de la justice.
rescuer ['reskjuər], *s.* **1.** Secoureur, -euse ; libérateur, -trice. **2.** (*From shipwreck*) Sauveteur *m*.
research [ri'səːrtʃ], *s.* Recherche *f* (*after, for,* de). **Piece of research,** enquête *f* scientifique. **Research work,** recherches, investigations ; travaux *mpl* de recherche. *Ind :* Research department, service *m* de recherches.
reseat [riː'siːt], *v.tr.* **1.** Rasseoir (qn) ; faire rasseoir (qn). **2.** Remettre un fond à (une chaise). **3.** To reseat a valve, roder le siège d'une soupape.
resect [ri'sekt], *v.tr.* *Surg :* Réséquer (un os).
resection [ri'sekʃ(ə)n], *s.* *Surg :* Résection *f*.
reseda [ri'siːda]. **1.** *s.* *Bot :* Réséda *m*. **2.** ['rezeda] *a. & s.* (Vert) réséda *inv*.
resell [riː'sel], *v.tr.* (resold [riː'sould] ; resold) Revendre.
resemblance [ri'zembləns], *s.* Ressemblance *f* (*to*, à, avec ; *between*, entre). *A strong r.,* une grande ressemblance. To bear a resemblance to sth., avoir de la ressemblance avec qch.
resemble [ri'zembl], *v.tr.* Ressembler à (qn qch.). To r. one another, se ressembler.
resent [ri'zent], *v.tr.* **1.** Être offensé, froissé, de (qch.) ; être irrité de (qch.). *You r. my being here* ma présence vous déplaît. **2.** S'offenser de (qch.). ressentir (une critique).
resentful [ri'zentful], *a.* **1.** Plein de ressenti-

ment; rancunier. **2.** Froissé, irrité (*of*, de).
-fully, *adv.* Avec ressentiment.
resentment [ri'zentmənt], *s.* Ressentiment *m*.
To cherish a secret r. against s.o., ressentir un dépit secret contre qn.
reservation [rezər'veiʃ(ə)n], *s.* **1.** (*a*) Réserve *f* (des places). *Rail:* Office for reservation of seats, garde-places *m inv.* (*b*) *U.S:* Place retenue. **2.** Réserve, restriction *f*. **To accept sth. without reservation,** accepter qch. sans réserve. **With reservations,** avec certaines réserves; *F:* sous bénéfice d'inventaire. **With this reservation,** à cette restriction près. *S.a.* MENTAL. **3.** *Jur:* Réservation *f* (d'un droit). **4.** *U.S:* Terrain réservé. **Indian reservation,** réserves indiennes.
reserve[1] [ri'zə:rv], *s.* **1.** (*a*) Réserve *f* (d'argent, d'énergie). *R. for doubtful debts,* réserve pour créances douteuses. **Cash reserves,** réserve de caisse. **Reserve fund,** fonds de réserve, de prévision. *S.a.* GOLD. (*b*) **To have sth. in reserve,** tenir qch. en réserve. *Mil:* **Horse in reserve,** cheval haut-le-pied. **2.** (*a*) *Mil:* **The reserves,** les réserves. (*b*) *Mil:* **The reserve,** la réserve (de l'armée active). **Reserve list,** cadre *m* de réserve. (*c*) *Sp:* (Joueur *m* de) réserve. **3.** Terrain réservé. *For:* Réserve. **4.** (*a*) Réserve, restriction *f*. **Without reserve,** sans réserve. *Not without some* (*mental*) *reserves,* non sans réserves; avec quelques réserves. (*b*) (*At sale*) **Reserve price,** prix *m* minimum; mise *f* à prix. **To be sold without reserve,** à vendre sans réserve. **5.** Réserve, discrétion *f*. *When he breaks through his r. . . .,* quand il sort de sa réserve. . . .
reserve[2], *v.tr.* Réserver (*sth. for s.o.*, qch. pour qn); mettre (qch.) en réserve. **To reserve a seat for s.o.,** retenir une place pour qn. **To reserve the right to do sth.,** se réserver de faire qch. *I consent, reserving the right to . . .,* je consens sauf à. . . . **reserved,** *a.* **1.** (Compartiment) réservé. **Reserved seats,** places réservées, louées. *Publ:* **All rights reserved,** tous droits (de reproduction) réservés. **2.** *Navy: etc:* **Reserved list,** cadre *m* de réserve. **3.** Réservé, renfermé; peu communicatif.
reservedly [ri'zə:rvidli], *adv.* Avec réserve.
reservist [ri'zə:rvist], *s.' Mil:* Réserviste *m*.
reservoir ['rezərvwɑ:r], *s.* Réservoir *m*.
reset [ri:'set], *v.tr.* (*p.t.* reset; *p.p.* reset; *pr.p.* resetting) **1.** Remettre en place; replacer; remonter (des pierres précieuses); replanter (des rosiers). **2. To reset one's watch,** remettre sa montre à l'heure. **3.** *Surg:* **To reset a limb,** remettre un membre. **4.** Raffûter (un outil). **5.** *Typ:* Recomposer (un livre).
resettle [ri:'setl]. **1.** *v.tr.* Réinstaller. **To resettle oneself,** se rasseoir; se réinstaller. **2.** *v.i.* (*a*) Se remettre (*to an occupation,* à une occupation); se réinstaller. (*b*) (*Of wine after transport*) Se reposer.
resharpen [ri:'ʃɑ:rp(ə)n], *v.tr.* Réaffûter, raffûter (un outil); retailler (un crayon).
reship [ri:'ʃip], *v.tr.* **1.** Rembarquer, réexpédier (des marchandises). **2.** Remonter (le gouvernail, l'hélice).
reshipment [ri:'ʃipmənt], *s.* Réembarquement *m*, réexpédition *f*.
reshoe [ri:'ʃu:], *v.tr.* Referrer (un cheval).
reshuffle [ri:'ʃʌfl], *v.tr.* **1.** Rebattre, remêler (les cartes). (*b*) *F:* Remanier (un personnel).
reside [ri'zaid], *v.i.* **1.** Résider (*in a place,* dans un endroit). **Permission to reside,** permis de séjour. **2.** (*Of quality*) Résider (*in sth.,* dans qch.).
residence ['rezidəns], *s.* **1.** Résidence *f*, de-

meure *f*, séjour *m*. *To have one's r. at . . .,* résider à. . . . *During my r. abroad,* pendant mon séjour à l'étranger. **To take up one's residence somewhere,** fixer sa résidence, établir sa demeure, quelque part. *Ecc:* **Canon in residence,** chanoine en résidence. *Sch:* **Residence of undergraduates,** internat *m* des étudiants. *S.a.* BOARD[1] **2. 2.** Demeure, maison *f*, habitation *f*. *Town and country residences for sale,* hôtels *m* et propriétés *f* à vendre.
residency ['rezidənsi], *s.* *Adm:* Résidence officielle du résident anglais (aux Indes et ailleurs); la Résidence.
resident [rezidənt]. **1.** *a.* (*a*) Résidant; qui réside. *To be r. in a place,* résider dans un endroit. *The r. population,* la population fixe. (*b*) (*In hospital*) **Resident physician,** interne *m*. *Sch:* **R. master,** maître à demeure (avec certaines fonctions de surveillant). **2.** *s.* (*a*) Habitant, -ante. (*b*) *Adm:* (Ministre) résident *m* (p.ex. aux colonies).
residential [rezi'denʃ(ə)l], *a.* **Residential district,** quartier d'habitation. *S.a.* HOTEL.
residual [ri'zidjuəl]. **1.** *a.* *Ph: etc:* Résiduel, résiduaire. **Residual magnetism,** magnétisme remanent. **2.** *s.* (*a*) *Ch:* Résidu *m.* (*b*) *Ar:* Reste *m*.
residuary [ri'zidjuəri], *a.* **1.** *Ch:* Résiduaire, résiduel. **2.** Qui reste; restant. **3.** *Jur:* **Residuary legatee,** légataire (à titre) universel.
residue ['rezidju:], *s.* **1.** *Ch:* Résidu *m.* **2.** Reste(s) *m(pl)* (d'une armée). **3.** *Jur:* Reliquat *m* (d'une succession). **4.** *Mth:* Résidu (d'une fonction).
residuum, *pl.* **-a** [ri'zidjuəm, -a], *s.* *Ch: etc:* Résidu *m*; reste *m*.
resign [ri'zain], *v.tr.* **1.** (*a*) Résigner (une fonction); donner sa démission de (son emploi); *abs.* démissionner. *Parl:* **Resign! resign!** démission! démission! (*b*) Abandonner (tout espoir); renoncer à (une tâche). (*c*) **To resign sth. to s.o.,** abandonner, céder, qch. à qn. **2.** (*a*) **To resign oneself to sleep,** s'abandonner au sommeil. *To r. oneself to s.o.'s guidance,* se laisser guider par qn. (*b*) **To resign oneself to doing sth.,** se résigner à faire qch.; en prendre son parti. **resigned,** *a.* Résigné (*to,* à). *To become r. to sth.,* prendre son parti de qch.; se résigner à qch.
resignation [rezig'neiʃ(ə)n], *s.* **1.** (*a*) Démission *f*. **To tender one's resignation,** donner sa démission. (*b*) Abandon *m* (d'un droit, etc.). **2.** Résignation *f* (*to,* à); soumission *f*.
resignedly [ri'zainidli], *adv.* Avec résignation.
resilience [ri'ziliəns], **resiliency** [ri'ziljənsi], *s.* **1.** (*a*) *Mec:* Résilience *f*; résistance vive. **Spring resilience,** bande *f* d'un ressort. (*b*) Élasticité *f* de tempérament. **2.** Rebondissement *m*.
resilient [ri'ziljənt], *a.* Rebondissant, élastique. *F:* (*Of pers.*) **To be resilient,** avoir du ressort.
re-silver [ri:'silvər], *v.tr.* Rétamer (un miroir).
resin[1] ['rezin], *s.* **1.** Résine *f*. **White resin,** galipot *m.* **2.** (*Also* rosin) Colophane *f*; poix sèche.
resin[2], *v.tr.* Résiner.
resinous ['rezinəs], *a.* Résineux. ·
resipiscence [resi'pisəns], *s.* Résipiscence *f*.
resist[1] [ri'zist], *s.* *Engr: Dy:* Réserve *f*.
resist[2], *v.tr.* **1.** (*a*) Résister à (une attaque). *A temptation too strong to be resisted,* une tentation trop forte pour que l'on pût y résister. (*b*) *I couldn't r. telling him what I thought of him,* je n'ai pas pu m'empêcher de lui dire son fait. *I can't r. chocolates,* je ne peux pas résister à la tentation d'une crotte de chocolat. **2.** (*a*) Résister

à, s'opposer à (un projet). *It's best not to r.*, mieux vaut ne pas offrir de résistance. (*b*) Repousser (une suggestion). *To r. the evidence*, se refuser à l'évidence. **3.** (*Of girder*) Résister à (une pression).

resistance [ri'zistəns], *s.* Résistance *f.* **1. To offer resistance**, résister (à la police, etc.) ; *F :* rouspéter. *She made no r.*, elle s'est laissé faire. **Weary of resistance**, de guerre lasse. **2.**(*a*) *Mec :* *Ph :* **Line of least resistance**, ligne de moindre résistance. *F : To take the line of least r.*, aller au plus facile. *Mec :* **Impact resistance**, résistance au choc. **High-resistance steel**, acier à haute résistance. (*b*)*El : Magn :* **Resistance coil**, bobine de résistance. (*c*) *El :* **Variable resistance**, résistance variable ; rhéostat *m.*

resistant, resistent [ri'zistənt], *a.* Résistant.

resistless [ri'zistləs], *a.* **1.** Irrésistible. **2.** Qui se laisse faire. **-ly,** *adv.* Irrésistiblement.

resold. *See* RESELL.

re-sole [riː'soul], *v.tr.* Ressemeler (des souliers).

resolute ['rezoljut], *a.* Résolu, déterminé. *R. tone*, ton résolu ; ton ferme. **-ly,** *adv.* Résolument ; avec détermination.

resoluteness ['rezoljutnəs], *s.* Résolution *f.*

resolution [rezo'ljuːʃ(ə)n], *s.* **1.** *Ch : Mth : Mus : etc :* Résolution *f.* **Resolution of water into steam**, résolution de l'eau en vapeur. *Mec :* **Resolution of forces**, décomposition *f* des forces. **2.** Résolution, délibération *f* (d'une assemblée) ; ordre *m* du jour. **To put a resolution to the meeting**, mettre une résolution aux voix. **3.** Résolution, détermination *f.* **Good resolutions**, bonnes résolutions. **4.** Résolution, fermeté *f*, décision *f.* **Lack of resolution**, manque *m* de caractère.

resolve[1] [ri'zɔlv], *s.* Résolution *f.* **To make a resolve to do sth.**, prendre la résolution de faire qch.

resolve[2]. I. *v.tr.* **1.** (*a*) Résoudre (qch. en ses éléments). *The water resolves itself into vapour*, l'eau se résout en vapeur. *Steam resolved into water*, vapeur résoute en eau. *Mec :* **To resolve a velocity into its components**, décomposer une vitesse en ses composantes. *Mus :* **To resolve a discord**, résoudre une dissonance. (*b*) *The House resolved itself into a committee*, la Chambre se constitua en commission. **2.** Résoudre (un problème) ; dissiper (un doute). **3.** (*a*) (*Of committee*) Résoudre, décider (de faire qch.). (*b*) (*Of individual*) **To resolve to do sth.**, prendre la résolution de faire qch. II. **resolve**, *v.i.* **1.** Se résoudre (en ses éléments). **2.** (*Of pers.*) Se résoudre (*upon sth.*, à qch.) ; résoudre (*upon sth.*, de faire qch.). **resolved,** *a.* Résolu, décidé (*to do sth.*, à faire qch.).

resonance ['rezonəns], *s.* Résonance *f.* *Mus :* Vibration *f* (de la voix).

resonant ['rezonənt], *a.* (*Of sound*) Résonnant. *R. voice*, voix sonore.

resorb [ri'sɔːb], *v.tr.* Résorber.

resorption [ri'sɔːrpʃ(ə)n], *s.* Résorption *f.*

resort[1] [ri'zɔːrt], *s.* **1.** (*a*) Ressource *f.* **To be the only resort**, être la seule ressource. (*b*) Recours *m.* **Without resort to compulsion**, sans avoir recours à la force. *Jur :* **Last resort**, dernier ressort. **2. Place of great resort**, lieu très fréquenté. **3.** (*a*) Lieu de séjour, de rendez-vous. *R. of thieves*, repaire *m* de voleurs. (*b*) **Health resort**, station climatique, thermale. **Seaside resort**, station balnéaire ; plage *f.* **Holiday resort**, (centre *m* de) villégiature *f.*

resort[2], *v.i.* **1.** Avoir recours, recourir (*to*, à) ; user (*to*, de). **To resort to force**, faire emploi de

la force. *To r. to violence*, recourir à la violence. **To resort to blows**, en venir aux coups. **2. To resort to a place**, (i) se rendre, affluer, dans un endroit ; (ii) fréquenter un lieu.

resound [ri'zaund], *v.i.* (*a*) Résonner ; retentir (*with cries*, de cris). (*b*) (*Of event*) Avoir du retentissement. **resounding**, *a.* Résonnant, retentissant ; (rire) sonore. **Resounding success**, succès bruyant. **-ly,** *adv.* D'une manière retentissante ; bruyamment ; avec fracas.

resource [ri'sɔːrs], *s.* **1.** Ressource *f.* **Man of resource**, homme de ressource. *Man of no r.*, homme sans moyens, incapable de se débrouiller. *S.a.* LAST[2] I. **1.** **2.** *pl.* **To be at the end of one's resources**, être au bout de ses ressources. **3.** Récréation *f*, distraction *f.*

resourceful [ri'sɔːrsful], *a.* Fertile en ressources ; *F :* débrouillard.

resourcefulness [ri'sɔːrsfulnəs], *s.* Ressource *f.*

respect[1] [ri'spekt], *s.* **1.** Rapport *m*, égard *m.* **To have respect to sth.**, avoir rapport à qch. **With respect to . . .**, en ce qui concerne . . . ; quant à . . . **In many respects**, à bien des égards. **In some respects**, sous quelques rapports ; par certains côtés. **In every respect**, sous tous les rapports. **In this respect**, à cet égard. **2.** (*Heed*) Égard. **To have respect to sth.**, tenir compte de qch. **Without respect of persons**, sans acception de personnes. **3.** (*a*) Respect *m* (*for the truth*, pour la vérité) ; considération *f* (*for s.o.*, pour, envers, qn). **To have respect for s.o.**, avoir du respect pour qn. *He can command r.*, il sait se faire respecter. **Worthy of respect**, respectable ; digne d'estime. **Out of respect for . . .**, par respect, par égard, pour . . . **With all due respect (to you)**, sauf votre respect. (*b*) **Respect for the law**, respect de la loi. **4.** *pl.* **Respects**, respects, hommages *m.* **To pay one's respects to s.o.**, rendre ses respects à qn.

respect[2], *v.tr.* Respecter. **1.** Honorer (qn) ; porter respect à (qn). **My respected colleague**, mon honoré confrère. **2.** Avoir égard à (qch.). (*a*) *To r. s.o.'s opinion*, respecter l'opinion de qn. (*b*) **To respect persons**, faire acception de personnes. (*c*) **To respect the law**, avoir le respect des lois. (*d*) *He was able to make himself respected*, il a su se faire respecter. **3.** Avoir rapport, avoir trait, à (qch.) ; concerner (qch.). **As respects . . .**, pour ce qui est de . . . ; quant à . . . **respecting,** *prep.* Relativement à ; quant à ; à l'égard de. *Questions r. a matter*, questions relatives à un sujet.

respectability [rispektə'biliti], *s.* Respectabilité *f*, honorabilité *f.*

respectable [ri'spektəbl], *a.* Respectable. **1.** Digne de respect. **2.** (*a*) Honorable, convenable. *The r. middle classes*, la bonne bourgeoisie. **Respectable society**, milieu *m* de gens respectables. *You don't look r.*, vous n'avez pas l'air convenable. **It isn't respectable**, ce n'est pas comme il faut. *Hardly r.*, peu honorable. (*b*) *F :* *She is of a respectable age*, elle est d'un âge canonique. **3.** Passable. **A respectable number of people**, un nombre respectable de gens. **-ably,** *adv.* **1.** Respectablement, honorablement, convenablement. **2.** Pas mal ; passablement.

respecter [ri'spektər], *s.* **To be no respecter of persons**, ne pas faire acception de personnes. *Death is no r. of persons*, la mort n'épargne personne.

respectful [ri'spektful], *a.* Respectueux (*to*, envers, pour). *To keep s.o. at a r. distance*, tenir qn en respect. **-fully,** *adv.* Respectueusement ;

avec respect. *Corr:* I remain yours respectfully, je vous prie d'agréer mes salutations très respectueuses.
respectfulness [ri'spektfulnəs], *s.* Caractère respectueux; respect *m.*
respective [ri'spektiv], *a.* Respectif. **-ly,** *adv.* Respectivement.
respirable ['respirəbl], *a.* Respirable.
respiration [respi'reiʃ(ə)n], *s.* Respiration *f.*
respirator ['respireitər], *s.* Respirateur *m*; masque *m* respiratoire; *Mil:* masque à gaz.
respiratory ['respireitəri], *a.* Respiratoire.
respire [ris'paiər], *v.tr. & i.* **1.** *Bot: etc:* Respirer. **2.** *F:* Reprendre haleine; respirer.
respite[1] ['respit], *s.* **1.** *Jur:* Sursis *m*, délai *m.* To get a r., obtenir un délai. **2.** Répit *m*, relâche *m.* To work without r., travailler sans relâche.
respite[2], *v.tr.* **1.** (*a*) Accorder un sursis à (un prévenu). (*b*) Remettre, différer (un jugement). **2.** Apporter du soulagement à (qn).
resplendence [ri'splendəns], **resplendency** [ri'splendənsi], *s.* Splendeur *f*, resplendissement *m*, éclat *m* (d'une cérémonie).
resplendent [ri'splendənt], *a.* Resplendissant, éblouissant. **-ly,** *adv.* Avec splendeur.
respond [ri'spɔnd], *v.i.* **1.** (*a*) Répondre; faire une réponse. To r. to a toast, répondre à un toast. (*b*) *Ecc:* Réciter les répons. **2.** Répondre, être sensible (à l'affection); se prêter (à une proposition). To respond to music, *F:* avoir la fibre de la musique. (*Of plane*) **To respond to the controls,** obéir aux gouvernes.
respondent [ri'spɔndənt], **1.** *a.* Répondant; qui répond. **2.** *s. Jur:* (i) (*Esp. in divorce case*) Défendeur, -eresse. (ii) (*Before Court of Appeal*) Intimé *m.*
response [ri'spɔns], *s.* **1.** (*a*) Réponse*f*, réplique*f.* (*b*) *Ecc:* Répons *m.* **To make the responses in the mass,** at mass, répondre la messe. **2.** (*a*) Réponse (à un appel). This appeal met with a generous r., il fut répondu largement à cet appel. To act in r. to the call of duty, répondre à l'appel du devoir. (*b*) Réaction *f*, réponse.
responsibility [rispɔnsi'biliti], *s.* Responsabilité *f.* **To assume a responsibility,** accepter une responsabilité. **To accept responsibility for sth.,** prendre la responsabilité de qch. To do sth. on one's own responsibility, faire qch. de son chef.
responsible [ri'spɔnsibl], *a.* **1.** (*a*) Chargé (d'un devoir). Person r. for doing sth., personne à qui il incombe de faire qch. **Responsible to s.o.,** responsable devant qn. Commission r. to a government, commission relevant d'un gouvernement. **To be responsible to s.o. for sth.,** avoir à rendre compte à qn de qch. He ·s not responsible for his actions, il n'est pas maître de ses actes. (*b*) Responsable (d'un accident). **To hold s.o. responsible (for sth.),** tenir qn responsable (de qch.). *Jur:* **To be responsible for s.o.'s actions,** être solidaire des actes de qn. **2.** Capable, compétent. **In responsible quarters,** dans les milieux autorisés. Situation for a r. man, situation pour homme sérieux. **3.** (Poste) plein de responsabilités.
responsive [ri'spɔnsiv], *a.* (*a*) Impressionnable; sensible (to, à). They are r. to affection, ils répondent à l'affection. (*b*) (Moteur) docile, nerveux, souple. *W.Tel:* (Détecteur) sensible. **-ly,** *adv.* Avec sympathie.
responsiveness [ri'spɔnsivnəs], *s.* **1.** Émotion *f* sympathique; sensibilité *f.* **2.** Flexibilité *f*, souplesse *f* (d'un moteur).
ressaldar [resal'dɑːr], *s.m.* (*Indian army*) Capitaine (indigène) de cavalerie.

rest[1] [rest], *s.* **1.** (*a*) Repos *m.* To go, retire, to rest, aller se reposer. **To have a good night's rest,** passer une bonne nuit. **At rest,** en repos. **To set a question at rest,** régler, vider, une question. **To set s.o.'s mind at rest,** calmer l'esprit de qn; dissiper les inquiétudes de qn. *S.a.* LAY[4] 3. (*b*) **To take a rest,** se donner du repos; se reposer; *Mil:* faire la pause. To travel with occasional rests, voyager à reposées *f.* **The day of rest,** le jour du Seigneur. (*c*) **To come to rest,** s'arrêter, s'immobiliser. **2.** *Mus:* Pause *f*, silence *m.* **Semibreve rest,** pause. **Crotchet rest,** soupir *m.* **Quaver rest,** demi-soupir *m.* **3.** Abri *m* (pour chauffeurs de taxis); foyer *m* (pour matelots). **4.** Support *m.* **Arm-rest** (*of chair*), accoudoir *m.* (Billiard-cue) rest, râteau *m.* **Telescope rest,** affût *m* de télescope. *Tp:* **Receiver-rest,** étrier *m* du récepteur. **'rest-camp,** *s. Mil:* Cantonnement *m* de repos. **'rest-cure,** *s.* Cure *f* de repos. **'rest-house,** *s.* Auberge *f*, hôtellerie *f.*
rest[2]. **I.** *v.i.* **1.** (*a*) Avoir du repos, de la tranquillité. He will not r. till he has succeeded, il n'aura (pas) de cesse qu'il n'ait réussi. **To rest in the Lord,** s'en remettre à Dieu. **Let him rest in peace,** qu'il repose en paix. The waves never rest, les vagues ne sont jamais tranquilles. (*b*) Se reposer. Let us rest here awhile, reposons-nous ici quelques instants. *Th: F:* **To be resting,** se trouver sans engagement. *S.a.* OAR[1]. (*c*) **So the matter rests,** l'affaire en reste là. I shall not let it r. at that, cela ne se passera pas ainsi. **2.** (*a*) Se poser, s'appuyer. His hand resting on the table, sa main posée, appuyée, sur la table. **To 'et one's glance rest on sth.,** reposer ses regards sur qch. A heavy responsibility rests upon them, une lourde responsabilité pèse sur eux. (*b*) Trade rests upon credit, le commerce repose sur le crédit. *Cf.* REST[4]. **II.** *v.tr.* (*a*) Reposer, faire reposer (qn). To r. one's men, faire reposer ses hommes. God rest his soul! Dieu donne le repos à son âme! (*b*) Appuyer (ses coudes sur la table); déposer (un fardeau par terre). **To rest sth. against sth.,** appuyer qch. contre qch. **resting,** *a.* (Homme, machine) au repos. **'resting-place,** *s.* (Lieu *m* de) repos *m*; gîte *m*, abri *m.* Last resting-place, dernière demeure.
rest[3], *s.* **1.** Reste *m*, restant *m.* **To do the rest,** faire le reste. **For the rest,** quant au reste; d'ailleurs. **2.** The rest, les autres *mf.* The rest of us, les autres d'entre nous.
rest[4], *v.i.* **1.** Rester, demeurer. **Rest assured that . . .,** soyez assuré que. . . . **2.** It rests with you (*to do sth.*), il dépend de vous, il ne tient qu'à vous (de faire qch.). It does not r. with me to . . ., il est en dehors de mes pouvoirs de. . . . It rests with France to decide, il appartient à la France de décider. *Cf.* REST[2].
rest[5], *s.* Lance *f*, lance en arrêt. **'rest-harrow,** *s. Bot:* Bugrane *f.*
restart [riː'stɑːrt]. **1.** *v.tr.* (*a*) Recommencer, reprendre (un travail). (*b*) (Re)mettre (une machine) en marche; relancer (un moteur). **2.** *v.i.* (*a*) (Of work) Recommencer, reprendre. (*b*) (*Of machine*) Se remettre en marche.
restaurant ['restərɔ̃, 'restorɑ̃(t)], *s.* Restaurant *m.* Rail: **Restaurant-car,** wagon-restaurant *m.*
restful ['restful], *a.* Qui repose; paisible, tranquille. R. spot, endroit reposant. **-fully,** *adv.* Paisiblement, tranquillement.
restfulness ['restfulnəs], *s.* Tranquillité *f.*
restitch [riː'stitʃ], *v.tr.* Repiquer (à l'aiguille).
restitution [resti'tjuːʃ(ə)n], *s.* Restitution *f.* **To make restitution of sth.,** restituer qch. *Jur:*

Restitution of conjugal rights, réintégration *f* du domicile conjugal.

restive ['restiv], *a.* **1.** (Cheval) rétif, quinteux; *F:* (personne) rétive, indocile. **2.** Inquiet, -ète; nerveux.

restiveness ['restivnəs], *s.* **1.** Humeur rétive. **2.** Humeur inquiète; nervosité *f.*

restless ['restləs], *a.* **1.** Sans repos. To have a restless night, passer une nuit blanche. **2.** (*a*) Agité. To be restless in one's sleep, avoir le sommeil agité, troublé. (*b*) (Enfant) remuant. **3.** Inquiet, agité. *R.* brain, cerveau en effervescence. *He's a r.* soul, c'est un agité. *R.* eye, regard inquiet. The audience was getting restless, l'auditoire s'impatientait. **-ly,** *adv.* **1.** Avec agitation. **2.** Nerveusement, fiévreusement.

restlessness ['restləsnəs], *s.* **1.** (*a*) Inquiétude *f*, agitation *f.* (*b*) Turbulence *f*; mouvement incessant (de la mer). **2.** Nervosité *f*; effervescence *f* (du peuple).

restock [riː'stɔk], *v.tr.* **1.** Repeupler (un étang). **2.** *Com:* Remonter, regarnir (un magasin).

restoration [restə'reiʃ(ə)n], *s.* **1.** Restitution *f* (de biens); remise *f* (d'objets trouvés). **2.** Restauration *f* (d'un monument); restitution (d'un texte). **3.** (*a*) Réintégration *f* (d'un fonctionnaire). (*b*) Rétablissement *m* de la santé. (*c*) Relèvement *m* (d'une fortune). **4.** Rétablissement sur le trône; restauration.

restorative [ri'stɔːrətiv], *a. & s. Med:* **1.** Fortifiant (*m*); reconstituant (*m*). **2.** Cordial (*m*), -aux.

restore [ri'stɔːər], *v.tr.* **1.** Restituer, rendre (qch.). To restore sth. to s.o., rendre qch. à qn. **2.** (*a*) Restaurer (un monument); réparer (un tableau); rénover (un meuble). (*b*) Reconstituer, restituer (un texte). **3.** (*a*) To restore sth. to its place, remettre en place. (*b*) Rétablir, réintégrer (qn dans ses fonctions). To restore the king (to the throne), rétablir le roi sur le trône. (*c*) To restore s.o. to health, rétablir la santé de qn. *Are you quite restored to health?* êtes-vous bien rétabli? To restore s.o. to life, ramener qn à la vie. **4.** (*a*) Rétablir (la liberté, la discipline); ramener (la confiance); faire renaître (le calme). *Public order is being restored,* l'ordre se rétablit. *To see calm restored,* voir renaître le calme. (*b*) To restore s.o.'s strength, redonner des forces à qn. To restore the circulation, réactiver la circulation.

restorer [ri'stɔːrər], *s.* **1.** Restaurateur, -trice (d'un tableau); rénovateur *m* (de meubles). **2.** Health restorer, fortifiant *m.*

restow [riː'stou], *v.tr.* Réarrimer (la cargaison).

restrain [ri'strein], *v.tr.* **1.** Retenir, empêcher (qn) (*from,* de). **2.** Contenir, refréner (ses passions); retenir (sa curiosité). To restrain oneself, se contraindre. To restrain one's mirth, se retenir de rire. To r. production, freiner la production. **restrained,** *a.* **1.** (*Of anger*) Contenu. In restrained terms, en termes mesurés. **2.** (*Of style*) Tempéré. *R.* drawing, dessin très sobre. **restraining,** *a.* Qui retient; restrictif. *Phot:* Restraining bath, bain ralentisseur.

restrainedly [ri'streinidli], *adv.* Avec retenue. *To speak r.,* parler avec contrainte.

restraint [ri'streint], *s.* **1.** (*a*) Contrainte *f*, entrave *f*, frein *m.* To put a restraint on s.o., tenir qn en contrainte. To fret, chafe, under restraint, (i) ronger son frein; (ii) ne pouvoir souffrir aucune contrainte. To break through every restraint, se donner libre cours. *To be under no r.,* avoir ses coudées franches. (*b*) Con-

trainte; réserve *f.* To put a restrain upon oneself, se contenir, se contraindre. Lack of restraint, abandon *m*; manque *m* de réserve. *To speak without r.,* parler en toute liberté. *To fling aside all r.,* ne garder aucune mesure. (*c*) Sobriété *f* (de style); mesure *f.* **2.** Contrainte par corps; interdiction *f* (d'un aliéné). To keep s.o. under restraint, tenir qn emprisonné. To put a lunatic under restraint, interner un aliéné.

restrict [ri'strikt], *v.tr.* Restreindre; réduire (les libertés publiques). *I am restricted to advising,* il ne m'est permis que de donner des conseils. To restrict the consumption of alcohol, restreindre la consommation de l'alcool. **restricted,** *a.* Restreint, limité. *R.* horizon, horizon borné. *R.* diet, régime sévère. *Adm:* Restricted area, zone *f* où l'allure des automobiles est limitée.

restriction [ri'strikʃ(ə)n], *s.* Restriction *f.* (*a*) Restriction of expenditure, réduction *f* des dépenses. (*b*) To place restrictions on the sale of . . ., apporter des restrictions à la vente de . . .

restrictive [ri'striktiv], *a.* Restrictif.

restring [riː'striŋ], *v.tr.* Recorder (une raquette).

result¹ [ri'zʌlt], *s.* **1.** Résultat *m* (*of,* de); aboutissement *m* (des efforts de qn). *His infirmity is the r. of an accident,* son infirmité est due à un accident. The result is that . . ., il en résulte que. . . . In the result . . ., finalement. . . . *What will be the r. of it all?* que sortira-t-il de tout cela? As a result of . . ., par suite de. . . . Without result, sans résultat. *To give out the results (of a competition),* donner le classement. *Gram:* 'Result' clause, proposition consécutive. **2.** *Ar:* Résultat.

result², *v.i.* **1.** Résulter, provenir (*from,* de). *It results from this that . . .,* il s'ensuit que. . . . *Damage resulting from an accident,* dommage consécutif à un accident. **2.** It resulted in nothing, il n'en est rien résulté; cela n'a mené à rien. It resulted in a large profit, cela a donné de gros bénéfices.

resultant [ri'zʌltənt], *a.* Résultant. *Mec:* Resultant force, *s.* resultant, force résultante; résultante *f. To find the r. of three forces,* composer trois forces.

resume [ri'zjuːm], *v.tr.* **1.** Reprendre, regagner (sa vigueur). To resume one's seat, se rasseoir. **2.** To resume a territory, reprendre possession d'un territoire. *S.a.* POSSESSION 1. **3.** (*a*) Reprendre (une conversation); renouer (des relations). To resume work, se remettre au travail. *If hostilities should be resumed,* si les hostilités reprenaient. (*b*) "This was a great mistake," he resumed, "c'était une grosse erreur," reprit-il. **4.** Reprendre, récapituler (les faits).

résumé ['rezjume], *s.* Résumé *m.*

resumption [ri'zʌmpʃ(ə)n], *s.* Reprise *f* (de négociations, des travaux). *Jur:* Resumption of residence, réintégration *f* de domicile.

resurrect [rezə'rekt], *v.tr.* Ressusciter, faire revivre (qn, *F:* une mode, etc.).

resurrection [rezə'rekʃ(ə)n], *s.* **1.** Résurrection *f* (des morts). **2.** *Eng.Hist: F:* Resurrection man, déterreur *m* de cadavres. **3.** *F:* Résurrection (d'une coutume); réchauffement *m* (d'un plat).

resurrectionist [rezə'rekʃənist], *s. Eng.Hist:* Déterreur *m* de cadavres (aux fins de dissection).

resuscitate [ri'sʌsiteit], *v.tr. & i.* Ressusciter.

resuscitation [risʌsi'teiʃ(ə)n], *s.* Ressuscitation *f.*

ret [ret], *v.tr.* (retted) Rouir (le lin). **retting,** *s.* Roui *m,* rouissage *m* (du lin).

retable [ri'teibl, 'riːteibl], *s. Ecc:* Retable *m.*

retail¹ ['ri:teil], *s. Com:* Détail *m* ; vente *f* au détail. **To sell goods retail,** vendre des marchandises au détail. **Wholesale and retail,** en gros et au détail. **Retail dealer,** détaillant. **Retail price,** prix de étail.

retail² [ri:'teil], *v.tr.* **1.** Détailler, vendre au détail (des marchandises). **Goods that retail at . . .,** marchandises qui se vendent au détail à. . . . **2.** *F:* Répéter, colporter (des commérages).

retailer [ri:'teilər], *s.* **1.** Détaillant *m* ; marchand *m* au détail. **2.** *F:* **Retailer of news,** colporteur *m* de nouvelles.

retain [ri'tein], *v.tr.* **1.** Retenir, maintenir (qch. dans une position). **2.** Engager, retenir (un domestique). **To retain s.o.'s services,** retenir, arrêter, les services de qn. **3.** Conserver, garder (un bien). *To r. all one's faculties,* conserver toutes ses facultés. **To retain hold of sth.,** ne pas lâcher (prise de) qch. *To r. control of one's car,* demeurer maître de sa voiture. **4.** Garder (qch.) en mémoire ; retenir (qch.) dans son souvenir. **retaining,** *a.* **1. Retaining wall,** mur de soutènement. **Retaining dam,** barrage de retenue. *Surg:* **Retaining bandage,** bandage contentif. **2. Retaining fee** = RETAINER 3.

retainer [ri'teinər], *s.* **1.** *(a)* Dispositif *m* de retenue. *(b) A brick is a r. of heat,* une brique conserve la chaleur. **2.** *Hist:* Serviteur *m,* suivant *m. A lord's retainers,* la suite, les gens *m,* d'un noble. **3.** *(a)* Arrhes *fpl. (b) Jur:* Honoraires versés à un avocat pour s'assurer son concours éventuel ; avance *f.*

retake¹ ['ri:teik], *s. Cin:* Réplique *f* (d'une prise de vues).

retake² [ri:'teik], *v.tr.* (**retook** [ri:'tuk] ; **retaken**) **1.** Reprendre (une place forte) ; rattraper (un prisonnier qui s'est sauvé). **2.** *Cin:* Tourner à nouveau (une scène). **retaking,** *s.* Reprise *f* d'une position.

retaliate [ri'talieit], *v.i.* **To retaliate on s.o.,** rendre la pareille (à qn) ; user de représailles (envers qn).

retaliation [ritali'ei∫(ə)n], *s.* Revanche *f,* représailles *fpl.* **In retaliation,** en revanche. **The law of retaliation,** la loi du talion.

retaliatory [ri'taliətəri], *a.* De représailles. **Retaliatory measures,** représailles *f.*

retard [ri'ta:rd], *v.tr.* Retarder. *I.C.E:* **To retard the spark,** retarder l'allumage. *Mec:* **Retarded acceleration,** accélération négative. *Med:* **Mentally retarded child,** enfant attardé.

retardation [ri:ta:r'dei∫(ə)n], *s.* **1.** *(a)* Retardement *m* ; retard *m. (b) Mus:* Ralentissement *m* (de la mesure). **2.** *Mec: Ph:* *(a)* Retardation *f* ; accélération négative. *(b)* Freinage *m.* **3.** *Nau:* Retard (des marées).

retardment [ri'ta:rdmənt], *s.* Retardement *m,* retard *m.*

retch [ret∫, ri:t∫], *v.i.* Faire des efforts pour vomir ; avoir des haut-le-cœur. **retching,** *s.* Efforts *mpl* pour vomir ; des haut-le-cœur *m.*

retell [ri:'tel], *v.tr.* (**retold** [ri:'tould] ; **retold**) Raconter de nouveau.

retemper [ri:'tempər], *v.tr. Metalw:* Retremper. **retempering,** *s.* Retrempe *f.*

retention [ri'ten∫(ə)n], *s.* **1.** *Med:* Rétention *f.* **2.** Conservation *f* (d'un usage). **To decide on the r. of sth.,** décider de garder, de conserver, qch.

retentive [ri'tentiv], *a.* **1.** *(a)* (Mémoire) tenace. *(b)* **To be retentive of sth.,** retenir, garder, qch. **Retentive soil,** sol qui retient l'eau. **2.** *Surg:* (Bandage) contentif.

retentiveness [ri'tentivnəs], *s.* **Retentiveness of memory,** fidélité *f,* ténacité *f,* de mémoire.

reticence ['retis(ə)ns], *s.* **1.** Réticence *f. To tell a story without any r.,* raconter les choses sans rien gazer, sans aucune réserve. **2.** Caractère peu communicatif.

reticent ['retis(ə)nt], *a.* Peu communicatif ; taciturne. **To be very reticent about an event,** faire grand mystère d'un événement. **-ly,** *adv.* Avec réticence ; avec réserve.

reticle ['retikl], *s. Opt:* Réticule *m* (de télescope).

reticular [re'tikjulər], *a.* Réticulaire ; en réseau.

reticulate [re'tikjuleit]. **1.** *v.tr.* Couvrir (une surface) d'un réseau ; diviser (une surface) en réseau. **2.** *v.i.* Former un réseau. **reticulated,** *a.* Réticulé ; rétiforme.

reticulation [retikju'lei∫(ə)n], *s.* Réticulation *f* ; structure maillée.

reticule ['retikju:l], *s.* **1.** Réticule *m* ; sac *m* à main. **2.** = RETICLE.

retiform ['ri:tifɔ:rm], *a.* Rétiforme.

re-tin [ri:'tin], *v.tr.* (re-tinned) Rétamer.

retina ['retinə], *s. Anat:* Rétine *f* (de l'œil).

retinue ['retinju:], *s.* Suite *f* (d'un prince).

retire [ri'taiər]. I. *v.i.* **1.** *(a)* Se retirer (*to a place,* dans un endroit). **To retire into oneself,** se replier sur soi-même. *(b)* **To retire from the room,** quitter la salle. **To retire for the night,** aller se coucher. **2.** Se démettre (de ses fonctions). **To retire from business,** se retirer des affaires. **To retire on a pension,** prendre sa retraite. **3.** *(a) Mil:* Reculer ; se replier. *(b) Sp:* **To retire from the race,** se retirer de la partie ; abandonner. *(c) Fenc:* Rompre. **4.** *Art:* (Of background) S'éloigner, fuir. II. **retire,** *v.tr.* **1.** *Adm:* Mettre (un fonctionnaire) à la retraite. **2.** *Com:* Retirer, rembourser (un effet). **retired,** *a.* **1.** *(a)* (Of life) Retiré. *(b)* (Endroit) retiré, peu fréquenté. **In a retired spot,** à l'écart. **2.** *(a)* (Commerçant) retiré des affaires ; (officier) retraité. *(b)* **Retired pay,** solde *f* de retraite. *Mil:* **Retired list,** cadre *m* de retraite. **On the retired list,** en retraite ; retraité.

retiring¹, *a.* **1.** (Of pers.) Réservé ; farouche. *He is of a r. disposition,* il aime à s'effacer. **2.** (Président) sortant. **retiring²,** *s.* **1. Retiring room,** cabinet particulier, vestiaire *m* (d'un magistrat). **2.** *(a)* **Retiring pension,** pension de retraite. *(b)* **R. from business,** cessation *f* de commerce.

retirement [ri'taiərmənt], *s.* **1.** *(a) Adm: Mil:* La retraite. **Compulsory retirement,** retraite d'office. *(b)* **To live in retirement,** vivre retiré du monde. **2.** *(a)* Retraite, repliement *m* (des troupes). *(b)* Abandon *m* de la partie ; *abs.* abandon. **3.** *Com:* Retrait *m,* remboursement *m* (d'un effet).

retold [ri:'tould]. See RETELL.

retort¹ [ri'tɔ:rt], *s.* Réplique *f* (*to,* à) ; riposte *f. To make an insolent r.,* répliquer par une insolence.

retort², *v.tr.* Répliquer, riposter, repartir. *"That's your business,"* he retorted, "ça c'est votre affaire," riposta-t-il.

retort³, *s. Ch: Ind:* Cornue *f.*

retouch¹ [ri:'tat∫], *s.* Retouche *f* (à un tableau).

retouch², *v.tr.* Retoucher (un travail).

retrace [ri'treis], *v.tr.* **1.** Remonter à l'origine de (qch.). **2.** Reconstituer (le passé). **3.** **To retrace one's steps,** revenir sur ses pas.

retract [ri'trakt], *v.tr.* *(a)* Rétracter ; tirer (qch.) en arrière. *Av:* **To retract the under-carriage,** escamoter le train d'atterrissage. *(b)* Rétracter (ce qu'on a dit). *Abs.* **To retract,** se rétracter ; se dédire. *Chess:* **To retract a move,** déjouer.

retractable [ri'traktəbl], *a.* *Av:* Retractable under-carriage, train d'atterrissage rentrant, escamotable.

retractation [ri:trak'teiʃ(ə)n], *s.* Rétractation *f* (de sa parole); désaveu *m* (d'une opinion).

retractile [ri'traktail], *a.* *Nat.Hist:* (Organe, etc.) rétractile.

retraction [ri'trakʃ(ə)n], *s.* **1.** Retrait *m*, rétraction *f* (des griffes). **2.** = RETRACTATION.

retranslation [ri:traːns'leiʃ(ə)n], *s.* *Sch:* Retranslation exercise, thème *m* où l'on part d'une traduction pour reconstituer l'original.

retransmission [ri:traːns'miʃ(ə)n], *s.* **1.** Réexpédition *f*, translation *f* (d'un télégramme). **2.** *W.Tel:* Retransmission *f*.

retransmit [ri:traːns'mit], *v.tr.* (retransmitted) Réexpédier (un télégramme).

retread [ri:'tred], *v.tr.* (p.t. & p.p. retreaded) *Aut:* Rechaper, surmouler (un pneu). **retreading,** *s.* Rechapage *m*, surmoulage *m*.

retreat[1] [ri'tri:t], *s.* **1.** *Mil:* (*a*) Retraite *f*. To be in retreat, battre en retraite. (*b*) (*Evening call*) La retraite. **2.** Retraite, recul *m* (des eaux, etc.); décrue *f* (d'un glacier). **3.** (*a*) Abri *m*, asile *m*; retraite. (*b*) Repaire *m* (de brigands).

retreat[2]. **1.** *v.i.* (*a*) Se retirer, s'éloigner (*to a place*, vers un endroit). *Box: Fenc:* Rompre. (*b*) *Mil:* Battre en retraite. **2.** *v.tr. Chess:* Ramener (une pièce en danger). **retreating,** *a.* **1.** (*a*) (Mer, etc.) qui se retire. (*b*) *Mil:* (Ennemi) en retraite. **2.** Retreating chin, menton fuyant.

retrench [ri'trenʃ], *v.tr.* Restreindre (ses dépenses). *Abs.* To retrench, restreindre sa dépense; faire des économies.

retrenchment [ri'trenʃmənt], *s.* **1.** (*a*) Réduction *f* (des dépenses). (*b*) Policy of retrenchment, politique d'économies. **2.** Suppression *f*, retranchement *m* (d'un passage littéraire, etc.). **3.** *Mil:* Retranchement.

retrial [ri:'traiəl], *s.* *Jur:* Nouveau procès.

retribution [retri'bju:ʃ(ə)n], *s.* Châtiment *m*; jugement *m*. Just retribution of, for, a crime, juste récompense *f* d'un crime.

retributive [ri'tribjutiv], *a.* Vengeur, *f.* vengeresse. Retributive punishment, punition justicière.

retrievable [ri'tri:vəbl], *a.* **1.** (Somme) recouvrable. **2.** (Perte, erreur) réparable.

retrieval [ri'tri:v(ə)l], *s.* **1.** Recouvrement *m* (de biens). **2.** Rétablissement *m*, relèvement *m* (de sa fortune). **3.** Réparation *f* (d'une perte, d'une erreur). Beyond retrieval, past retrieval, irréparable(ment).

retrieve [ri'tri:v], *v.tr.* **1.** (*a*) (*Of dog*) Rapporter (le gibier). (*b*) Recouvrer (des biens); retrouver (un objet perdu). **2.** (*a*) Relever, rétablir (la fortune de qn). To r. one's honour, to retrieve oneself, racheter son honneur; rétablir sa réputation. (*b*) To r. s.o. from ruin, arracher qn à la ruine. **3.** Réparer (une perte, une erreur).

retriever [ri'tri:vər], *s.* *Ven:* **1.** Chien rapporteur. **2.** (*Breed*) Retriever *m*.

retrim [ri:'trim], *v.tr.* (retrimmed) Regarnir.

retroaction [ri:tro'akʃ(ə)n], *s.* **1.** Réaction *f*; contre-coup *m*. **2.** Rétroaction *f* (d'une loi).

retroactive [ri:tro'aktiv], *a.* Rétroactif.

retrocede[1] [ri:tro'si:d], *v.i.* Rétrograder, reculer.

retrocede[2], *v.tr.* Rétrocéder (un territoire, etc.).

retrocession[1] [ri:tro'seʃ(ə)n], *s.* Recul *m*; mouvement *m* rétrograde.

retrocession[2], *s.* Rétrocession *f* (d'un droit).

retrogradation [retrogra'deiʃ(ə)n], *s.* **1.** *Astr:* Rétrogradation *f*; mouvement *m* rétrograde. **2.** Dégénérescence *f*; *Biol:* régression *f*.

retrograde[1] ['retrogreid], *a.* (*a*) Rétrograde. (*b*) *In r.* order, en ordre inverse.

retrograde[2], *v.i.* Rétrograder.

retrogress [ri:tro'gres], *v.i.* **1.** Rétrograder. **2.** *Mth:* (*Of curve*) Rebrousser.

retrogression [ri:tro'greʃ(ə)n], *s.* **1.** = RETROGRADATION. **2.** *Mth:* Rebroussement *m* (d'une courbe).

retrogressive [ri:tro'gresiv], *a.* **1.** Rétrogressif, rétrograde. **2.** *Biol:* Régressif; dégénérescent.

retrospect ['retrospekt, 'ri:-], *s.* Coup d'œil rétrospectif; examen rétrospectif.

retrospection [ri:tro'spekʃ(ə)n, retro-], *s.* Examen rétrospectif (des événements, etc.).

retrospective [ri:tro'spektiv, retro-], *a.* **1.** (Examen) rétrospectif. **2.** (Loi) avec effet rétroactif. **3.** (Vue) vers l'arrière.

retry [ri:'trai], *v.tr.* *Jur:* Juger à nouveau.

return[1] [ri'tə:rn], *s.* **1.** (*a*) Retour *m*. The return to school (*after the holidays*), la rentrée des classes. (Immediately) on my return, dès mon retour, à mon retour. On my r. home I found . . ., de retour à la maison j'ai trouvé. . . . He is on his return, il est sur la route du retour. By return of post, par retour du courrier. Many happy returns (of the day)! mes meilleurs vœux pour votre anniversaire! Return journey, voyage de retour. *Rail:* Return ticket, F: return, billet d'aller et retour. (*b*) Return stroke (*of piston*), course de retour. Return flue, tube de retour de fumée ou de flamme. Return angle, retour d'angle. *El.E:* Return current, contre-courant *m*. (*c*) *Arch:* Retour (d'un mur). **2.** *Com:* (*a*) *pl.* Returns, recettes *f.* Quick returns, un prompt débit. (*b*) Revenu *m*, profit *m*; rendement *m*. To bring (in) a fair r., rapporter un bénéfice raisonnable. **3.** (*a*) Renvoi *m*, retour (de marchandises avariées, etc.). On sale or return, (marchandises) en dépôt (avec reprise des invendus); à condition. *Post:* Return address, adresse de l'expéditeur. (*b*) Restitution *f* (d'un objet volé, etc.); ristourne *f* (d'une somme payée en trop). (*c*) *Pen given* in return for a pencil, plume donnée en échange d'un crayon. In return for which . . ., moyennant quoi. . . . If you will do sth. in return, si vous voulez bien faire qch. en retour. (*d*) *pl. Com:* Returns, rendus *m*; (*of books, newspapers*) invendus *m*, *F:* bouillon *m*. **4.** (*a*) Renvoi, répercussion *f* (d'un son). R. of a control lever, rappel *m* d'un levier. Return spring, ressort de rappel. (*b*) *Ten: etc:* Renvoi (de la balle); riposte *f*. **5.** (*a*) Récompense *f.* In return for this service . . ., en récompense, en retour, de ce service. (*b*) *Sp:* Return match, match retour. **6.** (*a*) État *m*, exposé *m*; compte rendu; relevé *m*, relèvement *m*; statistique *f.* Bank return, situation *f* de la Banque. Quarterly r., rapport trimestriel. (*b*) Return of income, déclaration *f* de revenu. **7.** *Pol:* Élection *f* (d'un député).

return[2]. **I.** *v.i.* **1.** (*Come back*) Revenir ; (*go back*) retourner. To r. from a journey, rentrer de voyage. To return (to one's) home, (i) rentrer (chez soi); (ii) regagner sa patrie. They have returned, ils sont de retour. To return from the dead, ressusciter d'entre les morts. Her colour returned, les couleurs lui revinrent. *Nau:* To return to port, rentrer au port. **2.** To return to a task, reprendre une tâche. Let us return to the subject, *F:* revenons à nos moutons. **3.** Retourner, revenir (à un état antérieur). **II.** return, *v.tr.* **1.** (*a*) Rendre (un livre emprunté); restituer (un objet volé); renvoyer (un cadeau); rembourser (un emprunt). (*b*) To return a book to its place, remettre un livre à sa place. **2.** Renvoyer (la lumière, une balle). **Spring to return the valve to its seat,** ressort pour ramener, rappeler, la soupape sur son siège. **3.** (a) Rendre (une visite, un compliment, un coup); renvoyer (une accusation). **To return like for like,** rendre la pareille. **To return s.o.'s love,** répondre à l'amour de qn; aimer qn en retour. *Cards:* **To return clubs,** rejouer du trèfle (après son partenaire). (b) Répondre, répliquer. **To return a denial,** opposer une dénégation. (c) **To return thanks to s.o.,** adresser des remerciements à qn. **4.** Rapporter, donner (un bénéfice). **5.** (a) Déclarer, rapporter; rendre compte de (qch.). **To return one's income at £400,** faire une déclaration de £400 de revenu. (b) *Jur:* **Prisoner was returned guilty,** l'accusé fut déclaré coupable. **6.** *Pol:* Élire (un député). **returned,** a. **1.** (*Of pers.*) De retour. **2. Returned letter,** lettre renvoyée à l'expéditeur. *Com:* **Returned article,** (i) rendu m; (ii) laissé-pour-compte m. **3.** *Sp:* **Returned time,** temps contrôlé, temps officiel.

returnable [ri'tə:rnəbl], a. Restituable. *R. goods,* marchandises de retour; marchandises en commission.

reunion [ri:'ju:njən], s. Réunion f, assemblée f.

reunite [ri:ju'nait]. **1.** v.tr. (a) Unir de nouveau; réunir. (b) Réunir, rassembler (ses partisans); réconcilier (une famille). **2.** v.i. Se réunir. (a) Se réconc lier. (b) (*Of edges of wound*) Se ressouder.

rev[1] [rev], s. *Aut: F:* (*Abbr. of revolution*) *Two thousand revs a minute,* deux mille tours m à la minute.

rev[2], v.tr. (revved) *Aut: F:* **To rev up the engine,** faire s'emballer le moteur.

revarnish [ri:'va:rniʃ], v.tr. Revernir.

reveal[1] [ri'vi:l], v.tr. (a) Révéler, découvrir (son jeu); faire connaître (un fait). **To reveal one's identity,** se faire connaître. (b) Laisser voir. (c) Révéler, découvrir, déceler (un objet caché); dévoiler (un mystère); faire voir, mettre à jour (qch.). **revealing,** a. Révélateur, -trice.

reveal[2], s. *Arch:* Jouée f; tableau m (de pied-droit); listel m d'encadrement (de baie).

reveille [ri'veli], s. *Mil:* Le réveil; la diane.

revel[1] ['rev(ə)l], s. *Often pl.* (a) Divertissement(s) m(pl); réjouissances fpl; ébats mpl. (b) Bacchanale f, orgie f. **Midnight revels,** orgies nocturnes.

revel[2], v. (revelled) **1.** v.i. (a) Se réjouir, se divertir. (b) Faire bombance, faire ripaille. (c) **To revel in sth., in doing sth.,** se délecter à qch., à faire qch.; faire ses délices de qch. **To r. in words,** s'enivrer de mots. **2.** v.tr **To revel away the time,** passer le temps en orgies.

revelation [revə'leiʃ(ə)n], s. **1.** Révélation f. **2.** *B:* **The Revelation, (the Book of) Revelations,** l'Apocalypse f.

reveller ['rev(ə)lər], s. (a) Joyeux convive. (b) Noceur, -euse, cascadeur, -euse, bambocheur, -euse.

revelry ['revəlri], s. (a) Divertissements mpl, ébats mpl. (b) Bacchanale f, orgie f, bombance f.

revenge[1] [ri'vendʒ], s. **1.** Vengeance f. **To take revenge for sth. on s.o.,** se venger de qch. sur qn. **To have one's revenge,** se venger. **In revenge,** pour se venger (*for* de). **Out of revenge,** par vengeance. **2.** (*Esp. in games*) Revanche f; contre-partie f.

revenge[2], v.tr. **1.** **To revenge oneself, to be revenged,** se venger (*on s.o.,* sur qn); tirer, prendre, vengeance (de qn). **To r. oneself for sth.,** e venger de qch. **2.** Venger (une injure). **3.** Venger (qn).

revengeful [ri'vendʒful], a. **1.** Vindicatif. **2.** Vengeur, -eresse. **-fully,** adv. Par vengeance.

revengefulness [ri'vendʒfulnəs], s. Caractère vindicatif; esprit m de vengeance.

revenger [ri'vendʒər], s. Vengeur, -eresse (*of,* de).

revenue ['revənju:], s. **1.** Revenu m, rentes fpl; rapport m (*from an estate,* d'une terre). **2.** **The Public Revenue,** (i) le revenu de l'État; le Trésor public; (ii) *Adm:* le fisc. **Revenue office,** (bureau m de) perception f. **Revenue officer,** employé m de la douane.

reverberate [ri'və:rbəreit]. **1.** v.tr. (a) Renvoyer, répercuter (le son). (b) Réverbérer, réfléchir (la lumière, la chaleur). **To be reverberated,** réverbérer. **2.** v.i. (*Of sound*) Retentir, résonner. (b) (*Of light, heat*) Réverbérer.

reverberation [rivə:rbə'reiʃ(ə)n], s. (a) Renvoi m, répercussion f (d'un son). (b) Réverbération f (de la lumière, de la chaleur).

reverberator [ri'və:rbəreitər], s. Réflecteur m.

reverberatory [ri'və:rbərətəri], a. & s. *Metall:* **Reverberatory (furnace),** four m à réverbère.

revere [ri'vi:ər], v.tr. Révérer, vénérer.

reverence[1] ['revərəns], s. **1.** Respect religieux; révérence f, vénération f. **To hold s.o. in reverence,** révérer qn; éprouver de la vénération pour qn. **To pay reverence to s.o.,** rendre hommage à qn. **2.** *A. & P:* **Saving your reverence,** sauf révérence. **3.** (*Esp. in Ireland*) **Your Reverence,** monsieur l'abbé.

reverence[2], v.tr. Révérer.

reverend ['revərənd], a. **1.** Vénérable. **2.** *Ecc:* (a) **The reverend gentleman,** le révérend abbé, père ou pasteur. (b) (*As title*) **The Rev. Ch. Black,** le révérend Ch. Black. (*Of dean*) **Very Reverend,** très révérend. (*Of bishop*) **Right Reverend,** très révérend. (*Of archbishop*) **Most Reverend,** révérendissime.

reverent ['revərənt], a. Respectueux; plein de vénération. **-ly,** adv. Avec respect.

reverential [revə'renʃ(ə)l], a. (Respect) révérenciel. **-ally,** adv. Avec respect; avec une crainte révérencielle.

reverie ['revəri], s. Rêverie f; *F:* songerie f.

revers [rə'veər, ri'vi:ərz], s.pl. *Cost:* Revers mpl.

reversal [ri'və:rs(ə)l], s. **1.** *Jur:* Réforme f, annulation f (d'un jugement). **2.** Renversement m (*Opt:* d'une image, *Log:* d'une proposition); inversion f. **Reversal of opinion,** revirement m d'opinion.

reverse[1] [ri'və:rs], a. Inverse, contraire, opposé (*to,* à). **In the reverse order,** en ordre inverse. **The reverse side of a medal,** le revers, l'envers m, d'une médaille. *The r. side of a picture,* le dos d'un tableau. **Reverse slope** of a hill, contre-pente f. **Reverse stroke,** contre-course f (du piston). *Mec:* **Reverse motion, action,** marche f arrière.

reverse[2], s. **1.** (a) Inverse m, contraire m, opposé m. **To be quite the reverse of s.o.,** être tout le contraire de qn. (b) *Mil:* **To take a position in reverse,** prendre une position à revers. (c) *Aut:* **To go into reverse,** mettre en marche arrière; renverser la marche. **2.** (a) Revers m (d'une médaille). (b) Verso m (d'un feuillet). **3.** Reverse of fortune, revers de fortune. **To suffer a reverse,** essuyer un revers, une défaite.

reverse[3], v.tr. **1.** Renverser. *Mil:* **To reverse arms,** renverser l'arme. **2.** (a) Retourner (un habit). (b) Renverser (un mouvement); intervertir (l'ordre). **To reverse a process,** avoir recours à une méthode inverse. *Phot:* **To reverse a negative,** invertir un cliché (de négatif en positif)

(c) *Aut:* To reverse one's car, *abs.* to reverse, faire marche arrière. **3.** *Jur:* Révoquer (une sentence); réformer (un jugement). **4.** *v.i. Danc:* Valser de gauche à droite. **reversed,** *a.* **1.** Renversé. *Mil:* With reversed arms, es armes renversées. **2.** Inverse, contraire, opposé. *El:* **Reversed current,** renverse *f* de courant. **reversing**[1], *a.* Réversible. **reversing**[2], *s.* **1.** Renversement *m.* **2.** Inversion *f. Mch: Aut:* Inversion de marche. *Mec.E:* **Reversing lever,** (levier *m* de) renvoi *m. El:* **Reversing switch,** inverseur *m* du courant.

reversible [ri'və:rsibl], *a.* **1.** (Flacon) renversable. **2.** (Drap) à deux endroits; (vêtement) à double face. **3.** (Procédé) réversible. **Reversible motion,** mouvement réciproque **4.** *Phot:* (Film) inversible.

reversion [ri'və:rʃ(ə)n], *s.* **1.** *Jur:* (a) Retour *m* (d'un bien); réversion *f.* (b) Substitution *f.* **Estate in reversion,** bien grevé de droit de retour. **2.** Survivance *f* (d'un bénéfice). **3.** Retour (à un état antérieur). *Biol:* Reversion to type, réversion (au type primitif). **4.** *Phot:* Inversion *f.*

reversionary [ri'və:rʃənəri], *a.* **1.** (Droit) de réversion. **Reversionary annuity,** (i) annuité *f* réversible; (ii) rente *f* à paiement différé. **2.** Atavique.

revert [ri'və:rt], *v.i.* (a) (Of property) Revenir, retourner (to, à). (Of estate) To r. to an ascendant, faire retour à un ascendant. (b) *Biol:* To revert to type, revenir au type primitif. (c) To revert to our subject, pour en revenir à notre sujet.

revetment [ri'vetmənt], *s. Const:* Revêtement *m.*

revictual [ri:'vit(ə)l] *v.* (revictualled) **1.** *v.tr.* Ravitailler, réapprovisionner. **2.** *v.i.* Se ravitailler. **revictualling,** *s.* Ravitaillement *m,* réapprovisionnement *m.*

review[1] [ri'vju:], *s.* **1.** *Jur:* Revision *f* (d'un procès). **2.** *Mil:* Revue *f.* To hold a review, passer une revue. *S.a.* ORDER[1] 3. **3.** Examen *m,* revue (du passé). **4.** Compte rendu (d'un livre). **Review copy,** exemplaire fourni au critique. **5.** *Publ:* Revue (périodique).

review[2], *v.tr.* **1.** Reviser (un procès). **2.** Passer (des faits) en revue. **3.** To review the troops, passer les troupes en revue. **4.** To review a book, faire la critique, le compte rendu, d'un livre.

reviewer [ri'vju:ər], *s.* Critique *m* (littéraire).

revile [ri'vail]. **1.** *v.tr.* Injurier; insulter à (qn). **2.** *v.i. To r. against s.o.,* invectiver contre qn.

revisal [ri'vaiz(ə)l], *s.* Revision *f,* révision *f.*

revise[1] [ri'vaiz]. *s. Typ:* Épreuve *f* de revision; seconde *f.*

revise[2], *v.tr.* **1.** Revoir, relire (un travail); corriger, reviser, réviser (des épreuves). **2.** (a) Reviser (les lois). (b) To revise a decision, revenir sur une décision.

revision [ri'viʒ(ə)n], .. Revision *f,* révision *f.* 'For revision,' 'à revoir.'

revisit [ri:'vizit], *v.tr.* Visiter de nouveau; revisiter; revenir voir (sa maison natale).

revival [ri'vaiv(ə)l], *s.* **1.** Renaissance *f* (des arts); reprise *f* (d'une pièce de théâtre); remise *f* en vigueur (d'une loi). The r. of trade, la reprise des affaires. *Hist:* The revival of learning, la renaissance des lettres; la Renaissance. **2.** (a) Retour *m* à la vie; retour des forces. (b) Reprise des sens. **3.** *Rel:* Réveil *m.* **Religious revival,** renouveau religieux.

revive [ri'vaiv]. **1.** *v.i.* (a) (Of pers.) Ressusciter; reprendre connaissance; reprendre ses sens. (b) (Of feelings) Se ranimer; renaître. His spirits revived, son courage se ranima. (c) (Of custom) Reprendre; (of arts) renaître. Industry is reviving,

l'industrie reprend. Credit is reviving, le crédit se rétablit. **2.** *v.tr.* (a) Faire revivre (qn); rappeler (qn) à la vie; ressusciter (qn). That will revive you, voilà qui vous remontera. (b) Ranimer (les espérances); réveiller (un désir); rappeler (un souvenir); renouveler (un usage); ressusciter (un parti politique). To r. an old charge, reproduire une accusation. To r. s.o.'s courage, remonter le courage de qn. (c) Remettre (une pièce) au théâtre; ressusciter (un périodique). (d) To r. leather, redonner de la souplesse au cuir.

revivify [ri'vivifai], *v.tr.* Revivifier.

revocable ['revokəbl], *a.* Révocable. R. post, emploi amovible.

revocation [revo'keiʃ(ə)n], *s.* Révocation *f;* abrogation *f* (d'un décret). **Revocation of driving licence,** retrait *m* du permis de conduire.

revoke[1] [ri'vouk], *s. Cards:* Fausse renonce.

revoke[2]. **1.** *v.tr.* (a) Révoquer (un ordre); rapporter (un décret); retirer (son consentement); rétracter (une promesse). (b) To revoke a driving licence, retirer un permis de conduire. **2.** *v.i. Cards:* Faire une fausse renonce.

revolt[1] [ri'voult], *s.* Révolte *f.* To rise in revolt, se soulever, se révolter (against, contre).

revolt[2]. **1.** *v.i.* Se révolter, s'insurger, se soulever, se rebeller (from, against, contre). **2.** *v.tr.* (Of action) Révolter, indigner (qn). **revolting,** *a.* **1.** Révoltant. **2.** The r. troops, les troupes insurgées, en révolte. **-ly,** *adv.* D'une façon révoltante.

revolution [revo'lju:ʃ(ə)n, -'lu:-], *s.* **1.** *Astr:* Révolution *f* (d'une planète). **2.** (a) Rotation *f* (autour d'un axe). (b) Tour *m,* révolution d'une roue. Maximum revolutions, régime *m* maximum. **Revolution counter,** compte-tours *m inv.* **3.** *Pol: etc:* Révolution.

revolutionary [revo'lju:ʃənəri, -'lu:-], *a. & s.* Révolutionnaire (mf).

revolutionist [revo'lju:ʃənist, -'lu:-], *s.* Partisan *m* de la révolution; révolutionnaire *mf.*

revolutionize [revo'lju:ʃənaiz, -'lu:-], *v.tr.* Révolutionner.

revolve [ri'vɔlv]. **1.** *v.tr.* (a) Retourner, ruminer (une pensée). (b) Faire tourner (les roues). **2.** *v.i.* (a) Tourner. To revolve on a spindle, pivoter, tourner, sur un axe. The earth revolves round the sun, la terre tourne autour du soleil. (b) The seasons revolve, les saisons font leur révolution, reviennent. **revolving,** *a.* **1.** En rotation. **2.** R. chair, fauteuil pivotant, tournant. R. bookcase, bibliothèque tournante. **Revolving light,** feu à éclats (d'un phare). **Revolving crane,** grue à pivot.

revolver [ri'vɔlvər], *s.* Revolver *m.*

revue [ri'vju:], *s. Th:* Revue *f.*

revulsion [ri'vʌlʃ(ə)n], *s.* **1.** Revirement *m* (de sentiments). R. from s.o., réaction *f* contre qn. **2.** *Med:* Révulsion *f.*

revulsive [ri'vʌlsiv], *a. & s. Med:* Révulsif (m).

reward[1] [ri'wɔːrd], *s.* **1.** Récompense *f.* A hundred pounds reward, cent livres de récompense. As a reward for . . ., en récompense de . . ., pour prix de. . . . **2.** *Publ:* Livre m de prix.

reward[2], *v.tr.* Récompenser, rémunérer (s.o. for sth., qn de qch.). That's how he rewards me for my zeal, voilà comment il me paie mon zèle.

re-wind [ri:'waind], *v.tr.* (re-wound [ri:'waund]) (a) Rebobiner (la soie). (b) Cin: Typewr: etc: Rembobiner (le film, le ruban). **re-winding,** *s.* (a) Rebobinage *m.* (b) Typewr: Rembobinage *m.*

rewrite [ri:'rait], *v.tr.* (rewrote [ri:'rout]; re-written [ri:'rit(ə)n]) Récrire (un article).

Rex [reks]. *Pr.n.m. Jur:* Rex v. Smith, le Roi en cause avec Smith.

rexine ['reksi:n], *s.* Similicuir *m* (de la marque Rexine).

Reynard ['renərd, 'rei-]. *Pr.n.m. Lit:* Reynard (the Fox), maître Renard ; compère le renard.

Rhaetian ['ri:ʃən], *a. Geog:* The Rhaetian Alps, les Alpes rhétiques.

rhapsodize ['rapsodaiz], *v.i. F:* To rhapsodize over sth., s'extasier sur qch.

rhapsody ['rapsodi], *s.* **1.** R(h)apsodie *f.* **2.** *F:* Transports *mpl.*

rhea ['ri:a], *s. Orn:* Rhée *f*, nandou *m.*

Rheims [ri:mz]. *Pr.n. Geog:* Reims *m.*

Rhenish ['reniʃ], *a.* Rhénan. Rhenish w.ne, vin du Rhin.

rheostat ['ri:ostat], *s. El.E:* Rhéostat *m*; résistance *f* à curseur.

rhetor ['ri:tɔːr], *s.* Rhéteur *m.*

rhetoric ['retorik], *s.* **1.** Rhétorique *f*, éloquence *f.* **2.** *Pej:* Rhétorique ; discours creux.

rhetorical [re'tɔrik(ə)l], *a.* (*a*) (Terme) de rhétorique. (*b*) *Pej:* (Style) ampoulé.

rhetorician [reto'riʃ(ə)n], *s.* (*a*) Rhétoricien *m.* (*b*) *Pej:* Rhéteur *m.*

rheumatic [ru'matik], *a.* (*Of pain*) Rhumatismal, -aux. *R. person, s.* **rheumatic,** rhumatisant, -ante. Rheumatic fever, rhumatisme articulaire aigu.

rheumaticky [ru'matiki], *a. F:* Rhumatisant.

rheumatics [ru'matiks], *s.pl. F:* Rhumatisme *m.*

rheumatism ['ru:mətizm], *s.* Rhumatisme *m.* Muscular rheumatism, myodynie *f.* To suffer from *r.*, être sujet au rhumatisme.

rheumatoid ['ru:mətɔid], *a.* Rhumatoïde. *S.a.* ARTHRITIS.

rheumy ['ru:mi], *a. R. eyes*, yeux chassieux.

Rhine (the) [ðə'rain]. *Pr.n.* Le Rhin.

Rhineland (the) [ðə'rainlənd]. *Pr.n.* Les pays rhénans ; la Rhénanie.

Rhinelander ['rainlandər], *s.* Rhénan, -ane.

Rhinestone ['rainstoun], *s.* **1.** Caillou *m* du Rhin (en cristal de roche). **2.** Faux diamant.

rhino¹ ['rainou], *s. P:* Argent *m*; *P:* galette *f.*

rhino², *s. F:* Rhinocéros *m.*

rhinoceros [rai'nɔsərəs], *s.* Rhinocéros *m.*

rhinoplasty ['rainoplasti], *s. Surg:* Rhinoplastie *f.*

rhizome ['raizoum], *s. Bot:* Rhizome *m.*

Rhodesia [ro'di:ziə]. *Pr.n. Geog:* Rhodésia *f.*

Rhodesian [ro'di:ziən], *a. & s.* Rhodésien, -ienne.

rhodium ['roudiəm], *s. Ch:* Rhodium *m.*

rhododendron, *pl.* **-ons, -a** [roudo'dendrən, -ənz, -ə], *s. Bot:* Rhododendron *m.*

rhomb [rɔm(b)], *s.* **1.** *Geom:* Losange *m*; rhombe *m.* **2.** *Cryst:* Rhomboèdre *m.*

rhombohedron, *pl.* **-a** [rɔmbo'hi:drən, -ə], *s. Cryst:* Rhomboèdre *m.*

rhombus, *pl.* **-uses, -i** ['rɔmbəs, -əsiz, -ai], *s. Geom:* Losange *m*; rhombe *m.*

rhubarb ['ru:baːrb], *s. Bot: Pharm:* Rhubarbe *f.*

rhumb [rʌm(b)], *s. Nau:* R(h)umb *m* (de 11° 15'). **'rhumb-line,** *s.* Ligne *f* de rumb ; (*on chart*) loxodromie *f.*

rhyme¹ [raim], *s.* **1.** *Pros:* Rime *f. Rhymes in couplets,* rimes plates, suivies. *Alternate rhymes,* rimes croisées, alternées. *F: Without rhyme or reason,* sans rime ni raison. *There's neither r. nor reason about it,* cela ne rime à rien. **2.** *Usu. pl.* Vers (rimés) ; poésie *f.* In rhyme, en vers.

rhyme². **1.** *v.i.* (*a*) Rimer ; faire des vers. (*b*) (*Of words*) Rimer (*with*, avec). **2.** *v.tr.* Faire rimer (des mots). **rhyming,** *s.* **1.** Recherche *f* de la rime. Rhyming dictionary, dictionnaire de rimes. **2.** *F:* Versification *f.*

rhymester ['raimstər], *s.* Rimailleur *m.*

rhythm [riðm], *s.* Rythme *m*, cadence *f.*

rhythmic(al) ['riðmik(ə)l], *a.* Rythmique, cadencé. *R. tread,* marche scandée. **-ally,** *adv.* Avec rythme ; avec cadence.

rib¹ [rib], *s.* **1.** *Anat:* Côte *f. F:* To smite s.o. under the fifth rib, poignarder qn. **2.** (*a*) Nervure *f* (d'une feuille) ; strie *f* (d'une coquille). (*b*) Nervure (d'une voûte). **3.** (*a*) Support *m*, étançon *m* (d'un échafaudage) ; baleine *f* (de parapluie) ; brin *m* (d'éventail). *Av:* Travée *f* (d'une aile). (*b*) *N.Arch:* Membre *m*, membrure *f.*

rib², *v.tr.* (ribbed) Garnir (qch.) de côtes, de nervures. **ribbed,** *a.* **1.** (Coquillage) strié ; (plafond) à nervures. **2.** (Bas, velours) à côtes, côtelé. Ribbed stitch, point à côtes. **3.** *Bot:* (*Of leaf*) A nervures, nervuré. **ribbing,** *s.* Côtes *fpl.*

ribald ['ribəld], *a.* Licencieux, impudique. *R. song,* chanson paillarde. *R. joke,* paillardise *f.*

ribaldry ['ribəldri], *s.* Paillardises *fpl.*

riband ['ribənd], *s.* = RIBBON.

ribband ['ribənd], *s.* **1.** *Av: N.Arch:* Lisse *f.* **2.** = RIBBON.

ribbon ['ribən], *s.* **1.** Ruban *m. Bunch of r.,* chou *m. Typewr:* Inking ribbon, ruban encreur. **2.** (*a*) Ruban (d'une décoration) ; cordon *m* (d'un ordre). Blue ribbon, ruban bleu. (*b*) *Navy:* Cap ribbon, ruban légendé (du béret). **3.** *pl.* Ribbons, guides *f.* **4.** (*a*) Ruban (de magnésium). (*b*) Steel ribbon, ruban d'acier ; feuillard *m.* **5.** Bande *f*, ruban (de route). Ribbon building, alignement *m* (de maisons) en bordure de route. **6.** *pl.* To tear sth. to ribbons, mettre qch. en lambeaux ; déchiqueter qch. **'ribbon-brake,** *s.* Frein *m* à ruban, à bande. **'ribbon-saw,** *s.* Scie *f* à ruban, à lame sans fin.

rice [rais], *s.* Riz *m.* Husked rice, riz décortiqué. Ground rice, farine *f* de riz. **'rice-paper,** *s.* Papier *m* de riz. **'rice-plantation,** *s.* Rizière *f.*

rice 'pudding, *s. Cu:* Riz *m* au lait. **rice 'shape,** *s. Cu:* Gâteau *m* de riz. **'rice-straw,** *s.* Paille *f* de riz. **'rice-swamp,** *s.* Rizière *f.* **'rice-water,** *s.* Eau *f* de riz.

rich [ritʃ], *a.* **1.** Riche. *R. people, s.* the rich, les riches *m. Extremely r., F:* richissime. The newly rich, les nouveaux riches. To grow rich, s'enrichir. **2.** (*Of soil*) Riche, fertile. *R. pastures,* gras pâturages. *Museum r. in paintings,* musée riche en tableaux. *R. in hope,* riche d'espérances. *S.a.* STRIKE² I. 7. **3.** (Toilette) magnifique ; (meubles) de luxe ; (festin) somptueux. **4.** (*a*) Rich food, nourriture (i) grasse, (ii) composée d'ingrédients de choix. (*b*) *I.C.E:* Rich mixture, mélange riche. **5.** *R. colour,* couleur chaude, riche. **6.** *F:* (*Of incident*) Très divertissant, impayable, épatant. **-ly,** *adv.* **1.** Richement ; avec opulence. **2.** (*a*) Richement, abondamment. (*b*) *F:* He r. deserves it, il l'a joliment bien mérité.

riches ['ritʃiz], *s.pl.* Richesse(s) *f(pl).* He had great r., il était très riche.

richness ['ritʃnəs], *s.* **1.** Richesse *f*, abondance *f.* **2.** Richesse (du sol) ; fertilité *f.* **3.** Somptuosité *f*, luxe *m.* **4.** (*a*) Richesse en principes nutritifs (d'un aliment). (*b*) *I.C.E:* R. of the mixture, richesse du mélange. **5.** Éclat *m* (d'une couleur) ; ampleur *f* (de la voix) ; richesse (du style).

rick¹ [rik], *s.* Meule *f* (de foin). **'rick-cloth,** *s.* Bâche *f* de meule. **'rick-yard,** *s.* Cour *f* de ferme ; pailler *m.*

rick²,³, *s. & v.tr.* = WRICK¹,².

ickets ['rikets], *s.pl.* Rachitisme *m*, nouure *f*. *To have r.*, être rachitique.

ickety ['riketi], *a.* **I.** *Med:* Rachitique, *F:* noué. **2.** *F:* **R.** *legs,* jambes chancelantes. **3.** *F:* (Escalier) branlant, délabré; (fauteuil) bancal. *R. table,* table boiteuse.

ickshaw ['rikʃɔ:, 'rikʃa], *s.* Pousse-pousse *m inv.*

icochet¹ ['rikoʃei], *s.* Ricochet *m*.

icochet², *v.i.* (ricochetted ['rikoʃeid, -ʃetid]) (Of *projectile*) Ricocher.

ictus ['riktəs], *s.* Rictus *m*.

id [rid], *v.tr.* (*p.t.* ridded, rid; *p.p.* rid) Débarrasser, délivrer (*s.o. of sth., qn de qch.*); débarrasser (*a place of sth.,* un endroit de qch.). *To rid one's estate of debt,* purger ses terres de dettes. *To get rid of sth.,* **to rid oneself of sth.,** se débarrasser, se défaire, de qch. *Com: Article hard to get rid of,* article d'écoulement difficile. *Mth: To get rid of* x, y, éliminer x, y. *To get rid of s.o.,* (i) se débarrasser de qn; (politely) éconduire qn; renvoyer (un domestique); (ii) faire disparaître qn; se défaire (d'un ennemi).

·iddance ['ridəns], *s.* (*a*) Débarras *m*. A good riddance! bon débarras! (*b*) Délivrance *f* (from, de).

·idden ['rid(ə)n]. *See* RIDE².

·iddle¹ [ridl], *s.* Énigme *f*, devinette *f*. To ask s.o. a riddle, poser une énigme à qn. *F:* To speak in riddles, parler par énigmes.

·iddle², *s.* Crible *m*, claie *f*.

·iddle³, *v.tr.* **I.** Cribler (le grain); passer (qch.) au crible. **2.** *F:* To riddle s.o. with bullets, cribler qn de balles. **riddling,** *s.* **I.** Criblage *m*. **2.** *pl.* Riddlings, refus *m* du crible.

·ide¹ [raid], *s.* **I.** (*a*) Course *f*, promenade *f*, trajet *m* (à cheval, à bicyclette). To go for a ride, aller se promener à cheval. The ride of the Valkyries, la chevauchée des Valkyries. (*b*) Promenade, voyage *m* (en automobile). To go for a ride in a carriage, aller se promener en voiture. *R. on a roundabout,* tour *m* de chevaux de bois. *It's a twopenny r. on the bus,* c'est un trajet de deux pence en autobus. *U.S: F:* To take s.o. for a ride, enlever qn (pour l'assassiner). **2.** (In forest) Allée cavalière; piste *f*; laie *f*.

·ide², *v.* (rode [roud]; ridden ['rid(ə)n]) **I.** *v.i.* **I.** (*a*) Chevaucher; se promener, monter, à cheval. To ride astride, monter à califourchon. He rides well, il monte bien (à cheval); il est bon cavalier. (*b*) To r. on an elephant, voyager à dos d'éléphant. To ride on a bicycle, aller, se promener, monter, à bicyclette. (Of child) To r. on s.o.'s knee, être à califourchon, à cheval, sur le genou de qn. (*c*) Did he walk or r.? est-il venu à pied ou à cheval? I rode all the way, j'ai fait tout le trajet à cheval. He rode straight at us, il lança son cheval contre nous. To ride like mad, chevaucher à une allure folle. *S.a.* FALL¹ I, HOUND¹, ROUGHSHOD. **2.** He rides twelve stone, il pèse 76 kilos en selle. **3.** Aller, se promener, en voiture; aller, venir, être, en autobus, etc. **4.** (*a*) The moon was riding high in the heavens, la lune voguait haut dans le ciel. (*b*) (Of ship) To ride at anchor, être mouillé. We were riding by the starboard anchor, nous étions sur l'ancre de tribord. To r. head to the land, être évité le cap sur la terre. **II.** ride, *v.tr.* **I.** To ride a race, courir une course. **2.** (*a*) To ride a horse, monter un cheval. *Turf:* Comet ridden by Jones, Comet monté par Jones. To r. an elephant, être monté à dos d'éléphant. To ride a bicycle, aller à bicyclette. *For sale: bicycle, never (been) ridden,* à vendre: bicyclette, jamais

roulée. (*b*) To ride one's horse at a fence, diriger son cheval sur une barrière. *F:* To ride an idea to death, être féru d'une idée. (*c*) Opprimer; (of nightmare) oppresser (qn). Ridden by fear, hanté par la peur. **3.** The ship rides the waves, le navire vogue sur les flots. **ride away,** *v.i.* Partir, s'éloigner (à cheval, etc.). **ride back,** *v.i.* (S'en) retourner, s'en revenir (à cheval, etc.). **ride behind,** *v.i.* **I.** Monter en croupe. **2.** Suivre à cheval. **ride by,** *v.i.* Passer (à cheval, etc.). **ride down,** *v.tr.* Écraser, piétiner. *The squadron rode them down,* l'escadron leur passa sur le corps. **ride in,** *v.i.* Entrer à cheval, etc.). **ride off,** *v.i.* Partir, s'éloigner (à cheval, etc.). **ride out.** **I.** *v.i.* Sortir (à cheval, etc.). **2.** *v.tr.* To ride out the storm, (i) Nau: étaler la tempête; (ii) *F:* surmonter la crise. **ridden,** *a.* Gang-ridden, infesté de gangsters. Family-ridden, (i) chargé de famille; (ii) tyrannisé par sa famille. **riding,** *s.* **I.** Équitation *f*; exercice *m* à cheval. Clever r. (of jockey), monte adroite. *S.a.* TRICK¹ 3. Riding costume, habit *m* de cavalier. **2.** *Nau:* Mouillage *m*. *S.a.* LIGHT¹ 2. **'riding-boots,** *s.pl.* Bottes *f* (à l'écuyère). **'riding-breeches,** *s.pl.* Culotte *f* de cheval. **'riding-coat,** *s.* Habit *m* de cheval. **'riding-gauntlet, -glove,** *s.* Gant *m* de buffle. **'riding-habit,** *s. Cost:* Amazone *f*. **'riding-hood,** *s. A:* Capuchon *m*. Little Red Riding Hood, le petit Chaperon rouge. **'riding-master,** *s.m.* **I.** Maître d'équitation. **2.** *Mil:* Écuyer instructeur. **'riding-school,** *s.* École *f* d'équitation; manège *m*. **'riding-whip,** *s.* Cravache *f*.

rider ['raidər], *s.* **I.** Cavalier, -ière; (in circus) écuyer, -ère. *Rac:* Jockey *m*. He is a good r., il monte bien à cheval. **2.** *pl.* N.Arch: Riders, porques *f*. **3.** (*a*). Ajouté *m*, annexe *f* (d'un document); avenant *m* (d'un verdict); clause additionnelle (d'un projet de loi). (*b*) *Mth:* Exercice *m* d'application (d'un théorème). **4.** Cavalier (d'une balance).

ridge [ridʒ], *s.* **I.** (*a*) Arête *f*, crête *f* (d'une chaîne de montagnes). Wind-cut ridge, arête vive. (*b*) Faîte *m*, faîtage *m*, crête (d'un comble). **2.** *Nau:* Banc *m* (de rochers). **2.** Chaîne *f*, rangée *f* (de coteaux). **3.** *Agr:* Billon *m*, butte *f*. **4.** Arête, strie *f* (sur une surface); ride *f* (sur le sable). **'ridge-bar, -board,** *s. Const:* Longeron *m*, longrine *f*, de faîtage. **'ridge-pole,** *s.* Poutre *f* de faîte. **'ridge-roof,** *s.* Comble *m* à deux pentes. **'ridge-tile,** *s.* (Tuile) faîtière *f*.

ridicule¹ ['ridikju:l], *s.* Moquerie *f*, raillerie *f*, risée *f*, dérision *f*. To hold s.o. up to ridicule, se moquer de qn; tourner qn en ridicule. To lay oneself open to r., s'exposer au ridicule.

ridicule², *v.tr.* Se moquer de, ridiculiser (qn, qch.).

ridiculous [ri'dikjuləs], *a.* Ridicule. *It is perfectly r.,* c'est d'un ridicule achevé. To make oneself ridiculous, se rendre ridicule. The r. side of the situation, le ridicule de la situation. **-ly,** *adv.* Ridiculement; (se conduire) d'une façon ridicule. **ridiculousness** [ri'dikjuləsnəs], *s.* Ridicule *m*.

rife [raif], *pred.a.* To be rife, (of disease) régner, sévir; (of rumour) courir les rues. Distress is r., la misère sévit partout. To wax rife, sévir de plus belle.

riff-raff ['rifraf], *s. Coll:* Canaille *f*, racaille *f*, gueusaille *f*. All the r.-r., tout le bas peuple.

rifle¹ [raifl], *v.tr.* Piller (un endroit); (fouiller à) vider (les poches de qn). *To r. a tomb*, violer, spolier, un tombeau.

rifle², *s.* **1.** Rayure *f* (d'un fusil). **2.** Fusil (rayé). Gallery rifle, carabine *f* de salon. Magazine rifle, fusil à répétition. Rifle shooting, tir *m* au fusil. Rifle sling, bretelle *f* de fusil. **3.** *pl.* Rifles, fusiliers *m*, fantassins *m*. **'rifle-club**, *s.* Société *f* de tir. **'rifle-green**, *a.* Vert foncé *inv* (de l'uniforme des *riflemen*). **'rifle-pit**, *s.* Trou *m* de tirailleur(s); tranchée-abri *f*. **'rifle-range**, *s.* **1.** = RIFLE-SHOT 1. **2.** (*a*) Champ *m* de tir. (*b*) Stand *m* (de tir). **'rifle-shot**, *s.* **1.** Within rifle-shot, à portée de fusil. **2.** Coup *m* de fusil.

rifle³, *v.tr.* Rayer (une pièce à feu). **rifled**, *a.* Rayé. Rifled bore, âme rayée. **rifling**, *s.* **1.** Rayage *m* (d'un fusil). **2.** *Coll.* Rayure(s) *f*.

rifleman, *pl.* **-men** ['raiflmən, -men], *s.m. Mil:* Chasseur à pied; fusilier.

rift [rift], *s.* (*a*) Fente *f*; fissure *f* (dans une roche); crevasse *f*. *R. in the clouds*, éclaircie *f*. (*b*) *F: A rift in the lute*, une fêlure dans le cristal de leur amitié.

rig¹ [rig], *s.* **1.** Gréement *m* (d'un navire). **2.** *F:* Rig(-out), toilette *f*, tenue *f*. *In full evening rig*, en grande tenue de soirée. To get a new rig-out, *F:* se requinquer. **3.** *Mec.E:* (*a*) Équipement *m*, installation *f*. (*b*) Mécanisme *m* de manœuvre.

rig², *v.tr.* (rigged) **1.** Gréer, équiper (un navire). **2.** Monter, mâter (un mât de charge). **rig out**, *v.tr. F:* Attifer, accoutrer (qn). **rig-'out**, *s.* **1.** *See* RIG¹ 2. **2.** (*a*) Trousseau *m*, équipement *m*. (*b*) Jeu complet (d'instruments). **rig up**, *v.tr.* Monter, installer (un appareil); mâter (un mât de charge). **rigging**, *s.* **1.** (*a*) Gréage *m* (d'un navire). (*b*) *Mec.E:* Équipage *m* ou montage *m* (d'une machine). **2.** Gréement *m*, agrès *mpl* (d'un vaisseau); capelage *m* (d'un mât). Main rigging, haubans *mpl* de grand mât. Standing rigging, manœuvres dormantes.

rig³, *v.tr.* **1.** To rig the market, provoquer une hausse ou une baisse factice. **2.** *Cards:* Apprêter, truquer (les cartes).

rigadoon [rigə'du:n], *s. Danc: A:* Rigodon *m*.

rigger ['rigər], *s. Nau:* **1.** Gréeur *m*, mâteur *m*; (*on board*) gabier *m*. **2.** Square-rigger, navire gréé en carré.

right¹ [rait]. **I.** *a.* **1.** *Geom:* (*a*) Right line, ligne droite. (*b*) Right angle, angle droit. To meet at right angles, se croiser à angle droit. **2.** Bon, honnête, droit. More than is right, plus que de raison. It is only right (and proper) *to tell you . . .*, il n'est que justice de vous dire. . . . *Would it be r. for me to . . .?* ferais-je bien de . . . ? I thought it right to . . ., j'ai cru devoir. . . . To take a right view of things, voir juste. To do the right thing, (i) se conduire honnêtement; (ii) faire ce qu'il fallait faire. To do the right thing by s.o., traiter qn honorablement. **3.** (*a*) Correct, juste, exact. *The r. use of words*, l'emploi correct des mots. *To give the r. answer*, répondre juste. *The sum is r.*, l'addition est exacte. *To put an account r.*, ajuster un compte. To put an error right, redresser, corriger, réparer, rectifier, une erreur. *Mistake that can be put r.*, erreur réparable. The right time, l'heure exacte, l'heure juste. My watch is right, ma montre est à l'heure. (*b*) To be right, avoir raison. *He was r. in his opinion*, il ne s'était pas trompé dans son opinion. *Are you r. in refusing?* êtes-vous fondé à refuser? (*c*) The right word, le mot juste. The right side of a fabric, l'endroit *m* d'une étoffe. Right side up, à l'endroit. *The plank is not the r. width*, la planche n'est pas de la largeur voulue.

Have you the right amount? avez-vous votr compte? Is that the right house? est-ce bien l maison? The r. train, le bon train, le train qu'i faut. *F: Am I right for Paris?* suis-je bien dan le train de Paris? To put s.o. right, (i) mettre qr sur la voie; (ii) détromper, désabuser, qn (iii) rectifier les dires de qn. (*d*) In the right place (i) bien placé; (ii) à sa place. The right man in the right place, l'homme de la situation. Yo came at the right moment, vous êtes venu au bor moment. *To do sth. in the r. way*, s'y bier prendre pour faire qch. The right thing to do ce qu'il y a de mieux à faire. The knack o saying the right thing, le don de l'à-propos *F:* He's one of the right sort, c'est un brave homme. That's right! c'est bien cela! à l bonne heure! Quite right! parfaitement *F:* Right! right you are! right ho! bon entendu! d'accord! He is on the right side of forty, il n'a pas encore quarante ans. To ge on the right side of s.o., s'insinuer dans les bonnes grâces de qn. **4.** (*a*) *F:* As right as a trivet, as right as rain, en parfait état. To be in one's right mind, être en possession de toutes ses facultés; avoir toute sa raison. He is not right in his head, il est un peu détraqué. That'll set you right, voilà qui vous remontera. To set things right, rétablir les choses. Things will come right, les affaires s'arrangeront. (*b*) All right. *Everything is all r.*, tout est très bien. It's all right, c'est parfait; tout va bien. All right! c'est bon! ça y est! *I'm all r. again now*, je suis tout à fait remis maintenant. I have made it all right for my family, j'ai pris des arrangements en faveur de ma famille. *F:* It's all right for you to laugh! permis à vous de rire! He's all right! c'est un bon type! **5.** (*Genuine*) Right whale, baleine franche. **6.** (Côté, etc.) droit. On the right side, à droite, sur la droite. On one's right hand, à sa droite. **-ly**, *adv.* **1.** *To act r.*, bien agir; agir sagement. **2.** (Expliquer) correctement. *To see r.*, voir juste. Rightly speaking, à bien prendre les choses. I cannot rightly say, je ne saurais dire au juste. Rightly or wrongly, *I think he is guilty*, à tort ou à raison je le juge coupable. **II. right**, *s.* **1.** Le droit; la justice; le bien. Might and right, la force et le droit. Right and wrong, le bien et le mal. *S.a.* WRONG¹ II. God defend the r.! Dieu protège le droit! To be in the right, avoir raison; être dans son droit. **2.** (*a*) Droit, titre *m*. To have a right to sth., avoir droit à qch. Right of way, (i) *Jur:* servitude *f* de passage; jouissance *f* de passage; (ii) *Aut:* priorité *f* de passage. He has no right to complain, il est mal venu à se plaindre. *With r. of transfer*, avec faculté de transfert. By what right . . .? de quel droit . . .? à quel titre . . .? To possess sth. in one's own right, posséder qch. de son chef; avoir qch. en propre. (*b*) *pl.* Rights, droits; droit. By rights, en toute justice. To be within one's rights, être dans son droit. **3.** (*a*) To set things to rights, rétablir les choses; réparer le désordre. (*b*) Not to know the rights of the case, ne pas savoir qui a tort et qui a raison. I want to know the rights of it, e voudrais en avoir le cœur net. **4.** (*a*) Droite *f*; côté droit. On the right, à droite. To keep to the right, tenir la droite. *Mth: etc:* From right to left, sinistrorsum. *Mil:* By the right! guide à droite! (*b*) *Box:* Coup *m* du droit. **III. right**, *adv.* **1.** (*a*) Droit. To go right on, continuer tout droit. *To do sth. right away*, faire qch. sur-le-champ. *I am going there r. away*, j'y vais de ce pas. Right away! *Rail:* en route! *Av:*

enlevez (les cales)! **2.** (*a*) To sink right to the bottom, couler droit au fond. *There was a wall* right round the house, il y avait un mur tout autour de la maison. (*b*) **Right at the top**, tout en haut. **Right in the middle**, au beau milieu. *He threw it r. in my face*, il me le jeta en pleine figure. *The wind was r. behind us*, nous avions le vent juste dans le dos. **3.** To know right well that . . ., savoir fort bien que. . . . Right reverend, très révérend. **4.** (*a*) To do right, bien faire; bien agir. *S.a.* SERVE I. 7. (*b*) (Répondre) correctement; (deviner) juste. If I remember right, si je me souviens bien. Nothing goes right with me, rien ne me réussit. *I got your letter* all right, *;'*ai bien reçu votre lettre. *F: He is coming right enough*, il va venir sans aucun doute. **5.** A droite. *He looks neither r. nor left*, il ne regarde ni à droite ni à gauche. He owes money right and left, il doit de l'argent de tous les côtés. *Mil:* Eyes right! tête à droite! Right turn! à droite! par le flanc droit! Right dress! à droite, alignement! **'right-about.** **I.** *s. Mil:* Demi-tour *m* à droite. *F:* To send s.o. to the right-about, envoyer promener qn. **2.** *adv. Mil:* Right-about turn! demi-tour à droite! *Nau:* To go right-about, virer court. **'right-angled,** *a.* A angle droit. Right-angled triangle, triangle rectangle. **'right-down.** *F:* **I.** *a.* Right-down thief, franc voleur. **2.** *adv.* He was right-down angry about it, il était tout à fait fâché. **'right-hand,** *attrib.a.* (*a*) (Pouce, gant) de la main droite. (*b*) *The r.-h. drawer*, le tiroir de droite. On the right-hand side, à droite. Right-hand man, *F:* bras droit (de qn). **'right-handed,** *a.* **I.** (*Of pers.*) Droitier. **2.** *Box:* Right-handed blow, punch, coup du droit. **'right-'hander,** *s. Box:* Coup *m* du droit. **'right-'minded,** *a.* **I.** Bien pensant. **2.** *F:* Sain d'esprit. **'right-'thinking,** *a.* Bien pensant. **ight²,** *v.tr.* **I.** Redresser (un canot); remettre (une auto) d'aplomb. (*Of boat*) To right itself, *v.i.* to right, se redresser. **2.** (*a*) Redresser, réparer (un tort). (*b*) Rendre justice à (qn). (*c*) *To r. oneself in the eyes of s.o.*, se justifier aux yeux de qn. **3.** Corriger, rectifier (une erreur). **ighteous** ['raitʃəs], *a.* **I.** Droit, juste; vertueux. **2.** Juste, justifié. *R. anger*, juste colère. **-ly,** *adv.* Avec droiture; vertueusement. **ighteousness** ['raitʃəsnəs], *s.* Droiture *f*, vertu *f.* **ightful** ['raitful], *a.* **I.** Rightful heir, héritier légitime. **2.** (*a*) (*Of claim*) Légitime, juste. (*b*) (*Of conduct*) Équitable. **-fully,** *adv.* Légitimement; à juste titre. **ightness** ['raitnəs], *s.* **I.** Rectitude *f*, droiture *f.* **2.** Justesse *f* (d'une décision). **igid** ['ridʒid], *a.* **I.** Rigide, raide. *R. member*, organe fixe (d'une machine). **2.** (*Of conduct*) Sévère, strict. *R. parsimony*, âpre parcimonie. *R. obligation*, obligation stricte. **-ly,** *adv.* **I.** Rigidement. **2.** Sévèrement. **igidity** [ri'dʒiditi], *s.* **I.** Rigidité *f*, raideur *f.* **2.** Sévérité *f*; intransigeance *f.* **igmarole** ['rigmaroul], *s.* Discours sans suite, incohérent. **igor** ['raigɔːr, 'ri-], *s. Med:* **I.** Frissons *mpl.* **2.** Rigor mortis, rigidité *f* cadavérique. **igorous** ['rigərəs], *a.* Rigoureux. **-ly,** *adv.* Rigoureusement; avec rigueur. **igour** ['rigər], *s.* **I.** Rigueur *f*, sévérité *f.* *The r. of the law*, la rigueur de la loi. **2.** Rigueur, âpreté *f* (du temps). **3.** Exactitude *f* (d'une preuve). **4.** Raideur *f*, austérité *f* (d'une doctrine). **ile** [rail], *v.tr. F:* Agacer, exaspérer (qn). **ill** [ril], *s.* Ruisselet *m*; petit ruisseau.

rim [rim], *s.* **I.** (*a*) Jante *f* (de roue). *Aut:* Well-base rim, jante à base creuse. (*b*) Cercle *m* (d'un tamis). **2.** Bord *m* (d'un vase); cordon *m*, listeau *m* (d'une pièce de monnaie); rebord *m* (d'une cartouche). Spectacle rims, monture *f* de lunettes. *Astr:* Rim of the sun, limbe *m* du soleil. **rime¹** [raim], *s.* Givre *m*; gelée blanche. **rime²,³,** *s. & v.* = RHYME¹,². **rimless** ['rimləs], *a.* (Lunettes) sans monture; (récipient) sans bordure (dépassante). **rimmed** [rimd], *a.* A bord; bordé. **rind** [raind], *s.* **I.** Écorce *f* (mince), peau *f* (d'arbre). **2.** Peau, pelure *f* (de fruit); pelure, croûte *f* (de fromage); couenne *f* (de lard). **rinderpest** ['rindəpest], *s.* Peste bovine. **ring¹** [riŋ], *s.* **I.** (*a*) (Finger-)ring, (*symbolical of rite, office*) anneau *m*; (*for adornment*) bague *f.* Wedding ring, anneau nuptial; alliance *f.* (*b*) Arm-ring, bracelet *m.* **2.** (*a*) Rond *m*, anneau (de métal, etc.); maille *f* (d'une cotte de mailles). Napkin ring, rond de serviette. Umbrella ring, rondelle *f* de parapluie. Split ring (*for keys*), anneau brisé. Ring and staple, anneau à happe. (*b*) (Binding-)ring, frette *f*; (*on gun*) plate-bande *f.* (*c*) *Mch:* I.C.E: Segment *m.* Split ring, segment fendu. **3.** (*a*) Anneau (d'une planète); cerne *m* (autour des yeux); aréole *f* (autour de la lune); rond (de fumée). *He has rings round his eyes*, il a les yeux cernés. *F:* To make rings round s.o., courir deux fois aussi vite que qn; battre qn à plate couture. (*b*) *Bot:* Annual ring (*of tree*), anneau annuel. (*c*) *Orn:* Collier *m* (d'un pigeon). **4.** Cercle *m* (de personnes). Sitting in a ring, assis en rond. **5.** (*a*) Groupe *m*, petite coterie (de personnes). (*b*) *Com:* (i) Syndicat *m*, cartel *m* (ii) *Pej:* Bande noire. (c) *St. Exch:* The Ring, le Parquet; le marché officiel. **6.** Arène *f*, piste *f* (de cirque). **7.** *Box: Wr:* (*a*) Cercle formé par les spectateurs. *F:* To keep, hold, the ring, laisser le champ libre aux adversaires. (*b*) Enceinte *f*, ring *m* (d'un match de boxe). (*c*) *F:* The ring, le pugilisme. **8.** *Turf:* The Ring, (i) l'enceinte (du pesage); (ii) les bookmakers *m.* **'ring-armour,** *s.* Armure *f* de mailles. **'ring-bolt,** *s.* (*a*) Anneau *m* à fiche. (*b*) Boucle *f*, bague *f*, d'amarrage. **'ring-craft,** *s.* Le pugilisme; la boxe. **'ring-dove,** *s.* (Pigeon) ramier *m*; palombe *f.* **'ring-fence,** *s.* Clôture *f* (enfermant une propriété). **'ring-finger,** *s.* Annulaire *m.* **'ring-master,** *s.m.* Maître de manège (d'un cirque). **'ring-ouzel,** *s. Orn:* Merle *m* à collier. **ring²,** *v.tr.* **I.** (*a*) Baguer (un pigeon). (*b*) Boucler, anneler (un taureau). **2.** To ring round, encercler; entourer. **ring³,** *s.* **I.** Son (clair); sonnerie *f* (de cloches); tintement *m* (de cloches, de pièces de monnaie); timbre *m* ou intonation *f* (de la voix). **2.** (*a*) Coup *m* de sonnette, de timbre. There is a ring at the door, on sonne (à la porte). (*b*) Ring on the telephone, appel *m* téléphonique. I'll give you a ring (up), je vous téléphonerai. **ring⁴,** *v.* (rang [raŋ], *occ.* rung [rʌŋ]; rung) **I.** *v.i.* (*a*) (*Of bell*) Sonner, tinter. To set the bells ringing, mettre les cloches en branle. *The electric bell rang*, le timbre électrique résonna. (*b*) (*Of coin*) To ring true, sonner clair. *F:* His answer did not r. true*, sa réponse a sonné faux. (*c*) Résonner, retentir (*with*, de). The air rang with their cries, l'air résonnait de leurs cris. (*d*) Words ringing with emotion, paroles vibrantes d'émotion. My ears are ringing, les oreilles me tintent. **2.** *v.tr.* (*a*) Sonner, faire sonner (une cloche).

42

Ring the bell! sonnez! *Abs.* **To ring at the door,** sonner à la porte. **To ring for the maid,** sonner la bonne. **Did you ring, madam?** madame a onné? **To ring for (church) service,** tinter l'office. **To ring the alarm,** sonner le tocsin. *S.a.* CHANGE[1] 5. (*b*) Faire sonner (une pièce de monnaie). (*c*) **To ring the bell,** (i) (*at fair*) faire sonner la sonnette de la tête de Turc ; (ii) *P :* réussir le coup. **ring down,** *v.tr. Th :* To ring down the curtain, sonner pour la chute du rideau. **ring off,** *v.tr.* I. *Tp : Abs.* To ring off, raccrocher (l'appareil) ; couper la communication. 2. *Nau :* 'Ring off the engines,' "terminé pour la machine." **ring out,** *v.i.* Sonner ; retentir. *A shot rang out,* un coup de fusil retentit. **ring up,** *v.tr.* I. *Th :* To ring up the curtain, sonner pour la levée du rideau. 2. To ring s.o. up (*on the telephone*), donner un coup de téléphone à qn. **ringing**[1], *a.* I. (*Of bell*) Qui tinte, qui résonne. 2. Sonore, retentissant. *In r. tones,* d'une voix vibrante. **ringing**[2], *s.* I. Son *m*, tintement *m* (de cloches). 2. (*a*) Tintement (dans les oreilles). (*b*) Retentissement *m*.

ringer ['riŋər], *s.* Sonneur *m* ; carillonneur *m*.

ringleader ['riŋliːdər], *s.* Chef *m* (d'attroupement) ; meneur *m* (de révolte) ; chef d'émeute.

ringlet ['riŋlet], *s.* I. Petit anneau. 2. Boucle *f* (de cheveux) ; frisette *f.* **To wear one's hair in ringlets,** porter des anglaises.

ringworm ['riŋwəːrm], *s. Med :* Teigne tonsurante, tondante.

rink [riŋk], *s.* I. **Skating-rink,** patinoire *f.* **Roller-skating rink,** salle *f* de patinage à roulettes.

rinse[1] [rins], *s.* **To give a bottle a rinse,** rincer une bouteille.

rinse[2], *v.tr.* Rincer (une bouteille, le linge).

riot[1] ['raiət], *s.* I. Émeute *f* ; rassemblement tumultueux. **The Riot Act,** la loi contre les attroupements. **To read the Riot Act,** faire les trois sommations légales. *F :* **To read the Riot Act to s.o.,** semoncer qn d'importance. 2. Orgie *f* (de couleurs, etc.). 3. **To run riot,** se déchaîner, ne plus connaître de frein ; (*of plants*) pulluler.

riot[2], *v.i.* (rioted) (*a*) Provoquer une émeute ; s'ameuter. (*b*) Faire du vacarme. **rioting,** *s.* Émeutes *fpl* ; troubles *mpl.*

rioter ['raiətər], *s.* I. Émeutier *m*, séditieux *m.* 2. Noceur *m*, *F :* chahuteur *m.*

riotous ['raiətəs], *a.* I. Séditieux ; tumultueux, turbulent. 2. (*Of pers.*) Tapageur, bruyant. *A few r. students,* quelques étudiants en rupture de ban. **-ly,** *adv.* I. Séditieusement ; tumultueusement. 2. D'une manière désordonnée.

riotousness ['raiətəsnəs], *s.* I. Turbulence *f* (de la foule). 2. Désordre *m.*

rip[1] [rip], *s.* Déchirure *f* ; fente *f.* **'rip-cord,** *s.* Corde *f* de déchirure (d'un ballon) ; corde d'ouverture (d'un parachute). **'rip-saw,** *s. Tls :* Scie *f* à refendre.

rip[2], *v.* (ripped) I. *v.tr.* Fendre (en long) ; déchirer. **To rip (sth.) open,** ouvrir (un paquet) en le déchirant ; (*of wild boar*) découdre (un chien). 2. *v.i.* (*a*) Se déchirer, se fendre. (*b*) *F :* **To rip (along),** aller à toute vitesse. (*Of pers.*) Let him rip! laissez-le faire à sa guise! (*Of motor-car*) Let her rip! laissez-la filer! **rip off,** *v.tr.* Arracher, déchirer (ce qui recouvre qch.). **rip out,** *v.tr. To rip out the lining of a coat,* arracher la doublure d'un habit. **rip up,** *v.tr.* Éventrer (qn) ; découdre (un vêtement, le ventre). **ripping,** *a.* I. Qui déchire, qui fend. 2. *P :* Épatant, fameux.

rip[3], *s. F :* (*a*) Mauvais garnement.' **An old rip,**

un vieux marcheur. (*b*) **He's a bit of a rip,** c'e un gaillard.

rip[4], *s.* Clapotis *m.*(du courant). *S.a.* TIDE-RI

riparian [rai'pɛəriən], *a. & s.* Riverain (*m*).

ripe [raip], *a.* I. (*a*) Mûr. **Ripe cheese,** fromag (bien) fait. **To grow ripe,** mûrir. (*b*) **Ripe scholar** savant accompli. **A ripe old age,** un bel âge 2. **Plan ripe for execution,** projet prêt à êtr exécuté ; projet mûr. **He is ripe for mischief,** est prêt à faire le mal.

ripen ['raip(ə)n]. I. *v.tr.* Mûr r ; faire mûri 2. *v.i.* Mûrir ; venir à maturité. *This cheese wi r.,* ce fromage se fera. **ripening,** *s.* Maturation *f* jaunissement *m* (du blé) ; affinage *m* (du fromage

ripeness ['raipnəs], *s.* Maturité *f* ; état mûr.

riposte[1] [ri'poust], *s.* Riposte *f.*

riposte[2], *v.i.* Riposter.

ripper ['ripər], *s.* I. *Hist :* **Jack the Ripper,** Jac l'Éventreur. 2. *P :* Type épatant ; chos épatante.

ripple[1] [ripl], *s.* I. (*a*) Ride *f* (sur l'eau) ondulation *f.* (*b*) Gazouillement *m* (d'un ruis seau). 2. (*In hair*) Ondulation. 3. Murmure[*m*(*pl*) (de conversation). **'ripple-mark,** s Ride laissée sur le sable (par la marée).

ripple[2]. I. *v.i.* (*Of lake*) Se rider. (*b*) (*Of cor* Onduler ; (*of hair*) former des ondulations (*c*) (*Of brook*) Murmurer ; (*of the tide*) clapoter (*of laughter*) perler. **Rippling laughter,** rire perlés. 2. *v.tr.* (*Of wind*) Rider (le sable).

rise[1] [raiz], *s.* I. (*a*) Ascension *f.* **Rise of day** l'aube *f. Th :* **Rise of the curtain,** lever *m* d rideau. (*b*) **To shoot a bird on the rise,** tirer u oiseau au cul levé. (*Of fish*) **To be on the rise,** monter à la mouche. *F :* **To get a rise out of s.o.** mystifier qn ; se payer la tête de qn. 2. (*a*) Mon tée *f*, côte *f* (de route) ; rampe *f.* **Rise in th** ground, exhaussement du terrain ; (*sharp* ressaut *m* de terrain. (*b*) Éminence *f*, élévation *i* 3. *Arch : Civ.E :* Flèche *f*, hauteur *f* sous cle (d'un arc). 4. (*a*) Crue *f* (des eaux) ; flot *m* flux *m* (de la marée) ; hausse *f* (du baromètre) élévation (de température) ; augmentation *f* (d pression). **The rise of the tide,** la montée de l'eau (*b*) Augmentation, hausse (de prix). **Rise in valu** *of a possession,* appréciation *f* d'un bien *St.Exch :* **To speculate on a rise,** jouer à 1 hausse. **To ask (one's employer) for a rise** demander une augmentation. (*c*) *Mus :* R. c half a tone, hausse d'un demi-ton. 5. Avance ment *m* ; élévation (en rang). **The rise c** Napoleon, l'essor *m* de Napoléon. *S.a.* IRISHMAN 6. (*Of river*) **To take its rise in . . .,** prendre s source dans. . . . **To give rise to sth.,** fair naître, engendrer, qch. *To give r. to dissatisfaction* provoquer le mécontentement.

rise[2], *v.i.* (rose [rouz] ; risen ['riz(ə)n]) I. (*a*) T rise (to one's feet), se lever ; se mettre debout (*after kneeling*) se relever. **To rise (up) from table** se lever de table. **The horse rose on its hind legs** le cheval se dressa sur ses pieds de derrière (*b*) **Parliament will rise next week,** le Parlemen doit s'ajourner la semaine prochaine. (*c*) **To ris** early, se lever tôt. (*d*) **To rise (again) from th** dead, ressusciter les morts. 2. **To rise (in revolt)** se soulever, se révolter (*against*, contre). **To ris** (up) in arms, prendre les armes. 3. (*a*) (*Of su* star) Se lever ; (*of smoke*) monter, s'élevei (*b*) **To rise off the ground,** quitter le sol. **To ris** to the surface, monter à la surface. (*c*) (*Of fish* **To rise to the bait,** monter à la mouche ; mordre *F :* (*Of pers.*) Se laisser provoquer He did not r. to it, il laissa passer l'occasion (*d*) (*Of game*) **To rise,** se lever, s'envoler

4. (a) (*Of ground*) Monter, s'élever; (*of dough*) lever; (*of sea*) (i) monter, (ii) devenir gros. The barometer is rising, le baromètre remonte, est à la hausse. (b) **In the distance rises a castle,** au loin s'élève, se dresse, un château. (c) **A picture rises in my mind,** une image se présente à mon esprit. (d) **The wind is rising,** le vent s'élève. **Her colour rose,** ses joues s'empourpraient. (e) **Prices are rising,** les prix sont à la hausse. **Everything has risen in price,** tout a augmenté de prix. **5.** (a) **To rise above vanity,** être au-dessus de la vanité. (b) *The horse rose at the fence,* le cheval s'enleva pour franchir l'obstacle. *F:* **To rise to the occasion,** se montrer à la hauteur de la situation. **6. To rise in the world,** faire son chemin. **To rise in s.o.'s esteem,** monter dans l'estime de qn. **He rose from nothing,** il est parti de rien. *S.a.* RANK¹ 1. **7.** (*Of river*) Prendre sa source (*at,* à; *in,* dans).

rising¹, *a.* **1.** (Soleil) levant. **2.** (a) (Route) qui monte; (baromètre) en hausse. **Rising ground,** élévation *f* de terrain. **Rising tide,** marée montante. (b) *Phot:* **Rising front,** objectif à décentration en hauteur. **3.** (a) (Vent) qui se lève; (colère) croissante. (b) **Rising market,** marché orienté à la hausse. **4. Rising man,** homme d'avenir. **5. The rising generation,** la nouvelle génération. **6. To be rising five,** (*of horse*) aller sur (ses) cinq ans. **rising**², *s.* **1.** (a) Lever *m* (du rideau). (b) **Upon the rising of the House,** quand la Chambre se leva. (c) **Not to like early rising,** ne pas aimer à se lever tôt. (d) **Rising from the dead,** résurrection *f.* **2.** Ameutement *m,* soulèvement *m.* **3.** (a) Lever (d'un astre). (b) *Ven:* Envol *m* (de gibier). **4.** Hausse *f* (du baromètre); crue *f* (des eaux); poussée *f* (de la sève). **Rising and falling,** mouvement de hausse et de baisse.

ˈiser [ˈraizər], *s.* **1. Early riser,** personne matinale. **2.** (Ais *m* de) contremarche *f* (d'un escalier). **3.** Canalisation ascendante; tuyau *m* de montée.

ˈisk¹ [risk], *s.* (a) Risque *m,* péril *m.* **The risks of an undertaking,** les aléas *m* d'une entreprise. **To run, incur, a risk,** courir un risque. **To take risks,** courir des risques. **It isn't worth the risk,** *F:* ça ne vaut pas le coup. **At one's own risk,** à ses risques et périls. (b) *Ins:* **Fire risk,** risque d'incendie.

ˈisk², *v.tr.* Risquer. (a) Aventurer, hasarder (qch.). *F:* **To risk one's own skin,** risquer sa peau; payer de sa personne. (b) **I'll risk it,** je vais risquer le coup. (c) **To risk defeat,** courir les chances d'une défaite.

ˈiskiness [ˈriskinəs], *s.* Risques *mpl* et périls *mpl* aléas *mpl* (d'une entreprise).

ˈisky [ˈriski], *a.* **1.** Hasardeux, chanceux, aléatoire. **2.** (*Of story*) Risqué, scabreux.

ˈissole [ˈrisoul], *s.* *Cu:* Rissole *f;* attignole *f.*

ˈite [rait], *s.* Rit(e) *m.* *Funeral rites, burial rites,* les rites funèbres.

ˈitual [ˈritjuəl]. **I.** *a.* Rituel; selon le rite. **2.** *s.* (a) Rites *mpl.* (b) (*Book*) Rituel *m.* **-ally,** *adv.* Selon les rites.

ˈitualism [ˈritjuəlizm], *s.* *Ecc:* Ritualisme *m.*

ˈitualist [ˈritjuəlist], *s.* Ritualiste *mf.*

ˈival¹ [ˈraiv(ə)l], *a. & s.* (a) Rival, -ale, *pl.* -aux, -ales; concurrent, -ente. (b) Émule *mf.*

ˈival², *v.tr.* (rivalled) (a) Rivaliser avec (qn). (b) Être l'émule de (qn).

ˈivaˈry [ˈraivəlri], *s.* (a) Rivalité *f.* *To enter into r. with s.o.,* entrer en rivalité avec qn; *F:* aller sur les brisées de qn. (b) Émulation *f.*

ˈive [raːiv], *v.tr.* (rived [raːivd]; riven [ˈriv(ə)n])

Fendre (le bois). *Trees riven by the lightning,* arbres éclatés par la foudre.

river [ˈrivər], *s.* **1.** Cours *m* d'eau; (*main r.*) fleuve *m;* (*small r.*) rivière *f.* **Down the river,** en aval. **Up the river,** en amont. **River port,** port fluvial. **2.** Coulée *f* (de lave, etc.); flot *m* (de sang). **3.** Diamond of the finest river, diamant de la plus belle eau. **river-ˈbank,** *s.* Bord *m* de la rivière, du fleuve; rive *f.* **riverˈbasin,** *s.* Bassin fluvial. **river-ˈbed,** *s.* Lit *m* de rivière. **river-ˈhead,** *s.* Source *f.*

riverain [ˈrivərein], *a. & s.* Riverain, -aine.

riverman, *pl.* **-men** [ˈrivərmən, -men], *s.m.* Batelier; marinier (d'eau douce).

riverside [rivərˈsaid], *s.* **1.** Bord *m* de l'eau; rive *f.* **2.** *Attrib.* [ˈrivərsaid] Riverside inn, auberge située au bord de la rivière. **Riverside police,** agents plongeurs.

rivet¹ [ˈrivit], *s.* **1.** Rivet *m;* (i) Rivet *m,* (ii) clou *m* à river. **To drive a rivet,** placer un rivet. **2.** (*For china*) Attache *f.* **ˈrivet-punch, -set, -snap,** *s.* Chasse-rivet(s) *m inv;* bouterolle *f.*

rivet², *v.tr.* (rivet(t)ed) (a) River, riveter. (b) *F:* **To rivet the attention,** fixer, capter, l'attention. **rivet(t)ing,** *s.* **1.** Rivetage *m,* **2.** Rivure, . **ˈriveting-machine,** *s.* Machine *f* à river.

Riviera (the) [ðəriviˈɛərə]. *Pr.n.* La Côte d'Azur.

rivulet [ˈrivjulet], *s.* Ruisseau *m.*

roach [routʃ], *s.* *Ich:* Gardon *m.*

road [roud], *s.* **1.** Route *f,* chemin *m,* voie *f;* (*in towns often* = *street*) rue *f.* (a) **Across the road,** de l'autre côté de la route ou de la rue. **High road, main road,** grand chemin, grande route. **Local road,** chemin vicinal. *Aut:* **The Great West Road,** l'Autostrade *f* de l'ouest. **Road transport,** transports routiers. (b) **To take the road,** se mettre en route; partir. **To be on the road,** (i) être en route; (ii) *Com: F:* être commi voyageur; (iii) *Com:* (*of traveller*) être en tournée. **He is on the right road,** il est dans la bonne voie. **The road to success,** la voie du succès. **There is no royal road to proficiency,** on n'arrive pas sans peine à la compétence. (c) **Voie, chemin.** *Rail:* **To whistle for the road,** demander la voie. **2.** Chaussée *f.* **Car that holds the road well,** voiture qui tient bien la route. **3.** *Nau:* Roads, rade *f.* **ˈroad-bed,** *s.* *Civ.E:* (a) Assiette *f,* encaissement *m* (de la route). (b) *Rail:* Superstructure *f* (de la voie). **ˈroad-book,** *s.* Itinéraire *m;* guide routier. **ˈroad-hog,** *s.* *F:* Écraseur *m,* chauffard *m.* **ˈroad-house,** *s.* Auberge *f,* hôtel *m;* *esp.* hôtellerie *f* en bord de route avec piscine, dancing, etc. **ˈroad-map,** *s.* Carte routière. **ˈroad-mender,** *s.* Cantonnier *m.* **ˈroad-metal,** *s.* Matériaux *mpl* d'empierrement pour routes. **ˈroad-race,** *s.* *Sp:* Course *f* sur route. **ˈroad-racer,** *s.* *Cy:* Bicyclette *f* de course sur route. **ˈroad-sense,** *s.* *Aut: etc:* Sens *m* pratique de la conduite sur route. **ˈroad-surveyor,** *s.* Agent voyer.

roadman, *pl.* **-men** [ˈroudmən, -men], *s.m.* Travailleur de la voirie; cantonnier.

roadside [roudˈsaid], *s.* **1.** Bord *m,* côté *m,* de la route, de la chaussée. **2.** *Attrib.* [ˈroudsaid] Roadside inn, auberge située au bord de la route. *Aut:* **Roadside repairs,** réparations *f* de fortune; dépannage *m.*

roadstead [ˈroudsted], *s.* *Nau:* Rade *f.* **Open roadstead,** rade foraine.

roadster [ˈroudstər], *s.* Bicyclette *f* ou voiture *f* de route; machine routière.

roadway ['roudwei], *s.* **1.** Chaussée *f.* **2.** Voie *f*, tablier *m* (de pont).

roam [roum]. **1.** *v.i.* Errer, rôder. *To r. about the world*, rouler par le monde; rouler sa bosse. **2.** *v.tr.* Errer par, parcourir (les rues). **roaming**[1], *a.* Errant, vagabond. **roaming**[2], *s.* Course errante.

roan[1] [roun]. **1.** *a.* Rouan. **2.** *s.* (Cheval) rouan *m*.

roan[2], *s. Bookb:* Basane *f.*

roar[1] ['rɔːər], *s.* **1.** (*a*) (*Of pers.*) Hurlement *m*; rugissement *m.* *Roars of laughter*, grands éclats de rire. *To set the table in a roar*, faire rire aux éclats la table. (*b*) Rugissement (du lion). **2.** Grondement *m* (de canon); mugissement *m* (de la mer).

roar[2]. **1.** *v.i.* (*a*) (*Of pers.*) Hurler, rugir. *To roar with pain*, hurler de douleur. *S.a.* LAUGHTER. (*b*) (*Of lion*) Rugir. (*c*) (*Of thunder*) Gronder; (*of sea*) mugir. *A motor car roared by*, une auto a passé en ronflant. (*d*) (*Of horse*) Corner. **2.** *v.tr.* *To roar (out) an order*, vociférer un ordre. **roaring**[1], *a.* **1.** (*a*) (Lion) rugissant. (*b*) (Tonnerre) grondant; (vent) mugissant. *We were sitting in front of a r. fire*, nous étions assis devant une belle flambée. *Nau:* *The roaring forties*, les parages océaniques situés entre les 40ᵉ et 50ᵉ degrés de latitude sud. **2.** *To do a roaring trade*, faire un gros commerce; faire des affaires superbes. **roaring**[2], *s.* **1.** = ROAR[1]. **2.** *Vet:* Cornage *m.*

roarer ['rɔːərər], *s.* (Cheval) cornard *m.*

roast[1] [roust], *s. Cu:* Rôti *m*, *F:* rosbif *m.* *A r. of veal*, un rôti de veau. *F:* *He rules the roast*, il fait la loi chez lui.

roast[2], *v.* (*p.p. in compound tenses* **roasted**, *as attrib. a.* **roast**) **1.** *v.tr.* Rôtir, faire rôtir (la viande); rôtir (des marrons). *Fire fit to roast an ox*, feu à rôtir un bœuf. *Ind:* Griller (le minerai). (*c*) Griller, torréfier (le café). (*d*) *F:* Railler, berner (qn). **2.** *v.i.* (*a*) (*Of meat, etc.*) Rôtir. (*b*) *I was roasting in the sun*, je grillais sous le soleil. **roast**[3], *a.* *R. meat*, viande rôtie. *Roast beef*, rôti *m* de bœuf; rosbif *m.* **roasting**, *s.* **1.** Rôtissage *m*, cuisson *f* (de la viande). **2.** Grillage *m*, calcination *f* (du minerai). **3.** Torréfaction *f* (du café). **'roasting-jack,** *s.* Tournebroche *m.*

rob [rɔb], *v.tr.* (**robbed**) Voler, détrousser (qn); piller (un verger); *abs. F:* brigander. *To rob s.o. of sth.*, (i) voler qch. à qn; (ii) escroquer qch. à qn. *To rob the till*, voler la caisse.

robber ['rɔbər], *s.* (*a*) Voleur, -euse. (*b*) *A:* Voleur de grand chemin; brigand *m.*

robbery ['rɔbəri], *s.* Vol qualifié. *A:* Highway robbery, vol de grand chemin; brigandage *m.*

robe[1] [roub], *s.* **1.** Robe *f* (d'office, de cérémonie). *Magistrates in their robes*, magistrats en robe. *The Coronation robes*, les robes et insignes du sacre (du roi). **2.** Vêtement *m.* (*Baby's*) long robe, maillot anglais.

robe[2]. **1.** *v.tr.* (*a*) Revêtir (qn d'une robe d'office. (*b*) *Lit:* Hills robed in verdure, collines couvertes de verdure. **2.** *v.i.* Revêtir sa robe.

Robert ['rɔbət]. **1.** *Pr.n.m.* Robert. **2.** *F:* Surnom donné aux agents de police.

Robin ['rɔbin]. **1.** *Pr.n.m.* Robin Goodfellow, lutin *m* domestique. Robin Hood, Robin des bois. **2.** *s.* (*a*) *Orn:* Robin (redbreast), rougegorge *m.* (*b*) *Bot:* Ragged robin, lychnide *f* des prés. (*c*) *See* ROUND ROBIN.

robot ['roubɔt], *s.* Automate *m.* *F:* Robot traffic-lights, feux de circulation automatiques.

robust [ro'bʌst], *a.* (*Of pers.*) Robuste, vigoureux,

solide. **Robust appetite**, appétit robuste. **-ly** *adv.* Robustement, vigoureusement.

robustious [ro'bʌstjəs], *a.* *F:* **1.** Robuste, vigoureux, solide. **2.** Violent, bruyant.

rochet ['rɔtʃet], *s.* *Ecc.Cost:* Rochet *m*; surplis *m* (à manches étroites).

rock[1] [rɔk], *s.* **1.** (*a*) Rocher *m*, roc *m.* Rock-face (to be climbed), varappe *f.* (*b*) *Geol:* Roche *f.* Volcanic rock, roche d'épanchement. **2.** A rock, un rocher, une roche. *F:* The Rock, le rocher de Gibraltar. *Nau:* To run upon the rocks, donner sur les écueils. *F:* To see rocks ahead, voir des obstacles devant soi. To be on the rocks, être à la côte; être dans la débine, dans la dèche. *S.a.* FIRM[2] 1. **'rock-alum,** *s.* Alun *m* de roche. **'rock-basin,** *s.* Bassin *m* géologique. **'rock-bottom,** *s.* (*a*) Fond rocheux. (*b*) *F:* Le fin fond. Rock-bottom price, prix le plus bas. **'rock-bound,** *a.* Entouré de rochers. *R.-b. coast*, côte hérissée de rochers. **'rock-cake,** *s. Cu:* Petit gâteau pour le thé à surface irrégulière. **'rock-climber,** *s.* Varappeur *m.* **'rock-climbing,** *s.* Varappe *f.* **'rock-crystal,** *s. Miner:* Cristal *m* de roche. **'rock-dove,** *s. Orn:* = ROCK-PIGEON. **'rock-garden,** *s.* Jardin *m* de rocaille; jardin alpin. **'rock-oil,** *s. Miner:* Huile *f* de roche; naphte minéral. **'rock-pigeon,** *s. Orn:* Biset *m*; pigeon *m* de roche. **'rock-plant,** *s.* Plante *f* des rochers. **'rock-salt,** *s.* Sel *m* gemme.

rock[2]. **1.** *v.tr.* (*a*) Bercer, balancer; basculer (un levier). *To rock a child*, bercer un enfant. *To rock a cradle*, balancer, faire aller, un berceau. *Ship rocked by the waves*, navire ballotté, balancé, par les flots. *Lever rocked by a cam*, levier basculé par une came. *Gold-Min:* To rock the ore, travailler le minerai au berceau. (*b*) The earthquake rocks the house, le tremblement de terre secoue, ébranle, la maison. **2.** *v.i.* (*a*) The cradle rocks, le berceau balance. (*b*) The house was rocking with the shock, la maison oscillait sous le choc. **rocking**[1], *a.* **1.** Oscillant; à bascule. **2.** Branlant. **'rocking-chair,** *s.* Fauteuil *m* à chaise *f*, à bascule. **'rocking-horse,** *s.* Cheval *m*, -aux, à bascule. **'rocking-lever,** *s.* = ROCKER-ARM. **'rocking-stone,** *s. Geol:* Rocher branlant. **rocking**[2], *s.* **1.** Balancement *m*, bercement *m*; oscillation *f.* *Mec.E:* Basculage *m.* Rail: Mouvement *m* de lacet. **2.** Tremblement *m*, branlement *m.*

rocker ['rɔkər], *s.* **1.** Bascule *f* (de berceau). *F:* To be off one's rocker, avoir l'esprit dérangé; être un peu fou. **2.** *Gold-Min:* etc: Berceau *m.* **3.** *I.C.E:* Culbuteur *m.* *Aut:* Valve-rocker shaft, rampe *f* des culbuteurs. **'rocker-arm,** *s.* (*a*) *Mec.E:* Basculeur *m.* *I.C.E:* Culbuteur *m.* (*b*) *Mch:* Balancier *m* de renvoi. **'rockershaft,** *s. Mch:* Arbre *m* de renversement de marche.

rockery ['rɔkəri], *s. Hor:* Rochers artificiels; jardin *m* de rocaille.

rocket[1] ['rɔket], *s. Bot:* Roquette *f.*

rocket[2], *s. Pyr:* Fusée *f.* Rocket signal, signal rocket, signal *m* à fusée; fusée de signaux. **'rocket-apparatus,** *s.* (Fusée *f*) porte-amarre *m inv.* **'rocket-stick,** *s.* Baguette *f* de direction (d'une fusée).

rocket[3], *v.i.* *a.* (*Of horse*) Se lancer comme un éclair. (*Of rider, etc.*) To rocket into s.o., foncer comme un éclair sur qn. (*b*) (*Of partridge*) Monter en chandelle.

Rockies ['rɔkiz]. *Pr.n.pl. Geog:* See ROCKY[1] 2.

rockiness ['rɔkinəs], *s.* Nature rocheuse, rocailleuse (*of*, de).

rocky¹ ['rɔki], a. **1.** Rocailleux; rocheux. **2.** De roche; rocheux. **The Rocky Mountains,** F: **the Rockies,** les montagnes Rocheuses.

rocky², a. F: Chancelant, instable.

rococo [rɔ'kouko], a. & s. (Style) rococo m inv).

rod [rɔd], s. **1.** Baguette f. **2.** Verge f. **To be beaten with rods,** être battu de verges. F: **To make a rod for one's own back, se préparer des ennuis. To have a rod in pickle for s.o.,** garder à qn un chien de sa chienne. Prov: **Spare the rod and spoil the child,** qui aime bien châtie bien. **3.** Verge (d'huissier). F: **To rule s.o. with a rod of iron,** mener qn à la baguette. **4.** (Fishing- rod, canne f à pêche; gaule f. **Rod and line,** ligne f de pêche. **5.** Meas: = PERCH¹ 2. **6.** (a) Tringle f. **Curtain rod,** tringle de rideau. **Stair rod,** tringle d'escalier. (b) **Copper rod,** barre f de cuivre. El: **Carbon rod, zinc rod,** crayon m de charbon, de zinc (de pile). (c) **Pump rod,** tige f de pompe. Aut: **Brake rod,** tige de frein; tirant m de frein. Ph: **Rod of a pendulum,** verge d'un pendule. **7.** Surv: Mire f. **'rod-fishing,** s. Pêche f à la ligne.

rode [roud]. See RIDE².

rodent ['roudənt]. **1.** a. Rongeur. **2.** s. Z: Rongeur m.

rodeo [rɔ'dejo], s. U.S: Concours m d'équitation des cowboys.

Roderick ['rɔdərik]. Pr.n.m. Rodrigue.

roe¹ [rou], s. Z: Roe(-deer), chevreuil m.

roe², s. (a) (Hard) roe, œufs mpl (de poisson). (b) **Soft roe,** laite f, laitance f.

roebuck ['roubʌk], s. Chevreuil m (mâle).

rogation [rɔ'geiʃ(ə)n], . Ecc: Usu. pl. Rogations fpl. **Rogation days,** Rogations.

Roger ['rɔdʒər]. Pr.n.m. Roger. A: **The Jolly Roger,** le pavillon noir (des pirates).

rogue [roug], s. **1.** Coquin, -ine; fripon, -onne; chenapan m. **2.** Malin, -igne; espiègle mf. **She's a little r.,** c'est une petite coquine, une petite friponne. **3.** Jur: A: Vagabond m. **4.** (Éléphant ou buffle) solitaire m.

roguery ['rougəri], s. **1.** Coquinerie f, friponnerie f, fourberie f. **2.** Malice f, espièglerie f (d'un enfant).

roguish ['rougiʃ], a. **1.** (Air) coquin, fripon, polisson; (ruses) de coquin, de fripon. **2.** (Air) malin, espiègle. **-ly,** adv. **1.** En fripon, en fourbe, en coquin. **2.** Avec espièglerie; malicieusement.

roguishness ['rougiʃnəs], s. = ROGUERY.

roisterer ['rɔistərər], s. Tapageur, -euse; fêtard, -arde.

roistering¹ ['rɔistəriŋ], a. Tapageur; bruyant; chahuteur.

roistering², s. Tapage m; chahut m; la noce, la fête.

Roland ['roulənd]. Pr.n.m. Roland. F: **To give s.o. a Roland for an Oliver,** rendre à qn la monnaie de sa pièce.

rôle [roul], s. Th. & F: Rôle m.

roll¹ [roul], s. **1.** (a) Rouleau m (de papier, etc.); pièce f (d'étoffe). Cin: Rouleau, galette f (de film pour prise de vues). (b) Arch: Volute f (de chapiteau ionique). (c) Cu: **Boiled jam roll,** pudding m dont la pâte a été enroulée après avoir été enduite de confiture. **Swiss roll,** bûche f. Bak: **Roll of bread,** petit pain. **French roll,** petit pain mollet. (d) **Coquille f** (de beurre). (e) U.S: **Liasse f** (de billets de banque). **2.** Adm: etc: Rôle m, contrôle m, liste f. Mil: Nau: **To put, enter, a man on the rolls,** porter un homme sur les contrôles. **To call the roll,** faire l'appel. **The roll of honour,** la liste de ceux qui sont morts pour la patrie. **To strike s.o. off the rolls,** Jur: rayer qn du tableau, du barreau; Mil: etc: rayer qn des états. **3.** Canon m, bâton m (de soufre); carotte f, boudin m (de tabac). **4.** Tail: Rabat m (de col d'habit). **5.** (Roller) (a) Rouleau, cylindre m (de laminoir, etc.). (b) pl. Rolls, train m (de laminoir). **'roll-call,** s. Mil: Sch: Appel (nominal). **'roll-collar,** s. Col roulé. **'roll-shutter,** s. Rideau m (de classeur, etc.). **'roll-top,** attrib. **Roll-top desk,** pupitre m à cylindre; bureau améri.cain.

roll², s. **1.** (a) Nau: Coup m de roulis. F: **To walk with a roll** (in one's gait), se dandiner en marchant. (b) **The roll of the sea,** la houle. **2.** (a) Roulement m (d'une balle, etc.). (b) **To have a roll on the grass,** se rouler par terre. (c) Av: Vol m en tonneau. **3.** Rou ement (de tambour, de tonnerre).

roll³. I. v.tr. **1.** Rouler (un tonneau, une bille). **To roll one's eyes,** rouler les yeux. **2.** **To roll one's r's,** rouler les r; grasseyer. **3.** (a) Rouler, passer au rouleau (le gazon); cylindrer (une route). (b) Laminer (les métaux); travailler (les métaux) au laminoir. (c) Cu: **To roll (out) paste,** étendre la pâte au rouleau. **To roll and fold,** feuilleter (la pâte). **4.** **To roll (up) paper,** (en)rouler du papier. **To r. (up) one's cape,** faire un rouleau de son manteau. **To roll cigarettes,** rouler des cigarettes. II. **roll,** v.i. Rouler. **1.** (a) **The ball rolls under the table,** la balle roule sous la table. S.a. BALL¹ 1. (Of pers.) **To roll downhill,** faire une roulade. **To r. downstairs,** débouler l'escalier. **The tears rolled down his cheeks,** les larmes coulaient sur ses joues. (b) **His eyes were rolling,** les yeux lui roulaient dans la tête. **2.** v.i. & pr. **To roll (oneself) from side to side,** se retourner, se rouler, de côté et d'autre. F: **To be rolling in wealth,** rouler sur l'or. **3.** (Of thunder) Gronder, rouler. **To hear the drums rolling,** entendre le roulement des tambours. **4.** (Of ship, aeroplane) Rouler; avoir du roulis. **To roll gunwale under,** rouler à faire cuiller; engager. F: **To roll in one's walk,** se dandiner, se balancer, en marchant. **roll by,** v.i. Passer (en roulant); (of time) s'écouler. **roll in.** I. v.tr. Hockey: **To roll in the ball,** remettre la balle en jeu. **2.** v.i. Entrer en roulant; (of carriage) entrer lourdement. **To watch the waves r. in,** regarder les vagues déferler sur le rivage. **'roll-in,** s. Hockey: Touche f. **roll on.** I. v.i. Continuer de rouler; (of time) s'écouler. **2.** v.tr. Passer (un vêtement) en le faisant rouler sur le corps. **Roll-on belt,** gaine f sans agrafes. **roll over.** I. v.tr. Retourner (qch.); culbuter (qn). **2.** v.i. Se retourner (en roulant). **To r. over and over,** rouler sur soi-même (plusieurs fois). **roll up.** I. v.tr.(a) Rouler, enrouler (une carte); (b) relever, retrousser (ses manches). (b) Envelopper (qch.). **To roll oneself up in a blanket,** s'enrouler dans une couverture. **2.** v.i. (a) (Of blind, etc.) S'enrouler. (Of kitten) **To roll up into a ball,** se mettre en boule. (b) P: (Of guests, etc.) Arriver, s'abouler. **rolled,** a. **1.** (Papier) en rouleau. **Rolled (up) leaf,** feuille enroulée. **2.** **Rolled iron,** fer laminé, cylindré. **Rolled gold,** doublé m. **Rolled-gold watch,** montre en plaqué or, en doublé.

rolling¹, a. **1.** Roulant. Prov: **A rolling stone gathers no moss,** pierre qui roule n'amasse pas mousse. F: **He is a r. stone,** il ne s'applique à rien; il roule sa bosse. **2.** **To have a rolling gait,** se balancer, se dandiner, en marchant. **3.** (a) **Rolling sea,** mer grosse, houleuse. (b) **Rolling country,** contrée ondulée, accidentée. **'rolling-stock,** s. Rail: Matériel roulant. **rolling²,** s.

1. Roulement *m*. **2.** *Metalw:* Laminage *m*, cylindrage *m*; travail *m* au laminoir. **3.** Roulis *m* (d'un navire). **4.** Roulement (du tambour, du tonnerre). **'rolling-mill,** *s. Metalw:* **1.** Usine *f* de laminage. **2.** Laminoir *m*. **'rolling-pin,** *s. Cu:* Rouleau *m*, bille *f* (pour pâtisserie). **roller** ['roulər], *s.* **1.** (*a*) Rouleau *m* (de pâtissier, etc.); enrouleur *m* (de store). *Typ:* Inking roller, rouleau encreur. *S.a.* BLIND³ **1.** (*b*) (*For roads*) (Rouleau) compresseur; cylindre compresseur. **Garden roller,** rouleau de jardin. (*c*) *Metalw:* Cylindre (lamineur); laminoir *m*. *Tex: Paperm:* Calandre *f*. (*d*) Roulette *f* (de fauteuil). (*e*) *Mec.E:* Galet *m*, rouleau. Roller ring, couronne *f* de galets. (*f*) Tourniquet *m*, tambour *m* (de cabestan). **2. Roller-bandage,** bande roulée. **3.** *Nau:* Lame *f* de houle. **4.** *Orn:* (*a*) Pigeon culbutant. (*b*) Rollier *m*; geai bleu. **roller-'bearing,** *s. Mec.E:* Coussinet *m*, palier *m*, roulement *m*, à rouleaux. **'roller-chain,** *s.* Chaîne *f* à galets. **'roller-map,** *s.* Carte *f* sur rouleau. **'roller-skate,** *v.i.* Patiner sur roulettes. **roller-skating,** *s.* Patinage *m* à roulettes. **'roller-skates,** *s.pl.* Patins *m* à roulettes. **roller-'towel,** *s.* Essuie-main(s) *m* à rouleau; serviette *f* sans fin.
rollick¹ ['rɔlik], *s.* **1.** Ébats *mpl*. **2.** Bamboche *f*, noce *f*.
rollick², *v.i.* Faire la fête, la noce, la bombe; rigoler. **rollicking,** *a.* D'une gaieté exubérante; rigoleur, -euse. *To lead a r. life,* mener une vie de patachon, de bâton de chaise.
Roman ['roumən], *a. & s.* Romain, -aine. (*a*) **Roman numerals,** chiffres romains. **Roman nose,** nez busqué, aquilin. (*b*) **The Holy Roman Empire,** le Saint Empire (romain). (*c*) *Typ:* **Roman type,** (caractère) romain. **'Roman 'Catholic,** *a. & s.* Catholique (*mf*).
romance¹ [ro'mans], *s.* **1. The Romance languages,** les langues romanes, néo-latines. **2.** (*a*) *Mediev.Lit:* Roman *m* de chevalerie, d'aventures, etc. **The age of romance,** les temps chevaleresques. (*b*) Histoire *f* romanesque; conte bleu. **It's quite a romance,** c'est tout un roman. *R. between two young people,* idylle *f* entre deux jeunes gens. (*c*) **Love of romance,** amour du romanesque. *The r. of the sea,* la poésie de la mer. **3.** *Mus:* Romance *f*.
romance², *v.i.* Exagérer; lâcher la bride à son imagination; inventer à plaisir.
Romanesque [roumə'nesk], *a. & s. Arch:* (Le) roman.
Romanic [ro'manik]. **1.** *a. & s. Ling:* (Le) roman. **2.** *a.* Romain; qui dérive des Romains.
romantic [ro'mantik]. **1.** *a.* (*a*) (Histoire, etc.) romanesque; qui tient du roman. *R. young woman,* jeune fille romanesque, exaltée. (*b*) *R. site,* site pittoresque. (*c*) *Art: Lit:* Romantique. **2.** *s.* = ROMANTICIST.
romanticism [ro'mantisizm], *s.* **1.** Idées *f* romanesques. **2.** *Art: Lit:* Romantisme *m*.
romanticist [ro'mantisist], *s.* Romantique *mf*.
Romany ['rɔməni], *s.* **1.** Romanichel, -elle; bohémien, -ienne. **2.** *Ling:* Le romanichel.
romaunt [ro'mɔːnt], *s. Mediev.Lit:* Roman *m*. **The Romaunt of the Rose,** le Roman de la Rose.
Rome [roum]. *Pr.n.* Rome *f*. *Prov:* When at Rome you must do as the Romans do, à Rome il faut vivre comme à Rome. **All roads lead to Rome,** tout chemin mène à Rome. *Ecc:* **The Church of Rome,** l'Église romaine; le catholicisme.
Romish ['roumiʃ], *a. Pej:* Catholique.

romp¹ [rɔmp], *s.* **1.** (*a*) Jeune fille garçonnière gamine *f*. (*b*) Enfant turbulent. **2.** Gambade *fpl*; jeu turbulent.
romp². *v.i.* **1.** S'ébattre (bruyamment). **2.** *Rac & F:* To romp in, home, gagner haut la main, arriver dans un fauteuil. **To romp through a examination,** passer un examen haut la main.
romper(s) ['rɔmpər(z)], *s.(pl.)* Tablier-com binaison *m* (pour enfants); barboteuse *f*.
rondo ['rɔndou], *s. Mus:* Rondeau *m*.
rood [ruːd], *s.* **1.** (*a*) *A:* The (Holy) Rood, Sainte Croix. (*b*) *Ecc:* Crucifix *m* (au centre du jubé). **2.** *Meas:* Quart *m* d'arpent. **'rood-loft,** *s.* (Galerie *f* du) jubé. **'rood-screen,** *s* Jubé *m*.
roof¹ [ruːf], *s.* **1.** Toit *m*, toiture *f*, comble *m* Tiled roof, toit en tuiles. **Flat roof,** toit en terrasse. **Pent roof, lean-to roof,** comble er appentis. *F:* To lift the roof, applaudir à tou caser. **2.** Voûte *f* (de tunnel, de caverne). Roo of the mouth, dôme *m* du palais; le palais **3.** *Aut:* Toit, capotage *m*. **Sliding roof,** toi découvrable. **4.** *Min:* Ciel *m*, plafond *m*, toi (d'une mine). **5.** *Mch:* Ciel (du foyer). **6.** *Av:* = CEILING 2. **'roof-garden,** *s.* Jardin *m* su un toit en terrasse. **'roof-lamp, -light,** *s* *Aut:* Plafonnier *m*. **'roof-tree,** *s.* **1.** Charpente *f* de toiture; faîtage *m*. **2.** *Lit:* Toit *m* demeure paternelle.
roof², *v.tr.* **1.** *Const:* Couvrir (une maison etc.). **Red-roofed,** à toit rouge; à toiture rouge **2.** To roof sth. (in, over), recouvrir qch. d'un toit. **roofing,** *s.* Toiture *f*, couverture *f* garniture *f* de comble. **Glass roofing,** vitrerie *j* de toits. *S.a.* FELT¹ **1.**
roofless ['ruːfləs], *a.* **1.** Sans toit, sans toiture à ciel ouvert. **2.** (*Of pers.*) Sans abri, sans asile.
rook¹ [ruk], *s.* **1.** *Orn:* Freux *m*; corneille *f* (chauve). **2.** *F:* Filou *m*, escroc *m*.
rook², *v.tr.* To refaire, rouler, (qn) au jeu *To r. s.o. of his money,* filouter son argent à qn.
rook³, *s. Chess:* Tour *f*.
rookery ['rukəri], *s.* **1.** Colonie *f* de freux; roukerie *f*. **2.** Seal rookery, colonie, roukerie, de phoques. **Penguin rookery,** *F:* pingouinière *f*.
rookie ['ruki], *s. Mil: P:* Recrue *f*, bleu *m*.
room¹ [rum, ruːm], *s.* **1.** (*a*) Place *f*, espace *m*. To take up a great deal of r., être très encombrant. There is plenty of r., ce n'est pas la place qui manque. You have plenty of r. here, vous êtes au large ici. There is still r., il y a encore de la place. To be cramped for room, être à l'étroit. R. taken up by a machine, encombrement *m* d'une machine. To make room for s.o., faire place à qn. (*b*) In s.o.'s room, in the room of s.o., au lieu de qn; à la place de qn. **2.** There is room for uneasiness at . . ., il y a lieu d'être inquiet de. . . . No r. for dispute, aucun sujet de désaccord. That leaves no room for doubt, le doute n'est plus permis. There is (much) room for improvement, cela laisse (beaucoup) à désirer. **3.** (*a*) (*In house*) Pièce *f*; (*public room*) salle *f*. (Bed)room, chambre *f* (à coucher). (Reception) room, salon *m*. **Reception rooms,** appartements *m* de réception. **Private room,** (*in restaurant*) cabinet particulier; (*in hotel*) salon réservé. (*b*) *pl.* (Set of) rooms, appartement *m*. To live in rooms, vivre en garni. **Bachelor's rooms,** garçonnière *f*. **4.** (*a*) *Ind:* Salle, hall *m*. *S.a.* BOILER-ROOM, ENGINE-ROOM. (*b*) *Nau:* Store-room, soute *f*. Torpedo-room, magasin *m* des torpilles. **'room-mate,** *s.* Compagnon, *f*. compagne, de chambre.
room², *v.i. U.S:.* (*a*) Vivre en garni. (*b*) Partager

un logement (*with s.o.*, avec qn). **To room to-gether**, partager un logement.

roomed [ruːmd], *a.* **Four-roomed flat**, appartement de quatre pièces.

roominess [ˈruːminəs], *s.* Ample espace *m*, dimensions spacieuses (d'une maison, etc.).

roomy [ˈruːmi], *a.* Spacieux ; (vêtement) ample, d'amples proportions. *This makes the cabin more r.*, cela donne plus de place dans la cabine.

roost[1] [ruːst], *s.* Juchoir *m*, perchoir *m*. **To go to roost**, (i) (*of hens*) se jucher ; (ii) *F :* (*of pers.*) aller se coucher. (*Of crime, etc.*) **To come home to roost**, retourner sur son auteur. **To rule the roost** = *to rule the roast.*

roost[2], *v.i.* (*Of hens*) Se percher (pour la nuit) ; se jucher. *F : Where do you r.?* où perchez-vous? **roosting**, *a.* Perché, juché.

rooster [ˈruːstər], *s. U.S :* Coq *m.*

root[1] [ruːt], *s.* **1.** Racine *f.* **To take root, strike root**, pousser des racines ; prendre racine. *F :* **To strike at the root of an evil**, couper un mal dans sa racine. **2.** Source *f*, fondement *m. To lie at the r. of . . .*, être la cause première de. . . . *Money is the root of all evil*, l'argent est la source de tous les maux. *He ha[s] the root of the matter in him*, il possède le fond de cette matière. **Root ideas**, idées fondamentales. **Root cause**, cause première. **3.** *Mth :* **Square root, cube root**, racine carrée, cubique. **4.** *Ling :* Racine (d'un mot). **5.** *Mus :* Base *f*, son fondamental (d'un accord). **'root-hair,** *s. Bot :* Poil *m* radiculaire. **'root-sign,** *s. Mth :* Signe radical. **'root-stock,** *s.* (*a*) *Bot :* Rhizome *m.* (*b*) *F :* Souche *f*, origine *f.* **'root-word,** *s. Ling :* Mot *m* racine, mot souche.

root[2]. **1.** *v.tr.* Enraciner. *F :* **To remain rooted to the spot**, rester cloué, figé, sur place. *Principles rooted in the public mind*, principes enracinés dans l'opinion publique. **2.** *v.i.* S'enraciner ; prendre racine. **root out, up,** *v.tr.* Déraciner, arracher (une plante) ; extirper (un abus). **rooted,** *a.* **1.** **Shallow-rooted tree**, arbre à enracinement superficiel. *S.a.* DEEP-ROOTED. **2.** *F :* (Préjugé) enraciné, invétéré.

root[3]. **1.** *v.i.* (*a*) (*Of swine*) Fouiller avec le groin. (*b*) *F :* (*Of pers.*) **To root among, in, papers**, fouiller dans des paperasses. **2.** *v.tr.* (*Of swine*) Fouiller (la terre). *F :* **To root sth. out, up,** dénicher qch.

rootedness [ˈruːtidnəs], *s.* Enracinement *m* (d'une opinion, etc.).

rope[1] [roup], *s.* **1.** (*a*) Corde *f*, cordage *m. Nau :* Filin *m. Hempen r.*, cordage en chanvre. **Three-, four-stranded rope**, filin en trois, en quatre. **Bell-rope**, cordon *m* de sonnette. **Wire rope**, câble *m* métallique. *Nau :* **Running ropes**, manœuvres courantes. *F :* **To know the ropes**, connaître son affaire ; *P :* être à la coule. **To put s.o. up to the ropes**, mettre qn au courant. **To give s.o. (plenty of) rope**, lâcher la bride à qn. *F :* **Crime worthy of the rope**, crime pendable, qui mérite la corde. (*b*) *Box : Rac :* **The ropes**, les cordes ; *F :* les ficelles *f.* **2.** Glane *f*, chapelet *m* (d'oignons) ; grand collier (de perles). **'rope-dancer,** *s.* Danseur de corde ; funambule *mf* ; équilibriste *mf.* **'rope-house,** *s.* Corderie *f.* **'rope-ladder,** *s.* Échelle *f* de corde. **'rope-maker,** *s.* Cordier *m.* **'rope-moulding,** *s. Arch :* Torsade *f.* **'rope-railway,** *s.* (Chemin *m* de fer) funiculaire *m.* **'rope's-'end,** *s.* Bout *m* de corde ; *Nau :* (i) bout de manœuvre ; (ii) garcette *f.* **'rope-walk,** *s.* Corderie *f.* **'rope-walker,** *s.* = ROPE-DANCER. **'rope-way,** *s.* Câble aérien ; transpor-

teur *m* par câbles ; téléphérique *m.* **'rope-yard,** *s.* Corderie *f.*

rope[2]. **I.** *v.tr.* **1.** Corder (un paquet). **2.** (*a*) **To rope s.o. to a tree**, lier qn à un arbre. (*b*) *Climbers roped together*, ascensionnistes en cordée. **3.** *Nau :* Ralinguer (une voile). **4.** *Rac :* Tirer (un cheval) (pour l'empêcher de gagner). **II. rope,** *v.i.* (*Of beer, etc.*) Devenir graisseux ; (*when poured*) filer. **rope in, round,** *v.tr.* **1.** Entourer (un terrain) de cordes. **2.** *F :* **To rope s.o. in,** (i) s'assurer le concours de qn ; (ii) prendre (un filou) dans une rafle. **rope off,** *v.tr.* Réserver (une partie de la salle) au moyen d'une corde tendue.

ropery [ˈroupəri], *s.* Corderie *f.*

ropiness [ˈroupinəs], *s.* Viscosité *f* ; (*in beer*) graisse *f.*

ropy [ˈroupi], *a.* (*Of liquid*) Visqueux ; (*of beer*) gras, graisseux ; (*when poured*) filant, qui file. (*Of wine*) *To become r.*, tourner à la graisse.

rorqual [ˈrɔːrkwəl], *s. Z :* Rorqual, -als *m.*

rosaceae [roˈzeisiiː], *s.pl. Bot :* Rosacées *f.*

rosary [ˈrouzəri], *s.* **1.** Rosaire *m.* **Lesser rosary** (*of 55 beads*), chapelet *m.* **To go through the r.**, dire le rosaire. **2.** = ROSERY.

rose[1] [rouz], *s.* **1.** Rose *f.* **Briar-rose, wild rose**, églantine *f.* **Life is not a bed of roses**, tout n'est pas rose(s) dans ce monde. *Prov :* **No rose without a thorn**, pas de rose sans épines. *Hist :* **The Wars of the Roses**, les guerres des Deux-Roses. *F :* **Under the rose**, en cachette ; en confidence ; sous le manteau. **2.** (*On hat, shoe*) Rosette *f.* **3.** (*On stag's horn*) Fraise *f.* **4.** Pomme *f* (d'arrosoir) ; crépine *f* (de pompe). *Mch :* Reniflard *m.* **5.** *El :* Ceiling rose, rosace *f* de plafond. **6.** *Tls :* Rose (countersink) bit, fraise champignon. **7.** *Med : F :* **The rose**, l'érysipèle *m.* **8.** (*Colour*) Rose *m. Dark t. materials*, étoffes (d'un) rose foncé. **9.** *Arch :* = ROSE-WINDOW. **10.** *Lap :* ROSE-DIAMOND. **'rose-bay,** *s. Bot :* **1.** Laurier-rose *m.* **2.** Rhododendron *m.* **'rose-bed,** *s.* Massif *m*, corbeille *f*, de rosiers. **'rose-bowl,** *s.* Coupe *f* à fleurs. **'rose-'burner,** *s.* Brûleur *m* à couronne (de réchaud à gaz). **'rose-bush,** *s.* Rosier *m.* **'rose-'campion,** *s. Bot :* Coquelourde *f* ; passe-fleur *f.* **'rose-coloured,** *a.* Rose, rosé ; couleur de rose *inv. F :* **To see things through rose-coloured spectacles**, voir tout en rose. **'rose-copper,** *s. Metall :* (Cuivre *m* de) rosette *f.* **'rose-diamond,** *s. Lap :* (Diamant taillé en) rose *f.* **'rose-engine,** *s.* Tour *m* à guillocher. **'rose-gall,** *s. Hort :* Bédégar *m*, éponge *f.* **'rose-garden,** *s.* Roseraie *f.* **'rose-laurel,** *s. Bot :* Laurier-rose *m.* **'rose-leaf,** *s.* Feuille *f* de rose ; pétale *m* de rose. **'rose mallow,** *s. Bot :* Rose trémière ; passe-rose *f.* **'rose-nail,** *s.* Clou *m* à tête de diamant. **'rose-pink.** (*a*) *s.* Rose *m.* (*b*) *a.* (Couleur de) rose ; rosé ; incarnat. **'rose-rash,** *s. Med :* = ROSEOLA. **'rose-red. 1.** *a.* Vermeil. **2.** *s.* Vermillon *m.* **'rose-tree,** *s.* Rosier *m.* **'rose-water,** *s.* Eau *f* de rose. **'rose-window,** *s. Arch :* Rosace *f*, rose *f.* **'rose-wine,** *s.* Vin rosé.

rose[2]. *See* RISE[2].

roseate [ˈrouziet], *a.* Couleur de rose *inv* ; rose, rosé.

rosebud [ˈrouzbʌd], *s.* Bouton *m* de rose. *F :* **Rosebud mouth**, bouche en cerise.

rosemary [ˈrouzməri], *s. Bot :* Romarin *m.*

roseola [roˈziːola], *s. Med :* Roséole *f.*

rosery [ˈrouzəri], *s.* Roseraie *f.*

rosette [roˈzet], *s.* **1.** Chou *m*, -oux (de ruban) ; cocarde *f* ; rosette *f* (de la Légion d'honneur). **2.** *Arch :* Rosace *f.*

rosewood ['rouzwud], s. Palissandre m.
rosin ['rɔzin], s. Colophane f.
rosolio [ro'zoulio], s. (Cordial) Rossolis m.
roster ['rɔstər, 'roustər], s. Mil: Navy:
(a) (Duty) roster, tableau m de service. By roster,
à tour de rôle. (b) Liste f. Adm: Promotion
roster, tableau d'avancement.
rostrum, pl. **-a, -ums** ['rɔstrəm, -a, -əmz], s.
(a) Rom.Ant: The Rostra, les rostres m. (b) Tribune f.
rosy ['rouzi], a. De rose; rose, rosé. R. cheeks,
joues vermeilles. F: To paint everything in rosy
colours, peindre tout en beau, en rose. A r.
prospect, une perspective souriante, attrayante.
S.a. -CHEEKED. **'rosy-'fingered**, a. Lit:
(L'Aurore) aux doigts de rose.
rot¹ [rɔt], s. **1.** Pourriture f, carie f. Vit: Brown
rot, mildew m, mildiou m. S.a. DRY-ROT, FOOT-
ROT. **2.** F: Blague f, bêtises fpl. That's all
(beastly) rot! tout ça c'est de la blague, des
sottises! To talk (utter) rot, dire des imbécillités.
What rot! quelle blague! allons donc! **3.** Démoralisation f. A rot set in, le moral (des joueurs,
des combattants) a flanché. To stop the rot,
parer à la démoralisation; enrayer la crise.
'rot-proof, a. Imputrescible.
rot², v. (rotted) **1.** v.i. (Se) pourrir; se décomposer, se putréfier, se carier. To rot off, away,
tomber en pourriture. **2.** v.tr. (a) Pourrir, faire
pourrir; décomposer, putréfier, carier. (b) F:
Railler, blaguer (qn). **rotting**, a. En pourriture.
'rot-gut, s. P: (Spirits) Tord-boyaux m.
rota ['routa], s. Liste f de roulement; tableau m
de service.
rotary ['routəri], a. Rotatif, rotatoire. (a) R.
motion, mouvement de rotation. Rotary traffic,
circulation giratoire. (b) Rotary crane, grue
pivotante. Rotary dryer, essoreuse centrifuge.
Rotary printing-press, rotative f.
rotate [ro'teit]. **1.** v.i. Tourner; (on pivot)
basculer, pivoter. **2.** v.tr. (a) Faire tourner;
faire basculer. (b) Remplir (des fonctions) à tour
de rôle. (c) Agr: Alterner, varier (les cultures).
rotating, a. Tournant, rotatif, à rotation.
Rotating body, corps en rotation.
rotation [ro'teiʃ(ə)n], s. **1.** (a) (Mouvement m de)
rotation f. (b) Basculage m. **2.** (a) Succession f
tour à tour. Rotation roll, (tableau m de) roulement m. By rotation, in rotation, par roulement;
à tour de rôle. (b) Agr: Rotation of crops,
assolement m. Three-course rotation, assolement
triennal. **3.** Rotation, tour m. Rotations per
minute, tours-minute mpl.
rotational [ro'teiʃən(ə)l], **rotative** ['routətiv], a.
Rotatif; de rotation; (of force, etc.) rotateur,
-trice.
rotatory ['routətəri], a. Rotatoire; de rotation.
rote [rout], s. Routine f. To say, learn, sth. by
rote, dire, apprendre, qch. mécaniquement, par
cœur. To do sth. by r., faire qch. par routine.
rotifera [ro'tifərə], s.pl. Ann: Rotifères m.
rotor ['routər], s. Mec.E: Rotor m. El.E: Rotor,
induit m.
rotten ['rɔt(ə)n], a. **1.** Pourri, carie. R. egg, œuf
pourri, gâté. F: He is rotten to the core, il est
pourri de vices. **2.** P: De mauvaise qualité;
F: lamentable; P: moche. R. weather, temps
de chien. R. job, sale besogne. I am feeling
rotten, je me sens patraque. Rotten luck! quelle
guigne! pas de veine! **-ly**, adv. P: D'une
façon pitoyable; abominablement. **'rotten(-)**
stone, s. Tripoli anglais; terre pourrie.
rottenness ['rɔt(ə)nnəs], s. État m de pourriture,
de décomposition.

rotter ['rɔtər], s. **1.** Raté m; propre m à rien.
2. Sale type m; P: vilain coco.
rotund [ro'tʌnd], a. **1.** Rond, arrondi. **2.** (Discours) emphatique; (style) ampoulé.
rotunda [ro'tʌnda], s. Arch: Rotonde f.
rotundity [ro'tʌnditi], s. **1.** Rondeur f, rotondité f. Hum: Embonpoint m. **2.** Grandiloquence f
(de style).
rouble [ru:bl], s. Num: Rouble m.
rouge¹ [ru:ʒ], s. **1.** (a) Toil: Rouge m, fard m,
carmin m. (b) Jewellers' rouge, rouge à polir.
2. Cards: Rouge et noir ['ru:ʒe'nwɑ:r], trente et
quarante m.
rouge², v.tr. To r. one's cheeks, se carminer les
joues. To rouge (oneself), mettre du rouge;
se farder.
rough¹ [rʌf]. I. a. **1.** (a) (Of surface, skin) Rêche,
rugueux, rude; (of cloth) revêche, grossier.
Rough to the touch, rude, âpre, au toucher.
Rough edges, tranches non ébarbées, non rognées
(d'un livre). R. glass, verre dépoli. Rough side
of a skin, côté chair. (b) (Of road) Raboteux,
rude; (of ground) inégal, accidenté. R. hair,
cheveux ébouriffés. (c) In the rough state, à
l'état brut. Rough casting, pièce brute de
fonderie. **2.** Grossier; brutal, -aux; (of wind)
violent. R. sea, mer agitée, mauvaise, houleuse
Nau: Rough weather, gros temps. To have a r
crossing, faire une mauvaise traversée. Rough
play, jeu brutal. F: Rough music, tintamarre m,
charivari m. To give s.o. a r. handling, malmener
houspiller, qn. To be r. with s.o., brutaliser
rudoyer, qn. S.a. TIME¹ 8. **3.** (Of manners)
Grossier, fruste; (of speech) bourru, rude; (o,
style) fruste. R. nursing, soins rudes, sommaires
4. Approximatif. Rough sketch, (i) ébauche f
esquisse f; (ii) plan m en croquis; premier jet
aperçu m. R. translation, traduction à peu près
Rough draft, brouillon m. Rough calculation
calcul approximatif. At a rough guess, pai
aperçu; approximativement. Rough estimate
évaluation en gros. **5.** (a) (Of voice) Rude, rêche
rauque. (b) Gram: Rough breathing, esprit r
rude. (c) (Of wine) Rude, âpre. **-ly**, adv
1. Rudement, brutalement, brusquement. Te
treat s.o. r., malmener, rudoyer, qn. **2.** R. painted
peint grossièrement. Roughly made, F: fait
coups de serpe. To sketch sth. r., faire un croqui
sommaire de qch. **3.** Approximativement;
peu près; en gros. Roughly speaking, er
général; généralement parlant. II. rough, adv
Rudement, grossièrement. To play r., joue
brutalement. III. rough, s. **1.** Terrain accidenté. Golf: To be in the rough, être dan
l'herbe longue. **2.** Crampon m (d'un fer à cheval)
3. One must take the rough with the smooth, i
faut prendre le bénéfice avec les charges; à la
guerre comme à la guerre. **4.** (Pers.) Voyou m
bandit m. **5.** (a) Wood in the rough, bois (
l'état) brut; bois en grume. (b) Statue in the
rough, statue brute; ébauche f d'une statue
'rough-and-'ready, a. **1.** Exécuté grossière
ment; fait à la hâte. Done in a r.-and-r. fashion
taillé à coups de hache. R.-and-r. installatior
installation de fortune. **2.** (Of pers.) Cava
lier; sans façon. **'rough-and-'tumble**
1. a. (a) (Combat, jeu) où l'on n'observ
pas de règles. (b) Rough-and-tumble life, vi
mouvementée. **2.** s. Mêlée f, bousculade f
corps-à-corps jovial. **'rough-cast¹**, s. **1.** Cons
Crépi m, gobetis m. **2.** Ébauche f (d'un plan
'rough-cast², v.tr. (rough-cast) **1.** Cons
Crépir, hourder, gobeter (un mur); ravaler (un
façade). **2.** Ébaucher (un plan). **'rough-cast**

ı. **I.** *Const:* Crépi, hourdé, gobeté. **2.** *Metall:*
Brut de fonte. **3.** (Plan) à l'état d'ébauche.
'rough-coated, *a.* (Cheval) hérissé, à long
poil; (chien) à poil dur. **'rough-dry,** *v.tr.*
Faire sécher (le linge) sans le repasser. **rough-**
'forged, *a.* Brut de forge. **'rough-grained,**
a. A grain grossier, à gros grain. **'rough-'hew,**
v.tr. (rough-hewed; rough-hewn) Ébaucher,
dégrossir (une statue, etc.). **'rough 'house,** *s.*
F: Chahut *m*, bousculade *f.* **'rough-rider,** *s.*
Dresseur *m* de chevaux. **'rough-spoken,** *a.*
I. Bourru. **2.** Au langage grossier.
ough², *v.tr.* **I.** To rough (up) the hair, ébouriffer
(les cheveux); faire hérisser (le poil). **2.** (*a*) Ferrer (un cheval) à glace. (*b*) Dépolir (le verre).
(*c*) *Const:* Piquer (un mur). **3.** *F:* To rough it,
(i) en voir de dures; manger de la vache enragée;
(ii) se passer des raffinements auxquels l'on est
habitué. **4.** Dégrossir (une lentille, etc.). **rough**
down, *v.tr.* Dégrossir (une pièce de forge).
rough out, *v.tr.* Ébaucher (un plan); dégrossir
(une pièce, une statue).
oughage ['rʌfedʒ], *s.* *Physiol:* Détritus *mpl*,
déchets *mpl* (de la nourriture).
oughen ['rʌf(ə)n]. **I.** *v.tr.* Rendre rude, rugueux.
2. *v.i.* (*a*) Devenir rude, rugueux. (*b*) (*Of* sea)
Grossir; devenir houleux.
oughness ['rʌfnəs], *s.* **I.** (*a*) Rudesse *f*, aspérité *f*,
rugosité *f.* (*b*) Rugosité, inégalité *f* (du sol).
2. (*a*) Grossièreté *f*, brusquerie *f*; manières
bourrues. (*b*) Agitation *f* (de la mer); rudesse
(du temps). **3.** Rudesse (de la voix); âpreté *f*
(de goût); qualité *f* fruste (du style).
oughshod ['rʌf'ʃɔd], *a.* (*a*) (Cheval) ferré à
glace. (*b*) *F:* To ride roughshod over s.o., fouler
qn aux pieds; traiter qn sans ménagement.
oulette [ru'let], *s.* **I.** (*Gaming*) Roulette *f.*
2. *Mil:* (Courbe) trochoïde *f.* **3.** *Tls:* Roulette
(de graveur, etc.); molette *f* (à perforer).
Roumania [ru'meinjə]. *Pr.n.* La Roumanie.
Roumanian [ru'meinjən], *a.* & *s.* Roumain,
-aine.
ound¹ [raund]. **I.** *a.* **I.** Rond, circulaire. The
Round Table, la Table ronde. **Round-table**
conference, conférence pour échange de vues
sur un pied d'entière égalité. To make round,
arrondir. Eyes r. with astonishment, yeux arrondis
par l'étonnement. Round shoulders, épaules
voûtées. **Round-hand,** (écriture) ronde; grosse *f.*
R. nut, écrou cylindrique. *S.a.* ARCH¹ **I.**
2. Round dance, danse en rond; ronde *f.*
U.S: Round trip, l'aller et le retour. **Round**
towel, essuie-main(s) à rouleau. **3.** (*a*) Round
dozen, bonne douzaine. In round figures, en
chiffres ronds. *R.* sum, compte rond. (*b*) Good
round sum, somme rondelette. To go at a good
round pace, aller bon train. (*c*) *R.* style, style
rond, coulant. *R.* voice, voix pleine, sonore.
Round oath, gros juron. **4.** *A:* To be round
with s.o., parler à qn franchement, rondement.
-ly, *adv.* **I.** Rondement, vivement. To go
roundly to work, mener rondement les choses;
s'y mettre avec entrain. **2.** *A:* (Parler) rondement, carrément. **II. round,** *s.* **I.** (*a*) Cercle *m*,
rond *m.* Cylinder out of round, cylindre ovalisé.
(*b*) *Art:* Statue in the round, statue en bosse.
To draw from the round, dessiner d'après la
bosse. **2.** (*a*) Barreau *m*, échelon *m* (d'échelle).
(*b*) *Arch:* Rond (de moulure). (*c*) *Cu:* Round
of beef, tranche grasse. Round of veal, rouelle *f*
de veau. *R.* of toast, rôtie *f.* **3.** *F:* The yearly r.
of the earth, la révolution annuelle de la terre.
F: The daily round, le train ordinaire des jours;
train-train quotidien. **One continual round of**

pleasures, une succession perpétuelle de plaisirs.
4. (*a*) Tour *m.* *Sp:* Circuit *m.* To go for a good
r., faire un grand tour (de promenade). To have
a round of golf, faire une tournée de golf. *F:* The
story went the round, l'histoire a passé de bouche
en bouche. (*b*) Tournée *f.* The postman's r., la
tournée du facteur. (Of doctor) To make his
rounds, to go (on) his rounds, faire sa tournée.
(*c*) *Mil:* Ronde *f* (d'inspection). (Of officer) To
go the rounds, faire sa ronde. **5.** (*a*) *Box:*
Round *m*, reprise *f.* (*b*) *Ten:* Tour, série *f* (d'un
tournoi). **6.** (*a*) To stand a round of drinks,
payer une tournée (générale). (*b*) *Cards:* Tour;
levée *f.* (*c*) *Mil:* A round of ten shots, une salve
de dix coups. *F:* Round of applause, salve
d'applaudissements. (*d*) *Mil:* Round of ammunition, cartouche *f.* (Of company) To fire a round,
tirer un coup (chacun). **7.** *Mus:* Canon *m.*
'round-'backed, *a.* = ROUND-SHOULDERED.
'round-'eyed, *a.* To stare round-eyed,
ouvrir de grands yeux étonnés. To listen in r.-e.
wonder, écouter les yeux ouverts tout rond.
'round-house, *s.* **I.** *Nau:* Roufle *m*; dunette *f.*
2. *Hist:* Corps m de garde. **'round 'robin,** *s.*
Pétition revêtue de signatures en rond (pour
ne pas révéler ·e chef de bande). **'round-**
'shouldered, *a.* Au dos voûté, bombé. To
be r.-s., avoir le dos rond.
round². **I.** *adv.* **I.** (*a*) To go round, tourner;
décrire un cercle. To turn round and round,
tournoyer. To turn round (about), se retourner.
(*b*) All the year round, (pendant) toute l'année.
Winter came round, l'hiver revint, arriva.
S.a. BRING ROUND, COME ROUND, etc. **2.** (*a*) Garden
with a wall right round, all round, jardin avec
un mur tout autour. To be six feet round, avoir
six pieds de tour. To show s.o. round, faire faire
à qn le tour de sa propriété, etc. *F:* Taken all
round, dans l'ensemble; en général. *S.a.* ALL-
ROUND. (*b*) All the country round (about), tout
le pays à l'entour. For a mile round, à un mille
à la ronde. **3.** To hand round the cakes, faire
passer, faire circuler, les gâteaux. Glasses round!
des verres pour tout le monde! There is not
enough to go round, il n'y en a pas pour tout le
monde. **4.** (*a*) It's a long way round, cela fait
un grand détour. To take the longest way
round, prendre par le plus long. (*b*) To order the
carriage round, commander qu'on amène la
voiture. *F:* To ask s.o. round for the evening,
inviter qn à venir passer la soirée. If you are r
this way, si vous passez par ici. *S.a.* GET ROUND,
GO ROUND, etc. **II. round,** *prep.* **I.** (*a*) Autou
de. Seated r. the table, assis autour de la table
There was a crowd r. the church, il y avait foule
aux abords de l'église. He is 36 inches r. the chest,
il a un tour de poitrine de 36 pouces. It will be
somewhere round a hundred pounds, cela vien
dans les cent livres. Round (about) midday, sur
les midi. (*b*) (Motion) To row, swim, r. the island,
faire le tour de l'île à la rame, à la nage. To go
r. the museums, visiter les musées. To go round
(and round) sth., tourner autour de qch. To write
a book round an incident, écrire un livre à propos
d'un incident. **2.** To go round an obstacle,
contourner un obstacle. You will find the grocer
r. the corner, vous trouverez l'épicerie en tournant
le coin. *S.a.* GET ROUND I (*c*).
round³. **I.** *v.tr.* (*a*) Arrondir; abattre (un angle).
Bookb: Endosser (un livre). (*b*) Contourner (un
obstacle). *Nau:* Doubler, franchir (un cap).
2. *v.i.* (*a*) S'arrondir. (*b*) To round on one's heel,
faire demi-tour. *F:* To round on s.o., (i) dénoncer qn; (ii) s'en prendre inopinément à qn.

round off, *v.tr.* Arrondir; adoucir (une arête). *To r. off one's sentences,* arrondir, perler, ses phrases. *To r. off the negotiations,* achever les négociations. **round up,** *v.tr.* Rassembler (du bétail); cerner, rabattre, rafler (des filous). **round-'up,** *s.* (a) *U.S:* Rassemblement *m* (du bétail); grande battue (à cheval). (b) Rafle *f* (de filous). **rounded,** *a.* Arrondi. *R. cheeks,* joues rebondies. *R. bank,* talus curviligne, bombé.

roundabout ['raundabaut]. I. *s.* I. (Manège *m* de) chevaux *mpl* de bois; carrousel *m.* 2. *Aut:* Sens *m* gyro; circulation *f* giratoire. II. **round-about,** *a.* (Chemin) détourné, indirect. *To take a roundabout way,* faire un détour; *F:* prendre le chemin des écoliers. *To lead up to a question in a r. way,* aborder de biais une question. *R. phrase,* circonlocution *f.*

roundel ['raundəl], *s. Her:* Tourteau *m.*

roundelay ['raundəlei], *s. A:* (a) Chanson *f* à refrain; rondeau *m.* (b) Chant *m* d'oiseau.

rounders ['raundərz], *s.pl. Games:* Balle *f* au camp.

Roundhead ['raundhed], *s. Hist:* Tête ronde (adhérent de Cromwell).

roundish ['raundiʃ], *a.* Rondelet.

roundness ['raundnəs], *s.* Rondeur *f.*

roundsman, *pl.* **-men** ['raundzmən, -men], *s.m.* Homme de tournée; livreur. **Milk roundsman,** laitier livreur.

roup [ru:p], *s.* Diphtérie *f* des poules; angine croupeuse.

rouse [rauz]. I. *v.tr.* I. (a) *Ven:* Faire lever (le gibier). (b) *To rouse s.o.* (from sleep), réveiller qn. *F: To rouse the sleeping lion,* réveiller le chat qui dort. *To r. the camp,* donner l'alerte au camp. *To r. s.o. from indolence,* to rouse s.o. up, secouer l'indifférence, l'énergie, de qn; *F:* secouer qn. *I tried to r. him,* je voulus le faire sortir de sa torpeur. *To rouse oneself,* se secouer; sortir de son apathie. *To rouse the masses,* remuer, activer, les masses. (c) Mettre (qn) en colère. *He is terrible when roused,* il est terrible quand il est monté. 2. Soulever (l'indignation); susciter (l'admiration, l'opposition). 3. *Nau: To rouse in the cable,* haler la chaîne. II. **rouse,** *v.i. To rouse* (up), (i) se réveiller; (ii) se secouer; sortir de sa torpeur. **rousing,** *a.* I. *R. cheers,* applaudissements chaleureux. *R. speech,* discours enlevant, vibrant. *R. chorus,* refrain entraînant. 2. (a) *F:* **Rousing lie,** gros mensonge. (b) *R. fire,* belle flambée.

rout¹ [raut], *s.* I. Bande *f* (de fêtards). 2. *A:* Raout *m*; réception (mondaine).

rout², *s. Mil:* Déroute *f*; débandade *f.* *To put troops to rout,* mettre les troupes en déroute. *To break into a rout,* se débander.

rout³, *v.tr. Mil:* Mettre (une armée) en déroute; disperser, défaire, enfoncer (une armée). **routed,** *a.* En déroute.

rout⁴, *v.tr. & i.* = ROOT³. **rout out,** *v.tr.* I. Dénicher (qn, qch.); tirer (qn) son lit, etc.; faire déguerpir (un renard). 2. (a) *Carp:* Évider (une rainure). (b) *Engr: Typ:* Échopper. **'routing-plane,** *s. Tls:* Guimbarde *f.*

route [ru:t], *s.* (a) Itinéraire *m*; route, voie *f.* **Trade routes,** routes commerciales. **Bus route,** (i) ligne *f* d'autobus; (ii) itinéraire, parcours *m,* d'un autobus. *Nau: To alter one's route,* changer de direction. (b) *Mil:* [raut] **Column of route,** colonne de route. **route-map** ['ru:tmap], *s.* Carte routière. **route-march** ['rautmɑ:rtʃ], *s. Mil:* Marche *f* d'entraînement.

routine [ru:'ti:n], *s.* I. Routine *f.* **The daily routine,** le train-train journalier. *Office r.,*

travail courant du bureau. *To do sth. as a mat of r.,* faire qch. d'office. **Routine work,** affai courantes; *Adm:* service de détail. 2. *M Navy:* Emploi *m* du temps. **Routine boa** tableau *m* de service.

rove¹ [ro:uv]. I. *v.i.* Rôder; vagabonder, err *To r. in every land,* rouler dans tous les pay rouler sa bosse. *His eyes roved over the pictur* son regard parcourait les tableaux. 2. *v.tr.* P courir (la campagne). *To r. the streets,* errer les rues. (*Of pirate, etc.*) *To rove the se* écumer les mers. **roving¹,** *a.* Vagabor nomade. **roving²,** *s.* Vagabondage *m.* **R.** *instincts,* instincts nomades.

rove². *See* REEVE².

rove-beetle ['rouvbi:tl], *s. Ent:* Staphylin *m.*

rover¹ ['rouvər], *s.* I. (a) Coureur *m*; vagabond (b) *Scouting:* Éclaireur chevalier. 2. *Croque* Corsaire *m.*

rover², *s. Nau:* Écumeur *m* de mer.

row¹ [rou], *s.* I. (a) Rang *m,* rangée *f*; ligne file *f* (de voitures). *Row of pearls,* rang de perl *Row of bricks,* assise *f* de briques. **Row of knittin** rang, tour *m,* de tricot. **In a row,** en rang, ligne. **In rows,** par rangs. *In two rows,* sur de rangs. (b) *Hort: Row of onions, of lettuces,* ran rayon *m,* d'oignons, de laitues. 2. (a) Rang (chaises, etc.). **In the front row,** au premier ran (b) *Row of houses,* ligne, rangée, de maisons.

row² [rou], *s.* I. Promenade *f* en canot; partie de canotage. *To go for a row,* faire une pr menade en canot. 2. *It was a long row,* il a fal ramer longtemps.

row³ [rou]. I. *v.i.* (a) Ramer. *Nau:* Nager. *row hard,* faire force de rames. *To row round t island,* faire le tour de l'île en canot, à la ram *To row a fast stroke,* ramer vite. **To row a rac** faire une course d'aviron. (b) Canoter; faire canotage. 2. *v.tr.* (a) Conduire (un batea à l'aviron. (b *To row s.o. over the river,* tran porter qn (en canot) sur l'autre rive. **rowing,** Conduite *f* (d'un bateau) à l'aviron. *Nau:* Nage *Sp:* Canotage *m.* *To go in for r.,* faire canotage, de l'aviron. **'row(ing)-boat,** Bateau *m* à rames; canot à l'aviron. **'rowing club,** *s.* Cercle *m* d'aviron. **'rowing-ma** *s.m.* Amateur de canotage. **'rowing-match,** Course *f* à l'aviron.

row⁴ [rau], *s.* I. Chahut *m,* tapage *m,* vacarme *To make, kick up, a row,* faire du chahu chahuter; faire du tapage, *P:* du boucan, c chambard. *F: To kick up the devil of a ro* faire un bacchanal, un charivari, de tous l diables. *P:* **Hold your row!** taisez-vous 2. Rixe *f,* dispute *f*; scène *f.* *To be always read for a row,* F: ne demander que plaies et bosse 3. Réprimande *f; F:* savon *m.* **To get into row,** se faire attraper; se faire laver la tête.

row⁵ [rau]. I. *v.tr. F:* Attraper, semoncer (qn 2. *v.i.* Se quereller (*with s.o.,* avec qn).

rowan ['rouən], *s. Bot:* I. **Rowan(-tree),** sorbier des oiseaux. 2. **Rowan(-berry),** sorbe *f.*

rowdiness ['raudinəs], *s.* Turbulence *f*; t page *m.*

rowdy ['raudi]. I. *a.* Tapageur. 2. *s.* (a) Chah teur *m.* (b) Voyou *m.*

rowdyism ['raudiizm], *s.* Chahutage *m*; d sordre *m.*

rowel¹ ['rauəl], *s.* I. Molette *f* (d'éperon 2. *Vet:* (Draining) rowel, séton *m* à, en, rouell **rowel²,** *v.tr.* (rowelled) Éperonner (un cheval labourer les flancs (d'un cheval).

rower ['rouər], *s.* Rameur, -euse; canotier *m Nau:* Nageur *m.*

owlocks ['rʌləks], *s.pl.* Dames *f* de nage; tolets *m*. **Swivel rowlocks,** tolets à fourche; systèmes (articulés).

oyal ['rɔiəl], *a.* (*a*) Royal, -aux. **His, Her, Royal Highness,** son Altesse royale. *The R. household,* la maison du roi. *With r. consent,* avec le consentement du roi. (*b*) Royal, princier; magnifique. *R. munificence,* munificence princière. *A r. feast,* un festin de roi. **To have a (right) royal time,** s'amuser follement. (*c*) *Nau:* Royal (sail), cacatois *m*. **-ally,** *adv.* Royalement; en roi.

oyalism ['rɔiəlizm], *s.* Royalisme *m*.

oyalist ['rɔiəlist], *a. & s.* Royaliste (*mf*).

oyalty ['rɔiəlti], *s.* **1.** Royauté *f*. **2.** (*a*) *pl.* **Royalties,** membres *m* de la famille royale. (*b*) *Coll.* **Hotel patronized by royalty,** hôtel fréquenté par les personnages royaux. **3.** *pl.* **Royalties,** (i) redevance (due à un inventeur, etc.); (ii) *Publ:* droits *m* d'auteur. **Mining royalties,** redevance tréfoncière.

ub¹ [rʌb], *s.* **1.** Frottement *m*; friction *f*. **To give sth. a rub (up),** donner un coup de torchon à qch.; frotter, astiquer (des cuivres). **2.** *Bowls:* Inégalité *f* (du terrain). *F:* **There's the rub!** c'est là le diable! voilà le hic! voilà le cheveu! **To come to the rub,** arriver au moment difficile.

ub², *v.* (rubbed) **I.** *v.tr.* (*a*) Frotter. *To rub one's leg with oil,* se frictionner la jambe avec de l'huile. **To rub one's hands (together),** se frotter les mains. *F:* **To rub shoulders with other people,** se frotter au monde; s'associer avec, frayer avec, d'autres gens. **To rub s.o. (up) the wrong way,** prendre qn à rebrousse-poil; contrarier, énerver, qn; *F:* échauffer la bile de qn. (*b*) **To rub sth. dry,** sécher qch. en le frottant. **To rub a surface bare,** dénuder une surface par le frottement. (*c*) **To rub sth. through a sieve,** passer qch. dans un tamis. *To rub sth. over a surface,* enduire une surface de qch. **To rub oil into s.o.,** faire une friction d'huile à qn; frictionner qn à l'huile. (*d*) **To rub an inscription,** prendre un frottis d'une inscription. **2.** *v.i.* (*a*) Frotter (*against,* contre); (*of pers.*) se frotter (contre). (*b*) (*Of clothes, etc.*) S'user. *Nau:* (*Of hawser, etc.*) Riper, raguer. **rub along,** *v.i. F:* Aller son petit bonhomme de chemin; se débrouiller. **We manage to rub along,** on va tant bien que mal. **rub down,** *v.tr.* **1.** (*a*) Panser, épousseter, (*with wisp*) bouchonner (un cheval). (*b*) Frictionner (qn) (après le bain). **2.** Adoucir (une surface); regratter (un mur); poncer (la peinture). **rub-'down,** *s.* Friction *f*. **To give s.o. a rub-down,** faire une friction à qn; frictionner qn. *To give a horse a rub-down,* bouchonner un cheval. **rub in,** *v.tr.* Faire pénétrer (un liniment, etc.) par des frictions. *F:* **Don't rub it in!** n'insistez pas davantage (sur ma gaffe, etc.). **rub off,** *v.tr.* Enlever (qch.) par le frottement. *To rub one's skin off,* s'écorcher légèrement; s'érafler la peau. **rub out,** *v.tr.* Effacer. **rub up. 1.** *v.tr.* Astiquer, frotter, fourbir. *F:* **To rub up one's memory,** rafraîchir sa mémoire. *To rub up one's Greek,* refaire du grec pour se dérouiller. **2.** *v.i.* **To rub up against other people,** se frotter au monde. **rubbed,** *a.* (*Of cloth*) Râpé; qui montre la corde. *R. furniture,* meubles dévernis.

rubbing, *s.* **1.** (*a*) Frottage *m*. *Mec:* Frictions *fpl*. **Rubbing compound,** pâte *f* à polir. (*b*) Frottement *m* (d'un organe de machine, etc.). **2.** Calque *m* par frottement; frottis *m*. **'rubbing-strake,** *s.* *N.Arch:* Bourrelet *m* de défense; liston *m*, listeau *m*.

rub-a-dub ['rʌbə'dʌb], *s.* Rataplan *m* (d'un tambour).

rubber¹ ['rʌbər], *s.* **1.** Frottoir *m*. **Kitchen rubber,** torchon *m*. **2.** (*Pers.*) (*a*) Frotteur, -euse. (*b*) Masseur, -euse (de hammam). **3.** (*a*) (India-) rubber (eraser), gomme *f* à effacer. (*b*) (India-) rubber, caoutchouc *m*. **Crêpe rubber,** crêpe *m* de latex. (India-)rubber band, (i) élastique *m*; (ii) courroie *f* en caoutchouc. **Rubber fabric,** tissu caoutchouté. *El.E:* **Rubber cable,** câble sous caoutchouc. **Rubber gloves,** gants en caoutchouc. (*c*) *pl.* (*Overshoes*) Caoutchoucs. **'rubber-covered,** *a.* (Câble) à revêtement en caoutchouc, sous (gaine de) caoutchouc. **'rubber-neck,** *s.* *U.S: P:* Badaud, -aude (qui regarde en l'air); touriste *mf*. **'rubber-tree,** *s.* *Bot:* Arbre *m* à gomme. **rubber-'tyred,** *a.* (*Of wheel*) Caoutchouté.

rubber², *s.* *Cards:* Robre *m*. *To play a r.,* faire un robre. **The rubber game,** la belle.

rubberize ['rʌbəraiz], *v.tr.* Caoutchouter; imprégner, enduire, (un tissu) de caoutchouc.

rubbish ['rʌbiʃ], *s.* **1.** (*a*) Immondices *fpl,* détritus *mpl*; (*of buildings*) décombres *mpl*. *Ind:* Rebuts *mpl*; déchets *mpl*. **Household rubbish,** ordures ménagères. **'Shoot no rubbish,'** "défense de déposer des immondices." (*b*) Fatras *m*; choses *fpl* sans valeur. (*c*) Camelote *f*. **2.** To talk rubbish, débiter des absurdités; dire des bêtises, des niaiseries. **(What) rubbish!** quelle blague! **'rubbish-bin,** *s.* Boîte *f* aux ordures. **'rubbish-cart,** *s.* Tombereau *m*. **'rubbish-heap,** *s.* (*a*) (*In garden*) Monceau *m* de détritus. (*b*) = RUBBISH-SHOOT. **'rubbish-shoot,** *s.* Dépôt *m* d'immondices; (lieu *m* de) décharge *f*.

rubbishy ['rʌbiʃi], *a.* Sans valeur (marchandises) de camelote.

rubble [rʌbl], *s.* *Const:* **1.** Rubble(-stone), moellons (bruts); libages *mpl*; blocaille *f*. **2.** Rubble(-work), moellonage *m*, blocage *m*; maçonnerie brute, en blocaille; *Arch:* rocaille *f*.

rubefacient [ru:bi'feiʃənt], *a. & s.* *Med:* Rubéfiant (*m*).

Rubicon ['ru:bikən]. *Pr.n. F:* **To cross the Rubicon,** franchir le Rubicon; sauter le pas.

rubicund ['ru:bikʌnd], *a.* Rubicond; rougeaud.

rubric ['ru:brik], *s.* *Typ: Ecc:* Rubrique *f*.

ruby ['ru:bi]. **1.** *s.* *Miner: Lap:* (*a*) Rubis *m*. **Balas ruby,** rubis balais. **Bohemian ruby,** rubis de Bohême. (*b*) **Ruby silver,** argent rouge. **2.** *a. & s.* Couleur de rubis; rouge (*m*). **Ruby lips,** lèvres vermeilles. *F:* **Ruby nose,** nez vineux.

ruche¹ [ru:ʃ], *s.* *Dressm:* Ruche *f*.

ruche², *v.tr.* *Dressm:* Rucher. **ruched,** *a.* À ruches; garni de ruches. **ruching,** *s.* Ruché *m*.

ruck¹ [rʌk], *s.* **1.** *Rac:* Peloton *m* (des coureurs). **2.** The (common) ruck, le commun (du peuple). **To get out of the ruck,** sortir du rang, de l'ornière.

ruck²,³, *s. & v.* = RUCKLE¹, ².

ruckle¹ ['rʌkl], *s.* (*In cloth*) Faux pli; godet *m*; froissure *f*.

ruckle², *v.* **To ruckle (up). 1.** *v.tr.* Froisser, chiffonner, friper (ses habits). **2.** *v.i.* (*Of garment*) (*a*) Se froisser. (*b*) Goder.

rucksack ['rʌksak], *s.* Sac *m* touriste.

ruction ['rʌk(ə)n], *s. F:* Désordre *m*, scène *f*. **There will be ructions,** il va y avoir du grabuge. *If you come home late, there'll be ructions,* si tu rentres tard, tu te feras attraper.

rudd [rʌd], *s.* *Ich:* Gardon *m* rouge.

rudder ['rʌdər], *s.* **1.** *Nau:* Gouvernail *m*. **2.** *Av:* Vertical *r.,* gouvernail de direction. **Horizontal r.,** gouvernail de profondeur.

3. Queue *f* (d'orientation) (de moulin à vent). **'rudder-bands, -braces,** *s.pl.* Pentures *f* du gouvernail. **'rudder-bar,** *s.* **1.** Barre *f* du gouvernail. **2.** *Av:* Palonnier *m.* **'rudder-post,** *s.* **1.** *N.Arch:* Étambot *m* arrière. **2.** *Av:* Axe *m* du gouvernail.

rudderless ['rʌdərləs], *a.* (Vaisseau) sans gouvernail, à la dérive.

ruddiness ['rʌdinəs], *s.* Coloration *f* du teint.

ruddle[1,2] [rʌdl], *s. & v.tr.* = REDDLE[1,2].

ruddy[1] ['rʌdi], *a.* (*a*) (Teint) coloré, haut en couleur, rouge de santé. *Large r. man,* gros rougeaud. (*b*) Rougeâtre. *R. glow* (*of fire*), lueur rouge, rougeoyante.

ruddy[2], *v.tr.* Rendre rouge.

rude [ruːd], *a.* **1.** (*a*) Primitif, rude; non civilisé. *R. style,* style fruste. *R. voice,* voix sans raffinement. (*b*) (Outil, etc.) grossier; rudimentaire. *R. beginnings,* commencements informes. *R. verses,* vers faits sans art. **2.** Violent, brusque. *R. shock,* choc violent; rude secousse. *S.a.* AWAKENING[2]. **3.** *R. health,* santé robuste. **4.** (*Of pers.*) Impoli, malhonnête; mal élevé. **To be rude to s.o.,** répondre grossièrement; dire des grossièretés à qn. *He was most r.,* il a été on ne peut plus grossier. *Would it be r. to inquire . . .,* peut-on demander sans indiscrétion. . . . **-ly,** *adv.* **1.** Primitivement; grossièrement. *R. fashioned,* fabriqué sans art. **2.** Violemment; brusquement. **3.** (Parler, etc.) impoliment, malhonnêtement, grossièrement.

rudeness ['ruːdnəs], *s.* **1.** Manque *m* de civilisation (d'un peuple); manque d'art; rudesse *f* (des mœurs). **2.** (*Of pers.* Impolitesse *f*, malhonnêteté *f*, grossièreté *f*.

rudiment ['ruːdimənt], *s.* **1.** *Biol:* Rudiment *m.* *R. of a thumb,* rudiment de pouce. **2.** *pl.* Rudiments, éléments *m,* premières notions (de grammaire, etc.).

rudimentary [ruːdi'mentəri], *a.* Rudimentaire.

rue[1] [ruː], *v.tr.* Regretter amèrement (une action); se repentir de (qch.). **You shall rue it,** vous vous en repentirez; il vous en cuira.

rue[2], *s. Bot:* Rue *f. Common rue,* rue odorante.

rueful ['ruːful], *a.* Triste, lugubre.

ruefulness ['ruːfulnəs], *s.* Tristesse *f;* air *m* triste, lugubre; ton *m* triste.

ruff[1] [rʌf], *s.* **1.** *A.Cost:* Fraise *f,* collerette *f.* **2.** *Z: Orn:* Collier *m,* cravate *f*

ruff[2], *s. Orn:* Combattant *m;* paon *m* de mer.

ruff[3], *v.tr. Whist: etc:* Couper (avec un atout).

ruffian ['rʌfjən], *s.* (*a*) Bandit *m,* brute *f.* *A:* Hired ruffian, spadassin *m* à gages. (*b*) *F: Little ruffians,* petits polissons.

ruffianly ['rʌfjənli], *a.* (Homme) brutal; (conduite) de brute. *R. appearance,* allure *f* de brigand, d'apache.

ruffle[1] [rʌfl], *s.* **1.** (*a*) *A:* Trouble *m,* agitation *f. Life without r.,* vie que rien n'est venu agiter. (*b*) *R. on the surface of the water,* rides *fpl* sur l'eau. **2.** (*a*) *Cost:* (At wrist) Manchette *f* en dentelle; (at breast) jabot plissé; (at neck) fraise *f.* (*b*) *Nat.Hist:* Collier *m;* cravate *f.*

ruffle[2], *v.tr.* (*a*) Ébouriffer (les cheveux); troubler, rider (la surface des eaux). **The bird ruffles (up) its feathers,** l'oiseau hérisse ses plumes. **To ruffle s.o.'s feelings,** froisser qn. **To ruffle s.o.'s temper,** contrarier qn. *Nothing ever ruffles him,* rien ne le trouble jamais. (*b*) Rucher (des manchettes); plisser (un jabot).

rug [rʌg], *s.* **1.** Couverture *f.* Travelling rug, motor rug, couverture de voyage; plaid *m.* **2.** Floor rug, carpette *f.* **Bedside rug,** descente *f* de lit.

Rugby ['rʌgbi]. *Pr.n.* **1.** (La grande école de Rugby. **2.** Rugby (football), le rugby.

rugged ['rʌgid], *a.* **1.** (*Of ground*) Raboteux, accidenté, inégal; (*of rock*) anfractueux; (*of bark*) rugueux. **2.** Rugged features, traits rudes, irréguliers. **3.** (*Of character*) Bourru, rude; (*of style*) raboteux, fruste. *R. independence,* indépendance farouche. *R. kindness,* tendresse bourrue.

ruggedness ['rʌgidnəs], *s.* **1.** Nature raboteuse, aspérité *f,* rugosité *f* (d'une surface); anfractuosités *fpl* (d'un rocher). **2.** Rudesse *f* (de caractère).

rugger ['rʌgər], *s. Fb: F:* Le rugby.

rugosity [ru'gɔsiti], *s.* Rugosité *f.*

ruin[1] ['ruin], *s.* **1.** Ruine *f;* renversement *m* (d'un État). **To go to ruin,** se délabrer; tomber en ruine. *S.a.* RACK[2]. *The r. of my hopes,* la ruine, l'effondrement *m,* de mes espoirs. *R. was staring him in the face,* la ruine se dressait devant lui. **To bring s.o. to ruin,** ruiner, perdre, qn. **2.** (*Often pl.*) Ruine(s). **Ramparts fallen in ruins,** remparts dégradés. *The building is a r.,* l'édifice est en ruines. **To lay a town in ruins,** détruire une ville de fond en comble. **3.** **To be, prove, the ruin of s.o.,** ruiner, perdre, qn.

ruin[2], *v.tr.* **Ruiner. 1.** (*a*) Abîmer (son chapeau, etc.). (*b*) *To r. one's prospects,* gâcher son avenir. *To r. one's health,* *F:* démolir sa santé. **To ruin s.o.'s reputation,** perdre qn de réputation. **2.** (*a*) *Her extravagance ruined him,* ses folles dépenses l'ont ruiné. *He is utterly ruined,* il est coulé. (*b*) Séduire, tromper (une jeune fille).

ruined, *a.* **1.** En ruines. **2.** Ruiné.

ruination [rui'neiʃ(ə)n], *s.* Ruine *f,* perte *f. It will be the r. of him,* ce sera sa ruine.

ruinous ['ruinəs], *a.* **1.** (Tombé) en ruines, délabré; ruineux. *R. old houses,* vieilles maisons qui menacent ruine. **2.** *R. expense,* dépenses ruineuses. (*Of undertaking*) To prove ruinous to s.o., être la ruine de qn.

rule[1] [ruːl], *s.* **1.** Règle *f.* (*a*) To set sth. down as a rule, établir qch. en règle générale. *As a (general) rule,* en règle générale; en thèse générale; en principe. **It is the rule to . . .,** il est de règle de. . . . **To do everything by rule,** tout faire suivant les règles. **Rule of thumb,** méthode *f* empirique; procédé *m* mécanique. *Mth:* Rule of three, règle de trois. (*b*) **To make it a rule to . . .,** se faire une règle de. . . . **Rules of conduct,** directives *f;* normes *f* de conduite. (*c*) **Rules and regulations,** statuts *m* et règlements *m.* **The rules of the game,** les règles, les lois, du jeu. *That is against the rules,* c'est contre les règles; ce n'est pas réglementaire. **The Rule of the Road,** (i) *Aut:* le code de la route; (ii) *Nau:* les règles du route. **2.** Empire *m,* autorité *f.* **To bear rule,** commander. **Under the rule of a tyrant,** sous l'empire d'un tyran. *Under British r.,* sous l'autorité britannique. **3.** *Jur:* Décision *f,* ordonnance *f.* **Rule of court,** décision du tribunal. **4.** (*a*) *Carp: etc:* Règle graduée; mètre *m.* **Folding rule,** mètre pliant. (*b*) *Surv:* Sighting rule, alidade *f.* **5.** *Typ:* (*a*) (Brass) rule, filet *m.* (*b*) (Em) rule, tiret *m.* **(En) rule,** trait *m* d'union.

rule[2]. I. *v.tr.* **1.** Gouverner, régir (un État). **To rule (over) a nation,** régner sur une nation. **To rule one's passions,** contenir, commander à, ses passions. **To be ruled by s.o.,** subir la loi de qn, être sous la coupe de qn. **2.** *Jur: etc:* Décider. **To rule sth. out of order,** déclarer que qch. n'est pas en règle. **3.** Régler, rayer (du papier). **To rule a line,** tracer une ligne à la règle. II. **rule,** *v.i.* **Prices are ruling high,** les prix restent levés. *The prices ruling in Manchester*, les prix qui se pratiquent à Manchester. **rule out**, *v.tr.* **1.** Écarter, éliminer (qch.). *Possibility that cannot be ruled out*, possibilité que l'on ne saurait écarter. **2.** Biffer, rayer (un mot). **ruling**[1], *a.* **1.** Souverain, dominant. **The ruling classes**, les classes dirigeantes. **Ruling passion**, passion dominante. **2.** Ruling price, cours pratiqué. **ruling**[2], *s.* **1.** Ordonnance *f*, décision *f*, (d'un juge, etc.) sur un point de droit. **To give a ruling in favour of s.o.**, décider en faveur de qn. **2.** Réglage *m*, réglure *f* (d'une feuille de papier). **~ler** [ru:lər], *s.* **1.** Souverain, -aine (*of*, *over*, de). *The rulers*, les dirigeants *m*. **2.** Règle *f*, mètre *m*. **~m**[1] [rʌm], *s. Dist*: Rhum *m*. **~m**[2], *a.* (rummer) *F*: Drôle, bizarre. *That's rum!* ça c'est pas ordinaire! **~umania** [ru'meinjə]. *Pr.n.* La Roumanie. **~umanian** [ru'meinjən], *a. & s.* Roumain, -aine. **~mble**[1] [rʌmbl], *s.* **1.** Grondement *m* (du tonnerre); roulement *m* (d'une charrette); gargouillement *m*, grouillement *m* (des entrailles). **2.** *Veh:* Siège *m* de derrière. **~mble**[2], *v.i.* (*Of thunder, etc.*) Gronder (sourdement); rouler, bruire; (*of bowels*) grouiller, gargouiller. *The cart rumbled off*, la charrette s'ébranla lourdement. **rumbling**, *s.* = RUMBLE[1] **1.** *Med:* **Rumblings in the bowels**, borborygmes *m*. **~men** ['ru:men], *s. Z:* Rumen *m*, panse *f* (d'un ruminant). **~minant** ['ru:minənt], *a. & s. Z:* Ruminant (*m*). **~minate** ['ru:mineit]. **1.** *v.i.* (*Of cow*) Ruminer. **2.** *v.i. & tr. F:* Ruminer, méditer. **~mination** [ru:mi'neiʃ(ə)n], *s.* **1.** *Physiol:* Rumination *f*. **2.** *F:* Rumination, méditation *f*. **~minative** ['ru:mineitiv], *a.* Méditatif. **~mmage**[1] ['rʌmedʒ], *s.* **1.** *Nau:* Changement *m* d'arrimage. **2.** (a) Recherches *fpl*, fouille *f* (dans le vieux documents, etc.). (b) *Cust:* Visite *f* (de douane (à bord). **3.** Vieilleries *fpl*; choses *fpl* de rebut. **Rummage sale**, (i) déballage *m*; (ii) vente *f* d'objets usagés (pour une charité). **~mmage**[2]. **1.** *v.tr.* Fouiller, farfouiller (une armoire, dans une armoire). **2.** *v.i.* To rummage in one's pockets, fouiller dans ses poches. **To rummage for sth.**, fouiller pour trouver qch. **To rummage about among old papers**, fouiller, fourrager, dans de vieux documents. **~mmer** ['rʌmər], *s.* Grand verre à boire. **~mmy**[1] ['rʌmi], *a. F:* = RUM[2]. **~mmy**[2], *s.* Jeu *m* de cartes (pour un nombre indéterminé de joueurs). **~mour**[1] ['ru:mər], *s.* Rumeur *f*, bruit *m* (qui court); on-dit *m inv.* **Rumour has it that . . .**, le bruit court que . . .; on dit que. . . . *Disquieting rumours are afloat*, il court des bruits peu rassurants. **~mour**[2], *v.tr.* **It is rumoured that . . .**, le bruit, la rumeur, court que . . . **~mp** [rʌmp], *s.* **1.** Croupe *f* (d'un quadrupède); croupion *m* (de volaille). *Cu:* Culotte *f*, cimier *m* (de bœuf). **2.** *F:* Restes *mpl*, restant *m* (d'un parti politique, etc.). **'rump-steak**, *s. Cu:* Rum(p)-steak *m*, romsteck *m*. **~mple** [rʌmpl], *v.tr.* (a) Chiffonner, friper, froisser (une robe, etc.); ébouriffer (les cheveux). (b) *F:* Contrarier, fâcher, chiffonner (qn). **~mpus** ['rʌmpəs], *s. F:* Chahut *m*, vacarme *m*. **To kick up, make, a rumpus**, (i) faire un chahut tout casser; (ii) faire du fracas, faire une

scène. **To have a rumpus with s.o.**, avoir une prise de bec avec qn.

run[1] [rʌn], *s.* **1.** (a) Action *f* de courir. **At a run**, au pas de course. **To break into a run**, se mettre à courir. **Prices have come down with a run**, les prix ont dégringolé. **She is always on the run**, elle est tout le temps à courir. *Mil:* **To keep the enemy on the run**, ne laisser aucun répit aux fuyards. *Nau:* **To lower the yards by the run**, amener les vergues en pagaïe. (b) Course *f*. *The horse had had a long run*, le cheval avait fourni une longue course. *F:* **To make a run for it**, s'enfuir, se sauver. **To have a run for one's money**, en avoir pour son argent. *We must give him a run for his money*, il faut lui en donner pour son argent. (c) Élan *m*. **To make a run at s.o.**, s'élancer sur qn. (d) *Cr:* **To make ten runs**, faire dix courses; marquer dix points. (e) *Fish:* Remonte *f*, montaison *f* (du saumon, etc.). **2.** (a) Course, promenade *f*, tour *m.* **To have a run, to go for a run**, faire une promenade. **Trial run**, (i) course d'essai (d'un navire, d'une locomotive); (ii) *Aut:* course d'essai que l'on fait faire à un client. (b) *Rail:* Trajet *m*. (c) *Nau:* Traversée *f*, parcours *m*. **Day's run**, course; distance parcourue. (d) *Mach:* Marche *f* (d'une machine). *Typ:* **Run of three thousand** (copies), tirage *m* à trois mille. **3.** (a) *N.Arch:* Formes *fpl* arrière (d'un navire); coulée *f* arrière; façons *fpl* de 'arrière. **Ship with a clean run**, vaisseau à l'arrière évidé. (b) **Run of sea, of tide**, courant *m* de marée. (c) Cours *m*, marche, suite *f* (des événements); rythme *m*, cadence *f* (des vers). **4.** **A run of luck**, une suite d'heureuses chances. *To have a run of luck*, être en veine. *A run of misfortune*, une suite de malheurs; *F:* la série noire. **Cards: Run of three**, séquence *f* de trois. **To have a long run**, (*of fashion*) avoir une longue vogue, rester longtemps en vogue; (*of play*) tenir longtemps l'affiche. **In the long run**, à la longue; en fin de compte. **5.** *Gaming:* **Run on the red**, série *f* à la rouge. **6.** Descente *f* (sur une banque); ruée *f* (sur des valeurs de bourse). *There was a run on the bank*, les guichets ont été assiégés. *There is a great run on that novel*, on demande beaucoup ce roman. **7.** **The common run of men**, le commun des hommes. **Above the common run**, au-dessus de l'ordinaire. **8.** Libre accès *m*. **To allow s.o. the run of one's library**, mettre sa bibliothèque à la disposition de qn. **To have the (free) run of the house**, avoir libre accès, pouvoir aller partout, dans la maison. **9.** (a) Sheep-run, pâturage *m* de moutons; bergerie *f*. **Pigeon-run**, volière *f*. (b) Toboggan-run, piste *f* de toboggan. **Ski run**, descente *f* à ski. **10.** *Mus:* Roulade *f*, tirade *f*, trait *m*.

run[2], *v.* (*p.t.* ran [ran]; *p.p.* run; *pr.p.* running) **I.** *v.i.* **1.** Courir. *F:* **To run like a hare, like the devil**, courir comme un lièvre, comme un Basque. **To run to meet s.o.**, courir au-devant de qn. *F:* **To run to meet one's troubles**, aller au-devant des ennuis. **To run upstairs**, monter l'escalier en toute hâte, quatre à quatre. *To run down the street*, descendre la rue en courant. *Rules so clear that he who runs may read*, règles si claires qu'elles se comprennent immédiatement. **To run a race**, courir, disputer, une course. *To run a mile*, courir, faire, un mille. *To run (about) the streets*, to run about the fields, courir les rues, les champs. **To run an errand, a message**, faire une course. **To run the blockade**, forcer le blocus. **2.** Fuir, s'enfuir, se sauver. **Now we must run for it!** maintenant sauvons-nous! **3.** **To run in a race**, courir, disputer, une épreuve, une course.

F: To run for office, se porter candidat (à une place). **4.** (*Of salmon, etc.*) Remonter les rivières ; faire la montaison. **5.** *Nau:* Courir, filer, faire route. **To run before the wind,** courir vent arrière ; fuir devant le vent. **To run free,** courir largue. **To run before the sea,** fuir devant la lame. *To run on the rocks,* donner sur les roches. *S.a.* AGROUND. **6.** (*a*) Aller marcher. *Vehicle that runs easily,* voiture qui roule bien. *Train running at fifty miles an hour,* train qui marche à cinquante milles à l'heure, qui fait cinquante milles à l'heure. *Trains running to Paris,* trains à destination de Paris. (*b*) Circuler. *Trains running between London and the coast,* trains qui font le service entre Londres et la côte. *This train is not running to-day,* ce train est supprimé aujourd'hui. *Boats that run daily,* bateaux qu font à traversée tous les jours. **7.** (*a*) *A whisper ran through the crowd,* un murmure courut dans la foule. *This error runs through all his work,* cette erreur se retrouve dans toute son œuvre. **The thought keeps running through my head,** cette idée me revient continuellement à l'esprit, me trotte dans la cervelle. **It runs in the family, in the blood,** cela tient de famille, cela est dans le sang. (*b*) **The talk ran on this subject,** la conversation a roulé sur ce sujet. *His life runs smoothly,* ses jours s'écoulent paisiblement. *Things must run their course,* il faut que les choses suivent leur cours. *The lease has only a year to run,* le bail n'a plus qu'un an à courir. *The play has been running for a year,* la pièce tient l'affiche depuis un an. (*c*) (*Of amount*) **To run to . . .,** se monter, s'élever, à. . . . *The interval sometimes runs to as much as half an hour,* l'entr'acte pousse parfois à la demi-heure. *The manuscript ran to a great length,* le manuscrit était très long. (*d*) **The money won't run to a car,** c'est une somme insuffisante pour acheter une auto. *F:* **I can't run to that,** c'est au-dessus de mes moyens. **8.** (*Of engine*) Fonctionner, marcher ; (*of wheel, etc.*) tourner. *The engine is running,* le moteur est en marche. **Apparatus that runs off the** (*electric*) **mains,** appareil qui se branche sur le secteur. *The drawer does not run easily,* le tiroir ne joue pas bien. **9.** (*Of colour in fabric*) Déteindre ; (*of ink on paper*) s'étendre ; (*of dye*) couler (au lavage). **10.** (*a*) (*Of liquid, etc.*) Couler. *River that runs for 200 miles,* rivière qui a 200 milles de cours. *River running into the sea,* rivière qui coule, se jette, dans la mer. **The tide runs strong,** le courant de marée est fort. **A heavy sea was running,** la mer était grosse. *The wine ran over the table,* le vin se répandit sur la table. *The rivers ran blood,* les rivières coulaient rouge, étaient teintes de sang. **Our stores are running low,** nos provisions s'épuisent, tirent à leur fin. *S.a.* BLOOD[1] I, DRY[1] I, HIGH II. 3, SHORT[1] I. 3. (*b*) **The floor was running with water,** le parquet ruisselait. *He was running with sweat,* il était en nage. **His nose was running, he was running at the nose,** le nez lui coulait. *Her eyes were running,* ses yeux pleuraient. *Ulcer that runs,* ulcère qui suppure. *Pen that runs,* plume qui bave, qui coule. *Casting that has run,* pièce qui a coulé. (*c*) *Vessel that runs,* vase qui coule, qui fuit. *F:* **Money runs through his fingers,** l'argent lui fond entre les mains. **11.** (*a*) *A gallery runs round the room,* une galerie court autour de la salle, fait le tour de la salle. **To run north and south,** être orienté du nord au sud. *The road runs quite close to the village,* la route passe tout près du village. (*b*) **So the story runs,** c'est ainsi que l'histoire est

racontée. *Thus the letter runs,* telle est la teneur d la lettre. *He runs to sentimentality,* il tombe dan la sentimentalité. **To run to seed,** (*of plant* monter en graine. (*Of pers.*) **To run to fa** prendre de la graisse. (*c*) *Apples run rathe big this year,* les pommes sont plutôt grosse cette année. **II. run,** *v.tr.* **I.** (*a*) Chasser (l renard, etc.). *S.a.* EARTH[1] 4. (*b*) **To run hard, close,** serrer qn de près. *You'll run m off my legs,* à ce train-là vous me romprez le jambes. *To run oneself out of breath,* s'essouffle (à force de courir). *S.a.* FINE[3] 6. **2.** (*a*) Mettr (un cheval) au galop. (*b*) Mettre (du bétail) a vert. **3.** (*a*) *To run the car into the garage,* rentre la voiture dans le garage. *To run s.o. up to tow* conduire qn en ville (en voiture). *To run a bo* ashore, atterrir une embarcation. **To run one'** **head against the door,** donner de la tête cont la porte. (*b*) *An express train is run betwee X and Y,* un train direct est en service entr X et Y. *They are running an extra train,* on fa chauffer un train supplémentaire. (*c*) Introduir (de l'alcool) en contrebande. **4.** (*a*) *I can't affor to run a car,* je n'ai pas les moyens d'entreten une auto. *To run a car at small cost,* faire u usage économique d'une voiture. (*b*) *Com:* W are running a cheap line, nous avons en magasi nous vendons, un article à bon march **5.** (*a*) Tenir (un magasin, un hôtel) ; exploite (une usine) ; diriger (un théâtre, une ferme) éditer, gérer (un journal). *To run the busines* faire marcher la maison. *To run s.o.'s house* tenir le ménage de qn. (*b*) *F:* **To run a (hig temperature,** faire de la température. **6.** *F:* **T run a horse,** faire courir un cheval. *F:* **T run a candidate,** (i) mettre en avant, (ii) appuye un candidat. **7.** Passer ; faire passer. *To run s.o sword through s.o., to run s.o. through with a swor* passer à qn une épée à travers le corps. *To r pipes through a wall,* faire passer des tuyaux travers un mur. *To run a thorn into one's finge* s'enfoncer une épine dans le doigt. **To run one fingers over a surface,** promener, faire glisse ses doigts sur une surface. *To run one's eye ov sth.,* jeter un coup d'œil sur qch. ; parcour qch. des yeux. **To run one's pen through a wor** rayer, biffer, un mot. **8.** *To run lead into a joi* couler du plomb dans un joint. **9.** Tracer (u ligne) (*round,* autour de). **run about,** *v.i. Courir de côté et d'autre. **'run-about,** *Aut:* Voiturette *f.* **run across,** *v.i.* **I.** Tr verser (la rue) en courant. **2.** Rencontrer (q par hasard) ; tomber sur (qn) inopinément. **ru after,** *v.i.* Courir après (qn). *She is much r after in society,* elle est très recherchée dans monde. **run against,** *v.i.* (*a*) Se heurter cont (qch.). (*b*) *This runs against my interests,* cela à l'encontre de mes intérêts. **run along,** *v* **I.** *Road that runs along the river,* chemin qui lon la rivière. *A ditch runs along the garden,* un fos borde le jardin. **2.** Run along! allez-vous-e filez ! **run at,** *v.i.* Courir sur, se jeter sur (q **run away,** *v.i.* (*a*) (*Of pers.*) S'enfuir, sauver ; s'échapper. *F:* **To run away from th** facts, se refuser à l'évidence des faits. (*b*) (O horse) S'emballer, s'emporter ; prendre le mo aux dents. (*c*) **To run away with s.o.,** enlever q **To run away with sth.,** emporter, enlever, q *F:* *Don't run away with the idea that . .* n'allez pas vous imaginer, n'allez pas croi que. . . . *That runs away with a lot of mone* cela mange beaucoup d'argent. **run dow** I. *v.i.* **I.** (*a*) Descendre en courant. (*b*) *The r ran down the windscreen,* la pluie ruisselait

.ong du pare-brise. *The sweat ran down his fore-head*, la sueur lui coulait sur le front. **2.** (*Of spring*) Se détendre; (*of clock*) s'arrêter (faute d'être remonté); (*of accumulator*) se décharger à plat; (*of dynamo*) se désamorcer. **II. run down,** *v.tr.* **1. To run down a ship,** (i) couler (à fond) un navire; (ii) laisser porter sur un navire. **To run s.o. down,** heurter, renverser, qn; (*of motorist*) écraser qn. **2.** (*a*) *Ven:* Mettre aux abois (un cerf). *F:* Attraper (qn) à la course. (*b*) *The police ran him down,* la police l'a dépisté. **3.** *F:* Dénigrer, déprécier, décrier, éreinter (qn); déblatérer contre (qn); éreinter (une pièce de théâtre). **run down,** *a.* **1.** (Accumulateur) à plat, déchargé. **2.** *F:* (*Of pers.*) *To get run down,* s'anémier; se débiliter. **run in,** *v.tr.* **1.** *F:* Conduire qn) au poste (de police); fourrer (qn) au bloc. *To be, get, run in,* se faire coffrer; se faire ramasser. **2.** *I.C.E:* Roder (un moteur). *Aut:* 'Running in,' "en rodage." *To run in the gears,* permettre aux engrenages de se faire. **run into. 1.** *v.i.* (*a*) *To run into debt,* faire des dettes; s'endetter. *To run into absurdity,* tomber dans l'absurdité. (*b*) (*Of colours*) **To run into one another,** se fondre l'une dans l'autre. (*c*) *To run into sth.,* entrer en collision avec qch.; (*of vehicle*) heurter, accrocher (un autre); (*of train*) tamponner (un autre); (*of ship*) aborder (un autre). (*Of pers.*) **To run into s.o.,** se trouver nez à nez avec qn. (*d*) *His income runs into thousands,* son revenu s'élève à des milliers de livres. *Book that has run into five editions,* livre dont on a publié cinq éditions. **2.** *v.tr.* (*a*) *To run one's car into a wall,* aller s'emboutir contre un mur. (*b*) **To run s.o. into debt,** faire faire des dettes à qn. **run off. 1.** *v.i.* Fuir, s'enfuir, se sauver. *To run off with the cash,* filer avec l'argent. **2.** *v.tr.* (*a*) Réciter (qch.) tout d'une haleine; rédiger (un article) au courant de la plume. *To run off a letter on the typewriter,* taper une lettre en moins de rien. (*b*) Faire écouler (un liquide). *To run off the water from a boiler,* vider l'eau d'une chaudière. (*c*) *Sp:* *To run off a heat,* courir une éliminatoire. **run on. 1.** *v.i.* (*a*) Continuer sa course. (*b*) (*Of time*) S'écouler; (*of contract, disease, etc.*) suivre son cours. (*c*) (*Of verse*) Enjamber. (*d*) *Typ:* (*Of words*) Se rejoindre; être liés; (*of text*) suivre sans alinéa. 'Run on,' "alinéa à supprimer." (*e*) Continuer à parler; *F:* en dégoiser. **2.** *v.tr.* *Typ:* *To run on the matter,* faire suivre sans alinéa. **run out. 1.** *v.i.* (*a*) Sortir en courant. (*b*) *The tide is running out,* la mer se retire. (*c*) (*Of liquid*) Couler, fuir; se répandre (sur la table). (*d*) (*Of period of time*) Se terminer, expirer. *Our lease has run out,* notre bail est expiré. (*e*) *Cards:* (*Of player*) Gagner la partie. (*f*) (*Of supplies*) Venir à manquer; faire défaut. *Our stores are running out,* nos provisions s'épuisent, tirent à leur fin. *F:* *His sands are running out,* il t.re à sa fin. *The sands are running out,* la dernière heure approche. (*Of pers.*) *To have run out of provisions,* avoir épuisé ses provisions; être à court, à bout, de provisions. *We ran out of food,* les vivres vinrent à nous manquer. (*g*) (*Of rope*) Filer, se dérouler. (*h*) *A strip of land runs out to sea,* une langue de terre s'avance dans la mer. **2.** *v.tr.* (*a*) *To run oneself out,* s'épuiser à force de courir. (*b*) (Laisser) filer (une corde). (*d*) *Nau:* Pousser dehors (une passerelle). (*d*) *Typ:* *To run out a line* (*into the margin*), sortir une ligne. **run over,** *v.i.* **1.** (*a*) Parcourir un document) du regard; passer en revue (les vénements). (*b*) *To run over the seams of a boat,*

vérifier les coutures d'une embarcation. *To run over s.o.'s pockets,* fouiller qn. (*c*) (*Of vehicle*) Passer sur le corps de, à (qn). *He has been run over,* il a été écrasé. **2.** (*Of vessel or contents*) Déborder. **run through. 1.** *v.i.* (*a*) Traverser (la salle) en courant. (*b*) Parcourir (un document) du regard; feuilleter (un livre). (*c*) *To run through a fortune,* dissiper, dévorer, une fortune. **2.** *v.tr.* See RUN[2] II. 7. **To run s.o. through** (and through), percer qn de part en part; transpercer, enfiler, qn. **run up. 1.** *v.i.* (*a*) Monter en courant. (*b*) Accourir. *To come running up,* arriver en courant. **To run up against s.o.,** rencontrer qn par hasard. (*c*) (*Of amount, price*) Monter, s'élever. **2.** *v.tr.* (*a*) Laisser grossir (un compte); faire monter (le prix de qch.); laisser accumuler (des dettes). (*b*) **To run up a flag,** hisser un pavillon. (*c*) Bâtir (une maison) à la va-vite; confectionner (une robe) à la hâte; faire un point à (une déchirure). **run,** *a.* **1.** *Tchn:* Price per foot run, prix par pied courant. **2.** (*Of dutiable goods*) Passé en contrebande. **3. Run butter,** beurre fondu pour conserve. **Run honey,** miel extrait des rayons. **running[1],** *a.* **1.** *Fb:* Running kick, coup de pied donné en courant. *Sp:* Running jump, saut avec élan. **To keep up a running fight,** (i) se battre en retraite; (ii) *Navy:* soutenir, appuyer, la chasse. **2. Running water,** eau courante, eau vive. (*In hotel*) Bedroom with r. water, chambre avec eau courante. **Running sore,** plaie qui suppure. **3.** (*a*) (Style) coulant. (*b*) Running hand, écriture cursive; (écriture) coulée f. **4.** (*a*) Continu. **Running accompaniment,** accompagnement soutenu. *Mil:* **Running fire,** feu roulant. *Typ:* **Running title,** titre courant. *S.a.* COMMENTARY. (*b*) *Meas:* **Running foot,** pied courant. (*c*) **Running expenses,** dépenses courantes. (*d*) (*Following the noun*) Consécutif; de suite. **Three days running,** trois jours de suite. **5.** (*a*) *Running block,* poulie mobile. (*b*) *Nau:* Running rigging, manœuvres courantes. **6.** *Needlew:* Running stitch, point devant, point droit. **running[2],** *s.* **1.** Course(s) *f(pl)*. *F:* **To make, take up, the running,** mener la course. **To be in the running,** avoir des chances d'arriver. **To be out of the running,** n'avoir plus aucune chance. **2.** (*a*) Marche *f*, fonctionnement *m* (d'une machine); roulement *m* (d'une voiture). Smooth *m*, allure régulière. **In running order,** prêt au service. (*b*) *To alter the r. of the trains,* modifier la marche des trains. (*c*) Direction *f* (d'un hôtel, etc.); exploitation *f* (des chemins de fer). (*d*) Introduction *f* (de 'alcool) en contrebande. *S.a.* GUN-RUNNING. **3.** Écoulement *m*, ruissellement *m* (de l'eau, etc.). *Med:* Suppuration *f*. **'running board,** *s.* **1.** *Aut:* Marchepied *m*. **2.** *Rail:* Tablier *m*.

runagate ['rʌnəgeit], *s.* A. & *Dial:* Vagabond, -onde.

runaway ['rʌnəwei], *attrib. a.* & *s.* **1.** (*a* Fuyard (*m*), fugitif (*m*). **Runaway slave,** esclave fugitif. (*b*) **Runaway horse,** cheval emballé. (*c*) *Rail:* Runaway truck, wagon parti à la dérive. **2.** (*a*) **To make a runaway match with s.o.,** enlever une jeune fille pour l'épouser; (*of girl*) se laisser enlever pour être épousée. (*b*) **Runaway victory,** victoire remportée haut la main.

rune [ruːn], *s.* *Pal:* Rune *f*.

rung[1] [rʌŋ]. *See* RING[4].

rung[2], *s.* **1.** Échelon *m*, barreau *m*, (barre *f* de) traverse *f* (d'une échelle); bâton *m* (d'une chaise).

runic ['ruːnik], *a.* Runique.

runnel ['rʌn(ə)l], *s.* Ruisseau *m*; rigole *f*.

runner ['rʌnər], s. I. (a) Coureur, -euse. Rac: Five runners, cinq partants m. (b) Messager m, courrier m. (c) Hist: (Bow-Street) runner, sergent m (de police). (d) Blockade-runner, forceur m de blocus. 2. Orn: Râle m d'eau. 3. Hort: (a) Coulant m, stolon m; traînée f (de fraisier). (b) Scarlet runner, runner-bean, haricot m d'Espagne. 4. Maille partie (d'un tricot). 5. (Meule) courante f (de moulin). 6. Patin m (de traîneau). Av: Glissoir m. 7. (a) Nau: Chaîne f de charge. (b) Anneau m mobile. 8. Curseur m. El: Runner resistance, résistance à curseur. 9. (a) Chariot m de roulement; trolley m. (b) Galet m (de roulement). (c) Roue f parasite, intermédiaire. (d) Roue mobile, couronne f mobile (d'une turbine). 10. Mec.E: Poulie f fixe. II. Metall: (a) Trou m, jet m, de coulée. (b) Jet, masselotte f. 12. (Table-) runner, chemin m de table; garde-nappe m. 13. Runner-up. (i) Sp: etc: Celui des deux joueurs (ou des deux coureurs) qui est battu dans l'épreuve finale; bon second. (ii) The runners-up, ceux qui dans la liste de classement d'un concours viennent en tête des refusés.

runt [rʌnt], s. I. Bœuf m ou vache f de race petite. 2. (Cheval) ragot m. 3. Pigeon romain. 4. F: Nain m, nabot m. 5. Trognon m (de chou).

runway ['rʌnwei], s. I. Mec.E: Chemin m de roulement. Crane runway, pont roulant. Overhead runway, transporteur aérien. 2. Aer: Coursive f (d'un dirigeable). 3. Av: Piste f d'envol.

rupee [rù:'pi:], s. Num: Roupie f.

rupture[1] ['rʌptjər], s. I. (a) Rupture f (de négociations, etc.); brouille f (entre amis). (b) El: Rupture of the arc, rupture de l'arc. 2. Med: (a) Rupture (d'une veine). (b) Hernie f.

rupture[2]. I. v.tr. (a) Rompre (des relations). (b) To r. a ligament, se rompre un tendon; claquer un tendon. 2. v.i. Se rompre. **ruptured**, a. I. Rompu. 2. (Intestin) hernié. (Of pers.) To be ruptured, avoir une hernie.

rural ['ruərəl], a. Rural, -aux; champêtre; de (la) campagne. R. site, site agreste. R. occupations, travaux des champs. Rural postman, facteur rural. Rural constable, garde m champêtre. -ally, adv. R. situated, situé à la campagne.

ruse [ru:z], s. Ruse f, stratagème m, piège m.

rush[1] [rʌʃ], s. I. Bot: Jonc m. Plantation of rushes, jonchaie f. Sweet rush, jonc odorant; lis m des marais. 2. F: Jonc ou paille f (pour fonds de chaises). 'rush-bed, a. Jonchaie f. 'rush-bottomed, a. (Chaise) à fond de paille. 'rush-'candle, -'dip, s. = RUSHLIGHT. 'rush-'mat, s. Natte f de jonc; paillasson m.

rush[2], s. I. (a) Course précipitée. To make a rush at s.o., se précipiter sur qn. Mil: To attack by rushes, attaquer par bonds. (b) General rush, ruée générale; bousculade f. There was a r. for safety, ce fut une ruée pour se mettre à l'abri. There was a r. to the doors, on se précipita vers les portes. The rush hours, (i) les heures d'affluence, les heures de pointe; (ii) (in business) le coup de feu. 2. Hâte f. We had a r. to get the job done, il a fallu nous hâter pour achever le travail. The r. of modern life, la vie fiévreuse d'aujourd'hui. Rush order, commande urgente. Rush-work, travail de première urgence. 3. A rush of air, un coup d'air, une chasse d'air. Rush of blood to the head, coup de sang. El.E: Rush of current, à-coup m de courant.

rush[3]. I. v.i. I. (a) Se précipiter; s'élancer. To rush about, courir çà et là. The river rushes along, la rivière précipite ses eaux. To rush int the room, faire irruption dans la chambre. F: T rush in where angels fear to tread, y aller ave audace sans se rendre compte du danger. To rus into an affair, se jeter étourdiment dans un affaire. F: To rush to conclusions, conclur trop hâtivement. (b) To rush out, s'élance dehors. To rush down, descendre impétueuse ment. To rush up, (i) monter à la hâte (ii) accourir. To r. upstairs, monter l'escalie quatre à quatre. To r. through France, traverse la France à la galopade. F: To rush throug one's prayers, expédier ses prières. (c) To rus at, on, s.o., se ruer, se jeter, sur qn; fondre su qn. 2. The wind rushes up the chimney, le ven s'engouffre dans la cheminée. The blood rushe to his face, le rouge lui monta au vis..ge. II. rusi v.tr. I. (a) Pousser ou entraîner violemmen To rush s.o. out of the room, chasser qn brusque ment de la chambre. They were rushed to hospita on les transporta d'urgence à l'hôpital. To r. s. into an undertaking, entraîner qn dans un entreprise sans lui donner le temps de réfléchi He rushed me through luncheon, il me fit déjeune au galop. I don't want to rush you, je ne voudra pas vous bousculer. Don't r. me, laissez-moi temps de souffler. To rush a bill through (th House), faire passer un projet de loi à la hât Th: To rush the ending, brusquer le dénoue ment. (b) F: To rush s.o. for sth., faire pay à qn un prix exorbitant pour qch. 2. Dépêche (un travail); exécuter (une commande) d'urgenc 3. The audience rushed the platform, le publ envahit l'estrade. Mil: To rush a positio prendre d'assaut une position. **rush up**, v.t I. Bâtir (une maison) à la hâte. To rush u the prices, se hâter de majorer les prix. 3. rush up reinforcements, faire venir du renfo en toute hâte.

rushlight ['rʌʃlait], s. Chandelle f à mèche jonc.

rusk [rʌsk], s. Cu: Biscotte f.

russet ['rʌset], I. s. (a A: Drap m de bure couleur brunâtre. (b) Hort: Reinette gris 2. a. & s. (Couleur f) roussâtre; feuille-mor (m) inv. Russet pear, rousselet m.

Russia ['rʌʃə]. Pr.n. La Russie Russia leathe cuir m de Russie.

Russian ['rʌʃən]. I. s. (a) Russe mf. Litt Russian, Petit(e) russe; Ruthène mf. (b) Lin Le russe. 2. a. De Russie; russe.

Russianize ['rʌʃənaiz], **Russify** ['rʌsifai], v. Russifier.

Russophil(e) ['rʌsofil], a. & s. Russophile (m

rust[1] [rʌst], s. I. Rouille f. To rub the rust o (i) enlever la rouille; (ii) F: se remettre courant (d'une science, etc.); se dérouille 2. Agr: Rouille. Black rust, charbon m d céréales; nielle f. 'rust-cement, s. Mastic de fonte. 'rust-preventer, s. Anti-roui m inv. 'rust-proof, a. Inoxydable; an rouille inv.

rust[2]. I. v.i. Se rouiller. F: To allow on knowledge to r., laisser rouiller ses connaissanc 2. v.tr. Rouiller. F: Idleness rusts the mir l'oisiveté rouille l'esprit. **rust in**, v.i. (Of scre Se rouiller dans son trou.

rustic ['rʌstik]. I. a. Rustique; agreste; paysa R. seat, banc rustique. 2. s. (a) Paysa -anne; campagnard, -arde. (b) Rustaud, -aud rustre m.

rusticate ['rʌstikeit]. I. v.i. Habiter la ca pagne; être en villégiature. 2. v.tr. Sch: Re voyer temporairement (un étudiant).

rustication ‚rʌsti'keiʃ(ə)n‚, s. **1.** Vie à la campagne. **2.** *Sch:* Renvoi *m* temporaire (d'un étudiant).

rusticity rʌs'tisiti], s. Rusticité *f*.

rustiness ['rʌstinəs], s. Rouillure *f*; rouille *f*; (*of clothing*) vétusté *f*.

rustle[1] [rʌsl], s. **1.** Bruissement *m*; frou-frou *m* (de la soie); froissement *m* (de papiers). **2.** *U.S:* = HUSTLE[1] 2.

rustle[2]. **1.** *v.i.* (*a*) (*Of leaves, paper*) Produire un bruissement; (*of leaves, wind*) bruire; (*of garment*) faire frou-frou. *I heard a deer r. through the bracken*, j'entendis un cerf froisser les fougères. (*b*) *U.S:* = HUSTLE[2] 2. **2.** *v.tr.* Faire bruire (les feuilles, des papiers); faire froufrouter (la soie); froisser (le papier). **rustling**[1], *a.* Bruissant; (jupon) froufroutant **rustling**[2], *s.* = RUSTLE[1].

rustless ['rʌstləs], *a.* **1.** Sans rouille. **2.** Inoxydable.

rusty[1] ['rʌsti], *a.* **1.** Rouille. **To get rusty, se** rouiller. *F: My French is r.*, mon français se rouille, est rouillé. **2.** Couleur de rouille; rouilleux; (vêtement) vétuste. *A r. black coat*, un habit d'un noir rouilleux. **3.** *Agr:* (Blé) rouillé. **-ily**, *adv.* **1.** *The door moved r. on its hinges*, la porte grinça sur ses gonds rouillés.

2. *To be r. clad*, porter des vêtements dont le noir tourne au roux.

rusty[2], *a.* Cheval) rétif, quinteux. *F: (Of pers.)* **To turn rusty, to cut up rusty, se rebiffer;** regimber.

rut[1] [rʌt], s. Ornière *f*. *F:* **To settle, sink, into a rut,** (*of pers.*) s'encroûter; (*of the mind*) se figer en routine. *To move in a rut*, être routinier. **To get out of the rut,** sortir de l'ornière; se désencroûter.

rut[2], *v.tr.* (rutted) Sillonner (un chemin) d'ornières.

rut[3], *s.* (*Of stags, etc.*) Rut *m*.

rut[4], *v.i.* (rutted) Être en rut. **Rutting season,** saison *f* du rut.

ruth ru:θ], *s.* *A:* Pitié *f*; compassion *f*.

ruthless ['ru:θləs], *a.* Impitoyable; sans pitié, sans merc ; (*of truth, act*) brutal, -aux. **-ly,** *adv.* Sans pitié, sans merci.

ruthlessness ['ru:θləsnəs], *s.* Nature impitoyable.

rutty ['rʌti], *a.* (Chemin) coupé d'ornières.

rye [rai], *s.* Seigle *m.* ' **ye-bread,** *s.* Pain *m* de seigle.

rye-grass ['raigrɑːs], *s.* Ivraie *f* vivace; ray-grass *m*.

ryot ['raiət], *s.* (*In India*) Ryot *m* paysan *m*.

S

S, s [es], *s.* **1.** (La lettre) S, s *f*; esse *f*. *Typ:* **Long s,** s allongée. **2.** (Courbe en) S; esse. **S curve,** courbure double. **S-shaped wall-anchor,** fer en S. **3.** (*Abbr. for Lt. 'solidus'*) Shilling *m*.

Saar [sɑːr]. *Pr.n. Geog:* **The Saar,** la Sarre.

Saarbruck ['sɑːrbruk]. *Pr.n.* Sarrebruck *m*.

Sabbatarian [sabə'tɛəriən], *s.* Observateur, -trice, du dimanche, *Jew:* du sabbat.

Sabbath ['sabəθ], *s.* **1.** (*a*) *Jew: B.Hist:* Sabbat *m.* (*b*) *Ecc:* Dimanche *m.* **To keep, break, the Sabbath,** observer, violer, le sabbat ou le dimanche. **2.** *A:* **Witches' sabbath,** sabbat. '**Sabbath-breaker,** *s.* Violateur, -trice, du sabbat ou du dimanche. '**Sabbath-'day,** *s.* = SABBATH 1. **Sabbath-day's journey,** voyage très court.

sabbatic(al) [sə'batik(əl)], *a. Jew.Rel:* Sabbatique. **Sabbatical year,** (i) *Jew.Rel:* année sabbatique; (ii) *U.S:* année de congé (accordée à un professeur pour voyager).

Sabine ['sabain], *a. & s. A.Hist:* Sabin, -ine. **The rape of the Sabines,** l'enlèvement *m* des Sabines.

sable[1] [seibl], *s.* **1.** *Z:* (Martre *f*) zibeline *f.* **2.** Sable (fur), zibeline. **3.** *Art:* **Sable (brush),** pinceau *m* en poil de martre.

sable[2]. **1.** *Her:* (*a*) s. Sable *m.* (*b*) *a.* (Écusson, etc.) de sable. **2.** *Poet:* (*a*) s. Noir *m. Esp. in pl.* **Sables,** vêtements *m* de deuil. (*b*) *a.* Noir; (vêtement) de deuil.

sabot ['sabou], *s.* **1.** *Cost:* Sabot *m.* **2.** Sabot (de pieu). *Artil:* Sabot (de projectile).

sabotage[1] [sabo'tɑːʒ, 'saboted₃], *s.* Sabotage *m. Continual acts of s.*, des sabotages continuels.

sabotage[2], *v.tr.* Saboter (l'outillage, un projet).

sabre[1] ['seibər], *s. Mil:* Sabre *m.* **Sabre cut,** (i) coup *m* de sabre; (ii) (*scar*) balafre *f.* '**sabre-rattler,** *s. F:* Traîneur *m* de sabre.

'**sabre-rattling,** *s.* Rodomontades *fpl*; menaces *fpl* de guerre.

sabre[2], *v.tr.* Sabrer.

sabretache ['sabrtaʃ], *s.* Sabretache *f*.

sabulous ['sabjuləs], *a. Med:* Graveleux.

sac [sak], *s. Nat.Hist:* Sac *m*, poche *f*.

sacchariferous [saka'rifərəs], *a.* Saccharifère.

saccharify [sa'karifai], *v.tr. Ch:* Saccharifier.

saccharimeter [saka'rimetər], *s.* Saccharimètre *m*.

saccharin(e) ['sakarin, -riːn], *s.* Saccharine *f*.

sacerdotal [sasər'dout(ə)l], *a.* Sacerdotal, -aux.

sachet ['saʃe], *s. Toil:* Sachet *m.* **Scent sachet,** sachet à parfums.

sack[1] [sak], *s.* **1.** (Grand) sac. *S. of coal*, sac de charbon. **2.** *P:* **To give s.o. the sack,** congédier (un employé, etc.); *F:* donner son paquet à qn; débarquer; *P:* balancer, saquer, qn; mettre qn à pied. **To get the sack,** recevoir son congé; *F:* se faire saquer. '**sack-race,** *s. Sp:* Course *f* en sacs.

sack[2], *v.tr.* **1.** Ensacher, mettre en sac (du charbon, etc.). **2.** *P:* **To sack s.o.** = *to give s.o. the sack.* **sacking**[1], *s.* **1.** Mise *f* en sac. **2.** *P:* Congédiement *m.* **3.** = SACKCLOTH 1.

sack[3], *s.* Sac *m*, pillage *m* (d'une ville, etc.).

sack[4], *v.tr.* Saccager, mettre à sac, mettre au pillage. **sacking**[2], *s.* Saccagement *m*; sac *m* (d'une ville, etc.).

sack[5], *s. A:* (Canary) sack, vin *m* des Canaries.

sackbut ['sakbət], *s. Mus: A:* **1.** Saquebute *f.* **2.** *B:* Sambuque *f*.

sackcloth ['sakklɔθ], *s.* **1.** *Tex:* Toile *f* à sacs; grosse toile; serpillière *f*; toile d'emballage. **2.** *B: etc:* Sac *m*; bure *f* (au sens figuré). **Sackcloth and ashes,** le sac et la cendre.

sackful ['sakful], *s.* Sachée *f*, plein sac.

sacral ['seikrəl], *a. Anat:* Sacré; du sacrum.

sacrament ['sakrəmənt], s. *Ecc:* Sacrement *m.*
The Holy Sacrament, the Blessed Sacrament, le
saint Sacrement (de l'autel); le Très Saint
Sacrement. **To receive, partake of, the sacrament,**
s'approcher des sacrements; communier. *To
give the last sacraments to a dying person,*
administrer les derniers sacrements à un mourant.
sacramental ['sakra'ment(ə)l], *a.* (*a*) Sacra-
mentel. (*b*) **Sacramental obligation,** obligation
sous serment; vœu *m.*
sacrarium, *pl.* **-ia** [sa'krɛəriəm, -ia], s. **I.** *Rom.
Ant:* Sacrarium *m.* **2.** *Ecc:* (*a*) Sanctuaire *m*
(d'une église). (*b*) *R.C.Ch:* Piscine *f.*
sacred ['seikrid], *a.* **I.** (*a*) Sacré. *Rom.Hist:* **The
Sacred Way,** la Voie sacrée. (*b*) **Tree sacred to**
. . ., arbre consacré à . . ., dédié à . . . **Sacred
to the memory of . . .,** consacré à la mémoire
de . . . **2.** (*a*) *Ecc:* Sacré, saint. **Sacred history,**
l'Histoire sainte. *S. books,* (i) livres d'Église;
(ii) livres saints. **Convent of the Sacred Heart,**
couvent du Sacré-Cœur. **The sacred orders,** les
ordres majeurs. (*b*) **S. music,** musique religieuse.
3. (*Of promise, etc.*) Sacré, inviolable. *S. duty,*
devoir sacré. **His Sacred Majesty,** la personne
sacrée du Souverain. *Nothing was s. to him,* il ne
respectait rien.
sacredness ['seikridnəs], s. **I.** Caractère sacré
(d'un lieu). **2.** Inviolabilité *f* (d'un serment).
sacrifice[1] ['sakrifais], s. **I.** (*a*) Sacrifice *m,*
immolation *f* (d'une victime). **To offer (up) sth.
as a sacrifice,** offrir qch. en sacrifice (*to,* à). *To
win a battle at a great sacrifice of life,* remporter
la victoire au prix de grands sacrifices. (*b*) Victime *f;* offrande *f.* **2.** *Theol:* Sacrifice (du
Christ). **The Sacrifice of the Mass,** le saint
sacrifice, le sacrifice de la messe. **3.** (*a*) Sacrifice,
abnégation *f* (de qch.); renoncement *m* (à qch.).
To make sacrifices to attain one's end, faire de
grands sacrifices pour arriver à ses fins. *To amuse
oneself at the sacrifice of one's studies,* s'amuser
aux dépens de ses études. *He succeeded at the s.
of his health,* il a réussi en sacrifiant sa santé.
S.a. SELF-SACRIFICE. (*b*) *Com:* Mévente *f;* vente *f*
à perte. **To sell sth. at a sacrifice,** vendre qch.
à perte. **Sacrifice prices,** prix au-dessous des
prix coûtants.
sacrifice[2], *v.tr.* **I.** Sacrifier, immoler, offrir en
sacrifice (une victime). *Abs.* **To sacrifice to idols,**
offrir des sacrifices aux idoles. **2.** (*a*) Sacrifier,
renoncer à (qch.); faire abnégation de (ses
intérêts, etc.). **To sacrifice oneself,** se sacrifier
(*for,* pour). (*b*) *Com:* Sacrifier, vendre à perte
(des marchandises).
sacrilege ['sakrilidʒ], s. Sacrilège *m.*
sacrilegious [sakri'lidʒəs] *a.* Sacrilège. *S.
person,* sacrilège *mf.* **-ly,** *adv* D'une manière
sacrilège.
sacrist ['seikrist], **sacristan** ['sakristən], s.
Ecc: Sacristain *m.*
sacristy ['sakristi], s. *Ecc:* Sacristie *f.*
sacrosanct ['sakrosaŋkt], *a.* Sacro-saint.
sacrum ['seikrəm], s. *Anat:* Sacrum *m.*
sad [sad], *a.* (**sadder**) **I.** (*a*) Triste. **To become sad,**
s'attrister. *To look sad,* avoir l'air triste, malheureux, affligé, mé.ancolique. **To make s.o. sad,**
attrister, contrister, qn. **To be sad at heart,** avoir
le cœur gros. **In sad earnest,** bien sérieusement.
A sadder and a wiser man, (i) *F:* un homme
instruit par le malheur; (ii) *Iron:* un homme
désillusionné. (*b*) (*Of news, etc.*) Affligeant; (*of
loss, etc.*) cruel; (*of place, etc.*) morne, ugubre.
He came to a sad end, il a fait une triste fin.
2. *A sad mistake,* une erreur déplorable. *She is a
sad flirt,* c'est une terrible coquette. **To make**

sad work of . . ., s'acquitter peu brillamment
de. . . . **-ly,** *adv.* **I.** Tristement. **2.** *Usu. iron.*
Déplorablement. *I was s. puzzled,* j'étais cruellement embarrassé. **3.** *Très;* beaucoup. *I need
it s.,* j'en ai bien besoin, grand besoin. *You are
s. mistaken,* vous vous trompez fort.
sadden ['sad(ə)n]. (*a*) *v.tr.* Attrister, affliger.
(*b*) *v.i.* S'attrister.
saddle[1] [sadl], s. **I.** (*a*) (i) Selle *f* (de cheval);
(ii) sellette *f* (de cheval de trait). **Hunting saddle,**
selle anglaise. **To rise in the saddle,** (i) se dresser
sur ses étriers; (ii) faire du trot enlevé. *To vault
into the s.,* sauter en selle. *To be in the s.,* être en
selle. *To be thrown out of the s.,* vider les arçons.
F: You are putting the s. on the wrong horse, votre
accusation porte à faux. (*b*) Selle (de bicyclette).
2. Col *m* (de montagne). **3.** *Cu:* Selle (de
mouton); râble *m* (de lièvre). **4.** *Tchn:* Reposoir *m* (d'un cric, etc.); chevalet *m* (de
chaudière). **5.** *Nau:* Croissant *m,* collier *m* (de gui,
de vergue). **'saddle-back. I.** s. (*a*) Toit *m* en
dos d'âne. (*b*) (*Of hill*) Ensellement *m.* (*c*) *Geol:*
Pli anticlinal. **2.** *a.* = SADDLE-BACKED. **'saddle-
backed,** *a.* (*a*) (Colline, toit) en dos d'âne.
(*b*) (Cheval) ensellé. **'saddle-bag,** s. **I.** *Cy:
etc:* Sacoche *f* (de selle). **2.** *Furn:* Moquette *f.*
'saddle-bow, s. *Harn:* Pontet *m,* arçon *m.*
'saddle-cloth, s. Housse *f* de cheval; couverture *f,* tapis *m,* de selle. **'saddle-horse,** s.
Cheval *m* de selle; monture *f.* **'saddle-
pin,** s. *Cy:* Tube *m* porte-selle. **'saddle-
room,** s. Sellerie *f.* **'saddle-tile,** s. Tuile *f*
en dos d'âne. **'saddle-tree,** s. Arçon *m;*
bois *m* de selle.
saddle[2], *v.tr.* (*a*) Seller (un cheval); embâter
(une bête de somme). (*b*) *F:* **To saddle s.o.
with sth., to saddle sth. on s.o.,** charger qn de
qch.; mettre qch. sur le dos de qn. *She is saddled
with five children,* elle a cinq enfants sur le dos.
Saddled with a tax, grevé d'un impôt.
saddler ['sadlər], s. Sellier *m;* bourrelier *m.*
saddlery ['sadləri], s. **I.** (*Trade*) Sellerie *f,*
bourrellerie *f.* **2.** = SADDLE-ROOM.
Sadducee ['sadjusi:], s. Saducéen, -enne.
sadism ['sadizm], s. Sadisme *m.*
sadist ['sadist], s. Sadique *mf.*
sadistic [sa'distik], *a.* Sadique.
sadness ['sadnəs], s. Tristesse *f,* mélancolie *f.*
safari [sa'fɑ:ri], s. (*In Africa*) Expédition *f* de
chasse. **On safari,** en expédition de chasse.
safe[1] [seif], s. **I.** Coffre-fort *m, pl.* coffres-forts.
2. Meat-safe, garde-manger *m inv.* **3. Rifle (set)
at safe,** carabine au cran de sûreté.
safe[2], *a.* **I.** (*a*) En sûreté; à l'abri. **Safe from
sth.,** à l'abri de, en sûreté contre, qch. (*b*) (Sain
et) sauf. **Safe and sound, safe in life and limb,**
sain et sauf. *We got s. into port,* nous sommes
arrivés à bon port. *To come s. home again,*
rentrer sans accident. **With a safe conscience,** en
toute sûreté de conscience. *His honour is safe,*
son honneur est à couvert, est sauf. **2.** (*a*) Sans
danger; sûr. **Safe retreat,** asile assuré, sûr. *To
put s.o., sth., in a s. place,* mettre qn, qch., en
lieu sûr. *S. beach, s. bathing,* plage sûre. *Nau:*
Safe anchorage, bon mouillage; mouillage sain.
(*b*) *Dog that is not safe,* chien dangereux. **Is it
safe to leave him alone?** est-ce qu'il n'y a pas
de danger à le laisser seul? *Tchn:* **Safe load,**
charge admissible; charge de sécurité. *Phot:*
Safe edge, cache *m.* **Safe light,** éclairage inactinique. (*c*) **To be on the safe side,** être du bon côté.
In order to be on the s. side, pour plus de sûreté.
The safest course would be to . . ., le plus sûr
serait de. . . . **To play a safe game,** avoir un

jeu sûr, serré. **It is safe to say that . . .**, on peut dire à coup sûr que. . . . **3.** (*Of critic, politician*) Prudent, circonspect. **-ly,** *adv.* **1.** Sans accident, sans dommage. **To arrive safely,** arriver sain et sauf, sans accident; (*of ship, etc.*) arriver à bon port. **To put sth. safely away,** mettre qch. en lieu sûr. **2.** Sûrement, sans danger, sans risque. **I can safely say that . . .**, je puis dire à coup sûr que.... **safe-'conduct,** *s.* Sauf-conduit *m,* *pl.* sauf-conduits. **safe-'keeping,** *s.* Bonne garde. **To be in safe-keeping,** être sous bonne garde, en sûreté.

safeguard[1] ['seifgɑːrd], *s.* **1.** *A:* Sauvegarde *f,* sauf-conduit *m.* **2.** Sauvegarde, garantie *f* (*against,* contre). **To obtain safeguards,** s'entourer de garanties.

safeguard[2], *v.tr.* Sauvegarder, protéger; mettre (ses intérêts) à couvert.

safeness ['seifnəs], *s.* **1. A feeling of safeness,** un sentiment de sécurité *f,* de sûreté *f.* **2.** Solidité *f* (d'un pont). **3.** Sûreté (d'un placement, etc.).

safety ['seifti], *s.* Sûreté *f,* sécurité *f;* salut *m.* **To seek safety in flight,** chercher son salut dans la fuite. **For safety's sake,** pour plus de sûreté. **In a place of safety,** en lieu sûr. **Road safety,** sécurité de la route. **Safety first!** prudence est mère de sûreté! la sécurité d'abord! **Safety-first policy,** politique de prudence. **To play for safety,** jouer au plus sûr. *Hist:* **Committee of Public Safety,** Comité de salut public. *Sm.a:* **To put one's rifle at safety,** mettre son fusil au cran de sûreté. *Ind:* **Safety factor,** coefficient *m* de sécurité. *Cin:* **Safety film,** film ininflammable. **'safety-bicycle,** *s.* *A:* Bicyclette *f.* **'safety-catch,** *s.* **1.** Fermoir *m* de sûreté (d'une agrafe). *Aut:* **Handle with a s.-c.,** poignée à condamnation. **2.** *Sm.a:* Cran *m* de sûreté. **'safety-lamp,** *s.* *Min:* Lampe *f* de sûreté. **'safety-pin,** *s.* Épingle anglaise; épingle de nourrice, de sûreté. **'safety-valve,** *s.* *Mch:* Soupape *f* de sûreté. *F:* **To sit on the safety-valve,** museler la presse; bâillonner l'opinion publique.

safflower ['saflauər], *s.* *Bot:* Carthame *m;* safran bâtard.

saffron ['safrən], *s.* **1.** Safran *m.* **2.** *a. & s.* Jaune safran *inv.*

sag[1] [sag], *s.* **1.** (*a*) Affaissement *m,* fléchissement *m* (d'un toit). (*b*) *Com:* Baisse *f* (des valeurs, etc.). **2.** Flèche *f,* ventre *m* (d'un cordage).

sag[2], *v.i.* (sagged) **1.** (*a*) (*Of roof, etc.*) S'affaisser, fléchir, arquer (sous un poids, etc.). (*b*) (*Of gate, etc.*) Pencher d'un côté; s'incliner; gauchir. (*c*) (*Of cheeks, breasts, etc.*) Pendre. (*d*) (*Of cable*) Se relâcher, se détendre; (*of rope, beam, etc.*) fléchir au milieu; faire ventre; faire guirlande; faire flèche. **2. Prices are sagging,** les prix fléchissent.

saga ['sɑːga], *s.* *Lit:* Saga *f.*

sagacious [sə'geiʃəs], *a.* Sagace, avisé; perspicace; entendu; (*of dog*) intelligent; (*of action*) plein de sagesse. **-ly,** *adv.* Avec sagacité.

sagaciousness [sə'geiʃəsnəs], **sagacity** [sə'gasiti], *s.* Sagacité *f;* intelligence *f* (d'un animal); sagesse *f* (d'une remarque).

sage[1] [seidʒ], **1.** *a.* *Lit:* Sage, prudent. **2.** *s.* Philosophe *m,* sage *m.* **The Seven Sages,** les sept Sages. **-ly,** *adv.* (*a*) *Lit:* Sagement, prudemment. (*b*) *F:* D'un ton doctoral.

sage[2], *s.* *Bot:* *Cu:* Sauge *f.* *a. & s.* **Sage green,** vert cendré *inv.*

sago ['seigo], *s.* *Cu:* Sagou *m.* **Sago pudding,** sagou au lait. **'sago-palm,** *s.* Sagoutier *m.*

Sahara (the) [ðəsa'hɑːra]. *Pr.n.* Le Sahara.

sahib ['sɑːib], *s.m.* Sahib.

said [sed]. *See* SAY[2].

sail[1] [seil], *s.* **1.** *Nau:* (*a*) Voile *f.* **To hoist, lower, a sail,** hisser, amener, une voile. **To take in a sail,** carguer une voile. **To carry all sails, to have all sails set,** porter tout dessus. (*b*) *Coll.* Voile(s), voilure *f,* toile *f.* **To make more s.,** augmenter de toile. **Ship under full sail,** navire toutes voiles dehors. **Vessel under sail,** vaisseau marchant à la voile. **To get under sail,** appareiller (à la voile). **To set sail,** mettre à la voile; prendre la mer; appareiller. **To strike sail,** amener les voiles. (*c*) (*Ship*) **Sail ho!** navire en vue! *Coll.* **A fleet of twenty sail,** une flotte de vingt voiles. **2.** Aile *f,* volant *m* (de moulin). **'sail-arm,** *s.* Châssis *m* de l'aile (d'un moulin à vent). **'sail-loft,** *s.* Voilerie *f.* **'sail-maker,** *s.* Voilier *m.*

sail[2], *s.* **1.** Excursion *f* en bateau à voiles; sortie *f* à la voile. **To go for a sail, to take a sail,** faire une promenade à la voile, en bateau. **2.** Voyage *m* sur mer. **It is a week's s. from Hull,** c'est à huit jours de traversée de Hull.

sail[3]. **1.** *v.i.* (*a*) (i) (*Of sailing-ship*) Aller à la voile; (ii) (*of sailing-ship or steamer*) naviguer; faire route. **To sail up the coast,** remonter la côte. **To sail round a cape,** contourner un promontoire. **To sail into harbour,** entrer dans le port. **To sail to, for, America,** faire route sur l'Amérique. **To sail (at) ten knots,** filer dix nœuds. (*b*) Partir, appareiller; prendre la mer. **To be about to sail,** être en partance. **2.** *v.tr. & ind.tr.* **To sail (on, over) the seas,** parcourir les mers; naviguer les mers. **3.** *v.i.* Planer (dans l air, etc.). *The clouds sailing by,* les nuages voguant dans le ciel. *F:* **She sailed into the room,** elle fit une entrée pleine de dignité. **4.** *v.tr.* Manœuvrer (un voilier); conduire (un vaisseau). **sailing**[1], *s.* **1. Fleet sailing,** flotte en mer. **2. Sailing-ship,** (navire) voilier *m;* bâtiment *m* à voiles. **Sailing-boat,** canot *m* à voiles. **3. Fast-sailing ship,** navire de bonne marche. **'sailing-barge,** *s.* Chaland *m* à voiles; gabare *f.* **'sailing-craft,** *s.* **1.** Petit bateau à voiles. **2.** *Coll.* Petits bateaux à voiles.

sailing[2], *s.* **1.** (*a*) Navigation *f.* **Plane sailing,** navigation plane, loxodromique. *F:* **It's (all) plain sailing,** cela va tout seul! tout cela ne fait pas un pli. (*b*) Marche *f,* allure *f* (d'un navire). **Fast sailing,** bonne marche. *Navy:* **Order of sailing,** ordre de marche. **2.** Départ *m,* appareillage *m.* **Port of sailing,** port de départ.

sailcloth ['seilklɔθ], *s.* Toile *f* à voile(s).

sailer ['seilər], *s.* *Nau:* **1.** (*Of sailing-ship*) Voilier *m.* **Good s., bad s.,** bâtiment bon, mauvais, voilier. **2.** (*Of any ship*) **Fast s., slow s.,** (navire) bon, mauvais, marcheur.

sailor ['seilər], *s.* (*a*) Marin *m* (officier ou matelot). **Sailors' home,** maison *f,* foyer *m,* du marin. (*b*) **To be a bad sailor,** être sujet au mal de mer. **To be a good sailor,** avoir le pied marin. **'sailor 'hat,** *s.* *Cost:* **1.** Canotier *m* (pour femmes). **2.** Jean-Bart *m* en paille (de petit garçon). **'sailor-'suit,** *s.* Costume marin (d'enfant).

sainfoin ['seinfoin], *s.* Sainfoin *m.*

saint[1] [seint]. **1.** (*a*) *s.* Saint, -e. **Saint's day,** fête *f* de saint. **All Saints' (Day),** la Toussaint. *F:* **To try the patience of a saint,** lasser la patience d'un saint. (*b*) [s(ə)nt] *Attrib.a.* (*abbr.* St *or* S.) **St Chrysostom,** saint Chrysostome. *Ellip.* **St Peter's,** (l'église *f*) Saint-Pierre. **2.** *s.* **The saints departed,** les fidèles trépassés. **Saint 'Bernard,** *s.* (Chien *m*) saint-bernard *inv.* **Saint He'lena** [he'liːna]. *Pr.n. Geog:* Sainte-Hélène *f.* **Saint 'John.** *Pr.n.m.* Saint Jean. **Saint John's day, Saint John's Eve,** la Saint-

Jean. **Saint 'Lawrence.** *Pr.n.* Le (fleuve) Saint-Laurent.

saint², *v.tr. Ecc:* Canoniser. **sainted,** *a.* **1.** Saint, canonisé; (*of place*) saint, sacré. **2.** (*Of pers.*) Saint, pieux.

saintliness ['seintlinəs], *s.* Sainteté *f.*

saintly ['seintli], *a.* (De) saint.

saith [seθ]. *See* SAY².

sake [seik], *s. Used only in the phr.* **For the sake of s.o., of sth.** *To do sth. for the sake of s.o., for s.o.'s sake,* faire qch. dans l'intérêt de qn, par égard pour qn, en considération de qn, à cause de qn. *I forgive you for her s.,* je vous pardonne à cause d'elle. *Do it for the s. of your family,* faites-le pour (l'amour de) votre famille. **Do it for my sake,** faites-le pour moi, pour me faire plaisir. **For God's sake, for goodness(') sake,** pour l'amour de Dieu. *For the s. of example,* pour l'exemple. **For old times' sake,** en souvenir du passé. **For old acquaintance(') sake,** en souvenir de notre vieille amitié. **For conscience(') sake,** par acquit de conscience. **To talk for talking's sake,** parler pour le plaisir de parler. **Art for art's sake,** l'art pour l'art.

saker et ['seikərət], *s. Orn:* Sacret *m.*

sal [sal], *s. A.Ch:* Sel *m.* **sal-am'moniac,** *s.* Sel ammoniac. **sal volatile** [salvo'latili], *s.* Sels volatils anglais; *F:* sels (à respirer).

salaam¹ [sa'lɑːm], *s. F:* Salamalec *m*; grand salut.

salaam², *v.tr. & i.* Faire des salamalecs, un grand salut (à qn).

salable ['seiləbl], *a.* = SALEABLE.

salacious [sa'leiʃəs], *a.* Lubrique, ordurier.

salaciousness [sa'leiʃəsnəs], **salacity** [sa'lasiti], *s.* Salacité *f,* lubricité *f.*

salad ['saləd], *s.* **1.** Salade *f.* Mixed salad, salade panachée.' **Fruit salad,** macédoine *f* de fruits. **'salad-basket,** *s.* Panier *m* à salade. **'salad-bowl,** *s.* Saladier *m.* **'salad days,** *s.pl. F:* Années *f* de jeunesse, d'inexpérience. **'salad-'dressing,** *s.* Sauce *f* genre mayonnaise (pour la salade). **'salad-'oil,** *s.* Huile *f* comestible, de table.

Salamanca [salaˈmaŋka]. *Pr.n.* Salamanque *f.*

salamander ['saləmandər], *s.* **1.** Salamandre *f.* **2.** *Cu:* Couvercle *m* à braiser; four *m* de campagne. **3.** Tisonnier ardent; allumoir *m.* **'salamander 'stove,** *s.* Salamandre *f.*

salary¹ ['saləri], *s.* Traitement *m,* appointements *mpl. S. of a member of Parliament,* indemnité *f* parlementaire. **To receive a salary,** être aux appointements.

salary², *v.tr.* Payer des appointements à (qn); faire un traitement à (qn). **salaried,** *a.* **1.** (Personnel) aux appointements. *High-salaried officials,* fonctionnaires à forts appointements. **2.** (*Of post*) Rétribué.

sale [seil], *s.* **1.** Vente *f.* (*a*) Débit *m,* mise *f* en vente (de marchandises). **Cash sale,** vente au comptant. **Credit sale,** vente à crédit. **Sale value,** valeur marchande. *Goods that command a sure s.,* marchandises de placement sûr. **House for sale,** maison à vendre. *To exhibit sth. for s.,* mettre qch. en vente. **On sale,** en vente. *Ind:* **The sales department,** le service commercial, le service ventes. **Sales-book,** livre de(s) vente(s); facturier *m.* (*b*) **Sale by auction,** sale to the highest bidder, vente à l'enchère, aux enchères; criée *f*; vente à la criée. *Jur:* **Compulsory sale,** adjudication forcée. (*c*) **Sale of work,** vente de charité. **2.** *Com:* **The sales are on,** c'est le moment des soldes *m.* **Sale goods,** soldes. **Sale price,** prix de

solde. **'sale-goer,** *s.* Chercheur, -euse, de soldes. **'sale-room,** *s.* Salle *f* de(s) vente(s).

saleable ['seiləbl], *a.* (*Of goods, etc.*) Vendable; de vente facile, courante.

salesman, *pl.* **-men** ['seilzmən, -men], *s.m.* **1.** (Commis) vendeur; employé à la vente. **2.** Courtier de commerce. **Travelling salesman,** voyageur de commerce; commis voyageur.

salesmanship ['seilzmənʃip], *s.* L'art *m* de vendre.

saleswoman, *pl.* **-women** ['seilzwumən, -wimen], *s.f.* Vendeuse.

Salic ['salik], *a. Hist:* **The Salic law,** la loi salique.

salicin ['salisin], *s. Ch:* Salicine *f.*

salicylate [sa'lisilet], *s. Ch:* Salicylate *m.*

salicylic [sali'silik], *a. Ch:* Salicylique.

salient ['seiliənt], *a.* **1.** (*a*) (*Of angle, etc.*) Saillant; en saillie. *Large s. eyes,* de gros yeux saillants. (*b*) *s. Mil:* Saillant *m.* **2.** (Trait) saillant, frappant.

salina [sa'laina], *s.* Marais salant.

saline. **1.** *a.* ['seilain] (*a*) Salin, sale. **Saline marshes,** marais salants. (*b*) (*Of medicine, etc.*) Salin. **2.** *s.* ['salain] Purgatif salin; sel purgatif. **3.** *s.* [sa'lain] = SALINA.

salinity [sa'liniti], *s.* Salinité *f.*

saliva [sa'laiva], *s.* Salive *f.*

salivary ['salivəri], *a.* Salivaire.

salivate ['saliveit], *v.i.* Saliver.

salivation [sali'veiʃ(ə)n], *s.* Salivation *f.*

sallow¹ ['salou, -o], *s. Bot:* Saule *m.*

sallow², *a.* (Teint) jaune, jaunâtre, olivâtre; *occ.* (teint) plombé, brouillé.

sallow³. **1.** *v.tr.* Jaunir, brouiller (le teint). **2.** *v.i. His complexion had sallowed,* son teint avait jauni.

sallowness ['salonəs], *s.* Ton *m* jaunâtre (du teint).

sally¹ ['sali], *s.* **1.** *Mil:* Sortie *f* (des assiégés). **2.** Excursion *f,* sortie. **3.** (*a*) Saillie *f,* élan *m* (d'activité, etc.). (*b*) **Sally (of wit),** saillie (d'esprit); boutade *f*; trait *m* d'esprit.

sally², *v.i.* **1.** *Mil:* **To sally (out),** faire une sortie. **2. To sally forth, out,** se mettre en route; partir en promenade.

sally³, *s.* Branle *m* (d'une cloche); mise *f* en branle.

Sally⁴. *Pr.n.f.* (*Dim. of Sarah*) Sarah. *S.a.* AUNT 2. **Sally Lunn,** *s. Cu:* Petit pain au lait (qui se mange au thé en rôtie beurrée).

sally⁵, *s. Bot:* = SALLOW¹. **'sally-garden,** *s.* Oseraie *f.*

sallyport ['salipɔːt], *s.* Poterne *f* de sortie (d'une place forte, etc.).

salmagundi [salma'gʌndi], *s. Cu:* Salmigondis *m.*

salmi ['salmi], *s. Cu:* Salmis *m.*

salmon ['samən], *s.* **1.** (*Usu. inv.*) Saumon *m.* **Young salmon,** saumoneau *m. River full of salmon,* rivière pleine de saumons. *Fish:* **Salmon ladder, salmon leap,** échelle *f* à saumon(s). **2.** *a. & s.* (*Colour*) Saumon *inv.* **'salmon-'trout,** *s.* Truite saumonée.

salon ['salɔ̃], *s.* **1.** (*a*) Salon *m.* (*b*) Réception *f* (de notabilités). **2.** (*a*) Salon d'exposition (d'une modiste, etc.). (*b*) *Art:* **The Salon,** le Salon.

Salonika [salo'niːka, -'naika]. *Pr.n.* Salonique *f.*

saloon [sa'luːn], *s.* **1.** (*a*) Salle *f,* salon *m.* **Billiard saloon,** salle de billard. **Hairdressing saloon,** salon de coiffure. **Dancing saloon,** dancing *m.* (*b*) *U.S:* Cabaret *m.* **Saloon keeper,** cabaretier *m.* **2.** *Nau:* Salon (de paquebot); la cabine. **Saloon passenger,** voyageur de première classe. **Saloon**

deck, pont de première classe. **3.** (a) *Rail:* **Saloon(-car, -carriage)**, wagon-salon *m*, *pl.* wagons-salons. (b) *Aut:* Saloon-car, voiture *f* à conduite intérieure. **sa'loon-bar**, *s.* Salle *f* de cabaret.

salsify ['salsifi], *s. Bot:* Salsifis *m.*

salt¹ [sɔlt]. I. *s.* **1.** (a) *Cu:* Sel (commun); *Ch:* chlorure *m* de sodium. *Cake of s.*, salignon *m.* **Rock salt**, sel gemme. **Kitchen salt**, sel de cuisine; gros sel. **Table salt**, sel de table; sel blanc. **Meat in salt**, viande en conserve, en train de mariner. **To eat salt with s.o.**, partager le pain et le sel avec qn. **To eat s.o.'s salt**, (i) recevoir l'hospitalité de qn; (ii) être à la charge de qn. *F:* **To take a story with a grain, a pinch, of salt**, croire à une histoire avec quelques réserves; prendre l'histoire avec un grain de sel. **He is not worth his salt**, il ne vaut pas le pain qu'il mange. *B:* **Ye are the salt of the earth**, vous êtes le sel de la terre. *A:* **Attic salt**, sel attique. (b) *A:* = SALT-CELLAR. **To sit (at table) above, below, the salt**, être assis au haut bout, au bas bout, de la table. (c) *F:* **Old salt**, loup *m* de mer; vieux matelot. **2.** (a) *Ch:* Sel. **Metal(lic) salt**, sel métallique. *Com:* **Spirit(s) of salts**, esprit *m* de sel; acide *m* chlorhydrique. (b) **Salt(s) of lemon**, sel d'oseille. **Rochelle salt(s)**, sel de Seignette. *S.a.* EPSOM. II. **salt**, *a.* Salé. **1.** (a) **Salt water**, eau salée; eau de mer. **Salt provisions**, vivres salés. *Lit:* **To weep salt tears**, pleurer à chaudes larmes. (b) (*Of food*) **Too salt**, trop salé. **2. Salt plant**, plante marine, salicole. **3.** (*Of rocks, ground*) Salifère. **'salt-box**, *s.* Boîte *f* à sel. **'salt-cellar**, *s.* **1.** Salière *f* (de table). **2.** *F:* *Salt-cellars*, salières (derrière les clavicules). **salt 'lake**, *s.* Lac salé; (*in N. Africa*) chott *m.* **Salt Lake City**, la ville du Grand Lac Salé. **'salt-marsh**, *s.* Marais salant. **'salt 'meadow**, *s.* Pré salé. **'salt-mine**, *s.* Mine *f* de sel. **'salt-pan**, *s.* = SALT-MARSH. **'salt-pit**, *s.* Saline *f*; mine *f* de sel. **'salt-spoon**, *s.* Cuiller *f* à sel; pelle *f* à sel. **'salt-tax**, *s. Hist:* La gabelle. **'salt-water**, *attrib.a.* Salt-water fish, poisson de mer. **'salt-works**, *s.* (a) Saunerie *f.* (b) Raffinerie *f* de sel.

salt², *v.tr.* **1.** (a) **To salt (down)** *meat, butter,* saler la viande, le beurre. (b) Saupoudrer (qch.) de sel. (c) Saler (un mets). **2.** *Vet:* Immuniser (un cheval). *F:* **An old salted veteran**, un vieux dur à cuire. **3.** (a) *Com: F:* Cuisiner, truquer (les livres de compte). (b) *F:* **To s. the bill**, saler l'addition. (c) *Min:* **To salt a mine**, saler une mine (d'or, etc.); tapisser le front d'une mine. **salting**, *s.* **1.** Salaison *f.* **2.** *Vet:* Immunisation *f.* **3.** *pl.* **Saltings**, prés salés. **'salting-tub**, *s.* Saloir *m.*

salter ['sɔltər], *s.* **1.** Fabricant *m* de sel; ouvrier *m* de saunerie; saunier *m.* **2.** = DRYSALTER. **3.** Saleur *m* (de poissons, etc.).

saltire ['saltaiər], *s. Her:* Sautoir *m*; croix *f* de Saint-André. **In saltire**, en sautoir.

saltish ['sɔltiʃ], *a.* Légèrement salé; saumâtre.

saltness ['sɔltnəs], *s.* Salure *f*, salinité *f.*

saltpetre [sɔlt'pi:tər], *s.* Salpêtre *m.* **Chile saltpetre**, nitre *m* de Chili; nitrate *m* de soude; caliche *m.* **Saltpetre bed**, nitrière *f.* **Saltpetre works**, salpêtrière *f.*

saltwort ['sɔltwə:rt], *s. Bot:* **1.** Soude *f.* **2. Black saltwort**, glaux *m.* **3.** Salicorne *f.*

salty ['sɔlti], *a.* **1.** Salty deposit, grumeaux *mpl* de sel. **2.** Salé, saumâtre.

salubrious [sə'lju:briəs, -lu:-], *a.* Salubre, sain.

salubrity [sə'lju:briti, -lu:-], *s.* Salubrité *f.*

saluki [sə'lu:ki], *s.* Sloughi *m*; lévrier *m* arabe.

salutary ['saljutəri], *a.* Salutaire (*to*, à).

salutation [salju'teiʃ(ə)n], *s.* Salutation *f.*

salute¹ [sə'lju:t, -lu:-], *s.* (a) Salut *m*, salutation *f.* *Fenc:* **Salute with foils**, salut des armes. (b) *Mil:* *Navy:* Salut. **To give a salute**, faire, exécuter, un salut. **To return, acknowledge, a salute**, rendre un salut. **To stand at (the) salute**, garder l'attitude du salut. **To beat a salute**, battre aux champs. (c *Mil: Navy:* **To fire a salute**, tirer une salve. **To fire a s. of ten guns**, saluer de dix coups.

salute², *v.tr.* Saluer (qn). **1.** (a) **To salute s.o. emperor**, saluer qn empereur. (b) **To salute s.o. with a smile, a kiss**, accueillir, saluer, qn par un sourire, un baiser. **2.** **To salute (s.o.) with the hand**, with the sword, saluer (qn) de la main, de l'épée. *Abs. Mil:* **To salute**, faire le salut militaire. **To salute with twenty guns**, saluer de vingt coups. **3.** **The first object that salutes the eye**, la première chose qui s'offre à, qui frappe nos regards.

salvable ['salvəbl], *a. Ins:* Qui peut être sauvé; susceptible de sauvetage.

salvage¹ ['salvedʒ], *s.* **1.** Indemnité *f*, droit *m*, prime *f*, de sauvetage. **2.** Sauvetage *m* (d'un vaisseau, etc.); assistance *f* maritime. **To make salvage of goods**, sauver des marchandises. **Salvage company**, société *f* de sauvetage (de marchandises). *Nau:* **Salvage plant**, appareils *mpl* de renflouage. **3.** Objets sauvés (d'un naufrage, d'un incendie). **'salvage-tug**, *s.* Remorqueur *m* de sauvetage.

salvage², *v.tr.* (a) = SALVE³. (b) Récupérer (une voiture, etc.). **Salvaged material**, matériel sauvé, récupéré.

salvation [sal'veiʃ(ə)n], *s.* Salut *m.* **To work out one's own salvation**, travailler à son (propre) salut; faire son salut. **To find salvation**, faire son salut. **To seek salvation in sth.**, chercher son salut dans qch. *S.a.* ARMY 1.

salvationist [sal'veiʃənist], *s.* Salutiste *mf.*

salve¹ [sɑːv], *s. Pharm:* Onguent *m*, baume *m*, pommade *f.*

salve², *v.tr.* Adoucir, apaiser, calmer (les sentiments). **To do sth. to salve one's conscience**, faire qch. par acquit de conscience.

salve³ [salv], *v.tr. Nau: etc:* Sauver, relever (un vaisseau); effectuer le sauvetage (des marchandises); sauver (des objets dans un incendie).

salver ['salvər], *s.* Plateau *m* (d'argent, etc.).

salvo, *pl.* **-oes** ['salvo, -ouz], *s.* Salve *f.* **To fire a salvo**, lancer, tirer, une salve. *F:* **Salvo of applause**, salve d'applaudissements.

salvor ['salvər], *s. Nau:* Sauveteur *m.*

Sam [sam]. *Pr.n.m.* Samuel. *F:* **Uncle Sam**, l'oncle Sam; les États-Unis. *F:* **To stand Sam**, régaler la compagnie; payer la tournée. **Upon my Sam**, parole d'honneur. **Sam Browne**, *s. Mil:* F: (Sam Browne (belt), ceinturon *m* et baudrier *m* (d'officier); *F:* bricole *f.*

Samaria [sə'mɛəriə]. *Pr.n.* La Samarie. *B:* **The woman of Samaria**, la Samaritaine.

Samaritan [sə'maritən], *a. & s.* Samaritain, -aine. *B:* **The good Samaritan**, le bon Samaritain.

sambo ['sambo], *s.* **1.** *Ethn:* Zambo *m.* **2.** *F:* Moricaud *m.*

same [seim]. **1.** *a. & pron.* (Le, la) même, (les) mêmes. **To repeat the s. words twice**, répéter deux fois les mêmes mots. **At the s. time that this was happening**, au moment même que cela se passait. **He is of the s. age as myself**, il est du même âge que moi. **They are sold the s. day as they come in**, ils sont vendus le jour même de leur arrivée. *All actuated by the s. impulse*, tous poussés par un même élan. **Of the same kind**, similaire. **In the same way**, de même. *A Happy New Year to you!*—**The same to you!** je vous souhaite une bonne année !—A vous de même, à vous pareillement. *He got up and I did the same*, il se leva et j'en fis autant, et je fis de même. (*Emphatic*) **The very same thing, one and the same thing**, une seule et même chose ; tout à fait la même chose. **At the same time,** (i) en même temps ; (ii) à la fois. **It is the same (thing) everywhere,** il en est de même partout. **It all amounts, comes, to the same thing,** tout cela revient au même. **It's all the same, it's just the same,** c'est tout un ; *F:* c'est tout comme. **It is all the same to me,** ça m'est égal. *If it is all the s. to you,* si cela ne vous fait rien ; si ça vous est égal. *It is the s. with me,* il en va de même pour moi. *You still look the s.,* vous n'avez pas changé. **It is much the same,** c'est à peu près la même chose. *He is much about the s.,* il va à peu près de même. *P:* The) same here! et moi aussi ! et moi de même ! **2.** *adv.* **To think, feel, act, the s.,** penser, sentir, agir, de même. *We like good things the same as you,* nous aimons les bonnes choses tout comme vous-même. **All the same**, malgré tout ; quand même ; tout de même. *All the s. it has cost us dear,* n'empêche que cela nous a coûté cher. *I feel anxious all the s.,* cela ne laisse pas (que) de m'inquiéter. *When I am away things go on just the same,* quand je suis absent tout marche comme d'habitude.

sameness ['seimnəs], *s.* **I.** (*a*) Identité *f* (with, avec). (*b*) Ressemblance *f* (with, à). **2.** Monotonie *f*, uniformité *f* (d'un paysage, etc.).

samite ['samait], *s. Tex: A:* Samit *m* ; brocart lamé.

samovar [samo'vɑːr], *s.* Samovar *m*.

Samoyed [samo'jed], **Samoyede** [samo'jiːd]. **I.** *a. & s.* Samoyède (*mf*). **2.** *s.* Chien *m* samoyède.

sampan ['sampan], *s. Nau:* Sampan *m*.

samphire ['samfaiər], *s. Bot:* **I.** C(h)ristemarine *f*. **2.** Salicorne *f*.

sample[1] [sɑːmpl], *s.* Échantillon *m* ; prise *f*, prélèvement *m* (de gaz, de minerai, de sang, etc.). **Up to sample**, pareil, conforme, à l'échantillon. **To be up to sample**, répondre à l'échantillon. **To send sth. as a sample**, envoyer qch. à titre d'échantillon. **To buy sth. from sample**, acheter qch. d'après l'échantillon. *F:* **To give a sample of one's knowledge**, donner un exemple de son érudition.

sample[2], *v.tr.* (*a*) *Com:* Prendre des échantillons de, échantillonner (une étoffe, etc.) ; déguster (un vin). (*b*) *F:* Goûter (un mets) ; essayer (un nouveau restaurant). **2.** Donner un échantillon de (qch.). **sampling,** *s.* Prise *f* d'échantillons ; échantillonnage *m*.

sampler[1] ['sɑːmplər], *s.* **I.** Modèle *m* de broderie (sur canevas) ; marquoir *m*. **2.** *For:* Arbre type (laissé debout).

sampler[2], *s.* (*Pers.*) Échantillonneur, -euse.

samurai ['samurai], *s.inv.* Samouraï *m*.

sanatorium [sana'tɔːriəm], *s.* Sanatorium *m*.

sanctification [saŋ(k)tifi'keiʃ(ə)n], *s.* Sanctification *f*.

sanctify ['saŋ(k)tifai], *v.tr.* Sanctifier ; consacrer. *F: Custom sanctified by time*, coutume consacrée par le temps. **sanctified,** *a.* (*a*) (*Of pers.*) Sanctifié, saint ; (*of thg*) consacré. (*b*) **Sanctified air,** air confit (en dévotion).

sanctimonious [saŋ(k)ti'mounjəs], *a.* Papelard, cagot, béat. *His s. air*, son air confit (en dévotion).

sanction[1] ['saŋ(k)ʃ(ə)n], *s.* **I.** *Jur:* Vindicatory sanction, punitive sanction, sanction pénale. **2.** Sanction *f*, consentement *m*, approbation *f*. **With the sanction of . . .,** avec le consentement de. . . . *F:* **Sanction of custom,** sanction de l'usage. **3.** *Hist:* Ordonnance *f*, décret *m*. **The Pragmatic Sanction,** la pragmatique sanction.

sanction[2], *v.tr.* Sanctionner. **I.** *Jur:* Attacher des sanctions (pénales) à (une loi, etc.). **2.** (*a*) *Jur:* Ratifier (une loi, etc.). (*b*) *F:* Approuver, autoriser (qch.). **Sanctioned by usage,** consacré par l'usage.

sanctity ['saŋ(k)titi], *s.* **I.** Sainteté *f*. *S.a.* ODOUR 2. **2.** Caractère sacré (d'un terrain, d'un serment) ; inviolabilité *f* (de la vie privée).

sanctuary ['saŋ(k)tjuəri], *s.* **I.** (*a*) Sanctuaire *m*, temple *m*. (*b*) (*Sacrarium*) Sanctuaire ; saint *m* des saints. **2.** *Ecc.Jur:* Asile (sacré) ; refuge *m*. **Rights of sanctuary,** droits *m* d'asile ; immunité *f*. **To take sanctuary,** chercher asile. **3.** *Ven:* Refuge d'oiseaux.

sanctum ['saŋ(k)təm], *s.* **I.** Sanctuaire *m*, sacrarium *m*. **2.** *F:* Sanctuaire ; cabinet privé ; *P:* turne *f*. *Lady's s.*, boudoir *m*.

sand[1] [sand], *s.* **I.** (*a*) Sable *m*. **Scouring sand, welding sand, fine sand,** sablon *m*. *To scour with s.*, sablonner. *Choked up with s.*, ensablé. *F:* **To build on sand,** bâtir sur le sable. (*b*) *sg. or pl.* Banc *m* de sable. (*c*) *Usu. pl.* Grain(s) *m*(*pl*) de sable. **As numerous as the sand(s on the sea-shore,** aussi nombreux que les grains de sable de la mer. **2.** *pl.* **Sands,** plage *f*, grève *f*. *S.a.* QUICKSAND. **'sand-bank,** *s.* Banc *m* de sable. **'sand-bar,** *s.* Somme *f* (à l'embouchure d'un fleuve). **'sand-blast,** *s.* Jet *m* de sable. **'sand-blast (machine),** *s.* **'sand-box,** *s. Metall:* Caisse *f* à sable. *Golf:* Boîte *f* à sable. *Rail:* Sablière *f* (de locomotive). **'sand-boy,** *s.m. In the phr.* As merry, as jolly, as a sand-boy, gai comme un pinson. **'sand-casting,** *s. Metall:* Coulée *f* en sable. **'sand-crack,** *s. Vet:* Seime *f*. **'sand-drift,** *s.* **I.** Mouvement *m* du sable. **2.** Sable mouvant. **'sand-eel,** *s. Ich:* Équille *f*, lançon *m*. **'sand filter,** *s. F:* Fontaine sablée. **'sand-fly,** *s. Ent:* Simulie *f*. *F:* moustique *m*. **'sand-glass,** *s.* Sablier *m*. **'sand-hill,** *s.* Dune *f*. **'sand-man,** *pl.* **-men,** *s.m.* Sablonnier. *Esp. F:* (*To children*) The sand-man has come, le marchand de sable passe. **'sand-martin,** *s.* Hirondelle *f* de rivage. **'sand-pit,** *s. Sablière f*, sablonnière *f*. **'sand-shoal,** *s.* = SAND-BANK. **'sand-shoes,** *s.pl.* **I.** Souliers *m* bains de mer (à semelles de caoutchouc). **2.** Sandales *f* ou espadrilles *f*. **'sand-spout,** *s.* Trombe *f* de sable. **'sand-storm,** *s.* Simoun *m* ; tempête *f* de sable.

sand[2], *v.tr.* **I.** Sabler (une allée). *To s. the floor,* répandre du sable sur le plancher. **2.** (*a*) *To sand (up),* ensabler (l'embouchure d'un fleuve). (*b*) *v.i. To sand up,* s'ensabler. **3.** Mettre du sable dans (le sucre). **4.** Sablonner ; nettoyer avec du sable.

sandal ['sand(ə)l], *s.* Sandale *f*. **Bathing sandals,** espadrilles *f*.

sandal(wood) ['sand(ə)l(wud)], *s.* (Bois *m* de) santal *m*.

sandarac ['sandarak], *s.* **I.** Réalgar *m*. **2.** (Gum) sandarac, sandaraque *f* ; vernis sec.

sandbag[1] ['sandbag], *s.* **I.** *Fort:* Sac *m* à terre.

2. Sac de lest. **3.** *P:* Assommoir *m*; boudin *m*. **4.** Bourrelet *m* (de porte, fenêtre); boudin. **andbag²**, *v.tr.* (sandbagged) **1.** (*a*) Protéger (un bâtiment, etc.) avec des sacs de terre ou de sable. (*b*) Mettre des bourrelets à (une porte). **2.** Assommer (qn) (d'un coup de boudin sur la nuque).

andpaper¹ ['sandpeipər], *s.* Papier *m* de verre.

andpaper², *v.tr.* Frotter (qch.) au papier de verre; poncer, doucir (une surface). **Sand-papering machine**, ponceuse *f*.

andpiper ['sandpaipər], *s. Orn:* Maubèche *f*, bécasseau *m*, chevalier *m*.

andstone ['sandstoun], *s. Geol:* Grès *m*. **Red sandstone**, grès rouge. **Sandstone quarry**, grésière *f*. **Sandstone wheel**, meule *f* en grès.

andwich¹ ['sandwitʃ], *s.* Sandwich *m*. **Ham sandwiches**, sandwichs au jambon. **'sandwich-board**, *s.* Panneau *m*. **'sandwich-man**, *pl.* **-men**, *s.m.* Homme-sandwich, homme-affiche.

andwich², *v.tr.* Serrer, intercaler (*between*, entre).

andy ['sandi], *a.* **1.** Sableux, sablonneux; (*of path*) sablé. *S. stretches of coast*, longues grèves de sable. **2.** (*Of hair*) Roux pâle *inv*; blond roux *inv*.

ane [sein], *a.* Sain d'esprit; sensé; (*of views, speech*) raisonnable, sensé. *To be s.*, avoir toute sa raison. **-ly**, *adv.* Raisonnablement.

ang [saŋ]. *See* SING.

sanguinary ['saŋgwinəri], *a.* **1.** (*a*) (*Of battle*) Sanguinaire, sanglant. (*b*) (*Of law*) Barbare. (*c*) Altéré de sang. **2.** *P: Euphemism for* BLOODY 2.

sanguine ['saŋgwin]. **1.** *a.* (*a*) (*Of complexion*) D'un rouge sanguin; rubicond. (*b*) (*Of temperament*) Sanguin. (*c*) Confiant, optimiste. *To be of a s. disposition*, être porté à l'optimisme. *To be, feel, sanguine about the future*, avoir confiance en l'avenir. **2.** *s. Art:* Sanguine *f* (crayon ou dessin).

Sanhedrim ['sanidrim], *s. Jew.Ant:* Sanhédrin *m*.

sanies ['seinii:z], *s. Med:* Sanie *f*.

sanify ['sanifai], *v.tr.* Assainir.

sanious ['seiniəs], *a. Med:* Sanieux.

sanitarian [sani'tɛəriən], *a. & s.* Hygiéniste (*mf*).

sanitary ['sanitəri], *a.* Hygiénique, sanitaire. *S. care*, précautions *f* hygiéniques. *Insufficient s. arrangements*, manque m d'hygiène. *To render s.*, assainir. **Sanitary inspector**, inspecteur du la salubrité publique.

anitation [sani'teiʃ(ə)n], *s.* **1.** Hygiène *f*; salubrité publique; système *m* sanitaire. *To improve the s. of a town*, assainir une ville. **2.** *F:* Aménagements *m* sanitaires.

sanity ['saniti], *s.* Santé *f* d'esprit; jugement sain; bon sens; rectitude *f* (du jugement).

sank [saŋk]. *See* SINK².

sanserif [san'serif], *s. Typ:* Caractères *mpl* sans obit et sans empattement.

Sanskrit ['sanskrit], *a. & s. Ling:* (Le) sanscrit.

Santa Claus ['santə'klɔ:z]. *Pr.n.m.* Le Bonhomme Noël; saint Nicolas.

sap¹ [sap], *s. Bot:* Sève *f*. *F:* **The sap of youth**, la sève de la jeunesse. **'sap-wood**, *s.* Aubier *m*. *Carp:* Aubour *m*.

sap², *s. Mil:* Sape *f*. **To drive a sap**, exécuter une sape.

sap³, *v.* (sapped) **1.** *v.tr. & 1. Mil:* Saper; approcher (d'un endroit) à la sape. **To sap forward**, pousser des approches. **2.** *v.tr.* Saper, miner (les fondements d'une doctrine, etc.).

sap⁴, *s. Sch: P:* Piocheur, -euse; bûcheur, -euse.

sap⁵, *v.i.* (sapped) *Sch: P:* Piocher, bûcher.

sapajou ['sapadʒu:], *s. Z:* Sapajou *m*.

sapience ['seipiəns], *s.* **1.** *A:* Sagesse *f*. **2.** Pédanterie *f*.

sapient ['seipiənt], *a.* **1.** *A:* Sage, savant. **2.** Pédant.

sapless ['sapləs], *a.* Sans sève; desséché; *F:* (*of pers.*) sans vigueur.

sapling ['sapliŋ], *s.* **1.** Jeune arbre *m*; plant *m*, baliveau *m*. *For:* **Sapling wood**, gaulis *m*. **2.** *F:* (*a*) Jeune homme *m*; adolescent *m*. (*b*) Jeune lévrier *m*.

saponaceous [sapo'neiʃəs], *a.* Saponacé, savonneux.

saponify [sa'pɔnifai]. **1.** *v.tr.* Saponifier (la graisse, etc.). **2.** *v.i.* Se saponifier.

sapper ['sapər], *s. Mil:* Sapeur *m*. **Engineer sapper**, sapeur du génie. *F:* **The sappers**, le génie.

sapphic ['safik]. *Pros:* **1.** *a.* (Strophe) saphique. **2.** *s.pl.* Sapphics, vers *m* saphiques.

sapphire ['safaiər], *s.* Saphir *m*. **Sapphire ring**, bague de saphirs.

sappy ['sapi], *a.* (*a*) Plein de sève. (*b*) (*Of timber*) Vert.

saprophyte ['saprofait], *s. Biol:* Saprophyte *m*.

saraband ['sarəband], *s. Danc:* Sarabande *f*.

Saracen ['sarəsən], *a. & s.* **1.** *Hist:* Sarrasin (*m*). **2.** **Saracen corn**, sarrasin *m*; blé noir. **Saracen's head**, *s. Her:* Tête de Maure.

saratoga [sarə'touga], *s.* **Saratoga trunk**, malle bombée; chapelière *f*.

sarcasm ['sɑ:rkazm], *s.* **1.** Ironie *f*; esprit *m* sarcastique. **2.** (Piece of) sarcasm, sarcasme *m*.

sarcastic [sɑr'kastik], *a.* Sarcastique; mordant. **Sarcastic remark**, sarcasme *m*. **-ally**, *adv.* D'une manière sarcastique; ironiquement.

sarcology [sɑr'kɔlodʒi], *s.* Sarcologie *f*.

sarcoma [sɑr'koumə], *s. Med:* Sarcome *m*.

sarcomatous [sɑr'koumatəs], *a.* Sarcomateux.

sarcophagus, *pl.* **-phagi** [sɑr'kɔfəgəs, -fadʒai], *s.* Sarcophage *m*.

sarcosis [sɑr'kousis], *s. Physiol:* Sarcose *f*.

sard [sɑ:rd], *s. Miner:* Sardoine *f*.

sardine [sɑr'di:n], *s. Ich:* Sardine *f*. **Tinned sardines**, sardines (conservées) à l'huile.

Sardinia [sɑr'diniə]. *Pr.n.* La Sardaigne.

Sardinian [sɑr'dinjən], *a. & s.* Sarde (*mf*).

sardonic [sɑr'dɔnik], *a. F:* (Expression, rire) sardonique. **-ally**, *adv.* Sardoniquement.

sardonyx ['sɑ:rdoniks], *s.* Agate *f* onyx; sardoine *f*.

sargasso [sɑr'gaso], *s.* Sargasse *f*. **The Sargasso Sea**, mer des Sargasses.

sark¹ [sɑ:rk], *s. Scot:* (*a*) Chemise *f*. (*b*) Chemise de nuit.

Sark². *Pr.n. Geog:* Sercq *m*.

sarmentose [sɑr'men'touse], **sarmentous** [sɑr'mentəs], *a. Bot:* Sarmenteux.

sarong [sɑ'rɔŋ], *s.* Pagne *m*, jupe *f* (des indigènes de la Malaisie).

sarsaparilla [sɑ:rsapa'rila], *s.* Salsepareille *f*.

sarsen ['sɑ:rsən], *s.* **1.** Monolithe *m* tumulaire (des plaines du Wiltshire). **2.** *Geol:* **Sarsen stone**, grès mamelonné.

sarsenet ['sɑ:rsnet], *s. Tex:* Taffetas léger; florence *m*.

sartorial [sɑr'tɔ:riəl], *a.* De tailleur.

Sarum ['sɛərəm]. *Pr.n. Ecc:* (Évêché *m* de) Salisbury.

ash¹ [saʃ], *s. Cost:* (*a*) Écharpe *f* ou ceinture *f* (d'étoffe) (portée par les officiers). (*b*) Large ceinture à nœud bouffant (de dame, d'enfant).

sash², *s. Const:* Châssis *m* mobile, cadre *m*

(d'une fenêtre à guillotine). **'sash frame,** s. (Châssis) dormant m (d'une fenêtre à guillotine). **sash-'window,** s. Fenêtre f à guillotine.

sassafras ['sasafras], s. Bot: Sassafras m.

Sassenach ['sasənax], a. & s. Scot: Irish: Anglais, -aise.

sat [sat]. See SIT.

Satan ['seit(ə)n]. Pr.n.m. Satan. F: It's like **Satan reproving sin,** les morveux veulent moucher les autres.

satanic [sa'tanik], a. Satanique, diabolique.

satchel ['satʃ(ə)l], s. Sacoche f. Sch: Cartable m, carton m (d'écolier). Cy: Saddle s., sacoche de selle.

sate [seit], v.tr. **1.** Assouvir (sa faim, ses passions); rassasier, satisfaire (qn, la faim). **2.** = SATIATE. **sated,** a. **1.** Rassasié (with, de). **2.** To become **sated,** se blaser (with, de).

sateen [sa'tiːn], s. Tex: Satinette f.

satellite ['satelait], s. Satellite m.

satiate ['seiʃieit], v.tr. Rassasier (qn) jusqu'au dégoût (with, de); blaser (with, de). **satiated,** a. Gorgé, rassasié.

satiety [sa'taiəti], s. Satiété f. To eat to satiety, F: manger jusqu'à plus faim.

satin[1] ['satin], s. **1.** Tex: Satin m. **2.** (White) satin = SATIN-FLOWER. **3.** Satin finish, apprêt satiné (du papier, etc.). **Satin paper,** papier satiné. **'satin-flower,** s. Bot: Lunaire f; monnaie f du pape. **'satin-stitch,** s. Needlew: Plumetis m. **'satin-wood,** s. Com: Bois satiné de l'Inde.

satin[2], v.tr. Satiner.

satinette [sati'net], s. (a) (Silk) Satinade f. (b) (Cotton) Satinette f.

satiny ['satini], a. Satiné.

satire ['sataiər], s. **1.** Lit: Satire f (on, upon, contre). **2.** Satire, sarcasme m.

satiric(al) [sa'tirik(əl)], a. **1.** Satirique. **2.** (Satirical) Sarcastique, ironique. **-ally,** adv. Satiriquement.

satirist ['satirist], s. **1.** (Auteur) satirique m. **2.** Esprit mordant, malicieux.

satirize ['satiraiz], v.tr. Satiriser.

satisfaction [satis'fakʃ(ə)n], s. **1.** (a) Acquittement m, paiemen. m, liquidation f (d'une dette); désintéressement m (d'un créancier); exécution f (d'une promesse). (b) **Satisfaction for an offence,** réparation f, expiation f, d'une offense. To demand s. for an insult, demander raison d'un affront. **To give s.o. satisfaction** (by a duel), faire réparation à qn (par les armes). **To make full satisfaction to s.o.,** dédommager qn entièrement. (c) Assouvissement m (de la faim, d'une passion). **2.** Satisfaction f, contentement m (at, with, de). **To give s.o. satisfaction,** donner du contentement à qn; satisfaire, contenter, qn. To express s. at a result, se féliciter d'un résultat; exprimer sa satisfaction. **I note with satisfaction that . . .,** je suis heureux de noter que. . . . The work will be done to your s., le travail sera fait de manière à vous satisfaire. **3.** That is a great satisfaction, c'est un grand motif de contentement.

satisfactoriness [satis'faktərinəs], s. Caractère satisfaisant (d'un travail, etc.).

satisfactory [satis'faktəri], a. Satisfaisant. S. pupil, élève qui donne satisfaction. **To bring negotiations to a satisfactory conclusion,** mener à bien des négociations. **To give a satisfactory account of one's movements,** justifier de ses mouvements. **-ily,** adv. De façon satisfaisante.

satisfy ['satisfai], v.tr. **1.** (a) S'acquitter (d'une dette, d'une obligation); exécuter (une promesse); faire droit à (une réclamation); remplir (une condition); désintéresser (ses créanciers). (b) Satisfaire (qn); faire réparation à, satisfaire à (l'honneur). To s. one's conscience, par acquit de conscience. **2.** (a) Satisfaire, contenter (qn); donner sujet de satisfaction à (qn). (b) Satisfaire, assouvir, donner satisfaction à (un désir, un appétit). To s. all requirements, suffire à tous les besoins. Abs. Food that satisfies, nourriture qui satisfait. **3.** Convaincre, satisfaire (qn); éclaircir (un doute, etc.). **To satisfy s.o. of a fact,** convaincre qn d'un fait. **I have satisfied myself that . . .,** je me suis assuré que. . . . **satisfied,** a. **1.** To be satisfied with sth., (i) être content, sat'sfait, de qch.; se louer de qch.; (ii) se contenter de qch. **To rest satisfied with an explanation,** se contenter d'une explication; se tenir pour satisfait. Cards: I am satisfied, je m'y tiens. **2.** Convaincu. **satisfying,** a. **1.** Satisfaisant; qui contente; (of food) nourrissant. **2.** (Argument, etc.) convaincant. **-ly,** adv. De façon satisfaisante.

saturate ['satjureit], v.tr. **1.** Saturer, tremper, imbiber (with, de). To become saturated with . . ., s'imprégner de. . . . **2.** Ch: Ph: Saturer (une solution). **saturated,** a. **1.** (Terrain, etc.) trempé. **2.** (Of solution, etc.) Saturé; (of vapour) saturant. **3.** (Of colour) Riche; intense.

saturation [satju'reiʃ(ə)n], s. **1.** Imprégnation f. **2.** Ch: Ph: Saturation f. **To dissolve a salt to saturation,** dissoudre un sel jusqu'à saturation, jusqu'à refus.

Saturday ['satərdi], s. Samedi m. **Saturday-to-Monday,** fin f de semaine. (For phrases cf. FRIDAY.)

Saturn ['satərn]. Pr.n. Astr: Myth: Saturne m.

Saturnalia [satər'neiljə], s.pl. Saturnales f.

saturnine ['satərnain], a. **1.** Taciturne, sombre. To be of a s. disposition, avoir du sombre dans l'âme. **2.** Saturnine poisoning, intoxication f par le plomb; saturnisme m.

satyr ['satər], s. Myth: Satyre m.

satyric [sa'tirik], a. Gr.Lit: Satyrique. S. drama, drame satyrique.

sauce[1] [sɔːs], s. **1.** (a) Sauce f. Tomato s., sauce tomate. Caper s., sauce aux câpres. (b) Assaisonnement m; condiment m. **To add a sauce to sth.,** relever le goût de qch. Prov: What is sauce for the goose is sauce for the gander, ce qui est bon pour l'un l'est aussi pour l'autre. **2.** P: (i) Impertinence f, insolence f; (ii) culot m, toupet m. **None of your sauce!** pas d'impertinences! **What sauce!** quel toupet! **'sauce-alone,** s. Bot: Alliaire f. **'sauce-boat,** s. Saucière f.

sauce[2], v.tr. P: Dire des impertinences à (qn); manquer de respect à (qn).

saucepan ['sɔːspən], s. Casserole f; poêlon m. **Double saucepan,** bain-marie m, pl. bains-marie.

saucer ['sɔːsər], s. **1.** (a) Soucoupe f. **2.** El: Godet m à couleur. **'saucer-eyed,** a. Aux yeux en soucoupe, en boules de loto.

saucerful ['sɔːsərful], s. Pleine soucoupe (of, de).

sauciness ['sɔːsinəs], s. (a) Impertinence f; toupet m. (b) Élégance f; chic m.

saucy ['sɔːsi], a. (a) Impertinent, effronté; répliqueur. A. & Lit: Saucy baggage, petite effrontée. (b) Fripon, gamin. S. smile, sourire aguichant. S. little nursemaid, petite bonne à l'air fripon. (c) S. little hat, petit chapeau coquet, chic. S. frigate, frégate pimpante et de crâne allure. **-ily,** adv. (a) D'un ton effronté. (b) D'un air gamin. (c) (Chapeau porté) coquettement, avec chic.

sauerkraut ['sauərkraut], s. Cu: Choucroute f.

Saul [sɔːl]. Pr.n.m. B.Hist: Saül.

saunter[1] ['sɔ:ntər], *s.* **1.** Promenade faite à loisir ; flânerie *f.* **2.** *To come along* at a saunter, s'amener tout doucement.

saunter[2], *v.i.* **To saunter (along),** flâner ; se balader ; déambuler. *To s. up to the hotel,* arriver à petits pas devant l'hôtel. *To s. across the road,* traverser la rue sans se presser. *To s. back home,* s'en revenir tout doucement chez soi.

saunterer ['sɔ:ntərər], *s.* Flâneur, -euse ; baladeur, -euse.

saurian ['sɔ:riən], *a. & s. Rept:* Saurien (*m*).

sausage ['sɔsedʒ], *s.* **1.** *Cu:* (*a*) (*Fresh, wet, eaten hot*) Saucisse *f.* **Paris sausage,** small sausage, chipolata *f.* **Frankfurt sausage,** saucisse de Francfort. (*b*) (*Preserved, hard, dry*) Saucisson *m.* **2.** (*a*) *Min: etc:* Boudin *m* (d'explosif). (*b*) *Mil:* **Sausage (balloon),** ballon *m* d'observation ; *F:* saucisse. **'sausage-meat,** *s.* Chair *f* à saucisse. **'sausage-'roll,** *s. Cu:* Saucisse enrobée (de pâte feuilletée).

savage[1] ['savedʒ]. **1.** *a.* (*a*) Sauvage, barbare ; non civilisé. (*b*) (*Animal, coup*) féroce ; (coup) brutal, -aux ; (visage) farouche. (*c*) *F:* (*Of pers.*) Furieux ; en rage. **To grow savage,** se fâcher (tout rouge). **To make a s. attack on s.o.,** s'attaquer férocement à qn. **2.** *s.* Sauvage *mf.* **-ly,** *adv.* Sauvagement, férocement ; furieusement.

savage[2], *v.tr.* (*Esp. of horse*) Attaquer, mordre (qn, les autres bêtes).

savageness ['savedʒnəs], **savagery** ['savedʒəri], *s.* **1.** Sauvagerie *f*, barbarie *f* (d'une race, etc.). *To live in savagery,* vivre à l'état sauvage. **2.** Férocité *f* ; brutalité *f* (d'un coup).

savanna(h) [sə'vana], *s.* Savane *f*.

save[1] ['seiv], *s.* **1.** *V. & Dial:* Économie *f.* **2.** *Fb:* Arrêt *m* (du ballon). **To effect a save,** parer à l'attaque.

save[2], *v.tr.* **1.** (*a*) Sauver. **To save s.o.'s life,** sauver la vie à qn. *He has saved several lives at sea,* il a fait plusieurs sauvetages en mer. *He was saved from the wreck,* il a réchappé du naufrage. **To save s.o. from death,** arracher qn à la mort. *To s. s.o. from s.o.'s anger,* préserver qn de la colère de qn. *To s. s.o. from falling,* empêcher qn de tomber. *Fb:* **To save the goal,** arrêter le ballon. (*b*) **To save one's soul,** sauver son âme. (*c*) Sauver, protéger, sauvegarder (son honneur, etc.). **To save the situation,** se montrer à la hauteur de l'occasion. **To save appearances,** sauver, sauvegarder, les apparences. **(God) save me from my friends!** Dieu me protège contre mes amis ! **God save the King!** Dieu sauve le Roi ! **Save us!** Dieu nous garde ! **2.** (*a*) Mettre (qch.) de côté. *S. a dance for me,* réservez-moi une danse. (*b*) Économiser, épargner, mettre de côté (de l'argent). *I have money saved,* j'ai de l'argent de côté. *To s. little by little,* économiser sou par sou. *Abs.* **To save (up),** économiser pour l'avenir ; thésauriser. *To s. up for one's old age,* amasser pour sa vieillesse. (*c*) *Ind:* Recueillir, capter (les sous-produits, etc.). **3.** Ménager (ses vêtements, etc.) ; éviter (une dépense, de la peine). **To save time,** gagner du temps ; faire une économie de temps. *Hours saved,* heures rescapées. *In this way you s. twenty per cent,* vous faites ainsi une économie de vingt pour cent. *I am saving my strength,* je me ménage. **To save oneself for sth.,** se réserver pour qch. **4.** **To save s.o. sth.,** éviter, épargner, qch. à qn. *This has saved him much expense,* cela lui a évité beaucoup de dépense. *They would be saved all this labour,* cela leur épargnerait tout ce travail. **To save s.o. the trouble of doing sth.,** épargner à qn la peine de faire qch. **saving**[1]. I. *a.* **1.** (*a*) Qui sauve ; qui

protège. (*b*) (Qualité) qui rachète des défauts. *S.a.* GRACE[1] 2. **2.** (*a*) (*Of pers.*) Économe, ménager (*of*, de). (*b*) (*Of system, etc.*) Économique. **3.** **Saving clause,** clause de sauvegarde ; clause restrictive ; réservation *f.* II. **saving.** **1.** *prep. & conj.* = SAVE[3]. **2.** *prep.* Sauf ; sans porter atteinte à. **Saving your presence,** sauf votre respect. **saving**[2], *s.* **1.** (*a*) Délivrance *f*, salut *m* (de qn, des âmes). *This was the s. of him,* cela a été son salut. (*b*) Sauvetage *m.* (*c*) Protection *f.* **2.** (*a*) Économie *f*, épargne *f.* (*b*) *pl.* **Savings,** économies. *To live on one's savings,* vivre de ses épargnes. **'savings-bank,** *s.* Caisse *f* d'épargne. **Post office savings-bank,** caisse (nationale) d'épargne postale.

save[3]. A. *& Lit:* **1.** *prep.* (*a*) Sauf, except., hormis ; à l'exception de ; exception faite de. *All, s. the doctor,* tous, à l'exception du docteur. *All is lost s. honour,* A: tout est perdu fors l'honneur. (*b*) **Save for** *a grazed arm he is unhurt,* il est indemne sauf une écorchure au bras. **2.** *conj.* (*a*) *A. & Lit:* **Save he be dead,** *he will return,* à moins qu'il ne soit mort, il reviendra. (*b*) *conj.phr.* **Save that . . .,** hormis que . . ., sauf que . . ., sinon que . . . .

saveloy ['savəlɔi], *s. Cu:* Cervelas *m.*

saver ['seivər], *s.* **1.** (*a*) Sauveur *m*, libérateur, -trice (de sa patrie, etc.). (*b*) Sauveteur *m* (de vie, de biens). **2.** Appareil économiseur. **3.** Personne *f* économe.

saviour ['seivjər], *s.* Sauveur *m. Theol:* **Our Saviour,** Notre Sauveur.

savory ['seivəri], *s. Bot: Cu:* Sarriette *f.*

savour[1] ['seivər], *s.* **1.** Saveur *f*, goût *m*, arome *m. F: The s. of his humour,* son humour savoureux. **2.** Trace *f*, soupçon *m*, pointe *f* (d'ail, d'hérésie).

savour[2]. **1.** *v.tr.* A: Savourer (un mets). **2.** *v.i.* (*Of thg*) **To savour of sth.,** sentir qch. ; tenir de qch. *Passion that savours of love,* passion qui tient de l'amour. *Doctrine that savours of heresy,* doctrine qui sent le fagot.

savouriness ['seivərinəs], *s.* Saveur *f*, succulence *f* (d'un mets, etc.).

savourless ['seivərləs], *a.* Fade ; sans saveur.

savoury ['seivəri]. **1.** *a.* (*a*) Savoureux, appétissant ; succulent. *To make a dish s.,* relever un plat. (*b*) (Mets) piquant ou salé. **Savoury herbs,** plantes aromatiques. **Savoury omelette,** omelette aux fines herbes. **2.** *s.* Entremets non sucré (de fin de repas).

Savoy [sa'vɔi]. **1.** *Pr.n. Geog:* La Savoie. **2.** *s.* (*a*) Chou frisé de Milan. (*b*) Biscuit *m* à la cuillère.

savvy[1] ['savi], *s. P:* Jugeotte *f*, gingin *m.*

savvy[2], *v.tr. P:* Savoir ; comprendre, *P:* piger. **Savvy?** compris ?

saw[1] [sɔ:], *s. Tls:* Scie *f.* **Hand-saw,** scie à main ; (small) égohine *f.* **Power saw,** scie mécanique ; scierie *f.* **Circular saw,** *U.S:* buzz-saw, scie circulaire. *Bookbinder's saw,* grecque *f.* **'saw-bench,** *s.* Scie *f* circulaire à table. **'saw-cut,** *s.* Trait *m* de scie. **'saw-fly,** *s. Ent:* Tenthrède *f* ; mouche *f* à scie. **'saw-frame,** *s.* Châssis *m*, monture *f*, de scie. **'saw-horse, -jack,** *s.* Chevalet *m* de sciage, de scieur. **'saw-pad,** *s. Tls:* Manche *m* porte-scies. **'saw-pit,** *s.* Fosse *f* de scieur de long. **'saw-set,** *s. Tls:* Tourne-à-gauche *m inv.* **'saw-tooth,** *s.* Dent *f* de scie. **Saw-tooth roof,** toit en dents de scie ; (toit en) shed *m.* **'saw-toothed,** *a.* En dents de scie ; (toit) en shed. **'saw-way,** *s.* Trait *m* de scie.

saw[2], *v.tr.* (*p.t.* sawed ; *p.p.* sawn, *F:* sawed)

1. Scier. **To saw up wood,** débiter du bois. **Sawn timber,** bois de sciage. **To saw off a piece of wood,** scier (et détacher, un morceau de bois. **Sawed-off shot-gun,** carab ne à canon tronçonné. **To saw out a piece,** découper un morceau de la scie ; chantourner un morceau. *F:* **To saw the air,** battre l'air (avec les bras). **To saw on the fiddle,** racler du violon. *Equit:* **To saw a horse's mouth,** gourmander la bouche d'un cheval ; scier du bridon. **2.** *Bookb:* Grecquer (les feuilles).

saw³, *s.* Adage *m*, proverbe *m*, maxime *f* ; dicton *m*. **Wise saw,** aphorisme *m*.

saw⁴. *See* SEE¹.

sawbones ['sɔːbounz], *s. F:* Carabin *m*.

sawdust ['sɔːdʌst], *s.* Sciure *f* (de bois).

sawfish ['sɔːfiʃ], *s. Ich:* Scie *f* (de mer).

sawmill ['sɔːmil], *s.* Scierie *f*.

sawn [sɔːn]. *See* SAW².

sawyer ['sɔːjər], *s.* Scieur *m* ; *esp.* scieur de long.

sax [saks], *s. Tls:* Hache *f* d'ouvrage (de couvreur).

saxatile ['saksətail], *a. Nat.Hist:* Saxatile.

saxhorn ['sakshɔːrn], *s. Mus:* Saxhorn *m*.

saxifrage ['saksifredʒ], *s. Bot:* Saxifrage *f*.

Saxon ['saksən], *a. & s.* Saxon, -onne.

Saxony ['saksəni]. *Pr.n. Geog:* La Saxe.

saxophone ['saksofoun], *s.* Saxophone *m*.

saxophonist ['saksofounist], *s.* (Joueur *m* de) saxophone *m*.

say¹ [sei], *s.* Dire *m*, parole *f*, mot *m*. **To have, say, one's say,** dire ce qu'on a à dire ; dire son mot. **To have one's say out,** dire ce que l'on a sur le cœur. *Let me have my say,* laissez-moi parler. **I have no say in the matter,** *F:* je n'ai pas voix au chapitre.

say², *v.tr.* (said [sed] ; said ; *3rd sg. pr. ind.* says [sez], *A:* sayeth ['seiəθ], saith [seθ]) Dire. **1.** (*a*) *To say a word,* dire un mot. *F:* **To ask s.o. to say a few words,** prier qn de prendre la parole, de faire une courte allocution. *To say good morning to s.o.,* dire bonjour à qn. *F:* **Who shall I say?** qui dois-je annoncer? **To say again,** répéter, redire. **It isn't said in good company,** cela ne se dit pas dans la bonne société. **What do you say?** que dites-vous? qu'est-ce que vous dites? **What did you say?** (i) qu'avez-vous dit? (ii) plaît-il? **To say yes, no,** dire (que) oui, (que) non. **To say yes to an invitation,** accepter une invitation. **What do you say to a drink?** si on buvait un verre? *What do you say to a game of bridge?* si on faisait un bridge? *He goes to the club.—So he says!* il va au cercle.—A l'en croire ! **Thus saith the Lord,** ainsi dit l'Éternel ; ainsi parle le Seigneur. **"I accept,"** said he, he said, "j'accepte," fit-il, dit-il. (*b*) (*Express orally or otherwise*) *All that can be said in a couple of words,* tout ça tient en deux mots. *As I said in my letter,* comme je vous l'ai dit dans ma lettre. *The Bible says . . ., it says in the Bible . . .,* il est dit dans la Bible. . . . *The text of the treaty says . . .,* le texte du traité porte ces mots. . . . *The church clock says ten o'clock,* le cadran de l'église marque dix heures. *Be it said (incidentally),* soit dit en passant. *Though I say it who should not,* bien que ce ne soit pas à moi de le dire. *As people say, as they say,* comme on dit. **So to say,** pour ainsi dire. **As one might say . . .,** comme qui dirait. . . . **One might as well say . . .,** autant dire. . . . **I must say . . .,** j'avoue . . . ; franchement . . . . *This news surprises me, I must say,* cette nouvelle me surprend, je l'avoue. *That is to say . . .,* c'est-à-dire . . . ; à savoir. . . . *Have you said anything about it to him?* lui en

avez-vous parlé? *I remember something was said about it,* je me souviens qu'il en a été parlé. *The less said the better,* moins nous parlerons, mieux cela vaudra. **Say no more!** n'en dites pas davantage ! **To say nothing of . . .,** sans parler de. . . . *He has plenty to say for himself,* (i) il n'a pas sa langue dans sa poche ; (ii) il sait se faire valoir, se mettre en avant. *At first they would have nothing to say to him,* d'abord on refusa de le reconnaître. *There is something to be said on both sides,* il y a du pour et du contre. *This much can be said at present, that . . .,* on peut affirmer dès maintenant que. . . . **There is much to be said for beginning now,** il y a de bonnes raisons pour s'y mettre dès maintenant. *That doesn't say much for his intelligence,* cela ne dénote pas beaucoup d'intelligence. **You don't say so!** allons donc ! pas possible ! *P:* **You don't say!** c'est-il possible ! (*c*) (*Report*) **They say that . . .,** it is said that . . ., on dit que. . . . *That is what people are saying,* voilà ce qu'on raconte. **He is said to have a large fortune,** on lui attribue une grande fortune. *He is said to be rich,* on le dit riche. (*d*) (*Opine*) **Anyone would say that he was asleep,** on dirait qu'il dort. *I should say she has intelligence,* autant que j'en puis juger elle est intelligente. **I should say not,** je ne crois pas ; je crois que non. *What say you?* et vous, qu'en dites-vous? **And so say all of us,** c'est ce que nous disons tous. *Didn't I say so!* quand je vous le disais ! (*e*) *It was you who said I was to,* c'est vous qui m'avez dit de le faire. (*f*) *Come and have lunch one of these days, say Sunday,* venez déjeuner un de ces jours, disons dimanche. *If I had an income of say a thousand a year,* si j'avais des rentes, mettons mille livres par an. *Three times round the track, say two miles,* trois tours de piste, soit deux milles. **Well, say it were true, what then?** eh bien, mettons que ce soit vrai, alors quoi? (*g*) (*Exclamatory*) **I say!** dites donc ! (*expressing surprise*) pas possible ! fichtre ! **2.** Dire, réciter (une leçon, une prière, etc.) ; faire (ses prières). **To say mass,** dire la messe. **say over,** *v.tr.* **1.** Repasser (un rôle). **2.** **To say a thing over and over again,** répéter qch. à satiété. **saying,** *s.* **1.** (*a*) Énonciation *f* (d'un fait, etc.) ; récitation *f* (d'une leçon, etc.). It goes without saying that . . ., il va de soi, cela va sans dire, que. . . . *That goes without saying,* cela va sans dire. (*b*) **There is no saying . . .,** (il est) impossible de dire (quand . . ., etc.). **2.** (*a*) Dit *m*. **Doings and sayings,** faits et dits. **Historical saying,** mot *m* historique. (*b*) (*Common*) **saying,** adage *m*, proverbe *m*, dicton *m*, aphorisme *m*. **As the saying goes,** comme dit le proverbe.

sbirro, *pl.* **sbirri** ['sbirro, 'sbirri], *s.* Sbire *m*.

scab¹ [skab], *s.* **1.** (*a*) *Vet:* Gale *f*, bouquet *m*. (*b*) (*Of plants*) Gale *f*. **2.** (*a*) (*On wound*) Croûte *f*, eschare *f.* (*b*) *Metall:* Dartre *f*. **3.** *P:* (*Pers.*) (*a*) *Ind:* Renard *m*, jaune *m*. (*b*) Canaille *f*, *P:* sale type *m* ; vilain coco. **'scab-wort,** *s. Bot:* Aunée *f* hélène.

scab², *v.i.* (scabbed) **1.** (*Of wound*) To scab (over), former une croûte ; se cicatriser. **2.** *Metall:* Dartrer.

scabbard ['skabərd], *s.* Fourreau *m* (d'une épée) ; gaine *f* (d'un poignard, etc.). *F:* **To throw away the scabbard,** jurer la guerre à outrance ; s'en remettre au sort des armes.

scabbiness ['skabinəs], *s.* **1.** État galeux. **2.** État croûteux (d'une blessure). **3.** *P:* Mesquinerie *f* ; pingrerie *f*.

scabby ['skabi], *a.* **1.** *Vet:* Galeux. **2.** (*Of sore*)

Croûteux, scabieux. **3.** *P:* (*a*) Mesquin, sordide, méprisable. (*b*) (*Of pers.*) Ladre, pingre.

scabies ['skeibiːz], *s. Med:* Gale *f.*

scabious ['skeibiəs]. **I.** *a.* = SCABBY 1, 2. **2.** *s. Bot:* Scabieuse *f.*

scabrous ['skeibrəs], *a.* **I.** Rugueux, raboteux. **2.** (*Of topic, etc.*) Scabreux, risqué.

scaffold[1] ['skafəld], *s.* **I.** *A:* (*a*) Échafaud *m*, estrade *f* (pour représentations). (*b*) Tribunes *fpl* (pour spectateurs). **2.** Échafaud (pour exécutions). To go to, to mount, the scaffold, monter à, sur, l'échafaud. **3.** *Const:* = SCAFFOLDING.

scaffold[2], *v.tr. Const:* Dresser un échafaudage autour de, contre (une maison). **scaffolding**, .. Échafaudage *m.* 'scaffolding-pole, *s. Const:* Écoperche *f*; perche *f* d'échafaudage. *Horizontal s.-p.*, tendière *f.*

scald[1] [skɔːld], *s.* Échaudure *f.*

scald[2], *v.tr.* **I.** Échauder, ébouillanter. *To s. one's foot*, s'échauder le pied. **2.** Faire chauffer (le lait) juste au-dessous du point d'ébullition. *Scalded cream*, crème échaudée. **scalding**[1], *a. Scalding hot*, tout bouillant. *F: Scalding tears*, larmes brûlantes. **scalding**[2], *s.* Échaudage *m*, ébouillantage *m.*

scale[1] [skeil], *s.* **I.** (*On fish, bud, etc.*) Écaille *f. Med:* (*On skin*) Écaille, squame *f. Lit:* The scales fell from his eyes, les écailles lui tombèrent des yeux. **2.** *Metalw:* (*a*) Barbure *f* (de pièce coulée); dartre *f.* (*b*) Écailles de fer; battitures *fpl*, pailles *fpl. Mill scale, roll scale*, scories *fpl* de laminoir. **3.** Incrustation *f*, dépôt *m*; tartre *m* (des dents). *Mch:* Boiler scale, tartre, incrustation; dépôt calcaire. *Scale preventer, remover*, désincrustant *m.*

scale[2]. **I.** *v.tr.* **I.** (*a*) Écailler (un poisson, etc.). (*b*) Détartrer, ruginer (les dents); piquer, décrasser, détartrer (une chaudière). **2.** Entartrer, incruster (une chaudière). **II. scale**, *v.i.* **I.** To scale (off), s'écailler; *Med:* (*of skin*) se desquamer; (*of bone, etc.*) s'exfolier. **2.** (*Of boiler*) S'entartrer, s'incruster. **scaling**[1], *s.* **I.** (*a*) Écaillage *m* (d'un poisson). (*b*) Détartrage *m* (des dents, d'une chaudière). **2.** Formation *f* du tartre; incrustation *f* (d'une chaudière).

scale[3], *s.* **I.** Plateau *m*, plat *m* (de balance). To throw sth. into the scale, jeter qch. dans la balance; mettre qch. en balance. To turn the scale, emporter, faire pencher, la balance. *F:* To turn the scale(s) at . . ., peser plus de. . . **2.** *pl.* (*Pair of*) scales, balance. *Platform scales*, bascule *f*; (*with steelyard*) bascule romaine. *Kitchen scales, shop scales*, balance à plateaux. *Letter-scales*, pèse-lettres *m inv. F:* To hold the scales even, tenir la balance égale. **3.** *pl. Astr:* The Scales, la Balance. 'scale-pan, *s.* = SCALE[3] 1.

scale[4], *v.i.* To scale six pounds, peser six livres. **scale in**, *v.i. Turf:* Passer au pesage.

scale[5], *s.* **I.** Échelle *f.* (*a*) Graduation *f*, graduations (d'un thermomètre, etc.); série *f*, suite *f* (de nombres, etc.). *Fahrenheit scale*, échelle de Fahrenheit. *Scale of salaries*, échelle, barème *m*, des traitements. *Com: Scale of prices*, échelle, gamme *f*, des prix. *F:* The social scale, l'échelle sociale. *S.a.* SLIDING[1]. (*b*) Cadran gradué. *W.Tel:* Wave-length scale, cadran des longueurs d'onde. (*c*) Règle (divisée). *Diagonal scale*, échelle de proportion. (*d*) Échelle (d'une carte, d'un plan, etc.). To draw sth. to scale, dessiner qch. à l'échelle. *Map on the scale of . . .*, carte (rapportée) à l'échelle de. . . . *On a large scale*, en grand. *S.a.* LARGE I. 1. *Reproduction on a*

small *s.*, reproduction en petit. (*e*) Envergure *f* (d'une entreprise, etc.); étendue *f* (d'une calamité). *To keep house on a small s.*, avoir un train de maison très simple. **2.** (*a*) *Mus:* Gamme *f.* To sing up the scale, monter la gamme. To practise scales, faire des gammes. (*b*) Scale of colours, of tones, échelle, gamme, de couleurs, de nuances. 'scale drawing, *s.* Dessin *m* à l'échelle.

scale[6], *v.tr.* **I.** Escalader. *To s. a mountain*, faire l'ascension d'une montagne. **2.** To scale a map, tracer une carte à l'échelle. To scale a building, établir le dessin d'un bâtiment à l'échelle. **3.** To scale wages up, down, augmenter, réduire, les gages à l'échelle. **scaling**[2], *s.* **I.** Escalade *f.* **2.** (*a*) Graduation *f* (des prix, des salaires, etc.). (*b*) Dessin *m* à l'échelle. 'scaling-ladder, *s.* Échelle *f* d'escalade.

scaled [skeild], *a.* Écailleux, squameux.

scalene [skei'liːn], *a.* (Triangle) scalène.

scaliness ['skeilinəs], *s.* Squamosité *f.*

scallion ['skaljən], *s. Bot:* (*a*) Ciboule *f.* (*b*) *Dial:* Échalote *f.*

scallop ['skɔləp], *s.* **I.** (*a*) *Moll:* Pétoncle *m*, peigne *m*; coquille *f* (de) Saint-Jacques. (*b*) *Cu:* Coquille (de poisson au gratin, etc.). **2.** *Needlew:* Feston *m*, dentelure *f. Skirt with scallops*, jupe avec découpes *f.*

scallop[2], *v.tr.* **I.** *Cu:* Faire cuire (du poisson, etc.) en coquille(s). **2.** *Needlew:* Festonner; découper, échancrer.

scallywag ['skaliwag,], *s.* *P:* **I.** Propre-à-rien *m inv*; bon-à-rien *m inv*; mauvais garnement. **2.** *U.S:* Bête mal venue.

scalp[1] [skalp], *s.* **I.** (*a* *Anat:* Épicrâne *m.* (*b*) *Anat:* Cuir chevelu. (*c*) Sommet pelé d'une montagne. **2.** (*In Amer. Indian warfare*) Scalpe *m. F:* To be out for scalps, être parti en campagne; chercher qui éreinter. 'scalphunter, *s.* Chasseur *m* de chevelures.

scalp[2], *v.tr.* a) (*Of Amer. Indians*) Scalper (un ennemi). (b, *F:* (*Of critic*) Éreinter (un auteur).

scalpel ['skalpəl], *s. Surg:* Scalpel *m.*

scaly ['skeili], *a.* Écailleux, squameux; (*of metal*) paillé, lamelleux; (*of boiler*) tartreux.

scammony ['skaməni], *s. Bot: Pharm:* Scammonée *f.*

scamp[1] [skamp], *s.* Vaurien *m*; mauvais sujet; garnement *m. F: My s. of a nephew*, mon garnement de neveu. (*Of child*) Young scamp, petit galopin, petit polisson.

scamp[2], *v.tr. F:* Bâcler, saboter (un travail); faire (un travail) par-dessous la jambe.

scamper[1] ['skampər], *s.* (*a*) Course *f* folâtre, allègre. (*b*) Course rapide.

scamper[2], *v.i.* (*a*) Courir allègrem., d'une manière folâtre. (*b*) To scamper away, off, détaler; se sauver à toutes jambes; *F:* prendre ses jambes. à son cou. (*c*) To scamper through France, traverser la France à la galopade.

scamper[3], *s. F:* Galopeur, -euse (de travail).

scan[1] [skan], *s.* Regard scrutateur.

scan[2], *v.tr.* (scanned) I. (*a*) Scander, mesurer (des vers). (*b*) (*Of verse*) Se scander (facilement, mal, etc.). *This line won't s.*, le vers est faux. **2.** (*a*) Examiner, scruter; sonder du regard. *To s. the horizon*, scruter l'horizon. *To s. the crowd*, promener ses regards sur la foule. (*b*) *To s. the newspaper*, parcourir rapidement le journal. (*c*) *Televis:* Balayer, explorer (l'image à transmettre).

scandal ['skand(ə)l], *s.* **I.** Scandale *m*; honte *f*; affaire scabreuse. To create a scandal, faire un scandale; faire de l'éclat. *Without any s.*, sans éclat. **2.** Médisance *f*; cancans *mpl.* To talk

scandal, cancaner. *Th:* The School for Scanda.., l'École de la Médisance. **3.** *Jur:* (a) Allégations *f* diffamatoires. (b) Atteinte *f* à la dignité du tribunal. **'scandal-monger,** *s.* Cancanier, -ière; médisant, -ante; mauvaise langue.

scandalize ['skandəla:iz], *v.tr.* Scandaliser, offusquer.

scandalous ['skandələs], *a.* **I.** Scandaleux, infâme, honteux. **2.** *Jur:* (Of statement) Diffamatoire, calomnieux. **-ly,** *adv.* Scandaleusement.

Scandinavia [skandi'neivjə]. *Pr.n.* La Scandinavie.

Scandinavian [skandi'neivjən], *a. & s.* Scandinave (mf).

scansion ['skanʃ(ə)n], *s. Pros:* Scansion *f*.

scansorial [skan'so:rial], *a. Orn:* Grimpeur.

scant [skant], *a.* (In certain phrases) Insuffisant, peu abondant, limité. **Scant weight,** poids bien juste. *F:* **In scant attire,** en tenue plutôt sommaire. **To be s.** of speech, être peu communicatif; être avare de paroles. **Scant of breath,** (i) hors d'haleine; (ii) poussif.

scantiness ['skantinəs], *s.* Insuffisance *f*, rareté *f* (de provisions, etc.); pauvreté *f* (de la végétation); étroitesse *f* (d'un vêtement). *The s.* of my resources, l'exiguïté *f* de mes ressources.

scantling ['skantlin], *s.* **I.** (a) Menu bois de sciage; volige *f*. (b) Bois d'équarrissage; madrier *m*. *N.Arch:* Ship heavy of scantling, navire fort en bois. **2.** Échantillon *m*, équarrissage *m*. *To have a s.* of two by four inches, avoir un équarrissage de deux pouces sur quatre. **3.** Chantier *m* (pour fûts).

scanty ['skanti], *a.* Insuffisant ou à peine suffisant; peu abondant; (of garment) étroit, étriqué. *S. hair,* cheveux rares. *A s. income,* un mince revenu; un revenu bien juste. *S. meal,* repas sommaire. *In s. attire,* en tenue (plutôt) sommaire. **-ily,** *adv.* Insuffisamment; peu abondamment. *S. clad,* à peine vêtu.

scape [skeip], *s.* **I.** *Arch:* Fût *m* (d'une colonne). **2.** (a) *Bot:* Hampe *f*. (b) *Orn:* Tuyau *m* (de plume).

scapegoat ['skeipgout], *s.* (a) *B:* Bouc *m* émissaire. (b) *F:* Souffre-douleur *m inv.*

scapegrace ['skeipgreis], *s.* **I.** Polisson *m*; mauvais sujet. **2.** Petit écervelé; enfant incorrigible.

scaphoid ['skafoid], *a. & s. Anat:* Scaphoïde (m).

scapula, *pl.* **-ae** ['skapjula, -i:], *s.* Omoplate *f*.

scapular ['skapjulər]. **I.** *a.* Scapulaire. *Anat:* **Scapular arch,** ceinture *f* thoracique. *Surg:* **Scapular bandage,** scapulaire *m*. **2.** *s.* = SCAPULARY.

scapulary ['skapjulᴀri], *s. Ecc:* Scapulaire *m*.

scar[1] [skɑ:r], *s.* **I.** Cicatrice *f*. *Long s.* (on face), balafre *f*. **2.** *Bot:* Cicatrice, hile *m*. **'scarface,** *s.* Balafré *m*. **'scar-tissue,** *s.* Tissu cicatriciel.

scar[2], *v.* **(scarred) I.** *v.tr.* Laisser une cicatrice sur (la peau); marquer d'une cicatrice; balafrer. **2.** *v.i.* (Of wound) To scar (over); se cicatriser.

scarred, *a.* (Of face, etc.) Couturé (de cicatrices); portant des cicatrices; balafré. **Face scarred by smallpox,** figure grêlée (par la petite vérole).

scar[3], *s.* (In mountain range) Rocher escarpé; muraille *f*.

scarab ['skarab], *s.* **I.** *Ent:* Scarabée sacré (de i'Égypte). **2.** *Lap:* Scarabée.

scarce [skɛərs]. **I.** *a.* Rare; peu abondant. *Good engravers are growing s.,* les bons graveurs se font rares. *F:* **To make oneself scarce,** s'es-

quiver, décamper, filer; *P:* se défiler. **2.** *adv.* = SCARCELY. **-ly,** *adv.* **I.** A peine; presque pas. *I have s.* any left, il ne m'en reste presque plus. *She could s.* speak, c'est à peine si elle pouvait parler. *He s.* thinks of anything else, il ne pense guère à autre chose. *You'll s.* believe it, vous aurez de la peine à le croire. *I s.* know what to say, je ne sais trop que dire. **Scarcely ever,** presque jamais. **2.** (Expressing incredulity) Sûrement pas. **Scarcely!** j'en doute!

scarceness ['skɛərsnəs], **scarcity** ['skɛərsiti], *s.* Rareté *f*; manque *m*, pénurie *f*. *S.* of rain, rareté des pluies. *S.* of labour, manque de main-d'œuvre.

scare [skɛər], *s.* Panique *f*, alarme *f*. **To create a scare,** semer l'alarme. **To raise a scare,** porter l'alarme dans le camp. *F:* **You did give me a scare,** vous m'avez fait rudement peur. *Journ:* **Scare headline,** manchette sensationnelle. **'scare-monger,** *s.* Alarmiste *mf*; *F:* paniquard *m*. **'scare-mongering,** *s.* Nouvelles *f* alarmistes.

scare[2], *v.tr.* Effrayer, effarer, alarmer; faire peur à (qn). **To scare away,** effaroucher (le gibier, etc.). **scared,** *a. S. look,* regard effaré; air épouvanté. **To be scared to death,** avoir une peur bleue. *They were s.* out of their wits, ils étaient affolés.

scarecrow ['skɛərkrou], *s.* **I.** Épouvantail *m*. **2.** *F:* (Of pers., (i) Épouvantail (ii) grand escogriffe.

scarf[1], *pl.* **scarfs, scarves** [skɑ:rf(s), skɑ:rvz], *s.* **I.** (Woman's) Écharpe *f*, fichu *m*; (man's) cache-co *m*; (in silk) foulard *m*. **2.** Écharpe (d'officier, de dignitaire). **'scarf-ring,** *s.* Coulant *m* de cravate. **'scarf-skin,** *s.* Cuticule *f*. **'scarf-wise,** *adv.* En écharpe.

scarf[2], *s.* (Also scarf-joint) **I.** Assemblage *m* à mi-bois, à entaille; joint *m* en sifflet; enture *f*. **2.** *Metalw:* Chanfrein *m* de soudure. **'scarfweld(ing),** *s.* Soudure *f* à chanfrein.

scarf[3], *v.tr.* **I.** *Carp: N.Arch:* Enter; assembler à mi-bois. **2.** Amorcer (deux bouts à souder).

scarify ['skarifai], *v.tr.* **I.** Scarifier (la peau, e sol); écroûter, ameublir le sol). **2.** *F:* Éreinter (un auteur, etc.).

scarlatina [skɑ:rlə'ti:nə], *s.* (Fièvre) scarlatine *f*.

scarlet ['skɑ:rlet], *a. & s.* Écarlate (f). *F:* **To blush scarlet, flush scarlet,** devenir cramoisi, rouge comme une pivoine. *Med:* **Scarlet rash,** roséole *f*. *R.C.Ch:* **To don the scarlet,** revêtir la pourpre card nalice. **Scarlet hat,** chapeau de cardinal. *A:* **To wear the King's scarlet,** porter l'uniforme. *S.a.* RUNNER 3. **'scarlet 'fever,** *s. Med:* (Fièvre) scarlatine *f*.

scarp [skɑ:rp], *s.* **I.** *Fort:* Escarpe *f*. **2.** Escarpement *m* (d'une colline).

scarus ['skɛərəs], *s. Ich:* Scare *m*; perroquet *m* de mer.

scathe [skeið], *s. A:* Dommage *m*, blessure. **Without scathe,** indemne; sain et sauf.

scatheless ['skeiðləs], *a.* Sans dommage, sans blessure; sain et sauf; indemne.

scathing ['skeiðin], *a.* Acerbe, mordant, cinglant, caustique. *S. retort,* réplique cinglante. *S. irony,* ironie âpre. *To write a s.* criticism of a play, soumettre une pièce à une critique sanglante. **-ly,** *adv.* D'une manière acerbe; d'un ton cinglant.

scatological [skato'lodʒik(ə)l], *a.* Scatologique.

scatology [ska'tolodʒi], *s.* Scatologie *f*.

scatter[1] ['skatər], *s.* (Of shot) Éparpillement *m*; dispersion *f*.

scatter[2]. **I.** *v.tr.* (a) Disperser, mettre en fuite;

(b) Éparpiller; semer (des graines) à la volée; disséminer (des nouvelles); (of surface) diffuser (la lumière). **To scatter the floor with paper,** oncher le plancher de morceaux de papier. Path scattered with roses, chemin jonché de roses. The region is scattered over with small towns, la région est parsemée de petites villes. (Of gun) **To scatter the shot,** abs. to scatter, éparpiller, écarter, le plomb. **2.** v.i. (Of crowd) Se disperser; (of party) se débander; (of clouds) se dissiper; (of shot) s'éparpiller, s'écarter. **scattered,** a. Dispersé, éparpillé; épars. Thinly s. population, population clairsemée. Ph: **Scattered light,** lumière diffuse. **scattering,** s. **1.** Dispersion f; eparpillement m; diffusion f (de la lumière). **2.** Petit nombre; petite quantité. He has a mere s. of followers, es adhérents sont peu nombreux et sans cohés on. 'scatter-brain, s. F: Étourd i, -ie; écervelé, -ée. 'scatter-brained, a. F: Étourdi, écervelé, évaporé.

caup [sko:p], s. Orn: Milouinan m.
cavenge ['skavəndʒ], v.tr. **1.** Ébouer, balayer (les rues). **2.** Artil: Écouvillonner (une pièce). **3.** I.C.E: **To scavenge the burnt gases,** balayer, refouler les gaz brûlés. **scavenging,** s. **1.** Ébouage m, balayage m (des rues); enlèvement de ordures. **2.** Artil: Écouvillonnage m à l'air. **3.** Évacuat on f, balayage (des gaz brûlés, de la vapeur).
cavenger ['skavəndʒər], s. **1.** Boueur m; balayeur m des rue. **Sewer scavenger,** égoutier m. **2.** Insecte ou animal nécrophage, coprophage.
'scavenger-beetle, s. Ent: Nécrophore m.
cenario [se'nɑ:rio], s. Scénario m; canevas m (d'une pièce. (Film) **scenario writer,** cinégraphiste m, scénariste m.
cend [send], v.i. = SEND².
cene [si:n]. s **1.** Th: A: = STAGE¹ 2. F: **To appear on the scene,** entrer en scène. **2.** (a) Th: (Place of action) Scène f. **The scene is laid in London,** l'action se passe à Londres. (b) Théâtre m, eu m (d'un événement). F: The scenes of his early exploits, les lieux de ses premiers exploits. On the s. of the disaster, sur le(s) lieu(x) du sinistre. **3.** (a) (Sub-division of a play) Scène. Second s. of Act III, deuxième scène du troisième acte. (b) Scène, incident m, spectacle m. Distressing scenes, des scènes affligeantes. That brings the s. before you, cela fait image. **4.** (a) Th: (Set) scene, décor m. **Behind the scenes,** derrière la toile; F: dans la coulisse. To know what is going on behind the scenes, savoir ce qui se passe dans la coulisse; voir le dessous des cartes. (b) A sylvan s., un paysage champêtre. The s. from the window, la vue de la fenêtre. **5.** F: **To make a scene,** faire une scène; faire de l'esclandre.
'scene-painter, s. Brosseur m de décors; peintre m de décors. 'scene-shifter, s. Th: Machiniste m.
cenery ['si:nəri], s. **1.** (a) Th: Décors mpl; la mise en scène. (b) F: You want a change of s., il vous faut du changement. **2.** Paysage m; vue f. A passion for s., la passion des beaux paysages.
cenic ['si:nik], a. **1.** (a) Scénique; théâtral, -aux. (b) (Of emotion, effect) Théâtral, exagéré. **2.** Scenic railway, montagnes f russes.
cent¹ [sent], s. **1.** (a) Parfum m, senteur f; odeur f agréable. (b) Bottle of scent, flacon m de parfum. To use scents, se parfumer. **2.** Ven: (a) Fumet m, vent m (de la bête). (b) Piste f, voie f, trace f. (Of hounds) **To get on the scent, to pick up the scent,** empaumer la voie. The hounds are on the s.,

les ch ens ont rencontré. F: To be on the right s., être sur la piste. To throw the hounds off the s., dépister les chiens; mettre les chiens en défaut. F: **To put s.o. on a false scent,** aiguiller qn sur une fausse piste. **3.** Odorat m, flair m (d'un chien). Dog that has no s., chien qui n'a pas de nez. 'scent-bottle, s. Flacon m de parfum; flacon à odeur. 'scent-spray, s. Vaporisateur m.
scent², v.tr. **1.** (Of hounds, etc.) **To scent (out)** game, flairer, éventer, le gibier. F: **To scent** trouble, flairer des désagréments, des ennuis. **2.** (a) (Of flower, etc.) Parfumer, embaumer (l'air). (b) To s. one's handkerchief, parfumer son mouchoir. **scented,** a. **1.** Parfumé (with, de); (of air) embaumé (with, de). **Lavender-scented** sachet, sachet à odeur de lavande. **2.** Odorant. **3.** Keen-scented dog, chien au nez fin.
scentless ['sentləs], a. Inodore; sans odeur.
sceptic ['skeptik], s. Sceptique mf.
sceptical ['skeptik(ə)l], a. Sceptique. **-ally,** adv. Sceptiquement; avec scepticisme.
scepticism ['skeptisizm], s. Scepticisme m.
sceptre ['septər], s. Sceptre m.
schedule¹ ['ʃedjul], s. **1.** (a) Annexe f (à une loi). (b) Bordereau m; note explicative. **2.** (a) Inventaire m (des machines, etc.); barème m (de prix). **Schedule of charges,** liste officielle des taux; tarif m. (b) Adm: Cédule f (d'impôts). **3.** Esp. U.S: Plan m (d'exécution d'un travail, etc.). F: Everything went off according to schedule, tout a marché selon les prévisions. **Up to schedule,** (train) à l'heure.
schedule², v.tr. **1.** (a) Ajouter (un article) comme annexe (à une loi, etc.). (b) Ajouter (une note) en bordereau. **2.** Inscrire (un article) sur une liste, sur l'inventaire. **3.** U.S: Dresser le programme de (qch.). The mayor is scheduled to make a speech, le maire doit prononcer un discours. The train is scheduled to arrive at noon, selon l'indicateur le train arrive à midi.
Scheldt (the) [ʃəskelt, ʃelt]. Pr.n. L'Escaut m.
schema, pl. **-ata** ['ski:ma, -ata], s. Schéma m, diagramme m.
schematic [ski:'matik], a. Schématique.
scheme¹ [ski:m], s. **1.** (a) Arrangement m, combinaison f. **Colour scheme,** schéma m, combinaison de(s) couleurs; coloris m. The colour s. is good, les couleurs sont bien agencées. **Rhyme scheme,** agencement m, disposition f, des rimes. (b) Jur: **Scheme of composition** (between debtor and creditors), concordat préventif (à la faillite). **2.** Résumé m, exposé m (d'un sujet d'étude); plan m (d'un ouvrage littéraire). **3.** (a) Plan, projet m. S. for a canal, étude f d'un canal. (b) Pej: Machination f, intrigue f, complot m, cabale f. Shady s., combinaison f louche. To lay a scheme, ourdir, tramer, une machination.
scheme². **1.** v.i. Intriguer, ruser, comploter. **To scheme in order to do sth.,** combiner de faire qch.; intriguer pour faire qch. **2.** v.tr. (a) Machiner, combiner (une conspiration, etc.). (b) Projeter (de faire qch.). **scheming¹,** a. Intrigant, tripoteur. **scheming²,** s. **1.** Plans mpl, projets mpl. **2.** Machinations fpl, intrigues fpl.
schemer ['ski:mər], s. **1.** Faiseur de projets; homme à projets. **2.** Pej: Intrigant, -ante; comploteur m.
schism [sizm], s. Schisme m.
schismatic [siz'matik], a. & s. Schismatique (mf).
schist [ʃist], s. Schiste m.
schizophrenia [skaizo'fri:nia], s. Psy: Schizophrénie f.
schizophyte ['skaizofait], s. Biol: Schizophyte m.

schnap(p)s [ʃnaps], *s.* Genièvre (allemand); schnaps *m.*

scholar [ˈskɔlər], *s.* **1.** (*a*) Élève *mf*, écolier, -ière (d'une école primaire). (*b*) Personne qui apprend. *At eighty he was still a s.*, à quatre-vingts ans il apprenait encore. **2.** Savant, lettré; homme d'étude; érudit; *esp.* humaniste *m. A fine s.*, un fin lettré. *A s. and a gentleman*, un homme cultivé et un gentleman. *Latin s.*, latiniste *mf. F:* He is no scholar, son éducation laisse à désirer. **3.** *Sch:* Boursier, -ière.

scholarly [ˈskɔlərli], *a.* Savant, érudit. *A very s. man*, un homme d'un grand savoir.

scholarship [ˈskɔlərʃip], *s.* **1.** Savoir *m*, science *f*; érudition *f*; *esp.* connaissance *f* du latin et du grec; humanisme *m.* **2.** *Sch:* Bourse *f* (d'études). **Open scholarship**, bourse accessible à tous.

scholastic [skoˈlastik]. **1.** *a.* (*a*) (Philosophie) scolastique. (*b*) (Année) scolaire. *The s. profession*, la carrière de l'enseignement. **Scholastic agency**, agence de placement pour professeurs et institutrices. (*c*) (*Of manner, etc.*) Pédant. **2.** *s. Phil:* Scolastique *m.*

scholiast [ˈskouliast], *s.* Scoliaste *m.*

school¹ [skuːl], *s.* **1.** (*a*) École *f.* **Infant school**, école maternelle, école enfantine. **Elementary school, primary school**, école primaire. **Secondary school**, établissement *m* d'enseignement secondaire. **High school**, (i) école secondaire de jeunes filles; (ii) *Scot:* école secondaire. **Central school**, école primaire supérieure. **Private school**, école libre. **Public school**, grande école d'enseignement secondaire. **Sunday school**, école du dimanche; (*in Fr.*) "le catéchisme." **What school were you at?** où avez-vous fait vos études? **School furniture**, matériel *m* scolaire. (*b*) *The s. was assembled*, on avait réuni tous les élèves. **The upper school**, les hautes, grandes, classes. **The middle, lower, school**, les moyennes classes; les petites classes. **2.** **To go to school**, (i) aller en classe; (ii) aller à l'école (primaire). *We were at s. together*, nous avons été à l'école ensemble. **To be in school**, être en classe. *S. begins at nine*, les classes commencent à neuf heures. **School children**, écoliers *m.* **School year**, année scolaire. **School report**, bulletin trimestriel. **3.** École, institut *m* (d'enseignement technique, etc.). **School of art**, école des beaux-arts. **School of dancing**, académie *f* de danse; cours *m* de danse. **School of music**, académie de musique; conservatoire *m.* **Fencing s.**, salle *f* d'escrime. **Evening school**, cours *mpl* du soir. **Technical school, trade school**, école des arts et métiers; école professionnelle. *F:* The school of adversity, l'école du malheur. *Lit:* The School for Wives, l'École des Femmes. **4.** *pl. Hist. of Phil:* The Schools, l'École; la philosophie scolastique (du moyen âge). **5.** (*In Universities*) Faculté *f.* The Arts School, la Faculté des lettres. **6.** (*a*) *Art:* The Flemish school, the Italian school, l'école flamande; l'école italienne. *Phil:* The Platonic school, l'école de Platon. (*b*) *F:* School of thought, école (de pensée, d'opinions). One of the old school, un homme de la vieille école, de la vieille roche. He founded no school, il n'a pas laissé de disciples; il n'a pas fait école. **'school-book**, *s.* Livre classique; livre de classe. **'school-dame**, *s.f.* (*a*) *A:* Maîtresse d'une école enfantine de village. (*b*) *Hum:* Maîtresse d'école. **'school-day**, *s.* **1.** Jour *m* de classe. **2.** *pl.* In my school-days, au temps où j'allais en classe; du temps que j'étais à l'école. **'school-house**, *s.* Maison *f* d'école; école *f.* **'school-**

miss, *s.f. F:* Pensionnaire. **'school-teacher**, *s.* Maître *m*, maîtresse *f*, d'école primaire; instituteur, -trice.

school², *v.tr.* **1.** Instruire (qn); faire l'éducation de (qn). **2.** Former (un enfant, un cheval, l'esprit de qn); discipliner (sa voix, son geste). **To school s.o. to do sth.**, entraîner, dresser, qn à faire qch. **To school oneself to patience**, apprendre patienter. *To s. s.o. in society ways*, styler qn aux usages du monde. **Well schooled servant**, domestique bien stylé. **Schooled in adversity**, formé à l'école du malheur. **schooling**, *s.* Instruction *f* éducation *f. He has had no s.*, il n'a pas reçu d'instruction.

school³, ⁴, *s. & v.i.* = SHOAL³, ⁴.

schoolboy [ˈskuːlbɔi], *s.m.* Écolier; élève.

schoolfellow [ˈskuːlfelo], *s.* Camarade *mf* de classe ou d'école; condisciple *m.*

schoolgirl [ˈskuːlgəːrl], *s.f.* Écolière; élève. *S. complexion*, teint frais de petite pensionnaire.

schoolman, *pl.* **-men** [ˈskuːlmən, -men], *s.m.* Scolastique. **The Schoolmen**, l'École *f.*

schoolmaster [ˈskuːlmɑːstər], *s.m.* (*a*) (*In elementary school*) Instituteur; maître d'école; (*in secondary school*) professeur. (*b*) Directeur (de l'école); chef d'institution.

schoolmistress [ˈskuːlmistres], *s.f.* (*a*) (*In elementary school*) Institutrice; maîtresse d'école (*in secondary school*) professeur *m.* (*b*) Directrice (de pensionnat).

schoolroom [ˈskuːlrum], *s.* (Salle *f* de) classe *f* (*in private house*) salle d'étude.

schooner¹ [ˈskuːnər], *s. Nau:* Schooner *m* goélette *f.* **Fore-and-aft schooner**, goélette franche. **Three-mast(ed) schooner**, trois-mâts *m* goélette.

schooner², *s.* **1.** *U.S:* Grande flûte (pour bière). **2.** (*In Engl. approx.*) Demi-litre *m* (de bière).

schorl [ʃɔːrl], *s. Miner:* Tourmaline noire.

sciagraph [ˈsaiagrɔːf, -graf], *s.* **1.** *Med:* etc. Radiographie *f*; skiagramme *m.* **2.** *Arch* Coupe verticale; sciagraphie *f.*

sciatic [saiˈatik], *a. & s. The s. nerve*, the sciatic le nerf sciatique.

sciatica [saiˈatika], *s. Med:* Sciatique *f.*

science [ˈsaiəns], *s.* Science *f.* **Physical science** les sciences physiques. **To study science**, étudie les sciences. **Man of science**, savant *m*; homme de science. **Social science**, économie sociale. **To reduce betting to a science**, ériger le pari en étude scientifique. **'science-master**, *s.m. Sch:* Professeur de sciences.

scienter [saiˈentər], *adv. Jur:* A bon escient.

scientific [saiənˈtifik], *a.* Scientifique. **Scientifi instruments**, instruments de précision. *S. men* hommes de science. **-ally**, *adv.* Scientifiquement.

scientist [ˈsaiəntist], *s.* Savant, -ante; homm de science.

scilicet [ˈsailiset], *adv.* A savoir; c'est-à-dire.

Scilly [ˈsili]. *Pr.n.* The Scilly Isles, les Sorlingues *f.*

scimitar [ˈsimitar], *s.* Cimeterre *m.*

scintilla [sinˈtila], *s.* Soupçon *m*, parcelle *f F:* miette *f.* Not a scintilla of truth, pas un atome de vérité. Not a s. of genius, pas un étincelle de génie.

scintillate [ˈsintileit], *v.i.* Scintiller, étinceler.

scintillation [sintiˈleiʃ(ə)n], *s.* Scintillation scintillement *m.*

sciolism [ˈsaiolizm], *s.* Demi-savoir *m*, dem science *f.*

sciolist [ˈsaiolist], *s.* Demi-savant *m*; prétend savant.

cion ['saiən], s. **1.** Hort: Scion m, ente f, greffon m. **2.** Descendant m. **Scion of a noble house,** rejeton m d'une famille noble.

cirrhous ['sirəs], a. Med: Squirreux.

cirrhus ['sirəs], s. Med: Squirre m.

cissile ['sisil], a. Miner: Scissile, fissile.

cission ['si∫(ə)n], s. **1.** Coupage m avec un instrument tranchant; cisaillement m. **2.** F: Scission f, division f (dans un parti).

cissiparous [si'sipərəs], a. Biol: Scissipare.

cissor[1] ['sizər], s. (a) **(Pair of) scissors,** ciseaux mpl. **Cutting-out scissors,** ciseaux de couturière. Journ: etc: **To work with scissors and paste,** travailler à coups de ciseaux. **Scissors-and-paste production,** ouvrage fait à coups de ciseaux; pure compilation. Sp: **Scissor jump,** saut en hauteur avec élan. Skiing: **Scissors stop,** arrêt en ciseaux. (b) Swim: **The scissors,** le coup de ciseaux.

'scissor-bill, s. Orn: F: Bec-en-ciseaux m.

'scissor-case, s. Étui m à ciseaux.

cissor[2], v.tr. Couper, découper, (qch.) avec des ciseaux.

ciuridae [sai'juəridi:], s.pl. Z: Sciuridés m, écureuils m.

clera ['skliərə], s. Anat: Sclérotique f; cornée f opaque; F: blanc m de l'œil.

cleritis [skliə'raitis], s. Med: Sclérotite f.

clerometer `skliə'rɔmetər], s. Ph: Scléromètre m.

cleroscope ['skliərɔskoup], s. Ph: Scléroscope m.

clerosed [skliə'roust], a. Scléreux sclérosé.

clerosis, pl. **-oses** [skliə'rousis, -ousi:z], s. Med: Sclérose f.

clerotic [skliə'rɔtik] Anat: **1.** a. Sclérotique. **2.** s. = SCLERA.

clerotitis [skliərɔ'taitis], s. Med: Sclérotite f.

clerous ['skliərəs], a. (Tissu) scléreux.

cobs [skɔbz], s.pl. **1.** Sciure f; copeaux mpl; limaille f. **2.** Scorie f, scories.

coff[1] [skɔf], s. **1.** Sarcasme m, brocard m, raillerie f. **2.** (Pers.) Objet m de risée. **To be the s. of the town,** la risée de la ville.

coff[2], v.i. Se moquer. **To scoff at s.o.,** se moquer, se gausser, de qn. **To scoff at dangers,** mépriser les dangers. **To be scoffed at,** recueillir des railleries. **scoffing**[1], a. Moqueur, -euse; railleur, -euse. **-ly,** adv. En raillant; par moquerie.

scoffing[2], s. Moquerie f, raillerie f.

coffer ['skɔfər], s. Moqueur, -euse; railleur, -euse.

cold[1] [skould], s.f. (Femme) criarde; mégère; F: bougonne, rabroueuse.

cold[2]. **1.** v.i. Gronder, criailler, ronchonner (at s.o., contre qn). **2.** v.tr. Gronder, réprimander, F: tancer (qn). **scolding**[1], a. Grondeur, -euse.

scolding[2], s. **1.** Gronderie f, réprimande f, semonce f. **To give s.o. a good scolding,** tancer qn; F: laver la tête à qn. **2.** Constant s., des criailleries f sans fin.

collop[1, 2] ['skɔləp], s. & v. = SCALLOP[1, 2].

colopendra `skɔlɔ'pendrɑ], s. Myr: Scolopendre f.

colopendrium [skɔlɔ'pendriəm], s. Bot: Scolopendre f, langue-de-cerf f.

comber ['skɔmbər], s. Ich: Scombre m, maquereau m.

conce[1] [skɔns], s. **1.** Bougeoir m. **2.** Applique f; candélabre fixé au mur. **Piano sconce,** flambeau m de piano. **3.** Bobèche f (d'un bougeoir).

conce[2], s. **1.** Fort détaché; blockhaus m, fortin m. **2.** Culot m du feu (d'une grande cheminée).

cone [skɔn, skoun], s. Scot: Pain m au lait cuit en galette (sur une plaque de fer).

scoop[1] [sku:p], s. **1.** (a) Nau: Épuisette f, écope f, puchet m. (b) Pelle f à main. **Grocer's scoop,** main f. (c) Surg: Curette f. (d) **Aural scoop,** cure-oreilles m inv. **2.** (a) Civ.E: Cuiller f, godet m (de drague). (b) I.C.E: Cuiller de graissage (de tête de bielle). Rail: Cuiller (de locomotive pour ramasser l'eau). **3.** (Coal) scoop, seau m à charbon (coupé en biseau).

'scoop-net, s. Fish: Drague f.

scoop[2], s. **1.** Creux m, excavation f. **2.** (a) Coup m de pelle. **At one scoop,** d'un seul coup. F: **A fine scoop!** une belle rafle! un joli coup de filet! (b) Journ: F: Primeur f d'une grosse nouvelle.

scoop[3], v.tr. **1.** **To scoop (out),** écoper (l'eau); excaver (la terre); évider (un navet, etc.); gouger (le bois). **To scoop up,** (i) ramasser (du charbon, etc.) avec la pelle; (ii) épuiser, écoper (l'eau). **2.** F: **To scoop a large profit,** faire une belle rafle. **To scoop in £100 a day,** ramasser cent livres par jour.

scooper ['sku:pər], s. **1.** Celui qui puise, qui évide, qui ramasse (à la pelle). **2.** Outil m à évider; gouge f. **3.** Orn: Avocette f.

scoot[1] [sku:t], s. P: Fuite précipitée. **To do a scoot,** filer.

scoot[2], v.i. P: **To scoot (off, away),** détaler; filer.

scooter ['sku:tər], s. Trottinette f, patinette f, scooter m.

scope [skoup], s. (a) Portée f, étendue f (d'une action, du savoir de qn); rayon m (d'une action). **That is beyond, outside, my scope,** cela n'est pas de, ne rentre pas dans, ma compétence, n'est pas dans mes moyens. **Undertaking of wide scope,** entreprise de grande envergure. To extend the s. of one's activities, élargir le champ de son activité. **To fall within the scope of a work,** rentrer dans le plan d'un ouvrage. **Scope of gunfire,** champ m d'action de l'artillerie. (b) Espace m, place f (pour les mouvements de qn, etc.). **To give s.o. scope for his abilities,** donner à qn une liberté d'action en rapport avec ses capacités. Subject that gives s. for eloquence, sujet qui donne carrière à l'éloquence. **To give full, free, scope to** (s.o., one's imagination, etc.), donner (libre) carrière à (qn, son imagination, etc.). To have free, full, scope to act, avoir toute latitude pour agir; avoir ses coudées franches.

scops [skɔps], s. **Scops(-owl),** petit duc.

scorbutic [skɔ:r'bju:tik], a. & s. Scorbutique (mf).

scorch [skɔ:rt∫]. **1.** v.tr. Roussir, brûler légèrement (le linge, etc.); (of sun) rôtir, flétrir, dessécher (l'herbe, etc.); (of frost) griller (les bourgeons). **2.** v.i. Roussir; brûler légèrement. **3.** v.i. F: **To scorch (along),** brûler le pavé; conduire ou pédaler comme un fou; aller un train d'enfer. **scorching**[1]. **1.** a. Brûlant, ardent. S. heat, chaleur torride. F: S. criticism, critique caustique. **2.** adv. **Scorching hot,** tout brûlant. **scorching**[2], s. **1.** Roussissement m; dessèchement m. **2.** Aut: Allure excessive; allure de chauffard. **To be had up for scorching,** se faire dresser une contravention pour excès de vitesse.

scorcher ['skɔ:rt∫ər], s. **1.** F: (a) Journée f torride. (b) Discours écrasant; riposte cinglante. **2.** F: (a) Aut: Chauffard m; Cy: cycliste m casse-cou. (b) **A real scorcher,** un homme qui va vite en affaires. **3.** P: Chose ou personne épatante.

score[1] ['skɔ:rər], s. **1.** (On skin) Éraflure f, entaille f; (on rock) strie f; (on cylinder) rayure f.

The scores in a bearing, les grippures *f* d'un palier. **2.** (*a*) Trait *m* de repère. (*b*) Gorge *f*, engoujure *f* (de poulie). **3.** (*a*) Encoche *f*; coche *f* (sur une taille de boulanger). (*b*) *F:* **To run a score at a public house,** *F:* avoir une ardoise à une taverne. **To pay one's score,** régler son compte. *F:* **To pay off old scores,** régler de vieux comptes; vider d'anciens griefs. **4.** (*a*) (Nombre *m* de) points *m* (dans une partie, un match). *Golf:* Compte *m* des points. *Fb:* Marque *f*, score *m*. *Fb:* **What's the score?** où en est le jeu? **There was no score,** aucun but n'a été enregistré. (*b*) *F:* (i) Réponse bien envoyée; (ii) coup *m* de fortune; aubaine *f*. **5.** *Mus:* Partition *f*. **Full score,** partition d'orchestre. **6.** (*a*) *Inv. in pl.* Vingt, vingtaine *f*. **A score of people,** une vingtaine de gens. *Some* **two score words,** une quarantaine de mots. **Four score years and ten,** quatre-vingt-dix ans. (*b*) *pl.* *F:* **Scores,** un grand nombre. **Scores of people,** une masse de gens. **7.** Point *m*, question *f*, sujet *m*. **Have no fear on that score,** n'ayez aucune crainte à cet égard, sur ce chapitre. **On more scores than one,** à plus d'un titre. *On the s. of ill-health,* pour cause, pour raison, de santé. **'score-card,** *s.* **1.** (*At shooting-range*) Carton *m*. **2.** *Golf:* Carte *f* du parcours. **'score-game,** *s.* *Golf:* Match *m* par coups. **'score-play,** *s.* *Golf:* Jeu *m* par coups.

score², *v.tr.* **1.** (*a*) Érafler; inciser (le cuir); strier; rayer. *Face scored with scars, with lines,* visage couturé de cicatrices, haché de rides. (*b*) Faire un trait de plume au-dessous de (qch.); souligner (un passage). **2.** (*a*) Entailler, (en)cocher. **To score a tally,** faire des coches à une taille. (*b*) *F:* **To score up the drinks,** inscrire les consommations à l'ardoise. **3.** *Games:* (*a*) Compter, marquer (les points). (*b*) Gagner (une partie); faire, marquer (trente points). *To fail to s.,* ne marquer aucun point. *Cr:* **To score a century,** faire une centaine. *Fb:* **To score a goal,** loger le ballon dans le but; marquer un but. *F:* **To score (a success),** remporter un succès. **That's where he scores,** c'est par là qu'il l'emporte; voilà où il est avantagé. **4.** *Mus:* (*a*) Noter (un air). (*b*) Orchestrer (une composition). **score off,** *v.tr.* **To score off s.o.,** (i) *Games:* marquer un point aux dépens de qn; (ii) *F:* river son clou à qn. **score out,** *v.tr.* Rayer, biffer (un mot).

scoring, *s.* **1.** Éraflement *m*; striation *f*; grippage *m* (d'un cylindre, etc.). **2.** *Games:* Marque *f* (des points). **Scoring board,** tableau *m*, boulier *m*. **3.** *Mus:* (*a*) Notation *f* (d'un air). (*b*) Orchestration *f*.

scorer ['skɔːrər], *s.* *Games:* Marqueur *m*.

scoria, *pl.* **-iae** ['skɔːriə, -iː], *s.* *Metall: etc:* Scorie *f*, mâchefer *m*, crasse *f*.

scorn¹ [skɔːrn], *s.* **1.** (*a*) Dédain *m*, mépris *m*. **To think scorn of s.o.,** dédaigner, mépriser, qn. (*b*) **He is the scorn of his friends,** il est devenu un objet de mépris pour ses amis.

scorn², *v.tr.* **1.** Dédaigner, mépriser. **To scorn a piece of advice,** faire fi d'un conseil. **2.** **To scorn to do sth.,** trouver indigne de soi de faire qch.

scorner ['skɔːrnər], *s.* Contempteur, -trice (*of,* de); railleur, -euse.

scornful ['skɔːrnful], *a.* Dédaigneux, méprisant. **To be scornful of sth.,** dédaigner, mépriser, qch. **-fully,** *adv.* Dédaigneusement; avec mépris.

scorpion ['skɔːrpjən], *s.* Scorpion *m*. **'scorpion-broom,** *s.* *Bot:* Épine fleurie. **'scorpion-fish,** *s.* Scorpène *f*.

scorzonera [skɔːrzoˈniːərə], *s.* Scorsonère *f* salsifis noir.

Scot¹ [skɔt], *s.* Écossais, -aise.

scot², *s.* **1.** Écot *m*. *To pay one's s.,* payer so écot. **2.** *Hist:* Scot and lot, taxes communale **'scot-'free,** *a.* **1.** **To get off scot-free,** s'e tirer indemne, sain et sauf. **2.** Sans frais.

scotch¹ [skɔtʃ], *s.* Cale *f*; sabot *m* d'arrêt (pla sous une roue).

scotch², *v.tr.* Caler (une roue).

scotch³, *s.* Entaille *f*; trait *m* (au couteau, etc.

scotch⁴, *v.tr.* **1.** Mettre (qn, une bête) hors d combat. **2.** Mettre à néant, faire avorter (u projet).

Scotch⁵. **1.** (*a*) *a.* Écossais; d'Écosse. Scotc **terrier,** terrier griffon. (*b*) *s.pl.* **The Scotch,** le Écossais. **2.** *s.* (*a*) *Ling:* L'écossais *m*. (*b*) ! Whisky écossais. **A glass of Scotch,** un whisky.

Scotchman, *pl.* **-men** ['skɔtʃmən, -men], *s.n* Écossais.

Scotchwoman, *pl.* **-women** ['skɔtʃwumə -wimen], *s.f.* Écossaise.

scoter ['skoutər], *s.* *Orn:* Macreuse *f*.

scotia ['skouʃiə], *s.* *Arch:* Scotie *f*, nacelle *f*.

Scotland ['skɔtlənd]. *Pr.n.* **1.** L'Écosse **2.** Scotland Yard, les bureaux centraux d police métropolitaine de Londres, en particuli de la police de sûreté.

Scots [skɔts], *a. & s.* = SCOTTISH. **To talk Scot** parler (en) écossais. *To write in S.,* écrire e écossais. Scots law, droit écossais. **The Sco Guards,** la Garde écossaise.

Scotsman, *pl.* **-men** ['skɔtsmən, -men], *s.n* Écossais. *Rail:* **The Flying Scotsman,** le rapi de Londres à Édimbourg.

Scotswoman, *pl.* **-women** ['skɔtswumə -wimen], *s.f.* Écossaise.

Scot(t)icism ['skɔtisizm], *s.* Mot écossai idiotisme écossais.

Scottie ['skɔti], *s.* *F:* Écossais *m*.

Scottish ['skɔtiʃ], *a. & s.* *Lit:* = SCOTCH⁵. Th Scottish Border, les marches *f* d'Écosse.

scoundrel ['skaundrəl], *s.* Chenapan *m*, coquin n scélérat *m*, gredin *m*. *That s. of a lawyer!* u gredin d'homme de loi! **Regular scoundre** franche canaille.

scoundrelism ['skaundrəlizm], *s.* **(Piece o scoundrelism,** canaillerie *f*, gredinerie *f*.

scoundrelly ['skaundrəli], *a.* Scélérat, v canaille. *A s. money-lender,* une canaille d'usurie

scour¹ ['skauər], *s.* **1.** (*a*) *F:* Nettoyage *n* récurage *m*. *To give a saucepan a goo s.,* récurer à fond une casserole. (*b*) *Hyd.E* (i) Chasse *f* (d'un réservoir, etc.); (ii) for érosive, force d'affouillement (d'un cours d'eau **2.** *Tex:* Dégraissant *m*. **3.** *Vet:* Diarrhée *f*.

scour², *v.tr.* **1.** (*a*) Nettoyer, essiver, frotter (plancher, etc.). **To scour out a saucepan,** récur une casserole. (*b*) *Tex:* Dessuinter, dégraiss (la laine). (*c*) Décaper, dérocher (une surfac métallique). **2.** (a) Donner une chasse d'eau (un égout, etc.). (*b*) (*Of river*) Affouiller, dégrad (les rives). (*c*) Purger.

scour³. **I.** *v.i.* **To scour about,** battre la can pagne. **To scour after s.o.,** courir à la poursui de qn. **To scour out of s.o.,** détaler, filer. **2.** *v.tr.* Pa couιrir, battre (la campagne); (*of pirates*) balaye écumer (la mer). **To scour a wood,** fouiller u bois.

scourge¹ [skəːrdʒ], *s.* **1.** *A:* Fouet *m*; *Ecc:* (*f self-flagellation*) discipline *f*. **2.** Fléau *m*. **Attil the Scourge of God,** Attila, le Fléau de Die *War is the greatest s.,* la guerre est e pire d fléaux.

scourge², *v.tr.* **I.** *A:* Fouetter, flageller. *Ecc:* To scourge oneself, se donner · la discipline. **2.** Châtier (un peup.e); être un fléau pour (la population).

scout¹ [skaut], *s.* **I.** (*a*) *Mil:* Écla reur *m.* (*b*) Boy scout, boy-scout *m, pl.* boys-scouts. (*c*) Scout employé par les associat.ons automobiles. **2.** *Navy:* Scout (ship), vedette *f*; (croiseur-)éclaireur *m.* **3.** *Mil:* To be, go, on the scout, être, aller, en reconnaissance.

scout², *v.i.* *Mil:* Aller en reconnaissance; éclairer la marche. Scouting party, reconnaissance *f.* *Navy:* Scouting vessel, éclaireur *m.*

scout³, *s.* Garçon *m* de service (à Oxford).

scout⁴, *v.tr.* Repousser (une proposition, etc.) avec mépris, avec dédain.

scoutmaster ['skautmɑːstər], *s.* Chef éclaireur; chef de troupe (de boys-scouts).

scow [skau], *s.* *Nau:* (*a*) Chaland *m.* (*b*) (Ferry) scow, toue *f.*

scowl¹ [skaul], *s.* Air menaçant, re(n)frogné; froncement *m* de(s) sourcils. To look at s.o. with a s., regarder qn de travers.

scowl², *v.i.* Se re(n)frogner; froncer les sourcils. To scowl at, on, s.o., regarder qn de travers, d'un air menaçant. **scowling**, *a.* Re(n)frogné, menaçant.

scrabble [skrabl], *v.i.* (*a*) To scrabble about, gratter (çà et là); jouer des pieds et des mains. (*b*) Chercher à quatre pattes (pour retrouver qch.).

scrag¹ [skrag], *s.* **I.** (*a*) Personne décharnée, maigre; bête efflanquée. (*b*) *P:* The scrag of the neck, la nuque. **2.** *Cu:* Scrag(-end) of mutton, bout saigneux.

scrag², *v.tr.* (scragged) *P:* **I.** Tordre le cou à (qn). **2.** *Fb:* Saisir (un adversaire) autour du cou.

scrag³, *s.* **I.** Tronçon *m,* souche *f* (d'un arbre); chicot *m.* **2.** Terrain rocailleux.

scragginess¹ ['skraginəs], *s.* Décharnement *m,* maigreur *f.*

scragginess², *s.* Rugosité *f,* anfractuosité *f* (d'un rocher, etc.); rabougrissement *m* (d'un arbre).

scraggy¹ ['skragi], *a.* Décharné, maigre; qui n'a que la peau et les os.

scraggy², *a.* (*Of rock, etc.*) Rugueux, anfractueux, raboteux; (*of tree*) rabougri.

scramble¹ [skrambl], *s.* **I.** Marche *f* ou ascension *f* difficile, à quatre pattes; escalade *f* à quatre pattes. **2.** Mêlée *f,* lutte *f,* bousculade *f.* The scramble for a living, la lutte pour l'existence. The scramble for office, la curée des places.

scramble². **I.** *v.i.* (*a*) To scramble up, down, in, out, monter, descendre, entrer, sortir, à quatre pattes; jouer des pieds et des mains. To scramble up a hill, grimper une colline à quatre pattes. To scramble through sth., jouer des pieds et des mains pour traverser qch. (*b*) To scramble for sth., se battre, se bousculer, pour avoir qch.; se battre à qui aura qch. **2.** *v.tr.* (*a*) Scrambled eggs, œufs brouillés. (*b*) *W.Tg:* Brouiller (un message).

scrap¹ [skrap], *s.* **I.** (*a*) Petit morceau; bout *m,* chiffon *m* (de papier); fragment *m* (de porcelaine, etc.); parcelle *f* (de terrain, etc.); brin *m* (d'étoffe). Tea without a s. of sugar, thé sans une parcelle de sucre. Not a s. of evidence, pas une parcelle de preuve. A little scrap of a man, un bout d'homme. To catch scraps of conversation, saisir des bribes de conversation. Scrap of comfort, fiche *f,* brin, de consolation. *F:* That won't benefit you a scrap, vous n'en tirerez pas le moindre avantage. (*b*) Découpure *f* (pour album); coupure *f* (de journal). **2.** *pl.*

Scraps (*left over*), restes *m,* reliefs *m* (d'un repas); déchets *m* (de papeterie, d'usine, etc.). To dine off scraps, dîner des restes de la veille. *Coll.* Mill scrap, déchets de fabrication. 'scrap-book, *s.* Album *m* (de découpures, etc.). 'scrap-heap, *s.* Tas *m* de ferraille. To throw sth. on the scrap-heap, mettre qch. au rebut. 'scrap-iron, -steel, *s.* Ferraille *f.*

scrap², *v.tr.* (scrapped) **I.** Mettre (qch.) au rebut; envoyer (un navire, etc.) à la ferraille; *Ind:* réformer (le matériel). Scrapped material, matériel hors de service. **2.** *F:* Mettre au rancart (une théorie, un projet).

scrap³, *s.* (*a*) *P:* Querelle *f,* rixe *f;* bagarre *f.* (*b*) *Box:* Match *m.* To have a scrap, (i) se battre; (ii) se quereller.

scrap⁴, *v.i.* (scrapped) *P:* Se battre; se prendre aux cheveux; se colleter.

scrape¹ [skreip], *s.* **I.** (*a*) Coup *m* de grattoir, de racloir. *F:* A scrape of the pen, (i) un trait de plume; (ii) quelques mots griffonnés; (iii) *F:* une signature, un parafe. To give a carrot a scrape, gratter, racler, une carotte. To give one's hand a s., s'érafler la main. (*b*) *F:* Révérence *f* gauche, courbette *f* (avec glissade). (*c*) *F:* Mince couche *f* (de beurre, de confitures). (*d*) *F:* Coup d'archet raclé (sur le violon). (*e*) Grincement *m* (d'un violon). **2.** *F:* Mauvaise affaire, mauvais pas. To get into a scrape, se mettre dans un mauvais pas, dans le pétrin, dans l'embarras; s'attirer des ennuis, une affaire. To get out of a scrape, se tirer d'affaire; se dépêtrer. We are in a nice scrape! nous voilà propres! nous voilà bien! nous sommes dans de beaux draps!

scrape². **I.** *v.tr.* **I.** Érafler, écorcher. To scrape one's shins, s'érafler les tibias. (*Of ship*) To scrape the bottom, sillonner le fond; talonner. *F:* Wine that scrapes the throat, vin qui racle le gosier. **2.** (*a*) Racler, gratter (qch.); *Cu:* gratter, ratisser (des navets, etc.); *Surg:* ruginer (un os). To scrape one's boots, s'essuyer les pieds. To scrape one's plate, gratter le fond de son assiette; *F:* nettoyer son assiette. (*b*) (*Smooth*) Riper (une sculpture); racler, raturer (le parchemin). **3.** (*a*) To scrape the bow across the fiddle, faire grincer l'archet sur le violon. *F:* To scrape the fiddle, *v.i.* to scrape on the fiddle, racler, gratter, du violon. To scrape one's feet along the floor, frotter, traîner, les pieds sur le plancher. (*b*) *Abs.* To scrape, faire une révérence (en glissant le pied). *S.a.* BOW¹ **I.** **4.** (*a*) To scrape acquaintance with s.o., trouver moyen de lier connaissance avec qn. (*b*) To scrape (together, up) a sum of money, amasser petit à petit, sou par sou, une somme d'argent. **II.** **scrape**, *v.i.* **I.** (*a*) Gratter. Branches that s. against the shutters, branches qui frottent les volets. (*b*) Grincer. **2.** (*a*) To scrape against, along, the wall, raser le mur; passer tout près du mur. (*b*) *F:* To scrape clear of prison, échapper tout juste à la prison; friser la prison. **scrape along**, *v.i.* *F:* Vivoter péniblement; joindre péniblement les deux bouts. **scrape away**, *v.tr.* Enlever (qch.) en frottant, en raclant. To scrape away the dirt from sth., décrotter qch. **scrape off**, *v.tr.* Enlever (qch.) au racloir. **scrape through**, *v.i.* Passer tout juste (une ouverture). *F:* To scrape through an examination, réussir de justesse (dans un examen); passer tout juste.

scraping¹, *a.* **I.** (*a*) Qui gratte. (*b*) Scraping bow, salut obséquieux. **2.** Avare, ladre. **scraping²** *s.* **I.** Éraflement *m.* **2.** (*a*) Raclage *m,*

grattage *m* (de qch.). **Scraping tool**, racloir *m*.
(*b*) Ripage *m*; raturage *m*. **3.** Grincement *m*.
4. (**Bowing and**) **scraping**, salamalecs *mpl*; courbettes *fpl*. **5.** *pl.* **Scrapings**. (*a*) Raclures *f*;
grattures *f*. (*b*) Sous amassés un à un; petites
économies.
scraper ['skreipər], *s.* **I.** (*Pers.*) Gratteur *m*,
racleur *m*. **2.** *Tls:* (*a* Racloir *m*, grattoir *m*,
racle *f*, rac ette *f*. (*b*) *Sculp:* Ripe *f*. *Surg:*
Bone-scraper, rugine *f*. (*c*) **Pipe(-bowl) scraper**,
nettoie-pipes *m inv.* *Mch:* **Tube-scraper**,
nettoie-tubes *m inv.* **Door-, shoe-scraper**, décrottoir *m*; gratte-pieds *m inv.* '**scraper-ring**,
s. I.C.E: (Segment) racleur *m* d'huile.
scrapper ['skrapər], *s. F:* Pugiliste *m*.
scrappy ['skrapi], *a.* **I.** Hétérogène, hétéroclite;
(*of speech, style*) décousu. **2.** *S.* education, éducation qui présente beaucoup de lacunes. *S.* knowledge, bribes *fpl* de connaissances. **3.** *S.* dinner,
dîner composé de rogatons, de restes.
scrapy ['skreipi], *a.* (*Of violin, etc.*) Discordant,
rauque.
scratch[1] [skratʃ], *s.* **I.** (*a*) Coup *m* d'ongle, de
griffe. Égratignure *f*, éraflure *f*. To go through
the war without a *s.*, sortir de la guerre indemne,
sans une égratignure. (*c*) Rayure *f*; striation *f*.
2. (*a*) Grattement *m* (de la peau). **To give one's
head a scratch**, se gratter la tête. (*b*) Grincement *m*
(d'une plume, d'un phonographe); frottement *m*
(d'une allumette). **3.** *Sp:* (*a*) Scratch *m*, ligne *f*
de départ (d'une course). **To start (at) scratch**,
partir scratch. **To come up to scratch**, (i) se
mettre en ligne; (ii) *F:* se montrer à la hauteur
(de l'occasion); s'exécuter. *F:* **To bring s.o.
up to the scratch**, (i) amener qn à se décider, à
s'exécuter; (ii) chauffer un candidat (pour
un examen). **When it comes to the scratch**,
quand on en vient au fait et au prendre.
(*b*) *F:* = SCRATCH-MAN. '**scratch-awl**, *s. Tls:*
Aiguille *f* à tracer; traçoir *m*. '**scratch-brush**, *s.*
Tls: Gratte-boësse *f*. '**scratch-man, -player**,
s. Sp: Scratch *m*; champion,-ionne. '**scratch-
weed**, *s. Bot:* Grateron *m*. '**scratch-work**,
s. Art: Sgraffite *m*; graffiti *mpl*.
scratch[2]. I. *v.tr.* **I.** (*a*) Égratigner, griffer;
donner un coup de griffe à (qn). Cat that
scratches, chat qui griffe. (*b*) Écorcher, érafler,
érailler (la peau). To s. one's hands, s'égratigner
les mains. (*c*) Rayer (le verre, un diamant, etc.);
strier (la roche). **To scratch a figure on ivory**,
graver (au trait) une figure sur l'ivoire. **2.** (*a*) Gratter; frotter (une allumette). **To scratch one's
head**, se gratter la tête. *F:* **To scratch s.o.'s
back**, gratter qn où ça le démange. (*b*) **To scratch
the surface**, (i) gratter la surface; (ii) *F:* ne pas
aller au fond (de la question, etc.). **3.** (*Of animal*)
Gratter (le sol). To s. a hole, creuser un trou avec
les griffes. **To scratch up a bone**, déterrer un os.
v.i. **To scratch at the door**, gratter à la porte.
4. **To scratch s.o. off a list**, rayer biffer, qn
d'une liste. *Turf: Sp:* (*Of entrant*) **To scratch
the race**, *abs.* **to scratch**, déclarer forfait. *Sp:* (*Of
organizers*) **To scratch a match**, décommander
un match. **5.** Griffonner (quelques mots, sa
signature). II. **scratch**, *v.i.* (*Of pen, etc.*)
Grincer, gratter. **scratch out**, *v.tr.* **I.** Rayer,
biffer, raturer (un mot); (*with penknife*) gratter,
effacer. **2.** *F:* **To scratch s.o.'s eyes out**,
arracher les yeux à qn.
scratch[3], *a.* (Repas, etc.) improvisé, sommaire.
A *s.* collection, une collection hétérogène; un
ramas (de bibelots). *Parl:* **Scratch vote, scratch
division**, vote par surprise. *Sp:* **Scratch team**,
équipe improvisée.

scratchy ['skratʃi], *a.* **I.** (*a*) (*Of drawing*) Au trait
maigre, peu assuré. (*b*) **Scratchy writing**, pattes *f*
d'araignée; pattes de mouche. (*c*) *Mus:* écrit:
S. performance, exécution qui manque d'ensemble. **2.** (*a*) (*Of pen, etc.*) (i) Qui gratte; (ii) qui
grince (sur le papier). (*b*) (*Of stuff*) Qu. gratte
la peau.
scrawl[1] [skrɔːl], *s.* Gr ffonnage *m*, gribouillage *m*;
pattes *fp* de mouche. His writing is a *s.*, il
écrit comme un chat.
scrawl[2], *v.tr.* Griffonner, gribouiller (une lettre).
scray [skrei], *s. Orn:* Hirondelle *f* de mer.
scream[1] [skriːm], *s.* **I.** (*a*) Cri perçant. *S.* of
anguish, cri d'angoisse. **To give a scream**, pousser
un cri aigu, un cri de terreur. (*b*) **Screams of
laughter**, de grands éclats de rire. **2.** *P:* Chose
amusante, grotesque. **It was a perfect scream**,
c'était tout ce qu'il y a de plus cocasse; c'était
à se tordre. In that part he is a (perfect, regular)
s., dans ce rôle il est tordant, impayable.
scream[2]. **I.** *v.i.* (*a*) Pousser un cri perçant;
pousser des cris; crier. **To scream (out) with
pain, for help**, hurler de douleur; crier au
secours. (*b*) *F:* **To scream with laughter**, rire
aux éclats. He made us s., il nous a fait tordre.
2. *v.tr.* **To scream oneself hoarse**, s'enrouer à
(force de) crier. **screaming**, *a.* **I.** Criard; (*of
sound*) perçant. **2.** *F:* (*Of farce, etc.*) Tordant.
-ly, *adv.* *F:* **Screamingly funny**, tordant,
crevant.
scree [skriː], *s.* Eboulis *m* (sur une pente de
montagne).
screech[1] [skriːtʃ], *s.* Cri perçant; cri rauque.
screech[2], *v.i.* Pousser des cris perçants, des cris
rauques; *F:* (*of singer*) chanter d'une voix
aiguë. '**screech-owl**, *s. Orn:* Effraie *f*;
chouette *f* des clochers.
screed [skriːd], *s.* (*a*) Harangue *f*; longue tartine.
(*b*) Longue liste (de réclamations, etc.). (*c*) Longue
missive.
screen[1] [skriːn], *s.* **I.** (*a*) *Furn:* Ecran *m*.
Draught screen, folding screen, paravent *m*.
(*b*) **Side-screens**, (i) *Nau:* écrans des feux de
côté; (ii) *Aut:* rideaux *m* de côté (d'une torpédo). (*c*) *Nau:* **Canvas screen**, cloison *f* en
toile; toile *f* abri. (*d*) *S.* of trees, rideau d'arbres.
F: **Under screen of night**, à l'abri de la nuit.
(*e*) **Wrought-iron s.**, grille *f*. *Ecc.Arch:* **Choir-
screen**, jubé *m*. (*f*) *Mec.E:* **Safety screen**, écran
de sécurité. *Mil: Navy:* **To form a screen**,
former un écran (against, contre). *S.a.* SMOKE-
SCREEN. **2.** *Cin:* Écran (de projection). **To put
a play on the screen**, mettre, présenter, une pièce
à l'écran. **Screen star**, vedette *f* de l'écran.
3. (*a*) *W.Tel:* **Anode screen**, écran de plaque.
Screen-grid, grille-écran *f*; grille blindée.
(*b*) *Phot:* **Colour screen**, écran coloré; écran de
sélection. *Phot.Engr:* **Ruled screen, half-tone
screen**, trame *f*, réseau *m*. **4.** Crible *m*; sas *m*.
Gravel screen, crible à gravier. **Revolving screen**,
trommel *m* (de criblage). '**screen-fire**, *s. Mil:* Tir *m* de
barrage.
screen[2], *v.tr.* **I.** (*a*) Munir (qch.) d'un écran. **To
screen off a corner of the room**, cacher un coin
de la chambre au moyen de paravents. (*b*) **To
screen sth. from view**, cacher, masquer, dérober,
qch. aux regards. **To screen oneself behind sth.**,
se cacher derrière qch. (*c*) Abriter, protéger;
mettre à couvert, à l'abri; blinder (une machine)
(against, contre); couvrir (qn) de sa protection.
To screen sth. from the wind, garantir qch. du
vent. *Mil:* To s. a battery from fire, dérober une
batterie. *W.Tel:* **To screen a valve**, blinder une
lampe. **2.** Tamiser, cribler (le gravier, etc.);

passer (du sable) au tamis, au crible ; sasser (le grain). **3.** *Cin:* Mettre (un roman, etc.) à l'écran. **screened,** *a.* **I.** *(a)* S. *window,* fenêtre jalousée. *W.Tel:* S. *valve,* lampe blindée. **Screened-grid valve,** valve à grille blindée. *(b)* Caché, dérobé, dissimulé ; voilé. *(c)* A *'abri (from,* de). **2.** (Charbon) criblé ; (sable) passé à la claie.

screw¹ [skru:], *s.* **I.** Vis *f.(a)* Right-handed screw, left-handed screw, vis à droite, à gauche. **Endless screw, worm screw,** vis sans fin. **Thumb screw, wing screw,** vis à ailettes ; papillon *m.* **Capstan screw,** vis à tête percée. **Bench screw,** étau *m* d'établi. **Screw joint,** joint vissé, joint à vis. **Screw-thread,** filet *m* de vis ; pas *m* de vis. *(b)* **Set screw,** vis d'arrêt ; vis de réglage, de rappel. *F:* To have a screw loose, avoir le timbre fêlé ; être timbré, toqué. There's a screw loose somewhere, il y a quelque chose qui cloche. *(c) A:* The screws, les poucettes *f. F:* To put the screws on s.o.; to tighten the screw, serrer les pouces, la vis, à qn ; mettre les poucettes à qn ; forcer la main à qn. **2.** *(a) Nau:* Screw(-propeller), hélice *f. Av:* Air-screw, hélice (propulsive). **3.** *(a)* Coup *m* de tournevis ; tour *m* de vis. *Give it another s.,* serrez-le encore un peu. *(b) Bill:* **Ten:** Effet *m.* To put *(a)* screw on the ball, (i) *Bill:* faire de l'effet (de côté) ; (ii) *Ten:* couper la balle. **4.** Cornet *m,* papillote *f* (de bonbons, de tabac, etc.). **5.** *P:* Avare *m; F:* grigou *m;* pingre *m.* **An old screw,** un vieux ladre. **6.** *F:* Mauvais cheval ; *F:* rosse *f,* carcan *m.* **7.** *P: (a)* Gages *mpl;* paye *f,* salaire *m.* *(b)* Appointements *mpl* (minimes). **'screw-auger,** *s. Tls:* Tarière rubanée ; tarière à vis. **'screw-bolt,** *s.* Boulon *m* à vis, à écrou. **'screw-'cap,** *s.* Couvercle *m* à vis (d'une bouteille). **'screw-coupling,** *s. Mec.E:* Manchon *m* à vis. **'screw-cutter,** *s.* **I.** *(Pers.)* Fileteur *m;* tourneur *m* de vis. **2.** Tour *m* à fileter ; taraudeuse *f.* **'screw-cutting,** *s.* Filetage *m,* taraudage *m,* décolletage *m.* **Screw-cutting machine,** machine à fileter, à décolleter. **'screw-driven,** *a.* (Paquebot) à hélice. **'screw-eye,** *s.* Piton *m.* **'screw-gear,** *s.* **I.** Engrenage hélicoïdal. **2.** Outillage *m* de vissage. **'screw-hook,** *s.* Crochet *m* à vis. **'screw-jack,** *s.* Vérin *m* à vis. **'screw-nail,** *s.* Vis *f* à bois. **'screw-plate,** *s.* Filière *f* à truelle. **'screw-plug,** *s.* Tampon *m* à vis ; bouchon fileté. **'screw-spike,** *s.* Tire-fond *m inv.* **'screw-steamer,** *s.* Navire *m* à hélice. **'screw-tap,** *s. Tls:* Taraud *m;* filière *f.* **'screw-wheel,** *s. Mec.E:* Roue *f* à dents hélicoïdales (engrenant avec une vis sans fin). **'screw-wrench,** *s. Tls:* Clef anglaise ; clef à molette.

screw². I. *v.tr.* **I.** Visser. To screw sth. (on) to sth., visser qch. à, sur, qch. The knobs screw into the drawer, les boutons se vissent sur le tiroir. *Screwed together,* assemblé(s) à vis. **2.** *(a)* To screw (up), visser ; (res)serrer (un tourniquet, les chevilles d'un violon). *To s. up a nut,* serrer un écrou. To screw sth. tight, visser qch. à bloc. *(b)* To screw s.o.'s neck, tordre le cou à qn. To screw one's face into a smile, grimacer un sourire. *(c* To screw (down) the peasantry, pressurer, opprimer, les paysans. *(d' Bill:* Donner de l'effet à (la bille). *Ten:* Couper (la balle). **3.** Fileter (une vis, un boulon) ; tarauder. II. **screw,** *v.i.* **I.** *(Of tap, etc.)* Tourner (à droite, à gauche, etc.). **2.** *F:* Faire des économies ; liarder. **screw back,** *v.i. Bill:* **I.** Faire de l'effet rétrograde ; *F:* faire un rétro. **2.** *(Of ball)* Revenir en arrière. **screw**

down, *v.tr.* Visser (un couvercle, un cercueil) ; fermer (une boîte) à vis. **screw on,** *v.tr.* *(a)* Visser, fixer. *F:* His head is screwed on the right way, il a de la tête, du bon sens ; c'est un homme de tête. *(b) The nozzle screws on to the head of the hose,* la lance se visse au bout du tuyau. **screw out,** *v.tr. F:* To screw the truth out of s.o., tirer la vérité de qn. To screw money out of s.o., arracher, extorquer, de l'argent à qn. *It is hard to s. money out of him,* il est dur à la détente. **screw up,** *v.tr.* **I.** Visser (une boîte, etc.); condamner (une porte). **2.** Tortiller (du papier, ses cheveux) ; tire-bouchonner (son mouchoir). To screw sth. up in a piece of paper, entortiller qch. dans un morceau de papier. To screw up one's eyes, plisser les yeux. To screw up one's lips, pincer les lèvres. *He screwed up his face,* il fit la grimace. **3.** *F:* To screw up one's courage, prendre son courage à deux mains. To screw oneself up to do sth., se forcer à faire qch. *(b)* To screw up the rents, majorer les loyers (d'une façon déraisonnable). **screwed,** *a.* **I.** Fileté, taraudé. **2.** *Pred. F:* Ivre ; *F:* gris, éméché. **screwdriver** ['skru:draivər], *s.* Tournevis *m.* **scribble¹** [skribl], *s.* **I.** Griffonnage *m.* **2.** *F:* Petit billet. **3.** Écriture *f* illisible. **scribble²,** *v.tr.* Griffonner (quelques mots à qn). *Abs.* To scribble, (i) barbouiller du papier ; *(ii)* faire du journalisme ; écrivailler. **scribbling,** *s.* Griffonnage *m.* **Scribbling paper,** papier à brouillon. **Scribbling block,** bloc mémento. **scribbler** ['skriblər], *s.* **I.** Griffonneur, -euse. **2.** *F:* Écrivailleur, -euse ; gratte-papier *m inv;* noircisseur *m* de papier. **scribe¹** [skraib], *s.* Scribe *m.* **scribe²,** *s. Tls:* Scribe(-awl), pointe *f* à tracer. **scribe³,** *v.tr.* **I.** *Carp:* Tracer, trusquiner (une ligne). **2.** *Mec.E: etc:* Repérer, pointer (le centre). **'scribing-block,** *s.* Trusquin *m* à équerre. **scriber** ['skraibər], *s.* = scribe². **scrim** [skrim], *s. Tex: Furn:* Canevas léger. **scrimmage** ['skrimedʒ], *s.* **I.** Mêlée *f;* bagarre *f,* bousculade *f.* **2.** *Rugby Fb:* Mêlée. **scrimshank** ['skrimʃaŋk], *v.i. Mil: P:* Tirer au flanc. **scrimshanking,** *s.* Tirage *m* au flanc. **scrimshanker** ['skrimʃaŋkər], *s. Mil: P:* Tireur *m* au flanc. **scrip¹** [skrip], *s. A:* Besace *f.* **scrip²,** *s. (No pl.) Fin:* **I.** Scrip (certificate), certificat *m* (d'actions) ; actions *f* provisoires), "scrip" *m.* **2.** *Coll. F:* Valeurs *fpl,* titres *mpl,* actions. **scripholder** ['skriphouldər], *s. Fin:* Détenteur, -trice, de .itres. **script** [skript], *s.* **I.** *(a,* Manuscrit *m. (b) Sch:* Copie *f* (d'examen). *(c) Jur:* (Document) original *m,* -aux. *(d) Cin:* Scénario *m.* **2.** *(a) (As opposed to print)* Écriture *f. (b) Typ:* Cursive *f.* **scriptural** ['skriptjurəl], *a.* Scriptural, -aux ; biblique ; des saintes Écritures. **scripture¹** ['skriptjər], *s.* **Holy Scripture, the Scriptures,** l'Écriture sainte ; les saintes Écritures. **Scripture history,** l'histoire sainte. **scrivener** ['skrivnər], *s. A:* **I.** *(a)* Scribe *m,* copiste *m;* écrivain public. *(b)* Notaire *m.* *c)* Changeur *m,* prêteur *m* (d'argent). **2.** Plumitif *m; F:* gratte-papier *m inv.* **scrofula** ['skrɔfjulə], *s. Med:* Scrofule *f;* écrouelles *fpl.* **scrofulous** ['skrɔfjuləs], *a.* Scrofuleux. **scroll** [skroul], *s.* **I.** Rouleau *m* (de parchemin, de papier). **2.** (a) *Art:* Banderole *f* à inscription. (b) *Her:* Listel *m*. **3.** (a) *Arch: etc:* Spirale *f*; volute *f* (de chapiteau ionique). (b) (*In writing*) Enjolivement *m*, arabesque *f*. (c) Crosse *f*, volute (de violon). **'scroll-saw,** s. *Tls:* Scie *f* à chantourner. **'scroll-work,** s. *Arch:* Ornementation *f* en volute.

scrotum, pl. **-ta** ['skroutəm, -ta], s. *Anat:* Scrotum *m*.

scrounge [skraundʒ]. *P:* **I.** v.tr. (a) (*Steal*) Chiper, chaparder (qch.). (b) (*Sponge*) Écornifler (un dîner, du tabac). **2.** v.i. To scrounge around for sth., aller à la recherche de qch.

scrounger ['skraundʒər], s. *P:* (a) Chipeur *m*, chapardeur *m*. (b) Écornifleur *m*.

scrub¹ [skrʌb], s. **I.** (a) Arbuste rabougri. (b) Broussailles *fpl*; brousse *f*. **2.** (a) Brosse *f* à soies courtes; brosse usée. (b) Barbe *f* de trois jours.

scrub², s. Friction *f* (à la brosse); nettoyage *m*. To give the table a good scrub, bien laver la table avec une brosse de chiendent. *The saucepan wants a s.*, la casserole a besoin d'être récurée.

scrub³, v.tr. (scrubbed) **I.** (a) Récurer (une casserole); laver, frotter, (le plancher) avec une brosse de chiendent. (b) *Nau:* (i) Goreter, (ii) briquer (le pont). **2.** *Ch:* Laver, épurer (un gaz). **'scrubbing-brush,** s. Brosse *f* de chiendent.

scrubber ['skrʌbər], s. **I.** Laveur, -euse (à la brosse de chiendent). **2.** (a) **Paint scrubber,** brosse *f* à peinture. (b) *Ch:* Épurateur *m*; flacon laveur. *Gasm:* Épurateur, scrubber *m*. **Air scrubber,** épurateur d'air.

scrubby¹ ['skrʌbi], a. **I.** Rabougri. **2.** (*Of land*) Couvert de broussailles. **3.** *F:* (*Of pers.*) Insignifiant; de piètre apparence.

scrubby², a. *F:* (*Of chin*) Mal rasé; (*of moustache*) hérissé. *S. beard,* barbe de trois jours.

scruff [skrʌf], s. Nuque *f*; peau *f* de la nuque. *Used in* To seize an animal by the scruff of the neck, saisir un animal par la peau du cou.

scrum(mage) ['skrʌm(edʒ)], s. = SCRIMMAGE. **'scrum-cap,** s. *Rugby Fb:* Protège-oreilles *m inv.* **'scrum-half,** s. Demi *m* de mêlée.

scrumptious ['skrʌm(p)ʃəs], a. *F:* Excellent, délicieux, épatant.

scrunch [skrʌnʃ], v.tr. & i. = CRUNCH².

scruple¹ [skru:pl], s. **I.** *Meas:* Scrupule *m* (de 20 grains). **2.** *A. & F:* Quantité *f* minime.

scruple², s. Scrupule *m* (de conscience). To have scruples about sth., about doing sth., éprouver des scrupules au sujet de qch.; se faire (un) scrupule de faire qch. To have no scruples, to make no scruple about sth., n'avoir aucun scrupule à faire qch.; ne pas hésiter à faire qch.

scruple³, v.i. To scruple to do sth., avoir des scrupules à faire ;ch. *He does not s. to . . .*, il n'hésite pas à . . .

scrupulous ['skru:pjuləs], a. **I.** Scrupuleux (*about, over, as to,* sur). To be s. in doing sth., être scrupuleux à faire qch. Not over-scrupulous in one's dealings, peu délicat en affaires. **2.** (*Of care, work*) Scrupuleux, exact, méticuleux, minutieux. **-ly,** adv. **I.** Scrupuleusement. **2.** Méticuleusem nt, minuticusement. *S. exact,* exact jusqu'au scrupule.

scrutineer [skru:ti'ni:ər], s. Scrutateur *m* (des votes, du scrutin).

scrutinize ['skru:tinaiz], v.tr. (a) Scruter; examiner (qch.) minutieusement. (b) To scrutinize votes, vérifier, pointer, des suffrages. **scrutinizing,** a. Scrutateu:, -trice; inquisiteur.

scrutiny ['skru:tini], s. (a) Examen minutieux. *His record does not bear s.*, son passé ne se supporte pas un examen rigoureux. (b) *Pol:* Vérification *f* (des bulletins de vote). To demand a scrutiny, contester la validité d'une élection.

scud¹ [skʌd], s. **I.** Course précipitée; fuite *f*. **2.** (a) (*Of clouds*) Diablotins *mpl*. (b) Rafale *f*. (c) Embrun *m*. **3.** *Sch:* *F:* Bon coureur.

scud², v.i. (scudded) **I.** Courir droit et vite; filer comme le vent. To scud away, off, s'enfuir, détaler. **2.** *Nau:* To scud before the wind, fuir vent arrière; avoir (le vent sous vergue; cingler.

scuff [skʌf]. **I.** v.tr. (a) Effleurer. (b) Frotter, racler, user (avec les pieds). (c) To scuff away the tread of the tyre, user la bande de roulement (par abus du frein). **2.** v.i. Traîner les pieds. **'scuff-plate,** s. *Aut:* Seuil *m* de portière.

scuffle¹ [skʌfl], s. Mêlée *f*, échauffourée *f*, bousculade *f*; (*between crowd and police*) bagarre *f*.

scuffle², v.i. **I.** Se battre, se bousculer. *To s. with s.o.*, se colleter avec qn. **2.** To scuffle through a task, accomplir une tâche tant bien que mal, à la hâte. **3:** Traîner les pieds.

scuffle³, s. *Tls:* Ratissoire *f*.

scuffle⁴, v.tr. **I.** Ratisser. **2.** Érafler.

scull¹ [skʌl], s. **I.** *Row:* (a) Aviron *m* de couple. (b) *F:* Aviron, rame *f*. **2.** Godille *f*.

scull². **I.** v.i. (a) Ramer, nager, en couple. (b) Godiller. (c) *F:* Ramer. **2.** v.tr. To scull a boat, faire avancer un bateau (i) à couple, (ii) à la godille, (iii) *F:* à la rame.

sculler ['skʌlər], s. **I.** (a) Rameur *m* de couple. (b) Godilleur *m*. **2.** (*Boat*) Double-sculler, outrigger *m* à deux rameurs de couple.

scullery ['skʌləri], s. Arrière-cuisine *f*. **'scullery maid,** s.f. Laveuse de vaisselle. **'scullery wench,** s.f. *A:* Souillon.

scullion ['skʌljən], s. *A:* Marmiton *m*.

sculptor ['skʌlptər], s. Sculpteur *m*.

sculptress ['skʌlptres], s.f. Femme sculpteur.

sculptural ['skʌlptjurəl], a. Sculptural, -aux. *S. beauty,* beauté sculpturale, plastique.

sculpture¹ ['skʌlptjər], s. Sculpture *f* (l'art ou l'œuvre).

sculpture², v.tr. **I.** Sculpter. *Abs.* Faire de la sculpture. *To s. a statue out of stone,* sculpter une statue dans la pierre. **2.** Orner de sculptures, de bas-reliefs.

sculpturesque [skʌlptju'resk], a. Sculptural, -aux; (beauté) plastique.

scum¹ [skʌm], s. **I.** (a) Écume *f*. *To take the s. off the pot,* écumer le pot. (b) *Metall:* Scories *fpl*, crasse(s) *f*(*pl*). **2.** *F:* The scum of society, le rebut de la société. *The s. of the people,* la lie du peuple.

scum², v. (scummed) **I.** v.tr. = SKIM² **I.** **2.** v.i. Écumer; se couvrir d'écume.

scumble¹ [skʌmbl], s. *Art:* Glacis *m*; frottis *m*.

scumble², v.tr. *Art:* **I.** Glacer, frotter (le ciel, le fond). **2.** Fondre, blaireauter (un ciel, etc.).

scummy ['skʌmi], a. **I.** Écumeux; couvert d'écume. **2.** Qui tient de l'écume.

scupper¹ ['skʌpər], s. *Nau:* Dalot *m* (de pont). **'scupper-pipes,** s.pl. Tuyaux *m* d'orgue (des dalots).

scupper², v.tr. (a) *Mil:* *Nau:* *P:* Surprendre et massacrer (des troupes, l'équipage). (b) *F:* Couler à fond (un navire, un projet); saborder (un navire).

scurf [skə:rf], s. Pellicules *fpl* (du cuir chevelu); farine *f* (d'une dartre); (*in boiler*) tartre *m*.

scurfy ['skə:rfi], a. (a) (*Of head, etc.*) Pelliculeux. (b) *S. affection of the skin,* dartre *f*.

scurrility [skʌ′riliti], *s.* **1.** Grossièreté *f*, obscénité *f* (de langage). **2.** *To indulge in scurrilities*, prononcer, publier, des grossièretés sur le compte de qn.

scurrilous [′skʌriləs], *a.* (*Of language, etc.*) Grossier, injurieux, ordurier ; (*of pers.*) ignoble, vil. *To make a s. attack on s.o.*, se répandre en injures contre qn. *S. little rag*, petite feuille de chou ordurière. **-ly,** *adv.* Grossièrement.

scurry[1] [′skʌri], *s.* **1.** Galopade *f* ; débandade *f*. *A regular s.*, un sauve-qui-peut général. *A general s. towards the door*, une bousculade vers la porte. **2.** Tourbillon *m* (de neige, etc.).

scurry[2], *v.i.* Courir à pas précipités ; se hâter. **To scurry off, away,** détaler, décamper. **To scurry through one's work,** expédier son travail.

scurvied [′skəːrvid], *a. Med :* Scorbutique.

scurvy[1] [′skəːrvi], *s. Med :* Scorbut *m*. **′scurvy-grass,** *s. Bot :* Cochléaria *m*.

scurvy[2], *a.* Bas, vil, vilain, indigne. *S. fellow*, goujat *m. S. trick*, rosserie *f*, vilain tour, goujaterie *f. To play s.o. a s. trick*, faire une crasse à qn.

scut [skʌt], *s.* **1.** Couette *f* (de lièvre, de lapin). **2.** *P :* Mufle *m* ; sale type *m*.

scutch [skʌtʃ], *v.tr. Tex :* Écanguer, teiller (le chanvre, le lin).

scutcheon [′skʌtʃ(ə)n], *s.* = ESCUTCHEON.

scutellum, *pl.* **-la** [skjuˈteləm, -la], *s. Nat.Hist :* Scutelle *f*.

scuttle[1] [skʌtl], *s.* Seau *m* à charbon.

scuttle[2], *s.* **1.** *Nau :* (*a*) Écoutillon *m* ; descente *f*. (*b*) Hublot *m* ; lentille *f* (de cabine). **2.** *Aut :* Bouclier *m* avant ; auvent *m*. **3.** *U.S :* Trappe *f* (de toit).

scuttle[3], *v.tr. Nau :* Saborder (un navire).

scuttle[4], *s.* Fuite *f* ; course précipitée ; débandade *f*.

scuttle[5], *v.i.* (*a*) Courir d'une façon affairée. **To scuttle off, away,** déguerpir, filer, détaler. (*b*) *Pol : F :* Renoncer à un mandat ; se retirer ; *F :* lâcher.

scuttler[1] [′skʌtlər], *s. Pol : F :* Lâcheur *m*.

scuttler[2], *s.* Assureur frauduleux qui saborde son navire.

scutum, *pl.* **-a** [′skjuːtəm, -a], *s.* **1.** *Rom.Ant :* Scutum *m*, bouclier *m*. **2.** *Ent :* Écusson *m*. **3.** *Anat :* Rotule *f*.

scythe[1] [saːið], *s. Tls :* Faux *f*. **′scythe-stone,** *s.* Pierre *f* à aiguiser (les faux).

scythe[2], *v.tr.* Faucher (le blé, etc.).

'sdeath [zdeθ], *int.* (*Euphemism for God's death!*) Mordieu ! morbleu !

sea [siː], *s.* **1.** Mer *f*. (*a*) *An arm of the sea*, un bras de mer. **On land and sea, by land and sea,** sur terre et sur mer. **By the sea,** au bord de la mer. **By sea,** par (voie de) mer. **Beyond, over, the sea(s),** outre-mer. *From beyond the sea*, d'outre-mer. *To smell of the sea*, sentir la mer, la marine. (*Of pers.*) **To put to sea,** s'embarquer. **To go to sea, to take to the sea, to follow the sea,** se faire marin. **To serve at sea,** servir sur mer. **Sea trip,** excursion *f* en mer. *A long sea journey*, une longue traversée. **Sea battle,** bataille navale. **Sea transport of goods,** messageries *f* maritimes. (*b*) **The open sea, the high seas,** le large, la haute mer. *On the high seas, out at sea*, en pleine mer. (*Of ship*) **To put (out) to sea,** prendre la mer, le large. *To remain at sea, to keep the sea* (*in heavy weather*), tenir la mer. **To stand out to sea,** gagner le large, prendre le large. **Head on to sea,** le cap au large. **Ship at sea,** navire en mer. *F :* **To be all at sea,** être tout désorienté ; n'y être pas du tout ; ne savoir sur quel pied danser. *I am quite at sea*, je ne m'y reconnais plus. (*c*) **Inland sea,** mer intérieure, mer fermée. **The four seas,** les mers qui entourent la Grande-Bretagne. *F :* **Within the four seas,** dans la Grande-Bretagne. **The seven seas,** toutes les mers du monde. (*d*) **To be in British seas,** être dans les eaux anglaises. **2.** (*a*) (*State of the sea*) **Heavy sea, strong sea,** grosse mer ; mer houleuse. *There is a sea, a heavy sea*, il y a de la mer. *In anything of a sea . . .*, pour peu qu'il y ait de la mer. . . . (*b*) **Lame** *f*, houle *f*. **To run before the sea,** gouverner l'arrière à la lame ; fuir devant la lame. **Head sea,** mer debout. **Beam sea,** mer de travers. (*c*) **Coup** *m* **de mer** ; paquet *m* de mer ; (grosse) vague. **To ship a (green) sea,** embarquer une lame, un coup de mer, un paquet de mer. *To be struck by a* (*heavy*) *sea*, essuyer un coup de mer. **To ship heavy seas,** embarquer d'énormes paquets de mer. **3.** *F :* Océan *m*, infinité *f*, multitude *f*. *A sea of faces, of corn*, un océan de visages, de blés. *A sea of cares*, une infinité, une multitude, de soucis. **′sea air,** *s.* Air *m* de la mer. **′sea-anchor,** *s. Nau :* Ancre flottante ; ancre de cape. **′sea-a′nemone,** *s.* Actinie *f* ; *F :* anémone *f* de mer. **′sea-arm,** *s.* Bras *m* de mer. **′sea-bathing,** *s.* Bains *mpl* de mer. **′sea-biscuit,** *s. Nau :* Biscuit *m* ; *F :* cassant *m*. **′sea-boat,** *s.* Good sea-boat, bon bateau de mer. *His tramp was a good sea-b.*, son cargo tenait bien la mer. **′sea-boots,** *s.pl.* Bottes *f* de marin, de mer. **′sea-born,** *a. Myth :* Né de la mer. **′sea-borne,** *a.* (*Of trade*) Maritime ; (*of goods*) transporté par mer. **′sea-′bottom,** *s.* Fond *m* de la mer. **′sea-bound,** *a.* (*Of land*) Borné par la mer. **′sea-breeze,** *s.* Brise *f* du large. **′sea-calf,** *s. Z :* Phoque commun ; veau marin. **′sea-captain,** *s.m.* **1.** Capitaine de la marine (marchande ou de guerre). **2.** Capitaine au long cours. **′sea-carrier,** *s. Jur :* Transporteur *m* par mer. **′sea-chart,** *s. Nau :* Carte marine. **′sea-chest,** *s.* Coffre *m* (de marin). **′sea-coal,** *s. A :* Houille *f* ; charbon *m* de terre. **′sea-coast,** *s.* Littoral *m*, -aux ; côte *f*. **′sea-cow,** *s. Z :* Vache marine (lamantin, dugong, morse, ou hippopotame). **′sea-craft,** *s.* **1.** Art *m* du navigateur. **2.** *Coll.* Petits bâtiments de mer. **′sea-dog,** *s.* **1.** *Z :* = SEA-CALF. **2.** *F :* An old sea-dog, un vieux marin ; un vieux loup de mer. **′sea-eagle,** *s. Orn :* Pygargue *m*, orfraie *f* ; *F :* grand aigle des mers. **′sea-eel,** *s. Ich :* Congre *m*. **′sea-elephant,** *s.* Éléphant *m* de mer ; phoque *m* à trompe. **′sea-fennel,** *s. Bot :* = SAMPHIRE 1. **′sea-fight,** *s.* Combat naval. **′sea-fish,** *s.* Poisson *m* de mer. **′sea-fishery,** *s.* Pêche *f* maritime. **′sea-floor,** *s. Oc :* Fond sous-marin. **′sea-′front,** *s.* **1.** Partie *f* de la ville qui fait face à la mer. **House on the sea-front,** maison qui donne sur la mer. **2.** Digue *f*, esplanade *f*. **′sea-girt,** *a. Lit :* Entouré, ceint, par la mer. **′sea-god,** *s.m.* Dieu marin ; triton. **′sea-going,** *a.* **1.** De haute mer ; affecté à la navigation maritime. **Sea-going ship,** navire de long cours ; navire allant en mer. **2.** (*Of pers.*) = SEAFARING[1]. **′sea-green,** *s. & a.* Vert (*m*) de mer *inv* ; vert d'eau *inv* ; glauque. **′sea-gull,** *s. Orn :* = GULL[1]. **′sea-horse,** *s.* **1.** *Z :* = WALRUS. **2.** *Myth : Z :* Hippocampe *m* ; cheval marin. **′sea-kale,** *s. Bot :* Crambé *m* (maritime) ; chou marin. **′sea-lawyer,** *s.* *F :* **1.** Requin *m* (féroce). **2.** Rouspéteur *m*, chicaneur *m*. **′sea legs,** *s.pl. F :* Pied marin. **To find, to get, one's sea-legs,** s'amariner. **′sea-letter,** *s. Nau :* Permis *m* de navigation.

'sea-level, s. Niveau (moyen) de la mer. Pressure corrected to sea-level, pression (barométrique) ramenée au niveau de la mer. **'sea-light,** s. Feu m (de port); balise f, phare m. **'sea-line,** s. (At sea) Ligne f d'horizon. **'sea-lion,** s. Z: Otarie f. **'sea-lord,** s. Lord m de l'Amirauté. First Sea-lord, Premier Lord Naval. **'sea-mark,** s. Nau: (a) Amer m. (b) Balise f. **'sea-otter,** s. Z: Loutre f de mer. **'sea-pass,** s. (For neutral ships in time of war) Permis m de navigation; laissez-passer m inv. **'sea-pie,** s. Cu: Nau: Pâté m (viande salée et légumes). **'sea-piece,** s. Art: = SEA-SCAPE. **'sea-plane,** s. = SEAPLANE. **'sea-plant,** s. Plante marine. **'sea-power,** s. Puissance f maritime. **'sea-risk,** s. M.Ins: Risque m de mer; fortune f de mer. **'sea-room,** s. Nau: (a) Évitage m; évitée f. (b) Eau f à courir. To have plenty of sea-room, (i) avoir de l'évitée; (ii) avoir une belle dérive. **'sea-'rover,** s. Corsaire m, pirate m, flibustier m. **'sea-scout,** s. Boy-scout m de mer. **'sea-serpent,** s. Serpent m de mer. **'sea-shell,** s. Coquille f de mer; coquillage m. **sea-'shore,** s. (a) Rivage m; bord m de la mer. (b) Plage f. **'sea-sick,** a. Qui a le mal de mer. To be s.-s., avoir le mal de mer. **'sea-sickness,** s. Mal m de mer; chanson f de mer. **'sea-song,** s. Chanson f de marin; chanson de mer. **'sea-speed,** s. Nau: Vitesse f de route. **'sea-squirt,** s. Moll: Ascidie f; outre f de mer. **'sea-trip,** s. (a) Promenade f en mer. (b) Croisière f d'agrément. **'sea-trout,** s. Ich: Truite saumonée. **'sea-urchin,** s. Echin: Oursin m; hérisson m de mer. **'sea-voyage,** s. Voyage m par mer; traversée f. **'sea-'wall,** s. Digue f. **'sea-washed,** a. Baigné par la mer. **'sea-water,** s. Eau f de mer. **'sea-way,** s. Nau: 1. Route f, sillage m (d'un navire). 2. Mer dure. Boat stiff in a sea-way, bateau dur à la mer. Ship that behaves well in a sea-way, vaisseau qui tient bien à la mer. **'sea-wife,** s. Ich: Vieille f. **'sea-wind,** s. Vent m de mer, du large. **'sea-wolf,** s. 1. Ich: Bar(s) m. 2. A: (a) = SEA-ROVER. (b) Viking m. **'sea-wrack,** s. Varech m.

seaboard ['si:bɔ:rd], s. Littoral m; rivage m (de la mer). Seaboard town, ville maritime.

seafarer ['si:fɛərər], s. (a) Homme m de mer; marin m. (b) She had been a great s., elle avait fait de nombreux voyages sur mer.

seafaring[1] ['si:fɛəriŋ], a. (Gens, etc.) de mer, qui naviguent. Seafaring man (officer or seaman), marin m.

seafaring[2], s. Voyages mpl par mer.

seal[1] [si:l], s. 1. Z: Phoque m; F: veau marin. Seal-oil, huile f de phoque. Seal-fishery, (i) pêche f des phoques; (ii) pêcherie f de phoques. 2. Com: Con(e)y seal, fourrure f genre loutre. 3. Leath: Phoque (pour gainerie). Cf. SEALSKIN.

seal[2], s. 1. (a) Sceau m; (on letter) cachet m. To break the s. of a letter, rompre le cachet d'une lettre. Given under my hand and seal, signé et scellé par moi. Under the seal of secrecy, sous le sceau du secret. To put one's seal to a document, marquer un document de son sceau. F: To set one's seal to sth., autoriser qch.; donner son approbation à qch. Book that bears the seal of genius, livre qui porte le sceau, le cachet, du génie. (b) Com: Cachet (de bouteille de vin, etc.). Jur: Official seal (affixed to property, etc.), scellé m. To affix, remove, the seals, apposer, lever, les scellés. Com: Leaden seal, plomb m (pour sceller une caisse). Custom-house seal, plomb de la douane. 2. (Instrument) Sceau, cachet. The

Great Seal, le grand sceau (employé pour les actes publics). 3. Tchn: (a) Dispositif m d'étanchéité; joint m étanche; tampon m. (b) (Liquide) obturateur m (d'un siphon). **'seal-ring,** s. Chevalière f.

seal[3], v.tr. 1. (a) Sceller (un acte); cacheter (une lettre). F: His fate is sealed, son sort est réglé c'en est fait de lui. (b) Cacheter (une bouteille de porto, etc.); plomber (un colis). Jur: Apposer les scellés sur (une porte, un meuble). 2. (a) To seal (up) a letter, fermer une lettre (b) To seal up the windows, fermer hermétiquement les fenêtres. (c) F: My lips are sealed, m'est défendu de parler. (d) Assurer l'étanchéité (d'un joint, etc.). To s. a puncture, boucher u trou (dans un pneu). **'sealing-wax,** s. Cire à cacheter.

sealer ['si:lər], s. 1. Navire armé pour la chass des phoques. 2. Chasseur m, pêcheur m, d phoques.

sealery ['si:ləri], s. Pêcherie f de phoques.

sealskin ['si:lskin], s. 1. Peau f de phoque 2. Com: (Fourrure f en) loutre f.

seam[1] [si:m], s. 1. (a) Couture f. Flat seam couture rabattue. Overcast seam, surjet m (b) (In metal pipe, etc.) Couture, joint m. Braze seam, brasure f. Welded seam, soldered seam joint soudé; soudure f. (c) Ship's seams, couture d'un navire. Lapped seam, couture à clin 2. (a) (On face, etc.) Cicatrice f, couture, balafre (b) (In wood, rock) Fissure f, gerçure f. 3. (a) Geol Ligne f de séparation (des couches). (b) Min Couche f, gisement m, gîte m, veine f.

seam[2], v.tr. 1. To seam up a garment, assemble un vêtement. 2. Couturer; marquer (un visage de cicatrices, (un rocher, etc.) de fissures.

seaman, pl. **-men** ['si:mən, -men], s.m. 1. Marin matelot. Navy: Matelot de l'État. Ordinar seaman, matelot de troisième classe; de pont Able(-bodied) seaman, F: A.B., gabier breveté matelot de deuxième classe. Leading seaman matelot (breveté) de première classe; quartier maître. 2. (a) Manœuvrier. (b) Navigateur. good s., un bon manœuvrier ou un bon navigateur

seamanlike ['si:mənlaik]. 1. a. De marin, d'u bon marin. 2. adv. En bon marin.

seamanship ['si:mənʃip], s. Manœuvre f e matelotage m; la manœuvre.

seamew ['si:mju:], s. Orn: = GULL[1].

seamless ['si:mləs], a. 1. Sans couture. 2. San soudure.

seamstress ['semstres], s.f. Ouvrière couturière

seamy ['si:mi], a. Qui montre les coutures F: The seamy side of life, l'envers m, les des sous m, de la vie.

séance ['seɔ:s], s. Séance f de spiritisme.

seaplane ['si:plein], s. Av: Hydravion m. Boa seaplane, avion m monocoque. Seaplane base hydroaéroport m.

seaport ['si:pɔ:rt], s. Port m de mer.

sear[1] [si:ər], s. Sm.a: Gâchette f (de fusil).

sear[2], v.tr. 1. (Of heat, frost) Flétrir, dessèche (les feuilles, le grain); faner (les feuilles) 2. (a) Cautériser (une blessure). F: Endurci (la conscience); dessécher (le cœur). (b) Mar quer au fer rouge. **'searing-iron,** s. Fer r à cautériser; cautère (actuel).

sear[3], a. = SERE.

search[1] [sɔ:rtʃ], s. 1. Recherche(s) f(pl). T make a search, faire des recherches. To make s. for s.o., (re)chercher qn. In search of ..., la recherche de. . . . 2. (a) Cust: Visite Right of search, droit de visite; (at sea) dro de recherche. (b) *Jur:* Perquisition *f.* **House-search**, visite domiciliaire ; perquisition à domicile. **Search warrant**, mandat *m* de perquisition. **'search-party**, *s.* Expédition *f* de secours. **'search-room**, *s.* (*At Record Office*) Salle *f* du public ; salle de travail. **earch².** **I.** *v.tr.* Inspecter (un endroit) ; chercher dans (un endroit, une boîte) ; fouiller dans (un tiroir) ; fouiller (un suspect, les poches de qn) ; scruter, sonder (un visage). *Cust:* **To search a ship,** s.o.'s trunks, visiter un vaisseau, les malles de qn. *Jur:* **To search a house,** faire une visite domiciliaire ; perquisitionner dans une maison. *Surg:* **To search a wound,** sonder une plaie. **To search men's hearts,** scruter, sonder, les cœurs. **2.** *v.i.* **To search into** *the cause of sth.*, rechercher la cause de qch. *To s. after truth,* rechercher la vérité. **To search for** *sth.,* (re)chercher qch. **searching,** *a.* (Examen) minutieux, attentif ; (regard) pénétrant, scrutateur ; (vent) pénétrant. **To give** s.o. a **searching look,** scruter qn du regard. *S. questions,* questions qui vont au fond des choses. **-ly,** *adv.* (Examiner, etc.) minutieusement ; (regarder qn, etc.) d'un œil scrutateur, pénétrant. **earcher** ['sǝ:rtʃǝr], *s.* **I.** (*a*) Chercheur, -euse, rechercheur, -euse (*after,* de). (*b*) *Cust:* Douanier *m* ; visiteur *m.* (*c*) *Jur:* Perquisiteur *m,* perquisitionneur *m.* **2.** *Surg:* Sonde *f.* **earchlight** ['sǝ:rtʃlait], *s.* (*a*) Projecteur *m. Armoured s.,* phare cuirassé. (*b*) (*Beam*) Projection *f* électrique. *To flash a s. on sth.,* donner un coup de projecteur sur qch. **eascape** ['si:skeip], *s.* *Art:* Marine *f.* **easide** [si:'said], *s.* **I.** Bord *m* de la mer. **2.** *Attrib.* ['si:said] **Seaside resort,** station *f* balnéaire ; plage *f* ; bains *mpl* de mer. **eason¹** ['si:z(ǝ)n], *s.* **I.** Saison *f.* (*a*) *The rainy s.,* la saison des pluies. **Late season,** arrière-saison *f.* **Holiday season, hunting season, season** des vacances, de la chasse. *Ven:* **Close season, open season,** chasse (ou pêche) fermée, ouverte. **The dull season, the dead season, the off season,** la morte-saison. **The busy season,** le fort de la saison. **Between-season,** demi-saison *f.* (*Of oysters, etc.*) **To be in season,** être de saison. *Com:* **To have a good season,** faire une bonne campagne. (*b*) **The** (**London**) **season,** la saison (où la haute société se trouve à Londres). *The s. is at its height,* la saison bat son plein. **2.** Période *f* temps *m. A s. of peace,* une période de tranquillité. **To last for a season,** durer pendant quelque temps. *It shall be done in due season,* cela se fera en temps voulu. **Word in season,** mot dit à propos. **Remark out of season,** remarque déplacée. **In season and out of season, in and out of season,** à tout propos et hors de propos ; à tout bout de champ. **3.** *F:* = SEASON-TICKET. **'(Season) all seasons, please!" "les abonnements,** s'il vous plaît !" **'season-'ticket,** *s.* Carte *f* d'abonnement. **Season-ticket holder,** abonné, -ée. **eason².** **I.** *v.tr.* (*a*) Assaisonner, relever (un mets). *F: Speech seasoned with irony,* discours assaisonné d'ironie. (*b*) Dessécher, étuver, conditionner (le bois) ; mûrir, laisser se faire (le vin). (*c*) Acclimater ; endurcir (qn) ; aguerrir (un soldat) ; amariner (un matelot). (*d*) *F:* Tempérer, modérer. *Justice seasoned with goodwill,* justice tempérée de bienveillance. **2.** *v.i.* (*Of wood, etc.*) Sécher ; (*of wine, etc.*) mûrir, se faire. **seasoned,** *a.* **I.** Assaisonné. **Highly s.** *dish,* plat de haut goût. **Highly seasoned anecdote,** anecdote relevée, épicée. **2.** (*a*) (*Of wood, cigar*) Sec, *f.* sèche ; (*of wine*) mûr, fait. (*b*) **To grow,**

become, **seasoned,** (*of soldier*) s'aguerrir, (*of sailor*) s'amariner. **seasoning,** *s.* **I.** (*a*) *Cu:* Assaisonnement *m.* (*b*) Séchage *m* ; maturation *f.* (*c*) Acclimatement *m* ; aguerrissement *m.* **2.** *Cu:* Assaisonnement, condiment *m.* **seasonable** ['si:z(ǝ)nǝbl], *a.* **I.** De (la) saison. *S. weather,* temps de saison. **2.** (*Of aid, advice*) Opportun, à propos. **-ably,** *adv.* Opportunément, à propos. **seasonableness** ['si:z(ǝ)nǝblnǝs], *s.* (*Of remark, etc.*) Opportunité *f.* **seasonal** ['si:z(ǝ)nǝl], *a.* (Changements, etc.) des saisons ; (commerce) saisonnier, qui dépend de la saison. **seat¹** [si:t], *s.* **I.** (*a*) Siège *m* ; banquette *f* (d'autobus, etc.) ; gradin *m* (d'amphithéâtre) ; selle *f* (de bicyclette) ; lunette *f* (de water-closet). **Driver's seat,** siège de cocher, de conducteur. **Folding seat,** pliant *m.* **Flap-seat, bracket-seat,** strapontin *m.* (*b*) **To take a seat,** s'asseoir. **To keep one's seat,** rester assis ; rester à sa place. (*c*) Place *f.* *Car with four seats,* voiture à quatre places. *Th: S. in the stalls,* fauteuil *m* d'orchestre. *I want two seats,* il me faut deux places assises. *Rail:* 'Take your seats!' "en voiture !" (*d*) *He has a s. in the House,* il siège au Parlement. *To vacate one's s.,* se démettre. **2.** (*a*) Siège, fond *m* (d'une chaise). *Rush s.,* siège en paille. (*b*) *F:* Postérieur *m,* derrière *m. He came down on his s.,* il s'est assis par terre. (*c*) Fond (de culotte). **3.** (*a*) Théâtre *m* (de la guerre) ; siège, centre *m* (du gouvernement, etc.) ; foyer *m* (d'une maladie, etc.). (*b*) **Country-seat,** château *m* ; maison *f* de campagne. **4.** *Equit:* Assiette *f,* assise *f.* **To keep one's seat,** conserver l'assiette. **To lose one's seat,** être désarçonné. (*Of rider*) **To have a good seat,** bien se tenir en selle ; avoir de l'assiette. **5.** *Tchn:* Siège (d'une soupape) ; chaise *f* (d'un coussinet) ; embase *f,* assiette, surface *f* d'appui (d'une machine). **'seat-box,** *s. Veh:* Caisson *m.* **'seat-holder,** *s. Th: etc:* Abonné, -ée. **'seat-stick,** *s.* Canne-siège *f.* **seat²,** *v.tr.* **I.** (Faire) asseoir (un enfant, etc.). **To seat oneself,** s'asseoir. **To ask, beg,** s.o. **to be seated,** faire asseoir qn. **Pray be seated,** donnez-vous la peine de vous asseoir. *To remain seated,* rester assis. *S.a.* DEEP-SEATED. **2.** (*a*) Placer (qn) ; trouver place pour (qn). (*b*) (*Of car, etc.*) **To seat six persons,** à six places (assises). *This table seats twelve,* on tient douze à cette table. **3.** (Re)-mettre le siège à (une chaise). **4.** *Hall seated to hold a thousand,* salle avec places assises pour mille personnes. **5.** (*a*) Asseoir, poser (une machine, etc.). *Mec.E:* Faire porter, caler, (une pièce) sur son siège. *I.C.E:* **To seat a valve,** ajuster l'assise d'une soupape. (*b*) (*Of part*) **To seat on . . .,** porter, reposer, sur. . . . **6.** *The trouble is seated in . . .,* le mal a son siège dans. . . . **seating,** *s.* **I.** (*a*) Allocation *f* des places. *The s. of the guests,* la disposition des invités. (*b*) Places assises ; bancs *mpl* et sièges *mpl.* **Seating capacity,** nombre *m* de places (assises). **2.** *Tchn:* Portage *m* ; ber *m,* berceau *m* (de chaudière) ; siège *m* (de soupape) ; embase *f,* lit *m* de pose (d'une machine) ; assiette *f,* logement *m.* **3.** Montage *m,* ajustage *m* (d'une pièce). **-seater** ['si:tǝr], *s. Aut:* **Two-seater,** voiture *f* à deux places. *Av:* **Single-seater, two-seater,** appareil *m* monoplace, biplace. **seaward** ['si:wǝrd]. **I.** *adv.* = SEAWARDS. **2.** *a.* (*a*) (*Of tide*) Qui porte au large. (*b*) **Seaward breeze,** brise du large. **3.** *s.* **To seaward,** vers le large.

seawards ['siːwərdz], *adv.* Vers la mer ; vers le large.

seaweed ['siːwiːd], *s.* Algue *f*, goémon *m.* *Agr :* Varech *m.*

seaworthiness ['siːwəːrðinəs], *s.* Bon état de navigabilité (d'un navire).

seaworthy ['siːwəːrði], *a.* (*Of ship*) En (bon) état de navigabilité ; capable de tenir la mer.

sebaceous [si'beiʃəs], *a.* (*Of gland*) Sébacé.

sec [sek], *s. P :* (= SECOND¹) Half a sec! attendez un instant !

secant ['sekənt, 'siːk-]. *Mth :* 1. *a.* Sécant. 2. *s.* Sécante *f.*

seccotine ['sekotiːn], *s.* (Colle forte de la marque) seccotine *f.*

secede [si'siːd], *v.i.* Faire scission, faire sécession (*from*, de) ; se séparer (d'un parti). **seceding**, *a.* Sécessionniste, scissionnaire.

seceder [si'siːdər], *s. Pol : etc :* Sécessionniste *m* ; scissionnaire *m. Rel :* Dissident *m.*

secession [si'seʃ(ə)n], *s.* Sécession *f* ; scission *f.*

seclude [si'kluːd], *v.tr.* Tenir (qn, qch.) retiré, éloigné, écarté (*from*, de). *To s. oneself from society*, se retirer du monde. **secluded**, *a.* (Endroit) écarté, retiré. *S. life*, vie retirée, cloîtrée.

seclusion [si'kluːʒ(ə)n], *s.* Solitude *f*, retraite *f.* *In seclusion*, retiré du monde. *To live in s.*, vivre retiré ; vivre dans la retraite.

second¹ ['sekənd], *s.* 1. Seconde *f* (de temps). *F : I'll be back in a s.*, je reviens dans un instant. *Timed to a split second*, chronométré à une fraction de seconde près. *F :* In a split second, en un rien de temps. 2. Seconde (de degré). **'second(s)-hand**¹, *s.* Aiguille *f* des secondes ; trotteuse *f.*

second². I. *a.* 1. Second, deuxième. (*a*) *Twenty-s.*, vingt-deuxième. *The s. of January*, le deux janvier. *To live on the second floor*, habiter au deuxième (étage) ; *U.S :* habiter au premier. **Charles the Second**, Charles Deux. *Every second day*, tous les deux jours. *S. marriage*, secondes noces. *Aut :* Second speed, deuxième vitesse. *s. F :* Silent second, prise silencieuse en deuxième. *S.a.* COUSIN. (*b*) **The second largest city in the world**, la plus grande ville du monde sauf une. **To travel second class**, voyager en deuxième classe, en seconde. *In intelligence he is second to none*, pour l'intelligence il ne le cède à personne. **To be second in command**, commander en second. 2. Second ; autre ; nouveau. *A s. Attila*, un nouvel Attila ; un second Attila. **Second nature**, seconde nature. **-ly**, *adv.* Deuxièmement ; en second lieu. II. **second**, *s.* 1. (Le) second, (la) seconde ; (le, la) deuxième. *To come in a good second (to so-and-so)*, arriver bon second (derrière un tel). 2. *Mus :* Major second, seconde majeure. 3. *pl. Com :* Seconds, articles m de deuxième qualité ; *Mill :* griot *m.* 4. (*a*) (*In duel*) Témoin *m.* (*b*) *Box :* Second *m* ; soigneur *m.* **'second-best**. 1. *a.* My s.-b. suit, mon complet numéro deux. *s.* It's a second-best, c'est un pis-aller. 2. *adv. F :* To come off 'second-'best, être battu ; *P :* écoper. **'second-class**, *a.* (Voyageur, wagon) de seconde classe, de seconde ; (marchandises) de deuxième qualité ; (hôtel) de second ordre. **second-'hand**². 1. *Adv.phr.* To buy sth. (at) second hand, acheter qch. de seconde main. 2. *a.* 'Second-hand, (nouvelle) de seconde main ; (marchandises) d'occasion. *S.-h. car*, voiture usagée. **Second-hand dealer**, brocanteur *m. S.-h. bookshop*, librairie d'occasion. **'second-rate**, *a.* Médiocre, inférieur *f* ; de qualité inférieure. *A s.-r.*

artist, un artiste de second ordre. **'second-'sight**, *s. Psy :* Seconde vue ; clairvoyance *f.*

second³, *v.tr.* 1. (*a*) Seconder (qn) ; appuyer soutenir (des troupes, etc.). (*b*) (*In debate*) T second a motion, appuyer une proposition 2. *Mil :* [se'kɔnd] Mettre (un officier) en di ponibilité, hors cadre. *To be seconded for servi with . . .*, être détaché auprès de. . . .

secondary ['sekəndəri], *a.* 1. Secondaire. . meaning of a word, sens dérivé d'un mo *S.a.* SCHOOL¹ 1. *El :* S. current, courant indui secondaire. **Secondary winding**, (enroulemen secondaire *m. Phil :* Secondary causes, cause secondes. 2. (Rôle, etc.) peu important, de pe d'importance. **Secondary road** = route départe mentale.

seconder ['sekəndər], *s.* (*a*) *To be the s. of proposal*, appuyer une proposition. (*b*) Propose and seconder (*of a candidate*), parrain m e deuxième parrain.

secrecy ['siːkrəsi], *s.* 1. Discrétion *f. To tell s.. sth. under pledge of secrecy*, dire qch. à qn sou le secret. 2. **In secrecy**, en secret. *There is no about it*, on n'en fait pas mystère.

secret ['siːkret]. 1. *a.* Secret, -ète ; cach **To keep sth. secret**, tenir qch. secret ; garder secret au sujet de qch. **The Secret Service**, le agents secrets du gouvernement. Secret doo porte dérobée. **The secret places of the hear** les replis *m* du cœur. (*b*) (*Of pers.*) Discret ; pe communicatif. (*c*) (*Of place*) Secret, caché, retir 2. *s.* (*a*) Secret *m. He can't keep a s.*, il ne pe pas garder le secret. *To tell each other secret* se faire les confidences *f.* **I make no secret of** je n'en fais pas mystère. **To let s.o. into th** secret, mettre qn dans le secret. **To be in the** secret, être dans le secret. **Open secret**, *F :* secr de Polichinelle. **To tell sth. as a secret**, dire qc en confidence. *As a great s.*, en grand secre (*b*) = SECRECY 2. **In secret**, en secret. **-ly**, *ad* Secrètement ; en secret, en cachette.

secretaire [sekri'tɛər], *s. Furn :* Secrétaire *m.*

secretarial [sekri'tɛəriəl], *a.* (Travail) de secr taire.

secretariat [sekri'tɛəriət], *s.* Secrétariat *m.*

secretary ['sekritəri], *s.* (*a*) Secrétaire m, occ. **Private secretary**, secrétaire particulier. (*b*) Secr tary of State, ministre *m* (à portefeuille). (*c*) Leg tion secretary, chancelier *m* de légatio *S.a.* FOREIGN 2, HOME III. 2. **'secretary-bir** *s.* Messager *m* ; serpentaire *m.*

secretaryship ['sekritəriʃip], *s.* Secrétariat m fonction *f* de secrétaire.

secrete¹ [si'kriːt], *v.tr.* (*Of gland*) Sécréter.

secrete², *v.tr.* Soustraire (qch.) à la vue ; cach *Jur :* Recéler (des objets volés).

secretion [si'kriːʃ(ə)n], *s. Physiol :* Sécrétion *f.*

secretive [si'kriːtiv, 'siːkrətiv], *a.* (*Of pers* Réservé, dissimulé ; *F :* cachottier.

secretory [si'kriːtəri], *a.* (*Of duct, etc.*) Sécréteu -trice.

sect [sekt], *s.* Secte *f.*

sectarian [sek'tɛəriən], *a. & s.* Sectaire (*m*).

sectarianism [sek'tɛəriənizm], *s.* Esprit sectaire.

section¹ ['sekʃ(ə)n], *s.* 1. Sectionnement section *f.* 2. (*a*) Tranche *f. Microscopic sectio* lame *f* mince ; lamelle *f.* (*b*) *Geom :* Con sections, sections coniques. (*c*) Coupe *f*, profil *Longitudinal section*, profil en long. *Verti* section, coupe verticale. **Machine shown** section, machine figurée en coupe. (*d*) *Civ.* *etc :* Profilé *m* (en métal). **Iron section**, fer pr filé ; profilé en fer. 3. (*a*) Section ; partie division *f* (d'une structure); tronçon *m* (de tube, etc.); compartiment *m* (d'un tiroir). *Made in sections*, démontable. *S. of a store*, rayon *m* d'un magasin. *All sections of the population*, toutes les sections de la population. (*b*) *Typ:* Section; paragraphe *m*, alinéa *m*. **Section mark** (§), paragraphe. (*c*) *Mil:* Groupe *m* de combat; escouade *f*.

section², *v.tr.* Diviser (qch.) en sections; diviser (une région) par sections; sectionner.

sectional ['sekʃənəl], *a.* **1.** (Dessin, etc.) en coupe, en profil. *Ind:* **Sectional iron,** fers profilés; profilés *mpl* en fer. **2.** En sections. **Sectional bookcase,** bibliothèque démontable.

sector ['sektər], *s.* **1.** (*a*) *Geom: Astr:* Secteur *m*. (*b*) *Mil:* Secteur. *Adm:* **Postal sector,** secteur postal. **2.** *Mec.E:* Secteur, couronne *f*. **Sector and gate,** secteur à grille. **3.** *Mth:* Compas *m* de proportion.

secular ['sekjulər], *a.* **1.** Séculier; (enseignement) laïque. *S. music,* musique profane. **The secular arm,** le bras séculier; la justice temporelle. **2.** Séculaire. (*a*) Qui a lieu tous les siècles. (*b*) Très ancien.

secularization [sekjulərai'zeiʃ(ə)n], *s.* Sécularisation *f*; désaffectation *f* (d'une église); laïcisation *f* (d'une école).

secularize ['sekjuləra:iz], *v.tr.* Séculariser; laïciser (une école). *Secularized church,* église désaffectée.

secure¹ [si'kjuər], *a.* **1.** Sûr; (avenir) assuré. *S. investments,* placements sûrs, de tout repos. *To feel secure of victory,* être assuré, certain, de la victoire. **2.** En sûreté; sauf. *Now we can feel s.,* nous voilà à l'abri, hors de danger. **Secure from, against, attack,** à l'abri de toute attaque. **3.** (*Of plank, etc.*) Fixé, assujetti; (*of foundations*) solide; (*of foothold*) ferme, sûr. **To make a plank secure,** assujettir une planche. **-ly,** *adv.* **1.** (*a*) Sûrement; avec sécurité. (*b*) Avec confiance. **2.** Fermement, solidement.

secure², *v.tr.* **1.** (*a*) Mettre en sûreté, à l'abri. **To secure s.o. from sth.,** garantir qn de qch. *To s. a pass,* garder un défilé. (*b*) Mettre (un prisonnier) en lieu sûr. **2.** Immobiliser; assujettir (qch. qui a du jeu); fixer, retenir (qch. à sa place). **To secure the door,** verrouiller la porte. *Nau:* **To secure the boats,** saisir les canots. **3.** *Jur:* Nantir (un prêteur). *Secured by pledges,* nanti de gages. **To secure a debt by mortgage,** garantir une créance par une hypothèque; hypothéquer une créance. **4.** Obtenir, acquérir; se procurer (qch.). *He has secured a good seat,* il s'est assuré une bonne place. *To s. a room (in an hotel),* retenir une chambre. *To s. acceptance of sth.,* faire accepter qch. **To secure s.o.'s services,** s'assurer de l'aide de qn.

security [si'kjuəriti], *s.* **1.** (*a*) Sécurité *f*, sûreté *f*. **In security,** en (toute) sécurité. **Security device,** dispositif de sûreté. (*b*) Solidité *f* (d'une ceinture, etc.). **2.** (Moyen *m* de) sécurité; sauvegarde *f*. **3.** *Com: Jur:* (*a*) Caution *f*, cautionnement *m*; (*collateral*) nantissement *m*. *S. for a debt,* garantie d'une créance. **To give sth. as (a) security,** donner qch. en gage. *To pay in a sum as a s.,* verser une provision; verser une somme par provision. *To lodge stock as additional s.,* déposer des titres en nantissement. **To lend money on security,** prêter de l'argent sur nantissement, sur gage. **Without security,** à découvert; sans couverture, sans garantie. (*b*) (*Pers.*) (Donneur *m* de) caution; garant *m*. *Jur:* Répondant *m*. **To stand security for s.o.,** se porter caution, se porter garant, pour qn.

(*c*) *pl.* **Securities,** titres *m*, valeurs *f*. *Government securities,* fonds d'État; fonds publics. *Registered securities,* titres nominatifs. *Transferable securities,* valeurs mobilières.

sedan [si'dan], *s.* **1.** = SEDAN-CHAIR. **2.** *Aut: U.S:* Voiture *f* à conduite intérieure. **se'dan-'chair,** *s. A:* Chaise *f* à porteurs.

sedate [si'deit], *a.* (*Of pers.*) Posé, reposé; (maintien) composé; (esprit) rassis. **-ly,** *adv.* Posément. *To step s. forward,* s'avancer à pas posés.

sedative ['sedətiv], *a. & s. Med:* Sédatif (*m*); calmant (*m*).

sedentary ['sedəntəri], *a.* (*a*) (*Of statue, posture*) Assis. (*b*) (Emploi, etc.) sédentaire.

sedge [sedʒ], *s. Bot:* L.-îche *f*. **Sweet sedge,** souchet odorant. (*b*) *F:* Joncs *mpl*, roseaux *mpl*. **'sedge-warbler,** *s. Orn:* Fauvette *f* des roseaux; rousserolle *f*.

sediment ['sedimənt], *s.* Sédiment *m*, dépôt *m*; boue *f* (d'un accu, d'un encrier); lie *f* (du vin). *S. in a boiler,* vidange(s) *f(pl)* d'une chaudière.

sedimentary [sedi'mentəri], *a. Geol:* (Couche) sédimentaire.

sedition [si'diʃ(ə)n], *s.* Sédition *f*.

seditious [si'diʃəs], *a.* Séditieux. **-ly,** *adv.* Séditieusement.

seduce [si'dju:s], *v.tr.* **1.** Séduire, corrompre (qn). *To seduce s.o. from his duty,* détourner qn de son devoir. **2.** Séduire (une femme).

seducer [si'dju:sər], *s.* Séducteur *m*.

seduction [si'dʌkʃ(ə)n], *s.* **1.** (*a*) Séduction *f*, corruption *f* (de qn). (*b*) Séduction (d'une femme). **2.** Attrait *m*, charme *m*, séduction (de qch.).

seductive [si'dʌktiv], *a.* Séduisant, attrayant. **-ly,** *adv.* D'une manière séduisante.

seductiveness [si'dʌktivnəs], *s.* Caractère séduisant (d'une offre); charmes *mpl* (d'une femme); séduction *f* (du style, etc.).

sedulous ['sedjuləs], *a.* (Travailleur) assidu, appliqué; (soin) assidu. *To be s. in doing sth.,* s'empresser à faire qch. **-ly,** *adv.* Assidûment; avec empressement.

see¹ [si:], *v.tr.* (saw [sɔ:]; seen [si:n]) **1.** Voir. (*a*) *I saw it with my own eyes,* je l'ai vu de mes (propres) yeux. **To see the sights of the town,** visiter les monuments de la ville. *There was not a house to be seen,* il n'y avait pas une maison de visible. **Nothing could be seen of him,** il restait invisible. *To see s.o. in the distance,* apercevoir qn dans le lointain. **'See page 8,' "voir page 8";** "se reporter à la page 8." **He is not fit to be seen,** il n'est pas présentable; *F:* il n'est pas voyable. (*b*) *Abs.* **As far as the eye can see,** aussi loin qu'on peut voir; à perte de vue. **It was too dark to see clearly,** il faisait trop noir pour bien distinguer. **We can't see to read,** on n'y voit pas assez clair pour lire. (*c*) **To see s.o. do sth.,** voir faire qch. à qn; voir qn faire qch. *I saw him fall,* je l'ai vu tomber. *He was seen to fall,* on le vit tomber. **To see s.o. coming,** voir venir qn. *I saw him taking the apples,* je l'ai vu qui prenait les pommes. *I saw it done,* je l'ai vu faire. *F:* **I'll see him damned first!** qu'il aille au diable! (*d*) **To see s.o. home,** reconduire qn jusque chez lui. *I'll see you to the door,* je vais vous accompagner jusqu'à la porte. (*e*) **He has seen a good deal of the world,** il connaît bien la vie. *F:* **He will never see forty again,** il a quarante ans sonnés. **2.** (*a*) Comprendre, saisir (une pensée); reconnaître (ses erreurs). **I don't see the point,** je ne saisis pas la nuance. **He cannot see a joke,** il n'entend pas la plaisanterie. **As far as I can see . . . ,** à ce que je vois . . . ; autant que j'en puis juger. . . . *I see what you are driving at,* je vois où vous voulez en venir. **I see!** je comprends! **You see . . .,** vous comprenez . . .; voyez-vous. . . . *(b)* Observer, remarquer (qch.); s'apercevoir de (qch.). *I see that it is time to go,* je m'aperçois qu'il est temps de partir. **See for yourself,** voyez par vous-même. **I can see no fault in him,** je ne lui connais pas de défaut. **I don't know what you can see in her,** je ne sais pas ce que vous pouvez trouver en elle. *S.a.* REMAIN² 1. *(c)* Voir, juger, apprécier (qch. d'une manière quelconque). **This is how I see it,** voici comment j'envisage la chose. *To see things wrong,* juger de travers. **If you see fit to . . .,** si vous jugez convenable, si vous trouvez bon, de. . . . **3.** Examiner (qch.); regarder (qch.) avec attention. *Let me see that letter again,* repassez-moi cette lettre (que je la relise). **See if this hat suits you,** voyez si ce chapeau vous va. *Abs.* **I'll go and see,** je vais y aller voir. **Let me see, (i)** attendez un peu; **(ii)** faites voir! **4. To see (to it) that** *everything is in order,* s'assurer que tout est en ordre. *See that he has all he needs,* ayez soin qu'il ait tout ce qu'il lui faut; voyez à ce qu'il ne manque de rien. *See that he comes in time,* faites en sorte qu'il arrive à temps. **I will see you righted,** je veillerai à ce qu'on vous fasse justice. **5.** *(a)* Fréquenter, avoir des rapports avec (qn). *He sees a great deal of the Smiths,* il fréquente beaucoup les Smith. *We see less of him in winter,* nous le voyons moins l'hiver. **I shall see you again soon,** à bientôt. *F:* **See you on Thursday!** à jeudi! *(b)* **To go and see s.o.,** aller trouver qn. **To call to see s.o.,** faire une visite à qn; passer chez qn. *I wanted to see you on business,* je voulais vous parler d'affaires. **To see the doctor,** consulter le médecin. *(c)* Recevoir (un visiteur). **see about,** *v.ind.tr.* S'occuper de (qch.); se charger de (qch.). **I'll see about it,** (i) je m'en occuperai; (ii) j'y réfléchirai. **see after,** *v.ind.tr.* = SEE TO. **see in,** *v.tr.* Voir arriver (une nouvelle époque, etc.). *S.a.* NEW YEAR. **see into,** *v.ind.tr.* **1.** Voir dans (l'avenir); pénétrer (les motifs de qn). **2. We must see into this,** il faudra examiner cette affaire à fond. **see off,** *v.tr.* **To see s.o. off (at the station),** accompagner qn jusqu'à la gare (pour lui dire adieu). **see out,** *v.tr.* **1.** Accompagner (qn) jusqu'à la porte; reconduire (qn). **2.** Assister à (un opéra, etc.) jusqu'au bout; voir la fin de (qch.). *S.a.* YEAR. **see through,** **1.** *v.i.* *(a)* Voir à travers (qch.). *(b)* *F:* Pénétrer les intentions de (qn); voir clair dans l'esprit de (qn); pénétrer (un mystère). *Tricks easily seen through,* finesses cousues de fil blanc. **2.** *v.tr.* **To see s.o. safely through,** soutenir qn jusqu'au bout. *He saw the operation through without wincing,* il assista à l'opération sans broncher. *To see a business through,* mener une affaire à bonne fin. *F:* **To see it through,** tenir jusqu'au bout. **see to,** *v.ind.tr.* S'occuper de (qn, qch.); veiller à (qch.). *To see to the house,* vaquer aux soins du ménage. **To see to everything,** avoir l'œil à tout. *It must be seen to,* il faut y aviser. **seeing¹. 1.** *a.* Voyant; qui voit. **2.** *Conj.phr.* **Seeing (that) . . .,** puisque . . ., attendu que . . ., vu que. . . . **seeing²,** *s.* Vue *f*; vision *f.* **Seeing is believing,** voir c'est croire. **It is worth seeing,** cela vaut la peine d'être vu. *Seeing distance,* portée *f* de la vue. **see²,** *s.* *Ecc:* Siège épiscopal; *(of bishop)* évêché *m*; *(of archbishop)* archevêché *m*, métropole *f.* **The Holy See,** le Saint-Siège.

seed¹ [si:d], *s.* **1.** *(a)* Graine *f. Tomato seeds,* graines de tomates. *Seeds of an apple, of a grape,*

pépins *m* d'une pomme, d'un grain de raisin. *F:* **The seeds of discord,** les germes *m* de discorde. *(b)* *Coll.* Semence *f*; graine(s). **Lawn seed,** graine pour gazon. **To go, run, to seed,** monter en graine; *(of land)* s'afficher. *(c)* Frai *m* (d'huître). **2.** *B. & Lit:* Descendance *f*, lignée *f.* **'seed-bed,** *s.* Couche *f* de semis. *For:* Semis *m*, pépinière *f.* **'seed-cake,** *s.* *Cu:* Gâteau au carvi ou à l'anis. **'seed-corn,** *s.* *Agr:* Grain *m* de semence. **'seed-drill,** *s.* *Agr:* Semoir *m.* **'seed-hole,** *s.* Poquet *m.* **'seed-oysters,** *s.pl.* Naissain *m.* **'seed-pearls,** *s.pl.* Semence *f* de perles. **'seed-po'tatoes,** *s.pl.* Pommes *f* de terre à semence. **'seed-shop,** *s.* Graineterie *f.* **'seed-time,** *s.* (Époque *f* des) semailles *f*; la semaison.

seed², **1.** *v.i.* *(Of plant)* *(a)* Monter en graine; porter semence. *(b)* *(Of cereals)* Grener; venir à graine. *(c)* S'égrener. **2.** *v.tr.* *(a)* Ensemencer, semer (un champ). *(b)* Enlever la graine (d'un fruit); épépiner (un concombre, etc.). **'seeding machine,** *s.* *Agr:* Semoir *m* mécanique. **seeder** ['si:dər], *s.* *Agr:* Semoir *m.* **seedling** ['si:dliŋ], *s.* *Hort:* (Jeune) plant *m*; élève *f.* *Arb:* Sauvageon *m.* **seedsman,** *pl.* **-men** ['si:dzmən, -men], *s.m.* Grainetier. **seedy** ['si:di], *a.* **1.** Monté en graine. **2.** *F:* (Vêtement) râpé, usé, *F:* miteux. *Seedy-looking individuals,* individus d'aspect minable. **3.** *(Of pers.)* Mal en train; *F:* patraque. **seek** [si:k], *v.tr.* (sought [sɔ:t]; sought) **1.** Chercher (un objet perdu); rechercher, quêter (de l'avancement, etc.). *To go and s. s.o.,* aller à la recherche de qn; aller chercher qn. **To seek employment,** être en quête d'un emploi. **To seek shelter,** se réfugier (sous un arbre, etc.). **To seek death,** se faire tuer. **The reason is not far to seek,** la raison est assez claire. **2.** *(a)* **To seek sth. from, of s.o.,** demander qch. à qn. **To seek advice,** demander conseil. *(b)* **To seek to do sth.,** essayer de, chercher à, faire qch. **seek after,** *v.ind.tr.* (Re)chercher, poursuivre (la gloire, etc.). *Much sought after,* très recherché, très couru. **seek for,** *v.ind.tr.* (Re)chercher (qch.). **seek out,** *v.tr.* Chercher et trouver (qn); *F:* dénicher (qn). **seeker** ['si:kər], *s.* Chercheur, -euse. **Pleasure-seekers,** gens en quête de plaisir(s). **seem** [si:m], *v.i.* Sembler, paraître. **1.** *(a)* *To s. tired,* paraître fatigué; avoir l'air fatigué. *How does it seem to you?* que vous en semble? *It seems like a dream,* on dirait un rêve; on croirait rêver. **There seems to be some difficulty,** il semble (i) qu'il y a, (ii) qu'il y ait, quelque difficulté. *(b)* *I s. to have heard his name,* il me semble avoir entendu son nom. *P:* **I don't seem to fancy it,** je ne sais pas pourquoi, mais ça me dit rien. **2.** *Impers.* **It seems (that) . . .,** it would seem that . . ., il paraît, il semble que. . . . **It seems to me that** *you are right,* il me semble que vous avez raison; à mon avis vous avez raison. **It seemed as though, as if . . .,** il semblait que + *sub.*; on aurait dit que + *ind.* **So it seems,** à ce qu'il paraît. **It seems not,** il paraît que non. **seeming,** *a.* Apparent; soi-disant. *With s. kindness,* avec une apparence de bonté. *A s. friend,* un soi-disant ami. **-ly,** *adv.* Apparemment; en apparence. *He was s. content,* il paraissait être satisfait. **seemliness** ['si:mlinəs], *s.* **1.** Décorum *m*; bienséance *f*, convenance(s) *f(pl)* agréable. **2.** Aspect *m*

seemly ['si:mli], *a.* **1.** Convenable, bienséant. *It*

is not s. for me to go alone, il n'est pas convenable que j'aille toute seule. **2.** Agréable à voir.
seen [si:n]. *See* SEE¹.
seep [si:p], *v.i.* Suinter; s'infiltrer.
seepage ['si:pedʒ], *s.* **1.** Suintement *m*; infiltration *f.* **2.** Fuite *f*, déperdition *f* (par infiltration).
seer ['si:ər], *s.* Prophète *m.*
see-saw¹ ['si:sɔ:]. **1.** *s.* Bascule *f*, balançoire *f*, tape-cul *m.* **2.** *a.* **See-saw motion,** (i) mouvement de bascule; (ii) va-et-vient *m.*
see-saw², *v.i.* **1.** Jouer à la bascule. **2.** *(Of machine-part, etc.)* Basculer; osciller; faire la bascule.
seethe [si:ð], *v.i.* *(a)* Bouillonner. *(b)* F: *(Of crowd, etc.)* S'agiter, grouiller. **The street is seething with people,** la foule grouille dans la rue. *Country seething with discontent,* pays en effervescence. **To be seething with anger,** bouillir, bouillonner, de colère. *The seething waters,* les eaux tourmentées.
segment¹ ['segmənt], *s.* Segment *m.* *S. of an orange,* loge *f*, tranche *f*, d'une orange. *El:* **Commutator segment,** segment, lame *f*, touche *f*, du commutateur. **'segment-gear,** *s.* Secteur denté. **'segment-rack,** *s.* Crémaillère *f* du secteur denté.
segment². **1.** *v.tr.* Couper, partager, en segments; segmenter. **2.** *v.i. Biol:* Se segmenter.
segmented, *a.* Segmentaire; formé de segments; (miroir) à facettes.
segmental [seg'ment(ə)l], *a.* Segmentaire. *Arch:* **Segmental arch,** arc surbaissé.
segmentation [segmən'teiʃ(ə)n], *s.* Segmentation *f.*
segregate ['segrigeit]. **1.** *v.tr.* Isoler, mettre à part (qch.). *To s. the sexes,* séparer les deux sexes. **2.** *v.i.* *(a)* Se désunir *(from,* de). *(b)* Se grouper à part *(from,* de).
segregation [segri'geiʃ(ə)n], *s.* Ségrégation *f*; séparation *f*, isolement *m.*
Seidlitz ['sedlits]. *Pr.n. Pharm:* **Seidlitz powder,** sel *m* de Sedlitz.
seigniory ['seinjəri], *s. Hist:* Seigneurie *f.*
seignorial [sei'njɔ:riəl], *a.* Seigneurial, -aux.
seine [sein], *s. Fish:* Seine *f*, senne *f.*
seise [si:z], *v.tr. Jur:* To seise s.o. of, with, an estate, mettre qn en possession d'un bien. **To be, stand, seised of a property,** posséder une propriété de droit.
seism [saizm], *s.* Séisme *m*; tremblement *m* de terre.
seismic ['saizmik], *a.* Séismique, sismique.
seismograph ['saizmogrɑ:f, -graf], *s.* Sismographe *m.*
seismology [saiz'molodʒi], *s.* Sismologie *f.*
seize [si:z]. **I.** *v.tr.* **1.** *Jur:* = SEISE. **2.** *(a)* *Jur:* Confisquer, saisir (qch.); opérer la saisie de (qch.). *To s. goods (in transit),* faire arrêt sur des marchandises. *(b)* **To seize s.o.,** appréhender qn (au corps). **3.** *(a)* Se saisir, s'emparer, de (qch.). *To s. an enemy ship,* capturer un vaisseau ennemi. *(b)* **To seize (hold of) s.o., sth.,** saisir, empoigner, s'emparer de, qn, qch. *To s. s.o. by the throat,* prendre qn à la gorge. *(c)* F: **To be seized with fear,** être saisi, frappé, d'effroi. *He was seized with a fit of rage,* il fut pris d'un accès de colère. **To be seized with a desire to do sth.,** être pris du désir de faire qch. **To seize the opportunity,** saisir l'occasion; F: prendre l'occasion aux cheveux, prendre la balle au bond. *(d)* *v.ind.tr. They seized upon the newcomer,* ils ont happé, accaparé, le nouvel arrivant. *To s. (up)on a pretext,* saisir un prétexte, se saisir d'un prétexte. **4.** *Nau:* Amarrer, faire un amarrage à, aiguilleter

(deux cordages). **II. seize,** *v.i. Mec.E: etc: (Of part)* Gripper, coincer. **To seize up,** (se) caler. **seizing,** *s.* **1.** *(a)* Saisie *f*; prise *f* (d'une forteresse); capture *f* (d'un vaisseau ennemi). *(b)* Empoignement *m.* **2.** *Nau:* Amarrage *m.* **3.** Grippage *m*, coincement *m*, calage *m* (d'un piston, etc.); blocage *m.*
seizure ['si:ʒər], *s.* **1.** *Jur:* *(a)* Appréhension *f* au corps; mainmise *f* (*of s.o.,* sur qn). *(b)* Saisie *f* (de marchandises). **2.** *Med:* (Apoplectic) seizure, attaque *f* d'apoplexie. **To have a seizure,** tomber en apoplexie.
seldom ['seldəm], *adv.* Rarement; peu souvent. *I s. see him now,* je ne le vois plus guère. **He seldom if ever goes out,** il sort rarement, pour ne pas dire jamais.
select¹ [si'lekt], *a.* **1.** Choisi. *(a)* Select passages from . . .,* morceaux choisis de. . . . *(b) Parl:* Select committee, commission d'enquête. **2.** De (premier) choix; d'élite; F: trié sur le volet. *S. club,* club très fermé; F: club select. *S. audience,* public choisi. **To be a select party,** F: être en petit comité.
select², *v.tr.* Choisir *(from,* parmi); trier (des minerais, etc.). **To select a specimen at random,** prélever un spécimen au hasard.
selection [si'lekʃ(ə)n], *s.* **1.** Choix *m*, sélection *f. Biol:* **Natural selection,** sélection naturelle. *Sp:* **Selection match,** critérium *m*, critère *m*; match *m* de sélection. **2.** *A good s. of wines,* un bon choix de vins fins. **To make a selection,** faire un choix. **Selections from Byron,** morceaux choisis de Byron. *Mus: S. from "Faust,"* fantaisie *f* sur "Faust." **Selections for the Derby,** pronostics *m* pour le Derby.
selective [si'lektiv], *a. W.Tel:* Sélectif. *Phot:* **Selective filters,** écrans sélecteurs.
selectivity [silek'tiviti], *s. W.Tel:* Sélectivité *f.*
selector [si'lektər], *s.* **1.** One of the selectors of the team, un de ceux qui choisissent l'équipe. **2.** *(a) Aut:* **Selector-rod,** baladeur *m.* *(b) W.Tel: Tp:* Sélecteur *m.*
selenite¹ ['selenait], *s. Miner:* Sélénite *f.*
Selenite² [se'li:nait], *s.* Sélénite *m*; habitant de la lune.
selenium [se'li:niəm], *s. Ch:* Sélénium *m.* **Selenium cell,** cellule au sélénium; cellule photo-résistante.
selenography [sele'nogrəfi], *s.* Sélénographie *f.*
self, *pl.* **selves** [self, selvz]. **1.** *s.* Le moi. *S. is his god,* il se fait un dieu de lui-même. **One's better self,** le meilleur côté de notre nature. **He is my second self,** c'est un autre moi-même. **He is quite his old self again,** il est complètement rétabli. *Smith became his silent s. again,* Smith rentra dans la taciturnité qui lui était propre. *Your own dear s.,* votre chère personne. **All by one's very self,** absolument tout seul. **Com: Your good selves,** vous-mêmes; vous. **2.** *pron. Com:* **Pay self, selves . . .,** payez à moi-même, à nous-mêmes. . . . **3.** *a.* **Wooden tool with self handle,** outil en bois avec manche de même. **Self carnation,** œillet de couleur uniforme. **4.** *(In compound pronouns) (a) (Emphatic)* **Myself,** moi(-même); **thyself,** toi(-même); **himself,** **herself, itself,** oneself, lui(-même), elle(-même), soi(-même); **yourself,** vous(-même); **ourselves,** nous(-mêmes); **yourselves,** vous(-mêmes); **themselves,** eux(-mêmes) *m*, elles(-mêmes) *f. I drive the car myself,* je tiens le volant moi-même. *I, myself, do not believe it,* (quant à) moi, pour ma part, je ne le crois pas. *They themselves continued to enjoy independence,* eux-mêmes continuèrent à jouir de l'indépendance. *Myself and my two*

brothers, mes deux frères et moi. *We saw John himself*, nous avons vu Jean en personne, lui-même. *I am not (quite) myself to-day*, je ne suis pas dans mon assiette aujourd'hui. *I am quite myself again*, je suis tout à fait rétabli. *She is kindness itself*, elle est la bonté même. (b) ⟨*Reflexive*⟩ **Myself**, me ; **thyself**, te ; **himself, herself, itself, oneself**, se ; **ourselves**, nous ; **yourself, -selves**, vous ; **themselves**, se. *I have hurt myself*, je me suis fait mal. *Are you enjoying yourself?* vous amusez-vous? (*Emphatic*) *Door that shuts itself*, porte qui se ferme d'elle-même. (c) (*After prep.*) *To say sth. to oneself*, (se) dire qch. à part soi. *To speak of oneself*, parler de soi. *She has to attend to herself*, elle doit pourvoir à ses propres besoins. *To look after oneself*, soigner son individu. **To keep oneself to oneself**, se tenir sur son quant-à-soi. *I am keeping it for myself*, je le garde pour moi(-même). *I am not speaking for myself*, je ne parle pas en mon nom. *He thinks for himself*, il pense de son chef. *See for yourselves*, voyez vous-mêmes. **Everyone for himself**, chacun pour soi. **To come to oneself**, revenir à soi. **The thing in itself**, la chose en elle-même. *The basin cracked ot itself*, la cuvette s'est fendue toute seule. *They came and apologized of themselves*, ils sont venus de leur propre initiative nous faire des excuses. *She lived by herself*, elle vivait seule. **To do sth. (all) by oneself**, faire qch. tout seul. (d) (*Reciprocal*) *They whispered among themselves*, ils chuchotaient entre eux. **self-a'basement**, *s.* Humiliation *f* de soi-même. **self-'acting**, *a.* (Appareil automatique, à mise en marche automatique. **self-a'pparent**, *a.* Évident ; de toute évidence. **self-a'ssertion**, *s.* Caractère impérieux ; affirmation *f* de sa volonté ; outrecuidance *f*. **self-a'ssertive**, *a.* Autoritaire ; impérieux ; outrecuidant. **self-a'ssurance**, *s.* Confiance *f* en soi ; assurance *f*; aplomb *m* ; sûreté *f* de soi(-même). **self-'centred**, *a.* Égocentrique. **'self-'colour**, *s.* **1.** Couleur uniforme. *Tex:* Self-colour material, tissu uni. **2.** Couleur naturelle. **self-co'mmand**, *s.* Maîtrise *f* de soi ; empire *m* sur soi-même. **self-co'mmunion**, *s.* Recueillement *m*. **self-com'placency**, *s.* Satisfaction *f* de soi-même ; (*of a man*) fatuité *f*. **self-com'placent**, *a.* Satisfait, content, de soi. **self-con'ceit**, *s.* Suffisance *f*, vanité *f*; infatuation *f* (de soi). *He is eaten up with self-conceit*, il est pétri d'amour-propre. **self-'confidence**, *s.* Confiance *f* en soi ; assurance *f*. *He is full of s.-c.*, il ne doute de rien. **self-'confident**, *a.* Sûr de soi ; plein d'assurance. **self-'conscious**, *a.* **1.** *Phil:* Conscient. **2.** Embarrassé, gêné ; (*of manner*) emprunté, contraint. **self-'consciousness**, *s.* **1.** *Phil:* Conscience *f*. **2.** Contrainte *f*, embarras *m*, gêne *f*. **self-con'tained**, *a.* **1.** (*Of pers.*) Peu communicatif. **2.** (Appareil) indépendant, complet par lui-même. **Self-contained flat**, appartement avec entrée particulière. **self-con'trol**, *s.* Sang-froid *m* ; empire *m* sur soi-même ; maîtrise *f* de soi. *To exercise self-control*, faire un effort sur soi-même. *To lose one's self-control*, ne plus se maîtriser. **self-de'ception**, *s.* Illusion *f*; déception *f* de soi-même. **self-de'fence**, *s.* Défense personnelle. *Jur:* Légitime défense. *The* (noble) *art of self-defence*, la boxe. **self-de'nial**, *s.* (a) Abnégation *f* de soi ; renoncement(s) *m(pl)*. (b) Frugalité *f*. **self-de'nying**, *a.* a) Qui fait abnégation de soi. (b) Frugal, -aux. **self-determi'nation**, *s.* *Right of peoples to s.-d.*, droit des peuples de disposer d'eux-mêmes.

self-'discipline, *s.* Subjugation *f* de soi-même. **self-'educated**, *a.* Autodidacte. **self-'energized**, *a.* *Aut:* (Frein) servo-moteur. **self-es'teem**, *s.* Respect *m* de soi ; amour-propre *m*. **self-'evident**, *a.* Évident en soi ; *F:* qui tombe sous les sens ; qui saute aux yeux. **self-exami'nation**, *s.* Examen *m* de conscience. **self-ex'planatory**, *a.* Qui s'explique de soi-même. **self-'feeding**, *a.* *Mec.E:* A alimentation automatique, continue. **self-fertili'zation**, *s.* *Bot:* Pollinisation directe. **self-'filling**, *a.* (Stylo) à remplissage automatique. **self-'governing**, *a.* (Colonie) autonome. **self-'government**, *s.* Autonomie *f*. **self-'heal**, *s.* *Bot:* Prunelle *f*. **self-'help**, *s.* Efforts personnels. **self-ig'nition**, *s.* *I.C.E:* Allumage spontané ; auto-allumage *m*. **self-im'portance**, *s.* Suffisance *f*, présomption *f*. **self-im'portant**, *a.* Suffisant, présomptueux, important. **self-im'posed**, *a.* (Tâche) dont on a pris de soi-même la responsabilité. **self-in'duction**, *s.* *El:* Self-induction *f*; auto-induction *f*; auto-inductance *f*. **Self-induction coil**, bobine *f* de self ; *F:* self *f*. **self-in'dulgence**, *s.* Satisfaction *f* égoïste de ses appétits. **self-in'dulgent**, *a.* Qui se dorlote ; qui ne se refuse rien. **self-in'struction**, *s.* Étude personnelle ; étude sans maître. **self-'interest**, *s.* Intérêt personnel. **self-'knowledge**, *s.* Connaissance *f* de soi. **self-'locking**, *a.* **1.** *Mec.E:* A blocage automatique. Self-looking nut, écrou indesserrable. **2.** A verrouillage automatique. **self-'love**, *s.* Égoïsme *m* ; amour *m* de soi. **self-'loving**, *a.* Égoïste. **'self-'made**, *a.* (Homme) qui est (le) fils de ses œuvres, qui est l'artisan de sa fortune, qui est arrivé par lui-même. **self-'murder**, *s.* Suicide *m*. **self-muti'lation**, *s.* Mutilation *f* volontaire. **self-o'pinionated**, *a.* Qui ne démord pas de ses opinions ; suffisant. **self-'portrait**, *s.* Portrait *m* de l'artiste par lui-même. **self-po'ssessed**, *a.* Maître de soi ; qui a beaucoup d'aplomb, de sang-froid. **self-po'ssession**, *s.* Aplomb *m*, sang-froid *m*, flegme *m*. *To lose one's self-possession*, perdre son aplomb. *To regain one's self-possession*, se ressaisir. **self-'praise**, *s.* Éloge *m* de soi-même. *Prov:* Self-praise is no recommendation, qui se loue s'emboue. **self-preser'vation**, *s.* Conservation *f* de soi-même. **self-pro'pelling**, *a.* *Veh:* Automoteur, -trice. **self-re'cording, 'registering**, *a.* (Appareil) enregistreur. **self-'reliance**, *s.* Indépendance *f*. **self-re'liant**, *a.* Indépendant. **self-re'spect**, *s.* Respect *m* de soi ; amour-propre *m*. **self-re'specting**, *a.* Qui se respecte, qui a de l'amour-propre. **self-re'straint**, *s.* Retenue *f*; modération *f*. *To exercise s.-r.*, se contenir. **self-'righteous**, *a.* Pharisaïque. **self-'righting**, *a.* (Canot) à redressement automatique ; inchavirable. **self-'sacrifice**, *s.* Abnégation *f* (de soi). **'self-'same**, *attrib. a.* Identique ; absolument le même. **self-satis'faction**, *s.* Contentement *m* de soi ; fatuité *f*, suffisance *f*. **self-'satisfied**, *a.* Content de soi ; suffisant. *S.-s. air*, air avantageux. **self-'seeking**[1], *a.* Égoïste, intéressé. **self-'seeking**[2], *s.* Égoïsme *m*. **self-'starter**, *s.* *Aut:* (Auto)démarreur *m*. **self-'styled**, *a.* Soi-disant *inv*, prétendu. **self-su'fficing**, *a.* Indépendant ; qui se suffit à soi-même. **self-su'pporting**, *a.* (*Of pers.*) Qui vit de son travail ; (*of business*) qui couvre ses frais. **self-'taught**, *a.* Autodidacte.

self-'timing, *a. Phot :* (Obturateur) comportant réglage automatique de temps de pose.

self-'toning, *a. Phot :* (Papier) auto-vireur.

self-'willed, *a.* Opiniâtre, volontaire.

selfish ['selfiʃ], *a.* Égoïste, intéressé. *To act from a s. motive,* agir dans un but intéressé. **-ly,** *adv.* Égoïstement ; en égoïste.

selfishness ['selfiʃnəs], *s.* Égoïsme *m.*

selfless ['selfləs], *a.* Désintéressé.

sell[1] [sel], *s. F :* Déception *f ; F :* attrape *f ; P :* carotte *f.*

sell[2], *v.tr.* (sold [sould] ; sold) **1.** (*a*) Vendre (*to,* à). **To sell back,** revendre. *Difficult to s.,* de vente difficile ; d'écoulement difficile. *What are you selling plums at to-day?* combien faites-vous les prunes aujourd'hui ? *He sold it me for ten shillings,* il me l'a vendu dix shillings. **To sell s.o. for a slave,** vendre qn comme esclave. (*b*) *Goods that sell easily,* marchandises qui se placent facilement, d'écoulement facile. *This book sells well,* ce livre est de bonne vente. *What are plums selling at?* combien valent les prunes ? à combien se vendent les prunes ? **Land to sell, to be sold,** terrain à vendre. **2.** (*a*) Vendre, trahir (un secret, etc.) ; trafiquer de (sa conscience). (*b*) *F :* Duper, tromper (qn). *You have been sold,* on vous a refait. *Sold again!* attrapé ! **sell off,** *v.tr.* Solder, écouler à bas prix (des marchandises) ; liquider (son écurie, etc.) ; *P :* bazarder (ses effets). **selling off,** *s.* Liquidation *f.* **sell out,** *v.tr.* (*a*) *Fin :* Réaliser (tout un portefeuille d'actions). (*b*) *Com :* Vendre tout son stock de (qch.). *The edition is sold out,* l'édition est épuisée. *We are sold out of this article,* nous sommes démunis de cet article. **sell up,** *v.tr.* Vendre, faire saisir (un failli). **selling,** *s.* Vente *f ;* écoulement *m,* placement *m* (de marchandises). **Selling price,** prix *m* de vente. *Turf :* **Selling race, plate,** course *f,* prix, à réclamer.

seller ['selər], *s.* **1.** (*a*) Vendeur, -euse. (*b*) Marchand, -ande ; débitant, -ante (*of,* de). **2.** *F :* (*Of book*) **Good seller,** livre *m* de bonne vente. *S.a.* BEST-SELLER.

seltzer ['seltsər], *s.* **Seltzer(-water),** eau *f* de seltz.

seltzogene ['seltsodʒi:n], *s.* = GASOGENE.

selvage, selvedge ['selvedʒ], *s. Tex :* Lisière *f ;* cordeau *m* (de lainages épais).

selves [selvz]. *See* SELF.

semantic [se'mantik], *a. Ling :* Sémantique.

semantics [se'mantiks], *s.pl.* = SEMASIOLOGY.

semaphore[1] ['semafɔːər], *s.* Sémaphore *m.*

semaphore[2], *v.tr.* Transmettre par sémaphore.

semasiology [semeisi'ɔlodʒi], *s. Ling :* Sémasiologie *f,* sémantique *f.*

semblance ['sembləns], *s.* Apparence *f,* semblant *m,* simulacre *m.* **To bear the semblance of** sth., ressembler à qch. **To put on a semblance** of gaiety, faire semblant d'être gai.

semester [si'mestər], *s. U.S :* Semestre *m.*

semi- ['semi], *pref.* **1.** Semi-. *Semi-historic,* semi-historique. **2.** Demi-. *Semicircle,* demi-cercle. *Semi-opaque,* demi-opaque. **3.** *Semi-civilized,* à moitié civilisé. *Semi-barbarous,* à demi barbare. *Semi-portable,* mi-fixe. **semi-'conscious,** *a.* A demi conscient. **semi-'darkness,** *s.* Pénombre *f ;* demi-jour *m.* **semi-de'tached,** *a.* **Semi-detached house,** maison jumelle ; maison faisant corps avec une autre dont elle n'est séparée que par un mur mitoyen. **semi-'final,** *s. Sp :* Demi-finale *f.* **semi-'invalid,** *s.* Demi-valétudinaire *mf.* **semi-'nude,** *a.* A moitié nu ; à demi nu. **semi-**

o'fficial, *a.* Semi-officiel ; officieux. **semi-o'paque,** *a.* Demi-opaque. **semi-'precious,** *a. Lap :* Fin. **semi-'profile,** *attrib.a.* (Portrait) de trois quarts. **semi-tran'sparent,** *a.* Semi-transparent, à demi transparent.

semibreve ['semibriːv], *s. Mus :* Ronde *f. S.a.* REST[1] 2.

semicircle ['semisəːrkl], *s.* Demi-cercle *m.*

semicircular [semi'səːrkjulər], *a.* Demi-circulaire, semi-circulaire ; en demi-cercle. *S.a.* ARCH[1] I.

semicolon ['semikoulən], *s.* Point *m* et virgule.

seminar [semi'naːr], *s. Sch :* Groupe *m* d'étudiants avancés qui se livrent à des travaux pratiques sous la direction du professeur.

seminary ['seminəri], *s.* **1.** *R.C.Ch :* Séminaire *m.* **2.** *A :* **Young ladies' seminary,** pensionnat *m* de jeunes filles.

semiquaver ['semikweivər], *s. Mus :* Double croche *f.*

Semitic [se'mitik], *a.* Sémitique.

semitone ['semitoun], *s. Mus :* Demi-ton *m.*

semivowel ['semivauəl], *s. Ling :* Semi-voyelle *f.*

semolina [semo'liːna], *s. Cu :* Semoule *f.*

sempiternal [sempi'təːrnəl], *a.* Sempiternel.

sempstress ['sem(p)stres], *s.f.* = SEAMSTRESS.

senate ['senet], *s.* Sénat *m.* (*At university*) Conseil *m* de l'université. **'senate-house,** *s.* Sénat *m.*

senator ['senətər], *s.* Sénateur *m.*

senatorial [senə'tɔːriəl], *a.* Sénatorial, -aux.

senatorship ['senətərʃip], *s.* Office *m* de sénateur.

send[1] [send], *v.tr.* (sent [sent] ; sent) **1.** (*a*) Envoyer (qn). *To s. a child to school,* envoyer, mettre, un enfant à l'école. **To send s.o. for,** after, sth., envoyer qn chercher qch. ; envoyer qn à la recherche de qch. (*b*) Envoyer, faire parvenir (qch.) ; expédier (un colis, etc.). *I am sending you by post the sum of ten pounds,* je vous fais tenir par la poste la somme de dix livres. **To send word to s.o.,** faire savoir qch. à qn. *To s. clothes to the wash,* donner du linge à blanchir. **2.** *It sent a shiver down my spine,* cela m'a fait passer un frisson dans le dos. *The blow sent him sprawling,* le coup l'envoya rouler. **3.** *God send that I may arrive in time,* Dieu veuille que j'arrive à temps. *(God)* **send him victorious,** que Dieu lui accorde la victoire. **4.** *Abs. If you don't s. I shall not come,* si vous ne me le faites pas dire je ne viendrai pas. **To send for s.o., sth.,** envoyer chercher qn, qch. **I shall send for it,** je vais l'envoyer prendre. *The doctor was sent for,* on fit venir le médecin. **send away,** *v.tr.* (*a*) Renvoyer, congédier (qn). (*b*) Expédier (qch.). **send back,** *v.tr.* Renvoyer. **send down,** *v.tr.* **I.** (*a*) Envoyer en bas ; faire descendre (qch.). (*b*) Envoyer de Londres en province. (*c*) *Sch :* (i) Expulser (un étudiant de l'université) ; (ii) renvoyer temporairement (un étudiant). **2.** *Nau :* Dégréer (une vergue). **send forth,** *v.tr.* (*a*) Répandre, exhaler (une odeur) ; lancer, jeter (des étincelles) ; émettre (des rayons). (*b*) (*Of plant*) Pousser (des feuilles). **send in,** *v.tr.* **I.** (*a*) Faire (r)entrer (qn). (*b*) *To s. in* one's card, faire passer sa carte. *To s. in one's name,* se faire annoncer. **2.** (*a*) Livrer, rendre (un compte) ; remettre (une demande). (*b*) **To send in one's resignation,** donner sa démission. **send off,** *v.tr.* (*a*) Envoyer (qn) (en mission, etc.). (*b*) Expédier (une lettre, etc.). **send-'off,** *s. F :* Démonstration *f* d'amitié (au départ de qn). **To give s.o. a good send-off,** assister en nombre au départ de qn (pour lui souhaiter bon voyage). *The press has given the play a good send-off,* la presse a été unanime à saluer de ses éloges la nouvelle pièce. **send on,** *v.tr.* (*a*) Faire suivre (une lettre). (*b*) Transmettre (un ordre). **send out,** *v.tr.* (*a*) Envoyer (qn) dehors; faire sortir (qn). (*b*) Lancer (des circulaires). (*c*) Jeter, vomir (des nuages de fumée, etc.). (*d*) Émettre (des signaux, de la chaleur). **send round,** *v.tr.* Faire circuler, faire passer (la' bouteille, etc.). **send up,** *v.tr.* **1.** (*a*) Faire monter. *To s. up a balloon,* enlever un ballon. (*b*) Envoyer de la province à Londres. **2.** *Nau:* Passer, guinder (un mât). **3.** Faire hausser (les prix, etc.). **sending,** *s.* **1.** Envoi *m*; expédition *f* (d'un colis, etc.). **2.** *W.Tel:* **Sending station,** poste émetteur, d'émission.

send², *v.i.* (sended) (*Of ship*) Tanguer fortement.

sender ['sendər], *s.* **1.** Envoyeur, -euse; expéditeur, -trice (d'une lettre). **2.** *Tg: Tp:* (*Device*) Manipulateur *m*, transmetteur *m*. **Morse sender,** clef *f* Morse.

Seneca ['seneka]. *Pr.n.m.* Sénèque.

Senegal [sene'gɔːl]. *Pr.n.* Le Sénégal.

Senegalese [senegə'liːz], *a. & s.* Sénégalais, -aise.

seneschal ['s
eneʃəl], *s. Hist:* Sénéchal *m*, -aux.

seneschalsy ['seneʃəlsi], *s. Hist:* Sénéchaussée *f*.

senile ['siːnail], *a.* Sénile.

senility [se'niliti], *s.* Sénilité *f*.

senior ['siːnjər]. **1.** *a.* (*a*) **Jones senior,** Jones aîné. **William Jones senior,** William Jones père. *He is two years s. to me,* il est mon aîné de deux ans. (*b*) **Senior in rank,** de grade supérieur. *To be s. to s.o.,* être l'ancien, le doyen, de qn. **The senior Service,** la marine. *Sch: The s. boys,* les grands (élèves); les (élèves) anciens. **Senior clerk,** premier commis, commis principal. **The senior officer,** le doyen des officiers. *My s. officer,* mon officier supérieur. *Sch:* **Senior master,** maître en premier. **2.** *s.* (*a*) Aîné, -ée; doyen, -enne (d'âge). (*b*) (Le plus) ancien, (la plus) ancienne. *To be s.o.'s s.,* être l'ancien, le doyen, de qn. *Sch:* **The seniors,** les anciens, les grands.

seniority [siːni'ɔriti], *s.* **1.** Priorité *f* d'âge; supériorité *f* d'âge. **2.** Ancienneté *f* (de grade). *To be promoted by seniority,* avancer à l'ancienneté.

senna ['sena], *s.* Séné *m*. **Senna tea,** tisane *f* de séné. **Senna pods,** follicules *m* de séné.

sensation [sen'seiʃ(ə)n], *s.* **1.** Sensation *f*; sentiment *m* (de malaise, etc.). *I had a s. of falling,* j'avais l'impression que je tombais. **2.** Sensation; effet sensationnel. **To create, make, a sensation,** faire sensation. *Book that made a s.,* livre qui a fait du fracas, du bruit.

sensational [sen'seiʃən(ə)l], *a.* Sensationnel; (roman) à sensation. **Sensational happening,** événement qui a fait sensation. *S. writer,* auteur à effets corsés.

sensationalism [sen'seiʃənəlizm], *s.* Recherche *f* du sensationnel, *F:* de l'épate.

sense¹ [sens], *s.* **1.** (*a*) Sens *m*. **The five senses,** les cinq sens. **To have a keen sense of smell, of hearing,** avoir l'odorat fin, l'ouïe fine. (*b*) Les sens. *Errors of s.,* erreurs des sens. **Sense organs,** organes des sens. **2.** *pl.* (*a*) **To be in one's senses,** être sain d'esprit. **Are you in your right senses?** avez-vous votre raison? **Any man in his senses,** tout homme jouissant de son bon sens. **Have you taken leave of your senses?** est-ce que vous perdez la tête? vous perdez la raison? **To bring s.o. to his senses,** ramener qn à la raison. **To frighten s.o. out of his senses,** effrayer qn jusqu'à lui faire perdre la raison. **To come to one's**

senses, revenir à la raison. (*b*) **To lose one's senses,** perdre connaissance. **To come to one's senses,** revenir à soi; reprendre ses sens. **3.** (*a*) Sensation *f*, sens. **A sense of pleasure,** une sensation de plaisir. *To labour under a s. of injustice,* nourrir un sentiment d'injustice. (*b*) Sentiment, conscience *f*. *S. of colour,* sentiment des couleurs. **To have a sense of time,** avoir le sentiment de l'heure. *Keen sense of humour,* sentiment très vif de l'humour. (*c*) **To take the sense of the meeting,** prendre l'opinion, le sentiment, de l'assemblée. **4.** **Bon sens,** intelligence *f*, jugement *m*. **Common sense,** bon sens, sens commun; bon sens. **To show good sense,** faire preuve de jugement. *To act against all sense,* agir en dépit du sens commun. **To talk sense,** parler raison. **There is no sense in that,** tout cela n'a pas le sens commun; cela ne rime à rien. **To have the (good) sense to** + *inf.,* avoir l'intelligence de + *inf.* **5.** Sens, signification *f* (d'un mot). *I can't make s. of this passage,* je n'arrive pas à comprendre ce passage. **In the literal sense,** au sens propre. **In the full sense of the word,** dans toute la force, l'acception, du terme. **To take a word in the wrong sense,** prendre un mot à contre-sens. **In a sense,** dans un (certain) sens; d'un certain point de vue.

sense², *v.tr.* **1.** Sentir (qch.) intuitivement; pressentir (qch.). **2.** *U.S:* *I had sensed as much,* c'est bien ce que j'avais compris.

senseless ['sensləs], *a.* **1.** (*Of pers.*) Sans connaissance; inanimé. **To fall senseless,** tomber sans connaissance. **To knock s.o. senseless,** assommer qn. **2.** Qui n'a pas le sens commun; insensé, stupide, déraisonnable. **A senseless remark,** une bêtise. **3.** Dépourvu de ses facultés, de sens; insensible. **-ly,** *adv.* Insensément, déraisonnablement, stupidement.

senselessness ['sensləsnəs], *s.* **1.** Manque *m* de bon sens; stupidité *f*. **2.** Insensibilité *f*.

sensibility [sensi'biliti], *s.* **1.** Sensibilité *f* (d'un organe, etc.). **2.** (*Emotional*) Sensibilité, émotivité *f*. *Mawkish s.,* sensiblerie *f*. **3.** *My s. of his many kindnesses,* la conscience que j'ai de tous ses bienfaits.

sensible ['sensibl], *a.* **1.** Sensible, perceptible. *S. heat,* chaleur sensible. **2.** (*Of difference, etc.*) Sensible, appréciable. **3.** Conscient (*of,* de). **To be sensible of one's danger,** se rendre compte du danger. *He became s. of a confused noise,* il eut conscience d'un bruit confus. *S. of an honour,* sensible à un honneur. **4.** Sensé, raisonnable; (choix) judicieux. *S. people,* les esprits sages. **Be sensible,** soyez raisonnable. **Sensible clothing,** vêtements pratiques. **-ibly,** *adv.* **1.** Sensiblement, perceptiblement. **2.** Sensément, raisonnablement, judicieusement. **To be sensibly dressed,** porter des vêtements pratiques.

sensitive ['sensitiv], *a.* **1.** *Bot:* **Sensitive plant,** sensitive *f*. **2.** (*a*) (*Of skin, tooth*) Sensible, sensitif. **Sensitive to sth.,** sensible à qch. (*Of pers.*) *To be s. to cold,* être frileux. (*b*) (*Of pers.*) Susceptible; impressionnable. *S. on questions of honour,* chatouilleux sur l'honneur. (*c*) **Sensitive scales,** balance sensible. *Com: Fin:* **Sensitive market,** marché prompt à réagir. *Phot:* **Sensitive plate,** plaque impressionnable. **Sensitive paper,** papier sensible, sensibilisé.

sensitiveness ['sensitivnəs], **sensitivity** [sensi'tiviti], *s.* **1.** Sensibilité *f*; faculté *f* de sentir; promptitude *f* à réagir. **2.** (*a*) Sensibilité (de caractère); susceptibilité *f*. (*b*) Sensibilité (d'une machine, etc.) (*to,* à, pour).

sensitize ['sensita:iz], *v.tr. Phot:* Sensibiliser. **sensitized**, *a.* (Papier, plaque) sensible, impressionnable. **sensitizing**, *a.* Sensibilisateur, -trice.

sensitizer ['sensitaizər], *s. Phot:* (Agent) sensibilisateur *m.*

sensory ['sensəri], *a. Physiol:* Sensoriel.

sensual ['sensjuəl,-ʃuəl], *a.* 1. Sensuel; (instinct) animal. 2. Sensuel; voluptueux. *S. enjoyment,* jouissances des sens; volupté *f.* -**ally,** *adv.* Avec sensualité; sensuellement.

sensualist ['senʃuəlist], *s.* Sensualiste *m*; jouisseur, -euse, voluptueux, -euse.

sensuality [senʃu'aliti], *s.* Sensualité *f.*

sensuous ['senʃuəs], *a.* (*Of pleasure*) Sybaritique, voluptueux; (*of charm*) capiteux. -**ly,** *adv.* Avec volupté.

sent [sent]. *See* SEND[1].

sentence[1] ['sentəns], *s.* 1. *Jur:* (*a*) Jugement *m*; sentence *f,* condamnation *f.* **Life sentence,** condamnation à vie. **Sentence of death,** arrêt *m,* sentence, de mort. *Under s. of death,* condamné à mort. **To pass** (*a*) **sentence,** prononcer une sentence. (*b*) Peine *f. While he was undergoing his s.,* pendant la durée de sa peine. 2. *Gram:* Phrase *f.*

sentence[2], *v.tr. Jur:* Condamner (qn). *To s. s.o. to a month's imprisonment, to death,* condamner qn à un mois de prison, à mort.

sententious [sen'tenʃəs], *a.* Sentencieux. -**ly,** *adv.* Sentencieusement.

sentient ['senʃjənt], *a.* Sentant, sensible.

sentiment ['sentimənt], *s.* 1. Sentiment *m.* (*a*) Mouvement *m* de l'âme. *Noble sentiments,* sentiments nobles. *My sentiments towards your sister,* mes sentiments pour (mademoiselle) votre sœur. (*b*) Opinion *f,* avis *m.* Those are my **sentiments,** voilà mon sentiment; *F:* voilà comme je pense. 2. Sentimentalité *f*; (*mawkish*) sensiblerie *f.*

sentimental [senti'ment(ə)l], *a.* (*a*) Sentimental, -aux. (*b*) D'une sensiblerie romanesque. -**ally,** *adv.* Sentimentalement.

sentimentalism [senti'mentəlizm], *s.* Sentimentalisme *m,* sensiblerie *f.*

sentimentalist [senti'mentəlist], *s.* Personne sentimentale.

sentimentality [sentimen'taliti], *s.* Sentimentalité *f,* sensiblerie *f.*

sentinel ['sentin(ə)l], *s.* (i) (*Guard*) Factionnaire *m*; (ii) (*outpost*) sentinelle *f.* **To stand sentinel,** monter la garde; être posté en sentinelle.

sentry ['sentri], *s.* 1. (*a*) (*Guard*) Factionnaire *m.* **To relieve a sentry,** relever qn de faction. (*b*) (*Outpost*) Sentinelle *f.* 2. Faction *f.* **To stand sentry; to be on sentry(-go),** faire sa faction; être en, de, faction; monter la garde. *F: To do s.-go before s.o.'s door,* faire les cent pas devant la porte de qn. **To force a sentry,** forcer la consigne. '**sentry-box,** *s. Mil:* Guérite *f.*

sepal ['sep(ə)l], *s. Bot:* Sépale *m.*

separable ['sepərəbl], *a.* Séparable (*from,* de).

separate[1] ['sepəret], *a.* (*a*) (*Of parts*) Séparé, détaché (*from,* de); *Mec.E:* (pièce) rapportée. (*b*) (*Of existence, etc.*) Distinct, indépendant; (*of room, etc.*) particulier. *Entered in a s. column,* inscrit dans une colonne à part. *S. cup for each soldier,* tasse individuelle pour chaque soldat. -**ly,** *adv.* Séparément; à part.

separate[2] ['sepəreit]. 1. *v.tr.* Séparer. (*a*) Désunir, détacher, décoller (*from,* de). *To s. truth from error,* dégager la vérité de l'erreur. *Husb:* To separate the milk, écrémer le lait. (*b*) Désunir (une famille, etc.). **He is separated from his wife**

il est séparé de sa femme. (*c*) *This river separates the two countries,* ce fleuve sépare les deux pays. 2. *v.i.* (*a*) (*Of thg*) Se séparer, se détacher, se désunir (*from,* de). (*b*) (*Of pers.*) *When we separated for the night,* quand nous nous sommes quittés pour la nuit. **To separate from s.o.,** se séparer de, rompre avec, qn. (*c*) (*Of man and wife*) Se séparer de corps et de biens.

separation [sepə'reiʃ(ə)n], *s.* 1. Séparation *f. Min:* Classement *m* (du minerai). **Separation from s.o.,** séparation d'avec qn. *Mil:* **Separation allowances,** allocations faites aux femmes (des soldats). **Judicial separation,** séparation de corps (et de biens); séparation judiciaire. **Separation order,** jugement *m* de séparation. 2. Écart *m,* distance *f.*

separator ['sepəreitər], *s.* (*Device*) Séparateur *m.* **Cream-separator,** (i) écrémeuse *f*; (ii) centrifugeur *m*; centrifugeuse *f.*

sepia ['si:pjə], *s. Art:* Sépia *f. Phot:* **Sepia paper,** papier bistre.

sepoy ['si:pɔi], *s.* Cipaye *m.*

sepsis ['sepsis], *s. Med:* (*a*) Putréfaction *f.* (*b*) Septicémie *f*; infection *f* putride.

September [sep'tembər], *s.* Septembre *m. In S.,* au mois de septembre. (*On*) *the fifth of S.,* le cinq septembre.

septennial [sep'tenjəl], *a.* Septennal, -aux. -**ally,** *adv.* Tous les sept ans.

septet(te) [sep'tet], *s. Mus:* Septuor *m.*

septic ['septik], *a. Med:* Septique. **Septic poisoning,** septicémie *f.*

septicaemia [septi'si:mia], *s.* Septicémie *f*; infection *f* putride.

septuagenarian [septjuadʒe'nɛəriən], *s. & a.* Septuagénaire (*mf*).

Septuagesima [septjua'dʒesima], *s. Ecc:* (Dimanche *f*) de la Septuagésime.

septuagint ['septjuadʒint], *s.* Version *f* (de la Bible) des Septante.

septum, *pl.* -**a** ['septəm, -ə], *s.* (*a*) *Anat:* Septum *m.* (*b*) *Bot:* Cloison *f.*

sepulchral [se'pʌlkrəl], *a.* Sépulcral, -aux.

sepulchre ['sepəlkər], *s.* Sépulcre *m,* tombeau *m.*

sepulture ['sepəltjər], *s.* Sépulture *f.*

sequel ['si:kwəl], *s.* Suite *f* (d'un roman, etc.). *Action that had an unfortunate s.,* acte qui entraîna des suites malheureuses. **In the sequel,** par la suite.

sequence ['si:kwəns], *s.* 1. (*a*) Succession *f*; ordre naturel. **In sequence,** en série; en succession. (*b*) Suite *f,* série *f* (d'événements, etc.). (*c*) *Gram:* Sequence of tenses, concordance *f* des temps. 2. *Cards:* Séquence *f.* 3. *Cin: F:* Scène *f* (de film).

sequester [se'kwestər]. 1. *v.pr.* **To sequester oneself** (*from the world, etc.*), se retirer (du monde, etc.). 2. *v.tr. Jur:* Séquestrer; mettre (un bien) sous séquestre. **sequestered,** *a.* 1. (*Of life, etc.*) Retiré, isolé; (*of spot, etc.*) retiré, perdu. 2. *Jur:* (*Of property*) Sous séquestre.

sequestrate [si'kwestreit, 'si:kwestreit], *v.tr. Jur:* = SEQUESTER 2.

sequestration [si:kwes'treiʃ(ə)n], *s.* 1. Retraite *f*; éloignement *m* du monde. 2. *Jur:* Séquestration *f*; mise *f* sous séquestre.

sequin ['si:kwin], *s.* Sequin *m.*

seraglio [se'ra:ljo], *s.* Sérail *m,* -ails.

seraph, *pl.* **seraphs, seraphim** ['seraf, -im], *s.* Séraphin *m.*

seraphic [se'rafik], *a.* Séraphique.

Serb [sə:rb], *a. & s.* = SERBIAN.

Serbia ['sə:rbia]. *Pr.n.* La Serbie.

Serbian ['sə:rbiən]. **I.** *a. & s.* Serbe (*mf*). **2.** *s. Ling :* Le serbe.

sere ['si:ər], *a. Poet :* Flétri, desséché, fané.

serenade¹ [sere'neid], *s.* Sérénade *f.*

serenade², *v.tr.* Donner une sérénade à (qn).

serenader [sere'neidər], *s.* Donneur *m*, joueur *m*, de sérénades.

serene [se'ri:n], *a.* **I.** Serein, calme, tranquille ; (ciel) clair. *F :* All serene! ça y est! c'est bien ! **2.** His Serene Highness, son Altesse sérénissime. **-ly**, *adv.* Tranquillement ; avec sérénité.

serenity [se'reniti], *s.* Sérénité *f*, calme *m*, tranquillité *f.*

serf [sə:rf], *s.* Serf, *f.* serve.

serfdom ['sə:rfdəm], *s.* Servage *m.*

serge [sə:rdʒ], *s. Tex :* Serge *f.*

sergeant, serjeant ['sɑ:rdʒənt], *s.m.* **I.** (*a*) *A :* Serjeant at law, avocat (d'un ordre supérieur du barreau). (*b*) Common Serjeant (at law), magistrat de la corporation de Londres. (*c*) *Parl :* Serjeant at Arms, huissier d'armes. **2.** (*Always* sergeant) (*a*) *Mil :* (*Infantry*) Sergent ; (*cavalry, artillery*) = maréchal des logis. (*b*) Police sergeant, brigadier. **sergeant-'major**, *s.m. Mil :* **I.** (*Infantry*) Sergent major ou adjudant. (*Mounted arms*) Maréchal des logis chef. **2.** Regimental sergeant-major = adjudant chef.

serial ['siəriəl], *a.* **I.** Serial number, numéro de série ; numéro matricule (d'un moteur, etc.). **2.** Serial story, *s.* serial, roman-feuilleton *m.* Serial writer, feuilletoniste *m.* Serial rights, droit de reproduction en feuilleton.

seriatim [siːəri'eitim], *adv.* Successivement ; au fur et à mesure.

seri(ci)culture [seri(si)'kʌltjər], *s.* Séri(ci)-culture *f.*

series ['siər(i)i:z, 'siəriz], *s.inv.* **I.** Série *f*, suite *f* ; échelle *f*, gamme *f* (de couleurs, etc.). *Mth :* Series of numbers, of terms, suite, série, de nombres, de termes. Infinite series, série infinie. **2.** *Adv.phr.* In series, en série, en succession. Reservoirs arranged in s., réservoirs en chapelet. *El :* To connect cells in s., grouper des éléments en série, en tension.

serif ['serif], *s. Typ :* (*At top of letter*) Obit *m* ; (*at foot*) empattement *m.*

seringa [se'riŋgə], *s. Bot :* Seringa *m.*

serious ['siəriəs], *a.* Sérieux. **I.** *S. wound,* blessure grave, grave blessure. *S. mistake,* grosse faute. **2.** (*a*) Serious promise, promesse sérieuse, sincère. (*b*) Réfléchi. I am serious, je ne plaisante pas. **-ly**, *adv.* Sérieusement. **I.** Seriously ill, gravement malade. *S. wounded,* grièvement blessé. **2.** To take sth. (too) seriously, prendre qch. (trop) au sérieux. **'serious-'minded**, *a.* Réfléchi, sérieux.

seriousness ['siəriəsnəs], *s.* **I.** Gravité *f* (d'une maladie, etc.). **2.** Sérieux *m* (de maintien, etc.). **3.** In all seriousness, sérieusement.

seriph ['serif], *s.* = SERIF.

serjeant ['sɑ:rdʒənt], *s. See* SERGEANT I.

sermon ['sə:rmən], '. **I.** *Ecc :* Sermon *m* ; *R.C.Ch :* prône *m.* B : The Sermon on the Mount, le Sermon sur la montagne. **2.** *F :* Sermon, semonce *f.*

sermonize ['sə:rmənaiz]. **I.** *v.i. Pej :* Sermonner, prêcher. **2.** *v.tr. F :* Sermonner, chapitrer (qn) ; faire la morale à (qn).

sermonizer ['sə:rmənaizər], *s. F :* Sermonneur, -euse.

serosity [si'rɔsiti], *s.* Sérosité *f.*

serous ['siːərəs], *a.* Séreux.

serpent ['sə:rpənt], *s.* (*a*) Serpent *m.* (*b*) *Pyr :* Serpenteau *m.*

serpentine ['sə:rpəntain], *a.* Serpentin ; (ruisseau, sentier) sinueux, tortueux, serpentant.

serrate ['sereit], **serrated** [se'reitid], *a.* Denté en scie ; dentelé.

serried ['serid], *a. Lit :* Serré. In serried ranks, en rangs serrés, en rangs pressés.

serum ['siːərəm], *s. Physiol :* Sérum *m.*

servant ['sə:rvənt], *s.* **I.** (*a*) (Domestic) servant, domestique *mf* ; servante *f*, bonne *f.* General servant, bonne à tout faire. To keep a servant, avoir une domestique. *Mil :* Officer's servant, valet *m* d'officier ; ordonnance *f.* (*b*) Serviteur *m*, servante (de Dieu, etc.). (*c*) *Corr :* Your (most) obedient servant, (*usual equivalent*) je vous prie d'agréer mes salutations empressées. Your humble servant, votre (très) humble serviteur. **2.** Employé, -ée (du chemin de fer, etc.). Civil servant, fonctionnaire *m* (de l'État). I am my own servant, je me sers moi-même. **'servant-girl**, *s.f.* Domestique, bonne.

serve [sə:rv]. **I.** *v.tr.* **I.** (*a*) (*Of pers.*) Serv.r (un maître, une cause, etc.). How can I serve you? comment, en quoi, puis-je vous être utile? *Abs.* To serve at table, servir à table. To serve in the army, servir dans l'armée ; être au service militaire. *To have served ten years,* avoir dix ans de service. *Jur :* To serve on the jury, être du jury. (*b*) To serve one's apprenticeship, faire son apprentissage. To have served one's time, (i) avoir fait son temps de service ; (ii) sortir d'apprentissage. To serve one's sentence, subir, purger, sa peine. **2.** (*a*) (*Of thg*) Être utile à (qn) ; suffire à (qn). It will serve the purpose, *abs.* it will serve, cela fera l'affaire. (*b*) If my memory serves me right, si j'ai bonne mémoire. **3.** Desservir. Localities served by a railway line, localités desservies par un chemin de fer. **4.** (*a*) To serve s.o. with a pound of butter, servir une livre de beurre à qn. Are you being served? est-ce qu'on vous sert? (*b*) *Tradesman who has served us for ten years,* marchand qui nous sert, qui fournit chez nous, depuis dix ans. (*c*) (*At table*) To serve s.o. with soup, servir du potage à qn. **5.** (*a*) To serve a dish, (i) servir un mets ; (ii) servir (aux convives) d'un mets. (*b*) *Ten :* To serve the ball, *abs.* to serve, servir (la balle). **6.** *Jur :* To serve a writ on s.o., to serve s.o. with a writ, délivrer, signifier, notifier, une assignation à qn. **7.** Traiter (qn) (bien, mal). *He served me very badly,* il a très mal agi envers moi. It serves you right! c'est bien fait ! vous ne l'avez pas volé ! It serves him right for being . . ., ça lui apprendra à être. . . . **II.** serve, *v.i.* **I.** To serve for sth., servir à qch. To serve as sth., ser.ir de qch. ; faire fonction de qch. To s. as a pretext, as an example, servir de prétexte, d'exemple. **2.** When occasion serves, lorsque l'occasion est favorable. **serve out**, *v.tr.* **I.** Distribuer (des provisions, etc.) ; servir (la soupe, etc.) à la ronde. **2.** *F :* To serve s.o. out for sth., revaloir qch. à qn ; se venger. **serve up**, *v.tr.* Servir, mettre sur la table (un plat). *F :* To s. up an old tale, resservir une vieille rengaine. **serving¹**, *a.* Servant ; (soldat) au service. **'serving-man**, *s.m. A :* Domestique. **'serving-woman**, *s.f. A :* Domestique. **serving²**, *s.* **I.** Service *m* (d'un maître). **2.** Service (du dîner, etc.). *Ten :* Service (d'une balle). **3.** *Nau :* Fourrage *m*, garniture *f* (d'un cordage). Serving-mallet, maillet *m* à fourrer ; mailloche *f.*

server ['sə:rvər], *s.* **I.** (*a*) Serveur, -euse. (*b*) *Ecc :* (*At mass*) Acolyte *m*, répondant *m.*

2. *pl.* Salad-servers, fish-servers, service *m* à salade, à poisson.
service[1] ['sə:rvis], *s.* **I.** Service *m. Length of s.*, ancienneté *f.* To do one's military service, faire son service militaire. To be on active service, être en activité (de service). To have seen long service, avoir vieilli dans le service. **2.** (*a*) Public services, services publics. Postal service, telegraph service, administration publique des postes, des télégraphes. Army Service Corps = service de l'Intendance; *F*: le Train. Army Medical Service, service de santé de l'armée. (*b*) Distribution *f*, installation *f* (de gaz, d'électricité, d'eau). *El.E*: Service tension, tension de distribution. (*c*) Entretien *m* et dépannage *m* (d'automobiles, etc.). **3.** (*a*) Emploi *m* (d'un fonctionnaire, etc.). The military and civil services, les emplois militaires et civils de l'État. To be in the civil service, être fonctionnaire (de l'État). To be in the customs service, être dans la douane. (*b*) The three services, l'armée *f*, la marine et l'armée de l'air. *Av*: Service pilot, pilote militaire. The senior service, la marine. **4.** (Domestic) service, service (domestique). To be in service, être en service, *F*: en condition. To go out to service, to go into service, entrer en service, en place. To take service with s.o., entrer au service de qn. **5.** (*a*) To render, do, s.o. a service, rendre (un) service à qn. *Exchange of friendly services*, échange de bons procédés. *His services to education*, les services qu'il a rendus à l'enseignement. (*b*) I am at your service, je suis à votre disposition. Always at your service, toujours à votre disposition, à votre service. (*c*) Utilité *f*. To be of some service, être de quelque utilité. To be of service to s.o., être utile à qn. (*Of thg*) To do service, servir. To do good service, faire un bon usage; faire de l'usage. **6.** *Ecc*: Office *m*; (*in Protestant churches*) ervice, culte *m*. **7.** *Ten*: Service. **8.** *Jur*: Délivrance *f*, signification *f* (d'un acte, d'une assignation). **9.** Tea service, service à thé. Toilet service, garniture *f* de toilette. **'service-hoist,** *s.* Monte-plats *m inv.* **'service-line,** *s.* *Ten*: Ligne *f* de service, de fond. **'service-pipe,** *s.* Branchement *m* (pour le gaz, etc.). **'service-rifle,** *s.* *Mil*: Fusil *m* d'ordonnance. **'service-station,** *s.* *Aut*: Station-service *f*; agence *f* stockiste. **'service-uniform,** *s.* *Mil: etc*: Uniforme *m* réglementaire.
service[2], *v.tr.* Entretenir et réparer (les automobiles, etc.).
service[3], *s.* *Bot*: Service(-tree), sorbier *m*, cormier *m*.
serviceable ['sə:rvisəbl], *a.* **I.** (*Of pers.*) Serviable. **2.** (*Of thg*) (*a*) En état de fonctionner; utilisable. (*b*) Utile; de bon usage; avantageux. (*c*) Pratique, commode.
serviette [sə:rvi'et], *s.* *F*: *V*: Serviette *f* de table.
servile ['sə:rvail], *a.* **I.** Servile; d'esclave. *S. imitation*, imitation servile. **2.** (*Of pers.*) Servile; bas, *f.* basse. **-ly,** *adv.* **I.** Servilement; avec servilité; bassement. **2.** (Traduire) servilement, trop exactement.
servility [sə:r'viljti], *s.* **I.** Servilité *f*, exactitude trop étroite (d'une copie, etc.). **2.** (*Of pers.*) Servilité; bassesse *f*.
servitude ['sə:rvitju:d], *s.* **I.** Servitude *f*, esclavage *m*. **2.** *Jur*: Penal servitude, travaux forcés; prison *f* cellulaire.
servo-brake ['sə:rvobreik], *s.* *Aut*: Servofrein *m*; frein *m* à servo.
servo-motor ['sə:rvomoutər], *s.* *Mec.E*: Servomoteur *m*.

45

sesame ['sesəmi], *s.* *Bot*: Sésame *m*.
sesquioxide [seskwi'oksaid], *s.* *Ch*: Sesquioxyde *m*.
sessile ['sesail], *a.* (*Of leaf, etc.*) Sessile.
session ['se∫(ə)n], *s.* **I.** *A*: Tenue *f* (d'une assemblée, des assises, etc.). **2.** Session *f*; séance *f*. To have a long session, faire une longue séance. *Parl*: The House is now in session, la Chambre siège actuellement. To go into secret session, se former en comité secret. **3.** (*a*) *Sch*: *U.S*: Trimestre *m* scolaire ou universitaire. (*b*) *U.S. & Scot*: Année *f* universitaire. **4.** *Jur*: *pl.* Petty sessions, session des juges de paix.
sestet [ses'tet], *s.* *Mus*: Sextuor *m*.
set[1] [set], *s.* **I.** Ensemble *m*. (*a*) Jeu *m* (d'outils, de dominos); équipage *m* (d'outils); série *f* (de casseroles); batterie *f* (d'ustensiles de cuisine); collection complète (des œuvres de qn); service *m* (de porcelaine). Set of golf-clubs, eu de crosses. Set of tyres, train *m* de pneus. Set of furniture, ameublement *m*. Set of apartments, appartement meublé. Set of fire-irons, garniture *f* de foyer. Toilet set, garniture de toilette. *El.E*: Generating set, groupe *m* électrogène. *Com*: Bill drawn in a set of three, lettre de change tirée à trois exemplaires. *S.a.* TOOTH[1] I. (*b*) Wireless set, poste *m* de radio. Receiving-set, poste récepteur. (*c*) *Ten*: Manche *f*, set *m*. (*d*) Groupe de (personnes). *A magnificent set of men*, un magnifique groupe d'hommes. *Set of thieves*, bande *f* de voleurs. *Literary set*, coterie *f* littéraire. The smart set, le monde élégant. *We don't move in the same set*, nous ne fréquentons pas les mêmes milieux. **2.** (*a*) *Poet*: At set of sun, au coucher du soleil. (*b*) *Ven*: (*Of dog*) Arrêt *m*. *F*: To make a set at s.o., (i) attaquer furieusement qn (à la tribune); (ii) (*of woman*) entreprendre la conquête d'un homme. (*c*) *Hairdr*: (Wave-)set, mise *f* en plis. **3.** (*a*) Assiette *f* (d'une poutre); tournure *f* (d'un vêtement); disposition *f* des plis (d'une draperie). Set of a saw, voie *f*, chasse *f*, d'une scie. *Nau*: Set of the sails, (i) orientation *f* des voiles; (ii) façon *f* dont les voiles sont établies. (*b*) Direction *f* (du courant); *Nau*: lit *m* (du vent). **4.** (*a*) *Hort*: Plant *m* à repiquer. (*b*) (Paving-)set, pavé *m* d'échantillon. (*c*) *Th*: Décor *m*; mise *f* en scène. Rehearsal on the set, répétition *f* sur le plateau. **5.** *Tls*: (*a*) Saw-set, tourne-à-gauche *m inv.* (*b*) Cold set, tranche *f* à froid.
set[2], *v.* (set; setting) **I.** *v.tr.* **I.** (*a*) Asseoir, placer (qn sur le trône). To set sth. above rubies, priser qch. plus que des rubis. (*b*) To set a hen, mettre une poule à couver. (*c*) (*a*) Mettre, poser (qch. sur qch., devant qn). *To set one's glass on the table*, poser son verre sur la table. *To set a dish on the table*, servir un plat. *To set one's seal to a document*, apposer son sceau à un acte. *S.a.* EYE[1] I, HAND[1] I, SPUR[1] I. (*b*) To set one's affections on s.o.*, fixer ses affections sur qn. *S.a.* HEART[1] 2 (*c*). **3.** (*a*) To set chairs (*for the company*), placer, avancer, des chaises. (*b*) To set the table, mettre, dresser, le couvert; dresser la table. To set (the table) for two, mettre deux couverts. **4.** (*a*) To set a piano too high, accorder un piano trop haut. (*b*) To set words to music, mettre des paroles en musique. To set 'Othello' to music, écrire une partition sur *Othello*. **5.** (*a*) To set a stake in the ground, enfoncer, planter, un pieu dans la terre. (*b*) To set seeds, planter des graines. **6.** (*a*) To set the clock, régler la pendule. *To set the alarm(-clock) for five o'clock*, mettre le réveille-matin sur cinq heures. *Aut*: To set the speedometer to zero, ramener

le compteur à zéro. *Navy:* To set a torpedo, régler une torpille. *Av:* To set the controls, régler, repérer, les commandes. (b *El.E:* *To set the brushes*, ajuster, caler, ,es balais. (c) To set the iron of a plane, régler, ajuster, le fer d'un rabot. To set (the teeth of) a saw, donner de la voie à une scie. (d) *To set one's head-dress*, ajuster sa coiffure. *S.a.* CAP[1] I. To set the hair, mettre les cheveux en plis. 7. (a) To set a butterfly, monter un papillon. (b) *Th:* To set a scene, monter un décor. (c) To set a gem, sertir, enchâsser, une pierre. *Ring set with rubies*, bague ornée de rubis. *Panes set in lead*, vitres serties de plomb. *Mec.E:* To set the shaft in its bearings, loger l'arbre dans les paliers. (d) *Nau:* To set a sail, déployer, établir, une voile. (With) all sails set, toutes voiles dehors. 8. (a) To set a snare, dresser, tendre, un piège. (b) To set the camera shutter, armer l'obturateur. 9. To set (the edge of) a razor, affiler un rasoir. *To set a chisel*, affûter un ciseau. 10. *Typ:* To set type, composer. II. To set a date, a day, fixer une date. To set limits to sth., assigner des limites à qch. *S.a.* WATCH[1] 4. 12. To set the fashion, fixer la mode ; donner le ton. *Row:* To set the stroke, régler l'allure. *Nau:* To set the course (*on the chart*), tracer la route. 13. To set a bone, remettre un os. 14. To set one's teeth, serrer les dents. 15. Cold sets jellies, le froid fait prendre les gelées. 16. To set s.o. on his way, mettre qn dans le bon chemin. 17. (a) To set s.o. doing sth., mettre qn à faire qch. *To set the dog barking*, faire aboyer le chien. *This incident set everybody's tongue wagging*, cet incident a mis toutes les langues en branle. (b) To set sth. going, mettre qch. en train. 18. To set a man to work, mettre un homme au travail. *S.a.* THIEF I. 19. To set a good example, donner un bon exemple. To set a problem, donner un problème à résoudre. *Sch:* To set a book, mettre un livre au programme (d'études). To set a paper, établir les questions d'une composition. II. set, *v.i.* I. (a) (*Of sun*) To set, se coucher. (b) (*Of fame*) S'éteindre. 2. (*Of dress*) To set well, badly, bien, mal, tomber. 3. (*Of broken bone*) Se ressouder ; *F:* se recoller. 4. (a) (*Of white of egg*) Se coaguler ; (*of blood*) se figer ; (*of milk*) (se) cailler ; (*of jelly*) prendre. (b) (*Of cement*) Faire prise. 5. *Ven:* (*Of dog*) Tomber en arrêt. 6. *Danc:* To set (to partners), balancer ; faire chassé-croisé. 7. (*Of current*) To set southwards, porter au sud. *F:* The tide has set in his favour, ses actions remontent. *Opinion is setting that way*, le courant de l'opinion prend cette direction. 8. To set to work, se mettre au travail, à l'œuvre. set about. I. *v.i.* (a) To set about doing sth., se mettre à faire qch. *I don't know how to set about it*, je ne sais pas comment m'y prendre. (b) *F:* To set about s.o., attaquer qn. 2. *v.tr.* To set a rumour about, donner cours à un bruit. set against, *v.tr.* (a) To set s.o. against s.o., prévenir qn contre qn. (b) To set one's face against sth., s'opposer résolument à qch. set apart, *v.tr.* I. To set the women apart, isoler les femmes. 2. Mettre (qch.) à part. set aside, *v.tr.* I. = SET APART 2. 2. (a) Rejeter ; mettre (qch.) au rebut. (b) Écarter (une proposition). *Setting aside my expenses . . .*, sans compter mes frais. . . . (c) To set a will aside, annuler un testament. set back, *v.tr.* I. (a) Renfoncer (une façade). *House set back* (*from the alignment*), maison en retrait. (b) (*Of horse*) To set back its ears, coucher les oreilles. 2. (a) *To set back the trip-recorder to* o, remettre le compteur de trajet

à o. (b) Retarder (la pendule, le travail, le progrès). 'set-back, *s.*(*pl.* set-backs *or* sets-back) (a) Recul *m* (dans les affaires). (b) Déconvenue *f* ; revers *m* de fortune. set before, *v.tr.* I. (a) To set a dish before s.o., servir un plat à qn. (b) To set a plan before s.o., exposer un projet à qn. 2. To set Vergil before Homer, préférer Virgile à Homère. set down, *v.tr.* I. Poser, déposer. (*Of train*) To set down passengers at . . ., laisser, débarquer, des voyageurs à. . . , 2. (a) To set sth. down (in writing), consigner, coucher, qch. par écrit. (b) To set sth. down to a cause, attribuer qch. à une cause. (c) To set s.o. down as an actor, prendre qn pour un acteur. set forth. I. *v.tr.* Énoncer ; exposer, faire valoir (ses raisons) ; avancer (une théorie). 2. *v.i.* Se mettre en route, en voyage ; partir (*for*, pour). set in, *v.i.* Commencer. *Before winter sets in*, avant le début de l'hiver. A reaction is setting in, une réaction se dessine. *If no complications set in*, s'il ne survient pas de complications. set off. I. *v.tr.* I. (a) To set off a debt, compenser une dette. (b) Faire ressortir, faire valoir (une couleur). *Jewelry sets off a handsome face*, la parure relève la bonne mine. *Her dress sets off her figure*, sa robe fait valoir sa taille. 2. *Surv:* Rapporter (un angle). 3. Faire partir (une fusée). This answer set them off laughing, cette réponse a déclenché les rires. II. set off, *v.i.* I. Partir ; se mettre en route, en voyage. 2. *Typ:* (*Of wet ink*) Maculer. 'set-off, *s.* I. Contraste *m*. Set-off to beauty, (i) ornement *m* de la beauté ; (ii) repoussoir *m* à la beauté. *As a set-off to . . .*, comme contraste à. . . . 2. (a) Compensation *f* (d'une dette). Book-k: Écriture *f* inverse. (b) *Jur:* (*Counter-claim*) Reconvention *f*. 3. *Typ:* Maculage *m*. set on, *v.tr.* To set a dog on s.o., lancer un chien contre qn. *I was set on by a dog*, j'ai été attaqué par un chien. set out. I. *v.tr.* I. Équiper (qn). 2. Arranger, disposer. *To set out one's ideas clearly*, ordonner clairement ses idées. 3. *Mth: Surv: etc:* To set out a curve, faire le tracé d'une courbe. 4. *Typ:* Espacer (les mots). II. set out, *v.i.* (i) Se mettre en route, en chemin ; (ii) s'embarquer ; Faire voile. *To set out in a small boat*, monter à, gagner, la terre dans une embarcation. *S.a.* JOURNEY[1]. To set out in pursuit of s.o., se mettre à la poursuite de qn. set to, *v.i.* I. Se mettre (résolument) au travail. *We must set to!* allons-y ! 2. *F:* (*Of two pers.*) En venir aux coups. set-'to, *s.* I. Assaut *m* (de boxe). 2. Lutte *f*, combat *m*. To have a set-to, en venir aux mains. set up[1]. I. *v.tr.* I. (a) Placer, fixer (un objet). (b) Élever, ériger (une statue) ; planter (un drapeau) ; monter (une machine) ; armer (un appareil). (c) *Typ:* To set up a MS., composer un MS. 2. Exalter, élever (qn). 3. (a) Instaurer (un culte). (b) Établir (une agence, une école, un record) ; fonder (une maison de commerce) ; monter (un magasin). To set up one's abode somewhere, établir son domicile quelque part. *S.a.* HOUSE[1] I. (c) Food that sets up irritation, aliment qui occasionne de l'irritation. (d) To set up a king, instaurer une monarchie. (e) To set s.o. up in business, établir qn dans un commerce. (f) To set s.o. up as a model, proposer qn comme modèle. To set up ridiculous pretentions, afficher des prétentions ridicules. To set up a claimant to the throne, mettre en avant un prétendant au trône. 4. To set up a shout, pousser une clameur. 5. Donner, rendre, de la vigueur à (qn). *This medicine will set you up*, ce remède va vous remettre d'aplomb. II. **set up**, *v.i.* **1.** To set up in business, s'établir dans le commerce. **2.** *v.i. & pr.* To set (oneself) up as a critic, se poser en critique. **set up²**, *a.* Well set up fellow, gaillard bien campé. Well set up girl, jeune fille bien tournée. **setting up,** *s.* **1.** (*a*) Montage *m*, installation *f*. (*b*) *Typ:* Composition *f*. **2.** Setting up of a new order, établissement *m*, instauration *f*, d'un nouveau régime. Setting up housekeeping, entrée *f* en ménage. **set upon,** *v.i.* To set upon the enemy, attaquer l'ennemi. **set³**, *a.* **1.** (*a*) Set face, visage immobile, aux traits rigides. Set smile, sourire figé. *S.a.* FAIR² I. 6. (*b*) (Ressort) bandé, tendu. *Sp:* (*To runners*) (Get) set! en position! *U.S:* *F:* To be all set, être prêt à commencer. (*c*) Hard set, ferme, figé. (*d*) The fruit is set, le fruit est formé, noué. **2.** (*a*) Set price, prix fixe. Set time, heure fixée. *At set hours,* à des heures réglées. Set purpose, ferme intention. *S.a.* PURPOSE¹ I. (*b*) Set phrase, cliché *m*; expression consacrée. *Set phrases,* expressions toutes faites. Set speech, discours composé à l'avance, discours en forme. (*c*) *Cu:* *Pyr:* Set piece, pièce montée. *Th:* Set scene, décor (monté). (*d*) Set task, tâche assignée. *Sch:* Set subject, sujet imposé aux candidats. The set books, les auteurs *m* du programme. **3.** To be set on sth., être résolu, déterminé, à qch. *Since you are set upon it . . .*, puisque vous y tenez. . . . *His mind is set*, son parti est pris. To be dead set against s.o., s'acharner contre qn. **'set square,** *s.* Équerre *f* (à dessin). **setting¹**, *a.* (Astre) baissant, couchant; (gloire) sur son déclin. **setting²**, *s.* **1.** (*a*) Mise *f*, pose *f* (de qch.). (*b*) Disposition *f*, arrangement *m*. Setting to music, mise en musique. (*c*) Plantation *f* (de graines). (*d*) Réglage *m*; mise à l'heure (d'une horloge); ajustage *m*. (*e*) Montage *m* (d'un spécimen); armement *m* (d'un piège); mise en plis (des cheveux). (*f*) Aiguisage *m*, affûtage *m* (d'un outil). (*g*) *Typ:* Composition *f*. Page-setting, mise en pages. ·(*h*) Fixation *f* (d'une date). (*i*) Réduction *f* (d'une fracture). (*j*) Imposition *f* (d'une tâche). **2.** (*a*) Coucher *m* (d'un astre). (*b*) Recollement *m* (d'un os brisé). (*c*) Nouure *f* (du fruit). (*d*) Prise *f* (du ciment); coagulation *f* (de l'albumine). **3.** (*a*) Cadre *m* (d'un récit). *Th:* Mise en scène. (*b*) Monture *f* (d'un diamant). (*c*) *Mus:* (i) Ton *m* (d'un morceau). (ii) Setting for piano, arrangement pour piano. **setaceous** [si'teiʃəs], *a.* *Nat.Hist:* Sétacé. **setiferous** [si:'tifərəs], **setigerous** [si:'tidʒərəs], *a.* Sétifère, sétigère. **setness** [ˈsetnəs], *s.* Rigidité *f* (des traits). Setness o purpose, détermination *f*. **seton** [ˈsiːtən], *s.* *Vet:* *Surg:* Séton *m* à mèche. **settee** [se'ti:], *s.* Canapé *m*, causeuse *f*. **ᵹet'teebed,** *s.* Lit-canapé *m*. **setter** [ˈsetər], *s.* **1.** (*Pers.*) (*a*) Monteur *m*, sertisseur *m* (de diamants). (*b*) Affûteur *m* (de scies). **2.** Chien *m* d'arrêt; setter *m*. **settle¹** [setl], *s.* Banc *m* à dossier. **settle²**. I. *v.tr.* **1.** *a*) Établir, installer (qn) (dans un pays). *b*) Coloniser (un pays). (*c*) Rendre stable. (*d*) Mettre bien en place. **2.** (*a*) To settle an invalid for the night, arranger un malade pour la nuit. (*b*) To settle one's children, établir ses enfants. (*c*) To settle one's affairs, mettre ordre à ses affaires. **3.** (*a*) Clarifier, laisser rasseoir (un liquide). (*b*) To s. s.o.'s doubts, dissiper les doutes de qn. **4.** Concerter (son visage); calmer (les nerfs). *Give me something to s. my stomach*, donnez-moi quelque chose pour me remettre

l'estomac. **5.** Fixer, déterminer (un jour, un endroit). *The terms were settled*, on convint des conditions. *It's as good as settled, F:* l'affaire est dans le sac. *It's all settled*, c'est une affaire faite. *That is settled then*, alors c'est dit. **6.** (*a*) Résoudre, décider (une question); trancher, aplanir (un différend); vider (une querelle); arranger, liquider (une affaire). *Questions not yet settled*, questions en suspens. That settles it! (i) voilà qui tranche la question! (ii) cela me décide! Settle it among yourselves, arrangez cela entre vous. *Jur:* To settle an affair out of court, transiger avant jugement. *Settled between the parties*, arrangé à l'amiable. (*b*) Conclure, terminer (une affaire); régler, solder (un compte); payer (une dette). *Abs.* To settle (up) with s.o., régler son compte avec qn. *F:* Now to settle with you! maintenant à nous deux! (*c*) To settle s.o., *F:* donner son reste à qn. *S.a.* HASH¹ 2. **7.** To settle an annuity on s.o., constituer une annuité à qn; asseoir une annuité sur qn. II. **settle,** *v.i. 1. v.i. & pr.* (*a*) To settle (down) in a locality, s'établir dans un lieu. (*b*) To settle (oneself) in an armchair, s'installer commodément dans un fauteuil. (*c*) (*Of bird*) Se percher, se poser (sur un arbre). (*d*) The snow is settling, la neige prend, ne fond pas. (*e*) The wind is settling in the north, le vent s'établit dans le nord. (*f*) To settle (down) to work, se mettre sérieusement au travail. **2.** (*Of liquid*) Se clarifier, déposer; (*of sediment*) se précipiter. To let (sth.) settle, laisser déposer (un précipité); laisser rasseoir (le vin). **3.** (*a*) (i) (*Of ground, pillar*) Prendre son assiette; (ii) (*of foundation*) s'affaisser. *F:* Things are settling into shape, (i) les choses commencent à prendre tournure; (ii) l'ordre se rétablit. (*b*) (*Of ship*) To settle (down), couler. **4.** (*Of passion*) S'apaiser, se calmer. *The weather is settling*, le temps se calme. **settle down,** *v.i.* **1.** *See* SETTLE² II. 1 (*a*), (*f*), 3 (*b*). **2.** (*a*) (*Of pers.*) Se ranger; devenir sérieux. *To s. down for life*, se marier; se caser. *Marriage has made him s. down*, le mariage l'a rangé. (*b*) *Since the war things have settled down*, depuis la guerre tout s'est tassé. **3.** He is beginning to settle down at school, il commence à s'habituer à l'école. **settle upon,** *v.i.* **1.** To settle upon sth., choisir qch. ; se décider pour qch. **2.** (*Of affections*) Se poser sur (qn). **settled,** *a.* **1.** (*a*) Invariable, sûr; (*of idea*) fixe, enraciné. Settled intention, intention bien arrêtée. Settled policy, politique continue. Settled weather, temps fait, fixe. (*b*) (*Of pers.*) Rassis, réfléchi. (*c*) (*Of pers.*) Rangé; *esp.* marié. **2.** (*a*, (*Of question*) Arrangé, décidé. (*b*) (*On bill*) 'Settled,' "pour acquit." **3.** (*Of pers.*) Domicilié, établi; (*of thg*) bien assis. **4.** (*Of country*) Colonisé. **settling,** *s.* **1.** = SETTLEMENT I. **2.** (*a*) Apaisement *m* (d'une agitation). (*b*) Clarification *f* (d'un liquide). (*c*) Précipitation *f* (du sédiment). (*d*) Tassement *m*; affaissement *m* (du terrain). **3.** = SETTLEMENT 2 (*a*). **4.** Conclusion *f*, terminaison *f* (d'une affaire). Settling (up), règlement *m* (d'un compte). **settlement** [ˈsetlmənt], *s.* **1.** (*a*) Établissement *m*; installation *f*. (*b*) Colonisation *f*, peuplement *m* (d'un pays). **2.** (*a*) Règlement *m* (d'une affaire); résolution *f* (d'une question). (*b*) *Com:* Règlement, payement *m* (d'un compte). In (full) settlement . . ., pour solde (à l'acquit). . . . (*c*) *They have reached a s.*, ils sont arrivés à un accord amical. (*d*) (*Deed of*) settlement, acte *m* de disposition; contrat *m* de constitution. Family settlement, pacte *m* de famille. Marriage settlement, contrat de mariage.

3. (*a*) Colonie *f* (de peuplement). (*b*) Œuvre sociale (dans les quartiers pauvres d'une grande ville).

settler ['setlər], *s.* **1.** Colon *m*, mmigrant *m* (dans un pays nouvellement découvert). **2.** *F:* Coup décisif ; argument décisif. *That was a s. for him,* ça lui a fermé le bec.

settlor ['setlər], *s.* *Jur:* Disposant *m*, constituteur *m* (d'une annuité, etc.).

seven ['sev(ə)n], *num. a. & s.* Sept (*m*). *Fourteen is seven times as much as two,* quatorze est le septuple de deux. *S.a.* SIX. (*For other phrases see* EIGHT.) **'seven-league(d),** *attrib.a.* Seven-league(d) boots, bottes de sept lieues (du Petit Poucet).

sevenfold ['sev(ə)nfould]. **1.** *a.* Septuple. **2.** *adv.* Sept fois autant.

seventeen [sev(ə)n'ti:n], *num.a. & s.* Dix-sept (*m*). *F: To be sweet s.,* être dans la fleur de ses dix-sept printemps.

seventeenth [sev(ə)n'ti:nθ]. **1.** *num. a. & s.* Dix-septième. **Louis the Seventeenth,** Louis Dix-sept. **2.** *s.* (*Fractional*) Dix-septième *m.*

seventh ['sev(ə)nθ]. **1.** *num. a. & s.* Septième. *F: To be in the seventh heaven (of delight),* être au septième ciel. (*For other phrases see* EIGHTH.) **2.** *s.* (*a*) (*Fractional*) Septième *m.* (*b*) *Mus:* Septième *f.* **-ly,** *adv.* Septièmement ; en septième lieu.

seventieth ['sev(ə)ntiəθ], *num. a. & s.* Soixante-dixième.

seventy ['sev(ə)nti], *num. a. & s.* Soixante-dix (*m*) ; *A. & Dial:* septante (*m*). **Seventy-one, -nine,** soixante et onze, soixante-dix-neuf.

sever ['sevər], *v.tr.* (*a*) Désunir, disjoindre (les parties d'un tout) ; rompre (une liaison). *To s. one's connections with s.o.,* se désassocier d'avec qn. (*b*) *To s. s.o.'s leg (from his body),* couper la jambe à qn.

several ['sevərəl], *a.* **1.** (*a*) Séparé ; différent. *The s. members of the committee,* les divers membres du comité. (*b*) *Jur:* (Bien) individuel. *S.a.* LIABILITY 1. (*c*) *Our s. rights,* nos droits respectifs. **2.** (*a*) Plusieurs, divers ; quelques. *He and several others,* lui et quelques autres. (*b*) *I have several,* j'en ai plusieurs. *Several of them,* plusieurs d'entre eux. **-ally,** *adv.* Séparément, individuellement. *S.a.* JOINTLY.

severance ['sevərəns], *s.* Séparation *f* (*from,* de) ; rupture *f* (des relations). *S. of communications,* interruption complète de communication.

severe [si'viːər], *a.* **1.** (*a*) Sévère, strict, rigoureux (*with,* envers). *S. sentence,* sentence rigoureuse. *Unduly s. regulations, F:* règlements draconiens. *A s. reprimand,* une verte réprimande. (*b*) *To be severe on s.o.'s failings,* être sévère pour les défauts de qn. **2.** (*a*) (Temps) rigoureux, dur. *The cold was s.,* le froid sévissait. (*b*) *S. blow,* coup rude. *S. pain,* vive douleur. **3.** (Style, etc.) sévère, austère. **-ly,** *adv.* **1.** Sévèrement ; avec sévérité. *I was left severely alone,* personne ne m'a accordé la moindre attention. **2.** Grièvement, gravement (blessé). **3.** *Severely plain,* d'une simplicité sévère.

severity [si'veriti], *s.* **1.** Sévérité *f,* rigueur *f.* *To use severity,* sévir. **2.** (*a*) Rigueur, inclémence *f* (du temps). (*b*) Gravité *f* (d'une maladie) ; violence *f* (d'une douleur). (*c*) Rigueur *f* (d'un examen). **3.** Sévérité, austérité *f* (de style).

sew [sou], *v.tr.* (sewed [soud] sewn [soun]) Coudre. *Bookb:* Brocher, coudre (les feuilles d'un livre). **sew on,** *v.tr.* Coudre, attacher (un bouton). **sew up,** *v.tr.* Coudre (un ourlet) ; faire (une couture). *Surg:* Coudre, suturer (les lèvres d'une plaie). **sewing,** *s.* **1.** Couture *f.* *Bookb:* Brochage *m.* **Plain sewing,** couture simple. **Sewing needle,** aiguille *f* à coudre. **Sewing cotton,** fil *m* à coudre. **2.** Ouvrage *m* (à l'aiguille). **'sewing-bee,** *s.* *U.S:* Réunion *f* pour couture en commun. **'sewing-machine,** *s.* Machine *f* à coudre. **'sewing-maid,** *s.f.* Couturière ; lingère. **'sewing-press,** *s.* *Bookb:* Cousoir *m.* **'sewing-woman,** *pl.* **-women,** *s.f.* Ouvrière à domicile ; (*in factory*) piqueuse à la machine.

sewage ['sjuːedʒ], *s.* Eau(x) *f(pl)* d'égout. **Sewage system,** système du tout-à-l'égout. **Sewage farm,** champs *mpl* d'épandage.

sewer[1] ['souər], *s.* *Bookb:* Brocheur, -euse.

sewer[2] ['sjuːər], *s.* *Civ.E:* Égout *m.* **Main sewer,** égout collecteur. **Sewer gases,** miasme égoutier. *F:* (Moral) sewer (*of vice*), cloaque *m* (de vice).

sewerage ['sjuːredʒ], *s.* **1.** Système *m* d'égouts. **2.** *F:* = SEWAGE.

sewerman, *pl.* **-men** ['sjuːərmən, -men], *s.m.* Égoutier.

sex [seks], *s.* Sexe *m.* (*a*) *F:* **Sex appeal,** attrait *m.* (*b*) **The fair sex,** le beau sexe. **The sterner sex,** le sexe fort.

sexagenarian [seksadʒe'neəriən], *a. & s.* Sexagénaire (*mf*).

sexed [sekst], *a.* Sexué.

sexennial [seks'enjəl], *a.* Sexennal, -aux.

sexless ['seksləs], *a.* Asexué.

sextant ['sekstənt], *s.* Sextant *m.*

sextet [seks'tet], *s.* *Mus:* Sextuor *m.*

sextillion [seks'tiljən], *s.* **1.** (*In Gr. Britain*) Dix à la trente-sixième puissance ; 10^{36}. **2.** (*U.S. & Fr.*) Sextillion *m* ; 10^{21}.

sexton ['sekstən], *s.* *Ecc:* (*a*) Sacristain *m.* (*b*) *F:* Sonneur *m.* (*c*) *F:* Fossoyeur *m.* **'sexton-beetle,** *s.* *Ent:* Nécrophore *m :* enfouisseur *m.*

sextuple[1] ['sekstjupl], *a. & s.* Sextuple *m*).

sextuple[2], *v.tr.* Sextupler.

sexual ['seksjuəl], *a.* Sexuel. **Sexual intercourse,** rapports sexuels. **-ally,** *adv.* **1.** D'une manière sexuelle. **2.** Quant au sexe.

sexuality [seksju'aliti], *s.* Sexualité *f.*

sgraffito, *pl.* **-ti** [sgraf'fiːto, -tiː], *s.* Sgraffite *m.*

sh [ʃ], *int.* Chut !

shabbiness ['ʃab nəs], *s.* **1.** État râpé, usé (d'un habit, etc.) ; état défraîchi (d'un meuble) ; apparence pauvre, *F:* miteuse (de qn). **2.** (*a*) Mesquinerie *f* (de conduite). (*b*) Parcimonie *f.*

shabby ['ʃabi], *a.* **1.** (Habit) râpé, usé ; (mobilier, etc.) pauvre, minable. *S. room,* chambre tristement meublée. (*Of pers.*) *To look s.,* avoir l'air râpé. *S.a.* GENTILITY 1. **2.** (*a*) Mesquin ; peu honorable. **To do s.o. a shabby turn,** faire une mesquinerie à qn. **2.** (*b*) Chiche ; parcimonieux. **-ily,** *adv.* **1.** Pauvrement. *S. dressed,* miteux, râpé. **2.** (*a*) (Se conduire) mesquinement. (*b*) Chichement. **'shabby-gen'teel,** *a.* Qui trahit la misère sous des apparences de dignité. **'shabby-looking,** *a.* De pauvre apparence ; minable.

shack [ʃak], *s.* *U.S:* Cabane *f,* hutte *f.*

shackle[1] ['ʃakl], *s.* **1.** *pl.* **Shackles,** fers *m* (d'un prisonnier). *F: The shackles of convention,* les entraves *f* des conventions sociales. **2.** Maillon *m* de liaison (d'une chaîne) ; anse *f* (d'un cadenas) ; cigale *f* (d'une ancre). **3.** *Tg:* Shackle(-insulator) *s.* isolateur *m* d'angle.

shackle[2], *v.tr.* **1.** Mettre les fers à, entraver (un prisonnier). **2.** Maniller, mailler (une chaîne) ; étalinguer (une ancre).

shad [ʃad], *s.* *Ich:* Alose *f.*

shaddock ['ʃadək], *s. Bot:* Pamp.emousse *m or f.*
shade[1] [ʃeid], *s.* **I.** (*a*) Ombre *f.* **Temperature in
the shade,** température à l'ombre. *F:* **To put
s.o.** in(to) the shade, éclipser qn; faire ombre à
qn. *A s. of annoyance on his face,* une ombre de
contrariété sur son visage. **The shades of night,**
les ombres de la nuit; les ténèbres *f.* **The Shades,**
(i) .e enfers *m;* (ii) *F:* le bar (d'un hôtel).
(*b*) *Art:* Ombre (dans un tableau). **2.** (*a*) Nuance *f*
(de couleur, d'opinion); teinte *f.* **There is a
shade of meaning,** il y a une nuance. (*b*) *F:* Nuance; petit peu. *He is a s. better,* il va un tout
petit peu mieux. **3.** (*a*) Pâle reflet *m,* ombre (de
qch.). (*b*) Ombre, fantôme *m* (d'un mort).
F: **Shades of Demosthenes!** par Démosthène!
4. (*a*) (Lamp-)shade, abat-jour *m inv. Opt:* **Lens
shade, sky shade,** parasoleil *m,* pare-soleil *m inv,*
cache-soleil *m inv. Opt:* **Eye-glass shade** (*of
telescope*), bonnette *f.* (*b*) Store *m* (de fenêtre).
(*c*) (*For clocks*) Globe *m.*
shade[2]. **I.** *v.tr.* (*a*) Ombrager; couvrir (qch.)
d'ombre. **To shade sth. from the sun,** abriter
qch. du soleil. **To shade one's eyes with one's
hand,** mettre la main en abat-jour. *To s. a
light,* (i) voiler, atténuer, une lumière; (ii) masquer une lumière. (*b*) Obscurcir, assombrir (le
visage). **2.** (*a*) Ombrer (un dessin). (*b*) *Draw:
Mapm:* Hachurer. **3.** Nuancer (une étoffe). **To
shade away, shade off,** colours, dégrader des
couleurs. **II. shade,** *v.i. Blue that shades* (*off*)
into green, bleu qui se fond en vert. **shaded,** *a.*
I. (*a*) *Art:* (Dessin) ombré. (*b*) *Mapm:* Hachuré.
2. (*Of embroidery, etc.*) Nuancé.
shadiness ['ʃeidinəs], *s.* **I.** Ombre *f,* ombrage *m*
(d'un sentier). **2.** *F:* Aspect *m* louche (d'une
affaire).
shadow[1] ['ʃadou], *s.* Ombre *f.* **I.** (*a*) Obscurité *f.*
The shadow of death, les ombres de la mort.
Under the shadow of *a terrible accusation,* sous
le coup d'une accusation terrible. (*b*) Noir *m*
(d'un tableau). **2. To cast a shadow,** projeter
une ombre; faire ombre. **Coming events cast
their shadows before,** les événements à venir se
font pressentir. **In the shadow of . . .,** à
l'ombre de. . . . **To quarrel with one's own
shadow,** se faire du mauvais sang à propos de
rien. **May your shadow never grow less!** tous
mes vœux pour votre prospérité! **3.** (*a*) Compagnon inséparable (de qn). (*b*) Ombre (d'un
mort). **To wear oneself to a shadow,** (i) se manger
les sangs; (ii) s'épuiser (de travail). **He's a mere
shadow of his former self,** il n'est plus que
l'ombre de lui-même. (*c*) *Agent m* de la police
secrète; filateur, -trice. **'shadow-boxing,** *s.
Box:* Assaut *m* d'entraînement contre un adversaire fictif.
shadow[2], *v.tr.* **I.** (*a*) *Poet:* Ombrager (qch.);
couvrir (qch.) de son ombre. (*b*) *Tex:* Chiner
(un tissu). **2.** Filer (qn). **shadowing,** *s.*
Filature *f* (d'une personne suspecte).
shadowy ['ʃadoui], *a.* (Songe) chimérique;
(projet) indécis, vague. *The s. form seen by X,*
l'ombre aperçue par X.
shady ['ʃeidi], *a.* **I.** (*a*) Qui donne de l'ombre;
ombreux. (*b*) Ombragé; couvert d'ombre. *S.
walk,* allée couverte. *F:* **To be on the shady
side of forty,** avoir dépassé la quarantaine. **2.** (*Of
transaction*) Louche. *S. public house,* cabaret
borgne. **Shady-looking customer,** individu *m* aux
allures louches; marque-mal *m inv.* **The shady
side of politics,** les dessous *m* de la politique.
shaft[1] [ʃɑːft], *s.* **I.** (*a*) Hampe *f,* bois *m* (d'une
lance). (*b*) Manche *m* (de club de golf).
2. (*a*) Flèche *f,* trait *m.* (*b*) *A:* Javelot *m. The*

shafts of Cupid, les traits de l'Amour. **3.** Rayon
m (de lumière). **4.** (*a*) Tige *f* (de plume d'oiseau).
Anat: Corps *m* (du tibia). (*b*) *Arch:* Tige,
fût *m* (d'une colonne). *Const: Ind:* Souche *f*
(de cheminée d'usine). **5.** *Mec.E:* Arbre *m.*
Driving shaft, arbre de transmission. **Driven
shaft,** arbre commandé. **6.** *Veh:* Brancard *m,*
limon *m.* **'shaft-horse,** *s.* Cheval *m* de
brancard; limonier *m.*
shaft[2], *s.* **I.** *Min:* Puits *m.* **Ventilating shaft,
air shaft,** puits d'aérage; cheminée *f* d'appe..
Hoisting shaft, puits d'extraction. **2.** Cage *f*
(d'un ascenseur). **'shaft-sinker,** *s. Min:*
Puisatier *m.*
shafting ['ʃɑːftiŋ], *s.* **I.** *Mec.E:* (Line of)
shafting, ligne *f* d'arbres; "les arbres." **Main
shafting,** transmission principale. **2.** *Arch:*
Fûts *mpl.*
shag[1] [ʃag], *s.* Tabac fort (coupé fin).
shag[2], *s. Orn:* Cormoran huppé.
shaggy ['ʃagi], *a.* Poilu; (poney) à longs poils,
à poils rudes; (barbe) hirsute, touffue; (sourcils)
en broussailles.
shagreen[1] [ʃa'griːn], *s. Leath:* (*a*) (Peau *f* de)
chagrin *m.* (*b*) Galuchat *m.*
shagreen[2], *v.tr.* Chagriner (le cuir).
shah [ʃɑː], *s.* Schah *m* (de Perse).
shake[1] [ʃeik], *s.* **I.** (*a*) Secousse *f.* **To give sth.
a good shake,** bien secouer, bien agiter, qch. *A
shake of the head,* un hochement de tête. *To
answer with a s. of the head,* répondre d'un
mouvement de tête. **Shake of the hand,** poignée *f*
de main. *P:* **In a shake, in a brace of shakes,**
en un rien de temps. (*b*) Tremblement *m. F:* **To
be all of a shake,** trembler de tous ses membres.
(*c*) *Mus:* Trille *m.* (*d*) **With a shake in his voice,**
d'une voix mal assurée. **2.** *U.S: F:* **Egg-shake,**
lait *m* de poule. **3.** (*In wood*) Gerçure *f.*
4. *P:* **To be no great shakes,** n'être pas grand'-
chose; ne pas valoir grand'chose.
shake[2], *v.* (shook [ʃuk]; shaken [ʃeikn]) **I.** *v.tr.*
I. Secouer; agiter (un liquide, etc.). **'Shake the
bottle,'** "agiter le flacon." **To shake one's head,**
(i) secouer, hocher, la tête; (ii) (*in dissent*) faire
non de la tête. **To shake one's fist at s.o.,**
menacer qn du poing. **To shake s.o. by the hand,
to shake hands with s.o.,** serrer la main à qn;
donner une poignée de main à qn. **They shook
hands on it,** ils ont topé. **To shake oneself free**
(**from sth.**), se dégager (de qch.) d'une secousse.
2. Ébranler. *Threats cannot s. my purpose,* les
menaces ne sauraient m'ébranler. *It has shaken
his health,* sa santé a reçu une secousse. *To feel
shaken after a fall,* se ressentir d'une chute.
Voice shaking with emotion, voix émue. **3.** *Mus:*
Triller (un passage). **II. shake,** *v.i.* **I.** Trembler; (*of building*) chanceler, branler; (*of voice*)
trembloter. *His hand was shaking,* la main lui
tremblait. *S.a.* LAUGHTER. **To shake all over,**
trembler de tout son corps. *F:* **To shake in one's
shoes,** trembler dans sa peau. **2.** *Mus:* Faire des
trilles. **3.** *Nau:* (*Of sail*) Ralinguer. **To keep
the sails shaking,** tenir les voiles en ralingue.
shake down. I. *v.tr.* Secouer, faire tomber
(des fruits). **2.** *v.i.* (*a*) S'installer. (*b*) Se tasser.
The team is shaking down, l'équipe se forme.
'shake-down, *s. F:* Lit improvisé. **shake
off,** *v.tr.* **I.** *F:* **To shake off the dust from one's
feet,** secouer la poussière de ses pieds. **To shake
off the yoke,** secouer le joug; s'affranchir du
joug. **To shake off a cold,** venir à bout d'un
rhume. **2.** *F:* Se débarrasser, se défaire, de (qn).
I can't shake him off, il ne me lâche pas d'un cran.
shake out, *v.tr.* **I.** (*a*) Secouer; faire sortir

(la poussière). (*b*) Vider (un sac) en le secouant.
2. *Nau:* To shake out a reef, larguer un ris.
shake up, *v.tr.* **1.** Secouer, brasser (un oreiller).
2. (*a*) Agiter (le contenu d'une bouteille).
(*b*) *F:* Éveiller, secouer, stimuler (qn). **shaking,** *s.* (*a*) Secouement *m.* To give sth. a good
shaking, bien secouer (un tapis, etc.). (*b*) Ébranlement *m* (d'une maison); tremblement *m* (du sol);
tremblotement *m* (de la voix).

shaker ['ʃeikər], *s.* **I.** *Rel.H:* Trembleur *m.*
2. (*a*) (Appareil *m*) secoueur. (*b*) Cocktail shaker,
frappe-cocktail *m.*

Shak(e)spearian [ʃeiks'piəriən], *a.* *Lit.Hist:*
Shak(e)spearien, -ienne; de Shak(e)speare.

shakiness ['ʃeikinəs], *s.* Manque *m* de stabilité;
tremblement *m* (de la main); chevrotement *m*
(de la voix).

shako ['ʃakou], *s.* *Mil.Cost:* Shako *m.*

shaky ['ʃeiki], *a.* (Bâtiment) peu solide; (santé)
faible, chancelante. *S.* hand, main tremblante.
S. writing, écriture tremblée. *S.* voice, voix mal
assurée. To be shaky on one's legs, avoir les
jambes branlantes. I feel shaky to-day, je ne
suis pas d'aplomb aujourd'hui. *His English is s.,*
il est faible en anglais. **-ily,** *adv.* Peu solidement; faiblement; (marcher) à pas chancelants; (écrire) d'une main tremblante.

shale [ʃeil], *s.* Schiste (argileux); argile schisteuse. Oil shale, schiste bitumineux. **'shale-
oil,** *s.* Huile *f* de schiste.

shall [ʃal, ʃ(ə)l], *modal aux. v.* (*pr.* shall, shalt
[ʃalt], shall; *p.t.* & *condit.* should [ʃud], shouldst
[ʃudst]. *No other parts.* *'Shall not' is often
contracted into* shan't [ʃɑːnt]) I. **1.** Denotes duty
or a command. (*a*) (*In general precepts*) Ships
shall carry three lights, les navires sont tenus de
porter trois feux. *Everybody should go to the poll,*
il convient que tout le monde prenne part au
vote. All is as it should be, tout est très bien.
Which is as it should be, ce qui n'est que justice.
(*b*) *He shall do it if I order it,* il devra le faire si
je l'ordonne. *He shall not die!* il ne faut pas
qu'il meure! *He shall not do it,* je défends qu'il
le fasse. *You 'shall do it!* vous le ferez, je le
veux! (*c*) *You should do it at once,* vous devriez
le faire tout de suite. *It was an accident that
should have been foreseen,* c'était un accident à
prévoir. *F:* You should have seen him! il
fallait le voir! *This inquiry should be taken up
anew,* c'est une question à reprendre. (*d*) *He
should have arrived by this time,* il devrait être
arrivé à l'heure qu'il est. *That should suit you!*
voilà qui fera sans doute votre affaire! I should
think so! je crois bien! **2.** Shall I open the window? voulez-vous que j'ouvre la fenêtre? *I'll
call the children, shall I?* je vais appeler les
enfants, hein? *Let us go in, shall we?* rentrons,
voulez-vous? **3.** (*With weakened force*) (*a*) *Why
should you suspect me?* pourquoi me soupçonner
(, moi)? **Whom should I meet but Jones!** voilà
que je rencontre Jones! *Who shall describe their
surprise?* comment décrire leur surprise? (*b*) *He
ordered that they should be released,* il ordonna
qu'on les relâchât. *Mistresses expect that their
maids shall wear caps,* les maîtresses de maison
demandent que les bonnes portent la coiffe.
(*c*) *If he should come* (you will) *let me know,* si par
hasard il vient faites-le-moi savoir. *Should I be
free I shall come,* si je suis libre je viendrai.
Should the occasion arise, should it so happen,
le cas échéant. In case he should not be there . . .,
au cas qu'il n'y soit pas . . .; dans le cas où il
n'y serait pas. . . . II. **shall** *used as an auxiliary
verb forming the future tenses.* **I.** (*Assurance,*

promise, menace) *You shan't have any!* tu n'en
auras pas! *You shall pay for this!* vous me le
payerez! **2.** (*Simple futurity*) (*Used in the 1st
pers. For the 2nd and 3rd pers. see* WILL³.)
To-morrow I shall go and he will arrive, demain,
moi je partirai et lui arrivera. *We shall hope to
see you again,* nous espérons avoir l'occasion de
vous revoir. *Will you be there?—I shall,* y
serez-vous?—Oui (, j'y serai). *No, I shall not;
F: no, I shan't,* non (, je n'y serai pas). *He had
promised that I should be there,* il avait promis que
je serais là. *I shall explain the situation to you and
you will listen,* je vais vous expliquer la situation
et vous allez m'écouter. (*b*) (*In interrogation*)
Shall you come to-morrow? vous viendrez
demain? (*Cp. Will you come to-morrow?* voulez-
vous venir demain?) **3.** *If he comes I shall speak
to him,* s'il vient je lui parlerai. *We should come
if we were invited,* nous viendrions si on nous
invitait. *I shouldn't do it if I were you,* à votre
place je n'en ferais rien. **4.** (*In softened affirmation*) *I should like a drink,* je prendrais bien
quelque chose. *I shouldn't be surprised* (*if . . .*),
cela ne me surprendrait pas (que . . .).

shallot [ʃə'lɔt], *s.* Échalote *f.*

shallow ['ʃalo, -ou]. **I.** *a.* (*a*) (*Of water*) Peu
profond, bas de fond; (*of dish*) plat. *Nau:*
Shallow water, hauts-fonds. Shallow draft, faible
tirant *m* (d'un navire). (*b*) *F:* (*Of mind, pers.*)
Superficiel, frivole. Shallow intellect, homme
qui a peu de fond; esprit superficiel. **2.** *s.* (*In
sea, river*) (*often in pl.*) Bas-fond *m,* haut-fond *m.*

shallowness ['ʃalonəs], *s.* (*a*) (Le) peu de profondeur (de l'eau, etc.). (*b*) *F:* Caractère superficiel; manque *m* de fond (de qn, de l'esprit).

sham¹ [ʃam]. **I.** *a.* (*Of illness*) Simulé, feint; (*of
jewel*) faux, postiche, en toc. Sham title, titre
d'emprunt. *A s. colonel,* un faux colonel. *Mil:*
Sham fight, combat d'exercice; simulacre *m* de
combat. **II. sham,** *s.* **1.** Feinte *f, F:* trompe-
l'œil *m inv, P:* chiqué *m.* That's all sham, tout
ça c'est de la frime. *His love was a mere s.,* son
amour était une imposture. He is all sham, tout
en lui est artificiel. **2.** (*Of pers.*) He's a sham,
c'est un imposteur.

sham², *v.tr.* (shammed) Feindre, simuler. To
sham sickness, feindre une maladie. *To s. sleep,*
faire semblant de dormir. He is only shamming,
tout ça c'est de la frime. He shammed dead, il
fit le mort.

shamble¹ [ʃambl], *s.* Démarche traînante.

shamble², *v.i.* To shamble (along), aller à pas
traînants; s'avancer en traînant e pas.

shambles ['ʃamblz], *s.pl.* (*With sg. const.*)
(*a*) Abattoir *m.* (*b*) Scène *f* de carnage, de
boucherie.

shame¹ [ʃeim], *s.* (*a*) Honte *f.* To put s.o. to
shame, (i) confondre qn; (ii) faire honte à qn.
Shame (up)on you! honte à vous! All the more
shame to you! c'est d'autant plus honteux à
vous! For shame! fi! quelle honte! Without
shame, éhonté. To be lost to all (sense of) shame,
avoir perdu toute honte. (*b*) *F:* It was a s. of
you to . . ., c'était honteux de votre part de . . .
It is a shame to laugh at him, ce n'est pas bien
de se moquer de lui. It's a (great) shame! c'est
honteux! It's a sin and a shame! c'est une
indignité! What a shame! quel dommage!
quelle pitié!

shame², *v.tr.* Faire honte à, humilier (qn);
couvrir (qn) de honte. To be shamed into doing
sth., faire qch. par amour-propre.

shamefaced ['ʃeimfeist], *a.* (A l'air) honteux;
embarrassé, penaud.

shamefacedly [ʃeim'feisidli], *adv.* D'une manière embarrassée ; honteusement ; d'un air penaud.

shameful [ʃeimful], *a.* Honteux, scandaleux, indigne. **-fully,** *adv.* Honteusement, scandaleusement.

shamefulness [ʃeimfulnəs], *s.* Honte *f*, infamie *f*.

shameless [ʃeimləs], *a.* **1.** (*Of pers., conduct*) Éhonté, effronté, cynique. **2.** (*Of action*) Honteux, scandaleux. **-ly,** *adv.* Immodestement, effrontément. *To lie s.,* mentir impudemment.

shamelessness [ʃeimləsnəs], *s.* **1.** Immodestie *f*, impudeur *f*. **2.** Effronterie *f*, impudence *f*.

shammer [ʃamər], *s.* Simulateur, -trice ; imposteur *m*.

shammy(-leather) [ʃami('leðər)], *s.* = CHAMOIS-LEATHER.

shampoo[1] [ʃam'puː], *s.* Schampooing *m.* *Dry shampoo,* friction *f.* *Shampoo powder,* schampooing en poudre.

shampoo[2], *v.tr.* To shampoo one's hair, se dégraisser les cheveux. *To s. s.o.,* donner, faire, un schampooing à qn.

shamrock [ʃamrɔk], *s.* Trèfle *m* d'Irlande.

shandrydan [ʃandridan], *s.* **1.** Carriole irlandaise. **2.** *F:* Patache *f*, berlingot *m*, bagnole *f*.

shandy(gaff) [ʃandi(gaf)], *s.* Mélange *m* de bière et de *ginger-beer* (*q.v.*) ; bière panachée.

shanghai [ʃaŋ'hai], *v.tr.* *F:* To shanghai a man, enivrer ou "endormir" un homme pour l'embarquer sur un navire à court d'équipage.

shank [ʃaŋk], *s.* **1.** (*a*) Shanks, jambes *f*, *P:* quilles *f.* *F:* To go, come, on Shanks's mare, prendre le train onze. (*b*) (i) Tibia *m*; (ii) *Farr:* canon *m* (du membre antérieur). (*c*) *Cu:* Manche *m* (de gigot de mouton). **2.** (*a*) Branche *f*, bras *m* (de ciseaux). (*b*) Tige *f* (de clef, etc.) ; fût *m* (d'une colonne) ; hampe *f* (d'hameçon) ; *Typ:* corps *m*, tige (de lettre). Anchor shank, verge *f* (d'ancre). (*c*) Queue *f* (d'un bouton). **'shank-bone,** *s.* Tibia *m.*

shan't [ʃɑːnt]. *See* SHALL.

shantung [ʃan'tʌŋ], *s.* *Tex:* Shant(o)ung *m.*

shanty[1] [ʃanti], *s.* Hutte *f*, cabane *f*, baraque *f.*

shanty[2] *s.* = CHANTY.

shape[1] [ʃeip], *s.* **1.** (*a*) Forme *f*, configuration *f*; façon *f*, coupe *f* (d'un habit, etc.). **What shape is his hat?** de quelle forme est son chapeau? **Trees of all shapes,** des arbres de toutes les formes. *My hat was knocked out of shape,* mon chapeau a été déformé. **To get out of shape, to lose shape,** se déformer ; (*of boots*) s'avachir. *Journ: etc:* **To put an article into shape,** mettre un article au point. *S.a.* LICK[2] I. ' (*b*) Taille *f*, tournure *f.* (*c*) Forme indistincte ; apparition *f.* **2. To take shape,** prendre forme. *Our plans are taking s.,* nos projets se dessinent. **3.** *No communication in any shape or form,* aucune communication de n'importe quelle sorte. **4.** (*a*) *Cu:* (i) (*For jellies, etc.*) Moule *m.* (ii) Rice shape, gâteau *m* de riz. (*b*) (i) Forme (pour chapeau) ; (ii) carcasse *f* (de chapeau). (*c*) *Phot:* Cutting shape, calibre *m* à découper.

shape[2], *v.* **1.** *v.tr.* (*a*) Façonner, modeler de l'argile) ; tailler (un bloc de pierre). *Cer:* Contourner (un vase). *To s. the clay into an urn,* donner à l'argile la forme d'une urne. **To shape a coat to the figure,** ajuster un habit à la taille. **To shape one's life,** régler sa vie. (*b*) Former, inventer (un plan). (*c*) **To shape one's course,** diriger ses pas, se diriger (*towards,* vers) ; *Nau:* faire route (*for,* sur). **To shape the course of public opinion,** imprimer une direction à

l'opinion. **2.** *v.i.* Se développer. **To shape well,** promettre. *The affair is shaping well,* l'affaire prend bonne tournure. **He is shaping well at Latin,** il mord au latin. *The crops are shaping well,* la récolte s'annonce bien. **shape up,** *v.i.* **To shape up to s.o.,** avancer sur qn en posture de combat.

shaped, *a.* **1.** Façonné, taillé. **2. Well-shaped,** ill-shaped, bien, mal, formé. **Heart-shaped,** wedge-shaped, en forme de cœur, de coin.

shaping, *s.* **1.** Façonnement *m*, façonnage *m* (d'un bloc de pierre) ; contournement *m* (d'un vase). **Shaping (of a coat) to the figure,** ajustage *m* à la taille. **2.** Formation *f*, conception *f* (d'un projet) ; mise *f* au point.

shapeless [ʃeipləs], *a.* Informe ou difforme. *S. legs,* jambes toutes d'une venue.

shapelessness [ʃeipləsnəs], *s.* Manque *m* de forme ; manque de galbe.

shapeliness [ʃeiplinəs], *s.* Beauté *f* de forme ; galbe *m.*

shapely [ʃeipli], *a.* Bien fait, bien tourné.

shard [ʃɑːrd], *s.* Tesson *m* (de poterie). *To break into shards,* se briser (en fragments).

share[1] [ʃɛər], *s.* Soc *m* (de charrue).

share[2], *s.* **1.** (*a*) Part *f*, portion *f.* *In equal shares,* par portions égales. **The lion's share,** la part du lion. **Share in profits,** participation *f* aux bénéfices ; tantième *m* (des bénéfices). **To go shares,** partager (*with,* avec). **To go half-shares with s.o.,** mettre qn de part à demi. **Share and share alike,** en partageant également. (*b*) (**Fair**) **share,** portion juste ; lot *m.* **To come in for one's full share of sth.,** avoir sa bonne part de qch. **To each one his due share,** à chacun ce qui lui revient. **2.** Contribution *f*, écot *m.* **To pay one's share,** payer sa (quote-)part, son écot. **To take a share in** *the conversation,* contribuer (pour sa part) à la conversation. **To bear one's share of the burden,** prendre sa part du fardeau. **He doesn't do his share,** il n'y met pas du sien. **To have a share in an undertaking,** avoir un intérêt dans une entreprise. **3.** *Com:* (*In a company*) Action *f*, titre *m.* **Ordinary share,** action ordinaire. **Qualification share,** action statutaire. **Founder's share,** part de fondateur. **To hold shares,** posséder, détenir, des actions. **'share-certificate,** *s.* *Fin:* Titre *m* d'action(s). **'share-list,** *s.* Cours *m* de la Bourse. **'share-pusher,** *s.* Courtier marron. **'share-warrant,** *s.* Titre *m* au porteur.

share[3]. **1.** *v.tr.* Partager. (*a*) Donner une partie de (ce que l'on a). *To s. sth. with s.o.,* partager qch. avec qn. (*b*) Avoir part à (qch.). **To share s.o.'s opinion,** partager l'avis de qn. **To share and share alike,** partager entre tous également. **2.** *v.tr. & ind.tr.* **To share (in) sth.,** prendre part à, participer à, qch. **To share (in) s.o.'s grief,** partager la douleur de qn. **share out,** *v.tr.* Partager, répartir (le butin). **sharing,** *s.* **1.** Partage *m.* **2.** Participation *f.*

shareholder [ʃɛərhouldər], *s.* Actionnaire *mf.*

sharer [ʃɛərər], *s.* Partageant, -ante ; participant, -ante.

shark [ʃɑːrk], *s.* **1.** *Ich:* Requin *m.* **Basking shark,** pèlerin *m.* **2.** *F:* (*a*) Escroc *m* ; requin. **Financial sharks,** les aigrefins *m* de la finance. (*b*) *U.S:* Racoleur *m* de main-d'œuvre. **'shark-skin,** *s.* Peau *f* de requin ; galuchat *m.*

sharp[1] [ʃɑːrp]. **I.** *a.* **1.** (*a*) Tranchant, aiguisé, affilé ; (*of point*) aigu, pointu. **Sharp edge of a sword,** tranchant *m* d'un sabre. (*b*) (*Of features*) Anguleux, tiré ; (*of angle*) saillant, aigu ; (*of curve*) prononcé. **Sharp edge,** vive arête. **Sharp turn,** tournant brusque. (*c*) (*Of outline, Phot:* of *image*) Net, *f*. nette. (*d*) **Sharp contrast**, contraste marqué. **2.** (*a*) (*Of pers.*) Fin, éveillé; (*of sense of hearing*) fin, subtil; (*of sight*) perçant; (*of glance*) pénétrant. **A sharp child**, un enfant vif, futé, affûté. **He is as sharp as a needle**, il est fin comme l'ambre. *S.a.* LOOK-OUT I. (*b*) (*Of pers., etc.*) Rusé, malin; peu scrupuleux. **Sharp practice(s)**, procédés peu honnêtes. **To be too sharp for s.o.**, être trop malin pour qn. **3.** (*a*) (*Combat*) vif, acharné. (*b*) (*Orage*) violent. *S. shower*, forte averse. (*c*) (*Hiver*) rigoureux; (*vent*) vif, perçant; (*froid*) pénétrant. *S. pain*, vive douleur. (*d*) Rapide; (*trot*) vif. **That was sharp work!** ça n'a pas pris longtemps! (*e*) *S. rebuke*, verte réprimande. **Sharp tongue**, langue acérée. **In a sharp tone**, d'un ton acerbe, cassant. **4.** (*Of sauce*) Piquant; (*of apple*) aigre, acide; (*of wine*) vert. **5.** (*a*) (*Of sound*) Pénétrant, aigu. **A sharp whistle**, un coup de sifflet perçant. (*b*) *Mus:* (Fa, etc.) dièse. (*c*) *Ling:* **Sharp consonant**, consonne forte. **-ly,** *adv.* **1.** *S. divided into two classes*, partagé nettement en deux classes. **2.** *The road dips s.*, la route plonge brusquement. **3.** (*a*) (Marcher) vivement; (geler) fort. (*b*) *He looked s. at her*, il dirigea sur elle un regard pénétrant. (*c*) (Réprimander) sévèrement. *To speak s. to s.o.*, rudoyer qn. **To answer sharply**, répondre avec brusquerie. **4.** (Sonner) sec. **II. sharp,** *s.* **1.** *Mus:* Dièse *m.* **2.** = SHARPER. **III. sharp,** *adv.* **1.** Sharp-cut outline, profil nettement découpé. **2.** (*a*) (S'arrêter) brusquement, court. (*b*) (Tourner) brusquement. **Turn sharp right**, prenez à droite à angle droit. **3.** Ponctuellement, exactement. **At four o'clock sharp**, à quatre heures sonnantes, précises. **4.** *F:* **Look sharp!** faites vite! *Now then, look s. about it!* allons, et plus vite que ça! **'sharp-'edged,** *a.* Tranchant, affilé. **'sharp-'eyed,** *a.* Aux yeux perçants, à la vue perçante. **'sharp-'faced,** *a.* A visage en lame de couteau. **'sharp-'featured,** *a.* **1.** Aux traits tirés, amaigris. **2.** = SHARP-FACED. **'sharp-'set,** *a.* **1.** To be sharp-set, avoir l'estomac creux. **2.** (*Of tool*) Bien aiguisé; affilé. **'sharp-'sighted,** *a.* **1.** A la vue perçante. **2.** *F:* Perspicace. **'sharp-'tongued,** *a.* Qui a la langue acérée. **'sharp-'toothed,** *a.* Aux dents aiguës. **'sharp-'witted,** *a.* Intelligent, éveillé, dégourdi.

sharp², *v.tr.* (*a*) *F:* Duper (qn). (*b*) *Abs.* Tricher (au jeu).

sharpen ['ʃɑːrp(ə)n], *v.tr.* **1.** (*a*) Affiler, affûter, aiguiser. *Razor that wants sharpening*, rasoir qui a perdu son fil. (*b*) Tailler en pointe, aiguiser (un bâton). **To sharpen a pencil**, tailler un crayon. *S.a.* CLAW¹ I. **2.** *F:* **To sharpen (the wits of) s.o.**, dégourdir qn. *The wine had sharpened his wits*, le vin lui avait éveillé l'esprit. **3.** Aviver, aggraver (la douleur). **4.** Relever (une sauce) (au vinaigre). **5.** *Mus:* Diéser (une note).

sharpener ['ʃɑːrpnər], *s.* Dispositif *m* d'affûtage; aiguisoir *m. S.a.* PENCIL-SHARPENER.

sharper ['ʃɑːrpər], *s.* **1.** Aigrefin *m*; chevalier *m* d'industrie. **2.** (*At cards*) Tricheur *m.*

sharpness ['ʃɑːrpnəs], *s.* **1.** (*a*) Acuité *f*, finesse *f* (du tranchant d'un couteau); acuité (d'une pointe). (*b*) *Nau:* Finesse (des formes d'un navire). (*c*) *Aut:* *S. of the turn*, raccourci *m* du virage. (*d*) Netteté *f* (des contours). (*e*) Caractère marqué (d'un contraste). **2.** (*a*) *S. of sight*, acuité de la vue. (*b*) Intelligence *f* (d'un enfant). **3.** (*a*) Acuité (de la douleur); (*b*) **There is a sharpness in the air**, il y a de l'aigre dans l'air. (*c*) Sévérité *f*, acerbité *f* (du ton). **4.** (Goût)

piquant *m* (d'une sauce); acidité *f*, aigreur *f* (d'une pomme). **5.** Acuité (d'un son).

sharpshooter ['ʃɑːrpʃuːtər], *s. Mil:* Tirailleur *m*; tireur *m* d'élite.

shatter ['ʃatər]. **I.** *v.tr.* (*a*) Fracasser; briser en éclats. *The glass was shattered*, le verre a volé en éclats.·(*b*) Briser (des espérances). (*c*) Détraquer (les nerfs). **2.** *v.i.* Se briser (en éclats); se fracasser. **shattering,** *a.* **1.** (Coup) écrasant. **2.** *Exp:* **Shattering charge,** charge brisante.

shave¹ [ʃeiv], *s.* **1.** To have a shave, (i) se faire raser; (ii) se raser. *Hair-cut or s., sir?* les cheveux ou la barbe? **2.** Coup effleurant, à fleur de peau. *F:* **To have a close, narrow, shave,** l'échapper belle. **It was a narrow shave!** *F:* il était moins cinq!

shave², *v.tr.* (*p.p. in comp. tenses* **shaved**; *as adj.* **shaven** ['ʃeiv(ə)n]) **1.** (*a*) Raser; faire la barbe à (qn). (*b*) **To shave (oneself)**, se raser, se faire la barbe. **2.** Planer (le bois). **3.** Friser, raser, effleurer (qch.). *Aut:* *To s. another car*, frôler une autre voiture. **shaven,** *a.* (*Of monk*) Tonsuré; (*of head, chin*) rasé. **shaving,** *s.* **1.** (*a*) Action *f* de raser ou de se raser. (*b*) Planage *m* (du bois). **2.** Copeau *m*, planure *f* (de bois, de métal). *pl.* Shavings, copeaux, raboture(s) *f.* **'shaving-basin, -dish,** *s.* Plat *m* à barbe. **'shaving-block,** *s. Toil:* Pierre *f* d'alun. **'shaving-brush,** *s.* Blaireau *m*; pinceau *m* à barbe. **'shaving-glass,** *s.* Miroir *m* à barbe. **'shaving-soap, -stick,** *s.* Savon *m* à barbe; bâton *m* de savon pour la barbe.

shaveling ['ʃeivliŋ], *s. A: F:* Tonsuré *m.*

shaven ['ʃeiv(ə)n]. *See* SHAVE².

shaver ['ʃeivər], *s.* **1.** Raseur *m*, barbier *m.* **2.** *F:* **Young shaver,** gosse *m*, gamin *m*, moutard *m.*

shaw [ʃɔː], *s. A. & Poet:* Taillis *m*, fourré *m.*

shawl [ʃɔːl], *s.* Châle *m* ou fichu *m.*

she [ʃi, ʃiː], *pers. pron. nom. f.* **1.** (*Unstressed*) Elle. (*a*) (*Of pers.*) *What is she doing?* que fait-elle? *Here she comes*, la voici qui vient. (*b*) *F:* (i) (*Of female animals, motor cars, etc.*) Elle. (ii) (*Of ships, etc.*) *She sails to-morrow*, il appareille demain. **2.** (*Stressed*) (*a*) Elle. *She and I*, elle et moi. *It is she*, c'est elle. (*Emphatic*) *'She knows nothing about it*, elle n'en sait rien, elle. (*b*) (*Antecedent to a rel. pron.*) (i) Celle. **She that, she who,** believes, celle qui croit. (ii) **It is she who did it,** c'est elle qui l'a fait. **3.** (*As substantive*) *F:* Femelle, femme. **She-ass,** ânesse *f.* **She-bear,** ours *m* femelle; ourse *f.* **She-goat,** chèvre *f*; *F:* bique *f.*

sheaf, *pl.* **-ves** [ʃiːf, -vz], *s.* **1.** Gerbe *f* (de blé). **Loose sheaf,** javelle *f.* **2.** Liasse *f* (de papiers).

shear¹ [ʃiːər], *s.* **1.** (Pair of) shears, cisaille(s) *f(pl)*; (grands) ciseaux. **Garden shears,** cisailles à haie. *Lit:* *The shears of Atropos*, les ciseaux de la Parque. **2.** *Mec.E:* Shears, shear-legs, bigue *f*; chèvre *f* à haubans. **'shear-hulk,** *s. Nau:* Ponton-mâture *m*; mâture flottante.

shear², *s.* **1.** Tonte *f* (de laine). **2.** *Mec:* (Effort de) cisaillement *m.*

shear³, *v.tr.* (*p.t.* **sheared;** *p.p.* **shorn** [ʃɔːrn], **sheared**) **1.** (*a*) To shear (off), couper (une branche). **To shear through sth.,** trancher qch. (*b*) *Metalw:* Cisailler (une tôle). **2.** Tondre (un mouton). *F:* **To be shorn of sth.,** être dépouillé, privé, de qch. **3.** *Mec:* Cisailler; faire subir un cisaillement à (une poutre). **shorn,** *a.* **1.** *A. & Poet:* (*Of head*) Rasé. **2.** (Mouton) tondu. *F:* *S. of all his belongings*, dépouillé de tout ce qu'il possédait. **shearing,** *s.* **1.** (*a*) Coupage *m* (d'une haie); cisaillement *m* (d'une tôle); tonte *f,* tondaison *f* (des moutons). (*b*) *Mec:* Shearing stress, (effort *m* de) cisaillement. **2.** *pl.* **Shearings,** tontes (de laine).

shearer ['ʃiːərər], *s.* Tondeur *m* (de moutons).

shearwater ['ʃiːərwɔːtər], *s. Orn:* Puffin *m.*

sheath [ʃiːθ], *s.* (*pl.* [ʃiːðz] *or* [ʃiːθs]) (*a*) Manchon protecteur; fourreau *m* (d'épée); étui *m* (de ciseaux); gaine *f* (de couteau). (*b*) *Anat:* Enveloppe *f* (d'un organe). 'sheath-knife, *s.* Couteau *m* à gaine.

sheathe [ʃiːð], *v.tr.* **1.** (Re)mettre au fourreau, rengainer (une épée). *Lit:* To sheathe the sword, cesser les hostilités. **2.** (*a*) Revêtir, recouvrir, doubler (un navire) (*with,* de, en). (*b*) *El.E:* Armer (un câble). **sheathing,** *s.* **1.** (*a*) Mise *f* au fourreau. (*b*) Armement *m* (d'un câble). **2.** (*a*) Revêtement *m* (de, en, métal). *N.Arch:* Doublage *m.* **Sheathing felt,** ploc *m.* (*b*) *Mec.E: etc:* Enveloppe *f*; chemise *f* (d'un cylindre). '(*c*) Armure *f* (d'un câble).

sheave [ʃiːv], *s.* Réa *m,* rouet *m* (de poulie).

sheaves [ʃiːvz]. *See* SHEAF.

shebeen [ʃiˈbiːn], *s. Irish:* Débit de boissons clandestin.

she'd [ʃiːd] = she had, she would.

shed[1] [ʃed], *s. Ph.Geog:* Ligne *f* de faîte.

shed[2], *s.* (*a*) Hangar *m.* **Lean-to shed,** appentis *m.* **Open shed,** auvent *m.* **Building shed,** atelier *m* de construction. (*b*) *Nau:* Tente *f* à marchandises. (*c*) Baraque *f.*

shed[3], *v.tr.* (*p.t.* & *p.p.* **shed**; *pr.p.* **shedding**) **1.** (*a*) Perdre (ses feuilles); (*of animal*) jeter (sa peau). *S.a.* HORN 1. (*b*) *F:* Se défaire de (qn). (*c*) To s. one's clothes, se dévêtir. **2.** Répandre, verser (des larmes, le sang). The lamp shed a soft light, la lampe versait une douce lumière. *F:* To shed (a) light on a matter, éclaircir une affaire. **shedding,** *s.* **1.** Perte *f,* chute *f* (des feuilles). (*Of animals*) S. of skin, mue *f.* **2.** Effusion *f* (de sang, etc.). *S. of tears,* pleurs *mpl.*

sheen [ʃiːn], *s.* Luisant *m,* lustre *m* (de la soie); chatoiement *m* (d'une étoffe). **To take the sheen off sth.,** délustrer qch.

sheeny ['ʃiːni], *s. P:* Youpin, -ine.

sheep [ʃiːp], *s.inv. in pl.* **1.** Mouton *m.* **Black s.,** brebis noire. *F:* **The black sheep** (*of the family*), la brebis galeuse. **They follow one another like sheep,** ce sont les moutons de Panurge. *S.a.* EYE[1] 1. **2.** *Bookb:* = SHEEPSKIN 2. 'sheep-dip, *s.* Bain *m* parasiticide (pour moutons). 'sheep-dog, *s.* Chien *m* de berger. 'sheep-farming, *s.* Élevage *m* de moutons. 'sheep-run, -walk, *s.* Pâturage *m* (pour moutons). 'sheep-wash, *s.* = SHEEP-DIP.

sheepfold ['ʃiːpfould], *s.* Parc *m* à moutons; bercail *m.*

sheepish ['ʃiːpiʃ], *a.* **1.** Penaud; interdit. *To look s.,* rester penaud. **2.** Timide; gauche. **-ly,** *adv.* **1.** D'un air penaud. **2.** D'un air timide.

sheepishness ['ʃiːpiʃnəs], *s.* **1.** Timidité *f*; fausse honte. **2.** Air penaud.

sheepshank ['ʃiːpʃæŋk], *s.* (Nœud *m* en) jambe *f* de chien.

sheepskin ['ʃiːpskin], *s.* **1.** Peau *f* de mouton. **2.** *Bookb:* Basane *f.* **3.** Parchemin *m.*

sheer[1] [ʃiːər], *s. Nau:* Embardée *f.*

sheer[2], *v.i. Nau:* Embarder. **sheer off,** *v.i.* **1.** *Nau:* Larguer les amarres. **2.** *F:* S'écarter; *F:* prendre le large.

sheer[3], *s. N.Arch:* Tonture *f* (du pont). 'sheer-rail, *s.* Liston *m,* listeau *m,* listel *m.*

sheer[4]. **1.** *a.* (*a*) Pur, véritable, franc. *It is s. robbery,* c'est un véritable vol. *A s. impossibility,* une impossibilité absolue. *A s. waste of time,*

une pure perte de temps. (*b*) Perpendiculaire; (rocher) à pic. *S. coast,* côte accore. **2.** *adv.* (*a*) Tout à fait; complètement. (*b*) *Hill that descends s. to the town,* colline qui descend abruptement à la ville.

sheer-hulk ['ʃiːərhʌlk], *s.* = SHEAR-HULK.

sheer-legs ['ʃiːərlegz], *s.pl.* = SHEAR[1] 2.

sheet[1] [ʃiːt], *s.* **1.** Drap *m* (de lit). *Hist:* **White sheet,** linge blanc dont se couvraient les pénitents. *S.a.* WHITE[1] I.2. **2.** (*a*) Feuille *f,* feuillet *m* (de papier). **Loose sheet,** feuille volante. *Com:* **Order sheet,** bulletin *m* de commande. (*b*) *F:* Journal *m,* -aux; feuille. **3.** Feuille (de verre, de plomb, etc.); tôle *f.* **4.** (*a*) Nappe *f* (d'eau). (*b*) Lame d'eau (embarquée à bord). 'sheet-copper, *s.* Cuivre *m* en tôles. 'sheet-glass, *s.* Verre *m* à vitres. 'sheet-iron, *s.* (Fer *m* en) tôle *f*; fer en feuilles. 'sheet-lead [led], *s.* Plomb laminé; plomb en feuilles. 'sheet-lightning, *s.* Éclairs *mpl* diffus; éclairs en nappe(s). 'sheet-rubber, *s. Ind:* Feuille anglaise.

sheet[2], *v.tr.* **1.** Couvrir, garnir, (qch.) d'un drap, d'une bâche. **2.** *River sheeted with ice,* rivière couverte de glace. **sheeting,** *s.* **1.** Toile *f* pour draps. **Waterproof sheeting,** drap *m* d'hôpital. **2.** *Coll.* Tôlerie *f*; tôles *fpl.*

sheet[3], *s. Nau:* **1.** Écoute *f.* **Sheet bend,** nœud *m* d'écoute. **2.** Stern-sheets, arrière *m,* chambre *f* (d'un canot).

sheet-anchor ['ʃiːtæŋkər], *s. Nau:* Ancre *f* de veille. *F:* **It is our sheet-anchor,** c'est notre ancre de salut.

sheikh [ʃeik, ʃiːk], *s.m.* Cheik, scheik.

shekel ['ʃek(ə)l], *s.* **1.** *A. Jew. Meas.* & *Num:* Sicle *m.* **2.** *pl. F:* Shekels, argent *m.*

sheldrake ['ʃeldreik], *s. Orn:* Tadorne *m.*

shelf[1], *pl.* **shelves** [ʃelf, ʃelvz], *s.* **1.** Tablette *f* (de rayonnage); planche *f* (d'armoire); rayon *m* (de bibliothèque). **Set of shelves,** étagère *f. F:* **To be on the shelf,** être au rancart. *She is on the s.,* elle a coiffé sainte Catherine. **2.** (*a*) Rebord *m,* corniche *f* (d'un rocher). (*b*) **Continental shelf,** plateau, banc, continental.

shelf[2], *s.* Haut-fond *m,* bas-fond *m*; banc *m* de sable.

shell[1] [ʃel], *s.* **1.** (*a*) Coquille *f* (de mollusque); carapace *f* (de tortue); écaille *f* (d'huître). (*Empty*) **shells,** coquillages *m. F:* **To come out of one's shell,** sortir de sa chrysalide ou de sa coquille. **To retire into one's shell,** rentrer dans sa coquille. (*b*) Coquille (d'œuf, de noix); coque *f* (d'œuf plein). *Ent:* Enveloppe *f* (de nymphe). (*c*) *F:* Forme *f* vide; simple apparence *f.* **2.** (*a*) *Mch:* Paroi *f,* coque (de chaudière). (*b*) Enveloppe extérieure. *Metall:* Manteau *m* (de moule). **3.** Carcasse *f,* coque (de navire). **4.** (*a*) Cercueil *m* provisoire. (*b*) **Lead(en) shell,** doublure *f* en plomb (pour cercueil). **5.** *Artil:* Obus *m.* **Live shell,** obus de combat. **High-explosive shell,** obus brisant. **6.** *Sch:* Classe *f* intermédiaire. 'shell-back, *s. Nau: P:* Gourganier *m*; vieux loup de mer. 'shell-fire, *s.* Tir *m* à obus. **To be under shell-fire,** subir un bombardement. 'shell-fish, *s.* **1.** (*a*) Testacé *m* (moule, etc.). *F:* coquillage *m.* (*b*) Crustacé *m* (homard, etc.). **2.** *Coll.* Mollusques *m* et crustacés. 'shell-hole, *s.* Trou *m* d'obus; cratère *m*; entonnoir *m.* 'shell-jacket, *s. Mil:* Veste *f* de petite tenue. 'shell-proof, *a.* Blindé; à l'épreuve des obus. 'shell-shock, *s. Med:* Psychose *f* traumatique; commotion cérébrale. *Suffering from s.-s.,* commotionné.

shell[2], *v.tr.* **1.** Écaler (des noix); écosser (des pois); écailler (des huîtres). *To s. green walnuts*, cerner des noix. **2.** *Mil:* Bombarder. **shell out,** *v.tr. F:* To shell out one's money, *abs.* to shell out, payer la note; débourser. **shelled,** *a.* **1.** A coquille; testacé. **2.** (*Of nuts*) Écalé; (*of peas*) écossé. **shelling,** *s.* **1.** Egrenage *m* (de pois); décorticage *m* (d'amandes); écaillage *m* (d'huîtres). **2.** *Mil:* Bombardement *m.*

she'll [ʃiːl] = she will.

shellac¹ [ʃe'lak], *s.* Laque *f* en écailles, en plaques.

shellac², *v.tr.* (shellacked) Gommelaquer.

shelter¹ ['ʃeltər], *s.* **1.** Lieu *m* de refuge; abri *m*; asile *m.* **Taxi-drivers' shelter**, kiosque-vigie *m.* **2.** Under shelter, à l'abri, à couvert. To take shelter, s'abriter, se mettre à l'abri (*under*, sous; *from*, de, contre). **'shelter-deck,** *s. Nau:* Pont-abri *m.*

shelter². **1.** *v.tr.* (*a*) Abriter. (*b*) Donner asile à, recueillir (un malheureux). **To shelter s.o. from blame**, tenir qn à l'abri de la censure. **2.** *v.i. & pr.* S'abriter, se mettre à l'abri (*from*, contre). *To s. from the rain*, se mettre à couvert (de la pluie). **sheltered,** *a.* Abrité (*against, from*, contre). **Sheltered industry,** industrie garantie contre la concurrence étrangère. **sheltering,** *a.* Protecteur, -trice.

shelve¹ [ʃelv], *v.tr.* **1.** Munir, garnir, (une bibliothèque) de rayons. **2.** *F:* Ajourner, enterrer (une question); mettre (qn) au rancart; remiser (qn). *My request has been shelved*, ma demande est restée dans les cartons. **shelving¹,** *s.* **1.** *F:* Enterrement *m*, ajournement *m* (d'une question); mise *f* au rancart (de qn). **2.** (Ensemble *m* de) rayons *mpl*; rayonnage *m.* *Adjustable s.*, rayons mobiles.

shelve², *v.i.* Aller en pente. *The shore shelves down to the sea*, le rivage s'incline vers la mer. **shelving²,** *a.* En pente; incliné.

shelves [ʃelvz]. *See* SHELF¹.

shepherd¹ ['ʃepərd], *s.m.* (*a*) Berger, pâtre. **Shepherd boy**, petit pâtre. **Shepherd girl**, bergère *f.* (*b*) The Good Shepherd, le bon Pasteur. *S.a.* PIE². **shepherd's 'plaid,** *s.* Plaid *m* en damier. **shepherd's 'purse,** *s. Bot: F:* Bourse-à-pasteur *f.*

shepherd², *v.tr.* **1.** Garder, soigner (les moutons). **2.** *F:* To shepherd school children through the town, piloter des écoliers à travers la ville.

shepherdess ['ʃepərdes], *s.f.* Bergère.

sherbet ['ʃəːrbət], *s.* Sorbet *m.*

shereef, sherif [ʃe'riːf], *s.* Chérif *m* (titre arabe).

sheriff ['ʃerif], *s.m.* **1.** *Eng.Adm:* Shériff. (Fonctions correspondant à celles du préfet). *S.a.* OFFICER¹ **1.** **2.** (Scot.) Premier président (d'un comté). **3.** *U.S:* Chef de la police (d'un comté). **sheriff 'substitute,** *s.m.* (Scot.) Juge de première instance (d'un comté).

sherry ['ʃeri], *s.* Vin *m* de Xérès; xérès *m.* **'sherry-glass,** *s.* Verre *m* à madère.

she's [ʃiːz] = she is, she has.

Shetland ['ʃetlənd]. *Pr.n.* The Shetland Islands, les îles Shetland. **'Shetland pony,** *s.* Poney shetlandais.

shew¹,² [ʃou], *s. & v.* = SHOW¹,².

shibboleth ['ʃiboleθ], *s.* (*a*) *B.Hist:* S(c)hibboleth *m.* (*b*) *F:* Mot *m* d'ordre (d'un parti).

shield¹ [ʃiːld], *s.* **1.** (*a*) Bouclier *m.* *Archeol:* Body-shield, pavois *m.* (*b*) *Her:* = ESCUTCHEON. *F:* The other side of the shield, le revers de la médaille. (*c*) Écusson (d'un canif). **2.** *Tchn:* Tôle protectrice. *Artil:* Bouclier (d'une pièce

d'artillerie). **3.** (*a*) *Z:* Carapace *f.* *Ent:* Écu *m*, écusson. (*b*) *Hort:* Écusson (de greffe). **'shield-bearer,** *s.* Écuyer *m.* **'shield-bud,** *s. Hort:* Écusson *m.* **'shield-shaped,** *a.* Scutiforme.

shield², *v.tr.* **1.** Protéger (*from, against*, contre); couvrir (qn) de sa protection. **2.** (*a*) To shield one's eyes, se protéger les yeux. (*b*) *El.E:* Blinder (un transformateur, etc.). **shielding,** *s.* Protection *f* (*against, from*, contre).

shieling ['ʃiːliŋ], *s. Scot:* **1.** Pâturage *m.* **2.** Abri *m* (pour moutons, chasseurs).

shier ['ʃaiər], **shiest** ['ʃaiəst]. *See* SHY³.

shift¹ [ʃift], *s.* **1.** (*a*) Changement *m* de position; renverse *f* (de la marée). **To make a shift**, changer de place. **Shift of the wind**, saute *f* du vent. *Nau:* Shift of cargo, désarrimage *m.* *Ling:* Consonant shift, mutation *f* consonantique. (*b*) *Mus:* (*In violin-playing*) Démanchement *m.* **2.** *Ind:* (*a*) Équipe *f*, poste *m* (d'ouvriers). **To work in shifts**, se relayer. (*b*) Journée *f* de travail. *They work an eight-hour s.*, ils se relaient toutes les huit heures. **3.** *A:* Chemise *f* (de femme). **4.** (*a*) Expédient *m.* **To be at one's last shift**, être aux abois, à sa dernière ressource. **To make shift to do sth.**, trouver moyen de faire qch. **To make shift with sth.**, s'arranger, s'accommoder, de qch. *I can make shift without it*, je peux m'en passer. (*b*) *Nothing but shifts and excuses*, rien que des échappatoires et des excuses. **'shift-key,** *s. Typewr:* Touche *f* de manœuvre.

shift². **I.** *v.tr.* (*a*) Changer (qch.) de place; déplacer. **To shift the furniture**, remuer, déplacer, les meubles. *F:* To shift the responsibility of sth. upon s.o., rejeter la responsabilité de qch. sur qn. (*b*) Changer. *Th:* To shift the scenery, changer le décor. *F:* To shift one's quarters, changer de résidence. (*c*) *Nau:* To shift a sail, changer une voile. (*d*) *Abs.* (*In violin playing*) Démancher. **II.** **shift,** *v.i.* **1.** (*a*) Changer de place; se déplacer. *Nau:* (*Of cargo*) se désarrimer. (*b*) Changer. **The scene shifts**, la scène change. **The wind has shifted**, le vent a tourné, sauté. **2.** *F:* To shift for oneself, se débrouiller. **He can shift for himself**, il est débrouillard. **shift about,** *v.tr. & i.* Changer continuellement de place. **shift round,** *v.i.* (*Of wind*) Virer. **shifting,** *a.* **1.** Qui se déplace. **Shifting sand**, sables mouvants. **2.** (*Of scene*) Changeant; (*of wind*) inégal, -aux.

shiftiness ['ʃiftinəs], *s.* Sournoiserie *f*; astuce *f.*

shiftless ['ʃiftləs], *a.* **1.** Paresseux; sans énergie. **2.** Peu débrouillard.

shiftlessness ['ʃiftləsnəs], *s.* **1.** Paresse *f*; manque *m* d'énergie. **2.** Manque de ressource, d'initiative.

shifty ['ʃifti], *a.* Roublard, retors; (regard) chafouin, sournois. **S. eyes**, yeux fuyants. *S.a.* CUSTOMER 2.

shikar [ʃi'kɑːr], *s.* (*Anglo-Indian*) (La) chasse.

shikaree [ʃi'kɑːriː], *s.* (*Anglo-Indian*) **1.** Guide *m* indigène. **2.** Chasseur *m* (indigène).

shillelagh [ʃi'leila], *s.* Gourdin irlandais.

shilling ['ʃiliŋ], *s.* Shilling *m* (vingtième de la livre sterling). *F:* To cut s.o. off with a shilling, déshériter qn. **To take the King's shilling**, s'engager.

shilly-shally¹ ['ʃiliʃali], *s. F:* Barguignage *m*, vacillation *f. No more s.-s.!* plus d'hésitations!

shilly-shally², *v.i. F:* Barguigner, lanterner, vaciller.

shimmer¹ ['ʃimər], *s.* Lueur *f*; chatoiement *m.* *The s. of the moon on the lake*, les reflets *m* de la lune sur le lac.

shimmer², *v.i.* Miroiter, luire, chatoyer.

shin[1] [ʃin], *s.* (*a*) *Anat:* Le devant du tibia, de la jambe. *S.a.* BARK[2]. (*b*) *Cu:* Jarret *m* (de bœuf). **'shin-bone,** *s. Anat:* Tibia *m.* **'shin-guard,** *s. Fb:* Jambière *f.*
shin[2], *v.i.* (shinned) *F:* To shin up a tree, grimper à un arbre (à la force des bras et des jambes).
shindy ['ʃindi], *s. F:* Tapage *m,* chahut *m,* boucan *m.* To kick up a shindy, chahuter ; faire du chahut, du tapage.
shine[1] [ʃain], *s.* **I.** Éclat *m,* lumière *f. F:* Rain or shine, par tous les temps. **2.** *F:* (*On boots*) Brillant *m ;* (*on material*) luisant *m. To give a s. to the brass-work,* faire reluire les cuivres. *P:* To take the shine out of s.o.,* éclipser, surpasser, qn.
shine[2], *v.i.* (shone [ʃɔn] ; shone) **I.** Briller ; reluire. The moon is shining, il fait clair de lune. The sun is shining, il fait du soleil. *Joy shines in his face,* la joie rayonne sur son visage. His face shone with happiness, sa figure rayonnait de bonheur. *F:* He does not shine in conversation, il ne brille pas dans la conversation. **2.** To shine on sth., éclairer, illuminer, qch.
shining, *a.* Brillant, (re)luisant. Shining example, exemple brillant, insigne (*of,* de). *S.a.* IMPROVE I.
shingle[1] [ʃingl], *s.* **I.** *Const:* Bardeau *m.* **2.** *Hairdr:* Coupe *f* à la garçonne.
shingle[2], *v.tr.* **I.** *Const:* Couvrir (un toit) de bardeaux. **2.** To shingle s.o.'s hair, couper les cheveux de qn à la garçonne.
shingle[3], *s.* Galets *mpl ;* (gros) cailloux *mpl.* Shingle beach, plage *f* de galets.
shingles [ʃinglz], *s.pl. Med:* Zona *m ; F:* ceinture *f.*
shingly ['ʃingli], *a.* Couvert de galets ; caillouteux. *S. beach,* plage *f* de galets.
shiny [ʃaini], *a.* (*a*) Brillant, luisant. (*b*) *Clothes made s. by long wear,* vêtements lustrés par l'usage.
ship[1] [ʃip], *s.* (*Usu. referred to as she, her*) Navire (marchand) ; vaisseau *m* (de guerre) ; bâtiment *m ; F:* bateau *m. Navy:* Capital ship, bâtiment de ligne cuirassé. His Majesty's ships, les vaisseaux de la marine royale. **H.M.S.** Hood, le Hood. Merchant ship, navire de commerce, navire marchand. Sailing ship, navire à voiles. Convict ship, bagne flottant. *S.a.* TAR[1] I. The ship's company, l'équipage *m.* On board ship, à bord. To take ship, (s')embarquer. *F:* When my ship comes home, dès que j'aurai fait fortune. *F:* The ship of the desert, le chameau. *S.a.* BOOK[1] 2, PAPER[1] 3, REGISTER[1] I. **ship('s) boy,** *s.m. Nau:* Mousse. **'ship-breaker,** *s.* Démolisseur *m* de navires. **'ship-broker,** *s.* Courtier *m* maritime. **'ship-canal,** *s.* Cana. *m* maritime, *pl.* canaux. **'ship-chandler,** *s.* Fournisseur *m,* approvisionneur *m,* de navires. **'ship-load,** *s.* Chargement *m ;* cargaison *f ;* fret *m.* **'ship-mate,** *s.* Compagnon *m,* camarade *m,* de bord. **'ship-owner,** *s.* Propriétaire *m* de navire ; armateur *m.* **ship's 'carpenter,** *s.* Charpentier *m* du bord. **'ship-shape.** *Nau. & F:* **I.** *a.* Bien tenu ; en bon ordre. *All is s.-s.,* tout est à sa place. **2.** *adv.* En marin ; comme il faut. **ship's 'time,** *s. Nau:* L'heure locale du navire. **'ship-worm,** *s. Moll:* Taret *m.*
ship[2], *v.* (shipped) I. *v.tr.* **I.** Embarquer (une cargaison, etc.). **2.** *Com:* (i) Mettre (des marchandises) à bord. (ii) Envoyer, expédier (des marchandises). **3.** To ship a sea, embarquer une lame. **4.** *Nau:* (*a*) Monter, mettre en place (l'hélice, etc.). (*b*) To ship oars, (i) armer les avirons ; (ii) rentrer les avirons. II. **ship,** *v.i.* (*a*) (*Of passenger*) S'embarquer. (*b*) (*Of sailor*) To ship on (board) a vessel, armer sur un vaisseau.

shipping, *s.* **I.** (*a*) Embarquement *m.* Shipping charges, frais de mise à bord. (*b*) *Com:* Expédition *f,* envoi *m* (de marchandises). (*c*) Montage *m,* mise *f* en place (de l'hélice, etc.). **2.** *Coll.* Navires *mpl,* vaisseaux *mpl* (d'un pays, d'un port). Idle shipping, tonnage désarmé. **3.** Dangerous for, to, shipping, dangereux pour la navigation. Shipping routes, routes de navigation. *S.a.* LINE[1] 5. **4.** Marine marchande. Shipping intelligence, shipping news, nouvelles *f* maritimes. **'shipping-agent,** *s.* Agent *m* maritime ; (*for goods*) expéditeur *m.* **'shipping-clerk,** *s.* Expéditionnaire *m.* **'shipping-office,** *s.* (*For sailors*) L'Inscription *f* maritime. **2.** Bureau *m* de réception des marchandises. **3.** Agence *f* maritime.
-ship, *s.suff.* **I.** État ou qualité. *Authorship,* qualité d'auteur. *Ownership,* propriété. **2.** (*a*) Emploi ou dignité ; ou période d'exercice de l'emploi. *Professorship,* professorat. *Clerkship,* place de commis. (*b*) *His Lordship,* Sa Seigneurie.
shipboard ['ʃipbɔːrd], *s.* Bord *m* (de navire). On shipboard, à bord.
shipbuilder ['ʃipbildər], *s.* Constructeur *m* de navires.
shipbuilding ['ʃipbildiŋ], *s.* Architecture navale ; construction navale.
shipmaster ['ʃipmɑːstər], *s.* **I.** Capitaine marchand. **2.** Patron *m.*
shipment ['ʃipmənt], *s.* **I.** (*a*) Embarquement *m ;* mise *f* à bord. (*b*) Expédition *f* (de marchandises) ; envoi *m* par mer. **2.** (*Goods shipped*) Chargement *m.*
shipper ['ʃipər], *s. Com:* **I.** Chargeur *m,* expéditeur *m.* **2.** Affréteur *m.*
shipwreck[1] ['ʃiprek], *s.* Naufrage *m.* (*Of ship*) To suffer shipwreck, faire naufrage. *F:* The shipwreck of one's hopes, le naufrage, la ruine, de ses espérances.
shipwreck[2], *v.tr.* Faire naufrager (un vaisseau) ; *F:* faire échouer (une entreprise). To be shipwrecked, faire naufrage. **shipwrecked,** *a.* Naufragé.
shipwright ['ʃiprait], *s.* Charpentier *m* de navires.
shipyard ['ʃipjɑːrd], *s. N.Arch:* Chantier *m* de construction.
shire [ʃaiər ; *termination* ʃər], *s.* Comté *m.* Ayrshire ['ɛərʃər], le comté d'Ayr. *F:* The shires, les comtés centraux (de l'Angleterre). **'shire horse,** *s.* Type de cheval anglais de gros trait.
shirk [ʃəːrk], *v.tr.* Manquer à, se dérober à (une obligation) ; esquiver (un devoir). *Mil:* Carotter (le service). *Abs.* Négliger son devoir. He is shirking, il se défile.
shirker ['ʃəːrkər], *s.* Carotteur, -euse ; *Mil:* (i) tireur *m* au flanc ; (ii) embusqué *m.* To be no shirker, être franc du collier.
shirt [ʃəːrt], *s.* Chemise *f* (d'homme). Soft shirt, chemise molle, souple. Dress shirt, starched shirt, *F:* boiled shirt, chemise empesée, de soirée. To put on a clean s., changer de chemise. To be in one's shirt-tails, être en bannière. *P:* Keep your shirt on! ne vous emballez pas ! ne vous fâchez pas ! *Turf:* To put one's shirt on a horse, parier tout ce qu'on possède sur un cheval. *Archeol:* Shirt of mail, chemise de mailles. **'shirt-'blouse,** *s. Cost:* Chemisier *m* (de femme). **'shirt-'button,** *s.* Bouton *m* de chemise. **'shirt-'collar,** *s.* Col *m* de chemise. **'shirt-'front,** *s.* Plastron *m.* **'shirt-maker,** *s.* Chemisier, -ière. **'shirt-'sleeve,** *s.* Manche *f* de chemise. To be in one's shirt-sleeves, être en bras de chemise.

shirting ['ʃəːrtiŋ], s. Toile f pour chemises; shirting m.

shirty ['ʃəːrti], a. P: Irritable; P: en rogne. To get shirty, se fâcher.

shiver¹ ['ʃivər], s. Éclat m, fragment m. To break into shivers, se briser; voler en éclats.

shiver². **1.** v.tr. Fracasser; briser (qch.) en éclats. S.a. TIMBER¹ 2. **2.** v.i. Se fracasser; voler en éclats.

shiver³, s. Frisson m. It sent cold shivers down my back, cela m'a donné froid dans le dos. F: To have the shivers, avoir la tremblote, le frisson.

shiver⁴. **1.** v.i. To shiver (with cold), frissonner, grelotter, trembler (de froid). To have a shivering fit, être pris de frissons. **2.** Nau: (a) v.i. (Of sail) Ralinguer. (b) v.tr. Faire ralinguer (les voiles).

shoal¹ [ʃoul]. **1.** a. Shoal water, eau peu profonde. Nau: To be in s. water, raguer le fond. **2.** s. Haut-fond m, bas-fond m.

shoal², v.i. The water shoals, le fond diminue.

shoal³, s. Banc voyageur (de poissons); F: grande quantité, tas m (de lettres).

shoal⁴, v.i. (Of fish) Se réunir en bancs; voyager par bancs.

shock¹ [ʃɔk], s. Agr: Moyette f, meulette f.

shock², s. Shock of hair, tignasse f; F: toison f. **'shock-headed**, a. À la tête ébouriffée.

shock³, s. **1.** (a) Choc m, heurt m; secousse f; à-coup m. (b) Geol: Séisme m. **2.** (a) Coup m, atteinte f. It gave me a dreadful s., cela m'a porté un coup terrible. The s. killed him, il mourut de saisissement. (b) Med: Choc; traumatisme m ou commotion f. (c) Electric shock, secousse électrique. **'shock-absorber**, s. Amortisseur m (de chocs). **'shock troops**, s.pl. Mil: Troupes f d'assaut, de choc.

shock⁴, v.tr. **1.** (a) Choquer, scandaliser (qn). Easily shocked, pudibond. (b) Bouleverser (qn). I was shocked to hear that . . ., j'ai été atterré, choqué, d'apprendre que. . . . (c) To shock the ear, blesser l'oreille. **2.** (a) Donner une secousse électrique à (qn). (b) Med: Surg: To be shocked, être commotionné. **shocking¹**, a. **1.** (Of spectacle) (i) Choquant; (ii) révoltant, affreux. Shocking news, nouvelle atterrante. How s.! quelle horreur! **2.** F: (Of weather) Abominable, exécrable. **-ly**, adv. **1.** Abominablement, affreusement. **2.** Shockingly dear, terriblement cher. **shocking²**, s. Électrisation f (de qn). **'shocking-coil**, s. Med.El: Bobine f d'induction.

shocker ['ʃɔkər], s. P: **1.** (Shilling) shocker, roman m à gros effets. **2.** Surprise f pénible; rude coup m.

shod [ʃɔd]. See SHOE².

shoddiness ['ʃɔdinəs], s. Mauvaise qualité.

shoddy¹ ['ʃɔdi], s. **1.** Tex: Drap m de laine d'effilochage. **2.** (Marchandises fpl de) pacotille f.

shoddy², a. **1.** (Of cloth) D'effilochage. **2.** (Marchandises) de pacotille; camelote f.

shoe¹ [ʃuː], s. **1.** Soulier m. (Ladies') evening shoes, souliers de bal. I buy my shoes at Smith's, je me chausse chez Smith. To put on one's shoes, se chausser. F: To put the shoe on the right foot, s'en prendre à celui qui le mérite. To step into s.o.'s shoes, prendre la place de qn. I should not like to be in his shoes, je ne voudrais pas être à sa place. To be waiting for dead men's shoes, attendre la mort de qn (pour le remplacer). That's another pair of shoes, ça c'est une autre paire de manches. S.a. BOOT¹ I, SHAKE² II. 1. **2.** Fer m (de cheval). To cast a shoe, perdre un

fer. My horse has a s. loose, mon cheval a un fer qui lâche. **3.** Tchn: Sabot m (d'un pieu, etc.); patin m (de traîneau). **'shoe-brake**, s. Veh: Frein m à sabots. **'shoe-brush**, s. Brosse f à souliers. **'shoe-buckle**, s. Boucle f de soulier. **'shoe-cream**, s. Crème-cirage f. **'shoe-horn**, s. Chausse-pied m; corne f. **'shoe-lace**, s. Lacet m; cordon m de soulier. F: He is not fit to tie your shoe-laces, il n'est pas digne de vous déchausser. **'shoe-shop**, s. Magasin m de chaussures. **'shoe-strap**, s. Barrette f de soulier. **'shoe-string**, s. = SHOE-LACE.

shoe², v.tr. (shod [ʃɔd]; shod; pr.p. shoeing) **1.** Chausser. To be well shod, être bien chaussé. **2.** Ferrer; mettre un fer à (un cheval). **3.** Garnir d'une ferrure, d'un sabot; armer (un pieu). **'shoeing-forge**, s. Forge f de maréchalerie. **'shoeing smith**, s. Maréchal ferrant.

shoeblack ['ʃuːblak], s. Décrotteur m, cireur m (de chaussures).

shoemaker ['ʃuːmeikər], s. Cordonnier m. S.a. LAST¹.

shoemaking ['ʃuːmeikiŋ], s. Cordonnerie f.

shone [ʃɔn]. See SHINE².

shoo¹ [ʃuː], int. (a) (To chickens) Ch-ch! (b) (To children) Allez! filez!

shoo², v.tr. To shoo (away, off) the chickens, chasser, faire enfuir, les poules.

shook [ʃuk]. See SHAKE².

shoot¹ [ʃuːt], s. **1.** Bot: Pousse f (d'une plante); rejeton m. Vit: Sarment m. **2.** (In river) Rapide m. **3.** (a) Ind: Couloir m; glissière f. Min: Ore-shoot, cheminée f à minerai. Ind: Coal-shoot, manche f à charbon; trémie f de chargement. (b) Dépôt m (d'immondices). **4.** Geol: Shoot of ore, colonne f de richesse. **5.** Jaillissement m. **6.** (a) Partie f de chasse. (b) Concours m de tir. **7.** Chasse gardée. To rent a s., louer une chasse.

shoot², v. (shot [ʃɔt]; shot) I. v.i. **1.** Se précipiter; se lancer. The dog shot past us, le chien passa près de nous comme un éclair. To shoot ahead, aller rapidement en avant. To s. ahead of s.o., devancer qn rapidement. **2.** (Of pain) Lanciner, élancer. My corns are shooting, mes cors m'élancent. **3.** (Of tree, bud) Pousser, bourgeonner; (of plant) germer. II. **shoot**, v.tr. **1.** Franchir (un rapide); passer rapidement sous (un pont). P: To shoot the moon, déménager à la cloche de bois. **2.** (a) Préc piter, lancer (qch.); pousser vivement (un verrou). F: To shoot one's cuffs, faire sortir ses manchettes. (b) Verser, décharger (des décombres). To shoot coal into the cellar, déverser du charbon dans la cave. (c) Fish: Jeter (un filet). **3.** Darder faire jaillir (des rayons). **4.** (a) Décocher (une flèche); lancer, tirer (une balle). To shoot a glance at s.o., lancer, décocher, un regard à qn. S.a. BOLT¹ I. (b) Décharger (un fusil). Abs. Don't shoot! ne tirez pas! To shoot straight, bien viser. To shoot wide of the mark, (i) mal viser; (ii) F: être loin de la vérité. To shoot at s.o., tirer, faire feu, sur qn. S.a. SUN¹. (c To shoot s.o. with a revolver, atteindre qn d'un coup de revolver. P: I'll be shot if . . . ., je diable m'emporte si. . . . (d) Tuer (qn) d'un coup de fusil; fusiller (un espion). To s. s.o. through the head, tuer qn d'une balle à la tête. Mil: To be (court-martial ed and) shot, passer par les armes. To s. a deserter, passer un déserteur par les armes. (e) Chasser (e gibier). To s. a partridge, abattre une perdrix. **5.** Phot: Prendre un instantané de (qn). Cin: To shoot a film, tourner un film. **6.** Fb: To shoot the ball, abs. to shoot shooter.

To shoot a goal, marquer un but. **shoot away,** *v.tr.* **I.** *He had an arm shot away,* il eut un bras emporté. **2.** *To shoot away all one's ammunition,* épuiser ses munitions. **shoot down,** *v.tr.* Abattre, descendre (le gib er, un avion). **shoot off. I.** *v.i.* Partir comme un trait. **2.** *v.tr.* He had a foot shot off, il eut un pied emporté par un obus. **3.** To shoot off for a prize, prendre part à l'épreuve finale (de tir). **shoot out. I.** *v.i.* Sortir comme un trait. *The sun shot out,* le soleil s'est montré tout à coup. *The flames were shooting out of the window,* les flammes jaillissaient de la fenêtre. **2.** *v.tr.* (a) Lancer (des étincelles). *The snake shoots out its tongue,* le serpent darde sa langue. (b) (Of tree) Pousser (des branches). **shoot up.** *v.i.* (a) (Of flame) Jaillir. (Of aeroplane) To shoot up like a rocket, monter en chandelle. (b) (Of prices) Augmenter rapidement. (c) (Of plant) Pousser. To shoot up into a young man, devenir jeune homme. **2.** *v.tr. Mil.Av:* Mitrailler, arroser (un aérodrome, etc.). **shot¹,** *a.* **I.** (Poisson) qui a déposé ses œufs. **2.** *F:* To fall like a shot rabbit, tomber raide. **3.** (a) *Tex:* Chatoyant. Shot silk, taffetas changeant; soie gorge-de-pigeon. (b) Beard shot with grey, barbe parsemée de gris. **shooting¹,** *a.* Qui s'élance; jaillissant. Shooting star, étoile filante. Shooting pains, douleurs lancinantes. **shooting²,** *s.* **I.** (a) Élancement *m* (d'une blessure, etc.). (b) Bourgeonnement *m.* **2.** Franchissement *m* (d'un rapide). **3.** Déchargement *m* (de décombres). *Fish:* Jet *m* (d'un filet). **4.** (a) Décochement *m* (d'une flèche); action *f* de tirer (un coup de revolver). Shooting affray, bagarre *f* avec coups de feu. (b) Tir *m* (au pistolet). Fusillade *f.* Rabbit shooting, chasse *f* aux lapins. Pigeon shooting, chasse *f* aux pigeons. To go shooting, aller à la chasse. The s. season has begun, la chasse est ouverte. **5.** *Cin:* The shooting of the film, la prise de vues. **'shooting-box,** *s.* Pavillon *m* de chasse. **'shooting-gallery,** *s.* Tir *m;* stand *m.* **'shooting-party,** *s.* Partie *f* de chasse. **'shooting-range,** *s.* (a) Champ *m* de tir; *F:* tir *m.* (b) Polygone *m* d'artillerie. **'shooting-stick,** *s.* **I.** *Ven:* Canne-siège *f.* **2.** *Typ:* Décognoir *m.*

hooter ['ʃuːtər], *s.* Chasseur, -euse.

hop¹ [ʃɔp], *s.* **I.** Magasin *m;* (small) boutique *f;* (for wine, tobacco) débit *m.* Grocer's shop, épicerie *f.* To keep a shop, tenir (un) magasin. To play at (keeping) shop, jouer à la marchande. Shop! il y a du monde! quelqu'un! *F:* You have come to the wrong shop, vous vous adressez mal; vous tombez mal. Everything was all over the shop, tout était en confusion. **2.** *Ind:* Atelier *m.* Pattern shop, atelier *m* de modelage. To go through the shops, suivre un cours d'apprentissage. **3.** *P:* (a) Bureau *m,* maison *f,* où l'on travaille; "la boîte." (b) To talk shop, parler affaires. **'shop-assistant,** *s.* Commis *m,* garçon *m,* demoiselle *f,* de magasin. **'shop-boy,** *s.m.* Garçon de boutique; petit commis. **'shop-case,** *s.* Vitrine *f.* **'shop-fitter,** *s.* Agenceur *m* de magasins. **'shop-foreman,** *s. Ind:* Chef *m* d'atelier. **'shop-front,** *s.* Devanture *f* de magasin. **'shop-girl,** *s.f.* Demoiselle de magasin; vendeuse. **'shop-lifter,** *s. F:* Voleur, -euse, à l'étalage. **'shop-lifting,** *s.* Vol *m* à l'étalage. **'shop-soiled,** *a.* (Article) défraîchi. **'shop-walker,** *s.* **I.** Chef *m* de rayon. **2.** Inspecteur, -trice (du magasin). **'shop-'window,** *s.* Vitrine *f;* devanture *f* (de magasin); étalage *m. The goods exposed in the s.-w.,* la montre.

shop², *v.* (shopped) **I.** *v.i.* Faire des achats, des emplettes. **2.** *v.tr. P:* Coffrer (qn). **shopping,** *s.* Achats *mpl,* emplettes *fpl.* To go shopping, faire ses emplettes; courir les magasins. *I have some s. to do,* j'ai des courses à faire. Shopping centre, quartier commerçant. Shopping bag, sac à provisions.

shopkeeper ['ʃɔpkiːpər], *s.* Boutiquier, -ière; marchand, -ande.

shopkeeping ['ʃɔpkiːpiŋ], *s.* La tenue d'une boutique; le (petit) commerce.

shopman, *pl.* **-men** ['ʃɔpmən, -men], *s.m.* Commis de magasin; vendeur.

shopper ['ʃɔpər], *s.* Acheteur, -euse.

shore¹ [ʃɔːr], *s.* (a) Rivage *m,* littoral *m;* bord *m* (de la mer, d'un lac). (b) *Nau:* The shore, la terre. On shore, à terre. Off shore, au large. In shore, près de la côte. (Of ship) To keep close to the s., côtoyer. *Nau:* Shore clothes, frusques *f* d'escale. (c) *pl. Poet:* Distant shores, de lointains rivages. *To return to one's native shores,* rentrer dans son pays natal. **'shore-boat,** *s. Navy:* Bateau *m* de passage.

shore², *s. Const: etc:* Étai *m,* étançon *m;* contre-boutant *m. Nau:* Béquille *f,* épontille *f.*

shore³, *v.tr.* To shore (up), étayer, étançonner; contre-bouter, arc-bouter (un mur). *Nau:* Épontiller (un navire).

shorn [ʃɔːrn]. *See* SHEAR².

short¹ [ʃɔːrt]. **I.** *a.* **I.** Court. *To go by the shortest road,* prendre par le plus court. A short way off, à peu de distance. *S. steps,* petits pas. *A s. man,* un homme de petite taille. To be short in the arm, avoir les bras courts. *Your coat is s. in the arms,* votre habit est trop court des manches. *S.a.* CUT¹ 9, HEAD¹ 1, SIGHT¹ 1. **2.** Court, bref. (a) De peu de durée. *Days are getting shorter,* les jours raccourcissent. For a short time, pour peu de temps. In a short time, sous peu; bientôt. *Ling:* Short vowel, voyelle brève. *Com:* Short bills, traites à courte échéance. *Deposit* at short notice, dépôt à court terme. To make short work of it, ne pas y aller par quatre chemins; mener rondement les choses. (b) Short story, nouvelle *f,* conte *m.* Short list, liste choisie (d'aspirants à un poste). In short . . ., bref . . ., en un mot . . ., en somme. . . . *He is called Bob* for short, on l'appelle Bob pour abréger. *S.a.* SHRIFT. (c) (Pouls) rapide. (d) (Style) concis, serré. (e) (Of reply) Brusque; sec, *f.* sèche. To be short with s.o., être sec, cassant, avec qn. Short temper, caractère brusque, vif. **3.** (a) (Of weight) Insuffisant. To give short weight, ne pas donner le poids. It is two francs s., il s'en faut de deux francs. I am twenty francs short, il me manque vingt francs. *Ind:* To be on short time, être en chômage partiel. *S.a.* COMMONS 2. Little, not far, short of it, peu s'en faut. It is little s. of folly, cela confine à la folie. Nothing short of violence would compel him, la violence seule le contraindrait. (b) To be short of sth., être à court de qch. *S. of petrol,* à bout d'essence. To be s. of hands, manquer de main-d'œuvre. *Com:* We are s. of that article, cet article nous manque. *Cards:* To be short of spades, avoir une renonce à pique. To go short of sth., se priver de qch. *We ran s. of butter,* le beurre vint à manquer. **4.** *Cu:* Short pastry, pâte croquante. **-ly,** *adv.* **I.** (Raconter qch.) brièvement, en peu de mots. **2.** (Répondre) brusquement, sèchement. **3.** Bientôt, prochainement; sous peu. **Shortly after** (-wards), peu (de temps) après; bientôt après. **II. short,** *s.* **I.** (a) The long and the short. *See* LONG¹ II. **I.** (b) *pl.* Shorts, culotte *f* de sport.

2. (a) *Pros:* (Syllabe) brève f. (b) *Ling:* Voyelle brève. (c) *Artil:* Coup court. **3.** *El:* = SHORT-CIRCUIT[1]. **III. short,** *adv.* **1. To stop short,** s'arrêter (tout) court. **To cut s.o. short,** couper la parole à qn. **2. To fall short of the mark,** ne pas atteindre le but. *F:* **To fall, come, short of** sth., être, rester, au-dessous de qch. *It falls far s. of it,* il s'en faut de beaucoup. *S. of burning it . . .,* à moins de le brûler. . . . **To stop short of crime,** s'arrêter au seuil du crime. **'short-'armed,** *a.* Aux bras courts. **short-'circuit[1],** *s. El:* Court-circuit m. **short-'circuit[2]. 1.** *v.tr. El:* Court-circuiter. **To short-circuit a resistance,** mettre une résistance hors circuit. **2.** *v.i. El.E:* (Of current) Se mettre en court-circuit. **'short-date(d),** *a. Fin:* (Billet) à courte échéance; (papier) court. **short-'handed,** *a.* A court de main-d'œuvre, de personnel. **short-'headed,** *a. Anthr:* Brachycéphale. **'short-'legged,** *a.* A jambes courtes. **'short-'lived,** *a.* (Of pers.) Qui meurt jeune; (of joy) éphémère, de courte durée. **'short-'range,** *attrib.a.* (Tir) à courte portée. **short-'sighted,** *a.* **1.** Myope; à la vue courte. *I am getting s.-s.,* ma vue baisse. **2.** *F:* Imprévoyant. **short-'sightedness,** *s.* **1.** Myopie f. **2.** *F:* Imprévoyance f. **short-'tempered,** *a.* Vif; d'un caractère emporté. **'short-term,** *attrib.a. Fin:* (Placement, etc.) à court terme. **short-'winded,** *a.* Poussif; à l'haleine courte.

short[2], *v.tr. & i. El.E:* = SHORT-CIRCUIT[2].
shortage ['ʃɔːrtedʒ], *s.* **1.** Insuffisance f, manque m (de poids). *S. of staff,* pénurie f de personnel. **2.** Crise f, disette f. *Food shortage,* disette. *The paper s.,* la crise du papier.
shortbread ['ʃɔːrtbred], *s. Cu:* (Sorte de) sablé m.
shortcoming [ʃɔːrt'kʌmiŋ], *s.* **1.** Shortcomings, défauts m, imperfections f (chez qn). **2.** Manque m, insuffisance f.
shorten [ʃɔːrtn]. **1.** *v.tr.* (a) Raccourcir, rapetisser; abréger (une tâche, *Pros:* une syllabe). *Mil:* **To shorten step,** raccourcir le pas. (b) *Nau:* **To shorten sail,** diminuer de voile. (c) **Baby not yet shortened,** petit enfant encore en vêtements longs. **2.** *v.i.* (Of days) Raccourcir, décroître.
shortening, *s.* Raccourcissement m; décroissance f (des jours).
shorthand ['ʃɔːrthand], *s.* Sténographie f. **Shorthand writing,** écriture f sténographique. **To take a speech down in shorthand,** sténographier un discours. (*Pers.*) **Shorthand typist,** sténodactylographe mf; *F:* sténodactylo mf.
shorthorn ['ʃɔːrthɔːrn], *s.* Bœuf m à cornes courtes.
shortness ['ʃɔːrtnəs], *s.* **1.** (a) Peu m de longueur. **Shortness of sight,** myopie f. (b) Brièveté f, courte durée (de la vie). **Shortness of memory,** manque m de mémoire. *Pros:* *S. of a vowel,* brièveté f d'une voyelle. (c) Brusquerie f (d'humeur). **2.** Manque, insuffisance f (de vivres).
shot[1]. *See* SHOOT[2].
shot[2] [ʃɔt], *s.* **1.** *Artil:* (a) *A:* Boulet m. *F:* *Without a s. in the locker,* sans ressources. (b) *Coll.* Projectiles mpl. **2.** *Sm.a:* (a) *A:* Balle f. *S.a.* POWDER[1]. (b) *Ven:* Plomb m. **Small shot,** menu plomb. **Bird shot, dust shot,** cendrée f. **3.** (a) Coup m de feu. **Pistol shot,** coup de pistolet. *Without firing a s.,* sans brûler une amorce. **To take a (flying) shot at a bird,** tirer un oiseau (au vol). *F:* **To be off like a shot,** partir comme un trait. *He accepted like a s.,* il accepta avec empressement. (b) (*Pers.*) Tireur, -euse.

He's a good shot, il est bon chasseur. *S.a.* DEAD I. 5. **4.** Coup. (a) *F:* **I'll have a shot (at it),** je vais essayer; je vais tenter le coup. **To make a shot at an answer,** répondre au petit bonheur. (b) *Fb:* **Shot (at the goal),** shot m. (c) *Cin:* Prise f de vue. (d) *P:* Piqûre f (à la morphine). **5.** *Min:* **To fire a shot,** tirer un coup de mine. **'shot-gun,** *s.* Fusil m de chasse. **'shot proof,** *a.* A l'épreuve des balles. **'shot tower,** *s.* Tour f à fondre la dragée (de chasse).
shot[3], *s.* = SCOT[2] I.
should [ʃud]. *See* SHALL.
shoulder[1] ['ʃouldər], *s.* **1.** (a) Épaule f. **Breadth of shoulders,** carrure f. *F:* **His shoulders are broad enough,** il a bon dos. **Slung across the shoulder,** en bandoulière. **To bring the gun to the shoulder,** épauler le fusil. **To hit out straight from the shoulder,** frapper directement, en plein; *F:* **I let him have it straight from the shoulder,** je ne le lui ai pas envoyé dire. **To stand head and shoulders above the rest,** dépasser le autres de la tête. **To stand s. to s.,** se soutenir les uns les autres. *F:* **To put one's shoulder to the wheel,** (i) pousser à la roue; (ii) se mettre à l'œuvre. *S.a.* COLD[1], HEAD[1] 2, RUB[2] 1. (b) *Cu:* Épaule (de mouton). *Nau:* **Shoulder of mutton sail,** (voile f à) houari m. (c) Épaulement m (de colline). **2.** Embase f (de boulon etc.); talon m (de lame d'épée); ressaut m (d'un projectile). **'shoulder-belt,** *s.* Baudrier m. **'shoulder-blade,** *s.* (i) Omoplate f; (ii) paleron m (de cheval). **'shoulder-knot,** s **'shoulder strap,** *s.* **1.** (a) Bretelle f; bandoulière f. *Shoulder-straps* (of knapsack), brassière f. (b) (Of women's underclothing) Bretelle. **2.** *Mil:* Patte d'épaule.
shoulder[2], *v.tr.* **1.** Pousser avec l'épaule. **To shoulder one's way through the crowd,** se frayer un chemin à travers la foule. **2.** **To shoulder one's gun,** mettre son fusil sur l'épaule. **To shoulder the responsibility,** endosser la responsabilité. **3.** *Mil:* **Shoulder arms!** portez armes!
shout[1] [ʃaut], *s.* (a) Cri m (de joie, etc.). **Shout of laughter,** éclats m de rire. (b) Clameur f **Shouts of applause,** acclamations f. *P:* **It's m shout,** c'est ma tournée.
shout[2]. 1. *v.i.* Crier; pousser des cris. *v.pr.* **To shout oneself hoarse,** s'enrouer à force de crier **2.** *v.tr.* Crier (qch.); vociférer (des injures) **shout down,** *v.tr.* Huer (un orateur). **shout out. 1.** *v.i.* Crier, s'écrier. **2.** *v.tr.* Crier (un nom). **shouting,** *s.* Cris mpl; acclamations fp
shove[1] [ʃʌv], *s. F:* Coup m (d'épaule); poussée f. **To give s.o. a shove off,** aider qn au départ, au démarrage.
shove[2], *v.tr. F:* Pousser. **To shove (one's way) through the crowd,** se frayer un chemin à travers la foule. **To shove sth. into a drawer,** fourre qch. dans un tiroir. **shove aside,** *v.tr.* Écarter d'une poussée; pousser (qch.) de côté. **shove away,** *v.tr. Abs.* Continuer à pousser. **Shove away!** poussez donc! allez-y! **shove back** *v.tr.* Repousser, faire reculer. **shove forward 1.** *v.tr.* Pousser en avant. **2.** *v.i.* (a) Se frayer u chemin. (b) Se pousser; faire son chemir **shove off,** *v.tr. Nau:* Pousser (une embarcation) au large. *Abs.* **Shove off!** laissez aller poussez! **shove out,** *v.tr.* Pousser dehors. *T s. out one's hand,* étendre le bras. **shoving,** s. Poussée f.
shovel[1] ['ʃʌv(ə)l], *s.* Pelle f. **Fire-shovel,** pelle feu. **shovel 'hat,** *s.* Chapeau m ecclésiastique
shovel[2], *v.tr.* (shovelled) Pell(et)er (le charbon

etc.); prendre ou jeter (le charbon, etc.) à la pelle. **shovel away**, *v.tr.* Enlever (qch.) à la pelle.

shovel-board ['ʃʌv(ə)lbɔːrd], *s.* Jeu *m* de galets.

shovelful ['ʃʌv(ə)lful], *s.* Pellée *f*, pelletée *f*.

shoveller ['ʃʌv(ə)lər], *s.* **1.** Pelleteur *m*. **2.** *Orn:* Shoveller (duck), souchet *m*.

show[1] [ʃou], *s.* **1.** Mise *f* en vue; étalage *m* (de qch.). Show of hands, vote *m* à main(s) levée(s). *F:* The show pupil of the class, l'élève qu'on met en avant. *Mus:* Show piece, morceau de facture. *Organ:* The show pipes, la montre. **2.** (*a*) Exposition *f* (de marchandises); exhibition *f* (d'animaux sauvages), comice *m* (agricole). Motor show, salon *m* de l'automobile. (*b*) Spectacle *m*. Wild-beast show, ménagerie *f*. *F:* To make a show of oneself, se donner en spectacle. *S.a.* DUMB. *P:* To go to a show, aller au spectacle. (*c*) Étalage *m*. Our furniture makes a poor s., notre mobilier fait triste figure. (*d*) *U.S:* To give s.o. a (fair) show, laisser franc jeu à qn. **3.** (*a*) (i) Apparence *f*; (ii) semblant *m*. With some show of reason, avec quelque apparence de raison. Show of resistance, simulacre *m* de résistance. *To make a great s. of friendship*, faire de grandes démonstrations d'amitié. (*b*) Parade *f*, ostentation *f*, affichage *m*. To be fond of show, aimer l'éclat, la parade. To make a show of learning, faire parade d'érudition. To do sth. for show, faire qch. pour faire parade. **4.** *F:* Affaire *f*. To run the show, diriger l'affaire. *S.a.* GIVE AWAY 3. **'show-bill**, *s.* Affiche *f* (de spectacle). **'show-boat**, *s.* *U.S:* Bateau-théâtre *m* (sur le Mississipi). **'show-card**, *s.* *Com:* **1.** Pancarte *f*. **2.** Étiquette *f* (de vitrine). **3.** Carte *f* d'échantillons. **'show-case**, *s.* *Com:* Montre *f*, vitrine *f*. **'show-ground**, *s.* Champ *m* de comice agricole. **'show-place**, *s.* Endroit *m*, monument *m*, d'intérêt touristique.

show[2], *v.* (*p.t.* showed [ʃoud]; *p.p.* showed, shown [ʃoun]) I. *v.tr.* **1.** Montrer. (*a*) Faire voir, exhiber (qch.). To show s.o. sth., montrer, faire voir, qch. à qn. To show the colours, déployer le pavillon. What can I show you, madam? madame désire? Picture shown at the Academy, tableau exposé au Salon de Londres. To show a picture on the screen, projeter une image (sur l'écran). To show one's passport, exhiber, (re)présenter, son passeport. To show one's cards, one's hand, (i) jouer cartes sur table; (ii) *F:* découvrir ses batteries. *Nau:* To show a light, porter un feu. To have sth. to show for one's money, en avoir pour son argent. He won't show his face here again, il ne se montrera plus ici. To show oneself, se montrer; (*at a reception*) faire acte de présence. (*Of thg*) To show itself, devenir visible; se révéler. *S.a.* HEEL[1] 1. (*b*) Représenter, figurer (qch.). Machine shown in section, machine figurée en coupe. (*c*) Indiquer. As shown in the illustration, comme l'indique l'illustration. (*Of watch*) To show the time, indiquer, marquer, l'heure. The indicator shows a speed of . . ., l'indicateur accuse une vitesse de. . . To show a profit, faire ressortir un bénéfice. **2.** (*a*) To show s.o. the way, indiquer, tracer, le chemin à qn. *S.a.* DOOR 1. (*b*) To show s.o. to his room, conduire qn à sa chambre. Let me s. you round, laissez-moi vous piloter. To show s.o. to his seat, placer qn. To show s.o. into a room, faire entrer qn dans une pièce. **3.** (*a*) *To s. intelligence*, faire preuve d'intelligence. To show an interest in s.o., témoigner de l'intérêt à qn. *His face showed his delight*, son visage annonçait sa joie. *Selection that shows s.o.'s tastes*,

choix qui déclare, qui accuse, les goûts de qn. He shows his age, il marque son âge. *To s. one's true character*, se démasquer. *Abs.* Time will show, qui vivra verra. *S.a.* FIGHT[1] 2, HOSPITALITY. (*b*) Révéler, montrer. *Garment that shows the figure*, vêtement qui dessine la taille. (*c*) To show s.o. to be a rascal, prouver la coquinerie de qn. *Abs.* I'll show you! je vous apprendrai! To show cause, reason, exposer ses raisons. II. show, *v.i.* Se montrer, (ap)paraître; se laisser voir. The buds are beginning to show, les bourgeons commencent à se montrer, à paraître. *He never shows at her at-homes*, il ne se montre jamais quand elle reçoit. **'show-down**, *s.* *U.S:* **1.** *Cards:* Étalement *m* de son jeu (sur la table). **2.** *F:* To call for a show-down, sommer qn de mettre cartes sur table. *If it comes to a s.-d.*, s'il faut en venir au fait et au prendre. **show in**, *v.tr.* Show him, them, in, faites entrer. **show off. 1.** *v.tr.* (*a*) Faire valoir, mettre en valeur (qch.). (*b*) Faire parade, étalage, de (qch.). **2.** *v.i.* Parader, poser; se pavaner. To show off before s.o., chercher à épater qn. **show out**, *v.tr.* Reconduire (qn); escorter (qn) jusqu'à la porte. **show through**, *v.i.* Transparaître. **show up. 1.** *v.tr.* **1.** *Sch:* Donner (sa copie). **2.** Démasquer (un imposteur); dévoiler (une imposture); révéler (un défaut). II. **show up**, *v.i.* **1.** Se détacher, ressortir (sur un fond). **2.** Se présenter; faire acte de présence. **showing**, *s.* Exposition *f*, mise *f* en vue (de qch.). On your own showing, à ce que vous dites vous-même.

shower[1] ['ʃauər], *s.* (*a*) Averse *f*. Heavy shower, ondée *f*. Sudden shower, averse; (*with hail or snow*) giboulée *f*. (*b*) *F:* Shower of stones, volée *f* de pierres. *S. of sparks*, gerbe *f* d'étincelles. **'shower-bath**, *s.* Bain-douche *m*; douche *f* (en pluie).

shower[2]. **1.** *v.tr.* (*a*) Verser; faire pleuvoir (de l'eau). (*b*) *F:* To shower blows, frapper dru (on s.o., sur qn). To shower invitations on s.o., accabler qn d'invitations. **2.** *v.i.* Pleuvoir.

showery ['ʃauəri], *a.* (Temps) de giboulées, d'ondées; (temps) pluvieux.

showiness ['ʃouinəs], *s.* Prétention *f*, clinquant *m*; luxe criard.

showman, *pl.* **-men** ['ʃoumən, -men], *s.m.* (*a*) Directeur (d'un spectacle de la foire); forain. (*b*) Montreur de curiosités (à la foire).

showmanship ['ʃoumənʃip], *s.* Art *m* de la mise en scène.

showroom ['ʃourum], *s.* Salle *f*, salon *m*, ou magasin *m* d'exposition (d'une maison de commerce); salle de démonstration (d'automobiles).

showy ['ʃoui], *a.* (*Of appearance*) Prétentieux, voyant. *S. hat*, chapeau à effet; chapeau criard. **-ily**, *adv.* (Habillé) d'une façon prétentieuse, avec ostentation.

shrank [ʃraŋk]. *See* SHRINK.

shrapnel ['ʃrapnəl], *s.* Shrapnel(l) *m*; obus *m* à balles.

shred[1] [ʃred], *s.* Brin *m*; lambeau *m*, fragment *m* (d'étoffe). **To tear sth. (in)to shreds**, déchiqueter qch.; mettre qch. en lambeaux. *Her dress was all in shreds*, sa robe était tout en lambeaux. *F:* There isn't a shred of evidence, il n'y a pas une parcelle d'évidence.

shred[2], *v.tr.* (shredded Couper (qch.) par languettes; déchirer (qch.) en lambeaux; effilocher; déchiqueter.

shrew[1]**-mouse**, *pl.* **-mice** ['ʃruː(maus, -mais)], *s.* *Z:* Musaraigne *f*; souris *f* d'eau.

shrew[2], *s.f.* Femme criarde, acariâtre; mégère.

shrewd [ʃruːd], *a.* **1.** Sagace, perspicace; qui

a du flair. *S. business man*, homme d'affaires très entendu. *S. reasoning*, raisonnement judicieux. **2.** *A:* (*a*) (*Of cold*) Sévère, âpre. (*b*) **Shrewd blow,** coup dur. **3.** *(Intensive)* **I have a shrewd idea that . . .,** je suis porté à croire que. . . . **-ly,** *adv.* Sagacement; avec finesse; avec perspicacité.

shrewdness ['ʃruːdnəs], *s.* Sagacité *f*; finesse *f*.

shrewish ['ʃruiʃ], *a.* (Femme) acariâtre, criarde.

shrewishness ['ʃruiʃnəs], *s.* Humeur acariâtre.

shriek[1] [ʃriːk], *s.* Cri déchirant; cri perçant. *S. of anguish,* cri d'angoisse. **Shrieks of laughter,** grands éclats de rire. **The shriek of a locomotive,** le cri strident d'une locomotive. **To give a shriek,** pousser un cri.

shriek[2]. **I.** *v.i.* Pousser des cris aigus; (*of locomotive*) déchirer l'air. **To shriek with !aughter,** rire aux éclats; *F:* s'esclaffer (de rire). **2.** *v.tr.* **To shriek out a warning,** avertir qn d'un cri.

shrieking, *s.* Cris stridents. **The s. of the wind,** les clameurs aiguës du vent.

shrievalty ['ʃriːvəlti], *s.* **I.** Fonctions *fpl* de shériff. **2.** Juridiction *f* du shériff.

shrift [ʃrift], *s.* *A:* Confession *f* et absolution *f*. *F:* **To give s.o. short shrift,** expédier vite son homme.

shrike [ʃraik], *s.* *Orn:* Pie-grièche *f*.

shrill[1] [ʃril], *a.* (*Of voice*) A note aiguë; aigu, strident. **In a shrill voice,** d'une voix perçante. *S. whistle,* coup de sifflet strident. **-lly** ['ʃrilli], *adv.* D'un ton aigu, criard.

shrill[2], *v.i.* *Lit:* Pousser un son aigu. *A whistle shrilled,* un coup de sifflet déchira l'air.

shrillness ['ʃrilnəs], *s.* Stridence *f*.

shrimp[1] [ʃrimp], *s.* Crevette (grise); crangon *m*; chevrette *f*. *F:* **Shrimp** (of a man), petit bout d'homme; gringalet *m*.

shrimp[2], *v.i.* Pêcher la crevette. **shrimping,** *s.* Pêche *f* à la crevette.

shrine[1] [ʃrain], *s.* **I.** Châsse *f*, reliquaire *m*. **2.** Tombeau *m* de saint ou de sainte. **3.** Chapelle *f* ou autel *m* consacrés à un saint.

shrine[2], *v.tr.* = ENSHRINE.

shrink [ʃriŋk], *v.* (shrank [ʃraŋk]; shrunk [ʃraŋk], *as adj.* shrunken ['ʃraŋk(ə)n]) **I.** *v.i.* (*a*) Se contracter; (se) rétrécir. His gums are shrinking, ses dents se déchaussent. **To shrink in the wash,** (se) rétrécir au lavage. (*b*) Faire un mouvement de recul; se dérober. **To shrink away,** s'éloigner timidement. **To shrink (back) from** (sth.), reculer devant (un danger). **To shrink from doing sth.,** répugner à faire qch. *His mind shrank from painful memories,* son esprit se dérobait aux souvenirs pénibles. (*c*) *F:* **To shrink into oneself,** rentrer dans sa coquille. **2.** *v.tr.* (R)étrécir (un tissu). **shrinking**[1], *a.* **I.** Qui se contracte. *S. capital,* capital qui diminue. **2.** Timide, craintif. **-ly,** *adv.* Timidement. **shrinking**[2], *s.* **I.** = SHRINKAGE. **2.** Shrinking (away, back) from sth., reculement *m* devant qch.

shrinkage ['ʃriŋkedʒ], *s.* **I.** Contraction *f* (du métal); rétrécissement *m* (d'une étoffe).

shrive [ʃraiv], *v.tr.* (shrove [ʃrouv]; shriven ['ʃriv(ə)n]) *A:* Confesser, absoudre (un pénitent).

shrivel ['ʃriv(ə)l], *v.* (shrive:led) **I.** *v.tr.* **To shrivel (up),** rider, ratatiner (la peau); (*of sun*) brûler, hâler (les plantes). **2.** *v.i.* **To shrivel (up),** se rider, se ratatiner.

shroud[1] [ʃraud], *s.* **I.** Linceul *m*, suaire *m*. *F:* **In a shroud of mystery,** enveloppé de mystère. **2.** *Mec.E:* Bouclier *m*, blindage *m*.

shroud[2], *s.* *Nau: Civ.E:* Hauban *m*.

shroud[3], *v.tr.* **I.** (*a*) Ensevelir; envelopper (un cadavre) d'un linceul. (*b*) *F:* Envelopper, voile[r] (qch.). **2.** *W.Tel:* Blinder (un transformateur).

shrouded, *a.* **I.** (*a*) Enveloppé d'un suaire. (*b*) Enveloppé, voilé (*in*, de). **Shrouded in gloom,** enténébré. **2.** *W.Tel:* (Transformateur) blindé.

shrove [ʃrouv]. **I.** *See* SHRIVE. **2. Shrove Tuesday,** (le) mardi gras.

Shrovetide ['ʃrouvtaid], *s.* Les jours gras.

shrub[1] [ʃrab], *s.* Arbrisseau *m*, arbuste *m*.

shrub[2], *s.* Grog *m* à l'orange ou au citron.

shrubbery ['ʃrabəri], *s.* Bosquet *m*; plantation *f* d'arbustes, massif *m* d'arbustes.

shrug[1] [ʃrag], *s.* Haussement *m* d'épaules. **Shrug of resignation,** geste *m* de résignation.

shrug[2], *v.tr.* (shrugged) **To shrug (one's shoulders),** hausser les épaules.

shrunk [ʃraŋk]. *See* SHRINK.

shrunken ['ʃraŋk(ə)n], *a.* Contracté; (*of hands*) ratatiné.

shuck[1] [ʃak]. *U.S:* **I.** *s.* Cosse *f*, gousse *f* (de pois). **2.** *int.* **Shucks!** allons donc! chansons!

shuck[2], *v.tr.* *U.S:* Écosser, écaler (des pois).

shudder[1] ['ʃadər], *s.* Frisson *m* (d'horreur); frémissement *m*. **A shudder passed over him,** il fut pris d'un frisson.

shudder[2], *v.i.* **To shudder with horror,** frissonner d'horreur; frémir d'horreur.

shuffle[1] ['ʃafl], *s.* **I.** (*a*) Mouvement traînant des pieds; marche traînante. (*b*) *Danc:* Frottement *m* de pieds. **2.** Battement *m*, mélange *m* (des cartes). **3.** (*a*) Tergiversation *f*, barguignage *m*. (*b*) Faux-fuyant *m*.

shuffle[2]. **I.** *v.tr. & i.* **To shuffle (one's feet),** traîner les pieds. **2.** *v.tr.* (*a*) (Entre)mêler (des papiers). (*b*) **To shuffle the dominoes,** brasser les dominos. (*c*) Battre, mêler (les cartes). **3.** *v.i.* Équivoquer, tergiverser, barguigner. **shuffle off. I.** *v.tr.* Ôter (ses vêtements) à la hâte, n'importe comment. *S.a.* COIL[3]. **2.** *v.i.* S'en aller en traînant le pas. **shuffling**[1], *a.* **I.** (*Of gait*) Traînant. **2.** (*Of pers.*) Tergiversateur, -trice; (*of conduct*) équivoque, évasif. **shuffling**[2], *s.* = SHUFFLE[1].

shuffle-board ['ʃaflbɔːrd], *s.* = SHOVEL-BOARD.

shuffler ['ʃaflər], *s.* Tergiversateur, -trice.

shun[1] [ʃan], *v.tr.* (shunned) Fuir, éviter (qn, qch.). **To s. everybody,** s'éloigner de tout le monde.

'shun[2], *int.* *Mil:* *F:* (= attention!) Garde à vous!

shunt[1] [ʃant], *s.* **I.** *Rail:* Garage *m*, manœuvre *f* (d'un train). **2.** *El:* Shunt *m*, dérivation *f*. **To put in shunt,** mettre en dérivation; shunter. **'shunt circuit,** *s.* *El:* Circuit dérivé. **'shunt line,** *s.* *Rail:* Voie *f* de garage. **'shunt-wound,** *a.* *El.E:* Excité en dérivation, en shunt.

shunt[2], *v.tr.* **I.** *Rail:* Garer, manœuvrer (un train). **'Shunt with care,'** "défense de tamponner." *F:* **To shunt s.o.,** mettre qn au rancart. **2.** *El:* Shunter, dériver (un circuit); monter (un condensateur) en dérivation. **shunting,** *s.* **I.** *Rail:* Garage *m*, manœuvre *f*; aiguillage *m*. **Shunting operations,** manœuvres de triage *m*. **Shunting yard,** chantier *m* de voies de garage et de triage. **2.** *El:* Dérivation *f*.

shunter ['ʃantər], *s.* **I.** *Rail:* Classeur *m* de trains. **2.** *El:* (*For arc-lamp*) Dérivateur *m*.

shut [ʃat], *v.* (*p.t.* shut; *p.p.* shut; *pr.p.* shutting) **I.** *v.tr.* (*a*) Fermer (une porte, une boîte). **To shut the door against s.o.,** refuser de recevoir q[n]. **To find the door shut,** trouver porte close; *F:* trouver visage de bois. *S.a.* EYE[1] I. **To shut one's mouth,** (i) fermer la bouche, (ii) *F:* se taire. **To keep one's mouth shut tight,** *F:* avoir la bouche cousue. *P:* **Shut your mouth!** ferme ton bec ! la ferme ! (b) To shut one's finger, one's dress, in the door, se pincer le doigt, laisser prendre sa robe, dans la porte. 2. v.i. (Of door) (Se) fermer. The door won't s., la porte ne ferme pas. shut down. 1. v.tr. (a) Rabattre (un couvercle). (b) Ind: Fermer (une usine). Tchn: Couper (la vapeur). 2. v.i. (Of lid) Se rabattre. shut in, v.tr. (a) Enfermer. (b) (Of hills) Entourer, encercler (un endroit). shut off, v.tr. 1. Couper, interrompre (la vapeur); fermer (l'eau). Aut: To shut off the engine, couper le moteur. 2. Séparer, isoler (from, de). shut out, v.tr. (a) Exclure (qn, l'air). The trees shut out the view, les arbres bouchent la vue. (b) To shut s.o. out (of doors), fermer la porte à qn. shut to. 1. v.tr. Fermer, clore (une porte). 2. v.i. (Of door) Se fermer. shut up. 1. v.tr. (a) Enfermer. To shut oneself up, se renfermer. (b) To shut s.o. up (in prison), emprisonner qn. (c) Clore (une maison). To shut up shop, fermer boutique. (d) P: Réduire (qn) au silence; clouer le bec à (qn). 2. v.i. P: Se taire; ne plus dire mot. Shut up! taisez-vous ! shutting, s. Fermeture f.

shutter ['ʃʌtər], s. 1. Volet m. Outside shutter, contrevent m. Venetian shutters, persiennes f. Folding shutters, volets brisés. To take down the shutters, enlever les volets (d'une boutique). To put up the shutters (of a shop), mettre les volets. F: We can put up our shutters, il n'y a plus qu'à fermer boutique. 2. Phot: Obturateur m. Diaphragm shutter, obturateur au diaphragme. Focal-plane shutter, obturateur de plaque. 'shutter-release, s. Phot: Déclancheur m d'obturateur.

shuttle [ʃʌtl], s. 1. Navette f. 2. Mec.E: Shuttle movement, mouvement alternatif. Line over which a s. service is run, ligne de chemin de fer exploitée en navette. 'shuttle-winder, s. Dévidoir m (de machine à coudre).

shuttlecock ['ʃʌtlkɔk], s. Games: Volant m.

shy¹ [ʃai], s. Écart m, faux bond (d'un cheval).
shy², v.i. (shied; shying) (Of horse) Faire un écart; broncher. To shy at sth., prendre ombrage de qch. shying, s. Écart m, bronchement m. Horse given to s., cheval ombrageux.
shy³, a. (shyer, shyest; occ. shier, shiest) Sauvage, farouche, timide; (of horse) ombrageux. To make s.o. shy, intimider qn. She's not at all shy, F: elle n'a pas froid aux yeux. To fight shy of sth., se défier, se méfier, de qch. To fight shy of a job, éviter une besogne. Don't pretend to be shy, ne faites pas la réservée. Day when the fish are shy, jour où les poissons ne mordent pas. S.a. BITE² 1. -ly, adv. Timidement.
shy⁴, s. F: 1. Jet m, lancement m (d'une pierre). (At fairs) Three shies a penny, trois coups m pour un penny. S.a. COCOA¹ 1. 2. Essai m, tentative f (pour atteindre qch.). To have a shy at doing sth., s'essayer à faire qch.
shy⁵, v. (shied; shying) F: 1. v.i. Lancer une pierre, une balle, etc. (at, à). 2. v.tr. To shy a stone at s.o., lancer une pierre à qn.

Shylock ['ʃailɔk], s. F: Créancier m impitoyable; usurier m.

shyness ['ʃainəs], s. Timidité f, réserve f; sauvagerie f (d'un animal, F: de qn).

shyster ['ʃaistər], s. U.S: P: Homme d'affaires véreux.

Siamese [saia'miːz], a. & s. Siamois, -oise. Siamese twins, frères siamois.

Siberia [sai'biəria]. Pr.n. La Sibérie.

Siberian [sai'biəriən], a. & s. Sibérien, -ienne. Siberian dog, chien de Sibérie.

sibilant ['sibilənt]. 1. a. Sifflant. 2. s. Ling: (Lettre) sifflante f.

sibyl ['sibil], s. Sibylle f.

Sibylline ['sibilain], a. Sibyllin.

sic [sik], Lt. adv. Sic, ainsi.

siccative ['sikətiv], a. & s. Siccatif (m).

Sicilian [si'siljən], a. & s. Sicilien, -ienne.

Sicily ['sisili]. Pr.n. La Sicile.

sick [sik], a. 1. Malade. s.pl. The sick, les malades. Mil: To report sick, se faire porter malade. 2. To be sick, vomir, rendre. To feel sick, avoir mal au cœur. 3. To be sick at heart, être abattu. He did ook sick! il en faisait une tête ! To be sick of sth., être las, dégoûté, de qch. I'm sick of it, j'en ai assez, j'en ai plein le dos. I'm s. and tired of telling you, je me tue à vous le dire. 'sick-allowance, s. Allocation f pour maladie. 'sick-'bay, s. Navy: Infirmerie f; poste m des malades. 'sick-'bed, s. Lit m de malade; lit de douleur. 'sick-'berth, s. = SICK-BAY. Sick-berth attendant, infirmier m. 'sick-'headache, s. Migraine f. 'sick-leave, s. Congé m de maladie, de réforme. 'sick-list, s. Mil: Rôle m des malades; état m des malades. To be on the sick-list, être porté malade; F: être malade. 'sick-nurse, s. Garde-malade mf. 'sick-room, s. Chambre f de malade.

sicken ['sik(ə)n]. 1. v.i. (a. Tomber malade (of, with, de). To be sickening for an illness, couver une maladie. (b) To sicken of sth., se lasser de qch. 2. v.tr. (a) Rendre malade; donner mal au cœur à (qn). His business methods s. me, ses procédés me soulèvent le cœur. (b) To sicken s.o. of sth., dégoûter qn de qch. sickening, a. Écœurant, navrant. Sickening fear, crainte qui serre le cœur.

sickener ['siknər], s. F: Déception f.

sickle [sikl], s. Agr: Faucille f. 'sickle-feather, s. Faucille f (de la queue du coq).

sickliness ['siklinəs], s. 1. État maladif. 2. Pâleur f (du teint). 3. Fadeur f (d'un goût); sentimentalité outrée (d'une romance).

sickly ['sikli], a. 1. (a) Maladif, souffreteux. (b) (Of light) Faible, pâle. A sickly white, un blanc terreux. (c) Sickly smile, sourire pâle. 2. (Of climate) Malsain, insalubre. 3. (Of taste) Fade.

sickness ['siknəs], s. 1. Maladie f. Bed of sickness, lit de malade, de misère. Is there any s. on board? avez-vous des malades à bord ? 2. Mal m, maladie. Mountain sickness, mal des montagnes. Air sickness, mal des aviateurs. 3. Mal de cœur; nausées fpl.

side¹ [said], s. Côté m. 1. (a) Flanc m. (Of animal) To lash its sides, se battre les flancs. By the side of s.o., à côté de qn. Side by side (with s.o.), côte à côte (avec qn). F: To split one's sides (with laughter), se tenir les côtes de rire. (b) Side of bacon, flèche f de lard. 2. Côté (d'un triangle); flanc m, versant m (d'une montagne); paroi f (d'un fossé); lisière f (d'une forêt). Side of a ship, bande f, bord m, flanc. 3. (Surface) (a) The right side, wrong side (of sth.), le bon, mauvais, côté (de qch.); l'endroit m, l'envers m (d'une étoffe). (Of garment) Right side out, à l'endroit. Wrong side out, à l'envers. Bookb: Cloth sides of a book, plats m toile d'un livre. S.a. BREAD. (b) F: The bright side of things, le bon côté des choses. The other side of the picture, le revers de la médaille. To get on the soft side of s.o., prendre qn par son endroit faible. To hear both sides (of a question), entendre le pour et le contre. The weather's on the cool

side, il fait plutôt froid. *S.a.* SEAMY. **4.** (*a*) On this side, de ce côté-ci. On the left-hand side, à (main) gauche. On both sides, des deux côtés, de part et d'autre. On all sides, de tous côtés. To be on the right side of forty, avoir moins de quarante ans. To move to one side, se ranger. To put sth. on one side, mettre qch. à l'écart. *S.a.* WRONG[1] I.3. (*b*) *F :* To put on side, se donner des airs ; poser ; *P :* faire sa poire. *He puts on s.*, il est poseur. (*c*) *U.S :* On the side, par-dessus le marché. **5.** (*a*) Parti *m.* He is on our side, il est de notre parti. To change sides, changer de camp. You have the aw on your side. vous avez la loi pour vous. Mistakes made on both sides. erreurs commises de part et d'autre. (*b*) Section *f*, division *f*. The modern side (*of a school*), les classes modernes. (*c*) *Games :* Camp *m*, équipe *f*. To pick sides, tirer les camps. *Rugby Fb :* No side, fin *f* de partie. (*d*) Well connected on his mother's side, de haute parenté par sa mère, du côté maternel. **6.** *Attrib.* Latéral, de côté. Side entrance, entrée de côté. Side door, porte latérale. *To enter a profession through the s.-door*, entrer dans une profession par la petite porte. Side street, rue latérale ou transversale. Side line, (i) *Rail :* voie *f* secondaire ; (ii) *Com :* article *m* à côté. *To keep poultry as a side line*, élever de la volaille comme occupation secondaire. Side issue, question d'intérêt secondaire. *S.a.* ARM² I. **'side-aisle,** *s. Ecc.Arch :* Nef latérale ; bas-côté *m.* **'side-altar,** *s. Ecc :* Autel latéral. **'side-car,** *s. Aut :* Voiturette *f* à remorque latérale ; sidecar *m.* **'side-dish,** *s.* Entremets *m* ; hors-d'œuvre *m inv.* **'side-drum,** *s.* Tambour *m.* **'side-face.** **1.** *s.* Profil *m.* **2.** *adv.* Taken *s.-f.*, photographié de profil. **'side-glance,** *s.* Regard *m* de côté ; coup *m* d'œil oblique. **'side-lamps,** *s.pl. Veh :* Lanternes *f* ; feux *m* de côté. **'side-pocket,** *s.* Poche *f* de côté. **'side-road,** *s.* Chemin *m* de traverse. **'side-saddle,** *s.* Selle *f* de dame. To ride side-saddle, monter en amazone. **'side-show,** *s.* **1.** Spectacle payant (à une foire). **2.** *F :* Affaire *f* d'importance secondaire. **'side-slip**[1], *s.* **1.** *Aut : Cy :* Dérapage *m*, dérapement *m.* **2.** *Av :* Glissade *f* sur l'aile. **'side-slip**[2], *v.i.* **1.** *Aut : Cy :* Déraper. **2.** *Av :* Glisser sur l'aile. **'side-step**[1], *s.* **1.** *Box : etc :* Pas *m* de côté. **2.** *Veh :* Marchepied *m* de côté. **'side-step**[2], *v.i.* Faire un pas de côté ; *Box :* esquiver. **'side-stroke,** *s. Swim :* Nage *f* sur le côté, à la marinière. **'side-table,** *s.* Petite table. **'side-track**[1], *s. Rail :* Voie *f* de garage ; voie secondaire. **'side-track**[2], *v.tr.* (*a*) Garer (un train). (*b*) *F :* Reléguer au second plan (un projet). **'side-view,** *s.* Vue *f* de profil, de côté. *S.-v. of the hotel*, l'hôtel vu de côté. **'side-walk,** *s.* **1.** Contre-allée *f.* **2.** Trottoir *m.* **'side-whiskers,** *s.pl.* Favoris *m.* **'side-wind,** *s.* Vent *m* de côté. *F : To hear of sth. by a s.-w.*, apprendre qch. indirectement.

side², *v.i.* To side with s.o., se ranger du côté de qn. **siding,** *s. Rail :* (*a*) Voie *f* de garage, de service. (*b*) Embranchement *m* ; voie privée. Goods siding, voie de chargement.

sideboard ['saidbɔːrd], *s. Furn :* Buffet *m.*

-sided ['saidid], *a.* Five-sided, à cinq faces, à cinq pans. Double-sided, à doubles côtés. Double-s. record (*for gramophone*), disque à double face.

sidelight ['saidlait], *s.* **1.** *Phot : etc :* Lumière *f* oblique. *F :* To throw a sidelight on a subject, donner un aperçu indirect sur un sujet. **2.** (*a*) Lanterne latérale (d'une voiture) ; lanterne à feu blanc. (*b*) *Nau :* Sidelights, feux *m* de côté.

sidelong ['saidlɔŋ]. **1.** *adv.* (Se mouvoir) obliquement, de côté. **2.** *a.* (Regard) oblique, en coulisse

sidereal [sai'diːəriəl], *a.* Sidéral, -aux. Siderea time, heure ' astronomique.

sidesman, *pl.* **-men** ['saidzmən, -men], *s.m Ecc :* Marguillier adjoint.

sideward ['saidwərd]. **1.** *a.* (Mouvement) de côté ; latéral, -aux. **2.** *adv* = SIDEWARDS.

sidewards ['saidwərdz], *adv.* (Regarder, etc.) de côté.

sideways ['saidweːiz], **sidewise** ['saidwaːiz] **1.** *adv.* De côté ; latéralement. To jump sideways, faire un saut de côté. To walk sideways, marcher en crabe. To stand sideways, s'effacer. **2.** *a.* Latéral, -aux ; de côté.

siding ['saidiŋ], *s. See* SIDE².

sidle [saidl], *v.i.* To sidle along, s'avancer de côté, de guingois. To sidle up to s.o., se couler auprès de qn.

siege [siːdʒ], *s. Mil :* Siège *m.* To lay siege to a town, assiéger une ville. **'siege-ar'tillery,** *s.* Artillerie *f* de siège.

Siena [si'ena]. *Pr.n. Geog :* Sienne *f.*

sienna [si'ena], *s.* Terre *f* de Sienne. Raw burnt, sienna, terre de Sienne naturelle, brûlée.

siesta [si'esta], *s.* Sieste *f*, méridienne *f.*

sieve [siv], *s.* **1.** Crible *m* ; tamis *m. Ind :* Sas *m*, crible. *S.a.* MEMORY I. **2.** *F :* Personne qui ne sait pas garder le secret.

sift [sift]. **1.** *v.tr.* (*a*) Passer (qch.) au tamis ou au crible ; tamiser ; vanner (le blé) ; sasser (la farine). (*b*) *Fr :* Examiner minutieusement. To sift a matter to the bottom, éplucher une affaire. To sift (out) the true from the false, dégager le vrai du faux. **2.** *v.i.* (*Of dust*) Filtrer (*through*, à travers). **sifting,** *s.* **1.** (*a*) Tamisage *m*, criblage *m.* (*b*) Examen minutieux (des preuves). **2.** *pl.* Siftings, criblure(s) *f(pl).*

sifter ['siftər], *s.* **1.** (*Pers.*) Tamiseur *m*, cribleur *m* ; *Ind :* sasseur *m.* **2.** (*a*) Tamis *m*, crible *m.* (*b*) Appareil *m* à cribler ; cribleuse *f. Mill :* Sasseur *m.* **3.** Saupoudroir *m* (à sucre).

sigh[1] [sai], *s.* Soupir *m.* To breathe a sigh, laisser échapper un soupir. To heave a sigh, pousser un soupir.

sigh[2], *v.i.* (*a*) Soupirer ; pousser un soupir. (*b*) To sigh for, after, sth., soupirer pour, après, qch. **sighing,** *s.* Soupirs *mpl.*

sight[1] [sait], *s.* **1.** (*Faculty of vision*) Vue *f.* (*a*) To have long sight, avoir la vue longue. Short sight myopie *f.* To lose one's sight, perdre la vue ; devenir aveugle. (*b*) To catch sight of s.o., apercevoir qn. To lose sight of s.o., perdre qn de vue. *Nau :* To lose sight of land, perdre terre. To lose sight of the fact that . . ., perdre de vue que. . . . I can't bear the sight of him, je ne peux pas le sentir. At sight, à vue. *To translate at s.*, traduire à livre ouvert. *To shoot s.o. at s.*, faire feu sur qn à première vue. *Com :* Sight bill, effe à vue. At first sight, à première vue ; au premier abord. To know s.o. by sight, connaître qn de vue. (*c*) To find favour in s.o.'s sight, trouver grâce devant qn. **2.** To come into sight, (ap)paraître. To be within sight, être à portée de la vue ; être en vue. Land in sight! terre ! My goal is in sight, j'approche de mon but. Keep him in sight, ne le perdez pas de vue. Out of sight, caché aux regards. He didn't let her out of his sight, il ne la perdait pas de vue. *Prov :* Out of sight, out of mind, loin des yeux, loin du cœur. **3.** *Surv :* Coup *m* de lunette. *Artil : Sm.a :* Visée *f. Nau :* To take a sight at the sun, observer le soleil. **4.** (*a*) Appareil *m* de visée ; œilleton *m* (de viseur) ; pinnule *f* d'une alidade).

b) Sm.a: Artil: (Back-)**sight**, hausse *f.* (Fore-)sight, (i) *Sm.a:* guidon *m*; (bouton *m* de) mire *f*; (ii) *Artil:* fronteau *m* de mire. **5.** (*a*) Spectacle *m*. *Sad s.*, spectacle navrant. *It is a s. to see*, cela vaut la peine d'être vu. *F:* **It was a sight for sore eyes**, c'était réjouissant à voir. (*b*) *F: His face was a s.*, si vous aviez vu son visage! **What a sight you are!** comme vous voilà fait! *c*) Chose digne d'être vue. **The sights**, les monuments *m*, les curiosités *f* (de la ville). **6.** *P:* **A sight of . . .**, énormément de. . . 'sight-**feed**, *s. Mch:* Débit *m* visible. 'sight-**reading**, *s.* Déchiffrement *m* (de la musique); lecture *f* à vue. 'sight-**rule**, *s. Surv:* Alidade *f* à pinnules. 'sight-**seeing**, *s.* **To go sight-seeing**, visiter les monuments, les curiosités d'une ville). 'sight-**seer**, *s.* (i) Curieux, euse; (ii) excursionniste *mf.* 'sight-**testing**, *.* Examen *m* de la vue.

ght², *v.tr.* **1.** Apercevoir, aviser (qn, qch.). *Nau:* **To sight land**, reconnaître la terre; viser la terre. **2.** Viser, observer (un astre). **3.** Pointer un fusil). **sighting**, *s.* **1.** Vue *f.* **2.** Visée *f*, pointage *m.* **Sighting-slit**, voyant *m* (d'un instrument scientifique). *Mil: etc:* **Sighting-shot**, coup préliminaire pour vérifier a visée. *S.a.* NOTCH¹ I, RULE¹ 4.

ghted ['saitid], *a.* **Weak-sighted**, à la vue faible. **Long-sighted, far-sighted**, (i) presbyte; (ii) prescient, prévoyant.

ghter ['saitər], *s. Phot:* Aiguille *f* de mire.

ghtless ['saitləs], *a.* Aveugle; privé de la vue. *S. eyes*, yeux éteints.

ghtlessness ['saitləsnəs], *s.* Cécité *f.*

ghtliness ['saitlinəs], *s.* Grâce *f*, beauté *f.*

ghtly ['saitli], *a.* Agréable à voir; avenant.

gillary ['sidʒiləri], *a.* Sigillaire.

gn¹ [sain], *s.* **1.** Signe *m.* (*a*) **To make a sign to s.o.**, faire (un) signe à qn. **To make an affirmative s.**, faire signe que oui. (*b*) *S. of recognition*, signe de reconnaissance. (*c*) *Tg:* **Call sign**, indicatif *m* d'appel. **2.** (*a*) Indice *m*, indication *f.* **Sure sign**, indice certain. *S. of rain*, signe de pluie. **Sign of the times**, marque *f*, signe, des temps. *There is no s. of his coming*, rien n'annonce sa venue. (*b*) Trace *f.* **No sign of . . .**, nulle, aucune, trace de. . . . **To show no sign of life**, ne donner aucun signe de vie. *There was no s. of him*, on ne l'a pas aperçu. **3.** (*a*) Enseigne *f* (d'auberge) (*b*) (Shop-)sign, enseigne. **Neon sign**, réclame *f* au néon. (*c*) **Sign of the Zodiac**, signe du zodiaque. **4.** (*Written sign*) *Mth: Mus: etc:* Symbole *m.* **Positive sign**, signe positif. **5. Sign of the cross**, signe de la croix. 'sign-**board**, *s.* Enseigne *f.* 'sign-**language**, *s.* Langage *m* mimique. **sign-'manual**, *s.* Seing *m*, signature *f.* 'sign-**painter**, *s.* Peintre *m* d'enseignes. 'sign-**post**, *s.* Poteau indicateur. 'sign-**writer**, *s.* Peintre *m* en lettres; peintre d'enseignes.

ign², *v.tr.* **1.** (*a*) Signer; marquer d'un signe. **To sign oneself**, se signer. (*b*) Signer (son nom); souscrire (une lettre de change). (*In shops*) **Sign please!** visa, s'il vous plaît! *S.a.* PLEDGE¹ 3. **2. To sign assent**, faire signe que oui. **sign away**, *v.tr.* Céder par écrit (une propriété). **sign off**, *v.i.* (*Of workmen*) Signer le registre (en quittant le travail). **sign on. I.** *v.tr.* Embaucher (un ouvrier); engager (un matelot). **2.** *v.i.* (*a*) (*Of workmen*) S'embaucher; (*of seamen*) s'engager. (*b*) Signer le registre (en arrivant au travail). **signing**, *s.* Signature (d'un document); souscription *f* (d'un acte).

signal¹ ['signəl], *s.* **1.** (*Sign*) Signal, -aux *m.* **To give the signal** (*for departure*), donner le signal (du départ). *Tp:* **Calling, signal**, signal d'appel. *W.Tel:* **Station signal**, indicatif *m* du poste. *S.a.* CONTROL¹ 1, READY I. 1. **2.** (*Apparatus*) (*a*) **Visual signal**, signal optique; voyant *m*. **Semaphore signal**, signal à bras. **Signal bell**, avertisseur *m.* (*b*) *Rail:* **Home signal**, signal d'arrivée. **Block signal**, disque *m* de fermeture. **3.** *Navy:* **Signal officer**, officier de transmissions. **Yeoman of the signals**, maître-timonier *m.* 'signal-**beacon**, *s.* Fanal *m*, -aux. 'signal-**book**, *s. Nau:* Code *m* de signaux. 'signal-**box, -cabin**, *s. Rail:* Cabine *f* à signaux; cabine d'aiguillage. 'signal-**cord**, *s. Rail:* Corde-signal *m.* 'signal-**flag**, *s. Navy:* Pavillon *m* pour signaux. 'signal-**lamp**, *s.* **1.** Lampe *f* de signal. **2.** *Ind:* Lampe indicatrice, lampe témoin. 'signal-**light**, *s. Nau: etc:* Fanal *m*, -aux. *pl.* **Signal-lights**, feux *m* de route. 'signal-**mast, -post**, *s.* Mât *m*, pylône *m*, de signaux. 'signal-**rocket**, *s.* Fusée *f* de signaux. 'signal-**station**, *s. Nau:* (*On board*) Poste *m* de timonerie; (*on land*) sémaphore *m.*

signal², *v.* (**signalled**) **1.** *v.i.* Donner un signal (*to*, à); signaler. *Aut:* **To signal before stopping**, mettre le bras avant de stopper. **2.** *v.tr.* (*a*) Signaler (un train). (*b*) *Aut:* **To s. a turn**, signaler un changement de direction. (*c*) **To signal to s.o. to stop**, faire signe à qn de s'arrêter. **signalling**, *s.* Signalisation *f*; transmission *f* de signaux. *Nau:* Timonerie *f.* **Signalling-flag**, fanion-signal *m.* **Diver's signalling-line**, corde de communication du scaphandrier. *Aut:* **Signalling device**, signalisateur *m.*

signal³, *a.* (Service) signalé, insigne; (succès) éclatant. **-ally**, *adv.* Remarquablement.

signalize ['signəlaiz], *v.tr.* Signaler, marquer (une victoire).

signaller ['signələr], *s.* Signaleur *m.*

signalman, *pl.* **-men** ['signəlmən, -men], *s.m.* **1.** *Rail:* Signaleur. **2.** *Navy:* Timonier.

signatory ['signətəri], *a. & s.* Signataire (*mf*).

signature ['signətjər], *s.* **1.** Signature *f*; *Adm:* visa *m.* **Stamped signature**, griffe *f. Com:* **The signature of the firm**, la signature sociale. **2.** *Typ:* (*a*) Signature *f* (d'un cahier). (*b*) *We are sending you the first four signatures*, nous vous envoyons les quatre premiers cahiers. **3.** *Mus:* **Key-signature**, armature *f*, armure *f* (de la clef). 'signature **tune**, *s. W.Tel:* Indicatif musical.

signet ['signet], *s.* **1.** Sceau *m*, cachet *m.* **2.** *Scot:* **Writer to the signet** = avoué *m.* 'signet-**ring**, *s.* (Bague ') chevalière *f.*

significance [sig'nifikəns], *s.* **1.** Signification *f.* **Look of deep significance**, regard très significatif. **2.** Importance *f*, conséquence *f.*

significant [sig'nifikənt], *a.* **1.** (Mot) significatif. **2.** *Ar:* **Significant figure**, chiffre significatif. **3.** (Événement) important, de grande portée. **-ly**, *adv.* (Regarder) d'une manière significative.

signification [signifi'kei∫(ə)n], *s.* Signification *f*, sens *m* (d'un mot, d'une phrase, etc.).

significative [sig'nifikətiv], *a.* Significatif (*of*, de).

signify ['signifai]. **1.** *v.tr.* Signifier. (*a*) Être (le) signe de (qch.). (*b*) Vouloir dire. *What does this word s.?* que signifie ce mot? (*c*) Déclarer, faire connaître (ses intentions). **2.** *v.i.* Importer. **It does not signify**, cela ne fait rien. *What does it s.?* qu'importe?

sikh [sik, si:k], *a. & s. Ethn:* Sikh, -e.

silence¹ ['sailəns], *s.* Silence *m.* (*a*) **Dead silence**,

silence absolu. **A breathless silence,** un silence
ému, anxieux. *Calls for s.,* des chut réitérés.
Silence! (faites) silence! du silence! (*notice in
reading-room*) défense *f* de parler. **Silence gives
consent,** qui ne dit mot consent. (*b*) **To pass over
sth. in silence,** passer qch. sous silence. (*c*) **The
silence of the night,** le silence de la nuit.
silence², *v.tr.* (*a*) Réduire (qn) au silence ; faire
taire (un adversaire) ; étouffer (les plaintes). **To
silence criticism,** fermer la bouche à la critique.
(*b*) Amortir, étouffer (un bruit). *Cin:* **To silence
the camera,** insonoriser la camera. *I.C.E:* **To
silence the exhaust,** assourdir l'échappement.
silencer ['sailənsər], *s.* Amortisseur *m* de son.
I.C.E: Silencieux *m* ; pot *m* d'échappement.
silene [sai'liːni], *s. Bot:* Silène *m.*
silent ['sailənt], *a.* **I.** Silencieux. (*a*) **To keep
silent,** (i) observer le silence ; (ii) garder le silence,
se taire (*about*, sur). **To become s.,** se taire. **Be
silent!** taisez-vous ! **Silent as the tomb,** muet
comme la tombe. (*b*) **A silent man,** un homme
silencieux, taciturne. **2.** (*a*) Silencieux, insonore.
S. running of the engine, allure silencieuse du
moteur. *Cin:* **To make the camera s.,** insonoriser
la caméra. (*b*) *Ling:* **Silent letter,** lettre muette.
-ly, *adv.* Silencieusement ; en silence.
silex ['saileks], *s. Miner:* Silex *m.*
silhouette¹ [silu'et], *s.* Silhouette *f.*
silhouette², *v.tr.* Silhouetter.
silica ['silika], *s. Ch:* Silice *f.*
silicate ['siliket], *s. Ch:* Silicate *m.*
siliceous [si'liʃəs], *a. Ch:* Siliceux.
silicic [si'lisik], *a. Ch:* (Acide) silicique.
silicon ['silikɔn], *s. Ch:* Silicium *m. Metall:*
Silicon bronze, bronze siliceux.
siliqua, *pl.* **-quae** ['silikwa, -kwiː], **silique**
[si'liːk], *s. Bot:* Silique *f.*
silk [silk], *s.* **I.** Soie *f.* (*a*) **Raw silk,** soie grège.
Thrown silk, soie moulinée ; organsin *m.*
Sewing silk, soie à coudre. **Silk stockings,** bas
de soie. **The silk trade,** la soierie. (*b*) *Tex:* **Oiled
silk,** taffetas *m* imperméable. **Artificial silk, rayon
silk,** soie artificielle ; rayonne *f.* **Silk fabrics,
silks,** soierie. *S.a.* HAT, PURSE¹ I, SOFT I. I.
2. To wear a black silk, porter une robe de soie
noire. *Jur: F:* **To take silk,** être nommé conseiller du roi. **'silk-'covered,** *a. El:* (Fil) isolé
à la soie. **'silk-'finish,** *v.tr. Tex:* Similiser.
'silk-'hatted, *a.* Coiffé d'un chapeau haut de
forme. **'silk-mercer,** *s.* Marchand, -ande, de
soieries. **'silk-moth,** *s: Ent:* Bombyx *m* du
ver à soie.
silken ['silk(ə)n], *a.* **I.** Soyeux. *S. tresses,*
boucles de soie. **2.** *F:* (*Of voice*) Doucereux.
silkiness ['silkinəs], *s.* **I.** Nature soyeuse (d'une
étoffe). **2.** *F:* Moelleux *m* (de la voix).
silkworm ['silkwəːrm], *s.* Ver *m* à soie. **Silkworm
breeder,** sériciculteur *m* ; magnanier, -ière.
silky ['silki], *a.* (*a*) Soyeux. (*b*) *S. voice,* voix
moelleuse. (*c*) *Pej:* Doucereux.
sill [sil], *s.* **I.** *Const:* = GROUNDSEL². **2.** (**Win-
dow-)sill,** tablette *f*, appui *m*, de fenêtre. **3.** *Min:*
Sole *f*, semelle *f* (d'une galerie). **4.** *Geol:* Filon-
couche *m.*
silliness ['silinəs], *s.* Sottise *f*, niaiserie *f.*
silly ['sili], *a.* **I.** Sot, *f.* sotte ; niais. *S. answer,*
réponse saugrenue. **You silly boy!** petit nigaud !
s. **You little silly!** petite niaise ! **Silly ass!**
imbécile ! gros bêta ! *To do a s. thing,* faire une
bêtise. *Journ: F:* **The silly season,** l'époque où
les journaux en sont réduits à publier des
niaiseries. *Cin:* **Silly symphonies,** symphonies
folâtres. **2. To knock s.o. silly,** étourdir, assommer, qn. **-ily,** *adv.* Sottement, bêtement.

silo ['sailou], *s. Agr:* Silo *m.*
silt¹ [silt], *s.* Dépôt (vaseux) ; vase *f. Geol:*
Apports *mpl* de ruissellement ; lais *m.*
silt², *v.* **To silt (up). I.** *v.tr.* Envaser, ensable
(un port). **2.** *v.i.* (*Of harbour*) S'envaser
s'ensabler. **silting (up),** *s.* Envasement *m.*
Silurian [sai'ljuəriən], *a. Geol:* Silurien.
silver¹ ['silvər], *s.* **I.** Argent *m.* **German silver
nickel silver,** maillechort *m.* **2.** *Attrib.* (*a*) D'ar
gent, en argent. *S.* **inkstand,** encrier en argent
S. **spoon,** cuiller d'argent. *F:* **He was born wit
a silver spoon in his mouth,** il est né coiffé
(*b*) *S.* **hair,** cheveux argentés. *Cin:* **Silver screen**
écran argenté. *S.a.* CLOUD¹ I. **3.** Argent mon
nayé. **Silver coin,** pièce *f* d'argent. **4.** = SILVER
PLATE¹. **'silver-'foil,** *s.* Feuille *f* d'argent
'silver 'fox, *s. Z:* Renard argenté. **'silver
gilt. I.** *s.* Vermeil *m.* **2.** *a.* En vermeil
'silver-'haired, *a.* Aux cheveux argentés
'silver-'headed, *a.* **I.** = SILVER-HAIRED
2. (Canne) à pomme d'argent. **'silver
mounted,** *a.* Monté en argent. **'silver
'paper,** *s.* *F:* "Papier d'argent" (en étain)
silver-'plate¹, *s. Coll.* Argenterie *f* ; vaisselle
d'argent. **silver-'plate²,** *v.tr.* Argenter. **sil
ver-'plated,** *a.* Argenté. *S.-p. wares,* doublé *n*
d'argent. **'silver-plating,** *s.* Argenture *f*
argentage *m.* **'silver-print,** *s. Phot:* Épreuv
sur papier aux sels d'argent. **'silver-side,** *s*
Cu: Gîte *m* à la noix. **'silver-toned,** *a*
(*Of voice*) Argentin. **'silver-'tongued,** *a*
F: Éloquent ; à la langue dorée. **'silver
'wedding,** *s.* Noces *fpl* d'argent. **'silver
work,** *s.* Orfèvrerie *f.*
silver². **I.** *v.tr.* (*a*) Argenter. (*b*) Étamer (ui
miroir). **2.** *v.i.* (*Of the hair*) S'argenter. **silver
ing,** *s.* **I.** (*a*) Argentage *m.* (*b*) Étamage *m* (d
miroirs). **2.** (*a*) Argenture *f.* (*b*) Tain *m* de
miroir).
silversmith ['silvərsmiθ], *s.* Orfèvre *m.*
silvery ['silvəri], *a.* (*a*) (Nuage) argenté
(écailles) d'argent. (*b*) (Rire) argentin.
simian ['simiən], *a. & s.* Simien (*m*)
similar ['similər], *a.* (*a*) Semblable, pareil (*to
à). *Geom:* **Similar triangles,** triangles sem
blables. (*b*) *Mth:* **Similar products,** produit
similaires. **-ly,** *adv.* Pareillement, semblable
ment.
similarity [simi'læriti], *s.* Ressemblance *f*, imi
larité *f. Geom:* Similitude *f* (de triangles).
simile ['simili], *s.* Comparaison *f*, image *f.*
similitude [si'militjuːd], *s.* Similitude *f.*
simmer¹ ['simər], *s. Cu:* **To keep sth.** at
simmer, on the simmer, (faire) mijoter qch.
simmer². **I.** *v.i.* (*a*) (*Of liquid*) Frémir ; (*of foo
in pot*) mijoter, bouillotter. **To let the soup s.
mitonner la soupe. (*b*) *F:* (*Of revolt, etc.*
Fermenter. (*Of pers.*) **To simmer down,** s'apaise
peu à peu. **2.** *v.tr.* (Faire) mijoter (un ragoût)
simmering, *s.* **I.** Frémissement *m* (d'u
liquide) ; bouillottement *m.* **2.** *F:* Ferment *n*
(de révolte).
Simon ['saimən]. *Pr.n.m.* Simon. *F:* **Simp
Simon,** niais *m*, nicodème *m.* **The (real) Simo
Pure,** la véritable personne.
simoniac [sai'mouniak], **simoniacal** sa.mo
'naiak(ə)l], *a. Ecc:* Simoniaque.
simony ['saiməni, 'si-], *s. Ecc:* Simonie *f.*
simoon [si'muːn], *s.* Simoun *m.*
simper¹ ['simpər], *s.* Sourire affecté, minaudè
simper², *v.i.* Minauder, mignarder. **simper
ing,** *s.* **I.** Minauder. **simpering²,** *s.* Minaud
derie(s) *f(pl)* ; grimaces *fpl.*
simple [simpl]. **I.** *a.* (*a* (*Of pers.*) Simple

naturel (de caractère) ; sans affectation. *S. folk,* es humbles, les petits. *A s. soul,* une bonne âme. (*b. Pej :* Naïf, *f.* naïve ; crédule, niais. *What a s. soul he is!* ce qu'il est candide, naïf. *S.a.* SIMON. (*c*) *S. problem,* prob ème simple, peu difficile. *F:* As simple as ABC, as shelling peas, simple comme bonjour. (*d*) *Com :* Simple interest, intérêts simples. *Gram :* Simple sentence, proposition indépendante. (*e*) *Jur :* Simple contract, convention verbale, tacite. (*f*) *F:* It's simple robbery, c'est e vol pur et simple. 2. *s. Med.Bot :* Simples, simples *m.* -ply, *adv.* 1. (Parler) simplement. 2. (*a*) Absolument. *You look s. lovely!* vous êtes absolumen parfaite! You simply must, il le faut absolument. (*b*) Uniquement ; tout simplement. *He did it s. to test you,* il l'a fait uniquement pour vous éprouver. *I s. observed that . . .,* je me suis borné à faire remarquer que. . . . simple-'hearted, *a.* Simple, ingénu. simple-'minded, *a.* Simple d'esprit ; naïf, *f.* naïve. simple-'mindedness, *s.* Simplicité *f* d'esprit ; naïveté *f* ; candeur *f.*
impleness ['simplnəs], *s.* = SIMPLICITY 1.
impleton ['simpltən], *s.* Nigaud, -aude ; niais, -aise.
implicity [sim'plisiti], . 1. ,*a*) Candeur *f,* simplicité *f* (d'un enfant). (*b*) Bêtise *f,* niaiserie *f.* 2. (*a*) Simplicité (d'un problème). *F:* It is simplicity itself, c'est simple comme bonjour. (*b*) Absence *f* de recherche ; simplicité (dans la mise).
implification [simplifi'keiʃ(ə)n], *s.* Simplification *f.*
implify ['simplifai], *v.tr.* Simplifier. *To become simplified,* se simplifier.
imply ['simpli], *adv. See* SIMPLE.
imulacrum, *pl.* -a [simju'leikrəm, -a], *s.* Simulacre *m,* semblant *m.*
imulate ['simjuleit], *v.tr.* Simuler, feindre (une maladie) ; affecter (de l'enthousiasme).
imulation [simju'leiʃ(ə)n], *s.* Simulation *f,* feinte *f.*
imulator ['simjuleitər], *s.* Simulateur, -trice.
imultaneous [siməl'teinjəs], *a.* (*a*) Simultané. (*b*) Simultaneous with . . ., qui a lieu en même temps que. . . . -ly, *adv.* (*a*) Simultanément. (*b*) En même temps (*with,* que).
in¹ [sin], *s.* (*a*) Péché *m.* Original sin, péché originel. The forgiveness of sins, le pardon des offenses *f.* To fall into sin, tomber dans le péché. *F:* For my sins, *I was appointed to . . .,* pour mes péchés je fus nommé à. . . . *P:* Like sin, furieusement, violemment. (*b*) *F:* Offense (contre les convenances). *Sin against good taste,* infraction *f* au bon goût.
sin², *v.i.* (sinned) (*a*) Pécher. Liable to sin, peccable. (*b*) *To sin against propriety,* manquer aux convenances. sinning, *s.* Le péché.
since [sins]. 1. *adv.* Depuis. (*a*) Ever since, depuis (lors). (*b*) (*Ago*) Many years since, il y a bien des années. Long since, (i) depuis longtemps ; (ii) il y a longtemps. How long is it since? il y a combien de cela ? 2. *prep.* Depuis. *He has been up s. dawn,* il était levé dès l'aurore. Since when *have you been here?* depuis quand êtes-vous ici ? Since that time, since then, depuis lors. 3. *conj.* (*a*) Depuis que ; que. *S. I have been here,* depuis que je suis ici. *It is just a week . he came,* il y a juste huit jours qu'il est arrivé. (*b*) Puisque. *S. he is not of age,* puisqu'il est mineur.
sincere [sin'si:ər], *a.* (*a*) Sincère ; franc, -che. (*b*) (Sentiment) sincère. -ly, *adv.* Sincèrement. Yours sincerely, cordialement à vous.

sincerity [sin'seriti], *s.* Sincérité *f* ; bonne foi. In all sincerity, de la meilleure foi du monde.
sine [sain], *s. Mth :* Sinus *m* (d'un angle). Sine wave, onde sinusoïdale.
sinecure ['sainekjuər], *s.* Sinécure *f.*
sinecurist ['sainekjuərist], *s.* Sinécuriste *mf.*
sinew ['sinju], *s.* 1. (*a*) Tendon *m.* (*b*) *F:* A man of sinew, un homme musclé ; un homme fort. 2. *pl. F:* Sinews, nerf *m,* force *f. The sinews of war,* le nerf de la guerre.
sinewy ['sinjui], *a.* 1. (*Of meat*) Tendineux. 2. *F:* (Bras) musclé, nerveux.
sinful ['sinful], *a. S. person,* pécheur, *f.* pécheresse. *S. pleasure,* plaisir coupable. *S. world,* monde de pécheurs. -fully, *adv.* D'une façon coupable.
sinfulness ['sinfulnəs], *s.* 1. Caractère criminel (d'un acte) ; culpabilité *f.* 2. Le péché.
sing [siŋ], *v.* (sang [saŋ] ; sung [sʌŋ]) 1. *v.tr.* Chanter. *F:* To sing small, (i) déchanter ; (ii) filer doux. To sing s.o. to sleep, endormir qn en chantant. *F:* To be always singing the same song, chanter toujours la même chanson. 2. *v.i.* (*Of the wind, etc.*) Siffler ; (*of the ears*) tinter, bourdonner. The kettle sings, la bouilloire chante. sing out, *v.tr. Nau : etc :* Crier (le fond, etc.). sing up, *v.i. F:* Chanter plus fort.
singing¹, *a.* (Oiseau) chanteur ; qui chante. 'singing-buoy, *s. Nau :* Bouée *f* sonore, à sifflet. singing², *s.* 1. Chant *m.* Singing lesson, leçon de chant. 2. Sifflement *m* (du vent, etc.). Singing in the ears, bourdonnement *m,* tintement *m,* d'oreilles. 'sing-song, *s.* 1. Chant *m* monotone ; psalmodie *f.* Sing-song accent, accent chantant. 2. *F:* Concert improvisé (entre amis).
Singapore [siŋga'pɔːr]. *Pr.n.* Singapour.
singe¹ [sindʒ], *s. Hairdr :* Brûlage *m,* flambage *m* (de la pointe des cheveux).
singe², *v.tr.* 1. Brûler (qch.) légèrement ; roussir (du linge, etc.). *F:* To singe one's wings, se brûler à la chandelle. 2. Passer (qch.) à la flamme ; flamber (une volaille). *Hairdr :* Brûler, flamber (la pointe des cheveux).
singer ['siŋər], *s.* 1. Chanteur ; *f.* chanteuse, (*professional*) cantatrice. *Ecc :* Chantre *m.* 2. *The singers of the past,* les chantres du passé.
single¹ [siŋgl], *s. Ten : Golf :* Partie *f* simple ; simple *m. Ten :* Men's singles, simple messieurs.
single², *a.* 1. (*a*) Seul, unique. Not a single one, pas un seul, pas un. *I haven't seen a s. soul,* je n'ai pas vu âme qui vive. *He hasn't a s. penny,* il n'a pas le premier sou. *Fin :* Single premium, prime unique. (*b*) Individuel, particulier. Every single day, *F:* tous les jours que Dieu fait. 2. (*a*) Single bed, lit à une place, pour une personne. Single bedroom, chambre à un lit. In single rank, sur un rang. (*b*) (*Of pers.*) Célibataire ; non marié(e). To lead a single life, vivre dans le célibat. 3. Sincère, honnête, simple. A single heart, un cœur sincère. -gly, *adv.* 1. Séparément ; un à un. 2. Seul ; sans aide. 'single-barrelled, *a.* (Fusil) à un canon, à un coup. 'single-breasted, *a. Cost :* (Veston) droit. 'single-cylinder, *attrib.a.* Monocylindrique. 'single-eyed, *a.* Qui ne vise qu'un but. single-'handed, *a.* 1. (Arme, instrument) qui se manie d'une main. 2. (Accomplir une tâche) seul, sans aide, *F:* tout seul. 'single-hearted, *a.* (*Of pers.*) Sincère, honnête, droit ; loyal, -aux. single-'heartedness, *s.* Sincérité *f* ; loyauté *f.* 'single-phase, *attrib.a. El.E :* Uniphasé, monophasé. single-

'seater, s. Aut: Av: Monoplace m. **'single-track,** attrib.a. Rail: (Ligne) à voie unique. **'single-wire,** attrib.a. El.E: Unifilaire. **single³,** v.tr. To single out s.o., sth., (i) choisir qn, qch., (ii) remarquer, distinguer, qn, qch. (for, pour; as, comme).

singleness ['singlnəs], s. **1.** Sincérité f, droiture f. **2.** Unicité f. **With singleness of purpose,** avec un seul but en vue. **3.** Célibat m.

singlestick ['singlstik], s. Sp: Canne f.

singlet ['singlet], s. **1.** Gilet m de corps. **2.** Sp: Maillot fin.

singleton ['singltən], s. Cards: Singleton m.

singular ['singjulər], a. **1.** (a) Gram: Singulier. s. **In the singular,** au singulier. (b) **All and singular,** tous et chacun. **2.** (a) Rare, remarquable, surprenant. (b) Singulier, bizarre. **-ly,** adv. Singulièrement. (a) Remarquablement. (b) Bizarrement.

singularity [singju'lariti], s. Singularité f. **1.** Particularité f. **2.** Bizarrerie f.

singularize ['singjuləra:iz], v.tr. Singulariser.

Sinhalese [sinhə'li:z], a. & s. inv. in pl. Cingalais, -aise.

sinister ['sinistər], a. **1.** Sinistre. **With a s. purpose,** dans un mauvais dessein. **A man of s. countenance,** un homme de mauvaise mine. **2.** Her: Sénestre.

sink¹ [sink], s. **1.** (a) Évier m (de cuisine). **Sink trap,** siphon m d'évier. **Sink basket,** passoire f de coin d'évier. (b) F: **Sink of iniquity,** cloaque m, bourbier m, sentine f, de tous les vices. **2.** = SINK-HOLE 2. **3.** Th: Trappe f (de plateau). **'sink-hole,** s. **1.** Souillard m (de dallage, etc.). **2.** Geol: Emposieu m, entonnoir m.

sink², v. (sank [sank]; sunk [sʌnk], A: & a. sunken ['sʌnkən]) I. v.i. **1.** Tomber au fond (des eaux); aller au fond; (of ship) couler au fond; couler bas; sombrer. (Of ship) **To sink by the bow,** couler de l'avant. F: **He was left to sink or swim,** il fut abandonné à la grâce de Dieu. **Here goes! sink or swim!** allons-y! advienne que pourra! **2. To sink into sth.** (a) S'enfoncer, pénétrer (dans la boue, etc.). **The dye must be allowed to s. in,** il faut donner à la teinture le temps de pénétrer. F: (Of words) **To sink into the memory,** se graver dans la mémoire. **His words begin to sink in,** ses paroles commencent à faire impression. (b) Tomber (dans le vice, dans l'oubli). **To s. deep(er) into crime,** s'enfoncer dans le crime. **To s. into insignificance,** devenir insignifiant. (c) **To sink in oneself,** rentrer en soi-même; se recueillir. **3.** (Subside) (a) **To sink (down),** s'affaisser; (of building) se tasser. (b) **The fire is sinking,** le feu baisse. (c) (Of pers.) **To sink (down) into a chair,** se laisser tomber, s'affaler, dans un fauteuil. **To sink on one's knees,** (se laisser) tomber à genoux. **His legs sank under him,** ses jambes se plièrent sous lui. **His heart sank,** son cœur se serra; le cœur lui manqua. **His spirits sank,** son courage s'abattit. **4.** Descendre; aller en descendant; s'abaisser. **To sink out of sight,** disparaître. **The sun is sinking,** le soleil baisse. **5.** Baisser (en valeur); diminuer; s'affaiblir, décliner. **The patient is sinking,** le malade baisse. **He has sunk in my estimation,** il a baissé, diminué, dans mon estime. II. **sink,** v.tr. **1.** (a) Couler, faire sombrer (un navire); envoyer (un navire) au fond. (b) Mouiller (une mine). **2.** Baisser (la voix); enfoncer (un pieu, etc.). **3.** (a) Creuser, foncer (un puits). (b) Engr: **To sink a die,** graver un coin en creux. **4.** Supprimer (une objection, etc.). **They sank their differences,** ils ont fait table rase de leurs dif-

férends. **5.** Fin: Éteindre, amortir (une dette). **6.** (a) **To sink money in an annuity,** placer de l'argent en viager. (b) **To s. money in an unfortunate undertaking,** enterrer, engloutir, de l'argent dans une entreprise malheureuse. **sunk,** a. **1.** (Navire) sombré, coulé; (terrain) submergé. F: **Sunk in thought,** plongé, abîmé, dans ses pensées. **S. in the mud,** enlisé dans la boue, embourbé. **To be s. in sloth,** croupir dans l'oisiveté. **Sunk in debt,** noyé de dettes. U.S: F: **He's sunk,** c'est un homme coulé. **2.** Sunk road, route encaissée. **Sunk garden,** jardin en caissé. **Sunk key,** clavette à rainure; clavette encastrée. **Sunk screw,** vis noyée. Phot: **Sunk mount** (of lens), monture noyée. El.E: **Sunk studs,** plots noyés. **sinking¹,** a. (Navire) qui coule; (navire) en perdition. **With sinking heart,** avec un serrement de cœur. **sinking²,** **1.** (a) Enfoncement m (des pieds dans la boue, etc.); enlisement m (de qn dans une fondrière); engloutissement m (d'un navire). (b) **The s. of the 'Lusitania,'** le torpillage du "Lusitania." **2.** Affaissement m, abaissement m (du sol, etc.); oppression f (du cœur). F: **That sinking feeling,** ce sentiment de défaillance. **3.** Affaiblissement m, déclin m (des forces, etc.); abaissement m (de la voix, etc.). **4.** Creusage m, foncement m (d'un puits). **5.** (a) Amortissement m, extinction f (d'une dette). (b) Placement m (d'une somme) à fond perdu. **'sinking-fund,** s. Caisse f d'amortissement.

sinkable ['sinkəbl], a. (Bateau) submersible.

sinker ['sinkər], s. **1.** Well-sinker, Min: shaft sinker, fonceur m de puits; puisatier m. **2.** (a) Navy: Crapaud m d'amarrage (d'une mine). (b) Plomb m (d'une ligne de pêche).

sinless ['sinləs], a. Sans péché; innocent.

sinner ['sinər], s. (a) Pécheur. f. pécheresse (b) F: Mauvais sujet.

sinter ['sintər], s. Geol: Travertin m.

sinuous ['sinjuəs], a. **1.** Sinueux. **2.** (Of pers.) Souple, agile.

sinus ['sainəs], s. Anat: Sinus m, antre m.

sip¹ [sip], s. Petit coup; petite gorgée; F: goutte f.

sip², v.tr. (sipped) Boire à petits coups, à petite gorgées.

siphon¹ ['saifən], s. Siphon m. (a) **Siphon barometer,** baromètre à siphon. (b) **Siphon(-bottle),** siphon à eau de seltz.

siphon², v.tr. Siphonner (un liquide).

sippet ['sipet], s. Cu: (For soup) Croûton m (for egg) mouillette f.

sir [sər, sər], s. **1.** (a) Monsieur m. **Yes, sir** (i) oui, monsieur; (ii) Mil: (to superior officer) oui, mon capitaine; oui, mon colonel, etc. (iii) Navy: oui, commandant; oui, amiral. **Dinner is served, sir,** monsieur est servi. (b) Corr: **Sir, (my) dear Sir,** Monsieur. **2.** Sir (titre d'un baronet ou d'un knight).

sire [saiər], s. **1.** (a) A. & Poet: Père m, aïeul m. (b) Breed: Père m (en parlant des quadrupèdes) esp. étalon m. **2.** (In addressing sovereigns) Sire m.

siren ['saiərən], s. **1.** (a) Myth: Sirène f. (b) F: Femme fatale; tentatrice f; sirène f. **2.** (a) (Acoustics) Sirène. (b) Nau: Sirène trompe f d'alarme.

sirloin ['sə:rloin], s. Cu: Aloyau m (de bœuf) faux-filet m.

sirocco [si'rɔko], s. Meteor: Siroc(o) m.

sirrah ['sira], s. A: **1.** = SIR. **2.** Pej: Maraud coquin!

sisal ['sisəl, 'saizəl], s. Bot: Agave f d'Amérique; sisal m.

sissy ['sisi], *s. U.S: F:* Mollasson *m*; poule mouillée.

sister ['sistər], *s.f.* **1.** Sœur. **2.** (*a*) *Ecc:* Religieuse; sœur. Sister Ursula, la sœur Ursule. (*b*) (*In hospital*) (Ward-)sister, surveillante; infirmière en chef. **3.** *Attrib.* Sister nations, nations sœurs. Sister ships, (i) bâtiments identiques, bâtiments de même série; (ii) navires appartenant au même armateur. 'sister-in-law, *s.f.* Belle-sœur, *pl.* belles-sœurs.

sisterhood ['sistərhud], *s.* Communauté religieuse.

sisterly ['sistərli], *a.* De sœur.

Sistine ['sistin], *a.* The Sistine chapel, ia chapelle Sixtine.

Sisyphus ['sisifəs]. *Pr.n.m. Myth:* Sisyphe.

sit [sit], *v.* (*p.t.* sat [sat]; *p.p.* sat; *pr.p.* sitting) I. *v.i.* **1.** (*a*) (*Of pers.*) S'asseoir; être assis, rester assis; se tenir (dans une pièce, etc.). *F:* She is a sit-by-the-fire, elle ne quitte pas le coin du feu. *To sit still*, rester sans bouger; rester tranquille. To sit with s.o., tenir compagnie à qn. To sit at home, se tenir chez soi. To sit at table, être à table. To sit over one's work, rester attablé à son travail. *To sit over a pipe*, rester (assis) à savourer une pipe. *To sit over a book*, s'absorber dans la lecture d'un livre. *F:* To sit tight, ne pas bouger de sa place; ne pas se laisser ébranler; ne pas céder. To sit on s.o., rabrouer qn; rabaisser le caquet à qn. *S.a.* EXAMINATION 2. (*b*) To sit for one's portrait, poser pour son portrait. To sit for an artist, poser chez un artiste. (*c*) To sit on the committee, on the jury, être du comité, du jury. To sit· in Parliament, siéger au parlement. **2.** (*Of assemblies*) Siéger; être en séance. **3.** (*a*) (*Of bird*) (Se) percher; être perché, posé. (*b*) (*Of hen*) To sit (on eggs), couver (des œufs). (*c*) To find a hare sitting, trouver un lièvre au gîte. To shoot a pheasant sitting, tirer sur un faisan à terre, un faisan posé. **4.** (*a*) How sits the wind? d'où vient le vent? This food sits heavy on the stomach, cette nourriture pèse sur l'estomac. *His responsibilities sit heavy upon him*, ses responsabilités lui sont à charge. (*b*) (*Of garments*) Tomber (bien, mal); (bien ou mal) aller. II. sit, *v.tr.* **1.** To sit a horse well, badly, se tenir bien, mal, à cheval; avoir une bonne, mauvaise, assiette. **2.** *To sit a child on the table*, asseoir un enfant sur la table. To sit oneself down, s'asseoir. sit down, *v.i.* S'asseoir; prendre un siège. Please sit down, asseyez-vous; veuillez vous asseoir. To sit down to table, s'attabler; se mettre à table. *F:* To sit down under an insult, empocher, avaler, une insulte. *U.S: F:* To sit down hard on a plan, s'opposer résolument à un projet. sit-down, *attrib.a. U.S:* Sit-down strike, grève *f* sur le tas. sit out, *v.tr.* **1.** Ne pas prendre part à (un jeu, etc.). To sit out a dance (with s.o.), causer une danse. **2.** (*a*) To sit a lecture out, rester (patiemment) jusqu'à la fin d'une conférence. (*b*) To sit s.o. out, rester jusqu'après le départ de qn. sit up, *v.i.* **1.** (*a*) Se tenir droit; se redresser (sur sa chaise). *F:* To make s.o. sit up, étonner qn. (*b*) To sit up (in bed), se mettre, se lever, sur son séant. **2.** To sit up late, veiller tard; se coucher tard. To sit up for s.o., (rester levé à) attendre qn. To sit up with a sick person, garder, veiller, un malade pendant la nuit. .**3.** To sit up to the table, approcher sa chaise de la table. **sitting**[1], *a.* **1.** Assis. **2.** (*Of tribunal, etc.*) En séance; siégeant. **3.** (*a*) (Gibier) posé, au repos. (*b*) Sitting hen, poule en train de couver. **sitting**[2], *s.*

1. (*a*) Posture assise. Sitting and standing room, places assises et places debout. (*b*) To paint a portrait in three sittings, faire un portrait en trois séances *f*. **2.** (*a*) To serve 500 people at one sitting, servir 500 personnes à la fois. *F: To write two chapters at one s.*, écrire deux chapitres d'un seul jet, d'arrache-pied. (*b*) Séance, réunion *f* (d'une commission, etc.); tenue *f* (d'une assemblée). *S. of a court*, audience *f.* **3.** Siège réservé (dans une église). **4.** Husb: (*a*) (*Of hen*) Couvaison *f*, incubation *f.* (*b*) Couvée *f* (d'œufs). 'sitting-room, *s.* **1.** Petit salon. Bed-sitting-room, pièce *f* unique (d'étudiant, etc.). **2.** (*Space*) Place *f* pour s'asseoir.

site [sait], *s.* **1.** Emplacement *m* (d'un édifice, d'une ville, etc.); assiette *f* (d'un camp). **2.** Building-site, terrain *m* à bâtir. On site, à pied d'œuvre.

sitter ['sitər], *s.* **1.** (*a*) Personne assise. (*b*) Voyageur assis. **2.** (Chez un peintre) (i) Modèle *m*; (ii) client, -ente. **3.** (*a*) (Poule) couveuse *f.* (*b*) To fire at a sitter, tirer sur le gibier posé. *F:* It was a sitter for me, c'était un coup tout fait.

situate ['sitjueit], *v.tr.* Situer (une maison, etc.). **situated**, *a.* **1.** Pleasantly s. house, maison bien située. **2.** (*Of pers.*) This is how I am s., voici la situation dans laquelle je me trouve.

situation [sitju·eiʃ(ə)n], *s.* **1.** Situation *f*, emplacement *m* (d'un édifice). **2.** Situation (politique, financière). **3.** Emploi *m*, place *f.* To get a situation, obtenir un emploi. To be out of a situation, être sans place; se trouver sans emploi. Situations vacant, offres *fpl* d'emplois.

six [siks], *num. a. & s.* Six (*m*). *I have six*, j'en ai six. *F: Two and six*, deux shillings et six pence. Coach and six, carrosse à six chevaux. (*At dominoes*) The double six, le double six. *Mil: To be on six months' leave*, être en semestre. *F:* It is six of one and half a dozen of the other, c'est bonnet blanc et blanc bonnet; *P:* c'est kif-kif. Everything is at sixes and sevens, tout est désorganisé, en désordre; tout est sens dessus dessous. (*For other phrases see* EIGHT.) 'six-eight, *s. Mus:* (Mesure *f* à) six-huit *m.* 'six-foot, *attrib.a. Rail:* The six-foot way, l'entre-voie *f.* six-'footer, *s. F:* Homme (haut) de six pieds. six-'shooter, *s.* Revolver *m* ou pistolet *m* à six coups.

sixfold ['siksfould]. **1.** *a.* Sextuple. **2.** *adv.* Six fois autant; au sextuple.

sixpence ['sikspəns], *s.* **1.** Six pence. **2.** Pièce *f* de six pence.

sixpenny ['sikspəni], *attrib.a.* (Journal, etc.) qui coûte, qui vaut, six pence; à, de, six pence. Sixpenny piece, bit, pièce *f* de six pence.

sixpennyworth [siks'peniwə:rθ], *s. To buy s. of chocolate*, acheter pour six pence de chocolat.

sixteen [siks'ti:n], *num. a. & s.* Seize (*m*). She is s., elle a seize ans. *For other phrases see* EIGHT.

sixteenth [siks'ti:nθ], *num. a. & s.* Seizième. *Louis the S.*, Louis Seize. (On) the sixteenth (of August), le seize (août).

sixth [siksθ]. **1.** *num. a. & s.* Sixième (*m*). *Sch:* The sixth (form), *approx.* = la classe de première. **2.** *s.* (*Fractional*) Sixième *m.* (*b*) *Mus:* Sixte (majeure, mineure). -ly, *adv.* Sixièmement.

sixtieth ['sikstiəθ], *num. a. & s.* Soixantième (*m*).

sixty ['siksti], *num. a. & s.* Soixante (*m*). Sixty-one, soixante et un. He is in the sixties, il a passé la soixantaine.

sizar ['saizər], *s. Sch:* Étudiant boursier.

sizarship ['saizər ip], *s. Sch:* Bourse *f* d'études.

size[1] [saiz], *s.* **1.** (*a*) Grandeur *f*, dimension *f*, grosseur *f*, volume *m.* To take the size of sth., mesurer qch. **All of a size,** tous de la même grosseur; tous de même taille. **Drawn full size,** dessiné à grandeur naturelle. *P:* **That's about the size of it,** c'est à peu près cela. *(b) Ind:* **To cut a piece to size,** tailler une pièce à la dimension, à la cote. **2.** *(a) (Of pers., horse, etc.)* Taille *f.* *(b) Com:* Numéro *m* (d'un article); taille (de vêtements); encolure *f* (de chemises); pointure *f* (de chaussures, de gants). **Small size,** petit modèle. **What size do you take?** *(in dresses, etc.)* quelle est votre taille? *(in shoes)* quelle pointure chaussez-vous? *(in hats)* du combien coiffez-vous? *(c)* Format *m* (d'un livre, etc.). *(d)* Calibre *m* (d'un fusil); grosseur (du plomb de chasse).

size², *v.tr.* **1.** Classer (des objets) par grosseur, par dimension. **2.** *Ind:* *(a)* Calibrer. *(b)* Mettre (une pièce) à la cote, à dimension. **size up,** *v.tr.* Jauger; prendre les dimensions de (qch.). *F:* **To size s.o. up,** classer, juger, qn. *I have sized him up,* j'ai pris sa mesure. **sized,** *a.* **Fair-sized,** assez grand. **Large-sized,** de grande taille; de grandes dimensions.

size³, *s.* *Tchn:* Apprêt *m.* *(a)* Colle *f.* **Animal size,** colle animale. *(b) Tex:* Empois *m.*

size⁴, *v.tr.* Apprêter (le papier, etc.).

sizeable ['saizəbl], *a.* *F:* D'une belle taille; assez grand.

sizzle¹ [sizl], *s.* Grésillement *m.*

sizzle², *v.i.* Grésiller; *(of gas)* chuinter. **Sizzling hot,** tout chaud.

skate¹ [skeit], *s.* *Ich:* Raie *f.*

skate², *s.* Patin *m.* *S.a.* ROLLER-SKATES.

skate³, *v.i.* Patiner. **skating,** *s.* Patinage *m.* **'skating-rink,** *s.* Skating *m*; piste *f* ou salle *f* de patinage.

skater ['skeitər], *s.* Patineur, -euse.

skedaddle¹ [ski'dadl], *s.* *F:* (i) Fuite précipitée; (ii) débandade *f.*

skedaddle², *v.i.* *F:* *(a)* Se sauver à toutes jambes; déguerpir. *(b)* S'enfuir à la débandade.

skein [skein], *s.* *(a)* Écheveau *m* (de fil de soie, de laine). *(b) F:* **Tangled skein,** confusion *f*, *F:* brouillamini *m.*

skeleton ['skelətən], *s.* **1.** Sque.ette *m*, oss.ture *f.* *F:* **The skeleton in the cupboard,** le secret honteux de la famille. **The skeleton at the feast,** le rabat-joie. **2.** *(a)* Charpente *f*, carcasse *f*, ossature (d'un navire, etc.). **Skeleton key,** crochet *m* (de serrurier); fausse clef; *F:* rossignol *m.* *(b)* Monture *f*, carcasse (d'un parapluie). *(c)* Canevas *m*, esquisse *f* (d'un sermon, etc.). **Skeleton map,** carte muette. *(d)* **Skeleton staff,** personnel réduit. **Skeleton army,** armée-cadre *f.*

skelp¹ [skelp], *s.* *Scot:* *F:* Taloche *f.*

skelp², *v.tr.* *Scot:* *F:* Administrer une taloche, une fessée, à (un enfant).

skep [skep], *s.* **1.** Panier *m.* **2.** *Ap:* Ruche *f* en paille.

sketch¹ [sketʃ], *s.* **1.** *(a)* Croqu s *m*, esquisse *f.* **Free-hand sketch,** dessin *m* à main levée. *(b) Mil:* Levé *m* topographique. *(c) Ind:* Dimensioned sketch, croquis coté. **2.** *(a)* **Sketch of procedure to be adopted,** exposé *m* de la procédure à adopter. *(b) Th:* Saynète *f.* **'sketch-book,** *s.* Cahier *m*, album *m*, de croquis.

sketch², *v.tr.* Esquisser, dessiner à grands traits, croquer (un paysage, etc.); faire le croquis de (qch.). **sketch in,** *v.tr.* Dessiner sommairement (les détails, etc.). **sketching,** *s.* Prise *f* de croquis; dessin m à main levée.

sketcher ['sketʃər], *s.* Dessinateur, -trice.

sketchy ['sketʃi], *a.* *F:* (Ouvrage) qui manque de précision, de perfection. **Sketchy knowledge,**

savoir rudimentaire, peu sûr. **-ily,** *adv.* D'une manière imprécise, incomplète, vague.

skew¹ [skju:], *s.* Biais *m*, obliquité *f* (d'un pont, d'une arche). **On the skew,** en biais; obliquement.

skew². **1.** *a.* *Arch:* *Mec:* *etc:* (Pont, mur) biais; (section) oblique. **2.** *adv.* En biais; de travers.

skew³. **1.** *v.i.* Biaiser, obliquer. **2.** *v.tr.* Couper en sifflet.

skewbald ['skju:bɔ:ld], *a.* (Cheval) blanc et roux.

skewer¹ ['skjuər], *s.* **1.** *Cu:* Brochette *f*, hâtelet *m.* **2.** *F:* Baïonnette *f*, épée *f.*

skewer², *v.tr.* Brocheter (une volaille); embrocher (un gigot).

ski¹, *pl.* **ski, skis** [ʃi:(z), ski:(z)], *s.* Ski *m.* **Ski-runner,** skieur, -euse.

ski², *v.i.* (ski'd; ski'd; *pr.p.* ski-ing, skiing) Faire du ski; skier. **ski-ing, skiing,** *s.* Le ski.

skid¹ [skid], *s.* **1.** *(a)* *Veh:* Skid(-pan), sabot *m* d'enrayement). *(b) Av:* Patin *m.* **2.** *Aut:* *etc:* *(a)* Dérapage *m.* *(b)* Embardée *f.*

skid², *v.i.* (skidded) *(a) Aut:* *etc:* ( ) *(Of wheel)* Déraper, glisser, patiner. (ii) *(Of car)* **To skid across the road,** faire une embardée. *(b) Av:* Glisser sur l'aile. **skidding,** *s.* **1.** Ensabotage *m*, enrayage *m.* **2.** *(a,* Dérapage *m*; patinage *m* (d'une roue). *(b)* Embardée *f.*

skier ['ʃi:ər, 'skiːər], *s.* Skieur, -euse.

skiff [skif], *s.* **1.** *Nau:* *(a)* Esquif *m*, yole *f.* *(b)* Youyou *m* (de bateau de commerce). **2.** *Row:* Skiff *m.*

skilful ['skilful], *a.* Adroit, habile. **-fully,** *adv.* Habilement, adro.tement.

skilfulness ['skilfulnəs], *s.* Habileté *f*, adresse *f.*

skill [skil], *s.* Habileté *f*, adresse *f*, dextérité *f.* **Skill in doing sth.,** talent *m* pour faire qch. **Want, lack, of skill,** maladresse *f.*

skilled [skild], *a.* Habile. **Skilled labour,** ma.nd'œuvre spécialisée, professionnelle. **To be skilled in an art, in business,** être fort en, versé dans, un art; se connaître en affaires.

skilly ['skili], *s.* *Cu:* Bouillie claire.

skim¹ [skim], *s.* **To take, have, a skim through a book,** parcourir rapidement un livre. **'skim-milk,** *s.* Lait écrémé.

skim², *v.tr. & i.* (skimmed) **1.** Écumer (le bouillon); écrémer (le .ait, etc.). *F:* **To skim the cream off sth.,** prendre la meil.eure partie de qch. **2.** Effleurer, raser (une surface). **To skim along,** passer légèrement; glisser. **To skim (over, through) a novel,** parcourir rapidement, feuilleter, un roman.

skimmer ['skimər], *s.* *(For soup)* Écumoire *f*; *(for milk)* écrémoir *m*, écrémeuse *f.*

skimp [skimp], *v.tr.* **1.** *(a)* **To skimp s.o. in food,** mesurer la nourriture à qn; compter les morceaux à qn. *(b)* **To skimp the food,** lés ner sur ia nourriture. **To s. the materia. in making a dress,** être parcimonieux d'étoffe; affamer une robe. *Skimped coat,* habit étriqué. **2.** *F:* **To skimp one's work,** saboter, bâcler, son ouvrage.

skimpiness ['skimp nəs], *s.* Insuffisance *f*; manque *m.*

skimpy ['skimpi], *a.* **Skimpy skirt,** jupe étriquée, (bien) juste. **Skimpy meal,** maigre repas. **-ily,** *adv.* Insuffisamment, parcimonieusement (meublé, etc.).

skin¹ [skin], *s.* **1.** Peau *f.* (i) **Outer skin,** épiderme *m.* (ii) **True skin,** derme *m.* *F:* **To have a thir skin,** être susceptible. *(Of snake, etc.)* **To cast, throw, its skin,** faire peau neuve. **Next (to) one's skin,** à même, sur, la peau. *F:* **He is nothing but skin and bone,** .l n'a que la peau et les os. **T**

come off with a whole skin, s'en tirer sain et sauf, indemne. **2.** (a) Dépouille f, peau (d un animal). **Fur skins,** pelleterie f. **Raw skins,** peaux vertes. (b) (For wine, etc.) Outre . (c) Feuille f (de parchemin). **3.** (a) Bot: Tunique f d'une graine); pellicule f (d'un grain de café). (b) **Orange skin,** peau d'orange. **Banana skin,** pelure f de banane. **Grape skin,** pellicule. Cu: **Potatoes boiled in their skins,** pommes de terre en robe de chambre. **4.** (a) Robe f (de saucisson). (b) Nau: Bordé extérieur (d'un canot). Av: Revêtement m (du fuselage). **5.** (a) Pellicule (sur le lait, etc.). (b) Metall: Croûte f (de la fonte). 'skin-dealer, s. Pelletier m, fourreur m. 'skin-'deep, a. (Of wound, emotions) A fleur de peau; superficiel. 'skin-disease, s. Maladie cutanée. 'skin-dresser, s. Peaussier m, pelletier m. 'skin-game, s. Escroquerie f; jeu m où d'avance l'un des joueurs doit perdre. 'skin-grafting, s. Med: Greffe f épidermique. 'skin-test, s. Med: Cuti-réaction f. 'skin-tight, a. (Vêtement) collant.

skin², v.tr. (skinned) **I.** (a) Écorcher, dépouiller, P: dépiauter (un lapin, etc.). F: **To skin s.o.,** dépouiller, écorcher, qn (au jeu). (b) Peler, éplucher (un fruit, etc.). **2.** (a) N.Arch: **To skin a ship,** revêtir un navire. (b) Nau: **To skin up a sail,** faire la chemise d'une voile. **skinned,** a. **Dark-skinned,** à peau brune; qui a la peau brune. **Clean-skinned,** qui a la peau saine. **skinning,** s. **I.** (a) Écorchement m (d'un lapin). (b) Épluchage m (d'un fruit). **2.** Desquamation f. **skinflint** ['skinflint], s. F: Ladre m; grigou m, -ous; rapiat m. **skinful** ['skinful], s. **I.** (Pleine) outre (de vin, etc.). **2.** P: **He's got a good skinful,** il a son plein (de boisson). **skinny** ['skini], a. **I.** Décharné; maigre. F: (Of child) Maigrichon, -onne; maigriot, -ote. **2.** Membraneux. **3.** Avare, ladre.

skip¹ [skip], s. **I.** (Petit) saut; gambade f. **2.** W.Tel: Zone f de silence.

skip², v. (skipped [skipt]) **I.** v.i. (a) Sauter, sautil er, gambader. **To skip for joy,** sauter de oie. (b) Sauter à la corde. (c) **To skip from one subject to another,** bondir d'un sujet à un autre; voleter de sujet en sujet. (d) U.S: F: **To skip (off),** filer; décamper. **2.** v.tr. & i. **To skip (over) a passage in a book,** sauter, passer, un passage d'un livre. Sch: **To skip a form,** sauter une classe. 'skipping-rope, s. Corde f à sauter.

skipjack ['skipdʒak], s. Ent: Élatère m, taupin m.

skipper¹ ['skipər], s. Sauteur, -euse.

skipper², s. **I.** Nau: Patron m (de bateau). **2.** Sp: F: Chef m d'équipe.

skirl [skə:rl], s. Scot: Son aigu (de la cornemuse). **To set up a skirl,** se mettre à jouer de la cornemuse.

skirmish¹ ['skə:rmiʃ], s. Mil: Escarmouche f, échauffourée f.

skirmish², v.i. (a) Escarmoucher. (b) Combattre en tirailleurs; tirailler (with, contre).

skirmisher ['skə:rmiʃər], s. Mil: Tirailleur m.

skirt¹ [skə:rt], s. **I.** Cost: (a) Jupe f (de femme). **Divided skirt,** jupe-culotte f. F: **To be always hanging on to s.o.'s skirts,** être toujours pendu à la ceinture de qn. (b) Pans mpl, basque f (de pardessus, etc.). (c) U.S: P: Femme f. **2.** pl. **Skirts,** bord m (d'un village, etc.); lisière f (d'un bois).

skirt², v.tr. & i. Contourner (un village, une colline); (of pers.) longer, serrer (le mur, etc.).

The path skirts (along, round) the wood, le sentier côtoie, contourne, le bois. **skirting,** s. (a) Bord m, bordure f. (b) Const: **Skirting (-board),** plinthe f.

skit¹ [skit], s. Lit: Th: Pièce f satirique; charge f; satire f (on, de).

skit², v.tr. (skitted) Parodier (un acteur); travestir (un ouvrage).

skittish ['skitiʃ], a. **I.** (a) (Cheval) ombrageux, peureux. (b) (Femme) capricieuse. **2.** (Femme) évaporée, folâtre, coquette. **-ly,** adv. D'un air ou d'un ton espiègle; en faisant a coquette.

skittle [skitl], s. **I.** Skittle(-pin), quille f. **2.** pl. (Game of) skittles, jeu m de quilles. **Skittle-alley,** (terrain m de) jeu de quilles.

skive [ska:iv], v.tr. Doler, drayer; fendre.

skiver ['ska:ivər], s. **I.** Tls: Doloir m. **2.** Bookb: Parchemin m mince; mouton scié.

skivvy ['skivi], s.f. P: Boniche; petite bonne a tout faire.

skrimshank ['skrimʃaŋk], v.i., **skrimshanker** ['skrimʃaŋkər], s. = SCRIMSHANK, SCRIMSHANKER.

skua ['skjua], s. Orn: Stercoraire m; mouette pillarde.

skulk¹ [skʌlk], s. Fainéant m. Mil: Tireur m au flanc; embusqué m.

skulk², v.i. **I.** Se cacher; se tenir caché. **2.** Rôder furtivement. **3.** P: Se défiler; fainéanter; se dérober (au devoir). Mil: Tirer au flanc.

skull [skʌl], s. Crâne m. **Skull and cross-bones,** tête f de mort et tibias (du pavillon des pirates). 'skull-cap, s. Calotte f (de prêtre, etc.).

-skulled [skʌld], a. **Thiok-skulled,** à l'esprit épais, obtus; à la tête dure.

skunk [skʌŋk], s. **I.** Z: Mouffette f. **2.** (Fur) Skunks m, skungs m. **3.** F: (Pers.) Mufle m, rosse f.

sky¹ [skai], s. **I.** Ciel m, pl. cieux, ciels. **Under the open sky,** au grand air; (dormir) à la belle étoile. F: **To laud, praise,** s.o. **to the skies,** élever, porter, qn aux nues. Th: **Sky pieces,** frises f. S.a. SHADE¹ 4. **2.** Ciel, pl. ciels; climat m. 'sky-blue, a. & s. Bleu m céleste; bleu (de) ciel. **2.** a. Azuré. **Sky-blue dresses,** robes f bleu (de) ciel. 'sky-'high, adv. (Faire sauter qn, qch.) jusqu'aux cieux, aux nues. 'sky-line, s. (Ligne f d')horizon m; profil m de l'horizon. 'sky-'pilot, s. F: Prêtre m, pasteur m. Nau: Aumônier m. Pyr: Fusée volante. 'sky-rocket, s. Pyr: Fusée volante. 'sky-scraper, s. **I.** Nau: Aile f de pigeon; (aile de) papillon m. **2.** U.S: F: Gratte-ciel m inv. 'sky-sign, s. Enseigne lumineuse. 'sky-writing, s. Av: Publicité aérienne.

sky², v.tr. (skied) skying) (a) Cr: Ten: etc: Lancer (la balle) en chandelle. (b) Art: F: Jucher (un tableau); exposer (un tableau) au plafond.

skylark¹ ['skaila:rk], s. Orn: Alouette f (des champs).

skylark², v.i. F: Rigoler; faire des farces.

skylarking, s. F: Rigolade f.

skylight ['skailait], s. Jour m d'en haut. (a) Châssis vitré; (hinged) abattant m; châssis à tabatière; (in cellar) soupirail, -aux m. (b) Nau: Claire-voie f.

skyward(s) ['skaiwərd(z)], adv. Vers le ciel.

slab [slab], s. **I.** (a) Plaque f, tranche f (de marbre); dalle f (de pierre). Metall: Brame f, lopin m (de fer). (b) **Slab of gingerbread,** pavé m de pain d'épice. S. of cake, grosse tranche de gâteau. **Slab of chocolate,** tablette f de chocolat. **2.** Marbre m (pour broyer les couleurs).

slack¹ [slak], *s.* (i) Menus *mpl* (de houille); charbonnaille *f*; (ii) poussier *m*.

slack², *s.* **I.** (*a*) Mou *m*, ballant *m*, étale *m* (d'un câble). To take up the slack in a cable, mettre un câble au raide. (*b*) *Mec.E:* Jeu *m*. To take up the slack, rattraper le jeu. **2.** *pl.* Slacks, pantalon *m* (de marin).

slack³, *a.* **I.** (*a*) (Cordage) mou, lâche, flasque; (pneumatique) dégonflé, détendu; (écrou) desserré. (*Of rope*) To hang slack, avoir du mou. (*b*) (Main, prise) faible, sans force. **2.** (*Of pers.*) Négligent; mou, *f.* molle; afflachi. To be slack at one's work, être mou au travail. To be slack in, about, doing sth., être lent, paresseux, à faire qch. **3.** (*a*) Peu vif; faible. Slack oven, four modéré. Slack business, affaires languissantes. Slack time, accalmie *f.* The slack season, la morte-saison. *Nau:* Slack water, mer étale; étale *m* de la marée. *Ind: etc:* Slack hours, heures creuses. (*b*) To spend a slack morning, passer une matinée désœuvrée. **-ly,** *adv.* **I.** (Agir) négligemment, nonchalamment; sans énergie. **2.** (Lier qch.) mollement, lâchement. **'slack-rope,** *s.* Corde *f* lâche; voltige *f.* Slack-rope gymnastics, voltige.

slack⁴. I. *v.tr.* (*a*) Détendre, relâcher (un cordage); desserrer (un écrou). (*b*) To slack lime, éteindre, amortir, la chaux. Air-slacked lime, chaux fusée. **2.** *v.i.* (*a*) (*Of cable, sail*) Prendre du lâche, du mou. (*b*) (*Of lime*) S'éteindre, s'amortir. (*c*) *F:* (*Of pers.*) Se relâcher; fainéanter. To slack (about), fainéanter. **slack off. I.** *v.tr.* Relâcher (la pression, etc.). **2.** *v.i.* Se relâcher; diminuer d'efforts; mollir. **slacking,** *s.* **I.** Relâchement *m.* **2.** Extinction *f* (de la chaux). **3.** *F:* Manque *m* d'application au travail; paresse *f.*

slacken [ˈslak(ə)n]. **I.** *v.tr.* (*a*) Ralentir (le pas, son ardeur). To slacken speed, diminuer de vitesse; ralentir. *Nau:* To slacken a ship's way, casser l'erre d'un navire. (*b*) Détendre, relâcher (un cordage); détendre (les muscles); desserrer (un écrou). To slacken the reins, lâcher la bride, les rênes. **2.** *v.i.* (*a*) (*Of pers.*) To slacken (off, up), se relâcher; devenir négligent. (*b*) (*Of rope*) Prendre du mou. (*c*) (*Of speed*) Ralentir; (*of energy, etc.*) diminuer. (*d*) (*Of the tide*) Mollir. **slackening,** *s.* Ralentissement *m*; diminution *f* (de zèle); relâchement *m* (d'un cordage); desserrage *m* (d'un écrou); détente *f* (des muscles, etc.).

slacker [ˈslakər], *s. F:* Paresseux, -euse; *F:* flémard, -arde.

slackness [ˈslaknəs], *s.* **I.** (*a*) Manque *m* d'énergie; négligence *f*, mollesse *f*; inexactitude *f* (à remplir ses devoirs); fainéantise *f.* (*b*) Désœuvrement *m.* (*c*) Relâchement *m* (de la discipline). **2.** Détente *f* (des muscles, etc.); mou *m* (d'un cordage). **3.** *Com:* Stagnation *f*, marasme *m* (des affaires).

slag [slag], *s. Metall:* Scorie(s) *f(pl)*, crasse(s) *f(pl)*, laitier *m*, mâchefer *m* (de haut fourneau). Slag-heap, crassier *m.* Slag wool, coton minéral, ouate minérale.

slain [slein]. *See* SLAY.

slake [sleik]. **I.** *v.tr.* (*a*) To slake one's thirst, étancher sa soif; se désaltérer. (*b*) = SLACK⁴ I (*b*). **2.** *v.i.* = SLACK⁴ 2 (*b*). **slaking,** *s.* **I.** Étanchement *m*, assouvissement *m* (de la soif). **2.** = SLACKING 2.

slam¹ [slam], *s.* Claquement *m* (d'une porte, etc.).

slam², *v.* (slammed) **I.** *v.tr.* To slam a door (to), claquer, faire claquer, une porte. **2.** *v.i.* Se fermer avec bruit; claquer.

slam³, *s. Cards:* (*At bridge*) Chelem *m*, schlem *m.* To make a slam, faire (le) chelem.

slander¹ [ˈslɑːndər], *s.* Calomnie *f.* Slander and libel, diffamation *f. S.a.* MONGER 2.

slander², *v.tr.* Calomnier. *Jur:* Diffamer.

slanderer [ˈslɑːndərər], *s.* Calomniateur, -trice. *Jur:* Diffamateur, -trice.

slanderous [ˈslɑːndərəs], *a.* (Propos) calomnieux. *Jur:* Diffamatoire. **-ly,** *adv.* Calomnieusement.

slang¹ [slaŋ], *s.* Argot *m.*

slang², *v.tr. F:* (*a*) Dire des sottises à (qn); injurier (qn). (*b*) Réprimander vivement (qn).

slanging, *s. F:* (*a*) Pluie *f* d'injures. (*b*) Verte réprimande.

slangy [ˈslaŋi], *a.* **I.** (*Of pers.*) Qui aime à s'exprimer en argot. **2.** (Style, langage) argotique; (terme) d'argot. **-ily,** *adv.* (S'exprimer, etc.) en termes d'argot.

slant¹ [slɑːnt], *s.* **I.** Pente *f*, inclinaison *f.* **2.** Biais *m*, biseau *m.* On the slant, en écharpe. Stuff cut on the slant, étoffe coupée en biais.

slant², *a.* Oblique; d'écharpe; en écharpe.

slant³. I. *v.i.* (*a*) Être en pente; (s')incliner. (*b*) Être oblique. **2.** *v.tr.* Incliner (qch.); mettre (qch.) en pente; déverser (un mur). **slanting,** *a.* (*a*) (Toit) en pente, incliné. (*b*) (Direction) oblique. Slanting rain, pluie qui tombe en oblique. Slanting hand(writing), écriture couchée, inclinée.

slantways [ˈslɑːntweiz], **slantwise** [ˈslɑːntwaiz], *adv.* Obliquement; de biais; en écharpe.

slap¹ [slap]. **I.** *s.* **I.** Claque *f*, tape *f.* Slap in the face, (i) soufflet *m*, gifle *f*; (ii) *F:* affront *m.* **2.** *I.C.E:* Piston slap, claquement *m* du piston. **II. slap,** *adv.* To run slap into sth., se heurter en plein contre qch. **'slap-bang,** *adv.* Brusquement; de but en blanc. **'slap-dash,** *a. & adv.* Sans soins. To do sth. slap-dash, faire qch. à la six-quatre-deux. **'slap-stick,** *s. U.S:* Batte *f* (d'Arlequin). **'slap-up,** *a. F:* Fameux, soigné, chic. Slap-up turn-out, équipage très chic.

slap², *v.* (slapped [slapt]) **I.** *v.tr.* Frapper (qn) avec la main (ouverte); donner une fessée à (un enfant, etc.). To slap s.o.'s face, gifler, souffleter, qn. To slap s.o. on the back, donner à qn une tape sur l'épaule. **2.** *v.i. I.C.E:* (*Of piston*) Claquer. **slapping,** *s.* **I.** (*a*) Claques *fpl*; jeu *m* de mains. (*b*) Fouettée *f,* fessée *f.* **2.** *I.C.E:* Claquement *m* (du piston).

slapjack [ˈslapdʒak], *s. Cu: U.S:* Crêpe *f.*

slash¹ [slaʃ], *s.* **I.** Estafilade *f*, entaille *f*; (*on the face*) balafre *f.* **2.** *Cost:* Crevé *m*, taillade *f.*

slash², *v.tr.* **I.** (*a*) Taillader (la chair); balafrer, écharper (le visage). (*b*) Cingler (un cheval, etc.) (d'un coup de fouet); fouailler (un cheval). (*c*) *Abs.* Frapper à droite et à gauche; ferrailler, sabrer. To cut and slash, frapper d'estoc et de taille. (*d*) *F:* (*Criticize*) Éreinter, esquinter (un ouvrage littéraire). (*e*) *F:* To slash a speech, faire des amputations dans un discours. **2.** *Cost:* Faire des crevés en, tailladés, dans (un vêtement). **3.** Faire claquer (un fouet). **slashed,** *a.* **I.** (Visage) balafré. **2.** *Cost:* (Pourpoint) à crevés, à tailladés. **slashing¹,** *a.* (*Of criticism, etc.*) Mordant, cinglant. (*b*) Slashing rain, pluie cinglante. **slashing²,** *s.* **I.** Tailladés *fpl*; coups *mpl* de sabre, de fouet. **2.** *Cost:* Crevé *m.* **3.** Critique incisive, cinglante.

slat [slat], *s.* Lame *f*, lamelle *l* (de jalousie, etc.); traverse *f* (de lit).

slate¹ [sleit], *s.* **I.** (*a*) *Geol:* Ardoise *j*; schiste ardoisier. (*b*) *Const:* (Feuille *f* d')ardoise *f.* To have a slate loose, être un peu toqué; avoir la tête fêlée. **2.** Ardoise (pour écrire). *F :* To clean the slate, passer l'éponge sur le passé. To start with a clean slate, commencer une nouvelle vie. **'slate-blue,** *a.* Bleu ardoise *inv.* **'slate-'clay,** *s. Geol :* Schiste argileux ; argile schisteuse. **'slate-coloured, -grey,** *a.* Ardoisé ; gris ardoise *inv.* **'slate-pencil,** *s.* Crayon *m* d'ardoise. **'slate-quarry,** *s.* Ardoisière *f.*

ate², *v.tr.* Ardoiser (un toit). Slated roof, toit en ardoise.

ate³, *v.tr. F :* **I.** Tancer, réprimander vertement (qn) ; laver la tête à (qn). **2.** Critiquer (qn) ; éreinter (un livre). **slating,** *s.* **I.** Verte réprimande ; *F :* savon *m.* **2.** Dure critique ; éreintement *m.*

ater ['sleitər], *s.* **I.** (*Pers.*) Couvreur *m* (en ardoises). **2.** *Crust :* Cloporte *m.*

attern ['slatərn], *s.* Femme mal soignée ; traîne-savates *f inv* ; souillon *f.*

atternly ['slatərnli], *a.* (*Of woman*) Mal soignée, mal peignée ; qui manque d'ordre.

aty ['sleiti], *a.* **I.** *Geol :* Ardoiseux, schisteux. **2.** (*Of colour*) Ardoisé.

aughter¹ ['slɔːtər], *s.* **I.** (*a*) Abattage *m* (de bêtes de boucherie). (*b*) Abattis *m* (de gibier). **2.** Tuerie *f,* carnage *m,* massacre *m.* **3.** *Com :* Vente *f* à sacrifice. **'slaughter-house,** *s.* Abattoir *m.*

aughter², *v.tr.* **I.** Abattre (des bêtes de boucherie). **2.** (*a*) Tuer, massacrer (des gens). (*b*) *Com :* Sacrifier (des marchandises). **slaughtering,** *s.* **I.** Abattage *m.* **2.** (*a*) Tuerie *f,* massacre *m.* (*b*) Vente *f* à sacrifice.

aughterer ['slɔːtərər], *s.* **I.** Tueur *m,* massacreur *m,* égorgeur *m.* **2.** = SLAUGHTERMAN.

aughterman, *pl.* **-men** ['slɔːtərmən, -men], *s.m.* Abatteur, assommeur (de bœufs, etc.).

lav [slɑːv]. **I.** *a.* & *s. Ethn :* Slave (*mf*). **2.** *s. Ling :* Le slave.

ave¹ [sleiv], *s.* Esclave *mf. F :* To be the slave of, a slave to, a passion, être l'esclave d'une passion. To be a slave to duty, ne connaître que son devoir. White-slave traffic, traite des blanches. **'slave-dealer,** *s.* Marchand *m* d'esclaves. **'slave-driver,** *s. F :* (i) Maître ou maîtresse qui traite durement ses domestiques ; (ii) patron ou patronne sans merci. **'slave-trade, -traffic,** *s.* Traite *f* des noirs, des nègres. **'slave-trader,** *s.* = SLAVE-DEALER.

ave², *v.i.* Travailler comme un nègre ; peiner, bûcher. To slave away at (sth.), s'échiner, s'éreinter à (un travail).

aver¹ ['slavər], *s.* **I.** Bave *f,* salive *f.* **2.** *F :* Flatterie grossière ; flagornerie *f.*

aver², *v.i.* Baver (*over,* sur). **slavering,** *a.* Baveur.

aver³ ['sleivər], *s.* **I.** *Nau :* (Bâtiment) négrier *m.* **2.** = SLAVE-DEALER.

averer ['slavərər], *s.* **I.** Baveur, -euse. **2.** *F :* Flagorneur, -euse.

avery ['sleivəri], *s.* **I.** Esclavage *m.* **2.** *F :* Asservissement *m* (à une passion). **3.** *F :* Travail tuant.

avey ['sleivi], *s. F :* Boniche *f* ; petite bonne *f* à tout faire.

avish ['sleiviʃ], *a.* (Soumission) d'esclave ; (imitation) servile. **-ly,** *adv.* (Obéir) en esclave ; imiter servilement.

lavonian [slə'vounjən]. **I.** *a.* & *s.* Slavon, -onne. **2.** *s. Ling :* Le slavon.

lavonic [slə'vɔnik], *a.* & *s. Ling :* Slave (*m*).

ay [slei], *v.tr.* (slew [sluː] ; slain [slein]) *Lit :*

Tuer ; mettre à mort. **slaying,** *s.* Tuerie *f* ; massacre *m.*

slayer ['sleiər], *s.* Tueur *m* ; meurtrier *m* (*of,* de).

sled¹, ² [sled], *s.* & *v. U.S :* = SLEDGE¹, ².

sledge¹ [sledʒ], *s.* Traîneau *m.*

sledge². **I.** *v.i.* Aller en traîneau. **2.** *v.tr.* Transporter (qch.) en traîneau.

sledge³ (-hammer) ['sledʒ(hamər)], *s.* Marteau *m* de forgeron ; marteau à deux mains ; marteau à frapper devant. *F :* Sledge-hammer argument, argument coup de massue.

sleek¹ [sliːk], *a.* **I.** Lisse ; luisant (de santé). Sleek hair, cheveux lisses. **2.** *F :* (*Of manner*) Mielleux ; onctueux.

sleek², *v.tr.* Lisser (les cheveux) ; polir.

sleekness ['sliːknəs], *s.* **I.** Luisant *m* (d'une peau, etc.). **2.** Onctuosité *f* (de ton).

sleep¹ [sliːp], *s.* **I.** Sommeil *m.* Short sleep, somme *m.* Sound sleep, sommeil profond. Winter sleep, sommeil hibernal (de certains animaux). To go, drop off, to sleep, s'endormir, s'assoupir. *He has gone to s.,* il dort. To send s.o. to sleep, endormir, assoupir, qn. To put a child to sleep, endormir un enfant. To put s.o.'s suspicions to sleep, endormir les soupçons de qn. I lose sleep over it, j'en perds le sommeil. To come out of one's sleep, s'éveiller. To rouse s.o. from his sleep, réveiller qn. To have a good sleep, faire un bon somme. I didn't have a wink of sleep all night, je n'ai pas fermé l'œil de (toute) la nuit ; j'ai passé une nuit blanche. To walk in one's sleep, être noctambule, somnambule. **2.** My foot has gone to sleep, 'ai le pied engourdi. **'sleep-walker,** *s.* Somnambule *mf,* noctambule *mf.* **'sleep-walking,** *s.* Somnambulisme *m,* noctambulisme *m.*

sleep², *v.i.* & *tr.* (slept [slept] ; slept) **I.** Dormir. (*a*) To sleep like a log, like a top, dormir à poings fermés ; dormir comme un sabot. To sleep soundly, dormir profondément ; (*without fear*) dormir sur les deux oreilles. I have not slept a wink all night, je n'ai pas fermé l'œil de (toute) la nuit. To sleep over, upon, a question ; to sleep over it, prendre conseil de son oreiller. (*b*) To sleep the sleep of the just, dormir du somme l du juste. **2.** Coucher. To sleep at an hotel, coucher à un hôtel. *To s. away from home,* découcher. **3.** To sleep in the churchyard, reposer dans le cimetière. **4.** (*Of top*) Dormir. **sleep away,** *v.tr.* Passer (le temps) à dormir. **sleep in,** *v.i.* (*a*) Être pensionnaire (dans une maison de commerce, etc. ; être logé dans la maison. (*b*) Ne pas se réveiller à l'heure. **sleep off,** *v.tr.* Faire passer (une migraine, etc.) en dormant. To sleep off the effects of wine, cuver son vin. **sleep out,** *v.i.* **I.** Découcher. **2.** (*Of servant*) Ne pas coucher à la maison. **sleeping¹,** *a.* **I.** Dormant, endormi. *Prov :* Let sleeping dogs lie, ne réveillez pas le chat qui dort. **2.** (*Of limb*) Engourdi. **3.** *Com :* Sleeping partner, (associé *m*) commanditaire *m* ; bailleur *m* de fonds. **sleeping²,** *s.* Sommeil *m.* Sleeping accommodation, logement *m.* **'sleeping apartments,** *s.pl.* Chambres *f* à coucher. *Com : etc :* Dortoirs *m.* **'sleeping-bag,** *s.* Sac *m* de couchage. **'sleeping-car,** *s. Rail :* Wagon-lit *m, pl.* wagons-lits ; *F :* sleeping *m.* **'sleeping draught,** *s.* Potion assoupissante, soporifique ; narcotique *m.* **'sleeping-quarters,** *s.pl. Mil :* Dortoir *m.* **'sleeping sickness,** *s.* Narcotomie *f* des nègres ; maladie *f* du sommeil. **'sleeping-suit,** *s.* Pyjama *m.*

sleeper ['sliːpər], *s.* **I.** Dormeur, -euse. To be a light, a heavy, sleeper, avoir le sommeil léger,

profond. **2.** (a) Poutre horizontale; sole f;
lambourde f (de parquet, etc.). (b) Rail: (Cross-)
sleeper, traverse f. **3.** Rail: F: = SLEEPING-CAR.
sleepiness ['sli:pinəs], s. **1.** Somnolence f.
2. Indolence f, léthargie f.
sleepless ['sli:pləs], a. **1.** Sans sommeil. Sleepless night, nuit blanche. **2.** (Of mind) Sans cesse
en éveil.
sleeplessness ['sli:pləsnəs], s. Insomnie f.
sleepy ['sli:pi], a. **1.** (a) Somnolent. To be, feel,
sleepy, avoir envie de dormir; avoir sommeil.
(b) Sleepy look, air endormi. F: Sleepy little
town, petite ville endormie. **2.** (a) Apathique,
engourdi. (b) Med: Sleepy sickness, encéphalite f
léthargique. **3.** (Of fruit) Blet, cotonneux.
-ily, adv. (Répondre, etc.) d'un air endormi,
somnolent. '**sleepy-head,** s. F: Endormi, -ie.
sleet¹ [sli:t], s. Neige à moitié fondue (qui tombe).
sleet², v.impers. It sleets, il tombe de la neige
fondue.
sleeve [sli:v], s. **1.** Manche f. False sleeves,
poignets m de manches. Dressm: Short sleeve,
mancheron m. S.a. SHIRT-SLEEVE. To put sth.
up one's sleeve, mettre qch. dans sa manche.
F: To have a plan up one's sleeve, avoir un
expédient en réserve. To have more than one
trick up one's sleeve, avoir plus d'un tour dans
son (bis)sac. **2.** (a) Mec.E: Manchon m,
douille f; bague f d'assemblage; virole f. Aut:
Axle sleeve, boîte f d'essieu. (b) (For punctured
tyre) Guêtre f. '**sleeve-board,** s. **1.** Laund:
Pied m à manches, à repasser; F: jeannette f.
2. Tail: Passe-carreau m. '**sleeve-nut,** s.
Manchon taraudé. '**sleeve-valve,** s. I.C.E:
Soupape f à fourreau; fourreau m de distribution.
sleeved [sli:vd], a. (Vêtement) à manches.
sleigh¹ [slei], s. Traîneau m. S.a. BOB-SLEIGH.
'**sleigh-bell,** s. Grelot m ou clochette f.
sleigh². **1.** v.i. Aller en traîneau. **2.** v.tr.
Transporter en traîneau.
sleight [slait], s. Sleight of hand,'prestidigitation f;
tours mpl de passe-passe.
slender ['slendər], a. **1.** Mince, ténu; (of figure)
svelte, élancé; (of finger) fuselé. To grow, become,
more s., s'amincir. **2.** (Of intelligence, etc.)
Maigre; (of hope, etc.) faible; (of income, etc.)
exigu; mince. Slender voice, filet m de voix.
Our slender means, nos ressources exiguës. **-ly,**
adv. **1.** Slenderly made, slenderly built, person,
personne fluette. **2.** Maigrement, faiblement.
slenderness ['slendərnəs], s. **1.** Minceur f,
ténuité f; sveltesse f. **2.** Exiguïté f (d'une
fortune, etc.); faiblesse f (des ressources).
slept [slept]. See SLEEP².
sleuth(-hound) ['slu:θ(haund)], s. **1.** Limier m.
2. U.S: F: The sleuths, la police de sûreté;
les limiers de la police.
slew¹ [slu:]. **1.** v.tr. To slew (over) a mast, dévirer,
trévirer un mât. **2.** v.i. Pivoter, virer. **slew
round.** **1.** v.tr. Faire pivoter (qch.). **2.** v.i.
(a) (Of crane, etc.) Pivoter, tourner. (b) Aut:
Faire (un) tête-à-queue.
slew². See SLAY.
slice¹ [slais], s. **1.** Tranche f; darne f (de gros
poisson). Round s. (of sausage, etc.), rond m,
rondelle f. Slice of bread and butter, tartine f
de beurre. F: Slice of (good) luck, coup m de
veine. **2.** (a) Cu: Fish-slice, truelle f (à poisson).
(b) = SLICE-BAR. **3.** Coup m en biseau ou en
sifflet. Golf: Coup qui fait dévier la balle à
droite. '**slice-bar,** s. Tls: Lance f à feu,
ringard m de chauffeur.
slice², v.tr. **1.** Découper (qch.) en tranches.
2. (a) Ten: Couper (la balle). (b) Abs. (i) Golf:

Faire dévier la balle à droite. (ii) Row: Attaqu
en sifflet. **slice off,** v.tr. Trancher, coupe
détacher (un morceau).
slicer ['slaisər], s. Machine f à trancher :e pai
etc. S.a. VEGETABLE.
slick [slik]. **1.** a. F: (a) Habile, adroit. (b) Bie
rangé; en bon ordre. (c) U.S: You'd bett
look slick about it, vous ferez bien de vou
dépêcher. **2.** adv. (a) Habilement, adroitemen
(b) To cut slick through sth., couper qch. ne
Slick in the middle, en plein milieu. (c) Preste
ment; vite.
slickenside(s) ['slikənsaid(z)], s.(pl.) Geo
Miroir m de faille.
slickness ['sliknəs], s. F: Habileté f, dextérité
adresse f.
slid [slid]. See SLIDE².
slide¹ [slaid], s. **1.** (a) Glissade f, glissement ι
(b) (Land-)slide, éboulement m. (c) Mus: Coulé m
2. (Slipway, runner) Glissière f, coulisse
3. (a) (On snow or ice) Glissoire f, glissadι
(b) Plan m de glissement; piste f en pentι
4. (a) Glissoire; coulant m (d'une bourse, etc.)
curseur m (d'un compas, etc.). Row: Glissièrι
Writing slide (of desk), tirette f. Slide of a slidι
rule, réglette f, tiroir m, d'une règle à calcuι
Opt: Focusing slide, draw-slide, tube m à tiragι
(b) Mec.E: = SLIDE-REST. (c) Mus: Coulisse (dι
trombone, etc.). **5.** (a) Microscopy: Object-slidι
(plaque f, lame f) porte-objet m inv; lamelle
(b) (Lantern-)slide, diapositive f de projectioι
vue f (de projection). Lecture with (lantern-)slidι
conférence avec projections. **6.** Phot: Daι
slide, châssis m porte-plaques. **7.** Toil: (Hair
slide, barrette f. '**slide-bar,** s. Coulisseau ι
1. Mch: Glissière f de crosse. **2.** Mec.Ε
Coulisse f, jumelle f (de tour). '**slide-block,**
Mch: Coulisseau m, glissoir m. '**slide-bridgı**
s. El: Pont m de Wheatstone. '**slide-carrieι**
s. Châssis m passe-vues (de lanterne à projeι
tions). '**slide-contact,** s. El: Curseur ι
frotteur m. '**slide-lathe,** s. Tour m à charioteι
'**slide-rest,** s. Mec.E: Support m à charioι
(of lathe) chariot m porte-outil(s). '**slide-rulι**
s. Règle f à calcul (logarithmique). '**slidι
valve,** s. Mch: Tiroir m (de distribution).
slide², v. (slid [slid]; slid) **I.** v.i. (a) Glisseι
coulisser. (b) (Of pers.) To slide (on ice), faiι
des glissades. (c) He slid on the floor and fell,
glissa sur le parquet et tomba. To slide inι
sin, glisser dans le péché. Abs. To slide, :ombε
dans l'erreur, dans le vice. (e) F: To let a thiι
slide, se désintéresser de qch. To let things slidι
laisser tout aller à vau-l'eau. **2.** v.tr. (Fairε
glisser. To slide sth. into s.o.'s hand, glisseι
qch. dans la main à qn. **slide away, by,** v.
(Of time) S'écouler, couler. **slide down,** v.
I. Descendre en glissant. **2.** To slide down thε
banisters, glisser le long de la rampe. To s. doẃ
the wall, se laisser couler ∴n bas du mur. **slidˊ
off,** v.i. F: Décamper; filer. **sliding¹,**
Glissant; coulissant. **Sliding door,** portε
glissières. **Sliding panel,** panneau mobilε
Sliding sash, châssis m à coulisse. Row: Slidiŋ
seat, banc à glissières à coulisses. Opt: Slidiŋ
tube, tube à tirage. El: Sliding contact, curseur ˊ
frotteur m. Wages on a sliding scale, salairε
calculés suivant une échelle mobile. **sliding²,**
(a) To go sliding, aller faire des glissadeι
(b) Coulissement m, glissement m.
slider ['slaidər], s. **1.** (Pers.) Glisseur, -eusι
2. Curseur m (d'une bobine électrique, etc.).
slight¹ [slait], a. **1.** Mince, ténu; (of figure) frêlε
menu, svelte. **2.** (Of pain, etc.) Léger, petit

(*of intelligence, etc.*) maigre, faible; (*of occasion, etc.*) de peu d'importance. **To make a slight gesture,** faire un léger geste; esquisser un geste. *There is a s. improvement,* il y a un léger mieux. **To some slight extent,** quelque peu. **Not the slightest danger,** pas le moindre danger. *To take offence at the slightest thing,* se piquer d'un rien. **Not in the slightest (degree),** pas le moins du monde. **-ly,** *adv.* **1.** Slightly built, (i) au corps frêle; (ii) à la taille mince, svelte. **2.** Légèrement, faiblement. **Slightly better,** un petit peu mieux. **I know him slightly,** je le connais un peu.

slight², *s.* Manque *m* de considération, d'égards; affront *m.* **To put, pass, a slight on s.o.,** infliger un affront à qn; manquer d'égards envers qn.

slight³, *v.tr.* Traiter (qn) sans considération; manquer d'égards envers (qn); négliger (qn). **slighting,** *a.* (Air) de mépris. **-ly,** *adv* Avec peu d'égards; dédaigneusement.

slightness ['slaitnəs], *s.* **1.** Minceur *f*, ténuité *f*; sveltesse *f* (de la taille). **2.** Légèreté *f*, petitesse *f* (d'une faute, etc.); peu *m* d'importance, insignifiance *f* (des dégâts, etc.).

slim¹ [slim], *a.* (slimmer) **1.** Svelte, élancé, délié, mince. **Slim-waisted,** à la taille svelte. **2.** *F:* Rusé; malin, -igne; astucieux.

slim², *v.* (slimmed) **1.** *v.tr.* Amincir. **Slimming remedy,** médicament *m* obésifuge. **2.** *v.i.* Suivre un régime amincissant.

slime [slaim], *s.* **1.** Limon *m*, vase *f.* *Gold-min:* The slimes, les schlamms *m.* **2.** Humeur visqueuse (qui couvre les poissons, etc.); bave *f* (de limace, etc.). **3.** Bitume *m* (liquide).

sliminess ['slaiminəs], *s.* **1.** (*a*) État vaseux. (*b*) Viscosité *f.* **2.** *F:* Servilité *f.*

slimness ['slimnəs], *s.* **1.** Taille *f* mince; sveltesse *f*, gracilité *f.* **2.** *F:* Astuce *f.*

slimy ['slaimi], *a.* **1.** (*a*) Limoneux, vaseux. (*b*) Visqueux, gluant. **2.** Couvert de vase, de limon. **3.** *F:* Servile, obséquieux. **Slimy-tongued,** doucereux.

sling¹ [sliŋ], *s.* **1.** Fronde *f.* **2.** (*a*) *Med:* Écharpe *f.* **To carry one's arm in a sling,** porter le bras en écharpe. (*b*) Bandoulière *f* (de harpe); courroie *f* (de bidon). **Sword-sling,** belière *f.* **Slings of a knapsack,** brassière *f* d'un havresac. (*c*) (*For hoisting*) Élingue *f* (pour barriques); cravate *f* (pour mât). *Nau:* **Boat slings,** pattes *f* d'embarcation; saisines *f.* **Yard sling,** suspente *f* de vergue. **'sling-cart,** *s.* *Artil:* Triqueballe *m* or *f.* **'sling-dog,** *s.* Patte *f* d'élingue.

sling², *v.tr.* (slung [slʌŋ]; slung) **1.** Lancer, jeter (avec une fronde, *F:* avec la main). **2.** Suspendre. **To sling a hammock,** suspendre, gréer, un hamac. **To sling (sth.) over one's shoulder,** jeter (son pardessus) sur l'épaule; passer la bandoulière (d'une harpe, etc.) sur son épaule; mettre (une harpe, etc.) en bandoulière. **3.** Élinguer, brayer (un fardeau).

sling³, *s.* Grog *m.*

slinger ['sliŋər], *s.* **1.** Frondeur *m.* **2.** Lanceur *m* (d'une pierre, etc.).

slink [sliŋk], *v.i.* (slunk [slʌŋk]; slunk) **To slink off, away,** partir furtivement, en catimini. **To slink in,** entrer furtivement. **slinking,** *a.* Furtif.

slip¹ [slip], *s.* **1.** (*a*) Glissade *f*, glissement *m*, faux pas. (*b*) **To give s.o. the slip,** se dérober à qn; faire faux bond à qn. (*c*) Faute *f* ou erreur *f* d'inattention; inadvertance *f.* **Slip of the tongue, of the pen,** lapsus *m* linguæ, lapsus calami. *It was a s. of the tongue,* la langue lui a fourché. (*d*) Écart *m* (de conduite); peccadille *f.* (*e*) Glissement, patinage *m.* *Aut:* Clutch slip, patinage

de l'embrayage. **Propeller slip,** (i) *N.Arch:* Av: recul *m* de l'hélice; (ii) *Av:* vent *m* de l'hélice. (*f*) *Geol:* (**Land**)**slip,** éboulement *m*; affaissement *m* de terrain. **2.** Laisse *f*, botte *f* (de chien de chasse) **3.** *Rail:* Slip(-portion), rame *f* remorque. **4.** Taie *f* d'oreiller. **5.** *Cost:* (*a*) **Princess slip,** combinaison *f* jupon. (*b*) *Sp:* Slip *m.* *Th:* Cache-sexe *m inv. pl.* (**Bathing-**)**slips,** caleçon *m* forme slip. (*c*) **Gym-slip,** tunique *f* (de femme athlète). **6.** (*a*) Cale *f* de chargement (pour bacs, etc.). (*b*) *N.Arch:* **Building slip,** cale, chantier *m* (de construction). **Ship on the slips,** navire sur cale(s), en chantier. (*c*) **Launching slip(s)** = SLIP-WAY 2. **7.** *pl. Th:* The slips, les coulisses *f.* *Cf.* SLIP³ 3. **'slip-carriage, -coach,** *s.* *Rail:* Voiture *f* remorque. **'slip-knot,** *s.* Nœud coulant. **'slip-mount,** *s.* *Phot: etc:* Carton *m* passe-partout. **'slip-noose,** *s.* Nœud coulant. **'slip-ring,** *s.* *El.E:* Bague collectrice (de dynamo, etc.); collecteur *m.* **'slip-stitch,** (*a*) *Knitting:* Maille glissée. (*b*) *Needlew:* Point perdu. **'slip-stream,** *s.* *Aut: Av:* Sillage *m*, remous *m* (d'air). **'slip-way,** *s.* **1.** Cale *f* (d'un bac). **2.** *N.Arch:* Cale (de lancement); slipway *m*, slip *m*; chantier *m* de construction.

slip², *v.* (slipped [slipt]) I. *v.i.* **1.** (*a*) Glisser; (*of knot*) couler; *Nau:* (*of rope*) choquer; (*of earth, etc.*) s'ébouler. *Mec.E:* (*Of belt, etc.*) Patiner, glisser. *His foot slipped,* son pied glissa. **To slip from s.o.'s hands, through s.o.'s fingers,** échapper des mains de qn; glisser entre les doigts de qn. (*b*) Se glisser, se couler. **To slip into the room,** se glisser dans la salle; entrer furtivement dans la salle. **To slip into bed,** se couler, se glisser, entre les draps, dans son lit. (*c*) *F:* **Just slip round to the post,** faites un saut jusqu'au bureau de poste. *Aut:* **We're slipping along!** ça gaze! (*d*) (*Of bolt*) **To slip home,** fermer à fond. **2.** (*a*) Faire une faute d'étourderie, une bévue. (*b*) Faire un écart de conduite. **3. To let slip,** lâcher (un lévrier); laisser échapper (une belle occasion, un secret). II. **slip,** *v.tr.* **1.** (*a*) Se détacher de (qch.). (*Of animal*) **To slip its chain,** se détacher. (*b*) *F:* **Your name has slipped my memory,** votre nom m'est sorti de la mémoire. **To slip s.o.'s notice,** échapper à l'attention de qn. **2.** (*a*) *Ven:* Lâcher, découpler (les chiens). **To slip the hounds,** laisser courre. (*b*) *Nau:* **To slip a cable,** larguer, filer, une amarre par le bout. **To slip one's moorings,** filer le corps-mort. (*c*) *Rail:* Décrocher (un wagon en marche). (*d*) *Husb:* (*Of animal*) **To slip its young,** mettre bas avant terme. **3.** Pousser (un verrou), couler, glisser (qch. dans la main de qn). **To slip the bolt home,** pousser le verrou à fond. **4.** *Aut:* **To slip the clutch,** laisser patiner l'embrayage. **slip away,** *v.i.* **1.** (*Of pers.*) Filer à l'anglaise; s'esquiver. **2.** (*Of time*) S'écouler, (se) passer, fuir. **slip by,** *v.i.* = SLIP AWAY 2. **slip down,** *v.i.* **1.** (*Of pers.*) Tomber (du fait d'avoir glissé). **2.** Descendre en glissant; se couler en bas (de l'arbre, etc.). **slip in,** *v.tr.* **To slip in a new film,** introduire un nouveau film dans l'appareil. **'slip-in,** *attrib.a.* (Album, etc.) passe-partout *inv.* **slip off,** *v.tr.* Enlever, ôter (un vêtement). **slip on,** *v.tr.* Enfiler, passer, mettre (une chemise, etc.). **Slip-on blouse,** blouse à enfiler. **slip out,** *v.i.* (*a*) S'échapper. *The secret slipped out,* le secret se fit jour. (*b*) *F:* Sortir (à la dérobée). **slip over,** *v.tr.* **To slip a dress over one's head,** enfiler une robe par-dessus la tête. **slip up,** *v.i.* *U.S:* **1.** Se tromper; faire une bourde. **2.** (*Of plan*) Échouer; ne pas aboutir.

slip³, s. **I.** (a) *Hort:* Bouture *f*, plançon *m*, plant *m*; (*for grafting*) ‹cion *m*. (b) *F:* **Slip of a girl**, jeune fille fluette. **Tall slip of a woman**, jeune femme élancée. **Fine slip of a girl**, beau brin de fille. (c) *Ich: Com:* Petite sole. **2.** (a) Bande étroite (de toile, de terre). **Slip of paper**, bande, fiche *f*, de papier; bout *m* de papier. **Detachable slip**, volant *m* (d'un carnet, etc.). **Tail:** **Vest slips**, transparents *m*, dépassants blancs (de gilet). (b) *F:* Billet *m*, bordereau *m*. (c *Typ:* (**Proof-**)**slip**, placard *m*. **To pull matter in slips**, placarder des épreuves. (d) **Table slip**, napperon *m*. **3.** *pl. Th:* Slips, couloir *m* du balcon. *Cf.* SLIP¹ 7.

slip⁴, *v.tr.* (**slipped**) Bouturer (une plante).

slip⁵, s. *Cer:* Barbotine *f*, engobe *m*. **To coat with slip**, engober.

slippage ['slipedʒ], s. *Mec.E: etc:* Glissement *m*, patinage *m*; décalage *m*. *El.E:* **Frequency slippage**, décalage de fréquence.

slipper ['slipər], s. **I.** Pantoufle *f*. **Bedroom slipper**, pantoufle en feutre; (*backless*) mule *f*. **Turkish slippers**, babouches *f*. **List slippers**, chaussons *m* (de lisière). **To take one's slipper to a child**, fesser un enfant (avec une pantoufle). **2.** (a) *Mec.E:* Patin *m*, savate *f* (de frein). (b) **Piston-rod slipper**, glissière *f* de bielle. **3.** *Med:* Bassin *m* de lit. **'slipper-bath**, s. Baignoire *f* en sabot.

slippered ['slipərd], a. En pantoufles. **Slippered ease**, le confort en pantoufles.

slipperiness ['slipərinəs], s. **I.** Nature glissante (du sol, etc.). **2.** Caractère rusé.

slipperwort ['slipərwɔːrt], s. *Bot:* Calcéolaire *f*.

slippery ['slipəri], a. **I.** Glissant. *It is s. walking*, on glisse en marchant. **2.** (a) Instable, incertain; sur lequel on ne peut compter. **To be on slippery ground**, être sur un terrain glissant. (b) (Sujet) délicat, scabreux. **3.** Fin, rusé, matois. **He's as slippery as an eel**, il est souple comme une anguille; il vous coule entre les doigts. **He's a slippery customer**, on ne sait par où le prendre.

slippy ['slipi], a. *P:* **To be, look, slippy**, se dépêcher.

slipshod ['slipʃɔd], a. **I.** En savates. **2.** (Travail) négligé, fait sans soin; (style, écrivain) négligé. **Slipshod English**, anglais peu correct.

slip-slop ['slipslɔp], s. **I.** (a) Aliments *m* liquides. (b) Lavasse *f*, ripopée *f*. **2.** Conversation *f* d'une sentimentalité fade; sensiblerie *f*.

slit¹ [slit], s. Fente *f*; fissure *f*, rainure *f*; (*between curtains*) entrebâillement *m*; (*made by surgeon*) incision *f*. **The slit of the letter-box**, le guichet de la boîte aux lettres. **To have slits of eyes**, avoir les yeux bridés. **Slit-eyed**, (i) aux yeux bridés; (ii) aux yeux en amande.

slit², *v.* (**slit**; **slit**; **slitting**) **I.** *v.tr.* (a) Fendre. **To slit s.o.'s throat**, couper la gorge à qn; **to slit open a sack**, éventrer un sac. (b) Faire une incision dans (les chairs, etc.). **The blow slit his cheek**, le coup lui a déchiré la joue. (c) Refendre (le cuir, le bois). **2.** *v.i.* Se fendre, se déchirer (en long). **slitting**, s. Fendage *m*. **'slitting-mill**, s. *Metalw:* Fenderie *f*.

slither¹ ['sliðər], s. Glissement *m*, glissade *f*; dégringolade *f*.

slither², **I.** *v.i.* (a) Glisser; manquer de tomber. *To s. into the room*, glisser en entrant dans la chambre. **To slither down a hill on one's heels**, *F:* descendre une pente sur le derrière. (b) (*Of snake, worm*) Ramper. **2.** *v.tr.* Traîner (les pieds).

slitter ['slitər], s. *Ind:* **I.** (*Pers.*) Fendeur *m*. **2.** *Tls:* Fendoir *m*.

sliver¹ ['slivər, 'slaivər] s. **I.** (a) Tranche *f*.

Esp. Fish: Tranche de poisson montée ‹n appât. (b) Éclat *m* (de bois). **2.** *Tex:* Ruban *m* (de lin cardé); mèche *f*.

sliver². **I.** *v.tr.* (a) Couper (qch.) en tranches. (b) *Tex:* Établir les rubans (de lin cardé). **2.** *v.i.* (*Of wood*) Éclater.

slobber¹ ['slɔbər], s. **I.** (a) Bave *f*. (b) *F:* Sentimentalité larmoyante. **2.** Boue *f*; limon *m*; neige à moitié fondue.

slobber². **I.** *v.i.* (a) Baver. (b) *F:* Larmoyer. **To slobber over s.o.**, témoigner une tendresse exagérée envers qn; s'attendrir sur qn. **2.** *v.tr.* (a) Couvrir de bave. (b) Gâcher, bousiller (une besogne).

sloe [slou], s. *Bot:* **I.** Prunelle *f*. **Sloe gin**, (liqueur *f* de) prunelle. **2.** Prunellier *m*; épine noire.

slog¹ [slɔg], s. *F:* **I.** Coup violent. **2.** Corvée *f*; *P:* turbin *m*.

slog², *v.* (**slogged**) *F:* **I.** *v.tr.* Cogner violemment; rouer (qn) de coups. *Abs. Box:* Cogner dur (mais sans science). **2.** *v.i.* (a) *Cr:* **To slog at the ball**, donner de grands coups de batte. (b) *P:* Turbiner. **To slog away at sth.**, travailler avec acharnement à qch. (c) **To slog along**, marcher d'un pas lourd.

slogan ['slougən], s. **I.** *Hist:* Cri *m* de guerre (de clan écossais). **2.** *F:* (a) Cri de guerre, mot *m* d'ordre (d'un parti politique). (b) *Com:* Devise *f*; slogan *m*.

slogger ['slɔgər], s. *F:* **I.** *Box:* Cr: Cogneur *m* (qui frappe au hasard). **2.** Travailleur acharné; bûcheur *m*.

sloop [sluːp], s. **I.** *Nau:* Sloop *m*. **2.** *Navy:* Aviso *m*.

slop¹ [slɔp], s. **I.** Boue *f*, bourbe *f*. **2.** *pl.* **Slops.** (a) Boissons renversées (sur la table, etc.). (b) (*Tasteless drink*) Lavasse *f*, ripopée *f*. (c) Aliments *m* liquides. (*Of invalid*) **To be on slops**, être réduit au bouillon. (d) Eaux ménagères; eaux sales. **3.** *F:* Sensiblerie *f*. **4.** *Cer:* = SLIP⁵. **'slop-basin**, s. Vide-tasses *m inv.* **'slop-pail**, s. (a) Seau *m* de ménage. (b) Seau de toilette; seau hygiénique.

slop², *v.* (**slopped**) **I.** *v.tr.* *To s. beer over the table*, répandre de la bière sur la table. *Coffee slopped in the saucer*, *F:* bain *m* de pieds. **2.** *v.i.* (a) **To slop (over)**, (i) (*of liquids*) déborder; (ii) se répandre en effusions de tendresse; faire de la sensiblerie. (b) **To slop about in the mud**, patauger dans la boue.

slop³, s. **I.** Blouse *f*; sarrau *m*. **2.** *pl.* **Slops.** (a) *A:* Pantalon *m* de marin. (b) Effets *m* (d'habillement), frusques *f* (d'un matelot). (c) Vêtements *m* de confection. **'slop-room**, s. *Nau:* Magasin *m* d'habillement.

slope¹ [sloup], s. **I.** (a) Pente *f*, inclinaison *f*. **Steep s.**, pente rapide. **Slope down**, descente *f*; déclivité *f*. **Slope up**, montée *f*. **Angle of slope**, angle de déclivité. **S. of a wall**, dévers *m* d'un mur. **Street on the slope**, rue en pente. *Mil:* **Rifle at the slope**, l'arme sur l'épaule. *Civ.E:* **Natural slope**, pente naturelle de talus. (b) Dégagement *m* (d'un outil). (c) **Cut on the slope**, coupé en biais. **2.** Pente; talus *m*; (*in railway*) rampe *f*; (*in road*) côte *f*. **Half-way down, up, the slope**, à mi-pente. *Mountain slopes*, versants *m* de montagne.

slope². **I.** *v.i.* (a) Être en pente; incliner, pencher. **To slope down**, descendre. **To slope up**, monter. (*Of writing*) **To slope forward, backward**, pencher à droite, à gauche. (b) Aller en pente. *The garden slopes down to the river*, le jardin dévale vers le fleuve. **2.** *v.tr.* (a) Couper (qch.) en pente. (b) To slope (out) the neck of a dress, échancrer le col d'une robe. (c) *Mil:* To slope arms, mettre l'arme sur l'épaule. To slope swords, reposer le sabre. **sloping,** *a.* (a) En pente ; incliné ; (jardin) en talus. Sloping approach *of a bridge,* rampe *f* d'accès d'un pont. Sloping shoulders, épaules tombantes. (b) En biais.

slope², *v.i.* *F:* 1. To slope about, flâner. 2. To slope (off), *s.* to do a slope, filer, se défiler.

sloppiness ['slɔpinəs], *s.* 1. (a) État détrempé. (b) The *s.* of the tables, les flaques de bière, etc., qui inondaient les tables. 2. (a) (Of pers.) Mollesse *f* ; avachissement *m*. *S.* of mind, manque *m* de netteté dans les idées. (b) Manque de soin ; négligence *f* (de style). (c) Sentimentalité larmoyante.

sloppy ['slɔpi], *a.* 1. (a) (Chemin) détrempé, bourbeux, plein de flaques. *S.* omelet, omelette baveuse. (b) (Plancher) encore mouillé ; (table) qui n'a pas été essuyée. 2. (a) (Of pers.) Mou, *f.* molle ; flasque. (b) (Travail) fait sans soin ; (style) négligé. (c) (Vêtement) mal ajusté. (d) (Roman) larmoyant. *S.* sentimentality, sensiblerie *f.*

slosh [slɔʃ], *v.tr.* *P:* 1. Flanquer un coup à (qn). 2. Flanquer une (bonne) pile à (qn).

slot¹ [slɔt], *s.* 1. Entaille *f*, encoche *f*, rainure *f*, mortaise *f* ; cannelure *f* ; fente *f* (de la tête d'une vis). Cotter slot, logement *m* de clavette. *El.E:* Slots between the commutator bars, fentes des segments du commutateur. To cut slots, mortaiser des rainures. Slot-drilling machine, fraiseuse *f* à rainer. To put a penny in the slot, introduire un penny dans la fente (d'un distributeur). 2. *Th:* Trappillon *m* (dans le plateau). **'slot-machine,** *s.* Distributeur *m* automatique. **'slot-meter,** *s.* Compteur *m* (à gaz) à paiement préalable ; *F:* taxigaz *m.* **'slot-winding,** *s.* *El.E:* Enroulement *m* (d'induit) à rainures.

slot², *v.tr.* (slotted) Tailler une fente, une rainure, dans (qch.) ; entailler, encocher, mortaiser. Slotted screw, vis à filets interrompus. *Av:* Slotted wing, aile à fente. **'slotting-machine,** *s.* Mortaiseuse *f.*

slot³, *s.* *Ven:* Foulées *fpl*, voies *fpl* (d'une bête).

sloth [slouθ], *s.* 1. Paresse *f*, fainéantise *f*, indolence *f.* To become sunk in sloth, s'avachir, s'aveulir. 2. *Z:* (a) Paresseux *m.* (b) Sloth(-bear), ours jongleur.

slothful ['slouθful], *a.* Paresseux, fainéant ; indolent. **-fully,** *adv.* Paresseusement ; avec indolence.

slotter ['slɔtər], *s.* 1. (Pers.) Mortaiseur *m.* 2. = SLOTTING-MACHINE.

slouch¹ [slautʃ], *s.* 1. (a) Lourdaud *m.* (b) Fainéant *m.* *U.S:* *F:* He's no slouch, il n'est pas empoté. 2. Démarche *f* mollasse ; lourdeur *f* d'allure. To walk with a slouch, traîner le pas. *S.* of the shoulders, épaules arrondies. **'slouch-'hat,** *s.* Grand chapeau mou ; sombrero *m.* '

slouch², *s.* 1. *v.i.* Se laisser aller en marchant ; manquer de tenue ; avoir une allure lourde. Don't *s.!* tenez-vous droit ! To slouch about, rôder. To slouch away, s'en aller d'un pas traînant, le dos courbé. 2. *v.tr.* Rabattre le bord de (son chapeau). **slouching,** *a.* (a) (Of pers.) (i) Qui traîne le pas ; (ii) aux épaules arrondies. (b) (Allure) mollasse.

slough¹ [slau], *s.* 1. (a) Bourbier *m*, fondrière *f.* *F:* The sloughs of vice, le bourbier du vice. *S.a.* DESPOND¹. (b) Terrain marécageux.

slough² [slʌf], *s.* 1. (Of reptile, insect) Dépouille *f*, mue *f.* (Of serpent) To cast its slough, quitter sa

peau ; jeter sa dépouille. 2. *Med:* Eschare *f*, croûte *f* (sur une plaie).

slough³ [slʌf]. 1. *v.i.* (a) (Of reptile, etc.) Se dépouiller ; muer. (b) (Of scab) To slough off, away, tomber ; se détacher. (c) (Of wound) Se couvrir d'une eschare. 2. *v.tr.* (Of reptile) To slough its skin, jeter sa dépouille.

sloughy ['slaui], *a.* (a) Marécageux. (b) Coupé de fondrières.

Slovak [slo'vak], *a. & s.* Slovaque (*mf*).

sloven ['slʌv(ə)n], *s.* 1. Mal peigné, -ée ; mal soigné, -ée ; maritorne *f* ; souillon *f.* 2. Gâcheur de besogne.

Slovene [slo'viːn], *a. & s.* Slovène (*mf*).

slovenliness ['slʌvənlinəs], *s.* 1. Négligence *f* (de mise) ; manque *m* de tenue. 2. Manque de soin.

slovenly ['slʌvənli], *a.* 1. (Of pers.) Mal peigné, mal soigné. *S.* gait, allure déhanchée ; (of soldier) allure peu martiale. 2. (a) Négligent ; sans soin. (b) (Travail) négligé, bousillé.

slow¹ [slou]. I. *a.* 1. (a) Lent. At a s. trot, au trot ralenti. *S.* speed, petite vitesse ; ralenti *m.* *Cin:* etc: Slow motion, ralenti. He was a s. speaker, il avait la parole lente. *F:* It is slow work, ça ne va pas vite. Slow and sure! hâtez-vous lentement ! *Cu:* Cook in a slow oven, faites cuire à feu doux. Rail: Slow train, train omnibus. (b) To be slow to start sth., in starting sth., être lent, être peu empressé, à commencer qch. To be s. to act, être lent à agir. He was not slow to . . ., il ne tarda pas à (agir, répondre, etc.). Slow to anger, lent à la colère. (c) Slow (of wit), à l'esprit lourd. He's frightfully s., il a l'intelligence très lourde. Slow child, enfant tardif, arriéré. (d) (Spectacle) ennuyeux, qui manque d'entrain. *S.* little village, petit trou endormi. Business is slow, les affaires traînent. (e) Games: (Terrain, billard, etc.) qui ne rend pas. 2. (Of clock) En retard. Your watch is five minutes slow, votre montre retarde de cinq minutes. **-ly,** adv. Lentement ; (écrire) à main posée. Engine running s., moteur au ralenti. Drive slowly! au pas ! ralentir ! II. **slow,** adv. (In certain set phrases) (a) Lentement. To go slower, ralentir sa marche. To go slow, (i) aller lentement ; (ii) *F:* ne pas agir à la hâte. To go slow with one's provisions, ménager ses vivres. *Nau:* Slow ahead ! en avant doucement ! (b) The clock goes slow, la pendule retarde, perd. **'slow-'acting,** *a.* A action lente. **'slow-'burning,** *a.* 1. A combustion lente. 2. Peu combustible. **'slow-coach,** *s.* *F:* (a) Lambin, -ine. (b) *Sch:* Élève lent d'esprit. **'slow-'motion,** attrib.a. 1. *Cin:* Slow-motion film, film tourné au ralenti. Slow-motion projection, ralentissement *m* de la projection. 2. *W.Tel:* Slow-motion knob, bouton démultiplicateur. **'slow-'witted,** *a.* A l'esprit lent, lourd.

slow². 1. *v.i.* (a) To slow down, to slow up, ralentir (son allure) ; diminuer de vitesse. *F:* I have slowed down somewhat, j'ai un peu ralenti de mes efforts. (b) To slow up (to a stop), s'arrêter. 2. *v.tr.* To slow sth. down, up, ralentir qch.

slowness ['slounəs], *s.* 1. (a) Lenteur *f.* *S.* to answer, lenteur à répondre. (b) Lourdeur *f*, lenteur (d'esprit). 2. Retard *m* (d'une pendule).

slow-worm ['slouwəːrm], *s.* Orvet *m* ; *F:* serpent *m* de verre.

sloyd [slɔid], *s.* *Sch:* Système suédois de travail manuel.

slub¹ [slʌb], *s.* *Tex:* Mèche *f*, boudin *m* (de laine cardée).

slub², *v.tr.* *Tex:* Boudiner (le fil). **'slubbing-machine**, *s.* Boudineuse *f.*

sludge [slʌdʒ], *s.* **I.** (*a*) *Metalw:* Boue *f* d'émoulage. *Min:* Schlamms *mpl.* (*b*) *Mch:* Tartres boueux; vidanges *fpl.* **2.** Glaçons à moitié pris (sur la surface de la mer).

sludgy ['slʌdʒi], *a.* **I.** Boueux. **2.** (Mer) pleine de glaçons.

slue [slu:], *v.tr.* & *i.* = SLEW¹.

slug¹ [slʌg], *s.* **I.** Limace *f.* **2.** *F:* Paresseux, -euse; *F:* flémard, -arde.

slug², *s.* **I.** *Sm.a:* Lingot *m.* **2.** *Typ:* (*a*) Lingot. (*b*) Ligne-bloc *f* (de linotype).

sluggard ['slʌgərd], *s.* Paresseux *m*, fainéant *m.*

sluggish ['slʌgiʃ], *a.* **I.** Paresseux, léthargique; (esprit) lourd, inerte. **2.** *S. river*, rivière lente, paresseuse. *Sluggish liver*, foie paresseux, engorgé. *Sluggish digestion*, digestion laborieuse. *Sluggish compass*, compas peu sensible. **-ly**, *adv.* **I.** Paresseusement. **2.** (*Of river*) *To flow s.*, couler lentement.

sluggishness ['slʌgiʃnəs], *s.* **I.** (*a*) Paresse *f.* (*b*) Lourdeur *f*, pesanteur *f* (de l'esprit). **2.** Lenteur *f* (d'une rivière); paresse (du foie, de l'intestin).

slughi ['slu:gi], *s.* (Chien) sloughi *m.*

sluice¹ [slu:s], *s.* **I.** *Hyd.E:* (*a*) Écluse *f*; bonde *f* (d'étang). *To open the sluices*, lâcher les écluses. (*b*) Canal *m*, -aux, de décharge. **2.** = SLUICE-VALVE. **3.** *F:* *To give* (sth.) *a sluice down*, laver (le plancher, etc.) à grande eau. **'sluice-gate**, *s.* Porte *f* d'écluse; vanne *f.* **'sluice-valve**, *s.* Vanne *f* (de communication). **'sluice-way**, *s.* Canal *m*, -aux, à vannes.

sluice², *v.tr.* (*a*) Vanner (un cours d'eau). (*b*) *To sluice out the water in a reservoir*, laisser échapper l'eau d'un réservoir (par les vannes). (*c*) Laver à grande eau; débourber (un égout).

slum¹ [slʌm], *s.* (*a*) Bas quartier. (*b*) Rue *f* ou impasse *f* sordide. (*c*) Taudis *m.* *Slum-clearance*, abolissement *m* des taudis.

slum², *v.i.* (slummed) *To slum*, *to go slumming*, faire des visites de charité dans les bas quartiers.

slumber¹ ['slʌmbər], *s.* Sommeil *m* (paisible); assoupissement *m*; somme *m.* *To fall into a slumber*, s'endormir, s'assoupir.

slumber². **I.** *v.i.* Sommeiller; être assoupi; dormir (paisiblement). **2.** *v.tr.* *To slumber away the golden hours*, passer à dormir des heures précieuses.

slummy ['slʌmi], *a.* (Quartier) de taudis.

slump¹ [slʌmp], *s.* *Com:* Baisse soudaine, effondrement *m* (des cours); *F:* crise *f.* *The s. in the book trade*, la crise du livre. *S. in the franc*, dégringolade *f* du franc. *F:* *The slump*, la crise économique.

slump², *v.i.* **I.** *Dial:* Tomber lourdement, comme une masse. *Com:* (*Of prices, etc.*) Baisser tout à coup; s'effondrer, dégringoler.

slung [slʌn]. *See* SLING².

slunk [slʌŋk]. *See* SLINK.

slur¹ [slər], *s.* **I.** (*a*) Affront *m.* *To put, cast, a slur on s.o.*, infliger un affront à qn. (*b*) Tache *f*, flétrissure *f.* *To cast a slur on s.o.'s reputation*, entamer, porter atteinte à, la réputation de qn. **2.** *Typ:* Frison *m*, macule *f.* **3.** *Mus:* (*a*) (*Sign*) Liaison *f.* (*b*) (*Slurred passage*) Coulé *m.* **4.** (*In speech*) Mauvaise articulation.

slur², *v.* (slurred) **I.** *v.tr.* (*a*) *To s. one's words* (*in speaking*), mal articuler ses mots; bredouiller. *To s. a word*, *v.i.* *to slur over a word*, bredouiller un mot; escamoter un mot. *To slur* (*over*) *a fact*, passer légèrement sur un fait; glisser sur un fait. (*b*) *Mus:* Lier (deux notes); couler un

passage). (*c*) *Typ:* Maculer, friser (une page). **2.** *v.i.* (*Of outline, etc.*) Se brouiller; s'estomper

slurred, *a.* (*a*) Brouillé, indistinct. (*b*) *Mu:* (*Passage*) coulé.

slush [slʌʃ], *s.* **I.** (*a*) Neige à demi fondue. *T: tramp through the s.*, patauger dans la neige (*b*) Fange *f*, bourbe *f.* **2.** (*a*) *Mec.E:* Graisse lubrifiante. (*b*) *Nau:* Graisse de coq. **3.** *F* Sensiblerie *f.*

slushy ['slʌʃi], *a.* (*a*) (i) Détrempé par la neige (ii) boueux. (*b*) *F:* *S. sentimentality*, sentimentalité fadasse.

slut [slʌt], *s.f.* Souillon; *F:* salope.

sluttish ['slʌtiʃ], *a.* (*Of woman*) Malpropre, sale mauvaise ménagère.

Sluys [slɔis]. *Pr.n.* *Geog:* L'Écluse *f.*

sly [slai], *a.* (slyer, slyest) **I.** (*a*) Matois, rusé madré. (*b*) Cauteleux, sournois; en dessous *F:* *Sly dog*, (i) fin matois; (ii) retors *m* (*c*) *s.* *F:* *To do sth. on the sly*, faire qch furtivement, à la dérobée. **2.** Malin, -igne malicieux, espiègle, futé. **-ly**, *adv.* **I.** (*a*) Avec finesse; adroitement. (*b*) Sournoisement, cauteleusement. **2.** D'une manière espiègle. **'sly-boots**, *s.* *F:* **I.** (*a*) Sournois(e). (*b*) Petit(e rusé(e); petite futée. **2.** Espiègle *mf.*

slyness ['slainəs], *s.* **I.** (*a*) Finesse *f.* (*b*) Sour-noiserie *f.* **2.** Malice *f*, espièglerie *f.*

smack¹ [smak], *s.* Léger goût; saveur *f*, soup-çon *m* (d'ail, etc.).

smack², *v.i.* *To smack of sth.*, avoir un léger goût de qch. *Opinions that s. of heresy*, opinion qui sentent l'hérésie.

smack³. **I.** *s.* **I.** Claquement *m*, clic-clac *m* (d'un fouet). **2.** Claque *f.* *Smack in the face*, (i) gifle *f* (ii) *F:* affront *m.* *He gave the ball a hard s.*, il frappa vigoureusement la balle. *F:* *To have a smack at sth.*, essayer de faire qch. **3.** *F:* Gro baiser retentissant. **II.** **smack**, *adv.* **I.** *Smack went the whip*, le fouet claqua. **2.** *F:* *He fell smack on the floor*, il est tombé paf! *Smack in the middle*, en plein milieu, vlan!

smack⁴. **I.** *v.tr.* (*a*) Faire claquer (un fouet) *To s. one's lips*, *F:* se lécher les babines. (*b*) Frap-per, taper (avec le plat de la main). *To smack s.o.'s face*, donner une gifle à qn. **2.** *v.i.* (*Of whip* Claquer. *Smacking kiss*, baiser retentissant.

smack⁵, *s.* (Fishing-)smack, bateau pêcheur.

small [smɔ:l]. **I.** *a.* Petit. **I.** (*a*) Menu. *S. pebbles*, menus cail:oux. *Small stature*, petite taille. *Dress that makes one look s.*, robe qu vous rapetisse. *To make oneself small*, se fai~e tou petit. *Small shot*, menu plomb. *He is a smal eater*, il n'est pas gros mangeur. *Ven:* *Small game*, menu gibier. *Typ:* *Small letters*, minus-cules *f.* *S.a.* ARM² I, END¹ I, HOUR 2. (*b*) *In small numbers*, en petit nombre. *S. party* réunion peu nombreuse. *S. committee*, comité restreint. **2.** (*a*) *Small wine*, vin léger; petit vin *Small beer*, petite bière. (*b*) *Small voice*, voi fluette. *S.a.* STILL¹ I. **3.** *S. resources*, faible ressources. *S. income*, mince revenu. *S. harvest* maigre récolte. *Not the smallest difference*, pas l moindre différence. *He failed*, *and s. blame to him* il échoua, et ce n'était nullement sa faute. *It is smal wonder that . . .*, ce n'est guère étonnant que + *sub.* *To pay but s. attention to sth.*, n'accorde que peu d'attention à qch. **4.** Peu important peu considérable. *Small change*, menue monnaie *The smaller industries*, la petite industrie. In small way, en petit; modestement. *Great an small*, les grands et les petits. **5.** Mesquin chétif. *S. mind*, petit esprit. *To look small*, avoi l'air penaud. *To make s.o. look small*, humilie

qn. II. **small,** *s.* Small of the back, creux *m* des reins. *Sm.a:* Small of the butt, poignée *f* de la crosse. III. **small,** *adv.* **I.** (Hacher) menu, :n petits morceaux. **2.** *See* SING I. **'small-clothes,** *s.pl.* A: Culotte (collante); pantalon collant. **small-'minded,** *a.* A l'esprit mesquin. **'small-sword,** *s.* Épée *f* d'escrime. **'small-toothed,** *a.* A petites dents Small-toothed comb, peigne fin.
smallish ['smɔːliʃ], *a.* Assez petit; plutôt petit.
smallness ['smɔːlnəs], *s.* **I.** Petitesse *f*; exiguïté *f*; faiblesse *f* (d'une somme). **2.** *The s. of his mind,* sa petitesse d'esprit.
smallpox ['smɔːlpɔks], *s.* Petite vérole; variole *f*.
smarm [smɑːrm], *v. P:* **I.** *v.tr.* To smarm one's hair down, s'aplatir les cheveux à la pommade. **2.** *v.i.* To smarm over s.o., flagorner qn.
smart[1] [smɑːrt], *s.* Douleur cuisante; cuisson *f* (d'une blessure); cinglure *f* (d'une lanière). **'smart-money,** *s.* Mil: Pension *f* pour blessure.
smart[2], *v.i.* (a) (Of wound, etc.) Cuire, brûler. My eyes are smarting, les yeux me picotent. (b) To smart under an injustice, souffrir sous le coup d'une injustice. He will make you smart for it, il vous le fera payer cher. You shall s. for this, il vous en cuira. **smarting,** *s.* Douleur cuisante.
smart[3], *a.* **I.** (Coup de fouet) cinglant; (coup de marteau) sec. S. box on the ear, bonne gifle. **2.** Vif; prompt; alerte. S. attack, vive attaque. F: That's smart work! vous allez vite en besogne! Look smart (about it)! dépêchez-vous! **3.** (a) Habile; à l'esprit éveillé. 'Smart lad wanted,' "on demande un jeune homme intelligent." F: He's a smart one, c'est une fine mouche. (b) Pej: Malin, madré. S.a. ALEC(κ). **4.** Élégant, distingué, chic. To make oneself s., se faire beau. Smart society, the smart set, le monde élégant; la haute gomme. He thinks it smart to . . ., il croit chic de. . . **-ly,** *adv.* **I.** Promptement, vivement. S. executed, fait vite et bien. **2.** Habilement, adroitement. **3.** (S'habiller) élégamment.
smarten ['smɑːrt(ə)n]. **I.** *v.tr.* (a) To smarten (up), accélérer (la production); animer (le dialogue). To smarten s.o. up, dégourdir qn. (b) To smarten oneself up, se faire beau. **2.** *v.i.* To smarten up. (a) S'animer. (b) Se dégourdir; prendre du chic.
smartness ['smɑːrtnəs], *s.* **I.** (a) Vivacité *f* (d'esprit); esprit débrouillard. (b) A-propos *m* (d'une réponse). **2.** Habileté peu scrupuleuse; finesse *f*. **3.** Élégance *f*, coquetterie *f* (de toilette); chic *m*.
smash[1] [smaʃ]. I. *s.* **I.** (a) F: Coup écrasant. He fell with an awful s., il est tombé comme une masse. (b) Ten: Coup écrasé; smash *m*. **2.** (a) Mise *f* en morceaux, en miettes; fracassement *m*. (b) Désastre *m*, sinistre *m* (de chemin de fer). **3.** Débâcle *f*; faillite (commerciale); krach *m* (d'une banque). II. **smash,** *adv.* **I.** To go smash, (i) (of firm) faire faillite, tomber en faillite; (of bank) sauter. **2.** To run smash into sth., se heurter de front contre qch.
smash[2]. I. *v.tr.* **I.** (a) To smash sth. against sth., heurter qch. contre qch. avec violence. (b) Ten: Écraser, massacrer, smasher (la balle). **2.** (a) To smash sth. to pieces, briser qch. en morceaux. To s. the door open, enfoncer la porte. Smash-and-grab raid, rafle *f* (de bijoux) après bris de devanture. (b) Détruire; écraser (une armée). (c) Ruiner (qn); faire échouer (un projet). II. **smash,** *v.i.* **I.** Se heurter violem-

ment (contre qch.). **2.** Éclater en morceaux; se briser. **3.** Faire faillite; (of bank) sauter. **smash up,** *v.tr.* Briser en morceaux; fracasser. **'smash-up,** *s.* **I.** Destruction complète. Rail: Collision *f*. **2.** Débâcle *f*; faillite *f*. **smashing,** *a.* (Coup) écrasant, assommant.
smasher[1] ['smaʃər], *s.* (a) Coup écrasant, assommant. (b) To come a smasher, faire une violente culbute.
smasher[2], *s.* P: Faux monnayeur.
smattering ['smatəriŋ], *s.* Légère connaissance (d'une langue, etc.). To have a smattering of sth., avoir des notions de (chimie).
smear[1] [smiːər], *s.* **I.** Tache *f*, souillure *f*. **2.** (For microscopic slide) Frottis *m* (de sang, etc.).
smear[2], *v.tr.* **I.** (a) Barbouiller, salir (with, de). (b) Enduire (with, de). Cheeks smeared with rouge, joues barbouillées de rouge. **2.** Maculer, barbouiller (une page écrite). (Of outline) To get smeared, s'estomper.
smell[1] [smel], *s.* **I.** (Sense of) smell, odorat *m*; flair *m* (d'un chien). To have a keen sense of s., avoir ∙'odorat fin. **2.** (a) Odeur *f*; parfum *m*. Unpleasant s., relent *m*. (Nice) s. of cooking, fumet *m* de cuisine. (b) Mauvaise odeur. **3.** To take a smell at sth., flairer qch.
smell[2], *v.* (p.t. & p.p. smelt, occ. smelled) **I.** *v.tr. & ind.tr.* (a) Flairer (qch.); sentir (une fleur). To s. a bottle of salts, respirer un flacon de sels. The dog smelt at my shoes, le chien flaira mes souliers. (b) Abs. Avoir de l'odorat. (c) Sentir l'odeur de (qch.); sentir (une odeur). (d) F: Sentir, flairer, pressentir (le danger). **2.** *v.i.* (a) (Of flower, etc.) Sentir. To smell nice, sentir bon. Room that smells damp, pièce qui sent l'humidité. F: To smell of the lamp, sentir l'huile. (b) Sentir (mauvais); avoir une forte odeur. **smell out,** *v.tr.* (a) (Of dog) Flairer, dépister (le gibier). (b) Découvrir (un secret).
'smelling-bottle, *s.* Flacon *m* de sels.
'smelling-salts, *s.pl.* Sels (volatils) anglais; F: sels.
smelly ['smeli], *a.* F: Malodorant.
smelt[1] [smelt], *s.* Metall: **I.** Fondre (le minerai). **2.** Extraire (le métal) par fusion.
smelting, *s.* (a) Fonte *f*, fonderie *f*, fusion *f*. (b) Extraction *f* (du métal). Smelting works, fonderie *f*.
smelt[2], *s.* Ich: Éperlan *m*.
smelt[3]. *See* SMELL[2].
smew [smjuː], *s.* Orn: Harle *m* piette.
smilax ['smailaks], *s.* Bot: Smilax *m*.
smile[1] [smail], *s.* Sourire *m*. Scornful s., sourire de mépris. With a s. on his lips, le sourire aux lèvres. To give a faint smile, sourire du bout des lèvres. To be all smiles, être tout souriant. Face wreathed in smiles, visage rayonnant.
smile[2]. **I.** *v.i.* Sourire. To smile (up)on, at, s.o., sourire à qn. To smile at s.o.'s vain endeavours, sourire des vains efforts de qn. (Of child) To s. in his sleep, F: rire aux anges. F: To keep smiling, garder le sourire. **2.** *v.tr.* (a) To smile a bitter smile, sourire amèrement. (b) To smile s.o.'s fears away, écarter d'un sourire les craintes de qn. (c) To smile a welcome to s.o., accueillir qn avec, par, un sourire. **smiling,** *a.* Souriant. He always comes up smiling, il garde toujours le sourire. **-ly,** *adv.* En souriant.
smirch[1] [smɔːrtʃ], *s.* Tache *f*; salissure *f*, souillure *f*.
smirch[2], *v.tr.* Tacher; salir, souiller.
smirk[1] [smɔːrk], *s.* Sourire affecté, minauder.
smirk[2], *v.i.* Sourire d'un air affecté; minauder.
smirking, *a.* Affecté; minauder.

47

smite [smait], *v.tr.* (smote [smout]; smitten [smitn]) Frapper. **1.** *Lit:* To s. one's thigh, se taper la cuisse avec la main. *S.a.* HIP¹ I. *F:* My conscience smote me, je fus frappé de remords. **2.** To be smitten with blindness, être frappé de cécité. *F:* To be smitten with a girl, être épris d'une jeune fille. Love-smitten, féru d'amour. **3.** *v.i.* A sound smote upon his ear, un son lui frappa l'oreille. **smite down,** *v.tr.* Abattre (qn).

smith [smiθ], *s.* Forgeron *m.* Shoeing smith, maréchal ferrant.

smithereens [smiðə'ri:nz], *s.pl.* *F:* Morceaux *m;* miettes *f.* To smash, knock, sth. (in)to smithereens, briser, réduire, qch. en éclats, en mille morceaux.

smithy ['smiði], *s.* Forge *f.*

smitten [smitn]. *See* SMITE.

smock [smɔk], *s.* Smock(-frock), blouse *f,* sarrau *m.*

smoke¹ [smouk], *s.* **1.** Fumée *f.* *F:* (Of project) To end in smoke, s'en aller en fumée; n'aboutir à rien. To go like smoke, aller comme sur des roulettes. **2.** (a) Action de fumer (du tabac). Will you have a smoke? voulez-vous fumer? (b) Quelque chose à fumer; cigare *m* ou cigarette *f.* Pass round the smokes, faites circuler les cigares. **'smoke-consumer,** *s.* *Ind:* (Appareil *m*) fumivore *m.* **'smoke-dried,** *a.* (Jambon, etc.) fumé. **'smoke-helmet,** *s.* Casque *m* à fumée; casque pare-fumée. **'smoke-producing,** *a.* (Appareil) fumigène. **'smoke-screen,** *s.* *Mil:* *Navy:* Rideau *m* de fumée; nuage artificiel. **'smoke-shell,** *s.* Obus *m* fumigène. **'smoke-stack,** *s.* Cheminée *f* de locomotive, d'usine).

smoke² **1.** *v.i.* Fumer. The lamp is smoking, la lampe fume, charbonne. **2.** *v.tr.* (a) Fumer (le jambon). (b) Noircir de fumée, enfumer (le plafond). (c) Fumer (du tabac); *F:* griller (une cigarette). *Abs.* Do you smoke? êtes-vous fumeur? Do you mind if I s.? la fumée vous gêne-t-elle? *S.a.* PIPE¹ 4. **smoke out,** *v.tr.* Enfumer (un guêpier). **smoking¹,** *a.* Fumant. **smoking²,** *s.* **1.** Émission *f* de fumée. **2.** Fumage *m* (du jambon). **3.** Action *f* ou habitude *f* de fumer (le tabac). No smoking (allowed), défense *f* de fumer. **'smoking-carriage, -compartment,** *s.* *Rail:* Compartiment *m* pour fumeurs. **'smoking-concert,** *s.* Concert *m* où il est permis de fumer. **'smoking-jacket,** *s.* Veston *m* d'intérieur. **'smoking-mixture,** *s.* Mélange *m* de tabacs pour la pipe. **'smoking-room, -saloon,** *s.* Fumoir *m.*

smokeless ['smouklǝs], *a.* (Houille, poudre) sans fumée.

smoker ['smoukǝr], *s.* **1.** Fumeur *m* (de tabac). Heavy smoker, grand fumeur. **2.** *F:* = SMOKING-COMPARTMENT.

smokiness ['smoukinǝs], *s.* Condition fumeuse (de l'atmosphère).

smoky ['smouki], *a.* **1.** (Of atmosphere) Fumeux; fuligineux; (of room) plein de fumée. **2.** (Plafond) noirci par la fumée. **3.** Smoky lamp, lampe qui fume, qui file.

smooth¹ [smu:ð], *a.* **1.** (a) (Surface) lisse; (chemin) uni, égal. Smooth as glass, poli, uni, comme la glace. S. forehead, front sans rides. S. skin, peau douce, satinée. Sea as smooth as a mill-pond, mer calme comme un lac; mer d'huile. (b) (Menton) glabre. **2.** (a) Doux, *f.* douce; sans heurts. Smooth running, marche douce d'une machine); roulement silencieux (d'une voiture). (b) S. voice, voix moelleuse. (c) Doucereux, mielleux. He has a smooth tongue, c'est un beau

parleur. **-ly,** *adv.* **1.** Uniment; sans inégalités. **2.** (Marcher, travailler) doucement. Everything is going on s., *F:* tout va comme sur des roulettes. **3.** (Parler) doucereusement. **'smooth-bore,** *a. & s.* (Canon *m*) à âme lisse. Smooth-bore gun, fusil *m* à canon lisse. **'smooth-chinned,** *a.* **1.** Au menton rasé de près. **2.** Imberbe. **'smooth-faced,** *a.* **1.** = SMOOTH-CHINNED. **2.** A l'air doucereux. **'smooth-running,** *a.* A marche douce, régulière. **'smooth-spoken, -tongued,** *a.* Aux paroles doucereuses.

smooth², *s.* **1.** To give one's hair a smooth, lisser ses cheveux. **2.** *Nau:* Accalmie *f,* embellie *f.* **3.** *See* ROUGH¹ III. 3.

smooth³, **smoothe,** *v.tr.* **1.** Lisser (ses cheveux); aplanir (une planche); égaliser (le terrain). To s. s.o.'s ruffled spirits, apaiser l'irritation de qn. *F:* To smooth the way for s.o., aplanir la voie pour qn. **2.** Adoucir (un angle). **smooth away,** *v.tr.* Aplanir (un obstacle). **smooth out,** *v.tr.* Faire disparaître (un faux pli). **smooth over,** *v.tr.* **1.** Aplanir (une difficulté). **2.** (a) Pallier (une faute). (b) To smooth things over, arranger les choses.

smoothness ['smu:ðnǝs], *s.* **1.** (a) Égalité *f* (d'une surface); satiné *m* (de la peau). (b) Calme *m* (de la mer). **2.** Douceur *f* (de la marche d'une machine). **3.** (Of pers.) Douceur feinte; air doucereux.

smote [smout]. *See* SMITE.

smother¹ ['smʌðǝr], *s.* (a) Fumée épaisse. (b) Brouillard épais. S. of foam, tourbillon *m* d'eau écumante.

smother², *v.tr.* (a) Étouffer (qn, le feu); suffoquer (qn). To smother a curse, étouffer un juron. (b) Recouvrir. Strawberries smothered with cream, fraises enrobées de crème. Pedestrian smothered in dust, piéton enfariné de poussière.

smothering, *s.* Étouffement *m,* suffocation *f.*

smoulder ['smouldǝr], *v.i.* (a) Brûler lentement, sans flamme. (b) (Of fire, rebellion) Couver (sous la cendre). **smouldering¹,** *a.* (a) Qui brûle sans fumée. (b) Qui couve (sous la cendre). **smouldering²,** *s.* Combustion lente.

smudge¹ [smʌdʒ], *s.* **1.** Tache *f* (de suie, etc.); noircissure *f;* bavure *f* de plume.

smudge², *v.tr.* Salir, souiller; barbouiller; maculer (son écriture).

smudgy ['smʌdʒi], *a.* **1.** Taché, souillé; (of writing) barbouillé, maculé. **2.** (Contour) estompé.

smug [smʌg], *a.* (Ton, air) suffisant; satisfait de soi-même. S. optimism, optimisme béat. **-ly,** *adv.* D'un air suffisant. **'smug-faced, -looking,** *a.* A l'air suffisant.

smuggle [smʌgl], *v.tr.* (Faire) passer (des marchandises) en contrebande, en fraude. *Abs.* Faire la contrebande. *F:* To s. sth. into the room, apporter qch. dans la salle furtivement. To smuggle sth. away, escamoter (une lettre, etc.).

smuggling, *s.* Contrebande *f;* fraude *f* (aux droits de douane).

smuggler ['smʌglǝr], *s.* Contrebandier *m;* fraudeur *m* (à la douane).

smugness ['smʌgnǝs], *s.* Suffisance *f;* béatitude *f.*

smut [smʌt], *s.* **1.** Parcelle *f* de suie; flocon *m* de suie. **2.** To talk smut, dire des saloperies **3.** *Agr:* Charbon *m,* nielle *f* (des céréales).

smuttiness ['smʌtinǝs], *s.* **1.** Noirceur *f,* saleté *f.* **2.** Obscénité *f.* **3.** *Agr:* État niellé, charbonné (du blé).

smutty ['smʌti], *a.* **1.** (a) Noirci; sali (de suie)

(b) (Of conversation) Malpropre, ordurier.
2. Agr: Niellé.
snack [snak], s. Léger repas; casse-croûte m inv.
To have a snack, casser la croûte; manger sur
le pouce. **'snack-bar,** s. Casse-croûte m inv.
snaffle[1] [snafl], s. Harn: (Also snaffle-bit) Filet m;
mors m de bridon. **'snaffle-'bridle,** s. Filet m,
bridon m.
snaffle[2], v.tr. P: S'emparer de (qch.); chiper
(qch.).
snag [snag], s. (a) Chicot m (d'arbre); souche f
au ras d'eau; entrave f à la navigation fluviale.
(b) F: Écueil m; obstacle caché. **To strike a
snag,** se heurter à un obstacle. **There's a snag,**
il y a un cheveu.
snail [sneil], s. Limaçon m, escargot m, colimaçon m. **Edible snail,** escargot comestible.
F: **To go at a snail's pace,** aller à pas de tortue.
snake [sneik], s. Serpent m. **Common snake,**
couleuvre f à collier; serpent d'eau. P: **To see
snakes,** avoir le delirium tremens. **'snake-bite,**
s. Morsure f de serpent. **'snake-charmer,** s.
Charmeur, -euse, de serpents. **'snake-root,** s.
Bot: Pharm: Serpentaire f.
snaky ['sneiki], a. **1.**(a) De serpent. (b) (Langue)
perfide, de vipère. **2.**(Of road) Serpentant.
snap[1] [snap]. I. s. **1.** (a) Coup m de dents. (Of
dog) **To make a snap at s.o.,** essayer de mordre
qn. (b) Coup sec, claquement m (des dents, d'un
fouet). The box shut with a s., la boîte se ferma
avec un coup sec. F: **I don't care a snap,** je m'en
soucie comme d'une guigne. **2.** Cassure f;
rupture soudaine. **3.** Cold snap, courte période
de temps froid. **4.** F: Énergie f, vivacité f. **Style
full of snap,** style vif, énergique. **Put some snap
into it!** un peu d'énergie! **5.** Cu: Biscuit
croquant. **6.** Snap(-fastener), fermoir m (de
valise); cadenas m (de bracelet); bouton m
(fermoir) à pression. El: Snap contact, contact
à languette. **7.** Phot: = SNAPSHOT[1]. **8.** Jeu de
cartes enfantin. II. **snap,** attrib.a. Instantané,
imprévu. Parl: **Snap division,** vote m de
surprise. III. snap, adv. Crac. **To go snap,**
se casser net. **'snap-hook,** s. Porte-mousqueton m inv. **'snap-lock,** s. Serrure f à ressort.
snap[2], v. (snapped [snapt]) I. v.i. **1.** (Of dog) **To
snap at s.o.,** chercher à mordre qn. F: **To snap
at an opportunity,** saisir vivement une occasion.
2. (Of whip) Claquer; faire un bruit sec; (of
fastener) se fermer avec un bruit sec; (of pistol)
partir. **3. To snap** (asunder), se casser net.
II. **snap,** v.tr. **1.** (Of dog) Happer (qch.).
2. (a) Faire claquer (un fouet). **To snap one's
fingers,** faire claquer ses doigts. F: **To snap
one's fingers at a threat,** se moquer d'une menace.
To snap one's fingers at s.o., narguer qn.
(b) Phot: **To snap s.o.,** prendre un instantané
de qn. **3.** Casser, rompre (une canne). **Snapped
tendon,** tendon claqué. **4. To snap out an order,**
donner un ordre d'un ton sec. **5.** Faire (qch.)
brusquement. Aut: **To snap in a gear,** changer
vivement de vitesse. **snap off. 1.** v.tr. (a) Enlever (qch.) d'un coup de dents. F: **Don't snap
my head off!** ne m'avalez pas! (b) Casser (le
bout d'une canne). **2.** v.i. Se détacher brusquement. **snap up,** v.tr. **1.** Saisir, happer (qch.).
To snap up a bargain, saisir une occasion.
2. F: Répondre (qn) vertement.
snapdragon ['snapdragən], s. **1.** Bot: = AN-
TIRRHINUM. **2.** Jeu m (de Noël) qui consiste à
happer des raisins secs dans du cognac flambant.
snapper ['snapər], s. Snapper-up of unconsidered
trifles, chipeur, -euse; escamoteur, -euse.
snappish ['snapiʃ], a. Irritable; hargneux.

snappishness ['snapiʃnəs], s. Humeur hargneuse; irritabilité f.
snappy ['snapi], a. **1.** = SNAPPISH. **2.** (Style)
vif, plein d'allant. S. phrase, locution pleine de
sel. **3.** Aut: (Moteur) nerveux. P: **Make it
snappy!** dépêchez-vous!
snapshot[1] ['snapʃɔt], s. **1.** Coup (de fusil) lâché
sans viser. **2.** Phot: F: Instantané m.
snapshot[2], v.tr. (snapshotted) Prendre un
instantané de (qch.). Abs. Faire de l'instantané.
snare[1] [snɛər], s. **1.**(a) Ven: Lacet m, collet m;
lacs m, filet m. (Of rabbit) **To be caught in a snare,**
être pris au lacet. (b) F: Piège m. (Of pers.) **To
be caught in the snare,** être pris au piège.
2. pl. **Snares of a drum,** timbre m d'un tambour.
'snare-drum, s. Tambour m à timbre; caisse
claire.
snare[2], v.tr. Prendre (un lapin) au collet, au lacet;
attraper (qn).
snarl[1] [snɑːrl], s. Grondement m, grognement m.
snarl[2], v.i. Grogner, gronder. **snarling**[1], a.
Hargneux. **snarling**[2], s. Grondement m,
grognement m.
snatch[1] [snatʃ], s. **1.** Mouvement vif pour saisir
qch. **To make a snatch at sth.,** chercher à saisir
qch. **2.** (a) Courte période. **Snatch of sleep,**
petit somme. **To work by snatches,** travailler à
bâtons rompus. (b) **Snatches of song,** fragments m de chanson. **'snatch-block,** s. Poulie
coupée; galoche f. **'snatch-crop,** s. Récolte
dérobée. **'snatch-hook,** s. Mousqueton m.
snatch[2], v.tr. & i. **1.** Saisir, empoigner (qch.).
He snatched (up) his revolver off the table, il saisit
son revolver sur la table. **To snatch (at) an
opportunity,** saisir une occasion. **To snatch a
meal,** manger un morceau sur le pouce. **2. To
snatch sth. out of s.o.'s hands,** arracher qch. des
mains de qn. **Snatch-and-grab robbery,** vol à
l'esbroufe.
sneak[1] [sniːk], s. **1.** Pleutre m; pied plat.
2. Sch: F: Cafard, -arde; mouchard m;
rapporteur, -euse.
sneak[2]. **1.** v.i. (a) **To sneak off, away,** partir
furtivement; s'éclipser. (b) Sch: F: Mou-
charder, cafarder. **2.** v.tr. P: Chiper, chaparder.
sneaking, a. **1.**(a) Furtif. **To have a sneaking
liking for sth.,** avoir un penchant inavoué pour
qch. (b) Sournois, dissimulé. **2.** Rampant,
servile. **-ly,** adv. **1.** (a) Furtivement, en
cachette. (b) Sournoisement. **2.** Servilement.
sneck[1] [snɛk], s. Scot: Loquet m (de porte).
sneck[2], v.tr. Scot: Fermer (la porte) au loquet.
sneer[1] [sniːər], s. **1.** Sourire m de mépris;
ricanement m. **2.** Sarcasme m.
sneer[2], v.i. Sourire, rire, d'un air moqueur;
ricaner. **To sneer at s.o.,** parler de qn d'un ton
méprisant. **To s. at riches,** dénigrer les richesses.
sneering[1], a. Ricaneur, -euse; moqueur,
-euse; sarcastique. **-ly,** adv: D'un air méprisant; en ricanant. **sneering**[2], s. **1.** Ricanerie f.
2. Sarcasme m.
sneeze[1] [sniːz], s. Éternuement m. **To stifle a
sneeze,** réprimer une envie d'éternuer.
sneeze[2], v.i. Éternuer. F: **That's not to be
sneezed at,** cela n'est pas à dédaigner.
snick[1] [snik], s. **1.** Entaille f, encoche f.
2. Coup m de ciseaux; entaille (dans l'étoffe).
snick[2], v.tr. Faire une entaille dans (le drap).
2. Cr: **To snick the ball,** couper légèrement
la balle.
sniff[1] [snif], s. Reniflement m. **To get a sniff of
fresh air,** prendre une bouffée d'air frais.
sniff[2], v.i. & tr. **1.** (a) Renifler. (b) **To sniff at
a dish,** renifler sur un p.at. The offer is not to

be **sniffed at**, l'offre n'est pas à dédaigner. **2.** (a) Flairer (un danger). (b) To s. (at) a bottle of salts, respirer un flacon de sels. **3.** Humer, renifler (une prise de tabac). Med: 'To be **sniffed up the nostrils**,' "pour être aspiré par les narines."

sniffle [snifl], v.i. F: Être enchifrené; renifler. **sniffling**, a. Enchifrené; enrhumé du cerveau. **sniffy** ['snifi], a. F: **1.** (a) Dédaigneux. (b) De mauvaise humeur. **2.** D'odeur suspecte.

snift [snift], v.i. (Of steam-engine) Tousser, cracher. **'snifting valve**, s. Mch: Reniflard m.

snigger[1] ['snigər], s. (a) Rire intérieur, en dessous; léger ricanement. (b) Petit rire grivois. **snigger**[2], v.i. Rire sous cape; ricaner tout bas. **sniggering**, s. Rires mpl en dessous; petits rires.

snip[1] [snip], s. **1.** Morceau coupé; petit morceau (de papier, de toile). **2.** (a) Petite entaille. (b) Coup m de ciseaux. **3.** P: (a) Certitude f. Turf: Gagnant sûr. (b) Affaire avantageuse. **snip**[2], v.tr. (snipped [snipt]) Couper avec des ciseaux.

snipe[1] [snaip], s. **1.** Bécassine f. The moor was full of snipe, la .ande abondait en bécassines. **2.** F: Gamin, -ine.

snipe[2], v.i. & tr. To snipe (at) the enemy, canarder l'ennemi. To be sniped at, essuyer les coups de feu de tireurs isolés. **sniping**, s. Tir m en canarderie.

sniper ['snaipər], s. Mil: Canardeur m; tireur d'élite embusqué.

snippet ['snipet], s. **1.** Bout m, morceau (coupé). **2.** Court extrait (de journal).

snippety ['snipeti], a. (Style) décousu.

snivel[1] ['sniv(ə)l], s. (a) Reniflement larmoyant. (b) Pleurnicherie f.

snivel[2], v.i. (snivelled) (a) Pleurnicher, larmoyer. (b) Y aller de sa larme; larmoyer hypocritement. **snivelling**[1], a. Pleurnicheur, -euse; larmoyant. **snivelling**[2], s. **1.** Reniflement m. **2.** Pleurnicherie f.

sniveller ['snivələr], s. **1.** Pleurnicheur, -euse. **2.** Faux bonhomme avec la larme à l'œil.

snob [snɔb], s. Personne qui dédaigne les humbles, qui admire les grands.

snobbery ['snɔbəri], s. Admiration f des grands.

snobbish ['snɔbiʃ], a. Admirateur, -trice, des grands, de la haute société.

snobbishness ['snɔbiʃnəs], s. = SNOBBERY.

snood [snu:d], s. Cost: Résille f.

snook [snu:k], s. P: Pied m de nez. To cock a snook at s.o., faire un pied de nez à qn.

snooker[1] ['snu:kər], s. Bill: (Jeu m de) "snooker" m.

snooker[2], v.tr. F: To snooker s.o., mettre qn dans une impasse.

snooze[1] [snu:z], s. F: Petit somme.

snooze[2], v.i. F: Sommeiller; faire un petit somme. **snoozing**, a. Endormi, assoupi.

snore[1] ['snɔ:ər], s. Ronflement m.

snore[2], v.i. Ronfler. **snoring**, s. Ronflement m.

snorer ['snɔ:rər], s. Ronfleur, -euse.

snort[1] [snɔ:rt], s. Reniflement m; ébrouement m (d'un cheval).

snort[2]. **1.** v.i. Renifler fortement; (of horse) s'ébrouer. **2.** v.tr. To snort defiance at s.o., lancer un défi à qn avec un reniflement de mépris. **snorting**, s. Reniflement m; ébrouement m.

snorter ['snɔ:rtər], s. P: (a) Chose épatante. (b) **Problem that is a regular snorter**, problème

qui va nous donner du fil à retordre. (c) Nau: Vent carabiné.

snot [snɔt], s. V: Morve f.

snotty ['snɔti]. **1.** a. V: (a) Morveux. (b) De mauvaise humeur; maussade. **2.** s. P: = MIDSHIPMAN.

snout [snaut], s. Museau m; mufle m (de taureau); groin m (de porc).

snow[1] [snou], s. **1.** (a) Neige f. **There has been a fall of snow**, il est tombé de la neige. **Driven snow**, neige vierge. (b) Ind: Carbonic acid 'snow,' neige carbonique. **2.** P: (Drug) Cocaïne f, P: coco f. **'snow-blind**, a. Atteint de la cécité des neiges. **'snow-blindness**, s. Cécité f des neiges. **'snow-blink**, s. Reflet m, clarté f, des glaces (sur l'horizon). **'snow-boots**, s.pl. Couvre-chaussures m, snow-boots m. **'snowbound**, a. (Of pers.) Retenu par la neige; (of road) bloqué par la neige. **'snow-capped**, **-clad**, **-covered**, a. Couronné, encapuchonné, de neige. **'snow-drift**, s. Amoncellement m de neige. **'snow-field**, s. Champ m de neige. **'snow-flake**, s. Flocon m de neige. **'snowflurry**, s. U.S: Rafale f de neige. **'snowleopard**, s. Z: Léopard m des neiges; once f. **'snow-line**, s. Limite f des neiges perpétuelles. **'snow-man**, pl. **-men**, s.m. Bonhomme de neige. **'snow-plough**, s. Chasse-neige m inv. **'snow-shoes**, s.pl. Raquettes f. **'snow-slide**, **-slip**, s. Avalanche f. **'snow-storm**, s. Tempête f de neige. **'snow-white**, a. D'un blanc de neige.

snow[2]. **1.** v. impers. Neiger. It is snowing, il neige; il tombe de la neige. **2.** To be snowed in, up, être retenu, bloqué, pris, par la neige. F: Snowed under with work, submergé de besogne.

snowball[1] ['snoubɔ:l], s. **1.** (a) Boule f, pelote f, de neige. (b) Cu: (Entremets sucré en forme de) boule de neige. **2.** Bot: Snowball(-tree), boule-de-neige f; rose f de Gueldre.

snowball[2], v.tr. To snowball s.o., lancer des boules de neige à qn.

snowdrop ['snoudrop], s. Bot: Perce-neige m or f inv; F: grelot blanc.

snowy ['snoui], a. Neigeux; de neige. F: Snowy hair, cheveux de neige. **Snowy white**, blanc comme neige.

snub[1] [snʌb], s. Mortification f, avanie f, rebuffade f. He got a good s., il a été mouché de belle façon.

snub[2], v.tr. (snubbed) (a) Faire sentir à (qn) qu'il a pris une liberté; remettre (qn) à sa place. (b) Infliger un affront à (qn).

snub[3], a. (Nez) camus, retroussé. **'snubnosed**, a. (Au nez) camus.

snuff[1] [snʌf], s. Tabac m à priser. **To take snuff**, priser. **A pinch of snuff**, une prise. P: To be up to snuff, être dégourdi, avisé; être à la hauteur. **'snuff-box**, s. Tabatière f. **'snuff-coloured**, a. (Couleur) tabac inv. **'snuff-taker**, s. Priseur, -euse.

snuff[2], v.i. Priser.

snuff[3], v.tr Moucher (une chandelle). **snuff out**. **1.** v.tr. Éteindre (une chandelle) avec les doigts. **2.** v.i. P: Mourir.

snuffer ['snʌfər], s. **1.** A: Moucheur (de chandelles). **2.** pl. (Pair of) snuffers, mouchettes f.

snuffle[1] [snʌfl], s. **1.** (a) Reniflement m. (b) pl. To have the snuffles, être enchifrené. **2.** Ton nasillard. Esp. Hypocritical snuffle, débit m hypocrite.

snuffle[2], v.i. **1.** (a) Renifler. (b) Être enchifrené.

2. Nasiller. **snuffling,** *a.* **1.** Qui renifle ; enchifrené. **2.** Nasillard.
snuffler ['snʌflər], *s.* (*a*) Nasilleur, -euse. (*b*) F: Cagot m ; tartufe m.
snug [snʌg], *a.* **1.** *Nau:* (Navire) paré (à tout événement). **2.** (*Of house*) Confortable ; (*of pers.*) bien abrité ; bien au chaud. *It is very s. in here,* on est bien ici. *To lie snug in bed,* être bien au chaud dans son lit. *P:* As snug as a bug in a rug, tranquille comme Baptiste. **3.** To lie snug, rester coi. **-ly,** *adv.* Confortablement, douillettement.
snuggery ['snʌgəri], *s.* Petit fumoir (du maître de maison) ; *P:* "turne" *f.*
snuggle [snʌgl]. **1.** *v.i.* To snuggle up to s.o., se pelotonner contre qn. To snuggle down in bed, se blottir dans son lit. **2.** *v.tr.* To snuggle a child close to one, serrer un enfant dans ses bras.
snugness ['snʌgnəs], *s.* Confortable *m.*
so [sou]. **I.** *adv.* **1.** (*a*) Si, tellement. *He is so (very) kind,* il est si aimable. *She isn't so very old,* elle n'est pas tellement vieille. *I am not so sure of that,* je n'en suis pas très sûr. So true it is that . . ., tant il est vrai que. . . . *He is not so feeble as he appears,* il n'est pas aussi faible qu'il n'en a l'air. *Would you be so kind as to* . . .? voudriez-vous avoir la bonté de . . .? *What man would be so mean as not to admire him?* quel est l'homme assez mesquin pour ne pas l'admirer? *Give me* ever so little, donnez-m'en si peu que vous voudrez, si peu que rien. *S.a.* NEVER. So greatly, so much, tellement, tant. I loved him so (much), je l'aimais tant. *We enjoyed ourselves* ever so much, on s'est joliment bien amusés. *Loving her so, he could not blame her,* l'aimant à ce point, il ne pouvait la blâmer. *S.a.* EVER 3, FAR¹ I, LONG¹ III. **1.** (*b*) *If it takes* so many men so long *to do* so much work . . ., s'il faut à tant d'hommes tant de temps pour faire tant de travail. . . . **2.** (*a*) Ainsi ; de cette façon ; de cette manière. Stand so, tenez-vous comme ça. So it was that he became a soldier, c'est ainsi qu'il devint soldat. Why do you cry so? pourquoi pleurez-vous ainsi? As X is to Y, so is Y to Z, comme X est à Y, Y est à Z. *As the father is so is the son,* tel père, tel fils. So many men so many minds, autant de têtes autant d'avis. They are so many rogues, ce sont autant de filous. *She so arranged things that* . . ., elle fit en sorte que + *ind. or sub.* It so happened that I was there, le hasard a voulu que je fusse là. And so forth, and so on, et ainsi du reste ; et ainsi de suite. So to say, so to speak, pour ainsi dire. So saying he departed, ce disant il partit. (*b*) I think so, je le crois. I suppose so, I expect so, je le suppose ; sans doute. I hope so, je l'espère bien. I fear so, j'en ai bien peur. *S.a.* SAY² I (*d*). So it seems, à ce qu'il paraît. I told you so! je vous l'avais bien dit! So much so that . . ., à tel point que . . . ; tellement que. . . . Much more so, bien plus encore. It is so ; so it is ; that's so, il en est ainsi ; parfaitement ; effectivement. Is that so? vraiment? It is not so, il n'en est rien. So be it! qu'il en soit ainsi ! soit! *Many people would have run away.* Not so he, beaucoup de gens se seraient sauvés, mais pas lui. (*c*) How so? comment cela? Why so? pourquoi cela? Perhaps so, cela se peut. Not so, pas du tout. Quite so! just so! très juste ! parfaitement ! A shilling or so, un shilling ou à peu près. A hundred pounds or so, une centaine de livres. *A week or so,* une semaine environ. (*d*) He's right and so are you,

il a raison et vous aussi. *He quickened his pace and so did I,* il hâta le pas et j'en fis autant. *I thought you were French.*—So I am, je pensais que vous étiez Français.—(Je le suis) en effet ; mais parfaitement ! (*e*) You're late.—So I am! vous êtes en retard.—C'est vrai ! **3.** *Conj.phr.* So that. (*a*) *He stepped aside so that I might enter,* il s'effaça pour que je pusse entrer. *Speak so that you are understood,* parlez de (telle) sorte qu'on vous comprenne. (*b*) *He tied me up so that I could not move,* il m'a ligoté de (telle) sorte que je ne pouvais pas bouger. **4.** *Conj.phr.* So as to. (*a*) Afin de. *We hurried so as not to be late,* nous nous sommes dépêchés pour ne pas être en retard. (*b*) *Speak so as to be understood,* parlez de (telle) sorte qu'on vous comprenne. *To behave so as to annoy one's neighbours,* se conduire de façon à incommoder ses voisins. **II.** **so,** *conj.* **1.** Donc ; c'est pourquoi. *He did not reappear and so he was thought dead,* il ne reparut plus, si bien qu'on le crut mort. **2.** So there you are! vous voilà donc ! *So you are not coming?* ainsi vous ne venez pas? So, my dear, I am reduced to . . ., enfin, ma fille, me voilà réduit à. . .
'so-and-so, *s. F:* (*a*) Mr So-and-so, Mrs So-and-so, Monsieur un tel, Madame une telle. (*b*) *I was asked to do so-and-so,* on me priait de faire ceci et cela. *She must have her coffee so-and-so,* il faut lui préparer son café de telle et telle manière. **'so-called,** *a.* **1.** Ainsi nommé. *The so-c. temperate zone,* la zone dite tempérée. **2.** A so-called doctor, un soi-disant docteur. So-called improvements, prétendus progrès. **'so so, 'so-so,** *a. & adv.* Médiocre(ment), comme ci comme ça. *I'm only so so,* ça ne va qu'à moitié. **Business is so so,** les affaires vont doucement.
soak¹ [souk], *s.* **1.** Trempe *f.* To put (sth.) in soak, tremper, mettre en trempe (le linge sale). **2.** *P:* Ivrogne *m.*
soak². **1.** *v.tr.* (*a*) Tremper, détremper. The rain soaked me to the skin, la pluie m'a trempé jusqu'aux os. (*b*) To soak sth. in sth., tremper qch. dans qch. *To s. a sponge,* imbiber une éponge. (*c*) *F:* Écorcher (un client). *To s. the rich,* faire payer les riches. **2.** *v.i.* (*a*) Baigner, tremper (*in sth.,* dans qch.). (*b*) S'infiltrer, s'imbiber (*into,* dans). (*c*) *P:* Boire comme une éponge ; s'ivrogner. **soak through,** *v.i.* S'infiltrer à travers (qch.). **soak up,** *v.tr.* Absorber, boire, imbiber. **soaked,** *a.* Trempé. Soaked to the skin, trempé jusqu'aux os. *S. ground,* sol détrempé. Oil-soaked rag, linge imbibé d'huile. **soaking¹,** *a.* **1.** Trempé. **2.** Soaking downpour, pluie battante. **soaking²,** *s.* (*a*) Trempage *m,* trempe *f.* (*b*) Trempée *f. F:* To get a soaking, se faire tremper.
soaker ['soukər], *s. F:* **1.** Biberon *m,* ivrogne *m.* **2.** Déluge *m* de pluie. *Yesterday was a (regular) s.,* hier il a plu du matin au soir.
soap¹ [soup], *s.* Savon *m.* Cake of soap, (pain *m* de) savon ; savonnette *f.* To wash sth. with soap, savonner qch The soap industry, l'industrie savonnière. **'soap-boiler,** *s.* Savonnier *m.* **'soap-box,** *s.* Caisse *f* à savon. *F:* Soap-box orator, orateur de carrefour. **'soap-bubble,** *s.* Bulle *f* de savon. **'soap-dish,** *s* Plateau *m* à savon. **'soap flakes,** *s.pl.* Savon *m* en paillettes. **'soap-maker,** *s.* Fabricant *m* de savon **'soap-stone,** *s. Miner:* Stéatite *f,* talc *m.* **'soap-suds,** *s.pl.* Eau *f* de savon. **'soap-works,** *s.pl.* Savonnerie *f.*
soap², *v.tr.* Savonner.
soapwort ['soupwəːrt], *s. Bot:* Sapona re *f.*

soapy ['soupi], a. 1. (a) Savonneux; couvert ou imprégné de savon. (b) S. taste, goût de savon. (c) S. potatoes, pommes de terre cireuses. 2. F: (Of pers.) Doucereux, onctueux.

soar ['sɔ:ər], v.i. (a) Prendre son essor; .monter, s'élever (dans les airs). F: Prices soared, les prix ont subi une hausse vertigineuse. Rents have soared, les loyers ont fait un bond. (b) To soar above the common herd, planer sur la foule. (c) Av: Faire du vol à voile. **soaring**[1], a. 1. (a) Qui monte dans les airs. (b) Soaring flight, vol plané 'd'un oiseau). 2. (Ambition) sans bornes. **soaring**[2], s. 1. (a) Essor m. (b) Hausse f (des prix). 2. Planement m (d'un oiseau). Av: Vol m à voile.

sob[1] [sɔb], s. Sanglot m. F: Sob-stuff, littérature f d'une sentimentalité larmoyante.

sob[2], v. (sobbed) 1. v.i. Sangloter; pousser des sanglots. 2. v.tr. (a) To sob (out) sth., dire qch. en sanglotant. (b) She was sobbing her heart out, elle pleurait à chaudes larmes.

sober[1] ['soubər], a. 1. (a) Sobre, modéré, tempéré. (b) Ca me, posé. As sober as a judge, sérieux comme un juge. Sober-paced, à pas mesurés. In sober earnest, bien sérieusement. (c) In his sober senses, ouissant de son bon sens. (d) Sober fact, fait réel. In sober fact, en réalité. (e) Sober colours, couleurs sobres, peu voyantes. 2. (a) Qui n'est pas ivre. He is never s., il est toujours ivre. To sleep oneself sober, cuver sa boisson, (in Fr.) son vin. (b) Qui ne s'enivre amais; tempérant. -ly, adv. (a) Sobrement, modérément. (b) Avec calme; tranquillement. **sober-'minded,** a. Sérieux; pondéré.

sober[2]. 1. v.tr. Dégriser, dessouler. This news sobered him, cette nouvelle l'a dégrisé. 2. v.i. To sober down. (a) S'assagir. (b) Se dégriser; se dessouler.

soberness ['soubərnəs], s. 1. (a) Sobriété f, modération f, tempérance f. (b) Calme m, tranquillité f. 2. To return to a state of s., se dessouler. **sobersides** ['soubərsaidz], s F: Personne grave, pondérée.

sobriety [so'braiəti], s. = SOBERNESS.

soccer ['sɔkər], s. F: Football-association m.

sociability [souʃə'biliti], s. Sociabilité f.

sociable ['souʃəbl], a. Sociable. To become more s., s'apprivoiser. **-ably,** adv. Sociablement, amicalement

sociableness ['souʃəblnəs], s. Sociabilité f.

social ['souʃ(ə)l], a. 1. Social, -aux. (a) Social problems, problèmes sociaux. Social reformer, réformateur f, -trice, de la société. Social service, œuvres fpl d'amélioration sociale. (b) Social events, mondanités f. Social gathering, (i) soirée f; (ii) réception f. S.a. ENGAGEMENT 1. (c) Social evening, petite soirée intime; réunion f. 2. Man is an essentially s. animal, l'homme est essentiellement sociable. **-ally,** adv. Socialement.

socialism ['souʃəlizm], s. Socialisme m. State socialism, étatisme m.

socialist ['souʃəlist], a. & s. Socialiste (mf).

socialistic [souʃə'listik], a. Socratique.

socialize ['souʃəla:iz], v.tr. Socialiser.

society [so'saiəti], s. 1. Société f. (a) Compagnie f (de qn). He is fond of s., il aime la compagnie. (b) Duties towards society, devoirs envers la société. (c) (High) society, la haute société. Fashionable society, le beau monde. To go into, move in, society, aller dans le monde. Society woman, mondaine f. Journ: Society news, mondanités f. 2. Société (de la Croix rouge, etc.); association f. Charitable society, œuvre f de bienfaisance.

sociological [souʃio'lɔdʒik(ə)l], a. Sociologique.

sociologist [souʃi'ɔlɔdʒist], s. Sociologue m.

sociology [souʃi'ɔlɔdʒi], s. Sociologie f.

sock[1] [sɔk], s. 1. Chaussette f. (Ladies') golf socks, ankle socks, socquettes f. S.a. PULL UP 1. 2. Semelle intérieure (en liège, etc.). 3. A.Th: Sock and buskin, le socque et le cothurne.

sock[2], s. P: Coup m, gnon m; (in the eye) pochon m. To give s.o. socks, flanquer à qn une bonne raclée.

sock[3], v.tr. & i. P: 1. To sock a brick at s.o., lancer un briqueton à qn. 2. To sock (into) s.o., flanquer une beigne à qn.

socket ['sɔket], s. 1. (a) Emboîture f, douille f; godet m (de pied de machine). El: Lamp socket, douille de lampe. (b) Crapaudine f (de gouvernail). (c) Bobèche f (de chandelle). (d) Emplanture f (d'aile d'avion). (e) Cuissard m (de jambe artificielle). 2. Anat: (a) Alvéole m or f (de dent). (b) Eye-socket, orbite f de l'œil; (of horse) salière f. (c) Cavité f articulaire, glène f (d'un os). S.a BALL[1] 1. '**socket-joint,** s. Joint m à rotule.

socle [sɔkl], s. Arch: Socle m.

Socrates ['sɔkratiːz]. Pr.n.m. Socrate.

Socratic [so'kratik], a. Socratique.

sod [sɔd], s. 1. Gazon m. F: Under the sod, enterré. 2. Motte f de gazon. To cut the first sod, enlever le premier coup de bêche.

soda ['soudə], s. 1. (a) Ch: Soude f. Caustic soda, soude caustique. (b) Com: Washing soda, common soda, soude du commerce; carbonate m de soude; F: cristaux mpl (de soude). (c) Cooking soda, baking soda, bicarbonate m de soude. 2. = SODA-WATER. '**soda-fountain,** s. Bar m pour glaces et rafraîchissements. '**soda-water,** s. Eau f de seltz; soda m.

sodden [sɔdn], a. 1. (a) (Of field) (Dé)trempé. (b) (Of bread) Mal cuit; pâteux. 2. Sodden with drink, abruti par l'alcool.

sodium ['soudiəm], s. Ch: Sodium m. Sodium nitrate, azotate m de soude. Sodium chloride, chlorure m de sodium.

soever [so'evər], adv. Lit: In any way soever, n'importe comment. How great soever it may be, quelque grand que ce soit.

sofa ['soufa], s. Furn: Sofa m, canapé m.

soffit ['sɔfit], s. Arch: Soffite m.

soft [sɔft]. I. a. 1. Mou, f. molle. (a) As soft as butter, mou comme le beurre. Soft pencil, crayon tendre. Com: Soft fruit, fruits rouges. S.a. CORN[2] 1, PALATE, ROE[2]. (b) Soft to the touch, mou, doux,. au toucher; moelleux. S. hair, cheveux flous. As soft as silk, doux comme du satin. Com: Soft goods, matières f textiles; tissus m. (c) Soft muscles, muscles mous, flasques. 2. Doux, f. douce. Soft rain, pluie douce. Soft water, eau qui n'est pas dure. Soft outline, contour mou, flou. Soft voice, voix douce. S.a. PEDAL[1] 2. Soft step, pas feutré, ouaté. Ling: Soft consonant, consonne douce. F: Soft job, emploi facile et agréable. To have a soft time of it, P: se la couler douce. U.S: Soft drinks, boissons non alcooliques. (b) Soft words, mots doux, tendres. Soft heart, cœur tendre. To have a soft place in one's heart for s.o., avoir un faible pour qn. F: To be soft on s.o., être épris de qn. S.a. SIDE[1] 3. 3. a. & s. Soft (person), niais, -aise. He's gone soft! il a perdu la boule! -ly, adv. 1. (a) Doucement. To tread s.) marcher sans bruit. (b) Tendrement. 2. Mollement. II. adv. Doucement. '**soft-'boiled,** a. (Œuf) mollet. '**soft-'headed,** a. Faible de cerveau, d'esprit. '**soft-'hearted,**

a. Au cœur tendre; compatissant. **'soft-'sawder**[1], *s.* *F:* Flatterie *f*, patelinage *m*. **soft-'sawder**[2], *v.tr.* *F:* Flatter, louanger (qn); faire du plat à (qn). **'soft-'soap,** *s.* **1.** Savon vert, noir. **2.** = SOFT-SAWDER[1]. **'soft-'spoken,** *a.* Mielleux, doucereux. **'soft-'tack,** *s.* *Nau:* Pain *m*. **'soft-'witted,** *a.* = SOFT-HEADED.

soften [sɔfn]. **1.** *v.tr.* (*a*) Amollir, ramollir. (*b*) Assouplir (le cuir). (*c*) Affaiblir, énerver. Troops softened by idleness, troupes amollies par l'oisiveté. (*d*) Adoucir (sa voix). *Curtains that s. the light,* rideaux qui tamisent la lumière. (*e*) Attendrir, émouvoir (qn). (*f*) Soulager (la douleur). **2.** *v.i.* (*a*) S'amollir, se ramollir. (*b*) S'attendrir. **softening,** *s.* (*a*) Amollissement *m*. Softening of the brain, ramollissement *m* du cerveau. (*b*) Assouplissement *m* (du cuir). (*c*) Adoucissement *m* du caractère. (*d*) Attendrissement *m*.

softness ['sɔftnəs], *s.* **1.** Douceur *f* (de la peau, du climat); tiédeur *f* (de l'air). **2.** (*a*) Mollesse *f* (de caractère); manque *m* d'énergie. (*b*) Flou *m* (des contours). **3.** Niaiserie *f*, simplicité *f*.

softy ['sɔfti], *s.* *F:* = SOFT I. 3.

soggy ['sɔgi], *a.* Détrempé; saturé d'eau.

soil[1] [sɔil], *s.* (*a*) Sol *m*, terrain *m*, terre *f*. *Rich s.*, terre grasse. **Artificial soil,** terres de rapport. Light soil, loose soil, terre meuble. (*b*) *Lit:* One's native soil, le sol natal. Son of the soil, fils de la terre.

soil[2], *v.tr.* (*a*) Souiller, salir. (*b*) Stuff that soils easily, étoffe qui se salit facilement. **soiled,** *a.* Souillé, sali, défraîchi. Soiled linen, linge sale.

sojourn[1] ['sɔdʒərn, 'sʌdʒərn], *s.* *A.* & *Lit:* **1.** Séjour *m*. **2.** Lieu *m* de séjour.

sojourn[2], *v.i.* *Lit:* Séjourner. **sojourning,** *s.* Séjour *m*.

sol [sɔl], *s.* *Mus:* Sol *m*. **'sol-'fa**[1], *s.* *Mus:* (*a*) Solmisation *f*. (*b*) Solfège *m*. **'sol-'fa**[2], *v.tr.* *Mus:* Solfier.

sola ['soulə], *s.* *Bot:* Æschynomène *f*. Sola topee, casque colonial.

solace[1] ['sɔles], *s.* *Lit:* Consolation *f*, soulagement *m*.

solace[2], *v.tr.* *Lit:* Conso·er (qn); soulager, adoucir (la douleur de qn).

solan(-goose) ['soulən('gu:s)], *s.* *Orn:* Fou *m*.

solanaceae [sɔlə'neisiï], *s.pl.* *Bot:* Solan(ac)ées *f*.

solar ['soulər], *a.* (Système) solaire.

solarize ['souləra:iz], *v.tr.* *Phot:* Solariser.

solatium [so'leiʃiəm], *s.* (Somme donnée à titre de) compensation *f*.

sold [sould]. *See* SELL[2].

solder[1] ['sɔldər, 'soudər, 'sɔdər], *s.* Soudure *f*. Soft solder, (i) soudure tendre; (ii) *F:* = SOFT-SAWDER[1].

solder[2], *v.tr.* Souder; ressouder. **'soldering-bit,** *s.* *Tls:* Fer *m* à souder; soudoir *m*. **'soldering-lamp,** *s.* Lampe *f* à souder à braser.

soldier[1] ['souldʒər], *s.* **1.** (*a*) Soldat *m*. *Three soldiers and two civilians,* trois militaires *m* et deux civils. Private soldier, simple soldat. Old soldier, ancien soldat; vétéran *m*. *S.a.* COME 8. Tin soldier, soldat de plomb. Soldier of fortune, soldat, officier *m*, de fortune. (*b*) Tacticien *m*, stratégiste *m*. (*c*) *Nau:* *F:* (i) Fainéant *m*; (ii) marin *m* d'eau douce. **2.** (*a*) *Ent:* Soldier (-ant), soldat des bois. (*b*) *Crust:* Soldier(-crab), soldat marin, bernard-l'ermite *m*. **3.** *P:* Hareng saur. **'soldier-man,** *pl.* **-men,** *s.* *F:* Soldat *m*; militaire *m*.

soldier[2], *v.i.* Faire le métier de soldat. **soldiering,** *s.* Le métier de soldat, des armes.

soldierly ['souldʒərli], *a.* De soldat. **Soldierly bearing,** allure martiale, militaire.

soldiery ['souldʒəri], *s.* *Coll.* **1.** Soldats *mpl*, militaires *mpl*. **2.** *Pej:* Soldatesque *f*.

sole[1] [soul], *s.* **1.** Plante *f* (du pied). **2.** Semelle *f* (de chaussure). **3.** Semelle (de rabot, de crosse de golf, etc.).

sole[2], *v.tr.* (*a*) Mettre une semelle à (un soulier). (*b*) Ressemeler. **soling,** *s.* (*a*) Mise *f* d'une semelle. (*b*) Ressemelage *m*.

sole[3], *s.* *Ich:* Sole *f*.

sole[4], *a.* Seul, unique. The sole management, l'entière direction. Sole right, droit exclusif. Sole agent, agent exclusif. Sole legatee, légataire universel. **-ly,** *adv.* Uniquement. Solely responsable, seul responsable.

solecism ['sɔlisizm], *s.* **1.** *Gram:* Solécisme *m*; faute *f* de grammaire. **2.** *S. in conduct,* so'écisme de conduite; faute contre le savoir-vivre.

solemn ['sɔləm], *a.* **1.** Solennel. Solemn fact, réalité sérieuse. Solemn duty, devoir sacré. Solemn ceremony, solennité *f*. It is the solemn truth, je vous jure que c'est vrai. **2.** Grave, sérieux. To keep a s. face, composer son visage. **-ly,** *adv.* **1.** Solennellement. **2.** Gravement, sérieusement.

solemnity [so'lemniti], *s.* **1.** (*a*) Solennité *f*. (*b*) Gravité *f* (de maintien). **2.** Fête solennelle.

solemnization [sɔləmnai'zei\(ə)n], *s.* Solennisation *f*; célébration *f* (d'un mariage).

solemnize ['sɔləmnaːiz], *v.tr.* **1.** Solenniser (une fête); célébrer (un mariage). **2.** Prêter de la solennité à (une occasion).

solenoid [so'liːnɔid], *s.* *El:* Solénoïde *m*.

solfatara [sɔlfa'taːra], *s.* *Geol:* Solfatare *f*.

solfeggio [sɔl'fedʒio], *s.* *Mus:* Solfège *m*.

solicit [so'lisit], *v.tr.* Solliciter (une faveur). To solicit s.o. for sth., solliciter qch. de qn. To solicit votes, solliciter, briguer, des voix. To s. a government post, postuler un emploi (de fonction-naire).

solicitation [solisi'tei\(ə)n], *s.* Sollicitation *f*.

solicitor [so'lisitər], *s.* *Jur:* Avoué *m*, solicitor *m*. The Solicitor General, le conseiller juridique de la Couronne.

solicitous [so'lisitəs], *a.* Soucieux, désireux (*of*, de). Solicitous about sth., préoccupé de qch. To be solicitous for s.o.'s comfort, avoir à cœur le confort de qn. To be solicitous of sth., désirer qch. **-ly,** *adv.* Avec sollicitude; soucieusement.

solicitousness [so'lisitəsnəs], **solicitude** [so'lisitjuːd], *s.* Sollicitude *f*, souci *m*.

solid ['sɔlid]. **1.** *a.* Solide. (*a*) Solid food, aliment solide. To become solid, se solidifier. (*b*) To build on solid foundations, bâtir sur le solide. Steps cut in the solid rock, escalier taillé dans la pierre vi·e. (*c*) Solid common sense, solide bon sens. (*d*) Plein, massif. Solid contents, volume plein. Solid mahogany table, table en acajou massif. Pond frozen solid, étang gelé jusqu'au fond. *Typ:* Matter set solid, texte non inter-ligné. Solid measures, mesures de volume. *S.a.* GEOMETRY. *F:* To sleep for nine solid hours, dormir neuf heures d'affilée. Solid vote, vote unanime. (*e*) En une seule pièce. Parts cast solid, parties (coulées) monobloc. **2.** *s.* Solide *m*. **-ly,** *adv.* **1.** Solidement. **2.** To vote solidly for sth., voter qch. à l'unanimité.

solidarity [sɔli'dariti], *s.* Solidarité *f*.

solidification [sɔlidifi'kei\(ə)n], *s.* (i) Solidifica-tion *f*; (ii) congélation *f* (de l'huile).

solidify [so'lidifai]. **1.** *v.tr.* Sol·difier; concréter

(l'huile). **2.** *v.i.* (i) Se solidifier ; (ii) se figer ;
se congeler.
solidity [so'liditi], *s.* Solidité *f.*
soliloquize [so'lilokwa:iz], *v.i.* Monologuer ; se
parler à soi-même.
soliloquy [so'lilokwi], *s.* Soliloque *m* ; monologue (intérieur).
solitaire [sɔli'teər], *s.* **1.** Solitaire *m* (diamant
de bague). **2.** *Games :* Solitaire.
solitary ['sɔlitəri], *a.* (*a*) Solitaire ; qui est ou
qui se sent seul. *F :* Not a solitary one, pas un
seul. *S.a.* CONFINEMENT 1. (*b*) (Lieu) solitaire,
retiré. **-ily,** *adv.* Solitairement.
solitude ['sɔlitjuːd], *s.* **1.** Solitude *f,* isolement *m.*
2. (*a*) Lieu *m* solitaire. (*b*) Lieu inhabité.
solo, *pl.* **-os, -i** ['soulo, -ouz, -iː], *s.* **1.** *Mus :*
Solo *m.* To play solo, jouer en solo. Violin solo,
solo de violon. Solo violin, violon solo. **2.** *Cards :*
Solo whist, whist *m* de Gand. To go solo, jouer
solo.
soloist ['soulɔist], *s.* *Mus :* Soliste *mf.*
Solomon ['sɔləmən]. *Pr.n.m.* Salomon. '**Solomon's 'seal,** *s. Bot :* Sceau *m* de Salomon.
solstice ['sɔlstis], *s.* *Astr :* Solstice *m.*
solubility [sɔlju'biliti], *s.* **1.** Solubilité *f* (d'un
sel). **2.** To question the s. of a problem, mettre
en doute s'il est possible de résoudre un
problème.
soluble ['sɔljubl], *a.* **1.** Soluble. **2.** (Problème)
soluble, résoluble.
solution [so'ljuːʃ(ə)n], *s.* Solution *f.* **1.** (*a*) Dissolution *f.* (*b*) *Ch :* Standard solution, liqueur
titrée ; solution normale. *Aut :* (Rubber) solution, (dis)solution (de caoutchouc). **2.** (*a*) (Ré)so-
lution *f* (d'une équation). (*b*) (*Answer*) Solution.
3. Solution of continuity, solution de continuité.
solvability [sɔlvə'biliti], *s.* **1.** Solvabilité *f* (d'un
commerçant). **2.** Résolubilité *f* (d'un problème).
solvable ['sɔlvabl], *a.* (Problème) réso'uble.
solve [sɔlv], *v.tr.* Résoudre (un problème). To
solve a riddle, trouver le mot d'une énigme.
solvency ['sɔlvənsi], *s.* Solvabilité *f.*
solvent ['sɔlvənt]. **I.** *a.* *Com :* So vable.
2. *a. & s.* Dissolvant (*m*).
solver ['sɔlvər], *s.* Celui qui trouve la solution
du problème.
Somaliland [so'mɑːliland]. *Pr.n.* La Somalie.
sombre ['sɔmbər], *a.* Sombre morne. **-ly,** *adv.*
Sombrement.
some¹ [sʌm]. ¹. *a.* **1.** Quelque, quelconque.
(*a*) *S. other solution will have to be found,* il
faudra trouver quelque autre solution. In some
form or (an)other, sous une forme ou sous une
autre. He will arrive some day, il arrivera un de
ces jours. Some way or another, d'une manière
ou d'une autre. To make some sort of reply,
répondre d'une façon quelconque. (*b*) *Give it to
s. lawyer or other,* remettez-le aux mains de
n'importe quel notaire. *To ask s. experienced
person,* se rapporter à l'avis de quelqu'un qui a,
qui ait, de l'expérience. **2.** (*Partitive*) De. To
drink some water, boire de l'eau. *To eat s. fruit,*
manger des fruits. *Can you give me s. lunch?*
pouvez-vous me donner à déjeuner ? **3.** (*a*) Quelque. Some distance away, à quelque distance de
là. To some degree, quelque peu ; à un certain
degré. After some time, après un certain temps.
It takes some time, cela prend pas mal de temps.
At some length, assez longuement. (*b*) (*In the pl.*)
There are some others, il y en a d'autres. Some
days ago, il y a quelques jours. Some days he is
better, certains jours il va mieux. **4.** *U.S :* *P :*
(*Intensive*) He's some doctor, c'est un médecin
à la hauteur. It was some dinner. c'était un

chouette dîner. **II. some,** *pron.* **1.** *Pers.* Certains.
Some agree with us, and some disagree, es uns
sont de notre avis, d'autres ne le sont pas. *We
scattered, some one way, some another,* on se
dispersa, qui d'un côté, qui de l'autre. **2.** I have
some, j'en ai. Take some! prenez-en ! *Give me
s. of that wine,* donnez-moi de ce vin. Some of
them, quelques-uns d'entre eux. *I agree with s.
of what you say,* je suis d'accord avec une partie
de ce que vous dites. *F :* *He's up to all the tricks
and then s.,* il les sait toutes et une par-dessus.
III. some, *adv.* **1.** (*a*) Environ, quelque *inv.*
Some twenty pounds, une vingtaine de livres.
S. five hundred people, environ cinq cents personnes ; quelque cinq cents personnes. (*b*) I
waited some few minutes, j'ai attendu quelques
minutes. **2.** *U.S :* *P :* *It amused me s.,* ça m'a
pas mal amusé.
somebody ['sʌmbodi], **someone** 'sʌmwʌn], *s.*
or pron. Quelqu'un. **1.** *S. told me so,* quelqu'un,
on, me l'a dit. Somebody is knocking, on frappe.
Somebody passing at the time, un passant.
Somebody or other has told him . . ., je ne sais
qui lui a dit. . . . Mr Somebody (or other),
Monsieur Chose. **2.** (*pl.* somebodies ['sʌmbodiz])
He's (a) somebody, c'est un personnage. He
thinks he's somebody, il se croit quelqu'un.
somehow ['sʌmhau], *adv.* **1.** De façon ou d'autre,
d'une manière ou d'une autre. **2.** I never liked
him somehow, je ne sais pourquoi mais il ne m'a
jamais été sympathique.
someone ['sʌmwʌn], *pron.* = SOMEBODY.
somersault ['sʌmərsɔlt], *s.* (*a*) (*Accidental*) To
turn a somersault, (*of pers.*) faire la culbute ; *Aut :*
Av : capoter, faire panache. (*b*) *Gym :* Saut
périlleux.
something ['sʌmθiŋ]. l. *s. or pron.* Quelque
chose *m.* **1.** (*a*) *Say s.,* dites quelque chose.
Something or other, une chose ou une autre.
S. or other went wrong, je ne sais quoi a cloché.
There's s. the matter with him, il a quelque chose.
Something to drink, de quoi boire. *To ask for
s. to drink,* demander à boire. *F :* Will you take
something? voulez-vous boire, manger, quelque
chose ? To give s.o. something for himself,
donner un pourboire à qn. To give s.o. something to live for, donner à qn une raison de vivre.
I have something else to do, j'ai autre chose à
faire. The four something train, le train de
quatre heures et quelque chose. (*b*) An indefinable something, un je ne sais quoi d'indéfinissable.
2. (*a*) To speak with something of a foreign
accent, parler avec un accent plus ou moins
étranger. He's something of a miser, il est un
peu, tant soit peu, avare. *Perhaps we shall see s.
of you now,* peut-être que maintenant on vous
verra un peu. (*b*) There's something in what
you say ; there's something in that, il y a un fond
de vérité dans ce que vous dites. There's something in him, il a du fond. Well, that's something! bon, c'est toujours quelque chose !
II. something, *adv.* (*a*) Quelque peu, tant soit
peu. Something after the French style, un peu
dans le style français. That's something 'like a
cigar! voilà un vrai cigare ! *S.a.* LIKE¹ I. 2. *He
is s. under forty,* il a un peu moins de quarante
ans. (*b*) *P :* He treated me something shocking,
il m'a traité d'une façon abominable.
sometime ['sʌmtaim], *adv.* **1.** Autrefois, jadis.
Mr X, my sometime tutor, M. X, autrefois mon
précepteur. **2.** Sometime (or other), tôt ou tard.
Sometime before dawn, avant l'aube. Sometime
last year, au cours de l'année dernière. Sometime
soon, bientôt.

sometimes ['sʌmtaimz], *adv.* Quelquefois, parfois. Sometimes the one, sometimes the other, tantôt l'un, tantôt l'autre.

someway ['sʌmwei], *adv.* F: De façon ou d'autre.

somewhat ['sʌmhwɔt]. **I.** *adv.* Quelque· peu ; un peu ; tant soit peu. It is somewhat difficult, c'est assez difficile. To be somewhat surprised, être passab'ement étonné. We treat him s. as he treated us, nous le traitons à peu près de la même façon qu'il nous a traités. **2.** *s.* He was somewhat of a coward, il était quelque peu poltron.

somewhere ['sʌmhwɛər], *adv.* **I.** Quelque part. S. near us, pas bien loin de chez nous. Somewhere in the world, de par le monde. Somewhere else, ailleurs ; autre part. Somewhere or other, je ne sais où. F: I will see him somewhere first! qu'il aille au diable ! **2.** He is somewhere about fifty, il a environ cinquante ans.

somnambulism [sɔm'nambjulizm], *s.* Somnambulisme *m*, noctambulisme *m*.

somnambulist [sɔm'nambjulist], *s.* Somnambule *mf*, noctambule *mf*.

somnolence ['sɔmnoləns], *s.* Somnolence *f*.

somnolent ['sɔmnolənt], *a.* Somnolent.

son [sʌn], *s.m.* Fils. How is your son? comment va votre fils? F: comment va votre garçon? S.a. MOTHER[1] I. **'son-in-law,** *s.m.* Gendre.

sonant ['sounənt]. *Ling:* **I.** *a.* Sonore. **2.** *s.* Consonne *f* sonore.

sonata [so'nɑːta], *s.* *Mus:* Sonate *f*.

sonatina [sɔnə'tiːna], *s.* *Mus:* Sonatine *f*.

song [sɔŋ], *s.* **I.** Chant *m*. To burst into song, se mettre tout à coup à chanter. **2.** (*a*) Chanson *f*. Give us a song, chantez-nous quelque chose. *Mus:* Song without words, romance *f* sans paroles. Marching song, chanson de route. F: To buy sth. for an old song, for a song, acheter qch. à vil prix. To make a song about sth., faire des embarras à propos de qch. (*b*) *Lit:* Song of victory, chant de victoire. The Song of Roland, la Chanson de Roland. *Gr.Ant:* Song of triumph, péan *m*. (*c*) The Song of Songs, le Cantique des Cantiques. **'song-bird,** *s.* Oiseau chanteur. **'song-book,** *s.* Recueil *m* de chansons ; chansonnier *m*. **'song-thrush,** *s.* Grive chanteuse. **'song-writer,** *s.* Chansonnier, -ière.

songster ['sɔŋstər], *s.m.* **I.** Chanteur. **2.** Oiseau chanteur.

sonnet ['sɔnet], *s.* *Pros:* Sonnet *m*. Sonnetwriter, sonnettiste *mf*.

sonny ['sʌni], *s.m.* F: Mon petit, mon fiston.

sonority [so'nɔriti], *s.* Sonorité *f*.

sonorous ['sɔ'nɔːrəs], *a.* Sonore. **-ly,** *adv.* D'un ton sonore.

sonorousness [so'nɔːrəsnəs], *s.* Sonorité *f*.

soon [suːn], *adv.* **I.** (*a*) Bientôt, tôt. Soon after, bientôt après ; peu après. See you again soon! à bientôt ! It will s. be three years since . . ., voici tantôt trois ans que. . . . How soon may I expect you? quand devrai-je vous attendre? How s. can you be ready? en combien de temps serez-vous prêt? Too soon, trop tôt ; avant le temps. I got out of the house none too soon, je m'éc'appa de la maison juste à temps. S.a. MEND[2] I. 3. (*b*) As soon as, so soon as, aussitôt que, dès que. As soon as possible, le plus tôt possible ; aussitôt que possible. (*c*) I would as soon stay, j'aime autant rester. **2.** (*a*) The sooner the better, le plus tôt sera le mieux. Sooner or later, tôt ou tard. No sooner said than done, aussitôt dit, aussitôt fait. No sooner had he finished than he was seized, à peine eut-il fini qu'il fut arrêté. (*b*) Death sooner than slavery,

plutôt la mort que ''escl.vage. I would sooner die, j'aimerais mieux mourir ; plutôt mourir !

soot[1] [sut], *s.* **I.** Suie *f*. **2.** *I.C.E:* Encrasment *m*, calamine *f*.

soot[2], *v.tr.* *I.C.E:* To soot up the plugs, encrasser, suiffer, les bougies. (O/ plugs) To soot up, s'encrasser.

sooth [suːθ], *s.* *A:* Vérité *f*. Sooth to say . . ., à vrai dire. . . .

soothe [suːð], *v.tr.* Ca·mer, apa·ser (la douleur) ; tranquilliser (l'esprit). **soothing,** *a.* Ca·mant, apaisan.. *Med:* Lénitif. **-ly,** *adv.* Avec douceur.

soothsayer ['suːθseiər], *s.* *Lit:* Devin *m*, *f.* devineresse.

soothsaying ['suːθseiiŋ], *s.* *Lit:* Divination *f*.

sooty ['suti], *a.* **I.** Couvert de suie ; noir de suie. **2.** Qui contient de la suie ; fuligineux. S. deposit, (i) dépôt *m* de suie ; (ii) dépôt de calamine.

sop[1] [sɔp], *s.* **I.** Morceau de pain trempé. **2.** (*a*) Pot-de-vin *m*. (*b*) F: Sop to Cerberus, don *m* propitiatoire.

sop[2], *v.tr.* (sopped [sɔpt]). **I.** Tremper (le pain). **2.** To sop up a liquid, éponger un liquide.

sopping, *a.* Sopping wet, tout trempé.

Sophia [so'faia]. *Pr.n.f.* Sophie.

sophism ['sɔfizm], *s.* Sophisme *m*.

sophist ['sɔfist], *s.* Sophiste *m*.

sophistic(al) [so'fistik(əl)], *a.* Sophistique ; (argument) captieux.

sophisticated [so'fistikeitid], *a.* Au goût perverti ; aux goûts compliqués ; blasé.

sophistry ['sɔfistri], *s.* **I.** Sophistique *f*. To indulge in s., sophistiquer. **2.** Sophisme *m*.

soporific [sɔpo'rifik], *a. & s.* Somnifère (*m*), soporifique (*m*), soporatif (*m*).

soppy ['sɔpi], *a.* **I.** (Terrain) détrempé. **2.** (*a*) (Of pers.) Mou, *f.* molle ; flasque. (*b*) (Of sentiment) Fadasse ; larmoyant.

sopranist [so'prɑːnist], *s.* *Mus:* Soprano *mf*.

soprano, *pl.* **-os, -i** [so'prɑːno, -ouz, -iː], *s.* *Mus:* Soprano *mf*. Soprano voice, voix de soprano.

sorb [sɔːrb], *s.* *Bot:* **I.** Sorb(-apple), sorbe *f*. **2.** Sorb(-apple) (tree), sorbier *m*, cormier *m*.

sorbet ['sɔːrbet], *s.* Sorbet *m*.

sorcerer ['sɔːrsərər], *s.m.* Sorcier ; magicien.

sorceress ['sɔːrsəres], *s.f.* Sorcière ; magicienne.

sorcery ['sɔːrsəri], *s.* Sorcellerie *f*.

sordid ['sɔːrdid], *a.* Sordide. (*a*) Sale, crasseux. (*b*) Bas, vil. **-ly,** *adv.* Sordidement.

sordidness ['sɔːrdidnəs], *s.* Sordidité *f*. (*a*) Saleté *f*. (*b*) Bassesse *f*. (*c*) Avarice *f* sordide.

sore[1] ['sɔːər]. I. *a.* **I.** (*a*) Douloureux, endolori. To be sore all over, avoir mal partout. (*b*) Enflammé, irrité. Sore eyes, yeux malades. *S.a.* SIGHT[1] 5. Sore throat, mal *m* de gorge. (*c*) Ulcéré. F: To put one's finger on the sore place, mettre le doigt sur la plaie. (*d*) F: That's his sore spot, c'est son endroit sensible. **2.** Chagriné. To be sore at heart, être désolé. To be sore about sth., être chagriné au sujet de qch. **3.** To be in sore need of sth., avoir grandement besoin de qch. S. trial, cruelle épreuve. S. temptation, tentation difficile à vaincre. **-ly,** *adv.* S. wounded, gravement, grièvement, blessé. Sorely tried, fort éprouvé ; cruellement éprouvé. II. *sore,* *adv.* Sore distressed, dans une grande détresse.

sore[2], *s.* (*a*) Plaie *f* ; (chafe) blessure *f*, écorchure *f*. F: To (re)open an old sore, évoquer un souvenir pénible ; raviver une ancienne plaie. (*b*) Ulcère *m*.

soreness ['sɔːrnəs], *s.* **I.** Endolorissement *m*.

2. (*a*) Chagrin *m*, peine *f*. (*b*) Sentiment *m* de rancune.

sorghum ['sɔːrgəm], *s*. Bot: Sorg(h)o *m*.

sorites [so'raitiːz], *s*. Log: Sorite *m*.

sorrel[1] ['sɔrəl], *s*. Bot: Oseille *f*. Salts of sorrel, sel *m* d'oseille.

sorrel[2], *a. & s.* (Cheval) alezan (*m*).

sorrow[1] ['sɔrou, 'sɔro], *s*. Peine *f*, chagrin *m*, tristesse *f*. To be sorrow-stricken. être accablé de douleur. To my sorrow, à mon regret.

sorrow[2], *v.i.* S'affliger, être affligé (*over, at, about, sth.*, de qch.). To sorrow after s.o., pleurer qn.

sorrowing, *a.* Affligé.

sorrowful ['sɔrəful], *a.* Affligé, chagriné; triste; (*of news, etc.*) attristant, pénible. **-fully,** *adv.* Tristement; avec chagrin.

sorry ['sɔri], *a.* **1.** (*a*) Fâché, chagriné, désolé, peiné.' *F:* You will be sorry for it, il vous en cuira. I am extremely s., je regrette infiniment. I'm sorry for that, j'en suis bien fâché. Sorry to have kept you, pardon de vous avoir retenu. Sorry! pardon! je regrette! Awfully sorry! je vous demande mille fois pardon! (*b*) I am sorry for him, je le plains. *F:* To look sorry for oneself, faire piteuse mine. **2.** Mauvais; misérable. *S. steed*, méchant cheval. *S. jest*, mauvaise plaisanterie. *S. excuse*, piètre excuse. To cut a sorry figure, faire piteuse figure.

sort[1] [sɔːrt], *s*. **1.** (*a*) Sorte *f*, genre *m*, espèce *f*. What sort of tree is it? quelle sorte d'arbre est-ce? Of all sorts, de toutes sortes. All sorts of men, des hommes de toutes sortes. *F:* These sort of people, les gens de cette espèce. *A strange s. of fellow*, un type bizarre. That's the sort of man he is, voilà comme il est. *F:* She's a (real) good sort, c'est une brave fille. *He looks a good s.*, il a l'air bon garçon. *F:* That's the sort of thing I mean, c'est à peu près ce que je veux dire. I can't stand that s. of thing, je ne peux pas souffrir tout ça. Something of that sort, quelque chose dans ce genre-là. Nothing of the sort, (i) rien de semblable; (ii) pas du tout! I shall do nothing of the s., je n'en ferai rien. A writer of some sort, quelque vague écrivain. To make some sort of excuse, faire des excuses quelconques. There is no sort of reason for this, il n'y a aucune raison pour cela. I have a sort of idea that . . ., j'ai comme une idée, j'ai une sorte d'idée, que. . . . A s. of sour taste, un goût plutôt aigre. *F:* I sort of feel that . . ., j'ai une sorte d'impression que. . . . *The good news s. of cheered him up*, cette bonne nouvelle l'a comme qui dirait ragaillardi. (*b*) *Pej:* We had coffee of sorts, of a sort, on nous a donné du soi-disant café. *A peace of sorts*, une paix telle quelle. (*c*) *Typ:* Sorte. Missing sort, short sort, sorte manquante. (*d*) To be out of sorts, (i) être indisposé; ne pas être dans son assiette; *F:* être patraque; (ii) être de mauvaise humeur. **2.** In some sort, à un certain degré; jusqu'à un certain point. *A translation* after a sort, ce qui peut passer pour une traduction.

sort[2], *v.tr.* (*a*) Trier, assortir; débrouiller (des papiers, etc.). To sort rags, séparer des chiffons; faire le tri des chiffons. To sort (out) articles, classifier, lotir, les articles. *Post:* To sort the letters, trier les lettres. (*b*) To sort out sth. from sth., faire le départ entre qch. et qch. *To s. out the bad ones*, trier les mauvais; faire le tri des mauvais. **sorting**, *s*. Triage *m*, tri *m*; classement *m*. *Post:* Sorting-office, bureau *m* de tri.

sorter ['sɔːrtər], *s*. (*a*) Trieur, -euse; classeur, -euse. *Post:* Letter sorter, trieur de lettres. (*b*) (*Device*) Trieur (de minerai).

sortie ['sɔːrtiː], *s*. Mil: Sortie *f*.

sot[1] [sɔt], *s*. Personne abrutie par l'alcool; ivrogne *m*; *P:* soûlard *m*.

sot[2], *v.i.* (sotted) S'abrutir (dans l'ivresse).

sottish ['sɔtiʃ], *a.* Abruti par .'alcool; (air) d'ivrogne.

sotto voce ['sɔtto'voutʃe], *adv.* (*a*) (Causer) tout bas, à demi-voix. (*b*) *Mus:* Sotto-voce; (chanter) à demi-voix; (jouer) à demi-jeu.

Soudan (the) [ðəsuː'dan]. *Pr.n.* Le Soudan.

Soudanese [sudɑ'niːz], *a. & s.* Soudanais, -aise.

sough[1] [sau, sʌf], *s*. Murmure *m*, susurration *f*, frémissement *m* (du vent, etc.).

sough[2], *v.i.* (*Of wind, etc.*) Murmurer, susurrer.

sought [sɔːt]. *See* SEEK.

soul [soul], *s*. Âme *f*. **I.** (*a*) With all my soul, de tout mon cœur; de toute mon âme. I cannot for the soul of me, je ne le ferais pour rien au monde. Upon my soul! sur mon âme! To 'make one's soul,' se recueillir (avant la confession). He has a soul above money, il est au-dessus des préoccupations d'argent. *S.a.* BODY 1, HEART[1] 2 (*d*), LIFE 1. (*b*) *He is the s.* of the enterprise, c'est lui qui est le premier mobile de l'entreprise. *S.a.* HONOUR[1] 3. **2.** Departed souls, les âmes des trépassés. God rest his soul! que Dieu ait son âme! **3.** (*a*) Population of a thousand souls, population de mille âmes. Ship lost with all souls, navire perdu corps et biens. Without meeting a living soul, sans rencontrer âme qui vive. (*b*) He's a good soul, c'est une bonne âme; *F:* c'est une bonne pâte (d'homme). Poor soul! pauvre créature*f*! 'soul-killing, *a.* (Emploi) abrutissant. 'soul-stirring, *a.* Qui remue l'âme; émouvant.

soulful ['soulful], *a.* (*a*) Plein d'âme. *S. eyes*, yeux expressifs. *S. music*, musique qui émeut l'âme. (*b*) Sentimental, -aux.

soulless ['soulləs], *a.* **1.** Sans âme; terre à terre. **2.** (Emploi) abrutissant.

sound[1] [saund], *s*. (*a*) Son *m*, bruit *m*. Not a sound was heard, on n'entendait pas le mo ndre bruit. (*b*) Within (the) sound of . . ., à portée du son de. . . . To catch the sound of sth., entendre qch. à demi; entr'ouïr qch. *F:* I don't like the sound of it, cela ne me dit rien qui vaille. (*c*) (The science of) sound, l'acoustique *f*. 'sound-absorbing, *a.* Amortisseur (de son). 'sound-board, *s*. (*a*) Table *f* d'harmonie (de piano). (*b*) Tamis *m* (d'orgue). 'sound-box, *s*. **I.** *Mus:* Caisse *f* de résonance (d'un instrument à cordes). **2.** Diaphragme *m* (de gramophone). 'sound-deadening, *a.* (*Of material*) Insonore. 'sound-detector, *s*. Géophone *m*. 'sound-hole, *s*. *Mus:* Ouïe *f* (de violon, de guitare). 'sound-post, *s*. L'âme *f* (d'un violon). 'sound-proof, *a.* Impénétrable au son; (*of telephone box*) isolant; (*of film studio*) insonore. 'sound-proofed, *a.* Insonorisé. 'sound-record, *s*. *Cin: etc:* Phonogramme *m*. 'sound-track, *s*. *Cin:* Piste *f* sonore (d'un film). 'sound-wave, *s*. Onde *f* sonore.

sound[2]. **I.** *v.i.* **1.** Sonner, résonner; retentir. *The garden bell, the electric bell, sounded*, la cloche du jardin tinta; le timbre électrique résonna, retentit. **2.** (*a*) *To s. like a drum*, avoir le son du tambour. To sound hollow, sonner creux; rendre un son creux. (*b*) Paraître, sembler. *Name that sounds French*, nom qui a une apparence française. *It sounded a long way off*, on aurait dit que cela venait de loin. That sounds well in a speech, cela fait bon effet dans un discours. *That sounds like heresy*, cela a l'air d'une hérésie. **II. sound,** *v.tr.* **1.** (*a*) Sonner (la cloche, le tocsin). *To s. the trumpet*, sonner de la trompette. *Aut:* **To sound the horn**, faire retentir l'avertisseur ; corner. (*b*) Proclamer (une vérité, etc.). *S.a.* PRAISE¹. **2.** Prononcer (une lettre). *To sound one's r's*, faire sonner les r. **3.** (*a*) *Med:* Ausculter ; (*by percussion*) percuter. (*b*) *Rail:* Vérifier (une roue) au marteau. **sounding¹,** *a.* **I.** (*Of style, etc.*) Sonore, pompeux ; ronflant. **2.** **Sharp-sounding,** au son aigu. *S.a.* HIGH-SOUNDING. **sounding²,** *s.* **I.** Résonnement *m* ; retentissement *m* (du tambour, etc.). **2.** *The s. of the retreat*, le signal de la retraite. **3.** *Med:* Auscultation *f* ; percussion *f*. **'sounding-board,** *s.* Abat-voix *m inv.*

sound³, *s. Surg:* Sonde *f*.

sound⁴. I. *v.tr* (*a*) *Nau:* Sonder. *Abs.* Prendre le fond. (*b*) *Surg:* Sonder (une plaie). (*c*) *F:* **To sound s.o.** (about sth.), questionner qn (relativement à qch.) ; *F:* tâter le pouls à qn. *To s. one's conscience*, interroger sa conscience. **2.** *v.i.* (*Of whale*) Faire la sonde ; foncer. **sounding³,** *s. Nau:* **I.** Sondage *m*. **2.** *pl.* (*a*) **To be in soundings,** être sur les sondes. **To be out of soundings,** être hors des sondes. (*b*) **To take soundings,** sonder ; prendre le fond. *What are the soundings?* quel est le fond ? **'sounding-balloon,** *s. Meteor:* Sonde aérienne. **'sounding-lead** [led], *s. Nau:* (Plomb *m* de) sonde *f*. **'sounding-machine,** *s. Nau:* Sondeur *m*.

sound⁵, *s.* (i) Détroit *m* ; goulet *m* ; (ii) bras *m* de mer. *Geog:* **The Sound,** le Sund.

sound⁶. I. *a.* **I.** (*a*) Sain. *S. constitution*, santé *f* solide, robuste. *Sound in body and mind*, sain de corps et d'esprit. **Of sound mind,** sain d'esprit. *Vet: S. horse*, cheval sans tare. *F:* (*Of pers.*) **To be sound in wind and limb,** avoir bon pied bon œil ; *F:* avoir le coffre solide. **I'm as sound as a bell,** je suis en parfaite santé. (*b*) En bon état ; non endommagé. *S. fruit*, fruits sains. **2.** (*a*) *S. financial position*, situation financière solide. **To be a sound man,** avoir du crédit sur la place ; être solide. *S. statesman*, homme d'état au jugement sain. (*b*) (Argument valide, irréfutable ; (raisonnement) juste. *It is a s. rule to . . .*, la bonne règle est de. . . . *It isn't s. finance*, ce n'est pas de la finance sérieuse. **3.** *Sound sleep*, sommeil profond. *To give s.o. a s. thrashing*, rosser qn d'importance. **-ly,** *adv.* **I.** Sainement ; judicieusement. *To argue s.*, raisonner avec justesse. **2. To sleep soundly,** dormir profondément, à poings fermés. **To thrash s.o. soundly,** rosser qn d'importance, de la belle manière. **II. sound,** *adv.* **To sleep sound,** dormir à poings fermés. *S.a.* ASLEEP I.

sounder¹ ['saundər], *s. Tg:* (*Device*) Parleur *m*, sonneur *m*.

sounder², *s. Nau:* (*Man or apparatus*) Sondeur *m*.

soundness ['saundnəs], *s.* **I.** État sain (de l'esprit) ; bon état (des poumons, des marchandises). **2.** Solidité *f* (d'une maison de commerce). **3.** Solidité (d'un argument) ; sûreté *f*, justesse *f* (d'un jugement).

soup [su:p], *s.* Soupe *f*, potage *m*. **Thick soup,** crème *f*, purée *f*. **Clear soup,** consommé *m*. *Meat s.*, soupe grasse. *Vegetable s.*, soupe maigre. *Onion s.*, soupe à l'oignon. *F:* **To be in the soup,** être dans le pétrin, dans la purée. **'soup-ladle,** *s.* Louche *f*. **'soup-plate,** *s.* Assiette creuse. **'soup-tureen,** *s.* Soupière *f*.

sour¹ ['sauər], *a.* **I.** (*a*) (*Fruit*) aigre, acide. *S.a.* GRAPE. (*b*) (*Lait*, pain) aigre, suri ; (vin) suret, verjuté. **To turn sour,** tourner à l'aigre ; surir. **To turn sth. sour,** (faire) aigrir qch. *To smell s.*, sentir l'aigre. (*c*) *Agr:* (Sol) trop humide.

2. (*Of pers.*) Revêche ; aigre. **She's a sour-face,** c'est une chipie. **-ly,** *adv.* (Répondre) avec aigreur, d'un ton revêche. **'sour-faced,** *a.* Au visage morose.

sour². I. *v.i.* (*a*) Surir ; (s')aigrir. (*b*) *Her temper has soured*, son caractère a aigri. **2.** *v.tr.* Aigrir (le lait, *F:* le caractère). *To s. s.o.'s life*, enfieller la vie de qn.

source [sɔːrs], *s.* Source *f* (d'un fleuve, de malheurs, etc.). *To trace a tradition back to its s.*, remonter aux sources, à l'origine, d'une tradition. **Source of infection,** foyer *m* d'infection. *Prov:* **Idleness is the source of all evil,** l'oisiveté est la mère de tous les vices. **I know it from a good source,** je le sais de bonne source, de bonne part.

sourish ['sauəriʃ], *a.* Aigrelet, suret.

sourness ['sauərnəs], *s.* **I.** Aigreur *f*, acidité *f* (d'un fruit). **2.** Aigreur (de qn) ; humeur *f* revêche.

souse¹ [saus], *s.* **I.** *Cu:* Marinade *f*. **2. To get a souse,** recevoir une saucée ; être trempé jusqu'aux os. **3.** *P:* Soûlerie *f*.

souse². I. *v.tr.* (*a*) *Cu:* Faire mariner (le poisson, etc.). (*b*) Plonger, immerger (*in*, dans). (*c*) Tremper, noyer (*with water*, d'eau). (*d*) **To souse water over sth.,** répandre de l'eau sur qch. **2.** *v.i.* Mariner. **soused,** *a.* **I.** *Cu:* Mariné. **Soused venison,** marinade *f* de chevreuil. **2.** *P:* **To be soused,** avoir une cuite.

south¹ [sauθ]. **I.** *s.* Sud *m*, midi *m*. **On the south,** to the south (of), au sud (de) ; du côté du sud. *To live in the s. of England*, demeurer dans le sud de l'Angleterre. **The South of France,** le Midi (de la France). **2.** *adv.* (*a*) Au sud. **To travel south,** voyager vers le sud. (*b*) **To go South,** aller dans le sud, dans le midi. **3.** *a.* Sud *inv* ; (vent) du sud ; (pays) du sud, méridional, -aux ; (mur) qui fait face au sud, exposé au midi. **South 'Africa.** *Pr.n.* L'Afrique australe. **The Union of South Africa,** l'Union sud-africaine. **South-'African,** *a. & s.* Sud-africain, -aine. **'South 'Downs (the),** *s.p* Les Collines *f* du sud (de l'Angleterre). **south-'east. I.** *s.* Sud-est *m*. **2.** *adv.* Vers le sud-est. **3.** *a.* Du sud-est. **south-'easterly,** **south-'eastern,** *a.* Du sud-est. **'South 'Sea (the).** *Pr.n.* Le Pacifique sud. **The South Sea Islands,** les îles du Pacifique ; l'Océanie *f*. **south-'west. I.** *s.* Sud-ouest *m*. **2.** *adv.* Vers le sud-ouest. **3.** *a.* Du sud-ouest. **south-'wester,** *Nau:* **sou' 'wester,** *s.* **I.** Vent *m* du sud-ouest ; le suroît. **2.** Chapeau *m* imperméable ; suroît *m*. **south-'westerly,** *a.* Du sud-ouest. **south-'western,** *a.* Du sud-ouest.

south², *v.i.* **I.** (*Of star*) Passer le méridien. **2.** *Of ship*) Faire route au sud. **southing,** *s.* **I.** *Astr:* Passage *m* au méridien. **2.** *Nau:* Chemin *m* sud.

southerly ['sʌðərli], *a.* (*a*) (i, (Vent) du sud, qui vient du sud ; (ii) (courant) qui se dirige vers le sud. (*b*) *S. aspect*, exposition au midi. *Nau: To steer a s. course*, faire route au sud, mettre le cap au sud.

southern ['sʌðərn], *a.* (Du) sud ; du midi ; méridional, -aux. *The s. counties*, les comtés du sud. **Southern lights,** aurore australe. *Astr:* **The Southern Cross,** la Croix du Sud.

southerner ['sʌðərnər], *s.* Habitant du sud ; (*in Fr.*) méridional.

southron ['sʌðrən], *a. & s. Scot: Pej:* Anglais, -aise.

southward ['sauθwərd]. **I.** *s.* **To the southward,** vers le sud. **2.** *a.* Au, du, sud ; du côté du sud.

southwards ['sauθwərdz], *adv.* Vers le sud.
souvenir [su:və'ni:ər], *s.* Souvenir *m*, mémento *m*.
sou'wester. *See* SOUTH-WESTER.
sovereign ['sɔvrən]. **I.** *a.* Souverain; suprême. **Sovereign** **rights,** droits de souveraineté. **The** **sovereign** **good,** le souverain bien. *F:* **Sovereign** **remedy,** remède souverain, infaillible. **2.** *s.* (*a*) Souverain, -aine. (*b*) *Num:* Souverain *m* (pièce d'or de la valeur de 20 shillings).
sovereignty ['sɔvrənti], *s.* Souveraineté *j.*
Soviet ['souviet] *s.* Soviet *m.* **Soviet union,** union soviétique. **The Union of Socialist Soviet** **Republics,** l'Union des Républiques socialistes soviétiques.
sow[1] [sou], *v.tr.* (sowed [soud]; sowed, sown [soun]) Semer (des graines, un champ). **To sow** **land with wheat,** ensemencer une terre en blé. *Abs.* **To sow broadcast,** semer à la volée, à tout vent. **To sow discord,** semer, répandre, la discorde. **The seeds of revolution were sowing,** la révolution se préparait. *S.a.* OAT, REAP. **sowing,** *s.* Semailles *fpl*, semis *m.* **'sowing-machine,** *s.* Semoir *m.* **'sowing-peas,** *s.pl.* Pois *m* à semence. **'sowing-time,** *s.* La semaison; le temps des semailles.
sow[2] [sau], *s.* **I.** (*a*) Truie *f*, coche *f*. *F:* **To get** **the wrong sow by the ear,** être loin de compte. (*b*) *Ven:* Laie *f* (sanglier femelle). **2.** *Metall:* (*a*) Gueuse *f*. (*b*) Sow(-channel), mère-gueuse *f*. **'sow(-bug),** *s.* *Crust:* Cloporte *m*; *F:* cochon *m* de St-Antoine.
sower ['souər], *s.* Semeur, -euse.
sow-thistle ['sauθisl], *s.* *Bot:* Laiteron *m.*
soy [sɔi], *s.* **I.** *Cu:* Sauce piquante (de soya). **2.** = SOYA-BEAN.
soya-bean [sɔia'bi:n], *s.* *Bot:* Soya *m*; pois chinois.
spa [spɑ:], *s.* **I.** Source minérale. **2.** Ville *f* d'eau; station thermale.
space[1] [speis], *s.* **I.** Espace *m*, intervalle *m* (de temps). **For a space,** pendant quelque temps. **2.** (*a*) L'espace. **Staring into space,** le regard perdu dans l'espace. (*b*) **In a confined space,** dans un espace restreint. **To take up a lot of** **space,** occuper beaucoup de place; être encombrant. **To leave space for . . .,** laisser de la place à. . . . (*c*) Étendue *f*; surface *f*. *The* *aerodrome occupies a large s.,* l'aérodrome occupe un vaste terrain. **3.** (*a*) Espace libre; espacement *m*, intervalle. **Space between two things,** écartement *m* de deux choses; (*between windows*) entre-deux *m* *inv*; (*between lines of writing, etc.*) entre-ligne *m*, interligne *m.* **Blank space,** blanc *m.* *To write one's name in the s. indicated,* écrire son nom dans la case indiquée. (*b*) *Typ:* Espace *f* (en métal); blanc *m.* *Thick* s., espace forte. *S.a.* LINE-SPACE. **'space-bar,** *s.* *Typewr:* Barre *f* d'espacement.
space[2], *v.tr.* (*a*) **To space (out),** espacer; disposer (des objets) de distance en distance; échelonner (des troupes, des paiements). *Typ:* **To space (out) the lines,** espacer les lignes. **To** **space out the matter,** blanchir la composition. (*b*) **To space off,** (sub)diviser (une ligne); répartir (des trous). **spaced,** *a.* **I.** Écarté; espacé. **2.** *Typ:* Close-spaced, aux espaces fines.
spacing, *s.* (*a*) Espacement *m*, écartement *m*; échelonnement *m* (des troupes, des paiements). *Typ:* Espacement. *Typewr:* **In single, double,** **spacing,** à interligne simple, double. (*b*) Pas *m*; répartition *f* (de rivets, etc.).
spacer ['speisər], *s.* **I.** *Typ:* Espace *f*. **2.** *Typewr:* Barre *f* d'espacement. *S.a.* LINE-

SPACER. **3.** *Mec.E:* Pièce *f* d'épaisseur; entretoise *f*.
spacious ['speiʃəs], *a.* (*a*) Spacieux, vaste. (*b*) Ample (vêtement).
spaciousness ['speiʃəsnəs], *s.* (*a*) Vaste étendue *f.* (*b*) Logeabilité *f* (d'un appartement, d'une voiture).
spade[1] [speid], *s.* **I.** *Tls:* Bêche *f*; (*child's*) pelle *f*. *F:* **To call a spade a spade,** appeler les choses par leur nom. **2.** *Artil:* Trail spade, bêche de crosse. **'spade-work,** *s.* **I.** Travaux *mpl* à la bêche; le gros travail. **2.** *F:* Travaux préliminaires, déblaiemen *m* de terrain (en vue d'une enquête, etc.).
spade[2], *v.tr.* Bêcher (la terre, etc.).
spade[3], *s.* *Cards:* Pique *m.* **Ace of spades,** as de pique. *To play a s.,* **to play spades,** jouer pique.
spadeful ['speidful], *s.* Pleine bêche; pelletée *f*.
spaghetti [spa'geti], *s.* *Cu:* Spaghetti *mpl.*
spahi ['spɑ:hi:], *s.* *Mil:* Spahi *m*.
Spain [spein]. *Pr.n.* L'Espagne *f*.
spake [speik]. *See* SPEAK.
spalpeen [spal'pi:n], *s.* (*Irish*) (*a*) Coquin *m*, fripon *m.* (*b*) Voyou *m*, -ous.
span[1] [span], *s.* **I.** (*a*) (i) Empan *m* (de la main); (ii) *Meas:* neuf *inches* (229 mm.). (*b*) Wing-span (*of bird, aeroplane*), envergure *f.* **2.** (*a*) Portée *f* (entre deux appuis); ouverture *f*, largeur *f* (d'une arche); écartement *m* (de deux piliers). **Sixty** **foot span,** soixante pieds de portée. (*b*) Travée *f* (d'un pont, d'un comble). **3.** (*a*) Petite étendue (de terre). (*b*) Court espace de temps. **Our** **mortal span,** notre séjour *m* terrestre. **'span-roof,** *s.* *Const:* Comble *m* à deux versants, à double pente.
span[2], *v.tr.* (**spanned**) **I.** Mesurer à l'empan. **2.** (*Of bridge, etc.*) Franchir, enjamber (une rivière, etc.). *F: His life spans nearly the whole* *century,* sa vie embrasse presque tout le siècle.
span[3], *s.* (*a*) *U.S:* Paire *f*, couple *m* (de chevaux, de bœufs). (*b*) *S. Africa:* Attelage *m* (de bœufs).
span[4], *v.tr.* (*Esp. S. Africa*) (*a*) **To span (in),** atteler (des chevaux, des bœufs). (*b*) **To span** **out,** dételer.
span[5]. *See* SPIN-.
spandrel ['spandrəl], *s.* *Arch:* Tympan *m.*
spangle[1] [spangl], *s.* *Tex:* Paillette *f*; (*large*) paillon *m.* **Gold spangles,** lamé *m* d'or.
spangle[2], *v.tr.* Pailleter (*with,* de). *Spangled with* *silver,* lamé d'argent.
Spaniard ['spanjərd], *s.* Espagnol, -ole.
spaniel ['spanjəl], *s.* Épagneul *m*.
Spanish ['spaniʃ]. **I.** *a.* Espagnol. **Spanish** **onion,** oignon d'Espagne. *Hist:* **The Spanish** **Main,** (i) la Terre-ferme; (ii) la mer des Antilles. **2.** *s.* *Ling:* L'espagnol *m.* **Spanish-A'meri-can,** *a.* Hispano-américain, ibéro-américain.
spank[1] [spaŋk], *v.tr.* Fesser (un enfant); administrer une fessée, une fouettée, à (un enfant). **spanking**[1], *s.* Fessée *f*.
spank[2], *v.i.* **To spank along,** aller bon train; filer à bonne allure. **spanking**[2], *a.* **I.** *F:* **To go at** **a spanking pace,** filer raide; brûler le terrain. **2.** *P:* chic, épatant. **2. To go at**... épatante.
spanker ['spaŋkər], *s.* **I.** *Nau:* Brigantine *f*. **2.** *P:* (*a*) Cheval *m* qui va bon train. (*b*) Chose épatante.
spanner ['spanər], *s.* **I.** Clef *f* (à écrous). **Bolt-spanner,** serre-écrou *m* *inv.* **Screw spanner,** clef anglaise; clef à molette. **2.** *Civ.E:* Entretoise *f*.
spar[1] [spɑ:r], *s.* **I.** *Nau:* (*a*) Espar(t) *m*, épar(t) *m*; bout *m* de mât. (*b*) *pl.* **The spars,** la mâture. **2.** *Av:* Wing spar, poutrelle *f*; bras *m* d'aile. **'spar-deck,** *s.* *Nau:* Pont volant; spardeck *m.*

par², *s.* *Miner:* Spath *m.* **Diamond spar, spath** adamantin.

par³, *s.* **1.** Combat *m* de coqs. **2.** *(a)* Assaut de boxe amical. *(b)* Assaut de paroles ; *F:* prise *f* de bec.

par⁴, *v.i.* (sparred) **1.** *(Of cocks)* Se battre. **2.** *(Of pers.)* **To spar with s.o.**, (i) faire un assaut de boxe amical avec qn ; (ii) s'escrimer contre qn. **To spar up to s.o.**, se mettre en posture de combat. **Sparring match**, (i) assaut de boxe amical, de démonstration ; (ii) *F:* prise *f* de bec. **Sparring partner**, partenaire *m* (d'un boxeur).

spare¹ ['spɛər], *a.* **1.** *(a) S. diet*, régime frugal. *(b) (Of pers.)* Sec, *f.* sèche ; maigre, fluet. **To be spare of build**, avoir une charnure sèche. **2. Spare time**, (i) temps disponible ; (ii) moments perdus ; loisir(s) *m(pl). S. capital*, fonds disponibles. **Spare bedroom**, chambre d'ami. *A yard of s. rope*, trois pieds de corde de reste, en surplus. **3. Spare parts**, *s.* **spares**, pièces *f* de rechange, de réserve ; rechanges *m. S. machine*, machine de remplacement. *Aut:* **Spare wheel**, roue de secours. *S. tyre*, pneu de rechange. *Mil:* **Spare horse**, cheval haut-le-pied. *Nau: S. bunker*, soute de réserve. **-ly**, *adv.* **1.** *(a)* (Manger) frugalement. *(b) (Of pers.)* **Sparely built**, sec, *f.* sèche ; mince. **2.** = SPARSELY.

spare², *v.tr.* **1.** Épargner, ménager. **To spare no expense**, ne pas regarder à la dépense. **To spare no pains**, ne pas ménager, ne pas marchander, sa peine. *He will s. no pains to do it*, rien ne lui coûtera pour le faire. **2.** *(a)* Se passer de (qch.). *Can you spare it?* pouvez-vous vous en passer ? je ne vous en prive pas ? **To have nothing to spare**, n'avoir que le strict nécessaire. *Three yards to s.*, neuf pieds de trop, de reste. **To have enough and to spare of sth.**, avoir plus qu'il n'en faut de qch. *He has money and to spare*, il a de l'argent de reste. *(b)* **I cannot spare the time**, le temps me fait défaut. **To have no time to spare**, (i) ne pas avoir de temps de libre ; (ii) n'avoir que juste le temps (pour attraper le train, etc.). *I have a minute to s.*, je peux disposer d'un instant. *(c)* **To spare s.o. sth.**, donner, céder, qch. à qn. *Can you s. me a few moments?* voulez-vous m'accorder quelques minutes ? **3.** *(a)* Faire grâce à (qn). **To spare s.o.'s life**, épargner la vie de qn. **If he is spared** *a few weeks longer*, s'il lui est donné de vivre encore quelques semaines. *Death spares no one*, la mort ne pardonne à personne. *The fire spared nothing*, le feu ne respecta rien. *F:* **He spares nobody**, il ne fait de quartier à personne. **To spare s.o.'s feelings**, ménager qn. *(b)* Ménager (qn, son cheval). *(c)* **To spare s.o. the trouble of doing sth.**, épargner, éviter, à qn la peine de faire qch. *S. me this journey*, dispensez-moi de ce voyage. **sparing**, *a.* **1.** Ménager, -ère ; économe. **To be sparing with the butter**, épargner, ménager, le beurre. *He is sparing of praise*, il est chiche, avare, de louanges. **Sparing of words**, sobre de paroles. **2. Sparing use of sth.**, emploi modéré, restreint, de qch. **-ly**, *adv.* Frugalement ; (manger) sobrement. *To use sth. s.*, ménager qch.

spare-rib ['spɛərrib], *s. Cu:* Côte (découverte) de porc.

spark¹ [spɑːk], *s. (a)* Étincelle *f* ; *(of fire)* flammèche *f.* **Spark of wit**, paillette *f*, bluette *f*, d'esprit. *F:* **He hasn't a spark of generosity in him**, il n'a pas pour deux sous de générosité. *(b) El:* Étincelle. **Spark resistance**, résistance de la distance explosive. **Spark discharge**, étincelle disruptive. *I.C.E:* **Spark ignition**, allumage par étincelle. **To advance the spark**, mettre de l'avance

à l'allumage. *(c) Nau: Av: F:* **Sparks**, l'opérateur *m* de T.S.F. ; *F:* le radio. **'spark-arrester**, *s.* **1.** *El.E:* Déchargeur *m* ; parafoudre *m.* **2.** = SPARK-CATCHER. **'spark-catcher**, *s. Rail: etc:* Pare-étincelles *m inv.* **'spark-control**, *s. I.C.E:* Commande d'allumage. **'spark-gap**, *s. El:* **1.** Distance explosive. **2.** Pont *m* d'éclatement. **'spark-tester**, *s. Aut:* Contrôleur *m* d'allumage.

spark², *v.i.* *(a)* Émettre des étincelles ; *(of dynamo, etc.)* cracher. *I.C.E:* **The car sparks well**, l'allumage fonctionne bien. *(b) (Of current)* **To spark across the terminals**, jaillir entre les bornes. **sparking**, *s. El:* **1.** Émission *f* d'étincelles ; *(accidental)* jaillissement *m* d'étincelles ; crachement *m.* **2.** Allumage *m* par étincelle électrique. **'sparking-distance**, *s.* Distance explosive. **'sparking-plug**, *s. I.C.E:* Bougie *f* (d'allumage).

spark³, *s.* **1.** Élégant *m* ; *A:* petit-maître *m.* **2. Gay spark**, gaillard *m* ; gai luron.

sparkle¹ [spɑːkl], *s.* **1.** Brève lueur ; bluette *f.* **2.** Étincellement *m* ; éclat *m*, pétillement *m* (des yeux) ; feux *mpl* (d'un diamant). **3.** Vivacité *f* d'esprit.

sparkle², *v.i.* **1.** *(a)* Étinceler, scintiller ; *(of jewel)* chatoyer, miroiter. *Book sparkling with wit*, livre qui pétille d'esprit. *(b) (Of wine)* Pétiller, mousser. **2.** *(Of fire)* Émettre des étincelles ; pétiller. **sparkling¹**, *a. (a)* Étincelant, brillant. *F:* **Sparkling wit**, vivacité *f* d'esprit. *S. conversation*, conversation pétillante d'esprit. *(b) (Vin)* mousseux ; (limonade) gazeuse. **Semi-sparkling wine**, vin pétillant. **-ly**, *adv.* Vivement ; avec vivacité. **sparkling²**, *s.* **1.** Étincellement *m* ; scintillement *m*, scintillation *f.* **2.** Pétillement *m.*

sparrow ['spæro], *s.* **1.** Moineau *m*, passereau *m* ; *F:* pierrot *m.* **2. Hedge-sparrow**, fauvette *f* des haies ; *F:* mouchet *m.* **'sparrow-hawk**, *s. Orn:* Épervier *m.*

sparse [spɑːs], *a.* Clairsemé, épars, éparpillé. *S. hair*, cheveux rares, clairsemés. **-ly**, *adv.* Peu abondamment. *S. populated*, qui a une population clairsemée.

Sparta ['spɑːtə], *Pr.n. A.Geog:* Sparte *f.*

Spartan ['spɑːtən], *a. & s.* Spartiate *(mf). F:* **To live a S. life**, vivre en Spartiate.

spasm [spæzm], *s.* **1.** *Med:* Spasme *m.* **2.** *(a)* **In a spasm of temper**, dans un mouvement de colère. *F:* **To work in spasms**, travailler par à-coups, par boutades.

spasmodic [spæz'mɔdik], *a.* **1.** *(a) Med:* Spasmodique. *(b)* (Saut) involontaire, convulsif. **2.** Qui se produit par saccades ; fait par à-coups. **-ally**, *adv.* (Travailler, etc.) par à-coups.

spastic ['spæstik], *a. Med:* Spasmodique.

spat¹ [spæt], *s.* Frai *m.* naissain *m* (d'huîtres, de moules).

spat², *v.i.* (spatted) *(Of oysters)* Frayer.

spat³, *s.* Demi-guêtre *f* ; guêtre *f* de ville.

spat⁴. See SPIT⁴.

spatchcock¹ ['spætʃkɔk], *s. Cu:* Poulet *m* à la crapaudine.

spatchcock², *v.tr.* **1.** *Cu:* Faire cuire (un poulet) à la crapaudine. **2.** *F: (a)* **To spatchcock a sentence into a report**, fourrer, faire entrer à la dernière minute, une phrase dans un rapport. *(b)* Faire une interpolation dans (une dépêche).

spate [speit], *s.* Crue *f.* **River in spate**, rivière en crue. *F:* **To have a s. of work**, être débordé de travail.

spathe [speið], *s. Bot:* Spathe *f.*

spatial ['speiʃ(ə)l], a. Spatial, -aux : dans l'espace.
spatter[1] ['spatər], s. Éclaboussure f.
spatter[2]. 1. v.tr. To spatter s.o. with mud, éclabousser qn de boue. 2. v.i. (Of liquid) Jaillir gicler.
spatterdash ['spatərdaʃ], s. A : Houseau m, guêtre f.
spatula ['spatjula], s. Spatule f.
spatulate ['spatjulet], a. Nat.Hist : Spatulé. S. fingers, doigts en spatule.
spavin ['spavin], s. Vet : Éparvin m.
spawn[1] [spɔːn], s. 1. Frai m; œufs mpl (de poisson, etc.). 2. F : Progéniture f; rejeton m. 3. Mushroom spawn, blanc m de champignon.
spawn[2], v.i. (a) (Of fish, etc.) Frayer. (b) F : Se multiplier. (c) F : To spawn from sth., naître de qch. **spawning**, s. Le frai. '**spawning-season**, s. Époque f du frai ; fraie f, fraieson f.
speak spiːk], v. (spoke [spouk], A : spake [speik] ; spoken) I. v.i. 1. (a) Parler. Without speaking, sans parler ; sans rien dire. (b) To speak to s.o., parler à qn ; adresser la parole à qn ; s'adresser à qn. I will speak to him about it, je lui en toucherai un mot. To s. rudely to s.o., tenir un langage grossier à qn. I know him to speak to, je le connais pour lui avoir été présenté. To speak with s.o., causer, s'entretenir, avec qn. Speaking for myself . . ., pour ma part . . . ; quant à moi. . . . Roughly speaking, approximativement. So to speak, pour ainsi dire. (c) The facts speak for themselves, ces faits se passent de commentaire. (d) (Of gun, organ) Parler. Suddenly the guns spoke, tout à coup le canon se fit entendre. (e) Ven : (Of dog) Aboyer ; donner de la voix. 2. Faire un discours ; prendre la parole. Mr X rose to speak, M. X a demandé la parole. II. speak, v.tr. 1. (a) Dire (un mot, ses pensées). To speak the truth, dire la vérité. Not to speak a word, ne pas dire, ne pas prononcer, un mot. (b) To speak one's mind, dire sa façon de penser ; avoir son franc parler. To his shame be it spoken, soit dit à sa honte. 2. Indiquer, accuser (qch.). Eyes that s. affection, yeux qui témoignent de l'amitié. 3. Parler (une langue). Do you speak French? parlez-vous français? 'English spoken,' "on parle anglais." 4. Nau : Héler, arraisonner (un navire). **speak for**, v.i. 1. (a) To speak for s.o., parler, plaider, pour qn. (b) That speaks well for your courage, cela en dit long sur votre courage ; cela fait honneur à votre courage. 2. That is already spoken for, cela est déjà réservé, retenu. **speak of**, v.i. 1. Parler de (qch.). Speaking of . . ., à propos de. . . . She has no voice to speak of, elle n'a pour ainsi dire pas de voix. To speak well, highly, of s.o., sth., dire du bien de qn ; parler en termes très flatteurs de qn ; vanter qch. 2. Être significatif de (qch.). His pinched features spoke of privation, ses traits hâves trahissaient les privations. **speak out**, v.i. (a) Parler à haute voix. (b) Parler franchement, sans détours ; trancher le mot. **speak to**, v.i. 1. Témoigner de (qch.). To speak to the truth of a statement, garantir la vérité d'une affirmation. 2. To speak to a point, parler sur un point. **speak up**, v.i. 1. Parler plus fort, plus haut. 2. To speak up for s.o., parler en faveur de qn. **spoken**, a. 1. The spoken word, la parole. S. language, langue parlée. 2. A well-spoken man, un homme à la parole courtoise. To be loud-spoken, avoir le verbe haut. S.a. PLAIN-SPOKEN. **speaking**[1], a. 1. (Of eyes, etc.) Expressif, éloquent. F : A

speaking likeness, un portrait parlant, vivant 2. Evil-speaking, médisant. English-speaking races, races de langue anglaise. **speaking**[2], 1. Parler m, discours m, parole f. To be c speaking terms, se connaître assez pour se parler S.a. DISTANCE 1. 2. Public speaking, l'éloquence f l'art m oratoire. '**speaking-trumpet**, Porte-voix m inv. '**speaking-tube**, s. Tube acoustique. Nau : etc : Porte-voix m inv (com muniquant avec la chambre des machines '**speak-easy**, s. U.S : P : Débit clandestin.
speaker ['spiːkər], s. 1. Parleur, -euse ; (a dialogue) interlocuteur, -trice. The last s., cel qui a parlé le dernier. 2. (In public) Orateur n To be a fluent s., avoir la parole facile. 3. Par The Speaker, le Président (des Communes 4. W.Tel : Speaker unit, haut-parleur m.
spear[1] ['spiːər], s. 1. (a) Lance f. (b) (Fo throwing) Javelot m, javeline f. 2. Fish : Foène trident m. '**spear-head**, s. Fer m, pointe de lance. '**spear-shaft**, s. Bois m, hampe de lance. '**spear-thrust**, s. Coup m de lance **spear**[2]. 1. v.tr. (a) (Trans)percer d'un coup d lance. (b) Prendre (un poisson) à la foène 2. v.i. (a) (Of mast, etc.) To spear up, se dresse comme une ance ; s'élancer. (b) (Of bull Pousser ; monter en tige.
spearmint ['spiːərmint], s. Bot : Menthe verte
spearwort ['spiːərwɔːrt], s. Bot : Renoncule langue ; douve f.
spec [spek], s. F : = SPECULATION 2.
special ['speʃ(ə)l]. 1. a. (a) Spécial, -aux ; par ticulier. S. feature, particularité f. S. tool, out façonné exprès. Com : Special price, prix d faveur. Post : U.S : 'By special delivery,' "pa exprès." S.a. CONSTABLE 2. (b) (Especia) T take special care over sth., apporter des soin particuliers à qch. Special friend, ami intime I have nothing special to tell you, je n'ai rien d particulier à vous dire. (c) Com : (Article) hor série. 2. s. (a) Train spécial. (b) Édition spécial (d'un journal). -**ally**, adv. Spécialement particulièrement ; surtout. I went there s. to se them, j'y ai été dans le seul but de les voir.
specialist ['speʃəlist], s. Spécialiste mf. Med Heart specialist, spécialiste des maladies de cœur
speciality [speʃi'aliti], s. 1. Spécialité f. To mak a speciality of sth., se faire une spécialité de qch 2. Qualité particulière ; particularité f. 3. Jur = SPECIALTY 1.
specialization [speʃəlai'zeiʃ(ə)n], s. Spécialisa tion f.
specialize ['speʃəlaiz]. 1. v.tr. (a) Particulariser spécialiser. (b) Désigner à un but spécial. Hos pital with specialized wards, hôpital où chaqu salle a sa spécialité. 2. v.i. Se spécialiser (in dans). To specialize in a subject, faire sa spé cialité d'un sujet.
specialty ['speʃəlti], s. 1. Jur : Contrat forme sous seing privé. 2. = SPECIALITY 1.
specie ['spiːʃiː, -ʃi], s. (No pl.) Espèces mon nayées ; numéraire m. To pay in specie, payer en espèces.
species ['spiːʃiːz, -ʃiz], s. inv. 1. (a) Nat.Hist Espèce f. The origin of species, 'origine de espèces. (b) Arb : Essence f. 2. (a) Spécifique m genre m.
specific [spe'sifik]. 1. a. (a) Spécifique. Ph Specific gravity, poids m spécifique. Jur : In each specific case, dans chaque cas d'espèce (b) (Of statement) Précis ; (of order) explicite Specific aim, but déterminé. 2. s. Med : Spéci fique m (for, contre). -**ally**, adv. 1. Spécifique ment. 2. Précisément.

specification [spesifi'keiʃ(ə)n], s. **1.** Spécification f (des détails, etc.). **2.** Devis descriptif. **Specifications of a patent,** mémoire descriptif d'une invention ; description f de brevet. *Specifications of a car,* caractéristiques f d'une voiture. **Specifications of a contract,** stipulations f d'un contrat.

specify ['spesifai], v.tr. Spécifier, déterminer ; préciser (des conditions). **Specified load,** charge prévue, prescrite. **Unless otherwise specified,** sauf indication contraire.

specimen ['spesimən], s. (a) Spécimen m. *The finest specimens in his collection,* les plus belles pièces de sa collection. (b) Exemple m, échantillon m. **Specimen page,** page spécimen ; page type. **Specimen copy** (of book), livre à l'examen. (c) F: (Of pers.) **Queer specimen,** drôle m de type.

specious ['spiːʃəs], a. (Of appearance) Spécieux, trompeur ; (of argument) captieux, spécieux.

speciousness ['spiːʃəsnəs], s. Spéciosité f ; apparence trompeuse.

speck [spek], s. **1.** Petite tache ; po nt m, goutte f (de couleur) ; moucheture f, tacheture f. **2.** (a) Grain m, atome m (de poussière). *S. on the horizon,* point noir à l'horizon. (b) **Not a speck of generosity,** pas un brin de générosité. **3.** Défaut m ; tavelure f (sur un fruit).

specked [spekt], a. Tacheté, moucheté ; (fruit) tavelé.

speckle [spekl], s. Petite tache ; point m (de couleur) ; moucheture f, tacheture f.

speckled [spekld], a. Tacheté, moucheté, tiqueté, truité ; (of plumage grivelé. *S. with white,* tacheté de blanc.

spectacle ['spektəkl], s. **1.** Spectacle m. **2.** pl. **Spectacles,** lunettes f. **Coloured spectacles,** conserves f. **'spectacle-case,** s. Étui m à lunettes. **'spectacle-maker,** s. Lunetier m, lunettier m.

spectacled ['spektəkld], a. Qui porte des lunettes ; à lunettes.

spectacular [spek'takjulər], a. Spectaculaire. *S. play,* pièce à grand spectacle.

spectator [spek'teitər], s. Spectateur, -trice ; assistant, -ante. *The spectators,* l'assistance f.

spectral ['spektrəl], a. Spectral, -aux.

spectre ['spektər], s. Spectre m, fantôme m, apparition f.

spectrometer [spek'trɔmetər], s. Opt: Spectromètre m.

spectroscope ['spektroskoup], s. Opt: Spectroscope m. **Grating spectroscope,** spectroscope à réseau.

spectroscopy [spek'trɔskopi, 'spektroskoupi], s. Spectroscopie f.

spectrum, pl. **-tra** ['spektrəm, -tra], s. Ph: Spectre m. *Solar s.,* spectre solaire. *The colours of the s.,* les couleurs spectrales. **'spectrum-a'nalysis,** s. Ch: Analyse spectrale.

specular ['spekjulər], a. (Minéral) spéculaire.

speculate ['spekjuleit], v.i. **1.** **To speculate** (up)on, about, sth., (i) spéculer, méditer, sur qch. ; (ii) faire des conjectures sur qch. **2.** Fin: Spéculer (in, sur). **To speculate on the Stock Exchange,** spéculer, jouer, à la Bourse. **speculating,** s. Spéculation f.

speculation [spekju'leiʃ(ə)n], s. **1.** (a) Spéculation f, méditation f (on, sur). (b) Conjecture f. **To be the subject of much speculation,** donner lieu à bien des conjectures. **2.** (a) Fin: Spéculation. **To buy sth. on speculation,** acheter qch. à titre de spéculation. *F:* **To do, buy, sth. on speculation,** *F:* **on spec,** faire, acheter, qch. à

tout hasard. (b) **Entreprise spéculative.** *Good s.,* bonne affaire.

speculative ['spekjulətiv], a. **1.** (a) Spéculatif, contemplatif. (b) Conjectural, -aux. **2.** *Fin:* Spéculatif ; fait par spéculation.

speculator ['spekjuleitər], s. Spéculateur m. *St.Exch:* Joueur m à la Bourse ; agioteur m.

speculum ['spekjuləm], s. **1.** *Surg:* Spéculum m. **2.** Miroir m (d'un télescope, etc.).

sped [sped]. *See* SPEED².

speech [spiːtʃ], s. **1.** (a) **(Faculty of) speech,** la parole. **To lose the power of speech,** perdre la parole. (b) **To be slow of speech,** parler lentement ; avoir l'articulation lente ; avoir un débit très lent. *Abruptness of s.,* brusquerie de langage. *S.a.* IMPEDIMENT I. (c) **Figure of speech,** figure f de rhétorique. *Gram:* **Parts of speech,** parties f du discours. **2.** Paroles, propos mpl. **Fair speeches,** belles paroles. **To have speech with s.o.,** s'entretenir avec qn. *Without further s.,* sans plus rien dire. **3.** Langue f (d'un peuple) ; parler m (d'une région), d'une classe sociale). **4.** Discours m, harangue f ; (to subordinates) allocution f. **To make, deliver, a speech,** faire, prononcer, un discours. **5.** *Gram:* **Direct speech,** discours direct. **Indirect, reported, speech,** discours oblique, indirect. **'speech-day,** *Sch:* Distribution f de prix. **'speech-making,** s. Discours mpl.

speechify ['spiːtʃifai], v.i. Discourir, pérorer ; *P:* laïusser. **speechifying,** s. Beaux discours.

speechless ['spiːtʃləs], a. **1.** Incapable de parler. **2.** Interdit, interloqué. **Speechless with surprise,** muet de surprise. *Emotion left him s.,* l'émotion lui coupa la parole.

speed¹ [spiːd], s. **1.** (a) Vitesse f ; marche f (rapide) ; rapidité f, célérité f. **To do sth. with all speed,** *F:* **at speed,** faire qch. au plus vite, *F:* en vitesse, à la vapeur. *To make all s. to a place,* se rendre en toute hâte à un endroit. **At the top of one's speed,** de toute sa vitesse. **At full speed, at top speed,** au plus vite ; (of car) à toute vitesse, à toute allure, à fond de train ; (of train, ship) à toute vapeur ; (of runner) à toutes jambes ; (of horseman) à bride abattue, ventre à terre, à franc étrier. *Nau:* **Full speed ahead!** en avant à toute vitesse ! **Maximum speed,** vitesse limite. *Av:* **Ground speed,** vitesse par rapport au sol. **Air speed,** vitesse aérodynamique. *Aut:* **Three-speed car,** voiture à trois vitesses. **To pick up speed,** prendre de la vitesse. *Aut: P:* **Speed-hog,** chauffard m. **Speed-cop,** agent chargé de dresser procès-verbal dans les cas d'excès de vitesse. (b) *Mec.E:* **Normal running speed,** vitesse de régime. *To attain s.,* atteindre sa vitesse de régime. *Keep to this s.,* gardez ce régime. (c) *Phot:* Rapidité f (d'une émulsion d'un objectif). **2.** *A:* **To wish s.o. good speed,** souhaiter bonne chance à qn. **'speed-boat,** s. *Sp:* Motoglisseur m ; hydroglisseur m. **'speed-indicator,** s. Compteur m (de tours) ; indicateur m de vitesse. **'speed-limit,** s. Vitesse f maxima. **'speed-trial,** s. Essai m de vitesse. **'speed-way,** s. **1.** *Rac:* Piste f (d'autodrome). **2.** Autostrade f.

speed², v. (sped [sped ; ; sped) **I.** v.i. Se hâter, se presser ; aller vite. **He sped down the street,** il descendit vite la rue. **To speed off,** partir à toute vitesse. **2.** v.tr. *A:* (a) **To speed the parting guest,** souhaiter bon voyage à l'hôte qui part. (b) **God speed you!** que Dieu vous fasse prospérer ! *S.a.* GOD-SPEED.

speed³, v. (speeded) **I.** v.tr. (a) **To speed an engine,** régler la vitesse d'une machine. (b) **To**

speed (up) the work, activer, accélérer, les travaux. **2.** *v.i. Aut: etc:* Faire de la vitesse. **speeding,** *s.* **1.** *Aut:* Excès *m* de vitesse. **2.** Speeding (up), speed-up, accélération *f* (d'un travail, d'un service).

speediness ['spi:dinəs], *s.* Rapidité *f*, célérité *f*.

speedometer [spi:'dometər], *s.* **1.** *Aut: etc:* Indicateur *m* de vitesse ; compteur *m.* **2.** *Mec.E:* Tachymètre *m.*

speedster ['spi:dstər], *s. F:* Chauffard *m.*

speedwell ['spi:dwel], *s. Bot:* Véronique *f.*

speedy ['spi:di], *a.* (*a*) Rapide, prompt. *S. revenge,* prompte vengeance. (*b*) *Sp: Very s. forwards,* avants très vites. **-ily,** *adv.* Vite ; promptement ; en toute hâte.

spelaeology [spi:li'ɔlɔdʒi], *s.* Spéléologie *f.*

spell[1] [spel], *s.* **1.** Incantation *f*; formule *f* magique. **2.** Charme *m*, maléfice *m.* **To cast a spell over s.o.,** to lay s.o. under a spell, jeter un sort sur qn ; ensorceler, envoûter, qn. *F:* **The spell of the abyss,** l'attirance *f* du gouffre. **Under a spell,** sous un charme ; ensorcelé. **'spell-bound,** *a.* Retenu par un charme ; magnétisé ; *F:* figé sur place. **To hold one's audience spell-bound,** tenir ses auditeurs sous le charme.

spell[2], *v.tr.* (spelt *or* spelled) **1.** Épeler ; (*in writing*) orthographier (un mot). **He can't spell,** il ne sait pas l'orthographe. **To spell badly,** faire des fautes d'orthographe. **To spell out sth.,** déchiffrer, lire, qch. péniblement. **Spelt in full,** écrit en toutes lettres. **How is it spelt?** comment cela s'écrit-il ? **2.** **What do these letters spell?** quel mot forment ces lettres ? **3.** Signifier. *That would s. disaster!* ce serait le désastre ! *Gaming spells ruination,* le jeu c'est la ruine. **spelling,** *s.* Épellation *f*; (*in writing*) orthographe *f.* Reformed spelling, néographie *f.* **'spelling-bee,** *s.* Concours (oral) d'orthographe. **'spelling-book,** *s.* Syllabaire *m*, alphabet *m.*

spell[3], *s.* **1.** Tour *m* (de travail, etc.). **To take spells at the pumps,** se relayer aux pompes. **Three hours at a spell,** trois heures de suite, d'arrache-pied. **2.** (Courte) période. **To rest for a (short) spell,** se reposer pendant quelque temps. **A long spell of cold weather,** une longue période de froid. *During the cold s.,* pendant le coup de froid.

speller ['spelər], *s.* **To be a good, a bad, speller,** savoir, ne pas savoir, l'orthographe.

spelter ['speltər], *s. Com:* Zinc *m.*

spend [spend], *v.tr.* (spent [spent] ; spent) **1.** Dépenser (de l'argent). **To spend money on s.o.,** faire des dépenses pour qn. **I am always spending,** j'ai toujours l'argent à la main. **Without spending a penny,** sans bourse délier, sans rien débourser. **2.** **To spend care, time, on sth.,** consacrer, employer, du soin, du temps, à qch. **3.** Passer, employer (son temps). *To s. Sunday in the country,* passer le dimanche à la campagne. **4.** **To spend oneself in a vain endeavour,** s'épuiser dans un vain effort. *The bullet had spent its force,* la balle avait perdu (de) sa force. **spent,** *a.* **1.** **The day was far spent,** c'était tard dans la journée. **2.** (*a*) Épuisé (de fatigue). *The horses are s.,* les chevaux n'en peuvent plus. (*b*) *The storm is s.,* l'orage est calmé. **Spent volcano,** volcan éteint. **Spent bullet,** balle morte. **Spent cartridge,** cartouche vide, brûlée. **spending,** *s.* Dépense *f.* *Pol.Ec:* Spending power, pouvoir d'achat.

spendthrift ['spendθrift], *s.* Dépensier, -ière ; gaspilleur, -euse ; *F:* panier percé.

spent [spent]. *See* SPEND.

sperm[1] [spə:rm], *s.* Sperme *m.*

sperm[2], *s.* Sperm(-whale), cachalot *m.* **'sperm oil,** *s.* Huile *f* de baleine ; huile de spermaceti.

spermaceti [spə:rmə'seti], *s.* Spermaceti *m*; blanc *m*, sperme *m*, de baleine.

spew [spju:]. **1.** *v.tr. & i.* (*a*) Vomir. *Lit:* **To spew out,** forth, rejeter (avec dégoût). (*b*) (*Of ship*) To spew oakum, cracher ses étoupes. **2.** *v.i.* (*Of gun*) S'égueuler.

sphacelate ['sfasileit], *s.* **1.** *v.tr.* Sphacéler, gangrener. **2.** *v.i.* Se sphacéler, se gangrener.

sphacelus ['sfasiləs], *s. Med:* Sphacèle *m*; gangrène sèche.

sphagnum ['sfagnəm], *s. Bot:* Sphaigne *f.*

sphenoid ['sfi:nɔid], *a. & s. Anat:* Sphénoïde (*m*).

sphenoidal [sfi'nɔid(ə)l], *a. Anat:* Sphénoïdal, -aux.

sphere [sfiːər], *s.* **1.** Sphère *f. S.a.* MUSIC. **2.** (*a*) Milieu *m*, sphère. **To be out of one's sphere,** être hors de sa sphère ; se sentir dépaysé. **In the mental sphere,** dans le domaine de l'esprit. (*b*) *To extend one's s. of activity,* étendre sa sphère d'activité, le champ de son activité. *Limited s.,* cadre restreint. *That does not come within my sphere,* cela ne rentre pas dans ma compétence ; cela n'est pas de mon domaine, de mon ressort. **Sphere of influence,** sphère, zone *f*, d'influence.

spherical ['sferik(ə)l], *a.* Sphérique. *Mec.E:* Spherical joint, joint à rotule.

sphericity [sfe'risiti], *s.* Sphéricité *f.*

spheroid ['sfiːərɔid], *s.* Sphéroïde *m.*

spherometer [sfe'rometər], *s.* Sphéromètre *m.*

spherule ['sferjuːl], *s.* Sphérule *f.*

sphincter ['sfiŋktər], *s. Anat:* Sphincter *m.*

sphinx [sfiŋks], *s. Myth: Ent:* Sphinx *m.* **'sphinx-like,** *a.* (Sourire, etc.) de sphinx.

sphygmograph ['sfigmogrɑːf, -graf], *s. Med:* Sphygmographe *m.*

sphygmometer [sfig'mometər], *s. Med:* Sphygmomètre *m.*

spica ['spaikə], *s.* **1.** *Bot:* Épi *m.* **2.** *Surg:* Spica-bandage, spica *m*, épi.

spicate ['spaiket], *a. Bot:* Épié ; en épi, à épi.

spice[1] [spais], *s.* (*Coll. sg. preferred to pl.*) **1.** Épice *f*, aromate *m.* **Mixed spice(s),** épices mélangées. **Poultry spice(s),** produits stimulants pour volaille. **2.** Teinte *f* (de fourberie) ; nuance *f* (d'hypocrisie) ; soupçon *m* (de jalousie). **3.** **To give spice to a story,** pimenter un récit. **'spice-box,** *s.* Boîte *f* aux épices. **'spice-cake,** *s.* Gâteau *m* aux quatre épices.

spice[2], *v.tr.* **1.** Épicer (un mets). **2.** *F:* Épicer, pimenter (un récit, etc.).

spiciness ['spaisinəs], *s.* **1.** Goût épicé. **2.** *F:* Piquant *m*, sel *m* (d'un récit).

spick and span ['spikən(d)'span], *adj.phr.* Reluisant de propreté ; propre comme un sou neuf ; (*of pers.*) tiré à quatre épingles.

spicule ['spikjuːl], *s.* Spicule *m* (d'éponge) ; épillet *m*, spicule (de fleur) ; aiguillon *m.*

spicy ['spaisi], *a.* **1.** Épicé (goût) relevé. **2.** Aromatique, parfumé. **3.** *F:* (*Of story, etc.*) (i) Piquant, croustillant ; (ii) salé, épicé, poivré. *S. expressions,* termes pimentés, égrillards.

spider ['spaidər], *s.* **1.** Araignée *f.* **2.** *El.E:* Spider armature, induit *m* à croisillon(s). **3.** *U.S:* Trépied *m.* **4.** *Veh:* Spider(-cart), spider *m*, araignée. **'spider-crab,** *s.* Araignée *f* de mer. **'spider-lines,** *s.pl. Opt:* Fils *m* d'araignée ; réticule *m.*

spidery ['spaidəri], *a.* **1.** Qui ressemble à une

araignée. **Spidery handwriting**, pattes *fpl* d'araignée. **2.** (Grenier) infesté d'araignées.
spigot[1] ['spigət], *s.* **1.** Fausset *m*, broche *f*, cannelle *f* (de tonneau). **2.** (*a*) Clef *f*, carotte *f* (de robinet). (*b*) Robinet *m*. **3. Pipe spigot,** bout *m* mâle (d'un tuyau). **'spigot-joint,** *s.* Assemblage *m* à emboîtement.
spigot[2], *v.i.* S'encastrer (*into,* dans).
spike[1] [spaik], *s.* **1.** Pointe *f* (de fer); piquant *m* (de fil barbelé); (*on railing*) lance *f*. **2.** (*a*) Spike (-nail), clou *m* à large tête; broche *f*. (*b*) *Rail: etc:* Crampon *m* (d'attache). **Screw spike,** tire-fond *m inv.* **3.** *Bot:* (*a*) Épi *m*. (*b*) **Spike(-lavender),** lavande commune; spic *m*. **Spike oil,** essence *f* de spic. **4.** *Ven:* Spike(-horn), dague *f* (de cerf de deux ans).
spike[2], *v.tr.* (*a*) Clouer, cheviller. (*b*) Armer (qch.) de pointes. (*c*) *Artil:* Enclouer (un canon). *F:* **I spiked his guns for him,** je lui ai damé le pion. **spiked,** *a.* Garni de pointes; barbelé. **Spiked shoes,** chaussures à pointes.
spikelet ['spaiklet], *s. Bot:* Spicule *m*.
spikenard ['spaiknɑːrd], *s.* Nard (indien).
spiky ['spaiki], *a.* A pointe(s) aiguë(s).
spile[1] [spail], *s.* **1.** Cheville *f*, fausset *m*, broche *f* (d'un tonneau). **2.** Pilot *m*, pieu *m*.
spile[2], *v.tr.* Piloter (les fondements d'un édifice).
spill[1] [spil], *s.* **To have a spill,** culbuter; (*in motor car*) faire panache; (*from bicycle, horse*) *F:* ramasser une pelle, une bûche.
spill[2], *v.* (spilt [spilt] *or* spilled) I. *v.tr.* **1.** Répandre, renverser; verser (du sang). *F:* **Much ink has been spilt about this question,** on a fait couler beaucoup d'encre autour de cette question. **2.** Désarçonner (un cavalier); verser (les occupants d'une voiture). II. **spill,** *v.i.* (*Of liquid*) Se répandre; s'épancher, s'écouler.
spill[3], *s.* Allume-feu *m inv* en papier roulé; papillote *f* en papier; *F:* fidibus *m*.
spillikin ['spilikin], *s.* Jonchet *m*. **To play (at) spillikins,** jouer aux jonchets.
spin[1] [spin], *s.* **1.** (*a*) Tournoiement *m*; (mouvement *m* de) rotation *f* (d'une balle). *Games:* **To put spin on the ball,** donner de l'effet à la balle. (*b*) *Av:* (Tail) spin, vrille *f*. **Flat spin,** tonneau *m*. **To get into a spin,** descendre en vrille. **2. To go for a spin,** aller faire une promenade (en auto, etc.); faire une randonnée.
spin[2], *v.* (*p.t.* span [span], spun [spʌn]; *pr.p.* spinning) I. *v.tr.* (*a*) Filer (la laine, etc.). *S.a.* YARN[1] 2. (*b*) **To spin a top,** faire aller une toupie. **To spin a coin,** jouer à pile ou face. **To spin s.o. round,** faire tourner, faire tournoyer, qn. (*c*) *Fish:* Pêcher dans (un étang) à la cuiller. *Abs.* **To spin for fish,** pêcher au lancer. (*d*) *Metalw:* Emboutir, repousser, au tour. **2.** *v.i.* (*a*) (*Of top, etc.*) Tourner; (*of aeroplane*) descendre en vrille; (*of compass*) s'affoler. **To spin round and round,** tournoyer; *F:* toupiller. **My head is spinning,** la tête me tourne. (*Of pers.*) **To spin round,** (i) pivoter, virevolter; (ii) se retourner vivement. **Blow that sent him spinning,** coup qui l'a envoyé rouler. (*b*) (*Of wheel*) Patiner (sur place). **spin along,** *v.i.* (*Of carriage, etc.*) Filer (à toute vitesse). **spin out,** *v.tr.* Délayer (un discours); faire traîner (une affaire) en longueur. *v.i.* **To make one's money spin out,** ménager son argent. **spun,** *a.* **1.** *Tex:* Câblé. (*b*) *Metalw:* (Cuivre) repoussé. *S.a.* GLASS I. **spinning,** *s.* **1.** (*a*) Filage *m* (au rouet). (*b*) *Ind:* Filature *f*. **2.** Tournoiement *m*; (mouvement *m* de) rotation *f*; affolement *m* (de l'aiguille magnétique). *Av:* Vrille *f*. **Spinning top,** toupie *f*. **3.** Pêche *f* au

lancer. **'spinning-frame,** *s.* Métier *m* à filer. **'spinning-mill,** *s.* Filature *f*. **'spinning-wheel,** *s.* Rouet *m*.
spinach ['spinedʒ], *s. Bot:* Épinard *m*; *Cu:* épinards *mpl*.
spinal ['spain(ə)l], *a.* Spinal, -aux. **Spinal column,** colonne vertébrale. *S.a.* CORD[1].
spindle [spindl], *s.* **1.** *Tex:* Fuseau *m*. **2.** *Mec.E: etc:* Mandrin *m*; axe *m* (de pompe); arbre *m*, broche *f* (de tour, etc.). **Valve spindle,** tige *f* de soupape. *Nau:* **Spindle of the capstan,** mèche *f* du cabestan. *Veh:* **Axle spindle,** fusée *f* d'essieu. **'spindle-berry,** *s. Bot:* Baie *f* du fusain. **'spindle-shanks,***s.pl. F:* **1.** Jambes *f* de fuseau; mollets *m* de coq. **2.** (*With sg. const.*) Type grand et maigre. **'spindle-shaped,** *a.* Fusiforme, fuselé. **'spindle-side,***s.* Le côté maternel (d'une famille); la quenouille. **'spindle-tree,** *s. Arb:* Fusain *m*.
spindrift ['spindrift], *s.* Embrun courant; poussière *f* d'eau; poudrin *m*.
spine [spain], *s.* **1.** *Nat.Hist:* Épine *f*; piquant *m* (de hérisson). **2.** *Anat:* Épine dorsale; colonne vertébrale.
spinel ['spin(ə)l], *s. Miner:* Spinelle *m*.
spineless ['spainləs], *a. F:* (*Of pers.*) Mou, *f.* molle; qui manque de caractère.
spinet ['spinet], *s. Mus:* Épinette *f*.
spinnaker ['spinakər], *s. Nau:* Spinnaker *m*. *S.a.* BOOM[1] 2.
spinner ['spinər], *s.* **1.** Araignée fileuse. **2.** *Tex:* Fileur, -euse. **Master spinner,** filateur *m*. **3.** Machine *f* à filer; métier *m* à filer. **4.** = SPINNERET.
spinneret ['spinəret], *s.* Filière *f* (de ver à soie, etc.).
spinney ['spini], *s.* Petit bois; bosquet *m*.
spinster ['spinstər], *s.f.* (*a*) Fille non mariée; *Adm:* célibataire *f*. (*b*) Vieille fille.
spinthariscope [spin'θariskoup], *s.* Spinthariscope *m*.
spinule ['spainjuːl], *s. Nat.Hist:* Spinule *f*.
spiny ['spaini], *a.* Épineux; couvert d'épines ou de piquants. *S.a.* LOBSTER.
spiracle ['spairəkl], *s.* (*a*) Évent *m* (d'un cétacé). (*b*) *Ent:* Stigmate *m*.
spiraea [spai'riːa], *s. Bot:* Spirée *f*.
spiral[1] ['spairəl]. **I.** *s.* (*a*) Spirale, hélice *f*. **In a s.,** en spirale. (*b*) Spire *f*; tour *m* (de spirale). **2.** *a.* Spiral, -aux; hélicoïdal, -aux; en spirale; vrillé; (ressort) en boudin; (mouvement) spiroïdal, -aux. *S. gear,* engrenage hélicoïdal. *S. curl of smoke,* volute *f* de fumée. *Surg:* **Spiral bandage,** bandage rampant. *S.a.* CONVEYOR, STAIRCASE. **-ally,** *adv.* En spirale, en hélice. **'spiral-wound,** *a.* Enroulé en spirale.
spiral[2], *v.i.* (spiralled) Former une spirale; tourner en spirale; monter en spirale; (*of smoke*) tire-bouchonner.
spirant ['spairənt], *s. Ling:* Spirante *f*.
spire[1] ['spaiər], *s.* Aiguille *f*, flèche *f* (d'église).
spire[2], *s.* Spire *f*, tour *m* (d'une hélice, etc.).
spirit[1] ['spirit], *s.* **1.** Esprit *m*, âme *f*. *He was vexed in spirit,* il avait l'esprit tourmenté. *Peace to his spirit,* la paix soit de son âme. **2.** (*a*) **The Holy Spirit,** le Saint-Esprit. **Evil spirit,** esprit malin, mauvais génie. *S.a.* MOVE[2] I. 3. (*b*) **To raise a spirit,** évoquer un esprit. *To believe in spirits,* croire aux esprits, aux revenants. **3.** (*Pers.*) *The discontented spirits of the regiment,* les esprits factieux du régiment. **The leading spirit,** (i) l'âme, le chef d'une entreprise); (ii) le meneur (d'une révolte). **4.** Esprit, disposition *f*

The spirit of the age, l'esprit de l'âge. Party spirit, esprit de parti. *S.a.* PUBLIC I. To follow out the spirit of s.o.'s instructions, se conformer à l'intention des ordres de qn. To take sth. in a wrong spirit, prendre qch. en mauvaise part, de travers. In a spirit of mischief, par espièglerie. To enter into the spirit of sth., entrer de bon cœur dans (la partie). 5. (a) Caractère *m*, cœur *m*, courage *m*; *F*: cran *m*. Man of spirit, homme de caractère. To show spirit, montrer du caractère, du courage. To catch s.o.'s spirit, être enflammé par le courage de qn. (b) Ardeur *f*, entrain *m*, fougue *f*. He went on playing with s., il continua de jouer avec entrain, avec brio. (c) He is full of spirits, il est très remuant, très diable. To be in good spirits, être gai, dispos; être de bonne humeur. To be in high spirits, être en train, en verve; être d'une gaieté folle. To be in low spirits, être abattu, accablé; se sentir tout triste. To keep up one's spirits, ne pas perdre courage; ne pas se laisser abattre. To recover one's spirits, reprendre courage; se remonter. *Their spirits rose,* ils reprenaient courage, leur moral se relevait. 6. *Usu. pl.* (a) Spiritueux *mpl*; liqueurs spiritueuses, alcooliques; alcool *m*. Raw spirits, alcool pur, naturel; *P*: casse-gueule *m*. Glass of spirits and water, verre d'eau-de-vie à l'eau. (b) Spirit(s) of salts, esprit de sel. Spirit of turpentine, essence *f* de térébenthine. 'spirit-lamp, *s.* Lampe *f* ou réchaud *m* à alcool, à esprit de vin. 'spirit-level, *s.* Niveau *m* à bulle d'air, à alcool. 'spirit-rapper, *s.* Médium *m* (spirite) (qui évoque des esprits frappeurs). 'spirit-stove, *s.* Réchaud *m* à alcool.

spirit², *v.tr.* (spirited) I. To spirit s.o. away, faire disparaître qn comme par enchantement. To spirit sth. away, *F*: subtiliser, escamoter, qch. 2. To spirit s.o. (up), animer, encourager, qn.

spirited ['spiritid], *a.* I. (High-)spirited, (of pers.) vif, animé; plein de verve, d'ardeur; (of horse) fougueux, ardent, vif. 2. (Of style) Chaleureux, entraînant, plein de verve. To give a s. performance, jouer avec verve. -ly, *adv.* Ardemment; avec verve, avec entrain.

spiritedness ['spiritidnəs], *s.* Ardeur *f*, entrain *m*, verve *f*; fougue *f*, ardeur (d'un cheval).

spiritless ['spiritləs], *a.* I. Sans vie; terne; qui manque d'entrain. 2. Sans courage, sans caractère; lâche. 3. Abattu, déprimé. 4. Sans force, sans vigueur; mou, *f.* molle. -ly, *adv.* Sans vigueur; sans entrain; mollement.

spiritual ['spiritjuəl]. I. *a.* (a) Spirituel; de l'esprit. Spiritual court, tribunal ecclésiastique. (b) Spiritual features, traits purs, raffinés. (c) Spirituel, immatériel. 2. *s.* Negro spirituals, chants religieux des nègres.

spiritualism ['spiritjuəlizm], *s.* I. *Psychics:* Spiritisme *m*. 2. *Phil:* Spiritualisme *m*.

spiritualist ['spiritjuəlist], *s. & a.* I. *Psychics:* Spirite (*mf*). 2. *Phil:* Spiritualiste (*mf*).

spirituous ['spiritjuəs], *a.* Spiritueux, alcoolique. *S.a.* LIQUOR I.

spirometer [spai'rɔmətər], *s.* Spiromètre *m*.

spirt¹ [spəːrt], *s.* I. Jaillissement *m*; rejaillissement *m*; jet *m*. *S. of petrol,* giclée *f* d'essence. 2. = SPURT².

pirt². I. *v.i.* To spirt up, jaillir. To spirt out, saillir, gicler. To spirt back, rejaillir. 2. *v.tr.* To spirt (out) a liquid, faire jaillir, faire gicler, un liquide. Pen that spirts, plume qui coule, qui crache. 3. *v.i.* = SPURT⁴.

spit¹ [spit], *s.* I. *Cu:* Broche *f*. 2. *Ph.Geog:*

Langue *f* de sable; digue *f*; pointe *f*, ras *m*, de terre. Shingle-spit, cordon *m*; levée *f* de galets. spit², *v.tr.* (spitted) (a) Embrocher, mettre à la broche (un rôti). (b) *F*: Embrocher (qn).

spit³, *s.* I. (a) Crachat *m*, salive *f*. *F*: He's the dead spit of his father, c'est son père tout craché. *P*: Spit and polish, fourbissage *m*; astiquage *m*. (b) Crachement *m*. 2. Crachin *m* (de pluie).

spit⁴, *v.* (spat [spat]; spat; spitting) I. *v.i.* Cracher. *I.C.E:* (Of engine) To spit back, avoir des retours de flamme (au carburateur). It is spitting (with rain), il crachine; il tombe quelques gouttes. *The bullets went spitting against the wall,* les balles allaient s'aplatir sur le mur. 2. *v.tr.* Cracher (du sang). To spit sth. out, cracher qch. *P*: Spit it out! dis-le!

spit⁵, *s.* Profondeur *f* de fer de bêche. To dig two-spit(s) deep, labourer la terre à deux fers de bêche.

spite¹ [spait], *s.* I. (a) Rancune *f*. (b) Malveillance *f*. (c) Pique *f*, dépit *m*. From spite, out of spite, (i) par rancune; (ii) par dépit; (iii) par malveillance, par méchanceté. To have a spite against s.o., en vouloir à qn; garder rancune à qn. 2. *Prep.phr.* In spite of . . ., en dépit de . . .; malgré. . .

spite², *v.tr.* Vexer, contrarier (qn).

spiteful ['spaitful], *a.* Rancunier, vindicatif; méchant, malveillant. *S. tongue,* langue venimeuse. -fully, *adv.* I. Par dépit; par rancune; par méchanceté. 2. Méchamment.

spitefulness ['spaitfulnəs], *s.* Méchanceté *f*; rancœur *f*; malveillance *f*.

spitfire ['spitfaiər], *s.* *F*: Rageur, -euse.

spittle [spitl], *s.* Salive *f*, crachat *m*; bave *f* (du crapaud).

spittoon [spi'tuːn], *s.* Crachoir *m*.

splash¹ [splaʃ], *s.* I. Éclaboussement *m*; clapotis *m* (des vagues). To fall into the water with a splash, tomber dans l'eau en faisant flac. *F*: To make a splash, faire de l'épate. 2. (a) Éclaboussure *f* (de boue, etc.). (b) Tache *f* (de couleur, de lumière). (c) Flaque *f* (d'eau). (d) *F*: Poudre *f* de riz. 'splash-board, *s.* *Veh:* (Tablier *m*) pare-boue *m inv*; garde-boue *m inv.* 'splash-lubrication, *s.* *Mec.E:* Graissage *m* par barbotage.

splash². I. *v.tr.* (a) Éclabousser (with, de). (b) To splash water about, faire rejaillir l'eau. *F*: To splash one's money about, prodiguer son argent. 2. *v.i.* (a) (Of liquid) Rejaillir en éclaboussures; (of waves) clapoter; (of tap) cracher. To splash up, gicler. (b) Barboter; patauger. To splash into the water, entrer dans l'eau en faisant rejaillir des éclaboussures. To splash about in the water, s'agiter dans l'eau.

splay¹ [splei], *s.* I. (a) *Arch:* Embrasure *f* (b) (Bevelled edge) Chanfrein *m*; coupe *f* oblique. 2. (Of bowl, etc.) Évasement *m*, évasure *f*.

splay². I. *v.tr.* (a) To s. the sides of a window, ébraser une fenêtre. To splay out an embrasure, épanouir une embrasure. (b) *Carp:* Couper en biseau, en sifflet; chanfreiner. (c) *Vet:* To splay a horse's shoulder, épauler un cheval; démettre l'épaule d'un cheval. 2. *v.i.* To splay out, s'évaser. splayed, *a.* I. (Of opening) Ébrasé, évasé. Splayed wheel, roue désaxée. 2. *Carp:* En sifflet.

splay³, *a.* Bricks cut splay, briques biaises. 'splay-footed, *a.* Aux pieds plats tournés en dehors.

spleen [spliːn], *s.* I. *Anat:* Rate *f*. 2. (a) Spleen *m*; humeur noire. In a fit of spleen, dans un moment d'humeur noire. (b) Mauvaise humeur.

To vent one's spleen (up)on s.o., décharger sa rate, sa bile, sur qn. **splendid** ['splendid], a. Splendide; superbe; magnifique. **She's simply splendid!** elle est vraiment merveilleuse! **That's splendid!** à la bonne heure! **-ly**, adv. Splendidement; magnifiquement. **I am getting on s.**, ça marche comme sur des roulettes. **splendour** ['splendər], s. Splendeur f; magnificence f, éclat m. **splenic** ['splenik], a. Anat: Splénique. **splice**[1] [splais], s. **1.** (In rope) Épissure f. (In wire cable) Ligature f; joint épissé. **2.** (a) Carp: Enture f. (b) Collure f, point m de collage (d'un film). (c) Soudure f (d'un pneu). **splice**[2], v.tr. **1.** Épisser (un cordage, un câble). S.a. MAIN-BRACE. **2.** Carp: Enter. **3.** Cin: Réparer (un film cassé). **4.** F: **To get spliced**, se marier. **spline**[1] [splain], s. Mec.E: **1.** (a) Languette f; clavette f linguiforme. (b) Saillie f (d'un arbre); ergot m. **2.** Cannelure f, rainure f. **Two-spline hole**, trou à deux rainures. **spline**[2], v.tr. Mec.E: **1.** Claveter. **2.** Canneler, rainurer. **splint**[1] [splint], s. **1.** Surg: Éclisse f, attelle f; (cradle-shaped) gouttière f. **To put a limb in splints**, éclisser un membre. **2.** Vet: Suros m. **'splint-bone**, s. **1.** Os métacarpien (du cheval). **2.** Anat: Péroné m. **'splint-coal**, s. Houille sèche à longue flamme. **splint**[2], v.tr. Surg: Éclisser (un membre fracturé). **splinter**[1] ['splintər], s. **1.** Éclat m (de bois, d'obus); picot m (de bois). **S. lodged under the skin**, écharde f. **2.** Surg: Esquille f (d'os). **'splinter-deck**, s. N.Arch: Pont m pare-éclats. **'splinter-proof**, a. **1.** A l'épreuve des éclats (d'obus). **2.** (Verre) se brisant sans éclats. **splinter**[2]. **1.** v.tr. (a) Briser en éclats; faire voler en éclats. (b) Éclater (un mât, etc.). **2.** v.i. (a) Voler en éclats. (b) Éclater. **splintered**, a. (Bois) en éclats; (os) en esquilles, esquilleux. **split**[1] [split], s. **1.** Fente f; fissure f; crevasse f (dans une roche); déchirure f; gerçure f (de la peau). **2.** Division f, séparation f; rupture f, scission f (dans un parti). **3.** Coupe m de bouteille; demi-bouteille f. **4.** **Devonshire split**, brioche fourrée à la crème. **5.** pl. Danc: **To do the splits**, faire le grand écart. **split**[2], v. (split; split; splitting) **1.** v.tr. (a) Fendre; refendre (l'ardoise); cliver (la roche). **To s. an apple**, couper une pomme en deux. Leath: **To split a hide**, dédoubler une peau. Ph: **To split the atom**, désintégrer l'atome. S.a. HAIR 1, SIDE[1] 1. (b) Déchirer (sa jupe, etc.). (c) Diviser; partager. (d) Pol: **To s. a party** (on a question), diviser un parti (sur une question); provoquer une rupture dans le parti. Fin: **To split shares**, fractionner, scinder, des actions. **2.** v.i. (a) Se fendre, se crevasser; (of rock) se cliver; (of paint, skin) se gercer. **The ship split in two**, le navire s'est cassé en deux. **To split open**, se fendre largement. (b) (Of cloth) Se déchirer. (c) F: **My head is splitting**, j'ai un mal de tête fou. (d) F: **To split on s.o.**, dénoncer qn; vendre (un complice); F: cafarder. **split up**. **1.** v.tr. Fractionner; décomposer (une fraction). **2.** v.i. Se fractionner. **The party split up into three groups**, le parti se divisa en trois groupes. **split**[3], a. **1.** Fendu. **Split cane**, bambou refendu. Tls: **Split key**, clef anglaise.

S.a. RING[1] 2, SECOND[1] 1. **2.** (a) F: **A split Vichy** un quart ou une demi-bouteille de Vichy. (b) Psy: **Split personality**, dédoublement m de la personnalité. **splotch**[1] [splɔtʃ], s. F: Tache f (de couleur, etc.). **splotch**[2], v.tr. Barbouiller (with, de); tacher. **splutter**[1] ['splʌtər], s. **1.** Bredouillement m. **2.** Crachement m (d'une plume); bafouillage m (d'un moteur). **splutter**[2]. **1.** v.tr. **To splutter (out) a threat**, bredouiller une menace. **2.** v.i. (a) Lancer de la salive (en parlant); P: envoyer des postillons. **Pen that splutters**, plume qui crache. (b) Bredouiller, bafouiller. (c) I.C.E: (Of engine) Bafouiller. **spoil**[1] [spɔil], s. **1.** (Usu. pl.) Dépouilles fpl; butin m. **Laden with the spoils of the chase**, chargé du produit de la chasse. **To make spoil of s.o.'s flowers**, piller les fleurs de qn. **2.** Min: etc: **Spoil(-earth)**, déblai(s) m(pl). **'spoil-bank**, **-dump**, s. Min: etc: Halde f. **spoil**[2], v. (p.t. & p.p. spoiled or (except in sense 2) spoilt) **1.** v.tr. (a) Gâter, endommager, abîmer (qch.); avarier (des marchandises). **To get spoiled, spoilt**, s'abîmer. **To s. a piece of work**, gâcher un travail. **To s. a lock**, fausser, mêler, une serrure. **To spoil the beauty of sth.**, s.o. déparer qch.; détruire la beauté de qn. **To s. a sauce**, manquer une sauce. **The news spoilt his appetite**, la nouvelle lui a coupé l'appétit. (b) Gâter (un enfant). B. & Lit: (a) Dépouiller, spolier (s.o. of sth., qn de qch.). F: **To spoil the Egyptians**, piller, dépouiller, l'ennemi (héréditaire). (b) Piller, saccager (une ville). **3.** v.i. (Of fruit, etc.) Se gâter, s'abîmer; s'avarier, s'altérer. F: **To be spoiling for a fight**, brûler du désir de se battre. **'spoil-sport**, s. F: Trouble-fête m inv, rabat-joie mf inv. **'spoil-trade**, s. F: Concurrent déloyal; gâte-métier m inv. **spoilage** ['spɔilidʒ], s. Typ: Déchets mpl de tirage. **spoke**[1] [spouk], s. **1.** (a) Rayon m, rais m (de roue). (b) Nau: Poignée f, manette f (de roue de gouvernail). **2.** (a) Échelon m (d'échelle). (b) Bâton m (à enrayer). F: **To put a spoke in s.o.'s wheel**, mettre des bâtons dans les roues à qn. **spoke**[2], v.tr. Enrayer (une roue). **spoke**[3], **spoken.** See SPEAK. **spokeshave** ['spoukʃeiv], s. Tls: Vastringue f, racloire f. **spokesman**, pl. **-men** ['spouksmən, -men], s. Porte-parole m inv. **To act as spokesman for one's fellow-citizens**, porter la parole pour ses concitoyens. **spokewise** ['spoukwaiz], adv. Radialement. **spoliation** [spouli'eiʃ(ə)n], s. **1.** (a) Spoliation f, dépouillement m. (b) Pillage m. **2.** Jur: Destruction f ou altération f (de documents probants). **spondaic** [spɔn'deiik], a. Pros: Spondaïque. **spondee** ['spɔndi:], s. Pros: Spondée m. **sponge**[1] [spʌndʒ], s. **1.** (a) Éponge f. **To throw up the sponge**, (i) Box: jeter l'éponge; abandonner; (ii) F: s'avouer vaincu; quitter la partie. (b) Artil: Écouvillon m. **2.** (a) Cu: Pâte molle. (b) Metall: Éponge métallique. S.a. PLATINUM. **3.** = SPONGER. **'sponge-bag**, s. Sac m à éponge. **'sponge-bath**, s. Tub m. **'sponge-cake**, s. Cu: **1.** Gâteau m de Savoie; gâteau mousseline. **2.** Madeleine f. **'sponge-cloth**, s. Tex: Tissu-éponge m. **'sponge-finger**, s. Biscuit m à la cuiller. **sponge**[2]. Coup m d'éponge. **To give sth. a sponge**, passer l'éponge sur qch.

sponge³. I. *v.tr.* (*a*) Éponger (qch.); nettoyer (qch.) avec une éponge. *To s. a child's face*, passer l'éponge sur le visage d'un enfant. (*b*) *Med:* Lotionner (une plaie). (*c*) *F:* Écornifler (un dîner, etc.). **2.** *v.i.* *F:* Écornifler; *F:* écumer la marmite. **To sponge on s.o.**, vivre aux crochets de qn. *To s. on s.o. for drinks*, se faire payer des tournées par qn. **sponge down,** *v.tr.* Passer l'éponge sur le corps de (qn); éponger (un cheval). **sponge off,** *v.tr.* Enlever (une tache) à l'éponge. **sponge out,** *v.tr.* **I.** Effacer (une tache) à l'éponge. **2.** *Artil:* Écouvillonner (une pièce) à l'eau. **sponging¹,** *a.* *F:* (*Of pers.*) Parasite, écornifleur. **sponging²,** *s.* **I.** (*a*) Nettoyage m à l'éponge. (*b*) *Med:* Lotionnement m. **2.** *F:* Écorniflage m. **'sponging-house,** *Hist:* Prison f provisoire pour dettes.

sponger ['spʌndʒər], *s.* *F:* Parasite m; écornifleur, -euse; pique-assiette m inv.

sponginess ['spʌndʒinəs], *s.* Spongiosité f.

spongy ['spʌndʒi], *a.* Spongieux.

sponsion ['spɔnʃ(ə)n], *s.* *Jur:* Garantie (personnelle) (*on behalf of*, en faveur de).

sponson ['spɔnsən], *s.* **I.** *N.Arch:* Paddle-box sponson, jardin m des tambours. **2.** *Av:* Stabilizing sponson, nageoire f.

sponsor¹ ['spɔnsər], *s.* **I.** Garant m, caution f, répondant m (*for s.o.*, de qn). **2.** (*a*) (*At baptism*) Parrain m, marraine f. **To stand sponsor to a child**, tenir un enfant sur les fonts (baptismaux). (*b*) (*Introducing new member to club, etc.*) Parrain.

sponsor², *v.tr.* Être le garant de, répondre pour (qn).

spontaneity [spɔntə'niːiti], *s.* Spontanéité f.

spontaneous [spɔn'teinjəs], *a.* Spontané; (i) (mouvement) automatique; (ii) (acte) volontaire. **-ly,** *adv.* Spontanément; (i) automatiquement; (ii) de son propre mouvement.

spontaneousness [spɔn'teinjəsnəs], *s.* Spontanéité f.

spoof¹ [spuːf], *s.* *P:* Attrape f; mystification f.

spoof², *v.tr.* Mystifier, duper (qn). *You've been spoofed*, on vous a eu.

spook [spuːk], *s.* *F:* Spectre m, revenant m, apparition f.

spool¹ [spuːl], *s.* **I.** *Tex:* Bobine f, can(n)ette f. *S. of a sewing-machine*, can(n)ette. *U.S:* *S. of thread*, bobine de coton (à coudre). **2.** *Fish:* Tambour m (de moulinet). **3.** Film-spool, *Phot:* bobine de film; *Cin:* bobine, rouleau m. *Typewr:* Ribbon spools, bobines du ruban. **'spool-box,** *Cin:* Carter m.

spool², *v.tr.* Bobiner; dévider ou envider (du fil, etc.).

spoon¹ [spuːn], *s.* **I.** Cuiller f, cuillère f. Teaspoon, cuiller à thé. Spoon and fork, couvert m. *Cu:* Basting spoon, louche f. **2.** *Metall:* etc: Assay spoon, éprouvette f. **'spoon-bit,** *s.* *Tls:* Mèche f à cuiller. **'spoon-feed,** *v.tr.* Nourrir (un enfant) à la cuiller. *F:* To spoon-feed a pupil, mâcher les morceaux à un élève. **'spoonnet,** *s.* *Fish:* Épuisette f.

spoon². I. *v.tr.* (*a*) To spoon (up) one's soup, manger sa soupe (avec la cuiller). To spoon off the cream, enlever la crème (avec la cuiller). (*b*) *Cr:* *Golf:* Prendre (la balle) en cuiller. **2.** *v.i.* *F:* (*Of couple*) Se faire des mamours.

spoonbill ['spuːnbil], *s.* *Orn:* Spatule f. Spoonbill duck, souchet m.

Spoonerism ['spuːnərizm], *s.* *F:* Contrepetterie f.

spoonful ['spuːnful], *s.* Cuillerée f. Two dessert-spoonfuls, deux cuillerées à dessert.

---

spoor¹ ['spuər], *s.* *Ven:* Foulées fpl, erre f (d'un cerf, etc.).

spoor², *v.tr.* *Ven:* Suivre (un animal) à la piste.

sporadic [spɔ'radik], *a.* **I.** Sporadique. **2.** Isolé; rare. **-ally,** *adv.* **I.** Sporadiquement. **2.** Dans des cas isolés; par-ci par-là.

sporangium, *pl.* **-ia** [spɔ'randʒiəm, -ia], *s.* *Bot:* Sporange m.

spore ['spɔːər], *s.* Spore f. **'spore-case,** *s.* *Bot:* Sporange m.

sporran ['spɔrən], *s.* *Scot:* Bourse en peau brute (portée par les Highlanders sur le devant du kilt).

sport¹ [spɔːrt], *s.* **I.** (*a*) Jeu m, divertissement m. In sport, pour rire; par plaisanterie; en badinant. **To make sport of . . .**, se moquer de . . ., se jouer de. . . . *They made a s. of baiting him*, ils se faisaient un jeu de le tourmenter. (*b*) **To have good sport,** (*hunting*) faire bonne chasse; (*fishing*) faire bonne pêche. **2.** Sport m. Athletic sports, sports athlétiques. **To go in for sports,** s'adonner aux sports. *Aut:* Sports model, machine grand sport. **3.** **To be the sport of fortune,** être le jouet de la fortune. **4.** *Biol:* Variété anormale; variation sportive. **5.** *F:* He's a (real) sport, (i) c'est un beau joueur; (ii) c'est un chic type. **Be a sport!** sois chic! **'sportsground,** *s.* Terrain m de jeux; stade m. **'sports-jacket,** *s.* Veston m tous sports.

sport². I. *v.i.* (*a*) Jouer; se divertir. (*b*) *Biol:* Produire une variété anormale. **2.** *v.tr.* *F:* Arborer (son huit-reflets); exhiber (un manteau de fourrure). *S.a.* OAK. **sporting¹,** *a.* **I.** Amateur de la chasse ou de la pêche. **2.** De sport; sportif. **Sporting man,** amateur m de sport. In a sporting spirit, sportivement. *S. conduct,* conduite digne d'un sportsman. **You have a sporting chance,** ça vaut la peine d'essayer le coup. *I'll make you a sporting offer*, je vais vous faire une offre à laquelle vous ne perdrez rien. **sporting²,** *s.* (*a*) La chasse; la pêche. Sporting gun, fusil de chasse. (*b*) Le sport. The sporting results, les résultats des courses.

sportive ['spɔːrtiv], *a.* Badin; folâtre. **-ly,** *adv.* En badinant; en plaisantant.

sportsman, *pl.* **-men** ['spɔːrtsmən, -men], *s.m.* **I.** Chasseur ou pêcheur. **2.** Amateur de sport. **3.** He's a real sportsman, il est animé de l'esprit sportif; c'est un beau joueur.

sportsmanlike ['spɔːrtsmənlaik], *a.* (Conduite) digne d'un sportsman.

sportsmanship ['spɔːrtsmənʃip], *s.* Habileté f, qualités fpl, de sport; pratique f des sports.

sporule ['spɔrjuːl], *s.* Sporule f.

spot¹ [spɔt], *s.* **I.** (*a*) Endroit m, lieu m. A rustic s., un petit coin rustique. *I was standing on the very s.*, je me trouvais sur les lieux mêmes. *The manager should always be on the s.*, le gérant doit toujours être là. (*b*) *U.S:* *P:* To put s.o. on the spot, assassiner qn. (*c*) *Adv.phr.* On the spot, sur-le-champ; immédiatement. **To be killed on the spot,** être tué sur place, raide. *To fall dead on the s.*, tomber raide mort. (*d*) *Com:* Spot cash, argent comptant. (*e*) **To put one's finger on a weak spot,** mettre le doigt sur un point faible. **To touch the spot,** aller jusqu'à la racine du mal. **2.** (*a*) Tache f, macule f. (*b*) *U.S:* (*Of fruit*) Bouton m. **3.** (*a*) Pois m (de couleur). Blue tie with red spots, cravate bleue à pois rouges. *A panther's spots*, la tacheture, la moucheture, d'une panthère. *F:* To knock spots off s.o., battre qn à plate(s) couture(s). (*b*) *Bill:* (i) Mouche f (sur la bille ou la table). (ii) Bille marquée d'une mouche. **4.** (*a*) Goutte f (de pluie). (*b*) *F:* Just a spot of

whisky, deux doigts de whisky. **A spot of trouble,** un petit ennui ; une anicroche.
spot², *v.tr.* (spotted) **I.** (*a*) Tacher, souiller (qch.). (*b*) Tacheter, moucheter (qch.). **2.** *F:* (*a*) Repérer ; apercevoir (qn, qch.). *He spotted me from his box,* il m'a repéré de sa loge. (*b*) Reconnaître. *Turf:* **To spot the winner,** prédire le gagnant.
spotted, *a.* **I.** (*a*) Tacheté, moucheté. (*b*) *Tex:* A pois. **2. Spotted fever,** méningite cérébro-spinale. **3.** *F:* **Spotted dog,** pouding *m* aux raisins de Corinthe. **spotting,** *s.* **I.** Taches *fpl* ; tachetures *fpl.* **2.** *Phot:* Repiquage *m* (des épreuves). **3.** (*a*) Repérage *m.* (*b*) *Artil:* **Aircraft spotting,** réglage *m* par avions.
spotless ['spɔtləs], *a.* Sans tache ; immaculé ; pur. *S. snow,* neige vierge. **-ly,** *adv.* **Spotlessly clean,** d'une propreté irréprochable.
spotlight ['spɔtlait], *s.* **I.** *Th: Cin:* (*a*) Feu *m* de projecteur. (*b*) Projecteur *m.* **2.** *Aut:* Projecteur auxiliaire orientable.
spotter ['spɔtər], *s.* *Av:* Avion *m* de réglage de tir.
spotty ['spɔti], *a.* Moucheté, tacheté ; (visage) couvert de boutons.
spouse [spauz], *s.* *Lit:* Époux, *f.* épouse.
spout¹ [spaut], *s.* **I.** (*a*) **Rain-water spout,** (i) tuyau *m* de décharge ; (ii) gargouille *f* (de gouttière). (*b*) Bec *m* (de théière) ; jet *m,* dégorgeoir *m* (de pompe). **2.** *P:* **To put one's watch up the spout,** mettre sa montre au clou. **3.** *Meteor:* Trombe *f.*
spout² **I.** *v.i.* (*a*) (*Of liquid*) Jaillir, rejaillir. (*b*) (*Of whale*) Souffler. **2.** *v.tr.* (*a*) Faire jaillir, lancer (de l'eau). (*b*) *P:* Dégoiser (des discours). *Abs.* **To spout,** parler à jet continu. **spouting,** *s.* **I.** Jaillissement *m.* **2.** *F:* Déclamation *f.*
spouter ['spautər], *s.* *F:* Déclamateur *m,* péroreur *m.*
sprag [sprag], *s.* *Veh:* (*a*) Cale *f.* (*b*) Bâton *m* (pour enrayer les roues). (*c*) *Aut:* Béquille *f* de recul.
sprain¹ [sprein], *s.* Entorse *f,* foulure *f.*
sprain², *v.tr.* **To sprain one's wrist,** se fouler le poignet. **To sprain one's ankle,** se donner une entorse.
sprang [spraŋ]. *See* SPRING².
sprat [sprat], *s.* **I.** *Ich:* Sprat *m,* harenguet *m.* **2.** *F:* Gringalet *m.*
sprawl [sprɔːl], *v.i.* (*a*) S'étendre, s'étaler. (*b*) **To go sprawling,** s'étaler par terre ; *P:* ramasser une pelle. **sprawling,** *a.* **I.** (*a*) Vautré. (*b*) Étendu les quatre fers en l'air. **2.** *S. handwriting,* grosse écriture informe.
spray¹ [sprei], *s.* **Spray of flowers,** rameau fleuri. **Spray of diamonds,** aigrette *f* de diamants.
spray², *s.* **I.** Poudroiement *m* d'écume ; embrun *m.* **2.** (*a*) Poussière *f* d'eau. (*b*) Jet pulvérisé (de parfum). **3.** (*a*) Liquide *m* pour vaporisation. (*b*) Coup *m* de vaporisateur ; jet (de parfum). (*c*) Gicleur *m* ; vaporisateur *m.* **'spray-cone,** *s.* *I.C.E:* Diffuseur *m.*
spray³, *v.tr.* **I.** Pulvériser, vaporiser, atomiser (un liquide). **2.** Asperger, arroser. *Hort:* **To spray a tree,** passer un arbre au vaporisateur. **spraying,** *s.* **I.** Pulvérisation *f,* vaporisation *f* (d'un liquide). **Spraying machine,** pulvérisateur *m,* vaporisateur *m.* **2.** Arrosage *m.*
sprayer ['spreiər], *s.* *Hort:* Vaporisateur *m* (d'insecticide) ; pulvérisateur *m,* atomiseur *m.*
spread¹ [spred], *s.* **I.** (*a*) Étendue *f* (de pays, etc.). (*b*) (*Of bird's wings, of aeroplane*) Envergure *f.* **2.** (*a*) Diffusion *f* (de l'éducation) ; propagation *f* (d'une doctrine) ; expansion *f* (des

idées). (*b*) *Ball:* Dispersion *f* (du tir). **3.** = BED-SPREAD. **4.** *F:* Régal *m,* festin *m.* **Cold spread,** repas froid.
spread², *v.* (spread ; spread) **I.** *v.tr.* **I.** Étendre. **To spread a net,** tendre un filet. **To spread the sails,** déployer les voiles. **To spread out goods for sale,** étaler des marchandises. **To** *s.* **oneself on a subject,** se répandre sur un sujet. **2.** (*a*) Répandre (du sable, des nouvelles, la terreur). **Spread it abroad!** qu'on se le dise ! (*b*) Instalments spread over several months, versements échelonnés sur plusieurs mois. **3.** **To spread butter on a slice of bread,** étendre du beurre sur une tranche de pain. **4. To spread a surface with** sth., couvrir une surface de qch. **To spread the table,** mettre la table; (*b*) mettre le couvert. **II. spread,** *v.i.* **I.** S'étendre, s'étaler. *Here the river spreads out,* ici la rivière s'élargit. **2.** (*Of news*) se disséminer ; se répandre ; (*of disease*) se propager. **The fire is spreading,** le feu gagne. *His fame had spread,* sa renommée s'était répandue. **3.** (*Of small shot*) S'écarter, se disperser. **spread-'eagle¹,** *s.* *Her:* Aigle éployée. **spread-'eagle²,** *v.tr.* Étaler (qch.). *F:* *Bathers lying spread-eagled on the sand,* baigneurs vautrés sur la plage. **spreading,** *s.* **I.** (*a*) Déploiement *m,* développement *m.* (*b*) Colportage *m* (d'une nouvelle) ; propagation *f* (d'une maladie) ; diffusion *f* (de l'éducation). **2.** (*a*) Extension *f* (d'une industrie). (*b*) Dispersion *f.*
spree [spriː], *s.* *F:* Partie *f* de plaisir ; bombe *f.* **To go on the spree,** faire la fête ; *Nau:* tirer une bordée. *Students out on the s.,* étudiants en bombe, en rupture de ban.
sprig [sprig], *s.* **I.** (*a*) Brin *m,* brindille *f;* petite branche. (*b*) *Needlew:* Ramage *m.* **2.** *F:* *Usu. Pej:* Rejeton *m* (d'une race illustre).
sprightliness ['spraitlinəs], *s.* Vivacité *f,* enjouement *m,* sémillance *f.*
sprightly ['spraitli], *a.* Éveillé, enjoué, sémillant.
spring¹ [spriŋ], *s.* **I.** (*a*) Source *f* (d'eau). **Hot spring,** source d'eau chaude. (*b*) Source, origine *f.* (*c*) *Arch:* Naissance *f* (de voûte) ; apophyge *f* (de colonne). **2.** Printemps *m.* **In (the) spring,** au printemps. *Spring is in the air,* on respire le printemps dans l'air. **Spring flowers,** fleurs printanières. *S.a.* ONION. **3.** Saut *m,* bond *m.* **To take a spring,** prendre son élan ; faire un bond. **4.** Élasticité *f.* **5.** (*a*) Ressort *m.* **Spiral spring,** ressort en boudin. *Cin:* **Spring-drive camera,** appareil avec moteur à ressort. **The springs of human action,** les mobiles *m* qui font agir les hommes. *S.a.* BINDING² (*b*). (*b*) *pl.* **Springs,** suspension *f* (d'une auto, etc.). *Cart without springs,* charrette non suspendue. **'spring-balance,** *s.* Peson *m* à ressort. **'spring-board,** *s.* *Gym:* Tremplin *m.* **'spring-cart,** *s.* Voiture suspendue ; jardinière *f.* **spring-'clean,** *v.tr.* Nettoyer à fond (au printemps). **spring-'cleaning,** *s.* Grand nettoyage (fait au printemps). **'spring-gun,** *s.* Piège *m* à fusil. **spring-'head,** *s.* Source *f.* **spring-'mattress,** *s.* Sommier *m* élastique. **spring-tide,** *s.* **I.** ['spriŋtaid] = SPRINGTIME. **2.** ['spriŋ'taid] Grande marée ; marée de syzygie ; vive-eau *f.* **'spring-water,** *s.* Eau *f* de source.
spring², *v.* (sprang [spraŋ] ; sprung [sprʌŋ]) **I.** *v.i.* **I.** (*a*) Bondir, sauter. **To spring to one's feet,** se dresser vivement sur ses pieds. **To spring over a ditch,** sauter un fossé. **To spring out of bed,** sauter du lit. **To spring at s.o.,** s'élancer sur qn. *F:* **Where did you spring from?** d'où sortez-vous ? (*b*) *P:* **If you could spring to a thousand pounds,** si vous pouviez aller jusqu'à

mille livres. (c) The lid sprang open, le couvercle se releva instantanément. **2.** (a) (Of water) Jaillir, sourdre. (b) The blood sprang to her cheeks, une rougeur subite lui monta aux joues. Hope springs eternal, l'espérance reste toujours vivace. To spring into existence, naître ; (ap)paraître (soudainement). (c) Sprung from the people, sorti du peuple. (d) (Of plant) Pousser. **3.** (Of mast) Craquer. II. **spring,** v.tr. **1.** (a) Fendre (une raquette) ; faire craquer (un aviron). (b) Nau : See LEAK¹ **1. 2.** (a) Faire jouer (un piège) ; faire sauter (une mine). (b) F : To spring a surprise on s.o., prendre qn à l'improviste. **3.** Suspendre (une voiture). **spring aside,** v.i. Faire un bond de côté. **spring back,** v.i. **1.** Faire un bond en arrière. **2.** Faire ressort. The branch sprang back, la branche se redressa. **spring up,** v.i. **1.** (a) Sauter en l'air. (b) Se lever précipitamment. **2.** (a) (Of plant) Pousser. (b) A breeze sprang up, une brise se leva. An intimacy sprang up between them, l'intimité s'établit entre eux. **sprung,** a. **1.** Aut : Sprung weight, poids suspendu. **2.** Nau : Sprung mast, mât craqué. **springing,** s. **1.** Bonds mpl, sauts mpl. **2.** (a) Jaillissement m (d'une source). (b) Germination f (de plantes). **3.** Craquement m (d'un mât). **4.** Suspension f (d'une voiture).

springbok ['spriŋbɔk], s. Z : Springbok m.

springe [sprindʒ], s. **1.** (For birds) Lacet m, lacs m. **2.** (For rabbits) Collet m.

springiness ['spriŋinəs], s. Élasticité f.

springlike ['spriŋlaik], a. Printanier.

springtime ['spriŋtaim], s. Printemps m.

springy ['spriŋi], a. Élastique ; qui fait ressort ; flexible.

sprinkle¹ ['spriŋkl], s. **1.** A sprinkle of rain, quelques gouttes f de pluie. **2.** A s. of salt, quelques grains m de sel ; une pincée de sel.

sprinkle², v.tr. (a) Répandre, jeter (de l'eau, du sel). (b) Asperger (with water, d'eau) ; saupoudrer (with salt, de sel). To s. the floor with sand, répandre du sable sur le plancher. Lawn sprinkled with dew, gazon parsemé de rosée. (c) Bookb : Jasper (les tranches). **sprinkling,** s. **1.** Aspersion f, arrosage m ; saupoudrage m. **2.** (a) Sprinkling of gravel, légère couche de gravier. (b) A sprinkling of knowledge, quelques connaissances f. **3.** Bookb : Jaspure f.

sprinkler ['spriŋklər], s. **1.** Appareil m d'arrosage. **2.** Ecc : Goupillon m.

sprint¹ [sprint], s. Pointe f de vitesse.

sprint², v.i. Faire une course de vitesse. **sprinting,** s. Course f de vitesse.

sprinter ['sprintər], s. Coureur, -euse, de vitesse ; "sprinter" m.

sprit [sprit], s. Nau : Livarde f, baleston m.

sprite [sprait], s. Lutin m ; esprit follet ; farfadet m.

spritsail ['spritseil, spritsl], s. Nau : Voile f à livarde ; voile à baleston.

sprocket ['sprɔket], s. **1.** Dent f (de pignon). **2.** Sprocket(-wheel), pignon m de chaîne. Sprocket-chain, chaîne f à barbotin.

sprout¹ [spraut], s. Bot : **1.** (a) Jet m, rejeton m, pousse f. (b) Germe m, bourgeon m. **2.** Brussels sprouts, choux m de Bruxelles.

sprout². **1.** v.i. (a) (Of plant) Pousser, pointer. (b) (Of branch) Bourgeonner. (c) (Of seed) Germer. **2.** v.tr. (Of animal) To sprout horns, pousser des cornes. **sprouting,** s. Germination f, pointement m, bourgeonnement m.

spruce¹ [spru:s], a. Pimpant ; soigné ; tiré à quatre épingles.

spruce², v.tr. To spruce oneself up, se faire beau, belle. All spruced up, sur son trente et un.

spruce³, s. (a) Bot : Spruce(-fir), sapin m épinette f. White spruce, sapinette f. Norway spruce, épicéa m. (b) Spruce beer, sapinette f.

spruceness ['spru:snəs], s. Mise pimpante.

sprung [sprʌŋ]. See SPRING².

spry [sprai], a. (spryer, spryest) Vif, actif ; plein d'allant ; plein d'entrain.

spud [spʌd], s. **1.** Petite bêche ; sarcloir m. **2.** F : Pomme f de terre.

spume [spju:m], s. Lit : Écume f (de a mer).

spumous ['spju:məs], **spumy** ['spju:mi], a. Lit : Écumeux ; spumeux.

spun [spʌn]. See SPIN².

spunk [spʌŋk], s. **1.** Amadou m. **2.** F : Courage m, cran m.

spunky ['spʌŋki], a. F : Qui a du cran.

spur¹ [spə:r], s. **1.** Éperon m. To win one's spurs, faire ses preuves. To set, put, clap, spur to one's horse, donner de l'éperon à son cheval piquer des deux. **2.** Coup m d'éperon ; stimulant m. The spur of necessity, l'aiguillon m de la nécessité. To do sth. on the spur of the moment faire qch. sous l'impulsion du moment. **3.** (a) Ergot m (de coq). (b) Éperon d'ergot (d'un coq de combat). **4.** (a) Éperon, contrefort m (d'une chaîne de montagnes). (b) Embranchement m (de chemin de fer). **5.** N.Arch : Arc-boutant m de soutien. **6.** Fort : Éperon.

spur², v.tr. (spurred) **1.** Éperonner (un cheval) donner de l'éperon à (un cheval). Abs. To spur on, piquer des deux. **2.** To spur s.o. on, aiguillonner, stimuler, qn. Spurred on by desire fouetté par le désir. **3.** Éperonner (un coq de combat).

spurge [spə:rdʒ], s. Bot : Euphorbe f. **'spurge-flax,** s. Bot : Sainbois m. **'spurge-laurel,** s Bot : Daphné m, lauréole f.

spurious ['spjuəriəs], a. **1.** Faux, f. fausse contrefait. Spurious coin, pièce de monnaie fausse. **2.** (Of writings) Apocryphe. **-ly,** adv Faussement ; par contrefaçon.

spuriousness ['spjuəriəsnəs], s. **1.** Fausseté f **2.** Caractère m apocryphe (d'un texte).

spurn [spə:rn], v.tr. **1.** Repousser, écarter, (qch. du pied. **2.** Rejeter (une offre) avec mépris traiter (qn) avec mépris.

spurrey, spurry ['spʌri], s. Bot : Spergule f.

spurt¹, ² [spə:rt], s. & v. = SPIRT¹, ².

spurt³, s. (a) Effort soudain ; coup m de collier (b) Sp : Emballage m, démarrage m. Row : Enle vage m. To put on a spurt, démarrer, emballer Final spurt, pointe finale.

spurt⁴, v.i. Sp : Emballer, démarrer.

sputter ['spʌtər]. **1.** v.tr. Débiter (qch.) er bredouillant. **2.** v.i. (a) Lancer des "postillons" en parlant ; bredouiller. (b) (Of pen) Cracher (c) (Of candle flame) Grésiller, crépiter. **sputtering,** s. **1.** Bredouillement m. **2.** Crachement m (d'une plume). **3.** Crépitement m.

sputum, pl. **-a** ['spju:təm, -a], s. Med : Crachat m ; expectorations fpl.

spy¹, pl. **spies** [spai, -a:iz], s. Espion, -onne F : mouchard m. To play the spy on s.o. espionner qn. The spy system, l'espionnage m

spy², v. (spied) spying) **1.** v.tr. Apercevoir remarquer, (qch.). To spy out the ground, explorer le terrain. **2.** v.i. Espionner. To spy (up)on s.o. espionner qn. **spying,** s. Espionnage m **'spy-glass,** s. Lunette f d'approche ; longue vue f. **'spy-hole,** s. (a) Trou m (dans ur rideau). (b) Judas m (de porte). (c) Regard m (de machine).

squab [skwɔb], s. **1.** Pigeonneau m sans plumes. **2.** Aut: Coussin m (de siège). **3.** (a) Ottomane f. (b) Pouf m.

squabble[1] [skwɔbl], s. Querelle f, chamaillerie f; prise f de bec.

squabble[2]. **1.** v.i. Se chamailler, se quereller. **2.** v.tr. Typ: Faire chevaucher (les caractères). **squabbling,** s. Chamaillerie f; querelles fpl.

squad [skwɔd], s. **1.** Mil: etc: Escouade f. Defaulters' squad, peloton m de punition; F: la pelote. Firing squad, peloton d'exécution. **2.** (a) Brigade f (de cheminots). (b) The Flying Squad (of Scotland Yard), la brigade mobile (de la police).

squadron ['skwɔdrən], s. **1.** (a) Mil: Escadron m. (b) Mil.Av: Escadrille f. **Squadron leader,** commandant m. **2.** Navy: Escadre f. Flying squadron, escadre volante.

squalid ['skwɔlid], a. Sale; misérable. S. dwellings, demeures sordides.

squall[1] [skwɔːl], s. Cri m (rauque).

squall[2], v.i. Crier, brailler, piailler. **squalling,** a. Criard, braillard.

squall[3], s. Nau: Grain m; coup m de vent; bourrasque f; rafale f. Light squall, risée f. F: Look out for squalls! veille au grain! gare la bombe!

squally ['skwɔːli], a. (Temps) à grains, à rafales.

squalor ['skwɔlər], s. Saleté f; misère f. Born in squalor, né dans la crasse. To die in squalor, mourir sur le fumier.

squama, pl. **-ae** ['skweimₐ, -iː],s. **1.** Z: Squame f. **2.** Bot: Pellicule f. **3.** Med: Squame.

squamose ['skweimous], **squamous** ['skweimₒs], a. Squameux.

squander ['skwɔndər], v.tr. Gaspiller, prodiguer (l'argent); dissiper (sa fortune). **squandering,** s. Gaspillage m.

squanderer ['skwɔndərər], s. Gaspilleur, -euse.

square[1] ['skweər]. I. s. **1.** Carré m. Mil: To form into a square, former le carré. **2.** (a) Carreau m (de figure quadrillée); case f (d'échiquier). To divide a map into squares, quadriller une carte. (b) Silk square, foulard m. **3.** (Of town) Place f; (with garden) square m. S.a. BARRACK SQUARE. **4.** Équerre f. Set square, équerre à dessin. T square, tee-square, équerre en T. Surv: Optical square, équerre d'arpenteur. To cut sth. on the square, couper qch. à angles droits. Out of square, hors d'équerre. F: To act on the square, agir carrément, honnêtement. **5.** Mth: Carré (d'une expression). II. **square,** a. **1.** Carré. (a) Square table, table carrée. Square game, partie à quatre. Square measure, mesure de surface. S.a. PEG[1] 1. (b) Square shoulders, épaules carrées. Square chin, menton carré. Square toe, carre f (de chaussure). **2.** Mth: Square root, racine carrée. **3.** To get things square, mettre tout en ordre. Square dealings, procédés honnêtes. He always gives you a s. deal, il est toujours loyal en affaires. To be square with s.o., être quitte envers qn. Golf: To be all square, être à égalité. F: To call it square, faire une cote mal taillée. **-ly,** adv. Carrément. III. **square,** adv. **1.** A angles droits (to, with, avec). Set s. upon its base, d'aplomb sur sa base. **2.** F: (Agir) honnêtement. **'square-'built,** a. **1.** Bâti en carré. **2.** (Of pers.) Trapu. **'square-'jawed,** a. Au menton carré. **'square-'shouldered,** a. Aux épaules carrées. **'square-'toed,** a. (Souliers) à bouts carrés.

square[2]. I. v.tr. **1.** (a) Carrer, équarrir (le bois).

(b) Nau: To square the yards, brasser carré. **2.** (a) How do you square it with your conscience? comment arrangez-vous cela avec votre conscience? (b) Balancer, régler (un compte). To square matters, arranger les choses. (c) F: Graisser la patte à (qn); acheter, suborner (qn). **3.** Mth: Élever (une expression) au carré. II. **square,** v.i. **1.** His practice does not square with his principles, ses actions ne s'accordent pas avec ses principes. **2.** Golf: To square with one's opponent, égaliser la marque. **square up.** **1.** v.tr. (a) Affranchir d'équerre (le bout d'une planche). (b) Abs. To square up with s.o., régler ses comptes avec qn. **2.** v.i. To square up to s.o., s'avancer vers qn en posture de combat.

squareness ['skweərnəs], s. **1.** Forme carrée. **2.** Honnêteté f, loyauté f (dans les affaires).

squash[1] [skwɔʃ], s. **1.** Écrasement m, aplatissement m. **2.** Cohue f, presse f. **3.** Pulpe f. His hand was just a s., sa main était en capilotade. S.a. LEMON-SQUASH. **'squash-'hat,** s. F: **1.** Chapeau mou. **2.** Gibus m. **'squash-'rackets,** s. Jeu m de balle au mur.

squash[2]. **1.** v.tr. (a) Écraser, aplatir (un fruit). (b) F: Aplatir, écraser (qn). (c) F: Remettre (qn) à sa place; P: s'asseoir sur (qn). **2.** v.i. (a) (Of fruit) S'écraser. (b) Se serrer, se presser.

squash[3], s. Hort: Courge f, gourde f.

squashy ['skwɔʃi], a. Mou et humide.

squat[1] [skwɔt], v.i. (squatted) **1.** (a) To squat (down), v.pr. to squat oneself (down), s'accroupir. (b) Ven: (Of game) Se tapir. **2.** To squat upon a piece of land, s'approprier un terrain. **squatting,** a. **1.** Accroupi. **2.** Qui occupe un terrain comme squatter.

squat[2], a. (Of pers.) Ramassé, trapu.

squatter ['skwɔtər], s. Squatter m (en Amérique).

squaw [skwɔː], s.f. Femme peau-rouge.

squawk[1] [skwɔːk], s. Cri m rauque; Mus: couac m.

squawk[2], v.i. (Of bird) Pousser des cris rauques; (on reed instrument) faire des couacs.

squeak[1] [skwiːk], s. Petit cri aigu; couic m (de souris); crissement m (de choses mal huilées). F: To have a narrow squeak, l'échapper belle.

squeak[2], v.i. (a) Pousser des cris aigus; (of mouse) faire couic; (of shoes) crier. Pen that squeaks in writing, plume qui grince sur le papier. (b) P: = SQUEAL[2] (b). **squeaking,** s. Couics mpl.

squeaker ['skwiːkər], s. **1.** (a) Celui qui pousse des petits cris. (b) P: = SQUEALER 2. **2.** Pratique f (de montreur de guignol).

squeal[1] [skwiːl], s. Cri aigu; cri perçant.

squeal[2], v.i. (a) Pousser des cris aigus. (b) F: Protester; pousser les hauts cris. (c) P: Trahir ses complices. To squeal on s.o., dénoncer qn.

squealing[1], a. Criard. **squealing**[2], s. Cris aigus; hauts cris.

squealer ['skwiːlər], s. **1.** Criard, -arde. **2.** P: Dénonciateur, -trice.

squeamish ['skwiːmiʃ], a. **1.** Sujet aux nausées. To feel squeamish, avoir mal au cœur. **2.** (a) Difficile, délicat, dégoûté. (b) Scrupuleux à l'excès. (c) Pudique à l'excès. Don't be so s.! ne faites pas tant de façons!

squeamishness ['skwiːmiʃnəs], s. **1.** Disposition f aux nausées. **2.** Délicatesse f exagérée.

squeegee [skwiː'dʒiː], s. **1.** Balai m en caoutchouc; racloir m. Nau: Râteau m de pont. **2.** Phot: etc: Raclette f.

squeeze[1] [skwiːz], s. **1.** (a) Compression f. (b) Étreinte f. To give s.o. a squeeze, serrer qn dans ses bras. **2.** Presse f, cohue f. It was a tight squeeze, on tenait tout juste. **3.** A squeeze of lemon, quelques gouttes *f* de citron. **4.** Empreinte *f* au carton mouillé (d'une médaille, etc.). **squeeze²**, *v.tr.* **1.** (*a*) Presser (une éponge). To squeeze s.o.'s hand, serrer la main à qn. *To s. one's finger*, se pincer le doigt (dans la porte). He was squeezed to death in the crowd, il fut étouffé dans la foule. (*b*) *F:* Embrasser, étreindre (qn). **2.** To squeeze sth. into a box, faire entrer qch. de force dans une boîte. To squeeze the juice out of a lemon, exprimer le jus d'un citron. To squeeze (oneself) through a hole in the fence, se faufiler par un trou dans la clôture. To squeeze up, se serrer, se tasser. **3.** (*a*) Exercer une pression sur (qn); *F:* serrer les pouces à (qn). (*b*) To squeeze money out of s.o., extorquer de l'argent à qn. **squeezing**, *s.* **1.** (*a*) Compression *f.* (*b*) Étreinte *f.* **2.** Expression *f* (du jus d'un citron). **3.** Extorsion *f*, exaction *f.*

squeezer ['skwi:zər], *s.* Machine *f* à compression. *S.a.* LEMON-SQUEEZER.

squelch¹ [skwelʃ], *s.* **1.** Giclement *m* (de boue). **2.** Lourde chute (sur qch. de mou).

squelch². **1.** *v.tr.* (*a*) Écraser (qch.) (en le faisant gicler). (*b*) *F:* Aplatir (qn); réprimer (une rébellion). **2.** *v.i.* *The water squelched in his shoes*, l'eau giclait dans ses chaussures.

squib [skwib], *s.* **1.** *Pyr:* Pétard *m*, serpenteau *m.* *F:* **Damp squib**, affaire ratée. **2.** Satire *f*, brocard *m.*

squid [skwid], *s.* *Moll:* Calmar *m.*

squiffy ['skwifi], *a.* *F:* Gris, ivre, éméché.

squill [skwil], *s.* **1.** (*a*) *Bot:* Scille *f*, squille *f.* (*b*) *Pharm:* Squills, scille. **2.** Squill(-fish), squille.

squint¹ [skwint], *s.* **1.** Strabisme *m*, louchement *m.* *He has a slight s.*, il louche légèrement. **2.** Coup d'œil furtif. **3.** *F:* Regard *m*; coup d'œil. *Let's have a s. at it!* faites voir !

squint², *v.i.* **1.** Loucher. **2.** To squint at sth., regarder qch. de côté, furtivement. **squinting¹**, *a.* Strabique, louche. **squinting²**, *s.* Strabisme *m*, louchement *m.*

squint³, *a.* Squint eyes, yeux louches. **'squint-eyed**, *a.* Au regard louche; strabique.

squinter ['skwintər], *s.* Loucheur, -euse.

squire¹ [skwaiər], *s.* **1.** *Hist:* Écuyer (attaché à un chevalier). *Hum:* Squire of dames, cavalier servant. **2.** *A. & F:* (*a*) Propriétaire terrien. (*b*) The squire, le châtelain (de l'endroit).

squire², *v.tr.* *F:* Servir de cavalier à (une dame).

squireen [skwaiə'ri:n], *s.* *F:* Hobereau *m.*

squirm [skwə:rm], *v.i.* (*a*) (*Of worm*) Se tordre, se tortiller. (*b*) *F:* Ne savoir comment se tenir; être au supplice. To make s.o. squirm, mettre qn au supplice.

squirrel ['skwirəl], *s.* **1.** Écureuil *m.* **2.** *Com:* Squirrel (fur), petit-gris; vair *m.*

squirt¹ [skwə:rt], *s.* **1.** Seringue *f*; (*toy*) clifoire *f.* **2.** Jet *m*, giclée *f* (de liquide).

squirt². **1.** *v.tr.* Faire jaillir, lancer en jet (un liquide). To squirt in oil, injecter de l'huile. **2.** *v.i.* (*Of liquid*) Jaillir, gicler.

stab¹ [stab], *s.* **1.** Coup *m* de poignard, de couteau. Stab in the back, (i) coup porté dans le dos, (ii) *F:* attaque déloyale. Stab of pain, élancement *m.* **2.** *Golf:* Stab shot, coup sec. **'stab-wound**, *s.* Estocade *f.*

stab², *v.* (stabbed) **1.** *v.tr.* (*a*) Poignarder; donner un coup de couteau à (qn). *F:* To stab s.o. to the heart, frapper qn au cœur. To stab s.o. in the back, poignarder qn dans le dos. (*b*) *Bookb:* Piquer (un cahier). Stabbed pamphlet' piqûre *f.* **2.** *v.i.* To stab at s.o., porter un coup de couteau de poignard, à qn. **stabbing,**

---

a. Qui perce, qui frappe. Stabbing pain, douleur lancinante.

stability [sta'biliti], *s.* Stabilité *f*, solidité *f* (d'une construction). Man of no stability, homme de peu de fermeté; homme inconstant.

stabilization [steibilai'zeiʃ(ə)n], *s.* Stabilisation *f.*

stabilize ['steibilaiz], *v.tr.* Stabiliser. **stabilizing,** *a.* Stabilisateur, -trice.

stabilizer ['steibilaizər], *s.* *Av:* Stabilisateur *m.*

stable¹ [steibl], *s.* **1.** Écurie *f.* **2.** Chevaux *mpl* d'une certaine écurie. **'stable-boy,** *s.m.* Valet, garçon, d'écurie. **'stable companion,** *s.* **1.** Cheval *m* de la même écurie. **2.** *F:* Membre *m* de la même entreprise. **'stable-keeper,** *s.* Loueur *m* de chevaux.

stable², *v.tr.* Loger (un cheval). *We can s. three horses*, nous avons de la place pour trois chevaux. **stabling,** *s.* **1.** Logement *m*, installation *f* (de chevaux). **2.** *Coll:* Écuries *fpl.*

stable³, *a.* **1.** Stable; solide, fixe. *To become s.*, se stabiliser. **2.** (*Of pers.*) Constant, ferme. **-bly,** *adv.* D'une manière stable.

stableman, *pl.* **-men** ['steiblmən, -men], *s.m.* Palefrenier.

staccato [sta'ka:to], *a.*, *adv.*, & *s.* (*a*) *Mus:* Staccato (*m*). Staccato note, note piquée. (*b*) *F:* Staccato style, style haché. In a staccato voice, d'une voix saccadée.

stack¹ [stak], *s.* **1.** (*a*) Meule *f* (de foin); (*of corn*) gerbier *m.* (*b*) Pile *f*, tas *m* (de bois). **2.** (*a*) Souche *f* (de cheminée). (*b*) Cheminée *f* (d'une locomotive, etc.).

stack², *v.tr.* **1.** Mettre (le foin) en meule. **2.** To stack (up), empiler, entasser.

stadium, *pl.* **-ia** ['steidiəm, -ia], *s.* Stade *m.*

staff¹ [sta:f], *s.* **1.** (*a*) Bâton *m.* Pilgrim's staff, bourdon *m* de pèlerin. *F:* Bread is the staff of life, le pain est le soutien de la vie. (*b*) Hampe *f* (de bannière). *Nau:* Mât *m* (de pavillon). (*c*) *Surv:* Jalon *m*, mire *f.* **2.** (*a*) *Mil:* Navy: État-major *m.* Staff College = École supérieure de Guerre. (*b*) Personnel *m.* The domestic s., les domestiques *m.* *Teaching s.*, personnel enseignant. *Adm:* Medical s., service *m* de santé, d'hygiène. *Journ:* Editorial s., la rédaction. **3.** *Mus:* (*pl.* staves [steivz]) Portée *f.* Staff notation, notation figurée sur la portée. **'staff officer,** *s.* Officier *m* d'état-major.

staff², *v.tr.* Pourvoir (un bureau) de personnel. To be over-staffed, avoir un personnel trop nombreux. To be under-staffed, manquer de personnel.

stag [stag], *s.* **1.** Cerf *m.* **2.** *St.Exch:* *F:* A stag, un loup. **'stag-beetle,** *s.* Cerf-volant *m.* **'stag-horn,** *s.* Corne *f* de cerf; *pl.* Staghorns, bois *mpl* de cerf. **'stag-hunt(ing),** *s.* Chasse *f* (au cerf). **'stag-party,** *s.* *U.S:* *F:* Réunion *f* entre hommes.

stage¹ [steidʒ], *s.* **1.** (*a*) Estrade *f*, échafaud *m*, échafaudage *m.* Hanging stage, échafaud volant. *Nau:* Floating stage, plate-forme flottante. *S.a.* LANDING-STAGE. (*b*) Platine *f* (d'un microscope). **2.** (*a*) *Th:* Scène *f*; *F:* les planches *f.* Front of the stage, avant-scène *f.* Up-stage, au second plan; à l'arrière-plan. To come on the stage, entrer en scène. To go on the stage, se faire acteur ou actrice. To put a play on the stage, monter une pièce. To write for the stage, écrire pour le théâtre. Stage lights, herses *f.* Stage directions, indications scéniques. *S.a.* HOLD² I. 3. (*b*) Champ *m* d'action. **3.** Phase *f*, période *f*, stade *m.* The stages of an evolution, les étapes *f*, les stades, d'une évolution. *W.Tel:* Stage of amplification, étage *m* d'amplification. **At this stage an interruption occurred,** à ce point une interruption se produisit. **To rise by successive stages,** monter par échelons. **4.** (*a*) Étape *f*. **To travel by easy stages,** voyager à petites étapes. (*b*) *A:* Relais *m.* (*c*) **Fare stage,** section *f* (de l'itinéraire d'un autobus). 'stage-box, *s. Th:* Loge *f* d'avant-scène. **stage-'carpenter,** *s. Th:* Machiniste *m.* 'stage-coach, *s.* Diligence *f.* 'stage-craft, *s. Th:* Technique *f* de la scène. **stage-'door,** *s. Th:* Entrée *f* des artistes. 'stage-effect, *s. Th:* Effet *m* scénique. 'stage-fright, *s. Th:* Trac *m.* 'stagehand, *s. Th:* Machiniste *m.* **stage-'manager,** *s. Th:* Régisseur *m.* 'stage-name, *s. Th:* Nom *m* de théâtre. 'stage-rights, *s.pl.* Droits *m* de production (d'une pièce). 'stagestruck, *a.* Entiché, enamouré, du théâtre. **stage-'whisper,** *s. Th:* Aparté *m.* **In a stage-whisper,** en aparté.

stage², *v.tr.* (*a*) Monter (une pièce); mettre (un roman) à la scène. (*b*) Organiser (une démonstration); monter (un coup). **staging,** *s.* **1.** Mise *f* à la scène (d'une pièce, d'un roman). **2.** (*a*) Échafaud *m*, échafaudage *m.* (*b*) *Nau:* Appontement *m* (d'un quai).

stager ['steidʒər], *s. F:* **Old stager,** vieux routier.

stagger¹ ['stagər], *s.* (*a*) Titubation *f.* (*b*) Allure chancelante.

stagger². I. *v.i.* Chanceler, tituber. **To stagger to one's feet,** se lever ou se relever en chancelant. II. **stagger,** *v.tr.* **1.** (*a*) Faire chanceler (qn). (*b*) Confondre, consterner (qn); frapper (qn) de stupeur. **To be staggered,** être saisi (d'étonnement). **2.** (*a*) *Av:* Décaler (les ailes). (*b*) *Mec.E:* Disposer (des rivets) en chicane. (*c*) *El:* Échelonner (les balais). **staggered,** *a.* Décalé; (of *rivets*) en chicane. **staggering¹,** *a.* **1.** (Pas) chancelant, titubant. **2.** *F:* (*a*) **Staggering blow,** coup d'assommoir. (*b*) (*of news*) Renversant, atterrant. **staggering²,** *s.* **1.** Titubation *f.* **2.** (*a*) Décalage *m.* (*b*) Disposition *f* en quinconce. (*c*) Échelonnement *m.*

staggerer ['stagərər], *s. F:* Chose renversante; coup *m* d'assommoir.

staghound ['staghaund], *s.* Lévrier *m* d'Écosse.

stagnancy ['stagnənsi], *s.* Stagnation *f.*

stagnant ['stagnənt], *a.* Stagnant; (*of trade*) en stagnation.

stagnate ['stagneit], *v.i.* (*Of water, trade*) Être ou devenir stagnant; (*of water*) croupir.

stagnation [stag'nei∫(ə)n], *s.* Stagnation *f.*

stagy ['steidʒi], *a.* Théâtral, -aux; histrionique. (*a*) De cabotin. (*b*) Peu sincère.

staid [steid], *a.* Posé, sérieux, sage. **-ly,** *adv.* Posément, sérieusement, sagement.

staidness ['steidnəs], *s.* Caractère posé, sérieux, sage; air posé.

stain¹ [stein], *s.* **1.** (*a*) Tache *f*, souillure *f.* (*b*) **He came out of the business without a stain on his character,** il est sorti de l'affaire sans atteinte à sa réputation. **To cast a stain on s.o.'s honour,** ternir l'honneur de qn. **2.** Couleur *f*, colorant *m.* **Wood-stain,** couleur pour bois.

stain², *v.tr.* **1.** (*a*) Tacher; souiller (*with*, de). **Hands stained with blood,** mains souillées de sang. **Stuff that stains easily,** étoffe qui se tache facilement. (*b*) Tacher, ternir (la réputation de qn). **2.** Teindre, teinter (le bois); peindre (le verre). **Stained floor,** parquet teinté. *S.a.* GLASS 1.

stainless ['steinləs], *a.* **1.** Sans tache; immaculé, pur. **2. Stainless steel,** acier inoxydable.

stair ['stɛər], *s.* **1.** Marche *f*, degré *m* (d'un escalier). **2.** (*Usu. pl.*) Escalier. **Spiral stairs,** escalier tournant, en vis. **To meet s.o. on the stairs,** rencontrer qn dans l'escalier. 'stair-carpet, *s.* Tapis *m* d'escalier. 'stair-rod, *s.* Tringle *f* d'escalier.

staircase ['stɛərkeis], **stairway** ['stɛərwei], *s.* (i) Cage *f* d'escalier; (ii) escalier *m.* **External staircase, turret staircase,** escalier hors d'œuvre. **Winding, spiral, corkscrew, staircase,** escalier tournant; escalier en vis, en (co)limaçon.

stake¹ [steik], *s.* **1.** (*a*) Pieu *m*, poteau *m*; (*rod*) jalon *m*, fiche *f. Hort:* Tuteur *m.* (*b*) *Surv:* Jalon, piquet *m.* **2.** (Poteau du) bûcher. **To perish at the stake,** mourir sur le bûcher. **3.** (*a*) *Gaming:* Mise *f*, enjeu *m.* **To lay the stakes,** faire le jeu. **Put down your stakes!** faites vos jeux! **To hold the stakes,** tenir les enjeux. *F:* **The interests at stake,** les intérêts en jeu. **To have a stake in sth.,** avoir des intérêts dans une affaire. *S.a.* HIGH I. 2 (*d*). (*b*) *pl. Turf:* **Stakes,** prix *m.* **Maiden Stakes,** prix de l'avenir. 'stake-holder, *s.* Celui qui tient les enjeux.

stake², *v.tr.* **1.** **To stake (off, out),** (i) jalonner (une concession); enclore (une concession) de pieux; (ii) *Surv:* jalonner (une ligne). **2.** Ramer (des haricots). **3.** (*Of horse*) **To be staked on a jump,** s'éventrer sur une haie. **4.** Mettre (une somme) en jeu; jouer (une somme). *P:* **To stake twenty francs,** miser vingt francs. **To stake one's all,** jouer son va-tout; y aller de son reste. **I'd s. my life on it,** j'y mettrais ma tête à couper.

stalactite ['stalaktait], *s.* Stalactite *f.*

stalagmite ['stalagmait], *s.* Stalagmite *f.*

stale¹ [steil], *a.* **1.** (*a*) (Pain) rassis. (*b*) (Œuf) qui n'est pas frais. (*c*) (Air) vicié, corrompu. **Stale smell,** odeur de renfermé (d'une chambre). **2.** (*a*) Vieux, *f.* vieille; passé. **Stale joke,** vieille plaisanterie; plaisanterie rebattue. **Stale news,** nouvelle déjà connue. (*b*) **Stale cheque,** chèque prescrit. **3.** (*Of athlete*) **To go stale,** se surentraîner.

stale². **1.** *v.tr.* Rendre (qch.) banal. **2.** *v.i.* (*a*) (*Of beer*) S'éventer. (*b*) (*Of news, etc.*) Perdre son intérêt. **Pleasure that never stales,** plaisir toujours nouveau.

stalemate¹ ['steilmeit], *s. Chess:* Pat *m.*

stalemate², *v.tr.* Faire pat (son adversaire).

staleness ['steilnəs], *s.* **1.** (*a*) État rassis (du pain). (*b*) Évent *m* (de la bière). (*c*) Odeur *f* de renfermé. **2.** Manque *m* de fraîcheur (d'une nouvelle).

stalk¹ [stɔ:k], *s.* **1.** Démarche fière. **2.** *Ven:* Chasse *f* d'un animal en affût.

stalk². **1.** *v.i.* **To stalk (along),** (i) marcher d'un pas majestueux; (ii) marcher à grands pas. **2.** *v.tr.* (*a*) Traquer (la bête) d'affût en affût. *Abs.* Chasser au tir sans chien. (*b*) *F:* **To stalk s.o.,** filer qn. **stalking,** *s. Ven:* = STALK¹ 2. *S.a.* DEER-STALKING. 'stalking-horse, *s.* **1.** *Ven:* Cheval *m* d'abri, masque *m.* **2.** *F:* Prétexte *m*, masque *m.*

stalk³, *s.* **1.** Tige *f* (de plante); queue *f* (de fruit); trognon *m* (de chou). **2.** Pied *m* (d'-verre à vin). **3.** = CHIMNEY-STALK.

stalker ['stɔ:kər], *s. Ven:* Chasseur *m* à l'affût.

stall¹ [stɔ:l], *s.* **1.** (*a*) Stalle *f* (d'écurie); case *f* (d'étable). **Garage stall,** box *m.* **2.** Étable *f.* (*b*) Étalage *m* (en plein vent); échoppe *f. Market stalls,** boutiques *f* en plein vent. **Newspaper stall,** kiosque *m.* **To have a stall** (*at a bazaar*), présider à un étalage. *S.a.* BOOKSTALL, COFFEE-STALL. **3.** (*a*) *Ecc:* Stalle *f.* chaise *f* de chœur. (*b*) *Th:* **(Orchestra) stalls,** fauteuils *m* d'orchestre.

Seat in the stalls, fauteuil. **'stall-fed,** a. Engraissé à l'étable. **'stall-holder,** s. **I.** Étalagiste mf. **2.** (At charity bazaar) Vendeuse f.

stall². **I.** v.tr. (a) Aut: etc: Caler, bloquer (le moteur). (b) Av: Mettre (l'appareil) en perte de vitesse. **2.** v.i. (a) Aut: (Of engine) (Se) caler, se bloquer. (b) Av: Se mettre en perte de vitesse; (of plane) s'engager. **stalling,** s. (a) Calage m, blocage m, arrêt m (du moteur). (b) Av: Perte f de vitesse. **Stalling point,** vitesse f minimum de sustentation.

stallion ['staljən], s. Étalon m; cheval entier.

stalwart ['stɔ:lwərt], a. **I.** Robuste, vigoureux. **2.** Vaillant, résolu.

stamen ['steimen], s. Bot: Étamine f.

stamina ['stamina], s. Vigueur f, résistance f. Man of great s., homme qui a du fond.

staminate ['staminet], a. Bot: Staminé.

stammer¹ ['stamər], s. (a) Bégaiement m. (b) Balbutiement m.

stammer². **I.** v.i. (a) Bégayer. (b) Balbutier. **2.** v.tr. To stammer (out) sth., bégayer, balbutier, qch. **stammering¹,** a. (Personne) bègue. **-ly,** adv. En bégayant. **stammering²,** s. = STAMMER¹.

stammerer ['stamərər], s. Bègue mf.

stamp¹ [stamp], s. **I.** Battement m de pied (d'impatience). **With a stamp (of the foot),** en frappant du pied. **2.** (a) Timbre m, empreinte f. Signature stamp, griffe f. Date-stamp, timbre à date. Self-inking stamp, timbre à encrage automatique. Rubber stamp, tampon m. (b) Découpoir m (à emporte-pièce). (c) Étampe f, poinçon m. (d) Minting: Coin m. **3.** (a) Timbre; marque (apposée). Official s., estampille officielle. (b) To bear the s. of genius, porter l'empreinte, le cachet, du génie. Men of his s., les hommes de sa trempe, de sa sorte, Pej: de son acabit. **4.** Revenue stamp, timbre du fisc. Adhesive stamp, timbre mobile. Embossed stamp, timbre à empreinte; timbre fixe. Postage stamp, timbre-(poste) m. Postage-due stamp, chiffretaxe m. **5.** Metalw: Étampeuse f. **6.** Min: Bocard m (pour écraser les minerais); pilon m; broyeuse f. **'stamp-album,** s. Album m de timbres-poste (de collectionneur). **'stamp-collector,** s. Collectionneur m de timbres-poste; philatéliste mf. **'stamp-dealer,** s. Marchand m de timbres-poste pour philatélistes. **'stamp-duty,** s. Impôt m du timbre. **'stamp-machine,** s. Distributeur m automatique de timbres-poste. **'stamp office,** s. Bureau m du timbre.

stamp², v.tr. **I.** (a) To stamp one's foot, frapper du pied. (b) Abs. To stamp (about), piétiner. **To stamp on sth.,** fouler qch. aux pieds. **2.** Frapper, imprimer, une marque sur (qch.).; frapper, estamper (la monnaie, une médaille, le cuir); Notepaper stamped with one's address, papier à lettres marqué à son adresse. **3.** Timbrer (un document); viser (un passeport); timbrer, affranchir (une lettre); estampiller (un document). The letter is insufficiently stamped, l'affranchissement est insuffisant. **4.** Min: Broyer, bocarder (le minerai). **5.** Metalw: Étamper, matricer (des objets en métal). **6.** His manners s. him a gentleman, ses manières indiquent un homme comme il faut. **7.** To stamp sth. on the mind, imprimer, empreindre, qch. sur l'esprit. **stamp out,** v.tr. **I.** Metalw: Découper (qch.) à la presse. **2.** To stamp out the fire, piétiner sur le feu pour l'éteindre. **To stamp out an epidemic,** étouffer, écraser, une épidémie. **stamped,** a. **I.** (a) Broyé, concassé. (b) Stamped earth, terre

battue. **2.** Stamped paper, papier timbré. S.a. SIGNATURE I. **3.** (Acier) estampé, embouti; (cuir) gaufré. **stamping,** s. **I.** Piétinement m. **2.** (a) Timbrage m (de documents); estampillage m. (b) Metalw: Estampage m, matriçage m. (c) Min: Bocardage m, broyage m (du minerai). **3.** Metalw: Pièce estampée, emboutie. **'stamping-mill,** s. Min: Moulin m à bocards; bocard m. **'stamping-press,** s. Estampeuse f, emboutisseuse f.

stampede¹ [stam'pi:d], s. **I.** (a) Fuite précipitée; panique f. (b) Débandade f (de troupes). **2.** Ruée f. There was a s. for the door, on se précipita vers la porte.

stampede². **I.** v.i. (a) Fuir en désordre, à la débandade. (b) Se ruer, se précipiter (for, towards, vers, sur). **2.** v.tr. Jeter la panique parmi (des bêtes).

stamper ['stampər], s. **I.** (Pers.) Timbreur m. **2.** (Machine) Estampeuse f.

stance [stans], s. Golf: Cr: Position f des pieds; posture f. **To take up one's stance,** se mettre en posture (pour jouer).

stanch [stɑ:nʃ], v.tr. **I.** Étancher (le sang). **2.** Étancher le sang (d'une blessure).

stanchion ['stɑ:nʃ(ə)n], s. **I.** Étançon m, étai m, béquille f. **2.** Nau: Épontille f (de cale).

stand¹ [stand], s. **I.** (a) Manière f de se tenir (debout). **To take a firm stand,** se camper solidement sur ses jambes. (b) Arrêt m, halte f. **To be brought to a stand,** être forcé de s'arrêter. **2.** Résistance f. **To make a stand against s.o.,** résister à qn. **3.** Situation f, position f. (a) To take one's stand near the door, se placer près de la porte. (b) To take one's stand on a principle, se fonder sur un principe. **4.** Station f, stationnement m (de voitures). **5.** Support m, pied m (de lampe); affût m (de télescope); dessous m (de carafe). Milliner's stand, champignon m. Liqueur-stand, service m. Motor-Cy: Back-wheel stand, béquille f. **6.** Étalage m, étal m (en plein air); (at exhibition) stand m. **7.** (a) Sp: Tribune f; stand. (b) Estrade f. **'stand-camera,** s. Phot: Appareil m à pied. **'stand-pipe,** s. Tuyau montant; colonne f d'alimentation (d'eau, d'essence).

stand², v. (stood [stud]; stood) I. v.i. **I.** (a) Être debout; se tenir debout; rester debout. **I could hardly stand,** je pouvais à peine me tenir. F: To stand on one's own legs, ne dépendre que de soi. **I didn't leave him a leg to stand on,** j'ai détruit ses arguments de fond en comble. For: To leave a tree standing, réserver un arbre. S.a. EASE¹ I, HAIR I, SENTRY 2. (b) To stand six feet high, avoir six pieds de haut. (c) Se lever. **2.** (a) Se trouver; être. The chapel stands upon a height, la chapelle se dresse sur une hauteur. The village stands against the hill, le village s'adosse à la colline. The tears stood in his eyes, il avait les larmes aux yeux. **To let sth. stand in the sun,** laisser qch. exposé au soleil. To buy the house as it stands, acheter la maison telle quelle. **Nothing stands between you and success,** rien ne s'oppose à votre succès. (b) A man stood in the doorway, un homme se tenait à la porte. **To stand talking,** rester à causer. He left her standing in the middle of the room, il la laissa plantée au milieu de la salle. **3.** S'arrêter; faire halte. **Stand!** halte! halte là! **Stand and deliver!** la bourse ou la vie! **4.** Rester, durer. **To stand fast,** tenir (pied); tenir bon. I shall s. or fall by the issue, je suis prêt à engager ma fortune sur le résultat. **5.** The contract stands, le contrat tient. The *objection stands*, cette objection subsiste. *S.a.* REASON[1] 3. **6.** (*a*) To stand convicted of . . ., être déclaré coupable de. . . . *S.a.* CONVICT[2]. To stand in need of . . ., avoir besoin de. . . . *You s. in danger of getting killed*, vous vous exposez à vous faire tuer. *S.a.* CORRECT[1] 3. To stand to lose nothing, n'avoir rien à perdre. (*b*) **To stand as security for a debt**, assurer une créance. **To stand as candidate**, se porter candidat. (*c*) *He stands first on the list*, il vient en tête de la liste. *The thermometer stood at* 90°, le thermomètre marquait 90°. (*d*) *The house does not s. in his name*, la maison n'est pas portée à son nom. (*e*) **The amount standing to your credit**, votre solde créditeur. **How do we stand?** où en sont nos comptes? *The matter stands thus*, voici, voilà, où en est l'affaire. **As matters stand, as it stands**, au point où en sont les choses. I don't know where I stand,- j'ignore quelle est ma position. To stand well with s.o., être estimé de qn. *S.a.* CEREMONY. **7.** *I'll s. by the window*, je me mettrai à la fenêtre. *Nau :* **To stand to the south**, avoir ou mettre le cap au sud. *S.a.* CLEAR[1] II. **8.** **To allow a liquid to stand**, laisser reposer un liquide. **To let the tea stand**, laisser infuser le thé. *Cabs may s. here*, les voitures peuvent stationner ici. II. **stand,** *v.tr.* **1.** Mettre, poser. *To s. sth. against the wall*, dresser qch. contre le mur. **2. To stand one's ground**, tenir bon, ferme. **3.** Supporter, subir. **To stand cold**, supporter le froid. *To s. a shock*, soutenir un choc. (*Of car*) *To s. rough handling*, résister à des manipulations brutales. *We had to* **stand the loss**, la perte a porté sur nous. *Utensils that will s. the fire*, ustensiles qui vont au feu. *F :* **I can't stand him at any price**, je ne peux pas le sentir. *I can't s. it any longer*, je n'y tiens plus ; j'en ai assez. **4.** *F :* Payer, offrir. **To stand s.o. a drink**, payer à boire à qn. *I am standing this one*, c'est ma tournée. **stand aside,** *v.i.* (*a*) Se tenir à l'écart. (*b*) S'écarter, se ranger. (*c*) *To s. aside in favour of s.o.*, se désister en faveur de qn. **stand away,** *v.i.* S'éloigner, s'écarter (*from*, de). **stand back,** *v.i.* (i) Se tenir en arrière ; (ii) reculer. **House standing back from the road**, maison en retrait (de la route). **stand by,** *v.i.* **1.** (*a*) Se tenir prêt. *Mil :* **The troops are standing by**, les troupes sont consignées. (*b*) *Nau :* Se tenir paré ; veiller. **Stand by below!** paré à manœuvrer! (*c*) *W.Tel :* **Stand by!** ne quittez pas l'écoute! (*d*) Se tenir là (sans intervenir). **2.** (*a*) Se tenir près de, à côté de (qn). (*b*) Soutenir, défendre (qn). (*c*) Rester fidèle à (sa promesse). **I stand by what I said**, j'en tiens, j'en suis, pour ce que j'ai dit. (*d*) *Nau :* **Stand by the anchors!** paré à mouiller! **'stand-by,** *s.* Ressource *f*. **Stand-by engine**, locomotive de réserve. **stand down,** *v.i.* **1.** (*Of witness*) Quitter la barre. **2.** Retirer sa candidature (*in favour of*, en faveur de). **stand for,** *v.ind.tr.* **1.** Défendre, soutenir (une cause). **2.** Tenir lieu de (qch.). **3.** Signifier, vouloir dire (qch.). **To stand for nothing**, ne compter pour rien. **stand in,** *v.i.* **1. To stand in with others**, s'associer à d'autres (pour une cotisation). **2.** *Nau :* **To stand in to land**, rallier la terre. **3.** Coûter. *These horses stood me in (at) three hundred*, ces chevaux m'ont coûté trois cents livres. **stand off,** *v.i.* (*a*) Se tenir éloigné, à l'écart. (*b*) S'éloigner. *Nau :* Courir au large. **To stand off and on**, (i) courir des bordées près de terre ; louvoyer ; (ii) *F :* louvoyer. (*c*) *Ind :* (*Of employee*) Chômer. **stand out,** *v.i.* **1.** Résister (*against*, à) ; tenir bon (*against*, contre). **2. To stand out for sth.,**

s'obstiner à demander qch. **3.** Faire saillie. **To stand out in relief**, ressortir. **To stand out against sth.**, faire contraste avec qch. *Mountains that s. out on the horizon*, montagnes qui se dessinent à l'horizon. **4.** *Nau :* **To stand out to sea**, gagner le large. **stand over,** *v.i.* **1.** Rester en suspens. *To let a question s. over*, remettre une question à plus tard. **To let an account stand over**, laisser traîner un compte. **2.** *If I don't s. over him he does nothing*, si je ne suis pas toujours sur son dos il ne fait rien. **stand to,** *v.i.* (*a*) *Nau :* **To stand to the south**, avoir le cap au sud. (*b*) *Mil :* **To stand to one's arms**, tenir sous les armes. (*c*) **To stand to one's promise**, ne pas renier sa promesse. **stand up,** *v.i.* **1.** (*a*) Se lever ; se mettre debout. (*b*) Se dresser, se tenir droit. **2.** (*a*) **To stand up against . . .**, résister à . . . ; tenir tête à. . . . (*b*) **To stand up for s.o.**, défendre qn ; prendre fait et cause pour qn. (*c*) **To stand up to s.o.**, affronter bravement qn ; tenir pied à qn. **To stand up to one's work**, être courageux au travail. **'stand-up,** *attrib.a.* **1.** *Cost :* **Stand-up collar**, col droit, montant. **2. Stand-up buffet**, buffet où l'on mange au comptoir. **3. Stand-up fight**, combat en règle. **standing',** *a.* **1.** (*a*) (Qui se tient) debout. *Rac :* *F :* **To leave a competitor standing**, brûler un concurrent. **To be left standing**, être laissé sur place. *S.a.* START[1] 2. (*b*) **Standing crops**, récoltes sur pied. **2.** (*a*) **Standing water**, eau stagnante, dormante. (*b*) *Typ :* **Standing type**, conservation *f*. **3.** (*a*) *Mil :* **Standing camp**, camp permanent. (*b*) *Tchn :* **Standing block**, poulie *f* fixe. *S.a.* RIGGING 2. **4.** *adv.phr. Nau :* **To be brought up all standing**, rester en panne. **5.** (*a*) *Com :* **Standing expenses**, frais généraux. (*b*) **Standing rule**, règle fixe. **Standing joke**, plaisanterie courante, traditionnelle. *S. custom*, coutume établie. *S.a.* ARMY I, INSTRUCTION 2. **'standing 'stone,** *s. Archeol :* Menhir *m*. **standing²,** *s.* **1.** Stationnement *m* (d'une voiture). **2.** Durée *f*. **Friend of long standing**, ami de longue main, de longue date. **Officer of six months' standing**, officier qui a six mois de service. **3.** Rang *m*, position *f*. **Social standing**, position sociale. **Man of high standing**, homme haut placé. *Man of good s.*, homme estimé. *Man of no s.*, homme sans consistance. **Standing of a firm**, importance *f* d'une maison. *Firm of recognized s.*, maison d'une honorabilité reconnue. **'standing 'room,** *s.* Place(s) *f(pl)* debout. **standard** ['standərd], *s.* **1.** Bannière *f*. *Mil :* Étendard *m*. *Nau :* Pavillon *m*. **2.** Étalon *m* (de poids). *The metre is the s. of length*, le mètre est le module des longueurs. *Fin :* **The gold standard**, l'étalon (d'or). **3.** Modèle *m*, type *m*. **Standard of living**, niveau *m* de vie. *Judged by that standard . . .*, à cette mesure. . . . (*a*) Degré *m* (d'excellence) ; qualité *f*. *The s. of wages*, le taux des salaires. *To aim at a high s.*, viser à un haut degré d'excellence. *Com :* **Up to standard**, conforme à l'échantillon. *Sch :* *Your papers are up to s.*, vos compositions sont à la hauteur. (*b*) **Standard (of purity) of gold**, titre *m* de l'or. **5.** (*In elementary schools*) Classe *f*. **6.** (*a*) Support *m* (d'un instrument scientifique) ; montant *m* (d'une machine). (*b*) Pylône *m* d'éclairage. *S.a.* LAMP 2. **7.** *Hort :* **Standard (tree)**, arbre *m* de plein vent. **8.** *Attrib.* **Standard measure**, mesure-étalon *f*. **Standard metre**, étalon *m* du mètre. **Standard gold**, or au titre. *Rail :* **Standard gauge**, voie normale. **Of standard size**, de taille courante. *Ind :* **Of standard** dimensions, de dimensions normales. **Car of standard model,** voiture de série. **The standard authors,** les auteurs classiques. **Standard English,** l'anglais courant. **'standard-bearer,** s. Mil: (In cavalry) Porte-étendard m inv.

standardization [standərdai'zeiʃ(ə)n], s. Étalonnage m, étalonnement m (des poids); unification f (des méthodes d'essai). Ind: Standardisation f (d'une machine). Ch: Titrage m.

standardize ['standərda:iz], v.tr. Étalonner, unifier (des méthodes d'essai). Ind: Standardiser (des voitures). Ch: Titrer (une solution).

stand-offish [stand'ɔfiʃ], a. F: (Of pers.) Peu accessible; distant, réservé.

stand-offishness [stand'ɔfiʃnəs], s. F: Raideur f, réserve f, morgue f.

standpoint ['standpɔint], s. Point m de vue.

standstill ['standstil], s. Arrêt m, immobilisation f. **To come to a standstill,** s'arrêter, s'immobiliser; (of motor car) rester en panne. **To bring a train to a standstill,** arrêter un train. Trade is at a s., le commerce ne va plus. Many mills are at a s., beaucoup d'usines chôment.

stank [staŋk]. See STINK².

stannate ['staneit], s. Ch: Stannate m.

stannic ['stanik], a. Ch: Stannique.

stanniferous [sta'nifərəs], a. Stannifère.

stanza, pl. **-as** ['stanza, -az], s. Stance f, strophe f.

staple¹ [steipl], s. **1.** Crampon m (à deux pointes). **Wire staple,** (i) (clou) cavalier m en fil de fer, clou à deux pointes; (ii) Bookb: etc: broche f (en fil métallique). **2.** (Bolt-)staple, gâche f, gâchette f; auberon m (de la serrure d'une malle). **'staple-press,** s. Bookb: Brocheuse f. **'staple-vice,** s. Étau m à pied.

staple², s. (a) Produit principal (d'un pays). **Staple commodities,** denrées principales. **Staple industry,** industrie principale. (b) Matière première, matière brute.

staple³, s. Tex: Brin m, fibre f (de laine); soie f (de coton). **Long-staple cotton,** coton longue soie.

star¹ [sta:r], s. **1.** Étoile f; astre m. **Shooting-star,** étoile filante. **The pole-star,** l'étoile polaire. F: **To be born under a lucky star,** naître sous une bonne étoile. I thank my stars that . . ., je bénis mon étoile de ce que + ind. **To see stars,** voir trente-six chandelles. **2.** (a) **Star of an order,** plaque f d'un ordre; décoration f. (b) Mil: Étoile (servant à indiquer les grades). **3.** (a) **The stars and stripes** (of the U.S.A.), la bannière étoilée. (b) (On horse's forehead) Étoile. (c) (Star-shaped crack) Étoile, étoilement m. (d) Typ: Astérisque m. **4.** Cin: Th: (Pers.) Étoile, vedette f. Th: **Star part,** rôle de vedette. **'Star-Chamber (the),** s. Hist: La Chambre étoilée. **'star-fish,** s. Echin: Astérie f; étoile f de mer. **'star-gazing,** s. Rêvasserie(s) f(pl). **'star-lit,** a. Star-lit night, nuit étoilée. **'star-shell,** s. Obus éclairant; obus à étoiles. **'star-shower,** s. Pluie f d'étoiles filantes. **'star-spangled,** a. (Par)semé d'étoiles. **The star-spangled banner,** la bannière étoilée (des États-Unis). **'star-thistle,** s. Chardon étoilé; chausse-trape f.

star², v. (starred) **1.** v.tr. (a) Étoiler; (par)semer d'étoiles. (b) Étoiler, fêler (une glace). **2.** v.i. (a) (Of glass) Se fêler, s'étoiler. (b) Th: Être en vedette; tenir le premier rôle. **starred,** a. Étoilé; parsemé d'étoiles.

starboard¹ ['sta:rbɔːrd, -bərd], s. Nau: Tribord m. On the s. side, to starboard, à tribord. **Starboard tack,** tribord amures. **On the starboard**

bow, par tribord devant. **Hard a-starboard!** droite toute!

starboard². Nau: **1.** v.tr. **To starboard the helm,** mettre la barre à tribord. **2.** v.i. (Of ship) Venir sur tribord.

starch¹ [sta:rtʃ], s. **1.** (a) Amidon m. **Rice starch,** amidon de riz. **Potato starch,** fécule f de pommes de terre. (b) Starch(-paste), colle f d'amidon. **2.** F: (a) Manières empesées, guindées; raideur f. (b) **To take the starch out of s.o.,** démonter qn.

starch², v.tr. Empeser, amidonner. **starched,** a. **1.** Empesé. S.a. SHIRT. **2.** F: (Of pers.) Empesé; guindé; raide.

stardom ['sta:rdəm], s. Cin: Divisme m. **To rise to stardom,** devenir une vedette de l'écran.

stare¹ [stɛər], s. Regard fixe; regard appuyé. **Glassy s.,** regard terne, vitreux. Set s., regard fixe. **Stony s.,** regard dur. **Vacant s.,** regard vague; regard ahuri. **To give s.o. a stare,** dévisager qn. **With a s. of astonishment,** les yeux écarquillés; les yeux ébahis. **With a s. of horror,** les yeux grands ouverts d'horreur.

stare². **1.** v.i. (a) Regarder fixement. **To s. into the distance,** regarder au loin. **To stare in s.o.'s face,** dévisager qn. (b) Écarquiller les yeux; ouvrir de grands yeux. **2.** v.ind.tr. **To stare at s.o.,** (i) regarder qn fixement; fixer ses yeux sur qn; fixer qn; (ii) regarder qn effrontément; dévisager qn; (iii) regarder qn d'un air hébété. **3.** v.tr. **To stare s.o. in the face,** dévisager qn. Ruin stares him in the face, sa ruine est imminente. F: **It's staring you in the face,** ça vous crève les yeux. **To stare s.o. out (of countenance),** faire baisser les yeux à qn; faire perdre contenance à qn. **staring,** a. **1.** S. eyes, (i) yeux fixes; (ii) yeux grands ouverts; yeux effarés; regard ébahi. **2.** (a) S. waistcoat, gilet aux couleurs criardes. (b) **Stark staring mad,** complètement fou. **'stare-cat,** s.f. P: Effrontée; curieuse.

stark [sta:rk]. **1.** a. Lit: (a) Raide, rigide. He lay s. in death, il gisait dans la rigidité de la mort. (b) Poet: Fort, vigoureux. (c) Poet: Résolu, inflexible. (d) S. nonsense, pure bêtise. **The s. desolation of the whole region,** l'absolue désolation de toute cette région. **2.** adv. **Stark naked,** tout nu; nu comme un ver, comme la main.

starless ['sta:rləs], a. Sans étoiles.

starlight ['sta:rlait], s. **1.** Lumière f des étoiles; lumière stellaire. **In the starlight, by starlight,** à la lueur, à la clarté, des étoiles. **2.** Attrib. A starlight night, une nuit étoilée.

starling¹ ['sta:rliŋ], s. Orn: Étourneau m; sansonnet m.

starling², s. Bec m, éperon m (de môle, de pile de pont); brise-glace m (en pilotis).

starry ['sta:ri], a. (Ciel) étoilé, (par)semé d'étoiles.

start¹ [sta:rt], s. **1.** (a) Tressaillement m, sursaut m, soubresaut m. **To wake with a start,** se réveiller en sursaut. He gave a start, il tressaillit, sursauta. To give a s. of joy, tressaillir de joie. **To give s.o. a start,** faire tressaillir qn. (b) Saut m; mouvement m brusque. S.a. FIT² **2.** (a) Commencement m, début m. **To make an early start,** commencer de bonne heure. You will work here for a start, vous travaillerez ici pour débuter. **At the start,** au début. **At the very start,** de prime abord. **From start to finish,** du commencement à la fin. F: **To give s.o. a start,** lancer qn (dans les affaires, etc.). To give an artist, a play, a good s., lancer un artiste, une pièce. **To make a good start,** bien commencer. **To make a fresh start (in life),** recommencer (sa vie). (b) Départ m. Av: Envol m. Sp: Envolée f (d'une course de bicyclettes);

start *m.* **To make an early start,** partir de bonne heure. *Rac:* **Flying start,** départ lancé. **Standing start,** départ arrêté. **False start,** faux départ. (*c*) *Sp:* **To give s.o. a start,** donner un peu d'avance à qn. **To get the start of s.o.,** prendre les devants ; devancer qn.

tart². I. *v.i.* **1.** (*a*) Tressaillir, tressauter, sursauter ; avoir un haut-le-corps ; (*of horse, etc.*) soubresauter. *The report made him s.,* la détonation le fit (sur)sauter. **To start out of one's sleep,** se réveiller en sursaut. (*b*) **To start aside,** se jeter de côté ; s'écarter brusquement ; (*of horse*) faire un écart. **To start back,** se jeter en arrière. **To start to one's feet,** se lever tout à coup. **To start from one's chair,** se lever vivement de sa chaise. *Tears started from his eyes,* les larmes jaillirent de ses yeux. *His eyes were starting out of his head,* les yeux lui sortaient de la tête. **2.** (*Of rivets*) Se détacher ; sauter. *Nau:* (*Of ship's seams*) Se délier, s'ouvrir. (*Of ship*) **To start at the seams,** cracher ses étoupes. **3.** (*a*) Commencer ; débuter. *To s. with soup,* commencer par un potage. *The play starts (off) with a prologue,* la pièce débute par un prologue. **To start at the beginning,** commencer par le commencement. *S.a.* END¹ 1. **To start afresh,** recommencer. **To start in life,** débuter dans la vie. **To start in business,** se mettre, se lancer, dans les affaires. *There were only six members to start with,* il n'y avait que six membres au début. *To s. with we must . . .,* en premier lieu il va falloir. . . . **To start by doing sth.,** commencer par faire qch. (*b*) **To start (away, off, out, on one's way),** partir ; se mettre en route. *We s. to-morrow,* nous partons demain. **He started back the next day,** il reprit le chemin de la maison le lendemain. *F:* **He started out to write a novel,** il se mit en devoir d'écrire un roman. *Rac:* **Only six horses started,** six chevaux seulement sont partis. (*c*) **To start (off),** (*of car*) démarrer ; (*of train*) s'ébranler. (*d*) **To start (up),** (*of engine*) se mettre en marche ; (*of injector, dynamo*) s'amorcer. *The engine won't s.,* le moteur refuse de partir. II. **start,** *v.tr.* **1.** Commencer (un travail) ; entamer (une conversation). *To s. a hole,* amorcer un trou. **To start (on) a fresh loaf,** entamer un nouveau pain. *To s. negotiations,* entamer, engager, des négociations. *To s. life afresh,* recommencer sa vie. *Fb: etc:* *To s. an attack,* amorcer une attaque. **To start doing sth.,** commencer à, de, faire qch. ; se mettre à faire qch. *To s. crying again,* se remettre à pleurer. *It's just started raining,* voilà qu'il commence à pleuvoir. **2.** (*a*) **To start (off) a horse at a gallop,** faire partir un cheval au galop. (*b*) *Rac:* Donner le signal du départ à (des coureurs). (*c*) *Ven:* Lancer (un cerf, un sanglier) ; lever, faire partir (une perdrix, etc.). **3.** (*a*) Lancer, donner le branle (à une entreprise) ; fonder (un commerce) ; fonder, lancer (un journal) ; ouvrir (une école) ; mettre en train (une affaire). (*b*) **To start a fire,** provoquer un incendie. **4.** (*a*) Mettre en marche, faire marcher (une horloge). (*b*) **To start (up) a machine,** mettre une machine en marche (up), en train. *Av:* **Start up!** mettez en route ! **5.** **To start s.o. on a career,** lancer qn dans une carrière. **Once you start him talking . . .,** quand on le met à causer. . . . **6.** Disjoindre (des tôles) ; faire craquer (les coutures d'un vêtement). **start up,** *v.i.* **1.** (*Of pers.*) Se lever brusquement ; se lever en sursaut. **2.** (*Of plant*) (*a*) Lever. (*b*) Pousser rapidement. *F:* *Mushroom villages starting up everywhere,* pareil à des villages qui surgissent du jour au lendemain. (*c*) Se produire ; naître. **starting,** *s.* **1.** Tressaille-

ment *m* ; sursaut *m*, soubresaut *m*. **2.** (*a*) Commencement *m*, début *m*. (*b*) Départ *m*. **3.** (*a*) Mise ƒ en train (d'une entreprise, etc.). (*b*) **Starting** (up), mise en mouvement, mise en marche, lancement *m* (d'une machine) ; amorçage *m* (d'une dynamo). **'starting-engine,** *s.* Moteur *m* de lancement. **'starting-gate,** *s.* *Rac:* Barrière ƒ. **'starting-gear,** *s.* Appareil *m* de démarrage ; mise ƒ en train. **'starting-handle,** *s.* Manivelle ƒ de mise en marche. **'starting-lever,** *s.* Levier *m* de mise en marche. **'starting-line,** *s.* *Sp:* Ligne ƒ de départ. **'starting-place,** **-point,** *s.* Point *m* de départ. *Rail: etc:* Tête ƒ de ligne. **'starting-post,** *s.* *Rac:* Poteau *m* de départ ; barrière ƒ. **'starting-price,** *s.* **1.** *Com:* Prix initial. **2.** *Rac:* Dernière cote avant le départ.

starter ['sta:rtər], *s.* **1.** (*a*) *You are an early starter,* vous partez de bonne heure. (*b*) *Sp:* Partant *m*. **2.** (*a*) *Rac:* Starter *m* (qui donne le signal du départ). (*b*) Auteur *m* (d'un projet, etc.) ; lanceur, -euse (d'une affaire, etc.). **3.** (*Device*) *Aut:* El.E: Appareil *m* de mise en marche ; démarreur *m*. **Starter-button,** bouton (-pressoir) *m* de mise en marche. *Aut:* **Self-starter,** mise ƒ en marche automatique ; démarreur automatique.

startle [sta:rtl], *v.tr.* Effrayer, alarmer (qn) ; faire tressaillir, faire sursauter (qn). **To startle s.o. out of his sleep,** éveiller qn en sursaut.

startling, *a.* Effrayant, saisissant ; *F:* renversant. *S. events,* événements sensationnels. *S. get-up,* toilette ébouriffante. *S. resemblance,* ressemblance saisissante.

starvation [sta:r'vei∫(ə)n], *s.* Privation ƒ de nourriture ; affamement *m.* *Med:* Inanition ƒ. **To die of starvation,** mourir de faim, d'inanition. **Starvation wages,** salaire de famine ; salaire de meurt-de-faim.

starve [sta:rv]. **1.** *v.i.* (*a*) **To starve to death,** mourir de faim. (*b*) **To starve,** Manquer de nourriture ; endurer la faim. *F:* **I am starving,** je meurs de faim. (*c*) *F:* **To be starving with cold,** être tout transi (de froid) ; être gelé. (*d*) (*Of tree, plant*) Dépérir ; s'étioler. **2.** *v.tr.* (*a*) Faire mourir (qn) de faim. **To s. out a town,** prendre, réduire, une ville par la famine. *Trade would have been starved out of existence,* le commerce serait mort d'inanition. (*b*) Priver (qn) de nourriture. *F:* **To starve a cold,** traiter un rhume par la diète. **starved,** *a.* (*a*) Affamé. **Starved-looking,** à l'aspect famélique. (*b*) **Starved of affection,** privé d'affection. **starving,** *a.* Mourant de faim ; famélique.

starveling ['sta:rvlin], *s.* Famélique *mf* ; *F:* meurt-de-faim *m inv.*

starwort ['sta:rwə:rt], *s.* *Bot:* Stellaire ƒ. **Sea-starwort,** aster *m*.

state¹ [steit], *s.* **1.** (*a*) État *m*, condition ƒ ; situation ƒ. *In a good s.,* en bon état ; en bonne condition. *Here's a nice, a pretty, state of things,* nous voilà bien ! c'est du joli, du propre ! *F:* **What a state you are in!** dans quel état vous êtes ! (*b*) **Body in a s. of rest,** corps à l'état de repos ; corps au repos. *S. of health,* état de santé. *People in a savage s.,* peuple à l'état sauvage. **The married state,** le mariage. **The single state,** le célibat. **State of mind,** disposition ƒ d'esprit. *F:* **To be in a great state,** être dans tous ses états. **2.** (*a*) Rang *m*, dignité ƒ. *In a style befitting his s.,* sur un pied digne de son rang. (*b*) Pompe ƒ, parade ƒ, apparat *m*. **To keep great state,** to live in state, mener grand train. **To travel in state,** voyager en grand apparat, en grand équipage. **To dine in state,** dîner en grand gala. (*Of body*) To lie in state, être exposé (sur un lit de parade). Lying in state, exposition *f* (d'un corps). *F:* To sit in state *in one's carriage*, se pavaner, se prélasser, dans sa voiture. *He was in his robes of state*, il était en costume d'apparat. Bed of state, lit de parade. (*c*) State carriage, state coach, voiture d'apparat; voiture de gala. State reception *of a prince*, réception solennelle d'un prince. State ball, grand bal officiel; grand bal de cour. State apartments, salons d'apparat. **3.** = ESTATE 3. *Fr.Hist:* The States General, les États généraux. **4.** (*a*) The State, l'État. Church and State, l'Église et l'État. Secretary of State, secrétaire d'État. Affairs of State, affaires d'État. State trial, procès politique. State forest, forêt domaniale; forêt de l'État. (*b*) État, nation *f. Every s. was represented*, tous les états étaient représentés. The United States of America, les États-Unis d'Amérique. **'State-aided,** *a.* Subventionné par l'État. **'State-managed,** *a.* (Théâtre, etc.) en régie. **'state-room,** *s.* **I.** Chambre *f* d'apparat; salle *f* de réception (d'un palais). **2.** *Nau:* Cabine *f* (de luxe).

state², *v.tr.* **I.** (*a*) Énoncer, déclarer, affirmer, faire connaître (qch.). *To s. sth. definitely*, spécifier qch. *This condition was expressly stated*, cette condition était énoncée expressément. Please state below . . ., veuillez noter en bas. . . . As stated above, ainsi qu'il est dit plus haut. *It should be so stated that* . . ., nous devons ajouter que. . . . *I have stated my opinion*, j'ai donné mon opinion. *He states positively that he heard it*, il affirme l'avoir entendu. *He is stated to have been found* . . ., on affirme l'avoir trouvé. . . . *I have seen it stated that* . . ., j'ai lu quelque part que. . . . (*b*) Exposer (une réclamation). *Jur:* To state the case, faire l'exposé des faits. To state a case, soumettre les faits au tribunal. (*c*) *Mth:* Poser, énoncer (un problème). **2.** Régler, arrêter, fixer (une heure, une date). **stated,** *a. At s. intervals*, à des époques fixées; à intervalles réglés. *On s. days*, à jours fixes.

statecraft ['steitkrɑːft], *s.* Habileté *f* politique; diplomatie *f.*

stateless ['steitləs], *a. Adm:* Stateless person, sans-patrie *mf inv.*

stateliness ['steitlinəs], *s.* Majesté *f;* aspect imposant; dignité *f.*

stately ['steitli], *a.* **I.** Majestueux; imposant. **2.** Plein de dignité; noble, élevé.

statement ['steitmənt], *s.* **I.** (*a*) Exposition *f*, exposé *m*, énoncé *m* (des faits); rapport *m*, compte rendu, relation *f.* Official statement (*to the press*), communiqué *m.* Certified statement, constatation *f.* To make, publish, a statement, émettre une déclaration. *Full s. of the position*, exposé complet de la situation. *According to his own s.*, suivant sa propre déclaration. *Jur:* The statements made by the witnesses, les dépositions *f* des témoins. Written statement of a case, instruction écrite; mémoire *m.* (*b*) Affirmation *f.* *To contradict a s.*, nier une affirmation. **2.** *Com:* Statement of account, état *m* de compte; relevé *m* de compte. Statement of affairs (*in bankruptcy*), bilan *m* de liquidation.

statesman, *pl.* **-men** ['steitsmən, -men], *s.m.* Homme d'État.

statesmanlike ['steitsmənlaik], *a.* D'homme d'État.

statesmanship ['steitsmənʃip], *s.* Science *f* du gouvernement.

statics ['statiks], *s.pl.* **I.** *Mec:* La statique. **2.** *W.Tel:* Perturbations *f* atmosphériques.

station¹ ['steiʃ(ə)n], *s.* **I.** (*a*) Position *f*, place *f*, poste *m.* To take up a station, (i) prendre une place; se placer; (ii) se rendre à un poste. *Navy:* Action stations, postes de combat. (*Of ship*) To be in station, out of station, être, ne pas être, à son poste. (*b*) Station *f*, poste. Naval station, station navale; port *m* de guerre. Ship on station, navire en station. Coaling station, dépôt *m* de charbon. Military station, poste militaire. *The battalion is about to change s.*, le bataillon va changer de garnison. Listening station, poste d'écoute. (*c*) (*In Australia*) (Sheep-station, élevage *m* de moutons. (*d*) Lifeboat station, station de sauvetage. Frontier station, poste de frontière. *El.E:* Transformer station, poste abaisseur de tension. *Hyd.E:* Pumping station, centrale *f* de pompage. **2.** Station, condition *f;* rang *m.* Station in life, situation sociale. To marry below one's station, se mésallier. Men of exalted s., hommes de haute position. **3.** (*a*) *Rail:* Gare *f.* Passenger station, gare de voyageurs. Goods station, gare de marchandises. Euston Station, la gare de Euston. Station hotel, hôtel de la gare. Station bus, voiture *f* de service d'hôtel. (*b*) Bus station, terminus *m* d'autobus. **4.** *Ecc:* The stations of the Cross, le chemin de la Croix.

station², *v.tr.* (*a*) Placer, mettre (qn dans un endroit). (*b*) *To s.* troops, poster des troupes. *Mil: Navy:* To s. the officers and men, désigner leurs postes aux officiers et aux hommes. (*c*) To be stationed at . . ., (i) *Mil:* être en garnison à . . .; (ii) *Navy:* être en station à . . .

stationary ['steiʃənəri], *a.* **I.** Stationnaire, immobile. *S. car*, auto en stationnement. **2.** (*a*) *S.* engine, machine fixe. (*b*) *S.* troops, troupes sédentaires.

stationer ['steiʃənər], *s.* Papetier *m.* Stationer's shop, papeterie *f.* Stationers' Hall, Hôtel *m* de Corporation des libraires, relieurs, et papetiers (à Londres). Entered at Stationers' Hall, (livre) déposé.

stationery ['steiʃənəri], *s.* Papeterie *f.* Office stationery, school stationery, fournitures *fpl* de bureau, d'école.

stationmaster ['steiʃənmɑːstər], *s.* Chef *m* de gare.

statistical [stə'tistik(ə)l], *a.* Statistique.

statistician [statis'tiʃ(ə)n], *s.* Statisticien, -ienne.

statistics [stə'tistiks], *s.pl.* La statistique.

stator ['steitər], *s.* Stator *m* (d'une turbine, d'un moteur électrique).

statuary ['statjuəri]. **I.** *a.* Statuaire. **2.** *s.* (*Pers*) Statuaire *mf.* **3.** *s.* (*a*) La statuaire; l'art statuaire. (*b*) *Coll.* Statues *fpl.*

statue ['statju], *s.* Statue *f.*

statuesque [statju'esk], *a.* Sculptural, -aux; plastique.

statuette [statju'et], *s.* Statuette *f.*

stature ['statjər], *s.* Stature *f;* taille *f.* To be short of stature, avoir la taille courte.

status ['steitəs], *s.* (*a*) Statut légal (de qn). Personal status, statut personnel. (*b*) *Adm:* Civil status, état civil. (*c*) Condition *f*, position *f;* rang *m.* Social status, rang social. *Without official s.*, sans titre officiel.

status quo ['steitəs'kwou], *s.* Statu quo *m inv.*

statute ['statjuːt], *s.* **I.** Acte *m* du Parlement; loi *f*, ordonnance *f.* The Statute of Limitations, la loi de prescription. *To bar a debt by the S.* Limitations, prescrire une dette. Statute measure, mesures légales. **2.** *pl.* Statuts *m*, règlements (d'une société, d'une compagnie). **3.** *Internat. Jur:* Personal statute, statut personnel. **'sta-tute-'barred,** *a.* (*Of interest, debt*) Prescrit, caduc. **'statute-book,** *s.* Code *m* (des lois). **'statute-law,** *s.* Droit écrit; jurisprudence *f.* **tatutory** ['statjutəri], *a.* **1.** Établi, imposé, par la loi; réglementaire; (*of offence*) prévu par la loi. **Statutory holiday,** fête légale. **Statutory declaration,** (i) attestation *f* (tenant lieu de serment); (ii) acte *m* de notoriété. **2.** Statutaire; conforme aux statuts.

taunch[1] [stɔːnʃ], *a.* **1.** (*Of pers.*) Sûr, dévoué; ferme. *S. friend,* ami à toute épreuve; ami solide. *S. courage,* courage inébranlable. **2.** (*Of ship*) Étanche. **-ly,** *adv.* Avec fermeté; avec résolution; avec dévouement.

taunch[2], *v.tr.* = STANCH.

taunchness ['stɔːnʃnəs], *s.* **1.** Fermeté *f*; dévouement *m.* **2.** Étanchéité *f.*

tave[1] [steiv], *s.* **1.** (*a*) *Coop:* Barrel staves, douves *f* pour tonneaux. (*b*) Bâton *m.* **2.** *Pros:* Stance *f,* strophe *f* (d'un poème). **3.** *Mus:* (*a*) Portée *f.* (*b*) (Barre *f* de) mesure *f.*

tave[2], *v.tr.* (*p.t.* staved; *p.p.* staved, *Nau:* stove [stoːuv]) **1.** *Coop:* Assembler les douves (d'un tonneau). **2.** = STAVE IN. **stave in,** *v.tr.* Défoncer, enfoncer (une barrique, un bateau). **stave off,** *v.tr.* Détourner, écarter (un ennui, etc.); prévenir (un danger); conjurer (un désastre). **To stave off hunger,** tromper la faim.

tay[1] [stei], *s.* **1.** Séjour *m*; visite *f* (chez un ami). *Fortnight's s.,* séjour de quinze jours. **2.** (*a*) *Lit:* Retard *m*; entrave *f. He will endure no s.,* il ne supportera aucun retard. (*b*) *Jur:* **Stay of proceedings,** suspension *f* d'instance. **Stay of execution,** sursis *m*; ordonnance *f* de surseoir (à un jugement).

tay[2]. I. *v.i.* **1.** (*a*) *A:* S'arrêter. (*b*) (*In imp.*) Stay! attendez! **2.** (*a*) Rester; demeurer sur les lieux. *S. here till I return,* restez ici jusqu'à ce que je revienne. **Stay there!** tenez-vous là! **To stay at home,** se tenir chez soi; rester à la maison. **To stay in bed,** rester au lit; garder le lit. **To stay in for dinner,** rester à dîner. *To make s.o. s. to lunch,* retenir qn à déjeuner. **He has come to stay,** il est venu (i) passer quelques jours, (ii) habiter, chez nous. (*b*) Séjourner, demeurer quelque temps (dans un endroit). **To stay at a hotel,** (i) descendre à un hôtel; (ii) être installé à un hôtel. **3.** *Rac:* **He was not able to stay,** il n'a pas pu soutenir l'allure. *He can s. three miles,* il peut fournir une course de trois milles. II. **stay,** *v.tr.* **1.** Arrêter (le progrès de qn); enrayer (une épidémie). **To stay s.o.'s hand,** retenir le bras de qn. **To stay one's hand,** se retenir. **2.** *Jur: etc:* Remettre, ajourner (une décision); surseoir à (un jugement). **stay away,** *v.i.* Ne pas venir; s'absenter. **stay in,** *v.i.* (*a*) Ne pas sortir; rester à la maison; garder le logis. (*b*) *Sch:* Être en retenue. **Stay-in strike,** grève *f* avec occupation (d'usine); *F:* grève sur le tas. **stay on,** *v.i.* Rester encore quelque temps. **stay out,** *v.i.* Rester dehors; ne pas rentrer. *To s. out all night,* découcher. **stay up,** *v.i.* Ne pas se coucher; veiller. **To stay up late,** veiller tard. **staying**[1], *s.* **1.** Séjour *m.* **2.** Staying power, résistance *f*; endurance *f.* (*Of horse*) *To have good s. power,* avoir du fond. **3.** (*a*) Enrayage *m.* (*b*) *Jur: etc:* Remise *f,* ajournement *m.* **'stay-at-home,** *a. & s.* Casanier, -ière.

tay[3], *s.* **1.** (*a*) Support *m,* soutien *m. F:* The stay of his old age, le soutien de sa vieillesse. (*b*) *Const: Mec.E:* Support, appui *m,* étai *m,*

étançon *m*; jambe *f* de force; arc-boutant *m*; accore *m* (de navire en construction). **2.** (*Brace, tie*) Tirant *m* (de chaudière); entretoise *f.* **3.** *pl. Cost:* Stays, corset *m.* **'stay-bar,** *s.* = STAY-ROD. **'stay-lace,** *s. Cost:* Lacet *m* (de corset). **'stay-maker,** *s.* Corsetier, -ière. **'stay-rod,** *s.* **1.** Jambe *f* de force. **2.** Tirant *m* de fixation.

stay[4], *v.tr.* **1.** Étayer, étançonner, arc-bouter (un mur, une maison); accorer (un navire). **2.** Entretoiser; ancrer (une cheminée). **staying**[2], *s.* **1.** Étayage *m.* **2.** Entretoisement *m.*

stay[5], *s.* **1.** Hauban *m.* **2.** (*Of ship*) To be in stays, to hang in stays, être pris vent devant. **To be slack in stays,** être lent à virer (de bord). **To go about in stays,** virer vent devant. **'stay-rope,** *s.* Hauban *m.*

stay[6]. **1.** *v.tr.* Hauban(n)er (un mât, un poteau). **2.** *Nau:* (*a*) *v.tr.* Faire virer de bord (un navire) vent devant. (*b*) *v.i.* Virer de bord vent devant.

stayer ['steiər], *s. Sp:* (*a*) Coureur *m* de fond; stayer *m.* (*b*) Cheval *m* qui a du fond.

staysail ['steiseil, steisl], *s. Nau:* Voile *f* d'étai.

stead [sted], *s.* **1.** To stand s.o. in good stead, être fort utile à qn; être d'un grand secours à qn. **2.** In s.o.'s stead, à la place de qn. *To act in s.o.'s s.,* remplacer qn.

steadfast ['stedfəst], *a.* Ferme; inébranlable. *S. in danger,* ferme en face du danger. *S. in love,* in adversity, constant en amour, dans l'adversité. **-ly,** *adv.* Fermement; avec constance.

steadfastness ['stedfəstnəs], *s.* Fermeté *f* (d'esprit); constance *f.* **Steadfastness of purpose,** ténacité *f* de caractère.

steadiness ['stedinəs], *s.* **1.** Fermeté *f. S. of hand,* sûreté *f* de main. **2.** Assiduité *f,* persévérance *f,* application *f. S. of gaze,* fermeté du regard. **3.** Stabilité *f. S. of prices,* tenue *f* des prix. **4.** (*Of pers.*) Conduite rangée; sagesse *f.*

steading ['stedin], *s. Scot:* (*a*) Ferme *f* et ses dépendances. (*b*) Dépendances *f* (d'une ferme).

steady[1] ['stedi]. **1.** *a.* (*a*) Ferme, solide; fixe, rigide. *To make a table s.,* caler une table. **To keep steady,** ne pas bouger; rester en place. **To have a steady hand,** avoir la main sûre. *With a s. hand, step,* d'une main assurée; d'un pas assuré. *Horse s. under fire,* cheval docile au feu. *Ship s. in a sea,* navire qui tient bien la mer. (*b*) Continu, soutenu; persistant; régulier; *To play a s. game,* avoir un jeu régulier. *S. progress,* progrès ininterrompus, soutenus. *S. pace,* allure réglée. *S. trot,* trot soutenu. **Steady pulse,** pouls égal. **Steady weather,** temps établi. *S. downpour,* pluie persistante. **Steady barometer,** baromètre stationnaire. *Com:* **Steady demand for . . .,** demande suivie pour. . . . (*d*) (*Of pers.*) Rangé, posé; sérieux, sage. **2.** *adv.* (*a*) **Steady!** (i) ne bougez pas! (ii) *Mil:* fixe! *F:* Steady (on)! doucement! du calme! (*b*) *Nau:* Steady (the helm)! droite la barre! **3.** *s.* (*a*) Support *m* (pour la main, etc.). (*b*) Lunette *f* (d'un tour). **-ily,** *adv.* **1.** Fermement. *To walk s.,* marcher d'un pas ferme. **2.** (*a*) Régulièrement; sans arrêt. *His health grows s. worse,* sa santé va (en) empirant. (*b*) Uniment; sans à-coups. **3.** Assidûment. *To work s. at sth.,* travailler assidûment, d'arrache-pied, à qch. **4.** (Se conduire) d'une manière rangée, posée; avec sagesse.

steady[2]. **1.** *v.tr.* (*a*) Raffermir, affermir. *To s. a table-leg,* caler le pied d'une table. *To s. one's hand,* assurer sa main. **To steady oneself against** sth., s'étayer contre qch. *To s. the running of a machine,* régulariser la marche d'une machine

To s. *the nerves*, raffermir les nerfs. (*b*) Assagir (un jeune homme). **2.** *v.i.* Se raffermir ; reprendre son aplomb. **steady down.** **1.** *v.tr.* Assagir (qn). **2.** *v.i.* *The market has steadied down,* le marché a repris son aplomb. *Young man who has steadied down,* jeune homme qui s'est rangé.

steak [steik], *s.* *Cu:* (*a*) Tranche *f* (de viande, de poisson) ; darne *f* (de saumon) ; côtelette *f* (de porc). (*b*) Bifteck *m* ; (*cut from the table*) entrecôte *f*. **Fillet steak,** tournedos *m.* **Bear steak,** bifteck d'ours.

steal [sti:l], *v.* (stole [stoul] ; stolen ['stoul(ə)n]) **1.** *v.tr.* (*a*) Voler, dérober, soustraire (*sth. from s.o.,* qch. à qn). *To s. money from the till,* voler de l'argent dans la caisse. (*b*) *F:* **To steal (away)** *s.o.'s heart,* séduire le cœur de qn. *To s. a few hours from one's studies,* dérober quelques heures à ses études. (*c*) **To steal a glance at** *s.o.,* jeter furtivement un regard à qn ; regarder qn à la dérobée, d'un œil furtif. (*d*) **To steal a march on the enemy,** *F:* **on s.o.,** gagner une marche sur l'ennemi ; devancer qn ; circonvenir qn. **2.** *v.i.* **To steal away, down, in, out,** s'en aller, descendre, entrer, sortir, à la dérobée, furtivement. *He stole away,* il s'esquiva. *He stole into the room,* il se faufila, se glissa, dans la chambre. **To steal along,** marcher à pas de loup. *A smile stole across her lips,* elle eut un sourire furtif.

stealing, *s.* Vol *m.*

stealer ['sti:lər], *s.* Voleur, -euse (*of,* de). **Sheep-stealer,** voleur de moutons.

stealth [stelθ], *s.* (*Only in the phr.*) **By stealth,** à la dérobée ; furtivement.

stealthiness ['stelθinəs], *s.* Caractère furtif (d'une action).

stealthy ['stelθi], *a.* Furtif. *S. glance,* regard dérobé. **-ily,** *adv.* A la dérobée ; furtivement. *To creep in s.,* entrer à pas de loup.

steam¹ [sti:m], *s.* (*a*) Vapeur *f* (d'eau) ; buée *f.* *Room full of s.,* salle remplie de buée. (*b*) *Ph:* *Mch:* **Wet steam,** vapeur mouillée. **Dry steam,** vapeur sèche. *Heated by s.,* chauffé à la vapeur. **To work by steam,** fonctionner à la vapeur. **To get up steam, to raise steam,** mettre (la chaudière) sous pression. **Steam is up,** nous sommes sous pression. **To keep up steam,** rester sous pression. **To let off, blow off, steam,** (i) lâcher la vapeur ; (ii) *F:* dépenser son superflu d'énergie ; (iii) *F:* épancher sa bile. **Engine under steam,** machine sous pression. *To put on full s.,* mettre à toute vitesse. **To make all steam,** pousser les feux. **At full steam,** à toute vapeur. *Nau:* **Full steam ahead!** en avant à toute vapeur! en avant toute! (*Of damaged ship*) **To proceed under its own steam,** marcher par ses seuls moyens. **'steam-'boiler,** *s.* Chaudière *f* (à vapeur) ; générateur *m.* **'steam-box, -chamber, -chest,** *s.* **1.** *Mch:* Chapelle *f* du tiroir ; boîte *f* de distribution de vapeur. **2.** Réservoir *m* de vapeur. **'steam-cock,** *s.* Prise *f* de vapeur. **'steam-'crane,** *s.* Grue *f* à vapeur. **'steam-driven,** *a.* Actionné par la vapeur ; à vapeur. **'steam-engine,** *s.* Machine *f* à vapeur. **'steam-gauge,** *s.* Manomètre *m* de pression. **'steam-'hammer,** *s.* Marteau-pilon *m* à vapeur. **'steam-heating,** *s.* Chauffage *m* à la vapeur. **'steam-'jacket,** *s.* *Mch:* Chemise *f* de vapeur. **'steam-port,** *s.* Orifice *m* de vapeur. *Mch:* Lumière *f* d'admission. **'steam-pressure,** *s.* Tension *f* de vapeur. **'steam-'roller,** *s.* *Civ.E:* Cylindre *m* compresseur à vapeur ; rouleau *m* compresseur. **'steam-shovel,** *s.* Pelle *f* à vapeur ; excavateur *m.* **'steam-tight,** *a.* Étanche (à la vapeur).

'steam-'whistle, *s.* Sifflet *m* à vapeur ; trompe *f.*

steam² **1.** *v.tr.* (*a*) *Cu:* Cuire (des légumes) à la vapeur, à l'étuvée. (*b*) Passer (qch.) à la vapeur ; vaporiser (un vêtement). *Tex:* Délustrer (? drap). **To steam open an envelope,** décacheter une lettre à la vapeur. **2.** *v.i.* (*a*) Jeter, exhaler de la vapeur ; fumer. *The soup steams on the table,* la soupe fume sur la table. *Horses steaming with sweat,* chevaux fumants (de sueur). (*b*) Marcher (à la vapeur). **To steam ahead,** (i) avancer (à la vapeur) ; (ii) *F:* faire des progrès rapides. **The train steamed away, steamed off,** le train partit. *The ship steamed out of port,* le vapeur sortit du port. **To steam at ten knots,** filer dix nœuds. *We can only s. with one boiler,* nous ne pouvons plus marcher qu'avec un chaudière. **steaming,** *a.* Fumant. **Steaming hot,** tout chaud.

steamboat ['sti:mbout], *s.* Bateau *m,* navire *m* à vapeur ; vapeur *m* ; steamboat *m.*

steamer ['sti:mər], *s.* **1.** = STEAMSHIP. **2.** *Cu:* Marmite *f* à vapeur.

steamship ['sti:mʃip], *s.* Navire *m* à vapeur ; vapeur *m* ; steamer *m.* **Screw-steamship,** vapeur à hélice(s). **Steamship line,** compagnie *f* de paquebots.

steamy ['sti:mi], *a.* Plein de vapeur, de buée (*of atmosphere*) humide.

stearate ['sti:əreit], *s.* *Ch:* Stéarate *m.*

stearic [sti'arik], *a.* *Ch:* Stéarique *m.*

stearin(e) ['sti:ərin], *s.* *Ch:* Stéarine *f.* **Stearin candle,** bougie *f* stéarique.

steed [sti:d], *s.* *Lit:* Coursier *m.*

steel¹ [sti:l], *s.* **1.** *Metall:* Acier *m.* **Heat-resisting s.,** acier indétrempable. **Rolled s.,** acier laminé. **Bar steel,** acier en barres. **Cold-drawn s.,** acier étiré à froid. **Tungsten steel,** acier au tungstène. **Steel pen,** plume métallique. **Steel edge** (*of a tool*) acérure *f.* *Electro-Ch:* **Steel bath,** bain d'aciérag *F:* **Grip of steel,** poigne d'acier. *S.a.* STAINLESS **2.** *Lit:* Fer *m,* épée *f* ; lame *f.* **To fight with cold steel,** se battre à l'arme blanche. **3.** (*a*) (*For sharpening knives*) Fusil *m* ; affiloir *m.* (*b*) (*For striking light*) Briquet *m.* **Flint and steel,** briquet à silex. **4.** Busc *m* (de corset). **5.** *Pharm:* **Tincture of steel,** teinture de perchlorure de fer. **Steel pills,** pilules ferrugineuses. **'steel-clad,** Couvert, revêtu, d'acier ; (*of ancient knight*) bardé de fer. **steel-en'graved,** *a.* Gravé sur acier. **'steel-engraver,** *s.* Graveur *m* sur acier. **steel-en'graving,** *s.* **1.** Gravure *f* sur acier. **2.** Estampe *f* sur acier. **'steel-faced,** *a.* surface aciérée. **'steel-'grey,** *a.* & *s.* Gris d'acier (*m inv*). **'steel-hearted,** *a.* Au cœur de fer. **steel-'plate,** *s.* **1.** Tôle *f* d'acier. **2.** *Engr:* Planche *f* d'acier. **steel-'plated,** *a.* Cuirassé. **'steel-works,** *s.pl.* Aciérie *f.*

steel², *v.tr.* **1.** (*a*) Aciérer, acérer, armer (un outil). (*b*) *Electro-Ch:* **To steel(-face) a copper plate,** aciérer une plaque de cuivre. **2.** *Metal:* Aciérer (le fer). **3.** *F:* **To steel oneself, to steel one's heart, to do sth.,** (i) s'endurcir à faire qch ; (ii) s'armer de courage pour faire qch. **To steel oneself against sth.,** se raidir, se cuirasser, contre qch. *Selfishness had steeled his heart,* l'égoïsme lui avait bronzé le cœur.

steelwork ['sti:lwə:rk], *s.* (*a*) Construction **steelwork,** profilés *mpl* pour construction (*b*) *Aut: etc:* Tôleries *fpl.*

steely ['sti:li], *a.* **1.** D'acier ; (fer) aciéreu **2.** *F:* D'acier ; dur, inflexible. *To direct a glance at s.o.,* lancer un regard d'acier à qn.

steelyard ['sti:ljɑ:rd], *s.* (Balance) romaine *f*; peson *m* à contrepoids.

steenbok ['sti:nbɔk], *s.* *Z*: Steinbock *m.*

steep[1] [sti:p]. **I.** *a.* (*a*) Escarpé; à pic; raide. *S. gradient*, forte pente; pente raide, rapide. **The slopes grow steeper**, les pentes s'escarpent. *S. path*, chemin ardu. *S. climb*, rude montée; montée raide. *Nau: S. shore*, côte accore. *Av: Steep start*, départ en chandelle. *Too s. a dive*, descente trop piquée. (*b*) *F*: **That's a bit steep!** c'est un peu fort! c'est un peu raide! **Steep price**, prix exorbitant; prix salé. **Steep story**, histoire incroyable, invraisemblable. **2.** *s.* Pente *f* rapide; escarpement *m*; à-pic *m.* **-ly**, *adv.* En pente rapide; à pic.

steep[2], *s.* *Ind:* **I.** = STEEPING. **To put sth. in steep**, mettre qch. en trempe. **2.** Bain *m* (de macération).

steep[3]. **I.** *v.tr.* (*a*) *Ind: etc:* Baigner, tremper; mettre (qch.) en trempe, à macérer; mouiller (le linge); infuser (des herbes) à froid. *To s. flax*, rouir le lin. (*b*) Saturer, imbiber (*sth. in sth.*, qch. de qch.). *F*: **To steep oneself in drink**, se noyer dans l'alcool. *Scholar steeped in the classics*, érudit nourri des auteurs classiques, saturé des disciplines antiques. **Steeped in ignorance, in prejudice**, croupi dans l'ignorance; imbibé de préjugés. *Steeped in piety*, confit en dévotion. **2.** *v.i.* (*Of soiled linen, etc.*) Tremper; (*of flax*) rouir; (*of herbs*) infuser (à froid). **steeping**, *s.* *Ind: etc:* Trempage *m*, macération *f*, trempe *f*; mouillage *m* (du linge); rouissage *m* (du chanvre); infusion *f* à froid.

steepen [sti:pn]. **I.** *v.i.* (*a*) (*Of road, etc.*) S'escarper; devenir plus raide. (*b*) (*Of prices*) Augmenter. **2.** *v.tr.* *F*: Augmenter, hausser (un prix, un impôt).

steeple [sti:pl], *s.* (*a*) Clocher *m.* (*b*) Flèche *f* (de clocher). **'steeple-jack**, *s.* Réparateur *m* de clochers, de cheminées d'usines.

steeplechase ['sti:pltʃeis], *s.* Steeple-chase *m*, *F*: steeple *m*; course *f* d'obstacles (à cheval).

steepled [sti:pld], *a.* (*Of church*) A clocher; surmonté d'un clocher.

steepness ['sti:pnəs], *s.* **I.** Raideur *f*, rapidité *f*, escarpement *m* (d'une pente). *Mth:* **Steepness of a curve**, degré *m* d'inclinaison d'une courbe.

steer[1] ['sti:ər], *v.tr.* Gouverner (un navire); conduire, diriger, mener (un bateau, une auto); barrer (un yacht). *Abs.* **To steer**, gouverner; tenir la barre, le gouvernail; *Row:* barrer. *To s. by the wind*, gouverner d'après le vent. **To steer the course**, faire route; gouverner en route. **To steer north**, faire route au nord. **To steer (one's course) for . . .**, faire route, mettre le cap, sur. . . . **To steer clear of sth.**, éviter, s'écarter de, qch. (*With passive force*) **Ship that steers well, badly**, navire qui gouverne bien, mal. **The ship refused to steer**, le navire ne gouvernait plus. **steering**, *s.* **I.** (*a*) Direction *f*, conduite *f* (d'un bateau, d'une auto). *Aut:* **Ease of steering**, facilité *f* de braquage. (*b*) = STEERING-GEAR. **2.** *Nau:* Manœuvre *f* de la barre. (*Of ship*) **To have lost steering control**, n'être plus maître de sa manœuvre. **'steering-column**, *s.* *Aut:* Colonne *f*, tube *m*, de direction. **'steering-compass**, *s.* *Nau:* Compas *m* de route. **'steering-engine**, *s.* *Nau:* Servo-moteur *m* de gouvernail. **'steering-gear**, *s.* Appareil *m* à gouverner. *Aut:* (i) Timonerie *f*; (ii) boîte *f* de direction. *Av:* Direction *f.* *Nau:* Servo-moteur *m* de gouvernail. **'steering-knuckle**, *s.* *Aut:* Rotule *f* de direction. **'steering-wheel**, *s.* **I.** (*a*) *Nau:* Roue *f* du gouvernail.

(*b*) *Aut:* Volant *m* (de direction). **2.** *Cy:* Roue directrice.

steer[2], *s.* **I.** Jeune bœuf *m*; bouvillon *m.* **2.** *U.S:* Bœuf; taureau *m.*

steerable ['sti:ərəbl], *a.* Dirigeable.

steerage ['sti:əredʒ], *s.* *Nau:* (*a*) Emménagements *mpl* pour passagers de troisième classe, pour émigrants; entrepont *m.* **To travel steerage**, faire la traversée en troisième classe. (*b*) *Navy:* Avant-carré *m.* **'steerage-way**, *s.* Erre *f* pour gouverner. (*Of ship*) **To have good steerage-way**, sentir la barre.

steersman, *pl.* **-men** ['sti:əzmən, -men], *s.m.* *Nau:* Homme de barre; timonier.

steeve [sti:v]. *Nau:* **I.** *v.tr.* Apiquer (le beaupré). **2.** *v.i.* (*Of bowsprit*) Être apiqué.

stele, *pl.* **-ae** ['sti:li, -i:], *s.* Stèle *f.*

stellar ['stelər], *a.* Stellaire.

stellate ['stelet], **stellated** ['steleitid], *a.* *Nat. Hist:* Étoilé; en étoile; radié.

stellenbosch ['stelənbɔʃ], *v.tr.* *Mil:* *F:* Renvoyer à la base (un général incompétent); *F:* limoger (un général).

stem[1] [stem], *s.* **I.** (*a*) *Bot:* Tige *f* (de plante, de fleur); queue *f* (de fruit, de feuille); pétiole *m*, hampe *f* (de fleur); tronc *m*, souche *f* (d'arbre); stipe *m* (de palmier). **Underground stem**, rhizome *m.* (*b*) Régime *m* (de bananes). (*c*) Dague *f* (de cerf de deux ans). **2.** (*a*) Pied *m*, patte *f* (de verre à boire); tige, queue (de soupape); tige (de vis); broche *f* (de serrure); tuyau *m* (de pipe de fumeur); arbre *m* (de grue). (*b*) *Mus:* Queue (d'une note). **3.** (*a*) Souche (de famille). *Descended from an ancient s.*, rejeton *m* d'une souche ancienne. (*b*) *Ling:* Thème *m*, radical *m* (d'un mot). **4.** *N.Arch:* Étrave *f*, avant *m*; *A. & Lit:* proue *f.* **Cutwater stem**, étrave à guibre. **From stem to stern**, de l'avant à l'arrière. **'stem-winder**, *s.* Montre *f* à remontoir.

stem[2], *v.tr.* (stemmed) Égrapper (des raisins); écôter (des feuilles de tabac).

stem[3], *v.tr.* **I.** Contenir, arrêter, endiguer (un cours d'eau); enrayer (une épidémie). *To s. the course of events*, endiguer la marche des événements. **2.** Aller contre, lutter contre (la marée); refouler, remonter (le courant); (*of ship*) étaler (le courant); refouler, résister à (une attaque). *F*: **To stem the tide of popular indignation**, endiguer le flot de l'indignation publique.

stemmed [stemd], *a.* **I.** (Fleur, etc.) à tige & queue; (verre) à pied, à patte. **2.** *Bot:* **Long-stemmed**, longicaule. **Thick-stemmed**, crassicaule.

stemson ['stemsən], *s.* *N.Arch:* Marsouin *m* (de l')avant (d'un navire en bois).

stench [stenʃ], *s.* Odeur infecte; puanteur *f.* **'stench-pipe**, *s.* Ventilateur *m.* **'stench-trap**, *s.* Siphon *m* (d'évier, etc.).

stencil[1] ['stensil], *s.* **I.** (*a*) Patron (ajouré); poncif *m* ou pochoir *m.* **Stencil-plate**, pochoir. (*b*) **Cipher-stencil**, grille *f.* **2.** Peinture *f*, décoration *f*, au poncif ou au pochoir. **3.** *Typewr: etc:* Cliché *m*; stencil *m.* **stencil-brush**, *s.* Pochon *m.* **'stencil-paper**, *s.* Papier *m* stencil.

stencil[2], *v.tr.* (stencilled) (*a*) Peindre, marquer, imprimer, (qch.) au patron ou au pochoir; passer (un dessin) au pochoir. *Ind:* Marquer (une caisse, un ballot). (*b*) Polycopier (une circulaire); tirer (une circulaire) au stencil.

stenographer [ste'nɔgrəfər], *s.* Sténographe *mf.*

stenography [ste'nɔgrəfi], *s.* Sténographie *f.*

Stentor ['stentɔr]. **I.** *Pr.n.m.* Stentor *m.* **2.** *s.* (*a*) *Prot:* Stentor *m.* (*b*) *Z:* Stentor (monkey), stentor.

49

stentorian [sten'tɔːriən], *a.* (Voix) de Stentor.
step[1] [step], *s.* **I.** Pas *m.* **To take a step,** faire un
pas. *To take a s.·back, forward,* faire un pas en
arrière, en avant. **To turn, bend, one's steps
towards** . . ., se diriger vers . . .; diriger ses
pas vers. . . . **Step by step,** pas à pas ; petit à
petit. *To fall back s. by s.,* reculer pied à pied.
Within a step of the house, à deux pas de la
maison. **It is a good step,** c'est un bon bout de
chemin ; il y a une bonne trotte. **That is a great
step forward,** c'est déjà un grand pas de fait.
F : **To tread in the steps of s.o.,** marcher sur les
traces de qn. **2.** (*a*) Pas, cadence *f. Mil : Mus :*
Quick step, pas redoublé ; pas accéléré. **To keep
step, to be in step,** marcher au pas ; être au pas.
To fall into step, se mettre au pas. **To break
step,** rompre le pas. (*b*) *El.E : Alternators in*
step, alternateurs accrochés, en phase. (*c*) **Waltz
step,** pas de valse. **3.** Démarche *f. Untimely s.,*
démarche inopportune. *To take a rash s.,* commettre une imprudence. *If you take such a s. . . .,*
si vous agissez de la sorte. . . . **To take the
necessary steps, all useful steps,** faire les démarches nécessaires ; prendre toutes les dispositions utiles. **To take steps to do sth.,** aviser, se
préparer, à faire qch. **The first step** *will be to . . .,*
la première chose à faire, ce sera de. . . . *His
first steps in this career,* ses débuts *m* dans cette
carrière. **4.** (*a*) Marche *f,* degré *m,* pas (d'un
escalier) ; échelon *m,* barreau *m* (d'une échelle) ;
marchepied *m* (d'un véhicule). **Cellar steps,**
descente *f.* **Top step** (*of a stair*), palière *f. The
steps of the altar,* le marchepied de l'autel. *The
steps of the throne,* les marches du trône. **Flight
of steps,** (i) escalier ; (ii) perron *m.* (*b*) Gradin *m,*
étage *m* (de cône-poulie). **5.** (Pair, set, of) **steps,**
escabeau *m* ; échelle *f* double. **Folding steps,**
échelle brisée. **6.** (*a*) Cran *m.* **Steps of a key,**
dents *f* d'une clef. (*b*) Redan *m* (d'hydroglisseur).
'step-'bearing, -box, *s. Mec.E :* Palier *m*
de pied (d'un arbre vertical) ; crapaudine *f.*
'step-cone, *s.* Cône-poulie *m* ; poulie *f* à
gradins ; poulie étagée. **'step-dance,** *s.* Danse *f*
de caractère. **'step-gable,** *s.* Pignon *m* à
redans. **'step-ladder,** *s.* Escabeau *m* ; échelle *f*
double.
step[2], *v.* (**stepped** [stept]) I. *v.i.* Faire un pas ou
des pas ; marcher pas à pas ; marcher, aller.
Step this way, venez par ici. II. *v.tr.*
I. (*a*) **To step (off, out)** a distance, mesurer une
distance au pas. (*b*) **To step a minuet,** danser
un menuet. *F :* **To step it with s.o.,** danser
avec qn. **2.** Disposer en échelons ; échelonner.
3. *Nau :* Mettre (un mât) dans son emplanture.
step across, *v.i.* Traverser (la rue, etc.). **step
aside,** *v.i.* **I.** S'écarter, se ranger. **2.** Se
détourner de son chemin. **step back,** *v.i.* Faire
un pas en arrière ; reculer. **step down.**
I. *v.i.* Descendre. **2.** *v.tr.* (*a*) *El.E :* **To step
down the current, the voltage,** réduire la tension ;
dévolter le courant. (*b*) *Mec.E :* **To step down
the gear,** démultiplier la transmission. **step
forward,** *v.i.* S'avancer ; faire un pas en avant.
step in, *v.i.* **I.** Entrer ; (*into carriage*) monter.
2. *F :* Intervenir ; s'interposer. **step-'in,** *s.*
Combinaison-pantalon *f,* combinaison-culotte *f.*
step off, *v.i.* (*a*) **To step off with the left foot,**
partir du pied gauche. (*b*) Descendre (de voiture,
d'autobus, etc.). **step on,** *v.i.* **I.** Mettre le
pied sur, marcher sur (qch.). *Someone stepped
on my foot,* on m'a marché sur le pied. *U.S : P :* **To
step on the gas,** to step on it, *Aut :* écraser l'accélérateur ; mettre tous les gaz ; *Av :* mettre toute
la sauce. *To step on the brakes,* donner un coup

de frein (au pied). **2.** *Nau :* **To step on board,**
monter à bord. **step out,** *v.i.* **I.** Sortir ;
descendre (de voiture). *As we stepped out into
the sunshine* . . ., tandis que nous débouchions
au soleil. . . . **2.** (*a*) Allonger le pas. (*b*) Marcher
avec entrain. **step over,** *v.i.* **I.** Franchir ;
enjamber (un obstacle). **2. To step over to s.o.'s
house,** faire un saut jusque chez qn (qui habite
en face). **step up. I.** *v.i.* (*a*) Monter. (*b*) S'approcher (*to, de*). **2.** *v.tr. El.E :* **To step up the
current,** survolter le courant ; augmenter la
tension. **Step-up transformer,** survolteur *m.*
stepped, *a.* A gradins, en gradins, à étages ;
échelonné, en échelons. **Stepped gear(ing),**
engrenage en échelon. **'stepping-stone,**
I. Marchepied *m.* **To take a post as a stepping-
stone** (*to a better position*), prendre un poste
comme tremplin. **2.** *pl.* **Stepping-stones,** pierres
de gué.
stepbrother ['stepbrʌðər], *s.m.* Frère consanguin ou utérin ; demi-frère.
stepchild, *pl.* **-children** ['steptʃaild, -tʃildrən],
s. Enfant *mf* d'un autre lit.
stepdaughter ['stepdɔːtər], *s.f.* Belle-fille (née
d'un lit antérieur), *pl.* belles-filles.
stepfather ['stepfɑːðər], *s.m.* Beau-père, *pl.*
beaux-pères.
Stephen ['stiːv(ə)n]. *Pr.n.m.* Étienne.
stepmother ['stepmʌðər], *s.f.* Belle-mère, *pl.*
belles-mères.
steppe [step], *s. Ph.Geog :* Steppe *m or f.*
stepper ['stepər], *s.* (*Of horse*) Stepper *m,* steppeur *m.* **To be a good stepper,** avoir de l'action,
de l'allure.
stepsister ['stepsistər], *s.f.* Sœur consanguine
ou utérine ; demi-sœur.
stepson ['stepsʌn], *s.m.* Beau-fils (né d'un lit
antérieur), *pl.* beaux-fils.
stereo, *pl.* **-os** ['sterio, -ouz], *s. F : =* STEREO-
TYPE[1] I.
stereograph ['steriogrɑːf, -graf], *s.* **I.** Stéréographe *m.* **2.** Vue *f* stéréoscopique.
stereographic [sterio'grafik], *a.* Stéréographique.
stereography [steri'ɔgrəfi], *s. Geom :* Stéréographie *f.*
stereophotography [steriofo'tɔgrəfi], *s.* Stéréo-
photographie *f.*
stereophotography [steriofo'tɔgrəfi], *s.* Stéréo-
photographie *f.*
stereoscope ['sterioskoup], *s. Opt :* Stéréoscope *m.*
stereoscopic [sterio'skɔpik], *a.* Stéréoscopique.
Stereoscopic camera, photo-jumelle *f, pl.* photos-
jumelles. **-ally,** *adv.* Stéréoscopiquement.
stereotype[1] ['steriotaip]. *Typ :* **I.** *s.* Cliché *m.*
2. *a.* Stéréotypé, cliché. *S. printing,* stéréotypie *f.*
stereotype[2], *v.tr. Typ :* Stéréotyper, clicher.
stereotyped, *a. Typ :* Stéréotypé. *F :* **Stereotyped phrase,** cliché *m.*
sterile ['sterail], *a.* **I.** Stérile. **2.** *Bac :* Stérile,
aseptique.
sterility [ste'riliti], *s.* Stérilité *f.*
sterilization [sterilai'zeiʃ(ə)n], *s.* Stérilisation *f.*
Sterilization of milk, pasteurisation *f* du lait.
sterilize ['sterilaiz], *v.tr.* Stériliser. **Sterilized
milk,** lait pasteurisé. **Sterilized gauze,** gaze
oxygénée.
sterling ['stəːliŋ], *a.* **I.** (Monnaie, or) de bon
aloi, d'aloi. **2.** Pound sterling, pound stg, livre *f*
sterling. **3.** *F :* De bon aloi, vrai, véritable, solide.
He's a sterling fellow, c'est une excellente nature.
Sterling qualities, qualités solides.
stern[1] [stəːrn], *a.* Sévère, rigide, dur. **Stern
countenance,** visage austère. **The sterner sex,** le
sexe fort. **-ly,** *adv.* Sévèrement, durement.

stern², *s.* **I.** *Nau :* (*a*) Arrière *m* ; *A :* poupe *f*. (*Of ship*) To sink stern foremost, couler par l'arrière. To go out stern first, appareiller en culant. To anchor by the stern, mouiller en croupière. To be (down) by the stern, être enfoncé par l'arrière. Stern ladder, échelle de poupe. (*b*) Arrière-bec *m* (d'un ponton). **2.** (*a*) *F. & Hum :* Postérieur *m*, derrière *m*. (*b*) *Ven :* Queue *f* (d'un chien courant, d'un loup). **'stern-chase,** *s. Navy :* Chasse *f* dans les eaux du navire chassé. **'stern-chaser,** *s. Navy :* Canon *m*, pièce *f*, de retraite. **'stern-fast,** *s. Nau :* Amarre *f* (de l')arrière ; croupière *f*. **'stern-light,** *s. Nau :* Feu *m* d'arrière ; feu de poupe. **'stern-oar,** *s.* Aviron *m* de queue ; godille *f*. **'stern-post,** *s. Nau :* Étambot *m*. **'stern-sheet(s),** *s. Nau :* Arrière *m*, chambre *f* (d'une embarcation). **'stern-way,** *s. Nau :* Marche *f* arrière ; culée *f*. To gather s.-*w.*, culer ; aller de l'arrière.

sternmost ['stə:rnmoust], *a.* Le plus à l'arrière ((i) à bord, (ii) de l'escadre).

sternness ['stə:rnnəs], *s.* Sévérité *f* ; austérité *f* ; dureté *f*.

sternum ['stə:rnəm], *s. Anat :* Sternum *m*.

sternutation [stə:rnju'teiʃ(ə)n], *s.* Sternutation *f*, éternûment *m*.

stertorous ['stə:rtərəs], *a. Med :* Stertoreux, ronflant.

stet¹ [stet], *Lt.imp. Typ :* Bon ; à maintenir.

stet², *v.tr.* (stetted) Maintenir (un mot sur l'épreuve, sur le MS.).

stethoscope ['steθoskoup], *s. Med :* Stéthoscope *m*. *Binaural s.*, stéthoscope binauriculaire.

stetson ['stets(ə)n], *s. F :* Chapeau mou (porté par les soldats australiens). (Du nom du fabricant.)

stevedore ['sti:vidɔ:ər], *s. Nau :* **I.** (*Labourer*) Arrimeur *m* ou déchargeur *m*. **2.** Entrepreneur *m* d'arrimage ; entrepreneur de chargement et de déchargement.

stew¹ [stju:], *s.* **I.** *A :* (*a*) Maison *f* de bains. (*b*) *pl.* Lieu *m* de débauche. **2.** (*a*) *Cu :* Ragoût *m* ; civet *m* (de chevreuil, etc.) ; *F :* miroton *m* ; *Mil : P :* ratatouille *f*, rata *m*. Mutton stew, ragoût de mouton ; navarin *m*. Irish stew, ragoût de mouton, de pommes de terre, et d'oignons. (*b*) *F :* To be in a stew, être sur des charbons ardents ; être dans tous ses états. (*c*) *F :* What a stew! quelle chaleur ici ! quelle étuve ! (*d*) *W.Tel :* Friture *f*, crachements *mpl*. **3.** *F :* (*Of pers.*) Piocheur *m*, bûcheur *m*.

stew². **I.** *v.tr. Cu :* Faire cuire (la viande) en ragoût, à la casserole. To stew some mutton, faire un ragoût de mouton. To s. a rabbit, fricasser un lapin. To stew fruit, faire cuire des fruits en compote. **2.** *v.i.* (*a*) *Cu :* Cuire à la casserole ; mijoter. *F :* To let s.o. stew in his own juice, laisser qn mijoter dans son jus. (*b*) *F :* Étouffer ; manquer d'air. (*c*) *F :* Piocher, bûcher. **stewed,** *a.* (*a*) Stewed mutton, ragoût *m* de mouton. *S. beef*, bœuf (à la) mode ; bœuf en daube. Stewed fruit, compote *f* de fruits ; fruits en compote. *S. prunes*, pruneaux au jus. *S. apples*, marmelade *f* de pommes. (*b*) Stewed tea, thé trop infusé.

stew³, *s.* **I.** Vivier *m*. **2.** Huîtrière *f* ; parc *m* à huîtres.

steward ['stjuərd], *s.* **I.** Économe *m*, régisseur *m*, intendant *m* (d'une propriété). *B :* The unjust steward, l'économe infidèle. **2.** (*a*) Maître *m* d'hôtel (d'une maison, d'un cercle). (*b*) *Nau :* Commis *m* aux vivres. Steward's room, cambuse *f*. (*c*) *Nau :* Garçon *m* (de cabine) ; steward *m*. Chief steward, maître d'hôtel. **3.** Commissaire *m*

(d'une réunion sportive, d'un bal). **4.** *Ind :* Shop steward, délégué *m* d'atelier ; délégué syndical.

stewardess ['stjuərdes], *s.f. Nau :* Femme de chambre (de bord) ; la stewardess.

stewardship ['stjuərdʃip], *s.* Économat *m*, intendance *f* ; charge *f* de régisseur. *F :* To give an account of one's stewardship, rendre compte de sa gestion.

stewpan ['stju:pan], *s.* Casserole *f* (à couvercle).

stewpot ['stju:pɔt], *s.* Braisière *f*, daubière *f*, cocotte *f*.

stick¹ [stik], *s.* **I.** (*a*) Bâton *m*. *F :* To cut one's stick, décamper, filer. To get the stick, recevoir des coups de bâton. The big stick, le recours à la force ; la politique de la force. *S.a.* CLEAVE¹ 1. *Hort :* Pea sticks, rames *f*. Hop sticks, vine sticks, échalas *m*. (*b*) Walking stick, canne *f*. Loaded stick, canne plombée. (*c*) Manche *m* (à balai) ; canne, manche (de parapluie) ; baguette *f* (de fusée volante). Stick of a violin bow, fût *m*, baguette, tige *f*, d'archet. *Av :* Direction stick, manche à balai. (*d*) *Sp :* Crosse *f* (de hockey). (*At hockey*) To give sticks, couper ; donner des crosses. (*e*) Morceau *m* de bois. To gather sticks, ramasser du bois sec, du petit bois. Cherry stick, bâtonnet *m* (pour cerise de cocktail). *S.a.* ORANGE-STICK. *F :* Not a stick was saved, on n'a pas sauvé une allumette. Without a stick of furniture, sans un meuble. (*f*) *Typ :* (Setting-)stick, composteur *m*. **2.** *F :* (*Of pers.*) (*a*) Queer stick, drôle de type, drôle d'oiseau. Old stick, vieille perruque. (*b*) Personne *f* sans entrain, sans talent ; acteur *m* au jeu raide ; *P :* godiche *mf*. **3.** Bâton (de sucre d'orge, de cire à cacheter, etc.) ; barre *f* (de chocolat) ; canon *m* (de soufre) ; *El :* baguette *f* (de charbon). Stick sulphur, soufre en canons. *S.a.* LIPSTICK, SHAVING-STICK. **4.** Stick of celery, branche *f* de céleri. Stick of rhubarb, tige *f* de rhubarbe. **'stick-insect,** *s. Ent :* Phasme *m*.

stick², *v.* (stuck [stʌk] ; stuck) I. *v.tr.* (*a*) Piquer, enfoncer (*into*, dans). To stick a dagger into s.o., percer qn d'un poignard. To stick a stake in the ground, ficher un pieu en terre. To stick a pin through sth., passer une épingle à travers qch. Cushion stuck full of pins, pelote pleine d'épingles. Cake stuck (over) with almonds, gâteau garni d'amandes. (*b*) *P :* To stick s.o., poignarder qn ; *P :* suriner qn. To stick s.o. with a bayonet, enfoncer une baïonnette dans le corps de qn. To stick a pig, égorger, saigner, un porc. (*c*) Planter, fixer (*sth. on a spike*, qch. sur une pointe). **2.** *F :* (= 'put,' 'place') To stick a rose in one's button-hole, mettre une rose à sa boutonnière. To stick one's hat on one's head, planter son chapeau sur sa tête. To stick a candle in a bottle, ficher une bougie dans une bouteille. Stick it in your pocket, fourrez-le dans votre poche. Stick in a few commas, mettez quelques virgules. **3.** Coller. To stick photographs in an album, fixer, coller, des photographies dans un album. Trunk stuck all over with labels, malle bardée d'étiquettes. *S.a.* BILL⁴ 3. **4.** *F :* Supporter, endurer, souffrir (qn, qch.). To stick it, tenir le coup ; tenir. I can't stick him, je ne peux pas le sentir. **5.** *Hort :* Ramer (des pois, etc.). II. **stick,** *v.i.* **I.** Se piquer, s'enfoncer, se ficher, se planter. *The arrows s. in the target*, les flèches se piquent dans la cible. **2.** (*a*) (Se) coller, s'attacher, tenir, adhérer (*to*, à) ; happer (aux lèvres, à la langue). The envelope will not stick, l'enveloppe ne veut pas (se) coller. *Dry clay sticks to the tongue*, l'argile sèche happe à la langue. *The vegetables have stuck to the pan*, les légumes ont attaché. *The name stuck to him*, ce nom lui (en) est resté. *It sticks like pitch*, cela colle comme poix. *To stick by, to, a friend*, s'attacher à un ami; ne pas abandonner un ami. *He has stuck to me*, il m'est resté fidèle. *To s. together*, faire preuve de solidarité. *To stick like a limpet, like a leech, like glue, like a burr* (*to s.o.*), se cramponner (à qn); cramponner (qn). *To stick to one's post*, rester à son poste. *To s. to one's duty*, s'attacher à remplir son devoir. *Stick to it!* persévérez! ne lâchez pas! *F: To stick to one's guns, to one's opinions*, ne pas en démordre. *To stick to* (the) *facts*, s'en tenir aux faits. *He sticks to it*, il ne veut pas en démordre. *S.a.* LAST[1]. (*b*) *To stick to sth.*, garder qch. pour soi. *S. to what you've got!* ne lâchez pas ce que vous avez! (*c*) *F:* Rester. *Here I am and here I stick*, j'y suis, j'y reste. *He sticks to his room*, il ne sort pas de sa chambre. **3.** (*a*) *To stick, to be stuck, to become stuck*, être pris, engagé; (*in mud, etc.*) s'embourber, être embourbé, s'enliser. *To get stuck in a bog*, s'embourber dans un marécage. *F: He's an old stick-in-the-mud*, c'est un vieux routinier. (*Of boat*) *To stick fast*, s'enliser. *To stick, to be stuck* (*in a speech*), *F:* rester en carafe, en panne. *v.tr. P:* **The problem sticks me**, ce problème-là me déroute. *Sch:* I got stuck in history, j'ai été collé en histoire. (*b*) (*To be caught, jammed*) Être pris, être engagé, rester pris, s'empêtrer; (*of machine parts*) (se) coincer, gommer; *Aut:* (*of valve, etc.*) rester collé. *It sticks in my throat*, je ne peux pas avaler ça. *The lift has stuck*, l'ascenseur est en détresse, en panne. *Aut:* **The switch was stuck**, le conjoncteur était collé. **stick at,** *v.i.* **I.** *To stick at a difficulty*, s'arrêter devant, achopper contre, une difficulté. *To stick at doing sth.*, se faire scrupule de faire qch. *To stick at nothing*, ne reculer devant rien. **2.** *To stick at a task for six hours*, travailler à qch. pendant six heures d'arrache-pied. **stick down,** *v.tr.* **I.** *F:* (*a*) *Stick it down anywhere*, mettez-le, collez-le, n'importe où. (*b*) *To stick sth. down in a note-book*, inscrire qch. sur un carnet. **2.** *To stick down an envelope*, fermer, coller, une enveloppe. **stick on. I.** *v.tr.* (*a*) Coller, fixer (un timbre, etc.). (*b*) *F: To stick it on*, (i) surfaire, saler, l'addition, la note; (ii) se donner de grands airs; faire l'important. **2.** *v.i.* Rester collé; adhérer; s'agripper. *Stick-on label*, étiquette adhésive. **stick out. I.** *v.tr.* (*a*) Faire dépasser (qch.); sortir (qch.). *To stick out one's tongue*, tirer la langue. *To stick out one's chest, one's figure*, bomber la poitrine; cambrer la taille. *Aut: To stick out one's arm before stopping*, mettre le bras avant de stopper. (*b*) *F: To stick it out*, tenir jusqu'au bout. **2.** *v.i.* (*a*) Faire saillie; ressortir. *To stick out beyond sth.*, dépasser qch. (*b*) *F: To stick out for sth.*, s'obstiner à demander qch. **stick up. I.** *v.tr.* (*a*) *F:* Dresser (une cible, etc.). *U.S: P:* Stick 'em up! haut les mains! (*b*) *To stick up a bill, a notice*, afficher un avis. **2.** *v.i.* (*a*) Se dresser; se tenir debout. *His hair sticks straight up*, il a les cheveux en brosse. *The end keeps sticking up*, le bout persiste à se relever. (*b*) *F: To stick up for s.o.*, prendre la défense de qn. (*c*) *To stick up to s.o.*, tenir tête à qn. **stuck-'up,** *a. F:* Prétentieux, guindé, poseur. **'sticking-plaster,** *s. Pharm:* Taffetas gommé; taffetas d'Angleterre. **'stick-jaw,** *s. P:* Bonbons collants; caramels *mpl.*

sticker ['stikər], *s.* **I.** Tueur *m* (de porcs).

2. (*a*) Couteau *m* de boucher. (*b*) Couteau de chasse. **3.** Colleur, -euse (d'affiches). *S.a.* BILL-STICKER. **4.** *F:* (*a*) Rude travailleur. (*b*) *Cr:* Batteur prudent, qui ne risque rien. **5.** *P:* (*Of pers.*) Crampon *m*. **6.** *Sch: F:* Colle *f*.

stickiness ['stikinəs], *s.* Viscosité *f*; nature gluante (d'un produit); adhésivité *f*.

stickleback ['stiklbak], *s. Ich:* Épinoche *f*.

stickler ['stiklər], *s.* Rigoriste *mf* (*for sth.*, à l'égard de qch.). *To be a stickler for etiquette*, être à cheval sur l'étiquette. *S. over trifles*, tatillon.

sticky ['stiki], *a.* **I.** Collant, gluant, visqueux, adhésif. *To make one's hand's s.*, s'engluer les mains. *F: To have sticky fingers* (*in money matters*), avoir de la poix aux mains. **2.** *P:* (*a*) Peu accommodant; difficile, désagréable. (*b*) *I had a s. ten minutes*, j'ai passé un mauvais quart d'heure. *He will come to a sticky end*, il finira mal.

stiff [stif]. **I.** *a.* **I.** (*a*) Raide, rigide, dur, inflexible. *Stiff shirt-front*, plastron empesé. *Phot:* Stiff film, film rigide. Stiff brush, brosse dure, rude. (*b*) *Stiff joint*, articulation ankylosée. (*Of joint*) *To grow stiff*, s'ankyloser. *To be quite stiff*, (i) (*with sitting still*) être engourdi; (ii) (*after exercise*) être tout courbaturé. *F:* (*Of pers.*) *Stiff as a poker*, raide, droit, comme un piquet. *The body was already s.*, le cadavre était déjà raide. (*c*) (*Of pers.*) Raide, contraint, guindé, compassé. *Stiff bow*, salut contraint, froid. *Stiff style*, style guindé, empesé. (*d*) (*Of pers.*) Inflexible, obstiné. *To offer a stiff resistance*, résister opiniâtrement. *Nau:* Stiff ship, navire très stable. **2.** (*a*) (*Of door-handle, etc.*) Qui fonctionne mal. *The handle is stiff*, le bouton est dur. (*b*) (*Of paste batter*) Ferme; (*of lubricant*) consistant; (*of soil*) tenace. (*c*) *Nau:* Stiff wind, forte brise. **3.** (*a*) Stiff climb, montée rude, pénible, raide. Stiff examination, examen difficile. Stiff piece of work, besogne ardue. *The book is very s. reading*, ce livre est dur à lire. (*b*) *F:* Stiff price, prix salé. *He tells some stiff yarns*, il en raconte de raides. **-ly,** *adv.* **I.** Raidement; avec raideur. **2.** D'un air guindé. **3.** (Résister) obstinément. **II. stiff,** *s.* **I.** *P:* Lettre *f* de change, billet *m* à ordre. **2.** *Med: P:* Cadavre *m* (pour dissection); machabée *m*. **stiff-'necked,** *a.* Obstiné, entêté, intraitable.

stiffen ['stif(ə)n]. **I.** *v.tr.* **I.** (*a*) Raidir, renforcer (une poutre, etc.); donner plus de rigidité à (qch.). *Aut: To s. the springs*, donner plus de raideur à la suspension. (*b*) Age has stiffened his joints, l'âge lui a noué les membres. (*c*) Raidir, rendre obstiné (qn). (*d*) *Nau: To stiffen a ship*, lester un navire. (*e*) *Mil: To stiffen a battalion*, renforcer un bataillon avec des éléments aguerris. **2.** (*a*) Donner de la consistance à (une pâte). (*b*) *To s. a drink*, corser une boisson. **3.** (*a*) Rendre (un examen) plus difficile, plus dur. **II. stiffen,** *v.i.* **I.** (*a*) (Se) raidir; devenir raide. *The body had stiffened*, le cadavre était déjà raide. (*b*) (*Of pers.*) Se raidir; se guinder. **2.** (*a*) (*Of paste etc.*) Prendre de la consistance. (*b*) *Nau:* (*Of wind*) Se carabiner. **3.** (*Of examination*) Devenir plus difficile.

stiffness ['stifnəs], *s.* **I.** (*a*) Raideur *f*, rigidité *f*. (*b*) Stiffness of manner, raideur, contrainte *f*, air guindé. (*c*) Obstination *f*, opiniâtreté *f*. **2.** Fermeté *f*, consistance *f* (d'une pâte); ténacité *f* (du sol). **3.** (*a*) Raideur (d'une pente). (*b*) Difficulté *f* (d'un examen).

stifle ['staifl]. **I.** *v.tr.* (*a*) Étouffer, suffoquer. *To be stifled by the smoke*, être asphyxié par la fumée. *To s. a revolt at birth*, étouffer une révolte dans son germe. (*b*) Étouffer (un son, les cris de qn)

To stifle a scandal, étouffer un scandale. (c) Réprimer (une émotion, un éternûment). *To s. one's laughter,* pouffer dans son mouchoir. **2.** *v.i.* Suffoquer, étouffer. **stifling,** *a.* Étouffant, suffocant. *It is stifling here!* on étouffe ici !
stifle², *s.* **1.** Stifle(-joint), grasset *m.* **2.** *Vet:* Affection *f* du grasset. **'stifle-bone,** *s.* Os *m* du grasset.

stigma, *pl.* **-as, -ata** ['stigma, -az, -ata], *s.* **1.** (*pl.* **stigmas**) (a) *A:* Flétrissure *f* (au fer rouge). (b) Stigmate *m,* tache *f;* flétrissure (morale). **2.** (*pl.* **stigmata**) (a) *Nat.Hist:* Stigmate (d'un insecte, etc.). (b) *Med:* Stigmate (de l'hystérie). (c) *pl.* Stigmates (d'un saint). **3.** *Bot:* (*pl.* **stigmas**) Stigmate (du pistil).
stigmatic [stig'matik]. **1.** *a.* *Opt:* (Objectif) stigmatique. **2.** *s.* *Rel.H:* Stigmatisé, -ée.
stigmatize ['stigmətaːiz], *v.tr.* **1.** Marquer de stigmates. **2.** Stigmatiser, flétrir (qn).
stile¹ [stail], *s.* Échalier *m.* *S.a.* DOG¹ **1.**
stile², *s.* Montant *m* (de porte, etc.).
stiletto, *pl.* **-os, -oes** [sti'leto, -ouz], *s.* **1.** (*Dagger*) Stylet *m.* **2.** *Needlew:* Poinçon *m.*
still¹ [stil]. **1.** *a.* Tranquille. (a) Immobile. **To keep still,** ne pas bouger ; se tenir tranquille. **To stand still,** (i) ne pas bouger ; (ii) s'arrêter. *Prov:* **There is no standing still,** qui n'avance pas recule. *His heart stood s.,* son cœur cessa de battre. (b) Silencieux. *In the still watches of the night,* pendant les veilles silencieuses de la nuit. *Still water,* eau tranquille. *S.a.* DEEP II. **1.** *F:* **The still small voice,** la voix de la conscience. (c) *Still wines,* vins non mousseux. (d) *Art:* *Still life,* nature morte. **2.** *s.* *In the still of the night,* dans le calme de la nuit. **'still-'born,** *a.* Mort-né, -ée, *pl.* mort-nés, -ées.
still². **1.** *v.tr.* (a) Tranquilliser, calmer, apaiser. *To s. s.o.'s fears,* calmer les craintes de qn. (b) *To s. one's songs,* taire, cesser, ses chants. **2.** *v.i.* Se calmer.
still³. **1.** *adv.* (a) Encore. *He is s. here,* il est encore ici. *I have s. five francs,* il me reste cinq francs. *In spite of his faults, I love him s.,* malgré ses fautes je l'aime toujours. (b) *Still more,* still less, encore plus, encore moins. **2.** *conj.* Cependant, pourtant, encore, toutefois, malgré cela. *S. the fact remains that . . .,* toujours est-il que. . . .
still⁴, *s.* Alambic *m,* cornue *f.* *Tar still,* cornue à goudron. **'still-room,** *s.* **1.** *A:* Laboratoire *m* de distillerie. **2.** Office *f.*
stilling ['stiliŋ], **stillion** ['stiljən], *s.* Chantier *m* (pour fûts).
stillness ['stilnəs], *s.* Tranquillité *f,* calme *m,* repos *m,* silence *m.*
stilt [stilt], *s.* **1.** Échasse *f.* **To be on stilts,** (i) être monté sur des échasses ; (ii) *F:* être guindé, ampoulé. **2.** *Civ.E:* Pilotis *m,* pieu *m.* **3.** Manche *m,* mancheron *m* (de charrue). **4.** The stilt birds, les échassiers *m.*
stilted [stiltid], *a.* **1.** (Arc) surhaussé, surélevé. **2.** (*Of style, etc.*) Guindé, tendu.
stiltedness ['stiltidnəs], *s.* Manière guindée ; air, ton, style, guindé ; emphase *f.*
Stilton ['stilt(ə)n], *s.* Fromage *m* de Stilton ; stilton *m.*
stimulant ['stimjulənt]. **1.** *a. & s.* *Med:* Stimulant (*m*) ; remontant (*m*). **2.** *s.* Surexcitant *m.*
stimulate ['stimjuleit], *v.tr.* (a). Stimuler ; aiguillonner, activer, exciter (*to,* à) ; aiguiser (l'esprit, l'appétit). **To stimulate s.o. to do sth.,** encourager qn à faire qch. *To s. production,* encourager, activer, la production. (b) *Med:* Stimuler (le foie, etc.).

stimulation [stimju'leiʃ(ə)n], *s.* Stimulation *f.*
stimulus, *pl.* **-i** ['stimjuləs, -ai], *s.* **1.** (a) Stimulant *m;* *F:* aiguillon *m.* **To give a stimulus to trade,** donner de l'impulsion *f* au commerce. *F:* **To give a stimulus to the circulation,** donner un coup de fouet à la circulation. (b) *Physiol:* Stimulus *m;* incitation motrice. **2.** *Bot:* Stimule *m.*
stimy ['staimi], *s.* *Golf:* Trou barré.
sting¹ [stiŋ], *s.* **1.** (a) Dard *m,* aiguillon *m* (d'abeille). (b) Dard ; poil piquant (d'ortie) ; poil urticant. (c) Crochet venimeux (d'un serpent). **2.** (a) Piqûre *f* (de guêpe, etc.). (b) *F:* Pointe *f* (d'une épigramme). **The sting of remorse,** l'aiguillon du remords. (c) Douleur cuisante (d'une blessure) ; cinglure *f* (d'une lanière). (d) Vigueur *f,* mordant *m* (d'une attaque). **'sting-bull,** *s.* *Ich:* Vive commune. **'sting-nettle,** *s.* Ortie brûlante.
sting², *v.* (stung [stʌŋ] ; stung) **1.** *v.tr.* (a) (*Of bees, nettles*) Piquer. *His conscience stings him,* sa conscience le tourmente. *That reply stung him (to the quick),* cette réponse l'a piqué (au vif). *Prov:* *Nothing stings like the truth,* il n'y a que la vérité qui offense. *Smoke that stings the eyes,* fumée qui picote les yeux. (b) *P:* **To sting s.o. for sth.,** faire payer qch. à qn un prix exorbitant. **2.** *v.i.* (*Of parts of the body*) Cuire ; sentir des élancements. *My eyes were stinging,* les yeux me cuisaient. **stinging,** *a.* Piquant, cuisant, mordant. **Stinging plant,** plante piquante, urticante. **Stinging blow,** coup cinglant, coup raide.
stinger ['stiŋər], *s.* *F:* Coup *m* raide, qui cingle.
stinginess ['stindʒinəs], *s.* Mesquinerie *f,* ladrerie *f.*
stingo ['stingo], *s.* *P:* **1.** Bière forte. **2.** Verve *f,* entrain *m,* brio *m.*
stingy ['stindʒi], *a.* Mesquin, chiche, ladre, regardant. *S. fellow,* pingre *m.* **-ily,** *adv.* Chichement, mesquinement.
stink¹ [stiŋk], *s.* **1.** (a) Puanteur *f;* odeur *f* fétide ; mauvaise odeur. (b) *P:* **To raise a stink,** faire de l'esclandre. **2.** *pl.* *Sch:* *F:* Stinks, la chimie. **'stink-alive,** *s.* *Ich:* Tacaud *m.* **'stink-bomb,** *s.* *P:* Obus *m* à gaz. **'stink-trap,** *s.* Siphon *m* (d'évier, etc.).
stink², *v.* (*p.t.* stank [staŋk], stunk [stʌŋk] ; *p.p.* stunk) **1.** *v.i.* Puer ; sentir mauvais ; *F:* empester. **To stink of garlic,** puer l'ail. **2.** *v.tr.* **To stink s.o. out,** chasser qn par la mauvaise odeur. *To s. out a fox,* enfumer un renard. **stinking,** *a.* Puant, nauséabond, empesté, infect. **Stinking nettle,** galéopsis *m.*
stinker ['stiŋkər], *s.* *P:* **1.** (a) Individu *m* méprisable. (b) Individu qui pue. **2.** (a) **To write s.o. a stinker,** écrire une lettre de sottises à qn. (b) *The algebra paper was a s.,* on a eu une sale composition d'algèbre.
stinkstone ['stiŋkstoun], *s.* *Geol:* Stinkal *m.*
stinkweed ['stiŋkwi:d], *s.* *Bot:* **1.** Diplotaxis *m.* **2.** *U.S.:* Datura *m* stramonium.
stint¹ [stint], *s.* **1.** Restriction *f.* **Without stint,** sans restriction ; sans limite ; à discrétion. *To spend money without s.,* dépenser sans compter. **2.** Besogne assignée. **To do one's daily stint,** accomplir sa tâche quotidienne.
stint², *v.tr.* **1.** Réduire (qn) à la portion congrue. **To stint oneself,** se refuser le nécessaire. *To s. oneself for one's children,* se priver pour ses enfants. **To stint s.o. of sth.,** priver qn de qch. ; refuser qch. à qn. *They s. me of fire and light,* on me mesure le feu et la lumière. *To s. one's horses of oats,* rationner l'avoine à ses chevaux.

2. Réduire (la nourriture) ; être chiche de (qch.) ; lésiner sur (qch.). **To give without stinting,** donner sans compter.
stintless ['stintləs], *a.* Prodigué ; donné sans compter. *S. charity,* aumônes larges.
stipend ['staipend], *s.* Traitement *m,* appointements *mpl* (d'un ecclésiastique, d'un magistrat).
stipendiary [stai'pendiəri], *a.* Qui reçoit des appointements fixes. *Esp. S. magistrate, s.* **stipendiary,** juge *m* d'un tribunal de simple police (à Londres et dans les grandes villes).
stipple[1] [stipl], *s. Art:* Pointillé *m* ; *Engr:* grenure *f.*
stipple[2], *v.tr.* (a) Figurer (un dessin) en pointillé. (b) *Engr:* Graver au pointillé ; grener (une planche).
stipulate ['stipjuleit]. I. *v.i.* To stipulate for sth., stipuler, énoncer expressément (une condition obligatoire). *To s. for a reward of a hundred pounds,* stipuler une récompense de cent livres. **2.** *v.tr.* **To stipulate (in writing) that . . .,** stipuler (par écrit) que. . . .
stipulation [stipju'leiʃ(ə)n], *s. Jur:* Stipulation *f* (d'une condition). **On the stipulation that . . .,** à condition que. . . .
stipule ['stipjul], *s. Bot:* Stipule *f.*
stir[1] [stə:r], *s.* I. Remuement *m.* **To give one's coffee, the fire, a stir,** remuer son café ; tisonner le feu. **2.** Mouvement *m.* **Stir of warm wind,** souffle *m* d'air chaud. **3.** (a) Remue-ménage *m inv. Place full of s. and movement,* endroit plein de vie et de mouvement. (b) Agitation *f,* émoi *m.* **To make a stir,** faire du bruit, de l'éclat ; faire événement ; faire sensation. *To create little s.,* avoir peu de retentissement.
stir[2], *v.* (stirred) I. *v.tr.* (a) Remuer, mouvoir. (*Usu. neg.*) *Not a breath stirs the leaves,* pas un souffle ne remue, ne fait trembler, les feuilles. *He could not stir a foot,* (i) il était incapable de faire un pas ; (ii) on ne lui laissait aucune liberté. **I will not stir a foot,** je ne bougerai pas d'ici. (b) Activer, tisonner, fourgonner (le feu) ; agiter (un mélange) ; *Cu:* tourner (une crème). **To stir one's tea,** remuer son thé. *F:* **To stir heaven and earth,** remuer ciel et terre. (c) Émouvoir, troubler (qn). **To stir s.o.'s wrath,** exciter, animer, la colère de qn. **To stir s.o. to pity,** émouvoir la compassion de qn. *Scents that stir the senses,* parfums qui troublent les sens. **2.** *v.i.* Bouger, remuer ; se mettre en mouvement. (*Usu. neg.*) *To sit without stirring,* rester assis sans bouger. *Don't stir from here,* ne bougez pas d'ici. *He did not stir out of the house,* il n'est pas sorti de la maison. **He is not stirring yet,** il n'est pas encore levé. **There is not a breath of air** stirring, on ne sent pas un souffle d'air. **stir about,** *v.i.* Se remuer. **stir up,** *v.tr.* I. Remuer, agiter (un liquide) ; ranimer, activer (le feu). **2.** Fomenter (les dissensions) ; ameuter (le peuple) ; exciter, animer (la curiosité, l'émotion) ; susciter (l'admiration). *To stir up hatred,* attiser les haines. *To stir up s.o.'s zeal,* réchauffer, exciter, le zèle de qn. *He wants stirring up,* il a besoin qu'on l'aiguillonne. **stir-'up,** *s. F:* Agitation *f,* commotion *f.*
stirring, *a.* I. Actif, remuant ; (enfant) turbulent. *To lead a s. life,* mener une vie très active. **Stirring times,** époque mouvementée. **2.** Émouvant, empoignant. *S. speech,* discours vibrant, entraînant.
stirk [stə:rk], *s. Dial:* Bouvillon *m.*
stirrer ['stə:rər], *s.* I. (*Pers.*) Stirrer(-up), incitateur, -trice ; instigateur, -trice (*of,* de). **Stirrer-up of strife,** fomentateur, -trice, de

dissensions. **2.** (*Device*) Agitateur *m. Cu:* Mouvette *f.* **3.** (*Pers.*) **To be an early stirrer,** être matinal.
stirrup ['stirəp], *s.* I. Étrier *m. To put one's feet in the stirrups,* chausser les étriers. **To lose one's stirrups,** vider les étriers. **2.** *Nau:* Étrier (de marchepied de vergue). **3.** Tire-pied *m* (de cordonnier). **4.** *Surg:* Étrier (de la table d'opération). **5.** (a) *Const:* Étrier (de fixation) armature *f* en étrier. (b) (*Of rowlock*) Lyre *f* (c) (*Of leaf-spring*) Bride *f* de ressort. **'stirrup-bone,** *s. Anat:* Étrier *m* (de l'oreille). **'stirrup-cup,** *s.* Coup *m* de l'étrier. **'stirrup-iron,** *s.* Étrier *m.* **'stirrup-leather,** *s.* Étrivière *f.*
stitch[1] [stitʃ], *s.* I. (a) *Needlew:* Point *m* piqûre *f.* **Darning stitch,** point de reprise. **Knot stitch,** point noué. *To put a few stitches in a garment,* faire un point à un vêtement. *Prov: A stitch in time saves nine,* un point à temps en épargne cent. *Nau:* **With every stitch of canvas** set, couvert de toile ; toutes voiles dehors. *F:* **He has not a dry stitch on him,** il est complètement trempé. (b) (*In knitting, crochet*) Maille *f.* **To drop a stitch,** sauter, laisser échapper, une maille. (c) *Surg:* (Point de) suture *f.* **To put stitches in** a wound, suturer, faire une suture à, une plaie. **2.** *Med:* Stitch (in the side), point de côté.
stitch[2], *v.tr.* I. (a) Coudre (un vêtement, etc.) (b) **To stitch leather,** piquer le cuir. **2.** *Surg:* Suturer (une plaie). **3.** *Bookb:* Brocher (un livre). **stitch down,** *v.tr. Needlew:* Rabattre (une couture). **stitch on,** *v.tr.* Coudre (qch. sur qch.) ; appliquer (une poche, etc.) ; coudre (qch.) en place. **stitch up,** *v.tr.* I. Recoudre (une déchirure, etc.) ; faire un point à (qch.). **2.** *Surg:* Suturer (une plaie). **stitched,** *a.* I. Piqué. **2.** *Bookb:* Broché. **stitching,** *s.* I. (a) *Needlew:* Couture *f.* *Leath:* Piqûre *f.* (b) *Surg:* Suture *f.* (c) *Bookb:* Brochage *m* brochure *f.* **2.** Points *mpl,* piqûres. **Ornamental stitching,** broderie *f.*
stiver ['staivər], *s. F:* Sou *m.* **He hasn't a stiver** il n'a pas le sou ; *P:* il n'a pas un radis.
stoa, *pl.* **-ae, -as** ['stouə, -i:, -az], *s. Gr.Ant:* Portique *m.*
stoat [stout], *s. Z:* Hermine *f* d'été.
stock[1] [stɔk], *s.* I. (a) *Bot:* Tronc *m* (d'arbre) (b) Souche *f* (d'arbre) ; bloc *m* ; souche, fût *m* (d'enclume). *F:* **To stand like a stock,** demeurer comme une souche. (c) *Hort:* Sujet *m,* ente *f* porte-greffe *m inv.* (d) Race *f,* famille *f,* lignée *f.* **True to stock,** fortement racé. *Of good Puritan s.,* de bonne lignée puritaine. *Man of the good old s. F:* homme de la vieille roche. **2.** (a) Fût, bois *m* monture *f* (de fusil) ; manche *m* (de fouet) **Anchor-stock,** jas *m* d'ancre. *The chain is round the s.,* l'ancre est surjalée. (b) **Bit-stock,** vilebrequin *m.* **Die-stock,** tourne-à-gauche *m inv* filière *f* (à coussinets). **3.** *pl. A:* Stocks, ceps *mp* pilori *m,* tabouret *m* (en place publique). **To put s.o. in the stocks,** mettre qn aux ceps **4.** *pl. N.Arch:* Stocks, chantier *m* ; cale *f* de construction. **Ship on the stocks,** navire en construction, sur cales. *F:* **To have a piece of work on the stocks,** avoir un ouvrage sur le chantier. **5.** (a) Provision *f,* approvisionnement *n S. of wood,* provision de bois. **Stock of plays,** répertoire *m.* **To lay in a stock of . . .,** faire (une provision de . . . ; s'approvisionner de. . . . *To lay in a good s. of linen,* se monter en linge (b) *Com:* Marchandises *fpl* ; stock *m.* **Old stock,** dead stock, fonds *mpl* de boutique ; vieux rossignols. **Surplus stock,** soldes *mpl.* **Stock hand,** stock-in-trade, marchandises en magasin

stock. To buy the whole stock of a business, acheter un fonds en bloc. **In stock,** en magasin, en stock, en dépôt. (*Of goods*) **To be out of stock,** manquer en magasin. **To take stock,** faire, dresser, l'inventaire. *F:* **To take stock of s.o.,** scruter, toiser, qn. (*c*) (*At cards, dominoes*) Talon *m.* (*d*) *Husb:* **Live-stock, grazing stock,** bétail *m;* bestiaux *mpl;* cheptel *m.* **Fat stock,** bétail de boucherie. *Breed:* **Stock mare,** jument de haras. (*e*) *Ind:* Dotation *f.* *Rail:* **Locomotive stock,** effectif *m,* dotation, en locomotives. **6.** (*a*) *Ind:* Matières premières. (*b*) *Cu:* **Soup-stock,** consommé *m,* bouillon *m.* **7.** *Fin:* Fonds *mpl,* valeurs *fpl,* actions *fpl.* **Government stock,** fonds d'État; fonds publics; rentes *fpl* (sur l'État). **Bank stock,** valeurs de banque. **Fully paid stock,** titres libérés. **Stocks and shares,** valeurs mobilières; valeurs de bourse. *F:* **His stock is going up, going down,** ses actions haussent, baissent. *U.S:* **To take no stock in s.o.,** faire peu de cas de qn. **8.** *Bot:* Stock(-gilly-flower), matthiole *f;* giroflée *f* des jardins. **9.** *Cost:* (*a*) *A:* Cravate *f* ample. (*b*) *Mil: A:* Col droit (d'uniforme); *F:* carcan *m.* (*c*) Col-cravate *m* (d'équitation). (*d*) Plastron en soie noire (des ecclésiastiques anglais). **10.** *Attrib.* (*a*) *Com:* **Stock size,** taille courante. **Stock car,** voiture de série. (*b*) *Th:* **Stock play,** pièce du répertoire. **Stock company,** troupe à demeure (dans une ville). *S.* argument, argument habituel, bien connu. **Stock phrase,** phrase toute faite; cliché *m.* **'stock-account,** *s.* *Book-k:* Compte *m* de capital. **'stock-book,** *s.* Livre *m* de magasin; magasinier *m.* **'stock-breeder,** *s.* Éleveur *m.* **'stock-breeding,** *s.* Élevage *m.* **'stock-broker,** *s.* *Fin:* Agent *m* de change. **Outside stock-broker,** coulissier *m.* **'stock-dove,** *s. Orn:* Petit ramier; colombin *m.* **'stock exchange,** *s.* Bourse *f* (des valeurs). **The Stock Exchange,** la Bourse (de Londres). **'stock-farm,** *s.* Élevage *m* (de bestiaux). **'stock-fish,** *s.* Stockfisch *m;* morue séchée; *Nau:* bacaliau *m.* **'stock-in-'trade,** *s.* **1.** *See* STOCK[1] 5 (*b*). **2.** (*a*) Outils essentiels (d'un artisan). (*b*) *F:* Fonds *m,* répertoire *m* (de phrases à effet, etc.). **'stock-keeper,** *s.* Magasinier *m.* **'stock-list,** *s.* **1.** *Com:* Inventaire *m.* **2.** *St.Exch:* Bulletin *m* de la cote. **'stock-market,** *s.* **1.** Marché *m* des valeurs; marché financier. **2.** Marché aux bestiaux. **'stock owl,** *s. Orn:* Grand-duc *m.* **'stock-pot,** *s. Cu:* Pot *m* à bouillon; pot-au-feu *m* inv. **'stock-raiser,** *s.* Éleveur *m.* **'stock-rais-ing,** *s.* Élevage *m.* **'stock-room,** *s.* **1.** *Ind:* Magasin *m.* **2.** (*In hotel*) Salle *f* de montre (des marchandises d'un commis voyageur). **'stock-saw,** *s.* Scie alternative à plusieurs lames. **'stock-solution,** *s.* *Ch: Phot:* Solution concentrée (et de bonne garde). **'stock 'still,** *a.* **To stand stock still,** rester complètement immobile, sans bouger; demeurer immobile. **'stock-taking,** *s.* *Com: Ind:* Inventaire *m.* **'stock-whip,** *s.* (*In Austr.*) Fouet *m* de bouvier (à manche court). **'stock-yard,** *s.* **1.** Parc *m* à bestiaux. **2.** Parc à matériau.

tock², *v.tr.* **1.** (*a*) Monter (un fusil). (*b*) *Nau:* Enjaler (une ancre). **2.** Garnir, stocker (un magasin) (*with,* de); monter (en); meubler (une ferme) de bétail; approvisionner (une maison) (*with,* de); empoissonner (un étang); peupler (une forêt). **Shop well stocked with . . .,** magasin bien monté en . . ., bien approvisionné de, en. . . . *Memory stocked with facts,* mémoire meublée de faits. **3.** Tenir, garder, (des mar-

chandises) en magasin, en dépôt; stocker (des marchandises).

stockade¹ [stɔ'keid], *s.* **1.** Palissade *f,* palanque *f.* **2.** Estacade *f.*

stockade², *v.tr.* **1.** Palissader, palanquer. **2.** Garnir (une berge) d'une estacade.

stocker ['stɔkər], *s.* Stockiste *m* (de pièces détachées d'automobiles, etc.).

stockholder ['stɔkhouldər], *s.* Actionnaire *mf;* porteur *m,* détenteur *m,* de titres.

stockinet(te) [stɔki'net], *s.* Jersey *m,* tricot *m,* de laine, de soie (pour sous-vêtements).

stocking ['stɔkin], *s.* **1.** *Cost:* Bas *m.* **Open-work stockings,** bas à jours. **Ribbed stockings,** bas à côtes. *Surg:* **Elastic stockings,** bas pour varices. *F:* **A well-lined stocking,** un bas de laine bien garni. *S.a.* BLUE-STOCKING. **2.** **White stocking** (*of a horse*), balzane *f.* **Horse with white stockings,** cheval balzan. **'stocking-frame, -loom,** *s.* Métier *m* à bas. **'stocking-stitch,** *s. Knitting:* Point *m* (de) jersey.

stockist ['stɔkist], *s.* *Com:* Stockiste *m.*

stockless ['stɔkləs], *a.* (Ancre) sans jas.

stockman, *pl.* **-men** ['stɔkmən, -men], *s.m.* (*In Austr.*) Gardeur de bestiaux; bouvier.

stocky ['stɔki], *a.* Trapu; ragot, -ote; (*of horse*) goussaut, ragot.

stodge¹ [stɔdʒ], *s.* *F:* **1.** (*a*) Aliment bourrant. (*b*) Littérature *f* indigeste. **2.** **To have a good s.,** s'en fourrer jusque-là.

stodge², *v.i. & pr.* *F:* Se bourrer de nourriture; bâfrer.

stodgy ['stɔdʒi], *a.* (Repas) lourd; (aliment) qui bourre; (livre) indigeste.

stoep [stu:p], *s.* (*In S. Africa*) Véranda *f.*

stoic ['stouik], *a. & s.* Stoïcien, -ienne; stoïque *mf.*

stoical ['stouik(ə)l], *a.* Stoïque. **-ally,** *adv.* Stoïquement.

stoicism ['stouisizm], *s.* Stoïcisme *m.*

stoke [stouk], *v.tr.* **1.** Charger (un foyer); chauffer (un four); entretenir, alimenter, le feu (d'un four); chauffer le foyer d'une machine à vapeur). **2.** *Abs.* **To stoke (up).** (*a*) Pousser les feux. (*b*) *Hum:* Manger, bouffer. **'stoke-hole,** *s.* **1.** (*a*) Ouverture *f* de foyer; tisard *m.* (*b*) *Nau:* Enfer *m* (devant le tisard). **2.** = STOKE-HOLD.

stokehold ['stoukhould], *s.* *Nau:* Chaufferie *f;* chambre *f* de chauffe.

stoker ['stoukər], *s.* *Nau: Rail:* **1.** (*Pers.*) Chauffeur *m.* **Head stoker,** chef *m* de chauffe. **2.** **Mechanical stoker,** chauffeur automatique; grille *f* mécanique.

stole¹ [stoul], *s.* **1.** *Rom.Ant:* Stole *f.* **2.** *Ecc:* Étole *f.* **3.** *Cost:* Écharpe *f* (de fourrure, etc.).

stole², *s.* = STOLON.

stole³. *See* STEAL.

stolen ['stoul(ə)n]. *See* STEAL.

stolid ['stɔlid], *a.* Lourd, lent, flegmatique, impassible. **-ly,** *adv.* Avec flegme.

stolidity [stɔ'liditi], **stolidness** ['stɔlidnəs], *s.* Flegme *m.*

stolon ['stoulən], *s.* *Bot: Biol:* Stolon *m; Bot: F:* coulant *m.*

stomach¹ ['stʌmək], *s.* **1.** Estomac *m.* **Pain in the s.,** mal *m* d'estomac. **On a full stomach,** aussitôt après un repas; au moment de la digestion. **To turn s.o.'s stomach,** soulever le cœur à qn; écœurer qn. **It makes my stomach rise,** cela me donne des nausées. **2.** *F:* (Euphémisme pour désigner le) ventre. **To crawl on one's s.,** ramper à plat ventre. **3.** (*a*) Envie *f,* goût *m* (*for,* de); inclination *f* (*for,* pour); cœur *m,* courage *m* (pour faire qch.). **It will put some**

stomach into them, cela leur mettra du cœur au ventre. (b) A: To be of a proud, of a high, stomach, être plein de morgue. 'stomach-ache, s. (a) Douleurs fpl d'estomac. (b) F: Mal m de ventre. 'stomach-cough, s. Toux f gastrique. 'stomach-pump, s. Med: Pompe stomacale.

stomach², v.tr. F: Endurer, supporter, tolérer (qch.); F: digérer (une insulte, etc.). He won't s. that affront, il n'avalera pas, ne digérera pas, cet affront.

stomachal ['stɔmək(ə)l], a. Stomacal, -aux.

-stomached ['stʌməkt], a. Weak-stomached, à la digestion faible.

stomacher ['stʌməkər], s. A.Cost: Pièce f d'estomac (d'un corsage de femme).

stone¹ [stoun], s. I. Pierre f. (a) Pebble stone, caillou, -oux m. Meteoric stone, aérolithe m. To leave no stone unturned (to . . .), ne rien négliger (pour . . .); mettre tout en œuvre, remuer ciel et terre, faire l'impossible (pour . . .). To throw, cast, stones at s.o., (i) lancer des pierres à qn; (ii) F: jeter des pierres dans le jardin de qn. To throw stones at a dog, lapider un chien. (b) Const: etc: Moellon m; pierre de taille. Not to leave a stone standing, ne pas laisser pierre sur pierre. (c) Typ: (Imposing-)stone, marbre m. (d) Meule f (à repasser, de moulin). Honing stone, oil-stone, pierre à huile. 2. Precious stones, pierres précieuses; pierreries f. 3. (Material) Pierre (à bâtir, etc.). Broken stone, pierraille f, cailloutis m. 4. Med: Calcul m, pierre (de la vessie, du rein). 5. (a) Noyau m (de fruit); pépin m (de raisin). (b) Hail-stone, grêlon m. 6. inv. Meas: Stone m (= 6·348 kg). He weighs 12 stone, il pèse 76 kilos. 7. Attrib. Stone jug, pot m, cruche f, de grès. 'stone-axe, s. I. Hache f de pierre. 2. Const: Marteau m à dresser. 'stone-'blind, a. Complètement aveugle. 'stone-break, s. Bot: Saxifrage f. 'stone-breaker, s. I. (Pers.) Casseur m de pierres. 2. (Machine) Concasseur m. 'stone-'broke, a. F: = STONY-BROKE. 'stone-coal, s. Anthracite m. 'stone-'cold, a. Froid comme (le) marbre. The tea is s.-c., le thé est complètement froid. 'stone-crusher, s. Civ.E: Concasseur m. 'stone curlew, s. Orn: Grand pluvier; courlis m de terre. 'stone-cutter, s. Tailleur m, équarrisseur m, de pierres. 'stone-'dead, a. Raide mort. 'stone-'deaf, a. Complètement sourd. 'stone-dresser, s. Dresseur m de pierres. 'stone falcon, s. Orn: Émerillon m. 'stone-fruit, s. Fruit m à noyau. 'stone-guard, s. Aut: Pare-radiateur m; pare-pierres m inv. 'stone-plover, s. Orn: = STONE CURLEW. 'stone-quarry, s. Carrière f de pierre. 'stone's throw, s. Jet m de pierre. F: Within a stone's throw, à quelques pas, à deux pas. stone wall, s. (a) Mur m de, en, pierre; mur en moellon. (b) Mur (d'enclos) en pierre sèche. 'Stone-wall countenance, visage impassible.

stone², v.tr. I. Lapider; assaillir (qn) à coups de pierres. To stone s.o. to death, lapider qn. 2. To stone fruit, enlever les noyaux des fruits; énoyauter, épépiner, les fruits. 3. Revêtir de pierres (un édifice); paver de pierres (une allée). 4. Empierrer, caillouter (une route).

stonechat ['stountʃat], s. Orn: I. Traquet m; tarier m saxicole. 2. F: = WHEATEAR.

stonecrop ['stounkrɔp], s. Bot: Orpin m.

stonemason ['stounmeis(ə)n], s. Maçon m.

stonewall [stoun'wɔːl], v.i. I. (a) Cr: Jouer un jeu prudent pour tenir jusqu'à la fin. (b) Fenc:

Parer au mur. 2. Parl: F: Faire de l'obstruction.

stonewaller [stoun'wɔːlər], s. I. Cr: Joueur prudent, qui ne risque rien. 2. Parl: F: Obstructionniste mf.

stoneware ['stounwɛər], s. Grès m (cérame) poterie f de grès.

stonework ['stounwəːrk], s. I. (a) Maçonnage m maçonnerie f. (b) Ouvrage m en pierre. 2. Typ Correction f sur le marbre.

stoniness ['stouninəs], s. I. Nature pierreuse (du sol, d'une poire). 2. Dureté f (de cœur).

stony ['stouni], a. I. (a) Pierreux; couvert ou rempli de pierres; rocailleux. (b) S. pear, poire pierreuse. 2. Dur comme la pierre. 3. S. heart cœur de roche, de marbre. S. look, regard glacial S. politeness, politesse glacée. 4. F: = STONY BROKE. -ily, adv. (Regarder) d'un air glacial 'stony-'broke, a. P: Dans la dèche; décavé à sec. I'm s.-b., je n'ai pas le sou. 'stony-'hearted, a. (Of pers.) Au cœur de roche, de marbre.

stood. See STAND².

stook [stuːk], s. Dial: Tas m de gerbes; meu lette f, moyette f.

stool¹ [stuːl], s. I. (a) Tabouret m. Folding stool pliant m. Piano stool, music stool, tabouret d piano. Stool of repentance, sellette f. F: To fal between two stools, demeurer entre deux selle (le cul à terre). (b) (Three-legged) Escabeau m 2. (a) A: Garde-robe f. Night-stool, clos stool, chaise percée. To go to stool, aller à l selle. (b) pl. Med: Stools, selles. 3. (a) For etc: Souche f (d'un arbre abattu). (b) Hort Pied m mère; plante f mère. 4. = STOOL PIGEON. 'stool-ball, s. Games: Balle f a camp. 'stool pigeon, s. I. Ven: Appeau m appelant; chanterelle f. 2. F: (a) Canard priv (de la police). (b) Compère m (d'un escroc).

stool², v.i. (Of plant) Pousser des rejetons (of tree) taller. 2. Med: Aller à la selle.

stoop¹ [stuːp], s. Inclination f en avant (du corps); attitude voûtée. To walk with a stoop marcher le dos voûté; marcher penché.

stoop². I. v.i. (a) Se pencher, se baisser. He ha to s. in order to get into the car, il lui fallait s baisser pour monter dans la voiture. (b) S'abaisser s'avilir, descendre (to do sth., à, jusqu'à, fair qch.). He stooped to a lie, il descendit jusqu'a mensonge. I refuse to s. to such a thing, je n veux pas déroger jusqu'à faire une chose pareille (c) Avoir le dos rond; être voûté. 2. v.t Pencher, incliner, courber (la tête); courbe arrondir (le dos); pencher. stooping, a. Penché, courbé voûté.

stoop³, s. U.S: Canada: (a) Terrasse surélevé (devant une maison). (b) Véranda f.

stop¹ [stɔp], s. I. (a) Arrêt m, interruption f. T put a stop to sth., arrêter, faire cesser, qch. mettre fin à qch. It ought to be put a stop t il faudrait y mettre fin. To be at a stop, trouver arrêté; être aheurté à un obstacle (b) Arrêt, halte f, pause f. Short stop, moment d'arrêt. Ten minutes' stop, dix minutes d'arrê To come to a stop, s'arrêter; faire halte; (o car) stopper. Traffic stop, arrêt de circulatio To bring sth. to a stop, arrêter qch. (c) Bus sto (point m d')arrêt d'autobus; halte. Regular sto arrêt fixe. Request stop, arrêt facultatif. (Aut (On long-distance flight) Terrain m d'escal 2. Signe m de ponctuation; point m. To put the stops, mettre les points et virgules. 3. Mus (a) Jeu m, registre m (d'orgue). To pull out stop, tirer un registre. (b) Trou m (de flûte, etc.

(c) Clé f (de clarinette, etc.). (d) Touche f, touchette f (de la guitare). (e) Barré m (sur la guitare, le violon), **4.** Dispositif m de blocage; arrêt, taquet m, butée f, toc m; heurtoir m (d'une porte, etc.); arrêtoir m (de vis, de boulon); (on moving part of machine) mentonnet m. Aut: etc: Shackle stop, butée de jumelle. Carp: Bench stop, crochet m, griffe f, d'établi. Typewr: Marginal stop, margin stop, régulateur m de marge. **5.** (a) Cards: Carte f d'arrêt. (b) Box: Coup bloqué. **6.** Opt: Phot: Diaphragme m (de l'objectif). **7.** Ling: Plosive f; explosive f. **8.** Nau: (a) (Frapping) Genope f. To break the stops (of a flag), casser les genopes. (b) Raban m de ferlage. **'stop-bath,** s. Phot: etc: Bain m d'arrêt. **'stop-block,** s. Rail: Taquet m d'arrêt; tampon m. **'stop-gap,** s. Bouche-trou m. It will serve as a s.-g., cela servira à boucher un trou. **'stop-gear,** s. Appareil m d'arrêt. **'stop-hit,** s. Fenc: Coup m d'arrêt. **'stop-light,** s. Aut: The stop-light, le feu "stop"; le signal d'arrêt. **'stop-point,** s. = STOPPING-PLACE. **'stop-press,** attrib.a. Journ: Stop-press news, informations de dernière heure. **'stop-screw,** s. Vis-butoir f; vis f de butée. **'stop-signal,** s. Rail: Signal m d'arrêt. **'stop-watch,** s. Montre f à arrêt; compte-secondes m inv; chronographe m à pointage.

stop², v. (stopped [stɔpt]) I. v.tr. **1.** Boucher, aveugler (une voie d'eau); plomber, obturer (une dent). To stop (up), boucher, fermer (un trou); obstruer, obturer (un tuyau). (Of pipe, etc.) To get stopped (up), super, s'obstruer. To stop one's ears, se boucher les oreilles. F: To stop one's ears against entreaties, rester sourd aux requêtes. To stop a gap, (i) boucher un trou; (ii) combler une lacune. To stop the way, fermer, barrer, le passage. 'Road stopped,' "rue barrée." **2.** (a) Arrêter (un cheval, une balle, etc.). To stop s.o. short, arrêter qn (tout) court. Stop thief! au voleur! To stop the traffic, interrompre la circulation. To stop s.o.'s breath, couper la respiration à qn. To stop a blow, parer un coup; Box: bloquer. Fb: To stop the ball, bloquer. Walls that stop sounds, murs qui étouffent, qui amortissent, le son. Curtains that stop the light, rideaux qui interceptent la lumière. (b) To stop s.o.'s doing sth., to stop s.o. from doing sth., empêcher qn de faire qch. To stop sth. being done, empêcher que qch. (ne) se fasse. There is no one to stop him, il n'y a personne pour l'en empêcher. Com: To stop (payment of) a cheque, bloquer, stopper, un chèque; frapper un chèque d'opposition. (c) Arrêter (une pendule); arrêter, stopper (une machine). (d) Mettre fin à (qch.); enrayer (un abus). It ought to be stopped, il faudrait y mettre fin. **3.** (a) Cesser (ses efforts, ses visites). Com: To stop payment, cesser ses paiements. To stop doing sth., s'arrêter de faire qch. To stop playing, cesser de jouer. She never stops talking, elle n'arrête jamais de parler. Stop that noise! assez de bruit! Stop it! assez! finissez! (b) Impers. It has stopped raining, il a cessé de pleuvoir; la pluie a cessé. **4.** To stop s.o.'s supply of electricity, couper l'électricité à qn. To stop s.o.'s wages, retenir les gages de qn. To stop s.o.'s allowance, couper les vivres à qn. Mil: All leave is stopped, toutes les permissions sont suspendues. **5.** Mus: To stop (down) a string, presser une corde. **6.** Nau: Genoper (un amarrage). **7.** Gram: Ponctuer. II. **stop,** v.i. **1.** (a) S'arrêter. Nau: (Of ship) Stopper. (Of pers.) To stop short, dead, s'arrêter (tout) court;

s'arrêter net. (Of car) To stop at the kerb, s'arrêter, F: stopper, le long du trottoir. 'Cars stop by request,' "arrêt facultatif." 'All cars stop here,' "arrêt fixe, obligatoire." Rail: How long do we stop at . . .? combien d'arrêt à . . .? To pass a station without stopping, brûler une gare. Nau: To stop at a port, faire escale à un port. (b) Cesser (de parler, de fonctionner, etc.). My watch has stopped, ma montre (s')est arrêtée. To work fifteen hours without stopping, travailler pendant quinze heures d'arrache-pied. To stop short in one's speech, rester court dans son discours. Once on this subject he never stops, une fois sur ce sujet il ne tarit pas. He did not stop at that, il ne s'en tint pas là. To stop for s.o., (rester à) attendre qn. Stop a moment, arrêtez un instant. Stop there! (i) restez-en là! (ii) demeurez là! restez là! The matter will not stop there, l'affaire n'en demeurera pas là. The rain has stopped, la pluie a cessé. **2.** F: = STAY² I. 2. **stop away,** v.i. **1.** Ne pas venir. **2.** S'absenter. **stop down,** v.tr. Phot: To stop down a lens, diaphragmer un objectif. **stopping,** s. **1.** (a) Arrêt m. Stopping device, dispositif d'arrêt (de mouvement). (b) Suspension f; cessation f. S. of a train, of a service, suppression f d'un train, d'un service. (c) Stopping of a cheque, arrêt de payement d'un chèque. (d) Stopping (up), obturation f. Stopping of a tooth, plombage m, obturation, d'une dent. (e) Gram: Ponctuation f. **2.** (a) Bouchon m, tampon m. (b) Dent: Plombage m, mastic m. (c) Aut: Cy: Tyre-stopping, mastic pour enveloppes. **'stopping-place,** s. (Point m d')arrêt m; halte f. Av: Terrain m d'escale.

stopcock ['stɔpkɔk], s. Robinet m d'arrêt, de fermeture.

stope¹ [stoup], s. Min: **1.** Gradin m. **2.** Chantier m en gradins.

stope², v.tr. Min: **1.** Exploiter (une mine) en gradins. **2.** Abattre (le minerai).

stoppage ['stɔpedʒ], s. **1.** Arrêt m; mise f au repos; suspension f (du travail, etc.). S. of the traffic, suspension de la circulation. S. of payments, suspension de payements. Stoppage of pay, retenue f sur les appointements; Mil: suppression f de solde. Mil: Stoppage of leave, consigne f; suppression des permissions. **2.** Obstruction f, engorgement m. Med: Intestinal stoppage, occlusion intestinale. **3.** Arrêt, pause f, halte f; interruption f (du travail).

stopper¹ ['stɔpər], s. **1.** (a) Bouchon m (en verre). Screw stopper, fermeture f à vis. (b) Obturateur m; pointeau m d'arrêt (de citerne). **2.** (a) Mec.E: Taquet m (d'arrêt de mouvement). F: To put a stopper on s.o.'s activities, enrayer les activités de qn. (b) Nau: Bosse f. Cat-head stopper, bosse de bout.

stopper², v.tr. **1.** Boucher (un flacon). **2.** Nau: Bosser.

storage ['stɔːredʒ], s. **1.** Emmagasinage m, emmagasinement m, entreposage m. To take a car out of storage, remettre une voiture en service. To take goods out of s., sortir des marchandises. Storage tank, réservoir d'emmagasinage. Hyd.E: Storage basin, réservoir de barrage. **2.** Caves fpl, greniers mpl; entrepôts mpl, magasins mpl (d'une maison de commerce); espace m disponible. **3.** Frais mpl d'entrepôt. **'storage bin,** s. Coffre m, récipient m. **'storage cell,** s. El: Élément m d'accumulateur.

storax ['stɔːraks], s. Bot: Styrax m.

store¹ ['stɔːr], *s.* **I.** (*a*) Provision *f*, approvisionnement *m*. (*b*) Abondance *f*. *Ind:* Store of energy, énergie disponible. **To lay in a store of** sth., faire une provision de qch. ; s'approvisionner de qch. *To lay in stores*, s'approvisionner. **To hold, keep, sth. in store**, tenir, garder, qch. en réserve. *What the future holds in s. for us*, ce que l'avenir nous réserve. *I have a surprise in s. for him*, je lui ménage une surprise. **That is a treat in store**, c'est un plaisir à venir. **To set great store by sth.**, faire grand cas de qch. ; attacher beaucoup de prix à qch. **To set little store by sth.**, faire peu de cas de qch. *Prov:* **Store is no sore**, abondance de biens ne nuit pas. *Husb:* **Store cattle**, bétail à l'engraissage. **2.** *pl.* (*a*) Stores, provisions, approvisionnements, vivres *m*. **War stores**, munitions *f*, matériel *m*, de guerre. (*b*) **Marine stores**, (i) approvisionnements, matériel ; (ii) maison *f* d'approvisionnements de navires. **Marine-store dealer**, approvisionneur, -euse. **3.** (*a*) Entrepôt *m*, magasin *m* ; (*for furniture*) garde-meuble *m*. *Mil: Navy:* Magasin ; (*for whole district*) manutention *f*. (*b*) *Esp. U.S:* Boutique *f*, magasin. **The village store**, l'épicerie *f* du village. (*c*) **The (departmental) stores**, les grands magasins. **'store-room**, *s.* (*a*) (*In private house*) Office *f*, dépense *f*. (*b*) *Ind:* Halle *f* de dépôt. (*c*) *Nau:* (i) Soute *f* aux vivres ; soute à provisions ; (ii) cambuse *f*.
store², *v.tr.* **I.** Pourvoir, munir, approvisionner (*with*, de). **To have a well-stored mind**, avoir la tête bien meublée. **2. To store sth.** (up), amasser, accumuler, qch. **To store up electricity, heat**, emmagasiner l'électricité, la chaleur. **3.** (*a*) Emmagasiner, mettre en dépôt (des meubles) ; mettre en grange (le foin, le blé). (*b*) Prendre en dépôt. **Stored car**, voiture en dépôt. **Stored furniture**, mobilier au garde-meuble.
storehouse ['stɔːrhaus], *s.* Magasin *m*, entrepôt *m*. *Mil:* Manutention *f*. *F:* **He is a storehouse of information**, c'est une vraie mine de renseignements.
storekeeper ['stɔːrkiːpər], *s.* **I.** (*a*) Garde-magasin *m*, *pl.* gardes-magasin ; magasinier *m*. (*b*) (*In hospital, convent, etc.*) Dépensier, -ière. *Nau:* Cambusier *m*. **2.** *U.S:* Boutiquier, -ière.
storey ['stɔːri], *s.* = STOREY².
storeyed ['stɔːrid], *a.* = STORIED².
storied¹ ['stɔːrid], *a.* **I.** *Arch:* Storied window, vitrail historié. **2.** *A:* Célébré dans l'histoire ou dans la légende.
storied², *a.* À étage(s). **Two-storied house**, maison à un étage ; *U.S:* maison à deux étages.
stork [stɔːk], *s. Orn:* Cigogne *f*. *F:* **A visit from the stork**, l'arrivée *f* d'un bébé.
storm¹ [stɔːrm], *s.* **I.** Orage *m*. *Meteor:* Tempête *f*, dépression *f*. **Rain storm**, tempête de pluie ; *Nau:* fort grain de pluie. **Magnetic storm**, orage magnétique. *F:* **A storm in a tea-cup**, une tempête dans un verre d'eau. *F:* **Political storm**, tourmente *f* politique. **To stir up a storm**, soulever une tempête. **2.** Pluie *f* (de projectiles) ; bordée *f* (de sifflets). **Storm of abuse, of applause**, tempête d'injures, d'applaudissements. **To bring a storm about one's ears**, s'attirer une véritable tempête d'ennuis ou d'indignation ; soulever un tollé général. **3. To take a stronghold by storm**, emporter, prendre d'assaut, une place forte. *F:* **To take the audience by storm**, emporter l'auditoire. **'storm-area**, *s.* Étendue *f* d'une dépression. **'storm-beaten**, *a.* Battu par les tempêtes. **'storm-bell**, *s.* Tocsin *m*. **'storm-belt**, *s.* Zone *f* des tempêtes. **'storm-bird**, *s.* Pétrel *m* des tempêtes. **'storm-bound**, *a.* Retenu par la tempête ; en relâche forcée.

'storm centre, *s.* (*a*) *Meteor:* Centre *m* du cyclone. (*b*) *F:* Foyer *m* d'agitation, de troubles. **'storm-cloud**, *s.* (*a*) Nuée *f* (d'orage). (*b*) *F:* Nuage *m* à l'horizon ; nuage menaçant. **'storm-cone**, *s. Nau:* Cône *m* de tempête. **'storm-jib**, *s. Nau:* Trinquette *f*, tourmentin *m*. **'storm-lantern**, *s.* Lanterne-tempête *f*, *pl.* lanternes-tempête. **'storm-proof**, *a.* **I.** A l'épreuve de la tempête. **2.** Inexpugnable. **'storm-sail**, *s. Nau:* Voile *f* de cape. **'storm-tossed**, *a.* Ballotté par la tempête. **'storm-troops**, *s.pl.* Troupes *f* d'assaut. **'storm-window**, *s.* Contre-fenêtre *f*.
storm². **I.** *v.i.* (*a*) (*Of wind, rain*) Se déchaîner ; faire rage. (*b*) *F:* (*Of pers.*) Tempêter, pester. **2.** *v.tr.* (i) Livrer l'assaut à (une place forte) ; (ii) prendre d'assaut, emporter d'assaut (une place forte). **storming**, *s.* **I.** Violence *f*, emportements *mpl*. **2.** *Mil:* (i) Assaut *m* ; (ii) prise *f* d'assaut. **'storming party**, *s. Mil:* Troupes *fpl* d'assaut.
stormer ['stɔːrmər], *s.* **I.** Membre *m* de la colonne d'assaut. **2.** *See* BARN-STORMER.
stormy ['stɔːrmi], *a.* (Vent) tempétueux ; (temps, ciel) orageux, d'orage. **S. sea**, mer démontée. *F:* **Stormy discussion**, discussion orageuse. *S. meeting*, réunion houleuse.
story¹ ['stɔːri], *s.* **I.** Histoire *f*, récit *m*, conte *m*. **Idle story**, conte en l'air. **To tell a story**, raconter, conter, une histoire. *According to his own s.*, à croire qu'il raconte ; d'après lui. **There is a story that . . .**, on raconte que. . . . *F:* **That is quite another story**, ça c'est une autre paire de manches. **It's the (same) old story**, c'est toujours la même rengaine, la même chanson. **It's a long story**, c'est toute une histoire. *The best of the s. is that . . .*, le plus beau de l'histoire, c'est que. . . . **These bruises tell their own story**, ces meurtrissures en disent long. *Have you read the s. of his life?* avez-vous lu l'histoire de sa vie ? **2.** *Lit:* **Short story**, nouvelle *f*, conte. **3.** Intrigue *f* (d'un roman, d'une pièce de théâtre). **4.** *F:* Conte ; mensonge *m*, menterie *f*. **To tell stories**, dire des mensonges ; raconter des blagues *f*. **5.** *A:* L'histoire ; la légende. **Famous in story**, célèbre dans l'histoire ou dans la fable. **'story-book**, *s.* Livre *m* de contes ; livre d'histoires. **'story-teller**, *s.* **I.** Conteur, -euse. **2.** *F:* Menteur, -euse.
story², *s.* Étage *m* (d'une maison). *To add a s. to a house*, exhausser une maison d'un étage. **On the third story**, *U.S:* on the fourth story, au troisième étage.
stoup [stuːp], *s.* **I.** *A:* Cruche *f*. **2.** *Ecc:* Bénitier *m*.
stout¹ [staut], *a.* **I.** (i) Fort, vigoureux ; (ii) brave, vaillant ; (iii) ferme, résolu. **Stout fellow**, (i) homme vaillant ; (ii) gaillard *m* solide. **To put up a stout resistance**, se défendre vaillamment. **Stout heart**, cœur vaillant. **2.** (*Of thg*) Fort, solide ; (*of cloth, etc.*) renforcé, résistant. *S. sole*, semelle forte. **3.** Gros, *f.* grosse ; corpulent. *To grow s.*, devenir adipeux ; engraisser ; prendre de l'embonpoint. **-ly**, *adv.* **I.** Fortement, vigoureusement, vaillamment. **To deny sth. stoutly**, nier qch. (fort et) ferme. *He s. maintained that . . .*, il affirmait énergiquement que. . . . **2.** Stoutly built, solidement bâti. **stout-hearted**, *a.* Intrépide, vaillant.
stout², *s.* **I.** *Brew:* bière stout *f*.
stoutish ['stautiʃ], *a.* **I.** Assez corpulent ; replet, -ète. **2.** Assez solide.
stoutness ['stautnəs], *s.* Embonpoint *m*, corpulence *f*.

stove[1] [sto:uv], s. I. (a) Poêle m, fourneau m; cheminée prussienne (d'appartement). **Slow-combustion stove**, calorifère m, salamandre f. S.a. GAS-STOVE. (b) Fourneau de cuisine; cuisinière f. 2. Ch: Ind: Étuve f, four m. 3. Hort: Serre chaude; forcerie f. 4. Chaufferette f (à charbon de bois). '**stove-enamelled**, a. Émaillé au four. '**stove-pipe**, s. I. Tuyau m de poêle. 2. F: Chapeau haut de forme; P: tuyau de poêle. '**stove-polish**, s. Vernis m pour poêles. '**stove-setter**, s. Poseur m de poêles; poêlier-fumiste m.

stove[2], v.tr. I. (a) Étuver (des émaux, etc.). (b) Étuver, désinfecter (des vêtements). 2. Élever (des plantes) en serre chaude.

stove[3]. See STAVE[2].

stow [stou], v.tr. I. To stow (away), mettre en place, ranger, serrer (des objets). F: We were stowed in an attic, on nous avait fourrés dans une mansarde. P: Stow it! ferme ça! la barbe! 2. Nau: Arrimer (des marchandises, le charbon). To stow the cargo, faire l'arrimage. To stow the anchor, the boats, mettre l'ancre à poste; saisir les canots. 3. To s. a waggon, charger une charrette.

stowage ['stoued3], s. Nau: (a) Arrimage m. (b) Capacité f utilisable pour marchandises. (c) Frais mpl d'arrimage.

stowaway[1] ['stouawei], s. Nau: Voyageur m de fond de cale; passager clandestin.

stowaway[2], v.i. To s. on board a ship, s'embarquer clandestinement à bord d'un navire.

stower ['stouər], s. Nau: Arrimeur m.

strabism ['streibizm], s. Strabisme m.

straddle[1] [stradl], s. I. (a) Écartement m des jambes. (b) Position f à califourchon. 2. Artil: Encadrement m (du but).

straddle[2]. I. v.i. Se tenir (debout) les jambes écartées. 2. v.tr. (a) Enfourcher (un cheval); mettre à califourchon sur (une chaise); chevaucher (un mur). Mil: To straddle a river, être à cheval sur un fleuve. (b) Artil: To straddle a target, encadrer un objectif. (c) To straddle (out) one's legs, écarter les jambes.

straggle [stragl], v.i. I. To straggle (along), marcher sans ordre, à la débandade. 2. Houses that s. round the lake, maisons qui s'éparpillent autour du lac. The guests straggle off, les invités s'en vont par petits groupes. **straggling**, a. I. Disséminé. S. village, village aux maisons éparses. **Straggling hairs**, cheveux épars. 2. Straggling plants, plantes qui traînent.

straggler ['straglər], s. Celui qui reste en arrière. Mil: Traînard m.

straight [streit]. I. a. I. (a) Droit, rectiligne. Straight as a ram-rod, droit comme un i. Straight line, ligne droite; droite f. Straight up and down, tout d'une venue. Straight hair, cheveux (i) plats, (ii) raides. Carp: Straight joint, assemblage à plat. Geom: Straight angle, angle de 180°. (b) (Mouvement) en ligne droite. 2. (a) Juste, honnête; loyal, -aux. Man who does a s. deal, homme sérieux et rond en affaires; homme loyal en affaires. Straight answer, réponse franche, sans équivoque. To be s. with s.o., agir loyalement avec qn. To play a straight game, jouer bon jeu bon argent. 3. Net, f. nette; tout simple. Pol: Straight fight, campagne électorale à deux candidats. Th: Straight play, pièce de théâtre proprement dite. Straight part, vrai rôle. 4. (a) Droit; d'aplomb. To put sth. straight, redresser, ajuster, qch. Your tie isn't s., votre cravate est de travers. (b) En ordre. To put the room straight, remettre de l'ordre dans

la chambre. To put things straight, arranger les choses; débrouiller l'affaire. The accounts are straight, les comptes sont en ordre. S.a. FACE[1] 2. II. **straight**, s. I. (a) To be out of the straight, n'être pas d'aplomb; être de travers. To cut material on the straight, couper une étoffe de droit fil. (b) F: To act on the straight, agir loyalement. 2. (a) Rac: The straight, la ligne droite. (b) Rail: Alignement droit. III. **straight**, adv. I. Droit. To shoot straight, tirer juste. Keep straight on, continuez tout droit. The bullet went s. through his leg, la balle lui a traversé la jambe de part en part. To read a book straight through, lire un livre d'un bout à l'autre. 2. Directement. I shall come straight back, je ne ferai qu'aller et (re)venir. To go straight to the point, aller droit au fait. To drink straight from the bottle, boire à même la bouteille. To walk straight in, entrer sans frapper. Straight away, immédiatement, aussitôt; tout de suite; (deviner) du premier coup. Straight off, sur-le-champ; tout de suite; d'emblée. 3. To go straight across the road, traverser la rue tout droit. Straight above sth., juste au-dessus de qch. To look s.o. straight in the face, regarder qn bien en face. I tell you straight, je vous le dis tout net. Straight out, franchement; sans détours, sans ambages. '**straight-'edge**, s. Règle f (à araser); limande f. '**straight-'eight**, s. Aut: F: Une huit-cylindres en ligne.

straighten ['streit(ə)n]. I. v.tr. (a) Rendre (qch.) droit; (re)dresser (qch.). To straighten (out) an iron bar, défausser, dégauchir, une barre de fer. (b) To straighten (up), ranger; mettre en ordre. To s. one's tie, arranger sa cravate. To straighten (out) one's affairs, mettre ses affaires en ordre. 2. v.i. Se redresser; devenir droit. (Of pers.) To straighten up, se redresser. I expect things will s. out, F: je pense que ça s'arrangera.

straightforward [streit'fɔ:rwərd], a. Loyal, -aux; franc, f. franche. To give a straightforward answer, répondre sans détours. **-ly**, adv. (Agir) avec droiture, loyalement; (parler) carrément, franchement, sans détours.

straightforwardness [streit'fɔ:rwərdnəs], s. Droiture f, honnêteté f, franchise f.

straightness ['streitnəs], s. I. Rectitude f (d'une ligne). 2. Droiture f, rectitude (de conduite).

straightway ['streitwei], adv. Lit: Immédiatement, tout de suite, aussitôt.

strain[1] [strein], s. I. Tension f, surtension f. The s. on the rope, la tension de la corde. To take the s. off a beam, soulager une poutre. Mec.E: Breaking strain, effort m de rupture. Bending strain, effort à la flexion. Parts under strain, pièces de fatigue. It would be too great a s. on my purse, ce serait trop demander à ma bourse. The s. of a long match, l'effort soutenu d'un match prolongé. The strain of modern life, la tension de la vie moderne. Mental strain, surmenage intellectuel. To write without s., écrire sans effort. 2. (a) Med: Entorse f, foulure f. S. in the back, tour m de reins. (b) Mec.E: Déformation f (d'une pièce). 3. pl. Poet: Accents mpl. Sweet strains, doux accords. 4. Ton m, sens m (d'un discours, etc.). He said much more in the same s., il s'est étendu longuement dans ce sens.

strain[2]. I. v.tr. I. Tendre, surtendre (un câble). To strain one's ears, tendre l'oreille. To strain one's eyes, se fatiguer, s'abîmer, les yeux (doing sth., à faire qch.). To strain the law, faire violence, donner une entorse, à la loi. To strain s.o.'s friendship, exiger trop de l'amitié de qn.

To **strain a point**, faire une exception ; faire violence à ses principes. *S.a.* NERVE¹ 3. 2. (*a*) *To s. one's back*, se donner un tour de reins. *To s. one's heart, one's shoulder*, se forcer le cœur ; se fouler l'épaule. (*b*) Forcer (un mât, une poutre). *Mec.E :* Déformer (une pièce). (*c*) To strain oneself, se surmener, *F :* s'éreinter (*doing sth.*, à faire qch.). 3. *Lit :* To strain s.o. to one's bosom, serrer qn sur son cœur. 4. (*a*) Filtrer, passer, couler (un liquide) (à travers un linge, etc.) ; passer au tamis ; tamiser. (*b*) To strain sth. out (of a liquid), enlever qch. d'un liquide (en se servant d'une passoire). To strain (off) the vegetables, faire égoutter les légumes. II. strain, *v.i.* I. Faire un (grand) effort. To strain at a rope, tirer sur une corde. To strain after sth., faire tous ses efforts pour atteindre qch. 2. (*Of beam, etc.*) Fatiguer, travailler. (*Of ship*) To strain in a seaway, fatiguer, bourlinguer, par une mer dure. 3. (*Of machine part*) Se déformer ; gauchir ; se fausser. **strained**, *a.* I. (*a*) Strained relations, rapports tendus. (*b*) Strained ankle, cheville foulée. 2. Strained laugh, rire forcé, contraint. **'straining-bag**, *s.* Chausse *f.* **'straining-screw**, *s.* Tendeur *m* à vis ; vis *f* de tension. **'straining-stay, -tie**, *s.* Hauban raidisseur.

strain³, *s.* I. Qualité héritée, inhérente ; tendance (morale). *A s. of weakness*, un héritage, un fond, de faiblesse. 2. Race *f*, lignée *f. There is in him a s. of Irish blood*, il y a en lui une trace de sang irlandais.

strainer ['streinər], *s.* I. (*a*) Filtre *m* ou tamis *m. Cu :* Passoire *f. Ind :* Épurateur *m.* Soup-strainer, passe-bouillon *m inv.* (*b*) Crépine *f* (d'une pompe). *Mch :* Reniflard *m.* (*Over drain-pipe*) Pommelle *f.* 2. Tendeur *m*, tenseur *m*, raidisseur *m. S.a.* WIRE-STRAINER.

strait [streit]. I. *a.* (*a*) *A :* Étroit. *B :* The strait gate, la porte étroite. (*b*) Strait jacket, strait waistcoat, camisole *f* de force. 2. *s.* (*a*) Détroit *m.* The Straits of Dover, le Pas de Calais. (*b*) To be in (great, dire) straits, être dans l'embarras, dans la (plus grande) gêne ; être aux abois. **'strait-'laced**, *a.* Prude, bégueule ; collet monté *inv.*

straitened ['streitnd], *a.* Straitened circumstances, gêne *f* pécuniaire. To be in straitened circumstances, être dans la gêne, dans le besoin, dans l'embarras ; être gêné d'argent.

strake [streik], *s.* Virure *f* (de bateau) ; lisse *f.* Binding strake (of deck), hiloire *f.*

stramonium [strə'mouniəm], *s.* I. *Bot :* Stramoine *f.* 2. *Pharm :* Stramonine *f.*

strand¹ [strand], *s.* Rive *f*, grève *f.*

strand². I. *v.tr.* Échouer (un navire) ; jeter (un navire) à la côte. 2. *v.i.* (*Of ship*) Échouer. **stranded¹**, *a.* I. (*Of ship*) Échoué. 2. *F :* To leave s.o. stranded, laisser qn en plan ; laisser qn le bec dans l'eau. To be stranded, être en panne.

strand³, *s.* I. (*a*) Brin *m*, toron *m* (de cordage) ; cordon *m* (d'aussière) ; brin (de fil à coudre). (*b*) Brin, corde *f.* Four-strand pulley-block, palan à quatre brins. 2. Fil *m* (de perles) ; tresse *f* (de cheveux).

stranded² ['strandid], *a.* A torons, à brins. Three-stranded rope, filin commis en trois ; corde à trois torons.

strange [streindʒ], *a.* I. (*a*) *A :* In a strange land, dans un pays étranger. (*b*) *This writing is strange to me*, je ne connais pas cette écriture. *S. faces*, visages nouveaux, inconnus. 2. Sin-gulier, bizarre, étrange. *S. beasts*, bêtes curieuses.

Strange to say . . ., chose étrange (à dire). . . . It is strange that he has not arrived yet, il est singulier, étonnant, qu'il ne soit pas encore arrivé. 3. I am strange to the work, je suis nouveau dans le métier. To feel strange, se sentir dépaysé. -ly, *adv.* Étrangement, singulièrement.

strangeness ['streindʒnəs], *s.* I. Étrangeté *f*, singularité *f.* 2. The s. of the work, la nouveauté du travail.

stranger ['streindʒər], *s.* I. Étranger, -ère ; inconnu, -ue. I am a stranger here, je ne suis pas d'ici. *He is quite a s. to me*, il m'est tout à fait étranger, inconnu. You are quite a stranger ! on ne vous voit plus ! vous vous faites rare ! He is a stranger to fear, il ne connaît pas la peur. *U.S :* Say, stranger ! pardon, monsieur ! 2. (*In candle*) Champignon *m.*

strangle ['straŋgl], *v.tr.* Étrangler ; serrer le cou à (qn). *To s. a sneeze*, réprimer un éternûment. *To s. evil at its birth*, étouffer le mal au berceau. Strangled voice, voix étranglée. **strangling**, *s.* Étranglement *m* ; *Jur :* strangulation *f.* **stranglehold** ['straŋlhould], *s.* To have a stranglehold on s.o., tenir qn à la gorge. **strangles** [straŋglz], *s.pl. Vet :* Gourme *f.* **strangulate** ['straŋgjuleit], *v.tr. Med :* Étrangler (l'intestin). Strangulated hernia, hernie étranglée ; étranglement *m* herniaire. **strangulation** [straŋgju'leiʃ(ə)n], *s.* Strangula-tion *f. Med :* Étranglement *m* (herniaire).

strap¹ [strap], *s.* I. (*a*) Courroie *f.* Watch strap, bracelet *m* en cuir pour montre. Harn : Stirrup-strap, étrivière *f.* (*b*) *F :* = TAWSE. 2. (*a*) Bande *f*, sangle *f* (de cuir, de toile). *Mec.E :* Driving strap, courroie d'entraînement. (*b*) *Cost :* Bande, patte *f* (d'étoffe). *Bootm :* Barrette *f* (de soulier). *A :* Trouser strap, sous-pied *m.* 3. (*a*) Lien *m*, attache *f*, armature *f*, plate-bande *f* (en métal) ; (*for pipe*) collier *m.* (*b*) *Mch :* Chape *f*, bride *f* (de bielle) ; bague *f* (d'excentrique). *Mec.E :* Ruban *m*, bande (de frein). **'strap brake**, *s.* Frein *m* à sangle, à bande, à ruban. **'strap-fork**, *s. Mec.E :* Fourche *f* de débrayage. **'strap-hang**, *v.i. F :* Voyager debout (en se tenant à la courroie). **'strap hinge**, *s.* Penture *f.* **'strap iron**, *s.* (Fer) feuillard *m.* **'strap-oil**, *s. F :* Huile *f* de cotret. To give s.o. a little strap-oil, administrer une raclée à qn.

strap², *v.tr.* (strapped [strapt]) I. To strap sth. (up), attacher, lier, qch. avec une courroie ; cercler (une caisse) ; sangler (un paquet). 2. *Scot :* Administrer une correction à (un enfant) avec le bout d'une courroie. 3. *Med :* Mettre des bandelettes, de l'emplâtre adhésif, à (une blessure). **strapping¹**, *a. F :* Strapping fellow, grand gaillard ; gaillard solide ; jeune homme bien découplé. Tall s. lass, beau brin de fille. **strapping²**, *s.* I. Correction (administrée avec une courroie). 2. (*a*) Courroies *fpl*, liens *mpl*, armatures *fpl.* (*b*) *Med :* Emplâtre adhésif. (*c*) *Dressm :* Bandes *fpl.*

straphanger ['straphaŋər], *s. F :* Voyageur *m* debout (dans un autobus, etc.).

strata ['streitə]. See STRATUM.

stratagem ['stratədʒem], *s.* Ruse *f* (de guerre) ; stratagème *m.*

strategic(al) [strə'ti:dʒik(əl)], *a.* Stratégique. -ally, *adv.* Stratégiquement.

strategist ['stratədʒist], *s.* Stratégiste *m.*

strategy ['stratədʒi], *s.* Stratégie *f.*

strathspey [straθ'spei], *s.* Branle écossais (dansé par deux personnes).

stratification [stratifi'keiʃ(ə)n], *s.* Stratifica-tion *f.*

stratify ['stratifai], *v.tr.* Stratifier.

stratosphere ['stratosfi:ər], *s.* Stratosphère *f.*

stratum, *pl.* **-a** ['streitəm, -a], *s. Geol :* Strate *f*, couche *f*, gisement *m* ; gîte *m* (de minerai, etc.). *F :* Social strata, étages *m* de la société ; couches sociales.

stratus ['streitəs], *s. Meteor :* Stratus *m.*

straw [strɔ:], *s.* **1.** Paille *f. Loose s.,* paille de litière. *F :* Man of straw, homme de paille, de carton. Straw roof, toiture en paille. Straw case (*for bottle*), paillon *m.* **2.** Paille ; chalumeau *m.* To drink lemonade through a straw, boire de la limonade avec une paille. *F :* It is not worth a straw, cela ne vaut pas un fétu. *F :* To cling to a straw, se raccrocher à un brin d'herbe. Straw in the wind, indication *f* d'où vient le vent. It's the last straw! c'est le comble ! il ne manquait plus que cela ! **'straw-board,** *s.* Carton *m* paille. **'straw-'bottomed,** *a.* A fond de paille ; (chaise) de paille. **'straw-coloured,** *a.* (Jaune) paille *inv.* **'straw 'hat,** *s.* Chapeau *m* de paille ; (*boating*) canotier *m*, régate *f.* **'straw 'mat,** *s.* Paillasson *m.* **'straw 'mattress,** *s.* Paillasse *f.* **'straw 'vote,** *s. Pol :* Vote *m* d'essai pour se rendre compte des tendances de l'opinion. **'straw-yard,** *s.* Pailler *m.*

strawberry ['strɔ:bəri], *s.* (i) Fraise *f* ;· (ii) (*plant*) fraisier *m.* Wild strawberry, (petite) fraise des bois. Strawberry jam, confiture de fraises. Strawberry ice, glace à la fraise. **'strawberry mark,** *s.* Fraise *f* (sur la peau) ; tache *f* de vin (congénitale). **'strawberry-tree,** *s.* Arbousier commun.

stray[1] [strei]. 1. *s.* **1.** (*a*) Animal égaré ; bête perdue. (*b*) Waifs and strays, enfants moralement abandonnés. **2.** *El :* (*a*) Dispersion *f.* (*b*) *pl. W.Tel :* Bruissements *m* parasites ; (bruits *m* de) friture *f.* II. **stray,** *a.* **1.** (*Of animal*) Égaré, errant. **2.** *S. bullets,* balles perdues. *S. thoughts,* pensées détachées. *A few s. houses,* quelques maisons isolées, éparses.

stray[2], *v.i.* (*a*) S'égarer, errer ; (*of sheep*) s'écarter du troupeau. *To s. from the right path,* s'écarter du bon chemin ; se dévoyer. To let one's thoughts stray, laisser vaguer ses pensées. (*b*) *El :* (*Of current*) Se disperser.

streak[1] [stri:k], *s.* **1.** Raie *f*, rayure *f*, bande *f*, strie *f* ; sillon *m* (de feu) ; trait *m*, filet *m* (de lumière) ; coulée *f* (de soleil). The first streak of dawn, la première lueur du jour. *F :* The silver streak, la Manche. Like a streak of lightning, comme un éclair. **2.** Streak of ore, bande, filon *m*, de minerai. There is in him a streak of Irish blood, il y a en lui une trace de ᵇsang irlandais. *There was a yellow streak in him,* il y avait de la lâcheté dans sa nature. A streak of irony, une pointe, un filet, d'ironie.

streak[2]. **1.** *v.tr.* Rayer, strier, zébrer. *Sky streaked with shooting stars,* ciel sillonné d'étoiles filantes. *Panes streaked with water,* vitres hachurées d'eau. **2.** *v.i. F :* Passer comme un éclair. *He streaked off,* il se sauva à toutes jambes.

streaky ['stri:ki], *a.* **1.** En raies, en bandes. **2.** Rayé, strié, zébré. *Tex :* Vergé. *Geol :* Rubané. **3.** (*Of bacon*) Entrelardé.

stream[1] [stri:m], *s.* **1.** (*a*) Cours *m* d'eau ; fleuve *m*, rivière *f.* (*b*) Ruisseau *m.* (*c*) Flot *m* (d'eau) ; ruissellement *m. In a thin s.,* en mince filet. **2.** Coulée *f* (de lave) ; flot(s), jet *m* (de lumière, de sang). *S. of abuse,* torrent *m* d'injures. *People entered in streams,* les gens entraient à flots. *S. of cars,* défilé ininterrompu de voitures. In one

continuous stream, à jet continu. **3.** Courant *m.* With the stream, dans le sens du courant ; au fil de l'eau. Against the stream, à contre-courant. **'stream-line**[1], *s.* **1.** Courant naturel (d'un fluide). **2.** *Aut : Av :* Ligne fuyante, fuselée. Stream-line body, carrosserie profilée, carénée. **'stream-line**[2], *v.tr.* Caréner (une auto, etc.). **stream-lined,** *a.* Caréné, fuselé, profilé. *S.-l. fuselage,* fuselage aérodynamique.

stream[2]. **1.** *v.i.* (*a*) (*Of liquid*) Couler (à flots) ; ruisseler. *The fugitives were streaming over the meadows,* les fuyards traversaient les prés à flot continu. (*b*) (*Of hair, banner*) Flotter (au vent). **2.** *v.tr.* (*a*) Verser à flots, laisser couler (un liquide). (*b*) *Nau :* Mouiller (une bouée). *S.a.* LOG[1] **2. stream forth,** *v.i.* Jaillir. **stream in,** *v.i.* (*Of sunlight*) Pénétrer à flots ; (*of crowd*) entrer à flots. **stream out,** *v.i.* Sortir à flots. **streaming,** *a.* Ruisselant. Face streaming with tears, visage inondé de larmes. To be streaming with perspiration, être en nage.

streamer ['stri:mər], *s.* Banderole *f. Nau :* Flamme *f.* (Paper) streamers, serpentins *m.*

street [stri:t], *s.* (*a*) Rue *f. The main streets,* les grandes artères. *F :* To turn s.o. into the streets, mettre qn sur le pavé. To walk the streets, courir les rues ; battre le pavé. The man in the street, l'homme moyen ; le grand public. *F :* Not to be in the same street with s.o., n'être pas de taille avec qn. He is streets above you, il vous dépasse du tout au tout. Street level, rez-de-chaussée *m inv.* Street accidents, accidents de la circulation. Street cries, cris des marchands ambulants. Street musician, musicien de carrefour. (*b*) (*Opposed to footway*) La chaussée. **street-'arab,** *s.* Gamin *m* des rues ; (*in Fr.*) gavroche *m.* **'street-'door,** *s.* Porte *f* sur la rue ; porte d'entrée. **'street-'guide,** *s.* Indicateur *m* des rues. **'street-'lamp,** *s.* Réverbère *m.* **street-'lighting,** *s.* Éclairage *m* des rues.

strength [streŋθ], *s.* **1.** (*a*) Force(s) *f(pl). S. of body,* force corporelle. *S. of a current,* force d'un courant ; *El :* intensité *f* d'un courant. *Art :* S. of a colour, intensité d'une couleur. Alcoholic strength, teneur *f* en alcool. *Ch :* Strength of a solution, titre *m* d'une solution. Strength of mind, fermeté *f* d'esprit. Strength of will, résolution *f.* By sheer strength, de vive force. To recover, regain, strength, reprendre des forces ; se retremper. On the strength of . . ., sur la foi de . . ., se fiant à. . . . (*b*) Solidité *f* ; rigidité *f*, résistance *f* (d'une poutre, etc.) ; robustesse *f* (d'un meuble). *Mec :* Breaking strength, ultimate strength, résistance à la rupture ; résistance limite. **2.** To be present in great strength, être présents en grand nombre. **3.** *Mil :* Effectif(s) *m(pl)* (d'un régiment). Fighting strength, effectif mobilisable. To bring a battalion up to strength, compléter un bataillon. Squadron at full strength, escadron au grand complet. To be taken on the strength, être porté sur les contrôles. Not on the strength, hors cadre. To strike s.o. off the strength, rayer qn des cadres.

strengthen ['streŋθ(ə)n], *v.tr.* Consolider, assurer (un mur) ; renforcer (une poutre) ; fortifier (qn, le corps) ; (r)affermir (l'autorité de qn). *To s. a solution,* augmenter la concentration d'une solution. **strengthening**[1], *a.* Fortifiant ; (*of drink, etc.*) remontant. **strengthening**[2], *s.* Renforcement *m*, renforçage *m* ; consolidation *f* ; armement *m* (d'une poutre, etc.). Strengthening piece, renfort *m.*

strenuous ['strenjuəs], *a.* **1.** (*Of pers.*) Actif, agissant, énergique. **2.** (Travail) acharné, ardu ; (effort) tendu. *S. profession,* métier où l'on peine beaucoup. *S. life,* vie toute d'effort. *To offer s. opposition,* faire une opposition vigoureuse (*to,* à). **-ly,** *adv.* Vigoureusement ; avec acharnement ; énergiquement.

strenuousness ['strenjuəsnəs], *s.* Ardeur *f,* vigueur *f ;* acharnement *m.*

stress[1] [stres], *s.* **1.** Force *f,* contrainte *f.* Stress of weather, gros temps. Under stress of poverty, poussé par la misère. **2.** (*a*) *Mec:* Effort (subi) ; tension *f,* travail *m.* **Stress diagram,** épure *f* des efforts. **Bending stress,** effort de flexion. (*Of beam*) **To be in stress,** travailler. (*b*) Period of storm and stress, période de trouble et d'agitation. **3.** (*a*) Insistance *f.* To lay stress on a faet, insister sur un fait ; faire ressortir un fait. *To lay s. on a word, on a syllable,* peser sur un mot ; appuyer sur une syllabe. (*b*) *Ling:* **Stress (-aceent),** accent *m* (d'intensité) ; accent tonique. **'stress-mark,** *s. Ling:* Accent écrit.

stress², *v.tr.* **1.** *Mec:* Charger, fatiguer, faire travailler (une poutre, etc.). **2.** Appuyer, insister, sur (qch.) ; faire ressortir (un fait) ; souligner, peser sur (un mot) ; accentuer (une syllabe). *Mus: To s. the melody,* faire sentir la mélodie ; faire ressortir le chant.

stretch[1] [stret∫], *s.* **1.** (*a*) Allongement *m,* extension *f. S. of the arm,* extension du bras. *Rac:* **At full stretch,** à toute allure ; ventre à terre. (*b*) Allongement ou élargissement *m* par traction ; tension *f,* étirage *m. F:* **By a stretch of the imagination,** par un effort d'imagination. (*c*) Étendue *f,* portée *f* (du bras, etc.). **Stretch of wing,** envergure *f.* (*d*) Élasticité *f.* **2.** (*a*) Étendue (de pays, d'eau). **Level stretch** (*of road*), palier *m. Rac:* The (home-)stretch, la ligne droite. (*b*) For a long stretch of time, longtemps. *F:* At a stretch, (tout) d'un trait, (tout) d'une traite ; d'arrache-pied, d'affilée. *He has been working for hours at a s.,* voilà des heures qu'il travaille sans désemparer, sans débrider. *P:* He is doing his stretch, il tire, fait, de la prison.

stretch². **1.** *v.tr.* (*a*) Tendre (de l'élastique) ; tendre, tirer, bander (un câble, un ressort) ; élargir (des souliers) ; détirer (le linge). (*b*) **To stretch** (oneself), s'étirer. **To stretch one's legs,** se dégourdir, se dérouiller, les jambes. **Stretched on the ground,** étendu de tout son long par terre. (*c*) Forcer (le sens d'un mot, etc.). *To s. a privilege,* abuser d'un privilège. **To stretch veraeity too far,** outrepasser les bornes de la vérité. *F:* **To stretch a point,** faire une concession. **2.** *v.i.* (*a*) S'élargir ou s'allonger ; (*of elastic*) s'étendre ; (*of gloves*) s'élargir. *Material that stretches,* étoffe qui prête. (*b*) S'étendre. *The valley stretches southward,* la vallée s'étend, se déroule, vers le sud. **stretch out.** **1.** *v.tr.* (*a*) Allonger (le bras). **To stretch s.o. out** (on the ground), (i) étendre qn par terre tout de son long ; (ii) assommer qn raide. (*b*) Tendre, avancer (la main). *Abs.* **To stretch out to reach sth.,** tendre la main pour atteindre qch. **2.** *v.i.* (*Of column on the march, etc.*) S'étirer.

stretcher ['stret∫ər], *s.* **1.** (*a*) Tendeur *m ;* tenseur *m* (de hauban). **Trouser-stretcher,** extenseur *m. S.a.* GLOVE-STRETCHER. (*b*) *Art:* Canvas-stretcher, châssis *m* (de toile). **2.** (*a*) Bois *m* d'écartement (de hamac) ; traverse *f* (de tente) ; arc-boutant (d'un parapluie). (*b*) Barreau *m,* bâton *m* (de chaise). **3.** Brancard *m,* civière *f.* **4.** *Row:* Marchepied *m,* barre *f* des pieds, traversin *m.* **5.** (*In masonry*) Carreau *m ;*

panneresse *f.* **Stretcher-bond,** appareil *m* en panneresses. **'stretcher-bearer,** *s.* Brancardier *m,* ambulancier *m.* **'stretcher-party,** *s.* Détachement *m* de brancardiers.

strew [stru:], *v.tr.* (*p.p.* strewed [stru:d] *or* strewn [stru:n]) **1.** To strew sand over the floor, jeter, répandre, du sable sur le plancher. *Fragments strewn about the pavement,* débris qui jonchent le pavé. **2.** To strew the floor with flowers, joncher, parsemer, le plancher de fleurs. *The ground was strewn with rushes,* une jonchée de roseaux recouvrait le sol.

stria, *pl.* **-ae** ['straia, -iː], *s.* Strie *f,* striure *f.*

striated [strai'eitid], *a.* Strié.

stricken [strikn]. See STRIKE².

strickle [strikl], *s.* **1.** *Meas:* Racloire *f.* **2.** *Metall:* Trousse *f,* gabarit *m.*

strict [strikt], *a.* **1.** Exact ; strict. (*a*) Précis. In the strictest sense of the word, au sens précis, dans le sens le plus étroit, du mot. (*b*) Rigoureux. *S. neutrality,* neutralité rigoureuse. **In strictest confidence,** à titre tout à fait confidentiel. **2.** *S. orders,* ordres formels. **Strict discipline,** discipline sévère. *S. etiquette,* étiquette rigide. *Jur:* **Strict time-limit,** délai péremptoire. **3.** (*Of pers.*) Sévère. **To be strict with s.o.,** être sévère avec, envers, pour, qn ; traiter qn avec beaucoup de rigueur. **-ly,** *adv.* **1.** Exactement, rigoureusement. **Strictly speaking,** à proprement parler. **2.** Étroitement ; strictement. **Smoking** (is) strictly prohibited, défense formelle, défense expresse, de fumer. *It is s. forbidden,* c'est absolument défendu. **3.** Sévèrement ; (élevé) avec rigueur.

strictness ['striktnəs], *s.* **1.** Exactitude rigoureuse, précision *f* (d'une traduction). **2.** Rigueur *f* (des règles) ; sévérité *f* (de la discipline).

stricture ['strikt∫ər], *s.* **1.** *Med:* Rétrécissement *m ;* étranglement *m* (de l'intestin). **2.** To pass strictures (up)on sth., exercer sa critique sur qch. ; trouver à redire à qch.

stride[1] [straid], *s.* (Grand) pas ; enjambée *f. F:* To make great strides, faire de grands progrès. **To take sth. in one's stride,** faire qch. sans le moindre effort. **To get into one's stride,** prendre son allure normale ; attraper la cadence (d'un travail).

stride², *v.* (strode [stroud] ; stridden [stridn]) **1.** *v.i.* (*a*) To stride along, avancer à grands pas, à grandes enjambées. **To stride away,** s'éloigner à grands pas. *To s. up and down the room,* arpenter la salle. *F: Science is striding ahead,* la science avance à pas de géant. (*b*) **To stride over** sth., enjamber qch. **2.** *v.tr.* (*a*) Arpenter (les rues). (*b*) Enjamber (un fossé).

stridency ['straidənsi], *s.* Stridence *f.*

strident ['straidənt], *a.* Strident.

stridulate ['stridjuleit], *v.i.* (*Of insect*) Striduler.

stridulation [stridju'leiʃ(ə)n], *s.* Stridulation *f.*

strife [straif], *s.* Lutte *f.* To be at strife, être en conflit, en lutte (*with,* avec). **To cease from strife,** mettre bas les armes.

strike[1] [straik], *s.* **1.** Coup (frappé). **2.** *Ind:* Grève *f.* To go, to come out, on strike, se mettre en grève. **To be on strike,** faire grève, être en grève. **3.** *Min:* Rencontre *f* (de minerai, de pétrole). *F:* **Lucky strike,** coup de veine. **4.** *Geol:* Direction *f* (d'un filon). **5.** = STRICKLE. **'strike-breaker,** *s. Ind:* Renard *m,* jaune *m.*

strike², *v.* (struck [strʌk] ; struck, *A:* stricken [strikn]) I. *v.tr. & ind.tr.* **1.** (*a*) Frapper. *Jur:* Porter la main sur (qn). **To strike at s.o.,** porter un coup à qn. *S.a.* BLOW⁵ **1.** (*Of ship*) To be struck by a heavy sea, essuyer un coup de mer.

Abs. **To strike home,** frapper juste ; porter coup. *To s. one's fist on the table,* frapper du poing sur la table. *Nau :* To strike the hour, piquer l'heure. *Prov :* Strike while the iron is hot, il faut battre le fer quand il est chaud. (*b*) Frapper (une monnaie, une médaille). (*c*) Frapper (les touches du piano) ; toucher de (la harpe). **To strike a chord,** plaquer un accord. (*d*) **To strike a bargain,** faire, conclure, un marché. **2.** (*a*) **To strike sparks from a flint,** faire jaillir des étincelles d'un silex. **To strike a match,** a light, frotter une allumette. (*b*) *El :* **To strike the arc,** amorcer l'arc (entre les charbons). **3.** (*a*) **To strike a knife into s.o.'s heart,** enfoncer un couteau dans le cœur de qn. *Abs.* (*Of serpent*) To strike, foncer. **To strike terror into s.o.,** frapper qn de terreur. **The plant strikes root,** abs. strikes, la plante prend racine ; la plante prend. (*b*) *Fish :* Ferrer, piquer (le poisson). **4. To strike s.o. with wonder,** frapper qn d'étonnement. *Struck with terror,* saisi d'effroi. *S.a.* DUMB I, LIGHTNING. **5.** Percer ; pénétrer. *The rays s. through the mist,* les rayons percent le brouillard. **6.** (*a*) **To strike (against) sth.,** heurter, donner, buter, contre qch. *His head struck the pavement,* sa tête a porté sur le trottoir. (*Of ship*) **To strike (the) bottom,** abs. to strike, toucher (le fond) ; talonner. *To s. a mine,* heurter une mine. *The ship strikes (on) the rocks,* le navire donne, touche, sur les écueils. *A sound struck my ear,* un bruit me frappa l'oreille. **The thought strikes me that . . .,** l'idée me vient que. . . . (*b*) **How did she strike you?** quelle impression vous a-t-elle faite ? *He strikes me as (being) sincere,* il me paraît sincère. *That is how it struck me,* voilà l'effet que cela m'a fait. *It strikes me that . . .,* il me semble, il me paraît, que. . . . (*c*) Faire impression à (qn) ; impressionner (qn) ; frapper (l'œil, l'imagination). *What struck me was . . .,* ce qui m'a frappé, c'est. . . . **To get struck on s.o.,** s'enticher de qn. **7.** Tomber sur, découvrir (une piste, etc.). **To strike oil,** (i) rencontrer, toucher, le pétrole ; (ii) *F :* faire une bonne affaire ; trouver le filon. *He has struck it rich,* il tient le filon. *I struck upon an idea,* j'ai eu une idée. **8.** (*a*) *Nau :* Amener (une voile) ; abaisser (un mât). **To strike one's flag,** one's colours, amener, baisser, son pavillon. (*b*) **To strike tents,** abattre, plier, les tentes. **To strike camp,** lever le camp. (*c*) *Const :* **To strike the centre of an arch,** décintrer une voûte. **9.** *Ind :* **To strike work,** abs. to strike, se mettre en grève. **10. To strike an attitude,** prendre une attitude dramatique ; poser. **11.** (*a*) Tirer (une ligne) ; décrire (un cercle). (*b*) **To strike an average,** établir, prendre, une moyenne. *S.a.* BALANCE[1] 3. **II. strike,** *v.i.* **1.** (*Of clock*) Sonner. *The clock struck six,* six heures sonnèrent. *It has just struck ten,* dix heures viennent de sonner. *His hour has struck,* son heure est sonnée, a sonné. **2. To strike across country,** prendre à travers champs. *To s. into the jungle,* s'enfoncer, pénétrer, dans la jungle. *The road strikes off to the right,* la route tourne à droite. **strike down,** *v.tr.* Abattre, renverser (d'un coup de poing, etc.). *He was struck down by apoplexy,* l'apoplexie l'a foudroyé. *Stricken down by disease,* terrassé par la maladie. **strike in. 1.** *v.tr.* Enfoncer (un clou). **2.** *v.i.* (*Of pers.*) S'interposer (dans une querelle). *She struck in with the remark that . . .,* elle est intervenue pour faire observer que. . . . **strike off,** *v.tr.* **1.** Trancher, abattre (la tête de qn). **2. To strike a name off a list,** rayer, radier, un nom d'une liste. *S.a.* ROLL[1] 2. **3.** *Typ :* Tirer

(tant d'exemplaires). **strike out. 1.** *v.tr.* (*a*) Rayer, radier, biffer, barrer (un mot) ; retrancher (un passage). (*b*) Faire jaillir (des étincelles). (*c*) Tracer, ouvrir (une route). **2.** *v.i.* (*a*) **To strike out at s.o.,** allonger un coup à qn. (*b*) **I struck out for the shore,** je me mis à nager dans la direction du rivage. (*c*) *F :* **To strike out for oneself,** voler de ses propres ailes. **strike up,** *v.tr.* **1.** Entonner (une chanson) ; commencer de jouer (un morceau). *Abs. On his arrival* the band struck up, à son arrivée la fanfare attaqua un morceau. **2. To strike up an acquaintance, a friendship, with s.o.,** lier connaissance avec qn ; se lier d'amitié avec qn. **stricken,** *a.* **1.** *Ven :* (Daim) blessé. **2.** Stricken with grief, accablé de douleur ; en proie à la douleur. *S. with fever,* atteint d'une fièvre. **3.** *A :* Stricken in years, avancé en âge ; *Lit :* écrasé sous le poids des ans. **4.** *A :* Stricken field, champ *m* de carnage. **5.** Stricken measure, mesure rase. **striking**[1], *a.* **1.** Striking clock, pendule à sonnerie ; horloge sonnante. **2.** (Spectacle) remarquable, frappant, saisissant ; (trait) saillant. **-ly,** *adv.* *S. beautiful,* d'une beauté frappante. **striking**[2], *s.* **1.** (*a*) Frappement *m* ; coups *mpl.* *Within striking distance,* à portée ; à (la) portée de la main. *Row:* Rate of striking, cadence *f* de nage. (*b*) Frappe *f* (de la monnaie). (*c*) *El :* Amorçage *m* (de l'arc). **2.** Striking camp, levée *f* du camp. **3.** Sonnerie *f* (d'une horloge). **Striking mechanism,** sonnerie.

striker ['straikər], *s.* **1.** Frappeur, -euse. *Ten :* Striker(-out), relanceur, -euse. **2.** *Ind :* Gréviste *mf.* **3.** (*Device*) (*Of clock*) Marteau *m* ; (*of fire-arm*) percuteur *m*.

string[1] [striŋ], *s.* **1.** (i) Ficelle *f* ; (ii) corde *f*, cordon *m.* *A ball of s.,* une pelote de ficelle. Bonnet-strings, cordons, brides *f*, de chapeau. *F :* **To have s.o. on a string,** (i) tenir qn en lisière ; (ii) se payer la tête de qn ; faire marcher qn. **To pull the strings,** tenir les fils, les ficelles. **2.** (*a*) *Strings in beans,* fils *m* des haricots. (*b*) *Anat :* Filet *m*, frein *m* (de la langue). *S.a.* HEART-STRINGS. **3.** (*a*) *Mus :* Corde. *Catgut s.,* corde à boyau. (*Of violin*) First string, E string, le mi ; la chanterelle. (*In orchestra*) The strings, les instruments *m* à cordes. (*b*) Corde (d'un arc, etc.). *Strings of a tennis-racquet,* cordes, cordage *m*, d'une raquette. *S.a.* BOW[1] 1. **4.** String of beads, (i) collier *m* ; (ii) *Ecc :* chapelet *m*. String of onions, chapelet d'oignons. String of medals, brochette *f* de décorations. *S. of vehicles,* file *f* de véhicules. *S. of barges,* train *m* de bateaux. *A long s. of tourists,* une longue procession de touristes. **'string 'bag,** *s.* Filet *m* à provisions. **'string-bean,** *s.* Haricot vert.

string[2], *v.tr.* (strung [strʌŋ] ; strung) **1.** (*a*) Mettre une ficelle, une corde, à (qch.) ; ficeler (un paquet). (*b*) Garnir (qch.) de cordes ; corder (une raquette). (*c*) Bander (un arc). *Highly strung* = HIGH-STRUNG. **3.** Enfiler (des perles). *F :* **To s. sentences together,** enfiler des phrases. **4.** *Cu :* Effiler (les haricots). **string up,** *v.tr.* **1.** Pendre (qn) haut et court. **2.** *F :* **To string oneself up to do sth.,** tendre toute sa volonté pour faire qch. **stringed,** *a.* *Mus :* (Instrument) à cordes.

stringency ['strindʒənsi], *s.* Rigueur *f*, sévérité *f* (des règles, etc.).

stringent ['strindʒənt], *a.* **1.** (Règlement) rigoureux, strict. **2.** *Fin :* (Argent) serré ; (marché) tendu.

stringer ['striŋər], *s.* **1.** (*Pers.*) Monteur *m* de cordes (d'un piano). **2.** (*a*) *Const :* Tirant *m*,

entrait *m* (d'une ferme de comble). (*b*) Longeron *m*, longrine *f*; sommier *m* (d'un pont).
stringy ['striŋi], *a.* **1.** Fibreux, filandreux. *S. meat*, viande tendineuse, filandreuse. **2.** (Liquide) visqueux, qui file.
strip[1] [strip], *s.* Bande *f* (d'étoffe, de papier). *Narrow s.*, bandelette *f. Metal s.*, ruban *m* métallique. *S. of land*, bande, langue *f*, de terrain. *Hort:* **Strip of onions**, planche *f* d'oignons. *Av:* Ground strip-signal, panneau *m. Mil:* Loading strip (*of machine-gun*), bandechargeur *f.* **'strip-iron**, *s.* (Fer) feuillard *m*; fer en barres. **'strip-wound** [waund], *a. Artil:* (Canon) rubané.
strip[2], *v.* (**stripped** [stript]) I. *v.tr.* **1.** Mettre (qn) tout nu; dépouiller (qn) de ses vêtements. **Stripped to the waist**, nu jusqu'à la ceinture; le torse nu. **2.** (*a*) To strip s.o. of sth., dépouiller qn de qch. *Trees stripped of their leaves, of their bark*, arbres dépouillés de leurs feuilles, dénudés de leur écorce. *To s. s.o. of his money*, dévaliser qn. (*b*) Dégarnir (un lit, une maison); démeubler (une maison). *El.E:* Dépouiller (un câble). *Aut:* **Stripped chassis**, châssis nu. *To s. a wall*, arracher le papier d'un mur. **Stripped tobaccoleaf**, tabac écôté. *Tex:* To strip flax, teiller le lin. *Mec.E:* To strip a nut, arracher le filet d'un écrou. *Metall:* To strip a casting, démouler une pièce coulée. **3.** To strip sth. off, from, sth., ôter, enlever, qch. de qch. II. **strip**, *v.i.* **1.** (*Of pers.*) Se dépouiller de ses vêtements; dépouiller ses vêtements; se dévêtir. **To strip to the skin**, *F:* se mettre à poil. **2.** (*Of bark, etc.*) To strip (off), s'enlever, se détacher.
stripe[1] [straip], *s.* (*a*) Raie *f*, barre *f* (d'une étoffe); raie, rayure *f*, zébrure *f* (sur le pelage). *Black with a red s.*, noir rayé de rouge. (*b*) Bande *f* (de pantalon). (*c*) *Mil: etc:* **Sergeant's stripes**, galons *m* de sergent. **Long-service stripe**, chevron *m.* **To lose one's stripes**, être dégradé.
stripe[2], *v.tr.* Rayer, barrer. **striped**, *a.* (*a*) (Chaussettes, etc.) à raies, à barres; (pelage) rayé. *Nat.Hist:* Zébré, rubané. (*b*) *Anat:* (Muscle) strié.
stripling ['striplin], *s.* Tout jeune homme; adolescent *m.*
strive [straiv], *v.i.* (**strove** [strouv]; **striven** [strivn]) **1.** To strive to do sth., tâcher, s'efforcer, de faire qch. To strive for sth., essayer d'obtenir qch. *What are you striving after?* à quoi tendent vos efforts? *To s. after effect*, rechercher l'effet. **2.** To strive with, against, s.o., lutter, se débattre, contre qn. *To . (with one another) for sth.*, se disputer qch.
strode [stroud]. *See* STRIDE[2].
stroke[1] [strouk], *s.* Coup *m.* **1.** *To receive twenty strokes*, recevoir vingt coups (de férule, etc.). **To fell a tree at a stroke**, abattre un arbre d'un seul coup. **Finishing stroke**, coup de grâce. **2.** (*a*) Coup (d'aile, d'aviron). *Bill:* etc: *Whose s. is it?* à qui de jouer? *Row:* To lengthen the stroke, allonger la nage. **'Keep stroke!'** "nagez ensemble!'' (*b*) *Swim:* Brassée *f.* **The swimming strokes**, les nages *f.* **Stroke's length**, nagée *f. S.a.* BACK-STROKE 3, BREAST-STROKE, OVERARM. (*c*) *Mec.E:* Mouvement *m*, course *f* (du piston). *I.C.E:* Two-stroke engine, moteur à deux temps. (*d*) *F: He hasn't done a s.* of work, il n'a pas fait œuvre de ses dix doigts. (*e*) **Stroke of good luck**, coup de bonheur. **Stroke of genius**, trait *m* de génie. **A good stroke of business**, une bonne affaire. **3.** Coup (d'horloge, etc.). **On the stroke of nine**, sur le coup de neuf heures; à neuf heures sonnant(es). **To arrive on the stroke (of**

time), arriver à l'heure juste. **4.** **Stroke of apoplexy**, attaque *f* d'apoplexie; coup de sang; congestion cérébrale. *F:* **To have a stroke**, tomber en apoplexie. **5.** Coup de crayon ou de pinceau; trait de plume. *Typ:* **Thin stroke**, délié *m* (d'une lettre). **Thick stroke**, plein *m.* **With a stroke of the pen**, d'un trait de plume. **6.** *Row:* (*a*) (Pers.) Chef *m* de nage. (*b*) **To row stroke**, donner la nage. **'stroke-play**, *s. Golf:* Concours *m* par coups.
stroke[2], *v.tr. Row:* To stroke a boat, être chef de nage d'un canot; donner la nage.
stroke[3], *s.* Caresse *f* de la main.
stroke[4], *v.tr.* Passer la main sur, caresser de la main (une fourrure, etc.). *To s. one's chin*, se flatter le menton. *F:* To stroke s.o. the wrong way, prendre qn à contre-poil, à rebrousse-poil. *F:* To stroke s.o. down, (i) à apaiser la colère de qn; (ii) câliner, cajoler, qn.
stroll[1] [stroul], *s.* Petit tour; bout *m* de promenade; *F:* balade *f.* **To take, go for, a stroll**, (aller) faire un tour.
stroll[2], *v.i.* Errer à l'aventure; flâner; déambuler; *F:* se balader. **strolling**, *a.* Vagabond, errant. **Strolling player**, comédien ambulant; acteur forain.
stroller ['stroulər], *s.* Flâneur, -euse; promeneur, -euse.
strong [strɔŋ], *a.* (**stronger** ['strɔŋgər]) Fort. **1.** (*a*) Solide. *S. cloth*, drap fort, solide, résistant, qui a du corps. *S. conviction*, ferme conviction. *Com:* *S. market*, marché ferme. *S. character*, caractère fort, ferme. (*b*) **Strong constitution**, tempérament robuste. **Strong nerves**, nerfs bien équilibrés. *He is not very s.*, il est peu robuste. **2.** (*a*) *S. fellow*, solide gaillard. *S. horse*, cheval vigoureux. **Strong voice**, voix forte, puissante. *S. memory*, bonne mémoire. **To be strong in the arm**, avoir le bras fort. **The strong arm of the law**, l'autorité publique. **Strong measures**, mesures énergiques. *He is s. enough to overthrow you*, il est de force, de taille, à vous renverser. **Strong in Greek**, fort en grec. **Politeness is not his strong point**, la politesse n'est pas son fort. **Strong in numbers**, en grand nombre. *Cards:* **Strong suit**, couleur longue. **Strong partisan**, partisan ardent. **He is strong against . . .**, il s'oppose énergiquement à. . . . **Company two hundred strong**, compagnie forte de deux cents hommes. **Strong evidence**, preuves convaincantes. *S. argument*, argument puissant. *S. reason*, forte raison. **Strong features**, traits accusés. *S. spring*, ressort puissant. **Strong wind**, grand vent. *El:* **Strong current**, courant intense. *Mus:* **Strong beat**, temps fort. *S.a.* LANGUAGE 2. (*b*) **Strong drink**, liqueurs fortes. **Strong solution**, solution concentrée. **Strong light**, vive lumière. (*c*) **Strong cheese**, fromage qui pique. **Strong butter**, beurre rance. (*Of food*) **To have a strong smell**, sentir fort. **3.** *Gram:* (Verbe, etc.) fort. **4.** *adv. F:* **Things are going strong**, tout marche à merveille. **Going strong?** ça marche? **-ly**, *adv.* Fortement. **1.** Solidement, fermement. **2.** Vigoureusement, énergiquement. **Strongly worded letter**, lettre en termes énergiques. **Strongly marked**, accentué, prononcé. **strong-'armed**, *a.* Aux bras forts. **'strong-box**, *s.* Coffre-fort *m.* **strong-'minded**, *a.* A l'esprit solide, résolu, décidé. *S.-m. person*, forte tête. **strong-'mindedness**, *s.* Force *f* de caractère. **'strong room**, *s.* Chambre blindée; cave *f* des coffres-forts. *Nau:* Soute *f* aux valeurs.
stronghold ['strɔŋhould], *s.* Forteresse *f*; place

forte. *F: S. of free trade*, citadelle *f* du libre-échange.

strontia ['strɔnʃja], *s. Ch:* Strontiane *f*.

strontium ['strɔnʃjəm], *s. Ch:* Strontium *m*.

strop¹ [strɔp], *s.* **1.** (Razor-)strop, cuir *m* (à rasoir). **2.** *Nau:* Estrope *f* (de poulie).

strop², *v.tr.* (stropped [strɔpt]) Affiler, repasser sur le cuir (un rasoir).

strophe ['stroufi], *s. Gr.Lit:* Strophe *f*.

strove [strouv]. *See* STRIVE.

struck [strʌk]. *See* STRIKE².

structural ['strʌktjurəl], *a.* **1.** De construction. Structural iron, steel, fer, acier, de construction; charpentes *f* métalliques. **Structural engineer,** ingénieur constructeur. **2.** Structural, -aux.

structure ['strʌktjər], *s.* **1.** Structure *f*; facture *f* (d'un drame). **2.** (*a*) Édifice *m*, structure, bâtiment *m*. (*b*) *Civ.E:* Ouvrage *m* d'art; travail, -aux *m*, d'art. *F:* **The social structure,** l'édifice social.

struggle¹ [strʌgl], *s.* Lutte *f*. **1.** *Desperate s.*, lutte désespérée; combat acharné. *He gave in without a struggle*, il n'a fait aucune résistance. **In the death struggle,** à l'agonie; dans les affres *f* de la mort. **2.** *Biol:* **The struggle for life,** la lutte pour l'existence; la concurrence vitale.

struggle², *v.i.* Lutter (*with, against,* avec, contre); se débattre, se démener. **To be struggling with adversity,** être aux prises avec l'adversité. **To struggle hard to succeed,** faire tous ses efforts, faire des pieds et des mains, pour réussir. *They s. for the prize*, ils se disputent le prix. *He struggled to his feet*, il réussit à se relever. *We struggled through*, nous avons surmonté tous les obstacles. **struggle in, out,** *v.i.* Se frayer un passage (à grand'peine). **struggling,** *a.* (Artiste) qui vit péniblement, qui cherche à percer.

struggler ['strʌglər], *s.* Lutteur *m*.

strum [strʌm], *v.tr.* (strummed) To strum, *v.i.* to strum on, the piano, the guitar, taper sur le piano; s'escrimer sur le piano; gratter de la guitare. *Abs.* To strum, pianoter. To strum a tune, tapoter un air (au piano).

struma, *pl.* **-ae** ['stru:ma, -i:], *s. Med:* Strume *f*, scrofules *fpl*; *F:* écrouelles *fpl*.

strumous ['stru:məs], *a. Med:* Strumeux, scrofuleux.

strung [strʌŋ]. *See* STRING².

strut¹ [strʌt], *s.* Démarche fière; pas mesuré.

strut², *v.i.* (strutted) To strut (about), se pavaner, se rengorger. **To strut along,** se carrer en marchant. **To strut in, out,** entrer, sortir, d'un air important.

strut³, *s.* Entretoise *f*, étrésillon *m*; montant *m*, cale *f*, support *m*, étai *m*, traverse *f*; (*spur*) arc-boutant *m*, jambe *f* de force; (*of roof-truss*) contre-fiche *f*.

strut⁴, *v.tr.* (strutted) *Const: etc:* Entretoiser, étrésillonner; étayer (une tranchée).

strychnin(e) ['strikni:n], *s.* Strychnine *f*.

stub¹ [stʌb], *s.* **1.** Souche *f* (d'arbre); chicot *m* (d'arbre, de dent); bout *m* (de crayon, de cigare); tronçon *m* (de mât); *F:* mégot *m* (de cigare). *Mec.E:* Stub teeth, denture tronquée. **2.** *Tchn:* Mentonnet *m* (de serrure). **3.** *U.S:* Souche, talon *m* (de chèque). **'stub-axle,** *s. Aut:* Fusée *f*. **'stub-iron,** *s.* Fer *m* de riblons. **'stub-mast,** *s.* Mât tronqué. **'stub-nail,** *s.* Caboche *f*.

stub², *v.tr.* (stubbed) **1.** To stub (up) roots, extirper des racines. To stub (out) a field, essoucher un champ. **2.** To stub one's toe

against sth., se cogner le pied, heurter du pied, contre qch.

stubble [stʌbl], *s.* **1.** Chaume *m*. **2.** *F:* (*a*) Barbe *f* de trois jours. (*b*) Cheveux coupés en brosse. **'stubble-field,** *s.* Chaume *m*.

stubbly ['stʌbli], *a.* **1.** (Champ) couvert de chaume. **2.** *F:* Stubbly beard, (i) barbe de trois jours; (ii) barbe courte et raide. *S. hair*, cheveux en brosse.

stubborn ['stʌbərn], *a.* **1.** Obstiné, opiniâtre, entêté, têtu; (volonté) tenace; (cheval) rétif. As stubborn as a mule, têtu comme un mulet, comme une mule. **2.** *S.* ore, minerai réfractaire. *S. fever*, fièvre rebelle. *S. soil*, terre ingrate. **-ly,** *adv.* Obstinément, opiniâtrement.

stubbornness ['stʌbərnnəs], *s.* Entêtement *m*, obstination *f*, opiniâtreté *f*; ténacité *f* (de volonté).

stubby ['stʌbi], *a.* (*Of plant, etc.*) Tronqué; (*of pers.*) trapu.

stucco¹ ['stʌko], *s. Const:* Stuc *m*. **'stucco-work,** *s.* Stucage *m*.

stucco², *v.tr.* (stuccoed) Stuquer; enduire de stuc, de stucage.

stuck [stʌk]. *See* STICK².

stud¹ [stʌd], *s.* **1.** (*a*) Clou *m* à grosse tête, clou doré (pour ornement). (*b*) Clou (de passage clouté). **2.** Collar-stud, bouton *m* de col. Shirt stud, bouton de plastron (de chemise). Stud-hole, boutonnière *f*. *S.a.* PRESS-STUD. **3.** *Tchn:* (*a*) Goujon *m*, tourillon *m*. Spring stud, verrou *m* à ressort. **Locking stud,** ergot *m* d'arrêt. (*b*) *El:* Plot *m* (de contact); goutte-de-suif *f*. **4.** *Const:* Poteau *m*, montant *m* (de cloison). **'stud-bolt,** *s.* Goujon *m*; (goujon) prisonnier *m*. **'stud-wall,** *s.* Cloison lattée et plâtrée.

stud², *v.tr.* (studded) **1.** Garnir de clous; clouter. **2.** *Const:* Établir la charpente (d'une cloison). **studded,** *a.* **1.** Garni de clous; clouté. **2.** Parsemé (*with*, de). Sky s. with stars, ciel piqué d'étoiles. *S. with jewels*, constellé de pierreries. *Style s. with metaphors*, style émaillé de métaphores.

stud³, *s.* **1.** Écurie *f* (de chasse, etc.). **2.** Breeding stud, haras *m*. **'stud-book,** *s.* Livre *m* généalogique, registre *m* (des chevaux, etc.); stud-book *m*. **'stud-farm,** *s.* Haras *m*. **'stud-horse,** *s.* Étalon *m*. **'stud-mare,** *s.* (Jument) poulinière *f*.

studding sail [stʌnsl], *s. Nau:* Bonnette *f*.

student ['stju:dənt], *s.* **1.** Étudiant, -ante. *Medical s.*, étudiant en médecine. **2. He is a great student,** il est très studieux; il étudie beaucoup.

studentship ['stju:dəntʃip], *s.* Bourse *f* d'études.

studio ['stju:dio], *s. Art:* Atelier *m*. *Cin:* Studio *m*; théâtre *m* de prise de vues. **Broadcasting studio,** studio d'émission. **Photographer's studio,** salon *m*, atelier, de pose.

studious ['stju:diəs], *a.* **1.** (*Of pers.*) Studieux, appliqué; adonné à l'étude. **2.** Studious to do sth., attentif à, empressé à, faire qch. **With studious politeness,** avec une politesse étudiée. **-ly,** *adv.* **1.** Studieusement. **2.** Avec empressement. *He studiously avoided me*, il s'étudiait à m'éviter.

studiousness ['stju:diəsnəs], *s.* **1.** Studiosité *f*; attachement *m* à l'étude. **2.** Empressement *m* (*in doing sth.*, à faire qch.).

study¹ ['stʌdi], *s.* **1.** Soin(s) *m(pl)*, attention *f*. *It shall be my whole s. to please you*, je mettrai tous mes soins à vous plaire. *He made a s. of my health*, il s'occupait soigneusement de ma santé. **2.** Brown study, rêverie *f*. **To be (lost) in a brown study,** être plongé, absorbé, dans ses réflexions,

50

dans de vagues rêveries. **3.** Étude *f. The s. of mathematics*, l'étude des mathématiques. **To make a study of sth.**, étudier qch. **To finish one's studies**, achever ses études. **4.** *Art: Mus:* Étude. **5.** (*a*) Cabinet *m* de travail. (*b*) *Sch:* Salle *f* d'étude.

study², *v.tr.* (studied) **I.** Étudier; observer (les astres); faire des études de (philologie). *He had studied under Bopp*, il avait suivi les cours de Bopp. **To study for the bar**, faire son droit. **To study for an examination**, préparer un examen. **2.** S'occuper de, se préoccuper de (qn, qch.). *To s. economy*, viser à l'économie. **3.** S'étudier, s'appliquer, chercher (*to do sth.*, à faire qch.). **studied**, *a.* **I.** Étudié, recherché; prémédité, calculé. *S. carelessness*, négligence voulue. **2.** (*Of pers.*) Instruit, versé (*in*, dans).

stuff¹ [stʌf], *s.* **I.** (*a*) Matière *f*, substance *f*, étoffe *f*. **Garden stuff**, légumes *mpl*, jardinage *m. Carp:* Thick stuff, planches *fpl* de doublage. *Nau:* Small stuff, merlin *m*. **He is of the stuff that heroes are made of**, il est du bois, de la pâte, dont on fait les héros. *You will see what s. I am made of*, vous verrez de quel bois je me chauffe. *There is good s. in him*, il a de l'étoffe. *F:* That's the stuff! c'est du bon! *That's the s. to give him!* c'est comme ça qu'il faut le traiter. *S.a.* HOT 1. (*b*) *F:* Fatras *m. Old s.*, vieilleries *fpl. Silly s.*, sottises *fpl*, balivernes *fpl*. **Stuff and nonsense!** quelle bêtise! allons donc! **2.** *Tex:* Étoffe *f*, tissu *m* (dè laine). *Jur:* A stuff gownsman, un avocat en second (qui ne porte pas de soie).

stuff², *v.tr.* **I.** (*a*) Bourrer (with, de); rembourrer (un meuble). *To s. a child with cakes*, bourrer un enfant de gâteaux. *F:* To stuff (oneself), se bourrer; bâfrer. (*b*) *Cu:* Farcir (une volaille). (*c*) *F:* To stuff s.o. for an exam, chauffer qn en vue d'un examen. (*d*) Empailler (un animal). **2.** *F:* To stuff s.o. (up), bourrer le crâne à qn; faire marcher qn. **3.** To stuff up a hole, boucher un trou. *My nose is stuffed up*, je suis enchifrené. **4.** To stuff sth. into sth., fourrer qch. dans qch. **stuffing**, *s.* **I.** (*a*) Bourrage *m*, rembourrage *m*. (*b*) Empaillage *m*. **2.** (*a*) Bourre *f. Mch:* Garniture *f*, étoupe *f. F:* To knock the stuffing out of s.o., flanquer une tripotée à qn. **To take the stuffing out of s.o.**, dégonfler qn. (*b*) *Cu:* Farce *f.* **'stuffing-box**, *s. Mch:* Boîte *f* à étoupe; presse-étoupe *m inv.*

stuffiness ['stʌfinəs], *s.* Manque *m* d'air; odeur *f* de renfermé.

stuffy ['stʌfi], *a.* **I.** Mal ventilé; mal aéré. *Room that smells s.*, pièce qui sent le renfermé. **2.** *F:* Collet monté *inv*; aux préjugés vieillots.

stultify ['stʌltifai], *v.tr.* **I.** Enlever toute valeur à (un argument); infirmer (un décret); rendre inutile (une mesure). **2.** Rendre ridicule (qn); faire ressortir l'absurdité (d'une action). *Jur:* To stultify oneself, se démentir.

stumble¹ [stʌmbl], *s.* Trébuchement *m*; faux pas; bronchement *m* (d'un cheval).

stumble², *v.i.* **I.** Trébucher; faire un faux pas; (*of horse*) broncher. **To stumble along**, avancer en trébuchant. **To stumble over sth.**, buter contre qch. *That is where all have stumbled*, voilà où tous ont achoppé. **2.** To stumble in one's speech, hésiter en parlant. *To s. through one's lesson*, ânonner sa leçon. **3.** To stumble across, upon, s.o., sth., rencontrer qn, qch., par hasard; tomber sur qn, qch. **'stumbling-block**, *s.* Pierre *f* d'achoppement.

stumer ['stju:mər], *s. F:* **I.** (*a*) Chèque *m* sans

provision. (*b*) Faux billet de banque. **2.** Chose qui ne vaut rien.

stump¹ [stʌmp], *s.* **I.** (*a*) Tronçon *m*, souche *f* (d'arbre); chicot *m* (de dent); moignon *m* (de bras, de jambe); bout *m* (de cigare, de crayon); tronçon (de queue, de mât); trognon *m* (de chou). (*b*) Jambe *f* de bois. **2.** *pl. F:* Jambes. **You must stir your stumps**, il faut vous remuer. **3.** *F:* To be on the stump, être en tournée électorale. **Stump orator**, orateur de carrefour; harangueur *m*. **4.** *Cr:* Piquet *m* (du guichet). **To draw stumps**, cesser la partie. **5.** *Draw:* Estompe *f*.

stump². **I.** *v.i.* To stump along, clopiner. **To stump in, out**, entrer, sortir, clopin-clopant. **2.** *v.tr.* (*a*) *F:* Coller (un candidat); réduire (qn) à quia. **This fairly stumped me**, sur le coup je n'ai su que répondre. (*b*) *Cr:* Mettre hors jeu (un batteur qui est sorti de son camp). (*c*) *Draw:* Estomper (un dessin). **stump up**, *v.i. F:* Payer, casquer, s'exécuter.

stumpy ['stʌmpi], *a.* (*Of pers.*) Trapu, ragot, ramassé. **Stumpy umbrella**, tom-pouce *m*.

stun [stʌn], *v.tr.* (stunned) **I.** Étourdir, assommer. **2.** *F:* Renverser, abasourdir. *The news stunned us*, ce fut un coup de massue. **stunning**, *a.* **I.** (*a*) (Coup) étourdissant, d'assommoir. (*b*) (Malheur) accablant. **2.** *F:* Renversant, épatant, mirifique.

stung [stʌŋ]. *See* STING².

stunner ['stʌnər], *s. F:* **I.** Type épatant. *She's a s.*, elle est épatante. **2.** Chose épatante.

stunt¹ [stʌnt], *v.tr.* Arrêter (qn, qch.) dans sa croissance; rabougrir. **stunted**, *a.* (Arbre) rabougri, chétif; (esprit) noué. **To become stunted, (se) rabougrir.**

stunt², *s. F:* **I.** Coup *m* d'épate; affaire *f* de pure réclame. **2.** Tour de force. *Av:* Stunt flying, vol de virtuosité. **To perform stunts**, faire des acrobaties (en vol).

stunt³, *v.i. Av:* Faire des acrobaties (en vol).

stuntedness ['stʌntidnəs], *s.* État rabougri.

stupefaction [stju:pi'fækʃ(ə)n], *s.* Stupéfaction *f*; (*with astonishment*) stupeur *f*, ahurissement *m*.

stupefy ['stju:pifai], *v.tr.* **I.** (*a*) *Med:* Stupéfier, engourdir. (*b*) Hébéter, abrutir. *Stupefied with grief*, hébété par la douleur. **2.** *F:* Abasourdir, stupéfier. *I am absolutely stupefied (by what has happened)*, je n'en reviens pas; les bras m'en tombent.

stupendous [stju'pendəs], *a.* Prodigieux; *F:* formidable. **-ly**, *adv.* Prodigieusement.

stupid ['stju:pid], *a.* **I.** Stupide; sot, *f.* sotte. *F:* bête. **My boys are very stupid**, mes élèves ont la tête dure. *F:* Don't be stupid! un faites pas la bête! *How s. of me!* que je suis bête! **To drink oneself stupid**, s'hébéter, s'abrutir, à force de boire. **-ly**, *adv.* Stupidement, sottement; *F:* bêtement.

stupidity [stju'piditi], *s.* Stupidité *f*. (*a*) Lourdeur *f* d'esprit. (*b*) Sottise *f*, niaiserie *f*, bêtise *f*.

stupor ['stju:pər], *s.* Stupeur *f*.

sturdiness ['stə:rdinəs], *s.* **I.** Vigueur *f*, robustesse *f*. **2.** Résolution *f*, fermeté *f*.

sturdy ['stə:rdi]. **I.** *a.* (*a*) Vigoureux, robuste. (*b*) (*Of opposition, etc.*) Hardi, résolu, ferme. (*c*) *A:* Sturdy beggar, truand *m*. **2.** *s. Vet:* Tournis *m*. **-ily**, *adv.* **I.** Fortement; avec robustesse. **2.** Hardiment, vigoureusement.

sturgeon ['stə:rdʒ(ə)n], *s. Ich:* Esturgeon *m*.

stutter¹ ['stʌtər], *s.* Bégaiement *m*.

stutter², *v.i. & tr.* Bégayer, bredouiller. **stuttering¹**, *a.* Bègue. **-ly**, *adv.* En bégayant.

stuttering², *s.* Bégaiement *m*.

stutterer ['stʌtərər], *s.* Bègue *mf.*

sty¹, *pl.* **sties** [stai, star:iz], *s.* (*a*) Étable *f* (à porcs); porcherie *f.* (*b*) *F:* Taudis *m.*

sty², **stye** [stai], *s. Med:* Orgelet *m*, hordéole *m*; *F:* grain-d'orge *m.*

Stygian ['stidʒiən], *a.* Stygien. *Lit: To visit the S. shores*, visiter les rives du Styx.

style¹ [stail], *s.* **1.** (*a*) *Ant:* Style *m* (pour écrire). (*b*) *Engr:* Style, burin *m.* (*c*) *Surg:* Stylet *m* (à bouton olivaire). (*d*) (*Of sun-dial*) Style, gnomon *m.* (*e*) *Bot:* Style. **2.** (*a*) Style, manière *f*, façon *f.* **Style of living**, manière de vivre ; train *m* de maison. **To live in (grand, great) style**, mener grand train. *They drove up in s.*, ils ont fait leur entrée en grand équipage. **In good style**, dans le bon genre ; de bon goût, de bon ton. **To win in fine style**, gagner haut la main. *That's the style!* bravo! à la bonne heure! *Furniture in the Empire s.*, meubles style Empire. *In the s. of the last century*, dans le goût du siècle dernier. (*b*) Style, genre ; type *m*, modèle *m* (d'une auto). *Made in three styles*, fabriqué en trois genres, sur trois modèles. **Something in that style**, quelque chose de ce genre ; quelque chose dans ce goût-là. (*c*) **In the latest style**, de la dernière mode ; *F:* dernier cri. **3.** Style ; manière d'écrire. *Written in a humorous s.*, écrit sur un ton de plaisanterie. **Writer who lacks style**, écrivain qui n'a pas de style. **4.** Ton *m*, chic *m*, cachet *m.* **She has style**, elle a de l'allure, du chic, du genre. *There is no s. about her*, elle manque de chic. **5.** Titre *m*, nom *m* ; *Com:* raison sociale ; firme *f.* *He had assumed the s. of Colonel*, il s'était intitulé "colonel."

style², *v.tr.* Dénommer ; appeler. **To style oneself Doctor**, se donner le titre de docteur ; se faire appeler docteur.

stylet ['stailet], *s.* Stylet *m.*

stylish ['stailiʃ], *a.* Élégant, chic ; coquet, -ette ; (chapeau) habillé, qui a du chic. **-ly**, *adv.* Élégamment ; avec chic.

stylishness ['stailiʃnəs], *s.* Élégance *f*, chic *m.*

stylist ['stailist], *s. Lit:* Styliste *mf.*

stylistic [stai'listik], *a.* Du style.

stylistics [stai'listiks], *s.pl.* Stylistique *f.*

stylize ['staila:iz], *v.tr. Art:* Styliser.

stylo ['stailo], *s. F:* = STYLOGRAPH.

stylobate ['stailobeit], *s. Arch:* Stylobate *m* ; soubassement *m* (d. colonnade).

stylograph ['stailograf, -graːf], *s.* Stylograph (pen), stylographe *m*, *F:* stylo *m.*

stylus ['stailəs], *s. Ant:* Engr: Style *m.*

stymie ['staimi], *s. Golf:* = STIMY.

styptic ['stiptik], *a. & s. Med:* Styptique (*m*).

styrax ['staiəraks], *s. Bot:* Styrax *m.*

suable ['sju:əbl], *a.* Poursuivable en justice.

suasion ['sweiʒ(ə)n], *s.* Persuasion *f.* **To subject s.o. to moral suasion**, agir sur la conscience de qn.

suave [sweiv], *a.* **1.** Suave ; doux, *f.* douce. **2.** (*a*) (Accueil) affable. (*b*) *Pej:* Suave manners, manières doucereuses. **-ly**, *adv.* **1.** Suavement. **2.** (*a*) Avec affabilité. (*b*) *Pej:* Doucereusement.

suavity ['swaviti], *s.* (*a*) Affabilité *f.* (*b*) *Pej:* Politesse mielleuse.

subacetate [sʌb'asiteit], *s. Ch:* Sous-acétate *m.*

subacid [sʌb'asid], *a.* **1.** Aigrelet, -ette. **2.** (Ton) aigre-doux.

subacute [sʌbə'kju:t], *a. Med:* Subaigu, -uë.

sub-agency [sʌb'eidʒənsi], *s.* Sous-agence *f.*

sub-agent [sʌb'eidʒənt], *s.* Sous-agent *m.*

subalpine [sʌb'alpain], *a.* Subalpin.

subaltern ['sʌbaltərn], *s.* **1.** *a.* Subalterne, subordonné. **2.** *s. Mil:* Lieutenant *m* ou sous-lieutenant *m* ; subalterne *m.*

subarctic [sʌb'aːrktik], *a.* Presque arctique.

sub-charter [sʌb'tʃaːrtər], *v.tr.* Sous-affréter (un navire).

subchloride [sʌb'klɔːraid], *s. Ch:* Sous-chlorure *m.*

subclass ['sʌbklaːs], *s. Nat.Hist:* Sous-classe *f.*

subcommittee ['sʌbkomiti], *s.* Sous-comité *m* ; sous-commission *f.*

subconscious [sʌb'kɔnʃəs], *a. Psy:* Subconscient. **The subconscious self**, l'inconscient *m.* **-ly**, *adv.* Inconsciemment.

subcontract¹ [sʌb'kɔntrakt], *s.* Sous-traité *m.*

subcontract² [sʌbkon'trakt], *v.tr.* Sous-traiter (une affaire).

subcontractor [sʌbkon'traktər], *s.* Sous-entrepreneur *m*, sous-traitant *m.*

subcutaneous [sʌbkju'teinjəs], *a.* Sous-cutané.

subdeacon [sʌb'di:kən], *s. Ecc:* Sous-diacre *m.*

sub-derivative [sʌbdi'rivətiv], *s. Ling:* Dérivé *m* secondaire.

subdivide [sʌbdi'vaid]. **1.** *v.tr.* Subdiviser. **2.** *v.i.* Se subdiviser.

subdivision [sʌbdi'viʒ(ə)n], *s.* Subdivision *f* ; sous-division *f.*

subdominant [sʌb'dɔminənt], *s. Mus:* Sous-dominante *f.*

subdue [sʌb'dju:], *v.tr.* **1.** Subjuguer, soumettre, assujettir (une tribu) ; maîtriser (un incendie) ; dompter (ses passions). **2.** Adoucir (la lumière, la voix) ; assourdir (une couleur) ; amortir, atténuer (la lumière, la douleur). **subdued**, *a.* **1.** (Peuple) vaincu, subjugué. **2.** (*Of pers.*) Déprimé. **3.** **Subdued light**, demi-jour *m* ; lumière tamisée, atténuée. **Subdued conversation**, conversation à voix basse. *In a s. voice*, à voix basse ; à mi-voix. *S. satisfaction*, satisfaction contenue.

sub-edit [sʌb'edit], *v.tr. Journ:* Corriger, mettre au point (un article).

sub-editor [sʌb'editər], *s. Journ:* Secrétaire *m* de la rédaction.

sub-equatorial [sʌbekwa'tɔ:riəl], *a.* Presque sous l'équateur.

suberose ['sju:bərous], **suberous** ['sju:bərəs], *a. Bot:* Subéreux.

sub-foundation [sʌbfaun'deiʃ(ə)n], *s. Arch:* Soubassement *m.*

sub-frame ['sʌbfreim], *s. Aut:* Faux châssis.

subfusc [sʌb'fʌsk], *a. Lit:* Sombre.

subgenus, *pl.* **-genera** ['sʌbdʒi:nəs, -dʒenərə], *s. Nat.Hist:* Sous-genre *m.*

sub-heading [sʌb'hedin], *s.* Sous-titre *m.*

sub-human [sʌb'hju:mən], *a.* **1.** Pas tout à fait humain. **2.** Presque humain.

subjacent [sʌb'dʒeis(ə)nt], *a.* Sous-jacent, subjacent.

subject¹ ['sʌbdʒekt], *s.* **1.** Sujet, -ette (d'un souverain). *British s.*, sujet britannique. **2.** *Gram:* Sujet (du verbe). **3.** (*a*) Sujet (de conversation, etc.) ; objet *m* (de méditation). **Subject picture**, tableau *m* de genre. *Let us return to our subject*, revenons au sujet, à notre texte, *F:* à nos moutons. *On the subject of . . .*, au sujet de . . . . *To change the subject*, parler d'autre chose ; changer de sujet. (*b*) *Sch:* *What subjects do you teach?* quelles matières enseignez-vous? **4.** *To be a s. of experiment*, servir de sujet d'expérience. **Good hypnotic subject**, sujet facile à hypnotiser. **'subject-matter**, *s.* Sujet *m* (d'un livre) ; contenu *m* (d'une lettre) ; objet *m* (d'un contrat réel).

subject², *a.* **1.** (Pays) assujetti, soumis (to, à) ; sous la dépendance (to, de). **Subject to the laws of nature**, soumis aux lois de la nature. *S. to*

military law, justiciable des tribunaux militaires.
2. (*a*) Sujet, exposé (à des accès de fièvre, etc.).
He is s. to extraordinary whims, il lui prend des
lubies impossibles. (*b*) **Prices subject to** 5%
discount, prix qui comportent 5% d'escompte.
Subject to stamp duty, passible du droit de timbre. *The plan is s. to modifications*, ce projet
pourra subir des modifications. **3.** (*Conditional*)
S. to ratification, sous réserve de ratification.
Subject to alteration, sauf nouvel avis ; sauf
correction.
subject³ [sʌb'dʒekt], *v.tr.* **1.** Assujettir, subjuguer (un peuple). **2.** *To s. s.o. to an operation*,
soumettre qn à une opération. **To subject s.o.**,
sth., to an examination, faire subir un examen
à qn ; soumettre qch. à un examen. **To subject**
s.o. to criticism, critiquer qn. **To be subjected**
to much criticism, être en butte à de nombreuses
critiques.
subjection [sʌb'dʒekʃ(ə)n], *s.* Sujétion *f*, soumission *f*, assujettissement *m* (*to*, à). **To hold**
s.o. in subjection, tenir qn sous sa dépendance.
To be in s. to s.o., être soumis à qn. **To bring**
into subjection, soumettre, assujettir.
subjective [sʌb'dʒektiv], *a.* **1.** *Phil :* Subjectif.
2. *Gram :* **The subjective case**, le cas sujet ; le
nominatif. **-ly,** *adv.* Subjectivement.
subjoin [sʌb'dʒɔin], *v.tr.* Ajouter, adjoindre
(une liste, etc.). *The subjoined details*, les détails
ci-joints.
subjugate ['sʌbdʒugeit], *v.tr.* Subjuguer, soumettre, assujettir (un peuple) ; dompter (un
animal, ses passions).
subjugation [sʌbdʒu'geiʃ(ə)n], *s.* Subjugation *f*,
assujettissement *m*.
subjunctive [sʌb'dʒʌŋktiv], *a. & s. Gram :*
Subjonctif (*m*). **In the subjunctive (mood)**, au
subjonctif.
sub-lease¹ ['sʌbliːs], *s.* Sous-bail *m*, sous-
location *f*.
sub-lease² [sʌb'liːs], *v.tr.* Sous-louer (un appartement) ; sous-affermer (une terre).
sub-lessee [sʌble'siː], *s.* Sous-locataire *mf*.
sub-let¹ ['sʌblet], *s.* Sous-bail *m*, sous-location *f*.
sub-let² [sʌb'let], *v.tr.* (-let ; -letting) Sous-louer
(un appartement) ; sous-affermer (une terre).
sub-librarian [sʌblai'breəriən], *s.* Sous-bibliothécaire *m*.
sub-lieutenant [sʌblef'tenənt], *s. Navy :* Enseigne *m* (de vaisseau).
sublimate¹ ['sʌblimet], *s. Ch :* Sublimé *m*.
Corrosive sublimate, sublimé corrosif.
sublimate² ['sʌblimeit], *v.tr.* **1.** Sublimer (le
soufre). **2.** Raffiner, idéaliser (un sentiment).
sublimation [sʌbli'meiʃ(ə)n], *s.* Sublimation *f*.
sublime [sʌ'blaim]. **1.** *a.* (*a*) Sublime. (*b*) *F :*
Sublime indifference, suprême indifférence. *S.*
impudence, impudence sans pareille. **2.** *s.* **The**
sublime, le sublime. **-ly,** *adv.* **1.** Sublimement.
2. *F :* **To be sublimely unconscious of . . .**,
être dans une ignorance absolue de. . . .
subliminal [sʌb'limin(ə)l], *a. Psy :* Subliminal,
-aux.
sublimity [sʌ'blimiti], *s.* Sublimité *f*.
sub-manager [sʌb'manedʒər], *s.* Sous-directeur *m*, sous-gérant *m*.
submarine ['sʌbmariːn]. **1.** *a.* Sous-marin.
2. *s.* (Navire) sous-marin *m*. **High-reserve**
submarine, submersible *m*.
submerge [sʌb'məːdʒ]. **1.** *v.tr.* (*a*) Submerger,
immerger. (*b*) Inonder, noyer (un champ).
2. *v.i.* (*Of submarine*) Plonger ; effectuer sa
plongée. **submerged,** *a.* **1.** (*a*) Submergé.
I.C.E : The jet is s., le gicleur est noyé. *S. vessel*,

vaisseau englouti par les flots. (*b*) **Submerged**
submarine, sous-marin en plongée. **Submerged**
speed, vitesse en plongée. (*c*) **Submerged reef**,
écueil sous-marin. **2.** *a. & s. F : The submerged*
(tenth), les déclassés *m*, les nécessiteux *m*.
submergence [sʌb'məːdʒəns], *s.* Submersion *f* ;
plongée *f* (d'un sous-marin).
submersible [sʌb'məːrsibl], *a.* Submersible.
submersion [sʌb'məːrʃ(ə)n], *s.* Submersion *f* ;
plongée *f*.
submission [sʌb'miʃ(ə)n], *s.* **1.** (*a*) Soumission *f*
(à une autorité) ; résignation *f* (à une défaite).
To starve s.o. into submission, réduire qn par la
famine. (*b*) Docilité *f* ; humilité *f*. **2.** Soumission
(d'une question à un arbitre). **3.** *Jur :* Plaidoirie *f*.
In my submission . . ., selon ma thèse. . . .
submissive [sʌb'misiv], *a.* Soumis, humble,
résigné. *S. to advice*, docile aux conseils donnés.
-ly, *adv.* D'un ton soumis ; avec docilité.
submissiveness [sʌb'misivnəs], *s.* Soumission *f*,
docilité *f*. *In all s.*, très humblement.
submit [sʌb'mit], *v.* (submitted) **1.** *v.i. & pr.*
Se soumettre (*to*, à) ; se plier (à une nécessité) ;
s'astreindre (à la discipline) ; se résigner (à un
malheur). **2.** *v.tr.* (*a*) Soumettre. **To submit**
sth. to s.o.'s inspection, soumettre, présenter,
qch. à l'inspection de qn. *To s. proofs of identity*,
présenter des pièces d'identité. **To submit a**
question to a court, saisir un tribunal d'une
question. (*b*) **To submit that . . .**, représenter,
alléguer, que . . . ; poser en thèse que. . . .
submultiple [sʌb'mʌltipl], *a. & s.* Sous-multiple
(*m*) (*of*, de).
subnormal [sʌb'nɔːrməl], *a.* (Température, etc.)
au-dessous de la normale.
sub-office ['sʌbɔfis], *s. Com :* Succursale *f* ;
filiale *f* ; bureau *m* auxiliaire.
suborder ['sʌbɔːrdər], *s. Nat.Hist :* Sous-
ordre *m*.
subordinate¹ [sʌ'bɔːrdinet]. **1.** *a.* (*a*) (Rang,
etc.) inférieur, subalterne ; (rôle) secondaire,
accessoire. (*b*) Subordonné (*to*, à). *Gram :*
Subordinate clause, proposition subordonnée.
2. *s.* Subordonné, -ée. **-ly,** *adv.* D'une façon
secondaire ; en sous-ordre.
subordinate² [sʌ'bɔːrdineit], *v.tr.* Subordonner
(*to*, à).
subordination [sʌbɔːrdi'neiʃ(ə)n], *s.* **1.** Subordination *f* (*to*, à). **2.** Soumission *f* (*to*, à).
suborn [sʌ'bɔːrn], *v.tr. Jur :* Suborner, corrompre, séduire (un témoin). **suborning,**
s. = SUBORNATION.
subornation [sʌbɔːr'neiʃ(ə)n], *s.* Subornation *f*,
corruption *f*, séduction *f* (de témoins).
suborner [sʌ'bɔːrnər], *s.* Suborneur *m*.
subpoena¹ [sʌb'piːna], *s. Jur :* Citation *f*,
assignation *f* (de témoins) (sous peine d'amende).
subpoena², *v.tr.* (subpoenaed) **To subpoena s.o.**
to appear, citer, assigner, qn à comparaître (sous
peine d'amende). *To s. a witness*, signifier une
assignation à un témoin.
subrent [sʌb'rent], *v.tr.* Sous-louer ; prendre
(un appartement) en sous-location.
subsalt ['sʌbsɔlt], *s. Ch :* Sous-sel *m*.
subscribe [sʌb'skraib], *v.tr.* **1.** (*a*) Souscrire
(son nom). *To s. one's name to a document*, apposer sa signature à un document. (*b*) *Abs.* To
subscribe to an opinion, souscrire à une opinion.
2. (*a*) **To subscribe ten pounds**, souscrire pour
(la somme de) dix livres. *Fin :* **To subscribe**
shares, souscrire des actions. *To s. to a loan*,
souscrire à un emprunt. **Subscribed capital**,
capital souscrit. (*b*) **To subscribe to a newspaper**,
(i) s'abonner, prendre un abonnement, à un

journal ; (ii) être abonné à un journal. (c) *Publ :* To subscribe a book, (i) (*of publisher*) offrir un livre en souscription ; (ii) (*of bookseller*) acheter un livre en souscription.

subscriber [sʌb'skraibər], *s.* **I.** Signataire *mf*, souscripteur *m* (d'un document). The subscriber, (i) le soussigné ; (ii) le contractant. **2.** Subscriber to a charity, for shares, souscripteur à une œuvre de charité, à des actions. **3.** Abonné, -ée (à un journal, etc.). Telephone subscriber, abonné au téléphone.

subscript ['sʌbskript], *a. Gr.Gram:* (Iota) souscrit.

subscription [sʌb'skripʃ(ə)n], *s.* **I.** (*a*) Souscription *f* (de son nom) ; signature *f.* (*b*) Adhésion *f* (*to*, à) ; approbation *f* (*to*, de). **2.** *To pay a s.*, verser une cotisation. To get up a subscription, se cotiser. *Fin:* Subscription to a loan, souscription à un emprunt. Subscription list, liste des souscripteurs. Subscription dance, bal par souscription. **3.** Abonnement *m* (à un journal, etc.). To take out a subscription to a paper, s'abonner à un journal. Subscription to a club, cotisation (annuelle) à un cercle.

subsequent ['sʌbsekwənt], *a.* (Chapitre, etc.) subséquent, qui suit. *At a s. meeting*, dans une séance ultérieure. Subsequent to . . ., postérieur, consécutif, à. . . . **-ly,** *adv.* Plus tard ; dans la suite ; postérieurement (*to*, à).

subserve [sʌb'sə:rv], *v.tr.* Aider à, favoriser (un but).

subservience [sʌb'sə:rviəns], *s.* **I.** Utilité *f* (*to*, à). **2.** Soumission *f*, servilité *f.* Subservience to fashion, asservissement *m* à la mode.

subservient [sʌb'sə:rviənt], *a.* **I.** Utile, qui aide (*to*, à). To make sth. s. to sth., faire servir qch. à qch. **2.** Subordonné (*to*, à). **3.** Obséquieux, servile.

subside [sʌb'said], *v.i.* **I.** (*a*) (*Of sediment*) Tomber au fond ; se précipiter. (*b*) (*Of liquid*) Déposer. **2.** (*Of ground, building*) S'affaisser, se tasser, s'enfoncer. *F:* To subside into an armchair, s'affaler, s'effondrer, dans un fauteuil. **3.** (*Of water, etc.*) Baisser. *The flood is subsiding*, la crue diminue. **4.** (*a*) (*Of storm, etc.*) S'apaiser, se calmer, tomber. (*b*) *F:* (*Of pers.*) Se taire.

subsidence ['sʌbsidəns, sʌb'saidəns], *s.* **I.** (*a*) Affaissement *m* ; dénivellation *f*, dénivellement *m* ; effondrement *m* ; tassement *m* (des fondations). (*b*) Décrue *f*, baisse *f* (d'une rivière). **2.** *Geol:* Effondrement.

subsidiary [sʌb'sidjəri], *a.* Subsidiaire, auxiliaire. *Fin:* Subsidiary company, filiale *f.* **-ily,** *adv.* Subsidiairement ; en second lieu.

subsidize ['sʌbsidaiz], *v.tr.* Subventionner ; primer (une industrie). To be subsidized by the State, recevoir une subvention de l'État.

subsidy ['sʌbsidi], *s.* Subvention *f* ; *Ind:* prime *f.*

subsist [sʌb'sist], *v.i.* Subsister. (*a*) Continuer d'être. *Custom that still subsists*, coutume qui existe encore, qui a persisté. (*b*) S'entretenir, vivre (*on*, de). To s. on vegetables, se nourrir de légumes.

subsistence [sʌb'sistəns], *s.* **I.** Existence *f.* **2.** *Means of s.*, moyens de subsistance *f.* A bare subsistence wage, un salaire à peine suffisant pour vivre.

subsoil ['sʌbsɔil], *s. Geol: Agr:* Sous-sol *m.* To sell soil and subsoil, vendre le fonds et le tréfonds.

subspecies ['sʌbspi:ʃi:z], *s. Nat.Hist:* Sous-espèce *f.*

substance ['sʌbstəns], *s.* **I.** *Phil: Ch:* Substance *f*, matière *f.* **2.** Substance, fond *m*, essentiel *m* (d'un article, d'un argument). **3.** Solidité *f. Book of s.*, livre solide. Argument of little substance, argument qui n'a rien de solide. **4.** Avoir *m*, bien *m*, fortune *f.* Man of substance, homme qui a de quoi, qui a du bien ; *F:* homme cossu.

substantial [sʌb'stanʃ(ə)l], *a.* **I.** Substantiel, réel. **2.** Important. Substantial reasons, raisons sérieuses. *S. proof*, preuve concluante. *A s. difference*, une différence appréciable, sensible. **3.** (*a*) *S. food*, nourriture substantielle. *S. meal*, repas copieux, solide. (*b*) Solide ; (drap) résistant. *S. furniture*, ameublement solide et riche. *Man of s. build*, homme bien taillé. **4.** (Bourgeois) cossu, qui a des écus ; (maison de commerce) bien assise. **-ally,** *adv.* Substantiellement. **I.** Réellement ; en substance. **2.** Solidement. **3.** Fortement. *This contributed s. to our success*, cela a contribué pour une grande part à notre succès.

substantiate [sʌb'stanʃieit], *v.tr.* Établir, justifier (une affirmation). To substantiate a claim, établir le bien-fondé d'une réclamation.

substantive ['sʌbstəntiv], **I.** *a.* (*a*) *Gram:* Substantif. (*b*) Réel, indépendant. *Jur:* Substantive law, droit positif. **2.** *s. Gram:* Substantif *m*, nom *m.* **-ly,** *adv.* Substantivement.

sub-station ['sʌbsteiʃ(ə)n], *s.* Sous-station *f* ; *El.E:* sous-centrale *f.*

substitute¹ ['sʌbstitju:t], *s.* **I.** (*Pers.*) (*a*) Suppléant, -ante ; intérimaire *mf* ; *Sp:* remplaçant. *To find a s.*, se faire suppléer. (*b*) Mandataire *mf* ; représentant. **2.** (*a*) (*Of food-stuffs, etc.*) Succédané *m* (*for*, de). *Rubber s.*, factice *m* de caoutchouc. (*b*) *Beware of substitutes*, se méfier des contrefaçons *f.*

substitute² ['sʌbstitju:t], *v.tr.* Substituer. To substitute margarine for butter, substituer la margarine au beurre ; remplacer le beurre par la margarine. **2.** *v.i.* To substitute for s.o., remplacer, suppléer, qn.

substitution [sʌbsti'tju:ʃ(ə)n], *s.* Substitution *f*, remplacement *m.* Substitution of margarine for butter, remplacement du beurre par la margarine ; substitution de la margarine au beurre.

substratum ['sʌbstreitəm, -a, -əmz], *s.* Couche inférieure ; sous-couche *f. Agr:* Sous-sol *m. F: A substratum of truth*, un fond de vérité.

substructure ['sʌbstrʌktʃər], *s. Const:* Substruction *f*, fondement *m* (d'un édifice). *Civ.E:* Infrastructure *f.* The social substructure, les bases *f* de la société.

subtangent ['sʌbtandʒənt], *s. Geom:* Soustangente *f.*

subtenant ['sʌbtenənt], *s.* Sous-locataire *mf.*

subtend [sʌb'tend], *v.tr. Geom:* Sous-tendre (un arc).

subterfuge ['sʌbtərfju:dʒ], *s.* Subterfuge *m* ; faux-fuyant *m. To resort to s.*, user de subterfuge.

subterranean [sʌbtə'reiniən], *a.* Souterrain.

subtilize ['sʌbtilaiz], **I.** *v.tr.* Subtiliser ; raffiner (son style) ; *Pej:* alambiquer (sa pensée). **2.** *v.i.* Subtiliser, raffiner ; discuter sur des vétilles.

sub-title ['sʌbtaitl], *s.* Sous-titre *m.*

subtle [sʌtl], *a.* Subtil. **I.** (*a*) (Parfum) pénétrant. (*b*) (Charme) qui échappe à l'analyse. Subtle distinction, distinction subtile. **2.** (*a*) (Esprit) fin, raffiné ; (dispositif) ingénieux. Subtle irony, fine ironie. (*b*) Rusé, astucieux. **-tly,** *adv.* Subtilement ; avec finesse.

subtlety ['sʌtlti], *s.* **I.** Subtilité *f.* (a) Raffinement *m*, finesse *f.* (b) Distinction subtile. **2.** Ruse *f*, astuce *f.*

subtract [sʌb'trakt], *v.tr.* *Mth:* Soustraire, retrancher (*from*, de).

subtraction [sʌb'trakʃ(ə)n], *s.* *Mth:* Soustraction *f.*

subulate ['sju:bjulet], *a.* *Nat.Hist:* Subulé.

suburb ['sʌbəːrb], *s.* Faubourg *m.* In the suburbs, dans la banlieue. Garden suburb, cité-jardin *f.*

suburban [sʌ'bəːrbən], *a.* Suburbain; (maison, train) de banlieue.

suburbanite [sʌ'bəːrbənait], *s.* *F:* Banlieusard, -arde.

Suburbia [sʌ'bəːrbia]. *Pr.n.* *F:* La banlieue.

subvention [sʌb'venʃ(ə)n], *s.* Subvention *f*; *Ind:* prime *f.*

subveutioned [sʌb'venʃənd], *a.* (Théâtre) subventionné; (industrie) primée.

subversion [sʌb'vəːrʃ(ə)n], *s.* Subversion *f*; renversement *m.*

subversive [sʌb'vəːrsiv], *a.* Subversif (*of*, de).

subvert [sʌb'vəːrt], *v.tr.* Renverser, subvertir.

subway ['sʌbwei], *s.* (a) Passage ou couloir souterrain. (b) *El.E:* Cable subway, tunnel *m* de câbles.

succedaneum, *pl.* **-ea** [sʌksi'deiniəm, -ia], *s.* Succédané *m.*

succeed [sʌk'siːd], *v.tr. & i.* **I.** (a) Succéder (à qn, à qch.). **To succeed to the throne**, succéder à la couronne. **To succeed to an estate**, hériter d'une propriété. *To s. a minister*, prendre la succession d'un ministre. *George III was succeeded by George IV*, George III eut pour successeur George IV. (b) **Day succeeds day**, les jours se suivent. *Winter is succeeded by spring*, le printemps suit l'hiver. **2.** *v.i.* Réussir; atteindre son but; venir à bien. **How to succeed**, le moyen de parvenir. **To succeed in doing sth.**, réussir, parvenir, arriver, à faire qch.; venir à bout de faire qch. **succeeding,** *a.* **I.** Suivant, subséquent. **2.** A venir; futur. **3.** Successif.

success [sʌk'ses], *s.* **I.** *A:* Succès *m*, issue *f* (d'une affaire). *S.a.* ILL-SUCCESS. **2.** (a) Succès, réussite *f*; issue heureuse. **To meet with success**, avoir, obtenir, remporter, du succès; réussir. *Man who has achieved s.*, homme qui a abouti. **Without success**, sans succès; sans y parvenir. (b) (*Of venture*) To be, turn out, a success, réussir; (*of play*) avoir du succès. *The evening was a great s.*, la soirée a été très réussie. He was **a success as Hamlet**, il était excellent dans le rôle de Hamlet. **To make a success of sth.**, réussir qch.

successful [sʌk'sesful], *a.* (Projet) couronné de succès; (résultat) heureux; (portrait) réussi. *S. play*, pièce qui a du succès. **To be entirely s.**, remporter un succès complet. **To be s. in doing sth.**, réussir à faire qch. *He is s. in everything*, tout lui réussit. **Successful candidates**, (i) candidats élus; (ii) *Sch:* candidats reçus. **-fully,** *adv.* Avec succès.

succession [sʌk'seʃ(ə)n], *s.* Succession *f.* **I.** (a) Suite *f.* In succession, successivement; à la file. *For two years in s.*, pendant deux années successives, consécutives. **In rapid succession**, coup sur coup. (b) Série *f*, suite (de victoires, etc.). *After a s. of losses*, après des pertes successives. **2.** (a) Succession (à la couronne, etc.). **In succession to s.o.**, en remplacement de qn. (b) *Jur:* Title by succession, titre par droit de succession. **Succession duties**, droits de succession, de mutation. (c) Héritage *m.* (d) Lignée *f*; descendance *f*, descendants *mpl.*

successive [sʌk'sesiv], *a.* Successif, consécutif. **-ly,** *adv.* Successivement; (i) à mesure; (ii) tour à tour.

successor [sʌk'sesər], *s.* Successeur *m* (*to, of,* de). *To appoint a s. to s.o.*, remplacer qn.

succin ['sʌksin], *s.* Succin *m*; ambre *m* (jaune).

succinct [sʌk'sin(k)t], *a.* Succinct, concis. **-ly,** *adv.* Succinctement; en peu de mots.

succour[1] ['sʌkər], *s.* *Lit:* Secours *m*; aide *f.*

succour[2], *v.tr.* *Lit:* Secourir, soulager (les pauvres); venir en aide à, venir à l'aide de (qn).

succulence ['sʌkjuləns], *s.* Succulence *f.*

succulent ['sʌkjulənt], *a.* (a) Succulent. (b) *Bot:* Succulent leaf, feuille charnue.

succumb [sʌ'kʌm], *v.i.* Succomber; céder. *To s. to temptation*, succomber à la tentation. *To s. to force*, succomber sous le nombre. **To succumb to one's injuries**, succomber à, mourir de, ses blessures.

such [sʌtʃ]. **I.** *a.* Tel, pareil, semblable. **I.** (a) *Poets s. as Keats*, poets as Keats, des poètes tels que Keats. *S. men as he and I*, des gens comme lui et moi. *S. food is very unwholesome*, les aliments de cette nature sont très malsains. **Such a man**, un tel homme. *S. things*, de telles choses. *In s. cases*, en pareils cas. **Did you ever see such a thing!** a-t-on jamais vu chose pareille! *All s. errors are to be avoided*, toutes les erreurs de ce genre sont à éviter. **Some such plan**, un projet de ce genre. **No such body exists**, il n'existe aucun corps de cette nature. *There are no s. things as fairies*, les fées n'existent pas. *I said no s. thing*, je n'ai rien dit de semblable, de la sorte. **No such thing!** il n'en est rien! pas du tout! *S.a.* ANOTHER 2. (b) *S. is not my intention*, ce n'est pas là mon intention. *S. is not the case*, il n'en est pas ainsi. *S. were his words*, tel fut son langage. *F:* Such is the world! ainsi va le monde! **2.** In such (and such) a place, en tel endroit. *We are told that on s. a date he lived in s. and s. a street*, on nous dit qu'à une certaine date il demeurait dans telle et telle rue. **Such a one**, un tel, une telle. **3.** In such a way that . . ., de telle sorte que . . .; de manière, de façon, que. . . . *His pain was s. that . . .*, telle était sa douleur que. . . . *S. is his strength*, tant il est fort. **To take such steps as shall be considered necessary**, prendre telles mesures qui paraîtront nécessaires. **Until such time as . . .**, jusqu'à ce que. . . . **4.** (*Intensive*) Such large houses, de si grandes maisons. *I had never heard s. good music*, je n'avais jamais entendu d'aussi bonne musique. **Such a clever man**, un homme si habile. *S. courage*, un tel courage; tant de courage. *S. an industrious person as yourself*, une personne aussi travailleuse que vous. **I had such a fright!** j'ai eu une de ces peurs! *You do use s. expressions!* vous avez de ces expressions! **II.** *such*, *pron.* **I.** We know of no such, nous n'en connaissons pas de cette espèce. *Down with traitors and all such*, à bas les traîtres et tous ceux qui leur ressemblent. *Dance bands and s.*, orchestres de danse et choses dans ce goût-là. **2.** Let (all) such as are of my opinion lift up their hands, que (tous) ceux qui sont de mon opinion lèvent la main. *I will send you such as I have*, ce que j'en ai je vous les enverrai. **3.** History as such is too often neglected, l'histoire en tant que telle est trop souvent négligée.

suchlike ['sʌtʃlaik]. **I.** *a.* *F:* Semblable, pareil; de ce genre. **2.** *pron.* *Usu. pl.* Beggars, tramps, and suchlike, mendiants, chemineaux et autres gens de la sorte, de cette espèce.

suck[1] [sʌk], *s.* **I.** (a) Action *f* de sucer. **To have,**

take, a suck at a sweet, sucer, suçoter, un bonbon. (b) *Hyd.E:* Succion *f*, aspiration *f* (d'une pompe). **2.** To give a child suck, donner à téter, la tétée, à un enfant. **3.** *pl. Sch: P:* Sucks, bonbons *m*. **4.** *P:* What a suck! quelle attrape! suck². **1.** *v.tr.* (*a*) Sucer (le lait, etc.). (*Of horse*) To suck wind, avaler de l'air. (*b*) Sucer, suçoter (des bonbons); mordiller (le coin de son mouchoir); sucer, tirer sur (sa pipe). *To s. one's fingers*, se sucer les doigts. To suck a raw egg, gober, humer, un œuf. To suck s.o.'s brains, exploiter les connaissances, l'intelligence, de qn. To suck s.o. dry, sucer qn jusqu'à la moelle, jusqu'au dernier sou. **2.** *v.i.* (*a*) (*Of pers.*) To suck at sth., sucer, suçoter (un bonbon); sucer, tirer sur (une pipe). (*b*) (*Of pump*) Super. suck down, *v.tr.* Engloutir; entraîner au fond. suck in, *v.tr.* (*a*) Sucer, absorber; aspirer. (*b*) Engloutir (dans un tourbillon). (*c*) Faire rentrer (ses joues). suck up. **1.** *v.tr.* Sucer, aspirer, pomper (un liquide, de l'air); (*of sponge*) absorber, boire (l'eau). **2.** *v.i. Sch: P:* To suck up to s.o., faire de la lèche à qn; lécher les bottes à qn. sucking¹, *a.* (Animal) qui tette. Sucking calf, veau de lait. Sucking child, enfant à la mamelle. *F:* Sucking poet, poète en herbe. 'sucking-fish, *s.* Rémora *m*. 'sucking-pig, *s.* Cochon *m* de lait. sucking², *s.* Succion *f*; aspiration *f*. *Nat.Hist:* Sucking disk, ventouse *f*.

sucker¹ ['sʌkər], *s.* **1.** Suceur, -euse. **2.** *F:* Écornifleur, -euse. **3.** (*a*) *Nat.Hist:* Suçoir *m*; ventouse *f* (de sangsue). (*b*) Piston *m* (de pompe aspirante). **4.** *Hort:* Rejeton *m*; drageon *m*, surgeon *m* (d'arbre); stolon *m* (de fraisier). Stem sucker, bouture *f*.

sucker², *v. Hort:* **1.** *v.tr.* Enlever les drageons (d'un arbre). **2.** *v.i.* (*Of plant*) Rejetonner; (*of tree*) pousser des drageons.

suckle [sʌkl], *v.tr.* Allaiter (un enfant, un petit); donner le sein, donner à téter, à (un enfant). suckling¹, *s.* Allaitement *m*.

suckling² ['sʌkliŋ], *s.* Nourrisson *m*; enfant à la mamelle.

suction ['sʌkʃ(ə)n], *s.* Succion *f*; aspiration *f* (de l'eau); appel *m* (d'air). *To adhere by s.*, faire ventouse. Suction-grip ash-tray, cendrier à ventouse. Suction apparatus, appareil aspirateur. 'suction-dredger, *s.* Drague *f* à succion; drague aspirante. 'suction-fan, *s.* Ventilateur aspirant; aspirateur *m*. 'suction-shaft, *s. Min:* Puits *m* d'appel d'air. 'suction-valve, *s.* Clapet *m* d'aspiration.

suctorial [sʌk'tɔ:riəl], *a. Nat.Hist:* Suceur.

Sudan [su'dan]. *Pr.n.* = SOUDAN.

sudden [sʌdn], *a.* (*a*) Soudain, subit. *S. shower*, averse inopinée. (*b*) (Mouvement) brusque. *S. turning*, tournant brusque. *Adv.phr.* All of a sudden, soudain, subitement; tout à coup. -ly, *adv.* Soudain, soudainement; subitement; tout à coup. *The door s. opened*, la porte s'ouvrit brusquement.

suddenness ['sʌdnnəs], *s.* (*a*) Soudaineté *f*. *With startling s.*, en coup de théâtre. (*b*) Brusquerie *f* (d'un départ).

sudoriferous [sju:do'rifərəs], *a.* Sudoripare.

sudorific [sju:do'rifik], *a. & s.* Sudorifique (*m*).

suds [sʌdz], *s.pl.* (Soap-)suds, eau *f* de savon; mousse *f* (de savon).

sue [sju:]. **1.** *v.tr.* (*a*) To sue s.o. at law, intenter un procès à qn; poursuivre qn en justice. To sue s.o. for damages, poursuivre qn en dommages-intérêts. (*b*) To sue for a writ, obtenir une ordonnance de la cour. To sue out a pardon for

s.o., obtenir la grâce de qn (à la suite d'une requête). **2.** *v.i.* To sue (to s.o.) for sth., solliciter qch. (de qn). *He sued for her hand*, il demanda sa main. To sue for peace, demander la paix.

suède [sweid], *s.* (i) (*For shoes*) Daim *m*. (ii) (*For gloves, etc.*) Peau *f* de suède; suède *m*.

suet ['sju:et], *s. Cu:* Graisse *f* de rognon; gras *m* de rognon. *F:* Suet face, visage terreux.

Suez ['sju:ez]. *Pr.n.* Suez. The Suez Canal, le canal de Suez.

suffer ['sʌfər]. I. *v.tr.* **1.** Éprouver, souffrir (une perte); subir (une peine, etc.). To suffer defeat, essuyer, subir, une défaite. To suffer death, subir la peine de mort. **2.** Permettre, supporter, tolérer. *He will s. no retort*, il ne souffre, ne supporte, aucune réplique. *S. me to tell you the truth*, permettez, souffrez, que je vous dise la vérité. *They suffered him to go, he was suffered to go*, on le laissa partir. II. suffer, *v.i.* **1.** Souffrir. To suffer from rheumatism, souffrir de rhumatismes; être affligé de rhumatismes. To suffer for one's misdeeds, supporter la conséquence de ses méfaits. *You will s. for it*, il vous en cuira. **2.** To suffer from neglect, pâtir d'un manque de soins. *Country suffering from labour troubles*, pays en proie à l'agitation ouvrière. **3.** Subir une perte, un dommage. *The battalion suffered severely*, le bataillon a essuyé de fortes pertes. *The vines have suffered from the frost*, les vignes ont souffert de la gelée. suffering¹, *a.* Souffrant; qui souffre. suffering², *s.* (*a*) Souffrance *f*. (*b*) *pl.* Sufferings, souffrances; douleurs *f*.

sufferance ['sʌfərəns], *s.* Tolérance *f*, souffrance *f* (*of, de*); permission *f* (tacite). *Esp.* On sufferance, par tolérance.

sufferer ['sʌfərər], *s.* Sufferers from a calamity, victimes *f* d'une calamité; sinistrés *m*; (*from accident*) accidentés *m*. Fellow-sufferer, compagnon *m* d'infortune.

suffice [sʌ'fais]. **1.** *v.i.* Suffire. *That will s. for me*, cela me suffira. Suffice it to say that . . ., qu'il (nous) suffise de dire que . . .; *F:* suffit que . . . **2.** *v.tr.* Suffire à (qn). *One meal a day suffices him*, il lui suffit d'un repas par jour.

sufficiency [sʌ'fiʃənsi], *s.* (*a*) Suffisance *f. A s. of provisions*, une quantité suffisante de vivres. (*b*) Fortune suffisante. To have a sufficiency, jouir de l'aisance; être dans l'aisance.

sufficient [sʌ'fiʃənt], *a. & s.* Assez; suffisant. *This is s. to feed them*, cela suffit pour les nourrir. *A hundred francs will be s.*, j'aurai assez de cent francs. *One lamp is s.*, il suffit d'une lampe. *F:* Have you had sufficient? avez-vous mangé à votre faim? *Prov:* Sufficient unto the day is the evil thereof, à chaque jour suffit sa peine. -ly, *adv.* Suffisamment; assez.

suffix ['sʌfiks], *s. Gram:* Suffixe *m*.

suffocate ['sʌfokeit]. **1.** *v.tr.* Étouffer, suffoquer, asphyxier. *In a suffocated voice*, d'une voix étranglée. **2.** *v.i.* Étouffer, suffoquer. suffocating, *a.* Suffocant, étouffant, asphyxiant. *It is s. in this room*, on étouffe dans cette pièce.

suffocation [sʌfo'keiʃ(ə)n], *s.* Suffocation *f*; étouffement *m*, asphyxie *f*.

suffragan ['sʌfrəgən], *a. & s. Ecc:* (Évêque) suffragant (*m*).

suffrage ['sʌfredʒ], *s.* Suffrage *m*. (*a*) Vote *m*, voix *f*. (*b*) Droit *m* de vote. Universal suffrage, suffrage universel.

suffragette [sʌfrə'dʒet], *s.f.* Suffragette; militante.

suffragist ['sʌfrədʒist], *s.* Partisan *m* du droit de vote des femmes.

suffuse [sʌ'fju:z], *v.tr.* Se répandre sur (qch.).

A blush suffused her cheeks, une rougeur se répandit sur ses joues. *Eyes suffused with tears,* yeux baignés de larmes. *Suffused with light,* inondé de lumière.

sugar[1] ['ʃugər], *s.* **1.** Sucre *m. Granulated s.,* sucre cristallisé. **Lump sugar,** sucre en morceaux, en tablettes. **Castor sugar,** sucre en poudre. **Brown sugar, moist sugar,** cassonade *f.* **Sugar and water,** eau sucrée. *Cu:* **Burnt sugar,** caramel *m.* **2.** (*a*) *A.Ch:* **Sugar of lead,** acétate *m* de plomb. (*b*) **Sugar of milk,** sucre de lait; lactose *f.* **'sugar-'almond,** *s.* Dragée *f;* amande lissée. **'sugar-basin,** *s.* Sucrier *m.* **'sugar-beet,** *s.* Betterave *f* à sucre. **sugar-'candy,** *s.* Sucre candi. **'sugar-cane,** *s.* Canne *f* à sucre. **'sugar-loaf,** *s.* Pain *m* de sucre. *F:* **Sugarloaf hat,** chapeau pointu. **'sugar-maple,** *s.* *Bot:* Érable *m* à sucre. **'sugar-pea,** *s.* *Hort:* Mange-tout *m inv.* **'sugar-plantation,** *s.* Plantation *f* de cannes à sucre. **'sugar-plum,** *s.* Bonbon *m.* **'sugar-refiner,** *s.* Raffineur *m* (de sucre). **'sugar-refinery,** *s.* Raffinerie *f* (de sucre). **'sugar-sifter,** *s.* Saupoudroir *m.* **'sugar-tongs,** *s.pl.* Pince *f* à sucre.

sugar[2]. **1.** *v.tr.* Sucrer; saupoudrer (un gâteau) de sucre; lisser (des amandes). *F:* **To sugar the pill,** dorer la pilule. **2.** *v.i.* *F:* Tirer au flanc; ne pas se la fouler.

sugariness ['ʃugərinəs], *s.* (*a*) Goût sucré. (*b*) Douceur mielleuse (d'un discours, etc.).

sugary ['ʃugəri], *a.* **1.** (*a*) Sucré; (gâteau) saupoudré de sucre. (*b*) Trop sucré. **2.** (Sourire) mielleux, sucré; (ton) doucereux. *S. eloquence,* éloquence mellifue.

suggest [sʌ'dʒest], *v.tr.* **1.** Suggérer, proposer (qch. à qn). *A solution suggested itself to me,* une solution me vint à l'esprit, se présenta à mon esprit. **2.** Inspirer, faire naître (une idée). *Prudence suggests a retreat,* la prudence conseille la retraite. **3.** Insinuer. *Do you s. that I am lying?* est-ce que vous insinuez que je mens? *Jur:* I suggest that . . ., n'est-il pas vrai que . . .? **4.** Évoquer. *His nose and ears s. a rabbit,* son nez et ses oreilles donnent, évoquent, l'idée d'un lapin.

suggestion [sʌ'dʒest∫(ə)n], *s.* **1.** Suggestion *f.* **To make, offer, a suggestion,** faire une suggestion, une proposition. *Suggestions for improvement,* suggestions en vue d'une amélioration. *Jur:* My suggestion is that . . ., n'est-il pas vrai que . . .? **2.** *It conveys the s. that . . .,* cela donne l'idée que. . . . *To speak with just a s. of a foreign accent,* parler avec une pointe d'accent étranger. *S. of regret,* nuance *f* de regret. **3.** **Hypnotic suggestion,** suggestion hypnotique.

suggestive [sʌ'dʒestiv], *a.* Suggestif; évocateur, -trice. *S. of sth.,* qui évoque qch.

suicidal [sjui'said(ə)l], *a.* *S. tendencies,* tendances au suicide. *F: It would be s. to do so,* ce serait un véritable suicide, ce serait courir à la ruine, que d'agir de la sorte.

suicide[1] ['sjuisaid], *s.* (*Pers.*) Suicidé, -ée.

suicide[2], *s.* (Crime *m* du) suicide. **To commit suicide,** se suicider. *To attempt s.,* attenter à ses jours. **Attempted suicide,** tentative *f* de suicide.

suint [swint], *s.* Suin(t) *m.*

suit[1] [sju:t], *s.* **1.** *Jur:* **Suit at law,** procès (civil); poursuites *fpl* (en justice). **To bring a suit against s.o.,** intenter un procès à qn. **To be a party to a suit,** être en cause. **2.** Prière *f,* demande *f,* requête *f.* **At the suit of s.o.,** à la requête de qn. **3.** Recherche *f,* demande *f* en mariage. **4.** *Cost:* (*a*) **Suit of clothes,** costume *m,* complet *m* (pour homme). **Lounge-suit,** complet veston. *S.a.* AR-MOUR[1] 1. (*b*) Ensemble *m* (pour femme).

(*c*) **Sailor-suit,** costume marin (pour enfant). **5.** *Nau:* **Suit of sails,** jeu *m* de voiles; voilure *f.* **6.** *Cards:* Couleur *f.* **To lead from one's long s.,** attaquer dans sa longue. *F:* **Politeness is not his long suit,** la politesse n'est pas son fort. **To follow suit,** (i) donner de la couleur; (ii) *F:* en faire autant, faire de même. **'suit-case,** *s.* Mallette *f,* valise *f.*

suit[2], *v.tr.* **1.** Accommoder, adapter, approprier (*to,* à). **To be suited to, for, sth.,** être adapté, apte, à qch.; être fait pour qch. *He is ill-suited to these parts,* ces rôles ne lui conviennent pas. **They are suited to each other,** ils sont faits l'un pour l'autre. *S.a.* ACTION 1. **2.** Convenir à, aller à, accommoder (qn). **The house does not suit me,** la maison n'est pas à ma convenance. *That suits me best,* c'est ce qui m'arrange le mieux. **I am not easily suited,** je suis difficile à satisfaire. *That just suits me,* ça me va à merveille; c'est juste mon affaire. *I shall do it when it suits me,* je le ferai quand cela me conviendra. **Suit yourself,** arrangez cela à votre gré; faites comme vous voudrez. **This climate does not suit me,** ce climat ne me va pas, ne me vaut rien. *This hat suits you,* ce chapeau vous va, vous coiffe bien. **3.** *Are you suited with a cook?* avez-vous trouvé une cuisinière qui vous convient? **suiting,** *s.* **1.** Adaptation *f,* appropriation *f* (de qch. à qch.). **2.** *pl.* **Gentlemen's suitings,** étoffes *f,* tissus *m,* pour complets.

suitability [sjuːtə'biliti], *s.* Convenance *f;* à-propos *m* (d'une remarque); accord *m* (de caractères). *S. of a candidate to, for, a post,* aptitude *f* d'un candidat à un poste.

suitable ['sjuːtəbl], *a.* **1.** Convenable, qui convient; (exemple) approprié. **Suitable marriage,** union sortable, bien assortie. *We have found nothing s.,* nous n'avons rien trouvé à notre convenance. *The most s. date,* la date qui conviendrait le mieux. *It seemed more s. to laugh,* il semblait plus à propos de rire. **2.** **Suitable to, for, sth.,** bon à qch.; propre, approprié, adapté, à qch. **Suitable to the occasion,** qui convient à la circonstance. **-ably,** *adv.* Convenablement; (répondre) à propos; (agir) comme il convient. *S. matched,* bien assortis.

suite [swiːt], *s.* **1.** Suite *f,* cortège *m* (d'un prince). **2.** (*a*) **Suite of rooms,** appartement *m;* pièces *fpl* en enfilade. (*b*) **Suite of furniture,** ameublement *m;* mobilier *m.* **Dining-room s.,** salle à manger. **3.** **Orchestral suite,** suite d'orchestre.

suitor ['sjuːtər], *s.* **1.** *Jur:* Plaideur, -euse. **2.** Prétendant *m,* soupirant *m.*

sulk[1] [sʌlk], *s.* *Usu. pl.* **To be in the sulks, to have (a fit of) the sulks,** bouder; faire la mine.

sulk[2], *v.i.* Bouder; faire la mine; être maussade.

sulkiness ['sʌlkinəs], *s.* Bouderie *f,* maussaderie *f.*

sulky[1] ['sʌlki], *a.* Boudeur, maussade. *To be s.,* bouder. *To look s.,* faire la mine. **To be sulky with s.o.,** bouder (contre) qn. **-ily,** *adv.* En boudant; d'un air boudeur ou maussade.

sulky[2], *s. Veh:* Sulky *m.*

sullage ['sʌledʒ], *s.* **1.** (*a*) Eaux *fpl* d'égout. (*b*) Vase *f* d'alluvion; limon *m.* **2.** *Metall:* Scories *fpl,* crasses *fpl.*

sullen ['sʌl(ə)n], *a.* (*Of pers.*) Maussade, renfrogné, morose; (*of thg*) sombre, morne. *S. silence,* silence obstiné. **-ly,** *adv.* D'un air maussade, renfrogné; (obéir) de mauvaise grâce.

sullenness ['sʌlənnəs], *s.* (*a*) Maussaderie *f;* air renfrogné. (*b*) Obstination *f* à ne pas parler.

sully ['sʌli], *v.tr.* Souiller, salir, ternir; flétrir, tacher (la réputation de qn).

sulphate¹ ['sʌlfet, -eit], s. **1.** *Ch:* Sulfate m. Iron sulphate, sulfate ferreux, de fer; vitriol vert. Copper sulphate, sulfate de cuivre. **2.** *Com:* Sulfate de soude.

sulphate² ['sʌlfeit]. **1.** *v.tr.* Sulfater. **2.** *v.i.* *El:* (Of battery) Se sulfater. *Sulphated accumulator,* accu encrassé de sulfate. **sulphating,** s. **1.** Sulfatage m. **2.** *El:* Sulfatation f (des plaques d'accumulateur).

sulphide ['sʌlfaid], s. *Ch:* Sulfure m. Hydrogen sulphide, hydrogène sulfuré; acide m sulfhydrique. *Phot:* Sulphide toning, virage au sulfure.

sulphite ['sʌlfait], s. *Ch:* Sulfite m. Sodium sulphite, sulfite de soude.

sulphocyanide [sʌlfo'saianaid], s. *Phot:* Sulfocyanure m.

sulphur¹ ['sʌlfər], s. Soufre m. Roll sulphur, stick sulphur, soufre en canon(s), en bâtons. Plastic sulphur, soufre mou. Flowers of sulphur, fleur(s) f de soufre. **sulphur-'match,** s. Allumette soufrée. **'sulphur mine,** s. Soufrière f. **'sulphur-spring,** s. *Geol:* Solfatare f. **'sulphur water,** s. Eau sulfureuse.

sulphur², *v.tr.* Soufrer. **sulphuring,** s. Soufrage m.

sulphureous [sʌl'fjuəriəs], a. (a) Sulfureux. (b) Couleur de soufre *inv*; soufré. (c) Bleuâtre (comme le soufre qui brûle).

sulphuretted ['sʌlfjuretid], a. *Ch:* Sulfuré.

sulphuric [sʌl'fjuərik], a. *Ch:* Sulfurique.

sulphurous [sʌl'fjuərəs], a. *Ch:* (Acide, etc.) sulfureux.

sultan ['sʌltən], s. **1.** Sultan m. **2.** *Bot:* Sweet sultan, ambrette f.

sultana [sʌl'tɑːna], s. **1.** Sultane f. **2.** Raisin sec de Smyrne; (raisin) sultana m.

sultriness ['sʌltrinəs], s. Chaleur étouffante; lourdeur f (de l'atmosphère).

sultry ['sʌltri], a. (Of heat, etc.) Étouffant, suffocant. *It is s.,* il fait très lourd.

sum¹ [sʌm], s. **1.** (a) Somme f, total m; montant m. To find the sum of the terms of a series, sommer les termes d'une série. (b) *F:* The sum and substance of the matter, le fond, l'essence f, de l'affaire. In sum . . ., en somme . . .; somme toute. . . . (c) Sum of money, somme d'argent. **2.** Problème m, exercice m (d'arithmétique). *To do a sum in one's head,* faire un calcul de tête. To do sums, faire du calcul, des problèmes. *I was very bad at sums,* j'étais très faible en calcul, en arithmétique. **'sum-'total,** s. Somme totale, globale.

sum², *v.tr.* (summed) (a) Additionner. *To sum a series,* sommer une série. **sum up,** *v.tr.* **1.** To sum up ten numbers, faire la somme de dix nombres. **2.** (a) Résumer, faire un résumé de, récapituler (les faits). To sum up the matter, *abs.* to sum up, en résumé. (b) *Jur:* (Of judge) To sum up (the case), résumer les débats. (c) To sum up the situation at a glance, se rendre compte de la situation d'un coup d'œil. *F:* To sum s.o. up, juger, classer, qn. **summing up,** s. (a) *Jur:* Résumé m des débats (par le juge). (b) Évaluation f (de la situation, etc.).

sumac(h) ['sjuːmak, 'ʃuːmak], s. *Bot:* Sumac m. Venetian sumac, (sumac) fustet m.

summarize ['sʌməraiz], *v.tr.* Résumer sommairement (un ouvrage). **summarized,** a. (Of report, etc.) Compendieux; en résumé.

summary ['sʌməri]. **1.** a. Sommaire. Summary account, (i) récit sommaire, succinct; (ii) récit récapitulatif. *Jur:* Summary proceedings, affaire f sommaire. **2.** s. Sommaire m, résumé m (d'un livre); récapitulation f, relevé m (d'opérations commerciales, etc.). **-ily,** *adv.* Sommairement.

summer¹ ['sʌmər], s. Été m. In summer, en été. A summer('s) day, un jour d'été. *Poet:* Maiden of twenty summers, jeune fille de vingt printemps. Summer clothes, habits d'été. Summer residence, résidence estivale; résidence d'été. The summer holidays, les grandes vacances. **'summer-house,** s. Pavillon m, kiosque m. **'summer-time,** s. **1.** L'été m. **2.** L'heure f d'été (en avance de soixante minutes sur l'heure normale).

summer², *v.i.* Passer l'été, estiver (au bord de la mer, etc.).

summer³, s. *Const:* Summer(-beam, -tree), poutre f de plancher.

summit ['sʌmit], s. Sommet m, cime f, faîte m (d'une montagne); point m de partage (d'un canal). *F:* The summit of greatness, le faîte, le comble, des grandeurs.

summon ['sʌmən], *v.tr.* **1.** (a) Appeler, faire venir (un domestique); mander (un ministre); convoquer (une assemblée). To be summoned to the peerage, être appelé à la pairie. (b) *Jur:* Sommer (qn) de comparaître. To summon a defendant, a witness, to attend, citer, assigner, un défendeur, un témoin. To summon s.o. for debt, assigner qn en paiement d'une dette. **2.** Sommer, requérir. To summon a town to surrender, sommer une place. **3.** To summon up one's courage, faire appel à, s'armer de, tout son courage.

summons¹, *pl.* **-ses** ['sʌmənz, -ziz], s. **1.** Appel (fait d'autorité); convocation urgente. **2.** *Jur:* Citation f (à comparaître); assignation f; mandat m de comparution; sommation f (de comparaître); *F:* procès-verbal m, *pl.* procès-verbaux. To serve a summons on s.o., signifier une citation, une assignation, à qn. To take out a summons against s.o., faire assigner qn. **3.** *Mil:* Summons to surrender, sommation f.

summons², *v.tr.* *Jur:* Citer (qn) à comparaître; assigner (qn); appeler (qn) en justice.

sump [sʌmp], s. **1.** (a) Puisard m. (b) Fosse f d'aisance. **2.** *Mec.E:* *Aut:* Fond m de carter (formant réservoir d'huile); cuvette f d'égouttage. Dry sump, carter sec.

sumpter ['sʌmptər], s. *A:* Bête f de somme, de charge; sommier m. Sumpter mule, mulet m de somme, de charge.

sumptuary ['sʌmptjuəri], a. (Of law) Somptuaire.

sumptuous ['sʌmptjuəs], a. Somptueux, fastueux. **-ly,** *adv.* Somptueusement.

sumptuousness ['sʌmptjuəsnəs], s. Somptuosité f, faste m; richesse f (du mobilier).

sun¹ [sʌn], s. (a) Soleil m. The sun is shining, il fait du soleil. *F:* His sun is set, son étoile a pâli. *Nau:* *F:* To take, shoot, the sun, observer le soleil; faire le point. With the sun, against the sun, de gauche à droite, de droite à gauche. (b) To have one's place in the sun, avoir sa place au soleil. *Full in the sun,* au grand soleil. To take a touch of the sun, prendre un coup de soleil. **'sun-baked,** a. Brûlé par le soleil; cuit au soleil. **'sun-bath,** s. Bain m de soleil. To take a sun-bath = SUN-BATHE. **'sun-bathe,** *v.i.* Prendre des bains de soleil; s'insoler. **sun-bathing,** s. Bains *mpl* de soleil; insolation f. **'sun-bonnet,** s. Capeline f. **'sun-deck,** s. *Nau:* Pont-promenade m. **'sun-dial,** s. Cadran m solaire. **'sun-dog,** s. Parhélie m; faux soleil. **'sun-dried,** a. (a) Séché au soleil. (b) (Fruit) confit au soleil. **'sun-fish,** s. Poisson-lune *m.* **'sun-glasses,** *s.pl.* Lunettes *f* contre le soleil ; conserves *f.* **'sun-hat,** *s.* Chapeau *m* à larges bords. **'sun-helmet,** *s.* Casque colonial. **'sun-proof,** *a.* (Tissu) inaltérable au soleil. **'sun-spot,** *s. Astr :* Tache *f* solaire. **'sun-up,** *s.* Lever *m* du soleil.

sun², *v.tr.* (sunned) Exposer au soleil ; insoler. **To sun** oneself, prendre le soleil ; se chauffer au soleil ; *F :* faire le lézard ; lézarder.

sunbeam ['sʌnbiːm], *s.* Rayon *m* de soleil.

sunburn ['sʌnbəːrn], *s.* **I.** Hâle *m.* **2.** *Med :* Coup *m* de soleil.

sunburned, -burnt ['sʌnbəːrnd, -bəːrnt], *a.* Brûlé par le soleil ; hâlé, basané. **To get sunburnt,** se hâler, se basaner.

sunburst ['sʌnbəːrst], *s.* Échappée *f* de soleil.

sundae ['sʌndei], *s.* Glace *f* aux fruits.

Sunday ['sʌndi], *s.* Dimanche *m.* **Sunday calm,** le repos dominical. **Sunday paper,** journal du dimanche. **In one's Sunday clothes, in one's Sunday best,** dans ses habits du dimanche ; endimanché. (*For other phrases cf.* FRIDAY.)

sunder ['sʌndər], *v.tr.* (*a*) Séparer, disjoindre (*from,* de). (*b*) Couper, fendre, (qch.) en deux.

sundew ['sʌndjuː], *s. Bot :* Drosère *f*, rossolis *m.*

sundown ['sʌndaun], *s.* = SUNSET.

sundry ['sʌndri]. **I.** *a.* Divers. **Sundry expenses,** frais divers. **On s. occasions,** à différentes occasions. **2.** *s.* (*a*) **All and sundry,** tous sans exception ; tout le monde et son père. *He told all and s. about it,* il le racontait à tout venant, au tiers et au quart. (*b*) *pl.* **Sundries,** (i) articles divers ; (ii) frais divers ; faux frais.

sunflower ['sʌnflauər], *s. Bot :* Hélianthe annuel ; tournesol *m*, soleil *m.*

sung [sʌŋ]. *See* SING.

sunk [sʌŋk]. *See* SINK².

sunken ['sʌŋk(ə)n]. **I.** *See* SINK². **2.** *a.* (*a*) (Rocher) noyé, submergé. (*b*) Affaissé, enfoncé. **Sunken cheeks,** joues hâves, creuses. (*c*) *S. road,* route encaissée.

sunlight ['sʌnlait], *s.* Lumière *f* du soleil. **In the sunlight,** au (grand) soleil. *Med :* **Sunlight treatment,** héliothérapie *f ;* traitement *m* solaire.

sunlit ['sʌnlit], *a.* Éclairé par le soleil ; ensoleillé.

sunny ['sʌni], *a.* **I.** (Journée de soleil ; (endroit) ensoleillé ; (côté) exposé au soleil. **It is sunny,** il fait du soleil. *F :* **The sunny side of the picture,** le bon côté de l'affaire. **2.** (Visage) radieux, rayonnant ; (caractère) heureux.

sunrise ['sʌnraiz], *s.* Lever *m* du soleil. **At sunrise,** au soleil levant ; au lever du soleil.

sunset ['sʌnset], *s.* Coucher *m* du soleil. **At sunset,** au soleil couchant ; au coucher du soleil. *F :* **The sunset of life,** le déclin de la vie.

sunshade ['sʌnʃeid], *s.* **I.** Ombrelle *f ;* (*for table, etc.*) parasol *m.* **2.** Parasoleil *m*, pare-soleil *m inv* (de télescope). **3.** *Aut :* Pare-soleil.

sunshine ['sʌnʃain], *s.* **I.** (Clarté *f*, lumière *f*, du) soleil. **In the sunshine,** au soleil. *In the bright s.,* au grand soleil ; en plein soleil. *F :* **Sunshine friend,** ami des beaux jours. **2.** Bonheur *m*, gaieté *f*, rayonnement *m* (du visage, de la vie).

sunstroke ['sʌnstrouk], *s. Med :* Insolation *f ;* coup *m* de soleil. **To get (a touch of) sunstroke,** attraper un coup de soleil.

sup¹ [sʌp], *s. Scot :* Petite gorgée. **To take a sup of soup,** prendre une goutte de bouillon. *S.a.* BITE¹ 3.

sup², *v.* (supped [sʌpt]) **I.** *v.tr. Esp. Scot :* Prendre à petites gorgées. **2.** *v.i.* Souper (*off, on,* de).

super ['sjuːpər], *s. F :* = SUPERNUMERARY 2.

superable ['sjuːpərəbl], *a.* Surmontable.

superabound [sjuːpərə'baund], *v.i.* Surabonder (*in, with,* de, en) ; foisonner (de).

superabundance [sjuːpərə'bʌndəns], *s.* Surabondance *f*, foisonnement *m*, pléthore *f* (*of,* de).

superabundant [sjuːpərə'bʌndənt], *a.* Surabondant, pléthorique.

superadd [sjuːpər'æd], *v.tr.* Surajouter.

superannuate [sjuːpər'ænjueit]. **I.** *v.tr* (*a*) Mettre (qn) à la retraite ; retraiter (qn). (*b*) *F :* Mettre au rancart (une vieille auto). **2.** *v.i.* Arriver à l'âge de la retraite. **superannuated,** *a.* **I.** Suranné ; démodé. **2.** En retraite ; retraité.

superannuation [sjuːpərənju'eiʃ(ə)n], *s.* Retraite *f* par limite d'âge. **Superannuation fund,** caisse *f* des retraites.

superb [sjuː'pəːrb], *a.* Superbe, magnifique. **-ly,** *adv.* Superbement, magnifiquement.

supercargo [sjuːpər'kaːrgo], *s. Nau :* Subrécargue *m.*

supercharged [sjuːpər'tʃaːrdʒd], *a. I.C.E :* (Moteur) suralimenté, surcomprimé, à compresseur.

supercharger [sjuːpər'tʃaːrdʒər], *s. I.C.E :* Compresseur *m.*

supercharging [sjuːpər'tʃaːrdʒiŋ], *s. I.C.E :* Suralimentation *f*, surcompression *f.*

supercilious [sjuːpər'siliəs], *a.* Sourcilleux, hautain ; (air) pincé, dédaigneux. **-ly,** *adv.* Avec une nuance de dédain.

superciliousness [sjuːpər'siliəsnəs], *s.* Hauteur *f ;* air dédaigneux.

supereminent [sjuːpər'eminənt], *a.* Suréminent, prééminent (*for,* par).

supererogation [sjuːpərero'geiʃ(ə)n], *s.* Surérogation *f ; F :* superfétation *f.*

superficial [sjuːpər'fiʃ(ə)l], *a.* Superficiel. **To have a superficial knowledge of sth.,** avoir des connaissances superficielles, une teinture, de qch. *His knowledge is entirely s.,* son savoir est tout en superficie. **-ally,** *adv.* Superficiellement.

superficies [sjuːpər'fiʃiiːz], *s.inv.* Superficie *f.*

superfine ['sjuːpərfain], *a.* **I.** Superfin ; *Com :* surfin. **2.** *S. distinctions,* distinctions raffinées.

superfluity [sjuːpər'fluiti], *s.* **I.** Superfluité *f. S. of good things,* embarras *m* de richesses. **2.** *To have a s. of hands,* avoir un excédent de main-d'œuvre. **To give one's superfluity,** donner de son superflu.

superfluous [sjuː'pəːrfluəs], *a.* Superflu.

superheat [sjuːpər'hiːt], *v.tr. Mch :* Surchauffer (la vapeur).

superheater [sjuːpər'hiːtər], *s. Mch :* Surchauffeur *m* (de vapeur).

superhet(erodyne) [sjuːpər'het(ərodain)], *s. W.Tel :* Superhétérodyne *m ; F :* super *m.*

superhuman [sjuːpər'hjuːmən], *a.* Surhumain.

superimpose [sjuːpərim'pouz], *v.tr.* Superposer, surimposer.

superimposition [sjuːpərimpo'ziʃ(ə)n], *s.* Superposition *f* (de couleurs, etc.).

superintend [sjuːpərin'tend], *v.tr.* Diriger, surveiller. *To s. an election,* présider au scrutin.

superintendence [sjuːpərin'tendəns], *s.* Direction *f*, surveillance *f*, contrôle *m ;* conduite *f* (des travaux).

superintendent [sjuːpərin'tendənt], *s.* **I.** Directeur, -trice ; surveillant, -ante ; chef *m* (des travaux). **2. Police superintendent,** officier *m* de paix. **Railway superintendent,** commissaire *m* des chemins de fer. **3.** *Hist :* Surintendant *m.*

superior [sjuː'piəriər]. **I.** *a.* (*a*) Supérieur, -eure. *To be s. in numbers to the enemy,* être supérieur en nombre à l'ennemi ; avoir la supériorité du nombre sur l'ennemi. *My gardener is a s. sort of* *man,* mon jardinier est d'une classe supérieure. *Thanks to your s. wealth,* grâce à la supériorité de vos richesses. **To be superior to flattery,** être au-dessus de la flatterie. *(b) (Of pers.)* Sourcilleux, superbe. *With a s. smile,* avec un sourire suffisant, condescendant. *(c) Typ:* **Superior letter,** lettre supérieure ; lettrine *f.* **Superior figure,** appel *m* de note. **2.** *s. (a)* Supérieur, -eure. *He is your s.,* il est votre supérieur. *(b) Ecc:* **The Father Superior,** le père supérieur. *S.a.* MOTHER[1] 3.

superiority [sjupi:əri'ɔriti], *s.* Supériorité *f. S. in talent,* supériorité de talent.

superlative [sju'pəːrlətiv]. **1.** *a.* Suprême ; d'une excellence suprême. **2.** *a. & s. Gram:* Superlatif *(m).* **In the superlative,** au superlatif. **-ly,** *adv. F:* Au suprême degré. *S. ugly,* d'une laideur sans pareille.

superman, *pl.* **-men** ['sju:pərman, -men], *s.m.* Surhomme.

supernatural [sju:pər'natjurəl], *a.* Surnaturel. *s.* The supernatural, le surnaturel.

supernormal [sju:pər'nɔːrm(ə)l], *a.* Au-dessus de la normale.

supernumerary [sju:pər'nju:mərəri]. **1.** *a.* Surnuméraire ; en surnombre. **2.** *s. (a)* Surnuméraire *m. (b) Th:* Figurant, -ante.

superpose [sju:pər'poːuz], *v.tr.* Superposer *(upon, on,* à) ; étager (des planchettes).

superposition [sju:pərpo'ziʃ(ə)n], *s.* Superposition *f.*

supersalt ['sju:pərsɔlt], *s. Ch:* Sursel *m.*

supersaturate [sju:pər'satjureit], *v.tr.* Sursaturer.

supersaturation [sju:pərsatju'reiʃ(ə)n], *s.* Sursaturation *f.*

superscribe [sju:pər'skraib], *v.tr.* **1.** Marquer d'une inscription. *Packet superscribed 'Glass with care,'* colis portant la mention "Fragile." **2.** Mettre l'adresse sur (une lettre).

superscription [sju:pər'skripʃ(ə)n], *s.* Inscription *f ; (on coin)* légende *f ; (on letter)* adresse *f,* suscription *f ; (on document)* en-tête *m.*

supersede [sju:pər'si:d], *v.tr. (a)* Remplacer. **To supersede an official,** relever un employé de ses fonctions. *Method now superseded,* méthode périmée. *(b)* Prendre la place de (qn) ; supplanter (qn).

supersensitive [sju:pər'sensitiv] *a.* Hypersensible.

supersession [sju:pər'seʃ(ə)n], *s.* Remplacement *m* (d'un employé, du gaz par l'électricité).

supersonic [sju:pər'sɔnik], *a. Ph:* Ultra-sonore.

supersports car [sju:pər'spɔ:rtska:r], *s. Aut:* Voiture *f* grand sport.

superstition [sju:pər'stiʃ(ə)n], *s.* Superstition *f.*

superstitious [sju:pər'stiʃəs], *a.* Superstitieux. **-ly,** *adv.* Superstitieusement.

superstructure ['sju:pərstraktʃər], *s.* **1.** Superstructure *f ;* tablier *m* (d'un pont). **2.** *N.Arch:* Accastillage *m.*

super-tax ['sju:pərtaks], *s. Adm:* Impôt *m* supplémentaire sur le revenu ; surtaxe *f.*

supertonic [sju:pər'tɔnik], *s. Mus:* Sous-médiante *f.*

supervene [sju:pər'vi:n], *v.i.* Survenir. *Lockjaw supervened (up)on the wound,* le tétanos se déclara à la suite de la blessure.

supervise ['sju:pərva:iz], *v.tr.* **1.** Avoir l'œil sur, surveiller (une entreprise). **2.** Diriger, conduire (une entreprise).

supervision [sju:pər'viʒ(ə)n],*s.* **1.** Surveillance *f.* Under police supervision, sous la surveillance de la police. **To keep s.o. under strict super-**

vision, exercer une surveillance sévère sur la conduite de qn. **2.** Direction *f* (d'une entreprise).

supervisor ['sju:pərvaizər], *s.* Surveillant, -ante ; directeur, -trice. *To act as s.,* exercer la surveillance.

supine[1] ['sju:pain], *a.* **1.** *(Of pers.)* Couché, étendu, sur le dos. *Med:* En supination. **2.** *F:* Mou, *f.* molle ; indolent, inerte.

supine[2], *s. Lt.Gram:* Supin *m.* **In the supine,** au supin.

supineness [sju'painnəs], *s.* Mollesse *f,* indolence *f,* inertie *f.*

supper ['sapər], *s.* Souper *m.* **To have supper,** souper. **The Last Supper,** la (Sainte) Cène. *Ecc:* **The Lord's Supper,** la communion, l'eucharistie *f.* '**supper-time,** *s.* Heure *f* du souper.

supplant [sa'plaːnt], *v.tr.* Supplanter ; prendre la place de (qn) ; évincer (qn).

supplanter [sa'plaːntər], *s.* Supplantateur, -trice.

supple[1] [sapl], *a.* Souple. **1.** Liant, pliable, flexible ; *(cordage)* maniable. *S. figure,* taille souple, déliée, libre. **To become supple,** s'assouplir. **2.** Obséquieux, complaisant. **-ply,** *adv.* Souplement ; avec souplesse. '**supple-jack,** *s.* **1.** Canne *f* souple ; jonc *m.* **2.** *U.S:* Pantin *m.*

supple[2], *v.tr.* Assouplir ; dresser (un cheval).

supplement[1] ['sapliment], *s.* Supplément *m ;* appendice *m* (d'un livre). *Geom:* Supplément (d'un angle). *Journ:* **Literary supplement,** supplément littéraire.

supplement[2] [sapli'ment], *v.tr.* Ajouter à (un livre, etc.). **To supplement one's income by journalism,** augmenter ses revenus en faisant du journalisme.

supplemental[sapli'ment(ə)l],*a. Geom:* (Angle) supplémentaire *(to, of,* de).

supplementary [sapli'mentəri], *a.* Supplémentaire *(to,* de) ; additionnel *(to,* à).

suppleness ['saplnəs], *s.* **1.** Souplesse *f,* flexibilité *f.* **2.** Complaisance *f,* obséquiosité *f.*

suppliant ['sapliənt]. **1.** *a.* Suppliant ; de supplication. **2.** *s.* Suppliant, -ante.

supplicant ['saplikənt], *s.* Suppliant, -ante.

supplicate ['saplikeit]. **1.** *v.i.* Supplier. **2.** *v.tr.* To supplicate s.o. to do sth., supplier qn de faire qch. *To s. protection,* solliciter humblement la protection de qn.

supplication [sapli'keiʃ(ə)n], *s.* **1.** Supplication *f.* **2.** Supplique *f.*

supplier [sa'plaiər], *s.* Fournisseur, -euse ; pourvoyeur, -euse *(of,* de) ; approvisionneur, -euse *(of, en,* de).

supply[1] [sa'plai], *s.* **1.** *(a)* Approvisionnement *m,* fourniture *f.* **Food supply,** approvisionnement. **Supply column,** convoi de ravitaillement. *Navy:* **Supply ship,** (transport) ravitailleur *m. El.E:* **Supply pressure,** tension *f* de distribution. *(b) Parl:* **Bill of Supply,** projet *m* de crédit supplémentaire. **To vote supplies,** voter des crédits *m. (c)* Occupation *f* (d'une place) par intérim ; provision *f. To hold a post on supply,* occuper une place par intérim. **2.** *(a)* Provision *f.* **To take in,** lay in, a supply of sth., se faire une provision, s'approvisionner, de qch. *To get (in) a fresh s. of sth.,* se remonter de qch. *Pol.Ec:* **Supply and demand,** l'offre *f* et la demande. *(b) pl.* **Supplies.** (i) Fournitures *f* (de photographie, etc.). *Typewriting supplies,* accessoires *m* de machines à écrire. (ii) **Supplies of a town,** approvisionnements d'une ville. **Food supplies,** vivres *m. To obtain, get, one's supplies from X,* s'approvisionner chez X ; se fournir chez X.

To cut off, stop, the enemy's supplies, couper les vivres à l'ennemi. (c) Suppléant, -ante; F: intérim m. **To arrange for a supply,** se faire suppléer. **su'pply-circuit,** s. El.E: The local supply-circuit, le secteur. **su'pply-main, -pipe,** s. Hyd.E: Canalisation f; tuyau m d'alimentation.

supply², v.tr. (supplied) **1.** (a) **To supply s.o. with sth.,** fournir, pourvoir, munir, approvisionner, qn de qch. **To s. s.o. with food,** alimenter qn. **To supply a town** (with provisions), approvisionner, ravitailler, une ville. **The tradesmen who s. us,** nos fournisseurs m. Com: **Families supplied daily,** livraisons f à domicile tous les jours. **To s. a machine** (with material, etc.), alimenter une machine. (b) **To supply sth.,** fournir, apporter, qch.; amener (l'eau, le gaz, etc.). **2.** (a) Réparer (une omission); remplir (une vacance); combler, pourvoir à (un déficit); répondre à (un besoin). **To supply s.o.'s needs,** fournir, pourvoir, subvenir, aux besoins de qn. (b) **To supply s.o.'s place,** abs. to supply for s.o., remplacer, suppléer, qn; assurer l'intérim.

supply³ ['sʌpli], adv. See SUPPLE¹.

support¹ [sʌ'pɔːrt], s. **1.** (a) Appui m, soutien m. **Moral support,** appui moral. **To give support to the proposal,** venir à l'appui de, appuyer, la proposition. **To get, obtain, no support,** ne trouver aucun appui. **Documents in support of an allegation,** pièces à l'appui d'une allégation. **Troops in support,** troupes de soutien. (b) Soutènement m (d'une voûte, etc.). (c) **Family dependent upon a son for s.,** famille qui n'a qu'un fils pour la faire vivre. **To be without means of support,** être sans ressources. **2.** (a) **The sole support of his old age,** son seul soutien dans sa vieillesse. (b) Appui, support m, soutien (d'une voûte, etc.); pied m (de sustentation); console f, soupente f (de treuil); assiette f (de pied de colonne, etc.); potence f. Mec.E: Mch: Chaise f. Hort: Tuteur m.

support², v.tr. **1.** (a) Supporter, soutenir, appuyer, maintenir (une voûte, etc.). (b) Mec.E: Supporter, résister à (un effort, une charge). **2.** Appuyer (qn); soutenir, corroborer (une théorie); patronner (qn, un bal de charité); faire une donation à (une œuvre de charité, etc.). **Proofs that s. a case,** preuves à l'appui d'une cause. Parl: **To support the motion,** soutenir la motion. **He supported my statement,** il est venu à l'appui de mon dire. **To be supported by s.o.** (in a proposal), être secondé par qn. **3.** Entretenir (la vie, la combustion, etc.). **To support a family,** faire vivre, faire subsister, une famille. **To support oneself,** se suffire (à soi-même); gagner sa vie. **4.** Supporter, tolérer (une injure, etc.). **5.** Soutenir (un rôle, un caractère). **supporting,** a. (Mur) d'appui, de soutènement. Th: **The supporting cast,** la troupe qui seconde les premiers rôles.

supportable [sʌ'pɔːrtəbl], a. Supportable, tolérable.

supporter [sʌ'pɔːrtər], s. **1.** (Device) Soutien m, support m. **2.** (Pers.) Défenseur m, tenant m (d'une opinion); adhérent m (d'une cause); partisan m (d'un homme politique).

suppose [sʌ'pouz], v.tr. Supposer. (a) Let us s. the two things equal, supposons les deux choses égales. **Suppose ABC an equilateral triangle,** soit ABC un triangle équilatéral. **Suppose you are right, supposing (that) you are right,** supposons, supposé, que vous ayez raison; en supposant, à supposer, que vous ayez raison. Supposing he came back, si par supposition il

revenait. F: **Suppose we change the subject,** si nous changions de sujet. (b) **That supposes the perfectibility of man,** cela (pré)suppose la perfectibilité humaine. (c) S'imaginer; croire, penser. **You will do it, I suppose,** je suppose que vous le ferez. I don't s. he will do it, je ne suppose pas, il est peu probable, qu'il le fasse. **Will you go?—I suppose so,** irez-vous?—Probablement; sans doute. I declined, **as you may suppose,** vous pensez bien que j'ai refusé. F: I don't s. I have ridden in a bus for two years, autant que je sache, voilà deux ans que je n'ai pris l'autobus. **He is supposed to be wealthy,** on le suppose riche; il est censé être riche. **I am not supposed to know,** je suis censé ne pas le savoir. **supposed,** a. Supposé, prétendu; soi-disant. **The s. culprit,** le présumé coupable.

supposedly [sʌ'pouzidli], adv. Censément; soi-disant.

supposition [sʌpo'ziʃ(ə)n], s. Supposition f, hypothèse f. **Why should I make such a s.?** pourquoi irais-je supposer cela?

supposititious [sʌpɔzi'tiʃəs], a. Faux, f. fausse. Jur: (Enfant) supposé, substitué; (testament) supposé.

suppository [sʌ'pozitəri], s. Pharm: Suppositoire m.

suppress [sʌ'pres], v.tr. **1.** (a) Réprimer (une révolte). (b) Supprimer (un journal); faire disparaître (un abus). **2.** Étouffer (un bâillement, un scandale); réprimer, refouler (ses sentiments); faire taire (un interrupteur). **3.** Cacher, dissimuler (qch.); ne pas révéler (un fait); taire (un nom). Jur: Supprimer (un fait). **suppressed,** a. S. anger, colère réprimée, rentrée, refoulée. **S. excitement,** agitation contenue. **In a s. voice,** en baissant la voix.

suppression [sʌ'preʃ(ə)n], s. **1.** Répression f (d'une émeute, d'un abus); suppression f (d'un livre). **2.** Étouffement m (d'un scandale); refoulement m (des émotions). **3.** Dissimulation f (de la vérité).

suppurate ['sʌpjureit], v.i. Suppurer.

suppuration [sʌpju'reiʃ(ə)n], s. Suppuration f.

supraliminal [sju:pra'limin(ə)l], a. Psy: Supraliminal, -aux.

supremacy [sju'preməsi], s. Suprématie f (over, sur).

supreme [sju'pri:m], a. Suprême. **To reign supreme,** régner en maître, en souverain absolu. Jur: **Supreme court,** cour souveraine. F: **S. happiness,** bonheur suprême. **To hold s.o. in supreme contempt,** avoir un souverain mépris pour qn. **-ly,** adv. Suprêmement; au suprême degré.

surah ['sjuərə], s. Tex: Surah m.

surbase ['sə:'beis], v.tr. Arch: Surbaisser.

surcharge¹ ['sə:tʃɑːrdʒ], s. **1.** (Overload) Surcharge f; charge excessive. **2.** Droit m supplémentaire; surtaxe f. **3.** Surcharge (sur un timbre-poste).

surcharge² [sər'tʃɑːrdʒ], v.tr. **1.** (Overload) Surcharger (with, de). **2.** (Sur)taxer (une lettre, etc.). **3.** Post: Surcharger (un timbre-poste).

surcingle ['sə:rsiŋgl], s. Harn: Surfaix m; sous-ventrière f.

surd [sə:rd], s. (a) Mth: Quantité f incommensurable; racine irrationnelle. (b) Ling: Consonne sourde.

sure ['ʃuər]. **I.** a. Sûr, certain. (a) **To be sure of sth.,** être sûr, certain, de qch. **I am s. of it,** j'en suis convaincu; j'en ai la certitude. **I am not so sure of that,** je n'en suis pas bien sûr. **To be sure of oneself,** être sûr de soi(-même). F: **I'm**

sure I don't know, ma foi, je ne sais pas. To make sure of a fact, s'assurer d'un fait. *To make s. of a seat*, s'assurer une place. To make s.o. sure of sth., assurer qch. à qn. (b) Infaillible; (jugement, tireur) sûr; (asile) assuré; (remède) sûr, infaillible. (c) Indubitable; (succès) sûr, assuré. *To make the result s.*, assurer le résultat. *F:* Sure thing, chose certaine; *Rac:* certitude *f. U.S:* P: Sure thing! bien sûr! *I do not know for sure*, je n'en suis pas bien sûr. To-morrow for sure, demain sans faute. (d) It is sure to be fine, il fera sûrement beau. He is sure to come, il viendra à coup sûr; il viendra sûrement. Be sure to come early, ne manquez pas d'arriver de bonne heure. Be sure not to lose it, prenez garde de le perdre. (Yes,) to be sure! certainement! bien sûr! It's John, to be sure! tiens, c'est Jean! Well, to be sure! tiens, tiens! par exemple! 2. *adv.* (a) *Dial. & U.S:* Vraiment; certainement. It sure was a cold night, il faisait vraiment froid cette nuit-là. (b) As sure as death, as fate; *F:* as sure as eggs is eggs, aussi sûr que deux et deux font quatre. Sure enough, *he was there*, il était bien là; c'était bien lui. *He will come s. enough*, il viendra à coup sûr. Sure enough! c'est (bien) vrai! bien sûr! assurément! *U.S:* Sure! mais oui! bien sûr! **-ly,** *adv.* **1.** Sûrement. To work slowly but surely, travailler lentement mais sûrement. **2.** (a) *Lit:* Assurément. (b) *F:* Surely you don't believe that! vous ne croyez pas cela, voyons! *I know something about it s.!* j'en sais quelque chose peut-être! **3.** *Will you help me?*—Surely! voulez-vous m'aider?—Assurément! **sure-'footed,** *a.* sure-'sighted, *a.* A l'œil juste.

sureness ['ʃuərnəs], *s.* **1.** Sûreté *f* (de main, de pied). **2.** Certitude *f.*

surety ['ʃuərti], *s.* **1.** *A:* Sûreté *f*, certitude *f.* **2.** (a) *A:* Garantie *f*, cautionnement *m.* (b) (*Pers.*) Caution *f*; garant, -ante; *Com:* donneur *m* d'aval. To stand, go, surety for s.o., se rendre caution de qn; se porter caution pour qn.

surf [səːrf], *s.* Barre *f* de plage; ressac *m*; brisants *mpl* sur la plage. **'surf-bathing,** *s.* **1.** (*Esp. in Austr.*) Bains *mpl* dans les brisants de la plage. **2.** = SURF-RIDING. **'surf-board,** *s. Sp:* Aquaplane *m.* **'surf-boat,** Pirogue *f* de barre. **'surf-rider,** *s. Sp:* Chevaucheur *m* de ressac. **'surf-riding,** *s.* Sport *m* de l'aquaplane.

surface¹ ['səːrfes], *s.* **1.** (a) Surface *f.* (Of submarine) To proceed on the s., marcher en surface. To break surface, revenir en surface. *Min:* Work at the surface, travail au jour. *Mec.E:* Bearing surface, working surface, surface d'appui; portée *f.* (b) *F:* Extérieur *m*, dehors *m.* On the surface everything was well, tout allait bien en apparence. His faults are all on the s., malgré des défauts apparents le fond est bon. He never goes below the s., il s'arrête à la surface des choses. **2.** (a) *Geom:* Surface of revolution, surface de révolution. (b) Aire *f*, étendue *f*, superficie *f.* **'surface-coated,** *a. Paperm:* (Papier) couché. **'surface-drain,** *s.* Tranchée *f* à ciel ouvert. **'surface-plate,** *s. Mec.E:* Marbre *m* à dresser; plaque *f* de dressage. **'surface-tension,** *s. Ph:* Tension superficielle, de surface.

surface², *v.tr.* **1.** Apprêter, polir, la surface de (qch.). *Paperm:* Calandrer, glacer (le papier). **2.** *Civ.E:* Revêtir (une route, etc.) (with, de). **-surfaced,** *a.* Mat-surfaced, à surface mate. Smooth-surfaced, à surface lisse.

surfaceman, *pl.* **-men** ['səːrfesmən, -men], *s.m.* **1.** *Min:* Ouvrier du jour. **2.** *Rail:* Cheminot.

surfeit¹ ['səːrfit], *s.* **1.** Surabondance *f.* **2.** (a) Réplétion *f*; satiété *f.* To have a surfeit of oysters, être rassasié d'huîtres. *F:* To have a s. of advice, être comblé, accablé, de conseils. (b) Dégoût *m*; nausée *f.*

surfeit². 1. *v.i.* Se gorger; se repaître. **2.** *v.tr.* Gorger, rassasier (s.o. with good cheer, qn de bonne chère); blaser (qn). To surfeit oneself with sth., se gorger de qch. jusqu'à la nausée.

surge¹ [səːrdʒ], *s.* **1.** (a) *Nau:* Levée *f* de la lame; houle *f.* (b) *El.E:* Surge of current, vague, de colère. (b) *El.E:* Surge of current, vague, à-coup *m*, de courant; onde *f* de surtension. **2.** *Nau:* Saut *m* (d'un cordage); choc *m*, coup *m* de fouet (au cabestan).

surge², *v.i.* **1.** (*Of sea*) Être houleux; (*of waters*) se soulever. *The crowd surged along the street*, la foule se répandit en flots dans la rue. *The blood surged to her cheeks*, le sang lui refluait au visage. **2.** *El.E:* The current surges, il y a des surtensions de courant. *I.C.E:* The engine surges, le moteur pompe, galope. **3.** (*Of wheel*) Glisser. *Nau:* (*Of cable*) Choquer brusquement. **surging,** *a. S.* sea, mer houleuse; forte mer. *A s. mass of people*, un flot (pressé) d'êtres humains.

surgeon ['səːrdʒən], *s.* **1.** Chirurgien, -ienne. *S.a.* DENTAL, VETERINARY. **2.** Médecin *m* militaire; major *m.* *Navy:* Médecin.

surgery ['səːrdʒəri], *s.* **1.** Chirurgie *f*; médecine *f* opératoire. **2.** Cabinet *m* de consultation (chez un médecin); dispensaire *m* (d'un hôpital); clinique *f* (de quartier pauvre). Surgery hours, heures de consultation.

surgical ['səːrdʒik(ə)l], *a.* Chirurgical, -aux. *S. instruments*, instruments de chirurgie.

surliness ['səːrlinəs], *s.* Air bourru; maussaderie *f.*

surly ['səːrli], *a.* (a) Bourru; (b) Hargneux, maussade. *S. disposition*, humeur rébarbative.

surmise¹ [sər'maiz], *s.* Conjecture *f*, supposition *f.*

surmise², *v.tr.* Conjecturer, deviner; soupçonner. I surmised as much, je m'en doutais bien.

surmount, *v.tr.* **1.** Surmonter. *Mountain surmounted with snow*, montagne coiffée, couronnée, de neige. **2.** Surmonter (un obstacle); triompher (d'une difficulté).

surmullet [sər'mʌlet], *s. Ich:* Surmulet *m.*

surname¹ ['səːrneim], *s.* Nom *m* de famille. Christian names and surname, nom et prénoms *m.*

surname², *v.tr.* **1.** He is surnamed Smith, son nom de famille est Smith. **2.** William surnamed Longsword, Guillaume surnommé Longue-Épée.

surpass [sər'pɑːs], *v.tr.* **1.** Surpasser. To s. s.o. in intelligence, surpasser qn par l'intelligence. You have surpassed yourself, vous avez été audessus de vous-même. **2.** The result surpassed my hopes, le résultat a excédé mes espérances, a dépassé mon attente. **surpassing,** *a.* Sans pareil. *Of s. beauty*, d'une beauté incomparable. **-ly,** *adv.* Extrêmement, excessivement. He was s. ugly, il était d'une laideur sans égale.

surplice ['səːrplis], *s.* Surplis *m.*

surpliced ['səːrplist], *a.* En surplis.

surplus ['səːrpləs], *s.* **1.** Surplus, excédent *m.* *Fin:* Boni *m.* To have a surplus of sth., avoir qch. en excès; avoir (des livres) en surnombre. **2.** *Attrib.* Surplus population, surplus, excédent, de la population. *Com:* Sale of surplus stock, vente de soldes *m.*

surprise[1] [sər'prɑːiz], s. Surprise f. **1.** To take s.o. by surprise, prendre qn à l'improviste, au dépourvu. *Mil:* Surprise attack, attaque brusquée; coup *m* de main. Surprise visit, visite à l'improviste. **2.** To give s.o. a surprise, faire une surprise à qn. *It was a great s. to me,* j'en ai été grandement surpris. **3.** Étonnement *m.* To my great surprise, much to my surprise, à ma grande surprise. *I paused in surprise,* je m'arrêtai surpris.

surprise[2], *v.tr.* Surprendre. **1.** Prendre (une place) par surprise, par coup de main. To surprise s.o. in the act, prendre qn sur le fait. **2.** Étonner. To be surprised at sth., être surpris de qch. *I am surprised to see you,* je m'étonne de vous voir. *I should not be surprised if . . .,* cela ne me surprendrait pas si. . . . *I am surprised at you!* vous m'étonnez! surprising, *a.* Surprenant, étonnant. It is surprising that *you (should) know it,* il est surprenant que vous le sachiez. **-ly,** *adv.* Étonnamment. *I found him looking s. young,* j'ai été surpris de lui trouver l'air si jeune.

surprisedly [sər'praizidli], *adv.* D'un air de surprise; avec surprise.

surrealist [sər'riːəlist], *a. & s.* Surréaliste.

surrender[1] [sʌ'rendər], s. **1.** (a) Reddition (d'une forteresse). (b) No surrender! on ne se rend pas! (c) *Jur:* Surrender of a defendant to his bail, décharge *f* de ses cautions par un accusé. **2.** Abandon *m*, abandonnement *m*, cession *f* (de biens); remise *f* (des armes à feu, etc.). *F:* To make a surrender of principle(s), transiger avec ses principes. **3.** *Ins:* Rachat *m* (d'une police).

surrender[2]. **1.** *v.tr.* (a) Rendre, livrer (une forteresse, etc.). (b) *Jur: etc:* Abandonner, céder (un droit, ses biens, etc.). *To s. one's office,* démissionner. *F:* To surrender all hope of sth., abandonner, renoncer à, tout espoir de qch. (c) *Ins:* Racheter (une police). **2.** *v.pr. & i.* To surrender (oneself), se rendre; *Mil:* faire (sa) soumission; rendre les armes. To surrender (oneself) to justice, se livrer à la justice.

surreptitious [sʌrep'tiʃəs], *a.* Subreptice, clandestin. **-ly,** *adv.* Subrepticement, clandestinement, furtivement.

surround[1] [sʌ'raund], s. Encadrement *m*, bordure *f.*

surround[2], *v.tr.* Entourer. (a) *To s. a town with walls,* entourer, ceinturer, ceindre, une ville de murs. Surrounded by, with, dangers, entouré, environné, de dangers. (b) *Mil:* Entourer, cerner (l'ennemi, etc.); investir (une ville, etc.).

surrounding, *a.* Entourant, environnant.

surroundings, *s.pl.* **1.** Entourage *m*, milieu *m*, ambiance *f.* **2.** Environs *mpl*, alentours *mpl* (d'une ville, etc.).

surtax[1] ['səːrtaks], s. Surtaxe *f.*

surtax[2], *v.tr.* Surtaxer.

surtout [səː'tuː], s. *Cost: A:* Surtout *m*, pardessus *m.*

surveillance [sər'veil(j)əns], s. *Adm:* Surveillance *f*, contrôle *m.*

survey[1] ['səːrvei], s. **1.** (a) Aperçu *m*; vue générale, exposé *m* sommaire (d'un sujet). (b) Examen attentif; étude *f* (de la situation). To take, make, a survey of sth., (i) jeter un coup d'œil sur qch.; (ii) se rendre compte de la situation actuelle, etc.). *Political s.,* tour *m* d'horizon politique. **2.** *Surv:* Levé *m* des plans; relevé *m.* (b) Plan *m*, levé (du terrain). Trigonometrical survey, levé trigonométrique. To make, effect, a survey, lever un plan. Survey

vessel, navire *m* hydrographe. **3.** Inspection *f*, visite *f*; expertise *f.*

survey[2] [sər'vei], *v.tr.* **1.** (a) Regarder, contempler, promener ses regards sur (le paysage, etc.). (b) Mettre (une question) à l'étude; passer (la situation) en revue. **2.** *Surv:* Relever, faire le (re)levé de, lever le(s) plan(s) de (la ville, etc.); arpenter (un champ). *To s. a railway,* faire les études d'une ligne de chemin de fer. *Nau: To s. a coast,* faire l'hydrographie d'une côte. *Civ.E:* To survey for quantities, métrer, toiser. **3.** Inspecter; visiter; faire l'expertise de l'état (d'un navire). surveying, s. **1.** *Surv:* Levé *m* de plans. **(Land-)surveying,** arpentage *m*, géodésie *f*; topographie *f.* Naval surveying, hydrographie *f.* **2.** Inspection *f*, visite *f*; expertise *f.*

surveyor [sər'veiər], s. **1.** (Land-)surveyor, arpenteur *m* (géomètre); ingénieur *m* géographe. Naval surveyor, (ingénieur) hydrographe *m.* Highways surveyor, agent *m* voyer. **2.** *Adm:* (a) Surveillant *m*, inspecteur *m.* Surveyor of taxes, contrôleur, inspecteur, des contributions directes. (b) Ship surveyor, visiteur *m*, inspecteur, de navires; expert *m.*

survival [sər'vaiv(ə)l], s. (a) Survivance *f.* Survival of the fittest, survivance des mieux adaptés, du plus apte. (b) *Jur: Ins:* Survie *f.*

survive [sər'vaiv]. **1.** *v.i.* (a) Survivre; *(of custom)* subsister; passer à la postérité. (b) *Jur: (Of estate)* To survive to X, passer aux mains de X (qui est le survivant). **2.** *v.tr.* (a) Survivre à (qn). (b) *To s. an injury,* survivre à une blessure. *To s. a disease, a shipwreck,* réchapper d'une maladie, d'un naufrage.

survivor [sər'vaivər], s. Survivant, -ante. *The survivors of the disaster,* les rescapé(e)s.

survivorship [sər'vaivərʃip], s. *Jur:* Survie *f.*

Susan ['suːz(ə)n, 'sjuː-]. *Pr.n.f.* Suzanne.

susceptibility [sʌsepti'biliti], s. **1.** (a) Susceptibilité *f* (magnétique). (b) Susceptibility to a disease, prédisposition *f* à une maladie. **2.** Sensibilité *f*, susceptibilité. *These people have their susceptibilities,* ces gens-là ont leurs délicatesses *f.* *To avoid wounding any susceptibilities,* éviter tout froissement.

susceptible [sʌ'septibl], *a.* **1.** (a) Susceptible of proof, susceptible d'être prouvé. (b) Susceptible to a disease, prédisposé à une maladie. **2.** (a) Sensible, impressionnable. *S. to good influences,* ouvert, sensible, accessible, aux bonnes influences. (b) Qui se froisse facilement; susceptible.

suspect[1] ['sʌspekt], *a. & s.* Suspect, -e. *A:* To hold s.o. suspect, tenir qn pour suspect.

suspect[2] [sʌ'spekt], *v.tr.* **1.** To suspect s.o. of a crime, soupçonner qn d'un crime. To be suspected, être en suspicion. *To be suspected by s.o. of sth.,* être suspect à qn de qch. *I s. him of drinking,* je le soupçonne d'être ivrogne. **2.** Soupçonner, s'imaginer (qch.). *I s. that he is, I s. him to be, the perpetrator of the joke,* j'ai idée que c'est lui l'auteur de cette farce. *I suspected as much,* je m'en doutais; j'en avais le soupçon. *To s. danger,* flairer le danger. *He suspects nothing,* il ne se doute de rien. *I s. he is inclined to be selfish,* je lui soupçonne un peu d'égoïsme.

suspend [sʌ'spend], *v.tr.* Suspendre. **1.** Pendre (un trophée, etc.). **2.** Suspendre (son jugement, les paiements, le travail). *Jur:* To suspend judgment, surseoir au jugement. **3.** Suspendre (un fonctionnaire); interdire (qn) de ses fonctions; mettre (un jockey) à pied. *Parl:* Exclure temporairement (un député). *Aut:* To suspend a licence, suspendre un permis de conduire.

uspended, *a.* Suspendu. **1.** *S. particles,* articules en suspension. **2.** (*a*) (*Of traffic*) interrompu. *Jur:* (*Of proceedings*) En suspens. **uspended animation,** arrêt momentané des onctions vitales; syncope *f.* (*b*) *Mus:* Suspended cadence, cadence suspendue.

spender [sʌs'pendər], *s.* (*a*) Suspensoir *m.* *b*) Stocking suspenders, jarretelles *f.* Sock uspenders, fixe-chaussettes *m.* *S.a.* BELT¹ 1. *c*) *U.S:* Suspenders, bretelles *f.*

spense [sʌs'pens], *s.* (*a*) Suspens *m.* To keep, old, s.o. in suspense, tenir qn en suspens. *b*) The question remains in suspense, la question este pendante.

spension [sʌs'penʃ(ə)n], *s.* **1.** *Mec.E:* etc: uspension *f.* Suspension cable, câble porteur. . (*a*) Suspension (de la circulation, etc.). To he suspension of all other business, toute affaire essante. (*b*) *Gram:* Points of suspension, points uspensifs. **3.** Suspension (d'un fonctionnaire, tc.); mise *f* en non-activité (d'un officier); ise à pied (d'un jockey). *Parl:* Exclusion *f* emporaire (d'un député). Suspension of a driving licence, retrait *m* temporaire d'un permis e conduire. **sus'pension-bridge,** *s.* Pont uspendu.

spensory [sʌs'pensəri], *a.* (*a*) *Anat:* (*Of gament, etc.*) Suspenseur *m.* (*b*) **Suspensory** andage, suspensoir *m.*

spicion [sʌs'piʃ(ə)n], *s.* **1.** Soupçon *m.* *Jur:* uspicion *f.* Not the shadow, not the ghost, of suspicion, pas l'ombre *f* d'un soupçon. With uspicion, avec défiance. My suspicion is that . . ., e soupçonne que . . ., j'ai dans l'idée que. . . . o have suspicions about s.o., avoir des doutes ur qn; soupçonner qn. To hold s.o in suspicion, tenir qn pour suspect. To cast suspicion n s.o.'s good faith, suspecter la loyauté de qn. 'o lay oneself open to suspicion, s'exposer aux oupçons. To arouse suspicion, éveiller, faire aître, les soupçons. To arouse, awaken, s.o.'s uspicions, éveiller la défiance de qn; donner éveil à qn. Above suspicion, au-dessus de tout oupçon. Evidence not beyond s., témoignages ujets à caution. To be right in one's suspicions, oupçonner juste. *Jur:* To arrest, detain, s.o. on uspicion, arrêter, détenir, qn préventivement. **. F:** I had my suspicions about it, je m'en outais. **3.** Très petite quantité, soupçon (*of,* .e).

spicious [sʌs'piʃəs], *a.* **1.** Soupçonnable, uspect; (*of conduct, etc.*) louche, équivoque. To ook suspicious, avoir l'air louche, suspect. **.** Méfiant, soupçonneux. To be, feel, s. about .o., of s.o., avoir des soupçons à l'endroit de qn, l'égard de qn. **-ly,** *adv.* **1.** D'une manière uspecte, équivoque, louche. *F:* It looks to me uspiciously like measles, ça m'a tout l'air d'être a rougeole. **2.** D'un air méfiant; soupçon-eusement.

spiciousness [sʌs'piʃnəs], *s.* **1.** Caractère uspect, louche, équivoque (*of,* de). **2.** Caractère oupçonneux; méfiance *f.*

stain [sʌs'tein], *v.tr.* Soutenir, supporter. **.** (*a*) Enough to sustain life, de quoi entretenir a vie; de quoi vivre. To sustain the body, utenir, sustenter, le corps. Evidence to sustain n assertion, témoignages pour soutenir une ffirmation. *Th:* To sustain a part, soutenir, enir, remplir, un rôle. *Mus:* To sustain a note, outenir, prolonger, une note. (*b*) *Jur:* (*Of court*) 'o sustain an objection, admettre une réclama-ion. **2.** (*a*) *Mil:* To sustain an attack, soutenir ne attaque. (*b*) To sustain a loss, éprouver,

essuyer, souffrir, subir, une perte. To sustain an injury, recevoir une blessure; être blessé. **sustained,** *a.* (*Of effort, attention, etc.*) Soutenu. *S.* applause, applaudissements prolongés, nourris. *Ph:* Sustained oscillations, oscillations entretenues. **sustaining,** *a.* Soutenant. **1.** Sustaining food, nourriture qui soutient (bien); nourriture fortifiante. **2.** *Mec:* Sustaining force, force portante.

sustenance ['sʌstinəns], *s.* (*a*) Sustentation *f.* Means of sustenance, moyens de subsistance; moyens de vivre. (*b*) Aliments *mpl,* nourriture *f.*

sutler ['sʌtlər], *s.* *Mil:* Cantinier, -ière.

suttee [sʌ'tiː], *s.* *Hindoo Rel:* Sâti *m,* suttee *m.*

suture ['sjuːtjər], *s.* *Anat:* *Bot:* *Surg:* Suture *f.*

suzerain ['sjuːzərein], *s.* Suzerain *m.*

suzeraine ['sjuːzərein], *s.f.* Suzeraine.

suzerainty ['sjuːzəreinti], *s.* Suzeraineté *f.*

swab¹ [swɔb], *s.* **1.** (*a*) Torchon *m.* (*b*) *Artil:* Écouvillon *m.* (*c*) *Nau:* Fauber(t) *m.* (*d*) *Surg:* Swab of cotton wool, tampon *m* d'ouate. *Med:* To take a swab (*of s.o.'s throat*), faire un pré-lèvement dans la gorge de qn. **2.** *P:* Lourdaud *m,* andouille *f;* propre *m* à rien. **3.** *Navy:* *P:* Épaulette *f.*

swab², *v.tr.* (swabbed) **1.** Nettoyer, essuyer (avec un torchon, etc.). *Nau:* Fauberter, essarder (le pont). **2.** *Artil:* To swab (out), écouvillonner (une pièce). **3.** To swab (down), laver à grande eau. **4.** To swab up, éponger (une flaque, etc.).

swaddle [swɔdl], *v.tr.* Emmailloter (*with,* de). **'swaddling-clothes,** *s.pl.* Maillot *m.*

swag [swag], *s.* **1.** Balancement *m,* ballotte-ment *m.* **2.** *Furn:* *Arch:* Bouillon *m,* guirlande *f.* **3.** *P:* (*a*) Rafle *f,* butin *m* (d'un cambrioleur). (*b*) (*In Austr.*) Baluchon *m,* paquet *m* (de chemineau).

swage¹ [swe:idʒ], *s.* *Tls:* Étampe *f,* emboutissoir *m.* Bottom swage, sous-chasse *f,* contre-étampe *f.*

swage², *v.tr.* Étamper, emboutir.

swagger¹ ['swagər], *a.* Élégant; ultra-chic.

swagger², *s.* **1.** (*a*) Air important. To walk with a swagger, marcher avec un air avantageux; faire la roue. (*b*) Air cavalier, désinvolte. **2.** Rodomon-tades *fpl;* crâneries *fpl.* **'swagger-cane, -stick,** *s.* *Mil:* (*a*) Jonc *m,* stick *m* (d'officier). (*b*) Petit jonc de tenue de sortie (de simple soldat); badine *f.* **'swagger-coat,** *s.* Man-teau *m* raglan trois-quarts.

swagger³, *v.i.* (*a*) Crâner, se pavaner; plas-tronner; poser (insolemment). (*b*) Fanfaronner; faire de l'esbrouffe. (*c*) To swagger in, out, entrer, sortir, d'un air important, glorieux. To swagger along, se carrer en marchant. **swag-gering,** *a.* (Air, etc.) important, crâneur, glorieux, conquérant.

swaggerer ['swagərər], *s.* Crâneur, -euse.

swain [swein], *s.m.* (*a*) *A. & Poet:* Jeune berger; amoureux (de pastorale). (*b*) *Hum:* Sou-pirant.

swallow¹ ['swɔlo], *s.* **1.** Gosier *m,* gorge *f.* **2.** Gorgée *f* (d'eau, etc.). To drink sth. at one swallow, boire qch. d'un seul coup. **'swallow-hole,** *s.* *Geol:* Bétoire *f;* perte *f* (d'un fleuve).

swallow², *v.tr.* **1.** To swallow sth. (down). (i) avaler, ingurgiter, qch.; (ii) gober (une huître). To swallow the bait, (i) (*of fish*) avaler l'appât; (ii) *F:* (*of pers.*) se laisser prendre à l'appât. *F:* To swallow one's tears, dévorer ses larmes. To swallow one's pride, mettre son orgueil dans sa poche. To swallow a story, gober, avaler, une histoire. To swallow an affront, avaler, boire, un affront. To swallow one's words, se rétracter. **2.** *Abs.* Avaler sa

salive (pour faire passer une émotion). **swallow up**, *v.tr.* (i) Dévorer, avaler (qch.); (ii) (*of the sea, etc.*) engloutir, engouffrer (qch.).
swallow³, *s.* Hirondelle *f.* Common swallow, hirondelle domestique. **House-swallow**, hirondelle rustique, de cheminée. *Prov:* One swallow does not make a summer, une hirondelle ne fait pas le printemps. **'swallow-fish**, *s. Ich:* Hirondelle *f* de mer; trigle *m* hirondelle. **'swallow-tail**, *s.* **1.** Queue fourchue; queue d'hirondelle. **2.** *Cost: F:* (*Often pl.*) Queue-de-morue *f.* **'swallow-tailed**, *a.* A queue fourchue.
swam [swam]. See SWIM².
swamp¹ [swɔmp], *s.* Marais *m*, marécage *m*, bas-fond *m.* **'swamp-fever**, *s.* Fièvre paludéenne.
swamp², *v.tr.* **1.** Inonder, submerger (un pré); *F:* inonder (une pièce, la cave). **2.** (*a*) Remplir d'eau (une embarcation). (*b*) *F: To be swamped with work*, être débordé de travail.
swampy ['swɔmpi], *a.* Marécageux.
swan [swɔn], *s.* Cygne *m. Lit:* The Swan of Avon, Shakespeare. **'swan-neck**, *s. Mec.E:* Cou *m*, col *m*, de cygne. **'swan-necked**, *a.* **1.** Au cou de cygne. **2.** *Tls: etc:* En col de cygne. **'swan's down**, *s.* **1.** Duvet *m* de cygne. **2.** *Tex:* Molleton *m.* **'swan-song**, *s.* Chant *m* du cygne. **'swan-upping**, *s.* Recensement annuel des cygnes de la Tamise.
swank¹ [swaŋk], *s. F:* **1.** Prétention *f*, gloriole *f*, épate *f.* **2.** = SWANKER.
swank², *v.i. F:* Se donner des airs; crâner; faire de l'épate.
swanker ['swaŋkər], *s. F:* Épateur, -euse; poseur, -euse; crâneur, -euse.
swanky ['swaŋki], *a. F:* Prétentieux, poseur.
swanskin ['swɔnskin], *s.* **1.** Peau *f* de cygne. **2.** *Tex:* Molleton *m.*
swap¹ [swɔp], *s.* (*a*) Troc *m*, échange *m.* (*b*) *pl.* (*In stamp-collecting*) Swaps, doubles *m.*
swap², *v.tr.* (swapped [swɔpt]) *F: To swap sth.* for sth., échanger, troquer, qch. contre, pour, qch. To swap places with s.o., changer de place avec qn. **swapping**, *s.* Échange *m*, troc *m.*
sward [swɔ:rd], *s.* (Tapis *m* de) gazon *m*; pelouse *f.*
sware [swɛər]. See SWEAR².
swarm¹ [swɔ:rm], *s.* Essaim *m*, jetée *f* (d'abeilles). (*Of bees*) To send out a swarm, jeter un essaim. *F:* Swarm of children, essaim, troupe *f*, *F:* ribambelle *f*, d'enfants.
swarm², *v.i.* **1.** (*a*) (*Of bees*) Essaimer; faire l'essaim. (*b*) (*Of pers.*) Accourir en foule, se presser (autour de, dans, qch.). (*c*) *F:* Pulluler, grouiller. **2.** To swarm with . . ., fourmiller, grouiller, de. . . . *The roads are swarming with people*, les rues grouillent, regorgent, de monde.
swarm³, *v.tr. & i.* To swarm (up) a tree, monter, grimper, à un arbre.
swarthiness ['swɔ:rθinəs, -ði-], *s.* Teint basané, bistré.
swarthy ['swɔ:rθi, -ði], *a.* (Teint) basané, bistré, boucané.
swash [swɔʃ]. **1.** *s.* Clapotage *m*, clapotement *m*, clapotis *m* (des vagues). **2.** *adv.* To fall swash, faire pouf en tombant (par terre).
swashbuckler ['swɔʃbʌklər], *s.* Rodomont *m*, brétailleur *m*, matamore *m.*
swashbuckling¹ ['swɔʃbʌkliŋ], *a.* Brétailleur, bretteur, fanfaron.
swashbuckling², *s.* Rodomontades *fpl*; fanfaronnades *fpl.*

swastika ['swastika, -wɔs-], *s.* Svastika *m* croix gammée.
swat [swɔt], *v.tr. U.S: P:* Frapper (qn, qch. *S. that fly!* écrasez donc cette mouche !
swath [swɔ:θ], *s. Husb:* Andain *m*, ondain *n* fauchée *f.*
swathe [sweːið], *v.tr.* Emmailloter; envelopp (*in*, de). **swathing**, *s.* **1.** Emmaillotement *n* enveloppement *m.* **2.** *pl.* Swathings, bandages *m* bandelettes *f* (de momie). **'swathing-band** *s.pl.* Langes *mpl*, maillot *m.*
swatter ['swɔtər], *s.* (Fly-)swatter, (balai *m* tue-mouches *m inv.*
sway¹ [swei], *s.* **1.** Balancement *m*, oscillation *f* mouvement *m* de va-et-vient. *Aut:* Roulis (de la voiture). **2.** Empire *m*, domination Under his sway, sous son empire; sous s influence. To bring a people under one's swa réduire un peuple sous sa puissance. To hol bear, sway over a people, régner sur un peuple exercer le pouvoir sur un peuple.
sway². **I.** *v.i.* (*a*) Se balancer; osciller; ballotte (*of drunkard*) vaciller. (*Of trees*) To s. in the win se balancer au vent. (*b*) Rester indécis; balance (*c*) (*Of balance, etc.*) Pencher; incliner. **2.** *v. (a*) Faire osciller; balancer, agiter (les arbre etc.). (*b*) Porter, tenir (le sceptre). (*c*) Go verner, diriger, influencer. (*d*) To sway s.o. from his course, détourner qn de ses projet (*e*) *Nau:* To sway up, hisser, guinder (un m de hune, etc.).
swear¹ [swɛər], *s.* Jurons *mpl. To indulge i to have, a good s.*, lâcher une bordée de juron **'swear-word**, *s. F:* Gros mot; juron *m.*
swear², *v.* (*p.t.* swore [swɔːər], *A:* sware [swɛər *p.p.* sworn [swɔːrn]) **I.** *v.tr.* (*a*) Jurer. To swea sth. on the Bible, jurer qch. sur la Bible. T swear to do sth., jurer de faire qch. We could ha sworn we heard cries, on aurait juré entendre d cris. (*b*) To swear (in) a witness, faire prêt serment, déférer le serment, à un témoin. (*juryman*) To be sworn (in), prêter serment. T swear s.o. to secrecy, faire jurer le secret à q (*c*) Déclarer (qch.) sous la foi du serment. **2.** *v* Jurer; proférer un juron. To swear like trooper, jurer comme un charretier. It's enoug to make a saint swear, il y a de quoi faire jur un saint. **swear at**, *v.ind.tr.* Maudire, injuri (qn). **swear away**, *v.tr.* To swear away s.o. life, envoyer qn à l'échafaud en portant un fau témoignage. **swear by**, *v.i.* **1.** To swear one's honour, jurer sa foi. **2.** Préconiser, vante **swear off**, *v.i.* Jurer de renoncer à (l'alcoo etc.). **swear to**, *v.ind.tr.* Attester, certifie (qch.) sous serment. *I s. to it*, j'en lève la mai *I would s. to it*, j'en jurerais. **sworn**, *a.* **1.** Swo official, fonctionnaire assermenté. Sworn enemie ennemis jurés, acharnés. **2.** Sworn statemen déclaration sous serment. **swearing**, *s.* **1.** (*a*) A testation *f* sous serment. (*b*) Prestation *f* serment. **2.** Swearing (in) of the jury, asse mentation *f* du jury. **3.** Jurons *mpl*; gros mot
sweat¹ [swet], *s.* **1.** Sueur *f*, transpiration By the sweat of one's brow, à la sueur de s front. To be in a sweat, (i) être trempé de sueu suer à grosses gouttes; (ii) être tout en émo **2.** To give a horse a sweat, donner une suée un cheval. **3.** *P:* Corvée *f*; suée *f.* **4.** *Mil: F* An old sweat, un vieux troupier. **'sweat-ban** *s.* Cuir intérieur (d'un chapeau). **'sweat cloth**, *s. Harn:* Tapis *m* de selle. **'swea gland**, *s. Anat:* Glande *f* sudoripare.
sweat². **I.** *v.i.* **1.** (*a*) Suer, transpirer; *F:* êt en nage. *To s. profusely*, suer à grosses goutte

(b) (*Of worker*) Peiner; *P:* turbiner. **2.** (*Of walls*) Suer, suinter. II. **sweat,** *v.tr.* **I.** (*a*) Suer (du sang). (*b*) Faire suer (qn). *Med:* Faire transpirer (qn). (*c*) Exploiter (la main-d'œuvre). **2.** Frayer (la monnaie d'or). **sweated,** *a.* (Travail) mal rétribué. **sweating**^{1}, *a.* En sueur; suant; (mur) suintant. **sweating**^{2}, *s.* **I.** (*a*) Transpiration *f*; *Med:* sudation *f*. (*b*) Suintement *m* (d'un mur). **2.** (*a*) *Med:* Suée *f*. (*b*) Exploitation *f* (de la main-d'œuvre). **The sweating system,** l'exploitation patronale. **sweater** ['swetər], *s.* **I.** *Cost:* Chandail *m*; tricot *m*. **2.** *Pej:* Exploiteur *m* (de main-d'œuvre).

swede [swiːd], *s.* **I.** Suédois, -oise. **2.** *Agr:* Rutabaga *m*; navet *m* de Suède.

Sweden ['swiːd(ə)n]. *Pr.n.* La Suède.

Swedish ['swiːdiʃ]. **I.** *a.* Suédois. **2.** *s. Ling:* Le suédois.

sweep^1 [swiːp], *s.* **I.** (*a*) Coup *m* de balai, de faux. **At one sweep,** d'un seul coup. (*b*) Balayage *m*. *F:* **To make a clean sweep of sth.,** faire table rase de qch. **To make a clean s.** *of one's staff,* faire place nette de son personnel. *Gaming:* **To make a clean sweep,** rafler le tout. **2.** Mouvement *m* circulaire (du bras, du regard). *With a wide* *s. of the arm,* d'un geste large. **Within the sweep of the net,** dans le cercle du filet. **3.** Course *f* rapide (d'un fleuve). **4.** (*a*) Courbe *f*; boucle *f* (d'une rivière); *Arch:* courbure *f* (d'un arc). *The car took a big s.,* l'auto prit un virage large. *S. of a* *motor car's lines,* galbe *m* d'une auto. (*b*) *Fine* **sweep of grass,** belle étendue de gazon. (*c*) *Artil:* Battage *m* (d'une pièce). *Within the s. of the* *guns,* à portée. (*d*) Envergure *f*. **5.** (i) Aviron *m* (de galère); (ii) aviron de queue (d'une embarcation). **6.** *Nau:* Câble balayeur; drague *f* (pour mines). **7.** (Chimney-)sweep, ramoneur *m*. **8.** *F:* = SWEEPSTAKE. **Sweep-ticket,** billet *m* de sweepstake.

sweep^2, *v.* (swept [swept]; swept) I. *v.tr.* **I.** (*a*) Balayer (une chambre); ramoner (une cheminée). *A storm swept the town,* un orage balaya la ville. **The deck was swept by a sea,** une grosse vague balaya le pont. **To sweep the horizon with a telescope,** parcourir l'horizon avec une lunette. **To sweep the seas of one's enemies,** purger la mer de ses ennemis. **To sweep the board,** faire rafle; faire table rase; *F:* remporter un succès complet. *S.a.* BROOM 2. (*b*) Draguer (un chenal). *Abs.* **To sweep for mines,** draguer des mines. **2.** (*a*) Balayer (la poussière). (*b*) Emporter, entraîner. *A wave swept him overboard,* une lame le jeta à la mer. *To be swept off one's* *feet by the tide,* être entraîné par la marée; perdre pied. **3.** **To sweep one's hand over sth.,** passer la main sur qch. II. **sweep,** *v.i.* **I.** *The plain* *sweeps (away) towards the north,* la plaine s'étend vers le nord. **2.** **To sweep (along),** avancer avec un mouvement rapide et uni. **She swept into the room,** elle entra dans la salle d'un air majestueux. (*Of car*) **To sweep round the corner,** tourner le coin de la rue en faisant un large virage. *The road sweeps round the lake,* la route décrit une courbe autour du lac. **sweep along,** *v.tr.* (*Of current*) Entraîner, emporter (qch.). **sweep aside,** *v.tr.* Écarter (les rideaux, etc.) d'un geste large. **sweep away,** *v.tr.* Balayer (la neige); supprimer, détruire (un abus). *Bridge* *swept away by the torrent,* pont emporté, balayé, par le torrent. **sweep by,** *v.i.* Passer (i) avec vitesse, (ii) majestueusement. **sweep down.** **I.** *v.tr. The current sweeps the logs down with it,* le courant entraîne, charrie, le bois. **2.** *v.i.* (*a*) *The*

enemy swept down upon us, l'ennemi s'abattit sur nous. (*b*) *Hills sweeping down to the sea,* collines qui dévalent vers la mer. **sweep off,** *v.tr.* Enlever, emporter, avec violence. **sweep on,** *v.i.* Continuer d'avancer (irrésistiblement). **sweep out,** *v.tr.* Balayer (une chambre). **sweep past,** *v.i.* = SWEEP BY. **sweep round,** *v.i. Nau:* Virer. **sweep up.** **I.** *v.tr.* (*a*) Balayer, ramasser (la poussière). (*b*) Rassembler (la poussière) en tas. (*c*) *Aut:* Swept-up chassis, châssis surélevé (à l'arrière). **2.** *v.i. The avenue sweeps up to the* *front door,* l'allée décrit une courbe jusqu'au perron. **sweeping**^{1}, *a.* **I.** (*Of stream*) Rapide, impétueux. **2.** (*a*) Sweeping gesture, geste large. Sweeping curtsy, révérence profonde. (*b*) Sweeping flight, vol plané (des grands oiseaux). (*c*) *Art:* The *s. lines of the drapery,* les lignes dégagées des draperies. **3.** Sweeping statement, déclaration par trop générale. Sweeping reform, réforme complète. Sweeping changes, changement de fond en comble. **sweeping**^{2}, *s.* **I.** Balayage *m*; ramonage *m* (d'une cheminée). **2.** *pl.* Sweepings, balayures *f*, ordures *f*. *F:* The sweepings of society, le rebut de la société. **'sweeping-machine,** *s.* Balayeuse *f* mécanique.

sweeper ['swiːpər], *s.* **I.** (*Pers.*) Balayeur, -euse. **2.** (*Machine*) Balayeuse *f* (mécanique).

sweepstake ['swiːpsteik], *s. Turf:* Poule *f*; sweepstake *m*.

sweet [swiːt]. I. *a.* Doux, *f.* douce. **I.** Sucré. **As sweet as honey,** doux comme (le) miel. Sweet **stuff,** bonbons *mpl*, friandises *fpl*. *My tea is too s.,* mon thé est trop sucré. **To have a sweet tooth,** aimer les douceurs. *F:* Sweet morsel, morceau succulent. *S.a.* OMELETTE, POTATO 2. **2.** Sweet violet, violette odorante. **To smell sweet,** sentir bon. *S.a.* HERB, PEA 2. **3.** (*Of food*) Frais, *f.* fraîche. Sweet breath, haleine saine, fraîche. **4.** (Son) doux, mélodieux. **5.** (*a*) Sweet temper, caractère doux, aimable. *Revenge is s.,* la vengeance est douce. (*b*) *F:* Charmant; gentil, *f.* gentille. That's very sweet of you! c'est bien gentil à vous! **To say sweet nothings to** s.o., dire des gentillesses, des douceurs, à qn. **6.** *F:* **To be sweet on s.o.,** être amoureux de qn. *I am not very s. on the suggestion,* cette proposition ne me dit rien. **7.** Sweet running (*of a machine*), fonctionnement doux. **-ly,** *adv.* **I.** (*a*) Doucement; avec douceur. (*b*) (Chanter) mélodieusement. **2.** Agréablement, *F:* gentiment. *S.a.* PRETTY I. **3.** (*Of machine*) *To run s.,* fonctionner sans à-coups; avoir une allure douce. II. **sweet,** *s.* **I.** (*a*) Bonbon *m*. Sweets, sucreries *f*, confiseries *f*. (*b*) (*At dinner*) Entremets sucré. **2.** *pl.* Sweets, douceurs *f* (de la vie). **sweet 'oil,** *s.* Huile douce; *esp.* huile d'olive. **'sweet-'scented,** *a.* Qui sent bon, qui embaume; au parfum délicieux. **'sweet-shop,** *s.* Confiserie *f*. **'sweet-'smelling,** *a.* = SWEET-SCENTED. **'sweet-'tempered,** *a.* Au caractère doux. **'sweet-'toothed,** *a.* Qui aime les douceurs, le sucre. **sweet-'william,** *s. Bot:* Œillet *m* de poète.

sweetbread ['swiːtbred], *s. Cu:* Ris *m* de veau, d'agneau.

sweeten ['swiːt(ə)n]. **I.** *v.tr.* (*a*) Sucrer (un plat). (*b*) Purifier (l'air, l'eau). (*c*) Adoucir (la vie). **2.** *v.i.* (*a*) S'adoucir. (*b*) (*Of gears*) Se faire. **sweetening,** *s.* **I.** Adoucissement *m*; sucrage *m*. **2.** Substance *f* pour sucrer.

sweetheart ['swiːthɑːt], *s.* **I.** Amoureux, -euse. **(My) sweetheart!** mon amour! **2.** Fiancé, -ée. **sweetish** ['swiːtiʃ], *a.* Douceâtre.

sweetmeat ['swi:tmi:t], s. Bonbon m. Sweet-meats, sucreries f. Sweetmeat box, bonbon-nière f.
sweetness ['swi:tnəs], s. I. Douceu: f. 2. F: Gentillesse f, charme m.
swell[1] [swel]. I. s. I. (a) Bosse f; renflement m. (b) Swell of ground, éminence f, ondulation f. (c) Mus: Crescendo m et diminuendo. Lit: The majestic s. of the organ, les accents majestueux du grand orgue. 2. Nau: Houle f; levée f (de la lame). There is a heavy s., il y a une forte houle. 3. Mus: Soufflet m (d'un orgue). S.a. PEDAL[1] 2. 4. (a) F: Élégant m; F: faraud m. (b) P: Gros personnage. The swells, les gens chics; la (haute) gomme. II. swell, a. F: (a) Chic, élégant. S.a. MOB[1] 3. (b) (Artiste) de premier ordre. (c) U.S: P: Épatant. 'swell-box, s. (Of organ) Caisse f d'expression; le récit. 'swell-manual, s. (Of organ) Clavier expressif.
swell[2], v. (p.t. swelled [sweld]; p.p. swollen ['swoulən], occ. swelled) I. v.tr. (a) (R)enfler, gonfler. Eyes swollen with tears, yeux gonflés de larmes. To swell the crowd, augmenter la foule. (b) Mus: Enfler (une note). 2. v.i. (a) To swell (up), (s')enfler, se gonfler; (of lime) foisonner; (of debt) augmenter, grossir. The murmur swells into a roar, le murmure s'enfle jusqu'à devenir un rugissement. To swell with importance, F: to swell like a turkey-cock, enfler, gonfler, le jabot. (b) (Of sea) Se soulever. Hate swelled up within him, la haine montait en lui. (c) To swell out, être bombé; bomber. swollen, a. Enflé, gonflé. I. (a) The river is s., la rivière est en crue. (b) To have a swollen face, avoir une fluxion à la joue. S.a. GLAND[1]. 2. P: To suffer from swollen head, from swelled head, être pénétré de sa propre importance; F: s'en faire accroire. 'swollen-headed, a. P: Vaniteux, suffisant. swelling[1], a. (Of sails) Enflé, gonflé. Arch: Swelling column, colonne renflée. F: S. with importance, gonflé d'importance. swelling[2], s. I. (a) Enfle-ment m, gonflement m; crue f (d'un fleuve). (b) Renflement m (d'une colonne). (c) Aut: Cy: Hernie f (du bandage). 2. Med: Tuméfaction f; boursouflement m (du visage). 3. Bosse f, enflure f (au front); fluxion f (à la joue). To have a s. on the neck, avoir une grosseur au cou.
swelter[1] ['sweltər], s. Chaleur lourde et humide. To be in a swelter, étouffer de chaleur; être en nage.
swelter[2], v.i. (a) Étouffer de chaleur. (b) Être en nage. sweltering, a. I. En nage. 2. Swelter-ing heat, chaleur étouffante, accablante.
swept [swept]. See SWEEP[2].
swerve[1] [swə:rv], s. Écart m, déviation f. Fb: Crochet m. Aut: Embardée f.
swerve[2], v.i. Faire un écart, un crochet; (of horse) se dérober; (of motor car) faire une em-bardée; (of footballer) crocheter.
swift [swift]. I. a. (a) Rapide; (coureur, cheval) vite. As swift as thought, rapide comme la pensée. (b) Prompt. Swift of wit, vif d'esprit; à la repartie prompte. Swift to action, prompt à agir. -ly, adv. Vite, rapidement. To fly s. away, s'envoler à tire-d'aile. II. swift, adv. Vite, rapidement. III. swift, s. Orn: (Black) swift, martinet (noir). 'swift-flowing, a. (Rivière) au cours rapide. 'swift-'footed, a. Au pied léger.
swiftness ['swiftnəs], s. I. Rapidité f, vitesse f. 2. Promptitude f.
swig[1] [swig], s. P: Grand trait, lampée f (de bière).
swig[2], v.tr. P: Boire (un verre) à grands traits, à grands coups.

swill[1] [swil], s. I. Lavage m à grande eau. ? give a pail a swill out, incer un sea 2. (a) Pâtée f pour les porcs; eaux grasse (b) P: Mauvaise boisson; rinçure f.
swill[2], v.tr. I. Laver (le plancher) à grande ea To swill out a basin, rincer une cuvett 2. P: (a) Boire avidement (qch.). (b) Ab Riboter.
swim[1] [swim], s. I. Action f de nager. To hav a swim, faire un peu de nage. The s. across t. river, la traversée du fleuve à la nage. 2. F: T be in the swim, être dans le mouvement, da le train.
swim[2], v. (swam [swam]; swum [swʌm]; pr. swimming) I. v.i. I. (a) Nager. F: To swi like a fish, nager comme un poisson. To sta to swim, se mettre à la nage. To swim und water, nager entre deux eaux. To swim acro a river, traverser une rivière à la nage. T swim with the tide, (i) nager dans le sens d courant; (ii) F: aller dans le sens de la foul S.a. SINK[2] I. I. (b) To swim a stroke, faire ur brasse. F: He can't swim a stroke, il nag comme un chien de plomb. (c) Meat swimmi in gravy, viande noyée dans la sauce. (d) Su nager, flotter. 2. Eyes swimming with tears, yeu inondés de larmes. 3. (a) My head is swimmin la tête me tourne. (b) Everything swam befo my eyes, tout semblait tourner autour de mo II. swim, v.tr. I. Traverser, passer, (ur rivière) à la nage. 2. Faire nager (un cheval
swimming[1], a. I. Swimming eyes, yeu noyés de larmes. 2. Swimming head, tête qu tourne. -ly, adv. F: Comme sur des roulettes; merveille. swimming[2], s. I. Nage f, natation 2. Swimming of the head, vertige m. 'swim ming-bath, s. Piscine f. 'swimming match, s. Concours m de natation. 'swim ming-pool, s. Piscine f (en plein air).
swimmer ['swimər], s. Nageur, -euse.
swindle[1] [swindl], s. I. Escroquerie f, filouterie 2. F: Duperie f. 3. F: Déception f.
swindle[2], v.tr. Escroquer, filouter (qn). T swindle s.o. out of sth., escroquer qch. à qn.
swindler ['swindlər], s. Filou m, escroc m.
swine [swain], s.inv. I. Cochon m, porc m pourceau m. 2. P: Dirty swine! sale cochon He's a s., c'est un salaud. 'swine-herd, s. A: Porcher; gardeur de cochons.
swing[1] [swiŋ], s. I. (a) Balancement m. To gi a hammock a s., faire aller un hamac. (b) Aut: T give the starting-handle a s., donner un tour à l manivelle de mise en marche. (c) Coup balanc Box: Swing m. (d) Golf: Upward s., downwar s., ballant ascendant, descendant. 2. (a) Oscilla tion f (d'un pendule). Pol: The swing of th pendulum, le flux et le reflux des partis. To b in full swing, (of fête) battre son plein; (of factory) être en plein travail. F: Sudden s. o public opinion, revirement inattendu de l'opinio publique. Swing-to of the door, rabattement r de la porte. (b) To give a child a swing, pousse un enfant sur l'escarpolette; balancer un enfant 3. (a) Amplitude f (d'une oscillation). (b) Nau Évitage m (d'un navire à l'ancre). 4. To wal with a swing, marcher d'un pas rythmé. Son that goes with a swing, chanson très rythmée chanson entraînante. F: Everything went wit a swing, tout a très b.en marché. When you hav got into the s. of things, quand vous serez a courant. 5. Escarpolette f, balançoire f. 'swing back[1], s. Phot: Bascule f arrière. 'swing bar, s. Av: Palonnier m de direction. 'swing boat, s. (At. fairs) Bateau m balançoire

balançoire f. **'swing-bridge,** s. Pont tournant, pivotant. **'swing-cot,** s. Bercelonnette f. **'swing-door,** s. Porte battante ; porte va-et-vient. **'swing-front.** Phot: Bascule antérieure. **'swing-gate,** s. **I.** Barrière battante, tournante. **2.** Counterpoise swing-gate, tape-cul m.

swing², v. (swung [swʌŋ] ; swung) I. v.i. **I.** (a) To swing to and fro, se balancer ; (of bell) branler ; (of pendulum) osciller. To set the bells swinging, mettre les cloches en branle. Door that swings to and fro in the wind, porte qui ballotte au vent. P: To swing for a crime, être pendu pour un crime. (b) Tourner, pivoter (sur un axe) ; basculer. The door swung on its hinges, la porte tourna sur ses gonds. (c) (Of ship) To swing (at anchor), éviter (sur l'ancre). (d) Games: Se balancer. **2.** Faire un mouvement de conversion ; changer de direction. (a) To swing round, faire volte-face. The car swung right round, la voiture a fait un tête-à-queue. (b) Mil: The whole line swung to the left, toute la ligne fit une conversion vers la gauche. (Of fleet) To swing to starboard, faire un crochet sur la droite. **3.** To swing along, marcher d'un pas rythmé. II. **swing,** v.tr. **I.** (a) (Faire) balancer (qch.) ; faire osciller (un pendule). To s. one's arms, balancer les bras (en marchant). S.a. CAT I, LEAD¹ 3. (b) P: To swing it on s.o., duper ou essayer de duper qn. **2.** (a) Nau: Boat swung out, embarcation parée au dehors. (b) To swing a car round, faire faire un brusque virage à une auto. (c) Faire tourner. Av: To swing the propeller, lancer, brasser, l'hélice. **3.** To s. a hammock, pendre, (ac)crocher un hamac. **4.** v.pr. & i. To swing (oneself) into the saddle, monter vivement à cheval, en selle. **swing back,** v.i. **I.** Basculer ; se rabattre. **2.** (Of pendulum) Revenir. **'swing-back²,** s. Retour m en arrière ; revirement m (d'opinion). **swinging¹,** a. **I.** Balançant, oscillant ; (bras) ballants. **S.** stride, allure rythmée, cadencée. **swinging²,** s. **I.** (a) Balancement m, oscillation f. (b) Mouvement m de bascule ou de rotation. (c) Nau: Évitage m. (d) Swinging round, tête-à-queue m inv. **2.** Av: Lancement m (de l'hélice).

swinish ['swaini∫], a. De cochon, de pourceau ; sale. **-ly,** adv. Salement ; comme un pourceau. **swinishness** ['swaini∫nəs], s. **I.** Saleté f, grossièreté f. **2.** Goinfrerie f.

swipe¹ [swaip], s. **I.** Cr: Golf: Coup m à toute volée. **2.** F: Taloche f.

swipe², v.tr. & ind.tr. Cr: etc: To swipe (at) the ball, frapper la balle à toute volée.

swipes [swaips], s.pl. F: Petite bière ; F: bibine f.

swirl¹ [swə:rl], s. Remous m (de l'eau). A s. of dust, un tourbillon de poussière.

swirl², v.i. Tournoyer, tourbillonner. (Of dust) To swirl up, monter en tourbillons.

swish¹ [swi∫], s. **I.** Bruissement m (de l'eau) ; froufrou m (d'une robe) ; sifflement m (d'un fouet) ; crissement m (d'une faux). **2.** Coup m de fouet.

swish². **I.** v.i. (Of water) Bruire ; susurrer. (Of wheels) To s. through the mud, faire gicler la boue. **2.** v.tr. (a) Fouetter. (b) Faire siffler (sa canne). (c) (Of animal) To s. its tail, battre l'air de sa queue. **swishing,** s. Sch: P: To get a swishing, recevoir une bonne correction.

Swiss [swis]. **I.** a. Suisse. **2.** s. Suisse, -esse. The Swiss, les Suisses.

switch¹ [swit∫], s. **I.** (a) Badine f ; houssine f (pour battre les meubles). **Riding switch,**

houssine (de cavalier). (b) Coup m de baguette. **2.** (a) Rail: Aiguille f ; changement m de voie. Cards: Changement m de couleur (dans les annonces). (b) El.E: Interrupteur m ; commutateur m. **Tumbler switch,** interrupteur à culbuteur. **Two-way switch,** commutateur à deux départs ; interrupteur d'escalier. Aut: The starting switch, le contacteur du démarreur. **Charging switch,** commutateur de charge. **3.** Tresse f de cheveux postiches. **'switch-bar,** s. Rail: Tringle f de manœuvre. **'switch-rail,** s. Rail: Rail m mobile.

switch², v.tr. **I.** (a) Donner un coup de badine à (qn) ; houssiner (des meubles). (b) (Of animal) To switch its tail, battre l'air de sa queue. **2.** To switch a train on to a branch line, aiguiller, dériver, un train sur un embranchement. **3.** Aut: See DIP² I. 3. **switch off,** v.tr. (a) El: Interrompre, couper (le courant) ; abs. ouvrir le circuit. **To switch off the light,** couper la lumière. I.C.E: **To switch off the ignition, the engine,** couper l'allumage. **To switch off the wireless,** abs. to switch off, tourner le bouton ; arrêter la T.S.F. Don't s. off, ne quittez pas l'écoute. (b) Tp: Couper la communication. **switch on,** v.tr. To s. on the current, abs. to switch on, donner du courant. **To switch on the light,** allumer (l'électricité). **To switch on the wireless,** tourner le bouton. Aut: **To switch on the ignition,** mettre l'interrupteur sur marche. **switch over,** v.tr. El: Commuter (le courant). Abs. W.Tel: To s. over (to another station), changer de réglage.

switchback ['swit∫bak], s. Montagnes f russes. **switchboard** ['swit∫bɔːrd], s. (a) El.E: Tableau m de distribution. (b) Tp: **Office switchboard,** standard m.

Swithin ['swiðin]. Pr.n.m. **St Swithin's day** (15th July) = la Saint-Médard (le huit juin).

Switzerland ['switsərlənd]. Pr.n. La Suisse.

swivel¹ ['swiv(ə)l], s. (a) Émerillon m ; maillon tournant. (b) Pivot m ; tourillon m. **Ball-swivel,** pivot à rotule. **Swivel block,** poulie f à émerillon. S.a. ROWLOCKS. **'swivel-eyed,** a. F: Louche, strabique. **'swivel-gun,** s. Canon m à pivot. **'swivel-seat, -chair,** s. Siège tournant.

swivel², v.i. (swivelled) Pivoter, tourner.

swizz(le) [swiz(l)], s. P: = SWINDLE¹.

swollen ['swoulən]. See SWELL².

swoon¹ [swuːn], s. Évanouissement m, défaillance f. Med: Syncope f. **To go off in a swoon,** s'évanouir ; tomber évanoui.

swoon², v.i. S'évanouir, défaillir ; se trouver mal. Med: Avoir une syncope. **swooning,** a. (a) Défaillant. (b) Évanoui.

swoop¹ [swuːp], s. Abat(t)ée f (d'un avion) (upon, sur) ; attaque brusquée. F: **At one (fell) swoop,** d'un seul coup (fatal).

swoop², v.i. To swoop down upon sth., s'abattre, foncer, sur qch.

swop¹·² [swɔp], s. & v.tr. = SWAP¹·².

sword [sɔːrd], s. (a) Épée f ; A. & Poet: glaive m. **To wear a sword,** porter l'épée. **To draw one's sword,** tirer son épée ; dégainer. F: **To draw the sword,** commencer les hostilités. **To cross swords with s.o.,** (i) croiser le fer avec qn ; (ii) F: mesurer ses forces avec qn. **To put the inhabitants to (the edge of) the sword,** passer les habitants au fil de l'épée. S.a. FIRE¹ I. (b) Sabre m. **With drawn sword,** sabre au clair. **'sword-arm,** s. Le bras droit. **'sword-bearer,** s. Officier municipal qui porte le glaive. **'sword-belt,** s. Ceinturon m. **'sword-cut,** s. Coup m de sabre ; (on face) balafre f. **'sword-dance,** s.

Danse *f* du sabre (les pas sont exécutés autour de deux sabres croisés sur le sol). **'sword-fish,** *s.* *Ich :* Espadon *m.* **'sword-knot,** *s.* Dragonne *f.* **'sword-play,** *s.* **1.** Maniement *m* de l'épée : escrime *f.* **2.** *F :* (Verbal) sword-play, joute *f* oratoire. **'sword-stick,** *s.* Canne *f* à épée. **'sword-thrust,** *s.* Coup *m* de pointe ; coup d'épée.

swordsman, *pl.* **-men** ['sɔːrdzmən, -men], *s.m.* Épéiste ; tireur d'épée. *Fine s.,* fine lame.

swordsmanship ['sɔːrdzmənʃip], *s.* Maniement *m* de l'épée ; escrime *f* (à l'épée).

swore [swɔːər], **sworn** [swɔːrn]. *See* SWEAR².

swot¹ [swɔt], *s.* *P :* **1.** (*a*) *Sch :* Travail *m* intense. (*b*) Corvée *f.* **2.** (*Pers.*) Bûcheur, -euse ; potâsseur *m.*

swot², *v.tr. & i.* (swotted) *Sch :* *P :* Bûcher, piocher. *To s. for an exam,* bûcher un examen. *To swot at mathematics,* bûcher les mathématiques.

swum [swʌm]. *See* SWIM².

swung [swʌŋ]. *See* SWING².

sybarite ['sibarait], *a. & s.* Sybarite (*mf*).

sybaritic [siba'ritik], *a.* Sybarite.

sycamore ['sikamɔːər], *s.* **1.** (Érable *m*) sycomore *m ;* faux platane. **2.** Figuier *m* d'Égypte.

syce [sais], *s.* (*In India*) Saïs *m ;* palefrenier *m.*

sycophancy ['sikofənsi], *s.* Flagornerie *f.*

sycophant ['sikofənt], *s.* **1.** *Gr.Ant :* Sycophante *m.* **2.** Flagorneur *m.*

syllabic [si'labik], *a.* Syllabique.

syllable ['siləbl], *s.* Syllabe *f.*

syllabus, *pl.* **-i** ['siləbəs, -ai], *s.* Programme *m,* sommaire *m* (d'un cours).

syllepsis, *pl.* **-es** [si'lepsis, -iːz], *s.* Syllepse *f.*

syllogism ['silɔdʒizm], *s.* Syllogisme *m.*

sylph [silf], *s.* **1.** Sylphe *m,* sylphide *f.* **2.** *F :* (*Applied to woman*) Sylphide. **'sylph-like,** *a.* *F :* (Taille, etc.) de sylphide.

sylvan ['silvən], *a.* (*a*) Sylvestre. (*b*) *Z :* Sylvicole.

sylviculturist [silvi'kʌltjurist], *s* Sylviculteur *m.*

symbiosis [simbi'ousis], *s.* *Biol :* Symbiose *f.*

symbol ['simb(ə)l], *s.* **1.** Symbole *m,* emblème *m.* **2.** *Ch : Mth :* Symbole.

symbolic(al) [sim'bɔlik(əl)], *a.* Symbolique. **-ally,** *adv.* Symboliquement.

symbolism ['simbolizm], *s.* Symbolisme *m.*

symbolize ['simbolaːiz], *v.tr.* Symboliser.

symmetrical [si'metrik(ə)l], *a* Symétrique. **-ally,** *adv.* Symétriquement.

symmetry ['simetri], *s.* Symétrie *f.*

sympathetic [simpa'θetik], *a.* **1.** (*a*) (*Of pain, nerve*) Sympathique. **The sympathetic nerve,** le grand sympathique. (*b*) **Sympathetic ink,** encre sympathique. **2.** (*a*) Qui marque la sympathie. *S. glance,* regard de sympathie. (*b*) *S. audience,* auditoire bien disposé. (*c*) Compatissant. *S. words,* paroles de condoléance, de sympathie. (*d*) Dicté par la solidarité. **-ally,** *adv.* **1.** Sympathiquement. **2.** D'une manière compatissante.

sympathize ['simpaθaːiz], *v.i.* **1.** To sympathize with s.o. (in his sorrow, etc.), (i) sympathiser avec qn ; (ii) avoir de la compassion pour qn. *The Smiths called to s.,* les Smith sont venus exprimer leurs condoléances. **2. To sympathize with s.o.'s point of view,** comprendre le point de vue de qn (sans l'approuver). **sympathizing,** *a.* Compatissant.

sympathizer ['simpaθaizər], *s.* **1.** *To be a s. in s.o.'s grief,* compatir au chagrin de qn. **2.** Partisan, -ane (*with a cause,* d'une cause).

sympathy ['simpaθi], *s.* **1.** Compassion *f.*

Accept my deep s., agréez mes condoléances. **2.** (*a*) Sympathie *f* (*for s.o.,* à l'égard de qn). **Popular sympathies are on his side,** il a l'opinion pour lui. *I know you are in s. with them,* je sais que vous êtes de leur côté. **To strike in sympathy,** se mettre en grève par solidarité. (*b*) **Prices went up in sympathy,** les prix sont montés par contre-coup. *Ph :* **String that vibrates in sympathy,** corde qui vibre par résonance.

symphonic [sim'fɔnik], *a.* Symphonique.

symphony ['simfoni], *s.* Symphonie *f.* **Symphony concert,** concert *m* symphonique.

symposium, *pl.* **-ia** [sim'pouziəm, -ia], *s.* **1.** (*a*) *Gr.Ant :* Banquet *m.* (*b*) *F :* Réunion *f* de convives. **2.** (*a*) Discussion *f* (académique). (*b*) Recueil *m* d'articles.

symptom ['simptəm], *s.* Symptôme *m ;* indice *m.* **To show symptoms of . . .,** présenter des indices de. . . .

symptomatic [simpto'matik], *a.* Symptomatique.

synaeresis [si'niːərisis], *s.* *Ling :* Synérèse *f.*

synagogue ['sinagɔg], *s.* Synagogue *f.*

synarthrosis, *pl.* **-oses** [sinɑːr'θrousis, -ousiːz], *s. Anat :* Synarthrose *f.*

synchromesh ['sinkromeʃ], *s.* *Aut :* (Boîte *f* de vitesses) synchromesh *m.*

synchronism ['sinkronizm], *s.* Synchronisme *m.* **In synchronism,** en synchronisme ; *El.E :* en phase.

synchronize ['sinkronaːiz]. **1.** *v.tr.* (*a*) Synchroniser (deux mouvements, deux horloges) ; *El.E :* coupler en phase. (*b*) Établir le synchronisme de (différents événements). **2.** *v.i.* (*a*) (*Of events*) Arriver, avoir lieu, simultanément. (*b*) *El.E : When the generators s. . . .,* lorsque les générateurs sont en phase. . . .

synchronous ['sinkronəs], *a.* Synchrone.

synchrony ['sinkroni], *s.* Synchronisme *m.*

synclinal [sin'klain(ə)l], *a. Geol :* Synclinal, -aux.

syncopate ['sinkopeit], *v.tr.* *Gram : Mus :* Syncoper.

syncopation [sinko'peiʃ(ə)n], *s.* *Mus :* Syncope *f.*

syncope ['sinkopi], *s.* *Med :* Syncope *f*

syndic ['sindik], *s.* Syndic *m.*

syndical ['sindik(ə)l], *a.* Syndical, -aux.

syndicate¹ ['sindiket], *s.* **1.** *Com :* Syndicat *m.* **2.** Conseil *m* de syndics.

syndicate² ['sindiket], *v.tr.* (*a*) Syndiquer (des ouvriers, une industrie). (*b*) Publier (un article) simultanément dans plusieurs journaux.

syndrome ['sindroum], *s. Med :* Syndrome *m.*

synergy ['sinərdʒi], *s.* Synergie *f.*

synod ['sinəd], *s. Ecc :* Synode *m,* concile *m.*

synonym ['sinonim], *s.* Synonyme *m.*

synonymous [si'nɔniməs], *a.* Synonyme (*with,* de).

synonymy [si'nɔnimi], *s.* Synonymie *f.*

synopsis, *pl.* **-opses** [si'nɔpsis, -ɔpsiːz], *s.* Résumé *m,* sommaire *m ;* tableau *m* synoptique. *S. of chemistry,* mémento *m* de chimie.

synoptic(al) [si'nɔptik(əl)], *a.* Synoptique.

synovia [si'nouvia, sai-], *s. Anat :* Synovie *f.*

synovial [si'nouvial, sai-], *a.* Synovial, -aux.

synovitis [sino'vaitis, sai-], *s. Med :* Synovite *f.*

syntactic(al) [sin'taktik(əl)], *a.* Syntactique, syntaxique.

syntax ['sintaks], *s.* Syntaxe *f.*

synthesis, *pl.* **-es** [sin'θesis, -iːz], *s.* Synthèse *f.*

synthesize ['sinθesaːiz], *v.tr.* Synthétiser.

synthetic(al) [sin'θetik(əl)], Synthétique. **-ally,** *adv.* Synthétiquement.

syntonic [sin'tɔnik], *a. W.Tel:* Syntonique.
syntonism ['sintɔnizm], *s. W.Tel:* Syntonie *f.*
syntony ['sintoni], *s.* Syntonie *f*, accord *m.*
sypher ['saifər], *v.tr. Carp:* Assembler à mi-bois.
'**sypher-joint,** *s.* Assemblage *m* à mi-bois.
Syria ['siriə]. *Pr.n.* La Syrie.
Syriac ['siriak], *s. Ling:* Le syriaque.
Syrian ['siriən], *a. & s.* Syrien, -ienne.
syringa [si'ringə], *s. Bot:* Seringa *m.*
syringe[1] ['sirindʒ], *s.* Seringue *f.*
syringe[2], *v.tr.* Seringuer (des fleurs, etc.). To
syringe (**out**) **the ears,** laver les oreilles avec une
seringue.
syrup ['sirəp], *s.* **1.** Sirop *m.* **2.** Golden syrup,
mélasse raffinée ; sirop de sucre.
syrupy ['sirəpi], *a.* Sirupeux.
system ['sistəm], *s.* **1.** (*a*) Système *m. The feudal*

s., le régime féodal. **To establish** sth. **on a system,**
établir qch. d'après un système. *Astr:* The solar
system, le système solaire. *Anat:* The digestive
system, l'appareil digestif. The system, l'organisme *m.* (*b*) Réseau ferré (de chemin de fer) ;
réseau télégraphique. **2.** Méthode *f* (de travail).
To lack s., manquer de méthode, d'organisation.
systematic [sistə'matik], *a.* (*a*) Systématique,
méthodique. *He is s.,* il a de l'ordre, de la
méthode. (*b*) *Pej: S. opposition,* opposition
systématique. **-ally,** *adv.* Systématiquement.
She does her work s., elle travaille avec méthode.
systematize ['sistəmataːiz], *v.tr.* Réduire en
système ; systématiser.
systole ['sistoli], *s. Physiol:* Systole *f.*
systolic [sis'tɔlik], *a.* Systolique.
syzygy ['sizidʒi], *s. Astr:* Syzygie *f.*

T

T, t [tiː], *s.* **1.** (La lettre) T, t *m.* To cross one's
t's, (i) barrer ses t ; (ii) *F:* mettre les points sur
les i. *Adv.phr.* **To a T,** exactement ; à la perfection. **That suits me to a T,** cela me va à
merveille. **2.** (*a*) *Mec.E:* Union T, union tee,
raccord *m* en T. (*b*) En (forme de) T. **T section,**
T iron, fer *m* à, en, T. **T-shaped,** en T, en
potence. *S.a.* SQUARE[1] I. 4.
ta [taː], *s. & int.* (*Nursery speech*) Merci (*m*).
tab [tab], *s.* **1.** (*a*) Patte *f* (de vêtement).
(*b*) Écusson *m*, insigne *m* (d'officier d'état-major).
F: **A red tab,** un officier breveté. (*c*) Shoe-lace
tab, ferret *m* de cordon de soulier. (*d*) (*For
hanging up coat*) Attache *f.* (*e*) Touche *f*, onglet *m*
(de dictionnaire, de fichier). **2.** Étiquette *f* (pour
bagages).
tabard ['tabərd], *s.* Tabar(d) *m* (de héraut).
tabbed [tabd], *a. Cost:* Garni de pattes.
tabby ['tabi], *s.* **1.** Tabby (cat), (i) chat moucheté ; (ii) *F:* chatte *f.* **2.** *F:* Vieille fille
cancanière ; vieille chipie.
tabernacle ['tabərnakl], *s.* Tabernacle *m.*
tabes ['teibiːz], *s. Med:* Tabes *m*, consomption *f.*
table[1] ['teibl], *s.* Table *f.* **1.** (*a*) Occasional table,
guéridon *m.* Nest of tables, table gigogne. Card-
table, gaming table, table de jeu. *Parl:* To lay
a measure on the table, déposer un projet de loi
sur le bureau. (*b*) Table à manger. To lay the
table, mettre la table ; dresser le couvert. *T. laid
for twelve,* table de douze couverts. To clear the
table, desservir. To sit down to table, se mettre
à table. *Separate tables (at restaurant)* (service *m*
par) petites tables. **Table wine,** vin ordinaire.
Ecc: **The Lord's Table,** the Communion table,
la Sainte Table. *S.a.* CLOTH 2. **2.** *pl. A:* Tables,
trictrac *m. F:* **To turn the tables on s.o.,**
renverser les rôles ; retourner la situation.
3. *Tchn:* Plaque *f* (de machine-outil) ; tablier *m*
(de laminoir). **4.** (*a*) Table (d'un diamant).
(*b*) Tablier (de pont à bascule). **5.** Plaque,
tablette *f* (de marbre). *B:* **The Tables of the
Law,** les Tables de la loi. **6.** (*List*) Table,
tableau *m.* **Table of weights and measures,** table
de poids et de mesures. **Multiplication table,**
table de multiplication. *Ch:* **Table of chemical
equivalents,** abaque *m* des équivalents chimiques.
Nau: **Tide table,** annuaire *m* des marées. *Rail:*
Table of fares, barème *m* des prix. '**table-**

centre, *s.* Rond *m*, carré *m*, de table. '**table-
cover,** *s.* Tapis *m* de table. '**table diamond,**
s. Diamant (taillé) en table. '**table-flap,** *s.*
Abattant *m* de table. '**table-fork,** *s.* Fourchette *f.* '**table-land,** *s. Ph.Geog:* Plateau
(élevé). '**table-leaf,** *s.* **1.** = TABLE-FLAP.
2. Rallonge *f* (de table). '**table-linen,** *s.*
Linge *m* de table. '**table-rapping,** *s. Psychics:*
Tables frappantes. '**table-spoon,** *s.* Cuiller *f*
à soupe, à bouche. '**table-talk,** *s.* Propos *mpl*
de table. '**table-tennis,** *s.* Tennis *m* de salon ;
ping-pong *m.* '**table-'top,** *s.* Dessus *m* de
table. '**table-turning,** *s. Psychics:* Tables
tournantes. '**table-water,** *s.* Eau minérale.
table[2], *v.tr.* **1.** (*a*) *Parl:* To table a bill, (i) saisir
la Chambre d'un projet de loi ; (ii) *U.S:* ajourner
(indéfiniment) un projet de loi. (*b*) *Cards:* To
table a card, jouer une carte. **2.** *Carp:* Emboîter. **3.** *Nau:* Doubler les bords (d'une
voile).
table d'hôte [taːblə'dout], *s.* Table *f* d'hôte ;
repas *m* à prix fixe.
tablespoonful ['teiblspuːnful], *s.* Cuillerée *f* à
bouche.
tablet ['tablet], *s.* **1.** Plaque commémorative.
Votive tablet, ex-voto *m inv.* **2.** (*a*) *Pharm: etc:*
Comprimé *m.* (*b*) **Tablet of soap,** pain *m* de
savon.
tabloid ['tablɔid], *s.* **1.** *Pharm:* Comprimé *m*
(de la marque Burroughs, Wellcome & Co.).
2. *F: News in t. form,* nouvelles en une ligne.
taboo[1] [ta'buː], *s.* **1.** *s.* Tabou *m*, -ous. **2.** *Pred. a.*
Interdit, proscrit (comme étant tabou). *It's t.,*
c'est une chose qui ne se fait pas.
taboo[2], *v.tr.* **1.** *Anthr:* Tabouer ; déclarer
tabou. **2.** *F:* Proscrire, interdire (qch.).
tabor ['teibər], *s. A:* Tambourin *m* ; tambour *m*
de basque.
tabular ['tabjulər], *a.* Tabulaire.
tabulate ['tabjuleit], *v.tr.* Disposer (des chiffres)
en forme de table(s) ; classifier (des résultats) ;
cataloguer.
tacheometer [taki'ɔmetər], *s. Surv:* Tachéomètre *m.*
tachometer [ta'kɔmetər], *s. Mec.E:* Tachymètre *m.* **Recording tachometer,** tachymètre
enregistreur.

tacit ['tasit], *a.* (Consentement) tacite, implicite. **-ly,** *adv.* Tacitement.

taciturn ['tasitə:rn], *a.* Taciturne.

taciturnity [tasi'tə:rniti], *s.* Taciturnité *f.*

Tacitus ['tasitəs]. *Pr.n.m.* Tacite.

tack[1] [tak], *s.* **I.** Petit clou; broquette *f*; *pl.* semence *f* (de tapissier). *F:* To get down to brass tacks, en venir au fait. **2.** *Needlew:* Long point (d'aiguille); point de bâti. *To take out the tacks,* enlever la faufilure. **3.** *Nau:* (a) (*Clew-line*) Amure *f.* Tacks and sheets *of a sail,* les lofs *m.* (b) To make a tack, courir un bord, une bordée. *F:* To be on the right tack, être sur la bonne voie. To try another tack, essayer une autre tactique.

tack[2]. **I.** *v.tr.* (a) To tack sth. (down), clouer qch. avec de la semence. *F:* To tack sth. (on) to sth., attacher qch. à qch. (b) *Needlew:* Faufiler, bâtir (un vêtement). **2.** *v.i. Nau:* To tack (about), (i) virer (de bord); (ii) tirer des bordées; louvoyer. **tacking,** *s.* **I.** (a) Clouage *m.* (b) *Needlew:* Bâtissage *m*; faufilure *f.* **2.** *Nau:* Virement *m* de bord.

tack[3], *s.* Nourriture *f*, aliment *m.* **Hard-tack,** biscuit *m* de mer. *S.a.* SOFT-TACK.

tackle[1] [takl], *s.* **I.** Attirail *m*, appareil *m*, engins *mpl.* Fishing tackle, articles *mpl* de pêche. **2.** Appareil de levage. Rope tackle, agrès *mpl,* apparaux *mpl. Nau:* Pulley tackle, les palans *m.* Boat tackles, garants *m* de canot. **3.** Action *f* de saisir (qn). *Fb:* Plaquage *m.* **'tackle-block,** *s.* Moufle *m or f.* **'tackle-fall,** *s.* Garant *m.*

tackle[2], *v.tr.* (a) Empoigner; saisir (qn) à bras le corps; s'attaquer à (une corvée); aborder (un problème). (b) *Rugby Fb:* Plaquer (un adversaire).

tacky ['taki], *a.* Collant; (vernis) presque sec.

tact [takt], *s.* **I.** Tact *m*, savoir-faire *m*; entregent *m. Without t.,* indiscret, -ète. **2.** *Mus:* = BEAT[1] I (b).

tactful ['taktful], *a.* (Homme) de tact; délicat. *To be t.,* avoir du tact. **-fully,** *adv.* Avec tact. *To deal t. with s.o.,* ménager qn.

tactical ['taktik(ə)l], *a.* **I.** Tactique. **2.** (*Of pers.*) Adroit.

tactician [tak'ti∫(ə)n], *s.* Tacticien *m.*

tactics ['taktiks], *s.pl.* Tactique *f.*

tactile ['taktail], *a.* Tactile, tangible.

tactless ['taktləs], *a.* (a) Dépourvu de tact; qui manque d'entregent. (b) *T. question,* question indiscrète. **-ly,** *adv.* Sans tact.

tactlessness ['taktləsnəs], *s.* Manque *m* de tact.

tadpole ['tadpoul], *s. Amph:* Têtard *m.*

taenia, *pl.* **-iae** ['ti:nia, -ii:], *s. Med:* Ténia *m*; ver *m* solitaire.

taffeta ['tafətə], *s.* Taffetas *m.*

taffrail ['tafreil], *s. N.Arch:* (Lisse *f* de) couronnement *m* (de la poupe).

tag[1] [tag], *s.* **I.** (a) Morceau *m* (d'étoffe) qui pend. (b) Attache *f*; tirant *m* (de botte). (c) Ferret *m* (de lacet). **2.** (a) Citation banale; cliché *m.* *One of his favourite tags,* une de ses expressions favorites. (b) Refrain *m.* **'tag-rag,** *s.* = RAG-TAG.

tag[2], *v.tr.* (tagged) **I.** To tag a shoe-lace, ferrer un lacet. **2.** To tag a speech with quotations, parsemer un discours de citations. **3.** To tag sth. on to sth., attacher, ajouter, qch. à qch.

Tahiti [ta:'hi:ti]. *Pr.n. Geog:* Taïti *m.*

tail[1] [teil], *s.* **I.** (a) Queue *f* (d'animal). (*Of peacock*) To spread its tail, faire la roue. With his tail between his legs, (i) (*of dog*) la queue entre les jambes; (ii) *F:* (*of pers.*) l'oreille basse. *F:* To keep one's tail up, ne pas se laisser abattre.

To turn tail, s'enfuir; tourner les talons. The sting is in the tail, à la queue gît le venin. (b) Queue (de note musicale); natte *f* (de cheveux); empennage *m* (d'avion). Tail of a shirt, pan *m* de chemise. *pl.* Tails of a coat, coat-tails, basques *f,* pans, d'un habit. To wear tails, porter l'habit à queue. *S.a.* SPIN[1] I. (c) Arrière *m* (d'une voiture). *There was another car close on my t.,* une autre voiture me suivait de près. Tail of a procession, queue d'un défilé. (d) Adhérents *mpl* (d'un chef politique). (e) *F:* The tail of the class, la queue de la classe. **2.** (*Of coin*) Pile *f,* revers *m.* *S.a.* HEAD[1] 8. **'tail-board,** *s. Veh:* Layon *m* (d'une charrette). **'tail-'coat,** *s.* Cost: Habit *m* à queue. **'tail-end,** *s.* Extrémité *f* arrière; queue *f* (d'un défilé); fin *f* (d'un orage, etc.). *Turf:* To come in at the tail-end, arriver dans les choux. **'tail-lamp, -light,** *s. Rail: etc:* Feu *m* (d')arrière; lanterne *f* arrière. **'tail-piece,** *s.* **I.** Queue *f*; empennage *m* (d'avion). **2.** Cordier *m* (de violon). **3.** *Typ:* Cul-de-lampe *m.* **'tail-plane,** *s. Av:* Plan stabilisateur. **'tail-shaft,** *s.* **I.** *N.Arch:* Extrémité *f* de l'arbre. **2.** Hampe *f* (de bombe aérienne). **'tail-skid,** *s. Av:* Béquille *f.* **'tail-slide,** *s. Av:* Glissade *f* sur l'empennage. **'tail-stock,** *s.* Contrepoupée *f* (de tour).

tail[2]. **I.** *v.tr.* To tail sth. on to sth., attacher qch. derrière qch. **2.** *v.tr.* Enlever les queues (des groseilles, etc.). **3.** *v.i.* To tail after s.o., (i) suivre qn de près; (ii) suivre qn à la queue leu leu. **tail off,** *v.i.* (*Of voice*) S'éteindre. **tailed,** *a.* A queue.

tail[3], *s. Jur:* Heir, estate, in tail, héritier par substitution; bien substitué.

tailor[1] ['teilər], *s.* **I.** Tailleur *m* (d'habits). Tailor-made costume, costume *m* tailleur; *F:* tailleur.

tailor[2], *v.tr.* Faire, façonner (un complet). *Well-tailored overcoat,* pardessus de facture soignée. *Tailored dress,* robe tailleur. **tailoring,** *s.* **I.** Métier *m* de tailleur. **2.** Ouvrage *m* de tailleur.

tailoress ['teilərəs], *s.f.* Tailleuse-couturière.

taint[1] [teint], *s.* **I.** (a) Corruption *f,* infection *f.* (b) The taint of sin, la tache, la souillure, du péché. **2.** Tare *f* héréditaire (d'insanité). **3.** Trace *f* (d'infection). *Meat free from taint,* viande fraîche.

taint[2], *v.tr.* **I.** Infecter, vicier (l'air); gâter, corrompre (la nourriture). **2.** (*With passive force*) Se corrompre; se gâter. **tainted,** *a.* Infecté, corrompu. Tainted meat, viande gâtée. Tainted heredity, hérédité chargée. To be tainted with insanity, être taré d'insanité. *Jur:* Tainted with fraud, entaché de dol.

take [teik], *v.* (**took** [tuk]; **taken** ['teik(ə)n]). Prendre. **I.** *v.tr.* **I.** (a) *To t. sth. on one's back,* prendre, charger, qch. sur son dos. (b) To take sth. from s.o., enlever, prendre, qch. à qn. *Someone has taken my umbrella,* on m'a pris mon parapluie. *To t. sth. from the table,* prendre qch. sur la table. *To t. a saucepan off the fire,* retirer une casserole du feu. *To t. the lid off sth.,* enlever, ôter, le couvercle de qch. To take a sum out of one's income, prélever une somme sur son revenu. Take your hands out of your pockets, ôtez, sortez, les mains de vos poches. (c) To take (hold of) s.o., saisir, empoigner, qn. He took her in his arms, il la prit dans ses bras. She took my arm, elle me prit le bras. To take an opportunity, saisir une occasion. *S.a.* CHANCE[1] 2, WHEEL[1] I. (d) Prendre (une ville). To take s.o. prisoner, faire qn prisonnier. The deuce take him! que le diable l'emporte! To be taken ill,

tomber malade. **He was very much taken with
the idea,** l'idée lui souriait beaucoup. **I was not
taken with him,** il ne m'a pas été sympathique;
il ne m'a pas fait bonne impression. *S.a.* ABACK.
e) **To take a passage from a book,** emprunter
un passage à un livre. *To t. an idea from an
author,* puiser une idée chez un auteur.
2. *(a)* Louer, prendre (une maison). *(b)* **To take
tickets,** prendre des billets. *(Of seat, table)*
Taken, "occupé." **To take (in) a paper,** acheter
régulièrement un journal. **To take paying
guests,** recevoir, prendre, des pensionnaires.
To take pupils, donner des leçons particulières.
S.a. WIFE 1. *(c)* Prendre (le train). **To take a seat,**
prendre un siège; s'asseoir. **Take your seats!**
prenez vos places! *Rail:* en voiture! *(d) T. the
turning on the left,* prenez à gauche. **To take
the wrong road,** se tromper de chemin. *Sp:* **To
take an obstacle,** franchir, sauter, un obstacle.
e) **To take legal advice** consulter un avocat.
f) **To take holy orders,** recevoir les ordres.
S.a. COURSE[1] I, 3, FIELD[1] I. **3.** *(a)* Gagner,
remporter (le prix). *Cards:* **To take a trick,**
faire une levée. *(b)* **To take one's degree,** prendre
ses diplômes. **To take an examination,** se présenter à un examen. *(c) Com:* **To take so much
a week,** se faire tant par semaine. **4.** Prendre (de
la nourriture). **To take a meal,** faire un repas.
I cannot take whisky, je ne supporte pas le
whisky. 'Not to be taken,' "médicament pour
l'usage externe." *P:* **I'm not taking any!** je ne
marche pas! **5.** *(a)* **To take a walk,** faire une
promenade. **To take a bath,** prendre un bain.
S.a. STEP[1] 3. *Mr X is taking the sixth form,*
M. X est chargé de la classe de première. *To t.
a print from a negative,* tirer une épreuve d'un
cliché. *Surv:* **To take an angle,** observer un
angle. **To take breath,** reprendre haleine. **To
take effect,** produire son effet. *S.a.* OATH 1,
PLACE[1] 2, PLUNGE[1], POSSESSION 1, STAND[1] 1, 3,
STOCK[1] 5. *(b)* **To take a photograph,** faire une
photographie. *To have one's likeness taken,* se
faire photographier. *(c)* **To take sth. apart,** en
pieces, démonter qch. **6.** *(a)* Prendre, recevoir.
Ten: **To take the service,** recevoir le service.
Take that (and that)! attrape (ça et ça)! **To
take no denial,** ne pas accepter de refus. **What
will you take for it?** combien en voulez-vous?
To take a bet, tenir un pari. **To take all responsibility,** assumer toute la responsabilité. **Taking
one thing with another,** l'un portant l'autre. *T. it
from me!* croyez-m'en! *I wonder how he will
t. it,* F: je me demande quelle tête il fera.
S.a. GIVE[2] I. 1, HINT[1] I, LAMB[1]. *(b)* **Bus that
takes twenty passengers,** autobus qui tient vingt
voyageurs. *(Of crane)* **To take heavy loads,**
supporter de fortes charges. *Mec:* **To take a
stress,** résister à une tension. **7.** *(a)* Prendre,
F: attraper (une maladie, un rhume). *(b)* **To
take a dislike to s.o.,** prendre qn en grippe.
S.a. EXCEPTION 2. **8.** *(a)* **We take the will for the
deed,** l'intention est réputée pour le fait. *How
old do you t. him to be?* quel âge lui donnez-vous?
I take it that . . ., je suppose que. . . . *(b) I took
you for an Englishman,* je vous croyais anglais.
F: **What do you take me for?** pour qui me
prenez-vous? **9.** *(Require)* *(a)* **That will take some
explaining,** voilà qui va demander des explications. *The work took some doing,* le travail a été
difficile, dur. **The journey takes five days,** le
voyage prend, demande, cinq jours. **It won't
take long,** ce sera tôt fait. *It took four men to hold
him,* il a fallu le tenir à quatre. **It takes a clever
man to do that,** bien habile qui peut le faire.

(b) Gram: **Verb that takes a preposition,** verbe
qui veut la préposition. *(c) I t. sixes (in gloves,
etc.),* j'ai six de pointure. **10.** *(a)* **To take s.o.
somewhere,** mener, conduire, qn dans un endroit.
To take s.o. over a house, faire visiter une maison
à qn. **To take s.o. out of his way,** écarter qn de
sa route. *F:* **What (ever) took him there?**
qu'allait-il faire dans cette galère? *(b)* **To take
sth. to s.o.,** porter qch. à qn. *To t. s.o. to the
hospital,* transporter qn à l'hôpital. **II. take,** *v.i.*
(a) Avoir du succès; réussir; prendre. *(b) Med:*
The vaccine has not taken, le vaccin n'a pas pris.
take about, *v.tr.* Faire visiter la ville à (des
parents de province). **take after,** *v.i.* Tenir
de (qn). *His daughter does not t. after him,* sa
fille n'a rien de lui. **take away,** *v.tr.* **1.** Enlever, emporter (qch.); emmener (qn). *(Of book
in library)* 'Not to be taken away,' "exclu du
prêt." **2.** *(a)* **To take away a knife from a child,**
ôter un couteau à un enfant. *(b)* **To take a child
away from school,** retirer un enfant du collège.
S.a. BREATH. **take back,** *v.tr.* **1.** *(a)* Reconduire
(qn). *(b) To take a book back to s.o.,* reporter un
livre à qn. **2.** *(a)* Reprendre (un employé).
(b) **I take back what I said,** je retire ce que j'ai
dit. **take down,** *v.tr.* **1.** *(a) To t. down a picture,* descendre, décrocher, un tableau. *(b)* **To
take down a machine,** démonter une machine.
(c) F: **To take s.o. down (a peg or two),**
remettre qn à sa place. **2.** Avaler, prendre (des
aliments). **3.** **To take down a few notes,** prendre
quelques notes. *To t. down in shorthand,* sténographier. **'take-down,** *s.* *F:* Mortification *f*,
humiliation *f*. **take in,** *v.tr.* **1.** *(a)* Faire entrer
(qn). **To take in s.o.'s card,** faire passer la carte
de qn. *(b)* **To take in the harvest,** rentrer la
moisson. *Nau:* **To take in (a supply of) water,**
faire de l'eau. *(Of boat)* **To take in water,** faire
eau; avoir une voie d'eau. *(c)* **To take in an
orphan,** recueillir un orphelin. **To take in
lodgers,** recevoir des locataires. **2.** *(a)* **To take
in a dress at the waist,** rentrer une robe à la
taille. *(b)* **To take in sail,** diminuer de voile(s).
3. Comprendre, inclure. *The empire took in all
these countries,* 'empire englobait tous ces pays.
4. *(a)* Comprendre, se rendre compte de (qch.).
To take in the situation, se rendre compte de la
situation; juger la situation. **To take in everything at a glance,** tout embrasser d'un coup d'œil.
(b) F: (Believe) **He takes it all in,** il prend tout
ça pour argent comptant. *(c) F: (Cheat)* Mettre
(qn) dedans; *F:* rouler (qn). **To be taken in,**
se laisser attraper. *He is easily taken in,* il est très
jobard. **I am not to be taken in!** ça ne mord pas,
ne prend pas! *To be taken in by appearances,* se
laisser tromper aux apparences. **'take-in,** *s.*
Duperie *f*; attrape *f*. **take into,** *v.tr.* **1.** **To
take s.o into one's confidence,** mettre qn dans
sa confidence. **2.** **To take it into one's head to
do sth.,** se mettre dans la tête de faire qch.
take off. **I.** *v.tr.* **1.** **To take s.o.'s attention
off sth.,** distraire l'attention de qn. **To take one's
eye off sth.,** quitter qch. des yeux. *S.a.* CHILL[1] 2.
2. *(a)* Enlever, ôter. *To t. off the lid,* enlever,
ôter, le couvercle. **To take off one's c othes,**
quitter ses vêtements; se déshabiller. *S.a.* HAT.
Tp: **To take off the receiver,** décrocher le récepteur. *(b)* Emmener (qn). **He was taken off to
gaol,** il fut emmené en prison. **To take oneself
off,** s'en aller, s'éloigner. *(c)* **To take so much off
(the price of sth.)** rabattre tant (sur le prix de
qch.). *(d)* **To take off a train,** supprimer un train.
(e) Imiter, singer (qn). **II. take off,** *v.i.*
Prendre son élan, s'élancer *(from,* de). *Av:* Dé-

coller, s'envoler. **'take-off,** *s.* (*a*) Élan *m.*
(*b*) *Av:* Décollage *m,* envolée *f.* **take on.**
1. *v.tr.* (*a*) Se charger de, entreprendre (un
travail). (*b*) Accepter le défi de (qn). *I'll t. you
on at billiards!* je vais vous faire une partie de
billard! To take on a bet, accepter un pari.
(*c*) Engager, embaucher (un ouvrier). (*d*) Prendre,
revêtir (une qualité). (*e*) (*Of train*) To take on
passengers, prendre des voyageurs. (*f*) Mener
(qn) plus loin, au delà de sa destination.
2. *v.i.* (*a*) *F:* **Don't take on so!** ne vous désolez
pas comme ça! (*b*) *F:* Devenir populaire;
réussir. *This fashion has taken on,* cette mode a
pris. **take out,** *v.tr.* **1.** (*a*) To take out one's
pipe, sortir sa pipe. To take out a tooth, arracher
une dent. To take out a stain, enlever, ôter, une
tache. (*b*) *F:* **I'll take out of him,** je me
vengerai. *The heat takes it out of me,* la chaleur
m'épuise. **2.** Faire sortir (qn). He is going to
take me out to dinner, il va m'emmener dîner.
3. Prendre, obtenir (un brevet). To take out an
insurance policy, contracter une assurance.
S.a. SUMMONS¹ 2. **4.** To take it out in goods, se
payer en marchandises. **take over,** *v.tr.*
1. To take over a business, prendre la suite des
affaires. To rent a flat and take over the furniture, louer un appartement avec une reprise de
meubles. To take over the liabilities, prendre les
dettes à sa charge. *Abs.* To take over from s.o.,
relever qn (dans ses fonctions). **2.** (*a*) Transporter (qn, qch.). (*b*) Passer (qn) (dans un
bateau). **take round,** *v.tr.* To take round the
plate, faire la quête. **take to,** *v.i.* **1.** To take
to flight, prendre la fuite. *To t. to the woods,*
gagner le taillis. *S.a.* BED¹ 1, HEEL¹ 1. **2.** To take
to drink, s'adonner à la boisson. **3.** (*a*) To take
to s.o., se prendre de sympathie pour qn;
prendre qn en amitié. (*b*) To take to a game,
prendre goût à un jeu. *I do not t. to the idea,*
cette idée ne me dit rien. *I shall never t. to it,*
e ne m'y ferai jamais. **take up.** I. *v.tr.*
1. (*a*) Relever, ramasser (qch.). (*b*) To take up
a carpet, enlever un tapis. To take up a street,
dépaver une rue. *S.a.* ARM² 1. (*c*) *Rail:* To stop
to take up passengers, s'arrêter pour embarquer
des voyageurs. (*d*) *Dressm:* To take up a sleeve,
raccourcir une manche. **2.** (*a*) Absorber (de
l'eau). (*b*) *Aut:* To take up the bumps, absorber
les chocs. **3.** (*a*) *Com:* To take up a bill, honorer
un effet. *St.Exch:* To take up an option, lever
une prime. To take up shares, souscrire à des
actions. (*c*) To take up a challenge, relever un
défi. (*c*) To take up an idea, adopter une idée.
4. (*a*) To take up a question, prendre une question en main. *To t. up a statement,* relever une
affirmation. *S.a.* REFERENCE 6. (*b*) Embrasser,
s'adonner à (une carrière); épouser (une querelle).
To t. up new studies, aborder de nouvelles études.
To t. up one's duties again, reprendre ses fonctions.
(*c*) Prendre (qn) sous sa protection. **5.** Arrêter
(qn); *F:* pincer (qn). *He was taken up by the
police,* il a été arrêté. **6.** To take s.o. up sharply,
reprendre qn vertement. To take s.o. up short,
couper la parole à qn. **7.** To take s.o. up wrongly,
mal comprendre les paroles de qn. **8.** Occuper.
(*a*) To take up too much room, occuper trop de
place. (*b*) To take up all s.o.'s attention, absorber
l'attention de qn. *It takes up all my evenings,*
cela remplit toutes mes soirées. (*c*) *He is entirely
taken up with his business,* il est tout à son commerce, il ne songe qu'à son commerce. *He is
quite taken up with her,* il ne pense plus qu'à elle.
II. **take up,** *v.i.* **1.** (*Of weather*) S'améliorer.
2. To take up with s.o., (i) se lier d'amitié avec

qn; (ii) se mettre à fréquenter (des vauriens).
take upon, *v.tr.* To take it upon oneself to d
sth., prendre sur soi de faire qch. *He takes ◁
good deal upon himself,* il se permet bien de
choses. **taking¹,** *a.* (Style) attrayant; (visage
séduisant. *T. manners,* manières engageantes
taking², *s.* **1.** Prise *f* (d'une ville); arrestation
(d'un voleur). **2.** *pl.* **Takings,** recette *f,* produit *m*
taker ['teikər], *s.* (*a*) Preneur, -euse (d'un bail
etc.). (*b*) Snuff-taker, priseur, -euse. (*c*) *St.Exch*
Taker of an option, optant *m.* Taker of a bill
preneur d'une lettre de change. (*d*) Taker of a
bet, tenant *m* d'un pari. *Turf:* The takers of
odds, les preneurs.
talc [talk], *s.* **1.** Talc *m.* **2.** *Com:* Mica *m.*
talcum ['talkəm], *s.* *Toil:* Talcum powder
(poudre *f* de) talc *m.*
tale [teil], *s.* **1.** Conte *m.* (*a*) Récit *m,* histoire *f*
Old wives' tales, contes de bonne femme. *His
drawn face told the t. of his sufferings,* ses traits
tirés en disaient long sur ses souffrances. *F:* I've
heard that tale before, je connais des paroles sur
cet air-là. (*b*) *Lit:* Nouvelle *f,* conte. **2.** *Pej :*
(*a*) Raconter *m. I've heard a fine t. about you,*
j'en ai appris de belles sur votre compte. (*b*) Rapport *m,* cafardage *m.* To tell tales (out of school),
rapporter; cafarder. *S.a.* DEAD I. 1. **3.** *A:*
Nombre *m;* quantité *f.*
talebearer ['teilbɛərər], *s.* Rapporteur, -euse ;
cafard, -arde. *He is a t.,* il rapporte.
talent ['talənt], *s.* **1.** *Gr.Ant:* Gold talent, silver
talent, talent d'or, d'argent. **2.** (*a*) Talent ;
capacité (naturelle); aptitude *f.* To have a talent
for doing the right thing, avoir le don d'agir à
propos. (*b*) Man of talent, homme de talent.
3. *Coll.* Gens *mpl* de talent. Exhibition of local t.,
exposition des œuvres d'artistes régionaux.
talented ['taləntid], *a.* Qui a du talent; doué.
talisman ['talizmən], *s.* Talisman *m.*
talk¹ [tɔ:k], *s.* **1.** (*a*) Paroles *fpl.* He is all talk
ce n'est qu'un bavard. *U.S: F:* That's the talk!
très bien! à la bonne heure! (*b*) Bruit *m,* dires
mpl racontages *mpl.* There is some talk of his
returning, il est question qu'il revienne. *S.a.* all
talk, ce ne sont que des on-dit. (*c*) Propos *mpl* ;
bavardage *m. Disjointed t.,* propos incohérents.
Idle talk, paroles en l'air. Small talk, menus
propos. To indulge in small talk, parler de la
pluie et du beau temps. To have plenty of small
talk, avoir de la conversation. **2.** (*a*) Entretien *m* ;
causerie *f.* To have a talk with s.o., causer,
s'entretenir, avec qn. (*b*) *W.Tel:* Causerie.
Weekly talk on . . ., feuilleton parlé hebdomadaire sur. . . . **3.** It is the talk of the town,
on ne parle, il n'est bruit, que de cela. *S.a.*
COMMON¹ 2.
talk². I. *v.i.* **1.** (*a*) Parler. *To learn to t.,*
apprendre à parler. (*b*) Parler, discourir. *It was
only for the sake of talking,* c'était histoire de
parler. To talk in riddles, parler par énigmes.
To talk big, se vanter. *P:* To talk through
one's hat, débiter des sottises. *It's easy to talk!*
cela vous plaît à dire! *P:* Now you're talking!
voilà qui s'appelle parler! *I am not talking of
you,* il ne s'agit pas de vous. Talking of that . . .
à propos de cela. . . . He knows what he is
talking about, il parle en connaissance de cause ;
il sait ce qu'il dit. *F:* Talk about luck! tu parles
d'une chance! (*c*) To talk of doing sth., parler
de faire qch. **2.** (*a*) To talk to, with, s.o., causer,
s'entretenir, avec qn. *To talk freely to s.o.,*
s'ouvrir à qn. To talk to oneself, se parler à
soi-même; monologuer. *F:* Who do you think
you are talking to! à qui croyez-vous donc parler?

(b) *F:* To talk (*severely*) to s.o., faire des remontrances à qn; réprimander qn. I'll talk to him! e vais ui dire son fait! **3.** (*a* Jaser, bavarder. (b) **To get oneself talked about,** faire par er de soi. *The whole town was talking about it,* toute la ville en glosait. II. **talk,** *v.tr.* **1.** (*a*) *To t.* French, parler français. (b) **To talk politics,** parler politique. **To talk (common) sense,** parler raison. *S.a.* RUBBISH 2, SCANDAL 2. **2.** (*a*) **To talk oneself hoarse,** s'enrouer à force de parler. (b) **To talk s.o. into doing sth.,** amener qn à faire qch. *S.a.* HEAD[1] 1. **talk at,** *v.i.* **To talk at s.o.,** faire des allusions voilées à qn (qui se trouve présent). **talk away. 1.** *v.tr.* Passer (le temps) à causer. **2.** *v.i.* Parler avec volubilité. **talk down. 1.** *v.i.* **To talk down to one's audience,** s'adapter à l'intelligence (bornée) de son auditoire. **2.** *v.tr.* Réduire (qn) au silence (en parlant plus haut et plus longtemps que lui). **talk on,** *v.i.* Continuer à parler. **talk over,** *v.tr.* **1.** Discuter, débattre (une question). **2.** = TALK ROUND 1. **talk round. 1.** *v.tr.* Enjôler (qn); amener (qn) à changer d'avis. *I talked them round at last,* j'ai fini par les persuader. **2.** *v.i.* **To talk round a question,** tourner autour du pot. **talking[1],** *a.* Parlant. *Cin:* Talking film, picture, film parlant, parlé. **talking[2],** *s.* **1.** Discours *mpl,* propos *mpl.* **A truce to talking!** c'est assez parlé! **2.** (*a*) Conversation *f.* (b) Bavardage *m.* **To do all the talking,** faire tous les frais de la conversation. **No talking please!** pas de bavardage! **3. To give s.o. a good talking-to,** semoncer qn.

talkative ['tɔːkətiv], *a.* Causeur; `aseur; loquace.

talkativeness ['tɔːkətivnəs], *s.* Loquacité *f.*

talker ['tɔːkər], *s.* **1.** Causeur, -euse; parleur, -euse. **2. To be a great talker,** être bavard; *F:* ne pas avoir sa langue dans sa poche; avoir du bagou(t).

talkie ['tɔːki], *s. Cin: F:* Film parlant, film parlé.

tall [tɔːl], *a.* **1.** (*Of pers.*) (*a*) Grand; de haute taille. (b) **How tall are you?** quelle est votre taille? *She is taller than I,* elle est plus grande que moi. *He was taller by a head than I,* il me dépassait de la tête. **She is growing tall,** elle se fait grande. **2.** (*Of thg*) Haut, élevé. *How t. is that mast?* quelle hauteur a ce mât? **Tall hat,** chapeau haut de forme. **3.** *F:* (Histoire) incroyable. **That's a tall story,** celle-là est raide. *S.a.* ORDER[1] 10.

tallboy ['tɔːlbɔi], *s. Furn:* (*a*) Commode *f* de hauteur élevée. (b) (Commode à) secrétaire *m.*

tallness ['tɔːlnəs], *s.* **1.** (*Of pers.*) Grande taille. (b) Hauteur *f* (d'un édifice).

tallow[1] ['talo], *s.* Suif *m. S.a.* CANDLE 1. **'tallow-'chandler,** *s.* Fabricant *m* ou marchand *m* de chandelles. **'tallow-drop,** *s.* **1.** Goutte *f* de suif. **2.** *Lap:* Cabochon *m.*

tallow[2] ['talo], *v.tr.* Suiffer; enduire de suif.

tally[1] ['tali], *s.* **1.** (*a*) Taille *f;* baguette *f* à encoches. (b) **The tally trade,** le commerce à tempérament. **2.** Entaille, coche (faite sur la taille). **3. To keep tally of goods,** pointer des marchandises (sur une liste). **4.** (*a*) Étiquette *f* (pour plantes, bagages). (b) Jeton *m* (de présence); marron *m* (de service). **'tally-clerk,** *s.* Pointeur *m.* **'tally-stick,** *s.* = TALLY[1] 1 (*a*).

tally[2]. 1. *v.tr.* Po nter, contrôler (des marchandises). **2.** *v.i.* Correspondre (*with,* à); s'accorder (*with,* avec). *These accounts do not t.,* ces comptes ne s'accordent pas.

tally-ho [tali'hou], *int. & s.* Taïaut (*m*).

tallyman, *pl.* **-men** ['talimən, -men], *s.m.* Drapier faisant la vente à tempérament à l'aide de démarcheurs.

talon ['talən], *s.* **1.** Serre *f* (d'oiseau de proie); griffe *f* (de lion). **2.** *Arch:* Talon *m,* doucine *f.* **3.** (*a*) Talon (d'une feuille de coupons); talon de souche. (b) (*At cards*) Talon.

tamarind ['tamarind], *s. Bot:* **1.** Fruit *m* du tamarinier. **2.** Tamarinier *m.*

tamarisk ['tamarisk], *s. Bot:* Tamaris *m.*

tambour ['tambuər], *s.* **1.** *Mus:* Grosse caisse. **2.** *Needlew:* Métier *m,* tambour *m,* à broder. **3.** Tambour (de vestibule . **'tambour-lace,** *s.* Dentelle *f* sur tulle.

tambourine [tambə'riːn], *s. Mus:* (*With jingles*) Tambour *m* de basque; (*without jingles*) tambourin *m.*

tame[1] [teim], *a.* **1.** (Animal) apprivoisé, domestiqué. **2.** *F:* (*a*) (*Of pers.*) Soumis, dompté. (b) (Style) monotone, terne. **-ly,** *adv.* **1.** *The story ends t.,* l'histoire se termine sur une note banale. **2.** (*Of pers.*) Sans résistance.

tame[2], *v.tr.* (*a*) Apprivoiser. (b) Domestiquer (une bête). (*c*) Mater (qn, une passion). **tame down. 1.** *v.tr.* Atténuer (son langage). **2.** *v.i.* (*a*) S'atténuer. (b) (*Of pers.*) S'adoucir, décolérer. **taming,** *s.* **1.** (*a*) Apprivoisement *m.* (b) Domestication *f.* **2.** Domptement *m. Lit:* **The Taming of the Shrew,** la Mégère mise à la raison.

tameable ['teiməbl], *a.* Apprivoisable ou domptable.

tameness ['teimnəs], *s.* **1.** (*a*) Nature douce (d'un animal). (b) Caractère soumis (de qn). **2.** *F:* (*a*) Pusillanimité *f.* (b) Monotonie *f,* fadeur *f* (du style, etc.); insipidité *f,* banalité *f* (d'un conte).

tamer ['teimər], *s.* Apprivoiseur, -euse; dompteur, -euse (d'animaux sauvages).

tammy ['tami], *s. F:* = TAM O' SHANTER.

tam o'shanter [tamo'ʃantər], *s.* Béret écossais.

tamp [tamp], *v.tr.* **1.** *Civ.E:* Damer, pilonner, tasser (la terre, etc.). **2.** Bourrer (un fourneau de mine).

tamper ['tampər], *v.i.* (*a*) **To tamper with sth.,** toucher (à un mécanisme); altérer (un document, une clef); falsifier (un registre); fausser, brouiller (une serrure). *To t. with the cash,* tripoter la caisse. (b) **To tamper with a witness,** suborner un témoin.

tamperer ['tampərər], *s.* Falsificateur, -trice (*with,* de).

tampion ['tampiən], *s. Artil:* Tampon *m* (de canon).

tampon ['tampən], *s.* (*a*) *Surg:* Tampon *m* (d'ouate). (b) *Hairdr:* Crêpé *m.*

tan[1] [tan], *s.* **1.** (*a*) Tan *m.* **Spent tan,** tannée *f.* (b) Couleur *f* du tan; (i) tanné *m;* (ii) hâle *m* (du teint). **2.** *a.* Tanné; tan inv. *Tan leather shoes,* souliers jaunes. **Black and tan dog,** chien noir et feu inv. **'tan-bark,** *s.* Écorce *f* à tan. **'tan-yard,** *s.* Tannerie *f.*

tan[2], *v.* (tanned) **1.** *v.tr.* (*a*) Tanner (les peaux). *F:* **To tan s.o., s.o.'s hide,** tanner le cuir à qn; étriller (qn). (b) (*Of sun*) Hâler, bronzer (la peau). **2.** *v.i.* (*Of complexion*) Se hâler, se basaner. **tanning,** *s.* **1.** Tannage *m.* **2.** *F:* Tannée *f,* raclée *f.*

tandem ['tandem], *s.* **1.** *Veh:* Tandem *m.* (b) Tandem (bicycle), tandem (de tourisme). **2.** *adv.* **To drive tandem,** conduire en flèche, en tandem.

tang[1] [tan], *s.* **1.** Soie *f* (d'un couteau, d'une épée); queue *f* (de lime). **2.** (*a*) Goût vif; saveur *f*. **Tang of the soil,** native tang, goût *m* de terroir. (*b*) **The tang of the morning air,** le piquant de l'air matinal. **tang²,** *s.* Son aigu, tintement *m* (d'une cloche). **tang³.** **I.** *v.tr.* Faire retentir, faire résonner (une cloche, etc.). **2.** *v.i.* (*Of bell*) Rendre un son aigu ; retentir.

tangency ['tandʒənsi], *s.* Tangence *f*.

tangent ['tandʒənt]. **I.** *a.* (Plan) tangent, tangentiel (*to*, à). **Tangent screw,** vis tangentielle ; vis sans fin. **2.** *s.* Tangente *f*. *F*: **To fly off at a tangent,** s'échapper par la tangente. *Trig*: **Tangent of an angle,** tangente d'un angle. **'tangent-scale,** *s.* **I.** Échelle *f* des tangentes. **2.** *Artil*: Hausse *f*.

tangential [tan'dʒenʃ(ə)l], *a.* *Geom*: Tangentiel, tangent (*to*, à).

tangerine [tandʒə'ri:n], *s.* Mandarine *f*.

tangible ['tandʒibl], *a.* **I.** Tangible. **Tangible assets,** valeurs matérielles. **2.** *F*: Réel. *T. difference,* différence sensible. **-ibly,** *adv.* **I.** Tangiblement. **2.** Sensiblement, manifestement.

Tangier(s) [tan'dʒiːər(z)]. *Pr.n.* Tanger *m*.

tangle¹ [taŋgl], *s.* *Algae*: Laminaire *f* ; ceinture *f* de Neptune.

tangle², *s.* Embrouillement *m* ; emmêlement *m* (de cheveux) ; fouillis *m* (de broussailles). *The string is all in a t.,* la ficelle est tout embrouillée. *F*: **To be in a tangle,** ne plus savoir où on en est. **To get into a tangle,** (i) s'embrouiller ; (ii) se mettre dans le pétrin. *It's a hopeless t.,* *F*: c'est le pot au noir.

tangle³. **I.** *v.tr.* **To tangle (up) sth.,** embrouiller, (em)mêler (des fils) ; embrouiller (une affaire). **To get tangled (up),** (*of thgs*) s'emmêler ; (*of thgs, pers.*) s'embrouiller ; *F*: (*of pers.*) se mettre dans le pétrin. *F*: **Tangled web,** trame compliquée. **2.** *v.i.* S'embrouiller, s'emmêler.

tanglefoot ['tanglfut], *s.* *U.S*: Whisky *m* ; *P*: casse-pattes *m*.

tango¹ ['taŋgo]. **I.** *s.* *Danc*: Tango *m*. **2.** *a.* (*Colour*) Tango *inv* ; orange *inv*.

tango², *v.i.* Danser le tango.

tank [taŋk], *s.* **I.** (*a*) Réservoir *m*. **Water tank,** réservoir à eau ; citerne *f* ; *Rail*: château *m* d'eau ; (*on locomotive*) caisse *f* à eau. *I.C.E*: **Petrol tank,** réservoir à essence. (*Of submarine*) **To blow the tanks,** chasser aux ballasts. (*b*) **Air tank,** caisson *m* à air. *Phot*: **Washing tank,** cuve *f* à lavage. *Cin*: *etc*: **Cooling tank,** cuvette *f* de refroidissement. **2.** *Mil*: *F*: Char *m* de combat, d'assaut ; tank *m*. **'tank-engine,** *s.* *Rail*: Locomotive *f* tender ; machine *f* tender. **'tank-steamer,** *s.* = TANKER.

tankard ['taŋkərd], *s.* Pot *m*, chope *f*, en étain.

tanker ['taŋkər], *s.* Bateau-citerne *m*, *pl.* bateaux-citernes.

tanner¹ ['tanər], *s.* Tanneur *m*.

tanner², *s.* *P*: (Pièce *f* de) six pence.

tannery ['tanəri], *s.* Tannerie *f*.

tannic ['tanik], *a.* *Ch*: Tannique.

tannin ['tanin], *s.* Tan(n)in *m*.

tansy ['tanzi], *s.* *Bot*: Tanaisie *f* ; sent-bon *m inv*.

tantalize ['tantəlaiz], *v.tr.* Infliger le supplice de Tantale à (qn) ; tantaliser, taquiner (qn) ; mettre (qn) au supplice. **tantalizing,** *a.* Qui tantalise ; (sourire) provocant. **-ly,** *adv.* (*a*) Cruellement. (*b*) D'un air provocant.

tantalum ['tantələm], *s.* *Ch*: Tantale *m*.

Tantalus ['tantələs]. **I.** *Pr.n.m.* Tantale. **2.** *s.* Cave à liqueurs anglaise.

tantamount ['tantəmaunt], *a.* Équivalent (*to*, à). **To be tantamount to sth.,** équivaloir à qch.

tantrum ['tantrəm], *s.* Accès *m* de mauvaise humeur, de colère. **To get into a tantrum,** se mettre en colère ; sortir de ses gonds.

tap¹ [tap], *s.* **I.** (*a*) Fausset *m* (de fût). (*b*) Robinet *m* ; (*of cask*) cannelle *f*. **To turn on, turn off, the tap,** ouvrir, fermer le robinet. (*c*) (*Of liquor*) **On tap,** (i) en perce, en vidange ; (ii) au tonneau. **Cask in tap,** tonneau en vidange. **2.** *F*: Boisson *f*, *esp.* bière *f*. **3.** = TAP-ROOM. **4.** *El*: Dérivation *f* (d'une canalisation) ; prise *f* intermédiaire (d'une bobine). **5.** *Tls*: **(Screw-)tap,** taraud *m* ; filière *f* (simple, à truelle). **6.** *Metall*: Coulée *f* (de métal fondu). **'tap-holder,** *s.* *Tls*: Porte-taraud *m*. **'tap-hole,** *s.* *Metall*: Trou *m* de coulée. **'tap-house,** *s.* Cabaret *m*, estaminet *m*. **'tap-room,** *s.* Estaminet *m*, buvette *f*. **'tap-root,** *s.* *Bot*: Racine pivotante, pivot *m*. **'tap-water,** *s.* Eau *f* du robinet ; eau de la ville.

tap², *v.tr.* (tapped) **I.** (*a*) Percer, mettre en perce (un fût). (*b*) **To tap a tree** (for resin), inciser, saigner, un arbre. *Metall*: **To tap the furnace,** percer le haut fourneau. *Surg*: **To tap a lung,** ponctionner, faire une ponction à, un poumon. *F*: **To tap s.o. for five pounds,** taper qn de cinq livres. (*c*) **To tap wine,** tirer du vin. (*d*) **To tap a stream,** faire une prise à un cours d'eau. **To tap a main,** brancher une conduite (de gaz, d'eau). **To tap a telegraph wire,** faire une prise sur un fil télégraphique ; capter un message. *El*: **To tap a coil,** faire des prises sur un enroulement. *F*: **To tap a new country,** ouvrir un nouveau pays au commerce. **2.** Tarauder, fileter. **tapping,** *s.* **I.** (*a*) Mise *f* en perce, perçage *m* (d'un tonneau) ; incision *f* (d'un arbre). *Surg*: Ponction *f*. (*b*) Tirage *m* (du vin). *El*: Dérivation *f* (d'une canalisation). **2.** Taraudage *m*.

tap³, *s.* Tape *f* ; petit coup. *There was a tap at the door,* on frappa doucement à la porte.

tap⁴, *v.* (tapped) **I.** *v.tr.* Frapper légèrement ; taper, tapoter. **2.** *v.ind.tr.* **To tap at, on, the door,** frapper doucement à la porte. **To tap in a nail,** enfoncer un clou à petits coups secs. **To tap off a message,** envoyer un message en Morse. **To tap out a pin,** chasser une goupille. **To tap out one's pipe,** débourrer sa pipe (sur son talon).

tape¹ [teip], *s.* **I.** (*a*) Ruban *m* de fil, de coton ; ganse *f* ; (*for parcels*) bolduc *m*. **Paper tape,** bande *f* de papier ; *esp.* bande de papier gommé. *El*: **Insulating tape,** ruban isolant ; chatterton *m*. *S.a.* RED TAPE. (*b*) *Sp*: Bande d'arrivée. (*c*) *Turf*: **The tapes** (at the starting-post), les rubans. **2.** **Steel tape,** ruban d'acier. **Surveyor's tape,** roulette *f* d'arpenteur. **3.** *Tg*: Bande, ruban, du récepteur. **'tape-machine,** *s.* Télégraphe imprimeur. **'tape-measure,** *s.* Mètre *m* en ruban.

tape², *v.tr.* **I.** *Dressm*: Garnir d'une ganse ; border (un vêtement). *Av*: *Aer*: Maroufler (une couture). *El*: Guiper (un conducteur). **2.** *Bookb*: Coudre sur ruban (les cahiers d'un livre). **3.** Mesurer (un terrain) au cordeau. *F*: (*Of pers.*) **I've got him taped,** j'ai pris sa mesure.

taper¹ ['teipər], *s.* Bougie filée. *Ecc*: Cierge *m*. **'taper-stand,** *s.* Bougeoir *m*.

taper², *s.* *Mec.E*: Conicité *f*.

taper³, *a.* **I.** *Poet*: (Doigt) effilé, fuselé. **2.** = TAPERED.

taper⁴. **I.** *v.tr.* Effiler ; tailler en cône. *Mec.E*: Ajuster en cône, côner (une fusée, etc.). **2.** *v.i.* **To taper (off, away),** s'effiler ; aller en diminuant.

tapered, *a. Mec.E: etc:* (Calibre, taraud) conique, diminué. **tapering,** *a.* En pointe; (doigt) effilé, fuselé. *Arch:* **Tapering column,** colonne diminuée.

tapestried ['tapestrid], *a.* Tendu de tapisseries.

tapestry ['tapestri], *s.* Tapisserie *f.* **To hang a wall with t.,** tendre un mur avec des tapisseries. **'tapestry-carpet,** *s.* Tapis bouclé. **'tapestry-weaver,** *s.* Tapissier, -ière. **'tapestry-work,** *s.* Tapisserie *f.*

tapeworm ['teipwə:rm], *s.* Ténia *m;* ver *m* solitaire.

tapioca [tapi'oukə], *s.* Tapioca *m.*

tapir ['teipər], *s. Z:* Tapir *m.*

tapnet ['tapnet], *s.* Cabas *m* (pour figues).

tappet ['tapet], *s. Mch:* Came *f* (de distribution); taquet *m,* heurtoir *m,* mentonnet *m. I.C.E:* Poussoir *m* de tige de culbuteur; tige *f* de poussoir. **'tappet-rod,** *s.* Tige-poussoir *f.*

tapster ['tapstər], *s.* **1.** Garçon *m* de cabaret. **2.** Cabaretier *m.*

tar[1] [tɑːr], *s.* **1.** (a) Goudron *m.* (b) *F:* Bitume *m,* brai *m.* **Wood tar, Stockholm tar,** goudron végétal; goudron de bois. *F:* **To spoil the ship for a ha'p'orth of tar,** faire des économies de bouts de chandelle. *S.a.* COAL-TAR. **2.** *Nau: F:* (Jack) tar, loup *m* de mer; *P:* mathurin *m.* **'tar-brush,** *s.* Brosse *f* à goudronner; *Nau:* guipon *m. F:* **To have a dash of the tar-brush,** avoir un peu de sang nègre dans les veines. **tar ma'cadam,** *s. Civ.E:* Tarmacadam *m.* **'tar-spraying,** *s.* Goudronnage *m.* **'tar-water,** *s. Med:* Eau *f* de goudron. **'tar-works,** *s.pl.* Goudronnerie *f.*

tar[2], *v.tr.* (tarred) Goudronner (une route, un cordage); bitumer (du carton); *Nau:* brayer (un vaisseau). *F:* **They are all tarred with the same brush,** ls sont tous taillés dans le même drap; ce sont des gens de (la) même farine, du même acabit. **Tarred felt,** carton bitumé. **tarring,** *s.* Goudronnage *m,* bitumage *m.*

tarantella [tarən'telɑ], *s.* Tarentelle *f.*

Taranto [tə'ranto]. *Pr.n.* Tarente *f.*

tarantula [tə'rantjula], *s.* Tarentule *f.*

tarboosh [tɑr'buːʃ], *s.* Tarbouch(e) *m;* chéchia *f.*

tardigrade ['tɑːrdigreid], *a. & s. Z:* Tardigrade (*m*).

tardiness ['tɑːrdinəs], *s.* **1.** Lenteur *f,* nonchalance *f* (*in doing sth.,* à faire qch.). **2.** (a) Tardiveté *f* (d'un fruit, etc.). (b) *U.S:* Manque *m* de ponctualité.

tardy ['tɑːrdi], *a.* **1.** Lent, nonchalant, paresseux. **2.** (a) Tardif. (b) *U.S:* (*Belated*) En retard. **-ily,** *adv.* **1.** Lentement, paresseusement. **2.** (a) Tardivement. (b) *U.S:* En retard.

tare[1] ['teər], *s. Bot:* **1.** Vesce *f.* **2.** *B. & F:* Ivraie *f.*

tare[2], *s.* (a) *Com:* Tare *f;* poids *m* à vide. **Allowance for tare,** la tare. (b) Poids net (des voitures automobiles).

target ['tɑːrget], *s.* **1.** *Archeol:* Targette *f;* petit bouclier. **2.** (a) Cible *f;* but *m,* objectif *m.* **Disappearing target, vanishing target,** cible, but, à éclipse. (b) *F:* **To be the target for popular ridicule,** être en butte aux risées de la foule. **3.** *X-rays:* Anticathode *f.* **4.** *Cu:* Épaulée *f* (d'agneau, de mouton).

tariff ['tarif], *s.* **1.** Tarif *m.* **Tariff walls,** barrières douanières. **2.** Tableau *m,* liste *f* des prix. **'tariff-reform,** *s. Pol:* Réforme *f* des tarifs douaniers.

tarlatan ['tɑːrlatən], *s. Tex:* Tarlatane *f.*

tarmac ['tɑːrmak], *s.* **1.** *Civ.E:* Tarmac *m.* **2.** *Av:* **The tarmac,** (i) ·'aire *f* d'embarquement; (ii) la piste d'envol.

tarn [tɑːrn], *s.* Petit lac (de montagne).

tarnish[1] ['tɑːrniʃ], *s.* Ternissure *f.*

tarnish[2]. **1.** *v.tr.* Ternir (un métal, la réputation de qn). **2.** *v.i.* (*Of metal, etc.*) Se ternir; (*of picture-frame*) se dédorer.

tarpaulin [tɑr'pɔːlin], *s. Nau:* (a) Toile goudronnée. (b) Bâche *f; Nau:* prélart *m;* banne *f. A:* **Tarpaulin hat,** chapeau en toile goudronnée.

tarpon ['tɑːrpɔn], *s. Ich:* Tarpon *m.*

tarragon ['taragən], *s.* Estragon *m.*

tarry[1] ['tɑːri], *a.* **1.** Goudronneux, bitumeux, bitumineux. **2.** Couvert, souillé, de goudron.

tarry[2] [tari], *v.i. Lit:* **1.** Rester, demeurer (dans un endroit). **To tarry for s.o.,** attendre qn. **2.** Tarder, s'attarder.

tarsus, *pl.* **-i** ['tɑːrsəs, -ai], *s. Anat:* Tarse *m.*

tart[1] [tɑːrt], *s.* **1.** *Cu:* (a) (*Open*) Tarte *f.* **Small jam t.,** tartelette *f* aux confitures. (b) (*Covered*) Tourte *f.* **2.** *P:* Fille *f,* cocotte *f,* grue *f.*

tart[2], *a.* (a) Au goût âpre, aigrelet; (*of wine*) vert, piquant. (b) *F:* (*Of answer*) Aigre *f,* mordant.

tartan[1] ['tɑːrtən], *s. Tex: Cost:* Tartan *m.*

tartan[2], *s. Nau:* Tartane *f.*

tartar[1] ['tɑːrtər], *s. Ch: Dent:* Tartre *m.*

Tartar[2]. **1.** *a. & s. Ethn:* Tatar, -e; Tartare. **2.** *s. F:* Homme *m* intraitable; (*of woman*) mégère *f.* **To catch a Tartar,** trouver à qui parler. **To have caught a Tartar,** tenir le loup par les oreilles.

tartaric [tɑr'tarik], *a. Ch:* Tartrique.

Tartary ['tɑːrtəri]. *Pr.n. A.Geog:* La Tartarie.

tartlet ['tɑːrtlet], *s. Cu:* Tartelette *f.*

tartness ['tɑːrtnəs], *s.* Acerbité *f;* verdeur *f* (d'un vin); *F:* acidité *f,* aigreur *f* (du ton).

tartrate ['tɑːrtret], *s. Ch:* Tartrate *m.*

task [tɑːsk], *s.* **1.** Tâche *f.* (a) *Sch:* (i) Devoir *m;* (ii) pensum *m.* (b) Travail, -aux *m,* ouvrage *m,* besogne *f.* **2. To take s.o. to task for sth.,** prendre qn à partie, réprimander qn, pour avoir fait qch.

taskmaster ['tɑːskmɑːstər], *s.m.* Chef de corvée; surveillant. *F:* **Hard taskmaster,** véritable tyran.

Tasmania [taz'meiniɑ]. *Pr.n.* La Tasmanie.

Tasmanian [taz'meinjən], *a. & s.* Tasmanien, -ienne.

tassel [tas(ə)l], *s.* **1.** *Cost: Furn: etc:* Gland *m* (de rideau, etc.); houppe *f* (de bonnet de coton). **2.** *Bookb:* Signet *m.*

tasselled [tasld], *a.* À glands; à houppes. **Tasselled fringe,** frange à houppes.

Tasso ['taso]. *Pr.n.m. Lit.Hist:* Le Tasse.

taste[1] [teist], *s.* **1.** (a) (*Sense of*) taste, goût *m.* (b) Saveur *f,* goût. **It has a burnt t.,** cela sent le brûlé. *This drink has no t.,* cette boisson n'a pas de goût, est insipide. (c) *F:* **A taste of sth.,** un petit peu (de fromage, etc.); une petite gorgée (de vin, etc.). (d) *F:* **He gave us a t.** of his illnature, il nous a donné un échantillon de sa méchanceté. **You'll get a t.** of it one of these days, vous en tâterez un de ces jours. **2.** Goût, penchant particulier, prédilection *f* (*for,* pour). **To have a taste for sth.,** avoir du goût pour qch.; avoir le goût de (la musique, etc.). **To have no taste for . . .,** n'avoir pas de goût pour . . .; *F:* être fermé à (la musique, etc.). **To acquire, develop, a taste for sth.,** prendre goût à qch.; acquérir le goût de qch. **To find sth. to one's taste,** trouver qch. à son goût. **Add sugar to taste,** on ajoute du sucre selon son goût, à volonté. *Prov:* **Tastes differ;** everyone to his taste, chacun (à) son goût. **3.** (*a*) To have taste in music, avoir du goût en matière de musique ; s'y connaître en musique. **People of taste,** les gens de goût. (*b*) **Costume in perfect taste,** costume d'un goût parfait. **It is (in) bad taste to . . .,** il est de mauvais goût de. . . .

taste². I. *v.tr.* **1.** Percevoir la saveur de (qch.) ; sentir (qch.). **2.** (*a*) (*Of cook*) Goûter (un mets). (*b*) Déguster (des vins, etc.) ; sonder (un fromage). **3.** (*a*) Goûter de, à (qch.) ; manger un petit morceau (d'un mets) ; tâter de (qch.) ; boire une petite gorgée (d'un liquide). **He had not tasted food for three days,** il ne s'était rien mis sous la dent depuis trois jours. (*b*) *To t. happiness, ill fortune,* connaître, goûter, le bonheur, la mauvaise fortune. *To t. power,* goûter, tâter, du pouvoir. II. **taste,** *v.i.* **To taste of** sth., avoir un goût de qch. **To taste like honey,** avoir un goût de miel.

tasteful ['teistful], *a.* De bon goût ; (vêtement) élégant. **-fully,** *adv.* (Habillé, etc.) avec goût.

tasteless ['teistləs], *a.* **1.** Sans saveur ; fade, insipide. **2.** (Ameublement) qui manque de goût, de mauvais goût.

tastelessness ['teistləsnəs], *s.* **1.** Insipidité *f*, fadeur *f* (d'un mets, etc.). **2.** Manque *m* de goût (dans l'habillement, etc.).

taster ['teistər], *s.* **1.** Dégustateur, -trice (de vins, de thés, etc.). **2. Wine-taster,** (i) tasse *f* à déguster ; (ii) sonde *f* à vin, tâte-vin *m inv.* **Cheese-taster,** sonde à fromage.

tastiness ['teistinəs], *s.* Saveur *f*, goût *m* agréable (d'un mets).

tasty ['teisti], *a.* (Mets) savoureux ; (morceau) succulent.

tat [tat], *v.tr. & i.* (tatted) *Needlew:* Faire de la frivolité. *Tatted insertion,* entre-deux en frivolité. **tatting,** *s.* Frivolité *f.*

ta-ta [ta'tɑ:], *int. Nursery & P:* Au revoir !

tatter ['tatər], *s.* Lambeau *m.* **Garment in tatters,** vêtement en lambeaux, en loques.

tatterdemalion [tatərdi'meiljən], *s.* Loqueteux, -euse ; déguenillé, -ée ; va-nu-pieds *mf inv.*

tattered ['tatərd], *a.* (Vêtement) dépenaillé, en loques ; (homme) déguenillé, loqueteux.

tattle¹ [tatl], *s.* **1.** Bavardage *m*, commérage *m.* **2.** Cancans *mpl* ; commérages.

tattle², *v.i.* **1.** Bavarder ; jaser ; commérer. **2.** Cancaner ; faire des cancans.

tattler ['tatlər], *s.* **1.** Bavard, -arde ; babillard, -arde. **2.** Cancanier, -ière.

tattoo¹ [ta'tu:], *s. Mil:* **1.** Retraite *f* (du soir). **To beat, sound, the tattoo,** battre, sonner, la retraite. *F:* **To beat the devil's tattoo** (*on the table,* etc.), tambouriner, pianoter (sur la table, etc.). **2.** (*a*) **Torchlight tattoo,** retraite aux flambeaux. (*b*) Carrousel *m*

tattoo², *s.* Tatouage *m.*

tattoo³, *v.tr.* Tatouer (le corps). **tattooing,** *s.* Tatouage *m.*

taught [tɔːt]. *See* TEACH.

taunt¹ [tɔːnt], *s.* Reproche méprisant ; injure *f* (en paroles) ; sarcasme *m*, brocard *m.*

taunt², *v.tr.* (*a*) Accabler (qn) de sarcasmes ; se gausser de (qn). (*b*) **To taunt** s.o. **with** sth., reprocher qch. à qn (avec mépris). **taunting,** *a.* (Ton, air) de sarcasme. **-ly,** *adv.* D'un ton, d'un air, de mépris provocant.

taut [tɔːt], *a. Nau: etc:* (*a*) (Cordage) tendu, raide, raidi. **To haul a rope taut,** raidir, embraquer, un cordage. *F:* **Taut situation,** situation tendue. (*b*) **Taut and trim,** (i) (navire) paré, en bon état ; (ii) (personne) à l'air soigné, tirée à quatre épingles.

tauten ['tɔːtən], *v.tr.* Raidir, embraquer (un câble) ; étarquer (une voile).

tautness ['tɔːtnəs], *s.* Raideur *f* (d'un câble).

tautology [tɔː'tɔlodʒi], *s.* Tautologie *f.*

tavern ['tavərn], *s.* Taverne *f*, cabaret *m.* **'tavern-keeper,** *s.* Cabaretier, -ière.

taw¹ [tɔː], *s. Games:* **1.** Grosse bille (de verre) ; cal(l)ot *m.* **2.** (Jeu *m* de) rangette *f.*

taw², *v.tr.* Mégir, mégisser, chamoiser (les peaux) ; préparer (les peaux) en blanc. **tawing,** *s.* Mégissage *f.*

tawdriness ['tɔːdrinəs], *s.* Clinquant *m* ; faux brillant.

tawdry ['tɔːdri], *a.* D'un mauvais goût criard. *T. jewellery,* clinquant *m*, toc *m. F: T. style,* style affublé d'oripeaux. **-ily,** *adv.* Avec un faux éclat ; avec un faux luxe criard.

tawer ['tɔːər], *s.* Mégissier *m.*

tawery ['tɔːəri], *s.* (Établissement *m* de) mégisserie *f.*

tawny ['tɔːni], *a.* (i) Tanné, basané ; (ii) fauve ; tirant sur le roux. **Old tawny port,** porto qui a jauni dans le fût.

tawse [tɔːz], *s. Sch:* (*Scot.*) Courroie *f* de cuir, à extrémité découpée en lanières (pour corriger les enfants).

tax¹ [taks], *s.* **1.** (*a*) Impôt *m*, contribution *f*, taxe *f.* **Direct taxes, assessed taxes,** contributions directes ; impôts. **Indirect taxes,** contributions indirectes. **Land tax,** impôt foncier. *Visitors' tax,* taxe de séjour. **Road Fund tax,** taxe de circulation. **Petrol tax,** droit *m* sur l'essence. **To lay, levy, a tax on** sth., mettre un impôt sur qch. ; frapper qch. d'un impôt ; imposer qch. *To collect a tax,* percevoir un impôt. *To reduce the tax on* sth., dégrever partiellement (un produit, etc.). **Free of tax, tax free,** exempt d'impôts. (*b*) *Hist:* Taille *f. Tax on income,* taille personnelle. **2.** Charge *f* ; fardeau (imposé à qn). **To be a tax on** s.o., être une charge pour qn ; être à charge à qn. **'tax-collector,** *s.* Percepteur *m* (des contributions directes) ; receveur *m* (des contributions indirectes). **'tax-payer,** *s.* Contribuable *mf.*

tax², *v.tr.* **1.** (*a*) Taxer (les objets de luxe, etc.) ; frapper (qch.) d'un impôt ; mettre un impôt sur (qch.). (*b*) Imposer (qn). (*c*) *F:* Mettre à l'épreuve (l'adresse, la patience, de qn). **2.** *Jur:* Taxer (les dépens d'un procès). **Taxed bill of costs,** mémoire taxé (par le juge). **Taxing-master,** (juge) taxateur *m.* **3. To tax** s.o. **with doing** sth. (i) taxer, accuser, qn, (ii) reprocher à qn, d'avoir fait qch.

taxable ['taksəbl], *a.* **1.** Imposable. *To make* sth. *t.,* imposer qch. **2.** *Jur:* **Costs taxable to** s.o., frais à la charge de qn.*

taxation [tak'sei∫(ə)n], *s.* **1.** (*a*) Imposition *f* (de la propriété, etc.). **The taxation authorities,** l'administration fiscale. (*b*) Charges fiscales ; prélèvement fiscal. (*c*) Revenu réalisé par les impôts ; les impôts *m.* **2.** *Jur:* **Taxation of costs,** taxation *f*, taxe *f*, des frais.

taxi¹ ['taksi], *s. F:* = TAXI-CAB. **'taxi-cab,** *s.* Fiacre *m* automobile ; taxi *m.* **'taxi-driver,** *s.* Conducteur *m*, chauffeur *m*, de taxi. **'taxi-rank,** *s.* Stationnement *m* (pour taxis).

taxi², *v.i.* **1.** (taxied ; taxying) **1.** Aller en taxi. **2.** (*Of aircraft*) Rouler sur le sol.

taxidermist ['taksidəːrmist], *s.* Empailleur *m*, naturaliste *m*, taxidermiste *m.*

taxidermy ['taksidəːrmi], *s.* Taxidermie *f.*

taximeter ['taksimiːtər], *s.* Taximètre *m.*

tea [tiː], *s.* **1.** Thé *m.* (*a*) **To drink tea,** boire, prendre, du thé. *Weak tea, strong tea,* thé léger, fort. (b) **Afternoon tea**, five-o'clock m. **High tea**, repas à la fourchette (arrosé de thé). **2.** Tisane f, infusion f. **'tea-basket,** s. Mallette f de camping. **'tea-caddy,** s. Boîte f à thé. **'tea-cake,** s. Brioche plate (se mange grillée et beurrée). **'tea-chest,** s. Caisse f à thé. **'tea-cloth,** s. **1.** Nappe f à thé ; napperon m. **2.** Torchon m (pour essuyer la vaisselle). **'tea-cosy,** s. Couvre-théière m. **'tea-cup,** s. Tasse f à thé. **'tea-fight,** s. F: (a) Five-o'clock m où il y a cohue. (b) Soirée f (de village, etc.) avec thé et limonades. **'tea-garden,** s. **1.** Établissement m où l'on sert le thé en plein air. **2.** Plantation f de thé. **'tea-gown,** s. Robe f d'intérieur ; déshabillé m. **'tea-infuser,** s. Boule f à thé. **'tea-kettle,** s. Bouilloire f. **'tea-leaf,** s. Feuille f de thé. **Used tea-leaves,** marc m de thé. **'tea-merchant,** s. Négociant m en thés. **'tea-party,** s. Thé m d'apparat. **To give a tea-party,** donner un thé. **'tea-plant,** s. Arbre m à thé. **'tea-planter,** s. Planteur m de thé. **'tea-pot,** s. Théière f. **'tea-room,** s. Salon m de thé. **'tea-rose,** s. Hort: Rose f thé, pl. roses thé. **'tea-service, -set,** s. Service m à thé. **'tea-shop,** s. Pâtisserie f (où l'on sert le thé) ; salon m de thé. **'tea-spoon,** s. Cuiller f à thé. **'tea-strainer,** s. Passe-thé m inv. **'tea-table,** s. Table f à thé. **'tea-things,** s.pl. Service m à thé. **'tea-time,** s. L'heure f du thé. **'tea-urn,** s. Fontaine f à thé.

teach [ti:tʃ], v.tr. (taught [tɔ:t] ; taught) Enseigner, instruire (qn) ; enseigner (qch.). **To teach s.o. sth.,** enseigner, apprendre, qch. à qn. **He is being taught all sorts of things,** on lui apprend toutes sortes de choses. **He teaches French,** il enseigne, il professe, le français. **The teaching staff,** le corps enseignant. **To teach s.o. (how) to do sth.,** apprendre à qn à faire qch. **To teach oneself sth.,** apprendre qch. tout seul. S.a. SELF-TAUGHT. I had been taught never to tell a lie, on m'avait inculqué qu'il ne faut jamais mentir. F: **To teach s.o. a lesson,** donner à qn une leçon (qu'il n'oubliera pas de si tôt). That will teach him! ça lui apprendra! **To teach s.o. a thing or two,** dégourdir qn. I'll teach you to speak to me like that! je vous apprendrai à me parler de la sorte! **teaching,** s. **1.** Enseignement m, instruction f. **To go in for teaching,** entrer dans l'enseignement. **2. The teachings of experience,** les leçons f de l'expérience. **3.** Doctrine f.

teachable ['ti:tʃəbl], a. **1.** Qui apprend facilement ; docile. **2.** (Sujet) enseignable.

teacher ['ti:tʃər], s. (i) Instituteur, -trice ; maître, f. maîtresse (d'école) ; (ii) professeur m ; (iii) maître (au sens large). **Pupil teacher, student teacher,** élève-maître, f. élève-maîtresse. The t. and his disciples, le maître et ses disciples.

teachership ['ti:tʃərʃip], s. Professorat m.

teak [ti:k], s. Chêne m des Indes ; teck m, tek m.

teal [ti:l], s.inv. Orn: Sarcelle f. The moorland is full of teal, la lande abonde en sarcelles.

team[1] [ti:m], s. **1.** (Inv. after numeral) Attelage m (de chevaux, de bœufs). A thousand team of cattle, mille attelages de bœufs. **Team driver,** conducteur m d'attelage. **2.** Équipe f (de joueurs, d'ouvriers) ; camp m (de joueurs). **Football team,** équipe f de football. **Team games,** jeux d'équipe. **The team spirit,** l'esprit d'équipe. **'team-work,** s. Travail m d'équipe ; collaboration f. Sp: Jeu m d'ensemble.

team[2]. **1.** v.tr. Atteler (des chevaux, des bœufs). **2.** v.i. F: **To team up with s.o.,** se joindre à

qn, F: s'atteler avec qn (pour accomplir un travail).

tear[1] ['ti:ər], s. Larme f. **To shed tears,** verser des larmes. To shed a perfunctory t., y aller de sa larme. **To burst into tears,** fondre en larmes ; être plein d'une crise de larmes. To weep tears of joy, pleurer de joie. **To move s.o. to tears,** attendrir qn (jusqu'aux larmes). To be easily moved to tears, avoir la larme facile. **She was (all) in tears,** elle était (tout) en larmes. These words brought tears to her eyes, ces paroles lui firent venir les larmes aux yeux. **To laugh till the tears come** rire (jusqu')aux larmes. **'tear-drop,** s. Larme f. **'tear-duct,** s. Conduit lacrymal. **'tear-gas,** s. Gaz m lacrymogène. **'tear-stained,** a. (Visage) portant des traces de larmes, barbouillé de larmes.

tear[2] ['teər], s. **1.** Déchirement m (d'une étoffe). **2.** Déchirure f, accroc m (dans un vêtement). **3.** F: (a) To go full tear, aller à toute vitesse, à fond de train. (b) Rage f, agitation f.

tear[3] ['teər], v. (tore ['tɔ:ər] ; torn [tɔ:rn]) **1.** v.tr. (a) Déchirer. **To tear sth. open,** ouvrir qch. en le déchirant ; éventrer (un paquet). S.a. PIECE[1] 1. **To tear a hole in sth.,** faire un trou, faire un accroc, à (un vêtement). **Stuff that tears easily,** étoffe qui se déchire facilement. Paperm: **To tear rags,** effilocher les chiffons. **To tear a muscle,** claquer un muscle. F: **Country torn by civil war,** pays déchiré par la guerre civile. Torn between two emotions, tiraillé entre deux émotions. (b) Arracher (from, à qn, de qch.). **To tear (out) one's hair,** s'arracher les cheveux. To t. a confession from s.o., arracher un aveu à qn. **2.** v.i. (a) **To tear at sth.,** déchirer ou arracher qch. avec des doigts impatients ; tirer de toutes ses forces sur qch. (b) F: **To tear along,** aller à toute vitesse, à fond de train ; brûler le pavé. He was tearing along (the road), il dévorait la route. **To tear upstairs,** monter l'escalier quatre à quatre. **To tear away,** partir à toute vitesse. **To tear back,** revenir en toute hâte. **tear away,** v.tr. Arracher. I could not tear myself away from this scene, je ne pouvais pas m'arracher de, à, cette scène. He could not t. himself away, il ne pouvait se décider à les quitter. **tear down,** v.tr. Arracher (une affiche, etc.). **tear off,** v.tr. Arracher. A shell tore off his arm, un obus lui emporta le bras. S.a. CALENDAR 1. **tear out,** v.tr. Arracher. **To tear s.o.'s eyes out,** arracher les yeux à qn. **tear up,** v.tr. **1.** Déchirer ; mettre en pièces. **2. To tear up a tree by the roots,** déraciner un arbre. **tearing**[1], a. **1.** Déchirant ; (vent) à écorner les bœufs. F: **Tearing rage,** rage à tout casser. **2.** F: **At a tearing rate,** à toute allure. **To be in a tearing hurry,** être terriblement pressé. **tearing**[2], s. **1.** Déchirement m. **2.** Tearing away, off, out, arrachement m. Mec: **Tearing strength,** résistance f à la déchirure.

tearful ['ti:ərful], a. Éploré ; tout en pleurs ; Pej: larmoyant. In a t. voice, (i) avec des larmes dans la voix ; (ii) Pej: en pleurnichant. **-fully,** adv. En pleurant ; les larmes aux yeux.

tease[1] [ti:z], s. **1.** Taquin, -ine. He's a tease, il est taquin. **2.** Taquinerie f.

tease[2], v.tr. **1.** (a) To tease (out), effiler, effilocher (un tissu) ; démêler (la laine). (b) = TEASEL[2]. (c) Carder (la laine). **2.** Taquiner, tourmenter. faire enrager (qn) ; faire des taquineries à (qn). **teasing**[1], a. Taquin ; (ton) railleur, persifleur. **teasing**[2], s. **1.** (a) Teasing (out), effilage m, effilochage m ; démêlage m (de la laine). (b) Cardage m. **2.** Taquinerie f, taquinage m.

teasel¹ [ˈtiːz(ə)l], *s.* **I.** *Bot:* Cardère *f.* *S.a.* FULLER¹. **2.** *Tex:* Carde *f.*

teasel², *v.tr.* (teaseled) *Tex:* Lainer, gratter (le drap).

teaser [ˈtiːzər], *s.* **I.** = TEASE¹I. **2.** *F:* Problème *m* difficile ; question embarrassante. *To ask a candidate teasers*, poser des colles *f* à un candidat.

teaspoonful [ˈtiːspuːnful], *s.* Cuillerée *f* à thé.

teat [tiːt], *s.* **I.** (*a*) Mamelon *m* ; bout *m* de sein ; tétin *m* (de femme) ; tette *f*, trayon *m* (de vache). (*b*) Tétine *f* (de biberon). **2.** *Tchn:* Téton *m.* **Teat-screw**, vis à téton.

teazle¹, ² [tiːzl], *s. & v.tr.* = TEASEL¹, ².

tec [tek], *s. P:* = DETECTIVE 2.

technical [ˈteknik(ə)l], *a.* **I.** Technique. **Technical institute**, école *f* des arts et métiers. *T. difficulty*, difficulté d'ordre technique. **Technical terms**, termes techniques ; termes de métier. *Jur: Judgment quashed on a t. point*, arrêt cassé pour vice de forme, de procédure. **2.** *Jur:* **Technical offence**, quasi-délit *m.* **-ally**, *adv.* Techniquement.

technicality [tekniˈkaliti], *s.* Détail *m* technique ; considération *f* d'ordre technique.

technician [tekˈniʃ(ə)n], *s.* Technicien *m.*

technics [ˈtekniks], *s.pl.* Technologie *f.*

technique [tekˈniːk], *s.* Technique *f.*

technological [teknoˈlɔdʒik(ə)l], *a.* Technologique.

technology [tekˈnɔlodʒi], *s.* Technologie *f.*

tectrices [tekˈtraisiːz], *s.pl. Orn:* (Plumes) tectrices *f.*

ted [ted], *v.tr.* (tedded) Faner, sauter (le foin).

tedder [ˈtedər], *s.* **I.** Faneur, -euse. **2.** (*Machine*) Faneuse *f.*

Teddy [ˈtedi]. *Pr.n.m.* (*Dim.*) = Édouard, Edmond, Théodore. **Teddy Bear**, ours *m* en peluche.

tedious [ˈtiːdiəs], *a.* (Travail) fatigant, pénible ; (discours) ennuyeux, fastidieux. *T. tale*, histoire à dormir debout.

tediousness [ˈtiːdiəsnəs], **tedium** [ˈtiːdiəm], *s.* Ennui *m* ; manque *m* d'intérêt (d'un travail).

tee¹ [tiː], *s.* (La lettre) té *m. S.a.* T 2.

tee², *s. Golf:* (*a*) Dé *m* (de sable) ; tee *m.* (*b*) = TEEING-GROUND.

tee³, *v.tr. Golf:* Surélever (la balle). *Abs.* **To tee up**, placer la balle sur le dé. **To tee off**, jouer sa balle (du tertre de départ). **ˈteeing-ground**, *s.* (Tertre *m* de) départ *m.*

teem [tiːm], *v.i.* Abonder (*with*, en) ; foisonner, regorger, fourmiller (*with*, de). *Streets that t. with people*, rues qui regorgent, qui grouillent, de monde. *His brain is teeming with new ideas*, son cerveau est fertile en idées neuves. **teeming**, *a. T. streets*, rues bondées de monde. *T. crowd*, foule grouillante.

teens [tiːnz], *s.pl. F:* L'âge *m* entre treize et vingt ans. **To be in one's teens**, être adolescent(e). **To be out of one's teens**, avoir plus de vingt ans.

teeny(-weeny) [ˈtiːni(ˈwiːni)], *a. F:* Minuscule ; tout petit.

teeth [tiːθ]. *See* TOOTH¹.

teethe [tiːð], *v.i.* (*Only in pr.p. and progressive tenses*) Faire ses (premières) dents. **teething**, *s.* Dentition *f.*

teetotal [tiːˈtout(ə)l], *a.* Antialcoolique ; qui ne boit que de l'eau.

teetotalism [tiːˈtoutəlizm], *s.* Abstention *f* des liqueurs alcooliques.

teetotal(l)er [tiːˈtout(ə)lər], *s.* Abstinent, -ente ; buveur, -euse, d'eau.

teetotum [tiːˈtoutəm], *s.* Toton *m.*

tegulated [ˈtegjuleitid], *a.* Imbriqué.

tegument [ˈtegjumənt], *s.* Tégument *m.*

telamon [ˈtelamən], *s.* (*pl.* **telamones** [telaˈmou-niːz]) *Arch:* Atlante *m*, télamon *m.*

telecommunication [telikɔmjuːniˈkeiʃ(ə)n], *s. Post:* Télégraphes *m* et téléphones.

teleferic [teliˈferik], *s.* Téléphérique *m*, téléférique *m.*

telegony [tiˈlegoni], *s. Biol:* Télégonie *f.*

telegram [ˈteligram], *s.* Télégramme *m* ; dépêche *f.* **Wireless telegram**, radio télégramme, radiotélégramme *m.*

telegraph¹ [ˈteligraf, -grɑːf], *s.* **I.** Télégraphe *m.* **Recording telegraph**, télégraphe enregistreur **Printing telegraph**, typotélégraphe *m.* **Telegraph office**, bureau télégraphique. **2.** *Nau:* (Ship's telegraph, transmetteur *m* d'ordres. **Engine-room telegraph**, cadran *m.* **3.** *Sp:* **Telegraph (board)**, tableau *m* d'affichage (des résultats) **ˈtelegraph boy, messenger**, *s.m.* Facteur télégraphiste ; petit télégraphiste. **ˈtelegraph operator**, *s.* Télégraphiste *mf.* **ˈtelegraph-pole**, *s.* Poteau *m* télégraphique.

telegraph². I. *v.i.* Télégraphier ; envoyer un télégramme, une dépêche. *His son was telegraphed for*, on télégraphia pour faire venir son fils. **2.** *v.tr.* (*a*) Télégraphier (une nouvelle, etc.) (*b*) **To telegraph s.o. to come**, envoyer une dépêche à qn pour lui dire de venir ; appeler qn par télégramme.

telegraphese [teligraˈfiːz], *s.* Style *m* télégraphique.

telegraphic [teliˈgrafik], *a.* Télégraphique.

telegraphist [tiˈlegrəfist], *s.* Télégraphiste *mf.*

telegraphy [tiˈlegrəfi], *s.* Télégraphie *f. S.a.* WIRELESS¹.

teielens [ˈtelilenz], *s. Phot:* Téléobjectif *m.*

telemechanics [telimeˈkaniks], *s.pl.* Télémécanique *f.*

telemeter [tiˈlemetər], *s.* Télémètre *m.* (*Stereoscopic t.*, stéréotélémètre *m.*

teleological [teliɔˈlɔdʒik(ə)l], *a.* Téléologique.

teleology [teliˈɔlodʒi], *s.* Téléologie *f.*

telepathic [teliˈpaθik], *a.* Télépathique.

telepathy [tiˈlepaθi], *s.* Télépathie *f.*

telephone¹ [ˈtelifoun], *s.* Téléphone *m.* **Desk telephone**, poste *m* mobile. **Are you on the telephone?** avez-vous le téléphone ? *You are wanted on the t.*, on vous demande au téléphone **Telephone number**, numéro *m* de téléphone ; numéro d'appel. *S.a.* CALL¹ 2, EXCHANGE¹ 1. **ˈtelephone-box**, *s.* Cabine *f* téléphonique. **ˈtelephone girl**, *s.f.* Demoiselle du téléphone. **ˈtelephone operator**, *s.* Téléphoniste *mf.*

telephone². I. *v.i.* Téléphoner (*to*, à). **2.** *v.tr.* (*a*) Téléphoner (un message). (*b*) Téléphoner à (qn).

telephonic [teliˈfɔnik], *a.* Téléphonique.

telephonist [tiˈlefonist], *s.* Téléphoniste *mf.*

telephony [tiˈlefoni], *s.* Téléphonie *f. S.a.* WIRELESS¹.

telephotography [telifoˈtɔgrəfi], *s.* Téléphotographie *f* ; photographie *f* au téléobjectif.

teleprinter [ˈteliprintər], *s. Tg:* (Appareil) télétype *m.*

telescope¹ [ˈteliskoup], *s.* (*a*) **Refracting telescope**, lunette *f* (d'approche) ; longue-vue *f* ; *Astr:* réfracteur *m.* (*b*) **Reflecting telescope**, télescope *m* ; réflecteur *m.*

telescope². I. *v.tr.* Télescoper (un train, etc.) **2.** *v.i.* (*a*) (Of trains, cars, etc.) (Se) télescoper. (*b*) Parts made to t., pièces qui s'emboîtent.

telescopic [telisˈkɔpik], *a.* **I.** Télescopique. *Phot:* **Telescopic lens**, téléobjectif *m.* **2.** **Telescopic leg** (*of tripod*), branche coulissante, à coulisse.

televise ['teliva:iz], *v.tr.* Téléviser.
television [teli'viʒ(ə)n], *s.* Télévision *f.*
televisor ['telivaizər], *s.* Téléviseur *m.*
telewriter ['teliraitər], *s. Tg:* Télautographe *m.*
tell [tel], *v.* (told [tould]; told) I. *v.tr.* **1.** (*a*) Dire (une nouvelle, etc.). *S.a.* LIE[1], TRUTH I. (*b*) To tell s.o. sth., dire, apprendre, qch. à qn; faire savoir qch. à qn. I cannot tell you how pleased I am, je ne saurais vous dire combien je suis content. *I have been told that* . . ., on m'a dit que. . . . I tell you no! je vous dis que non! Don't let me have to tell you that again, tenez-vous cela pour dit. I told you so! je vous l'avais bien dit! quand je vous le disais! I'll tell you what! écoute(z)! (*c*) Raconter, conter (une histoire). *I will t. you what happened*, je vais vous raconter ce qui est arrivé. *He told his adventures*, il nous a fait le récit de ses aventures. *F:* Tell me another! à d'autres! More than words can tell, au delà de tout ce qui peut se dire. To hear tell that . . ., entendre dire que. . . . To hear tell of . . ., entendre parler de. . . . (*d*) Annoncer, proclamer (un fait); révéler (un secret). *The sign-post tells the way to* . . ., le poteau indique le chemin pour aller à. . . . (*Of clock*) To tell the time, marquer l'heure. *To t. the quarters*, sonner les quarts. *S.a.* FORTUNE I. **2.** (*a*) To tell s.o. about s.o., parler de qn à qn. *He told us of foreign lands*, il nous décrivait des pays étrangers. (*b*) (*Emphatic*) *It is not so easy, let me tell you*, ce n'est pas si facile, je vous assure. *He will be furious, I (can) t. you!* il va être furieux, je vous en réponds! **3.** To tell s.o. to do sth., ordonner, dire, à qn de faire qch. *Do as you are told*, faites comme on vous l'ordonne, comme on vous dit. I told him not to, je le lui ai défendu. **4.** (*a*) Discerner, distinguer, reconnaître. To tell right from wrong, discerner le bien du mal. You can't tell her from her sister, elle ressemble à sa sœur à s'y tromper. One can tell him by his voice, on le reconnaît à sa voix. One can tell she is intelligent, on la devine intelligente. (*b*) Savoir. How can I tell that he will do it? quelle certitude ai-je qu'il le fera? Who can tell? qui sait? You never can tell, il ne faut (jamais) jurer de rien; on ne sait jamais. I cannot tell, je n'en sais rien. **5.** *Abs.* To tell of sth., annoncer, révéler, qch. *The lines on his face told of suffering*, son visage sillonné de rides accusait, révélait, ses souffrances. **6.** To tell (over), compter (un troupeau, etc.); compter, énumérer (les voix). All told, tout compris; somme toute. *There were twenty people all told*, il y avait en tout vingt personnes. *S.a.* BEAD[1] I. II. **tell**, *v.i.* (*a*) Produire son effet; porter (coup). Blood will tell, bon sang ne peut mentir. *Words that tell*, mots à l'emporte-pièce. *Every shot tells*, chaque coup porte. It tells (up)on his health, cela affecte sa santé. *These drugs tell upon one in time*, l'effet de ces drogues se fait sentir à la longue. (*b*) This tells in his favour, cela milite en sa faveur. *Everything told against him*, tout témoignait contre lui. **tell off**, *v.tr.* **1.** Désigner, affecter (qn pour une corvée). To tell off one's men, désigner leurs postes à ses hommes. **2.** *P:* Rembarrer, moucher (qn); dire son fait à qn. **telling**[1], *a.* Fort, efficace; qui fait de l'effet. Telling blow, coup qui porte; coup bien asséné. Telling style, style énergique. With t. effect, avec un effet marqué. **-ly**, *adv.* Efficacement; d'une manière impressionnante.
telling[2], *s.* **1.** Récit *m*; narration *f* (d'une histoire). **2.** Divulgation *f* (d'un secret). **3.** There is no telling, on ne sait pas; qui sait? **4.** Telling

(over), dénombrement *m*; énumération *f* (des votes). **'tell-tale**, *s.* **1.** (*a*) Rapporteur, -euse; *Sch:* *F:* cafard, -arde. (*b*) Tell-tale signs, signes révélateurs. *T.-t.* blush, rougissement dénonciateur. **2.** *Mec.E:* *etc:* Aiguille indicatrice; indicateur *m. Aut:* Petrol-tank tell-tale, indicateur jauge d'essence. *El.E:* *Ind:* Tell-tale (lamp), lampe témoin. **3.** *Nau:* (*a*) Axiomètre *m* (du gouvernail). (*b*) Compas renversé.
teller ['telər], *s.* **1.** (Ra)conteur, -euse; narrateur, -trice. **2.** (*a*) Caissier *m*, payeur *m* (de banque). (*b*) *Parl:* Scrutateur *m*; recenseur *m.*
telluric [te'ljuərik], *a.* Tellurique.
tellurium [te'ljuəriəm], *s. Ch:* Tellure *m.*
telpher[1] ['telfər], *a. Ind:* Telpher (rail)way, *s.* telpher, ligne *f* de telphérage; (ligne) téléphérique *m.*
telpher[2], *v.tr.* Telphérer, téléphérer.
telpherage ['telfəredʒ], *s.* Telphérage *m*, téléphérage *m.*
temerity [ti'meriti], *s.* Témérité *f*, audace *f.*
temper[1] ['tempər], *s.* **1.** *Metall:* Coefficient *m* de dureté (de l'acier); trempe *f.* To draw, let down, the temper (of a tool), recuire après trempe. (*Of steel*) To lose its t., se détremper. **2.** (*Of pers.*) Sang-froid *m.* To keep one's temper, rester calme; garder, conserver, son sang-froid. To lose one's temper, perdre son sang-froid; s'emporter, se fâcher. To be out of temper, être de mauvaise humeur. To try s.o.'s temper, énerver qn. **3.** Humeur *f.* (*a*) Caractère *m*, tempérament *m.* Even t., caractère égal, calme. To have a good temper, avoir bon caractère. To have a bad temper, *F:* to have a temper, avoir le caractère mal fait. (*b*) To show (ill) temper, montrer de l'humeur. In a vile temper, d'une humeur massacrante. To be in a good, a bad, temper, être de bonne, de mauvaise, humeur. (*c*) Mauvaise humeur. Outburst of temper, mouvement *m* d'humeur. To be in a temper, être en colère. To get s.o.'s temper up, mettre qn en colère; fâcher qn.
temper[2], *v.tr.* **1.** (*a*) Gâcher, délayer, broyer (le mortier, etc.); broyer (les couleurs). (*b*) *Metall:* (i) Tremper; donner la trempe à (l'acier). (ii) Recuire, adoucir (un métal). **2.** Tempérer; modérer (son ardeur, une passion). *To t. severity with gentleness*, tempérer la sévérité par la douceur. **tempered**, *a.* **1.** (Acier) trempé ou recuit. **2.** *Mus:* Equally tempered scale, gamme tempérée. **3.** Mild-tempered, d'une disposition douce. *S.a.* BAD-TEMPERED, *etc.*
tempera ['tempərə], *s. Art:* = DISTEMPER[3] I.
temperament ['tempərəmənt], *s.* **1.** (*Of pers.*) Tempérament *m*, humeur *f*, complexion *f.* **2.** *Mus:* Tempérament. Equal t., even t., tempérament égal.
temperamental [tempərə'ment(ə)l], *a.* (*a*) Capricieux, fantasque. (*b*) Qui s'emballe ou se déprime facilement.
temperance ['tempərəns], *s.* Tempérance *f.* **1.** Modération *f*, retenue *f.* **2.** (*a*) Sobriété *f* (à table). (*b*) Abstention *f* des boissons alcooliques. Temperance society, ligue *f* antialcoolique.
temperate ['tempərət], *a.* **1.** (*a*) (*Of pers.*) Tempérant, sobre. *T. habits*, habitudes de sobriété. (*b*) (*Of language*) Modéré, mesuré. **2.** (*Of climate*) Tempéré. **-ly**, *adv.* Sobrement, avec modération.
temperateness ['tempərətnəs], *s.* **1.** Modération *f*, retenue *f*; sobriété *f.* **2.** Douceur *f* (du climat).
temperature ['temp(ə)rətʃər], *s.* Température *f.* Fall in temperature, refroidissement *m* du temps.

Med : **To have a high temperature,** *F :* **To have, to run, a temperature,** avoir de la température, de la fièvre.

tempest ['tempest], *s.* Tempête *f*, tourmente *f*.

tempestuous [tem'pestjuəs], *a.* **1.** Tempétueux; de tempête. **2.** *F :* (*Of meeting*) Orageux.

Templar ['templər], *s.* **1.** *Hist :* (Knight) Templar, templier *m*; chevalier *m* du Temple. **2. Good Templars,** sociétés de tempérance (quasi secrètes).

template ['templet], *s.* = TEMPLET.

temple[1] [templ], *s.* Temple *m*.

temple[2], *s. Anat :* Tempe *f*.

templet ['templet], *s.* **1.** Gabarit *m*, calibre *m*, patron *m*, jauge *f*. **2.** *Const :* Sablière *f*.

tempo, *pl.* **-i** ['tempo, -iː], *s. Mus :* Tempo *m*.

temporal[1] ['tempərəl], *a. Anat :* (Os, etc.) temporal, -aux.

temporal[2], *a.* Temporel. **The lords spiritual and temporal,** les lords spirituels et les lords temporels. *Ecc :* **Temporal power,** puissance temporelle. *T. affairs,* les affaires séculières.

temporary ['tempərəri], *a.* (*a*) Temporaire, provisoire. *T. officer,* officier temporaire, intérimaire. **Temporary appointment,** emploi amovible. *T. apparatus,* installation de fortune. (*b*) Momentané. *The improvement is but t.,* l'amélioration n'est que passagère. **-ily,** *adv.* (*a*) Temporairement, provisoirement. (*b*) Momentanément; pour le moment.

temporization [tempɔraiˈzeiʃ(ə)n], *s.* **1.** Temporisation *f*. **2.** Transaction *f*; compromis *m*.

temporize ['tempɔraiz], *v.i.* **1.** Temporiser; chercher à gagner du temps. **2.** Transiger provisoirement (*with*, avec).

temporizer ['tempɔraizər], *s.* Temporisateur *m*.

tempt [tem(p)t], *v.tr.* Tenter. **1.** To tempt s.o. to do sth., induire qn à faire qch.; tenter qn pour lui faire faire qch. **To allow oneself to be tempted,** se laisser tenter; céder à la tentation. *I was greatly tempted,* l'occasion était bien tentante. *I am strongly tempted to accept,* j'ai bien envie d'accepter. **2.** (*a*) *A :* Mettre (qn) à l'épreuve. *B : God did t. Abraham,* Dieu tenta Abraham. (*b*) **To tempt God, providence,** tenter Dieu, la providence. **tempting,** *a.* Tentant, alléchant; (*of offer*) séduisant, attrayant; (*of dish*) ragoûtant, appétissant.

temptation [tem(p)ˈteiʃ(ə)n], *s.* Tentation *f*. **To throw temptation in s.o.'s way,** exposer qn à la tentation. **To yield to temptation,** succomber à la tentation; se laisser tenter.

tempter ['tem(p)tər], *s.* Tentateur *m*; séducteur *m*.

temptress ['tem(p)tres], *s.f.* Tentatrice.

ten [ten], *num. a. & s.* **1.** Dix (*m*). *About ten years ago,* il y a une dizaine d'années. *To count in tens,* compter par dizaines. *F :* **Ten to one he'll find it out,** je vous parie qu'il le découvrira. (*For other phrases see* EIGHT.) **2.** *Aut :* *F :* **A ten,** une dix chevaux.

tenable ['tenəbl], *a.* (Position) tenable; (théorie) soutenable.

tenace ['tenes], *s. Cards :* Tenace *f*; (*in dummy*) fourchette *f*, impasse *f*.

tenacious [tiˈneiʃəs], *a.* Tenace. **To be tenacious of one's opinion,** tenir à son opinion. **-ly,** *adv.* Obstinément; avec ténacité.

tenacity [tiˈnasiti], *s.* Ténacité *f*.

tenancy ['tenənsi], *s.* **1.** Location *f*. *Expiration of t.,* expiration de bail. **2.** *During my t.,* pendant que j'étais locataire. **3. To hold a life tenancy of a house,** jouir viagèrement d'une maison.

tenant[1] ['tenənt], *s.* Locataire *mf*. **Under-tenant,**

sous-locataire *mf*. **Tenant for life,** usufruitier *m*. **Tenant's repairs,** réparations locatives. **tenant-'farmer,** *s.* Tenancier *m*; cultivateur *m* à bail.

tenant[2], *v.tr.* Habiter (une maison) comme locataire.

tenantry ['tenəntri], *s. Coll.* **1.** Locataires *mpl.* **2.** Les tenanciers *m* et fermiers *m* (d'un domaine).

tench [tenʃ], *s. Ich :* Tanche *f*.

tend[1] [tend]. **1.** *v.tr.* Soigner (un malade); panser (un blessé); surveiller (des enfants, une machine); garder (les moutons); entretenir (un jardin). **2.** *v.i.* **To tend (up)on s.o.,** servir qn; *esp.* servir qn à table.

tend[2], *v.i.* **1.** (*a*) (*Of course, etc.*) Tendre, se diriger (*towards*, vers). *The road tends downwards,* la route va en descendant. *F :* **Where do these plans tend?** à quoi tendent ces projets? **Doctrine that tends towards socialism,** doctrine qui penche vers le socialisme. **Blue tending to green,** bleu tirant sur le vert. (*b*) *Examples that t. to undermine morality,* exemples qui tendent à ébranler les mœurs. **To tend to the success of an enterprise,** contribuer au succès d'une entreprise. **2. To tend to do sth.,** être sujet à faire qch. *Woollens that t. to shrink,* lainages qui ont tendance à rétrécir.

tendency ['tendənsi], *s.* Tendance *f*, inclination *f*, disposition *f* (*to,* à). **Tendency to drink,** penchant *m* à la boisson. *There is a t. for the weak vowels to disappear,* les voyelles faibles tendent à disparaître. **Rheumatic tendency,** diathèse rhumatismale. *Com :* **Strong upward t.,** forte poussée vers la hausse.

tendential [tenˈdenʃ(ə)l], **tendentious** [tenˈden-ʃəs], *a.* Tendanciel, tendancieux.

tender[1] ['tendər], *s.* **1.** *Esp. U.S :* Garde *m*, gardien *m* (d'un pont à bascule, etc.). **Bar-tender,** garçon *m* de comptoir. **2.** (*a*) *Nau :* Bateau *m* annexe; tender *m*. **Aircraft tender,** ravitailleur *m* d'hydravions. (*b*) *Rail :* Tender.

tender[2], *a.* **1.** Tendre; peu résistant. **Tender meat,** viande tendre. **2.** Tendre, sensible. **Tender to the touch,** sensible, douloureux, au toucher. **Horse with a tender mouth,** cheval qui a la bouche sensible, délicate. **Tender heart,** cœur tendre, sensible. **3.** (*a*) (*Of plant, etc.*) Délicat, fragile. (*b*) Jeune, tendre. **Child of tender years,** enfant en bas âge. **4.** (*Of pers.*) Tendre, affectueux. *T. parents,* parents aimants, indulgents. *To have a t. recollection of s.o.,* conserver un souvenir ému de qn. **5.** Soigneux, soucieux, jaloux (*of,* de). **-ly,** *adv.* **1.** (*Toucher qch.*) doucement. **2.** Tendrement; avec tendresse. **'tender-'hearted,** *a.* Compatissant; au cœur tendre, sensible. **'tender-'heartedness,** *s.* Sensibilité *f*.

tender[3], *s.* **1.** *Com :* Soumission *f*, offre *f*. **To invite tenders for a piece of work,** mettre un travail en adjudication. **To make, put in, send in, a tender for sth.,** faire une soumission pour qch.; soumissionner un travail. **By tender, put in a tender for sth.,** soumission pour qch. **2. Legal tender,** cours légal; monnaie *f* libératoire. (*Of money*) *To be legal t.,* avoir cours; avoir force libératoire.

tender[4]. **1.** *v.tr.* (*a*) *Jur :* **To tender an oath to s.o.,** déférer le serment à qn. (*b*) Offrir (ses services, une somme, etc.). *To t. one's resignation,* offrir de démissionner. **2.** *v.i. Com :* **To tender for sth.,** soumissionner (pour) qch.; faire une soumission pour qch.

tenderer ['tendərər], *s.* **1.** Offreur *m* (*of,* de). **2.** *Ind : etc :* Soumissionnaire *m*. *Successful t.,* adjudicataire *m*.

tenderness ['tendərnəs], *s.* **1.** Sensibilité *f* (de la peau, etc.). **2.** Délicatesse *f*, fragilité *f* (d'une plante, etc.). **3.** Tendresse *f* (des sentiments); affection *f* (*for*, pour).

tendon ['tendən], *s. Anat:* Tendon *m*.

tendril ['tendril], *s. Bot:* Vrille *f*.

tenement ['tenimənt], *s.* **1.** *Jur:* Fonds *m* de terre. **2.** (*a*) Appartement *m* dans une maison de rapport. (*b*) *Scot:* Maison de rapport. '**tenement house,** *s.* Maison *f* de rapport; logements ouvriers.

tenet ['ti:net, 'te-], *s.* (*a*) Doctrine *f*, dogme *m*; principe *m*. (*b*) *F:* Opinion *f*.

tenfold ['tenfould]. **1.** *a.* Décuple. **2.** *adv.* Dix fois autant; au décuple. *To increase t.*, décupler.

tennis ['tenis], *s.* **1.** (Lawn-)tennis, (lawn-)tennis *m*. **2.** (Jeu *m* de) paume *f*. '**tennis-ball,** *s.* Balle *f* de tennis. '**tennis-court,** *s.* **1.** (*a*) Court *m* (de tennis). (*b*) (Terrain *m* de) tennis *m*. **2.** ((i) Salle *f*, (ii) terrain *m*, de) jeu *m* de paume.

tenon[1] ['tenən], *s.* **1.** *Carp:* Tenon *m*; goujon *m*. **2.** *Metalw:* Ailette *f*.

tenon[2], *v.tr. Carp: etc:* Tenonner; assembler à tenon (des pièces de bois). **To tenon and mortise,** assembler à tenon et mortaise.

tenor ['tenər], *s.* **1.** (*a*) *Jur:* Copie *f* conforme. (*b*) Teneur *f* (d'un acte); contenu *m*, sens général (d'une lettre). (*c*) Cours *m*, marche *f* (des affaires, de la vie). **2.** *Mus:* (*a*) Ténor *m*. **Tenor voice,** voix de ténor. **Tenor clef,** clé d'ut quatrième ligne. (*b*) **Tenor (bell),** bourdon *m* (d'une sonnerie).

.**tense**[1] [tens], *s. Gram:* Temps *m*. **In the future tense,** au (temps) futur.

.**tense**[2], *a.* **1.** Tendu, rigide, raide. **2.** *F:* (*Of nerves, relations, etc.*) Tendu. **Tense moment,** moment angoissant. **Tense silence,** silence impressionnant. **Tense voice,** voix étranglée (par l'émotion).

tenseness ['tensnəs], *s.* **1.** Rigidité *f*; (état *m* de) tension *f* (des muscles). **2.** Tension (de relations, etc.).

tensile ['tensail, -sil], *a.* **1.** Extensible, élastique; (*of metal*) ductile. **2.** *Mec:* **Tensile stress, load,** effort *m* de traction. **Tensile stretch,** allongement *m* (à l'essai). **High-tensile steel,** acier de, à, haute tension.

tension ['tenʃ(ə)n], *s.* **1.** (*a*) Tension *f*, raideur *f*, rigidité *f* (d'une corde, des muscles, etc.). (*b*) *F:* Tension, état tendu (des nerfs, etc.). (*c*) Tension, pression *f* (d'un gaz). (*d*) *El:* Tension, voltage *m*. **High-, low-tension circuit,** circuit de haute, basse, tension. **2.** *Mec.E:* Traction *f*. **To be in tension, under stress of tension,** travailler à la traction. **3.** (*Device*) Tendeur *m* (d'une machine à coudre). '**tension-pulley, -roller,** *s. Mec.E: etc:* Galet tendeur, de tension.

tent[1] [tent], *s.* Tente *f*. **To pitch (the) tents,** dresser les tentes. '**tent-peg,** *s.* Piquet *m*, broche *f*, de tente.

tent[2], *s. Surg:* Mèche *f*, tampon *m*.

tentacle ['tentəkl], *s. Nat.Hist:* (*a*) Tentacule *m*. (*b*) Cirre *m*.

tentacular [ten'takjulər], *a.* Tentaculaire.

tentative ['tentətiv]. **1.** *a.* Expérimental, -aux; d'essai. **Tentative offer,** offre pour entamer les négociations. **2.** *s.* Tentative *f*, essai *m*. **-ly,** *adv.* En guise d'essai; expérimentalement.

tenter[1] ['tentər], *s. Tex:* Élargisseur *m*. '**tenter-hook,** *s. Tex:* (Clou *m* à) crochet *m*. *F:* **To be on tenter-hooks,** être au supplice, sur des charbons ardents. **To keep s.o. on tenter-hooks,** faire mourir qn à petit feu.

52

tenter[2], *s. Ind:* Soigneur *m* (de machines); machiniste *m*.

tenth [tenθ]. **1.** *num. a. & s.* Dixième. **2.** *s.* (*Fractional*) Dixième *m.* (*a*) *F:* **Nine tenths of the voters,** la majeure partie des électeurs. (*b*) *Hist:* Dîme *f*. **-ly,** *adv.* Dixièmement; en dixième lieu; décimo.

tenuity [te'njuiti], **tenuousness** ['tenjuəsnəs], *s.* **1.** Ténuité *f*, finesse *f* (d'un fil). **2.** Ténuité (d'un liquide); raréfaction *f* (de l'air, d'un gaz).

tenuous ['tenjuəs], *a.* **1.** Ténu; délié; mince. **2.** (*a*) (Gaz) raréfié. (*b*) *T. distinctions,* distinctions subtiles.

tenure ['tenjər], *s.* **1.** *Hist. & Jur:* Tenure (féodale). **2.** *Jur:* (Période *f* de) jouissance *f*, (période d')occupation *f*. **Fixity of tenure,** (i) bail assuré; (ii) stabilité *f* d'un emploi.

tepid ['tepid], *a.* Tiède. **-ly,** *adv.* Tièdement; sans ardeur.

teratological [terato'lɔdʒik(ə)l], *a.* Tératologique.

teratology [tera'tɔlodʒi], *s.* Tératologie *f*.

tercel ['tə:rs(ə)l], **tercelet** ['tə:rs(ə)let], *s. Orn:* Tiercelet *m*; faucon *m* mâle.

tercentenary [tə:rsen'ti:nəri, -'tenəri], *a. & s.* Tricentenaire (*m*).

tercet ['tə:rset], *s.* **1.** *Pros:* Tercet *m*. **2.** *Mus:* Triolet *m*.

teredo [te'ri:do], *s. Moll:* Taret **(naval);** perce-bois *m inv*.

tergiversate ['tə:rdʒivərseit], *v.i.* Tergiverser.

tergiversation [tə:rdʒivər'seiʃ(ə)n], *s.* Tergiversation *f*. **1.** Changements *mpl* de front. **2.** Recours *m* aux équivoques.

term[1] [tə:rm], *s.* **1.** (*a*) Terme *m*, borne *f*, fin *f*, limite *f*. **To set, put, a term to sth.,** fixer une limite à qch.; assigner une fin, un terme, à qch. (*b*) *Com:* (Terme d')échéance *f* (d'une lettre de change). **2.** (*a*) Terme, période *f*, durée *f*. *Banishment* **for a term of years,** banissement à temps. **During his term of office,** pendant sa période d'activité. **To owe a term's rent,** devoir trois mois de loyer; devoir un terme. **Long-term, short-term, transaction,** opération à long, à court, terme. (*b*) *Sch:* Trimestre *m*. **During term,** pendant la période des cours, des classes. **To keep one's terms,** (i) (*in universities*) *approx.* = prendre ses inscriptions; (ii) (*of law students*) remplir les obligations matérielles et pécuniaires incombant à un étudiant. (*c*) *Jur:* Session *f*. **3.** *pl.* **Terms.** (*a*) Conditions *f*; clauses *f*, termes, teneur *f* (d'un contrat). *Fin: Terms and conditions of an issue,* modalités *f* d'une émission. *On* **these terms I accept,** à ces conditions j'accepte. **I'll take it on your own terms,** je le prends à vos conditions. **Make, name, your own terms,** faites vos conditions vous-même. **By the terms of article 49 . . .,** aux termes de l'article 49. . . . **To dictate terms,** imposer des conditions. **To come to terms, make terms,** en venir à un accommodement; s'accorder (*with*, avec). *S.a.* REFERENCE 1. (*b*) **Terms of payment,** conditions de paiement. '**Terms inclusive,**' "tout compris." **To buy sth. on easy terms,** acheter qch. avec facilités de paiement. *Not on any terms,* à aucun prix. **4.** *pl.* Relations *f*, termes, rapports *m*. **To be, live, on friendly, on good, terms** with s.o., vivre en bonne intelligence, en bons termes, avec qn. **To be on bad terms with** s.o., être mal avec qn. **To be on the best of terms** with s.o., être au mieux, dans les meilleurs termes, avec qn. **5.** (*a*) Terme (d'une équation, d'un syllogisme). *To express one quantity in terms of another,* exprimer une quantité en fonction d'une autre. *F:* To reckon happiness in terms of worldly success, mesurer le bonheur en fonction du succès. (*b*) Terms of a problem, énoncé *m* d'un problème. 6. (*a*) Terme, mot *m*, expression *f*, appellation *f*. Legal terms, termes de droit, de pratique, du Palais. (*b*) *pl.* Langage *m*, termes. *How dare you use such terms to me?* c'est à moi que vous osez tenir un pareil langage? 'term-time, *s.* *Sch:* Période *f* des cours.

term², *v.tr.* Appeler, désigner, nommer. *He termed himself a professor,* il se qualifiait de professeur.

Termagant ['tə:rmagənt]. 1. *Pr.n.m. Mediev. Lit:* Tervagant. 2. *s.f.* Mégère, virago.

terminable ['tə:rminəbl], *a.* Terminable; (*of contract*) résiliable.

terminal ['tə:rmin(ə)l]. I. *a.* 1. Qui borne, qui termine (une région, etc.). 2. (*a*) *Nat.Hist:* Terminal, -aux; distal, -aux. (*b*) *Geol:* Terminal moraine, moraine frontale. (*c*) *Rail:* (Gare) terminus, de tête de ligne. (*d*) *El: Tg:* (Isolateur, poteau) d'arrêt. (*e*) (*Of letter, etc.*) Final, -als; dernier. (*f*) *W.Tel:* Terminal amplifier, ampli terminal, de sortie. 3. Trimestriel. -ally, *adv. Sch:* Par trimestre; tous les trimestres. II. terminal, *s. El:* Borne *f* (de prise de courant); borne d'attache.

terminate ['tə:rmineit]. I. *v.tr.* Terminer. 1. (*Of boundary*) Délimiter (une région). 2.(*a*) Résoudre, résilier (un contrat, etc.); mettre fin à (un engagement). (*b*) Être à la fin de (qch.). II. terminate, *v.i.* 1. (*Of word, etc.*) Se terminer, finir (*in,* en, par). 2. Aboutir (*in, at,* à).

termination [tə:rmi'neiʃ(ə)n], *s.* 1. Terminaison *f*, fin *f* (d'un procès, etc.); cessation *f* (de relations). To put a termination to sth., mettre fin à qch. 2. *Gram:* Terminaison, désinence *f*.

terminator ['tə:rmineitər], *s.* (*a*) Celui qui met ou a mis fin à qch. (*b*) Celui qui a achevé (un ouvrage posthume, etc.).

terminological [tə:rmino'lɔdʒik(ə)l], *a.* Terminologique. Terminological inexactitude, inexactitude de termes.

terminology [tə:rmi'nɔlɔdʒi], *s.* Terminologie *f*.

terminus ['tə:rminəs], *s.* 1. (Gare *f*) terminus *m*; (gare de) tête *f* de ligne. 2. *Sculp:* Terme *m*; dieu *m* Terme.

termite ['tə:rmait], *s. Ent:* Termite *m*; fourmi blanche.

tern [tə:rn], *s. Orn:* Sterne *m*; hirondelle *f* de mer.

ternary ['tə:rnəri], *a.* Ternaire.

terrace¹ ['teres], *s.* 1. *Const:* Terrasse *f*; terre-plein *m, pl.* terre-pleins. 2. (i) Rangée de maisons formant terrasse; (ii) rangée de maisons de style uniforme.

terrace², *v.tr.* Disposer (un jardin, etc.) en terrasse(s). terraced, *a.* (Jardin) suspendu, étagé, en terrasse.

terra-cotta ['terə'kɔta], *s.* Terre cuite.

terra firma ['terə'fə:rma], *s.* Terre *f* ferme; *F:* le plancher des vaches.

terrapin ['terəpin], *s.* Tortue *f* aquatique d'Amérique.

terrestrial [te'restriəl], *a.* Terrestre.

terrible ['teribl], *a.* (*a*) Terrible. (*b*) Terrible, affreux, épouvantable; atroce. *To die in t. agonies,* mourir dans d'atroces souffrances. *He's a t. talker,* c'est un terrible bavard. -bly, *adv.* (*a*) Terriblement, affreusement, atrocement. (*b*) *F:* T. dangerous, excessivement dangereux. T. rich, diablement riche.

terrier ['teriər], *s.* (Chien *m*) terrier *m*. Bull-terrier, bull-terrier *m*.

terrific [te'rifik], *a.* 1. Terrifiant, épouvantable. 2. *F:* Terrible; énorme. *T. pace,* allure vertigineuse. -ally, *adv.* 1. D'une manière terrifiante. 2. *F:* Terriblement.

terrify ['terifai], *v.tr.* Terrifier, effrayer, épouvanter. To terrify s.o. into doing sth., faire faire qch. à qn sous le coup de la peur. To terrify s.o. out of his wits, rendre qn fou de terreur. terrifying, *a.* Terrifiant, terrible, épouvantable.

terrine [te'ri:n], *s.* Terrine *f*.

territorial [teri'tɔ:riəl]. 1. *a.* (*a*) Territorial, -aux. (*b*) Terrien, foncier. 2. *s. Mil:* Territorial *m*.

territory ['teritəri], *s.* 1. Territoire *m*. 2. *Austr:* The Northern Territory, l'Australie septentrionale. 3. *F:* Commercial traveller's territory, région assignée à un commis voyageur.

terror ['terər], *s.* 1. Terreur *f*, effroi *m*, épouvante *f*. To be in terror, être dans la terreur. To be in terror of one's life, craindre pour sa vie. *F:* To go in terror of s.o., avoir une peur bleue de qn. To have a holy terror of sth., craindre qch. comme le feu. *Fr.Hist:* The (Reign of) Terror, la Terreur. 2. (*a*) He was the terror of the countryside, c'était la terreur du pays. (*b*) *F:* He's a little terror, a holy terror, c'est un enfant terrible. *He was a t. for always being late,* il était d'une inexactitude désespérante. 'terror-stricken, -struck, *a.* Saisi de terreur; épouvanté.

terrorism ['terərizm], *s.* Terrorisme *m*.

terrorize ['terəra:iz], *v.tr.* Terroriser.

terry ['teri], *a. Tex:* (Velours, etc.) bouclé, épinglé, frisé.

terse [tə:rs], *a.* (*Of style, language*) Concis, net; élégant et précis. -ly, *adv.* Avec concision.

terseness ['tə:rsnəs], *s.* Concision *f*; netteté *f* (de style).

tertiary ['tə:rʃiəri], *a.* Tertiaire.

tertius ['tə:rʃiəs], *a. Sch:* Smith tertius, Smith (numéro) trois.

Tesla ['teslα]. *Pr.n.m. El:* Tesla coil, bobine *f* de Tesla.

tessellated ['teseleitid], *a.* (Pavage) en mosaïque ou disposé en damier.

tessellation [tese'leiʃ(ə)n], *s.* Arrangement *m* en damier; mosaïque *f*.

test¹ [test], *s.* 1. (*a*) Épreuve *f*. To put s.o. to the test, through a test, mettre qn à l'épreuve, à l'essai. To pass, stand, the test, soutenir, supporter, l'épreuve; subir victorieusement l'épreuve. (*b*) *Ind: Ch:* Essai *m*, épreuve. Boiler test, épreuve des chaudières. Endurance test, épreuve d'endurance. Control test, check test, essai contradictoire; contre-épreuve *f*. The acid test, l'épreuve à la pierre de touche; *F:* l'épreuve concluante. Blood test, examen *m* du sang. *Aut:* Test run, course d'essai. Test engine, test car, moteur, voiture, d'étude. (*c*) *Ch:* Réactif *m* (*of, for,* de). 2. (*a*) Examen. Eye test, examen visuel. *Navy:* To fail to pass the eye *t.*, être refusé, réformé, pour la vue. *Aut:* Driving test, examen pour permis de conduire. (*b*) *Sch:* Weekly test, composition *f*. Oral test, épreuve orale. (*c*) *Psy: Ind:* Test *m*. Intelligence test, test de capacité intellectuelle, d'intelligence pratique. 3. *Eng.Hist:* The Test, le Serment du Test. 4. *Ch:* Têt *m*, test (de coupellation); coupelle *f*. 'Test Act, *s. Eng.Hist:* Test Act *m*; loi *f* du Test. 'test-bar, *s. Mec.E:* Metall: Barrette *f* d'essai; éprouvette *f*. 'test-bench, *s.* Banc *m* d'essai; banc d'épreuve. 'test case, *s. Jur:* Cas *m* dont la solution fait jurisprudence. **'test-match,** s. *Cr :* Rencontre internationale, grand match (entre l'Angleterre et l'Australie, etc.). **'test-paper,** s. **1.** *Ch :* Papier réactif. **2.** *Sch :* Composition (faite dans les mêmes conditions qu'à l'examen envisagé). **'test-piece,** s. *Mus :* Morceau imposé (dans un concours de fanfares, d'orphéons). **'test-tube,** s. *Ch :* Éprouvette f.

test², v.tr. **1.** (a) Éprouver ; mettre (qn, qch.) à l'épreuve, à l'essai. (b) Essayer (un ciment, une machine) ; contrôler, vérifier (des poids et mesures) ; examiner (la vue de qn, etc.) ; expérimenter (un procédé) ; analyser (l'eau, etc.). *To t. a boiler,* éprouver une chaudière. **2.** (a) Coupeller (l'or). (b) *Ch :* Déterminer la nature (d'un corps) au moyen d'un réactif. *To t. with litmus paper,* faire la réaction au papier de tournesol.

test³, s. *Nat.Hist :* Test m (d'un oursin, d'une graine) ; carapace f (du tatou).

testacean [tes'teiʃən], s. *Z :* Testacé m.

testaceous [tes'teiʃəs], a. *Z :* Testacé.

testament ['testəmənt], s. **1.** *A :* Testament m ; dernières volontés. **2.** *B :* **The Old, the New, Testament,** l'Ancien, le Nouveau, Testament.

testamentary [testə'mentəri], a. Testamentaire.

testate ['testet], a. & s. (Personne) qui est morte en laissant un testament valable.

testator [tes'teitər], s.m. Testateur.

testatrix [tes'teitriks], s.f. Testatrice.

tester¹ ['testər], s. *A. Furn :* Baldaquin m, ciel m (de lit). **'tester-bed,** s. Lit m à baldaquin.

tester², s. **1.** *Ind :* (Pers.) Essayeur, -euse ; contrôleur, -euse. **2.** Appareil contrôleur ; machine f à essayer. Battery tester, vérificateur m de voltage et d'ampérage (pour accus).

tester³, s. *Num :* A : (a) Teston m. (b) Pièce f de six pence.

testicle ['testikl], s. Testicule m.

testifier ['testifaiər], s. Témoin m.

testify ['testifai]. **1.** v.tr. Témoigner (son regret, sa foi). **2.** *Jur :* (a) v.tr. Déclarer, affirmer (qch.) (sous serment). *Abs.* **To testify in s.o.'s favour,** rendre témoignage en faveur de qn. **To testify against s.o.,** déposer contre qn. (b) v.ind.tr. **To testify to a fact,** attester un fait ; se porter garant d'un fait ; témoigner d'un fait.

testimonial [testi'mounjəl], s. **1.** Certificat (délivré par une maison, un chef) ; (lettre de) recommandation f. *To show one's testimonials,* exhiber ses certificats. **2.** Témoignage m d'estime ; cadeau (offert à qn par cotisation).

testimony ['testiməni], s. Témoignage m (des sens) ; *Jur :* attestation f ; déposition f (d'un témoin). **To bear testimony to sth.,** rendre témoignage de qch. **In testimony whereof . . .,** en foi de quoi. . . . *Jur :* **To produce testimony of, to, a statement,** apporter des preuves testimoniales à l'appui d'une affirmation.

testiness ['testinəs], s. (a) Irritabilité f, irascibilité f. (b) Susceptibilité f.

testudo [tes'tju:do], s. **1.** Tortue f. **2.** *Rom.Ant :* (a) Tortue (de siège). (b) Tortue (de boucliers).

testy ['testi], a. (a) Irritable, irascible ; peu endurant. (b) Susceptible. **-ily,** adv. D'un air irrité ; avec humeur.

tetanus ['tetənəs], s. *Med :* Tétanos m.

tetchy ['tetʃi], a. = TESTY.

tête-à-tête ['teitɑ:'teit]. **1.** adv. Tête-à-tête. **2.** s. (pl. tête-à-têtes) Tête-à-tête m inv.

tether¹ ['teðər], s. Longe f, attache f (d'un cheval, etc.). **To be at the end of one's tether,** (i) être à bout de forces ; n'en plus pouvoir ; (ii) être à bout de ressources ; *F:* être au bout de son rouleau.

tether², v.tr. Attacher, mettre à l'attache (un cheval, etc.).

tetrachord ['tetrəkɔ:rd], s. *Mus :* Tétracorde m.

tetragon ['tetragən], s. Tétragone m, quadrilatère m.

tetragonal [te'tragənəl], a. Tétragone, quadrilatère. *Cryst :* Quadratique.

tetrahedron [tetrə'hi:drən], s. Tétraèdre m.

tetralogy [te'tralodʒi], s. *Gr.Th :* Tétralogie f.

tetrameter [te'trametər], s. Tétramètre m.

tetrarch ['tetrɑ:rk, 'ti:trɑ:rk], s. Tétrarque m.

tetrarchy ['tetrɑ:rki], s. Tétrarchie f.

tetrasyllabic ['tetrasi'labik], a. *Gram :* Tétrasyllabe, tétrasyllabique.

tetravalent [tetrə'veilənt], a. *Ch :* Tétravalent.

tetrode ['tetroud], s. Lampe f à quatre électrodes ; tétrode f.

Teucrian ['tju:kriən], a. & s. Troyen, -enne.

Teuton ['tju:tən]. **1.** s. Teuton, -onne. **2.** a. = TEUTONIC.

Teutonic [tju:'tɔnik], a. Teuton, teutonique.

text [tekst], s. **1.** Texte m (d'un manuscrit, d'un auteur). *To restore a t.,* restituer un texte. **2. Scripture text,** citation tirée de l'Écriture sainte. *F:* *The t. of his speech,* le sujet de son discours. **To stick to one's text,** ne pas s'écarter de la question ; s'en tenir au sujet. **'text-book,** s. *Sch :* Manuel m. *A t.-b. on, of, algebra,* une algèbre.

textile ['tekstail]. **1.** a. Textile. **2.** s. (a) Tissu m, étoffe f. **The textile industry,** l'industrie textile. (b) Matière f textile ; textile m.

textual ['tekstjuəl], a. (a) Textuel. (b) **Textual error,** erreur de texte.

texture ['tekstjər], s. Texture f (d'une étoffe) ; texture, grain m (de la peau, du bois). *F:* *T. of a speech,* trame f d'un discours.

thalassic [θə'lasik], a. Thalassique.

thallium ['θaliəm], s. *Ch :* Thallium m.

thallus ['θaləs], s. *Bot :* Thalle m.

Thames (the) [ðə'temz]. *Pr.n.* La Tamise. *F:* **He will never set the Thames on fire,** il n'a pas inventé la poudre.

than [ðan]. **1.** conj. (a) (In comparison of inequality) Que ; (with numbers) de. *I have more, less, t. you,* j'en ai plus, moins, que vous. *More t. twenty,* plus de vingt. **More than once,** plus d'une fois. **You had better speak to him than write,** vous feriez mieux de lui parler que de lui écrire. *She would do anything* **rather than** *let him suffer,* elle ferait n'importe quoi plutôt que de le laisser souffrir. **No sooner had we entered than the music began,** nous étions à peine entrés que la musique commença. (b) *Any person other* **than** *himself,* tout autre que lui. **2.** quasi-prep. *A man* **than** *whom no one was more respected,* un homme qui était plus respecté que personne, que quiconque.

thane [θein], s. *Hist :* Thane m, comte m.

thank¹ [θaŋk], s. **Thanks,** remerciement(s) m. **Give him my best thanks,** présentez-lui tous mes remerciements. *F:* **Thanks! =** thank you, q.v. under THANK² **1.** **To give thanks to s.o. for sth.,** rendre grâces à qn de qch. **To return thanks,** dire des grâces (après le repas). **To pass a vote of thanks to s.o.,** voter des remerciements à qn. **Thanks be to God!** rendons grâces à Dieu ! **Thanks to . . .,** grâce à. . . . *F:* **That's all the thanks I get!** voilà comme on me remercie !

'thank-offering, s. *B:* Sacrifice m d'actions de grâces.

thank², v.tr. **1.** (a) Remercier (qn) ; exprimer ses remerciements, dire merci, à (qn) ; rendre grâce(s) à (Dieu). **To thank s.o. for sth.,** remercier qn de qch. *To t. s.o.* **effusively,** se confondre

en remerciements. **Thank God! thank heaven!
thank goodness!** Dieu merci! grâce au ciel!
S.a. STAR¹ I. (*b*) (I) thank you, je vous remercie;
merci. *Will you have some tea?*—No, thank you,
prenez-vous du thé?—Merci! **2. I will thank
you to close the door,** je vous serai obligé de
vouloir bien fermer la porte. **I'll thank you to
mind your own business!** occupez-vous donc
de ce qui vous regarde! **3. To have s.o. to thank
for sth.,** devoir qch. à qn. *F:* **You have only
yourself to thank for it,** c'est à vous seul qu'il
faut vous en prendre.

thankful ['θaŋkful], *a.* Reconnaissant. *Let us be
t. that our lives have been spared,* félicitons-nous
de ce que nous avons la vie sauve. **-fully,** *adv.*
Avec reconnaissance.

thankfulness ['θaŋkfulnəs], *s.* Reconnaissance *f*,
gratitude *f*.

thankless ['θaŋkləs], *a.* Ingrat. **A thankless
task,** une tâche ingrate, une vraie corvée.

thanklessness ['θaŋkləsnəs], *s.* **1.** Ingratitude *f.*
2. Caractère ingrat ou peu profitable (d'une
tâche).

thanksgiving [θaŋks'giviŋ], *s.* Action *f* de
grâce(s).

that¹ [ðat]. I. *Dem. pron., pl.* those [ðo:uz].
1. Cela, *F:* ça; ce. (*a*) **Give me that,** donnez-
moi cela. **What is that?** qu'est-ce (que c'est)
que cela, que ça? **Who is that?** qui est-ce là?
That's Mr. Smith, c'est M. Smith. *Are those your
children?* sont-ce là vos enfants? *T. is my opinion,*
voilà mon avis. *After that,* après cela. *With that
she sobbed into her handkerchief,* là-dessus elle
sanglota dans son mouchoir. **What do you mean
by that?** qu'entendez-vous par là? **They all
think that,** c'est ce qu'ils pensent tous. **Have
things come to that?** les choses en sont-elles
arrivées là? *S.a.* ALL I. 1, FOR¹ I. 9. **That is . . .,**
c'est-à-dire. . . . (*b*) (*Stressed*) *And so 'that is
settled,* alors quant à cela, c'est décidé. *He is
only a fiddler,* **and a poor one at that,** ce n'est
qu'un violoneux, et encore assez piètre. *F:* **Will
you help me?**—That I will! voulez-vous m'aider?
—Volontiers! *They are fine chaps.*—**They are
that!** ce sont des gaillards.—En effet! **That's
right! that's it!** c'est cela! **That's all,** voilà
tout. **That's curious!** voilà qui est curieux!
And that's that! et voilà! **And that was that,**
plus rien à dire. **2.** (*Opposed to 'this', 'these'*)
Celui-là, *f.* celle-là; *pl.* ceux-là, *f.* celles-là. *This
is new and t. is old,* celui-ci est neuf et celui-là est
vieux. *S.a.* THIS I. 2. **3.** Celui, *f.* celle; *pl.* ceux,
f. celles. *All those that I saw,* tous ceux que j'ai
vus. *Those of whom I speak,* ceux dont je parle.
There are those who think that . . ., certains
pensent que. . . . *There was that in her which
commanded respect,* il y avait en elle quelque
chose qui imposait le respect. II. **that,** *dem.a.,
pl.* those. (*a*) Ce, (*before vowel or h 'mute'*) cet;
f. cette; *pl.* ces; (*for emphasis and in opposition to 'this', 'these'*) ce. . . -là. **That book,
those books,** ce livre(-là), ces livres(-là). **That
one,** celui-là, celle-là. *Everybody is agreed on t.
point,* tout le monde est d'accord là-dessus. *I
only saw him that once,* je ne l'ai vu que cette
fois-là. *S.a.* THIS II. (*b*) (*Followed by 'of mine',
'of his', etc.*) *F: Hum:* or *Pej:* **Well, how's
that leg of yours?** eh bien, et cette jambe?
(*c*) *Those people who take an interest in these
things,* les gens, ceux, qui s'intéressent à ces
choses-là. *I am not one of those people who . . .,*
je ne suis pas de ceux qui. . . . III. **that,**
dem.adv. F: 'That high, aussi haut que ça.'
S.a. MUCH 3.

that² [ðət], *rel. pron. sg. & pl.* **1.** (*For subject*)
Qui; (*for object*) que. **The house that stands
at the corner,** la maison qui se trouve au coin.
The letter (that) I sent you, la lettre que je vous
ai envoyée. **This is he that brought the news,**
voici celui qui a apporté la nouvelle. **Wretch that
I am!** malheureux que je suis! **2.** (*Governed
by prep.*) Lequel, *f.* laquelle; *pl.* lesquels, *f.* lesquelles. **The envelope (that) I put it in,** l'enveloppe dans laquelle je l'ai mis. **The man (that)
we are speaking of, about,** l'homme dont nous
parlons. **No one has come that I know of,**
personne n'est venu que je sache. **3.** Où; que.
The night (that) we went to the theatre, le soir
où nous sommes allés au théâtre. *During the
years t. he had languished in prison,* pendant les
années qu'il avait langui en prison.

that³ [ðat, ðət], *conj.* **1.** (*Introducing subordinate
clause*) Que. (*a*) *It was for this t. they fought,*
c'est pour cela qu'on s'est battu. **Not that,** *see*
NOT 4. **But that,** *see* BUT 1. (*b*) *I hope (that) you
will have good luck,* j'espère que vous aurez de
la chance. (*c*) (Afin) que, pour que, + *sub.* **Come
nearer t. I may see you,** approchez, que je vous
voie. *I am telling you,* (so) that you may know,
je vous préviens pour que vous soyez au courant.
2. (*a*) **That he should behave like this!** dire
qu'il se conduit comme cela! (*b*) **O that it were
possible!** oh, si c'était possible!

thatch¹ ['θatʃ], *s.* Chaume *m* (de toiture).

thatch², *v.tr.* Couvrir (un toit) de, en, chaume.

thatched, *a.* (Toit) de chaume. **Thatched
cottage,** chaumière *f.*

thatcher ['θatʃər], *s.* Couvreur *m* en chaume.

thaumaturgy ['θɔ:mətə:rdʒi], *s.* Thaumaturgie *f.*

thaw¹ [θɔ:], *s.* Dége *m*; fonte *f* des neiges.
Silver thaw, verglas *m.* **The thaw is setting in,**
le temps est au dégel.

thaw². **1.** *v.tr.* Dégeler; décongeler (la viande
frigorifiée). *Aut:* **To thaw out the radiator,**
dégeler le radiateur. **2.** *v.i.* (*a*) (*Of snow*) Fondre;
(*of frozen meat*) se décongeler. (*b*) *Impers.* **It is
thawing,** il dégèle. **thawing,** *s.* **1.** Dégèlement *m*
(des conduites d'eau); décongélation *f* (de la
viande). **2.** Dégel *m* (des neiges).

the¹ [ðə; *before vowel* ði], *def. art.* **1.** Le, *f.* la;
(*before vowel or h 'mute'*) l'; *pl.* les. (*a*) (*Particularizing*) **The father and (the) mother,** le père et
la mère. *On the other side,* de l'autre côté. *The
Alps,* les Alpes. *I spoke to the coachman,* j'ai parlé
au cocher. *Give that to the woman,* donnez cela
à la femme. *He has gone to the fields,* il est allé
aux champs. *The roof of the house,* le toit de la
maison. *The arrival of the guests,* l'arrivée des
invités. *The Smiths,* les Smith. **Edward the
Seventh,** Édouard Sept. *P:* **The wife,** ma femme.
Well, how's the throat? et cette gorge?
(*b*) *He is not the person to do that,* ce n'est pas une
personne à faire cela. *The impudence of it!*
quelle audace! *He hasn't the patience to wait,*
il n'a pas assez de patience pour attendre. (*c*) *The
beautiful,* le beau. *Translated from the Russian,*
traduit du russe. *Coll.* **The poor,** les pauvres.
(*d*) *F:* **He has the toothache, the measles,** il a
mal aux dents; il a la rougeole. (*e*) (*Generalizing*)
The dog is. our best friend, le chien est notre
meilleur ami. (*f*) (*Distributive*) **Sixpence the
pound,** six pence la livre. *To be employed by the
day,* travailler à la journée. *Twenty-five miles to
the gallon,* quarante kilomètres pour quatre litres
et demi. **2.** (*Demonstrative in French*) Ce, cet,
f. cette, *pl.* ces. *I was absent at the time,* j'étais
absent à cette époque. *I shall see him during the
summer,* je le verrai cet été. *The ladies are in*

the drawing-room, ces dames sont au salon. **3.** (*Stressed*) [ðiː] *Her father is Professor X*, '*the Professor X*, son père est le professeur X, le grand, le célèbre, professeur X. *He is* '*the surgeon here*, c'est lui le grand chirurgien ici. **Smith's is** '*the shop for furniture*, la maison Smith est la meilleure pour les meubles.

the², *adv*. (*Preceding an adj. or adv. in the comparative degree*) (*a*) *It will be the easier for you as you are young*, cela vous sera d'autant plus facile que vous êtes jeune. (*b*) **The** *sharper the point the better the needle*, les aiguilles sont d'autant meilleures que leur pointe est plus fine. **The sooner the better**, le plus tôt sera le mieux. *The less said about it the better*, moins on en parlera mieux cela vaudra. *S.a.* MORE 4, WORSE 1.

theatre ['θiːətər], *s*. **1.** (*a*) Théâtre *m*; salle *f* de spectacle. (*b*) **Picture theatre**, grand cinéma. **News theatre**, ciné-actualités *m*. (*c*) **The theatre**, l'art *m* dramatique; le théâtre. **2.** (*a*) (*In universities*) Amphithéâtre *m*. (*b*) = OPERATING-THEATRE. **3.** *F:* **The theatre of war**, le théâtre de la guerre. '**theatre-goer**, *s* Amateur, -trice, du théâtre.

theatrical [θiˈatrik(ə)l], *a*. **1.** Théâtral, -aux. *T. performance*, représentation théâtrale. **Theatrical company**, troupe *f* d'acteurs. **2.** (*Of attitude*) Théâtral, histrionique. **-ally**, *adv*. **1.** Théâtralement (parlant). **2.** Avec affectation.

theatricals [θiˈatrik(ə)lz], *s.pl*. **Amateur theatricals**, spectacle *m* d'amateurs.

thee [ðiː], *pers. pron., objective case*. *A. & Poet:* **1.** Te; (*before a vowel sound*) t'. *We beseech t.*, nous te supplions. *I adore t.*, je t'adore. *S.a.* GET I. 9. **2.** (*Stressed*) Toi. *He thinks of t.*, il pense à toi.

theft [θeft], *s*. (*a*) Vol *m*. (*b*) *Jur:* **Aggravated theft**, vol qualifié. **Petty theft**, larcin *m*.

their [ðɛər], *poss.a*. **1.** (*a*) Leur, *pl*. leurs. *T. father and mother*, leur père et leur mère. (*b*) **Their Majesties**, leurs Majestés. **2.** *F:* **Nobody in their senses . . .**, personne jouissant de son bon sens.

theirs [ðɛərz], *poss.pron*. Le leur, la leur, les leurs. *This house is t.*, cette maison est la leur, leur appartient. **He is a friend of theirs**, c'est un de leurs amis.

them [ðem], *pers. pron., pl., objective case*. **1.** (*a*) (*Direct*) Les *mf*; (*indirect*) leur *mf*. *I like them*, je les aime. *I shall tell them so*, je le leur dirai. *Call them*, appelez-les. *Speak to them*, parlez-leur. (*b*) (*Refl.*) *They took the keys away with them*, ils ont emporté les clefs avec eux. **2.** (*Stressed*) Eux, *f*. elles. **Them** *I do not admire*, 'e ne les admire pas, eux. **3. Many of them**, plusieurs d'entre eux. *Both of them saw me*, ils m'ont vu tous (les) deux. *Give me half of them*, donnez-m'en la moitié. *Every one of them was killed*, ils furent tous tués. **Neither of them**, ni l'un ni l'autre. **None of them**, aucun d'eux. *Prepare the tables and put some flowers on them*, préparez les tables et mettez-y des fleurs. **4.** *F:* **It's them**, ce sont eux, c'est eux; les voilà! **5.** *F:* **When anyone comes she says to them . . .**, quand quelqu'un vient elle lui dit

theme [θiːm], *s*. **1.** Sujet *m*, thème *m* (d'un discours). **2.** *Sch:* Dissertation *f*; exercice *m* littéraire. **3.** *Mus:* Thème, motif *m*.

themselves [ðemˈselvz], *pers. pron*. *See* SELF 4.

then [ðen]. **I.** *adv*. **1.** (*a*) Alors; en ce temps-là. **The then existing system**, le système qui existait à cette époque. **Then and there**, séance tenante. (*b*) **Now good, then bad**, tantôt bon, tantôt

mauvais. *S.a.* NOW I. 1. **2.** Puis, ensuite, alors. *They travelled in France and then in Spain*, ils voyagèrent en France et ensuite en Espagne. **What then?** et puis? et (puis) après? **3.** D'ailleurs; aussi (bien); et puis. *I haven't the time, and then it isn't my business*, je n'ai pas le temps, d'ailleurs, aussi bien, ce n'est pas mon affaire. **II. then**, *conj*. En ce cas, donc, alors. **Go, then**, soit, allez. **But then . . .**, mais c'est que. *. . . You knew all the while then?* vous le saviez donc d'avance? *S.a.* NOW I. 2. **III. then**, *quasi-s*. Ce temps-là; cette époque-là. **Before then**, avant cela. **By then** *they had gone*, ils étaient déjà partis. **Till then**, (i) jusqu'alors; (ii) jusque-là. **(Ever) since then**, dès lors; depuis ce temps-là. **Between now and then**, d'ici là. '**then**'**-clause**, *s*. *Gram:* Apodose *f*.

thence [ðens], *adv*. *A. & Lit:* **1.** De là. **2.** Pour cette raison; par conséquent.

thenceforth ['ðensfɔːrθ], **thenceforward** [ðensˈfɔːrwərd], *adv*. Dès lors; désormais.

Theobald ['θiːɔbɔːld]. *Pr.n.m.* Thibau(l)t.

theocracy [θiˈɔkrəsi], *s*. Théocratie *f*.

theocratic [θiɔˈkratik], *a*. Théocratique.

theodicy [θiˈɔdisi], *s*. *Phil:* Théodicée *f*.

theodolite [θiˈɔdəlait], *s*. *Surv:* Théodolite *m*.

theogony [θiˈɔgəni], *s*. Théogonie *f*.

theologian [θiɔˈloudʒiən], *s*. Théologien *m*.

theological [θiɔˈlɔdʒik(ə)l], *a*. Théologique.

theology [θiˈɔlɔdʒi], *s*. Théologie *f*.

theorem ['θiɔrem], *s*. Théorème *m*.

theoretic(al) [θiɔˈretik(əl)], *a*. Théorique. **Theoretical chemistry**, chimie pure. **-ally**, *adv*. Théoriquement.

theoretician [θiɔreˈtiʃ(ə)n], *s*. Théoric en *m*.

theorist ['θiːorist], *s*. **1.** = THEORETICIAN. **2.** = THEORIZER.

theorize ['θiːoraiz], *v.tr. & i*. Théoriser.

theorizer ['θiːoraizər], *s*. Théoriste *mf*.

theory ['θiːori], *s*. Théorie *f*. **In theory**, en théorie. *Plan which is all right in t.*, *F:* projet qui est beau sur le papier.

theosophist [θiˈɔsofist], *s*. Théosophe *mf*.

theosophy [θiˈɔsofi], *s*. Théosophie *f*.

therapeutic(al) [θeraˈpjuːtik(əl)], *a*. *Med:* Thérapeutique.

therapeutics [θeraˈpjuːtiks], *s.pl*. La thérapeutique.

therapeutist [θeraˈpjuːtist], *s*. *Med:* Thérapeutiste *m*, thérapeute *m*.

there [ðɛər]. **I.** *adv*. **1.** (*a*) Là, y. **Put it there**, mettez-le là. *He is still t.*, il y est toujours. **We are there**, nous voilà rendus. *F:* **To be all there**, être avisé, dégourdi. *He's all t.*, c'est un homme capable; c'est un malin. **He is not all there**, il n'a pas toute sa tête. *S.a.* HERE 6, THEN I. 1. (*b*) *I am going t.*, j'y vais. **A hundred miles there and back**, cent milles aller et retour. *S.a.* GET II. 2. (*c*) *F:* (*Emphatic*) -là. *That man t. always comes*, cet homme-là vient toujours. **Hurry up there!** dépêchez-vous là-bas! (*d*) (*Calling attention to s.o., sth.*) **There is, are . . .**, voilà. . . . **There's the bell ringing**, voilà la cloche qui sonne. **2.** (*Unstressed*) (*a*) **There is, are . . .**, il est, il y a. . . . **There was once a king . . .**, il était, il y avait, une fois un roi. . . . **There was singing and dancing**, on a chanté et dansé. *T. is a page missing*, il manque une page. (*b*) **There comes a time when . . .**, il arrive un moment où. . . . **3.** (*Stressed*) Quant à cela; en cela. **There you are mistaken**, quant à cela vous vous trompez. **There we differ**, sur ce sujet nous ne sommes pas d'accord. *F:* **There you have me!** ça, ça me dépasse. **II. there**, *int*. (*Stressed*) **Voilà!**

There now! (i) voilà! (ii) allons bon! There, take this book, tenez! prenez ce livre. There! there! don't worry. là là, ne vous inquiétez pas! But there, *what is the good of talking!* mais à quoi bon en parler! III. **there,** *quasi-s.* He left there *last night,* il est parti (de là) hier soir. In there, là-dedans; là.

thereabout(s) ['ðɛərəbaut(s)], *adv.* **I.** Près de là; dans le voisinage. Somewhere thereabout, quelque part par là. **2.** A peu près; environ. *It is four o'clock or t.,* il est à peu près quatre heures.

thereafter [ðɛər'ɑːftər], *adv.* A. *& Lit:* Après (cela); par la suite.

thereat [ðɛər'at], *adv.* A. *& Lit:* Là-dessus; à ce sujet.

thereby ['ðɛərbai], *adv.* Par ce moyen; de ce fait; de cette façon.

therefore ['ðɛərfɔːr], *adv.* Donc; par conséquent. I think, therefore I am, je pense, donc je suis.

therefrom [ðɛər'frɔm], *adv.* A. *& Lit:* De là.

therein [ðɛər'in], *adv.* A. *& Lit:* **I.** En cela; à cet égard. *T. you are mistaken,* en cela vous faites erreur. **2.** (Là-)dedans.

thereof [ðɛər'ɔv, ðɛər'ɔf], *adv.* A. *& Lit:* De cela; en. *He ate t.,* il en mangea.

thereon [ðɛər'ɔn], *adv.* A. *& Lit:* (Là-)dessus.

thereto [ðɛər'tuː], *adv.* A. *& Lit:* He put his *signature t.,* il y apposa sa signature.

thereupon [ðɛərə'pɔn, 'ðɛərəpɔn], *adv.* **I.** Sur ce. **2.** *Lit:* There is much to be said t., il y aurait beaucoup à dire là-dessus, à ce sujet.

therewith [ðɛər'wið, -'wiθ], *adv.* A. *& Lit:* **I.** Avec cela. **2.** = THEREUPON I. **3.** En outre.

therm [θəːrm], *s.* (a) A: (= British thermal unit, B.T.U.) = 252 grandes calories. (b) (*In gas industry*) = 100 000 B.T.U.

thermal ['θəːrm(ə)l], *a.* **I.** Thermal, -aux. Thermal baths, thermes *m.* **2.** *Ph:* Thermal, thermique.

thermic ['θəːrmik], *a.* *Ph:* = THERMAL 2.

thermionic [θəːrmi'ɔnik], *a.* *W.Tel:* Thermionic tube, lampe *f* thermoïonique.

thermite ['θəːrmait], *s.* Thermite *f.*

thermo-cautery [θəːrmo'kɔːtəri], *s.* Thermo-cautère *m.*

thermochemistry [θəːrmo'kemistri], *s.* Thermo-chimie *f.*

thermo-couple, *s.* Élément *m* thermo-électrique; thermo-couple *m.*

thermodynamics [θəːrmodai'namiks], *s.pl.* Thermo-dynamique *f.*

thermo-electric(al), *a.* Thermo-électrique.

thermo-electricity, *s.* Thermo-électricité *f.*

thermogene ['θəːrmodʒiːn], *s.* Ouate *f* thermogène.

thermogenic [θəːrmo'dʒenik], *a.* *Physiol:* Thermogène.

thermometer [θər'mɔmetər], *s.* Thermomètre *m.* Alcohol t., thermomètre à alcool. The t. stood at 100° (*Fahrenheit*), le thermomètre indiquait 38° (centigrades).

thermometric(al) [θəːrmo'metrik(əl)], *a.* Thermométrique.

thermopile ['θəːrmopail], *s.* Pile *f* hermo-électrique; thermopile *f.*

thermos ['θəːrmɔs], *s. & a.* Thermos flask, *F:* thermos, bouteille isolante; thermos *m.*

thermostat ['θəːrmostat], *s.* Thermostat *m.*

thesaurus [θi'sɔːrəs], *s.* Thesaurus *m*; trésor *m* (de la langue grecque, etc.).

these [ðiːz]. *See* THIS.

thesis, *pl.* **theses** ['θiːsis, 'θiːsiːz], *s.* (a) Thèse *f* (b) *Sch:* Dissertation *f* (d'élève).

thews [θjuːz], *s.pl.* Muscles *m*; *F:* nerfs *m.* He has thews of steel, il a des nerfs d'acier.

they [ðei]. **I.** *Pers. pron. nom. pl.* (a) Ils *f.* elle. *T. are dancing,* ils, elles, dansent. Here t. come les voici (qui viennent). *T. are rich people,* ce sont des gens riches. (b) (*Stressed*) Eux, *f.* elles It is they, ce sont eux; *F:* c'est eux. If I were they, (si j'étais) à leur place. *They know nothing about it,* quant à eux, ils n'en savent rien. (c) They who believe, ceux, celles, qui croient. **2.** (a) *Indef pron.* On. They say that . . ., on dit que. . . (b) *F:* Nobody ever admits they are to blame, on ne veut jamais reconnaître ses torts.

they'd [ðeid] = they had, they would.

they'll [ðeil] = they will.

they're [ðeiər] = they are.

thick [θik]. I. *a.* **I.** Épais, *f.* épaisse; (*of book thread*) gros, *f.* grosse. Wall that is two feet thick, mur, qui a deux pieds d'épaisseur. *F:* To have a thick skin, être peu sensible, peu susceptible. *Typ: etc:* Thick stroke, plein *m S.a.* SPACE[1] 3. **2.** (*Of forest, etc.*) Épais, serré touffu. *T. eyebrows,* sourcils touffus *T. beard* barbe fournie. *Bodies lay t. on the ground,* le so était encombré de cadavres. **3.** (a) (*Of liquid*) Épais, consistant; (*of wine*) trouble; (*of mist* dense, épais; (*of weather*) couvert; (*of darkness* profond. *T. mud,* boue grasse. *Cu:* Thick sauce sauce courte. Thick soup, potage *m* crème (b) (*of voice*) Empâté. To be thick of speech, avoir le parler gras. (c) *F:* (*of pers.*) Obtus **4.** *F:* To be very thick with s.o., être très lié être à tu et à toi, avec qn. They are as thick as thieves, ils s'accordent comme larrons en foire. **5.** *P:* That's a bit thick! ça c'est raide! -ly, *adv.* **I.** En couche épaisse. **2.** Snow fell t., la neige tombait dru. **3.** (Parler) d'une voix empâtée. II. **thick,** *s.* **I.** (a) (La) partie charnue, le gras (de la jambe etc.). (b) In the thick of the fight, au (plus) for de la mêlée. **2.** To stick to s.o. through thick and thin, rester fidèle à qn à travers toutes les épreuves. III. **thick,** *adv.* **I.** En couche épaisse. Don't spread the butter too t., ne mettez pas trop de beurre sur les tartines. To cut the bread thick, couper le pain en tranches épaisses. *S.a.* LAY ON 2. **2.** His blows fell thick and fast, il frappait à coups redoublés; les coups pleuvaient dru. **'thick-'headed,** *a.* *F:* Bête, stupide; à l'esprit obtus. **'thick-'lipped,** *a.* Lippu; à grosses lèvres. **'thick-'set,** *a.* **I.** (*Of hedge*) Épais, *f.* épaisse; dru. **2.** (*Of pers.*) (Short and) thick-set, trapu. **'thick-'skinned,** *a.* **I.** A la peau épaisse; *Z:* pachyderme. **2.** *F:* (*Of pers.*) Peu sensible; peu susceptible. *He is t.-s.,* il ne sent pas les affronts.

thicken ['θik(ə)n]. **I.** *v.tr.* Épaissir; lier (une sauce). **2.** *v.i.* (a) (S')épaissir. (b) (*Of sauce*) Se lier. *The crowd thickens,* la foule augmente. (c) (*Of plot*) Se compliquer, se corser.

thicket ['θiket], *s.* Hallier *m*, fourré *m.*

thickness ['θiknəs], *s.* **I.** (a) Épaisseur *f* (d'un mur); grosseur *f* (des lèvres). (b) Épaisseur (d'une forêt); abondance *f* (de la chevelure). (c) Consistance *f* (d'un liquide); épaisseur (du brouillard). **2.** Couche *f* (de papier).

thief, *pl.* **thieves** [θiːf, θiːvz], *s.* **I.** Voleur, -euse. Hotel t., *F:* rat m d'hôtel. Thieves (as a class) *F:* la pègre. Stop thief! au voleur! *Prov:* Set a thief to catch a thief, à voleur, voleur et demi. Honour among thieves, foi *f* de bohème.

S.a. KITCHEN I, THICK I. 4. **2.** F: (In candle) Champignon m, larron m.
thieve [θiːv], v.tr. Voler (qch.). Abs. Être voleur; voler. **thieving**[1], a. Voleur, -euse. **thieving**[2], s. Vol m, volerie f. **Petty thieving**, larcin(s) m(pl).
thievish ['θiːviʃ], a. Voleur, -euse. **-ly,** adv. En voleur.
thievishness ['θiːviʃnəs], s. Penchant m au vol.
thigh [θai], s. Cuisse f. S.a. HIP[1] I. **'thigh-bone,** s. Fémur m. **'thigh-boots,** s.pl. Bottes cuissardes.
thill [θil], s. Veh: Limon m, brancard m. **'thill-horse,** s. Limonier m; cheval m de brancard.
thimble [θimbl], s. **1.** Dé m (à coudre). **Tailor's thimble,** dé ouvert. **2.** Mch: Bague f; virole f. **3.** Nau: Cosse f (de câble). **'thimble-case,** s. Étui m à dé.
thimbleful ['θimblful], s. F: Doigt m, plein un dé à coudre (de cognac, etc.).
thimblerigger ['θimblrigər], s. **1.** Escamoteur m. **2.** F: Escroc m.
thimblerigging ['θimblrigiŋ], s. F: Escroquerie f.
thin[1] [θin], a. (thinner) **1.** (a) Peu épais; (of paper) mince; (of thread) ténu; (of stuff) léger. To cut the bread thin, couper le pain en tranches minces. Typ: **Thin stroke,** délié m. Phot: **Thin negative,** cliché faible. (b) (Of pers.) Maigre, mince. **To grow thinner,** maigrir; s'amaigrir. F: **As thin as a lath,** maigre comme un clou. S.a. ICE[1] I. **2.** (Of hair, population) Clairsemé, rare. **3.** (a) (Of liquid) Fluide, clair; (of blood) appauvri. (b) **Thin voice,** voix fluette, grêle. **4.** F: (a) Peu convaincant. **Thin excuse,** pauvre excuse. That's a bit thin! c'est peu convaincant! (b) **To have a thin time of it,** passer un temps peu agréable. **5.** s. See THICK II. **2.** **-ly,** adv. **1.** A peine. **Thinly clad,** vêtu insuffisamment. **Thinly veiled allusion,** allusion à peine voilée. **2.** D'une manière éparse. **To sow thinly,** semer clair. **Country t. populated,** pays peu peuplé. **'thin-'lipped,** a. Aux lèvres minces. **'thin-'skinned,** a. **1.** A la peau mince. **2.** A l'épiderme sensible; susceptible; qui se froisse facilement.
thin[2], v. (thinned) **1.** v.tr. (a) Amincir. **To thin (down) a board,** amincir, alléger, une planche. (b) **To thin (down) the paint, a sauce,** délayer la peinture; allonger une sauce. (c) Éclaircir (les arbres). **To thin (out) seedlings,** éclaircir, repiquer, les jeunes plants. **2.** v.i. (a) Maigrir. (b) S'amincir, s'effiler. (c) (Of crowd) S'éclaircir.
thinning, s. **1.** Thinning (down), amincissement m. **2.** Thinning (out), éclaircissage m, repiquage m (de jeunes plants).
thine [ðain]. A. & Poet: **1.** Poss.pron. (a) Le tien, la tienne, les tiens, les tiennes. (b) (Thy kindred) **For thee and thine,** pour toi et les tiens. (c) (Thy property) **What is mine is thine,** ce qui est à moi est à toi. **2.** Poss.a. **When I look into thine eyes,** quand je regarde dans tes yeux.
thing [θiŋ], s. **1.** Chose f. (a) Objet m, article m. **T. of beauty,** objet de beauté. **To go the way of all things,** aller où va toute chose; mourir. (b) F: **What's that thing?** qu'est-ce que c'est que ce machin-là? (c) Usu. pl. **Tea things,** service m à thé. **To clear away the things,** desservir. To wash up the tea things, the dinner things, laver la vaisselle. (d) pl. **Vêtements m,** effets m. **To take off one's things,** se déshabiller. (e) pl. Affaires f, effets. **To pack up one's things,**

faire ses malles. To put one's things away, serrer ses affaires. **2.** F: Être m, créature f. **Poor little things!** pauvres petits êtres! P: **I say, old thing!** dis donc, mon vieux, ma vieille! **3.** (a) You take the t. too seriously, vous prenez la chose trop sérieusement. **To expect great things** of the new treatment, attendre grand bien du nouveau traitement. **To be all things to all men,** être tout à tous. **To talk of one thing and another,** parler de choses et d'autres. That's the very thing, c'est juste ce qu'il faut. That's the t. for me, voilà mon affaire. **The thing is to find a substitute,** le difficile, c'est de trouver un remplaçant. F: **The play's the thing,** la pièce avant tout. **The thing is this,** voici ce dont il s'agit. **Neither one thing nor another,** ni l'un ni l'autre; mi-figue, mi-raisin. **What with one thing and another . . .,** tant et si bien que. . . . **For one thing,** it is too good to be true, en premier lieu c'est trop beau pour être vrai. **He makes a good thing out of it,** ça lui rapporte pas mal. S.a. GOOD I. 1 (d). **I don't know a thing about algebra,** je ne sais pas un mot d'algèbre. F: **To know a thing or two,** en savoir plus d'un(e). To put s.o. up to a t. or two, mettre qn à la page. S.a. FIRST I. 1, LAST[2] I. 1, RIGHT[1] I. 2. (b) pl. **Things are going badly,** les affaires vont mal. Since that is how things are . . ., puisqu'il en est ainsi. . . . F: **How are things?** comment ça va? **4.** The latest thing in ties, cravate(s) dernier cri. **5.** F: **The thing (to do),** l'usage m. **It's not the thing,** cela ne se fait pas. **It's quite the thing,** c'est tout à fait correct. **He is not feeling quite the thing this morning,** il ne se sent pas dans son assiette ce matin.
thingamy ['θiŋəmi], **thingumbob** ['θiŋəmbɔb], **thingummy** ['θiŋəmi], s. P: Chose m, machin m.
think[1] [θiŋk], s. **To have a quiet think,** réfléchir.
think[2], v. (thought [θɔːt]; thought) I. v.tr. & i. **1.** Penser, réfléchir. **He thinks for himself,** il pense par lui-même. To t. hard, réfléchir profondément. He does not say much, but he thinks a lot, il ne dit pas grand'chose mais il n'en pense pas moins. I know what you are thinking, je connais vos pensées. **To act without thinking,** agir sans réflexion. **Think before you speak,** pesez vos paroles. Give me time to t. (and remember), laissez-moi me reprendre. His name was—let me think—there, I've forgotten! il s'appelait—voyons—tiens, j'ai oublié! **To think again,** se raviser. F: **Think again!** réfléchissez! S.a. TWICE. **2.** Songer, s'imaginer. **I can't think what you mean,** je ne peux pas m'imaginer ce que vous voulez dire. **One would have thought that . . .,** c'était à croire que. . . . Anyone would t. that he was asleep, on dirait qu'il dort. **Who'd have thought it!** qui l'aurait dit? **Only think!** songez donc! To t. that he is only twenty! et dire qu'il n'a que vingt ans! **3.** (a) I have been thinking that . . ., l'idée m'est venue que. . . . **Thinking to . . .,** dans l'intention de. . . . (b) **Did you think to bring any money?** avez-vous pensé à apporter de l'argent? **4.** (a) **Then you t. that . . .,** il vous semble donc que. . . . **It is better, don't you think, to get it over?** il vaut mieux, n'est-ce pas, en finir? **What do you t. I ought to do?** que pensez-vous que je doive faire? I thought all was over, je me disais que tout était fini. He thinks he may do anything, il se croit tout permis. **I think she is pretty,** je la trouve jolie. Everyone thought he was mad, on le jugeait fou. **I think so,** je pense que oui. **I should hardly think so,** c'est peu probable. **I should (just)**

think so! je crois bien! *P:* I don't think!
jamais de la vie! (*b*) *Pred.* Juger, trouver, penser.
I think her pretty, je la trouve jolie. *I hardly t.
it likely that . . .*, il n'est guère probable que +
sub. You thought her (to be) a fool, vous l'avez
prise pour une sotte. *They were thought to be
rich,* ils passaient pour (être) riches. *S.a.* BEST¹ 2.
5. I little thought to see him again, je ne m'attendais guère à le revoir. I thought as much,
I thought so, je m'y attendais; je m'en doutais
(bien). II. **think of, about,** *v.ind.tr.* **1.** Penser
à (qn, qch.); songer à (qch.). *We are thinking
of you,* nous pensons à vous. One can't think of
everything, on ne s'avise jamais de tout; on ne
saurait penser à tout. *I have so much to t. about,
of,* j'ai tant de choses auxquelles il me faut
songer. *I can't t. of the right word,* le mot propre
m'échappe. The best thing I can think of, ce
que je vois de mieux. That is worth thinking
about, cela mérite réflexion. What am I thinking
about? où ai-je la tête? **2.** S'imaginer, se figurer,
songer. *T. of me having to beg!* dire que je
suis obligé de mendier! *F:* Think of that!
ça, c'est pas banal! **3.** Considérer. *To t. of
s.o.'s feelings,* avoir égard aux sentiments de qn.
To think of the expense, regarder à la dépense.
4. To think of, about, doing sth., méditer
de faire qch.; penser à faire qch. I couldn't
think of it! il n'y a pas à y songer! **5.** (*a*) *v.tr.*
Penser (qch.) de (qch., qn). What do you think
of it, about it? qu'en pensez-vous? To think
too much of oneself, s'en faire accroire. *To t.
too much of sth.,* attacher trop d'importance à
qch. I told him what I thought of him, je lui ai
dit son fait. (*b*) To think well of s.o., estimer qn.
To think ill of s.o., tenir qn en médiocre estime.
He is thought well of, il est bien vu. *S.a.* BETTER¹ 3,
MUCH 3 (*c*). **think out,** *v.tr.* **1.** Imaginer,
méditer (qch.). To think out a plan, élaborer
un plan. *Carefully thought-out answer,* réponse
bien pesée. *That wants thinking out,* cela demande mûre réflexion. **2.** *He thinks things out for
himself,* il juge des choses par lui-même. **think
over,** *v.tr.* Réfléchir sur, aviser à (une question).
T. it over, réfléchissez-y bien. *This wants thinking
over,* cela mérite réflexion. **thinking**¹, *a.* Pensant; qui pense. **thinking**², *s.* Pensée(s) *f(pl)*,
réflexion(s) *f(pl)*. *F:* To put on one's thinking-
cap, méditer une question. To my thinking,
à mon avis. That is my way of thinking, voilà
ma façon de penser.

thinkable ['θiŋkəbl], *a.* Concevable, imaginable.
Is it thinkable that . . .? est-il admissible que
+ *sub.*

thinker ['θiŋkər], *s.* Penseur, -euse.

thinness ['θinnəs], *s.* **1.** (*a*) Peu *m* d'épaisseur;
minceur *f*; légèreté *f* (d'un voile). (*b*) Maigreur *f*.
2. Rareté *f* (des cheveux). **3.** Fluidité *f* (d'un
liquide); manque *m* de corps (d'un vin).
4. *F:* Faiblesse *f* (d'une excuse).

thinnish ['θiniʃ], *a. F:* **1.** (*a*) Plutôt mince.
(*b*) Assez maigre. **2.** (Cheveux) assez rares.
3. (Voix) fluette.

thiosulphate [θaio'sʌlfet], *s. Ch:* Thiosulfate *m*,
hyposulfite *m*.

third [θəːrd], **1.** *Num.a.* Troisième. Third
person, (i) *Jur:* tierce personne, tiers *m*;
(ii) *Gram:* troisième personne. Edward the
Third, Édouard Trois. (On) the third of March,
le trois mars. *Rail:* To travel third, voyager en
troisième (classe). *S.a.* DEGREE 2. **2.** *s.* (*a*) *Mus:*
Tierce *f*. (*b*) *Com:* Third of exchange, troisième *f*
de change. (*c*) *Aut: F:* Troisième vitesse *f*.
3. *s.* (*Fractional*) Tiers *m.* **-ly,** *adv.* Troisième-

ment; en troisième lieu. **'third-class,** *a.*
(*a*) (Wagon) de troisième (classe). (*b*) De qualité
inférieure; (hôtel) d'ordre inférieur. **'third-
'hand,** *adv.phr.* Information at third hand,
renseignements de troisième main. **'third-
'rate,** *a.* De troisième qualité; très inférieur.

thirst¹ [θəːrst], *s.* Soif *f. Great t.,* altération *f.
S.a.* QUENCH 3. The thirst for knowledge, la soif
de la science.

thirst², *v.i.* *A:* Avoir soif; être altéré. *Lit:* To
thirst after sth., avoir soif de qch. *To t. for
blood,* être altéré de sang. **thirsting,** *a.* Altéré.
assoiffé (*for,* de).

thirsty ['θəːrsti], *a.* **1.** Altéré. To be thirsty,
avoir soif. To make s.o. thirsty, donner soif à
qn; altérer qn. *F:* So much talking is thirsty
work, de tant parler, cela donne soif. Thirsty
for blood, for riches, assoiffé, avide, de sang, de
richesses. **2.** (*Of earth*) Desséché; sec, *f.* sèche.
-ily, *adv.* Avidement.

thirteen [θəːr'tiːn], *num. a.* & *s.* Treize (*m*).

thirteenth [θəːr'tiːnθ]. **1.** *Num. a.* & *s.* Treizième. (On) the thirteenth of May, le treize mai.
2. *s.* (*Fractional*) Treizième *m.*

thirtieth ['θəːrtiəθ], *num. a.* & *s.* Trentième (*m*).
(On) the thirtieth of June, le trente juin.

thirty ['θəːrti], *num. a.* & *s.* Trente (*m*). Thirty-
one, trente et un. Thirty-first, trente et unième.
The thirty-first of March, le trente et un mars.
Thirty-two, trente-deux. *About t. persons,* une
trentaine de personnes.

this [ðis]. I. *Dem.pron., pl.* these [ðiːz]. **1.** Ceci;
ce. This I knew, ceci je le savais. Who is this?
quelle est cette personne? You will be sorry for
this, vous le regretterez. *It ought to have been
done before t.,* cela devrait être déjà fait. This is
a free country, ce pays est libre. This is curious,
voici qui est curieux. This is Mr Smith, je vous
présente M. Smith. *T. is where he lives,* c'est
ici qu'il demeure. It was like this, voici comment
les choses se sont passées. The thing is this,
voici ce dont il s'agit. **2.** (*Opposed to 'that'*) Will
you have this or that? voulez-vous ceci ou cela?
F: To put this and that together, rapprocher
les faits. Speaking of this and that, parlant de
choses et d'autres. **3.** Celui-ci, *f.* celle-ci,
pl. ceux-ci, *f.* celles-ci. *I prefer these to those,* je
préfère ceux-ci à ceux-là. II. this, *dem.a.,
pl.* these. (*a*) Ce, (*before vowel or h 'mute'*) cet,
f. cette, *pl.* ces; (*for emphasis*) ce (*etc.*) . . .-ci.
T. book, these books, ce livre(-ci), ces livres(-ci).
In these days, de nos jours. This day last year,
l'an dernier à pareil jour. *To run this way and
that,* courir de-ci, de-là. *S.a.* ONE III. (*b*) I've
been watching you these ten minutes, voilà dix
minutes que je vous observe. III. **this,** *dem.adv.*
This high, aussi haut que ceci, que ça. This far,
jusqu'ici. *S.a.* MUCH 3.

thistle [θisl], *s. Bot:* Chardon *m.* Scotch thistle,
acanthe *f* sauvage. **'thistle-down,** *s.* Duvet *m*
de chardon.

thither ['ðiðər]. A. & *Lit:* **1.** *adv.* (*Expressing
motion*) Là; y. To run hither and thither, courir
çà et là. **2.** *a.* Plus lointain. On the t. side of the
mountains, de l'autre côté des montagnes.

tho' [ðou], *adv.* & *conj.* = THOUGH.

thole(-pin) ['θoul(pin)], *s.* **1.** *Nau:* (*a*) Tolet *m.*
(*b*) *pl.* = ROWLOCKS. **2.** *Veh:* Cheville *f* (de brancard).

thong [θɔŋ], *s.* (*a*) Lanière *f* de cuir; courroie *f.*
(*b*) Lanière, longe *f* (de fouet).

thoracic [θɔ'rasik], *a.* Thoracique.

thorax ['θɔːraks], *s, Anat: Ent:* Thorax *m*

thorite ['θɔːrait], *s. Miner:* Thorite *f.*

thorium ['θɔ:riəm], s. *Ch:* Thorium *m.*
thorn [θɔ:rn], s. (a) Épine *f.* *F:* **To be on thorns,** être sur des épines, être au supplice. **A thorn in the flesh,** une épine au pied. (b) Arbrisseau épineux ; épine. *S.a.* BLACKTHORN, HAWTHORN. **'thorn-apple,** s. Pomme épineuse ; stramoine *f.* **'thorn-bush,** s. = THORN (b). **'thorn-hedge,** s. Haie *f* d'épines ; *esp.* haie d'aubépine.
thornback ['θɔ:rnbak], s. *Ich:* Raie bouclée.
thorny ['θɔ:rni], a. Épineux.
thorough ['θʌrə], a. (a) (*Of search*) Minutieux ; (*of knowledge*) profond ; (*of work*) consciencieux. *T. enquiry,* enquête approfondie. *To give a room a t. cleaning,* nettoyer une chambre à fond. (b) A thorough Frenchman, un vrai Français. *A t. republican,* un républicain convaincu. *A t. scoundrel,* un coquin achevé. **-ly,** adv. (Épuiser) tout à fait ; (comprendre) parfaitement ; (renouveler) complètement ; (nettoyer) à fond. *To know sth. t.,* savoir qch. à fond. **'thorough-paced,** a. (*Of rascal*) Accompli, fieffé. *He is a t.-p. scoundrel,* c'est un scélérat consommé.
thoroughbred ['θʌrəbred]. **I.** a. (Cheval) pur sang *inv* ; (chien) de (pure) race. **2.** s. (a) Cheval pur sang. (b) Animal de race. (*Of pers.*) *She is a real t.,* elle est très racée.
thoroughfare ['θʌrəfɛər], s. Voie *f* de communication. **Public thoroughfare,** voie publique. *One of the main thoroughfares of the town,* une des rues principales de la ville. *Busy t.,* rue très passante. '**No thoroughfare,'** "interdiction de passage."
thoroughgoing ['θʌrəgouiŋ], a. **I.** = THOROUGHPACED. **2.** (Travailleur, etc.) consciencieux.
thoroughness ['θʌrənəs], s. Caractère approfondi (des recherches) ; perfection *f* (du travail).
those [ðo:uz]. *See* THAT¹ I., II.
thou [ðau], *pers. pron. A. & Poet:* (a) Tu. *T. seest,* tu vois. (b) (*Stressed*) Toi. **Thou and I,** toi et moi.
though [ðou]. I. conj. **I.** Quoique, bien que, encore que, + *sub.* *T. he is poor he is generous,* quoiqu'il soit pauvre, quoique pauvre, il est généreux. *I am sorry for him, t. he is nothing to me,* je le plains, encore qu'il ne me soit rien. *T. I am a father . . .,* tout père que je suis. . . . *T. small he is none the less brave,* pour être petit il n'en est pas moins brave. **2.** *Esp. A. & Lit:* (*With sub.*) (a) **Strange though it may appear . . .,** si étrange que cela paraisse. . . . *Vice is infamous t. it be in a prince,* le vice est infâme fût-ce chez un prince. *I will do it* (even) **though** *it cost me my fortune,* je le ferai quand (bien même) cela me coûterait toute ma fortune. *Even t. I could . . .,* alors même que je le pourrais. . . . (b) **What though** *the way be long* ! qu'importe que le chemin soit long ! **3. As though,** comme si. **It looks as though he had gone,** il semble qu'il soit parti. *As t. nothing had happened . . .,* comme si de rien n'était. . . . II. **though,** adv. (a) Cependant, pourtant. (b) (*Exclamatory*) **Did he though!** vraiment ! il a dit, fait, cela ?
thought¹ [θɔ:t], s. (La) pensée. **I.** *T. is free,* la pensée est libre. **Capable of thought,** capable de penser. **2.** (a) Idée *f.* **Happy thought,** heureuse idée. (b) *Gloomy thoughts,* pensées sombres ; *F:* papillons noirs. *F:* **A penny for your thoughts,** à quoi pensez-vous ? **To read s.o.'s thoughts,** lire dans la pensée de qn. (c) **The mere thought of it,** rien que d'y penser. **I did not give it another thought,** je n'y ai pas repensé. (d) *pl.* Esprit *m,* pensée. **To collect one's thoughts,** rassembler ses idées, ses esprits. **Her thoughts** were elsewhere, son esprit etait ailleurs. **3.** (a) Réflexion *f,* considération *f.* **To take thought how to do sth.,** réfléchir comment faire qch. **Want of thought,** irréflexion *f.* **After much thought,** après mûre réflexion. **He has no thought for his mother,** il n'a pas de considération pour sa mère. **On second thoughts,** (toute) réflexion faite. (b) Pensées, rêverie *f,* méditation *f,* recueillement *m.* **4.** (a) Intention *f,* dessein *m.* **To have thoughts of doing sth.,** avoir la pensée de faire qch. ; songer à faire qch. **I had no thought of offending you,** je n'avais pas l'intention de vous offenser. **His one thought** *is to get money,* il ne pense qu'à l'argent. **With the thought of . . .,** dans le dessein de. . . . (b) (*Usu. neg.*) **I had no thought of meeting you here,** je ne m'attendais pas à vous rencontrer ici. **5.** *Adv.phr.* *F:* **A thought,** un tout petit peu. *The ribbon is a t. too blue,* le ruban est d'un rien trop bleu. **'thought-reader,** s. Liseur, -euse, d'âmes. **'thought-reading,** s. Lecture *f* de la pensée ; télépathie *f.* **'thought-transference,** s. Télépathie *f.*
thought², v. *See* THINK².
thoughtful ['θɔ:tful], a. **I.** (a) Pensif, méditatif ; rêveur, -euse. (b) Réfléchi, prudent. **2.** Prévenant (*of,* pour). **To be thoughtful of others,** être plein d'égards pour les autres. *He was so t. as to notify me,* il a eu la prévenance de m'avertir. **3.** (*Of book*) Profond. **-fully,** adv. **I.** Pensivement. **2.** D'une manière réfléchie. **3.** Avec prévenance.
thoughtfulness ['θɔ:tfulnəs], s. **I.** Méditation *f,* recueillement *m.* **2.** Réflexion *f,* prudence *f.* **3.** Prévenance *f,* égards *mpl* (*of,* pour, envers).
thoughtless ['θɔ:tləs], a. **I.** Irréfléchi, mal avisé ; étourdi. **Thoughtless action,** étourderie *f.* **2. Thoughtless of others,** peu soucieux des autres. **-ly,** adv. Étourdiment ; (agir) à la légère.
thoughtlessness ['θɔ:tləsnəs], s. **I.** Irréflexion *f* ; étourderie *f.* **2.** Manque *m* d'égards (*of,* pour, envers).
thousand ['θauz(ə)nd], *num. a. & s.* Mille (*m*) *inv* ; s. millier *m.* *A t. men,* mille hommes. *Com:* *A t. needles,* un mille d'aiguilles. **About a thousand men,** un millier d'hommes ; quelque mille hommes. *F:* **I paid five thousand pounds for it,** je l'ai payé cinq mille livres. **The year 4000 B.C.,** l'an quatre mille avant J.-C. **A thousand years,** un millénaire. **Thousands of people,** des milliers de gens. **Thousands upon thousands,** des milliers. **He is one in a thousand,** c'est un homme entre mille. **A thousand apologies!** (je vous demande) mille fois pardon ! mille pardons ! *No, no,* **a thousand times no!** non, non, et cent fois non !
thousandth ['θauzəndθ], *num. a. & s.* Millième.
thraldom ['θrɔ:ldəm], s. Esclavage *m,* servitude *f.*
thrall [θrɔ:l], s. **I.** Esclave *m,* serf *m* (*of, to,* de). **2.** = THRALDOM.
thrash [θraʃ], *v.tr.* **I.** (a) Battre (qn) ; *F:* rosser, étriller (qn). (b) Battre (un adversaire) à plates coutures. **2.** (a) *Husb:* = THRESH. (b) *Swim:* **To t. the water,** battre l'eau (avec les jambes). **3.** *Abs.* (a) *Nau:* **To thrash to windward,** marcher vent debout. (b) *Mec.E:* Vibrer. **thrash out,** *v.tr.* Débattre, creuser (une question). **thrashing,** s. **I.** (a) Rossée *f,* correction *f.* **To give s.o. a thrashing,** administrer une raclée à qn. (b) *Sp:* Défaite *f.* **2.** (a) *Husb:* = THRESHING. (b) Battement *m* (de la pluie). (c) *Mec.E:* Vibration (d'un vilebrequin) due à la torsion.
thread¹ [θred], s. **I.** Filament *m,* fil *m* (de soie).

F: **To hang by a thread,** ne tenir qu'à un fil. **2.** (*a*) *Needlew:* Fil (de coton); *esp.* fil de lin. **Sewing thread,** fil à coudre. **Lisle thread,** fil d'Écosse. **Gold thread,** fil d'or. (*b*) *Tex:* Fil (de trame ou de chaîne). *F:* **The thread of life,** la trame de la vie. **To lose the thread of one's discourse,** perdre le fil de son discours. (*c*) (*Length of*) **thread,** brin *m*, bout *m* (de coton). **3.** *Tchn:* Filet *m*, filetage *m*, pas *m* (de vis). **Worn t.,** filetage usé, mangé. **4.** (*a*) *Geol:* Veinule *f* (de minerai). (*b*) Filet (de vinaigre, etc.). **'thread-cutter,** *s. Metalw:* Tour *m* à fileter; tarau-deuse *f.* **'thread-like,** *a.* Filiforme.

thread², *v.tr.* **1.** (*a*) Enfiler (une aiguille). (*b*) Enfiler (des perles) (*on,* sur). (*c*) Enfiler (une ficelle dans un œillet). (*d*) **To thread one's way** *through the crowd,* se faufiler à travers la foule. **2.** Fileter (une vis); tarauder (un tuyau).

threadbare ['θredbɛər], *a.* (*a*) (*Of clothes*) Râpé; qui montre la corde. (*b*) (*Of argument*) Usé (jusqu'à la corde).

threadworm ['θredwəːrm], *s.* **1.** *Ann:* Néma-tode *m.* **2.** *Med:* Ascaride *m,* trichine *f.*

threat [θret], *s.* Menace *f.* (*a*) **To utter a threat,** proférer une menace. **To be under the threat of expulsion,** être sous le coup d'un arrêté d'expul-sion. (*b*) **There is a threat of rain,** la pluie menace.

threaten ['θret(ə)n], *v.tr.* **1.** Menacer. *Jur:* Intimider. **To threaten s.o. with sth.,** menacer qn de qch. *He threatened him with dismissal,* il menaça de le renvoyer. **To threaten to do sth.,** menacer de faire qch. **2.** *The sky threatens rain,* le ciel annonce la pluie. *Abs.* **A storm is threaten-ing,** la tempête (ou l'orage) menace. **threaten-ing,** *a.* (Ton) menaçant. **Threatening letter,** lettre de menaces; *Jur:* lettre comminatoire. **The weather looks threatening,** le temps menace. *To put a t. tone into one's voice,* grossir sa voix. **-ly,** *adv.* D'une manière menaçante.

three [θriː], *num. a. & s.* Trois (*m*). *T. weeks,* trois semaines. *Number t.,* le numéro trois. **To enter three by three,** entrer par trois. *S.a.* R. (*For other phrases see* EIGHT.) **'three-act,** *attrib.a. Th:* (Pièce) en trois actes. **'three-ball,** *attrib.a. Golf:* **Three-ball match,** partie à trois balles. **'three-colour(ed),** *a. Phot:* Tri-chrome. **'three-'cornered,** *a.* Triangulaire; (*of hat*) tricorne. *Pol: T.-c. fight,* élection *f* triangulaire. *S.a.* FILE¹ **1. 'three-'decker,** *s. Nau: A:* Trois-ponts *m.* **'three-element,** **'three-e'lectrode,** *attrib.a. W.Tel:* (Lampe) triode. **'three-'engined,** *a. Av:* (Avion) trimoteur. **'three-'footed,** *a.* A trois pieds. **'three-'four,** *a. Mus:* **Three-four time,** trois-quatre *m.* **'three-'handed,** *a. Cards:* **Three-handed game,** partie à trois. **'three-'legged,** *a.* **Three-legged race,** course à trois pieds. **'three-'masted,** *a. Nau:* (Vaisseau) à trois mâts. **'three-'master,** *s. Nau:* Trois-mâts *m.* **'three-pair,** *attrib.a.* **Three-pair back,** chambre *f* au troisième donnant sur la cour. **'three-phase,** *attrib.a. El.E:* Triphasé. **'three-piece,** *attrib.a.* En trois pièces. (*Lady's*) **three-piece suit,** trois-pièces *m.* **'three-ply,** *attrib.a.* **1.** Three-ply wood, contre-plaqué *m* à trois épaisseurs. **2.** (*Of wool*) A trois fils, à trois brins. **three-'quarter,** *attrib.a.* (Por-trait) de trois quarts. **Three-quarter fiddle,** trois-quarts *m. Fb:* **Three-quarter back,** *s.* three-quarter, trois-quarts. **'three-'speed,** *attrib.a.* A trois vitesses. **'three-square,** *a.* Triangulaire. **'three-way,** *attrib.a.* (Soupape, robinet) à trois voies. *El:* (Commutateur) à

trois directions. **'three-wheeled,** *a.* A trois roues. **Three-wheeled motor car,** tri-car *m.*

threefold ['θriːfould]. **1.** *a.* Triple. **2.** *adv.* Trois fois autant. **To increase threefold,** tripler.

threepence ['θripəns, 'θrʌ-], *s.* (La somme de) trois pence *m.*

threepenny ['θripəni, 'θrʌ-], *attrib.a.* (Article) coûtant trois pence. **Threepenny bit,** *s. F:* three-penny, pièce *f* de trois pence.

threescore ['θriːskɔːr], *a. Lit:* Soixante.

threesome ['θriːsəm], *s. Golf:* Partie *f* de trois.

thresh [θreʃ], *v.tr.* **1.** Battre (le blé). **2.** (*Of ship's screw*) **To thresh the water,** battre l'eau. **threshing,** *s.* Battage *m* (des blés). **'thresh-ing-floor,** *s.* Aire *f.* **'threshing-machine,** *s.* Batteuse *f.*

thresher ['θreʃər], *s.* **1.** *Husb:* (*a*) Batteur *m* en grange. (*b*) (*Machine*) Batteuse *f.* **2.** *Ich:* Renard marin.

threshold ['θreʃould], *s.* **1.** Seuil *m,* pas *m* (d'une porte). **To cross the threshold,** franchir le seuil. **2.** *Psy:* (*Of impression*) **Above the threshold,** supraliminal, -aux. *W.Tel:* **Threshold of oscillation,** limite *f* d'entretien (d'un circuit).

threw [θruː]. *See* THROW².

thrice [θrais], *adv.* **1.** Trois fois. *T. as great,* trois fois plus grand. **2.** **Thrice-told tale,** histoire rebattue.

thrift [θrift], *s.* **1.** Économie *f,* épargne *f.* **2.** *Bot:* Statice *m.* **Sea-thrift,** gazon *m* d'Olympe.

thriftiness ['θriftinəs], *s.* Économie *f.*

thriftless ['θriftləs], *a.* **1.** Dépensier, prodigue. **2.** Sans soin; imprévoyant.

thriftlessness ['θriftləsnəs], *s.* **1.** Prodigalité *f.* **2.** Manque *m* de soin; imprévoyance *f.*

thrifty ['θrifti], *a.* Économe, ménager. **-ily,** *adv.* Avec économie. *To live t.,* vivre frugalement.

thrill¹ [θril], *s.* (*a*) Frisson *m,* tressaillement *m.* (*b*) (Vive) émotion. **It gave me quite a thrill,** ça m'a fait quelque chose.

thrill². **1.** *v.tr.* (*a*) Faire frissonner, faire frémir (qn). **To be thrilled with joy,** frissonner de joie. (*b*) Émouvoir, empoigner (qn); *F:* électriser (son auditoire). *To be thrilled at the sight of sth.,* ressentir une vive émotion à la vue de qch. **2.** *v.i.* Tressaillir, frissonner, frémir. *We thrilled at the news,* la nouvelle nous fit battre le cœur. **thrilling,** *a.* (Spectacle) empoignant, émou-vant; (roman) sensationnel. *Rac:* **Thrilling finish,** arrivée palpitante.

thriller ['θrilər], *s. P:* Roman sensationnel; pièce *f* mélodramatique, à gros effets.

thrive [θraiv], *v.i.* (*p.t.* throve [θrouv], thrived; *p.p.* thriven ['θriv(ə)n], thrived) (*a*) (*Of child, plant*) Se (bien) développer; (*of plant*) réussir, bien venir; (*of business*) bien marcher. **Children who thrive on milk,** enfants à qui le lait profite bien. *Plant that thrives in all soils,* plante qui s'accommode de tous les sols. *He thrives on it,* il s'en trouve bien. (*b*) (*Of pers.*) Prospérer. **thriving,** *a.* Vigoureux; (*of pers., business*) prospère.

throat [θrout], *s.* **1.** (*a*) *Anat:* Gorge *f.* **To grip s.o. by the throat,** empoigner qn à la gorge. **To cut s.o.'s throat,** couper la gorge à qn; égorger qn. *F:* **He is cutting his own throat,** il travaille à sa propre ruine. (*b*) Gorge, gosier *m.* *To have a fish-bone in one's t.,* avoir une arête dans le gosier. **I have a sore throat,** j'ai mal à la gorge. **To clear one's throat,** s'éclaircir le gosier, la voix. *F:* **To moisten one's throat,** s'humecter le gosier. **To thrust sth. down s.o.'s throat,** imposer une opinion à qn. *S.a.* JUMP² I. 1, STICK² II. 3. **2.** (*a*) Rétrécissement *m,* gorge (dans un cours d'eau). (b) Nau: Mâchoire f (de corne). **3.** Gueulard m (de haut fourneau).

throatiness ['θroutinəs], s. Qualité gutturale (de la voix).

throaty ['θrouti], a. (Of voice) D'arrière-gorge; guttural, -aux. **-ily,** adv. Gutturalement.

throb¹ [θrɔb], s. Pulsation f, battement m (du cœur); vrombissement m (d'une machine).

throb², v.i. (throbbed) (a) (Of heart) Battre fort; palpiter; (of engine, etc.) vrombir. **His heart throbbed with joy,** son cœur tressaillit de joie. (b) **My finger is throbbing,** mon doigt lancine.

throbbing, s. (a) Battement m, pulsation f (du cœur); vrombissement m (d'une machine). (b) Lancination f, élancement m (d'un panaris).

throes [θro:uz], s.pl. Douleurs fpl, angoisse f, agonie f. **The throes of death,** les affres f de la mort; l'agonie. F: England was in the throes of a general election, l'Angleterre était au beau milieu d'une élection.

thrombosis [θrɔm'bousis], s. Med: Thrombose f.

thrombus ['θrɔmbəs], s. Med: Thrombus m; caillot sanguin.

throne [θroun], s. Trône (royal ou épiscopal). **To come to the throne; to mount the throne,** venir au trône; monter sur le trône.

throng¹ [θrɔŋ], s. (a) Foule f, affluence f. (b) Cohue f.

throng², **1.** v.i. S'assembler en foule; affluer (à, dans, un endroit). **To throng round s.o.,** se presser autour de qn. People t. to her at-homes, on se presse à ses jours de réception. **2.** v.tr. Encombrer (les rues). **thronged,** a. (Of street, etc.) Plein de gens; (of hall) comble, bondé. **Everywhere was thronged,** la foule se pressait partout. **thronging,** a. (Of crowd) Serré, compact.

throstle [θrɔsl], s. **1.** Grive chanteuse. **2.** Tex: Métier continu.

throttle¹ [θrɔtl], s. **1.** F: Gosier m. **2.** Throttle (-valve), soupape f de réglage. (a) Mch: Registre m de vapeur. (b) I.C.E: Étrangleur m; obturateur m d'air. **To open out the throttle,** mettre les gaz. **To give full throttle,** marcher à pleins gaz. **'throttle-chamber,** s. I.C.E: Boisseau m (d'étranglement). **'throttle-control,** s. I.C.E: Contrôleur m de marche.

throttle², v.tr. **1.** Étrangler; serrer (qn) à la gorge. **2.** Mch: I.C.E: Étrangler (la vapeur, le moteur). Abs. **To throttle down,** mettre le moteur au ralenti; fermer le(s) gaz. **throttling,** s. Étranglement m.

through [θru:]. **I.** prep. **1.** (a) A travers; par. T. a hedge, au travers d'une haie. A narrow path leads t. the forest, un chemin étroit traverse la forêt. **To look t. a telescope,** regarder dans un télescope. F: **To go through, s.o.'s pockets,** fouiller qn. F: **He's been through it,** il en a vu de dures. **To speak through one's nose,** parler du nez. **He is through his examination,** il a été reçu à son examen. **I am half through this book,** j'ai lu la moitié de ce livre. **I have got through this book,** j'ai fini ce livre. S.a. PUT² I. 5. (b) Pendant, durant. **All through his life,** sa vie durant. **2. Through s.o.,** par qn; par l'entremise de qn. **To send sth. through the post,** envoyer qch. par la poste. **3.** (a) En conséquence de, à cause de (qch.). **Through ignorance,** par ignorance. **Absent through illness,** absent par suite de maladie. **To act through fear,** agir sous le coup de la peur. (b) Par l'action de (qn, qch.). **It all happened through him,** il est cause de tout. **II. through,** adv. **1.** (a) A travers. The water

poured t., l'eau coulait à travers. **To let s.o. through,** laisser passer qn. (b) **Through (and through),** de bout en bout; de part en part. **To run s.o. through** (with one's sword), transpercer qn (de part en part). S.a. WET¹ I. (c) D'un bout à l'autre; jusqu'au bout. **To see sth. through,** mener qch. à bonne fin. **The lesson is half through,** la leçon est à moitié finie. **I am through with you,** j'en ai fini avec vous. S.a. SEE THROUGH 2. **2.** (a) **The train runs through to Paris,** le train va directement à Paris. (b) Tp: **To get through to s.o.,** obtenir la communication avec qn. I'm putting you t. to the secretary, je vous passe le secrétaire. **You are through,** vous êtes en communication. **III. through,** attrib.a. Rail: **Through carriage for . . .,** voiture directe pour. . . . **Through traffic,** transit m. **'through-communi'cation,** s. Rail: Intercommunication f (entre wagons). **'throughstone,** s. Const: Parpaing m.

throughout [θru:'aut]. **I.** prep. (a) **Throughout the country,** dans tout le pays; partout dans le pays. (b) **Throughout the year,** pendant toute l'année. **2.** adv. (a) **House with electric light t.,** maison avec lumière électrique dans toutes les pièces. **Leather-lined t.,** doublé entièrement en peau. (b) Tout le temps.

throve [θro:uv]. See THRIVE.

throw¹ [θrou], s. **1.** (a) Jet m, lancement m, lancée f (de qch.). **Throw of dice,** coup m de dés. (b) Long t., jet d'une longue portée. S.a. STONE'S THROW. (c) Wr: Mise f à terre (de l'adversaire). **2.** Geol: Rejet m (dans une stratification). **3.** Mec.E: (a) **Throw of the piston,** course f, volée f, du piston. (b) Bras m de manivelle. **Two-throw crank-shaft,** arbre à deux coudes.

throw², v.tr. (threw [θru:]; thrown [θroun]) **1.** (a) Jeter, lancer (une balle). Abs. **He can throw a hundred yards,** il est capable de lancer à cent mètres. **To throw s.o. a kiss,** envoyer un baiser à qn. **To throw a glance at s.o.,** jeter un coup d'œil à, sur, qn. **To throw oneself backwards,** se rejeter en arrière. **To throw temptation in s.o.'s way,** exposer qn à la tentation. **To throw the blame on s.o.,** rejeter la faute sur qn. S.a. MONEY I, MUD, WATER¹ I. (b) **To throw a sheet over sth.,** couvrir qch. d'un drap. **To throw oneself into the fray,** s'élancer à l'assaut. **To throw oneself on s.o.'s generosity,** s'en remettre à la générosité de qn. **To be thrown upon one's own resources,** n'avoir plus à compter que sur soi-même. **To throw two rooms into one,** de deux pièces n'en faire qu'une. **To throw open the door,** ouvrir la porte toute grande. S.a. GEAR¹ 3, WORK¹ 4. **2.** (a) Projeter (des éclaboussures). (b) **To throw a picture on the screen,** projeter une image sur l'écran. **To throw a lustre over sth.,** ajouter du lustre à qch. **3.** F: **To throw a fit,** tomber en convulsions; piquer une attaque de nerfs. **4.** (a) Wr: **To throw an opponent,** terrasser un adversaire. (b) (Of horse) **To throw its rider,** démonter son cavalier. (Of rider) **To be thrown,** être désarçonné. **5.** Cer: Tourner (un pot). **throw about,** v.tr. **1.** Jeter (des objets) çà et là; éparpiller. **To throw one's money about,** gaspiller son argent. **2.** (a) **To throw one's arms about,** faire de grands gestes. **To throw oneself about,** se démener. (b) **To be thrown about,** être ballotté ou cahoté. **throw aside,** v.tr. Jeter (qch.) de côté. **throw away,** v.tr. **1.** Jeter (son cigare); rejeter (qch.); mettre (qch.) au rebut. **2.** Donner (qch.) inutilement; gaspiller. **To throw away a chance,** laisser passer une occasion. **To throw away one's**

life, se sacrifier inutilement. (*Of girl*) **To throw herself away,** se marier avec un homme indigne d'elle. **throw back.** **I.** *v.tr.* (*a*) Rejeter (un poisson dans l'eau) ; renvoyer (une balle) ; réverbérer (la lumière). (*b*) *To t. back one's shoulders,* effacer les épaules. (*c*) Retarder (un travail). (*d*) **To be thrown back upon s.o.,** être forcé de se rabattre sur qn. **2.** *v.i.* (*Of breed*) Retourner à un type antérieur. **'throw-back,** *s.* **I.** Recul *m* (dans le progrès) ; échec *m*. **2.** *Biol:* Retour *m* atavique. **throw down,** *v.tr.* **I.** (*a*) Jeter (qch.) de haut en bas. (*b*) Jeter (qch.) à terre ; abattre (ses cartes). (*c*) **To throw down one's arms,** (i) abandonner ses armes ; (ii) se rendre. *Ind:* **To throw down one's tools,** se mettre en grève. **2.** *River that throws down mud,* rivière qui dépose de la vase. **throw in,** *v.tr.* **I.** Jeter dedans. **2.** (*a*) Ajouter (qch.) ; donner (qch.) par-dessus le marché. (*b*) Intercaler (un mot). **3.** **To throw in one's lot with s.o.,** partager le sort de qn. **4.** (*a*) **To throw in one's hand, one's cards,** abandonner la partie. (*b*) *Fb:* **To throw in,** remettre en touche. **'throw-in,** *s.* *Fb:* Remise *f* en jeu, en touche. **throw off,** *v.tr.* **I.** (*a*) Jeter, rendre (de la vapeur). (*b*) Enlever, quitter (ses vêtements) ; se débarrasser de (qn, qch.) ; abandonner (un déguisement). *To t. off a bad habit,* se défaire d'une mauvaise habitude. *S.a.* YOKE[1] 1. **2.** (*a*) **To throw a train off the rails,** faire dérailler un train. (*b*) **To throw the dogs off the scent,** dépister les chiens. *S.a.* GUARD[1] 1. **throw out,** *v.tr.* **I.** Jeter dehors ; expulser (qn). **2.** Répandre, émettre (de la chaleur). **3.** (*a*) Rejeter (un projet de loi) ; écarter (des articles défectueux). (*b*) *Aut:* **To throw out the clutch,** débrayer. **4.** (*a*) **To throw out one's chest,** bomber la poitrine. (*b*) *Mil:* **To throw out skirmishers,** envoyer des tirailleurs en avant. **5.** Lancer, laisser entendre (des insinuations). **6.** Déconcerter (un orateur). **'throw-outs,** *s.pl.* *Com:* Écarts *m*, rebuts *m*. **throw over,** *v.tr.* **I.** Abandonner (ses confédérés). **2.** *Mec.E:* Renverser (un levier). *S.a.* POINT[1] II. 4. **throw together,** *v.tr.* **I.** Assembler (qch.) à la hâte. **2.** *Chance had thrown us together,* le hasard nous avait réunis. **throw up,** *v.tr.* **I.** Jeter (qch.) en l'air. *S.a.* SPONGE[1] 1. **2.** Vomir, rejeter, rendre. **3.** Lever haut, mettre haut (les mains). **4.** Construire à la hâte (une maison). **5.** Renoncer à, abandonner. **To throw up one's situation,** se démettre de son poste. **thrower** ['θrouər], *s.* Lanceur, -euse. **thrum**[1] [θrʌm], *s.* *Tex:* (*Usu. pl.*) Penne(s)*f*(*pl*) ; bouts laissés à la fin de la pièce. **thrum**[2], *v.tr. & i.* **To thrum** (**on**) **a guitar,** pincer de la guitare. *To t. on the piano,* tapoter le piano. *To t. on the window-pane,* tambouriner sur les vitres. **thrush**[1] [θrʌʃ], *s.* *Orn:* Grive *f*. **thrush**[2], *s.* **I.** *Med:* Muguet *m*. **2.** *Vet:* Teigne *f* ; échauffement *m* de la fourchette (du cheval). **thrust**[1] [θrʌst], *s.* **I.** (*a*) Poussée *f*. (*b*) Coup *m* de pointe. *Fenc:* Coup d'estoc. **Thrust and parry,** la botte et a parade. **Lance thrust,** coup de lance. *F:* **A shrewd thrust,** un trait, une critique, qui frappe juste. **2.** (*a*) *Arch: Mec:* Poussée, butée *f*. (*b*) *Geol:* Chevauchement *m* (des plissements). **'thrust-block,** *s.* Palier *m* de butée. **thrust**[2], *v.* (thrust ; thrust) **I.** *v.tr.* (*a*) Pousser (avec force). **To thrust one's hands into one's pockets,** fourrer les mains dans ses poches. **To thrust a dagger into s.o.'s back,** enfoncer un

poignard dans le dos de qn. (*b*) **To thrust oneself upon s.o.,** s'imposer à qn, chez qn. (*c*) **To thrust** (**one's way**) **through the crowd,** se frayer un chemin à travers la foule. **To thrust past s.o.,** écarter qn pour passer. **2.** *v.i.* **To thrust at s.o.,** porter un coup de pointe à qn ; *Fenc:* porter, pousser, une botte à qn. *To t. in tierce,* tirer en tierce. **thrust aside, away,** *v.tr.* Repousser, écarter (qn, qch.). **thrust back,** *v.tr.* Repousser violemment (la porte). **thrust forward,** *v.tr.* **I.** Pousser (qn, qch.) en avant ; avancer (la main). **2.** **To thrust oneself forward,** (i) se mettre en avant ; (ii) s'ingérer dans une affaire. **thrust out,** *v.tr.* **I.** *To t. out one's head,* passer la tête dehors. **To thrust out one's tongue,** tirer la langue. **2.** **To thrust out one's hand,** avancer la main. **thruster** ['θrʌstər], *s.* (*a*) Chasseur *m* à courre qui pousse de l'avant. (*b*) *F:* Arriviste *mf*. **thud**[1] [θʌd], *s.* Bruit sourd ; son mat ; floc *m*. **thud**[2], *v.i.* (thudded) Tomber avec un bruit sourd ; émettre un bruit mat. **thug** [θʌg], *s.* **I.** *Hist:* Thug *m*, étrangleur *m*. **2.** *U.S:* *F:* Apache *m*, assassin *m*, bandit *m*. **thumb**[1] [θʌm], *s.* Pouce *m*. *To hold sth.* **between finger and thumb,** tenir qch. entre le pouce et l'index. *F:* **His fingers are all thumbs,** il est maladroit de ses mains. **To be under s.o.'s thumb,** être sous la domination, sous la coupe, de qn. **To bite one's thumbs,** se ronger les poings de dépit. *P:* **Thumbs up!** (i) chic alors ! (ii) on les a eus ! *S.a.* RULE[1] 1. **'thumb-index,** *s.* **I.** Bound with thumb-index, relié avec encoches. **2.** Répertoire *m* à onglets. **'thumb-nail,** *s.* Ongle *m* du pouce. **Thumb-nail sketch,** croquis *m* minuscule. **'thumb-piece,** *s.* Poucier *m*, poussoir *m* (d'un loquet). **'thumb-screw,** *s.* **I.** Vis *f* à ailettes ; papillon *m*. **2.** *Hist:* Poucettes *fpl* (de torture). **'thumb-stall,** *s.* Poucier *m* (de cordonnier). **thumb**[2], *v.tr.* **I.** Manier (qch.) maladroitement. **2.** *Well-thumbed book,* livre fatigué ; livre souvent feuilleté. **thump**[1] [θʌmp], *s.* **I.** Coup sourd ; cognement *m* (d'un mécanisme). **2.** Coup de poing ; bourrade *f*. **thump**[2], *v.tr. & i.* Bourrer (qn) de coups. *To t.* (**on**) *the table,* cogner sur la table. **To thump out a tune,** taper un air (au piano). **My heart was thumping,** mon cœur battait fort. **thumping,** *a.* *F:* Énorme. **Thumping lie,** mensonge énorme. *This is a t. lie,* le mensonge est de taille. **thumper** ['θʌmpər], *s.* *P:* (*a*) Chose *f* énorme. *Isn't it a t.!* il (elle) est de taille ! (*b*) **To. tell thumpers,** en conter de fortes. **thunder**[1] ['θʌndər], *s.* **I.** (*a*) Tonnerre *m*. **Peal of thunder,** coup *m* de tonnerre. **There is thunder in the air,** le temps est à l'orage. (*b*) *F:* **Thunder of applause,** tonnerre d'applaudissements. **2.** *A. & Lit:* (*a*) La foudre. (*b*) **The thunders of Jupiter,** les foudres *m* de Jupiter. *F:* **To steal s.o.'s thunder,** couper l'herbe sous le pied à qn. *S.a.* BLACK[1] I.1. **'thunder-clap,** *s.* Coup *m* de tonnerre. **'thunder-cloud,** *s.* Nuage orageux. **'thunder-shower,** *s.* Pluie *f* d'orage. **'thunder-storm,** *s.* Orage *m*. **thunder**[2], *v.i. & tr.* **I.** Tonner. *It is thundering,* il tonne. *The sea thunders under our windows,* la mer gronde sous nos fenêtres. **2.** *F:* **To thunder** (**out**) **threats,** tonner, fulminer, des menaces. **To thunder out an order,** donner un ordre d'une voix tonnante. **thundering**[1], *a.* **I.** Tonnant ; fulminant. **2.** *F:* **To be in a thundering rage,** être dans une rage à tout casser.

What a t. nuisance! ce que c'est embêtant !
adv. **A thundering great fish,** un poisson formidable. **thundering²,** ⸫. **1.** Tonnerre *m.*
2. *F:* Bruit retentissant.
thunderbolt ['θʌndərboult], *s.* **1.** (Coup *m* de)
foudre *f. S.a.* JOVE. **2.** *F:* Nouvelle foudroyante.
3. *A:* Météorite *m.*
thunderous ['θʌndərəs], *a.* **1.** Orageux. **2.** (*Of
voice*) Tonnant ; (*of applause*) à tout rompre.
thunderstruck ['θʌndərstrʌk], *a.* Confondu,
abasourdi, sidéré. **To be thunderstruck,** tomber
des nues ; être atterré.
thurible ['θjuəribl], *s. Ecc:* Encensoir *m.*
thurifer ['θjuərifər], *s. Ecc:* Thuriféraire *m.*
Thursday ['θəːrzdi], *s.* Jeudi *m.* (*For phrases cf.*
FRIDAY.)
thus [ðʌs], *adv.* **1.** AINSI ; de cette façon. *If you
do it t.,* si vous le faites comme ceci, comme cela.
2. Ainsi, donc. **Thus, when he arrived . . .,**
donc, lorsqu'il arriva. . . . **3.** **Thus far,**
jusqu'ici ; jusque-là. *T. much is certain :
that . . .,* ce qui est certain, c'est que. . . .
thuya ['θjuːja], *s. Bot:* Thùya *m.*
thwack¹, ² [θwak], *s. & v.tr.* = WHACK¹, ².
thwart¹ [θwɔːrt], *s.* Banc *m* de nage (d'une
embarcation).
thwart², *a.* Transversal, -aux ; transverse.
thwart³, *v.tr.* Contrecarrer (qn) ; déjouer les
menées de (qn). *To t. s.o.'s plans,* se mettre en
travers des projets de qn ; circonvenir les projets
de qn. **To be thwarted,** essuyer un échec.
thy [ðai], *poss.a.* (*thine before a vowel sound*)
A. & Lit: Ton, *f.* ta, *pl.* tes. *Thy service,* ton
service. *Thy glory,* ta gloire. *Thy friendship,* ton
amitié *f. Thine own son,* ton propre fils.
thyme [taim], *s. Bot:* Thym *m.* **Wild thyme,**
serpolet *m.*
thymol ['θaiməl], *s. Pharm:* Thymol *m.*
thymus ['θaiməs], *s.* Thymus (gland), thymus *m.*
thyroid ['θairɔid], *a.* Thyroïde. *Pharm:* **Thyroid gland extract,** extrait *m* thyroïde.
thyroidism ['θairɔidizm], *s. Med:* Thyroïdisme *m.*
thyself [ðai'self], *pron. See* SELF 4.
tiara [ti'ɑːra], *s.* Tiare *f.*
Tiber (the) [ðə'taibər]. *Pr.n.* Le Tibre.
Tiberius [tai'biːriəs]. *Pr.n.m. Hist:* Tibère.
Tibet [ti'bet]. *Pr.n. Geog:* Le T(h)ibet.
Tibetan [ti'bet(ə)n], *a. & s.* T(h)ibétain, -aine.
tibia, *pl.* **-ae** ['tibia, -iː], *s.* Tibia *m.*
tic [tik], *s. Med:* **1.** Tic *m.* **2.** Tic douloureux.
tick¹ [tik], *s.* **1.** (*a*) Tic-tac *m. F:* **On the tick,**
à l'heure sonnante. *You are here on the t.,* vous
êtes à la minute. (*b*) *F:* Moment *m,* instant *m.
I should be recognized* **in a tick,** je serais reconnu
en un instant. *I am coming* **in a tick,** j'arrive
dans un instant. **Half a tick!** un instant ! *He'll
do it* **in two ticks,** il fera ça en moins de rien.
2. Marque *f,* pointage *m,* trait *m.* **To put a tick
against a name,** faire une marque à un nom ;
pointer un nom. **'tick-'tack, 'tick-'tock,** *s.*
Tic-tac *m.*
tick². **1.** *v.i.* (*Of clock*) Faire tic-tac. **2.** *v.tr.*
= TICK OFF 1. **tick off,** *v.tr.* **1.** Pointer (une
liste). *To t. off a name,* faire une marque à un
nom. **2.** *F:* Rembarrer (qn). **tick out,** *v.tr.*
(*Of telegraph*) Enregistrer (un message). **tick
over,** *v.i. I.C.E:* (*Of engine*) Tourner au
grand ralenti. **ticking¹,** *s.* Tic-tac *m.*
tick³, *s.* 1. *Arach:* Tique *f* (du bétail). **2.** *Ent:*
Mouche *f* araignée. **Dog tick(-fly),** mouche des
chiens.
tick⁴, *s. P:* Crédit *m.* **To buy sth. on tick,** acheter
qch. à crédit, à l'œil.

tick⁵, *s.* **1.** Enveloppe *f,* toile *f* (à matelas).
2. = TICKING².
ticker ['tikər], *s.* **1.** (*a*) *F:* Montre *f; P:* tocante *f.* (*b*) *F:* Le cœur. **2.** Télégraphe imprimeur.
ticket¹ ['tiket], *s.* **1.** Billet *m* (de chemin de fer) ;
ticket *m* (d'autobus). **Complimentary ticket,**
billet de faveur. **Soup ticket,** bon *m* de soupe.
Th: **Box ticket,** coupon *m* de loge. *Your
cloak-room ticket,* votre numéro *m* de vestiaire.
Rail: **Single ticket,** billet simple. **Return
ticket,** billet d'aller et retour. **Luggage ticket,**
bulletin *m* (d'enregistrement) de bagages. **Left-
luggage ticket, cloak-room ticket,** bulletin,
ticket, de consigne. **Platform ticket,** billet de
quai ; laissez-passer *m inv.* **2.** *Com:* (**Price-**)
ticket, étiquette *f;* fiche *f.* **3.** *Pol:* *U.S:* *F:*
The democratic ticket, le programme du parti
démocrate. **4.** (*a*) *Mil:* *Nau:* **To get one's**
ticket, recevoir son congé définitif. (*b*) *Nau:* *F:*
To get one's (master's) ticket, passer capitaine.
Av: **To get one's (pilot's) ticket,** obtenir son
brevet de pilote. (*c*) *See* LEAVE¹ 2. **5.** *P:* **That's
the ticket!** voilà qui fera l'affaire ! à la bonne
heure ! **'ticket-collector,** *s. Rail:* Contrôleur *m* (de billets). **'ticket-holder,** *s.* Voyageur,
spectateur, muni d'un billet. **Season-ticket-
holder,** abonné. **'ticket-inspector,** *s.* Contrôleur *m* (d'autobus). **'ticket-office,** *s. U.S:*
= BOOKING-OFFICE. **'ticket-punch,** *s. Rail:*
Poinçon *m* de contrôleur.
ticket², *v.tr.* (ticketed) Étiqueter, marquer (des
marchandises). **ticketing,** *s.* Étiquetage *m.*
ticking² ['tikiŋ], *s.* Toile *f,* coutil *m,* à matelas.
tickle¹ ['tikl], *s.* Chatouillement *m.* **To give s.o.
a t.,** chatouiller qn.
tickle². **1.** *v.tr.* (*a*) Chatouiller. *F:* (*Of food*) **To
tickle the palate,** chatouiller le palais. **To tickle
s.o.'s fancy,** amuser qn. (*b*) *F:* Amuser. **To be
tickled to death at sth.,** se tordre de rire à l'idée
de qch. (*c*) *Aut:* **To tickle the carburettor,**
presser à plusieurs reprises le bouton de noyage
du carburateur. (*d*) Pêcher (la truite) à la main.
2. *v.i. My hand tickles,* j'ai des chatouille-
ments à la main. **tickle up,** *v.tr. F:* Exciter,
stimuler qn. **tickling¹,** *a.* Chatouillant. **Tickling
cough,** toux d'irritation. **tickling²,** *s.* **1.** Chatouillement *m.* **2.** *Fish:* Pêche *f* à la main.
tickler ['tiklər], *s.* **1.** *I.C.E:* Bouton *m* de
noyage (du carburateur). **2.** (*a*) Question embarrassante. (*b*) Sujet délicat.
ticklish ['tikliʃ], *a.* **1.** Chatouilleux, -euse.
2. (*a*) (*Of pers.*) Susceptible. (*b*) (*Of task*)
Délicat ; (*of undertaking*) scabreux. **A ticklish
subject,** un sujet délicat.
ticklishness ['tikliʃnəs], *s.* **1.** Sensibilité *f* au
chatouillement. **2.** (*a*) Susceptibilité *f.* (*b*) Délicatesse *f* (d'une tâche).
tidal ['taid(ə)l], *a.* **1.** Qui relève de la marée.
Tidal wave, (i) raz *m* de marée ; vague *f* de
fond ; (*in estuary*) mascaret *m;* (ii) vague
(d'enthousiasme, d'indignation). **2.** (*Of river,
harbour*) A marée. **Tidal basin,** bassin à flot.
tid-bit ['tidbit], *s.* = TIT-BIT.
tiddler ['tidlər], *s. F:* = STICKLEBACK.
tiddlywinks ['tidliwiŋks], *s.* Jeu *m* de la puce.
tide¹ [taid], *s.* **1.** *A:* Temps *m,* époque *f,* saison *f.
S.a.* CHRISTMAS-TIDE, EASTERTIDE. **2.** Marée *f.*
Flood tide, marée montante ; *Nau:* (marée de)
flot *m.* **High tide,** marée haute ; haute marée.
Low tide, marée basse. **Against the tide,** à
contre-marée. **To go with the tide,** suivre le
courant. **To go against the tide,** prendre le
contre-sens de la marée. **The tide of battle**

turned, la fortune de la bataille tourna. **'tide-gate**, *s.* Porte ׀ à flot; écluse *f* (de bassin). **'tide-gauge**, *s.* Échelle *f* de marée. **'tide-mark**, *s.* (*a*) Ligne *f* de marée haute. (*b*) Laisse *f* de haute mer. **'tide-race**, *s.* Raz *m* de marée. **'tide-rip**, *s.* 1. Revolin *m* de lame; clapotis *m* de marée. 2. Raz *m* de marée. **'tide-waiter**, *s.* *A*: Douanier *m* (de port).

tide². 1. *v.tr. Drift-wood tided up the river*, bois flottant porté en amont par la marée. 2. *v.i. Nau*: To tide (it) into port, out of port, entrer au port, sortir du port, grâce à la marée. **tide over**, *v.tr.* Venir à bout (d'une difficulté). *This sum will tide us over*, cette somme nous permettra de surmonter nos difficultés.

tideless ['taidləs], *a.* Sans marée.

tideway ['taidwei], *s.* Lit *m* de la marée.

tidiness ['taidinəs], *s.* Bon ordre; (*of dress*) bonne tenue.

tidings ['taidiŋz], *s.pl.* Nouvelle(s) *f*(*pl*).

tidy¹ ['taidi], *a.* 1. (*a*) (*Of room, etc.*) Bien rangé, en bon ordre; (*of dress*) bien tenu. *Make yourself t.*, faites-vous propre. (*b*) (*Of pers.*) Ordonné; qui a de l'ordre. 2. *F*: Assez bon; passable. *At a tidy pace*, à un bon petit train. *A tidy fortune*, une jolie fortune. *A tidy sum*, une somme rondelette. **-ily**, *adv.* Proprement; avec ordre. *T. dressed*, soigneusement mis; mis avec soin.

tidy², *s.* Vide-poche(s) *m inv.*

tidy³, *v.tr.* Ranger; mettre de l'ordre dans, arranger (une chambre). *To tidy one's hair*, s'arranger les cheveux. *To tidy oneself (up)*, faire un brin de toilette. *To tidy away the books*, ranger les livres. *T. up the room a bit*, mettez un peu d'ordre dans la chambre. *Abs. To tidy up*, tout remettre en place.

tie¹ [tai], *s.* 1. (*a*) Lien *m*; attache *f*. *F*: *Ties of friendship*, liens d'amitié. (*b*) Assujettissement *m*. *Her children are a tie on her*, ses enfants sont pour elle une entrave continuelle. 2. (*a*) Lien (de corde, etc.). (*b*) *Nau*: Itague *f*. (*c*) Lacet *m*, cordon *m* (de soulier). (*d*) (Neck-)tie, nœud *m*, cravate *f*. *Wearing a white tie*, en cravate blanche. *Woman's fur tie*, cravate de fourrure. 3. *Const: etc*: Chaîne *f*, ancre *f*, moise *f*, entretoise *f*; tirant *m*. 4. *Mus*: Liaison *f*. 5. (*a*) *Sp*: Match *m* ou course *f* à égalité. *Tie award*, prix ex æquo. (*b*) Match de championnat. *S.a.* CUP-TIE. (*c*) *The election ended in a tie*, les candidats obtinrent un nombre égal de suffrages. **tie-beam**, *s. Const:* Moise *f*; tirant *m.* **'tie-clip**, *s.* Pince *f* à cravate. **'tie-pin**, *s.* Épingle *f* de cravate. **'tie-rod**, *s.* Tirant *m*; barre *f* d'accouplement. *Const:* Entrait *m* (de toit).

tie², *v.* (**tied**; **tying**) I. *v.tr.* 1. (*a*) Attacher; lier (qn à un poteau). *F*: *To tie s.o.'s hands*, enlever à qn toute liberté d'action. *To be tied and bound*, (i) être ligoté; (ii) *F*: avoir les mains liées. *To be tied to one's bed*, être cloué au lit (par la maladie). *To be tied to one's work*, être toujours à l'attache. (*b*) Lier, nouer (un lacet, etc.); faire (un nœud, sa cravate). *To tie an artery*, ligaturer une artère. 2. Renforcer (une chaudière, etc.) avec des tirants; entretoiser. 3. *Mus:* Lier (deux notes). II. **tie**, *v.i. Sp: etc:* Être, arriver, à égalité (*with*, avec). *Sch:* *To tie for first place*, être premier ex æquo (*with*, avec). **tie down**, *v.tr.* 1. Immobiliser (qn) en l'attachant contre terre, sur son lit; assujettir (qch.). 2. *Tied down to one's duties*, assujetti à ses fonctions. *To tie s.o. down to a task*, asservir, astreindre, qn à une tâche. **tie on**, *v.tr.* Attacher avec une ficelle. **Tie-on label**, étiquette *f*

à œillets. **tie up**, *v.tr.* 1. Attacher, ficeler (un paquet); bander, panser (un bras blessé). 2. Attacher (un cheval); mettre (un cheval) à l'attache. 3. *F*: Rendre (un legs) inaliénable; immobiliser (ses capitaux). **tied**, *a.* 1. *To keep s.o. close tied*, ne laisser aucune liberté à qn. 2. *Tied (public-)house*, débit de boissons qui est astreint à ne vendre que les produits d'une certaine brasserie. 3. *Mus:* Tied notes, notes liées.

tier [ti:ər], *s.* Rangée *f* (de sièges, etc.); étage *m.* *Ground tier*, plan inférieur. *Tiers of an amphitheatre*, gradins *m* d'un amphithéâtre. *In tiers*, en amphithéâtre. *To arrange in tiers*, disposer par étages; étager. *To rise in tiers*, s'étager. *Th:* First tier box, loge de premier rang, de premier balcon.

tierce [ti:əs], *s. Cards: Fenc:* Tierce *f.*

tiered ['ti:ərd], *a.* A gradins, à étages. **Three-tiered cake**, pièce montée à trois étages.

tiff [tif], *s.* Petite querelle; fâcherie *f.* *They have had a t.*, il y a entre eux de la fâcherie.

tiffin ['tifin], *s.* (*Anglo-Indian*) Déjeuner *m* (de midi).

tig¹ [tig], *s.* (Jeu *m* du) chat *m.*

tig², *v.tr.* (**tigged**) Toucher (qn) (au jeu du chat).

tiger ['taigər], *s.* 1. (*a*) Tigre *m.* (*b*) *F*: A tiger at the card-table, homme âpre au jeu. 2. *A*: Tigre, groom *m*, petit laquais. **'tiger-cat**, *s.* Chat-tigre *m*; serval, -als *m*; ocelot *m.* **'tiger-eye**, *s. Lap:* Œil-de-chat *m.* **'tiger-lily**, *s.* Lis tigré.

tight [tait]. I. *a.* 1. Imperméable (à l'eau, etc.); à l'épreuve (du gaz, etc.); (*of ship, container*) étanche; (*of joint*) hermétique. *S.a.* AIR-TIGHT, WATERTIGHT. 2. (*Of cord, etc.*) Raide, tendu. *To draw a cord tight*, serrer un cordon. *F*: *To keep a tight hand, a tight hold, over s.o.*, tenir qn serré; tenir qn de court. (*b*) (*Of clothes*) (Skin-)tight, collant. (Too) tight, étriqué; trop juste. *My shoes are too t.*, mes souliers me gênent. *F*: *To be in a tight corner*, être en mauvaise passe; n'en pas mener large. *S.a.* FIT³. (*c*) (*Of mortise, etc.*) Bien ajusté; (*of knot, screw*) serré. *The nut is t.*, l'écrou est serré à bloc, à refus. 3. *A*: Propret, gentil, coquet. *A t. little house*, une petite maison bien construite et commode. 4. (*Of money*) Resserré, rare. 5. *P*: To be tight, être ivre, gris, soûl; être en ribote. *To get tight*, prendre une cuite. **-ly**, *adv.* 1. *Eyes t. shut*, yeux bien fermés. 2. (*a*) (Tendre, etc.) fortement. (*b*) Étroitement. *To hold sth. t.*, tenir qch. serré; serrer qch. dans ses mains, dans ses bras. *To fit t.*, être bien ajusté. II. **tight**, *adv.* 1. Hermétiquement. *Shut tight*, tight shut, (porte) hermétiquement close; (yeux) bien fermés. 2. (*a*) Fortement, fermement. *To hold sth. tight*, tenir qch. serré; serrer qch. dans ses bras. *To screw a nut up tight*, serrer un écrou à bloc, à refus. *To pump the tyres tight*, mettre les pneus au rond. *S.a.* HOLD² II. 1, SIT I. 1. (*b*) Étroitement. *To fit tight*, être bien ajusté. **'tight-'fisted**, *a.* *F*: Serré; ladre; dur à la détente. **'tight-fitting**, *a.* 1. (Vêtement) collant. 2. (*Of joint, etc.*) Bien ajusté. **'tight-'laced**, *a.* 1. Serré dans son corset. 2. *F*: Collet monté inv; guindé. **'tight rope**, *s.* Corde tendue; corde raide. *Tight-rope walker*, danseur de corde; funambule *mf.*

tighten ['tait(ə)n]. 1. *v.tr.* (*a*) Serrer, resserrer (une vis, un nœud); retendre (une courroie, un ressort); raidir (un cordage). *Aut:* To tighten up the steering-gear, rattraper le jeu de la direction. *F*: To tighten one's belt, se serrer le ventre ; se boucler la ceinture. (b) **To tighten (up) a blockade, restrictions,** renforcer un blocus, des restrictions. **2.** v.i. (a) Se (res)serrer. (b) (Of cable, etc.) Se tendre ; raidir.

tightness ['taitnəs], s. **1.** Étanchéité ƒ (d'un vaisseau) ; imperméabilité f. **2.** (a) Tension f, raideur ƒ (d'un cordage). (b) Med : To feel a t. across the chest, avoir la poitrine oppressée. (c) Étroitesse ƒ (d'un lien, d'un vêtement). **3.** Fin : Resserrement m, rareté ƒ (de l'argent).

tights [taits], s.pl. Th : Collant m, maillot m. Flesh-coloured tights, maillot chair.

tigress ['taigres], s.f. Tigresse.

Tigris (the) [ðəˈtaigris]. Pr.n. Geog : Le Tigre.

tike [taik], s. = TYKE.

tile[1] [tail], s. **1.** Tuile ƒ (de toiture). Crest tile, tuile faîtière. F : He spends his nights on the tiles, il traîne dehors toute la nuit. P : To have a tile loose, être toqué, timbré. **2.** P : Chapeau m ; esp. chapeau haut de forme. **3.** Carreau m. Paving tile, brique ƒ à paver ; carreau de carrelage. **4.** Chimney-flue tile, boisseau m.

tile[2], v.tr. **1.** Couvrir (un comble) de tuiles, en tuiles. **2.** Carreler (un plancher, etc.). **tiled,** a. **1.** (Toit) de, en, tuiles. **2.** (Pavage) carrelé, en carreaux ; (paroi) à carreaux vernissés. **tiling,** s. **1.** (a) Pose ƒ des tuiles. (b) Carrelage m. **2.** Coll. (a) Couverture ƒ en tuiles. (b) Carreaux mpl.

till[1] [til], v.tr. Labourer, cultiver. **tilling,** s. Labour m, culture ƒ.

till[2], s. Com : Tiroir-caisse m. F : To be caught with one's hand in the till, être pris sur le fait.

till[3]. **1.** prep. (a) Jusqu'à. Till now, till then, jusqu'ici, jusque-là. From morning till night, du matin au soir. Good-bye till Thursday! à jeudi ! (b) Not till, pas avant. He will not come till after dinner, il ne viendra qu'après le dîner. He did not begin till 1880, ce ne fut qu'en 1880 qu'il commença. **2.** conj. (a) Jusqu'à ce que + sub. Till the doors are shut, jusqu'à ce que les portes soient fermées. To laugh till one cries, rire aux larmes. (b) Not till, pas avant que + sub. He will not come till you invite him, till he is invited, il ne viendra pas avant que vous (ne) l'invitiez, avant d'être invité.

tillable ['tiləbl], a. Labourable, arable.

tillage ['tilidʒ], s. Labour m, labourage m, culture ƒ. Land in tillage, terre en labour.

tiller[1] ['tilər], s. Nau : Barre franche (de direction). To put the tiller hard over, donner un brusque coup de barre. **'tiller-lines,** s.pl. Row : Tire-v(i)eilles f. **'tiller-rope,** s. Drosse ƒ (du gouvernail). **'tiller-wheel,** s. Roue ƒ du gouvernail. **'tiller-yoke,** s. Row : Barre ƒ à tire-v(i)eilles.

tiller[2], s. Laboureur m, cultivateur m.

tiller[3], s. Agr : Hort : Talle ƒ.

tiller[4], v.i. Agr : Hort : Taller.

tilt[1] [tilt], s. **1.** Inclinaison ƒ, pente ƒ ; dévers m. To be on the tilt, être penché, incliné. To give a cask a tilt, incliner un tonneau. **2.** (a) A : Joute ƒ, tournoi m. (b) A : Coup m de lance. F : To have a tilt at s.o., jouter avec qn (dans un débat) ; allonger une botte à qn. (c) (At) full tilt, à toute vitesse. To run full tilt into sth., se jeter tête baissée, à corps perdu, contre qch. To ride (at) full tilt, aller à franc étrier, à bride abattue. **'tilt-hammer,** s. Metall : Martinet m ; marteau m à bascule. **'tilt-yard,** s. A : Lice ƒ ; champ clos.

tilt[2]. **1.** v.i. **1.** To tilt (up), s'incliner ; pencher. To tilt backwards, incliner vers l'arrière. To tilt over, (i) se pencher, s'incliner ; (ii) se renverser.

(Of bench) To tilt up, basculer. **2.** A : (a) Jouter (avec qn). (b) To tilt at s.o., (i) courir sur qn la lance en arrêt ; (ii) F : allonger une botte à qn. **II. tilt,** v.tr. (a) Pencher, incliner. To tilt one's chair back, se balancer, se renverser, sur sa chaise. Aut : To t. back a seat, rabattre un siège. To tilt over a table, renverser une table. (b) Culbuter, faire basculer (une charrette). To tilt stones out of a cart, verser les pierres d'une charrette.

tilting[1], a. (i) Incliné ; (ii) inclinable ; (iii) (mouvement) basculaire. **Tilting seat,** strapontin m ; siège basculant, à bascule. **tilting**[2], s. **1.** Inclinaison f, pente ƒ. **2.** A : Joute ƒ. Tilting at the ring, jeu m de bagues. **'tilting-lance,** s. Lance courtoise.

tilt[3], s. Veh : Bâche ƒ, banne ƒ. Nau : Tendelet m.

tilt[4], v.tr. Couvrir d'une bâche ; bâcher (une charrette) ; couvrir (une embarcation) d'un tendelet.

tilth [tilθ], s. **1.** Labour m, culture ƒ. **2.** Couche ƒ arable.

timber[1] ['timbər], s. **1.** (a) Bois m d'œuvre. Building timber, bois de construction, de charpente. (b) Standing timber, bois sur pied ; arbres mpl de haute futaie. **2.** (a) Piece of timber, F : timber, poutre f, madrier m. (b) N.Arch : Couple m, membre m. (c) pl. P : Jambes ƒ de bois. A : Shiver my timbers! mille tonnerres ! **'timber-cart,** s. Triqueballe m or ƒ. **'timber-hitch,** s. Nœud m de bois, d'anguille. **'timber-toes,** s. F : Homme à la jambe de bois. **'timber-tree,** s. Arbre m de haute futaie. **'timber-work,** s. **1.** Construction ƒ en bois. **2.** Charpente ƒ. **'timber-yard,** s. Chantier m (de bois de charpente).

timber[2], v.tr. Boiser, blinder, cuveler (un puits de mine, etc.). **timbered,** a. (a) (Maison, etc.) en bois. (b) (Of land) Boisé. **timbering,** s. **1.** Boisage m. **2.** (i) Blindage m (d'un puits de mine) ; (ii) armature ƒ (de bois).

timbrel ['timbrəl], s. B : Tambourin m.

Timbuktu [timbʌk'tu:]. Pr.n. Tombouctou.

time[1] [taim], s. **1.** Temps m. Work of time, ouvrage de longue haleine. (Father) Time, le Temps. Time will show, qui vivra verra. In (the course of) time, in process of time, as time goes on, avec le temps ; à la longue. It was a race against time, il était de toute importance d'agir vite. **2.** In a short time, en peu de temps ; sous peu. In three weeks' time, dans trois semaines. F : To do sth. in no time, faire qch. en un rien de temps, en moins de rien. Within the required time, dans le délai prescrit. To take a long time over sth., mettre un temps interminable à faire qch. For a long time to come, d'ici à longtemps. We haven't seen him for a long time past, voilà longtemps que nous ne l'avons vu. For some time past, depuis quelque temps. For some time to come, pendant quelque temps. A short time after, peu (de temps) après. After a short time, (i) après un temps assez court ; (ii) peu après. After a long time, (i) au bout d'un temps assez long ; (ii) longtemps après. All the time, (i) pendant tout ce temps ; (ii) continuellement. Sp : Official time, temps chronométré. **3.** (a) My time is my own, je ne suis pas sujet à l'heure. To have time on one's hands, avoir du temps de reste. To have no time to do sth., ne pas avoir le temps de faire qch. P : I've no time for him, il m'embête ; ce n'est pas un type intéressant. F : You have heaps of time, vous avez tout le temps voulu. To lose time, perdre du temps. To make up for lost time, rattraper le temps perdu. To lose no time in doing sth., s'empresser, se hâter, de faire qch. *Sp: etc:* **To play for time,** gagner du temps. **It takes time,** cela prend du temps. **To take one's time over sth.,** mettre le temps à faire qch. **Take your time,** prenez votre temps. *F:* It will take you all your time to . . .**, vous aurez fort à faire pour. . . . **To stay beyond one's time doing sth.,** s'attarder à faire qch. **Time's up!** l'heure a sonné! *Box:* **Time!** allez! (*In public house*) **Time, gentlemen, please!** on ferme! (*b*) *P:* **To do time,** faire de la prison. **To serve one's time** (*of apprenticeship*), faire son apprentissage. **The house will last our time,** la maison durera autant que nous. **4.** *Usu. pl.* Époque *f.* (*a*) **A sign of the times,** un signe de l'époque. **In times past, in olden times,** autrefois, jadis. **The good old times,** le bon vieux temps. **Those were happy times,** c'était le bon temps. **In times to come,** à l'avenir; dans l'avenir. **In my time** *it was different,* de mon temps c'était différent. **In our time,** de nos jours. **The times we live in,** notre époque. (*b*) **To be behind the times,** être en retard sur son siècle; être arriéré, attardé. **As times go,** par le temps qui court. **5.** Moment *m.* (*a*) **At the time of delivery,** au moment de la livraison. *I was absent at the time,* j'étais absent alors, à ce moment. **At that time,** en ce temps-là. **At the present time,** à l'heure qu'il est; actuellement. **At a given time,** à un moment donné. **At the time fixed,** à l'heure dite. **At one time . . .,** **at another time . . .,** tantôt . . . tantôt. . . . **At one time** *it used not to be so,* autrefois, dans le temps, il n'en était pas ainsi. **At one time priest of this parish,** ancien prêtre de cette paroisse. *Lit:* **Time was when . . .,** il fut un temps où. . . . **At no time,** jamais; à aucun moment. **At times,** parfois. **At various times,** à diverses reprises. **At all times,** (i) en tout temps; (ii) à n'importe quel moment. **Between times,** entre temps. **(At) any time (you like),** n'importe quand. **He may turn up at any time,** il peut arriver d'un moment à l'autre. **Some time or other,** un jour ou l'autre. **This time next year,** l'an prochain à pareille époque. **By the time (that) I got there . . .,** (i) lorsque je suis arrivé . . .; (ii) lorsque je serais arrivé. . . . **From time to time,** de temps en temps. **From that time,** dès lors; depuis lors. **To do sth. when the time comes,** faire qch. en son temps, en temps utile. **At the proper time and place,** en son lieu et place. **Now is the time to . . .,** voilà le moment pour. . . . **To choose one's time,** choisir son heure. **This is no time for trifling,** ce n'est pas le moment de badiner. (*b*) **In due time and place,** en temps et lieu. **You will hear from me in good time,** je vous écrirai en temps utile. **In his own good time,** à son heure. **6.** Heure *f.* (*a*) **Greenwich mean time,** l'heure de Greenwich. **Standard time,** l'heure légale. **Summer time,** l'heure d'été. (*b*) **What is the time?** quelle heure est-il? **To look at the time,** regarder (à) sa montre. **Watch that keeps (good) time,** montre qui est exacte, qui est bien réglée. **At any time of the day or night,** à n'importe quelle heure du jour ou de la nuit. *F:* **To pass the time of day with s.o.,** échanger quelques mots avec qn. **At this time of day,** à l'heure actuelle. (*c*) **Dinner-time,** l'heure du dîner. **To be before (one's) time,** être en avance; être avant l'heure. **To be behind (one's) time,** être en retard. **To arrive up to time, on time,** arriver à l'heure. *To arrive in t. for dinner,* arriver à temps pour dîner. **I was just in time to see it,** je suis arrivé juste à temps pour le voir. **To start in good time,** se mettre

en route de bonne heure. *F:* **And about time too!** c'est pas trop tôt! (*d*) **Time of the year,** époque de l'année; saison *f.* **At my time of life,** *F:* of day, à mon âge. **Sowing time,** la saison des semailles. **In the day-time,** de jour. **In the night-time,** de nuit. (*e*) **To die before one's time,** mourir avant l'âge. **7.** *Ind:* **To be paid by time,** être payé à l'heure. **8.** *F:* **To have a good time** (of it), se donner du bon temps; *F:* se la couler douce. *We had a good t.,* on s'est bien amusé. **To have a bad time, a rough time, of it,** (i) souffrir; en voir de dures, de grises; (ii) passer un mauvais quart d'heure. **9.** Fois *f.* **Five times,** cinq fois. **Next time,** la prochaine fois. **The first time I saw him,** la première fois que je l'ai vu. *To do sth.* several times over, faire qch. à plusieurs reprises, plusieurs fois. **Time and time again, time after time,** à maintes reprises; maintes et maintes fois. **To do two things at a time,** faire deux choses à la fois. **To run upstairs four at a time,** monter l'escalier quatre à quatre. **For weeks at a time,** des semaines durant. **Four times two is eight,** quatre fois deux font huit. **Three times as big as . . .,** trois fois plus grand que. . . . **10.** *adv.phr.* **At the same time.** (*a*) En même temps. *Prov:* You cannot be in two places at the same time, on ne peut pas se trouver dans deux endroits à la fois. (*b*) **At the same time you must not forget . . .,** d'autre part il ne faut pas oublier. . . . **11.** (*a*) *Mus:* Durée *f* (d'une note). (*b*) *Mus:* Mesure *f.* **Common time,** (i) (*also* quadruple time) mesure à quatre temps; (ii) (*also* duple time) mesure à deux temps. **To beat time,** battre la mesure. (*c*) **In strict time,** en mesure. **To keep time,** suivre la mesure, la cadence. *To get out of t.,* perdre la mesure. *I.C.E:* **The ignition is out of time,** l'allumage est déréglé, décalé. (*d*) *Mus:* To quicken the t., presser le tempo, le mouvement. *Gym:* **To march in quick time,** marcher au pas accéléré. '**time-allowance,** *s. Rac:* Rendement *m* de temps. '**time-ball,** *s. Nau:* Boule *f* horaire. '**time-bargain,** *s.* Marché *m* à terme. '**time-belt,** *s. Chr:* (Standard) time-belt, fuseau *m* horaire. '**time-clause,** *s. Gram:* Proposition temporelle. '**time-expired,** *a.* (Soldat) qui a servi son temps. '**time-exposure,** *s. Phot:* Pose *f.* '**time-fuse,** *s.* Fusée fusante; fusée à temps. '**time-honoured,** *a.* Consacré (par l'usage). '**time-keeper,** *s.* **1.** *Sp: etc:* Chronométreur *m.* **2.** Good time-keeper, (i) montre *f* qui est toujours à l'heure; (ii) personne qui est toujours à l'heure. '**time-lag,** *s. El.E:* Retard *m.* '**time-limit,** *s.* **1.** Limite de temps (imposée à un orateur, etc.). **2.** Délai *m* (de payement, etc.). '**time-server,** *s.* Complaisant *m* (envers le pouvoir, etc.); opportuniste *m.* '**time-serving,** *s.* Basse complaisance (envers le pouvoir); opportunisme *m.* '**time-sheet,** *s. Ind:* Feuille *f* de présence. '**time-signal,** *s. W.Tel: etc:* Signal *m* horaire; *pl.* signaux horaires. '**time-switch,** *s.* Minuterie *f* (d'escalier, etc.). '**time-table,** *s.* **1.** Horaire *m*; indicateur *m* (des chemins de fer). **2.** *Sch:* Emploi *m* du temps. '**time-work,** *s.* Travail *m* à l'heure. '**time-worker,** *s.* Ouvrier, -ère, qui travaille à l'heure. '**time-worn,** *a.* **1.** Usé par le temps. **2.** Séculaire, vénérable.

time², *v.tr.* **1.** (*a*) Fixer l'heure de (qch.). (*b*) **To time a blow,** choisir le moment de porter un coup; mesurer un coup. **Well-timed remark,** observation opportune, à propos. **Well-timed stroke,** coup bien calculé, bien jugé. (*c*) Régler (une horloge). (*d*) *I.C.E:* Régler, ajuster

(l'allumage, etc.) ; caler (la magnéto). (e) *Row :* To time the stroke, régler la nage. **2.** Calculer la durée de (qch.). **3.** *Sp : etc :* Chronométrer (qn, une course). To time how long it takes s.o. to do sth., mesurer le temps que qn met à faire qch. **timing,** *s.* **I.** (a) *I.C.E :* Réglage *m* (de l'allumage). *Mch :* Calage *m* (d'une soupape). (b) *I.C.E :* Distribution *f.* Timing gear, (engrenage(s) *m(pl)* de) distribution. **2.** *Phot :* Calcul *m* (du temps de pose). **3.** *Sp :* Chronométrage *m.*
timeless ['taimləs], *a.* Éternel ; sans fin.
timeliness ['taimlinəs], *s.* Opportunité *f ;* à-propos *m* (d'une intervention, etc.).
timely ['taimli], *a.* Opportun, à propos.
timepiece ['taimpiːs], *s.* Pendule *f* ou montre *f.*
timid ['timid], *a.* Timide, timoré, peureux. **-ly,** *adv.* Timidement.
timidity [ti'miditi], *s.* Timidité *f.*
timorous ['timərəs], *a.* Timoré, peureux, craintif. **-ly,** *adv.* Peureusement, craintivement.
timpani ['timpani], *s.pl. Mus :* Timbales *f.*
tin[1] [tin], *s.* **I.** Étain *m.* **2.** (a) = TIN-PLATE[1]. (b) Boîte *f* (en fer-blanc). **Petrol-tin,** bidon *m* à essence. **Cake-tin,** moule *m* à gâteaux. **Baking tin,** plat *m* à rôtir. **Tin loaf,** pain cuit au moule. **3.** *P :* (*Money*) Galette *f,* braise *f.* **'tin-bearing,** *a.* Stannifère. **tin-'hat,** *s. Mil : P :* Casque *m* de tranchée ; bourguignotte *f.* **'tinopener,** *s.* Ouvre-boîte(s) *m inv.* **'tin-plate**[1], *s.* Fer-blanc *m* ; ferblanterie *f.* **tin-'plate**[2], *v.tr. Metalw :* Étamer (le fer). **tin-'pot. I.** *s. Cu :* Marmite *f* en fer-blanc. **2.** *Attrib.a. F :* Mesquin, misérable, méprisable. **'tin-tack,** *s.* Broquette *f* ; clou *m* de tapisserie. **Tin-tacks,** semence *f.* **'tin-ware,** *s.* Articles *mpl* en fer-blanc ; ferblanterie *f.* **tin-'whistle,** *s. F :* Flageolet *m.* **tin-work,** *s.* **I.** Ferblanterie *f.* **2.** *pl.* Tin-works, ferblanterie.
tin[2], *v.tr.* (tinned) **I.** Étamer. **2.** Mettre (des sardines, etc.) en boîtes de fer-blanc. **tinned,** *a.* **I.** Étamé. **2.** Conservé (en boîtes métalliques). **Tinned foods,** conserves *f* alimentaires (en boîte). *U.S : P :* Tinned music, musique enregistrée.
tinctorial [tiŋk'tɔːriəl], *a.* Tinctorial, -aux.
tincture[1] ['tiŋktjər], *s.* **I.** *Pharm :* Teinture *f* (d'iode, etc.). **2.** (a) *A :* Teinte *f,* nuance *f.* (b) To have but a tincture of Latin, n'avoir qu'une teinture de latin. **3.** *Her :* Émail *m,* -aux ; teinture.
tincture[2], *v.tr.* Teindre, teinter.
tinder ['tindər], *s.* Mèche *f* de briquet. German tinder, amadou *m.* **'tinder-box,** *s.* Briquet *m* (à silex).
tine [tain], *s.* **I.** Dent *f,* fourchon *m* (de fourche). **2.** Andouiller *m* (de bois de cerf).
tinfoil ['tinfoil], *s.* **I.** Feuille *f* d'étain. **2.** Papier *m* (d'étain) ou papier simili-étain.
ting[1] [tiŋ], *s.* Tintement *m* (d'une cloche).
ting[2], *v.i.* Tinter.
ting-a-ling ['tiŋəliŋ], *s.* Drelin din din *m.*
tinge[1] [tindʒ], *s.* Teinte *f,* nuance *f.*
tinge[2], *v.tr.* Teinter, nuancer. *F :* Words tinged with malice, paroles teintées de malice.
tingle[1] [tiŋgl], *s.* **I.** Tingle in the ears, tintement *m* d'oreilles. **2.** Picotement *m,* fourmillement *m* (de la peau). To have a t. in one's legs, avoir des fourmis dans les jambes.
tingle[2], *v.i.* **I.** (*Of ears*) Tinter. **2.** Picoter. To tingle with impatience, vibrer d'impatience. Her cheeks tingled, les joues lui picotaient, lui cuisaient. *My eyes are tingling,* les yeux me cuisent. **My fingers are tingling to box his ears,**

la main me démange de lui flanquer une gifle.
tingling, *s.* = TINGLE[1].
tinker[1] ['tiŋkər], *s.* (a) Chaudronnier ambulant ; rétameur *m.* (b) *Scot :* = GIPSY. (c) *F :* Bousilleur *m,* savetier *m* ; gâcheur *m* (d'ouvrage).
tinker[2]. **I.** *v.tr.* To tinker (sth.) up, retaper, rafistoler (une machine, etc.) ; replâtrer (un contrat, etc.). To *t.* up a car, faire à une auto des réparations de fortune. **2.** *v.i.* Bricoler.
tinkering, *s.* **I.** (Petite) chaudronnerie ; rétamage *m.* **2.** (a) Petites besognes d'entretien, de réparation. (b) Rafistolage *m.*
tinkle[1] [tiŋkl], *s.* Tintin *m,* tintement *m,* drelin *m.*
tinkle[2]. **I.** *v.i.* Tinter. **2.** *v.tr.* Faire tinter (une sonnette). **tinkling,** *s.* = TINKLE[1].
tinkler ['tiŋklər], *s. Scot :* = GIPSY.
tinner ['tinər], *s.* Étameur *m.*
tinniness ['tininəs], *s.* Timbre grêle, métallique, fêlé (d'un piano, etc.).
tinny ['tini], *a.* **I.** (*Of earth, etc.*) Stannifère. **2.** (Goût) d'étain. **3.** To sound tinny, sonner grêle ; rendre un son fêlé.
tinsel[1] ['tins(ə)l], *s.* **I.** (a) *Dressm :* Lamé *m,* paillettes *fpl.* (b) Clinquant *m.* (c) *F :* Faux éclat, clinquant (du style). **2.** *Attrib.* Faux, *f.* fausse ; de clinquant.
tinsel[2], *v.tr.* (inselled) **I.** Garnir (une robe) de lamé, de paillettes. **Tinselled finery,** oripeaux *mpl.* **2.** Donner un faux éclat à (son style, etc.).
tinsmith ['tinsmiθ], *s.* Ferblantier *m.*
tint[1] [tint], *s.* **I.** Teinte *f,* nuance *f.* To paint tint upon tint, peindre ton sur ton. *S.a.* FLESH-TINTS, HALF-TINT. **2.** (*In line engraving*) Grisé *m.*
'tint-drawing, *s.* **I.** Camaïeu *m.* **2.** (Épure *f* au lavis.
tint[2], *v.tr.* **I.** Teinter, colorer. **2.** *Engr :* Ombrer ; hachurer.
tiny ['taini], *a.* Minuscule. A tiny bit, un tout petit morceau.
tip[1] [tip], *s.* **I.** Bout *m,* extrémité *f,* pointe *f ;* dard *m* (de flamme). On the tips of the toes, sur la pointe des pieds. Artist to the finger-tips, artiste jusqu'au bout des ongles. To have sth. on the tip of one's tongue, avoir qch. sur le bout, le bord, de la langue. *El :* Platinum tip, grain *m* de platine. *Cu :* Asparagus tips, pointes d'asperges. **2.** (a) Bout ferré, embout *m* (d'une canne, etc.) ; *Bootm :* bout (de fer, de caoutchouc). (b) *Bill :* Procédé *m* (de la queue). **'tip-tilted,** *a.* À bout relevé ; (nez) retroussé. **'tip-top.** *F :* **I.** *s.* Sommet *m,* faîte *m.* **2.** *a.* De premier ordre ; excellent, extra. That's tip-top! ça c'est tapé ! à la bonne heure !
tip[2], *v.tr.* (tipped [tipt]) Mettre un bout à (un soulier) ; embouter, mettre un embout à (une canne, etc.). **tipped,** *a.* Gold-tipped, silver-tipped, à bout doré, d'argent.
tip[3], *s.* **I.** Pente *f,* inclinaison *f.* **2.** Coup léger ; tape *f.* **3.** (a) Pourboire *m,* gratification *f.* (b) *F :* Don *m* d'argent de poche (à un neveu, etc.). **4.** *Turf : etc :* Tuyau *m.* If you take my tip . . ., si vous m'en croyez. . . . **5.** *Civ.E : etc :* (a) Chantier *m* de versage. Rubbish tip, fosse *f* à ordures. (b) Tas *m,* monceau *m* (de déblais, etc.). **'tip-cart,** *s.* Tombereau *m* (à bascule). **'tip-cat,** *s. Games :* Bâtonnet *m.* **'tip-truck,** *s.* Wagonnet *m,* wagon *m,* à bascule.
tip[4], *v.* (tipped [tipt]) **I.** *v.tr.* (a) To tip (over), renverser (qch.), chavirer, verser (un canot, etc.). (b) To tip (up), soulever (un strapontin) ; faire basculer (une charrette). (c) To tip (out), déverser, décharger. To tip one's passengers into the ditch, verser, renverser, ses passagers dans le fossé. (d) Faire pencher, faire

53

incliner. **To tip the scale(s) at a hundred pounds,** peser tout juste cent livres. **To tip one's hat over one's eyes,** rabattre son chapeau sur ses yeux. **2.** (a) Toucher légèrement, effleurer (qch. du pied). **Tip-and-run raid,** raid de surprise avec fuite précipitée. (b) *P:* Donner, passer, lancer (qch. à qn). (c) Donner un pourboire, une gratification, à (qn); donner la pièce à (un domestique, etc.). **3.** *Turf: etc:* Tuyauter (qn). **II. tip,** *v.i.* (a) To tip (over), se renverser, basculer; (of boat, etc.) chavirer, verser. (b) To tip (up), (of plank, etc.) se soulever, basculer. **'tip-up,** *attrib.a.* (Charrette, cuvette, etc.) à bascule, à renversement. **Tip-up seat,** strapontin m. **tipping[1],** *a.* Basculant, culbutant, à bascule. **tipping[2],** *s.* **I.** (a) Inclinaison f. (b) Tipping (over), renversement m; chavirement m (d'un canot). (c) Basculage m. **2.** (Système m des) pourboires m; distribution f de pourboires. **3.** *Turf:* Tuyautage m.

tippet ['tipet], *s. Cost:* **I.** Pèlerine f. **2.** Écharpe f en fourrure.

tipple[1] [tipl], *s.* Boisson f (alcoolique).

tipple[2], *v.i.* Se livrer à la boisson. **tippling,** *s.* Ivrognerie f.

tippler ['tiplər], *s.* Ivrogne m; *F:* poivrot m.

tipsiness ['tipsinəs], *s.* Ivresse f.

tipstaff, *pl.* **-staffs, -staves** ['tipstɑːf, -stɑːfs, -steːivz], *s. Jur:* Huissier m.

tipster ['tipstər], *s. Turf: etc:* Tuyauteur m.

tipsy ['tipsi], *a.* **I.** Gris, ivre. **To get t.,** se griser. **2.** (Rire, etc.) d'ivrogne. **-ily,** *adv.* D'une voix, avec une démarche, qui accuse l'ivresse. **'tipsy-cake,** *s.* Gâteau m au madère.

tiptoe[1] ['tiptou], *s. & adv.* (On) tiptoe, sur la pointe des pieds. *F:* **To be (up)on the tiptoe of expectation,** être dans l'angoisse de l'attente; attendre fiévreusement qch.

tiptoe[2], *v.i.* Marcher sur la pointe des pieds. **To tiptoe in, out,** entrer, sortir, sur la pointe des pieds.

tirade [ti'reid], *s.* Tirade f. **Tirade of invective,** tirade, bordée f, d'injures. **A violent tirade against s.o.,** une diatribe contre qn.

tire[2] ['taiər]. **I.** *v.tr.* (a) Fatiguer, lasser. (b) To tire s.o. out, (i) épuiser, pomper, qn de fatigue; (ii) excéder qn. **2.** *v.i.* Se fatiguer, se lasser. **To tire of sth.,** se lasser, se fatiguer, de qch. **tired,** *a.* Fatigué. (a) Las, f. lasse. **Tired out, tired to death,** rompu de fatigue; exténué, éreinté, fourbu. (b) (Sleepy) To be tired, être fatigué, avoir sommeil. *F:* **You make me tired,** tu m'ennuies; tu m'embêtes. (c) To be tired of sth., être las de qch. **To get, grow, tired of doing sth.,** se lasser de faire qch.

tire[2], *s. A:* (a) Atours mpl. (b) Coiffure f. **'tire-woman,** *pl.* **-women,** *s.f. A:* Demoiselle, dame, d'atour.

tire[3], *v.tr. A:* Parer. **'tiring-room,** *s. A:* Chambre f d'atours.

tire[4,5], *s. & v.tr. U.S:* = TYRE[1,2].

tiredness ['taiərdnəs], *s.* Lassitude f, fatigue f.

tireless ['taiərləs], *a.* Inlassable, infatigable. **-ly,** *adv.* Infatigablement, inlassablement.

tiresome ['taiərsəm], *a.* **I.** Fatigant, lassant; (discours) fastidieux, ennuyeux. **2.** Exaspérant; (of child) fatigant, assommant. **How tiresome!** quel ennui!

tiro, *pl.* **-o(e)s** ['tairo, -ouz], *s..* Novice mf; commençant, -ante.

'tis [tiz] = *it is.*

tissue ['tisju, 'tiʃju], *s.* **I.** Tissu m (de coton, etc.); étoffe f. (b) *F:* **Tissue of lies,** tissu de

mensonges. **2.** *Biol:* Tissu (musculaire, etc.). **'tissue-paper,** *s.* (a) Papier m de soie. (b) Papier pelure.

tit[1] [tit], *s. Orn:* = TITMOUSE.

tit[2], *s. In the phr.* Tit for tat, un prêté pour un rendu. **To give s.o. tit for tat,** rendre à qn la pareille.

Titan ['taitən], *s. Myth:* Titan m. *Const:* **Titan crane,** grue f titan.

titanic [tai'tanik], *a.* Titanique, titanesque.

tit-bit ['titbit], *s.* Morceau friand; friandise f.

tithe[1] [taːið], *s.* **I.** Dîme f. **2.** Dixième m. *F:* I don't believe a tithe of what he says, je ne crois pas le dixième, le quart, de ce qu'il dit.

tithe[2], *v.tr.* **I.** Payer la dîme de (ses récoltes). **2.** Soumettre (un champ, qn) à la dîme. **tithing,** *s.* (a) Paiement m de la dîme. (b) Prélèvement m de la dîme; levée f de la dîme.

Titian ['tiʃjən]. *Pr.n.m.* Le Titien.

titillate ['titileit], *v.tr.* (a) Titiller, chatouiller. (b) Chatouiller (le palais); émoustiller (les sens).

titillation [titi'leiʃ(ə)n], *s.* (a) Titillation f, chatouillement m. (b) Émoustillement m.

titivate ['titiveit]. **I.** *v.tr.* Faire (qn) beau; attifer, pomponner (qn). **2.** *v.i. & pr.* Se faire beau; faire un brin de toilette.

titlark ['titlɑːrk], *s. Orn:* Pipit m. **Meadow titlark,** farlouse f.

title[1] ['taitl], *s.* **I.** (a) Titre m. **To have a title,** avoir un titre, une qualification. **To deprive s.o. of his title,** dépouiller qn. (b) Titre de noblesse. **Persons of title,** les nobles m; la noblesse. **2.** Titre (d'un livre); intitulé m (d'un journal, d'un acte). *Typ:* **Bastard title,** faux titre. *S.a.* HALF-TITLE. **3.** (a) Titre, droit m. **Title to property,** titre de propriété. **Clear title,** titre incontestable. **To have a title to sth.,** avoir droit, avoir des titres, à qch. *F:* **Titles to fame,** titres de gloire. (b) = TITLE-DEED. **4.** Titre (de l'or). **'title-deed,** *s. Jur:* Titre (constitutif) de propriété. **'title-page,** *s. Typ:* Page f de titre; titre m. **'title-part, -rôle,** *s. Th:* Rôle m qui donne le titre à la pièce.

title[2], *v.tr.* Intituler (un livre, etc.). **titled,** *a.* Titré; *I* noticed several t. people, j'ai remarqué (dans l'assistance) plusieurs personnes titrées.

titmouse, *pl.* **-mice** ['titmaus, -mais], *s. Orn:* Mésange f. **Great titmouse,** (mésange) charbonnière f; mésangère f. **Coal titmouse,** (mésange) petite charbonnière; mésange noire. **Crested titmouse,** mésange huppée.

titrate ['taitreit], *v.tr.* Titrer, doser (une solution).

titter[1] ['titər], *s.* **I.** Rire étouffé. **2.** = GIGGLE[1].

titter[2], *v.i.* **I.** Avoir un petit rire étouffé. **2.** = GIGGLE[2]. **tittering,** *s.* Petits rires.

tittle [titl], *s.* **I.** *A:* Point m. **2.** La moindre partie. **Not one tittle,** pas un iota. **To a tittle,** exactement; trait pour trait.

tittle-tattle[1] ['titltatl], *s.* Potins mpl, cancans mpl, racontars mpl, caquetage m, commérages mpl. **The tittle-tattle of the day,** la chronique scandaleuse du jour.

tittle-tattle[2], *v.i.* Potiner, cancaner.

tittup ['titəp], *v.i.* (Of horse) Aller au petit galop; fringuer.

titubation [titju'beiʃ(ə)n], *s. Med:* Titubation f.

titular ['titjulər], *a.* (a) (Évêque, etc.) titulaire. (b) *Of function, etc.:*) Nominal, -aux. (c) Titular possessions, terres attachées à un titre.

tmesis ['tmiːsis], *s. Gram:* Tmèse f.

to [tu(ː)]. **I.** *prep.* A, à. **I.** (a) They go to church, ils vont à l'église. **What school do you go to?**

à quelle école allez-vous? *He went to France, to Japan, to India*, il est allé en France, au Japon, aux Indes. *She returned home to her family*, elle est rentrée auprès de sa famille. *I am going to the grocer's*, je vais chez l'épicier. *From town to town, from flower to flower*, de ville en ville, de fleur en fleur. *Air-lines to and from the Continent*, lignes aériennes à destination ou en provenance du Continent. (*b*) *The road to London*, la route de Londres. *The road to ruin*, le chemin de la ruine. *It is twenty miles to London*, il y a vingt milles d'ici Londres. **To horse!** à cheval! **2.** (*a*) Vers, à. *To the east*, vers l'est. (*At marine station*) '*To the boat*,' "vers le bateau." *To the right*, à droite. (*b*) *Feet to the fire*, les pieds au feu. **3.** Elbow to elbow, coude à coude. *To fight man to man*, se battre homme à homme. *To clasp s.o. to one's heart*, serrer qn sur son cœur. **4.** (*Of time*) (*a*) **From morning to night**, du matin au soir. **From day to day**, de jour en jour. (*b*) **Ten minutes to six**, six heures moins dix. **5.** (*a*) **Wet to the skin**, trempé jusqu'aux os. *Shaken to the foundations*, ébranlé jusque dans les fondements. *To see s.o. to the end of the street*, accompagner qn jusqu'au bout de la rue. *To this day*, jusqu'à ce jour. *To count up to ten*, compter jusqu'à dix. **Killed to a man**, tués jusqu'au dernier. (*b*) **To a high degree**, à un haut degré. **Generous to a fault**, généreux à l'excès. **Accurate to a milli-metre**, exact à un millimètre près. *A year to the day*, un an jour pour jour. **6.** (*a*) **To this end**, à cet effet, dans ce but. *To come to s.o.'s aid*, venir à l'aide de qn. **To sentence s.o. to death**, condamner qn à mort. (*b*) **To my despair**, à mon grand désespoir. *To the general surprise*, à la surprise de tous. **7.** (*a*) En. **To run to seed**, monter en graine. **To go to ruin**, tomber en ruine. **To put to flight**, mettre en fuite. (*b*) **To take s.o. to wife**, prendre qn pour femme. **8.** *To take wine to one's lunch*, prendre du vin à déjeuner, avec son déjeuner. *To sing sth. to the tune of . . .*, chanter qch. sur l'air de. . . . **9.** *Charles brother to John*, Charles frère de Jean. *Heir to s.o.*, *to an estate*, héritier de qn, d'une propriété. **Ambassador to the King of Sweden**, ambassadeur auprès du roi de Suède. *Secretary to the manager*, secrétaire du directeur. **10.** (*a*) (*Effecting a comparison*) **Superior to**, supérieur à. *That's nothing to what I have seen*, cela n'est rien auprès de, à côté de, ce que j'ai vu. (*b*) *Three is to six as six is to twelve*, trois est à six ce que six est à douze. *Six votes to four*, six voix contre quatre. *Three goals to nil*, trois buts à zéro. *To bet ten to one*, parier dix contre un. *One house to the square mile*, une maison par mille carré. **To the dozen, the dozen**, treize à la douzaine. **11. To all appearances**, selon les apparences. **To write to s.o.'s dictation**, écrire sous la dictée de qn. **To the best of my remembrance**, autant qu'il m'en souvienne. **12.** *Hail to thee!* salut à toi! *To build an altar to s.o.*, ériger un autel à qn. *To drink to s.o.*, boire à la santé de qn. **13.** (*a*) (*Concerning*) *What did he say to my suggestion?* qu'est-ce qu'il a dit de ma proposition? *That's all there is to it*, c'est tout ce qu'il y a à dire. *There's nothing to it*, ça ne vaut pas la peine; cela ne rapporte rien. (*b*) (*On bill*) To repairing boiler . . ., réparations à la chaudière. . . . *To taking out jets . . .*, pour avoir démonté les gicleurs. . . . **14.** (*Used to form the dative*) (*a*) *To give sth. to s.o.*, donner qch. à qn. *The man I gave it to*, l'homme à qui je l'ai donné. *What is that to you?* qu'est-ce que cela vous fait? *What is life to me?* que m'importe la vie? *I said to myself . . .*, je me

suis dit (en moi-même). . . . (*b*) Envers, pour. *Favourable to s.o.*, favorable à qn. *Good to all*, bon pour tous, envers tous. *Kind to me*, aimable à mon égard; aimable pour, envers, moi. (*c*) *Known to the ancients*, connu des anciens. **II. to.** *With the infinitive.* **1.** (*a*) (*Purpose, result*) Pour. *He came to help me*, il est venu pour m'aider. *We must eat (in order) to live*, il faut manger pour vivre. **So to speak**, pour ainsi dire. *I have not done anything to rouse his anger*, je n'ai rien fait pour provoquer sa colère. (*b*) *Happy to do it*, heureux de le faire. *Ready to listen*, prêt à écouter. *Old enough to go to school*, assez âgé pour aller à l'école. *You are foolish to believe that*, vous êtes bien sot de croire cela. *What a queer chap to be a mayor!* quel drôle d'homme pour un maire! **Good to eat**, bon à manger. *Too hot to drink*, trop chaud pour qu'on puisse le boire. (*c*) (i) **To look at her** one would never imagine that . . ., à la voir on ne s'imaginerait pas que. . . . (ii) (*Expressing subsequent fact*) *I woke to find the lamp still burning*, en s'éveillant il trouva la lampe encore allumée. *These times are gone never to return*, ces temps sont passés et ne reviendront plus. **2.** (*a*) *To have a letter to write*, avoir une lettre à écrire. *To have much to do*, avoir beaucoup à faire. *Nothing to speak of*, rien qui vaille la peine qu'on en parle. *There is no one to see us*, il n'y a personne qui puisse nous voir. *He is not a man to forget his friends*, il n'est pas homme à oublier ses amis. *He is not a man to be trusted*, ce n'est pas un homme à qui on puisse se fier. *The first to complain*, le premier à se plaindre. *The third to arrive*, le troisième à venir. *House to be sold*, maison à vendre. *The English Plato is still to be*, un Platon anglais est encore à naître. (*b*) *Tendency to do sth.*, tendance à faire qch. *Desire to do sth.*, désir de faire qch. *This is the time to do it*, c'est le moment de le faire. **3.** *To be or not to be* . . ., être ou ne pas être. . . . *To lie is shameful, it is shameful to lie*, il est honteux de mentir. **4.** *I wish him to do it*, je veux qu'il le fasse. *You would like it to be true*, vous voudriez bien que cela soit vrai. **5.** (*Expressing futurity, obligation*) (*In headline*) *A hundred employees to go*, cent employés vont recevoir leur congé. **6.** (*With ellipsis of verb*) *I did not want to look*, I 'had to, je ne voulais pas regarder mais il le fallut bien, mais je ne pus m'en défendre. *Take it; it would be absurd not to*, prenez-le; ce serait absurde de ne pas le faire, de manquer l'occasion. *You ought to*, vous le devriez. *I want to*, je voudrais bien. **III. to**, *adv.* (*Stressed*) **1.** *Ship moored head to* (= *to the wind*), navire amarré vent debout. **To put the horses to** (= *to the carriage*), atteler les chevaux. **To come to** (= *to one's senses*), reprendre connaissance. **2. To and fro.** *To go to and fro*, aller et venir. *The busy hurrying to and fro*, le va-et-vient affairé. *Two journeys to and fro*, deux voyages d'aller et retour. *Mec.E:* **To-and-fro movement**, mouvement *m* de va-et-vient. **to-'be**, *s.* **The to-be**, l'avenir *m*. **to-'do**, *s.* *F:* Remue-ménage *m.* **To make a to-do**, faire des histoires, des chichis. **What a to-do!** quelle affaire!

toad [toud], *s.* **1.** (*a*) Crapaud *m.* *F:* **To treat s.o. like a toad under the harrow**, fouler qn aux pieds. (*b*) *P:* Type répugnant; sale type. **2.** *Cu:* **Toad in the hole**, morceau de viande cuit dans la pâte. **'toad-eater**, *s.* Patelineur *m*, flagorneur *m*; lécheur *m* de bottes. **'toad-flax**, *s.* *Bot:* Linaire *f.* **'toad-spit**, *s.* Crachat *m* de coucou.

toadstone ['toudstoun], *s.* Crapaudine *f.*

toadstool ['toudstu:l], *s.* Champignon vénéneux.
toady[1] ['toudi], *s.* = TOAD-EATER.
toady[2], *v.tr. & i.* (toadied) To toady (to) s.o., lécher les bottes à qn; flagorner qn.
toadyism ['toudiizm], *s.* Flagornerie *f.*
toast[1] [toust], *s.* **I.** Pain grillé. **Piece, round, of toast,** rôtie *f.* Anchovies on toast, anchois sur canapé. *P:* To have s.o. on tcast, avoir qn à sa merci; tenir qn. **2.** (*a*) (i) Personne à qui on porte un toast; *esp.* (ii) *Hist:* beauté *f* à la mode. (*b*) Toast *m.* **To give, propose, a toast,** porter un toast; boire à la santé de qn. **'toast-list,** *s.* Liste *f* des toasts (à un banquet). **'toast-master,** *s.* Annonceur *m* des toasts. **'toast-rack,** *s.* Porte-rôties *m inv.* **'toast-water,** *s.* Eau panée.
toast[2]. **I.** *v.tr.* (*a*) Rôtir, griller (du pain). *F:* To toast one's feet (before the fire), se chauffer les pieds. (*b*) To toast s.o., porter un toast à (la santé de) qn; boire à la santé de qn. **2.** *v.i.* Rôtir, griller. **'toasting-fork,** *s.* Fourchette *f* à rôtir le pain; grille-pain *m inv.*
toaster ['toustər], *s.* Grille-pain *m inv.*
tobacco, *pl.* -os [to'bako, -ouz], *s.* Tabac *m* (à fumer). **Cut tobacco,** tabac haché. **to'bacco-heart,** *s.* Maladie de cœur due à l'abus du tabac. **to'bacco-jar,** *s.* Pot *m* à tabac. **to'bacco-pouch,** *s.* Blague *f* à tabac. **to'bacco-shop,** *s.* Débit *m* de tabac. **to'bacco-stopper,** *s.* Bourre-pipe *m.*
tobacconist [to'bakonist], *s.* Marchand *m* de tabac. **Tobacconist's (shop),** débit *m* de tabac.
toboggan[1] [to'bogan], *s.* Toboggan *m.* **to'boggan-run, -shoot,** *s.* Piste *f* de toboggan.
toboggan[2], *v.i.* Faire du toboggan.
tobogganer [to'bogonər], *s.* Tobogganniste *mf;* lugeur, -euse.
Toby ['toubi]. **I.** *Pr.n.m.* Tobie. **2.** *s.* Pot *m* à bière (en forme de gros bonhomme à tricorne). **3.** Chien (vivant) du guignol anglais.
toc [tok], *s. Mil. Tg. & Tp:* La lettre T. **Toc H** [tok'eitʃ], (lettres initiales de *Talbot House*) association pour l'étude des problèmes religieux et sociaux.
tocsin ['toksin], *s.* Tocsin *m.*
to-day [tu'dei], *adv. & s.* Aujourd'hui (*m*). **To-day week,** d'aujourd'hui en huit. *To-day's paper,* le journal d'aujourd'hui, du jour. *F:* **He is here to-day and gone to-morrow,** il est comme l'oiseau sur la branche.
toddle[1] [todl], *s.* **I.** Allure chancelante (d'un enfant). **2.** *F:* Petite promenade.
toddle[2], *v.i.* **I.** Marcher à petits pas chancelants. **2.** Marcher à petits pas; trottiner. To toddle in, out, entrer, sortir, à petits pas. *After toddling round to see old friends* . . ., après ses petites trotteries chez de vieux amis. . . . **To toddle off,** *F:* se trotter. *F:* **I must be toddling,** il faut que je me trotte.
toddler ['todlər], *s.* Enfant qui commence à marcher. **The toddlers,** les tout petits.
toddy ['todi], *s.* **I.** Toddy *m* (de palme). **2.** Grog chaud.
toe[1] [tou], *s.* **I.** Orteil *m;* doigt *m* de pied. **Great toe, big toe,** gros orteil. **Little toe,** petit orteil. *To come down on (the points of) one's toes,* retomber sur la pointe des pieds. **To stand on the tips of one's toes,** se dresser sur la pointe des pieds. *P:* **To turn up one's toes,** mourir. **2.** (*a*) Bout *m,* pointe *f* (de soulier, chaussette, etc.). (*b*) *Farr:* Pince *f* (de sabot ou de fer à cheval). (*c*) *Golf:* Pointe (de la crosse). **3.** (*a*) *Mch:* Touche *f* (de distribution Corliss). (*b*) Ergot (actionné par une

came). **4.** Éperon *m,* saillie *f* (d'un arc-boutant). **'toe-cap,** *s.* *Bootm:* Bout rapporté. **'toe-clip,** *s.* *Cy:* Cale-pied(s) *m inv.* **'toe-nail,** *s.* Ongle *m* d'orteil.
toe[2], *v.tr.* **I.** To toe a sock, (i) tricoter, (ii) refaire, la pointe d'une chaussette. **To toe a shoe,** mettre ou remettre un bout à un soulier. **2.** To toe the line, the mark, (i) s'aligner; (ii) *F:* s'aligner avec son parti; se conformer au mot d'ordre. **3.** *F:* To toe and heel it, danser. **4.** (*a*) *Fb:* Botter (le ballon) avec la pointe du pied. (*b*) *F:* Enlever le ballon à (qn); botter (qn). **5.** *Golf:* Frapper (la balle) avec la pointe de la crosse. **toed,** *a.* **I.** Two-toed, three-toed, à deux, trois, orteils. **2.** (Soulier) à bout rapporté.
toff [tof], *s.* *P:* Dandy *m,* aristo *m.* **The toffs,** la haute gomme; les gens huppés.
toff[2], *v.tr.* *F:* To toff oneself up, out, se faire beau.
toffee ['tofi], *s.* Caramel *m* au beurre. **Almond toffee, walnut toffee,** caramel aux amandes, aux noix.
tog [tog], *v.tr. & i.* (togged) *F:* Attifer, habiller. **To tog (oneself) up, out,** se faire beau; s'attifer. **To get togged out anew,** renouveler son trousseau; *F:* se requinquer.
toga ['touga], *s. Rom.Ant:* Toge *f.*
together [tu'geðər], *adv.* Ensemble. (*a*) **To go together, belong together,** aller ensemble. **We stand or fall together,** nous sommes tous solidaires. (*Of ships*) **To sail together,** naviguer de conserve. **Together with,** avec. (*b*) **To gather together,** (i) réunir, rassembler; (ii) se réunir, se rassembler. **To strike two things together,** frapper deux choses l'une contre l'autre. **To bring together,** rassembler, réunir. (*c*) **To act together,** agir de concert. **All together,** tous à la fois. *Art: F:* **To pose for the 'all together,'** poser pour l'ensemble *m.* (*d*) **For months together,** pendant des mois entiers.
toggle [togl], *s.* **I.** *Nau:* Cabillot *m* (d'amarrage). **2.** (*a*) Barrette *f* (de chaîne de montre). (*b*) **Brake toggle,** clef *f* de frein. (*c*) **Halter-rope toggle,** billot *m* de longe de licou. **'toggle-joint,** *s.* *Mec.E:* Rotule *f;* (joint *m* à) genou *m.* **'toggle-lever,** *s.* Levier articulé; *I.C.E:* levier-bascule *m* (du carburateur). **'toggle-pin,** *s.* ═ TOGGLE I.
Togoland ['tougoland]. *Pr.n. Geog:* Le Togo.
togs [togz], *s.pl.* *F:* Nippes *f,* frusques *f.* *Nau:* **Harbour togs, long togs,** frusques d'escale.
toil[1] [toil], *s.* Travail dur, pénible; labeur *m,* peine *f.* **After great toil,** à force de labeur. **'toil-worn,** *a.* Usé par le travail.
toil[2], *v.i.* Travailler, peiner; se donner du mal. **To toil and moil,** peiner; travailler dur. **To toil up a hill,** gravir péniblement une colline.
toiler ['toilər], *s.* Travailleur, -euse.
toilet ['toilet], *s.* **I.** Toilette *f.* *To make one's t.,* faire sa toilette. **2.** (*In hotels, etc.*) Les toilettes, les cabinets *m.* **'toilet-case,** *s.* Nécessaire *m* de toilette. **'toilet-paper,** *s.* Papier *m* hygiénique. **'toilet-roll,** *s.* Rouleau *m* de papier hygiénique. **'toilet-set, -service,** *s.* Garniture *f* de toilette. **'toilet-soap,** *s.* Savon *m* de toilette. **'toilet-table,** *s.* Table *f* de toilette.
toils [toilz], *s.pl.* *Ven:* Filet *m,* lacs *m.* **To be taken, get caught, in the toils,** se laisser prendre au filet; se laisser prendre au piège. **Caught in his own toils,** pris dans ses propres lacets.
toilsome ['toilsəm], *a.* Pénible, fatigant.
token ['touk(ə)n], *s.* **I.** Signe *m,* marque *f,* témoignage *m* (d'amitié, de respect, etc.). **token of . . ., as a token of . . .,** en signe

de . . ., en témoignage de . . ., comme marque de. . . . **It gives token of intelligence,** cela annonce, indique, de l'intelligence. **By the token** . . ., de plus. . . . *F:* **More by token** . . ., et la preuve c'est que. . . . **Token payment,** paiement symbolique. **2.** (*a*) *To show a glove for a t.*, montrer un gant comme signe. *Love* **token,** gage *m* d'amour. (*b*) Jeton *m.* (*c*) *Book* **tokens,** bons *m* de livres. **'token-money,** *s.* Monnaie *f* fiduciaire.

tolbooth ['toulbuːθ], *s. Scot: A:* (*a*) Hôtel *m* de ville. (*b*) Prison *f.*

told [tould]. *See* TELL.

Toledo [tɔ'liːdo]. **I.** *Pr.n.* Tolède. **2.** *s. A:* Lame *f* de Tolède.

tolerable ['tɔlərəbl], *a.* (*a*) Tolérable, supportable. (*b*) Passable; assez bon. *They enjoy a t. amount of freedom,* ils jouissent d'une assez grande liberté. **-ably,** *adv.* **I.** Tolérablement. **2.** Passablement. **It is tolerably certain that** . . ., il est à peu près certain que. . . .

tolerance ['tɔlərəns], *s.* **I.** *Med:* Tolérance *f* (d'une drogue, d'un remède). **2.** Tolérance (religieuse, etc.). *To show great t.,* faire preuve de beaucoup de tolérance, d'une grande indulgence. **3.** *Mec.E: T. of two thousandths,* tolérance de deux millièmes (de pouce).

tolerant ['tɔlərənt], *a.* Tolérant (*of*, à l'égard de).

tolerate ['tɔləreit], *v.tr.* Tolérer, supporter (la douleur, la contradiction).

toleration [tɔlə'reiʃ(ə)n], *s.* Tolérance *f* (en matière de religion).

toll[1] [toul], *s.* **I.** (*a*) Droit *m* de passage; péage *m.* *Town toll,* octroi *m.* **To pay toll,** payer un droit de passage. **To pay the toll,** acquitter le péage. (*b*) Droit de place (au marché). **2. Rent takes heavy toll of one's income,** le loyer mange une grande partie de nos revenus. **The toll of the roads,** la mortalité sur les routes. **'tcll-bar,** *s.* Barrière *f* (de péage). **'toll-booth,** *s. Scot:* = TOLBOOTH. **'toll-bridge,** *s.* Pont *m* à péage. **'toll-call,** *s. Tp:* Conversation interurbaine (entre villes peu éloignées). **'toll-collector,** *s.* Péager, -ère. **'toll-gate,** *s.* = TOLL-BAR. **'tollhouse,** *s.* Bureau *m* de péage; péage *m.* **'toll-keeper,** *s.* Péager, -ère.

toll[2], *s,* Tintement *m,* son *m* (de cloche).

toll[3]. **I.** *v.tr.* Tinter, sonner (une cloche). *Abs.* **To toll for the dead,** sonner pour les morts. **To toll s.o.'s death,** sonner le glas (pour la mort de qn). **2.** *v.i.* (*Of bell*) (*a*) Tinter, sonner. (*b*) Sonner le glas. **tolling,** *s.* (*a*) Tintement *m* (de cloche). (*b*) Glas *m.*

Tom [tɔm]. **I.** *Pr.n.m.* (*Dim. of Thomas*) Thomas. *F:* **Any Tom, Dick, or Harry,** tout le monde; le premier venu. **2. Tom cat,** *F:* **a tom,** matou *m.* **tom-'noddy,** *s. F:* Dadais *m,* nigaud *m.* **Tom 'Thumb.** *Pr.n.m.* Le petit Poucet; Tom Pouce. **tom-'tit,** *s. Orn:* Mésange azurée.

tomahawk[1] ['tɔməhɔːk], *s.* Hache *f* de guerre (des Peaux-Rouges); tomahawk *m.* *F:* **To bury the tomahawk,** enterrer la hache de guerre.

tomahawk[2], *v.tr.* Frapper (qn) avec un tomahawk; assommer (qn).

tomato, *pl.* -oes [tə'maːto, -ouz], *s.* Tomate *f.* **Tomato sauce,** sauce *f* tomate.

tomb [tuːm], *s.* Tombe *f;* (*with monument*) tombeau *m.*

tomboy ['tɔmbɔi], *s.* Fillette *f* d'allures gaı çonnières. **She's a regular tomboy,** c'est un garçon manqué; elle est très diable.

tombstone ['tuːmstoun], *s.* Pierre tombale.

tome [toum], *s.* Tome *m;* gros volume.

tomfool[1] [tɔm'fuːl]. **I.** *s.* Nigaud *m,* serin *m.*

2. *Attrib.a.* Stupide, idiot. *T. scheme,* projet insensé.

tomfool[2], *v.i.* Faire, dire, des sottises; *F:* faire l'idiot.

tomfoolery [tɔm'fuːləri], *s.* Nigauderie(s) *f*(*pl*): bouffonnerie(s) *f*(*pl*).

Tommy ['tɔmi]. **I.** *Pr.n.m.* (*Dim. of Thomas*) Thomas. **2.** *Pr.n. F:* **Tommy Atkins,** sobriquet du soldat anglais. *s.* **A tommy,** un simple soldat. **3.** *s. P:* (*a*) Pain *m,* mangeaille *f.* (*b*) *Ind:* Provisions fournies par l'économat de l'usine; paiement *m* en nature. (*c*) = TOMMY-SHOP. **4.** *s. Tls:* = TOMMY-BAR. **'tommy-bar,** *s. Tls:* **I.** Broche *f* (à visser). **2.** (*Crow-bar*) Pince *f.* **'tommy-nut,** *s.* Écrou *m* à trous (se vissant à la broche). **tommy-'rot,** *s. F:* Bêtises *fpl,* inepties *fpl.* **'tommy-shop,** *s. Ind:* Cantine *f* (dirigée par l'économat de l'usine).

to-morrow [tu'mɔro, -ou], *adv. & s.* Demain (*m*). *To-m. morning,* demain matin. **To-morrow week,·** de demain en huit. *The day after to-m.,* aprèsdemain. **Event without a to-morrow,** événement sans lendemain.

tompion ['tɔmpiən], *s.* = TAMPION.

tomtom ['tɔmtɔm], *s.* Tam-tam *m.*

ton [tʌn], *s. Meas:* **I.** Tonne *f.* **Long ton, gross ton** (*of* 2240 *lb.*), tonne forte. **Short ton, net ton** (*of* 2000 *lb.*), tonne courte. **Metric ton** (*of* 1000 *kg.* or 2204.6 *lb.*), tonne métrique. *F:* **There's tons of it,** il y en a des tas. **2.** *Nau:* (*a*) Tonneau *m* (de jauge); tonne (de 100 pieds cubes). **Per net register ton,** par tonne de jauge nette. (*b*) **Measurement ton, measured ton,** tonne d'arrimage, d'encombrement (de 40 pieds cubes).

tonal ['toun(ə)l], *a. Ac: Mus:* Tonal, -aux.

tonality [to'naliti], *s.* Tonalité *f.*

tone[1] [toun], *s.* **I.** Son *m,* accent *m;* timbre *m* (de la voix, d'une cloche). **Tone quality,** qualité *f* de la note (d'un instrument). **2.** (*a*) Ton *m,* voix *f. In an impatient t.,* d'un ton d'impatience. *F:* **To alter one's tone,** changer de ton, de note. (*b*) **To give a serious tone to a discussion,** donner un ton sérieux à une discussion. *Fin:* **The prevailing tone,** la tendance générale. **The tone of the market,** la tenue, l'allure *f,* du marché. (*c*) *Med:* Tonicité *f* (des muscles). **Want of tone,** atonie *f.* (*Of pers.*) **To lose tone,** se déprimer. **To recover tone,** se retremper. **3.** *Mus: Ac:* Ton. **Whole tone,** ton entier. **4.** Ton, nuance *f* (d'une couleur). *Warm tones,* tons chauds. *S.a.* HALF-TONE. **5.** *Ling:* Ton; accent *m* tonique. **'tone-arm,** *s.* Bras *m* acoustique (d'un phonographe). **'tone-poem,** *s. Mus:* Poème *m* symphonique.

tone[2]. **I.** *v.tr.* (*a*) Régler la tonalité (d'un instrument). (*b*) Modifier la tonalité (d'un tableau). (*c*) *Phot:* Virer (une épreuve). (*d*) Tonifier (la peau, etc.). **2.** *v.i.* **To tone (in) with sth.,** s'harmoniser avec qch. **tone down. I.** *v.tr.* Adoucir, atténuer (une expression, un contraste, une couleur). **2.** *v.i.* S'adoucir; le prendre sur un ton plus doux. **tone up. I.** *v.tr.* Tonifier (le système nerveux); retremper, *F:* remonter (qn). **2.** *v.i.* Se tonifier. **toned,** *a.* **Low-toned, high-toned,** à ton bas, élevé. *Low-toned picture,* tableau dans les tonalités basses. *Low-toned conversation,* conversation à voix basse. **Fulltoned voice,** voix grave. **toning,** *s. Phot:* Virage *m.* **Toning-bath,** bain de virage.

toneless ['tounləs], *a.* **I.** (*Couleur*) sans éclat. **2.** (Personne, voix) veule; (voix) blanche, atone.

tonga[1] ['tɔŋgə], *s.* Charrette légère à deux roues (en usage aux Indes).

Tonga². *Pr.n.* The Tonga Islands, l'archipel *m* de Tonga ; les îles *f* des Amis.

tongs [tɔŋz], *s.pl.* **I**. (Fire-)tongs, pincettes *f*. **2**. *Ind :* Pince(s) *f*, tenailles *fpl*.

tongue¹ [tʌŋ], *s.* **I**. Langue *f*. (*a*) To put out one's tongue, montrer, tirer, la langue (*at s.o.*, à qn). (*b*) To have a ready, a glib, tongue, avoir la langue bien pendue. To keep a watch on one's tongue, surveiller sa langue. To curb, bridle, one's tongue, tenir sa langue ; mesurer ses paroles ; se retenir (de parler). To find one's tongue again, retrouver la parole. *F :* To keep a civil tongue in one's head, rester courtois. *To* compliment *s.o.* with one's tongue in one's cheek, faire des compliments à qn par moquerie, en blaguant. *He continually has his t. in his cheek*, il ne fait que blaguer. (*Of hounds*) To give tongue, donner de la voix. **2**. Langue, idiome *m* (d'un peuple). The German tongue, la langue allemande. The gift of tongues, le don des langues. **3**. Langue, languette *f* (de terre) ; langue, dard *m* (de feu) ; patte *f*, languette (de soulier) ; battant *m* (de cloche) ; ardillon *m* (de boucle) ; soie *f* (de couteau, de lime). *Mus :* Languette, anche *f* (de hautbois). *Carp :* Languette de bois. **'tongue-rail**, *s.* *Rail :* Aiguille *f*. **'tongue-tied**, *a.* Qui a la langue liée. **I**. Muet, -ette (d'étonnement, etc.) ; interdit. **2**. Engagé au silence. **'tongue-twister**, *s.* *F :* Mot *m* ou phrase *f* difficile à prononcer.

tongue², *v.tr.* (*a*) *Carp :* Langueter (le bord d'une planche). *S.a.* GROOVE². (*b*) *Mus :* To tongue a passage (*on the flute, etc.*), détacher les notes d'un passage. **tongued**, *a.* A langue, à languette.

tonic ['tɔnik]. **I**. *a.* (*a*) *Med :* Tonique, remontant, réconfortant. (*b*) *Gram :* (Accent) tonique. (*c*) *Mus :* (Note) tonique. (*d*) *Med :* Tonic spasm, convulsion *f* tonique. **2**. *s.* (*a*) *Med :* Tonique *m*, reconstituant *m*, fortifiant *m*. *F :* (*Of news, etc.*) To act as a tonic on s.o., réconforter qn ; remonter qn. (*b*) *Mus :* Tonique *f*.

tonicity [to'nisiti], *s.* Tonicité *f*.

to-night [tu'nait], *adv. & s.* Cette nuit ; ce soir.

Tonka ['tɔŋka], *s.* Tonka (bean), tonka *f*.

Tonkin [tɔŋ'kin], **Tongking** [tɔŋ'kiŋ]. *Pr.n.* Le Tonkin.

tonnage ['tʌnedʒ], *s.* **I**. *Nau :* Tonnage *m*, jauge *f*. Register(ed) tonnage, tonnage enregistré ; jauge nette. Gross tonnage, tonnage brut. **2**. Tonnage (d'un port, d'un pays).

tonsil ['tɔnsil], *s.* Amygdale *f*. *Med :* Enlarged tonsils, hypertrophie *f* des amygdales.

tonsillitis [tɔnsi'laitis], *s.* *Med :* Angine *f* (tonsillaire) ; amygdalite *f*.

tonsorial [tɔn'sɔːriəl], *a.* *F : Hum :* De barbier.

tonsure¹ ['tɔnʃər], *s.* Tonsure *f*.

tonsure², *v.tr.* Tonsurer.

tontine [tɔn'tiːn], *s.* *Ins :* Tontine *f*.

tonus ['tounəs], *s.* *Med :* **I**. Tonicité *f*, tonus *m*. **2**. Convulsion *f* tonique.

Tony¹ ['touni]. *Pr.n.m.* (*Dim. of Antony*) Antoine.

tony², *a.* *F :* Dans le ton ; chic, élégant.

too [tuː], *adv.* **I**. Trop, par trop. *Too difficult a job*, un travail (par) trop difficile. Too much money, trop d'argent. To work too much, too little, travailler trop, trop peu. Ten shillings too much, dix shillings de trop. The task is too much for me, la tâche est au-dessus de mes forces. He was too much, *F :* one too many, for me, il était trop fort pour moi. *The hole was too narrow for a rat to come in by*, le trou était trop étroit

pour qu'un rat entrât par là. *I know him all too well*, je ne le connais que trop. **2**. (*Also*) Aussi ; également. *I too want some*, il m'en faut également ; moi aussi il m'en faut. **3**. (*Moreover*) D'ailleurs ; de plus ; en outre. *The prisoner, too, inspired little sympathy*, le prisonnier, d'ailleurs, inspirait peu de sympathie.

took [tuk]. *See* TAKE.

tool¹ [tuːl], *s.* **I**. Outil *m* ; instrument *m*, ustensile *m*. Garden tools, gardening tools, instruments, ustensiles, de jardinage. A bad workman always finds fault with his tools, à méchant ouvrier point de bon outil. **2**. *F :* Instrument, créature *f*. To make a tool of s.o., se servir de qn (dans un but intéressé). *He was a mere t. in their hands*, il était devenu leur créature. **'tool-bag**, *s.* Sac *m* à outils ; (*of car, etc.*) sacoche *f*. **'tool-basket**, *s.* Cabas *m*. **'tool-box**, **-chest**, *s.* Coffre *m* à outils. **'tool-holder**, *s.* Porte-outil(s) *m inv*. **'tool-outfit**, *s.* Outillage *m*. **'tool-rest**, *s.* Support *m* d'outil ; porte-outil(s) *m inv* (de tour).

tool², *v.tr.* (*a*) *Bookb :* Ciseler, dorer (une tranche, une reliure). (*b*) *Stonew :* Bretteler (une pierre). (*c*) Usiner, travailler (une pièce venue de fonte). **2**. *F :* Conduire (une voiture). *Abs.* To tool along, rouler. **tooling**, *s.* **I**. (*a*) Ciselage *m*. (*b*) Usinage *m*. **2**. *Bookb :* Ciselure *f*, dorure *f* (du dos ou des plats). Blind tooling, dorure à froid. Gold tooling, dorure à chaud.

toot¹ [tuːt], *s.* **I**. Son *m*, appel *m*, de clairon, etc. **2**. *Nau :* Coup *m* de sirène. *Aut :* Coup de trompe, de klaxon ; cornement *m*.

toot². **I**. *v.tr.* *F :* To toot a horn, a trumpet, sonner du cor, de la trompette. *Aut :* To toot the horn, corner ; donner un coup de klaxon. **2**. *v.i.* (*Of pers.*) Sonner du cor. *Aut :* Corner ; avertir. To toot on the trumpet, sonner de la trompette.

tooth¹, *pl.* **teeth** [tuːθ, tiːθ], *s.* **I**. Dent *f*. Second teeth, dentition définitive. Front teeth, dents de devant. A fine set of teeth, une belle denture. False teeth, fausse dent. Set of (false) teeth, dentier *m*, *F :* râtelier *m*. To cut one's teeth, faire, percer, ses dents. *He has lost a few front teeth, F :* il est brèche-dent. To have a tooth out, se faire arracher une dent. To knock a tooth out of s.o.'s mouth, faire sauter une dent à qn ; édenter qn. *F :* To cast, throw, sth. in s.o.'s teeth, reprocher qch. à qn. In the teeth of all opposition, malgré, en dépit de, toute opposition. *F :* To show one's teeth, montrer les dents. Armed to the teeth, armé jusqu'aux dents. To fight tooth and nail, se battre avec acharnement. *He went at it t. and nail*, il y allait de toutes ses forces. To set one's teeth, serrer les dents. To say sth. between one's teeth, grommeler qch. entre ses dents. To be long in the tooth, n'être plus jeune. He has a dainty tooth, c'est une fine bouche. **2**. Dent (de scie, de peigne, de fourche) ; dent, alluchon *m* (de roue d'engrenage). The teeth of a wheel, la denture. Pin teeth, denture à fuseaux. *To break the teeth of a comb*, édenter un peigne. **3**. *Const :* = TOOTHING-STONE. **4**. Grain *m* (du papier). **'tooth-brush**, *s.* Brosse *f* à dents. **'tooth-like**, *a.* Dentiforme. **'tooth-paste**, *s.* Pâte *f* dentifrice. **'tooth-pick**, *s.* Cure-dents *m inv*. **'tooth-powder**, *s.* Poudre *f* dentifrice.

tooth². **I**. *v.tr.* (*a*) Denter, créneler. (*b*) Bretteler (une pierre). **2**. *v.i.* (*Of cog-wheels*) S'engrener. **toothed**, *a.* **I**. Toothed wheel, roue dentée ; roue d'engrenage. Toothed plate (*of safety razor, etc.*), peigne *m*. **2**. *Bot :* Dentelé. **3**. White-

toothed, aux dents blanches. **Broken-toothed,** édenté. **toothing,** s. (a) Dents fpl (d'une roue); crénelage m. (b) Const: Arrachement m, harpes fpl. (c) Stonew: Bretture f. **'toothingstone,** s. Const: Pierre f d'attente, d'arrachement; harpe f.

toothache ['tu:θeik], s. Mal m de dents. **To have toothache,** avoir mal aux dents.

toothful ['tu:θful], s. F: Goutte f (de vin, etc.).

toothless ['tu:θləs], a. Sans dents; édenté.

toothsome ['tu:θsəm], a. Savoureux; agréable au goût. **Toothsome morsel,** morceau friand, succulent.

tootle¹ [tu:tl], v.i. Hum: To tootle on the flute, flûter; seriner un air de flûte.

tootle², v.i. Aut: F: To tootle along, aller son petit bonhomme de chemin.

top¹ [tɔp]. I. s. **1.** Haut m, sommet m, cime f, faîte m (d'une montagne, d'un arbre); haut (de la tête). **At the top of the tree,** en haut de l'arbre. **From top to bottom,** de haut en bas; de fond en comble. **From top to toe,** de la tête aux pieds; de pied en cap. **To put the best apples on top,** mettre les plus belles pommes sur le dessus du panier. **To come out on top,** avoir le dessus. **We are on top,** nous avons le dessus. F: **One thing happens on top of another,** les événements se précipitent. **To go to bed on top of one's supper,** se coucher sitôt dîné. **On top of it all** he wanted . . ., en sus de tout cela il a voulu. . . . Mil: **To go over the top,** franchir le parapet; monter à l'assaut. **2.** Surface f (de l'eau, de la terre); dessus m (d'une table, etc.); impériale f (d'un tramway, etc.). **To climb on top,** monter à l'impériale. **Oil always comes to the top,** l'huile surnage toujours. **3.** Dessus (d'un soulier); revers m (d'une botte, d'un bas); scion m (d'une canne à pêche); capote f (d'une voiture). **4.** Tête f (de page, etc.). Bookb: **Gilt top,** tête dorée. **5.** Haut bout (de la table). **The top of the street,** le haut de la rue. Sch: **To be at the top of the form,** être à la tête de la classe. **6. To shout at the top of one's voice,** crier à tue-tête, à pleine gorge. **I was feeling on top of my form,** je me sentais tout à fait en train, en pleine forme. **To enjoy oneself to the top of one's bent,** s'amuser tout son soûl. Aut: F: **To climb a hill on top,** prendre une montée en prise directe. (Cf. TOPGEAR 2.) Nau: **The top of the flood, of the tide,** le haut de l'eau; l'étale m du flot. **7.** Bot: **Flowering top,** sommité fleurie. Hort: **Turnip tops, carrot tops,** fanes f de navets, de carottes. **8.** Nau: Hune f. **Main top,** grand'hune f. **Fore top,** hune de misaine. Navy: **Director top,** hune de télépointage. **II. top,** attrib.a. **1.** Supérieur; du dessus, du haut, d'en haut. **The top stones,** les pierres de faîte (d'un mur). **The top floor,** le plus haut étage; le dernier étage. **Top stair,** dernière marche (en montant). **A top garment,** un vêtement de dessus. Cu: **Top ribs** (of beef), plat m de côtes; côtes plates. S.a. HAT. **2.** Premier; principal, -aux. Sch: **The top boy,** le premier de la classe. **'top-'boots,** s.pl. Bottes f à revers. **'top-'coat,** s. Pardessus m. **top 'dog,** s. F: Vainqueur m. **To be top dog,** avoir le dessus. **top-'dressing,** s. Agr: Fumure f en surface. **'top-end,** s. Haut bout (de la table, etc.). Bot: **Top-end shoot,** pousse terminale. **'top-gear,** s. **1.** Nau: Manœuvres hautes. **2.** Aut: **Top-'gear,** prise directe. **'top-'hamper,** s. Superstructure f (d'un pont, etc.). Nau: Fardage m. **'top-'hatted,** a. En chapeau haut de forme. **'top-'heavy,** a. Trop lourd du haut; peu stable. (Of ship) Trop

chargé dans les hauts. **top-'hole,** a. P: Épatant, chic; excellent. **We had a top-hole time,** on s'est joliment amusé. **'top-notch,** attrib.a. P: **The top-notch people of Paris society,** le gratin de la société parisienne. **'top-'note,** s. Plus haute note (d'un registre). **The top-notes,** les notes hautes. **'top-'sawyer,** s. **1.** Scieur m de long de dessus. **2.** Chef m (d'une entreprise, etc.); un personnage. **top 'story,** s. Dernier étage.

top², v.tr. (topped [tɔpt]) **1.** Écimer, élaguer, étêter (un arbre). **2.** (a) Surmonter, couronner, coiffer (with, de). **A statue tops the column,** une statue surmonte la colonne. (b) **He topped off his dinner with a cup of coffee,** il a couronné son dîner d'une tasse de café. **And to top it all** . . ., et pour comble. . . . **3.** Dépasser, surpasser. **To top sth. in height,** dépasser qch. en hauteur. **The takings have topped a thousand pounds,** les recettes dépassent mille livres. **To top s.o. by a head,** dépasser qn de la tête. **4. To top a hill,** atteindre le sommet d'une colline. **The squadron topped the ridge,** l'escadron franchit l'arête. **5. To top a list, a class,** être à la tête d'une liste, de la classe. **6.** Golf: Calotter, topper (la balle). **top up,** v.tr. Remplir (complètement). **2.** (a) Reniveler (un accumulateur); ramener (l'électrolyte) à niveau. Aer: Renflouer (un ballon). **-topped,** a. **Cloud-topped peaks,** sommets couronnés de nuages. **Ivory-topped walking stick,** canne à pomme d'ivoire. **topping,** a. P: Excellent, chic. **A topping idea,** une riche idée. **That's topping!** ça c'est fameux! **A topping dinner,** un dîner à la hauteur. **Topping weather,** temps superbe. **We had a topping time,** on s'est fameusement amusé. **'topping-lift,** s. Nau: Balancine f, cartahu m.

top³, s. (Spinning, peg) top, toupie f. **To spin a top,** faire aller une toupie.

topaz ['toupaz], s. Topaze f. **Pink topaz,** topaze brûlée.

tope [toup], v.i. F: Boire, riboter.

topee [to'pi:], s. = TOPI.

toper ['toupər], s. F: Ivrogne m, buveur m.

topgallant [top'galənt], a. & s. Nau: (Voile f, mât m) de perroquet.

topi [to'pi:], s. Casque colonial.

topic ['tɔpik], s. Matière f (d'un écrit, d'une discussion); sujet m, thème m (de conversation). **Topics of the day,** questions f d'actualité.

topical ['tɔpik(ə)l], a. **1.** Qui se rapporte au lieu; topique; local, -aux. **2. Topical allusion,** allusion aux événements du jour. **Topical song,** chanson d'actualités. W.Tel: **Topical talk,** journal parlé. **Topical film,** film d'actualités.

topknot ['tɔpnɔt], s. **1.** A.Cost: Fontange f. **2.** (a) Huppe f (d'un oiseau). (b) Chignon (porté sur le front); toupillon m.

topman, pl. **-men** ['tɔpmən, -men], s.m. **1.** Nau: Gabier m. **2.** = TOP-SAWYER.

topmast ['tɔpmɑːst], s. Mât m de hune; mât de flèche.

topmost ['tɔpmoust], a. Le plus haut; le plus élevé. **Having reached the t. height** . ., arrivé au faîte. . .

topographer [to'pɔgrəfər], s. Topographe m.

topography [to'pɔgrəfi], s. Topographie f.

topper ['tɔpər], s. F: **1.** Type épatant, chose épatante. **2.** = top hat, q.v. under HAT.

topple [tɔpl]. **1.** v.i. (a) **To topple (down, over),** tomber, s'écrouler, culbuter. **To bring the Government toppling down,** faire tomber le gouvernement. (b) Chanceler, vaciller, branler. **2.** v.tr. **To topple sth. down, over,** faire tomber qch.; jeter qch. à bas.

topsail ['tɔpseil, tɔpsl], s. Nau: Hunier m; (of cutter) flèche f. **Main topsail**, grand hunier.

topside ['tɔpsaid], s. Cu: Tendre m de tranche (du bœuf).

topsides ['tɔpsaidz], s.pl. Nau: Hauts m, œuvres mortes, accastillage m (d'un navire).

topsy-turvy ['tɔpsi'tə:rvi], adv. & adj. Sens dessus dessous. **To turn sth. topsy-turvy**, mettre qch. sens dessus dessous; renverser qch. **To turn everything t.-t.**, tout bouleverser. **Everything is t.-t.**, tout est en désarroi.

topsy-turvydom ['tɔpsi'tə:rvidəm], s. F: Le monde à l'envers.

toque [touk], s. Cost: Toque f.

tor [tɔ:r], s. Pic m, éminence f conique (dans le sud-ouest de l'Angleterre).

torch [tɔ:rʃ], s. **1.** Torche f, flambeau m. **To hand on the torch**, transmettre le flambeau (à la génération suivante). **2.** Electric torch, lampe f électrique de poche; torche électrique. **'torchbearer**, s. Porte-flambeau m inv. **'torchlight**, s. Lumière f de(s) flambeaux. **Torch-light procession, tattoo**, retraite f aux flambeaux; défilé m aux flambeaux.

tore¹ ['tɔ:r], s. = TORUS 1.

tore². See TEAR³.

toreador [tɔria'dɔ:r], s. Toréador m.

torment¹ ['tɔ:rment], s. Tourment m, torture f, supplice m. The torments of jealousy, les tourments de la jalousie. He suffered torments, il souffrait le martyre. **To be in torment**, être au supplice. F: **That child is a positive torment**, cet enfant est assommant.

torment² [tɔ:r'ment], v.tr. Tourmenter, torturer (qn). **To be tormented by hunger**, éprouver les tourments de la faim. Tormented with remorse, tourmenté par les remords; en proie aux remords. Tormented with suspense, angoissé par l'attente.

tormentil ['tɔ:rməntil], s. Bot: Tormentille f.

tormentor [tɔ:r'mentər], s. (a) Hist: Tourmenteur m, bourreau m. (b) The dog and its tormentors, le chien et les gamins qui étaient après.

torn [tɔ:rn]. See TEAR³.

tornado, pl. **-oes** [tɔ:r'neido, -ouz], s. Tornade f, ouragan m, cyclone m. F: Political t., ouragan politique. **tor'nado-lamp**, s. Lanterne f de tempête.

torpedo¹, pl. **-oes** [tɔ:r'pi:do, -ouz], s. **1.** Ich: Torpille f. **2.** Navy: Mil.Av: Torpille. **Aerial torpedo**, torpille aérienne. **To make a t. attack**, attaquer à la torpille. **tor'pedo boat**, s. A: Torpilleur m. S.a. DESTROYER 2. **tor'pedo-body**, s. Aut: Torpédo m or f. **tor'pedo-net**, s. Filet m pare-torpilles. **tor'pedo-plane**, s. Av: Avion m porte-torpille(s). **tor'pedo-tube**, s. Navy: (Tube m) lance-torpille m; tube de lancement.

torpedo², v.tr. Torpiller (un vaisseau). F: **To torpedo the negotiations**, faire échouer les pourparlers.

torpid ['tɔ:rpid], a. (a) Engourdi, inerte. (b) F: Engourdi, nonchalant, léthargique. **Torpid liver**, foie paresseux.

torpidity [tɔ:r'piditi], **torpidness** ['tɔ:rpidnəs], s. Engourdissement m, inertie f, torpeur f; F: léthargie f, lenteur f.

torpor ['tɔ:rpər], s. Torpeur f. **To arouse oneself from one's t.**, sortir de sa torpeur.

torps [tɔ:rps], s. Navy: F: Officier m torpilleur.

torque¹ [tɔ:rk], s. Archeol: Torque f (des Gaulois).

torque², s. Mec: Couple m de torsion; couple moteur. **Starting torque**, couple de démarrage. El: **Armature torque**, couple d'induit.

torrefaction [tɔri'fakʃ(ə)n], s. Torréfaction f.

torrefy ['tɔrifai], v.tr. Torréfier.

torrent ['tɔrənt], s. Torrent m. Hill t., torrent de montagne. (Of rain) **To fall in torrents**, tomber à torrents, à verse. F: **Torrent of abuse, of tears**, torrent d'injures, de larmes.

torrential [tɔ'renʃ(ə)l], a. Torrentiel.

torrid ['tɔrid], a. Torride.

torridity [tɔ'riditi], s. Chaleur f torride (of, de).

torsade [tɔ:r'seid], s. Torsade f.

torsion ['tɔ:rʃ(ə)n], s. Torsion f. **'torsion-balance**, s. Ph: Balance f de torsion. **'torsion-elec'trometer**, s. El: Balance f de Coulomb.

torsional ['tɔ:rʃən(ə)l], a. Mec: De torsion. **Torsional stress, strain**, effort m de torsion.

torso, pl. **-os** ['tɔ:rso, -ouz], s. Art: Torse m.

tort [tɔ:rt], s. Jur: Acte m dommageable; dommage m; préjudice m.

torticollis [tɔ:rti'kɔlis], s. Med: Torticolis m.

tortious ['tɔ:rʃəs], a. Jur: Dommageable, préjudiciable.

tortoise ['tɔ:rtəs], s. **1.** Z: Tortue f. F: Tortoise gait, pas de tortue. **2.** Rom.Ant: Tortue (de boucliers). **'tortoise-shell**, s. Écaille f (de tortue). Imitation t.-s., simili-écaille f. Tortoise-shell spectacles, lunettes en écaille. Tortoise-shell cat, chat écaille de tortue.

Tortuga [tɔ:r'tu:ga]. Pr.n. (L'île f de) la Tortue.

tortuous ['tɔ:rtjuəs], a. Tortueux. T. descent, descente sinueuse. T. style, style contourné.

torture¹ [tɔ:rtjər], s. **1.** Hist: Torture f, question f. **To put s.o. to the torture**, mettre qn à la torture; appliquer la question à qn. **2.** Torture, tourment m, supplice m. Gout is a real t., la goutte est un supplice.

torture², v.tr. **1.** (a) Hist: Appliquer la question à (qn); mettre (qn) à la question. (b) Torturer (qn); mettre (qn) à la torture, au supplice. Tortured mind, esprit à la torture. **Tortured by remorse**, tenaillé par le remords. **2.** To t. s.o.'s words into a confession of guilt, dénaturer les paroles de qn pour en tirer un aveu.

torturer ['tɔ:rtjurər], s. **1.** Hist: Bourreau m. **2.** Harceleur m.

torus, pl. **-i** ['tɔ:rəs, -ai], s. **1.** Arch: Tore m. **2.** Bot: Tore, réceptacle m.

Tory ['tɔ:ri], a. & s. Pol: Tory (m).

Toryism ['tɔ:riizm], s. Pol: Toryisme m.

tosh [tɔʃ], s. F: Bêtises fpl, blague(s) f(pl).

toss¹ [tɔs], s. **1.** Action f de jeter (qch.) en l'air. (a) Lancement m, jet m (d'une balle, etc.). (b) Coup m de pile ou face. Sp: Tirage m au sort. **To win the toss**, gagner (à pile ou face); Sp: gagner le toss. **2.** Toss of the head, mouvement de tête impatient, dédaigneux. **3.** Chute f de cheval. **To take a toss**, faire une chute de cheval; vider les arçons.

toss², v. (tossed [tɔst]) **I.** v.tr. (a) Lancer, jeter, (une balle, etc.) en l'air; (of bull) lancer (qn) en l'air; (of horse) démonter (un cavalier). **To toss sth. to s.o.**, jeter qch. à qn. **To toss s.o. in a blanket**, berner qn; F: passer qn à la couverture. Nau: **To toss (the) oars**, mâter les avirons. (b) **To toss (up) a coin**, jouer à pile ou face. Abs. **To toss for sth.**, jouer qch. à pile ou face. **To toss for sides**, choisir les camps (à pile ou face). (c) **To toss one's head**, relever la tête d'un air dédaigneux, méprisant. (Of horse) **To toss its head**, hocher de la tête; encenser. (d) Agiter, secouer, ballotter. Tossed on the waves, ballotté par les flots. **2.** v.i. (a) **To toss (about) in bed**, se tourner et se retourner dans son lit. **To toss in one's sleep**, s'agiter dans son sommeil. (b) **To toss on the waves**, être ballotté par les flots. (Of ship) **To pitch and toss**, tanguer. (c) (Of the waves) S'agiter. **toss aside, away,** v.tr. Jeter (qch.) de côté. **toss off**, v.tr. Avaler d'un trait, lamper (un verre de vin); expédier (une tâche); écrire (un article) au pied levé. **toss-'up**, s. **1.** (Of coin) Coup m de pile ou face. **2.** Affaire f à issue douteuse. **It is a toss-up, les chances sont égales. tossing,** s. **1.** Lancement m en l'air. **2.** Agitation f, ballottement m. *We got a t. in the Channel,* nous avons été secoués en Manche.

tosspot ['tɔspɔt], s. A: Ivrogne m.

tot[1] [tɔt], s. **1.** Tout(e) petit(e) enfant. **Tiny tot,** baby m; bambin, -ine. **2.** F: Goutte f, petit verre (de whisky, etc.).

tot[2], s. Colonne f de chiffres à additionner; addition f.

tot[3], v. (totted) **1.** v.tr. **To tot up a column of figures,** additionner une colonne de chiffres. **2.** v.i. (Of expenses, etc.) **To tot up,** s'élever (to, à).

total[1] ['tout(ə)l]. **1.** a. Total, -aux; complet, -ète; global, -aux. (a) **Total amount,** somme totale, globale. **Total tonnage,** tonnage global (d'un port, etc.). (b) *The t. loss of his fortune,* la perte totale de sa fortune. *They were in total ignorance of it,* ils l'ignoraient complètement. **Total failure,** échec complet. *Astr:* **Total eclipse,** éclipse totale. **2.** s. Total m; montant m; tout m. **Grand total,** total global. *The t. amounts to a hundred pounds,* la somme s'élève à cent livres. **-ally,** adv. Totalement, entièrement, complètement.

total[2], v.tr. & i. (totalled) **1.** Totaliser, additionner (les dépenses). **2. To total up to . . .,** to total . . ., s'élever à, se monter à (une somme, un nombre).

totality [to'taliti], s. **1.** Totalité f. **2.** *Astr:* Obscuration totale.

totalizator ['toutəlaizeitər], s. *Turf:* Totaliseur m, totalisateur m (des paris).

totalize ['toutəlaiz], v.tr. Totaliser, additionner.

tote [tout], s. F: = TOTALIZATOR.

totem ['toutəm], s. *Anthr:* Totem m.

t'other, tother ['tʌðər], a. & pron. F: = the other.

totter[1] ['tɔtər], s. Chancellement m.

totter[2], v.i. **1.** (Of pers.) (a) Chanceler. **To totter to one's feet,** se relever en chancelant. **To totter in, out,** entrer, sortir, d'un pas mal assuré, d'un pas chancelant. (b) Tituber (sous le coup de l'ivresse). **2.** Menacer ruine; chanceler, branler. **tottering,** a. Chancelant; (of drunken pers.) titubant. *T. steps,* pas mal assurés. **Tottering empire,** empire qui menace ruine, qui croule.

toucan [tu'ka:n, 'tu:k(ə)n], s. *Orn:* Toucan m.

touch[1] [tʌtʃ], s. **1.** (a) Attouchement m. **To give s.o. a touch,** toucher qn. *I felt a t. on my arm,* je sentis qu'on me touchait le bras. (b) *Mil:* **Touch of elbows,** tact m des coudes. **2.** (Le sens du) toucher; tact. **To know sth. by the touch,** reconnaître qch. au toucher. **3.** (Feel) *The cold t. of marble,* le toucher froid du marbre. **4.** (a) Léger coup. *To give one's horse a t. of the spurs,* picoter son cheval. (b) Touche f (de pinceau); coup m (de crayon). **To add a few touches to a picture,** faire quelques retouches f à un tableau. **To give the finishing touch(es), the final touch, to sth.,** mettre la dernière main à qch. **5.** (a) *Sculptor* **with a bold touch,** sculpteur au ciseau hardi. **Delicate touch** (with the brush), coup de pinceau délicat. **To write with a light touch,** avoir la plume légère, le style léger. (b) *Mus:*

Toucher m. *Typewr:* Frappe f. **6.** (a) **Touch of salt, of garlic,** pointe f de sel, d'ail. **Touch of satire,** pointe de satire. *T. of rouge,* soupçon m de rouge. *The first touches of autumn,* les premières atteintes de l'automne. *There was a t. of bitterness in his reply,* il répondit avec une nuance d'amertume. **Touch of nature,** trait naturel. (b) **Touch of fever, of flu, of gout,** soupçon de fièvre; un peu de grippe; légère attaque de goutte. **7.** Contact m. **To be in touch with s.o.,** être en contact avec qn; être en rapport avec qn. **To get in touch with the police,** se mettre en communication avec la police. **To put s.o. in touch with s.o.,** mettre qn en relations avec qn. **To lose touch with s.o.,** perdre qn de vue; perdre contact avec qn. **The personal touch,** les rapports personnels (avec les clients, etc.). **To be in touch with the situation,** être au courant de la situation. **8.** *Fb:* Touche. **Kick into touch,** envoi m en touche. **9.** *F:* **It was a near touch,** cela n'a tenu qu'à un fil. **'touch-hole,** s. *Artil:* Lumière f (du canon). **'touch-in-'goal,** s. *Rugby Fb:* Touche f de but. **'touch-line,** s. *Fb:* Ligne f de touche. **'touch-paper,** s. Papier m d'amorce.

touch[2]. I. v.tr. **1.** (a) Toucher. *To t. sth. with one's finger,* toucher qch. du doigt. *To t. s.o. on the shoulder,* toucher qn à l'épaule. **To touch one's hat,** porter, mettre, la main à son chapeau. *He touched his hat to me,* il m'a salué. *F:* **Touch wood!** touche du bois! *Don't t. those eggs,* ne touchez pas à ces œufs. **To touch land,** atterrir, aborder. *S.a.* BARGE-POLE, BOTTOM[1] 1, GROUND[2] 1. (b) *His garden touches mine,* son jardin touche au mien. (c) Effleurer (les cordes de la harpe). **To touch a spring,** faire jouer un ressort. (d) *v.ind.tr.* **To touch on a subject,** toucher, effleurer, un sujet. (e) Toucher, atteindre. *The law can't touch him,* la loi ne peut rien contre lui. *F:* **No one can touch him in comedy,** personne ne peut l'approcher dans la comédie. (f) **I never touch wine,** jamais je ne bois de vin. **2.** (a) Produire de l'effet sur (qch.). *The file will not t. it,* la lime ne mord pas dessus. *S.a.* RAW II. (b) *I could not t. the history paper,* je n'ai pas pu répondre à la moindre question en histoire. **3.** Toucher, émouvoir (qn). **To be touched by s.o.'s kindness,** être touché de la bonté de qn. **4.** *The question touches you nearly,* la question vous touche de près. **5. Flowers touched by the frost,** fleurs atteintes par la gelée. **6.** *F:* **To touch s.o. for a fiver,** taper qn de cinq livres. **II. touch,** v.i. **1.** (Of persons, thgs) Se toucher. (a) Être en contact. (b) Venir en contact. **2.** *Nau:* **To touch at a port,** faire escale à un port. **touch down,** v.tr. *Rugby Fb:* Toucher dans les buts. **touch-'down,** s. Touché m. **touch off,** v.tr. **1.** Esquisser (qch.) rapidement. **2.** Faire jouer, faire exploser (une mine). **touch up,** v.tr. Faire des retouches à (un tableau). **touched,** a. *F:* Toqué, timbré. *He is slightly t.,* il a un grain (de folie). **touching. 1.** a. Touchant, émouvant, attendrissant. **2.** prep. Touchant, concernant. **-ly,** adv. D'une manière touchante. **'touch and 'go,** s. It was touch and go whether we should catch the train, nous courions grand risque de manquer le train. **That was touch and go!** *F:* il était moins cinq!

touchiness ['tʌtʃinəs], s. Susceptibilité f, irascibilité f.

touchstone ['tʌtʃstoun], s. Pierre f de touche.

touchwood ['tʌtʃwud], s. Amadou m.

touchy ['tʌtʃi], a. Susceptible, ombrageux. **To**

be t., se piquer facilement. *He is very t. on that point*, il n'entend pas raillerie là-dessus. *To be t. on a point of honour*, être chatouilleux sur le point d'honneur.
tough [tʌf], a. **1.** Dur, résistant. **Tough meat,** viande coriace. **2.** (*Of pers.*) Fort, solide. *To become t.* (*through training*), s'endurcir. **3.** (*Of pers.*) Raide, inflexible. *F:* **He's a tough customer!** il est peu commode! **4.** *F:* (*a*) (*Of task*) Rude, difficile. (*b*) *That's t.!* c'est dur pour vous! **5.** *s. U.S:* *F:* Apache *m*, bandit *m*. **-ly,** *adv.* **1.** Avec ténacité. **2.** Vigoureusement. **3.** Avec opiniâtreté.
toughen ['tʌf(ə)n]. **1.** *v.tr.* (*a*) Durcir. (*b*) Endurcir (qn). **2.** *v.i.* (*a*) Durcir. (*b*) (*Of pers.*) S'endurcir.
toughish ['tʌfiʃ], a. **1.** Plutôt dur; (*of meat*) peu tendre. **2.** (Travail) assez dur, peu facile.
toughness ['tʌfnəs], s. **1.** Dureté *f*; résistance *f*; (*of meat*) coriacité *f*. **2.** (*a*) Force *f*, solidité *f*. (*b*) Résistance *f* à la fatigue. **3.** Caractère *m* peu commode (de qn). **4.** Difficulté *f* (d'un travail).
tour[1] ['tuər], s. **1.** Tour *m*; voyage *m* circulaire. **Conducted tours,** excursions accompagnées. *To start on a t.,* partir en voyage. **Walking tour,** excursion à pied. **To be on tour,** être en voyage ou en randonnée. **2.** *Tour of inspection,* tournée *f* de visite. *Th:* To take a company on tour, emmener une troupe en tournée.
tour[2], *v.tr. & i.* **To tour** (through, about) a country, faire le tour d'un pays; voyager dans un pays. *Touring party,* groupe *m* de touristes. *Th:* **Touring company,** troupe *f* en tournée. **'touring-car,** s. Automobile *f* de tourisme. **Open touring-car,** torpédo *m* or *f*.
tourer ['tuərər], s. *F:* = TOURING-CAR.
tourist ['tuərist], s. Touriste *mf*. **'tourist agency,** s. Bureau *m* de tourisme. **'tourist ticket,** s. Billet *m* d'excursion; billet circulaire.
touristic [tuə'ristik], a. Touristique.
tourmalin(e) ['tuərməlin, -iːn], s. Tourmaline *f*.
tournament ['tuərnəmənt], s. **1.** *Hist:* (*a*) Tournoi *m*. (*b*) Carrousel *m*. **2.** Tennis tournament, tournoi de tennis. **Chess tournament,** concours *m* d'échecs.
tourniquet ['tuərnike(t)], s. *Surg:* Tourniquet *m*.
tousle [tauzl], *v.tr.* **1.** Houspiller, tirailler (qn). **2.** Ébouriffer (les cheveux). **tousled,** a. T. dress, robe chiffonnée. **Tousled hair,** cheveux ébouriffés.
tout[1] [taut], s. **1.** Racoleur *m*; (*for hotels*) rabatteur *m*, pisteur *m*. **2.** *Turf:* Espion *m*.
tout[2], *v.i.* **1.** *Turf:* Espionner dans les écuries. **2.** To tout for customers, courir après la clientèle; pister des clients.
tow[1] [tou], s. **1.** (Câble *m* de) remorque *f*. **2.** To take a boat in tow, prendre un bateau à la remorque. **To be taken in tow,** se mettre à la remorque. **3.** (*a*) (*Vessel towed*) Remorque. (*b*) A tow of barges, une rame de péniches. **'tow-boat,** s. Remorqueur *m*. **'tow-line, -rope,** s. Remorque *f*; corde *f* de halage. **'tow-path,** s. Chemin *m* de halage.
tow[2], *v.tr.* Remorquer (un navire); touer (un chaland); (*from tow-path*) haler (un chaland). **towing,** s. Remorque *f*; touage *m*; (*from tow-path*) halage *m*.
tow[3], s. Étoupe (blanche); filasse *f*. **'tow-headed,** a. *F:* Aux cheveux blond filasse.
toward ['touərd]. **1.** a. (*Pred.*) Proche; tout près. **2.** *prep. Lit:* = TOWARDS.
towards ['touərdz, tɔːrdz], *prep.* **1.** (*Of place*)

Vers; du côté de. **2.** Envers, pour, à l'égard de (qn). *His feelings t. me,* ses sentiments envers, pour, moi. **3.** Pour. **To save towards the children's education,** économiser pour l'éducation des enfants. **4.** (*Of time*) Vers, sur. *T. noon,* vers midi. *T. the end of his life . . .,* sur la fin de sa vie. . . .
towel[1] ['tauel], s. **1.** Serviette *f* (de toilette); essuie-mains(s) *m inv.* *A clean t.,* une serviette blanche. **Turkish towel,** serviette éponge. **2.** Sanitary towel, serviette hygiénique. **'towel-horse,** s. Chevalet *m*. **'towel-rail,** s. Porte-serviettes *m inv.*
towel[2], *v.tr.* (towelled) Essuyer, frotter, avec une serviette. **towelling,** s. **1.** Friction *f* avec une serviette. **2.** Toile *f* pour serviettes; tissu-éponge *m*.
tower[1] ['tauər], s. **1.** (*a*) Tour *f*. (*b*) **Church tower,** clocher *m*. **Observation tower,** belvédère *m*. (*c*) *F:* **He is a tower of strength,** c'est un puissant appui. **2.** *Civ.E:* Pylône *m* (de réseau électrique, etc.). **Tower-crane,** grue à pylône.
tower[2], *v.i.* **1.** Dominer. **He towered above the others,** il dominait les autres par la taille. **2.** (*a*) Monter très haut (en l'air). (*b*) (*Of bird*) Planer. **towering,** a. **1.** (*a*) Très haut. A towering height, une très grande hauteur. (*b*) Towering ambition, ambition sans bornes. **2.** *F:* In a towering passion, rage, au paroxysme de la colère.
towered ['tauərd], a. **1.** Surmonté d'une tour, de tours. **2.** High-towered, aux tours élevées.
town [taun], s. **1.** Ville *f*; cité *f*. **Country town,** ville de province. **2.** (*a*) To live in town, habiter Londres. **A man about town,** un mondain; (*in Fr.*) un boulevardier. (*b*) He is out of town, il est à la campagne. (*At Oxford and Cambridge*) **Town and gown,** les bourgeois et les étudiants. **3.** Town water supply, adduction des eaux de ville. **Town gas,** gaz de ville. **Town residence,** hôtel *m*. **Town life,** vie urbaine. **town-'clerk,** s. Greffier municipal. **'town-'council,** s. Conseil municipal. **'town-'councillor,** s. Conseiller municipal. **town-'hall,** s. Hôtel *m* de ville. **'town-house,** s. Hôtel *m* (d'une famille). **'town-plan,** *v.tr.* (-planned) Aménager (une ville) selon les principes de l'urbanisme.
town-planning, s. Urbanisme *m*; aménagement *m* des villes.
township ['taunʃip], s. Commune *f*.
townsman, *pl.* **-men** ['taunzmən, -men], *s.m.* Habitant de la ville; bourgeois, citadin. *Fellow t.,* concitoyen *m*.
townspeople ['taunzpiːpl], *s.pl.* **1.** Habitants *m* de la ville; bourgeois *m*. **2.** Concitoyens *m*.
toxic ['tɔksik], a. & s. *Med:* Toxique (*m*); intoxicant.
toxicology [tɔksi'kɔlɔdʒi], s. Toxicologie *f*.
toxin ['tɔksin], s. Toxine *f*.
toy[1] [tɔi], s. **1.** Jouet *m*; *F:* joujou *m*, -oux. **2.** *Attrib.* (*a*) Toy trumpet, trompette d'enfant. **Toy theatre,** théâtre de marionnettes. (*b*) Tout petit. **Toy dog,** chien de salon. (*c*) A toy army, une petite armée pour rire. **'toy-book,** s. Livre *m* d'images. **'toy-'railway,** s. Chemin *m* de fer mécanique (d'enfant). **toy-shop,** s. Magasin *m* de jouets.
toy[2], *v.i.* **1.** To toy with sth., s'amuser, jouer, avec qch. **To toy with one's food,** manger du bout des dents. **To toy with an idea,** caresser une idée. **2.** To toy with s.o., badiner avec qn.
trace[1] [treis], s. **1.** (*Usu. pl.*) Trace(s) *f(pl)* (de qn, d'un animal); empreinte *f* (d'un animal). **2.** Trace, vestige *m*. **To find a trace of s.o.,**

retrouver trace de qn. **There is no trace of it,** il n'en reste pas trace.

trace², *v.tr.* **1.** Tracer (un plan). **To trace out a scheme,** esquisser un projet. **2.** (*a*) **To trace (out) a plan,** faire le tracé d'un plan. (*b*) Calquer (un dessin). **3. To trace an animal,** suivre la piste d'une bête. *He has been traced to Paris,* on a suivi sa piste jusqu'à Paris. **To trace lost goods,** recouvrer des objets perdus. **4.** *I cannot t. any reference to the event,* je ne trouve trace d'aucune mention du fait. **5.** Suivre (un chemin). **trace back,** *v.tr.* **To trace sth. back to its source,** remonter jusqu'à l'origine de qch. *To t. one's family back to the Conqueror,* faire remonter sa famille à Guillaume le Conquérant. **tracing,** *s.* **1.** (*a*) Tracé *m.* (*b*) Calquage *m.* **2.** Dessin calqué; calque *m.* **'tracing-cloth, -paper,** *s.* Toile *f,* papier *m,* à calquer. **'tracing-linen,** *s.* = TRACING-CLOTH. **'tracing-wheel,** *s.* *Dressm:* Roulette *f* (à piquer).

trace³, *s.* *Harn:* Trait *m.* **In the traces,** attelé. *F:* (*Of pers.*) **To kick over the traces,** (i) s'insurger; (ii) s'émanciper. **'trace-horse,** *s.* Cheval *m* de renfort.

traceable ['treisəbl], *a.* Que l'on peut suivre à la trace.

tracer ['treisər], *s.* *Mil:* **Tracer shell, tracer bullet,** obus traceur; balle traceuse.

tracery ['treisəri], *s.* **1.** *Arch:* Réseau *m* (d'une rosace); découpures *fpl.* **2.** Réseau, nervures *fpl* (d'une feuille).

trachea, *pl.* **-eae** [tra'ki:a, -i:i:], *s.* (*a*) *Anat:* Trachée-artère *f*; *F:* trachée *f.* (*b*) Trachée (d'insecte).

tracheotomy [traki'ɔtomi, trei-], *s* *Surg:* Trachéotomie *f.*

track¹ [trak], *s.* **1.** (*a*) Erre *f,* trace(s) *f(pl),* piste *f* (d'une bête). (*b*) Trace(s), piste (de qn); sillage *m* (d'un navire). **To follow in s.o.'s track,** suivre la voie tracée par qn. **To be on s.o.'s track,** être sur la trace de qn. **To keep track of s.o.,** ne pas perdre de vue qn. **To throw s.o. off the track,** dépister qn. **To cover up one's tracks** (*from the police*), dépister la police. *P:* **To make tracks,** filer, s'éclipser. **2.** (*a*) Mule track, piste muletière. **Sheep track,** sentier battu par les moutons. **Wheel track,** voie charretière. *S.a.* BEATEN 1. (*b*) *Mec.E:* Chemin *m,* piste (de glissement). **3.** Route *f,* chemin. **To put s.o. on the right track,** mettre qn sur la voie. **4.** *Rac:* Piste. **Motor-racing track,** autodrome *m.* **5.** *Rail:* Voie (ferrée). **The train left the track,** le train a déraillé. **6.** Chenille *f* (de tracteur). **'track-gauge,** *s.* *Rail:* Gabarit *m.* **'track-racing,** *s.* Courses *fpl* sur piste.

track², *v.tr.* Suivre (une bête) à la piste; traquer (un malfaiteur). **To track down,** dépister (le gibier, un malfaiteur).

tracker ['trakər], *s.* Traqueur *m* (de gibier).

trackless ['trakləs], *a.* Sans chemins. **Trackless forest,** forêt vierge.

tract¹ [trakt], *s.* **1.** Étendue *f* (de pays); nappe *f* (d'eau); région (montagneuse). **2.** *Anat:* Respiratory tract, appareil *m* respiratoire.

tract², *s.* Petit traité; brochure *f*; *esp.* petite brochure de piété.

tractability [trakta'biliti], **tractableness** ['traktəblnəs], *s.* Humeur *f* traitable; docilité *f.*

tractable ['traktəbl], *a.* **1.** (*Of pers.*) Docile; traitable. **2.** (*Of material*) Facile à ouvrer; ouvrable.

traction ['trakʃ(ə)n], *s.* Traction *f,* tirage *m.* **Motor traction,** traction automobile. **Traction wheels,** roues motrices (d'une locomotive).

'traction-engine, *s.* Machine routière; tracteur *m.*

tractive ['traktiv], *a.* Tractif; (force) de traction.

tractor ['traktər], *s.* **1.** Tracteur *m.* *S.a.* PLOUGH¹ 1. **2.** *Av:* Tractor propeller, hélice tractive.

trade¹ [treid], *s.* **1.** État *m,* emploi *m*; métier manuel; commerce *m.* **To carry on a trade,** exercer un métier, un commerce. **To put s.o. to a trade,** apprendre un métier à qn. *He is a grocer by trade,* il est épicier de son état. **Everyone to his trade,** chacun son métier. *S.a.* JACK¹ II. 1. **2.** Commerce, négoce *m,* affaires *fpl.* **Trade in cotton,** commerce du coton. **Foreign trade,** commerce étranger, extérieur. *Nau:* **Coasting trade,** cabotage *m.* **To be in trade,** être dans le commerce; *esp.* tenir boutique. *S.a.* FREE TRADE, ROARING¹ 2. **3.** Commerçants *mpl.* **4.** *pl.* **Trades** = TRADE-WINDS. **5.** *Attrib.* **Trade bank,** banque de commerce. **Trade card,** carte d'affaires. **Trade expenses,** frais de bureau. **Trade price,** prix marchand. **'trade allowance,** *s.* Remise *f,* escompte *m.* **'trade-mark,** *s.* Marque *f* de fabrique. **Registered trade-mark,** marque déposée. **trade-'union,** *s.* Syndicat ouvrier. **trade-'unionism,** *s.* Syndicalisme (ouvrier). **trade-'unionist,** *s.* Syndiqué, -ée; syndicaliste *mf.* **'trade-wind,** *s.* Vent alizé; alizé *m.*

trade², **1.** *v.i.* (*a*) Faire le commerce, le négoce (*in,* de); trafiquer (*in,* en). (*b*) **To trade on s.o.'s ignorance,** exploiter l'ignorance de qn. **2.** *v.tr.* (*b*) **To trade sth. for sth.,** troquer qch. contre qch. **trading,** *s.* Commerce *m,* négoce *m.* **Trading town,** ville commerçante. **Trading concern,** entreprise commerciale. **Trading vessel,** navire marchand. *Fin:* **Trading capital,** capital de roulement. *Book-k:* **Trading year,** exercice *m.*

trader ['treidər], *s.* **1.** Négociant, -ante; commerçant, -ante; marchand, -ande. **2.** Navire marchand.

tradesfolk ['treidzfouk], *s.pl.* Commerçants *m.*

tradesman, *pl.* **-men** ['treidzmən, -men], *s.m.* **1.** Marchand, boutiquier, fournisseur. **Tradesmen's entrance,** entrée des fournisseurs. **2.** *Scot:* Artisan *m.*

tradition [tra'diʃ(ə)n], *s.* Tradition *f.*

traditional [tra'diʃən(ə)l], *a.* Traditionnel. **-ally,** *adv.* Traditionnellement.

traduce [tra'dju:s], *v.tr.* Calomnier, diffamer.

traducer [tra'dju:sər], *s.* Calomniateur, -trice.

traffic¹ ['trafik], *s.* **1.** Trafic *m,* négoce *m,* commerce *m.* *Pej:* **Traffic in arms,** trafic des armes. **Ocean traffic,** navigation *f* au long cours. **2.** Mouvement *m,* circulation *f.* **Road traffic,** circulation routière. **Block in the traffic,** embouteillage *m.* **Congested t.,** circulation embarrassée. **Road carrying a great deal of t.,** route à circulation intense. **Traffic accident,** accident de circulation. **'Beware of traffic!'** "attention aux voitures!" **Traffic regulations,** règlements sur la circulation. **Road fit for traffic,** route viable. **3.** **Railway traffic,** trafic de chemin de fer. *S.a.* POLICEMAN, THROUGH III. **'traffic-indicator,** *s.* *Aut:* Signalisateur *m*; indicateur *m* de direction. **'traffic-manager,** *s.* *Rail:* Chef *m* de mouvement. **'traffic-signals,** *s.pl.* = traffic lights, *q.v.* under LIGHT¹ 2.

traffic², *v.* (trafficked ['trafikt]) **1.** *v.i.* Trafiquer (*in,* en); faire le commerce (*in,* de). **2.** *v.tr.* *Usu. Pej:* Trafiquer de (qch.). **To traffic away one's honour,** vendre son honneur.

trafficator ['trafikeitər], s. Aut: Indicateur m de direction.
trafficker ['trafikər], s. **1.** Trafiquant m (in, de, en). **2.** Drug-trafficker, trafiqueur m de, en, stupéfiants.
tragacanth ['tragakanθ], s. See GUM TRAGACANTH.
tragedian [tra'dʒi:djən], s. **1.** Auteur m tragique. **2.** Th: Tragédien, -ienne.
tragedienne [traʒe'djen], s.f. Th: Tragédienne.
tragedy ['tradʒedi], s. (a) Tragédie f. (b) The final t. of his death, le drame final de sa mort. What a tragedy! quelle tragédie!
tragic(al) ['tradʒik(əl)], a. Tragique. **-ally**, adv. Tragiquement. To take things tragically, prendre les choses au tragique.
tragi-comedy [tradʒi'kɔmedi], s. Tragi-comédie f.
tragi-comic(al) [tradʒi'kɔmik(əl)], a. Tragi-comique.
trail¹ [treil], s. **1.** (a) Traînée f (de fumée). T. of fire (of rocket), sillon m de feu. T. of a meteor, queue f d'un météore. (b) Av: Ball: Traînée réelle (d'une bombe). (c) Artil: Flèche f, crosse f (d'affût). **2.** (a) Piste f, trace f (d'une bête). To pick up the trail, retrouver la piste. False trail, fausse piste. (b) Sentier (battu); piste (dans une forêt). **'trail-bridge,** s. (Bac m à) traille f. **'trail-net,** s. Fish: Chalut m. **'trail-rope,** s. **1.** Artil: Prolonge f. **2.** Aer: Guide-rope m.
trail². I. v.tr. **1.** (a) To trail sth. (along), traîner qch. après soi; (of car) remorquer (une voiturette). F: To trail one's coat, chercher noise à tout le monde; traîner son sabre. (b) Mil: To trail arms, porter l'arme avec le canon parallèle au sol. **2.** Traquer (une bête). II. **trail,** v.i. **1.** (a) Traîner. (b) With a boat trailing behind, avec un bateau à la traîne. **2.** (Of pers.) To trail along, se traîner. Her voice trailed off in the distance, sa voix se perdit dans le lointain. **3.** (Of plant) Grimper ou ramper. **trailing,** a. **1.** (Of plant) Grimpant ou rampant. **2.** Rail: Trailing wheel, roue porteuse arrière (de locomotive). Av: Trailing edge, bord (d'aile) postérieur.
trailer ['treilər], s. **1.** (Pers.) Traqueur m. **2.** Veh: Baladeuse f (d'auto). Trailer car, voiturette f remorque.
train¹ [trein], s. **1.** Traîne f, queue f (d'une robe). **2.** (a) Suite f, équipage m (d'un prince). To be in s.o.'s train, être à la suite de qn. (b) Mil: Baggage train, train m des équipages. (c) War brings famine in its t., la guerre amène la disette. **3.** (a) Train, convoi m (de wagons); succession f, série f (d'événements). Train of thought, chaîne f d'idées. (b) Min: To fire a train, allumer une traînée de poudre. (c) F: To set sth. in train, mettre qch. en train. **4.** Tchn: Système m d'engrenages; rouage(s) m(pl) (d'une montre). Wheel train, train de roues. **5.** Rail: (a) Train. Slow train, train omnibus. Main-line train, train de grande ligne. Workmen's t., train ouvrier. Cattle t., convoi m de bestiaux. To go by train, aller par le train, par le chemin de fer. To get into the t., monter en wagon. We had dinner on the t., nous avons dîné dans le train. The t. is in, le train est en gare, à quai. S.a. EXPRESS¹ I, FAST³ I. 2, GOOD II. 2. (b) Rame f (du Métro). **'train-bearer,** s. (Pers.) Porte-queue m inv.
train². I. v.tr. **1.** (a) Former, instruire (qn); former, exercer (des conscrits); dresser (un animal); exercer (l'oreille). To train (up) a child, élever un enfant. Engineers who have been

trained at . . ., les ingénieurs sortis de. . . . To t. a youth for the navy, préparer un jeune homme pour la marine. To train s.o. to business, rompre qn aux affaires. (b) Sp: Entraîner (un coureur). Box: He is being trained by so-and-so, c'est le poulain d'un tel. (c) Hort: Diriger, conduire (une plante); palisser (un arbre fruitier). **2.** Pointer (un canon), braquer (une lunette) (on, sur). Navy: Orienter (un canon). II. **train,** v.i. (a) S'exercer. Mil: Faire l'exercice. (b) Sp: S'entraîner. (Of athlete) To train down, réduire son poids. **trained,** a. **1.** (a) (Soldat) instruit; (chien) dressé; (domestique) stylé; (œil) exercé. Well-trained child, enfant bien élevé. Trained nurse, infirmière diplômée. (b) Sp: Entraîné. **2.** (Rosier) palissé, mis en espalier. **training,** s. **1.** (a) Éducation f, instruction f. Character training, formation f du caractère. Physical training, éducation physique. To have had a business training, être formé aux affaires. (b) Military training, dressage m militaire. To keep troops in training, tenir des troupes en haleine. Navy: Training squadron, escadre d'instruction. (c) Sp: Entraînement m (d'un boxeur, etc.). To go into training, s'entraîner. To be out of training, ne plus être en forme. (d) Dressage (d'un animal). **2.** Hort: Palissage m. **3.** Artil: Pointage m en direction. **'training-college,** s. Sch: École normale. **'training-ship, -vessel,** s. Navire m école; vaisseau-école m.
trainer ['treinər], s. **1.** Dresseur m (d'animaux). **2.** Sp: Entraîneur m.
train-oil ['treinɔil], s. Huile f de baleine; thran m.
trait [trei], s. Trait m (de caractère).
traitor ['treitər], s. Traître m. To turn traitor, passer à l'ennemi; se vendre.
traitorous ['treitərəs], a. Traître, f. traîtresse; perfide. **-ly,** adv. En traître; traîtreusement.
traitress ['treitres], s.f. Traîtresse.
trajectory [tra'dʒektəri], s. Trajectoire f.
tram¹ [tram], s. **1.** = TRAM-CAR. Tram driver, conducteur m de tramway; wattman m. Tram conductor, receveur m. **2.** = TRAMWAY. **3.** Min: Benne f, berline f. **'tram-car,** s. (Voiture f de) tramway m. **'tram-track,** s. Voie f de tramway.
tram², v.i. (trammed) F: To tram (it), voyager en tramway; prendre le tramway.
trammel¹ ['træm(ə)l], s. **1.** Fish: Trammel(-net), tramail m, -ails. **2.** pl. F: The trammels of etiquette, les entraves f de l'étiquette.
trammel², v.tr. (trammelled) Entraver.
tramp¹ [tramp], s. **1.** Bruit m de pas marqués. I heard the (heavy) t. of the guard, j'entendis le pas lourd de la garde. **2.** (a) Marche f; promenade f à pied. (b) To be on the tramp, P: être sur le trimard. **3.** (Pers.) Chemineau m, vagabond m. **4.** Nau: (Ocean) tramp, tramp steamer, navire m, cargo m, sans ligne régulière; F: chemineau.
tramp², v.i. **1.** Marcher à pas marqués; marcher lourdement. **2.** = TRAMPLE I **3.** (a) Marcher; voyager à pied. v.tr. To tramp the country, parcourir le pays à pied. They had to tramp it, ils furent obligés de faire le trajet à pied. (b) Vagabonder. v.tr. To tramp the streets, battre le pavé.
trample [trampl]. I. v.i. To trample on sth., s.o., piétiner, écraser, qch., qn. To trample on s.o.'s feelings, fouler aux pieds les susceptibilités de qn. **2.** v.tr. To trample sth. under foot, fouler qch. aux pieds. To t. down the grass,

fouler, piétiner, l'herbe. **trampling,** *s.* Piétinement *m*; bruit *m* de pas.

tramway ['tramwei], *s.* Voie *f* de tramway.

trance [trɑːns], *s* (*a*) *Med:* (i) Extase *f*; (ii) catalepsie *f.* **To fall into a trance,** tomber en extase. (*b*) (**Hypnotic**) **trance,** transe *f*, hypnose *f.*

tranquil ['traŋkwil], *a.* Tranquille (et serein); calme, paisible. **-illy,** *adv.* Tranquillement, paisiblement; avec sérénité.

tranquillity [traŋ'kwiliti], *s. Lit:* Tranquillité *f*, calme *m*, sérénité *f.*

tranquillize ['traŋkwilɑːiz], *v.tr. Lit:* Tranquilliser, calmer, apaiser.

transact [trɑːn'zakt], *v.tr.* **To transact business with s.o.,** faire des affaires avec qn ; traiter une affaire, une opération, avec qn.

transaction [trɑːn'zakʃ(ə)n], *s.* **1.** Conduite *f* (d'une affaire). **The transaction of business,** le commerce, les affaires *f.* **2.** Opération (commerciale). **Cash transaction,** opération au comptant. **3.** *pl.* **Transactions,** (i) transactions *f*, (ii) procès-verbaux *m* des séances (d'une société savante).

transalpine [trɑːns'alpain], *a.* Transalpin.

transatlantic [trɑːnsat'lantik], *a.* Transatlantique.

transcend [trɑːn'send], *v.tr.* **1.** Dépasser les bornes de (la raison); aller au delà de (ce que l'on peut concevoir). **2.** Surpasser (qn).

transcendence [trɑːn'sendəns], **transcendency** [trɑːn'sendənsi], *s.* Transcendance *f.*

transcendent [trɑːn'sendənt], *a.* Transcendant.

transcendental [trɑːnsen'dent(ə)l], *a.* **1.** *Phil:* Transcendantal, -aux. **2.** *Mth:* (*Of quantity*) Transcendant.

transcribe [trɑːn'skraib], *v.tr.* Transcrire.

transcriber [trɑːn'skraibər], *s.* Transcripteur *m.*

transcript ['trɑːnskript], *s.* Transcription *f*, copie *f.*

transcription [trɑːn'skripʃ(ə)n], *s.* Transcription *f.*

transept ['trɑːnsept], *s. Ecc.Arch:* Transept *m.*

transfer[1] ['trɑːnsfəːr], *s.* **1.** (*a*) Translation *f*, transport *m* (de qch. à un autre endroit); déplacement *m* (d'un fonctionnaire). *Rail:* **Transfer ticket,** billet de correspondance. *Fb:* **Transfer fee,** somme payée pour le transfert d'un joueur. (*b*) *Jur:* Transfert *m* (d'un droit); mutation *f* (de biens). *St.Exch:* **Transfer of shares,** transfert, assignation *f*, d'actions. (*c*) *Book-k:* Transport (d'une somme). *Bank:* **Transfer of funds,** virement *m* de fonds. **2.** *Jur:* (**Deed of**) **transfer,** acte *m* de cession. **3.** (*a*) *Lith:* Report *m*. *Phot:* (*In carbon process*) **Temporary transfer,** transfert provisoire. (*b*) *Needlew:* Décalque *m*. (*c*) **Transfer(-picture),** décalcomanie *f.* **'transfer-paper,** *s.* **1.** Papier *m* à décalquer. **2.** *Lith: Phot:* Papier à report.

transfer[2] [trɑːns'fəːr], *v.tr.* (**transferred**) **1.** Transférer. (*a*) **To t.** *a civil servant,* déplacer un fonctionnaire. **To t.** *a soldier,* muter un soldat. (*b*) *Jur:* Transmettre, céder (une propriété). (*c*) *Book-k:* Contre-passer (une écriture). *Bank:* Virer (une somme). **2.** (*a*) *Lith: Phot:* Reporter. (*b*) *Needlew: etc:* Calquer.

transferable ['trɑːnsfərəbl], *a.* Transmissible. *Jur:* (Droit) cessible. *Fin:* **T. securities,** valeurs mobilières. **'Not transferable,'** (*on railway ticket*) strictement personnel.

transferee [trɑːnsfə'riː], *s. Jur:* Cessionnaire *mf.*

transference ['trɑːnsfərəns], *s.* Transfert *m.*

transferor ['trɑːnsfərər, -rɔːr], *s.* Cédant, -ante.

transfiguration [trɑːnsfigjuˈreiʃ(ə)n], *s.* Transfiguration *f.*

transfigure [trɑːnsˈfigər], *v.tr.* Transfigurer.

transfix [trɑːnsˈfiks], *v.tr.* **1.** Transpercer. **2.** *F:* **He stood transfixed (with fear),** il resta cloué au sol (par la peur).

transform [trɑːnsˈfɔːrm], *v.tr.* **1.** Transformer; *F:* métamorphoser. **2.** (*a*) *Ch: etc:* Convertir (*into,* en). **To t.** *heat into energy,* convertir la chaleur en énergie. (*b*) *El.E:* Transformer (le courant). **transforming,** *s.* Transformation *f*, conversion *f* (*into,* en).

transformable [trɑːnsˈfɔːrməbl], *a.* **1.** Transformable. **2.** Convertissable (*into,* en).

transformation [trɑːnsfərˈmeiʃ(ə)n], *s.* **1.** (*a*) Transformation *f*; *F:* métamorphose *f*. *Th:* **Transformation scene,** apothéose *f* (d'une féerie). (*b*) *T. of heat into energy,* conversion *f* de la chaleur en énergie. **2.** *Hairdr:* Faux toupet; transformation.

transformer [trɑːnsˈfɔːrmər], *s.* *El.E:* Transformateur *m* (de tension). **Transformer station,** poste *m* de transformateurs.

transfuse [trɑːnsˈfjuːz], *v.tr.* (*a*) Transfuser (du sang). (*b*) Faire une transfusion à (un malade).

transfusion [trɑːnsˈfjuːʒ(ə)n], *s.* **Blood transfusion,** transfusion *f* de sang.

transgress [trɑːnsˈgres], *v.tr.* Transgresser, enfreindre (la loi). *Abs.* Pécher. **To t.** *a rule,* violer une règle.

transgression [trɑːnsˈgreʃ(ə)n], *s.* (*a*) Transgression *f*, violation *f* (d'une 'loi); infraction *f* (*of the law,* à la loi). (*b*) Péché *m*, faute *f.*

transgressor [trɑːnsˈgresər], *s.* Transgresseur *m*; pécheur, *f.* pécheresse.

tranship [trɑːnˈʃip]. **1.** *v.tr.* Transborder (des voyageurs). **2.** *v.i.* (*Of passenger*) Changer de vaisseau.

transhipment [trɑːnˈʃipmənt], *s.* Transbordement *m.*

transient ['trɑːnsiənt], *a.* (*a*) Transitoire; (bonheur) passager. (*b*) (Espoir) momentané. (*c*) *Mus:* **Transient note,** note de passage. **-ly,** *adv.* Transitoirement, passagèrement.

transire [trɑːnˈsaiər], *s. Cust:* Passavant *m*, passe-debout *m inv*, laissez-passer *m inv.*

transit ['trɑːnsit], *s.* **1.** Passage *m* (à travers un pays). **2.** Transport *m* (de marchandises). **Damage in transit,** avarie(s) *f(pl)* en cours de route. **3.** *Cust:* Transit *m*. **4.** *Astr:* Passage ((i) d'une planète sur le disque du soleil, (ii) d'un astre au méridien). **'transit-compass,** *s.* *Surv:* Théodolite *m* à boussole.

transition [trɑːnˈsiʒ(ə)n], *s.* **1.** Transition *f*; passage *m* (du jour à la nuit). **Transition period,** période de transition. **2.** *Mus:* Modulation *f.*

transitive ['trɑːnsitiv], *a.* *Gram:* (Verbe) transitif. **-ly,** *adv.* Transitivement.

transitory ['trɑːnsitəri], *a.* Transitoire; (bonheur) fugitif.

translatable [trɑːnsˈleitəbl], *a.* Traduisible.

translate [trɑːnsˈleit], *v.tr.* **1.** Traduire. (*a*) **Book translated from (the) German,** livre traduit de l'allemand. **How do you t.** *his silence?* comment interprétez-vous son silence? (*b*) **To t.** *one's thoughts into words,* reproduire ses pensées en paroles. **2.** (*a*) Transférer (un évêque) (*to,* à). (*b*) **Enoch was translated (to heaven),** Enoch fut enlevé au ciel.

translation [trɑːnsˈleiʃ(ə)n], *s.* **1.** (*a*) Traduction *f.* (*b*) Traduction; ouvrage traduit. *Sch:* Version (latine, etc.). **2.** (*a*) Translation *f* (d'un évêque). (*b*) *Mec:* **Movement of translation,** mouvement de translation. (*c*) *B:* Enlèvement *m* au ciel.

translator [trɑːnsˈleitər], *s.* Traducteur *m.*

translucence [trɑːnsˈluːsəns], s. Translucidité f.
translucent [trɑːnsˈluːsənt], a. Translucide.
transmigrate [ˈtrɑːnsmigreit, -mai-], v.i. Trans-migrer.
transmigration [trɑːnsmiˈgreiʃ(ə)n, -mai-], s. **I.** Transmigration f (d'un peuple, etc.). **2.** Métempsycose f.
transmissible [trɑːnsˈmisibl], a. Transmissible.
transmission [trɑːnsˈmiʃ(ə)n], s. **I.** Transmission f (d'un ordre). Ph: Transmission (de la chaleur, etc.). El.E: **Transmission of power,** transport m de force. **2.** Mec.E: Système m d'arbres de transmission.
transmit [trɑːnsˈmit], v.tr. (transmitted) Transmettre (un ordre, etc.). Ph: Transmettre (la lumière, etc.). El.E: Transporter (la force). **transmitting,** a. (a) Transmetteur. (b) W.Tel: **Transmitting station,** poste émetteur.
transmittal [trɑːnsˈmit(ə)l], s. Transmission f.
transmitter [trɑːnsˈmitər], s. (a) **T. of motive power,** communicateur m de mouvement. (b) Tg: Transmetteur m. (c) W.Tel: (Poste) émetteur m. (d) Microphone m (d'un téléphone).
transmogrification [trɑːnsmɔgrifiˈkeiʃ(ə)n], s. F: Métamorphose f.
transmogrify [trɑːnsˈmɔgrifai], v.tr. F: Transformer, métamorphoser.
transmutation [trɑːnsmjuˈteiʃ(ə)n], s. Transmutation f (des métaux).
transmute [trɑːnsˈmjuːt], v.tr. (a) Transformer (into, en). (b) Transmuer (un métal).
transom [ˈtrɑːnsəm], s. **I.** Const: (a) Traverse f, linteau m (de fenêtre, de porte). (b) Meneau horizontal (de croisée). **2.** N.Arch: (Barre f d')arcasse f. **3.** = TRANSOM-WINDOW. **'transom-window,** s. **I.** Fenêtre f à meneau horizontal. **2.** U.S: Vasistas m, imposte f (de porte).
transparency [trɑːnsˈpɛərənsi], s. **I.** (a) Transparence f (du verre). (b) Limpidité f (de l'eau). **2.** (a) (Picture) Transparent m. (b) Phot: Diapositive f (de projection).
transparent [trɑːnsˈpɛərənt], a. **I.** Transparent; (eau) limpide. T. window-panes, vitres claires. **2.** F: Évident, clair. **T. deception,** tromperie facile à pénétrer. **-ly,** adv. D'une manière transparente; clairement.
transpierce [trɑːnsˈpiərs], v.tr. Transpercer.
transpiration [trɑːnspiˈreiʃ(ə)n], s. Transpiration f.
transpire [trɑːnˈspaiər]. **I.** v.tr. (Of plants, etc.) Transpirer (un fluide); exhaler (une odeur). **2.** v.i. (a) Transpirer. (b) (Of news) Transpirer, s'ébruiter. (c) His account of what transpired, sa version de ce qui s'était passé.
transplant [trɑːnsˈplɑːnt], v.tr. (a) Transplanter, repiquer (des plants). (b) Transplanter (une population). (c) Surg: Greffer (du tissu).
transplantation [trɑːnsplɑːnˈteiʃ(ə)n], s. Transplantation f.
transpontine [trɑːnsˈpɔntain], a. Transpontin. Esp (In London) De la rive droite. A: **The Transpontine drama,** le mélodrame à gros effets.
transport¹ [ˈtrɑːnspɔːt], s. **I.** Transport m (de marchandises). **Transport worker,** employé m des entreprises de transport. **Transport agent,** transitaire m. S.a. SEA I. **2.** (a) Nau: Transport (-vessel), (bâtiment m) de transport. Av: Transport plane, (avion m) de transport. (b) Mil: Les charrois m. **3.** Transport (de joie, de colère); élancement m (de l'esprit). **She was in transports (of joy),** elle était dans le ravissement.
transport² [trɑːnsˈpɔːt], v.tr. **I.** Transporter. **2. To be transported with joy,** être transporté de joie; être ravi.

transportation [trɑːnspɔːrˈteiʃ(ə)n], s. Jur: A: Déportation f; (for life) relégation f. **Convict sentenced to t.,** relégué m.
transporter [trɑːnsˈpɔːrtər], s. Transporteur m. **Transporter-bridge,** (pont) transbordeur m.
transposable [trɑːnsˈpouzəbl], a. Transposable.
transpose [trɑːnsˈpouz], v.tr. Transposer. **transposing¹,** a. Mus: Transpositeur. **transposing²,** s. Mus: Transposition f.
transposition [trɑːnspoˈziʃ(ə)n], s. Transposition f.
trans-ship [trɑːnsˈʃip], v.tr. = TRANSHIP.
trans-shipment [trɑːnsˈʃipmənt], s. = TRANSHIPMENT.
transubstantiation [trɑːnsʌbstænʃiˈeiʃ(ə)n], s. Theol: Transsubstantiation f.
transude [trɑːnˈsjuːd], v.tr. & i. Transsuder.
transversal [trɑːnzˈvəːrs(ə)l], a. Transversal, -aux.
transverse [trɑːnzˈvəːrs], a. Transversal, -aux; en travers. **Transverse muscle,** s. **transverse,** (muscle) transverse m. **-ly,** adv. Transversalement.
trap¹ [trap], s. **I.** (a) Piège m; (for big game) trappe f; (for wolves) chausse-trape f; (for small game) traquenard m; (for hares, etc.) panneau m. **To set a trap,** dresser, armer, tendre, un piège. **To catch an animal in a trap,** prendre une bête au piège. (b) F: Piège, ruse f. Aut: **Police-trap,** zone f de contrôle de vitesse. **To be caught in the trap,** se laisser prendre au piège. **2.** (a) = TRAP-DOOR. (b) Th: Trappe. **3.** Boîte f de lancement (pour pigeons vivants). **4.** Tchn: (a) Collecteur m (d'huile). Mch: **Steam-trap,** purgeur m de vapeur. (b) (Air-, gas-)trap, siphon m, coupe-air m inv (d'un égout, etc.). **5.** Veh: Charrette anglaise; cabriolet m. **'trap-'door,** s. **I.** Trappe f. **Trap-door spider,** mygale f. **2.** Min: Porte f d'aérage. **'trap-shooting,** s. Sp: Tir m aux pigeons (artificiels ou vivants). **'trap-valve,** s. Soupape f à clapet.
trap², v.tr. (trapped) **I.** (a) Prendre (une bête) au piège. F: **Trapped by the flames,** cerné par les flammes. (b) Tendre des pièges dans (un bois). (c) Abs. Trapper. **2.** Fb: Bloquer (le ballon) avec la plante du pied. **3.** Tchn: **To trap a drain,** disposer un siphon dans une conduite d'eaux ménagères. **trapped,** a. Pris dans un piège; pris au piège.
trap³, s. Geol: Trapp m.
trape(s) [treip(s)], v.i. Traîner çà et là; balader.
trapeze [traˈpiːz], s. Trapèze m. **Flying trapeze,** trapèze volant. **Performer on the flying t.,** voltigeur, -euse.
trapezium [traˈpiːziəm], s. Geom: Trapèze m.
trapezoid [ˈtrapizɔid], s. Geom: Quadrilatère irrégulier.
trapper [ˈtrapər], s. Ven: Trappeur m.
trappings [ˈtrapinz], s.pl. **I.** Harnachement m, caparaçon m. **2.** F: Atours mpl; apparat m.
trappist [ˈtrapist], s. Ecc: Trappiste m.
traprock [ˈtraprɔk], s. Geol: = TRAP³.
traps [traps], s.pl. F: Effets (personnels). **To pack up one's traps,** faire son paquet, sa malle.
trash [traʃ], s. (a) Chose(s) f(pl) sans valeur; camelote f. (b) Littérature f de camelote. (c) U.S: **White trash,** les pauvres m de race blanche.
trashy [ˈtraʃi], a. (Marchandises) sans valeur; (littérature) de camelote.
traumatic [trɔːˈmatik], a. Med: (Fièvre, choc) traumatique.
travail [ˈtraveil], s. **I.** A: Dur travail. **2.** A: &

Lit: Douleurs *fpl* de l'enfantement; enfantement *m.* **Woman in travail,** femme en travail. **travel**[1] ['trav(ə)l], *s.* **I.** (a) Voyages *mpl.* *To be fond of t.,* aimer à voyager. **Travel agency,** bureau *m* de tourisme. (b) *pl.* *Is he still on his travels?* est-il toujours en voyage? **2.** *Aut:* **Clutch travel,** course *f* de l'embrayage. **travel**[2], *v.i.* (travelled) **I.** (a) Voyager; faire des voyages. *He is travelling,* il est en voyage. **To travel round the world,** faire le tour du monde. **To travel over a country,** parcourir un pays. *To t. a long way,* faire un long trajet. (b) Aller, marcher; (of news) circuler. *Light travels faster than sound,* la lumière va, se propage, plus vite que le son. *Train travelling at sixty miles an hour,* train qui marche à soixante milles à l'heure. *Aut:* *We travelled two hundred miles in one day,* nous avons fait une étape de deux cents milles. **2.** Être voyageur de commerce. **To travel in lace,** être représentant en dentelles. **3.** *Mec.E:* (Of part) Se mouvoir, se déplacer. **travelled,** *a.* (Of pers.) (Much-, well-)travelled, qui a (beaucoup) voyagé. **travelling**[1], *a.* **I.** *Rail:* Travelling post-office, bureau ambulant. **Travelling kitchen,** voiture-cuisine *f.* **2.** **Travelling staircase,** escalier roulant. *Ind:* **Travelling apron,** tablier mobile. **travelling**[2], *s.* Voyages *mpl.* **Travelling bag,** sac de voyage. **Travelling expenses,** frais de voyage. *S.a.* RUG I.
traveller ['trav(ə)lər], *s.* **I.** Voyageur, -euse. **Fellow-traveller,** compagnon de voyage. **Traveller's cheque,** chèque de voyage. **2.** (Commercial) traveller, voyageur de commerce; commis voyageur. **Traveller in lace,** représentant en dentelles. **Town traveller,** placier, -ière. **3.** Curseur *m* (de règle à calcul). **'traveller's 'joy,** *s.* *Bot:* Clématite *f* des haies.
traverse[1] ['travərs], *s.* **I.** (a) *Mountaineering:* Traverse *f* (sur la face d'un escarpement); vire *f.* (b) Translation latérale (d'un chariot de tour, etc.). (c) *Artil:* Pointage *m* en direction. **2.** *Geom:* (Ligne) transversale *f.* **3.** *Mec.E:* Traverse, entretoise *f* (de châssis). **4.** (a) *Fort:* Traverse. (b) *Mil:* Pare-éclats *m inv* (de tranchée).
traverse[2], *v.tr.* **I.** (a) Traverser, passer à travers (une région); passer (la mer). (b) *Abs.* *Mountaineering:* Prendre une traverse. **2.** *Artil:* Braquer, pointer en direction (un canon). **3.** *F:* Contrarier, traverser (un dessein).
travertin(e) ['travərtin], *s.* *Geol:* Travertin *m.*
travesty[1] ['travəsti], *s.* Parodie *f*; travestissement *m.*
travesty[2], *v.tr.* Parodier, travestir.
trawl[1] [trɔːl], *s.* **I.** *Fish:* Trawl(-net), chalut *m*, traille *f*; filet *m* à la trôle. **2.** (For mines) Câble balayeur.
trawl[2]. **I.** *v.i.* *Fish:* Pêcher au chalut; chaluter. **2.** *v.tr.* Traîner (un chalut). **trawling,** *s.* Pêche *f* au chalut.
trawler ['trɔːlər], *s.* Chalutier *m.*
tray [trei], *s.* **I.** (a) Plateau *m.* (b) **Hawker's tray,** éventaire *m.* (c) Châssis *m* (d'une malle, etc.); tablette *f* mobile (d'un classeur). **Letter-tray,** boîte *f* à correspondance. **2.** *Phot:* Developing tray, cuvette *f* pour développement. *S.a.* ASH-TRAY. **3.** Tambour *m* de mitrailleuse Lewis). **'tray-cloth,** *s.* Dessus *m* . napperon *m*, de plateau.
treacherous ['tretʃərəs], *a.* (Homme) traître; (action) perfide. *T* memory, mémoire infidèle. **-ly,** *adv.* (Agir) en traître, perfidement.
treachery ['tretʃəri], *s.* Trahison *f*, perfidie *f.* **An act of treachery,** une perfidie.

treacle [triːkl], *s.* Mélasse *f.*
tread[1] [tred], *s.* **I.** (a) Pas *m.* *The sound of a heavy t.,* le bruit d'un pas lourd. *The measured t. of a policeman,* la démarche mesurée d'un agent. (b) Bruit *m* de pas. **2.** (a) Tread of a stair, giron *m* d'une marche d'escalier. (b) Semelle *f* (d'un soulier). (c) Échelon *m* (d'échelle). (d) *Aut:* Bande *f* de roulement, chape *f* (d'un pneu). **Non-skid tread,** roulement antidérapant. **3.** *Cy:* Distance *f* entre pédales. **4.** *Veh:* Largeur *f* de voie; voie *f.*
tread[2], *v.* (trod [trɔd]; trodden [trɔdn]) **I.** *v.i.* Marcher; poser les pieds. *To t. softly,* marcher doucement, à pas feutrés. **To tread on sth.,** marcher sur qch.; mettre le pied sur qch. *S.a.* CORN[2] I, DELICATE 2, FOOTSTEP 2, RUSH[2] I. I. **2.** *v.tr.* (a) Well-trodden path, chemin battu. **To tread sth. under foot,** écraser qch. du pied; fouler qch. aux pieds. (b) *A:* **To tread a measure,** danser. (c) **To tread (out) grapes,** fouler la vendange. *Swim:* **To tread water,** nager debout. **tread down,** *v.tr.* Écraser du pied, fouler aux pieds; opprimer (le peuple). **treading,** *s.* (a) Piétinement *m.* (b) Foulage *m* (des raisins). (c) Treading water, nage *f* debout.
treadle [tredl], *s.* Pédale *f* (de tour, etc.).
treadmill ['tredmil], *s.* (a) *A:* (In prisons) Écureuil *m*; treadmill *m.* (b) *F:* Besogne ingrate quotidienne; le collier de misère.
treason ['triːz(ə)n], *s.* *Jur:* Trahison *f.* **To talk treason,** tenir des propos séditieux. **High treason,** haute trahison; lèse-majesté *f.*
treasonable ['triːz(ə)nəbl], *a.* **I.** De trahison. **2.** Traître, perfide. **-ably,** *adv.* Traîtreusement.
treasure[1] ['treʒər], *s.* Trésor *m.* **To hoard treasure,** thésauriser. **Art treasures,** objets *m* d'art qui sont des trésors. **'treasure-house,** *s.* Trésor *m.* **'treasure-ship,** *s.* *A:* Galion *m.* **'treasure-'trove,** *s.* *Jur:* Trésor (découvert par hasard).
treasure[2], *v.tr.* **I.** Priser, tenir beaucoup à (qch.). **2.** (a) **To treasure sth. (up),** garder qch. soigneusement. (b) **To treasure up wealth,** amasser des richesses.
treasurer ['treʒərər], *s.* Trésorier, -ière; économe *m* (d'un collège). **Treasurer's office,** trésorerie *f.*
treasury ['treʒəri], *s.* **I.** Trésor (public); trésorerie *f.* **The Treasury,** la Trésorerie (britannique); (in *Fr.*) le Trésor (public). **First Lord of the Treasury** = Président *m* du Conseil (des ministres). *S.a.* BENCH I. **2.** **Treasury of verse,** anthologie *f* poétique. **'treasury-bill,** *s.* Billet *m* du Trésor. **'treasury-note,** *s.* *Fin:* Coupure *f* de dix shillings ou d'une livre).
treat[1] [triːt], *s.* **I.** (a) Régal *m*, -als; festin *m*; fête *f.* (b) *F:* This is my treat, c'est moi qui régale. **I'll stand treat all round,** je paie une tournée générale. **2.** *F:* Plaisir *m.* It is quite a treat to me *to listen to him,* cela m'est un vrai régal de l'écouter. **To give oneself a treat,** faire un petit extra. **A treat in store,** un plaisir à venir.
treat[2]. **I.** *v.i.* **I.** **To treat with s.o.,** traiter, négocier, avec qn. **To treat for peace,** traiter la paix. **2.** **To treat of a subject,** traiter d'un sujet. **II.** **treat,** *v.tr.* **I.** Traiter. *To t. s.o. well,* se conduire bien avec qn; bien agir avec qn. *Is that how you t. him?* est-ce ainsi que vous en agissez avec lui? **To treat sth. as a joke,** considérer qch. comme une plaisanterie. **2.** Régaler (qn); payer à boire à (qn). *F:* **To treat oneself to an ice,** s'offrir, se payer, une glace. **I'm treating,** c'est moi qui paie. **3.** (a) *Med:* Traiter (un malade). **To treat s.o. for rheumatism,**

soigner qn pour le rhumatisme. *(b) Ch:* To **treat a metal with an acid**, traiter un métal par un acide. **4.** Traiter (un thème).

treatise ['tri:tiz], *s.* Traité *m (on,* de).

treatment ['tri:tmənt], *s.* **1.** *(a)* Traitement *m* (de qn). *His t. of his friends,* sa manière d'agir envers ses amis. *Handsome t.,* belle façon d'agir. *(b)* Traitement (d'un sujet). **2.** Traitement médical. **Fresh air treatment,** cure *f* d'air.

treaty ['tri:ti], *s.* **1.** Traité *m* (de paix); convention *f.* **Treaty obligations,** obligations conventionnelles. **Treaty-port,** port ouvert (au commerce étranger). **2.** *(a)* Accord *m,* contrat *m.* **To sell sth. by private treaty,** vendre qch. à l'amiable. *(b)* **To be in treaty with s.o. for . . .,** être en pourparlers avec qn pour. . . .

treble[1] [trebl]. **I.** *a.* **1.** Triple. **2.** *Mus:* **Treble voice,** (voix *f* de) soprano *m.* **Treble clef,** clef *f* de sol. **II. treble,** *adv.* Trois fois autant. *He earns t. my salary,* il gagne trois fois plus que moi. **III. treble,** *s.* **1.** Triple *m.* **2.** *Mus:* *(a)* *To sing the t.,* chanter le dessus. *(b)* *(Pers., voice)* Soprano *m.*

treble[2]. **1.** *v.tr.* Tripler. **2.** *v.i.* (Se) tripler.

trebly ['trebli], *adv.* Triplement; trois fois autant.

tree [tri:], *s.* **1.** *(a)* Arbre *m.* **Timber tree,** arbre de haute futaie. *To climb a t.,* grimper sur, monter à, un arbre. *F:* **To be at the top of the tree,** être au haut de l'échelle. *To get to the top of the t.,* arriver. *P:* **To be up a tree,** être dans le pétrin. *(b)* **The tree of life,** l'arbre de vie. *S.a.* BARK[4] **1.** **2. Family-tree,** arbre généalogique. **3.** *A:* **Gallows-tree,** gibet *m,* potence *f.* **4.** *Const:* Poutre *f.* *Min:* Étai *m,* butte *f.* **'tree-calf,** *s.* *Bookb:* Veau raciné. **'tree-fern,** *s.* Fougère arborescente. **'tree-frog,** *s.* *Amph:* Rainette *f.* **'tree-trunk,** *s.* Tronc *m* d'arbre.

treeless ['tri:ləs], *a.* Dépourvu d'arbres; sans arbres. *T. hill tops,* cimes nues ou dénudées.

treenail ['tri:neil, trenl], *s.* *Nau:* Gournable *f.*

trefoil ['tri:foil, 'tre-], *s.* **1.** *Bot:* Trèfle *m.* **Bird's-foot trefoil,** lotier *m.* **Marsh trefoil,** trèfle d'eau. **2.** *Arch:* Trèfle.

trek[1] [trek], *s.* *(In S. Africa)* **1.** Étape *f* (d'un voyage en chariot). **2.** *(a)* Voyage *m* en chariot. *(b)* Migration *f.*

trek[2], *v.i.* *(In S. Africa)* Voyager en chariot. *F:* Faire route. **2.** *F:* Plier bagage; déguerpir.

trellis[1] ['trelis], *s.* Treillis *m,* treillage *m.* **'trellis-work,** *s.* Treillis *m,* treillage *m.*

trellis[2], *v.tr.* Treillisser, treillager.

tremble[1] [trembl], *s.* Frisson *m; (in voice)* tremblotement *m.* *F:* **To be all of a tremble,** être tout tremblant.

tremble[2], *v.i.* **1.** Trembler, vibrer. **2.** Trembler, frissonner. **To tremble before s.o.,** trembler devant qn. **I tremble for his sanity,** je tremble qu'il ne devienne fou. **trembling**[1], *a.* Tremblant, tremblotant. *Bot:* **Trembling poplar,** (peuplier *m*) tremble *m.* **Trembling bog,** tourbière flottante. *El.E:* **Trembling bell,** sonnerie trembleuse. **trembling**[2], *s.* Tremblement *m;* tremblotement *m.* *F:* **In fear and trembling,** tout tremblant.

trembler ['tremblər], *s.* *El.E:* Trembleur *m.*

tremendous [tri'mendəs], *a.* **1.** Terrible, épouvantable. **2.** *F:* Immense, énorme. *There was a t. crowd,* il y avait un monde fou. *T. success,* succès formidable. *T. blow,* coup assommant. **-ly,** *adv.* **1.** Terriblement. **2.** *F:* Énormément; démesurément.

tremolo ['tremolo], *s.* *Mus:* Tremolo *m.* **Tremolo notes,** notes tremblées.

tremor ['tremər], *s.* **1.** Tremblement *m,* frémissement *m.* **2.** Trépidation *f* (des vitres). *Meteor:* **Earth tremor,** secousse *f* sismique. **Preliminary tremor,** choc avant-coureur (d'un séisme).

tremulous ['tremjuləs], *a.* Tremblotant, frémissant. *T. smile,* sourire timide. *T. voice,* voix chevrotante. *T. writing,* écriture tremblée. **-ly,** *adv.* En tremblant; timidement.

trench[1] [trenʃ], *s.* **1.** *(a)* *Agr:* Tranchée *f,* fossé *m;* saignée *f.* *(b)* *El.E:* **Covered-in trench** *(for wiring),* canalisation *f.* **2.** *Mil:* Tranchée. **Communication trench,** boyau *m.* **Zigzag trench,** chicane *f.* **'trench-coat,** *s.* *Mil:* Manteau *m* imperméable; trench-coat *m.* **'trench-fever,** *s.* *Med:* Fièvre récurrente. **'trench-foot, -feet,** *s.* *Med:* Pieds gelés. **'trench-mortar,** *s.* Lance-bombes *m inv;* *P:* crapouillot *m.*

trench[2]. **1.** *v.tr.* *(a)* Creuser un fossé, une tranchée, dans (le sol). *Abs.* **To trench,** creuser des fossés. *(b)* *Hort:* Planter (le céleri) dans une rigole. **2.** *v.i.* **To trench (up)on s.o.'s property, s.o.'s rights,** empiéter sur la propriété, sur les droits, de qn.

trenchant ['trenʃənt], *a.* **1.** *Poet:* *(Of sword)* Tranchant, coupant. **2.** *(a)* *(Ton)* tranchant, incisif. *(b)* *(Réponse)* mordante, caustique. **-ly,** *adv.* D'une manière tranchante.

trencher ['trenʃər], *s.* **1.** *Cu:* Tranchoir *m,* tailloir *m.* **2.** *Sch:* *T:* Toque universitaire (anglaise); toque à plateau.

trencherman, *pl.* **-men** ['trenʃərmən, -men], *s.* (Good) trencherman, (grand, gros) mangeur.

trend[1] [trend], *s.* Direction *f* (d'un cours d'eau); tendance *f* (de l'opinion publique). *The t. of my thoughts,* le cours de mes pensées.

trend[2], *v.i.* Se diriger, tendre *(to, towards,* vers).

Trentino (the) [ɔːtren'tiːno]. *Pr.n.* Le Trentin.

trepan[1] [tre'pan], *s.* *Surg:* *Min:* Trépan *m.*

trepan[2], *v.tr.* (trepanned) Trépaner. **trepanning,** *s.* Trépanation *f.*

trepang [tre'pan], *s.* *Echin:* Tripang *m,* trépang *m;* *F:* bêche-de-mer *f.*

trephine[1] [tre'fiːn, -'fain], *s.* *Surg:* Tréphine *f.*

trephine[2], *v.tr.* *Surg:* Opérer avec la tréphine. **trephining,** *s.* *Surg:* Térébration *f.*

trepidation [trepi'deiʃ(ə)n], *s.* Trépidation *f.*

trespass[1] ['trespəs], *s.* **1.** *(a)* Contravention *f* de la loi; délit *m.* *(b)* *Theol:* Offense *f,* péché *m.* **2.** *Jur:* Violation *f* des droits de qn; trouble *m* de jouissance.

trespass[2], *v.i.* **1.** *A. & Lit:* Pécher *(against,* contre). *To t. against the law,* enfreindre la loi. **2.** *(a)* **To trespass (up)on s.o.'s rights,** violer les droits de qn. *(b)* **To trespass (up)on s.o.'s property,** *abs.* **to trespass,** s'introduire sans autorisation sur la propriété de qn. *F:* **To trespass on s.o.'s preserves,** empiéter sur le champ d'activité de qn. *(c)* *To t. (up)on s.o.'s kindness,* abuser de la bonté de qn.

trespasser ['trespəsər], *s.* **1.** *Theol:* Transgresseur *m.* **2.** Auteur *m* d'une violation de propriété (foncière). **'Trespassers will be prosecuted,'** "défense de passer, d'entrer, sous peine d'amende."

tress [tres], *s.* *(a)* Tresse *f,* boucle *f* (de cheveux). *(b)* *pl.* Tresses, chevelure *f* (d'une femme).

trestle [tresl], *s.* Tréteau *m,* chevalet *m.* **'trestle-bed,** *s.* Lit *m* de sangle. **'trestle-bridge,** *s.* Pont *m* sur chevalets. **'trestle-table,** *s.* Table *f* à tréteaux.

trews [truːz], *s.pl.* Pantalon *m* en tartan (de certains régiments écossais).

trey [trei], *s.* *Cards:* *Dice:* (Le) trois.

triad ['traiad], *s.* Triade *f.* *Ch:* Élément trivalent. *Mus:* Accord *m* sans l'octave.

trial ['traiəl], *s.* **I.** *Jur:* (*a*) Jugement *m* (d'un litige, d'un accusé). **To bring s.o. to trial,** faire passer qn en jugement. **They were sent for trial,** ils furent renvoyés en jugement. **Trial by jury,** jugement par jury. *S.a.* COMMIT 2. (*b*) Procès *m.* **Famous trials,** causes *f* célèbres. (*c*) *Hist:* **Trial by combat,** combat *m* judiciaire. **2.** Essai *m.* (*a*) Épreuve *f.* *Lit:* **To make trial of s.o.'s courage,** mettre à l'épreuve le courage de qn. *Sp:* **Trial game,** match *m* de sélection. (*b*) **To give sth. a trial,** faire l'essai de qch. **On trial,** à l'essai. *Mth:* **To proceed by trial and error,** appliquer la règle de fausse position. *Com:* **Trial order,** commande d'essai. *Book-k:* **Trial balance,** balance de vérification. *Av:* **Trial flight,** vol d'essai. *Nau: etc:* **Speed trial,** essai de vitesse. *Artil:* **Gun trials,** expériences *f* de tir. (*c*) **Sheepdog trials,** concours *m* de chiens de berger. **3.** Épreuve douloureuse. *He has met with sad trials,* il a été cruellement éprouvé. *That child is a great trial to his parents,* cet enfant fait le martyre de ses parents.

triangle ['traiaŋgl], *s.* **I.** Triangle *m.* *F:* **The eternal triangle,** le ménage à trois. **2.** *Mus:* Triangle.

triangular [trai'aŋgjulər], *a.* Triangulaire; en triangle. *Nau:* **T. flag,** triangle *m.*

triangulation [traiaŋgju'leiʃ(ə)n], *s.* *Surv:* Triangulation *f.*

trias ['traias], *s.* *Geol:* Trias *m.*

triassic [trai'asik], *a.* *Geol:* Triasique.

tribal ['traib(ə)l], *a.* **I.** (*Of race*) Qui vit en tribus. **2.** Qui appartient à la tribu; de tribu.

tribasic [trai'beisik], *a.* *Ch:* Tribasique.

tribe [traib], *s.* **I.** Tribu *f.* *F:* *Father with a whole t. of children,* père avec toute une smala d'enfants. **2.** *Nat.Hist:* Tribu, espèce *f.* *F:* **The scribbling tribe,** la gent écrivassière.

tribesman, *pl.* **-men** ['traibzmən, -men], *s.m.* Membre de la tribu.

tribrach ['traibrak], *s.* *Pros:* Tribraque *m.*

tribulation [tribju'leiʃ(ə)n], *s.* Tribulation *f,* affliction *f;* épreuves *f pl.*

tribunal [trai'bju:n(ə)l, tri-], *s.* Tribunal *m,* -aux. **I.** Siège du juge. **2.** Cour *f* de justice; la cour.

tribune[1] ['tribju:n], *s.* **I.** *Rom.Hist:* Tribun *m.* **2.** *F:* Tribun, démagogue *m.*

tribune[2], *s.* Tribune *f* (d'orateur).

tributary ['tribjutəri]. **I.** *a.* Tributaire. **2.** *s.* (*a*) Tributaire *m.* (*b*) Affluent *m* (d'un fleuve); tributaire.

tribute ['tribju:t], *s.* **I.** Tribut *m.* **To pay tribute,** payer tribut (*to,* à). **2.** Tribut, hommage *m.* *To pay a last t. of respect to s.o.,* rendre à qn les derniers devoirs.

tricar ['traika:r], *s.* *Veh:* Tri-car *m;* (*commercial*) triporteur *m.*

trice[1] [trais], *s.* *Only in the phr.* **In a trice,** en un clin d'œil, en moins de rien.

trice[2], *v.tr.* *Nau:* **To trice (up) a sail,** hisser, remonter, une voile.

trichina, *pl.* **-ae** [tri'kaina, -i:], *s.* *Med:* Trichine *f.*

trichromatic [traikro'matik], *a.* *Phot: etc:* (Procédé) trichrome.

trick[1] [trik], *s.* **I.** (*a*) Tour *m,* ruse *f;* supercherie *f.* **To play a trick on s.o.,** jouer un tour à qn. **To obtain sth. by a trick,** obtenir qch. par ruse. (*b*) Truc *m.* **Tricks of writing,** artifices *m* de style. **The tricks of the trade,** les trucs du métier. *He knows a trick or two, he's up to every trick,* il est roublard. *I know a trick worth two*

of that, je connais un truc encore meilleur que celui-là. **To know the trick of it,** avoir le truc. *That'll do the trick,* ça fera l'affaire. **2.** Farce *f,* tour. **Shabby trick, scurvy trick,** vilain tour. **To play a trick on s.o.,** faire une farce à qn. *You have been up to your old tricks,* vous avez encore fait des vôtres. **3.** Tour d'adresse. **Card trick,** tour de cartes. *F:* **The whole bag of tricks,** toute la boutique; tout le bataclan. *F:* **To do the trick,** réussir le coup. **Trick-riding,** voltige *f.* *S.a.* FLYING[2] I, PARLOUR. **4.** Manie *f,* habitude *f;* tic *m.* *He has a trick of (doing sth.),* il a la manie de (faire qch.). **5.** *Cards:* Levée *f.* **The odd trick,** le trick, le tri. **To take a trick,** faire une levée. **6.** *Nau:* **Trick at the wheel,** tour de barre.

trick[2], *v.tr.* **I.** Attraper, duper (qn). *Fb:* Mystifier (un adversaire). *I've been tricked,* on m'a refait. **To trick s.o. out of sth.,** escroquer qch. à qn. **2.** *F:* **To trick s.o. out,** parer qn (*with, in,* de).

trickery ['trikəri], *s.* Fourberie *f,* tricherie *f.* **Piece of trickery,** fraude *f,* supercherie *f.*

trickiness ['trikinəs], *s.* **I.** Fourberie *f.* **2.** *F:* Nature compliquée, difficile (d'un mécanisme).

trickle[1] ['trikl], *s.* Filet *m* (d'eau). **'tricklecharger,** *s.* *El.E:* Chargeur *m* (d'accu) par filtrage, à régime lent.

trickle[2]. **I.** *v.i.* (*a*) Couler (goutte à goutte). *Waters that t. from the rock,* eaux qui sourdent de la roche. *Tears trickled down her cheeks,* les larmes coulaient le long de ses joues. **To trickle in,** s'infiltrer. (*b*) *The ball just trickled into the hole,* la balle roula tout doucement dans le trou. **2.** *v.tr.* Laisser dégoutter (un liquide); laisser tomber (un liquide) goutte à goutte. **trickling,** *s.* Dégouttement *m;* écoulement *m* goutte à goutte.

trickster ['trikstər], *s.* Fourbe *m,* escroc *m.*

tricky ['triki], *a.* **I.** Rusé, astucieux, fin. **2.** *F:* (Mécanisme) d'un maniement délicat.

tricolo(u)r ['traikələr]. **I.** *a.* Tricolore. **2.** *s.* **The Tricolour,** le drapeau tricolore (français).

tricycle ['traisikl], *s.* Tricycle *m.* **Carrier-tricycle,** triporteur *m.*

tridactyl(ous) [trai'daktil(əs)], *a.* *Z:* Tridactyle.

trident ['traidənt], *s.* Trident *m* (de Neptune).

tried [traid]. *See* TRY[2].

triennial [trai'enjəl], *a.* **I.** Trisannuel. **2.** Triennal. *Triennial plants, s.* triennals, plantes triennales.

trier ['traiər], *s.* **I.** *F:* He's a trier, il fait toujours de son mieux. **2.** *Tail:* Trier-on, essayeur, -euse.

trifle[1] ['traifl], *s.* **I.** (*a*) Bagatelle *f,* vétille *f.* *The merest t. puts him out,* il se fâche pour un rien. *Ten pounds, a mere t.!* dix livres, une misère! *To stick at trifles,* s'arrêter à des vétilles. *It's no trifle,* ce n'est pas une petite affaire. (*b*) *He gave the beggar a trifle,* il donna quelques sous au mendiant. (*c*) *Adv.phr.* **A trifle,** un tout petit peu. *A t. too narrow,* un soupçon trop étroit. **2.** *Cu:* Charlotte *f* russe sur biscuit de Savoie imbibé de xérès.

trifle[2]. **I.** *v.i.* (*a*) Jouer, badiner (*with,* avec). **To trifle with s.o.,** se jouer de qn. *To t. with one's health,* jouer avec sa santé. (*b*) **To trifle with sth.,** manier nonchalamment (sa canne). *To t. with one's food,* manger du bout des dents. (*c*) Vétiller; s'occuper à des riens. **2.** *v.tr.* **To trifle one's time away,** gâcher son temps. **trifling,** *a.* **I.** (*Of pers.*) Futile, léger. **2.** (*Of thg*) Insignifiant; peu important. *T. incidents,* menus incidents. **Of trifling value,** d'une valeur minime.

trifling, *s.* **I.** Légèreté *f* d'esprit; manque *m* de sérieux. **2.** Futilités *f pl.*

trifler ['traiflər], s. Personne f frivole.

trig[1] [trig], s. **1.** Cale f (pour empêcher une roue, un tonneau, de rouler). **2.** Sabot m d'enrayage.

trig[2], v.tr. **(trigged) 1.** Caler (une roue, un tonneau). **2.** Enrayer (une roue).

trig[3], v.tr. **(trigged)** To trig oneself out, se mettre sur son trente et un ; s'endimancher.

trig[4], s. Sch: P: Trigonométrie f.

trigger ['trigər], s. (a) Poussoir m à ressort. Aut: T. of the hand-brake, manette f du frein. Trigger action, déclenchement m. (b) Sm.a: Détente f; F: gâchette f. **'trigger-finger,** s. Index m (de la main droite). **'trigger-guard,** s. Sm.a: Pontet m; sous-garde f.

triglyph ['traiglif], s. Arch: Triglyphe m.

trigonometric(al) [trigonoʹmetrik(əl)], a. Trigonométrique. **-ally,** adv. Trigonométriquement.

trigonometry [trigoʹnɔmetri], s. Trigonométrie f. Plane trigonometry, trigonométrie rectiligne.

trigynous ['tridʒinəs], a. Bot: Trigyne.

trihedral [traiʹhi:drəl, -ʹhedrəl], a. & s. (Angle) trièdre ; trièdre m.

trill[1] [tril], s. **1.** Mus: (a) Trille m. (b) Cadence perlée. **2.** Chant perlé (des oiseaux). **3.** Ling: Consonne roulée.

trill[2]. **1.** v.i. (a) Mus: Faire des trilles. (b) (Of bird) Perler son chant. **2.** v.tr. (a) Mus: Triller (une note). (b) Ling: Rouler (les r).

trillion ['triljən], s. **1.** Quintillion m (10[18]). **2.** U.S: Trillion m (10[12]).

trilobate [traiʹloubet], a. Bot: etc: Trilobé.

trilogy ['trilɔdʒi], s. Trilogie f.

trim[1] [trim], s. **1.** Bon ordre. (a) Everything was in perfect trim, tout était en parfait état. Ship in fighting trim, navire prêt pour le combat. (b) To be in good trim, être gaillard ; (of boxer) être en forme. **2.** Nau: Assiette f, arrimage m (d'un navire). Av: Équilibrage m. **3.** Hairdr: Coupe f.

trim[2], a. Soigné ; en bon état ; tiré à quatre épingles. A t. figure, une tournure élégante. **-ly,** adv. En bon ordre ; proprement.

trim[3], v.tr. **(trimmed) 1.** (a) Arranger ; mettre en ordre. (b) Tailler (une haie) ; émonder (un arbre) ; dégrossir (le bois) ; rafraîchir (la barbe). Phot: Calibrer (une épreuve). To trim one's nails, se faire les ongles. To trim a lamp, couper¹ a mèche d'une lampe. Bookb: **To trim (down) the edges of a book,** rogner les tranches d'un livre. Cu: **To trim meat,** parer la viande. **2.** Dressm: etc: Orner, parer (with, de). Underclothes trimmed with lace, linge de corps garni de dentelles. **3.** Nau: (a) Équilibrer (un navire). **Trimmed by the head,** chargé sur nez. **To trim the cargo,** arrimer le chargement. (b) Orienter, appareiller (les voiles). **trim up,** v.tr. **1.** Garnir à neuf (un chapeau). **To trim oneself up,** faire un brin de toilette. **2.** Carp: Dresser (une poutre). **trimming,** s. **1.** (a) Arrangement m, mise f en état (de qch.). (b) Taille f (des haies). Phot: Calibrage m (des épreuves). Bookb: **Trimming (down) of the edges,** ébarbage m des tranches. **2.** (a) Garnissage m (de chapeaux). (b) Garniture f, ornement m (de vêtements, de chapeaux). **Bead trimming,** motif perlé. **Lace trimming,** garniture de dentelles. **3.** Nau: Arrimage m. **4.** pl. **Trimmings.** (a) Rognures fpl (de papier) ; parure f (de viande). (b) Passementerie f (pour vêtements) ; fournitures fpl (pour chapeaux). Cu: Accompagnements mpl, garniture d'un gigot, etc.).

trimeter ['trimetər, 'trai-], a. & s. Pros: Trimètre (m).

trimmer ['trimər], s. **1.** (a) Ind: Appareilleur m (b) Lamp-trimmer, lampiste m. (c) Garnisseur -euse (de chapeaux). (d) Nau: Arrimeur m Coal-trimmer, soutier m. (e) Pol: F: Opportuniste m. **2.** (a) Machine f à trancher. Bookb. Massicot m. (b) Const: Chevêtre m.

trimness ['trimnəs], s. Air soigné, air bien tenu (de qn) ; élégance f (de mise). The t. of her figure sa jolie tournure.

tringle [tringl], s. Arch: Furn: Tringle f.

Trinidad ['trinidad]. Pr.n. (Ile de) la Trinité.

trinitrotoluene ['trainaitroʹtɔljui:n], s. Exp Trinitrotoluène m.

Trinity ['triniti], s. **1.** (a) Theol: The (blessed) Trinity, la (sainte) Trinité. **Trinity Sunday** (fête f de) la Trinité. (b) F: Groupe m de trois (personnes). **2.** Nau: **Trinity House,** corporation chargée de l'entretien des phares, du balisage et du pilotage.

trinket ['trinket], s. (a) Petit objet de parure ; breloque f. (b) Bibelot m.

trinomial [traiʹnoumiəl], a. & s. Mth: Trinôme (m).

trio, pl. **-os** ['tri:ou(z)], s. Trio m.

triolet ['tri:olet], s. Pros: Triolet m.

trip[1] [trip], s. **1.** Excursion f; voyage m d'agrément. **Honeymoon trip,** voyage m de noces. To go for a short sea t., faire une sortie en mer. **Cheap trip,** excursion à prix réduit. Aut: **Trip recorder** (of speedometer), (totalisateur) journalier m. Nau: **Maiden trip,** première sortie (d'un navire). **Round trip,** croisière f. **2.** (a) Faux pas ; trébuchement m. (b) F: Faute f; faux pas. (c) Croc-enjambe m. Box: Enlaçage m de jambe. **'trip-gear,** s. Mec.E: Déclic m ; modificateur instantané. **'trip-hammer,** s. Marteau m à bascule. **'trip-wire,** s. Mil: Fil tendu (en guise de traquenard ou d'avertisseur).

trip[2], v. **(tripped** [tript]) **1.** v.i. (a) **To trip (along),** aller d'un pas léger. (b) Trébucher ; faire un faux pas. (c) F: Se tromper ; commettre une faute. **To catch s.o. tripping,** prendre qn en défaut, en erreur. (d) (Of anchor) Déraper. **2.** v.tr. (a) **To trip s.o. (up),** (i) donner un croc-en-jambe à qn ; (of obstacle) faire trébucher qn ; (ii) F: prendre qn en défaut. (b) Nau: **To trip the anchor,** déraper l'ancre.

tripe [traip], s. **1.** (a) Cu: Tripe(s) f(pl) ; grasdouble m. (b) P: Fatras m, bêtises fpl. To publish t., publier des ouvrages sans valeur, de la littérature de camelote. **2.** pl. P: (i) Entrailles f, intestins m ; (ii) panse f. **'tripe-dealer, -seller,** s. Tripier, -ière.

triphase ['traife:iz], a. El: (Courant) triphasé.

triplane ['traiplein], a. & s. Av: Triplan (m).

triple[1] ['tripl], a. Triple. Mth: **Triple ratio,** raison triple. Mus: **Triple time,** mesure ternaire, à trois temps. Hist: **The Triple Alliance,** la Triplice ; la triple Alliance. **Triple-expansion engine,** machine à triple expansion. **Triplescrew steamer,** vapeur à trois hélices. **-ply,** adv. Triplement.

triple[2]. **1.** v.tr. Tripler. **2.** v.i. (Se) tripler.

triplet ['triplet], s. **1.** Trio m ; réunion f de trois personnes, de trois choses. Esp. (a) Mus: Triolet m. (b) Pros: Tercet m. (c) Opt: **Triplet lens,** triplet m. **2.** Trijumeau, -elle. To give birth to triplets, mettre au monde trois jumeaux.

triplex ['tripleks, 'trai-], a. (Planche) en trois épaisseurs ; (machine) à trois cylindres.

triplicate[1] ['tripliket]. **1.** a. Triplé ; triple. Mth: **Triplicate ratio,** raison triplée. **2.** s. Triple m ; triplicata m. Agreement in triplicate, traité en triple exemplaire, en triple expédition.

triplicate² ['triplikeit], *v.tr.* **1.** Tripler. **2.** Rédiger (un document) en triple expédition.

tripod ['traipɔd], *s.* Trépied *m*; pied *m* (à trois branches). *Folding t.*, pied à brisures; pied pliant. **Tripod stand,** pied à trois branches; support *m* à trois pieds. *Nau:* Tripod mast, (mât) tripode *m*.

Tripoli ['tripoli]. **1.** *Pr.n.* (a) Tripoli *m*. (b) La Tripolitaine. **2.** *s.* Tripoli (powder), tripoli *m*; terre pourrie.

tripos ['traipɔs], *s. Sch:* Examen de Bachelier-ès-Arts (à Cambridge), spécialisé en mathématiques, langues classiques, etc.

tripper ['tripər], *s.* Excursionniste *mf*.

triptych ['triptik], *s. Art:* Triptyque *m*.

triptyque ['triptik], *s. Aut:* Triptyque *m* (pour passage en douane).

trireme ['trairi:m], *s. Gr.Ant:* Trirème *f*.

trisect [trai'sekt], *v.tr. Geom: etc:* Triséquer. **trisecting,** *a.* Trisecteur, -trice.

trisection [trai'sekʃ(ə)n], *s.* Trisection *f*.

Tristram ['tristrəm]. *Pr.n.m. Lit:* Tristan.

trisyllabic [traisi'labik], *a.* Tris(s)yllabique, tris(s)yllabe.

trisyllable [trai'siləbl], *s.* Tris(s)yllabe *m*.

trite [trait], *a.* Banal, -aux. **Trite subject,** sujet usé, rebattu. **-ly,** *adv.* Banalement.

triteness ['traitnəs], *s.* Banalité *f*.

Triton ['trait(ə)n]. **1.** *Pr.n.m. Myth:* Triton. **2.** *s. F:* To be a triton among the minnows, éclipser tout son entourage.

tritone ['traitoun], *s. Mus:* Triton *m*.

triturate ['tritjureit], *v.tr.* Triturer.

trituration [tritju'reiʃ(ə)n], *s.* Trituration *f*.

triumph¹ ['traiəmf], *s.* **1.** *Rom.Ant:* Triomphe *m*. **2.** (a) Triomphe, succès *m*. **To achieve great triumphs,** remporter de grands succès. (b) Air *m* de triomphe; jubilation *f*.

triumph², *v.i.* **1.** *Rom.Ant:* Triompher. **2.** Triompher; remporter un succès éclatant. **To triumph over one's enemies,** triompher de ses ennemis; l'emporter sur ses ennemis.

triumphal [trai'ʌmf(ə)l], *a.* Triomphal, -aux; de triomphe. **Triumphal arch,** arc *m* de triomphe.

triumphant [trai'ʌmfənt], *a.* Triomphant. **The Church Triumphant,** l'Église triomphante. **-ly,** *adv.* Triomphalement; d'un air, d'un ton, de triomphe.

triumvir, *pl.* **-virs, -viri** [trai'ʌmvər, -vərz, -virai], *s. Rom.Hist:* Triumvir *m*.

triumvirate [trai'ʌmviret], *s.* Triumvirat *m*.

triune ['traiju:n], *a.* D'une unité triple. *Esp.* **Triune godhead,** divinité *f* une en trois personnes.

trivalent ['trivələnt], *a. Ch:* Trivalent.

trivet ['trivet], *s.* Trépied *m*, chevrette *f* (pour bouilloire, etc.). *S.a.* RIGHT¹ I. 4.

trivial ['trivial], *a.* **1.** (a) Insignifiant; sans importance. (b) (Of pers.) Superficiel, léger, futile. **2.** Banal, -aux; trivial, -aux. **The trivial round,** le train-train de tous les jours.

triviality [trivi'aliti], *s.* (a) Insignifiance *f* (d'une perte, d'une offense, etc.). (b) Banalité *f* (d'une observation, etc.).

tri-weekly [trai'wi:kli], **1.** (a) *a.* De toutes les trois semaines. (b) *adv.* Toutes les trois semaines. **2.** (a) *a.* Trihebdomadaire. (b) *adv.* Trois fois par semaine.

troat¹ [trout], *s. Ven:* Bramement *m* (du cerf).

troat², *v.i. Ven:* (Of stag) Bramer.

trocar ['troukar], *s. Surg:* Trocart *m*.

trochaic [tro'keiik], *a. & s. Pros:* Trochaïque (*m*).

troche [trouk, trou(t)ʃ, 'trouki:], *s. Pharm:* Trochisque *m*, tablette *f*.

trochee ['trouki:], *s. Pros:* Trochée *m*.

trochlea, *pl.* **-eae** ['trɔklia, -ii:], *s. Anat:* Trochlée *f*.

trochoid ['troukɔid]. **1.** *a.* (a) *Anat:* (Articulation) trochoïde. (b) *Geom:* Cycloïdal, -aux. **2.** *s. Geom:* (i) *A:* Cycloïde *f*, roulette *f*. (ii) Courbe cycloïdale.

trod [trɔd], **trodden** [trɔdn]. See TREAD².

troglodyte ['trɔglodait], *s.* Troglodyte *m*.

Trojan ['troudʒən], *a. & s.* Troyen, -enne; de Troie. **The Trojan War,** la guerre de Troie. *F:* **To work like a Trojan,** travailler comme un nègre.

troll¹ [troul], *s.* **1.** Chanson *f* à reprises; canon *m*. **2.** Moulinet *m* (de canne à pêche).

troll². **1.** *v.tr.* (a) *A:* Chanter (un air) en canon. (b) Chantonner (un air); *abs.* chantonner. **2.** *v.i. Fish:* To troll for pike, pêcher le brochet à la cuiller. **trolling,** *s. Fish:* Pêche *f* à la cuiller. **'trolling-spoon,** *s. Fish:* Cuiller *f*.

troll³, *s. Norse Myth:* Troll *m*.

trolley ['trɔli], *s.* **1.** (a) *Veh:* (Four-wheeled) Fardier *m*, chariot *m*; (two-wheeled) diable *m*. **Porter's luggage trolley,** chariot à bagages. (b) **Dinner trolley,** serveuse *f*. **2.** *Ind:* **Overhead trolley,** chariot, baladeur *m* ou transporteur aérien (de pont roulant, etc.). **3.** (a) Moufle *m* or *f* (de transport sur câble aérien). (b) *El.E:* (Poulie *f* de) trolley *m*; poulie de contact (d'un tramway). **'trolley-bus,** *s.* Autobus *m* à trolley; trolleyautobus *m*. **'trolley-pole,** *s.* Perche *f* de trolley. **'trolley-wheel,** *s.* Roulette *f* de trolley. **'trolley-wire,** *s.* Câble conducteur.

trollop ['trɔləp], *s.f.* Souillon, guenipe.

trolly ['trɔli], *s.* = TROLLEY.

trombone [trɔm'boun], *s.* Trombone *m*. **Valve trombone,** trombone à pistons.

troop¹ [tru:p], *s.* **1.** Troupe *f*, bande *f* (de personnes). **In troops,** par bandes. **2.** *Mil:* (a) *pl.* **Troops,** -troupes. **To raise troops,** lever des soldats. *S.a.* STORM-TROOPS. (b) Peloton *m* (de cavalerie). **To get one's troop,** passer capitaine. **3.** Troop of boy scouts, troupe de boys-scouts. **'troop-ship,** *s.* Transport *m*. **'trooptrain,** *s.* Train *m* régimentaire.

troop². **1.** *v.i.* (a) To troop together, s'attrouper, s'assembler. (b) To troop in, out, off, entrer, sortir, partir, en troupe, en bande. **2.** *v.tr. Mil:* To troop the colour(s), faire la parade du drapeau; présenter le drapeau. **trooping,** *s.* **1.** Trooping (together), attroupement *m*, assemblement *m*; rassemblement *m* (de troupes). **2.** *Mil:* Trooping the colour(s), parade *f* du drapeau; salut *m* au drapeau.

trooper ['tru:pər], *s. Mil:* (a) Cavalier *m*; soldat *m* de cavalerie. *Pej:* Old trooper, soudard *m*. *S.a.* SWEAR² 2. (b) *F:* Cheval *m* de cavalerie.

trope [troup], *s. Rh:* Trope *m*.

trophy ['troufi], *s.* Trophée *m*.

tropic ['trɔpik]. **1.** *s.* (a) *Astr: Geog:* Tropique *m*. (b) The tropics, les tropiques; les pays chauds. *In the tropics,* sous les tropiques. **2.** *a.* Tropical, -aux.

tropical ['trɔpik(ə)l], *a.* **1.** *Astr:* (Année) tropique. **2.** (Climat) tropical, -aux; des tropiques.

trot¹ [trɔt], *s.* Trot *m*. **Gentle trot,** petit trot. **Full trot,** grand trot. **Close trot,** trot assis. **To go at a trot,** aller au trot. *At a slow t., at an easy t.,* au petit trot. **To break into a trot,** se mettre au trot. *F:* To keep s.o. on the trot, faire trotter qn. *S.a.* JOG-TROT.

trot², *v.* (trotted) **1.** *v.i.* (a) Trotter; aller au trot. **To trot away, off,** partir au trot. *To t. five miles,* faire cinq milles au trot. **To trot short,** trottiner. (*b*) (*Of pers.*) Trotter ; (*of child, etc.*) trottiner ; (*of athlete*) courir au pas gymnastique. (*c*) *F:* **Now I must be trotting,** maintenant il faut que je file, que je me trotte. **2.** *v.tr.* (*a*) Faire trotter (un cheval). (*b*) *F:* **To trot s.o. round,** balader qn ; faire voir la ville à qn ; servir de guide à qn. **trot out. 1.** *v.i.* Allonger le pas ; aller au grand trot. **2.** *v.tr.* (*a*) **To trot out a horse,** faire trotter un cheval (devant un client). (*b*) *F:* **To trot out one's knowledge,** exhiber, faire étalage de, ses connaissances.

troth [trouθ], *s. A. & Lit:* **1.** Foi *f.* **By my troth!** sur ma foi ! *S.a.* PLIGHT[2]. **2. In troth,** en vérité.

trotter ['trɔtər], *s.* **1.** (*a*) Cheval *m* de trot ; trotteur *m.* (*b*) (*Pers.*) Trotteur ; (*of child*) *S.a.* GLOBE-TROTTER. **2.** *pl. Cu:* **Sheep's trotters, pigs' trotters,** pieds *m* de mouton, de cochon ; pieds panés.

trouble[1] [trʌbl], *s.* **1.** Peine *f*, chagrin *m* ; affliction *f*, malheur *m.* **To be in trouble,** être dans la peine ; avoir du chagrin. (*Cp.* 2 (*b*).) *They are in great t.,* ils sont tout désemparés. *His troubles are over,* il est au bout de ses peines. **2.** Ennui *m*, difficulté *f.* (*a*) **Money troubles** soucis *m* d'argent. **Family troubles,** ennuis de famille. **The trouble is that . . .,** l'ennui, la difficulté, c'est que. . . . **You will have trouble with him,** il vous donnera du fil à retordre. *The child must be a great t. to you,* l'enfant doit vous donner bien du tracas. *Prov:* **Troubles never come singly,** un ennui ne vient jamais seul. (*b*) **To get into trouble,** s'attirer une mauvaise affaire, des désagréments, des ennuis. **To get into trouble with the police,** avoir affaire à la police. **To get s.o. into trouble, to make trouble for s.o.,** créer, susciter, des ennuis à qn. **To get out of trouble,** se tirer d'affaire. *To get s.o. out of t.,* tirer qn d'affaire. **To be in trouble,** avoir des ennuis (avec la police, etc.). **He is looking for trouble,** il fait tout ce qu'il faut pour s'attirer une affaire ; il se prépare des ennuis. (*c*) **To make trouble,** semer la discorde, la mésintelligence. *If you do not consent he will make t.,* si vous ne consentez pas il va se montrer désagréable. **3.** Dérangement *m*, peine. **To take the trouble to do sth. ; to go to, be at, the trouble of doing sth.,** prendre, se donner, la peine de faire qch. **It is not worth the trouble,** ce n'est pas la peine ; cela n'en vaut pas la peine. **To give s.o. trouble, to put s.o. to trouble,** déranger qn. *I am putting you to a lot of t.,* je vous donne beaucoup d'embarras. **To put oneself to a lot of trouble, to give oneself a lot of trouble, to take a great deal of trouble,** se donner beaucoup de mal, beaucoup de peine. **To spare no trouble in order to . . .,** ne pas ménager sa peine pour. . . . **He thinks nothing too much trouble,** rien ne lui coûte. **To have some trouble to do sth.,** avoir quelque peine à faire qch. **It is no trouble to make,** cela ne donne aucun mal ; cela se fait tout seul. *F:* **It is no trouble,** cela ne me coûte aucune peine. *It will be but little t. to copy it again,* il n'en coûtera guère de le recopier. **To have (had) all one's trouble for nothing, for one's pains,** en être pour sa peine. **4.** (*a*) *Med:* Dérangement, trouble *m*, troubles. *Eyesight t.,* troubles de vision. *Eye t.,* affection *f* de l'œil. *Digestive troubles,* embarras digestifs. **To have heart trouble,** être malade du cœur. **What is the trouble?** de quoi vous plaignez-vous ? où avez-vous mal ? (*b*) *Aut: etc:* **Engine trouble,** panne *f*

du moteur. (*c*) *Ind:* **Labour troubles,** conflits entre ouvriers et patrons.

trouble[2]. **1.** *v.tr.* (*a*) Affliger, tourmenter, chagriner (qn) ; inquiéter, préoccuper, soucier (qn). **To be troubled about s.o.,** se tourmenter au sujet de qn. *He has been much troubled about his son,* son fils lui a causé bien du tourment. *That does not t. him much,* cela le, lui, soucie fort peu ; cela ne le préoccupe guère. (*b*) (*Of disease, ailment*) Affliger, faire souffrir (qn). (*c*) Déranger, incommoder, gêner, ennuyer, embarrasser (qn) ; donner de la peine à (qn). *I am so sorry to t. you,* toutes mes excuses pour la peine que je vous donne. *I shall not t. you with the details,* je ne vous importunerai pas de tous les détails. **May I trouble you to shut the door?** cela vous dérangerait-il de fermer la porte ? puis-je vous prier de (vouloir bien) fermer la porte ? **To trouble oneself about sth.,** se mettre en peine de qch. **To trouble oneself to do sth.,** se donner la peine de faire qch. **2.** *v.i.* (*a*) S'inquiéter, *F:* se tracasser (*about,* au sujet de, à propos de). **Don't trouble about it,** ne vous inquiétez pas de cela ; que cela ne vous inquiète pas. (*b*) Se déranger ; se mettre en peine. **Don't trouble to write,** ne vous donnez pas la peine d'écrire. **troubled,** *a.* **1.** (*Of liquid*) Trouble. *F:* **To fish in troubled waters,** pêcher en eau trouble. *S.a.* OIL[1] 1. **2.** (*a*) Inquiet ; agité. (*b*) *T. period* (*of history*), époque de troubles.

troubler ['trʌblər], *s.* Perturbateur, -trice.

troublesome ['trʌblsəm], *a.* **1.** Ennuyeux, gênant, incommode, embarrassant. *T. child,* enfant fatigant, énervant. *T. rival,* rival gênant. *T. asthma,* asthme pénible. **How troublesome!** quel ennui ! **2.** (*Tâche*) difficile, pénible.

troublous ['trʌbləs], *a. A:* Troublé, agité. **Troublous times,** époque *f* de troubles.

trough [trɔf], *s.* **1.** Auge *f* ; baquet *m* ; (*small*) auget *m*, augette *f. Husb:* **Drinking trough,** abreuvoir *m.* **Feeding trough,** auge. *Ph:* **Mercury trough,** cuvette *f*, cuve *f*, à mercure. **Accumulator trough,** bac *m* d'accumulateur. *S.a.* HORSE-TROUGH, KNEADING-TROUGH. **2.** Caniveau *m* (en bois, etc.) ; chéneau *m.* **3.** *Geol:* Fond *m* de bateau. **4. Trough of the sea,** creux *m* de la lame. *Ph:* **Trough of a wave,** point bas, creux, d'une onde. **'trough-battery,** *s. El:* Pile *f* à auge.

trounce [trauns], *v.tr.* **1.** (*a*) Rosser, étriller (qn) ; rouer (qn) de coups. (*b*) *Games:* Écraser (ses adversaires) ; battre (ses adversaires) à plates coutures. **2.** Réprimander, semoncer. **trouncing,** *s.* Raclée *f* ; étrillage *m.* **To give s.o. a trouncing,** (i) administrer une raclée à qn ; étriller qn ; (ii) battre (un adversaire) à plates coutures.

troupe [tru:p], *s.* Troupe *f* (de comédiens, etc.).

trouser ['trauzər], *s.* (Pair of) trousers, pantalon *m.* **Turn-up trousers,** pantalon à bords relevés. **'trouser-clip,** *s.* Pince *f* à pantalon (pour cycliste, etc.). **'trouser-press,** *s.* Presse *f* pour pantalons ; presse-pantalon *m.* **'trouser-stretcher,** *s.* Tendeur *m* pour pantalon(s).

trousseau ['tru:sou], *s.* Trousseau *m.*

trout [traut], *s.inv. Ich:* Truite *f. River full of trout,* rivière pleine de truites. **Trout stream,** ruisseau à truites. *S.a.* SALMON-TROUT, SEA-TROUT. **'trout-coloured,** *a.* (Cheval) truité. **'trout-fly,** *s.* **1.** *Ent:* Éphémère *m.* **2.** *Fish:* Mouche *f* pour la pêche à la truite.

trow [trau], *v.tr. A:* Croire, penser.

trowel ['trauəl], *s.* **1.** Truelle *f. S.a.* LAY ON 2. **2.** *Hort:* Déplantoir *m*, houlette *f.*

trowelful' ['trauəlful], s. Clapée f (de mortier); truellée f.

troy¹ [trɔi], s. Troy (weight), poids m troy (pour la pesée de l'or et de l'argent). S.a. OUNCE¹ I.

Troy². Pr.n. A.Geog: Troie f.

truant ['truːənt], a. & s. Élève absent de l'école sans permission. **To play truant,** faire l'école buissonnière. F: My t. thoughts, ma pensée qui était ailleurs; mes pensées vagabondes.

truce [truːs], s. Trêve f. Hist: **The Truce of God,** la trêve de Dieu. F: **A truce to jesting!** trêve de plaisanteries! S.a. FLAG⁴ I. **'truce-bearer,** s. Mil: Parlementaire m. **'truce-breaker,** s. Violateur m de la trêve.

truck¹ [trʌk], s. I. Troc m, échange m. 2. Hist: Truck Act, loi f interdisant le paiement des ouvriers en nature. 3. F: **I have no truck with him,** (i) je n'ai pas affaire à lui; (ii) je n'ai rien à faire avec lui. 4. (a) Articles divers. (b) Camelote f.

truck², s. I. (a) (Four-wheeled) Fardier m, camion m, chariot m. (b) Min: Benne f. (c) Porter's luggage truck, (four-wheeled) chariot à bagages; (two-wheeled) diable m. 2. Rail: Wagon m (à marchandises); truck m. **Flat truck,** wagon en plate-forme. S.a. CATTLE-TRUCK. 3. Rail: **Bogie-truck, radial truck,** bog(g)ie m (de locomotive ou de wagon). 4. Nau: Pomme f (de mât).

truckful ['trʌkful], s. Plein wagon, plein camion (of, de).

truckle ['trʌkl], v.i. **To truckle to s.o.,** ramper, s'abaisser, devant qn; faire des platitudes à qn.

truckle-bed ['trʌklbed], s. Lit bas à roulettes.

truckler ['trʌklər], s. Flagorneur m; plat valet.

truculence ['trʌkjuləns], **truculency** ['trʌkjulənsi], s. Férocité f; truculence f.

truculent ['trʌkjulənt], a. Féroce; brutal, -aux; truculent. **-ly,** adv. Férocement; avec truculence.

trudge¹ [trʌdʒ], s. Marche f pénible.

trudge², v.i. Marcher lourdement, péniblement; clopiner.

trudgen ['trʌdʒən], s. Swim: Trudgen (stroke), trudgeon m; coupe indienne.

true¹ [truː]. I. a. I. Vrai; exact. **If it be true that . . .,** s'il est vrai que + sub.; si tant est que + sub. **So true is it that . . .,** tant il est vrai que + ind. **True!** c'est (bien) vrai! c'est juste! **To come true,** se réaliser; se vérifier. **The same holds true in respect of . . .,** il en est de même pour. . . . S.a. BILL⁴ 6, LIFE I. 2. Véritable; vrai, réel, authentique. **To form a true estimate of the situation,** se faire une idée juste de la situation. Nau: **True longitude,** longitude vraie. 3. Mec.E: etc: Juste, droit; rectifié, ajusté. **To make a piece true,** ajuster une pièce. 4. (a) Fidèle, loyal, -aux (to, à). (b) T. repentance, repentir sincère. (c) A: (Of pers.) Honnête, sincère. 5. (Of voice, instrument) Juste. 6. Biol: **True to type,** conforme au type ancestral. II. **true,** adv. I. Vraiment; F: vrai. **Tell me true,** F: dites-moi pour de vrai. 2. (a) **To sing true,** chanter juste. **To aim true,** viser juste. (b) **To breed true,** se reproduire suivant un type invariable. III. **true,** s. Adj. phr. & adv. phr. **Out of true,** (i) (of vertical post, etc.) hors d'aplomb; (ii) (of horizontal member, etc.) dénivelé; (iii) (of metal plate) gauchi, gondolé; (of wheel) voilé; (of axle) faussé, dévoyé; (of timber) déjeté, dévié; (iv) (of cylinder, etc.) ovalisé; (of wheel) décentré, excentré. **To run out of true,** être décentré; tourner à faux. **'true-born,** a. **A true-born Englishman,** un vrai Anglais

d'Angleterre. **'true-'hearted,** a. (a) Au cœur fidèle; loyal, -aux. (b) Sincère, honnête. **'true-love 'knot,** s. Lacs m d'amour.

true², v.tr. To true (up), ajuster (les pièces d'une machine); défausser, dégauchir (un essieu, etc.); rectifier, (re)dresser (une surface); dégauchir (une planche, etc.).

truffle [trʌfl], s. Truffe f.

truffled [trʌfld], a. Cu: Truffé; aux truffes.

truism ['truːizm], s. Truisme m, axiome m; F: vérité f de La Palisse.

truly ['truːli], adv. I. (a) Vraiment, véritablement. **I am truly grateful,** je vous suis sincèrement reconnaissant. (b) Corr: **(I am) yours (very) truly,** je vous prie de croire à ma parfaite considération. F: **No one knows it better than yours truly,** personne ne le sait mieux que votre serviteur. 2. En vérité. T., I should be puzzled to say . . ., en vérité, je serais embarrassé de dire. . . . 3. (Servir qn, etc.) fidèlement, loyalement. 4. Avec vérité; justement.

trump¹ [trʌmp], s. A. & Lit: Trompette f. **The last trump, the trump of doom,** la trompette du jugement dernier.

trump², s. I. Cards: Atout m. **To play trumps,** jouer atout. **To call no trumps,** appeler, demander, sans-atout. F: **He always turns up trumps,** la chance le favorise sans cesse. 2. F: (a) Bon type; brave garçon, brave fille. (b) Chic type.

trump³, v.tr. I. Cards: Couper (une carte). Abs. **To trump,** jouer atout. 2. **To trump up an excuse,** inventer, forger, une excuse. **To t. up a charge against s.o.,** forger une accusation contre qn.

trumpery ['trʌmpəri]. I. s. (a) Friperie f, camelote f. (b) Bêtises fpl, fadaises fpl. 2. a. (a) (Marchandises) sans valeur, de camelote, de pacotille. (b) (Argument, etc.) mesquin, spécieux.

trumpet¹ ['trʌmpet], s. I. Trompette f. **Valve trumpet,** trompette à pistons. **Flourish of trumpets,** fanfare f de trompettes. F: **To publish sth. with a flourish of trumpets,** publier qch. à cor et à cri. 2. (a) (Ear-)trumpet, cornet m acoustique. S.a. SPEAKING-TRUMPET. (b) Pavillon m (de phonographe, etc.). **'trumpet-call,** s. Coup m de trompette; sonnerie f de trompette. **'trumpet-'major,** s. Mil: Trompette-major m. **'trumpet-shell,** s. Moll: Triton m ou buccin m.

trumpet², v. (trumpeted) I. v.i. (a) Sonner de la trompette. (b) (Of elephant) Barrir. 2. v.tr. F: Publier (qch.) à son de trompe. **To trumpet forth, abroad, s.o.'s great deeds,** proclamer les hauts faits de qn. **trumpeting,** s. I. Sonnerie f de trompette. 2. (Of elephant) Barrit m, barrissement m.

trumpeter ['trʌmpetər], s. (a) Mil: Trompette m. (b) (By profession) Trompettiste m.

truncate ['trʌŋkeit], v.tr. Tronquer (un arbre, etc.). **truncated,** a. Tronqué. Geom: **Truncated cone,** tronc m de cône; cône tronqué.

truncheon ['trʌnʃ(ə)n], s. Bâton m (d'agent de police).

trundle¹ ['trʌndl], s. I. Roulette f (de meuble). 2. Mec.E: (a) Trundle(-wheel), (roue f à) lanterne f. (b) (Stave) Fuseau m (de lanterne). 3. Binart m, fardier m. 4. Transport m sur fardier; roulage m.

trundle², v.tr. (a) Faire rouler, faire courir (un cerceau, etc.). Cr: F: Bôler (la balle). (b) Pousser (une brouette).

trunk [trʌŋk], s. I. (a) Tronc m (d'arbre).

(b) Tronc (du corps). (c) *Rail:* Artère principale (d'un réseau). *Tp:* Trunk **connections,** relations interurbaines. (d) *Arch:* Fût m (d'une colonne). **2.** Malle f, coffre m. Wardrobe trunk, malle-armoire f. **To pack one's trunk,** faire sa malle. *S.a.* CABIN-TRUNK. **3.** Trompe f (d'éléphant). **4.** *pl.* **Trunks,** (i) = TRUNK-HOSE; (ii) = TRUNK-DRAWERS. **'trunk-call,** s. *Tp:* Appel interurbain; appel à longue distance. **'trunk-drawers,** s.pl. *Cost:* Caleçon court. **'trunk-hose,** s. *A.Cost:* Haut-de-chausse(s) m. **'trunk-line,** s. **1.** *Rail:* Ligne principale. **2.** *Tp:* Ligne interurbaine. **'trunk-maker,** s. Malletier m, layetier m. **'trunk-road,** s. Grande route.

trunnion ['trʌnjən], s. Tourillon m.

truss¹ [trʌs], s. **1.** Botte f (de foin). **2.** (a) *Const:* (i) Armature f (de poutre, etc.); (ii) ferme f (de comble, de pont); (iii) cintre m (de voûte). (b) *Arch:* Console f, encorbellement m. **3.** *Nau:* Drosse f (de vergue). **4.** *Med:* Bandage m herniaire. **'truss-bridge,** s. Pont m métallique à poutres armées. **'truss-girder,** s. Poutre armée.

truss², v.tr. **1.** Botteler (le foin); mettre (le foin) en bottes. **2.** *Const:* Armer, renforcer (une poutre). Trussed roof, comble m sur fermes. **3.** *Cu:* Trousser, brider (une volaille); *F:* ligoter (qn).

trust¹ [trʌst], s. **1.** Confiance f (in, en). To put one's trust in s.o., avoir confiance en qn; mettre sa confiance en qn. To take sth. on trust, (i) accepter qch. de confiance; (ii) ajouter foi à qch. sans examen. **2.** Espérance f, espoir m. **3.** *Com:* To supply goods on trust, fournir des marchandises à crédit. **4.** (a) Responsabilité f, charge f. Position of trust, poste de confiance. To desert one's trust, manquer à son devoir. (b) Garde f; dépôt m. To commit sth. to the trust of s.o., confier qch. à qn, aux soins de qn, à la garde de qn. *S.a.* BREACH¹ 1. **5.** *Jur:* Fidéicommis m. To hold sth. in trust, tenir qch. par fidéicommis. **6.** *Ind:* Trust m, syndicat m, cartel m. **'trust-deed,** s. *Jur:* Acte m de fidéicommis. **'trust-house,** s. Auberge f ou hôtel m régis par un "trust" ou syndicat. (Les gérants n'ont aucun intérêt à pousser à la consommation des spiritueux.)

trust². **1.** v.tr. (a) Se fier à (qn, qch.); mettre sa confiance en (qn). He is not to be trusted, on ne peut pas se fier à lui. If we may t. his statement, s'il faut en croire son affirmation. I can scarcely trust my own eyes, my own ears, c'est à n'en pas croire mes yeux, mes oreilles. To trust s.o. with a task, se fier à qn du soin de qch. To trust s.o. with sth., confier qch. à qn. To trust s.o. to do sth., se fier à qn pour que qch. se fasse. Trust him! laissez-le faire! *F:* She won't trust him out of her sight, elle ne le perd jamais de vue. (b) To trust sth. to, with, s.o., confier qch. à qn. aux soins de qn. (c) *Com:* *F:* Faire crédit à (un client). (d) Espérer (que + *ind.*); exprimer le vœu (que + *sub.*). *Corr:* I trust to hear from you soon, j'espère avoir de vos nouvelles sous peu. **2.** v.i. (a) Se confier (in, en); se fier (in, à); mettre sa confiance (in, en). (b) Mettre ses espérances, son espoir (to sth., en qch.). To trust to chance, to luck, se confier au hasard. Trusting to the future, confiant en l'avenir. **trusted,** a. (Serviteur, etc.) de confiance. **trusting,** a. Plein de confiance. **-ly,** adv. Avec confiance.

trustee [trʌs'ti:], s. **1.** *Jur:* (a) (Of estate) Fidéicommissaire m; curateur, -trice. The Public Trustee, le curateur de l'État aux suc-

cessions. (b) Dépositaire m, consignataire m. (c) (With powers of attorney) Mandataire m. **2.** Administrateur m, curateur (d'un musée, etc.). Board of trustees, conseil m d'administration.

trusteeship [trʌs'ti:ʃip], s. **1.** Fidéicommis m **2.** Administration f, curatelle f.

trustful ['trʌstful], a. Plein de confiance; confiant. **-fully,** adv. Avec confiance.

trustfulness ['trʌstfulnəs], s. Confiance f.

trustiness ['trʌstinəs], s. Fidélité f, loyauté f.

trustworthiness ['trʌstwə:rðinəs], s. **1.** (Of pers.) Loyauté f, fidélité f. **2.** Crédibilité f, exactitude f (d'un témoignage, etc.).

trustworthy ['trʌstwə:rði], a. **1.** (Of pers.) Digne de confiance, digne de foi; honnête, fidèle. Trustworthy witness, témoin irrécusable. **2.** (Renseignement, etc.) croyable, exact; (témoignage) irrécusable.

trusty ['trʌsti], a. *A:* Sûr, fidèle; loyal, -aux.

truth [tru:θ], s. (a) Vérité f. The truth (of the matter) is, to tell the truth, I forgot it, pour dire la vérité, à dire vrai, je l'ai oublié. Truth to say, truth to tell, *A:* in truth, of a truth, en vérité, vraiment; à vrai dire. There is some truth in what you say, il y a du vrai dans ce que vous dites. Truth will out, tôt ou tard la vérité se découvre, se fait jour. (b) Vérité; chose vraie. To tell s.o. some home truths, dire ses quatre vérités à qn; dire son fait à qn.

truthful ['tru:θful], a. **1.** (Of pers.) Véridique. **2.** (Témoignage, etc.) vrai; (portrait, etc.) fidèle. **-fully,** adv. **1.** Véridiquement; sans mentir. **2.** Fidèlement.

truthfulness ['tru:θfulnəs], s. **1.** (Of pers.) Véracité f, véridicité f. **2.** Véracité f (d'une assertion, etc.); fidélité f (d'un portrait, etc.).

try¹ [trai], s. **1.** Essai m, tentative f. To have a try at (doing) sth., s'essayer à qch.; essayer de faire qch. Let's have a try! essayons toujours! At the first try, du premier coup. **2.** *Rugby Fb:* Essai. To score a try, marquer un essai. To convert a try, transformer un essai.

try², v. (tried [traid]) I. v.tr. **1.** (a) Éprouver (qn); mettre (qn, qch.) à l'épreuve. To be tried and found wanting, ne pas supporter l'épreuve. (b) Éprouver; affliger. A people sorely tried, une nation durement éprouvée. (c) To try one's eyes by reading too much, se fatiguer les yeux à trop lire. **2.** Essayer, expérimenter (qch.); faire l'essai de (qch.). To try a dish, goûter un mets. To try (out) a medicine upon an animal, faire l'essai d'un médicament sur une bête. **3.** Vérifier (un mécanisme); ajuster (des poids); essayer (un cordage, une voiture). **4.** *Jur:* Juger (une cause, un accusé). To be tried for theft, passer en correctionnelle pour vol; être jugé pour vol. **5.** Essayer, tenter. To try one's strength against s.o., se mesurer avec qn. Try how far you can throw the ball, essayez (pour) voir à quelle distance vous pouvez lancer la balle. **6.** To try to do sth., *F:* to try and do sth., tâcher, essayer, de faire qch. She tried to smile, elle essaya, s'efforça, de sourire. He tried his best, his hardest, to save them, il a fait tout son possible pour les sauver. To try again, tenter un nouvel effort; essayer de nouveau. *F:* You had better not try! ne vous en avisez pas! II. **try,** v.i. To try for sth., tâcher d'obtenir qch. **try on,** v.tr. **1.** Essayer (un vêtement). **2.** *F:* To try it on with s.o., chercher à mettre qn dedans; bluffer. **try-'on,** s. *F:* **1.** Tentative f de déception; bluff m. **2.** Ballon m d'essai. **try out,** v.tr. (a) Essayer à fond (une machine, etc.); soumettre (qn, une invention) à une épreuve

prolongée. (b) *Ind:* Épurer, affiner (un métal).
try over, *v.tr.* Essayer (un morceau de musique, etc.). **tried,** *a.* Éprouvé. **Well-tried remedy,** remède éprouvé. **trying**[1], *a.* **I.** Difficile, pénible, rude, dur. *A t. position,* une position pénible. **2.** Vexant; contrariant. **3.** Trying light, lumière fatigante (pour la vue). **trying**[2], *s.* **I.** Essai *m,* épreuve *f.* **2.** *Jur:* Jugement *m* (d'une cause). **'try(ing)-plane,** *s. Tls:* Varlope *f.* **'try-square,** *s. Tls:* Équerre *f* à lame d'acier.
trysail ['traiseil, traisl], *s. Nau:* Voile *f* goélette. **Main trysail,** grande voile goélette.
tryst [trist, traist], *s. Lit:* Rendez-vous *m.* **Lovers' tryst,** assignation amoureuse.
trysting-place ['tristiŋpleis], *s.* (Lieu *m* de) rendez-vous *m.*
tsar [zɑːr], *s.,* **tsarevitch** ['zɑːrevitʃ], *s.,* **tsarina** [zɑːˈriːna], *s.* = CZAR, CZAREVITCH, CZARINA.
tsetse ['tsetsi], *s. Ent:* Tsetse(-fly), (mouche *f*) tsé-tsé *f.*
tub[1] [tʌb], *s.* **I.** (a) Baquet *m,* bac *m. Nau:* Baille *f. F:* A tale of a tub, un conte à dormir debout; un coq-à-l'âne *inv.* (b) (**Wash-)tub,** baquet, cuvier *m* (à lessive). **2.** (a) (**Bath-)tub,** tub *m.* (b) **To have a tub,** prendre un bain (dans un tub). **3.** *Min:* (a) Benne *f.* (b) Berline *f,* truck *m,* wagonnet *m.* **4.** (a) *Nau: F:* Old tub (of a boat), vieille coque, vieux sabot. (b) *Row:* Canot *m* d'entraînement. **'tub-seat,** *s. Aut: etc:* Baquet *m.* **'tub-thumper,** *s. F:* Orateur *m* de carrefour.
tub[2], *v.* (tubbed) **I.** *v.tr.* (a) Encaisser (une plante). (b) Donner un tub à (qn). **2.** *v.i.* Prendre un tub.
tuba ['tjuːba], *s. Mus:* (a) (*Organ*) Trompette *f.* (b) Contrebasse *f* à vent; bombardon *m,* tuba *m.*
tubby ['tʌbi], *a. F:* (Of *pers.*) Boulot; gros et rond; pansu.
tube[1] [tjuːb], *s.* **I.** (a) Tube *m,* tuyau *m. W.Tel:* Lead-in tube, pipe *f* d'entrée (de l'antenne). (b) Tube (de pâte dentifrice, etc.). (c) *W.Tel: Rad.-A:* Lampe *f,* ampoule *f,* tube. (d) *Aut: Cy:* Inner tube, chambre *f* à air (de pneu). (e) *Surg:* Drain *m* (de plaie profonde). **2.** *Anat:* Tube; canal,-aux *m;* conduit *m.* **3.** *F:* = TUBE-RAILWAY. **We came in the tube, by tube** = nous avons pris le Métro. **'tube-railway,** *s. Rail:* Voie souterraine tubulaire. **'tube-station,** *s.* = Station *f* du Métro.
tube[2], *v.tr. Civ.E:* Tuber, garnir de tubes (un sondage). *Surg:* Tuber (le larynx); drainer (une plaie profonde). **tubing,** *s.* **I.** Tubage *m.* **2.** (a) *Coll.* Tuyautage *m,* tuyauterie *f,* tubes *mpl.* (b) Tube *m,* tuyau *m.* **Rubber tubing,** tuyau en caoutchouc.
tuber ['tjuːbər], *s.* **I.** *Bot:* (a) (i) Racine tubéreuse; (ii) tubercule *m.* (b) Tubéracée *f,* truffe *f.* **2.** (a) *Anat:* Tubérosité *f.* (b) *Med:* Tubercule.
tubercle ['tjuːbərkl], *s.* Tubercule *m.*
tubercular [tjuˈbəːrkjulər], *a. Bot:* Tuberculeux.
tuberculosis [tjuːbəːrkjuˈlousis], *s. Med:* Tuberculose *f.*
tuberculous [tjuˈbəːrkjuləs], *a.* Tuberculeux.
tuberosity [tjuːbəˈrɔsiti], *s.* Tubérosité *f.*
tuberous ['tjuːbərəs], *a. Bot:* Tubéreux.
tubular ['tjuːbjulər], *a.* (a) Tubulaire. *Mus:* Tubular bells, carillon *m* (d'orchestre). (b) *Mch:* (Chaudière) tubulaire, tubulaire, à tubes.
tuck[1] [tʌk], *s.* **I.** *Dressm:* (Petit) pli; rempli *m,* plissé *m;* (to shorten a garment) troussis *m.* **To make, take up, a tuck in a garment,** faire un

rempli à un vêtement; (to shorten) faire un troussis à un vêtement. **2.** *Sch: F:* Gâteaux *mpl,* friandises *fpl;* mangeaille *f.* **Tuck box,** boîte à provisions. **'tuck-shop,** *s. Sch: F:* Pâtisserie-confiserie *f.*
tuck[2], *v.tr.* **I.** *Dressm:* (a) Faire des plis à, remplier (un vêtement); plisser, froncer (l'étoffe). (b) Raccourcir (un vêtement). **2.** Replier, rentrer, serrer, mettre; *F:* fourrer. **To tuck a rug round s.o.,** envelopper qn d'une couverture. **To t. a table-napkin under one's chin,** rentrer un coin de sa serviette sous son menton. **To tuck (away) sth. in a drawer,** serrer qch. dans un tiroir. **Village tucked away at the far end of the valley,** village relégué au fond de la vallée. **tuck in.** **I.** *v.tr.* (a) Serrer, rentrer; replier (le bord d'un vêtement, etc.). **To tuck in a flap** (in folding document, etc.), rentrer un quartier. **To tuck in the bed-clothes,** border le lit. (b) **To tuck s.o. in,** border qn (dans son lit). **2.** *v.i. F:* Manger à belles dents. **Tuck in!** allez-y! **tuck-'in,** *s. F:* Bombance *f.* **To have a good tuck-in,** s'en mettre jusqu'au menton. **tuck into,** *v.i. F:* **To tuck into a pie,** attaquer un pâté. **tuck up,** *v.tr.* (a) Relever, retrousser (sa jupe). **To t. up one's dress** (at the girdle), se trousser. (b) Border (qn) (dans son lit). **To tuck oneself up in bed,** se blottir dans son lit.
tuck[3], *s. A:* **I.** Fanfare *f* (de trompettes). **2.** *Scot:* Roulement *m* de tambour.
tucker ['tʌkər], *s. A.Cost:* Fichu *m,* guimpe *f,* chemisette *f. S.a.* BIB 2.
tucket ['tʌket], *s. A:* Fanfare *f* (de trompettes).
Tuesday ['tjuːzdi], *s.* Mardi *m.* (For phrases *cf.* FRIDAY.) *S.a.* SHROVE 2.
tufa ['tjuːfa], *s. Geol:* (a) Tuf *m* calcaire. (b) = TUFF.
tuff [tʌf], *s. Geol:* Tuf *m* volcanique.
tuffet ['tʌfet], *s.* **I.** Pouf *m.* **2.** *Dial:* = TUFT I (a).
tuft [tʌft], *s.* **I.** (a) Touffe *f* (d'herbe). (b) Touffe (de plumes); houppe *f* (de soie); mèche *f,* flocon *m* (de laine); huppe *f,* aigrette *f* (d'un oiseau). **2.** (a) Barbiche *f.* (b) Toupet *m* (de cheveux). **3.** (a) Gland *m,* houppe (d'un bonnet); pompon *m.* (b) *A:* Étudiant *m* noble (qui portait un gland en or à sa toque). **'tuft-hunter,** *s. A:* Celui qui recherchait la compagnie des étudiants nobles. (b) Adulateur *m* des grands; sycophante *m.* **'tuft-hunting,** *s.* Sycophantisme *m.*
tufted ['tʌftid], *a.* **I.** (a) Garni de houppes, de glands. (b) En touffe, en houppe; houppé. **2.** *Orn:* Muni d'une aigrette; huppé.
tug[1] [tʌg], *s.* **I.** (a) Traction (subite); saccade *f.* **To give a good tug,** tirer fort; (of horse, etc.) donner un bon coup de collier. **Tug of war,** (i) *Sp:* lutte *f* de traction à la corde; (ii) *F:* lutte décisive. **Tug-of-war rope,** corde *f* de traction; jarretière *f.* (b) *F:* **To feel a tug at one's heart-strings,** avoir un serrement de cœur. **2.** = TUG-BOAT. **Salvage tug,** remorqueur *m* de sauvetage. **3.** *Harn:* Trait *m* (d'attelage). (b) Porte-brancard *m.* **'tug-boat,** *s.* (Bateau) remorqueur *m.*
tug[2], *v.* (tugged [tʌgd]) **I.** *v.tr. & i.* Tirer avec effort. **To tug sth. along,** traîner qch. **To tug at sth.,** tirer sur qch. **To tug at the oars,** tirer sur les rames; souquer (ferme). *F:* **The recollection tugged at his heart-strings,** ce souvenir lui déchirait le cœur. **2.** *v.tr. Nau:* Remorquer (un vaisseau).
tuition [tjuˈiʃ(ə)n], *s.* Instruction *f,* enseignement *m. Esp.* **Private tuition,** leçons particulières.
tulip ['tjuːlip], *s.* Tulipe *f*

tulle [tu:l, tju:l], s. *Tex:* Tulle m.
tumble[1] [tʌmbl], s. **1.** Culbute f, chute f, dégringolade f. **2.** *Gym:* Culbute (d'acrobate). **3.** Désordre m; masse confuse. **Everything was in a tumble,** tout était en désordre.
tumble[2]. **1.** v.i. (a) **To tumble (down, over),** tomber (par terre); faire une chute; faire la culbute. **Building that is tumbling down,** édifice qui s'écroule, qui tombe en ruine. **Her hair came tumbling down,** ses cheveux ːe déroulèrent. (b) **To tumble (about),** s'agiter. **To toss and tumble in bed,** s'agiter dans son lit. (c) Se jeter (précipitamment) (*into,* dans). **To tumble into bed,** *F:* **to tumble in,** se jeter dans son lit; se mettre au lit. **To tumble into one's clothes,** enfiler ses vêtements à la hâte. **To tumble out,** (i) tomber (de la voiture, par la fenêtre, etc.); (ii) *F:* sauter du lit. *F:* **To tumble on sth.,** trouver qch. par hasard. (d) (*Of acrobat, pigeon*) Faire des culbutes. (e) *F:* **To tumble to an idea,** comprendre, saisir, une idée. **2.** v.tr. (a) **To tumble sth. down, over,** culbuter, jeter à bas, renverser, qch. (b) Bouleverser, déranger; mettre en désordre. *Don't t. my hair,* ne m'ébouriffez pas. **'tumble-down,** attrib.a. *F:* Croulant, délabré; qui menace ruine. *Old t.-d. house,* maison qui tombe en ruines.
tumbler [tʌmblər], s. **1.** *A:* Jongleur m, acrobate mf. **2.** *Orn:* Tumbler pigeon, pigeon culbutant. **3.** Verre m (à boire) sans pied; gobelet m. **4.** (*Device*) (a) *El.E:* Culbuteur m (d'interrupteur, etc.). (b) Gorge f (mobile), arrêt m (de serrure). **Tumbler lock,** serrure à gorge(s).
tumbrel ['tʌmbrə., **tumbril** ['tʌmbril], s. Tombereau m.
tumefaction [tju:miˈfakʃ(ə)n], s. Tuméfaction f.
tumefy ['tju:mifai]. **1.** v.tr. Tuméfier. **2.** v.i. Se tuméfier.
tumid ['tuːmid], a. **1.** *Med:* Enflé, gonflé. **2.** (*Style*) ampoulé.
tummy ['tʌmi], s. *F:* (a) Estomac m, ventre m. (b) Bedaine f.
tumour ['tju:mər], s. Tumeur f.
tumult ['tju:mʌlt], s. **1.** Tumulte m; fracas m. **2.** Tumulte, agitation f, trouble m, émoi m (des passions).
tumultuous [tjuˈmʌltjuəs], a. Tumultueux.
tumulus, pl. **-i** ['tju:mjuləs, -ai], s. Tumulus m.
tun [tʌn], s. **1.** Tonneau m, fût m. **2.** *Brew:* Cuve f (de fermentation).
tundra ['tundrə], s. *Ph.Geog:* Toundra f.
tune[1] [tju:n], s. **1.** Air m (de musique). *F:* **Give us a tune!** faites-nous un peu de musique! *S.a.* PIPER. **To change one's tune,** changer de ton, de langage. *F:* **The tune the old cow died of,** une vieille rengaine. **To be fined to the tune of fifty pounds,** être mis à l'amende pour la somme pas mal salée de cinquante livres. **2.** (a) Accord m. **The piano is in tune,** le piano est d'accord. **The piano is out of tune,** le piano est désaccordé. **To get out of tune,** se désaccorder; perdre l'accord. (*Of singer*) **To be out of tune,** détonner. *To sing in t., out of t.,* chanter juste, faux. (b) **Engine in perfect tune,** moteur au point. **3.** (a) Accord, harmonie f. **To be in tune with one's surroundings,** être en bon accord avec son milieu. (b) *W.Tel:* **To be in tune,** être en résonance. **To get into tune,** accrocher la longueur d'onde.
tune[2], v.tr. **1.** Accorder, mettre d'accord (un instrument). **2.** *El.E: W.Tel:* **To tune one circuit to another,** accorder, syntoniser, un circuit sur un autre. *W.Tel:* **To tune in (to) a station,** accrocher, capter, un poste. *Abs* **To tune in,**

syntoniser le poste; accorder le récepteur. **To tune out a station,** éliminer un poste émetteur. **3.** *I.C.E: Mch: etc:* **To tune (up),** caler, régler, (re)mettre au point (un moteur). **tune up,** v.i. (*Of orchestra*) S'accorder. **tuning,** s. **1.** *Mus:* Accordage m, accord m (d'un piano, etc.). **2.** *I.C.E: Mch:* Tuning (up), calage m, réglage m, (re)mise f au point. **3.** *W.Tel:* Tuning (in), accordage, réglage, syntonisation f. **'tuning condenser,** *W.Tel:* Condensateur m d'accord, de syntonisation. **'tuning-fork,** s. *Mus:* Diapason m. **'tuning-hammer,** s. *Mus:* Accordoir m; clef f d'accordage, d'accordeur. **'tuning-slide,** s. *Mus:* Pompe f d'accord (d'un instrument à vent).
tuneful ['tju:nful], a. Mélodieux, harmonieux. **-fully,** adv. Mélodieusement, harmonieusement.
tuneless ['tju:nləs], a. Discordant; sans harmonie.
tuner ['tju:nər], s. Accordeur m (de pianos, etc.).
tungsten ['tʌŋstən], s. *Ch:* Tungstène m. **Tungsten-steel,** acier m au tungstène.
tunic ['tju:nik], s. **1.** *Cost:* Tunique f. **2.** *Nat. Hist:* Tunique, enveloppe f (d'un organe).
Tunis ['tju:nis]. *Pr.n.* **1.** La Tunisie. **2.** Tunis.
tunnel[1] ['tʌn(ə)l], s. Tunnel m; passage souterrain. *Rail:* Tunnel. *Min:* Galerie f (d'accès) à flanc de coteau. **To drive a tunnel through . . .,** percer un tunnel à travers, sous. . . . *Mec:* **Wind tunnel,** tunnel aérodynamique.
tunnel[2], v.tr. & i. (tunnelled [tʌnld]) **To tunnel a hill;** to tunnel through, into, a hill, percer un tunnel à travers, dans, sous, une colline. **tunnelling,** s. Percement m d'un tunnel, de tunnels.
tunny(-fish) ['tʌni(fiʃ)], ɔ. *Ich:* Thon m.
tup [tʌp], s. *Husb:* Bélier m.
tuppence ['tʌp(ə)ns], s. *F:* = TWOPENCE.
tuppenny ['tʌp(ə)ni], a. *F:* = TWOPENNY.
turban ['tə:rbən], s. *Cost:* Turban m.
turbid ['tə:rbid], a. **1.** (Liquide) trouble, bourbeux. **2.** (Esprit) trouble. *T. utterances,* langage confus.
turbidity [tə:r'biditi], **turbidness** ['tə:rbidnəs], s. Turbidité f.
turbinate ['tə:rbinet], a. *Nat.Hist:* Turbiné.
turbine ['tə:rbain, -bin], s. (a) Turbine f. **Steam turbine,** turbine à vapeur. (b) Turbine à vapeur; turbo-moteur m. **'turbine-chamber,** s. Chambre f d'eau. **'turbine-driven,** a. A turbines.
turbo-dynamo ['tə:rbo'dainəmo], s. *El.E:* Turbo-dynamo f.
turbo-generator ['tə:rbo'dʒenəreitər], s. *El.E:* Turbo-générateur m.
turbo-motor ['tə:rbomoutər], s. *Mch:* Turbo-moteur m.
turbot ['tə:rbət], s. *Ich:* Turbot m. **'turbot-kettle,** s. *Cu:* Turbotière f.
turbulence ['tə:rbjuləns], s. **1.** (a) Turbulence f, trouble m tumulte m. (b) Indiscipline f. **2.** *I.C.E:* (High) turbulence combustion chamber, chambre de combustion à (haute) turbulence.
turbulent ['tə:rbjulənt], a. **1.** (a) Turbulent, tumultueux. (b) Insubordonné. **2.** *I.C.E:* Turbulent cylinder-head, culasse à turbulence.
Turcoman, pl. **-mans** [tə:r'kɔmən, -mənz], s. **1.** *Ethn:* Turcoman m. **2.** *Ling:* Le turcoman.
tureen [tjuˈri:n], s. Soupière f.
turf [tə:rf], pl. **turves, turfs** [tə:rf, tə:rvz, tə:rfs], s. **1.** (a) Gazon m. (b) Motte f de gazon. **2.** (a) (*In Ireland*) Tourbe f. (b) **A turf of peat,** une motte de tourbe. **3.** *Rac:* **The turf,** le turf; ɪe monde

des courses. '**turf-cutter,** s. *Tls:* **1.** Tranche-gazon *m inv.* **2.** Louchet *m* (pour couper les mottes de tourbe).

turf², *v.tr.* **1.** Gazonner (un terrain). **2.** *F:* To turf s.o. out, flanquer qn dehors.

turgescence [tə:r'dʒes(ə)ns], *s.* **1.** Turgescence *f.* **2.** Emphase *f.*

turgescent [tə:r'dʒes(ə)nt], *a.* **1.** Turgescent. **2.** (Style) emphatique, boursouflé.

turgid ['tə:rdʒid], *a.* **1.** Turgide, enflé gonflé. **2.** (Style) boursouflé, ampoulé.

turgidity [tə:r'dʒiditi], *s.* **1.** Enflure **2.** Emphase *f* (de style).

Turk [tə:rk], *s.* Turc, *f.* Turque. *F:* He's a young Turk, c'est un enfant terrible. '**Turk's head,** *s.* *F:* **1.** (Long broom) Tête-de-loup *f.* **2.** *Nau:* Turk's head knot, nœud *m* de bonnet turc ; tête *f* de Maure.

Turkey¹ ['tə:rki]. *Pr.n.* La Turquie. '**Turkey carpet,** *s.* Tapis *m* d'Orient, de Smyrne. '**Turkey 'leather,** *s.* Cuir chamoisé. '**Turkey red,** *s. & a.* Rouge (*m*) d'Andrinople.

turkey², *s.* **1.** Dindon *m.* **Hen-turkey,** dinde *f.* Young turkey, dindonneau *m.* **2.** *Cu:* Dinde, dindonneau. '**turkey-cock,** *s.m.* Dindon. '**turkey-hen,** *s.f.* Dinde.

Turkish ['tə:rkiʃ]. **1.** *a.* Turc, *f.* turque ; de Turquie. Turkish cigarettes, cigarettes d'Orient. **2.** *s. Ling:* Le turc. '**Turkish de'light,** *s.* Rahat loukoum *m.*

turmeric ['tə:rmərik], *s.* Curcuma *m.*

turmoil ['tə:rmɔil], *s.* (*a*) Trouble *m,* tumulte *m,* agitation *f.* (*b*) Remous *m* (des eaux) ; tourbillon *m.*

turn¹ [tə:rn], *s.* **1.** Tour *m,* révolution *f* (d'une roue). With a quick turn of the wrist, avec un tour de poignet. Meat done to a turn, viande cuite à point. *F:* To give another turn to the screw, serrer la vis à qn. **2.** (*a*) Changement *m* de direction. *Aut:* Virage *m.* **To make, take, a turn to the right,** tourner à droite. **Turn of the wind,** saute *f* de vent. *F:* At every turn, à tout moment, à tout propos. (*b*) Tournure *f* (des affaires). The affair was taking a tragic turn, l'affaire tournait au tragique. Things are taking a turn for the better, les affaires prennent meilleure tournure, une meilleure allure. **To give a favourable turn to a business,** donner un bon pli à une affaire. (*c*) Turn of the tide, étale *m,* changement, de la marée. The tide is on the turn, la mer est étale ; la marée change. The milk is on the turn, le lait est en train de tourner. Turn of the scale, trait *m* de balance. (*d*) This sight gave me quite a turn, ce spectacle m'a donné un (vrai) coup ; *F:* ça m'a fait un effet de voir ça ; cela m'a émotionné. (*e*) She had one of her turns yesterday, elle a eu une de ses crises, une de ses attaques, hier. You gave me such a t.! vous m'avez fait une belle peur ! **3.** To take a turn in the garden, faire un tour dans le jardin. **4.** (*a*) Tour (de rôle). It is your turn, c'est votre tour. *It is your t.* (to play), c'est à vous de jouer. It will be my turn some day, (i) mon tour viendra un de ces jours ; (ii) je prendrai ma revanche un jour. In turn, by turns, tour à tour ; à tour de rôle. To speak in one's turn, parler à son tour. To play out of one's turn, jouer avant son tour. Turn and turn about, chacun son tour. To take turns in, at, doing sth., faire qch. à tour de rôle. To take it in turns to steer, se relayer à la barre. To take one's turn (at work, etc.), prendre son tour. (*b*) Music-hall turn, numéro *m* de music-hall. **5.** (*a*) (Bon ou mauvais) procédé. To do

s.o. a (good) turn, rendre un service, rendre service, à qn. To do s.o. a bad turn, jouer un mauvais tour à qn ; desservir qn. *Prov:* One good turn deserves another, à beau jeu beau retour ; à charge de revanche. (*b*) Intention *f,* but *m.* It will serve my turn, cela fera mon affaire pour le moment. **6.** (*a*) Disposition *f* d'esprit. His turn of mind, son tour d'esprit. To have a turn for mathematics, for business, avoir des dispositions pour les mathématiques, pour le commerce. (*b*) Turn of a sentence, tournure *f* d'une phrase. English turn of speech, anglicisme *m.* The turn of her arm, les contours *m* de son bras ; le galbe de son bras. (*c*) Car with a good turn of speed, auto rapide. **7.** (*a*) Tournant *m,* coude *m* (d'un chemin, etc.). *Sudden t.,* sharp t., crochet *m,* virage *m.* The path is full of twists and turns, le sentier fait beaucoup de tours et de détours. (*b*) Tour (d'une corde) ; tour, spire *f* (d'une spirale). *Nau:* Take a turn round the cleat! tournez au taquet ! **8.** *Mus:* Gruppetto *m,* *pl.* gruppetti. **9.** *Typ:* Caractère retourné ; blocage *m.* '**turn-buckle,** *s.* *Mec.E:* Lanterne *f* (de serrage) ; tendeur *m.* '**turn-table,** *s.* **1.** *Rail:* Plaque tournante. **2.** Plateau *m* (tourne-disques) (de phonographe).

turn², **I.** *v.tr.* **1.** Tourner, faire tourner (une roue). To turn the key in the lock, donner un tour de clef à la porte. To turn the knife in the wound, retourner le fer dans la plaie. To turn the light low, mettre la lumière en veilleuse. **2.** To turn (over) a page, tourner une page. Newly turned soil, terre fraîchement retournée. To turn a garment inside out, retourner un vêtement. To turn the hay, retourner le foin. *F:* Without turning a hair, sans sourciller, sans broncher. **3.** To turn one's horse, faire faire demi-tour à son cheval. He turned his steps homewards, il dirigea ses pas vers la maison. He never turned a beggar from the door, jamais il ne renvoya un mendiant. To turn a blow, faire dévier un coup ; détourner un coup. To turn the conversation, donner un autre tour à la conversation. **4.** Tourner, retourner (la tête) ; diriger (les yeux) (towards, vers). To turn a telescope on a star, braquer une lunette sur une étoile. **5.** To turn the laughter against s.o., retourner les rires contre qn. To turn s.o.'s argument against himself, retorquer, rétorquer, un argument contre qn. **6.** (*a*) To turn the corner, tourner le coin. (*b*) He is, has, turned forty, il a passé la quarantaine. It is turned seven o'clock, il est sept heures passées. **7.** (*a*) Changer, convertir, transformer (into, en). *His love was turned to hate,* son amour a tourné en haine. To turn Latin into English, mettre du latin en anglais. *To t. a sentence into French,* traduire une phrase en français. (*b*) Faire devenir ; rendre. The storm has turned the milk (sour), l'orage a fait tourner le lait. (*c*) Success has turned his head, le succès lui a tourné la tête. **8.** Tourner, façonner au tour (un pied de table, etc.). *F:* Well-turned leg, jambe qui a du galbe. Well-turned sentence, phrase bien tournée. **II.** **turn,** *v.i.* **1.** Tourner. (*a*) *The wheel turns,* la roue tourne. My head turns, la tête me tourne. (*b*) Everything turns on your answer, tout dépend de, roule sur, votre réponse. The conversation turned on a variety of subjects, la conversation a roulé sur une variété de sujets. **2.** (*a*) To toss and turn in bed, se tourner et se retourner dans son lit. (*b*) To turn upside down, (i) (of boat) chavirer ; (ii) (of vehicle) capoter, se retourner. **3.** Se tourner, se retourner. To turn short, se retourner tout à coup. *Mil:* **Right turn!** left turn! à droite! à gauche! par le flanc droit, gauche! **4.** (*a*) Tourner, se diriger. *He turned to the left*, il tourna, il prit, à gauche. *Nau: To t. to the east*, venir cap à l'est. **To turn sixteen points**, to turn a half-circle, virer de bord cap pour cap; venir de seize quarts. **The wind is turning**, le vent change. (*b*) Se diriger (vers qch.); s'adresser (à qn). **My thoughts often turn to this subject**, mes réflexions se portent souvent sur ce sujet. **To turn to a document**, se reporter à un document. **I don't know which way, where, to turn**, je ne sais de quel côté (me) tourner; je ne sais (plus) où donner de la tête. **To turn to s.o.**, recourir à qn, à l'aide de qn; avoir recours à qn. **5.** (*a*) **The tide is turning**, la marée change. **His luck has turned**, sa chance a tourné. (*b*) **To turn against s.o.**, se retourner contre qn. **6.** (*a*) Se changer, se convertir, se transformer (*into*, en). **It is turning to rain**, le temps se met à la pluie. **Everything he touches turns to gold**, tout ce qu'il touche se change en or. **The affair was turning to tragedy**, l'affaire tournait au tragique. (*b*) **To turn acid**, tourner au vinaigre. **The milk has turned (sour)**, le lait a tourné. **His head has turned with success**, le succès lui a tourné la tête. **The leaves are beginning to turn**, les feuilles commencent à tourner, à jaunir. *F:* **To turn all the colours of the rainbow**, passer par toutes les couleurs de l'arc-en-ciel. (*c*) **To turn socialist**, devenir socialiste; embrasser le socialisme. **To turn soldier**, se faire soldat. **turn about. I.** *v.i.* (*a*) Se tourner, se retourner. (*b*) Se tourner d'un côté et de l'autre; s'agiter. **2.** *v.tr.* Tourner (qch.) dans l'autre sens. **turn aside. I.** *v.tr.* Détourner, écarter (qch., qn). **2.** *v.i.* Se détourner, s'écarter. **turn away. I.** *v.tr.* (*a*) Détourner (les yeux, la colère). (*b*) Renvoyer, congédier (qn). **2.** *v.i.* Se détourner. **turn back. I.** *v.tr.* (*a*) Faire revenir ou faire retourner (qn) sur ses pas. (*b*) Relever, retrousser (ses manches); rabattre (le col de son pardessus, etc.). (*c*) *Nau:* Dévirer (le treuil, etc.). **2.** *v.i.* S'en retourner; retourner sur ses pas; rebrousser chemin; (*of horseman*) tourner bride. **turn down.** *v.tr.* **I.** (*a*) Rabattre. (*b*) Faire un pli, une corne, à (une page). **2.** Retourner (une carte) (face à la table). **3.** Baisser (le gaz). **4.** *F:* **To turn down a candidate, a claim**, refuser un candidat; écarter une réclamation. **To turn down an offer**, repousser une offre. **'turn-down**, *attrib.a.* **Turn-down collar**, col rabattu. **turn in. I.** *v.tr.* (*a*) Rentrer (les bouts de qch.); replier (le bord d'un vêtement, etc.). (*b*) **To turn one's toes in**, tourner les pieds en dedans. **2.** *v.i.* (*a*) **His toes turn in**, il a les pieds tournés en dedans. (*b*) *F:* **To turn in**, (aller) se coucher. **turn off. I.** *v.tr.* **I.** Fermer, couper (l'eau, le gaz); éteindre (le gaz); fermer (un robinet). **2.** Renvoyer, congédier, débaucher (un employé). **3.** Enlever (les inégalités, etc.) au tour. **II. turn off**, *v.i.* **I.** Changer de route; tourner (à droite, à gauche). **2. The car turned off the main road**, l'auto quitta la grande route. **turn on. I.** *v.tr.* (*a*) Donner (la vapeur); ouvrir, faire couler (l'eau); allumer, ouvrir (le gaz). **To turn on the fountains**, faire jouer les eaux. (*b*) *F:* **To turn s.o. on to sth.**, mettre qn à faire qch. **2.** *v.i.* (*Prep. use*) **To turn on s.o.**, se jeter sur qn; attaquer qn. **turn out. I.** *v.tr.* **I.** (*a*) **To turn s.o. out (of doors)**, mettre qn dehors, à la porte. **To turn out a tenant**, déloger, évincer, un locataire. **To turn out a servant**, congédier, chasser, un domestique. **To turn out the govern-**

ment, renverser le gouvernement. (*b*) Mettre (le bétail) au vert. *S.a.* GRASS[1] 2. (*c*) *Nau:* Réveiller (les hommes). *Mil:* Alerter (les troupes). **To turn out the guard**, faire sortir la garde. (*d*) *Cu:* Démouler (une crème, etc.). **2.** Vider (un tiroir, ses poches); retourner (ses poches); nettoyer (une chambre) à fond. **3.** Produire, fabriquer (des marchandises). **Turned out to order**, confectionné sur demande. **4.** (*Of pers., carriage, etc.*) **Well turned out**, élégant, pimpant; (*of pers.*) soigné dans sa mise. **5.** Couper, éteindre (le gaz). **6. To turn out one's toes**, tourner les pieds en dehors. **II. turn out**, *v.i.* **I.** (*a*) Sortir; paraître en public. **Guard turn out!** aux armes! (*b*) (*Of workmen*) **To turn out (on strike)**, se mettre en grève. (*c*) *F:* Sortir du lit; se lever. **2. His toes turn out**, il a les pieds tournés en dehors. **3.** (*a*) **Things have turned out well**, les choses ont bien tourné. *It will t. out all right*, cela s'arrangera. *I don't know how it will t. out*, je ne sais pas quelle en sera l'issue. **As it turned out . . .**, comme il arriva . . .; en l'occurrence. . . . **His son turned out badly**, son fils a mal tourné. **The weather has turned out fine**, le temps s'est mis au beau. (*b*) *The dog turned out to be mine*, il se trouva que le chien m'appartenait. **It turns out that . . .**, il apparaît, il se trouve, que. . . . **turn-'out**, *s.* **I.** Concours *m*, assemblée *f* (de gens). **2.** *Ind:* Grève *f*. **3.** (*a*) Tenue *f*, uniforme *m* (d'un régiment, etc.). (*b*) Attelage *m*, équipage *m*. **turn over. I.** *v.tr.* (*a*) Retourner (qch.); tourner (une page). **To turn over the pages, the leaves, of a book**, feuilleter un livre. *S.a.* LEAF[1] 2. *Agr:* **To turn over the soil**, retourner le sol. *Metalw:* **To turn over the edges of a plate**, rabattre, tomber, les bords d'une tôle. **To turn an idea over in one's mind**, ruminer une idée. (*b*) **He turns over £500 a week**, son chiffre d'affaires est de 500 livres par semaine. (*c*) **To turn sth. over to s.o.**, transférer, référer, qch. à qn. (*d*) *Typ:* **To turn a word, a letter, over**, faire sauter un mot, une lettre. **2.** *v.i.* Se tourner, se retourner; (*of vehicle*) verser, capoter; (*of aeroplane*) capoter. **To turn right over**, faire un panache complet. **'turn-over**, *s.* **I.** (*a*) Renversement *m*, culbute *f*. (*b*) *Parl: etc:* **Turn-over of four votes**, déplacement *m* de quatre voix. **2.** *Com:* (*a*) Chiffre *m* d'affaires; roulement *m*. (*b*) **Rapid turn-over of goods**, écoulement *m* rapide des marchandises. **3.** *Cu:* **Apple turn-over**, chausson *m* aux pommes. **turn round. I.** *v.tr.* Retourner. **2.** *v.i.* (*a*) Tourner; (*of crane, etc.*) virer, pivoter. **To turn round and round**, tourner, tournoyer; (*on one's toes*) pirouetter. (*b*) Se retourner; faire volte-face; (*in one's opinions, etc.*) tourner casaque. (*c*) (*Of ship in port*) Se retourner (pour repartir). (*d*) *F:* **To turn round on s.o.**, se retourner contre qn; s'en prendre à qn. **turn to**, *v.i.* *F:* Se mettre au travail; s'y mettre. **turn up. I.** *v.tr.* **I.** (*a*) Relever (le col de son pardessus); retrousser (ses manches). **Turned-up nose**, nez retroussé. *F:* **To turn up one's nose at sth.**, renifler sur qch.; faire le dégoûté. **To turn up one's eyes**, montrer le blanc des yeux; *F:* faire des yeux de carpe. *Metalw:* **To turn up a flange on a sheet**, tomber un collet sur une tôle. (*b*) Retourner (le sol). *The gardener turned up some human bones*, le jardinier a déterré des ossements humains. (*c*) Trouver, se reporter à (une citation). **To turn up a word in the dictionary**, consulter le dictionnaire. **2.** Remonter (une lampe). **II. turn up**, *v.i.* **I.** Se relever, se retrousser; se replier.

2. (a) *The ten of diamonds turned up*, le dix de carreau est sorti. (b) Arriver, se présenter (inopinément) ; faire son apparition. **To turn up at s.o.'s house**, arriver (à l'improviste) chez qn. *He turned up ten minutes late*, il est arrivé avec un retard de dix minutes. *He will t. up one of these days*, il reparaîtra un de ces jours. **Something is sure to turn up**, il se présentera sûrement une occasion. **'turn-up**, *s.* (a) Bord relevé (d'un pantalon, etc.). **Turn-up trousers**, pantalon à bords relevés, à bas américains. (b) (*At cards*) Retourne f. **turned**, *a.* **1.** (Lathe-, machine-) turned, façonné au tour ; fait au tour ; tourné. **2.** Retourné. **turning**[1], *a.* Tournant ; qui tourne ; giratoire, rotatif. **turning**[2], *s.* **1.** (a) Mouvement m giratoire ; rotation f, giration f. (b) Virage m (d'une auto, etc.) ; changement m de direction. (c) Retournage m (d'un vêtement, de la terre). (d) **Turning of the tide**, renversement m de la marée. (e) Changement, conversion f (*into*, en). **2.** Travail m au tour ; tournage m. **3.** Tournant m (d'une route) ; coude m. *Aut:* Virage. *Take the t. on the left*, prenez à gauche. *Take the first t. to the right*, prenez la première (route, rue) à droite. **Turnings and twistings**, tours. m et détours m. **4.** *pl.* Tournure f ; copéaux m de tour. **'turning-chisel**, *s. Tls:* Fermoir m de tour ; plane f. **'turning-lathe**, *s.* = LATHE 1. **'turning-point**, *s.* Point décisif ; moment m critique. **The turning-points of history**, les tournants m de l'histoire. **'turn-screw**, *s. Tls:* = SCREWDRIVER.
turncoat ['tə:rkout], *s.* Renégat m, apostat m. *Don't be a t.*, n'allez pas tourner casaque.
turncock ['tə:rnkɔk], *s. Adm:* Fontainier m ; l'employé m de la compagnie des eaux.
turner ['tə:rnər], *s. Ind:* Tourneur m.
turnery ['tə:rnəri], *s.* **1.** (a) Tournage m ; travail m au tour. (b) Articles façonnés au tour. **2.** Atelier m de tourneur ; tournerie f.
turnip ['tə:rnip], *s.* Navet m. **Swedish turnip**, chou-navet m. **'turnip-cabbage**, *s.* Chourave m ; turnep(s) m. **'turnip-tops**, *s.pl.* Fanes f de navets.
turnkey ['tə:rnki:], *s.* Guichetier m (d'une prison) ; porte-clefs m inv.
turnpike ['tə:rnpaik], *s. Hist:* **1.** Barrière f de péage. **2.** Route f à barrière, à péage.
turnsole ['tə:rnsoul], *s. Bot:* Tournesol m.
turnspit ['tə:rnspit], *s. A:* Tournebroche m.
turnstile ['tə:rnstail], *s.* Tourniquet(-compteur) m (pour entrées).
turpentine ['tə:rpəntain], *s.* Térébenthine f. **Oil of turpentine**, essence f de térébenthine. **'turpentine tree**, *s.* Térébinthe m.
turpitude ['tə:rpitjuːd], *s.* Turpitude f.
turps [tə:rps], *s. Com:* Essence f de térébenthine.
turquoise ['tə:rk(w)ɔːiz], *s.* **1.** Turquoise f. **2.** *a. & s.* Turquoise(-blue), turquoise (m) inv.
turret ['tʌret], *s.* **1.** *Arch:* Tourelle f. **Bell-turret**, clocheton m. **2.** *Mil: Navy:* (Gun-) turret, tourelle. **Twin turret-guns**, pièces couplées en tourelles. **3.** *Mec.E:* Tourelle f ; (porte-outil(s)) revolver m. **'turret-ship**, *s.* Cuirassé m à tourelles.
turtle [tə:rtl], *s.* Tortue f de mer. *S.a.* MOCK TURTLE. *F:* **To turn turtle**, (i) (*of boat*) chavirer ; faire capot ; capoter ; (ii) (*of car, etc.*) capoter ; faire un panache complet. *Nau:* **Turtle-back (deck)**, pont m en carapace de tortue. **turtle-'soup**, *s.* Potage m à la tortue.
turtle-dove ['tə:rtldʌv], *s. Orn:* Tourterelle f.
Tuscan ['tʌskən], *a. & s.* Toscan, -ane.
Tuscany ['tʌskəni]. *Pr.n.* La Toscane.

tush [tʌʃ], *int. A:* Bah ! chansons !
tusk [tʌsk], *s.* **1.** Défense f (d'éléphant, etc.) ; croc m (de loup, etc.). **2.** (a) *Carp:* Renfort m (de tenon). (b) Dent f (d'une herse, etc.).
tusker ['tʌskər], *s.* Éléphant m ou sanglier m adulte, qui a ses défenses.
tussle[1] [tʌsl], *s.* Lutte f, mêlée f, corps-à-corps m. *F:* **Verbal tussle**, passe f d'armes ; prise f de bec. **To have a tussle**, en venir aux mains (avec qn) ; (*of women*) se prendre aux cheveux.
tussle[2], *v.i.* **To tussle with s.o.**, lutter avec qn ; s'escrimer contre qn.
tussock ['tʌsək], *s.* Touffe f d'herbe.
tussore (silk) ['tʌsɔːr(silk)], *s. Tex:* Tussor(e) m.
tut [tʌt], *int.* (a) Quelle bêtise ! allons donc ! Tut, tut! ta, ta, ta ! (b) (*Of impatience*) Zut !
tutelage ['tjuːtiledʒ], *s.* Tutelle f.
tutelar ['tjuːtilər], **tutelary** ['tjuːtiləri], *a.* Tutélaire.
tutor[1] ['tjuːtər], *s.* **1.** Directeur m des études d'un groupe d'étudiants (à certaines universités). **2.** Private tutor, family tutor, précepteur m. **Army tutor**, préparateur m aux écoles militaires. **3.** Méthode f (de piano, etc.).
tutor[2], *v.tr.* Instruire (qn). **To tutor a boy in Latin**, donner à un élève des leçons particulières de latin. **To tutor oneself to endure poverty**, se discipliner à supporter la pauvreté.
tutorial [tjuːˈtɔːriəl]. **1.** *a.* (Cours) d'instruction. **2.** *s. Sch:* Cours individuel fait par le directeur d'études.
tu-whit, tu-whoo [tuˈhwit tuˈhwuː]. **1.** *int.* Hou hou ! **2.** *s.* Ululement m (du hibou).
tuxedo [tʌkˈsiːdo], *s. Cost: U.S:* Smoking m.
tuyere ['twiːər, 'twaiər], *s. Metall:* Tuyère f.
twaddle[1] ['twɔdl], *s.* Fadaises fpl ; futilités fpl. **To talk twaddle**, débiter des balivernes ; parler pour ne rien dire.
twaddle[2], *v.i.* Dire, conter, des sottises, des balivernes, des fadaises ; radoter.
twain [twein], *a. & s. Poet:* Deux. **In twain**, en deux. *To cleave a giant in t.*, pourfendre un géant.
twang[1] [twaŋ], *s.* **1.** Bruit sec (de la corde d'un arc) ; son aigu (d'un banjo). **2.** Nasal twang, ton nasillard. *To speak with a t.*, parler du nez ; nasiller.
twang[2]. **1.** *v.tr.* Faire frémir, faire résonner (les cordes d'une harpe). **To twang a guitar**, *v.i.* to twang a guitar, pincer, *F:* gratter, de la guitare. **2.** *v.i.* (a) (*Of string*) Vibrer, résonner, frémir. (b) (*Of pers.*) Nasiller.
'twas [twɔz] = *it was*.
tweak [twiːk], *v.tr.* Pincer ; serrer entre les doigts (en tordant). *To t. a boy's ears*, tirer les oreilles à un gamin.
tweed [twiːd], *s.* **1.** *Tex:* Étoffe f de laine à couleurs mélangées ; tweed m ; cheviote écossaise. **2.** *pl.* Tweeds, complet m, costume m, de cheviote.
'tween [twiːn], *adv. & prep. A. & Poet:* = BETWEEN. **'tween-decks**. *Nau:* **1.** s. Le faux-pont ; l'entrepont m. **2.** *adv.* Dans l'entrepont.
tweet[1] [twiːt], *s.* Pépiement m, gazouillement m.
tweet[2], *v.i.* (*Of bird*) Pépier ; gazouiller.
tweezers ['twiːzərz], *s.pl.* Petite pince ; brucelles fpl ; pince à épiler.
twelfth [twelfθ]. **1.** *num. a. & s.* Douzième. *F:* **The Twelfth**, le douze août (ouverture de la chasse à la "grouse"). **Louis the Twelfth**, Louis Douze. **2.** *s.* (*Fractional*) Douzième m.
'Twelfth-cake, *s.* Gâteau m des Rois.
'Twelfth-day, *s.* Jour m des Rois. **'Twelfth-**

night, s. Veille f des Rois. **To celebrate, keep, Twelfth-night,** faire les Rois.

twelve [twelv], num. a. & s. Douze (m). **Twelve o'clock,** (i) midi m ; Adm : Rail : douze heures ; (ii) minuit m. **Half past twelve,** midi, minuit, et demi. *About t. handkerchiefs,* une douzaine de mouchoirs. (*For other phrases see* EIGHT.)

twelvemo ['twelvmo], a. & s. Typ : In-douze (m) inv.

twelvemonth ['twelvmʌnθ], s. Année f. This day twe'vemonth, (i) d'aujourd'hui en un an ; (ii) il y a un an aujourd'hui.

twentieth ['twentiəθ], num. a. & s. Vingtième (m).

twenty ['twenti], num. a. & s. Vingt (m). **Twenty-one,** vingt et un. *T.-two,* vingt-deux. **Twenty-first,** vingt et unième. *The t.-first of May,* le vingt et un mai. *About t. people,* une vingtaine de gens. (*For other phrases see* EIGHT.)

twice [twais], adv. Deux fois. **Twice as big as . . .,** deux fois aussi grand que. . . . **I am twice your age,** j'ai deux fois votre âge ; j'ai le double de votre âge. *T. as slow,* plus lent du double. **Twice over,** à deux reprises. F : **To think twice before doing sth.,** y regarder à deux fois avant de faire qch. *That made him think twice,* cela lui a donné à réfléchir. **He did not have to be asked twice,** il ne se fit pas prier ; il ne se fit pas tirer l'oreille.

twiddle [twidl], v.tr. & i. Tourner (ses pouces) ; tortiller (sa moustache). **To twiddle (with) one's watch-chain,** jouer avec, tripoter, sa chaîne de montre.

twig[1] [twig], s. **1.** Brindille f (de branche) ; ramille f. **2.** (Dowser's hazel) twig, baguette f de sourcier. **To work the twig,** faire de l'hydroscopie, de la radiesthésie.

twig[2], v.tr. (twigged) P : Comprendre, saisir ; P : piger. *Now I twig it!* j'y suis maintenant !

twilight ['twailait], s. **1.** Crépuscule m, demi-jour m. **In the (evening) twilight,** au crépuscule ; entre chien et loup ; à la brune. **2.** Attrib. Crépusculaire.

twilit ['twailit], a. Crépusculaire ; éclairé par le crépuscule.

twill [twil], s. Tex : Croisé m ; twil m.

'twill [twil] = it will.

twin [twin], a. & s. **1.** Jumeau, -elle. **Twin(-)brother, (-)sister,** frère jumeau, sœur jumelle. **The Siamese twins,** les frères siamois. *Astr :* **The Twins,** les Gémeaux m. **2.** a. (a) **Twin beds,** lits jumeaux. **Twin tyres,** pneus jumelés. **Twin ships,** frères m. **3.** Bot : Géminé. **3.** Cryst : Macle f. **twin-'cylinder,** s. Aut : Moteur m à deux cylindres. **'twin-engine,** attrib.a. Av : **Twin-engine machine,** appareil bimoteur. **'twin-screw,** attrib.a. **Twin-screw steamer,** vapeur à hélices jumelles, à deux hélices.

twine[1] [twain], s. **1.** Ficelle f. **2.** *Twines of a snake,* replis m d'un serpent. *Twines of a river,* sinuosités f, méandres m, d'une rivière.

twine[2]. **1.** v.tr. Tordre, tortiller (des fils) ; entrelacer. **To twine sth. round sth.,** (en)rouler qch. autour de qch. **2.** v.i. (a) Se tordre, se tortiller. **To twine round sth.,** s'enrouler, s'enlacer, autour de qch. (b) (Of road) Serpenter.

twining, a. (a) Bot : Volubile. (b) (Sentier) sinueux.

twinge[1] [twindʒ], s. (a) Élancement m (de douleur) ; légère atteinte (de goutte, etc.). (b) *Twinge of conscience,* remords m.

twinge[2], v.i. (a) Élancer. *His finger twinges,* le doigt lui élance. (b) *His conscience twinges,* sa conscience le tourmente. **twinging,** a. (Of pain) Lancinant, cuisant.

twinkle[1] [twiŋkl], s. **1.** Scintillement m, clignotement m (des étoiles). **2.** Pétillement m (du regard). *A mischievous twinkle in the eye,* une éclair, une lueur, de malice dans les yeux.

twinkle[2], v.i. **1.** (Of light) Scintiller, papilloter ; clignoter. **2.** His eyes twinkled (with mischief) ses yeux pétillaient (de malice). **Twinkling eyes,** yeux pétillants d'esprit, de malice. **twinkling** s. = TWINKLE[1] I. **In a twinkling, in the twinkling of an eye,** en un clin d'œil, en un tour de main.

twirl[1] [twəːrl], s. **1.** Tournoiement m ; (of dancer) pirouette f. Fenc : Moulinet m. **2.** Volute f (de fumée, etc.). Conch : Spire f. (In writing) Enjolivure f en spirale ; fioriture f.

twirl[2]. **1.** v.tr. (a) Faire tournoyer ; faire des moulinets avec (une canne, etc.). (b) Tortiller, friser (sa moustache). **To twirl one's thumbs,** se tourner les pouces. **2.** v.i. Toupiller, tournoyer ; (of dancer) pirouetter.

twist[1] [twist], s. **1.** (a) Fil m retors ; cordon m ; cordonnet m. (b) **Twist of hair,** torsade f de cheveux. **Twist of paper,** tortillon m, cornet m de papier ; papillote f. (c) **Twist(-tobacco),** tabac (mis) en corde. **Twist of tobacco,** rouleau m, boudin m, de tabac. **2.** (a) (Effort m de) torsion f. **To give sth. a twist,** exercer une torsion sur qch. **To give one's ankle a twist,** se fouler la cheville ; se donner une entorse. (b) Tors m, torsion (des brins d'un cordage). *Sm.a :* Pas m (des rayures). (c) Effet (donné à une balle). *With a t. of the wrist,* avec un tour de poignet. F : **To learn the twist of the wrist,** apprendre le tour de main. **3.** (a) Spire f. **T. of rope round a post,** tour m de corde autour d'un poteau. *The twists of a serpent,* les replis m d'un serpent. (b) *The road takes a t.,* la route fait un coude. **Twists and turns,** tours et retours. **4.** (a) Dévers m, gauchissement m (d'une pièce de bois) ; gondolage m (d'une tôle). (b) Perversion f (du sens d'un texte). (c) (i) Prédisposition f (à qch.). **Criminal twist,** prédisposition au crime. (ii) **Mental twist,** perversion, déformation f, d'esprit. *His queer t. of mind,* sa singulière tournure d'esprit. **5.** F : **To have a twist,** avoir l'estomac creux ; F : avoir la fringale.

'twist-bit, s. Tls : Mèche hélicoïdale.

twist[2]. **1.** v.tr. (a) Tordre, tortiller. *Tex :* Retordre (le fil). **To twist together,** torsader, câbler (des fils). **To twist (up) one's handkerchief,** tire-bouchonner son mouchoir. **To twist flowers into a garland,** tresser des fleurs en guirlande. **To twist sth. round sth.,** rouler, entortiller, qch. autour de qch. F : **She can twist him round her little finger,** elle lui fait faire ses quatre volontés. (b) Se tordre (le bras, etc.). **To twist one's ankle,** se donner une entorse ; se fouler la cheville. **To twist s.o.'s arm,** tordre le bras à qn. *Face twisted by pain,* visage tordu par la douleur. (c) Dénaturer, altérer, fausser (le sens d'un texte). **To twist the truth,** donner une entorse à la vérité. (d) Donner de l'effet à (une balle). **2.** v.i. (a) (Of worm, etc.) Se tordre ; se tortiller. (b) Former une spirale ; (of smoke) former des volutes ; (of tendril, rope) vriller. (c) (Of road) Tourner ; faire des détours, des lacets. **To twist and turn,** serpenter ; décrire de nombreuses boucles. **twisted,** a. Tordu, tors ; *Tex :* (fil) retors. *T. hair,* cheveux m en torsade. *El.E :* **Twisted joint,** joint par torsade. **twisting,** a. (Sentier) tortueux, en lacet.

twister ['twistər], s. **1.** Tordeur, -euse (de chanvre, etc.). **2.** P : Faux bonhomme. *He's a twister,* il est ficelle. **3.** P : Question déconcertante. *That's a twister for you!* voilà qui vous donnera du fil à retordre.

twit [twit], *v.tr.* (twitted) **1.** Taquiner (qn); railler (qn) d'une manière sarcastique. **2.** To twit s.o. with sth., reprocher qch. à qn; railler qn de qch.

twitch¹ [twitʃ], *s.* **1.** Saccade *f*; petit coup sec. **2.** Élancement *m* (de douleur). **Twitch of conscience,** remords *m.* **3.** (a) Crispation nerveuse (des mains); mouvement convulsif. (b) **Facial twitch,** tic (convulsif). **4.** *Vet:* Serre-nez *m inv,* tord-nez *m inv.*

twitch². **1.** *v.tr.* (a) Tirer vivement; donner une saccade à (qch.). (b) Contracter (ses traits); crisper (les mains). *He twitches his leg,* il a un mouvement nerveux de la jambe. *Horse that twitches its ears,* cheval qui dresse les oreilles. **2.** *v.i.* (a) (*Of face*) Se contracter nerveusement; (*of hands*) se crisper nerveusement. (b) *His face twitches,* il a un tic. *That made him t.,* ça l'a fait tiquer.

twitch³, *s.* *Bot:* Chiendent officinal.

twitter¹ ['twitər], *s.* **1.** Gazouillement *m,* gazouillis *m.* **2.** *F:* To be all of a twitter, être tout en émoi.

twitter², *v.i.* Gazouiller. **twittering,** *s.* Gazouillement *m.*

'twixt [twikst], *prep. A:* = BETWIXT I.

two [tu:], *num. a. & s.* Deux (*m*). *Gym:* One two! une deux! To break sth. in two, casser qch. en deux. To walk in twos, two by two, two and two, marcher deux à deux, deux par deux. *F:* To put two and two together, tirer ses conclusions (après avoir rapproché les faits). *S.a.* GAME¹ I, MIND¹ 2. (*For other phrases see* EIGHT.) **'two-edged,** *a.* (Épée, *F:* argument) à deux tranchants, à double tranchant. **'two-faced,** *a.* = DOUBLE-FACED. **'two-footed,** *a.* Bipède. **'two-'handed,** *a.* **1.** (Épée) à deux mains. **2.** *Z: etc:* Bimane. **3.** *Cards:* (Jeu) qui se joue à deux. **'two-legged,** *a.* Bipède. **'two-phase,** *attrib.a. El.E:* (Courant) biphasé, diphasé. **'two-piece,** *attrib.a.* En deux pièces. **(Lady's)** two-piece costume, deux-pièces *m.* **'two-ply,** *attrib.a.* **1.** (Cordage) à deux brins. **2.** Two-ply wood, contre-plaqué *m* à deux épaisseurs. **'two-pole,** *attrib.a. El:* Bipolaire. **two-'seater,** *s.* Avion *m* ou voiture *f* à deux places; *F:* un biplace. **'two-speed,** *attrib.a.* A deux vitesses. **'two-step,** *s. Danc:* Pas *m* de deux. **'two-stroke,** *attrib.a. I.C.E:* (Moteur) bitemps *inv,* à deux temps. **'two-way,** *attrib.a.* (a) (Robinet) à deux voies. (b) Two-way street, rue à deux sens. *S.a.* SWITCH¹ 2. **'two-'yearly,** *a.* Biennal, -aux.

twofold ['tu:fould]. **1.** *a.* Double; (cordage) à deux brins. **2.** *adv.* Doublement. *Kindnesses returned t.,* bontés rendues au double.

twopence ['tʌpəns], *s.* Deux pence *m. F:* It isn't worth twopence, ça ne vaut pas deux sous.

twopenny ['tʌp(ə)ni], *a.* A, de, deux pence. **'twopenny-'halfpenny,** *attrib.a. F:* Insignifiant; sans importance; de quatre sous.

twyer ['twiːər, 'twaiər], *s. Metall:* Tuyère *f.*

Tyburn ['taibəːrn]. *Pr.n. Hist:* Carrefour *m* de Londres où se dressait la potence.

tying ['taiiŋ] *See* TIE².

tyke [taik], *s. P:* **1.** Vilain chien. **2.** Rustre *m.* **3.** (Yorkshire) tyke, homme *m* du Yorkshire.

tympan ['timpən], *s.* Tympan *m.*

tympanist ['timpənist], *s. Mus:* Timbalier *m.*

tympanum, *pl.* **-a** ['timpənəm, -a], *s.* Tympan *m.*

type¹ [taip], *s.* **1.** Type *m. T. of Italian beauty,* type de la beauté italienne. *People of this t.,* les individus de ce genre. **2.** *Typ:* (a) Caractère *m,* type. (b) *Coll.* Caractères. **Printed, displayed, in bold type,** en vedette. **To set type,** composer. *S.a.* STANDING¹ 2. **'type area,** *s. Typ:* Justification *f.* **'type-caster, -founder,** *s.* Fondeur *m* en caractères d'imprimerie. **'type-metal,** *s.* Alliage *m* pour caractères d'imprimerie. **'type-script,** *s.* Manuscrit dactylographié. **'type-setter,** *s. Typ:* Compositeur *m.* **'type-setting,** *s. Typ:* Composition *f.*

type², *v.tr.* Écrire à la machine; dactylographier.

typewrite ['taiprait], *v.tr. p.p.* typewritten; *no p.t.*) = TYPE². *Typewritten document,* document transcrit à la machine. **typewriting,** *s.* Dactylographie *f.*

typewriter ['taipraitər], *s.* Machine *f* à écrire.

typhlitis [ti'flaitis], *s. Med:* Typhlite *f.*

typhoid ['taifɔid], *a. Med:* Typhoïde. **Typhoid fever,** *s.* typhoid, fièvre *f* typhoïde.

typhoon [tai'fuːn], *s. Meteor:* Typhon *m.*

typhus ['taifəs], *s. Med:* Typhus *m.*

typical ['tipik(ə)l], *a.* Typique. *The t. Frenchman,* le vrai type français. *That is t. of him,* c'est bien de lui. *That is t. of France,* c'est un trait caractéristique de la France. **-ally,** *adv.* D'une manière typique.

typify ['tipifai], *v.tr.* **1.** Représenter (qch.); symboliser (qch.). **2.** Être caractéristique de (sa classe); être le type de (l'officier militaire, etc.).

typist ['taipist], *s.* Dactylographe *mf, F:* dactylo *mf.* **Typist's error,** erreur de machine. *S.a.* SHORTHAND.

typographer [tai'pɔgrəfər, ti-], *s.* Typographe *m.*

typographic(al) [taipo'grafik(ə)l, ti-], *a.* Typographique.

typography [tai'pɔgrəfi, ti-], *s.* Typographie *f.*

tyrannical [ti'ranik(ə)l, tai-], *a.* Tyrannique. **-ally,** *adv.* Tyranniquement; en tyran.

tyrannize ['tirənaiz], *v.i.* Faire le tyran. **To tyrannize over s.o.,** tyranniser qn.

tyrannous ['tirənəs], *a.* Tyrannique.

tyranny ['tirəni], *s.* Tyrannie *f.*

tyrant ['tairənt], *s.* Tyran *m.*

tyre¹ ['taiər], *s.* (a) Bandage *m,* cercle *m* (de roue). *Rail:* Flanged tyre, bandage à boudin. (b) *Aut:* *Cy:* Rubber tyre, bandage en caoutchouc. Pneumatic tyre, (bandage) pneumatique *m; F:* pneu *m.* **Balloon tyre,** pneu ballon, pneu confort. Non-skid tyre, (pneu) antidérapant *m. S.a.* PRESSURE I. **'tyre-cement,** *s. Aut: Cy:* Dissolution *f.* **'tyre-cover,** *s.* Enveloppe *f* (pour pneu). **'tyre-gauge,** *s.* Manomètre *m* (pour pneus). **'tyre-inflator, -pump,** *s.* Gonfleur *m,* pompe *f* (pour pneus). **'tyre-lever,** *s.* Démonte-pneus *m inv.*

tyre², *v.tr.* Poser un bandage à (une roue); cercler (une roue). **tyred,** *a.* **Solid-tyred,** à bandage(s) plein(s). *S.a.* RUBBER-TYRED.

tyro ['tairo], *s.* = TIRO.

Tyrolese [tiro'liːz], *a. & s.* Tyrolien, -ienne.

tzigane [tsi'gaːn], *a. & s.* Tzigane (*mf*).

U, u [juː], *s.* (La lettre) U, u *m.* *F:* It's all U.P. ['juːˈpiː] (= *up*), tout est perdu. It's all U.P. with him, son affaire est faite. **U-bolt,** boulon *m* en U. **'U-boat,** *s.* *F:* Sous-marin allemand.

ubiquitous [juˈbikwitəs], *a.* Qui se trouve partout; que l'on rencontre partout.

ubiquity [juˈbikwiti], *s.* Ubiquité *f.*

udder [ˈʌdər], *s.* Mamelle *f*, pis *m* (de vache).

udometer [juˈdɔmetər], *s.* Udomètre *m.*

ugh [ʌχ, uh], *int.* **1.** Pouah! **2.** Ugh, it's cold! brrr, il fait froid!

ugliness [ˈʌglinəs], *s.* Laideur *f.*

ugly [ˈʌgli], *a.* Laid; disgracieux. Ugly person, laideron, -onne. To grow ugly, enlaidir. *U.* piece of furniture, vilain meuble. *P:* To cut up ugly, se fâcher.

uhlan [ˈ(j)uːlən], *s.* Uhlan *m.*

ukase [juˈkeis], *s.* Ukase *m*, oukase *m.*

ukulele [juːkəˈleili], *s.* *Mus:* Ukulele *m.*

ulcer [ˈʌlsər], *s.* Ulcère *m.*

ulcerate [ˈʌlsəreit]. **1.** *v.tr.* Ulcérer. **2.** *v.t.* S'ulcérer. **ulcerated,** *a.* Ulcéré, ulcéreux.

ulceration [ʌlsəˈrei(ə)n], *s.* Ulcération *f.*

ulcerous [ˈʌlsərəs], *a.* Ulcéreux.

ulex [ˈjuːleks], *s.* *Bot:* Ulex *m*; *F:* ajonc *m.*

ullage [ˈʌledʒ], *s.* *Winem:* *Dist:* **(Dry)** ullage, vidange *f*, coulage *m*; *Cust:* manquant *m.*

ulna [ˈʌlna], *s.* *Anat:* Cubitus *m.*

ulnar [ˈʌlnər], *a.* *Anat:* Ulnaire; cubital, -aux.

ult. [ʌlt], *adv.* *Com:* = ULTIMO.

ulterior [ʌlˈtiːəriər], *a.* **1.** Ultérieur, -eure. **2.** Ulterior motive, motif secret, caché. *Without u.* motive, sans arrière-pensée. **-ly,** *adv.* Ultérieurement; plus tard.

ultimate [ˈʌltimet], *a.* (*a*) Final, -als. *U.* purpose, but final. *U.* decision, décision définitive. (*b*) *Mth:* Ultimate ratio, dernière raison. (*c*) *U.* truth, vérité fondamentale. (*d*) (*Of syllable, etc.*) Ultime, dernier. **-ly,** *adv.* A la fin; en fin de compte.

ultimatum, *pl.* **-tums, -ta** [ʌltiˈmeitəm, -təmz, -ta], *s.* Ultimatum *m.*

ultimo [ˈʌltimo], *adv.* Du mois dernier.

ultra [ˈʌltra]. **1.** *a.* Extrême. **2.** *s.* *Pol:* Ultra *m.*

ultra-fashionable, *a.* Tout dernier cri.

ultramarine [ʌltraməˈriːn]. **1.** *a.* (Pays, etc.) d'outre-mer. **2.** *a.* & *s.* (Bleu *m* d')outremer *m inv.*

ultramontane [ʌltraˈmɔntein], *a.* & *s.* *Theol:* *Pol:* Ultramontain, -aine.

ultra-violet [ʌltraˈvaiolet], *a.* *Opt:* Ultraviolet, -ette.

ultra vires [ʌltraˈvairiːz], *Lt.adj.* & *adv.phr.* Au delà des pouvoirs. Action ultra vires, excès *m* de pouvoir.

ululate [ˈjuːljuleit], *v.i.* (*Of owl*) Ululer, huer; (*of jackal*) hurler.

ululation [juːljuˈlei(ə)n], *s.* Ululation *f*, ululement *m* (du hibou); hurlement *m* (du chacal).

Ulysses [juˈlisiːz]. *Pr.n.m.* Ulysse.

umbel [ˈʌmb(ə)l, -bel], *s.* *Bot:* Ombelle *f.*

umbellate [ˈʌmbelet], *a.* (Fleur) ombellée, en ombelle.

umbellifer [ʌmˈbelifər], *s.* *Bot:* Ombellifère *f.*

umbelliferous [ʌmbeˈlifərəs], *a.* *Bot:* Ombellifère.

umber[1] [ˈʌmbər], *s.* *Ich:* Ombre *m.*

umber[2], *s.* *Paint:* Terre *f* d'ombre.

umbilical [ʌmˈbilik(ə)l], *a.* *Anat:* Ombilical, -aux.

umbra, *pl.* **-ae** [ˈʌmbra, -iː], *s.* *Astr:* (*a*) Cône *m*

d'ombre (dans une éclipse). (*b*) Obscurité centrale (d'une tache solaire).

umbrage [ˈʌmbredʒ], *s.* Ombrage *m*, ressentiment *m.* He took no u. at their friendship, il ne s'offensait pas de leur amitié.

umbrella [ʌmˈbrela], *s.* (*a*) Parapluie *m.* Stumpy umbrella, tom-pouce *m.* **Carriage** umbrella, grand parapluie (de portier d'hôtel). (*b*) Parasol *m* (de chef de tribu nègre). **um'brella-frame,** *s.* Monture *f*, carcasse *f*, de parapluie. **um'brella-stand,** *s.* Porte-parapluies *m inv.* **um'brella-stick,** *s.* Manche *m*, canne *f*, de parapluie. **um'brella-tree,** *s.* *Bot:* Magnolier *m* (en) parasol.

Umbria [ˈʌmbria]. *Pr.n.* *Geog:* L'Ombrie *f.*

umlaut [ˈumlaut], *s.* *Ling:* Umlaut *m.*

umph [mh], *int.* Hum! hmm!

umpire[1] [ˈʌmpaiər], *s.* Arbitre *m*, juge *m.*

umpire[2], *v.tr.* Arbitrer (un différend, *Sp:* un match). **umpiring,** *s.* Arbitrage *m.*

umpteen [ˈʌmptiːn], *a.* & *s.* *P:* Je ne sais combien. To have u. reasons for doing sth., avoir trente-six raisons de faire qch.

un [ən], *pron.* *P:* (= *one*) A little 'un, un petit.

unabashed [ʌnəˈbaʃt], *a.* **1.** Sans perdre contenance. *U., he replied* . . ., il répondit sans aucune confusion. . . . **2.** Aucunement ébranlé.

unabated [ʌnəˈbeitid], *a.* Non diminué. With u. speed, toujours avec la même vitesse.

unabating [ʌnəˈbeitiŋ], *a.* Persistant, soutenu.

unable [ʌnˈeibl], *a.* Incapable. Unable to do sth., impuissant à faire qch.; hors d'état de faire qch. We are u. to help you, nous ne pouvons pas vous aider. 'Unable to attend," "empêché."

unabridged [ʌnəˈbridʒd], *a.* Non abrégé. *U.* edition, édition intégrale.

unaccented [ʌnakˈsentid], *a.* Sans accent; (*of syllable*) non accentué; atone.

unacceptable [ʌnakˈseptəbl], *a.* Inacceptable; (théorie) irrecevable. *A glass of beer wouldn't be u.*, un verre de bière ne serait pas de refus.

unaccommodating [ʌnəˈkɔmodeitiŋ], *a.* Peu accommodant; désobligeant.

unaccompanied [ʌnəˈkʌmpənid], *a.* **1.** Non compagné, seul; sans escorte. **2.** *Mus:* Sans accompagnement.

unaccomplished [ʌnəˈkɔmpliʃt], *a.* (*a*) (Projet) inaccompli, non réalisé. (*b*) (Travail, etc.) inachevé.

unaccountable [ʌnəˈkauntəbl], *a.* (*a*) (Phénomène) inexplicable. *It is u.*, explique cela qui pourra. (*b*) (Conduite) bizarre. **-ably,** *adv.* Inexplicablement.

unaccounted [ʌnəˈkauntid], *a.* Unaccounted for. **1.** (Phénomène) inexpliqué. **2.** *Five of the passengers are still u. for*, on reste sans nouvelles de cinq passagers.

unaccredited [ʌnəˈkreditid], *a.* (Agent) non accrédité, sans pouvoirs.

unaccustomed [ʌnəˈkʌstəmd], *a.* **1.** (Evénement) inaccoutumé. **2.** (*Of pers.*) Unaccustomed to sth., peu habitué à qch.

unacknowledged [ʌnakˈnɔledʒd], *a.* **1.** (*a*) (Enfant) non reconnu. (*b*) (Péché) non avoué. **2.** (Lettre) demeurée sans réponse.

unacquainted [ʌnəˈkweintid], *a.* **1.** To be unacquainted with s.o., ne pas connaître qn. **2.** To be unacquainted with sth., ignorer (un fait, etc.).

unadaptable [ʌnə'daptəbl], a. (Of pers.) Qui ne s'accommode pas aux circonstances ; qui manque de liant.

unadapted [ʌnə'daptid], a. Mal adapté, peu adapté (to sth., à qch.).

unaddressed [ʌnə'drest], a. (Colis) sans adresse, qui ne porte pas d'adresse.

unadorned [ʌnə'dɔːrnd], a. Sans ornement ; naturel. Beauty unadorned, la beauté sans parure, sans fard. U. truth, la vérité pure, sans fard.

unadulterated [ʌnə'dʌltəreitid], a. Pur ; sans mélange.

unadvisable [ʌnəd'vaizəbl], a. (a) (Of action) Peu sage ; imprudent. (b) Alcohol is u. for heart patients, l'alcool est à déconseiller aux cardiaques.

unadvisedly [ʌnəd'vaizidli], adv. Imprudemment ; sans réflexion.

unaffected [ʌnə'fektid], a. 1. Sans affectation. (a) Véritable, sincère. (b) (Of pers.) Sans pose. U. style, style sans recherche. 2. Unaffected by air, inaltérable à l'air. Metal u. by acids, métal inattaquable par les acides. Organism u. by poison, organisme réfractaire au poison. -ly, adv. Sans affectation. (a) Sincèrement. (b) Simplement.

unaffectedness [ʌnə'fektidnəs], s. Absence f de toute affectation.

unaffiliated [ʌnə'filieitid], a. Non affilié (to, à).

unaided [ʌn'eidid], a. Sans aide. He did it u., il l'a fait tout seul. To see sth. with the unaided eye, voir qch. à l'œil nu.

unallayed [ʌnə'leid], a. (Of grief) Inapaisé ; sans soulagement.

unallotted [ʌnə'lɔtid], a. 1. (Temps) disponible. 2. Unallotted shares, actions non réparties.

unalloyed [ʌnə'lɔid], a. (Métal) pur, sans alliage. U. happiness, bonheur pur, sans mélange.

unalterable [ʌn'ɔltərəbl], a. Immuable, invariable. -ably, adv. Immuablement, invariablement.

unaltered [ʌn'ɔltərd], a. Toujours le même ; sans changement ; tel quel.

unambiguous [ʌnam'bigjuəs], a. Qui ne prête à aucune équivoque. U. terms, termes précis, clairs.

unambitious [ʌnam'biʃəs], a. 1. Sans ambition. 2. (Projet) sans prétention.

unamended [ʌnə'mendid], a. Sans modification ; tel quel.

unamiable [ʌn'eimjəbl], a. Peu aimable.

unanimity [juna'nimiti], s. Unanimité f. With unanimity, d'un commun accord.

unanimous [ju'nanimos], a. Unanime. -ly, adv. A l'unanimité ; unanimement.

unannounced [ʌnə'naunst], a. He marched in u., il entra sans se faire annoncer.

unanswerable [ʌn'ɑːnsərəbl], a. Qui n'admet pas de réponse ; (argument) sans réplique.

unanswered [ʌn'ɑːnsərd], a. 1. Sans réponse. 2. Irréfuté.

unanticipated [ʌnan'tisipeitid], a. Imprévu.

unappalled [ʌnə'pɔːld], a. To remain unappalled, ne pas s'émouvoir ; rester impassible.

unappeasable [ʌnə'piːzəbl], a. (Faim) inapaisable ; (appétit) insatiable ; (haine) implacable.

unappeased [ʌnə'piːzd], a. Inapaisé ; (of passion) inassouvi.

unappetizing [ʌn'apetaiziŋ], a. Peu appétissant.

unappreciated [ʌnə'priːʃieitid], a. Inapprécié ; peu estimé. U. poet, poète méconnu.

unappreciative [ʌnə'priːʃjətiv], a. (Public) insensible ; (compte rendu) peu appréciateur.

unapproachable [ʌnə'proutʃəbl], a. 1. Inac-

cessible ; (côte) inabordable ; (of pers.) inabordable, distant. 2. Incomparable ; sans pareil.

unappropriated [ʌnə'prouprieitid], a. 1. (Argent) inutilisé, disponible. U. funds, fonds sans application déterminée. 2. (Siège) libre.

unapt [ʌn'apt], a. 1. Qui ne convient pas ; (mot) peu juste. 2. U. for business, inapte aux affaires.

unarmed [ʌn'ɑːrmd], a. Sans armes.

unascertainable [ʌnasər'teinəbl], a. Non vérifiable ; indéterminable.

unascertained [ʌnasər'teind], a. Non vérifié. U. facts, faits non établis.

unashamed [ʌnə'ʃeimd], a. Sans honte ; éhonté ; sans pudeur ; cynique.

unasked [ʌn'ɑːskt], a. To do sth. unasked, faire qch. spontanément.

unassailable [ʌnə'seiləbl], a. (Droit) inattaquable ; (conclusion) indiscutable.

unassertive [ʌnə'səːrtiv], a. Modeste, timide.

unassimilated [ʌnə'simileitid], a. (Aliment) inassimilé.

unassisted [ʌnə'sistid], a. = UNAIDED.

unassuaged [ʌnə'sweidʒd], a. (Souffrance) que rien ne vient calmer ; (appétit) inassouvi.

unassuming [ʌnə'sjumiŋ], a. Sans prétention(s) ; simple, modeste.

unattached [ʌnə'tatʃt], a. 1. Qui n'est pas attaché (to, à) ; indépendant (to, de). 2. (Officier) disponible. F: Unattached young lady, jeune fille libre de tout engagement.

unattainable [ʌnə'teinəbl], a. Inaccessible (by, à) ; hors de la portée (by, de).

unattended [ʌnə'tendid], a. (a) Seul ; sans escorte. (b) Sport not unattended by danger, sport non dépourvu de danger.

unattractive [ʌnə'traktiv], a. Peu attrayant ; (personne) peu sympathique.

unauthorized [ʌn'ɔːθəraizd], a. (a) Inautorisé ; sans autorisation ; (commerce) illicite. (b) (Fonctionnaire) sans mandat.

unavailing [ʌnə'veiliŋ], a. Inutile ; (of tears) vain ; (of efforts) infructueux. -ly, adv. En vain.

unavoidable [ʌnə'vɔidəbl], a. (a) Inévitable. (b) (Événement) qu'on ne peut prévenir. -ably, adv. 1. Inévitablement. 2. Unavoidably absent, absent pour raison majeure ; "empêché."

unavowed [ʌnə'vaud], a. Inavoué.

unaware [ʌnə'weər], a. Ignorant, non informé (of sth., de qch.). To be unaware of sth., ignorer qch. I am not unaware that . . ., je ne suis pas sans savoir que + ind.

unawares [ʌnə'weərz], adv. 1. Inconsciemment ; par inadvertance. 2. To take s.o. unawares, prendre qn à l'improviste.

unbaked [ʌn'beikt], a. (Of brick) Cru.

unbalance [ʌn'baləns], v.tr. Déranger, déséquilibrer (l'esprit de qn).

unbalanced [ʌn'balənst], a. 1. (a) Ph: En équilibre instable. (b) (Esprit) déséquilibré, dérangé. 2. Unbalanced forces, forces non équilibrées.

unbearable [ʌn'beərəbl], a. Insupportable, intolérable. Unbearable agony, douleur atroce. -ably, adv. Insupportablement.

unbeatable [ʌn'biːtəbl], a. Imbattable, invincible.

unbeaten [ʌn'biːtn], a. 1. Non battu. Unbeaten path, sentier non battu, non frayé. 2. Unbeaten champion, champion qui n'a pas encore été battu.

unbecoming [ʌnbi'kʌmiŋ], a. 1. Peu convenable ; déplacé. Unbecoming of s.o., déplacé chez qn. 2. (Of garment) Peu seyant. -ly, adv. D'une manière peu séante.

unbeknown [ʌnbi'noun], 1. a. Inconnu (to, de).

2. *adv.* To do sth. unbeknown to anyone, faire qch. à l'insu de tous.

unbelief [ʌnbi'li:f], *s.* Incrédulité *f.*

unbelievable [ʌnbi'li:vəbl], *a.* Incroyable.

unbeliever [ʌnbi'li:vər], *s.* Incrédule *mf.*

unbelieving [ʌnbi'li:viŋ], *a.* Incrédule.

unbend [ʌn'bend], *v.* (unbent [ʌn'bent]; unbent) I. *v.tr.* **1.** Détendre, débander (un arc); *F:* détendre (son esprit). **2.** Rendre (qch.) droit; redresser. **3.** *Nau:* Défrapper (un câble). II. **unbend**, *v.i.* S'abandonner un petit peu; se détendre. He never unbends, son caractère ne se déraidit jamais. **unbending**, *a.* Inflexible, ferme, raide.

unbeseeming [ʌnbi'si:miŋ], *a.* Malséant; peu convenable. Action unbeseeming a priest, action qui sied mal à un prêtre.

unbias(s)ed [ʌn'baiəst], *a.* Impartial, -aux; sans parti pris; sans prévention.

unbidden [ʌn'bid(ə)n], *a.* **1.** Non invité; (hôte) intrus. **2.** Spontané.

unbind [ʌn'baind], *v.tr.* (unbound [ʌn'baund]; unbound) *(a)* Délier. *(b)* Dénouer (ses cheveux).

unbleached [ʌn'bli:tʃt], *a.* *Tex:* Écru.

unblemished [ʌn'blemiʃt], *a.* Sans défaut; sans tache; immaculé. Unblemished career, carrière sans tache.

unblock [ʌn'blɔk], *v.tr.* **1.** *(a)* Dégager, désencombrer. *(b)* *Cards:* To unblock a suit, affranchir une couleur. **2.** Décaler (une roue).

unblushing [ʌn'blʌʃiŋ], *a.* Sans vergogne; éhonté. **-ly**, *adv.* Sans vergogne; (mentir) impudemment, cyniquement.

unbolt [ʌn'boult], *v.tr.* **1.** Déverrouiller (la porte). **2.** Déboulonner.

unborn [ʌn'bɔ:rn, 'ʌn-], *a.* Qui n'est pas encore né. Generations yet unborn, générations à venir; générations futures.

unbosom [ʌn'bu:zəm], *v.tr.* Découvrir, révéler (ses sentiments). To unbosom oneself to s.o., ouvrir son cœur à qn.

unbound [ʌn'baund]. I. *See* UNBIND. II. **unbound**, *a.* **1.** *(a)* Délié. To come unbound, se délier. *(b)* *(Of hair)* Dénoué, flottant. **2.** *(Of book)* Non relié; broché.

unbounded [ʌn'baundid], *a.* Sans bornes; illimité; *(of conceit)* démesuré.

unbraid [ʌn'breid], *v.tr.* Détresser (ses cheveux).

unbreakable [ʌn'breikəbl], *a.* Incassable.

unbreathable [ʌn'bri:ðəbl], *a.* Irrespirable.

unbribable [ʌn'braibəbl], *a.* Incorruptible.

unbridled [ʌn'braidld], *a.* *(Of passion)* Débridé, effréné; sans retenue.

unbroken [ʌn'brouk(ə)n], *a.* **1.** *(a)* Non brisé, non cassé. *(b)* Intact. Unbroken spirit, courage inentamé. *(Cp.* 2 *(b).)* *(c)* *(Of rule)* Toujours observé. *Sp:* Record still unbroken, record qui n'a pas été battu. *(d)* *(Of silence)* Ininterrompu, continu; *(of ground)* non accidenté. Unbroken sheet of ice, nappe de glace continue. **2.** *(a)* *(Cheval)* Non rompu, non dressé. *(b)* Unbroken spirit, esprit insoumis, indompté. *(Cp.* 1 *(b).)* **3.** *Agr:* Unbroken ground, terre vierge.

unbrotherly [ʌn'brʌðərli], *a.* Peu fraternel.

unbuckle [ʌn'bʌkl], *v.tr.* Déboucler.

unburden [ʌn'bə:rd(ə)n], *v.tr.* **1.** *(a)* Alléger (qn) d'un fardeau. *(b)* To unburden the mind, soulager, alléger, l'esprit. To unburden oneself, se délester le cœur. To u. oneself of a secret, se soulager du poids d'un secret. **2.** To unburden one's sorrows to s.o., épancher ses chagrins dans le sein de qn.

unburied [ʌn'berid], *a.* **1.** Déterré. **2.** Sans sépulture; non enterré.

unbusinesslike [ʌn'biznəslaik], *a.* **1.** Peu commerçant. **2.** Unbusinesslike proceeding, procédé irrégulier. To conduct one's affairs in an u. way, manquer de méthode.

unbutton [ʌn'bʌt(ə)n], *v.tr.* Déboutonner. *(Of pers.)* All unbuttoned, tout débraillé.

uncalled [ʌn'kɔ:ld], *a.* **1.** Uncalled capital, capitaux non appelés. **2.** Uncalled for, *(of remark)* déplacé; *(of rebuke)* immérité.

uncanny [ʌn'kani], *a.* D'une étrangeté inquiétante; mystérieux, -euse. Uncanny noise, bruit inquiétant. U. light, lueur sinistre. **-ily**, *adv.* D'une manière étrange.

uncared-for [ʌn'keərdfɔ:r], *a.* Peu soigné. U.-for child, enfant délaissé. To leave a garden u.-for, laisser un jardin à l'abandon.

unceasing [ʌn'si:siŋ], *a.* *(a)* Incessant, continu. *(b)* *(Travail)* assidu; *(effort)* soutenu. **-ly**, *adv.* Sans cesse.

uncensored [ʌn'sensərd], *a.* **1.** *(Article)* qui n'a pas été soumis à la censure. **2.** *(Passage)* non expurgé *(par la censure).*

unceremonious [ʌnsere'mounjəs], *a.* *(Of pers.)* Sans façon, sans gêne. **-ly**, *adv.* **1.** Sans cérémonie. **2.** Sans façons.

uncertain [ʌn'sə:rt(ə)n], *a.* Incertain. **1.** *(a)* *(Of time, amount)* Indéterminé. *(b)* *(Résultat)* douteux. *(c)* Uncertain outline, contour mal défini. **2.** *(a)* Uncertain steps, pas mal assurés. Uncertain temper, humeur inégale. Uncertain health, santé vacillante. *(b)* To be u. of, as regards, the future, être incertain de l'avenir. To be uncertain whether . . ., ne pas savoir au juste si. . . . **-ly**, *adv.* D'une façon incertaine.

uncertainty [ʌn'sə:rtənti], *s.* **1.** Incertitude *f.* To remove any uncertainty . . ., pour dissiper toute équivoque. . . . **2.** To prefer a certainty to an uncertainty, préférer le certain à l'incertain.

uncertificated [ʌnsə:r'tifikeitid], *a.* Sans diplôme, non diplômé.

unchain [ʌn'tʃein], *v.tr.* Déchaîner; délivrer (un prisonnier). *F:* To unchain one's passions, donner libre cours à ses passions.

unchallenged [ʌn'tʃalendʒd], *a.* **1.** *(a)* Que personne ne vient contredire. To continue u., continuer sans être contredit. *(b)* *(Droit)* indisputé. To let (sth.) go, pass, unchallenged, ne pas relever (une affirmation). **2.** *Mil:* To let s.o. pass unchallenged, laisser passer qn sans interpellation.

unchangeable [ʌn'tʃeindʒəbl], *a.* Immuable.

unchanged [ʌn'tʃeindʒd], *a.* Inchangé; toujours le même.

unchanging [ʌn'tʃeindʒiŋ], *a.* Invariable, immuable.

uncharitable [ʌn'tʃaritəbl], *a.* Peu charitable.

uncharted [ʌn'tʃɑ:rtid], *a.* **1.** *(Of island)* Non porté sur la carte. **2.** *(Of sea)* Inexploré.

unchecked [ʌn'tʃekt], *a.* **1.** Auquel rien n'a été opposé; sans frein. Unchecked advance, libre marche en avant. Unchecked anger, colère non contenue. **2.** *(Of account)* Non pointé ou non vérifié.

unchivalrous [ʌn'ʃivəlrəs, -'tʃi-], *a.* Peu chevaleresque; peu courtois ou peu loyal.

unchristened [ʌn'kris(ə)nd], *a.* **1.** Non baptisé. **2.** Sans nom.

unchristian [ʌn'kristjən], *a.* **1.** Infidèle, païen. **2.** Peu chrétien.

uncial ['ʌnʃjəl], *a.* *(Of letter)* Oncial, -aux.

uncircumcised [ʌn'sə:rkəmsaizd], *a.* Incirconcis.

uncivil [ʌn'sivil], *a.* Incivil, impoli. **-illy,** *adv.* Impoliment.

uncivilized [ʌn'sivilaizd], *a.* Incivilisé, barbare.

unclaimed [ʌn'kleimd], *a.* Non réclamé. *U. right,* droit non revendiqué. *Post:* Unclaimed letter, lettre de rebut.

unclasp [ʌn'klɑːsp], *v.tr.* (*a*) Dégrafer, défaire (un bracelet). (*b*) Desserrer (le poing).

uncle [ʌŋkl], *s.* **1.** Oncle *m.* Yes, uncle! oui, mon oncle! To talk to s.o. like a Dutch uncle, faire la morale à qn. **2.** *P:* My watch is at my uncle's, ma montre est chez ma tante, au clou.

unclean [ʌn'kliːn], *a.* **1.** Impur, immonde. **2.** Malpropre, sale.

uncleared [ʌn'kliːərd], *a.* **1.** Uncleared ground, terrain indéfriché. **2.** (*a*) (*Of debt*) Non acquitté. (*b*) (Chèque) non compensé.

unclench [ʌn'klenʃ], *v.tr.* Desserrer (le poing, les dents).

uncloak [ʌn'klouk], *v.tr.* (*a*) Dépouiller (qn) de son manteau. (*b*) Découvrir (des projets); démasquer, dévoiler (une imposture).

unclothe [ʌn'klo:uð]. **1.** *v.tr.* Déshabiller, dévêtir (qn); mettre (qn) à nu. **2.** *v.i.* Se déshabiller.

unclothed [ʌn'klo:uðd], *a.* **1.** Déshabillé. **2.** Nu; sans vêtements.

unclouded [ʌn'klaudid], *a.* (*Of sky*) Sans nuage; (*of vision*) clair; (*of liquid*) limpide.

uncock [ʌn'kɔk], *v.tr.* Désarmer (un fusil).

uncoil [ʌn'kɔil]. **1.** *v.tr.* Dérouler. *Nau:* Délover. **2.** *v.i.* (*Of snake*) Se dérouler.

uncoloured [ʌn'kʌlərd], *a.* (*a*) Non coloré. *U. account of sth.,* rapport fidèle de qch. (*b*) Incolore.

uncombed [ʌn'koumd], *a.* (*Of hair*) Non peigné, mal peigné, ébouriffé; (*of wool*) non peigné.

uncomely [ʌn'kʌmli], *a.* Peu gracieux; disgracieux; laid.

uncomfortable [ʌn'kʌmfərtəbl], *a.* **1.** Peu confortable; (chaleur) incommode. This is a very *u. bed,* on est très mal dans ce lit. **2.** (*a*) Désagréable. To make things uncomfortable for s.o., créer des ennuis à qn; faire des histoires à qn. It makes things u., c'est très gênant. (*b*) (*Of news*) Inquiétant. **3.** To feel uncomfortable, être mal à l'aise. To be, feel, uncomfortable about sth., être inquiet au sujet de qch. **-ably,** *adv.* **1.** Peu confortablement; incommodément. **2.** Désagréablement. The enemy were uncomfortably near, la proximité de l'ennemi était inquiétante.

uncommon [ʌn'kɔmən]. **1.** *a.* Peu commun. (*a*) Uncommon word, mot rare, peu usité. (*b*) Peu ordinaire; singulier. **2.** *adv. F:* = UNCOMMONLY 2. **-ly,** *adv.* **1.** Not uncommonly, assez souvent. **2.** Singulièrement. Uncommonly good, excellent.

uncommunicative [ʌnkə'mju:nikətiv], *a.* Peu communicatif; taciturne.

uncompanionable [ʌnkəm'panjənəbl], *a.* Peu sociable.

uncomplaining [ʌnkəm'pleiniŋ], *a.* Qui ne se plaint pas; patient, résigné. **-ly,** *adv.* Sans se plaindre.

uncomplimentary [ʌnkɔmpli'mentəri], *a.* Peu flatteur, -euse.

uncompromising [ʌn'kɔmprəmaiziŋ], *a.* Intransigeant; intraitable. *U. sincerity,* sincérité absolue.

unconcealed [ʌnkən'siːld], *a.* Qui n'est pas caché; fait à découvert. *U. opinions,* opinions avouées.

unconcern [ʌnkən'səːrn], *s.* Insouciance *f;* indifférence *f. Smile of u.,* sourire détaché.

unconcerned [ʌnkən'səːrnd], *a.* Insouciant, indifférent. *U. air,* air dégagé. *U., he went on speaking,* sans se troubler, il continua de parler.

unconcernedly [ʌnkən'səːrnidli], *adv.* D'un air indifférent, dégagé; avec insouciance.

unconciliatory [ʌnkən'siliətəri], *a.* Inconciliant; raide (en affaires).

unconditional [ʌnkən'diʃən(ə)l], *a.* Inconditionnel. (*a*) Absolu. *U. refusal,* refus catégorique. (*b*) *U. acceptance,* acceptation sans conditions. **-ally,** *adv.* To accept u., accepter sans réserve. *To surrender u.,* se rendre à discrétion.

unconfirmed [ʌnkən'fəːrmd], *a.* (*Of news*) Qui n'est pas confirmé; sujet à caution.

uncongenial [ʌnkən'dʒiːnjəl], *a.* **1.** (*Of pers.*) Peu sympathique. **2.** (*a*) (Climat) peu favorable (*to,* à). (*b*) *U. job,* travail ingrat.

unconnected [ʌnkə'nektid], *a.* (*a*) Sans rapport, sans lien. The two events are totally u., les deux événements n'ont aucun rapport entre eux. (*b*) (Style) décousu, sans suite.

unconquerable [ʌn'kɔŋkərəbl], *a.* Invincible; (curiosité) irrésistible; (défaut) incorrigible.

unconscionable [ʌn'kɔnʃənəbl], *a.* **1.** Sans conscience. *U. rogue,* coquin fieffé. **2.** To take an unconscionable time doing sth., mettre un temps déraisonnable à faire qch.

unconscious [ʌn'kɔnʃəs], *a.* **1.** Inconscient. To be unconscious of sth., (i) ne pas avoir conscience de qch.; (ii) ignorer qch. He remained blissfully *u. of it all, F:* il n'y a vu que du bleu. **2.** Sans connaissance; évanoui. To become unconscious, perdre connaissance. **-ly,** *adv.* Inconsciemment.

unconsciousness [ʌn'kɔnʃəsnəs], *s.* **1.** Inconscience *f,* non-conscience *f* (*of,* de). **2.** Évanouissement *m.*

unconsidered [ʌnkən'sidərd], *a.* **1.** (*Of remark*) Inconsidéré, irréfléchi. **2.** (Petit objet) auquel on n'attache aucune valeur.

unconstitutional [ʌnkɔnsti'tjuːʃən(ə)l], *a.* Inconstitutionnel.

unconstrained [ʌnkən'streind], *a.* Non contraint; libre; (acte) spontané. *U. manner,* allure aisée, désinvolte.

unconstrainedly [ʌnkən'streinidli], *adv.* Sans contrainte, sans aucune gêne; librement.

uncontested [ʌnkən'testid], *a.* (Droit) incontesté. *Pol:* Uncontested seat, siège (à la Chambre) qui n'est pas disputé.

uncontradicted [ʌnkɔntrə'diktid], *a.* Non contredit; incontroversé.

uncontrollable [ʌnkən'trouləbl], *a.* **1.** (Pouvoir) absolu. **2.** (Enfant) ingouvernable; (désir) irrésistible. *U. laughter,* fou rire. Fits of u. *temper,* emportements *m* de colère. **-ably,** *adv.* Irrésistiblement.

uncontrolled [ʌnkən'trould], *a.* **1.** Indépendant; (monarque) irresponsable. **2.** *U. liberty,* liberté absolue. *U. passions,* passions effrénées.

unconventional [ʌnkən'venʃən(ə)l], *a.* Qui va à l'encontre des conventions; original, -aux. **-ally,** *adv.* A l'encontre des conventions.

unconversant [ʌnkən'vərsənt], *a.* Unconversant with sth., peu versé dans (une science, etc.); peu familier avec (un sujet).

unconvinced [ʌnkən'vinst], *a.* Sceptique (*of,* à l'égard de).

unconvincing [ʌnkən'vinsiŋ], *a.* (Récit) peu probant, peu convaincant.

uncooked [ʌn'kukt], *a.* (Aliment) non cuit, inapprêté, cru.

uncork [ʌn'kɔːrk], *v.tr.* Déboucher (une bouteille).

uncorrected [ʌnkə'rektid], *a.* **1.** (*Of proof*) Non

corrigé. **2.** (*Of error*) Non rectifié. *Ph:* Result uncorrected for temperature and pressure, résultat brut.

uncouple [ʌn'kʌpl], *v.tr.* **1.** Découpler (les chiens). **2.** Débrayer (une machine); désaccoupler (des piles). *Rail:* Dételer, découpler (des wagons).

uncouth [ʌn'ku:θ], *a.* **1.** Grossier, rude. **2.** Malappris, gauche. **-ly,** *adv.* **1.** Grossièrement. **2.** (Se conduire) gauchement.

uncouthness [ʌn'ku:θnəs], *s.* **1.** Rudesse *f* (de mœurs). **2.** Gaucherie *f*, lourdeur *f*.

uncover [ʌn'kʌvər], *v.tr.* (*a*) Découvrir (son visage); mettre à découvert. *To u. one's head, abs.* to uncover, se découvrir; ôter son chapeau. (*b*) *Chess:* To uncover a piece, dégarnir une pièce.

uncovered [ʌn'kʌvərd], *a.* **1.** Mis à découvert; découvert. To remain uncovered, garder son chapeau à la main. **2.** *Com:* (Achat) à découvert. Uncovered balance, découvert *m.*

uncritical [ʌn'kritik(ə)l], *a.* Dépourvu de sens critique; sans discernement. *U. audience,* auditoire peu exigeant.

uncrossed [ʌn'krɔst], *a.* **1.** Uncrossed cheque, chèque non barré; chèque ouvert. **2.** Que personne n'a franchi.

uncrowned [ʌn'kraund], *a.* **1.** Découronné. **2.** Non couronné.

unction ['ʌŋkʃ(ə)n], *s.* (*a*) Onction *f.* (*b*) *F:* To speak with unction, parler avec onction. (*c*) *To relate a scandal with u.,* raconter un scandale avec saveur.

unctuous ['ʌŋktjuəs], *a.* **1.** Onctueux, graisseux. **2.** (Prédicateur) onctueux. **-ly,** *adv.* Onctueusement.

unctuousness ['ʌŋktjuəsnəs], *s.* Onctuosité *f.*

uncultivated [ʌn'kʌltiveitid], *a.* (Terrain) inculte; (personne) sans culture.

uncultured [ʌn'kʌltjərd], *a.* (Esprit) incultivé, inculte; (personne) sans culture.

uncurbed [ʌn'kə:rbd], *a.* (*a*) Libre; (autorité) sans restriction. (*b*) (*Of passion*) Débridé; sans frein.

uncut [ʌn'kʌt], *a.* **1.** Uncut crops, récoltes sur pied. **2.** (*Of hedge*) Non taillé. Uncut diamond, diamant brut. Uncut book, (i) livre non coupé; (ii) *Bookb:* livre non rogné.

undamaged [ʌn'dæmedʒd], *a.* Non endommagé; indemne. *U. reputation,* réputation intacte.

undamped [ʌn'dæmpt], *a.* **1.** *Ph:* Non amorti. *W.Tel:* Undamped waves, ondes entretenues. **2.** (Courage) persistant, soutenu.

undated [ʌn'deitid], *a.* Non daté; sans date.

undaunted [ʌn'dɔ:ntid], *a.* (*a*) Intrépide. (*b*) Aucunement intimidé. **-ly,** *adv.* Intrépidement.

undecaying [ʌndi'keiiŋ], *a.* Impérissable.

undeceive [ʌndi'si:v], *v.tr.* Désabuser (*of,* de); détromper (qn). To undeceive oneself, se désabuser.

undeceived [ʌndi'si:vd], *a.* **1.** Désabusé; détrompé. **2.** Aucunement trompé (*by,* par).

undecided [ʌndi'saidid], *a.* Indécis. (*a*) (*Of colour*) Mal défini. (*b*) (*Of pers.*) Irrésolu, hésitant.

undecipherable [ʌndi'saifərəbl], *a.* Indéchiffrable.

undeciphered [ʌndi'saifərd], *a.* Indéchiffré.

undefeated [ʌndi'fi:tid], *a.* Invaincu.

undefended [ʌndi'fendid], *a.* **1.** Sans défense. **2.** Undefended suit, cause où le défendeur s'abstient de plaider.

undefiled [ʌndi'faild], *a.* Pur; sans souillure.

undefinable [ʌndi'fainəbl], *a.* Indéfinissable.

undefined [ʌndi'faind], *a.* **1.** Non défini. **2.** Indéterminé; vague.

undelivered [ʌndi'livərd], *a.* Non délivré. Undelivered letter, lettre de rebut. *If u. please return to sender,* en cas de non-délivrance prière de retourner à l'expéditeur.

undemonstrative [ʌndi'mɔnstrətiv], *a.* Peu expansif, peu démonstratif; réservé.

undeniable [ʌndi'naiəbl], *a.* Indéniable, incontestable. **-ably,** *adv.* Incontestablement.

undenominational [ʌndinɔmi'neiʃən(ə)l], *a.* Non confessionnel; (école) laïque.

under ['ʌndər], I. *prep.* **1.** Sous; au-dessous de. (*a*) Under water, sous l'eau. *S.a.* SWIM² I.1. Put it under that, mettez-le là-dessous. *The village lies u. the mountain,* le village est situé au pied de la montagne. *S.a.* FOOT¹ 1 (*c*), NOSE¹ 1. (*b*) To speak under one's breath, parler à demi-voix. He is under thirty, il a moins de trente ans. **2.** (*a*) Under lock and key, sous clef. Visible under the microscope, visible au microscope. *To be under sentence of death,* être condamné à mort. Under the circumstances, dans les circonstances. Under the terms of the treaty, aux termes du traité. Under his father's will, d'après le testament de son père. To be under the necessity of . . ., être dans la nécessité de. . . . *S.a.* FIRE¹ 4, OBLIGATION, SAIL¹ 1 (*b*), SPELL¹ 2, WAY¹ 9. (*b*) To be under s.o., être sous le commandement de qn. Under government control, assujetti au contrôle de l'État. *F:* To be u. the doctor, être traité par le médecin. (*c*) To be under a violent emotion, être en proie à une violente émotion. **3.** (*a*) Under repair, en (voie de) réparation. Patients under treatment, malades en traitement. (*b*) *Agr:* Field under corn, champ mis en blé. II. *under,* *adv.* **1.** (Au-)dessous. As under, comme ci-dessous. *S.a.* DOWN³ I. 2. **2.** To keep s.o. under, tenir qn dans la soumission. *S.a.* KEEP UNDER. **3.** (*In compounds*) Trop peu; insuffisamment. To underpay, mal rétribuer. III. *under, attrib. a. & comb.fm.* **1.** De dessous; inférieur; Under-strata, couches inférieures. Underlip, lèvre inférieure. Undervest, gilet *m* de dessous. **2.** Subalterne. Under-gardener, aide-jardinier *m.* Under-servant, sous-domestique *mf.* **3.** Insuffisant. **'under-body, -carriage,** *s.* **1.** *Av:* Châssis *m*, train *m* (d'atterrissage). **2.** *Aut:* Dessous *m* (de la voiture). **under-de'veloped,** *a.* **1.** *Phot:* (Cliché) insuffisamment développé. **2.** (Enfant) arrêté dans sa croissance. **under-'estimate,** *v.tr.* (*a*) Sous-estimer. *Artil:* To under-estimate the range, apprécier court. (*b*) *To u.-e. the importance of . . .,* faire trop peu de cas de. . . . **under-ex'posure,** *s.* *Phot:* Sous-exposition *f*; manque *m* de pose. **'under-garment,** *s.* Sous-vêtement *m.* **under-in'flation,** *s.* Gonflage insuffisant (d'un pneu). **'under-jaw,** *s.* Mâchoire inférieure. **'under-keeper,** *s.* Garde-chasse *m* auxiliaire, *pl.* gardes-chasse(s). **under-'nourished,** *a.* Insuffisamment nourri; mal nourri. **under-'ripe,** *a.* Pas assez mûr. **'under-secretary,** *s.* Sous-secrétaire *m.* Permanent under-secretary, directeur général (d'un Ministère). **under-'sized,** *a.* D'une taille au-dessous de la moyenne. **'under-skirt,** *s.* Jupon *m*; sous-jupe *f.* **under-sub'scribed,** *a.* *Fin:* (Emprunt) non couvert. **under-'tenancy,** *s.* Sous-location *f.* **'under-tenant,** *s.* Sous-locataire *mf.* **'under-trick,** *s.* *Cards:* Levée manquante.

underbid [ʌndər'bid], *v.tr.* (underbid; underbid(den)) **1.** *Com:* Demander moins cher que

(qn). **2.** *Cards:* To underbid one's hand, appeler au-dessous de ses moyens.
underbred ['ʌndərbred], *a.* Mal appris; mal élevé.
underbrush ['ʌndərbrʌʃ], *s.* = UNDERGROWTH.
undercall [ʌndər'kɔːl], *v.tr. Cards:* = UNDER-BID 2.
undercharge [ʌndər'tʃɑːrdʒ], *v.tr.* Ne pas faire payer assez à (qn).
underclothes ['ʌndərkloːuðz], *s.pl.*, **underclothing** ['ʌndərkloːuðiŋ], *s.* Vêtements *mpl* de dessous; linge *m* de corps; (*for women*) lingerie *f.*
undercrust ['ʌndərkrʌst], *s. Cu:* Croûte *f* de dessous; abaisse *f.*
undercurrent ['ʌndərkʌrənt], *s.* **1.** Courant *m* de fond; (*in sea*) courant sous-marin. **2.** Undercurrent of discontent, courant profond de mécontentement.
undercut[1] ['ʌndərkʌt], *s.* **1.** *Cu:* Filet *m* (de bœuf). **2.** *Box:* Coup *m* de bas en haut; undercut *m.*
undercut[2] [ʌndər'kʌt], *v.tr.* (undercut; undercut; undercutting) **1.** *Sculp:* Fouiller (une sculpture); creuser. **2.** *Golf:* Couper (la balle). **3.** (*a*) Faire des soumissions plus avantageuses que (qn). (*b*) Vendre moins cher que (qn).
underdog ['ʌndərdɔg], *s.* To plead for the underdog(s), plaider la cause des opprimés.
underdone [ʌndər'dʌn], *a.* **1.** Pas assez cuit. **2.** Pas trop cuit; (bœuf) saignant.
underfeed [ʌndər'fiːd], *v.tr. (p.t. & p.p.* underfed [-fed]) Nourrir insuffisamment; mal nourrir.
underfed, *a.* Mal nourri; sous-alimenté.
underfeeding, *s.* Sous-alimentation *f.*
underfoot [ʌndər'fut], *adv.* See FOOT[1] 1 (*c*).
undergo [ʌndər'goːu], *v.tr.* (underwent [-went]; undergone [-gɔn]) **1.** (*a*) Passer par, subir (un changement). Undergoing repairs, en réparation. (*b*) Subir (une épreuve). To undergo an operation, se soumettre à une intervention chirurgicale; *F:* être opéré. **2.** Supporter, (des souffrances); essuyer, éprouver (une perte).
undergraduate [ʌndər'gradjuet], *s.* Étudiant, -ante (qui n'a pas encore pris de grade).
underground [ʌndər'graund]. **1.** *adv.* (*a*) Sous terre. To work underground, travailler sous (la) terre. To rise from underground, surgir de dessous terre. (*b*) Secrètement; sous main. **2.** *a.* ['ʌndərgraund] Qui est sous le sol. Underground dwelling, habitation sous terre. Underground railway, chemin de fer souterrain. Underground gallery, souterrain *m.* Underground worker, travailleur du sous-sol; *Min:* ouvrier du fond. **3.** *s. F:* The Underground = le Métro.
undergrown ['ʌndərgroun], *a.* **1.** (*Of child*) Mal venu; chétif; rabougri. **2.** (*Of forest-land*) U. with scrub, plein de broussailles.
undergrowth ['ʌndərgrouθ], *s. For:* Broussailles *fpl*; sous-bois *m.*
underhand [ʌndər'hand]. **1.** *adv.* (*a*) *Cr: Ten:* (Bôler, servir) par en dessous. (*b*) (Agir) sous main, sournoisement. **2.** *a.* ['ʌndərhand] (*a*) *Ten: etc:* Underhand service, service par en dessous. (*b*) Secret, -ète; (*of pers.*) sournois. Underhand dealings, agissements clandestins. Underhand trick, sournoiserie *f.*
underhung [ʌndər'hʌŋ], *a.* Underhung jaw, menton *m* prognathe; *F:* menton en galoche.
underlay ['ʌndərlei], *s.* **1.** *Typ:* Hausse *f.* **2.** *Furn:* Assise *f* de feutre (pour tapis).
underlease ['ʌndərliːs], *s.* Sous-bail *m*, sous-location *f.*

underlessee [ʌndərle'siː], *s.* Sous-locataire *mf.*
underlet [ʌndər'let], *v.tr. (p.t. & p.p.* underlet; *pr.p.* underletting) Sous-louer (un appartement).
underlie [ʌndər'lai], *v.tr.* (underlay [-lei]; underlain [-lein]; underlying) **1.** Être sous (qch.); être au-dessous de (qch.). **2.** Être à la base de (qch.). **underlying,** *a.* **1.** Au-dessous; (*of rock*) sous-jacent. **2.** (Principe) fondamental, -aux. Underlying causes of an event, raisons profondes d'un événement.
underline [ʌndər'lain], *v.tr.* Souligner.
underlinen ['ʌndərlinen], *s.* Linge *m* de corps, de dessous.
underling ['ʌndərliŋ], *s. Usu. Pej:* Subalterne *m*; subordonné, -ée.
undermanned [ʌndər'mand], *a.* A court de personnel. *Nau:* A court d'équipage.
undermentioned [ʌndər'menʃ(ə)nd], *a.* Mentionné ci-dessous; sous-mentionné.
undermine [ʌndər'main], *v.tr.* Miner, saper (une muraille); (*of river*) affouiller (les berges). To undermine one's health, s'abîmer lentement la santé.
undermost ['ʌndərmoust], *a.* Le plus bas, *f.* la plus basse; inférieur.
underneath [ʌndər'niːθ]. **1.** *prep.* Au-dessous de; sous. From underneath sth., de dessous qch. **2.** *adv.* Au-dessous; dessous; par-dessous. **3.** *a.* De dessous; inférieur.
underpaid [ʌndər'peid], *a.* Mal rétribué.
underpin [ʌndər'pin], *v.tr.* (underpinned) **1.** Étayer; étançonner (un mur). **2.** Reprendre en sous-œuvre (des fondations); rechausser. **underpinning,** *s.* **1.** (*a*) Étayage *m*, étançonnement *m.* (*b*) Reprise *f* en sous-œuvre. **2.** (*a*) Étais *mpl.* (*b*) Maçonnerie *f* en sous-œuvre.
underrate [ʌndər'reit], *v.tr.* Mésestimer, sous-estimer (l'importance de qch.).
undersell [ʌndər'sel], *v.tr. (p.t. & p.p.* undersold [-sould]) Vendre à meilleur marché, moins cher, que (qn).
undershot ['ʌndərʃɔt], *a.* **1.** *Hyd.E:* Undershot wheel, roue en dessous, à aubes. **2.** = UNDER-HUNG.
undersigned [ʌndər'saind], *a. & s.* Soussigné, -ée. I, the undersigned . . ., je, soussigné. . . .
underslung ['ʌndərslʌŋ], *a.* (Ressort) sous l'essieu, surbaissé. Underslung car, voiture à châssis surbaissé.
undersold [ʌndər'sould]. See UNDERSELL.
understand [ʌndər'stand], *v.tr. (p.t. & p.p.* understood [-stud]) **1.** Comprendre. (*a*) I don't understand French, je ne comprends pas le français. To understand one's business, bien connaître son affaire. To understand business, s'entendre aux affaires. To understand horses, se connaître en chevaux. To understand driving a car, s'entendre à, savoir, conduire une auto. To understand sth., se rendre compte de qch. *Abs.* Now I understand! je comprends, j'y suis, maintenant! I am at a loss to understand it, je n'y comprends rien. I can't u. why . . ., je ne m'explique pas pourquoi. . . . That's easily understood, cela se comprend facilement. (*b*) To give s.o. to understand sth., donner à entendre qch. à qn. Am I to understand that . . .? ai-je bien compris que . . .? I u. that he will consent, je crois savoir qu'il consentira. Now understand me, I am resolved to . . ., sachez-le bien, je suis résolu à . . . . **2.** *Gram:* Sous-entendre (un mot). **3.** *v.i.* To understand about an affair, savoir ce qu'il faut faire à propos d'une affaire.
understood, *a.* **1.** Compris. **2.** Convenu. It

is an understood thing that . . ., il est bien entendu que. . . . That is understood, cela va sans dire. **3.** *Gram:* Sous-entendu. **understanding,** *s.* **1.** Entendement *m*, appréhension *f*, compréhension *f*. **To have reached the age of understanding,** être arrivé à l'âge de discernement *m*. **A person of good understanding,** quelqu'un d'intelligent. *His u. of the problems of life,* son intelligence *f* des problèmes de la vie. **2.** (*a*) Accord *m*, entente *f*. **Friendly understanding,** entente cordiale. (*b*) Arrangement *m*. **To have an understanding with s.o.,** avoir un arrangement, être d'intelligence, avec qn. **To come to an understanding with s.o.,** s'accorder, s'entendre, avec qn. (*c*) **On the understanding that . . .,** à condition que. . . .

understandable [ʌndər'standəbl], *a.* Compréhensible. *That is u.,* cela se comprend.

understate [ʌndər'steit], *v.tr.* Amoindrir (les faits).

understatement [ʌndər'steitmənt], *s.* **1.** Amoindrissement *m* (des faits). **2.** Affirmation *f* qui reste au-dessous de la vérité.

understrapper ['ʌndərstrapər], *s.* *F:* = UNDERLING.

understudy[1] ['ʌndərstʌdi], *s.* *Th:* Doublure *f.*

understudy[2] [ʌndər'stʌdi], *v.tr.* Doubler (un rôle).

undertake [ʌndər'teik], *v.tr.* (undertook [-tuk]; undertaken [-teik(ə)n]) **1.** Entreprendre (un voyage). **2.** (*a*) Se charger de, s'imposer (une tâche). (*b*) **To undertake to do sth.,** se charger de faire qch.; se faire fort de faire qch. **undertaking,** *s.* **1.** (*a*) Entreprise *f* (de qch.). (*b*) Entreprise de pompes funèbres. **2.** Entreprise (commerciale). *F:* **It is quite an undertaking,** c'est toute une affaire. **3.** Engagement *m*, promesse *f.*

undertaker ['ʌndərteikər], *s.* Entrepreneur *m* de pompes funèbres.

undertone ['ʌndərtoun], *s.* **To speak in an undertone,** parler bas; parler à demi-voix.

undertook [ʌndər'tuk]. *See* UNDERTAKE.

undertow ['ʌndərtou], *s.* **1.** Contre-marée *f*; courant *m* de fond. **2.** Ressac *m.*

undervalue [ʌndər'valju], *v.tr.* **1.** Sous-estimer, sous-évaluer. **2.** Mésestimer, faire trop peu de cas de (qn).

underwear ['ʌndərwɛər], *s.* = UNDERCLOTHES.

underwent [ʌndər'went]. *See* UNDERGO.

underwood ['ʌndərwud], *s.* Sous-bois *m*, broussailles *fpl*, taillis *m.*

underworld ['ʌndərwə:rld], *s.* **1.** (Les) enfers *m.* **2.** (Le) monde des apaches; (les) bas-fonds *m* de la société.

underwrite [ʌndər'rait], *v.tr.* (underwrote [-rout]; underwriting [-rit(ə)n]) (*a*) *Fin:* Garantir, souscrire (une émission). (*b*) *Ins:* **To underwrite a risk,** souscrire un risque. **underwriting,** *s.* **1.** *Fin:* Garantie *f* d'émission; souscription éventuelle à forfait. **2.** (*a*) Souscription *f* (d'une police d'assurance). (*b*) Assurance *f* maritime.

underwriter ['ʌndərraitər], *s.* **1.** *Fin:* Membre *m* d'un syndicat de garantie. **The underwriters,** le syndicat de garantie. **2.** *Ins:* Assureur *m*; *esp.* assureur maritime.

undescribable [ʌndis'kraibəbl], *a.* Indescriptible.

undeserved [ʌndi'zə:rvd], *a.* Immérité.

undeservedly [ʌndi'zə:rvidli], *adv.* A tort; injustement.

undeserving [ʌndi'zə:rviŋ], *a.* (*a*) Peu méritant; sans mérite. (*b*) **Undeserving of attention,** indigne d'attention. *U. case,* cas peu intéressant.

undesigned [ʌndi'zaind], *a.* (*Of action*) Involontaire, imprémédité.

undesirable [ʌndi'zaiərəbl], *a. & s.* Indésirable (*mf*); peu désirable.

undetected [ʌndi'tektid], *a.* **1.** Qui a échappé à l'attention. (*Of mistake*) **To pass undetected,** passer inaperçu. **2.** (*Malfaiteur*) insoupçonné.

undetermined [ʌndi'tə:rmind], *a.* **1.** (*Of quantity*) Indéterminé, incertain. **2.** (*Of question*) Indécis.

undeterred [ʌndi'tə:rd], *a.* Non découragé, aucunement ébranlé (*by*, par).

undeveloped [ʌndi'veləpt], *a.* **1.** Non développé. Undeveloped land, terrains inexploités. *Industry still u.,* industrie encore dans son enfance. **2.** *Phot:* **Undeveloped image,** image latente.

undeviating [ʌn'di:vieitiŋ], *a.* **1.** (Cours, chemin) droit, direct. **2.** Constant; (honnêteté) rigide. **-ly,** *adv.* **1.** Sans dévier; directement. **2.** Constamment, rigidement.

undevout [ʌndi'vaut], *a.* Indévot, -ote.

undid [ʌn'did]. *See* UNDO.

undies ['ʌndiz], *s.pl.* *F:* Lingerie *f* (de femme).

undigested [ʌndi'dʒestid, -dai-], *a.* (Mets, ouvrage) mal digéré. **Undigested knowledge,** connaissances indigestes, confuses.

undignified [ʌn'dignifaid], *a.* (*a*) Peu digne. (*b*) **To be undignified,** manquer de dignité, de tenue.

undiluted [ʌndai'ljutid, -di-], *a.* Non dilué; non étendu (d'eau); (vin) pur; (acide) concentré.

undine ['ʌndi:n], *s.f.* *Myth:* Ondine.

undiplomatic [ʌndiplo'matik], *a.* Peu diplomatique; *F:* peu politique, peu adroit.

undiscernible [ʌndi'zə:rnibl, -'sə:rn-], *a.* Imperceptible; invisible.

undiscerning [ʌndi'zə:rniŋ, - sə:rn-], *a.* (Esprit) sans discernement, peu pénétrant.

undischarged [ʌndis'tʃɑ:rdʒd], *a.* **1.** *Jur:* **Undischarged bankrupt,** failli non réhabilité. **2.** **Undischarged debt,** dette inacquittée. **3.** (Devoir) inaccompli.

undisciplined [ʌn'disiplind], *a.* Indiscipliné.

undiscovered [ʌndis'kʌvərd, 'ʌn-], *a.* Non découvert; caché. *Land at that time u.,* terre inconnue à cette époque.

undiscriminating [ʌndis'krimineitiŋ], *a.* (*Of pers.*) Sans discernement; (*of taste*) peu averti. *U. praise,* éloges prodigués sans discernement.

undisguised [ʌndis'gaizd], *a.* (*Of voice*) Non déguisé; (*of feelings*) non dissimulé. **To show undisguised satisfaction,** témoigner franchement sa satisfaction.

undisheartened [ʌndis'hɑ:rt(ə)nd], *a.* Sans se laisser abattre; aucunement découragé.

undismayed [ʌndis'meid, 'ʌn-], *a.* Sans peur, sans terreur; aucunement ébranlé.

undisputed [ʌndis'pju:tid, 'ʌn-], *a.* Incontesté, indisputé, incontroversé.

undistinguishable [ʌndis'tiŋgwiʃəbl], *a.* **1.** Indistinguible (*from*, de). **2.** Imperceptible; que l'on peut à peine distinguer.

undistinguished [ʌndis'tiŋgwiʃt], *a.* Médiocre; banal, -aux. **To live undistinguished,** vivre dans l'obscurité.

undisturbed [ʌndis'tə:rbd], *a.* **1.** (*Of pers.*) Tranquille; (*of sleep, etc.*) paisible. **2.** (*Of peace*) Que rien ne vient troubler; (*of the ground*) qui n'a pas été remué. *We found everything u.,* rien n'avait été dérangé.

undivided [ʌndi'vaidid], *a.* **1.** Indivisé; entier. **2.** Non partagé. **Undivided profits,** bénéfices non répartis. **Give me your undivided attention,** donnez-moi toute votre attention. **3.** **Undivided opinion,** opinion unanime.

undo [ʌn'duː], *v.tr.* (undid [-'did]; undone [-'dʌn]) **1.** Détruire (une œuvre). **To undo the mischief,** réparer le mal. **2.** Défaire, dénouer (un nœud, ses cheveux). **To undo one's dress,** dégrafer, défaire, sa robe. **3.** Perdre, ruiner (qn). **undoing,** *s.* **1.** Action *f* de défaire. **2.** Ruine *f,* perte *f.*

undone [ʌn'dʌn]. **I.** *See* UNDO. **II. undone,** *a.* **1.** (*a*) Défait. **To come undone,** (of button) se défaire. *My shoe has come u.,* le lacet de mon soulier est défait. (*b*) Ruiné; perdu. **2.** Inaccompli; non accompli. *To leave some work u.,* laisser du travail inachevé. **To leave nothing undone which might help,** ne rien négliger qui puisse être utile.

undoubted [ʌn'dautid], *a.* (Fait) indiscutable, incontestable. **-ly,** *adv.* Indubitablement, assurément. **Undoubtedly he is wrong,** sans aucun doute il a tort.

undraped [ʌn'dreipt], *a.* Sans draperies; (of human figure) nu.

undreamt [ʌn'dremt], *a.* **Undreamt of,** (i) dont on ne s'avisera jamais; (ii) qui passe l'imagination.

undress[1] [ʌn'dres], *s.* **1.** (*For women*) Déshabillé *m,* négligé *m.* **2.** *Mil: Navy:* Undress (uniform), petite tenue.

undress[2], *v.* (undressed [ʌn'drest]) **1.** *v.i. & pr.* Se déshabiller, se dévêtir. **2.** *v.tr.* Déshabiller, dévêtir.

undressed [ʌn'drest], *a.* **1.** (*a*) Déshabillé, dévêtu. (*b*) En déshabillé; en négligé. **2.** (*a*) Non préparé; brut. '**Undressed leather,** cuir inapprêté. (*b*) *Agr:* (Terre) qui n'a reçu aucune façon.

undrinkable [ʌn'driŋkəbl], *a.* Imbuvable, impotable.

undue [ʌn'djuː], *a.* (*a*) **Undue influence,** influence *f* illégitime; intimidation *f;* (*upon testator*) manœuvres *f* captatoires. (*b*) (*Of haste*) Exagéré, indu. **Undue optimism,** optimisme excessif, peu justifié.

undulate ['ʌndjuleit]. **1.** *v.tr.* Onduler. **2.** *v.i.* Onduler, ondoyer. **undulating,** *a.* Onduleux; (blé) ondoyant. *U. country,* pays ondulé, vallonné.

undulation [ʌndju'leiʃ(ə)n], *s.* Ondulation *f;* accident *m* de terrain.

undulatory ['ʌndjulətəri], *a.* **1.** Ondulatoire. **2.** Ondulé, onduleux.

unduly [ʌn'djuːli], *adv.* **1.** (*a*) (Réclamer) indûment. (*b*) Sans raison. **2.** A l'excès, outre mesure. **Unduly high price,** prix exagéré.

undutiful [ʌn'djuːtiful], *a.* Qui ne remplit pas ses devoirs (filiaux, conjugaux). **-fully,** *adv.* D'une façon indigne (d'un fils, d'un mari).

undying [ʌn'daiiŋ], *a.* Immortel, impérissable.

unearned [ʌn'əːrnd], *a.* **1.** (*Of reward*) Immérité. **2.** Non gagné par le travail.

unearth [ʌn'əːrθ], *v.tr.* (*a*) Déterrer, exhumer. (*b*) **To unearth an old manuscript,** déterrer, dénicher, un vieux manuscrit.

unearthly [ʌn'əːrθli], *a.* (*a*) Qui n'est pas de ce monde; surnaturel. (*b*) **Unearthly pallor,** pâleur mortelle. *U. light,* lueur sinistre, blafarde. (*c*) *F:* **At an unearthly hour,** à une heure indue. **Unearthly din,** vacarme de tous les diables.

uneasiness [ʌn'iːzinəs], *s.* **1.** Gêne *f,* malaise *m.* **2.** Inquiétude *f.*

uneasy [ʌn'iːzi], *a.* (*a*) Mal à l'aise; gêné. **Uneasy feeling,** sentiment de malaise. (*b*) Inquiet, -ète; anxieux. **Uneasy conscience,** conscience agitée. **To be uneasy in one's mind about . . .,** avoir l'esprit inquiet au sujet de. . . . *To pass an u. night,* passer une nuit tourmentée. **Uneasy sleep,**

---

sommeil agité. (*c*) (*Of situation*) Incommode, gênant. **-ily,** *adv.* (*a*) D'un air gêné. (*b*) Avec inquiétude.

uneatable [ʌn'iːtəbl], *a.* Immangeable.

uneducated [ʌn'edjukeitid], *a.* **1.** (*Of pers.*) Sans instruction; ignorant. **2.** (*Of pronunciation*) Vulgaire.

unembarrassed [ʌnem'barəst], *a.* **1.** Peu embarrassé, peu gêné; désinvolte. **2.** = UN-ENCUMBERED.

unemotional [ʌni'mouʃən(ə)l], *a.* Peu émotif. **-ally,** *adv.* Avec impassibilité.

unemployed [ʌnem'ploid], *a.* **1.** (*Of pers.*) (*a*) Désœuvré. (*b*) *Ind:* Sans travail; sans emploi. **The unemployed,** les chômeurs *m,* les sans-travail *m.* **2.** (*Of capital*) Inemployé.

unemployment [ʌnem'ploimənt], *s. Ind:* Chômage *m* (involontaire); manque *m* de travail. **Unemployment fund,** caisse *f* contre le chômage. **Unemployment benefit,** secours *m* de chômage.

unencumbered [ʌnen'kʌmbərd], *a.* **1.** Non encombré (by, with, de). **2.** Non embarrassé (by, with, par). **Unencumbered estate,** propriété franche d'hypothèques.

unended [ʌn'endid], *a.* Inachevé.

unending [ʌn'endiŋ], *a.* **1.** Interminable. **Unending complaints,** plaintes sans fin. **2.** Éternel.

unendurable [ʌnen'djuərəbl, 'ʌn-], *a.* Insupportable, intolérable.

un-English [ʌn'ingliʃ], *a.* Peu anglais; contraire à l'esprit anglais.

unenterprising [ʌn'entərpraiziŋ], *a.* Peu entreprenant; (homme) mou.

unenviable [ʌn'enviəbl], *a.* Peu enviable.

unequal [ʌn'iːkwəl], *a.* **1.** (*a*) Inégal, -aux. (*b*) **To be unequal to the task,** être au-dessous de la tâche. **To be unequal to doing sth.,** ne pas être de force à faire qch. **2.** Inégal, irrégulier. **-ally,** *adv.* Inégalement.

unequalled [ʌn'iːkwəld], *a.* Inégalé; sans égal.

unequivocal [ʌni'kwivək(ə)l], *a.* (*Of language*) Clair, net; sans équivoque. **-ally,** *adv.* Sans équivoque.

unerring [ʌn'əːriŋ], *a.* (Jugement) infaillible, sûr. *To fire with u. aim,* ne jamais manquer le but. **-ly,** *adv.* Infailliblement, sûrement.

unessential [ʌne'senʃ(ə)l], *a.* Non essentiel; peu important. *s.* **The unessential(s),** l'accessoire *m.*

uneven [ʌn'iːv(ə)n], *a.* **1.** Inégal, -aux. (*a*) Rugueux; (chemin) raboteux. (*b*) (Terrain) accidenté; (contour) anfractueux. (*c*) Irrégulier. **Uneven temper,** humeur inégale. **2.** (Nombre) impair. **-ly,** *adv.* **1.** Inégalement. **2.** Irrégulièrement.

unevenness [ʌn'iːvənnəs], *s.* **1.** Inégalité *f.* (*a*) Caractère raboteux (d'une route). (*b*) Irrégularité *f* (du pouls). **2.** *To take advantage of an u. in the ground,* profiter d'un accident de terrain.

uneventful [ʌni'ventful], *a.* Sans incidents. **Uneventful life,** vie calme, unie.

unexampled [ʌneg'zɑːmpld], *a.* Sans exemple, sans égal, sans pareil; unique.

unexcelled [ʌnek'seld], *a.* Qui n'a jamais été surpassé.

unexceptionable [ʌnek'sepʃ(ə)nəbl], *a.* Irréprochable; (conduite) inattaquable; (témoignage) irrécusable. *U. person,* personne tout à fait convenable.

unexciting [ʌnek'saitiŋ], *a.* Insipide; peu passionnant. *U. life,* vie monotone.

unexpected [ʌneks'pektid], *a.* (*a*) (Visiteur) inattendu; (résultat) imprévu; (secours, etc.) inespéré. **Unexpected meeting,** rencontre inopinée. **-ly,** *adv.* De manière inattendue.

unexpired [ʌneks'paiərd], *a.* (Bail) non expiré ; (passeport, billet) non périmé, encore valable.

unexplained [ʌneks'pleind], *a.* Inexpliqué ; (mystère) inéclairci.

unexploded [ʌneks'ploudid], *a.* (Obus) non éclaté.

unexplored [ʌneks'plɔ:rd], *a.* (Pays) inexploré, encore inconnu.

unexposed [ʌneks'po:uzd], *a.* **1.** *Phot :* (Plaque) vierge. **2.** *U. crime*, crime caché.

unexpurgated [ʌn'ekspərgeitid], *a.* (Livre) non expurgé. **Unexpurgated edition**, édition intégrale.

unfading [ʌn'feidiŋ], *a.* Qui ne se fane pas. **Unfading glory**, gloire impérissable.

unfailing [ʌn'feiliŋ], *a.* **1.** Qui ne se dément pas ; (moyen) infaillible, sûr. *U. good humour*, bonne humeur inaltérable. **2.** (Source) intarissable, inépuisable (*of*, de). **-ly**, *adv.* **1.** Infailliblement. **2.** Intarissablement.

unfair [ʌn'fɛər], *a.* **1.** (*Of pers.*) Injuste ; peu équitable. **It's unfair!** ce n'est pas juste ! **2.** (*a*) Inéquitable. *U. price*, prix déraisonnable. (*b*) **Unfair play**, jeu déloyal. **-ly**, *adv.* **1.** Injustement ; inéquitablement. **2.** *To act u.*, commettre une déloyauté.

unfairness [ʌn'fɛərnəs], *s.* **1.** Injustice *f* ; partialité *f*. **2.** Déloyauté *f* ; mauvaise foi.

unfaithful [ʌn'feiθful], *a.* Infidèle. (*a*) Déloyal, -aux (*to*, envers). *U. to one's master*, infidèle à son maître. **To be unfaithful to one's wife**, tromper sa femme. (*b*) (Compte rendu) inexact.

unfaithfulness [ʌn'feiθfulnəs], *s.* Infidélité *f*. **1.** Déloyauté *f* (*to*, envers). **2.** Inexactitude *f*.

unfaltering [ʌn'fɔltəriŋ], *a.* **Unfaltering voice**, voix ferme, résolue. **Unfaltering steps**, pas assurés.

unfamiliar [ʌnfa'miljər], *a.* **1.** Peu familier. *U. face*, visage étranger, inconnu. **2.** (*Of pers.*) **To be unfamiliar with sth.**, être peu familier avec qch. *To be u. with the customs*, ne pas être au fait des usages.

unfamiliarity [ʌnfamili'ariti], *s.* **1.** Caractère étranger (d'un lieu). **2.** Ignorance *f* (*with*, de).

unfashionable [ʌn'faʃənəbl], *a.* (Vêtement) démodé, qui n'est pas de mode.

unfasten [ʌn'fɑ:sn], *v.tr.* **1.** **To unfasten sth. from sth.**, détacher qch. de qch. **2.** Défaire (un vêtement) ; ouvrir, déverrouiller (la porte).

unfathomable [ʌn'faðəməbl], *a.* (Abîme) insondable ; (mystère) impénétrable.

unfathomed [ʌn'faðəmd], *a.* Insondé. **Unfathomed depths**, profondeurs inexplorées.

unfavourable [ʌn'feivərəbl], *a.* Défavorable, peu favorable ; (vent) impropice ; (*of terms*) désavantageux (*to*, à).

unfeasible [ʌn'fi:zibl], *a.* Irréalisable, impraticable.

unfeeling [ʌn'fi:liŋ], *a.* Insensible, impitoyable. *U. heart*, cœur sec, indifférent. *U. language*, langage froid. **-ly**, *adv.* Sans pitié ; froidement.

unfeigned [ʌn'feind], *a.* Sincère ; non simulé.

unfeignedly [ʌn'feinidli], *adv.* Sincèrement ; vraiment.

unfettered [ʌn'fetərd], *a.* Libre de tous liens ; (cheval) sans entraves.

unfilial [ʌn'filjəl], *a.* Peu filial, -aux.

unfinished [ʌn'finiʃt], *a.* **1.** Inachevé ; (ouvrage) imparfait. **2.** (*a*) *Ind :* Brut ; non façonné. (*b*) Qui manque de fini.

unfit¹ [ʌn'fit], *a.* **1.** (*a*) Impropre, peu propre (*for*, à). **Unfit to drink**, impropre à boire. *Story u. for publication*, histoire qu'on ne peut moralement publier. **Road unfit for motor traffic**, chemin impraticable aux automobiles. (*b*) *U.*

for military service, inapte au service militaire. **Unfit to rule**, indigne de régner. **2.** (*a*) **To be unfit**, être en mauvaise santé. (*b*) Faible de constitution. *Mil :* **To be discharged as unfit**, être réformé.

unfit², *v.tr.* (**unfitted**) Rendre (qn) inapte (*for sth.*, à qch.).

unfitness [ʌn'fitnəs], *s.* **1.** Manque *m* d'à-propos (d'une observation). **2.** Unfitness for sth., inaptitude *f* à qch. **3.** Mauvaise santé.

unfitted [ʌn'fitid], *a.* **1.** Impropre (*for sth.*, *to do sth.*, à qch., à faire qch.) ; inapte (à faire qch.). **2.** Non équipé (*with*, de) ; (*of dressing-case*) non garni.

unfitting [ʌn'fitiŋ], *a.* Peu convenable ; peu séant ; mal à propos ; déplacé.

unfix [ʌn'fiks], *v.tr.* Détacher, défaire. *Mil :* **To unfix bayonets**, remettre la baïonnette.

unflagging [ʌn'flagiŋ], *a.* (Courage, vigueur) inlassable, infatigable ; (intérêt) soutenu.

unflattering [ʌn'flatəriŋ], *a.* Peu flatteur, -euse.

unfledged [ʌn'fledʒd], *a.* **1.** (Oiseau) sans plumes. **2.** *F :* Sans expérience de la vie ; jeune.

unflinching [ʌn'flinʃiŋ], *a.* **1.** Qui ne recule pas ; qui ne bronche pas. **2.** Stoïque ; impassible. **-ly**, *adv.* **1.** Sans reculer ; sans broncher. **2.** Stoïquement.

unfold [ʌn'fould], **1.** *v.tr.* (*a*) Déplier (un journal). (*b*) Dérouler, déployer. (*c*) Exposer (une doctrine, un projet). **To unfold one's plans to s.o.**, dérouler ses plans à qn. **2.** *v.i. & pr.* Se déployer, se dérouler. **The landscape unfolds (itself) before us**, le paysage se déroule devant nous.

unforbearing [ʌnfər'bɛəriŋ], *a.* Peu endurant ; impatient, intolérant ; sans indulgence.

unforced [ʌn'fɔ:rst], *a.* Naturel, spontané. *U. mirth*, franche gaieté. *U. laugh*, rire franc.

unfordable [ʌn'fɔ:rdəbl], *a.* Inguéable.

unforeseen [ʌnfər'si:n], *a.* Imprévu, inattendu, inopiné.

unforgettable [ʌnfər'getəbl], *a.* Inoubliable.

unforgivable [ʌnfər'givəbl], *a.* Impardonnable.

unforgiving [ʌnfər'giviŋ], *a.* Implacable.

unforgotten [ʌnfər'gɔtn], *a.* Inoublié.

unfortified [ʌn'fɔ:rtifaid], *a.* Sans fortifications. **Unfortified town**, ville ouverte.

unfortunate [ʌn'fɔ:rtjunet], **1.** *a.* (*a*) Malheureux, infortuné. *To be u.*, avoir de la malchance. (*b*) (Événement) malencontreux ; (erreur) regrettable. **It is unfortunate that . . .**, il est fâcheux, malheureux, que + *sub*. **How unfortunate!** quel malheur ! quel dommage ! **2.** *s.* Malheureux, -euse. **-ly**, *adv.* Malheureusement ; par malheur.

unfounded [ʌn'faundid], *a.* (Accusation) sans fondement, sans base. *U. rumour*, bruit dénué de fondement. *U. supposition*, supposition gratuite.

unfrequented [ʌnfri'kwentid], *a.* Peu fréquenté ; (chemin) impratiqué. *U. spot*, endroit écarté, solitaire.

unfriendliness [ʌn'frendlinəs], *s.* Manque *m* d'amitié (*towards*, pour) ; hostilité *f* (*towards*, contre).

unfriendly [ʌn'frendli], *a.* (Ton) peu amical, -aux. **Unfriendly action**, acte hostile. **To be unfriendly towards s.o.**, être mal disposé pour, envers, qn.

unfrock [ʌn'frɔk], *v.tr.* Défroquer (un prêtre).

unfruitful [ʌn'fru:tful], *a.* **1.** Stérile, infécond. **2.** *U. labour*, travail peu fructueux.

unfulfilled [ʌn'fulfild], *a.* (*a*) *U. prophecy*, prophétie inaccomplie. (*b*) (Désir) non satisfait, inassouvi. (*c*) *U. promise*, promesse inexécutée.

unfurl [ʌn'fəːrl], *v.tr. Nau:* Déferler (une voile) ; déployer (un drapeau).

unfurnished [ʌn'fəːrniʃt], *a.* **1.** Non fourni, dépourvu (*with*, de). **2.** (Appartement) non meublé. **Room to let unfurnished**, chambre non meublée à louer.

ungainly [ʌn'geinli], *a.* Gauche, lourd ; dégingandé.

ungallant [ʌn'galənt], *a.* Peu galant ; indigne d'un galant homme.

ungenerous [ʌn'dʒenərəs], *a.* Peu généreux. (*a*) Peu magnanime. (*b*) Illibéral, -aux.

ungentlemanly [ʌn'dʒentlmənli], *a.* Peu comme il faut ; (homme) mal élevé. **Ungentlemanly conduct**, conduite indélicate. *It is u. to . . .*, il n'est pas poli de.

un-get-at-able [ʌnget'atəbl], *a. F :* Inaccessible.

unglazed [ʌn'gleːizd], *a.* **1.** (*Of window*) Non vitré ; sans vitres. **2.** (*a*) (Fil, papier) non glacé, non lustré. *Phot:* **Unglazed paper**, papier mat. (*b*) *Cer:* Non verni. **Unglazed china**, biscuit *m.*

ungodliness [ʌn'gɔdlinəs], *s.* Impiété *f.*

ungodly [ʌn'gɔdli], *a.* Impie.

ungovernable [ʌn'gʌvərnəbl], *a.* (Désir) irrésistible. *U. passion*, passion effrénée, deréglée.

ungraceful [ʌn'greisful], *a.* Disgracieux ; gauche. **-fully,** *adv.* Sans grâce ; gauchement.

ungracious [ʌn'greiʃəs], *a.* Malgracieux ; peu aimable. **It would be ungracious to refuse,** il serait de mauvaise grâce de refuser. **-ly,** *adv.* Malgracieusement.

ungraciousness [ʌn'greiʃəsnəs], *s.* Mauvaise grâce.

ungrammatical [ʌngra matik(ə)l], *a.* Peu grammatical, -aux ; incorrect. **-ally,** *adv.* Incorrectement.

ungrateful [ʌn'greitful], *a.* Ingrat. (*a*) Peu reconnaissant. *U. for favours*, ingrat aux bienfaits. (*b*) *U. soil*, sol ingrat. **-fully,** *adv.* Avec ingratitude.

ungratefulness [ʌn'greitfulnəs], *s.* Ingratitude *f.*

ungratified [ʌn'gratifaid], *a.* (Désir) inassouvi, non satisfait ; (vœu) inexaucé.

ungrounded [ʌn'graundid], *a.* = UNFOUNDED.

ungrudging [ʌn'grʌdʒiŋ], *a.* **1.** Donné de bon cœur. *To give s.o. u. praise*, ne pas ménager ses louanges à qn. **2.** Libéral, -aux ; généreux. **-ly,** *adv.* De bonne grâce ; libéralement.

unguarded [ʌn'goːrdid], *a.* **1.** (*a*) Non gardé ; sans garde ; (ville) sans défense. (*b*) *Cards:* (Roi) sec, non gardé. **2.** (*Of pers.*) Qui n'est pas sur ses gardes ; (*of speech*) indiscret. **In an unguarded moment**, dans un moment d'inattention. **-ly,** *adv.* Inconsidérément.

unguent ['ʌŋgwənt], *s.* Onguent *m.*

unguiferous [ʌŋ'gwifərəs], *a. Nat.Hist:* Unguifère.

ungulate ['ʌŋgjulet], *a. & s. Z:* Ongulé (*m*).

unhallowed [ʌn'haloud], *a.* **1.** Imbéni, profane. **2.** (*Of joy, etc.*) Impie.

unhampered [ʌn'hampərd], *a.* Libre (de ses mouvements). *U. by rules*, sans être gêné, qui n'est pas gêné, par des règles.

unhand [ʌn'hand], *v.tr. A. & Lit:* Lâcher. **Unhand me, sir!** lâchez-moi, monsieur !

unhandy [ʌn'handi], *a.* **1.** (*Of pers.*) Maladroit, gauche. **2.** (Outil) peu maniable, incommode. **-ly,** *adv.* Gauchement, maladroitement.

unhanged [ʌn'haŋd], *a.* Non pendu. **One of the greatest rogues unhanged,** un des plus grands coquins qui aient échappé à la potence.

unhappiness [ʌn'hapinəs], *s.* **1.** Chagrin *m* ; soucis *mpl.* **2.** Inopportunité *f* (d'une expression).

unhappy [ʌn'hapi], *a.* **1.** Malheureux, triste ; infortuné. *To make s.o. u.*, causer du chagrin à qn. *To be u. at leaving s.o.*, s'affliger de quitter qn. **2.** Mal inspiré ; peu heureux. **In an unhappy hour,** dans un moment funeste. **-ily,** *adv.* **1.** (*a*) Malheureusement ; par malchance. (*b*) Tristement. *To live u. together*, faire mauvais ménage. **2.** Thought unhappily expressed, pensée mal exprimée.

unharmed [ʌn'hɑːrmd], *a.* Sain et sauf ; indemne.

unharness [ʌn'hɑːrnəs], *v.tr.* (*a*) Déharnacher (un cheval). (*b*) Dételer (un cheval).

unhealthiness [ʌn'helθinəs], *s.* **1.** Insalubrité *f* (du climat). **2.** (*a*) Mauvaise santé ; état maladif. (*b*) **Unhealthiness of mind**, esprit malsain ; morbidité *f* d'esprit.

unhealthy [ʌn'helθi], *a.* **1.** Malsain, insalubre ; (travail) peu hygiénique. **2.** (*a*) (*Of pers.*) Maladif. *U. complexion*, visage terreux. (*b*) *U. influence*, influence malsaine. *U. curiosity*, curiosité morbide.

unheard [ʌn'həːrd], *a.* **1.** *To condemn s.o. unheard*, condamner qn sans l'entendre. **2. Unheard of,** (i) inouï ; (ii) (auteur) inconnu, ignoré.

unheeded [ʌn'hiːdid], *a.* (*Of warning*) Négligé, dédaigné. **To pass unheeded,** passer inaperçu.

unheeding [ʌn'hiːdiŋ], *a.* **1.** Insouciant, distrait. **2.** Inattentif (*of*, à) ; insouciant (*of*, de).

unhelped [ʌn'helpt], *a.* Sans aide, sans secours. **To do sth. unhelped,** faire qch. tout seul.

unhesitating [ʌn'heziteitiŋ], *a.* Qui n'hésite pas ; ferme, résolu. *U. reply*, réponse faite sans hésitation ; réponse prompte. **-ly,** *adv.* Sans hésiter.

unhindered [ʌn'hindərd], *a.* Sans encombre, sans obstacle, sans empêchement ; librement.

unhinge [ʌn'hindʒ], *v.tr.* **1.** Enlever (une porte) de ses gonds. **2.** Ébranler, détraquer (l'esprit). **His mind is unhinged,** il a le cerveau détraqué.

unholy [ʌn'houli], *a.* **1.** Profane. **Unholy desires,** convoitises *f.* **2.** *F:* **Unholy muddle,** désordre invraisemblable, affreux.

unhonoured [ʌn'ɔnərd], *a.* Sans être honoré ; qui n'est pas honoré ; dédaigné.

unhook [ʌn'huk], *v.tr.* (*a*) Décrocher. (*b*) Dégrafer (un vêtement).

unhoped [ʌn'houpt], *a.* **Unhoped for,** inespéré.

unhorse [ʌn'hɔːrs], *v.tr.* Désarçonner, démonter (un cavalier). **To be unhorsed,** vider les arçons, les étriers.

unhurt [ʌn'həːrt], *a.* **1.** (*Of pers.*) Sans mal ; indemne. **To escape unhurt,** s'en tirer sans aucun mal ; s'en tirer sain et sauf. **2.** (*Of thg.*) Intact.

Uniate ['juːniet], *s. & a.* Uniate (*m*).

unicellular [juːni'seljulər], *a.* Unicellulaire.

unicolor [juːni'kʌlər], **unicoloured** [juːni-'kʌlərd], *a.* Unicolore.

unicorn ['juːnikɔːrn], *s.* (*a*) *Myth:* Licorne *f.* (*b*) *Z:* **Sea-unicorn,** licorne de mer.

unidentified [ʌnai'dentifaid], *a.* Non identifié.

unidirectional [juːnidai'rekʃən(ə)l, -di-], *a. El:* (Courant) continu, redressé.

unification [juːnifi'keiʃ(ə)n], *s.* Unification *f.*

uniform ['juːnifɔːrm]. **1.** *a.* Uniforme. **Uniform temperature,** température constante. **Uniform velocity,** vitesse uniforme. **2.** *s.* (*a*) Uniforme *m.* **Field-service uniform,** tenue *f* de campagne. **In uniform,** en uniforme. (*b*) Costume *m* (d'infirmière). **-ly,** *adv.* Uniformément.

uniformity [juːni'fɔːrmiti], *s.* (*a*) Uniformité *f*, unité *f* (de style). (*b*) Régularité *f* (de fonctionnement).

unify ['juːnifai], *v.tr.* Unifier.

unilateral [juːni'latərəl], *a.* Unilatéral, -aux.

unimaginable [ʌni'madʒinəbl], *a.* Inimaginable.

unimaginative [ʌni'madʒineitiv, -ətiv], *a.* Dénué d'imagination ; peu imaginatif.

unimpaired [ʌnim'pɛərd], *a.* Non affaibli. Unimpaired health, santé non altérée ; santé intacte. *U.* strength, forces non diminuées. With faculties unimpaired, en possession de toutes ses facultés.

unimpassioned [ʌnim'paʃənd], *a.* Sans passion ; tranquille. *U.* speech, discours mesuré.

unimpeachable [ʌnim'piːtʃəbl], *a.* (*a*) Incontestable. I have it from an unimpeachable source, je le tiens de source sûre. (*b*) (Témoignage) inattaquable, irrécusable.

unimpeded [ʌnim'piːdid], *a.* Libre ; aucunement entravé ; sans empêchement.

unimportant [ʌnim'pɔːrtənt, 'ʌn-], *a.* Sans importance ; peu important. It is quite u., cela ne tire pas à conséquence.

unimpressed [ʌnim'prest], *a.* I was u. by his speech, son discours m'a laissé froid.

unimpressive [ʌnim'presiv], *a.* Peu émouvant ; (discours) terne.

uninformed [ʌnin'fɔːrmd], *a.* **1.** To be uninformed on a subject, ne pas connaître un sujet. **2.** (Homme) ignorant ; (esprit) inculte.

uninhabitable [ʌnin'habitəbl], *a.* Inhabitable.

uninhabited [ʌnin'habitid], *a.* Inhabité, désert.

uninitiated [ʌni'niʃieitid], *a.* Non initié (*in*, dans). *s.* The uninitiated, les profanes *m.*

uninjured [ʌn'indʒərd], *a.* **1.** (*Of pers.*) Sain et sauf ; sans mal ; indemne. **2.** (*Of thg*) Intact ; sans dommage.

uninspired [ʌnin'spaiərd], *a.* Sans inspiration ; (style) banal, qui rampe.

unintelligent [ʌnin'telidʒənt], *a.* Inintelligent ; à l'esprit borné.

unintelligible [ʌnin'telidʒibl], *a.* Inintelligible. **-ibly,** *adv.* D'une manière peu intelligible.

unintentional [ʌnin'tenʃən(ə)l], *a.* Involontaire ; fait sans intention. **-ally,** *adv.* Involontairement ; sans le vouloir.

uninterested [ʌn'int(ə)restid], *a.* Non ntéressé ; indifférent.

uninteresting [ʌn'int(ə)restiŋ], *a.* Peu intéressant ; sans intérêt.

uninterrupted [ʌnintə'rʌptid], *a.* **1.** Ininterrompu. **2.** Continu. Uninterrupted correspondence, correspondance suivie. **-ly,** *adv.* Sans interruption.

uninvited [ʌnin'vaitid], *a.* Sans être invité. Uninvited guest, hôte inconvié ; *F:* resquilleur, -euse.

uninviting [ʌnin'vaitiŋ], *a.* (*Of appearance*) Peu attrayant, peu engageant ; (*of food*) peu appétissant.

union ['juːnjən], *s.* **1.** Union *f.* (*a*) Union of a province with France, réunion *f* d'une province à la France. (*b*) (*Marriage*) Well-assorted u., union bien assortie. (*c*) Concorde *f*, harmonie *f.* **2.** (*a*) The American Union, l'Union américaine. (*b*) = TRADE-UNION. Union regulations, règles syndicales. (*c*) *Adm:* Union workhouse, *F:* Union, asile *m* des pauvres (à l'usage de plusieurs communes). To die in the Union, mourir à l'hôpital. **3.** (*a*) Soudure *f* (des os) ; raccordement *m* (de fils). (*b*) *Mec.E: etc:* Union(-joint), raccord *m* ; union. 'Union 'flag, 'jack, *s.* Le pavillon britannique.

unionist ['juːnjənist], *s.* **1.** *Pol:* Unioniste *mf.* **2.** *Ind:* = TRADE-UNIONIST.

uniparous [juːˈnipərəs], *a.* *Biol:* Unipare.

unipersonal [juːniˈpəːrsən(ə)l], *a.* *Gram:* (Verbe) unipersonnel.

uniphase ['juːnifeːiz], *a.* *El.E:* Monophasé.

unipolar [juːniˈpoulər], *a.* *El:* Unipolaire ; (lampe) à plot central.

unique [juːˈniːk], *a.* Unique ; seul en son genre. **-ly,** *adv.* Uniquement.

unisexed [juːniˈsekst], **unisexual** [juːniˈseksjuəl], *a.* *Biol:* Unisexué, unisexuel.

unison ['juːnizən, -sən], *s.* **1.** *Ph:Mus:* Unisson *m.* In unison, à l'unisson (*with*, de). **2.** To act in unison with s.o., agir de concert avec qn.

unissued [ʌnˈiʃjud, -ˈisjud], *a.* Unissued shares, actions non encore émises ; actions à la souche.

unit ['juːnit], *s.* **1.** Unité *f.* *Com:* Unit price, prix unitaire. **2.** (*a*) Unité (de longueur, etc.). Standard unit, module *m.* (*b*) *Mil:* Self-contained unit, fraction constituée. (*c*) *Mec.E:* Élément *m*, bloc *m.* Motor unit, bloc moteur.

Unitarian [juːniˈtɛəriən], *a. & s. Rel.H:* Unita(i)rien, -ienne.

unite [juːˈnait]. **I.** *v.tr.* (*a*) Unir (une chose à une autre). *Surg:* To unite a wound, suturer une blessure. (*b*) Mettre (les gens) d'accord ; unifier (un parti). (*c*) Unir en mariage. **2.** *v.i.* (*a*) S'unir, se joindre (*with*, à). (*b*) (*Of companies*) S'amalgamer ; (*of states*) se confédérer ; (*of rivers*) se mêler, confluer. *Ch:* (*Of atoms*) S'unir, se combiner. To unite in doing sth., se mettre d'accord pour faire qch. *Pol:* To unite against a party, faire bloc contre un parti. **united,** *a.* Uni, réuni. United efforts, efforts concertés. To present a united front, faire front unique. *Geog:* The United Kingdom, le Royaume-Uni. The United States, les États-Unis (d'Amérique). **-ly,** *adv.* Ensemble ; d'accord.

unity ['juːniti], *s.* Unité *f.* **1.** *Mth:* To reduce a coefficient to unity, réduire un coefficient à l'unité. **2.** Concorde *f*, accord *m.* National u., unité nationale. *Prov:* Unity is strength, l'union fait la force. **3.** *Lit:* The dramatic unities, les unités dramatiques. Unity of place, unité de lieu.

univalent [juːniˈveilənt, juːˈnivələnt], *a.* *Ch:* Univalent, monovalent.

universal [juːniˈvəːrs(ə)l]. **I.** *a.* Universel. He is a universal favourite, tout le monde l'aime. *S.a.* JOINT[1] **1.** **2.** *s. Log:* Proposition universelle. **-ally,** *adv.* Universellement.

universe ['juːnivəːrs], *s.* Univers *m.* The wonders of the u., les merveilles de la création.

university [juːniˈvəːrsiti], *s.* Université *f.* To have had a university education, avoir fait des études supérieures. University lecture, conférence de faculté. University professor, professeur de faculté. University town, ville universitaire.

unjust [ʌnˈdʒʌst], *a.* **1.** Injuste (to, envers, avec, pour). My suspicions were u., mes soupçons étaient mal fondés. **2.** Unjust weight, faux poids. **-ly,** *adv.* Injustement.

unjustifiable [ʌnˈdʒʌstifaiəbl], *a.* Injustifiable, inexcusable.

unjustified [ʌnˈdʒʌstifaid], *a.* Non justifié ; (*of verdict*) non motivé.

unkempt [ʌnˈkempt, ˈʌn-], *a.* **1.** (*Of hair*) Mal peigné ; (*of appearance*) dépeigné. **2.** (*Of garden, etc.*) Peu soigné ; mal tenu.

unkind [ʌnˈkaind], *a.* (i) Dur ; cruel ; (ii) peu aimable. Unkind fate, sort cruel. That's very unkind of him, c'est peu aimable de sa part. Her aunt is u. to her, sa tante la traite mal. He was u. enough to . . ., il a eu la méchanceté de. . . . **-ly,** *adv.* (i) Méchamment, durement ; (ii) sans bienveillance. Don't take it unkindly if I . . ., ne le prenez pas en mauvaise part si. . . .

unkindly², *a.* **1.** Peu aimable, peu bienveillant. **2.** (Temps) peu favorable ; (climat) rude.

unkindness [ʌn'kaindnəs], *s.* **1.** Méchanceté *f* ; rudesse *f* (du climat). **2.** Manque *m* de bienveillance.

unknot [ʌn'nɔt], *v.tr.* (unknotted) Dénouer.

unknowing [ʌn'nouiŋ], *a.* Ignorant (*of*, de). **-ly**, *adv.* Inconsciemment ; sans le savoir.

unknown [ʌn'noun]. **1.** *a.* (*a*) Inconnu (*to*, à, de) ; ignoré (*to*, de). Unknown writer, écrivain obscur. *adv.* He did it unknown to me, il l'a fait à mon insu. (*b*) *Mth:* Unknown quantity, inconnue *f.* **2.** *s.* (*a*) (*Pers.*) Inconnu, -ue. (*b*) *Mth:* Inconnue *f.* (*c*) The unknown, l'inconnu.

unlaboured [ʌn'leibərd], *a.* (Style) facile, spontané, coulant.

unlace [ʌn'leis], *v.tr.* Délacer, défaire (ses souliers, etc.) ; délacer (qn).

unladen [ʌn'leid(ə)n], *a.* *Nau:* Sans charge.

unladylike [ʌn'leidilaik], *a.* Indigne d'une femme bien élevée ; peu distingué.

unlaid [ʌn'leid], *a.* Unlaid ghost, esprit non exorcisé.

unlatch [ʌn'latʃ], *v.tr.* Ouvrir (la porte).

unlawful [ʌn'lɔ:ful], *a.* (*a*) Illégal, -aux. *S.a.* ASSEMBLY I. (*b*) (Moyen) illicite. **-fully**, *adv.* (*a*) Illégalement. (*b*) Illicitement.

unlearn [ʌn'lə:rn], *v.tr.* (*p.t. & p.p.* unlearnt [-lə:rnt] *or* unlearned) Désapprendre. To u. a habit, se défaire d'une habitude.

unlearned [ʌn'lə:rnid], *a.* **1.** Ignorant ; illettré. **2.** [ʌn'lə:rnd] *a.* (*a*) Peu versé (*in*, dans). (*b*) To leave a lesson u., ne pas apprendre une leçon.

unleash [ʌn'li:ʃ], *v.tr.* Lâcher, découpler (des chiens).

unleavened [ʌn'lev(ə)nd], *a.* (Pain) sans levain, azyme. *Jew.Rel:* The feast of unleavened bread, la fête des azymes.

unless [ʌn'les]. **1.** *conj.* A moins que + *sub.* U. it be you . . ., à moins que ce ne soit vous. . . . You will be late u. you start at once, vous arriverez trop tard à moins de partir sur-le-champ. Unless I am mistaken . . ., si je ne me trompe (pas). . . . Unless I hear to the contrary, à moins d'avis contraire. **2.** *prep.* Sauf, excepté. No other mineral, u. iron . . ., aucun autre minéral, sauf peut-être le fer. . . .

unlettered [ʌn'letərd], *a.* Peu lettré ; indocte.

unlicensed [ʌn'laisənst], *a.* (*a*) Non autorisé ; illicite. (*b*) Sans patente.

unlicked [ʌn'likt], *a.* *F:* (Rustre) mal léché.

unlike [ʌn'laik], *a.* Différent, dissemblable. (*a*) *Mth:* 'Unlike quantities, quantités dissemblables. (*b*) Unlike (to) sth., dissemblable à qch. Portrait quite u. the sitter, portrait peu ressemblant. Not unlike s.o., assez ressemblant à qn. He, unlike his father . . ., lui, à la différence de son père. . . . (*c*) That was very unlike him! je ne le reconnais pas là !

unlikelihood [ʌn'laiklihud], **unlikeliness** [ʌn'laiklinəs], *s.* Invraisemblance *f*, improbabilité *f.*

unlikely [ʌn'laikli], *a.* **1.** (*a*) Invraisemblable ; peu probable. Most unlikely, très peu probable. It is not at all unlikely that . . ., il se pourrait bien que + *sub.* (*b*) *F:* He is unlikely to come, il est peu probable qu'il vienne. **2.** The most unlikely man to do such a thing, l'homme le moins fait pour agir de la sorte.

unlimber [ʌn'limbər], *v.tr.* *Artil:* Décrocher l'avant-train (d'une pièce). *Abs.* Mettre en batterie.

unlimited [ʌn'limitid], *a.* Illimité ; sans bornes.

unload [ʌn'loud], *v.tr.* **1.** (*a*) Décharger (un bateau, des marchandises). *Abs.* (*Of carman*) Décharger sa voiture. (*b*) To u. one's heart of a secret, se soulager, se délester, le cœur d'un secret. **2.** Enlever la charge ; décharger (un fusil).

unloading, *s.* Déchargement *m.*

unloaded [ʌn'loudid], *a.* **1.** (*a*) Déchargé. (*b*) (Fusil) désarmé. **2.** (*a*) Non chargé. (*b*) (Fusil) sans charge.

unlock [ʌn'lɔk], *v.tr.* **1.** Ouvrir (la porte) ; faire jouer la serrure de (la porte). **2.** (*a*) Débloquer (une roue). *Typ:* Desserrer (la forme). (*b*) *Aut:* To unlock the steering-gear, déverrouiller la direction.

unlocked [ʌn'lɔkt], *a.* Qui n'est pas fermé à clef.

unlooked [ʌn'lukt], *a.* Unlooked for, (événement) inattendu, imprévu.

unloose [ʌn'lu:s], **unloosen** [ʌn'lu:s(ə)n], *v.tr.* **1.** To unloosen one's hold, lâcher prise. To unloose(n) one's tongue, délier sa langue. **2.** Délier, dénouer (ses souliers).

unlov(e)able [ʌn'lʌvəbl], *a.* Peu aimable ; peu sympathique.

unlovely [ʌn'lʌvli], *a.* Sans charme, disgracieux. U. prospect, perspective morne.

unlucky [ʌn'lʌki], *a.* **1.** (*a*) Malheureux, infortuné. To be unlucky, ne pas avoir de chance ; jouer de malheur. (*b*) (*Of thg*) Malheureux, malencontreux. Unlucky day, jour néfaste. How u. that he came! quelle malchance qu'il soit venu ! **2.** Unlucky star, étoile maléfique. It is unlucky, cela porte malheur. Unlucky omen, mauvais augure. **-ily**, *adv.* Malheureusement.

unmaidenlike [ʌn'meidnlaik], **unmaidenly** [ʌn'meidnli], *a.* Qui ne sied pas à une jeune fille ; immodeste.

unman [ʌn'man], *v.tr.* (unmanned) (*a*) Amollir (une nation). (*b*) Attendrir (qn). (*c*) Abattre, décourager (qn).

unmanageable [ʌn'manedʒəbl], *a.* **1.** Intraitable ; (*of child*) indocile ; (*of ship*) difficile à manœuvrer. **2.** Difficile à manier.

unmanliness [ʌn'manlinəs], *s.* (*a*) Manque *m* de virilité ; mollesse *f.* (*b*) Lâcheté *f.*

unmanly [ʌn'manli], *a.* Indigne d'un homme ; peu viril.

unmannerliness [ʌn'manərlinəs], *s.* Mauvaises manières ; impolitesse *f*, grossièreté *f.*

unmannerly [ʌn'manərli], *a.* Qui a de mauvaises manières ; malappris ; grossier.

unmarketable [ʌn'mɑ:rketəbl], *a.* Invendable ; d'un débit difficile.

unmarriageable [ʌn'maredʒəbl], *a.* (Fille) que l'on n'arrive pas à marier.

unmarried [ʌn'marid, 'ʌr-], *a.* Célibataire ; non marié. Unmarried state, célibat *m.* Unmarried mother, fille-mère *f.*

unmask [ʌn'mɑ:sk]. **1.** *v.tr.* (*a*) Démasquer. (*b*) To unmask a conspiracy, dévoiler un complot. **2.** *v.i.* Se démasquer.

unmatched [ʌn'matʃt], *a.* **1.** Sans égal, *pl.* sans égaux ; incomparable. **2.** Désassorti, dépareillé.

unmeaning [ʌn'mi:niŋ], *a.* Qui ne signifie rien ; vide de sens.

unmeant [ʌn'ment], *a.* (*Of insult*) Involontaire ; fait sans intention.

unmeasured [ʌn'meʒərd], *a.* **1.** (*a*) Non mesuré. (*b*) Infini, immense. **2.** (Langage) qui manque de retenue.

unmentionable [ʌn'menʃ(ə)nəbl]. **1.** *a.* (Mot) qu'on n'ose pas prononcer ; (chose) dont il ne faut pas parler. **2.** *s.pl.* *F:* Unmentionables, pantalon *m.*

unmerciful [ʌnˈməːrsiful], a. Impitoyable ; sans pitié. **-fully,** adv. Impitoyablement.

unmerited [ʌnˈmeritid], a. Immérité.

unmethodical [ʌnmeˈθɔdik(ə)l], a. **1.** Peu méthodique ; (travail) décousu. **2.** (Of pers.) Brouillon, -onne.

unmindful [ʌnˈmaindful], a. **Unmindful of one's duty,** oublieux de son devoir. U. of one's own interests, sans penser à ses propres intérêts.

unmistakable [ʌnmisˈteikəbl], a. (a) Qui ne prête à aucune erreur ; clair ; évident. (b) Facilement reconnaissable. **-ably,** adv. Nettement, évidemment ; à ne pas s'y méprendre.

unmitigated [ʌnˈmitigeitid], a. **1.** (Mal) non mitigé. **2.** F: Dans toute la force du terme. **Unmitigated ass,** parfait imbécile. **Unmitigated lie,** mensonge éclatant. **Unmitigated scoundrel,** coquin fieffé.

unmixed [ʌnˈmikst, ˈʌn-], a. Sans mélange ; pur. **It is not an unmixed blessing,** cela ne va pas sans quelques inconvénients.

unmolested [ʌnmɔˈlestid], a. Sans être molesté ; (voyager) sans obstacle.

unmoor [ʌnˈmuər], v.tr. Nau: Démarrer (un navire). **unmooring,** s. Démarrage m.

unmotherly [ʌnˈmʌðərli], a. Peu digne d'une mère ; peu maternel.

unmounted [ʌnˈmauntid], a. Non monté. **1.** (a) (Of gem) Non serti. (b) (Of photograph) Non collé. **2.** (Soldat) à pied.

unmoved [ʌnˈmuːvd], a. Impassible. **Unmoved by sth.,** aucunement ému, touché, de, par, qch. He remained u. by all entreaties, il resta inflexible à toutes les prières.

unmusical [ʌnˈmjuːzik(ə)l], a. **1.** Peu mélodieux. **2.** (Of ear) Peu musical, -aux.

unnamed [ʌnˈneimd], a. **1.** Au nom inconnu ; anonyme. **2.** Innom(m)é ; sans nom.

unnatural [ʌnˈnatjurəl], a. Non naturel. (a) Anormal, -aux. (b) Contre nature ; monstrueux. **Unnatural father,** père dénaturé. (c) U. laugh, rire forcé.

unnaturalized [ʌnˈnatjurəlaːizd], a. (Of alien) Non naturalisé.

unnavigable [ʌnˈnavigəbl], a. Innavigable.

unnecessary [ʌnˈnesesəri], a. Peu nécessaire ; inutile, superflu. **(It is) unnecessary to say that . . .,** inutile de dire que. . . . **-ily,** adv. **1.** Sans nécessité ; inutilement. **2.** Plus que de raison.

unneeded [ʌnˈniːdid], a. Inutile ; dont on n'a pas besoin.

unneighbourly [ʌnˈneibərli], a. Peu obligeant ; (conduite) de mauvais voisin. To behave in an u. manner, se conduire en mauvais voisin.

unnerve [ʌnˈnəːrv], v.tr. Faire perdre son courage, son sang-froid, à (qn) ; effrayer (qn). Entirely unnerved, tout à fait démonté.

unnoticed [ʌnˈnoutist], a. **1.** Inaperçu, inobservé. **To pass unnoticed,** passer inaperçu. **2.** To let an interruption pass u., ne pas relever une interruption. To leave a fact u., passer un fait sous silence.

unnumbered [ʌnˈnʌmbərd], a. **1.** (a) Qui n'est pas compté. (b) Sans nombre ; innombrable. **2.** Non numéroté.

unobjectionable [ʌnɔbˈdʒekʃ(ə)nəbl], a. (Personne) à qui on ne peut rien reprocher ; (chose) à laquelle on ne peut trouver à redire.

unobservant [ʌnɔbˈzəːrvənt], **unobserving** [ʌnɔbˈzəːrviŋ], a. Peu observateur, -trice.

unobserved [ʌnɔbˈzəːrvd, ˈʌn-], a. Inobservé, inaperçu. To go out u., sortir sans être vu.

unobstructed [ʌnɔbˈstrʌktid], a. **1.** Inobstrué ; (of street) non encombré ; (of view) libre. **2.** Sans rencontrer d'obstacles.

unobtainable [ʌnɔbˈteinəbl], a. Impossible à obtenir.

unobtrusive [ʌnɔbˈtruːsiv], a. Discret, -ète ; (rôle) effacé, modeste. **-ly,** adv. Discrètement.

unoccupied [ʌnˈɔkjupaid], a. Inoccupé. **1.** Sans occupation. **Unoccupied time,** temps libre. **2.** Inhabité. **3.** (Of seat) Libre, disponible.

unoffending [ʌnɔˈfendiŋ], a. Innocent.

unofficial [ʌnɔˈfiʃəl], a. Non officiel ; (i) (renseignement) officieux ; (ii) (nouvelle) non confirmée. **-ally,** adv. À titre officieux.

unopened [ʌnˈoupənd], a. Qui n'a pas été ouvert ; (of letter) non décacheté.

unopposed [ʌnɔˈpouzd, ˈʌn-], a. Sans opposition.

unorthodox [ʌnˈɔːrθɔdɔks], a. Peu orthodoxe.

unostentatious [ʌnɔstenˈteiʃəs], a. **1.** (Of pers.) Peu fastueux ; simple. **2.** Fait sans ostentation. U. wedding, mariage sans faste. **-ly,** adv. Sans ostentation, sans faste.

unpack [ʌnˈpak], v.tr. **1.** Déballer, dépaqueter (des objets). **2.** Défaire (une malle). Abs. Défaire sa malle, sa valise.

unpaid [ʌnˈpeid], a. Non payé. **1.** Qui ne reçoit pas de salaire ; (of post) non rétribué. U. secretary, secrétaire sans traitement. **Unpaid services,** services à titre gracieux. **2.** (Of bill) Impayé ; (of debt) non acquitté ; (of letter) non affranchi.

unpalatable [ʌnˈpalətəbl], a. (a) D'un goût désagréable. (b) F: (Of truth) Désagréable.

unparalleled [ʌnˈparaleld], a. Incomparable ; sans pareil, sans égal ; (of action) sans précédent.

unpardonable [ʌnˈpɑːrd(ə)nəbl], a. Impardonnable.

unparliamentary [ʌnpɑːrləˈmentəri], a. (Langage) (i) antiparlementaire, (ii) F: grossier, injurieux.

unpatriotic [ʌnpatriˈɔtik], a. (Of pers.) Peu patriote ; (of action) peu patriotique ; antipatriotique. To be u., être mauvais patriote.

unperceivable [ʌnpərˈsiːvəbl], a. Imperceptible.

unperceived [ʌnpərˈsiːvd], a. Inaperçu.

unperforated [ʌnˈpəːrfoːreitid], a. Non perforé.

unperturbed [ʌnpərˈtəːrbd], a. **1.** Impassible. **2. Unperturbed by this event,** peu ému de cet événement.

unpin [ʌnˈpin], v.tr. (unpinned) **1.** Décheviller (un assemblage) ; dégoupiller (un écrou). **2.** Désépingler, défaire (un châle).

unpitying [ʌnˈpitiiŋ], a. Impitoyable.

unplaced [ʌnˈpleist, ˈʌn-], a. **1.** (Cheval) non placé ; (candidat) non classé. **2.** (Of pers.) Sans poste ; sans place.

unplayable [ʌnˈpleiəbl], a. Injouable.

unpleasant [ʌnˈplez(ə)nt], a. Désagréable, déplaisant. **-ly,** adv. Désagréablement.

unpleasantness [ʌnˈplez(ə)ntnəs], s. **1.** Caractère m désagréable (de qch.). **2.** Désagrément m, ennui m. **There has been some unpleasantness,** F: il y a eu de la brouille.

unpleasing [ʌnˈpliːziŋ], a. Peu agréable ; qui manque de grâce.

unplumbed [ʌnˈplʌmd], a. Lit: **Unplumbed depths,** profondeurs insondées.

unpoetic(al) [ʌnpouˈetik(əl)], a. Peu poétique.

unpolished [ʌnˈpɔliʃt], a. **1.** Non poli ; mat ; (of stone) brut. **2.** Rude, grossier. **Unpolished style,** style fruste.

unpolluted [ʌnpɔˈljuːtid], a. Non pollué ; pur ; (atmosphère) vierge de fumée.

unpopular [ʌnˈpɔpjulər], a. Impopulaire. **To**

make oneself unpopular with everybody, se faire mal voir de tout le monde.

unpopularity [ʌnpɔpju'lariti], s. Impopularité f.

unpopulated [ʌn'pɔpjuleitid], a. Non peuplé ; sans population.

unpractical [ʌn'praktik(ə)l], a. **I.** (Of pers.) Peu pratique. **2.** (Projet) impraticable.

unpractised [ʌn'praktist], a. Inexercé, inexpert (in, à, dans) ; inexpérimenté (in, dans).

unprecedented [ʌn'presidentid], a. (i) Sans précédent ; (ii) sans exemple ; inouï.

unprejudiced [ʌn'predʒudist], a. Sans préjugés, sans préventions ; impartial, -aux ; désintéressé.

unpremeditated [ʌnpri'mediteitid], a. (Départ) inopiné. Jur : (Délit) non prémédité.

unprepared [ʌnpri'peərd], a. **I.** (Of food) Inapprêté. **Unprepared speech**, discours improvisé. Sch : **Unprepared translation**, traduction à livre ouvert. **2. To catch s.o. unprepared**, prendre qn au dépourvu. **3.** Sans préparatifs.

unprepossessing [ʌnpri:po'zesiŋ], a. (Of pers.) Peu engageant. **A man of unprepossessing appearance**, un homme de méchante mine.

unpresuming [ʌnpri'zju:miŋ], a. Modeste ; sans présomption.

unpretentious [ʌnpri'tenʃəs], a. Sans prétentions ; modeste. **-ly**, adv. Modestement.

unprincipled [ʌn'prinsipld], a. (Of pers.) Sans principes ; sans mœurs.

unprintable [ʌn'printəbl], a. Que l'on rougirait d'imprimer.

unprocurable [ʌnpro'kjuərəbl], a. Impossible à obtenir ; que l'on ne peut se procurer.

unproductive [ʌnpro'dʌktiv], a. Improductif ; (travail) stérile ; (capital) dormant.

unprofessional [ʌnpro'feʃən(ə)l], a. **Unprofessional conduct**, manquement m aux devoirs de la profession.

unprofitable [ʌn'prɔfitəbl], a. Improfitable ; peu lucratif ; sans profit ; (travail) inutile. **-ably**, adv. Sans profit ; inutilement.

unpromising [ʌn'prɔmisiŋ], a. Qui promet peu. (Of weather) **To look unpromising**, s'annoncer mal.

unprompted [ʌn'prɔm(p)tid], a. (Of answer) Spontané. **To do sth. unprompted**, faire qch. spontanément, sans y être incité.

unpronounceable [ʌnpro'naunsəbl], a. Imprononçable.

unpropitious [ʌnpro'piʃəs], a. Impropice, défavorable, peu favorable (to, à).

unprotected [ʌnpro'tektid], a. **I.** Inabrité ; sans protection, sans défense. **2.** Ind : (Of moving part) Exposé ; nu ; sans carter.

unproved [ʌn'pru:vd], **unproven** [ʌn'prouv(ə)n], a. **I.** (Of accusation) Improuvé ; non prouvé. **2.** (Of fidelity) Inéprouvé.

unprovided [ʌnpro'vaidid], a. **Unprovided with sth.**, dépourvu, dénué de qch. **To be left unprovided for**, être laissé sans ressources.

unprovoked [ʌnpro'voukt], a. Improvoqué ; fait sans provocation. S.a. ASSAULT¹ 2.

unpublished [ʌn'pʌbliʃt], a. **I.** Inédit ; non publié. **2.** The u. facts, les faits qui n'ont pas été livrés au public.

unpunctual [ʌn'pʌŋktjuəl], a. (a) Inexact ; peu ponctuel. (b) En retard ; pas à l'heure.

unpunctuality [ʌnpʌŋktju'aliti], s. Inexactitude f ; manque m de ponctualité.

unpunished [ʌn'pʌniʃt], a. Impuni. **To go unpunished**, (i) (of pers.) échapper à la punition ; (ii) (of crime) rester impuni.

unqualified [ʌn'kwɔlifaid], a. **I.** (a) Incompétent. Jur : **Unqualified to vote**, inhabile à voter.

(b) (Médecin) sans diplômes ; F : (médecin) marron. **2. Unqualified denial**, dénégation catégorique. **Unqualified praise**, éloges sans réserve.

unquenchable [ʌn'kwenʃəbl], a. (Feu, soif) inextinguible ; (cupidité) inassouvissable.

unquenched [ʌn'kwenʃt], a. (Feu) non éteint ; (désir, etc.) inassouvi. U. thirst, soif non étanchée.

unquestionable [ʌn'kwestʃənəbl], a. Indiscutable, indubitable. **Unquestionable fact**, fait hors de doute. **-ably**, adv. Indubitablement, incontestablement.

unquestioned [ʌn'kwestʃ(ə)nd], a. **I.** (Droit) indisputé, incontesté. **2. To let a statement pass u.**, laisser passer une affirmation sans la relever.

unquestioning [ʌn'kwestʃəniŋ], a. (Obéissance) aveugle, sans question. **-ly**, adv. Aveuglément ; sans question.

unquiet [ʌn'kwaiet], a. Inquiet, -ète ; agité. U. soul, âme trouble. U. times, temps de trouble.

unquoted [ʌn'kwoutid], a. **I.** Non cité. **2.** St. Exch : **Unquoted securities**, valeurs non cotées.

unratified [ʌn'ratifaid], a. (Traité, etc.) sans ratification ; qui n'a jamais été ratifié.

unravel [ʌn'rav(ə)l], v. (unravelled) **I.** v.tr. (a) Effiler, effilocher (un tissu). (b) Débrouiller, démêler (des fils). **2.** v.i. (a) (Of cloth) S'effiler. (b) (Of tangle) Se débrouiller, se démêler.

unravelling, s. **I.** Effilage m, effilochement m (d'un tissu). **2.** Débrouillement m, démêlement m.

unread [ʌn'red], a. **I.** Non lu. **To leave sth. unread**, ne pas lire qch. **2.** (Of pers.) Sans instruction ; illettré.

unreadable [ʌn'ri:dəbl], a. Illisible.

unreal [ʌn'ri:əl], a. Irréel ; sans réalité.

unreasonable [ʌn'ri:z(ə)nəbl], a. Déraisonnable. **I. Don't be unreasonable**, soyez raisonnable. **2.** (a) **Unreasonable demands**, demandes immodérées, exorbitantes. (b) **At this unreasonable hour**, à cette heure indue. **-ably**, adv. Déraisonnablement ; d'une manière peu raisonnable.

unreasoning [ʌn'ri:zəniŋ], a. Qui ne raisonne pas. **Unreasoning hatred**, haine aveugle.

unrecognizable [ʌn'rekognaizəbl], a. Méconnaissable.

unrecognized [ʌn'rekogna:izd], a. **I.** (Of genius) Méconnu. **2.** (Of ruler) Non reconnu (by, par).

unrecorded [ʌnri'kɔ:rdid], a. Non enregistré ; dont on ne trouve aucune mention.

unredeemed [ʌnri'di:md], a. **I.** (Péché) irracheté. Town of u. ugliness, ville uniformément laide. **2.** (a) **Unredeemed promise**, promesse inaccomplie. (b) Watch u. (from pawn), montre non dégagée.

unrefined [ʌnri'faind], a. **I.** Brut ; (sucre) non raffiné. **2.** (Homme) peu raffiné, grossier.

unrefreshed [ʌnri'freʃt], a. **I.** Non rafraîchi. **2.** To wake u., se réveiller peu reposé.

unregenerate [ʌnri'dʒenəret], a. (Of pers.) Non régénéré ; inconverti.

unregistered [ʌn'redʒistərd], a. Non enregistré, non inscrit. **Unregistered birth**, naissance non déclarée.

unregretted [ʌnri'gretid], a. **To die unregretted**, mourir sans laisser de regrets.

unrehearsed [ʌnri'hə:rst], a. (Discours, etc.) inapprêté. U. play, pièce jouée sans répétitions préalables. **Unrehearsed effect**, effet non préparé.

unrelated [ʌnri'leitid], a. (a) (Of phenomena) Sans rapport (one to another, l'un avec l'autre). (b) (Of pers.) **They are entirely u.**, il n'y a aucun lien de parenté entre eux.

unrelaxing [ʌnri'laksiŋ], a. (Assiduité) sans relâche; (effort) assidu, soutenu.

unrelenting [ʌnri'lentiŋ], a. (a) (Of pers.) Implacable, impitoyable (towards, à, pour, à l'égard de). (b) (Of persecution) Acharné.

unreliability [ʌnrilaiə'biliti], s. 1. Inexactitude f (des résultats d'une expérience, etc.). 2. Instabilité f (de qn).

unreliable [ʌnri'laiəbl], a. (Homme) sur lequel on ne peut pas compter; (renseignement) sujet à caution; (machine) d'un fonctionnement incertain. U. map, carte peu fidèle.

unrelieved [ʌnri'liːvd], a. 1. (a) (Of pers.) Qui reste sans secours. (b) (Of pain) Non soulagé. 2. Qui manque de relief; monotone. Plain u. by the smallest hillock, plaine ininterrompue par la moindre colline.

unremitting [ʌnri'mitiŋ], a. 1. Ininterrompu; sans intermission. U. efforts, efforts soutenus. 2. He was u. in his attentions, son assiduité ne s'est pas démentie un instant. -ly, adv. Sans cesse, sans relâche.

unremunerative [ʌnri'mjuːnərətiv], a. Peu rémunérateur; peu lucratif; improfitable.

unrepentant [ʌnri'pentənt], **unrepenting** [ʌnri'pentiŋ], a. Impénitent. To die unrepentant, mourir dans son péché.

unrequited [ʌnri'kwaitid], a. 1. (Of service) Non récompensé. 2. Unrequited love, amour non payé de retour, non partagé.

unreserved [ʌnri'zə:rvd], a. 1. Sans réserve. (a) Franc, f. franche; expansif. (b) (Of approval) Complet, -ète; entier. 2. Unreserved seats, places non réservées.

unreservedly [ʌnri'zə:rvidli], adv. Sans réserve. (a) Franchement; à cœur ouvert. (b) Entièrement; sans restriction.

unresisting [ʌnri'zistiŋ, ʌn-], a. Qui ne résiste pas; soumis, docile.

unresponsive [ʌnri'spɔnsiv], a. (a) Difficile à émouvoir; froid. (b) I.C.E: Unresponsive engine, moteur peu sensible, mou, plat.

unrest [ʌn'rest], s. 1. Inquiétude f. 2. The social unrest, le malaise social. Labour unrest, agitation ouvrière.

unrestrained [ʌnri'streind], a. Non restreint; libre; intempéré. U. laughter, rires immodérés.

unrestrainedly [ʌnri'streinidli], adv. Librement; sans contrainte.

unrestricted [ʌnri'striktid, ʌn-], a. Sans restriction; (pouvoir) absolu. Unrestricted prospect, vue dégagée. Unrestricted road, voie publique sans restriction de vitesse.

unretentive [ʌnri'tentiv], a. Unretentive memory, mémoire courte, peu fidèle.

unrevenged [ʌnri'vendʒd], a. Invengé. 1. Sans être vengé. 2. Sans s'être vengé.

unrewarded [ʌnri'wɔ:rdid], a. Sans récompense.

unrighteous [ʌn'raitʃəs], a. 1. Impie. 2. Inique, injuste, improbe. -ly, adv. Iniquement, injustement.

unrighteousness [ʌn'raitʃəsnəs], s. Iniquité f, injustice f, improbité f.

unripe [ʌn'raip], a. (Of fruit) Vert; qui n'est pas mûr; (of corn) en herbe; (of scheme) insuffisamment médité.

unrivalled [ʌn'raiv(ə)ld], a. Sans rival; sans pareil; incomparable. Our goods are u., nos articles sont sans concurrence.

unroll [ʌn'roul]. 1. v.tr. Dérouler. 2. v.i. & pr. Se dérouler.

unromantic [ʌnro'mantik], a. Peu romanesque; terre à terre inv.

unruffled [ʌn'rʌfld], a. 1. (Of temper) Calme, serein, placide. An u. composure, un calme imperturbable. 2. (Of sea) Calme, uni.

unruly [ʌn'ru:li], a. (Of child) Indiscipliné, insoumis, mutin; (of horse) fougueux; (of tongue, passions) déréglé.

unsaddle [ʌn'sadl], v.tr. 1. Desseller (un cheval) 2. (Of horse) Désarçonner (le cavalier).

unsafe [ʌn'seif], a. 1. (Of action) Dangereux; (of ice) peu sûr; (of undertaking) hasardeux; (of business house) véreux. Nau: Unsafe anchorage, mauvais mouillage. 2. Exposé au danger.

unsaid [ʌn'sed]. 1. See UNSAY. 2. a. To leave sth. unsaid, passer qch. sous silence.

unsalaried [ʌn'salərid], a. 1. (Fonctionnaire) sans traitement. 2. (Emploi) non rétribué.

unsaleable [ʌn'seiləbl], a. (Of goods) Invendable.

unsanitary [ʌn'sanitəri], a. Non hygiénique; insalubre.

unsated [ʌn'seitid], **unsatiated** [ʌn'seiʃieitid], a. Inassouvi; non rassasié.

unsatisfactory [ʌnsatis'faktəri], a. Peu satisfaisant; qui laisse à désirer; (of explanation) peu convaincant. -ily, adv. D'une manière peu satisfaisante.

unsatisfied [ʌn'satisfaid], a. 1. Mécontent, peu satisfait (with, de). 2. Inconvaincu. 3. (Of appetite) Inassouvi.

unsatisfying [ʌn'satisfaiiŋ], a. 1. Peu satisfaisant; peu convaincant. 2. (Of meal) Peu rassasiant.

unsavoury [ʌn'seivəri], a. 1. (a) (Goût) désagréable; (plat) d'un goût désagréable. (b) U. smell, mauvaise odeur. 2. (Scandale) répugnant. U. business, vilaine affaire.

unsay [ʌn'sei], v.tr. (unsaid [-'sed]; unsaid) Se dédire, se rétracter (ses paroles).

unscathed [ʌn'skeiðd], a. = SCATHELESS.

unscholarly [ʌn'skɔlərli], a. 1. Indigne d'un savant. 2. Peu savant; illettré.

unscientific [ʌnsaiən'tifik], a. (a) Non scientifique. (b) Peu scientifique.

unscratched [ʌn'skratʃt], a. Sans égratignure.

unscreened [ʌn'skri:nd], a. 1. (a) (Of place) Exposé. (b) Sans écran. El: (Condensateur) non blindé. 2. (Of coal) Non criblé.

unscrew [ʌn'skru:], v.tr. Dévisser.

unscrupulous [ʌn'skru:pjuləs], a. Peu scrupuleux; sans scrupules. Man of u. ambition, arriviste m. -ly, adv. Peu scrupuleusement; sans scrupule.

unseal [ʌn'si:l], v.tr. 1. Desceller (un acte); décacheter (une lettre). 2. F: To unseal s.o.'s lips, rendre à qn la liberté de parole. To unseal s.o.'s eyes, dessiller les yeux à, de, qn.

unseasonable [ʌn'si:z(ə)nəbl], a. 1. (Of fruit, etc.) Hors de saison. U. weather, temps qui n'est pas de saison. 2. (Of action) Inopportun; déplacé. -ably, adv. 1. Hors de saison. 2. Mal à propos.

unseasoned [ʌn'si:z(ə)nd], a. 1. (Of food) Non assaisonné. 2. (a) U. timber, bois vert. (b) Inacclimaté; (of troops) inaguerri.

unseat [ʌn'si:t], v.tr. 1. Désarçonner (un cavalier). 2. Invalider (un membre élu); Parl: faire perdre son siège à (un député).

unseaworthy [ʌn'si:wɔ:rði], a. (Navire) hors d'état de prendre la mer; incapable de tenir la mer.

unsecured [ʌnsi'kjuərd], a. 1. Mal assujetti; non assujetti. 2. (Of loan) Non garanti; à découvert.

unseeing [ʌn'si:iŋ], a. Qui ne voit pas; aveugle.

unseemliness [ʌn'si:mlinəs], s. Inconvenance f, messéance f (de conduite).

unseemly [ʌn'siːmli], a. (Of behaviour) Inconvenant ; peu convenable.

unseen [ʌn'siːn], a. (a) Inaperçu, invisible. (b) Sch : **Unseen translation,** s. unseen, passage m à traduire à livre ouvert.

unselfish [ʌn'selfiʃ], a. (Of pers.) Généreux ; sans égoïsme. U. motive, motif désintéressé. **-ly,** adv. Généreusement.

unselfishness [ʌn'selfiʃnəs], s. Générosité f ; désintéressement m.

unserviceable [ʌn'səːrvisəbl], a. (a) (Cadeau) inutilisable. (b) (Vêtement) de mauvais service, peu pratique. (c) Hors d'état de servir.

unset [ʌn'set], a. **1.** (Of diamond) Non serti ; hors d'œuvre. **2.** Cement still u., ciment qui n'a pas encore pris.

unsettle [ʌn'setl], v.tr. Ébranler (les convictions) ; troubler le repos de (qn). **unsettling,** a. (Of news) Troublant.

unsettled [ʌn'setld], a. **1.** (Pays, gouvernement) troublé ; (temps) variable ; (esprit) (i) inquiet, (ii) dérangé. The u. state of the weather, l'incertitude f du temps. **2.** (Of pers.) Sans domicile fixe. **3.** (Esprit) indécis. **4.** (a) (Of question) Indécis. (b) (Of bill) Impayé, non réglé. **5.** (Pays) non colonisé.

unshackle [ʌn'ʃakl], v.tr. **1.** Désentraver (un cheval, etc.) ; ôter les fers à (un prisonnier). **2.** Démaniller (une chaîne) : détalinguer (une ancre).

unshackled [ʌn'ʃakld], a. Libre ; sans entraves.

unshakeable [ʌn'ʃeikəbl], a. Inébranlable ; (amitié) à toute épreuve.

unshaken [ʌn'ʃeik(ə)n], a. Inébranlé, ferme ; (of faith) inentamé ; (of perseverance) constant. (Of troops) To remain u., tenir bon.

unshapely [ʌn'ʃeipli], a. **1.** Mal fait ; difforme, disgracieux. **2.** Informe.

unshaven [ʌn'ʃeiv(ə)n], a. Non rasé.

unsheathe [ʌn'ʃiːð], v.tr. Dégainer.

unsheltered [ʌn'ʃeltərd], a. Sans abri, non abrité (from, contre) : exposé (from the wind, au vent).

unship [ʌn'ʃip], v.tr. (unshipped [-ʃipt]) Nau : **1.** Décharger (les marchandises). **2.** (a) Enlever (un mât) ; démonter (le gouvernail, etc.). (b) Unship oars ! rentrez !

unshod [ʌn'ʃod], a. **1.** (Of pers.) Déchaussé. (Of horse) Déferré. **2.** (a) (Of pers.) Nu-pieds inv. (b) (Of horse) Sans fers.

unshrinkable [ʌn'ʃriŋkbl], a. (Of cloth) Irrétrécissable.

unshrinking [ʌn'ʃriŋkiŋ], a. Hardi ; qui ne bronche pas. **-ly,** adv. Hardiment ; sans broncher.

unshriven [ʌn'ʃriv(ə)n], a. To die unshriven, mourir sans confession ; mourir inabsous.

unsightly [ʌn'saitli], a. Peu agréable à la vue ; laid, vilain.

unsigned [ʌn'saind], a. Non signé ; sans signature.

unsinkable [ʌn'siŋkəbl], a. (Of boat) Insubmersible.

unskilful [ʌn'skilful], a. Malhabile, inhabile (in, at, à).

unskilled [ʌn'skild], a. (Of pers.) Inexpérimenté (in, à) ; inexpert (in, dans, en). Ind : Unskilled workman, manœuvre m. Unskilled labour, main-d'œuvre non spécialisée.

unslaked [ʌn'sleikt], a. **1.** Unslaked lime, chaux vive, non éteinte. **2.** (Of thirst) Non étanché.

unsleeping [ʌn'sliːpiŋ], a. Lit : Toujours en éveil ; vigilant.

unsling [ʌn'sliŋ], v.tr. (p.t. & p.p. unslung [-'slʌŋ]) Nau : **1.** Dégréer, décrocher (un hamac). **2.** Enlever les élingues (d'un ballot).

unsmirched [ʌn'sməːrtʃt], a. (Of reputation) Sans tache, sans souillure.

unsociable [ʌn'souʃəbl], a. Insociable ; sauvage, farouche.

unsoiled [ʌn'sɔild], a. Propre ; sans tache. Com : A l'état (de) neuf.

unsold [ʌn'sould], a. Invendu. Journ : Unsold copies, invendus m, bouillon m.

unsoldierly [ʌn'souldʒərli], a. Peu martial, -aux ; peu militaire.

unsolicited [ʌnso'lis.tid], a. Non sollicité ; (of action) volontaire, spontané. Unsolicited testimonial, lettre d'attestation spontanée.

unsolved [ʌn'sɔlvd], a. (Problème) non résolu ; (mystère) impénétré.

unsophisticated [ʌnso'fistikeitid], a. **1.** Non frelaté. **2.** (Of pers.) Ingénu, naïf, simple, candide ; F : innocent.

unsound [ʌn'saund], a. **1.** (a) (Of pers.) Malsain, maladif. Of unsound mind, non sain d'esprit ; qui a le cerveau dérangé. Vet : Unsound horse, cheval taré. (b) Gâté ; en mauvais état. **2.** (a) (Of ice) Peu solide ; (of position) mal affermi ; (of business) périclitant. (b) Unsound opinions, opinions perverties. Theory that is fundamentally unsound, théorie qui pèche par la base. Ins : Unsound life, mauvais sujet d'assurance. **-ly,** adv. Défectueusement ; (raisonner) à faux.

unsoundness [ʌn'saundnəs], s. **1.** (a) Unsoundness of mind, faiblesse f d'esprit. (b) Mauvais état (du bois, des fruits). **2.** (a) Manque m de solidité (d'un bâtiment). (b) Fausseté f (d'une doctrine).

unsparing [ʌn'spɛəriŋ], a. **1.** Prodigue (of, de). U. in one's efforts, infatigable. To be unsparing of one's strength, prodiguer ses forces. **2.** U. of others, impitoyable pour les autres. **-ly,** adv. **1.** Avec prodigalité ; généreusement. To use sth. u., ne pas ménager qch. **2.** Impitoyablement.

unspeakable [ʌn'spiːkəbl], a. **1.** (Douleur) inexprimable. U. confusion, désordre sans nom. **2.** F : Détestable, inqualifiable. It is unspeakable ! ça n'a pas de nom ! **-ably,** adv. Ineffablement, indiciblement.

unspecified [ʌn'spesifaid], a. Non spécifié.

unsplinterable [ʌn'splintərəbl], a. (Verre) se brisant sans éclats.

unspoiled [ʌn'spɔild], a. (a) (Of child) Non gâté ; bien élevé. (b) U. countryside, campagne non encore profanée.

unspoken [ʌn'spouk(ə)n], a. Non prononcé ; (accord) tacite.

unsportsmanlike [ʌn'spɔːrtʃmənlaik], a. Indigne d'un sportsman ; antisportif ; peu loyal, -aux.

unstable [ʌn'steibl], a. **1.** Instable ; (of position) peu sûr. Mec : Unstable equilibrium, équilibre instable. **2.** (Of pers.) Peu consistant ; (of character) muable, inconstant.

unstained [ʌn'steind], a. **1.** Propre ; sans tache. **2.** Non teint, non mis en couleur. **3.** (Of reputation) Sans tache.

unstamped [ʌn'stampt], a. (a) (Of letter) Sans timbre ; non affranchi. (b) (Of document) Non estampillé.

unsteadiness [ʌn'stedinəs], s. **1.** Instabilité f ; manque m d'aplomb (d'une table) ; manque de sûreté (de la main). **2.** (a) Irrésolution f, indécision f. (b) Manque de conduite. **3.** Irrégularité f, variabilité f (du vent, des prix).

unsteady [ʌn'stedi], a. **1.** (Of table) Peu stable, peu solide ; (of footsteps) chancelant ; (of voice) mal assuré. *F:* To be unsteady on one's legs, avoir une démarche chancelante. **2.** (*a*) (*Of purpose*) Vacillant, irrésolu. (*b*) (*Of pers.*) Dissipé ; déréglé. **3.** Irrégulier ; (*of barometer*) variable. **-ily,** *adv.* **1.** (Marcher) d'un pas chancelant. **2.** D'une façon irrégulière, inégale.

unstick [ʌn'stik], *v.tr.* (*p.t. & p.p.* unstuck [-stʌk]) Décoller (qch.). **To come unstuck, (i)** se décoller ; (ii) *F:* (*of plan*) s'effondrer.

unstinted [ʌn'stintid], *a.* (*a*) (*Of supplies*) Abondant ; à discrétion. (*b*) To give s.o. unstinted praise, ne pas ménager ses louanges à qn.

unstitch [ʌn'stitʃ], *v.tr.* Dépiquer, découdre (un vêtement). To come unstitched, se découdre.

unstop [ʌn'stɔp], *v.tr.* (unstopped [-stɔpt]) **1.** Déboucher, dégorger (un tuyau). **2.** *Nau:* Laisser filer (un cordage).

unstopped [ʌn'stɔpt], *a.* **1.** (*a*) Débouché, dégorgé. (*b*) (*Of tooth*) To come unstopped, se déplomber. **2.** (Tuyau) non bouché ; ouvert.

unstrap [ʌn'strap], *v.tr.* (unstrapped [-strapt]) Déboucler (une malle).

unstressed [ʌn'strest], *a.* (*Of syllable*) Sans accent ; inaccentué ; atone.

unstring [ʌn'striŋ], *v.tr.* (*p.t. & p.p.* unstrung [-strʌŋ]) **1.** (*a*) Enlever les ficelles de (qch.). (*b*) Débander (un arc). **2.** Défiler, désenfiler (des perles). **3.** Ébranler, détraquer (les nerfs).

unstudied [ʌn'stʌdid], *a.* **1.** Unstudied in . . ., ignorant de. . . . **2.** (Style) inapprêté, sans apprêt ; (langage) naturel ; (charme) inétudié.

unsubdued [ʌnsʌb'dju:d], *a.* Non subjugué ; (*of horse, passion*) non maîtrisé ; indompté.

unsubmissive [ʌnsʌb'misiv], *a.* Insoumis, indocile.

unsubsidized [ʌn'sʌbsidaizd], *a.* Non subventionné ; sans subvention, sans prime.

unsubstantial [ʌnsʌb'stanʃ(ə)l], *a.* = INSUBSTANTIAL.

unsuccess [ʌnsʌk'ses], *s.* Insuccès *m* ; non-réussite *f*.

unsuccessful [ʌnsʌk'sesful], *a.* **1.** Non réussi ; vain. *U. attempt,* tentative sans succès ; *F:* coup manqué, raté. *The negotiations were u.,* les pourparlers n'ont pas abouti. **2.** (*Of pers.*) Qui n'a pas réussi ; qui a échoué ; (*of candidate*) refusé, (*at election*) non élu. To be unsuccessful, échouer ; ne pas réussir. **-fully,** *adv.* Sans succès ; vainement.

unsuitableness [ʌn'sju:təblnəs], *s.* **1.** Inaptitude *f* (de qn) (*to, for,* à) ; incapacité *f*. **2.** Disconvenance *f* (du climat, etc.) ; inopportunité *f* (d'une observation) ; caractère mal assorti (d'un mariage).

unsuitable [ʌn'sju:təbl], *a.* **1.** (*Of pers.*) Peu fait (*to, for,* pour) ; inapte (à). **2.** (*Of thg*) Impropre, mal adapté (à) ; (*of remark*) déplacé ; inopportun ; (*of marriage*) mal assorti. Suitable to the occasion, qui ne convient pas à la circonstance. **-ably,** *adv.* D'une manière qui ne convient pas. *U. matched,* mal assorti(s).

unsuited [ʌn'sju:tid], *a.* Unsuited to, for, sth., (*of pers.*) peu fait pour qch. ; inapte à qch. ; (*of thg*) impropre, mal adapté, mal approprié, à qch.

unsullied [ʌn'sʌlid], *a.* Sans souillure ; sans tache ; immaculé.

unsurpassed [ʌnsər'pɑ:st], *a.* Qui n'a jamais été surpassé ; sans égal, -aux ; sans pareil.

unsuspected [ʌnsʌs'pektid, 'ʌn-], *a.* Insoupçonné (*by,* de) ; (i) non suspect ; (ii) dont on ne soupçonnait pas l'existence.

~suspecting [ʌnsʌs'pektiŋ], *a.* **1.** Qui ne se ~te de rien ; sans soupçons ; sans défiance.

2. Naturally unsuspecting, peu soupçonneux. **-ly,** *adv.* Sans rien soupçonner ; sans défiance.

unsuspicious [ʌnsʌs'piʃəs], *a.* **1.** = UNSUSPECTING. **2.** To be unsuspicious of sth., ne pas se douter de qch.

unsweetened [ʌn'swi:t(ə)nd], *a.* Non sucré.

unswerving [ʌn'swə:rviŋ], *a.* **1.** Constant, ferme. **2.** *U. flight,* vol rectiligne, qui ne s'écarte pas de la ligne droite. To pursue an unswerving course, ne pas s'écarter de son chemin, du but. **-ly,** *adv.* Sans s'écarter du but.

unsymmetrical [ʌnsi'metrik(ə)l], *a.* Asymétrique.

unsympathetic [ʌnsimpə'θetik], *a.* Peu compatissant ; froid ; indifférent. **-ally,** *adv.* D'un air peu compatissant ; froidement.

unsystematic [ʌnsistə'matik], *a.* Sans système ; sans méthode. **-ally,** *adv.* Sans système ; sans méthode.

untainted [ʌn'teintid, 'ʌn-], *a.* Non gâté ; non corrompu ; (*of food*) frais, *f.* fraîche.

untalented [ʌn'taləntid], *a.* Sans talents.

untam(e)able [ʌn'teiməbl], *a.* Inapprivoisable ; indomptable.

untamed [ʌn'teimd], *a.* Inapprivoisé, sauvage ; indompté.

untapped [ʌn'tapt], *a.* (*Of barrel*) Non mis en perce. Untapped resources, ressources inutilisées.

untarnishable [ʌn'tɑ:rniʃəbl], *a.* Internissable.

untarnished [ʌn'tɑ:rniʃt], *a.* **1.** Non terni. **2.** (Réputation) sans tache, sans souillure.

untaught [ʌn'tɔ:t], *a.* (*a*) (*Of pers.*) Sans instruction ; illettré, ignorant. (*b*) (*Of skill*) Naturel.

unteachable [ʌn'ti:tʃəbl], *a.* (*Of pers.*) Incapable d'apprendre ; à qui l'on ne peut rien apprendre.

untearable [ʌn'tɛərəbl], *a.* Indéchirable.

untempting [ʌn'tem(p)tiŋ], *a.* Peu tentant. **1.** Peu appétissant. **2.** Peu séduisant ; peu attrayant.

untenable [ʌn'tenəbl], *a.* **1.** (*Of position*) Intenable. **2.** (*Of theory*) Insoutenable.

untenanted [ʌn'tenəntid], *a.* Sans locataire(s) ; inoccupé ; inhabité.

untested [ʌn'testid], *a.* Inessayé, inéprouvé ; qui n'a pas encore été mis à l'épreuve.

untether [ʌn'teðər], *v.tr.* Détacher (un cheval).

unthinkable [ʌn'θiŋkəbl], *a.* Inimaginable. *It is u. that he should be acquitted,* il est inconcevable qu'il soit acquitté.

unthinking [ʌn'θiŋkiŋ], *a.* Irréfléchi, étourdi. In an unthinking moment, dans un moment d'abstraction ; par étourderie. **-ly,** *adv.* Sans réflexion ; étourdiment ; (prendre un engagement) à la légère, à l'étourdie.

unthread [ʌn'θred], *v.tr.* Désenfiler (une aiguille, des perles).

untidiness [ʌn'taidinəs], *s.* Désordre *m* ; manque *m* d'ordre, de soin.

untidy [ʌn'taidi], *a.* (*a*) (*Of room*) En désordre ou mal tenu ; (*of hair*) ébouriffé ; mal peigné. Untidy dress, tenue négligée, débraillée. (*b*) (*Of pers.*) Qui manque d'ordre ; sans ordre ; sans soin. **-ily,** *adv.* Sans ordre, sans soin.

untie [ʌn'tai], *v.tr.* (untied ; untying) Dénouer (sa ceinture) ; défaire, délier (un nœud, un paquet) ; délier, détacher (un chien) ; déficeler (un paquet). To come untied, se défaire, se déficeler.

until [ʌn'til], *prep. & conj.* = TILL³.

untilled [ʌn'tild, 'ʌn-], *a.* (*Of land*) **1.** Inculte, incultivé. **2.** Non labouré ; en friche.

untimely[1] [ʌn'taimli], *a.* **1.** (*a*) Prématuré. To come to an untimely end, mourir avant l'âge. (*b*) (*Of fruit*) Précoce. **2.** (*Of rain, etc.*) Hors de saison. **3.** (*Of action*) Inopportun, intempestif, mal à propos. **4. At an untimely hour,** à une heure indue.

untimely² [ʌnˈtaɪmli], adv. **1.** Prématurément; avant l'heure. **2.** Inopportunément; mal à propos.

untinged [ʌnˈtɪndʒd], a. Sans teinte (with, de). *Joy* not untinged *with gloom*, joie mêlée de tristesse.

untiring [ʌnˈtaɪərɪŋ], a. Inlassable, infatigable; (travail) assidu. **-ly,** adv. Inlassablement, infatigablement.

unto [ˈʌntu], prep. A. & B.Lit: (= 'to' in certain uses) **1.** *Unto us a child is born,* un enfant nous est né. *To liken sth. unto sth.,* comparer qch. à, avec, qch. *To be like unto sth.,* ressembler à qch. *And I say unto you* . . ., et je vous dis. . . . *Let us unto our ships,* allons à nos vaisseaux. **2.** Vers. *To turn unto s.o.,* se tourner vers qn. *To come nigh unto sth.,* s'approcher de qch. **3.** Jusqu'à. *Unto this day,* jusqu'à ce jour même.

untold [ʌnˈtould], a. **1.** Non compté; (richesse, etc.) immense, énorme. *It is worth untold gold,* cela vaut une somme fabuleuse. *U. losses,* pertes incalculables. *U. suffering,* souffrances inouïes. **2.** *(Of tale, etc.)* Non raconté; passé sous silence.

untouchable [ʌnˈtʌtʃəbl], a. *(In India)* Hors caste. s. **The untouchables,** les hors-caste *mf*; les tchandals *m.*

untouched [ʌnˈtʌtʃt], a. **1.** *(a)* Non manié. *(b) He had left the food u.,* il n'avait pas touché à la nourriture. **2.** *(a)* To leave sth. untouched, laisser qch. intact. *(b) (Of pers.)* Sain et sauf. **3.** *(Of subject)* Untouched (upon), non mentionné; non discuté. **4.** *(Of pers.)* Non ému; indifférent; insensible (by, à).

untoward [ʌnˈtouərd], a. **1.** *(Of pers.)* Insoumis, indocile; rétif; *(of thg)* incommode; difficile (à façonner). **2.** (Événement) fâcheux, malencontreux, malheureux. **I hope nothing untoward has happened,** il n'est pas arrivé un malheur, j'espère. **3.** *(Of season)* Impropice. **4.** *(Of behaviour)* Malséant.

untraceable [ʌnˈtreisəbl], a. Introuvable.

untrained [ʌnˈtreɪnd, ˈʌn-], a. Inexpert, inexercé, inexpérimenté; (animal, domestique) non dressé, non formé.

untrammelled [ʌnˈtraməld], a. Sans entraves, sans contrainte; non empêtré (by, de); libre (by, de).

untransferable [ʌnˈtrɑːnsfərəbl], a. Intransférable. *Jur:* (Droit, propriété) incessible, inaliénable. *(On ticket)* Strictement personnel.

untranslatable [ʌntrɑːnsˈleitəbl], a. Intraduisible.

untravelled [ʌnˈtravəld], a. **1.** *(Of pers.)* Qui n'a jamais voyagé. **2.** (Pays) inexploré, peu connu.

untried [ʌnˈtraid], a. **1.** Inessayé; non essayé. *We will no remedy u.,* il n'y a pas de remède qu'on n'ait essayé. **2.** Qui n'a pas été mis à l'épreuve. *U. troops,* troupes qui n'ont pas encore vu le feu.

untrodden [ʌnˈtrɒd(ə)n], a. (Chemin) impratiqué, non frayé; (région) inexplorée. **Untrodden forest,** forêt vierge. *U. snow,* neige immaculée, vierge.

untroubled [ʌnˈtrʌbld], a. Calme, tranquille, paisible.

untrue [ʌnˈtruː], a. **1.** *(Of statement, etc.)* Faux, *f.* fausse; mensonger ou erroné; contraire à la vérité. **2.** *Tchn:* Inexact, faux; qui n'est pas juste. *U. grindstone,* meule gauchie. **3.** *(Of pers.)* Infidèle, déloyal, -aux (to, à).

untrustworthiness [ʌnˈtrʌstwəːðinəs], s. **1.** *(Of pers.)* Manque *m* de probité. **2.** Caractère douteux (d'un renseignement).

untrustworthy [ʌnˈtrʌstwəːði], a. **1.** *(Of pers.)*

Indigne de confiance; (témoin) récusable. *U. memory,* mémoire infidèle, peu sûre. **2.** (Renseignement) douteux, peu sûr, sujet à caution.

untruth [ˈʌntruːθ], s. Mensonge *m.* **To tell an untruth,** dire, faire, un mensonge.

untruthful [ʌnˈtruːθful], a. **1.** *(Of pers.)* Menteur; peu véridique. **2.** *(Of news, etc.)* Mensonger; faux, *f.* fausse; dénué de vérité. **-fully,** adv. Menteusement, mensongèrement.

untruthfulness [ʌnˈtruːθfulnəs], s. **1.** *(Of pers.)* Caractère menteur. **2.** Fausseté *f,* caractère mensonger (d'une histoire).

untuck [ʌnˈtʌk], v.tr. Déborder (un lit); détrousser (ses manches). *F: He untucked his legs from under him,* il déplia ses jambes de dessous lui.

untuned [ʌnˈtjuːnd], a. **1.** *Mus:* Non accordé; discordant. **2.** *F: (Of pers.)* Peu disposé (to, à).

untuneful [ʌnˈtjuːnful], a. Peu harmonieux.

unturned [ʌnˈtəːrnd], a. Non (re)tourné. *S.a.* STONE¹ **1.**

untutored [ʌnˈtjuːtərd], a. **1.** *(a)* Sans instruction; illettré, ignorant; (esprit, goût) non formé. *(b) To be u. in the art of* . . ., ignorer l'art de. . . . **2.** (Talent) naturel.

untwist [ʌnˈtwist], **1.** v.tr. Détordre (un cordage); détortiller. **To come untwisted,** se détordre; se détortiller. **2.** v.i. Se détordre; se détortiller.

unusable [ʌnˈjuːzəbl], a. Inutilisable.

unused [ʌnˈjuːzd], a. **1.** *(a)* (i) Inutilisé; non employé; (ii) hors d'usage. *U. building,* bâtiment inhabité. *(b)* Qui n'a pas encore servi; neuf ou à l'état de neuf. **2.** *(Of pers.)* Peu habitué, inhabitué (to, à). **To get unused to sth.,** se désaccoutumer, se déshabituer, de qch.

unusual [ʌnˈjuːʒuəl], a. *(a)* Peu commun; exceptionnel; insolite; qui sort de l'ordinaire. **It is unusual,** (i) cela se fait peu; (ii) c'n'est pas l'usage; (ii) cela se voit rarement. **Nothing unusual,** rien d'anormal. *(b)* (Mot) peu usité. **-ally,** adv. *U. tall,* d'une taille exceptionnelle. *He was u. attentive,* il s'est montré plus attentif que d'habitude.

unusualness [ʌnˈjuːʒuəlnəs], s. Nature exceptionnelle, extraordinaire, insolite (of, de); rareté *f.*

unutilized [ʌnˈjuːtilaizd], a. Inutilisé.

unutterable [ʌnˈʌtərəbl], a. Inexprimable, indicible. *F: U. fool,* parfait imbécile. **-ably,** adv. Indiciblement.

unvanquished [ʌnˈvaŋkwiʃt], a. Invaincu.

unvaried [ʌnˈvɛərid], a. Uniforme, constant; (nourriture) sans variété, qui manque de variété.

unvarnished [ʌnˈvɑːrniʃt], a. **1.** Non verni; *(of pottery)* non vernissé. *Plain u. wood,* bois cru. **2.** *F: (Of statement)* Simple. **To tell a plain unvarnished tale,** raconter les choses sans fard.

unvarying [ʌnˈvɛəriiŋ], a. Invariable; uniforme, constant.

unveil [ʌnˈveil], v.tr. Dévoiler. **To unveil a statue,** inaugurer une statue. **unveiling,** s. Inauguration *f* (d'une statue).

unverifiable [ʌnˈverifaiəbl], a. Invérifiable.

unverified [ʌnˈverifaid], a. Invérifié.

unversed [ʌnˈvəːrst], a. Peu versé (in, dans); ignorant (de).

unvoiced [ʌnˈvɔist], a. *Ling:* *(Of vowel, consonant)* Sourd, soufflé, dévoisé.

unwanted [ʌnˈwɒntid], a. **1.** Non désiré, non voulu. **2.** Superflu.

unwariness [ʌnˈwɛərinəs], s. Imprudence *f,* imprévoyance *f;* manque *m* de précaution.

unwarrantable [ʌnˈwɒrəntəbl], a. (Action) injustifiable, inexcusable; (assertion) insoutenable; (conduite) peu qualifiable.

unwarranted [ʌnˈwɒrəntid], a. **1.** Sans garantie.

2. Injustifié ; peu justifié ; inautorisé. *U. insult*, injure gratuite. *U. remark*, observation déplacée. *U. familiarities*, familiarités indues. **I should be unwarranted in supposing that . . .,** je serais mal venu à supposer que. . . .

unwary [ʌn'wɛəri], *a.* Imprudent, imprévoyant ; irréfléchi. **-ily,** *adv.* Imprudemment ; sans précaution.

unwashed [ʌn'wɔʃt], *a.* (*Of pers.*) Non lavé ; malpropre, sale. *s. F:* **The Great Unwashed,** les prolétaires ; les crasseux.

unwavering [ʌn'weivəriŋ], *a.* Constant, ferme, résolu. *U. fortitude*, fermeté qui ne se dément jamais. *U. policy*, politique ferme et suivie.

unwearied [ʌn'wiːərid], *a.* (*a*) Non fatigué. (*b*) Infatigable.

unwearying [ʌn'wiːəriiŋ], *a.* Inlassable, infatigable.

unwedge [ʌn'wedʒ], *v.tr.* **I.** Décaler (un meuble, etc.). **2.** Décoincer (une pièce, un mât).

unwelcome [ʌn'welkəm], *a.* (*a*) (Visiteur) mal venu, importun. *A not unwelcome visit*, une visite opportune. (*b*) Unwelcome news, nouvelle fâcheuse, désagréable. *A not u. addition to our stores*, un surcroît de provisions très utile.

unwell [ʌn'wel], *a.* Indisposé ; souffrant.

unwholesome [ʌn'houlsəm], *a.* (*a*) (Aliment) malsain ; (climat) insalubre ; (air) vicié. (*b*) *U. doctrines*, doctrines malsaines, pernicieuses.

unwieldiness [ʌn'wiːldinəs], *s.* Lourdeur *f* ; pesanteur *f* (d'un colis, etc.).

unwieldy [ʌn'wiːldi], *a.* **I.** (*Of pers.*) Lourd, gauche ; à la démarche lourde. **2.** (Outil, colis) peu portatif ; peu maniable ; incommode à porter ou à manier.

unwilling [ʌn'wiliŋ], *a.* **I.** Inserviable ; de mauvaise volonté. **2. To be unwilling to do sth.,** être peu disposé à faire qch. *U. acquiescence*, assentiment donné à contre-cœur. **I was unwilling for my wife to accept the invitation,** je ne voulais pas que ma femme acceptât l'invitation. **-ly,** *adv.* A contre-cœur ; de mauvais cœur, de mauvaise grâce ; à regret.

unwillingness [ʌn'wiliŋnəs], *s.* **I.** Mauvaise volonté ; manque *m* de bonne volonté. **2.** Répugnance *f* (à faire qch.).

unwind [ʌn'waind], *v.tr.* (unwound [ʌn'waund]) Dérouler. *Tex:* Dévider (un cocon). *El:* Débobiner (une bobine). **To come unwound,** se dérouler.

unwise [ʌn'waiz], *a.* **I.** (*Of pers.*) Imprudent ; peu prudent, peu circonspect ; malavisé. **2.** (*Of action*) Peu sage ; malavisé. **-ly,** *adv.* Imprudemment.

unwitting [ʌn'witiŋ], *a.* **I.** Inconscient (*of*, de). **2.** (*Of action*) Fait sans dessein. **-ly,** *adv.* Sans le savoir ; sans le vouloir ; inconsciemment.

unwomanly [ʌn'wumənli], *a.* Peu féminin ; peu digne d'une femme.

unwonted [ʌn'wountid], *a.* Inaccoutumé, inhabituel ; (événement) peu commun, insolite.

unworkable [ʌn'wəːkəbl], *a.* **I.** (Projet) inexécutable, impraticable. **2.** (*a*) *Min:* (Gisement) inexploitable. (*b*) *U. material*, matière rebelle.

unworked [ʌn'wəːkt], *a.* **I.** (Métal, etc.) non ouvré, non travaillé. **2.** *Min:* (Gisement) inexploité.

unworldly [ʌn'wəːrldli], *a.* **I.** (*a*) Peu mondain ; détaché de ce monde. (*b*) Simple, candide. **2.** Céleste ; (beauté) qui n'est pas de ce monde.

unworthiness [ʌn'wəːrðinəs], *s.* **I.** Peu *m* de mérite (de qn). **2.** Caractère *m* méprisable, peu digne (d'une action).

unworthy [ʌn'wəːrði], *a.* Indigne. **I. Unworthy of sth., to do sth.,** indigne de qch., de faire qch. *U. of notice*, qui ne mérite pas qu'on y fasse attention. **2.** (Conduite) méprisable. **3.** (Travail) peu méritoire.

unwounded [ʌn'wuːndid], *a.* Non blessé ; sans blessure ; indemne ; sain et sauf.

unwrap [ʌn'rap], *v.tr.* (unwrapped) Défaire, désenvelopper (un paquet) ; enlever l'enveloppe de (qch.).

unwrinkled [ʌn'riŋkld], *a.* Sans rides ; lisse. *U. forehead*, front uni.

unwritten [ʌn'rit(ə)n], *a.* Non écrit ; inécrit ; (*of tradition*) oral, -aux. *F:* **The unwritten law,** (i) le droit coutumier ; *esp.* (ii) le droit de tuer pour venger son honneur ou celui d'une femme.

unwrought [ʌn'rɔːt], *a.* (Métal, etc.) brut, non ouvré, non façonné.

unyielding [ʌn'jiːldiŋ], *a.* Qui ne cède pas ; raide, ferme ; (*of pers.*) inébranlable, opiniâtre ; inflexible. *U. grip*, prise indesserrable.

unyoke [ʌn'jouk], *v.tr.* (*a*) Dételer, découpler (des bœufs). (*b*) *Abs. F:* Cesser le travail ; *F:* dételer.

up¹ [ʌp]. **I.** *adv.* **I.** (*a*) En montant ; vers le haut. **To go up,** monter. **Up went his stick,** il leva son bâton. **My room is three flights up,** ma chambre est au troisième palier. **To throw sth. up (in the air),** jeter qch. en l'air. **All the way up,** jusqu'au haut (de la colline, etc.) ; jusqu'en haut (de l'escalier). **Half-way up,** jusqu'à mi-hauteur. *S.a.* HAND¹ **I.** (*b*) **To walk up and down,** se promener de long en large. **To go up north,** aller dans le nord. **To go up to town,** aller à la capitale ; se rendre à Londres. **To go up to the university,** aller à l'université. **To go up for an examination,** se présenter à un examen. (*c*) *Nau:* **Hard up with the helm!** la barre au vent toute ! (*d*) **From five pounds up,** à partir de cinq livres. **From my youth up,** dès ma jeunesse. **2.** (*a*) Haut ; en haut. *What are you doing up there?* que faites-vous là-haut ? **Up above,** en haut. **Up above sth.,** au-dessus de qch. **The moon is up,** la lune est levée. *Bill:* **Game of a hundred up,** partie en cent. **The blinds are up,** on a relevé les stores. *The shops had their shutters up,* les magasins avaient leurs volets mis. *Turf:* **Comet with Jones up,** Comet monté par Jones. **The tide is up,** la marée est haute. **'Road up,'** "route en réfection, en réparation." (*b*) En dessus. **Face up,** face en dessus. *On packing-case:* **This side up,** haut ; dessus ; ne pas renverser. (*c*) **Up in London,** à Londres. **Up in Yorkshire,** au nord, dans le Yorkshire. *Relations up from the country,* parents de province en visite à la ville. **3.** (*a*) **To go up in price,** subir une hausse de prix. **Bread is up again,** le pain a encore augmenté. **The thermometer has gone up,** le thermomètre a monté, haussé. **To be one game up,** être en avance d'une partie. *Fb:* **To be one goal up,** mener par un but. (*b*) **To screw up,** visser, serrer (un tourniquet, etc.). *Mch:* **Steam is up,** nous sommes sous pression. **His blood was up,** il était monté ; le sang lui bouillait. (*c*) **To be well up in a subject,** connaître un sujet à fond ; être versé dans une matière. *To be well up in geography,* être fort, *F:* calé, en géographie. (*d*) (*Intensive*) **To praise s.o.,** vanter, prôner, qn. **To speak up,** parler plus fort, plus haut. **Sing up!** plus fort ! **4.** *Put it up beside, close up to, the other one,* mettez-le tout près de l'autre. **To follow s.o. up,** suivre qn de près. **To be up with sth.,** être au niveau de qch. **He came up with me,** il me rejoignit. **5.** (a) Debout, levé. **To get up,** (*from bed*) se lever; (*from seat*) se lever, se mettre debout. **To be up and a)out,** être sur pied. **Let us be up and doing,** mettons-nous à la besogne. **Hold yourself up!** tenez-vous droit! **Up, guards!** debout, les gardes ! (b) *At midnight I was still up,* à minuit je n'étais pas encore couché. **To be up all night,** ne pas se coucher de la nuit. **To stay, wait, up,** veiller. (c) **You are up against a strong man,** vous avez affaire à forte partie. **To be up against difficulties,** se heurter à, être aux prises avec, des difficultés. *F :* **To be up against it,** avoir la déveine, la guigne. **6.** (a) **To stir up** sediment, remuer, agiter, un dépôt. **To be up in arms, in revolt,** être en révolte. (b) *F :* **What's up?** que se passe-t-il? qu'y a-t-il? de quoi retourne-t-il? **There is something up,** il y a quelque chose. **What's up with you?** qu'est-ce qui vous prend? **7. Time is up,** il est l'heure (de finir, de fermer). **His time is up,** il a fini son temps (de service militaire, etc.). **His leave is up,** sa permission est expirée. *F :* **The game is up,** it's all up, tout est perdu. **It's all up with him,** son affaire est faite ; *P :* il est fichu, flambé. *I thought it was all up with me,* j'ai pensé mourir. **8. Up to.** (a) *They advanced up to the walls of the city,* ils s'avancèrent jusque devant les murs de la ville. **To come, go, up to s.o.,** s'approcher de, s'avancer vers, qn. **I am up to you,** je vous ai rattrapé. **To blush up to the ears,** rougir jusqu'aux oreilles. *S.a.* EAR¹ I, NECK I. (b) **Up to now, up to here,** jusqu'ici. **Up to this day,** jusqu'à ce jour. **Up to £500,** jusqu'à concurrence de 500 livres. **To live up to one's income,** dépenser tout son revenu. (c) **To be up to sth.,** être capable de qch. *F :* **She is up to anything,** elle n'a pas froid aux yeux. **To be up to a job,** être à la hauteur d'une tâche. **I don't feel up to it,** je ne m'en sens pas le courage, la force. **To be up to s.o., to s.o.'s tricks,** être de force à lutter avec qn. (d) **What are you up to?** qu'est-ce que vous faites? qu'est-ce que vous mijotez? **He is up to something,** il a quelque chose en tête. (e) *F :* **It is up to him to . . .,** c'est à lui de . . . ; c'est affaire à lui de. . . . *It's up to you to accept,* il ne tient qu'à vous d'accepter. **II. up,** *prep.* **1. To go up the stairs, a hill,** monter l'escalier, une colline. *The cat is up the tree,* le chat est en haut de l'arbre. **2.** (a) **Up the river,** en remontant le fleuve ; en amont. **Further up the street,** plus loin dans la rue. **To walk up and down the platform,** faire les cent pas sur le quai ; arpenter le quai. (b) **Up the yard,** au fond de la cour. *S.a.* COUNTRY 1, STAGE¹ 2. **III. up,** *attrib.a.* **Up motion,** mouvement de montée. *Rail :* **Up line,** voie descendante, paire ; la voie en direction de Londres. **Up train,** train descendant, de retour. **IV. up,** *s.* **Ups and downs,** ondulations *f* (du terrain). *F :* **The ups and downs of life,** les vicissitudes *f*, les péripéties *f*, de la vie. **A life of ups and downs,** une vie cahotée, mouvementée. **'up-and-down,** *attrib.a.* Up-and-down motion, (i) mouvement de haut en bas et de bas en haut ; (ii) jeu vertical (d'une pièce). **up-'end,** *v.tr.* Dresser (qch.) debout ; mettre (un tonneau) à cul. **'up-grade. 1.** *s.* Pente ascendante ; rampe *f*, montée *f* (d'une route). *F :* **To be on the up-grade,** (i) (*of prices*) monter ; tendre à la hausse ; (ii) (*of business*) reprendre, se relever. **2.** *Attrib.a.* (Traction, etc.) en rampe. **'up-'river. 1.** *Attrib.a.* D'amont. **2.** *adv.* En amont. **'up-'stream. 1.** *adv.* (a) En amont. (b) En remontant le courant ; à contre-fil de l'eau. **2.** *Attrib.a.* (a) (Bief, etc.) d'amont.

(b) (Vent) d'aval. **'up-stroke,** *s.* **1.** (*In writing*) Délié *m.* **2.** (*Of violin bow*) Poussé *m.* **3.** *Mch :* Course ascendante, levée *f* (du piston). **'up-to-date,** *attrib.a.* *F :* **1.** (*Of pers.*) Moderne ; de son temps ; *F :* à la page. **2.** Au goût du jour ; moderne. **Up-to-date hat,** chapeau dernier cri, à la mode. *More up-to-d. model,* modèle plus nouveau. *S.a.* DATE².

up², *v.* (upped) **1.** *v.tr.* (a) **To up the swans,** recenser les cygnes. (b) *F :* Lever (son bâton, etc.). **2.** *v.i.* *F :* **He ups with his stick,** il lève son bâton.

upas ['ju:pəs], *s.* *Bot :* Upas *m.*

upbeat ['ʌpbiːt], *s.* *Mus :* Levé *m* ; temps *m* faible.

upbraid [ʌp'breid], *v.tr.* Reprocher, faire des reproches à (qn). **To upbraid s.o. with, for, sth.,** reprocher vertement qch. à qn.

upbringing ['ʌpbriŋiŋ], *s.* Éducation *f* (d'un enfant). *What sort of (an) u. has he had?* comment a-t-il été élevé?

upheaval [ʌp'hiːv(ə)l], *s.* **1.** *Geol :* (a) Soulèvement *m.* (b) Commotion *f*, bouleversement *m.* **2.** *F :* Bouleversement, agitation *f*. **Political upheaval,** convulsion *f* politique.

up(-)hill. 1. *a.* ['ʌphil] (a) (*Of road, etc.*) Montant ; en rampe. (b) (*Of task*) Ardu, rude. **2.** *adv.* [ʌp'hil] **To go uphill,** monter ; aller en montant. *S.a.* HILL 1.

uphold [ʌp'hould], *v.tr.* (upheld [-held] ; upheld) Supporter, soutenir, maintenir. **To uphold the law,** faire observer la loi. **To uphold s.o.** (*in an action*), prêter son appui à qn. **To uphold a decision,** confirmer une décision.

upholder [ʌp'houldər], *s.* Partisan *m* (d'un usage, etc.) ; défenseur *m* (d'une opinion).

upholster [ʌp'houlstər], *v.tr.* (i) Capitonner, garnir, rembourrer, (ii) tapisser, couvrir (un canapé, etc.) (*with, in,* de).

upholsterer [ʌp'houlstərər], *s.* Tapissier *m* (en ameublement).

upholstery [ʌp'houlstəri], *s.* **1.** Capitonnage *m*, rembourrage *m* (d'un fauteuil, etc.). **2.** (i) Tapisserie *f* d'ameublement ; (ii) garniture *f* d'intérieur (d'une voiture). **Leather upholstery,** garniture en cuir. **3.** Métier *m* de tapissier ; tapisserie.

upkeep ['ʌpkiːp], *s.* (Frais *mpl* d')entretien *m.*

upland ['ʌplənd]. **1.** *s.* *Usu. pl.* Région montagneuse (de l'intérieur). **The uplands,** le haut pays ; les hautes terres. **2.** *Attrib.a.* (Village, etc.) des montagnes.

uplander ['ʌpləndər], *s.* Montagnard, -arde.

uplift¹ ['ʌplift], *s.* **1.** Élévation *f* (du terrain). *Geol :* Soulèvement *m.* **2.** *F :* Moral uplift, élévation morale.

uplift² [ʌp'lift], *v.tr.* **1.** Soulever, élever (qch.) ; hausser (les sourcils). **2.** *F :* Élever (l'âme, la voix).

upon [ə'pɔn], *prep.* = ON I.

upper ['ʌpər]. **I.** *a.* **1.** (a) Supérieur, -eure ; (plus) haut, (plus) élevé ; de dessus ; d'au-dessus. **The upper jaw,** la mâchoire supérieure. **Upper part of sth.,** dessus *m* de qch. *S.a.* DECK¹ 1, LIP 1. (b) **Upper end of a hall,** fond *m* d'une salle. **Upper waters of a river,** amont *m* d'une rivière. **The upper Rhine,** le haut Rhin. **Upper Egypt,** la Haute-Égypte. **2.** Supérieur (en rang, etc.). **Upper end of the table,** haut bout de la table. *Parl :* **The upper House,** la Chambre Haute. **The upper classes,** *F :* the upper ten (thousand), les hautes classes ; *F :* la haute volée. **To get, gain, have, the upper hand,** prendre, avoir, le dessus ; prédominer, prévaloir ; *F :* tenir la corde. *To allow s.o. to get the u. hand,* se laisser tyranniser, subjuguer, par qn. **To get the upper hand of s.o.,** avoir raison de qn. *Sch:* The upper forms, les grandes classes. II. **uppers,** *s.pl. Bootm:* (a) Empeignes f. (b) Tiges f (de bottes). *F:* **To be (down) on one's uppers,** être dans la débine, dans la dèche.

uppermost ['ʌpərmoust]. **1.** a. (a) Le plus haut, le plus élevé. (b) De la plus grande importance; premier. **To be uppermost,** prédominer; tenir le premier rang; avoir l'avantage. **2.** adv. (a) (Le plus) en dessus. **Face uppermost,** face en dessus. (b) **His friend's fate was uppermost in his thoughts,** le sort de son ami occupait la première place dans ses pensées.

uppish ['ʌpiʃ], a. *F:* Présomptueux, arrogant, rogue; suffisant. **Don't be so uppish!** ne le prenez pas de si haut!

uppishness ['ʌpiʃnəs], s. *F:* Présomption f, arrogance f; suffisance f.

upright ['ʌprait]. I. a. **1.** Vertical, -aux; perpendiculaire; droit. **Upright joint,** joint montant. **To set sth. upright,** mettre qch. debout, d'aplomb. 'To be kept upright,' "tenir debout." *Sitting up on his chair,* assis raide sur sa chaise. **2.** (*Of conduct*) Droit, intègre, honnête, probe. **-ly,** adv. Avec droiture; intègrement, honnêtement. II. **upright,** s. **1. Out of upright,** hors d'aplomb. **2.** *Const:* Montant m; pied-droit m, pl. pieds-droits; jambage m. *Fb:* **The uprights,** les montants de but.

uprightness ['ʌpraitnəs], s. Droiture f, intégrité f, rectitude f, honnêteté f.

uprising [ʌp'raiziŋ], s. **1.** Lever m (de qn). **2.** Soulèvement m (du peuple); insurrection f.

uproar ['ʌprɔːər], s. Vacarme m, tapage m, grand bruit; *F:* chahut m, bacchanal m. **The town is in an uproar,** la ville est en tumulte, en rumeur.

uproarious [ʌp'rɔːəriəs], a. Tumultueux, tapageur. **To burst into u. laughter,** partir d'un grand éclat de rire. **-ly,** adv. Tumultueusement. *S.a.* LAUGH¹ 1.

uproot [ʌp'ruːt], v.tr. Déraciner, extirper, arracher (une plante, *F:* un mal). **To uproot s.o. from his home,** arracher qn de son foyer.

uprush ['ʌprʌʃ], s. Montée soudaine (d'eau, etc.).

upset¹ ['ʌpset], s. **1.** Renversement m (d'une voiture); chavirement m (d'un bateau). **2.** (a) Désorganisation f, bouleversement m, désordre m; remue-ménage m inv. (b) Anicroche f, ennui m. (c) Bouleversement (d'esprit). *She has had a dreadful u.,* elle vient d'essuyer un coup terrible. (d) Dérangement m (de corps).

upset² [ʌp'set], v. (upset; upset; upsetting) I. v.tr. (a) Renverser (un vase, etc.); (faire) verser (une voiture); (faire) chavirer (un bateau); culbuter (qn). (b) Désorganiser, bouleverser, déranger (les plans de qn); tromper (les calculs de qn). (c) Troubler, bouleverser, démonter (qn); mettre (qn) en émoi. **He is easily upset,** il s'émeut d'un rien. **Don't upset yourself,** ne vous laissez pas émouvoir; ne vous impressionnez pas. (d) Indisposer (qn); dérégler, déranger (l'estomac); troubler (la digestion). **Beer upsets me,** la bière me rend malade, ne me vaut rien. **2.** v.i. (*Of cup, etc.*) Se renverser; (*of carriage*) verser; (*of boat*) chavirer. **upset**³, a. **1.** (a) Bouleversé, ému. *Don't be so u.,* ne vous désolez pas comme cela. **To get upset,** se laisser démonter. *He looked very much u.,* il avait le visage renversé, défait. (b) **My digestion is upset,** j'ai l'estomac dérangé. **2.** (*At auction*) Upset ['ʌpset] price, mise f à prix; prix de départ; prix demandé.

upshot ['ʌpʃot], s. Résultat m, issue f, dénouement m (d'une affaire, etc.). **What will be the**

---

upshot of it? à quoi cela aboutira-t-il? quelle en sera l'issue?

upside down ['ʌpsaid'daun]. **1.** adv.phr. (a) Sens dessus dessous; la tête en bas. *He was holding the barometer u. d.,* il tenait le baromètre renversé, à l'envers. (b) *F:* En désordre; bouleversé. **To turn everything upside down,** tout bouleverser; tout mettre sens dessus dessous. **2.** a. Renversé. *U.-d. ideas,* idées biscornues, paradoxales.

upsides ['ʌpsaidz], adv. *F:* **To get upsides with s.o.,** prendre sa revanche.

upstairs [ʌp'stɛərz]. **1.** adv. En haut (de l'escalier). **To go upstairs,** monter (l'escalier); aller en haut. **To call s.o. u.,** faire monter qn. **2.** a. (*Of room, etc.*) D'en haut; situé à l'étage supérieur.

upstanding ['ʌpstandiŋ], a. **1.** Debout inv; (*of hair, etc.*) dressé, hérissé. *A fine u. fellow,* un gaillard bien campé. **2.** *F:* (*Of pers.*) Honnête, probe, sincère. **3.** (*Of wages*) Fixe; qui ne varie pas.

upstart ['ʌpstɑːt], s. Nouveau riche; parvenu, -ue.

upsweep ['ʌpswiːp], s. *Aut:* Surélévation f (du châssis).

upswept ['ʌpswept], a. Qui remonte en courbe; *Aut:* (châssis) surélevé.

uptake ['ʌpteik], s. **1.** *Scot. & F:* **To be slow in the uptake,** avoir la compréhension difficile. *He is quick in the u.,* il a l'esprit vif, éveillé. **2.** Uptake pipe, tuyau ascendant, montant. *Min:* Uptake (shaft), puits m de retour d'air.

upthrow ['ʌpθrou], s. *Geol:* Rejet m en haut.

upthrust ['ʌpθrʌst], s. *Geol:* Soulèvement m.

upturned ['ʌptəːrnd], a. (Bord) relevé; (nez) retroussé; (yeux) tournés vers le ciel. *I looked into the child's upturned face,* je regardai le visage que l'enfant levait vers moi.

upward ['ʌpwərd]. **1.** a. Upward movement, mouvement ascensionnel; ascendant. **Upward gradient,** rampe f. **Prices show an upward tendency,** les prix sont à la hausse. **2.** adv. = UPWARDS. *Faces turned u.,* visages levés vers le ciel.

upwards ['ʌpwərdz], adv. **1.** De bas en haut; vers le haut; en montant. **The road runs upwards,** la route va en montant. **2.** En dessus. *To lay sth. face upwards on the table,* mettre qch. à l'endroit sur la table. **To look upwards,** regarder en haut, en l'air. **3.** Au-dessus. **£100 and upwards,** cent livres et au-dessus, et au delà. **Upwards of fifty pupils,** plus de cinquante élèves. **From ten years of age upwards,** à partir de dix ans.

uraemia [juˈriːmia], s. *Med:* Urémie f.

Ural ['juərəl]. *Pr.n.* The Ural (river), l'Oural m. **The Ural mountains,** les monts Ourals.

uranium [juˈreiniəm], s. *Ch:* Uranium m. **Uranium oxide,** urane m.

urban ['əːrbən], a. Urbain.

urbane [əːrˈbein], a. Courtois, poli, civil. **-ly,** adv. Courtoisement; avec urbanité.

urbanity [əːrˈbaniti], s. Urbanité f; courtoisie f.

urbanization [əːrbənaiˈzeiʃ(ə)n], s. Aménagement m et assainissement m des agglomérations urbaines.

urchin ['əːrtʃin], s. **1.** *F:* (a) Galopin, gamin; petit polisson. (b) Gosse m f; marmot m; *P:* moutard m. **2.** = SEA-URCHIN.

Urdu ['uərduː], s. *Ling:* L'ourdou m.

urea ['juəriə], s. *Ch:* Urée f.

ureter [juˈriːtər], s. *Anat:* Uretère m.

urethra [juˈriːθra], s. *Anat:* Urètre m.

urge[1] [əːrdʒ], *s.* Incitation *f*, impulsion *f*; poussée *f*. **To feel an urge to do sth.**, se sentir poussé à faire qch. *U. to write*, démangeaison *f* d'écrire.

urge[2], *v.tr.* **1.** (*a*) **To urge s.o. (on)**, encourager, exhorter, exciter, qn. **To urge a horse forward, on**, pousser, animer, talonner, un cheval. **To urge s.o. to do sth.**, pousser, exhorter, qn à faire qch.; prier instamment qn de faire qch. (*b*) Hâter, pousser; activer (le feu). **To urge on, forward, a piece of work**, hâter, activer, un travail. **2.** Mettre en avant, alléguer, objecter (une raison); faire valoir (une excuse); insister sur (un point). **3.** Conseiller fortement, recommander (une démarche). **To urge that sth. should be done**, insister pour que qch. se fasse.

urgency [ˈəːrdʒənsi], *s.* **1.** Urgence *f*; extrémité *f* (d'un besoin). **2.** Besoin pressant; nécessité urgente.

urgent [ˈəːrdʒənt], *a.* **1.** Urgent, pressant. *U. need*, besoin pressant. *The matter is u.*, l'affaire presse. *It is most urgent that the doctor should come*, il y a grande urgence à ce que le docteur vienne. *U. entreaty*, prière instante. **2.** *They were u. for him to start at once*, ils ont beaucoup insisté pour qu'il parte aussitôt. **-ly**, *adv.* Avec urgence; avec instance. *A doctor is u. required*, on demande instamment un médecin.

uric [ˈjuərik], *a.* (Acide, etc.) urique.

urinal [ˈjuərin(ə)l], *s.* **1.** *Med:* Bed urinal, urinal *m*, -aux. **2.** Urinoir *m*.

urine [ˈjuərin], *s.* Urine *f*.

urn [əːrn], *s.* **1.** Urne *f*. **2.** (Tea-)urn, fontaine *f* (à thé).

urticaceae [əːrtiˈkeisiiː], *s.pl.* Urticacées *f*.

urticaria [əːrtiˈkɛəriə], *s. Med:* Urticaire *f*.

urus [ˈjuərəs], *s.* *Z:* Urus *m*, aurochs *m*.

us [ʌs], *pers.pron.*, *objective case.* **1.** (*a*) Nous. *He sees us*, il nous voit. *Give us some*, donnez-nous-en. *There are three of us*, nous sommes trois. (*b*) (*Refl.*) *We will take the boxes with us*, nous prendrons les boîtes avec nous. **2.** (*Stressed*) Nous. *Between you and us*, entre vous et nous. *You cannot deceive 'us engineers*, on ne peut pas nous tromper, nous autres ingénieurs. **3.** (*Stressed: as a nominative*) *F:* *He would not believe that it was us*, il ne voulait pas croire que c'était nous. **4.** (*With sg. meaning*, = *me*) (*a*) (*Of majesty*) Nous. *Cf.* WE 2. (*b*) *F:* Let us, let's, have a look, laissez-moi regarder.

usable [ˈjuːzəbl], *a.* Utilisable.

usage [ˈjuːzedʒ], *s.* **1.** (*Usu. pej.*) Traitement *m*. *Book damaged by rough u.*, livre qui a été maltraité. *His usage of me*, sa manière d'agir envers moi. **2.** (*a*) Usage *m*, coutume, *f*; pratique consacrée. (*b*) *Jur:* Droit *m* de passage. **3.** Emploi *m*, usage (d'un mot, etc.).

usance [ˈjuːz(ə)ns], *s.* *Com:* Usance *f*.

use[1] [juːs], *s.* **1.** (*a*) Emploi *m*, usage *m*. *A new use for wireless*, une nouvelle utilisation de la radio. **To find a use for sth.**, trouver un moyen de se servir de qch. **To make use of sth.**, se servir de qch.; faire usage de qch.; tirer parti, tirer profit, de qch. **To make good, bad, use of sth.**; put sth. to good use, to (a) bad use, faire bon usage, mauvais usage, de qch. *To put advice to use*, profiter d'un conseil. **To put an article into use**, mettre un article en usage. **Article of everyday use**, article d'usage courant. **Word in everyday use**, mot très usité. **Not in use**, hors d'usage. *Machine that has been in use for ten years*, machine qui sert depuis dix ans. **Out of use**, hors de service; hors d'usage; (mot) désuet, tombé en désuétude. **Fit for use**, en état

de servir. **Ready for use**, prêt à servir. **For the use of schools**, à l'usage des écoles. '**Directions for use**,' "mode *m* d'emploi." (*b*) **To improve with use**, s'améliorer à l'usage. **2.** Jouissance *f*, usage. (*a*) **To have the full use of one's faculties**, jouir de toutes ses facultés. *He has lost the use of his left leg*, il est impotent de la jambe gauche. (*b*) **To have the use of the bathroom**, avoir l'usage, le droit de faire usage, de la salle de bains. *I should like to have the use of it*, je voudrais pouvoir en disposer. (*c*) *Jur:* Full right of use of sth., plein usufruit de qch.; pleine jouissance de qch. **3.** Utilité *f*. **To be of use (for sth.)**, être utile (à qch.). **Can I be of any use (to you)?** puis-je vous être utile en rien? *It is of no use*, cela ne sert à rien. *That will be of little use*, of great use, cela ne servira pas à grand'chose; cela sera d'une grande utilité. *F:* My servant is no use, ma bonne est incapable. **To have no use for sth.**, n'avoir que faire, ne savoir que faire, de qch. **To have no further use for sth.**, n'avoir plus besoin de qch. **It is no use discussing the question**, rien ne sert de, inutile de, discuter la question. *It is no use his writing to me*, il est inutile qu'il m'écrive. **What's the use of, in, making plans?** à quoi sert de faire des projets? à quoi bon faire des projets? **4.** Usage, coutume *f*, habitude *f*. **According to use and wont**, suivant l'usage; selon l'usage. *He called as was his use*, il était venu comme de coutume.

use[2] [juːz], *v.tr.* **1.** (*a*) Employer, se servir de (qch.). *Are you using this knife?* vous servez-vous de ce couteau? (*Of thg*) To be used for sth., servir à qch.; être employé à qch. *I used the money to rebuild my house*, j'ai utilisé l'argent à rebâtir ma maison. *Word no longer used*, mot désuet. *Book no longer used*, livre hors d'usage. **To use sth. as, for, sth.**, employer qch. comme qch. *I use that as a hammer*, cela me sert de marteau. **You may use my name (as a reference)**, vous pouvez vous réclamer de moi. (*b*) **To use force**, user de force. **To use discretion**, agir avec discrétion. **To use every means**, mettre en œuvre tous les moyens. **To use one's influence**, user de son influence. **2.** **To use s.o. well, ill**, en user bien, mal, avec qn; bien, mal, agir envers qn. **To use s.o. roughly**, maltraiter, rudoyer, qn. **3.** **To use sth. (up).** (*a*) User, épuiser, qch. **To use up all one's provisions**, consommer toutes ses provisions. *It is all used up*, il n'en reste plus. (*b*) **To use up the scraps**, tirer parti des restes. (*c*) **To use up one's horse**, surmener, épuiser, son cheval. **4.** (*As aux., only in p.t.; often translated by imperfect.*) *As children we used* [juːst] *to play together*, quand nous étions petits nous jouions ensemble. *I used to do it*, j'avais 'habitude, j'avais coutume, de le faire. *Things aren't what they used to be*, ce n'est plus comme autrefois. *You don't practise as much as you used to*, vous ne vous exercez pas autant que vous en aviez l'habitude. *She used not to like tobacco*, autrefois elle n'aimait pas le tabac. **used**, *a.* **1.** [juːzd] Usagé; (timbre-poste) oblitéré. **Used cars**, voitures d'occasion. **Hardly used**, à l'état de neuf. **2.** [juːst] To be used to sth., to doing sth., être habitué, accoutumé, à qch., à faire qch. *I am not used to it*, je n'en ai pas l'habitude. **To get used to sth.**, s'habituer, s'accoutumer, à qch. *You will get u. to it in time*, vous vous y ferez à la longue.

useful [ˈjuːsful], *a.* **1.** Utile; (vêtement, etc.) pratique. *This book was very u. to me*, ce livre m'a été d'une grande utilité, m'a rendu grand service. **To make oneself useful**, se rendre utile.

2. (*a*) *P:* *He's pretty u. with his fists,* il sait se servir de ses poings. (*b*) *F:* *He made a u. goalkeeper,* il s'est très bien acquitté comme gardien de but. **-fully,** *adv.* Utilement.

usefulness ['ju:sfulnəs], *s.* Utilité *f.*

useless ['ju:sləs], *a.* **1.** Inutile; bon à rien; (effort) vain. **To be useless,** ne servir à rien. *U. regrets,* regrets superflus. *U. remedy,* remède inefficace. **2.** *F:* **To feel useless,** se sentir mal en train, avachi. **-ly,** *adv.* Inutilement; en vain, en pure perte.

uselessness ['ju:sləsnəs], *s.* Inutilité *f.*

user[1] ['ju:zər], *s.* **1.** Usager, -ère (d'une bicyclette, etc.). **2.** *Jur:* Usufruitier *m.*

user[2], *s.* *Jur:* Droit *m* d'usage continu. **Full right of user of sth.,** plein usufruit de qch.

usher[1] ['ʌʃər], *s.* **1.** (*a*) (Gentleman) **usher,** huissier *m*; introducteur *m* (à une réception). (*b*) **Theatre usher,** ouvreuse *f.* (*c*) (*At wedding*) *The ushers,* les garçons d'honneur. **2.** *Sch:* *A:* Surveillant *m* d'études; *F:* pion *m.*

usher[2], *v.tr.* **To usher s.o. in, into a drawing-room,** introduire qn, faire entrer qn, dans un salon. *F:* **To usher in a new epoch,** inaugurer une époque. **To usher s.o. out,** reconduire qn (jusqu'à la porte).

usherette [ʌʃə'ret], *s.f.* *Cin:* Ouvreuse.

usual ['ju:ʒuəl], *a.* Usuel, habituel, ordinaire. *At the u. hour,* à l'heure accoutumée. *The u. terms,* les conditions d'usage. **It is usual to pay in advance,** il est d'usage de payer d'avance. *It is the u. practice,* c'est la pratique courante. **Earlier than usual,** plus tôt que de coutume, que d'habitude, que d'ordinaire. **As usual,** comme à l'ordinaire, comme d'ordinaire, comme d'habitude; comme d'usage. **-ally,** *adv.* Ordinairement, habituellement; d'ordinaire, d'habitude; à l'ordinaire. **He was more than usually polite,** il s'est montré encore plus poli que d'habitude.

usufruct ['ju:zjufrʌkt], *s.* *Jur:* Usufruit *m* (*of,* de).

usufructuary [ju:zju'frʌktjuəri], *a. & s.* *Jur:* Usufruitier, -ière.

usurer ['ju:ʒurər], *s.* Usurier *m.*

usurious [ju'ʒuəriəs], *a.* **1.** (Intérêt) usuraire. **2.** (Banquier, etc.) usurier.

usurp [ju'zə:rp]. **1.** *v.tr.* Usurper (*from,* sur); voler (un titre) (*from,* à). **2.** *v.i.* **To usurp (up)on s.o.'s rights,** empiéter, usurper, sur les droits de qn. **usurping,** *a.* Usurpateur, -trice.

usurpation [ju:zər'peiʃ(ə)n], *s.* Usurpation *f.*

usurper [ju'zə:rpər], *s.* Usurpateur *m.*

usury ['ju:ʒuri], *s.* Usure *f.* **To practise usury,** pratiquer l'usure. **To repay a service with usury,** rendre un bienfait avec usure.

utensil [ju'tensil], *s.* (*a*) Ustensile *m.* **Household utensils,** ustensiles de ménage. **Set of kitchen utensils,** batterie *f* de cuisine. (*b*) Outil *m,* instrument *m.*

utilitarian [jutili'tɛəriən], *a.* Utilitaire.

utilitarianism [jutili'tɛəriənizm], *s.* Utilitarisme *m.*

utility [ju'tiliti], *s.* **1.** (*a*) Utilité *f.* *To be of great u.,* être d'une grande utilité. **General utility waggon,** chariot à toutes fins. (*b*) **Public utility undertaking,** entreprise *f* de service public, de service de ville. **2.** *Th:* **To be a utility (man),** jouer les utilités.

utilizable ['ju:tilaizəbl], *a.* Utilisable.

utilization [ju:tilai'zeiʃ(ə)n], *s.* Utilisation *f;* mise *f* en valeur; exploitation *f* (d'une invention).

utilize ['ju:tilaiz], *v.tr.* Utiliser, se servir de (qch.); tirer parti de, tirer profit de, mettre en valeur (qch.).

utmost ['ʌtmoust]. **1.** *a.* Extrême; dernier. **The utmost ends of the earth,** les (derniers) confins, les extrémités *f,* de la terre. *To make the u. efforts to . . .,* faire tout son possible pour. . . . **It is of the utmost importance that . . .,** il est de toute importance, de la dernière importance, que + *sub.* **With the u. ease,** avec la plus grande facilité. **2.** *s.* Dernière limite; dernier degré. **To the utmost,** le plus possible; au suprême degré. *I shall assist you* **to the utmost of my ability,** je vous aiderai dans la pleine mesure de mes moyens. *Fifty* **at the utmost,** cinquante au plus, tout au plus. **To do one's utmost to . . .,** faire tout son possible, faire l'impossible, pour. . . .

Utopia [ju'toupjə]. **1.** *Pr.n.* L'Utopie *f.* **2.** *s.* **To create utopias,** créer des utopies.

Utopian [ju'toupjən], *a.* Utopique; d'utopie.

utricle ['ju:trikl], *s.* *Nat.Hist:* Utricule *m.*

utricularia [jutrikju'lɛəria], *s.* *Bot:* Utriculaire *f.*

utter[1] ['ʌtər], *a.* Complet, -ète; absolu. *He is an* **utter stranger** *to me,* il m'est complètement étranger. *U. fool,* sot achevé; maître sot. *U. want of breeding,* manque complet de savoir-vivre. **-ly,** *adv.* Complètement, absolument, tout à fait.

utter[2], *v.tr.* **1.** (*a*) Pousser, faire entendre (un cri, etc.); prononcer, proférer (un mot); lancer (un juron). **Not to utter a word,** ne pas sonner mot. (*b*) Dire; exprimer (ses sentiments); débiter (des mensonges). **2.** Émettre, mettre en circulation (de la fausse monnaie).

utterance ['ʌtərəns], *s.* **1.** Expression *f* (des sentiments, etc.); émission *f* (d'un son). **To give utterance to one's feelings,** exprimer ses sentiments. **2.** Articulation *f,* prononciation *f.* *To have a clear u.,* avoir la parole nette. **3.** *pl.* **Utterances,** propos *m,* paroles *f* (de qn).

uttermost ['ʌtərmoust], *a. & s.* = UTMOST.

uvula ['ju:vjulə], *s.* Uvule *f;* luette *f.*

uvular ['ju:vjulər], *a.* Uvulaire. *Ling:* **Uvular r,** r vélaire.

uxorious [ʌk'sɔ:riəs], *a.* Uxorieux; (mari) dominé par sa femme.

V

V, v [vi:], *s.* (La lettre) V, v *m.* **V-shaped,** en (forme de) V. *I.C.E:* **V-type engine,** moteur (à cylindres) en V. *Mec.E:* **V gear,** engrenage à chevrons. *Dressm:* **V neck,** décolleté en pointe.

vac [vak], *s.* *Sch:* *F:* = VACATION 1.

vacancy ['veikənsi], *s.* **1.** Vide *m,* vacuité *f.* To stare into vacancy, regarder dans le vide, dans le vague. **2.** Nullité *f* d'esprit; absence *f* d'idées. **3.** Vacance *f;* poste vacant.

vacant ['veikənt], *a.* **1.** Vacant, vide, libre. *V. space,* place vide. *V. room,* chambre libre, inoccupée. *S.a.* POSSESSION 1, SITUATION 3.

2. (Esprit) inoccupé; (regard) distrait, vague, sans expression. **Vacant expression**, air hébété. **-ly,** *adv.* D'un air distrait, d'un regard perdu.

vacate [va'keit], *v.tr.* (a) Quitter (un emploi). **To vacate office**, se démettre; donner sa démission. (b) Quitter, laisser libre (un siège); évacuer (un appartement); (*at hotel*) quitter (une chambre). *Jur:* **To vacate the premises**, vider les lieux.

vacating, *s.* (a) **Vacating of office**, démission *f.* (b) Évacuation *f* (d'une maison).

vacation [va'keiʃ(ə)n], *s.* **1.** Vacances *fpl.* *Jur:* Vacations *fpl.* (*At university*) **The long vacation**, les grandes vacances. **2.** = VACATING.

vaccinate ['vaksineit], *v.tr.* Vacciner (contre la variole).

vaccination [vaksi'neiʃ(ə)n], *s.* Vaccination *f* (contre la variole).

vaccinator ['vaksineitər], *s.* Vaccinateur *m.*

vaccine ['vaksi:n], *s.* Vaccin *m.* **Vaccine point**, plume *f* pour vaccination.

vacillate ['vasileit], *v.i.* Vaciller; hésiter (entre deux opinions). **vacillating,** *a.* Vacillant, irrésolu.

vacillation [vasi'leiʃ(ə)n], *s.* Vacillation *f*, hésitation *f.*

vacuity [va'kjuiti], *s.* **1.** Vacuité *f*, vide *m* (de l'espace, de la pensée). **2.** Espace *m* vide; vide.

vacuole ['vakjuoul], *s.* *Biol:* Vacuole *f.*

vacuous ['vakjuəs], *a.* Vide de pensée, d'expression. *V. remark*, observation dénuée de bon sens. *V. laugh*, rire niais, bête. *V. look*, air hébété.

vacuum, *pl.* **-ua, -uums** ['vakjuəm, -juə, -juəmz], *s.* *Ph:* Vide *m.* *Very high v.*, vide très poussé. *Aut:* **Vacuum(-feed) tank**, réservoir à élévateur. **'vacuum-brake,** *s.* Frein *m* à vide. **'vacuum-cleaning,** *s.* Nettoyage *m* par le vide; dépoussiérage *m* par aspirateur. **'vacuum-cleaner,** *s.* Aspirateur *m* (de poussière); dépoussiéreur *m.* **'vacuum-fan,** *s.* Ventilateur négatif; ventilateur aspirant. **'vacuum-flask,** *s.* Bouteille isolante; bouteille thermos. **'vacuum-lamp,** *s.* *El:* Lampe *f* à vide. **'vacuum-pump,** *s.* Pompe *f* à vide.

vagabond ['vagəbɔnd]. **1.** *a.* Vagabond, errant. **2.** *s.* (a) Vagabond, -onde; chemineau *m.* (b) *F:* Homme sans aveu; vaurien *m.*

vagabondage ['vagəbɔndedʒ], *s.* Vagabondage *m.*

vagary [va'gɛəri, 'veigəri], *s.* Caprice *m*, fantaisie *f*, lubie *f.* *The vagaries of fashion*, les caprices, l'inconstance *f*, de la mode.

vagrancy ['veigrənsi], *s.* (a) *Jur:* Vagabondage *m*; mendicité *f.* (b) Vie *f* de vagabond.

vagrant ['veigrənt]. **1.** *a.* Vagabond, errant. *V. basket-makers*, vanniers ambulants. **2.** *s.* (a) *Jur:* Vagabond, -onde. (b) Homme sans aveu; chemineau *m.*

vague [veːig], *a.* Vague; imprécis; (*of outline*) indécis, estompé, flou. **I haven't the vaguest idea**, je n'en ai pas la moindre idée. **-ly,** *adv.* Vaguement.

vagueness ['veignəs], *s.* Vague *m*, imprécision *f.*

vain [vein], *a.* Vain. **1.** (*Of hope, etc.*) Mensonger, creux. **Vain promises**, vaines promesses. **2.** Inutile, infructueux. **Vain efforts**, efforts vains, futiles, stériles. *It is v.* (*for you*) *to try*, vous aurez beau essayer, vous n'y arriverez jamais. **3.** Vaniteux, glorieux. **She was vain of her beauty**, elle était fière, vaine, de sa beauté. **4. In vain**, en vain. (a) Vainement. *We protested in v.*, *it was in v. that we protested*, *the tree was cut down*, nous avons eu beau protester, l'arbre a été abattu. *To labour in v.*, travailler inutilement; perdre sa peine. (b) **To**

take God's name in vain, prendre le nom de Dieu en vain; blasphémer le nom de Dieu. **-ly,** *adv.* **1.** Vainement, en vain, inutilement. **2.** Vaniteusement; avec vanité.

vainglorious [vein'glɔːriəs], *a.* Vaniteux, glorieux, orgueilleux. **-ly,** *adv.* Vaniteusement.

vainglory [vein'glɔːri], *s.* Vaine gloire; gloriole *f.*

vainness ['veinnəs], *s.* Vanité *f.*

vair ['vɛər], *s.* *Her:* Vair *m.*

valance ['valəns], *s.* **1.** *Furn:* Frange *f* de lit; soubassement *m*; tour *m* de lit; lambrequin *m* (d'un ciel de lit). **2.** *Aut:* Bavolet *m.*

vale[1] [veil], *s.* **1.** *Poet:* Vallon *m*; val *m*, *pl.* vals. **This vale of tears**, cette vallée de larmes, de misère. **2.** *Tchn:* Gouttière *f*, chéneau *m.*

vale[2] ['veili], *s.* & *int.* Adieu (*m*).

valediction [vali'dikʃ(ə)n], *s.* Adieu(x) *m*(*pl*).

valedictory [vali'diktəri], *a.* (Allocution, dîner) d'adieu.

valence[1] ['veiləns], *s.* = VALENCY.

valence[2] ['valəns], *s.* = VALANCE.

valency ['veilənsi], *s.* *Ch:* Valence *f.*

Valentine ['valəntain]. **1.** *Pr.n.* **Saint Valentine's day**, la Saint-Valentin (le 14 février). **2.** *s.* Carte envoyée le jour de la Saint-Valentin (soit comme gage d'amour, soit par plaisanterie).

valerian [va'liːəriən], *s.* *Bot:* Valériane *f.*

valet[1] ['valit], *s.* Valet *m* de chambre.

valet[2], *v.tr.* (**valeted** ['valetid, 'valeid]) **1.** Servir (qn) comme valet de chambre. **2.** Remettre en état (un vêtement d'homme). **Valeting company**, maison *f* pour la remise en état des vêtements d'hommes.

valetudinarian [valitju:di'nɛəriən], *a.* & *s.* Valétudinaire (*mf*).

valiant ['valjənt], *a.* Vaillant, valeureux, brave. **-ly,** *adv.* Vaillamment.

valid ['valid], *a.* (Contrat, etc.) valide, viable; (passeport) régulier; (argument) solide. **Ticket valid for three months**, billet bon pour trois mois.

validate ['valideit], *v.tr.* Valider; rendre valable.

validity [va'liditi], *s.* Validité *f* (d'un contrat, d'un passeport, etc.). *V. of an argument*, justesse *f*, force *f*, d'un argument.

valise [va'liːz, va-], *s.* *U.S:* **1.** Valise *f.* **2.** *Mil:* Portemanteau *m.*

Valkyrie ['valkiri], *s.f.* Walkyrie.

valley ['vali], *s.* **1.** Vallée *f*; (*small*) vallon *m*; val *m*, *pl.* vals. **The Rhone Valley**, la vallée du Rhône. **2.** *Const:* Noue *f*, cornière *f* (de toit). **Valley tile**, tuile cornière.

vallum ['valəm], *s.* *Rom.Ant:* Vallum *m.*

valorous ['valərəs], *a.* *Lit:* Valeureux, vaillant.

valour ['valər], *s.* *Lit:* Valeur *f*, vaillance *f.*

valuable ['valjuəbl]. **1.** *a.* (a) Précieux; de valeur, de prix. *Jur:* **For a valuable consideration**, à titre onéreux. (b) Évaluable. **2.** *s.pl.* **Valuables**, objets *m* de valeur, de prix.

valuation [valju'eiʃ(ə)n], *s.* **1.** (a) Évaluation *f*, estimation *f.* *Jur:* Expertise *f.* **At a valuation**, à dire d'expert. **To make a valuation of the goods**, faire l'expertise des marchandises. (b) Inventaire *m.* **2.** Valeur estimée. (a) **To set too high a valuation on goods**, surestimer des marchandises. (b) **To take s.o. at his own valuation**, estimer, coter, qn selon l'opinion qu'il a de lui-même.

value[1] ['valju], *s.* Valeur *f.* **1. To be of value**, avoir de la valeur. **To be of little value**, valoir peu de chose. **Of no value**, sans valeur. *He doesn't seem to know the value of time*, il semble ignorer le prix du temps. **To set a low value on sth.**, attacher peu de prix à qch. **To set a high value on sth.**, faire grand cas de qch., attacher un grand prix à qch. *Com:* **Increase in value,** plus-value *f.* **Decrease in value,** moins-value *f.* **2. To pay s.o. the value of the lost umbrella,** rembourser à qn le prix du parapluie perdu. *Com:* **For value received,** valeur reçue. **To get good value for one's money,** *F:* en avoir pour son argent. *This article is very good v.,* cet article est très avantageux.

value², *v.tr.* **I.** *Com:* **To value goods,** évaluer, estimer, priser, des marchandises; faire l'appréciation des marchandises. **2.** (a) **Estimer, faire grand cas de** (qn, qch.). **To value one's life,** tenir à la vie. *He doesn't v. his skin,* il fait bon marché de sa peau. (b) **To value oneself on one's achievements,** tirer vanité de ses exploits. **3.** *v.i. Com:* **To value upon s.o.,** disposer, tirer, sur qn. **valued,** *a.* Estimé, précieux.

valueless ['valjuləs], *a.* Sans valeur.

valuer ['valjuər], *s.* Estimateur *m,* commissaire-priseur *m,* expert *m.*

valve [valv], *s.* **I.** Soupape *f.* (a) **Ball-valve,** clapet *m* sphérique. **Needle-valve,** soupape à pointeau. **Clack-valve, flap-valve,** soupape à clapet, à charnière. *S.a.* AIR-VALVE, CHECK-VALVE, SAFETY-VALVE, *etc.* (b) *I.C.E:* **Mushroom valve, poppet** *m,* soupape en champignon; soupape circulaire; clapet. (c) **Stop-valve,** obturateur *m.* **Butterfly valve,** (soupape à) papillon *m;* vanne *f;* volet *m* (de carburateur). **Water valve,** vanne d'eau. (d) *Mch:* **Slide-valve,** tiroir *m.* (e) *Aut: Cy:* Valve *f* (de pneumatique). **2.** Valvule *f* (du cœur, etc.). **3.** (a) *El:* **Rectifying valve,** soupape électrique; valve redresseuse (de courant). (b) *W.Tel: etc:* Lampe *f* radio-électrique; lampe valve; tube *m.* **Valve set,** appareil *m,* poste *m,* à lampes. *Cin:* **Light-valve recording** (of sound), enregistrement par valve de lumière. **4.** *Bot: Moll:* Valve. **5.** *Hyd.E:* (**Gate-, sluice-)valve,** vanne (de communication).

'valve-box, -case, -chest, *s.* **I.** *Hyd.E:* Boîte *f* à clapet. **2.** *Mch:* (Of slide-valve) Boîte à vapeur; boîte de distribution (de vapeur). **'valve-cap,** *s.* Capuchon *m,* chapeau *m* (d'une valve de pneu). **'valve-gear,** *s.* **I.** *Mch:* (Steam) valve-gear, mécanisme *m* de distribution (de la vapeur). **2.** *I.C.E:* (Organes *mpl* de) distribution *f.* **'valve-holder,** *s.* *W.Tel:* Douille *f,* support *m,* de lampe. **'valve-rocker,** *s. I.C.E:* Culbuteur *m.*

valvular ['valvjulər], *a.* Valvulaire.

valvule ['valvjul], *s.* Valvule *f.*

vamoose [va'muːs], *v.i. U.S: P:* Décamper à la sourdine; filer.

vamp¹ [vamp], *s.* **I.** *Bootm:* Empeigne *f,* claque *f.* **2.** *Mus: F:* Accompagnement tapoté, improvisé. **vamp²,** *v.tr.* **I.** *Bootm:* Remonter (un soulier). **2.** *Mus: F:* Tapoter au piano (un accompagnement ad hoc). **vamp up,** *v.tr. F:* **I.** Rapiécer, rafistoler (qch.). **2.** **Vamped-up piece of scandal,** potin inventé à plaisir.

vamp³, *s.f. F:* (Abbrev. of vampire) (a) Aventurière; femme fatale. (b) Flirteuse.

vamp⁴, *v.tr. F:* (a) (Of woman) Ensorceler, envoûter (un homme). (b) *Abs.* Flirter.

vampire ['vampaiər], *s.* **I.** (a) *Myth:* Vampire *m;* strige *f.* (b) *F:* Vampire; extorqueur, -euse. **2.** *Z:* Vampire(-bat), vampire.

van¹ [van], *s.* (a) **Avant-garde** *f.* (b) **Front** *m* (de bataille). *F:* **To be in the van of progress,** être un pionnier du progrès.

van², *s. Veh:* **I.** (a) Fourgon *m.* **Furniture van, removal van,** voiture *f* de déménagement. **Delivery van,** (i) voiture de livraison; tapissière *f;* (ii) *Aut:* camion *m* de livraison; (light)

camionnette *f.* (b) **Gipsy van,** roulotte *f.* **2.** (a) *Cin:* **Recording van,** camion d'enregistrement. (b) *W.Tel:* **Van for broadcasting open-air events,** car de radio-reportage. **3.** *Rail:* Wagon *m,* fourgon *m.* **Luggage van, fourgon à bagages.** **'van-dwellers,** *s.pl.* Romanichels *m.* **'van-man,** *pl.* **-men,** *s.m.* Livreur.

van³, *s. Ten:* **Van in, out** = *advantage in, out, q.v. under* ADVANTAGE¹ I.

vanadium [va'neidiəm], *s.* *Ch:* Vanadium *m.*

vandal ['vand(ə)l], *s. Hist. & F:* Vandale *m.*

vandalism ['vandəlizm], *s.* Vandalisme *m.* **Piece of vandalism,** acte *m* de vandalisme.

vane [vein], *s.* **I.** (a) (**Wind-, weather-)vane,** girouette *f.* (b) Moulinet *m* (d'un anémomètre, etc.); turbine *f* (d'un compteur à eau). **2.** Bras *m* (de moulin à vent); aube *f,* ailette *f* (de turbine); ailette, pale *f* (de ventilateur). **3.** *Surv:* (**Sight-)vane,** pinnule *f* (d'une alidade); viseur *m* (de compas).

vanguard ['vangɑːrd], *s. Mil:* Tête *f* d'avant-garde. *F:* **To be in the vanguard of a movement,** être un des pionniers d'un mouvement.

vanilla [va'nila], *s.* Vanille *f.* **Vanilla ice,** glace à la vanille.

vanish ['vaniʃ], *v.i.* Disparaître; (of visions, suspicions, etc.) se dissiper, s'évanouir. *Mth:* (i) Tendre vers zéro; (ii) s'évanouir. *F:* **At the moment of danger he vanished,** au moment du danger il s'est éclipsé. **vanishing,** *s.* Disparition *f.* *Art:* **Vanishing line,** ligne d'horizon; ligne de fuite. *Toil:* **Vanishing cream,** crème *f* de jour.

vanity ['vaniti], *s.* **I.** Vanité *f,* vide *m* (des grandeurs humaines, etc.); futilité *f* (d'une tentative). **All is vanity,** tout est vanité. **Vanity Fair,** la foire aux vanités. **2.** Vanité; orgueil *m.* **To do sth. out of vanity,** faire qch. par vanité. **Vanity bag,** (petit) sac de dame (pour soirée).

vanquish ['vankwiʃ], *v.tr.* Vaincre.

vanquisher ['vankwiʃər], *s.* Vainqueur *m.*

vantage ['vɑːntedʒ], *s.* **I.** (**Coign, point, of**) **vantage,** position avantageuse; avantage *m* du terrain. **2.** *Ten:* = VAN³.

vapid ['vapid], *a.* Plat, insipide; (of conversation, etc.) fade. **-ly,** *adv.* Insipidement.

vapidity [va'piditi], **vapidness** ['vapidnəs], *s.* Fadeur *f,* insipidité *f.*

vaporization [veipərai'zeiʃ(ə)n], *s.* **I.** Vaporisation *f.* **2.** Pulvérisation *f* (d'un liquide).

vaporize ['veipəraiz], *v.tr.* (a) Vaporiser, gazéifier. (b) Pulvériser (un liquide); vaporiser. *I.C.E:* Carburer (le combustible). **2.** *v.i.* Se vaporiser, se gazéifier.

vaporizer ['veipəraizər], *s.* (Device) (a) Vaporis(at)eur *m.* (b) Pulvérisateur *m;* atomiseur *m.*

vaporous ['veipərəs], *a.* Vaporeux.

vapour¹ ['veipər], *s.* **I.** Vapeur *f;* buée *f* (sur les vitres). **2.** *pl. Med: A:* Vapeurs *f.* **'vapour-bath,** *s.* **I.** Bain *m* de vapeur. **2.** Étuve *f* humide (de hammam).

vapour², *v.i.* **I.** S'évaporer; se vaporiser. **2.** *F:* Débiter des fadaises; parler pour ne rien dire. **vapouring,** *s. F:* Platitudes *fpl;* paroles *fpl* en l'air.

variability [veəri'biliti], *s.* Variabilité *f* (du temps, etc.). *Biol:* Inconstance *f* (de type).

variable ['veəriəbl], *I. a.* (a) Variable; changeant, inconstant. *Mth:* **Variable quantity,** quantité variable. (b) *Mec.E:* Réglable. **2.** *s. Mth:* Variable *f.*

variance ['veəriəns], *s.* Désaccord *m;* discorde *f.* **To be at variance with s.o.,** être en désaccord avec qn; être brouillé avec qn. **To set two people**

at **variance**, mettre la discorde entre deux personnes. **Theory at variance with the facts,** théorie en désaccord, en contradiction, avec les faits.

variant ['vɛəriənt]. **1.** *a. Lit:* **Variant reading,** variante *f.* **2.** *s.* Variante *f.*

variation [vɛəri'eiʃ(ə)n], *s.* **1.** Variation *f*, changement *m. El:* **Current variation,** variation de courant. *Magn:* **Magnetic variation,** déclinaison magnétique (locale). **2.** Différence *f;* écart *m.* **3.** *Mus:* **Theme with variations,** thème varié ; thème avec variations.

vari(-)coloured ['vɛərikʌləˑrd], *a.* Diversicolore.

varicose ['varikous], *a. Med:* **1.** Variqueux. **Varicose vein,** varice *f.* **2.** **Varicose stocking,** bas *m* à varices.

variegate ['vɛərigeit], *v.tr.* **1.** Varier, diversifier (les couleurs). **2.** Bigarrer, barioler ; diaprer.

variegated, *a.* **1.** Varié ; divers. **2.** Bigarré, bariolé ; diapré. *Nat.Hist:* Panaché.

variegation [vɛəri'geiʃ(ə)n], *s.* Diversité *f* de couleurs ; bigarrure *f. Bot:* Panachure *f,* diaprure *f.*

variety [və'raiəti], *s.* **1.** (a) Variété *f*, diversité *f.* **To lend variety** *to the menu,* donner de la variété au menu. (b) **A variety of patterns,** un assortiment d'échantillons. **2.** (a) *Nat.Hist:* Variété (de fleur, etc.). (b) *Th:* **Variety entertainment, varieties** (*at hotel, etc.*), attractions *f.* **Variety turns,** numéros *m* de music-hall. **Variety theatre,** théâtre de variétés.

variola [və'raiola], *s. Med:·* Variole *f; F:* petite vérole.

variometer [vɛəri'ɔmətər], *s. El:* Variomètre *m.*

various ['vɛəriəs], *a.* **1.** Varié, divers. **Of various kinds,** de diverses sortes. **To talk about v. things,** parler de chose(s) et d'autre(s). **2.** (a) Différent, dissemblable ; divers. *Lit:* **Various reading,** variante *f.* (b) Plusieurs ; plus d'un. **For various reasons,** pour plusieurs raisons. **At various times,** à différentes reprises. **-ly,** *adv.* Diversement ; de diverses manières.

varlet ['vɑːrlet], *s.m.* **1.** *Hist:* Varlet, page. **2.** *F:* Coquin ; vaurien.

varletry ['vɑːrletri], *s. A:* Valetaille *f.*

varmint ['vɑːrmint], *s. P:* **1.** (a) Vermine *f.* (b) *Ven:* Renard *m.* **2.** **Young varmint,** petit polisson.

varnish[1] ['vɑːrniʃ], *s.* **1.** Vernis *m.* **Spirit varnish,** vernis à l'alcool. *Toil:* **Nail varnish,** vernis pour les ongles. **2.** (Enduit *m* de) vernis ; vernissure *f.* **'varnish-remover,** *s.* Décapant *m* pour vernis.

varnish[2], *v.tr.* **1.** Vernir ; vernisser (la poterie). **2.** *F:* **To varnish (over),** farder (les faits) ; glisser sur, vernir (les défauts de qn). **varnishing,** *s.* Vernissage *m.* **'varnishing-day,** *s.* Vernissage *m* (au Salon de peinture).

varsity ['vɑːrsiti], *s. F:* = UNIVERSITY.

vary ['vɛəri]. **1.** *v.tr.* Varier, diversifier ; faire varier. **To v.** *one's methods,* varier de méthode. **2.** *v.i.* (a) Varier, changer ; être variable. (b) **To vary from . . .,** dévier, s'écarter, de . . . ; différer de. . . . (c) Différer (d'avis). **As to the date,** *authors v.,* quant à la date, les auteurs ne sont pas d'accord. **varied,** *a.* Varié ; divers. **varying,** *a.* Variable, changeant ; varié, divers.

vascular ['vaskjulər], *a.* Vasculaire.

vasculum, *pl.* **-a** ['vaskjuləm, -a], *s.* **1.** *Bot:* Ascidie *f.* **2.** Boîte *f* en fer blanc (de botaniste).

vase [vɑːz], *s.* Vase *m.* **Flower vase,** vase à fleurs.

vaseline[1] ['vazəliːn, 'vas-], *s.* Vaseline *f.*

vaseline[2], *v.tr.* Frotter, graisser, avec de la vaseline ; enduire de vaseline.

vasiform ['veizifɔːrm, 'veis-], *a.* Vasiforme.

vaso-motor ['veiso'moutər], *a. & s. Anat:* Vaso-moteur (*m*).

vassal ['vas(ə)l], *a. & s.* Vassal (*m*), -aux ; feudataire (*m*) (to, de).

vassalage ['vasəledʒ], *s.* (a) Vassalité *f*, vasselage *m.* (b) *F:* Sujétion *f.*

vast[1] ['vɑːst], *a.* Vaste, immense. **To spend a v. amount of money,** dépenser énormément d'argent. **-ly,** *adv.* Vastement ; immensément.

vast[2], *int. Nau:* = AVAST.

vastness ['vɑːstnəs], *s.* Vastitude *f,* immensité *f.*

vat[1] [vat], *s.* Cuve *f;* (*small*) cuveau *m*; bac *m*; bain *m.* **Tan vat,** fosse *f* de tannage.

vat[2], *v.tr.* Mettre en cuve ; encuver.

vatful ['vatful], *s.* Cuvée *f.*

Vatican ['vatikən], *s.* **The Vatican,** le Vatican.

vaticinate [va'tisineit], *v.i.* Vaticiner ; prophétiser.

vaticination [vatisi'neiʃ(ə)n], *s.* Vaticination *f.*

vaticinator [va'tisineitər], *s.* Vaticinateur *m.*

vaudeville ['voudəvil], *s. Th:* **1.** Vaudeville *m.* **2.** Spectacle *m* de music-hall.

vault[1] [vɔlt], *s.* **1.** (a) Voûte *f.* **Barrel vault,** tunnel vault, (voûte en) tonnelle *f*; berceau *m.* **Semi-circular vault,** voûte à plein cintre. **Basket-handle vault,** voûte en anse de panier. *F:* **The vault of heaven,** le dôme des cieux ; la voûte céleste. (b) *Const:* Chapelle *f* (de four de boulangerie) ; voûte (d'un fourneau). **2.** (a) Souterrain *m.* (*Of bank, etc.*) **Safety vault,** chambre forte. (b) **Wine-vault,** cave *f,* cellier *m.* (c) **Sepulchral vault,** caveau *m.* **Family vault,** caveau de famille.

vault[2], *v.tr.* **To vault (over) a cellar,** voûter une cave. **vaulted,** *a.* Voûté, voussé ; en voûte. **vaulting,** *s.* **1.** Construction *f* de voûtes. **2.** *Coll:* Voûte(s) *f(pl).*

vault[3], *s. Gym: etc:* Saut *m* (de barrière, etc.) ; saut au cheval-arçons.

vault[4]. **1.** *v.i.* (a) **To vault over a gate,** sauter une barrière, franchir une barrière d'un saut (en s'aidant des mains). **To v.** *over a stream,* sauter un ruisseau à la perche. (b) **To vault into the saddle,** sauter en selle. **2.** *v.tr.* Sauter (une barrière, etc.). **vaulting**[2], *a. Lit:* **Vaulting ambition,** ambition qui vise trop haut. **vaulting**[3], *s. Gym:* Exercice *m* du saut ; voltige *f* (sur le cheval-arçons). *S.a.* HORSE 3.

vaunt[1] [vɔːnt], *s. Lit:* Vanterie *f*; fanfaronnade *f.*

vaunt[2], *v.tr. Lit:* (a) Vanter (qch.). (b) Se vanter de (qch.) ; se faire gloire de (qch.). **vaunting,** *a.* Vantard. **vaunting**[2], *s.* Vanterie *f*; jactance *f.*

veal [viːl], *s. Cu:* Veau *m. S.a.* LEG[1] 2.

vector ['vektər], *s.* **1.** *Mth:* Vecteur *m.* **Radius vector,** rayon vecteur. **2.** *Med:* Porteur, -euse (d'une maladie).

vectorial [vek'tɔːriəl], *a. Mth:* Vectoriel.

veer[1] [viːər], *s.* **1.** Changement *m* de direction, saute *f* (de vent). **2.** (*Of ship*) Virage *m* vent arrière. **3.** *F:* Revirement *m* (d'opinion).

veer[2]. **1.** *v.i.* (a) (*Of wind*) Tourner, sauter. **To veer aft, abaft,** adonner. **To veer ahead,** venir debout. **To veer forward,** refuser. (b) (*Of ship*) Virer (vent arrière) ; changer de bord. (c) *F:* (*Of pers.*) **To veer round,** changer d'opinion. **2.** *v.tr.* (Faire) virer (un navire) vent arrière.

veer[3], *v.tr. Nau:* **To veer out the cable,** filer du câble.

vegetable ['vedʒitəbl]. **1.** *a.* Végétal, -aux.

Vegetable oil materials, matières végétales oléagineuses. **2.** s. (a) Bot: Végétal m, -aux. (b) Légume m. **Early vegetables,** primeurs f. **Vegetable garden,** (jardin) potager m; jardin légumier. **Vegetable-slicer,** taille-légumes m inv. **'vegetable-dish,** s. Légumier m.

vegetal ['vedʒit(ə)l], a. & s. Bot: Végétal (m), -aux.

vegetarian [vedʒi'tɛəriən], a. & s. Végétarien m.

vegetarianism [vedʒi'tɛəriənizm], s. Végétarisme m.

vegetate ['vedʒiteit], v.i. Végéter. F: To vegetate in an office, moisir, végéter, dans un bureau.

vegetation [vedʒi'teiʃ(ə)n], s. Végétation f.

vegetative ['vedʒiteitiv], a. Végétatif.

vehemence ['vi:əməns], s. Véhémence f.

vehement ['vi:əmənt], a. Véhément; (vent) impétueux. **-ly,** adv. Véhémentement; impétueusement.

vehicle ['vi:ikl], s. **1.** Véhicule m, voiture f. **2.** Air is the v. of sound, l'air est le véhicule du son. The newspaper as a v. for advertising, le journal comme moyen de réclame. Med: V. of disease, agent vecteur.

vehicular [vi'hikjulər], a. **Vehicular traffic,** circulation f des voitures.

veil[1] [veil], s. **1.** (a) Voile m (de religieuse, de deuil). Bridal v., voile de mariée. Ecc: To take the veil, prendre le voile. (b) Hat-veil, eye veil, voilette f. **2.** A: Voile, rideau m. Lit: Beyond the veil, au delà de la tombe. **3.** F: To draw, throw, a veil over sth., jeter un voile sur qch. **4.** Phot: Voile faible.

veil[2], v.tr. **1.** Voiler. **2.** Voiler, cacher, dissimuler (ses sentiments). **veiled,** a. **1.** Voilé; couvert d'un voile. **2.** Voilé, caché, dissimulé. Hardly v. hostility, hostilité à peine déguisée. **veiling,** s. Coll. Voile(s) m(pl). S.a. NUN'S VEILING.

vein[1] [vein], s. **1.** Anat: Veine f. **2.** Nervure f (de feuille). **3.** Geol: Min: Veine, filon m. **4.** (In wood, marble) Veine. **5.** Veine, disposition f, humeur f. The poetic vein, la veine poétique. To be in the vein for doing sth., être en veine, en humeur, de faire qch.

vein[2], v.tr. Veiner, marbrer (une porte).

veined [veind], a. **1.** Veiné; à veines. **2.** Bot: Ent: Nervuré.

velar ['vi:lər], a. & s. Ling: Vélaire (f).

veld(t) [velt], s. (In S. Afr.) Veld(t) m.

velleity [ve'li:iti], s. Velléité f.

vellum ['veləm], s. Vélin m. **Rough vellum,** parchemin m en cosse. **'vellum paper,** s. Papier m vélin.

velocipede [vi'lɔsipi:d], s. A: Vélocipède m.

velocity [vi'lɔsiti], s. Vitesse f. Mec: **Accelerated velocity,** vitesse accélérée.

velour(s) [və'luər], s. Com: **1.** Tex: Velouté m; velours m de laine. **2.** Velours hat, chapeau (en feutre) taupé.

velum ['vi:ləm], s. Anat: Voile m du palais.

velvet ['velvet], s. **1.** Tex: Velours m. **Plain velvet,** velours plain, uni. **Uncut v.,** terry velvet, velours bouclé. **Ribbed velvet, corduroy velvet,** velours à côtes. F: To be on velvet, être sur le velours. **2.** Nat.Hist: Velouté m. **3.** Attrib: V. coat, habit de velours. **Velvet-surface paper,** papier velouté.

velveteen [velve'ti:n], s. **1.** Tex: Velours m lisse de coton; velours de chasse. **Ribbed velveteen, corduroy velveteen,** velours (de coton) côtelé, à côtes. **2.** pl. Velveteens, (i) pantalon m en velours de chasse; (ii) F: (with sg. const.) le garde-chasse.

velvety ['velveti], a. Velouté. **Velvety wine,** vin velouté, vin moelleux.

venal ['vi:nəl], a. Vénal, -aux; mercenaire. **-ally,** adv. Vénalement.

venality [vi'naliti], s. Vénalité f.

vend [vend], v.tr. (a) Jur: Vendre. (b) Faire le commerce de (choses de peu de valeur); vendre (des journaux).

Vendean [ven'di:ən], a. & s. Vendéen, -éenne.

vendetta [ven'detə], s. Vendetta f.

vendible ['vendibl], a. Vendable.

vendor ['vendɔːr], s. Vendeur, -euse. Fin: **Vendor's shares,** actions d'apport, de fondation.

veneer[1] [və'ni:ər], s. **1.** (a) Placage m, revêtement m (de bois mince). (b) Bois m de placage. **2.** F: Masque m; apparence extérieure; vernis m (de connaissances). A mere v. of politeness, une politesse toute en surface.

veneer[2], v.tr. Plaquer (le bois).

venerability [venərə'biliti], s. Vénérabilité f.

venerable ['venərəbl], a. Vénérable.

venerate ['venəreit], v.tr. Vénérer.

veneration [venə'reiʃ(ə)n], s. Vénération f (for, pour). **To hold s.o. in veneration,** avoir de la vénération pour qn.

venery ['venəri], s. A: Vénerie f; la chasse.

Venetian [vi'ni:ʃən], a. & s. Geog: Vénitien, -ienne. Needlew: **Venetian lace,** point m de Venise. S.a. BLIND[3] I, SHUTTER I.

vengeance ['vendʒəns], s. Vengeance f. To take vengeance on s.o., se venger sur qn; se venger de qn. **Crime that cries for vengeance,** crime qui crie vengeance. F: **With a vengeance,** furieusement; à outrance; pour de bon. It is raining with a v., voilà qui s'appelle pleuvoir. He's a gambler with a v., c'est un joueur s'il en fut jamais.

vengeful ['vendʒful], a. Vindicatif.

venial ['vi:niəl], a. (Péché) véniel. (Of fault) Léger, pardonnable, véniel.

veniality [vi:ni'aliti], s. Caractère léger, véniel (d'une faute).

Venice ['venis]. Pr.n. Venise f.

venison ['ven(i)z(ə)n], s. Venaison f. **Haunch of venison,** quartier m de chevreuil.

vennel ['ven(ə)l], s. Scot: Ruelle f, venelle f.

venom ['venəm], s. (a) Venin m. (b) F: Tongue full of v., mauvaise langue; langue de vipère.

venomous ['venəməs], a. **1.** Venimeux. **2.** F: Venomous tongue, langue de vipère. **-ly,** adv. D'une manière venimeuse; méchamment.

venomousness ['venəməsnəs], s. **1.** Nature venimeuse (d'un animal). **2.** Méchanceté f (de langue).

venous ['vi:nəs], a. Veineux.

vent[1] [vent], s. **1.** (a) Trou m, orifice m, lumière f, passage m (pour laisser entrer ou échapper l'air); évent m. (b) Lumière (d'une arme à feu). (c) Vents of a flute, trous d'une flûte. (d) Cheminée f (de volcan). **2.** To give vent to one's grief, to one's anger, donner libre cours à sa douleur, à sa colère. To give vent to a sigh, laisser échapper un soupir. **'vent-hole,** s. Trou m de fausset (d'un tonneau); évent m (d'un volcan).

vent[2], v.tr. To vent one's anger on s.o., décharger sa colère sur qn.

vent[3], s. Cost: Fente f (derrière un pardessus).

ventilate ['ventileit], v.tr. **1.** Aérer (une chambre); ventiler (un tunnel). **Ventilating-fan,** ventilateur m. **2.** F: Agiter (une question) (au grand jour).

ventilation [venti'leiʃ(ə)n], s. **1.** Aération f, aérage m, ventilation f. Ind: **Ventilation plant,**

installation *f* d'aérage. **2.** Mise *f* en discussion publique (d'une question). **venti'lation-shaft,** *s. Min:* Puits *m* d'aérage.

ventilator ['ventileitər], *s.* **1.** Ventilateur *m*; ventouse *f* (d'une cheminée); soupirail, -aux *m* (d'une cave). *Nau:* Manche *f* à ventilation. **2.** (*Over door*) Vasistas *m.* **3.** *Aut:* Volet *m* d'aération (de capot).

Ventimiglia [venti'miʎa]. *Pr.n. Geog:* Vintimille.

ventricle ['ventrikl], *s.* Ventricule *m* (du cœur).

ventriloquial [ventri'loukwiəl], *a.* Ventriloque, de ventriloque.

ventriloquism [ven'trilokwizm], *s.* Ventriloquie *f.*

ventriloquist [ven'trilokwist], *s.* Ventriloque *mf.*

ventriloquy [ven'triloʌkwi], *s.* Ventriloquie *f.*

venture¹ ['ventʃər], *s.* **1.** Entreprise risquée *To be ready for any venture,* être prêt aux entreprises les plus hasardeuses. **2.** *Com:* Entreprise, spéculation *f.* **3.** *At a venture,* à l'aventure, au hasard. *To answer at a venture,* répondre au petit bonheur. *F: To draw a bow at a venture,* plaider le faux pour savoir le vrai.

venture². **1.** *v.tr.* (*a*) To venture to do sth., oser faire qch.; se risquer à faire qch. I will venture to affirm that . . ., j'ose affirmer que. . . . *I v. to write to you,* je me permets de vous écrire. (*b*) To venture a guess, hasarder une conjecture. (*c*) Hasarder, aventurer, risquer (sa vie, son argent). **2.** *v.i.* (*a*) To venture upon sth., se risquer à faire qch. *To v. on an opinion,* hasarder une opinion. (*b*) To venture into an unknown country, s'aventurer dans un pays inconnu. *To v. out of doors,* se risquer à sortir.

venturesome ['ventʃərsəm], *a.* **1.** Aventureux, osé. **2.** (*Of action*) Aventuré, risqué.

venturesomeness ['ventʃərsəmnəs], *s.* Esprit aventureux.

venue ['venju:], *s.* **1.** *Jur:* Lieu *m* du jugement; juridiction *f. To change the venue* (*of a trial*), renvoyer l'affaire devant une autre cour (pour assurer l'ordre public, etc.). **2.** Lieu de réunion; rendez-vous *m.*

Venus ['vi:nəs]. *Pr.n.f.* Vénus. **'Venus's fly-trap,** *s. Bot:* Dionée *f* gobe-mouches.

veracious [ve'reiʃəs], *a.* Véridique. **-ly,** *adv.* Véridiquement; avec véracité.

veraciousness [ve'reiʃəsnəs], **veracity** [ve'rasiti], *s.* Véracité *f.*

veranda(h) [ve'randa], *s.* Véranda *f.*

verb [və:rb], *s. Gram:* Verbe *m.*

verbal ['və:rb(ə)l], *a.* **1.** (*a*) Verbal, -aux; oral, -aux. Verbal agreement, convention verbale. (*b*) *V. dispute,* dispute de mots. (*c*) (*Of translation*) Mot à mot, mot pour mot; littéral, -aux. **2.** *Gram:* Verbal noun, nom verbal. **-ally,** *adv.* **1.** Verbalement; de vive voix. **2.** Littéralement.

verbatim [vər'beitim]. **1.** *adv.* Mot pour mot; textuellement. **2.** *a.* **Verbatim report of the proceedings,** sténogramme *m* des débats.

verbena [vər'bi:na], *s.* Verveine *f.*

verbiage ['və:rbiedʒ], *s.* Verbiage *m.*

verbose [vər'bous], *a.* Verbeux, diffus, prolixe. **-ly,** *adv.* Avec verbosité.

verboseness [vər'bousnəs], **verbosity** [vər'bositi], *s.* Verbosité *f,* prolixité *f.*

verb. sap. ['və:rb'sap]. *Lt.phr.* (= *verbum sapienti sat est*) A bon entendeur salut.

verdant ['və:rdənt], *a.* **1.** Vert, verdoyant. **2.** *Hum:* Inexpérimenté, naïf.

verderer ['və:rdərər], *s. Hist:* Verdier *m.*

verdict ['və:rdikt], *s.* **1.** *Jur:* (*a*) Verdict *m*; réponse *f* du jury. **To return a verdict,** prononcer,

rendre, un verdict. (*b*) (*In coroner's court*) The jury returned a v. *of suicide,* le jury a conclu au suicide. **Open verdict,** jugement *m* qui conclut au crime sans désigner le coupable. **2.** Jugement, décision *f. To stick to one's verdict,* maintenir le bien-fondé de son jugement.

verdigris ['və:rdigris, -gri:s], *s.* Vert-de-gris *m. To become coated with v.,* se vert-de-griser.

verdure ['və:rdjər], *s.* (*a*) Verdure *f*; (i) couleur verte; (ii) herbage *m,* feuillage *m.* (*b*) *Lit:* Verdeur *f,* jeunesse *f,* vigueur *f.*

Verey ['veri]. *Pr.n.* = **VERY** .

verge¹ [və:rdʒ], *s.* **1.** (*a*) Bord *m* (d'un fleuve); orée *f* (d'une forêt). (*b*) Bordure *f* (d'une plate-bande). (*c*) To be on the verge of forty, friser la quarantaine. *He is on the v. of ruin,* il est sur le penchant de la ruine, à deux doigts de la ruine. On the verge of war, à la veille de la guerre. **On the verge of bursting into tears,** sur le point d'éclater en larmes. **2.** *Ecc:* Verge (portée devant l'évêque).

verge², *v.i.* (*a*) To verge on sth., toucher à, être contigu à, qch. (*b*) *That verges on disingenuousness,* cela frise la mauvaise foi.

verger ['və:rdʒər], *s.* (*a*) *Ecc:* Porte-verge *m inv*; bedeau *m.* (*b*) Huissier *m* à verge.

veridical [ve'ridik(ə)l], *a.* Véridique. **-ally,** *adv.* Véridiquement.

verification [verifi'keiʃ(ə)n], *s.* Vérification *f,* contrôle *m.*

verify ['verifai], *v.tr.* **1.** (*Of evidence*) Confirmer (un fait). *Subsequent events verified his suspicions,* les événements postérieurs ont donné raison à ses soupçons. **2.** Vérifier, contrôler (des renseignements, des comptes).

verily. *See* VERY¹ I.

verisimilitude [verisi'militju:d], *s.* Vraisemblance *f.*

veritable ['veritəbl], *a.* Véritable. **-ably,** *adv.* Véritablement.

verity ['veriti], *s. Lit:* Vérité *f.* **1.** The eternal verities, les vérités éternelles. **2.** Fait réel.

verjuice ['və:rdʒu:s], *s. Cu: A:* Verjus *m.*

vermicelli [və:rmi'seli, -'tʃeli], *s.* Vermicelle *m.*

vermicular [və:r'mikjulər], *a.* Vermiculaire, vermiforme.

vermiform ['və:rmifoʌrm], *a.* Vermiforme.

vermifuge ['və:rmifju:dʒ], *a. & s.* Vermifuge (*m*), anthelminthique (*m*).

vermilion [və:r'miljən]. **1.** *s.* Vermillon *m,* cinabre *m.* **2.** *a.* (De) vermillon; vermeil.

vermin ['və:rmin], *s.* **1.** (*Body parasites, etc.*) Vermine *f.* **2.** (*Weasels, etc.*) Bêtes puantes.

verminous ['və:rminəs], *a.* Couvert de vermine; *F:* grouillant de vermine.

verm(o)uth ['və:rmu:t, -mu:θ], *s.* Vermout(h) *m.*

vernacular [və:r'nakjulər]. *Ling:* **1.** *a.* Vernaculaire; indigène; (idiome) national. **Vernacular Arabic,** l'arabe vulgaire. **2.** *s.* (*a*) Vernaculaire *m*; idiome national. (*b*) La langue vulgaire. *F: Langage m* (d'un métier).

vernal ['və:rn(ə)l], *a.* Printanier; du printemps. *Astr: Bot:* Vernal, -aux.

vernier ['və:rniər], *s.* Vernier *m.* **Vernier calliper,** jauge *f* micrométrique.

veronal ['veronəl], *s. Pharm:* Vérona `m.`

veronica [ve'ronikə], *s.* Véronique *f.*

versant ['və:rsənt], *s.* **1.** Versant *m* (d'une montagne). **2.** Pente *f* (de terrain).

versatile ['və:rsətail], *a.* **1.** (*a*) Aux talents variés. *He is a v. writer,* il écrit dans tous les genres. (*b*) *V. mind,* esprit souple. **2.** (*a*) Pivotant; capable de tourner. (*b*) *Nat.Hist:* Versatile.

versatility [və:rsə'tiliti], *s.* **1.** Souplesse *f,*

univesalité *f* (d'esprit). **2.** *Nat.Hist:* Versa-tilité *f.*

verse [vɜːrs], *s.* **1.** Vers *m.* **2.** *(Of song)* Cou-plet *m*; *(of poem)* strophe *f.* **3.** *Coll.* Vers *mpl.*
Light verse, poésie légère. **4.** *Ecc:* Verset *m* (de la Bible). *S.a.* CHAPTER 1.

versed[1] [vɜːrst], *a.* Versé (*in*, en, dans). To be well v. in business matters être entendu aux affaires.

versed[2], *a. Mth:* **Versed sine**, sinus *m* verse.

versification [vɜːrsifiˈkeiʃ(ə)n], *s.* Versifica-tion *f.*

versify [ˈvɜːrsifai], *v.tr. & i.* Versifier; mettre en vers.

version [ˈvɜːrʃ(ə)n], *s.* **1.** *(a)* Version *f*, traduc-tion *f.* *(b) Sch:* (Scot.) Thème latin. **2.** Version (des faits); interprétation *f* (d'un fait). According to his v., selon son dire . . .; d'après lui. . . .

verso [ˈvɜːrso], *s.* Verso *m* (d'une page); revers *m* (d'une médaille).

versus [ˈvɜːrsəs], *Lt.prep. Esp. Jur:* Contre. Smith v. Robinson, Smith c. Robinson.

vert [vɜːrt], *s. Her:* Sinople *m*, vert *m.*

vertebra, *pl.* **-ae** [ˈvɜːrtibra, -iː], *s.* Vertèbre *f.*

vertebral [ˈvɜːrtibrəl], *a.* Vertébral, -aux.

vertebrate [ˈvɜːrtibret], *a. & s.* Vertébré (*m*).

vertex, *pl.* **-tices** [ˈvɜːrteks, -tisiːz], *s.* Sommet *m* (d'un angle, d'une courbe).

vertical [ˈvɜːrtik(ə)l]. **I.** *a.* *(a)* Vertical, -aux. Vertical elevation, altitude *f.* *V.* cliff, falaise à pic. *(b)* Du zénith; situé au zénith. *(c)* Vertical angles, angles opposés par le sommet. **2.** *s.* Ver-ticale *f.* **-ally**, *adv.* Verticalement; d'aplomb.

vertices [ˈvɜːrtisiːz], *s.pl. See* VERTEX.

vertiginous [vɜːrˈtidʒinəs], *a.* Vertigineux.

vertigo [ˈvɜːrtigo, vɜːrˈtaigo], *s. Med:* Vertige *m.*

vervain [ˈvɜːrvein], *s. Bot:* Verveine *f.*

verve [vɜːrv], *s.* Verve *f.* To play, act, with v., jouer avec verve.

very[1] [ˈveri]. **I.** *a.* **1.** Vrai, véritable. The veriest fool knows that, le plus parfait nigaud sait cela. **2.** *(a)* Même. He lives in this very place, il habite ici même. You are the v. man I wanted to see, vous êtes justement l'homme que je voulais voir. We shall appoint X, he is the very man, nous nom-merons X, il est tout indiqué. At that very moment, à cet instant même. It was a year ago to the very day, c'était il y a un an jour pour jour. These are his v. words, ce sont là ses propres paroles. *S.a.* THING 3. *(b)* At the very beginning, tout au commencement. He knows our v. thoughts, il connaît jusqu'à nos pensées. The v. children knew of it, les enfants mêmes le savaient. *(c)* The very thought frightens me, la seule pensée m'effraie. **-ily**, *adv.* B: For verily I say unto you . . ., car je vous dis en vérité. . . . **II. very**, *adv.* **1.** Très; fort, bien. Very good, (i) très bon, fort bon; (ii) très bien, fort bien. You are not very polite, vous êtes peu poli. Not v. well pleased, médiocrement satisfait. That's very nice of you, c'est bien gentil de votre part. Not so very small, déjà pas si petit. So very little, si peu. It isn't so very difficult, ce n'est pas tellement difficile. He wore a v. pleased expression, il avait l'air tout à fait satisfait. I was very much surprised, *F:* very surprised, j'en ai été très surpris. I feel very much better, je me sens beaucoup mieux. **2.** The very first, le tout premier. The very best, le meilleur de tous. I did the v. best I could, j'ai fait tout mon possible. The v. next day, dès le lendemain. At the very most, tout au plus. At the very latest, au plus tard. The very same, absolument le même.

Very[2]. *Pr.n. Mil:* **Very light**, étoile éclairante.

Very(-light) pistol, pistolet *m* à fusée; pistolet Very.

vesical [ˈvesik(ə)l], *a.* Vésical, -aux.

vesicatory [ˈvesikeitəri, veˈsikətəri], *a. & s.* Vésicatoire (*m*), vésicant (*m*).

vesicle [ˈvesikl], *s.* Vésicule *f*; *Med:* phlyc-tène *f.*

vesper [ˈvespər]. **1.** *s. Poet:* Le soir. **2.** *s.pl.* Vespers, vêpres *f.*

vessel [ˈves(ə)l], *s.* **1.** Vaisseau *m*, vase *m*, récipient *m.* **2.** Vaisseau, navire *m*, bâtiment *m.* **3.** *Anat: Bot:* Vaisseau. **4.** *B.Lit. & F:* Vais-seau, vase, instrument *m.* **Chosen vessel**, vase d'élection. Weaker vessel, vaisseau plus fragile.

vest[1] [vest], *s.* **1.** Gilet *m.* **Sleeved vest**, gilet à manches. **2.** (Under)vest, gilet de dessous; *(knitted)* gilet de tricot; *(for women)* chemise *f* (de tricot). *Sp:* (Running) vest, maillot *m.* **'vest-'pocket**, *s.* **1.** Poche *f* du gilet. **2.** *Attrib.* De petites dimensions. **Vest-pocket camera**, appareil vest-pocket.

vest[2]. **1.** *v.tr.* *(a)* To vest s.o. with authority, investir, revêtir, qn de l'autorité. *Jur:* To vest s.o. with an inheritance, saisir qn d'un héritage. *(b)* Right vested in the Crown, droit dévolu à la Couronne. Authority vested in the people, auto-rité exercée par le peuple. *Jur:* Vesting order, envoi *m* en possession. *(c)* Vêtir, revêtir (un dignitaire, le prêtre, etc.). **2.** *v.i.* *(Of property)* To vest in s.o., échoir à qn. **vested**, *a.* Dévolu. *Jur. & F:* Vested interests, droits acquis.

Vesta [ˈvestə]. **1.** *Pr.n.f. Rom.Myth:* Vesta. **2.** *s.* **(Wax)** vesta, allumette-bougie *f.*

vestal [ˈvest(ə)l], *a. & s. Rom.Ant:* Vestal (virgin), vestale *f.*

vestibule [ˈvestibjuːl], *s.* Vestibule *m*, anti-chambre *f.* *S.a.* CONCERTINA.

vestige [ˈvestidʒ], *s.* Vestige *m*, trace *f.* *F:* Not a vestige of . . ., pas la moindre trace de . . .; pas un grain de (bon sens, etc.).

vestment [ˈvestmənt], *s.* **1.** Vêtement *m* (de cérémonie). *Ecc:* Chasuble *f.* (Priestly) vest-ments, vêtements sacerdotaux. **2.** *Ecc:* Nappe *f* d'autel.

vestry [ˈvestri], *s. Ecc:* **1.** Sacristie *f.* **2.** Con-seil *m* d'administration de la paroisse. **Vestry-meeting**, réunion *f* du conseil de fabrique. **'vestry-clerk**, *s.* Secrétaire *m* du conseil de fabrique.

vestryman, *pl.* **-men** [ˈvestrimən, -men], *s.m. Ecc:* Marguillier; membre du conseil d'admini-stration.

Vesuvius [veˈsjuːviəs, -suː-]. *Pr.n.* Le Vésuve.

vet[1] [vet], *s. F:* = *veterinary surgeon*, *q.v.* under VETERINARY.

vet[2], *v.tr.* (vetted) *F:* *(a)* Examiner, traiter (une bête). To have a horse vetted, soumettre un cheval à l'examen d'un vétérinaire. *(b)* Examiner (qn) médicalement. *(c)* Revoir, corriger (l'œuvre littéraire de qn).

vetch [vetʃ], *s. Bot:* Vesce *f.*

vetchling [ˈvetʃliŋ], *s. Bot:* Gesse *f* des prés.

veteran [ˈvetərən]. **1.** *s.* Vétéran *m*; *F:* vieux *m* de la vieille. **2.** *a.* De(s) vétéran(s); aguerri. A veteran golfer, un vétéran du golf.

veterinary [ˈvetərinəri], *a.* Vétérinaire. Veteri-nary surgeon, *s.a.* veterinary, vétérinaire *m.*

veto[1], *pl.* **-oes** [ˈviːto, -ouz], *s.* Veto *m.* To put a veto on sth., mettre le veto, son veto, à qch. To have the right of veto, avoir le veto.

veto[2], *v.tr.* Mettre son veto à (qch.); interdire (qch.).

vex [veks], *v.tr.* **1.** Vexer, fâcher, chagriner. **2.** *Lit:* Troubler, tourmenter, agiter. **vexed**, *a.*

1. Vexé, contrarié, chagrin. **To be vexed at sth.**, être vexé, fâché, de qch. **To be vexed with s.o.**, être fâché contre qn. **To be vexed with oneself**, s'en vouloir. *He was v. that he could not find out anything*, il se dépitait de ne rien découvrir. **2. Vexed question**, question très débattue, non résolue. **vexing**, *a.* Vexant, ennuyeux, chagrinant.

vexation [vek'seiʃ(ə)n], *s.* **1.** Vexation *f*, tourment *m*. **Vexation of spirit**, tourment. **2.** (*a*) Contrariété *f*, ennui *m*. (*b*) Chagrin *m*, dépit *m*.

vexatious [vek'seiʃəs], *a.* **1.** Fâcheux, ennuyeux, contrariant. **2.** *Jur:* Vexatoire. **-ly**, *adv.* **1.** D'une manière contrariante. **2.** A seule fin de contrarier.

via ['vaiə], *prep.* Via; par la voie de; par (une route). *Post:* 'Via Marseilles', "voie Marseille."

viability[1] [vaiə'biliti], *s.* Viabilité *f*; aptitude *f* à vivre.

viability[2], *s.* Viabilité *f*, bon état (d'une route).

viable[1] ['vaiəbl], *a.* Viable; apte à vivre.

viable[2], *a.* (Route) viable, en bon état.

viaduct ['vaiədʌkt], *s.* Viaduc *m*.

vial ['vaiəl], *s.* Fiole *f*. *F:* To pour out the vials of one's wrath, lâcher la bonde à sa colère.

viand ['vaiənd], *s. Lit:* Mets *m*. *Usu.pl.* Viands, aliments *m*.

viaticum [vai'atikəm], *s.* **1.** *Ecc:* Viatique *m*. **2.** Provisions *fpl* (en vue d'un voyage); viatique.

vibrant [vaibrənt], *a.* Vibrant.

vibrate [vai'breit, 'vaibreit]. **1.** *v.i.* (*a*) Vibrer; trépider. (*b*) *Ph:* Vibrer, osciller. **2.** *v.tr.* Faire vibrer. **vibrating**, *a.* Vibrant; (mouvement) vibratoire, oscillant. **Voice vibrating with emotion**, voix vibrante d'émotion.

vibration [vai'breiʃ(ə)n], *s.* **1.** Vibration *f*; oscillation *f*. **2.** *Mch:* Trépidation *f*.

vibrator [vai'breitər], *s. El.E:* Vibrateur *m*; trembleur *m* (de bobine). *W.Tel:* Oscillateur *m*.

vibratory ['vaibrətəri], *a.* Vibratoire.

viburnum [vai'bə:rnəm], *s. Bot:* Viorne *f*.

vicar ['vikər], *s.* **1.** (*a*) Ecclésiastique préposé à l'administration d'une paroisse et titulaire du bénéfice, mais non de la dîme; curé *m*. *F:* Vicar of Bray, opportuniste *m*. (*b*) *Lit:* The Vicar of Wakefield, le Vicaire de Wakefield. (Erreur de traduction.) **2.** *R.C.Ch:* Vicar apostolic, vicaire apostolique. 'vicar-'general, *s. Ecc:* Vicaire général; grand vicaire.

vicarage ['vikəredʒ], *s.* Presbytère *m*; cure *f*.

vicarious [vai'keəriəs, vi-], *a.* **1.** (*Of authority*) Délégué. **2.** (*a*) (Châtiment) souffert (i) par un autre, (ii) pour un autre. (*b*) (Méthode) de substitution. **-ly**, *adv.* **1.** Par substitution. **2.** A la place d'un autre.

vice[1] [vais], *s.* **1.** Vice *m*. (*a*) To live in vice, vivre dans le vice. (*b*) *Avarice is a vice*, l'avarice est un vice. **2.** Défaut *m*. **3.** Vice (d'un cheval). **Stable vice**, tic *m*. 'vice-squad, *s. Adm:* Brigade *f* des mœurs.

vice[2], *s. Tls:* Étau *m*. **Bench-vice**, étau d'établi.

vice[3], *s. F:* = VICE-CHAIRMAN, VICE-PRESIDENT.

vice[4] ['vaisi], *prep.* A la place de (qn). *Treasurer: Mr B, vice Mr A, resigned*, trésorier: M. B, qui succède à M. A, démissionnaire.

vice-admiral [vais'admirəl], *s.* Vice-amiral, -aux *m*.

vice-chairman, *pl.* **-men**, *s.* Vice-président *m*.

vice-chairmanship, *s.* Vice-présidence *f*.

vice-chancellor, *s.* **1.** Vice-chancelier *m*. **2.** Recteur *m* (d'une université).

vice-chancellorship, *s.* **1.** Fonction *f*, dignité *f*, de vice-chancelier. **2.** Rectorat *m* (d'université).

vice-consul, *s.* Vice-consul *m*.

vice-consulate, *s.* Vice-consulat *m*.

vice-governor, *s.* Sous-gouverneur *m*.

vice-marshal, *s. Mil.Av:* Air vice-marshal, général *m*, -aux, de division.

vicennial [vi'senjəl], *a.* Vicennal, -aux.

vice-presidency, *s.* Vice-présidence *f*.

vice-president, *s.* Vice-président *m*.

vice-principal, *s. Sch:* Sous-directeur, -trice; sous-principal, -aux *m*; préfet *m* des études.

viceregal [vais'ri:g(ə)l], *a.* Du vice-roi.

viceroy ['vaisrɔi], *s.m.* Vice-roi.

vice versa ['vaisi'və:rsa], *Lt.adv.phr.* Vice versa; réciproquement.

vicinage ['visinedʒ], *s.* **1.** = VICINITY. **2.** *The v.*, les voisins *m*.

vicinity [vi'siniti], *s.* **1.** Voisinage *m*, proximité *f* (*to, with*, de). **2.** Abords *mpl*, alentours *mpl* (d'un lieu). **In the vicinity of . . .**, à proximité de . . .; *Nau:* dans les parages de. . . .

vicious ['viʃəs], *a.* **1.** Vicieux, corrompu. *V. tastes*, goûts pervers. **2.** (*Of horse*) Vicieux, hargneux, rétif. **3.** (*Of language*) Vicieux, défectueux. *S.a.* CIRCLE[1] 1. **4.** (i) *V. criticism*, critique méchante. (ii) To give a vicious tug at the bell, tirer rageusement la sonnette. **-ly**, *adv.* **1.** Vicieusement. **2.** Incorrectement. **3.** Méchamment; rageusement.

viciousness ['viʃəsnəs], *s.* **1.** Nature vicieuse; vice *m*. **2.** Méchanceté *f*.

vicissitude [vi'sisitju:d], *s.* Vicissitude *f*; *F:* péripétie *f*. *The vicissitudes of fortune*, les retours *m* de la fortune.

victim ['viktim], *s.* **1.** Victime (offerte en sacrifice) **2.** To be the victim of s.o., être la victime de qn. **Victim of an accident**, accidenté, -ée. *To fall a v. to s.o.'s charm*, succomber au charme de qn. *F:* To make a victim of oneself, se poser en victime.

victimization [viktimai'zeiʃ(ə)n], *s.* **1.** Oppression *f*, tyrannisation *f*. **2.** A case of victimization, une duperie.

victimize ['viktimaiz], *v.tr.* **1.** Prendre (qn) comme victime; exercer des représailles contre (les meneurs d'une grève, etc.). **2.** Tromper, escroquer (qn).

victor ['viktər], *s.* Vainqueur *m*.

Victoria [vik'tɔ:ria]. *Pr.n.f.* Victoire. **Queen Victoria**, la reine Victoria. **Vic'toria 'Cross**, *s.* (*Abbr.* V.C. ['vi:'si:]) Croix *f* de Victoria (décernée pour un acte de bravoure insigne).

Victorian [vik'tɔ:riən], *a. & s.* Victorien, -ienne; du règne de la reine Victoria. *S.a.* EARLY I.1 (*b*).

victorious [vik'tɔ:riəs], *a.* Victorieux; vainqueur *m*. **To be victorious over s.o.**, être victorieux de qn. **-ly**, *adv.* Victorieusement; en vainqueur.

victory ['viktəri], *s.* Victoire *f*. **To gain a victory, the victory**, remporter la victoire (*over*, sur). *S.a.* PYRRHIC[2].

victual ['vit(ə)l], *v.* (victualled ['vitld]) **1.** *v.tr.* Approvisionner; ravitailler (un navire). **2.** *v.i.* Se ravitailler. **victualling**, *s.* Approvisionnement *m*, ravitaillement *m*.

victualler ['vitlər], *s.* (*a*) Pourvoyeur *m*; fournisseur *m* de vivres. (*b*) **Licensed victualler**, (hôtelier) débitant *m* de boissons.

victuals ['vit(ə)lz], *s.pl.* (*a*) Vivres *m*, provisions *f*. (*b*) Victuailles *f*.

vicuña [vi'ku:nja], *s.* Vigogne *f*.

videlicet [vai'di:liset] *adv.* A savoir . . .; c'est-à-dire. . . .

vie [vai], *v.i.* (vied: vying) Le disputer (*with s.o.*, à qn); rivaliser (with s.o., avec qn). To vie with s.o. in politeness, faire assaut de politesse avec qn. They vie with one another as to who shall speak, c'est à qui parlera.

view¹ [vju:], s. Vue f. **I.** Regard m; coup m d'œil. At first view, à première vue. I should like to get a nearer v. of it, je voudrais l'examiner de plus près. On view, exposé; ouvert au public. Private view, entrée f sur invitation personnelle. **2.** (a) Exposed to view, exposé aux regards; à la vue de tous. He passed from our v., nous le perdîmes de vue. In view, en vue. At last a hotel came into view, enfin nous aperçûmes un hôtel. We were in v. of land, nous étions en vue de la terre. Land in view! terre! (b) Field of view (of telescope), champ m. **3.** (Prospect) (a) Vue, perspective f. Front view of the hotel, l'hôtel vu de face. You will get a better v. from here, vous verrez mieux d'ici. It was worth while coming up for the v., le panorama valait le déplacement. Point of view, point m de vue. (b) Arch: Front view, élévation f du devant. (c) To keep sth. in view, ne pas perdre qch. de vue. **4.** To offer a general v. of the subject, donner un aperçu général de la question. **5.** Manière f de voir; opinion f. To take a right view of things, voir juste. To hold extreme views, avoir des idées extrémistes. To have very decided views on . . ., avoir des idées arrêtées au sujet de. . . . What are your views on the matter? comment envisagez-vous la question? In my view, à mon avis. To share s.o.'s views, partager les sentiments de qn. **6.** In view of . . ., en considération de . . .; eu égard à. . . . In v. of these facts . . ., en présence de ces faits. . . . In v. of the distance . . ., vu l'éloignement. . . . **7.** Vue, intention f. To fall in with s.o.'s views, entrer dans les vues de qn. Will this meet your views? cela vous conviendra-t-il? To have sth. in view, avoir qch. en vue; méditer (un voyage). With a special object in view, en vue d'un objet spécial. Negotiations with a view to an alliance, négociations visant une alliance. **'view-finder,** s. Phot: Viseur m; iconoscope m. **'view-halloo,** s. Ven: "Vue f" du renard) (cri ou fanfare). **'view-point,** s. Point m de vue; (of beauty-spot) belvédère m.

view², v.tr. **I.** Regarder (qn, qch.); examiner, inspecter (qn, qch.); visiter (une maison à louer). **2.** Envisager (qch.). **3.** Voir, apercevoir. To view the fox away, voir débucher le renard.

vigil ['vidʒil], s. **I.** Veille f. To keep vigil, veiller. **2.** Ecc: Vigile f.

vigilance ['vidʒiləns], s. Vigilance f. U.S: Vigilance committee, comité de surveillance des mœurs.

vigilant ['vidʒilənt], a. Vigilant, éveillé, alerte. **-ly,** adv. Avec vigilance.

vignette¹ [vi'njet, -'net], s. **I.** Vignette f. **2.** Phot: Buste m sous cache dégradé.

vignette², v.tr. Phot: Dégrader (un portrait). Iris vignetting mask, dégradateur m iris.

vigorous ['vigərəs], a. Vigoureux robuste. Vigorous blow, coup de poing solide. **-ly,** adv. Vigoureusement.

vigour ['vigər], s. **I.** Vigueur f, énergie f. To die in the full vigour of manhood, mourir dans la force de l'âge. **2.** (a) Vigour of colouring, vigueur de coloris. (b) Mus: Brio m.

vile [vail], a. **I.** Vil; sans valeur. To render vile, avilir. S.a. DURANCE. **2.** Vil; bas, infâme. The vilest of men, le dernier des hommes. **3.** F: Abominable, exécrable. Vile weather, un sale temps. He's in a v. temper, il est d'une

humeur exécrable. **-ly,** adv. **I.** Vilement; bassement. **2.** D'une manière abominable.

vileness ['vailnəs], s. **I.** Bassesse f, caractère m ignoble (de qn, d'un sentiment). **2.** F: The v. of the weather, le temps abominable.

vilification [vilifi'keiʃ(ə)n], s. Dénigrement m, détraction f (de qn).

vilifier ['vilifaiər], s. Détracteur, -trice.

vilify ['vilifai], v.tr. Vilipender, diffamer, dénigrer (qn); dire des infamies de (qn).

villa ['vilə], s. **I.** Villa f; maison f de campagne. **2.** Petite maison (de banlieue).

village ['viledʒ], s. Village m ou bourgade f. Village inn, auberge de campagne.

villager ['viledʒər], s. Villageois, -oise.

villain ['vilən], s. (a) Scélérat m; bandit m, gredin m. F: You little v.! petit coquin! (b) Th: The villain (of the piece), le traître.

villainous ['vilənəs], a. **I.** Vil, infâme; de scélérat. V. deed, action scélérate. V. face, vilain visage. **2.** F: = VILE 3. **-ly,** adv. **I.** D'une manière infâme; en scélérat. **2.** F: D'une manière exécrable.

villainy ['viləni], s. **I.** Scélératesse f, infamie f (d'une action). **2.** Action scélérate; infamie.

villein ['vilən], s. Hist: Vilain m; serf m.

villose ['vilous], **villous** ['viləs], a. Villeux.

villosity [vi'lɔsiti], s. Anat: Villosité f.

vim [vim], s. F: Vigueur f, énergie f. Full of vim, plein de sève, d'énergie.

vinculum, pl. **-la** ['viŋkjuləm, -la], s. **I.** Lien m. **2.** Typ: (a) = BRACE¹ 6. (b) Mth: Barre tirée au-dessus d'un groupe de symboles.

vindicate ['vindikeit], v.tr. **I.** Défendre, soutenir (qn, sa foi); justifier (qn, sa conduite); prouver, maintenir (son dire). To v. one's character, se justifier. **2.** To vindicate one's rights, revendiquer ses droits.

vindication [vindi'keiʃ(ə)n], s. **I.** Défense f, apologie f. In vindication of his conduct, pour justifier sa conduite. **2.** Revendication f (d'un droit).

vindicative ['vindikeitiv], a. Justificatif.

vindicator ['vindikeitər], s. Défenseur m.

vindicatory ['vindikeitəri], a. = VINDICATIVE.

vindictive [vin'diktiv], a. **I.** Vindicatif; vengeur, -eresse. **2.** (Of pers.) Vindicatif, rancunier. **-ly,** adv. Vindicativement; avec une méchanceté rancunière.

vindictiveness [vin'diktivnəs], s. Esprit m de vengeance; esprit rancunier.

vine [vain], s. **I.** (Grape-)vine, vigne f. Wild vine, lambruche f, lambrusque f. **2.** Sarment m, tige f (de houblon). **'vine-arbour,** s. Treille f. **'vine-branch,** s. Branche f de vigne. Poet: Pampre m. **'vine-dresser,** s. Vigneron m. **'vine-grower,** s. Viticulteur m; vigneron m; propriétaire mf de vignes. **'vine-growing¹,** a. (Pays) vignoble, vinicole. **'vine-growing²,** s. Viticulture f. **'vine-leaf,** s. Feuille f de vigne. **'vine-plant, -stock,** s. Cep m de vigne.

vinegar ['vinigər], s. Vinaigre m. (a) Tarragon vinegar, vinaigre d'estragon. Cu: Vinegar sauce, vinaigrette f. F: Vinegar countenance, visage revêche. Toilet-vinegar, aromatic vinegar, vinaigre de toilette. **'vinegar-cruet,** s. Burette f à vinaigre; vinaigrier m. **'vinegar-faced,** a. F: Au visage revêche.

vinegarish ['vinigəriʃ], **vinegary** ['vinigəri], a. F: (Visage) revêche; (ton) acerbe, aigre.

vinery ['vainəri], s. Serre f à vignes.

vineyard ['vinjərd], s. Clos m de vigne; vigne f, vignoble m. The best vineyards, les meilleurs crus.

vinous ['vainəs], *a.* **1.** (*a*) (Goût) vineux. (*b*) Couleur *inv* de vin. **2.** (*a*) Aviné. (*b*) Ivrogne.

vintage ['vintedʒ], *s.* **1.** (*a*) Récolte *f* du raisin; vendanges *fpl*. (*b*) (*Crop*) Vendange. (*c*) Temps *m* de la vendange. **2.** Année *f* (de belle récolte). Of the vintage of 1906, de l'année 1906. Vintage year, année de bon vin; année honorable. Vintage wine, vin de marque; vin fin; grand vin.

vintager ['vintedʒər], *s.* Vendangeur, -euse.

vintner ['vintnər], *s.* Négociant *m* en vins.

viol ['vaiəl], *s. Mus: A:* Viole *f.* Bass-viol, basse *f* de viole.

viola¹ [vi'oulə], *s. Mus:* Alto *m* (à cordes). Viola player, altiste *mf.*

viola² ['vaiələ], *s. Bot:* **1.** Pensée *f* (unicolore). **2.** (*Genus*) Violacée *f.*

violate ['vaioleit], *v.tr.* Violer (un serment); profaner (un sanctuaire); manquer à (une règle). To violate the law, violer, enfreindre, la loi.

violation [vaio'lei∫(ə)n], *s.* Violation *f* (d'un serment); profanation *f* (d'un sanctuaire). *V. of an order,* infraction *f* à un ordre. *V. of s.o.'s privacy,* intrusion *f* auprès de qn.

violator ['vaioleitər], *s.* Violateur, -trice. Violator of the law, contrevenant, -ante.

violence ['vaioləns], *s.* **1.** (*a*) Violence *f*, intensité *f* (du vent). (*b*) **To die by violence,** mourir de mort violente. *To do v. to one's conscience,* violenter sa conscience. *To do v. to one's feelings,* se faire violence. **2.** *Jur:* **To resort to violence,** se livrer, se porter, à des voies de fait. Robbery with violence, vol *m* à main armée.

violent ['vaiolənt], *a.* **1.** Violent. *Aut:* V. braking, freinage brutal. **To lay violent hands on s.o.,** attaquer brutalement qn. *V. abuse,* injures violentes. **To lay violent hands on oneself,** attenter à ses jours. **To become violent,** se livrer à des actes de violence; s'emporter. **2.** (*a*) Violent, aigu, fort. *V. dislike,* vive aversion. *In a v. hurry,* extrêmement pressé. **Violent cold,** gros rhume. (*b*) Violent colours, couleurs criardes, crues. **-ly,** *adv.* **1.** Violemment; avec violence. **2.** Vivement; extrêmement. *To fall v. in love with s.o.,* tomber follement amoureux de qn.

violet ['vaiolet]. **I.** *s. Bot:* Violette *f.* **2.** *a. & s.* (*Colour*) Violet (*m*). **'violet-coloured,** *a.* Violet; de couleur violette. **'violet-powder,** *s.* Poudre *f* de riz à la violette. **'violet-scented,** *a.* A la violette.

violin [vaio'lin], *s.* Violon *m.*

violinist [vaio'linist], *s.* Violoniste *mf.*

violoncellist [vaiolon't∫elist], *s.* Violoncelliste *mf.*

violoncello [vaiolon't∫elo], *s.* Violoncelle *m.*

viper ['vaipər], *s.* (*a*) Vipère *f.* Young viper, vipereau *m. S.a.* BUGLOSS 2. (*b*) *F:* (*Of pers.*) Vipère.

viperine ['vaipərain], *a.* Vipérin.

viperish ['vaipəri∫], *a. F:* Viperish tongue, langue de vipère.

virago [vi'reigo], *s.f.* Mégère.

virgin ['vɜːdʒin]. **I.** *s.* Vierge *f.* The Blessed Virgin, la Sainte Vierge. *Ap:* Virgin queen, reine non fécondée. **2.** *a.* (*a*) De vierge; virginal, -aux. (*b*) Virgin forest, forêt vierge.

virginal ['vɜːdʒin(ə)l], *a.* Virginal, -aux.

Virginia [vər'dʒinjə]. **1.** *Pr.n.* Virginie *f. Bot:* Virginia creeper, vigne *f* vierge. **2.** *s.* Tabac *m* de Virginie; virginie *m.*

virginity [vər'dʒiniti], *s.* Virginité *f.*

virile ['virail], *a.* Viril, mâle. *A v. old age,* une mâle vieillesse.

virility [vi'riliti], *s.* Virilité *f.*

virtu [vər'tu:], *s.* Articles of virtu, objets *m* d'art.

virtual ['vɜːtjuəl], *a.* **1.** De fait; en fait. *He is the v. head of the business,* c'est lui le vrai chef de la maison. *This was a v. admission of guilt,* de fait, c'était un aveu. **2.** *Tchn:* Virtuel. *Opt:* Virtual image, image virtuelle. **-ally,** *adv.* Virtuellement; de fait; en pratique. . . . *I am v. certain of it,* j'en ai la quasi-certitude.

virtue ['vɜːtju], *s.* **1.** Vertu *f.* Woman of easy virtue, femme de mœurs faciles. **To make a virtue of necessity,** faire de nécessité vertu. **2.** Qualité *f*; avantage *m.* **3.** Plants that have healing virtues, plantes qu ont des propriétés curatives. **4.** *Prep.phr.* By virtue of, en vertu de; en raison de. *By v. of one's office,* à titre d'office.

virtuosity [vɜːtju'ositi], *s.* Virtuosité *f.*

virtuoso [vɜːtju'ouso], *s.* **1.** Amateur *m* des arts; connaisseur *m.* **2.** *Mus:* Virtuose *mf.*

virtuous ['vɜːtjuəs], *a.* Vertueux. **-ly,** *adv.* Vertueusement.

virulence ['virjulans], *s.* Virulence *f.*

virulent ['virjulant], *a.* Virulent. **-ly,** *adv.* Avec virulence.

virus ['vairəs], *s.* **1.** *Med:* Virus *m.* **2.** *F:* Venin *m*; poison (moral).

visa¹, ² ['vizə], *s. & v.tr.* = VISÉ¹, ².

visage ['vizedʒ], *s. Lit:* Visage *m,* figure *f.*

vis-à-vis ['vizzɑːviː]. **I.** *s. Danc: etc:* Vis-à-vis *m.* **2.** *adv.* Vis-à-vis (to, with, de).

viscera ['visərə], *s.pl.* Viscères *m.*

visceral ['visərəl], *a.* Viscéral, -aux.

viscid ['visid], *a.* Visqueux.

viscidity [vi'siditi], *s.* Viscidité *f*, viscosité *f.*

viscose [vis'kous], *s. Tex:* Viscose *f.* Viscose silk, soie artificielle.

viscosity [vis'kositi], *s.* Viscosité *f.*

viscount ['vaikaunt], *s.m.* Vicomte.

viscountcy ['vaikauntsi], *s.* Vicomté *f.*

viscountess ['vaikauntes], *s.f.* Vicomtesse.

viscounty ['vaikaunti], *s.* Vicomté *f.*

viscous ['viskəs], *a.* Visqueux; mucilagineux; gluant.

visé¹ ['viːze], *a. Adm:* Visa *m.*

visé², *v.tr.* (*p.t. & p.p.* viséd *or* visé'd ['viːzeid]) Viser; apposer un visa à (un passeport).

visibility [vizi'biliti], *s.* Visibilité *f. Nau:* Good visibility, bonne visibilité. (*In car*) Good v., vue dégagée.

visible ['vizibl], *a.* Visible. To become v., apparaître. Visible horizon, horizon visuel. Visible signal, signal optique. *Typewr:* Visible writer, machine à écriture visible. **-ibly,** *adv.* Visiblement, manifestement; (grandir) à vue d'œil.

Visigoth ['vizigoθ], *s. Hist:* Wisigoth *m.*

vision ['viʒən], *s.* **1.** (*a*) Vision *f,* vue *f.* Within the range of vision, à portée de vue. Beyond our v., au delà de notre vue. Field of vision, champ visuel. (*b*) Man of vision, homme d'une grande pénétration, qui voit loin dans l'avenir. **2.** (*a*) Imagination *f,* vision. Visions of wealth, visions de richesses. (*b*) Apparition *f,* fantôme *m.* He sees visions, il a des visions.

visionary ['viʒənəri]. **1.** *a.* (*a*) (*Of pers.*) Visionnaire. (*b*) (Projet) chimérique, fantastique. (*c*) (Mal) imaginaire. **2.** *s.* Visionnaire *mf*; idéologue *m.*

visit¹ ['vizit], *s.* **1.** (*a*) (Social) visit, visite *f.* Courtesy visit, visite de politesse. **To return s.o.'s visit,** rendre sa visite à quelqu'un. (*b*) *V. of a commercial traveller,* passage *m* d'un commis voyageur. **2.** Visite, séjour *m.* **To be on a visit to friends,** être en visite chez des amis. **3.** Tournée *f* d'inspection ; visite d'inspection. *Jur :* Domiciliary visit, visite domiciliaire.

visit², *v.tr.* **1.** (*a*) Rendre visite à (qn) ; aller voir (qn). (*b*) **To visit the poor,** visiter les pauvres. (*c*) *Com :* (*Of traveller*) Passer chez (un client). (*d*) Visiter, aller voir (un endroit). *We visited the museums,* nous avons vu les musées. **2.** (*Of official*) Visiter, inspecter. **3.** *To v. the sins of the fathers upon the children,* punir les enfants pour les péchés des pères ; faire retomber sur les enfants les péchés des pères. **visiting¹,** *a.* **1.** En visite. *Sp :* Visiting team, les visiteurs *m.* **2.** *Sch :* **Visiting master,** maître externe. **visiting²,** *s.* Visites *fpl.* **To be on visiting terms with s.o.,** être en relations de visites avec qn. **Visiting hours** (*at hospital*), heures de visite. **'visiting-card,** *s.* Carte *f* de visite.

visitation [vizi'teiʃ(ə)n], *s.* **1.** (*a*) Visite *f* (d'inspection). (*b*) Tournée *f* (d'inspection). **2.** Visitation of the sick, visites aux malades. **3.** (*a*) Visitation of God, affliction *f,* épreuve *f.* (*b*) *F :* Visite fâcheuse, trop prolongée. (*c*) Calamité *f.* **4.** Apparition (surnaturelle).

visitor ['vizitər], *s.* (*a*) Visiteur, -euse. *She has visitors,* elle a du monde. (*b*) **Summer visitors, winter visitors,** *at a seaside resort,* estivants *m,* hivernants *m,* d'une station balnéaire. **Visitors' book,** livre des voyageurs (à un hôtel) ; registre *m* des visiteurs (à un musée).

vison ['vaiz(ə)n], *s. Z :* Vison *m.*

visor ['vaizər], *s.* **1.** *Archeol :* Visière *f* (de casque). **2.** *Aut :* Paresoleil *m inv* ; parasol *m.*

vista ['vista], *s.* **1.** Échappée *f* de vue ; (*in forest*) percée *f,* éclaircie *f,* trouée *f.* **2.** *A long v. of beech-trees,* une longue perspective de hêtres. *F :* **To open up new vistas,** ouvrir de nouvelles perspectives.

visual ['viʒuəl, 'viz-], *a.* **1.** Visuel ; perceptible à l'œil. *V. distance,* distance de visibilité. *Mil : Nau :* **Visual signalling,** télégraphie optique. **2.** *Anat :* **The visual nerve,** le nerf optique. **-ally,** *adv.* Visuellement.

visualize ['viʒuəla:iz, 'viz-], *v.tr.* **1.** Rendre (qch.) visible. **2.** Se représenter (qch.) ; évoquer l'image de (qch.).

vital ['vait(ə)l]. I. *a.* **1.** Vital, -aux ; essentiel à la vie. **Vital force,** force vitale. **2.** Essentiel ; capital, -aux. **Question of vital importance,** question d'une importance vitale. **3.** *V. wound,* blessure mortelle. **V. error,** erreur fatale, irrémédiable. **4.** *Adm :* **Vital statistics,** statistique de vie. **-ally,** *adv.* D'une manière vitale. II. **vitals,** *s.pl.* **1.** Parties vitales. **2.** *Nau :* Œuvres vives.

vitality [vai'taliti], *s.* **1.** Vitalité *f* (d'un tissu) ; vitalité, vigueur *f* (d'une race). **2.** Vie *f,* animation *f,* vigueur (de style).

vitalize ['vaitəla:iz], *v.tr.* Vitaliser, vivifier.

vitamin ['vitəmin], *s. Bio-Ch :* Vitamine *f.*

vitellus, *pl.* **-i** [vi'teləs, -ai], *s. Biol :* Vitellus *m.*

vitiate ['viʃieit], *v.tr.* **1.** Vicier, corrompre. **2.** *Jur :* Vicier (un contrat). *To v. a transaction,* rendre une opération nulle.

vitiation [viʃi'eiʃ(ə)n], *s.* Viciation *f.*

viticultural [viti'kʌltjurəl], *a.* Viticole.

viticulture ['vitikʌltjər], *s.* Viticulture *f.*

vitreous ['vitriəs], *a.* **1.** Vitreux ; hyalin. **2.** *Anat :* **Vitreous body,** corps vitré (de l'œil).

vitrify ['vitrifai]. **1.** *v.tr.* Vitrifier. **2.** *v.i.* Se vitrifier.

vitriol ['vitriol], *s.* **1.** Vitriol *m.* **Blue vitriol,** vitriol bleu ; sulfate *m* de cuivre. **2.** (Oil of) vitriol, (huile *f* de) vitriol ; acide *m* sulfurique. **Vitriol-throwing,** vitriolage *m.*

vitriolic [vitri'ɔlik], *a. F :* Vitriolic pen, plume trempée dans du vitriol.

vituperate [vai'tju:pəreit], *v.tr.* Injurier, vilipender (qn).

vituperation [vaitju:pə'reiʃ(ə)n], *s.* Injures *fpl,* insultes *fpl,* invectives *fpl.*

vituperative [vai'tju:pərətiv], *a.* Injurieux ; mal embouché.

Vitus ['vaitəs]. *Pr.n.m. Med :* **Saint Vitus's dance,** chorée *f* ; danse *f* de Saint-Guy.

viva ['vaiva], *s. F : =* VIVA VOCE 3.

vivacious [vai'veiʃəs], *a.* Vif, animé, enjoué. **-ly,** *adv.* Avec enjouement ; avec verve.

vivaciousness [vai'veiʃəsnəs], **vivacity** [vai-'vasiti], *s.* Vivacité *f* ; animation *f* ; enjouement *m.*

vivat ['vaivat], *int. & s.* Vivat (*m*).

viva voce ['vaiva'vousi]. **1.** *adv.* De vive voix ; oralement. **2.** *a.* Oral, -aux. **3.** *s. Sch :* Examen oral ; épreuves orales.

vivid ['vivid], *a.* **1.** Vif, éclatant. *V. flash of lightning,* éclair aveuglant. **2.** *V. imagination,* imagination vive. **Vivid description,** description vivante. **-ly,** *adv.* **1.** Vivement ; avec éclat. **2.** *To describe sth. v.,* décrire qch. d'une manière vivante.

vividness ['vividnəs], *s.* **1.** Vivacité *f,* éclat *m* (des couleurs). **2.** *The v. of his style,* la vigueur de son style.

vivify ['vivifai], *v.tr.* Vivifier, animer.

vivipara [vi'vipara], *s.pl.* Vivipares *m.*

viviparous [vi'viparəs], *a.* Vivipare.

vivisect ['vivisekt], *v.tr.* Pratiquer des vivisections sur (des animaux). *Abs.* Faire de la vivisection.

vivisection [vivi'sekʃ(ə)n], *s.* Vivisection *f.*

vixen ['viks(ə)n], *s.f.* **1.** *Z :* Renarde. **2.** *F :* Mégère ; femme acariâtre ; *P :* teigne.

vixenish ['viksəniʃ], *a.* **1.** (*Of woman*) Acariâtre, méchante. **2.** (*Of disposition*) De mégère.

viz., *adv. =* VIDELICET.

Vizier [vi'zi:ər], *s.* Vizir *m.*

vocable ['voukəbl], *s.* Vocable *m.*

vocabulary [vo'kabjuləri], *s.* Vocabulaire *m.*

vocal ['vouk(ə)l], *a.* **1.** (*a*) Vocal, -aux. *Anat :* **Vocal cords,** cordes vocales. (*b*) **Vocal communication,** communication orale. (*c*) *Ling :* = VOICED 2. **2.** (*a*) Doué de voix ; capable de produire des sons. (*b*) Bruyant, sonore. *The vocal hills,* les collines retentissantes. **-ally,** *adv.* **1.** Vocalement, oralement. **2.** Par des chants ; à l'aide du chant.

vocalic [vo'kalik], *a.* **1.** (Langue) qui a beaucoup de voyelles. **2.** (Son) vocalique.

vocalist ['voukəlist], *s.* Chanteur *m,* cantatrice *f.*

vocalization [voukəlai'zeiʃ(ə)n], *s.* Vocalisation *f.*

vocalize ['voukəla:iz]. **1.** *v.tr.* (*a*) Prononcer (un mot) ; chanter (un air). (*b*) *Ling :* Vocaliser (une consonne). **2.** *v.i. Mus :* Faire des vocalises.

vocation [vo'keiʃ(ə)n], *s.* **1.** (*a*) Vocation *f* (*to the ministry,* au sacerdoce). (*b*) **A vocation for literature,** une inclination pour les lettres ; la vocation des lettres. **2.** Vocation, profession *f.* **To miss one's vocation,** manquer sa vocation.

vocative ['vɔkətiv], *a. & s. Gram :* Vocative (case), (cas) vocatif *m.* **In the vocative, au** vocatif.

vociferate [vo'sifəreit], *v.i. & tr.* Vociférer, crier (*against,* contre).

vociferation [vosifə'reiʃ(ə)n], *s.* **1.** Cri *m,* clameur *f.* **2.** Vociférations *fpl,* cris, clameurs.

vociferous [vo'sifərəs], *a.* Vociférant, bruyant,

criard, braillard. **-ly,** *adv.* En vociférant;
bruyamment.

vogue [voug], *s.* Vogue *f*, mode *f*. **To be in vogue,**
être en vogue, à la mode ; avoir de la vogue.

voice¹ [vɔis], *s.* **I. To raise one's voice,**
hausser la voix. **In a gentle voice,** d'une voix
douce. **In a low voice,** à voix basse ; à mi-voix ;
à demi-voix. **He likes to hear his own voice,** il
aime à s'entendre parler. *S.a.* RAISE 4, TOP¹ I. 6.
2. (*a*) Voix, suffrage *m*. (*b*) **To give voice to
one's indignation,** exprimer son indignation. **We
have no voice in the matter,** nous n'avons pas
voix au chapitre. **3.** *Gram:* Voix (du verbe). **In
the active voice,** à la voix active ; à l'actif.

voice², *v.tr.* **I.** Exprimer, énoncer (une opinion).
2. *Ling:* Voiser (une consonne). **voiced,** *a.*
I. Sweet-voiced, low-voiced, à la voix douce,
la voix basse. **2.** *Ling:* Voisé ; (consonne)
sonore.

voiceless ['vɔisləs], *a.* **I.** Sans voix ; muet.
2. *Ling:* Sourd ; non voisé.

void [vɔid]. I. *a.* **I.** Vide. **Void space,** espace
vide. **2.** (*Of office*) Vacant, inoccupé. **3.** *Jur:*
(*Of deed*) Nul, *f.* nulle. **To make a clause void,**
annuler une clause. *S.a.* NULL. **4.** *Poet:* Vain,
inutile. **5.** Dépourvu, dénué (*of, de*). *Proposal v.
of reason,* proposition dénuée de raison. II. **void,**
s. Vide *m.* **To fill the void,** combler le vide.
F: **To have an aching void,** avoir l'estomac
creux, dans les talons.

voile [vɔil], *s.* *Tex:* Voile *m.*

volatile ['vɔlətail], *a.* **I.** *Ch:* Volatil, gazéifiable.
2. (*a*) Vif, gai. (*b*) Volage, inconstant.

volatility [vɔlə'tiliti], *s.* *Ch:* Volatilité *f.*

volatilize [vɔ'latilaːiz]. **I.** *v.tr.* Volatiliser.
2. *v.i.* Se volatiliser.

volcanic [vɔl'kanik], *a.* Volcanique.

volcano, *pl.* **-oes** [vɔl'keino, -ouz], *s.* Volcan *m.*
Active volcano, volcan en activité.

vole [voul], *s.* *Z:* (**Field-)vole,** campagnol *m.*
Water vole, rat *m* d'eau.

volition [vo'liʃ(ə)n], *s.* Volition *f*, volonté *f.* **To
do sth. of one's own volition,** faire qch. de son
propre gré.

volley¹ ['vɔli], *s.* **I.** Volée *f*, salve *f* (d'armes à
feu) ; grêle *f* (de pierres). **2.** *F:* Volée, bordée *f*
(d'injures). **To let fly a volley of oaths,** lâcher
une bordée de jurons. **3.** *Ten:* (Balle prise de)
volée. **'volley-firing,** *s.* Feu *m* de salve ; feu
de peloton.

volley². **I.** *v.tr.* (*a*) *Mil:* Tirer une volée, une
salve, de (projectiles). *F:* **To volley (forth)
abuse,** lâcher une bordée d'injures. (*b*) *Ten:* **To
volley the ball,** *abs.* to volley, reprendre la balle
de volée. **2.** *v.i.* (*a*) (*Of guns*) Partir ensemble.
(*b*) *F:* Tonner.

volplane¹ ['vɔlplein], *s.* *Av:* Vol plané.

volplane², *v.i.* *Av:* **I.** Faire du vol plané ;
planer. **2.** Descendre en vol plané.

volt¹ [vɔlt, voult], *s.* *Equit:* *Fenc:* Volte *f.*

volt², *s.* *El.Meas:* Volt *m.* **volt-'ampere,** *s.*
El: Voltampère *m* ; watt *m.* **'volt-rise,** *s.*
El: Surtension *f.*

voltage ['vɔltedʒ, 'voultedʒ], *s.* *El.E:* Voltage *m* ;
tension *f* (en volts). **High voltage,** haute tension.
Voltage drop, perte *f* de charge. **Voltage recorder,**
voltmètre enregistreur.

voltaic [vɔl'teiik], *a.* *El:* Voltaïque ; de Volta.

volte [vɔlt, voult], *s.* = VOLT¹.

voltmeter ['vɔltmiːtər, 'voult-], *s.* *El:* Voltmètre *m.*

volubility [vɔlju'biliti], *s.* Volubilité *f.*

voluble ['vɔljubl], *a.* (*Of speech*) Facile, aisé ;
(langue) déliée, bien pendue. **To be a v. talker,**
parler avec beaucoup de volubilité. **-bly,** *adv.*
Avec volubilité.

volume ['vɔljum], *s.* **I.** Volume *m*, livre *m.*
Large v., tome *m.* **Volume one,** volume premier.
F: **It speaks volumes for him,** cela en dit long
en sa faveur. **2.** *pl.* **Volumes of smoke,** nuages *m*
de fumée. **Volumes of water,** flots *m* d'eau.
3. (*a*) *Ch:* *Ph:* Volume. **Densities for equal
volumes,** densités à volume égal. (*b*) **The v. of
the brain,** le volume du cerveau. **V. of a reservoir,**
cubage *m* d'un réservoir. **V. of a tone,** ampleur *f* (de la voix). *Mus:* **To give v. to the
tone,** nourrir le son.

volumetric(al) [vɔlju'metrik(əl)], *a.* *Ch:*
(Analyse) volumétrique.

voluminous [vo'ljuːminəs], *a.* **I.** (Auteur)
volumineux, abondant. **2.** (Paquet) volumineux.

voluntary ['vɔləntəri]. **I.** *a.* (*a*) Volontaire,
spontané. *V. offer,* offre spontanée. **Voluntary
confession of guilt,** confession volontaire ; aveu
spontané. **Voluntary discipline,** discipline librement consentie. (*b*) **Voluntary organization,**
organisation bénévole. (*c*) **Voluntary army,** armée
de volontaires. **2.** *s.* *Ecc.Mus:* Morceau d'orgue
(joué avant, pendant, ou après le service). **Outgoing voluntary,** sortie *f.* **-ily,** *adv.* Volontairement, spontanément ; de (son) plein gré.

volunteer¹ [vɔlən'tiːər], *s.* (*a*) *Mil:* Volontaire *m.*
(*b*) **To call for volunteers,** demander des
hommes de bonne volonté.

volunteer². **I.** *v.tr.* Offrir volontairement, spontanément (ses services). *Abs.* S'offrir (pour une
tâche). **To volunteer some information,** donner
spontanément des renseignements. **2.** *v.i.* *Mil:*
S'engager comme volontaire.

voluptuary [vo'lʌptjuəri], *s.* Voluptueux, -euse ;
sybarite *m* ; épicurien *m.*

voluptuous [vo'lʌptjuəs], *a.* Voluptueux. **-ly,**
adv. Voluptueusement.

voluptuousness [vo'lʌptjuəsnəs], *s.* Sensualité *f.*

volute [vo'ljuːt], *s.* Volute *f.*

voluted [vo'ljuːtid], *a.* **I.** A volutes. **2.** Enroulé
en spirale.

vomit¹ ['vɔmit], *s.* Matières vomies ; vomissement *m.*

vomit², *v.tr. & i.* (*a*) Vomir, rendre. *He began
to v.,* il fut pris de vomissements. (*b*) (*Of chimney*)
To vomit smoke, vomir de la fumée. **vomiting,**
s. Vomissement *m.*

vomitory ['vɔmitəri]. **I.** *a. & s.* *Med:* Vomitif (*m*).
2. *s.* *Rom.Ant:* Vomitoire *m* (d'amphithéâtre).

voodoo¹ ['vuːduː], *s.* *Anthr:* **I.** Vaudou *m* ;
envoûtement *m.* **2.** **Voodoo (doctor, priest),**
vaudou, *pl.* **-ous** ; sorcier *m* (nègre).

voodoo², *v.tr.* *Anthr:* Envoûter.

voracious [vo'reiʃəs], *a.* Vorace, dévorant.
Voracious appetite, appétit de loup. **Voracious
reader,** lecteur vorace. **-ly,** *adv.* Avec voracité ;
goulûment.

voraciousness [vo'reiʃəsnəs], **voracity** [vo'ra-
siti], *s.* Voracité *f.*

vortex, *pl.* **-ices, -exes** ['vɔːteks, -isiːz, -eksiz],
s. (*a*) *Ph:* Tourbillon *m.* **Vortex ring,** vortex *m.*
(*b*) Tourbillonnement *m* (d'air) ; tourbillon (de
fumée). (*c*) (*Whirlpool*) Tourbillon, gouffre *m.*
F: **The vortex of pleasure,** le tourbillon des
plaisirs.

vortical ['vɔːtik(ə)l], *a.* Tourbillonnaire.

vortiginous [vɔːr'tidʒinəs], *a.* Tourbillonnant.

votaress ['voutəres], *s.f.* Dévouée (*of, à*) ;
adoratrice (*of, de*) ; sectatrice (de).

votary ['voutəri], *s.* Dévoué, -e (*of, à*) ; adorateur, -trice (de) ; sectateur, -trice. *F* : **Votary of art**, partisan zélé des arts.

vote¹ [vout], *s.* **I.** (*a*) Vote *m*, scrutin *m*. **Secret vote**, scrutin secret. **Popular vote**, consultation *f* populaire. **Vote of an assembly**, délibération *f* d'une assemblée. **To put a question to the vote**, mettre une question aux voix. **To take the vote**, procéder au scrutin. (*b*) **(Individual) vote**, voix *f*, suffrage *m*. **To give one's vote to, for**, s.o., donner sa voix à qn. **To have a vote**, avoir le droit de vote. **To record one's vote**, voter. **2.** (*a*) Motion *f*, résolution *f*. **Vote of censure**, motion de censure. **To carry a vote**, adopter une résolution. *S.a.* CONFIDENCE 1. (*b*) *Parl* : Crédit *m*. **The Army vote**, le crédit militaire.

vote². **I.** *v.i.* Voter (*for, against*, pour, contre) ; donner sa voix, son vote (*for sth.*, pour qch.) ; *abs.* prendre part au vote. **2.** *v.tr.* (*a*) **To vote a sum**, voter une somme ; *Parl* : voter un crédit. (*b*) *F* : **I vote that we go**, je propose que nous y allions. **voting**, *s.* (Participation *f* au) vote ; scrutin *m* ; (*by white or black balls*) ballottage *m*. **Result of the v.**, vote. **Voting paper**, bulletin *m* de vote.

voter ['voutər], *s.* (*a*) Votant *m*. (*b*) Électeur, -trice.

votive ['voutiv], *a.* Votif. **Votive offering**, offrande votive ; ex-voto *m*.

vouch [vautʃ]. **I.** *v.tr.* (*a*) Affirmer, garantir (qch.). (*b*) Prouver, confirmer (une affirmation). **2.** *v.i.* **To vouch for the truth of sth.**, témoigner de, répondre de, la vérité de qch. **To vouch for s.o.**, répondre de qn ; se rendre garant de qn.

voucher ['vautʃər], *s.* (*a*) Justification produite à l'appui de dépenses ; pièce justificative. *Book-k* : Pièce comptable. (*b*) *Com* : Fiche *f* ; reçu *m*, bon *m*. **Cash voucher**, bon de caisse. *Adm* : **Issue voucher**, facture *f* de sortie. (*c*) *Th* : Contre-marque *f*.

vouchsafe [vautʃ'seif], *v.tr.* (*a*) **To vouchsafe s.o. sth.**, accorder, octroyer, qch. à qn. (*b*) **To vouchsafe to do sth.**, daigner faire qch.

voussoir ['vu:swɔ:r], *s.* *Arch* : Voussoir *m*, vousseau *m*, claveau *m*. **Centre voussoir**, clef *f* (de voûte).

vow¹ [vau], *s.* Vœu *m*, serment *m*. **Monastic vows**, vœux monastiques. **Lovers' vows**, serments d'amoureux. **To be under a vow to do sth.**, avoir fait le vœu de faire qch. **To fulfil a vow**, accomplir un vœu.

vow², *v.tr.* Vouer, jurer. **To vow obedience**, jurer obéissance. **To vow vengeance against s.o.**, faire vœu de se venger de, sur, qn. *Abs.* **To vow and protest**, jurer ses grands dieux.

vow³, *v.tr. A* : Affirmer, déclarer (*that*, que).

vowel ['vauəl], *s.* Voyelle *f*. **Vowel sound**, son *m* vocalique.

voyage¹ ['vɔiedʒ], *s.* Voyage *m* sur mer. **On the voyage out, home**, à l'aller, au retour.

voyage², *v.i.* Voyager sur mer ; naviguer. **voyaging**, *s.* Voyage(s) *m(pl)* sur mer.

voyager ['vɔiedʒər], *s.* Voyageur, -euse, par mer ; passager, -ère ; navigateur *m*.

vulcanite ['vʌlkənait], *s.* Vulcanite *f*, ébonite *f*.

vulcanization [vʌlkənai'zeiʃ(ə)n], *s.* *Ind* : Vulcanisation *f* (du caoutchouc).

vulcanize ['vʌlkənaiz]. **I.** *v.tr.* *Ind* : Vulcaniser (le caoutchouc). *Aut* : **To v. a repair**, vulcaniser une réparation (de pneu). **2.** *v.i.* Se vulcaniser. **vulcanizing**, *s.* Vulcanisation *f*.

vulgar ['vʌlgər], *a.* **I.** Vulgaire, commun ; de mauvais goût. **V. display of wealth**, gros luxe de mauvais goût. **The vulgar herd**, s. **the vulgar**, le vulgaire ; le commun des hommes. **2.** (*a*) Vulgaire ; communément reçu. **V. errors**, erreurs très répandues. (*b*) **The vulgar tongue**, la langue commune, la langue vulgaire. (*c*) *Ar* : **Vulgar fraction**, fraction ordinaire. **-ly**, *adv.* **I.** Vulgairement, grossièrement. **2.** Vulgairement, communément.

vulgarian [vʌl'geəriən], *s.* (*a*) Personne vulgaire, commune. (*b*) Parvenu(e) mal décrassé(e).

vulgarism ['vʌlgərizm], *s.* Expression *f* vulgaire.

vulgarity [vʌl'gariti], *s.* Vulgarité *f*, trivialité *f*. **To lapse into v.**, donner dans le vulgaire.

vulgarization [vʌlgərai'zeiʃ(ə)n], *s.* Vulgarisation *f*.

vulgarize ['vʌlgərai:z], *v.tr.* **I.** Vulgariser (une science). **2.** Vulgariser, trivialiser (son style).

vulnerability [vʌlnərə'biliti], *s.* Vulnérabilité *f*.

vulnerable ['vʌlnərəbl], *a.* (*a*) Vulnérable. **That is his v. spot**, c'est son talon d'Achille. (*b*) *Cards* : (*At bridge*) Vulnérable.

vulpine ['vʌlpain], *a.* **I.** Qui a rapport au renard. **2.** Qui tient du renard ; rusé, astucieux.

vulture ['vʌltjər], *s.* **I.** *Orn* : Vautour *m*. **2.** *F* : Homme *m* rapace.

vying ['vaiiŋ]. *See* VIE.

W

W, w ['dʌblju:], *s.* (La lettre) W, w *m*.

wad¹ [wɔd], *s.* **I.** (*a*) Tampon *m*, bouchon *m* (d'ouate, etc.). (*b*) *Esp. U.S* : Liasse *f* (de billets de banque). **2.** Bourre *f* (de cartouche).

wad², *v.tr.* (**wadded**) *Dressm* : Ouater, capitonner (un vêtement). **wadding**, *s.* **I.** Ouatage *m*, rembourrage *m*. **2.** (*a*) Ouate *f* (pour vêtements) ; bourre *f* (pour armes à feu). (*b*) Tampon *m* d'ouate.

waddle¹ [wɔdl], *s.* Dandinement *m* ; tortillement *m* des hanches ; démarche *f* de canard.

waddle², *v.i.* Se dandiner (comme un canard) ; tortiller les hanches.

wade [weid]. **I.** *v.i.* Marcher (avec effort) dans l'eau. (*Of child*) **To wade in the sea**, patauger dans la mer. **To wade across a stream**, passer à gué

un cours d'eau. *F* : **To wade through a book**, venir péniblement à bout d'un livre. **2.** *v.tr.* Passer à gué (un cours d'eau). **wading**, *a.* *Orn* : **Wading bird** = WADER I.

wader ['weidər], *s.* **I.** *Orn* : Échassier *m*. **2.** Personne *f* qui marche dans l'eau. **3.** *pl.* **Waders**, bottes cuissardes imperméables.

wadi ['wɔdi], *s.* Oued *m*, ravin *m* (dans le Sahara).

wafer ['weifər], *s.* **I.** *Cu* : Gaufrette *f* ; (*rolled into a cone*) plaisir *m*, oublie *f*. **2.** *Ecc* : Hostie *f*. **Unconsecrated wafer**, pain *m* à chanter. **3.** (*a*) *A* : Pain à cacheter. (*b*) Disque *m* de papier rouge (collé sur un document en guise de cachet). **4.** *Pharm* : Cachet *m* (de quinine).

waffle [wɔfl], *s.* *Cu* : Gaufre (américaine).

waffle-iron, *s.* Gaufrier *m* ; moule *m* à gaufres.

waft¹ [wɑːft], *s.* **1.** Bouffée *f*, souffle *m* (de vent). **2.** Coup *m* d'aile (d'un oiseau).

waft², *v.tr.* *Lit.* & *Poet :* To waft a sound, a scent, through the air, porter, transporter, un son, un parfum, dans les airs. *Music wafted on the breeze,* musique qui flotte sur la brise. *Lit :* (*Of the wind*) To waft the ship along, faire avancer le navire.

wag¹ [wag], *s.* **1.** Farceur *m*, blagueur *m* ; *P :* loustic *m.* **2.** *Sch :* *P :* To play (the) wag (from school), faire l'école buissonnière.

wag², *s.* Agitation *f*, mouvement *m* (de la queue) ; hochement *m* (de la tête). (*Of dog*) With a wag of its tail, en remuant la queue.

wag³, *v.* (wagged) **1.** *v.tr.* Agiter, remuer (le bras). (*Of dog*) To wag its tail, remuer, agiter, la queue. To wag one's tongue, jaser ; jacasser. To wag one's finger at s.o., menacer qn du doigt. To wag one's head, hocher la tête. *S.a.* CHIN. **2.** *v.i.* (*a*) S'agiter, se remuer. His tongue was beginning to wag, sa langue se déliait. To set (people's) tongues wagging, faire aller les langues. (*b*) How wags the world? comment vont les choses? So the world wags, ainsi va le monde.

wage¹ [weidʒ], *s.* *Usu. pl.* (*a*) Gages *mpl* (de domestique) ; salaire *m*, paye *f* (d'ouvrier). To receive one's day's wage(s), toucher sa journée. To earn good wages, être bien rétribué. A living wage, un salaire qui permet de vivre. (*b*) *Lit :* Prix *m*, salaire. The wages of sin is death, la mort est le salaire du péché. **'wage-earner,** *s.* **1.** Salarié, -ée. **2.** Le gagne-pain *inv* (de la famille). **'wage(s)-sheet,** *s.* *Ind :* Feuille *f* des salaires ; feuille de paye.

wage², *v.tr.* To wage war, faire la guerre (*with, on,* à).

wager¹ [ˈweidʒər], *s.* Pari *m* ; gageure *f.* To lay, make, wager, faire un pari ; parier.

wager², *v.tr.* Parier, gager. I'll wager that . . ., je parie, je gage, que. . . .

waggish [ˈwagiʃ], *a.* Plaisant, badin ; blagueur, facétieux. *W.* remarks, facéties *f.* **-ly,** *adv.* Plaisamment, facétieusement.

waggishness [ˈwagiʃnəs], *s.* Caractère blagueur ; disposition *f* à la plaisanterie.

waggle [wagl], *v.tr.* & *i.* *F :* = WAG³.

Wagnerian [vɑːgˈniːəriən], *a.* & *s.* Wagnérien.

wag(g)on [ˈwag(ə)n], *s.* **1.** Charrette *f* (à quatre roues) ; chariot *m* ; camion *m.* *U.S :* *F :* To be on the (water) waggon, s'abstenir des boissons alcooliques. **2.** *Mil :* Fourgon *m.* Ammunition waggon, caisson *m* à munitions. **3.** *Rail :* Wagon découvert (à marchandises). Covered goods waggon, fourgon. **'wag(g)on-load,** *s.* Charretée *f*, enlevée *f* (de foin, etc.). *Rail :* (Charge *f* de) wagon *m.* **'wag(g)on-train,** *s.* *Mil :* Train *m* des équipages ; les fourgons *m.*

wag(g)oner [ˈwagənər], *s.* Roulier *m*, voiturier *m*, charretier *m.*

wag(g)onette [wagəˈnet], *s.* *Veh :* Wagonnette *f*, break *m.*

wagtail [ˈwagteil], *s.* *Orn :* Hochequeue *m*, branle-queue *m*, bergeronnette *f.*

waif [weif], *s.* *Jur :* Épave *f.* *F :* The waifs of society, les épaves de la société. Waifs and strays, (enfants) abandonnés.

wail¹ [weil], *s.* (*a*) Cri plaintif ; plainte *f*, gémissement *m.* (*b*) Vagissement *m* (de nouveau-né).

wail², *v.i.* (*a*) Gémir ; (*of new-born child*) vagir. (*b*) To wail over sth., se lamenter sur qch. **wailing,** *a.* (Cri) plaintif ; (*of pers.*) gémissant.

wain [wein], *s.* **1.** Charrette *f* (à quatre roues). **2.** *Astr :* Charles's Wain, le Grand Chariot.

wainscot¹ [ˈweinskot], *s.* Lambris *m* (de hauteur) ; boiserie *f* (d'une salle).

wainscot², *v.tr.* Lambrisser. Wainscot(t)ed room, chambre ambrissée, boisée. **wainscot(t)ing,** *s.* **1.** Lambrissage *m.* **2.** = WAINSCOT¹.

waist [weist], *s.* **1.** (*a*) (*Of pers.*) Taille *f*, ceinture *f.* Down to the waist, up to the waist, jusqu'à mi-corps. Waist measurement, tour *m* de taille. To put one's arm round s.o.'s waist, prendre qn par la taille. *Wr :* Grip round the waist, la ceinture. (*b*) Étranglement *f* (d'un sablier, d'un violon). (*c*) *Nau :* Embelle *f*, passavant *m.* **2.** *Dressm :* Dress with a short waist, robe à taille courte. **'waist-belt,** *s.* *Mil :* Ceinturon *m.* **'waist-cloth,** *s.* = LOIN-CLOTH. **'waist-'deep, -'high,** *adv.* Jusqu'à la ceinture ; jusqu'à mi-corps. **'waist-lock,** *s.* *Wr :* Ceinture *f.*

waistband [ˈweistband], *s.* Ceinture (de jupe).

waistcoat [ˈweis(t)kout], *s.* **1.** Gilet *m.* *S.a.* POCKET¹ **1. 2.** Strait waistcoat, camisole *f* de force.

waisted [ˈweistid], *a.* Long-waisted, short-waisted, long, court, de taille.

waistline [ˈweistlain], *s.* *Dressm :* Taille *f.*

wait¹ [weit], *s.* **1.** (*a*) Attente *f* ; (*of train*) arrêt *m.* We had a long wait at the station, nous avons dû attendre longtemps à la gare. *Twenty minutes' w. between the two trains,* battement *m* de vingt minutes entre les deux trains. (*b*) To lie in wait, se tenir en embuscade ; être à l'affût. To lie in wait for s.o., se tenir à l'affût (for qn). *Jur :* Lying in wait, guet-apens *m.* **2.** *pl.* Waits, chanteurs *m* de noëls (qui vont de porte en porte).

wait². **1.** *v.i.* (*a*) Attendre. Wait a moment, *F :* wait a bit, attendez un moment. To keep s.o. waiting, faire attendre qn. He is keeping us waiting, il se fait attendre. To wait for s.o., attendre qn. Not to w. for s.o., brûler la politesse à qn. We are waiting to be served, nous attendons qu'on nous serve. He did not wait to be told twice, il ne se le fit pas dire deux fois. *Parcel waiting (to be called for) at the station,* colis en souffrance à la gare. *Com :* Repairs while you wait, réparations à la minute. *Prov :* Everything comes to him who waits, tout vient à point à qui sait attendre. Wait and see! il faudra voir ! attendez voir ! (*b*) To wait at table, servir (à table) ; faire le service. **2.** *v.tr.* (*a*) Attendre, guetter (une occasion). (*b*) To wait a meal for s.o., différer un repas jusqu'à l'arrivée de qn. **wait on, upon,** *v.ind.tr.* (*a*) Servir (qn). To wait on s.o. hand and foot, être aux petits soins pour, avec, qn. Waiting-maid, femme de chambre. (*b*) Se présenter chez (un supérieur). (*c*) Être la conséquence de (qch.) ; suivre (qch.). *The ills that w. on intemperance,* les maux qui découlent de l'intempérance. **wait up,** *v.i.* To wait up for s.o., rester levé à attendre qn.

waiting, *s.* **1.** Attente *f.* We shall lose nothing by w., nous ne perdrons rien pour attendre. **2.** Service *m.* In waiting, de service. Lady in waiting, dame d'honneur. **'waiting-room,** *s.* Salle *f* d'attente ; antichambre *f* (chez un médecin).

waiter [ˈweitər], *s.* **1.** Garçon *m* (de restaurant). Head waiter, maître d'hôtel. Waiter! garçon ! **2.** Plateau *m.*

waitress [ˈweitres], *s.f.* Fille de salle (de restaurant) ; serveuse. Waitress! mademoiselle !

waive [weiv], *v.tr.* Renoncer à, abandonner (ses

prétentions); déroger à (un principe); ne pas insister sur (une condition).

waiver ['weivər], *s. Jur:* Waiver of a right, abandon *m* d'un droit. *W. of a claim,* désistement *m* (de revendication).

wake[1] [weik], *s. (a) Nau:* Sillage *m,* houache *f.* To be in the wake of a ship, être dans les eaux d'un bâtiment. *(b) F:* To follow in s.o.'s wake, marcher à la suite de, sur les traces de, qn.

wake[2], *s. (In Ireland)* Veillée *f* mortuaire.

wake[3], *v. (p.t.* woke [wouk], waked [weikt]; *p.p.* woke, waked, woken ['wouk(ə)n]) **I.** *v.i. (a)* Être éveillé. Waking or sleeping, *that thought never left her,* éveillée ou endormie, cette pensée ne la quittait jamais. *(b)* To wake (up), se réveiller. Come, wake up! allons, réveillez-vous! To wake up with a start, se réveiller en sursaut. *F:* To wake up to find oneself famous, se réveiller célèbre. He is waking up to the truth, la vérité se fait jour dans son esprit. **2.** *v.tr. (a)* To wake s.o. (up), réveiller qn. *He wants something to w. him up,* il lui faut quelque chose qui l'émoustille. *(b) F:* To wake the dead, réveiller, ranimer, les morts. *(c) (In Ireland)* Veiller (un mort).

waking[1], *a.* Éveillé. Waking hours, heures de veille. *S.a.* DREAM[1]. **waking**[2], *s.* **I.** Veille *f.* Between sleeping and waking, entre la veille et le sommeil. **2.** Réveil *m.* On waking, au réveil.

wakeful ['weikful], *a.* **I.** *(a)* Éveillé; peu disposé à dormir. *(b)* Sans sommeil. Wakeful night, nuit blanche. **2.** Vigilant. **-fully,** *adv.* **I.** Sans dormir. **2.** Avec vigilance.

wakefulness ['weikfulnəs], *s.* **I.** *(a)* Insomnie *f.* *(b)* État *m* de veille. **2.** Vigilance *f.*

waken ['weik(ə)n]. **I.** *v.tr. (a)* Éveiller, réveiller (qn). *(b)* Éveiller, exciter (une émotion). **2.** *v.i.* Se réveiller, s'éveiller. **wakening,** *s.* Réveil *m.*

waker ['weikər], *s.* To be an early waker, se réveiller (habituellement) de bonne heure.

Waldenses [wɔl'densi:z], *s.pl. Rel.H:* Vaudois *m.*

wale[1] [weil], *s.* Marque *f,* trace *f* (d'un coup de fouet); vergeture *f.*

wale[2], *v.tr.* Marquer (d'un coup de fouet); zébrer (de coups de fouet).

Wales [weilz]. *Pr.n.* Le pays de Galles. North Wales, la Galles du Nord. *S.a.* NEW SOUTH WALES. The Prince of Wales, le Prince de Galles.

walk[1] [wɔ:k], *s.* **I.** Marche *f.* It is half an hour's walk from here, c'est à une demi-heure de marche d'ici. *It's only a short w. (from here),* ce n'est qu'une promenade. **2.** *(a)* Promenade (à pied). To go for a walk, aller se promener; faire un tour, une promenade. To take s.o. for a walk, emmener qn en promenade. *(b) Post:* Tournée *f* (du facteur). **3.** *(a)* Démarche *f.* I know him by his walk, je le reconnais à sa marche, à sa démarche. *(b) (Of horse)* To fall into a walk, se mettre au pas. **4.** *(a)* Allée *f* (de jardin); avenue *f,* promenade. *(b)* Trottoir *m.* *(c)* Allée couverte; promenoir *m.* **5.** Walk of life, (i) position sociale; (ii) métier *m,* carrière *f.*

walk[2]. **I.** *v.i.* **I.** Marcher, cheminer. To walk on the road, cheminer sur la chaussée. To walk on to the road, s'engager sur la chaussée. To walk in one's sleep, être somnambule, noctambule. To walk with s.o., accompagner qn. *W. a little way with me,* faites-moi un bout de conduite. **2.** *(a) (As opposed to ride, drive)* Aller à pied. To walk home, rentrer à pied. *I had to w.,* j'ai dû faire le trajet à pied. You can walk it in ten minutes, vous en avez pour dix minutes à pied. *(b) (For pleasure)* Se promener (à pied). To be out walking, être en promenade. **3.** *(Of horse, etc.)* Aller au pas. **4.** *(Of ghost)* Revenir.

II. walk, *v.tr.* **I.** To walk the streets, courir les rues; battre le pavé. *(Of sentry)* To walk one's round, faire sa faction. *F:* To walk the boards, être sur les planches; être acteur. *S.a.* HOSPITAL I, PLANK[1]. **2.** *(a)* Faire marcher (un stupéfié). *(b)* To walk s.o. off his legs, exténuer qn à force de le faire marcher. *(c)* To walk a horse, conduire, promener, un cheval (au pas). **walk about,** *v.i.* Se promener; circuler. **walk along,** *v.i.* **I.** Marcher; s'avancer. **2.** *To w. along the kerb,* suivre le bord du trottoir. **walk away,** *v.i.* S'en aller; partir. *Sp: F:* To walk away from a competitor, distancer facilement un concurrent. **walk in,** *v.i.* Entrer. To ask s.o. to walk in, faire entrer qn. *(On office door)* (Please) walk in, entrez sans frapper. **walk into,** *v.i.* **I.** To walk into the room, entrer dans la salle. **2.** *F: (a)* Se heurter à (qch.); se trouver nez à nez avec (qn). *(b)* S'attaquer à (qch.). *(c)* To walk into one's food, manger goulûment sa nourriture. **walk off.** **I.** *v.i.* S'en aller; partir. *F:* To walk off with sth., décamper avec (un objet volé, etc.). **2.** *v.tr. (a)* To walk s.o. off to prison, emmener qn en prison. *(b)* To walk off one's lunch, faire une promenade de digestion. **walk out.** **I.** *v.i. (a)* Sortir. *(b) (Of servant girl)* To walk out with a young man, sortir avec un jeune homme; être bien avec un jeune homme. **2.** *v.tr. (Of young man)* To walk out his girl, faire sortir sa bonne amie. **walk over,** *v.i. Sp:* To walk over (the course), gagner d'office (en l'absence d'autres concurrents). **'walk-over,** *s. Sp:* Victoire *f* facile. **walk round,** *v.i.* **I.** Faire le tour de (qch.). **2.** Faire le tour; faire un détour. **walk up.** **I.** *v.i.* To walk up to s.o., s'avancer vers qn; s'approcher de qn. To walk up and down, se promener de long en large. **2.** *v.tr.* To walk a horse up and down, promener un cheval. **walking**[1], *a.* **I.** (Voyageur) ambulant. **2.** *Th:* Walking gentleman, figurant *m.* **walking**[2], *s.* Marche *f;* promenades *fpl* à pied; le footing. *To like w.,* aimer la marche. It is within ten minutes' walking distance, vous en avez pour dix minutes à pied. It is within walking distance, on peut aisément s'y rendre à pied. **'walking-boots,** *s.pl.* Chaussures *f* de marche. **'walking-pace,** *s.* Allure *f* du pas. *Aut:* To drive at a w.-p., conduire, rouler, au pas. **'walking-race,** *s.* Match *m* de marche, de footing. **'walking-stick,** *s.* Canne *f.*

walker ['wɔ:kər], *s.* **I.** Marcheur, -euse; promeneur, -euse; piéton *m.* He is a fast walker, il marche vite. To be a good walker, être bon marcheur. **2.** *Th:* Walker-on, figurant, -ante.

wall[1] [wɔ:l], *s.* **I.** *(a)* Mur *m.* Main walls, gros murs. Blank wall, mur plein. *Surrounding w.,* mur d'enceinte. Dry wall, perré *m.* Wall for fruit trees, espalier *m. El.E:* Wall switchboard, tableau de distribution mural. To leave only the bare walls standing, ne laisser que les quatre murs. *F:* To run one's head against a (brick) wall, donner la tête contre un mur; se buter à l'impossible. *F:* He can see through a brick wall, plus fin que lui n'est pas bête. *F:* To go to the wall, succomber; perdre la partie. The weakest always goes to the wall, le plus faible est toujours écrasé. *(b)* Muraille *f. W. of rocks,* muraille de rochers. Within the walls (of the town), dans la ville; intra muros. The Great Wall of China, la muraille de Chine. *Pol.Ec:* High tariff walls, hautes murailles douanières. **2.** Paroi *f* (de la poitrine, d'une cellule). *Geol:* Wall of a lode, paroi, éponte *f,* d'un filon.

'**wall-bracket,** *s.* Console murale. '**wall-clock,** *s.* Cartel *m*; pendule murale; (*round*) œil-de-bœuf *m*, *pl.* œils-de-bœuf. '**wall-face,** *s.* **1.** Surface *f* d'un mur. **2.** *Min:* Paroi *f* (d'une galerie). '**wall fern,** *s.* Polypode *m* vulgaire. '**wall-fruit,** *s.* Fruit *m* d'espalier. '**wall-map,** *s.* Carte murale. '**wall-painting,** *s.* Peinture murale. '**wall-paper,** *s.* Papier peint; (papier) tenture *f.* '**wall-seat,** *s.* Banquette *f.*

wall², *v.tr.* **1.** To wall (in), entourer de murs; murer. **2.** Murailler (un talus, etc.). **wall up,** *v.tr.* To wall up the windows of a house, murer les fenêtres d'une maison. **walled,** *a.* **1.** Walled (in), muré; clos de murs. **2.** Brick-walled house, maison aux murs en briques.

wallaby ['wɔlabi], *s.* Kangourou *m* de petite taille; wallaby *m.*

wallah ['wɔla], *s.* (*Anglo-Indian*) Employé *m*, garçon *m.* Punkah-wallah, tireur *m* de panka.

wallet ['wɔlet], *s.* **1.** (i) Bissac *m*; (ii) besace *f* (de mendiant). **2.** Sacoche *f* (de bicyclette); giberne *f* (de musicien). **3.** Portefeuille *m.*

wall-eyed ['wɔːl'aid], *a.* (*Of horse*) Vairon.

wallflower ['wɔːlflauǝr], *s.* **1.** *Bot:* Giroflée *f* des murailles; ravenelle *f.* **2.** *F:* (*At a dance*) To be a wallflower, faire tapisserie.

Walloon [wɔ'luːn]. **1.** *a.* & *s.* Wallon, -onne. **2.** *s.* *Ling:* Le wallon.

wallop¹ ['wɔlǝp], *s.* *F:* **1.** Gros coup; *P:* torgn(i)ole *f.* **2.** And down he went with a wallop! et patatras, le voilà qui tombe!

wallop², *v.tr.* *P:* Rosser (qn); flanquer une tournée à (qn). **walloping¹,** *a.* *P:* Énorme; épatant. **walloping²,** *s.* *P:* Volée *f* (de coups); rossée *f.*

wallow¹ ['wɔlo, -ou], *s.* Trou bourbeux (où se roulent les buffles); souille *f* (de sanglier).

wallow², *v.i.* (*Of animals*) Se vautrer; se rouler dans la boue. *F:* (*Of pers.*) To wallow in blood, se baigner dans le sang. To wallow in vice, croupir dans le vice.

walnut ['wɔːlnʌt], *s.* **1.** Noix *f.* Green walnut, cerneau *m.* *Tex:* Walnut dye, racinage *m.* **2.** *Bot:* Noyer *m.* **3.** (Bois *m* de) noyer. '**walnut-juice,** *s.* Brou *m* de noix. '**walnut-shell,** *s.* Coquille *f* de noix. '**walnut-stain,** *s.* Brou *m* de noix. '**walnut-tree,** *s.* *Bot:* Noyer *m.*

walrus ['wɔːlrʌs], *s.* *Z:* Morse *m.* *F:* Walrus moustache, moustache tombante.

Walter ['wɔːltǝr]. *Pr.n.m.* Gauthier.

waltz¹ [wɔːls], *s.* **1.** Valse *f.* **2.** *Mus:* Air *m* de valse.

waltz², *v.i.* Valser. *I waltzed with Miss X,* j'ai fait valser Mlle X. **waltzing,** *s.* Valse *f.*

wampum ['wɔmpǝm], *s.* *Anthr:* Wampoum *m.*

wan [wɔn], *a.* Pâlot, -otte; blême. Wan light, lumière blafarde. Wan smile, pâle sourire. **-ly,** *adv.* (Sourire) d'un air triste.

wand [wɔnd], *s.* **1.** Baguette *f* (de fée). **2.** (*Staff of office*) Bâton *m* (de commandement); verge *f* (d'huissier).

wander ['wɔndǝr]. **1.** *v.i.* (*a*) Errer (sans but); se promener au hasard. To wander about, aller à l'aventure; vaguer. To let one's thoughts wander, laisser vaguer ses pensées. (*b*) To wander from the right way, s'écarter du droit chemin. To wander (away) from the subject, s'écarter du sujet. My thoughts were wandering, je n'étais pas à la conversation. (*c*) (*Of pers.*) To wander in one's mind, divaguer; avoir le délire. **2.** *v.tr. Lit:* To wander the world, errer par le monde.

wandering¹, *a.* **1.** (*a*) Errant, vagabond. *W. tribes,* nomades *m.* (*b*) (Esprit) distrait. **2.** (*a*) *Med:* Qui a le délire. (*b*) (Discours) incohérent. **wandering²,** *s.* **1.** Vagabondage *m*, nomaderie *f.* To recount one's wanderings, *F:* raconter son odyssée *f.* **2.** (*a*) Rêverie *f.* (*b*) *Med:* Égarement *m* (de l'esprit). *In his wanderings,* dans ses divagations. **3.** *W. from the subject,* déviation *f* du sujet.

wanderer ['wɔndǝrǝr], *s.* **1.** Vagabond, -onde. Our wanderer has returned, notre voyageur nous est revenu. **2.** Celui qui s'écarte (*from the right way,* du droit chemin).

wane¹ [wein], *s.* Déclin *m.* Moon on the wane, lune à son décours. To be on the wane, (*of moon*) décroître; *F:* (*Of pers.*) être à, sur, son déclin. *F:* His star is on the wane, son étoile pâlit.

wane², *v.i.* (*Of the moon, of power, etc.*) Décroître, décliner; (*of beauty*) être sur le retour; (*of enthusiasm*) s'attiédir. **waning,** *s.* Décours *m* (de la lune); déclin *m.*

wangle¹ [wæŋgl], *s.* *P:* Moyen détourné; truc *m.*

wangle², *v.tr. P:* **1.** Obtenir (qch.) par subterfuge. To wangle a week's leave, carotter huit jours de congé. **2.** Cuisiner (des comptes).

wangling, *s.* Carottage *m.*

wangler ['wæŋglǝr], *s.* *P:* Carotteur, -euse.

wanness ['wɔnnǝs], *s.* Pâleur *f.*

want¹ [wɔnt], *s.* **1.** (*a*) Manque *m*, défaut *m.* Want of judgment, défaut de jugement. **Want of imagination,** manque d'imagination. **For want of sth.,** faute de qch.; par manque de (prévoyance, etc.). **For want of something better,** faute de mieux. For w. of something to do, par désœuvrement. To make up for the w. of sth., suppléer à l'absence de qch. (*b*) **To be in want of sth.,** avoir besoin de qch. To be in w. of money, être à court d'argent. *I am in w. of . . .,* il me manque . . . **2.** Indigence *f*, misère *f.* **To be in want,** être dans le besoin, dans la gêne. **To be living in want,** vivre dans la misère. **3.** Besoin *m.* To attend to s.o.'s wants, pourvoir aux besoins de qn. A long-felt want, une lacune à combler.

want². **1.** *v.i.* (*a*) Manquer (*for,* de); être dépourvu (de). To want for nothing, ne manquer de rien. (*b*) His family will see to it that he does not want, sa famille veillera à ce qu'il ne se trouve pas dans le besoin. **2.** *v.tr.* (*a*) Manquer de, ne pas avoir (qch.). **To want patience,** manquer de patience. *Impers.* It wants six minutes to ten o'clock, il est dix heures moins six. *It wanted but a few days to Christmas,* Noël n'était éloigné que de quelques jours. (*b*) (*Of pers.*) Avoir besoin de (qch.); (*of thg*) exiger, réclamer (qch.). **To want rest,** avoir besoin de repos. **That work wants a lot of patience,** ce travail exige beaucoup de patience. **Have you all you want?** avez-vous tout ce qu'il vous faut? *You shall have as much as you w.,* vous en aurez autant que vous voudrez. I've had all I want(ed), j'en ai assez. That's the very thing I want, c'est juste ce qu'il me faut; c'est juste mon affaire. **To want a situation,** être en quête d'un emploi. **Wanted, a good cook,** on demande une bonne cuisinière. (*c*) **Your hair wants cutting,** vous avez besoin de vous faire couper les cheveux. **It wants some doing,** ce n'est pas (si) facile à faire. (*d*) Désirer, vouloir. He knows what he wants, il sait ce qu'il veut. *How much for this armchair?*—I want five pounds, combien ce fauteuil?—J'en demande cinq livres. *Iron:* You don't want much! tu n'es pas dégoûté! **You are wanted,** on vous demande. *We are not wanted here,* nous sommes de trop ici. We don't w. you, nous n'avons que faire de vous. **What**

does he want with me? que me veut-il? I want to tell you that . . ., je voudrais vous dire que. . . . To want to see s.o., to speak to s.o., demander qn; avoir à parler à qn. I want him to come, je désire qu'il vienne. I don't want it known, je ne veux pas que cela se sache. **wanted,** *a.* **1.** Désiré, voulu, demandé. **2.** (Criminel) que la police recherche. **wanting,** *pred.a.* (*a*) Manquant, qui manque. To be wanting, faire défaut. One sheet is wanting, il manque une feuille. There is something w., le compte n'y est pas. (*b*) Wanting in intelligence, dépourvu d'intelligence. He was tried and found wanting, il ne supporta pas l'épreuve. (*c*) *F:* Faible d'esprit. He is slightly wanting, il lui manque un petit quelque chose.

wanton[1] [ˈwɔntən]. **1.** *a.* (*a*) (*Of woman*) Licencieuse, impudique. (*b*) Wanton winds, vents folâtres. (*c*) Gratuit; sans motif. Wanton cruelty, cruauté gratuite. Wanton destruction, destruction pour le simple plaisir de détruire. **2.** *s.f.* Femme impudique. **-ly,** *adv.* **1.** Impudiquement. **2.** De gaieté de cœur. **3.** (Blesser, insulter) gratuitement.

wanton[2], *v.i.* Folâtrer; s'ébattre.

wantonness [ˈwɔntənnəs], *s.* **1.** Libertinage *m.* **2.** To do sth. in sheer wantonness, faire qch. de gaieté de cœur, par étourderie.

wapiti [ˈwɔpiti], *s.* *Z:* Wapiti *m.*

war[1] [wɔːr], *s.* Guerre *f.* Naval war, guerre maritime. To go to war, se mettre en guerre. To make war on s.o., faire la guerre à, contre, qn. War of the elements, conflit *m* des éléments. War of words, dispute *f* de mots. *F:* You look as if you had been in the wars, vous avez l'air de vous être battu. On a war footing, sur le pied de guerre. War preparations, armements *m.* War zone, zone militaire. *S.a.* ARTICLE[1] 2, BOND[1] 3, MEMORIAL 2. **ˈwar-cloud,** *s.* *F:* Menace *f* de guerre. **ˈwar-correspondent,** *s.* Correspondant *m,* journaliste *m,* aux armées. **ˈwar-cry,** *s.* Cri *m* de guerre. **ˈwar-dance,** *s.* Danse guerrière. **ˈwar-fever,** *s.* Psychose *f* de la guerre. **ˈwar-horse,** *s.* **1.** *A:* Destrier *m;* cheval *m* de bataille. **2.** *F:* An old war-horse, (i) un vieux soldat; (ii) un vétéran de la politique. **ˈwar-loan,** *s.* *Fin:* Emprunt *m* de guerre. **ˈwar-lord,** *s.* Généralissime *m;* chef *m* suprême (de l'armée). **ˈwar-monger,** *s.* Agitateur *m* qui pousse à la guerre; belliciste *m.* **ˈwar-mongering,** *s.* Propagande *f* de guerre. **ˈwar-paint,** *s.* **1.** Peinture *f* de guerre (des Peaux-Rouges). **2.** *F:* Decked out in all one's war-paint, en grande toilette; sur son trente et un. **ˈwar-path,** *s.* *F:* To be on the war-path, (i) être parti en campagne; (ii) être après tout le monde; chercher noise à tout le monde. The boss is on the w.-p., le patron est d'une humeur massacrante. **ˈwar-plane,** *s.* Avion *m* de guerre. **ˈwar-time,** *s.* Temps *m* de guerre. War-time regulations, règlements de guerre. **ˈwar-weary,** *a.* Fatigué, las, de la guerre. **ˈwar-worn,** *a.* Usé par la guerre.

war[2], *v.i.* (warred) To war against s.o., mener une campagne contre qn; lutter contre qn. To war against abuses, faire la guerre aux abus.

warring, *a.* Warring nations, nations en guerre. Warring interests, intérêts contraires.

warble[1] [wɔːrbl], *s.* Gazouillement *m,* ramage *m* (des oiseaux).

warble[2]. **1.** *v.i.* (*a*) Gazouiller. (*b*) *F:* (*Of pers.*) Chanter. **2.** *v.tr.* Chanter (qch.) en gazouillant.

warbling, *s.* = WARBLE[1].

warbler [ˈwɔːrblər], *s.* **1.** Oiseau chanteur; *F:* chanteur *m.* **2.** *Orn:* Fauvette *f;* bec-fin *m.*

ward[1] [wɔːrd], *s.* **1.** (*a*) Guet *m.* To keep watch and ward, faire le guet; faire bonne garde. (*b*) (*Pers.*) Pupille *mf.* *Jur:* Ward in Chancery, pupille sous tutelle judiciaire. **2.** (*a*) Hospital ward, salle *f* d'hôpital. *S.a.* CASUAL 2. (*b*) Quartier *m* (d'une prison). **3.** Arrondissement *m,* quartier (d'une ville). **4.** Wards of a lock, gardes *f* d'une serrure. **ˈward-room,** *s.* *Navy:* Carré *m* des officiers.

ward[2], *v.tr.* (*a*) *A. & Lit:* Garder (*from,* de); défendre (*from,* contre). (*b*) To ward off a blow, parer un coup. To w. off an illness, prévenir une maladie.

warden [ˈwɔːrd(ə)n], *s.* **1.** (*a*) Directeur *m* (d'une institution). (*b*) *Freemasonry:* Surveillant *m.* (*c*) Gardien *m.* (*d*) Gouverneur *m* (d'une ville). **2.** = CHURCHWARDEN 1.

warder [ˈwɔːrdər], *s.* Gardien *m* (de prison). Female warder, gardienne *f.*

wardress [ˈwɔːrdres], *s.f.* Gardienne de prison.

wardrobe [ˈwɔːrdroub], *s.* **1.** *Furn:* Armoire *f* (pour garde-robe). **2.** (Ensemble *m* de) vêtements *mpl.* An ample w., une riche garde-robe. Wardrobe dealer, marchand, -e, de toilette, à la toilette.

ware[1] [weər], *s.* **1.** *Coll.* (*a*) Articles fabriqués. Toilet ware, ustensiles *mpl* de toilette. (*b*) Faïence *f.* China ware, porcelaine *f.* **2.** *pl.* Wares, marchandise(s) *f.*

ware[2], *v.tr.* *Ven:* Ware wire! gare le fil de fer! Ware wheat! attention au blé!

warehouse[1] [ˈweərhaus], *s.* **1.** Entrepôt *m;* magasin *m.* Bonded warehouse, entrepôt de douane. *Com:* Ex warehouse, à prendre en entrepôt. **2.** Italian warehouse, magasin de comestibles; épicerie *f.* **3.** Furniture warehouse, garde-meuble *m.*

warehouse[2], *v.tr.* **1.** (Em)magasiner; mettre en magasin. **2.** To warehouse one's furniture, mettre son mobilier au garde-meuble. **warehousing,** *s.* (*a*) (Em)magasinage *m;* mise *f* en magasin. (*b*) *Cust:* Entreposage *m* (de marchandises).

warehouseman, *pl.* **-men** [ˈweərhausmən, -men], *s.m.* **1.** Garde-magasin; garçon de magasin. **2.** Italian warehouseman, marchand de comestibles; épicier.

warfare [ˈwɔːrfeər], *s.* La guerre. Trench warfare, la guerre de tranchées. Naval warfare, guerre maritime. Aerial warfare, guerre aérienne.

wariness [ˈweərinəs], *s.* Circonspection *f,* prudence *f;* défiance *f.*

warlike [ˈwɔːrlaik], *a.* (Maintien) guerrier (air) martial; (peuple) belliqueux.

warm[1] [wɔːrm], *a.* **1.** (*a*) Chaud (mais non brûlant). *W.* water, eau chaude. W. night, nuit tiède. To be warm, (i) (*of water*) être chaud; (ii) (*of pers.*) avoir chaud. I can't get w., je ne peux pas me réchauffer. (At games) You are getting warm! vous brûlez! To keep oneself warm, se tenir, se vêtir, chaudement. *Com:* 'To be kept in a warm place,' "tenir au chaud". *S.a.* FIRE[1] 1. (*b*) (Vêtement) chaud. (*c*) (*Of the weather*) It is warm, il fait chaud. (*d*) *Ven:* Warm scent, piste toute chaude. **2.** (*a*) Chaleureux; ardent. W. thanks, remerciements chaleureux. (*b*) Warm heart, cœur généreux, chaud. To meet with a warm reception, (i) être accueilli chaleureusement; (ii) *Iron:* être accueilli par des huées. (*c*) The argument was getting warm, la discussion s'animait. Warm contest, lutte acharnée, chaude. *F:* It is warm work, c'est une rude besogne. To make it warm for s.o., en faire voir de dures à qn. (d) (Of colour) Warm tints, tons chauds. -ly, adv. 1. (Vêtu) chaudement. 2. (a) (Applaudir) chaudement. To thank s.o. warmly, remercier qn chaleureusement, en termes chaleureux. (b) (Répondre) vivement, avec chaleur. warm-'blooded, a. Z: (Animal) à sang chaud. warm-'hearted, a. Au cœur chaud, généreux.

warm², s. F: Action f de chauffer. Come and have a w., venez vous réchauffer. To give sth. a warm, chauffer qch.

warm³. 1. v.tr. (a) Chauffer. To w. a bed, bassiner un lit. To warm oneself at the fire, in the sun, se chauffer au feu, au soleil. To w. oneself walking, se réchauffer en marchant. (b) That will warm the cockles of your heart, voilà qui vous réchauffera. F: To warm s.o.'s jacket, flanquer une tripotée à qn. 2. v.i. (a) (Se) chauffer; se réchauffer. (b) F: S'animer. The lecturer was warming to his subject, le conférencier s'échauffait peu à peu. warm up. 1. v.tr. (a) Chauffer; réchauffer. The wine will w. him up, le vin le réchauffera. (b) (Faire) réchauffer (la soupe, etc.). 2. v.i. (a) S'échauffer; s'animer. The game was warming up, la partie s'animait. (b) (Of company) Devenir plus cordial; F: se dégeler. warming, s. 1. Chauffage m. 2. F: Rossée f, raclée f. 'warming-pan, s. Bassinoire f.

warmth [wɔːrmθ], s. 1. Chaleur f. 2. (a) Ardeur f, zèle m; chaleur. (b) Cordialité f, chaleur (d'un accueil). (c) Emportement m, vivacité f.

warn [wɔːrn], v.tr. Avertir. 1. Prévenir. To warn s.o. of a danger, prémunir qn contre un danger; avertir qn d'un danger. To warn s.o. against sth., mettre qn en garde contre qch. He warned her not to go, il lui conseilla fortement de ne pas y aller. You have been warned! vous voilà prévenu! I shall not w. you again, tenez-vous-le pour dit. 2. To warn the police, alerter la police. Mil: To warn s.o. for guard, désigner qn pour une faction. warn off, v.tr. Turf: To warn s.o. off the course, exclure qn des champs de course. warning¹, a. (Geste) avertisseur, d'avertissement. Aut: Warning sign, plaque f, écriteau m, d'avertissement. Navy: Warning shot, coup m de semonce. warning², s. Avertissement m. 1. Action f d'avertir. Danger warning, signalisation f des dangers. Warning device, avertisseur m. 2. (a) Avis m, préavis m. To give warning of danger to s.o., avertir qn d'un danger. Without warning, sans préavis. (b) To give s.o. fair warning, dònner à qn un avertissement formel. (c) Let this be a warning to you, que cela vous serve de leçon, d'exemple. (d) Aut: Street warning, écriteau m, plaque f, d'avertissement. Road warnings, signaux m de route. 3. (a) To send a warning to the police, avertir la police. (b) Warning to leave, congé m. To give an employee warning, donner congé à un employé. To give a servant a week's w., donner ses huit jours à une domestique.

warp¹ [wɔːrp], s. 1. Tex: Chaîne f; (for tapestry) lisse f, lice f. 2. Nau: Amarre f; touée f. 3. Geol: Dépôt m alluvionnaire; lais m. 4. Voilure f, courbure f (d'une planche). 'warp-end, s. Tex: Fil m de chaîne.

warp². I. v.tr. 1. (a) Déjeter, (faire) voiler (le bois, une tôle). (b)F: Fausser, pervertir (l'esprit). (c) Av: Gauchir (les ailes). 2. Tex: Ourdir (l'étoffe). 3. Nau: Haler, touer (un navire). To warp off a ship, déhaler un navire. II. warp, v.i. 1. Se déformer; (of timber) se déjeter, gauchir; (of wheel) se voiler. 2. Nau: To warp out of

port, sortir du port à la touée; déhaler. warped, a. (a) (Bois) déjeté, gauchi. W. wheel, roue voilée. (b) (Esprit) perverti, faussé. W. nature, caractère mal fait.

warrant¹ ['wɔrənt], s. 1. Garantie f. A warrant for s.o.'s good behaviour, une garantie pour la bonne conduite de qn. 2. Autorisation f; justification f. 3. (a) Mandat m, ordre m. Warrant of arrest, mandat d'arrêt, mandat d'amener. A warrant is out against him, il est sous le coup d'un mandat d'amener. (b) Autorisation écrite; autorité f. (c) Certificat m. Warehouse, dock, warrant, certificat d'entrepôt; warrant m. To issue a warehouse w. for goods, warranter des marchandises. (d) Warrant for payment, ordonnance f de payement. (e) Brevet m. Royal warrant, brevet de fournisseur du roi. Warrant-officer, (i) Mil: sous-officier; (ii) Navy: maître principal.

warrant², v.tr. 1. Garantir, certifier (qch.). F: It won't happen again, I warrant you! cela n'arrivera pas deux fois, je vous en réponds! 2. Justifier. Nothing can warrant such conduct, rien ne justifie une pareille conduite. warranted, a. 1. Com: Garanti. Colours warranted fast, couleurs garanties bon teint. 2. We are w. in ascribing an effect to a cause, nous sommes autorisés à attribuer un effet à une cause.

warrantor ['wɔrəntɔːr], s. Jur: Répondant m, garant m.

warranty ['wɔrənti], s. 1. Autorisation f; justification f (for doing sth., pour faire qch.). 2. Garantie f. Jur: Warranty of title, attestation f du titre.

warren ['wɔrən], s. (Rabbit-)warren, garenne f.

warrior ['wɔriər], s. Lit: Guerrier m, soldat m. The Unknown Warrior, le Soldat inconnu. Warrior tribes, tribus guerrières.

Warsaw ['wɔːrsɔː]. Pr.n. Varsovie f.

warship ['wɔːrʃip], s. Vaisseau m de guerre.

wart [wɔːrt], s. Verrue f; F: poireau m. 'wart-hog, s. Z: Phacochère m.

wary ['wɛəri], a. (a) Avisé, prudent, circonspect. To keep a wary eye on s.o., surveiller qn attentivement. (b) To be wary of sth., se méfier de qch. -ily, adv. Avec circonspection; prudemment.

was [wɔz, wəz]. See BE.

wash¹ [wɔʃ], s. 1. (a) Lavage m, savonnage m. To give sth. a wash, laver qch. (b) (Of pers.) Ablutions fpl. F: To have a wash and brush-up, faire un bout de toilette. (c) Lessive f, blanchissage m. To send clothes to the wash, envoyer du linge au blanchissage. Linen fresh from the w., linge blanc de lessive. F: It will all come out in the w., ça se tassera. 2. (a) Hair-wash, lotion f capillaire. (b) Hort: Lessive (insecticide). 3. (a) Colour wash (for walls), badigeon m. (b) Couche légère (de couleur sur une surface). (c) Art: Lavis m (d'aquarelle). Wash-drawing, épure f au lavis. 4. (a) The wash of the waves, le bruit des flots qui passent. (b) Nau: Sillage m, houache f, remous m (d'un navire). Av: Propeller wash, souffle m de l'hélice. 'wash-basin, s. Cuvette f (de lavabo). 'wash-house, s. (a) Buanderie f. (b) Lavoir m (public). 'wash-leather, s. Peau f de chamois. Wash-leather gloves, gants chamois. 'wash-tint, s. Art: Lavis m. 'wash-tub, s. Cuvier m; baquet m (à lessive).

wash². I. v.tr. 1. (a) Laver. To wash sth. clean, nettoyer qch. à grande eau. To wash one's face, se débarbouiller. To wash one's hands, se laver les mains. F: To wash one's hands of sth., se

laver les mains de qch. (b) v.pr. & i. To wash (oneself), se laver. (c) Med: Lotionner (une plaie). 2. (a) Blanchir, lessiver, laver (le linge). (b) Material that washes well, étoffe très lavable. Material that won't wash, étoffe qui ne se lave pas, qui déteint. F: That story won't wash! cette histoire-là ne passe pas ! 3. Ind: Débourber (le minerai). 4. (a) To wash the walls, badigeonner les murs (with, de). (b) To wash a metal with gold, dorer un métal au trempé. (c) Art: Laver (un dessin). 5. (Of river, sea) Baigner, arroser (les côtes, un pays). 6. (Of sea) To wash sth. ashore, rejeter qch. sur le rivage. Sailor washed overboard, matelot enlevé, balayé, par une lame. II. wash, v.i. The waves washed over the deck, les vagues balayaient le pont. **wash away,** v.tr. **I.** Enlever (une tache) par le lavage. **2.** (a) River-bank washed away, berge affouillée, dégradée. (b) Emporter, entraîner. Washed away by the tide, emporté par la mer. **wash down,** v.tr. **I.** Laver (les murs) à grande eau. **2.** F: To wash down one's dinner with a glass of beer, arroser son dîner d'un verre de bière. **wash off,** v.tr. Enlever, effacer, (qch.) par le lavage. It will wash off, cela s'effacera à l'eau. **wash out,** v.tr. **I.** (a) Enlever (une tache). Lit: To wash out an insult in blood, laver un affront dans le sang. F: We must w. out the whole business, le mieux sera d'oublier toute cette affaire. You can wash that right out, il ne faut pas compter ·là-dessus. (b) Laver, rincer (une bouteille). (c) Min: To wash out the gold, extraire l'or (en lavant le sable). 2. (Of stain) Partir au lavage. **'wash-out,** s. F: (a) Fiasco m, four m. The business is a wash-out, l'affaire est manquée. The play was a wash-out, la pièce a fait four. (b) (Of pers.) He is a wash-out, c'est un raté. **washed out,** a. **I.** (a) (Of colour) Délavé. (b) F: Washed-out complexion, teint de papier mâché. 2. F: (Of pers.) Flapi, vanné. To feel washed out, se sentir à plat. **wash up,** v.tr. (a) To wash up the dishes, abs. to wash up, to do the washing-up, laver la vaisselle ; faire la vaisselle. (b) (Of sea) Rejeter (qn, qch.) sur le rivage. **washing¹,** a. Washing frock, washing silk, robe, soie, lavable, qui se lave. **washing²,** s. **I.** (a) Lavage m. Colour that won't stand any washing, couleur qui ne se lave pas. (b) Ablutions fpl. **2.** (a) Blanchissage m, lessive f (du linge). To do a little w., faire un petit savonnage. Washing is included, le blanchissage est compris. (b) Linge (à blanchir ou blanchi) ; le blanchissage. **3.** She takes in washing, elle fait le blanchissage. **3.** Ind: (a) Débourbage m (du minerai). (b) Lavée f (du minerai, de la laine). (c) pl. Washings, produits m de lavage. 4. (a) Badigeonnage m. (b) Art: Lavis m (d'un dessin). **'washing-bottle,** s. Ch: Flacon laveur. **'washing-crystals,** s.pl. Soude f du commerce ; F: cristaux mpl (de soude). **'washing-day,** s. Jour m de lessive. **'washing-glove,** s. Gant-éponge m. **'washing-machine,** s. Laund: Laveuse f mécanique. **'washing-soda,** s. See SODA I. **'wash-hand,** attrib.a. Wash-hand basin, cuvette f (de lavabo) ; lavabo m. Wash-hand stand, lavabo. **'wash-in,** s. Av: Augmentation f de l'incidence à l'extrémité de l'aile.
washable ['wɔʃəbl], a. Lavable.
washer¹ ['wɔʃər], s. **I.** (Pers.) (a) Laveur, -euse. (b) Washer-up, laveur, -euse, de vaisselle ; (in restaurant) plongeur m. **2.** (a) Laund: Laveuse f mécanique. (b) Phot: Plate-washer, print-washer, cuve f de lavage.
washer², s. Mec.E: etc: Rondelle f ; bague f

d'appui. Tap washer, rondelle de robinet. Spring washer, rondelle à ressort.
washerwoman, pl. -women ['wɔ\ərwumən, -wimen], s.f. Blanchisseuse, lavandière.
washstand ['wɔ\stand], s. Furn: Lavabo m.
washy ['wɔʃi], a. F: Fade, insipide. This coffee's pretty w.! quelle lavasse que ce café !
wasp [wɔsp], s. Guêpe f. Wasps' nest, guêpier m. **'wasp-waisted,** a. A taille de guêpe.
waspish ['wɔspiʃ], a. F: Méchant ; acariâtre. W. tone, ton aigre. **-ly,** adv. Méchamment.
waspishness ['wɔspiʃnəs], s. F: Méchanceté f.
wastage ['weistedʒ], s. **I.** (a) Déperdition f, perte f (de chaleur). (b) Gaspillage m. **2.** Coll: Déchets mpl, rebuts mpl.
waste¹ [weist], a. **I.** (a) Waste land, waste ground, (i) terre f inculte ; (ii) (in town) terrains m vagues. (Of ground) To lie waste, rester en friche. (b) To lay waste, dévaster, ravager (un pays). **2.** (a) (Matière) de rebut. Waste products of nutrition, déchets m de la nutrition. **Waste paper,** papier de rebut ; vieux papiers. **Waste-paper basket,** corbeille f à papier(s). Typ: Waste sheets, maculatures f. (b) Mch: Waste steam, vapeur perdue. S.a. WOOL I.
waste², s. **I.** Région f inculte ; désert m. **2.** Gaspillage m (d'argent). House where there is a lot of waste, maison où on gaspille beaucoup. Waste of time, perte f de temps. To run to waste, (i) (of liquids) se perdre, se dissiper ; (ii) (of garden) se couvrir d'herbes ; (of land) s'affricher. **3.** (a) Déchets mpl, rebut m. Cotton waste, déchets, bourre f, de coton ; chiffons mpl de nettoyage. Printing waste, maculatures fpl. (b) Hyd.E: Trop-plein m. **'waste-pipe,** s. Hyd.E: etc: Tuyau m d'écoulement du trop-plein ; (tuyau de) trop-plein. **'waste-weir,** s. Déversoir m.
waste³. I. v.tr. **I.** Consumer, user, épuiser (le corps). Patient wasted by disease, malade amaigri par la maladie. **2.** Gaspiller ; gâcher (du papier). Nothing is wasted, rien ne se perd. To waste one's time, perdre son temps. Wasted life, vie manquée. All my advice was wasted on him, je l'ai conseillé en pure perte. F: To waste words, parler en pure perte. Waste not, want not, qui épargne gagne. II. waste, v.i. **I.** Se perdre ; s'user. **2.** (Of living being) To waste (away), dépérir ; (of pers.) se miner, se décharner ; maigrir. Wasting disease, maladie de langueur ; consomption f. **wasted,** a. **I.** (Pays) dévasté, ravagé. **2.** (Malade) affaibli, amaigri. **3.** (Argent) gaspillé. Time wasted, temps perdu. Tchn: Wasted energy, dépense f à vide. **wasting,** s. **I.** Gaspillage m, perte f (de ses ressources). **2.** Wasting (away), dépérissement m, marasme m ; atrophie f (d'un membre) ; Med: consomption f.
wasteful ['weistful], a. Gaspilleur, -euse ; prodigue. W. expenditure, gaspillage m. W. habits, habitudes de gaspillage. **-fully,** adv. Avec prodigalité ; (dépenser une somme) en pure perte.
wastefulness ['weistfulnəs], s. Prodigalité f ; (habitudes fpl de) gaspillage m.
waster ['weistər], s. (Pers.) (a) Gaspilleur, -euse. Time-waster, perdeur, -euse, de temps. (b) F: = WASTREL.
wastrel ['weistrəl], s. F: Rebut m de la société ; vaurien m ; propre m à rien.
watch¹ [wɔtʃ], s. **I.** A: Veille f. In the watches of the night, pendant les heures de veille. **2.** Garde f ; surveillance f. To be on the watch, (i) être en observation ; se tenir aux aguets ; (ii) être sur ses gardes. To be on the watch for

s.o., guetter qn. To keep watch, monter la garde. To keep (a) good watch, faire bonne garde. To keep a close watch on s.o., surveiller qn de près. To set a watch on s.o., faire surveiller qn. **3.** *Hist:* The watch, la garde, le guet; la ronde de nuit. **4.** *Nau:* (a) Quart *m.* To set the watches, régler les quarts. The officer of the watch, l'officier de quart. To have watch and watch, faire le quart par bordées. *S.a.* RELIEVE 4. (b) (*Men*) Bordée *f.* The *w.* on deck, la bordée de quart. **5.** Montre *f.* Keyless watch, montre à remontoir. It is six by my watch, il est six heures à ma montre. **'watch-case,** *s.* Boîtier *m* de montre. **'watch-chain,** *s. See* CHAIN[1] I. **'watch committee,** *s.* Comité *m* qui veille au maintien de l'ordre et à l'éclairage de la commune. **'watch-dog,** *s.* Chien *m* de garde. **'watch-fire,** *s.* Feu *m* de bivouac. **'watch-glass,** *s.* Verre *m* de montre. **'watch-guard,** *s.* Chaîne *f* de gilet. **'watch-keeper,** *s. Nau:* **I.** Homme *m* de quart. **2.** Chef *m* de quart. **'watch-key,** *s.* Clef *f* de montre. **'watch-maker,** *s.* Horloger *m.* **'watch-making,** *s.* Horlogerie *f.* **'watch-night,** *s. Ecc:* Office *m* de minuit (à la veille du jour de l'an); veillée *f* du 31 décembre. **'watch-pocket,** *s. Cost:* Gousset *m* (de montre). **'watch-spring,** *s.* Ressort *m* de montre. **'watch-stand,** *s.* Porte-montre *m inv.* **'watch-tower,** *s.* Tour *f* d'observation, de guet.

watch[2]. **I.** *v.i.* (a) Veiller. *I watched all night,* j'ai veillé jusqu'au jour. (b) To watch by a sick person, veiller un malade. To watch over a flock, garder un troupeau. (c) To watch, *F:* to watch out, être aux aguets; être sur ses gardes. Watch out! ouvrez l'œil! prenez garde! (d) To watch for s.o., attendre qn; guetter qn. **2.** *v.tr.* (a) Veiller (un mort); garder, veiller sur (qn, qch.). (b) Observer; regarder attentivement. To watch s.o. narrowly, surveiller qn de près; ne pas quitter qn des yeux. We are being watched, on nous observe. (c) We shall have to watch the expenses, il nous faudra avoir l'œil sur la dépense. *I had to w. my step throughout the discussion,* pendant toute la discussion il m'a fallu éviter tout faux pas. (d) Regarder; voir. *I watched her working,* je la regardais travailler. To watch a football match, assister à un match de football. *Jur:* To watch a case, veiller (en justice) aux intérêts de qn. (e) To watch one's opportunity, one's time, guetter l'occasion.

watcher ['wɔtʃər], *s.* **I.** Veilleur, -euse (d'un malade). **2. Bird watcher,** observateur des mœurs des oiseaux.

watchful ['wɔtʃful], *a.* Vigilant; alerte; attentif. *To be w.,* être sur ses gardes. To keep a watchful eye on, over, s.o., surveiller qn de près. **-fully,** *adv.* Avec vigilance.

watchfulness ['wɔtʃfulnəs], *s.* Vigilance (méfiante).

watchman, *pl.* **-men** ['wɔtʃmən, -men], *s.m.* Gardien, garde. *Nau:* Homme de garde (au mouillage). *Ind:* Night watchman, veilleur de nuit.

watchword ['wɔtʃwərd], *s.* Mot *m* d'ordre.

water[1] ['wɔtər], *s.* Eau *f.* **I.** (a) Cold *w.,* eau fraîche. Fresh water, eau douce. *F:* To throw cold water on a scheme, décourager un projet. Drinking water, eau potable. Wine and water, vin coupé d'eau; eau rougie. To take the horses to water, conduire les chevaux à l'abreuvoir. To take in water, (of locomotive, etc.) faire de l'eau. (Of ship) To make water, (leak) avoir une voie d'eau. *S.a.* HOLD[2] 7, HOT I. (b) (For domestic

needs) Eaux ménagères. To turn on the water, ouvrir l'eau. To have the water laid on, faire mettre l'eau courante. Water supply, service *m* des eaux, distribution *f* d'eau (de la ville). The Water Company, la Compagnie des eaux. (c) To wash sth. in two or three waters, laver qch. dans deux ou trois eaux. **2.** *Usu. pl.* Iron waters, eaux ferrugineuses. To take, drink, the waters, prendre les eaux. *To take the waters at Bath,* faire la cure à Bath. **3.** (a) *The waters of the Danube,* les eaux du Danube. *Pirate-infested waters,* parages infestés par les pirates. (b) On land and water, sur terre et sur mer. By water, par eau; en bateau; *Com:* par voie d'eau. (*Of swimmer,* etc.). To take the water, se mettre à la nage. *S.a.* FISH[1] I, TREAD[2] 2. (c) To be under water, (of land) être inondé, submergé. To swim under water, nager entre deux eaux. Above water, à flot; surnageant. To keep one's head above water, (i) se maintenir à la surface; (ii) *F:* faire face à ses engagements. (d) High water, marée haute; haute mer. High-water mark, (i) = TIDE-MARK; (ii) *F:* apogée *m* (de la carrière de qn). Low water, marée basse. *F:* He is in low water, (i) il est dans la gêne; (ii) il est dans le marasme; il est déprimé. (e) *Nau:* Shallow water, hauts fonds. In Home waters, dans les eaux de la Métropole. (f) *Nau:* What water does the ship draw? quel est le tirant d'eau du navire? *There are a hundred fathoms of w.,* il y a cent brasses de fond. **4.** (a) Strong waters, eau-de-vie *f.* (b) *Med:* Water on the brain, hydrocéphalie *f.* Water on the knee, hydarthrose *f* du genou; épanchement *m* de synovie. *S.a.* BLISTER[1]. (c) To bring the water to one's eyes, faire venir les larmes aux yeux. (d) It brings the water to one's mouth, cela fait venir l'eau à la bouche. (e) To make water, uriner. **5.** Transparence *f,* eau (d'un diamant). *The w. of a pearl,* l'orient *m* d'une perle. **'water-bag,** *s.* Outre *f,* gourde *f,* à eau. **'water-bailiff,** *s.* Garde-pêche *m.* **'water-ballast,** *s. Nau:* Lest *m* d'eau; lest liquide. **'water-bath,** *s. Ch: Cu:* Bain-marie *m.* **'water-bearer,** *s.* = WATER-CARRIER. **'water-bed,** *s. Med:* Matelas *m* à eau. **'water-biscuit,** *s.* Biscuit *m* de carême. **'water-borne,** *a.* (Of goods) Transporté par voie d'eau. *W.-b.* transport, transport par eau. **'water-bottle,** *s.* **I.** Carafe *f* (de toilette). **2.** Gourde *f.* *Mil:* Bidon *m.* **3.** Hot-water bottle, bouillotte *f;* boule *f* (of earthenware) cruchon *m.* **'water-butt,** *s.* Tonneau *m* pour recueillir l'eau de pluie. **'water-can,** *s.* Broc *m.* **'water-carriage,** *s. Com:* Transport *m* par voie d'eau. **'water-carrier,** *s.* Porteur, -euse, d'eau. **'water-cart,** *s.* Tonneau *m* d'arrosage. **'water-cask,** *s. Nau:* Baril *m* de galère. **'water-closet,** *s.* (Abbr. W.C. ['dʌblju'si:]) Cabinet *m;* les cabinets; water-closet *m;* (in hotel) le numéro zéro. **'water-colour,** *s. Art:* **I.** *pl.* Water-colours, couleurs *f* à l'eau. To paint in water-colours, peindre à l'aquarelle. *Painter in water-colours,* aquarelliste *mf.* **2. A water-colour (painting),** une peinture à l'aquarelle; une aquarelle. **'water-cooled,** *a. I.C.E:* (Moteur) à refroidissement d'eau. **'water-crane,** *s. Rail:* Grue *f* d'alimentation. **'water-cress,** *s.* Cresson *m* de fontaine. **'water-cure,** *s. Med:* Hydrothérapie *f.* **'water-diviner, -finder,** *s.* Sourcier *m,* radiesthésiste *m.* **'water-finding,** *s.* Radiesthésie *f.* **water-'front,** *s.* Partie *f* de la ville faisant face à l'eau, à la mer. **'water-gate,** *s.* **I.** Porte *f* d'écluse; vanne *f* (d'écluse). **2.** Grille *f* d'accès donnant sur le fleuve. **'water-gauge,** s. (Indicateur m de) niveau m d'eau; hydromètre m; (in river) échelle f d'étiage. **'water-glass,** s. Com: Silicate m de potasse ou de soude; F: verre m soluble. **'water-hen,** s. Poule f d'eau. **'water-hole,** s. Mare f (dans un cours d'eau à sec). **'water-ice,** s. Cu: Sorbet m. **'water-jacket,** s. I.C.E: etc: Chemise f d'eau. **'water-jug,** s. I. Pot m, cruche f, à eau. **2.** Toil: Broc m. **'water-jump,** s. Rac: Douve f, brook m. **'water-level,** s. (a) Niveau m d'eau. (b) Geol: Niveau piézométrique. **'water-lily,** s. Nénuphar m; lis m d'eau. White water-lily, nymphée f. Yellow water-lily, nuphar m, lis jaune. **'water-line,** s. Nau: (Ligne f de) flottaison f. **'water-main,** s. Hyd.E: Conduite principale (d'eau). **'water-mark,** s. I. Nau: Laisse f (de haute marée). **2.** (In paper) Filigrane m. **'water-marked,** a. (Papier) à filigrane. **'water-meadow,** s. Prairie susceptible d'être inondée; noue f. **'water-melon,** s. Melon m d'eau; pastèque f. **'water-mill,** s. Moulin m à eau. **'water-nymph,** s. Myth: Naïade f. **'water-ouzel,** s. Orn: Merle m d'eau. **'water-parting,** s. = WATERSHED. **'water-pipe,** s. Tuyau m d'eau, conduite f d'eau. **'water-polo,** s. Sp: Water-polo m; polo m nautique. **'water-pot,** s. = WATERING-POT. **'water-power,** s. Force f hydraulique; énergie f hydraulique; F: houille blanche. **'water-rat,** s. Z: Rat m d'eau; campagnol nageur. **'water-rate,** s. Taux m de l'abonnement aux eaux de la ville. **'water-rights,** s.pl. Droits m de captation d'eau. **'water-softener,** s. I. Adoucisseur m d'eau. **2.** Ind: Installation f d'épuration chimique de l'eau. **'water-softening,** attrib.a. Ind: W.-s. plant, épurateur m d'eau. **'water-spout,** s. I. Tuyau m, descente f (d'eau). **2.** Gouttière f, gargouille f. **3.** Meteor: Trombe f. **'water-sprite,** s. Ondin, -ine. **'water-system,** s. Canalisation f d'eau. **'water-tower,** s. Hyd.E: Château m d'eau. **'water-way,** s. Voie f d'eau; voie navigable. **'water-wheel,** s. Roue f hydraulique; turbine f hydraulique; roue à aubes. **'water-wings,** s.pl. Flotteur m de natation. **'water-worn,** a. Geol: Usé par l'eau.

water². I. v.tr. (a) Arroser. Egypt is watered by the Nile, l'Égypte est abreuvée par le Nil. (b) To water one's wine, mouiller, couper, son vin. Fin: To water the capital, diluer le capital (d'une société). (c) Faire boire, abreuver (des bêtes). (d) Tex: Moirer (la soie). (a) **I.** v.i. (a) My right eye is watering, mon œil droit pleure, larmoie. S.a. MOUTH¹ I. (b) Nau: (Of ship) Faire de l'eau; faire provision d'eau. (c) (Of horses, etc.) Être à l'abreuvoir. **water down,** v.tr. (a) = WATER² I (b). (b) F: To water down an expression, a statement, atténuer une expression, une affirmation. **watered,** a. I. Arrosé. **2.** Étendu d'eau. **3.** Tex: Watered silk, soie moirée, ondée. **watering,** s. I. (a) Arrosage m. (b) Irrigation f. **2.** Dilution f (d'un breuvage). Fin: Watering of stock, dilution f du capital (social). **3.** Abreuvage m (des bêtes). **4.** Tex: Moirage m. **5.** Watering of the eyes, larmoiement m. **'watering-can,** s. = WATERING-POT. **'watering-cart,** s. = WATER-CART. **'watering-place,** s. I. (For cattle) Abreuvoir m. **2.** Station f balnéaire. (a) Ville f d'eau. (b) Bains mpl de mer; plage f. **'watering-pot,** s. Arrosoir m.

watercourse ['wɔːtərkɔːrs], s. I. Cours m d'eau. **2.** Conduite f d'eau; conduit m. **waterfall** ['wɔːtərfɔːl], s. Chute f d'eau; cascade f. **waterfowl** ['wɔːtərfaul], s. (a) Oiseau m aquatique. (b) Coll. Gibier m d'eau; sauvagine f. **waterless** ['wɔːtərləs], a. Sans eau. **waterlogged** ['wɔːtərlɔgd], a. I. (a) Nau: (Navire) plein d'eau, entre deux eaux. (b) (Bois) alourdi par absorption d'eau. **2.** (Terrain) imbibé d'eau. **Waterloo** ['wɔːtər'luː]. Pr.n. The battle of Waterloo, la bataille de Waterloo. F: To meet one's Waterloo, arriver au désastre. **waterman,** pl. -men ['wɔːtərmən, -men], s.m. Batelier, marinier. **waterproof¹** ['wɔːtərpruːf]. I. a. (Tissu) imperméable (à l'eau), imbrifuge, caoutchouté. Waterproof varnish, vernis hydrofuge. S.a. SHEETING I. **2.** s. Cost: Waterproof m; imperméable m. **waterproof²,** v.tr. Imperméabiliser; hydrofuger (un enduit); caoutchouter (un vêtement). **watershed** ['wɔːtərʃed], s. Ph.Geog: Ligne f de partage des eaux; ligne de faîte. **watertight** ['wɔːtərtait], a. (Cloison) étanche (à l'eau). (Of vessel) To be w., retenir l'eau. F: W. regulations, règlement qui a prévu tous les cas. **waterworks** ['wɔːtərwəːrks], s.pl. I. Usine f de distribution d'eau. The town w., le service des eaux de la ville. **2.** A: Jeux mpl d'eau. F: To turn on the waterworks, se mettre à pleurer. **watery** ['wɔːtəri], a. I. (a) Aqueux; qui contient de l'eau; noyé d'eau. Watery clouds, nuages aqueux. Watery eyes, yeux larmoyants. W. potatoes, pommes de terre aqueuses. (b) (Temps) pluvieux. Watery sky, ciel chargé de pluie. (c) Poet: To find a watery grave, trouver la mort dans les eaux. **2.** (a) (Of soup) Peu consistant; "à l'eau." (b) (Of colour) Pâle, déteint. **watt** [wɔt], s. El.Meas: Watt m; voltampère m. **'watt-hour,** s. El.E: Watt-heure m. Watthour meter, wattmètre m. **wattage** ['wɔtedʒ], s. El.E: Puissance f ou consommation f en watts; wattage m. **wattle¹** [wɔtl], s. (a) Wattle(-work), clayonnage m. (b) Claie f. **wattle²,** v.tr. Clayonner. **wattle³,** s. Caroncule f (d'un dindon); fanon m (d'un porc, d'un dindon).; barbillon m, barbe f (d'un poisson); barbe f (d'un coq). **wattmeter** ['wɔtmiːtər], s. El.E: Wattmètre m. **wave¹** [weiv], s. I. (a) Vague f; Nau: lame f. (b) The waves, Lit: les flots m. (c) F: Wave of enthusiasm, vague d'enthousiasme. S.a. BRAIN-WAVE, HEAT-WAVE. **2.** Ph: Onde f. Long waves, grandes ondes. Short waves, petites ondes; W.Tel: ondes courtes. **3.** Ondulation f (des cheveux). To have a natural wave in one's hair, avoir les cheveux ondulés naturellement. Hairdr: To have a wave, se faire onduler. S.a. SET¹ 2. **4.** (a) Balancement m, ondoiement m. (b) With a wave of his hand, d'un geste, d'un signe, de la main. **'wave-detector,** s. W.Tel: Détecteur m d'ondes. **'wave-length,** s. Ph: Longueur f d'onde. **'wave-meter,** s. Ondemètre m. **'wave-setting,** s. Hairdr: Ondulation f. **'wave-trap,** s. W.Tel: Ondemètre m d'absorption.

wave². I. v.i. I. S'agiter; (of flag) flotter (au vent); (of plume) ondoyer, onduler. **2.** To wave to s.o., faire signe à qn (en agitant le bras). **3.** My hair waves naturally, mes cheveux ondulent naturellement. II. **wave,** v.tr. I. Agiter (un mouchoir); brandir (un parapluie). **To wave**

one's hand, faire signe de la main. **To wave
one's arms about,** battre des bras. **2.** (a) He
waved us good-bye, il nous fit un signe d'adieu.
(b) **To wave s.o. aside,** carter qn d'un geste.
He waved us on, de la main il nous fit signe de
continuer. **To wave aside an objection,** écarter
une objection. **3.** *Hairdr:* Onduler (les cheveux).
To have one's hair waved, se faire onduler.
waved, a. Ondé, ondulé. **waving,** s. **I.** (a) Agitation *f* (d'un mouchoir). *W. of the hand,* geste *m*
de la main. (b) Ondoiement *m* (du blé). **2.**
Hairdr: Ondulation *f* (des cheveux).
'waving-iron, s. Fer *m* à friser, à onduler.
wavelet ['weivlet], s. Petite vague.
waver ['weivər], v.i. Vaciller. **I.** (Of flame)
Trembloter. **2.** (a) Hésiter; être indécis; (of the
voice) se troubler; (of courage) défaillir. (b) (Of
troops) Fléchir. **wavering**[1], a. **I.** (Of flame)
Vacillant, tremblotant. **2.** (a) (Homme) irrésolu, hésitant; (voix) défaillante. (b) **Wavering
line of battle,** ligne de bataille flottante. **-ly,** adv.
Avec indécision; irrésolument. **wavering**[2], s.
I. Tremblement *m*, vacillement *m* (d'une
flamme). **2.** (a) Vacillation *f*, irrésolution *f* (de
l'esprit); défaillance *f* (du courage). (b) Flottement *m* (d'une ligne de troupes).
waverer ['weivərər], s. Indécis, -ise; irrésolu, -ue.
waviness ['weivinəs], s. Caractère onduleux,
ondulé (d'une surface, des cheveux).
wavy ['weivi], a. Onduleux. **Wavy line,** ligne
tremblée. **Wavy hair,** chevelure ondoyante.
wax[1] [waks], s. **I.** Cire *f*. *S.a.* BEESWAX. **2.** Fossil
wax, mineral wax, cire fossile, minérale; ozoké-
rite *f*. **'wax-bill,** s. *Orn:* Bec-de-cire *m*.
'wax 'candle, s. Bougie *f* de cire; (in church)
cierge *m*. **'wax-cloth,** s. Toile cirée. **'wax
'doll,** s. Poupée *f* de cire ou à tête en cire.
'wax-'end, s. *Bootm:* Fil poissé. **'wax-'light,**
s. Bougie *f* de cire. **'wax-myrtle,** s. *Bot:*
Cirier *m*. **'wax-paper,** s. Papier ciré. **'wax
sheet,** s. *Typew:* Papier *m* stencil. **'wax
'taper,** s. **I.** Rat *m* de cave; (small) queue-de-
rat *f*. **2.** *Ecc:* Cierge *m*. **'wax-tree,** s. Cirier *m*.
wax[2], v.tr. **I.** Cirer, enduire de cire, encaustiquer
(un meuble). **2.** *Bootm:* Empoisser (le fil).
waxed, a. **I.** Ciré; enduit de cire. **Waxed
moustache,** moustache cosmétiquée. **2.** Waxed
thread, fil poissé.
wax[3], v.i. **I.** (Of the moon) Croître. **To wax and
wane,** croître et décroître. **2.** *Lit. & Hum:*
Devenir, se faire. **He waxed indignant,** il
s'indigna. **waxing,** s. Croissement *m* (de la
lune).
wax[4], s. *F:* Rage *f*, colère *f*. **To be in a wax,**
être en colère. **To get into a wax,** se mettre en
colère.
waxen ['waks(ə)n], a. (a) De cire, en cire.
(b) Cireux. **Waxen pallor,** pâleur cireuse.
waxwing ['wakswiŋ], s. *Orn:* Jaseur *m*; *F:* becfigue *m*.
waxwork ['waxwə:rk], s. **I.** Modelage *m* en cire.
2. (a) Figure *f* de cire. (b) *pl.* Waxworks,
(musée *m* de) figures de cire.
waxy[1] ['waksi], a. Cireux. **Waxy potatoes,**
pommes de terre cireuses.
waxy[2], a. *F:* En colère; *P:* en rogne.
way[1] [wei], s. **I.** Chemin *m*, route *f*, voie *f*. **The
public way,** la voie publique. **Over, across, the
way,** de l'autre côté de la route, de la rue. **The
house across the way,** la maison d'en face. *Rail:*
Six-foot way, entre-voie *f*. *S.a.* COMPANION[2],
PERMANENT. **2.** (a) **The way to the station,** le
chemin de la gare. **To show s.o. the way,** montrer
la route à qn. **To ask one's way,** demander son

chemin. **To lose one's way,** s'égarer, se perdre.
To go the wrong way, to mistake the way, se
tromper de chemin; faire fausse route. **To go the
shortest way,** prendre par le plus court. **To know
one's way about (a house),** connaître les êtres.
F: He knows his way about, il sait se débrouiller.
To prepare the way, préparer les voies. **To start
on one's way,** se mettre en route. **On the way,**
chemin faisant; en chemin. *On my way home,*
en revenant chez moi; en rentrant. *F:* **He is
on the way to the workhouse,** il prend le chemin
de l'hôpital. **To go the way of all things,** aller
où va toute chose; mourir. **To go one's way,**
passer son chemin. **To go one's own way,**
faire à sa guise. *F:* To go out of one's way to
oblige s.o., se déranger pour être agréable à qn.
He seems to go out of his way to get hurt, il semble
prendre à tâche de se faire blesser. **Village that
is rather out of the way,** village un peu écarté.
His talent is nothing out of the way, son talent
n'est pas hors ligne. (b) **Way in,** entrée *f*. **Way
out,** sortie *f*. **Way through,** passage *m*. **Way up,**
montée *f*. **Way down,** descente *f*. *To find a way
in,* trouver moyen d'entrer. *To find a way out,*
trouver une issue. (c) **To find one's way to a
place,** parvenir à un endroit. **To make one's
way into . . .,** s'introduire dans. . . . **To make one's
way towards a place,** se diriger vers un endroit.
To make one's way through the crowd, se frayer
un chemin à travers la foule. **To make one's way
back,** retourner, revenir. **To make a way for
oneself,** se faire jour. **How to make one's way
in the world,** le moyen de parvenir. **To work
one's way up,** s'élever à force de travail. **To pay
one's way,** se suffire. **To see one's way to do
sth.,** se croire à même de faire qch. *Couldn't
you see your way to do it?* ne trouveriez-vous pas
moyen de le faire? *S.a.* CLEAR[2] I. 3, FEEL[2] I,
WEND. (d) **To stand in s.o.'s way,** être dans le
chemin de qn; faire obstacle à qn. **To put
difficulties in s.o.'s way,** créer des difficultés à
qn. **To get in one another's way,** se gêner (les
uns les autres). **To be in s.o.'s way,** gêner,
embarrasser, qn. *F:* **To put s.o. out of the way,**
se débarrasser de qn; faire disparaître qn. **To
get out of the way,** se ranger, s'effacer. **Get out
of the way!** laissez passer! rangez-vous! **To
keep out of the way,** se tenir à l'écart. **To keep
out of s.o.'s way,** se cacher de qn; éviter qn.
To make way for s.o., faire place à qn. *S.a.* HARM[1].
(e) *See* RIGHT[1] II. 2. **3.** *To accompany s.o. a little
way,* accompagner qn un bout de chemin. **All
the way,** tout le long du chemin; jusqu'au bout.
I flew part of the way, j'ai fait une partie du
trajet en avion. **It's a long way from here,** c'est
loin d'ici. **To have a long way to go,** avoir
beaucoup de chemin à faire. **A little, a short,
way off,** à peu de distance; pas trop loin. *F:* **He
will go a long way,** il ira loin; il fera son chemin.
His name goes a long way, son nom est d'un
grand poids. *A little sympathy goes a long way,*
un peu de sympathie fait grand bien. **To make a
penny go a long way,** savoir ménager les sous.
By a long way, de beaucoup. **Not by a long way,**
pas à beaucoup près; il s'en faut de beaucoup.
You are a long way out, vous êtes loin de compte.
4. (a) Côté *m*, direction *f*. *Which way is the wind
blowing?* d'où vient le vent? **This way out,** par
ici la sortie. *Which way did you come?* par où
êtes-vous venu? **This way and that,** de-ci de-là.
F: **Not to know which way to look,** être tout
décontenancé. **To look the other way,** détourner
les yeux. **I have nothing to say one way or the
other,** je n'ai rien à dire pour ou contre. **I am**

going your way, je vais de votre côté. *F:* **Down
our way,** chez nous. **He lived Hampstead way,**
il habitait du côté de Hampstead. **Such people
have not often come my way,** je n'ai pas souvent
eu affaire à des gens pareils. *I undertake* **anything
that comes my way,** j'entreprends n'importe quoi.
If the opportunity comes your way, si vous en
trouvez l'occasion. *S.a.* INCLINED 2, PARTING² 1.
(*b*) Sens *m.* (**In**) **the wrong way,** à contre-sens.
The wrong way up, sens dessus dessous; à
l'envers. *S.a.* WRONG¹ I. 3. **Right way up,**
dans le bon sens. (*c*) **Two-way cock,** robinet à
deux voies. *El.E:* **Two-way wiring system,** va-et-
vient *m. S.a.* THREE-WAY, TWO-WAY. **5.** Moyen *m.*
To find a way, trouver (le) moyen (*to, de*).
Adm: **Ways and means,** voies et moyens. *Parl:*
Committee of Ways and Means = Commission *f*
du Budget. *S.a.* WILL¹ 1. **6.** (*a*) Façon *f,* manière *f.*
In this way, de cette façon. **In a friendly way,**
en ami; amicalement. **Speaking in a general
way,** en thèse générale. **Without in any way
wishing to criticize . . . ,** sans aucunement vouloir critiquer. . . . **That's the way the money
goes!** voilà comme l'argent file! **That's the way!**
à la bonne heure! **To go the right way to work,**
s'y prendre bien. **In one way or another,** de
façon ou d'autre. **There are no two ways about
it,** il n'y a pas à discuter. **To go on the same
old way,** aller toujours son train. **The way things
are going,** l'allure *f* des affaires. **Well, it is this
way,** voici ce que c'est. *Our way of living,* notre
train *m,* genre *m,* de vie. *His way of looking at
things,* sa manière de voir. **That's his way,** voilà
comme il est. **That is always the way with him,**
il est toujours comme ça. **To do things in one's
own way,** faire les choses à sa guise. **He is a genius
in his way,** c'est un génie dans son genre. **I help
them in my small way,** je les aide dans la mesure
de mes moyens. **To be in the way of doing sth.,**
avoir l'habitude de faire qch. **To get into the
way of doing sth.,** (i) prendre l'habitude de faire
qch.; (ii) apprendre à faire qch. *You will get
into the way of it,* vous vous y ferez. (*b*) **Engaging
ways,** petites façons engageantes; gentillesses *f.*
I know his little ways, je connais ses petites
manies. **He has a way with him,** il est insinuant.
(*c*) **Ways and customs,** us *m* et coutumes *f. The
ways of good society,* l'usage *m* du monde. (*d*) **To
have, get, one's** (**own**) **way,** agir à sa guise;
suivre sa volonté. *He wants his own way,* il veut
(en) faire à sa tête. *He had it all his own way,*
il n'a pas rencontré de résistance. *S.a.* YOUTH 1.
7. In many ways, à bien des égards. **In some
ways . . . ,** à certains points de vue. . . . *He
was a gentleman in every way,* c'était un parfait
gentleman. *She is certainly clever in a way,* elle
ne manque pas d'une certaine adresse. **8.** Cours *m,*
course *f.* **I have him in the ordinary way of
business,** je l'ai rencontré dans le courant, au
cours, de mes affaires. **In the ordinary way,** *I am
home by five o'clock,* de coutume je suis rentré à
cinq heures. **9.** (*a*) **The flood is making way,**
l'inondation fait des progrès. (*b*) Erre *f* (d'un
navire). **Ship under way,** navire en marche,
faisant route. **To get (a ship) under way,**
appareiller; se mettre en route. **To gather way,**
prendre de l'erre. (*In rowing*) **Give way** (starboard)! avant (tribord)! (*Cp.* GIVE² I. 10.)
10. (*a*) **To be in a good way,** être bien en point.
Things seem in a bad way, les choses ont l'air
d'aller mal. *He is in a bad way of health,* sa santé
est chancelante; *F:* il file un mauvais coton.
He is in a bad way of business, il est mal dans ses
affaires. (*b*) *F:* **He is in a fine way about it,** (i) il

ne décolère pas; (ii) il a pris la chose très à
cœur. (*c*) **In a fair way to succeed,** en bonne
voie pour réussir. **This is not in my way,** ce
n'est pas de ma compétence. **II. Way of business,** genre *m* d'affaires; métier *m.* **To be in a
small way of business,** avoir un petit commerce.
He lives in a small way, il vit petitement, modestement. **12.** (*a*) **By the way.** (i) Chemin faisant;
en route. (ii) Incidemment; en passant. **All this
is by the way,** tout ceci est par parenthèse.
(iii) A (ce) propos. **By the way!** ah, j'y pense!
(*b*) **By way of.** (i) Par la voie de, par (un endroit).
(ii) En guise de, à titre de. *Boxes by way of
chairs,* des caisses en guise de chaises. **By way of
warning,** à titre d'avertissement. *F: He is by way
of being an artist,* c'est une manière d'artiste.
13. *pl. N.Arch:* **Ways,** couettes *f.* **'way-bill,**
s. Com: Lettre *f* de voiture; feuille *f* de route;
bordereau *m.* **'way-leave,** *s.* **1.** *Min:* Droit *m*
de passage. **2.** *Av:* Droit de survol (*over a
territory,* d'un territoire).

way², *adv. U.S: F:* = AWAY. **It was way back
in 1890,** cela remonte à 1890.

wayfarer ['weifɛərər], *s* Voyageur *m* (à pied);
passant *m.*

waylay [wei'lei], *v.tr.* (**waylaid** [wei'leid]; **waylaid**) **1.** Attirer (qn) dans une embuscade; tendre
un guet-apens à (qn). **2.** Arrêter (qn) au passage.

wayside ['weisaid], *s.* = ROADSIDE 1. **Wayside
flowers,** fleurs qui croissent en bordure de route.

wayward ['weiwərd], *a.* (*a*) Volontaire, rebelle.
(*b*) Capricieux, fantasque. **Wayward imagination,**
imagination vagabonde.

waywardness ['weiwərdnəs], *s.* (*a*) Entêtement *m,*
obstination *f.* (*b*) Caractère *m* fantasque.

W.C. ['dʌblju'si:], *s. F:* = WATER-CLOSET.

we [wi(:)], *pers. pron. nom. pl.* **1.** (*a*) Nous. *We
are playing,* nous jouons. **Here we are,** nous voici.
(*b*) (*Stressed*) **We and they,** nous et eux. **We
lawyers,** nous autres avocats. (*c*) On. **As we say,**
comme on dit. *We are sure to catch it,* on est
sûrs de se faire gronder. **2.** (*Plural of majesty*)
We are persuaded that . . . , nous sommes
persuadé que . . .

weak [wi:k], *a.* **1.** Faible; (*of health*) débile;
(*of body*) infirme, chétif. **To have w. eyes,** avoir
la vue faible. **Weak stomach,** estomac peu solide.
To grow weak, s'affaiblir. **The weaker sex,** le
sexe faible. **W. style,** style sans vigueur. **2.** (*a*) **Weak decision,** décision qui dénote de la
faiblesse. (*b*) **Weak character,** caractère faible.
S.o's weak side, le côté faible, la faible, de qn.
3. (*a*) (*Of solution*) Dilué, étendu. **W. tea,** thé
léger. (*b*) *I.C.E:* **Weak mixture,** mélange pauvre.
4. *Gram:* **Weak conjugation,** conjugaison faible.
-ly, *adv.* (*a*) Faiblement; sans force. (*b*) Sans
résolution. **weak-'eyed,** *a.* Qui a les yeux
faibles. **weak-'headed,** *a.* Faible d'esprit.
weak-'hearted, *a.* Sans courage. **weak-
'kneed,** *a. F:* Sans caractère. **weak-
'minded,** *a.* **1.** (*a*) Faible d'esprit. (*b*) (*Action*)
qui dénote de la faiblesse d'esprit. **2.** (*Action*)
manque de résolution. **weak-'sighted,** *a.* A
la vue faible.

weaken ['wi:k(ə)n]. **1.** *v.tr.* Affaiblir; amollir
(l'esprit). *I.C.E:* **To weaken the mixture,**
appauvrir le mélange. **2.** *v.i.* S'affaiblir, faiblir;
(*of current*) fléchir. **weakening¹,** *a.* **1.** Affaiblis-
sant; *Med:* anémiant. **2.** Faiblissant; qui
faiblit. **weakening²,** *s.* Affaiblissement *m,*
amollissement *m;* fléchissement *m* (de courant).
I.C.E: Appauvrissement *m* (du mélange).

weakling ['wi:kliŋ], *s.* (*a*) Être *m* faible, débile.
(*b*) Homme faible de caractère.

weakly ['wi:kli], a. (Enfant) débile, faible (de santé).

weakness ['wi:knəs], s. (a) Faiblesse f. The w. of his argument, le peu de solidité de son argument. I.C.E: Weakness of the mixture, pauvreté f du mélange. (b) To have a weakness for sth., s.o., avoir un faible pour qch., qn.

weal¹ [wi:l], s. Weal and woe, bonheur et malheur. For weal or (for) woe, quoi qu'il arrive; advienne que pourra. The general weal, le bien commun.

weal², s. = WALE¹.

weal³, v.tr. = WALE².

wealth [welθ], s. 1. Richesse(s) f(pl); opulence f. He is rolling in wealth, il roule sur l'or. 2. Abondance f, profusion f (de détails, etc.). Her w. of hair, sa chevelure abondante.

wealthy ['welθi], a. Riche, opulent. W. heiress, grosse héritière. s. The wealthy, les riches m.

wean [wi:n], v.tr. 1. Sevrer (un nourrisson). 2. To wean s.o. from his bad habits, détacher qn de ses mauvaises habitudes. **weaning**, s. Sevrage m.

weapon ['wepən], s. Arme f. To beat s.o. with his own weapons, battre qn avec ses propres armes.

wear¹ ['wɛər], s. 1. (a) Usage m. Frocks for evening wear, toilettes pour le soir. Ladies' wear, articles m pour dames. Foot-wear, chaussures f pl. (b) Stuff that will stand hard wear, étoffe d'un bon usage. (Of dress, etc.) To be the worse for wear, être usé, défraîchi. 2. Usure f; fatigue f (d'une machine); dégradation f (d'une route). Wear and tear, (i) usure; avaries f pl; (ii) frais mpl d'entretien. Jur: Fair wear and tear, usure naturelle, normale.

wear², v. (wore ['wɔːr]; worn [wɔːrn]) 1. v.tr. Porter (un vêtement). He was wearing a large hat, il portait un grand chapeau. To wear black, porter du noir. To have nothing fit to wear, n'avoir rien de mettable. What shall I w.? qu'est-ce que je vais mettre? A lounge suit may be worn, le veston est, sera, de mise. To wear one's hair long, porter les cheveux longs. To wear a sour look, avoir un air revêche. 2. v.tr. User. To wear one's coat threadbare, user son veston jusqu'à la corde. To wear sth. into holes, to wear holes in sth., faire des trous à qch. (à force d'usage). To wear oneself to death, se tuer à force de travail. 3. (With passive force) (a) (Of garment) To wear into holes, se trouer. (Of stone) To wear smooth, se lisser par le frottement. (b) To wear well, (i) (of material) être de bon usage; (ii) (of pers.) bien porter son âge. This friendship has worn well, cette amitié s'est soutenue. Tyres that wear for ever, pneus inusables. 4. v.i. (Of time) Traîner. The year was wearing to its close, l'année tirait à sa fin. **wear away. 1.** v.tr. (a) User, ronger. He is worn away to a shadow, il n'est plus que l'ombre de lui-même. (b) Effacer, détruire. **2.** v.i. (a) S'user. (b) S'effacer. (c) (Of pain) Passer, s'assoupir. (d) (Of time) S'écouler. **wear down. 1.** v.tr. User. To wear one's heels down, éculer ses souliers. To wear down the enemy's resistance, user à la longue la résistance de l'ennemi. **2.** v.i. S'user. **wear off. 1.** v.tr Faire disparaître (par l'usure). **2.** v.i. S'effacer, disparaître. The novelty of the sight soon wore off, la nouveauté de ce spectacle passa vite. **wear on**, v.i. (Of time) S'écouler (lentement). As the evening wore on . . ., à mesure que la soirée s'avançait. . . . **wear out. 1.** v.tr. (a) User (ses habits). To wear oneself out, s'user, s'épuiser. Worn out with work, usé par le travail. (b) Épuiser, lasser (la

patience de qn). (c) To w. out one's days in captivity, passer le reste de ses jours dans la captivité. **2.** v.i. S'user. Stuff that cannot w. out, étoffe inusable. **worn out**, a. **1.** Usé. W. out shoes, souliers usés, finis. **2.** (Of pers.) (i) Épuisé; exténué; (ii) usé (par le travail). The horses are w. out, les chevaux n'en peuvent plus. **3.** (Of idea) Rebattu. **wearing**¹, a. **1.** Fatigant, lassant, épuisant. **2.** Destructeur, -trice. **3.** Wearing parts (of a machine), organes sujets à l'usure. **4.** Good-wearing material, étoffe de bon usage. **wearing**², s. **1.** Action f de porter (des vêtements). Wearing apparel, vêtements mpl, habits mpl. **2.** Usure f. Wearing surface, surface d'usure.

wear³, v. (wore; wore) Nau: **1.** v.i. (Of ship) Virer (un) pour lof; virer vent arrière. **2.** v.tr. Virer (un navire) lof pour lof.

wearable ['wɛərəbl], a. (Vêtement) mettable.

wearer ['wɛərər], s. Personne qui porte qch. (sur elle).

weariness ['wi:ərinəs], s. **1.** Lassitude f, fatigue f. **2.** Dégoût m, lassitude.

wearisome ['wi:ərisəm], a. Ennuyeux, fastidieux; F: assommant. W. task, tâche ingrate. **-ly**, adv. Ennuyeusement.

weary¹ ['wi:əri], a. **1.** Fatigué; las, f. lasse. F: A weary Willie, un fainéant, un traîne-la-patte. **2.** Las, dégoûté (of, de). To grow w. of sth., se dégoûter de qch. **3.** Fatigant, obsédant. To have a w. time, s'ennuyer à mourir. **-ily**, adv. **1.** D'un air ou d'un ton las, fatigué. **2.** Avec fatigue; (cheminer) péniblement.

weary², v. (wearied) **1.** v.i. (a) Se lasser, se fatiguer. To weary of s.o., se fatiguer de la compagnie de qn. (b) Trouver le temps long. (c) To weary for sth., désirer ardemment qch.; languir après qch. **2.** v.tr. (a) Lasser, fatiguer. (b) To w. s.o. with one's prayers, importuner qn de ses sollicitations. **wearied**, a. Las, f. lasse; fatigué. **wearying**, a. Ennuyeux, fastidieux, F: assommant.

weasel ['wi:z(ə)l], s. Z: Belette f. **'weasel-faced**, a. A la mine chafouine.

weather¹ ['weðər], s. **1.** Temps m (qu'il fait). In all weathers, par tous les temps. It is settled weather, le temps est au beau fixe. In this, in such, weather, par le temps qu'il fait. In the hot w., pendant les grandes chaleurs. It is awful w., F: il fait un temps de chien. (Wind and) weather permitting, si le temps le permet. If there is a break in the weather, si le temps se gâte. What is the w. like? quel temps fait-il? (Of ship) To make heavy weather, bourlinguer. (Of pers.) To be under the weather, être indisposé, malade. Journ: The Weather, la Température. S.a. CLERK 3. **2.** Attrib. (a) The Weather Bureau, le Bureau météorologique. Weather conditions, conditions atmosphériques. (b) Nau: Du côté du vent. On the weather-beam, par le travers au vent. **'weather-beaten**, a. **1.** Battu des vents; battu par la tempête. **2.** (a) (Of countenance) Bronzé, hâlé, basané. (b) (Of thg) Dégradé par le temps. **'weatherbound**, a. Retenu, arrêté, par le mauvais temps. **'weather-chart**, s. Carte f météorologique; carte du temps. **'weather-deck**, s. Nau: Partie du pont non recouverte par des roufs. **'weather-eye**, s. F: To keep one's weather-eye open, veiller au grain. **'weather-forecast**, s. Bulletin m météorologique; prévisions f pl du temps. Journ: To-day's w.-f., probabilités f pl pour aujourd'hui. **'weather-ga(u)ge**, s. Nau: Avantage m du vent. **'weather-glass**, s.

Baromètre *m* (à cadran). **'weather-lore,** *s.* Connaissance *f* des signes qui présagent le temps. **'weather-proof,** *a.* A l'épreuve du gros temps ; (vêtement) imperméable ; (édifice) étanche. **'weather-prophet,** *s.* Personne *f* qui se pique de prédire le temps. **'weather-shore,** *s. Nau :* Côte *f* du vent. **'weather-side,** *s.* **1.** Côté (d'une maison) exposé au vent. **2.** *Nau :* Bord *m* du vent. **'weather-stained,** *a.* Délavé. **'weather-wise,** *a.* Qui sait prévoir le temps ; qui se connaît au temps. **'weather-worn,** *a.* Usé, rongé, par les intempéries. **weather².** I. *v.tr.* **1.** *Geol :* Weathered rocks, roches altérées par les intempéries. *Furn :* Weathered oak, chêne patiné. **2.** *Nau :* (*a*) To weather a headland, doubler un cap (à la voile). To weather a ship, passer au vent d'un navire. (*b*) To weather (out) a storm, survivre à une tempête. (*c*) *F :* To weather through, se tirer d'affaire. II. **weather,** *v.i.* **1.** (*Of rock*) Se désagréger, s'altérer. **2.** (*Of bronze*) Prendre la patine. **weathering,** *s.* (*a*) Altération *f*, désagrégation *f* (des roches) ; effet *m* de l'air (sur la pierre). (*b*) Patine *f*.

weatherboard ['weðərbɔːrd], *s.* (*a*) (*For roofs*) Planche *f* à recouvrement. (*b*) (*For window*) Jet *m* d'eau.

weathercock ['weðərkɔk], *s.* (*a*) Girouette *f*. (*b*) *F :* Personne inconstante ; girouette.

weave¹ [wiːv], *s. Tex :* **1.** Armure *f*. **2.** Tissage *m*. **weave²,** *v.* (wove [wouv] ; woven ['wouv(ə)n]) **1.** *v.tr.* (*a*) *Tex :* Tisser (une étoffe). *Abs.* Faire le métier de tisserand. (*b*) *F :* To weave a plot, tramer un complot. (*c*) Tresser (une guirlande, un panier) ; entrelacer (des fils, des fleurs). **2.** *v.i.* The road weaves through the valleys, la route serpente à travers les vallées. **wove,** *a. Only in* Wove paper, (papier) vélin *m*. Cream-wove paper, vélin blanc. **woven,** *a.* Tissé. Closely w., d'un tissu serré. **weaving,** *s.* **1.** Tissage *m*. Hand-loom weaving, tissage à la main. Power-loom weaving, tissage mécanique. **2.** Entrelacement *m* (de rameaux).

weaver ['wiːvər], *s.* **1.** (*a*) Tisserand *m*. (*b*) *F :* A weaver of rhymes, un faiseur, un tisseur, de vers. **2.** Weaver(-bird), tisserin *m*.

web [web], *s.* **1.** *Tex :* Tissu *m*. *F :* Web of lies, tissu de mensonges. **2.** Spider's web, toile *f* d'araignée. **3.** *Nat.Hist :* Palmure *f*, membrane *f* (d'un palmipède). **4.** *Tchn :* Joue *f*, flasque *m* (de manivelle) ; âme *f* (d'une poutre, d'un rail) ; panneton *m* (de clef). **5.** Pièce *f*, rouleau *m* (d'étoffe). **'web-fingered,** *a. Z :* Syndactyle. **'web-footed, -toed,** *a.* Palmipède ; aux pieds palmés.

webbed [webd], *a.* Palmé, membrané. Webbed feet, pattes palmées.

webbing ['webiŋ], *s.* **1.** Sangles *fpl* (de chaise). **2.** Toile *f* à sangles ; ruban *m* à sangles.

wed [wed], *v.* (wedded) **1.** *v.tr.* (*a*) Épouser (qn) ; se marier avec (qn). (*b*) (*Of priest*) To wed a couple, marier un couple. (*c*) Unir (to, with, à). To be wedded to an opinion, être obstinément attaché à une opinion. To become wedded to an opinion, se fixer à une opinion. **2.** *v.i.* Se marier. **wedded,** *a.* **1.** Marié. My wedded wife, mon épouse légitime. **2.** Wedded life, la vie conjugale. **wedding,** *s.* **1.** Noce(s) *f(pl)* ; mariage *m*. Church wedding, mariage à l'église. **2.** *Attrib.* Nuptial, -aux ; de noce(s) ; de mariage. **'wedding-breakfast,** *s.* Repas *m* de noces. **'wedding-cake,** *s.* Gâteau *m* de noces. **'wedding-card,** *s.* (Carte *f* de) faire-part *m inv* de mariage. **'wedding-day,** *s.* **1.** Jour *m*

des noces. **2.** Anniversaire *m* du mariage. **'wedding-guest,** *s.* Invité, -ée (à un mariage). **'wedding-march,** *s.* Marche nuptiale. **'wedding-present,** *s.* Cadeau *m* de noces. **'wedding-ring,** *s.* Alliance *f*.

wedge¹ [wedʒ], *s.* Coin *m*. **1.** (*a*) Fixing wedge, coin de serrage ; cale *f* de fixation ; *Mec.E :* clavette *f*, clef *f*. *Artil :* Recoil wedge, coin de recul. (*b*) Splitting wedge, coin à fendre. To drive in a wedge, enfoncer un coin. *F :* It is the thin end of the wedge, c'est un premier empiétement ; c'est un pied de pris. **2.** Chose de forme triangulaire. Wedge of a tennis racket, cœur *m* d'une raquette. W. of cake, morceau *m* (triangulaire) de gâteau. **'wedge-shaped,** *a.* En (forme de) coin.

wedge², *v.tr.* **1.** Coincer, assujettir ; caler (des rails) ; claveter (une roue sur son axe). **2.** To wedge (up) a piece of furniture, caler un meuble. To wedge a door open, maintenir une porte ouverte avec une cale. **3.** To wedge sth. in sth., enclaver, *F :* insérer, implanter, enfoncer, serrer, qch. dans qch. Traveller wedged in between two fat women, voyageur coincé entre deux grosses femmes.

wedged [wedʒd], *a.* Cunéiforme ; en forme de coin.

wedlock ['wedlɔk], *s.* (*a*) *Lit. & Jur :* Mariage *m*. Born in, out of, wedlock, (enfant) légitime, illégitime. (*b*) La vie conjugale.

Wednesday ['we(d)nzdi], *s.* Mercredi *m*. Ash Wednesday, le mercredi des Cendres. (*For phrases see* FRIDAY.)

wee [wiː], *a. F :* Petit ; tout petit ; minuscule. A wee (little) bit, un tout petit peu.

weed¹ [wiːd], *s.* **1.** *Bot :* Mauvaise herbe ; herbe folle. *Prov :* Ill weeds grow apace, mauvaise herbe croît toujours. **2.** (*a*) The weed, le tabac. (*b*) *F :* Cigare *m*. **3.** *F :* Personne étique, malingre, chétive. **weed²,** *v.tr.* Arracher les mauvaises herbes (d'un champ, etc.) ; sarcler. **weed out,** *v.tr.* **1.** Éclaircir (des laitues, etc.). **2.** *F :* Éliminer ; extirper (des préjugés, etc.). **weeding,** *s.* Sarclage *m* ; extirpation *f* des mauvaises herbes.

weeder ['wiːdər], *s.* **1.** Sarcleur, -euse. **2.** *Tls :* Sarcloir *m*.

weediness ['wiːdinəs], *s.* *F :* Maigreur *f* ; apparence *f* malingre.

weeds [wiːdz], *s.pl.* Vêtements *m* de deuil (de veuve).

weedy ['wiːdi], *a.* **1.** Couvert de mauvaises herbes. **2.** *F :* (Homme) malingre, poussé en asperge.

week [wiːk], *s.* Semaine *f*. **1.** (*a*) What day of the week is it? quel jour de la semaine sommes-nous ? Twice a week, deux fois par semaine. *P :* To knock s.o. into the middle of next week, donner à qn un fameux coup. Week in week out, d'un bout de la semaine à l'autre. I haven't seen him for weeks, je ne l'ai pas vu depuis des semaines. *F :* A week of Sundays, of weeks, (i) sept semaines ; (ii) une éternité. (*b*) *F :* Huit jours. Once a week, une fois par semaine ; tous les huit jours. Every week, tous les huit jours. Within the week, dans la huitaine. A week from now, this day week, to-day week, d'aujourd'hui en huit. To-morrow week, Tuesday week, de demain, de mardi, en huit. In a week or so, dans une huitaine. **2.** What I can't get done in the w. I do on Sundays, ce que je n'arrive pas à faire en semaine je le fais le dimanche. **'week-'end,** *s.* Fin *f* de semaine ; week-end *m*. To have one's week-ends free, être libre le samedi et le dimanche ;

faire la semaine anglaise. *I stayed with them over the week-end*, je suis resté chez eux du samedi au lundi. Week-end trip, excursion de fin de semaine. **week-'ender,** s. Touriste m de fin de semaine.

weekday ['wi:kdei], s. Jour m ouvrable ; jour de semaine. On weekdays, en semaine.

weekly ['wi:kli]. **I.** a. (a) (Salaire) de la semaine ; (visite, payement) hebdomadaire. The weekly rest-day Act, la loi sur le repos hebdomadaire. (b) (Pensionnaire) à la semaine. **2.** s. Journal m ou revue f hebdomadaire. **3.** adv. Par semaine ; tous les huit jours. Twice weekly, deux fois par semaine.

ween [wi:n], v.tr. A : I ween, j'imagine.

weep¹ [wi:p], s. Pleurs mpl. To have a good, a hearty, weep, pleurer à chaudes larmes ; pleurer tout son soûl. **'weep-hole,** s. Chantepleure f (dans un mur).

weep², v. (wept [wept]) **I.** v.i. (a) Pleurer. *To w. bitterly,* pleurer à chaudes larmes. To weep for joy, pleurer de joie. *That's nothing to weep over, about,* (i) il n'y a pas de quoi pleurer ; (ii) *Iron:* tant mieux ! *I could have wept to see them . . .,* je gémissais de les voir. . . . (With cogn. acc) To weep tears, répandre, verser, des larmes. (b) (Of wall, etc.) Suinter, suer ; (of tree) pleurer ; (of sore) couler, exsuder. Weeping willow, saule pleureur. **2.** v.tr. To weep oneself to sleep, s'endormir en pleurant, dans les larmes. To weep one's heart, one's eyes, out, pleurer à chaudes larmes. To weep away the time, passer son temps à pleurer. **weeping,** s. **I.** Pleurs mpl, larmes fpl. **2.** Suintement m ; exsudation f.

weeper ['wi:pər], s. **I.** Pleureur, -euse. **2.** pl. A : Crêpe m de deuil ; voile m de deuil.

weepy ['wi:pi], a. F : (a) (Ton, air) larmoyant. (b) To feel w., se sentir envie de pleurer.

weevil ['wi:vil], s. Ent: Charançon m.

weevil(l)ed ['wi:vild], **weevil(l)y** ['wi:vili], a. (Blé, etc.) charançonné.

weft [weft], s. **I.** Tex: (a) Trame f. (b) = WEFT-YARN. **2.** Traînée f (de nuage). **'weft-yarn,** s. Tex: Fil m de trame.

weigh¹ [wei], s. Nau: Under weigh = under way, q.v. at WAY¹ 9 (b).

weigh². **I.** v.tr. (a) Peser (un paquet, etc.); faire la pesée de (qch.). To w. sth. in one's hand, soupeser qch. (b) To weigh one's words, peser, mesurer, ses paroles. To weigh sth. (up) in one's mind, considérer qch. To weigh (up) the consequences of sth., calculer les conséquences de qch. To weigh the pros and cons, peser le pour et le contre. (c) Nau: To weigh anchor, lever l'ancre ; appareiller. **2.** v.i. (a) 'Peser ; avoir du poids. To weigh heavy, light, peser lourd inv ; peser peu. How much does the parcel weigh? combien pèse le paquet ? (b) The debt is weighing on his mind, cette dette le tracasse, lui pèse sur l'esprit. Fate weighs heavily on us, la fatalité s'appesantit sur nous. (c) The point that weighs with me is . . ., ce qui a du poids pour moi c'est. . . . **weigh down,** v.tr. **I.** Peser plus que (qch.) ; l'emporter en poids sur (qch.). **2.** Faire pencher (la balance). **3.** Surcharger. *Branch weighed down with fruit,* branche surchargée de fruits. *F:* Weighed down with sorrow, accablé de chagrin, par le chagrin. **weigh in,** v.i. (a) (Of jockey) Se faire peser avant la course. The weighing-in room, le pesage. (b) F: To weigh in (with an argument), intervenir avec un argument. **weigh out,** v.tr. Peser (du sucre, etc.) en petites quantités.

weighing, s. **I.** Pesée f (de denrées, etc.).

Turf: Pesage m. **2.** Nau: Levage m (de l'ancre) ; appareillage m. **'weighing-bottle,** s. Ch: Flacon m à tare. **'weighing-enclosure,** s. Turf: (Enceinte f du) pesage ; enceinte des balances. **'weighing-machine,** s. Appareil m de pesage ; bascule f (de pesage). **'weigh-beam,** s. **I.** Fléau m, verge f (d'une balance romaine). **2.** Balance romaine. **'weigh-bridge,** s. Pont m à bascule.

weighman, pl. -men ['weimən, -men], s.m. Peseur.

weight¹ [weit], s. **I.** (a) Poids m. To sell by weight, vendre au poids. To give good weight, faire bon poids. Two pounds in weight, d'un poids de deux livres. *F:* It is worth its weight in gold, cela vaut son pesant d'or. (Of pers.) To lose weight, perdre de son poids. To gain weight, prendre du poids. *P:* To throw one's weight about, faire de l'esbrouffe. To pull one's weight, (i) Row: fournir un effort en rapport avec son poids ; (ii) *F:* y mettre du sien. (b) Poids, pesanteur f. To try, feel, the weight of sth., soupeser qch. Specific weight, poids spécifique, pesanteur spécifique. Atomic weight, poids atomique. **2.** (a) Poids (en cuivre, etc.). Set of weights, série f de poids. Weights and measures, poids et mesures. (b) Corps lourd. Letter-weight, paper-weight, presse-papiers m inv, serre-papiers m inv. Gym: Heavy weight, gueuse f d'athlétisme. *F:* To hang a weight round one's own neck, se mettre la corde au cou. **3.** Charge f. To put the w. on a beam, charger une poutre. *F:* That's a weight off my mind, voilà qui me soulage l'esprit. The weight of years, le fardeau, le faix, le poids, des ans, des années. **4.** Force f (d'un coup). Blow with no weight behind it, coup sans force. **5.** Importance f. To give weight to an argument, donner du poids à un argument. His word carries weight, sa parole a du poids, de l'autorité. People of weight, gens influents. Of no weight, (i) sans conséquence, sans importance ; (ii) (of pers.) sans influence. **'weight-lifting,** s. Gym: (Travail m aux) poids et haltères.

weight², v.tr. **I.** Attacher un poids à (qch.); charger, alourdir, (qch.) d'un poids ; lester, plomber (un filet, etc.); plomber (une canne). **2.** Paperm: Charger (le papier).

weightiness ['weitinəs], s. **I.** Pesanteur f, lourdeur f (d'un paquet, etc.). **2.** *F:* Importance f, force f (d'une opinion).

weighty ['weiti], a. **I.** Pesant, lourd. **2.** (Motif, etc.) grave, important, sérieux. *W.* arguments, arguments puissants, d'un grand poids. For w. reasons, pour des raisons graves. -ily, adv. **I.** Pesamment. **2.** (Raisonner) avec force.

weir [wi:ər], s. **I.** Barrage m (dans un cours d'eau). **2.** Déversoir m (d'un étang, etc.).

weird¹ [wi:ərd], s. Scot: Sort m ; destin m.

weird², a. **I.** Myth: The weird Sisters, les Parques f. **2.** (a) Surnaturel ; mystérieux ; d'une étrangeté inquiétante. (b) *F:* Étrange, singulier. -ly, adv. Étrangement.

weirdness ['wi:ərdnəs], s. **I.** Étrangeté inquiétante (d'un spectacle, etc.). **2.** *F:* Caractère singulier (d'un costume, etc.).

Welch [wel(t)ʃ], a. (Used in regimenta names) = WELSH¹.

welcome¹ ['welkəm], a. **I.** (a) Bienvenu. To make s.o. welcome, faire bon accueil à qn. (b) As int. Welcome (to you)! soyez le bienvenu ! To bid, wish, s.o. welcome, souhaiter la bienvenue à qn. **2.** (Of thg) Agréable ; acceptable. A welcome change, un changement agréable. *This cheque is* *most w.*, ce chèque tombe à merveille. **3.** You are welcome to try, libre à vous d'essayer. You are welcome to it, (i) c'est à votre service, à votre disposition ; (ii) *Iron :* je ne vous l'envie pas ; grand bien vous fasse ! *F : Thank you very much.* —You're welcome, merci bien, monsieur.—Il n'y a pas de quoi.

welcome², *s.* (*a*) Bienvenue *f.* To overstay one's welcome, lasser l'amabilité de ses hôtes. (*b*) Accueil *m.* To give s.o. a hearty welcome, faire bon accueil à qn. To give *s.o. an enthusiastic w.*, faire à qn un accueil enthousiaste. To find a kind welcome, trouver, recevoir, bon accueil. To meet with a cold welcome, être reçu froidement.

welcome³, *v.tr.* **1.** Souhaiter la bienvenue à (qn) ; faire bon accueil à (qn). **2.** (*a*) Recevoir avec plaisir. *To w. a piece of news,* se réjouir d'une nouvelle. (*b*) To w. *s.o. with joy,* accueillir qn avec joie.

weld¹ [weld], *s.* Soudure *f* ; joint *m*, ligne *f*, de soudure.

weld². **1.** *v.tr.* (*a*) Souder (deux pièces) au blanc soudant ; unir (deux pièces) à chaud. (*b*) Corroyer (l'acier). (*c*) *F :* Unir, joindre, étroitement. *To w. the parts into a homogeneous whole,* amalgamer les parties en une unité homogène. **2.** *v.i.* (*Of metals*) (i) Se souder ; (ii) se.corroyer.

welding, *s.* Soudage *m*, soudure *f.* (Oxy)acetylene welding, soudure autogène, à l'autogène. Welding heat, (température *f* du) blanc soudant.

weldless ['weldləs], *a.* (Tube, etc.) sans soudure, sans couture.

welfare ['welfɛər], *s.* Bien-être *m* ; prospérité *f.* Public welfare, le salut public. Child welfare, infant welfare, puériculture sociale. Welfare work, assistance sociale. Welfare centre, dispensaire *m.* Welfare worker, personne qui se consacre à l'assistance sociale.

welkin (the) [ðə'welkin], *s. Poet :* Le firmament ; la voûte céleste. To make the welkin ring, retentir.

well¹ [wel], *s.* **1.** Puits *m.* To drive, sink, a well, forer, creuser, un puits. *Geol :* Hot well, source chaude. *F :* Well of knowledge, source de savoir ; (*of pers.*) puits de science. **2.** (*a*) (*Shaft*) Puits, cage *f* (d'un ascenseur). (*b*) Partie encaissée, creux *m* (de qch.). *Nau :* Vivier *m* (d'un bateau de pêche). *Aut :* Spare-wheel well (*in running board*), baignoire *f.* (*c*) Well of a yacht, cockpit *m* d'un·yacht. (*d*) Fond *m* de carter, etc. (formant réservoir d'huile). (*e*) *Nau :* Puisard *m*, archipompe *f*, sentine *f* (d'un navire). **3.** Ink-well, (i) encrier *m* (pour pupitre d'écolier) ; (ii) réservoir, *m* (d'un encrier). **'well-base,** *s. Aut :* Gorge *f* (d'une roue). **'well-boring,** *s.* (i) Sondage *m*, forage *m.* (ii) fonçage *m*, de puits. **'well-deck,** *s. N.Arch :* Coffre *m.* **'well-decked,** *a.* (Navire) à coffre. **'well-seat,** *s. Av :* Baquet *m.* **'well-sinker,** *s.* Puisatier *m.* **'well-sinking,** *s.* Fonçage *m* de puits.

well², *v.i.* To well (up, out, forth), (*of liquid*) jaillir ; (*of spring*) sourdre ; (*of tears*) jaillir. **welling,** *s.* Jaillissement *m.*

well³. (*Comp.* better, *sup.* best, *q.v.*) I. *adv.* Bien. **1.** (*a*) To work well, bien travailler. This lad will do well, ce garçon fera son chemin, ira loin. To do as well as one can, faire de son mieux. Well done ! bravo ! très bien ! *F :* To do oneself well, bien se soigner ; bien se nourrir. You would do well to be quiet, vous feriez bien de vous taire. He accepted, as well he might, il accepta, et rien d'étonnant. One might as well say *that* . . ., autant dire que. . . . You may (just) as well stay, (i) autant vaut rester ; (ii) vous

n'êtes pas de trop. You could just as well have stayed till to-morrow, vous auriez tout aussi bien pu rester jusqu'à demain. Very well ! très bien ! (c'est) entendu ! (*b*) To receive s.o. well, faire bon accueil à qn. It speaks well for . . ., cela fait honneur à. . . . To do well by s.o., se montrer généreux envers qn. She deserves well of you, elle mérite bien votre reconnaissance. Well intended, fait à bonne intention. (*c*) (*Happily*) You are well out of it, soyez heureux d'en être quitte. To come off well, (i) avoir de la chance ; (ii) (*of event*) se bien passer. Well met! soyez le bienvenu ! **2.** (*Intensive*) It is well worth trying, cela vaut bien la peine d'essayer. It is well on six, il est presque six heures. Well on into the small hours, bien avant, fort avant, dans la nuit. Well on in years, avancé en âge. To be well up in a subject, bien posséder un sujet. **3.** (*With qualifying adv.*) Pretty well all, presque tout. *F :* It serves him jolly well right, c'est joliment bien fait pour lui. **4.** (*a*) As well, aussi. *Take me as well,* emmenez-moi aussi. I want some as well, il m'en faut également. (*b*) As well as, de même que ; comme ; non moins que. *By day as well as by night,* de jour comme de nuit. **5.** (*a*) (*To introduce a remark*) Well, as I was telling you . . ., donc, comme je vous disais. . . . *Well, who was it?* eh bien, qui était-ce ? (*b*) (*Expressing relief, etc.*) Well I never ! pas possible ! *Well, it cannot be helped,* ma foi ! on n'y peut rien. Well, well! (i) que voulez-vous ! (ii) vous m'en direz tant ! (*c*) (*Summarizing*) Well then, *why worry about it?* eh. bien, alors, pourquoi vous faire de la bile ? II. **well,** *pred.a.* **1.** To be well, être en bonne santé, être bien portant. Well and strong, robuste ; *F :* vaillant. Not to feel well, ne pas se sentir bien. **2.** (*a*) (*Advisable*) It is well to . . ., il est opportun de. . . . It would be well to . . ., il serait bon, utile, recommandable, de. . . . It would be just as well if you were present, il y aurait avantage à ce que vous soyez présent. (*b*) (*Lucky*) It was well that you were there, c'est bien heureux que vous vous soyez trouvé là. (*c*) (*Satisfactory*) All's well that ends well, *tout est bien qui finit bien.* All's well ! *Mil :* tout va bien ! *Nau :* bon quart ! (*d*) That's all very well, but . . ., tout cela est bel et bon, mais. . . . It is all very well for you to say that . . ., libre à vous, permis à vous, de dire que. . . . He is all very well in his way, but . . ., il n'y a rien à dire contre lui, mais. . . . Well and good ! soit ! bon ! That's all very well and good, but . . ., tout ça c'est très bien, mais. . . . III. **well,** *s.* **1.** *pl.* The well and the sick, les bien portants et les malades. **2.** To wish s.o. well, vouloir du bien à qn ; être bien disposé (en)vers qn. **well ad'vised,** *pred.a.* (*a*) (*Of pers.*) Bien avisé. (*b*) (*Of action*) Sage, prudent, judicieux. **well-being,** *s.* Bien-être *m.* **well-be'loved,** *a. & s.* Bien-aimé, -ée. **well 'born,** *a.* Bien né ; de bonne famille. **well-'bred,** *a.* **1.** (*Of pers.*) Bien élevé, bien appris. **2.** (*Of dog, etc.*) De (bonne) race. **well-'chosen,** *a.* In a few well-chosen words, en quelques mots bien choisis. **well-con'ducted,** *a.* **1.** Qui se conduit bien ; sage. **2.** (*Commerce*) Bien dirigé ; (expérience) bien menée. **well di'rected,** *a.* (Tir, etc.) bien ajusté. **well dis'posed,** *a.* **1.** Bien arrangé, bien disposé. **2.** (*Of pers.*) Bien disposé, bien porté (to, towards, envers). **well-'doing,** *s.* **1.** Bien faire *m* ; le bien. **2.** Prospérité *f*, succès *m.* **well 'earned,** *a.* Bien mérité. **well 'educated,** *a.* Instruit. **'well 'found,** *a.* (*Of ship, etc.*) Bien équipé.

bien pourvu (*in*, de). **'well 'founded,** *a.* Bien fondé; (appréhension) légitime. **'well-'grown,** *a.* (Enfant) bien venu. **well in'formed,** *a.* (*Of pers.*) Bien renseigné, bien informé, instruit; (*of committee*) documenté. *To keep well i.*, se tenir au courant. **To be well informed on a subject,** connaître un sujet à fond. **In well-informed quarters,** en lieu compétent. **'well 'judged,** *a.* Judicieux; bien estimé, bien calculé. **'well 'kept,** *a.* (*a*) (*Of garden*) Bien tenu. (*b*) (*Of secret*) Bien gardé. **'well-'knit,** *a.* (*a*) Compact, solide, bien bâti. *Well-knit play,* pièce (de théâtre) bien charpentée. (*b*) (Homme, corps) bien bâti, bien découplé. **'well 'known,** *a.* (Bien) connu; célèbre; réputé; renommé (*for, pour*). *As is well known,* comme tout le monde le sait. **'well 'made,** *a.* **I.** (Homme) bien découplé. **2.** (Habit) de coupe soignée. **well-'mannered,** *a.* (*a*) Qui a de bonnes manières; (enfant) bien élevé. (*b*) *Well-m.* horse, cheval sage. **'well 'marked,** *a.* (*Of change*) Bien marqué; très évident; accusé. *Well-m.* differences, différences tranchées. **Well-marked outlines,** contours nets. **'well-'matched,** *a.* (Ménage) bien assorti. *The two teams are well-m.*, les deux équipes sont de force (égale). **well-'meaning,** *a.* Bien intentionné. **'well-'meant,** *a.* Fait avec une bonne intention. **well 'minded,** *a.* **I.** Bien disposé; bien pensant. **2.** D'un bon naturel. **'well-nigh,** *adv. Lit:* Presque. **well off,** *adj. phr.* **I.** (*a*) To be well off, être dans l'aisance, à l'aise; être riche. *To be well enough off,* avoir suffisamment de bien. *Well-off* people, gens aisés. (*b*) Prospère. *You don't know when you are well off,* vous ne savez pas quand vous êtes bien. **2.** To be well off for sth., être bien pourvu, bien fourni, de qch. **well-'ordered,** *a.* Bien ordonné; (*of mind*) méthodique. **'well 'read,** *a.* **I.** (*Of pers.*) Instruit; qui a de la lecture. **2.** (Volume) qui porte les traces de nombreuses lectures. **well-'regulated,** *a.* = WELL-ORDERED. **well 'spent,** *a.* (*Of money, etc.*) Bien utilisé; bien employé. **well-'spoken,** *a.* **I.** (*a*) Qui parle bien. (*b*) A la parole affable. **2.** To be well spoken of, avoir une bonne réputation. **well 'timbered,** *a.* **I.** Bien charpenté; solidement construit. **2.** (*Of country*) (Bien) boisé. **'well-to-'do,** *a.* To be well-to-do, être dans l'aisance; être à son aise. *Well-to-do folk,* gens cossus. *Well-to-do appearance,* air prospère. **'well-wisher,** *s.* Ami, -ie, partisan *m* (de qn, d'une cause). "Your well-wisher," "une personne qui vous veut du bien." **'well-'worn,** *a.* (*a*) (Vêtement) fortement usagé. (*b*) (Argument) rebattu, usé jusqu'à la corde.
Wellingtons ['weliŋtənz], *s.pl. Cost:* (*Also* **Wellington boots**) (i) Bottes *f* qui montent jusqu'aux genoux; demi-bottes *f*; (ii) bottes en caoutchouc (pour femmes ou enfants).
Welsh¹ [welʃ]. **I.** *a.* Gallois; du pays de Galles. **2.** *s.* (*a*) *pl.* The Welsh, les Gallois *m*. (*b*) *Ling:* Le gallois.
welsh², *v.i.* (*Of bookmaker*) Décamper, filer; lever le pied.
welsher ['welʃər], *s. Turf:* Bookmaker marron.
Welshman, *pl.* **-men** ['welʃmən, -men], *s.m.* Gallois.
Welshwoman, *pl.* **-women** ['welʃwumən, -wimen], *s.f.* Galloise.
welt¹ [welt], *s.* **I.** (*a*) *Bootm:* Trépointe *f* (de semelle). (*b*) Bordure *f* (de gant). **2.** = WALE¹.
welt², *v.tr.* **I.** (*a*) Mettre des trépointes à (des souliers). (*b*) Border un gant). **2.** *F:* Rosser,

battre (qn). **welted,** *a.* (Soulier, semelle) à trépointes. **welting,** *s. F:* Rossée *f*, raclée *f*.
welter¹ ['weltər], *s. F:* **I.** Confusion *f*, désordre *m*. **2.** Masse confuse, fouillis *m* (de choses disparates); ramassis *m*, fatras *m* (d'idées)..
welter², *v.i.* Se vautrer, se rouler (dans la boue, etc.). **To be weltering in one's blood,** baigner dans son sang.
welter³ weight ['weltərweit], *s. Box:* Poids mi-moyen.
wen [wen], *s. Med:* **I.** Kyste sébacé; *F:* loupe *f*. **2.** *F:* Goitre *m*.
wench [wenʃ], *s.f.* (*a*) *A. & Dial:* Jeune fille, jeune femme. *Strapping w.*, grande gaillarde. (*b*) Jeune fille du peuple. *Kitchen w.*, fille de cuisine.
wend [wend], *v.tr. Lit:* To wend one's way, porter, diriger, ses pas (*to*, vers). *To w. one's way back,* s'en revenir.
went. *See* GO².
wept [wept]. *See* WEEP².
were [wəər, wəːr]. *See* BE.
we're [wiːr] = we are.
werewolf, *pl.* **-wolves** ['wiːərwulf, 'wəːr-, -wulvz], *s.* Loup-garou *m*, *pl.* loups-garous.
wert [wəːrt]. *See* BE.
Wesleyan ['wezliən], *a. & s.* Wesleyen, -enne.
west¹ [west]. **I.** *s.* (*a*) Ouest *m*, occident *m*, couchant *m*. House facing (the) west, maison exposée à l'ouest. **On the west, to the west,** à l'ouest au couchant (*of*, de). (*b*) The West, l'Occident. (*c*) *U.S:* The West, les États occidentaux (des États-Unis). The Far West, les États des Montagnes Rocheuses et du littoral du Pacifique. **2.** *adv.* A l'ouest, à l'occident. To travel west, voyager vers l'ouest. To go west, (i) se diriger vers l'ouest; (ii) *P:* mourir; *Mil:* passer l'arme à gauche. **3.** *a.* Ouest *inv*; (vent) d'ouest; (pays) de l'ouest, occidental, -aux; (mur, fenêtre) qui fait face à l'ouest. **'West 'end.** **I.** *s.* The West end, le quartier des grands magasins, le quartier chic (de Londres). **2.** *Attrib.a.* Élégant, chic. **West 'Indian,** *a.* Des Antilles; antillais.
west², *v.i.* (*Of sun, ship*) Passer à l'ouest.
westing, *s. Nau:* Marche *f*, route *f*, vers l'ouest; chemin *m* ouest.
wester ['westər], *v.i.* **I.** (*Of sun, moon, stars*) Passer à l'ouest. *The westoring sun,* le soleil couchant. **2.** (*Of wind*) Sauter à l'ouest.
westerly ['westərli]. **I.** *a.* Westerly wind, vent d'ouest, qui vient de l'ouest. *W. current,* courant qui se dirige vers l'ouest. *The w. regions of a country,* les régions ouest d'un pays. **2.** *adv.* Vers l'ouest.
western ['westərn], *a.* Ouest, de l'ouest; occidental, -aux. The Western Empire, l'Empire d'Occident. Western Europe, l'Europe occidentale. The Western Church, l'Église d'Occident.
westerner ['westərnər], *s.* Occidental, -ale.
westward ['westwərd]. **I.** *s.* Direction *f* de l'ouest. **2.** *a.* A l'ouest, de l'ouest. To westward, vers l'ouest. **2.** *a.* A l'ouest, de l'ouest.
westwards ['westwərdz], *adv.* Vers l'ouest, à l'ouest.
wet¹ [wet], *a.* (wetter) **I.** (*a*) Mouillé, humide; imbibé d'eau. To get wet, se mouiller. **To get one's feet wet,** se mouiller les pieds. **To be wet through,** wet to the skin, dripping wet, être trempé (jusqu'aux os). Wringing wet, sopping wet, soaking wet, (*of clothes, etc.*) mouillé à tordre; (*of pers.*) trempé comme une soupe, jusqu'aux os. **Ink still wet,** encre encore fraîche. (*b*) **Wet weather,** temps humide, pluvieux; temps de

pluie. *It is going to be wet*, il va pleuvoir. *We had three wet days*, nous avons eu trois jours de pluie. **The wet season**, la saison des pluies; la saison humide. (c) *Ch :* **Wet process**, (procédé d'analyse par) voie *f* humide. *El :* **Wet cell**, pile à élément humide. **2.** *F :* (*Of country*) Qui permet la vente des boissons alcooliques. **'wet 'blanket,** *s. F :* **1.** **To throw a wet blanket over the meeting**, jeter un froid sur l'assemblée. **2.** Rabat-joie *m inv*, trouble-fête *m inv*. **'wet-bulb,** *attrib. a.* **Wet-bulb thermometer**, thermomètre à boule mouillée. **'wet 'nurse,** *s.* Nourrice *f.* **'wet 'plate,** *s. Phot :* Plaque *f* au collodion humide. **wet²,** *s.* **1.** Humidité *f.* **2.** Pluie *f.* **3.** *P :* **To have a wet**, boire un coup; se rincer la dalle. **wet³,** *v.tr.* (wetted) **1.** Mouiller, humecter; (une éponge). *F :* **To wet the tea**, infuser le thé. **2.** *F :* **To wet a deal**, arroser une affaire; *F :* boire le vin du marché. **wetting,** *s.* Mouillage *m*; infusion *f* (du thé). **To get a wetting**, se faire tremper.

wether ['weðər], *s. Husb :* Bélier châtré; mouton *m*.

wetness ['wetnəs], *s.* Humidité *f.*

whack¹ [hwak]. **1.** *s.* (*a*) Coup (de bâton) bien appliqué. (*b*) Action de battre (qch.). *F :* **To have a whack at sth.**, (i) tenter l'aventure; essayer de faire qch.; (ii) s'attaquer à (un pâté, etc.). (*c*) *P :* Part *f*, portion *f*; (grand) morceau. *To give s.o. a w. of rum*, donner à qn une bonne rasade de rhum. **2.** *int. F :* V'lan !

whack², *v.tr. F :* (*a*) Donner des coups à (qn, qch.); fesser (un enfant). (*b*) Battre (ses adversaires) à plates coutures. (*c*) **To whack her up to twenty knots**, pousser l'allure à vingt nœuds. **whacking,** *a. P :* Énorme; colossal, -aux. **Whacking lie**, mensonge de taille. **whacking²,** *s. F :* Rossée *f*, raclée *f.*

whacker ['hwakər], *s. P :* **1.** Quelque chose de colossal; chose énorme. **2.** Gros mensonge. *What a w. !* en voilà une forte !

whale¹ [hweil], *s.* **1.** *Z :* Baleine *f*; cétacé *m*. **Right whale**, baleine franche. **White whale**, bél(o)uga *m*. **Whale calf**, baleineau *m. S.a.* KILLER 1. **2.** *U.S :* *F :* **He's a whale at tennis**, au tennis c'est un as. **'whale-boat,** *s.* Baleinière *f.* **'whale-oil,** *s.* Huile *f* de baleine.

whale², *v.i.* Faire la pêche à la baleine. **whaling,** *s.* Pêche *f* à la baleine. **Whaling ship**, baleinier *m.* **Whaling industry**, industrie baleinière. **'whaling-ground,** *s.* Parages fréquentés par les baleines.

whaleback ['hweilbak], *s. Nau :* **Whaleback deck**, pont *m* en dos de baleine.

whalebone ['hweilboun], *s.* Fanon *m* de baleine; baleine *f* (d'un corset, etc.).

whaler ['hweilər], *s.* **1.** Baleinier *m*; pêcheur *m* de baleines. **2.** (*a*) (*Ship*) Baleinier. (*b*) (*Boat*) Baleinière *f.*

wharf¹ [hwɔːrf], *s. Nau :* Appontement *m*, débarcadère *m*, embarcadère *m*; wharf *m*, quai *m. Com :* **Ex wharf**, à prendre sur quai. **'wharf-rat,** *s.* **1.** *Z :* Surmulot *m.* **2.** *P :* Rôdeur *m* (qui fréquente les quais).

wharf², *v.tr.* **1.** (*a*) Déposer (des marchandises) sur le quai. (*b*) Débarquer (les marchandises). **2.** *v.i.* (*Of ship*) Amarrer à quai.

wharfage ['hwɔːrfedʒ], *s.* Quayage *m*; droits *mpl* de quai.

wharfinger ['hwɔːrfindʒər], *s.* (*a*) Propriétaire *m* d'un quai, d'un wharf. (*b*) Gardien *m* du quai.

what [hwɔt]. **I.** *a.* **1.** (*Relative*) (Ce, la chose) que, qui. *He took away from me what little I had left*, il m'a pris le peu qui me restait. *He*

traded with what capital he had, il faisait le commerce avec ce qu'il possédait de capital. **2.** (*Interrogative*) Quel, *f.* quelle. **What time is it?** quelle heure est-il? *Tell me what time it is*, dites-moi l'heure qu'il est. *What right has he to give orders?* de quel droit donne-t-il des ordres? **What good is this?** à quoi cela est-il bon? **What news?** quoi de nouveau? **What day of the month is it?** le combien sommes-nous? **3.** **What an idea!** quelle idée! *What a fool he is!* qu'il est bête! *What silly fools we have all been!* comme nous avons tous été bêtes! *What a lot of people!* que de gens! **II.** **what,** *pron.* **1.** (*Relative*, = *that which*) Ce qui, ce que. **What is done cannot be undone**, ce qui est fait est fait. **What I like is music**, ce que j'aime c'est la musique. *What is most remarkable is that . . .*, ce qu'il y a de plus remarquable c'est que. . . . *He had a key, and what is more, he has it still*, il avait une clef, et qui plus est, il l'a encore. *This is what it is all about*, voici ce dont il s'agit. **Come what may**, advienne que pourra. **Say what he will . . .**, quoi qu'il dise . . .; il a beau dire. . . . *What with golf and what with tennis, I have no time to write*, entre le golf et le tennis, il ne me reste pas une minute pour écrire. **Not a day but what it rains**, il ne se passe pas un jour qu'il ne pleuve. *P :* **To give s.o. what for**, laver la tête à qn; flanquer une bonne raclée à qn. **2.** (*Interrogative*) (*a*) Qu'est-ce qui? qu'est-ce que? quoi? **What on earth are you doing here?** qu'est-ce que vous pouvez bien faire ici? **What is it?** (i) qu'est-ce? qu'est-ce que c'est? (ii) qu'est-ce qu'il y a? **What is that?** qu'est-ce que cela? qu'est-ce que c'est que ça? **What is the matter?** qu'y a-t-il? de quoi s'agit-il? **What is that to you?** qu'est-ce que cela vous fait? **What's the good, the use?** à quoi bon? **What is to be done?** comment faire? que faire? **What the better are they for that?** en quoi s'en trouvent-ils mieux? **What do seven and eight make?** combien font sept et huit? **What is he like?** comment est-il? **What do you take me for?** pour qui me prenez-vous? **What's it all about?** de quoi s'agit-il? **What about a game of bridge?** si on faisait une partie de bridge? **What about you?** et vous? **Well, what about it?** (i) eh bien, quoi? et puis après? (ii) eh bien, qu'en dites-vous? **What is that for?** à quoi sert cela? **What (on earth) for?** mais pourquoi donc? **What then?** et après? et alors? **What though we are poor?** qu'importe que nous soyons pauvres? **What (did you say)?** plaît-il? pardon? *F :* comment? **What of that?** qu'est-ce que cela fait? (*b*) (*Indirect*) Ce qui, ce que. **Tell me what is happening**, dites-moi ce qui se passe. *I don't know what to do*, je ne sais que faire. *Tell me what you are crying for*, dites-moi pourquoi vous pleurez. *I'll tell you what . . .*, je vais vous dire . . .; écoutez. . . . *He knows what's what*, il en sait long; il s'y connaît; c'est un malin. **3.** (*a*) *What he has suffered!* ce qu'il a souffert! **What next!** par exemple! **(b) What! you can't come!** comment! vous ne pouvez pas venir! *P :* Nice little girl, what! joli brin de fille, hein ! **'what-d'ye-call-'em, -her, -him, -it,** *s. P :* Machin *m*; (*of pers.*) mistenflûte *m*, chose *mf.* **Mr What-d'ye-call-him**, monsieur Machin. **what-'ho,** *int. P :* Eh bien! qu'est-ce que ça veut dire ! **'what-not,** *s.* Étagère *f.*

whatever [hwɔt'evər]. (*Cf.* '*what ever*' *under* EVER 3.) **I.** *pron.* (*a*) (*Relative*) **Whatever you like**, tout ce qui vous plaira; tout ce que vous voudrez; n'importe quoi. (*b*) Quoi qui, quoi que + *sub.* **Whatever it may be . . .**, quoi que ce soit. . . . **2.** *a.* (*a*) Quelque . . . qui, que + *sub.* **Whatever ambition moves him,** quelque ambition qui l'agite. **Every treaty of whatever character . . .,** tout traité de quelque nature que ce soit. . . . (*b*) (i) Aucun. **He has no chance whatever,** il n'a aucune chance. **None whatever,** pas un seul. **Nothing whatever,** absolument rien. *He won't say anything whatever,* il refuse de dire quoi que ce soit. (ii) **Has he any chance whatever?** a-t-il une chance quelconque?

whatsoever [hwɔtsoˈevər], *pron. & a.* = WHATEVER.

wheat [hwiːt], *s.* Blé *m*, froment *m*. **Grain of wheat,** grain de blé. **Wheat-growing land,** terre à blé. **'wheat-sheaf,** *s.* Gerbe *f* de blé. **'wheat-stalk, -straw,** *s.* Chaume *m*, tige *f*, de blé.

wheatear ['hwiːtiːər], *s. Orn:* Cul-blanc *m*.

wheaten ['hwiːt(ə)n], *a.* (Pain) de froment, de blé. **Fine wheaten bread,** pain de gruau.

wheatmeal ['hwiːtmiːl], *s.* Grosse farine (de froment).

Wheatstone ['hwiːtstoun]. *Pr.n. El:* **Wheatstone bridge,** pont *m* de Wheatstone.

wheedle [hwiːdl], *v.tr.* Enjôler, cajoler, embobeliner (qn). **To wheedle money out of s.o.,** soutirer de l'argent à qn. **wheedling,** *a.* (Of manner) Enjôleur, câlin. *W. voice,* voix pateline. *W. ways,* câlineries *f*.

wheedler ['hwiːdlər], *s.* Enjôleur -euse; patelin, -ine.

wheel¹ [hwiːl], *s.* **I.** Roue *f*; (= *roller*) roulette *f* (*a*) *Veh:* **Back wheel,** roue arrière. **To run on wheels,** (i) marcher sur des roues; (ii) *F:* aller comme sur des roulettes. *Av:* **Ground wheels, landing wheels,** roues de train (d'atterrissage). *S.a.* DISK, FLY¹ (*a*), SHOULDER¹ 1, TRACK¹ 2. (*b*) *Mec.E:* **Fixed wheel,** roue calée. **Loose wheel,** roue folle, décalée. **Toothed wheel,** roue dentée; roue d'engrenage. *F:* **There are wheels within wheels,** il y a toutes sortes de forces en jeu. **The wheels of government,** les rouages *m* de l'administration. *S.a.* SPROCKET 2. (*c*) *Aut:* *Av:* **Steering-wheel, control-wheel,** volant *m* (de direction, de commande). *Nau: The steering w.,* 'the wheel,' la roue du gouvernail; *F:* la barre. **To take the wheel,** *Aut:* se mettre au volant; *Nau:* prendre la barre. (*d*) (**Grinding-)wheel,** meule *f*. **Carborundum wheel,** meule en carborundum. (*e*) *See* POTTER¹. (*f*) **Cutting-wheel,** molette *f* (à couper la pâte, le verre). (*g*) *Toys:* **Wheel of life,** zootrope *m*. **2.** *Hist:* **To break s.o. on the wheel,** rouer qn. *F:* **To break a butterfly on the wheel,** prendre un pavé pour écraser une mouche. **3.** *U.S: F:* Bicyclette *f*. **4.** *Mil:* Conversion *f*. **Left wheel,** conversion à gauche. **'wheel-base,** *s. Veh: Rail:* Empattement *m*; distance *f* entre les deux essieux. **'wheel-chair,** *s.* Fauteuil roulant; voiture *f* de malade. **'wheel-gear,** *s. Mec.E:* Transmission *f* par engrenage(s). **'wheel-house,** *s. Nau:* Kiosque *m* de la barre; la timonerie. **'wheel-lock,** *s. Aut:* Angle *m* de braquage (des roues avant). **'wheel-track,** *s.* **1.** Ornière *f*. **2.** Trace *f* de roues. **'wheel-train,** *s. Mec.E:* Train *m* de roues. **'wheel-window,** *s. Arch:* Rosace *f*, rose *f*.

wheel². **I.** *v.tr.* (*a*) Tourner; faire pivoter. **To wheel round one's chair,** faire pivoter sa chaise. (*b*) Rouler (une brouette); pousser (une bicyclette) à la main. **2.** *v.i.* (*a*) Tourner en rond; tournoyer. (*b*) *Mil:* (i) Faire une conversion. **To wheel about,** faire la roue. (ii) **Left wheel!**

par file à gauche, gauche! (*c*) (*Of pers.*) **To wheel round,** faire demi-tour; se retourner (brusquement).

wheelbarrow ['hwiːlbaro], *s.* Brouette *f*.

wheeled [hwiːld], *a.* A roues; muni de roues.

wheeler ['hwiːlər], *s.* Cheva *m* de derrière; timonier *m*.

wheelwright ['hwiːlrait], *s.* Charron *m*.

wheeze¹ [hwiːz], *s.* **1.** Respiration asthmatique, sifflante. **2.** *P:* Truc *m*. **A good wheeze,** une heureuse dée.

wheeze². **1.** *v.i.* (*a*) Respirer péniblement, en asthmatique. (*b*) (*Of horse*) Corner. **2.** *v.tr.* **To wheeze out sth.,** dire qch. d'une voix asthmatique.

wheezing, *s.* (*a*) Respiration *f* asthmatique. (*b*) (*Of horse*) Cornage *m*.

wheezy ['hwiːzi], *a.* (*a*) (*Of pers.*) Asthmatique; *F:* poussif. (*b*) (*Of horse*) Cornard.

whelk [hwelk], *s. Moll:* Buccin *m*.

whelp¹ [hwelp], *s.* **1.** *A. & Lit:* (*a*) = PUPPY. (*b*) Petit *m* d'un fauve. **Lion's whelp,** lionceau *m*. (*c*) *F:* Mauvais garnement; drôle *m*. **2.** *Nau:* Flasque *m*, taquet *m* (de cabestan).

whelp². **1.** *v.i.* (*Of lion, etc.*) Mettre bas. **2.** *v.tr.* Mettre bas (des petits).

when [hwen]. **I.** *adv.* Quand? *W. will you go?* quand partirez-vous? *I wonder when he will go,* je me demande quand il partira. **When is the meeting?** pour quand est la réunion? **When ever, when on earth,** will *he* come? quand donc viendra-t-il? **II. when,** *conj.* **I.** Quand, lorsque. *When I entered the room . . .,* lorsque j'entrai dans la pièce. . . *When he was born, married,* lors de sa naissance, de son mariage. *When I was young,* du temps que j'étais jeune. *When one is young,* quand on est jeune; lorsqu'on est jeune. *He will speak when I have done,* il parlera après que j'aurai fini. *He looks in when passing,* il nous fait une petite visite en passant. **When at school . . .,** lorsque j'étais à l'école. . . . **2.** (*Relative*) (*a*) **The day when** *I met you,* le jour où je vous ai rencontré. **One day when** *I was on duty . .,* un jour que j'étais de service. . . . **At the very time when . . .,** alors même que . . .; au moment même où. . . . **Now is when I need him most,** c'est maintenant que j'ai le plus besoin de lui. (*b*) (= *and then*) **The king will arrive on the 10th, when he will open the new building,** le roi arrivera le dix, et il inaugurera le nouvel édifice. **III. when,** *s.* Tell me the **when and the how of it,** dites-moi quand et comment la chose est arrivée. **The hows and whens of life,** les occasions qui se présentent dans la vie.

whence [hwens], *adv. A. & Lit:* D'où. **Do you know (from) whence he comes?** savez-vous d'où il vient? *The land w. ye are come,* la terre d'où vous êtes venus. **Whence I conclude that . . .,** d'où je conclus que. . . .

whenever [hwenˈevər], *adv.* (*a*) Toutes les fois que; chaque fois que. *I go w. I can,* j'y vais aussi souvent que cela m'est possible. (*b*) **You may come whenever you like,** vous pouvez venir à n'importe quel moment.

where ['hwɛər], *adv.* **I.** (*Interrogative*) (*a*) Où? **Where am I?** où suis-je? *Tell me w. he is,* dites-moi où il est. **Where ever have you been?** où diable étiez-vous (donc)? mais d'où venez-vous? *W. did we leave off (reading, etc.)?* où en sommes-nous restés? (*b*) **Where is the way out?** par où sort-on? (*c*) **Where do you come from?** (i) d'où venez-vous? (ii) de quel pays êtes-vous? **Where are you going to?** où allez-vous? **2.** (*Relative*) (*a*) (There) where, (là) où. I shall stay where I am, je resterai (là) où je suis. *Go w. you like,* allez où vous voudrez. (b) **That is where we've got to,** voilà où nous en sommes. **That is where you are mistaken,** voilà où vous vous trompez. *W. you are mistaken is . . .,* ce en quoi vous vous trompez c'est. . . . (c) *He came to where I was fishing,* il est venu à l'endroit où je pêchais. *I can see it* from *where we stand,* je le vois d'où nous sommes. (d) **The house where I was born,** la maison où, dans laquelle, je suis né. **3.** *s.* **The where and when** *of his birth are unknown,* on ne sait ni le lieu ni la date de sa naissance. *S.a.* ANYWHERE, ELSEWHERE, EVERYWHERE, NOWHERE, SOMEWHERE.

whereabout ['hwεərabaut], *adv.* **1.** Là-dessus ; à ce propos. **2.** *A :* = WHEREABOUTS 1.

whereabouts ['hwεərabauts]. **1.** *adv.* Où (donc)? **Whereabouts are you?** où donc êtes-vous ? **2.** *s.* Lieu *m* où se trouve qn, qch. **No one knows his whereabouts,** personne ne sait où il demeure, où il est.

whereafter [hwεər'ɑːftər], *rel.adv.* Après quoi ; à la suite de quoi.

whereas [hwεər'az], *conj.* **1.** Attendu que, vu que, puisque + *ind.* ; *Jur :* considérant que + *ind.* **2.** Alors que, tandis que, au lieu que + *ind.*

whereat [hwεər'at], *adv.* A quoi, sur quoi, de quoi, etc. *He said something, whereat everyone laughed,* il a dit quelque chose, sur quoi tout le monde a ri.

whereby [hwεər'bai], *adv.* **1.** Par quoi ? par quel moyen ? **2. Decision whereby . . .,** décision par laquelle. . . .

wherefore ['hwεərfɔːr]. **1.** *adv.* (a) Pourquoi ? pour quelle raison ? *W. do you laugh?* pourquoi riez-vous ? (b) = THEREFORE. **2.** *s.* **The whys and wherefores,** les pourquoi et les parce que ; les causes et les raisons.

wherefrom [hwεər'frɔm], *adv.* D'où.

wherein [hwεər'in], *adv.* **1.** En quoi ? *W. have we offended you?* en quoi vous avons-nous offensé ? **2.** Dans lequel ; où. *The room w. they slept,* la chambre dans laquelle ils dormaient. *The month w. the event took place,* le mois où l'événement eut lieu.

whereof [hwεər'ɔv], *adv.* **1.** En quoi ? de quoi ? *W. is it made?* en quoi est-ce fait ? **2.** De quoi ; dont. *Metals w. jewellery is made,* métaux dont on fait les bijoux.

whereon [hwεər'ɔn], *adv.* **1.** Sur quoi ? **2.** Sur quoi, sur lequel **That is whereon we differ,** c'est sur quoi nous ne sommes pas du même avis.

wheresoever [hwεərso'evər], *adv.* = WHEREVER.

whereupon [hwεərə'pɔn], *adv.* **1.** = WHEREON 1. **2.** (a) = WHEREON 2. (b) *W. he left us,* sur quoi il nous quitta.

wherever [hwεər'evər], *adv.* (Cp. 'where ever' under EVER 3.) **1.** Partout où . . . ; n'importe où. . . . *W. I go I see . . .,* partout où je vais je vois. . . . *I will go wherever you want me to,* j'irai où vous voudrez. **2.** Wherever they come from *they have done very well,* d'où qu'ils viennent ils se sont très bien acquittés (de leur tâche, etc.).

wherewith [hwεər'wið], *adv.* **1.** Avec quoi ? **2.** (a) Avec lequel ; avec quoi ; au moyen duquel. (b) = WHEREUPON 2 (b).

wherewithal [hwεərwiðɔːl]. **1.** *adv.* *A :* = WHEREWITH. **2.** *s.* **The wherewitha',** le nécessaire ; les moyens *m.* *I hadn't the w.* to pay for a dinner, je n'avais pas de quoi me payer un dîner. *To have the time and the w.,* avoir le temps et l'argent, et les moyens.

wherry ['hweri], *s.* Bachot *m* (de rivière).

wherryman, *pl.* **-men** ['hweriman, -men], *s.m.* Bachoteur.

---

whet[1] [hwet], *s.* *F :* (a) Stimulant *m,* aiguillon *m,* excitant *m.* *Whet to the appetite,* stimulant de l'appétit. (b) Apéritif *m* ou petit verre.

whet[2], *v.tr.* (whetted) **1.** Aiguiser, affûter, affiler, repasser (un outil). **2.** *F :* Stimuler, aiguiser, exciter, aiguillonner (l'appétit, les désirs, etc.).

whether ['hweðər], *conj.* **1.** (*Introducing an indirect question*) Si. *I don't know w. it is true,* je ne sais pas si c'est vrai. *It depends upon w. you are in a hurry or not,* cela dépend de s vous êtes pressé ou non. *The question was w. or not to take Nedda with him,* la question était de savoir si, oui ou non, il devait emmener Nedda. **2.** **Whether it rains or (whether it) blows,** *he always goes out,* soit qu'il vente, soit qu'il pleuve, il sort toujours. *We shall all die, w. to-day or to-morrow,* nous mourrons tous, soit aujourd'hui, soit demain. *W. he comes or not, or no, we shall leave,* qu'il vienne ou non, qu'il vienne ou qu'il ne vienne pas, nous allons partir. **Whether or not . . .,** qu'il en soit ainsi ou non. . . .

whetstone ['hwetstoun], *s.* Pierre *f* à aiguiser.

whew [hiuː], *int.* **1.** (*Of fatigue, relief*) Ouf ! **2.** (*Astonishment*) Fichtre !

whey [hwei], *s.* Petit lait. **'whey-faced,** *a.* *F :* A figure de papier mâché.

which [hwitʃ]. **I.** *a.* **1.** (*Interrogative*) Quel, *f.* quelle ; *pl.* quels, *f.* quelles? *W. colour do you like best?* quelle couleur aimez-vous le mieux ? **Which way do we go?** par où allons-nous ? **Which way is the wind?** d'où vient le vent ? **Which one?** lequel ? laquelle ? **Which ones?** lesquels ? lesquelles ? *W. one of us?* lequel d'entre nous ? **2.** (*Relative*) Lequel, *f.* laquelle ; *pl.* lesquels, lesquelles. *He was armed with a revolver, which weapon I had not observed before,* il était armé d'un revolver, laquelle arme je n'avais pas remarquée jusque-là. **Look which way you will . . .,** de quelque côté que vous regardiez. . . . **II.** **which,** *pron.* **1.** (*Interrogative*) Lequel? **Which have you chosen?** lequel avez-vous choisi ? *W. of the ladies has come?* laquelle des dames est venue ? *W. of you can answer?* lequel d'entre vous peut répondre ? **To which, of which,** is he speaking? auquel, duquel, parle-t-il ? **Tell me which is which,** dites-moi comment les distinguer. **I don't mind which,** cela m'est égal. **2.** (*Relative*) (a) (*Adj. clauses*) Qui ; que ; lequel. **The house which is to be sold,** la maison qui est à vendre. *The books w. I possess,* les livres que je possède. *B:* Our Father, which art in Heaven, notre père qui êtes aux cieux. (b) (*Continuative clauses*) Ce qui, ce que. *He looked like a retired clerk which* indeed *he was,* il avait l'air d'un commis retraité, ce qu'il était en effet. *If this happens, w. God forbid . . .,* si cela arrive, ce qu'à Dieu ne plaise. . . . *She tickles my neck, w. I hate,* elle me chatouille le cou, chose que je déteste. **3.** (*Relative pron. governed by a prep.*) (a) **To which, at which,** auquel, *f.* à laquelle, *pl.* auxquels, auxquelles. **Of which, from which,** duquel, *f.* de laquelle ; *pl.* desquels, desquelles ; dont. *The house of w. I speak,* la maison dont je parle. *The countries to w. we are going, w. we are going to,* les pays où nous irons. *The hotels at which we stayed,* les hôtels où nous sommes descendus. (b) (*Continuative clauses*) He demands that actors should have talent, **in which he is right,** il exige que les acteurs aient du talent, (ce) en quoi il a raison. *There are no trains on Sunday,* **which I hadn't thought of,** il n'y a pas de trains le dimanche, à quoi je n'avais pas pensé. **After which** *he went out,* après quoi il est sorti.

whichever [hwitʃ'evər], *rel. pron. & a.*
1. (*a*) *pron.* Celui qui, celui que, n'importe lequel. *Take w. you like best,* prenez celui que vous aimez le mieux; prenez n'importe lequel. (*b*) *a.* Le . . . que; n'importe quel. *Take w. book you like best,* prenez le livre que, n'importe que, livre, vous aimez le mieux. **2.** *a.* N'importe quel; quelque . . . que. *W. way he turned he saw nothing but sand,* de quelque côté qu'il se tournât, n'importe de quel côté il se tournait, il ne voyait (rien) que du sable.

whiff¹ [hwif], *s.* **1.** (*a*) Bouffée *f* (de vent, de fumée, etc.); halenée *f* (de vin, etc.). *There wasn't a w. of wind,* il n'y avait pas une haleine, pas un souffle, de vent. *To go out for a w. of fresh air,* sortir pour respirer un peu, pour prendre l'air. (*b*) Whiff of grape-shot, décharge *f* de mitraille. **2.** Petit cigare; médianito *m.* **3.** *Row:* Skiff *m.*

whiff². **1.** *v.i.* Souffler par bouffées. **2.** *v.tr.* To whiff smoke, émettre des bouffées de fumée. To whiff away, whiff off, *the dust,* souffler la poussière.

whig [hwig], *s. Hist:* Whig *m*; libéral *m*, -aux (de vieille roche).

while¹ [hwail] ,*s.* **1.** (*a*) (Espace *m* de) temps *m.* After a while, après quelque temps. In a little while, sous peu; avant peu. For a (short) while, pendant quelque temps. A little while ago, il n'y a pas bien longtemps; il y a peu de temps. A long while, longtemps. For a long while past, depuis longtemps. A good while, pas mal de temps. *It will be a good w. before you see him again,* vous ne le reverrez pas de si tôt. *It will take me quite a while to do,* cela me prendra pas mal de temps. *Stay* a (little) while, restez un (petit) peu. (*b*) *Adv.phr.* The while, en attendant; pendant ce temps. **2.** To be worth (one's) while, valoir la peine. *I will come if it is worth* (*my*) *w.,* je viendrai si cela en vaut la peine. I will make it worth your while, vous serez bien payé de votre peine. *It is perhaps worth w. pointing out that . . .,* il n'est peut-être pas oiseux de faire remarquer que . . . .

while², *v.tr.* To while away, faire passer (le temps); tuer (une heure, le temps).

while³, *conj.* **1.** (*a*) Pendant que, tandis que. While he was here, while here, *he studied a great deal,* pendant qu'il était ici il a beaucoup étudié. He died while eating his dinner, il est mort en mangeant son dîner. *W. reading I fell asleep,* tout en lisant, je me suis endormi. While this was going on, sur ces entrefaites. (*b*) (*As long as*) Tant que. While I live *you shall lack nothing,* tant que je vivrai vous ne manquerez de rien. **2.** (*Concessive*) Quoique, bien que, tout en. . . . While I admit, while admitting, the thing is difficult, *I do not think it impossible,* quoique j'admette, tout en reconnaissant, que la chose est difficile, je ne la crois pas impossible. **3.** (*Whereas*) Tandis que.

whilom ['hwailəm], *a. Lit:* Ancien, ci-devant; d'autrefois, d'antan. *Our w. friends,* nos ci-devant amis.

whilst [hwailst], *conj.* = WHILE³.

whim [hwim], *s.* **1.** Caprice *m*; fantaisie *f*, lubie *f.* A mere w., une simple lubie. Passing whim, toquade *f. It is a sudden w. of his,* c'est un caprice qui lui a pris. *His every w. must be complied with,* il faut faire ses quatre volontés. As the whim takes her, selon son caprice. To satisfy one's whim for sth., se passer la fantaisie de qch. **2.** *Min: etc:* (Horse-)whim, whim(-gin), cabestan *m* à cheval; treuil *m* d'extraction à manège. **3.** *Veh:* Trique-balle *m.*

whimbrel ['hwimbrəl], *s. Orn:* Petit courlis; turlu(i) *m.*

whimper¹ ['hwimpər], *s.* (i) Pleurnicherie *f,* pleurnichement *m*; (ii) geignement *m*, plainte *f.*

whimper². **1.** *v.i.* (*a*) Pleurnicher, geindre. (*b*) (*Of dog*) Faire entendre une plainte. **2.** *v.tr.* Dire (qch.) en pleurnichant. **whimpering,** *s.* = WHIMPER¹.

whimperer ['hwimpərər], *s.* Pleurnicheur *m.*

whimsical ['hwimzik(ə)l], *a.* **1.** Capricieux, fantasque; lunatique. **2.** (*Of thg*) Bizarre, baroque. **-ally,** *adv.* Capricieusement, bizarrement.

whimsicality [hwimzi'kaliti], *s.* **1.** Caractère *m* fantasque. **2.** Bizarrerie *f* (de caractère).

whin [hwin], *s. Bot:* Genêt *m* d'Angleterre; ajonc commun. **'whin-bush,** *s* (Arbuste *m* d')ajonc *m.*

whin², *s.* = WHINSTONE.

whinchat ['hwintʃat], *s. Orn:* Tarier *m.*

whine¹ [hwain], *s.* **1.** Plainte *f*; cri dolent; geignement *m.* **2.** *F:* Jérémiade *f.*

whine². **1.** *v.i.* (*Of pers.*) Se plaindre; (*of infant*) pleurnicher, piauler; (*of dog*) geindre. **2.** *v.tr.* Dire (qch.) d'un ton dolent, plaintif, pleurard.

whining¹, *a.* (*a*) Geignant; (enfant) pleurnicheur; (ton) plaintif, pleurard; (voix) dolente. (*b*) *F:* Geignard. **whining**², *s.* (*a*) Geignement *m. The w. of the shells,* le sifflement plaintif des obus. (*b*) *F:* Jérémiades *fpl*; plaintes *fpl.* **Stop your whining!** assez de jérémiades!

whinny¹ ['hwini], *s.* Hennissement *m* (de cheval).

whinny², *v.i.* (*Of horse*) Hennir.

whinstone ['hwinstoun], *s. Geol:* Trapp *m.*

whip¹ [hwip], *s.* **1.** Fouet *m. S.a.* HORSEWHIP¹, RIDING-WHIP. **2.** Cocher *m*, conducteur *m* (d'un mail-coach, etc.). **To be a good, a bad, whip,** bien, mal, conduire. **3.** *Parl:* (*a*) (Membre désigné par un parti comme) chef *m* de file; whip *m.* (*b*) Appel *m* aux membres d'un groupe. Four-line whip, appe urgent souligné quatre fois. **4.** Fouettement *m*, coup *m* de fouet (d'un câble, etc.). **5.** Aile *f*, bras *m* (de moulin à vent). **6.** *Nau:* Cartahu *m*; palan *m.* **'whip-hand,** *s.* Main *f* du fouet; main droite. *F:* **To have the whip-hand,** avoir l'avantage. **To have the whip-hand of s.o.,** avoir la haute main sur qn. **'whip-lash,** *s.* Mèche *f* de fouet. *F:* **Tongue like a whip-lash,** langue qui cingle. **'whip-stitch,** *s. Needlew:* (*a*) Point *m* de surjet. (*b*) Point roulé. **'whip-stock,** *s.* Manche *m* de fouet. **'whip-top,** *s. Toys:* Sabot *m.*

whip², *v.* (whipped [hwipt]) **I.** *v.tr.* **1.** (*a*) Fouetter; donner le fouet à (un enfant). **To whip a top,** fouetter, faire aller, un sabot. *The rain whipped the window-panes,* la pluie fouettait, cinglait, les vitres. (*b*) *Cu:* Battre (les œufs); fouetter, faire mousser (la crème). Whipped cream, crème fouettée. (*c*) *Fish:* Fouetter (un cours d'eau). **2.** (*a*) *Nau:* Surlier, garnir (un cordage). (*b*) Ligaturer (un brancard, etc.). (*c*) To whip a seam, surjeter une couture; faire un surjet. **3.** Mouvoir vivement (qch.). He whipped the revolver out of his pocket, il sortit vivement le revolver de sa poche. **4.** *Nau:* Hisser (une vergue) avec un cartahu. **II.** whip, *v.i.* **1.** Fouetter. The rain whipped against the panes, la pluie fouettait, cinglait, contre les vitres. **2.** (*Of pers.*) To whip behind the door, se jeter derrière la porte. **To whip round the corner,** tourner vivement e coin. **3.** *Mec.E:* (*Of shaft, etc.*) Fouetter. **whip back,** *v.i.* (*Of cable, etc.*) Fouetter. **whip in,** *v.tr. Ven:* Ramener, rassembler (les chiens) (avec le fouet). *Abs.* To **whip in**, être piqueur. **whip off**, *v.tr.* Enlever vivement (qch. de la table, etc.). **To whip off one's hat**, se découvrir d'un geste rapide. **whip round.** 1. *v.tr. Abs.* **To whip round for subscriptions**, faire passer à la ronde une invitation à participer à une souscription. 2. *v.i.* (*Of pers.*) Se retourner vivement ; (*of horse*) faire (un) tête-à-queue. **whip up**, *v.tr.* 1. Activer, stimuler (un cheval). 2. *Parl:* Faire passer un appel urgent (aux membres d'un parti). *F:* To **whip up one's friends**, rallier ses amis. **whipping**, *s.* 1. (*a*) Fouettage *m*. (*b*) Fouettée *f*. *Jur:* (Châtiment *m* du) fouet ; peine *f* du fouet. **To give a child a whipping**, donner le fouet à un enfant. **To get a whipping**, être fouetté. 2. (*a*) Fouettement *m* (de la pluie, etc.). (*b*) *Mec.E:* Fouettement. **'whip-poor-'will**, *s. Orn:* Engoulevent *m* de la Virginie.

whipcord ['hwipkɔːrd], *s.* 1. (*a*) Mèche *f* de fouet. (*b*) Corde *f* à fouet. 2. *Tex:* Whipcord *m* ; fil *m* de fouet.

whipper ['hwipər], *s.* Fouetteur *m*.

whipper-in ['hwipərin], *s. Ven:* Piqueur *m*.

whipper-snapper ['hwipərsnapər], *s. F:* Freluquet *m*, paltoquet *m* ; jeune fat.

whippet ['hwipit], *s.* 1. (*Dog*) Whippet *m*. 2. *Mil:* Char *m* d'assaut de modèle léger.

whir[1, 2] [hwəːr], *s. & v.i.* = WHIRR[1, 2].

whirl[1] [hwəːrl], *s.* (*a*) Mouvement *m* giratoire, giration *f* (d'une roue, etc.). (*b*) Tourbillon *m*, tourbillonnement *m*, tournoiement *m*. *A w. of dead leaves*, un tourbillon de feuilles mortes. *F:* A whirl of pleasures, un tourbil.on de plaisirs. *My head is in a whirl*, la tête me tourne.

whirl[2]. 1. *v.i.* (*a*) To whirl (round), tourbillonner, tournoyer ; (*of dancer*) pirouetter. *Whirling dervish*, derviche tourneur. *F: My head whirls*, la tête me tourne ; 'a le vertige. (*b* To whirl along, rouler, filer, à toute vitesse, à toute allure. **To come whirling down**, descendre en tournoyant. 2. *v.tr.* (*a*) Faire tournoyer, faire tourbillonner (les feuilles mortes, etc.). *To w. a stone at s.o.*, lancer une pierre à qn avec une fronde. (*b*) The train whirled us along, le train nous emportait à toute vitesse.

whirligig ['hwəːrligig], *s.* 1. (*a*) *Toys:* Tourniquet *m*. (*b*) Manège *m* de chevaux de bois. 2. Pirouette *f. F:* **The whirligig of life**, le tourbillon de la vie.

whirlpool ['hwəːrlpuːl], *s.* Tourbillon *m* (d'eau) ; remous *m* ; gouffre *m*, maelström *m*.

whirlwind ['hwəːrlwind], *s.* Tourbil'on *m* (de vent) ; trombe *f. F:* **To come in like a whirlwind**, entrer en trombe, en coup de vent.

whirr[1] [hwəːr], *s.* Bruissement *m* (d'ailes) ; bruit ronflant, ronflement *m*, ronronnement *m* (de machines) ; sifflement *m* (d'obus) ; vrombissement *m* (d'une hélice d'avion).

whirr[2], *v.i.* (*Of machinery, etc.*) Tourner à toute vitesse ; ronfler, ronronner ; (*of air-screw, etc.*) vrombir ; (*of shell*) siffler.

whisht [hwiʃt], *int. Scot:* Chut !

whisk[1] [hwisk], *s.* 1. Mouvement *m* en coup de fouet. **A whisk of the tail, of a duster**, un coup de queue, de torchon. 2. Dusting-whisk, époussette *f*. Furniture-whisk, houssoir *m* ; plumeau *m*. *S.a.* EGG-WHISK

whisk[2]. 1. *v.i.* S'élancer. **To whisk away**, filer comme un trait. **To whisk past**, passer comme le vent. 2. *v.tr.* (*a*) (*Of cow*) To whisk its tail, agiter sa queue ; se battre les flancs avec sa queue. (*b*) To whisk sth. away, off, enlever qch. d'un geste rapide ; escamoter qch. *To w. away*

a fly, chasser une mouche. *I was whisked up in the lift*, l'ascenseur m'emporta rapidement. (*c*) *Cu:* Battre (des œufs) ; fouetter (la crème).

whisker ['hwiskər], *s. Usu. pl.* **Whiskers**, favoris *m* (d'homme) ; moustache(s) *f* (de chat, de souris, etc.).

whiskered ['hwiskərd], *a.* (Homme) à favoris ; (chat, etc.) à moustaches.

whisk(e)y ['hwiski], *s.* Whisk(e)y *m* ; eau-de-vie *f* de grain. **Whisky and soda**, whisky à l'eau.

whisper[1] ['hwispər], *s.* 1. (*a*) Chuchotement *m*. **To speak in a whisper, in whispers**, parler bas. **To say sth. in a w.**, chuchoter qch. ; dire qch. tout bas. *This was said in a w.*, ceci fut dit dans un souffle. *S.a.* STAGE-WHISPER. (*b*) *F:* Bruissement *m* (des feuilles) ; murmure *m* (de l'eau). 2. Rumeur *f*, bruit *m* (que l'on se transmet à voix basse). **There is a whisper that . . .**, il court un bruit que . . .

whisper[2]. 1. *v.i.* Chuchoter ; parler bas ; (*of leaves*) susurrer ; (*of water*) murmurer. **To whisper to s.o.**, chuchoter à l'oreille de qn ; dire, souffler, qch. à l'oreille de qn. 2. *v.tr.* (*a*) To whisper a word to s.o., dire, glisser, souffler, un mot à l'oreille de qn. **Whispered conversation**, conversation à voix basse. (*b*) It is wh spered that . . ., il court un bruit que. . . . **whispering**, *s.* 1. (*a*) Chuchotement *m*. (*b*) *Pej:* Chuchoterie(s) *f(pl)*. 2. Bruissement *m* ; murmure *m*. **'whispering-gallery**, *s.* 1. Galerie *f* à écho. 2. *F:* Centre *m* d'intrigues.

whisperer ['hwispərər], *s.* Chuchoteur, -euse.

whist [hwist], *s.* Whist *m.* **Dummy whist**, whist à trois avec un mort. **Whist drive**, tournoi *m* de whist. *S.a.* SOLO 2.

whistle[1] [hwisl], *s.* 1. Sifflement *m* ; coup *m* de sifflet. *The blackbird's w.*, le sifflement du merle. 2. (*a*) Sifflet *m*. 'Pea' whistle, sifflet à roulette. **To blow a whistle**, donner un coup de sifflet. (*b*) *A:* Penny whistle = TIN-WHISTLE. 3. *P:* **To wet one's whistle**, s'humecter le gosier ; se rincer la dalle.

whistle[2]. 1. *v.i.* (*a*) Siffler. **To whistle for one's dog, for a taxi**, siffler son chien, un taxi. *F:* **He may whistle for his money**, il peut courir après son argent. *The bullet whistled past his ear*, la balle passa en sifflant près de son oreille. (*b*) Donner un coup de sifflet. *Rail:* **To whistle for the road**, demander la voie ; siffler au disque. 2. *v.tr.* (*a*) Siffler, siffloter (un air, etc.) (*b*) To whistle (up) a cab, siffler un fiacre.

whistler ['hwislər], *s.* 1. (*a*) Siffleur, -euse. (*b*) Cheval cornard. 2. Oiseau siffleur.

whit[1] [hwit], *s.* Brin *m*, iota *m*, petit morceau. (*Only in a few adv. phrs.*) He is not a whit the better for it, il ne s'en porte aucunement mieux. *He is no whit the happier for it*, il n'en est pas plus heureux (pour ça). *He is every whit as good as you*, il vous vaut bien.

Whit[2], *a.* Whit Sunday, (dimanche *m* de) la Pentecôte. **Whit Monday**, le lundi de la Pentecôte.

white[1] [hwait]. I. *a.* 1. Blanc, *f.* blanche. **He is going white**, il commence à blanchir. *Cu:* White sauce, sauce blanche. *Com:* White goods, articles de blanc. *Geog:* **The White Sea**, la Mer Blanche. (*a*) De couleur claire. White bread, pain blanc. White wine, vin blanc. White glass, verre transparent, sans couleur. **To have white hands**, avoir les mains blanches. (*b*) The white races, les races blanches. **A white man**, (i) un blanc ; (ii) *U.S:* un homme loyal. (*c*) White with fear, blanc de peur. **To turn, go, white**, pâlir, blêmir. **As white as a ghost, as a sheet**, pâle comme la mort. In a white rage, dans une colère blanche; blême de colère. 3. (Of reputation, etc.) Sans tache. S.a. LIE¹. II. white, s. 1. Blanc m; couleur blanche. Dead white, blanc mat. 2. Com: Zinc white, blanc de zinc. 3. Dressed in white, habillé en blanc, de blanc. Com: White sale, vente de blanc; vente de lingerie. Sp: Whites, pantalon m de flanelle blanche. 4. (Pers.) Blanc, f. blanche; homme, femme, de la race blanche. 5. (a) White of egg, blanc d'œuf. (b) White of the eye, blanc de l'œil; cornée f. F: To turn up the whites of one's eyes, faire des yeux de carpe pâmée. 'white-caps, s.pl. F: Vagues f à têtes d'écume; moutons m. 'white-'haired, a. Aux cheveux blancs. 'white-'headed, a. 1. Z: A tête blanche. 2. (Of pers.) (a) Aux cheveux blancs. (b) F: The white-headed boy, l'enfant gâté, le chouchou, de la famille. 'white-heart, attrib.a. See CHERRY 1. 'white 'hot, a. Metall: Chauffé à blanc; porté au blanc. 'white-'lipped, a. 1. Aux lèvres pâles. 2. Blême, livide (de peur). 'white-'livered, a. F: Poltron. To be w.-l., P: avoir les foies (blancs). 'white 'metal, s. 1. Métal blanc. 2. Antifriction f, régule m. 'white-tail, s. Orn: Dial: = WHEATEAR. 'white 'vine, s. Bot: 1. Vigne blanche. 2. Clématite f des haies. 'white ware, s. Faïence fine.

white², v.tr. Blanchir. Now only in Whited sepulchre, sépulcre blanchi.

whitebait ['hwaitbeit], s. Cu: Blanchaille f. A dish of w., une friture.

whitebeam ['hwaitbiːm], s. Bot: Alisier blanc.

whitefish ['hwaitfiʃ], s. Com: Poisson m à chair blanche, esp. le merlan et l'aiglefin m.

Whitehall ['hwaitɔːl]. (a) Pr.n. Rue f et quartier m des Ministères (à Londres). (b) F: L'Administration f.

whiten ['hwait(ə)n]. 1. v.tr. (a) Blanchir. F: To w. s.o.'s reputation, blanchir la réputation de qn. (b) Blanchir à la chaux; badigeonner en blanc. (c) Metalw: Étamer (un métal). 2. v.i. (a) Blanchir. (b) (Of pers.) Pâlir, blêmir. whitening, s. 1. Blanchiment m (du linge, d'un mur, etc.). 2. Blanchissement m (des cheveux, etc.); albescence f (du ciel au petit jour). 3. = WHITING¹.

whiteness ['hwaitnəs], s. (a) Blancheur f. (b) Pâleur f (du teint, du visage, etc.).

whitethorn ['hwaitθɔːrn], s. Bot: Aubépine f.

whitewash¹ ['hwaitwɔʃ], s. Blanc m de chaux, lait m de chaux; badigeon blanc. Whitewash brush, badigeon m.

whitewash², v.tr. (a) Badigeonner en blanc; blanchir à la chaux. (b) F: Blanchir, disculper (qn); réhabiliter (un failli). whitewashing, s. Peinture f à la chaux; badigeonnage m en blanc.

whitewood ['hwaitwud], s. Com: Bois blanc.

whither ['hwiðər], adv. 1. Où? vers quel lieu? W. will all this lead? où tout cela nous mènera-t-il? 2. (Là) où. I shall go w. Fate leads me, j'irai là où me mènera le Destin.

whithersoever [hwiðərso'evər], adv. N'importe vers quel endroit; n'importe où; où que + sub.

whiting¹ ['hwaitiŋ], s. Com: Blanc m d'Espagne.

whiting², s. Ich: Merlan m.

whitish ['hwaitiʃ], a. Blanchâtre.

whitlow ['hwitlou], s. Med: Panaris m.

Whitsun(tide) ['hwits(ə)n(taid)], s. (Fête f de) la Pentecôte.

whittle ['hwitl], v.tr. To whittle (down), amenuiser (un bâton, etc.). F: To whittle down, away, s.o.'s allowance, rogner la pension de qn.

whizz' [hwiz]. 1. int. Pan! 2. s. F: Sifflement m (d'une balle).

whizz², v.i. (Of bullet, etc.) Siffler. To whizz past, passer en sifflant; (of motor cycle) passer à toute vitesse. He is there.—Who? il est là. Fb: Whizzing shot, shoot foudroyant.

who [huː], pron. nom. 1. (a) Qui? qui est-ce qui? Who is that lady? qui, quelle, est cette dame? F: Who on earth is it? qui cela peut-1 bien être? Ask him who found it, demandez-lui qui l'a trouvé. He is there.—Who? il est là.—Qui ça? qui donc? Tell me who's who, dites-moi les noms des personnes présentes. Publ: Who's Who, annuaire m des notabilités; Bottin mondain. F: Who does he think he is? pour qui se prend-il? Who are in the running? quels sont les candidats ayant des chances? Who of us can still remember . . .? lesquels d'entre nous se rappellent encore . . . ? S.a. ELSE 2, EVER 3. (b) F: (= 'whom') Who do you want? qui voulez-vous? Who against? contre qui? Who should I meet but Betty? si je n'ai pas rencontré Betty! 2. (Relative) (a) Qui. Those who do not know their lessons . . ., ceux qui ne sauront pas leurs leçons. . . . My friend who came yesterday, mon ami qui est venu hier. (b) (In official language, and to avoid ambiguity) Lequel. Three witnesses were called, who declared . . ., ont comparu trois témoins, lesquels ont déclaré. . . . The father of this girl, who is very rich, le père de cette jeune fille, lequel est très riche. (c) Who eats must pay, celui qui mange doit payer. Deny it who may . . ., Je nie qui voudra. . . .

whoa [wou], int. (a) (To horse) Ho! (signal d'arrêt). (b) F: (To pers.) Doucement! attendez!

whoever [hu'evər], pron. nom. (Cp. 'who ever' under EVER 3.) 1. Celui qui; quiconque. Whoever finds it may keep it, celui qui le trouvera, quiconque le trouvera, pourra le garder. 2. Qui que + sub. W. you are, speak! qui que vous soyez, parlez! W. wrote that letter is a fool, qui que ce soit qui ait écrit cette lettre, c'est un sot. 3. F: = WHOMEVER.

whole [houl]. I. a. 1. (a) A: Sain; en bonne santé. B: His hand was made whole, sa main fut guérie. (b) (Of pers.) Sain et sauf; (of thg) intact. 2. (a) Intégral, -aux; entier; complet, -ète. Ox roasted whole, bœuf rôti entier. He swallowed it whole, (i) il l'a avalé sans le mâcher; (ii) F: il a pris ça pour de l'argent comptant. Mth: Whole number, nombre entier. Whole length, longueur totale. Whole coffee, café en grains. Whole-leather binding, reliure pleine peau. (b) To tell the whole truth, dire toute la vérité. The w. world, le monde entier. To last a whole week, durer toute une semaine. W. families died of it des familles entières en sont mortes. wholly ['houlli], adv. 1. Tout à fait; complètement, entièrement. 2. Intégralement; en totalité. W. or partly, en tout ou en partie. II. whole, s. Tout m, totalité f, ensemble m. The whole of the school, l'école entière; toute l'école. Nearly the w. of our resources, la presque totalité de nos ressources. The whole amounts to . . ., le total se monte à . . . As a whole, dans son ensemble; en totalité. Taken as a whole, pris dans sa totalité. (Up)on the whole, à tout prendre; en somme; somme toute. The work on the w. is good, dans l'ensemble le travail est bon. 'whole-coloured, a. (Of cloth) De teinte uniforme; unicolore. 'whole-'hearted. See -HEARTED. 'whole-'length, attrib. a. (Portrait) en pied. 'whole-meal, attrib. a. (Pain) complet. **'whole-time,** *attrib. a.* Whole-time work, travail qui occupe (i) la journée entière, (ii) la semaine entière.

wholesale ['houlseil]. **I.** *s.* (Vente *f* en) gros *m.* **Wholesale and retail,** gros et détail. **2.** *a.* (*a*) **Wholesale trade,** commerce de gros, en gros. **Wholesale warehouse,** maison / de gros. **Wholesale dealer,** commerçant *m* en gros; grossiste *m.* **Wholesale price,** prix de, en, gros. (*b*) *F:* **A wholesale s aughter,** une tuerie en masse. **3.** *adv.* (Vendre, acheter) en gros.

wholesaler ['houlseilər], *s.* Commerçant *m* en gros; grossiste *m.*

wholesome ['houlsəm], *a.* (Aliment) sain; (air, climat) salubre; (remède) salutaire.

wholesomeness ['houlsəmnəs], *s.* Nature saine (de la nourriture, d'un jeu); salubrité *f* (du climat).

wholly ['houlli], *adv. See* WHOLE I.

whom [hum], *pron., objective case, used of pers.* **I.** Qui? *W. did you see?* qui avez-vous vu? qui est-ce que vous avez vu? *Of w. are you speaking?* de qui parlez-vous? *Whom else?* qui d'autre? **2.** (*Relative*) (*a*) (*Direct obj.*) Que; lequel, *f.* laquelle; *pl.* lesquels, *f.* lesquelles. *The man w. you saw,* l'homme que vous avez vu. (*b*) (*Indirect obj. and after prep.*) Qui. *The beggar to w. you gave a penny,* le mendiant à qui vous avez donné deux sous. *The two officers between w. she was sitting,* les deux officiers entre lesquels elle était assise. **The friend of whom I speak,** l'ami dont je parle. *These two men,* both of whom *were quite young,* ces deux hommes, qui tous deux étaient tous jeunes. (*c*) *Here is Mr X,* than whom *no one could advise you better,* voici Monsieur X, qui est plus autorisé que personne à vous donner des conseils. **3.** Celui que; qui. **Whom the gods love die young,** qui est aimé des dieux meurt jeune.

whom(so)ever [hum(so)'evər], *pron.* **I.** Celui (quel qu'il soit) que. . . . *W.* they choose will *have the right to* . . ., celui qu'on choisira aura le droit de. . . . **2.** N'importe qui que . . .; qui que ce soit que. . . .

whoop[1] [hu:p]. **I.** *int.* Houp! **2.** *s.* (*a*) Houp *m.* *Ven:* Huée *f.* (*b*) *Med:* Quinte *f* (de la coqueluche).

whoop[2], *v.i.* **I.** Pousser des houp. *Ven:* Huer. **2.** *Med:* Faire entendre la toux convulsive de la coqueluche. **'whooping-cough,** *s. Med:* Coqueluche *f.*

whoopee [hu:'pi:, 'hwu:pi], *s. P:* **To make whoopee,** (i) faire la noce, la bombe; (ii) bien s'amuser.

whop[1] [hwɔp], *s. F:* Coup (retentissant).

whop[2], *v.tr.* (whopped) *F:* (*a*) Rosser, battre (qn). (*b*) Battre, rouler (une équipe, etc.).

whopping[1, 2], *a. & s. P:* = WHACKING[1, 2].

whopper ['hwɔpər], *s. P:* = WHACKER.

whore [hɔ:ər], *s.f.* Prostituée.

whorl [hwə:rl], *s.* **I.** *Bot:* Verticille *m.* **2.** Tour *m* (d'une spirale); spire *f*, volute *f.*

whorled [hwə:rld], *a. Bot:* Verticillé. *Conch:* Turbiné. *Arch: etc:* Voluté.

whortleberry ['hwə:rtlbəri], *s.* Airelle *f* myrtille.

whose [hu:z], *poss.pron.* **I.** De qui? (*ownership*) à qui? **Whose are these gloves?** à qui sont ces gants? **Whose daughter are you?** de qui êtes-vous la fille? *W. book did you take?* quel livre avez-vous pris? **2.** (*Relative*) (*a*) Dont. *The pupil w. work I showed you,* l'élève dont je vous ai montré le travail. (*b*) (*After prep.*) De qui; duquel, *f.* de laquelle; *pl.* desquels, *f.* desquelles.

The man to w. wife I gave the money, l'homme à la femme de qui, duquel, i'ai donné l'argent.

whosoever [hu:so'evər], *pron.* = WHOEVER.

why [hwai]. **I.** *adv.* (*a*) Pourquoi? pour quelle raison? *Why didn't you say so?* que ne le disiez-vous? il fallait le dire! *Why not?* pourquoi pas? *Why so?* pourquoi cela? (*b*) *That is* (the reason) why . . ., voilà pourquoi . . .; c'est ce qui fait que. . . . *Why he should always be late I do not understand,* qu'il soit toujours en retard, je ne me l'explique pas. **2.** *s.* (*pl.* whys) Pourquoi *m. S.a.* WHEREFORE 2. **3.** *int.* Why, it's Jones! tiens, mais c'est Jones! **Why, you are not afraid, are you?** voyons, vous n'avez pas peur? *Why, what's the matter?* mais qu'avez-vous donc?

wick [wik], *s.* Mèche *f* (d'une lampe, etc.). **'wick-trimmer,** *s.* Mouchettes *fpl.*

wicked ['wikid], *a.* **I.** (*Of pers.*) Mauvais, méchant, pervers. **2.** *F:* (*a*) (*Of temper, etc.*) Méchant, dangereux; (*of weather, etc.*) très mauvais; affreux; (*of pain*) cruel. *It's a w. climate,* le climat est atroce. (*b*) Malicieux, espiègle, fripon. *Her w. little heart,* son petit fripon de cœur. **-ly,** *adv.* **I.** Méchamment. **2.** *F:* (*a*) Terriblement, affreusement. (*b*) Malicieusement.

wickedness ['wikidnəs], *s.* Méchanceté *f.*

wicker ['wikər]. **I.** *s.* = WICKERWORK. **2.** *Attrib.* D'osier, en osier. *W. garden-chairs,* chaises de jardin en vannerie. *S.a.* BOTTLE[1] I.

wickerwork ['wikərwə:rk], *s.* (*a*) Vannerie *f;* osier tressé. (*b*) *Fort: etc:* Clayonnage *m.*

wicket ['wikit], *s.* **I.** Guichet *m* (d'une porte, etc.). **2.** (*a*) (*In large door*) Porte à piétons. (*b*) (*Into garden, etc.*) Petite porte à claire-voie; barrière *f.* (*c*) Portillon *m* (de passage à niveau, etc.). **3.** *Cr:* Guichet. **Wickets pitched at twelve o'clock,** la partie commence à midi. **'wicket-gate,** *s.* = WICKET 2.

wide [waid]. **I.** *a.* **I.** Large. **The road is twelve feet wide,** la route a douze pieds de large, de largeur; la route est large de douze pieds. *How w. is the room?* quelle est la largeur de la pièce? **2.** (*Of range, etc.*) Étendu, vaste, ample. **The wide world,** l'univers *m.* **There is a wide difference between** . . ., il y a une grande différence entre. . . . **3.** (*a*) (*Vêtement*) ample, large. (*b*) (Opinions) larges, libérales, sans étroitesse. **4.** (*a*) Éloigné, loin. **To be wide of the mark,** être loin de compte. *S.a.* BERTH[1] I. (*b*) *Cr:* Wide ball, balle écartée. **-ly,** *adv.* Largement. **Widely read newspaper,** journal très lu, à grande circulation. **To be widely read,** (i) (*of author*) avoir un public très étendu; (ii) (*of pers.*) avoir de la lecture. *W. known,* très connu. *W. held opinion,* opinion largement répandue. **He has travelled widely,** il a beaucoup voyagé. *W. different versions,* versions qui diffèrent du tout au tout. **II. wide,** *adv.* **I.** Loin. **Far and wide,** *see* FAR[1] I. **Wide apart,** espacé. **2.** (Ouvrir, etc.) largement. **To yawn wide,** bâiller en ouvrant largement la bouche. **To fling the door open wide,** ouvrir la porte toute grande. **'wide-awake,** *a. & s.* **I.** Chapeau *m* en feutre à larges bords. **2.** *See* AWAKE[2] I. **'wide-'mouthed,** *a.* **I.** (*a*) (*Of pers.*) A la bouche grande. (*b*) (*Of receptacle*) Évasé. **2.** *F:* (*Of pers.*) Bouche béante; bouche bée. **'wide 'open,** *a.* (Tout) grand ouvert. **To fling the gates wide open,** ouvrir les portes toutes grandes, à deux battants. *W.-o. eyes,* yeux grands ouverts, écarquillés. **'wide-spread,** *a.* **I.** Étendu. **2.** Répandu; universel; général, -aux. *W.-s. opinion,* opinion largement répandue.

widen [ˈwaid(ə)n]. I. v.tr. (a) Élargir; agrandir en large; donner plus d'ampleur à (un vêtement). (b) Évaser (un trou). (c) Étendre (les limites de qch.). **To widen the terms of a law,** donner plus d'extension aux termes d'une loi. **2.** v.i. S'élargir; s'agrandir (en large). **The breach is widening,** la rupture s'accentue. **widen out,** v.i. S'élargir; s'évaser; s'épanouir.

widgeon [ˈwidʒən], s. Orn: (Canard) siffleur m.

widow [ˈwidou], s.f. Veuve. **Mrs Green, widow of the late A. B. Green,** Mme veuve Green. S.a. GRASS WIDOW.

widowed [ˈwidoud], a. (Homme) veuf; (femme) veuve. She was w. early, elle devint veuve de bonne heure. He lives with his w. mother, il habite avec sa mère qui est veuve.

widower [ˈwidouər], s.m. Veuf.

widowhood [ˈwidohud], s. Veuvage m.

width [widθ], s. I. Largeur f; ampleur f (d'un vêtement); grosseur f (d'un pneu). The footpath is four feet in w., le trottoir a quatre pieds de large. **2.** F: Largeur (de vues, d'idées). **3.** Tex: Lé m, largeur. Double width, grande largeur.

wield [wiːld], v.tr. Manier (l'épée, la plume); tenir (le sceptre). **To wield power,** exercer le pouvoir.

wife, pl. **wives** [waif, waːivz], s.f. I. Femme, épouse. She was his second wife, il l'avait épousée en secondes noces. The general's wife, (Madame) la générale. The farmer's wife, la fermière. **To take a wife,** se marier; F: prendre femme. **To take s.o. to wife,** prendre qn pour femme; épouser qn. P: The wife, la ménagère, la bourgeoise. **2.** A: Femme. The Merry Wives of Windsor, les Joyeuses Commères de Windsor. S.a. FISHWIFE, HOUSEWIFE, MIDWIFE, OLD I.

wifely [ˈwaifli], a. (Qualités, devoirs) d'épouse, qui conviennent à une femme mariée.

wig [wig], s. I. (a) Perruque f. Bob-wig, perruque à marteaux. (b) Postiche m. **2.** F: Chevelure f; tignasse f. Curly wig, chevelure frisée. ˈwig-block, -stand, s. Tête f à perruque; champignon m. ˈwig-maker, s. Perruquier m.

wigged [wigd], a. (Juge, etc.) à perruque, portant (une) perruque.

wigging [ˈwigiŋ], s. F: Verte semonce; P: savon m. **To give s.o. a good wigging,** tancer vertement qn. **To get a good wigging,** se faire laver la tête; se faire attraper.

wight [wait], s. A: Être m, individu m. A sorry wight, un pauvre hère.

wigwam [ˈwigwæm], s. Wigwam m.

wild [waild], a. I. Sauvage. Wild country, pays inculte, désert. (Of plants) To run wild, retourner à l'état sauvage. **2.** (a) (Vent) furieux, violent; (torrent) impétueux. It was a wild night, c'était une nuit de tempête. (b) (Cheval, etc.) farouche, inapprivoisé. F: Wild horses wouldn't draw it out of me, rien au monde ne me le ferait dire. (c) (Of pers.) Dissipé, dissolu; (of conduct) déréglé. **To lead a wild life,** mener une vie déréglée, P: une vie de patachon, de bâton de chaise. **To run wild,** (i) faire des farces; s'émanciper; (ii) (of children) courir en liberté. **3.** (a) (Of pers.) Affolé. Wild eyes, yeux égarés. Wild with joy, fou, éperdu, de joie. **To be wild to do sth.,** avoir une envie folle de faire qch. I: makes, drives, me wild, cela me fait rager. F: To be w. with s.o., être furieux contre qn. (b) (Idée) fantasque; (projet) insensé; (conjecture) au hasard. Wild talk, propos en l'air. Wild exaggeration, exagération insensée. **4.** s.pl. Wilds, région sauvage. **To go out into the wilds,** pénétrer dans des régions inexplorées. **-ly,** adv. I. D'une

manière extravagante. **To talk wildly,** dire des folies. **To clap wildly,** applaudir frénétiquement. Her heart was beating w., son cœur battait à se rompre. **2.** (Répondre) au hasard, au petit bonheur. **wild beast,** s. Bête f sauvage. S.a. SHOW[1] **2.** ˈwild-cat, attrib. a. F: Wild-cat scheme, projet dénué de bon sens. Wild-cat finance, finance extravagante. ˈwild-fowl, s. Coll. (a) Gibier m à plume. (b) Gibier d'eau.

wildebeest [ˈvildəbeist], s. Z: Gnou m.

wilderness [ˈwildərnəs], s. Désert m; lieu m sauvage; pays m inculte. F: To preach in the wilderness, prêcher dans le désert.

wildfire [ˈwaildfaiər], s. A: Feu grégeois. F: To spread like wildfire, se répandre comme une traînée de poudre.

wilding [ˈwaildiŋ], s. I. Plante f sauvage; Arb: sauvageon m. **2.** Pommier m sauvage.

wildness [ˈwaildnəs], s. I. État m sauvage (d'un pays, d'un animal). **2.** (a) Fureur f (du vent); déchaînement m (de la tempête). (b) Dérèglement m (de mœurs); égarements mpl (de conduite). **3.** Extravagance f (d'idées, de paroles).

wile[1] [wail], s. Usu. pl. Ruses f, artifices m, finasseries f.

wile[2], v.tr. Séduire, charmer (qn). To w. s.o. into a place, attirer qn dans un endroit.

wilful [ˈwilful], a. I. (Of pers.) Entêté, volontaire. **2.** (Of action) Fait exprès, de propos délibéré, à dessein. Jur: Wilful murder, homicide volontaire, prémédité. **-fully,** adv. I. Exprès, à dessein, avec intention. **2.** Avec entêtement; volontairement.

wilfulness [ˈwilfulnəs], s. I. Obstination f, entêtement m. **2.** Préméditation f.

wiliness [ˈwailinəs], s. Astuce f.

will[1] [wil], s. I. (a) Volonté f. Will of iron, iron will, volonté de fer. He has a will of his own, il est volontaire. Man lacking strength of will, homme qui manque de caractère. To exercise one's will, faire acte de volonté. The will to victory, to win, la volonté de vaincre. **To take the will for the deed,** accepter l'intention f pour le fait. Where there's a will there's a way, vouloir c'est pouvoir; qui veut la fin veut les moyens. S.a. FREE WILL. (b) **To work with a will,** travailler de bon cœur, avec ardeur, avec courage. **2.** (a) Décision f; volonté. The will of God, le vouloir de Dieu; ce que Dieu veut. Thy will be done, que votre volonté soit faite. It is my w. that you should do it, je veux, j'ordonne, que vous le fassiez. **To work one's will upon s.o.,** faire à sa guise avec qn. (b) Bon plaisir; gré m. Such is our will and pleasure, tel est notre bon plaisir. At will, à volonté; à discrétion. **To have one's will,** (i) obtenir ce qu'on veut; (ii) faire à sa tête, à sa guise. Carried at the will of the wind, porté au caprice des vents. **To do sth. of one's own free will,** faire qch. de son plein gré. I did it against my will, je l'ai fait malgré moi, à contre-cœur. **To act against s.o.'s will,** aller à l'encontre des volontés de qn. **3.** Good will, ill will, bonne, mauvaise, volonté. S.a. GOODWILL, ILL-WILL. **4.** Jur: Testament m. The last will and testament of . . ., les dernières volontés de. . . . **To make one's will,** faire son testament. **To mention s.o. in one's will,** mettre, coucher, qn sur son testament. ˈwill-power, s. Volonté f. Lack of will-power, atonie f de la volonté; aveulissement m.

will[2], v.tr. (p.t. willed [wild]; p.p. willed) I. (a) God has willed it so, Dieu l'a voulu ainsi. Fate willed (it) that he should die, le sort voulut qu'il mourût. When I will to move my arm . . ., lorsque je remue le bras par un effort de ma volonté. . . . *Those who willed the war*, ceux qui ont voulu la guerre. **As we will the end we must will the means**, qui veut la fin veut les moyens. (*b*) **To will s.o. to do, into doing, sth.**, faire faire qch. à qn par un acte de volonté; (*in hypnotism*) suggestionner qn. *He willed the genie into his presence*, il évoqua le génie. **2.** Léguer (qch.); disposer de (qch.) par testament. **To will one's property away from s.o.**, déshériter qn.

will³, *modal aux. v. def.* (*Used only as follows*: I will, thou wilt [wilt], he, we, etc., will; *p.t. & condit.* would [wud], *thou* wouldst [wudst] *or* wouldst ['wudəst]) I. Vouloir. **1.** (*a*) *A: What wilt thou?* que désires-tu? *What would they?* que désirent-ils? (*b*) **Do as you will**, faites comme vous voudrez, comme vous l'entendrez. *The place where I would be*, l'endroit où je voudrais être. *What would you have me do?* que voulez-vous que je fasse? *Say what you will, you will not be believed*, quoi que vous disiez, vous aurez beau dire, on ne vous croira pas. *Look which way you will . . .*, de quelque côté que vous regardiez. . . . (*c*) (*Optative*) (I) **would (that) I were a bird!** je voudrais être un oiseau! **Would to God, would to heaven,** *it were not true!* plût à Dieu, plût au ciel, que cela ne fût pas vrai! **2.** (*Consent*) **The great 'I will,'** le grand oui. *I will not have it said that . . .*, je ne veux pas qu'on dise que. . . . **He could if he would,** il le pourrait s'il le voulait. *The wound would not heal*, la blessure ne voulait pas se cicatriser. *The engine won't start*, le moteur ne veut pas démarrer. **Just wait a moment, will you?** voulez-vous bien attendre un instant? **Would you kindly pass the mustard?** voudriez-vous bien me passer la moutarde? **He will have none of it,** (i) il n'en veut à aucun prix; (ii) il refuse d'en entendre parler. *I will not have it!* je ne le veux pas! **Won't you sit down?** veuillez (donc) vous asseoir. **'Will you hold your tongue!** voulez-vous bien vous taire! **3.** (*Emphatic*) **Accidents 'will happen,** on ne peut pas éviter les accidents. **He 'will have it that** *I was mistaken*, il veut absolument que je me sois trompé. **He 'will have his little joke, will the doctor,** il aime à plaisanter, le docteur. *I quite forgot!*—**You 'would (forget)!** j'ai oublié!—C'est bien de vous (d'avoir oublié)! **4.** (*Habit*) *This hen will lay up to six eggs a week*, cette poule pond jusqu'à six œufs par semaine. *She would often return home exhausted*, elle rentrait souvent très fatiguée. **5.** (*Of conjecture*) *This will be your cousin?* c'est là sans doute votre cousin? **II. will** *as an auxiliary forming the future tenses*. **1.** (*Still expressing something of the speaker's will. So used in the 1st pers.*) *I will not be caught again*, on ne m'y reprendra plus. **2.** (*Expressing simple futurity. Used in the 2nd and 3rd persons. For the 1st pers. see* SHALL.) (*a*) *Will he be there?*—He will, y sera-t-il?—Oui (, il y sera). *No, he will not, no. he won't,* non (, il n'y sera pas). *But I shall starve!*—No, *you won't*, mais je mourrai de faim!—Pas du tout. *You won't forget, will you?* vous n'oublierez pas, hein? *You will write to me, won't you?* vous m'écrirez, n'est-ce pas? *He told me he would be there*, il m'a dit qu'il serait là. (*b*) (*Immediate future*) *I shall dictate and you will write*, je vais dicter et vous allez écrire. (*c*) (*In injunctions*) *You will be here at three o'clock*, soyez ici à trois heures. **3.** *He would come if you invited him*, il viendrait si vous l'invitiez. **willing**, *a.* **1.** (*a*) De bonne volonté;

bien disposé; serviable. *A few w. men*, quelques hommes de bonne volonté. *W. hands*, mains empressées. (*b*) Consentant. **2.** *Used pred.* **to be willing to do sth.**, vouloir bien faire qch. *W. to oblige*, prêt à rendre service; complaisant. **I am willing that you should come**, je veux bien que vous veniez. **To be able and willing**, avoir à la fois le pouvoir et la volonté. **Willing or not**, bon gré mal gré. **God willing**, s'il plaît à Dieu. **-ly**, *adv.* **1.** Spontanément; de plein gré. **2.** De bon cœur; volontiers.

Will⁴. *Pr.n.m.* (*Dim. of William*) Guillaume.

'will-o'-the-'wisp, *s.* Feu follet.

willed [wild], *a.* **1.** Disposé (à faire qch.). **2. Strong-willed**, de forte volonté; volontaire.

William ['wiljəm]. *Pr.n.m.* Guillaume.

willingness ['wiliŋnəs], *s.* **1.** Bonne volonté. *With the utmost w.*, de très bon cœur. **2.** Consentement *m*.

willow ['wilou], *s.* **1.** *Bot:* Willow(-tree), saule *m*. **Weeping willow**, saule pleureur. **Water willow**, osier *m*. **2.** *Cr: F:* **The willow**, la batte. **'willow-bed**, *s.* Saulaie *f*. **'willow-pattern**, *s. Cer:* Décoration chinoise en teinte bleue à motif de saule pleureur. **'willow-warbler**, *s. Orn:* Pouillot *m*.

willowy ['wiloui], *a.* Souple, svelte, élancé.

willy-nilly ['wili'nili], *adv.* Bon gré mal gré; de gré ou de force.

wilt [wilt], *v.i.* (*a*) (*Of plant*) Se flétrir, se faner. (*b*) (*Of pers.*) Dépérir, languir; sécher sur pied. (*c*) *P:* Perdre contenance; se dégonfler.

wily ['waili], *a.* Rusé, astucieux; *F:* malin, -igne; *P:* ficelle. *He's a wily old bird*, c'est un vieux roublard.

wimple¹ [wimpl], *s.* **1.** Guimpe *f* (de religieuse). **2.** (*Of stream*) Méandre *m*.

wimple², *v.i. Scot:* (*Of stream*) (*a*) Se rider. (*b*) Serpenter. (*c*) Couler en murmurant.

win [win], *v.tr. & i.* (*p.t. & p.p.* won [wʌn]; *pr.p.* winning) I. Gagner; remporter (une victoire). **To win the prize**, remporter le prix. *Rac:* **To win by a length**, gagner d'une longueur. **2.** Acquérir (de la popularité); captiver (l'attention). **To win glory**, (re)cueillir des lauriers. **To win a reputation**, se faire une réputation. *This gallant action won him the cross*, cette action d'éclat lui a valu la croix. **To win s.o.'s love**, se faire aimer de qn. **3.** **To win all hearts**, gagner, conquérir, se concilier, tous les cœurs. **4.** **To win one's way to . . .**, parvenir à (un endroit). **To win home**, (i) regagner son chez-soi (en dépit des obstacles); (ii) parvenir à son but. **5.** Extraire (le charbon, le minerai). *S.a.* HARVEST¹ 1. **win back**, *v.tr.* **1.** Reconquérir (*from*, sur). **2.** Regagner (son argent). **win over**, *v.tr.* Gagner (qn); capter la bienveillance de (qn). *To win over the audience*, se concilier les auditeurs. **win through**, *v.i.* Venir à bout de (ses difficultés); parvenir à son but. **winning¹**, *a.* **1.** Winning number, numéro gagnant; (*in lottery*) numéro sortant. Winning stroke, coup décisif. **2.** Attrayant, séduisant; (sourire) engageant. **winning²**, *s.* **1.** Victoire *f* (au jeu, etc.); acquisition *f* (de qch.). *The w. of the war*, le fait d'avoir gagné la guerre. **2.** *pl.* Winnings, gains *m* (au jeu). **'winning-post**, *s. Turf:* Poteau *m* d'arrivée.

wince¹ [wins], *s.* Crispation (nerveuse, de douleur); tressaillement *m*. **Without a wince**, sans sourciller.

wince², *v.i.* Faire une grimace de douleur; tressaillir de douleur. **Not to wince**, ne pas sourciller; ne pas broncher.

winch [winʃ], s. 1. Manivelle f. 2. Treuil m (de hissage). Hand-winch, treuil à bras.

wind¹ [wind, *Poet :* waind], s. 1. Vent m. (a) The north wind, le vent du nord ; *Lit :* l'aquilon m, la bise. A north-east. wind, un vent de nord-est. High wind, vent fort, violent. *The w. is high,* il fait grand vent. How is the wind? d'où vient le vent ? *F :* To see which way the wind blows, regarder de quel côté vient le vent. *F :* There's something in the wind, il se manigance quelque chose. *F :* To go like the wind, aller comme le vent. To sow the wind and reap the whirlwind, semer le vent et récolter la tempête. *P :* To raise the wind, se procurer de l'argent ; battre monnaie. To have, get, the wind up, avoir le trac, la frousse ; avoir une peur bleue. (b) *Nau :* Head wind, vent debout. To sail, run, before the wind, courir vent arrière. To sail with wind and tide, avoir vent et marée. In the teeth of the wind, contre le vent. To sail into the wind, venir, aller, au lof. To sail off the wind, naviguer vent largue. To sail on a wind, close to the wind, pincer, serrer, le vent ; courir au plus près. *F :* To sail close to the wind, friser l'indécence ou la malhonnêteté. *F :* To take the wind out of s.o.'s sails, déjouer les plans de qn ; couper l'herbe sous le pied de qn. Between the wind and the water, à fleur d'eau. (c) *F :* Chose vaine. *These promises are merely w.,* ce sont des promesses en l'air. 2. *Ven :* To have the wind of one's game, avoir le vent de son gibier. *F :* To get wind of sth., avoir vent de qch. ; éventer (un secret). 3. *Med :* Vent(s) ; flatuosité f. To break wind, lâcher un vent. To bring up wind, roter. 4. Souffle m, respiration f, haleine f. To be in good wind, avoir la plenty of wind, être en haleine ; avoir du souffle, de l'haleine. To get one's second wind, reprendre haleine. 5. *Mus :* The wind, les instruments m à vent. *S.a.* WOOD-WIND. **'wind-bound,** a. *Nau :* Retenu par des vents contraires. **'wind-brace**¹, s. *Const :* Contrevent m. **'wind-brace**², v.tr. Contreventer. **'wind-chest,** s. Sommier m (d'un orgue). **'wind-cone,** s. *Av : =* WIND-SLEEVE. **'wind-egg,** s. Œuf non fécondé ; *F :* œuf clair. **'wind-engine,** s. *Mec.E :* Moteur m à vent ; éolienne f ; aéromoteur m. **'wind-flower,** s. Anémone f. **'wind-gauge,** s. Anémomètre m. **'wind-instrument,** s. *Mus :* Instrument m à vent. **'wind-jammer,** s. *Nau : F :* Voilier m. **'wind-sail,** s. *Nau :* Manche f à vent, à air (en toile). **'wind-sleeve,** s. *Av :* Sac m à vent (de l'aérodrome). **'wind-spout,** s. *Meteor :* Trombe f. **'wind-storm,** s. Tempête f de vent ; tourbillon m. **'wind-sucker,** s. *Vet :* Cheval m qui avale de l'air ; cheval cornard. **'wind-swept,** a. (Endroit) balayé par le vent, venteux. **'wind-tight,** a. Imperméable à l'air. **'wind-tunnel,** s. Tunnel m aérodynamique.

wind², v.tr. 1. [waind] (p.t. & p.p. winded ['waindid] or wound [waund]) To wind the horn, sonner du cor. 2. [wind] (winded ['windid]) (a) (Of hounds) Éventer, flairer (le gibier) ; avoir vent (du gibier). (b) Couper la respiration, le souffle, à (qn) ; essouffler (qn, un cheval). (c) Laisser souffler (un cheval). winded ['windid], a. 1. Hors d'haleine ; essoufflé ; à bout de souffle. 2. See LONG-WINDED, SHORT-WINDED.

wind³ [waind], v. (p.t. & p.p. wound [waund]) I. v.i. Tourner ; faire des détours ; (of path, river) serpenter ; (of staircase) monter en colimaçon. *The plant winds round the pole,* la plante s'enroule,

s'entortille, autour de la perche. *The road winds up, down, the hill,* le chemin monte, descend, en serpentant. II. **wind,** v.tr. 1. Enrouler. *Tex :* Dévider (le fil). To wind the wool into a ball, enrouler la laine en peloton. To wind cotton on a reel, bobiner du coton. *Fish :* To wind in the line, ramener la ligne. *She wound a blanket round him,* elle l'enveloppa d'une couverture. 2. To wind a bobbin, enrouler le fil sur une bobine. *El.E :* To wind a dynamo, armer une dynamo. 3. To wind the clock, remonter l'horloge. 4. *Min :* Hisser, remonter (le minerai). **wind up.** 1. v.tr. (a) Enrouler (un cordage). (b) Bander, remonter (un ressort) ; remonter (l'horloge). (c) Terminer (qch.) ; *Com :* liquider (une société) ; régler, clôturer (un compte). *To w. up the debate,* terminer les débats. 2. v.i. (a) Finir ; terminer. *How does the play w. up?* comment la pièce se dénoue-t-elle ? quel est le dénouement ? (b) *The company wound up,* la société se mit en liquidation. **winding**¹, a. (Chemin) sinueux, plein de détours, qui serpente ; (route) en lacet. *W. streets,* rues tortueuses. *S.a.* STAIRCASE. **winding**², s. 1. Mouvement sinueux ; cours sinueux ; replis mpl. 2. *Tex :* Bobinage m. *El :* Enroulement m, bobinage. *S.a.* COIL¹ 3. 3. Remontage m (d'une horloge) ; bandage m (d'un ressort). 4. (a) pl. Windings, sinuosités f, replis, méandres m (d'une rivière) ; lacets m (d'un chemin). (b) Spires fpl, enroulement (d'une bobine). Armature winding, enroulement d'induit. **'winding-gear,** s. 1. *Min :* Machine f d'extraction. 2. Treuil m (d'un ascenseur). **'winding-plant,** s. Chevalement m (de puits de mine). **'winding-shaft,** s. *Min :* Puits m d'extraction. **'winding-sheet,** s. Linceul m, suaire m.

windbag ['windbag], s. 1. Outre f (d'une cornemuse). 2. *F :* Orateur verbeux. *He's a w.,* il parle pour ne rien dire.

winder ['waindər], s. (a) *Tex :* Bobinoir m, dévidoir m. (b) *Fish :* Plior m. (c) Remontoir m (d'une montre à remontoir). (d) *Aut :* Lève-glace(s) m inv (de portière).

windfall ['windfɔ:l], s. 1. (a) Bois gisant ; chablis m. (b) Fruit abattu par le vent ; fruit tombé. 2. *F :* Aubaine f ; bonne fortune.

windhover ['windhɔvər, -hʌvər], s. *Orn :* Crécerelle f, émouchet m.

windlass ['windləs], s. Treuil m, vindas m ; (on dray, etc.) pouliot m. *Nau :* Guindeau m.

windmill ['windmil], s. Moulin m à vent ; (for pumping) aéromoteur m, éolienne f. *F :* To tilt at windmills, se battre contre des moulins à vent.

window ['windo, -ou], s. 1. (a) Fenêtre f. To look out of the window, regarder par la fenêtre. Attic window, fenêtre en mansarde. *To break the windows,* casser les vitres, les carreaux. *Jur :* To block up the windows, condamner les vues. *S.a.* BOW-WINDOW, FRENCH WINDOW, etc. (b) Stained-glass window, verrière f ; vitrail, -aux m (d'église). (c) Guichet m (d'un bureau de délivrance de billets). (d) *Com :* Vitrine f, devanture f, montre f. To put sth. in the window, mettre qch. à l'étalage, en montre. 2. *Rail : Veh :* Glace f. To lower, open, the w., baisser la glace. To raise, close, the w., remonter la glace. 3. Fenêtre (d'une enveloppe). **'window-box,** s. Caisse f, bac m, à fleurs. **'window-display,** s. Étalage m. **'window-dresser,** s. Étalagiste mf. **'window-dressing,** s. 1. Art m de l'étalage. 2. *F :* That's all window-dressing, tout ça, c'est du camouflage, du truquage, un trompe-l'œil. **'window-envelope,** s. Enveloppe f à fenêtre, à panneau transparent. **'window-frame,** s. Dormant m, châssis m, de fenêtre ; chambranle m. **'window-ledge,** s. Rebord m, appui m, de fenêtre. **'window-pane,** s. Vitre f, carreau m. **'window-raiser,** s. Aut : Lève-glace(s) m inv. **'window-sash,** s. Châssis m (de fenêtre à guillotine). **'window-seat,** s. Banquette f (dans l'embrasure d'une fenêtre). **'window-sill,** s. Appui m, rebord m, tablette f, de fenêtre.

windpipe ['windpaip], s. Anat : Trachée-artère f ; F : gosier m.

windrow ['windrou], s. Agr : Andain m.

windscreen ['windskri:n], s. **1.** (a) Abri m contre le vent. (b) Hort : Abat-vent m inv, brise-vent m inv. **2.** Aut : Pare-brise m inv.

windward ['windwǝd]. **I.** a. & adv. Au vent. **2.** s. Côté m au vent. Nau : To work to windward, louvoyer. To fetch to windward, gagner (dans) le vent, au vent. To (the) w. of . . ., au vent de. . . .

windy ['windi], a. **1.** Venteux. W. day, journée de grand vent. It is very w., il fait beaucoup de vent. **2.** (Of place) Balayé par le vent ; exposé aux quatre vents. **3.** F : To keep on the windy side of the law, se tenir hors de l'atteinte de la loi. **4.** (a) Med : Venteux, flatueux. (b) P : To feel windy, avoir le trac, la frousse. **5.** (Of speech) Ampoulé, enflé, verbeux.

wine[1] [wain], s. Vin m. (a) Dry w., sweet w., vin sec, doux. W. and water, eau rougie. To take (a glass of) wine with s.o., trinquer avec qn. F : To be in wine, être pris de vin. Prov : Good wine needs no bush, à bon vin point d'enseigne. (b) Pharm : Quinine wine, vin de quinquina. **'wine-bibber,** s. Lit : Buveur m ; F : sac m à vin. **'wine-bin,** s. Porte-bouteilles m inv. **'wine-butler,** s. Sommelier m. **'wine-cellar,** s. Cave f au vin. **'wine-coloured,** a. Couleur de vin ; lie de vin inv. **'wine-cooler,** s. Seau m à frapper ; glacière f. **'wine-cooper,** s. (i) Embouteilleur m, (ii) dégustateur m, (iii) goûtant m, de vins. **'wine-glass,** s. Verre m à vin. **'wine-glassful,** s. Plein verre à vin. **'wine-grower,** s. Viticulteur m ; vigneron m. **'wine-growing,** s. Viticulture f. **'wine-list,** s. (At restaurant) Carte f des vins. **'wine-merchant,** s. Négociant m en vins ; marchand m de vins en gros. **'wine-press,** s. Pressoir m. **'wine-vault(s),** s.(pl.) **1.** Cave f, caveau m (à vin). **2.** Cabaret m (en sous-sol). **'wine-waiter,** s. Sommelier m.

wine[2], v.tr. To (dine and) wine s.o., fêter qn.

wing[1] [wiŋ], s. **1.** Aile f. Fear lent him wings, la peur lui donnait des ailes. F : To take s.o. under one's wing, prendre qn sous sa protection, sous sa tutelle. **2.** Vol m, essor m. To shoot a bird on the wing, tirer un oiseau au vol, à la volée. (Of bird) To be on the wing, voler. To take wing, s'envoler ; prendre son vol, son essor. **3.** (a) Battant m (d'une porte). (b) Aile (d'un bâtiment) ; pavillon m (d'un hôpital). **4.** (a) Aile (d'un avion, d'une auto, etc.). Av : The wings, la voilure. Upper wing, plan supérieur. (b) Oreille f, ailette f (d'une vis à main). **5.** Th : The wings, les coulisses. In the wings, (i) dans la coulisse ; (ii) à la cantonade. **6.** Fb : (Pers.) Ailier m. **'wing-beat,** s. Coup m d'aile. **'wing-case,** s. Ent : Élytre m. **'wing-commander,** s. Mil.Av : Lieutenant-colonel m. **'wing-flap,** s. Av : Aileron m. **'wing-float,** s. Av : Ballonnet m (d'hydravion). **'wing-game,** s. Gibier ailé ; gibier à plumes. **'wing-rib,** s. Cu : Côte f

d'aloyau. **'wing-span, -spread,** s. Envergure f. **'wing-tip,** s. Av : Bec m d'aile.

wing[2], v.tr. **1.** (a) Empenner (une flèche). (b) Lit : Fear winged his flight, la peur lui donnait des ailes. (c) (Of bird) To wing the air, its way, voler. Winging towards the south, volant vers le sud. **2.** Frapper, blesser, (un oiseau) à l'aile. F : I have winged him, je lui ai mis du plomb dans l'aile. **winged,** a. **1.** (a) Ailé. Ven : Winged game, gibier à plumes, gibier ailé. Mil : Winged bomb, bombe empennée. (b) White-winged, aux ailes blanches. **2.** (Of bird) To be winged, être blessé à l'aile ; en avoir dans l'aile.

winger ['wiŋǝr], s. Fb : Ailier m.

wingless ['wiŋləs], a. Sans ailes ; aptère.

wink[1] [wiŋk], s. Clignement m d'œil ; clin m d'œil. To give the wink to s.o., F : to tip s.o. the wink, faire signe de l'œil à qn. With a w., en clignant de l'œil. Without a wink of the eyelid, sans sourciller. F : To have forty winks, faire un petit somme ; faire une courte sieste.

wink[2]. **1.** v.i. (a) Cligner les yeux. (b) To wink at s.o., cligner de l'œil, faire signe de l'œil, F : faire de l'œil, à qn. (c) F : To wink at an abuse, fermer les yeux sur un abus. (d) (Of light) Vaciller, clignoter. **2.** v.tr. (a) To wink one's eye, cligner de l'œil. (b) To wink assent, signifier son assentiment par un clin d'œil. **winking,** s. Clignement m de l'œil. F : Like winking, en un clin d'œil ; en un rien de temps.

winkle [wiŋkl], s. Moll : = PERIWINKLE[2].

winner ['winǝr], s. (a) Gagnant, -ante. The w. of the race, le vainqueur de l'épreuve. Every time a winner! à tous les coups l'on gagne ! (b) P : Roman m, pièce f, à grand succès.

winnow ['wino, -ou], v.tr. (a) Vanner (le grain). (b) Éplucher, examiner minutieusement (des preuves, etc.). To winnow (out) the true from the false, séparer, démêler, le vrai d'avec le faux. **winnowing,** s. **1.** (a) Vannage m. Winnowing-basket, van m. (b) Examen minutieux. **2.** pl. Winnowings, vannure f. **'winnowing-machine,** s. = WINNOWER 2.

winnower ['winouǝr], s. **1.** (Pers.) Vanneur, -euse. **2.** (Machine) Vanneuse f ; sasseur m mécanique ; tarare m.

winsome ['winsǝm], a. Captivant, séduisant.

winter[1] ['wintǝr], s. Hiver m. In winter, en hiver. Winter clothing, vêtements d'hiver. Winter resort, station hivernale. Winter visitors, hivernants m. Winter sports, sports d'hiver. Mil : Winter quarters, quartiers d'hiver ; hivernage m. **'winter-time,** s. Saison f d'hiver.

winter[2], v.i. Hiverner, passer l'hiver (at, à). **wintering,** s. Hivernage m.

wintergreen ['wintǝgri:n], s. Bot : Gaulthérie f du Canada. Pharm : Oil of wintergreen, essence f de wintergreen.

wintry ['wintri], a. D'hiver ; hivernal, -aux. F : Wintry smile, sourire décourageant. W. reception, accueil glacial.

wipe[1] [waip], s. **1.** (a) Coup m de torchon, de mouchoir, d'éponge. To give sth. a wipe, essuyer qch. (b) Cin : (Fermeture f en) fondu m. **2.** F : Tape f, taloche f. P : Mouchoir m. **'wipe-joint,** s. Plumb : Soudure f à nœud.

wipe[2], v.tr. **1.** (a) Essuyer. To w. the blackboard, passer une éponge sur le tableau. To wipe one's face, s'essuyer la figure. To wipe one's nose, se moucher. To wipe one's eyes, s'essuyer les yeux. F : To wipe s.o.'s eye, couper l'herbe sous le pied à qn. To wipe sth. dry, bien essuyer qch. S.a. FLOOR[1] I. (b) El.E : Wiping contact,

contact à frottement. **2.** *Plumb:* Ébarber (un joint). **3.** *v.i. P:* To wipe at s.o. with one's stick, allonger un coup de canne à qn. **wipe away,** *v.tr.* Essuyer (ses larmes). **wipe off,** *v.tr.* (a) Enlever, essuyer (une éclaboussure); régler, liquider (une dette). (b) *Phot:* Essorer (un cliché). **wipe out,** *v.tr.* (a) Liquider, amortir (une dette); effacer (une injure). He has wiped out his past, il a liquidé, racheté, son passé. (b) *F:* Exterminer (une armée, etc.).

wiper ['waipər], *s.* **1.** Torchon *m,* tampon *m,* ou éponge *f;* (*for hands*) essuie-main(s) *m inv.* Windscreen wiper, essuie-glace *m. S.a.* PEN-WIPER. **2.** *Mec.E:* Came *f,* mentonnet *m;* levée *f;* alluchon *m. I.C.E:* Ignition wiper, came d'allumage. **3.** Wiper lubrication, graissage *m* par frotteur. 'wiper-shaft, *s. Mec.E:* Arbre *m* à cames.

wire¹ ['waiər], *s.* **1.** Fil *m* métallique; *F:* fil de fer. (a) Copper wire, fil de laiton. Stranded wire, câble *m* métallique. Wire mattress, sommier métallique. *Mil:* Wire entanglement, réseau(x) *m(pl)* de fil de fer barbelé. (b) Cheese-wire, fil à couper le beurre. Telegraph wires, fils télégraphiques. Puppet-wires, fils de marionnettes. *F:* To pull the wires for s.o., intriguer pour qn. *Aut:* Wire of a tyre, tringle *f* d'un pneu. *S.a.* LIVE¹ 2, PIANO-WIRE, etc. **2.** Télégramme *m,* dépêche *f.* To send s.o. a wire, aviser qn par télégramme. Reply by wire, réponse télégraphique. 'wire-cutter, *s. Tls:* **1.** Coupe-fil *m inv.* **2.** (Pair of) wire-cutters, pince(s) coupante(s); cisaille(s) *f(pl);* coupe-fil. 'wire-draw, *v.tr.* **1.** *Metalw:* Tréfiler; travailler (un métal) à la filière. **2.** *Mch:* Étrangler, laminer (la vapeur). **3.** *F:* Alambiquer, subtiliser (son style, etc.). 'wire 'edge, *s.* Morfil *m,* bavure *f* (d'un outil). 'wire-glass, *s.* Verre armé; verre à fil de fer noyé. 'wire-haired, *a.* (Chien terrier) à poil dur. 'wire-mark, *s. Paperm:* Vergeure *f.* 'wire-mill, *s.* Tréfilerie *f.* 'wire-'netting, *s.* Treillis *m* métallique; treillage *m* en fil de fer. 'wire-puller, *s. F:* Intrigant, -ante. 'wire-pulling, *s.* Art *m* de tirer les ficelles; intrigues *fpl.* 'wire-strainer, *s.* Tendeur *m* pour fil de fer; raidisseur *m.* 'wire-tapping, *s.* Captation *f* de messages télégraphiques. 'wire-wove, *a.* (Papier) vergé.

wire², *v.tr.* **1.** (a) Munir (qch.) d'un fil métallique. (b) Rattacher (une pièce) avec du fil de fer. (c) Monter (des fleurs) sur fil de fer. (d) Grillager (une ouverture). **2.** *El.E:* Canaliser (une maison). To wire a station on to a circuit, embrocher un poste. **3.** *F:* Transmettre (un ordre) par le télégraphe, par fil; télégraphier (une nouvelle). To wire to s.o., télégraphier à qn. To wire for s.o., envoyer une dépêche pour faire venir qn. **wire in,** *v.tr.* **1.** *v.tr.* Grillager (un terrain). **2.** *v.i. F:* S'y mettre de tout son cœur. **To wire into a meal,** *abs.* to wire in, s'attaquer à un repas. **wire up,** *v.tr. El.E:* Monter, accoupler (des piles). **wired,** *a.* **1.** Monté sur fil de fer. **2.** (*Of enclosure*) Grillagé, grillé. **3.** *Aut:* Wired-on tyre, bandage à tringles. **wiring,** *s.* (a) Montage *m* sur fil de fer. (b) *El.E:* Pose *f* de fils électriques; canalisation *f.* (c) *W.Tel:* Montage (du poste).

wireless¹ ['waiərləs], *a.* Sans fil. Wireless telegraphy, s. wireless, télégraphie *f* sans fil, *abbr.* T. S. F.; radiotélégraphie *f; F:* la radio. Wireless telegram, radiotélégramme *m. W. message,* message *m* par radio; radio *m. Nau:*

Wireless room, poste *m* de T. S. F. Wireless telephony, *s. F:* wireless, téléphonie *f* sans fil. To talk on the wireless, parler au micro. Wireless set, poste *m* de T. S. F. Wireless enthusiast, sans-filiste *mf. S.a.* OPERATOR 1.

wireless², *v.tr.* Envoyer (un message) par la radio. *Abs.* To wireless to s.o., aviser qn par la radio.

wirework ['waiərwəːrk], *s.* **1.** Tréfilerie *f,* tréfilage *m.* **2.** *pl.* Wireworks, tréfilerie.

wireworm ['waiərwəːrm], *s. Ent:* Larve *f* de taupin.

wiriness ['waiərinəs], *s.* (a) Raideur *f* (des cheveux). (b) Vigueur (alliée à un corps sec).

wiry ['waiəri], *a.* (a) (*Of hair*) Raide, rude. (b) (*Of pers.*) Sec et nerveux.

wisdom ['wizdəm], *s.* Sagesse *f.* To have the wisdom of the serpent, avoir la prudence du serpent. Wisdom tooth, dent de sagesse.

wise¹ [waiz], *a.* **1.** Sage; prudent; sagace. The seven wise men, les sept sages. The Wise Men of the East, les (Rois) Mages *m. He would be a w. man that could tell,* bien avisé qui saurait le dire. To grow wise(r), (i) s'assagir; (ii) acquérir de l'expérience. *S.a.* SAD 1, WORD¹ 1. **2.** (a) To look wise, prendre un (petit) air entendu. (b) He is none the wiser (for it), il n'en est pas plus avancé. To do sth. without anyone being the wiser, faire qch. à l'insu de tout le monde. *If you hold your tongue no one will be any the wiser,* si tu te tais, ni vu ni connu. (c) *U.S: F:* To get wise to a fact, saisir un fait. *Put me w. about it,* expliquez-moi ça; mettez-moi au courant. **-ly,** *adv.* Sagement; prudemment. 'wise-crack, *s. U.S:* Bon mot.

wise², *s.* Manière *f,* façon *f;* guise *f.* In no wise, en aucune manière, d'aucune façon; nullement. In some wise, en quelque manière. *The letter ran in this wise,* la lettre était ainsi conçue.

wiseacre ['waizeikər], *s.* Prétendu sage; pédant *m.*

wish¹ [wiʃ], *s.* (a) Désir *m;* vœu *m.* He has a great wish to go, il éprouve un grand désir d'y aller. *Everything succeeds according to his wishes,* tout lui réussit à souhait. *You shall have your w.,* votre désir sera exaucé. (b) Souhait *m,* vœu. To send all good wishes to s.o., adresser tous ses vœux de bonheur à qn. 'wish-bone, *s.* Lunette *f,* fourchette *f* (d'une volaille).

wish². **1.** *v.ind.tr.* To wish for sth., désirer, souhaiter, qch. To wish everything one can wish for, avoir tout à souhait. What more can you wish for? que voudriez-vous de plus? **2.** *v.tr.* Vouloir. (a) I do not wish it, je ne le veux pas; je n'y tiens pas. To wish to do sth., désirer, vouloir, faire qch. (b) I wish I were in your place, je voudrais bien être à votre place. *I w. I had seen it!* j'aurais bien voulu voir cela! *I w. I hadn't left so soon,* je regrette d'être parti si tôt. *I w. he would come!* que ne vient-il? (c) It is to be wished that . . ., il est à souhaiter que. . . . *I w. you may succeed,* je vous souhaite de réussir. *F:* I w. you may get it! je vous en souhaite! (d) He wishes me well, il est bien disposé envers moi. He wishes nobody ill, il ne veut de mal à personne. To wish s.o. good night, souhaiter une bonne nuit à qn; dire bonsoir à qn. *S.a.* JOY. **wishing,** *s.* Désirs *mpl,* souhaits *mpl.* 'wishing-bone, *s.* = WISH-BONE.

wishful ['wiʃful], *a.* Désireux (*of sth.,* de qch.). **-fully,** *adv.* Avec désir.

wishy-washy ['wiʃi'wɔʃi], *a. F:* Fade, insipide.

wisp [wisp], *s.* (a) Bouchon *m,* poignée *f* (de paille). (b) Tortillon *m,* toron *m* (de paille). Wisp of smoke, traînée *f* de fumée. Wisp of hair, mèche folle. *F:* **Little wisp of a man,** tout petit bout d'homme. (c) **Époussette** *f.*

wist [wist]. See WIT³.

wistaria [wis'tɛəria], *s.* Bot: **Glycine** *f.*

wistful ['wistful], *a.* (Regard, air) plein d'un vague désir ou d'un vague regret. W. *smile,* (i) sourire désenchanté; (ii) sourire pensif. **-fully,** *adv.* D'un air songeur et triste; avec un désir silencieux.

wit¹ [wit], *s.* **1.** (*Often pl.*) Esprit *m*, entendement *m*; intelligence *f.* **He has slow wits, quick wits,** il a l'esprit lent, vif. **To be out of one's wits, to have lost one's wits,** avoir perdu l'esprit, la raison. **To collect one's wits, se ressaisir. To sharpen s.o.'s wits,** aiguiser l'intelligence de qn; *F:* **dessaler qn. To have, keep, one's wits about one,** avoir, conserver, toute sa présence d'esprit. **To be at one's wit's end,** ne plus savoir de quel côté se tourner, à quel saint se vouer. **To have a battle of wits,** jouer au plus fin. **To live by one's wits,** vivre d'expédients. **To set one's wits to work** to *extricate oneself,* s'ingénier à se tirer d'affaire. **2.** (Vivacité *f* d')esprit. **Flash of wit,** trait *m* d'esprit.

wit², (*Pers.*) **Bel esprit;** homme *m,* femme *f,* d'esprit.

wit³, *v.tr.* A: (*The only parts used are:* pr. ind. I wot, thou wottest, he wot; *p.t.* wist; *pr.p.* witting) Savoir. *Jur:* **To wit . . .,** à savoir . . .; c'est-à-dire. . . . *F:* **God wot,** en vérité.

witting, *a.* (*Of insult, etc.*) Fait de propos délibéré. **-ly,** *adv.* .Sciemment; à dessein.

witch¹ [witʃ], *s.f.* (a) **Sorcière.** (b) *F:* **Old witch,** vieille bonne femme (déplaisante). (c) *F:* **Jeune charmeuse; ensorceleuse.** '**witch-broom,** 'witches'-broom, *s.* Bot: **Balai** *m* **de sorcière.** '**witch-doctor,** *s.* Anthr: **Sorcier guérisseur.**

witch², *v.tr.* **Ensorceler, fasciner, envoûter.**

witching, *a.* **1.** Enchanteur, -eresse; charmant, séduisant. **2.** Magique.

witchcraft ['witʃkrɑ:ft], *s.* **Sorcellerie** *f;* **magie noire.**

witchery ['witʃəri], *s.* **1.** = WITCHCRAFT. **2.** (a) **Ensorcellement** *m,* **enchantement** *m.* (b) *F:* **Fascination** *f;* **charme** *m* **magique.**

witch-hazel ['witʃheiz(ə)l], *s.* Bot: **Hamamélis** *m.*

with [wið], *prep.* **Avec. 1.** (a) *To travel, work, with s.o.,* voyager, travailler, avec qn. *He is staying with friends,* il est chez des amis. *Is there someone with you?* êtes-vous accompagné? *He was there* along with *his wife,* il y était avec sa femme. **With the colours,** sous les drapeaux. **I shall be with you in a moment,** je serai à vous dans un moment. **Question that is always with us,** question qui est toujours d'actualité. (b) **Knife with a silver handle,** couteau à manche d'argent. **Girl with blue eyes,** jeune fille aux yeux bleus. **He was speaking with his hat on,** il parlait le chapeau sur la tête. **With your intelligence,** *you will easily understand that* . . ., intelligent comme vous l'êtes, vous comprendrez facilement que. . . . (c) **With child,** enceinte. (*Of animal*) **With young,** pleine. (d) **To leave a child with s.o.,** laisser un enfant à la garde de qn, aux soins de qn. **This decision rests, lies, with you,** c'est à vous de décider. **He rests with God,** il repose en Dieu. (e) (*In spite of*) **With all his faults** . . ., malgré tous ses défauts. . . . **2.** (a) **To trade with France,** faire le commerce avec la France. **To have to do with s.o.,** avoir affaire avec qn. **To have nothing to do with s.o.,** n'avoir rien à faire avec qn. **I can do nothing with him,** je ne peux rien en faire. **To be patient with s.o.,** être patient

avec qn. **To be sincere with oneself,** être sincère envers soi-même. **It is a habit with me,** c'est une habitude chez moi. **To be in favour with the queen,** être en faveur auprès de la reine. **The difficulty, with poetry, is to read it well,** le plus difficile, en ce qui concerne la poésie, c'est de bien la lire. (b) **I sympathize with you,** je sympathise avec vous. **I do not agree with you,** ie ne suis pas de votre avis. **I am with you there!** j'en conviens! **To vote with a party,** voter avec un parti. (c) **With these words he dismissed me,** là-dessus, ce disant, il me congédia. (d) **To wrestle with s.o.,** lutter avec qn. **To fight with s.o.,** se battre contre qn. **3.** *To part with sth.,* se dessaisir, se défaire, de qch. **4.** (a) **To cut sth. with a knife,** couper qch. avec un couteau, au couteau. **To walk with (the aid of) a stick,** marcher avec une canne. **To fight with swords,** se battre à l'épée. **To take sth. with both hands,** prendre qch. à deux mains. *To look at sth.* with **the naked eye,** regarder qch. à l'œil nu. *To strike* with *all one's might,* frapper de toutes ses forces. (b) **To tremble with rage,** trembler de rage. **To be stiff with cold,** être engourdi par le froid. **To be ill with typhoid fever,** être malade de la fièvre typhoïde. (c) **To fill a vase with water,** remplir un vase d'eau. **Endowed with beauty,** doué de beauté. **It is pouring with rain,** il pleut à verse. **5.** **To work with courage,** travailler avec courage. *To advance with great strides,* (s')avancer à grands pas. **To receive s.o. with open arms,** recevoir qn à bras ouverts. **With all due respect,** sauf votre respect. **With the object of** . . ., dans le but de. . . . **I say so with regret,** je le dis à regret. **With a few exceptions,** à part quelques exceptions; à peu d'exceptions près. **6.** (*Elliptical*) **Away with care!** bannissons les soucis!

withal [wi'ðɔ:l], *adv.* A: **Aussi, en même temps;** d'ailleurs, en outre, de plus.

withdraw [wið'drɔ:], *v.* (withdrew [-dru:]; withdrawn [-drɔ:n]) **1.** *v.tr.* (a) **Retirer (sa main); enlever (un étai);** tirer (le rideau). (b) **Ramener (des troupes) en arrière;** faire replier (des troupes). **To withdraw s.o. from an influence,** soustraire qn à une influence. (c) **To withdraw coins from circulation,** retirer des pièces de la circulation. **To withdraw a sum of money,** retirer une somme d'argent (de la caisse d'épargne, etc.). (d) Retirer (une offre, une promesse); reprendre (sa parole); revenir sur (une décision); renoncer à (une réclamation). **To withdraw a charge,** se rétracter. **To withdraw an order,** Com: annuler une commande; Adm: rapporter un décret. *Jur:* **To withdraw an action,** abandonner un procès; retirer sa plainte. **2.** *v.i.* **Se retirer** (*from,* de); s'éloigner. *Mil:* (*Of outposts*) **Se replier.** (*Of candidate*) **To withdraw in favour of s.o.,** se désister en faveur de qn. **To withdraw into oneself,** into silence, se renfermer en soi-même, dans le silence.

withdrawal [wið'drɔ:əl], *s.* **1.** (a) **Retrait** *m* (de troupes, d'une somme d'argent). W. *of capital,* retrait de fonds. (b) **Rappel** *m* (d'un décret); **rétractation** *f* (d'une promesse); retrait (d'une plainte). **2.** (a) **Retraite** *f.* Mil: **Repli** *m,* repliement *m* (des troupes). (b) **Withdrawal of a candidate,** désistement *m* d'un candidat.

withe [wiθ, wið, waːið], *s.* **Brin** *m* **d'osier.**

wither ['wiðər]. **1.** *v.i.* **To wither (up, away),** (*of plant*) se dessécher, dépérir; (*of flowers, beauty*) se passer; (*of pers.*) dépérir. **2.** *v.tr.* (a) **Dessécher, flétrir, faner, faire dépérir** (une plante, etc.). (b) *F:* **To wither s.o. with a look,** foudroyer qn du regard. **withering**¹, *a.* (a) Qui dessèche qui flétrit ; (vent) desséchant. (b) F : (Regard) foudroyant, écrasant. **-ly,** adv. F : D un regard foudroyant ; d'un ton de mépris. **withering²,** s. Dessèchement m.

withers ['wiðərz], s.pl. Garrot m (du cheval).

withershins ['wiðər∫inz], adv. Scot : A contresens ; de droite à gauche.

withhold [wið'hould], v.tr. (withheld [-held] ; withheld) **1.** (a) Refuser (son consentement) (from s.o., à qn). (b) **To withhold the truth from s.o.,** cacher la vérité à qn. (c) To withhold so much out of s.o.'s pay, retenir tant sur la paye de qn. (d) To withhold property, détenir des biens. **2.** To withhold s.o. from doing sth., retenir, empêcher, qn de faire qch.

within [wi'ðin]. **1.** adv. (a) A. & Lit : A l'intérieur ; dans la maison, chez soi. **Within and without,** à l'intérieur et à l'extérieur. **To go within,** entrer dans la maison, dans la chambre. **Make me pure within,** purifiez mon âme, mon cœur. (b) Th : A la cantonade. (c) Seen from within, vu de l'intérieur, du dedans. **2.** prep. (a) A l'intérieur de, en dedans de. Within four walls, entre quatre murs. Within the frontier, en deçà des frontières. A voice w. me said . . ., une voix intérieure me disait. . . . Within the committee, au sein de la commission. (b) To keep within the law, rester dans (les bornes de) la légalité ; F : se tenir dans les marges du code. **Within the meaning of the Act,** selon les prévisions de l'Acte. **To keep, live, within one's income,** ne pas dépasser son revenu. **To be well within the truth,** être en deçà, au-dessous, de la vérité. Weight within a pound, poids à une livre près. (c) Within sight, en vue. Within call, à (la) portée de·la voix. Situated within two miles of the town, situé à moins de deux milles de la ville. Within a radius of ten miles, dans un rayon de dix milles. **Within an inch of death,** à deux doigts de la mort. (d) Within an hour, dans, avant, une heure. Within the week, avant la fin de la semaine. Within a year of his death, (i) moins d'un an avant sa mort ; (ii) moins d'un an après sa mort. W. the next five years, d'ici cinq ans. W. the required time, dans le délai prescrit. Within a short time, (i) à court délai ; (ii) peu de temps après. They are within a few months of the same age, ils sont du même âge à quelques mois près. Within the memory of man, de mémoire d'homme.

without [wi'ðaut]. **1.** adv. A. & Lit : A l'extérieur, au dehors. Within and without, à l'intérieur et à l'extérieur. Seen from without, vu de l'extérieur, du dehors. **2.** prep. (a) A. & Lit : En dehors de. Without the walls, en dehors des murailles ; hors des murs. (b) Sans. To be without friends, être sans amis. To be without food, manquer de nourriture. He arrived without money or luggage, il arriva sans argent ni bagages. Not without difficulty, non sans difficulté. Without end, sans fin. He passed by without seeing me, without being seen, il passa sans me voir, sans être vu. It goes without saying that . . ., il va sans dire que. . . . That goes without saying, cela va sans dire. A year never passes without his writing to us, il ne se passe jamais une année sans qu'il nous écrive. To go, do, without sth., se passer de qch.

withstand [wið'stand, wið-], v.tr. (withstood [-stud] ; withstood) Résister à (qn, la douleur). To withstand pressure, supporter, résister à, la pression. Mil : To withstand an attack, soutenir une attaque.

withy ['wiði], s. **1.** Osier m. **2.** = WITHE.

witless ['witləs], a. (a) Sans intelligence ; sot, f. sotte. (b) Imbécile ; faible d'esprit.

witness¹ ['witnəs], s. **1.** Témoignage m. **To bear witness to, of, sth.,** rendre, porter, témoignage de qch. ; témoigner de qch. ; attester qch. In witness whereof, en témoignage de quoi, en foi de quoi. I call you to w., j'en appelle à votre témoignage. **2.** (Pers.) (a) Témoin m (d'un incident). (b) **Witness to a document,** témoin à un acte. (c) Témoin judiciaire. To call s.o. as a witness, citer qn comme témoin. The first w. was the wife of the accused, le premier témoin a été la femme de l'accusé. **3.** They are not all stay-at-homes, witness the three brothers who went to America, ils ne sont pas tous casaniers ; témoin les trois frères qui sont allés en Amérique. **'witness-box,** s. Jur : = Barre f des témoins.

witness², **1.** v.tr. (a) Être spectateur, témoin (d'une scène) ; assister à (une entrevue, etc.). She witnessed him do it, elle fut témoin de son action. (b) Attester (un acte) ; certifier (une signature). **2.** v.i. To witness to sth., témoigner de qch. To witness against s.o., témoigner contre qn.

-witted ['witid], a. Slow-witted, quick-witted, à l'esprit lourd, vif.

witticism ['witisizm], s. Trait m d'esprit ; bon mot.

wittiness ['witinəs], s. Esprit m ; sel m (d'une observation, etc.).

wittingly ['witiŋli]. See WIT³.

witty ['witi], a. (Of pers.) Spirituel ; (of remark) spirituel, piquant. **-ily,** adv. Spirituellement ; avec esprit.

wives [wa:ivz]. See WIFE.

wizard ['wizərd], s. Sorcier m, magicien m.

wizardry ['wizədri], s. Sorcellerie f, magie f.

wizened ['wizənd], a. Desséché, ratatiné ; (of cheeks, etc.) parcheminé ; (of face) vieillot.

wo [wou], int. (To horse) Ho !

woad [woud], s. **1.** Bot : (Dyer's) woad, pastel m des teinturiers ; guède f. **2.** Guède ; teinture bleue.

wobble¹ [wɔbl], s. **1.** (a) Branlement m, oscillation f ; tremblement m ; dandinement m (d'une roue). Aut : Front-wheel wobble, shimmy m. (b) (Of singer) Chevrotement m. **2.** F : Vacillation f, hésitation f.

wobble², v.i. **1.** (a) Ballotter ; (of pers. or car in motion) zigzaguer, tanguer ; (of pers.) tituber ; (of jelly, etc.) trembler ; (of table) branler. (b) (Of voice) Chevroter. **2.** F : (Of pers.) Hésiter, vaciller. **wobbling,** s. = WOBBLE¹.

wobbler ['wɔblər], s. Tergiversateur, -trice ; personne f aux opinions instables.

wobbly ['wɔbli], a. Branlant, vacillant ; hors d'aplomb. Wobbly chair, chaise bancale. Wobbly voice, voix tremblante, chevrotante. My legs are w., mes jambes flageolent.

woe [wou], s. Poet. & F : Malheur m, chagrin m, peine f. To tell one's tale of woe, faire le récit de ses malheurs, de ses infortunes ; conter ses doléances. Woe is me! pauvre de moi ! Woe to the vanquished! malheur aux vaincus ! **'woebegone¹,** a. (Of looks) Triste, désolé, abattu ; (of pers.) à l'air désolé, abattu.

wo(e)ful ['wouful], a. **1.** (Of pers.) Triste, affligé, malheureux. **2.** (Époque) de malheur, de misère ; (nouvelle) déplorable, attristante. **-fully,** adv. Tristement.

woke [wouk]. See WAKE³.

wold [would], s. Plaine onduleuse, vallonnée. The Wolds, les régions vallonnées (du comté d'York, etc.).

wolf¹, *pl.* **wolves** [wulf, wulvz], *s.* Loup *m.*
She-wolf, louve *f.* Wolf('s) cub, louveteau *m.*
Prairie wolf, coyote *m.* *F:* To cry wolf, crier
au loup. **To have the wolf by the ears**, tenir le
loup par les oreilles. **That will keep the wolf
from the door**, cela vous mettra à l'abri du besoin.
A wolf in sheep's clothing, un loup déguisé en
brebis. **'wolf-dog, 'wolf-hound,** *s.* **1.** Chien *m*
de chasse au loup; *esp.* lévrier *m* d'Irlande.
2. (*Alsatian*) Chien-loup *m.* **'wolf's-bane,** *s.*
Bot: Aconit *m.* **'wolf-tooth,** *s.* Surdent *f,*
dent *f* de loup (d'un cheval).
wolf², *v.tr.* To wolf (down) one's food, avaler sa
nourriture à grosses bouchées.
wolfish ['wulfiʃ], *a.* De loup; rapace, vorace, ou
cruel.
wolfram ['wulfrəm], *s.* (*a*) *Miner:* Wolfram *m*;
galène *f* de fer. (*b*) Tungstène *m.*
wolverine ['wulvəriːn], *s. Z:* Glouton *m.*
wolves [wulvz]. *See* WOLF¹.
woman, *pl.* **women** ['wumən, 'wimen], *s.f.*
1. Femme. (*a*) A young woman, une jeune
femme; (*unmarried*) une jeune personne. An
old woman, une vieille femme; *F:* une vieille.
F: Old woman's remedy, remède de bonne
femme. There's a woman in it, cherchez la
femme. To be always (running) after women,
courir les filles. (*b*) The new woman, la femme
des temps nouveaux. **2.** *Attrib.* Woman doctor,
pl. woman doctors *or* women doctors, femme
médecin. Woman friend, woman driver, amie;
chauffeuse. **3.** Milk-woman, laitière. Apple-
woman, marchande de pommes. Frenchwoman,
Française. **'woman-hater,** *s.* Misogyne *m.*
womanhood ['wumənhud], *s.* **1.** État *m,*
qualité *f,* de femme. She had now grown to w.,
c'était maintenant une femme (faite). **2.** *Coll.*
Les femmes.
womanish ['wuməniʃ], *a.* Efféminé.
womankind ['wumənkaind], *s.* **1.** Les femmes *f.*
2. One's womankind, les femmes de sa famille;
ses parentes *f.*
womanlike ['wumənlaik]. **1.** *a.* De femme.
2. *adv.* En femme; comme une femme.
womanliness ['wumənlinəs], *s.* (*a*) Caractère *m*
de femme; caractère féminin; féminité *f.*
(*b*) Charme féminin.
womanly ['wumənli], *a.* De femme, des femmes;
féminin. W. self-sacrifice, abnégation digne d'une
femme. She is so womanly, elle est si femme.
womb [wuːm], *s. Anat* Matrice *f.* *F:* In earth's
womb, dans le sein, dans les entrailles, de la terre.
women ['wimen]. *See* WOMAN.
womenfolk ['wimenfouk], *s.pl.* = WOMANKIND 2.
won [wʌn]. *See* WIN.
wonder¹ ['wʌndər], *s.* **1.** Merveille *f,* prodige *m.*
To work, do, wonders, faire, accomplir, des
merveilles, des prodiges. The seven wonders of
the world, les sept merveilles du monde. A
nine-days' wonder, la merveille d'un jour. It is
a wonder (that) he has not lost it, il est étonnant,
c'est miracle, qu'il ne l'ait pas perdu. The
wonder is that he found it, ce qu'il y a d'étonnant
c'est qu'il l'ait retrouvé. No wonder, little wonder,
that the scheme, failed, il n'est guère étonnant
que la chose n'ait pas réussi. For a wonder he
was in time, chose remarquable, par extraordinaire, il était à l'heure. He is ill, and no wonder,
il est malade, et rien d'étonnant. **2.** (i) Étonnement *m,* surprise *f.* (ii) Émerveillement *m.* To
fill s.o. with wonder, émerveiller qn; étonner
qn. **'wonder-struck,** *a.* Émerveillé. **'won-
der-worker,** *s.* Faiseur *m* de prodiges.

wonder². **1.** *v.i.* S'étonner, s'émerveiller (*at*, de).
I do not wonder at it, cela ne m'étonne pas.
That isn't to be wondered at, ce n'est pas
étonnant; rien d'étonnant à cela. I shouldn't
wonder, cela ne m'étonnerait pas. That set me
wondering, cela m'a intrigué. **2.** *v.tr.* (*a*) I wonder
he didn't kill you, je m'étonne qu'il ne vous ait
pas tué. (*b*) Se demander. I wonder whether he
will come, je me demande, je voudrais savoir,
s'il viendra. *I w. who invented that*, je suis curieux
de savoir qui a inventé celà. Their son will help
them.—I wonder! leur fils leur viendra en aide.
—Est-ce bien sûr? **wondering,** *a.* Étonné,
émerveillé. **-ly,** *adv.* D'un air étonné; avec
étonnement.
wonderful ['wʌndərful], *a.* Merveilleux, prodigieux, admirable. **Wonderful to relate . . . ,**
chose étonnante, chose remarquable. . . . It was
wonderful! *F:* c'était épatant! **-fully,** *adv.*
Merveilleusement. Wonderfully well, à merveille.
wonderland ['wʌndərland], *s.* Pays *m* des
merveilles.
wonderment ['wʌndərmənt], *s.* Étonnement *m*;
F: ébahissement *m.*
wondrous ['wʌndrəs], *a.* Étonnant; merveilleux. W. dexterity, dextérité prestigieuse. **-ly,**
adv. Merveilleusement. W. well, à merveille.
wont¹ [wount], *pred.a.* To be wont to do sth.,
avoir coutume, avoir l'habitude, de faire qch.
wont², *s.* Coutume *f,* habitude *f.* Use and wont,
l'usage *m*; les us *m* et coutumes. It is my wont
to . . . , c'est mon habitude de. . . . Oftener
than was his w., plus souvent que d'habitude, que
de coutume.
wont³, *aux.v.* (*p.t.* wont; *p.p.* wont *or* wonted)
A. & Lit: To wont to do sth., avoir coutume,
avoir l'habitude, de faire qch. **wonted,** *a.*
Habituel, accoutumé.
won't [wount]. *F:* = will not.
woo [wuː], *v.tr.* **1.** Faire la cour à, courtiser (une
femme); rechercher (une femme) en mariage.
2. Rechercher, courtiser (la fortune). **3.** Solliciter
(*s.o. to do sth.*, qn de faire qch.). **wooing,** *s.*
Cour *f*; recherche *f* en mariage.
wood [wud], *s.* **1.** Bois *m.* For: Crowded w.,
peuplement serré. Pine wood, bois de pins.
F: You can't see the wood for the trees, les
arbres empêchent de voir la forêt. We are not
yet out of the wood, nous ne sommes pas encore
tirés d'affaire. To take to the woods, s'enfuir; se
sauver; gagner le taillis. Wood folk, habitants
des bois. Wood lily, muguet des bois. **2.** (*Material*) Bois. Small wood (*for fires*), ramilles *fpl*;
ramée *f.* Wood pavement, pavage en bois. Wood
ash, cendre de bois. *F:* Touch wood! touchez
du bois! **3.** *Wine-m:* The wood, le tonneau,
la pièce, le fût. Wine in the wood, vin en pièce,
en cercles. Beer (*drawn*) from the wood, bière
tirée au fût. **4.** *Bowls:* Boule *f.* **'wood-
'block,** *s.* **1.** *Engr:* Planche *f,* bois *m.* **2.** Pavé *m*
de bois. **'wood-carving,** *s.* Sculpture *f* sur
bois. **'wood-cutter,** *s.* Bûcheron *m.* **'wood-
cutting,** *s.* **1.** Coupe *f* des bois. **2.** Gravure *f*
sur bois. **'wood-engraver,** *s.* Graveur *m* sur
bois. **'wood-engraving,** *s.* (*Process or print*)
Gravure *f* sur bois. **'wood-louse,** *pl.* **-lice,** *s.*
Cloporte *m*; *F:* porcelet *m.* **'wood-nymph,**
s.f. Nymphe des bois; hamadryade ou dryade
f. **'wood-pigeon,** *s. Orn:* (Pigeon *m*) ramier *m*;
palombe *f.* **'wood-pile,** *s.* Tas *m,* monceau *m,*
de bois. *S.a.* NIGGER. **'wood-pulp,** *s. Paperm:*
Pâte *f* de bois. **'wood-shed,** *s.* Bûcher *m.*
'wood-spirit, *s.* Esprit *m* de bois; alcool *m*

méthylique. **'wood-stack,** *s.* = WOOD-PILE.
'wood-wind [wind], *s. Mus:* Les bois *m.*
woodbine ['wudbain], *s.* **I.** *Bot:* (*a*) Chèvre-feuille *m* des bois. (*b*) *U.S:* Vigne *f* vierge. **2.** *P:* Cigarette *f* (à bon marché); cibiche *f*, sèche *f.*
woodchuck ['wudtʃʌk], *s.* Marmotte *f* d'Amé-rique.
woodcock ['wudkɔk], *s.* (*Usu. inv.*) Bécasse *f.*
woodcraft ['wudkrɑ:ft], *s.* Connaissance *f* (i) de la forêt, (ii) de la chasse à courre.
woodcraftsman, *pl.* **-men** ['wudkrɑ:ftsmən, -men], *s.m.* Trappeur; veneur.
woodcut ['wudkʌt], *s.* Gravure *f* sur bois; *F:* bois *m*; estampe *f.*
wooded ['wudid], *a.* Boisé, arbreux.
wooden ['wud(ə)n], *a.* **I.** De bois, en bois. **Wooden shoes,** sabots *m.* **2.** *F:* (*a*) (*Of movement, etc.*) Raide, gauche. (*b*) Sans intelligence; à l'esprit obtus. **'wooden-'headed,** *a.* Stupide. **'wooden 'spoon,** *s. Cu:* Mouvette *f.*
woodenness ['wudənnəs], *s.* Maintien compassé; raideur *f.*
woodland ['wudlənd], *s.* **I.** Pays boisé; bois *m.* **2.** *Attrib.* Des bois; sylvestre.
woodlander ['wudləndər], *s.* Habitant *m* des bois; forestier *m.*
woodman, *pl.* **-men** ['wudmən, -men], *s.m.* Bûcheron.
woodpecker ['wudpekər], *s. Orn:* Pic *m.* **Green woodpecker,** pivert *m.*
woodruff ['wudrʌf], *s. Bot:* Aspérule odorante.
woodsman, *pl.* **-men** ['wudzmən, -men], *s.m. Esp. U.S:* Chasseur (en forêt); trappeur; homme des bois.
woodwork ['wudwə:rk], *s.* **I.** Travail *m* du bois. (*a*) Construction *f* en bois; charpenterie *f.* (*b*) Menuiserie *f*, ébénisterie *f.* **2.** Bois travaillé. (*a*) Boiserie *f*, charpente *f.* (*b*) Menuiserie, ébénisterie *f; Veh:* carrosserie *f.*
woody ['wudi], *a.* **I.** Boisé, arbreux. *W. tract,* région couverte de bois. **2.** *Bot:* Ligneux.
wooer ['wu:ər], *s.* Amoureux *m*; prétendant *m.*
woof [wu:f], *s.* = WEFT I.
wool [wul], *s.* **I.** Laine *f.* (*a*) **Waste wool,** ploc *m. Tex:* Dyed in the wool, wool dyed, teint en laine. *U.S: F:* A **dyed-in-the-wool Irishman,** un Irlandais pur sang. **Wool cloth,** étoffe de laine. **The wool trade,** le commerce des laines. **Wool mill,** fabrique *f* de lainages. (*b*) **Knitting wool,** laine à tricoter. **2.** (*a*) Pelage *m* (d'animal). (*b*) *Bot:* Laine, duvet *m.* (*c*) Cheveux crépus, laine (des nègres). **3. Mineral wool,** coton minéral; laine de scorie(s). **Steel wool,** laine d'acier. *S.a.* COTTON-WOOL, GLASS-WOOL. **'wool-bearing,** *a.* Lanifère. **'wool-fat,** *s.* **I.** Suint *m.* **2.** *Com:* Lanoline *f.* **'wool-fell,** *s.* Peau *f* de mouton. **'wool-gathering.** *F:* (*a*) *s.* Rê-vasserie *f.* **Your wits have gone wool-gathering,** vous rêvassez; *F:* vous êtes dans la lune. *You've been w.-g.,* vous avez l'air de revenir de Pontoise. (*b*) *a.* Distrait. *You're w.-g.,* vous rêvassez. **'wool-hall,** *s.* Marché *m* aux laines. **'wool-waste,** *s.* Bourre *f* de laine.
woollen ['wulən], *a.* De laine. *W. stockings,* bas de laine. **Woollen cloth,** drap *m.* **Woollen goods,** *s.* **woollens,** lainages *m.*
woolliness ['wulinəs], *s.* **I.** Nature laineuse (*of,* de). **2.** *F:* Imprécision *f* (de raisonnement, etc.); manque *m* de netteté. **Woolliness of outline,** flou *m.*
woolly ['wuli]. **I.** *a.* (*a*) Laineux; de laine. *F:* **Woolly hair,** cheveux laineux, crépus. **Woolly clouds,** nuages ouatés. (*b*) (*Of fruit*)

Cotonneux. (*c*) (*Of style*) Mou; lâche. *W. out-lines,* contours flous, gras. *W.Tel:* Woolly reproduction, reproduction peu nette. **2.** *s.* (Vête-ment *m* en) tricot *m.*
woolsack ['wulsak], *s.* **I.** Sac *m* de laine. **2.** *Parl:* The **Woolsack,** le siège du Lord Chancelier.
woolwork ['wulwə:rk], *s.* Tapisserie *f.*
wop [wɔp], *s. U.S: P:* Immigrant italien; *F:* métèque *m.*
word[1] [wə:rd], *s.* **I.** Mot *m.* (*a*) Vocable *m.* **Word for word,** (répéter qch.) mot pour mot; (traduire qch.) mot à mot. **In a word,** en un mot; bref; pour tout dire. **In other words,** en d'autres termes. I told him in so many words that . . ., je lui ai dit en termes propres, en termes exprès, que. . . . **Bad is not the word for it,** mauvais n'est pas assez dire. (*b*) **Spoken words,** paroles *f.* **In the words of . . .,** selon l'expression de. . . . **To put a wish into words,** formuler un souhait. **To call upon s.o. to say a few words,** prier qn de prendre la parole. **A man of few words,** un homme qui parle peu, un homme sobre de paroles. **He never said a word,** il n'a pas soufflé mot. **I can't get a word out of him,** je ne peux pas le faire parler. **To put one's word in,** inter-venir; placer son mot. **Without a word,** sans mot dire. **With these words** he dismissed me, ce disant, là-dessus, il me congédia. **You have taken the words out of my mouth,** c'est justement ce que j'allais dire. *Conduct beyond words,* conduite inqualifiable, qui n'a pas de nom. He is too silly for words, il est d'une bêtise indicible. **Fair words, fine words,** belles paroles; *F:* eau bénite (de cour). *S.a.* LAST[2] I. **I.** (*c*) I want (to have) a word with you, j'aurais un mot à vous dire; j'ai affaire à vous. *I'll have a w. with him about it,* je lui en toucherai deux mots. **To say a good word for s.o.,** dire, glisser, un mot en faveur de qn. He never has a good word for anyone, il ne peut s'empêcher de dire du mal de son prochain. **A word in season,** un conseil opportun. *Prov:* A word to the wise (is sufficient), à bon entendeur salut. (*d*) **To have words with s.o.,** avoir une altercation avec qn; se disputer avec qn. **Words passed between them,** ils ont eu une dispute. **Words ran high,** la querelle s'échauffait. **2.** (*Speech*) **In word or in thought,** par la parole ou par la pensée. **By word of mouth,** de vive voix; verbalement. **To send s.o. word of** sth., faire dire, faire savoir, qch. à qn; prévenir qn de qch. **Word came that . . .,** on apporta la nouvelle, on nous manda, que. . . . **To bring word of** sth. to s.o., venir dire qch. à qn. **To leave word that . . .,** faire dire (à qn) que. . . . **4.** **To give s.o. one's word,** donner sa parole à qn. **To keep one's word,** to be as good as one's word, tenir (sa) parole. **To break one's word,** manquer à sa parole. **I give you my word for it, (you may) take my word for it,** croyez-m'en; je vous en réponds. *I take your w. for it,* je le crois sur votre parole; je m'en rapporte à vous. **He is a man of his word,** c'est un homme de parole. **To take s.o. at his word,** prendre qn au mot. **His word is as good as his bond,** sa parole vaut sa signature; il n'a qu'une parole. **Upon my word!** ça c'est trop fort! ça c'est raide! **My word!** fichtre! **5. Word of command,** ordre *m*, commandement *m.* **To give the word (to do** sth.), (i) donner l'ordre, (ii) donner le signal (de faire qch.). **The word has gone round,** on s'est passé le mot. *F:* **Sharp's the word!** (faites) vite! **6.** *Theol:* (*a*) **The Word of God,** la parole de Dieu. (*b*) **The Word was made flesh,** le Verbe s'est fait chair. **'word-book,** *s.* Vocabulaire *m*, lexique *m.*

'**word-'perfect,** *a.* Qui connaît parfaitement son rôle, sa leçon. '**word-picture,** *s.* Description imagée. '**word-play,** *s.* Jeu *m* sur les mots. **word²,** *v.tr.* Formuler par écrit; énoncer (un problème); rédiger (un télégramme); libeller (un document). **Thus worded,** ainsi conçu. **Well worded,** bien exprimé. **wording,** *s.* **1.** Rédaction *f*, libellé *m* (d'un document); énoncé *m* (d'un problème). **2.** Mots *mpl*; langage *m*; termes *mpl* (d'un acte, etc.). **Form of wording** *for a cheque*, formule *f* de chèque.
wordiness ['wɔːrdinəs], *s.* Verbosité *f*.
wordy ['wɔːrdi], *a.* **1.** Verbeux, prolixe, diffus; (style) délayé. **2. Wordy warfare,** lutte *f* oratoire.
wore ['wɔːr]. *See* WEAR².
work¹ [wɔːrk], *s.* **1.** Travail *m*. **To be at work,** être au travail; travailler. **The forces at work,** les forces en jeu. **To set to work,** se mettre au travail, à l'œuvre, à l'ouvrage. **To set s.o. to work,** mettre qn à l'ouvrage. **To set a machine to work,** mettre une machine en marche. **To go the right way to work,** s'y prendre bien. **Health work,** services *mpl* d'hygiène. *The w. is suspended,* on a suspendu les travaux. **2.** *(Work to be done)* (*a*) Travail, ouvrage *m*, besogne *f*, tâche *f*. **I have so much work to do,** j'ai tellement (de travail) à faire. **A piece of work,** un travail, un ouvrage, une œuvre. **The brandy had done its work,** l'eau-de-vie avait fait son effet. **I have my work cut out,** j'ai de quoi faire. *You have your w. cut out with him,* il vous donnera du fil à retordre. **To do s.o.'s dirty work,** faire les sales besognes de qn. **Day's work,** (travail d'une) journée. *F:* It's all in a day's work, c'est l'ordinaire de mon existence. (*b*) **It was bloody work,** ç'a été une sanglante affaire. **It was thirsty work,** c'était un travail qui donnait soif. *S.a.* SHORT¹ I. 2. **3.** (*a*) **The works of God,** les œuvres *f* de Dieu. **Good works,** (les) bonnes œuvres. (*b*) Ouvrage, œuvre. **A historical work,** un ouvrage historique. **The works of Shakespeare,** les œuvres *f* de Shakespeare; l'œuvre *m* de Shakespeare. **A work of art,** une œuvre d'art. **4. To be out of work,** être sans travail, sans emploi; chômer. **To throw s.o. out of work,** priver qn de travail; réduire qn au chômage. **5.** *pl. Mil:* **Defensive works,** ouvrages défensifs. **Field works,** travaux de campagne. **6.** *pl. Civ.E:* **Constructive works,** ouvrages d'art. **Public works,** travaux publics. **7.** *pl.* Rouages *mpl*, mécanisme *m*, mouvement *m* (d'une horloge). **8.** *pl.* *(Often with sg. const.)* Usine *f*, atelier *m*. **Gas-works,** usine à gaz. *Dye-works,* teinturerie *f*. *Steel-works,* aciérie *f*. **9. Chased work,** ouvrage ciselé. **Stucco work,** ouvrage de stuc. **Bright work,** parties polies (d'une machine). **10.** *Nau:* **Upper works,** œuvres mortes, le(s) haut(s). '**work-bag,** *s.* Sac *m* à ouvrage. '**work-basket,** *s.* Corbeille *f*, nécessaire *m*, à ouvrage. '**work-bench,** *s.* Établi *m*. '**work-box,** *s* Boîte *f* à ouvrage. '**work-day,** *s.* Jour *m* ouvrable. '**work-room,** *s.* (*a*) Atelier *m*. (*b*) *(For needlework)* Ouvroir *m* (d'une communauté). '**work-shy,** *a. F:* Qui boude à la besogne; *P:* qui a un poil (dans la main). '**work-table,** *s.* Table *f* à ouvrage.
work², *v.* (*p.t. & p.p.* worked [wɔːrkt], *A: and in a few set phrases* wrought [rɔːt]) I. *v.i.* **1.** (*a*) Travailler. **To work hard,** travailler dur, ferme. **To work like a nigger, like a horse,** travailler comme un nègre; peiner comme un cheval. *I am working at a shawl,* je travaille à un châle. **To work at music,** travailler la musique. (*b*) **To work for an end,** travailler pour atteindre un but. **Working**

from the principle that . . ., partant du principe que. . . . **2.** (*a*) *(Of machine, etc.)* Fonctionner, aller. **System that works well,** système qui fonctionne bien. *The pump isn't working,* la pompe ne marche pas. *Wireless set working on all voltages,* appareil marchant sur tous courants. **These tools work by compressed air,** ces outils sont actionnés par l'air comprimé. (*b*) **Drug that works,** médicament qui produit son effet, qui agit. **His scheme did not work,** son plan a échoué, n'a pas réussi. **3.** *(Of yeast, etc.)* Fermenter. **4.** (*a*) **His mouth was working,** i tordait la bouche; sa bouche se crispait. (*b*) *(Of sailing ship)* **To w. southwards,** remonter vers le sud (contre ie vent). *(Of angler)* **To work upstream,** remonter le courant. II. **work,** *v.tr.* **1.** Faire travailler. *He works his men too hard,* il surmène ses hommes. **To work oneself to death,** se tuer à force de travailler. **2.** (*a*) Faire fonctionner, faire marcher (une machine); faire jouer (un ressort); actionner (le frein). *(Of machine)* **To be worked by electricity,** marcher à l'électricité. (*b*) Diriger (un service de voitures). (*c*) **To work a scheme,** mettre un plan à exécution. **3.** (*a*) Faire, opérer (un miracle); opérer (une guérison); amener (un changement). **To work mischief,** semer la discorde. *The destruction wrought by the fire,* la dévastation causée par l'incendie. *F:* **I will work it if I can,** je vais tâcher de manigancer ça. (*b*) **To work a sum,** faire un calcul; résoudre un problème. **4.** Broder (un dessin). **Worked with silver,** lamé d'argent. **5.** (*a*) **To work an incident into a book,** introduire un incident dans un livre. (*b*) **To work one's hands free,** parvenir à dégager ses mains. (*c*) **He worked his way to the front of the crowd,** il se fraya un chemin jusqu'au premier rang de la foule. **6.** (*a*) Travailler, façonner (le bois); ouvrer (les métaux précieux). (*b*) **To work the iron into a horseshoe,** façonner, forger, le fer en fer à cheval. (*c*) **He worked himself into a rage,** il se mit à peu en colère. **7.** (*a*) Exploiter (une mine). (*b*) **Traveller working the south-eastern district,** commis voyageur qui fait le sud-est. **8.** *Nau:* **To work one's passage,** gagner son passage par son travail. **work down,** *v.i.* **His stockings are working down,** ses bas descendent, tombent. **work in. 1.** *v.tr.* Faire entrer (qch.) peu à peu. **2.** *v.i.* Pénétrer peu à peu. **work off. 1.** *v.tr.* Se dégager de (qch.); cuver (sa colère). **To work off one's fat,** se débarrasser de sa graisse par le travail. **To work off one's bad temper on s.o.,** passer sa mauvaise humeur sur qn. **2.** *v.i.* *(Of nut, etc.)* Se détacher. **work on,** *v.i.* **1.** Continuer à travailler. **2.** (*a*) *We have no data to w. on,* nous n'avons pas de données sur lesquelles nous baser. (*b*) **To work on s.o.,** agir sur qn. **work out. 1.** *v.tr.* (*a*) Mener à bien. **To work out one's salvation,** faire son salut. **To work out one's time,** *(of apprentice)* finir son temps. (*b*) Développer (une idée); élaborer (un projet). *The plan is being worked out,* le projet est à l'étude. (*c*) Supputer (un compte); résoudre (un problème). *Nau:* **To work out one's position,** calculer le point. **2.** *v.i.* (*a*) Sortir peu à peu. (*b*) *It worked out very well for me,* je m'en suis bien trouvé. (*c*) **How much does it work out at?** par combien cela se chiffre-t-il? **The total works out at six pounds,** le total s'élève à six livres. **work up. 1.** *v.i.* (*a*) *(Of garment)* Remonter. (*b*) **What are you working up to?** à quoi voulez-vous en venir? *S.a.* CLIMAX 2. **2.** *v.tr.* (*a*) Préparer (la matière première). *Phot:* **To work up a negative,** travailler, retoucher, un cliché. (*b*) Développer (une situation dramatique); élaborer (un article). **To work up a connexion,** se faire une clientèle. (c) Préparer (un sujet). (d) Exciter, émouvoir (qn). *To be worked up,* être emballé. **wrought up,** a. *Lit:* Excité, agité. **wrought,** a. (a) Travaillé, ouvré, façonné. (b) (*Of metals*) Ouvré, forgé, battu. **Wrought-iron pipe,** tuyau en fer forgé. **working**[1], a. **1.** (a) Qui travaille; ouvrier. **The working classes,** la classe ouvrière. **Working man,** ouvrier *m* ou homme *m* de peine. **Working woman,** ouvrière *f.* (b) *Mil:* **Working party,** atelier *m,* équipe *f.* **2.** Qu. fonctionne. (a) **Working parts of a machine,** parties ouvrières, actives, d'une machine. (b) **Working loom,** métier battant. **Not working,** hors d'action. *S.a.* SURFACE[1] 1. (c) **Working agreement,** modus vivendi *m.* **Working majority,** majorité suffisante. **Working theory,** théorie qui donne des résultats. **working**[2], s. **1.** Travail *m.* **Working clothes,** vêtements de travail. **Working day** = WORK-DAY. **2.** (a) Manœuvre *f* (d'une machine). **Working gear,** organes *mpl* de manœuvre. (b) Mise *f* en œuvre (d'un procédé); exploitation *f* (d'une mine). **Working expenses,** frais généraux. **Working capital,** capital d'exploitation. **Working drawing,** épure *f.* (c) Fonctionnement *m.* **Difficult in the working,** difficile dans la pratique. **3.** Marche *f,* fonctionnement (d'un mécanisme). **To alter the working of the trains,** modifier la marche des trains. *El.E:* **Working voltage,** tension *f* de régime. **In working order,** en état de service. **To be in good working order,** bien fonctionner. **4.** The workings of the mind, le travail de l'esprit. **5.** *pl. Min:* **Workings,** chantiers *m* d'exploitation.

workable ['wə:rkəbl], a. **1.** (Bois) ouvrable. **2.** (Mine) exploitable. **3.** (Projet) réalisable. **workaday** ['wə:rkədei], a. (a) De tous les jours. (b) This workaday world, ce monde prosaïque.

worker ['wə:rkər], s. **1.** (a) Travailleur, -euse. *To be a hard w.,* travailler dur; *F:* être un piocheur. (b) Ouvrier, -ère. **The workers,** les classes laborieuses. *Adm:* **Workers,** employés et ouvriers. *S.a.* BLACK-COATED. **2.** **Worker-bee,** abeille ouvrière. **3.** **Worker of miracles,** faiseur *m* de miracles.

workhouse ['wə:rkhaus], s. Asile *m* des pauvres; hospice *m.* **To end one's days in the workhouse,** finir ses jours à l'hôpital. *To bring s.o. to the w.,* *F:* mettre qn sur la paille.

workman, *pl.* **-men** ['wə:rkmən, -men], *s.m.* Ouvrier, artisan. **Workmen's dwellings,** habitations ouvrières.

workmanlike ['wə:rkmənlaik], a. **1.** Bien fait, bien travaillé. **2.** **To do sth. in a workmanlike manner,** faire qch. en bon ouvrier.

workmanship ['wə:rkmənʃip], s. *Ind:* Exécution *f;* fini *m* de l'exécution; façon *f.* *Sound w.,* construction soignée. **Of fine workmanship,** d'un beau travail.

workpeople ['wə:rkpi:pl], *s.pl.* Ouvriers *m;* ouvriers et ouvrières.

workshop ['wə:rkʃop], s. Atelier *m.*

workwoman, *pl.* **-women** ['wə:rkwumən, -wimen], s. Ouvrière.

world [wə:rld], s. Monde *m.* **1.** (a) In this world, en ce monde; ici-bas. **The other world, the next world, the world to come,** l'autre monde. **He is not long for this world,** il n'en a pas pour long-temps à vivre. **To go to a better world,** partir pour l'autre monde. **World without end,** jusqu'à la fin des siècles. (b) **To be alone in the world,** être seul au monde. **Nothing in the world,** rien au monde; rien du tout. *What in the w. is the*

matter with you? mais qu'est-ce que vous avez donc? **I would not do it for (all) the world,** je ne le ferais pour rien au monde. **He was for all the world like . . .,** il avait exactement l'air de. ... **I would give the world to know . . .,** je donnerais n'importe quoi pour savoir. . . . **2. To go round the world,** faire le tour du monde. **He has seen the world,** il a vu du pays. *F:* **To knock about the world,** rouler sa bosse. **Map of the world,** carte universelle; (*in two hemi-spheres*) mappemonde *f.* **All the world over,** dans le monde entier. **How small the world is!** que le monde est petit! **World congress,** congrès mondial. **3.** **It's the way of the world,** ainsi va le monde. **Man of the world,** homme qui connaît la vie. **He has gone down in the world,** il a connu des jours meilleurs. **To have the world before one,** avoir toute sa carrière devant soi. **What will the world say?** qu'en dira-t-on? **4.** (a) **The theatrical world,** le milieu du théâtre. **The sporting world,** le monde du sport. (b) **The animal world,** le monde animal. **5.** *F:* **A world of money,** un argent fou. **To give oneself a world of trouble,** se donner un mal de chien. **To think the world of s.o.,** avoir une très haute opinion de qn. **'world-'famous,** a. De renommée mondiale. **'world-politics,** *s.pl.* Politique mondiale. **'world-power,** *s. Pol:* Puissance mondiale. **'world-'war,** *s.* Guerre mondiale. **'world-weary,** a. Fatigué du monde. **'world-'wide,** a. Universel; répandu partout; mon-dial, -aux.

worldliness ['wə:rldlinəs], s. Mondanité *f.*

worldling ['wə:rldliŋ], s. Mondain, -aine.

worldly ['wə:rldli], a. **1.** Du monde, de ce monde, d'ici-bas. **Worldly wisdom,** la sagesse du monde, du siècle. **Worldly interests,** soucis matériels. **2.** Mondain. **'worldly-'minded,** a. Attaché aux choses matérielles.

worm[1] [wə:rm], s. Ver *m.* **1.** (a) Earthworm, ver de terre; lombric *m.* *F:* **The worm has turned,** il en a assez de se laisser mener par le bout du nez. **He is a worm,** c'est un piètre personnage. (b) *Ent:* (i) Larve *f;* (ii) mite *f.* *F:* **The worm of conscience,** le ver rongeur. *S.a.* BLIND-WORM, BOOK-WORM, SILKWORM, etc. (c) *Med: Vet:* **To have worms,** avoir des vers. **2.** (a) Filet *m* (de vis). (b) Vis *f* sans fin. **Worm and sector,** vis et secteur. **Conveyor worm,** hélice transporteuse. (c) Serpentin *m* (d'alambic). **'worm-bit,** *s. Tls:* Mèche *f* à vis. **'worm-cast,** *s.* Déjection *f* de ver de terre. **'worm-drive,** *s. Aut: etc:* Transmission *f* par vis sans fin. **'worm-eaten,** a. Rongé des vers, piqué des vers; (*of wood*) vermoulu. **'worm-gear,** *s. Mec.E:* Engrenage *m* à vis sans fin. **'worm-hole,** *s.* (*In cloth, wood*) Piqûre *f.* **'worm-like,** a. Vermiforme, vermiculaire. **'worm-powder,** *s.* Poudre *f* vermifuge.

worm[2], *v.tr.* (a) **To worm (oneself, one's way) through the undergrowth,** se glisser, se faufiler, à travers les buissons. **To worm oneself into s.o.'s favour,** s'insinuer dans les bonnes grâces de qn. (b) **To worm a secret out of s.o.,** tirer un secret de qn. *I'll w. it out of him,* je vais lui tirer les vers du nez.

wormwood ['wə:rmwud], s. *Bot:* Armoise amère; absinthe *f.* *F:* **Life to him was gall and wormwood,** la vie pour lui n'était qu'amertume et dégoût.

worn [wo:rn]. *See* WEAR[2].

worry[1] ['wʌri], s. Ennui *m,* tracasserie *f,* tracas *m.* **Money worries,** soucis *m* d'argent. *He has always been a w. to me,* il a fait le tourment de ma vie.

F: **What's your worry?** qu'est-ce qu'il y a qui cloche?

worry², *v.* (worried) I. *v.tr.* (*a*) (*Of dog*) Harceler, piller (les moutons); prendre avec les dents et secouer (un rat). (*b*) *F:* **To worry out a problem,** s'évertuer à résoudre un problème. (*c*) Tourmenter, tracasser, harceler, *P:* asticoter (qn). *Baby has a cough and it rather worries me,* mon bébé tousse, cela me taquine, m'inquiète. **To worry oneself,** se tourmenter, se tracasser; se faire du mauvais sang, de la bile. *He worries me to death,* il est assommant. 2. *v.i.* Se tourmenter, se tracasser, s'inquiéter; se faire de la bile, du mauvais sang. **Don't (you) worry!** soyez tranquille! *P:* vous en faites pas! **Don't worry about me,** ne vous tracassez pas sur mon compte; ne vous inquiétez pas de moi. **We'll worry along somehow,** on se débrouillera. **worried,** *a.* **To be** *w.,* (i) être en proie à l'inquiétude; (ii) avoir du tracas, des ennuis. *To look w.,* avoir l'air soucieux.

worse [wəːrs]. I. *a. & s.* Pire; plus mauvais. *I am a worse player than he,* je joue plus mal que lui. *In w. condition,* dans un plus mauvais état. *This is worse and worse,* c'est de mal en pis. **To make matters worse . . .,** par, pour, surcroît de malheur. . . . *It might have been worse,* ce n'est qu'un demi-mal. **He escaped with nothing worse than a fright,** il en fut quitte pour la peur. *He is in a worse way than you,* il est plus malade que vous. **So much the worse for him,** tant pis pour lui. *He escaped none the worse,* il s'en est tiré sans aucun mal. *I think none the w. of him because he accepted,* je n'ai pas moins bonne opinion de lui parce qu'il a accepté. *S.a.* DRINK¹ 3, LUCK I, WEAR¹ I. 2. *s.* (*a*) **But there was worse to come,** mais il y eut plus grave. **I have been through worse than that,** j'en ai vu bien d'autres. (*b*) **To change for the worse,** s'altérer. *S.a.* BETTER¹ 2. 3. *adv.* (*a*) Pis; plus mal. *He behaves worse than ever,* il se conduit plus mal que jamais. **You might do worse,** vous pourriez faire pis. **To think worse of s.o.,** avoir plus mauvaise opinion de qn. *He is worse off than before,* sa situation a empiré. (*b*) *The noise went on w. than ever,* le vacarme recommença de plus belle.

worsen ['wəːrs(ə)n]. I. *v.tr.* Empirer (un mal); aggraver. 2. *v.i.* Empirer; (*of evil*) s'aggraver.

worship¹ ['wəːrʃip], *s.* I. Culte *m,* adoration *f.* **Worship of images,** idolâtrie *f.* **Divine worship,** le culte divin. **Public worship,** l'exercice *m* du culte. **Hours of worship,** heures des offices. **Place of worship,** édifice *m* du culte; église *f,* temple *m.* *F:* **To be an object of worship,** être un objet d'adoration. 2. **His Worship the Mayor,** son Honneur le maire. **Yes, your Worship,** oui, monsieur le maire, monsieur le juge.

worship², *v.tr.* (worshipped) I. Rendre un culte à, adorer (un dieu). 2. Adorer (qn); aimer (qn) à l'adoration. *To w. money,* faire son idole de l'argent. *He worships the ground she treads on,* il baise la trace de ses pas. 3. *Abs.* **Where does he w.?** à quel temple va-t-il?

worshipful ['wəːrʃipful], *a.* Honorable.

worshipper ['wəːrʃipər], *s.* Adorateur, -trice. **The worshippers** (*in a church*), les fidèles *m.*

worst¹ [wəːrst]. I. *a.* (Le) pire, (le) plus mauvais. *His w. mistake,* sa plus grave erreur. *His w. enemy,* son pire ennemi. 2. *s.* **The worst of the storm is over,** le plus fort de la tempête est passé. **That's the worst of cheap shoes,** c'est le désavantage des souliers bon marché. **When things are at their worst,** quand les choses sont au pire. **To get the worst of it** (*in a fight*), avoir le dessous. **If the**

worst comes to the worst, en mettant les choses au pis. **Do your worst!** faites du pis que vous pourrez! **The worst is soon over,** le plus mauvais moment est vite passé. 3. *adv.* (Le) pis, (le) plus mal. *The w. educated,* le moins instruit.

worst², *v.tr.* Battre, vaincre. **To be worsted,** succomber; avoir le dessous.

worsted ['wustid], *s. Tex:* (*a*) Laine peignée; estame *f.* (*b*) Laine à tricoter, à tapisserie.

worth¹ [wəːrθ]. I. *pred. a.* Valant. (*a*) **To be worth so much,** valoir tant. *That is worth something,* cela a de la valeur. *It is not worth much,* cela n'a pas grande valeur. *Whatever it may be worth,* vaille que vaille. **Worth the money,** avantageux. *I tell you this for what it is worth,* je vous passe ce renseignement sans y attribuer grande valeur. *It would be as much as my life is worth,* ce serait risquer ma vie. (*b*) **It is not worth the trouble,** cela ne, n'en, vaut pas la peine. **Is it worth while?** *F:* is it worth it? cela (en) vaut-il la peine? **Book worth reading,** livre qui mérite d'être lu. **A thing worth having,** une chose précieuse. *It is w. thinking about,* cela mérite réflexion. *It's w. knowing,* c'est bon à savoir. (*c*) **He is worth money,** il a de l'argent. **To die worth a million,** mourir en laissant un million. *That is all I am w.,* voilà tout mon avoir. *F:* **For all one is worth,** de toutes ses forces. 2. *s.* Valeur *f.* **Persons of (sterling) worth,** personnes de valeur, de mérite. **Give me two shillings' worth of chocolate,** donnez-moi pour deux shillings de chocolat. **To want one's money's worth,** en vouloir pour son argent.

worth², *v.i. A. & Poet:* (*Only in*) **Woe worth the day!** maudit soit le jour!

worthiness ['wəːrðinəs], *s.* Mérite *m.*

worthless ['wəːrθləs], *a.* Sans valeur, de nulle valeur; mauvais. *W. fellow,* vaurien *m.*

worthlessness ['wəːrθləsnəs], *s.* Peu *m* de valeur; nature *f* méprisable (de qn).

worthy ['wəːrði]. I. *a.* Digne. (*a*) *A w. man,* un digne homme; un homme estimable. *F:* **Our worthy friend,** notre brave ami. (*b*) **To be worthy of sth.,** être digne de qch. **To be worthy of death,** mériter la mort. **It is worthy of note that . . .,** il est à noter que . . . (*c*) **Foeman worthy of my steel,** ennemi digne de mon épée. 2. *s.* (*a*) *A:* Personnage éminent. (*b*) *F. & Hum:* Personnage (de l'endroit). **The village worthies,** les gros bonnets du village. **-ily,** *adv.* I. Dignement. 2. A juste titre.

wot [wɔt], *v.i. See* WIT³.

would [wud]. *See* WILL³. **'would-be,** *a.* Prétendu, soi-disant.

wound¹ [wuːnd], *s.* (*a*) Blessure *f. Slight w. in the arm,* atteinte *f* au bras. (*b*) Plaie *f. The w. is festering,* la plaie s'envenime. **'wound-stripe,** *s. Mil:* Chevron *m* de blessé.

wound², *v.tr.* Blesser; faire une blessure à (qn). *Wounded in the shoulder,* atteint à l'épaule. **To wound s.o. in his pride,** blesser qn dans son orgueil. *To w. s.o.'s feelings,* froisser qn. **The wounded,** les blessés.

wound³ [waund]. *See* WIND²ʼ³.

wove [wouv], **woven** ['wouv(ə)n]. *See* WEAVE².

wrack [rak], *s.* I. Varec(h) *m.* 2. Laisse (déposée sur le rivage).

wraith [reiθ], *s.* (*a*) Apparition spectrale (d'un mort). (*b*) Double spectral d'une personne (présage de sa mort).

wrangle¹ [raŋgl], *s.* Dispute *f,* querelle *f.*

wrangle², *v.i.* Se disputer, se quereller. **wrangling,** *s.* Disputes *fpl,* querelles *fpl.*

wrangler ['raŋglər], *s.* I. Querelleur, -euse.

2. (*At Cambridge University*) Étudiant sorti dans la première classe à l'examen de mathématiques. **wrap**[1] [rap], *s.* (*a*) (*Usu. pl.*) Wraps, couvertures *f* (de voyage); châles *m.* (*b*) Pèlerine *f*; manteau *m.* (*c*) Morning wrap, saut-de-lit *m.* Evening wrap, manteau du soir; sortie *f* de bal. **wrap**[2], *v.tr.* (wrapped [rapt]) **1.** (*a*) Envelopper. To wrap sth. (up) in paper, envelopper qch. dans du papier. (*b*) To wrap oneself up, *abs.* to wrap up, se couvrir de vêtements chauds; s'emmitoufler. (*c*) To wrap up one's meaning in obscure language, envelopper sa pensée de paroles obscures. **2.** To wrap sth. round sth., enrouler qch. autour de qch. **3.** To wrap a tyre, bandeler un pneu. *El.E:* To wrap a cable (in cotton), guiper un câble. **wrapped,** *a.* **1.** (*a*) *W. in paper*, roulé dans du papier. (*b*) (*Of pers.*) Wrapped up, bien enveloppé; emmitouflé. (*c*) Affair wrapped in mystery, affaire enveloppée de mystère. **2.** (*a*) Wrapped in meditation, plongé dans ses pensées; absorbé dans ses réflexions. (*b*) To be wrapped up in s.o., vivre entièrement pour qn. *He is w. up in his work*, il est entièrement absorbé par son travail. **wrapping,** *s.* (*a*) Enveloppe *f*, couverture *f*. (*b*) Papier *m*, toile *f*, d'emballage. (*c*) (*Of momie.*) Bandelettes *f* (de momie). **'wrapping-paper,** *s.* Papier *m* d'emballage.

wrapper ['rapər], *s.* **1.** Toile *f* d'emballage; feuille *f* de papier d'emballage. **2.** (*a*) Chemise *f* (d'un dossier). (*b*) Couverture *f* (d'un livre); couvre-livre *m.* **3.** Bande *f* (de journal). **4.** *Tchn:* Couvre-joint *m*; fourrure *f*. **5.** Robe *f* de chambre (de dame); saut-de-lit *m.*

wrath [rɔ:θ], *s. Lit:* Colère *f*; courroux *m.*

wrathful ['rɔ:θful], *a. Lit:* Courroucé.

wreak [ri:k], *v.tr.* To wreak one's wrath upon s.o., décharger sa colère sur qn. To wreak vengeance on s.o., se venger de qn.

wreath [ri:θ, *pl.* ri:ðz], *s.* **1.** Couronne *f*, guirlande *f* (de fleurs). Funeral wreath, couronne mortuaire. **2.** Volute *f*, panache *m* (de fumée).

wreathe [ri:ð]. **1.** *v.tr.* (*a*) Enguirlander; couronner de fleurs (le front de qn). Mountain wreathed with mist, montagne couronnée de brouillard. Face wreathed in smiles, visage rayonnant. (*b*) Entrelacer, tresser (des fleurs). (*c*) To wreathe sth. round sth., enrouler qch. autour de qch. **2.** *v.i.* (*Of smoke*) Tourbillonner.

wreck[1] [rek], *s.* **1.** (*a*) *Jur:* Wreck of the sea, épaves *fpl* de mer. (*b*) Navire naufragé; épave. *Ins:* Total wreck, navire entièrement perdu. *F:* The building is a mere wreck, le bâtiment n'est qu'une ruine. He is a perfect wreck, sa santé est ruinée. To be a nervous wreck, avoir les nerfs détraqués. *To collect the w. of one's fortune,* recueillir les débris de sa fortune. **2.** Naufrage *m* (d'un navire). To suffer wreck, faire naufrage. *To be saved from the w.,* échapper au naufrage.

wreck[2], *v.tr.* (*a*) Faire faire naufrage à (un navire); causer le naufrage d'un navire. To be wrecked, faire naufrage. (*b*) Faire dérailler (un train); démolir, détruire, ruiner (un édifice). To wreck one's digestion, se détraquer l'estomac. (*c*) Faire échouer, *F:* saboter (une entreprise); détruire, ruiner (les espérances de qn). **wrecked,** *a.* (Vaisseau) naufragé, qui a fait naufrage; (marin) naufragé. *W. life,* existence brisée. *W. health,* santé ruinée. **wrecking,** *s.* Destruction *f* (d'un navire); déraillement *m* (d'un train); ruine *f* (des espérances de qn). Wrecking policy, politique de sabotage.

wreckage ['rekedʒ], *s.* Épaves éparses; débris *mpl.* Piece of wreckage, épave.

wrecker ['rekər], *s.* **1.** Naufrageur *m*; pilleur *m* d'épaves. **2.** Destructeur *m* (*of*, de); dérailleur *m* (de trains).

wren [ren], *s. Orn:* **1.** Troglodyte mignon; *F:* roitelet *m.* **2.** Golden-crested wren, roitelet huppé.

wrench[1] [renʃ], *s.* **1.** Mouvement violent de torsion. To give sth. a wrench, tordre qch. violemment. *With a w. he pulled off the knocker,* d'un effort violent il arracha le marteau. He gave his ankle a wrench, il s'est donné une entorse. It will be a wrench to leave them, il m'en coûtera de les quitter. **2.** *Tls:* Clef *f* (à écrous); tourne-à-gauche *m inv.*

wrench[2], *v.tr.* **1.** (*a*) Tordre; tourner violemment. To wrench the lid open, forcer le couvercle. To wrench off, out, arracher, enlever (avec un violent effort de torsion). (*b*) To wrench sth. from s.o., arracher qch. à qn. *She wrenched herself free,* d'une secousse elle se dégagea. (*c*) To wrench one's ankle, se donner une entorse. *To w. one's shoulder,* se fouler, se forcer, l'épaule. **2.** Forcer, fausser (le sens d'un passage).

wrest[1] [rest], *s. Mus:* Clef *f* d'accordeur. **'wrest-block,** *s.* Sommier *m* (de piano). **'wrest-pin,** *s.* Cheville *f* (d'accordage) (d'un piano).

wrest[2], *v.tr.* **1.** Arracher (*from*, à). **2.** Forcer, fausser, tordre (le sens d'un passage); *F:* donner une entorse à (la vérité).

wrestle[1] [resl], *s.* Lutte *f* (corps à corps); assaut *m* de lutte. *To have a w. with s.o.,* lutter avec, contre, qn.

wrestle[2]. **1.** *v.i.* (*a*) To wrestle with s.o., lutter avec, contre, qn. *To w. for a prize,* disputer un prix à la lutte. (*b*) To wrestle with sth., lutter contre (les difficultés); résister (à la tentation); être aux prises avec (l'adversité); s'attaquer à (un problème); s'escrimer à (un sujet). To wrestle in prayer, prier avec ferveur. **2.** *v.tr.* Lutter avec, contre (qn). To wrestle a fall with s.o., faire un assaut de lutte avec qn. **wrestling,** *s.* Sport *m* de la lutte; lutte (corps à corps). All-in wrestling, combat *m* en lutte libre. Wrestling match, assaut *m* (de lutte).

wrestler ['reslər], *s.* Lutteur *m.*

wretch [retʃ], *s.* **1.** Malheureux, -euse; infortuné, -ée. Poor wretch, pauvre diable *m.* **2.** (*a*) Scélérat, -ate. You wretch! misérable! (*b*) You little wretch! petit fripon!

wretched ['retʃid], *a.* **1.** (*Of pers.*) Misérable, malheureux, infortuné. To feel wretched, être mal en train; *P:* avoir le cafard. To look wretched, avoir l'air malheureux; faire triste mine. **2.** (*a*) Pitoyable; tout à fait mauvais; lamentable. *This coffee is w. stuff,* ce café est une abomination. What wretched weather! quel temps de chien! (*b*) *W. lodgings,* appartement minable. *W. little shop,* petite boutique de rien du tout. *He is a w. singer,* il chante à faire pitié. (*c*) I can't find that wretched umbrella! je ne retrouve pas ce diable de parapluie! **-ly,** *adv.* **1.** (Vivre) misérablement. **2.** (S'acquitter de) façon pitoyable, lamentable. **3.** *To be w. poor,* être dans la misère. *On board she was w. ill,* à bord elle a été malade à faire pitié.

wretchedness ['retʃidnəs], *s.* Misère *f*, malheur *m*, infortune *f*.

wrick[1] [rik], *s.* To give oneself a wrick, se donner, attraper, un effort. Wrick in the neck, torticolis *m.*

wrick[2], *v.tr.* To wrick oneself, a muscle, se

donner, attraper, un effort. *To w. one's ankle*, se fouler la cheville ; se donner une entorse.

wriggle¹ [rigl], s. **I.** Tortillement *m* (du corps). **2.** Détour *m*, sinuosité *f.*

wriggle². **I.** *v.i.* (*a*) (*Of worm*) Se tortiller ; (*of fish*) frétiller ; (*of pers.*) se tortiller, s'agiter, se remuer. *To w. through a hedge*, se faufiler à travers une haie (en se tortillant). (*b*) *To wriggle into s.o.'s favour*, s'insinuer dans les bonnes grâces de qn. **To wriggle out of a difficulty**, se tirer, s'extraire, d'une position difficile. *To try to w. out of it*, chercher une échappatoire. (*c*) *F:* Tortiller ; tergiverser. **2.** *v.tr.* (*a*) *To w. one's body, one's legs*, remuer, tortiller, le corps ; agiter les jambes. (*b*) **To wriggle one's way into . . .**, se faufiler, s'insinuer, dans. . . .

wriggling, s. **I.** Tortillement *m.* **2.** *F:* Tergiversation *f.*

wright [rait], s. (*Now only in compounds, as shipwright, wheelwright*) Ouvrier *m*, artisan *m.*

wring¹ [riŋ], s. **I.** (Mouvement *m* de) torsion *f.* **To give the clothes a wring**, tordre le linge. **2.** He gave my hand a wring, il m'étreignit la main. **'wring-bolt**, s. *N.Arch:* Serre-joint *m.*

wring², *v.tr.* (wrung [rʌŋ] ; wrung) **I.** Tordre. **To wring (out)** the linen, tordre, essorer, le linge. **To wring s.o.'s hand**, étreindre la main de qn. **To wring one's hands in despair**, se tordre les mains, les bras, de désespoir. **To wring a bird's neck**, tordre le cou à une volaille. **It wrings my heart to . . .**, cela me déchire le cœur de. . . . **2. To wring** sth. out of, from, sth., s.o., exprimer, faire sortir (l'eau d'un vêtement mouillé) ; arracher (un secret à qn) ; arracher, extorquer (de l'argent à qn). **3.** (*a*) Forcer, déformer (une plaque métallique, etc.). (*b*) *Lit:* Donner une entorse à (la vérité). **To wring s.o.'s words into an admission of guilt**, dénaturer en aveu les paroles de qn. **wringing**, *a.* Wringing wet, (*of clothes*) mouillé à tordre ; (*of pers.*) trempé comme une soupe ; trempé jusqu'aux os. **'wringing-machine**, s. Essoreuse *f* (à rouleaux).

wringer ['riŋər], s. = WRINGING-MACHINE.

wrinkle¹ [riŋkl], s. **I.** (*a*) (*On face*) Ride *f.* (*b*) Rugosité *f* ; (*of ground*) plissement *m*, sillon *m* ; (*on water*) ondulation *f*, ride. (*c*) (*In garment*) Faux pli. *Dress that fits without a wrinkle*, robe qui ne fait pas un pli. **2.** *F:* Renseignement *m* utile ; *F:* tuyau *m*. **To give s.o. a wrinkle, to put s.o. up to a wrinkle**, indiquer à qn la bonne recette ; donner un tuyau à qn.

wrinkle². **I.** *v.tr.* Rider, plisser. **To wrinkle one's forehead**, froncer les sourcils *Her stockings were wrinkled*, ses bas faisaient des plis. **2.** *v.i.* **To wrinkle (up)**, se rider ; se plisser ; faire des plis. *The skin of these apples wrinkles*, la peau de ces pommes se ratatine.

wrist [rist], s. **I.** Poignet *m.* **2.** = WRIST-PIN. **'wrist-bone**, s. *Anat:* Os *m* du carpe ; le carpe. **'wrist-pin**, s. **I.** *Mch:* Tourillon *m* de crosse. **2.** Bouton de manivelle, de bielle ; maneton *m*. **'wrist-watch**, s. Montre-bracelet *f* ; montre *f* de poignet.

wristband ['ristband], s. *Cost:* Poignet *m*, manchette *f.*

wristlet ['ris(t)let], s. **I.** (*a*) Bracelet *m.* Wristlet watch, montre *f* de poignet ; montre-bracelet *f.* (*b*) Woollen wristlet, miton *m.* **2.** *pl.* Wristlets, menottes *f.*

writ¹ [rit], s. **I.** Holy writ, les saintes Écritures ; l'Écriture sainte. **2.** *Jur:* Acte *m* judiciaire ; mandat *m*, ordonnance *f.* **Writ of summons**,

assignation *f*, citation *f.* **To serve a writ on s.o.**, assigner qn (en justice) ; signifier une assignation, un exploit, à qn. **A writ is out for his arrest**, il est sous le coup d'un mandat d'arrêt.

writ². *See* WRITE.

write [rait], *v.tr.* (*p.t.* wrote [rout] ; *p.p.* written ['rit(ə)n], *A:* writ) **I.** (*a*) Écrire. *That was not written by me*, cela n'est pas écrit de ma main. **How is it written?** comment cela s'écrit-il ? **He writes a good hand**, il a une belle écriture, une belle main. *F: His guilt was written in his eyes*, on lisait dans ses yeux qu'il était coupable. **There's detective written all over him**, il sent son policier d'une lieue. **Writ large**, écrit en gros. *The bailiff was writ large on his person*, il sentait l'huissier à plein nez. **He writes himself Doctor**, il se qualifie de docteur. (*b*) *M.Ins:* = UNDERWRITE (*b*). **2.** Écrire (un roman, une lettre) ; rédiger (un article). **To write for a paper**, faire du journalisme. **He writes**, il fait profession d'écrire ; il est écrivain. *F:* That's nothing to write home about, ce n'est pas bien extraordinaire, bien épatant. *He wrote to me, F:* he wrote me, *yesterday*, il m'a écrit hier. **I have written to him to come**, je lui ai écrit de venir. **I will write (off) for it at once**, je vais le commander tout de suite. **write back**, *v.tr.* **I.** *Abs.* Répondre (par écrit). **2.** *Book-k:* Contrepasser, ristourner (un article). **write down**, *v.tr.* **I.** Coucher, consigner, (qch.) par écrit ; inscrire (son nom) ; marquer, noter. *F:* I wrote him down as a shrewd fellow, je l'estimai très entendu. **2.** *F:* Décrier, *F:* éreinter (qn, une pièce). **3.** *Fin:* Réduire (le capital). **write in**, *v.tr.* Insérer (un mot). **write off**, *v.tr.* **I.** Écrire (un article) d'un trait, au courant de la plume. **2.** (*a*) *Fin:* To write off capital, réduire le capital ; amortir du capital. (*b*) *Com:* Défalquer (une mauvaise créance). **To write so much off for wear and tear**, déduire tant pour l'usure. **write out**, *v.tr.* **I.** Transcrire (qch.) ; mettre (une copie) au net. **2. To write sth. out in full**, écrire qch. en toutes lettres. **3.** (*a*) *Med:* Formuler, rédiger (une ordonnance). (*b*) Libeller, remplir (un chèque). **I'll write you (out) a cheque**, *F:* je vais vous faire un chèque. **write up**, *v.tr.* **I.** *Journ:* (*a*) Écrire, rédiger (un fait-divers). (*b*) Prôner, *F:* faire mousser (qn, qch.). **2.** Mettre (son agenda) au courant, à jour. **written**, *a.* Écrit. **Written consent**, consentement par écrit.

writing, s. **I.** Écriture *f.* (*a*) **The art of writing**, l'art d'écrire. **At the time of writing**, au moment où j'écris. *Give me* writing materials, donnez-moi de quoi écrire. (*b*) *His w. is bad*, il a une mauvaise écriture. *To answer in writing*, répondre par écrit. *Jur:* Evidence in writing, preuve littérale. **2.** (*a*) **The writing profession**, le métier d'écrivain. (*b*) Ouvrage *m* littéraire. *pl.* The writings of Bossuet, les écrits *m* de Bossuet. **'writing-book**, s. Cahier *m* (d'écriture). **'writing-cabinet**, s. Bureau *m* ; secrétaire *m*. **'writing-case**, s. Nécessaire *m* (contenant ce qu'il faut pour écrire). **'writing-desk**, s. Pupitre *m*, bureau *m*. **'writing-pad**, s. **I.** Sous-main *m*, buvard *m*. **2.** Bloc-notes *m*. **'writing-paper**, s. Papier *m* à écrire. **'writing-table**, s. Bureau *m*.

writer ['raitər], s. **I.** Public writer, écrivain public. **To be a good, bad, writer**, avoir une belle, une mauvaise, écriture. **2. The (present) writer**, celui qui écrit ; l'auteur *m* de cette lettre. **3.** (*a*) Auteur (d'un roman, etc.). (*b*) Écrivain *m.* **Woman writer**, femme auteur ; femme écrivain.

4. (a) Commis *m* (aux écritures). (b) *Scot:* = SOLICITOR. *S.a.* SIGNET

writhe [raːið], *v.i.* (a) Se tordre (de douleur) ; se tortiller ; se crisper. (b) *He writhed under the insult*, il ressentit vivement cette injure, **To make s.o. writhe**, donner des crispations a qn. **writhing,** *s.* Contorsions *fpl.*

written. *See* WRITE.

wrong[1] [rɔŋ]. **I.** *a.* **1.** Mauvais ; mal *inv.* **It is wrong to steal,** *stealing is w.*, c'est mal de voler. **That was very wrong of you!** c'était très mal de votre part ! *P:* **A wrong 'un,** un mauvais sujet ; un vaurien. **2.** (a) Incorrect, inexact : erroné ; faux, *f.* fausse. **My watch is wrong,** ma montre n'est pas à l'heure. *A w. calculation*, un calcul faux. **W. use of a word**, emploi abusif, vicieux, d'un mot. *His ideas are all w.*, il a des idées toutes de travers. (b) (*Of pers.*) To be wrong, avoir tort ; se tromper. **You were wrong to contradict him,** vous avez eu tort de le contredire. **3.** "Qu'il ne faut pas." (a) **To be in the wrong place,** n'être pas à sa place. *Picture in the w. light*, tableau dans un faux jour. **To drive on the wrong side of the road,** circuler à contre-voie. *F:* **To get out of bed on the wrong side,** se lever du pied gauche. **The wrong side of a material,** l'envers *m* d'une étoffe. **Your shirt is wrong side out,** votre chemise est à l'envers. **To bᵒ wrong side up,** être sens dessus dessous. **To brush a hat the wrong way,** brosser un chapeau à rebours, à contre-poil. *S.a.* END[1] **1.** *You set about it in the wrong way,* vous vous y prenez mal. (*Of food*) *It went down the w. way*, je l'ai avalé de travers. *F:* **To be on the wrong side of forty,** avoir (dé)passé la quarantaine. *S.a.* LAUGH[2] **1.** (b) I went to the wrong house, je me suis trompé de maison. *That is the w. book,* ce n'est pas le livre qu'il faut. **To take the wrong road,** se tromper de chemin. *I was sent the w. way,* on m'a mal dirigé. **To be on the wrong track,** suivre une mauvaise piste. **To do, say, the wrong thing,** commettre une gaffe. *Tp:* **Wrong number,** erreur *f* de numéro. **You have been given the wrong number,** on vous a mal branché. *Mus:* **Wrong note,** fausse note. *Typ:* **Wrong fount,** lettre *f* d'un autre œil. *S.a.* SHOP[1] **1.** **4.** (*Amiss*) **What's wrong with you?** quel est votre mal ? qu'avez-vous ? **Something is wrong,** il y a quelque chose qui ne va pas. **There's something wrong somewhere,** il y a quelque chose qui cloche. **I hope there is nothing wrong,** j'espère qu'il n'est rien arrivé (de malheureux).

Things are all wrong, tout va mal, de travers. *F:* **What's wrong with that?** qu'avez-vous à redire à cela ? **-ly,** *adv.* **1.** A tort, à faux. **Rightly or wrongly,** à tort ou à raison. **2.** Mal. **II. wrong,** *s.* **1.** Mal *m.* *To know right from w.*, distinguer le bien et le mal. **Two wrongs do not make a right,** deux noirs ne font pas un blanc. **2.** (a) Tort *m*, injustice *f.* **Right and wrong, le** juste et l'injuste. **To labour under a sense of wrong,** nourrir un sentiment d'injustice. (b) *Jur:* Dommage *m*, préjudice *m.* **3.** **To be in the wrong,** être dans son tort ; avoir tort. **To put s.o. in the wrong,** mettre qn dans son tort. *S.a.* LOSER **2.** **III. wrong,** *adv.* Mal. **1.** (a) Inexactement, incorrectement. **To answer wrong** répondre mal, de travers. (b) A tort ; à faux. **You did wrong,** vous avez mal agi. **You took me up wrong,** vous avez mal pris mes paroles. **2.** **To go wrong.** (a) (i) Faire fausse route ; (ii) se tromper ; (iii) *F:* tomber dans le vice. (b) (*Of mechanism*) Se déranger, se détraquer ; (*of business*) aller mal. *Something went w. with the electric light*, nous avons eu une panne d'électricité. *Things are going wrong*, les affaires se gâtent. **'wrong-doer,** *s.* (a) Auteur *m* d'une injustice. *Wrong-doers*, les méchants. (b) Celui qui commet une infraction à la loi. **'wrong-doing,** *s.* (a) Mal *m* ; injustice *f.* (b) Infraction *f* à la loi. **'wrong-headed,** *a.* Qui a l'esprit pervers, mal fait. **'wrong-'headedness,** *s.* Perversité *f* de jugement.

wrong[2], *v.tr.* (a) Faire (du) tort à (qn) ; faire injure à (qn) ; léser (qn). (b) Être injuste pour, envers (qn) ; faire tort à (qn).

wrongful ['rɔŋful], *a.* **1.** Injuste. **Wrongful dismissal,** renvoi injustifié (d'un employé). **2.** *Jur:* Illégal, -aux. **-fully,** *adv.* Injustement : à tort.

wrote [rout]. *See* WRITE.

wroth [rouθ, rɔθ], *pred.a.* *Lit:* Courroucé, en colère (*at*, contre). **To wax wroth,** entrer en courroux.

wrought [rɔːt]. *See* WORK[2]

wrung [rʌŋ]. *See* WRING[2].

wry [rai], *a.* Tordu, tors ; de travers **To pull a wry face,** faire la grimace. *He gave a wry smile*, il grimaça un sourire.

wryneck ['rainek], *s.* *Orn:* Torcol *m.*

wych-elm ['witʃelm], *s.* *See* ELM.

Wykehamist ['wikəmist], *a. & s.* (Élève *m* ou ancien élève) du collège de Winchester.

wyvern ['waivərn], *s.* *Her:* Dragon *m.*

X

X, x [eks], *s.* **1.** (La lettre) X, x *m.* *Mth:* **The x-axis,** l'axe *m* des abscisses. **2.** **Treble X, XXX,** bière extra-forte. **3.** *Ph:* **X rays,** rayons *m* X. **4.** *pl.* *W.Tel:* **X's,** bruits *m* parasites. **X-'ray**[1], *attrib.a.* (Appareil) radiologique. **X-ray examination,** examen radiographique. **X-ray photograph, radiogramme** *m.* **X-'ray**[2], *v.tr.* *Med:* Radiographier (qn) ; *F:* passer (qn) aux rayons X.

xanthin ['zanθin], *s.* *Ch:* Xanthine *f.*

xebec ['ziːbek], *s.* *Nau:* Chébec *m.*

xenon ['zenɔn], *s.* *Ch:* Xénon *m.*

xenophobe ['zenofoub], *a. & s.* Xénophobe (*mf*).

xenophobia [zeno'foubiə], *s.* Xénophobie *f.*

xeranthemum [ziːə'ranθiməm], *s.* *Bot:* Xéranthème *m.*

xerasia [ziːə'reiziə], *s.* *Med:* Xérasie *f.*

xeroderm(i)a [ziːərə'dəːrm(i)ə], *s.* *Med:* Xérodermie *f* ; ichtyose *f.*

xi [ksai], *s.* *Gr.Alph:* Xi *m.*

xiphias ['zifiəs], *s.* *Ich:* Xiphias *m*, espadon *m.*

xiphoid ['zifɔid], *a.* *Anat:* Xiphoïde.

Xmas ['krisməs, *F:* 'eksməs], *s.* *F:* (= *Christmas*) Noël *m.*

xylograph ['zailograf, -graːf], *s.* Xylographie *f* ; gravure *f* sur bois ; estampe *f.*

xylography [zai'lɔgrəfi], *s.* Xylographie *f.*

xylonite ['zailonait], *s.* Xylonite *f.*

xylophone ['zailofoun], *s.* *Mus:* Xylophone *m.*

xyster ['zistər], *s.* *Surg:* *Dent:* Xystre *m*, rugine *f.*

Y, y [wai], s. (La lettre) Y, y m; i grec. Mth: The y-axis, l'axe m des ordonnées. Tchn: **Y joint**, raccord m en Y. Hyd.E: **Y branch**, culotte f. **'Y-shaped,** a. Fourchu; à fourche; en Y.

yacht¹ [jɔt], s. Yacht m. Pleasure yacht, yacht de plaisance. **'yacht-club,** s. Yacht-club m.

yacht², v.i. Faire du yachting. **yachting,** s. Yachting m; navigation f de plaisance. Yachting cruise, croisière f en yacht. Yachting cap, casquette f de yachtman.

yachtsman, pl. **-men** ['jɔtsmən, -men], s.m. Yachtman, pl. yachtmen.

yachtsmanship ['jɔtsmənʃip], s. Qualités fpl du bon yachtman; habileté f à manier un yacht.

yah [jɑː], int. **1.** (Disgust) Pouah! **2.** (Derision) Oh, là là!

yahoo [jə'huː], s. F: Homme bestial; personnage m immonde. (Voir les "Voyages de Gulliver," de Swift.)

yak [jak], s. Z: Ya(c)k m; vache f de Tartarie.

Yale lock ['jeil'lɔk], s. Serrure f de la marque Yale; F: serrure à pompe.

yam [jam], s. Bot: Igname f.

yank¹ [jaŋk], s. U.S: Secousse f, saccade f.

yank², v.tr. U.S: Tirer (d'un coup sec). To y. the bed-clothes off s.o., découvrir qn d'une secousse. To yank out a tooth, arracher une dent d'un seul coup.

Yankee ['jaŋki], s. P: Américain, -aine (des États-Unis); Yankee m.

yap¹ [jap], s. Jappement m (d'un chien).

yap², v.i. (yapped) (a) Japper. (b) F: (Of pers.) Criailler; en dégoiser. **yapping,** s. = YAP¹.

yarborough ['jɑːrbərə], s. Cards: Main f qui ne contient aucune carte au-dessus du neuf.

yard¹ [jɑːrd], s. **1.** Meas: Yard m (o mètre 914). How many yards do you want? quel métrage désirez-vous? F: Words a yard long, mots longs d'une toise. Face a yard long, figure longue d'une aune. **2.** Nau: Vergue f. **'yard-arm,** s. Nau: Bout m de vergue. **'yard-measure,** s. Mesure f d'un yard. **'yard-stick,** s. Yard m (en bois, en métal). F: To measure others by one's own yard-stick, mesurer les autres à son aune.

yard², s. **1.** (a) Cour f (de maison); Sch: cour, préau m. Back-yard, cour de derrière. (b) Scotland Yard, F: the Yard, see SCOTLAND 2. **2.** (a) Chantier m. N.Arch: Repair yard, chantier de radoub. Naval (dock)yard, arsenal m maritime, pl. arsenaux. (b) Dépôt m. Coal yard, dépôt de charbon. Rail: Goods yard, cour, dépôt, de marchandises. S.a. MARSHALLING 2.

yard(s)man, pl. **-men** ['jɑːrd(z)mən, -men], s.m. **1.** Manœuvre de chantier. **2.** Rail: Gareur, classeur, de trains. **3.** (In stables) Garçon d'écurie.

yarn¹ [jɑːrn], s. **1.** (a) Tex: Fil m; filé m (de coton). Woollen yarn, laine filée; filé de laine. (b) Nau: Spun yarn, bitord m. **2.** F: (i) Histoire f, conte m, de matelot; (ii) longue histoire. To spin a yarn, raconter, débiter, une histoire.

yarn², v.i. F: Débiter des histoires.

yarrow ['jaro], s. Bot: Mille-feuille f.

yashmak ['jaʃmak], s. Cost: Yachmak m.

yataghan ['jatəgan], s. Yatagan m.

yaw¹ [jɔː], s. (a) Nau: Embardée f. (b) Av: Mouvement m de lacet.

yaw², v.i. (a) Nau: Embarder; faire des embardées. (b) Av: Faire un mouvement de lacet.

yawl [jɔːl], s. Nau: Yole f (à rames).

yawn¹ [jɔːn], s. Bâillement m. To give a yawn, bâiller. To stifle a y., étouffer un bâillement.

yawn². **1.** v.i. (a) Bâiller (de sommeil). (b) Être béant. The gulf yawned at his feet, le gouffre s'ouvrait à ses pieds. **2.** v.tr. F: To yawn one's head off, bâiller à se décrocher la mâchoire. **yawning¹,** a. (Gouffre) béant, ouvert. **yawning²,** s. Bâillement m.

yclept [i'klept], a. A. & Hum: Appelé; nomme.

ye [jiː], pers.pron. A: Vous. Where were ye? où étiez-vous? S.a. GOD 1. F: How d'ye do? comment allez-vous?

yea [jei], adv. Lit: (a) Oui. (b) En vérité; voire. The remedy is useless, yea harmful, ce remède est inutile, voire (même) pernicieux.

year [jiːər, jəːr], s. An m, année f. (a) Usu. An. In the year 1850, en l'an 1850. Sentenced to ten years' imprisonment, condamné à dix ans de prison. A y. last September, il y a eu un an au mois de septembre. Last year, l'an dernier; l'année dernière. To have a thousand a year, avoir mille livres de rente. To be ten years old, avoir dix ans. To see the old year out, réveillonner. (b) Usu. Année. Financial year, année d'exercice; exercice (financier). School year, année scolaire. He is in my y., il est de ma promotion. To hire sth. by the year, louer qch. à l'année. From year's end to year's end, d'un bout de l'année à l'autre. Year in (and) year out, year after year, une année après l'autre. Years ago, il y a bien des années. In after years, dans la suite. From his earliest years, dès son âge la plus tendre. Old for his years, plus vieux que son âge; (enfant) précoce. Disparity in years, différence f d'âge. To be getting on in years, to advance in years, prendre de l'âge; tirer sur l'âge. Advanced in years, âgé. **'year-book,** s. Annuaire m; almanach m (du Stock Exchange, etc.); recueil annuel (de jurisprudence).

yearling ['jiːərliŋ, 'jəːr-], a. & s. (Animal m) d'un an. Esp. Yearling colt, poulain m d'un an.

yearly ['jiːərli, 'jəːr-]. **1.** a. Annuel. (a) Qui se fait, qui revient, chaque année. (b) Qui dure un an. Yearly letting, location annale. **2.** adv. Annuellement; (i) une fois par an; (ii) tous les ans.

yearn [jəːrn], v.i. To yearn for, after, sth., languir pour, après, qch. To y. for the sight of one's native land, brûler de revoir son pays natal. To yearn to do sth., avoir bien envie de faire qch. **yearning¹,** a. (Désir) vif, ardent; (regard) plein d'envie. **-ly,** adv. Avec envie.

yearning², s. Désir ardent; envie f (for, de).

yeast [jiːst], s. Levure f.

yell¹ [jel], s. Hurlement m; cri aigu. To give a yell, pousser un cri.

yell². **1.** v.i. Hurler; crier à tue-tête. To yell with laughter, rire aux éclats; s'esclaffer. **2.** v.tr. To y. out abuse, vociférer, hurler, des injures. **yelling,** s. Hurlements mpl.

yellow¹ ['jelou]. **1.** a. Jaune. F: Yellow as a guinea, jaune comme un coing. To turn, go, yellow, jaunir. Yellow hair, cheveux blonds. Yellow metal, cuivre m jaune; laiton m. The yellow races, les races jaunes. Lemon yellow, jaune citron inv. S.a. LEAD¹ 2. (b) U.S: F: Poltron, lâche. S.a. STREAK¹ 2. **2.** s. Jaune m. Chrome yellow, jaune de chrome. **'yellow-**

back, s. F: Livre broché (français). **'yellow-'bunting,** s. = YELLOW-HAMMER. **'yellow 'fever,** s. Fièvre f jaune. **'yellow-hammer,** s. Orn: Bruant m jaune. **'yellow 'jack,** s. **1.** Nau: Pavillon m de quarantaine. **2.** F: = YELLOW FEVER. **'yellow 'soap,** s. Savon m de Marseille.

yellow², v.tr. & i. Jaunir.

yellowish ['jelouiʃ], a. Jaunâtre.

yellowness ['jelounəs], s. Ton m jaune, teinte f jaune (de qch.); teint m jaune (de qn).

yelp¹ [jelp], s. Jappement m, glapissement m.

yelp², v.i. Japper, glapir. **yelping,** s. Jappement m, glapissement m.

yeoman, pl. **-men** ['jouman, -men], s.m. **1.** Petit propriétaire; franc-tenancier; gros fermier. F: To do yeoman('s) service, fournir un effort précieux. **2.** Yeoman of the Guard = BEEF-EATER. **3.** Navy: Gardien; magasinier. S.a. SIGNAL¹ 3.

yeomanry ['joumənri], s. Coll. Corps de cavalerie composé de petits propriétaires fonciers qui fournissent leurs montures.

yes [jes], adv. (a) Oui; parfaitement; (contradicting negation) si; si fait. To answer yes or no, répondre par oui ou non. Yes, certainly, mais oui. You did not hear me?—Yes, I did, vous ne m'avez pas entendu?—Si (fait). (b) (Interrogatively) Yes? (i) vraiment? (ii) et puis après?

yesterday ['jestədei], adv. & s. Hier (m). The day before yesterday, avant-hier (m). Yesterday week, il y a eu hier huit jours. Y. was the sixteenth, c'était hier le seize. Yesterday morning, hier (au) matin.

yet [jet]. I. adv. **1.** (a) Encore. I can see him yet, je le vois encore. (b) Yet more, encore plus. Yet again, encore une fois. **2.** Déjà; jusqu'ici. Need you go yet? faut-il que vous partiez déjà? Not yet, pas encore. It will not happen just yet, nous n en sommes pas encore là. As yet nothing has been done, jusqu'à présent, jusqu'ici, on n'a rien fait. **3.** Malgré tout. He will win yet, malgré tout il gagnera. I'll do it yet! j'y arriverai! II. yet conj. Néanmoins, cependant; tout de même. And yet I like him, et cependant, et malgré tout, il me plaît.

yew [ju:], s. Bot: Yew(-tree), if m.

Yiddish ['jidiʃ], a. & s. Ling: Judéo-allemand (m).

yield¹ [ji:ld], s. **1.** Production f (d'une mine); rapport m (d'un arbre fruitier); rendement m, récolte f (d'un champ). If there is a good y. of wheat this year, si les blés donnent cette année. The y. on these shares is large, ces actions rapportent beaucoup. Net yield, revenu net. **2.** Fléchissement m. **'yield-point,** s. Mec: Limite f de résistance.

yield². I. v.tr. (a) Rendre, donner. (b) Rapporter, produire. Land that yields no return, terre qui ne rend rien. Money that yields interest, argent qui rapporte. Abs. Ground that yields well, terre qui donne un bon rendement. (c) Céder (une forteresse, un droit). To yield ground, céder le terrain. **2.** v.i. (a) Se rendre; faire sa soumission; céder (to, à). To yield to temptation, succomber à la tentation. The frost is yielding, la gelée s'adoucit. To yield to nobody in courage, ne le céder à personne en courage. (Of ship) To yield to the helm, obéir à la barre. (b) S'affaisser, fléchir, plier. The plank yielded under our weight, la planche manqua sous nos pieds. **yielding¹,** a. **1.** (Of pers.) Facile, complaisant. In a y. moment, dans un moment de faiblesse. **2.** (a) Mou, f. molle. Y. ground, sol mou, peu résistant. (b) Souple, élastique.

yielding², s. **1.** Rendement m. **2.** (a) Soumission f. (b) Reddition f (d'une forteresse); cession f (d'un droit). **3.** Affaissement m, fléchissement m.

yod [jɔd], s. Ling: Yod m.

yodel¹ ['joud(ə)l], s. Mus: Ioulement m.

yodel², v.i. (yodel(l)ed) Mus: Iouler; chanter à la tyrolienne.

yo-heave-ho ['jouhi:v'hou], **yoho** [jo'hou], int. Nau: O(h), hisse!

yoicks [jɔiks], int. Ven: = Taïaut.

yoke¹ [jouk], s. **1.** Joug m. Yoke oxen, bœufs d'attelage. Yoke of oxen, couple f, attelage m (de bœufs). F: To throw off, cast off, the yoke, secouer le joug; s'affranchir du joug. **2.** (For carrying two pails) Palanche f. **3.** Dressm: Empiècement m; (of chemise) tour m de gorge. **4.** (a) El: Culasse f (d'aimant); carcasse f, bâti m (de dynamo). (b) Mch: (Cross-head) Joug. **'yoke-fellow,** s. **1.** Compagnon m de travail. **2.** F: Époux, -ouse.

yoke², v.tr. **1.** Accoupler (des bœufs); mettre (des bœufs) au joug; atteler (des bœufs) (to the plough, à la charrue). **2.** Accoupler (les pièces d'un appareil). **3.** F: Unir (en mariage).

yokel ['jouk(ə)l], s. Rustre m; campagnard m.

yolk¹ [jouk], s. Jaune m d'œuf. **'yolk-bag, -sac,** s. Biol: Membrane vitelline.

yolk², s. Suint m.

yon [jɔn], a. & adv. A: = YONDER.

yonder ['jɔndər]. **1.** adv. Over yonder, là-bas. **2.** a. Ce . . . -là, f. cette . . . -là, pl. ces . . . -là. Yonder elms, ces ormes là-bas.

yore ['jɔːr], s. A: Of yore, (d')autrefois. In days of yore, au temps jadis; autrefois.

Yorkshire ['jɔːrkʃər]. Pr.n. Le comté d'York. Yorkshire pudding, pâte cuite au-dessous du rôti.

you [ju(:)], pers. pron. (i) Vous; (ii) sg. (addressing relatives, children, etc.) tu, te, toi. **1.** (a) (Nom.) Vous; tu. You are very kind, vous êtes bien aimable(s); tu es bien aimable. There you are, vous voilà, te voilà. Tp: Are you there? allô! (b) (as object) Vous; te. I hope to see you to-morrow, j'espère vous voir, te voir, demain. I will give you some, je vous en donnerai; je t'en donnerai. (c) Between you and me, (i) entre vous et moi, entre toi et moi; (ii) entre nous soit dit. There's a fine apple for you! regardez-moi ça, si ce n'est pas une belle pomme! Away with you! allez-vous-en! va-t'en! **2.** (a) You and I will go by train, vous et moi, nous irons par le train. It is you, c'est vous, toi. If I were you, (si j'étais) à votre place. You are the master, c'est vous le maître. Hi! you there! eh! dites donc, là-bas! (b) (In the imperative) Now you make a speech, à votre tour de parler. Never you mind! ça c'est mon affaire! (c) You lawyers, you Englishmen, vous autres avocats, vous autres Anglais. You idiot (, you)! idiot que vous êtes! **3.** Get you gone, allez-vous-en. **4.** (Indefinite) On. You never can tell, on ne sait jamais. The joy you feel when you meet a friend, la joie qui vous saisit quand on rencontre un ami.

young [jʌŋ]. **1.** a. (a) Jeune; (of animal) petit. Younger, plus jeune. Younger son, younger daughter, fils cadet, fille cadette. When I was twenty years younger, quand j'avais vingt ans de moins. We are only young once, jeunesse n'a qu'un temps. I am not so young as I was, (when walking) je n'ai plus mes jambes de vingt ans. Young men, jeunes gens m. S.a. LADY 1, 4, MAN¹ 3. Young Mr Smith, (i) M. Smith fils; (ii) le jeune M. Smith. (b) To grow young again, to grow younger, rajeunir. You are looking years

younger! comme vous avez rajeuni! (c) **The night is still young,** la nuit n'est que peu avancée. (d) **Young England,** l'Angleterre d'aujourd'hui; la nouvelle génération. **2.** s. pl. inv. (a) Les jeunes gens; la jeunesse. **Old and young,** les grands et les petits. (b) **Animal and its young,** animal et ses petits.

youngish ['jʌŋiʃ], a. Assez jeune.

youngster ['jʌŋstər], s. (a) Jeune personne f; esp. jeune homme m. (b) Petit, -ite; F: gosse mf.

your ['iuər], poss.a. **1.** (i) Votre, pl. vos; (ii) sg. (when addressing relatives, children, etc.) ton, f. ta, pl. tes. Your house, votre maison, ta maison. Your friends, vos ami(e)s, tes ami(e)s. Is it the most recent of your books? c'est votre livre le plus récent? Have you hurt your hand? vous vous êtes fait mal à la main? Games: **Your turn!** à vous! **Your Worship,** monsieur le juge. **2.** (Indefinite. Cf. YOU 4.) Son, f. sa, pl. ses. **You cannot alter your nature,** on ne peut pas changer son caractère. **3.** (Ethic) Your true reformer is unconscious of distinctions, le vrai réformateur ne sait pas distinguer.

yours ['juərz], poss.pron. (i) Le vôtre; (ii) sg. (when addressing relatives, children, etc.) le tien, la tienne. (a) **This is yours,** ceci est à vous, à toi. The idea is yours, l'idée est de vous. I should like to read something of yours, je voudrais bien lire quelque chose de vous. **He is a friend of yours,** c'est un de vos amis. That pride of yours,

votre orgueil. S.a. FAITHFULLY 1, OBEDIENTLY, TRULY 1. (b) **You and yours,** vous et les vôtres; toi et les tiens.

yourself [juər'self], **yourselves** [juər'selvz], pers. pron. See SELF 4.

youth [ju:θ, pl. ju:ðz or ju:θs], s. **1.** Jeunesse f, adolescence f, jeune âge m. **From youth upwards he showed talent,** dès sa jeunesse, il a fait preuve de talent. Myth: **The fountain of Youth,** la Fontaine de Jouvence. Prov: **Youth will have its way,** il faut que jeunesse se passe. **2.** Jeune homme, adolescent m. **3.** Coll. Jeunes gens m (garçons et filles); jeunesse (du village, etc.).

youthful ['ju:θful], a. **1.** Jeune. To look v., avoir l'air jeune. **2.** (Erreur) de jeunesse. **-fully,** adv. En jeune homme, en jeune fille.

youthfulness ['ju:θfulnəs], s. Jeunesse f; juvénilité f; air m de jeunesse.

you've [ju:v] = you have.

yowl[1] [jaul], s. Hurlement m (de chien); miaulement m (de chat).

yowl[2], v.i. (Of dog) Hurler; (of cat) miauler.

yttrium ['itriəm], s. Ch: Yttrium m

yucca ['jʌkə], s. Bot: Yucca m.

Yugoslav [jugo'slɑːv], a. & s. = JUGOSLAV.

Yugoslavia [jugo'slɑːviə] Pr.n = JUGOSLAVIA.

Yule [ju:l], s. A: Noël m. **'yule-log,** Bûche f de Noël. **'yule-tide,** s. L'époque f de Noël; les fêtes f de Noël.

Z

Z, z [zed], s. (La lettre) Z, z m.

Zambezi (the) [ðəzam'biːzi]. Pr.n. Le Zambèze.

zany ['zeini], s. **1.** A.Th: Zan(n)i m, bouffon m. **2.** A: Sot, f. sotte; niais, -aise.

zariba [za'riːba], s. (In Africa) Clôture (fortifiée de ronces); camp m de fortune.

zeal [zi:l], s. Zèle m, ardeur f; empressement m. To make a show of z., faire du zèle.

Zealand ['zi:lənd]. Pr.n. La Zélande.

zealot ['zelot], s. **1.** Hist: Zélateur, -trice; zélote m. **2.** F: Fanatique mf, zélateur (for, de).

zealous ['zeləs], a. Zélé; empressé. **Zealous for sth.,** plein de zèle pour qch. **-ly,** adv. Avec zèle.

zebra ['zi:bra], s. Zèbre m. **Striped like a zebra,** zébré. **Zebra-markings,** zébrure f.

zebu ['zi:bju], s. Z: Zébu m; bœuf m à bosse.

zemindar [ze'miːndɑːr], s. (India) Zémindar m; propriétaire foncier.

zenana [ze'nɑːna], s. (India) Zénana m, harem m. Tex: **Zenana cloth,** zénana.

zenith ['zeniθ], s. Astr: Zénith m. F: **At the zenith of his fame,** à l'apogée de sa gloire.

zenithal ['zeniθ(ə)l], a. Zénithal, -aux.

zephyr ['zefər], s. **1.** (Wind) Zéphire m, zéphyr(e) m. **2.** Tex: Zephyr (wool), laine f zéphire.

zeppelin ['zepəlin], s. Aer: Zeppelin m.

zero ['ziːəro], s. Zéro m. Ph: **Absolute zero,** zéro absolu. Mth: Surv: **Zero point,** point m zéro, (point) origine f. **Determination of the z. point,** zérotage m. **Zero tension,** tension nulle. **'zero hour,** s. Mil: L'heure f (de l'attaque); l'heure H.

zest [zest], s. (a) Enthousiasme m, entrain m. To fight with z., combattre avec élan. To eat with z., manger avec appétit. (b) Saveur f, goût m. To

add z. to the adventure. donner du piquant à l'aventure.

zeta ['ziːta], s. Gr.Alph: (D)zêta m.

Zeus [zjuːs]. Pr.n.m. Myth: Zeus.

zigzag[1] ['zigzag], s. Zigzag m. **In zigzags,** en zigzag. Nau: **To steer a zigzag course,** faire route en zigzag, en zigzaguant; faire des zigzags. **Zigzag riveting,** rivetage en quinconce. S.a. TRENCH[2]. adv. **The road runs zigzag,** le chemin fait des zigzags.

zigzag[2], v. (zigzagged) **1.** v.i. Zigzaguer; faire des zigzags. **2.** v.tr. Disposer (des rivets) en quinconce.

zinc [ziŋk], s. Zinc m. **1.** To cover a roof with zinc, zinguer un toit. S.a. OINTMENT. **2.** Zinc block, zincogravure f; F: zinc. **zinc-'plate,** s. Com: Zinc m en feuilles. **'zinc-trade,** s. Zinguerie f. **'zinc-ware,** s. Zinguerie f. **'zinc-worker,** s. Zingueur m. **'zinc-works,** s. Zinguerie f.

zincograph ['ziŋkograf], s. Phot.Engr: Zincogravure f; gravure f sur zinc.

zincography [ziŋ'kɔgrəfi], s. Phot.Engr: Zincographie f. **To reproduce by z.,** zincographier (un dessin).

Zion ['zaiən]. **1.** Pr.n. Sion m ((i) la colline; (ii) Jérusalem). **2.** s. Chapelle f, temple m (non-conformiste).

Zionist ['zaiənist], a. & s. Pol: Sioniste (mf).

zip[1] [zip], s. **1.** Sifflement m (d'une balle). **2.** F: Énergie f. **Put a zip into it,** mettez-y du nerf. **3.** Zip fastener, fermeture f éclair inv; fermeture à curseur.

zip[2], v.i. (zipped) Siffler (comme une balle). (Of car) **To zip past,** passer comme un éclair.

zircon ['zə:rkɔn], *s. Miner:* Zircon *m.*
zither(n) ['ziθər(n)], *s. Mus:* Cithare *f.*
zoantharia [zouan'θɛəria], *s.pl. Coel:* Zoanthaires *m.*
zodiac ['zoudiak], *s. Astr:* Zodiaque *m.*
zodiacal [zo'daiək(ə)l], *a.* Zodiacal, -aux.
zonal ['zoun(ə)l], *a.* Zonal, -aux.
zonaria [zou'neəria], *s. Algae:* Zonaire *f.*
zone [zoun], *s.* **1.** Zone *f. Geog:* The torrid zone, la zone torride. *Mil:* **Evacuating zone,** zone de l'arrière. **2.** *A. & Poet:* Ceinture *f.*
zoo [zu:], *s. F:* Jardin *m* zoologique; *esp.* the **Zoo,** le Jardin zoologique de Londres.
zoobiology [zouobai'ɔlodʒi], *s.* Zoobiologie *f.*
zoochemistry [zouo'kemistri], *s.* Zoochimie *f.*
zoolite ['zouolait], *s. Paleont:* Zoolit(h)e *m.*
zoological [zouo'lɔdʒik(ə)l, *F:* zu'lɔdʒikl], *a.* Zoologique. **The Zoological** [zu-] **Gardens,** = THE Zoo.
zoologist [zou'ɔlodʒist], *s.* Zoologiste *m.*
zoology [zou'ɔlodʒi], *s.* Zoologie *f.*
zoom¹ [zu:m], *s.* **1.** Bourdonnement *m;* vrombissement *m.* **2.** *Av:* Montée *f* en chandelle.

zoom², *v.i.* **1.** Bourdonner; vrombir. **2.** *Av:* Monter en chandelle; (se) cabrer.
zoophaga [zou'ɔfaga], *s.pl.* Zoophages *m.*
zoophagous [zou'ɔfagəs], *a.* Zoophage.
zoophyta [zouo'faita], *s.pl. Biol:* Zoophytes *m.*
zoophyte ['zouofait], *s. Biol:* Zoophyte *m.*
zoospore ['zouospɔ:ər], *s. Biol:* Zoospore *f.*
zostera ['zɔstərə], *s. Bot:* Zostère *f.*
zouave [zwɑ:v], *s.* Zouave *m.*
zounds [zaundz], *int. A:* Morbleu!
Zulu ['zu:lu], *a. & s. Ethn:* Zoulou *m, pl.* -ous.
Zululand ['zu:luland]. *Pr.n.* Le Zoulouland.
Zuyder Zee (the) [ðəzaidər'zi:]. *Pr.n.* Le Zuyderzée.
zygoma, *pl.* **-ata** [zai'goumɑ, -atɑ], *s. Anat:* Zygoma *m;* os *m* malaire; os de la pommette.
zygomatic [zaigo'matik], *a. Anat:* Zygomatique.
zygote ['zaigout], *s. Biol:* Zygote *m.*
zymase ['zaimeis], *s. Ch:* Zymase *f.*
zymosis [zai'mousis], *s.* Fermentation *f.*
zymotic [zai'mɔtik], *a.* (Maladie) zymotique.

A.B., *Nau: Able(-bodied) seaman.*
a/c, *Com: Account (current).*
A.D., *Anno Domini.*
A.D.C., *Aide-de-camp.*
Adjt, *Mil: Adjutant.*
ad lib., *Ad libitum, q.v.*
Adm., *Admiral.*
A.I.Mech.E., *Associate of the Institute of Mechanical Engineers.*
Ald., *Alderman.*
a.m., *Ante meridiem, q.v.*
A.M.I.C.E., *Associate Member of the Institute of Civil Engineers.*
A.M.I.E.E., *Associate Member of the Institution of Electrical Engineers.*
amp(s), *El: Ampere(s).*
A.R.A., *Associate of the Royal Academy of Arts.*
A.R.A.M., *Associate of the Royal Academy of Music.*
A.R.C.M., *Associate of the Royal College of Music.*
A.R.C.O., *Associate of the Royal College of Organists.*
A.T.S., *Auxiliary Territorial Service.*

B.A., *Bachelor of Arts.* V. BACHELOR 3.
Bart, *Baronet.*
Bart's, *St Bartholomew's Hospital (London).*
B.B.C., *British Broadcasting Corporation.*
B.C., *Before Christ.* V. BEFORE 2 (b).
B.Com., *Bachelor of Commerce.*
B/F, b/f, *Book-k: Brought forward.*
B'ham, *Geog: Birmingham.*
B.M.A., *British Medical Association.*
B.Mus., *Bachelor of Music.*
B/O, b/o, *Com: Brought over.*
Boro', *Borough.*
bro(s), *Brother(s).*
B.S., *Bachelor of Surgery.*
B.Sc., *Bachelor of Science.* V. BACHELOR 3.
B.S.T., *British summer-time.*
Bt, *Baronet.*

C., *Ph: Centigrade.*
c., 1. *Circa.* **2.** *Num: (a) Cent. (b) Centime.*
C.A., *Chartered Accountant.*
c. & f., *Com: Cost and freight.*
Cantab., *Sch: Cantabrigiensis, de l'Université de Cambridge.*
C.B., 1. *Companion of the Order of the Bath.* **2.** *Mil: Confinement to barracks.* V. BARRACK[1] I.
C.B.E., *(i) Commander, (ii) Companion, of the Order of the British Empire.*
c.c., *Meas: Cubic centimetre(s).*
C/D, c/d, *Book-k: Carried down.*
Cent., *Ph: Centigrade.*
cent., *Century, siècle.*
C/F, c/f, *Book-k: Carried forward.*
cf., *Confer, conferatur, voir.*
cg., *Meas: Centigramme.*
C.G.S., *Centimetre-gramme-second.*
C.H., *Companion of Honour.*
ch., *Chapter.*
Chas., *Charles.*
Ch. B., *Baccalaureus Chirurgiæ.*
C.I.D., *Criminal Investigation Department.*

C.I.E., *Companion of the Order of the Indian Empire.*
c.i.f., *Cost, insurance and freight.*
C.-in-C., *Mil: Commander-in-chief.*
cm., *Meas: Centimetre(s).*
C.M.G., *Companion of the Order of St Michael and St George.*
C.O., *Mil: Commanding officer.*
Co., 1. *Com: Company. X & Co., X et Cie.* **2.** *Adm: County.*
c/o, *Care of.* V. CARE[1] 3.
C.O.D., *Com: Cash on delivery.*
C. of E., *Church of England.*
Col., *Mil: Colonel.*
con., *Contra.*
cp., *Compare.*
Cpl, *Mil: Corporal.*
cr., *Book-k: (a) Credit. (b) Creditor.*
C.S., *Clerk to the Signet, avoué.*
C.S.I., *Companion of the Order of the Star of India.*
C.S.M., *Mil: Company Sergeant-major.*
cu., *Cubic.*
C.V.O., *Commander of the Royal Victorian Order.*
cwt(s), *Meas: Hundredweight(s), q.v.*

d., *Denarius, denarii, penny, pence.*
D.B.E., *Dame of the Order of the British Empire.*
D.C.L., *Jur: Doctor of Civil Law.*
D.C.M., *Distinguished Conduct Medal.*
D.D., *Divinitatis Doctor.*
deb., *Fin: Debenture.*
def., *Fin: Deferred.*
D.F.C., *Distinguished Flying Cross.*
D.F.M., *Distinguished Flying Medal.*
dg., *Meas: Decigramme.*
dis(c)., disct., *Com: Discount.*
div., *Fin: Dividend.*
D.Lit., *Sch: Doctor of Literature.*
dm., *Meas: Decimetre(s).*
do, *Ditto.*
doz., *Com: Dozen.*
Dr, 1. *Doctor.* **2.** *Com: Debtor.*
D.S.C., *Navy: Distinguished Service Cross.*
D.Sc., *Sch: Doctor of Science.*
D.S.M., *Navy: Distinguished Service Medal.*
D.S.O., *Distinguished Service Order.*
D.V., *Deo volente, si Dieu le permet.*
dwt, *Meas: Pennyweight, q.v.*

E. & O.E., *Com: Errors and omissions excepted.*
e.g., *Exempli gratia, par exemple; p.ex.*
e.m.f., *El.E: Electromotive force.*
esp., *Especially.*
Esq., V. ESQUIRE.
ex cp., *Fin: Ex coupon.*
ex off., *Ex officio, q.v.*

F., *Ph: Fahrenheit.*
f., *Phot: Focal distance.*
Fah(r)., *Fahrenheit.*
f.a.q., *Com: Free alongside quay.*
f.a.s., *Com: Free alongside ship.*
F.C.A., *Fellow of the Institute of Chartered Accountants.*

F.M., *Mil: Field Marshal.*
f.o.b., *Com: Free on board.*
f.o.r., *Com: Free on rail.*
f.o.w., *Com: Free on wharf.*
f.oz., *Pharm: Fluid ounces. V.* OUNCE[1] 2.
F.R.C.M., *Fellow of the Royal College of Music.*
F.R.C.O., *Fellow of the Royal College of Organists.*
F.R.C.P., *Fellow of the Royal College of Physicians.*
F.R.C.S., *Fellow of the Royal College of Surgeons.*
F.R.G.S., *Fellow of the Royal Geographical Society.*
F.R.S., *Fellow of the Royal Society.*
f.-s., *Mec: Foot-second(s).*
ft, *Meas: Foot, feet. Mec:* **ft-lb.**, *foot-pound.*
F.Z.S., *Fellow of the Zoological Society.*

gal(l)., *Meas: Gallon(s), q.v.*
G.B., *Great Britain.*
G.B.E., *Grand Cross of the British Empire.*
G.C., *George Cross.*
G.C.B., *Grand Cross of the Order of the Bath.*
G.C.M.G., *Grand Cross of the Order of St Michael and St George.*
G.C.S.I., *Grand Commander of the Order of the Star of India.*
G.C.V.O., *Grand Cross of the Royal Victorian Order.*
Gen., *Mil: General.*
Geo., *George.*
G.H.Q., *Mil: General Head-quarters.*
G.M.T., *Greenwich mean time.*
G.O.C., *Mil: General officer commanding.*
G.P., *Med: General practitioner.*
G.P.O., *General Post Office.*
G.R., *Georgius Rex.*
gr., **1.** *Com: Gross.* **2.** *(a) Gramme(s). (b) Grain(s).*

H.C.F., *Mth: Highest common factor.*
H.E., **1.** *(a) His Eminence. (b) His Excellency.* **2.** *High explosive.*
H.G., *His Grace, sa Grandeur.*
hl., *Meas: Hectolitre.*
H.M., *His (Her) Majesty.*
hm., *Meas: Hectometre.*
H.M.S., *His (Her) Majesty's Ship.*
H.M.S.O., *His Majesty's Stationery Office.*
Hon., **1.** *V.* HONOURABLE 2. **2. Hon. Sec.**, *Honorary Secretary.*
Hons, *Sch: Honours. V.* HONOUR[1] 5.
h.p., *Horse-power.*
H.Q., *Mil: etc: Head-quarters.*
hr(s), *Hour(s).*
H.R.H., *His (Her) Royal Highness.*
h.t., *El: High tension.*

id., *Idem.*
i.e., *Id est, c'est-à-dire; c.-à-d.*
I.L.O., *International Labour Office.*
I.L.P., *Pol: Independent Labour Party.*
Inc., *Incorporated, q.v.*
incl., *Inclusive.*
inst., *Instant. V.* INSTANT[1] 2.
I.O.U., *See page 404.*

J., *Ph.Meas: Joule.*
J.C., **1.** *Jesus Christ.* **2.** *Hist: Julius Cæsar.*
Jno., *John.*
jnr., *Junior.*
J.P., *Justice of the Peace. V.* PEACE 2.
jun., *Junior.*

K.B.E., *Knight of the British Empire.*

K.C., *Jur: King's Counsel. V.* COUNSEL[1] 4.
K.C.B., *Knight Commander of the Bath.*
K.C.I.E., *Knight Commander of the Indian Empire.*
K.C.M.G., *Knight Commander of the Order of St Michael and St George.*
K.C.S.I., *Knight Commander of the Star of India.*
K.C.V.O., *Knight Commander of the Royal Victorian Order.*
K.G., *Knight of the Order of the Garter.*
kg., *Meas: Kilogram.*
km., *Meas: Kilometre(s).*
K.P., *Knight of the Order of St Patrick.*
K.T., *Knight of the Order of the Thistle.*
Kt, *Knight.*
K.V.A., **kva.**, *El: Kilovolt-ampere(s).*
K.W., **kw.**, *El: Kilowatt.*

L., **£**, *Num: Libra, libræ, pound(s) (sterling).*
lb(s)., *Libra, libræ, pound(s) (avoirdupois).*
L.C.M., *Mth: Least common multiple.*
L.D.S., *Licentiate in Dental Surgery.*
Lieut., *Mil: Lieutenant.*
lit., *Meas: Litre.*
LL.B., *Legum Baccalaureus.*
LL.D., *Legum Doctor.*
L.R.A.M., *Licentiate of the Royal Academy of Music.*
L.R.C.P., *Licentiate of the Royal College of Physicians.*
L.R.C.S., *Licentiate of the Royal College of Surgeons.*
l.t., *El: Low tension, basse tension.*
Lt., *Mil: Lieutenant.*
Ltd., *Com: Limited.*

m., *Metre(s), mètre(s); m.*
M.A., *Magister Artium, Master of Arts.*
ma., *El: Milliampere(s).*
Maj., *Mil: Major, commandant.*
M.B., *Medicinæ Baccalaureus.*
M.B.E., *Member of the Order of the British Empire.*
M.C., **1.** *Master of Ceremonies. V.* MASTER[1] 1. **2.** *Magister Chirurgiæ, Master of Surgery.* **3.** *U.S: Member of Congress.* **4.** *Military Cross.*
M.C.C., *Cr: Marylebone Cricket Club.*
M.Ch., *Magister Chirurgiæ.*
M.D., *Medicinæ Doctor.*
mfd, *El: Microfarad.*
M.F.H., *Master of Foxhounds.*
mg., *Meas: Milligram(me).*
Mgr, *R.C.Ch: Monsignor.*
M.I.C.E., *Member of the Institution of Civil Engineers.*
M.I.E.E., *Member of the Institute of Electrical Engineers.*
M.I.Mech.E., *Member of the Institution of Mechanical Engineers.*
ml., *Meas: Millilitre.*
M.M., *Military Medal.*
mm., *Meas: Millimetre(s).*
M.O., *Medical officer. V.* MEDICAL.
M.O.H., *Medical Officer of Health. V.* MEDICAL.
mort(g)., *Mortgage.*
M.P., *Member of Parliament.*
M.P.S., *Member of the Pharmaceutical Society.*
M.R.C.P., *Member of the Royal College of Physicians.*
M.R.C.S., *Member of the Royal College of Surgeons.*
M.R.I.B.A., *Member of the Royal Institute of British Architects.*

M.S., *Master of Surgery.*
M.Sc., *Master of Science.*
Mus. B(ac)., *Musicæ Baccalaureus.*
Mus. D(oc)., *Musicæ Doctor.*
M.V.O., *Member of the Royal Victorian Order.*

N.B., **1.** *Nota bene.* **2.** *North Britain,* Écosse.
N.C.O., *Mil : Non-commissioned officer.*
nem. con., *See page* 505.
N.S.P.C.C., *National Society for the Prevention of Cruelty to Children.*

ob., *Obiit.*
O.B.E., *(Officer of the) Order of the British Empire.*
O.C., *Mil : Officer commanding.*
O.H.M.S., *Post: On His Majesty's Service.* *V.* MAJESTY.
O.M., *Order of Merit.*
O.S., **1.** *Nau : Ordinary seaman.* **2.** *Com : (a) Out of stock. (b) Out size, q.v.*
O.T.C., *Officers' Training Corps. V.* OFFICER[1] 2.
Oxon., **1.** *Geog : Oxfordshire.* **2.** *Sch : Oxoniensis,* de l'Université d'Oxford.
oz., *Meas : Ounce(s).*

p.a., *Per annum.*
pat., *Patent,* breveté.
P.C., **1.** *Police Constable.* **2.** *(a) Privy Council. (b) Privy Councillor.*
p.c., **1.** *Postcard.* **2.** *Per cent.*
per an., *Per annum.*
per pro., *Per procurationem.*
Ph.D., *Philosophiæ Doctor.*
P/L, *Book-k : Profit and loss.*
P.M., **1.** *Prime Minister.* **2.** *Postmaster.*
p.m., *Post meridiem, q.v.*
P.M.G., *Postmaster General.*
P.O., **1.** *Post office.* **2.** *Postal order.* **3.** *Navy : Petty officer.*
p.p., p. pro., *Per procurationem.*
Preb., *Ecc : Prebendary.*
pref., *Fin : Preference.*
pro tem., *Pro tempore. V.* PRO[1] 3.
prox. = PROXIMO.
prox. acc., *Proxime accessit.*
P.S., *Postscript.*
P.T., **1.** *Pupil teacher.* **2.** *Physical training.*
Pte., *Mil : Private.*
P.T.O., *Please turn over. V.* OVER II. 3 *(b).*

Q.E.D., *Geom : Quod erat demonstrandum.*
Q.M.S., *Quartermaster sergeant.*
qr., *Meas : Quarter.*
qto, *Paperm : Quarto,* in-quarto.
q.v., *Quod vide.*

r., *Num : Rupee.*
R.A., *(a) Royal Academy. (b) Royal Academician.*
R.A.F., *Royal Air Force.*
R.C., *Roman Catholic.*
R.D., R/D, *Bank : Referred to drawer. V.* REFER 1.
recd, *Received.*
ref., *Com.Corr : Reference . . ., mention. . .*
regd, *Registered.*
Rev., **1.** *B : Revelation(s).* **2.** *Ecc : See* REVEREND 2.

R.I., *Rex Imperator, Regina Imperatrix.*
R.I.P., *Requiescat in pace.*
R.M., **1.** *Royal Mail.* **2.** *Resident magistrate.*
R.N., *Royal Navy.*
R.N.V.R., *Royal Naval Volunteer Reserve.*
r.p.m., *Revolutions per minute.*
R.R., **1.** *Right Reverend. V.* REVEREND 2. **2.** *U.S : Railroad.* **3.** *Phot : Rapid rectilinear lens.*
R.S.M., *Mil : Regimental Sergeant-major.*
R.S.P.C.A., *Royal Society for the Prevention of Cruelty to Animals.*
Rt Hon., *Right Honourable. V.* HONOURABLE 2.
Rt Rev., *Right Reverend. V.* REVEREND 2.

S., **1.** *Saint.* **2.** *Num : Solidi, shillings.*
Salop., *Geog : Shropshire.*
s.d., *Sine die,* indéfiniment.
sec., **1.** *Secretary.* **2.** *Second.*
sen(r)., *Senior.*
Sergt, *Mil : Sergeant.*
S.M., *Mil : Sergeant-major, q.v.*
Soc., *Society.*
S.O.S., *Nau :* Signal de détresse ; S.O.S.
sp. gr., *Ph : Specific gravity.*
sq., *Square.* **sq. ft**, *square feet.*
S.S., *Nau : Steamship,* vapeur.
St, **1.** *Street.* **2.** *Saint.*
st., *Meas : Stone.*
stg, *Sterling.*
s.v., *Sub voce,* voir sous le mot.

T.B., *Med : (Also* **Tb.**) *Tuberculosis.*
Thos., *Thomas.*
T.U.C., *Trades Union Congress.*

U.K., *Geog : The United Kingdom.*
ult., *Ultimo, q.v.*
U.S.(A), *Geog : United States (of America).*
U.S.S.R., *The Union of Socialist Soviet Republics.*

v., **1.** *Vide,* voir. **2.** *B : Verse.* **3.** *El : Volt.*
va., *El.Meas : Volt-ampere(s).*
V.A.D., *Voluntary Aid Detachment.*
V.C., *Victoria Cross.*
Ven., *Ecc : Venerable.*
vid., *Vide.* Vid. inf., *vide infra.*
Vis(ct), *Viscount,* vicomte.
vol(s), *Volume(s).*

w., *El.Meas : Watt.* **w.-hr.**, *watt-hour.*
W.A.A.F., *Women's Auxiliary Air Force.*
W.C., *Water-closet.*
Wm., *William.*
W.P., *Weather permitting.*
W.R.N.S., *Women's Royal Naval Service.*
W.S., *Jur : (Scot.) Writer to the Signet.*
wt, *Weight,* poids.

X., *Cross. Charing X, Charing Cross.*
xd., *Fin : Ex dividend.*

yd(s). *Meas : Yard(s),* yard(s).
Y.M.C.A., *Young Men's Christian Association.*
Y.W.C.A., *Young Women's Christian Association.*

SUPPLEMENT
PART TWO
ENGLISH—FRENCH

PART TWO
ENGLISH—FRENCH

absenteeism [absən'tiːizm], s. Absentéisme m.
ack-ack ['ak'ak], s. Mil: Défense f contre-avions, abbr., D.C.A., défense antiaérienne.
advertisement, s. **2.** (a) Classified advertise-ments, petites annonces.
age-group, s. Mil: etc.: Classe f.
air¹, s. **I.** (b) Av: **The Fleet Air Arm,** = l'Aéro-nautique Navale, l'Aéronavale f. **The Royal Air Force** = L'Armée f de l'air. **Air chief marshal,** Général m d'armée aérienne. **Air marshal,** Général de Corps d'armée aérienne. **Air vice marshal,** Général de division aérienne. **Air commodore,** Général de brigade aérienne.
airborne ['ɛərbɔːrn], a. Aéroporté. **Airborne radar,** radar m d'avion.
aircraft, s. Av: **2.** Avion m. **Torpedo-carrying aircraft,** avion torpilleur.
aircraftman ['ɛərkrɑːftmən], s.m. Soldat m. **A. First-class,** soldat de première classe. **Leading a.,** caporal.
aircraftwoman ['ɛərkrɑːftwumən], s.f. Femme soldat de la W.R.A.F. **Leading a.,** Femme caporal de la W.R.A.F.
aircrew ['ɛərkruː], s. Équipage m d'avion.

airfield ['ɛərfiːld], s. Champ m d'aviation.
'air-hostess, s. Av: Hôtesse f de l'air.
air-lift ['ɛərlift], s. Av: Pont aérien.
'air-mail, s. Courrier m par avion.
airstrip ['ɛərstrip], s. Av: **I.** Terrain m d'atter-rissage.
all-clear, s. (Signal m de) fin d'alerte.
allergic ['alə:rdʒik], a. Med: Allergique.
allergy ['alə:rdʒi], s. Med: Allergie f.
amount², v.i. **2.** (Be equivalent) Se résumer, se borner, se ramener (to, à).
amplifier, s. **2.** W.Tel: Haut-parleur m.
announcer, s. **2.** W.Tel: Annonceur m, speaker m, speakerin f.
anti-freeze, s. Aut: Anti-gel m. inv.
appeasement, s. (c) A. policy, Munichisme m.
Arabia. Pr.n. Geog: **Saudi Arabia,** l'Arabie Séoudite.
arm², s. usu. pl. **I.** F: To be up in arms, se gendarmer (against, contre).
armour¹, s. **2.** (c) Unités blindées, blindés.
asdic [azdik], s. Asdic m.
atom, s. Mil: **Atom bomb,** bombe f atomique.
auto-cycle, s. Cyclomoteur m.

B

baby-sitter, s. Garde-bébé mf.
bacteriological [baktiːəri'ɔlədzikal], a. Bac-tériologique.
ball-point, s. **Ball-point pen,** stylo m à bille.
barrage¹, s. **2.** (b) **Barrage balloon,** ballon m de protection.
bashing, s. F: Mil: etc.: To take, get, a b., prendre quelque chose.
basic, a. **I.** B. pay, salaire m de base.
'battle-dress, s. Mil: Tenue f de campagne.
bazooka [ba'zuːkɑ], s. Artil: Bazooka m.
belt¹, s. **3.** Green b., ceinture f de verdure.
Benelux ['benelʌks]. Pr.n. Geog: Bénélux.
benzedrine ['benzidriːn]. **5.** Benzédrine f.
better¹. 2. (a) **That's better!** A la bonne heure!
bind¹, s. **3.** F: Scie f, casse-pieds m. inv.
bipod ['baipɔd], s. Mil: Bipied m.
birthday, s. B. party, réunion d'anniversaire.
biscuit, s. **I.** (a) **Biscuit factory,** biscuiterie f.
'black-out, s. **2.** Civil Defence: Black-out m; extinction f des lumières.
'black-out, v. **I.** v.i. Éteindre les lumières, faire le black-out. v.tr. To b.-o. a house, faire le black-out dans une maison.
blah [blɑː], s. F: **I.** Boulette f, gaffe f. **2.** Bêtises f.pl.
blimp, s. Aer: Vedette aérienne.

blitz¹ [blits], s. F: Bombardement aérien.
blitz², v.tr. The house was blitzed, la maison a été endommagée, détruite par un bombardement.
'blitzkrieg [blitskriːg], s. Guerre éclair.
blood, s. **I.** To spit b., voir rouge.
'blood-bank, s. Banque f de sang.
'blood-donor, s. Donneur, -euse, de sang.
'blood-group, s. Groupe sanguin.
blow out. 2. v.i. (d) The paper blew out of the window, le journal s'est envolé par la fenêtre.
'blue(-)print, s. Dessin négatif; photocalque m; F: bleu m; F: plan m, projet m.
booby-trap, s. Mil: Piège m; mine-piège f.
boy, s.m. **I.** (f) F: **Barrow boy** = marchand m des quatre saisons.
bra [brɑ], s. F: = BRASSIÈRE.
breeze-block, s. Parpaing m.
Bren-gun ['brenɡʌn], s. Mil: = Fusil mitrail-leur. **Bren-gun carrier** = chenillette f.
brief¹, v.tr. **3.** Donner une mission à; munir d'instructions, fournir des directives à.
brief-case, s. Serviette f.
briefing, s. **I.** B. of a case, constitution f du dossier d'une affaire. **2.** Instructions f, direc-tives f.
II. broadcast, s. Televis: Live b., prise de vue directe.

943

brown off, *v.tr.* *F:* Décourager (qn). **To be browned off,** avoir le cafard, être découragé.
bull-dozer [buldozər], *s.* **1.** *Metalw:* Machine *f* à refouler, à cintrer. **2.** *Civ.E:* Bull-dozer *m.*

bunker[1], *s.* **2.** *Mil:* Blockhaus; abri fortifié.
bush-shirt, *s.* = Saharienne *f.*
butane [bjutɛin], *s:* *Ch:* Butane *m.*
by-election, *s.* *Pol:* Élection partielle.

C

cableway [keiblwei], *s.* Blondin *m.*
call-up, *s.* *Mil:* *Navy:* Appel *m* sous les drapeaux.
camera, *s.* **1.** (*a*) *Televis:* Camera *f,* caméra *f.*
camper, *s.* **2.** Campeur, -euse.
candy-striped, *a.* Pékiné.
cannibalize [kanibalaːiz], *v.tr.* Cannibaliser, démonter (pour utiliser les pièces détachées). **To c. an engine,** démonter un moteur.
canoeing, *s.* Canoéisme *m.*
canoeist [ka'nuist], *s.* Canoéiste *mf.*
care[2], *v.i.* **1.** *F:* *I couldn't care less,* je m'en fiche.
carrier-borne, *a.* *Av:* *Nav:* Embarqué. **Carrier-borne aircraft,** l'aviation embarquée.
cartoon[1]. **2.** (*c*) *Cin:* Dessin animé, cartoon *m.*
cassette [ka'set], *s.* *Phot:* Chargeur *m.*
catapult[2], *v.tr.* *Av:* Catapulter.
catapulting, *s.* *Av:* Catapultage *m.*
'cat's-eye, *s.* *Opt:* Cataphote *m.* Catadioptre *m.*
cave[1], *s.* *Art:* (*attrib. use*) **Cave art,** art *m* rupestre. **Cave hunting,** spéléologie *f.*
chain-work, *s.* Travail *m* à la chaîne.
character, *s.* **5.** (*a*) *Th:* **Characters in order of appearance,** distribution *f* (par ordre d'entrée en scène).
cheese[1], *s.* **1.** **Blue cheese,** (fromage) bleu. **Processed cheese,** fromage industriel.
cheese-off, *v.tr.* *P:* Décourager (qn). **To be cheesed-off,** avoir le cafard, être découragé.
choc-ice ['tʃɔkais], *s.* *F:* Esquimau *m,* chocolat glacé.
chocolate. **1.** *s.* **Cooking chocolate,** chocolat *m* à cuire. **Fondant chocolate,** chocolat fondant.
choosy ['tʃuːzi], *a.* *F:* Difficile.
clear[2], *v.* **I.** **3.** **To c. of mines,** déminer.
clearance, *s.* **1.** *Mil:* *Bomb, shell c.,* désobusage *m.* *Mine c.,* déminage *m.*
clementine [klemən'tain], *s.* *Hort:* Clémentine *f*
climb, *s.* **2.** **Steep c.,** grimpette *f.*
climbing-irons. *s.pl.* Grimpettes *f.*
clip[1], *s.* **1.** *Jewellery:* Clip.
clipper, *s.* **3.** *Av:* Clipper *m.*
clippie ['klipi], *s.f.* *F:* Receveuse *f* (*in bus*).
clue, *s.* **2.** *F:* **He hasn't a c.,** il ne sait rien de rien.
clueless ['kluːles], *a.* *F:* **He's quite c.,** il ne sait jamais rien.
coat[1], *s.* **1.** (*b*) (*For women*) **house coat,** robe *f* d'intérieur, déshabillé *m.*

coco(a)-nut, *s.* **Coco(a)-nut plantation,** cocoteraie *f.*
column, *s.* **3.** *Pol:* **Fifth column,** cinquième colonne *f.*
combined, *a.* *Mil:* *Nav:* *Av:* **Combined operation,** opération *f* amphibie.
commando [ko'mando], *s.* *Mil:* Corps franc.
commonwealth, *s.* (*c*) **The British Commonwealth of Nations,** le Commonwealth Britannique.
communistic [kɔmju'nistik], *a.* Communisant.
compensation, *s.* **War damage compensation,** les dommages *m* de guerre.
concession, *s.* *Com:* Réduction *f.*
cone, *s.* **1.** (*b*) **Ice(cream) cone,** cornet *m* de glace, de crème glacée.
consumer, *s.* *Pol.Ec:* **Consumer goods,** biens *m* de consommation.
contact[1], *s.* **2.** (*a*) **Contact man,** employé *m* de liaison.
contact[2], *v.tr.* Contacter (qn), s'aboucher, se mettre en relation, avec qn.
container, *s.* (*b*) *Rail:* **(Freight) container,** cadre *m* de déménagement.
'continuity-girl, *s.* *Cin:* Script-girl *f.*
controlled [kɔn'trould], *a.* Dirigé. **Sold at the c. price,** vendu à la taxe. **To fix a c. price for a food-product,** taxer une denrée.
cook[1], *s.* (*b*) *Mil:* *F:* Cuistot *m.*
cornflakes [kɔːrnfleikʒ], *s.* *pl.* = Paillettes *f* de maïs.
councillor, *s.* *County c.* = conseiller général.
counsellor, *s.* *Dipl:* Conseiller *m* d'ambassade.
counter[1], *s.* **4.** (*b*) *F:* **To sell under the counter,** vendre en cachette.
II. crack, *v.i.* **5.** *F:* **To get cracking,** s'y mettre. **Get cracking!** grouille-toi!
crackers, *a.* *F:* **He's c.,** il est cinglé.
crock[2], *s.* **2.** (*Of motor-car, etc.*) Tacot *m,* vieille guimbarde.
crooner, *s.* Chanteur, -euse, de charme.
cruiser, *s.* **Light cruiser,** contre-torpilleur *m.*
cup[1], *s.* **1.** *F:* **That's just my cup of tea,** c'est tout à fait dans mes cordes.
currency, *s.* **3.** *Pol.Ec:* **Hard currency,** monnaie forte.
curtain[1], *s.* **1.** (*a*) *Pol:* *Hist:* **Iron curtain,** rideau de fer.
cut[1], *s.* **1.** (*a*) **(Electricity) cut,** coupure *f* (de courant).

D

day, *s.* **1.** (*a*) **Day in day out,** à longueur *f.* de journée. *F:* **Let's call it a day,** tenons-nous-en là.
decontrol [diːkon'troul], *v.tr.* (*a*) Libérer (le commerce, etc.) des contraintes du gouverne-

ment. (*b*) *Adm:* **To decontrol the price of meat,** détaxer la viande.
defer[1], *v.tr.* *Mil:* Mettre en sursis (d'appel). **To d. s.o. on medical grounds,** ajourner qn.
de-ice [diː'ais], *v.tr.* *Av:* Dégivrer.

delinquency, *s.* **1.** *Juvenile d.,* criminalité *f* juvénile.

demister [di:ˈmistər], *s.* *Aut:* (Dispositif) anti-buée *m.*

deration [ˈdi:raʃ(ə)n], *v.tr.* Dérationner.

desk-ˈpad, *s.* Sous-main *m.inv.*; bloc-notes *m.*

deviationism [di:ˈviˈeiʃ(ə)nizm], *s.* *Pol:* Déviationnisme *m.*

deviationist [di:viˈeiʃ(ə)nist], *a. & s.* Déviationniste (*mf*).

dial², *v.tr.* **1.** (*a*) *Tp:* Appeler à l'automatique. To dial 999, téléphoner à la police, appeler Police Secours. (*b*) *v.i.* *Tp:* Composer, chiffrer, un numéro.

disk, *s.* (*b*) *Aut:* Wheel-disk, enjoliveur *m.*

dive-ˈbomb, *v.tr.* *Av:* Bombarder, attaquer en piqué.

dive-ˈbomber, *s.* *Av:* Bombardier *m* en piqué.

dive-ˈbombing, *s.* *Av:* Bombardement *f,* attaque *f,* en piqué.

do¹. I. *v.tr.* **1.** (*a*) *F:* That's done it! ça c'est le bouquet, c'est la fin de tout. I will have nothing to do with him, je ne veux pas avoir affaire à lui.

doodle-bug [ˈdudlbʌg], *s.* *F:* *Mil:* Bombe volante.

draft², *v.tr.* **2.** *Mil* Affecter.

drop¹, *s.* **2.** (*a*) *Av:* Ouverture *f.* Delayed d., ouverture retardée (d'un parachute).

drunk, *a.* *D.* as an owl, saoûl comme une bourrique.

duck¹, *s.* **1.** (*b*) That's like pouring water on a duck's back, c'est comme si on chantait. **3.** *Mil:* Crabe *m.*

E

economy, *s.* **2.** *Pol.Ec:* Planned economy, économie planifiée.

escapism [isˈkeipizm], *s.* Évasion *f* (de la réalité).

evacuee [iˈvakjui:], *s.* Évacué, -ée.

ever, *adv.* **2.** (*a*) (*Intensive*) I have been here e. since lunch, je suis là depuis le déjeuner. **3.** Worst ever, best ever, sans précédent.

extension, *s.* **3.** (*a*) *Tp:* Extension 35, poste *m* 35.

F

fair². I. (*a*). (*c*) Fair enough! Ça va! D'accord!

fellow-ˈtraveller, *s.* Communisant, -te. *Communists and their fellow-travellers,* les communistes et leurs compagnons de route.

fibrositis [faibroˈsaitis], *s.* *Med:* = Cellulite *f.*

ˈfilm-script, *s.* Scénario *m,* script *m.*

ˈfilm-strip, *s.* Film *m* fixe (d'enseignement).

fission [fiʃ(ə)n], *s.* **1.** *Biol:* Fissiparité *f.* **2.** *Ph:* Fission *f,* division *f,* désintégration. Nuclear fission, fission de l'atome.

flap¹, *s.* **3.** *F:* Affolement *m.* To get into a flap, ne plus savoir où donner de la tête.

flare¹, *s.* **1.** (*b*) *Av:* Brûlot *m.*

flashing², *s.* *Const:* Bande *f* de solin *m.*

flavour². **1.** *v.tr.* Aromatiser.

flicker¹, *s.* (*c*) *Televis:* Papillotement *m.*

flood-light², *v.tr.* *F:* Embraser (un monument).

ˈflying-ˈbomb, *s.* *Mil:* Bombe volante.

ˈflying-ˈcolumn, *s.* Police *f* du roulage.

foldable [ˈfouldəbl], *a.* Pliable.

fondant [ˈfɔndənt], *s.* Fondant *m.*

ˈfood-processing, *s.* The f.-p. industry, l'industrie *f* alimentaire.

foot¹, *pl.* **feet,** *s.* **1.** (*a*) *P:* My foot! mon œil.

freeze. **2.** *v.tr.* To f. wages, figer, bloquer, les solaires.

freight¹, *s.* **2.** (*b*) *Av:* Freight plane, avion *m* de transport.

fridge, frig [fridʒ]. *F:* = REFRIGERATOR.

frogman [ˈfrɔgman], *s.* Homme-grenouille *m.*

fuel-oil, *s.* Gaz-oil *m.*

G

gangsterism [ˈgaŋstərizm], *s.* Gangstérisme *m.*

garden¹, *s.* (*a*) Garden of remembrance = cimetière *m.*

germ, *s.* **2.** *G.* warfare, guerre *f* bactériologique.

Gestapo [geˈsta:pou], *s.* Gestapo *f.*

glass-house, *s.* **2.** *F:* Prison *f* militaire.

go-ˈslow, *a.* Go-slow policy, travail *m* au ralenti, grève perlée.

gore⁴, *v.tr.* Gored skirt, jupe *f* en forme, jupe à panneaux.

gratuitousness [graˈtjui:təsnəs], *s.* Gratuité *f.*

ˈgroin-vault, *s.* *Arch:* Voûte *f* d'arêtes.

ground², *s.* **5.** (*a*) *Av:* Ground staff, personnel rampant, non-navigant.

'half-'shaft, *s. Aut:* Demi-arbre *m.*
'half-'timbered, *a.* Half-timbered house, maison *f* en colombage *m.*
'half-'track, *s.* Chenille *f.* Half-track vehicle, autochenille *f.*
'hang-'over, *s. P: To have a h.-o.,* avoir mal aux cheveux.
haywire ['heiwaiər], *a. He's gone h.,* il ne tourne plus rond. *His plans have gone h.,* c'est une affaire loupée.
head¹, *s.* **6.** *(b) (Pers.)* Head teacher, directeur, -trice, d'école primaire.
'hedge-hop, *v.i. Av:* Voler en rase-mottes.

high-grade, *attrib. a.* **2.** *H.-g. petrol* supercarburant *m.*
hiker, *s. F:* Randonneur, -euse (à pied).
'hitch-hike, *v.i.* Faire de l'auto-stop.
'hitch-hiker ,*s.* Personne *f* qui fait de l'auto-stop.
'hitch-hiking, *s.* Auto-stop *m.*
holder, *s.* **2.** *(Device) (b)* Tooth-brush holder, (i) *(fixture)* porte-brosses *m* à dents, (ii) étui *m* à brosse à dents.
holiday, *s. (c)* Holidays with pay, congé payé.
hoot². **1.** *v.i. (c) Aut:* Klaxonner.
housework, *s.* Travaux *m* domestiques, de ménage. To do the housework, faire le ménage.

I

icy, *a.* **1.** Icy road, route verglacée.
indelible, *a. I. pencil,* crayon à encre indélébile.
infantile, *a.* **2.** *Med:* Infantile paralysis, poliomyélite *f.*
infiltration, *s.* **2.** *Communist i.,* noyautage *m.*
insurance, *s.* **1.** *(a)* Unemployment insurance,

assurance *f* chômage. Workmen's compensation insurance, assurance *f* contre les accidents du travail.
inter-war, *a.* The inter-war years, l'entre-deux guerres *m.*
Israeli [izreili], *a. & s. Geog:* Israëlien, -ienne.

J

jacket¹, *s.* **1.** *(a) Cost:* Sheepskin jacket, canadienne *f.* Lumberman's jacket, lumber jacket, blouson *m.* **2.** *(b)* Jacquette *f* (de livre).
jeep [dʒiːp], *s. Aut:* Jeep *f.*
Jerry. **2.** *s. F: (a)* Fritz *m,* Fridolin *m,* doryphore *m.*
'Jerry-can, *s.* Jerricane *f.*

jet², *s.* **3.** *Av: etc.:* Jet engine, moteur *m* à réaction, réacteur *m,* turboréacteur *m.* Jet plane, jet-propelled aircraft, avion *m* à réaction. Jet liner, avion (commercial) à réaction.
jig-saw, *s.* Jig-saw puzzle, puzzle *m.*
jump². **II.** *v.tr.* **1.** *To j. the queue,* passer avant son tour.

K

key², *v.tr.* **2.** *F:* Keyed up, gonflé à bloc.
kidnap, *v.tr.* Kidnapper.

II. knock off, *v.i. Ind: F: (Of workman)* Débaucher, *(at end of day)* débrayer.

L

lance-sergeant, *s. Mil: (a)* Caporal-chef *m.* *(b) (Mounted arms),* brigadier-chef *m.*
land², **2.** *v.i. (a) Nav: Av: To land (on deck of aircraft carrier),* apponter.
landing², *s.* **1.** *(c) Av:* Parachute landing, parachutage *m.*
'landing-barge, *s.* Péniche *f* de débarquement.
'landing-craft, *s.* Bâtiment *m* de débarquement.
'landing-strip, *s. Av:* Piste *f* d'atterrissage.
lay on, *v.tr.* **4.** *(b) F:* Arranger, préparer, organiser.
lease-'lend, *s. Pol.Ec:* Prêt-bail *m.*
leftism ['leftizm], *s.* Politique *f* de gauche.

leftist ['leftist], *a. Pol:* De gauche.
level out, *v.tr.* Égaliser.
light¹, *s.* **2.** *(c) Av: Boundary l.,* feu *m,* borne *f* de balisage. *Adm:* Traffic lights, signaux lumineux (de croisement).
linotype, *s.* Linotype operator, linotypiste *m.*
lipstick, *s. Toil:* Crayon-lèvres *m.*
living-room, *s.* Salle *f* de séjour.
load¹, *s.* **2.** *El: To shed the l.,* délester.
loopy ['luːpi], *a. P:* Toqué, dingo.
'lorry-borne, *a. Mil:* Porté.
'lumber-jacket *s.* Blouson *m.*
lung, *s. (a) Med:* Iron lung, poumon *m* d'acier.

machine-gun, *v.tr.* Mitrailler.
maladjustment, *s.* Inadaptation *f. Emotional m.,* déséquilibre émotif.
Malaya [ma'leija]. *Pr.n. Geog:* Malaisie *f.*
manœuvrability [ma'nuːvrəbiliti], *s. Av:* Maniabilité *f,* manœuvrabilité *f.*
maquis ['makiː], *s. Pol:* Maquis *m.* **To take to the maquis,** prendre le maquis. *Member of the m.,* maquisard *m.*
marker, *s.* **3.** (*a*) *Av: Boundary m.,* feu *m,* borne *f,* de balisage.
market¹, *s.* (*a*) **Black market,** marché *m* noir.

'milk-float, *s.* Voiture *f* de laitier.
'mine-sweeping, *s. Navy:* Balayage *m* de mines.
misfit, *a. & s.* Inadapté, (ée).
mistress, *s.f.* **1.** (*d*) *Sch: Kindergarten m.,* jardinière *f* d'enfants.
monitoring ['mɔnitəriŋ], *s. W.Tel:* **Monitoring station,** station *f* d'écoute.
'moth-proof, *a.* Anti-mite.
motor-cycle, *s. Lightweight m.-c.,* vélomoteur *m.*
motor-'scooter, *s.* Scooter *m.*
music, *s.* **Hot music,** jazz *m.*

N

nannie, nanny ['nani], *s.f.* Bonne d'enfant, nurse *f.*
Nazi ['naːtsi], *s.* Nazi.
Naz(i)ism ['naːts(i)izm], *s. Pol:* Nazisme *m.*
non-'resident, *a. & s.* **2.** (*Hotel*) Hôte de passage. **Open to non-residents,** repas servis aux voyageurs de passage.
nut, *s.* **1.** (*b*) *P: He is nuts,* il est cinglé.
nylon ['nailɔn], *s. Tex:* Nylon *m. N. stockings,* des bas *m* nylon.

O

occupation, *s.* **2.** (*b*) *Adm: To be in a reserved o.,* être affecté spécial, avoir une affectation spéciale.
occupational [ɔkju'peiʃən(ə)l], *a.* **Occupational disease,** maladie professionnelle. *O. therapy,* thérapie rééducative.
officer, *s.* **2.** (*c*) *Mil.Av: Flying o.,* lieutenant *m. Pilot o.,* sous-lieutenant *m. Acting pilot o.,* aspirant *m.*
  II. **on,** *adv.* **1.** (*a*) **Not on,** pas moyen. **It's simply not on,** il n'y a pas moyen.

onion, *s.* **2.** *P: She knows her onions,* elle connaît son affaire.
oomph [umf], *s. F:* Sex appeal *m.*
operator, *s.* **1.** *Wireless o.,* radio *m* (à bord d'un navire).
organ, *s.* **1.** *Mus:* (*d*) **Theatre organ,** orgue *m* de cinéma.
out. I. **3.** (*d*) *An all-out attack,* une attaque à fond, *F:* à tout casser, avec tous ses moyens.
out-of-'school, *a.* Extra-scolaire.
overnight, *adv.* Du jour au lendemain.

P

pain¹, *s.* **1.** (*a*) *F: He gives me a pain in the neck,* il me tape sur le système.
Pakistan [paki'staːn]. *Pr.n. Geog:* Pakistan *m.*
pancake¹, *s.* **1.** *Av:* **Pancake landing,** atterrissage *m* sur le ventre.
parachute¹. **2.** *attrib.* Parachutiste.
parachute², *v.i. & v.tr. Av:* Parachuter.
parachuting [parə'ʃuːtin], *s.* Parachutage *m.*
paratrooper [parə'truːpər], *s.* (Soldat) parachutiste *m.*
paratroops [parə'truːps], *s.pl.* (Soldats) parachutistes *m.*
  II. **pass³,** *v.tr.* **3.** (*a*) *F: To pass the buck,* se débrouiller sur le voisin.
pay², *v.tr.* **1.** (*a*) *Pay as you earn* = retenue *f* de l'impôt à la base, à la source.
phone¹, *s. F:* **Phone box,** cabine *f* téléphonique.

photocopy [fouto'kɔpi], *s.* Photocopie *f.*
photo-'finish. *Sp:* Photo *f* à l'arrivée, décision *f* par photo
photographer, *s.* **Street photographer** photo-stoppeur *m.*
picture¹, *s. F: To be in the p.,* être à la page, être tout à fait au courant.
pilot¹, *s.* **1.** (*c*) *Av: Ferry pilot,* pilote convoyeur, pilote de convoyage. **Test pilot,** pilote d'essais.
pincers, *s.* **3.** *attrib. Mil:* **Pincer(s) movement,** manœuvre *f* en tenailles.
'pin-up girl, *s. F:* Pin-up *f.*
pipe down, *v.i. F:* (i) Changer de ton, (ii) mettre une sourdine. (iii) *V:* **Pipe down!** boucle-la !
planning [planin], *s.* **1.** Tracé *m* (d'un plan).

2. Conception *f*, organisation *f* (d'un complot, *etc*.). **3.** *Pol.Ec:* Dirigisme *m*, planification *f*.
plastic. 3. *s. Ind:* Plastics, plastique *m*.
playlet ['pleilət], *s.* Piécette *f*.
prawn, *s.* Dublin bay prawn, langoustine *f*.
precaution, *s.* Air raid precautions, défense passive.
prefabricated [pri:'fabrikeitəd], *a.* Préfabriqué.
prefabrication [pri:fabri'keiʃ(ə)n], *s.* Préconstruction *f*.

pressure-cooker, *s. Cu:* Marmite *f* souspression.
pretty. **1.** *a.* (*a*) To be sitting pretty, être bien placé.
problem, *s.* Problem child, enfant *mf* difficile.
process², *v.tr.* **1.** *Ind:* Traiter; transformer.
processing [prou'sesiŋ], *s.* Traitement *m* d'une matière première.
publicize ['pʌblisai:z], *v.tr.* Faire connaître au public.

Q

quadruplet, *s.* **1.** *pl.* Quadruplets, quadruplé(e)s.
quads ['kwɔdz], *s.pl.* *F:* = QUADRUPLETS.

quins ['kwinz], *s.pl.* = QUINTUPLETS.
quintuplet, *s.* **2.** *pl.* Quintuplets, quintuplé(e)s.

R

radar ['reidɑːr], *s.* Radar *m*.
radiodetection ['reidioudi'tekʃ(ə)n], *s.* Radiodétection *f*.
radiolocation ['reidioulokeiʃ(ə)n], *s.* Radiorepérage *m*.
ration¹, *s. Adm:* Off the ration, sans tickets, en vente *f* libre.
record¹, *s.* **2.** (*a*) *F:* Off the record, en secret, entre nous.
refit, *s.* Réaménagement *m*.
refit, *v.tr.* **3.** Réaménager.
reflector, *s.* Catadioptre *m*, cataphote *m*.
refrigerator, *s.* (*a*) Réfrigérateur *m*.
register². **1.** *v.tr.* (*a*) *Mil:* Recenser. **2.** *v.i. Adm:* To r. with a tradesman, s'inscrire chez un commerçant.
registration, *s.* **1.** *Mil:* Recensement *m*.
rehabilitation, *s.* **3.** Rééducation *f*.
rehousing [ri:'hauziŋ], *s.* Recasement *m*.

release¹, *s.* **1.** (*a*) *Mil:* Mise *f* en disponibilité; *Adm:* démobilisation *f*.
resettlement [ri:'setlmənt], *s.* **3.** Recasement *m*.
resident. **2.** *s.* (*a*) Pensionnaire *mf*.
rest¹, *s.* **3.** Rest centre, centre *m* d'accueil.
ride¹, *s.* **1.** (*b*) *F:* To take s.o. for a ride, (ii) faire marcher, duper qn.
robot, *s.* Robot *m*.
rocket², *s. Mil. Av:* Rocket (propelled) fighter, chasseur-fusée *m*.
rocket³, *v.i.* (*c*) *Pol.Ec:* Rocketing prices, des prix qui montent en flèche.
rocket-gun, *s.* Lance-fusées *m*.
roof¹, *s.* **3.** *Aut:* Sunshine roof, toit ouvrant.
rotary, *a.* (*b*) Rotary printer, rotativiste *m*.
rough-handle [rʌf'handl], *v.tr.* Malmener.
roundabout. **I.** *s.* **2.** *Aut:* Rond-point *m*; *Adm:* sens *m* giratoire.

S

salvage¹. **2.** Salvage vessel, navire *m* de relevage.
San Marino [sanmɑ'riːnou]. *Pr.n. Geog:* (La république de) Saint-Marin.
saucer, *s.* (*a*) *F: Av:* Flying saucer, soucoupe volante.
sausage, *s.* **1.** (*a*) *P:* Not a s., nib de nib.
saving², *s.* **2.** (*b*) Savings certificate = bon *m* d'épargne.
scare¹, *s. War* s., psychose *f* de guerre.
school¹, *s.* **1.** (*a*) Secondary Grammar School = Collège *m*. Secondary Modern School = Collège moderne. Government school, école publique.
scram [skram], *v.i.* *P:* Partir, filer; décamper; fiche le camp.
screen², *v.tr.* **4.** (*b*) To screen (s.o.), examiner et interroger (qn).

'script-writer, *s.* Scénariste *mf*.
scullery, *s.* Laverie *f*.
second². **I.** *a.* **1.** (*b*) To take second place, passer second.
self-'criticism, *s.* Autocritique *f*.
self-'service, *s. Com:* Libre service *m*.
sergeant, *s.m.* **2.** (*a*) *Mil.Av:* Flight s., sergent-chef.
service¹, *s.* **5.** (*b*) Social services, institutions sociales.
serviceman ['sɔ:rvismən], *s.m.* Soldat mobilisé *m*. National serviceman, soldat (qui fait son service militaire).
set¹, *s.* **1.** (*b*) *Television* set, télérécepteur *m*.
shadow¹, *s.* **4.** *Pol:* S. government, gouvernement *m* fantôme.
shaver, *s.* **1.** Electric shaver, rasoir électrique.

shoot², II. *v.tr.* **1.** *Aut:* To s. *the traffic lights*, brûler les signaux. **2.** (*b*) *F:* To s. *a line*, exagérer.
'show-down, *s.* **2.** Déballage *m.*
'ski-lift, 'ski-train, *s.* Remonte-pentes *m.inv.*
smasher¹, *s.* (*c*) *F:* **She's a smasher**, elle est formidable.
snoop [snuːp], *v.i.* Fureter, fouiner.
snooper [snuːpər], *s.* *F:* Inquisiteur, -euse.
'speed-indicator, *s.* *Av:* Badin *m.*
spin¹. **1.** (*b*) *Av:* **Steep** s., vrille serrée. *F:* To *get into a flat s.*, ne pas savoir où donner de la tête.
spiv [spiv], *s.* (*a*) Profiteur ; trafiquant du marché noir. (*b*) Parasite *m.*
splice², *v.tr.* **2.** (*b*) *Tex:* **Nylon spliced**, renforcé nylon.
squad, *s.* **2.** (*c*) **Rescue squad**, équipe *m* de secours.
squadron, *s.* **1.** (*b*) *Mil. Av:* S. **leader**, commandant *m* de groupe.
staggered, *a.* **S. holidays**, congés échelonnés.
stateless ['steitlis], *a.* *Jur:* **Stateless person**, apatride *mf.*

station¹, *s.* **1.** (*b*) *Av:* Escadre aérienne.
stockpile¹ ['stɔkpail], *s.* Stock *m* de réserve.
stockpile². **1.** *v.i.* Stocker, constituer des stocks de réserve. **2.** *v.tr.* Stocker.
stockpiling ['stɔkpailiŋ], *s.* Stockage *m.*
stimy², *v.tr.* *Golf:* Barrer le trou à (son adversaire). *F:* To be stimied, rester le bec dans l'eau.
stooge¹ [stuːdʒ], *s.* *F:* Nègre *m.*
stooge², *v.i.* *F:* (*a*) Faire le nègre. (*b*) To stooge around, faire un tour, flâner.
stop-press, *attrib.a.* *Journ:* Dernière heure.
stratocruiser ['stratɔkruːzər], **stratoliner** ['stratɔlainər], *s.* Avion *m* (de ligne) stratosphérique.
'strip-'tease, *s.* Acte *m* de déshabillage *m.*
sub-'machine-gun, *s.* Mitraillette *f.*
'sun-glasses, *s.pl.* Lunettes fumées, verres fumés.
surrealism [sər'riːəlizm], *s.* Surréalisme *m.*
Swiss. **1.** *a.* Helvétique. **The Swiss Government**, le Gouvernement helvétique.
switchboard, *s.* (*b*) *Tp:* S. **operator**, standardiste *mf.*

T

tap², *v.tr.* **1.** (*b*) Drainer.
tax¹, *s.* **1.** (*a*) *Adm:* **Purchase tax** = taxe *f* de luxe.
'tax-evasion, *s.* Fraude fiscale.
tea, *s.* **1.** (*a*) **China, Indian, tea**, thé de Chine, de Ceylan. (*b*) **(Afternoon) tea** = goûter *m.*
teleprinter, *s.* Téléimprimeur *m*, téléscripteur *m.*
televiewer ['teli'vjuər], *s.* Téléspectateur, -trice.
television, *s.* **Television set**, téléviseur *m.*
temporary, *a.* (*a*) *T.* **measures**, mesures *f* transitoires. *T.* **post**, situation *f* intérimaire, par intérim.
therapist ['θerapist], *s.* **Occupational therapist**, spécialiste de thérapie rééducative.
therapy ['θerəpi], *s.* Thérapie *f.*
thumb², *v.tr.* **3.** *F:* **To thumb a lift**, faire de l'auto-stop.
tight-fisted, *a.* *F:* **To be tight-fisted**, être très près de ses sous.

'time-bomb, *s.* Bombe *f* à retardement.
title¹, *s.* **2.** *Cin:* **Credit titles**, générique *m.*
token, *s.* **1.** **Token strike**, grève *f* d'avertissement.
'tommy-gun, *s.* Mitraillette *f.*
'touch-typist, *s.* Dactylo accomplie.
'town-planning, *s.* Urbanification *f.*
trade, *s.* **5.** *Attrib.* **Trade cycle**, cycle *m* économique.
'traffic-jam, *s.* Encombrement *m* (de circulation), embouteillage *m.*
trailer, *s.* **3.** *Cin:* Film *m* annonce.
trough, *s.* **5.** (*Of low pressure, of depression*) Dépression *f*, zone *f* dépressionnaire.
truncheon, *s.* **Rubber truncheon**, matraque *f* en caoutchouc.
tuxedo [tʌk'siːdou], *s.* Smoking blanc.

U

under-developed, *a.* **3.** *Pol.Ec:* **U.-d. countries**, pays sous-développés.
underground. **1.** *adv.* (*c*) *F:* **To go underground**, prendre le maquis. **2.** *a.* (*b*) Clandestin. **Underground forces**, armée clandestine.
unrationed [ʌn'raʃ(ə)nd], *a.* *Adm:* En vente libre.

use¹, *s.* **3.** **For all the use it is to me**, pour ce que j'en fais.
utility, *s.* **1.** (*a*) *Adm:* **Utility goods**, articles *m* d'utilité sociale. (*b*) **Public utility services**, services publics. (*c*) **Utility car**, voiture *f* à carrosserie canadienne.

V

van², *s.* **2.** (*b*) **Police loud-speaker van**, camionnette *f* de police.
view², **4.** *v.i.* *Televis:* Regarder.

viewer ['vjuːər], *s.* **1.** *Televis:* Téléspectateur, -trice.
vulnerable, *a.* (*a*) *Mil:* Perméable.

wage¹, s. (a) Pol.Ec: Living wage, minimum vital.

wait². I. v.i. (a) Wait-and-see policy, attentisme m.

walkie-talkie ['wɔːki'tɔki], s. W.Tel: F: Émetteur-récepteur m. ; poste de radio portatif.

war¹, s. Total war, guerre totale. Cold war, guerre froide. War of nerves, guerre des nerfs.

warden¹, s. I. (e) Air-raid warden, chef m d'îlot.

warning², s. I. (Air-raid) warning, alerte f.

wash down, s. Toilette complète.

washer¹, s. 2. (a) Laund: F: Electric washer, machine à laver électrique.

'water-heater, s. Chauffe-eau m.inv.

'water-skiing, s. Ski m nautique.

welfare, s. Welfare State, (i) État social, (ii) Iron: État providence.

whinberry ['hwinːberi], s. Bot: Airelle f, myrtille f.

'whitlow-grass, s. Drave printanière.

'wide-'eyed, a. Les yeux grands ouverts, les yeux écarquillés. en écarquillant les yeux. He looked at me in wide-eyed amazement, il m'a regardé les yeux écarquillés par la stupeur.

windbreaker ['windbrekər], **wind-cheater** ['wind'tʃitər], s. Blouson m.

window-box, s. Jardinière f.

'wind-proof, a. A l'épreuve du vent.

'wind-sock, s. Av: Manche f à air, biroute f.

'wing-chair, s. Furn: Fauteuil m à oreillettes.

wishful, a. F: Wishful thinking, pensée née du désir.

wizard, a. F: Épatant, excellent, chic, P: au poil.

woolly. I. a. (d) F: Vaseux.

workshop, s. Mobile workshop, camion-atelier m.

wrapper, s. 2. (b) Book wrapper, liseuse f.

Y

'yes-man, s. F: Beni-Oui-oui m.inv.

| **yodel²,** v.i. Mus: Yodler.

Z

zebra, s. Zebra (crossing), passage clouté.

| **zoo,** s. F: Zoo m.

A.A., *Anti-Aircraft* = D.C.A., Défense contre avions.
A.F.C., *Air Force Cross.*
A.F.M., *Air Force Medal.*
A.P., *Associated Press.*
A.T.C., *Av: Air Training Corps* = P.M.S., préparation militaire supérieure (pour l'aviation).
B.E.A., *British European Airways.*
B.E.M., *British Empire Medal.*
B.Litt., *Baccalaureus Litterarum, Bachelor of Letters.*
B.O.A.C., *British Overseas Airways Corporation.*
B.R., *British Railways.*
B.U.P., *British United Press.*
C.B.S., *U.S: Columbia Broadcasting Service.*
C.D., 1. *Civil Defence* = D.P., Défense passive. **2.** *Corps Diplomatique.*
C.M.S., *Church Missionary Society.*
D.D.T., *Dichloro-diphenyl-trichloroethane.*
D.P., *Displaced person,* personne déplacée.
D.V., En principe.
E.P.(N.S.), *Electro-plated (nickel silver).*
E.R.P., *European Recovery Programme.*
F.B.I., *U.S: Federal Bureau of Investigation.*
F.R.I.B.A., *Fellow of the Royal Institute of British Architects.*
G.C.E., *General Certificate of Education* = Baccalauréat.
G.I., *U.S. Army: General issue,* mobilisé.
G.M., *George Medal.*
G.S.O., *Mil: General Staff Officer.*
H.G., *Home Guard.*
H.M.I., *Her Majesty's Inspector* = Inspecteur d'Académie.
L.A.C., *Leading Aircraftman* = caporal.
L.S.D., *Librae, Solidi, Denarii, pounds, shillings and pence;* cash.
m., 2. *Million.*
M.T.B., *Motor Torpedo Boat,* vedette ancetorpilles.
N.A.A.F.I., *Navy, Army and Air Force Institutes.*
N.A.T.O., *North Atlantic Treaty Organisation.*
N.C.B., *National Coal Board.*
N.F.S., *National Fire Service.*
N.I.B., *National Institute for the Blind.*

No., *Number.*
N.U.R., *National Union of Railwaymen.*
N.U.S., *National Union of Students.*
N.U.T., *National Union of Teachers.*
O.C.T.U., *Mil: Officer Cadet Training Unit.*
O.E.E.C., *Organisation for European Economic Co-operation.*
P.A., *Personal Assistant.*
P.A.Y.E., *Pay as You Earn* = Retenue de l'impôt à la source, à la base.
P.O.W., *Prisoner of war* = P.G., prisonnier de guerre.
R.A., (c) *Royal Artillery.*
R.A.C., *Royal Armoured Corps.*
R.A.O.C., *Royal Army Ordnance Corps.*
R.A.S.C., *Royal Army Service Corps.*
R.E., *Royal Engineers.*
R.E.M.E., *Royal Electrical and Mechanical Engineers.*
R.I., 2. *Royal Institute of Painters in Water Colours.*
S.C.M., *Student Christian Movement.*
S.H.A.P.E., SHAPE, *Supreme Headquarters Allied Powers in Europe.*
S.T.C., *Mil: Senior Training Corps* = P.M.S., préparation militaire supérieure.
T.N.T., *TriNitro Toluol.*
T.V., *Television.*
T.W.A., *Transworld Airlines.*
U.N., *United Nations.*
U.N.E.S.C.O., *United Nations Educational, Scientific and Cultural Organisation.*
U.N.O., *United Nations Organisation* = O.N.U., Organisation des Nations unies.
V.D., *Venereal Disease*
V.I.P.s, *F: Very Important Persons,* les huiles (*f.pl.*).
W.R.A.C., *Women's Royal Army Corps* = A.F.A.T., Auxiliaire féminine de l'armée de terre.
W.R.A.F., *Women's Royal Air Force.*
W.T.A., *Worker's Travel Association.*
W.V.S., *Women's Voluntary Services.*
Y.H.A., *Youth Hostels Association.*